Concordance to the Bible

Concordance to the Bible

(Douay Version)

Rev. Newton Thompson, S.T.D.
and
Raymond Stock

Roman Catholic Books
Post Office Box 2286, Fort Collins, CO 80522

NIHIL OBSTAT:
Sti. Ludovici, die 20 Jan., 1942
G. H. Guyot, C.M.
Censor Deputatus

IMPRIMATUR:
Sti. Ludovici, die 21 Jan., 1942
Joannes J. Glennon
Archiepiscopus

ISBN 0-912141-85-9

PREFACE

The Old Testament portions of this CONCORDANCE were prepared by Dr. Thompson; the New Testament portions by Mr. Stock, who also supervised the preparation of the manuscript and read the proofs.

To reduce the bulkiness of the volume and to avoid the use of excessively fine print, some keywords, recurring hundreds of times, have been omitted.

All numbers (cardinal and ordinal), except *one* and *first,* will be found at the end of the volume, arranged numerically.

CONCORDANCE TO THE BIBLE

A

Aaronites 1 Pa 27 17 over the A., Sadoc: over Juda
Aaron's Exod 7 12 but A. rod devoured their rods
Exod 28 3 that they may make Aaron's vestments
30 which shall be on Aaron's breast when
29 28 they shall fall to Aaron's share and
Lev 2 2 remnant of the sacrifice shall be A.
10 whatsoever is left, shall be Aaron's
7 31 the breast shall be A. and his sons'
8 12 he poured it upon Aaron's head, and he
23 he touched the tip of A. right ear, and
24 9 they shall be Aaron's and his sons'
Aasbai 2 K 23 34 Eliphelet the son of Aasbai the
Abaddon Apoc 9 11 angel of bottomless pit . . . A.
Abana 4 K 5 12 are not the A. and the Pharphar
abandoned Eze 6 14 a. from the desert of Deblatha
Eze 36 35 and the cities that were abandoned
Amos 9 14 they shall build the abandoned cities
Abarim Num 27 12 into this mountain A. Deut 32:49
Num 33 47 they came to the mountains of Abarim
48 departing from the mountains of Abarim
Abaron 1 Ma 2 5 Eleazar who was surnamed Abaron
abase Dan 4 34 walk in pride he is able to abase
abasement Eccu 20 11 is an a. because of glory
abashed Eccu 21 25 man of experience will be a.
abated Gen 8 1 earth, and the waters were abated
Gen 8 3 began to be abated after 150 days
Lev 27 18 and the price shall be abated. And if
abateth Wisd 16 24 creature . . . a. its strength
Eccu 25 31 a wicked woman abateth the courage and
Abba Mark 14 36 Abba, Father, all things are
Rom 8 15 of sons, whereby we cry: Abba Father
Gal 4 6 into your hearts, crying: Abba Father
Abda 3 K 4 6 Adoniram the son of Abda over the
2 Es 11 17 and Abda the son of Samua the son of
Abdeel Jer 36 26 Selemias the son of Abdeel to take
Abdemelech Jer 38 7 A. the Ethiopian, an eunuch
Jer 38 8 Abdemelech went out of the king's house
10 then the king commanded Abdemelech the
11 Abdemelech taking the men with him
12 A. . . . said to Jeremias: Put these old
39 15 go and tell Abdemelech the Ethiopian
Abdenago Dan 1 7 names . . . to Azarias, Abdenago
Sidrach, Misach, and Abdenago; *see* **Sidrach**
Abdi 1 Pa 6 44 the son of Cusi the son of Abdi the
2 Pa 29 12 Cis the son of Abdi, and Azarias the
1 Es 10 26 Jehiel and A. and Jerimoth and Elia
Abdias 3 K 18 3 Achab called Abdias the governor
3 K 18 3 now Abdias feared the Lord very much
5 Achab said to Abdias: Go into the land
6 Achab went one way, and Abdias another
7 as Abdias was in the way, Elias met him
16 Abdias therefore went to meet Achab
1 Pa 27 19 Jesmaias the son of Abdias: over the
2 Pa 17 7 sent of his princes Benhail and Abdias
34 12 overseers of the workmen . . . Abdias
Abdi 1 the vision of Abdias. Thus saith the
Abdiel 1 Pa 5 15 the sons of Abdiel the son of Guni
Abdon Josu 21 30 of tribe of Aser . . . A. 1 Pa 6:74
Judg 12 13 after him Abdon, the son of Illel a
1 Pa 8 23 and Abdon and Zechri and Hanan
30 his firstborn son Abdon, and Sur. 9:36
2 Pa 34 20 Abdon the son of Micha, and Saphan the
Abed 1 Es 8 6 of the sons of Adan, Abed the son of
Abel Gen 4 2 she brought forth his brother Abel
Gen 4 2 and Abel was a shepherd, and Cain a
4 Abel also offered of the firstlings of
4 the Lord had respect to Abel and to his
8 Cain said to Abel his brother: Let us
8 Cain rose up against his brother Abel
9 said to Cain: Where is thy brother Abel
25 another seed, for Abel whom Cain slew
Judg 11 33 Abel, which is set with vineyards
1 K 6 18 to the great Abel whereon they set down
Mat 23 35 from the blood of Abel. Luke 11:51
Heb 11 4 by faith A. offered to God a sacrifice
12 24 which speaketh better than that of Abel
Abela 2 K 20 14 unto A. and Bethmaacha: and all
2 K 20 15 they came and besieged him in Abela
18 that inquire, let them inquire in Abela
Abeldomum 3 K 15 20 Dan and A. Maacha and all
4 K 15 29 and took Aion and Abeldomum Maacha
Abelmaim 2 Pa 16 4 they took . . . Dan and Abelmaim
Abelmehula Judg 7 23 the border of A. in Tebbath
3 K 4 12 Jezrael from Bethsan unto Abelmehula
Abelmeula 3 K 19 16 the son of Saphat of Abelmeula
Abelsatim Num 33 49 from Bethsimoth even to A.
Abenboen Josu 18 18 and it goeth down to Abenboen
Abes Josu 19 20 Abes and Rameth and Engannim and
Abesalom 2 Ma 11 17 John and A. who were sent from
Abesan Judg 12 8 Abesan of Bethlehem judged Israel
Abessalom 3 K 15 2 Maacha daughter of Abessalom. 10
Abgatha Esth 1 10 Harbona and Bagatha and Abgatha
abhor Exod 23 7 to death because I abhor the wicked
Lev 26 30 my soul shall abhor you. Insomuch that
Deut 7 26 shalt utterly abhor it as uncleanness
23 7 shalt not abhor the Edomite, because
Job 9 31 filth, and my garments shall abhor me
30 10 they abhor me and flee far from me and
Ps 5 7 the deceitful man the Lord will abhor
Prov 24 24 people, and the tribes shall abhor them
29 27 the just abhor the wicked man: and the
Wisd 12 3 whom thou didst abhor because they did
Eccu 38 4 and a wise man will not abhor them. Was
Mich 3 9 you that abhor judgment and pervert all
abhorred Lev 20 23 therefore I abhorred them. But
Job 19 17 my wife hath abhorred my breath, and I
19 sometime my counsellors, have a. me
Ps 105 40 and he abhorred his inheritance. And he
106 18 their soul abhorred all manner of meat
118 163 I have hated and abhorred iniquity; but
Eccu 16 9 but a. them for the pride of their word
Isa 49 7 to the nation that is abhorred, to the
Jer 14 19 hath thy soul abhorred Sion? Why then
Amos 5 10 and have a. him that speaketh perfectly
2 Ma 1 27 look upon them that are despised and a.
abhorrest Isa 7 16 land which thou a. shall be
Rom 2 22 thou that abhorrest idols, committest
abhorreth Deut 12 31 abominations which the Lord a.
Deut 18 12 for the Lord abhorreth all these things
25 16 thy God abhorreth him that doth these
Eccu 50 27 two nations which my soul abhorreth
Abi 4 K 18 2 the name of his mother was Abi the
Abia 1 K 8 2 name of the second was Abia, judges
3 K 14 1 Abia the son of Jeroboam fell sick

1 Pa 2 24 Hesron also had to wife Abia who bore
3 10 whose son Abia begot Asa. And his son
6 28 Samuel: the firstborn Vasseni, and Abia
7 8 Abia and Anathoth and Almath: all
24 10 the eighth to Abia, the ninth to Jesua
2 Pa 11 20 who bore him Abia and Ethai and Ziza
22 he put at the head of them Abia the son
12 16 and Abia his son reigned in his stead
13 1 Abia reigned over Juda. Three years
2 was war between Abia and Jeroboam
3 and when Abia had begun battle and had
4 and Abia stood upon mount Semeron, which
15 all Israel that stood against Abia and
17 and Abia and his people slew them with a
19 and Abia pursued after Jeroboam and took
20 to resist any more, in the days of A.
21 Abia, being strengthened in his kingdom
22 the rest of the acts of Abia and of
14 1 and Abia slept with his fathers, and
29 1 the name of his mother was Abia, the
2 Es 10 7 Mosollam, Abia, Miamin, Maozia, Belgia
12 4 went up with Zorobabel . . . Abia, Miamin
17 of Abia, Zechri: of Miamin and Moadia
Mat 1 7 Roboam begot Abia. And Abia begot Asa
Luke 1 5 Zachary of the course of Abia: and his
Abialbon 2 K 23 31 Abialbon the Arbathite
Abiam 3 K 14 31 A. his son reigned in his stead
3 K 15 1 Abiam reigned over Juda. He reigned
7 the rest of the words of Abiam and all
7 was war between Abiam and Jeroboam
8 and Abiam slept with his fathers, and
Abiasaph Exod 6 24 sons also of Core . . . Abiasaph
1 Pa 6 23 Elcana his son, Abiasaph his son
37 Asir the son of Abiasaph, the son of
9 19 Abiasaph the son of Core, with his
Abiathar 1 K 22 20 whose name was A., escaped
1 K 22 22 David said to Abiathar: I knew that
23 6 when Abiathar . . . fled to David to Ceila
9 he [David] said to Abiathar. 30:7
30 7 Abiathar brought the ephod to David
2 K 8 17 Achimelech the son of A. 1 Pa 18:16
15 24 Abiathar went up, till all the people
27 Jonathan the son of A. 36; 3 K 1:42
29 Sadoc and Abiathar carried back the ark
35 thou hast with thee Sadoc and Abiathar
35 shalt tell it to Sadoc and Abiathar
17 15 Chusai said to Sadoc and Abiathar
19 11 king David sent to Sadoc and Abiathar
20 25 Sadoc and Abiathar, priests. 3 K 4:4
3 K 1 7 he conferred . . . with A. the priest
19 and invited . . . Abiathar the priest. 25
2 22 and hath Abiathar the priest and Joab
26 king said also to Abiathar the priest
27 so Solomon cast out Abiathar from being
35 Sadoc the priest he put in place of A.
1 Pa 15 11 David called Sadoc and Abiathar the
24 6 Ahimelech the son of Abiathar and the
27 34 after Achitophel was . . . Abiathar. And
Mark 2 26 under Abiathar the high priest, and did
Abida Gen 25 4 of Madian was born . . . Abida and
1 Pa 1 33 sons of Madian . . . Abida and Eldaa
Abidan Num 1 11 Abidan the son of Gedeon. 2:22
Num 7 60 Abidan the son of Gedeon offered a
65 this was the offering of Abidan the son
10 24 the prince was Abidan the son of Gedeon
abide Gen 19 2 no, but we will abide in the street
Exod 29 46 Egypt, that I might abide among them
Lev 19 13 not abide with thee until the morning
33 dwell in your land and a. among you
Num 31 23 whatsoever cannot abide the fire, shall
35 3 that they may abide in the towns and the
25 he shall abide there until the death of
Deut 2 29 Seir, and the Moabites, that abide in Ar
4 18 of fishes, that abide in the waters
25 and grandsons and abide in the land
5 8 that abide in the waters under the earth
14 9 you eat of all that abide in the waters
16 11 and the widow, who abide with you: in
33 12 as in a bride chamber shall he abide
Judg 9 41 would not suffer them to abide in it
1 K 1 22 the Lord, and may abide always there
19 2 thou shalt abide in a secret place and
22 5 abide not in the hold, depart and go
23 abide thou with me, fear not: for he
29 4 this man return and abide in his place
30 21 ordered them to abide at the torrent
2 K 2 18 like one of the roes that a. in the
11 11 of my lord a. upon the face of the earth
16 18 all Israel, and with him will I abide
3 K 22 26 let him [Micheas] abide with Ammon the
4 K 4 10 when he cometh to us, he may a. there
Tob 4 20 that all thy counsels may abide in him
8 23 Raguel adjured Tobias to abide with him
31 13 if I have despised to abide judgment
37 8 his covert, and shall abide in his den
Ps 5 6 nor shall the unjust abide before thy
90 1 shall abide under the protection of the
Prov 7 11 quiet, not able to abide still at home
14 9 but among the just grace shall abide
15 31 shall abide in the midst of the wise
19 23 he shall abide in fulness without being
21 16 shall a. in the company of the giants
Cant 1 12 to me, he shall a. between my breasts
7 11 let us abide in the villages. Let us
Wisd 1 5 shall not abide when iniquity cometh in
Eccu 6 8 he will not abide in day of thy trouble
10 he will not abide in day of distress
11 22 abide not in the works of sinners. But
12 14 for an hour he will abide with thee
21 31 and he that shall abide with him shall
24 11 I shall abide in the inheritance of
25 23 more agreeable to abide with a lion
43 3 who can abide his burning heat? As one
Isa 1 13 and other festivals I will not abide
11 6 lion and the sheep shall abide together
Jer 4 14 shall hurtful thoughts abide in thee
10 10 not be able to abide his threatening
21 9 he that shall abide in this city, shall
40 10 and abide in your cities which you hold
49 19 like to me? And who shall abide me
33 no man shall abide there, nor son of
Dan 13 57 of Juda would not abide your wickedness
1 Ma 10 73 wilt thou be able to abide the horsemen
2 Ma 9 12 could not now abide his own stench, he
Mat 10 11 there abide. Mark 6:10; Luke 9:4
Luke 8 27 neither did he abide in a house, but in
19 5 for this day I must abide in thy house
John 14 16 that he may abide with you forever. The
17 shall a. with you and shall be in you
15 4 abide in me and I in you. As the branch
4 unless it abide in the vine, so neither
4 neither can you unless you abide in me
6 if any one abide not in me, he shall be
7 if you a. in me and my words a. in you
9 I also have loved you. Abide in my love
10 you shall abide in my love; as I also
10 commandments and do a. in his love
Acts 16 15 into my house, and abide there. And she
Rom 11 22 if thou abide in goodness, otherwise
23 if they abide not still in unbelief
1 C 3 14 if any man's work abide, which he hath
7 20 let every man abide in the same calling
24 wherein he was called, therein abide
16 6 with you perhaps I shall abide, or even
7 that I shall abide with you some time
Phil 1 24 to abide still in the flesh is needful

25 I know that I shall abide and continue
Heb 13 1 charity of the brotherhood abide in you
1 J 2 24 heard from the beginning, abide in you
24 if that a. in you which you have heard
24 you also shall abide in the Son and in
27 have received from him, abide in you
27 and as it hath taught you, abide in him
28 and now, little children, abide in him
3 17 doth the charity of God abide in him
4 13 we abide in him and he in us: because
abideth Num 13 30 Chanaanite abideth by the sea
Num 30 17 or that abideth in her father's house
Deut 27 26 that a. not in the words of this law
29 11 stranger that a. with thee in the camp
Job 17 2 not sinned, and my eye a. in bitterness
39 28 she abideth among the rocks and dwelleth
Ps 60 8 he abideth forever in the sight of God
Eccu 11 17 the gift of God abideth with the just
abiding Num 24 2 saw Israel abiding in their tents
Num 35 34 be cleansed, myself abiding with you
Judg 21 2 a. before him till the evening, lifted
1 Pa 2 55 and making melody and abiding in tents
17 6 and in a tent, abiding with all Israel
Jdth 13 20 both going hence and abiding with him
Prov 30 1 strengthened by God, abiding with him
John 5 38 you have not his word abiding in you
14 25 I have spoken to you, abiding with you
1 J 3 15 no murderer hath eternal life abiding
Abiel 1 K 9 1 Cis the son of Abiel the son of
1 K 14 51 the father of Abner, was son of Abiel
1 Pa 11 32 A. an Arbathite, Azmoth a Bauramite
Abiezer Judg 6 34 called together the house of A.
Judg 8 2 better than the vintages of Abiezer
2 K 23 27 Abiezer of Anathoth, Mabonnai of
1 Pa 7 18 named Queen bore Goodlyman and A.
11 28 Acces a Thecuite, A. an Anathothite
27 12 for the ninth month, was Abiezer, an
Abigabaon 1 Pa 8 29 and at Gabaon dwelt Abigabaon
Abigail 1 K 25 3 name of his wife was Abigail
1 K 25 14 but one of the servants told Abigail
18 Abigail made haste and took 200 loaves
23 when Abigail saw David she made haste
32 David said to Abigail: Blessed be
36 and Abigail came to Nabal: and behold
39 David sent and treated with Abigail
40 David's servants came to Abigail
42 Abigail arose and made haste and got
27 3 wives, Achinoam . . . and Abigail. 2 K 2:2
30 5 Achinoam the Jezrahelitess and Abigail
2 K 3 3 his second Cheleab of Abigail the wife
17 25 who went in to Abigail the daughter of
1 Pa 2 16 their sisters were Sarvia and Abigail
17 Abigail bore Amasa, whose father was
3 1 the second Daniel of Abigail, the
Abihaiel Num 3 35 Suriel the son of Abihaiel
Abihail 1 Pa 2 29 name of Abisur's wife was A.
1 Pa 5 14 these were the sons of Abihail
2 Pa 11 18 Roboam took to wife . . . Abihail
Esth 2 15 Esther the daughter of Abihail. 9:29
Abilina Luke 3 1 Lysanias tetrarch of Abilina
ability 4 K 23 35 of every man according to his a.
1 Pa 29 2 I with all my ability have prepared
1 Es 2 69 according to their ability, they gave
2 Es 5 8 have redeemed according to our ability
Tob 4 8 according to thy ability be merciful
Eccu 3 22 search not into things above thy a.
11 12 wanteth help and is very weak in a.
14 13 do good . . . according to thy ability
35 12 do according to the ability of thy hands
Mat 25 15 to every one according to his proper a.
Acts 11 29 according to his ability purposed to
Abimael Gen 10 28 Jectan begot . . . A. 1 Pa 1:22
Abimelech Gen 20 2 A. the king of Gerara sent and
Gen 20 3 and God came to Abimelech in a dream by
4 Abimelech had not touched her, and he
8 Abimelech forthwith rising up in the
9 Abimelech called also for Abraham and
14 A. took sheep and oxen and servants
17 God healed Abimelech and his wife and
18 had closed every womb of the house of A.
21 25 he reproved Abimelech for a well of
26 Abimelech answered: I knew not who did
27 sheep and oxen and gave them to A.
29 Abimelech said to him: What mean these
33 Abimelech and Phicol the general of
26 1 Isaac went to Abimelech king of the
8 Abimelech king of the Palestines looking
10 A. said: Why hast thou deceived us? Some
16 A. himself said to Isaac: Depart from
26 when A. and Ochozath his friend and
Judg 8 31 bore him a son, whose name was Abimelech
9 1 Abimelech the son of Jerobaal went
3 inclined their hearts after Abimelech
6 they went and made Abimelech king, by
16 in appointing Abimelech king over you
18 made A. the son of his handmaid king
19 rejoice ye this day in Abimelech, and
20 from town of Mello and devour A.
21 dwelt there for fear of Abimelech his
22 so Abimelech reigned over Israel for
23 evil spirit between Abimelech and the
24 crime the shedding of their blood upon A.
25 and it was told Abimelech. And Gaal the
27 banquets and cups they cursed A.
28 who is A., and what is Sichem that we
29 it was said to Abimelech: Gather together
29 that I might remove A. out of the way
31 sent messengers privately to Abimelech
34 A. therefore arose with all his army
35 Abimelech rose up and all his army with
38 who is Abimelech that we should serve
39 fought against Abimelech, who chased
41 Abimelech sat down in Ruma: but Zebul
42 it was told Abimelech. And he took his
45 and A. assaulted the city all that day
47 A. also hearing that the men of the tower
50 A. departing from thence came to the
52 A. coming near the tower, fought stoutly
53 dashed it against the head of Abimelech
56 the evil that Abimelech had done against
10 1 after A. there arose a ruler in Israel
1 Thola son of Phua the uncle of A., a
2 K 11 21 who killed A. the son of Jerobaal? Did
Abinadab 1 K 7 1 carried it into the house of A.
1 K 16 8 Isai called Abinadab and brought him
17 13 firstborn, and the second A. 1 Pa 2:13
31 2 they slew Jonathan and Abinadab and
2 K 6 3 out of the house of A. 4; 1 Pa 13:7
3 the sons of Abinadab drove the new cart
1 Pa 8 33 Melchisua and A. and Esbaal. 9:39
10 2 they killed Jonathan and Abinadab and
Abinoem Judg 4 6 Barac the son of Abinoem. 5:1
Judg 5 12 hold of thy captive, O son of Abinoem
Abiram 3 K 16 34 in A. his firstborn he laid its
Abiron Num 16 1 Dathan and A. the sons of Eliab. 12; Deut 11:6
Num 16 24 from tents of Core and Dathan and A.
25 arose and went to Dathan and Abiron
27 Dathan and Abiron coming out stood in
26 9 his sons were Namuel and Dathan and A.
9 Dathan and Abiron the princes of the
Ps 105 17 and covered the congregation of Abiron
Eccu 45 22 men that were with Dathan and Abiron
Abisag 3 K 1 3 and they found Abisag a Sunamitess
3 K 1 15 Abisag the Sunamitess ministered to him
2 17 give me Abisag the Sunamitess to wife

21 let Abisag . . . be given to Adonias thy
22 why dost thou ask A. the Sunamitess
Abisai 1 K 26 6 A. the son of Sarvia the brother
1 K 26 6 Abisai said: I will go with thee. So
7 David and Abisai came to the people by
8 Abisai said to David: God hath shut up
9 and David said to Abisai: Kill him not
2 K 2 18 sons of Sarvia were there, Joab and A.
24 Joab and Abisai pursued after Abner
3 30 Joab and Abisai his brother slew Abner
10 10 he delivered to Abisai his brother
14 they fled also before A. and entered
16 9 Abisai . . . said to the king: Why should
11 king said to Abisai . . . Behold, my son
18 2 a third part under the hand of Abisai
5 king commanded Joab and A. and Ethai
12 king charged thee and Abisai and Ethai
19 21 Abisai . . . said: Shall Semei for these
20 6 and David said to Abisai: Now will Seba
10 Joab and Abisai his brother pursued
21 17 Abisai the son of Sarvia rescued him
23 18 Abisai . . . was chief among three: and
1 Pa 2 16 sons of Sarvia: Abisai, Joab, and Asael
11 20 Abisai . . . was chief of three, and he
18 12 Abisai . . . slew of the Edomites in the
19 11 he delivered into the hand of Abisai
15 they likewise fled from Abisai his
Abisue 1 Pa 6 4 begot A., and A. begot Bocci
1 Pa 6 50 Phinees his son, Abisue his son, Bocci
8 4 sons of Bale . . . Abisue and Naaman and
1 Es 7 5 Bocci the son of Abisue, the son of
Abisur 1 Pa 2 28 sons of Semei: Nadab and Abisur
Abisur's 1 Pa 2 29 name of A. wife was Abihail
Abital 2 K 3 4 fifth Saphathia, the son of Abital
1 Pa 3 3 Saphatias of A., the sixth Jethrahem
Abitob 1 Pa 8 11 Behusim begot Abitob and Elphaal
Abiu Exod 6 23 who bore him Nadab and Abiu and
Exod 24 1 thou and Aaron, Nadab and Abiu and
9 Moses and Aaron, Nadab and Abiu and
28 1 Aaron, Nadab, and Abiu, Eleazar and
Lev 10 1 Nadab and Abiu . . . taking their. Num 3:4
Num 3 2 sons of Aaron . . . Abiu. 1 Pa 6:3; 24:1
26 60 of Aaron were born Nadab and Abiu and
Abiud 1 Pa 8 3 sons of Bale . . . Abiud and Abisue
Mat 1 13 Zorobabel begot A. A. begot Eliacim
abject Ps 83 11 I have chosen to be an abject
Isa 53 3 despised and the most abject of men
abjection Ps 24 18 see my a. and my labor: and
Ps 118 92 I had then perhaps perished in my a.
Eze 16 5 in the abjection of thy soul, in the
Abner 1 K 14 50 captain of his army was Abner
1 K 14 51 of Saul, and Ner the father of Abner
17 55 said to Abner the captain of the army
55 family is this young man descended, A.
55 Abner said . . . I know not. And the king
57 Abner took him and brought him in before
20 25 and Abner sat by Saul's side, and
26 5 wherein Saul slept, and Abner the son of
7 Abner and the people sleeping round
14 David cried to the people and to Abner
14 wilt thou not answer, Abner? And
14 Abner answering, said: Who art thou
15 David said to Abner: Art not thou a man
2 K 2 8 but Abner . . . took Isboseth the son of
12 Abner . . . went out from the camp to
14 Abner said to Joab: Let the young men
17 and Abner was put to flight with the men
19 Asael pursued after Abner and turned not
19 nor to the left from following Abner
20 Abner looked behind him and said: Art
22 Abner said to Asael: Go off and do not
23 Abner struck him with his spear with a
24 Joab and Abisai pursued after Abner
25 gathered themselves together to Abner
26 Abner cried out to Joab and said: Shall
29 Abner and his men walked all that night
30 Joab returning, after he had left Abner
31 and of the men that were with Abner
3 6 Abner the son of Ner ruled the house of
7 Isboseth said to Abner: Why didst thou
9 so do God to A., and more also, unless
12 A. therefore sent messengers to David
16 Abner said to him: Go and return. And
17 Abner also spoke to the ancients of
19 and Abner spoke also to Benjamin. And
20 David made a feast for A. and his men
21 when David had brought A. on his way
22 Abner was not with David in Hebron
24 behold Abner came to thee: Why didst
25 knowest thou not Abner the son of Ner
26 sent messengers after A. and brought
27 when Abner was returned to Hebron, Joab
28 are innocent . . . of the blood of Abner
30 Joab and Abisai his brother slew Abner
31 and mourn before the funeral of Abner
32 when they had buried Abner in Hebron
32 voice and wept at the grave of Abner
33 mourning and lamenting over Abner
33 not as cowards . . . hath Abner died. Thy
37 that Abner the son of Ner was slain
4 1 heard that Abner was slain in Hebron
12 buried in sepulcher of Abner in Hebron
3 K 2 5 to Abner the son of Ner and to Amasa
32 A. the son of Ner, general of the army
1 Pa 26 28 son of Cis, and Abner the son of Ner
27 21 over Benjamin Jasiel the son of Abner
aboard Acts 20 13 aboard ship, sailed to Assos
Acts 21 2 we went aboard and set forth. And when
Abobus 1 Ma 16 11 Ptolemee the son of Abobus was
1 Ma 16 15 son of A. received them deceitfully
abode Gen 13 12 Lot a. in the towns that were
Gen 19 30 Lot . . . abode in the mountain, and his
26 6 so Isaac abode in Gerara. And when he
8 and he [Isaac] abode there, Abimelech
37 12 and when his brethren abode in Sichem
Exod 2 15 sight, and abode in the land of Madian
12 40 and the abode of the children of Israel
Num 9 18 the cloud abode over the tabernacle
11 34 they came unto Haseroth and abode there
20 1 the people abode in Cades. And Mary died
25 1 Israel at that time abode in Settim
Deut 1 4 Og . . . who abode in Astaroth and in
46 you abode in Cadesbarne a long time
3 29 we abode in the valley over against the
Josu 3 1 and they abode there for three days
5 10 the children of Israel abode in Galgal
6 11 returning into the camp, abode there
8 9 abode between Bethel and Hai on the
9 6 abode in the camp at Galgal. 10:6
11 11 cut off all the souls that abode there
Judg 5 17 the seashore, and abode in the havens
11 17 he abode therefore in Cades, and went
17 11 he was content and abode with the man
19 2 abode with him four months. And her
20 47 they abode in the rock Remmon four
Ruth 1 2 the country of Moab, they abode there
1 K 7 2 ark of the Lord a. in Cariathiarim
14 2 Saul abode in uttermost part of Gabaa
22 4 abode with him all the days that David
6 whilst Saul abode in Gabaa and was in
23 14 David a. in the desert in strongholds
18 David abode in the wood: but Jonathan
25 and abode in the wilderness of Maon
26 3 David a. in the wilderness. And seeing
30 24 and of him that abode at the baggage
31 those places in which David had abode

2 K 1 1 Amalecites, and a. two days in Siceleg
2 3 and they abode in the towns of Hebron
11 days that David abode, reigning in
6 11 abode in the house of Obededom the
19 32 sustenance when he abode in the camp
3 K 17 19 into the upper chamber where he abode
19 9 was come thither, he abode in a cave
4 K 2 18 he [Eliseus] abode at Jericho, and he
19 36 and he returned and abode in Ninive
1 Pa 4 23 for his works, and they abode there
9 27 and they abode in their watches round
34 heads of the Levites . . . a. in Jerusalem
12 16 to the hold in which David abode. And
Tob 5 8 I have abode with Gabelus our brother
Jdth 5 8 in which she a. shut up with her maids
16 28 abode in her husband's house 105 years
Ps 54 8 and I abode in the wilderness. I waited
75 3 and his abode in Sion. There hath he
Eccu 24 16 and my abode is in the full assembly of
Dan 4 9 the fowls of the air had their abode
18 birds of the air had their abode in its
1 Ma 2 1 he abode in the mountain of Modin. And
30 they a. there, they and their children
2 Ma 14 23 Nicanor abode in Jerusalem and did no
Mat 17 21 when they abode together in Galilee
Luke 1 56 Mary abode with her about three months
21 37 he abode in mount that is called Olivet
John 1 39 they came and saw where he abode and
3 22 there he abode with them and baptized
4 40 he abode there two days. And many
10 40 John was baptizing, and there he abode
11 54 and there he abode with his disciples
14 23 will make our abode with him. He that
Acts 1 13 where abode Peter and John, James
9 43 he [Peter] a. many days in Joppe
12 19 to Caesarea, he [Herod] abode there
14 3 long time they abode there [Iconium]
27 a. no small time with the disciples
20 6 [Troas] where he abode seven days
21 7 we abode one day with them. And the
8 we abode with him [Philip]. And he
1 C 4 11 have no fixed abode; and we labor
Heb 11 9 by faith he abode in the land, dwelling
abolish Deut 9 14 a. their name from under heaven
Ps 73 8 let us abolish all the festival days
Eccu 47 24 he will not . . . abolish his own works
Dan 3 34 and abolish not thy covenant. And take
1 Ma 3 42 the people and utterly abolish them
abolished Deut 25 6 that his name be not a. out
Eccu 10 21 God hath a. the memory of the proud
45 31 that their good things might not be a.
Isa 28 18 your league with death shall be a.
Eze 6 6 and your altars shall be abolished
Dan 9 24 an end and iniquity may be abolished
2 Ma 2 23 restored the laws that were abolished
abolishing 2 Ma 4 11 a. those things which had
abominable Gen 34 14 with us is unlawful and a.
Lev 11 20 upon four feet, shall be a. to you
41 creepeth upon the earth shall be a.
42 you shall not eat, because it is a.
Deut 22 5 doeth these things is a. before God
24 4 and is become a. before the Lord: lest
3 K 21 26 he became a. insomuch that he followed
Job 15 16 how much more is man abominable and
33 20 bread becometh abominable to him in
Ps 13 1 are become abominable in their ways
52 2 they are corrupted and become a. in
Prov 11 20 a perverse heart is a. to the Lord
15 8 victims of the wicked are a. to the
16 12 that act wickedly are a. to the king
17 15 both are abominable before God. 20:10
21 27 the sacrifices of the wicked are a.
Wisd 14 27 the worship of a. idols is the cause
Jer 44 4 do not commit this abominable thing
1 Ma 1 57 king Antiochus set up the a. idol of
2 Ma 4 13 a. and unheard of wickedness of Jason
10 34 and cast forth abominable words. But
Acts 10 28 how a. it is for a man that is a Jew
Titus 1 16 being abominable and incredulous, and
Apoc 21 8 and the abominable and murderers and
abomination Gen 46 34 have all shepherds in a.
Lev 11 10 shall be an abomination to you. 23
18 22 with womankind because it is an a.
20 13 both have committed an abomination
14 neither shall so great an a. remain
Deut 7 25 it is an abomination to the Lord. 17:1
13 14 that this a. hath been really committed
17 4 and that the a. is committed in Israel
23 18 these are an abomination to the Lord
27 15 and molten thing, the a. of the Lord
Judg 20 6 and so great an a. committed in Israel
12 why hath so great an a. been found
4 K 23 13 abomination of the children of Ammon
Job 11 20 their hope the abomination of the soul
Ps 87 9 they have set me an a. to themselves
Prov 3 32 every mocker is an abomination to the
11 1 a deceitful balance is an abomination
12 22 lying lips are an a. to the Lord: but
15 9 way of the wicked is an abomination
26 evil thoughts are an abomination to the
16 5 every proud man is an a. to the Lord
20 23 diverse weights are an abomination
24 9 the detracter is the abomination of men
28 9 his prayer shall be an abomination. He
Wisd 14 11 creatures of God are turned to an a.
Eccu 1 26 to sinners wisdom is an abomination
32 the worship of God is an a. to a sinner
13 24 and as humility is an a. to the proud
15 13 Lord hateth all abomination of error
17 23 injustice and greatly hate abomination
Isa 1 13 vain: incense is an abomination to me
41 24 that hath chosen you is an abomination
66 17 that did eat swine's flesh and the a.
Jer 2 7 and made my inheritance an abomination
6 15 confounded, because they committed a.
8 12 because they have committed a.: yea
32 35 that they should do this abomination
Eze 8 10 the a. and all the idols of the house
18 12 his eyes to idols, that committeth a.
22 11 every one hath committed abomination
Dan 9 27 in the temple the a. of desolation
11 31 and they shall place there the a. unto
12 11 the a. unto desolation shall be set up
Mala 2 11 a. hath been committed in Israel and
1 Ma 6 7 that they had thrown down the a. which
Mat 24 15 abomination of desolation. Mark 13:14
Luke 16 15 is high to men is an a. before God
Apoc 17 4 full of the a. and filthiness of her
21 27 defiled or that worketh abomination
abominations Exod 8 26 sacrifice the a. of the
Lev 18 25 defiled: the a. of which I will visit
26 and do not any of these abominations
29 soul that shall commit any of these a.
Deut 12 31 they have done to their gods all the a.
18 9 mind to imitate the a. of those nations
12 for these a. he will destroy them at
20 18 lest they teach you to do all the a.
29 17 you have seen their abominations and
32 16 stirred him up to anger with their a.
3 K 14 24 did according to all the abominations
4 K 17 12 they worshipped a., concerning which
21 11 hath done these most wicked a., beyond
21 he served the a. which his father had
23 24 a. that had been in the land of Juda
2 Pa 33 2 according to all the a. of the nations
34 33 Josias took away all the a. out of

36 8 the acts of Joakim and his abominations
14 all the abominations of the Gentiles
1 Es 9 1 people of the lands, and from their a.
11 other lands, with their abominations
14 with the people of these abominations
Eccu 41 8 of sinners become children of a. and
49 3 and he took away the a. of wickedness
Isa 66 3 and their soul is delighted in their a.
Jer 7 10 because we have done all these a. Is
30 they have set their a. in the house in
13 27 thy a., upon the hills in the field
16 18 filled my inheritance with their a.
44 22 abominations which you have committed
Eze 5 9 will do no more because of all thy a.
11 all thy offences and with all thy a.
6 9 they have committed in all their a.
11 a. of the evils of the house of Israel
7 3 and I will set all thy a. against thee
4 thy a. shall be in the midst of thee. 9
20 have made of it the images of their a.
8 6 a. that the house of Israel committeth
6 shalt see greater abominations. 13, 15
9 and see the wicked a. which they commit
17 that they should commit these a. which
9 4 men that sigh and mourn for all the a.
11 18 all the a. thereof from thence. And I
21 walketh after their scandals and a.
14 6 turn away your faces from all your a.
16 2 make known to Jerusalem her a. And thou
22 after all thy a. and fornications
36 with the idols of thy abominations
43 to thy wicked deeds in all thy a.
50 they were lifted up and committed a.
51 hast justified thy sisters by all thy a.
18 24 do iniquity according to all the a.
20 4 declare to them the a. of their fathers
8 did not every man cast away the a. of
30 you commit fornications with their a.
22 3 shalt show her all her a. and shalt
33 26 on your swords, you have committed a.
29 desolate, for all their abominations
37 23 more with their idols nor with their a.
43 8 by the a. which they committed: for
Nah 3 6 and I will cast abominations upon thee
Zach 9 7 I will take . . . his a. from between his
1 Ma 1 51 defiled with all uncleannesses and a.
Apoc 17 5 fornications and the a. of the earth
abortive Num 12 12 as an a. that is cast forth
abound Deut 28 11 make thee a. with all goods
Deut 30 9 will make thee abound in all the works
Job 12 6 the tabernacles of robbers abound, and
22 26 then shalt thou abound in delights in
Ps 61 11 if riches abound, set not your heart
64 14 and the vales shall abound with corn
Ecce 2 1 I will go and abound with delights and
25 so feast and abound with delights as
Eccu 15 10 and shall abound in a faithful mouth
12 16 a wise man shall abound like a flood
23 3 lest . . . my sins a. and I fall before
24 36 who maketh understanding to abound as
34 11 surprised, shall abound with subtlety
Isa 60 5 then shalt thou see and abound and
Jer 30 10 rest, and abound with all good things
Mat 5 20 unless your justice abound more than
13 12 and he shall abound. 25:29; Luke 19:26
Luke 15 17 in my father's house a. with bread
Rom 5 20 the law entered in that sin might a.
20 where sin abounded, grace did more a.
6 1 we continue in sin that grace may a.
14 5 let every man abound in his own sense
15 13 that you may abound in hope and in
1 C 14 12 seek to a. unto edifying of the church
2 C 1 5 as the sufferings of Christ a. in us
5 also by Christ doth our comfort abound
4 15 may a. in thanksgiving unto the glory
7 4 I exceedingly abound with joy in all
8 7 as in all things you abound in faith
7 so in this grace also you may abound
9 8 God is able to make all grace a. in you
8 may abound in every good work, as it is
11 that you may a. unto all simplicity
Phil 1 9 more and more abound in knowledge
26 that your rejoicing may a. in Christ
4 12 be brought low and I know how to abound
12 hungry; both to a. and to suffer need
17 but I seek the fruit that may abound
18 but I have all and abound: I am filled
1 Th 3 12 make you a. in charity towards one
4 1 walk, that you may abound the more
10 we entreat you . . . that you abound more
2 P 1 8 if these things be with you and abound
abounded 2 Es 9 25 a. with delight in thy great
Ps 49 19 thy mouth hath abounded with evil and
Wisd 11 5 children of Israel a. therewith and
Osee 10 1 his land he hath abounded with idols
1 Ma 3 30 he had a. more than the kings that had
Mat 24 12 because iniquity hath a., the charity
Rom 3 7 if the truth of God hath more abounded
5 15 and the gift . . . hath a. unto many
20 where sin a., grace did more abound
2 C 8 2 their very deep poverty hath a. unto
1 Tim 1 14 the grace of our Lord hath abounded
aboundeth Eccu 6 5 gracious tongue in a good man a.
Eccu 10 30 he that laboreth and a. in all things
19 21 than he that a. in understanding and
21 15 but there is a wisdom that a. in evil
2 C 3 9 the ministration of justice aboundeth
9 12 aboundeth also by many thanksgivings
2 Th 1 3 the charity . . . towards each other a.
abounding Ps 72 12 and yet a. in the world they
Ps 143 13 in young, a. in their goings forth
1 Ma 6 1 renowned and a. in silver and gold
1 C 15 58 abounding in the work of the Lord
2 C 4 15 that the grace abounding through many
Col 2 7 abounding in him in thanksgiving
about Gen 41 25 Pharao what he is about to do
Deut 31 21 I know . . . what they are about to do
1 K 17 49 fetching it about struck the Philistine
2 K 12 27 the city of waters is about to be taken
15 32 where he was about to adore the Lord
3 K 16 18 that the city was about to be taken
above Gen 27 39 dew of heaven from above, shall
Gen 49 25 with the blessings of heaven above
Exod 20 4 that is in heaven above or in the earth
26 12 one curtain that is over and above
13 over and above in the length of the
28 32 above shall be a hole for the head and
40 18 bars underneath, and the oracle above
Lev 26 19 I will make to you the heaven above
27 15 part of the estimation over and above
Num 3 48 the price of them that are above. Moses
49 took the money of them that were above
5 7 the fifth part over and above, to him
Deut 4 39 the Lord he is God in heaven above and
5 8 any things, that are in heaven above
28 13 shalt be always above, and not beneath
33 27 his dwelling is above, and underneath
Josu 2 11 he is God in heaven above and in the
3 13 and those that come from above, shall
16 the waters that came down from above
Judg 9 53 casting a piece of a millstone from a.
2 K 11 20 darts are thrown from above off the
24 at thy servants from off the wall above
18 26 and crying aloud from above, he said
3 K 7 11 above there were costly stones of equal
20 chapiters in the top of the pillars a.

25 east, and the sea was above upon them
29 and in the joinings likewise above
8 7 the ark, and the staves thereof above
23 no God like thee in heaven above or
1 Pa 4 41 and those whose names are written above
2 Pa 34 22 and they spoke to her the words above
Job 3 4 let not God regard it from above, and
18 16 and his harvest destroyed above. Let
31 2 what part should God from above have
36 28 from the clouds that cover all above
30 and lighten with his light from above
Ps 49 4 he shall call heaven from above and
77 23 he had commanded the clouds from above
Prov 8 28 when he established the sky above, and
15 24 the path of life is above for the wise
25 3 heaven above and . . . is unsearchable
Wisd 9 17 and send thy Holy Spirit from above
Isa 7 11 depth of hell, or unto the height above
45 8 drop down dew . . . from above, and let
Jer 4 28 the heavens shall lament from above
Lam 1 13 from above he hath sent fire into my
Bar 6 62 the fire also being sent from above
Eze 1 22 stretched out over their heads above
26 appearance of a man above upon it. And
13 11 to fall violently from above, and a
42 5 were the store chambers lower above
5 which appeared above out of them from
6 therefore did they appear above, and
Amos 2 9 I destroyed his fruit from above, and
1 Ma 6 37 valiant men who fought from above; and
10 41 all that is above, which they that
Mat 5 37 that which is over and above these, is
10 24 disciple is not a. the master. Luke 6:40
24 nor the servant above his lord. It is
John 3 31 he that cometh from above is above all
6 13 which remained over and above to them
8 23 you are from beneath, I am from above
19 11 unless it were given thee from above
Acts 4 22 the man was above forty years old, in
26 13 above the brightness of the sun shining
1 C 4 6 be not puffed up . . . a. that which is
10 13 tempted above that which you are able
2 C 1 8 pressed out of measure a. our strength
11 23 in stripes above measure, in deaths
12 2 I know a man . . . above fourteen years
6 above that which he seeth in me, or
11 them that are above measure apostles
Gal 1 14 I made progress . . . above many of my
4 26 that Jerusalem which is above, is free
Eph 3 3 as I have written above in a few words
Phil 2 9 him a name which is above all names
Col 3 1 seek the things that are above; where
2 mind the things that are above, not the
Heb 4 7 as it is above said: Today if you shall
James 1 17 every perfect gift is from above
3 15 this is not wisdom, descending from a.
17 wisdom that is from a. . . . is chaste

Abraham Gen 17 5 but thou shalt be called Abraham
Gen 17 9 again God said to Abraham: And thou
15 God said also to Abraham: Sarai thy
17 Abraham fell upon his face and laughed
19 God said to Abraham: Sara thy wife
22 with him, God went up from Abraham
23 A. took Ismael his son and all that
24 A. was 99 years old when he circumcised
26 selfsame day was Abraham circumcised
18 6 A. made haste into the tent to Sara
13 Lord said to A.: Why did Sara laugh
16 A. walked with them, bringing them on
17 can I hide from A. what I am about to
22 Abraham as yet stood before the Lord
27 A. answered and said: Seeing I have
33 after he had left speaking to Abraham
33 and Abraham returned to his place
19 27 Abraham got up early in the morning and
29 remembering A., he delivered Lot out
20 1 A. removed from thence to the south
9 Abimelech called also for A. and said
11 Abraham answered: I thought within
14 and handmaids and gave to Abraham
17 when A. prayed, God healed Abimelech
21 3 Abraham called the name of his son whom
7 who would believe that A. should hear
8 A. made a great feast on the day of
9 she said to Abraham: Cast out this
11 A. took this grievously for his son
14 A. rose up in the morning and taking
22 said to A.: God is with thee in all
24 A. said: I will swear. And he reproved
27 A. took sheep and oxen and gave them
28 A. set apart seven ewe lambs of the
33 Abraham planted a grove in Bersabee
22 1 God tempted A. and said to him: A.
3 A. rising up in the night, saddled
8 A. said: God will provide himself a
11 called to him, saying: A., A. And he
13 A. lifted up his eyes and saw behind
15 angel of the Lord called to Abraham
19 A. returned to his young men, and they
20 it was told A. that Melcha also had
23 2 A. came to mourn and weep for her
7 Abraham rose up and bowed down to the
12 A. bowed down before the people of
16 when A. had heard this, he weighed out
18 was made sure to Abraham. 20
19 A. buried Sara his wife in a double
24 1 A. was old, and advanced in age: and
6 A. said: Beware thou never bring my
9 put his hand under the thigh of A.
12 the God of my master Abraham, meet me
12 show kindness to my master Abraham
15 wife to Nachor the brother of A.
27 blessed be Lord God of my master A.
34 I am the servant of Abraham. And the
42 God of my master A., if thou hast
48 blessing the Lord God of my master A.
25 1 A. married another wife named Cetura
5 A. gave all his possessions to Isaac
12 generations of Ismael the son of A.
19 generations of Isaac the son of A.
19 Abraham begot Isaac. 1 Pa 1:34
26 1 which had happened in the days of A.
3 the oath which I swore to Abraham thy
5 because Abraham obeyed my voice and
15 servants of his father A. had digged. 18
24 I am the God of Abraham. Exod 3:6
28 4 give the blessings of Abraham to thee
13 I am the Lord God of Abraham thy
31 42 the God of my father Abraham. 32:9
53 the God of Abraham . . . judge between us
35 12 the land which I gave to Abraham and
27 wherein Abraham and Isaac sojourned
48 15 in whose sight my fathers A. and Isaac
16 names of my fathers Abraham and Isaac
49 30 double cave . . . which Abraham bought
50 13 double cave which Abraham had bought
Exod 2 24 covenant which he made with Abraham.
4 K 13:23; 1 Pa 16:16
3 15 God of Abraham . . . hath sent me to you
16 God of Abraham . . . hath appeared to. 4:5
6 3 I am the Lord that appeared to Abraham
8 the land . . . to give it to Abraham
32 13 remember Abraham, Isaac, and Israel
33 1 land concerning which I swore to A.
Lev 26 42 covenant that I made with . . . Abraham
Deut 1 8 the Lord swore to your fathers Abraham

6 10 swore to thy fathers A. 29:13; 30:20
9 5 promised . . . to thy fathers Abraham
27 remember thy servants A., Isaac, and
34 4 for which I swore to Abraham, Isaac
Josu 24 2 Thare the father of Abraham, and Nachor
3 and I took your father Abraham from
3 K 18 36 God of Abraham . . . show this day that
1 Pa 1 27 Abram, this is Abraham. And the sons of
28 the sons of Abraham, Isaac, and Ismahel
29 18 God of Abraham . . . keep forever this
2 Pa 20 7 gavest it to the seed of Abraham thy
30 6 turn again to the Lord the God of A.
2 Es 9 7 and gavest him the name of Abraham
Tob 6 22 that in the seed of Abraham thou mayst
7 15 the God of Abraham . . . be with you
Jdth 8 22 how our father Abraham was tempted and
Esth 13 15 God of Abraham have mercy on thy people
14 18 but in thee, O Lord the God of Abraham
Ps 46 10 are gathered together with God of A.
104 6 ye seed of Abraham his servant; ye
9 which he made to Abraham: and his oath
42 he had spoken to his servant Abraham
Eccu 44 20 A. was the great father of a multitude
24 for the sake of Abraham his father. The
Isa 29 22 of Jacob, he that redeemed Abraham
41 8 the seed of Abraham, my friend, in whom
51 2 look unto Abraham your father and to
63 16 Abraham hath not known us, and Israel
Jer 33 26 to be rulers of the seed of Abraham
Bar 2 34 with an oath to their fathers, A., Isaac
Eze 33 24 Abraham was one, and he inherited the
Dan 3 35 for the sake of Abraham thy beloved
Mich 7 20 truth to Jacob, the mercy to Abraham
1 Ma 2 52 was not Abraham found faithful in
12 21 that they are of the stock of Abraham
2 Ma 1 2 his covenant that he made with Abraham
Mat 1 1 the son of David, the son of Abraham
2 Abraham begot Isaac. And Isaac begot
17 generations from Abraham to David are
3 9 we have A. for our father. Luke 3:8
9 able to raise up children to A. Luke 3:8
8 11 shall sit down with Abraham and Isaac
22 32 I am the God of A. Mark 12:26; Acts 7:32
Luke 1 55 as he spoke to our fathers, to A. and
73 oath which he swore to A. our father
3 34 Isaac who was of Abraham, who was of
13 16 ought not this daughter of Abraham whom
28 when you shall see A. and Isaac and
16 23 he saw Abraham afar off, and Lazarus
24 father Abraham, have mercy on me, and
25 A. said to him: Son, remember that
29 A. said to him: They have Moses and the
30 father Abraham: but if one went to them
19 9 house, because he also is a son of A.
20 37 he called the Lord, the God of Abraham
John 8 33 we are the seed of Abraham, and we have
37 I know that you are the children of A.
39 and said to him: A. is our father
39 you be children of A., do works of A.
40 this Abraham did not. You do the works
52 Abraham is dead, and the prophets: and
53 art thou greater than our father A.
56 A. your father rejoiced that he might
57 years old, and hast thou seen Abraham
58 before Abraham was made, I am. They
Acts 3 13 God of A. . . . hath glorified his Son
25 saying to A.: And in thy seed shall all
7 2 God of glory appeared to our father A.
16 the sepulcher that Abraham bought for
17 near, which God had promised to Abraham
13 26 children of the stock of Abraham, and
Rom 4 1 shall we say then that A. hath found
2 if Abraham were justified by works
3 A. believed God. Gal 3:6; James 2:23
9 unto A. faith was reputed to justice
12 in the uncircumcision of our father A.
13 was the promise to A. or to his seed
16 which is of the faith of Abraham, who
9 7 all they that are the seed of Abraham
11 1 am an Israelite of the seed of Abraham
2 C 11 22 they are the seed of Abraham: so am I
Gal 3 7 the same are the children of Abraham
8 told unto A. before: In thee shall all
9 shall be blessed with faithful Abraham
14 that the blessing of Abraham might come
16 to Abraham were the promises made and
18 but God gave it to Abraham by promise
29 then are you the seed of Abraham, heirs
4 22 that Abraham had two sons: the one by
Heb 2 16 of the seed of Abraham he taketh hold
6 13 God making promise to Abraham, because
7 1 met A. returning from the slaughter
2 to whom Abraham divided the tithes
4 to whom A. the patriarch gave tithes
5 also came out of the loins of Abraham
6 received tithes of A. and blessed him
9 who received tithes, paid tithes in A.
11 8 he that is called Abraham obeyed to
17 A. when he was tried, offered Isaac
James 2 21 was not A. our father justified by
1 P 3 6 as Sara obeyed A., calling him lord
Abraham's Gen 18 19 for A. sake the Lord may
Gen 20 18 on account of Sara, Abraham's wife
22 23 did Melcha bear to Nachor A. brother
24 52 which when Abraham's servant heard
59 and her nurse and Abraham's servant
25 7 and the days of A. life were 175 years
26 24 thy seed for my servant A. sake
28 9 the daughter of Ismael, Abraham's son
1 Pa 1 32 sons of Cetura, Abraham's concubine
Luke 16 22 by the angels into Abraham's bosom
Abram Gen 11 26 Thare . . . begot A. and Nachor. 27
Gen 11 29 and Abram and Nachor married wives
31 Thare took Abram, his son, and Lot the
31 Sarai . . . the wife of Abram his son
12 1 the Lord said to Abram: Go forth out
4 A. went out as the Lord had commanded
4 Abram was 75 years old when he went
6 Abram passed through the country into
7 the Lord appeared to Abram and said to
9 and Abram went forward, going and
10 Abram went down into Egypt to sojourn
14 and when Abram was come into Egypt the
16 they used Abram well for her sake. And
18 Pharao called Abram and said to him
20 gave his men orders concerning Abram
13 1 Abram went up out of Egypt, he and his
5 but Lot also, who was with Abram, had
7 strife between the herdsmen of Abram
8 Abram therefore said to Lot: Let there
12 Abram dwelt in the land of Chanaan; and
14 Lord said to Abram, after Lot was
18 Abram removing his tent came and dwelt
14 13 one that had escaped told Abram the
13 for these had made league with Abram
14 which when Abram had heard, to wit, that
19 blessed be Abram by the most high God
21 the king of Sodom said to Abram: Give
23 lest thou say I have enriched Abram
15 1 the word of the Lord came to Abram by
1 fear not, Abram, I am thy protector
2 Abram said: Lord God, what wilt thou
3 Abram added: But to me thou hast not
6 Abram believed God, and it was reputed
11 and Abram drove them away. And when the
12 a deep sleep fell upon Abram, and a

18 God made a covenant with Abram, saying
16 1 Sarai, the wife of Abram, had brought
5 Sarai said to Abram: Thou dost unjustly
6 and Abram made answer and said to her
15 Agar brought forth a son to Abram: who
16 Abram was fourscore and six years old
17 3 Abram fell flat on his face. And God
5 shall thy name be called any more Abram
1 Pa 1 27 Abram, this is Abraham. And the sons of
2 Es 9 7 Lord God, art he who chosest Abram
Abram's Gen 11 29 the name of A. wife was Sarai
Gen 12 17 grievous stripes for Sarai A. wife
14 12 Lot also, the son of Abram's brother
Abran Josu 19 28 to A. and Rohob and Hamon and
abridge 2 Ma 2 24 have attempted to a. in one book
abridged Isa 10 22 the consumption abridged shall
abridging 2 Ma 2 27 in undertaking this work of a.
2 Ma 10 10 abridging the account of the evils that
abridgment Isa 10 23 make a consumption and an a.
2 Ma 2 32 to be granted to him that maketh an a.
abroad Gen 4 8 his brother: Let us go forth abroad
Gen 10 18 of the Chanaanites were spread abroad
11 4 before we be scattered abroad into all
9 the Lord scattered them abroad upon the
15 5 brought him [Abram] forth abroad and
27 30 Jacob being now gone out abroad, Esau
28 14 thou shalt spread abroad to the west
45 16 fame was abroad in the king's court
Exod 9 19 all things that shall be found abroad
12 19 if he rise again and walk abroad upon
29 14 and the dung, thou shalt burn abroad
Lev 18 9 whether born at home or abroad. Thou
Josu 2 20 betray us and utter this word abroad
Judg 12 9 daughters, whom he sent abroad, and
2 K 22 43 I shall crush them and spread them a.
3 K 2 42 walk abroad any whither, know that thou
1 Pa 14 13 Philistines . . . spread themselves a.
26 29 for the business abroad over Israel to
2 Pa 26 8 his name was spread abroad even to the
15 his name went forth far abroad, for
29 16 carried it out abroad to the torrent
31 5 when it was noised abroad in the ears
2 Es 1 8 I will scatter you a. among the nations
Tob 14 6 our brethren that are scattered abroad
Job 4 11 the young lions are scattered abroad
Ps 44 3 grace is poured abroad in thy lips
58 16 they shall be scattered abroad to eat
Prov 5 16 let thy fountains be conveyed abroad
7 12 now abroad, now in the streets, now
23 32 will spread a. poison like a basilisk
29 18 the people shall be scattered abroad
Wisd 2 3 our spirit shall be poured abroad as
5 15 a smoke that is scattered a. by the
Eccu 25 34 to a wicked woman liberty to gad abroad
29 28 than sumptuous cheer abroad in another
29 and hear the reproach of going abroad
47 17 thy name went abroad to the islands
Isa 3 9 they have proclaimed abroad their sin
24 1 scatter abroad the inhabitants thereof
42 2 neither shall his voice be heard abroad
Jer 6 11 pour it out upon the child abroad and
8 2 shall spread them abroad to the sun
50 11 you are spread abroad as calves upon
Lam 1 20 abroad the sword destroyeth, and at
Eze 34 21 horns, till they were scattered abroad
Haba 1 8 their horsemen shall be spread abroad
1 Ma 11 4 and the bodies that were cast abroad
2 Ma 4 39 the rumor of it was spread abroad
8 7 fame of his valor was spread abroad
Mat 9 26 the fame hereof went abroad into all
31 spread his fame abroad into all that
Mark 1 45 publish and to blare abroad the word
4 22 secret, but that it may come abroad
Luke 1 65 all these things were noised abroad
15 13 went a. into a far country and there
20 9 he was abroad for a long time. And at
Acts 2 6 when this was noised a. the multitude
2 C 9 9 it is written: He hath dispersed abroad
James 1 1 the 12 tribes which are scattered a.
Absalom 2 K 3 3 the third A. the son of Maacha
2 K 13 1 Amnon . . . loved the sister of Absalom
4 Thamar the sister of my brother A.
20 Absalom her brother said to her: Hath
20 pining away in the house of Absalom
22 but Absalom spoke not to Amnon neither
22 for Absalom hated Amnon because he had
23 and A. invited all the king's sons
25 the king said to Absalom: Nay, my son
26 Absalom said: If thou wilt not come
27 Absalom pressed him so that he let
27 and Absalom made a feast as it were
28 and Absalom had commanded his servants
29 servants of Absalom did to Amnon as
Absalom had commanded
30 A. hath slain all the king's sons
32 he was appointed by the mouth of A.
34 but Absalom fled away: and the young
37 but Absalom fled and went to Tholomai
38 king David ceased to pursue after A.
14 1 the king's heart was turned to Absalom
21 fetch back the boy Absalom. And Joab
23 and brought Absalom to Jerusalem. But
24 so Absalom returned into his house and
25 so exceedingly beautiful as Absalom
27 there were born to Absalom three sons
28 Absalom dwelt two years in Jerusalem
30 servants of A. set the corn on fire
30 servants of Absalom have set on fire
31 Joab arose and came to Absalom to his
32 Absalom answered Joab: I sent to thee
33 Absalom was called for, and he went in
33 before him: and the king kissed Absalom
15 1 Absalom made himself chariots and
2 Absalom rising up early stood by the
2 Absalom called him to him and said: Of
3 Absalom answered him: Thy words seem
3 Absalom said: O that they would make
7 Absalom said to king David: Let me go
10 Absalom sent spies into all the tribes
10 say ye: Absalom reigneth in Hebron
11 went with Absalom two hundred men out
12 Absalom also sent for Achitophel the
12 the people . . . increased with Absalom
13 with their whole heart followeth A.
14 not escape else from the face of A.
31 also was in the conspiracy with Absalom
34 wilt say to Absalom: I am thy servant
37 city, and Absalom came into Jerusalem
16 8 the kingdom into the hand of Absalom
15 Absalom and all his people came into
16 when Chusai . . . was come to Absalom
17 Absalom said to him: Is this thy
18 Chusai answered Absalom: Nay, for I
20 Absalom said to Achitophel: Consult
21 Achitophel said to Absalom: Go in to
22 so they spread a tent for Absalom on
23 and when he [Achitophel] was with A.
17 1 Achitophel said to A.: I will choose
4 and his saying pleased Absalom and all
5 Absalom said: Call Chusai the Arachite
6 Chusai was come to A., A. said to him
7 Chusai said to Absalom: The counsel
9 slaughter among people that followed A.
14 Absalom and all the men of Israel
14 the Lord might bring evil upon Absalom
15 thus did Achitophel counsel Absalom

18 certain boy saw them and told Absalom
24 Absalom passed over the Jordan, he and
25 Absalom appointed Amasa in Joab's stead
26 and Israel camped with Absalom in the
18 5 saying: Save me the boy Absalom. 12
5 charge to all the princes concerning A.
9 that Absalom met the servants of David
10 I saw Absalom hanging upon an oak. And
14 thrust them into the heart of Absalom
17 they took Absalom and cast him into a
18 Absalom had reared up for himself in
18 it is called the hand of Absalom to
29 is the young man Absalom safe. 32
33 my son A., A. my son: would to God
33 die for thee, A., my son, my son A.
19 4 my son Absalom, O Absalom my son. Then
6 if Absalom had lived, and all we had
9 is fled out of the land for Absalom
10 Absalom, whom we anointed over us, is
20 6 do us more harm than did A.: take thou
3 K 1 6 beautiful, next in birth after Absalom
2 7 when I fled from the face of Absalom
1 Pa 3 2 the third Absalom the son of Maacha
2 Pa 11 20 Maacha the daughter of Absalom. 21
Ps 3 1 fled from the face of his son Absalom
142 1 David when his son Absalom pursued him
1 Ma 11 70 Mathathias the son of Absalom and
13 11 he sent Jonathan the son of Absalom
Absalom's 2 K 17 20 when A. servants were come
absence Luke 22 6 him in the a. of the multitude
Phil 2 12 only, but much more now in my absence
absent Gen 34 5 his sons being a. and employed in
Deut 29 15 all that are present and that are a.
Wisd 11 12 whether absent or present, they were
14 17 honor as present, him that was absent
1 C 5 3 absent in body but present in spirit
2 C 5 6 in the body we are absent from the Lord
8 will to be absent rather from the body
9 we labor, whether absent or present
10 1 but being absent, am bold toward you
11 as we are in word by epistles when a.
13 2 and foretell as present and now absent
10 I write these things, being absent
Phil 1 27 see you or, being a., may hear of you
Col 2 5 though I be absent in body, yet in
absolute Wisd 12 17 not believe thee to be a. in
absolutely 1 C 5 1 it is absolutely heard that
abstain Num 6 3 they shall abstain from all sin
Tob 1 10 to fear God and to abstain from all sin
Eccu 3 32 a wise heart . . . will abstain from sins
Acts 15 29 abstain from things sacrificed to idols
1 Th 4 3 that you should a. from fornication
1 Tim 4 3 to abstain from meats, which God hath
abstaineth Wisd 2 16 he a. from our ways as from
abstinence Num 30 14 to afflict her soul by a.
2 P 1 6 in knowledge, a.: and in a., patience
abuilding 1 Pa 3 20 when the ark was abuilding
abundance Gen 26 33 whereupon he called it A.
Gen 27 28 God give thee . . . abundance of corn
41 30 the abundance before shall be forgotten
48 all the a. of grain was laid up in
49 there was so great abundance of wheat
Exod 8 3 shall bring forth abundance of frogs
Num 20 11 came forth water in great abundance
Deut 8 9 eat thy bread and enjoy abundance of
28 47 gladness of heart for the a. of all
33 19 shall suck as milk the a. of the sea
23 Nephtali shall enjoy abundance, and
Judg 3 22 was closed up with the abundance of
1 K 1 16 out of the abundance of my sorrow and
3 K 10 10 no more such abundance of spices or
18 41 there is a sound of abundance of rain
1 Pa 12 40 oil and oxen and sheep in abundance
22 3 David prepared in abundance iron for
14 the abundance surpasseth all account
15 hast also workmen in abundance, hewers
29 2 and marble of Paros in great abundance
2 Pa 2 9 to provide me timber in abundance. For
9 1 abundance of gold and precious stones
9 talents of gold and spices in great a.
11 23 he gave them provisions in abundance
14 13 and they took abundance of spoils
18 2 killed sheep and oxen in abundance for
31 5 offered in abundance the firstfruits
10 have been filled, and abundance is left
32 4 should come and find a. of water. He
2 Es 9 25 and oliveyards and fruit trees in a.
Tob 11 18 an abundance of money of his wife's
Jdth 2 8 sufficient for the armies in abundance
10 of the king's house in great abundance
Esth 1 7 wine also in a. and of the best was
Job 5 26 thou shalt enter into the grave in a.
38 24 that an a. of waters may cover thee
Ps 29 7 in my abundance I said: I shall never
32 17 he be saved by the a. of his strength
36 11 and shall delight in a. of peace. The
51 9 trusted in the abundance of his riches
71 7 abundance of peace, till the moon be
77 25 he sent them provisions in abundance
121 6 and abundance for them that love thee
7 strength: and abundance in thy towers
144 7 the memory of the a. of thy sweetness
Prov 1 33 shall enjoy abundance without fear
3 10 and thy barns shall be filled with a.
14 23 in much work there shall be abundance
21 5 the industrious always bring forth a.
Eccu 18 25 remember poverty in the time of a. and
51 36 and possess abundance of gold by her
Isa 7 22 for the a. of milk he shall eat butter
66 11 delights from the a. of her glory
Eze 16 49 pride, fulness of bread, and abundance
47 9 and there shall be fishes in abundance
Dan 8 25 in the a. of all things he shall kill
Zach 14 14 and silver and garments in great a.
Mala 3 10 and pour you out a blessing even to a.
1 Ma 3 41 they took silver and gold in a., and
15 26 and gold and abundance of furniture
16 11 he had abundance of silver and gold
Mat 12 34 out of the a. of the heart. Luke 6:45
Mark 12 44 they did cast in of their abundance
Luke 12 15 doth not consist in the a. of things
21 4 have of their abundance cast into the
Rom 5 17 more they who receive a. of grace
15 29 abundance of the blessing of the gospel
2 C 8 2 they have had abundance of joy; and
14 let your a. supply their want that their a. also may supply your want
20 lest any man should blame us in this a.
James 1 21 all uncleanness and a. of naughtiness
abundant Prov 15 5 in a. justice there is the
Wisd 11 8 thou gavest to thine abundant water
1 C 12 23 about these we put more a. honor; and
23 parts have more abundant comeliness
24 that which wanted the more a. honor
Eph 2 7 the abundant riches of his grace in
abundantly 1 Pa 29 21 everything prescribed most a.
Tob 4 9 if thou have much, give abundantly
Job 37 10 and again the waters are poured out a.
Ps 30 10 will repay them a. that act proudly
Eccu 24 42 I will water abundantly the fruits of
John 10 10 life and may have it more abundantly
1 C 15 10 I have labored more a. than all they
2 C 1 12 and more abundantly towards you. For
2 4 the charity I have more a. towards you
7 13 we did the more abundantly rejoice for
15 and his bowels are more a. towards you

10 15 magnified in you according to our rule a.
Gal 1 14 more a. zealous for the traditions of
Eph 3 20 to do all things more a. than we desire
Col 3 16 word of Christ dwell in you abundantly
1 Th 2 17 hastened the more a. to see your face
3 10 more a. praying that we may see your
5 13 esteem them more abundantly in charity
1 Tim 6 17 who giveth us a. all things to enjoy
Titus 3 6 whom he hath poured forth upon us a.
Heb 6 17 meaning more a. to show to the heirs
James 1 5 God who giveth to all men abundantly
2 P 1 11 entrance shall be ministered to you a.
abuse Gen 19 8 a. you them as it shall please you
Gen 34 31 should they abuse our sister as a
39 14 hath brought in a Hebrew to abuse us
17 came to me to abuse me. And when he
Judg 19 22 that we may abuse him. And the old man
Ps 30 19 against the just with pride and abuse
Eccu 25 36 thy flesh, lest she always abuse thee
26 13 finding an opportunity she a. herself
Jer 38 19 their hands, and they should abuse me
Bar 6 27 their priests sell and abuse: in like
Dan 11 7 he shall abuse them and shall prevail
1 C 9 18 that I abuse not my power in the gospel
abused Judg 19 25 they had a. her all the night
Judg 20 5 a. my wife with an incredible fury
Lam 5 13 they abused the young men indecently
Eze 22 7 they have abused father and mother in
1 Ma 7 34 despised them and abused them: and he
9 26 took vengeance of them and abused them
2 Ma 8 17 which had been shamefully abused
abuses 2 Ma 14 42 to suffer abuses unbecoming his
abuseth Job 24 23 and he abuseth it unto pride
abyss Eccu 1 2 earth and the depth of the abyss
Luke 8 31 not command them to go into the abyss
Apoc 11 7 the beast that ascendeth out of the a.
Acan Gen 36 27 Balaan and Zavan and Acan. And
Accain Josu 15 57 Accain, Gabaa, and Thamna: ten
Accaron Josu 13 3 unto borders of A. northward
Josu 15 11 northward to a part of Accaron at the
45 Accaron with the towns and villages
46 from Accaron even to the sea: all
Judg 1 18 Ascalon and Accaron with their confines
1 K 5 10 they sent the ark of God into Accaron
10 when the ark of God was come into A.
6 16 and they returned to A. the same day
17 for Accaron one: and the golden mice
7 14 restored to Israel, from A. to Geth
17 52 the valley and to the gates of Accaron
52 as far as Geth and as far as Accaron
4 K 1 2 Beelzebub, the god of A. 3, 6, 16
Jer 25 20 Ascalon and Gaza and Accaron and the
Amos 1 8 I will turn my hand against Accaron
Soph 2 4 Accaron shall be rooted up. Woe to you
Zach 9 5 and A. because her hope is confounded
7 in Juda, and Accaron as a Jebusite
1 Ma 10 89 he gave him A. and all the borders
Accaronites Josu 13 3 the Gethites and the A.
1 K 5 10 the Accaronites cried out, saying
accept Exod 22 11 owner shall accept of the oath
Deut 16 19 thou shalt not accept person nor gifts
1 K 26 19 against me let him accept of sacrifice
Tob 12 4 that he would vouchsafe to accept. 5
Job 13 8 do you accept his person, and do you
10 because in secret you accept his person
32 21 I will not accept the person of man
42 8 pray for you: his face I will accept
Ps 50 21 shalt thou a. the sacrifice of justice
81 2 and accept the persons of the wicked
Prov 6 35 nor will he a. for satisfaction ever
18 5 not good to a. the person of the wicked
Eccu 4 26 accept no person against thy own person
7 11 high God, he will not a. thy offerings
35 16 Lord will not accept any person against
42 1 and accept no person to sin thereby
Eze 20 41 I will accept of you for an odor of
Mala 1 13 shall I accept it at your hands, saith
2 13 neither do I accept any atonement at
Acts 24 3 we accept it always and in all places
acceptable Lev 1 4 and it shall be acceptable and
Lev 4 7 incense most acceptable to the Lord
22 20 not offer it, neither shall it be a.
21 it without blemish, that it may be a.
23 11 that it may be acceptable for you, and
Deut 33 24 let him be acceptable to his brethren
1 K 18 5 he was a. in the eyes of all the people
Tob 12 13 because thou wast acceptable to God
14 17 so that they were acceptable both to
Jdth 9 16 have the proud been a. to thee: but
10 16 thou wilt be most acceptable to his
Job 21 33 hath been a. to the gravel of Cocytus
Ps 103 34 let my speech be acceptable to him
111 5 a. is the man that showeth mercy and
118 108 offerings of my mouth make a., O Lord
Prov 10 32 lips of the just consider what is a.
14 35 wise servant is acceptable to the king
15 8 the vows of the just are acceptable
16 5 this is more a. with God than to offer
17 8 that expecteth, is a most a. jewel
Wisd 3 14 most acceptable lot in the temple of
9 10 that I may know what is a. with thee
12 so shall my works be acceptable and
Eccu 2 5 a. men in the furnace of humiliation
15 16 perform a. fidelity forever, they shall
34 21 the mockeries of the unjust are not a.
35 9 sacrifice of the just is acceptable
Isa 49 8 in an a. time I have heard thee and
58 5 fast, and a day acceptable to the Lord
60 7 they shall be offered upon my a. altar
61 2 to proclaim the a. year of the Lord
Jer 6 20 your holocausts are not acceptable nor
Dan 4 24 let my counsel be acceptable to thee
Agge 1 8 the house: and it shall be a. to me
1 Ma 6 60 proposal was a. in the sight of the
Luke 4 19 preach the acceptable year of the Lord
Acts 7 20 [Moses] was acceptable to God: who was
10 35 he that . . . worketh justice is a. to
Rom 12 2 the a. and the perfect will of God
15 16 oblation of the Gentiles may be made a.
31 the oblation of my service may be a.
2 C 6 2 behold, now is the acceptable time
Phil 4 18 an a. sacrifice, pleasing to God. And
1 Tim 2 3 this is good and a. in the sight of God
5 4 this is acceptable before God. But she
Titus 2 14 might cleanse to himself a people a.
1 P 2 5 offer up spiritual sacrifices a. to God
acceptation 1 Tim 1 15 and worthy of all a. 4:9
accepted Job 42 9 and the Lord a. the face of Job
Eccu 35 20 that adoreth God with joy, shall be a.
Jer 37 19 let my petition be a. in thy sight: and
Dan 3 39 and humble spirit let us be accepted
Mala 2 9 and have accepted persons in the law
1 Ma 6 60 make peace: and they accepted of it
9 71 and he accepted it willingly and did
14 47 and Simon accepted thereof and was
Luke 4 24 no prophet is a. in his own country
2 C 6 2 in an a. time have I heard thee: and
8 12 if the will be forward, it is accepted
17 indeed he [Titus] a. the exhortation
accepteth Deut 10 17 a. no person nor taketh
Job 34 19 who a. not the persons of princes
accepting Heb 11 35 were racked not a. deliverance
Acces 2 K 23 26 Hira the son of Acces. 1 Pa 27:9
1 Pa 11 28 Ira the son of Acces a Thesuite
access Job 39 28 stony hills, where there is no a.
2 Ma 14 3 no safety for him, nor a. to the altar

Rom 5 2 we have a. through faith into this
Eph 2 18 by him we have access . . . to the Father
3 12 in whom we have boldness and access
accessible 1 K 24 3 which are a. only to wild
Accho Judg 1 31 destroyed not inhabitants of A.
acclamation Acts 12 22 the people made acclamation
acclamations 1 Ma 5 64 to them with joyful a. Then
accompanied Gen 35 3 a. me in my journey. So they
Acts 10 23 some of the brethren from Joppe a. him
20 4 there a. him Sopater the son of Pyrrhus
accompany Gen 33 12 I will a. thee in thy journey
Gen 33 15 may stay to accompany thee in the way
4 K 4 16 this same hour, if life a., thou shalt
Tob 5 21 in your way and his angel a. you
27 that the good angel of God doth a. him
2 Ma 2 4 and the ark should accompany him till
accompanying Gen 18 10 will return . . . life a. 14
accomplish Gen 11 6 till they a. them in deed
Exod 36 8 to a. the work of the tabernacle, made
Lev 16 27 to accomplish the atonement, they shall
Num 30 12 shall a. whatsoever she had promised
32 24 and accomplish what you have promised
Deut 9 5 that the Lord might a. his word which
2 Es 5 13 every man that shall not a. this word
Job 5 12 hands cannot a. what they had begun
36 11 shall accomplish their days in good
Jer 11 5 that I may a. the oath which I swore
23 20 and till he a. the thought of his heart
Eze 5 13 I will a. my fury and will cause my
6 12 and I will a. my indignation upon them
7 8 I will accomplish my anger in thee: and
13 15 I will a. my wrath upon the wall and
20 8 and a. my wrath against them in the
21 to accomplish my wrath in them in the
Dan 2 10 that can a. thy word, O king, neither
2 Ma 11 17 requested that I would a. those things
15 5 he prevailed not to a. his design. So
Luke 9 31 spoke of his decease that he should a.
Rom 7 18 to a. that which is good, I find not
Phil 2 13 in you both to will and to accomplish
1 Th 3 10 may a. those things that are wanting
accomplished Gen 28 15 till I shall have a. all
Lev 8 34 the rite of the sacrifice might be a.
Num 8 25 have a. the fiftieth year of their age
28 26 after the weeks are a., you shall offer
Josu 4 10 till all things were a. which the Lord
11 15 a. all: he left not one thing undone
Ruth 3 18 until we have a. what he hath said
3 K 8 15 with his own hands hath accomplished
2 Pa 6 4 who hath a. in deed that which he spoke
10 the Lord therefore hath a. his word
15 hast a. in fact what thou hast spoken
29 36 because the ministry of the Lord was a.
34 16 hath committed to thy servants is a.
35 16 all the service of the Lord was duly a.
1 Es 9 1 after these things were a., the princes
Jdth 6 5 imaginest these my words cannot be a.
Prov 13 19 the desire that is a., delighteth the
Wisd 10 10 and accomplished his labors. In the
Jer 25 34 slaughter and your dispersion are a.
29 10 the seventy years shall begin to be a.
39 16 they shall be a. in thy sight in that
44 29 that my words shall be accomplished
Lam 4 11 the Lord hath accomplished his wrath
22 thy iniquity is a., O daughter of Sion
Eze 4 6 and when thou hast a. this, thou shalt
5 13 when I shall have a. my indignation
12 28 word that I shall speak shall be a.
Dan 9 2 that seventy years should be a. of the
10 3 till the days of three weeks were a.
11 36 and shall prosper till the wrath be a.
12 7 band of the holy people shall be a.
Mark 1 15 the time is accomplished, and the
Luke 1 1 the things that have been a. among us
23 after the days of his office were a.
45 those things shall be a. that were
2 6 her days were accomplished, that she
21 after eight days were a. that the child
22 days of her purification . . . were a.
12 50 and how am I straitened until it be a.
18 31 things shall be a. which were written
John 7 8 because my time is not accomplished
19 28 knowing that all things were now a.
Acts 2 1 and when the days of Pentecost were a.
14 25 unto the work which they accomplished
Rom 15 28 when I shall have accomplished this
2 Tim 4 17 by me the preaching may be accomplished
2 P 1 2 grace to you and peace be accomplished
accomplishing Luke 9 51 of his assumption were a.
Heb 6 11 the accomplishing of hope unto the end
9 6 accomplishing the offices of sacrifices
accomplishment Acts 21 26 notice of the a. of the
accord Exod 25 2 that offereth of his own accord
Exod 35 26 hair, giving all of their own accord
36 2 such as of their own accord had offered
Lev 7 16 or of his own accord offer a sacrifice
22 18 or offering of his own accord. 21
25 11 that grow in the field of their own a.
4 K 12 4 which of their own accord and of their
1 Es 1 6 they had offered on their own accord
7 16 priests shall offer of their own accord
Jdth 4 9 cried to the Lord . . . with one accord
6 14 prayers with one accord to the Lord
7 4 praying with one accord, that the God
15 that we may of our own accord yield
10 12 would not of their own accord yield
Wisd 10 20 and they praised with one accord thy
2 Ma 6 4 women thrust themselves of their accord
Acts 2 46 daily with one accord in the temple
4 24 with one a. lifted up their voice to
5 12 all with one accord in Solomon's porch
7 56 and with one a. ran violently upon him
8 6 the people with one accord were attentive
12 20 but they with one a. came to him and
18 12 Jews with one accord rose up against Paul
19 29 rushed with one accord into the theater
Phil 2 2 having the same charity, being of one a.
according Wisd 18 10 sounded an ill according cry
Accos 1 Pa 24 10 the seventh to Accos, the eighth
1 Es 2 61 the children of Accos. 2 Es 7:63
account Gen 25 34 making little a. of having sold
Num 4 32 shall receive by account all the vessels
Deut 1 37 was angry with me also on your account
3 26 Lord was angry with me on your account
Josu 20 6 to give an account of his fact, and
22 11 messengers had brought them an account
2 K 20 12 who passed might not stop on his a.
3 K 10 21 nor was any account made of it in days
1 Pa 22 14 the abundance surpasseth all account
2 Pa 9 20 no account was made of silver in those
Tob 5 25 that we might account it as riches that
Job 39 24 make account when the noise of trumpet
Ps 68 7 them not be confounded on my account
143 3 that thou makest account of him? Man
Ecce 7 28 that I might find out the account
Bar 6 6 will demand an account of your souls
Dan 6 2 governors might give an a. to them
11 37 he shall make no account of the God
1 Ma 6 9 and he made account that he should die
10 42 received from the account of the holy
45 shall be given out of the king's a.
13 15 money that he owed in the king's a.
2 Ma 3 6 not belong to the a. of the sacrifices
8 35 of whom he had made no account, laying
9 15 not account worthy to be so much as
10 10 abridging the a. of the evils that

Mat 12 36 they shall render an account for it
18 23 who would take account of his servants
24 when he had begun to take the account
Luke 16 2 give an account of thy stewardship
Acts 19 40 no man guilty of whom we may give a.
22 1 hear ye the account which I now give
Rom 3 28 we a. a man to be justified by faith
14 13 every one of us shall render a. to God
1 C 4 1 let a man so account of us as of the
Phil 4 17 the fruit that may abound to your a.
Philem 18 in thy debt, put that to my account
Heb 13 17 watch as being to render an account
James 5 11 we a. them blessed who have endured
1 P 4 5 who shall render account to him, who
2 P 3 15 a. longsuffering of our Lord, salvation
accounted Lev 13 49 it shall be a. the leprosy, and
Deut 2 20 it was accounted a land of giants: and
2 K 18 3 thou alone art accounted for 10,000
1 Pa 5 1 he was not accounted for the firstborn
2 the first birthright was a. to Joseph
2 Pa 26 18 this thing shall not be a. to thy glory
Ps 118 119 I have a. all the sinners of the earth
Bar 3 36 no other be a. of in comparison of him
Osee 8 12 laws, which have been a. as foreign
1 Ma 10 38 let them be accounted with Judea: that
Luke 20 35 they that shall be accounted worthy of
21 36 you may be accounted worthy to escape
Acts 5 41 that they were a. worthy to suffer
Rom 8 36 we are a. as sheep for the slaughter
9 8 children of the promise are a. for the
accounting Heb 11 19 a. that God is able for the
accounts 1 Ma 10 40 silver, out of the king's a.
Accub 1 Pa 3 24 sons of Elioenai . . . Accub and
1 Pa 9 17 the porters were Sellum and Accub and
1 Es 2 42 the children of Accub. 45; 2 Es 7:46
11 19 and the porters, Accub, Telmon and
12 25 Accub, were keepers of the gates and of
accursed Num 24 9 curseth thee shall be reckoned a.
Deut 21 23 he is accursed of God that hangeth on
Eccu 28 15 and the double-tongued is accursed: for
Isa 65 20 being a hundred years old shall be a.
John 7 49 that knoweth not God, are accursed
Accus 2 Es 3 3 the son of Urias the son of Accus
accusation Gen 43 18 may bring upon us a false a.
1 Es 4 6 an a. against the inhabitants of Juda
7 letter of accusation was written in
18 the accusation which you have sent to
5 5 give satisfaction concerning that a.
Eccu 26 6 the accusation of a city, and the
2 Ma 4 43 accusation was laid against Menelaus
Luke 6 7 they might find accusation against him
John 18 29 what a. bring you against this man
Acts 25 18 they brought no a. of things which I
1 Tim 5 19 against a priest receive not an a. but
accusations 2 Ma 4 47 acquitted by him of the a.
2 Ma 14 27 provoked with this man's accusations
accuse Gen 30 33 goats, shall accuse me of theft
Prov 30 10 accuse not a servant to his master
Isa 1 18 then come and accuse me, saith the
Wisd 12 12 who shall accuse thee, if the nations
Eccu 46 22 of any man and no man did accuse him
1 Ma 10 61 themselves against him to accuse him
Mat 12 10 that they might accuse him. Mark 3:2
Mark 15 4 behold in how many things they a. thee
Luke 11 54 lying in wait . . . that they might a. him
23 2 they began to accuse him, saying: We
14 those things wherein you accuse him
John 5 45 not that I will a. you to the Father
8 6 tempting him that they might a. him
Acts 19 38 proconsuls: let them accuse one another
24 2 Tertullus began to accuse him, saying
8 all these things whereof we accuse him
13 the things whereof they now accuse me
19 to be present before thee and to a. if
25 5 go down with me and a. him if there be
11 of these things whereof they accuse me
28 19 I had anything to accuse my nation of
Rom 8 33 who shall a. against the elect of God
1 P 3 16 who falsely a. your good conversation
accused Gen 37 2 a. his brethren to his father
2 K 19 27 he hath also a. me thy servant to thee
Ecce 11 8 the things past shall be a. of vanity
Wisd 10 14 them to be liars that had accused him
Dan 3 8 Chaldeans came and accused the Jews
6 24 men were brought that had accused Daniel
1 Ma 7 6 they accused the people to the king
25 king, and accused them of many crimes
2 Ma 6 10 women were a. to have circumcised their
10 13 being accused for this to Eupator by
21 a. those men that they had sold their
14 37 now Razias . . . was accused to Nicanor
Mat 27 12 when he was a. by the chief priests and
Mark 15 3 the chief priests a. him in many things
Luke 16 1 was a. unto him, that he had wasted his
John 8 10 where are they that accused thee? Hath
Acts 22 30 for what cause he was a. by the Jews
23 29 whom I found to be accused concerning
25 16 who is a. have his accusers present
26 2 the things whereof I am a. by the Jews
7 for which hope, O king, I am accused
Titus 1 6 children not accused of riot or unruly
Apoc 12 10 who a. them before our God day and
accuser Prov 18 17 the just is first a. of himself
2 Ma 4 5 not to be an accuser of his countrymen
Apoc 12 10 the a. of our brethren is cast forth
accusers 1 Ma 10 64 so when his a. saw his glory
Acts 23 30 signifying also to his accusers to
35 hear thee, said he, when thy a. come
24 8 commanding his a. to come to thee: of
25 16 who is accused have his a. present
18 when the a. stood up, they brought no
Titus 2 3 not false a., not given to much wine
accuseth John 5 45 there is one that a. you, Moses
accusing Deut 19 16 a. him of transgression, both
Eccu 41 7 among the dead there is no a. of life
Luke 23 10 scribes stood by, earnestly accusing
Rom 2 15 a. or also defending one another, in
accustomed Exod 5 18 shall deliver the a. number
Num 22 30 on which thou hast been always a. to
29 6 holocaust with the a. libations. With
Judg 2 19 by which they were accustomed to walk
8 24 were a. to wear golden earlets. They
1 K 17 39 he [David] was not accustomed to it
2 Pa 9 14 the merchants were accustomed to bring
23 8 which were a. to succeed one another
Eccu 23 9 let not my mouth be a. to swearing. 17
20 the man that is a. to opprobrious words
Jer 2 24 a wild ass a. to the wilderness in the
48 33 not sing the accustomed cheerful tune
Dan 3 19 than it had been a. to be heated. And
6 10 he had been accustomed to do before
2 Ma 14 31 that were offering the a. sacrifices
Mat 27 15 the governor was a. to release to the
Mark 10 1 as he was a., he taught them again
Heb 10 25 forsaking our assembly, as some are a.
Achab 3 K 16 28 A. his son reigned in his stead
3 K 16 29 A. the son of Amri reigned over Israel
30 Achab the son of Amri did evil in the
33 Achab did more to provoke the Lord
17 1 Elias the Thesbite . . . said to Achab
18 1 go show thyself to Achab that I may
2 Elias went to show himself to Achab
3 Achab called Abdias the governor of his
5 Achab said to Abdias: Go into the land
6 Achab went one way, and Abdias another
9 me thy servant into the hand of Achab

12 I shall go in and tell Achab, and he
16 Abdias therefore went to meet Achab
16 and Achab came to meet Elias. And when
20 Achab sent to all the children of Israel
41 Elias said to Achab: Go up, eat and
42 Achab went up to eat and drink: and
44 say to Achab: Prepare thy chariot and
45 Achab getting up went away to Jezrahel
46 ran before A. till he came to Jezrahel
19 1 Achab told Jezabel all things Elias had
20 2 sending messengers to Achab king of
13 and behold a prophet coming to Achab
14 Achab said: By whom? And he said to him
21 1 a vineyard near the palace of Achab
2 Achab spoke to Naboth, saying: Give me
4 and Achab came into his house angry and
15 that she said to Achab: Arise and take
16 Achab heard this, to wit, that Naboth
18 go down to meet Achab king of Israel
20 Achab said to Elias: Hast thou found
21 will kill of Achab him that pisseth
24 if Achab die in the city, the dogs
25 there was not such another as Achab
27 when Achab had heard these words, he
29 hast thou not seen Achab humbled before
22 20 who shall deceive Achab. 2 Pa 18:19
39 but the rest of the acts of Achab and
40 so Achab slept with his fathers, and
41 in fourth year of Achab king of Israel
50 Ochozias the son of Achab said to
52 Ochozias the son of Achab began to
4 K 1 1 against Israel after the death of Achab
3 1 Joram the son of Achab. 8:16, 25, 28, 29; 9:29; 2 Pa 22:5, 6
5 when A. was dead, he broke the league
8 18 the daughter of Achab was his wife: and
9 8 and I will cut off from Achab him that
25 sitting in a chariot followed Achab
10 1 Achab had seventy sons in Samaria: so
17 he slew all that were left of Achab
18 Achab worshipped Baal a little, but I
21 3 made groves, as A. the king of Israel
2 Pa 18 1 and was joined by affinity to Achab
2 Achab at his coming killed sheep and
3 Achab king of Israel said to Josaphat
21 6 for his wife was a daughter of Achab
Jer 29 21 to Achab the son of Colias and to
22 make thee like Sedecias and like Achab

house of Achab 4 K 8 18 as the h. . . . had walked
4 K 8 27 he walked in the ways of the h. . . .
27 did evil before the Lord as did h. . . .
27 he was the son-in-law of the h. . . .
9 7 thou shalt cut off the h. . . . thy master
8 I will destroy all the house of Achab
9 will make h. . . . like house of Jeroboam
10 10 which Lord spoke concerning the h. . . .
11 Jehu slew all that were left of h. . . .
30 hast done to the h. . . . according to all
21 13 line of Samaria and weight of h. . . .
2 Pa 21 6 ways of king of Israel as h. . . . had
13 imitating the fornication of h. . . .
22 3 also walked in the ways of the h. . . .
4 evil in sight of the Lord, as h. . . .
7 had anointed to destroy the h. . . .
8 when Jehu was rooting out the h. . . .
Mich 6 16 of Amri, and all the works of the h. . . .

Achab's 3 K 21 8 she wrote letters in A. name and
4 K 10 1 them that brought up Achab's children

Achad Gen 10 10 Babylon and Arach and Achad

Achaia Acts 18 12 when Gallio was proconsul of A.
Acts 18 27 [Apollo] was desirous to go to Achaia
19 21 had passed through Macedonia and A.
Rom 15 26 hath pleased them of Macedonia and A.
1 C 16 15 that they are the firstfruits of Achaia
2 C 1 1 all the saints that are in all Achaia
9 2 A. also is ready from the year past
11 10 broken off in me in the regions of A.
1 Th 1 7 all that believe in Macedonia and in A.
8 not only in Macedonia and in Achaia

Achaicus 1 C 16 15 and of Fortunatus and of A.
1 C 16 17 I rejoice in the presence of . . . A.

Achan Josu 7 1 Achan the son of Charmi. 18
Josu 7 19 Josue said to Achan: My son, give glory
20 Achan answered Josue and said to him
24 with him took Achan the son of Zare
22 20 did not A. the son of Zare transgress

Achar 1 Pa 2 7 sons of Charmi: Achar, who troubled
1 Pa 2 27 the sons of Ram . . . Jamin and Achar

Achaz 4 K 15 38 Achaz his son reigned. 2 Pa 27:9
4 K 16 1 reigned Achaz the son of Joatham king
2 Achaz was 20 years old when. 2 Pa 28:1
5 they besieged Achaz, but were not able
7 A. sent messengers to Theglathphalasar
19 now the rest of the acts of Achaz, which
20 Achaz slept with his fathers. 2 Pa 28:27
17 1 in the twelfth year of Achaz king of
18 1 Ezechias the son of Achaz king of Juda
20 11 already gone down in the dial of Achaz
23 12 the top of the upper chamber of Achaz
1 Pa 3 13 begot Achaz, the father of Ezechias
2 Pa 28 19 Lord had humbled Juda because of Achaz
21 Achaz stripped the house of the Lord
24 Achaz having taken away all the vessels
Isa 1 1 days of Ozias, Joathan, A. Osee 1:1
7 1 it came to pass in the days of Achaz
3 said to Isaias: Go forth to meet Achaz
10 the Lord spoke again to Achaz, saying
12 Achaz said: I will not ask, and I will
38 8 now gone down in the sun dial of Achaz
Mich 1 1 in the days of Joathan, Achaz, and
Mat 1 9 Joatham begot A. A. begot Ezechias

king Achaz 4 K 16 10 king Achaz went to Damascus
4 K 16 10 king Achaz sent to Urias the priest
11 that king Achaz had commanded. 16
11 until king Achaz came from Damascus
15 king Achaz commanded Urias the priest
17 king Achaz took away the graven bases
2 Pa 28 16 king Achaz sent to king of the Assyrians
22 king Achaz himself by himself sacrificed
29 19 king Achaz in his reign had defiled
Isa 14 28 in the year that king Achaz died, was

Achazib Judg 1 31 of Ahalab and of Achazib and

acheth 4 K 4 19 said to his father: My head acheth

Achia 1 Pa 2 25 Aram and Asom and Achia. And
1 Pa 8 7 Naaman and Achia and Gera he removed

Achias 1 K 14 3 A. the son of Achitob brother of
1 K 14 18 Saul said to Achias: Bring the ark of
1 Pa 26 20 Achias was over the treasures of the

achieved Deut 8 17 of my own hand have a. all
1 Ma 16 23 worthy deeds which he bravely achieved

Achim Mat 1 14 Sadoc begot A. A. begot Elius. And

Achimaas 1 K 14 50 Achinoam the daughter of A.
2 K 15 27 let Achimaas thy son and Jonathan
36 A. the son of Sadoc, and Jonathan
17 17 Jonathan and A. stayed by the fountain
20 where is Achimaas and Jonathan? And
18 19 Achimaas the son of Sadoc said. 22
23 Achimaas running by a nearer way passed
27 seemeth to me like the running of A.
28 Achimaas crying out, said to the king
29 Achimaas said: I saw a great tumult
3 K 4 15 Achimaas in Nephtali: he also had
1 Pa 6 8 Sadoc begot A. A. begot Azarias
53 Sadoc his son, Achimaas his son. And

Achiman Num 13 23 Hebron, where Achiman and

Achimelech 1 K 21 1 David came to Nobe to A. the

1 K 21 1 A. was astonished at David's coming
2 David said to A. the priest: The king
8 David said to Achimelech: Hast thou
22 9 I saw the son of Isai in Nobe with A.
11 the king sent to call for Achimelech
12 Saul said to Achimelech: Hear, thou
14 Achimelech answering the king, said
16 dying thou shalt die, Achimelech, thou
20 one of sons of Achimelech . . . escaped
23 6 Abiathar the son of Achimelech fled
26 6 David spoke to Achimelech the Hethite
30 7 to Abiathar the priest the son of A.
2 K 8 17 and A. . . . were the priests. 1 Pa 18:16
Ps 33 1 he changed his countenance before A.
51 2 David went to the house of Achimelech
Achimoth 1 Pa 6 25 of Elcana: Amasai and Achimoth
Achinoam 1 K 14 50 the name of Saul's wife was A.
1 K 25 43 David took also A. of Jezrahel: and
27 3 David with his two wives, Achinoam the
30 5 captives, Achinoam the Jezrahelitess
2 K 2 2 wives, Achinoam the Jezrahelitess and
3 2 the firstborn was Ammon of A. 1 Pa 3:1
Achior Tob 11 20 A. and Nabath the kinsmen of
Jdth 5 5 Achior captain of all the children of
28 that Achior therefore may know that he
6 1 in a violent passion, said to Achior
7 commanded his servants to take Achior
9 tied Achior to a tree hand and foot
12 Achior related in the midst of the
13 Achior also himself to be put to death
14 when Achior had declared all these
16 was concluded, they comforted Achior
11 7 it is known also what Achior said, nor
13 27 Achior being called for, came, and
29 Achior seeing the head of Holofernes
14 6 Achior seeing the power that the God
Achis 1 K 21 10 and came to A. the king of Geth
1 K 21 11 servants of A., when they saw David
12 exceedingly afraid at the face of Achis
14 Achis said to his servants: You saw
27 2 men that were with him, to Achis the
3 David dwelt with Achis at Geth, he and
5 David said to Achis: If I have found
6 then Achis gave him Siceleg that day
9 apparel and returned and came to Achis
10 Achis said to him: Whom hast thou gone
12 Achis believed David, saying: He hath
28 1 Achis said to David: Know thou now
2 David said to Achis: Now thou shalt
2 Achis said to David: And I will appoint
29 2 his men were in the rear with Achis
3 princes of the Philistines said to A.
3 and Achis said to the princes of the
6 Achis called David and said to him
8 David said to Achis: But what have I
9 Achis answering said to David: I know
3 K 2 39 servants of Semei ran away to Achis
40 went to Achis to Geth to seek his
Achisamech Exod 31 6 the son of A. 35:34; 38:23
Achitob 1 K 14 3 Achias the son of Achitob brother
1 K 22 9 Achimelech the son of A. 11, 20
12 to Achimelech: Hear thou son of Achitob
2 K 8 17 the son of Achitob. 1 Pa 18:16; 1 Es 7:2
1 Pa 6 7 Amarias begot A. A. begot Sadoc. 11
52 Amarias his son, Achitob his son
9 11 Maraioth the son of Achitob. 2 Es 11:11
Jdth 8 1 Raphaim the son of Achitob the son of
Achitophel 2 K 15 12 Absalom also sent for A. the
2 K 15 31 that A. also was in the conspiracy with
31 infatuate . . . the counsel of Achitophel
34 shalt defeat the counsel of Achitophel
16 15 into Jerusalem, and A. was with him
20 Absalom said to Achitophel: Consult
21 Achitophel said to Absalom: Go in to
23 so was all the counsel of Achitophel
17 1 A. said to Absalom: I will choose me
6 A. hath spoken after this manner: Shall
7 counsel that A. hath given this time
14 better than the counsel of Achitophel
14 counsel of Achitophel was defeated
15 thus and thus did Achitophel counsel
21 of counsel has A. given against you
23 Achitophel seeing that his counsel was
23 34 Eliam son of Achitophel the Galonite
1 Pa 27 33 Achitophel was the king's counsellor
34 after Achitophel was Joiada the son of
Achobor Gen 36 38 Balanan the son of A. 1 Pa 1:49
4 K 22 12 A. the son of Micha, and Saphan and
14 A. and Saphan and Asaia went to Holda
Jer 26 22 Elnathan the son of Achobor. 36:12
Achor Josu 7 24 brought them to the valley of A.
Josu 7 26 place was called the valley of Achor
15 7 borders of Debara from valley of Achor
Isa 65 10 valley of Achor into a place for the
Osee 2 15 valley of Achor for an opening of hope
Achsa 1 Pa 2 49 the daughter of Caleb was Achsa
Achsaph Josu 11 1 Semeron and to the king of A.
Josu 12 20 the king of Achsaph one, the king of
Achziba Josu 19 29 sea from the portion of Achziba
acknowledge Deut 21 17 shall a. son of the hated
2 K 19 20 for I thy servant acknowledge my sin
Jdth 9 19 may acknowledge that thou art God and
Eccu 12 12 at the last thou a. my words, and be
Jer 3 13 but yet acknowledge thy iniquity, that
14 20 we a., O Lord, our wickedness, the
acknowledged Ps 31 5 I have a. my sin to thee and
Wisd 12 27 they acknowledged him the true God whom
13 1 have a. who was the workman: but have
18 13 they a. the people to be of God. For
Eccu 44 26 he a. him in his blessings and gave him
Dan 11 39 with a strange God, whom he hath a.
13 14 a. their lust; and then they agreed
acknowledging Gen 37 33 the father a. it, said
Gen 38 26 he acknowledging the gifts, said: She
Titus 1 1 a. of truth, which is according to
acknowledgment Eccu 27 9 in day of a. thou shalt
Philem 6 the a. of every good work that is in you
acoming Mat 24 48 lord is long acoming. Luke 12:45
acquaint Gen 31 27 why . . . not a. me, that I might
Eccu 8 9 acquaint thyself with their proverbs
acquaintance Job 19 13 my a. like strangers have
Ps 30 12 and a fear to my acquaintance. They
87 9 thou hast put away my a. far from me
19 put far from me: and my acquaintance
Dan 13 33 her friends and all her a. wept. But
Eccu 13 25 thrust away even by his acquaintance
Luke 2 44 among their kinsfolks and a. And not
23 49 all his a. and the women that had
acquainted Isa 53 3 sorrows, and a. with infirmity
2 Ma 14 20 captain had a. the multitude with it
acquire Gen 36 6 all that he was able to acquire
Ps 68 36 dwell there and a. it by inheritance
Prov 18 15 a wise heart shall acquire knowledge
acquired 2 Pa 17 5 he a. immense riches and much
acquisition Eph 1 14 unto the redemption of a.
acquit Wisd 1 6 and will not a. the evil speaker
Nah 1 3 and will not cleanse and a. the guilty
acquitted Eccu 32 2 when thou hast a. thyself of
2 Ma 4 47 evil was a. by him of the accusations
Acrabathane 1 Ma 5 3 and them that were in A.
acre 1 K 14 14 within half an acre of land which
acres Isa 5 10 ten acres of vineyard shall yield
Acron Josu 19 43 Elon and Themna and Acron
act Gen 34 7 and committed an unlawful act in
Gen 39 8 no wise consenting to that wicked act
Lev 18 3 neither shall you act according to the

1 Pa 22 13 take courage and act manfully, fear not
28 20 act like a man and take courage and
Ps 24 4 be confounded that act unjust things
30 24 repay them abundantly that act proudly
74 5 said to the wicked: Do not act wickedly
Prov 16 12 they that act wickedly are abominable
Eccu 6 11 shall act with confidence among them
2 Ma 6 8 also should act in like manner against
15 2 do not act so fiercely and barbarously
2 P 2 6 those that should after act wickedly
acted Num 25 18 they also have acted like enemies
2 K 18 13 if I should have acted boldly against
3 K 16 25 and acted wickedly above all that were
4 K 17 15 they followed vanities and acted vainly
Ps 13 3 their tongues they acted deceitfully
93 1 the God of revenge hath acted freely
105 6 we have acted unjustly, we have wrought
Jer 29 23 because they have acted folly in Israel
Bar 2 12 done wickedly, we have acted unjustly
Soph 3 4 have acted unjustly against the law
acting 2 Ma 4 17 acting wickedly against the laws
action Eccu 8 2 lest he bring an a. against thee
Eccu 37 20 and steady counsel before every action
38 25 that is less in action, shall receive
active Wisd 7 22 active, undefiled, sure, sweet
Wisd 7 24 wisdom is more a. than all a. things
acts 3 K 14 19 the rest of the acts of. 14:29; 15:23, 31; 16:5, 14, 20, 27; 22:39, 46; 4 K 1:18; 8:23; 10:34; 12:19; 13:8, 12; 14:15, 18, 28; 15:6, 11, 15, 21, 26, 31, 36; 16:19; 20:20; 21:17, 25; 23:28; 24:5; 2 Pa 9:29; 13:22; 20:34; 25:26; 26:22; 27:7; 32:32; 33:18; 35:26; 36:8; 1 Ma 16:23
4 K 23 19 the acts that he had done in Bethel
1 Pa 11 22 of Cabseel, who had done many acts: he
29 29 the acts of king David first and last
2 Pa 12 15 the acts of Roboam first and last are
Ps 144 6 speak of the might of thy terrible acts
150 2 praise ye him for his mighty acts
Eccu 18 3 who shall search out his glorious acts
1 Ma 3 4 in his acts he was like a lion and
8 2 of their battles and their noble acts
9 22 of the noble acts that he did and of
10 15 worthy acts that he and his brethren
14 35 the people seeing the acts of Simon
2 Ma 10 10 now we will relate the acts of Eupator
acute Dan 1 4 acute in knowledge and instructed
Ada Gen 4 19 wives, the name of the one was Ada
Gen 4 20 Ada brought forth Jabel: who was the
23 Lamech said to his wives Ada and Sella
36 2 Ada the daughter of Elon the Hethite
4 Ada bore Eliphaz: Basemoth bore Rahuel
12 are the sons of Ada the wife of. 16
16 of Edom, and these the sons of Ada
Adad Gen 36 35 Adad the son of Badad reigned in
Gen 36 36 when Adad was dead, there reigned in his
3 K 11 14 Adad the Edomite of the king's seed
17 then Adad fled, he and certain Edomites
17 Egypt, and Adad was then a little boy
19 Adad found great favor before Pharao
21 and when Adad heard in Egypt that David
25 this is the evil of Adad and his hatred
1 Pa 1 46 Adad the son of Badad reigned in his
47 when Adad was dead, Semla of Masreca
50 also died, and Adad reigned in his stead
51 after the death of Adad, there began
Adada Josu 15 22 Cina and Dimona and Adada and
Adadremmon Zach 12 11 like the lamentation of A.
Adaia 1 Pa 6 41 Zara the son of Adaia the son of
1 Pa 8 21 and Adaia and Baraia and Samareth
1 Es 10 29 Melluch and Adaia, Jasub and Saal
2 Es 11 5 Hazia the son of A. the son of Joiarib
12 Adaia the son of Jeroham the son of
12 16 of Adaia, Zacharia: of Genthon
Adaias 1 Pa 9 12 Adaias the son of Jeroham the son
2 Pa 23 1 of Obed and Maasias the son of Adaias
1 Es 10 39 Salmias and Nathan and Adaias
Adali 2 Pa 28 12 Amasa the son of Adali, stood up
Adalia Esth 9 8 Phoratha and A. and Aridatha
Adam Gen 2 19 brought them to Adam to see what he
Gen 2 19 for whatsoever Adam called any living
20 Adam called all the beasts by their
20 for Adam there was not found a helper
21 Lord God cast a deep sleep upon Adam
22 built the rib which he took from Adam
22 a woman: and brought her to Adam
23 Adam said: This now is bone of my bones
25 both naked: to wit, Adam and his wife
3 8 Adam and his wife hid themselves from
9 Lord God called Adam and said to him
17 to Adam he said: Because thou hast
20 Adam called the name of his wife Eve
21 God made for Adam and his wife garments
22 behold Adam is become as one of us
24 and he cast out Adam; and placed
4 1 and Adam knew Eve his wife: who
25 Adam also knew his wife again: and she
5 1 the book of the generation of Adam
2 called their name Adam, in the day
3 Adam lived 130 years, and begot a son
4 the days of Adam after he begot Seth
5 all the time that Adam lived were
11 5 tower which the children of Adam were
Deut 32 8 when he separated the sons of Adam
Josu 14 15 Adam the greatest among the Enacims
2 K 7 19 for this is the law of Adam, O Lord
1 Pa 1 1 Adam, Seth, Enos, Cainan, Malaleel
Tob 8 8 thou madest Adam of the slime of the
Ecce 3 21 if the spirit of the children of Adam
Eccu 33 10 earth, from whence Adam was created
49 19 above every soul Adam in the beginning
Jer 32 19 all the ways of the children of Adam
Osee 6 7 they, like Adam, have transgressed the
11 4 I will draw them with the cords of Adam
Zach 13 5 for Adam is my example from my youth
Luke 3 38 Seth who was of Adam, who was of God
Rom 5 14 but death reigned from Adam unto Moses
14 similitude of the transgression of Adam
1 C 15 22 as in Adam all die, so also in Christ
45 first Adam was made into a living soul
45 the last Adam into a quickening spirit
1 Tim 2 13 for Adam was first formed; then Eve
14 and Adam was not seduced; but the woman
Jude 14 Enoch also, the seventh from Adam
Adama Gen 10 19 Sodom and Gomorrha and Adama
Gen 14 8 king of Adama and the king of Seboim
Deut 29 23 destruction of Sodom and Gomorrha, A.
Osee 11 8 how shall I make thee as Adama, shall
adamant Eze 3 9 I have made thy face like an a.
Zach 7 12 made their heart as the adamant stone
Adami Josu 19 33 and Elon to Saananim and Adami
Adan 1 Es 8 6 of the sons of Adan, Abed the son
Adar Gen 36 39 dead, Adar reigned in his place
Num 34 4 shall go out to the town called Adar
1 Es 6 15 until the third day of the month of A.
Esth 3 7 month which is called A. 13; 9:1; 16:20
8 12 thirteenth of the twelfth month Adar
9 15 fourteenth day of the month Adar. 19
Adarezer 2 K 8 3 David defeated also A. 1 Pa 18:3
2 K 8 5 of Damascus came to succor Adarezer
7 which the servants of Adarezer wore
8 out of Beroth, cities of Adarezer
9 David had defeated all the forces of A.
10 because he had fought against Adarezer
10 Thou was enemy to Adarezer. 1 Pa 18:10
12 spoils of Adarezer the son of Rohob

10 16 Adarezer sent and fetched the Syrians
16 the captain of the host of Adarezer
19 the kings that were auxiliaries of A.
3 K 11 23 who had fled from his master Adarezer
1 Pa 18 5 Damascus came also to help Adarezer
7 quivers which servants of Adarezer had
8 Thebath and Chun, cities of Adarezer
9 had defeated all the army of Adarezer
10 had defeated and overthrown Adarezer
19 16 Sophach, general of army of Adarezer
19 and when the servants of Adarezer saw
Adarsa 1 Ma 7 40 Judas pitched in A. with 3,000
Adazer 1 Ma 7 45 one day's journey from Adazer
Adbeel Gen 25 13 Cedar and A. and. 1 Pa 1:29
add Gen 32 20 ye shall add: Thy servant Jacob
Exod 30 15 rich man shall not add to half a sicle
Lev 5 16 add the fifth part. 22:14; 27:19, 27, 31
27 13 he shall add above the estimation the
Deut 1 11 add to this number many thousands and
4 2 you shall not add to the word that I
12 32 neither add anything nor diminish
19 9 thou shalt add to thee other three
20 8 they shall add the rest and shall speak
Ruth 1 17 so and so to me, and add more also if
1 K 3 17 do so and so to thee and add so and so
14 44 do so and so to me, and add still more
20 13 and so to Jonathan and add still more
25 22 and add more to the foes of David if I
2 K 12 8 I shall add far greater things unto
19 13 so do God to me and add more, if thou
3 K 2 23 so may God do to me, and add more, if
12 11 but I will add to your yoke. 14
19 2 the gods do to me, and add still more
20 10 gods do to me, and more may they add
21 19 thou shalt add: Thus saith the Lord
4 K 6 31 so and so to me, and may he add more
20 6 I will add to thy days fifteen years
1 Pa 17 18 what can David add more, seeing thou
2 Pa 10 11 yoke, and I will add more weight to it
28 13 why will you add to our sins and heap
1 Es 10 10 wives, to add to the sins of Israel
Job 29 22 to my words they durst add nothing and
34 32 spoken iniquity, I will add no more
39 35 another, to which I will add no more
Ps 60 7 wilt add days to the days of the king
68 28 add thou iniquity upon their iniquity
70 14 hope; and will add to all thy praise
113 14 may the Lord add blessings upon you
Prov 3 2 they shall add to thee length of days
16 23 mouth: and shall add grace to his lips
19 19 take away, he shall add another thing
30 6 add not anything to his words, lest
Ecce 3 14 we cannot add anything, nor take away
Eccu 3 29 and the sinner will add sin to sin
5 5 and add not sin upon sin: and say not
18 15 anything, add not grief by an evil word
Isa 30 1 spirit, that you might add sin upon sin
38 5 I will add to thy days fifteen years
Jer 7 21 add your burnt offerings to your
Osee 1 6 I will not add any more to have mercy
1 Ma 8 30 have a mind to add to these articles
30 whatsoever they shall add or take away
Mat 6 27 can add to his stature one. Luke 12:25
Apoc 22 18 if any man shall add to these things
18 God shall add unto him the plagues
Addar Josu 15 3 reacheth into Esron, going up to A.
1 Pa 8 3 sons of Bale were Addar and Gera and
added Gen 15 3 Abram added: But to me thou hast
1 K 12 19 we have added to all our sins this evil
3 K 2 14 he added: I have a word to speak with
7 36 to be engraven but added round about
22 19 he added and said: Hear thou therefore
2 Pa 2 12 he added, saying: Blessed be the Lord
Job 27 1 Job also added, taking up his. 29:1
Ps 68 27 have added to the grief of my wounds
77 17 they added yet more sin against him
119 3 what shall be added to thee, to a
Prov 1 9 that grace may be added to thy head
9 9 man, and wisdom shall be added to him
11 years of life shall be added to thee
Eccu 15 15 he added his commandments and precepts
18 5 nothing may be taken away nor added
42 21 and to him nothing may be added nor
45 25 and he added glory to Aaron and gave
47 12 to the festivals he added beauty and
Isa 29 1 year is added to year: the solemnities
Jer 36 32 were added besides many more words than
45 3 the Lord hath added sorrow to my sorrow
Dan 4 33 and greater majesty was added to me
1 Ma 10 30 the 3 cities that are added thereto
38 three cities that are added to Judea
Mat 6 33 shall be added unto you. Luke 12:31
Luke 3 20 he added this also above all, and shut
19 11 he added and spoke a parable, because
Acts 2 41 were added in that day about 3,000
11 24 great multitude was added to the Lord
24 9 the Jews also added and said that these
Gal 2 6 that seemed to be something a. nothing
addeth Job 34 37 he addeth blasphemy upon his sins
Ecce 1 18 he that addeth knowledge, a. also labor
Gal 3 15 no man despiseth nor addeth to it
Addi Luke 3 28 Melchi who was of Addi who was of
adding Gen 45 23 adding besides ten he asses to
Lev 9 17 adding in the sacrifice the libations
Deut 5 22 a loud voice, adding nothing more
Judg 10 6 the children of Israel adding new sins
Addo 3 K 4 14 Abinadab the son of Addo was chief
1 Pa 6 21 Joah his son, Addo his son, Zara his
2 Pa 9 29 and in the vision of Addo the seer
12 15 in the books of . . . Addo the seer, and
13 22 in the book of Addo the prophet
1 Es 5 1 Zacharias the son of Addo. 6:14
2 Es 12 4 Addo, Genthon, Abia, Miamin, Madia
Zach 1 1 son of Barachias the son of Addo. 7
Addon 2 Es 7 61 Cherub, Addon, and Emmer
address Job 5 8 to the Lord, and a. my speech to
Addus 1 Ma 13 13 Simon pitched in Addus over
Adeodatus 2 K 21 19 A. the son of the Forrest
1 Pa 20 5 A. the son of Saltus a Bethlehemite
adhere Deut 4 4 you that adhere to the Lord your
Deut 10 20 to him thou shalt adhere and shalt
30 20 and obey his voice and adhere to him
Ps 72 28 it is good for me to adhere to my God
Isa 14 1 and shall adhere to the house of Jacob
56 6 of the stranger that a. to the Lord
adhered Ps 24 21 and the upright have a. to me
Isa 2 6 and have adhered to strange children
Acts 8 13 being baptized, he adhered to Philip
adherents 1 Ma 9 60 sent secretly letters to his a.
adhereth Isa 56 3 stranger, that a. to the Lord
adhering Acts 17 34 a. to him [Paul], did believe
Adiada 1 Ma 12 38 Simon built Adiada in Sephela
Adiel 1 Pa 4 36 Asaia and Adiel and Ismiel and
1 Pa 9 12 of Adiel the son of Jezra the son of
27 25 treasures was Azmoth the son of Adiel
Adin 1 Es 2 15 the children of Adin, 454. The
2 Es 7 20 children of Adin, 655. The children of
10 16 Adonia, Begoai, Adin, Ater, Hezecia
Adina 1 Pa 11 42 A. the son of Siza, a Rubenite
Adithaim Josu 15 36 Saraim and Adithaim and Gedera
adjoining 3 K 21 2 it is nigh and a. to my house
Mich 1 11 the house a. shall receive mourning
2 Ma 12 16 a pool adjoining of two furlongs broad
Acts 18 7 house was adjoining to the synagogue
adjure Num 5 19 he shall a. her and shall say
3 K 22 16 I adjure thee again and again that

Cant 2 7 I adjure you, O ye daughters of Jerusalem. 3:5; 5:8; 8:4
Mat 26 63 I adjure thee by the living God, that
Mark 5 7 I adjure thee by God that thou torment
adjured Exod 13 19 [Joseph] had a. the children
1 K 14 24 and Saul adjured the people, saying
27 when his father adjured the people
2 Pa 34 32 he a. all that were found in Jerusalem
Tob 8 23 Raguel adjured Tobias to abide with
9 5 thou seest how Raguel hath adjured me
Cant 5 9 beloved that thou hast so adjured us
Jer 42 19 know certainly that I have adjured you
adjuring Tob 9 5 whose adjuring I cannot despise
Adli 1 Pa 27 29 the valleys Saphat the son of Adli
Admatha Esth 1 14 Sethar and A. and Tharsis
administer Eph 4 29 may a. grace to the hearers
administered 2 C 8 19 grace which is a. by us
2 C 8 20 in this abundance which is a. by us
administereth 1 Pa 4 11 the power which God a.
administration 2 C 9 12 the a. of this office
admirable Ps 8 2 how admirable is thy name in. 10
Eccu 43 2 at his rising, an admirable instrument
31 great, and his power is a. Glorify the
2 Ma 15 13 another man, a. for age and glory
admiration Tob 5 10 his father being in a., desired
Isa 29 14 I will proceed to cause an admiration
2 Ma 7 18 and things worthy of a. are done to us
Mat 7 28 were in a. at his doctrine, 22:33; Mark 6:2; 11:18
Luke 11 14 spoke: and the multitude were in a. at
Apoc 13 3 all the earth was in a. after the beast
17 6 when I had seen her, with great a.
admire Eccu 27 26 mouth, and will admire thy words
Eccu 43 26 hear with our ears, we shall admire
admired Jdth 10 7 and a. her beauty exceedingly
Jdth 11 18 they admired her wisdom and they said
Wisd 8 11 shall be a. in the sight of the mighty
11 15 him they admired in the end, when they
13 4 or if they a. their power and their
Eccu 24 3 and shall be a. in the holy assembly
2 Ma 7 20 now the mother was to be admired above
admireth Eccu 43 20 eye a. at the beauty of the
admiring Eccu 9 11 a. the beauty of another man's
Acts 13 12 a. at the doctrine of the Lord. Now
Jude 16 admiring persons for gain's sake. But
admitted Josu 22 30 a. most willingly the words
Tob 6 20 be a. into the society of the holy
Bar 6 55 how then can it be supposed or a. that
Mark 5 19 he admitted him not, but saith to him
37 he admitted not any man to follow him
admonish 2 Es 9 29 didst a. them to return to thy
Wisd 11 11 thou didst a. and try them as a father
Eccu 19 15 a. thy friend: for there is often a
17 a. thy neighbor before thou threaten
Acts 20 31 I ceased not with tears to admonish
Rom 15 14 so that you are able to a. one another
1 C 4 14 but I a. you as my dearest children
1 Th 5 12 are over you in the Lord and a. you
2 Th 3 15 enemy, but admonish him as a brother
2 Tim 1 6 for which cause I admonish thee, that
Titus 3 1 admonish them to be subject to princes
Jude 5 I will therefore admonish you, though
admonished Num 16 40 wherewith they should be a.
Judg 1 14 husband a. her to ask a field of her
2 Es 9 26 who a. them earnestly to return to thee
2 Ma 9 11 being admonished by the scourge of God
admonishest Wisd 12 2 a. them and speakest to
admonishing 2 Pa 36 15 early and daily a. them
Tob 10 13 admonishing her to honor her father
Isa 30 21 word of one a. thee behind thy back
Col 1 28 we preach, a. every man and teaching
3 16 teaching and a. one another in psalms
2 Tim 2 25 a. them that resist the truth: if
admonition Titus 3 10 after the first and second a.
2 P 3 1 I stir up by way of a. your sincere
admonitions Deut 21 20 he slighteth hearing our a.
Tob 1 15 and gave them wholesome admonitions
ado Gen 33 11 [Esau] took it with much ado at his
Mark 5 39 why make you this ado and weep? The
Acts 27 8 with much ado sailing by it, we came
Adom Josu 3 16 from the city that is called Adom
Adommim Josu 15 7 is opposite to the ascent of A.
Josu 18 18 over against the ascent of Adommim
Adon 1 Es 2 59 Cherub and Adon and Emer. And they
Adonai Exod 6 3 my name Adonai I did not show them
Jdth 16 16 O Adonai, Lord, great art thou, and
Adonia 2 Es 10 16 Adonia, Begoai, Adin, Ater
Adonias 2 K 3 4 Adonias the son of Haggith. 3 K 1:5
3 K 1 8 strength of David's army was not with A.
9 Adonias having slain rams and calves
11 not heard that Adonias . . . reigneth and
13 why then doth Adonias reign? And while
18 and behold now Adonias reigneth, and
24 let Adonias reign after me, and let him
25 and saying: God save king Adonias: but
41 Adonias and all that were invited by
42 Adonias said to him: Come in, because
43 Jonathan answered Adonias: Not so: for
49 all the guests of Adonias were afraid
50 A. fearing Solomon, arose and went and
51 behold Adonias, fearing king Solomon
2 13 and Adonias . . . came to Bethsabee the
19 to speak to him for Adonias: and the
21 be given to Adonias thy brother to wife
22 ask Abisag the Sunamitess for Adonias
23 if Adonias hath not spoken this word
24 Adonias shall be put to death this day
28 because Joab had turned after Adonias
1 Pa 3 2 the fourth Adonias the son of Aggith
2 Pa 17 8 Adonias and Tobias and Thobadonias
Adonias's 3 K 1 7 who furthered Adonias's side
Adonibezec Judg 1 5 and they found A. in Bezec
Judg 1 6 A. fled: and they pursued after him
7 and A. said: Seventy kings having their
Adonicam 1 Es 2 13 the children of Adonicam, 666
1 Es 8 13 sons of Adonicam, who were the last
2 Es 7 18 children of Adonicam, 667. The children
Adoniram 3 K 4 6 A. the son of Abda over the
3 K 5 14 and Adoniram was over this levy. And
Adonis Eze 8 14 women sat there mourning for A.
Adonisedec Josu 10 1 when A. king of Jerusalem had
Josu 10 3 Adonisedec king of Jerusalem sent to
adopted Exod 2 10 she adopted him for a son and
adoption Rom 8 15 have received the spirit of a.
Rom 8 23 waiting for the a. of the sons of God
9 4 Israelites to whom belongeth the a.
Gal 4 5 that we might receive the a. of sons
Eph 1 5 hath predestinated us unto the a. of
Ador 1 Ma 13 20 by the way that leadeth to Ador
Adoram 1 Pa 1 21 Adoram and Usal and Decla
1 Pa 18 10 he sent Adoram his son to king David
adore Exod 20 5 thou shalt not a. them. Deut 5:9
Exod 23 24 thou shalt not adore their gods nor
24 1 you shall a. afar off. And Moses alone
34 14 adore not any strange god. The Lord his
Lev 26 1 remarkable stone in your land, to a. it
Deut 4 19 by error thou adore and serve them
8 19 strange gods, and serve and adore them
11 16 strange gods and adore them. 17:3; 3 K 9:6; 2 Pa 7:19
30 17 thou a. strange gods and serve them
Josu 23 7 their gods, and serve them and adore
1 K 1 3 to adore and to offer sacrifice to the
15 25 with me that I may adore the Lord. 30
2 K 15 32 where he was about to adore the Lord
3 K 12 30 the people went to adore the calf as

4 K 17 35 nor shall you adore them nor worship
36 him shall you fear and him shall you a.
1 Pa 16 29 adore the Lord in holy becomingness
2 Pa 6 32 adore in this place: hear thou from
34 adore thee towards the way of this city
38 adore thee towards the way of their own
Tob 11 7 forthwith adore the Lord thy God: and
13 14 gifts and shall adore the Lord in thee
Jdth 12 6 to a. her God as she pleased for three
16 22 came to Jerusalem to adore the Lord
Ps 21 28 kindreds of the Gentiles shall a. in
28 2 a. ye the Lord in his holy court. 95:9
44 12 Lord thy God, and him they shall adore
65 4 let all the earth adore thee and sing
71 11 all kings of the earth shall adore him
15 him they shall always adore: they shall
80 10 neither shalt thou adore a strange god
85 9 nations . . . shall come and a. before
94 6 come let us adore and fall down: and
96 7 adore him, all you his angels: Sion
98 5 adore his footstool, for it is holy
9 adore at his holy mountain: for the
131 7 we will adore in the place where his
Wisd 16 28 adore thee at the dawning of the light
Eccu 50 19 faces, to adore the Lord their God
Isa 2 20 which he had made for himself to adore
27 13 they shall adore the Lord in the holy
49 7 and princes shall rise up and adore
66 23 shall come to adore before my face
Jer 7 2 in at these gates, to adore the Lord
13 10 to serve them and to adore them. 25:6
26 2 come, to adore in the house of the Lord
Eze 46 2 he shall adore upon the threshold of
3 shall adore at the door of that gate
9 goeth in by the north gate to adore
Dan 3 5 adore the golden statue. 10, 12, 14, 18
6 man shall not fall down and adore. 11
15 and adore the statue which I have made
15 if you do not adore, you shall be cast
95 nor adore any god except their own God
14 3 went every day to adore him: but Daniel
3 to him: Why dost thou not adore Bel
23 a living God: adore him therefore. And
24 I adore the Lord my God: for he is the
Osee 13 2 sacrifice men, ye that adore calves
Mich 5 12 shalt no more adore the works of thy
Soph 1 5 them that adore and swear by the Lord
2 11 they shall adore him every man from
Zach 14 16 up from year to year to adore the King
17 to Jerusalem to adore the King the Lord
Mat 2 2 in the east and are come to adore him
8 that I also may come and adore him
4 9 if falling down thou wilt adore me
10 the Lord thy God shalt thou adore, and
Luke 4 7 if thou therefore wilt adore before me
8 thou shalt adore the Lord thy God, and
John 4 20 Jerusalem is place where men must adore
21 nor in Jerusalem adore the Father. You
22 you adore that which you know not: we
22 we adore that which we know; for
23 shall adore the Father in spirit and
23 Father also seeketh such to adore him
24 that adore him, must adore him in spirit
12 20 certain Gentiles who came up to adore
Acts 7 43 figures which you made to adore them
8 27 had come to Jerusalem to a. And he
24 11 twelve days since I went up to adore
1 C 14 25 he will adore God, affirming that God
Heb 1 6 let all the angels of God adore him
Apoc 3 9 I will make them to come and adore
9 20 should not adore devils and idols of
11 1 the altar and them that adore therein
13 12 to adore the first beast, whose wound
15 not adore image of the beast should be
14 7 adore ye him that made heaven and earth
9 if any man shall adore the beast and
15 4 all nations shall come and shall adore
19 10 I fell down before his feet to a. him
22 8 I fell down to adore before the feet of
9 the prophecy of this book. Adore God

adored Gen 18 2 tent and adored down to the ground
Gen 24 26 bowed himself down, and adored the Lord
48 falling down I a. the Lord, blessing
52 down to the ground he adored the Lord
47 31 Israel adored God, turning to the bed's
Exod 4 31 affliction, and falling down they adored
12 27 the people bowing themselves, adored
32 8 a molten calf, and have adored it, and
34 15 their gods, and have a. their idols
Num 25 2 they ate of them, and adored their gods
Deut 29 26 strange gods and a. them. Josu 23:16
Judg 2 12 round about them and they adored them
7 15 he [Gedeon] adored and returned to the
1 K 1 28 they adored the Lord there. And Anna
15 31 and Saul adored the Lord. And Samuel
20 41 his face to the ground, adored thrice
25 23 on her face and adored upon the ground
28 14 with his face to the ground and adored
2 K 1 2 he fell upon his face and adored. And
14 22 adored, and blessed the king: and Joab
3 K 1 47 the king adored in his bed. And he said
9 9 followed strange gods and adored them
11 33 hath forsaken me and hath a. Astarthe
16 31 went and served Baal and adored him
4 K 17 16 a. all the host of heaven. 21:3; 2 Pa 33:3
21 21 father had served, and he adored them
2 Pa 7 3 they a. and praised the Lord: because
22 and adored them and worshipped them
20 18 ground before the Lord and adored him
25 14 a. them and burnt incense to them
15 why hast thou adored gods that have not
29 28 and all the multitude adored, and the
29 were with him bowed down and adored
30 great joy, and bowing the knee adored
2 Es 8 6 and they bowed down and adored God with
9 3 they confessed and adored the Lord their
Tob 1 6 and there adored the Lord God of Israel
11 12 when they had adored God and given him
Jdth 13 22 and they all adored the Lord and said
Ps 21 30 have eaten and have adored: all they
105 19 Horeb, and they adored the graven thing
Isa 2 8 they have adored the work of their own
44 15 of the rest he made a god and adored it
Jer 1 16 have adored the work of their own hands
8 2 and whom they have sought and adored
16 11 gods and served them and adored them
22 9 and have adored strange gods and served
Bar 6 5 thou oughtest to be adored, O Lord
Dan 3 7 and adored the golden statue which king
6 10 adored and gave thanks before his God
14 3 but Daniel adored his God. And the king
1 Ma 4 55 and adored and blessed up to heaven
Mat 2 11 and falling down they adored him; and
8 2 a leper came and adored him, saying
9 18 a certain ruler came up and adored him
14 33 that were in the boat came and a. him
15 25 she came and adored him, saying: Lord
28 9 took hold of his feet and adored him
17 seeing him, they a.: but some doubted
Mark 5 6 seeing Jesus afar off, he ran and a.
15 19 bowing their knees, they adored him
John 4 20 our fathers adored on this mountain
9 38 Lord. And falling down, he adored him
Acts 10 25 [Cornelius] falling at his feet, adored
Heb 11 21 and [Jacob] adored the top of his rod
Apoc 4 10 adored him that liveth forever. 5:14

7 11 faces, and adored God, saying: Amen
11 16 fell on their faces and adored God
13 4 they adored the dragon, which gave power
4 they adored the beast, saying: Who is
8 that dwell upon the earth adored him
14 11 have adored the beast and his image
16 2 and upon them that adored the image
19 20 seduced them . . . who adored his image
20 4 who had not adored the beast nor his
adorers John 4 23 when true a. shall adore the
adoreth 2 Es 9 6 the host of heaven adoreth thee
Eccu 35 20 he that adoreth God with joy, shall
Isa 44 17 he boweth down before it and a. it
20 ashes: his foolish heart adoreth it
adoring Exod 34 8 adoring, said: If I have found
Deut 26 10 a. the Lord thy God. And thou shalt
Judg 2 17 with strange gods, and adoring them
19 gods, serving them and adoring them
Tob 14 9 rejoice in it, a. the King of Israel
Jdth 6 14 upon their faces, adoring the Lord
Bar 6 5 behind and before, adoring them
Mat 20 20 adoring and asking something of him
Luke 24 52 they adoring, went back into Jerusalem
adorn Gen 24 47 earrings on her to adorn her face
Exod 25 7 and precious stones to adorn the ephod
Judg 5 30 is heaped together to adorn the necks
Bar 6 10 of the harlots, they adorn their gods
2 Ma 9 16 promiseth to adorn with goodly gifts
Mat 23 29 and adorn the monuments of the just
Titus 2 10 that they may a. the doctrine of God
adorned Exod 39 24 wherewith high priest went a.
Judg 8 21 camels of kings are wont to be adorned
4 K 9 30 a. her head and looked out of a window
2 Pa 24 7 adorned the temple of Baal with all the
Jdth 10 3 adorned herself with all her ornaments
Job 26 13 his spirit hath adorned the heavens
Ps 143 12 daughters decked out, a. round about
Prov 25 23 an earthen vessel a. with silver dross
Eccu 50 10 of gold a. with every precious stone
Isa 57 9 thou hast adorned thyself for the king
61 10 and as a bride adorned with her jewels
Jer 31 4 shalt again be a. with thy timbrels
Eze 16 13 thou wast adorned with gold and silver
23 40 wast adorned with women's ornaments
1 Ma 2 17 city and adorned with sons and brethren
4 57 they a. the front of the temple with
2 Ma 3 25 adorned with a very rich covering: and
Luke 21 5 that it was adorned with goodly stones
1 P 3 5 a. themselves, being in subjection to
Apoc 21 2 prepared as a bride a. for her husband
19 a. with all manner of precious stones
adorneth Prov 15 2 tongue of the wise a. knowledge
adorning Exod 35 9 stones, for the a. of the ephod
4 K 25 17 second pillar had the like adorning
2 Ma 2 30 seek out fit things for the a. of it
1 Tim 2 9 adorning themselves with modesty and
1 P 3 3 whose a. let it not be the outward
Adramelech 4 K 17 31 burnt their children . . . to A.
4 K 19 37 Adramelech and Sarasar . . . slew him. 38
Adria Acts 27 27 as we were sailing in A., about
Adrumentum Acts 27 2 on board a ship of Adrumentum
Adullam Josu 15 35 and Jerimoth and Adullam, Socho
adulterating 2 C 2 17 a. the word of God. 4:2
adulterer Lev 20 10 to death, both the a. and the
Deut 22 22 both die . . . the a. and the adulteress
Job 24 15 the eye of the a. observeth darkness
Prov 6 32 an adulterer for the folly of his mind
Isa 27 3 seed of the adulterer and of the harlot
8 near me and hast received an adulterer
adulterers Ps 49 18 and with a. thou hast been a
Wisd 3 16 children of adulterers shall not come
Jer 9 2 because they are all adulterers. Osee 7:4
23 10 because the land is full of adulterers
14 I have seen the likeness of adulterers
Mala 3 5 witness against sorcerers and a. and
Luke 18 11 unjust, a., as also is this publican
1 C 6 9 neither fornicators nor idolaters nor a.
Heb 13 4 fornicators and a. God will judge. Let
James 4 4 a., know you not that the friendship
adulteress Lev 20 10 death, both adulterer and a.
Deut 22 22 both die . . . the adulterer and the a.
Prov 18 22 he that keepeth an adulteress is foolish
Eze 16 32 but as an a. that bringeth in strangers
Osee 3 1 beloved of her friend, an adulteress
Rom 7 3 she shall be called an adulteress if
3 she is not an a. if she be with another
adulteresses Eze 16 38 and I will judge thee as a.
Eze 23 45 these shall judge them as a. are judged
45 are judged: because they are a., and
Osee 4 13 and your spouses shall be adulteresses
adulteries Jer 13 27 I have seen thy adulteries
Eze 23 43 that were worn out in her adulteries
Osee 2 2 and her a. from between her breasts
Mat 15 19 come forth evil thoughts, murders, a.
Mark 7 21 of men proceed evil thoughts, a.
adulterous Prov 30 20 also the way of an a. woman
Mat 12 39 and a. generation seeketh a sign. 16:4
Mark 8 38 words in this a. and sinful generation
adultery Gen 39 10 and he [Joseph] refused the a.
Num 5 13 but the adultery is secret and cannot
13 because she was not found in the a.
15 and an oblation searching out adultery
27 despised her husband, be guilty of a.
Wisd 14 24 through envy or grieveth him by a.
26 and the irregularity of adultery and
Eccu 23 33 she hath fornicated in adultery and
Jer 5 7 they committed adultery and rioted in
29 23 a. with the wives of their friends and
Eze 23 37 because they have committed adultery
Osee 4 2 and theft and adultery have overflowed
Mat 5 28 hath already committed adultery with
32 marry her that is put away, committeth adultery. 19:9
19 9 marry another, committeth a. Mark 10:11
Mark 10 12 married to another, she committeth a.
Luke 16 18 and marrieth another, committeth a.
18 away from her husband, committeth a.
John 8 3 bring unto him a woman taken in a.
4 this woman was even now taken in a.
Rom 2 22 should not commit a., committest a.
2 P 2 14 having eyes full of adultery and sin
commit adultery Exod 20 14 thou shalt not c. a.
Lev 20 10 if any man c. a. with the wife of
Deut 5 18 neither shalt thou commit adultery
Jer 7 9 to steal, to murder, to commit adultery
Osee 4 14 your spouses when they shall c. a.
Mat 5 27 thou shalt not c. a. 19:18; Mark 10:19; Luke 18:20; Rom 13:9
32 maketh her to commit adultery: and he
Mark 10 19 do not commit adultery, do not kill, do
Rom 2 22 that sayest that men should not c. a.
James 2 11 he that said, Thou shalt not c. a.
11 if thou do not c. a. but shalt kill
Apoc 2 22 they that c. a. with her shall be in
Aduram Gen 10 27 Jectan begot . . . Aduram and Uzal
2 K 20 24 but Aduram over the tributes: and
3 K 12 18 king Roboam sent Aduram. 2 Pa 10:18
2 Pa 11 9 he [Roboam] built Aduram and Lachis
advance 1 K 13 23 to a. further in Machmas
Eccu 15 8 be found with her, and shall advance
20 29 a wise man shall advance himself with
1 Ma 14 35 he sought . . . to advance his people
advanced Gen 18 11 far a. in years. Josu 13:1; 23:2; 1 K 4:18
Gen 24 1 Abraham was old; and advanced in age
Josu 13 1 thou art grown old and advanced in age

Judg 19 8 till the day be farther advanced
1 K 2 26 the child Samuel advanced and grew on
3 K 1 1 king David was old and a. in years
Job 21 7 are they a. and strengthened with riches
Eze 16 13 and wast advanced to be a queen. And
Dan 2 48 the king advanced Daniel to a high
2 Ma 6 18 Eleazar . . . a man advanced in years
Luke 1 7 they were both well advanced in years
18 my wife is advanced in years. And the
2 36 she [Anna] was far advanced in years
52 Jesus a. in wisdom and age and grace
advancedst Eze 16 7 a. and camest to woman's
advanceth 1 Es 5 8 and advanceth in their hands
advancement Eccu 11 17 his a. shall have success
advantage Judg 17 9 I shall find a place to my a.
4 K 18 31 that which is for your advantage, and
Esth 2 12 for setting them off to advantage, it
Ps 88 23 the enemy shall have no advantage over
Ecce 4 9 they have the a. of their society
7 12 wisdom . . . bringeth more advantage to
Wisd 5 8 what a. hath the boasting of riches
Eccu 39 15 if he rest, it shall be to his a.
Isa 36 16 do with me that which is for your a.
Rom 3 1 what advantage then hath the Jew or
advantaged Luke 9 25 what is a man a. if he gain
adversaries Exod 15 7 thou hast put down thy a.
Num 33 55 they shall be your adversaries in the
Josu 5 13 art thou one of ours, or of our a.
1 K 2 10 the a. of the Lord shall fear him
2 K 24 13 shalt flee three months before thy a.
Esth 9 1 and to revenge themselves of their a.
Ps 3 8 hast struck all them who are my a.
Wisd 11 3 and revenged themselves of their a.
9 exalt thine and didst kill their a.
18 8 as thou didst punish the adversaries
Eccu 23 3 lest . . . I fall before my adversaries
46 7 in the descent he destroyed the a.
47 8 and extirpated the Philistines the a.
Isa 1 24 I will comfort myself over my a.: and I
59 18 to repay wrath to his adversaries and
Jer 18 19 and hear the voice of my adversaries
Lam 1 5 her adversaries are become her lords
2 17 and hath set up the horn of thy a.
Bar 4 6 you are delivered to your adversaries
Nah 1 2 the Lord taketh vengeance on his a.
2 Ma 10 21 having let their adversaries escape
26 and to be . . . an adversary to their a.
14 17 with the sudden coming of the a.
15 16 wherewith thou shalt overthrow the a.
Luke 13 17 all his adversaries were ashamed: and
21 15 all your a. shall not be able to resist
1 C 16 9 door is opened unto me: and many a.
Phil 1 28 in nothing be ye terrified by the a.
1 Th 2 15 Jews who . . . are a. to all men
Heb 10 27 a fire which shall consume the a.
adversary Judg 6 31 that is his a., let him die
Judg 16 24 hath delivered our a. into our hands
1 K 29 4 lest he be an adversary to us when we
2 K 2 16 his sword into side of his adversary
3 K 5 4 and there is no adversary nor evil
11 14 Lord raised up an a. to Solomon, Adad
23 raised up against him an a., Razon
25 and he was an adversary to Israel all
Esth 9 24 the enemy and adversary of the Jews
Job 27 7 and my adversary as the wicked one
Ps 73 10 is the adversary to provoke thy name
Eccu 36 9 take away the adversary, and crush the
Isa 50 6 who is my adversary? Let him come near
Lam 2 4 he hath fixed his right hand as an a.
4 12 the a. and the enemy should enter in
Zach 3 1 stood on his right hand to be his a.
2 Ma 10 26 to be . . . an a. to their adversaries
Mat 5 25 be at agreement with thy adversary
25 lest perhaps a. deliver thee to the
Luke 12 58 when thou goest with thy a. to the
18 3 avenge me of my adversary. And he
1 Tim 5 14 give no occasion to the adversary
1 P 5 8 your a. the devil . . . goeth about seeking
adversity Eccu 12 8 enemy shall not be hidden in a.
Eccu 12 9 and a friend is known in his adversity
2 Ma 6 16 though he chastise his people with a.
12 30 even in the times of their adversity
advertise 3 J 10 I will advertise his works
advice 2 Pa 10 14 according to a. of the young men
Eccu 6 24 counsel and cast not away my advice
2 C 8 10 herein I give my advice; for this is
advise Eccu 8 20 a. not with fools, for they
advised Eccu 22 19 established by a. counsel
advocate 1 J 2 1 we have an a. with the Father
Aen Josu 15 32 Selim and Aen and Remmon: all the
1 Pa 4 32 their towns also were Etam and Aen
afar Deut 28 49 bring upon thee a nation from afar
Deut 29 22 the strangers that shall come from afar
Tob 13 14 nations from afar shall come to thee
Prov 31 14 she bringeth her bread from afar. And
Wisd 14 17 brought their resemblance from afar
Isa 10 3 the calamity which cometh from afar
30 27 the name of the Lord cometh from afar
43 6 bring my sons from afar, and my
49 1 hearken, ye people from afar. The Lord
12 behold these shall come from afar and
60 4 thy sons shall come from afar, and thy
9 that I may bring thy sons from afar
Jer 5 15 will bring upon you a nation from afar
31 3 the Lord hath appeared from afar to me
Bar 4 15 brought a nation upon them from afar
Eze 23 40 they sent for men coming from afar, to
Haba 1 8 for their horsemen shall come from afar
Zach 10 9 and from afar they shall remember me
afar off Gen 22 4 he saw the place afar off
Gen 24 63 his eyes, he saw camels coming afar off
37 18 when they saw him afar off, before he
Exod 2 4 his sister standing afar off, and
20 18 struck with fear, they stood afar off
21 the people stood afar off. But Moses
24 1 of Israel, you shall adore afar off
11 upon those . . . that retired afar off
33 7 pitched it without the camp afar off
Num 9 10 or shall be in a journey afar off in
Deut 13 7 nations . . . that are near or afar off
Josu 3 4 that you may see it afar off and know
16 the waters . . . were seen afar off from
1 K 26 13 stood on the top of the hill afar off
2 K 15 17 king . . . stood afar off from the house
2 Pa 5 13 the sound was heard afar off, so that
6 36 to a land either afar off or near at
20 24 they saw afar off all the country for a
1 Es 3 13 shout and the voice was heard afar off
2 Es 12 42 the joy of Jerusalem was heard afar off
Tob 10 7 if possible see him coming afar off
11 5 from whence she might see afar off
6 she saw him afar off and presently
Jdth 13 13 and Judith from afar off cried to the
Job 2 12 had lifted up their eyes afar off, they
36 25 see him, every one beholdeth afar off
39 25 ha, ha, he smelleth the battle afar off
29 prey, and her eyes behold afar off
Ps 9 1 why, O Lord, hast thou retired afar off
37 12 they that were near me stood afar off
64 6 of the earth and in the sea afar off
137 6 and the high he knoweth afar off. If
138 3 hast understood my thoughts afar off
Prov 27 10 that is near, than a brother afar off
Eccu 21 8 by a bold tongue is known afar off, but
24 44 and I will declare it afar off. I will
27 22 he is gone afar off, he is fled, as a

Isa 5 26 lift up a sign to the nations afar off
8 9 and give ear, all ye lands afar off
13 5 them that come from a country afar off
23 7 shall carry her afar off to sojourn
46 12 justice near, it shall not be afar off
66 19 and Greece, to the islands afar off
Jer 23 23 saith the Lord, and not a God afar off
30 10 will save thee from a country afar off
31 10 in the islands that are afar off and
46 27 I will save thee from afar off, and thy
51 50 remember the Lord afar off, and let
Eze 12 27 this man prophesieth of times afar off
Mich 4 3 and rebuke strong nations afar off
Mat 26 58 Peter followed him afar off. Mark 14:54; Luke 22:54
27 55 many women afar off. Mark 15:40
Mark 5 6 seeing Jesus afar off, he ran and adored
8 3 for some of them came from afar off
11 13 when he had seen afar off a fig tree
Luke 14 32 whilst the other is yet afar off, sending
16 23 he saw Abraham afar off and Lazarus in
17 12 that were lepers, who stood afar off
18 13 the publican standing afar off would
23 49 the women . . . stood afar off beholding
Acts 22 21 unto Gentiles afar off will I send thee
Eph 2 13 you, who some time were afar off, are
17 preached peace to you that were afar off
Heb 11 13 beholding them afar off, and saluting
Apoc 18 10 standing afar off for fear of her
15 merchants . . . shall stand afar off from
17 every shipmaster . . . stood afar off
affable Eccu 4 7 make thyself affable to the
affair Eccu 42 3 of the affair of companions and
affairs 1 Ma 3 32 to oversee the affairs of the
1 Ma 6 56 to take upon him the a. of the kingdom
57 to take order for the a. of the kingdom
10 20 thou be of one mind with us in our a.
37 shall be set over the a. of the kingdom
41 were over the a. the years before
11 63 to remove him from the affairs of the
13 15 a. which he had the management of
2 Ma 3 7 who had the charge over his affairs
4 21 excluded from the a. of the kingdom
23 concerning certain necessary affairs
8 8 to send aid to the king's affairs
10 11 he appointed over the a. of his realm
11 1 had chief charge over all the affairs
19 if . . . will keep yourselves loyal in a.
26 comfort, and look to their own affairs
13 2 had charge over the a. of the realm
23 Philip, who had been left over the a.
14 14 to be the welfare of their affairs
affect Eccu 13 14 affect not to speak with him as
affected 2 Ma 14 24 he was well a. to the man
affection Ps 72 7 passed into the a. of the heart
Wisd 14 21 men serving either their affection
2 Ma 14 37 for his a. was called the father of
Rom 1 31 foolish, dissolute, without affection
Phil 2 20 with sincere a. is solicitous for you
2 Tim 3 3 men shall be . . . without affection
affections Rom 1 26 delivered them up to shameful a.
affinity Lev 18 14 who is joined to thee by a.
Lev 25 49 his kinsman by blood or by affinity
3 K 3 1 and he made affinity with Pharao the
2 Pa 18 1 and was joined by affinity to Achab
Gal 4 25 which hath affinity to that Jerusalem
affirm Rom 3 8 and as some affirm that we say
1 Tim 1 7 understanding . . . nor whereof they a.
Titus 3 8 I will have thee affirm constantly
affirmed Luke 22 59 a. . . . this man was also with
Acts 12 15 but she affirmed that it was so. Then
25 19 deceased whom Paul affirmed to be alive
affirming 2 Pa 32 11 a. that . . . God shall deliver

Acts 5 36 Theodas, a. himself to be somebody
9 22 at Damascus, a. that this is the Christ
1 C 14 25 will adore God, a. that God is among
afflict Gen 15 13 shall . . . afflict them 400 years
Gen 19 9 we will afflict thee more than them
31 50 if thou afflict my daughters, and if
Exod 1 11 works, to afflict them with burdens
22 21 not molest a stranger nor afflict him
23 22 and will afflict them that afflict thee
Lev 16 29 you shall afflict your souls. 31; 23:27, 32; 29:7
25 17 do not afflict your countrymen, but
43 afflict him not by might, but fear thy
52 he shall not afflict him violently in
Num 30 14 to afflict her soul by fasting or
Deut 8 2 to afflict thee and to prove thee and
28 22 may the Lord a. thee with miserable
Josu 24 20 he will turn and will afflict you and
Judg 16 5 to bind and afflict him [Samson]: which
1 K 1 8 why dost thou [Anna] a. thy heart? Am
2 K 7 10 neither shall children of iniquity a.
12 18 how much more will he a. himself if we
13 20 afflict not thy heart for this thing
21 he would not a. the spirit of his son
3 K 8 37 if their enemy afflict them, besieging
11 39 I will for this a. the seed of David
2 Pa 6 26 from their sins, when thou dost a. them
1 Es 8 21 that we might afflict ourselves before
Job 2 3 that I should afflict him without cause
19 2 how long do you afflict my soul, and
Ps 3 2 why . . . are they multiplied that a. me
22 5 before me, against them that afflict me
43 3 didst a. the people, and cast them out
8 hast saved us from them that afflict us
59 14 shall bring to nothing them that a. us
68 21 in thy sight are all they that afflict
118 157 they that persecute me and afflict me
142 12 will cut off all them that a. my soul
Prov 10 3 Lord will not a. the soul of the just
22 23 will a. them that have afflicted his
Ecce 10 15 the labor of fools shall afflict them
Eccu 4 3 afflict not the heart of the needy
30 22 a. not thyself in thy own counsel. The
Isa 24 1 shall a. the face thereof and scatter
58 5 a man to afflict his soul for a day
60 14 the children of them that afflict thee
64 12 hold thy peace and a. us vehemently
Jer 10 18 I will a. them so that they may be
22 3 a. not the stranger, the fatherless
25 6 and I will not afflict you. And you
30 20 I will visit against all that a. them
31 28 to scatter and destroy and afflict
Dan 10 12 to a. thyself in the sight of thy God
Nah 1 12 and I will afflict thee no more. And
Zach 8 14 as I purposed to a. you, when your
Mala 3 8 shall a man a. God? For you a. me. And
8 said: Wherein do we afflict thee? In
9 cursed with want, and you a. me, even
2 Ma 5 22 left also governors to a. the people
Acts 12 1 Herod . . . to a. some of the church
Apoc 16 8 was given unto him to a. men with heat
afflicted Gen 16 6 when Sarai a. her, she ran away
Exod 1 13 Egyptians . . . afflicted them and mocked
5 22 why hast thou afflicted this people
23 he [Pharao] hath afflicted thy people
7 18 afflicted when they drink the water
Lev 23 29 every soul that is not a. on this day
26 39 shall be a. for sins of their fathers
Num 11 11 why hast thou afflicted thy servant
15 that I be not afflicted with so great
20 15 Egyptians a. us and our. Deut 26:6
Deut 8 3 he a. thee with want and gave thee
16 after he had afflicted and proved thee

29 22 wherewith the Lord hath afflicted it
Judg 2 18 heard the groanings of the afflicted
6 9 of all the enemies that afflicted you
10 8 they were a. and grievously oppressed
Ruth 1 21 and the Almighty hath afflicted? So
1 K 1 6 her rival also afflicted her [Anna]
5 6 destroyed them and afflicted Azotus
12 not die, were a. with the emerods: and
10 18 hand of all the kings who afflicted you
30 6 David was greatly afflicted: for the
3 K 17 20 hast thou a. also the widow with whom
4 K 17 20 Lord . . . a. them and delivered them into
2 Pa 28 20 the Assyrians, who also afflicted him
2 Es 9 27 hands of their enemies, and they a.
Tob 9 4 one day more, his soul will be a.
10 9 and their spirit is grievously afflicted
Job 19 6 hath not a. me with an equal judgment
20 26 he shall be a. when left in his
30 11 opened his quiver and hath a. me and
25 I wept heretofore for him that was a.
31 39 if I . . . have a. the souls of the tillers
Ps 16 9 face of the wicked who have a. me. My
30 10 have mercy on me, O Lord, for I am a.
37 9 I am afflicted and humbled exceedingly
50 19 a sacrifice to God is an afflicted
55 2 he hath afflicted me fighting against
77 42 from hand of him that afflicted them
93 5 they have afflicted thy inheritance
105 11 the water covered them that a. them
32 and Moses was afflicted for their sakes
42 their enemies a. them: and they were
106 39 they were a. through the trouble of
Prov 11 15 shall be a. with evil, that is surety
22 23 will afflict them that a. his soul
Wisd 3 5 a. in few things, in many they shall be
5 1 against those that have afflicted them
14 15 a father being a. with bitter grief
19 15 a. them whom they had received with
Eccu 4 4 reject not the petition of the a.: and
30 14 rich man who is weak and a. with evils
Isa 51 13 presence of his fury who afflicted thee
53 4 as one struck by God and afflicted. But
58 10 and shalt satisfy the afflicted soul
63 10 afflicted the spirit of his Holy One
Jer 8 21 I am afflicted and made sorrowful
14 3 they were confounded and afflicted and
17 virgin daughter of my people is a.
Lam 2 5 and hath multiplied . . . the afflicted
3 33 he hath not willingly afflicted nor
49 my eye is afflicted and hath not been
Bar 4 31 the wicked that have afflicted thee
Eze 22 29 they afflicted the needy and poor, and
Mich 4 6 and her whom I had afflicted. And I
7 that hath been a., a mighty nation
Nah 1 12 I have a. thee, and I will afflict thee
Soph 3 19 I will cut off all that have afflicted
Zach 10 2 thus shall be a. because they have no
1 Ma 9 68 and they afflicted him exceedingly, for
10 46 he had afflicted them exceedingly. And
2 Ma 8 32 who had many ways a. the Jews. And when
Mat 24 9 deliver you up to be afflicted, and
Acts 7 19 this same . . . afflicted our fathers
Heb 11 25 Moses . . . rather choosing to be a. with
37 being in want, distressed, afflicted
James 4 9 be afflicted and mourn and weep: let
afflicteth Ps 41 10 whilst my enemy afflicteth me
Ps 42 2 I go sorrowful whilst my enemy a. me
Prov 13 12 hope . . . deferred afflicteth the soul
19 26 that afflicteth his father and chaseth
afflicting Job 6 10 a. me with sorrow, he spare
affliction Gen 16 11 because Lord hath heard thy a.
Gen 29 32 Ruben, saying: The Lord saw my a.: now
31 42 God beheld my a. and the labor of my
35 3 who heard me in the day of my a., and
42 21 therefore is this affliction come upon
Exod 2 11 [Moses] went out . . . and saw their a.
3 7 I have seen the affliction of my people
9 I have seen their a. wherewith they
17 bring you forth out of the a. of Egypt
4 31 and that he had looked upon their a.
Deut 4 29 if thou seek him with . . . all the a.
16 3 shalt thou eat . . . the bread of a.
26 7 looked down upon our affliction and
1 K 1 11 wilt look down on the a. of thy servant
22 2 all that were . . . under a. of mind
2 K 16 12 the Lord may look upon my affliction
22 19 prevented me in day of my affliction
24 16 the Lord had pity on the affliction
3 K 22 27 and feed him with bread of affliction
4 K 14 26 the Lord saw the affliction of Israel
1 Es 9 5 I [Esdras] rose up from my affliction
2 Es 1 3 are in great affliction and reproach
2 17 you know the affliction wherein we are
9 9 sawest the affliction of our fathers
Job 6 21 and now seeing my a. you are afraid
7 11 I will speak in the a. of my spirit
10 15 being filled with affliction and misery
30 16 and the days of affliction possess me
27 days of affliction have prevented me
36 15 and shall open his ear in affliction
Ps 17 7 in my a. I called upon the Lord, and I
19 they prevented me in the day of my a.
43 20 humbled us in the place of affliction
80 8 thou calledst upon me in affliction
106 13 they cried to Lord in their a. 19, 28
135 23 he was mindful of us in our affliction
Prov 10 22 neither shall affliction be joined to
27 10 thy brother's house in day of thy a.
Ecce 5 13 they are lost with very great a.: he
8 6 business and great affliction for man
12 1 before the time of affliction come and
12 and much study is an a. of the flesh
Wisd 11 13 a double affliction came upon them
Eccu 3 17 in day of a. thou shalt be remembered
4 19 will scourge him with the a. of her
11 29 the a. of an hour maketh one forget
25 20 any a., but the a. from them that hate
27 6 trial of affliction [trieth] just men
35 26 mercy of God . . . in time of affliction
40 9 famine and affliction and scourges
Isa 63 9 in all their a. he was not troubled
Jer 2 27 in the time of their a. they will say
28 deliver thee in the time of thy a.
8 21 for the a. of the daughter of my people
11 12 not save them in the time of their a.
14 their cry to me in the time of their a.
14 17 my people is afflicted with a great a.
15 11 I shall help thee in the time of a.
17 17 art my hope in the day of affliction
18 bring upon them the day of affliction
19 3 I will bring an a. upon this place
24 9 them up to vexation and affliction
28 8 prophesies . . . of war and of affliction
29 11 thoughts of peace and not of a., to give
18 I will give them up unto affliction to
30 15 why criest thou for thy affliction? Thy
51 2 on every side in the day of her a. Let
64 she shall not rise up from the a. that
Lam 1 3 her dwelling place because of her a.
4 her virgins are in affliction, and she
7 hath remembered the days of her a. and
9 behold, O Lord, my affliction, because
Bar 5 1 garment of thy mourning and affliction
Eze 7 5 one a., behold an a. is come. An end is
35 5 sword in the time of their affliction
Osee 6 1 in their a. they will rise early to me

Amos 6 6 not concerned for the a. of Joseph
Jon 2 3 I cried out of my a. to the Lord, and
Nah 1 9 there shall not rise a double affliction
Acts 7 34 I have seen the a. of my people which
2 C 2 4 out of much affliction . . . I wrote to
Phil 1 17 supposing they raise a. to my bands
1 P 5 9 the same a. befalls your brethren who
afflictions Deut 28 60 on thee all the a. of Egypt
Deut 31 17 all evils and a. shall find them, so
21 after many evils and a. shall have come
3 K 8 35 by occasion of their afflictions: then
2 Pa 20 9 we will cry to thee in our afflictions
Jdth 8 20 our blood of the a. of our enemies, and
Ps 33 20 many are the afflictions of the just
65 11 thou hast laid afflictions on our back
Eccu 51 5 from the gates of a. which compassed
1 Ma 2 30 because a. increased upon them. And it
Acts 20 23 a. wait for me at Jerusalem. But I fear
2 Tim 3 11 hast fully known my . . . afflictions
Heb 10 32 you endured a great fight of a. And on
affrighted Josu 2 11 hearing these things were a.
Job 4 14 all my bones were affrighted: and when
41 16 and being a., shall purify themselves
Wisd 17 4 visions appearing to them, a. them
Jer 51 32 fire, and the men of war are affrighted
Dan 4 2 I saw a dream that affrighted me: and my
7 15 I Daniel was affrighted at these things
Mark 16 6 be not affrighted; you seek Jesus of
Luke 24 22 certain women also of our company a. us
affront Heb 10 29 offered an a. to the Spirit of
afraid Gen 3 10 I was afraid because I was naked
Gen 18 15 I did not laugh: for she was afraid
19 30 he [Lot] was afraid to stay in Segor
26 7 he was afraid to confess that she was
32 7 then Jacob was greatly afraid: and in
11 I am greatly afraid of him Esau: lest
38 11 he was afraid lest he also might die
43 18 they being much afraid, said there one
Lev 26 6 there shall be none to make you afraid
Deut 1 29 fear not, neither be ye afraid of them
2 4 in Seir, and they will be afraid of you
21 21 all Israel hearing it may be afraid
28 60 of Egypt, which thou wast afraid of
Josu 10 2 [Adonisedec] was exceedingly afraid
Judg 7 10 if thou be afraid to go alone, let Phara
8 20 for he was afraid, being yet a boy
Ruth 3 8 the man was afraid and troubled: and
1 K 21 12 exceedingly afraid at the face of Achis
28 5 Saul saw the army . . . and was afraid
2 K 6 9 David was afraid of the Lord that day
22 5 floods of Belial have made me afraid
3 K 19 3 Elias was afraid and, rising up, he
2 Es 6 13 that I being afraid should do this
Tob 6 3 and Tobias being afraid of him, cried
15 I am afraid lest the same things should
7 11 when Raguel heard this he was afraid
Jdth 12 12 let not my good maid be afraid to go in
Job 3 25 which I was afraid of, hath befallen me
5 22 shalt not be afraid of the beasts of
6 21 now seeing my affliction you are afraid
11 19 there shall be none to make thee afraid
21 6 I am afraid and trembling taketh hold
30 10 and are not afraid to spit in my face
31 34 if I have been a. at a very great
32 6 I was afraid to show you my opinion
Ps 26 1 of my life: of whom shall I be afraid
63 10 troubled: and every man was afraid. And
64 9 borders, shall be afraid at thy signs
90 5 thou shalt not be afraid of the terror
118 120 fear: for I am afraid of thy judgments
Ecce 12 5 and they shall be afraid in the way
Wisd 8 15 terrible kings hearing shall be a. of
17 3 being horribly afraid and troubled with
18 25 gave place, and was afraid of them: for
Eccu 26 5 my heart hath been afraid, and at the
30 9 his way, and he shall make thee afraid
34 16 and shall not be a.: for he is his hope
Isa 7 4 let not thy heart be afraid of the two
8 12 neither fear ye their fear nor be a.
17 2 none to make them afraid. Mich 4:4; Nah 2:11; 1 Ma 14:12
19 16 they shall be amazed and afraid because
20 5 they shall be afraid and ashamed of
31 4 nor be afraid of their multitude: so
9 his princes fleeing shall be afraid
33 14 the sinners in Sion are a., trembling
51 12 that thou shouldst be a. of a mortal
13 hast been afraid continually all the
57 11 hast thou been solicitous and afraid
Jer 3 8 sister Juda was not afraid, but went
17 18 let them be a., and let not me be a.
26 21 Urias heard it and was afraid and fled
38 19 I am afraid because of the Jews that
42 11 of whom you are greatly afraid: fear
16 and the famine, whereof you are afraid
49 37 Elam to be afraid before their enemies
Bar 6 4 that you imitate not . . . and be afraid
Eze 2 6 neither be thou afraid of their words
18 14 is afraid, and shall not do the like
32 10 kings shall be horribly a. for thee
Amos 3 6 a city and the people not be afraid
Abdi 9 men of the south shall be afraid, that
Haba 3 2 have heard thy hearing, and was afraid
Mala 2 5 and he was afraid before my name. The
1 Ma 1 19 but Ptolemee was a. at his presence
4 8 neither be ye afraid of their assault
5 41 if he be afraid to pass over and camp
7 30 he was much afraid of him and would not
16 22 he heard it he was exceedingly afraid
2 Ma 8 13 and some of them being afraid and
14 18 afraid to try the matter by the sword
15 24 that they may be afraid, who come with
Mat 2 22 [Joseph] was afraid to go thither: and
14 30 seeing the wind strong, he was afraid
21 26 we are afraid of the multitude: for all
25 25 being afraid, I went and hid thy talent
Luke 8 25 being afraid, wondered, saying . . . Who
12 4 not a. of them who kill the body
John 14 27 let not your heart . . . be afraid
Acts 22 29 tribune also was a. after he understood
Rom 13 3 wilt thou then not be a. of the power
Gal 4 11 I am afraid of you lest perhaps I have
Titus 2 8 who is on the contrary part, may be a.
be not afraid Gen 45 5 b. . . . and let it not seem
Deut 20 3 be not afraid, do not give back, fear
4 K 19 6 b. . . . for the words which thou hast
25 24 be not afraid to serve the Chaldees
2 Pa 32 7 be not afraid nor dismayed for the king
2 Es 4 14 be not afraid of them. Remember the
Tob 7 12 be not afraid to give her to this man
Ps 48 17 be not thou afraid, when a man shall be
Prov 3 25 be not afraid of sudden fear, nor of the
Eccu 18 22 be not afraid to be justified even to
Isa 10 24 be not afraid of the Assyrian: he shall
37 6 be not afraid of the words that thou
51 7 and be not afraid of their blasphemies
Jer 1 8 be not a. at their presence: for. 17
10 2 be not afraid of the signs of heaven
John 6 20 it is I, be not afraid. They were willing
1 P 3 14 be not afraid of their fear, and be not
were afraid Gen 20 8 all the men were . . . afraid
Gen 50 15 his brethren were afraid and talked one
Exod 34 30 Aaron and . . . were afraid to come near
Num 12 8 why then were you not afraid to speak
Josu 8 15 making as if they were afraid, and
1 K 4 7 the Philistines were afraid, saying

7 7 they were afraid of the Philistines
13 7 that followed him were greatly afraid
17 11 were dismayed and greatly afraid. Now
2 K 10 19 by Israel, were afraid and fled away
19 all the Syrians were afraid to help the
3 K 1 49 all the guests of Adonias were afraid
4 K 10 4 they were exceedingly afraid and said
2 Es 6 16 which were round about us were afraid
Jdth 4 1 were exceedingly afraid of him. Dread
Job 32 15 they were afraid and answered no more
Ps 76 17 waters saw thee: and they were afraid
Eccu 29 10 but they were afraid to be defrauded
Jer 36 24 heard all these words were not afraid
41 18 for they were afraid of them, because
Dan 5 19 trembled and were afraid of him: whom
Jon 1 5 the mariners were afraid, and the men
10 the men were greatly afraid and they
1 Ma 8 12 heard their name, were afraid of them
16 6 people were afraid to go over the river
2 Ma 13 11 they were afraid to be deprived of the
Mat 17 6 the disciples . . . were very much afraid
27 54 were sore afraid, saying: Indeed this
Mark 5 15 well in his wits, and they were afraid
9 31 they were afraid to ask him. Luke 9:45
10 32 to Jerusalem . . . and following were a.
16 8 nothing to any man; for they were a.
Luke 8 35 in his right mind; and they were afraid
9 34 were afraid when they entered the cloud
24 5 and as they were afraid and bowed down
John 6 19 they see Jesus walking . . . they were a.
Acts 9 26 all were afraid of him [Paul], not
16 38 were afraid, hearing they were Romans
Africa Isa 66 19 I will send of them . . . into A.
Nah 3 9 Africa and the Libyans were thy helpers
afterbirths Deut 28 57 the filth of the a. that
afternoon Gen 3 8 in paradise at the a. air
Agabus Acts 11 28 one of them named Agabus rising
Acts 21 10 from Judea a certain prophet named A.
Agag Num 24 7 Agag his king shall be removed, and
1 K 15 8 he took Agag the king of Amalec alive
9 Saul and the people spared Agag and the
20 have brought Agag the king of Amalec
32 Samuel said: Bring hither to me Agag
32 Agag was presented to him very fat and
32 Agag said: Doth bitter death separate
Esth 3 1 Aman . . . of the race of Agag. 10; 9:24
Agagite Esth 8 3 that the malice of Aman the A.
Esth 9 6 beside the ten sons of Aman the Agagite
against Mat 12 30 not with me is a. me. Luke 11:23
Mark 9 39 is not against you is for you. Luke 9:50
Rom 8 31 if God be for us, who is against us
Agar Gen 16 1 having a handmaid . . . named Agar
Gen 16 3 took Agar the Egyptian her handmaid
8 Agar . . . whence comest thou? And whither
15 Agar brought forth a son to Abram
16 old when Agar brought him forth Ismael
21 9 son of Agar the Egyptian playing with
17 angel of God called to A. from heaven
17 what art thou doing, Agar? Fear not
25 12 A. the Egyptian, Sara's servant, bore
Bar 3 23 the children of Agar also, that search
Gal 4 24 the one from mount Sina . . . which is A.
Agarai 1 Pa 11 38 Mibahar the son of Agarai. Selec
Agarene 1 Pa 27 31 over the sheep, Jaziz and A.
Agarens Ps 82 7 made a covenant . . . Moab and the A.
Agarites 1 Pa 5 10 they fought against the A. 19
1 Pa 5 20 Agarites were delivered into their
agate Exod 28 19 in the third . . . an a. 39:12
age Gen 21 5 at this age of his father was Isaac
Gen 24 1 Abraham was old and advanced in age
35 29 being spent with age he [Isaac] died
43 33 and the youngest according to his age
48 10 eyes were dim by reason of his great age
Num 8 25 fiftieth year of their age, they shall
19 2 bring unto thee a red cow of full age
30 4 and but yet a girl in age: if her father
17 that is as yet but a girl in age
Deut 8 4 covered, hath not decayed for age
29 5 shoes of your feet consumed with age
Josu 9 5 old shoes, which for a show of age were
13 1 thou art grown old and advanced in age
Judg 8 21 strength of a man is according to his a.
Ruth 1 12 for I am now spent with age and not fit
1 K 17 12 of great age among men. And his three
2 K 19 32 Berzellai . . . was of a great age, that is
3 K 14 4 his eyes were dim by reason of his age
1 Pa 7 40 were of the age that was fit for war
23 3 numbered from the age of thirty years
26 32 his brethren of stronger age, 2,700
29 28 and he [David] died in a good age, full
2 Pa 36 17 man or even him that stooped for age
Job 32 7 I hoped that greater age would speak
Prov 17 22 a joyful mind maketh age flourishing
Ecce 6 3 many years and attain to a great age
Eccu 17 25 go to the side of the holy age with
24 46 their offspring even to the holy age
26 22 is the beauty of the face in a ripe age
41 4 who is in a decrepit age and that is
42 9 lest she pass away the flower of her a.
Isa 46 9 remember the former age, for I am God
Eze 13 18 for the heads of persons of every age
Dan 5 1 every one drank according to his age
2 Ma 4 40 far gone both in age and in madness
5 24 to kill all that were of perfect age
6 23 began to consider the dignity of his age
24 it doth not become our age, said he, to
24 at the age of fourscore and ten years
7 27 thee and brought thee up unto this age
15 13 another man, admirable for age and glory
Luke 2 52 Jesus advanced in wisdom and age and
3 23 beginning about the age of thirty years
John 9 21 ask himself: he is of age, let him speak
23 parents say: He is of age, ask himself
1 C 7 36 that she is above the age, and it must
Eph 4 13 of the age of the fulness of Christ
1 Tim 5 9 no less than threescore years of age
Heb 11 11 conceive seed even past the time of age
old age Gen 15 15 be buried in a good old age
Gen 21 2 [Sara] bore a son in her old age, at
7 whom she bore to him in his old age
24 36 borne my master a son in her old age
25 8 [Abraham] died in a good old age, and
37 3 because he had him in his old age: and
44 20 young boy, that was born in his old age
Deut 33 25 thy youth, so also shall thy old age be
Judg 8 32 the son of Joas died in a good old age
Ruth 4 15 comfort thy soul and cherish thy old age
3 K 15 23 in time of his old age he was diseased
Tob 5 23 hast taken the staff of our old age
6 15 I should bring down their old age with
10 4 light of our eyes, staff of our old age
14 15 found them in health in a good old age
Ps 70 9 cast me not off in the time of old age
18 unto old age and gray hairs: O God
91 11 my old age in plentiful mercy. My eye
15 shall still increase in fruitful old a.
Prov 16 31 old age is a crown of dignity, when it
Wisd 3 17 last old age shall be without honor
4 8 venerable old age is not that of long
9 a spotless life is old age. He pleased
Eccu 3 14 support the old age of thy father, and
8 7 despise not a man in his old age; for
25 5 how shalt thou find them in thy old age
30 26 pensiveness will bring old age before
46 11 strength continued even to his old age
Isa 46 4 even to your old age I am the same, and

Dan 13 50 hath given thee the honor of old age
2 Ma 6 25 a stain and a curse upon my old age
27 shall show myself worthy of my old age
Luke 1 35 hath conceived a son in her old age
Age 2 K 23 11 Semma the son of Age of Arari. And
aged Lev 19 32 honor the person of the aged man
Job 12 20 taketh away the doctrine of the aged
15 10 there are with us also aged and ancient
32 9 they that are aged are not the wise
Wisd 2 10 nor honor the ancient gray hairs of a.
Eccu 25 7 how comely is wisdom for the aged, and
27 is to the feet of the aged, so is a
42 8 the unwise and foolish and the aged
Isa 9 15 the aged and honorable, he is the head
2 Ma 8 30 and the widows, yea and the aged also
Titus 2 2 that the aged men be sober, chaste
3 the aged women in like manner in holy
ages Tob 13 1 and thy kingdom is unto all ages
Job 22 15 dost thou desire to keep path of ages
Ps 73 12 God is our king before ages: he hath
144 13 thy kingdom is a kingdom of all ages
148 6 established them . . . for ages of ages
Ecce 1 10 before in the ages that were before us
Wisd 8 8 done and the events of times and ages
Eccu 36 19 thou art God the beholder of all ages
Isa 58 12 places that have been desolate for ages
Dan 2 21 he changeth times and ages: taketh
3 52 praised and exalted above all in all a.
Eph 2 7 he might show in the ages to come the
Col 1 26 mystery which hath been hidden from a.
1 Tim 1 17 to the king of ages, immortal, invisible
Heb 9 26 now once at the end of ages he hath
Jude 25 empire and power before all ages and
25 now and for all ages of ages. Amen
Apoc 15 3 and true are thy ways, O King of ages
Aggeus 1 Es 5 1 Aggeus . . . prophesied to the Jews
1 Es 6 14 according to the prophecy of Aggeus
Ps 111 1 of the returning of Aggeus and
145 1 alleluia, of Aggeus and Zacharias
Agge 1 1 came by the hand of Aggeus. 3; 2:2
12 to the words of Aggeus the prophet
13 A. the messenger of the Lord . . . spoke
2 11 the word of the Lord came to Aggeus the
14 Aggeus said: If one that is unclean by
15 Aggeus answered and said: So is this
21 came a second time to Aggeus in the
Aggi Num 26 15 Aggi, of him is the family of the
Aggites Num 26 15 of him is the family of the A.
Aggith 1 Pa 3 2 fourth Adonias the son of Aggith
ago 1 K 9 20 asses which were lost three days ago
1 K 30 13 I began to be sick three days ago. For
1 Es 5 11 that was built these many years ago
Jdth 5 22 some years ago when they had revolted
Isa 22 11 a distance, that wrought it long ago
agony 2 Ma 3 21 high priest who was in an agony
Luke 22 43 being in an agony, he prayed the longer
agree 3 K 21 15 who would not agree with thee
2 Es 5 10 let us all agree not to call for it
Eccu 25 2 man and wife that agree well together
1 Ma 8 1 agree to all things that are requested
2 Ma 11 14 that he would agree to all things that
Mat 20 13 didst thou not agree with me for a
Mark 14 59 their witness did not agree. And the
Acts 15 15 to this agree the words of the prophets
agreeable Exod 15 23 name also a. to the place
Prov 5 19 be thy dearest hind and most a. fawn
Wisd 9 9 knew what was agreeable to thy eyes
12 15 not a. to thy power to condemn him who
Eccu 1 34 and that which is agreeable to him is
25 23 be more a. to abide with a lion and a
Eze 33 32 sung with a sweet and agreeable voice
Osee 10 1 branches, the fruit is agreeable to it
Nah 3 4 the harlot that was beautiful and a.
2 Ma 14 22 so they made an agreeable conference
agreed Gen 16 2 [Abram] agreed to her request
Gen 34 24 they all agreed, and circumcised all
37 27 his brethren agreed to his words. And
Judg 18 20 he agreed to their words and took the
4 K 16 9 he agreed to his desire: for the king
23 3 and the people agreed to the covenant
2 Pa 30 21 with instruments that agreed to their
1 Es 5 5 it was agreed that the matter should
Jer 34 18 which they agreed to in my presence
Dan 13 14 they agreed upon a time, when they
Amos 3 3 walk together except they be agreed
1 Ma 8 7 and that which was agreed upon, and
2 Ma 14 28 the articles that were agreed upon
Mat 20 2 having agreed with the laborers for a
John 9 22 agreed . . . if any man should confess him
Acts 5 9 why have you agreed together to tempt
23 20 the Jews have agreed to desire thee
28 25 when they agreed not . . . they departed
agreeing Gen 40 5 interpretation a. to themselves
Mark 14 56 and their evidences were not agreeing
Phil 2 2 being of one accord, a. in sentiment
agreement Eccu 13 3 what a. shall the earthen pot
1 Ma 6 58 let us come to an a. with these men
2 Ma 12 25 would restore them according to the a.
Mat 5 25 be at agreement with thy adversary
2 C 6 16 what a. hath the temple of God with
agreeth Luke 5 36 piece . . . a. not with the old
Agrippa Acts 25 13 Agrippa and Bernice came. 23
Acts 25 22 A. said to Festus: I would also hear
24 Festus saith: King A. and all ye men
26 brought him . . . before thee, O king A.
26 1 A. said to Paul: Thou art permitted to
2 I think myself happy, O king Agrippa
19 O king Agrippa, I was not incredulous
27 believest thou the prophets, O king A.
28 A. said to Paul: In a little thou
32 A. said to Festus: This man might have
aground Acts 27 41 they run the ship aground; and
ah Isa 1 24 ah! I will comfort myself over my
Jer 1 6 ah, ah, ah, Lord God: behold I cannot
14 13 I said: Ah, ah, ah, O Lord God.
Eze 4:14; 20:49
Joel 1 15 to the Lord: Ah, ah, ah, for the
aha Isa 44 16 aha, I am warm, I have seen the
Eze 26 2 hath said of Jerusalem: Aha, the gates
36 2 aha, the everlasting heights are given
Ahalab Judg 1 31 of Ahalab and of Achazib and
Ahara 1 Pa 8 1 Benjamin begot . . . Ahara the third
Aharehel 1 Pa 4 8 Cos begot . . . the kindred of A.
Ahasthari 1 Pa 4 6 Naara bore him . . . Ahasthari
Ahava 1 Es 8 15 river, which runneth down to Ahava
1 Es 8 21 there a fast by the river Ahava, that
31 we set forward from the river Ahava
Ahaz 1 Pa 8 35 sons of Micha . . . Ahaz. 9:41
1 Pa 8 35 Ahaz begot Joada: and Joada begot
9 42 Ahaz begot Jara: and Jara begot
Ahazi 2 Es 11 13 Azreel the son of Ahazi the son
Aher 1 Pa 7 12 Hasim the sons of Aher. And the
Ahi 1 Pa 7 34 sons of Somer: Ahi and Roaga
Ahia 3 K 4 3 and Ahia, the sons of Sisa, scribes
1 Pa 11 36 Ahia a Phelonite, Hesro a Carmelite
Ahialon Judg 12 11 to him succeeded Ahialon a
Ahiam 1 Pa 11 34 Ahiam the son of Sachar an
Ahias 3 K 11 29 the prophet Ahias the Silonite
3 K 11 30 Ahias taking his new garment wherewith
12 15 spoken in the hand of Ahias. 15:29
14 2 go to Silo where Ahias the prophet is
4 Silo and came to the house of Ahias
5 Lord said to Ahias: Behold the wife
6 Ahias heard the sound of her feet
18 spoke by the hand of his servant Ahias
15 27 Baasa the son of A. 33; 21:22; 4 K 9:9

2 Pa 9 29 in the books of Ahias the Silonite
10 15 he had spoken by the hand of Ahias
Ahicam 4 K 22 12 commanded . . . Ahicam. 2 Pa 34:20
4 K 22 14 so Helcias the priest and Ahicam
25 22 Godolias the son of Ahicam. Jer 39:14; 41:1, 2, 6, 10, 16, 18; 43:6
Jer 26 24 hand of Ahicam the son of Saphan
Ahiezer Num 1 12 A. the son of Ammisaddai. 2:25; 7:66, 71; 10:25
1 Pa 12 3 the chief was Ahiezer, and Joas, the
Ahilud 2 K 8 16 Josaphat the son of Ahilud was recorder. 20:24; 3 K 4:3; 1 Pa 18:15
3 K 4 12 Bana the son of Ahilud, who governed
Ahimam 1 Pa 9 17 Accub and Telmon and Ahimam
Ahiman Josu 15 14 sons of Enac, Sesai and Ahiman
Judg 1 10 slew Sesai and Ahiman and Tholmai
Ahimelech 1 Pa 24 3 A. of the sons of Ithamar
1 Pa 24 6 and Ahimelech the son of Abiathar
31 Ahimelech and the princes of the
Ahinadab 3 K 4 14 Ahinadab . . . was chief in Manaim
Ahio 2 K 6 3 Oza and Ahio . . . drove the new cart
2 K 6 4 Ahio having care of the ark of God
1 Pa 8 14 Ahio and Sesac and Jerimoth and
31 and Gedor and Ahio and Zacher and
9 37 Ahio and Zacharias and Macelloth and
Ahion 3 K 15 20 and they smote Ahion and Dan and
2 Pa 16 4 they took Ahion and Dan and Abelmaim
Ahira Num 1 15 Ahira the son of Enan. 2:29; 7:78, 83; 10:27
Ahiram Num 26 38 A. of whom is the family of the
Ahiramites Num 26 38 of whom is the family of the A.
Ahisahar 1 Pa 7 10 Zethan and Tharsis and Ahisahar
Ahisar 3 K 4 6 and Ahisar governor of the house
Ahiu 1 Pa 7 19 the sons of Semida were Ahiu
Ahiud Num 34 27 of the tribe of Aser, Ahiud the
1 Pa 8 7 removed them and begot Oza and Ahiud
Ahobban 1 Pa 2 29 Abihail, who bore him Ahobban
Ahod Gen 46 10 sons of Simeon . . . Ahod. Exod 6:15
1 Pa 8 6 these are the sons of Ahod, heads of
Ahoe 1 Pa 8 4 Abisue and Naaman and Ahoe
Ahohite 2 K 23 9 Eleazar the son of Dodo the A.
2 K 23 28 Selmon the Ahohite, Maharai the
1 Pa 11 12 Eleazar his uncle's son the Ahohite
29 Ilai an Ahohite, Maharai a Netophathite
27 4 was under Dudia, an Ahohite, and after
Ahumai 1 Pa 4 2 Jahath, of whom were born Ahumai
Aia Gen 36 24 sons of Sebeon: Aia and Ana. 1 Pa 1:40
2 K 3 7 Respha, daughter of Aia. 21:8, 10, 11
Aialon Josu 10 12 thou, O moon, toward valley of A.
Josu 19 42 Selebin and Aialon and Jethela, Elon
21 24 and Aialon and Gethremmon, with their
Judg 1 35 in Aialon and Salebim. And the hand
1 K 14 31 Philistines from Machmas to Aialon
1 Pa 8 13 their kindreds that dwelt in Aialon
2 Pa 11 10 A. and Hebron, which are in Juda
28 18 and they took Bethsames and Aialon and
Aiath Isa 10 28 he shall come into Aiath, he shall
aid Num 14 9 all aid is gone from them: the Lord is
Josu 8 10 environed with aid of the fighting men
Judg 20 14 together in Gabaa to aid them and
4 K 15 19 to aid him and to establish him in
1 Pa 12 33 there came fifty thousand to his aid
19 9 the kings that were come to their aid
1 Es 8 22 I was ashamed to ask the king for aid
Jdth 7 25 if after five days . . . there come no aid
8 10 if within five days there come no aid
Ps 82 9 are come to the aid of the sons of Lot
90 1 dwelleth in the aid of the most High
Isa 13 15 every one that shall come to their aid
17 3 and aid shall cease from Ephraim, and
31 2 against aid of them that work iniquity
63 5 I sought, and there was none to give aid
1 Ma 8 28 given to them that come to their aid
10 24 that they may be with me to aid me. And
15 19 no aid to them that fight against them
26 sent to him 2,000 chosen to aid him
16 18 he should send him an army to aid him
2 Ma 8 8 to send aid to the king's affairs. And
Heb 4 16 mercy, and find grace in seasonable aid
aided Judg 9 24 of the Sichemites, who aided him
Acts 26 22 aided by the help of God, I stand unto
Aila 4 K 16 6 A. to Syria and drove the men of Juda out of A.; and the Edomites came into A.
Ailath 3 K 9 26 fleet in Asiongaber, which is by A.
2 Pa 8 17 Solomon went to Asiongaber and to A.
26 2 he built Ailath and restored it to the
ailed Ps 113 5 what ailed thee, O thou sea, that
aileth Josu 15 18 to her: What a. thee. Judg 1:14
Judg 18 23 said to Michas: What aileth thee? Why
24 and do you say: What aileth thee? And
1 K 11 5 what aileth the people that they weep
4 K 6 27 the king said to her: What aileth thee
Isa 22 1 what aileth thee also, that thou too
ain Ps 118 121 ain. Lam 1:16; 2:17; 3:49, 50, 51; 4:17
Ain Josu 19 7 Ain and Remmon and Athor and Asan
Josu 21 16 and Ain and Jeta and Bethsames, with
Aion 4 K 15 29 king of Assyria and took A. and
air 4 K 15 29 to every fowl of the air and to all
Gen 3 8 walking in paradise at the afternoon air
Exod 9 8 let Moses sprinkle it in the air in the
10 Moses sprinkled it in the air: and there
Num 11 31 they flew in the air two cubits high
Deut 28 22 with heat and with corrupted air and
3 K 8 37 pestilence or corrupt air or blasting
19 12 after a fire a whistling of a gentle a.
Job 37 21 the air on a sudden shall be thickened
41 7 not so much as any air can come between
Ps 17 12 dark waters in the clouds of the air
Prov 30 19 the way of an eagle in the air, the way
Wisd 2 3 shall be poured abroad as soft air, and
5 11 as when a bird flieth through the air
11 sound of the wings beating the light a.
12 divided air presently cometh together
7 3 being born I drew in the common air
13 2 imagined . . . the wind or the swift air
17 9 denying that they saw the air, which
Jer 8 7 kite in the air hath known her time
9 10 from the fowl of the air to the beasts
Lam 4 19 were swifter than the eagles of the air
Osee 7 12 bring them down as the fowl of the air
2 Ma 5 2 were seen horsemen running in the air
Acts 22 23 garments and cast dust into the air
1 C 9 26 I so fight, not as one beating the air
14 9 you shall be speaking into the air
Eph 2 2 the prince of the power of this air
1 Th 4 16 the clouds to meet Christ, into the air
Apoc 9 2 the sun and the air were darkened
16 17 angel poured his vial upon the air
birds of the air; *see* **birds**
fowls of the air; *see* **fowls**
akin Lev 20 20 uncover the shame of his near akin
Num 27 11 given to them that are the next akin
Ruth 4 6 I yield up my right of next akin: for
2 Es 13 4 Eliasib . . . was near akin to Tobias
Jer 32 7 thy right to buy it, being next akin
alabaster 1 Pa 29 2 onyx stones and stones like a.
Mat 26 7 woman having an a. box. Mark 14:3
Mark 14 3 breaking the a. box, she poured it out
Luke 7 37 brought an a. box of ointment; and
Alam 1 Es 8 7 of the sons of Alam, Isaias the son
Alamath 1 Pa 8 36 Joada begot Alamath and Azmoth
1 Pa 9 42 Jara begot Alamath and Azmoth and
alarm Joel 2 1 sound an alarm in my holy mountain
Soph 1 16 a day of the trumpet and alarm against
1 Ma 4 40 they sounded with the trumpets of a.
alarmed Judg 7 19 the watchmen being alarmed, they

alas Num 24 23 alas, who shall live when God shall
Josu 7 7 Josue said: Alas, O Lord God, why
Judg 6 22 alas, my Lord God: for I have been
11 35 alas, my daughter, thou hast deceived
3 K 13 30 saying: Alas, alas, my brother. And
4 K 3 10 the king of Israel said: Alas, alas
6 5 alas, alas, alas, my lord, for this
Jer 4 10 alas, alas, alas, O Lord God, hast thou
22 18 alas, my brother, and alas, sister
18 alas, my Lord, or, alas, the noble
30 7 alas, for that day is great, neither
32 16 alas, alas, alas, O Lord God, behold
34 5 alas, Lord: for I have spoken the word
Eze 6 11 alas, for all the abominations of
9 8 alas, alas, alas, O Lord God, wilt. 11:13
Amos 5 16 they shall say: Alas, alas! And they
Apoc 18 10 alas, alas, that great city. 19
Alcimus 1 Ma 7 5 A. was at the head of them who
1 Ma 7 9 the wicked Alcimus he made high priest
12 there assembled to A. and Bacchides
20 he committed the country to Alcimus
21 Alcimus did what he could to maintain
23 Judas saw all the evils that Alcimus
25 A. saw that Judas and they that were
9 1 he sent again Bacchides and A. into
54 A. commanded the walls of the inner
55 Alcimus was struck: and his works were
56 A. died at that time in great torment
57 and Bacchides saw that Alcimus was dead
2 Ma 14 3 one Alcimus, who had been chief priest
13 and to make Alcimus the high priest
26 Alcimus seeing the love they had one
aleph Ps 118 1 aleph. Lam 1:1; 2:1; 3:1, 2, 3; 4:1
Alexander 1 Ma 1 1 A. the son of Philip the
1 Ma 1 8 A. reigned twelve years, and he died
10 1 A. the son of Antiochus, surnamed
4 before he make one with A. against us
23 Alexander hath prevented us to gain the
47 and their inclinations were towards A.
49 Alexander pursued after him and pressed
51 Alexander sent ambassadors to Ptolemee
88 when A. the king heard these words
11 1 and he sought to get the kingdom of A.
8 and he devised evil designs against A.
9 will give thee my daughter whom A. hath
12 and alienated himself from Alexander
15 when A. heard of it, he came to give
16 and A. fled into Arabia, there to be
39 brought up Antiochus the son of A.
Mark 15 21 the father of Alexander and of Rufus
Acts 4 6 John and Alexander and as many as
19 33 they drew forth A. out of the multitude
33 A. beckoning with his hand for silence
1 Tim 1 20 of whom is Hymeneus and Alexander, whom
2 Tim 4 14 A. the coppersmith hath done me much
king Alexander 1 Ma 6 2 shields which k. A. had
1 Ma 10 15 king Alexander heard of the promises
18 k. A. to his brother Jonathan, greeting
48 king A. gathered together a great army
58 king Alexander met him and he gave him
59 king Alexander wrote to Jonathan that
68 king Alexander heard of it and was much
11 2 king A. had ordered them to go forth
14 king Alexander was in Cilicia at that
Alexander's 1 Ma 11 17 took off A. head and sent
1 Ma 11 39 Tryphon who been of A. party before
Alexandria Jer 46 25 visit upon the tumult of A.
Eze 30 14 and will execute judgments in A. And I
15 and will cut off the multitude of A.
16 and Alexandria shall be laid waste and
Nah 3 8 art thou better than the populous A.
Acts 18 24 Apollo, born at Alexandria, an eloquent
27 6 the centurion finding a ship of A.
28 11 we sailed in a ship of Alexandria that
Alexandrians Acts 6 9 arose some of . . . the A.
Aliam 2 K 23 33 Aliam the son of Sarar the
Alian 1 Pa 1 40 sons of Sobal: Alian and Manahath
Alicamassus 1 Ma 15 23 things were written to . . . A.
alien Job 19 15 I have been like an alien in their
Ps 68 9 and an alien to the sons of my mother
alienated Ps 57 4 the wicked are a. from the womb
Eze 23 18 my soul was a. from her, as my soul was a. from her sister
48 14 firstfruits of the land be alienated
Osee 9 10 and a. themselves to that confusion
1 Ma 6 24 of our nation are alienated from us
11 12 alienated himself from Alexander, and
53 and alienated himself from Jonathan
15 27 and alienated himself from him. And he
Eph 4 18 being a. from the life of God through
Col 1 21 you were some time a. and enemies in
aliens Ps 107 10 the aliens are become my friends
Lam 5 2 our inheritance is turned to aliens
1 Ma 5 66 to go into the land of the aliens and
11 74 fell of the aliens in that day 3,000
Eph 2 12 a. from the conversation of Israel and
alike Deut 12 22 unclean shall eat of them alike
Deut 15 22 and the unclean shall eat them alike
1 K 30 24 baggage, and they shall divide alike
Ps 138 12 the light thereof are alike to thee
Prov 27 15 day and a contentious woman are alike
Ecce 2 14 I learned that they were to die both a.
Wisd 7 3 fell upon the earth, that is made alike
11 12 or present, they were tormented alike
14 9 and his wickedness are hateful alike
18 9 should receive both good and evil a.
12 all alike had innumerable dead, with
Eccu 5 18 justify alike the small and the great
Lam 1 20 and at home there is death alike
Eze 10 10 their appearance, all four were alike
42 11 fashions, and their doors were alike
Alima 1 Ma 5 26 in Alima and in Casphor and in
alive Gen 46 30 seen thy face, and leave thee a.
Exod 1 16 child, kill it: if a woman, keep it a.
22 of the female, ye shall save alive
4 18 that I may see if they be yet alive
21 21 if the party remain alive a day or two
22 4 which he stole be found with him, alive
Lev 14 6 the other that is alive he shall dip
16 10 he shall present alive before the Lord
20 14 he shall be burnt alive with them
Num 16 30 they go down alive into hell, you shall
33 and they went down alive into hell
Deut 4 4 are all alive until this present day
Josu 8 23 took the king of the city of Hai alive
10 33 his people, so as to leave none alive
1 K 2 6 the Lord killeth and maketh alive, he
15 8 he took Agag the king of Amalec alive
27 9 left neither man nor woman alive: and
2 K 8 2 to put to death, and one to save alive
12 18 when the child was yet alive we spoke
21 weep for the child while it was alive
22 while the child was yet alive, I fasted
3 K 3 22 thy child is dead, and mine is alive
23 the one saith: My child is alive, and
26 woman whose child was alive, said to
26 give her the child alive, and do not
20 18 they come for peace, take them a.; or whether they come to fight, take them a.
32 if he be yet alive he is my brother
21 15 for Naboth is not alive, but dead. And
4 K 7 12 out of the city, we shall take them a.
10 14 take them a. And they took them a. and
Prov 1 12 let us swallow him up alive like hell
Ps 54 16 and let them go down alive into hell
57 10 swalloweth them up, as alive, in his

123 3 perhaps they had swallowed us up alive
Eccu 17 27 whilst thou art alive and in health
Eze 13 19 to save souls a. which should not live
18 27 justice: he shall save his soul alive
Dan 2 30 that I have more than all men alive
1 Ma 1 7 kingdom among them while he was yet a.
8 7 took him alive and appointed to him
14 2 to take him alive and bring him to him
2 Ma 6 26 I not escape . . . neither alive nor dead
7 5 commanded him, being yet alive, to be
24 when the youngest was yet alive, did
10 36 gates and to burn the blasphemers alive
12 35 and when he would have taken him alive
Mat 27 63 seducer said, while he was yet alive
Mark 16 11 and they hearing that he was alive, did
Luke 24 23 vision of angels who say that he is a.
Acts 1 3 to whom also he showed himself alive
7 19 to the end they might not be kept alive
9 41 and the widows, he presented her alive
20 12 they brought the youth [Eutychus] alive
25 19 deceased, whom Paul affirmed to be alive
Rom 6 11 reckon that you are . . . alive unto God
13 as those that are alive from the dead
1 C 15 22 so also in Christ all shall be made a.
1 Th 4 14 we who are alive, who remain unto the
16 we who are alive, who are left, shall be
Apoc 1 18 First and Last, and alive and was dead
2 8 and the Last, who was dead and is alive
3 1 hast the name of being alive: and thou
19 20 these two were cast alive into pool of
allay Eccu 38 7 cure and shall allay their pains
allege Gen 44 16 or be able justly to allege? God
Isa 41 21 hither if you have anything to allege
Mat 27 13 testimonies they allege against thee
alleging Wisd 18 22 a. the oaths and covenant made
allegory Gal 4 24 which things are said by an a.
alleluia Tob 12 33 a. shall be sung in its streets
Ps 104 1 a. Give glory to the Lord. 105:1; 106:1
110 1 alleluia, I will praise thee, O Lord
111 1 alleluia, of the returning of Aggeus
112 1 alleluia. Praise the Lord. 135:1; 147:12
113 1 alleluia. When Israel went out of Egypt
114 1 alleluia. I have loved, because the Lord
115 10 alleluia. I have believed, therefore have
116 1 alleluia. O praise the Lord, all ye
117 1 alleluia. Give praise to the Lord
118 1 alleluia. Aleph. Blessed are the
134 1 alleluia. Praise ye the name of the
145 1 alleluia, of Aggeus and Zacharias
146 1 a. Praise ye the Lord. 148:1; 150:1
147 20 not made manifest to them. Alleluia
148 14 a people approaching to him. Alleluia
149 1 alleluia. Sing ye to the Lord a new
9 this glory is to all his saints. A.
150 5 every spirit praise the Lord. A.
Apoc 19 1 saying: Alleluia. 3, 4, 6
alliance 1 Ma 8 20 to make a. and peace with you
1 Ma 8 22 for a memorial of the peace and a.
12 3 to renew the amity and a. as it was
8 was mention made of the a. and amity
16 with them the former amity and alliance
14 18 to renew the friendship and alliance
15 17 to renew the former friendship and a.
2 Ma 4 11 to Rome to make amity and alliance
5 11 that the Jews would forsake the a.
allied Gen 34 15 we may be allied with you if you
Wisd 8 17 to be allied to wisdom is immortality
Jer 15 12 shall iron be allied with the iron
allies 1 Ma 8 31 yoke heavy upon our friends and a.
1 Ma 12 14 to you nor to the rest of our allies
Allon 1 Pa 4 37 Sephei the son of Allon the son of
allotted Num 36 12 possession that had been a.
1 Ma 5 20 now 3,000 men were allotted to Simon

allow Exod 5 10 saith Pharao: I allow you no straw
1 K 11 3 allow us seven days that we may send
3 K 5 9 thou shalt allow me necessaries, to
2 Pa 20 10 through whose lands thou didst not a.
Eze 46 5 what sacrifices his hand shall allow
2 Ma 9 16 allow out of his revenues the charges
11 24 allow them to live after their own
allowance Gen 47 22 certain a. of food was given
4 K 25 30 appointed him a continual allowance
2 Es 5 14 I . . . did not eat the yearly allowance
18 I did not require my yearly allowance
1 Ma 10 36 a. shall be made them as is due to all
2 Ma 4 14 games, and of the unlawful allowance
allowed Lev 25 53 his wages being allowed for
3 K 5 11 Solomon a. Hiram 20,000 measures of
10 16 he a. 600 sicles of gold for the plates
Tob 3 21 shall be allowed to come to thy mercy
Eccu 19 28 a judgment that is not a. to be good
Jer 52 34 continual provision was allowed him
Dan 6 8 nor any man be a. to transgress it
2 Ma 3 3 allowed out of his revenues all the
11 15 concerning the Jews, the king a. of
alloweth Job 9 18 he a. not my spirit to rest
Rom 14 22 not himself in that which he alloweth
allowing Gen 47 12 allowing food to every one
2 K 20 3 put them in ward, a. them provisions
all-seeing Eccu 14 22 think of the a. eye of God
allure Deut 17 17 wives, that may a. his mind
Osee 2 14 I will allure her and will lead her
2 P 2 18 a. by desires of fleshly riotousness
allured James 1 14 being drawn away and allured
allurements Prov 9 13 full of a. and knowing
allureth Prov 16 29 an unjust man a. his friend
alluring 2 P 2 14 alluring unstable souls, having
Almath 1 Pa 6 60 of the tribe of Benjamin . . . A.
1 Pa 7 8 sons of Bechor . . . Abia and Almath
almighty Gen 17 1 I am the Almighty God: walk
Gen 28 3 God almighty bless thee and make thee
35 11 send to him: I am God Almighty, increase
43 14 may my almighty God make him favorable
48 3 God Almighty appeared to me at Luza
49 25 the Almighty shall bless thee with the
Exod 6 3 by the name of God Almighty; and my
15 3 as a man of war, Almighty is his name
Num 24 4 hath beheld the vision of the Almighty
16 and seeth the visions of the Almighty
Ruth 1 20 the Almighty hath quite filled me with
21 and the Almighty hath afflicted? So
Tob 13 4 that there is no other almighty God
Jdth 16 7 but the almighty Lord hath struck him
20 the Lord Almighty will take revenge
Job 8 3 doth the Almighty overthrow that which
5 and wilt beseech the Almighty: if thou
11 7 wilt find out the Almighty perfectly
13 3 but yet I will speak to the Almighty
15 25 strengthened himself against the A.
21 15 who is the A., that we should serve him
20 shall drink of the wrath of the A.
22 17 looked upon the A. as if he could do
23 if thou wilt return to the Almighty
25 Almighty shall be against thy enemies
26 shalt thou abound in delights in the A.
23 16 and the Almighty hath troubled me. For
24 1 times are not hid from the Almighty
27 2 the A. who hath brought my soul to
10 can he delight himself in the Almighty
11 the hand of God, what the A. hath
13 which they shall receive of the A.
29 5 when the Almighty was with me: and my
31 2 what inheritance the A. from on high
35 that the Almighty may hear my desire
32 8 inspiration of A. giveth understanding
33 4 breath of the Almighty gave me life

34 10 wickedness, and iniquity from the A.
12 neither will the A. pervert judgment
35 13 the Almighty will look into the causes
Wisd 7 25 emanation of the glory of the a. God
11 18 thy almighty hand, which made the
18 15 thy a. word leapt down from heaven
Eccu 1 8 is one most high Creator Almighty
35 22 the Almighty will not have patience
43 30 the A. himself is above all his works
46 19 called upon the name of the Lord A.
47 6 he called upon the Lord the Almighty
Bar 3 1 Lord almighty, the God of Israel. 4
Eze 10 5 as the voice of God Almighty speaking
2 Ma 1 25 who alone art just and almighty and
3 22 called upon a. God to preserve the
24 spirit of the almighty God gave a
30 when the almighty Lord appeared, was
5 20 forsaken in the wrath of almighty God
6 26 not escape the hand of the Almighty
7 35 the judgment of the almighty God who
38 wrath of the Almighty . . . shall cease
8 11 which was to follow him from the A.
18 we trust in the almighty God, who at a
24 the A. being their helper, they slew
11 13 relied upon the help of the a. God
12 28 when they had invocated the Almighty
15 8 to hope for victory from the almighty
32 the holy house of the almighty God
2 C 6 18 be my sons . . . saith the Lord Almighty
Apoc 1 8 I am Alpha and Omega . . . the Almighty
4 8 holy, Lord God Almighty, who was and
11 17 Lord God Almighty, who art and who wast
15 3 Lord God Almighty, just and true. 16:7
16 14 against the great day of the a. God
19 6 Lord our God the Almighty hath reigned
15 wrath of God the Almighty. And he hath
21 22 Lord God Almighty is the temple thereof
Almon Josu 21 18 and Anathoth and Almon, with their
almond Gen 30 37 took green rods . . . of almond
Ecce 12 5 the almond tree shall flourish, the
almonds Gen 43 11 myrrh, turpentine, and almonds
Num 17 8 the leaves, were formed into almonds
almost Josu 9 13 worn out and almost consumed
Josu 10 20 slaughter and a. utterly consumed
Judg 8 1 him sharply and a. offered violence
Ps 72 2 my feet were almost moved: my steps
93 17 helper, my soul had a. dwelt in hell
118 87 they had almost made an end of me upon
Prov 5 14 I have almost been in all evil, in the
Eze 16 47 hast done almost more wicked things
1 Ma 5 13 they have slain there almost 1,000 men
22 fell of the heathens almost 3,000 men
34 them in that day almost 8,000 men
7 32 fell of Nicanor's army almost 5,000 men
10 85 were slain . . . were almost 8,000 men
2 Ma 14 46 when he was now almost without blood
Luke 8 42 an only daughter, almost 12 years old
23 44 it was a. the sixth hour; and there
Acts 13 44 the whole city almost came together
19 26 not only of Ephesus but a. of all Asia
Heb 9 22 almost all things . . . are cleansed with
alms Tob 2 16 gavest alms and buriedst the dead
Tob 2 22 to nothing, and thy alms now appear
4 7 give alms out of thy substance and
11 alms deliver from all sin and from
12 alms shall be a great confidence before
12 8 prayer is good with fasting and alms
9 alms delivereth from death, and the
Eccu 3 33 a flaming fire and alms resisteth sins
4 1 son, defraud not the poor of alms, and
7 10 neglect not to pray and to give alms
12 3 occupied in evil, and that giveth no a.
17 18 the alms of a man is as a signet with
29 15 shut up alms in the heart of the poor
31 11 the church . . . shall declare his alms
Dan 4 24 redeem thou thy sins with alms, and
Mat 6 3 when thou dost alms let not thy left
4 that thy alms may be in secret, and thy
Luke 11 41 that which remaineth, give alms; and
12 33 sell what you possess and give alms
Acts 3 2 that he might ask alms of them that
3 asked to receive an alms. But Peter
10 that it was he who sat begging alms
10 2 giving much alms to the people and
4 thy alms are ascended for a memorial
24 17 I came to bring alms to my nation and
almsdeed Mat 6 2 when thou dost an a., sound not
almsdeeds Tob 9 9 that feareth God and doth a.
Tob 14 11 that they do justice and almsdeeds
Acts 9 36 was full of good works and almsdeeds
aloes Prov 7 17 perfumed my bed with myrrh, aloes
Cant 4 14 and aloes with all the chief perfumes
Eccu 24 21 and galbanum and onyx and aloes
John 19 39 bringing a mixture of myrrh and aloes
Alohes 2 Es 3 12 Sellum the son of Alohes, lord of
2 Es 10 24 Alohes, Phalea, Sobec, Rehum, Hasebna
alone Gen 2 18 it is not good for man to be alone
Gen 32 24 he remained alone: and behold a man
42 38 brother is dead, and he is left alone
44 20 and he alone is left of his mother
Exod 18 14 why sittest thou alone, and all the
18 strength, thou alone canst not bear it
23 11 seventh year thou shalt let it alone
24 2 Moses alone shall come up to the Lord
32 10 let me alone, that my wrath may be
Lev 13 46 he shall dwell alone without the camp
20 4 let alone the man that hath given
Num 11 14 I am not able alone to bear all this
17 and thou mayest not be burthened alone
23 9 this people shall dwell alone and shall
Deut 1 10 I alone am not able to bear you: for
12 I a. am not able to bear your business
8 3 not in bread alone doth man live
9 14 let me alone that I may destroy them
22 25 lie with her, he alone shall die
27 she was alone in the field: she cried
32 12 the Lord alone was his leader: and
39 see ye that I alone am, and there is
33 28 Israel shall dwell in safety and alone
Josu 11 22 Azotus, in which alone they were left
22 20 would to God he alone had perished
Judg 3 20 he was sitting in a summer parlor alone
7 10 but if thou be afraid to go alone, let
Ruth 1 5 and the woman [Noemi] was left alone
1 K 21 1 why art thou alone, and no man with thee
2 K 16 10 let him alone and let him curse: for
11 let him alone that he may curse as the
17 2 I will kill the king who will be left a.
18 3 thou alone art accounted for 10,000
24 saw a man running alone. And crying out
25 the king said: If he be alone, there
26 I see another man running alone. And
3 K 11 29 and they two were alone in the field
19 10 I alone am left, and they seek. 14
4 K 4 27 let her alone, for her soul is in
19 11 canst thou alone be delivered? Have the
15 thou alone art the God of all the kings
23 18 let him alone, let no man move his bones
1 Pa 29 1 whom alone God hath chosen, is as yet
1 Es 4 3 we ourselves alone will build to the
2 Es 4 2 will the Gentiles let them alone? Will
9 6 O Lord alone, thou hast made heaven and
Tob 1 5 he alone fled the company of all and
8 19 that thou a. art God in all the earth
10 5 having all things together in thee a.
Jdth 13 3 and Judith was alone in the chamber

Job 1 15 a. have escaped to tell thee. 16, 17, 19
9 8 who alone spreadeth out the heavens
12 2 are you then men alone, and shall
15 19 to whom alone the earth was given, and
23 13 he is alone, and no man can turn away
31 17 if I have eaten my morsel alone, and
Ps 24 16 mercy on me: for I am alone and poor
70 16 I will be mindful of thy justice alone
71 18 who alone doth wonderful things. And
82 19 thou alone art the most High over all
85 10 wonderful things: thou art God alone
101 8 as a sparrow all alone on the housetop
135 4 who alone doth great wonders: for his
140 10 in his net: I am alone until I pass
148 13 for his name alone is exalted. The
Prov 5 17 keep them to thyself alone, neither let
9 12 scorner, thou alone shalt bear the evil
Ecce 4 10 woe to him that is alone, for when he
11 how shall one alone be warmed? And if
Wisd 10 1 when he was created alone. And she
11 22 great power belonged to thee alone
Ecce 3 21 great is the power of God alone, and
11 19 and now I will eat of my goods alone
24 8 I alone have compassed the circuit of
45 16 but only his children alone and his
Isa 2 11 and the Lord alone shall be exalted
17 Lord alone shall be exalted in that day
5 8 shall you alone dwell in the midst of
28 19 vexation a. shall make you understand
37 16 thou alone art the God of all the
44 24 that alone stretch out the heavens
49 21 I was destitute and alone: and these
51 2 I called him alone and blessed him
63 3 I have trodden the winepress alone
Jer 15 17 I sat alone, because thou hast filled
49 31 gates nor bars: they dwell alone. And
Bar 4 16 have left me all alone without children
19 go your way: for I am left alone. I
Eze 14 18 themselves alone shall be delivered
Dan 10 7 and I Daniel alone saw the vision: for
8 and I being left alone saw this great
13 14 time when they might find her alone
36 as we walked in the orchard alone, this
Osee 4 17 a partaker with idols, let him alone
8 9 to Assyria, a wild ass alone by himself
Mich 7 14 them that dwell alone in the forest
1 Ma 10 70 thou alone standest against us, and I
13 4 for Israel's sake, and I am left alone
2 Ma 1 24 merciful, who alone art the good king
25 alone art glorious, who alone art just
7 37 mayst confess that he alone is God
8 35 came alone to Antioch, being rendered
Mat 4 4 not in bread alone doth man live, but
14 23 he went into a mountain alone to pray
23 when it was evening, he was there alone
15 14 let them alone; they are blind and
18 15 rebuke him between thee and him alone
24 36 no one knoweth . . . but the Father alone
Mark 4 10 when he was alone, the twelve . . . asked
6 47 himself alone on the land. And seeing
14 6 Jesus said: Let her alone. John 12:7
Luke 4 4 man liveth not by bread alone, but by
34 let us alone, what have we to do with
5 21 who can forgive sins but God alone
9 18 as he was alone, praying, his disciples
36 Jesus was found alone. And they held
10 40 my sister hath left me alone to serve
13 8 let it alone this year also until I
18 19 none is good but God alone. Thou
John 5 44 glory which is from God alone you do
6 15 fled again into mountain himself alone
22 his disciples were gone away alone
8 9 Jesus alone remained, and the woman
16 I am not alone, but I and the Father
29 is with me and he hath not left me a.
11 48 if we let him alone so, all will
12 25 itself remaineth alone. But if it die
16 32 shall leave me a.; and yet I am not a.
Acts 5 38 let them alone; for if this council
15 34 and Judas alone departed to Jerusalem
Rom 11 3 I am left alone and they seek my life
1 Th 3 1 thought it good to remain at Athens a.
Heb 9 7 into the second, the high priest alone
along Gen 2 14 passeth along by the Assyrians
Exod 9 23 lightning running along the ground
Deut 2 27 we will go along by the highway: we
Josu 15 4 from thence passing along into Asemona
16 6 passeth along on the east side to Janoe
18 12 going along by the side of Jericho
13 passing along southward by Luza, the
18 it passeth along to the hills that
19 13 it passeth along from thence to the
27 and passeth along to Zabulon and to
34 passeth along to Zabulon southward
Judg 1 3 that I also may go along with thee
3 18 his companions that came along with
1 K 6 12 they went along the way, lowing as they
28 20 Saul fell all along on the ground, for
Jer 41 6 weeping all along as he went: and when
1 Ma 15 11 he fled along by the seacoast and
aloud Num 10 9 sound aloud with the trumpets
2 K 18 26 and crying aloud from above, he said
Job 19 7 I shall cry aloud, and there is none
Ps 80 2 sing aloud to the God of Jacob. Take a
Prov 8 1 doth not wisdom cry aloud, and prudence
Jer 4 5 cry aloud and say: Assemble yourselves
11 6 proclaim aloud all these words in the
Dan 4 11 he cried aloud and said thus: Cut down
5 7 the king cried out aloud to bring in
Alpha Apoc 1 8 I am Alpha and Omega. 21:6; 22:13
Alpheus Mat 10 3 and James the son of Alpheus
Mark 2 14 he saw Levi the son of Alpheus sitting
3 18 and James of Alpheus and Thaddeus and
Luke 6 15 James the son of Alpheus and Simon
Acts 1 13 James of A. and Simon Zelotes and
already Num 16 46 already wrath is gone out from
Num 32 19 because we have already our possession
32 we have a. received our possession
Josu 18 7 have a. received their possessions
Judg 15 5 corn that was already carried together
4 K 20 11 had a. gone down in the dial of Achaz
2 Es 5 5 some of our daughters are bondwomen a.
Tob 2 8 once already commandment was given
3 10 as thou hast already killed seven
Jdth 11 10 they are already to be counted among
Prov 8 24 as yet, and I was already conceived
Ecce 1 10 for it hath already gone before in the
3 15 things that shall be, have already been
6 10 he that shall be, his name is a. called
Eze 30 22 strong arm, which is already broken
2 Ma 4 39 quantity of gold being a. carried away
Mat 17 12 Elias is already come, and they knew
Mark 15 14 wondered that he should be a. dead
44 asked him if he were already dead
John 3 18 that doth not believe is already judged
4 35 for they are white already to harvest
9 22 Jews had a. agreed among themselves
27 I have told you a. and you have heard
11 17 he had been four days a. in the grave
16 11 prince of this world is already judged
19 33 when they saw that he was already dead
1 C 5 3 present in spirit, have already judged
6 7 a. there is plainly a fault among you
Phil 3 12 I had a. attained or were a. perfect
2 Th 2 7 the mystery of iniquity already worketh
1 Tim 5 15 some are a. turned aside after Satan

2 Tim 2 18 saying, that the resurrection is past a.
1 J 4 3 Antichrist . . . is now a. in the world
altar Gen 8 20 Noe built an altar unto the Lord
Gen 8 20 offered holocausts upon the altar
12 7 [Abram] built there an altar. 12:8
13 4 place of the altar which he had made
22 9 where he [Abraham] built an altar
9 he laid him [Isaac] on the altar upon
26 25 he [Isaac] built there an altar: and
33 20 [Jacob] raising an altar there, he
35 1 and make there an altar to God, who
3 that we may make there an altar to God
7 he built there an altar and called
Exod 17 15 Moses built an altar: and called the
20 24 you shall make an altar of earth unto
25 if thou make an altar of stone unto me
26 not go up by steps unto my altar, lest
21 14 shalt take him away from my altar
24 4 built an altar at the foot of the mount
6 the rest he poured upon the altar
27 1 make also an altar of setim wood which
5 under the hearth of the altar: and the
6 two bars for the altar of setim wood
7 shall be on both sides of the altar
28 43 when they approach to the altar to
29 12 put it upon the horns of the altar
13 offer a burnt offering upon the altar
16 and pour round about the altar: and
18 for a burnt offering upon the altar
20 thou shalt pour the blood upon the a.
21 of the blood that is upon the altar
25 shalt burn them upon the altar for a
36 thou shalt cleanse the altar when
37 seven days shalt thou expiate the altar
38 what thou shalt sacrifice upon the a.
43 the a. shall be sanctified by my glory
44 I will sanctify . . . with the altar
30 1 make also an altar to burn incense
4 that . . . the altar be carried. 37:27
6 set the altar over against the veil
18 tabernacle of the testimony and the a.
20 when they are come to the altar to
32 5 he [Aaron] built an altar before it
35 15 the altar of incense and the bars
37 25 he made also the altar of incense of
38 7 stood out in the sides of the altar
7 the altar itself was not solid, but
30 the altar of brass with the grate
39 37 the altar of gold and the ointment
39 altar of brass, the grate, the bars
40 5 the altar of gold whereon the incense
7 laver between the a. and the tabernacle
24 he set also the altar of gold under
28 tabernacle of the testimony and the a.
30 and went to the altar as the Lord had
31 round about the tabernacle and the a.
Lev 1 5 pouring it round about the altar, which
7 shall put fire on the altar, having
9 priest shall burn them upon the altar. 3:11, 16; 7:5
11 immolate it at the side of the altar
11 blood thereof upon the a. 3:8, 13; 17:6
13 burn it all upon the altar for a
15 the priest shall offer it at the altar
15 blood run down upon the brim of the a.
16 feathers he shall cast beside the a.
17 shall burn it upon the altar. 2:9; 4:19, 31, 35; 5:12; 6:15
2 2 shall put it a memorial upon the altar
12 they shall not be put upon the altar
3 2 pour the blood round about upon the a.
5 they shall burn them upon the altar
4 7 same blood upon horns of the altar. 18
5 9 he shall sprinkle the side of the altar
6 9 it shall be burnt upon the altar, all
9 the fire shall be of the same altar
10 putting them beside the altar, shall
12 the fire on the altar shall always burn
13 fire which shall never go out on the a.
14 before the Lord and before the altar
22 it shall be wholly burnt on the altar
7 2 shall be poured round about the altar
31 shall burn the fat upon the altar, but
8 11 sprinkled the altar seven times, he
15 he touched the horns of the altar
16 with their fat he burnt upon the a.
19 [Moses] poured the blood . . . upon the a.
21 whole ram he burnt upon the altar
24 the rest he poured on the altar round
30 blood thereof round about upon the a.
9 7 said to Aaron: Approach to the altar
8 Aaron, approaching to the altar
9 and touched the horns of the altar
10 are for sin, he burnt upon the altar
12 he poured round about on the altar
13 which he burnt with fire upon the a.
15 expiating the altar, he offered the
17 burning them upon the altar, besides
18 which he poured upon the altar round
20 after the fat was burnt upon the altar
24 and the fat that was upon the altar
10 12 eat it without leaven beside the altar
15 the fat that is burnt on the altar
14 20 put it on the altar with the libations
16 12 with the burning coals of the altar
18 when he is come out to the altar that
20 and the tabernacle and the altar
25 for sins, he shall burn upon the altar
33 tabernacle of the testimony and the a.
17 11 you may make atonement with it upon a.
21 23 nor approach to the altar, because he
22 22 anything of them upon the Lord's altar
Num 3 26 whatsoever belongeth to rite of the a.
4 11 they shall wrap up the golden altar
13 they shall cleanse the altar also from
14 shall cover all the vessels of the a.
26 all things that pertain to the altar
5 25 and shall put it upon the altar: yet so
26 a handful . . . and burn it upon the altar
7 1 the altar likewise and all the vessels
10 princes offered for dedication of the a.
10 anointed, their oblation before the a.
11 gifts for the dedication of the altar
84 in the dedication of the altar. 88
16 38 plates and fasten them to the altar
39 into plates, fastening them to the altar
46 putting fire in it from the altar, put
18 3 shall not come nigh . . . the altar, lest
5 sanctuary and in the ministry of the a.
7 that pertain to the service of the a.
17 blood only shalt thou pour upon the a.
23 30 laid on every altar a calf and a ram
Deut 12 27 the flesh, and the blood upon the altar
27 thou shalt pour on the altar, and the
16 21 no grove nor any tree near the altar
27 5 thou shalt build there an altar to the
33 10 thy wrath and holocaust upon thy altar
Josu 8 31 an altar of unhewn stones which iron
9 27 service of all the people and of the a.
22 10 they built an altar immensely great
11 had built altar in the land of Chanaan
16 building a sacrilegious altar and
22 we have set up this altar, let him not
26 us build an altar, not for holocausts
29 by building an altar to offer holocausts
34 called the altar which they had built

Judg	6	25	thou shalt destroy the altar of Baal
		26	cut down grove that is about the altar
		28	they saw the altar of Baal destroyed
		28	second bullock laid upon the altar
		30	he hath destroyed the altar of Baal
		31	on him that hath cast down his altar
	13	20	when the flame from the altar went up
	21	4	early the next day, they built an altar
1 K	2	28	to go up to my altar and burn incense
		33	take away a man of thee from my altar
3 K	1	50	and took hold on the horn of the altar
		51	hath taken hold of the horn of the a.
		53	and brought him out from the altar
	2	28	and laid hold on the horn of the altar
		29	was by the altar: and Solomon sent
	3	4	did Solomon offer upon that altar in
	6	20	the altar also he covered with cedar
		22	altar of the oracle he covered also with
	7	48	altar of gold and the table of gold
	8	22	and Solomon stood before the altar
		31	come because of the oath before thy a.
	9	25	peace offerings upon the altar which
	12	32	going up to the altar, he did in like
		33	and he went up to the altar which he
		33	went upon the altar to burn incense
	13	1	when Jeroboam was standing upon the a.
		2	he cried out against the altar in the
		2	O altar, altar, thus saith the Lord
		3	behold the altar shall be rent and the
		4	had cried out against the altar in
		4	stretched forth his hand from the altar
		5	the altar also was rent and the ashes
		5	the ashes were poured out from the a.
		32	word of Lord against a. that is in
	16	32	he set up an altar for Baal in the
	18	26	and they leaped over the altar that
		32	and he built with the stones an altar
		32	of two furrows round about the altar
		35	the water run round about the altar
4 K	11	11	unto the left side of the altar and
		18	they slew also Mathan . . . before the a.
	12	9	set it by the altar at the right hand
	16	10	when he had seen the altar of Damascus
		11	and Urias the priest built an altar
		12	he saw the altar and worshipped it
		13	which he had offered upon the altar
		14	altar of brass that was before the Lord
		14	from the place of the altar and from
		14	and he set it at the side of the altar
		15	upon the great altar offer the morning
		15	altar of brass shall be ready at my
	18	22	worship before this altar in Jerusalem
	23	15	the altar also that was at Bethel and
		15	altar and the high place he broke down
		16	and burnt them upon the altar and
		17	thou hast done upon the altar of Bethel
1 Pa	6	49	burnt offerings upon the altar of holocausts and upon the altar of incense
	16	40	upon the a. of holocausts continually
	21	22	that I may build therein an altar to
		26	fire from heaven upon the altar of the
		29	altar of holocausts was at that time
		30	David could not go to the altar there
	22	1	the altar for the holocaust of Israel
	28	18	for the altar of incense, he gave the
2 Pa	1	5	and the altar of brass which Beseleel
		6	went up thither to the brazen altar
	4	1	he made also an altar of brass twenty
		19	the golden altar and the tables, upon
	5	12	standing on the east side of the altar
	6	22	bind himself with curse before altar
	7	7	the brazen altar which he had made
		9	dedication of the altar seven days
	23	10	before the altar and the temple
	26	16	to burn incense upon altar of incense
		19	in house of Lord at altar of incense
	29	22	the blood and poured it upon the altar
		22	their blood they poured also upon a.
		22	lambs and poured the blood upon the a.
		24	sprinkled their blood before the altar
		27	should offer holocausts upon the altar
	32	12	you shall worship before one altar
1 Es	3	2	they built the altar of the God of
		3	set the altar of God upon its bases
	7	17	offer them upon the altar of the temple
Jdth	9	11	with their sword the horn of thy altar
Esth	14	9	the glory of thy temple and altar, that
Ps	25	6	and will compass thy altar, O Lord
	42	4	I will go in to the altar of God: to
	50	21	shall they lay calves upon thy altar
	117	27	boughs, even to the horn of the altar
Wisd	9	8	altar in the city of thy dwelling place
Eccu	35	8	maketh the altar fat and is an odor
	47	11	and he set singers before the altar
	50	12	when he went up to the holy altar, he
		13	priests, he himself stood by the altar
		15	finishing his service, on the altar
		17	he poured out at the foot of the altar
Isa	6	6	had taken with the tongs off the altar
	27	9	shall have made all the stones of the a.
	36	7	you shall worship before this altar
	56	7	victims shall please me upon my altar
	60	7	be offered upon my acceptable altar
Lam	2	7	the Lord hath cast off his altar, he
Eze	8	5	on north side of the gate of the altar
		16	between the porch and the altar, were
	9	2	went in and stood by the brazen altar
	40	46	that watch over the ministry of the a.
		47	a. that was before face of the temple
	41	22	altar of wood was three cubits high
	43	13	these are the measures of the altar
		13	and this was the trench of the altar
		18	these are the ceremonies of the altar
		22	they shall expiate the altar, as they
		26	seven days shall they expiate the altar
		27	shall offer your holocausts upon the a.
	45	19	on the four corners of brim of the a.
	47	1	temple to the south part of the altar
Osee	3	4	without sacrifice and without altar and
Joel	2	17	between the porch and the altar the
Amos	2	8	upon garments laid to pledge by every a.
	9	1	I saw the Lord standing upon the altar
Zach	9	15	as bowls, and as the horns of the altar
	14	20	shall be as the phials before the altar
Mala	1	7	you offer polluted bread upon my altar
		10	will kindle the fire on my altar gratis
1 Ma	1	23	and took away the golden altar and
		57	idol of desolation upon the altar of God
		62	sacrificed upon the a. of the idol that was over against the a. of God
	2	23	sacrifice to the idols upon the altar
		24	upon him, he slew him upon the altar
		25	pulled down the altar and showed zeal
	4	38	desolate and the altar profaned and
		44	considered about the a. of holocausts
		47	built a new a. according to the former
		49	brought in the candlestick and the a.
		50	and they put incense upon the altar and
		53	upon the new altar of holocausts which
		56	kept the dedication of the a. eight
		59	day of the dedication of the a. should
	5	1	the altar and the sanctuary were built
	6	7	which he had set up upon the altar in
	7	36	and stood before the face of the altar
2 Ma	1	18	after the temple and the a. was built
		19	took privately the fire from the altar

32 by the light that shined from the altar
2 5 and the ark and the altar of incense
20 temple and the dedication of the altar
3 15 prostrated themselves before the altar
4 14 occupied about the offices of the altar
6 5 a. also was filled with unlawful things
10 3 they made another a.; and taking fire
26 lying prostrate at foot of the altar
13 8 many sins against the altar of God
14 3 no safety for him nor access to the a.
33 ground and will beat down the altar
15 31 the priests to the altar, he sent also
Mat 5 23 if thou offer thy gift at the altar
24 leave there thy offering before the a.
23 18 shall swear by the a., it is nothing
19 whether is greater, the gift or the a.
20 that sweareth by the a., sweareth by it
35 you killed between the temple and the a.
Luke 1 11 standing on right side of the altar of
11 51 was slain between the a. and the temple
Acts 17 23 found an a. also on which was written
1 C 9 13 that serve the a., partake with the a.
10 18 of the sacrifices partakers of the a.
Heb 7 13 of which no one attended on the altar
13 10 we have an altar, whereof they have
James 2 21 offering up Isaac his son upon the a.
Apoc 6 9 I saw under the a. the souls of them
8 3 angel came and stood before the altar
3 of all saints upon the golden altar
5 filled it with the fire of the altar
9 13 from four horns of the golden altar
11 1 measure the temple of God and the altar
14 18 another angel came out from the altar
16 7 I heard another from the altar, saying
altar of holocaust Exod 35 16 a. . . . and its grate of brass
Exod 38 1 he made also the a. . . . of setim wood
40 6 before it the a. . . . : the laver between
10 anoint . . . the altar of holocaust and
27 a. . . . in the entry of the testimony
Lev 4 7 rest of the blood at foot of a. . . .
10 and he shall burn them upon the a. . . .
18 he shall pour at the foot of the a. . . .
25 therewith the horns of the a. . . . and
30 shall touch the horns of the a. . . . 34
8 28 and burnt them upon the a. . . . because
2 Pa 29 18 the house of the Lord and the a. . . .
altar of the Lord Deut 26 4 set it before a. . . .
Josu 22 19 by building an altar beside the a. . . .
28 behold the a. . . . which our fathers made
29 sacrifices and victims beside the a. . . .
3 K 8 54 [Solomon] arose from before the a. . . .
18 30 near unto him, he repaired the a. . . .
4 K 23 9 came not up to the a. . . . in Jerusalem
2 Pa 6 12 stood before the a. . . . in presence
8 12 holocausts to the Lord upon the a. . . .
15 8 he [Asa] dedicated the a. . . . which was
29 19 are all set forth before the a. . . .
21 of Aaron, to offer them upon the a. . . .
33 16 he repaired the a. . . . and sacrificed
35 16 and offering holocausts upon the a. . . .
2 Es 10 34 to burn upon the altar of the Lord our
Jdth 4 8 the a. . . . they covered with haircloth
Isa 19 19 there shall be an a. . . . in the midst
Bar 1 10 and offerings for sin at the a. . . .
Mala 2 13 you have covered the a. . . . with tears
altar to the Lord Gen 13 18 which is in Hebron: and he built there an a. . . .
Josu 8 30 Josue built an a. . . . the God of Israel
Judg 6 24 Gedeon built there an a. . . . and called
26 thou shalt build an a. . . . thy God
1 K 7 17 [Samuel] built also there an a. . . .
14 35 Saul built an altar to the Lord: and he then first began to build an a. . . .
2 K 24 18 go up and build an altar to the Lord
21 and build an a. . . . , that the plague
25 David built there an a. . . . 1 Pa 21:26
1 Pa 21 18 to go up and build an a. . . . God in
altars Exod 30 27 the a. of incense and of. 31:8
Exod 34 13 destroy their altars, break. Deut 7:5
Num 3 31 a. and the vessels of the sanctuary
23 1 build me here seven a. and prepare. 29
4 I have erected seven altars and have
14 Balaam built seven altars and laying
Deut 12 3 overthrow their altars and break down
Judg 2 2 but should throw down their altars
3 K 14 23 also built them altars and statues
19 10 they have thrown down thy altars, they
14 they have destroyed thy altars, they
4 K 11 18 temple of Baal and broke down his a.
17 11 they burnt incense there upon altars
18 22 and altars Ezechias hath taken away
21 3 set up altars to Baal and made groves
4 altars in the house of the Lord. 2 Pa 33:4
5 built a. for all the host of heaven
23 8 he broke down the altars of the gates
12 the altars that were upon the top of
12 the altars which Manasses had made
20 slew all the priests . . . upon the a.
2 Pa 14 2 destroyed the altars of foreign worship
5 he took away . . . the altars and temples
23 17 they broke down his a. and his idols
17 they slew Mathan . . . before the altars
24 made himself a. in all the corners
28 25 in all the cities of Juda he built a.
30 14 and destroyed the altars that were in
31 1 high places and destroyed the altars
32 12 destroyed his high places and his a.
33 3 built altars to Baalim and made groves
15 altars also which he had made in the
34 4 a. of Baalim and demolished the idols
5 of the priests on the a. of the idols
7 when he had destroyed the altars and
Ps 83 4 thy altars, O Lord of hosts, my king
Isa 17 8 he shall not look to the altars which
36 7 high places and a. Ezechias hath taken
Jer 11 13 hast set up altars of confusion, altars to offer sacrifice to Baalim
17 1 upon the horns of their altars. When
2 their children shall remember their a.
Eze 6 4 I will throw down your altars and
5 scatter your bones round about your a.
6 and your altars shall be abolished and
13 against your idols, round about your a.
Osee 8 11 Ephraim hath made many altars to sin
11 altars are become to him unto sin. I
10 1 he hath multiplied altars, according
2 he shall destroy their altars. For now
8 thistle shall grow up over their altars
12 11 their altars also are as heaps in the
Joel 1 13 howl, ye ministers of the altars: go
Amos 3 14 I will visit . . . upon the a. of Bethel
14 horns of the altars shall be cut off
1 Ma 1 50 he commanded altars to be built and
57 they built altars throughout all the
2 45 they threw down the altars and they
5 68 he threw down their a. and he burnt
10 2 threw down the a. which the heathens
Rom 11 3 they have dug down thy altars; and I
alter Num 22 18 I cannot alter the word of the
1 Es 6 11 if any . . . shall alter this commandment
Wisd 4 11 lest wickedness should alter his
alteration James 1 17 no change nor shadow of a.
alterations Wisd 7 18 the a. of their courses and

altered Cant 1 5 the sun hath altered my color
Dan 3 94 singed nor their garments altered nor
6 8 Medes and Persians may not be altered
15 which the king hath made, may be a.
Luke 9 29 shape of his countenance was altered
altogether Gen 44 14 a. fell down before him
Lev 5 8 neck, and be not altogether broken off
26 44 I did not cast them off altogether
Deut 4 31 not leave thee nor a. destroy thee
7 22 wilt not be able to destroy them a.
1 K 2 33 I will not a. take away a man of thee
2 K 14 14 that is cast off should not a. perish
Ps 118 51 the proud did iniquitously altogether
Jer 5 5 have altogether broken the yoke more
Amos 8 8 and rise up altogether as a river and
1 Ma 12 10 we should become strangers to you a.
2 Ma 10 17 slew altogether no fewer than 20,000
15 30 Judas, who was a. ready in body and
Alus Num 33 13 they camped in Alus. And departing from Alus, they pitched
Alva Gen 36 40 duke Alva, duke Jetheth. 1 Pa 1:51
Alvan Gen 36 23 the sons of Sobal: Alvan and
am Mat 16 15 whom do you say that I am. Mark 8:29; Luke 9:20
Mark 14 62 Jesus said to him: I am. And you shall
Luke 9 18 whom do the people say that I am? But
22 70 Son of God? Who said: You say that I am
John 7 28 you know whence I am, and I am not come
29 because I am from him, and he hath
33 yet a little while I am with you. 13:33
34 where I am you cannot come. 36
8 18 I am one that give testimony of myself
23 you are from beneath, I am from above
58 before Abraham was made, I am
12 26 where I am there also shall my minister
13 13 you say well, for so I am. If then I
14 3 that where I am you also may be. And
10 I am in the Father. 11, 20
17 10 I am glorified in them. And now I
24 I will that where I am, they . . . may be
18 35 Pilate answered: Am I a Jew? Thy own
Acts 9 5 I am Jesus whom thou persecutest. 22:8; 26:15
10 behold I [Ananias] am here, Lord. And
18 10 because I am with thee; and no man
23 6 men, brethren, I am a Pharisee, the son
26 29 should become such as I also am except
27 23 angel of God, whose I am . . . stood by
1 C 15 10 by the grace of God I am what I am
2 C 11 22 they are Hebrews; so am I. They are Israelites; so am I. They are the seed of Abraham; so am I
23 are ministers of Christ . . . I am more
12 10 when I am weak, then am I powerful
Gal 4 12 be ye as I, because I also am as you
Phil 4 11 in whatsoever state I am, to be content
Apoc 1 8 I am Alpha and Omega. 21:6; 22:13
18 I am living forever and ever, and have
19 10 I am thy fellow-servant and of thy
I am he Josu 13 6 I am he that will cut them off
1 K 4 16 I am he that came from the battle, and
Isa 43 25 I am, I am he that blot out thy
Jer 7 11 I am he: I have seen it, saith the
Mat 13 6 come . . . saying: I am he. Luke 21:8
John 4 26 I am he who am speaking with thee. And
8 24 if you believe not that I am he, you
28 then shall you know that I am he and
9 9 he is like him. But he said: I am he
13 19 to pass, you may believe that I am he
18 5 Jesus saith to them: I am he. And
6 as he had said to them: I am he; they
8 I have told you that I am he. If
Acts 10 21 I am he whom you seek; what is the
I am not Judg 12 5 if he said: I am not
Luke 22 58 Peter said: O man, I am not. And after
John 1 20 and he confessed: I am not the Christ
21 art thou Elias? And he said: I am not
3 28 witness that I said, I am not the Christ
8 16 because I am not alone, but I and the
23 I am not of this world. Therefore I
16 32 I am not alone, because the Father is
17 14 as I also am not of the world. I pray
18 17 man's disciples? He saith: I am not
25 he denied it and said: I am not
Acts 13 25 I am not he whom you think me to be
I am the Gen 15 7 I am the Lord who brought thee
Gen 17 1 I am the almighty God: walk before me
26 24 I am the God of Abraham thy father; do
28 13 I am the Lord God of Abraham thy father
31 13 I am the God of Bethel, where thou didst
46 3 I am the most mighty God of thy father
Exod 3 6 I am the God of thy father, the God of
6 2 I am the Lord, that appeared to Abraham
6 I am the Lord who will bring you out
7 shall know that I am the Lord. 7:5; 14:4, 18; 16:12; 29:46
8 I am the Lord. 29; 12:12; Lev 18:5, 6, 21; 19:12, 14, 16, 18, 28, 30, 32, 37; 21:12; 22:2, 3, 8, 30, 31, 33; 26:2, 45; Num 3:13, 41, 45
7 17 shalt know that I am the Lord. 8:22
10 2 you may know that I am the Lord. 31:13
15 26 upon thee: for I am the Lord thy healer
20 2 I am the Lord thy God. 5; Deut 5:6, 9; Isa 41:13; 43:3; Osee 13:4
Lev 11 44 I am the Lord your God. 18:2, 4, 30; 19:3, 4, 10, 25, 31, 34, 36; 20:7, 24; 23:22, 43; 24:22; 25:17, 38; 26:1, 13; Num 10:10; 15:41; Deut 29:6; Judg 6:10; Eze 20:5, 7, 19; 34:30; Joel 2:27
45 I am the Lord who brought you out of
20 8 I am the Lord that sanctify you. 23:32
21 15 for I am the Lord who sanctify him
23 I am the Lord who sanctify them. 22:9, 16
26 44 I am the Lord their God. Zach 10:6
Num 35 34 I am the Lord that dwell among the
Judg 6 15 I am the least in my father's house
1 K 9 19 I am the seer, go up before me to
17 58 I am the son of thy servant Isai the
Isa 41 4 I the Lord, I am the first and the last
43 11 I am, I am the Lord: and there is no
13 from the beginning I am the same, and
15 I am the Lord your Holy One, the
44 6 I am the first and I am the last. 48:12
24 I am the Lord, that make all things
45 5 I am the Lord, and there is none else. 6; 47:8
18 I am the Lord, and there is no other. 22
Jer 17 10 I am the Lord who search the heart and
32 27 I am the Lord the God of all flesh
Mala 3 6 I am the Lord and I change not: and you
Mat 22 32 I am the God of Abraham. Mark 12:26
John 1 23 I am the voice of one crying in the
6 35 I am the bread of life: he that cometh
41 I am the living bread which came. 51
48 I am the bread of life. Your fathers did
8 12 I am the light of the world. 9:5
10 7 I am the door of the sheep. All others
9 I am the door. By me, if any man enter
11 I am the good shepherd. The good
14 I am the good shepherd; and I know mine
36 because I said, I am the Son of God
11 25 I am the resurrection and the life
14 6 I am the way and the truth and the life

15 1 I am the true vine; and my Father is
5 I am the vine; you the branches: he
19 21 that he said: I am the King of the Jews
Acts 7 32 I am the God of thy fathers; the God of
Apoc 1 17 I am the First and the Last, and alive
22 16 I am the root and stock of David, the
Amaad Josu 19 26 Elmelech and Amaad and Messal
Amadathi Esth 3 1 Aman the son of Amadathi. 10; 9:24; 12:6; 16:10
Amai 1 Pa 7 8 Amai and Jerimoth and Abia and
amain Judg 5 22 stoutest of the enemies fled amain
Amal 1 Pa 7 35 and Jemna and Selles and Amal
Amalec Exod 17 8 Amalec came and fought against
Exod 17 9 and go out and fight against Amalec
10 he fought against Amalec; but Moses
11 let them down a little, Amalec overcame
13 Josue put A. and his people to flight
14 I will destroy the memory of Amalec
16 war of the Lord shall be against Amalec
Num 13 30 Amalec dwelleth in the south, the
24 20 when he saw A., he took up his parable
20 Amalec the beginning of nations, whose
Deut 25 17 remember what Amalec did to thee in
Judg 3 13 to him the children of Ammon, and A.
5 14 he destroyed them into Amalec, and
14 of Benjamin, into thy people, O Amalec
6 3 A. and the rest of the eastern nations
33 A. and the eastern people were gathered
7 12 Amalec and all the eastern people lay
10 12 and Amalec and Chanaan oppress you
1 K 14 48 he defeated Amalec and delivered Israel
15 2 all that Amalec hath done to Israel
3 now therefore go and smite Amalec and
5 when Saul was come to city of Amalec
6 get ye down from Amalec; lest I destroy
6 the Cinite departed from midst of A.
7 and Saul smote Amalec from Hevila until
8 he took Agag the king of Amalec alive
12 spoils which he had brought from Amalec
15 they have brought them from Amalec: for
18 go, and kill the sinners of Amalec and
20 have brought Agag the king of Amalec, and Amalec I have slain
32 hither to me Agag the king of Amalec
28 18 wrath of his indignation upon Amalec
2 K 1 13 I am the son of a stranger of Amalec
8 12 of A. and of the spoils of Adarezer
1 Pa 1 36 by Thamna, Amalec. The sons of Seir
18 11 from the Philistines and from Amalec
Jdth 4 12 who overcame Amalec that trusted in
Ps 82 8 Gebal and Ammon and Amalec: the
Amalech Gen 36 12 bore him Amalech. These are the
Gen 36 16 duke Core, duke Gatham, duke Amalech
Judg 12 15 land of Ephraim in the mount of Amalech
3 K 22 26 Joas the son of Amalech. 2 Pa 18:25
Amalecite Num 14 25 A. and the Chanaanite dwell
Num 14 43 A. and the Chanaanite are before you
45 and the Amalecite came down, and the
1 K 30 13 of Egypt, the servant of an Amalecite
2 K 1 8 and I said to him: I am an Amalecite
Amalecites Gen 14 7 smote all the country of the A.
1 K 27 8 pillaged Gessuri and Gerzi and the A.
30 1 the Amalecites had made an invasion
18 recovered all that the A. had taken
2 K 1 1 returned from the slaughter of the A.
1 Pa 4 43 they slew the remnant of the Amalecites
Amam Josu 15 26 Amam, Sama, and Molada, and
Aman Esth 3 1 king Assuerus advanced Aman, the
Esth 3 2 bent their knees and worshipped Aman
4 they told A., desirous to know whether
5 when Aman had heard this and had proved
7 lot was cast into an urn . . . before A.
8 Aman said to king Assuerus: There is a
10 from his own hand and gave it to Aman
12 and they wrote, as Aman had commanded
15 the king and Aman feasting together
4 7 how Aman had promised to pay money into
5 4 and Aman with thee to the banquet which
5 call ye Aman quickly, that he may obey
5 the king and Aman came to the banquet
8 let the king and A. come to the banquet
9 Aman went out that day joyful and merry
6 4 Aman was coming into the inner court
5 Aman standeth in the court, and the king
6 Aman thinking in his heart and supposing
11 Aman took the robe and the horse, and
12 and Aman made haste to go to his house
7 1 so the king and Aman went in, to drink
6 it is this Aman that is our adversary
6 Aman hearing this was forthwith
7 Aman also rose up to entreat Esther
8 he found Aman was fallen upon the bed
10 so Aman was hanged on the gibbet which
8 1 the house of Aman, the Jews' enemy
2 commanded to be taken again from Aman
3 that the malice of Aman the Agagite
5 that the former letters of Aman the
9 6 besides the ten sons of Aman. 12
13 the ten sons of Aman may be hanged
14 and the ten sons of Aman were hanged
24 Aman . . . had devised evil against them
10 7 but the two dragons are I and Aman
12 6 Aman . . . was in great honor with the
13 3 and was second after the king, Aman
6 that all whom Aman shall mark out, who
12 I refused to worship the proud Aman
15 2 Aman . . . hath spoken against us unto
16 10 Aman . . . was received, being a stranger
Amana Cant 4 8 shalt be crowned from top of Amana
Aman's Esth 7 9 standeth in Aman's house, being
Esth 8 7 I have given Aman's house to Esther
14 17 that I have not eaten at Aman's table
Amaria 1 Es 10 42 Sellum, Amaria, Joseph
2 Es 12 2 Amaria, Melluch, Hattus, Sebenias
13 of Amaria, Johanan: of Milicho
Amarias 1 Pa 6 7 Maraioth begot A., and A. begot
1 Pa 6 11 Azarias begot A., and A. begot Achitob
52 Meraioth his son, Amarias his son
23 19 Jeriau the first, A. the second. 24:23
2 Pa 19 11 Amarias the priest your high priest
31 15 Jesue and Semeias and Amarias
1 Es 7 3 the son of Amarias, the son of Azarias
2 Es 10 3 Pheshur, Amarias, Melchias, Hattus
11 4 son of Amarias, the son of Saphatias
Soph 1 1 the son of Amarias, the son of Ezechias
Amasa 2 K 17 25 A. in Joab's stead over the army
2 K 17 25 Amasa was the son of a man who was
19 13 say ye to Amasa: Art not thou my bone
20 4 king said to Amasa: Assemble to me all
5 Amasa went to assemble the men of Juda
8 Amasa coming met them. And Joab had
9 Joab said to Amasa: God save thee, my
9 he took Amasa by the chin with his
10 Amasa did not take notice of the sword
11 stopping at the dead body of Amasa
12 Amasa imbrued with blood, lay in the
12 he removed Amasa out of the highway into
3 K 2 5 A. the son of Jether: whom he slew
32 A. the son of Jether, general of the
1 Pa 2 17 Abigail bore Amasa, whose father was
2 Pa 28 12 and Amasa the son of Adali stood up
Amasai 1 Pa 6 25 sons of Elcana: Amasai and
1 Pa 6 35 the son of Amasai the son of Elcana
45 the son of Amasai the son of Helcias
46 the son of Amasai the son of Boni
12 18 upon Amasai the chief among thirty

15 24 Amasai and Zacharias and Banaias and
2 Pa 29 12 Mahath the son of Amasai, and Joel the
Amasias 4 K 12 21 A. his son reigned. 2 Pa 24:27
4 K 13 12 wherewith he fought against Amasias
14 1 reigned A. son of Joas king of Juda
8 then Amasias sent messengers to Joas
9 Joas king of Israel sent again to A.
11 but Amasias did not rest satisfied
11 he and A. king of Juda saw one another
13 Joas . . . took Amasias. 2 Pa 25:23
15 he fought against Amasias king of Juda
17 Amasias . . . lived after the. 2 Pa 25:25
18 rest of the acts of Amasias. 2 Pa 25:26
21 made him king instead of his father A.
23 in the fifteenth year of A. son of Joas
15 1 reigned Azarias son of Amasias king of
3 all that his father Amasias had done
1 Pa 3 12 and his son Amasias begot Azarias
4 34 Josa the son of Amasias, and Joel and
2 Pa 17 16 after him was A. the son of Zechri
25 1 Amasias was five and twenty years old
5 A. therefore gathered Juda together
9 Amasias said to the man of God: What
10 then Amasias separated the army that
11 Amasias taking courage led forth his
13 that army which Amasias had sent back
14 but A. after he had slain the Edomites
15 the Lord being angry against Amasias
17 Amasias . . . taking very bad counsel
20 A. would not hearken to him, because
21 Amasias king of Juda was in Bethsames
26 1 made him king in the room of Amasias
4 to all that Amasias his father had done
Amos 7 10 Amasias the priest of Bethel sent to
12 and Amasias said to Amos: Thou seer, go
14 Amos answered and said to Amasias: I
Amassai 2 Es 11 13 Amassai the son of Azreel the
Amath 1 Ma 12 25 met them in the land of Amath
Amathi 4 K 14 25 Jonas the son of Amathi. Jon 1:1
amazed 1 K 14 15 gone out to plunder were amazed
Jdth 10 14 her face, and their eyes were amazed
Wisd 5 2 shall be a. at the suddenness of their
Isa 13 8 every one shall be a. at his neighbor
19 16 and they shall be amazed and afraid
21 4 my heart failed, darkness amazed me
Jer 4 9 and the prophets shall be amazed. And
Eze 21 14 that maketh them stand a. and languish
32 10 I will make many people to be amazed
1 Ma 4 27 he was amazed and discouraged: because
Mat 12 23 the multitudes were amazed and said
Mark 1 27 were all amazed, insomuch that
Acts 2 7 they were all amazed and wondered
9 7 stood a., hearing indeed a voice, but
amazement Eze 26 16 with a. shall wonder at thy
Acts 3 10 were filled with wonder and amazement
ambassador Prov 13 17 a faithful a. is health
Jer 49 14 an ambassador is sent to the nations
Abdi 1 hath sent an ambassador to the nations
1 Ma 12 8 and Onias received the a. with honor
2 Ma 4 11 Eupolemus who went ambassador to Rome
Eph 6 20 for which I am an ambassador in a
ambassadors Jdth 3 1 sent their a., who coming
Ps 67 32 ambassadors shall come out of Egypt
Isa 18 2 that sendeth ambassadors by the sea
Eze 17 15 and sent ambassadors to Egypt, that
1 Ma 9 70 he sent a. to him to make peace with
10 51 Alexander sent a. to Ptolemee king of
11 9 he sent a. to Demetrius, saying: Come
14 21 the a. that were sent to our people
22 a. of the Jews, came to us to renew
40 had received Simon's a. with honor
15 17 a. of the Jews our friends came to us
2 Ma 11 34 Quintus Memmius and Titus Manilius, a.
2 C 5 20 for Christ therefore we are a., God as
amber Eze 1 4 the resemblance of amber. 27
Eze 8 2 brightness, as the appearance of amber
ambitious 1 C 13 5 is not ambitious, seeketh not
ambitiously 2 Ma 4 7 Jason . . . a. sought the high
ambush Josu 8 2 lay an a. for the city behind it
Josu 8 4 lay an ambush behind the city: and go
7 you shall arise out of the ambush and
9 they went to the place of the ambush
12 to lie in ambush between Bethel and Hai
14 not knowing that there lay an ambush
19 a. that lay hid, rose up immediately
Judg 9 25 they set an ambush against him on the
16 12 there being an ambush prepared for him
20 37 that were in ambush arose on a sudden
4 K 6 9 for the Syrians are there in ambush
Ps 9 8 he sitteth in ambush with the rich in
9 he lieth in ambush that he may catch
1 Ma 9 40 from the place where they lay in a.
10 80 Jonathan knew that there was an ambush
11 68 laid an ambush for him in the mountains
69 they that lay in ambush rose out of
ambushes Num 32 17 fear of a. of the inhabitants
Judg 9 34 and laid a. near Sichem in four places
35 with him from the places of the a.
43 laid ambushes in the fields. And seeing
20 29 set ambushes round about the city of
33 the a. also which were about the city
36 that they might come to the ambushes
38 sign to them whom they had laid in a.
1 K 15 5 he laid ambushes in the torrent. Saul
4 K 6 8 and such a place let us lay ambushes
2 Es 4 8 against Jerusalem and to prepare a.
Jer 51 12 set up the watchmen, prepare the a.
Acts 23 30 when I was told of ambushes that they
ambushment 2 Pa 13 13 Jeroboam caused an a. to
ambushments 2 Pa 20 22 Lord turned their a. upon
Amelech Jer 36 26 Jeremiel the son of Amelech and
Jer 38 6 dungeon of Melchias the son of Amelech
amen Deut 27 15 people shall answer and say: Amen
Deut 27 16 all the people shall say: Amen (and so to verse 26)
3 K 1 36 and let all the people say Amen, and a
2 Es 5 13 and all the multitude said: Amen. And
8 6 all the people answered, Amen, amen
13 31 remember me, O my God, unto good. Amen
Tob 9 12 when all had said, Amen, they went to
13 23 he reign over it forever and ever, a.
Isa 25 1 thy designs of old faithful, amen. For
65 16 shall be blessed in God, amen: and he
16 shall swear by God, amen: because the
Jer 11 5 and I answered and said: Amen, O Lord
28 6 the prophet said: Amen, the Lord do so
Mat 6 13 temptation. But deliver us from evil. A.
Luke 24 53 temple, praising and blessing God. Amen
Rom 1 25 Creator, who is blessed forever. Amen
11 36 to him be glory forever. Amen
15 33 be with you all. Amen. 16:24; 2 C 13:13; 2 Th 3:18; Titus 3:15; Heb 13:25; Apoc 22:21
16 27 forever and ever. Amen. Gal 1:5; 1 Tim 1:17; 2 Tim 4:18; Heb 13:21; 1 P 4:11; 5:11; Apoc 1:6; 7:12; 11:15
1 C 14 16 shall he . . . say Amen to thy blessing
16 24 be with you all in Christ Jesus. Amen
2 C 1 20 by him, amen to God, unto our glory
Eph 3 21 world without end. Amen. Phil 4:20
6 24 Lord Jesus Christ in incorruption. Amen
1 Th 3 13 Jesus Christ with all his saints. Amen
5 28 be with you. Amen. Col 4:18; 2 Tim 4:22
1 Tim 6 16 honor and empire everlasting. Amen
21 the faith. Grace be with thee. Amen
1 P 5 14 all you, who are in Christ Jesus. Amen

2 P 3 18 now and unto the day of eternity. Amen
1 J 5 21 keep yourselves from idols. Amen
Jude 25 now and for all ages of ages. Amen
Apoc 1 7 shall bewail themselves. Even so. Amen
3 14 these things saith the Amen, the
5 14 the four living creatures said: Amen
7 12 adored God, saying: Amen. Benediction
19 4 upon the throne saying: Amen; Alleluia
22 20 I come quickly. Amen. Come, Lord Jesus
amen, amen I say to thee John 3 3 a. . . . unless a man be born again. 5
John 13 38 a. . . . the cock shall not crow till thou
21 18 a. . . . when thou wast younger, thou
amen, amen I say to you John 1 51 a. . . . you shall see the heaven opened
John 3 11 a. . . . that we speak what we know, and
5 19 a. . . . the Son cannot do anything of
24 a. . . . that he who heareth my word and
25 a. . . . that the hour cometh and now is
6 26 a. . . . you seek me not because you have
32 a. . . . Moses gave you not bread from
47 a. . . . he that believeth in me, hath
54 a. . . . except you eat the flesh of the
8 34 a. . . . that whosoever committeth sin
51 a. . . . if any man keep my word, he shall
58 a. . . . before Abraham was made, I am
10 1 a. . . . he that entereth not by the door
7 a. . . . I am the door of the sheep. All
12 24 a. . . . unless the grain of wheat falling
13 16 a. . . . the servant is not greater than
20 a. . . . he that receiveth whomsoever I
21 a. . . . one of you shall betray me. The
14 12 a. . . . he that believeth in me, the
16 20 a. . . . that you shall lament and weep
23 a. . . . if you ask the Father anything
amen I say to thee Mat 5 26 a. . . . thou shalt not go out from thence
Mat 26 34 a. . . . that in this night before the
Mark 14 30 a. . . . today even in this night, before
Luke 23 43 a. . . . this day thou shalt be with me
amen I say to you Mat 5 18 a. . . . till heaven
Mat 6 2 a. . . . they have received their. 5, 16
8 10 a. . . . I have not found so. Luke 7:9
10 15 a. . . . it shall be more tolerable for
23 a. . . . you shall not finish all the
42 a. . . . he shall not lose his. Mark 9:40
11 11 a. . . . there hath not risen among the
13 17 a. . . . many prophets and just men have
16 28 a. . . . there are some that. Mark 8:39
17 19 a. . . . if you have faith as a grain of
18 3 a. . . . unless you be converted and
13 a. . . . he rejoiceth more for that
18 a. . . . whatsoever you shall bind upon
19 23 a. . . . that a rich man shall hardly
28 a. . . . that you who have followed me
21 21 a. . . . if you shall have faith and
31 a. . . . that the publicans and harlots
23 36 a. . . . all these things shall come upon
24 2 a. . . . there shall not be left here a
34 a. . . . that this generation shall not pass. Mark 13:30; Luke 21:32
47 a. . . . he shall place him over all his
25 12 a. . . . I know you not. Watch ye
40 a. . . . as long as you did it to one of
45 a. . . . long as you did it not to one
26 13 a. . . . wheresoever this gospel. Mark 14:9
21 a. . . . that one of you is about to
Mark 3 28 a. . . . that all sins shall be forgiven
8 12 a. . . . a sign shall not be given to
10 15 a. . . . whosoever shall not. Luke 18:17
29 a. . . . there is no man who. Luke 18:29
11 23 a. . . . whosoever shall say to this
12 43 a. . . . this poor widow hath cast in more
14 18 a. . . . one of you that eateth with me
25 a. . . . that I will drink no more of the
Luke 4 24 a. . . . that no prophet is accepted in
12 37 a. . . . that he will gird himself and
amend Lev 26 23 if even so you will not amend
Jer 26 13 amend your ways and your doings and
amended Wisd 12 26 were not amended by mockeries
amendment Jdth 8 27 have happened for our a. and
Prov 29 20 to be looked for, than his amendment
amends Prov 25 8 mayst not be able to make amends
amethyst Exod 28 19 in the third . . . an a. 39:12
Apoc 21 20 a jacinth; the twelfth, an amethyst
Ami 1 Es 2 57 of Asebaim, the children of Ami
amiable 2 K 1 26 exceeding beautiful and a. to me
2 K 12 25 called his name, Amiable to the Lord
Prov 18 24 a man amiable in society shall be more
Aminadab Exod 6 23 Elizabeth the daughter of A.
Num 1 7 the son of A. 2:3; 7:12, 17; 10:14
Ruth 4 19 Aram begot A. A. begot Nahasson
1 Pa 2 10 Ram begot A. A. begot Nahasson
6 22 sons of Caath, Aminadab his son
15 10 sons of Oziel, Aminadab the chief
11 the Levites . . . Eliel and Aminadab
Cant 6 11 troubled me for the chariots of A.
Mat 1 4 Aram begot A. A. begot Naasson
Luke 3 33 Naasson who was of A. who was of Aram
amiss Wisd 14 29 though they swear amiss, they
James 4 3 receive not because you ask amiss
Amital 4 K 23 31 the name of his mother was Amital. 24:18; Jer 52:1
amity 1 Ma 8 1 they have made amity with them
1 Ma 8 12 with their friends . . . they kept amity
17 to Rome to make a league of amity and
12 1 and to renew the amity with them: and
3 to renew the amity and alliance as it
8 mention made of the alliance and amity
16 to renew with them the former amity
2 Ma 4 11 to Rome to make amity and alliance
Amizabad 1 Pa 27 6 A. his son commanded his company
Amma Josu 19 30 and Amma and Aphec and Rohob
Ammaus 1 Ma 9 50 that was in Jericho and in A.
Ammiel Num 13 13 Ammiel the son of Gemalli
2 K 9 4 Machir the son of Ammiel. 5
1 Pa 3 5 Bethsabee the daughter of Ammiel
26 5 Ammiel the sixth, Issachar the
Ammihel 2 K 17 27 Machir the son of Ammihel of
Ammisaddai Num 1 12 Ahiezer the son of Ammisaddai. 7:66, 71; 10:25
Num 2 25 was Ahiezar the son of Ammisaddai
Ammiud Num 1 10 Elisama the son of Ammiud. 2:18; 7:48, 53; 10:22
Num 34 20 of Simeon, Samuel the son of Ammiud
28 of Nephtali, Phedael the son of Ammiud
2 K 13 37 son of Ammiud the king of Gessur
1 Pa 7 26 son was Ammiud, who begot Elisama
9 4 the son of Ammiud, the son of Amri
Ammon Gen 19 38 she called his name Ammon, that is
Judg 11 14 commanded them to say to the king of A.
2 K 3 2 his firstborn was Ammon of Achinoam
3 K 11 1 women of Moab and of Ammon and of Edom
22 26 let him abide with A. the governor
1 Pa 18 11 from Moab and from the sons of Ammon
2 Es 13 23 wives, women of Azotus and of Ammon
Jdth 5 2 princes of Moab and the leaders of A.
Ps 82 8 Gebal and Ammon and Amalec: the
Jer 25 3 Josias the son of Ammon king of Juda
children of Ammon Num 21 24 the Jeboc and to the confines of the c. . . .
Num 22 5 by the river of the land of the c. . . .
Deut 2 19 comest nigh the frontiers of the c. . . .
19 not give thee of the land of the c. . . .
37 except land of the children of Ammon

3 11 which is in Rabbath of the c. . . .
16 which is the border of c. . . . Josu 12:2
Josu 13 10 Hesebon unto the borders of the c. . . .
25 Galaad, and half the land of the c. . . .
Judg 3 13 he joined to him the c. . . . and
10 6 of Sidon and of Moab and of the c. . . .
7 into hands of Philistines and of c. . . .
9 c. . . . passing over the Jordan, wasted
11 the c. . . . and the Philistines, the
17 c. . . . shouting together, pitched their
18 first begin to fight against the c. . . .
11 4 the c. . . . made war against Israel. And
6 fight against the children of A. 11:8
9 I should fight for you against c. . . .
12 he sent messengers to the king of c. . . .
15 of Moab nor the land of the c. . . .
27 decide this day between Israel and c. . . .
28 king of the c. . . . would not hearken
29 passing over from thence to the c. . . .
30 if thou wilt deliver the c. . . . into my
31 when I return in peace from the c. . . .
32 Jephte passed over to the c. . . . to
33 c. . . . were humbled by the children of
12 1 thou wentest to fight against c. . . .
2 were at great strife with the c. . . .
3 passed over against the c. . . . , and the
1 K 12 12 that Naas king of the c. . . . was come
14 47 against Moab and against the c. . . .
2 K 8 12 Syria and of Moab and of the c. . . .
10 1 the king of the c. . . . died. 1 Pa 19:1
2 were come into land of c. . . . 1 Pa 19:2
3 the princes of c. . . . said. 1 Pa 19:3
6 the c. . . . seeing that they had done an
8 c. . . . came out and set their men in
10 set them in array against the c. . . .
11 if the c. . . . are too strong for thee
14 c. . . . seeing that the Syrians. 1 Pa 19:15
14 Joab returned from the c. . . . and came
19 Syrians were afraid to help the c. . . .
11 1 and they spoiled the children of Ammon
12 9 hast slain him with sword of the c. . . .
26 fought against Rabbath of the c. . . .
31 so did he to all the cities of c. . . .
17 27 the son of Naas of Rabbath of the c. . . .
3 K 11 7 Moloch the idol of the children of Ammon
33 Moab, and Moloch the god of the c. . . .
4 K 23 13 Melchom the abomination of the c. . . .
24 2 of Moab and the rovers of the c. . . .
1 Pa 19 1 Naas king of the c. . . . died, and his son
3 princes of the c. . . . said to Hanon
6 c. . . . saw that they had done an injury
7 the c. . . . gathered themselves together
9 c. . . . came out and put their army in
11 they went against the children of Ammon
12 if the c. . . . be too strong for thee
19 Syria would not help the c. . . . any more
20 1 and wasted the land of the c. . . .
3 dealt with all the cities of c. . . .
2 Pa 20 1 c. . . . were gathered together to fight
10 behold the c. . . . and of Moab and mount
22 of the c. . . . and of Moab and of mount
23 c. . . . and of Moab rose up against the
27 5 he fought against the king of c. . . .
5 c. . . . gave him at that time 100 talents
Jdth 5 5 then Achior captain of all the c. . . .
7 8 c. . . . and Moab came to Holofernes
Isa 11 14 c. . . . shall be obedient. And the Lord
Jer 9 26 upon the c. . . . and upon Moab and
25 21 Edom and Moab and the c. . . . And all
27 3 to the king of c. . . . and to the king
40 11 that were in Moab and among the c. . . .
14 Baalis the king of the c. . . . hath sent
41 10 and he departed, to go over to c. . . .
15 face of Johanan, and went to the c. . . .
49 1 against the c. . . . Thus saith the Lord
2 to be heard in Rabbath of the c. . . .
6 cause the captives of the c. . . . to
Eze 21 20 sword may come to Rabbath of the c. . . .
28 saith the Lord God concerning the c. . . .
25 2 set thy face against the c. . . . , and
3 thou shalt say to the c. . . . : Hear ye
5 the c. . . . a couching place for flocks
10 the people of the east with the c. . . .
10 no more any remembrance of the c. . . .
Dan 11 41 and the principality of the c. . . .
Amos 1 13 for three crimes of the c. . . . and for
Soph 2 8 and the blasphemies of the c. . . . with
9 as Sodom, and the c. . . . as Gomorrha
1 Ma 5 6 then he passed over to the c. . . .
Ammoni 2 K 23 37 Selec of Ammoni, Nahari the
Ammonite Deut 23 3 A. and the Moabite, even to
1 K 11 1 Naas the Ammonite came up and began
2 Naas the Ammonite answered them: On
1 Pa 11 39 Selec an A., Naharai a Barothite
2 Es 2 10 Tobias the servant, the Ammonite. 19
4 2 Tobias the A. who was by him said
Ammonites Gen 19 38 he is the father of the A.
Num 21 24 borders of the A. were kept with a
Deut 2 20 whom the Ammonites call Zomzommims
1 K 11 11 he slew the A. until the day grew hot
3 K 11 5 and Moloch the idol of the Ammonites
2 Pa 20 1 of the Ammonites, were gathered
26 7 dwelt in Gurbaal, and against the A.
8 and the Ammonites gave gifts to Ozias
1 Es 9 1 the A. and the Moabites. 2 Es 13:1
2 Es 4 7 A. and the Azotians heard that the
2 Ma 4 26 a fugitive into the country of the A.
5 7 fled again into the country of the A.
Ammonitess 3 K 14 21 name was Naama an A. 31
2 Pa 12 13 his mother was Naama an Ammonitess
24 26 Zabad the son of Semmaath an A. and
ammunition 1 Ma 14 10 should be furnished with a.
Amnon 2 K 13 1 A. the son of David loved the sister
2 K 13 3 now Amnon had a friend, named Jonadab
4 Amnon said to him: I am in love with
6 so Amnon lay down and made as if he
6 Amnon said to the king: I pray thee
7 come to the house of thy brother Amnon
8 Thamar came to the house of Amnon her
9 Amnon said: Put out all persons from
10 Amnon said the Thamar: Bring the mess
10 brought them in to her brother Amnon
15 then Amnon hated her with an
15 Amnon said to her: Arise and get thee
20 hath thy brother Amnon lain with thee
21 not afflict the spirit of his son Amnon
22 but Absalom spoke not to Amnon neither
22 for Absalom hated Amnon because he had
26 not come, at least let my brother A.
27 he let Amnon and all the king's sons go
28 take notice when Amnon shall be drunk
29 the servants of Absalom did to Amnon
32 are slain: Amnon only is dead. 33
38 comforted concerning the death of Amnon
1 Pa 3 1 the firstborn Amnon of Achinoam the
4 20 the sons also of Simon, Amnon and
Amoc 2 Es 12 6 Joiarib, Idaia, Sellum, A., Helcias
2 Es 12 20 of Amoc, Heber: of Helcias, Hasebia
Amon 4 K 21 18 Amon his son reigned in his stead
4 K 21 19 two and twenty years old when Amon
24 that had conspired against king Amon
25 the rest of the acts of Amon which he
1 Pa 3 14 Manasses begot A. the father of Josias
2 Pa 18 25 carry him to Amon the governor of the
33 20 his son Amon reigned in his stead
21 Amon was two and twenty years old

25 slew them that had killed Amon, and
2 Es 7 59 born of Sabaim the son of Amon
Jer 1 2 Josias the son of Amon. Soph 1:1
Mat 1 10 Manasses begot A. A. begot Josias
Amona Eze 39 16 name of the city shall be Amona
amorous Jer 5 8 they are become as a. horses
Amorrhean Gen 14 7 smote . . . the A. that dwelt in
Amorrhite Gen 10 16 the Jebusite and the A. Num 13:30; Josu 3:10; 1 Pa 1:14
Gen 14 13 dwelt in the vale of Mambre the A.
48 22 which I took out of the hand of the A.
Exod 3 8 the Hethite and the A. 17; 13:5; Deut 20:17; Josu 9:1; 12:8; Judg 3:5; 2 Es 9:8
23 23 the A. and the Hethite. 33:2; Josu 11:3
34 11 the A. and the Chanaanite. Deut 7:1
Num 21 13 Arnon . . . on the borders of the A.
25 dwelt in the cities of the Amorrhite
31 dwelt in the land of the Amorrhite
22 2 that Israel had done to the Amorrhite
Deut 1 19 by the way of the mountain of the A.
20 you are come to mountain of the A.
27 might deliver into the hand of the A.
44 and the Amorrhite . . . chased you
2 24 Sehon king of Hesebon the Amorrhite
Josu 7 7 to deliver us into the hand of the A.
10 12 in the day that he delivered the A.
13 4 Apheca and the borders of the A.
24 8 I brought you into the land of the A.
11 against you, the Amorrhite and the
18 he hath cast out . . . the Amorrhite
Judg 1 34 the A. straitened the children of Dan
36 border of the Amorrhite was from the
10 8 beyond the Jordan in land of the A.
11 21 and possessed all the land of the A.
23 God of Israel destroyed the Amorrhite
Eze 16 3 thy father was an Amorrhite, and thy
45 was a Cethite, and your father an A.
Amos 2 9 I cast out the A. before their face
10 might possess the land of the Amorrhite
Amorrhites Gen 15 21 A. and the Chanaanites
Num 21 13 dividing Moabites and the Amorrhites
32 29 wasted it, cutting off the Amorrhites
Deut 1 7 come to the mountain of the Amorrhites
3 9 Sidonians call Sarion, and the A. Sanir
Josu 24 15 rather serve . . . or the gods of the A.
Judg 6 10 fear not the gods of the Amorrhites
10 11 Egyptians and the Amorrhites. 1 Es 9:1
1 K 7 14 was peace between Israel and the A.
2 K 21 2 of Israel, but the remains of the A.
3 K 9 20 that were left of the A. 2 Pa 8:7
21 26 idols which the Amorrhites had made
4 K 21 11 beyond all that the Amorrhites did
Jdth 5 20 overthrew the king . . . of the A.
kings of the Amorrhites Deut 3 8 the two k. . . . that were. 4:47; Josu 2:10; 9:10
Deut 31 4 did to Sehon and Og the kings of the A.
Josu 5 1 the kings of the Amorrhites who dwelt
10 5 five kings of the A. being assembled
6 all the kings of the A. are gathered
24 12 their palaces the two kings of the A.
Sehon king of the Amorrhites Num 21 21 Israel sent messengers to S. . . . Judg 11:19
Num 21 26 Hesebon was the city of S. . . . , who
29 his daughters into captivity to S. . . .
34 do to him as thou didst to S. . . .
32 33 the kingdom of S. . . . and the kingdom
Deut 1 4 after that he had slain S. . . . who
3 2 as thou hast done to S. . . . that dwelt
4 46 temple of Phogor, in land of S. . . .
Josu 12 2 S. . . . who dwelt in Hesebon and had
13 10 all the cities of S. . . . who reigned
21 all the kingdoms of S. . . . that reigned
3 K 4 19 land of Galaad, in the land of S. . . .
Ps 134 11 slew mighty kings: S. . . . and Og king of
135 19 S. . . . : for his mercy endureth forever
Amos 4 K 19 2 Isaias . . . the son of Amos. 20; 20:1; 2 Pa 26:22; 32:20
Tob 2 6 the Lord spoke by Amos the prophet
Isa 1 1 Isaias the son of Amos. 2:1; 13:1; 20:2; 27:2, 21; 38:1
Amos 1 1 the words of Amos, who was among the
7 8 what seest thou, Amos? And I. 8:2
10 Amos hath rebelled against thee in the
11 thus saith Amos: Jeroboam shall die
12 Amasias said to Amos: Thou seer, go
14 Amos answered and said to Amasias: I
Luke 3 25 who was of Amos who was of Nahum
Amosa Josu 18 26 Mesphe and Caphara and Amosa
amounting 2 Pa 3 8 amounting to about 600 talents
Amphipolis Acts 17 1 passed through Amphipolis
Ampliatus Rom 16 8 salute A., most beloved
Amram Exod 6 18 the sons of Caath: Amram. Num 3:19; 1 Pa 6:2, 18; 23:12
Exod 6 20 Amram took to wife Jochabed his aunt
Num 26 58 Caath begot Amram: who had to wife
59 she bore to her husband Amram sons
1 Pa 6 3 the children of Amram: Aaron, Moses
23 13 the sons of Amram, Aaron and Moses
24 20 there was of the sons of Amram, Subael
1 Es 10 34 of the sons of Bani, Maaddi, Amram
Amramites Num 3 27 come the families of the A.
1 Pa 26 23 with the Amramites and Isaarites and
Amram's Exod 6 20 years of Amram's life were 137
Amraphel Gen 14 1 A. king of Sennaar . . . made war
Gen 14 9 against . . . Amraphel king of Sennaar
Amri 3 K 16 16 all Israel made Amri their king
3 K 16 17 Amri went up, and all Israel with him
21 him king: and one half followed Amri
22 people that were with Amri prevailed
22 and Thebni died, and Amri reigned. In
23 Amri reigned over Israel twelve years
25 Amri did evil in the sight of the Lord
27 the rest of the acts of Amri and the
28 and Amri slept with his fathers, and
29 Achab the son of Amri reigned over
30 Achab the son of Amri did evil in
4 K 8 26 Athalia daughter of Amri. 2 Pa 22:2
1 Pa 9 4 the son of Amri the son of Omrai the
27 18 over Issachar, Amri the son of Mishael
2 Es 3 2 to them built Zachur the son of Amri
Mich 6 16 thou hast kept the statutes of Amri
Amsi 2 Es 11 12 Phelelia the son of Amsi the
Amthar Josu 19 13 goeth out to Remmon, Amthar
Ana Gen 36 2 Oolibama the daughter of Ana. 14, 18
Gen 36 20 sons of Seir . . . Ana. 1 Pa 1:38
24 sons of Sebeon: Ain and Ana. 1 Pa 1:40
24 this is Ana that found the hot waters
29 duke Ana, duke Dison, duke Eser
4 K 18 34 where is the god of Sepharvaim, of Ana
19 13 where is the king . . . of Ana and of
1 Pa 1 40 the son of Ana: Dison. The sons of
Isa 37 13 king of city of Sepharvaim, of Ana
Anab Josu 11 21 from Hebron and Dabir and Anab
Josu 15 50 Anab and Istemo and Anim, Gosen and
Anaharath Josu 19 19 Seon and Anaharath
Anaia 2 Es 10 22 Pheltia, Hanan, Anaia, Osee
Anamelech 4 K 17 31 Adramelech and A. the gods of
Anamim Gen 10 13 Mesraim begot . . . A. 1 Pa 1:11
Anan 2 Es 10 26 Echaia, Hanan, Anan, Melluch
Anani 1 Pa 3 24 and Dalaia and Anani, seven
Anania 2 Es 11 32 at Anathoth, Nob, Anania, Asor
Ananias 2 Es 3 8 built A. the son of the perfumer
2 Es 3 23 Maasias the son of Ananias over against
Tob 5 18 I am Azarias the son of the great A.
Dan 1 6 Daniel, Ananias, Misael, and Azarias
7 names . . . To Ananias, Sidrach; to

11 appointed over Daniel, Ananias, Misael
19 among them all such as Daniel, Ananias
2 17 told the matter to Ananias and Misael
3 88 Ananias, Azarias, and Misael, bless
1 Ma 2 59 Ananias and Azarias . . . were delivered
Acts 5 1 man named Ananias with Saphira his
3 A., why hath Satan tempted thy heart
5 A. hearing these words, fell down and
9 10 disciple at Damascus, named Ananias
10 Lord said to him in a vision: Ananias
12 he saw a man named Ananias, coming in
13 Ananias answered: Lord, I have heard by
17 A. went his way and entered into the
22 12 Ananias, a man according to the law
23 2 high priest A. commanded them that
24 1 A. came down with some of the ancients
Anath Judg 3 31 Samgar the son of Anath. 5:6
anathema Num 21 3 place Horma, that is to say, A.
Deut 7 26 lest thou become an anathema like it
26 and filth, because it is an anathema
13 17 nothing of that a. stick to thy hand
Josu 6 17 let this city be an anathema, and all
7 1 took to their own use of the anathema
1 tribe of Juda took something of the a.
11 and they have taken of the anathema
12 them: because he is defiled with the a.
13 the anathema is in the midst of thee
Judg 1 17 was called Horma, that is, Anathema
1 Pa 2 7 sinned by the theft of the anathema
Zach 14 11 there shall be no more an anathema
Mala 4 6 lest I . . . strike the earth with a.
Rom 9 3 I wished myself to be an anathema from
1 C 12 3 saith Anathema to Jesus. And no man
16 22 let him be anathema, maranatha. The
Gal 1 8 have preached to you let him be a.
9 you have received, let him be a.
Anathoth Josu 21 18 and Anathoth and Almon, with
2 K 23 27 Abiezer of Anathoth, Mabonnai of
3 K 2 26 go to Anathoth to thy lands, for
1 Pa 6 60 A. also with its suburbs: all their
7 8 Jerimoth and Abia and Anathoth
1 Es 2 23 the men of Anathoth, 128. 2 Es 7:27
2 Es 10 19 Hareph, Anathoth, Nebai, Megphias
11 32 children of Benjamin . . . at Anathoth
Isa 10 30 attend, O Laisa, poor Anathoth
Jer 1 1 of the priests that were in Anathoth
11 21 saith the Lord to the men of Anathoth
23 evil upon the men of Anathoth
32 7 my field which is in Anathoth. 8
9 field of Hanameel . . . that is in A.
Anathothia 1 Pa 8 24 Hanania and Elam and A.
Anathothite 1 Pa 11 28 a Thecuite, Abiezer an A.
1 Pa 12 3 and Jehu an Anathothite. And Samaias
27 12 Abiezer an A. of the sons of Jemini
Jer 29 27 not rebuked Jeremias the Anathothite
ancestors Gen 47 30 in the buryingplace of my a.
Lev 26 40 iniquities of their a., whereby they
4 K 15 7 they buried him with his ancestors in
2 Pa 21 19 of burning, as they had done for his a.
1 Ma 10 52 am set in the throne of my ancestors
2 Ma 11 25 live according to the custom of their a.
ancestors' Lev 27 22 not of a man's a. possession
2 Ma 14 7 being deprived of my ancestors' glory
anchor Heb 6 19 which we have as an a. of the soul
anchors Acts 27 29 they cast four anchors out of
Acts 27 30 as though they would have cast anchors
40 and when they had taken up the anchors
ancient Lev 25 28 owner and to the a. possessor
Deut 33 15 of the tops of the ancient mountains
Judg 1 11 a. name of which was Cariath-Sepher
Job 12 12 in the ancient is wisdom, and in length
15 10 are with us also aged and ancient men
32 6 and you are more ancient: therefore
Ps 88 50 Lord, where are thy ancient mercies
Prov 22 28 pass not beyond the ancient bounds
Wisd 2 10 nor honor the a. gray hairs of the aged
12 3 those a. inhabitants of thy holy land
13 10 stone the work of an ancient hand. Or
Eccu 4 7 humble thy soul to the ancient and bow
8 9 discourse of them that are a. and wise
16 8 the a. giants did not obtain pardon
Isa 3 2 and the cunning man and the ancient
5 shall make a tumult against the ancient
19 11 son of the wise, the son of a. kings
44 7 since I appointed the ancient people
46 10 from a. times the things that as yet
47 6 upon the a. thou hast laid thy yoke
51 9 days of old, in the a. generations
61 4 and shall raise up ancient ruins and
Jer 5 15 a strong nation, an ancient nation
6 11 shall be taken, the ancient and he
18 15 stumbling in their ways, in a. paths
Lam 4 16 neither had they pity on the ancient
5 12 did not respect the persons of the a.
Bar 4 16 who have neither reverenced the a. nor
Eze 9 6 they began at the ancient men who were
16 55 shall return to their ancient state
55 shall return to your ancient state
Dan 7 9 the Ancient of days sat: his garment
13 and he came even to the Ancient of days
22 till the Ancient of days came and
13 5 iniquity came . . . from the a. judges
Haba 3 6 the a. mountains were crushed to pieces
Mala 3 4 days of old and in the ancient years
1 Ma 14 9 the ancient men sat all in the streets
2 Ma 6 23 dignity of his age and his a. years
1 Tim 5 1 an ancient man rebuke not, but entreat
1 P 5 1 who am myself also an ancient and a
2 J 1 the ancient to the lady Elect and her
3 J 1 the a. to the dearly beloved Gaius
ancients Gen 50 7 all the a. of Pharao's house
Exod 4 29 they assembled all the ancients of the
12 21 and Moses called all the ancients of
24 14 said to the ancients: Wait ye here
Lev 4 15 a. of the people shall put their hands
Num 11 16 thou knowest to be ancients and masters
22 7 a. of Moab and the elders of Madian
Deut 19 12 the ancients of his city shall send
21 2 thy ancients and judges shall go out
3 ancients of that city which they shall
6 the ancients of that city shall come
19 bring him to the ancients of his city
22 15 the tokens of her virginity to the a.
17 shall spread the cloth before the a.
18 the a. of that city shall take that man
25 7 and call upon the ancients and say
9 woman shall come to him before the a.
28 50 that will show no regard to the a. nor
29 10 and tribes and ancients and doctors
31 28 gather unto me all the ancients of your
Josu 8 10 with the a. in the front of the army
33 the a. and the princes and judges
9 11 our ancients and all the inhabitants of
20 4 shall speak to the ancients of that city
24 1 called for the ancients and princes and
31 a. that had lived a long time after
Judg 2 7 all his days and the days of the a.
8 16 so he took the ancients of the city
11 5 the a. of Galaad went to fetch Jephte
21 16 the ancients said: What shall we do
Ruth 4 2 Booz taking ten men of the ancients
4 and before the ancients of my people
9 he said to the ancients and to all the
11 and the a. answered: We are witnesses
1 K 11 3 ancients of Jabes said to him: Allow
15 30 yet honor me now before the ancients

16 4 and the ancients of the city wondered
30 26 sent presents of prey to the a. of Juda
2 K 12 17 and the ancients of his house came to
19 11 speak to the ancients of Juda, saying
3 K 20 7 king of Israel called all the ancients
8 ancients and all the people said to him
21 8 his ring and sent them to the ancients
11 a. and nobles that dwelt with him
4 K 6 32 house, and the ancients sat with him
32 he said to the ancients: Do you know
10 1 chief men of the city and to the a.
5 ancients and the tutors sent to Jehu
19 2 the ancients of the priests covered with
23 1 all the ancients of Juda and Jerusalem
1 Pa 21 16 and the ancients clothed in haircloth
26 15 of the house was the council of the a.
2 Pa 10 6 he took counsel with the ancients, who
8 he forsook the counsel of the ancients
13 leaving the counsel of the ancients
34 29 called together all the ancients of Juda
1 Es 3 12 ancients that had seen the former temple
5 5 eye of their God was upon the ancients
9 we asked those ancients and said to
6 7 governor of the Jews and by their a.
8 be done by those ancients of the Jews
14 and the ancients of the Jews built and
10 8 counsel of the princes and the ancients
14 with them the ancients and the judges
Jdth 2 2 he called all the ancients and all the
6 12 related in the midst of the ancients
20 and all the ancients were invited, and
8 9 sent to the ancients Chabri and Charmi
21 as you are the a. among the people of
28 Ozias and the ancients said to her: All
10 6 Ozias and the ancients of the city
13 14 they called the ancients of the city
15 9 with all his ancients to see Judith
Job 32 9 neither do the a. understand judgment
Ps 104 22 and teach his ancients wisdom. And
106 32 praise him in the chair of the ancients
118 100 I have had understanding above ancients
Wisd 8 10 honor with the a. though I be young
Eccu 6 35 stand in the multitude of ancients
7 15 be not full of words in multitude of a.
8 11 let not discourse of the a. escape thee
9 24 the word of the ancients for the sense
25 6 for ancients to know counsel! O how
32 13 when the ancients are present, speak
39 1 will seek out the wisdom of all the a.
Isa 3 14 into judgment with the a. of his people
24 23 shall be glorified in sight of his a.
37 2 the ancients of the priests covered
Jer 19 1 take of the ancients of the people and
of the ancients of the priests
26 17 some of the ancients of the land arose
29 1 the a. that were carried into captivity
Lam 1 19 and my ancients pined away in the city
2 10 the ancients of the daughter of Sion
5 14 the ancients have ceased from the gates
Bar 1 4 and in the hearing of the ancients
Eze 7 26 from the priest, and counsel from the a.
8 1 as the ancients of Juda sat before me
11 seventy men of the ancients of the house
12 what the a. of the house of Israel do
27 9 ancients of Gebal and the wise men
Dan 13 5 there were two of the ancients of the
5 the a. judges that seemed to govern the
Joel 1 14 gather together the ancients, all the
2 16 assemble the ancients, gather together
1 Ma 1 27 the princes and the ancients mourned
12 6 high priest and the a. of the nations
35 called together the a. of the people
13 36 to the ancients and to the nation of
14 20 and to the ancients and the priests and
28 princes of the nation and the a. of the
2 Ma 4 44 three men were sent from the ancients
13 13 he with the a. determined, before the
14 37 Razias, one of the a. of Jerusalem, was
Mat 15 2 transgress traditions of the ancients
26 57 where the scribes and a. were assembled
28 12 being assembled together with the a.
Mark 7 3 holding the tradition of the ancients
5 walk according to the tradition of a.
8 31 and be rejected by the a. Luke 9:22
14 53 scribes and the a. assembled together
Luke 7 3 he sent unto him the a. of the Jews
Acts 4 5 their princes and ancients and scribes
8 princes of the people and ancients, hear
5 21 together the council and all the a.
6 12 stirred up the people and the ancients
11 30 sending it to the a. by the hands of
20 17 he called the ancients of the church
21 18 all the ancients were assembled. Whom
22 5 doth bear me witness and all the a.
24 1 Ananias came down with some of the a.
Heb 11 2 by this the a. obtained a testimony
1 P 5 1 the a. therefore that are among you
5 young men, be subject to the ancients
Apoc 4 4 and upon the seats, 4 and 20 ancients
10 the 4 and 20 ancients fell down. 5:8, 14; 11:16; 19:4
5 5 and one of the a. said to me: Weep not
6 in the midst of the ancients, a Lamb
11 living creatures and the ancients. 14:3
7 11 about the throne, and the ancients
13 one of the a. answered and said to me

ancients of Israel Exod 3 16 gather together the ancients of Israel
Exod 3 18 thou shalt go in, thou and the a. . . .
17 5 and take with thee of the a. . . .
6 Moses did so before the a. . . . : and he
18 12 all the a. . . . came, to eat bread with
24 1 Abia and seventy of the a. . . . 9
Lev 9 1 Aaron and his sons and the a. . . .
Num 11 16 gather unto me seventy men of the a. . . .
24 assembled seventy men of the a. . . .
30 Moses returned with the a. . . . into the
16 25 the a. . . . following him, he said to
Deut 27 1 Moses with the a. . . . commanded the
31 9 covenant of the Lord and to all a. . . .
Josu 7 6 and all the a. . . . : and they put dust
1 K 4 3 and the a. . . . said: Why hath the Lord
8 4 a. . . . being assembled, came to Samuel
2 K 3 17 Abner also spoke to the a. . . . , saying
5 3 the a. . . . came to the king. 1 Pa 11:3
17 4 pleased Absalom and all the a. . . .
15 Achitophel counsel Absalom and a. . . .
3 K 8 1 the a. . . . with the princes of the
3 all the a. . . . came, and the priests
1 Pa 15 25 David and all the a. . . . and the captains
2 Pa 5 2 [Solomon] gathered together the a. . . .
4 all the a. . . . were come, the Levites
Eze 14 1 some of the a. . . . came to me and sat
20 1 came men of the a. . . . to inquire of
3 speak to the a. . . . and say to them
1 Ma 11 23 he chose some of the a. . . . and of the

apostles and ancients; *see* **apostles**
chief priests and ancients; *see* **chief**
chief priests and scribes and ancients; *see* **chief**

Andrew Mat 4 18 saw . . . A. his brother. Mark 1:16
Mat 10 2 names of the twelve . . . A. his brother
Mark 1 29 they came into the house of Simon and A.
3 18 Andrew and Philip and Bartholomew
13 3 and John and Andrew asked him apart
Luke 6 14 he chose twelve . . . Andrew his brother
John 1 40 A. . . . was one of the two who had heard

44 Bethsaida, the city of A. and Peter
6 8 A. . . . saith to him: There is a boy here
12 22 Philip cometh and telleth Andrew. Again Andrew and Philip told Jesus
Acts 1 13 where abode Peter . . . and Andrew, Philip
Andronicus 2 Ma 4 31 leaving A. . . . for his deputy
2 Ma 4 32 out of the temple, gave them to A.
34 Menelaus coming to A., desired him to
38 commanded A. to be stripped of his purple
5 23 in Gazarim, Andronicus and Menelaus
Rom 16 7 salute A. and Junias, my kinsmen
Anem 1 Pa 6 73 Anem with its suburbs. And out of
Aner Gen 14 13 of Escol and the brother of Aner
Gen 14 24 that came with me, Aner, Escol, and
1 Pa 6 70 out of the half tribe of Manasses, Aner
anew Jer 4 3 break up anew your fallow ground
1 Ma 4 54 was it dedicated anew with canticles
Ange Jdth 2 12 came to the great mountains of Ange
angel Gen 21 17 angel of God called to Agar from
Gen 24 7 he will send his angel before thee
40 will send his angel with thee and will
31 11 angel of God said to me in my sleep
48 16 the angel that delivereth me from all
Exod 14 19 angel of God who went before the camp
23 20 I will send my angel, who shall go
23 my angel shall go before thee. 32:24
33 2 I will send an angel before thee, that
Num 20 16 he heard us and sent an angel, who
22 23 the ass seeing the angel standing in
24 the angel stood in a narrow place
26 the angel going on to a narrow place
27 when the ass saw the angel standing
31 he saw the angel standing in the way
32 the angel said to him: Why beatest
35 the angel said: Go with these men and
Judg 13 6 having the countenance of an angel
9 when she saw the angel, she made haste
16 the angel answered him: If thou press
1 K 29 9 good in my sight as an angel of God
2 K 14 17 as an a. of God so is my lord the king
20 according to the wisdom of an angel
19 27 my lord the king art as an a. of God
24 16 said to the angel that slew the people
17 when he saw angel striking the people
3 K 13 18 an angel spoke to me in the word of
1 Pa 21 15 he sent an angel to Jerusalem to strike
15 and said to the angel that destroyed
20 when Ornan looked up and saw the angel
27 and the Lord commanded the angel: and
2 Pa 32 21 the Lord sent an angel, who cut off
Tob 5 6 not knowing that he was an a. of God
15 the angel said to him: I will conduct
17 Raphael the angel answered: Dost thou
20 the angel said to him: I will lead thy
21 and his angel accompany you. Then all
27 good angel of God doth accompany him
6 4 the angel said to him: Take him by the
5 the angel said to him: Take out the
7 Tobias asked the angel and said to him
8 the angel answering, said to him: If
11 the angel answering, said: Here is one
16 the angel Raphael said to him: Hear me
7 6 the angel said to Raguel: Tobias
12 the angel said to him: Be not afraid
8 3 then the angel Raphael took the devil
9 1 Tobias called the angel to him, whom
11 2 the angel said: Brother Tobias, thou
12 15 I am the angel Raphael, one of the
17 the angel said to them: Peace be to you
Jdth 13 20 his angel hath been my keeper both
Job 33 23 if there shall be an angel speaking
Prov 17 11 cruel angel shall be sent against him
Ecce 5 5 say not before the angel: There is no
Isa 33 3 at voice of the angel the people fled
63 9 the angel of his presence saved them
Bar 6 6 my angel is with you: and I myself
Dan 3 95 hath sent his angel and delivered his
6 22 my God hath sent his angel and hath
15 55 a. of God having received the sentence
Osee 12 3 by his strength he had success with a.
4 he prevailed over the angel and was
Zach 1 9 the angel that spoke in me. 13, 14; 2:3; 4:1, 4, 5; 5:10; 6:4
19 I said to the angel that spoke to me
2 3 and another angel went out to meet him
3 3 he stood before the face of the angel
5 5 the angel went forth that spoke in me
6 5 the angel . . . said to me: These are the
Mala 3 1 I send my angel, and he shall prepare
1 a. of the testament, whom you desire
1 Ma 7 41 an angel went out and slew of them
2 Ma 11 6 would send a good angel to save Israel
15 22 didst send thy a. in time of Ezechias
23 thy good angel before us, for the fear
Mat 11 10 I send my angel. Mark 1:2; Luke 7:27
28 5 angel answering said to the women
Luke 1 13 angel said to him: Fear not, Zachary
18 Zachary said to the angel: Whereby
19 angel said to him: I am Gabriel who
26 angel Gabriel was sent from God into
28 angel being come in, said unto her
30 the angel said to her; Fear not, Mary
34 Mary said to the angel: How shall
35 angel answering said to her: The Holy
38 the angel departed from her. And Mary
2 10 angel said to them: Fear not, for
13 there was with the angel a multitude of
21 Jesus, which was called by the angel
22 43 angel from heaven, strengthening him
John 12 29 others said: An angel spoke to him
Acts 6 15 as if it had been the face of an angel
7 30 an angel in a flame of fire in a bush
35 by hand of the angel who appeared to
38 the angel who spoke to him [Moses]
10 3 angel of God coming in unto him and
7 when angel who spoke to him was departed
22 received an answer of an holy angel
11 13 he told us how he had seen an angel
12 8 the angel said to him: Gird thyself
9 was true which was done by the angel
10 the angel departed from him. And Peter
11 the Lord hath sent his angel and hath
15 then said they: It is his angel. But
23 8 no resurrection, neither a. nor spirit
9 if spirit hath spoken to him or an a.
27 23 an angel of God, whose I am, and
2 C 11 14 transformeth himself into a. of light
12 7 flesh, an angel of Satan to buffet me
Gal 1 8 angel from heaven preach a gospel to
4 14 received me as an angel of God, even
Apoc 1 1 sending by his angel to his servant
2 1 to the angel of the church of. 8, 12, 18; 3:1, 7, 14
5 2 I saw a strong angel, proclaiming with
7 2 I saw another angel. 10:1; 14:6; 18:1
8 3 another angel came and stood before the
4 before God from the hand of the angel
5 the angel took the censer and filled it
7 angel sounded the trumpet. 8, 10, 12; 9:1, 13; 11:15
9 11 king, the angel of the bottomless pit
14 the sixth angel, who had the trumpet
10 5 angel whom I saw standing upon the sea
7 in days of the voice of the seventh a.
8 the book . . . from the hand of the a. 10
9 I went to the angel, saying unto him

14 8 another angel followed, saying: That
9 the third angel followed them, saying
15 another angel came out from the. 17, 18
19 angel thrust in his sharp sickle into
16 2 angel poured out. 3, 4, 8, 10, 12, 17
5 I heard the angel of the waters saying
17 7 angel said to me: Why dost thou wonder
18 21 a mighty angel took up a stone, as it
19 17 and I saw an angel coming down from heaven
21 17 measure of a man, which is of an angel
22 6 sent his angel to show his servants
8 to adore before the feet of the angel
16 I Jesus have sent my angel to testify
angel of the Lord Gen 16 7 a. . . . having found her
Gen 16 9 a. . . . said to her Agar: Return to thy
22 11 an a. . . . from heaven called to him
15 a. . . . called to Abraham a second time
Num 22 22 a. . . . stood in the way against Balaam
Judg 2 1 a. . . . went up from Galgal to the place
4 when the a. . . . spoke these words to all
5 23 curse ye land of Meroz, said a. . . .
6 11 an a. . . . came and sat under an oak
12 the a. . . . appeared to him and said: The
20 the a. . . . said to him: Take the flesh
21 the a. . . . put forth the tip of the rod
21 the a. . . . vanished out of his sight
22 Gedeon seeing that it was the a. . . .
22 I have seen the a. . . . face to face
13 3 an a. . . . appeared again to his wife
13 the a. . . . said to Manue: From all the
15 Manue said to the a. . . . I beseech thee
16 and Manue knew not it was the a. . . .
20 the a. . . . ascended also in the flame
21 and the a. . . . appeared to them no more
21 Manue understood that it was an a. . . .
2 K 24 16 the a. . . . had stretched out his hand
16 the a. . . . was by the thrashingfloor of
3 K 19 5 an a. . . . touched him and said to him
7 the a. . . . came again the second time
4 K 1 3 angel of the Lord spoke to Elias. 15
19 35 an a. . . . came and slew in the camp of
1 Pa 21 12 the a. . . . destroying in all the coasts
15 the a. . . . stood by the thrashingfloor
16 the a. . . . standing between heaven and
18 the a. . . . commanded Gad to tell David
30 great fear, seeing the sword of a. . . .
Tob 3 25 the holy angel of the Lord be with you
10 11 holy angel of the Lord be with you
Ps 33 8 angel of the Lord shall encamp round
34 5 let angel of the Lord straiten them
6 let the angel of the Lord pursue them
Eccu 48 24 the angel of the Lord destroyed them
Isa 37 36 a. . . . went out and slew in the camp
Dan 3 49 a. . . . went down with Azarias and his
13 59 the a. . . . waiteth with a sword to cut
14 33 a. . . . said to Habacuc: Carry the dinner
35 a. . . . took him by the top of his head
38 the a. . . . presently set Habacuc again
Zach 1 11 they answered the angel of the Lord
12 a. . . . answered and said: O Lord of
3 1 high priest standing before the a. . . .
5 him with garments, and the a. . . . stood
6 the a. . . . protested to Jesus, saying
12 8 an angel of the Lord in their sight
Mala 2 7 he is the angel of the Lord of hosts
Mat 1 20 a. . . . appeared to him in his sleep
24 as the a. . . . had commanded him [Joseph]
2 13 a. . . . appeared in sleep to Joseph. 19
28 2 an a. . . . descended from heaven and
Luke 1 11 a. . . . standing on the right side of
2 9 a. . . . stood by them, and the brightness
John 5 4 a. . . . descended at certain times into
Acts 5 19 an a. . . . by night opening the doors of
8 26 a. . . . spoke to Philip, saying: Arise
12 7 an a. . . . stood by him [Peter]: and a
23 an a. . . . struck him [Herod], because
angel's Tob 8 2 Tobias remembering the a. word
angels Gen 19 1 the two angels came to Sodom
Gen 19 15 the angels pressed him, saying: Arise
28 12 the angels also of God ascending and
32 1 angels of God met him. And when he
Job 4 18 and in his angels he found wickedness
41 16 raise him up, the angels shall fear
Ps 8 6 made him a little less than the angels
77 25 man ate the bread of angels: he sent
49 trouble, which he sent by evil angels
90 11 hath given his angels charge over thee
96 7 adore him, all you his angels: Sion
102 20 bless the Lord, all ye his angels: you
103 4 who makest thy angels spirits: and thy
137 1 praise to thee in the sight of the a.
148 2 praise ye him, all his angels: praise
Wisd 16 20 thy people with the food of angels
Isa 18 2 go, ye swift angels, to a nation rent
33 7 angels of peace shall weep bitterly
Dan 3 58 ye angels of the Lord, bless the Lord
Mat 4 6 hath given his angels charge. Luke 4:10
11 angels . . . ministered to him. Mark 1:13
13 39 the reapers are the angels. Even as
41 the Son of man shall send his angels
49 the a. shall go out and shall separate
16 27 Son of man shall come . . . with his a.
18 10 their a. in heaven always see the face
22 30 as angels of God in heaven. Mark 12:25
24 31 he shall send his angels. Mark 12:25
36 no one knoweth, not the a. Mark 31:32
25 31 majesty, and all the angels with him
41 prepared for the devil and his angels
26 53 more than twelve legions of angels
Mark 8 38 when he shall come . . . with the holy a.
12 25 married, but are as the a. in heaven
Luke 2 15 after the angels departed from them
9 26 in his majesty . . . and of the holy a.
12 8 Son of man confess before the a. of God
9 shall be denied before the a. of God
15 10 shall be joy before the angels of God
16 22 beggar died and was carried by the a.
20 36 for they are equal to the angels and
24 23 they had also seen a vision of angels
John 1 51 a. of God ascending and descending
20 12 she saw two angels in white, sitting
Acts 7 53 the law by the disposition of angels
Rom 8 38 nor a. nor principalities nor powers
1 C 4 9 a spectacle to the world and to angels
6 3 know you not that we shall judge a.
11 10 power over her head, because of the a.
13 1 if I speak with tongues of men and of a.
Gal 3 19 ordained by a. in hand of a mediator
Col 2 18 willing in humility and religion of a.
2 Th 1 7 from heaven with the a. of his power
1 Tim 3 16 appeared unto a., hath been preached
5 21 and Christ Jesus and the elect angels
Heb 1 4 made so much better than the angels
5 to which of the angels hath he said. 13
6 let all the angels of God adore him
7 he that maketh his angels spirits and
7 to the angels indeed he saith: He that
2 2 if the word spoken by angels became
5 not subjected unto angels the world
7 made him a little lower than the a. 9
16 nowhere doth he take hold of the a.
12 22 company of many thousands of angels
13 2 not aware of it, have entertained a.
1 P 1 12 on whom the angels desire to look
3 22 the a. and powers and virtues being
2 P 2 4 if God spared not the a. that sinned

11 11 angels who are greater in strength and
Jude 6 angels who kept not their principality
Apoc 1 20 the seven stars are the angels of the
3 5 before my Father and before his angels
5 11 I heard the voice of many angels round
7 1 I saw four angels standing on the four
2 he cried with loud voice to the four a.
11 all the a. stood round about the throne
8 2 I saw seven angels standing in the
6 the seven angels who had the seven
13 rest of the voices of the three angels
9 14 loose the four angels who are bound
15 the four angels were loosed, who were
12 7 Michael and his angels fought with the
7 and the dragon fought and his angels
9 his angels were thrown down with him
14 10 in the sight of the holy angels and
15 1 seven angels having the seven last
6 the seven angels came out of the temple
7 gave to the seven angels seven golden
8 till the seven plagues of the seven a.
16 1 saying to the seven a.: Go and pour
17 1 came one of the seven angels. 21:9
21 12 in the gates twelve angels, and names
anger Exod 15 8 with the blast of thy anger the
Exod 32 12 let thy anger cease, and be appeased
Num 32 10 and he swore in his anger, saying
Deut 9 19 I feared his indignation and anger
29 28 cast them out of their land in anger
32 16 and stirred him up to anger with their
Judg 2 12 and they provoked the Lord to anger
1 K 11 6 his anger was exceedingly kindled
20 34 Jonathan rose from table in great anger
2 K 12 5 David's anger being exceedingly kindled
24 1 anger of the Lord was again kindled
3 K 14 9 to provoke me to anger. 21:22; Jer 7:18
16 7 to provoke him to anger by the works
26 provoke Lord the God of Israel to anger
4 K 23 26 wherewith his anger was kindled against
2 Pa 28 13 anger of the Lord hangeth over Israel
33 6 to provoke him to anger. He set also
Jdth 8 15 nor be inflamed to anger like the
Esth 5 10 dissembling his anger, and returning
Job 5 2 anger indeed killeth the foolish, and
36 18 let not anger overcome thee to oppress
Ps 2 5 then shall he speak to them in his a.
7 7 rise up, O Lord, in thy anger: and be
20 10 oven of fire in the time of thy anger
34 20 speaking in the anger of the earth
36 8 cease from anger, and leave rage; have
55 8 in thy anger thou shalt break the people
68 25 let thy wrathful anger take hold of
76 10 will he in his a. shut up his mercies
77 38 many a time did he turn away his anger
50 he made a way for a path to his anger
58 they provoked him to anger on their
84 4 thou hast mitigated all thy anger: thou
5 savior: and turn off thy anger from us
88 47 end? Shall thy anger burn like fire
89 11 who knoweth the power of thy anger
101 11 because of thy anger and indignation
Prov 12 16 a fool immediately showeth his anger
14 35 good for nothing shall feel his anger
17 25 foolish son is the anger of the father
19 12 so also is the anger of a king: and
21 14 a secret present quencheth anger: and
24 who in anger worketh pride. Desires
22 8 with rod of his a. he shall be consumed
26 10 putteth fool to silence, appeaseth a.
17 so is he that passeth by in anger
27 3 the anger of a fool is heavier than
4 anger hath no mercy, nor fury when
Ecce 7 4 anger is better than laughter: because
10 anger resteth in the bosom of a fool
11 10 remove anger from thy heart and put
Wisd 10 3 unjust went away from her in his anger
Eccu 4 5 thy eyes from the poor for fear of a.
19 28 rebuke in the anger of an injurious man
25 23 no anger above the anger of a woman
29 a woman's anger and impudence and
26 25 and the third bringeth anger upon me
27 33 anger and fury are both of them
28 3 man to man reserveth anger, and doth
5 he that is but flesh, nourisheth anger
12 man's strength is, so shall his a. be
12 to his riches he shall increase his a.
30 26 envy and anger shorten a man's days
40 4 continual anger and strife, and in
46 5 was not the sun stopped in his anger
Isa 5 25 his anger is not turned away. 10:4
10 5 he is the rod and the staff of my anger
65 3 that continually provoke me to anger
5 these shall be smoke in my anger, a
Jer 2 35 let thy anger be turned away from me
4 8 anger of the Lord is not turned away
7 19 do they provoke me to anger, saith the
25 7 that you might provoke me to anger
37 because of the fierce a. of Lord. 38
32 37 I have cast them out in my anger and
42 18 as my a. and my indignation hath been
Lam 1 12 spoke in the day of his fierce anger
2 1 his footstool in the day of his anger
3 he hath broken in his fierce anger
3 66 thou shalt persecute them in anger
4 11 he hath poured out his fierce anger
Eze 2 7 they provoke me to anger. But thou
5 15 shall have executed judgments . . . in a.
7 8 I will accomplish my anger in thee
8 17 have turned to provoke me to anger
13 13 be an overwhelming shower in my anger
32 9 I shall provoke to anger the heart of
38 19 have spoken . . . in the fire of my anger
Jon 3 9 will turn away from his fierce anger
Nah 1 6 shall resist in the fierceness of his a.
Haba 3 12 in thy anger thou wilt tread the earth
Soph 2 2 before the fierce anger of the Lord
3 8 to pour upon them . . . all my fierce anger
Zach 1 15 I am angry with a great anger
1 Ma 7 35 swore in anger, saying: Unless Judas
2 Ma 4 38 [Antiochus] being inflamed to anger
40 their minds being filled with anger
7 39 the king being incensed with anger
9 4 swelling with a. he thought to revenge
Mark 3 5 looking . . . on them with anger, being
Luke 4 28 the synagogue . . . were filled with a.
Acts 19 28 they were full of anger and cried out
Rom 10 19 by a foolish nation I will anger you
1 C 13 5 charity . . . is not provoked to anger
Eph 4 26 not the sun go down upon your anger
31 anger and indignation . . . be put away
5 6 cometh anger of God upon the children
6 4 provoke not your children to anger
Col 3 8 anger, indignation, malice, blasphemy
1 Tim 2 8 without anger and contention. In like
Titus 1 7 bishop . . . must be . . . not subject to a
James 1 19 let every man be . . . slow to anger
20 a. of man worketh not the justice of
angered Deut 32 21 a. me with their vanities
Prov 18 14 that is easily angered, who can bear
angereth Eccu 3 18 that angereth his mother
angry Gen 4 6 said to him: Why art thou angry
Gen 18 30 be not angry . . . if I speak. 32
30 2 Jacob being angry with her, answered
31 35 let not my lord be a. that I cannot
36 Jacob being angry, said in a chiding
39 19 was very angry. And cast Joseph into

40 2 Pharao being angry with them . . . sent
41 10 the king being angry with his servants
44 18 be not angry with thy servant: for
45 24 be not angry in the way. And they
Exod 4 14 the Lord being angry at Moses, said
15 14 nations rose up and were angry
16 20 Moses was angry with them. Now every
32 19 being very angry, he threw the tablets
Lev 10 16 being angry with Eleazar and Ithamar
Num 11 1 when the Lord heard it he was angry
12 9 being angry with them he went away
16 15 Moses therefore being very angry, said
22 22 God was angry. And an angel of the
27 who being angry beat her sides more
24 10 and Balac being angry against Balaam
25 3 Lord being angry, said to Moses: Take
31 14 Moses being a. with the chief officers
32 13 Lord being a. against Israel. Judg 2:14
Deut 1 34 he was angry and swore and said: Not
37 Lord was angry with me. 3:26; 4:21
9 8 he was angry and would have destroyed
11 17 the Lord being angry shut up heaven
Josu 7 1 Lord was angry against the children of
Judg 3 8 Lord being angry with Israel, delivered
9 30 was very angry, and sent messengers
10 7 Lord being angry with them, delivered
1 K 17 28 he was angry with David, and said
20 7 if he be angry, know that his malice
30 Saul being angry against Jonathan, said
29 4 princes of the Philistines were angry
2 K 11 20 if thou see him [David] to be angry
19 42 why art thou angry for this matter
22 8 shaken, because he was angry with them
3 K 8 46 and thou being angry deliver them up
11 9 and the Lord was angry with Solomon
21 4 Achab came into his house angry and
4 K 5 11 Naaman was angry and went away, saying
13 19 the man of God was angry with him and
17 18 the Lord was very angry with Israel
24 20 the Lord was angry against Jerusalem
1 Pa 13 10 and the Lord was angry with Oza and
2 Pa 6 36 and thou be angry with them and deliver
16 10 and Asa was angry with the seer and
25 15 the Lord being angry against Amasias
26 19 Ozias was angry, and holding in his
28 9 being angry with Juda, hath delivered
1 Es 9 14 art thou angry with us unto utter
2 Es 4 1 were building the wall, he was angry
Tob 1 21 being angry slew many of the children
2 22 at these words his wife being angry
3 13 when thou hast been angry, wilt show
5 19 be not angry that I desired to know thy
Jdth 1 12 then king Nabuchodonosor being angry
5 26 all the great men of Holofernes were a.
6 13 how Holofernes himself being angry had
11 17 and because God is angry with them
Job 32 2 was angry and was moved to indignation
2 he was angry against Job because he
3 he was angry with his friends because
Ps 2 12 lest at any time the Lord be angry
4 5 be ye angry, and sin not: the things
7 12 and patient: is he angry every day
17 8 moved, because he was angry with them
59 3 thou hast been a., and hast had mercy
77 21 Lord heard and was angry: and a fire
78 5 how long, O Lord, wilt thou be angry
79 5 how long wilt thou be angry against
84 6 wilt thou be angry with us forever
88 39 thou hast been angry with thy anointed
98 1 hath reigned, let the people be angry
102 9 will not always be angry: nor will he
111 10 the wicked shall see and shall be angry
Prov 22 14 whom the Lord is a. with shall fall
24 be not a friend to an angry man, and
26 21 so an angry man stirreth up strife
29 9 whether he be angry or laugh, he shall
Ecce 5 5 lest God be angry at thy words and
Eccu 20 1 is it to reprove than to be angry
28 8 and be not angry with thy neighbor
Isa 8 21 shall be hungry, they will be angry
12 1 for thou wast angry with me: thy wrath
28 21 he shall be angry as in the valley
47 6 I was angry with my people, I have
54 9 sworn not to be angry with thee and
57 6 shall I not be angry at these things
16 neither will I be angry unto the end
17 of his covetousness I was angry and I
17 I hid my face from thee and was angry
64 5 thou art angry, and we have sinned
9 be not very angry, O Lord, and remember
66 14 he shall be angry with his enemies
Jer 3 5 wilt thou be angry forever or wilt
12 I will not be angry forever. But yet
37 14 the princes were angry with Jeremias
Eze 16 42 and I will cease and be angry no more
Dan 14 7 the king being angry called for his
18 19 the king was angry. And he took the
Jon 4 1 exceedingly troubled and was angry
4 think thou hast reason to be angry. 9
9 I am angry with reason even unto death
Nah 1 2 and he is angry with his enemies. The
Haba 3 2 when thou art angry thou wilt remember
8 wast thou angry, O Lord, with the rivers
Zach 1 12 Juda, with which thou hast been angry
15 I am angry with a great anger with
15 I was angry a little, but they helped
Mala 1 4 with whom the Lord is angry forever
1 Ma 3 27 he was angry in his mind: and he sent
6 28 when the king heard this, he was angry
9 69 he was angry with the wicked men that
11 22 when he heard it, he was angry: and
2 Ma 5 17 did not consider that God was angry
7 3 the king being a. commanded fryingpans
33 our God is angry with us a little while
13 25 being angry for fear they should break
Mat 5 22 whosoever is angry with his brother
18 34 his lord being angry, delivered him
22 7 he was angry, and sending his armies
Luke 13 14 being angry that Jesus had healed on
14 21 the master of the house being angry
15 28 and he was angry and would not go in
John 7 23 are you angry at me because I have
Acts 12 20 [Herod] was angry with the Tyrians
Eph 4 26 be angry, and sin not. Let not the sun
Apoc 11 18 nations were angry against the woman
12 17 the dragon was angry against the woman

exceeding angry Gen 34 7 they were e. a. because he had done a
Exod 11 9 and he went out from Pharao e. angry
Deut 9 20 he was exceeding angry against Aaron
Judg 14 19 e. a. he went up to his father's house
1 K 18 8 Saul was exceeding angry, and this word
Zach 1 2 Lord hath been e. a. with your fathers
1 Ma 5 1 built up as before, that there were e. a.
15 36 he had seen, and the king was e. a.
Mat 2 16 deluded by the wise men, was e. a.

exceedingly angry Gen 4 5 Cain was e. a., and his countenance fell
1 K 19 21 Saul being e. a., went also himself to
2 K 3 8 and he [Abner] was e. a. for the words
2 Es 4 7 to be closed, that they were e. a.
5 6 I was e. a. when I heard their cry
Job 32 5 were not able to answer, he was e. a.
Ps 105 40 and the Lord was e. a. with his people
Lam 5 22 rejected us, thou art e. a. against us

anguish Gen 42 21 seeing the anguish of his soul

Exod 6 9 not hearken to him, for a. of spirit
2 K 1 9 for anguish is come upon me [Saul]
4 K 4 27 let her alone for her soul is in a.
Esth 4 1 showing the anguish of his mind. And
15 8 bright eyes, hid a mind full of anguish
Job 6 7 now, through anguish, are my meats
Ps 31 4 I am turned in my anguish whilst the
60 3 when my heart was in anguish, thou
118 143 trouble and anguish have found me: thy
142 4 my spirit is in anguish within me: my
Wisd 5 3 groaning for anguish of spirit: these
Isa 21 3 anguish hath taken hold of me, as the anguish of a woman in labor
Jer 6 24 anguish hath taken hold of us, as a
49 24 anguish and sorrows have taken her
50 43 anguish hath taken hold of him, pangs
Bar 3 1 the soul in anguish, and troubled
John 16 21 remembereth no more the a., for joy
Rom 2 9 anguish upon every soul of man that
2 C 2 4 out of much affliction and a. of heart
anguishes Jer 4 31 a. as of a woman in labor of
Ani 1 Pa 15 18 Ani and Eliab and Banaias and
1 Pa 15 20 Ani and Eliab and Maasias and Banaias
Ania 2 Es 8 4 Ania and Uria and Helcia and
Aniam 1 Pa 7 19 and Sechem and Leci and Aniam
Anim Josu 15 50 Anab and Istemo and Anim, Gosen
animals Lev 11 2 the animals which you are to eat
Lev 11 27 all animals which go on all four, shall
Ps 67 11 in it shall thy animals dwell; in thy
Wisd 19 20 wasted not the flesh of corruptible a.
animosities 2 C 12 20 envyings, a., dissensions
anise Mat 23 23 because you tithe mint and anise
ankles 2 K 22 37 me: and my ankles shall not fail
Eze 47 3 me through the water up to the ankles
Anna 1 K 1 2 two wives, the name of one was Anna
1 K 1 2 but Anna had no children. And this man
5 to Anna he gave one portion with sorrow because he loved Anna
7 but Anna wept and did not eat. Then
8 Anna, why weepest thou? And why dost
9 so Anna arose after she had eaten and
10 as Anna had her heart full of grief
13 Anna spoke in her heart, and only her
15 Anna answering said: Not so, my lord
19 and Elcana knew Anna his wife: and the
20 Anna conceived and bore a son and
22 but Anna went not up; for she said to
26 Anna said: I beseech thee, my lord, as
28 and Anna prayed and said: My heart hath
2 21 Lord visited Anna, and she conceived
Tob 1 9 he took to wife Anna of his own tribe
2 19 Anna his wife went daily to weaving
7 2 said to Anna his wife: How like is
8 A. his wife and Sara their daughter
18 Raguel called to him Anna his wife and
8 16 Raguel and Anna his wife blessed the
10 3 sad, both he and Anna his wife with him
11 5 but Anna sat beside the way daily, on
Luke 2 36 and there was one Anna, a prophetess
Annas Luke 3 2 under high priests A. and Caiphas
John 18 13 and they led him away to Annas first
24 Annas sent him bound to Caiphas the
Acts 4 6 Annas the high priest and Caiphas the
annoyed 1 Ma 15 14 they annoyed the city by land
Anob 1 Pa 4 8 Cos begot Anob and Soboba and the
anoint Gen 31 13 where thou didst anoint the stone
Exod 29 36 and shalt anoint it to sanctify it
30 26 thou shalt anoint the tabernacle. 40:9
30 thou shalt anoint Aaron and his sons
Judg 9 8 the trees went to anoint a king over
Ruth 3 3 a. thee and put on thy best garments
1 K 9 16 thou shalt anoint him to be ruler over
15 1 sent me to anoint thee king over his
16 3 shalt a. him whom I shall show to thee
12 arise and anoint him, for this is he
3 K 1 34 prophet a. him there king over Israel
19 15 shalt a. Hazael to be king over Syria
16 thou shalt anoint Jehu the son of Namsi
16 thou shalt a. to be prophet in thy room
4 K 4 2 my house but a little oil to anoint me
Tob 11 8 immediately a. his eyes with this gall
Amos 6 6 a. themselves with the best ointments
Mat 6 17 when thou fastest, anoint thy head and
Mark 14 8 to anoint my body for the burial. Amen
16 1 that coming, they might anoint Jesus
Luke 7 46 my head with oil thou didst not anoint
Apoc 3 18 anoint thy eyes with eyesalve that thou
anointed Exod 29 2 wafers also unleavened anointed
Exod 29 29 that they may be anointed, and their
30 32 the flesh of man shall not be anointed
Lev 2 4 unleavened wafers, a. with oil. 7:12
4 3 if the priest that is anointed shall sin
16 the priest that is anointed shall carry
8 10 with which he anointed the tabernacle
11 altar seven times, he anointed it
12 anointed and consecrated him [Aaron]
16 32 priest that is a., and whose hands are
Num 3 3 the priests that were anointed and
6 15 wafers without leaven anointed with oil
7 1 had anointed and sanctified it with all
10 on the day when it was anointed, their
88 dedication of the altar, when it was a.
35 25 that is anointed with the holy oil. If
Deut 28 40 and shalt not be anointed with the oil
1 K 2 35 he shall walk all days before my a.
10 1 Lord hath anointed thee to be prince
12 3 before Lord and before his anointed
5 his anointed is witness this day that
15 17 and the Lord anointed thee to be king
16 6 is the Lord's anointed before him? And
13 took the horn of oil and anointed him
24 7 such thing to my master the Lord's a.
7 because he is the Lord's anointed. 11
26 9 his hand against the Lord's anointed
11 not my hand upon the Lord's anointed
16 not kept your master, the Lord's a.
23 my hand against the Lord's anointed
2 K 1 14 out thy hand to kill the Lord's a.
16 I have slain the Lord's anointed. And
21 as though he had not been a. with oil
2 4 men of Juda came and a. David there
7 house of Juda hath a. me to be their
3 39 I as yet am tender, though a. king
5 3 they a. David to be king over Israel
17 that they had a. David to be king
12 7 I anointed thee king over Israel, and
20 washed and anointed himself: and when
14 2 mourning apparel, and be not a. with
19 10 Absalom, whom we a. over us, is dead
21 because he cursed the Lord's anointed
22 51 showing mercy to David his anointed
3 K 1 39 the priest took . . . and a. Solomon
45 have a. him [Solomon] king in Gihon
5 1 heard that they had anointed him king
4 K 9 3 I have a. thee king over Israel. 6, 12
11 12 they made him king and anointed him
23 30 they a. him and made him king in his
1 Pa 11 3 and they anointed him king over Israel
14 8 that David was anointed king over all
16 22 touch not my anointed: and do no evil
29 22 they anointed the second time Solomon
22 they a. him to the Lord to be prince
2 Pa 6 42 God, turn not away the face of thy a.
22 7 whom the Lord had anointed to destroy
23 11 high priest and his sons anointed him
28 15 anointed them because of their labor

Tob 11 13 the gall of the fish, a. his father's
Jdth 10 3 anointed herself with the best ointment
16 10 she anointed her face with ointment
Ps 17 51 showing mercy to David his anointed
19 7 that the Lord hath saved his anointed
22 5 thou hast anointed my head with oil
26 1 the psalm of David before he was a.
27 8 protector of the salvation of his a.
44 8 hath a. thee with the oil of gladness
88 21 with my holy oil I have anointed him
39 thou hast been angry with thy anointed
52 have reproached the change of thy a.
104 15 touch ye not my anointed: and do no
131 10 turn not away the face of thy anointed
17 I have prepared a lamp for my anointed
Eccu 45 18 Moses . . . anointed him with holy oil
46 16 and anointed princes over his people
22 he protested before the Lord and his a.
Isa 45 1 thus saith the Lord to my a. Cyrus
61 1 the Lord hath a. me: he hath sent
Eze 16 9 and I anointed thee with oil. And I
Dan 9 24 the saint of saints may be anointed
10 3 neither was I anointed with ointment
Mich 6 15 but shalt not be anointed with the oil
2 Ma 1 10 of the stock of the anointed priests
Mark 6 13 anointed with oil many that were sick
Luke 4 18 he hath a. me to preach the gospel
7 38 and anointed them with the ointment
46 but she with ointment hath a. my feet
John 9 11 made clay and anointed my eyes and
11 2 Mary was she that anointed the Lord
12 3 anointed the feet of Jesus and wiped
Acts 4 27 child Jesus, whom thou hast anointed
10 38 Jesus of Nazareth: how God a. him with
2 C 1 21 that hath anointed us, is God: who
Heb 1 9 God hath a. thee with oil of gladness
anointedst Eccu 48 8 who a. kings to penance, and
anointing Lev 6 20 in the day of the a.: they
Lev 7 35 this is the anointing of Aaron and his
Tob 6 9 gall is good for anointing the eyes
James 5 14 a. him with oil in name of the Lord
another's Gen 11 7 not understand one a. speech
Lev 20 17 have discovered one another's nakedness
Luke 16 12 faithful in that which is another's
1 C 10 24 his own, but that which is another's
answer (noun) Gen 23 10 Ephron made a. to Abraham
Gen 38 21 when they all made answer: There was
41 16 God shall give Pharao a prosperous a.
Num 24 12 Balaam made answer to Balac: Did I
Josu 1 16 and they made answer to Josue and said
Judg 5 29 returned this a. to her mother-in-law
19 28 but as she made no answer, perceiving
2 K 24 13 see what answer I shall return to him
1 Es 5 4 in answer to which we gave them the
Tob 7 11 and gave no answer to his petition
Job 19 16 called my servant, and he gave me no a.
21 34 your answer is shown to be repugnant
32 3 they had not found a reasonable answer
Prov 15 1 a mild answer breaketh wrath: but a
27 11 that thou mayst give an answer to him
Ecce 8 5 understandeth time and answer. There
Eccu 5 13 and return a true answer with wisdom
8 12 and to give an answer in time of need
32 11 let thy answer be short. In many things
Jer 43 2 made answer, saying to Jeremias: Thou
44 20 people which had given him that answer
Dan 2 27 Daniel made answer before the king
5 17 Daniel made answer and said before the
Mich 3 7 because there is no answer of God. But
1 Ma 4 46 should come a prophet and give answer
12 18 you shall do well to give us an answer
13 35 king Demetrius in a. to this request
Mat 2 12 having received an answer in sleep
8 8 centurion making answer, said: Lord
11 4 Jesus making answer, said to them: Go
13 37 made answer . . . He that soweth the good
14 28 Peter making answer, said: Lord, if it
Luke 2 26 received an answer from the Holy Ghost
20 26 wondering at his answer they held their
John 1 22 that we may give an answer to them that
19 9 art thou? But Jesus gave him no answer
Acts 3 12 Peter seeing, made answer to the people
10 22 received an answer of an holy angel
25 8 Paul making answer for himself: Neither
16 have liberty to make his a., to clear
26 1 began to make his answer. I think
24 made his answer, Festus said with a
Rom 11 4 what saith the divine answer to him
2 C 1 9 we had in ourselves the answer of death
2 Tim 4 16 at my first answer no man stood with me
Heb 11 7 by faith Noe, having received an answer
answers 2 Ma 4 23 and to bring answers from him
Luke 2 47 astonished at his wisdom and his a.
ant Prov 6 6 go to the ant, O sluggard, and
Antichrist 1 J 2 18 you have heard that A. cometh
1 J 2 22 this is A. who denieth the Father and
4 3 this is A. of whom you have heard, that
2 J 7 this is a seducer and an antichrist
Antichrists 1 J 2 18 there are become many A.
Antioch 1 Ma 3 37 and went forth from Antioch
1 Ma 4 35 he went to Antioch and chose soldiers
6 63 returned to A., where he found Philip
10 68 was much troubled and returned to A.
11 13 Ptolemee entered into Antioch and set
44 sent him 3,000 valiant men to Antioch
56 and made himself master of Antioch
2 Ma 4 33 himself in a safe place at Antioch
36 the Jews that were at Antioch, and also
5 21 he went back in all haste to Antioch
6 1 the king sent a certain man of Antioch
8 35 he came alone to Antioch, being rendered
11 36 for we are going to Antioch. And
13 23 left over the affairs, had rebelled at A.
26 appeased the people and returned to A.
14 27 Machabeus prisoner in all haste to A.
Acts 6 5 and Nicolas, a proselyte of Antioch
11 19 far as Phenice and Cyprus and Antioch
20 when they were entered into Antioch
Antiochians 2 Ma 4 9 that were at Jerusalem, A.
Antiochis 2 Ma 4 30 to A., the king's concubine
Antiochus 1 Ma 1 11 wicked root, A. the Illustrious
1 Ma 1 17 the kingdom was established before A.
21 and after Antiochus had ravaged Egypt
2 17 and they that were sent from Antiochus
3 33 to bring up his son Antiochus. 6:55
6 15 that he should go to Antiochus his son
17 he set up Antiochus his son to reign
7 2 the army seized upon A. and Lysias, to
8 6 how Antiochus the great king of Asia
10 1 Antiochus, surnamed the Illustrious
11 39 Emalchuel the Arabian who brought up A.
54 and with him Antiochus the young boy
57 and young Antiochus wrote to Jonathan
12 16 Numenius the son of Antiochus. 14:22
15 10 A. entered into the land of his fathers
13 A. camped above Dora with 120,000 men
2 Ma 1 14 A. with his friends came to the place
16 shut the temple, when A. was come in
2 21 wars against Antiochus the Illustrious
4 7 A. who was called the Illustrious. 10:9
21 Antiochus understood that he was wholly
37 A. therefore was grieved in his mind
5 1 A. prepared for a second journey into
5 false rumor, as though A. had been dead
17 Antiochus going astray in mind, did not
21 when A. had taken away out of the temple

24 Antiochus, thinking himself despised
9 1 A. returned with dishonor out of Persia
2 A. being put to flight returned
19 A. king and ruler wisheth much health
25 have appointed my son Antiochus king
29 out of fear of the son of Antiochus
10 9 this was the end of Antiochus that was
10 Eupator, the son of that wicked A.
13 coming over to A. the Illustrious, had
13 1 that Antiochus Eupator was coming with
3 besought A., not for the welfare of
4 stirred up the mind of A. against the
14 2 master of the countries against A. and
king Antiochus 1 Ma 1 11 Antiochus the Illustrious,
the son of king Antiochus
1 Ma 1 43 king A. wrote to all his kingdoms, that
44 according to the word of king A. 52
57 king A. set up the abominable idol of
63 according to the commandment of king A.
2 15 that were sent from king Antiochus came
19 although all nations obey king A., so
22 not hearken to the words of king A.
25 the man whom king Antiochus had sent
33 do according to the edict of king A.
3 27 when king A. heard these words, he was
6 1 king A. was going through the higher
16 king Antiochus died there in the year
55 king A. while he lived had appointed
12 39 to stretch out his hand against king A.
13 31 journey with the young king Antiochus
15 1 k. A. the son of Demetrius sent letters
2 king Antiochus to Simon the high priest
11 king Antiochus pursued after him and he
25 king Antiochus moved his camp to Dora
2 Ma 11 22 king Antiochus to Lysias his brother
27 king A. to the senate of the Jews and
Antipas Apoc 2 13 when A. was my faithful witness
Antipater 1 Ma 12 16 A. the son of Jason. 14:22
Antipatris Acts 23 31 brought him by night to A.
antiquity Isa 23 7 gloried from of old in her a.
ants Prov 30 25 the ants, a feeble people, which
anvil Job 41 15 stone, and as firm as a smith's a.
Eccu 38 29 so doth the smith sitting by the anvil
anxiety 1 Ma 6 10 my heart is cast down for a.
anxious Ps 101 1 poor man, when he was anxious
Eccu 5 10 be not a. for goods unjustly gotten
Aod Judg 3 15 raised them up a savior called Aod
Judg 3 20 Aod went in to him: now he was sitting
21 Aod put forth his left hand and took
23 Aod carefully shutting the doors of
26 but Aod, while they were in confusion
4 1 did evil . . . after the death of Aod
1 Pa 7 10 Aod and Chanana and Zethan and
apace 2 K 18 25 as he was coming apace and drawing
Eccu 43 14 he maketh the snow to fall apace and
Jer 46 5 they fled apace, and they looked not
Apadno Dan 11 45 he shall fix his tabernacle A.
Apamea Jdth 3 14 all Syria Sobal and all Apamea
apart Gen 21 28 Abraham set apart seven ewe lambs
Gen 21 29 ewe lambs which thou hast set apart
32 13 he set apart of the things which he
43 32 for Joseph apart and for his brethren
apart, for the Egyptians also apart
Exod 13 12 shall set apart all that openeth the
36 16 five of which he joined apart, and
the other six apart
Lev 14 10 for a sacrifice, and a sextary of oil a.
Num 16 16 stand apart before the Lord tomorrow,
and Aaron apart
Judg 7 5 thou shalt set apart by themselves: but
1 K 9 23 commanded thee to set it apart by thee
4 K 15 5 and he dwelt in a free house apart
1 Pa 19 9 to their aid stood apart in the field
2 Pa 26 21 dwelt in a house apart, being full of
Eze 48 8 firstfruits which you shall set a. 9
20 shall be set apart for the firstfruits
Zach 1 21 have scattered Juda, every man apart
12 12 families and families apart. 14
12 families of the house of . . . apart. 13
12 and their women apart. 13, 14
13 the families of Semei apart, and their
1 Ma 11 34 be set apart to all them that sacrifice
Mat 14 13 into desert place a. Mark 6:32; Luke 9:10
17 1 into a high mountain apart. Mark 9:1
20 17 Jesus took the twelve disciples apart
Mark 4 34 apart he explained all things to his
6 31 come apart into a desert place and rest
7 33 taking him from the multitude apart, he
13 3 asked him apart: Tell us when shall
John 20 7 but apart, wrapped up into one place
Gal 2 2 a. to them who seemed to be something
apartments 3 K 10 5 and the a. of his servants
Apelles Rom 16 10 salute A., approved in Christ
apes 3 K 10 22 and apes and peacocks. 2 Pa 9:21
Aphara Josu 18 23 and Avim and Aphara and Ophera
Apharsachites 1 Es 6 6 your counsellors the A.
Apharsathacites 1 Es 4 9 the Dinites and the A.
Aphec Josu 12 18 the king of Aphec one, the king
Josu 19 30 Amma and Aphec and Rohob: 22 cities
Judg 1 31 of Helba and of Aphec and of Rohob
1 K 4 1 the Philistines came to Aphec and put
29 1 were gathered together to Aphec: and
3 K 20 26 and went up to Aphec, to fight against
30 they that remained fled to Aphec, into
4 K 13 17 thou shalt strike the Syrians in Aphec
Apheca Josu 13 4 Maara of the Sidonians as far as A.
Josu 15 53 Janum and Beththaphua and Apheca
Apherema 1 Ma 11 34 three cities, Apherema, Lydda
Aphia 1 K 9 1 Bechorath the son of Aphia the son
Aphonite 1 Pa 27 27 wine cellars, Zabdias an A.
Aphses 1 Pa 24 15 the eighteenth to Aphses, the
Aphuthites 1 Pa 2 53. A. and Semathites and
apiece Num 7 86 mortar . . . weighing ten sicles **a.**
John 2 6 containing two or three measures a.
Apollo Acts 18 24 A., born at Alexandria, an
Acts 19 1 while Apollo was at Corinth, that Paul
1 C 1 12 I am of Apollo, and I of Cephas, and
3 4 of Paul; and another, I am of Apollo
4 what then is Apollo, and what is Paul
6 I have planted, Apollo watered, but God
22 whether it be Paul or Apollo or Cephas
4 6 transferred to myself and to Apollo
16 12 touching our brother Apollo, I give you
Titus 3 13 send forward Zenas the lawyer and A.
Apollonia Acts 17 1 passed through Amphipolis and A.
Apollonius 1 Ma 3 10 A. gathered together the
1 Ma 3 12 and Judas took the sword of Apollonius
10 69 king Demetrius made A. his general
74 when Jonathan heard the words of A.
75 a garrison of Apollonius was in Joppe
77 A. heard of it and he took 3,000
79 Apollonius left privately in the camp
2 Ma 3 5 he went to A. the son of Tharseas who
7 now when A. had given the king notice
4 4 A., who was the governor of Celesyria
21 A. the son of Mnestheus was sent into
5 24 he sent that hateful prince Apollonius
12 2 Timotheus and A. the son of Genneus
Apollophanes 2 Ma 10 37 brother of Chereas and A.
Apollyon Apoc 9 11 is Abaddon, and in Greek A.
apostasy Jer 2 19 the apostasy shall rebuke thee
apostate Job 34 18 to the king: Thou art an a.
Prov 6 12 a man that is an a., an unprofitable
Isa 30 1 woe to you, apostate children, saith
apostle John 13 16 is a. greater than he that sent
Rom 1 1 Paul . . . called to be an a. 1 C 1:1

11 13 as long as I am the a. of the Gentiles
1 C 9 1 am not I an apostle? Have not I seen
2 if unto others I be not an apostle, but
15 9 who am not worthy to be called an a.
2 C 1 1 Paul, an a. of Jesus Christ. Eph 1:1;
Col 1:1; 1 Tim 1:1; 2 Tim 1:1; Titus 1:1
Gal 1 1 Paul, an a. not of men, neither by men
Phil 2 25 and fellow soldier, but your apostle
1 Tim 2 7 I am appointed . . . an a. 2 Tim 1:11
Heb 3 1 consider the apostle and high priest
1 P 1 1 Peter, an apostle of Jesus Christ, to
2 P 1 1 Simon Peter, servant and a. of Jesus
apostles Mat 6 30 a. coming together unto Jesus
Mat 10 2 the names of the twelve apostles are
Luke 6 13 whom also he named apostles; Simon
9 1 calling together the 12 a., he gave
10 a., when they were returned, told him
11 49 I will send to them prophets and a.
17 5 a. said to the Lord: Increase our faith
22 14 sat down and the 12 apostles with him
24 10 who told these things to the apostles
Acts 1 2 by the Holy Ghost to the apostles
26 and he was numbered with the eleven a.
2 37 said to Peter and to the rest of the a.
42 persevering in doctrine of the apostles
43 signs were done by the a. in Jerusalem
4 33 with great power did the apostles give
35 it down before feet of the a. 37; 5:2
36 Joseph who by the apostles was surnamed
5 12 by the hands of the a. were many signs
18 they laid hands on the apostles and put
29 Peter and the a. answering said: We
40 calling in the apostles, after they
6 6 these they set before the apostles
8 1 of Judea and Samaria except the a.
14 a., who were in Jerusalem, had heard
18 saw that by imposition of hands of the a.
9 27 took him and brought him to the a.
11 1 a. and brethren who were in Judea
14 4 held with the Jews, but some with the a.
13 when the a. Barnabas and Paul had heard
15 2 should go up to the apostles and priests
Rom 16 7 who are of note among the apostles, who
1 C 4 9 God hath set forth us apostles, the
9 5 as well as the rest of the apostles
12 28 first apostles, secondly prophets
29 are all apostles? Are all prophets? Are
15 7 was seen by James, then by all the a.
9 I am the least of the apostles, who am
2 C 8 23 our brethren, the a. of the churches
11 5 done nothing less than the great a.
13 for such false apostles are deceitful
13 transforming themselves into a. of
12 11 short of them that are above measure a.
Gal 1 17 neither went I to Jerusalem to the a.
19 but other of the apostles I saw none
Eph 2 20 built upon the foundation of the a.
3 5 it is now revealed to his holy apostles
4 11 he gave some a. and some prophets and
1 Th 2 7 might have been burdensome as apostles
2 P 3 2 that you may be mindful . . . of your a.
Jude 17 which have been spoken before by the a.
Apoc 2 2 who say they are apostles and are not
18 20 ye holy apostles and prophets; for God
21 14 names of the 12 apostles of the Lamb
apostles and ancients Acts 15 4 were received by
the church and by the a. . . .
Acts 15 6 the a. . . . assembled to consider of this
22 it pleased the a. . . . to choose men
23 a. . . . , brethren, to the brethren of the
41 to keep the precepts of the a. . . .
16 4 that were decreed by the a. . . . who
apostleship Acts 1 25 place of his ministry and a.

Rom 1 5 by whom we have received grace and a.
1 C 9 2 you are the seal of my a. in the Lord
2 C 12 12 the signs of my a. have been wrought
Gal 2 8 in Peter to the a. of the circumcision
apothecary Eccu 38 7 the a. shall make sweet
apparel Gen 38 19 putting off the a. which she had
Deut 22 5 shall not be clothed with man's apparel
5 neither shall a man use woman's apparel
Judg 17 10 double suit of apparel and thy victuals
1 K 27 9 the asses and the camels and the a.
2 K 12 20 when he had changed his apparel, he
14 2 and put on mourning apparel, and be not
3 K 10 5 order of his ministers and their a.
2 Pa 9 4 of his officers and their apparel
Esth 5 1 Esther put on her royal apparel and
6 8 to be clothed with the king's apparel
8 15 Mardochai . . . shone in royal apparel
14 2 had laid away her royal apparel, she
15 4 wore, and put on her glorious apparel
Eccu 11 4 glory not in apparel at any time, and
Isa 3 22 changes of apparel and short cloaks
4 1 own bread and wear our own apparel
63 2 why then is thy apparel red and thy
3 I have stained all my apparel. For the
Soph 1 8 such as are clothed with strange a.
2 Ma 3 26 in comely apparel, who stood by him
Luke 7 25 they that are in costly apparel and
24 4 two men stood by them in shining a.
Acts 10 30 a man stood before me in white apparel
12 21 Herod being arrayed in kingly apparel
20 33 coveted any man's silver, gold, or a.
1 Tim 2 9 women also in decent apparel: adorning
James 2 2 having a golden ring, in fine apparel
3 that is clothed with the fine apparel
1 P 3 3 of gold, or the putting on of apparel
apparition Mat 14 26 troubled saying: It is an a.
Mark 6 49 thought it was an a., and they cried
appeal Acts 25 11 I appeal to Caesar. Then Festus
Acts 28 19 was constrained to appeal to Caesar
appealed Acts 25 12 hast thou a. unto Caesar? To
Acts 25 25 he himself hath a. to Augustus, I have
26 32 been set at liberty if he had not a.
appealing Acts 25 21 Paul appealing to be reserved
appear Gen 1 9 let the dry land appear. And it
Gen 9 14 my bow shall appear in the clouds: and
37 20 then it shall appear what his dreams
30 the boy doth not appear and whither
Exod 10 5 that nothing thereof may appear, but
23 15 thou shalt not appear empty before me
17 all thy males appear before the Lord
30 36 in the place where I will a. to thee
34 20 neither shalt thou a. before me empty
23 all the males shall appear in the sight
24 and appear in the sight of the Lord
Lev 9 4 for today the Lord will appear to you
6 do it, and his glory will appear to you
13 10 the living flesh itself shall appear
14 when the live flesh shall a. in him
38 if a whiteness appear in the skin of a
57 and if after this there appear in those
16 2 I will a. in a cloud over the oracle
Num 12 6 I will appear to him in a vision, or I
Deut 13 3 that it may appear whether you love him
16 16 shall all thy males a. before the Lord
16 no one shall appear with his hands empty
23 14 let no uncleanness appear therein lest
31 11 to appear in the sight of the Lord thy
Judg 6 31 let him die before tomorrow light a.
1 K 1 22 that he may appear before the Lord
2 27 did I not plainly a. to thy father's
16 7 man seeth those things that appear
2 K 6 22 I [David] shall appear more glorious
2 Es 2 2 seeing thou dost not appear to be sick

4 21 rising of the morning, till the stars a.
Tob 2 22 come to nothing, and thy alms now a.
Job 6 3 this would appear heavier: therefore
15 14 of a woman that he should appear just
24 17 if the morning suddenly appear, it is
25 4 that is born of a woman appear clean
33 32 for I would have thee to appear just
Ps 16 15 I will a. before thy sight in justice
15 be satisfied when thy glory shall a.
41 3 when shall I come and a. before the
91 8 all the workers of iniquity shall a.
Prov 7 18 the desired embraces, till the day a.
25 6 appear not glorious before the king
Cant 6 4 as a flock of goats that a. from Galaad
Wisd 6 6 horribly and speedily will he a. to you
Eccu 7 5 desire not to a. wise before the king
23 2 that their sins may not appear: lest my
35 6 not appear empty in the sight of the
39 4 he shall . . . appear before the governor
Isa 1 12 when you came to a. before me, who
41 3 no path shall appear after his feet
Eze 42 6 therefore did they appear above out of
Haba 2 3 it shall appear at the end and shall
2 Ma 2 8 majesty of the Lord shall appear, and
Mat 6 16 they may appear unto men just. Amen
18 that thou a. not to men to fast, but
23 27 which outwardly a. to men beautiful
28 you also outwardly indeed a. to men just
24 30 then shall a. the sign of the Son of man
Luke 11 44 you are as sepulchers that a. not, and
Acts 26 16 those things wherein I will a. to thee
Rom 7 13 but sin, that it may appear sin, by
2 C 13 7 not that we may appear approved, but
Col 3 4 when Christ shall appear, who is your
4 you also shall appear with him in glory
Heb 9 24 that he may a. now in presence of God
28 the second time he shall a. without sin
11 1 the evidence of things that appear not
1 P 4 18 the ungodly and the sinner appear
5 4 when the prince of pastors shall appear
1 J 2 28 that when he shall appear, we. 3:2
Apoc 3 18 shame of thy nakedness may not appear
appearance Lev 13 26 a. of the leprosy be somewhat
Num 9 15 a. of fire until the morning. So it
16 and by night as it were the a. of fire
Esth 14 16 in the days of my public appearance
Bar 6 68 is no manner of a. that they are gods
Eze 1 5 this was their appearance: there was
7 sparkled like the a. of glowing brass
13 their a. was like that of burning coals
13 like the appearance of lamps. This was
16 the a. of the wheels . . . was like the
a. of the sea
16 their appearance and their work was
18 size and a height and a dreadful a.
22 as the a. of crystal terrible to behold
26 as the appearance of the sapphire stone
26 as the a. of a man above upon it. And
27 of amber as the a. of fire within it
28 as the appearance of the rainbow when
28 the a. of the brightness round about
8 2 a likeness as the appearance of fire
2 from the a. of his loins and downward
2 a. of brightness, as the a. of amber
10 1 as the a. of the likeness of a throne
9 a. of the wheels was to the sight like
10 as to their a., all four were alike
40 3 man whose a. was like the a. of brass
43 3 vision according to the a. which I had
3 and the a. was according to the vision
Dan 8 15 before me as it were the a. of a man
10 6 his face as the appearance of lightning
6 like in appearance to glittering brass

8 a. of my countenance was changed in me
Joel 2 4 the a. of them is as the a. of horses
2 Ma 4 24 he had magnified the a. of his power
John 7 24 judge not according to the a., but judge
2 C 10 7 things that are according to outward a.
1 Th 5 22 from all a. of evil refrain yourselves
2 Tim 3 5 having an a. indeed of godliness, but
appeared Gen 8 5 tops of the mountains appeared
Gen 12 7 the Lord appeared to Abram and said
7 to the Lord who had appeared to him
15 17 there appeared a smoking furnace and
17 1 the Lord appeared to him. 18:1; 26:2, 24;
Exod 3:2; 3 K 9:2; 2 Pa 7:12
18 2 eyes, there appeared to him three men
24 45 Rebecca appeared coming with a pitcher
30 37 were pilled, there appeared whiteness
35 1 who a. to thee when thou didst flee
7 there God appeared to him when he fled
9 God appeared again to Jacob after
38 27 there appeared twins in her womb: and
48 3 God Almighty appeared to me at Luza
Exod 3 16 hath a. to me, saying: Visiting I
4 1 the Lord hath not appeared to thee
5 God of Jacob, hath appeared to thee
6 3 I am the Lord, that a. to Abraham
16 10 glory of the Lord appeared. Lev 9:23;
Num 14:10; 16:19, 43; 20:6
14 it appeared in the wilderness small
19 16 was come, and the morning appeared
Num 12 10 Mary a. white as snow with a leprosy
21 16 the well appeared whereof the Lord said
Deut 31 15 Lord a. there in the pillar of a cloud
33 2 he hath appeared from mount Pharan
16 blessing of him that a. in the bush
Judg 6 12 angel of the Lord a. to him and said
13 3 an angel of the Lord appeared to her
9 angel of the Lord a. again to his wife
10 the man hath a. to me whom I saw before
21 angel of the Lord a. to them no more
1 K 3 21 and the Lord again appeared in Silo
9 2 he [Saul] a. above all the people. And
20 25 and David's place appeared empty. 27
2 K 1 2 a. a man who came out of Saul's camp
13 36 the king's sons also a. and coming in
18 31 Chusai a.: and coming up he said: I
22 16 the overflowings of the sea appeared
3 K 3 5 Lord a. to Solomon in a dream by night
7 31 that which a. without was of one cubit
9 2 as he had appeared to him in Gabaon
11 9 who had appeared to him twice and
4 K 6 33 the messenger a. who was coming to him
8 5 the woman a. whose son he had restored
2 Pa 1 7 behold that night God appeared to him
Jdth 10 4 so that she appeared to all men's eyes
16 13 howled when my lowly ones appeared
Ps 17 16 then the fountains of waters appeared
Prov 27 25 the green herbs have a., and the hay
30 32 hath a. a fool after he was lifted up
Cant 2 12 the flowers have appeared in our land
Wisd 17 6 there a. to them a sudden fire, very
19 7 water was before, dry land appeared
Eccu 26 28 two sorts of callings have a. to me
Isa 59 15 Lord saw, and it a. evil in his eyes
Jer 13 26 and thy shame hath appeared. I have
31 3 the Lord hath a. from afar to me
Eze 1 15 there a. upon the earth by the living
10 1 a. over them as it were the sapphire
8 there appeared in the cherubims the
20 5 a. to them in the land of Egypt and
21 24 your sins have a. in all your devices
42 5 which appeared above out of them from
Dan 1 15 their faces appeared fairer and fatter
5 5 the same hour there appeared fingers

8 1 a vision appeared to me. I Daniel
10 20 there a. the prince of the Greeks
1 Ma 4 19 part of them a. looking forth from
2 Ma 1 33 hid the fire, there appeared water
3 25 there appeared to them a horse with a
26 there appeared two other young men
34 spoken thus, they appeared no more
10 29 there a. to the enemies from heaven
35 when the fifth day appeared, twenty
11 8 there a. at Jerusalem a horseman going
15 13 appeared also another man admirable
Mat 1 20 angel of the Lord appeared. 2:13, 19
2 7 the time of the star which a. to them
13 26 fruit, then appeared also the cockle
17 3 a. to them Moses and Elias. Mark 9:3
27 53 into the holy city and a. to many
Mark 16 9 appeared first to Mary Magdalen, out
12 he a. in another shape to two of them
14 a. to the eleven as they were at table
Luke 1 11 there a. to him [Zachary] an angel of
9 8 but by other some, that Elias had a.
22 43 there a. to him an angel from heaven
24 34 is risen indeed and hath a. to Simon
Acts 2 3 there a. to them parted tongues as it
7 2 God of glory a. to our father Abraham
30 a. to him in the desert of mount Sina
35 angel who appeared to him in the bush
9 17 he that a. to thee [Paul] in the way
26 16 to this end have I a. to thee [Paul]
27 20 neither sun nor stars appeared for
Rom 10 20 I a, openly to them that asked not
1 Tim 3 16 a. unto angels, hath been preached
Titus 2 11 hath a. to all men; instructing us
Heb 9 26 he hath a. for the destruction of sin
1 J 1 2 with the Father, and hath a. to us
3 2 and it hath not yet a. what we shall be
5 that he appeared to take away our sins
8 the Son of God a. that he might destroy
4 9 the charity of God appeared towards us
Apoc 12 1 a great sign a. in heaven: A woman
appeareth Gen 38 24 she a. to have a big belly
Gen 44 28 and hitherto he appeareth not. If you
Lev 13 19 ulcer, there appeareth a white scar
1 K 26 21 for it a. that I have done foolishly
Job 23 8 if I go to the east, he appeareth not
Eccu 43 2 sun when he a. showing forth at his
Mat 24 27 of the east and a. unto the west
James 4 15 it is a vapor which a. for a little
appearing Job 30 8 not a. at all upon the earth
Wisd 17 4 and visions a. to them affrighted them
Luke 9 31 were Moses and Elias, a. in majesty
Acts 1 3 for forty days appearing to them and
1 P 1 7 and honor at the a. of Jesus Christ
appears Lev 13 3 where the leprosy appears lower
appease Gen 32 20 I will a. him with the presents
Lev 14 29 that he may appease the Lord for him
1 K 29 4 how can he otherwise a. his master
2 Pa 28 23 and I will appease them with victims
Eccu 39 34 they shall a. the wrath of him that
48 10 to appease the wrath of the Lord, to
2 Ma 4 31 went in all haste to appease them
appeased Exod 32 12 be a. upon the wickedness of
Exod 32 14 the Lord was a. from doing the evil
Judg 8 3 said this, their spirit was appeased
1 K 2 25 God may be appeased in his behalf: but
13 12 I have not a. the face of the Lord
19 6 he was a. with the words of Jonathan
2 K 14 21 I am a. and have granted thy request
4 K 24 4 therefore the Lord would not be a.
Prov 25 15 by patience a prince shall be appeased
Eccu 45 29 he appeased God for Israel. Therefore
Jer 42 10 I am a. for the evil that I have done
Dan 9 19 O Lord, be appeased, hearken and do
Mich 6 7 the Lord be a. with thousands of rams
2 Ma 13 26 a. the people and returned to Antioch
Acts 19 35 town clerk had appeased the multitudes
appeasest Ps 88 10 a. the motion of the waves
appeaseth Prov 15 18 that is patient a. those
Prov 26 10 putteth a fool to silence, a. anger
Eccu 6 5 multiplieth friends and a. enemies
43 25 with his thought he a. the deep
appeasing Eccu 46 9 and a. the wicked murmuring
appertain Lev 14 32 that a. to his cleansing
Heb 5 1 in the things that appertain to God
2 P 1 3 which appertain to life and godliness
appertained 2 Pa 31 13 to whom all things a.
2 Ma 4 28 to him a. the gathering of the taxes
appertaineth Num 3 7 a. to the service of the
appetite Job 38 39 and satisfy the a. of her whelps
Wisd 19 11 being led by their appetite they asked
Apphaim 1 Pa 2 30 sons of Nadab were Saled and A.
1 Pa 2 31 the son of Apphaim was Jesi: and Jesi
Apphus 1 Ma 2 5 Jonathan who was surnamed Apphus
Appia Philem 2 to Appia, our dearest sister, and
Appii Acts 28 15 meet us as far as Appii Forum
apple Deut 32 10 kept him as the apple of his eye
Ps 16 8 keep me as the apple of thy eye
Prov 7 2 and my law as the apple of thy eye
Cant 2 3 as the apple tree among the trees of
5 1 and eat the fruit of his apple trees
8 5 under the apple trees I raised thee up
Eccu 17 18 grace of a man as the apple of the eye
Lam 2 18 let not the apple of thy eye cease
Joel 1 12 the palm tree and the apple tree
Zach 2 8 toucheth you, toucheth the a. of my eye
apples Prov 25 11 like a. of gold on beds of silver
Cant 2 5 flowers, compass me about with apples
7 8 and the odor of thy mouth like apples
application Ecce 2 18 I hated all my a. wherewith
applied Judg 5 17 Dan applied himself to ships
Ecce 2 15 that I have a. myself more to the study
8 9 and applied my heart to all the works
16 and I applied my heart to know wisdom
Osee 7 6 have applied their heart like an over
apply Job 40 14 made him, he will apply his sword
Prov 22 17 and apply thy heart to my doctrine
23 12 let thy heart a. itself to instruction
Ecce 7 22 do not apply thy heart to all words
Eccu 6 33 if thou wilt apply thy mind, thou shalt
21 18 hear, and will apply it to himself
2 Ma 11 23 apply themselves diligently to their
applying Eccu 38 39 craft, applying their soul
appoint Gen 30 28 a. thy wages which I shall give
Gen 34 11 whatsoever you shall appoint I will
41 34 that he may appoint overseers over all
Exod 18 21 appoint of them rulers of thousands
19 12 thou shalt appoint certain limits to
21 13 I will appoint thee a place to which
29 42 where I will a. to speak unto thee
Lev 27 14 according to price which he shall a.
Num 1 50 appoint them over the tabernacle of the
3 10 thou shalt appoint Aaron and his sons
4 19 they shall appoint every man his work
14 4 let us appoint a captain, and let us
Deut 1 13 that I may appoint them your rulers
16 18 shalt appoint judges and magistrates
Josu 20 2 appoint cities of refuge, of which I
1 K 8 12 he will a. of them to be his tribunes
28 2 I will a. thee to guard my life forever
2 K 7 10 I will a. a place for my people Israel
3 K 1 35 I will a. him to be ruler over Israel
1 Pa 15 16 to appoint some of their brethren to be
1 Es 7 25 appoint judges and magistrates that
Job 14 13 a. me a time when thou wilt remember me
Ps 9 21 appoint, O Lord, a lawgiver over them
117 27 appoint a solemn day, with shady boughs

Wisd 11 25 thou didst not appoint or make anything
Isa 61 3 to appoint to the mourners of Sion and
Jer 49 19 whom I may appoint over her. 50:44
Eze 39 14 shall a. men to go continually about
45 6 you shall appoint the posession of the
Dan 4 14 he will appoint the basest man over it
Osee 1 11 they shall appoint themselves one head
1 Ma 11 57 I a. thee ruler over the four cities
14 42 should appoint rulers over their works
Mat 24 51 and a. his portion with the hypocrites
Luke 12 46 a. him his portion with unbelievers
Acts 6 3 whom we may appoint over this business
appointed Gen 14 14 in his house, 318 well a.
Gen 27 37 I have appointed him thy lord and have
41 41 I have appointed thee over the whole
Exod 2 14 who hath a. thee prince and judge over
7 1 behold I have a. thee the God of Pharao
9 5 and the Lord appointed a time, saying
18 25 he appointed them rulers of the people
29 30 that shall be appointed high priest
Lev 7 38 which the Lord appointed to Moses in
26 15 those things which are appointed by me
Num 30 17 the laws which the Lord a. to Moses
31 5 12,000 men well appointed for battle
32 20 go on well appointed for war before the
27 all well a. will march on to the war
35 26 cities that are a. for the banished
Deut 1 15 appointed them rulers, tribunes, and
3 18 go ye well a. before your brethren
28 36 king, whom thou shalt have appointed
32 8 he appointed the bounds of people
Josu 20 7 and they appointed Cedes in Galilee
8 east of Jericho, they appointed Bosor
9 these cities were appointed for all
Judg 18 16 before the door, a. with their arms
1 K 1 3 upon the appointed days, to adore and
2 19 which she brought to him on the a. days
8 1 he a. his sons to be judges over Israel
13 11 was not come according to the days a.
21 2 I have a. my servants to such and such
29 4 in his place, which thou hast a. him
2 K 7 11 from the day that I a. judges over my
13 32 for he was a. by the mouth of Absalom
15 3 there is no man a. by the king to hear
17 25 Absalom a. Amasa in Joab's stead over
18 1 a. over them captains of thousands and
20 5 the set time which the king had a. him
23 1 the man to whom it was a. concerning
24 15 from the morning unto the time a., and
3 K 1 43 king David hath appointed Solomon king
2 15 for it was appointed him by the Lord
35 the king a. Banaias the son of Joiada
4 28 the king was according as it was a.
9 23 and had charge over the appointed works
10 9 hath a. thee king to do judgment and
11 18 a. him victuals and assigned him land
12 12 the third day as the king had appointed
32 and he a. a feast in the eighth month
14 14 Lord hath a. himself a king over Israel
22 48 and there was then no king a. in Edom
4 K 7 17 king a. that lord on whose hand he
8 6 king a. her an eunuch, saying: Restore
21 6 a. pythons and multiplied soothsayers
23 5 the kings of Juda had a. to sacrifice
24 17 he a. Matthanias his uncle in his stead
25 30 he a. him a continual allowance, which
1 Pa 6 48 the Levites, who were appointed for all
9 22 and Samuel the seer a. in their trust
12 24 sons of Juda . . . 6,800 well a. to war
33 and stood in array well a. with armor
38 men of war well appointed to fight
15 17 they appointed Levites, Hemam the son
16 4 he a. Levites to minister before the ark
17 he appointed the same to Jacob for a
38 and Hosa he appointed to be porters
22 2 out of them he appointed stonecutters
25 1 serving in their appointed office
2 Pa 8 14 he a. according to the order of David
19 8 in Jerusalem also Josaphat a. Levites
20 21 appointed the singing men of the Lord
23 18 Joiada appointed overseers in the house
19 he appointed also porters in the gates
24 6 the money that was appointed by Moses
9 the money which Moses . . . appointed for
11 he whom the high priest had appointed
25 5 and appointed them by families and
31 2 Ezechias a. companies of the priests
19 there were men appointed to distribute
32 6 he appointed captains of the soldiers
33 14 and he appointed captains of the army
1 Es 3 8 they a. Levites from 25 years old and
5 14 Sassabasar, whom also he a. governor
10 14 let rulers be a. in all the multitude
14 come at the times appointed, and with
15 and Jaasia the son of Thecua were a.
2 Es 12 31 I a. two great choirs to give praise
43 they a. also in that day men over the
45 there were chief singers a. to praise
13 30 I appointed the courses of the priests
31 for the offering of wood at times a.
Tob 10 3 not return to them on the day appointed
Jdth 2 9 he appointed corn to be prepared out of
4 6 the priest of the Lord Eliachim had a.
8 13 of the Lord and you have a. him a day
12 1 he appointed what should be given her
Job 12 5 the lamp . . . is ready for the time a.
14 5 hast a. his bounds which cannot be
24 16 in the day they had a. for themselves
30 23 where a house is a. for every one that
34 13 what other hath he a. over the earth
Ps 2 6 I am appointed king by him over Sion
24 12 he hath a. him a law in the way he hath
103 20 thou hast a. darkness, and it is night
104 10 and he a. the same to Jacob for a law
Wisd 9 2 by thy wisdom hast a. man, that he
14 15 and appointed him rites and sacrifices
Eccu 17 20 and hath a. to them the lot of truth
24 34 he a. to David his servant to raise
36 28 him, as a robber well appointed, that
46 10 they two being a., were delivered out
Isa 15 4 shall the well a. men of Moab howl, his
44 7 since I appointed the ancient people
62 6 O Jerusalem, I have a. watchmen all the
Jer 6 17 I appointed watchmen over you, saying
20 1 who was a. chief in the house of the
Bar 5 7 God hath a. to bring down every high
Eze 4 6 yea a day for a year I have a. to thee
21 25 hath been a. in the time of iniquity
29 whose appointed day is come in the
23 24 shall come upon the well appointed
Dan 1 5 the king a. them a daily provision of
10 king, who hath a. you meat and drink
11 prince of the eunuchs had a. over Daniel
2 49 and he appointed Sidrach, Misach, and
5 11 appointed him prince of the wise men
6 1 he a. over the kingdom 120 governors
7 12 times of life were appointed them for
9 26 the end of the war the a. desolation
11 29 at the time a. he shall return and he
35 made white even to the appointed time
12 4 and seal the book, even to the time a.
9 and sealed until the appointed time
13 go thou thy ways until the time a.
13 5 ancients of the people appointed judges
Haba 1 12 thou hast appointed him for judgment
1 Ma 1 53 a. rulers over the people that should

3 55 Judas a. captains over the people, over
4 41 Judas appointed men to fight against
5 27 they had a. to bring their army on the
6 55 a. to bring up his son Antiochus and
8 7 took him alive and appointed to him
10 34 new moons and the days appointed and
36 shall be a. to be in the fortresses
14 10 a. that they should be furnished with
15 38 king appointed Cendebeus captain of
16 11 Ptolemee . . . was appointed captain in
2 Ma 3 4 who was a. overseer of the temple
14 on the day he had appointed, Heliodorus
4 20 the money was appointed by him that
8 22 he a. his brethren captains over each
36 they followed the laws a. by him
9 23 a. who should reign after him: to the
25 I have a. my son Antiochus king, whom
10 11 he a. over the affairs of his realm
13 3 that he should be a. chief ruler. But
14 21 a. a day upon which they might commune
Mat 24 45 lord hath appointed over his family
26 15 but they a. him 30 pieces of silver
19 disciples did as Jesus appointed to
27 10 potter's field, as the Lord appointed
28 16 unto the mountain where Jesus had a.
Luke 3 13 nothing more than that which is a. you
10 1 the Lord a. also other seventy-two and
12 14 who hath appointed me judge or divider
John 15 16 and have a. you that you should go and
Acts 1 23 they a. two, Joseph, called Barsabas
7 10 appointed him governor over Egypt and
27 who hath a. thee [Moses] prince. 35
12 21 upon a day appointed, Herod being
17 26 determining appointed times and the
31 hath a. a day wherein he will judge
31 by the man whom he hath appointed
20 13 so he [Paul] had appointed, himself
28 23 and when they had a. him [Paul] a day
1 C 4 9 last, as it were men appointed to death
Gal 4 2 until the time appointed by the Father
1 Th 3 3 know that we are appointed thereunto
5 9 God hath not appointed us unto wrath
1 Tim 2 7 I am appointed a preacher. 2 Tim 1:11
Titus 1 5 priests in every city as I also a. thee
Heb 1 2 whom he hath appointed heir of all
8 3 every high priest is appointed to offer
9 27 it is appointed unto men once to die
appointeth Ps 67 15 that is in heaven a. kings
appointing Judg 9 16 in a. Abimelech king over
appointment Gen 18 14 according to a. I will return
1 K 13 8 days according to the a. of Samuel
20 35 field, according to the a. with David
Job 2 11 they had made an appointment to come
Jer 47 7 there hath made an appointment for it
apprehend Deut 19 6 should pursue and apprehend him
Mat 26 4 by subtilty they might apprehend Jesus
55 swords and clubs to a. me. Mark 14:48
John 7 30 they sought therefore to a. him: and no
32 sent ministers to apprehend him. Jesus
11 56 tell, that they might apprehend him
2 C 11 32 city of the Damascenes to apprehend me
Phil 11 32 if I may by any means apprehend wherein
apprehended 2 K 4 10 I a. and slew him in Siceleg
Ps 118 39 turn away my reproach, which I have a.
1 Ma 9 61 he a. of the men of the country that
16 22 and he a. the men that came to kill him
2 Ma 7 1 together with their mother, were a.
13 4 that he should be a. and put to death
Mat 14 3 Herod had apprehended John. Mark 6:17
John 7 44 some of them would have apprehended him
Acts 1 16 was the leader of them that a. Jesus
12 4 when he had a. him, he cast him into
24 6 we having a., would also have judged
26 21 having a. me, went about to kill me
Phil 3 12 wherein I am also apprehended by Christ
13 I do not count myself to have a. But
apprehendeth Num 35 19 as soon as he a. him, he
apprehending Luke 22 54 a. him, they led him to
Acts 16 19 a. Paul and Silas, brought them into
approach Exod 28 43 when they a. to the altar
Lev 9 7 said to Aaron: Approach to the altar
10 3 I will be sanctified in them that a.
18 6 no man shall a. to her that is near
14 neither shalt thou approach to his wife
19 not a. to a woman having her flowers
21 18 neither shall he approach to minister
21 shall not approach to offer sacrifices
23 not within the veil nor a. to the altar
Num 8 19 if they should presume to approach unto
16 5 choose, they shall approach to him. Do
10 sons of Levi to approach unto him
18 7 stranger shall a., he shall be slain
22 that the children of Israel may not a.
Deut 5 27 approach thou rather: and hear all
33 3 they that approach to his feet shall
Josu 8 5 will approach on the contrary side
Judg 15 14 wont to be consumed at the a. of fire
2 K 11 20 why did you a. so near to the wall to
Eccu 35 20 his prayer shall a. even to the clouds
41 27 his handmaid, and approach not her bed
Isa 58 2 they are willing to approach to God
Jer 30 21 setteth his heart to approach to me
Eze 42 13 that approach to the Lord into the holy
43 19 of the race of Sadoc, who a. to me
Amos 6 3 and that a. to the throne of iniquity
9 10 who say: The evils shall not approach
approached Deut 2 37 to which we approached not
1 Ma 3 16 and they a. even as far as Bethoron
42 that the armies a. to their borders
6 26 they have a. this day to the castle
31 a. to Bethsura and fought many days
13 23 when he a. to Bascama, he slew Jonathan
2 Ma 10 35 approached manfully to the wall, and
approacheth Lev 22 3 that a. to those things
Num 3 10 stranger that approacheth to minister
17 13 whosoever a. to the tabernacle of the
Eccu 11 40 what time shall pass and that death a.
approaching Lev 9 8 Aaron a. to the altar
Judg 9 52 a. to the gate, endeavored to set fire
Ps 148 14 children of Israel, a people a. to him
2 Ma 11 5 a. to Bethsura, which was in a narrow
Heb 10 25 more as you see the day approaching
approve Mich 6 9 tribes, and who shall approve it
1 C 16 3 whomsoever you shall approve by letters
Phil 1 10 that you may approve the better things
approved Deut 1 13 whose conversation is approved
2 Es 13 13 for they were approved as faithful
Eccu 25 1 which are approved before God and men
39 40 all shall be well a. in their time
42 8 well approved in the sight of all men
Lam 3 36 judgment, the Lord hath not approved
Acts 2 22 a man approved of God among you, by
Rom 14 18 pleaseth God and is approved of men
16 10 salute Apelles, approved in Christ
1 C 11 19 that they also who are approved may be
2 C 10 18 not he who commendeth himself is a.
13 7 not that we may appear approved, but
1 Th 2 4 as we were approved by God that the
2 Tim 2 15 to present thyself approved unto God
Heb 11 39 being approved by the testimony of faith
approvest Rom 2 18 a. the more profitable things
approveth Eccu 34 23 a. not the gifts of the wicked
approving 2 C 8 8 a. also the good disposition of
appurtenances 3 K 6 38 and in all the a. thereof
aprons Gen 3 7 fig leaves and made themselves a.
Acts 19 12 to the sick, handkerchiefs and aprons

apt Wisd 19 20 food, which was apt to melt as ice
2 Tim 2 24 apt to teach, patient, with modesty
aqueduct 2 K 2 24 came as far as the hill of the a.
2 Es 2 14 fountain and to the king's aqueduct
Jdth 7 6 ran through an a. without the city on
6 and he commanded their a. to be cut off
Eccu 24 41 like an aqueduct, came out of paradise
Aquila Acts 18 2 finding a certain Jew named A.
Acts 18 18 and with him, Priscilla and Aquila
26 when Priscilla and Aquila had heard
Rom 16 3 salute Prisca and Aquila. 2 Tim 4:19
1 C 16 19 Aquila and Priscilla salute you much
Ar Num 21 15 that they might rest in Ar and lie
Num 21 28 and hath consumed Ar of the Moabites
Deut 2 9 I have given Ar to the children of Lot
18 borders of Moab the city named Ar
29 the Moabites, that abide in Ar: until
Isa 15 1 in the night Ar of Moab is laid waste
Ara 1 Pa 5 26 to Lahela and to Habor and to Ara
1 Pa 7 38 Jether: Jephone and Phaspha and Ara
Araas 4 K 22 14 Thecua the son of Araas keeper of
Arab Josu 15 52 Arab and Ruma and Esaan and Janum
Arabella 1 Ma 9 2 Masaloth, which is in Arabella
Arabia 3 K 10 15 all the kings of Arabia. 2 Pa 9:14
Ps 71 15 shall be given of the gold of Arabia
Isa 21 13 the burden in Arabia. In the forest at
Jer 25 24 all the kings of Arabia and all the
Eze 27 21 Arabia and all the princes of Cedar
1 Ma 11 16 Alexander fled into Arabia, there to be
Gal 1 17 but I went into Arabia, and again I
4 25 Sina is a mountain in Arabia, which
Arabian 2 Es 2 19 and Gossem the A. heard of it
2 Es 6 1 Gossem the Arabian and the rest of our
Isa 13 20 neither shall the Arabian pitch his
1 Ma 11 17 Zabdiel the A. took off Alexander's head
39 Emalchuel the Arabian who brought up
Arabians 2 Pa 17 11 the A. brought him cattle
2 Pa 21 16 the A., who border on the Ethiopians
22 1 rovers of the Arabians, who had broke
26 7 the Arabians that dwelt in Gurbaal
2 Es 4 7 and Tobias and the Arabians and the
Ps 71 10 the kings of the Arabians and of Saba
Eze 27 8 and the Arabians were thy rowers: thy
1 Ma 5 39 have hired the Arabians to help them
12 31 Jonathan turned upon the Arabians that
2 Ma 5 8 shut up by Aretas the king of the A.
12 10 and 500 horsemen of the A. set upon
11 the rest of the Arabians being overcome
Acts 2 11 and proselytes, Cretes and Arabians
Arach Gen 10 10 Arach and Achad and Chalanne
Arachite 2 K 15 32 Chusai the A. came to meet him
2 K 17 5 Absalom said: Call Chusai the Arachite
14 the counsel of Chusai the A. is better
1 Pa 27 33 Chusai the Arachite, the king's friend
Aracite Gen 10 17 Hevite and the Aracite. 1 Pa 1:15
Arad Num 21 1 when king Arad the Chanaanite
Num 33 40 king Arad the Chanaanite, who dwelt
Judg 1 16 lot, which is at the south side of Arad
Eze 27 11 the men of Arad were with thy army
Arada Num 33 24 they came to Arada. From thence
Aradian Gen 10 18 the A., the Samarite. 1 Pa 1:16
Aradus 1 Ma 15 23 Side and Aradus and Rhodes
Araia 2 Es 3 8 Eziel the son of A. the goldsmith
Aram Gen 10 22 Arphaxad and Lud and A. 1 Pa 1:17
Gen 10 23 the sons of Aram: Us and Hull and
36 28 Disan had sons: Hus and Aram. These
Num 23 7 hath brought me from Aram, from the
Ruth 4 19 Esron begot Aram, Aram begot Aminadab
1 Pa 2 23 he took Gessur and Aram the towns of
25 Ram his firstborn, and Buna and Aram
7 34 Ahi and Roaga and Haba and Aram
Mat 1 3 Esron begot Aram. Aram begot Aminadab
Arama Josu 19 36 and Edema and Arama, Asor and Cedes
1 K 30 30 that were in Arama and that were in
Aran Gen 11 26 Abram and Nachor and Aran. 27
Gen 11 27 Aran begot Lot. And Aran died before
29 Nachor's wife, Melcha, the daughter of A.
31 Lot the son of Aran, his son's son
1 Pa 1 42 sons of Disan: Hus and Aran. Now these
23 9 Salomith and Hosiel and Aran, three
Arapha 2 K 21 16 Jesibibenob who was of race of A.
2 K 21 18 slew Saph of the race of Arapha of the
22 these four were born of Arapha in Geth
Ararat Isa 37 38 they fled into the land of Ararat
Jer 51 27 against her the kings of Ararat, Menni
Arari 2 K 23 11 was Semma the son of Age of Arari
Ararite 1 Pa 11 33 Jonathan the son of Sage an A.
1 Pa 11 34 Ahiam the son of Sachar an Ararite
Arbathite 2 K 23 31 Abialbon the A., Azmaveth
1 Pa 11 32 Abiel an A., Azimoth a Bauramite
Arbatis 1 Ma 5 23 that were in Galilee and in A.
Arbe Josu 21 11 the city of Arbe the father of
Arbee Gen 23 2 [Sara] died in the city of Arbee
Gen 35 27 the city of Arbee, this is Hebron
Arbi 2 K 23 35 Hesrai of Carmel, Pharai of Arbi
arbiters Exod 21 22 require and as a. shall award
arch 1 K 15 12 erected for himself a triumphant a.
archangel 1 Th 4 15 with voice of an archangel
Jude 9 Michael the a. disputing with the devil
Archelaus Mat 2 22 hearing that Archelaus reigned
archer Gen 21 20 and became a young man, an a.
Job 41 19 the archer shall not put him to flight
archers 1 K 31 3 the a. overtook him [Saul]
1 K 31 3 was grievously wounded by the archers
2 K 11 24 the archers shot their arrows at thy
1 Pa 8 40 and a. of great strength, valiant men
10 3 the archers reached him and wounded
2 Pa 35 23 [Josias] was wounded by the archers
Jdth 2 7 mustered . . . 12,000 archers, horsemen
11 with the chariots and horsemen and a.
Isa 21 17 residue of the number of strong archers
Jer 4 29 voice of the horsemen, and the archers
1 Ma 9 11 slingers and the a. went before the army
Archi Josu 16 2 and passeth the border of Archi
Archippus Col 4 17 say to Archippus: Take heed to
Philem 2 to Archippus, our fellow soldier, and
architect Isa 3 3 the counsellor and the architect
1 C 3 10 as a wise architect, I have laid the
Arcturus Job 9 9 who maketh Arcturus and Orion
Job 38 31 thou stop the turning about of A.
Amos 5 8 seek him that maketh A. and Orion
ardent 3 K 11 2 joined with a most ardent love
Ardon 1 Pa 2 18 sons were Jaser and Sobab and A.
are Mat 2 18 not be comforted, because they are not
Luke 13 25 I know you not, whence you are. 27
1 C 1 28 things that are not that he might bring
to nought the things that are
6 19 and you are not your own? For you are
Heb 2 10 for whom are all things and by whom are
Apoc 1 19 and which are and which must be done
Area 1 Es 2 5 the children of Area, 775. The
2 Es 6 18 Sechenias the son of Area, and Johanan
7 10 children of Area, 652. The children of
Arebba Josu 15 60 the city of woods, and Arebba
Arecon Josu 19 46 and Mejarcon and Arecon, with
Ared Gen 46 21 and Mophim and Ophim and Ared
Aree 1 Pa 7 39 sons of Olla: Aree and Haniel
Areli Gen 46 16 Esebon and Heri and Arodi and Areli
Arem 2 Es 7 42 children of Arem, 1017. The Levites
Areopagite Acts 17 34 among whom was Dionysius the A.
Areopagus Acts 17 19 they brought him to the A.
Acts 17 22 Paul standing in the midst of the A.
Aretas 2 Ma 5 8 having been shut up by A. the king
2 C 11 32 governor of the nation under Aretas
Areuna 2 K 24 16 was by the thrashingfloor of A.
2 K 24 18 to the Lord in the thrashingfloor of A.

20 Areuna looked and saw the king and his
22 Areuna said to David: Let my lord the
23 things A. as a king gave to the king
23 Areuna said to the king: The Lord thy
Argob Deut 3 4 the country of A. 13, 14; 3 K 4:13
4 K 15 25 in tower of king's house near Argob
arguments Wisd 8 8 and the solutions of a.: she
Ariarathes 1 Ma 15 22 to A. and to Arsaces and to
Aridai Esth 9 9 Phermesta and Arisai and Aridai
Aridatha Esth 9 8 Phoratha and Adalia and A.
Arie 4 K 15 25 king's house near Argon and near A.
Ariel Num 26 17 Ariel, of him is the family of
1 Es 8 16 so I sent Eliezer and Ariel and Semeias
Isa 29 1 woe to Ariel, to Ariel the city which
2 I will make a trench about Ariel and
2 it shall be to me as Ariel. And I will
7 nations that have fought against Ariel
Eze 43 15 the Ariel itself was four cubits: and
15 from the Ariel upward were four horns
16 and the Ariel was twelve cubits long
Arielites Num 26 17 of him is the family of the A.
ariels 1 Pa 11 22 he slew the two ariels of Moab
aright Ps 77 8 that set not their heart aright
Eccu 38 10 from sin and order thy hands aright
Arimathea Mat 27 57 a certain rich man of A.
Mark 15 43 Joseph of A., a noble counsellor, who
Luke 23 51 of Arimathea, a city of Judea; who also
John 19 38 Joseph of Arimathea, because he was a
Arioch Gen 14 1 and Arioch king of Pontus and
Gen 14 9 and Arioch king of Pontus: four kings
Dan 2 14 Arioch the general of the king's army
15 when A. had told the matter to Daniel
24 after this Daniel went in to Arioch
25 Arioch in haste brought in Daniel
Arisai Esth 9 9 Arisai and Aridai and Jezatha
arise Gen 13 17 arise and walk through the land
Gen 19 14 arise: get you out of this place
15 arise, take thy wife and the two
21 18 arise, take up the boy, and hold him by
27 19 arise, sit, and eat of my venison
31 arise, my father, and eat of thy son's
43 arise and flee to Laban thy brother
31 13 arise and go out of this land and
35 1 arise, and go up to Bethel and dwell
3 arise, and let us go up to Bethel
44 4 arise, and pursue after the men: and
Exod 9 13 arise in the morning and stand before
12 31 arise and go forth from among my people
13 17 if they should see wars arise against
24 14 if any question shall arise, you shall
32 1 arise, make us gods, that may go before
Lev 13 2 in whose skin or flesh shall arise a
Num 10 35 arise, O Lord, and let thy enemies be
22 20 to call thee, arise and go with them
Deut 2 24 arise ye, and pass the torrent Arnon
9 12 arise and go down from hence quickly
17 8 arise, and go up to the place, which
32 38 let them arise and help you, and
Josu 1 2 arise and pass over this Jordan, thou
7 10 and the Lord said to Josue: Arise
13 arise, sanctify the people, and say
8 1 arise and go up to the town of Hai
7 you shall arise out of the ambush
Judg 4 14 arise, for this is the day wherein
5 12 arise, arise, O Debbora, arise, arise
12 arise, Barac, and take hold of thy
7 9 arise and go down into the camp
15 arise, for the Lord hath delivered
8 20 his eldest son: Arise and slay them
9 32 arise, and let us go up to them: for
19 28 said to her: arise, and let us be
1 K 9 3 and arise, go, and seek the asses
26 arise, that I may let thee go
16 12 arise, and anoint him, for this is he
23 4 arise and go to Ceila: for I will deliver
29 10 arise in the morning, thou and the
2 K 13 15 said to her: Arise and get thee gone
15 14 arise and let us flee: for we shall not
17 1 I will arise and pursue after David
21 arise and pass quickly over the river
19 7 arise and go out and speak to the
3 K 3 12 like thee before thee nor shall arise
8 37 if a famine arise in the land or a
14 2 arise and change thy dress that thou be
12 arise thou therefore and go to thy house
17 9 arise and go to Sarephta of the
19 5 arise and eat. He looked and behold
7 arise and eat: for thou hast yet a great
21 7 arise and eat bread and be of good
15 arise and take possession of the
21 18 arise and go down to meet Achab king
4 K 1 3 arise and go up to meet the messengers
8 1 arise and go thou and thy household
23 25 neither . . . did there arise any like
1 Pa 22 16 arise then and be doing and the Lord
19 arise and build a sanctuary to the Lord
2 Pa 6 28 if a famine arise in the land or a
41 now therefore arise, O Lord God into
16 9 from this time wars shall arise against
1 Es 10 4 arise, it is thy part to give orders
2 Es 9 5 arise, bless the Lord your God from
Tob 8 4 Sara, arise and let us pray to God today
Job 7 4 I shall say: When shall I arise? And
8 5 yet if thou wilt arise early to God
11 17 shall arise to thee at evening: and
25 3 upon whom shall not his light arise
Ps 3 7 arise, O Lord; save me, O my God. For
7 7 arise, O Lord my God, in the precept
9 12 arise, O Lord God, let thy hand be
20 a., O Lord, let not man be strengthened
11 6 now will I arise, saith the Lord
16 13 arise, O Lord, disappoint him and
34 23 arise and be attentive to my judgment
43 23 arise, why sleepest thou, O Lord? Arise
26 arise, O Lord, help us and redeem us
56 9 arise, O my glory, arise psaltery and
9 I will arise early, I will give praise
67 2 let God arise, and let his enemies be
73 22 arise, O God, judge thy own cause
81 8 arise, O God, judge thou the earth
101 14 thou shalt arise and have mercy on Sion
107 3 arise, my glory; arise, psaltery and
3 I will arise in the morning early
131 8 arise, O Lord, into thy resting place
Cant 2 10 arise, make haste, my Love, my dove
13 arise, my love, my beautiful one, and
4 16 arise, O north wind, and come, O south
Eccu 31 25 eat much, arise, go out, and vomit
37 21 four manner of things arise, good
Isa 21 5 arise, ye princes, take up the shield
23 12 arise and sail over to Cethim, there
51 9 arise, arise, put on strength, O thou
9 arise as in the days of old, in the
17 arise, arise, stand up, O Jerusalem
52 1 arise, arise, put on thy strength
2 arise, sit up, O Jerusalem: loose
58 8 and thy health shall speedily arise
60 1 arise, be enlightened, O Jerusalem
2 but the Lord shall arise upon thee and
Jer 1 17 arise and speak to them all that I
2 27 they will say: Arise and deliver us
28 let them arise and deliver thee in the
6 4 arise and let us go up at midday
5 arise and let us go up in the night
13 4 arise, go to the Euphrates and hide
6 arise, go to the Euphrates and take

18 2 arise and go down into the potter's
31 6 arise, and let us go up to Sion to
46 16 arise, and let us return to our own
49 28 arise and go ye up to Cedar and waste
31 arise and go up to a nation that is
Lam 2 19 arise, give praise in the night in the
Bar 5 5 arise, O Jerusalem, and stand on
Dan 7 5 said to it: Arise, devour much flesh
17 kingdoms, which shall arise out of
8 23 shall arise a king of a shameless
Osee 10 14 a tumult shall arise among thy people
Joel 3 12 let them arise, and let the nations
Abdi 1 arise and let us rise up to battle
Jon 1 2 arise and go to Ninive the great. 3:2
Mich 2 10 arise ye and depart, for there is
4 13 arise and tread, O daughter of Sion
6 1 arise, contend thou in judgment
7 8 I shall arise when I sit in darkness
Haba 2 19 to the dumb stone: Arise: can it teach
Mala 4 2 the Sun of justice shall arise and
1 Ma 9 8 let us arise and go against our enemies
44 let us arise and fight against our
14 41 there should arise a faithful prophet
Mat 2 13 saying: Arise and take the child. 20
9 5 or to say: Arise and walk. Mark 2:9; Luke 5:23
6 arise, take up thy bed. Mark 2:11; Luke 5:24; John 5:8
17 7 said to them, Arise and fear not
24 24 there shall arise false Christs and
Mark 5 41 damsel, I say to thee, arise. Luke 8:54
10 49 better comfort: arise, he calleth thee
Luke 6 8 arise and stand forth in the midst
7 14 said: Young man, I say to thee, arise
15 18 I will arise and will go to my father
17 19 arise, go thy way; for thy faith hath
22 46 why sleep you? Arise, pray, lest you
24 38 why do thoughts arise in your hearts
John 14 31 so do I: Arise, let us go hence
Acts 3 6 in name of Jesus Christ of Nazareth, a.
8 26 arise, go towards the south to the way
9 7 arise and go into the city, and there
11 arise and go into the street that is
34 healeth thee: arise and make thy bed
40 body, he said: Tabitha, arise
10 13 arise, Peter; kill and eat. 11:7
20 arise, get thee down and go with them
26 saying: Arise, I myself am also a man
12 7 arise quickly, And the chains fell off
20 30 shall arise men speaking perverse things
22 10 arise and go to Damascus; and there it
Eph 5 14 arise from the dead: and Christ shall
1 Tim 6 4 from which arise envies, contentions
2 P 1 19 until . . . the day star arise in your
Apoc 11 1 arise and measure the temple of God
ariseth Ps 103 22 sun a., and they are gathered
Mat 13 21 there ariseth tribulation. Mark 4:17
Heb 7 15 Melchisedech there ariseth another priest
arising Gen 26 31 a. in the morning, they swore
Gen 28 18 Jacob, arising in the morning, took
Judg 19 5 a. early in the morning, he desired
Luke 8 24 he arising, rebuked the wind and the
Aristarchus Acts 19 29 having caught Gaius and A.
Acts 20 4 of the Thessalonians, Aristarchus
27 2 A., the Macedonian of Thessalonica
Col 4 10 A. my fellow prisoner, saluteth you
Philem 24 Mark, Aristarchus, Demas, and Luke my
Aristobolus 2 Ma 1 10 to A. the preceptor of king
Aristobulus' Rom 16 11 that are of A. household
Arius 1 Ma 12 7 long ago to Onias . . . from Arius
1 Ma 12 20 Arius king of the Spartans to Onias
ark Gen 6 14 make thee an ark of timber planks
Gen 6 14 thou shalt make little rooms in the ark
15 length of the ark shall be 300 cubits
16 thou shalt make a window in the ark
16 door of the ark thou shalt set in the
18 thou shalt enter into the ark, thou and
19 bring two of a sort into the ark, that
7 1 in thou and all thy house into the ark
7 into the ark because of the waters of
9 went in to Noe into the ark, male and
13 his sons with them, went into the ark
15 went in to Noe into the ark two and two
17 lifted up the ark on high from the earth
18 the ark was carried upon the waters
23 they that were with him in the ark
8 1 cattle which were with him in the ark
4 the ark rested in the seventh month
6 Noe, opening the window of the ark
9 returned to him into the ark: for the
9 caught her and brought her into the ark
10 again sent forth the dove out of the ark
13 Noe opening the covering of the ark
16 go out of the ark, thou and thy wife
19 went out of the ark. And Noe built an
9 10 that are come forth out of the ark and
18 sons of Noe who came out of the ark
Exod 25 10 frame an ark of setim wood, the length
12 put at the four corners of the ark
14 rings that are in the sides of the ark
16 shalt put in the ark the testimony
20 wherewith the ark is to be covered
30 26 the ark of the testament and the table
35 12 ark and the staves, the propitiatory
37 1 Beseleel made also the ark of setim
5 rings that were at the sides of the ark
39 34 the ark, the bars, the propitiatory, the
40 3 and shalt put the ark in it, and shalt
18 and he put the testimony in the ark
19 had brought the ark into the tabernacle
Lev 16 2 with which the ark is covered, lest he
Num 3 31 they shall keep the ark, and the table
7 89 the propitiatory that was over the ark
10 35 when the ark was lifted up, Moses said
14 44 but the ark of the testament of the
Deut 10 1 and thou shalt make an ark of wood
2 and thou shalt put them in the ark
3 I made an ark of setim wood. And when
5 put the tables into the ark, that I
Josu 3 4 between you and ark the space of 2,000
4 take care you come not near the ark
13 when the priests that carry the ark
4 10 the priests that carried the ark stood
6 9 common people followed the ark. 13
8 33 stood on both sides of the ark, before
1 K 6 13 they saw the ark and rejoiced to see it
2 K 6 4 went before the ark. But David and all
3 K 8 3 the priests took up the arm and carried
5 went with him before the ark, and they
7 their wings over the place of the ark, and covered the ark
9 in the ark there was nothing else but
21 I have set there a place for the ark
1 Pa 6 31 after that the ark was placed. And they
13 3 let us bring again the ark of our God
9 put forth his hand to hold up the ark
10 because he had touched the ark; and
15 23 and Elcana were doorkeepers of the ark
24 and Jehias were porters of the ark
27 all the Levites that carried the ark
16 37 to minister in the presence of the ark
2 Pa 5 4 the Levites took up the ark and brought
6 were gathered together before the ark
8 the place in which the ark was set
8 covered the ark itself and its staves
9 staves wherewith the ark was carried

9 so the ark has been there unto this
10 there was nothing else in the ark but
6 11 and I have put in it the ark wherein
41 thou and the ark of thy strength: let
35 3 put the ark in the sanctuary of the
Ps 131 8 the ark, which thou hast sanctified
2 Ma 2 4 tabernacle and the ark should accompany
5 in thither the tabernacle and the ark
Mat 24 38 Noe entered into the ark. Luke 17:27
Heb 9 4 and the ark of the testament covered
11 7 framed the ark for the saving of his
1 P 3 20 when the ark was abuilding: wherein
Apoc 11 19 ark of his testament was seen in his
ark of God 1 K 3 3 where the ark of God was
1 K 4 11 and the ark of God was taken: and the
13 his heart was fearful for the a. . . .
17 are dead: and the ark of God is taken
18 when he had named the ark of God, he
19 news that the ark of God was taken
21 because the ark of God was taken. 22
5 1 Philistines took the ark of God. 2
10 they sent the ark of God into Accaron
10 when ark of God was come into Accaron
6 1 the ark of God was in the land of the
3 if you send back the ark of the God of
11 they laid the ark of God upon the cart
15 the Levites took down the ark of God
14 18 for the ark of God was there that day
2 K 6 2 of Juda, to fetch the ark of God, upon
3 laid the ark of God upon a new cart
4 Ahio having care of the ark of God
6 Oza put forth his hand to the a. . . .
7 he died there before the ark of God
12 that he had, because of the ark of God
12 brought away the a. . . . out of the house
7 2 the ark of God is lodged within skins
11 11 a. . . . and Israel and Juda dwell in tents
15 24 and they set down the ark of God: and
25 carry back the a. . . . into the city
29 carried back the a. . . . into Jerusalem
1 Pa 13 5 to bring the a. . . . from Cariathiarim
7 carried the ark of God upon a new cart
12 how can I bring in the ark of God
14 the ark of God remained in the house
15 1 and built a place for the ark of God
2 no one ought to carry the ark of God
3 that the ark of God might be brought
15 the sons of Levi took the ark of God
24 sounded with trumpets before the a. . . .
16 1 so they brought the ark of God and
2 Pa 1 4 David had brought the ark of God, and
ark of the covenant Num 10 33 a. . . . went before
Deut 10 8 the tribe of Levi, to carry the a. . . .
31 9 who carried the a. . . . 25; Josu 3:14, 17; 4:9, 18; 8:33; 1 Pa 15:26
26 book and put it in the side of a. . . .
Josu 3 3 when you shall see the a. . . . of the
6 take up the a. . . . and go before the
8 the priests that carry the a. . . . 4:16
11 behold the a. . . . of the Lord of all
4 7 waters of Jordan ran off before the a. . . .
6 4 and shall go before the a. . . . : and you
6 take the a. . . . : and let seven other
8 the seven trumpets before the a. . . .
Judg 20 27 time the a. . . . of the Lord was there
1 K 4 3 let us fetch unto us the a. . . . of the
4 they brought from thence the a. . . .
4 Ophni and Phinees were with the a. . . .
5 when the a. . . . of the Lord was come
2 K 6 15 brought the a. . . . of the Lord with joyful shouting. 1 Pa 15:28
15 24 Levites with him carrying the a. . . .
3 K 3 15 [Solomon] stood before the a. . . . of the
6 19 in the inner part, to set there a. . . .
8 1 that they might carry the a. . . . of the
6 priests brought in the a. . . . of the
1 Pa 15 25 went to bring the a. . . . of the Lord out
29 when the a. . . . was come to the city
16 6 trumpet continually before the a. . . .
37 [David] left there before the a. . . .
17 1 the a. . . . of the Lord is under skins
22 19 that the a. . . . of the Lord may be
28 18 their wings, and covering the a. . . .
2 Pa 5 2 to bring the a. . . . of the Lord out of
7 priests brought in the a. . . . into its
Jer 3 16 they shall say no more: The a. . . . of the
ark of the God of Israel 1 K 5 7 a. . . . shall not stay with us
1 K 5 8 said: What shall we do with the a. . . .
8 let the a. . . . be carried about. And
10 they have brought the a. . . . to us, to
11 send away the a. . . . and let it return
6 3 if you send back the a. . . . , send it
ark of the Lord Josu 4 5 go before the a. . . . your
Josu 4 11 the ark also of the Lord passed over
6 6 and march before the ark of the Lord
7 armed, marching before the a. . . .
11 a. . . . went about the city once a day
12 the priests took the ark of the Lord
13 they went before the ark of the Lord
7 6 fell flat on the ground before the a. . . .
1 K 4 6 that the a. . . . was come into the camp
5 3 face on the ground before the a. . . .
4 his face on the earth before the a. . . .
6 2 what shall we do with the a. . . . ? Tell
8 take the a. . . . and lay it on the cart
18 they set down the ark of the Lord
19 because they had seen the a. . . . : and
21 Philistines have brought back the a. . . .
7 1 came and fetched up the a. . . . and
1 Eleazar his son, to keep the a. . . .
2 ark of the Lord abode in Cariathiarim
14 18 Saul said to Achias: Bring the a. . . .
2 K 6 9 how shall the a. . . . come to me [David]
10 he would not have the a. . . . brought
11 a. . . . abode in the house of Obededom
13 when they that carried the a. . . . had
16 when the a. . . . was come into the city
17 they brought the a. . . . and set it in
3 K 2 26 because thou didst carry the a. . . .
8 4 carried the a. . . . the God of Israel to
15 12 bring the a. . . . the God of Israel to
14 were sanctified to carry the a. . . .
16 4 Levites to minister before the a. . . .
28 2 to have built a house, in which a. . . .
2 Pa 8 11 sanctified; because a. . . . came into it
ark of the testimony Exod 25 22 cherubims which shall be upon the a. . . .
Exod 26 33 within it thou shalt put the a. . . .
34 set the propitiatory upon the a. . . .
30 6 the veil that hangeth before the a. . . .
31 7 the a. . . . and the propitiatory that is
40 5 incense is burnt, before the a. . . .
Num 4 5 and shall wrap up the a. . . . in it
arm Gen 24 18 let down the pitcher upon her arm
Exod 6 6 redeem you with a high arm and great
15 16 in the greatness of thy arm, let them
Num 31 3 arm of you men to fight, who may take
Deut 33 20 seized upon arm and top of the head
1 K 2 31 I will cut off thy arm and the arm of thy father's house
2 K 1 10 bracelet that was on his arm, and have
2 Pa 32 8 with him is an arm of flesh; with us
1 Es 4 23 and hindered them with arm and power
Jdth 9 11 lift up thy arm as from the beginning
Job 22 8 in the strength of thy arm thou didst
26 2 the arm of him that has no strength
31 22 let thy arm with its bones be broken

35 9 for the violence of the arm of tyrants
38 15 away and the high arm shall be broken
40 4 hast thou an arm like God, and canst
Ps 9 15 break thou the arm of the sinner
43 4 neither did their own arm save them
4 but thy right hand and thy arm and the
70 18 until I show forth thy arm to all
76 16 with thy arm thou hast redeemed thy
78 11 according to the greatness of thy arm
88 11 with the arm of thy strength thou hast
14 thy arm is with might. Yet thy hand
22 him: and my arm shall strengthen him
97 1 him salvation, and his arm is holy
Prov 31 17 and hath strengthened her arm. She
Cant 8 6 as a seal upon thy arm, for love is
Wisd 5 17 with his holy arm he will defend them
18 and he will arm the creature for the
11 22 shall resist the strength of thy arm
16 16 scourged by the strength of thy arm
Eccu 21 24 like a bracelet upon his right arm
36 7 glorify thy hand and thy right arm
38 33 he fashioneth the clay with his arm
Isa 8 11 he hath taught me with a strong arm
9 20 shall eat the flesh of his own arm
17 5 his arm shall gather the ears of corn
30 30 and shall show the terror of his arm
33 2 be thou our arm in the morning, and our
40 10 and his arm shall rule: behold his reward
11 together the lambs with his arm, and
44 12 wrought with the strength of his arm
48 14 his arm shall be on the Chaldeans
51 5 and shall patiently wait for my arm
9 put on strength, O thou arm of the Lord
52 10 the Lord hath prepared his holy arm
53 1 to whom is arm of the Lord revealed
59 16 his own arm brought salvation to him
62 8 hand, and by the arm of his strength
63 5 my own arm hath saved for me, and my
12 by the arm of his majesty: that divided
Jer 17 5 and maketh flesh his arm, and whose heart
21 5 with a strong arm and in fury and in
48 25 is cut off, and his arm is broken
Bar 2 11 with a mighty arm, and hast made thee a
Eze 4 7 thy arm shall be stretched out: and
10 7 one cherub stretched out his arm from
17 9 and this without a strong arm, or many
22 6 hath employed his arm in thee to shed
30 21 I have broken the arm of Pharao king
22 I will break in pieces his strong arm
31 17 the arm of every one shall sit down
Dan 11 6 not obtain the strength of the arm
Zach 11 17 the sword upon his arm and upon his
17 his arm shall quite wither away, and
2 Ma 15 23 and dread of the greatness of thy arm
Luke 1 51 hath showed might in his arm: he hath
John 12 38 the arm of the Lord been revealed
Acts 13 17 with an high arm brought them out
stretched out arm Deut 4 34 and s. . . . and horrible
Deut 5 15 thence with a strong hand and a s. . . .
7 19 the s. . . . with which the Lord thy God
9 29 by thy great strength and in thy s. . . .
11 2 great doings and strong hand and s. . . .
26 8 out of Egypt with strong hand and s. . . .
3 K 8 42 thy mighty hand and thy s. . . . , so when
4 K 17 36 Egypt with great power and a s. . . .
2 Pa 6 32 and thy s. . . . , and adore in this place
Ps 135 12 with a mighty hand and with a s. . . .
Jer 27 5 by my s. . . . : and I have given it to whom
32 17 by thy s. . . . : no word shall be hard to
21 with a strong hand and a s. . . . , and
Eze 20 33 with a s. . . . , and with fury poured. 34
Armagedon Apoc 16 16 which in Hebrew is called Armagedon
armed Exod 13 18 children of Israel went up armed
Num 20 18 I will come out armed against thee
32 17 we ourselves will go armed and ready
29 children of Gad . . . all armed for war
30 if they will not pass armed with you
32 we will go armed before the Lord into
Deut 1 41 when you went ready armed unto the
Josu 1 14 but pass you over armed before your
4 12 armed before the children of Israel
6 7 go, and compass the city, armed
9 all the armed men went before, the rest
13 the armed men went before them, and the
Judg 1 19 had many chariots armed with scythes
4 13 his 900 chariots armed with scythes
1 K 17 38 armed him [David] with a coat of mail
2 K 12 31 drove over them chariots armed with
23 7 he must be armed with iron and with
2 Pa 17 17 and with him 200,000 armed with bow
Jdth 9 6 the Egyptians, when they pursued armed
15 2 were coming armed upon them, and fled
6 their chosen young men armed after them
Job 5 5 armed men shall take him by violence
15 26 raised up, and is armed with a fat neck
39 21 he goeth forward to met armed men
Prov 6 11 and poverty as a man armed. But if
24 34 a runner, and beggary as an armed man
Jer 51 3 that is armed with a coat of mail
Eze 23 24 they shall be armed against thee on
38 4 armed with spears and shields and
1 Ma 14 32 armed the valiant men of his nation
2 Ma 4 40 Lysimachus armed about 3,000 men, and
5 2 armed with spears, like bands of soldiers
26 through the city with armed men, he
8 9 him no fewer than 20,000 armed men of
13 2 and 300 chariots armed with hooks
15 11 he armed every one of them, not with
Luke 11 21 strong man armed keepeth his court
1 P 4 1 be you armed with the same thought
Armenia Gen 8 4 of the month, upon mountains of Armenia
Armenians 4 K 19 37 fled into the land of the A.
armies Josu 10 5 went up . . . they and their armies
1 K 17 26 defy the armies of the living God
45 the God of the armies of Israel, which
28 1 Philistines gathered together their a.
3 K 20 29 both sides set their armies in array
2 Pa 16 4 he sent the captains of his armies
Jdth 2 4 Holofernes the general of his armies
8 provisions sufficient for the armies
5 27 and his armies, men unarmed, and without
Ps 26 3 if armies in camp should stand together
43 10 wilt not go out with our armies. Thou
45 8 the Lord of armies is with us. 12
59 12 thou, O God, go out with our armies
107 12 thou, O God, go forth with our armies
Eccu 43 9 an instrument of the armies on high
Isa 34 2 his fury upon all their armies: he hath
Jer 3 19 inheritance of the a. of the Gentiles
34 21 hands of the armies of king of Babylon
Joel 2 11 his armies are exceeding great, for
1 Ma 3 42 that the a. approached to their borders
6 5 how the armies that were in the land of
33 the armies made themselves ready for
7 43 and the armies joined battle on the
9 13 earth shook at the noise of the armies
Mat 22 7 sending his armies, he destroyed those
Heb 11 34 put to flight the armies of foreigners
Apoc 19 14 and the armies that are in heaven
19 their a. gathered together to make war
Armon Amos 4 3 you shall be cast forth into Armon
Armoni 2 K 21 8 bore to Saul, A. and Miphiboseth
armor 1 K 14 1 young man that bore his armor. 6
1 K 17 39 girded his sword upon his armor, began
39 to try if he could walk in armor: for
54 but his armor he put in his tent. Now

31 9 and stripped him [Saul] of his armor
10 put his armor in the temple of Astaroth
3 K 10 25 garments and armor and spices. 2 Pa 9:24
22 30 take armor and go into the battle and
4 K 10 2 and horses and fenced cities and armor
1 Pa 10 10 his armor they dedicated in the temple
12 33 well appointed with armor for war
Cant 4 4 upon it, all the armor of valiant men
Wisd 5 18 his zeal will take a., and he will arm
1 Ma 1 36 and they stored up armor and victuals
3 3 girt his warlike armor about him in
4 6 only, who neither had armor nor swords
6 6 were grown strong by the armor and
41 the rattling of the armor, for the army
14 33 where the a. of the enemies was before
42 should appoint rulers over . . . the a.
15 7 and all the armor that had been made
2 Ma 3 25 upon him, seemed to have armor of gold
5 3 and glittering of golden armor and of
11 8 with golden armor, shaking a spear
15 21 and the divers preparations of armor
28 that Nicanor was slain in his armor
Luke 11 22 he will take away all his armor wherein
Rom 13 12 darkness, and put on the armor of light
2 C 6 7 by the armor of justice on the right
Eph 6 11 put you on the armor of God, that you
13 take unto you the armor of God, that you
armorbearer Judg 9 54 he called hastily to his a.
1 K 14 7 and his a. said to him: Do all that
12 spoke to Jonathan and to his a., and
12 Jonathan said to his a.: Let us go up
13 and his a. after him. And some fell
13 others his a. slew as he followed him
14 slaughter which Jonathan and his a. made
17 that Jonathan and his a. were not there
16 21 and made him his armorbearer. And Saul
17 7 and his armorbearer went before him
41 nigh against David, and his a. before
31 4 Saul said to his a.: Draw. 1 Pa 10:4
4 his armorbearer would not. 1 Pa 10:4
5 and when his a. saw this. 1 Pa 10:5
6 and his armorbearer and all his men
2 K 23 37 a. of Joab the son of Sarvia. 1 Pa 11:39
1 Ma 4 30 Jonathan the son of Saul and of his a.
armorbearers 2 K 18 15 ten young men, a. of Joab
armory 3 K 14 28 them back to the armory of the
2 Pa 9 16 the king put them in the armory, which
11 12 in every city he made an armory of
12 11 brought them back again to their armory
Isa 22 8 the armory of the house of the forest
Jer 50 25 the Lord hath opened his armory, and
armpit Prov 19 24 hideth his hand under his a. 25:15
arms Gen 27 3 take thy arms, thy quiver, and
Gen 49 24 the bands of his arms and his hands
Exod 38 25 of 603,550 men able to bear arms
Deut 33 27 underneath are the everlasting arms
Judg 7 11 where was the watch of men in arms
18 11 men furnished with arms for war, and
16 before door, appointed with their arms
1 K 8 12 and to make him arms and chariots
20 40 Jonathan gave his arms to the boy
2 K 8 7 and David took the arms of gold, which
22 35 maketh my arms like a bow of brass
4 K 11 10 the arms of king David, which were in
1 Pa 12 37 thousand, furnished with arms for war
2 Pa 9 18 two arms one on either side, and two
lions standing by the arms
23 7 every man with his arms; and if other
32 5 and made all sorts of arms and shields
27 of arms of all kinds, and of vessels
Jdth 7 5 taking their arms of war, they posted
14 2 let every man take his arms and rush
7 and every man took his arms, and they
16 23 all the arms of Holofernes, which the
Esth 15 11 holding her up in his arms, till she
Job 18 13 let the firstborn death consume his a.
22 9 arms of the fatherless thou hast broken
Ps 17 35 hast made my arms like a brazen bow
34 2 take hold of arms and shield: and rise
36 17 the arms of the wicked shall be broken
103 25 sea, which stretcheth wide its arms
Prov 22 5 arms and swords are in the way of the
Wisd 18 22 nor with force of arms, but with a
Eccu 7 33 and purify thyself with thy arms. Give
9 20 upon the arms of them that are grieved
Isa 49 22 shall bring thy sons in their arms
51 5 my arms shall judge the people: the
Jer 38 12 under thy arms, and upon the cords: and
47 3 at the noise of the marching of arms
Eze 13 20 I will tear them off from your arms
26 9 shall destroy thy towers with his arms
30 24 will strengthen arms of the king. 25
24 I will break the arms of Pharao, and
25 and the arms of Pharao shall fall
Dan 2 32 but the breast and the arms of silver
10 6 his arms and all downward even to the
11 15 arms of the south shall not withstand
22 arms of the fighter shall be overcome
31 arms shall stand on his part, and they
Osee 7 15 strengthened their arms: and they have
11 3 I carried them in my arms: and they
1 Ma 8 5 rest that had borne arms against them
26 or furnish them with wheat or arms or
28 either wheat or arms or money or ships
10 6 to make arms, and that he should be
21 army, and made a great number of arms
11 51 threw down their arms and made peace
12 27 to be in arms all night long ready to
13 29 by the arms ships carved, which might
2 Ma 5 11 mind, he took the city by force of arms
25 he commanded his men to take arms
8 27 they had gathered together their arms
31 carefully gathered together their arms
9 2 the multitude running together to arms
10 23 having good success in arms and in all
24 would take Judea by force of arms
27 taking their arms, they went forth
30 covered him on every side with their a.
11 7 Machabeus himself, first taking his a.
15 5 I command to take arms and to do the
21 not according to the power of their a.
Luke 2 28 [Simeon] took him into his arms, and
army Gen 21 22 Phicol general of his army. 33
Gen 39 1 chief captain of the army, an Egyptian
Exod 7 4 will bring forth my army and my people
12 17 I will bring forth your army out of the
41 all the army of the Lord went forth
14 4 in all his army: and the Egyptians shall
7 Egypt: and captains of the whole army
9 the whole army were in Phihahiroth
24 the Lord looking upon the Egyptian army
28 covered the chariots . . . of all the army
15 4 his army he hath cast into the sea
Num 1 16 and the chiefs of the army of Israel
52 man by his troops and bands and army
2 3 pitch his tents by bands of his army
8 all the army of fighting men of his
11 whole army of his fighting men. 13, 15,
19, 21, 23, 26, 28, 30; 26:11
32 of their army divided according to the
10 22 in whose army the prince was Elisama
25 in whose army the prince was Ahiezer
21 23 gathering an army, went forth to meet
31 14 angry with the chief officers of the a.
21 spoke to the men of the army that had
32 the spoil which the army had taken

48 the commanders of the army and the
Deut 20 1 numbers of enemy's army greater than
2 the priest shall stand before the army
5 in hearing of the army: What man is there
9 captains of the army shall hold their
25 18 slew the hindmost of the army, who sat
Josu 8 3 all the army of fighting men with him
10 with ancients in the front of the army
14 went out with all the army of the city
10 7 Josue went up from Galgal, and all the a.
21 and all the army returned to Josue in
24 [Josue] said to chiefs of the army
31 investing it with his army, besieged
11 7 Josue came, and all the army with him
Judg 4 2 had general of his army named Sisara
6 and lead an army to mount Thabor, and
7 Sisara the general of Jabin's army
13 and all his army from Haroseth of the
16 after the fleeing chariots and the a.
5 11 and army of the enemies was choked
14 out of Zabulon they that led the army
8 6 that we should give bread to thy army
10 were resting with all their army. For
9 29 gather together multitude of an army
34 Abimelech arose with all his army
35 Abimelech rose up and all his army
43 he took his army and divided it into
50 surrounded and besieged with his army
11 21 Lord delivered him with all his army
15 9 jawbone where their army was spread
20 10 to bring victuals for the army, that we
18 in our army the first to go to the
22 set their army in array in same place
30 drew up their army against Benjamin
33 set their army in battle array in the
39 killing thirty men of their army, and
21 5 came not up with the army of the Lord
8 were found not to have been in that a.
1 K 4 2 put their army in array against Israel
12 out of the army and came to Silo the
10 26 went with him a part of the army, whose
12 9 Sisara, captain of the army of Hasor
23 the army of the Philistines went out
14 48 gathering together an army, he defeated
50 name of captain of his army was Abner
17 2 they set the army in array to fight
20 to the army, which was going out to fight
36 dared to curse army of the living God
46 I will give the carcasses of the army
55 he said to Abner the captain of the army
26 5 the captain of the army, and Saul
28 5 Saul saw the army of the Philistines
19 Lord will also deliver army of Israel
29 6 and thy coming is with me in the army
2 K 2 8 general of Saul's army, took Isboseth
28 army stood still and did not pursue
3 23 Joab and all the army that was with him
5 24 to strike a. of Philistines. 1 Pa 14:15
8 16 Sarvia was over the army. 1 Pa 18:15
10 7 sent Joab and whole army of warriors
16 the river, and brought over their army
18 smote Sobach the captain of the army
12 31 and David returned with all the army
17 25 Amasa in Joab's stead over the army
18 7 were defeated there by David's army
19 13 chief captain of the army before me
20 23 Joab was over all the army of Israel
24 2 said to Joab the general of his army
4 of the captains of the army: and Joab
3 K 1 8 of David's army was not with Adonias
19 and Joab the general of the army: but
25 sons, and the captains of the army
2 5 did to the two captains of the army
32 of Ner, general of the army of Israel
32 of Jether, general of the army of Juda
35 over the army, and Sadoc the priest
4 4 of Joiada over the army: and Sadoc and
11 15 Joab the general of the army was gone
21 Joab the general of the army was dead
15 20 sent the captains of his army against
16 15 the army was besieging Gebbethon a city
20 19 and the rest of the army followed
24 remove all the kings from thy army
22 19 a. of heaven standing by him. 2 Pa 18:18
34 and carry me out of the army, for I am
36 herald proclaimed through all the army
4 K 3 9 and there was no water for the army
4 13 to the king or to general of the army
5 1 Naaman, general of army of the king
6 14 the strength of an army: and they came
15 and saw an army round about the city
24 gathered together all his army and went
7 6 of a very great army, and they said one
9 5 the captains of the army were sitting
11 15 centurions that were over the army
18 17 with a strong army to Jerusalem, and
24 14 all the valiant men of the army, to the
25 1 he and all his army against Jerusalem
5 the army of the Chaldees pursued after
8 Nabuzardan commander of the army. 11
10 army of the Chaldees, which was with
15 general of the army took away. 20
18 the general of the army took Seraias
19 and Sopher the captain of the army
20 Nabuzardan the general of the army. Jer 39:9; 41:10; 52:12
1 Pa 11 26 the most valiant men of the army, were
12 14 sons of Gad, captains of the army
21 and were made commanders in the army
22 a great number, like the army of God
23 chiefs of the army who came to David
14 16 defeated the army of the Philistines
18 9 had defeated all the army of Adarezer
19 8 [David] sent Joab and all the army
9 put their army in array before the gate
16 Sophach, general of the army of Adarezer
17 put his army in array against them
18 and Sophach the general of the army
20 1 Joab gathered together an army and the
25 1 David and the chief officers of the army
27 4 who commanded a part of the army of four
34 general of the king's army was Joab
28 1 the bravest of the army at Jerusalem
2 Pa 8 10 chief captains of king Solomon's army
13 3 Jeroboam put his army in array against
12 God is the leader in our army, and his
13 who perceived it not with his army
14 8 Asa had in his army of men that bore
9 came out against them with his army of
10 set his army in array for battle in the
13 and his army fought against them, and
16 7 army of the king of Syria escaped
17 14 in Juda captains of the army, Ednas the
20 21 to go before the army and with one voice
23 14 going out to . . . chiefs of the army
24 23 the army of Syria came up against him
25 7 let not the army of Israel go out with
8 consist in the strength of the army
10 then Amasias separated the army, that
13 that army which Amasias had sent back
26 13 and the whole army under them 307,500
14 for the whole army, shields and spears
28 9 to meet the army that came to Samaria
32 6 captains of the soldiers of the army
9 with all his army was besieging Lachis
21 the captains of the army of the king

	33	11	the army of the king of the Assyrians
		14	and he appointed captains of the army
Jdth	1	4	in the force of his army and in the
	2	11	he went forth he and all the army
	3	15	all the troops of his army to be united
	4	12	in his army and in his shields and in
	5	1	general of the army of the Assyrians
		9	army of them could not be numbered
		13	an innumerable army of the Egyptians
	7	1	gave orders to his army, to go up
		17	into the hand of the army of Holofernes
	10	13	without the loss of one man of his army
	13	19	Holofernes the general of the army
	14	11	were come, and all the chiefs of the a.
		17	the chiefs of the army of the Assyrians
	15	1	all the army heard that Holofernes was
Job	29	25	as a king with his army standing about
	39	25	captains, and the shouting of the army
Ps	32	16	the king is not saved by a great army
Cant	6	3	terrible as an army set in array. 9
Eccu	48	24	he overthrew the army of the Assyrians
Isa	36	2	to king Ezechias with a great army
	43	17	the army and the strong: they lay down
Jer	34	1	and all his army, and all the kingdoms
		7	the army of the king of Babylon fought
	35	11	from the face of army of the Chaldeans
		11	from the face of the army of Syria
	37	4	army of Pharao was come out of Egypt
		6	the army of Pharao, which is come forth
		9	if you should even beat all the army
		10	when the army of the Chaldeans was gone
		10	from Jerusalem, because of Pharao's a.
	38	3	hand of the army of the king of Babylon
	39	1	and all his army to Jerusalem and they
		5	army of the Chaldeans pursued. 52:8
	40	2	the general of the army taking Jeremias
		5	general of the army gave him victuals
		7	captains of army that were scattered
		13	captains of the army, that had been
	46	2	against the army of Pharao Nechao king
		22	they shall hasten with an army, and with
	51	3	not her young men, destroy all her army
	52	14	army of the Chaldeans that were with
		25	and a scribe, an officer of the army
Eze	1	24	like the noise of an army, and when they
	17	17	not with a great army, nor with much
	27	10	Libyans were thy soldiers in thy army
		11	the men of Arad were with thy army
	29	18	made his army to undergo hard service
		18	no reward given him nor his army for
		19	and it shall be wages for his army
	32	29	with their army are joined with them
		31	Pharao and all his army, saith the Lord
	37	10	upon their feet, an exceeding great a.
	38	4	I will bring thee forth and all thy a.
		15	a great company and a mighty army. And
		22	brimstone upon him and upon his army
Dan	2	14	Arioch the general of the king's army
	3	20	strongest men that were in his army
	11	7	he shall come with an army, and shall
		13	he shall come in haste with a great a.
		25	against king of the south with great a.
		26	his army shall be overthrown: and many
Joel	2	11	his voice before the face of his army
Abdi		11	strangers carried away his army captive
		13	shalt not be sent out against his army
Nah	2	3	the men of the army are clad in scarlet
Zach	4	6	not with an army nor by might, but by
1 Ma	1	4	a very strong army: and his heart was
	2	31	to the army that was in Jerusalem in
		44	they gathered an army and slew the
		66	let him be the leader of your army
	3	10	great army from Samaria, to make war
		13	Seron captain of the army of Syria
		17	when they saw the army coming to meet
		19	is not in the multitude of the army
		27	his kingdom, an exceeding strong army
		34	he delivered to him half the army
		35	he should send an army against him
		37	the king took half of the army that
	4	4	the army was dispersed from the camp
		9	when Pharao pursued them with great army
		10	will destroy this army before our face
		16	Judas returned again with his army
		18	Gorgias and his army are near us in the
		21	Judas and his army in the plain ready
		30	they saw that the army was strong
		31	shut up this army in the hands of thy
		34	fell of the army of Lysias 5,000 men
		37	all the army assembled together and
	5	27	to bring their army on the morrow near
		28	Judas and his army suddenly turned
		37	Timotheus gathered another army, and
		38	Judas sent men to view the army: and
		38	unto him an army exceeding great: and
		40	Timotheus said to captains of his army
		40	when Judas and his army come near the
		45	army exceeding great, to come into the
		50	the men of the army drew near, and he
		58	gave charge to them that were in his a.
	6	28	the captains of his army, and them that
		30	number of his army was 100,000 footmen
		38	with trumpets to stir up the army
		40	part of king's army was distinguished
		41	the army was exceeding great and strong
		42	Judas and his army drew near for battle
		42	there fell of the king's army 600 men
		47	the fierceness of his army, turned
		48	the king's army went up against them
		48	the king's army pitched their tents
		51	turned his army against the sanctuary
		56	with the army that went with him, and
		57	to the king and to captains of the a.
	7	2	that the army seized upon Antiochus
		4	so the army slew them. And Demetrius
		10	with great army into the land of Juda
		11	that they were come with a great army
		27	came to Jerusalem with a great army
		32	there fell of Nicanor's army almost
		35	unless Judas and his army be delivered
		38	be avenged of this man and his army
		39	and an army of Syria joined him. But
		42	destroy this army in our sight today
		43	the army of Nicanor was defeated, and
		44	when his army saw that Nicanor was
	8	6	a very great army, was routed by
	9	1	that Nicanor and his army were fallen
		1	the right wing of his army with them
		3	they brought the army to Jerusalem
		6	they saw the multitude of the army
		7	Judas saw that his army slipped away
		11	the army removed out of the camp, and
		11	and the archers went before the army
		14	stronger part of the army of Bacchides
		34	he came himself with all his army
		60	he arose to come with a great army
	10	2	gathered together an exceeding great a.
		6	to gather together an army. 8
		21	he gathered together an army, and made
		36	let there be enrolled in the king's a.
		48	Alexander gathered together a great a.
		49	the army of Demetrius fled away, and
		53	he and his army have been destroyed
		69	he gathered together a great army
		72	and so great an army in the plain
		77	took 3,000 horsemen and a great army

80 they surrounded his army and cast
82 then Simon drew forth his army, and
86 Jonathan removed his army from thence
11 1 king of Egypt gathered together an army
15 king Ptolemee brought forth his army
38 except the foreign army which he had
39 seeing that all the army murmured
43 me: for all my army is gone from me
63 with a great army, purposing to remove
67 Jonathan and his army encamped by the
68 the army of the strangers met him in
70 of Calphi, chief captain of the army
12 24 with a greater army than before to
42 that Jonathan came with a great army
45 the army and all that have any charge
46 sent away his army, and they departed
49 sent an army and horsemen into Galilee
13 1 gathering together a very great army
11 with him a new army into Joppe, and he
12 removed from Ptolemais with a great a.
20 Simon and his army marched to every
14 1 king Demetrius assembled his army, and
3 and defeated the army of Demetrius
15 3 I have chosen a great army and have
38 gave him army of footmen and horsemen
39 to march with his army towards Judea
41 he placed there horsemen and an army
16 5 very great army of footmen and horsemen
8 Cendebeus and his army were put to
18 should send him an army to aid him
2 Ma 1 13 and with him a very great army, he
4 22 returned with his army into Phenicia
5 24 Apollonius with an army of two and
8 22 captains over each division of his a.
24 disabled greater part of Nicanor's a.
35 unhappy by the destruction of his army
9 9 of his smell was noisome to the army
23 led an army into the higher countries
10 11 Lysias, general of army of Phenicia
12 27 [Judas] removed his army to Ephron
38 Judas having gathered together his army
13 13 before the king should bring his army
14 he placed his army about Modin. And
19 marched with his army to Bethsura
21 but Rhodocus, one of the Jews' army
15 20 the army was set in array, the beasts
22 didst kill 185,000 of a. of Sennacherib
Luke 2 13 a multitude of the heavenly army
21 20 Jerusalem compassed about with an army
23 11 Herod with his army set him at nought
Acts 23 27 by them, I rescued, coming in with an a.
Apoc 9 16 the number of the army of horsemen
19 19 that sat upon the horse, and with his a.
Arnan 1 Pa 3 21 his son was Arnan, of whom was
Arnon Num 21 13 and encamped over against Arnon
Num 21 13 Arnon is the border of Moab, dividing
14 so will he do in the streams of Arnon
24 his land from the Arnon unto the Jeboc
26 of his dominions, as far as the Arnon
28 inhabitants of the high places of the A.
22 36 situate in the uttermost borders of A.
Deut 2 24 arise ye, and pass the torrent Arnon
36 Aroer which is upon the bank of the torrent Arnon. 3:12; Josu 12:2; 13:9, 16
3 8 torrent A. unto mount Hermon. Josu 12:1
16 land of Galaad as far as torrent Arnon
Judg 11 13 from the confines of the Arnon unto
18 camped on the other side of the Arnon
22 from the Arnon to the Jaboc, and from
4 K 10 33 Aroer, which is upon the torrent Arnon
Isa 16 2 daughters of Moab be in passage of A.
Jer 48 20 ye it in Arnon, that Moab is wasted
Arod Num 26 17 Arod, of him is the family of the
1 Pa 8 15 and Zabadia and Arod and Heder and
Arodi Gen 46 16 Esebon and Heri and Arodi and Areli
Arodites Num 26 17 of him is the family of the A.
Aroer Num 32 34 sons of Gad built . . . Aroer
Deut 2 36 cities which we took: from Aroer, which
3 12 the land at that time from Aroer, which
4 48 from Aroer, which is situate upon the
Josu 12 2 had dominion from Aroer, which is
13 9 from Aroer, which is upon the bank
16 their border was from Aroer, which is
25 Aroer which is over against Rabba
Judg 11 26 in Aroer and its villages, and in all
33 smote them from Aroer till you come
1 K 30 28 and to them that were in Aroer and
2 K 24 5 they came to Aroer to the right side
4 K 10 33 from Aroer, which is upon the torrent
1 Pa 5 8 Joel, dwelt in Aroer as far as Nebo
Isa 17 2 cities of Aroer shall be left for
Jer 48 19 and look out, O habitation of Aroer
aromatical 4 K 20 13 the house of his a. spices
2 Pa 2 4 and to perfume with aromatical spices
Cant 3 6 a pillar of smoke of aromatical spices
4 10 of thy ointments above all a. spices
16 let the aromatical spices thereof flow
5 1 gathered my myrrh with my a. spices
13 his cheeks are as beds of a. spices
6 1 to the bed of aromatical spices, to
8 14 hart upon the mountains of a. spices
Eccu 24 20 aromatical balm: I yielded a sweet odor
Isa 39 2 storehouses of his aromatical spices
Arorite 2 K 23 33 Aiam the son of Sarar the Arorite
1 Pa 11 27 Sammoth an Arorite, Helles a Phalonite
44 Jehiel the son of Hotham an Arorite
arose Gen 13 7 arose strife between the herdsmen
Gen 15 17 there arose a dark mist, and there
21 33 arose and returned to the land of the
24 54 in the morning the servant arose and
31 55 Laban a. in the night and kissed his
37 7 my sheaf arose as it were and stood
38 19 she arose and went her way: and putting
44 3 when the morning arose, they were sent
Exod 1 8 there arose a new king over Egypt
2 7 Moses arose and defending the maids
12 30 Pharao arose in the night, and all his
30 there arose a great cry in Egypt: for
19 18 the smoke arose from it as out of a
Num 11 1 there arose a murmuring of the people
16 25 Moses arose and went to Dathan and
42 when there arose a sedition, and the
22 21 Balaam arose in the morning, and
Deut 34 10 there arose no more a prophet in Israel
Josu 8 3 Josue arose and all the army of the
24 9 Moab arose and fought against Israel
Judg 2 10 there arose others that knew not the
4 9 Debbora therefore arose and went with
5 7 until Debbora arose, a mother arose
6 21 there arose a fire from the rock, and
9 34 Abimelech therefore arose with all his
43 [Abimelech] arose and set upon them
10 1 there arose a ruler in Israel, Thola
12 1 there arose a sedition in Ephraim
19 9 the young men arose to set forward
27 the man arose and opened the door
20 18 they a. and came to the house of God
37 there were in ambush arose on a sudden
Ruth 1 6 she arose to go from the land of Moab
2 15 she arose from thence to glean the
3 14 she arose before men could know one
1 K 1 9 so Anna arose after she had eaten and
3 6 Samuel arose and went to Heli and said
8 [Samuel] arose up and went to Heli
5 3 when the Azotians a. early the next
9 26 Saul arose; and they went out both

13 15 Samuel arose and went up from Galgal
14 19 there arose a great uproar in the camp
17 20 David therefore arose in the morning
48 when the Philistine a. and was coming
20 25 Jonathan arose, and Abner sat by Saul's
43 David arose and departed: and Jonathan
21 10 David arose and fled that day from the
23 13 David and his men arose and departing
16 arose and went to David into the wood
24 they a. and went to Ziph before Saul
24 5 David a. and secretly cut off the hem
25 41 [Abigail] arose and bowed herself
42 Abigail arose and made haste and got
26 2 and Saul arose and went down to the
5 David arose secretly and came to the
27 2 David arose and went away, both he and
28 23 he arose from the ground and sat upon
29 11 David and his men arose in the night
31 12 most valiant men arose and walked all
2 K 2 15 arose and went over 12 in number of
6 2 and David arose and went, with all the
11 2 David arose from his bed before noon
12 20 David a. from the ground and washed and
13 39 all the king's sons arose and got up
14 23 Joab arose and went to Gessur and
31 Joab arose and came to Absalom to his
15 9 he [Absalom] arose and went to Hebron
17 22 David arose, and all the people that
23 arose and went home to his house and to
19 8 the king arose and sat in the gate
24 11 David arose in the morning, and the
3 K 1 49 they all arose and every man went his
50 Adonias fearing Solomon, arose and went
2 19 the king arose to meet her [Bethsabee]
40 and Semei arose and saddles his ass and
11 18 they arose out of Madian and came into
40 but he [Jeroboam] arose and fled into
14 17 the wife of Jeroboam arose and departed
17 10 he [Elias] arose and went to Sarephta
18 44 a little cloud arose out of the sea
19 8 he arose and ate and drank and walked
21 16 he [Achab] arose and went down to the
4 K 1 15 [Elias] arose therefore and went down
4 30 he arose therefore and followed her
7 5 they arose in the evening to go to the
7 they arose and fled away in the dark
12 he arose in the night and said to his
8 2 she arose and did according to the word
21 he [Joram] arose in the night and
9 6 he arose and went into the chamber
10 12 he [Jehu] arose and went to Samaria
11 1 arose and slew all the royal seed
12 20 his servants arose and conspired among
19 35 when he arose early in the morning
1 Pa 10 12 all the valiant men of them arose
20 4 after this there arose a war at Gazer
2 Pa 29 12 the Levites arose, Mahath the son of
30 14 they arose and destroyed the altars
36 16 until the wrath of the Lord a. against
1 Es 2 63 till there arose a priest learned and
10 5 Esdras arose and made the chiefs of the
2 Es 2 12 I arose in the night, and I and some
3 1 Eliasib the high priest arose and his
Tob 8 6 so they both arose and prayed earnestly
Jdth 12 15 and she arose and dressed herself out
Job 30 12 my calamities forthwith arose: they
Ps 75 10 when God arose in judgment, to save all
106 25 word, and there arose a storm of wind
Cant 5 5 I arose up to open to my beloved
Eccu 47 1 Nathan the prophet arose in the days
14 after him arose up a wise son and
Isa 37 36 they arose in the morning, and behold
Jer 41 2 arose, and the ten men that were with
Dan 8 22 broken, there arose up four for it
13 19 the two elders arose and ran to her
14 15 the king arose early in the morning
38 Daniel arose and ate. And the angel
Jon 3 3 and Jonas arose and went to Ninive
4 7 when the morning arose on the following
Nah 3 17 the sun arose, and they flew away
1 Ma 2 1 in those days arose Mathathias the son
4 52 they arose before the morning on the
7 10 they arose and came with a great army
9 4 they arose and went to Berea with twenty
60 he arose to come with a great army
16 5 they arose in the morning and went
2 Ma 14 45 being inflamed in mind he arose: and
Mat 2 14 who arose and took the child. 21
8 15 and she arose and ministered to them
24 a great tempest arose in the sea, so
9 7 he a. and went into his house. Luke 5:28
9 he arose up and followed him. Mark 2:14
25 the hand. And the maid arose. And the
25 7 virgins arose and trimmed their lamps
27 52 bodies of the saints that had slept a.
Mark 2 12 he arose; and taking up his bed, went
4 37 there arose a great storm of wind
9 26 Jesus lifted him up; and he arose
Luke 8 55 and she arose immediately. And he bid
John 3 25 a. a question between some of John's
6 18 sea arose by reason of a great wind
7 43 a. a dissension. Acts 15:39; 23:7, 10
Acts 6 1 arose a murmuring of the Greeks against
9 arose some of that which is called the
7 18 till another king arose in Egypt, who
9 8 Saul arose from the ground; and when
34 bed. And immediately he [Eneas] arose
10 23 he [Peter] arose and went with them
41 after he arose again from the dead
11 19 persecution that a. on occasion of
15 5 arose some of the sect of Pharisees
19 23 there arose no small disturbance about
23 9 and there arose a great cry. And some
27 14 arose against it a tempestuous wind
1 C 15 12 that he arose again from the dead
Apoc 9 2 and the smoke of the pit arose, as the
Arphad 4 K 18 34 god of Emath and of A. Isa 36:19
4 K 19 13 the king of Arphad, and the. Isa 37:13
Isa 10 9 and Emath as Arphad? Is not Samaria
Jer 49 23 Emath is confounded and Arphad: for
Arphasachites 1 Es 5 6 the A., who dwelt beyond
Arphaxad Gen 10 22 sons of Sem . . . A. 1 Pa 1:17
Gen 10 24 but Arphaxad begot Sale of. 1 Pa 1:18
11 10 when he begot Arphaxad, two years after
11 Sem lived after he begot Arphaxad
12 A. lived 35 years and begot Sale
13 and Arphaxad lived after he begot Sale
1 Pa 1 24 Sem, Arphaxad, Sale, Heber, Phaleg
Jdth 1 1 A. king of the Medes had brought many
5 fought against A. and overcame him
Luke 3 36 Cainan, who was of Arphaxad, who was of
array Gen 14 8 against them in battle array in the
Josu 8 13 rest of the army went in battle array
1 K 4 2 [Philistines] put their army in array
17 21 Israel had put themselves in array
2 K 10 9 put them in array against the Syrians
1 Pa 12 33 and stood in array well appointed
19 9 put their army in array before the
17 [David] put his army in array against
2 Pa 13 3 Jeroboam put his army in array against
Jer 43 12 shall array himself with the land
set in array Josu 8 14 set it in battle array
Judg 20 22 Israel . . . set their army in array
33 set their army in battle array in the
1 K 17 2 they set the army in array to fight
2 K 10 8 came out and set their men in array

10 Abisai . . . who set them in array
17 Syrians set themselves in array against
3 K 20 29 both sides set their armies in array
2 Pa 14 10 Asa . . . set his army in array for
Cant 6 3 terrible as an army set in array. 9
2 Ma 15 20 the army was set in array, the beasts
arrayed Mat 6 29 a. as one of these. Luke 12:27
Acts 12 21 Herod being arrayed in kingly apparel
arrive Tob 5 26 our son will arrive thither safe
arrived Tob 11 18 all the family arrived safe
Acts 20 15 day we arrived at Samos; and the day
arrogance Prov 8 13 I hate arrogance and pride
arrogancies James 4 16 you rejoice in your a.
arrogancy Esth 16 12 was so far puffed with a.
Isa 13 11 will bring down the a. of the mighty
16 6 his pride and his arrogancy and his
Jer 48 29 his arrogancy and his pride and the
49 16 thy arrogancy hath deceived thee, and
2 Ma 6 29 thought were uttered out of arrogancy
arrogant Job 40 6 behold every a. man and humble
Prov 21 24 proud and the a. is called ignorant
Isa 2 12 and upon every one that is arrogant
arrogantly Soph 1 9 every one that entereth a.
arrow 1 K 20 36 show another a. beyond the boy
1 K 20 37 came to the place of the arrow which
37 arrow is there further beyond thee
2 K 1 22 arrow of Jonathan never turned back
4 K 9 24 the arrow went out through his heart
13 17 Eliseus said: Shoot an arrow. And he
17 the arrow of the Lord's deliverance
17 arrow of the deliverance from Syria
18 strike with an arrow upon the ground
19 32 nor shoot an arrow into it. Isa 37:33
2 Pa 18 33 shot an arrow at a venture, and struck
Jdth 5 16 they went in without bow and arrow
Job 34 6 my arrow is violent without any sin
Ps 90 6 of the arrow that flieth in the day
Prov 7 23 till the arrow pierce his liver: as if
25 18 like a dart and a sword and a sharp a.
Wisd 5 12 as when an arrow is shot at a mark
Eccu 19 12 arrow that sticketh in a man's thigh
26 15 open her quiver against every arrow
Isa 49 2 and hath made me as a chosen arrow
Jer 6 23 shall lay hold on arrow and shield
9 8 their tongue is a piercing arrow, it
arrows Exod 19 13 shall be shot through with a.
Num 24 8 their bones, and pierce them with a.
Deut 32 23 and will spend my arrows among them
42 I will make my a. drunk with blood
1 K 20 20 I will shoot three arrows near it
21 he go and fetch me the arrows. 36
22 the arrows are on this side of thee
22 behold the arrows are beyond thee
38 Jonathan's boy gathered up the arrows
2 K 11 24 and the archers shot their arrows
22 15 he shot arrows and scattered them
4 K 13 15 bring a bow and arrows. And when he
15 had brought him a bow and arrows, he
18 and he said: Take the arrows. And when
1 Pa 10 3 and wounded him [Saul] with arrows
12 2 shooting arrows: of the brethren of Saul
2 Pa 26 15 to shoot arrows and great stones: and
Jdth 7 8 nor in their arrows, but the mountains
9 9 in their arrows, and glory in their
Job 6 4 the arrows of the Lord are in me, the
Ps 7 14 he hath made ready his arrows for them
10 3 they have prepared their arrows in the
17 15 and he sent forth his arrows, and he
37 3 thy arrows are fastened in me: and thy
44 6 thy arrows are sharp: under thee shall
56 5 whose teeth are weapons and arrows
63 8 the arrows of children are their wounds
76 18 for thy arrows pass: the voice of thy
119 4 the sharp arrows of the mighty, with
126 4 as arrows in the hand of the mighty
143 6 shoot out thy arrows, and thou shalt
Prov 26 18 as he is guilty that shooteth arrows
Isa 5 28 their arrows are sharp, and all their
7 24 with arrows and with bows they shall go
13 18 with their arrows they shall kill the
Jer 46 9 the Lydians that take and shoot arrows
50 9 their arrows, like those of a mighty
14 fight against her, spare not arrows
51 11 sharpen the arrows, fill the quivers
Lam 3 12 and set me as a mark for his arrows
Eze 5 16 upon them the grievous arrows of famine
21 21 seeking divination, shuffling arrows
39 3 I will cause thy arrows to fall out of
9 spears, the bows and the arrows, and
Haba 3 11 in the light of thy arrows, they shall
1 Ma 6 51 and pieces to shoot arrows, and slings
Arsa 3 K 16 9 drunk in the house of Arsa the
Arsaces 1 Ma 14 2 A. the king of Persia and Media
1 Ma 14 3 took him and brought him to Arsaces
15 22 and to Ariarathes and to Arsaces and
art Gen 40 17 that are made by the art of baking
Exod 30 25 compounded after the art of the
36 8 work, and the art of embroidering: the
39 6 graven by the art of a lapidary, with
3 K 7 17 wreathed together with wonderful art
2 Pa 15 14 were made by the art of the perfumers
Jdth 5 27 and without skill in the art of war
14 9 endeavoring by art to break his rest
Wisd 13 10 silver, the inventions of art, and the
11 with his art diligently formeth a
13 by the skill of his art fashioneth it
14 4 though a man went to sea without art
19 all his art to make the resemblance
17 7 delusions of their magic art were put
Eccu 38 35 and every one is wise in his own art
49 1 smell made by the art of a perfumer
Mat 11 3 art thou he that art to. Luke 7:19, 20
Acts 17 29 the graving of art, and device of man
Apoc 11 17 who art and who wast and who. 16:5
17 and who art to come: because thou hast
18 22 no craftsman of any art whatsoever
Artaxerxes 1 Es 4 7 in the days of Artaxerxes
1 Es 4 7 wrote to A. the king of the Persians
11 to Artaxerxes the king, thy servants
23 copy of the edict of king Artaxerxes
6 14 and Artaxerxes king of the Persians
7 1 in the reign of Artaxerxes king of the
7 in the seventh year of Artaxerxes
11 which king Artaxerxes gave to Esdras
12 Artaxerxes king of kings to Esdras
21 I Artaxerxes the king have ordered
8 1 from Babylon in the reign of A. the
2 Es 2 1 in the twentieth year of Artaxerxes
5 14 of Artaxerxes the king for twelve years
13 6 two and thirtieth year of A. king of
Esth 11 2 in the second year of the reign of A.
12 2 to lay violent hands on king Artaxerxes
13 1 Artaxerxes the great king who reigneth
16 1 great king Artaxerxes, from India to
Artemas Titus 5 12 I shall send to thee Artemas
artful Wisd 8 6 who is a more artful worker than
artfully Judg 20 32 they a. feigning a flight
3 K 6 18 the joints thereof artfully wrought
articles 1 Ma 8 29 according to these a. did the
1 Ma 8 30 shall have a mind to add to these a.
2 Ma 14 28 that he should make void the articles
artificer Gen 4 22 who was a hammerer and a. in
Exod 38 23 was an excellent artificer in wood
3 K 7 14 artificer in brass and full of wisdom
4 K 24 14 every a. and smith: and none were left
Wisd 14 18 the singular diligence also of the a.

Jer 10 9 the work of the artificer, and of the
artificers Deut 27 15 the work of the hands of a.
4 K 24 16 artificers and the smiths a thousand
1 Pa 4 14 Joab father of Valley of a., for a. were
29 5 to be made by hands of the artificers
2 Pa 2 7 with the a. which I have with me in
14 with thy a. and with the a. of my lord
24 12 hired with it stonecutters and a.
34 11 they gave it to the artificers and to
17 it is given to the overseers of the a.
Eccu 9 24 praised for the hand of the artificers
Jer 10 9 all these things are the work of a.
Bar 6 46 artificers themselves that make them
artificial 2 P 1 16 by following artificial fables
artificially Exod 28 28 and the joining a. wrought
Exod 35 33 whatsoever can be devised artificially
36 1 to know how to work artificially, made
artist Wisd 13 11 if an a., a carpenter, hath cut
Eccu 45 13 of twisted scarlet the work of an a.
Jer 10 14 every a. is confounded in his graven
arts 2 Pa 33 6 gave himself up to magic arts
Acts 19 19 them who had followed curious arts
Aruboth 3 K 4 10 Benhesed in Aruboth: his was
Arum 1 Pa 4 8 kindred of Aharehel the son of Arum
Asa 3 K 15 8 Asa his son reigned in his. 2 Pa 14:1
3 K 15 9 of Israel reigned Asa king of Juda
11 and Asa did that which was right in the
14 heart of Asa was perfect with. 2 Pa 15:17
16 was war between Asa and Baasa. 32
17 of the side of Asa king of Juda. Then
18 then Asa took all the silver and gold
23 the rest of all the acts of Asa, and all
25 reigned over Israel second year of Asa
28 in the third year of Asa king of. 33
16 8 in the sixth and twentieth year of Asa
10 seven and twentieth year of Asa. 15
23 in the one and thirtieth year of Asa
29 the eighth and thirtieth year of Asa
22 41 Josaphat the son of Asa began to reign
43 walked in all the way of Asa his father
47 effeminate, who remained in days of Asa
1 Pa 3 10 whose son Abia begot Asa. And his son
9 16 Asa the son of Elcana, who dwelt in the
2 Pa 14 2 and Asa did that which was good and
8 Asa had in his army of men that bore
10 Asa went out to meet him [Zara] and
12 terrified the Ethiopians before Asa
13 Asa and the people that were with him
15 2 he [Azarias] went out to meet Asa
2 hear ye me, Asa, and all Juda and
8 and when Asa had heard the words, and
10 in fifteenth year of the reign of Asa
19 and thirtieth year of kingdom of Asa
16 1 out or come in of the kingdom of Asa
2 then Asa brought out silver and gold
7 Hanani the prophet came to Asa king of
10 and Asa was angry with the seer, and
11 but the works of Asa the first and last
12 and Asa fell sick in the nine and
17 2 Ephraim, which Asa his father had taken
20 32 walked in the way of his father Asa
21 12 nor in the ways of Asa king of Juda
Mat 1 7 Abia begot Asa. Asa begot Josaphat
king Asa 3 K 15 20 Benadad hearkening to king A.
3 K 15 22 but king Asa sent work into all Juda
22 and with them king Asa built Gabaa of
2 Pa 15 16 moreover Maacha the mother of king Asa
16 6 then king Asa took all Juda, and they
Jer 41 9 is the same that king Asa made, for fear
Asaa 2 Pa 34 20 and Asaa the king's servant, saying
Asael 2 K 2 18 there, Joab and Abisai and Asael
2 K 2 18 Asael was a most swift runner, like one
19 Asael pursued after Abner, and turned
20 looked behind him and said: Art thou A.
21 Asael would not leave off following him
22 Abner said to Asael: Go off and do not
23 place where Asael fell down and died
30 of David's servants 19 men, beside Asael
32 they took Asael and buried him in the
3 27 in revenge of the blood of Asael his
30 because he had killed their brother A.
23 24 Asael the brother of Joab was one of the
2 Pa 17 8 Asael and Semiramoth and Jonathan and
31 13 and Nahath and Asael and Jerimoth and
Asahel 1 Pa 11 26 valiant men of the army were A.
1 Pa 27 7 for the fourth month, was Asahel the
Asaia 4 K 22 12 and A. the king's servant, saying
4 K 22 14 and Saphan and Asaia went to Hold
1 Pa 4 36 Asaia and Adiel and Ismiel and Benaia
6 30 Haggia his son, Asaia his son. These
9 5 of Siloni: Asaia the firstborn, and his
15 6 of the sons of Merari, Asaia the chief
11 the Levites, Uriel, Asaia, Joel, Semeia
Asalelphuni 1 Pa 4 3 name of their sister was A.
Asan Josu 15 42 Labana and Ether and Asan, Jephtha
Josu 19 7 Ain and Remmon and Athar and Asan
1 K 30 30 and that were in the lake Asan, and
1 Pa 4 32 Remmon and Thochen and Asan, five cities
6 59 Asan also and Bethsames, with their
Asana 1 Pa 9 7 of Oduia the son of Asana: and
Asaph 4 K 18 18 Joahe the son of A. 37; Isa 36:3, 22
1 Pa 6 39 his brother Asaph, who stood on his
39 Asaph the son of Barachias the son of
9 15 the son of Zechri the son of Asaph
15 17 and of his brethren Asaph the son of
19 the singers, Heman, Asaph, and Ethan
16 5 Asaph, the chief, and next after him
5 and Asaph sounded with cymbals: but
7 made Asaph the chief to give praise
37 Asaph and his brethren to minister in
25 2 under the hand of Asaph prophesying
6 to wit, Asaph and Idithun and Heman
9 came forth to Joseph, who was of Asaph
2 Pa 5 12 both they that were under Asaph and
29 30 with words of David and Asaph the seer
35 15 Asaph stood in their order, according
1 Es 2 41 singing men: the children of Asaph, 128
2 Es 2 8 Asaph the keeper of the king's forest
7 45 children of Asaph, 148. The porters
11 17 the son of Zebedei the son of Asaph
12 24 the son of Zechur the son of Asaph
45 in the days of David and Asaph from
Ps 49 1 a psalm for Asaph. 72:1; 75:1; 78:1; 80:1; 81:1; 82:1
73 1 understanding for Asaph. 79:1
74 1 a psalm of a canticle for Asaph. We will
76 1 for Idithun, a psalm of Asaph. I cried
77 1 understanding for Asaph. Attend, O my
sons of Asaph 1 Pa 25 1 for ministry of s. . . .
1 Pa 25 2 of the s. . . . : Zacchur and Joseph and
2 Nathania and Asarela, sons of Asaph
26 1 the son of Core of the sons of Asaph
2 Pa 20 14 son of Mathanias, Levite of the s. . . .
29 13 of the sons of Asaph, Zacharias and
35 15 the singers the s. . . . stood in their
1 Es 3 10 Levites the sons of Asaph with cymbals
2 Es 11 22 of the sons of Asaph, were the singing
Asaramel 1 Ma 14 27 Simon the high priest at A.
Asarela 1 Pa 25 2 Asarela, sons of Asaph: under
Asarhaddon 4 K 19 37 A. his son reigned. Isa 37:38
Asarmoth Gen 10 26 and Saleph and A. 1 Pa 1:20
Asasonthamar Gen 14 7 Amorrhean that dwelt in A.
2 Pa 20 2 behold they are in A., which is Engaddi
Asbel Gen 46 21 A. and Gera and Naaman. Num 26:38
1 Pa 8 1 Bale his firstborn, Asbel the second
Asbelites Num 26 38 whom is the family of the A.

Ascalon Judg 1 18 and A. and Accaron with their
Judg 14 19 he went down to Ascalon and slew there
1 K 6 17 for Ascalon one, for Geth one, for
2 K 1 20 publish it not in streets of Ascalon
Jer 25 20 Ascalon and Gaza and Accaron and the
47 5 Ascalon hath held her peace with the
7 hath given it a charge against Ascalon
Amos 1 8 him that holdeth the scepter from A.
Soph 2 4 Ascalon shall be a desert, they shall
7 in houses of Ascalon they shall rest
Zach 9 5 Ascalon shall see and shall fear, and
5 Ascalon shall not be inhabited. And the
1 Ma 10 86 camped against Ascalon: and they went
11 60 he came to Ascalon, and they met him
12 33 and came as far as Ascalon, and the
Ascalonites Josu 13 3 the A., the Gethites, and
ascend Ps 23 3 who shall a. into the mountain of
Ps 83 6 he hath disposed to ascend by steps
103 8 the mountains a. and the plains descend
138 8 if I ascend into heaven, thou art there
Ecce 3 21 a. upward, and if the spirit of the
10 4 ascend upon thee, leave not thy place
Isa 14 13 in thy heart: I will ascend into heaven
14 I will ascend above the height of the
19 1 Lord will ascend upon a swift cloud
Joel 2 20 and his stench shall ascend and his
John 6 63 ascend up where he was before? It is
20 17 say to them: I ascend to my Father
Rom 10 6 who shall ascend into heaven? That is
Apoc 14 11 smoke of their torments shall ascend
ascended Judg 13 20 a. also in the flame. And
Judg 20 40 and that the flames ascended on high
Ps 17 11 he a. upon the cherubim and he flew
46 6 God is ascended with jubilee and the
67 19 thou hast a. on high, thou hast led
Prov 30 4 who hath ascended up into heaven, and
John 3 13 no man hath ascended into heaven but
20 17 for I am not yet ascended to my Father
Acts 2 34 David ascended not into heaven; but he
10 4 thy prayers and thy alms are ascended
Eph 4 9 now that he ascended, what is it, but
10 that ascended above all the heavens
Apoc 8 4 ascended up before God from the hand of
ascendeth Josu 15 3 and a. into Cadesbarne, and
Josu 19 12 Dabereth, and ascendeth towards Japhie
Ps 67 5 for him who ascendeth upon the west
73 23 the pride of them that hate thee a.
Apoc 11 7 beast that a. out of the abyss, shall
19 3 her smoke ascendeth forever and ever
ascending Gen 28 12 angels of God ascending and
Josu 15 8 ascending to the top of the mountain
1 K 28 13 I saw gods ascending out of the earth
Isa 9 18 be wrapped up in smoke a. on high
John 1 51 angels of God ascending and descending
Eph 4 8 a. on high, he led captivity captive
Apoc 7 2 angel ascending from rising of the sun
Ascenez Gen 10 3 sons of Gomer: Ascenez. 1 Pa 1:6
ascension Amos 9 6 that buildeth his a. in heaven
ascent Num 34 4 the ascent of the Scorpion. Josu 15:3; Judg 1:36
Josu 10 10 the way of the ascent to Beth-horon
15 7 opposite to the ascent of Adommim
18 18 over against the ascent of Adommim
1 K 9 11 when they went up the a. to the city
2 K 15 30 David went up by the a. of mount Olivet
1 Pa 26 16 which leadeth to the way of the ascent
2 Pa 20 16 will come up by the ascent named Sis
Isa 15 5 by the ascent of Luith they shall go up
Jer 48 5 by the a. of Luith shall the mourner
ascents 1 K 14 4 there were between the ascents
Jdth 4 5 should take possession of the ascents
ascribed 2 K 12 28 the victory be a. to my name
Asebaim 1 Es 2 57 of Phochereth, which were of A.
Asedoth Josu 10 40 of Asedoth, with their kings
Josu 12 3 side that lieth under Asedoth, Phasga
8 in Asedoth and in the wilderness and
13 20 and Asedoth, Phasga, and Bethiesimoth
Asel 1 Pa 8 37 was born Elasa, who begot Asel
1 Pa 8 38 Asel had six sons whose names. 9:44
38 these were the sons of Asel. 9:44
9 43 begot Elasa; of whom was born Asel
Asem Josu 19 3 Hasersual, Bala, and Asem and
Asemona Num 34 4 and shall reach as far as Asemona
Num 34 5 limits shall fetch a compass from A.
Josu 15 4 passing along into A. and reaching the
Asena Josu 15 33 Estaol and Sarea and Asena and
1 Es 2 50 the children of Asena, the children of
Asenaphar 1 Es 4 10 and glorious A. brought over
Aseneth Gen 41 45 he gave him to wife Aseneth
Gen 41 50 whom Aseneth the daughter of. 46:20
Aser Gen 30 13 therefore she called him Aser
Gen 35 26 Gad and Aser: these are the sons of
49 20 Aser, his bread shall be fat, and he
Exod 1 4 Dan and Nephtali, Gad and Aser. And
6 24 the sons also of Core: Aser and Elcana
Num 1 13 of Aser, Phegiel the son of Ochran
26 46 name of the daughter of Aser was Sara
Deut 27 13 Ruben, Gad, and Aser, and Zabulon, Dan
33 24 to Aser he said: Let Aser be blessed
Josu 17 7 the border of Manasses was from Aser
11 in Issachar and in Aser, was Bethsan
19 24 fell to tribe of the children of Aser
31 possession of the children of Aser
34 and to Aser westward, and to Juda
21 6 of the tribes of Issachar and of Aser
Judg 1 31 Aser destroyed not the inhabitants of
5 17 Aser dwelt on the seashore and abode
6 35 and other messengers into Aser and
7 23 shouting from Nephtali and Aser and
3 K 4 16 Baana the son of Husi, in Aser and in
1 Pa 2 2 Benjamin, Nephtali, Gad, and Aser. The
7 30 the children of Aser were Jemna and
12 36 of Aser 40,000 going forth to fight
2 Pa 30 11 some men of Aser and of Manasses and
2 Es 3 19 next to him Aser the son of Josue
Eze 48 2 side of the sea, one portion for Aser
34 gate of Gad one, the gate of Aser one
sons of Aser Gen 46 17 the sons of Aser: Jamne
Num 1 40 hundred. Of the sons of Aser, by their
7 72 the prince of the sons of Aser, Phegiel
26 44 the sons of Aser by their kindreds
47 these are the kindreds of the s. . . .
1 Pa 7 40 all these were sons of Aser, heads of
tribe of Aser Num 2 27 t. . . . pitched their tents
Num 13 14 of the t. . . . Sthur the son of Michael
34 27 of the tribe of Aser, Ahiud the son of
Josu 17 10 joined together in the tribe of Aser
21 30 of the tribe of Aser, Masal and Abdon
1 Pa 6 62 out of the tribe of Aser, and out of
74 tribe of Issachar, and out of t. . . .
Luke 2 36 of tribe of Aser; she was far advanced
Apoc 2 36 of the tribe of Aser, 12,000 signed
Asergadda Josu 15 27 Asergadda and Hassemon and
ashamed Gen 2 25 and his wife: and were not ashamed
Lev 26 41 until their uncircumcised mind be a.
Num 12 14 ought she not to have been ashamed
Judg 3 25 waiting long time till they were ashamed
1 Es 8 22 I was ashamed to ask the king for aid
9 6 and ashamed to lift up my face to thee
Job 19 3 and are not ashamed to oppress me
Ps 6 11 let all my enemies be ashamed and be
11 turned back, and be a. very speedily
24 2 I put my trust: let me not be ashamed
20 I shall not be a., for I have hoped in
30 18 let the wicked be ashamed, and be
34 4 let them be confounded and a. 39:15

26 let them blush: and be ashamed together
39 15 let them be turned backward and be a.
68 7 let not them be ashamed for me, who
69 3 let them be confounded and ashamed
82 18 let them be ashamed and troubled for
118 46 before kings: and I was not ashamed
78 let the proud be ashamed, because they
Joel 1 11 the husbandmen are ashamed, the
Wisd 13 17 he is not a. to speak to that which
Eccu 4 24 soul be not ashamed to say the truth
30 be a. of the lie of thy ignorance
31 be not ashamed to confess thy sins
22 31 I will not be a. to salute a friend
41 21 be a. of fornication before father
28 be ashamed of upbraiding speeches
42 1 be not a. of any of these things
8 be not a. to inform the unwise and
11 she make thee ashamed before all the
Isa 1 29 you shall be ashamed of the gardens
20 5 and ashamed of Ethiopia their hope
23 4 be thou ashamed, O Sidon: for the sea
24 23 blush, and the sun shall be ashamed
29 22 neither shall his countenance now be a.
41 11 shall be confounded and ashamed, they
44 9 nor understand, that they may be a.
45 16 they are all confounded and ashamed
17 you shall not be a. forever and ever
46 8 remember this and be ashamed: return
Jer 2 36 thou shalt be ashamed of Egypt, as thou
36 Egypt, as thou wast ashamed of Assyria
12 13 you shall be ashamed of your fruits
15 9 she is confounded and ashamed: and the
22 22 and ashamed of all thy wickedness
31 19 I am confounded and ashamed, because
48 13 Moab shall be ashamed of Chamos, as the
13 house of Israel was ashamed of Bethel
Eze 16 27 that are ashamed of thy wicked way
61 shalt remember thy ways and be ashamed
36 32 confounded and a. at your own ways
43 10 them be ashamed of their iniquities
11 and be a. of all that they have done
Dan 13 11 for they were ashamed to declare to one
27 the servants were greatly ashamed
Soph 3 11 thou shalt not be a. of all thy doings
Mark 8 38 that shall be a. of me, and. Luke 9:26
38 Son of man will be a. of him. Luke 9:26
Luke 13 17 his adversaries were ashamed: and all
16 3 dig I am not able; to beg I am ashamed
Rom 1 16 I am not ashamed of the gospel. For
6 21 in those things of which you are now a.
2 C 9 4 should be ashamed in this matter
10 8 your destruction, I should not be a.
Gal 4 20 voice: because I am ashamed for you
2 Th 3 14 that he may be ashamed: yet do not
2 Tim 1 8 not ashamed of testimony of our Lord
12 but I am not ashamed. For I know whom
16 and hath not been ashamed of my chain
2 15 workman that needeth not to be ashamed
Heb 2 11 he is not a. to call them brethren
11 16 not ashamed to be called their God
1 P 3 16 they may be a. who falsely accuse your
4 16 if as a Christian, let him not be a.
ashes Gen 18 27 Lord, whereas I am dust and ashes
Gen 19 28 he saw the ashes rise up from the earth
Exod 9 8 take to you handfuls of ashes out of
10 they took ashes out of the chimney
27 3 uses thereof pans to receive the ashes
Lev 1 16 ashes were wont to be poured out. 4:12
6 10 and he shall take up the ashes of that
Num 4 13 cleanse the altar also from the ashes
19 9 shall gather up the ashes of the cow
10 he that carried the ashes of the cow
17 shall take of the ashes of the burning
Deut 28 24 let ashes come down from heaven upon
2 K 13 19 and she put ashes on her head, and rent
3 K 13 3 ashes that are upon it shall be poured
5 ashes were poured out from the altar
4 K 23 4 he carried the ashes of them to Bethel
12 cast the ashes of them into the torrent
Jdth 4 15 and with ashes upon their head. And
7 4 putting ashes upon their heads, praying
9 1 laid ashes on her head: and falling
Esth 4 1 strewing ashes on his head: and he cried
3 many using sackcloth and ashes for their
14 2 she covered her head with ashes and
Job 13 12 remembrance shall be compared to ashes
16 16 and have covered my flesh with ashes
21 18 ashes which the whirlwind scattereth
30 19 and am likened to embers and ashes
34 15 and man shall return into ashes. If
42 6 myself, and do penance in dust and ashes
Ps 101 10 I did eat ashes like bread, and mingled
147 16 like wool scattered mists like ashes
Wisd 2 3 our body shall be ashes, and our spirit
15 10 his heart is ashes, and his hope vain
Eccu 10 9 man. Why is earth and ashes proud
17 31 heaven: and all men are earth and ashes
40 3 him that is humbled in earth and ashes
Isa 1 31 your strength shall be as ashes of tow
5 24 so shall their root be as ashes, and
29 5 small dust: and as ashes passing away
33 12 people shall be as ashes after a fire
44 20 part thereof is ashes: his foolish heart
58 5 and to spread sackcloth and ashes? Wilt
61 3 to give them a crown for ashes, the oil
Jer 6 26 and sprinkle thee with ashes: make thee
25 34 and sprinkle yourselves with ashes
31 40 valley of dead bodies and of ashes
Lam 3 16 one by one, he hath fed me with ashes
Eze 4 12 as barley bread baked under the ashes
15 4 the midst thereof is reduced to ashes
27 30 heads and shall be sprinkled with ashes
28 18 will make thee as ashes upon the earth
Dan 9 3 with fasting and sackcloth and ashes
14 13 they brought ashes, and he sifted them
Osee 7 8 become as bread baked under the ashes
Amos 2 1 bones of the king of Edom even to ashes
Job 3 6 clothed with sackcloth and sat in ashes
Mala 4 3 when they shall be ashes under the sole
1 Ma 3 47 put ashes upon their heads: and. 4:39
2 Ma 4 41 and some threw ashes upon Lysimachus
13 5 having a heap of ashes on every side
6 to be thrown down into the ashes, all
8 the fire and ashes of which were holy
8 holy: he was condemned to die in ashes
Mat 11 21 in sackcloth and ashes. Luke 10:13
Heb 9 13 the ashes of an heifer being sprinkled
2 P 2 6 into ashes, condemned them to be
Ashur 1 Pa 2 24 Abia who bore him Ashur the
Asia 1 Ma 8 6 Antiochus the great king of Asia
1 Ma 11 13 head, that of Egypt and that of Asia
12 39 a design to make himself king of Asia
13 32 [Tryphon] put on the crown of Asia
2 Ma 3 3 Seleucus king of Asia allowed out of
10 24 and assembled horsemen out of Asia
Acts 2 9 and Cappadocia, Pontus and Asia, Phrygia
6 9 of Cilicia and Asia disputing with
16 6 Holy Ghost to preach the word in Asia
19 10 who dwelt in Asia heard the word of the
22 he himself remained for a time in Asia
26 of all Asia, saying: They are not gods
27 whom all Asia and the world worshippeth
31 some of the rulers of Asia . . . sent unto
20 4 and Timothy; and of Asia, Tychicus and
16 in Asia. For he hasted, if it were
18 the first day that I came into Asia

21 27 those Jews that were of Asia when they
24 19 certain Jews of Asia who ought to be
27 2 meaning to sail by the coasts of Asia
Rom 16 5 is the firstfruits of Asia in Christ
1 C 16 19 such. The churches of Asia salute you
2 C 1 8 tribulation which came to us in Asia
2 Tim 1 15 in Asia are turned away from me: of
1 P 1 1 through Pontus, Galatia, Cappadocia, A.
Apoc 1 4 seven churches which are in Asia. 11
aside Gen 18 5 therefore are you come aside to
Exod 23 6 not go aside in the poor man's judgment
35 5 set aside with you firstfruits to the
22 every vessel of gold was set aside
Lev 10 14 for they are set aside for thee and thy
19 31 go not aside after wizards, neither ask
20 6 that shall go aside after magicians
Num 5 20 hast gone aside from thy husband, and
29 if a woman hath gone aside from her
21 22 we will not go aside into the fields
22 26 where there was no way to turn aside
Deut 2 27 we will not turn aside neither to the
4 41 Moses set aside three cities beyond
5 32 you shall not go aside neither to the
14 22 set aside the tithes of all thy fruits
16 19 and not go aside to either part. Thou
31 29 will quickly turn aside from the way
Josu 23 6 turn not aside from them neither to the
Judg 14 8 he went aside to see the carcass of
17 2 which thou hast put aside for thyself
8 had turned aside a little into the
18 15 when they had turned a little aside
Ruth 4 1 turn aside for a little while and sit
1 here. He turned aside and sat down
1 K 6 12 turned not aside neither to the right
8 3 they turned aside after lucre, and took
12 21 turn not aside after vain things which
17 30 he [David] turned a little aside from
18 11 David stept aside out of his presence
2 K 3 27 Joab took him [Abner] aside to the
6 6 oxen kicked and made it lean aside
1 Pa 13 13 carried it aside into the house of
Tob 12 5 took him aside and began to desire him
Ps 13 3 they are all gone aside, they are become
52 4 all have gone aside, they are become
Prov 4 15 pass not by it: go aside and forsake it
Eccu 2 7 go not aside from him, lest ye fall
16 and have gone aside into crooked ways
38 20 in withdrawing aside sorrow remaineth
Isa 41 10 turn not aside, for I am thy God: I have
53 6 hath turned aside into his own way
56 11 all have turned aside into their own
Lam 3 11 he hath turned aside my paths and hath
35 to turn aside the judgment of a man
Dan 13 56 having put him aside, he commanded
1 Ma 9 45 there is no place for us to turn aside
2 Ma 6 21 taking him aside, desired that flesh
Luke 9 10 and taking them, he went aside into a
John 5 13 Jesus went aside from the multitude
Acts 4 15 to go aside out of the council; and
23 19 hand, went aside with him privately
26 31 when they were gone aside, they spoke
1 Tim 1 6 are turned aside unto vain babbling
5 15 some are already turned aside after
Heb 7 18 setting aside of the former commandment
12 1 laying aside every weight and sin which
2 P 3 17 led aside by the error of the unwise
Asiel 1 Pa 4 35 son of Saraia, the son of Asiel
Asima 4 K 17 30 and the men of Emath made Asima
Asiongaber Num 33 35 they camped in Asiongaber
Deut 2 8 plain from Elath and from Asiongaber
3 K 9 26 Solomon made a fleet in Asiongaber
22 49 not go. For the ships were broken in A.
2 Pa 8 17 then Solomon went to Asiongaber, and to
20 36 and they made the ships in Asiongaber
Asir 1 Pa 3 17 the sons of Jechonias were Asir
1 Pa 6 22 his son, Core his son, Asir his son
23 his son Abiasaph his son, Asir his son
37 Thahath, the son of Asir, the son of
ask Mat 6 8 needful for you before you ask him
Mat 7 7 ask and it shall be given. Luke 11:9
9 if his son shall ask bread, will he
10 if he shall ask him a fish, will he
11 give good things to them that ask him
14 7 to give her whatsoever she would ask
18 19 whatsoever they shall ask, it shall be
20 22 you know not what you ask. Mark 10:38
21 22 whatsoever you shall ask in prayer
24 I will ask you one word. Mark 11:29; Luke 20:3
22 46 day forth ask him any more questions
26 53 thinkest thou that I cannot ask my
27 20 that they should ask Barabbas, and make
Mark 6 22 ask of me what thou wilt and I will
23 whatsoever thou shalt ask I will give
24 said to her mother, What shall I ask
9 31 they were afraid to ask him. Luke 9:45
10 35 whatsoever we shall ask thou wouldst
11 24 things, whatsoever you ask when ye pray
Luke 6 9 ask you if it be lawful on the sabbath
30 taketh away thy goods, ask them not
11 11 he ask his father bread, will he give
12 if he shall ask an egg, will he reach
13 give good Spirit to them that ask him
19 31 if any man shall ask: Why do you loose
20 40 that they durst not ask him any more
22 68 if I shall also ask you, you will not
John 1 19 priests and Levites to him, to ask him
4 9 dost thou, being a Jew, ask of me to
9 21 ask himself; he is of age, let him. 23
11 22 whatsoever thou wilt ask of God, God
14 13 ask the Father in my name, that. 15:16
14 if you shall ask me anything in my
16 I will ask the Father and he shall give
15 7 you shall ask whatever you will, and it
16 19 knew that they had a mind to ask him
23 that day you shall not ask me anything
23 if you ask the Father anything in my
24 ask and you shall receive; that your
26 that I will ask the Father for you
30 needest not that any man should ask
18 21 ask them who have heard what I have
21 12 durst ask him: Who art thou? knowing
Acts 3 2 that he might ask alms of them that
10 29 I ask for what cause you have sent
1 C 14 35 let them ask their husbands at home
James 1 5 want wisdom, let him ask of God, who
6 let him ask in faith, nothing wavering
4 2 and you have not, because you ask not
3 receive not; because you ask amiss
1 J 3 22 and whatsoever we shall ask we shall. 5:14
5 15 he heareth us whatsoever we ask: we
16 let him ask, and life shall be given to
16 for that I say not that any man ask
asked Mat 16 13 asked his disciples: Whom. Mark 8:27
Mat 27 58 asked the body of Jesus. Then Pilate
Mark 9 20 he asked his father: How long time is
14 60 high priest . . . asked Jesus, saying
Luke 11 16 asked of him a sign from heaven. But
15 26 and asked what these things meant. And
17 20 asked by Pharisees, when the kingdom
18 36 passing by, he asked what this meant
23 6 Galilee, asked if the man were of
John 4 10 thou perhaps wouldst have asked of him
52 he asked therefore of them the hour
16 24 you have not asked anything in my name
18 19 priest asked Jesus of his disciples

Acts 3 3 the temple, asked to receive an alms
4 7 they asked: By what power or by what
9 2 asked of him letters to Damascus
10 18 they asked, if Simon who is surnamed
23 34 had asked of what province he was, and
Rom 10 20 openly to them that asked not after me
asked him Mat 12 10 a. him, saying: Is it lawful
Mat 16 1 they asked him to show them a sign
17 10 disciples asked him, saying: Why then
22 23 no resurrection: and asked him. Mark 12:18
35 doctor of law asked him, tempting him
27 11 governor asked him: Art thou the king
Mark 4 10 with him asked him the parable. 7:17
5 9 asked him: What is thy name. Luke 8:30
7 5 asked him: Why do not thy disciples
17 his disciples asked him the parable
8 23 him, he asked him if he saw anything
9 10 they asked him, saying: Why then do
27 disciples secretly asked him: Why
10 2 asked him: Is it lawful for a man to put
10 disciples asked him concerning the same
17 asked him: Good master, what shall I
12 28 well, asked him which was the first
13 3 and Andrew asked him apart: Tell us
14 61 high priest asked him, and said to him
15 2 Pilate asked him: Art thou. Luke 23:3
4 Pilate asked him, saying: Answerest thou
44 he asked him if he were already dead
Luke 3 10 the people asked him, saying: What then
14 the soldiers asked him, saying: And
8 9 disciples asked him what this parable
18 18 certain ruler asked, saying: Good
40 and when he was come near, he asked him
20 21 they asked him, saying: Master, we know
27 any resurrection, and they asked him
21 7 they asked him, saying: Master, when
22 64 they asked him, saying: Prophesy
John 1 21 they asked him: What then? Art thou
25 they asked him . . . Why then dost thou
4 12 they asked him therefore: Who is that
9 2 disciples asked him: Rabbi, who hath
15 asked him how he had received his sight
Acts 1 6 they . . . asked him, saying: Lord, wilt
23 19 asked him: What is it that thou hast to
25 20 question, asked him whether he would go
asked them Mat 22 41 Jesus asked them, saying: What
Mark 8 5 he asked them: How many loaves have
9 15 he asked them: What do you question
32 he asked them: What did you treat of
Luke 9 18 he asked them: Whom do the people say
John 9 19 asked them, saying: Is this your son
18 7 he asked them: Whom seek ye? And they
Acts 5 27 and the high priest asked them, saying
askest Judg 13 18 why askest thou my name, which
1 K 28 16 Samuel said: Why askest thou me, seeing
Dan 2 11 the thing that thou askest, O king
Mat 19 17 why a. thou me concerning. John 18:21
asketh Deut 15 9 to lend him that which he asketh
Wisd 13 19 he asketh him that is unable to do
Mat 5 42 give to him that asketh. Luke 6:30
7 8 every one that a. receiveth. Luke 11:10
Luke 11 29 it a. a sign, and a sign shall not be
John 16 5 none of you a. me: Whither goest thou
Rom 8 26 the Spirit himself asketh for us with
27 he asketh for the saints according to
1 P 3 15 that a. you a reason of that hope which
asking 2 Pa 28 16 sent to the Assyrians a. help
Ps 77 18 by asking meat for their desires. And
Dan 13 14 asking one another the cause, they
Mat 20 20 sons, adoring and asking something of
Mark 8 11 asking him a sign from heaven, tempting
Luke 2 46 hearing them and a. them questions
John 8 7 when they continued a. him, he lifted
1 C 10 25 a. no question for conscience' sake. 27
asleep Gen 2 21 when he [Adam] was fast asleep
Gen 41 21 I awoke and then fell asleep again
Josu 2 8 that were hidden were not yet asleep
1 K 26 12 but they were all asleep, for a deep
2 K 4 5 was cleansing wheat, was fallen asleep
3 K 3 20 was asleep and laid it in her bosom
18 27 perhaps he is asleep and must be awaked
19 6 ate and drank, and he fell asleep again
Jdth 13 4 Holofernes lay on his bed, fast asleep
Job 3 13 now I should have been asleep and still
14 12 when he is fallen asleep shall not rise
Prov 23 34 as a pilot fast asleep, when the stern
Eccu 22 9 speaketh with one that is asleep, who
Jon 1 6 why art thou fast asleep? Rise up, call
Haba 2 16 drink thou also and fall fast asleep
2 Ma 12 45 that they who had fallen asleep with
Mat 8 24 covered with waves, but he was asleep
13 25 while men were asleep his enemy came
26 40 findeth them asleep and he. Mark 14:37
28 13 stole him away while we were asleep
Mark 14 40 he found them again asleep, for their
Acts 7 59 he [Stephen] fell asleep in the Lord
1 C 15 6 this present, and some are fallen a.
18 also that are fallen asleep in Christ
1 Th 4 12 concerning them that are asleep, that
Aslia 4 K 22 3 Saphan the son of Aslia, the son
Asmodeus Tob 3 8 devil named A. had killed them
Asnaa 2 Es 3 3 fish gate the sons of A. built
Asom 1 Pa 2 15 the sixth Asom, the seventh David
1 Pa 2 25 and Buna and Aram and Asom and Achia
4 29 and in Bala and in Asom and in Tholad
Asor Josu 11 1 Jabin king of Asor had heard these
Josu 11 10 presently turning back he took Asor
10 now Asor of old was head of all these
13 burned: only Asor that was very strong
12 19 king of Madon one, the king of Asor one
15 23 and Cades and Asor and Jethnam, Ziph
25 New Asor and . . . Hesron, which is Asor
19 36 and Arama, Asor and Cedes and Edri
Judg 4 2 king of Chanaan, who reigned in Asor
4 K 15 29 and Asor and Galaad, and Galilee, and
1 Es 4 2 since the days of Asor Haddan king of
2 Es 11 33 Asor, Rama, Gethaim, Hadid, Seboim, and
Jer 49 28 Cedar and against the kingdoms of Asor
30 sit in deep holes, you that inhabit A.
33 Asor shall be a habitation for dragons
1 Ma 11 67 they were ready in the plain of Asor
Asoth 1 Pa 7 33 Asoth: these are the sons of Jephlat
asp Ps 57 5 like the deaf asp that stoppeth her
Ps 90 13 thou shalt walk upon the asp and the
Isa 11 8 shall play on the hole of the asp: and
aspersion Num 19 9 and for a water of a.: because
Asphar 1 Ma 9 33 pitched by water of the lake A.
Asphenez Dan 1 3 the king spoke to Asphenez the
asps Deut 32 33 venom of asps, which is incurable
Job 20 14 turned into the gall of asps within him
16 he shall suck the head of asps, and the
Ps 13 3 the poison of asps is under their lips
139 4 the venom of asps is under their lips
Isa 59 5 they have broken the eggs of asps, and
Rom 3 13 the venom of asps is under their lips
Asrael 1 Pa 4 16 Ziph and Sipha, Thiria and Asrael
Asriel Num 26 31 and Asriel of whom is the family
Asrielites Num 26 31 of whom is family of the A.
ass Gen 22 3 saddled his ass: and took with him
Gen 22 5 stay you here with the ass: I and the
49 11 his ass, O my son, to the vine. He shall
14 Issachar shall be a strong ass lying
Exod 4 20 set them upon an ass: and returned into
13 13 firstborn of an ass thou shalt change
20 17 nor his ass, nor anything that is his
21 33 not, and an ox or an ass fall into it

22 4 found with him alive, either ox or ass
9 to do any fraud, either in ox or ass
10 if a man deliver ass, ox, sheep, or any
23 5 see the ass of him that hateth thee
12 that thy ox and thy ass may rest: and
34 20 firstlings of an ass thou shalt redeem
Num 16 15 taken of them so much as a young ass
22 21 and saddling his ass, went with them
22 Balaam, who sat on the ass and had two
23 the ass seeing the angel standing in
25 the ass seeing him, thrust herself close
27 when the ass saw the angel standing
28 Lord opened the mouth of the ass, and
30 the ass said: Am not I thy beast, on
32 why beatest thou thy ass these three
33 unless the ass had turned out of the
Deut 5 14 nor thy ass nor any of thy beasts nor
21 nor his ass nor anything that is his
22 3 shalt do in like manner with his ass
4 if thou see thy brother's ass or his ox
10 not plow with an ox and an ass together
28 31 may thy ass be taken away in thy sight
Josu 15 18 she sighed as she sat on her ass. And
Judg 1 14 as she sighed sitting on her ass, Caleb
10 4 sons that rode on thirty ass colts
12 14 grandsons, mounted upon 70 ass colts
15 15 the jawbone of an ass which lay there
16 with the jawbone of an ass, with the
19 opened a great tooth in jaw of the ass
19 28 took her up and laid her upon his ass
1 K 12 3 I have taken any man's ox or ass: if
15 3 suckling, ox and sheep, camel and ass
16 20 Isai took an ass laden with bread, and
22 19 and ox and ass, and sheep with the edge
25 20 when she had gotten upon an ass, and
23 made haste and lighted off the ass, and
42 and got upon an ass, and five damsels
2 K 17 23 saddled his ass, and arose and went home
19 26 spoke to him to saddle his ass, and
3 K 2 40 Semei arose and saddled his ass and
13 13 he said to his sons: Saddle me the ass
23 he saddled his ass for the prophet, whom
24 and the ass stood by him, and the lion
27 he said to his sons: Saddle me an ass
28 and the ass and lion standing by the
28 eaten of the dead body, nor hurt the ass
29 and laid it upon the ass, and going
4 K 4 22 an ass that I may run to the man of God
24 and she saddled an ass, and commanded
6 25 head of an ass was sold for fourscore
Job 6 5 will the wild ass bray when he hath
24 3 driven away the ass of the fatherless
39 5 who hath sent out the wild ass free
Prov 26 3 and a snaffle for an ass, and a rod for
Eccu 13 23 the wild ass is the lion's prey in the
33 25 a wand and a burden are for an ass
Isa 1 3 the ass his master's crib: but Israel
21 7 a rider upon an ass, and a rider upon
30 24 the ass colts that till the ground
32 20 thither the foot of the ox and the ass
Jer 2 24 wild ass accustomed to the wilderness
22 19 be buried with the burial of an ass
Osee 8 9 a wild ass alone by himself: Ephraim
Zach 9 9 he is poor, and riding upon an ass
9 riding upon a colt the foal of an ass
14 15 of the camel and of the ass and of all
Mat 21 2 you shall find an ass tied, and a colt
5 sitting upon an ass, and a colt the foal
7 they brought the ass and the colt, and
Luke 13 15 loose his ox or his ass from the manger
14 5 shall have an ass or an ox fall into
19 30 you shall find the colt of an ass tied
John 12 14 Jesus found a young ass and sat upon it

assault Exod 21 32 if he assault a bondman or a
Num 22 3 were not able to sustain his assault
Judg 20 20 Benjamin, began to assault the city
3 K 22 32 making a violent assault they fought
4 K 24 11 the city with his servants to a. it
Jdth 2 13 he took by assault the renowned city
14 2 down beneath, but as making an assault
Wisd 18 20 touched by an assault of death, and
23 stood between and stayed the assault
Eccu 46 7 made violent assault against the nation
1 Ma 4 8 neither be ye afraid of their assault
5 30 to take the fortress and assault them
49 that they should make an assault every
Acts 14 5 assault made by the Gentiles and the
assaulted Judg 9 45 Abimelech a. the city all that
Eccu 46 6 when the enemies assaulted him on every
1 Ma 5 16 trouble, and were assaulted by them
35 to Maspha and assaulted and took it
50 he assaulted that city all the day
11 65 and a. it many days and shut them up
2 Ma 5 5 suddenly assaulted the city: and though
12 15 of Josue, fiercely assaulted the walls
assaulting Judg 9 44 a. and besieging the city
1 Ma 11 50 the Jews cease from assaulting us, and
15 25 assaulting it continually and making
2 Ma 10 17 a. them with great force, won the holds
Assedim Josu 19 35 the strong cities are Assedim
Assem 1 Pa 11 33 of Assem a Gezonite, Jonathan the
assemble Num 20 8 assemble the people together
Judg 11 40 daughters of Israel assemble together
2 K 20 4 assemble to me all the men of Juda
5 Amasa went to assemble the men of Juda
1 Es 10 7 captivity, that they should a. together
Jdth 7 15 assemble ye all that are in the city
Ps 101 23 when the people assemble together, and
Isa 11 12 shall assemble the fugitives of Israel
44 11 they shall all assemble together, they
45 20 assemble yourselves and come and draw
48 14 a. yourselves together, all you, and
Jer 4 5 assemble yourselves, and let us go
8 14 a. yourselves and let us enter into
12 9 assemble yourselves, all ye beasts
Eze 11 17 and assemble you out of the countries
39 17 assemble yourselves, make haste, come
Dan 11 10 they shall a. a multitude of great
Joel 2 16 the church, assemble the ancients
Amos 3 9 a. yourselves upon the mountains of
Mich 2 12 I will a. and gather together all of
Nah 3 15 assemble together like the bruchus
Soph 2 1 a. yourselves together, be gathered
3 8 my judgment is to a. the Gentiles, and
assembled Exod 4 29 they a. all the ancients of
Num 1 18 a. them on the first day of the second
11 24 assembled seventy men of the ancients
Deut 10 4 when the people were assembled: and he
33 5 the princes of the people being a.
Josu 22 12 they all assembled in Silo, to go up
1 K 8 4 ancients of Israel being a., came to
13 5 the Philistines also were a. to fight
17 1 a. at Socho of Juda, and camped between
2 K 2 30 assembled all the people: and there were
3 K 8 1 were a. to king Solomon in Jerusalem
2 and all Israel a. themselves to king
5 that were a. unto him went with him
22 6 the king of Israel a. the prophets
4 K 23 1 Juda and Jerusalem were assembled to him
1 Pa 13 5 so David a. all Israel from Sihor of
28 1 David a. all the chief men of Israel
2 Pa 10 1 all Israel were a. to make him king
20 26 they were a. in the valley of Blessing
24 5 assembled the priests and the Levites
29 4 and assembled them in the east street
20 assembled all the rulers of the city

30 13 much people were assembled to Jerusalem
1 Es 9 4 were a. to me all that feared the God
2 Es 7 5 I a. the princes and magistrates and
Ps 47 5 behold the kings of the earth assembled
Eze 38 7 thy multitude that is a. about thee
1 Ma 2 42 was a. to them the congregation of
3 13 heard that Judas had a. a company of
58 these nations that are a. against us to
5 15 and of Sidon were a. against them, and
38 are a. unto him an army exceeding great
64 people assembled to them with joyful
7 12 then there a. to Alcimus and Bacchides
10 61 a. themselves against him to accuse
11 55 there a. unto him all the hands which
13 2 went up to Jerusalem and a. the people
14 1 Demetrius a. his army and went into
15 10 all the forces assembled to him, as
2 Ma 8 1 they assembled six thousand men. And
10 21 he a. the rulers of the people and
24 assembled horsemen out of Asia, came
14 15 nations were assembled against them
Mat 26 57 where scribes and ancients were assembled
28 12 a. with the ancients, taking counsel
Acts 4 31 place was moved wherein they were a.
14 26 they had a. the church, they related
15 6 apostles and ancients a. to consider
16 13 we spoke to the women that were a.
20 7 when we were a. to break bread, Paul
8 upper chamber where we were assembled
21 18 and all the ancients were assembled
28 17 when they were a., he [Paul] said to
assembled together Deut 9 10 people were a. t.
Deut 31 12 the people being all assembled together
Josu 10 5 kings of the Amorrhites being a. t.
11 5 all these kings assembled together
18 1 children of Israel assembled together
Judg 10 17 the children of Israel a. themselves t.
16 23 princes of the Philistines a. t. to
2 Es 4 8 they all assembled themselves together
Ps 30 14 while they asesmbled together against
Isa 43 9 all the nations are a. together, and
1 Ma 3 46 they a. together and came to Maspha
4 37 all the army assembled together, and
5 9 a. themselves t. against the Israelites
11 45 that were of the city a. themselves t.
Mark 5 21 multitude a. t. unto him, and he was
7 1 there a. t. unto him the Pharisees
14 53 and the scribes and the ancients a. t.
Acts 4 26 the princes a. t. against the Lord
27 a. t. in this city against thy holy
15 25 being a. t. to choose out men, and to
assemblies Eccu 10 16 disgraced the a. of the
Eccu 18 32 take no pleasure in riotous a., be they
Isa 1 13 not abide, your assemblies are wicked
Amos 5 21 will not receive the odor of your a.
assembling Mat 2 4 and a. together all the chief
assembly Gen 49 6 nor my glory be in their a.
Exod 12 3 speak ye to the whole assembly of the
19 his soul shall perish out of the a.
47 all the assembly of the children of
16 10 when Aaron spoke to all the assembly
35 4 Moses said to all the assembly of the
Num 13 27 to all the a. of the children of Israel
16 2 in the time of assembly were called by
27 22 and all assembly of the people, and
Deut 16 8 because it is the a. of the Lord thy
18 16 when the assembly was gathered together
31 30 in the hearing of the whole assembly
Judg 20 2 in the assembly of the people of God
1 K 17 47 all this assembly shall know that the
3 K 8 14 blessed all the a. of Israel: for all
the a. of Israel stood
22 in the sight of the assembly of Israel
55 he stood and blessed all the assembly
12 20 they gathered an assembly, and sent and
1 Pa 13 2 [David] to all the assembly of Israel
28 8 now then before all the assembly of
29 1 king David commanded all the assembly
20 all the assembly blessed the Lord the
2 Pa 1 5 Solomon and all the assembly sought it
5 6 king Solomon and all the a. of the
7 9 on the eighth day a solemn assembly
20 5 Josaphat stood in midst of the a. of
30 2 and all the assembly of Jerusalem
25 and all the assembly that came out of
1 Es 10 1 of Israel an exceeding great assembly
2 Es 5 7 I gathered together a great assembly
8 17 assembly of them that were returned
18 in the eighth day a solemn assembly
Jdth 6 19 Ozias, after the assembly was broken up
7 18 lamentation of all in the assembly
Esth 10 13 the people gathered into one assembly
Ps 25 5 I have hated the a. of the malignant
63 3 protected me from a. of the malignant
85 14 a. of the mighty have sought my soul
88 8 who is glorified in a. of the saints
Prov 26 26 shall be laid open in the public a.
Eccu 23 34 woman shall be brought into the a.
24 3 shall be admired in the holy assembly
16 my abode is in the full a. of saints
38 37 they shall not go up into the assembly
Jer 9 2 are all adulterers, a. of transgressors
15 17 I sat not in the assembly of jesters
26 17 spoke to all the assembly of the people
30 20 their a. shall be permanent before me
50 9 against Babylon an a. of great nations
Eze 31 6 a. of many nations dwelt under his
Dan 13 60 all the a. cried out with a loud voice
Joel 1 14 sanctify ye a fast, call an assembly
2 15 sanctify a fast, call a solemn assembly
Mich 2 5 cord of a lot in the a. of the Lord
1 Ma 3 44 the a. was gathered that they might be
14 19 were read before the a. in Jerusalem
28 in a great assembly of the priests
44 to call together an a. in the country
Acts 19 32 the assembly was confused, and the
39 it may be decided in lawful assembly
40 these things, he dismissed the assembly
Heb 10 25 not forsaking our assembly, as some are
James 2 2 if there shall come into your assembly
assented 2 Ma 14 26 Nicanor a. to the foreign
asses Gen 12 16 and he asses and menservants and
Gen 12 16 maidservants and she asses and camels
24 35 and womenservants, camels and asses
30 43 and menservants, camels and asses. But
32 5 I have oxen and asses and sheep and
15 twenty she asses, and ten of their foals
34 28 their herds and their asses, wasting
36 24 when he fed the asses of Sebeon his
42 26 having loaded their asses with the corn
43 18 make slaves of us and our asses
24 and he gave provender to their asses
44 3 they were sent away with their asses
13 loading their asses again, returned
45 23 ten he asses to carry of all the riches
23 and as many she asses, carrying wheat
47 17 asses: and he maintained them that year
Exod 9 3 murrain upon thy horses and asses and
Num 31 28 of persons as of oxen and asses and
30 head of persons and of oxen and asses
34 oxen; 61,000 asses: and 32,000 persons
39 out of the 30,500 asses, 61 asses: out
45 out of the 30,500 asses, and out of the
Josu 6 21 the sheep and the asses they slew with
7 24 his oxen and asses and sheep, the tent
9 4 laying old sacks upon their asses, and

Judg 5 10 speak, you that ride upon fair asses
6 4 of life, nor sheep nor oxen nor asses
15 16 with the jaw of the colt of asses I
19 3 with him a servant and two asses: and
10 leading with him asses laden, and his
19 and hay for provender of the asses
21 and gave provender to his asses: and
1 K 8 16 and your asses he will take away, and
9 3 asses of Cis, Saul's father, were lost
3 arise, go, and seek the asses. And
5 lest perhaps my father forget the asses
20 as for the asses, which were lost three
10 2 father thinking no more of the asses
14 they answered: To seek the asses: and
16 he told us that the asses were found
25 18 cakes of dry figs, and laid them upon a.
27 9 and the asses and the camels and the
2 K 16 1 came to meet him with two asses, laden
2 the asses are for the king's household
4 K 7 7 asses in the camp, and fled, desiring
10 but horses and asses tied, and the
1 Pa 5 21 and of asses two thousand, and of men a
12 40 brought loaves on asses, and on camels
27 30 over the asses, Jadias a Meronathite
1 Es 2 67 their asses 6,720. And some. 2 Es 7:69
2 Es 13 15 lading asses with wine and grapes, and
Job 1 3 and five hundred she asses, and a
14 and the asses feeding beside them, and
24 5 others like wild asses in the desert
42 12 yoke of oxen, and a thousand she asses
Ps 103 11 wild asses shall expect in their thirst
Isa 32 14 a joy of wild asses, the pastures of
Jer 14 6 the wild asses stood upon the rocks
Eze 23 20 whose flesh is as the flesh of asses
Dan 5 21 his dwelling was with the wild asses
Assideans 1 Ma 2 42 the congregation of the A.
1 Ma 7 13 A. that were among the children of
2 Ma 14 6 among the Jews that are called A., of
assigned Num 4 27 to what burden he must be a.
Deut 29 26 for whom they had not been assigned
3 K 11 18 appointed him victuals and a. him land
assist Judg 12 2 I called you to assist me, and
Jdth 9 3 assist, I beseech thee, O Lord God, me
Wisd 19 20 but didst assist them at all times
2 Ma 12 11 and to assist him in other things. And
Rom 16 2 you assist her [Phebe] in whatsoever
assistance Ps 69 2 O God, come to my assistance
1 Ma 11 47 the king the Jews to his assistance
assisted 2 Es 12 43 priests and Levites that a.
Ps 88 44 sword: and hast not a. him in battle
93 18 moved: thy mercy, O Lord, assisted me
Rom 16 2 for she also hath assisted many, and
associate Eccu 13 20 shall a. himself to his like
associated Jdth 6 6 shalt be a. to their people
Eze 37 19 tribes of Israel that are a. with him
Acts 17 4 were associated to Paul and Silas; and
associates Eze 37 16 the children of Israel his a.
Eze 37 16 all the house of Israel and of his a.
Asson Acts 27 13 when they had loosed from Asson
Assos Acts 20 13 sailed to Assos, being there to
Acts 20 14 he [Paul] had met with us at Assos, we
ass's Job 11 12 born free like a wild ass's colt
John 12 15 king cometh, sitting on an ass's colt
assuage Eccu 18 16 shall not the dew a. the heat
assuaged Gen 27 44 till wrath of thy brother be a.
Assuerus 1 Es 4 6 in the reign of Assuerus, in the
Esth 1 1 in the days of Assuerus, who reigned
3 6 that were in the kingdom of Assuerus
7 twelfth year of the reign of Assuerus
Dan 9 1 Darius the son of Assuerus of the seed
king Assuerus Esth 1 9 where k. A. was used to
Esth 1 15 commandment of king Assuerus, which he
16 in all the provinces of king Assuerus
17 king Assuerus commanded that queen
2 1 wrath of king Assuerus was appeased
16 she was brought to chamber of king A.
3 1 king Assuerus advanced Aman, the son of
8 Aman said to king Assuerus: There is a
12 in the name of king Assuerus: and the
6 2 who sought to kill king Assuerus. And
7 5 king Assuerus answered and said: Who is
8 1 king Assuerus gave the house of Aman
7 king Assuerus answered Esther the queen
13 subject to the empire of king Assuerus
9 30 in the 127 provinces of king Assuerus
10 1 king A. made all the land and all the
3 was next after king A.: and great among
assumption Luke 9 51 when the days of his a. were
Assur Gen 10 11 out of the land came forth Assur
Gen 10 22 the sons of Sem: Elam and A. 1 Pa 1:17
Num 24 22 for Assur shall take thee captive. And
1 Pa 4 5 Assur the father of Thecua had two
5 26 spirit of Thelgathphalnasar king of A.
2 Es 9 32 from the days of the king of Assur
Eze 27 23 Saba, Assur, and Chelmad sold to thee
32 22 Assur is there, and all his multitude
assurance Eccu 4 17 his generation shall be in a.
assured Josu 6 22 hers, as you assured her by oath
2 K 23 5 firm in all things and assured. For
Tob 11 8 for be assured that his eyes shall be
Jdth 10 16 be a. of this, that when thou shalt
Wisd 7 23 steadfast, assured, secure, having all
2 Ma 7 24 also assured him with an oath, that he
Acts 16 10 being assured that God had called us
Rom 15 14 am assured of you, that you are full
2 P 1 14 being a. that the laying away of this
assuredly 1 K 28 1 know thou now assuredly that
3 K 13 32 a. the word shall come to pass which
Wisd 18 6 a. knowing what oaths they had trusted
Eccu 12 2 if not of him, assuredly of the Lord
Jer 15 11 a. it shall be well with thy remnant
11 a. I shall help thee in the time of
Assurim Gen 25 3 children of Dadan were Assurim
1 Pa 1 32 and the sons of Dadan: Assurim and
Assyria 4 K 15 29 carried them captives into Assyria
4 K 17 23 away out of their land to Assyria
18 11 carried away Israel into Assyria, and
Isa 7 18 and for the bee that is in land of A.
Jer 2 36 Egypt as thou was ashamed of Assyria
Osee 8 9 they are gone up to Assyria, a wild
10 6 itself also is carried into Assyria
14 4 Assyria shall not save us, we will not
Mich 5 6 they shall feed the land of Assyria
7 12 that day they shall come even from A.
Soph 2 13 upon the north, and will destroy A.
Zach 10 11 the pride of Assyria shall be humbled
king of Assyria 4 K 15 29 came Theglathphalasar k. . . . , and took
4 K 18 33 their land from the hand of the k. . . .
23 29 king of Egypt went up against k. . . .
1 Es 4 2 since the days of Asor Haddan k. . . .
6 22 turned the heart of the k. . . . to them
Isa 10 12 fruit of the proud heart of the k. . . .
Jer 50 17 first the king of Assyria devoured him
18 as I have visited the king of Assyria
Nah 3 18 thy shepherds have slumbered, O k. . . .
Assyrian Jdth 16 5 A. came out of the mountains
Ps 82 9 the Assyrian also is joined with them
Isa 10 5 woe to the Assyrian, he is the rod
24 be not afraid of the Assyrian: he shall
14 25 I will destroy the A. in my land, and
19 23 the Assyrian shall enter into Egypt
23 Egyptians shall serve the Assyrian
24 the third to the Egyptian and the A.
25 the work of my hands to the Assyrian
23 13 the Assyrian founded it: they have led

30 31 the Assyrian shall fear being struck
31 8 the Assyrian shall fall by the sword
52 4 and the Assyrian hath oppressed them
Eze 31 3 the A. was like a cedar in Libanus
Osee 5 13 Ephraim went to the Assyrian, and sent
11 5 the Assyrian shall be his king: because
Mich 5 5 when the A. shall come into our land
6 he shall deliver us from the A., when
Assyrians Gen 2 14 same passeth along by the A.
Gen 25 18 Egypt, to them that go towards the A.
Num 24 24 they shall overcome the Assyrians, and
4 K 19 11 what the kings of the A. have done
17 kings of the A. have destroyed nations
35 slew in camp of the Assyrians 185,000
2 Pa 32 4 lest the kings of the A. should come
Jdth 2 7 and officers of the power of the A.
12 passed through the borders of the A.
5 1 general of the army of the Assyrians
6 3 by the sword of the A., and all Israel
10 that the Assyrians had left him bound
7 13 not speak peaceably with the A., and
8 10 to give up the city to the Assyrians
9 6 look upon the camp of the A. now, as
10 11 watchmen of the Assyrians met her, and
12 11 looked upon as shameful among the A.
13 19 general of the army of the Assyrians
14 10 into chamber of the general of the A.
17 the chiefs of the army of the A. had
15 4 because the A. were not united together
7 went into the camp of the A. and took
7 spoils which the A. in their flight
13 to gather up the spoils of the A. But
16 13 then the camp of the Assyrians howled
Ps 75 1 for Asaph: a canticle to the Assyrians
Eccu 48 24 he overthrew the army of the A., and the
Isa 11 11 which shall be left from the A. 16
19 23 a way from Egypt to the Assyrians, and
23 the Egyptian to the Assyrians, and the
27 13 shall come from the land of the A.
37 11 that the kings of the A. have done
18 kings of the A. have laid waste lands
36 slew in the camp of the Assyrians a
Jer 2 18 thou to do with the way of the A., to
Lam 5 6 given our hand to Egypt and to the A.
Eze 16 28 also committed fornication with the A.
23 5 her lovers, on the A. that came to her
7 chosen men, all sons of the Assyrians
9 into the hands of the sons of the A.
12 prostituting herself to children of A.
23 princes all the sons of the Assyrians
Osee 7 11 called upon Egypt, they went to the A.
9 3 hath eaten unclean things among the A.
11 11 like a dove out of the land of the A.
12 1 he hath made a covenant with the A.
13 7 as a leopard in the way of the A. I
Zach 10 10 and will gather them from among the A.
king of the Assyrians 4 K 15 19 and Phul k. . . . came
into the land, and
4 K 15 20 to give the k. . . . each man fifty sicles
20 the k. . . . turned back and did not stay
16 7 messengers to Theglathphalasar k. . . .
8 he sent it for a present to the k. . . .
9 the k. . . . went up against Damascus, and
10 Damascus to meet Theglathphalasar k. . . .
18 into temple of Lord because of the k. . . .
17 3 against him came up Salmanasar k. . . .
4 and when the k. . . . found that Osee
4 that he might not pay tribute to k. . . .
6 k. . . . took Samaria and carried Israel
24 k. . . . brought people from Babylon and
26 it was told the k. . . . and it was said
27 k. . . . commanded, saying: Carry thither
18 7 [Ezechias] rebelled against the k. . . .
9 Salmanasar k. . . . came up to Samaria
11 k. . . . carried away Israel into Assyria
13 Sennacherib k. . . . came up against the
14 king of Juda sent messengers to k. . . .
14 the k. . . . put a tax upon Ezechias king
16 [Ezechias] and gave them to the k. . . .
17 k. . . . sent Tharthan and Rabsaris
19 thus saith the great k. . . . What is this
23 come over to my master the k. . . . , and I
28 the words of the great king, the k. . . .
30 not be given into hand of the k. . . .
31 thus saith the k. . . . Do with me that
19 4 k. . . . his master hath sent to reproach
6 servants of the k. . . . have blasphemed
8 found the k. . . . besieging Lobna: for he
10 not be delivered into hands of k. . . .
20 made to me concerning Sennacherib k. . . .
32 thus saith the Lord concerning k. . . .
36 Sennacherib k. . . . departing went away
20 6 and this city out of hand of k. . . .
1 Pa 5 6 Thelgathphalnasar k. . . . carried away
26 stirred up the spirit of Phul k. . . .
2 Pa 28 16 king Achaz sent to the k. . . . asking
20 against him Thelgathphalnasar k. . . .
21 Achaz . . . gave gifts to the k. . . . , and
30 6 that have escaped the hand of k. . . .
32 1 Sennacherib k. . . . came and entered into
7 not afraid nor dismayed for the k. . . .
9 Sennacherib k. . . . sent his servants
10 saith Sennacherib k. . . . In whom do you
11 deliver you from hand of the k. . . .
21 captains of the army of k. . . . 33:11
22 out of the hand of Sennacherib k. . . .
Tob 1 2 in the days of Salmanasar k. . . . , even
Jdth 1 5 Nabuchodonosor k. . . . fought against
10 Nabuchodonosor k. . . . sent messengers
2 1 in house of Nabuchodonosor k. . . . , that
14 11 all the chiefs of the army of k. . . .
Isa 7 17 of Ephraim from Juda with k. . . . And
20 by king of the A., the head and the hairs
8 4 shall be taken away before the k. . . .
7 the k. . . . , and all his glory: and he
20 1 when Sargon the k. . . . had sent him, and
4 so shall the k. . . . lead away the
6 to deliver us from face of the k. . . .
36 1 Sennacherib k. . . . came up against all
2 the k. . . . sent Rabsaces from Lachis to
4 thus saith the great king, the k. . . .
8 deliver thyself up to my lord the k. . . .
13 words of the great king, the k. . . .
15 not be given into the hands of k. . . .
16 thus said the king of the Assyrians
18 their land out of the hand of k. . . .
37 4 whom the k. . . . his master hath sent to
6 servants of k. . . . have blasphemed me
8 found the k. . . . besieging Lobna. For
10 not be given into hands of the k. . . .
21 made to me concerning Sennacherib k. . . .
33 thus saith Lord concerning the k. . . .
37 the k. . . . went out and departed, and
38 6 and this city out of hand of the k. . . .
Astaroth Deut 1 4 who abode in Astaroth, and in
Josu 9 10 Og king of Basan, that was in Astaroth
12 4 the Raphaims who dwelt in Astaroth
13 12 who reigned in Astaroth and Edrai, he
31 half Galaad and Astaroth and Edrai
Judg 2 13 him, and serving Baal and Astaroth
3 7 served Baalim and Astaroth. 1 K 12:10
10 6 served idols, Baalim and Astaroth
1 K 7 3 strange gods . . . Baalim and Astaroth
4 put away Baalim and Astaroth, and
31 10 put his armor in temple of Astaroth
4 K 23 13 Solomon . . . built to Astaroth the idol

Astarothcarnaim Gen 14 5 smote the Raphaim in A.
Astarothite 1 Pa 11 44 Ozia an Astarothite
Astarthe 3 K 11 5 Solomon worshipped Astarthe
3 K 11 33 forsaken me and hath adored Astarthe
Astharoth 1 Pa 6 71 to the sons of Gersom . . . A.
astonish Haba 3 12 thou wilt astonish the nations
astonished Gen 27 33 struck with fear and a.
Gen 42 28 they were astonished and troubled
35 all being astonished together, their
Lev 26 32 your enemies shall be astonished at it
Deut 28 34 be astonished at the terror of those
1 K 21 1 Achimelech was a. at David's coming
3 K 9 8 shall be a. and shall hiss. Jer 50:13
2 Pa 7 21 and they shall be astonished and say
9 4 no more spirit in her, she was so a.
Jdth 10 7 when they saw her they were astonished
Job 17 8 the just shall be astonished at this
18 20 come after him shall be a. at his day
21 5 hearken to me and be astonished, and
Eccu 43 20 the heart is a. at the shower thereof
Isa 10 29 Rama was astonished, Gabaath of Saul
29 9 be astonished and wonder, waver and
32 11 be astonished, ye rich women, be
41 5 ends of the earth were astonished
52 14 as many have been astonished at thee
59 16 he stood a., because there is none
Jer 2 12 be astonished, O ye heavens, at this
4 9 and the priests shall be astonished
18 16 shall be astonished and wag his head
19 8 pass by it shall be astonished and
49 17 that shall pass by it, shall be a.
Eze 26 18 now shall the ships be astonished
27 35 of the islands are a. at thee: and all
28 19 shall be astonished at thee: thou art
32 10 they shall be astonished on a sudden
Dan 3 91 Nabuchodonosor the king was a. and rose
8 27 I was astonished at the vision, and
Mich 1 13 tumult of chariots hath astonished the
Haba 1 5 wonder and be astonished: for a work
1 Ma 15 32 he was a. and told him the king's
Mark 1 22 were a. at his doctrine. Luke 4:32
5 42 they were astonished with a great
6 51 wind ceased: and they were far more a.
9 14 all the people seeing Jesus, were a.
10 24 disciples were astonished at his words
32 Jesus went before them and they were a.
16 5 with a white robe: and they were a.
Luke 2 47 were a. at his wisdom and his answers
5 9 was wholly a., and all that were with
26 all were a., and they glorified God
8 56 her parents were astonished, whom he
9 44 all were a. at the mighty power of God
24 4 as they were astonished . . . two men
Acts 2 12 they were all astonished in their mind
8 13 being a., wondered to see the signs
9 6 a., said: Lord, what wilt thou have me
21 all that heard him [Paul] were a. and
10 45 a. for that the grace of the Holy Ghost
12 16 they saw him [Peter] and were a.
astonishing Jer 5 30 a. and wonderful things have
astonishment Judg 15 8 in a. they laid the calf of
Wisd 17 3 and troubled with exceeding great a.
Jer 8 21 astonishment hath taken hold on me
19 8 I will make this city an astonishment
25 9 make them an a. and a hissing and
11 land shall be a desolation and an a.
18 to make them a desolation and an a.
29 18 to be a curse and an astonishment and
36 16 they looked upon one another with a.
42 18 you shall be an execration and an a.
44 22 land is become a desolation and an a.
51 37 Babylon . . . an a. and a hissing because
41 how is Babylon become an astonishment
43 her cities are become an astonishment
Eze 5 15 an a. amongst the nations that are
26 16 and be clothed with astonishment: they
39 11 shall cause a. in them that pass by
Zach 12 4 I will strike every house with a.
Mark 5 42 they were astonished with a great a.
astray Exod 23 4 enemy's ox or ass going astray
Num 5 12 whose wife shall have gone astray
15 39 eyes going astray after divers things
Deut 22 1 brother's ox or his sheep go astray
Ps 57 4 they have gone astray from the womb
118 176 I have gone astray like a sheep that is
Prov 10 17 he that forsaketh reproofs goeth astray
13 13 deceitful souls go astray in sins: the
Wisd 12 24 they went astray for a long time in
Eccu 4 22 if he go astray, she will forsake him
Isa 19 13 princes of Memphis are gone astray
28 7 they have gone astray for a long time in
53 6 all we like sheep have gone astray
Jer 50 6 have caused them to go astray, and
Bar 1 19 going a. we turned away from hearing
4 28 was your mind to go astray from God
Eze 14 11 may go no more astray from me nor
44 10 children of Israel went a. 15; 48:11
48 11 went not astray when the children of
11 as the Levites also went astray. And
Osee 4 16 Israel hath gone astray like a wanton
18 they have gone astray by fornication
2 Ma 5 17 Antiochus going astray in mind, did not
Mat 18 12 and one of them should go astray
12 to seek that which is gone astray
13 the ninety-nine that went not astray
1 Tim 1 6 from which things some going astray
1 P 2 25 you were as sheep going astray; but
2 P 2 15 they have gone astray, having followed
astrologers Isa 47 13 let now the a. stand and
Astyages Dan 13 65 king A. was gathered to his
asunder Num 5 21 thy belly swell and burst asunder
Num 16 31 earth broke asunder under their feet
4 K 2 11 fiery horses parted them both asunder
Ps 2 3 let us break their bonds asunder: and
Isa 58 6 free, and break asunder every burden
Jer 10 4 hammers, that it may not fall asunder
Dan 13 52 when they were put asunder one from
14 26 mouth, and the dragon burst asunder
Nah 1 13 and I will burst thy bonds asunder
Zach 11 10 and I cut it asunder to make void my
Mat 19 6 let no man put asunder. Mark 10:9
Acts 1 18 [Judas] burst asunder in the midst
Heb 11 37 they were stoned, they were cut asunder
Asyncritus Rom 16 14 salute Asyncritus, Phlegon
Atad Gen 50 10 came to the threshingfloor of Atad
Atara 1 Pa 2 26 married another wife, named Atara
Ataroth Num 32 3 A. and Dibon and Jazer and
Num 32 34 sons of Gad built Dibon and Ataroth
Josu 16 2 passeth border of Archi, to Ataroth
7 it goeth down from Janoe into Ataroth
Ataroth-addar Josu 16 5 A. unto Beth-horon the
Josu 18 13 it goeth down into Ataroth-addar to
ate Gen 19 3 baked unleavened bread and they ate
Gen 24 54 they ate and drank together and lodged
25 28 Esau because he ate of his hunting
34 he [Esau] ate and drank and went his
27 33 and I ate of all before thou camest
31 46 made a heap and they ate upon it. And
39 6 other thing, but the bread which he ate
40 17 and that the birds ate out of it
43 32 the Egyptians also that ate with him
Exod 16 3 flesh pots and ate bread to the full
35 children of Israel ate manna forty years
34 28 he neither ate bread nor drank water
Lev 22 14 fifth part with that which he ate
Num 11 5 we remember the fish that we ate in

25 2 their sacrifices. And they ate of them
Deut 32 38 of whose victims they ate the fat
Josu 5 11 they ate on the next day unleavened
12 ceased after they ate of the corn
12 they ate of the corn of the present
Judg 14 9 he gave them of it, and they ate: but
19 6 sat down together and ate and drank
8 mayest depart. And they ate together
Ruth 2 14 and ate and was filled and took the
1 K 1 18 the woman went on her way and ate
9 24 and Saul ate with Samuel that day
14 32 the people ate them with the blood
2 K 9 13 he ate always of the king's table
12 20 he [David] called for bread and ate
3 K 13 19 so he ate bread and drank water in his
17 15 he [Elias] ate, and she and her house
19 6 he ate and drank, and he fell asleep
8 he arose and ate and drank and walked
21 and gave to the people and they ate
4 K 4 44 they ate, and there was left according
6 23 they ate and drank, and he let them go
29 so we boiled my son and ate him. And
7 8 they went into one tent and ate and
23 9 but only ate of the unleavened bread
25 29 he ate bread always before him all the
1 Pa 29 22 and they ate and drank before the Lord
2 Pa 30 18 ate the phase otherwise than it is
22 they ate during the seven days of the
1 Es 10 6 he ate no bread and drank no water
2 Es 9 25 they ate and were filled and became
Tob 1 12 when all ate of the meats of the
2 5 he ate bread with mourning and fear
Jdth 12 19 she took and ate and drank before him
Job 30 4 they ate grass and barks of trees
42 11 they ate bread with him in his house
Ps 40 10 in whom I trusted, who ate my bread
77 25 man ate the bread of angels: he sent
105 28 and ate the sacrifices of the dead
Jer 41 1 and they ate bread there together in
52 33 and he ate bread before him always
Eze 34 3 you ate the milk, and you clothed
Dan 1 15 children that ate of the king's meat
10 3 I ate no desirable bread, and neither
14 14 and they ate and drank up all. And
38 Daniel arose and ate. And the angel
Amos 7 4 and ate up a part at the same time
Mat 13 4 birds of the air came and ate them up
Mark 1 6 he ate locusts and wild honey. And he
2 16 seeing that he ate with publicans and
4 4 birds of the air came and ate it up
Luke 4 2 and he ate nothing in those days
6 4 took and ate the bread of proposition
Apoc 10 10 and I took the book . . . and ate it up
Ater 1 Es 2 42 the children of Ater. 2 Es 7:21, 46
2 Es 10 17 Ater, Hezecia, Azur, Odaia, Hasum
Atach 1 K 30 30 Asan, and that were in Atach
Esth 4 5 she called for Atach the eunuch whom
6 Atach going out went to Mardochai
9 and Atach went back and told Esther
Athaias 2 Es 11 4 of the children of Juda, Athaias
Athalai 1 Es 10 28 Johanan, Hanania, Zabbai, A.
Athalìa 4 K 8 26 name of his mother was A. 2 Pa 22:2
4 K 11 1 A. the mother of Ochozias seeing that
2 and hid him from the face of Athalia
3 A. reigned over the land. 2 Pa 22:12
13 A. heard noise of the people. 2 Pa 23:12
20 A. was slain with the sword. 2 Pa 23:21
2 Pa 22 10 A. his mother seeing that her son was
11 therefore Athalia did not kill him
24 7 for that wicked woman Athalia and her
Athalias 1 Es 8 7 Isaias the son of Athalias
Athanai 1 Pa 6 41 Melchia the son of Athanai
Athar Josu 19 7 Ain and Remmon and Athar and

Athenians 2 Ma 9 15 to make equal with the A.
Acts 17 21 A. and strangers that were there
Athenobius 1 Ma 15 28 he sent to him Athenobius
1 Ma 15 32 A. the king's friend came to Jerusalem
35 Athenobius answered him not a word
Athens Acts 17 15 brought him as far as Athens
Acts 17 16 whilst Paul waited for them at Athens
22 ye men of Athens, I perceive that in all
18 1 departing from A., he came to Corinth
1 Th 3 1 thought it good to remain at A. alone
Ather 1 Es 2 16 the children of Ather, who were of
Athersatha 1 Es 2 63 A. said to them. 2 Es 7:65
2 Es 7 70 Athersatha gave into the treasure
8 9 Nehemias, he is A., and Esdras the
10 1 the subscribers were Nehemias, A.
Athmatha Josu 15 54 Athmatha and Cariath Arbe
atonement Exod 30 10 and shall make a. upon it
Lev 5 13 praying for him and making atonement
6 30 to make atonement in the sanctuary
16 27 the sanctuary, to accomplish the a.
32 in his father's stead, shall make a.
17 11 that you may make atonement, it shall
23 27 shall be the day of atonement, it shall
Num 25 13 hath made a. for the wickedness of the
28 22 buck goat for sin, to make a. for you
2 K 21 3 what shall be the atonement for you
2 Es 10 33 atonement might be made for Israel
Isa 43 3 I have given Egypt for thy atonement
Eze 45 15 offerings, to make atonement for them
Mala 2 13 neither do I accept any a. at your
atonements 1 Ma 1 47 a. to be made in the temple
atoning Exod 29 33 may be an atoning sacrifice
Num 5 8 for expiation, to be an a. sacrifice
attack 2 Pa 18 31 surrounded him to attack him
1 Ma 4 3 to attack the king's forces that
2 Ma 10 16 made a strong a. upon the strongholds
attacked Judg 20 34 a. inhabitants of the city
1 Ma 5 65 and attacked the children of Esau
10 82 forth his army and attacked the legion
attacus Lev 11 22 the bruchus in its kind, the a.
attain Prov 16 21 shall attain to greater things
Ecce 6 3 attain to a great age, and his soul
Phil 3 11 I may attain to the resurrection which
attained 2 K 23 19 to the three first he a. not
2 K 23 23 he attained not to the first. 1 Pa 11:21
1 Pa 11 25 to the three he [Banaias] a. not
Luke 1 3 having diligently attained to all
Rom 9 30 not after justice, have a. to justice
Phil 3 12 not as though I had already attained
1 Tim 4 6 good doctrine which thou hast a.
attaining 2 Tim 3 7 never a. to the knowledge of
Attalia Acts 14 24 they went down into Attalia
Attalus 1 Ma 15 22 to king Demetrius and to A.
attempt 2 Ma 4 41 perceived the a. of Lysimachus
attempted Judg 11 26 a. nothing about this claim
2 K 21 16 with a new sword, a. to kill David
2 Ma 2 24 we have a. to abridge in one book
9 2 attempted to rob the temple and to
10 15 of Jerusalem and a. to make war
13 18 a. to take the strong places by policy
Acts 16 7 they attempted to go into Bithynia
19 13 a. to invoke over them that had evil
attempting Heb 11 29 Egyptians a., were swallowed
attend Deut 27 9 attend, and hear, O Israel: This
2 Pa 20 15 attend ye, all Juda, and you that dwell
31 4 that they might attend to the law of
Job 13 6 and attend to the judgment of my lips
33 31 attend, Job, and hearken to me: and
Ps 16 1 attend to my supplication. 141:7
37 23 attend unto my help, O Lord, the God
58 6 attend to visit all the nations: have
68 19 attend to my soul, and deliver it
77 1 attend, O my people, to my law: incline

85 6 and attend to the voice of my petition
Prov 4 1 attend that you may know prudence
5 1 my son, attend to my wisdom, and incline
7 24 and attend to the words of my mouth
Wisd 10 9 from sorrow them that attend upon her
Eccu 6 33 if thou wilt attend to me, thou shalt
13 16 a. diligently to what thou hearest
16 24 attend to my words in thy heart. 25
Isa 10 30 attend, O Laisa, poor Anathoth, Medemena
42 23 that will attend and hearken for times
Lam 1 12 attend and see if there be any sorrow
Eze 44 5 son of man, attend with thy heart
Acts 16 14 a. to these things which were said
1 C 7 35 give you power to attend upon the Lord
1 Tim 4 13 till I come, attend unto reading
2 P 1 19 whereunto you do well to attend, as
attendance 2 Pa 9 4 and the a. of his officers
attended Ps 65 19 a. to voice of my supplication
Ps 67 18 chariot of the Lord is a. by ten
Jer 8 6 I attended and hearkened; no man
Heb 7 13 of which no one a. on the altar. For
attending Wisd 13 1 neither by a. to the works
attentive 2 Pa 6 3 all the multitude stood a.
2 Pa 6 40 let thy ears be a. to prayer. 2 Es 1:11
7 15 and ears attentive to the prayer of him
2 Es 1 6 let thy ears be a. and thy eyes open
8 3 ears of all the people were a. to the
Job 29 21 being a. held their peace at my counsel
Ps 34 23 arise, and be attentive to my judgment
39 2 waited for the Lord, and he was a. to
54 3 be attentive to me and hear me. I am
60 2 be attentive to my prayer. To thee have
129 2 let thy ears be attentive to the voice
Luke 19 48 the people were very a. to hear him
Acts 8 6 were a. to those things which were said
11 they were attentive to him [Simon]
attentively Josu 22 5 so that you observe a. and
Job 37 2 hear ye a. the terror of his voice
Lam 4 17 we looked a. towards a nation that
attestation Gen 43 3 with the a. of an oath
attire 2 K 1 24 gave ornaments of gold for your a.
Prov 7 10 woman meeteth him in harlot's attire
Eccu 19 27 attire of the body and the laughter
45 9 and crowned him with majestic attire
1 Tim 2 9 pearls or costly attire, but as it
Titus 2 3 aged women in like manner in holy a.
James 2 2 come in also a poor man in mean attire
attributed Judg 4 9 victory shall not be a. to thee
attributeth Eccu 29 21 a sinner a. to himself the
audacious 2 P 2 10 audacious, self-willed, they
audience Acts 25 23 entered into the hall of a.
aught Lev 11 43 nor touch aught thereof lest you
Josu 6 18 lest you touch aught of those things
Ruth 1 17 if aught but death part me and thee
1 K 12 4 nor taken aught at any man's hand
25 7 neither was there aught missing to
Mark 11 25 if you have aught against any man
Acts 4 32 any one say that aught of the things
augment Num 32 14 to a. the fury of the Lord
Augusta Acts 27 1 named Julius, of the band A.
Augustus Luke 2 1 went out decree from Caesar A.
Acts 25 21 to be reserved unto the hearing of A.
25 he himself hath appealed to Augustus
aunt Exod 6 20 Amram took to wife Jochabed his a.
Lev 20 19 not uncover nakedness of thy aunt by thy mother and of thy aunt by thy father
Auran Eze 47 16 which is by the border of Auran
Ausitis Jer 25 20 all the kings of the land of A.
austere Luke 19 21 because thou art an austere man
Luke 19 22 knewest that I was an austere man
author Judg 6 29 inquired for the a. of the fact
Wisd 13 3 the first author of beauty made all
Eccu 27 30 shall be rolled back upon the author
2 Ma 2 31 is the duty of the author of a history
7 31 hast been the author of all mischief
Acts 3 15 the author of life you killed, whom
24 5 a. of the sedition of the sect of the
Heb 2 10 to perfect the a. of their salvation
12 2 the author and finisher of faith, who
authority 3 K 21 7 thou art of great a. indeed
2 Pa 9 26 exercised authority over all the kings
15 16 Maacha . . . he deposed from the royal a.
1 Es 5 9 who hath given you authority to build
7 24 you have no authority to impose toll
Eccu 20 8 he that taketh authority to himself
Dan 3 3 great men that were placed in authority
1 Ma 10 6 gave him a. to gather together an army
8 had given him a. to gather together an
38 no other a. but that of the high priest
2 Ma 4 50 Menelaus continued in a., increasing in
Mat 8 9 I am a man subject to a. Luke 7:8
21 23 by what a. dost. Mark 11:28; Luke 20:2
23 given thee this a. Mark 11:28; Luke 20:2
24 I will tell you by what a. Mark 11:29
27 neither do I tell you by what authority. Mark 11:33; Luke 20:8
Mark 13 34 gave authority to his servants over
Luke 4 36 with a. and power he commandeth the
9 1 authority over all devils and to cure
20 20 deliver him up to the a. and power of
Acts 8 27 eunuch of great authority under Candace
9 14 hath a. from the chief priests to bind
26 10 having received a. of the chief priests
12 with authority and permission of the
1 Tim 2 12 not a woman to teach nor to use a.
Titus 2 15 rebuke with all authority. Let no man
authors 1 Ma 9 61 the principal a. of the mischief
2 Ma 2 29 leaving to the a. the exact handling of
autumn Isa 28 4 before the ripeness of autumn
Mich 7 1 as one that gleaneth in a. the grapes
Jude 12 trees of the autumn unfruitful, twice
auxiliaries 2 K 10 19 the kings that were a. of
Jdth 3 8 from all the cities he took auxiliaries
Ava 4 K 18 34 where is the god of Ana and of Ava
4 K 19 13 the king . . . of Ana and of Ava. Isa 37:13
Avah 4 K 17 24 from Cutha and from Avah and
avail Gen 25 32 what will the first birthright a.
Gen 37 20 shall appear what his dreams avail him
Prov 17 16 what doth it a. a fool to have riches
Ecce 2 15 what doth it avail me that I have
Eccu 34 30 again, what doth his washing avail
Haba 2 18 what doth the graven thing avail
availed 2 Pa 28 21 it a. him [Achaz] nothing
availeth Prov 17 10 reproof a. more with a wise
Gal 5 6 neither circumcision a. anything. 6:15
James 5 16 prayer of a just man availeth much
avarice Exod 18 21 there is truth and that hate a.
Isa 33 15 that casteth away a. by oppression
Rom 1 29 a., wickedness, full of envy, murder
avenge Lev 26 25 sword that shall a. my covenant
1 Ma 13 6 I will avenge then my nation and the
Luke 18 3 a. me of my adversary. And he would not
5 I will avenge her, lest continually
avenged 1 K 18 25 to be a. of the king's enemies
1 Ma 7 38 be avenged of this man and his army
Acts 7 24 he a. him who suffered the injury
avenger Num 35 27 by him that is the a. of blood
Josu 20 3 kinsman, who is the avenger of blood
5 when the avenger of blood shall pursue
Ps 8 3 mayst destroy the enemy and the a.
Rom 13 4 an a. to execute wrath upon him that
avengers Judg 6 31 are you the avengers of Baal
avengest Ps 17 48 who a. me and subduest the people
avenging Osee 5 13 sent to the avenging king
Osee 10 6 a present to the avenging king: shame
aversion Job 31 3 a. to them that work iniquity

Avim Josu 18 23 and Avim and Aphara and Ophera
Avith Gen 36 35 name of his city was A. 1 Pa 1:46
avoid Lev 11 11 their carcasses you shall avoid
Ecce 2 3 to wisdom, and might avoid folly
2 Ma 2 32 to avoid nice declarations of things
Rom 16 17 avoid them. For they that are such
1 Tim 4 7 avoid foolish and old wives' fables
5 11 the younger widows avoid. For when
2 Tim 2 23 a. foolish and unlearned questions
3 5 now these avoid. For of these sort are
4 15 whom do thou also avoid, for he hath
Titus 3 9 a. foolish questions and genealogies
10 a man that is a heretic . . . avoid
avoided Lev 11 13 which are to be avoided by you
Judg 11 3 [Jephte] avoided them and dwelt in
Wisd 17 9 which could by no means be avoided
avoiding Job 1 1 fearing God and a. evil. 8; 2:3
2 C 8 20 a. this, lest any man should blame
1 Tim 6 20 a. the profane novelties of words
awake Jdth 14 9 door of the chamber to awake him
Jdth 14 12 to the chamberlains: go in and awake
Job 8 6 he will presently awake unto thee
14 12 he shall not awake nor rise up out of
Ps 72 20 as the dream of them that awake
Prov 23 35 when shall I awake, and find wine again
Cant 2 7 nor make the beloved to awake till she
3 5 nor awake my beloved till she please
8 4 nor awake my love till she please
Eccu 13 17 were in sleep, and thou shalt awake
Isa 26 19 awake and give praise, ye that dwell
29 8 when he is awake, his soul is empty
8 after he is awake, is yet faint with
Jer 51 29 the Lord against Babylon shall awake
39 everlasting sleep, and awake no more
57 and shall awake no more, saith the
Dan 12 2 in the dust of the earth, shall awake
Joel 1 5 awake, ye that are drunk, and weep
Haba 2 19 woe to him that saith to wood: Awake
Zach 13 7 awake, O sword, against my shepherd
Mark 4 38 they awake him and say to him: Master
John 11 11 I go that I may awake him [Lazarus]
1 C 15 34 awake ye just, and sin not. For some
awaked Gen 28 16 when Jacob awaked out of sleep
Gen 41 7 Pharao awaked after his rest: and when
45 26 he [Jacob] awaked as it were out of
1 K 26 12 no man saw it or knew it or awaked
3 K 3 15 Solomon a. and perceived that it was a
18 27 perhaps he is asleep and must be awaked
Ps 77 65 the Lord was awaked as one out of sleep
Eccu 33 16 I awaked last of all, and as one that
Jer 31 26 I was as it were awaked out of a sleep
Eze 7 6 it hath awaked against thee: behold it
Mat 8 25 awaked him, saying: Lord, save us
Luke 8 24 awaked him, saying: Master, we perish
awakest Prov 6 22 when thou a., talk with them
awaketh Wisd 6 15 that awaketh early to seek her
awaking Gen 9 24 Noe awaking from the wine, when
Judg 16 14 awaking out of his sleep he drew out
20 a. from sleep, he said in his mind
Acts 16 27 keeper of the prison awaking out of
award Exod 21 22 damage . . . as arbiters shall award
aware Prov 11 15 he that is aware of the snares
Jer 50 24 Babylon, and thou wast not aware of it
Luke 11 44 and men that walk over are not aware
Heb 13 2 not a. of it, have entertained angels
away Mat 5 40 if a man will take away thy coat
Mat 5 42 that would borrow of thee, turn not a.
9 15 when the bridegroom shall be taken away
16 it taketh away the fulness thereof
11 12 the violent bear it away. For all the
13 6 they had not root, they withered away
12 from him shall be taken away that also
19 cometh the wicked one and catcheth away
36 having sent away the multitudes. 14:15
15 23 send her away, for she crieth after us
21 19 immediately the fig tree withered away
20 how is it presently withered away
24 39 the flood came and took them all away
26 42 if this chalice may not pass away
27 20 should ask Barabbas and make Jesus away
31 led him away to crucify him. And going
Luke 23 18 away with this man and release unto
John 19 15 they cried out: Away with him; away
Acts 21 36 crying: Away with him. And as Paul
22 22 away with such an one from the earth
awe Ps 32 8 inhabitants of world be in awe of him
Ps 118 161 my heart hath been in awe of thy words
Wisd 6 8 neither will he stand in awe of any
awful Judg 13 6 countenance of an angel, very a.
awl Exod 21 6 shall bore his ear through with an a.
Deut 15 17 thou shalt take an awl and bore through
awoke Gen 41 4 so Pharao awoke. He slept again
Gen 41 21 I awoke and then fell asleep again
Axa Judg 1 12 to him will I give my daughter Axa
Josu 15 16 I will give him Axa my daughter to
17 gave him Axa his daughter. Judg 1:13
Axaph Josu 19 25 Chali and Beten and Axaph
axe Deut 19 5 cutting down the tree the axe slipped
Judg 9 48 taking an axe, he cut down the bough of
1 K 13 20 to sharpen every man . . . his axe and
3 K 6 7 there was neither hammer nor axe nor
4 K 6 5 head of the axe fell into the water
Ps 73 6 with axe and hatchet they have brought
Isa 10 15 shall the axe boast itself against him
Jer 10 3 a tree out of the forest with an axe
Bar 6 14 hath in his hand a sword or an axe
Mat 3 10 the axe is laid to the root. Luke 3:9
axes Deut 20 19 country round about with axes
1 K 13 21 their forks and their axes were blunt
Ps 73 5 as with axes in a wood of trees
Jer 46 22 with axes they shall come against her
axletree Eccu 33 5 thoughts are like a rolling a.
axletrees 3 K 7 30 four wheels and a. of brass
3 K 7 33 their axletrees and spokes and strakes
Aza 1 Pa 7 28 as far as Aza with her daughters
1 Es 2 49 the children of Aza. 2 Es 7:51
Azael Amos 1 4 I will send a fire into house of A.
Azahel 1 Es 10 15 Jonathan the son of Azahel, and
Azanias 2 Es 10 9 Josue the son of Azanias
Azanotthabor Josu 19 34 westward to Azanotthabor
Azareel 1 Pa 12 6 Jesia and Azareel and Joezer
1 Pa 25 18 the eleventh to Azareel, to his sons
2 Es 12 35 his brethren Semeia and Azareel
Azaria 2 Pa 21 2 Azaria and Michael and Saphatias
Azarias 3 K 4 2 A. the son of Sadoc the priest
3 K 4 5 Azarias the son of Nathan over them
4 K 14 21 all the people of Juda took Azarias
15 1 reigned Azarias the son of Amasias
6 the rest of the acts of Azarias and
7 and Azarias slept with his fathers
8 in eight and thirtieth year of Azarias
13 nine and thirtieth year of Azarias. 17
23 in the fiftieth year of Azarias king
27 in the two and fiftieth year of Azarias
1 Pa 2 8 sons of Ethan: Azarias, and the sons of
38 Jehu begot A. A. begot Helles, and
3 12 and his son Amasias begot Azarias
12 Joathan the son of Azarias begot Achaz
6 9 Achimaas begot A., A. begot Johanan
10 Johanan begot Azarias. This is he that
11 Azarias begot Amarias, and Amarias
13 Helcias begot A., A. begot Saraias
36 Johel the son of Azarias, the son of
9 11 Azarias the son of Helcias, the son of
2 Pa 15 1 the spirit of God came upon Azarias
8 the prophecy of Azarias the son of Oded

21 2 sons of Josaphat, Azarias and Jahiel
23 1 Azarias the son of Jeroham, and
1 Azarias the son of Obed, and Maasias
26 17 Azarias the priest going in after him
20 A. the high priest and all the rest of
28 12 of the sons of Ephraim, Azarias the
29 12 Joel the son of Azarias of the sons of
12 son of Abdi, and A. the son of Jalaleel
31 10 A. the chief priest of the race of Sadoc
13 Jehiel and Azarias and Nahath and
13 Azarias the high priest of the house
1 Es 7 1 Saraias the son of Azarias, the son of
3 Amarias the son of Azarias, the son of
2 Es 3 23 after him built Azarias the son of
24 from the house of A. unto the bending
7 7 Nehemias, Azarias, Raamias, Nahamani
8 7 Azarias, Jozabed, Hanan, Phalaia
10 2 Saraias, Azarias, Jeremias, Pheshur
12 33 Azarias, Esdras, and Mosollam, Judas
Tob 5 18 I am A. the son of the great Ananias
6 7 I beseech thee, brother Azarias, tell
9 1 brother Azarias, I pray thee hearken
Jer 43 2 A. the son of Osaias, and Johanan
Dan 1 6 Ananias, Misael, and A. 11, 19; 2:17
7 them names . . . to Azarias, Abdenago
3 25 A. standing up prayed in this manner
49 angel of the Lord went down with A.
88 Ananias, Azarias, and Misael. 1 Ma 2:59
5 18 he left Joseph . . . and Azarias captains
56 and Azarias captain of the soldiers
60 Joseph and Azarias were put to flight
Azaricam 2 Es 11 15 Hasub the son of Azaricam
Azau Gen 22 22 Cased and Asau and Pheldas and
Azaz 1 Pa 5 8 Bala the son of Azaz, the son of
Azbai 1 Pa 11 37 Naarai the son of Azbai, Joel the
Azboc 2 Es 3 16 Nehemias the son of Azboc, lord of
Azeca Josu 10 10 cut them off all the way to A.
Josu 10 11 stoned from heaven as far as Azeca
15 35 Socho and Azeca and Saraim and
2 Es 11 30 at Azeca and the villages thereof
Azecha 1 K 17 1 camped between Socho and Azecha
2 Pa 11 9 and Aduram and Lachis and Azecha
Jer 34 7 against Lachis and against Azecha
Azgad 1 Es 2 12 the children of Azgad, 1,222
1 Es 8 12 of the sons of Azgad, Joanan the son of
2 Es 7 17 children of Azgad, 2,322. The children
10 15 Bonni, Azgad, Bebai, Adonia, Begoai
Aziam 2 Es 11 4 Athaias the son of Aziam, the son
Aziaza 1 Es 10 27 Jerimuth and Zabad and Aziaza
Azmaveth 2 K 23 31 Azmaveth of Beromi, Eliaba of
1 Es 2 24 the children of Azmaveth, forty-two
2 Es 12 29 the countries of Geba and Azmaveth
Azmoth 1 Pa 8 36 Joaba begot Alamath and Azmoth
1 Pa 9 42 Jara begot Alamath and Azmoth and
11 32 A. a Bauramite, Eliaba a Salabonite
12 3 Jaziel and Phallet the sons of Azmoth
27 25 over the king's treasures was Azmoth
Azor Mat 1 13 Eliacim begot A., A. begot Sadoc
Azotians Josu 13 3 the Azotians, the Gethites, and
1 K 5 3 when the Azotians arose early the next
6 hand of Lord was heavy upon the A.
2 Es 4 7 A. heard that the walls of Jerusalem
Azotus Josu 11 22 cities of Gaza and Geth and A.
Josu 15 46 all places that lie towards Azotus
47 Azotus with its towns and villages
1 K 5 1 carried it from Stone of help into A.
5 on the threshold of Dagon in Azotus
6 and afflicted Azotus and the coasts
7 men of A. seeing this kind of plague
6 17 for Azotus one, for Gaza one, for
2 Pa 26 6 wall of Jabnia and the wall of Azotus
6 he built towns in Azotus and among
2 Es 13 23 Jews that married wives, women of A.
24 spoke half in the speech of Azotus
Isa 20 1 year that Tharthan entered into Azotus
1 and he had fought against Azotus and
Jer 25 20 Accaron, and the remnant of Azotus
Amos 1 8 I will cut off the inhabitant from A.
3 9 publish it in the houses of Azotus
Soph 2 4 they shall cast out Azotus at noonday
Zach 9 6 and the divider shall sit in Azotus
1 Ma 4 15 to the plains of Idumea and of Azotus
5 68 Judas turned to Azotus into the land
9 15 pursued them even to the mount Azotus
10 78 he went to Azotus as one that was
78 Jonathan followed after him to Azotus
83 about the plain, fled into Azotus and
84 Jonathan set fire to A. and the cities
11 4 when he came near to Azotus, they
showed him . . . Azotus and the suburbs
14 34 Gazara, which bordereth upon Azotus
16 10 towers that were in the fields of A.
Acts 8 40 but Philip was found in Azotus; and
Azreel 2 Es 11 13 Amassai the son of Azreel the
Azuba 3 K 22 42 of his mother was A. 2 Pa 20:31
1 Pa 2 18 son of Hesron took a wife named Azuba
19 when Azuba was dead, Caleb took to
Azur 2 Es 10 17 Ater, Hezecia, Azur, Odaia, Hasum
Jer 28 1 Hananias the son of Azur, a prophet
Eze 11 1 Jezonias the son of Azur, and Pheltias
Azymes Mat 26 17 the first day of the Azymes
Mark 14 1 feast of the pasch and of the Azymes
Acts 12 3 now it was in the days of the Azymes
20 6 from Philippi after the days of the A.
Azzi 2 Es 11 22 Azzi the son of Bani the son of
2 Es 12 19 of Jodaia, Azzi: of Sellai, Celai: of
41 Eleazar and Azzi and Johanan and

B

Baal Num 22 41 him to the high places of Baal
Judg 2 13 forsaking him and serving Baal and
6 25 thou shalt destroy the altar of Baal
28 they saw the altar of Baal destroyed
30 he hath destroyed the altar of Baal
31 are you the avengers of Baal, that you
8 33 and they made a covenant with Baal, that
3 K 16 31 went and served Baal and adored him
32 altar for Baal in the temple of Baal
18 19 the prophets of Baal 450, and the
21 but if Baal, then follow him. And the
22 but the prophets of Baal are 450 men
25 then Elias said to the prophets of Baal
26 they called on the name of Baal . . . saying: O Baal, hear us
40 take the prophets of Baal, and let not
19 18 knees have not been bowed before Baal
22 54 he [Ochozias] served also Baal and
4 K 3 2 he took away the statues of Baal, which
10 18 Achab worshipped Baal a little, but I
19 call to me all the prophets of Baal and
19 I have great sacrifice to offer to Baal
19 might destroy the worshippers of Baal
20 he said: Proclaim a festival for Baal
21 and all the servants of Baal came
21 went into the temple of Baal. 11:18
21 and the house of Baal was filled from
22 garments for all the servants of Baal
23 went to the temple of Baal and said to the worshippers of Baal
23 that there be the servants of Baal only
25 into the city of the temple of Baal
27 they destroyed also the temple of Baal
28 so Jehu destroyed Baal out of Israel
11 18 slew also Mathan priest of B. 2 Pa 23:17
17 16 and they served Baal. And consecrated
21 3 he [Manasses] set up altars to Baal
23 4 vessels that had been made for Baal

5 them also that burnt incense to Baal
1 Pa 4 33 round about these cities as far as Baal
5 5 Baal his son, Beera his son, whom
23 from the borders of Basan unto Baal
8 30 Abdon and Sur and Cis and Baal. 9:36
2 Pa 23 17 into the house of Baal and destroyed it
24 7 adorned the temple of Baal with all
Jer 2 8 the prophets prophesied in Baal and
12 16 have taught my people to swear by Baal
23 13 they prophesied in Baal, and deceived
27 as their fathers forgot my name for B.
32 29 they offered sacrifice to Baal and
35 they have built the high places of B.
Osee 2 8 they have used in the service of Baal
10 14 by the house of him that judged Baal
13 1 he sinned in Baal and died. And now
Soph 1 4 out of this place the remnant of Baal
Rom 11 4 have not bowed their knees to Baal
Baal Hermon Judg 3 3 mount Baal Hermon to the
Baal Pharisim 2 K 5 20 and David came to B. P.
2 K 5 20 name of place was called Baal Pharisim
Baala Josu 15 9 it bendeth towards Baala which is
Josu 15 10 from Baala westward unto mount Seir
11 to Sechrona and passeth mount Baala
29 Baala and Jim and Esem and Eltholad
Baalath Josu 19 8 to Baalath Beer Ramath to the
3 K 9 18 B. and Palmira in the land of the
Baalberith Judg 9 4 silver out of temple of B.
Baalgad Josu 11 17 up to Seir as far as Baalgad
Josu 12 7 from Baalgad in the field of Libanus
13 5 from Baalgad under mount Hermon to the
Baalhasor 2 K 13 23 were shorn in Baalhasor which
Baali Osee 2 16 she shall call me no more Baali
Baaliada 1 Pa 14 7 born to him [David] . . . Baaliada
Baalim Judg 2 11 and they served Baalim. And they
Judg 3 7 served Baalim and Astaroth. 1 K 12:10
8 33 committed fornication with Baalim. And
10 6 served idols, Baalim and Astaroth and
10 and have served Baalim. And the Lord
1 K 7 3 strange gods . . . Baalim and Astaroth
4 put away Baalim and Astaroth and served
3 K 18 18 and have followed Baalim. Nevertheless
2 Pa 17 3 and trusted not in Baalim, but in the
28 2 also he cast statues for Baalim. It was
33 3 he [Manasses] built altars to Baalim
34 4 broke down . . . the altars of Baalim
Jer 2 23 I have not walked after Baalim? See
7 9 to swear falsely, to offer to Baalim
9 14 have gone after . . . Baalim, which their
11 13 altars to offer sacrifice to Baalim
17 to provoke me, offering sacrifice to B.
19 5 have built the high places of Baalim
5 children . . . for a holocaust to Baalim
Osee 2 13 I will visit upon her the days of B.
17 I will take away the names of Baalim
11 2 they offered victims to Baalim, and
Baalis Jer 40 14 B. king of the children of Ammon
Baalmaon Josu 13 17 and the town of Baalmaon and
Baalmeon Num 32 38 Nabo and Baalmeon, their names
Baalpharasim 1 Pa 14 11 when they were come to B.
1 Pa 14 11 the name of that place was called B.
Baal's 4 K 10 26 the statue out of Baal's temple
Baalsalisa 4 K 4 42 a certain man came from B.
Baalthamar Judg 20 33 place which is called B.
Baana 2 K 4 2 name of the one was Baana, and the
2 K 4 5 Rechab and Baana coming, went into
6 Rechab and Baana his brother stabbed
9 David answered Rechab and Baana his
23 29 Heled the son of Baana. 1 Pa 11:30
3 K 4 16 Baana the son of Husi, in Aser and in
1 Es 2 2 Mesphar, Beguai, Rehum, Baana. The
2 Es 3 4 next to them built Sadoc the son of B.
7 7 Mespharath, Begoia, Nahum, Baana. The
10 27 Hanan, Anan, Melluch, Haran, Baana
Baasa 3 K 15 16 was war between Asa and Baasa. 32
3 K 15 17 B. king of Israel went up against Juda
19 break thy league with Baasa king of
21 when Baasa had heard this, he left off
22 wherewith Baasa had been building, and
27 Baasa . . . conspired against him and slew
28 Baasa slew him in the third year of Asa
33 Baasa the son of Ahias reigned over all
16 1 word of the Lord came against B. 7
3 I will cut down the posterity of Baasa
4 him that dieth of Baasa in the city
5 the rest of the acts of Baasa and all
6 so Baasa slept with his fathers and
8 Ela the son of Baasa reigned over Israel
11 [Zambri] slew all the house of Baasa
12 Zambri destroyed all the house of Baasa
12 that he had spoken to Baasa in the hand
13 for all the sins of Baasa and the sins
21 22 like the house of Baasa. 4 K 9:9
2 Pa 16 1 Baasa . . . came up against Juda and built
3 thou mayst break thy league with Baasa
5 when Baasa heard of it, he left off
6 the timber that Baasa had prepared for
Jer 41 9 for fear of Baasa the king of Israel
babbler Eccu 20 7 b. and a fool will regard no time
babbling Eccu 20 7 hateth b., extinguisheth evil
1 Tim 1 6 are turned aside unto vain babbling
babblings 2 Tim 2 16 shun profane and vain b.
babe Exod 2 3 put the little babe therein and
Exod 2 7 a Hebrew woman to nurse the babe? She
Heb 11 23 they saw he [Moses] was a comely babe
Babel Gen 11 9 the name thereof was called Babel
babes Exod 2 6 is one of the babes of the Hebrews
Wisd 18 5 thought to kill the babes of the just
1 P 2 2 as newborn babes desire rational milk
1 J 2 14 I write unto you, babes, because you
Babylon Gen 10 10 beginning of his kingdom was B.
4 K 17 24 brought people from Babylon and from
30 the men of Babylon made Sochothbenoth
20 14 country they came to me out of Babylon
17 shall be carried into Babylon: nothing
24 15 he carried away Joachin into Babylon
15 into captivity from Jerusalem into B.
16 led them captives into Babylon. And he
25 7 him with chains and brought him to B.
13 kings that were with him in B. Jer 52:32
1 Pa 9 1 and they were carried away to Babylon
2 Pa 32 31 in embassy of the princes of Babylon
33 11 bound with chains and fetters to B.
36 6 led him bound in chains into Babylon
10 brought him to Babylon, carrying away
18 treasures . . . he carried away to Babylon
20 escaped the sword, was led into Babylon
1 Es 1 11 that came up from the captivity of B.
2 1 had carried away to Babylon and who
5 12 and carried away the people to Babylon
14 brought them to the temple of Babylon
14 Cyrus brought out of the temple of B.
17 the king's library, which is in Babylon
6 1 the books that were laid up in Babylon
5 Nabuchodonosor . . . brought to Babylon
7 6 this Esdras went up from Babylon and
9 [Esdras] began to go up from Babylon
16 find in all the province of Babylon
8 1 who came up with me from Babylon in the
Ps 86 4 I will be mindful of Rahab and of B.
136 1 upon the rivers of Babylon, there we
8 daughter of Babylon, miserable: blessed
Isa 13 1 the burden of Babylon which Isaias the
19 that Babylon, glorious among kingdoms
14 22 I will destroy the name of Babylon and
21 4 Babylon my beloved is become a wonder

9 Babylon is fallen, she is fallen, and
39 3 they came to me, from Babylon. And he
6 shall be carried away into Babylon
43 14 for your sake I sent to Babylon and
47 1 virgin daughter of Babylon, sit on the
48 14 he will do his pleasure in Babylon and
20 come forth out of Babylon, flee ye from
Jer 20 4 and he shall carry them away to Babylon
5 they shall . . . carry them to Babylon
6 and thou shalt go to Babylon. 34:3
24 1 Jerusalem, and had brought them to B.
27 16 short time be brought again from B.
18 in Jerusalem, may not go to Babylon
20 the king of Juda from Jerusalem to B.
22 they shall be carried to Babylon, and
28 3 from this place and carried them to B.
4 captives of Juda, that are gone to B.
6 all the captives may return out of B.
29 1 carried away from Jerusalem to B. 4
3 Sedecias king of Juda sent to Babylon
10 when the seventy years . . . in Babylon
15 hath raised us up prophets in Babylon
20 I have sent out from Jerusalem to B.
22 captivity of Juda, that are in Babylon
28 he hath also sent to us in Babylon
32 5 and he shall lead Sedecias to Babylon
39 7 with fetters, to be carried to Babylon
9 away captive to Babylon the remnant of
40 1 were carried to B. And the general of
4 it please thee to come with me to B.
4 not please thee to come with me to B.
7 not been carried away captive to B.
43 3 us to be carried away captives to B.
50 1 that the Lord hath spoken against B.
2 conceal it not: say: Babylon is taken
8 remove out of the midst of Babylon and
9 will bring against B. an assembly of
13 every one that shall pass by Babylon
14 prepare yourselves against Babylon
16 destroy the sower out of Babylon, and
23 how is Babylon turned into a desert
24 a snare, and thou art taken, O Babylon
28 have escaped out of the land of Babylon
29 declare to many against Babylon, to all
34 to disquiet the inhabitants of Babylon
35 sword is . . . upon the inhabitants of B.
42 battle against thee, O daughter of B.
45 which he hath taken against Babylon
46 at the noise of the taking of Babylon
51 1 a pestilential wind against Babylon
2 I will send to Babylon fanners and they
6 flee ye from the midst of Babylon, and
7 Babylon hath been a golden cup in the
8 B. is suddenly fallen and destroyed
9 we would have cured Babylon, but she
11 his mind is against B. to destroy it
12 upon walls of B. set up the standard
12 he spoke against the inhabitants of B.
24 I will render to Babylon . . . all their
29 the design of the Lord against Babylon
29 to make the land of Babylon desert and
30 valiant men of Babylon have forborne
33 daughter of B. like a thrashing-floor
35 the wrong done to me . . . be upon Babylon
37 Babylon shall be reduced to heaps
41 how is Babylon become an astonishment
42 the sea is come up over Babylon: she
44 I will visit against Bel in Babylon
44 the wall also of Babylon shall fall
47 and I will visit the idols of Babylon
48 in them shall give praise for Babylon
49 as B. caused that there should fall
49 of Babylon there shall fall slain in
53 if Babylon should mount up to heaven
54 the noise of a cry from Babylon and
55 because the Lord hath laid B. waste
56 spoiler is come upon her . . . upon B.
58 broad wall of Babylon shall be utterly
59 he went with king Sedecias to Babylon
60 all the evil that was to come upon B.
60 all these words are written against B.
61 to Saraias: When thou shalt come into B.
64 shalt say: Thus shall Babylon sink and
52 11 brought him [Sedecias] into Babylon
Bar 1 9 brought them bound to Babylon. And they
6 1 were to be led away captives into B.
1 shall be carried away captives into B.
2 when you are come into Babylon, you
3 you shall see in Babylon gods of gold
Eze 12 13 I will bring him into Babylon. 17:20
17 12 and carry them with him to Babylon
16 in the midst of Babylon shall he die
23 15 the likeness of the sons of Babylon
17 when the sons of B. were come to her
23 children of B. and all the Chaldeans
Dan 2 12 the wise men of Babylon should be put
14 forth to kill the wise men of Babylon
18 with the rest of the wise men of B.
24 orders to destroy the wise men of B.
24 destroy not the wise men of Babylon
48 governor over all the provinces of B.
48 over all the wise men of Babylon. And
49 over works of the province of B. 3:12
3 1 the plain of Dura of the province of B.
97 promoted Sidrach . . . in province of B.
4 3 that all the wise men of B. should
26 was walking in the palace of Babylon
27 is not this the great Babylon which I
5 7 and said to the wise men of Babylon
13 1 there was a man that dwelt in Babylon
5 iniquity came out from Babylon from
14 33 carry the dinner . . . into Babylon to
34 Lord, I never saw Babylon, nor do I
35 set him in Babylon over the den in the
Mich 4 10 and shalt come even to Babylon, there
Zach 2 7 that dwellest with the daughter of B.
6 10 son of Sophonias, who came out of B.
Mat 1 11 in the transmigration of B. 12:17
Acts 7 43 I will carry you away beyond Babylon
1 P 5 13 the church that is in Babylon, elected
Apoc 14 8 great Babylon is fallen, is fallen
16 19 great Babylon came in remembrance
17 5 a mystery; B. the great, the mother
18 2 Babylon the great is fallen, is fallen
10 alas! that great city Babylon, that
21 shall B., that great city, be thrown

king of Babylon 4 K 20 18 shall be eunuchs in the palace of the k. . . .
4 K 24 7 k. . . . had taken all that had belonged
12 Joachin king of Juda went out to k. . . .
12 the k. . . . received him [Joachin] in
16 the k. . . . led them captives into B.
20 Sedicias revolted from k. . . . Jer 52:3
25 6 brought him [Sedecias] to the k. . . .
8 the nineteenth year of the k. . . . , came
8 a servant of the k. . . . , into Jerusalem
11 fugitives that had gone over to k. . . .
20 carried them to k. . . . to Reblatha
21 the k. . . . smote them and slew them at
23 the k. . . . had made Godolias governor
24 stay in the land and serve the k. . . .
27 Evilmerodach k. . . . lifted up the head
1 Es 5 13 the first year of Cyrus the king of B.
2 Es 13 6 and thirtieth year of Artaxerxes k. . . .
Isa 14 4 this parable against the king of B.
39 1 Merodach Baladan . . . king of Babylon

7 shall be eunuchs in palace of k. . . .
Jer 20 4 all Juda into the hand of the k. . . .
21 4 with which you fight against the k. . . .
10 shall be given into the hand of k. . . .
25 11 all these nations shall serve k. . . .
12 will punish the k. . . . and that nation
27 8 his neck under the yoke of the k. . . .
9 you shall not serve the k. . . . 14
11 their neck under yoke of the k. . . .
12 your necks under yoke of the k. . . .
13 nation that will not serve the k. . . .
28 2 I have broken the yoke of the k. . . .
4 I will break the yoke of the k. . . .
29 22 whom the k. . . . fried in the fire
32 2 army of the k. . . . besieged Jerusalem
3 this city into the hand of the k. . . .
4 delivered into hands of k. . . . 36; 37:16
28 this city into hands of k. . . . 34:2
34 3 thy eyes shall see the eyes of k. . . .
7 army of k. . . . fought against Jerusalem
21 into hands of the armies of the k. . . .
36 29 k. . . . shall come speedily and shall lay
37 18 said: The k. . . . shall not come against
38 3 into hand of the army of the k. . . .
17 and go out to the princes of the k. . . .
18 wilt not go out to princes of k. . . .
22 brought out to the princes of k. . . .
23 be taken by the hand of the k. . . .
39 3 all the princes of the k. . . . came in
3 all the rest of the princes of k. . . .
6 k. . . . slew sons of Sedecias. 52:10
6 the k. . . . slew all the nobles of Juda
13 the nobles of the k. . . . sent and took
40 5 whom the k. . . . hath made governor over
7 the k. . . . had made Godolias the son of
9 dwell in the land and serve the k. . . .
11 heard that k. . . . had left a remnant
41 2 whom k. . . . had made governor. 18
42 11 fear not because of the king of B.
50 18 I will visit the k. . . . and his land
43 k. . . . hath heard the report of them
51 31 to tell k. . . . that his city is taken
9 they carried him [Sedecias] to k. . . .
11 the k. . . . brought him into Babylon
12 who stood before k. . . . in Jerusalem
15 that were fled over to the king of B.
26 brought them to the k. . . . to Reblatha
27 k. . . . struck them and put them to death
31 Evilmerodach k. . . . in the first year
34 provision was allowed him by the k. . . .
Bar 2 21 and your neck and serve the k. . . .
22 to serve the k. . . . : I will cause you
24 thy voice, to serve the king of Babylon
Eze 17 12 k. . . . cometh to Jerusalem: and he shall
19 9 brought him in chains to the k. . . .
21 19 for the sword of the k. . . . to come
21 k. . . . stood in the highway at the head
24 2 the k. . . . hath set himself against
30 24 strengthen the arms of the k. . . . 25
25 my sword into the hand of the k. . . .
32 11 sword of the k. . . . shall come upon thee
Dan 7 1 in the first year of Baltasar k. . . .
Nabuchodonosor (the) king of Babylon 4 K 24 1 in his days N. . . . came up, and Joakim
4 K 24 10 the servants of N. . . . came up against
11 N. . . . came to the city with his servants
25 1 N. . . . came, he and all his. Jer 52:4
22 in land of Juda, which N. . . . had left
1 Es 2 1 captivity which N. . . . had carried away
5 12 delivered them into the hands of N. . . .
2 Es 7 6 whom N. . . . had carried away and who
Esth 2 6 time that N. . . . carried away Jechonias
11 4 whom N. . . . had carried away from
Jer 21 2 N. . . . maketh war against us: if so be
7 into hand of N. . . . , and into. 22:25
24 1 N. . . . had carried away Jechonias the
25 1 the same is the first year of N. . . .
9 I will send and take . . . N. . . . 43:10
27 6 all these lands into the hand of N. . . .
8 and kingdom that will not serve N. . . .
20 which N. . . . did not take when he carried
28 3 which N. . . . took away from this place
11 even so will I break the yoke of N. . . .
14 of all these nations, to serve N. . . .
29 3 king of Juda sent to Babylon to N. . . .
21 deliver them up into hands of N. . . .
34 1 when N. . . . and all his army and all the
35 11 when N. . . . came up to our land, we said
37 1 whom N. . . . made king in land of Juda
39 1 came N. . . . and all his army to Jerusalem
5 they brought him [Sedecias] to N. . . .
11 N. . . . had given charge to Nabuzardan
44 30 king of Juda into the hand of N. . . .
46 2 whom N. . . . defeated in the fourth year
13 how N. . . . should come and strike the
26 will deliver them . . . into hand of N. . . .
49 28 kingdoms of Asor, which N. . . . destroyed
30 N. . . . hath taken counsel against you
50 17 last this N. . . . hath broken his bones
51 34 N. . . . hath eaten me up, he hath devoured
52 12 same is the nineteenth year of N. . . .
Bar 1 9 that N. . . . had carried away Jechonias
11 pray ye for the life of N. . . . , and for
12 we may live under the shadow of N. . . .
6 1 away captives into Babylon by N. . . .
Eze 26 7 behold I will bring against Tyre N. . . .
29 18 N. . . . hath made his army to undergo
19 I will set N. . . . in the land of Egypt
30 10 of Egypt to cease by hand of N. . . .
Dan 1 1 N. . . . came to Jerusalem and besieged it
Babylonia Bar 1 1 book which Baruch . . . wrote in B.
Bar 1 4 the greatest of them that dwelt in B.
1 Ma 6 4 sadness and returned towards Babylonia
2 Ma 8 20 had fought against the Galatians in B.
Babylonians 4 K 20 12 son of Baladan, king of B.
1 Es 4 9 Reum Beelteem and . . . the Babylonians
Dan 14 2 the Babylonians had an idol called Bel
22 and the Babylonians worshipped him
27 when the Babylonians had heard this
Bacbacar 1 Pa 9 15 Bacbacar the carpenter and
Bacbuc 1 Es 2 51 the children of Bacbuc. 2 Es 7:53
Bacchides 1 Ma 7 8 the king chose B., one of his
1 Ma 7 12 then there assembled to Alcimus and B.
19 B. removed the camp from Jerusalem and
20 so Bacchides went away to the king: but
9 1 sent again B. and Alcimus into Judea
12 and Bacchides was in the right wing
14 stronger part of the army of B. was on
24 and all their country yielded to B.
25 B. chose the wicked men and made them
26 friends of Judas, and brought them to B.
29 against our enemies, B. and them that
32 B. had knowledge of it and sought to
34 B. understood it and he came himself
43 B. heard it and he came on sabbath day
47 stretched forth his hand to strike B.
57 Bacchides saw that Alcimus was dead
58 let us bring Bacchides hither, and he
63 when B. knew it, he gathered together
68 they fought against Bacchides, and he
10 12 in the strongholds which B. had built
2 Ma 8 30 that were with Timotheus and Bacchides
Bacchides' 1 Ma 9 49 there fell of B. side that
Bacchus 2 Ma 6 7 when the feast of Bacchus was
2 Ma 6 7 crowned with ivy in honor of Bacchus
14 33 I will dedicate this temple to Bacchus

Bacenor's 2 Ma 12 35 Dositheus . . . one of B. band
back Gen 22 13 saw behind his back a ram amongst
Exod 26 12 cover the back parts of the tabernacle
23 in corners at the back of the tabernacle
28 26 that . . . look towards the back parts
33 8 and they beheld the back of Moses, till
23 and thou shalt see my back parts: but
Josu 8 14 that there lay an ambush behind his back
15 Josue and all Israel gave back, making
1 K 10 9 had turned his back to go from Samuel
2 K 2 23 with his spear with a back stroke in
22 41 hast made to turn their back to me
3 K 12 10 is thicker than the back of my father
14 9 anger, and hast cast me behind thy b.
4 K 19 21 hath wagged her head behind thy back
Job 39 22 he turneth not his back to the sword
Ps 17 41 hast made my enemies turn their back
20 13 thou shalt make them turn their back
43 11 made us turn our back to our enemies
65 11 thou hast laid afflictions on our back
67 14 of her back with the paleness of gold
68 24 and their back bend thou down always
80 7 he removed his back from the burdens
128 3 the wicked have wrought upon my back
Prov 10 13 rod on back of him that wanteth sense
26 3 an ass, and a rod for the back of fools
Eccu 4 5 ask of thee to curse thee behind thy b.
21 18 he will cast it behind his back. The
35 22 that he may crush their back. And he
Isa 30 21 one admonishing thee behind thy back
38 17 hast cast all my sins behind thy back
Jer 2 27 they have turned their back to me, and
9 22 as grass behind the back of the mower
18 17 I will show them the back, and not the
48 37 upon every back there shall be haircloth
Eze 9 11 linen, that had the inkhorn at his back
23 35 and hast cast me off behind thy back
41 15 which was separated at the back of it
Dan 13 18 went out by a back door to fetch what
26 they rushed in by the back door to see
Osee 5 8 behind thy back, O Benjamin. Ephraim
Amos 8 10 sackcloth upon every back of yours
Nah 1 13 his rod with which he struck thy back
1 Ma 9 16 followed after Judas . . . at their b.
11 55 against Demetrius, who turned his back
Mat 2 12 back another way into their country
28 2 an angel . . . rolled back the stone
Mark 13 16 not turn back to take up his garment
Rom 11 10 not see: and bow down their back always
Philem 12 Onesimus . . . whom I have sent back to
James 5 4 by fraud has been kept back by you
2 P 2 21 turn back from that holy commandment
backbiteth Ecce 10 11 he is nothing better that b.
backbiting Prov 25 23 sad countenance a b. tongue
backs Gen 14 10 and king of Gomorrha turned their b.
Exod 23 27 will turn the backs of all thy enemies
Deut 33 11 strike the backs of his enemies, and
Josu 7 4 men: who immediately turned their backs
8 seeing Israel turning their backs to
8 5 we will flee and turn our backs, as we
Judg 20 37 whilst Benjamin turned their backs to
41 turned their backs and began to go
1 K 4 2 Israel turned their backs to the
2 K 19 3 would do that hath turned their backs
2 Pa 29 6 and turned their backs. They have shut
2 Es 9 26 and threw thy law behind their backs
Isa 45 1 to turn the backs of kings and to open
Jer 32 33 they have turned their backs to me and
46 5 dismayed, and turning their backs
49 8 flee and turn your backs, go down into
Eze 8 16 having their backs towards the temple
backward Gen 9 23 going b., covered the nakedness
Gen 49 17 heels that his rider may fall backward
19 he himself shall be girded backward
Ps 39 15 let them be turned backward. 69:4
Eccu 48 26 in his days the sun went backward, and
Isa 28 13 that they may go and fall backward
38 8 with the sun . . . ten lines backward
44 25 that turn the wise backward and that
59 14 and judgment is turned away backward
Jer 7 24 went backward and not forward from the
15 6 thou art gone backward; and I will
Lam 1 8 but she sighed and turned backward
John 18 6 went backward and fell to the ground
backwards 1 K 4 18 he fell from his stool backwards
4 K 20 11 brought the shadow ten degrees b.
Isa 1 4 they are gone away b. For what shall I
1 Ma 9 47 but he turned away from him backwards
bad Exod 33 4 people hearing these very bad things
Lev 27 12 who judging whether it be good or bad
14 consider it whether it be good or bad
33 not be chosen neither good nor bad
Num 13 20 the land . . . whether it be good or bad
1 K 25 3 her husband was churlish and very bad
4 K 2 19 but the waters are very bad, and the
2 Pa 25 17 then Amasias . . . taking very bad counsel
Jer 24 2 the other basket had very bad figs
2 not be eaten, because they were bad
3 and the bad figs, very bad, which
3 cannot be eaten because they are bad. 8
8 as the very bad figs that cannot be
29 17 I will make them like bad figs that
17 not be eaten because they are very bad
48 34 waters also of Nemrim shall be very bad
49 23 they have heard very bad tidings
2 Ma 6 3 very bad was this invasion of evils
9 24 any bad tidings should be brought
Mat 5 45 sun to rise upon the good and bad
13 48 the bad they cast forth. So shall it
22 10 gathered together . . . both bad and good
Badacer 4 K 9 25 Jehu said to B. his captain: Take
Badad Gen 36 35 Adad the son of Badad. 1 Pa 1:46
Badaias 1 Es 10 35 of the sons of Bani . . . Badaias
Badan 1 K 12 11 Lord sent Jerobaal and Badan and
bade Tob 5 22 Tobias bade his father and his mother
Tob 7 18 and bade her prepare another chamber
Jdth 12 1 bade her tarry there and be appointed
13 11 and bade her put it into her wallet
Dan 13 18 they did as she bade them: and they shut
1 Ma 11 23 he bade them besiege it still: and he
2 Ma 1 21 then he bade them draw it up and bring
Baden 1 Pa 7 17 the son of Ulam, Baden. These are
bag Deut 25 13 not have divers weights in thy bag
Tob 8 2 took out of his bag part of the liver
Job 14 17 up my offences as it were in a bag
Prov 7 20 he took with him a bag of money: he
16 11 his work all the weights of the bag
Isa 46 6 you that contribute gold out of the bag
Mich 6 11 and the deceitful weights of the bag
Agge 1 6 wages, put them into a bag with holes
Bagatha Esth 1 10 B. and Abgatha and Zethar
Esth 12 1 with B. and Thara the king's eunuchs
Bagathan Esth 2 21 B. and Thares, two of the king's
Esth 6 2 the treason of Bagathan and Thares the
baggage 1 K 17 22 under care of keeper of the b.
1 K 25 13 two hundred remained with the baggage
30 24 and of him that abode at the baggage
2 Ma 12 21 other baggage before him into a fortress
bags Gen 43 22 cannot tell who put it in our bags
1 K 9 7 the bread is spent in our bags: and we
4 K 5 23 bound two talents of silver in two bags
Luke 12 33 to yourselves bags which grow not old
Bahurim 2 K 3 16 followed her, weeping as far as B.
2 K 16 5 and king David came as far as Bahurim
17 18 into house of certain man in Bahurim
19 16 the son of Jemini of Bahurim. 3 K 2:8

bake Gen 11 3 brick, and bake them with fire
Lev 23 17 you shall bake for the firstfruits
24 5 and shalt bake twelve loaves thereof
26 26 ten women shall bake your bread in one
baked Gen 19 3 baked unleavened bread and they ate
Gen 27 17 delivered him bread that she had baked
Exod 12 39 and they baked the meal, which a little
Lev 2 4 offerest a sacrifice baked in the oven
7 9 of flour that is baked in the oven
1 K 28 24 baked some unleavened bread, and set
Isa 44 15 and he kindled it and baked bread: but
19 and I have baked bread upon the coals
Eze 4 12 barley bread baked under the ashes
Osee 7 8 become as bread baked under the ashes
baker Gen 40 1 butler and the baker . . . offended
Gen 40 2 was chief butler, the other chief b.
41 10 commanded me and the chief baker to be
16 chief baker seeing that he had wisely
20 remembered chief butler and the chief b.
Osee 7 4 like an oven heated by the baker: the
bakers 1 K 8 13 and to be his cooks and bakers
baking Gen 40 17 are made by the art of baking
Osee 7 6 he slept all the night baking them
Bala Gen 14 2 the king of Bala, which is Segor. 8
Gen 29 29 her father gave Bala for her servant
30 3 I have here my servant Bala; go in unto
4 and she gave him Bala in marriage: who
7 again Bala conceived and bore another
35 22 Ruben went and slept with Bala, the
25 the sons of Bala, Rachel's handmaid
37 2 he [Joseph] was with the sons of Bala
46 25 these are the sons of Bala whom Laban
Josu 19 3 Molada and Hasersual, Bala, and Asem
1 Pa 4 29 in Bala and in Asom and in Tholad
5 8 and Bala the son of Azaz the son of
7 13 and Jezer and Sellum, sons of Bala
Balaam Num 22 5 sent messengers therefore to B.
Num 22 7 and when they were come to Balaam
8 while they stayed with Balaam, God came
12 God said to Balaam: Thou shalt not go
14 Balaam would not come with us. Then he
16 when they were come to Balaam, said
18 Balaam answered: If Balac would give
20 God therefore came to Balaam in the
21 B. arose in the morning and saddling
22 stood in the way against Balaam, who
23 when Balaam beat her and had a mind to
29 Balaam answered: Because thou hast
31 the Lord opened the eyes of Balaam and
34 Balaam said: I have sinned, not knowing
37 he said to Balaam: I sent messengers to
40 he sent presents to Balaam and to the
23 1 Balaam said to Balac: Build me here
2 had done according to the word of B.
3 Balaam said to Balac: Stand a while
4 Balaam speaking to him, said: I have
11 Balac said to Balaam: What is this that
14 Balaam built seven altars, and laying
25 Balac said to Balaam: Neither curse
29 Balaam said to him: Build me here seven
30 Balac did as Balaam had said: and he
24 1 when Balaam saw that it pleased the Lord
3 Balaam the son of Beor hath said. 15
10 and Balac being angry against Balaam
12 Balaam made answer to Balac: Did I not
25 Balaam rose and returned to his place
31 8 B. also the son of Beor they killed
16 that deceived . . . by the counsel of B.
Deut 23 4 because they hired against thee Balaam
5 the Lord thy God would not hear Balaam
Josu 13 22 B. also the son of Beor the soothsayer
24 9 he sent and called for Balaam son of
1 Pa 6 70 its suburbs, Balaam and its suburbs
2 Es 13 2 and they hired against them Balaam to
Mich 6 5 what B. the son of Beor answered
2 P 2 15 followed the way of Balaam of Bosor
Jude 11 after the error of Balaam they have
Apoc 2 14 them that hold the doctrine of Balaam
Balaan Gen 36 27 sons of Eser: Balaan. 1 Pa 1:42
Balaath Josu 19 44 Balaath and Jud and Bane and
2 Pa 8 6 Balaath also and all the strong cities
Balac Num 22 2 Balac the son of Sephor, seeing
Num 22 7 and had told him all the words of Balac
10 Balac . . . hath sent to me [Balaam]
14 the princes returning, said to Balac
16 thus saith Balac the son of Sephor
18 if Balac would give me his house. 24:13
36 when Balac heard it he came forth to
40 when Balac had killed oxen and sheep
23 1 Balaam said to Balac: Build me here
3 Balaam said to Balac: Stand a while
5 return to B., and thus shalt thou. 16
6 he found Balac standing by his burnt
7 B. king of the Moabites hath brought me
11 Balac said to Balaam: What is this that
13 Balac therefore said: Come with me to
15 he said to Balac: Stand here by thy
17 Balac said to him: What hath the Lord
18 stand, O Balac, and give ear: hear thou
25 Balac said to Balaam: Neither curse
27 B. said to him: Come, and I will bring
30 Balac did as Balaam had said: and he
24 10 and Balac being angry against Balaam
12 Balaam made answer to Balac: Did I not
25 Balac also returned the way that he
Josu 24 9 and Balac . . . fought against Israel
Judg 11 25 unless perhaps thou art better than B.
Apoc 2 14 taught Balac to cast a stumblingblock
Balach Mich 6 5 what B. the king of Moab purposed
Baladan 4 K 20 12 Berodach B. the son of B. Isa 39:1
Balan 1 Pa 7 10 and the son of Jadihel: Balan
1 Pa 7 10 the sons of Balan: Jehus and Benjamin
Balanam 1 Pa 27 28 was Balanam a Gederite
Balanan Gen 36 38 B. . . . succeeded to the kingdom
1 Pa 1 49 Balanan the son of Achobor reigned in
balance Lev 19 36 let the balance be just and the
Job 6 2 that I suffer were weighed in a balance
31 6 let him weigh me in a just balance
Prov 11 1 a deceitful balance is an abomination
16 11 weight and balance are judgments of
20 23 a deceitful balance is not good. The
Wisd 11 23 is as the least grain of the balance
Eccu 21 28 of the wise shall be weighed in a b.
28 29 make a balance for thy words, and a just
42 4 of exactness of balance and weights
Isa 40 12 in scales, and the hills in a balance
15 counted as the smallest grain of a b.
Eze 5 1 and take thee a balance to weigh in
Dan 5 27 Thecel: thou art weighed in the balance
Osee 12 7 there is a deceitful b. in his hand
2 Ma 9 8 heights of the mountains in a balance
balanced Prov 8 29 when he b. the foundations of
balances Ps 61 10 sons of men are liars in the b.
Jer 32 10 weighed him the money in the balances
Eze 45 10 you shall have just balances and a
Amos 8 5 and may convey in deceitful balances
Mich 6 11 shall I justify wicked balances and
bald Lev 13 40 from his head, he is bald and clean
Lev 13 41 forehead, he is bald before and clean
42 if in the bald head or in the bald
forehead there be risen a white
43 leprosy which is risen in the bald part
4 K 2 23 him, saying: go up, thou bald head, go
Isa 3 17 will make bald the crown of the head
Jer 16 6 nor make themselves bald for them. And
48 37 every head shall be bald, and every

Eze 27 31 they shall shave themselves bald for
29 18 every head was made bald, and every
Mich 1 16 make thee bald, and be polled for thy
1 C 11 6 to a woman to be shorn or made bald
Baldad Job 2 11 Baldad the Suhite. 8:1; 18:1; 25:1; 42:9
baldness Deut 14 1 nor make any b. for the dead
Isa 3 24 and instead of curled hair, baldness
15 2 on all their heads shall be baldness
22 12 to mourning, to b. and to girding with
Jer 47 5 baldness is come upon Gaza. Ascalon
Eze 7 18 face, and baldness upon all their heads
Amos 8 10 and baldness upon every head: and I
Mich 1 16 enlarge thy baldness as the eagle: for
Bale 1 Pa 1 43 Bale the son of Beor: and the name
1 Pa 1 44 Bale died, and Jobab the son of Zare
8 1 now Benjamin begot Bale his firstborn
3 the sons of Bale were Addar and Gera
bales Eze 27 24 with bales of blue cloth and of
ball Isa 22 18 he will toss thee like a ball into
balls Isa 3 20 and sweet balls and earrings and
Dan 13 17 bring me oil and washing balls, and
balm Gen 37 25 carrying spices and balm and
Gen 43 11 a little balm and honey and storax
Eccu 24 20 smell like cinnamon and aromatical b.
21 my odor is as the purest balm. I have
Jer 8 22 is there no balm in Galaad? Or is
46 11 go up into Galaad and take balm, O
51 8 howl for her, take balm for her pain
Eze 27 17 they set forth balm and honey and oil
Baloth Josu 15 24 Ziph and Telem and Baloth
3 K 4 16 the son of Husi in Aser and in Baloth
Baltasar Dan 5 1 B. the king made a great feast
Dan 5 9 king Baltasar was much troubled, and
22 Baltasar, hast not humbled thy heart
30 Baltasar the Chaldean king was slain
7 1 in the first year of Baltasar king of
8 1 the third year of the reign of king B.
Baltassar Dan 1 7 gave them names: to Daniel, B.
Dan 2 26 Daniel, whose name was B. 4:16
4 5 Daniel . . . whose name is Baltassar
6 Baltassar, prince of the diviners
15 B., tell me quickly the interpretation
16 Baltassar, let not the dream and the
5 12 Daniel, whom the king named Baltassar
10 1 word was revealed to Daniel surnamed B.
Balthasar Bar 1 11 and for the life of B. his son
Bar 1 12 under the shadow of Balthasar his son
Bamoth Num 21 19 Nahaliel: from Nahaliel unto B.
Num 21 20 from Bamoth is a valley in the country
Bamothbaal Josu 13 17 Dibon also and Bamothbaal
Bana 3 K 4 12 Bana the son of Ahilud, who
Banaa 1 Pa 8 37 begot Mosa, and Mosa begot B. 9:43
Banai 1 Pa 11 31 the sons of Benjamin, Banai
Banaia 2 K 23 30 Banaia the Pharathonite, Heddai
1 Pa 4 36 Asaia and Adiel and Ismiel and Banaia
1 Es 10 43 Zabina, Jeddu, and Joel, and Banaia
Banaias 2 K 8 18 Banaias the son of Joiada was over the. 20:23; 1 Pa 18:17
2 K 23 20 Banaias the son of Joiada a most valiant man. 1 Pa 11:22
22 these things did Banaias. 1 Pa 11:24
3 K 1 8 Sadoc the priest and Banaias. 26
10 Nathan the prophet and Banaias. 32, 44
36 B. the son of Joiada answered the king
38 the prophet went down, and Banaias
2 25 Solomon sent by the hand of Banaias
29 sent Banaias the son of Joiada, saying
30 and Banaias came to the tabernacle
30 Banaias brought word back to the king
34 so Banaias the son of Joiada went up
35 and the king appointed Banaias the son
46 king commanded B. the son of Joiada
4 4 B. the son of Joiada over the army
1 Pa 15 18 and Eliab and Banaias and Maasias
20 and Eliab and Maasias and Banaias
24 Amasai and Zacharias and Banaias
16 5 and Eliab and Banaias and Obededom
6 B. and Jaziel the priests to sound the
27 5 for the third month was Banaias the
6 B. the most valiant among the thirty
14 for the eleventh month, was Banaias
34 was Joiada the son of B., and Abiathar
2 Pa 20 14 Zacharias the son of Banaias the son
31 13 Mahath and Banaias, overseers under
1 Es 10 30 Edna and Chalol, Banaias and Maasias
Eze 11 1 and Pheltias the son of Banaias, princes
13 that Pheltias the son of Banaias died
band Deut 20 5 shall proclaim through every band
1 Pa 12 18 and made them captains of the band
Dan 4 12 and let it be tied with a band of iron
12 7 scattering of band of the holy people
Osee 5 13 saw his sickness, and Juda his band
13 be able to take off the band from you
2 Ma 8 23 himself leading the first band, he
12 22 when the first band of Judas came in
24 into the hands of the band of Dositheus
35 Dositheus . . . one of Bacenor's band
Mat 27 27 gathered . . . the whole band. Mark 15:16
John 18 3 Judas having received a b. of soldiers
12 then the hand and the tribune and the
Acts 10 1 of that which is called the Italian b.
21 31 it was told the tribune of the band
27 1 named Julius, of the band Augusta
bands Gen 49 24 bands of his arms and his hands
Num 1 52 camp every man by his troops and bands
2 3 pitch his tents by the bands of his
Deut 20 9 shall prepare their bands to fight. If
Josu 4 13 men by their troops and bands marched
Judg 15 14 the bands with which he was bound were
16 9 he [Samson] broke the bands. 12
1 K 17 8 he cried out to the bands of Israel and
10 I have defied the bands of Israel this
23 3 against the bands of the Philistines
2 K 4 2 Saul had two men captains of his bands
15 18 bands of Cerethi. 4 K 11:19; 1 Pa 18:17
3 K 7 29 as it were bands of brass hanging down
Prov 30 27 yet they all go out by their bands
Ecce 7 27 heart is a net, and her hands are bands
Wisd 10 14 and in bands she left him not, till she
Eccu 6 26 be not grieved with her bands. Come to
31 and her bands are a healthful binding
28 23 and hath not been bound in its bands
24 iron: and its bands are bands of brass
Isa 58 6 loose the bands of wickedness, undo the
Jer 2 20 my yoke, thou hast burst my bands
27 2 make thee bands and chains: and thou
30 8 off thy neck, and burst his bands
Eze 3 25 behold they shall put bands upon thee
4 8 I have encompassed thee with bands
17 21 fugitives with all his b. shall fall
20 37 bring you into bands of the covenant
38 6 Gomer and all his bands and many people
39 4 thou and all thy b. and thy nations
Osee 11 4 cords of Adam, with the bands of love
2 Ma 5 2 armed with spears, like b. of soldiers
12 20 and divided them by bands, went forth
John 11 44 bound feet and hands with winding bands
Acts 16 26 opened and the bands of all were loosed
20 23 bands and afflictions wait for me at
23 29 worthy of death or of bands. 26:31
26 29 such as I also am, except these bands
27 40 sea, loosing withal the rudder bands
Phil 1 7 that in my bands and in the defence
13 so that my bands are made manifest in
14 confident by my bands, are much more

17 that they raise affliction to my bands
Col 2 19 the whole body by joints and bands
4 18 be mindful of my bands. Grace be with
2 Tim 2 9 wherein I labor even unto bands, as an
Philem 10 I have begotten in my bands, Onesimus
13 ministered to me in the bands of the
Heb 10 34 compassion on them that were in bands
11 36 moreover also of bands and prisons
13 3 remember them that are in bands, as if
Bane Josu 19 45 and Jud and Bane and Barach and
Banea 1 Es 10 25 Eliezer and Melchia and Banea
Baneas 1 Es 10 35 Baneas and Badaias, Cheliau
Bani 1 Es 2 10 the children of Bani, 642. The
1 Es 10 29 and of the sons of Bani, Mosollam and
34 of the sons of Bani, Maaddi, Amram
38 Bani and Bennui, Semei and Salmias
2 Es 8 7 Josue and Bani and Serebia, Jamin
9 4 upon step of the Levites, Josue and B.
10 13 Serebia, Sabania, Odaia, Bani, Baninu
14 Elam, Zethu, Bani, Bonni, Azgad, Bebai
11 22 was Azzi, the son of Bani, the son of
Baninu 2 Es 10 13 Sabania, Odaia, Bani, Baninu
banished Num 35 26 that are appointed for the b.
Num 35 32 the banished and fugitives before
banishment 1 Es 7 26 unto death or unto b. or to
Bar 2 25 by famine and by the sword and in b.
banishments Lam 2 14 thee false revelations and b.
bank Gen 41 3 fed on the very bank of the river
Gen 41 17 methought I stood upon the bank of the
Exod 7 15 to meet him on the bank of the river
Deut 2 36 upon the bank of the torrent Arnon. 3:12; 4:48; Josu 12:2; 13:9, 16
4 K 2 13 he stood upon the bank of the Jordan
Eccu 40 16 and at the bank of the river, shall be
Eze 47 6 me to turn to the bank of the torrent
7 on bank of torrent were very many trees
Dan 12 5 on this side upon the bank of the river
5 side, on the other bank of the river
1 Ma 9 42 they returned to the bank of the Jordan
43 to the b. of the Jordan with a great
Luke 19 23 not give my money into the bank that
bankers Mat 25 27 committed my money to the bankers
banks Josu 3 15 had filled the b. of its channel
Josu 22 10 were come to the banks of the Jordan
11 Chanaan upon the banks of the Jordan
1 Pa 12 15 when it is used to flow over its banks
Isa 8 7 channels and shall overflow all his b.
19 6 streams of the b. shall be diminished
37 25 foot all the rivers shut up in banks
Eze 47 12 by the torrent on the banks thereof
1 Ma 9 45 and banks and marshes and woods: and
banner Isa 13 2 upon dark mountain lift ye up a b.
Bannui 2 Es 7 15 the children of Bannui, 648
banquet Gen 24 54 a banquet was made and they
Gen 40 20 at the banquet remembered the chief
Num 10 10 if at any time you shall have a b. and
Tob 8 22 and a banquet to be prepared for all
Esth 5 4 Aman with thee to the banquet which
5 the king and Aman came to the banquet
8 let the king and Aman come to the b.
12 no other to the banquet with the king
14 full of joy with the king to the b.
7 7 and went from the place of the banquet
8 entered into the place of the banquet
14 17 nor hath the king's banquet pleased me
Eccu 31 41 rebuke not thy neighbor in a banquet
32 7 a concert of music in a banquet of wine
49 2 mouth, and as music at a b. of wine
Dan 5 10 came into the banquet house: and she
Osee 4 18 their banquet is separated, they have
banqueting 1 Ma 16 16 entered into the b. place
banquetings Deut 21 20 and to debauchery and b.
1 P 4 3 excess of wine, revellings, banquetings

banquets Judg 9 27 their b. and cups they cursed
Esth 9 17 celebrate it with feasting, joy, and b.
19 fourteenth day of month of Adar for b.
19 send one another portions of their b.
Eccu 30 27 for his b. are prepared with diligence
Jude 12 these are spots in their b., feasting
baptism Mat 3 7 Sadducees coming to his baptism
Mat 21 25 b. of John, whence. Mark 11:30; Luke 20:4
Mark 1 4 preaching the baptism of penance. Luke 3:3; Acts 13:24
10 38 the baptism wherewith I am baptized. 39
Luke 7 29 being baptized with John's baptism
12 50 I have a baptism wherewith I am to be
Acts 1 22 from the baptism of John until the day
10 37 after the baptism which John preached
18 25 knowing only the baptism of John. This
19 3 baptized? Who said: In John's baptism
4 baptized the people with b. of penance
Rom 6 4 are buried together with him by baptism
Eph 4 5 one Lord, one faith, one baptism. One
Col 2 12 buried with him in baptism, in whom
1 P 3 21 baptism being of the like form, now
baptisms Heb 6 2 of the doctrine of baptisms and
Baptist; *see* **John**
baptize Mat 3 11 I baptize you in water. Mark 1:8; Luke 3:16; John 1:26
Mat 3 11 he shall b. you in Holy Ghost. Mark 1:8
John 1 25 why then dost thou baptize if thou be
33 he who sent me to baptize with water
4 2 Jesus himself did not baptize, but his
1 C 1 17 Christ sent me not to b., but to preach
baptized Mat 3 6 were b. by him in Jordan. Mark 1:5
Mat 3 13 unto John to be baptized by him. But
14 I ought to be baptized by thee, and
16 Jesus being baptized forthwith. Luke 3:21
Mark 1 8 I have baptized you with water; but
9 and was baptized by John in the Jordan
10 38 be baptized with the baptism wherewith I am baptized
39 wherewith I am b., you shall be b.
16 16 believeth and is b., shall be saved
Luke 3 7 that went forth to be baptized by him
12 the publicans also came to be baptized
21 when all the people were baptized, that
7 29 being baptized with John's baptism
30 the Pharisees . . . being not b. by him
12 50 baptism wherewith I am to be baptized
John 3 22 there he abode with them and baptized
23 they came and were baptized. For John
Acts 1 5 John indeed b. with water but you shall be b. with the Holy Ghost. 11:16
2 38 do penance and be baptized every one
41 they that received his word, were b.
8 12 they were baptized, both men and women
13 and being b., he adhered to Philip
16 they were only b. in name of Lord Jesus
36 what doth hinder me from being baptized
38 and the eunuch: and he baptized him
9 18 and rising up, he [Paul] was baptized
10 47 that these should not be baptized, who
48 and he commanded them to be baptized
16 15 when she [Lydia] was baptized and her
33 himself was baptized and all his house
18 8 hearing, believed and were baptized
19 3 in what then were you baptized? Who
4 John b. the people with the baptism
5 they were b. in the name of the Lord
22 16 rise up and be baptized and wash away
Rom 6 3 b. in Christ Jesus, are b. in his death
1 C 1 13 were you baptized in the name of Paul
14 I b. none of you but Crispus and Caius
15 should say that you were b. in my name
16 I b. also the household of Stephanus

16 I know not whether I b. any other. For
10 2 all in Moses were b. in the cloud and
12 13 for in one Spirit were we all baptized
15 29 they do that are baptized for the dead
29 why are they then baptized for them
Gal 3 27 as they have been baptized in Christ
baptizeth John 1 33 that b. with the Holy Ghost
John 3 26 behold he b. and all men come to him
4 1 disciples, and b. more than John
baptizing Mat 28 19 b. them in the name of the
Mark 1 4 John was in the desert baptizing and
John 1 28 beyond the Jordan, where John was b.
31 therefore am I come b. with water. And
3 23 John also was b. in Ennom near Salim
10 40 that place where John was b. first
bar Exod 36 33 he made also another bar, that
Isa 27 1 shall visit leviathan the bar serpent
Amos 1 5 and I will break the bar of Damascus
Bara Gen 14 2 made war against Bara king of Sodom
1 Pa 8 8 he sent away Husim and Bara his wives
Barabbas Mat 27 16 prisoner that was called B.
Mat 27 17 that I release to you B. or Jesus that
20 persuaded people that they should ask B.
21 released unto you? But they said, B.
26 he released to them Barabbas. Mark 15:15
Mark 15 7 there was one called Barabbas, who was
11 that he should rather release Barabbas
Lûke 23 18 this man, and release unto us Barabbas
John 18 40 saying: Not this man, but Barabbas. Now
Barabbas was a robber
Barac Judg 4 6 [Debbora] sent and called Barac
Judg 4 8 Barac said to her: If thou wilt come
9 arose and went with Barac to Cedes
12 Barac . . . was gone up to mount Thabor
14 Debbora said to Barac: Arise, for this
15 edge of the sword at the sight of B.
16 B. pursued after the fleeing chariots
22 Barac came pursuing after Sisara: and
5 1 Debbora and Barac son of Abinoem sung
12 arise, Barac, and take hold of thy
15 and followed the steps of Barac, who
Heb 11 32 me to tell of Gedeon, Barac, Samson
Barach Josu 19 45 Jud and Bane and Barach and
Barachel Job 32 2 Eliu the son of B. the Buzite. 6
Barachia 1 Pa 9 16 Barachia the son of Asa the
Barachias 1 Pa 3 20 Ohol and B. and Hasadias
1 Pa 6 39 Asaph the son of Barachias the son of
15 23 Barachias and Elcana were doorkeepers
2 Pa 28 12 Barachias the son of Mosollamoth
2 Es 3 4 Mosollam the son of Barachias. 30; 6:18
Isa 8 2 Zacharias the son of B. Zach 1:1, 7
Mat 23 35 the blood of Zacharias the son of B.
Barad Gen 16 14 same is between Cades and Barad
Baraia 1 Pa 8 21 B. and Samareth the sons of
Barasa 1 Ma 5 26 many of them were shut up in B.
barbarian 1 C 14 11 to him to whom I speak a b.
1 C 14 11 he that speaketh, a barbarian to me
Col 3 11 barbarian nor Scythian, bond nor free
barbarians 2 Ma 10 4 not be delivered up to b.
Acts 28 1 barbarians showed us no small courtesy
4 and when the barbarians saw the beast
Rom 1 14 to the Greeks and to the barbarians
barbarous Ps 113 1 house of Jacob from a b. people
2 Ma 2 22 and put to flight the b. multitude
5 22 more b. than he that set him there
barbarously 2 Ma 15 2 not act so fiercely and b.
barber Judg 16 19 she called a b. and shaved his
bare Gen 27 16 and covered the bare of his neck
Lev 13 45 clothes hanging loose, his head bare
Deut 32 42 of the bare head of the enemies. Praise
Job 33 21 that were covered shall be made bare
Eccu 13 6 live with thee and will make thee bare
Isa 19 7 channel of the river shall be laid bare
47 2 make b. thy legs, pass over the rivers
Jer 2 25 keep thy foot from being bare, and thy
49 10 I have made Esau bare, I have revealed
Eze 13 14 foundation thereof shall be laid bare
Joel 1 7 he hath stripped it bare and cast it
Mich 1 6 and will lay her foundations bare. And
Haba 3 13 thou hast laid bare his foundations
1 C 15 37 bare grain as of wheat, or of some of
bared Jer 13 26 also bared thy thighs against thy
Bared 1 Pa 7 20 Suthala, Bared his son, Thahath
barefoot 2 K 15 30 weeping, walking b., and with
Isa 20 2 he did so and went naked and barefoot
3 Isaias hath walked naked and barefoot
4 young and old, naked and barefoot, with
bargain Gen 30 33 when time of the b. shall come
Baria 1 Pa 3 22 Baria and Naaria and Saphat
1 Pa 7 30 Jessui and Baria, and Sara their sister
31 the sons of Baria: Haber and Melchiel
8 13 and Baria and Sama were heads of their
16 Jesphia and Joha, the sons of Baria
23 10 and Ziza and Jaus and Baria: these
11 Jaus and Baria had not many children
Bar-Jesu Acts 13 6 a Jew, whose name was B. Who
Bar-Jona Mat 16 17 blessed art thou, Simon B.
bark Gen 30 37 when the bark was taken off, in the
Jdth 11 15 there shall not so much as one dog b.
Cant 6 6 cheeks are as the bark of a pomegranate
Wisd 13 11 and skilfully taken off all the bark
Isa 56 10 dumb dogs not able to bark, seeing vain
Joel 1 7 hath pilled off the bark of my fig tree
barks Job 30 4 they ate grass and barks of trees
barley Exod 9 31 flax and the barley were hurt
Exod 9 31 were hurt because the barley was green
Lev 27 16 be sowed with 30 bushels of barley, let
Num 5 15 tenth part of a measure of barley meal
Deut 8 8 a land of wheat and b. and vineyards
Judg 7 13 as if a hearth cake of barley bread
Ruth 1 22 in the beginning of the barley harvest
2 17 about the measure of an ephi of barley
23 till all the barley and the wheat were
3 2 this night he winnoweth barley in the
15 he measured six measures of barley and
17 hath given me six measures of barley
2 K 14 30 my field, that hath a crop of barley
17 19 as it were to dry sodden barley: and
28 barley and meal and parched corn and
21 9 when the barley began to be reaped. And
3 K 4 28 they brought barley also and straw for
4 K 4 42 twenty loaves of barley, and new corn
7 1 two bushels of barley for a stater. 16
18 bushels of barley shall be for a stater
1 Pa 11 13 field of that country was full of b.
2 Pa 2 10 of wheat and as many cores of barley
15 the barley and the oil and the wine
27 5 wheat and as many measures of barley
Jdth 8 2 died in the time of the barley harvest
Job 31 40 wheat, and thorns instead of barley
Prov 27 22 when pestle striketh upon sodden barley
Isa 28 25 and put wheat in order and barley and
Jer 41 8 stores in the field, of wheat and b.
Eze 4 9 take to thee wheat and b. and beans
12 thou shalt eat it as barley bread baked
13 19 violated me . . . for a handful of barley
45 13 sixth part of an ephi of a core of b.
Osee 3 2 a core of b. and for half a core of b.
Joel 1 11 howled for the wheat and for the barley
John 6 9 boy here that hath five barley loaves
13 the fragments of the five b. loaves
Apoc 6 6 thrice two pounds of barley for a penny
barn Deut 28 17 cursed shall be thy b. and cursed
Mat 3 12 his wheat into the barn. Luke 3:17
13 30 but the wheat gather ye into my barn
Luke 12 24 neither have they storehouse nor barn

Barnabas Acts 4 36 by the apostles was surnamed B.
Acts 9 27 B. took him and brought him to the
11 22 they sent Barnabas as far as Antioch
25 Barnabas went to Tarsus to seek Saul
30 by the hands of Barnabas and Saul
12 25 B. and Saul returned from Jerusalem
13 1 and doctors, among whom was Barnabas
2 separate me Saul and B. for the work
7 sending for Barnabas and Saul, desired
43 followed Paul and B.: who speaking
46 then Paul and B. said boldly: To you it
50 raised persecution against Paul and B.
14 11 they called Barnabas, Jupiter: but Paul
13 when the apostles B. and Paul had heard
19 [Paul] departed with Barnabas to Derbe
15 2 Paul and B. had no small contest with
2 determined that Paul and B. and certain
12 they heard Barnabas and Paul telling
22 to send to Antioch with Paul and B.
25 with our well beloved Barnabas and
35 Paul and Barnabas continued at Antioch
36 Paul said to Barnabas: Let us return
37 B. would have taken with them John also
39 Barnabas taking Mark, sailed to Cyprus
1 C 9 6 I only and B., have not we power to do
Gal 2 1 I went up again to Jerusalem with B.
9 gave to me and B. the right hands of
13 so that B. also was led by them into
Col 4 10 Mark, the cousin german of Barnabas
barnfloor Num 18 30 had given firstfruits of the b.
Deut 15 14 out of thy barnfloor and thy winepress
16 13 gathered in thy fruit of the barnfloor
Ruth 3 3 garments and go down to the barnfloor
6 she went down to the barnfloor and did
4 K 6 27 can I save thee? Out of the barnfloor
13 7 as dust by thrashing in the barnfloor
Job 39 12 seed and gather it into thy barnfloor
barnfloors Num 15 20 separate firstfruits of your b.
Num 18 27 firstfruits, as well of the barnfloors
barns Gen 41 34 gather into barns the fifth part
Gen 41 47 gathered together into the b. of Egypt
56 Joseph opened all the barns, and sold
Deut 28 5 blessed shall be thy barns and blessed
Ruth 2 23 the wheat were laid up in the barns
1 K 23 1 against Ceila, and they rob the barns
Prov 3 10 thy b. shall be filled with abundance
Joel 1 17 the barns are destroyed, the storehouses
Mat 6 25 nor do they reap nor gather into barns
Luke 12 18 I will pull down my barns and will
barred Judg 9 51 shut and strongly barred the gate
barrels Luke 16 6 said: An hundred barrels of oil
barren Gen 11 30 Sarai was barren and had no
Gen 25 21 for his wife, because she was barren
29 31 womb, but her sister remained barren
31 38 thy ewes and goats were not barren, the
Exod 23 26 one fruitless nor barren in thy land
Num 13 21 the ground, fat or barren, woody or
Deut 7 14 no one shall be barren among you of
Judg 13 2 Manue, and his wife was barren. And an
3 thou art barren and without children
1 K 2 5 so that the barren hath borne many
4 K 2 19 waters are very bad, and the ground b.
Job 15 34 congregation of the hypocrite is barren
30 3 b. with want and hunger, who gnawed
39 6 and his dwellings in the barren land
Ps 112 9 who maketh a barren woman to dwell in
Cant 4 2 there is none barren among them. 6:5
Wisd 3 13 is cursed, for happy is the barren
Eccu 42 10 herself or at the least become barren
Isa 49 21 I was barren and brought not forth
54 1 praise, O thou barren, that bearest not
66 9 shall I . . . be barren, saith the Lord
Jer 22 30 write this man barren, a man that shall
Mala 3 11 shall the vine in the field be barren
Luke 1 7 for that Elizabeth was barren, and they
23 29 they will say: Blessed are the barren
Gal 4 27 rejoice, thou barren, that bearest not
Heb 11 11 Sara, being barren, received strength
barrenness Gen 26 1 that b. which had happened
4 K 2 21 no more in them death or barrenness
Ps 106 34 a fruitful land into barrenness, for
Isa 47 8 widow, and I shall not know barrenness
9 in one day barrenness and widowhood
49 20 the children of thy b. shall still say
bars Exod 25 13 shalt make bars also of setim wood
Exod 25 27 that the bars may be put through them
28 the bars also themselves thou shalt
26 26 shalt make also five bars of setim wood
29 for the bars to hold together the
29 which bars thou shalt cover with plates
27 6 shalt make also two bars for the altar
30 4 that the bars may be put into them
5 shalt make the bars also of setim wood
35 13 the table with the bars and the vessels
15 altar of incense and the bars and the
16 with the bars and vessels thereof
36 31 he made also bars of setim wood. 37:4
32 five other bars at the west side of the
34 through which the bars might be drawn
34 the bars themselves with plates of gold
37 15 the bars also themselves he made. 28
27 that the bars might be put into them
38 5 at the top, to put in bars to carry it
6 and he made the bars of setim wood and
39 32 rings, the boards, the bars, the pillars
34 the bars, the propitiatory, the table
39 the altar of brass, the grate, the bars
40 16 the boards and the sockets and the bars
18 in the ark, thrusting bars underneath
Num 3 36 the bars and the pillars and their
4 6 shall put in the bars. 8, 10, 11, 14
12 of violet skins and put in the bars
31 the bars thereof, the pillars and their
1 K 23 7 into a city, that hath gates and bars
2 Pa 8 5 walled cities with gates and bars and
14 7 them with towers and gates and bars
2 Es 3 3 set up . . . locks and the b. 6, 13, 14, 15
Job 38 10 around it and made it bars and doors
Ps 106 16 gates of brass and burst iron bars
Prov 18 19 judgments are like the bars of cities
Eccu 28 28 and make doors and bars to thy mouth
49 15 and set up the gates and the bars, who
Isa 15 5 the bars thereof shall flee unto Segor
43 14 and have brought down all their bars
45 2 brass, and will burst the bars of iron
Jer 49 31 they have neither gates nor bars: they
51 30 places are burnt, her bars are broken
Lam 2 9 he hath destroyed, and broken her bars
Bar 6 17 the priests secure the doors with bars
Eze 38 11 a wall, they have no bars nor gates
Jon 2 7 the bars of the earth have shut me up
Nah 3 13 enemies, the fire shall devour thy bars
1 Ma 9 50 with high walls and gates and bars
12 38 fortified it and set up gates and bars
13 33 and great walls and gates and bars
Barsabas Acts 1 23 appointed two, Joseph called B.
Barsaith 1 Pa 7 31 Melchiel: he is father of B.
Acts 15 22 to send . . . Judas who was surnamed B.
Bartholomew Mat 10 3 Philip the Bartholomew. Mark 3:18; Luke 6:14
Acts 1 13 Philip and Thomas, B. and Matthew
Bartimeus Mark 10 46 B. the blind man, the son of
Baruch 2 Es 3 20 Baruch the son of Zachai built
2 Es 10 6 Daniel, Genthon, Baruch, Mosollam, Abia
11 5 Maasia the son of Baruch, the son of
Jer 32 12 I gave the deed of the purchase to B.

13 and I charged Baruch before them, saying
16 delivered the deed of purchase to B.
36 4 so Jeremias called Baruch the son of
4 Baruch wrote from the mouth of Jeremias
5 Jeremias commanded Baruch, saying: I am
8 B. the son of Nerias did according to
10 Baruch read out of the volume. 13
14 to Baruch, saying: Take in thy hand
14 Baruch . . . took the volume in his hand
15 and Baruch read in their hearing. And
16 they said to Baruch. We must fell the
18 Baruch said to them: With his mouth he
19 princes said to Baruch: Go and hide
26 to take up Baruch the scribe and
27 the words that Baruch had written from
32 another volume and gave it to Baruch
43 3 Baruch . . . setteth thee on against us
6 Jeremias the prophet and Baruch the
45 1 Jeremias the prophet spoke to Baruch
2 the God of Israel to thee, Baruch
Bar 1 1 the words of the book which Baruch
3 and Baruch read the words of this book
Basaia 1 Pa 6 40 son of Michael the son of Basaia
Basan Num 21 33 and went up by the way of Basan
Deut 3 1 we turned and went by the way of Basan
4 kingdom of Og in B. 10; Josu 13:12, 31
10 all the land of Galaad and Basan as far
13 B. the kingdom of Og to the half tribe
13 all Basan is called the Land of giants
14 and he called Basan by his own name
4 43 Golan in Basan, which is in the tribe
32 14 of the rams of the breed of Basan
33 22 he shall flow plentifully from Basan
Josu 12 4 Hermon and in Salecha and in all B.
13 11 Hermon and all Basan as far as Salecha
30 all Basan and all the kingdoms of Og
30 villages of Jair, which are in Basan
17 1 had for possession Galaad and Basan
5 beside the land of Galaad and Basan
20 8 Gaulon in B. of the tribe of Manasses
21 6 of the half tribe of Manasses in Basan
27 Gaulon in Basan, one of the cities
22 7 Moses had given a possession in Basan
3 K 4 13 country of Argob, which is in Basan
4 K 10 33 torrent Arnon and Galaad and Basan
1 Pa 5 11 in the land of Basan as far as Selcha
12 second: and Janai and Saphat in Basan
16 they dwelt in Galaad and in Basan and
23 from the borders of Basan unto Baal
6 62 and out of tribe of Manasses in Basan
71 Gaulon, in Basan, and its suburbs
Ps 67 23 Lord said: I will turn them from Basan
Isa 2 13 Libanus and upon all the oaks of Basan
33 9 desert: and Basan and Carmel are shaken
Jer 22 20 lift up thy voice in Basan and cry to
Eze 27 6 cut thy oars out of the oaks of Basan
Mich 7 14 they shall feed in Basan and Galaad
Nah 1 4 desert. Basan languisheth and Carmel
Zach 11 2 howl, ye oaks of Basan, because the
Og king of Basan; *see* **Og**
Bascama 1 Ma 13 23 when he approached to Bascama
Bascath Josu 15 39 Lachis and Bascath and Eglon
base 3 K 7 27 every base was four cubits in length
3 K 7 30 every b. had four wheels and axletrees
32 which were at the four corners of base
32 joined one to another under the base
34 undersetters that were at every corner of each base, were of the base itself
35 in the top of the base there was a
38 upon every base, in all ten, he put as
Job 30 8 the children of foolish and base men
Wisd 15 10 earth, and his life more base than clay
Isa 3 5 and the base against the honorable
Jer 2 36 how exceeding base art thou become
Mala 2 9 made you contemptible and base before
1 C 1 28 the base things of the world, and the
baseborn 1 K 17 4 there went out a man baseborn
1 K 17 23 that b. man whose name was Goliath
Basemath Gen 26 34 and B. the daughter of Elon
Gen 36 3 Basemath the daughter of Ismael
4 Basemath bore Rahuel: Oolibama bore
10 Rahuel the son of Basemath his wife
13 these were the sons of Basemath the
17 the sons of Basemath the wife of Esau
3 K 4 15 had B. the daughter of Solomon to wife
bases 3 K 7 27 he made ten bases of brass, every
3 K 7 28 work itself of the b. was intergraven
37 after this manner he made ten bases
38 one laver contained four bases and was
39 and he set the ten bases, five on the
43 ten bases and the ten lavers on the b.
4 K 16 17 king Achaz took away the graven bases
25 13 and the bases and the sea of brass
16 the bases which Solomon had made in the
2 Pa 4 14 he made also bases and lavers, which he set upon the bases
1 Es 3 3 they set the altar of God upon its b.
Job 38 6 upon what are its bases grounded? Or
Ps 103 5 founded the earth upon its own bases
Cant 5 15 marble, that are set upon bases of gold
Eccu 26 23 as golden pillars upon bases of silver
Jer 27 19 to the b. and to the rest of the vessels
52 17 the bases and the sea of brass that was
20 oxen of brass that were under the bases
basest Dan 4 14 will appoint the b. man over it
bashfulness Eccu 20 25 for b. promiseth to his
basilisk Ps 90 13 walk upon the asp and the b.
Prov 23 32 will spread abroad poison like a b.
Isa 11 8 his hand into the den of the basilisk
14 29 shall come forth a basilisk, and his
30 6 lion, the viper and the flying basilisk
59 5 brought out, shall be hatched into a b.
basilisks Jer 8 17 will send among you serpents, b.
basin John 13 5 he putteth water into a basin and
basins 3 K 7 40 made caldrons and shovels and b.
3 K 7 45 caldrons and the shovels and the b.
Jer 52 19 censers and the pots and the basins
basis Zach 5 11 and set there upon its own basis
basket Gen 40 17 in one b. which was uppermost
Exod 2 3 she took a basket made of bulrushes
5 when she saw the basket in the sedges
29 3 thou shalt put them in a basket and
23 basket of unleavened bread. Lev 8:26; Num 6:17
32 the loaves also that are in the basket
Lev 8 2 a basket with unleavened bread and
31 consecration that are laid in the b.
Num 6 15 b. also of unleavened bread tempered
19 one unleavened cake out of the basket
Deut 26 2 thy fruits and put them in a basket
4 priest taking the basket of thy hand
Judg 6 19 putting the flesh in a basket and the
Jer 6 9 as a grapegatherer into the basket
24 2 one basket had very good figs, like the
2 and the other basket had very bad figs
Acts 9 25 the wall, letting him down in a basket
2 C 11 33 in a basket was I let down by the wall
baskets Gen 40 16 I had three baskets of meal upon
Gen 40 18 the three baskets are yet three days
4 K 10 7 put their heads in b. and sent them
Ps 80 7 burdens: his hands had served in baskets
Jer 24 1 behold two baskets full of figs, set
Mat 14 20 twelve full baskets. Mark 6:43; Luke 9:17; John 6:13
15 37 they took up seven baskets. Mark 8:8
16 9 how many b. took you up. 10; Mark 8:19, 20

Bason Jer 50 19 he shall feed on Carmel and Bason
bastard Wisd 4 3 b. slips shall not take deep root
bastards Heb 12 8 then are you b. and not sons
bat Lev 11 19 its kind, the houp also and the bat
Deut 14 18 their kind: the hoop also and the bat
bate Eze 45 10 and a just ephi and a just bate
Eze 45 11 the ephi and the bate shall be equal
11 bate may contain tenth part of a core
14 bate of oil is the tenth part of a core
bates 3 K 7 26 it contained two thousand bates
1 Es 7 22 and unto a hundred bates of wine and unto a hundred bates of oil
Eze 45 14 ten b. make a core: for ten b. fill a
Bathuel Gen 22 23 B. of whom was born Rebecca
Gen 24 15 Rebecca out, the daughter of Bathuel
24 I am the daughter of Bathuel. 47
50 Laban and Bathuel answered: The word
25 20 took to wife Rebecca the daughter of B.
28 2 the house of B. thy mother's father
5 to Laban the son of Bathuel the Syrian
1 Pa 4 30 in Bathuel and in Horma and in Siceleg
bats Isa 2 20 for himself to adore, moles and bats
battering Eze 4 2 place b. rams round about it
Eze 21 22 for Jerusalem, to set battering rams
26 9 and battering rams against thy walls
1 Ma 6 20 battering slings and engines. 51
battle Gen 14 8 themselves against them in b. array
Exod 32 17 noise of battle is heard in the camp
Num 31 5 say, 12,000 men well appointed for b.
14 centurions that were come from the b.
28 them that fought and were in the battle
36 given to them that had been in the b.
42 for them that had been in the battle
32 17 will go armed and ready for battle
Deut 2 9 neither go to battle against them: for
19 against them nor once move to battle
20 2 when the b. is now at hand, the priest
3 you join battle this day against your
5 to his house, lest he die in the b. 6
Josu 8 13 rest of the army went in battle array
14 set it in battle array toward desert
Judg 7 8 with the 300 gave himself to the battle
8 13 returning from the b. before the sun
20 18 in our army the first to go to the b.
23 go up against them and join battle
33 set their army in battle array, in the
34 battle grew hot against the children of
39 children of Israel saw this in the b.
1 K 4 2 when they had joined battle, Israel
16 I am he that came from the battle and
7 10 the Philistines began the b. against
13 22 when the day of battle was come, there
17 1 gathering together their troops to b.
13 eldest sons followed Saul to the battle
13 his three sons that went to the battle
20 out to fight, and shouted for the b.
22 [David] ran to the place of the battle
28 thou art come down to see the battle
47 it is his battle, and he will deliver
26 10 he shall go down to battle and perish
29 4 let him not go down with us to battle
9 shall not go down with us to the battle
30 24 portion of him that went down to battle
31 3 weight of battle was turned upon Saul
2 K 1 4 the people are fled from the battle
25 how are the valiant fallen in battle
2 17 there was a very fierce battle that day
3 30 brother Asael at Gabaon in the battle
5 24 pear trees, then shalt thou join battle
10 9 Joab seeing that the battle was prepared
11 15 set ye Urias in the front of the battle
18 told David all things concerning the b.
19 hast told all the words of the battle
18 6 battle was fought in forest of Ephraim
8 and the battle there was scattered
19 3 backs and fled away from the battle
10 anointed over us is dead in the battle
21 17 shalt go no more out with us to battle
18 there was also a second battle in Gob
19 there was a third battle in Gob against
20 a fourth battle was in Geth: where there
22 40 hast girded me with strength to battle
23 9 were there gathered together to battle
3 K 20 29 on seventh day the battle was fought
22 4 come with me to battle to Ramoth Galaad
15 shall we go to Ramoth Galaad to battle
30 take armor and go into the battle and
30 changed his dress and went into the b.
35 and the battle was fought that day and
4 K 3 7 come with me against him to battle. And
18 20 counsel, to prepare thyself for battle
1 Pa 5 20 they called upon God in the battle
22 slain: for it was the battle of the Lord
10 3 the battle grew hard against Saul, and
11 13 were gathered to that place to battle
12 33 of Zabulon such as went forth to battle
35 of Dan also 28,600 prepared for battle
36 forth to fight, and challenging in b.
14 15 then shalt thou go out to battle. For
19 7 out of their cities and came to battle
10 that the battle was set against him
14 went against the Syrians to the battle
20 1 the time that kings go out to battle
5 another battle was fought against the
6 there was another battle also in Geth
2 Pa 13 3 and when Abia had begun battle and had
14 they saw the battle coming upon them
14 10 set his army in array for b. in the vale
17 17 after him was Eliada valiant in battle
18 29 dress, and so I will go to the battle
29 changed his dress, went to the battle
33 carry me out of the battle, for I am
20 15 for the battle is not yours, but God's
22 6 many wounds in the foresaid battle
25 5 young men that could go out to battle
13 they should not go with him to battle
35 23 carry me [Josias] out of the battle
Jdth 7 9 mayst overcome them without joining b.
14 3 to awake their prince for the battle
16 14 they perished in b. before the face of
Job 5 20 in battle, from the hand of the sword
15 24 as a king that is prepared for the b.
38 23 against the day of battle and war? By
39 25 ha, ha: he smelleth the battle afar off
40 27 remember the battle and speak no more
Ps 17 40 hast girded me with strength unto b.
23 8 the Lord mighty in battle. Lift up your
26 3 if a battle should rise up against me
75 4 the shield, the sword, and the battle
77 9 have turned back in the day of battle
88 44 and hast not assisted him in battle
139 8 overshadowed my head in day of battle
Prov 21 31 horse is prepared for the day of battle
Ecce 9 11 the swift, nor the battle to the strong
Eccu 40 7 as if he had escaped in the day of b.
Isa 3 25 sword, and thy valiant ones in battle
21 15 from the face of a grievous battle
22 2 not slain by the sword nor dead in b.
27 4 make me a thorn and a brier in battle
28 6 that return out of the b. to the gate
42 25 indignation of his fury and a strong b.
Jer 4 19 sound of the trumpet, the cry of battle
8 6 course, as a horse rushing to the b.
18 21 men be stabbed with the sword in battle
46 3 shield and buckler, and go forth to b.
48 14 we are valiant and stout men in battle

49 14 against her, and let us rise up to b.
Eze 7 14 yet there is none to go to the battle
13 5 to stand in battle in day of the Lord
Dan 11 10 he shall join battle with his forces
20 be destroyed, not in rage nor in battle
25 shall be stirred up to battle with many
Osee 1 7 by bow nor by sword nor by battle
10 9 the b. in Gabaa against the children
14 that judged Baal in the day of battle
Joel 2 5 as a strong people prepared to battle
Amos 1 14 with shouting in the day of battle and
Abdi 1 let us rise up to battle against him
Zach 10 3 as the horse of his glory in the battle
4 the pin, out of him the bow of battle
5 under foot the mire of the ways in b.
14 2 all nations to Jerusalem to battle and
3 as when he fought in the day of battle
1 Ma 2 35 they made haste to give them battle
38 they gave them battle on the sabbath
3 2 with cheerfulness the battle of Israel
44 that they might be ready for battle
59 it is better for us to die in battle
4 13 they went out of the camp to battle
14 they joined battle: and the Gentiles
34 they joined battle: and there fell of
5 31 cry of the battle went up to heaven
42 behind: but let all come to the battle
59 went out of the city to give them b.
6 4 and they rose up against him in battle
30 thirty-two elephants, trained to battle
33 made themselves ready for the battle
42 Judas and his army drew near for battle
7 43 and the armies joined battle on the
43 he himself was first slain in the b.
8 5 that they had defeated in battle Philip
9 1 Nicanor and his army were battle in b.
7 away, and the battle pressed upon him
13 the battle was fought from morning even
17 and the battle was hard fought. 10:50
45 the battle is before us, and the water
46 and they joined battle. And Jonathan
10 53 have joined battle with him, and both
78 him to Azotus, and they joined battle
11 4 graves of them that were slain in b.
15 he came to give him battle, and king
69 rose out of their places and joined b.
72 Jonathan turned again to them to battle
12 28 Jonathan and his men were ready for b.
41 with 40,000 men chosen for battle, and
50 one another, and went out ready for b.
13 14 that he meant to join battle with him
2 Ma 8 20 battle that they had fought against
23 first band, he joined b. with Nicanor
10 28 sun was risen, both sides joined battle
28 making their rage their leader in b.
12 34 when they had joined b., it happened
36 to be their helper and leader of the b.
14 17 had joined battle with Nicanor, but was
15 19 for them that were to be engaged in b.
28 when the battle was over, and they were
1 C 14 8 who shall prepare himself to the battle
Heb 11 34 became valiant in battle, put to flight
Apoc 9 7 like unto horses prepared unto battle
9 chariots and many horses running to b.
12 7 and there was a great battle in heaven
16 14 to gather them to battle against the
20 7 and shall gather them together to battle
battlement Deut 22 8 make a b. to the roof round
battlements Judg 9 51 they stood upon the b. of
battles 1 K 8 20 our king . . . fight our b. for us
1 K 18 17 and fight the battles of the Lord
25 28 fightest the battles of the Lord: let
3 K 16 5 acts of Baasa . . . and his battles, are
27 acts of Amri and the battles he fought
22 46 works which he did and his battles
1 Pa 5 18 and trained up to battles, four and
22 8 and fought many battles, so thou canst
26 27 and the spoils won in battles, which
2 Pa 25 8 if thou think that battles consist in
Jdth 5 22 they were destroyed in battles by many
Ps 139 3 all the day long they designed battles
Isa 30 32 in great battles he shall overthrow
1 Ma 1 2 he [Alexander] fought many battles
3 3 his warlike armor about him in battles
26 all nations told of the b. of Judas
5 7 [Judas] fought many battles with them
21 fought many battles with the heathens
56 heard of the good success and the b.
8 2 they heard of their battles, and their
9 30 chosen thee . . . to fight our battles
10 15 they told him of the battles, and the
13 3 you know what great battles I and my
9 fight thou our battles, and we will do
2 Ma 15 9 in the mind of the b. they had fought
be Mat 4 3 if thou be the son of God, command
Mat 4 6 him: if thou be the son of God, cast
14 28 if it be thou, bid me come to thee
27 49 let be, let us see whether Elias will
Mark 9 18 how long shall I be with you? How long
Luke 2 49 I must be about my Father's business
23 43 thou shalt be with me in paradise
beaks Zach 4 12 that are by the two golden beaks
beam 1 K 17 7 like a weaver's beam. 2 K 21:19; 1 Pa 11:23; 20:5
1 Es 6 11 a beam shall be taken from his house
Esth 5 14 order a great beam to be prepared
Mat 7 3 seest not the beam. Luke 6:41, 42
4 and behold a beam is in thy own eye
5 cast out first the beam. Luke 6:42
beams 3 K 6 6 and he put beams in the house
3 K 6 36 stones, and one row of beams of cedar
7 5 over the pillars were square beams
2 Pa 3 7 the beams thereof . . . of the finest
Job 41 21 beams of the sun shall be under him
Cant 1 16 the beams of our houses are of cedar
Wisd 2 3 is driven away by the beams of the sun
Eccu 43 4 shining with his beams, he blindeth
Bar 6 18 but they are like beams in the house
54 shall be burnt in the midst like beams
Bean 1 Ma 5 4 the malice of the children of Bean
beans 2 K 17 28 corn and beans and lentils and
Eze 4 9 beans and lentils and millet and
bear (noun) 1 K 17 34 there came a lion or a bear
1 K 17 36 have killed both a lion and a bear
37 lion, and out of the paw of the bear
2 K 17 8 as a bear raging in the wood when her
Prov 17 12 better to meet a bear robbed of her
28 15 as a roaring lion and a hungry bear
Eccu 25 24 darkeneth her countenance as a bear
Isa 11 7 the calf and the bear shall feed
Lam 3 10 is become to me as a bear lying in wait
Dan 7 5 another beast like a bear stood up
Osee 13 8 I will meet them as a bear that is
Amos 5 19 of a lion, and a bear should meet him
Apoc 13 2 his feet were as the feet of a bear
bear (verb) Gen 13 6 the land able to bear them
Gen 17 19 Sara thy wife shall bear thee a son
18 13 who am an old woman bear thee a son
22 23 these eight did Melcha bear to Nachor
30 3 that she may bear upon my knees, and I
36 7 able to bear them, for the multitude
38 5 she ceased to bear any more. And Juda
Exod 18 18 strength, thou alone canst not bear it
23 shalt be able to bear his precepts
25 28 them with gold to bear up the table
28 12 Aaron shall bear their names before

29 Aaron shall bear the names of the
30 he shall bear the judgment of the
38 Aaron shall bear the iniquities of
35 14 the candlestick to bear up the lights
38 25 of 603,550 men able to bear arms
Lev 5 1 not utter it, he shall b. his iniquity
10 17 that you may bear the iniquity of the
12 2 shall bear a man child, she shall be
5 if she shall bear a maid child, she
17 16 his body, he shall bear his iniquity
19 8 shall bear his iniquity because he
20 17 they shall bear their iniquity. Eze 44:12
19 flesh, both shall bear their iniquity
20 near akin, both shall bear their sin
22 16 lest perhaps they bear the iniquity
24 15 that curseth God, shall bear his sin
Num 5 28 not be hurt and shall bear children
31 and she shall bear her iniquity
9 13 in due season: he shall bear his sin
11 12 and bear them into the land, for which
14 not able alone to bear all this people
17 they may bear with thee the burden
14 33 and shall bear your fornication until
15 31 destroyed, and shall bear his iniquity
18 1 bear the iniquity of the sanctuary
1 shall bear the sins of your priesthood
23 bear the sins of the people. It shall
30 16 he knew it, he shall bear her iniquity
Deut 1 10 I alone am not able to bear you: for
12 alone am not able to bear your business
Judg 13 3 shalt conceive and bear a son. 5, 7; Isa 7:14
Ruth 1 12 conceive the night and bear children
4 13 gave her to conceive to bear a son
1 K 15 25 but now bear, I beseech thee, my sin
16 16 and thou mayest bear it more easily
2 K 13 13 I shall not be able to bear my shame
18 20 but shalt bear tidings another day
20 I will not have thee bear tidings
4 K 18 14 thou shalt put upon me, I will bear
19 30 root downward, and bear fruit upward
2 Pa 2 2 numbered out 70,000 men to bear burdens
Job 9 13 they stoop that bear up the world
31 23 his weight I was not able to bear
Ps 39 16 them immediately bear their confusion
90 12 in their hands they shall bear thee up
Prov 9 12 scorner, thou alone shalt bear the evil
12 24 the hand of the valiant shall bear rule
18 14 that is easily angered, who can bear
27 4 and who can bear the violence of one
29 2 when the wicked shall bear rule, the
30 21 and the fourth it cannot bear: by a
Wisd 6 6 shall be for them that bear rule
23 all ye that bear rule over peoples
10 7 the trees bear fruits that ripen not
Eccu 1 29 a patient man shall bear for a time
22 18 and mass of iron is easier to bear
31 happen to me by him, I will bear it
Isa 30 27 wrath burneth and is heavy to bear
37 31 and shall bear fruit upward: for out
46 4 I have made you, and I will bear: I
7 they bear him on their shoulders and
53 11 and he shall bear their iniquities
64 3 we shall not bear them: thou didst
Jer 10 19 is my own evil, and I will bear it
20 9 wearied, not being able to bear it
29 6 and let them bear sons and daughters
30 6 ask ye, and see if a man bear children
44 22 so that the Lord could no longer bear
50 44 and who shall bear up against me
Eze 4 5 shalt bear the iniquity of the house
14 10 and they shall bear their iniquity
16 52 do thou also bear thy confusion, thou
52 also confounded and bear thy shame
54 that thou mayest bear thy shame and
17 8 bring forth branches and bear fruit
23 into branches and shall bear fruit
18 20 son shall not bear the iniquity of
20 father shall not bear the iniquity
19 11 make scepters for them that bear rule
23 35 bear thou also thy wickedness and
49 you shall bear the sins of your idols
34 29 shall they bear any more the reproach
36 7 shall themselves bear their shame
15 nor shalt thou bear the reproach of
30 that you bear no more the reproach
39 26 they shall bear their confusion and
44 13 they shall bear their shame and their
47 12 shall grow all trees that bear fruit
Amos 7 10 is not able to bear all his words
Mich 6 16 you shall bear the reproach of my
7 9 I will bear the wrath of the Lord
Zach 6 13 he shall bear the glory and shall
1 Ma 11 33 good will which they bear towards us
Mat 3 11 whose shoes I am not worthy to bear
4 6 shall they bear thee up. Luke 4:11
11 12 violence, and the violent bear it away
Luke 1 13 wife Elizabeth shall bear thee a son
11 46 with burdens which they cannot bear
13 9 if happily it bear fruit: but if not
John 15 4 as the branch cannot bear fruit of
16 12 but you cannot bear them now. But when
Acts 15 10 fathers nor we have been able to bear
18 14 I should with reason bear with you
27 15 could not bear up against the wind
Rom 15 1 ought to bear the infirmities of the
1 C 6 20 glorify and bear God in your body
9 12 but we bear all things lest we should
10 13 issue, that you may be able to bear it
15 49 let us bear the image of the heavenly
2 C 6 14 bear not the yoke with unbelievers
11 1 would to God you could bear with some
1 little of my folly: but do bear with me
4 received; you might well bear with him
Gal 5 10 troubleth you, shall bear the judgment
6 2 bear ye one anothers burden; and so
5 every one shall bear his own burden
17 I bear the marks of the Lord Jesus
Col 4 13 I bear him [Epaphras] testimony that
1 Tim 5 14 younger shall marry, bear children
James 3 12 the fig tree, my brethren, bear grapes
Apoc 2 2 thou canst not bear them that are evil

bear witness Exod 20 16 not bear false witness
Exod 23 1 to bear false witness for a wicked
Deut 5 20 neither shalt thou bear false witness
3 K 21 10 let them bear false witness: that he
Job 9 19 no man dare bear witness for me. If I
16 9 my wrinkles bear witness against me
Dan 13 21 we will bear witness against thee
Mat 19 18 thou shalt not bear false witness. Luke 18:20; Rom 13:9
Mark 10 19 bear not false witness, do no fraud
Luke 11 48 you bear witness that you consent to
John 3 28 you yourselves do bear me witness that
5 31 if I bear witness of myself, my witness
Acts 22 5 as the high priest doth bear me witness
23 11 must thou bear witness also at Rome
Rom 10 2 I bear them witness that they have a
2 C 8 3 to their power, I bear them witness
Gal 4 15 I bear you witness that if it could
1 J 1 2 and we have seen and do bear witness

beard Lev 13 29 break out in the head or the b.
Lev 13 30 is the leprosy of the head and the b.
14 9 shave the hair of his head and his b.
19 27 roundwise; nor shave your beard
21 5 they shave their head nor their beard
1 K 21 13 his spittle ran down upon his beard

2 K 19 24 washed his feet nor trimmed his beard
1 Es 9 3 off the hairs of my head and my beard
Ps 132 2 upon the beard, the beard of Aaron
Isa 7 20 hairs of the feet and the whole beard
15 2 every beard shall be shaven. Jer 48:37
Eze 5 1 to pass over thy head and over thy b.
beards 2 K 10 4 shaved off one half of their b.
2 K 10 5 at Jericho, till your beards be grown
1 Pa 19 4 Hanon shaved the heads and beards of
5 stay at Jericho till their beards grew
Jer 41 5 fourscore men, with their beards shaven
Bar 6 30 and their heads and beards shaven
bearer 2 K 18 22 wilt not be b. of good tidings
2 Es 4 10 the strength of the bearer of burdens
bearers 2 Ma 4 19 b. thereof desired it might not
bearest Isa 54 1 O thou barren, that bearest not
Rom 11 18 if thou boast, thou b. not the root
Gal 4 27 rejoice, thou barren, that bearest not
beareth Gen 1 12 and the tree that beareth fruit
Gen 9 15 every living soul that beareth flesh
Lev 12 7 law for her that beareth a man child
Deut 17 6 when only one beareth witness against
Job 24 21 he hath fed the barren that b. not
Prov 13 8 he that is poor beareth not reprehension
25 18 a man that beareth false witness
Wisd 17 10 beareth witness of its condemnation
Eccu 11 24 swift hour his blessing beareth fruit
28 13 tongue that b. witness bringeth death
40 4 weareth purple and beareth the crown
Mat 13 23 beareth fruit and yieldeth the one an
John 1 15 John beareth witness of him and crieth
5 32 is another that beareth witness of me
15 2 every branch in me that b. not fruit
2 every one that b. fruit, he will purge
5 I in him, the same beareth much fruit
Rom 13 4 for he beareth not the sword in vain
1 C 13 7 beareth all things, believeth all things
bearing Gen 1 29 given you every herb b. seed
Gen 16 2 Lord hath restrained me from bearing
29 35 called him Juda. And she left bearing
30 9 perceiving that she had left off b.
Num 10 17 set forward, bearing it. And the sons
1 Pa 5 18 fighting men bearing shields and
19 24 sons of Juda bearing shield and spear
Prov 7 11 not bearing to be quiet, not able to
30 17 the labor of his mother in bearing him
Eccu 30 20 bearing the reward of his iniquity
Isa 1 14 I am weary of bearing them. And when
1 Ma 2 56 Caleb, for bearing witness before the
2 Ma 6 20 he was come to it, patiently bearing
9 8 b. witness to the manifest power of God
John 19 5 came forth, b. the crown of thorns
17 bearing his own cross, he went forth
Rom 2 15 their conscience b. witness to them
9 1 I lie not, my conscience b. me witness
2 C 4 10 b. about in our body the mortification
Col 3 13 bearing with one another and forgiving
Heb 2 4 God also bearing them witness by signs
13 13 without the camp, b. his reproach
James 5 7 patiently b. till he receive the early
Apoc 22 2 was the tree of life b. twelve fruits
bears 4 K 2 24 there came forth two bears out of
Wisd 11 18 to send upon them a multitude of bears
Eccu 47 3 with bears he did in like manner as
Isa 59 11 we shall roar all of us like bears
beast Gen 7 14 every beast according to its kind
Gen 7 23 upon the earth from man even to beast
9 5 your lives at the hand of every beast
31 39 show thee that which the b. hath torn
37 33 an evil wild beast hath eaten him, a beast hath devoured Joseph
42 27 his sack, to give his beast provender
44 28 and you said: A beast devoured him
Exod 9 25 were in the field, both man and beast
11 7 least noise, from man even to beast
12 12 every firstborn . . . both man and beast
19 13 it be beast or man, he shall not live
20 10 nor thy beast nor the stranger that
22 5 vineyard and put in his beast to feed
10 or any b. to his neighbor's custody
13 if it were eaten by a beast, let him
19 copulateth with a beast shall be put to
Lev 5 2 that which hath been killed by a beast
7 if he be not able to offer a beast
7 21 touched the uncleanness of man or of b.
24 beast that was caught by another beast
11 26 beast that hath a hoof, but divideth
39 if any beast die, of which it is lawful
17 13 wild beast or a bird, which is lawful
15 itself, or has been caught by a beast
18 23 thou shalt not copulate with any beast
20 15 he that shall copulate with any beast
15 him die: the beast also ye shall kill
16 woman that shall lie under any beast
25 separate the clean beast from the
22 8 and that which was taken by a beast
24 beast that hath the testicles bruised
24 18 he that killeth a beast . . . shall give beast for beast
21 he that striketh a beast, shall render
27 9 a beast that may be sacrificed to the
11 unclean b., which cannot be sacrificed
27 if it be an unclean b., he that offereth
28 to the Lord, whether it be man or beast
Num 3 13 of man and beast, they are mine
18 15 every beast that is unclean thou shalt
22 30 ass said: Am not I thy beast, on which
31 26 take the sum . . . both of man and beast
Deut 14 6 every beast that divideth not the hoof
27 21 cursed be he that lieth with any beast
2 Es 2 12 no b. with me but the b. that I rode
14 for the beast on which I rode to pass
Job 37 8 the beast shall go into the covert
Ps 72 23 I am become as a beast before thee
79 14 singular wild beast hath devoured it
134 8 firstborn . . . from man even unto beast
Ecce 3 19 and man hath nothing more than beast
Wisd 13 14 or the resemblance of some beast
Eccu 13 19 every beast loveth its like: so also
40 8 to all flesh, from man even to beast
Isa 35 9 nor shall any mischievous beast go up
43 20 beast of the field shall glorify me
63 14 as a beast that goeth down in the field
Jer 32 43 there remaineth neither man nor beast
33 10 because there is neither man nor beast
10 desolate . . . and without beast. 12
36 29 cause to cease from thence man and b.
50 3 dwell therein, from man even to beast
51 62 neither man nor beast to dwell therein
Eze 14 13 will destroy man and beast out of it
17 and I destroy man and beast out of it
19 to cut off from it man and beast: and
21 to destroy out of it man and beast
25 13 will take away out of it man and beast
29 8 and cut off man and beast out of thee
44 31 that is dead of itself or caught by a b.
Dan 7 5 another beast like a bear stood up
6 the b. had four heads, and power was
7 a fourth beast, terrible and wonderful
11 and I saw that the beast was slain
19 learn concerning the fourth beast
23 fourth b. shall be the fourth kingdom
Osee 13 8 the beast of the field shall tear them
Joel 1 18 why did the beast groan, why did the
Soph 1 3 I will gather man and beast, I will
1 Ma 6 35 in order were chosen for every beast

36 wheresoever the beast was, they were
37 upon the beast . . . strong wooden towers
37 above; and an Indian to rule the beast
2 Ma 4 25 tyrant and the rage of a savage beast
Luke 10 34 setting him upon his own beast, brought
Acts 28 4 saw the beast hanging on his hand, they
5 shaking off the beast into the fire
Heb 12 20 beast shall touch the mount, it shall
2 P 2 16 the dumb beast used to the yoke, which
Apoc 11 7 the beast . . . shall make war against
13 1 I saw a beast coming up out of the sea
2 beast which I saw was like to a leopard
3 earth was in admiration after the b.
4 the dragon which gave power to the b.
4 they adored the beast. 14:11; 20:4
4 who is like to the beast? And who
11 I saw another beast coming up out of
12 executed all the power of the former b.
12 cause the earth to adore the first b.
14 given him to do in sight of the beast
14 they should make the image of the b. 15
17 the name of the beast or the number of
18 let him count the number of the beast
14 9 if any man shall adore the beast and
15 2 and them that had overcome the beast
16 2 the character of the beast. 19:20
10 poured out his vial upon seat of the b.
13 dragon and from the mouth of the beast
16 ten horns which thou sawest in the b.
17 that they give their kingdom to the b.
19 19 I saw the b. and the kings of the earth
20 the beast was taken, and with him the
20 9 beast and the false prophet shall be
beast's Dan 4 13 let a beast's heart be given him
beasts Gen 1 26 fowls of the air and the beasts
Gen 2 20 called all the beasts by their names
6 7 I will destroy . . . from man even to b.
20 and of beasts in their kind, and
7 2 of all clean beasts take seven and
3 of the beasts that are unclean two
8 of beasts clean and unclean and of fowls
21 of fowl and of cattle and of beasts
8 17 all flesh, as well in fowls as in b.
13 5 had flocks of sheep and herds of beasts
29 2 for the beasts were watered out of it
45 17 load your beasts and go into the land
Exod 8 17 came sciniphs on men and on beasts
18 sciniphs as well on men as on beasts
9 6 all the beasts of the Egyptians died
6 the beasts of the children of Israel
9 swelling blains both in men and b. 10
19 men and beasts and all things that
22 upon men and upon beasts and upon
11 5 mill, and all the firstborn of beasts
12 38 and herds and beasts of divers kinds
13 2 well of men as of beasts: for they
15 firstborn of man to the first born of b.
17 3 children and our beasts with thirst
21 34 pit shall pay the price of the beasts
22 31 flesh that beasts have tasted of before
23 29 and the beasts multiply against thee
34 19 shall be mine. Of all beasts, both of
Lev 7 26 not eat the blood . . . of birds or b.
11 3 cheweth the cud among the beasts, you
35 any of these dead beasts shall fall
46 this is the law of beasts and fowls
19 19 to gender with beasts of any other kind
20 25 defile not your souls with beasts or
25 7 that grow shall be meat to thy beasts
26 6 I will take away evil beasts: and the
Num 8 17 both of men and of beasts are mine
18 15 or of beasts, shall belong to thee
31 11 they had taken both of men and of b.
30 of all beasts, and thou shalt give
32 1 their substance in beasts was infinite
4 fertile soil for the feeding of beasts
24 folds and stalls for your sheep and b.
35 3 suburbs may be for their cattle and b.
Deut 4 17 the similitude of any beasts that are
5 14 ox nor thy ass nor any of thy beasts
14 4 these are the beasts that you shall eat
28 26 of the air and the beasts of the earth
32 24 I will send the teeth of b. upon them
Josu 14 4 suburbs to feed their beasts and flocks
Judg 20 48 city to the sword, both men and beasts
2 K 21 10 them by day nor the beasts by night
3 K 4 28 and straw for the horses and beasts
33 he discoursed of beasts and of fowls
18 5 that the beasts may not utterly perish
4 K 3 9 no water for the army and for the b.
17 you and your families and your beasts
14 9 b. of the forest that are in Libanus
2 Pa 25 18 b. that were in the wood of Libanus
28 15 upon b. and brought them to Jericho
32 28 stalls for all beasts, and folds for
1 Es 1 6 and gold, with goods and with beasts
2 Es 9 37 over our bodies and over our beasts
Tob 9 3 to take with thee beasts and servants
11 3 together with thy wife and with the b.
Jdth 15 8 no numbering of their cattle and b.
Esth 16 24 unpassable both to men and beasts
Job 12 7 ask now the beasts, and they shall
18 3 why are we reputed as beasts and counted
Ps 8 8 moreover the beasts also of the fields
35 7 men and beasts thou wilt preserve
48 13 he is compared to senseless beasts
21 hath been compared to senseless beasts
49 10 all the beasts of the woods are mine
73 19 deliver not up to beasts the souls that
103 20 shall all the b. of the woods go about
146 9 who giveth to beasts their food: and
148 10 beasts and all cattle: serpents and
Prov 12 10 regardeth the lives of his beasts
30 30 a lion, the strongest of beasts, who
Ecce 3 18 them and show them to be like beasts
19 the death of man and of beasts is one
21 if the spirit of the beasts descend
Wisd 11 16 dumb serpents and worthless beasts
16 upon them a multitude of dumb beasts
19 unknown beasts of a new kind, full of
12 9 under the just by war or by cruel b.
24 which are the most worthless among b.
13 10 of art, and the resemblances of beasts
15 19 can any man see good of these beasts
16 1 were destroyed by a multitude of beasts
5 when the fierce rage of beasts came
18 that the b. which were sent against
17 9 scared with the passing by of beasts
18 not be seen of beasts playing together
Eccu 10 13 he shall inherit serpents and beasts
17 4 he had dominion over beasts and fowls
39 36 for vengeance. The teeth of beasts
43 27 wonderful works: a variety of beasts
Isa 30 6 the burden of the beasts of the south
6 carry their riches upon shoulders of b.
40 16 nor the b. thereof sufficient for a
46 1 their idols are put upon beasts and
56 9 to devour, all ye beasts of the forest
Jer 7 20 upon men and upon beasts and upon
9 10 from the fowl of the air to the beasts
12 the beasts and the birds are consumed
21 6 men and beasts shall die of a great
27 5 the beasts that are upon the face of
31 27 of man and with the seed of beasts
Bar 3 16 they that rule over the beasts that are
32 filled it with cattle and fourfooted b.

6 67 beasts are better than they, which can
Eze 4 14 died of itself or was torn by beasts
5 17 in upon you famine and evil beasts
14 15 if I shall bring mischievous beasts
15 none that can pass because of the b.
21 the famine and the mischievous beasts
29 11 neither shall the foot of beasts go
31 6 b. of the forest brought forth their
32 4 I will fill the beasts of all the earth
13 I will destroy also all the b. thereof
13 neither shall the hoof of b. trouble
33 27 be given to the beasts to be devoured
34 25 evil beasts to cease out of the land
36 11 you abound with men and with beasts
Dan 3 81 ye beasts and cattle, bless the Lord
4 9 under it dwelt cattle and beasts, and
11 let the b. fly away that are under it
5 21 his heart was made like the beasts
7 3 four great beasts, different one from
7 and it was unlike to the other beasts
12 power of the other beasts was taken
17 these four great b. are four kingdoms
8 4 no beasts could withstand him nor be
Joel 1 17 the beasts have rotted in their dung
2 22 fear not, ye beasts of the fields: for
Amos 5 22 will I regard the vows of your fat b.
Jon 3 7 men nor beasts, oxen nor sheep, taste
8 let men and beasts be covered with
4 11 city in which there are . . . many b.
Mich 5 8 as a lion among the b. of the forests
Haba 2 17 the ravaging of beasts shall terrify
Soph 2 14 midst thereof, all the b. of the nations
15 a place for beasts to lie down in
Agge 1 11 upon men and upon beasts and upon
Zach 2 4 the multitude of men and of the beasts
8 10 men, neither was there hire for beasts
14 15 and of the ass and of all the beasts
1 Ma 1 50 to be immolated, and unclean beasts
6 35 they distributed the beasts by legions
43 saw one of the beasts harnessed with
43 it was higher than the other beasts
2 Ma 11 9 also the fiercest b. and walls of iron
15 20 the beasts and the horsemen ranged
21 armor, and the fierceness of the b.
Mark 1 13 and he was with beasts, and the angels
Acts 10 12 were all manner of fourfooted beasts
11 6 beasts and creeping things and fowls
23 24 provide beasts that they may set Paul
Rom 1 23 and of birds and of fourfooted beasts
1 C 15 32 I fought with beasts at Ephesus, what
39 another of beasts, another of birds
Titus 1 12 Cretians are always liars, evil beasts
Heb 13 11 the bodies of those beasts, whose blood
James 3 7 every nature of beasts and of birds
2 P 2 12 but these men, as irrational beasts
Jude 10 they naturally know, like dumb beasts
Apoc 18 13 and sheep and horses and chariots
beasts of the earth Gen 1 24 b. . . . according to their kinds. 25
Gen 1 30 to all b. . . . and to every fowl of the
2 19 formed out of the ground all the b. . . .
3 1 was more subtle than any of the b. . . .
14 art cursed among all cattle and b. . . .
9 2 dread of you be upon all the b. . . .
10 in all birds as in cattle and b. . . .
10 out of the ark, and in all the b. . . .
Deut 7 22 lest perhaps the b. . . . should increase
28 26 the fowls of the air and the b. . . .
1 K 17 44 birds of the air and to the b. . . . 46
Job 5 22 thou shalt not be afraid of the b. . . .
23 the b. . . . shall be at peace with thee
35 11 who teacheth us more than the b. . . .
Ps 78 2 the flesh of thy saints for the b. . . .
Isa 18 6 birds of the mountains and the b. . . .
6 all the b. . . . shall winter upon them
Jer 7 33 fowls of the air and for the b. . . . 16:4; 19:7
12 9 assemble yourselves, all ye b. . . .
15 3 the b. . . . to devour and to destroy
28 14 also I have given him the b. . . . And
34 20 to fowls of the air and to the b. . . .
Eze 29 5 have given thee for meat to the b. . . .
34 28 neither shall the b. . . . devour them
39 4 fowl, and to the b. . . . to be devoured
Apoc 6 8 and with death and with the b. . . .
beasts of the field Exod 23 11 let the b. . . . eat
Lev 26 22 and I will send in upon you the b. . . .
Jdth 11 5 also the beasts of the field obey him
Job 39 15 upon them that the b. . . . may break them
40 15 grass: there all the b. . . . shall play
Ps 103 11 all the beasts of the field shall drink
Isa 56 9 all ye b. . . . come to devour, all ye
Jer 27 6 b. . . . I have given him to serve him
Eze 31 13 all the b. . . . were among his branches
34 5 they became the prey of all the b. . . .
8 are become a prey to all the b. . . .
38 20 birds of the air and the b. . . . and
39 17 to all the birds and to all the b. . . .
Dan 2 38 of men and the b. . . . do dwell
4 18 under which the b. . . . dwelt, and the
Osee 2 12 the b. . . . shall devour her. And I will
18 a covenant with them, with the b. . . .
4 3 in it shall languish with the b. . . .
Joel 1 20 and the b. . . . have looked up to thee
wild beasts Ps 67 31 rebuke the wild b. of the
Wisd 7 20 rage of wild beasts, the force of winds
17 18 the roaring voice of wild beasts or a
Eccu 12 13 or any that come near wild beasts
Isa 13 21 wild beasts shall rest there, and their
Eze 39 4 I have given thee to the wild beasts
Dan 4 12 let its portion be with the wild beasts
20 let his feeding be with the wild beasts
22 thy dwelling . . . with the wild b. 29
2 Ma 5 27 and there lived amongst wild beasts
9 15 to be devoured by the birds and wild b.
10 6 when they were . . . in dens like wild b.
beat Exod 32 20 burnt it and beat it to powder
Num 11 8 in a mill, or beat it in a mortar
16 38 let him beat them into plates and
39 beat them into plates, fastening them
22 6 if by any means I may beat them and
23 when Balaam beat her and had a mind to
25 foot of the rider. But he beat her again
27 beat her sides more vehemently with a
33 52 beat down their pillars, and break in
Deut 22 18 city shall take that man and beat him
Judg 7 13 and beat it down flat to the ground
2 K 22 43 I shall beat them as small as the dust
3 K 12 11 my father beat you with whips, but I will beat you with scorpions. 14
4 K 13 25 by war, three times did Joas beat him
1 Pa 4 41 they beat down their tents and slew
2 Pa 10 11 my father beat you with scourges. 14
2 Es 13 25 I beat some of them, and shaved off
Jdth 9 11 to beat down . . . the horn of thy altar
Ps 17 43 I shall beat them as small as the
Prov 23 14 thou shalt beat him with the rod and
Eccu 30 12 beat his sides while he is a child
47 5 he beat down the boasting of Goliath
Jer 37 9 if you should even beat all the army
14 they beat him and cast him into the
Jon 4 8 the sun beat upon the head of Jonas
Mich 4 3 and they shall beat their swords into
13 thou shalt beat in pieces many peoples
2 Ma 14 33 ground, and will beat down the altar
Mat 7 25 beat upon that house. 27; Luke 6:48, 49

21 35 beat one and killed another and
Mark 4 37 the waves beat into the ship so that
12 3 beat him and sent him away empty. And
5 of whom some they beat and others they
Luke 19 44 beat thee flat to the ground, and thy
20 11 but they beat him also, and treating
Acts 18 17 beat him before the judgment seat; and
22 19 beat in every synagogue them that
beaten Exod 5 16 we thy servants are b. with whips
Exod 16 14 and as it were beaten with a pestle
25 18 make also two cherubims of beaten gold
31 make also a candlestick of beaten work
36 shall be of the same beaten work of
27 20 of the olives and beaten with a pestle
29 40 of flour tempered with beaten oil
30 36 when thou hast beaten all into very
37 7 two cherubims also of beaten gold
17 candlestick of b. work of the finest
22 all beaten work of the purest gold
Num 8 4 candlestick it was of beaten gold
10 2 make thee two trumpets of beaten silver
20 19 we will go by the beaten way: and if
Deut 25 2 and shall cause him to be beaten before
Judg 20 43 and were beaten down on the east side
4 K 14 10 hast beaten and prevailed over Edom
Prov 10 8 precepts: a fool is beaten with lips
10 the foolish in lips shall be beaten
33 35 thou shalt say: They have beaten me
Eccu 50 18 they sounded with beaten trumpets
Isa 28 27 gith shall be beaten out with a rod
Osee 4 14 doth not understand shall be beaten
Soph 3 6 and their towers are beaten down
Mark 13 9 in synagogues you shall be beaten
Luke 12 47 shall be beaten with many stripes. But
48 shall be beaten with few stripes. And
Acts 16 22 commanded them to be beaten with rods
37 have beaten us publicly, uncondemned
2 C 11 25 thrice was I beaten with rods, once I
beatest Num 22 32 why beatest thou thy ass these
beating Ruth 2 17 beating out with a rod and
Wisd 5 11 sound of the wings b. the light air
Isa 25 4 like a whirlwind b. against a wall
Luke 20 10 who beating him, sent him away empty
Acts 21 32 they left off beating Paul. Then the
1 C 9 26 I so fight, not as one beating the air
beautified Eccu 16 27 he b. their works forever
Eccu 42 21 he hath b. the glorious works of
beautiful Gen 12 11 that thou art a b. woman
Gen 12 14 saw the woman that she was very b.
24 16 most b. virgin and not known to man
29 17 well favored and of a b. countenance
39 6 Joseph was of a beautiful countenance
41 2 came up seven kine very b. and fat
4 whose bodies were very beautiful and
18 exceeding beautiful and full of flesh
26 the seven beautiful kine and the
49 12 his eyes are more beautiful than wine
Num 24 5 how beautiful are thy tabernacles
Deut 21 11 in number of the captives a b. woman
Ruth 1 20 call me not Noemi, that is, beautiful
1 K 15 9 that was b. and would not destroy
16 12 he was ruddy and beautiful to behold
2 K 1 26 Jonathan: exceeding b. and amiable to
11 2 the woman was very b. And the king
13 1 very b., and her name was Thamar
14 25 and so exceedingly b. as Absalom
27 name was Thamar, and she was very b.
3 K 1 3 so they sought a beautiful young woman
4 the damsel was exceeding beautiful and
6 he [Adonias] also was very beautiful
1 Es 8 27 of the best shining brass, b. as gold
2 Es 8 15 branches of b. wood, branches of
Tob 5 5 Tobias going forth found a b. young man
Jdth 8 7 and she was exceedingly beautiful
10 18 Hebrews, who have such beautiful women
Job 42 15 women so b. as the daughters of Job
Ps 44 3 thou art beautiful above the sons of
64 13 the b. places of the wilderness shall
Prov 3 17 her ways are b. ways, and all her paths
15 26 pure words most b. shall be confirmed
22 18 which shall be b. for thee if thou
23 8 and shalt loose thy beautiful words
24 4 with all precious and most b. wealth
Cant 1 4 I am black but b., O ye daughters of
9 thy cheeks are b. as the turtle-dove's
2 10 my dove, my beautiful one, and come
13 arise, my love, my beautiful one, and
4 1 how beautiful art thou! Thy eyes are
10 how beautiful are thy breasts, my
10 thy breasts are more b. than wine, and
5 9 O thou most beautiful among women. 17
6 3 thou art beautiful, O my love, sweet
7 1 how beautiful are thy steps in shoes
6 how beautiful art thou and how comely
Wisd 4 1 how b. is the chaste generation with
7 29 she is more beautiful than the sun and
13 3 the Lord of them is more b. than they
Eccu 35 26 the mercy of God is b. in the time of
43 12 is very beautiful in its brightness
45 15 before there were none so beautiful
Isa 10 18 glory of his forest and of his b. hill
27 10 the beautiful city shall be forsaken
44 13 a beautiful man dwelling in a house
52 7 how b. upon the mountains are the
63 1 this b. one in his robe, walking in
Jer 6 2 to a beautiful and delicate woman
9 10 and for the b. places of the desert
11 16 olive tree, fair, fruitful, and b.
13 20 that is given thee, thy b. cattle
46 20 Egypt is like a fair and b. heifer
48 17 the strong staff broken, the b. rod
49 19 the Jordan, against the strong and b.
50 44 of the Jordan to the strong and b.
Lam 2 2 not spared, all that was b. in Jacob
Eze 16 12 and a beautiful crown upon thy head
13 and wast made exceeding beautiful
17 thou tookest thy beautiful vessels
23 6 beautiful youths, all horsemen, mounted
23 of the Assyrians, beautiful young men
42 and beautiful crowns on their heads
31 7 and he was most b. for his greatness
9 I made him b. and thick set with many
Dan 4 9 its leaves were most beautiful, and its
18 branches thereof were most beautiful
13 2 b. woman and one that feared God
31 was exceeding delicate and beautiful
Joel 1 19 fire hath devoured the b. places. 20
2 22 the b. places of the wilderness are
3 5 and my desirable and most b. things
Amos 1 2 b. places of the shepherds have mourned
Mich 1 11 that dwellest in the Beautiful place
Nah 3 4 the harlot that was b. and agreeable
Soph 2 13 he will make the b. city a wilderness
Zach 9 17 what is his beautiful thing, but the
2 Ma 3 26 other young men beautiful and strong
Mat 23 27 sepulchers . . . appear to men beautiful
Acts 3 2 gate of the Temple, which is called B.
10 sat begging alms at the Beautiful gate
Rom 10 15 how b. are the feet of them that preach
beautifulness Eccu 44 6 men in virtue, studying b.
beautify Isa 60 13 to b. the place of my sanctuary
beauty Gen 26 7 would kill him because of her b.
Gen 41 7 devoured all the beauty of the former
24 they devoured the beauty of the former
49 21 hart let loose and giving words of b.
Exod 28 2 thy brother for glory and for beauty

40 girdles and miters for glory and beauty
Deut 33 17 his beauty as of the firstling of a
2 Pa 3 6 most precious marble, of great beauty
Jdth 10 4 and the Lord also gave her more beauty
4 the Lord increased this her beauty so
7 and admired her beauty exceedingly
14 they wondered exceedingly at her b.
11 19 not such another woman . . . in beauty
16 8 weakened him with the b. of her face
11 her beauty made his soul her captive
Esth 1 11 to show her beauty to all the people
2 15 her incredible beauty made her appear
Job 5 3 and I cursed his beauty immediately
24 visiting thy beauty thou shalt not sin
18 13 let it devour the beauty of his skin
40 5 clothe thyself with beauty, and set
Ps 20 6 and great b. shalt thou lay upon him
25 8 loved, O Lord, the b. of thy house
29 8 thou gavest strength to my beauty. Thou
44 5 with thy comeliness and thy b. set out
12 the king shall greatly desire thy b.
46 5 beauty of Jacob which he hath loved
49 2 out of Sion the loveliness of his b.
11 with me is the beauty of the field
67 13 b. of the house shall divide spoils
77 61 their b. into the hands of the enemy
92 1 hath reigned, he is clothed with beauty
95 6 praise and beauty are before him
103 1 thou hast put on praise and beauty
Prov 6 25 let not thy heart covet her beauty
31 25 strength and beauty are her clothing
30 favor is deceitful, and b. is vain
Wisd 5 17 crown of beauty at the hand of the Lord
7 10 I loved her above health and beauty
8 2 and I became a lover of her beauty
13 3 with whose b., if they being delighted
3 the first author of beauty made all
5 by the greatness of the beauty and of
14 20 carried away by the beauty of the work
Eccu 4 28 hide not thy wisdom in her beauty. For
6 31 in her is the beauty of life, and her
9 5 lest her beauty be a stumblingblock to
8 gaze not about upon another's beauty
9 have perished by the b. of a woman
11 admiring the b. of another man's wife
11 2 praise not a man for his beauty
25 28 look not upon a woman's beauty, and
desire not a woman for beauty
26 21 so is the beauty of a good wife for the
22 is the beauty of the face in a ripe age
31 6 beauty thereof hath been their ruin
36 24 the beauty of a woman cheereth the
40 22 thy eye desireth favor and beauty
42 12 behold not everybody's beauty: and
43 1 the firmament on high is his beauty
1 b. of heaven with its glorious show
10 glory of the stars is the b. of heaven
20 admireth at the b. of the whiteness
45 14 delightful to the eyes for its beauty
47 12 and to the festivals he added beauty
Isa 32 18 my people shall sit in the b. of peace
33 17 eyes shall see the king in his beauty
35 2 the beauty of Carmel and Saron, they
2 of the Lord and the beauty of our God
53 2 is no beauty in him nor comeliness
Jer 25 30 shall roar upon the place of his beauty
31 23 Lord bless thee, the beauty of justice
50 7 against the Lord the beauty of justice
Lam 1 6 all her beauty is departed: her princes
2 15 is this the city of perfect beauty
Bar 5 1 put on the beauty and honor of that
Eze 16 14 forth among the nations for thy beauty
14 thou wast perfect through my beauty
15 trusting in thy beauty, thou playedst
25 hast made thy beauty to be abominable
39 shall take away the vessels of thy b.
23 12 and to young men all of great beauty
27 3 thou hast said: I am of perfect beauty
4 built thee, have perfected thy beauty
11 round about: they perfected thy beauty
28 7 swords against the b. of thy wisdom, and
they shall defile thy beauty
12 full of wisdom and perfect in beauty
13 emerald: gold the work of thy beauty
17 thy heart was lifted up with thy b.
17 hast lost thy wisdom in thy beauty
31 8 paradise of God was like him in his b.
32 19 whom dost thou excel in beauty? Go
Dan 13 32 they might be satisfied with her beauty
56 beauty hath deceived thee, and lust
Osee 9 13 was a Tyre founded in beauty: and
10 11 I passed over upon the b. of her neck
Zach 11 7 two rods, one I called Beauty, and the
10 I took my rod that was called Beauty
1 Ma 1 27 the beauty of the women was changed
2 12 our b. and our glory is laid waste
2 Ma 15 13 environed with great b. and majesty
James 1 11 beauty of the shape thereof perished
Bebai 1 Es 2 11 the children of Bebai, 623
1 Es 8 11 of the sons of Bebai, Zacharias the son of
Bebai
10 28 and of the sons of Bebai, Johanan
2 Es 7 16 children of Bebai, 628. The children
10 15 Bonni, Azgad, Bebai, Adonia, Begoai
became Mat 28 4 terror, and became as dead men
Mark 9 2 and his garments became shining and
25 out of him, and he became as dead
Luke 9 29 his raiment became white and glittering
13 19 and it grew and became a great tree
18 23 became sorrowful; for he was very rich
22 44 his sweat became as drops of blood
Acts 1 19 b. known to all the inhabitants. 19:17
Rom 1 21 but became vain in their thoughts, and
22 themselves to be wise, they b. fools
1 C 9 20 I became to the Jews a Jew, that I
22 to the weak I became weak, that I might
22 I became all things to all men, that
13 11 when I became a man, I put away the
2 C 8 9 being rich he became poor for our
1 Th 1 6 you became followers of us and of the
2 7 we became little ones in the midst of
Heb 2 2 word spoken by angels b. steadfast
10 it became him, for whom are all things
5 9 he became to all that obey him, the
10 33 you became companions of them that were
11 34 became valiant in battle, put to flight
Apoc 6 12 the sun became black as sackcloth of
12 and the whole moon became as blood
8 8 the third part of the sea became blood
11 third part of the waters b. wormwood
16 10 his kingdom became dark, and they
Becbecia 2 Es 11 17 and Becbecia the second, one
2 Es 12 9 Becbecia and Hanni and their brethren
25 and Becbecia . . . keepers of the gates
Becher Num 26 35 the sons of Ephraim . . . Becher
Becherites Num 26 35 of whom is the family of B.
Bechor Gen 46 21 sons of Benjamin . . . B. 1 Pa 7:6
1 Pa 7 8 the sons of Bechor were Zamira and
Bechorath 1 K 9 1 Seror the son of Bechorath
beck Job 26 11 tremble and dread at his beck
2 Ma 8 18 who at a beck can utterly destroy both
beckoned Luke 5 7 they beckoned to their partners
John 13 24 Peter b. to him and said to him: Who
Acts 21 40 [Paul] b. with his hand to the people
beckoning Acts 12 17 [Peter] b. to them with his
Acts 19 33 Alexander beckoning with his hand

become Mat 18 3 and become as little children
Mat 21 42 is become the head of the corner. Mark 12:10; Luke 20:17; Acts 4:11
23 26 that the outside may become clean
Mark 1 17 I will make you to b. fishers of men
3 21 they said: He is become mad. And the
9 49 if the salt become unsavory, wherewith
Luke 18 24 Jesus seeing him become sorrowful, said
22 26 let him become as the younger; and he
John 4 14 shall become in him a fountain of water
9 27 will you also become his disciples
39 and they who see, may become blind
15 8 much fruit and become my disciples
Acts 1 20 let their habitation become desolate
7 40 we know not what is b. of him [Moses]
12 18 what was b. of Peter. And when Herod
26 28 persuadest me to become a Christian
29 should become such as I also am except
Rom 3 12 they are become unprofitable together
6 22 free from sin and become servants of God
7 4 you also are become dead to the law
13 might become sinful above measure. For
1 C 3 18 let him become a fool that he may be
4 8 you are now become rich; you reign
8 9 your liberty become a stumblingblock
9 27 I myself should become a castaway
10 7 neither become ye idolaters as some of
11 13 doth it become a woman to pray unto
13 1 I am become as sounding brass or a
14 20 do not become children in sense but in
2 C 12 11 am become foolish: you have compelled
Gal 4 16 am I then become your enemy, because
Eph 5 17 become not unwise, but understanding
1 Th 2 8 you were become most dear unto us
14 you are b. followers of the churches
1 Tim 6 9 they that will become rich, fall into
Titus 2 1 things that become sound doctrine
Heb 2 17 that he might become a merciful and
5 11 because you are become weak to hear
12 you are become such as have need of
6 12 we desire that you become not slothful
James 2 4 are become judges of unjust thoughts
10 offend in one point, is b. guilty of
11 thou art become a transgressor of the
2 P 2 20 latter state is become unto them worse
1 J 2 18 there are become many Antichrists
Apoc 11 15 kingdom of this world is b. our Lord's
18 2 is become the habitation of devils
becomes Luke 11 26 state of that man b. worse
becometh Mat 3 15 it b. us to fulfil all justice
Mat 13 22 up the word and he becometh fruitless
32 and becometh a tree, so that the birds
Mark 4 32 b. greater than all herbs and shooteth
Rom 16 2 receive her in the Lord as b. saints
Eph 5 3 as be named among you, as b. saints
1 Tim 2 10 as it b. women professing godliness
James 4 4 friend of this world b. an enemy of
becoming Phil 2 8 becoming obedient unto death
James 1 25 not b. a forgetful hearer, but a doer
becomingness 1 Pa 16 29 adore the Lord in holy b.
bed Gen 19 4 before they went to bed, the men of
Gen 38 27 when she was ready to be brought to bed
48 2 being strengthened he sat on his bed
49 4 thou wentest up to thy father's bed
32 drew up his feet upon the bed and died
Exod 8 3 upon thy bed and into the houses of
21 18 and he die not, but keepeth his bed
Lev 15 4 every bed on which he sleepeth shall
5 if any man touch his bed, he shall
22 he that toucheth her bed shall wash
24 every bed on which he shall sleep
26 every bed on which she sleepeth, and
Num 5 19 defiled by forsaking thy husband's bed
Deut 3 11 his bed of iron is shown, which is in
27 20 father's wife and uncovereth his bed
Judg 21 12 that had not known the bed of a man
1 K 9 25 he prepared a bed for Saul on the top
19 13 took an image and laid it on the bed
15 bring him [David] to me in the bed
16 they found an image upon the bed, and
28 23 from the ground and sat upon the bed
2 K 4 5 he was sleeping upon his bed at noon
7 was sleeping upon his bed in a parlor
11 slain an innocent man . . . upon his bed
11 2 David arose from his bed after noon
13 5 lie down upon thy bed and feign thyself
3 K 1 47 and the king adored in his bed: and he
17 19 [Elias] laid him upon his own bed
21 4 casting himself upon his bed, he turned
4 K 1 4 from the bed on which thou art gone. 16
6 thou shalt not come down from the bed
4 10 and put a little bed in it for him
21 laid him upon the bed of the man of
32 behold the child lay dead on his bed
1 Pa 5 1 as he defiled his father's bed, his
2 Pa 16 14 and they laid him [Asa] on his bed
24 25 they slew him in his bed, and he died
Jdth 13 4 Holofernes lay on his bed, fast asleep
6 Judith stood before the bed praying
Esth 4 3 using sackcloth and ashes for their bed
7 8 he found Aman was fallen upon the bed
11 12 seen this and arose out of his bed
14 15 and abhor the bed of the uncircumcised
Job 7 13 if I say: My bed shall comfort me
17 13 and I have made my bed in darkness
33 19 he rebuketh also by sorrow in the bed
Ps 6 7 every night I will wash my bed: I will
35 5 he hath devised iniquity on his bed
40 4 Lord help him on his bed of sorrow
62 7 if I have remembered thee upon my bed
131 3 if I shall go up into the bed wherein
Prov 7 16 I have woven my bed with cords, I have
17 I have perfumed my bed with myrrh
22 27 should take the covering from thy bed
26 14 so doth the slothful upon his bed
30 26 which maketh its bed in the rock: the
Cant 1 15 and comely. Our bed is flourishing
3 1 in my bed by night I sought him whom
7 surrounded the bed of Solomon? All
6 1 garden to the bed of aromatical spices
Wisd 3 13 that hath not known bed in sin: she
16 seed of unlawful bed shall be rooted
Eccu 9 12 wife, nor repose upon the bed with her
23 25 man that passeth beyond his own bed
40 5 in the time of rest upon his bed, the
41 27 handmaid, and approach not her bed
48 6 pieces, and the glorious from their bed
Isa 28 20 the bed is straitened, so that one must
57 2 let him rest in his bed that hath
7 lofty mountain thou hast laid thy bed
8 thou hast enlarged thy bed and made a
8 hast loved their bed with open hand
Eze 23 17 were come to her to the bed of love
41 thou sattest on a very fine bed, and
32 25 have set him a bed among all his people
Dan 2 28 the visions of thy head upon thy bed
29 didst begin to think in thy bed, what
4 2 thoughts in my bed, and the visions
7 this was the vision of my head in my bed
10 in the vision of my head upon my bed
7 1 vision of his head was upon his bed
Joel 1 20 as garden bed that thirsteth after rain
2 16 let bridegroom go forth from his bed
Amos 3 12 that dwell in Samaria, in piece of a bed
1 Ma 1 6 he fell down upon his bed and knew that
28 the bride that sat in the marriage bed

6 8 he laid himself down upon his bed
Mat 9 2 one sick of the palsy lying in a bed
6 take up thy bed. Mark 2:9, 11; Luke 5:24; John 5:8, 11, 12
Mark 2 4 they let down the bed wherein the
12 and taking up his bed, went his way
4 21 candle come in to be put under a bed
7 30 she found the girl lying upon the bed
Luke 5 18 brought in a bed a man who had the
19 down through the tiles with his bed
25 he took up the bed on which. John 5:9
8 16 or putteth it under a bed; but setteth
11 7 and my children are with me in bed
17 34 there shall be two men in one bed; the
John 5 10 not lawful for thee to take up thy bed
Acts 9 33 Eneas, who kept his bed for eight years
34 healeth thee: arise and make thy bed
Heb 13 4 honorable in all, and the bed undefiled
Apoc 2 22 I will cast her into a bed: and they
bedchamber Exod 8 3 thy b. and upon thy bed
4 K 11 2 out of the bedchamber with his nurse
2 Pa 22 11 hid him with his nurse in a bedchamber
bed's Gen 47 31 Israel . . . turning to the b. head
Jdth 13 8 the pillar that was at his bed's head
beds 2 K 17 28 brought him beds and tapestry
Esth 1 6 the beds also were of gold and silver
Job 33 15 and they are sleeping in their beds
Ps 4 5 be sorry for them upon your beds
149 5 they shall be joyful in their beds
Prov 25 11 like apples of gold on beds of silver
Cant 5 13 his cheeks are as beds of aromatical
Wisd 4 6 children that are born of unlawful beds
Osee 7 14 heart, but they howled in their beds
Amos 6 4 you that sleep upon beds of ivory and
Mich 2 1 unprofitable, and work evil in your b.
Mark 6 55 they began to carry about in beds those
7 4 and of brazen vessels and of beds
Acts 5 15 laid them on beds and couches, that
bee Eccu 11 3 the bee is small among flying things
Isa 7 18 the bee that is in the land of Assyria
beef 2 K 6 19 and piece of roasted beef. 1 Pa 16:3
Beelmeon 1 Pa 5 8 as far as Nebo and Beelmeon
Eze 25 9 land of Bethiesimoth and Beelmeon
Beelphegor Num 25 3 Israel was initiated to B.
Num 25 5 that have been initiated to Beelphegor
Deut 4 3 Lord hath done against Beelphegor
Josu 22 17 that you sinned with Beelphegor, and
Ps 105 28 they also were initiated to B.: and ate
Osee 9 10 but they went in to Beelphegor, and
Beelsephon Exod 14 1 which is . . . over against B.
Exod 14 9 army were in Phihahiroth before B.
Num 33 7 Phihahiroth which looketh towards B.
Beelteem 1 Es 4 9 Reum B. and Samsai the scribe
1 Es 4 17 the king sent word to Reum Beelteem
23 was read before Reum Beelteem and
Beelzebub 4 K 1 2 B. the god of Accaron. 3, 6, 16
Mat 10 25 called the goodman of the house B.
12 24 casteth not out devils but by Beelzebub
27 if I by B. cast out devils. Luke 11:19
Mark 3 22 said: He hath Beelzebub, and by
Luke 11 15 he casteth out devils by Beelzebub
18 you say that through B. I cast out
Beer Josu 19 8 Baalath Beer Ramath to the south
Beera 1 Pa 5 6 Baal his son, Beera his son
Beeri Gen 26 34 Judith the daughter of Beeri
Osee 1 1 that came to Osee the son of Beeri
bees Deut 1 44 meeting you, chased you, as bees do
Judg 14 8 swarm of bees in mouth of the lion
Ps 117 12 they surrounded me like bees, and they
beeves Lev 22 19 of the beeves or of the sheep
Lev 22 21 whether of beeves or of sheep, shall
Mat 22 4 my beeves and fatlings are killed, and
befall Gen 42 38 if any mischief b. him in the
Gen 44 29 and anything befall him in the way
49 1 that shall befall you in the last days
Prov 12 21 whatsoever shall befall the just man
Eccu 37 11 other side to see what shall befall thee
Jer 5 13 these things therefore shall b. them
Dan 10 14 what things shall befall thy people
Jon 4 5 might see what would befall the city
Soph 2 10 this shall befall them for their pride
Mark 10 32 the things that should befall him
Acts 20 22 the things which shall befall me there
befallen Gen 42 29 all things that had b. them
Exod 3 16 all that hath befallen you in Egypt
18 8 which had befallen them in the journey
32 1 we know not what has befallen him. And
23 we know not what is befallen him. And
2 K 19 7 than all the evils that have b. thee
Tob 2 13 because the evil of blindness hath b.
Job 2 11 heard all the evil that had b. him
3 25 which I was afraid of, hath b. me
Eccu 5 4 and what harm hath befallen me? For
1 Ma 1 12 for them, many evils have befallen us
befalleth Job 21 21 what b. his house after him
befalls 1 P 5 9 same affliction b. your brethren
befell Josu 2 23 told him all that befell them
Acts 20 19 b. me by the conspiracies of the Jews
before Mat 14 8 instructed before by her mother
Mark 11 9 they that went before and they that
Luke 15 18 against heaven and before thee. 21
19 4 running before, he climbed up into a
28 he went before, going up to Jerusalem
John 1 15 preferred b. me; because he was b. me
Acts 3 18 which God before had showed by the
8 9 Simon, who before had been a magician
20 5 these going before, stayed for us at
Rom 1 2 which he had promised before by his
2 C 1 15 I had a mind to come to you before
7 3 we have said before that you are in our
9 5 they would go to you before and prepare this blessing before promised
12 21 that sinned before and have not done
13 2 I have told before and foretell as
2 to them that sinned before and to all
Gal 1 9 as we said before, so now I say again
17 to the apostles who were before me
20 to you, behold, before God, I lie not
3 8 told unto Abraham before. In thee
Eph 1 12 we who before hoped in Christ: in whom
Phil 3 13 forth myself to those that are before
Col 1 17 he is before all, and by him all things
1 Th 2 2 having suffered many things before
4 6 as we have told you before and have
1 Tim 1 13 who before was a blasphemer and a
18 the prophecies going before on thee
5 24 are manifest, going before to judgment
Heb 10 8 in saying before, Sacrifices and
2 P 3 2 those words which I told you before
5 ignorant of, that the heavens were b.
17 knowing those things before, take heed
Jude 17 have been spoken before by the apostles
Apoc 4 6 living creatures, full of eyes before
beforehand Gen 15 13 know thou b. that thy seed
Ecce 7 15 and beware beforehand of the evil day
Eccu 31 2 the thinking b. turneth away the
Mat 24 25 I have told it to you beforehand
Mark 13 11 be not thoughtful b. what you shall
14 8 she is come b. to anoint my body for
beg Tob 3 15 I beg, O Lord, that thou loose me
Jdth 8 14 with many tears let us beg his pardon
Ps 108 10 be carried about vagabonds and beg
Prov 20 4 he shall beg therefore in the summer
Bar 2 19 prayers, and beg mercy in thy sight
Luke 16 3 I am not able; to beg I am ashamed
Phil 4 2 I beg of Evodia and I beseech Syntyche

Col 1 9 to beg that you may be filled with the
beget Gen 17 20 he shall beget twelve chiefs
Deut 4 25 if you shall beget sons and grandsons
28 41 thou shalt beget sons and daughters
4 K 20 18 issue from thee, whom thou shalt beget
Ecce 6 3 if a man beget a hundred children and
Isa 39 7 whom thou shalt beget, they shall take
Jer 29 6 take ye wives and beget sons and
Eze 18 10 if he beget a son that is a robber
14 if he beget a son who, seeing all
47 22 that shall beget children among you
2 Tim 2 23 knowing that they beget strifes. But
begettest Isa 45 10 to his father: Why b. thou
begetteth James 1 15 sin when it is completed b.
beggar Deut 15 4 shall be no poor nor b. among
Ps 39 18 but I am a beggar and poor: the Lord is
108 17 persecuted the poor man and the beggar
Luke 16 20 certain beggar named Lazarus, who lay
22 the beggar died and was carried by the
John 9 8 seen him before that he was a beggar
beggary Prov 30 8 give me neither b. nor riches
begged Jdth 4 16 all begged of God with all their
2 Ma 3 31 begged of Onias that he would call
Mark 15 43 begged the body of Jesus. Luke 23:52
John 9 8 is not this he that sat and begged
begging Eccu 35 3 a begging of pardon for sins
Eccu 40 32 b. will be sweet in the mouth of the
Mark 10 46 sat by the wayside begging. Luke 18:35
Acts 3 10 who sat b. alms at the Beautiful gate
2 C 8 4 with much entreaty b. of us the grace
beginning Gen 10 10 b. of his kingdom was Babylon
Gen 44 12 searched, beginning at the eldest
49 3 Ruben . . . the beginning of my sorrow
Exod 12 2 be to you the beginning of months
Lev 23 32 b. on the ninth day of the month
27 17 from the year of jubilee that is b.
Num 24 20 Amalec the beginning of nations, whose
Josu 13 30 the beginning whereof is this: from
15 2 its b. was from the top of most salt
5 the b. shall be the most salt sea
Judg 7 19 at the beginning of the midnight watch
4 K 7 8 were come to the beginning of the camp
1 Pa 17 9 of iniquity waste them, as at the b.
Tob 4 14 from it all perdition took its b.
Job 40 14 he is the beginning of the ways of God
42 12 latter end of Job more than his b.
Ps 110 10 fear of the Lord is the beginning of
wisdom. Prov 1:7; 9:10; Eccu 1:16
118 160 the beginning of thy words is truth
136 6 if I make not Jerusalem the b. of my
Prov 4 7 the beginning of wisdom, get wisdom
16 5 the b. of a good way is to do justice
17 14 b. of quarrels is as when one letteth
Ecce 7 9 the end of a speech than the beginning
10 13 the beginning of his words is folly
Wisd 6 18 the b. of her is the most true desire
7 5 none of the kings had any other b.
18 b. and ending and midst of the times
12 16 thy power is the beginning of justice
14 12 b. of fornication is devising of idols
27 the beginning and end of all evil
Eccu 10 14 the b. of the pride of man is to fall
15 pride is the beginning of all sin
25 16 the fear of God is the b. of his love
16 b. of faith is to be fast joined into
33 from the woman came the b. of sin
Isa 38 12 whilst I was yet but beginning, he
52 4 into Egypt at the b. to sojourn there
Dan 9 21 whom I had seen in the vision at the b.
Osee 1 2 the b. of the Lord's speaking by Osee
Mich 1 13 it is the b. of sin to the daughter of
2 Ma 1 23 Jonathan b., and the rest answering
4 13 this was not the b., but an increase
8 27 distilling the b. of mercy upon them
12 37 b. in his own language and singing
Mat 20 8 b. from the last even to the first
24 8 are the beginning of sorrows. Mark 13:8
Mark 1 1 the beginning of the gospel of Jesus
Luke 3 23 Jesus himself was b. about the age of
23 5 beginning from Galilee to this place
24 27 beginning at Moses and all the prophets
47 unto all nations, beginning at Jerusalem
John 2 11 this beginning of miracles did Jesus
8 9 went out one by one, b. at the eldest
25 the beginning who also speak unto you
Acts 1 22 beginning from the baptism of John
8 35 beginning at this scripture, preached
18 14 when Paul was b. to open his mouth
Col 1 18 who is the beginning, the firstborn
Heb 3 14 if we hold the b. of his substance
6 1 leaving the word of the b. of Christ
7 3 having neither b. of days nor end of
James 1 18 that we might be some beginning of his
Apoc 1 8 the beginning and the end. 21:6; 22:13
3 14 who is the b. of the creation of God
from the beginning Gen 2 8 had planted a paradise
of pleasure f. . . .
Deut 11 12 his eyes are on it f. . . . of the year
1 K 18 30 f. . . . of their going forth, David
2 K 21 10 upon the rock f. . . . of the harvest
4 K 19 25 thou not heard what I have done f. . . .
1 Es 7 5 the son of Aaron the priest f. . . .
2 Es 12 45 f. . . . there were chief singers appointed
Jdth 9 10 our God, who destroyest wars f. . . .
11 lift up thy arm as f. . . . and crush
16 nor f. . . . have the proud been acceptable
Job 20 4 this I know f. . . . since man was placed
36 3 I will repeat my knowledge f. . . . and
Ps 73 2 which thou hast possessed f. . . . The
76 12 will be mindful of thy wonders f. . . .
77 2 I will utter propositions f. . . . How
118 152 I have known f. . . . concerning thy
Prov 8 22 ways, before he made anything f. . . .
Ecce 3 11 which God hath made f. . . . to the end
Wisd 6 24 will seek her out f. . . . of her birth
9 8 which thou hast prepared f. . . . : and
19 have pleased thee, O Lord, f. . . .
12 11 it was a cursed seed f. . . . : neither
14 6 and f. . . . also when the proud giants
13 neither were they f. . . . neither shall
19 6 was fashioned again as f. . . . obeying
Eccu 15 14 God made man f. . . . and left him in the
16 25 that God hath put upon his works f. . . .
26 of God are done in judgment f. . . .
24 14 f. . . . and before the world was I
31 35 wine was created f. . . . to make men
36 13 and thou shalt inherit them as f. . . .
17 to them that are thy creatures f. . . .
39 30 things were created for the good f. . . .
38 therefore f. . . . I was resolved, and I
43 35 who shall magnify him as he is f. . . .
44 2 glory through his magnificence f. . . .
45 15 were none so beautiful, even f. . . .
51 28 I possessed my heart with her f. . . .
Isa 40 21 hath it not been told you f. . . .
41 4 things, calling the generations f. . . .
26 who hath declared f. . . . that we may
43 13 f. . . . I am the same, and there is none
45 21 who hath declared this f. . . . , who
46 10 who show f. . . . the things that shall be
48 16 I have not spoken in secret f. . . .
Jer 7 7 which I gave to your fathers f. . . .
12 in Silo, where my name dwelt f. . . .
17 12 a high and glorious throne f. . . . is
28 8 been before me and before thee f. . . .
30 20 and their children shall be as f. . . .

33 7 and I will build them as f. . . . And I
Lam 5 21 converted: renew our days, as f. . . .
Bar 3 26 those renowned men that were f. . . .
Eze 36 11 and I will settle you as f. . . . and
11 you greater gifts than you had f. . . .
Dan 9 23 f. . . . of thy prayers the word came
Joel 2 2 the like to it hath not been f. . . .
Mich 5 2 and his going forth is f. . . . , from
Haba 1 12 wast thou not f. . . . O Lord my God, my
Mat 19 4 who made man f. . . . , Made them male and
8 your wives, but f. . . . it was not so
Mark 10 6 but f. . . . of the creation God made them
13 19 tribulations, as were not f. . . . of the
Luke 1 2 who f. . . . were eyewitnesses and
3 attained to all things f. . . . , to write
70 of his holy prophets who are f. . . .
John 6 65 Jesus knew f. . . . who they were that did
8 44 he was a murderer f. . . . , and he stood
15 27 because you are with me f. . . .
16 5 but I told you not these things f. . . .
Acts 26 4 f. . . . among my own nation in Jerusalem
5 having known me f. . . . , if they will
2 P 3 4 all things continue as they were f. . . .
1 J 1 1 that which was f. . . . which we have
2 7 old commandment which you had f. . . .
13 you have known him who is f. . . .
24 have heard f. . . . 3:11; 2 J 6
3 8 for the devil sinneth f. . . . For this
2 J 5 but that which we have had f. . . .
from the beginning of the world Ps 24 6 and thy mercies that are f. . . .
Eccu 51 11 Lord, and thy works which are f. . . .
Isa 64 4 f. . . . they have not heard nor perceived
Mat 24 21 tribulation such as hath not been f. . . .
John 9 32 f. . . . it hath not been heard that any
Acts 3 21 by the mouth of his holy prophets f. . . .
15 18 to Lord was his own work known f. . . .
Heb 9 26 he ought to have suffered often f. . . .
Apoc 13 8 of the Lamb, which was slain f. . . .
in the beginning Gen 1 1 i. . . . God created
Ruth 1 22 into Bethlehem i. . . . of the barley
1 Es 4 6 of Assuerus, i. . . . of his reign, they
Ps 101 26 i. . . . O Lord, thou foundest the earth
Prov 8 22 Lord possessed me i. . . . of his ways
20 21 the inheritance gotten hastily i. . . .
Eccu 49 19 men: and above every soul Adam i. . . .
Isa 60 9 for me, and the ships of the sea i. . . .
63 19 we are become as i. . . . when thou didst
Jer 26 1 i. . . . of the reign of Joakim. 27:1
28 1 i. . . . of the reign of Sedecias. 49:34
Lam 2 19 in the night, i. . . . of the watches
Eze 40 1 i. . . . of the year, the tenth day of the
Dan 8 1 after what I had seen i. . . . saw in my
Joel 2 23 rain to come down to you as i. . . .
Amos 7 1 formed i. . . . of the shooting up of
Zach 12 7 the tabernacles of Juda, as i. . . .
John 1 1 in the beginning was the Word, and the
2 same was i. . . . with God. All things
Acts 11 15 them, as upon us also in the beginning
Phil 4 15 i. . . . of the gospel, when I departed
Heb 1 10 i. . . . , O Lord, didst found the earth
beginnings Exod 29 28 b. of their peace victims
Job 28 1 silver hath beginnings of its veins
Eccu 16 26 distinguished their parts and their b.
Begoai 2 Es 7 7 Begoai, Nahum, Baana. The number
2 Es 10 16 Adonia, Begoai, Adin, Ater, Hezecia
begone Mat 4 10 saith to him: Begone, Satan
begot Gen 5 3 begot a son to his own image and
Gen 5 4 begot sons and daughters. 7, 10, 13, 16, 19, 22, 26, 30; 11:11, 13, 15, 17, 19, 21, 23, 25; 1 Pa 14:3
7 lived after he begot. 13, 16, 19, 22, 26, 30; 11:11, 13, 15, 17, 19, 21, 23, 25
Deut 32 18 hast forsaken the God that begot thee
2 Pa 11 21 [Roboam] begot eight and twenty sons
13 21 Abia . . . begot two and twenty sons
Job 38 28 or who begot the drops of dew? Out
Ps 109 3 before the day star I begot thee
Prov 23 22 hearken to thy father, that begot thee
Mat 1 2 Abraham b. Isaac, and Isaac b. Jacob
16 Jacob b. Joseph, the husband of
Acts 7 8 so he b. Isaac and circumcised him
8 Isaac b. Jacob, and Jacob the twelve
29 land of Madian where he b. two sons
1 J 5 1 every one that loveth him who begot
begotten Gen 22 2 take thy only begotten son Isaac
Gen 22 12 hast not spared thy only b. son. 16
Num 11 12 conceived all this multitude or b. them
Ps 2 7 my son, this day have I begotten thee
Prov 23 24 he that hath b. a wise son, shall have
Ecce 5 13 he hath b. a son, who shall be in
Isa 49 21 who hath begotten these? I was barren
Jer 2 27 to a stone: Thou hast begotten me
Osee 5 7 they have begotten children that are
John 1 14 of the only begotten of the Father
3 16 the world as to give his only b. Son
Acts 13 33 this day have I b. thee. Heb 1:5; 5:5
1 C 4 15 in Christ Jesus by the gospel I have b.
Philem 10 I have begotten in my bands, Onesimus
Heb 1 6 when he bringeth in the first begotten
11 17 offered up his only begotten son; to
James 1 18 hath he b. us by the word of truth
1 J 4 9 sent his only b. Son into the world
Apoc 1 5 the first begotten of the dead and the
Beguai 1 Es 2 2 Mesphar, Beguai, Rehum, Baana
1 Es 2 14 the children of Beguai, 2,056. The
2 Es 7 19 children of Beguai, 2,067. The children
Begui 1 Es 8 14 of the sons of Begui, Uthai and
beguile Wisd 4 11 lest . . . deceit beguile his soul
behave 1 K 4 9 take courage and behave like men
1 Pa 19 13 and let us behave ourselves manfully
2 Pa 32 7 behave like men and take courage: be
Tob 10 13 govern the house, and to b. herself
1 Ma 2 64 and behave manfully in the law: for
2 Ma 9 27 he will behave with moderation and
1 Tim 3 15 know how thou oughtest to behave
Heb 13 18 being willing to behave ourselves well
behaved 1 K 18 5 [David] b. himself prudently
1 K 18 14 David behaved wisely in all his ways
30 David behaved himself more wisely
4 K 18 7 he [Ezechias] behaved himself wisely
Mich 3 4 they have behaved wickedly in their
2 Ma 2 22 that behaved themselves manfully on the
12 14 behaved in a more negligent manner
14 30 he behaved himself in a rough manner
behavior Eccu 30 13 lest his lewd b. be an offence
2 Ma 14 30 that this rough b. came not of good
1 Tim 3 2 sober, prudent, of good behavior
beheaded Jdth 15 1 heard that Holofernes was b.
Mat 14 10 sent and beheaded John in the prison
Mark 6 16 John whom I beheaded, he is risen again
28 and he beheaded him in the prison
Luke 9 9 and Herod said: John I have beheaded
Apoc 20 4 and the souls of them that were b.
behemoth Job 40 10 behold behemoth whom I made
beholder Eccu 36 19 thou art God the b. of all ages
behoved Luke 24 46 thus it b. Christ to suffer
Acts 13 46 to you it b. us first to speak the
Heb 2 17 it b. him in all things to be made like
behoveth Rom 12 3 more wise than it b. to be wise
1 Tim 3 2 it behoveth a bishop to be blameless
Col 3 18 be subject to your husbands as it b.
being Ps 103 33 praise to my God while I have my b.
Ps 138 16 thy eyes did see my imperfect being
Isa 40 17 as if they had no being at all and are
41 24 your work of that which hath no being

Bel Isa 46 1 Bel is broken, Nebo is destroyed
Jer 50 2 Babylon is taken, Bel is confounded
51 44 I will visit against Bel in Babylon
Bar 6 40 they present him to Bel, entreating
Dan 14 2 Babylonians had an idol called Bel
3 why dost thou not adore Bel? And he
5 doth not Bel seem to thee to be a living
8 if you can show that Bel eateth these
8 because he hath blasphemed against Bel
9 now the priests of Bel were seventy
9 went with Daniel into the temple of Bel
10 priests of Bel said: Behold we go out
11 findest not that Bel hath eaten up
13 the king set the meats before Bel and
17 great art thou, O Bel, and there is not
21 delivered Bel into the power of Daniel
27 he hath destroyed Bel, he hath killed
Bela Gen 36 32 the kings were . . . Bela the son of
Gen 36 33 Bela died, and Jobab the son of Zara
46 21 the sons of Benjamin: Bela. Num 26:38; 1 Pa 7:6
Num 26 40 the sons of Bela: Hered. 1 Pa 7:7
Belaites Num 26 38 of whom is the family of the B.
Belga 1 Pa 24 14 the fifteenth to Belga, the
2 Es 12 5 Miamin, Madia, Belga, Semeia, and
18 of Belga, Sammua of Semaia, Jonathan
Belgia 2 Es 10 8 Miamin, Maazia, Belgia, Semeia
Belial Deut 13 13 children of Belial are gone out
Judg 19 22 the men of that city, sons of Belial
1 K 1 16 for one of the daughters of Belial
2 12 sons of Heli were children of Belial
10 27 the children of Belial said: Shall this
25 17 he [Nabal] is a son of Belial, so that
2 K 16 7 man of blood, and thou man of Belial
20 1 happened to be there a man of Belial
22 5 floods of Belial have made me afraid
3 K 21 10 and suborn two men, sons of Belial
2 Pa 13 7 gathered to him . . . children of Belial
Nah 1 15 Belial shall no more pass through thee
2 C 6 15 what concord hath Christ with Belial
belief Jdth 13 7 b. that it might be done by thee
Jer 5 23 of this people is become hard of b.
belieth Wisd 1 11 mouth that b., killeth the soul
believe Gen 21 7 who would believe that Abraham
Exod 4 5 that they may believe, saith he, that
8 will believe the word of the latter
19 9 to thee and may believe thee forever
Jdth 8 27 believe that these scourges of the Lord
Wisd 12 2 they may believe in thee, O Lord. For
Eccu 50 26 that Israel may b. that the mercy of
Isa 43 10 that you may know and believe me and
Eze 13 19 lies to my people that believe lies
Haba 1 5 which no man will believe when it
Mat 18 6 little ones that b. in me. Mark 9:41
21 32 even repent that you might believe him
27 42 down from the cross and we will b. him
Mark 9 22 thou canst b., all things are possible
15 32 cross that we may see and believe
16 13 rest: neither did they believe them
Luke 8 13 they b. for a while and in time of
16 31 neither will they b. if one rise again
24 25 O foolish and slow of heart to believe
John 1 7 that all men might believe through him
5 46 did b. Moses you would perhaps b. me
6 30 that we may see and may believe thee
7 5 neither did his brethren believe in him
9 35 dost thou believe in the Son of God
36 who is he, Lord, that I may b. in him
10 38 that you may b. that the Father is in
11 15 was not there, that you may believe
40 if thou believe, thou shalt see the
42 that they may b. that thou sent me
48 if we let him alone so, all will b.
13 19 that you may believe that I am he
14 29 it shall come to pass, you may believe
17 20 who through their word shall b. in me
21 world may b. that thou hast sent me
19 35 he saith true that you also may believe
20 31 these are written that you may believe
Acts 10 43 remission of sins, who believe in him
14 1 of the Jews and of the Greeks did b.
15 7 Gentiles should hear . . . and believe
17 34 adhering to him [Paul], did believe
19 4 should b. in him who was to come after
21 25 but as touching the Gentiles that b.
Rom 10 9 for if thou . . . believe in thy heart
14 how shall they b. him whom they have
Eph 1 19 who believe according to the operation
Phil 1 29 not only to b. in him but also to
1 Th 1 7 pattern to all that b. in Macedonia
2 Th 2 10 the operation of error, to b. lying
1 Tim 1 16 shall b. in him to life everlasting
Titus 3 8 they who b. in God may be careful to
Heb 11 6 cometh to God must believe that he is
James 2 19 the devils also believe and tremble
1 P 2 6 believe in him shall not be confounded
7 to you therefore that b., he is honor
8 stumble at the word neither do believe
1 J 3 23 we should b. in the name of his Son
5 13 who b. in the name of the Son of God
believe (imperative) 2 Pa 20 20 b. in the Lord
2 Pa 20 20 b. his prophets and all things shall
Eccu 2 6 believe God, and he will recover thee
8 ye that fear the Lord, believe him
Mark 1 15 is at hand: repent and b. the gospel
5 36 fear not, only believe. Luke 8:50
11 23 b. that whatsoever he saith shall be
24 pray, believe that you shall receive
John 4 21 woman, b. me, that the hour cometh
10 38 will not believe me, believe the works
12 36 whilst you have the light, b. in the
14 12 otherwise b. for the very works' sake
Acts 16 31 they said: Believe in the Lord Jesus
believe not (not believe) Gen 45 26 yet did not believe them
Exod 4 1 they will not believe me nor hear my
8 if they will not believe thee, saith
9 if they will not even believe these
Num 14 11 how long will they not believe me
Deut 1 32 you did not believe the Lord your God
9 23 your God, and did not believe him
3 K 10 7 I did not believe them that told me
2 Pa 9 6 I did not believe them that told it
32 15 and do not believe him [Ezechias]. For
Job 9 16 I should not b. that he had heard my
15 31 he shall not b., being vainly deceived
Ps 67 19 for those also that do not believe
Wisd 12 17 when men will not believe thee to be
18 13 they would not believe anything before
Eccu 2 15 are fainthearted, who believe not God
13 14 believe not his many words: for by
19 16 believe not every word. There is one
Jer 12 6 believe them not when they speak good
Mich 7 5 b. not a friend, and trust not in a
Mat 21 26 why did you not believe him. Mark 11:31; Luke 20:5
32 John came . . . and you did not b. him
24 23 here is Christ, or there, do not believe. Mark 13:21
26 behold he is in the closets, b. it not
Mark 16 11 that he was alive . . . did not believe
14 because they did not believe them
Luke 22 67 if I shall tell you, you will not b.
24 11 as idle tales: they did not b. them
John 3 12 and you b. not; how will you believe
18 doth not believe, is already judged

4 48 see signs and wonders you believe not
5 38 whom he hath sent, him you believe not
47 but if you do not believe his writings
6 36 also have seen me, and you believe not
65 but there are some of you that b. not
65 who they were that did not believe
8 24 if you believe not that I am he, you
45 if I say the truth, you believe me not
46 if I say the truth, why do you not b. me
9 18 Jews then did not b. concerning him
10 25 I speak to you, and you believe not
26 you do not b. because you are not of my
37 works of my Father, believe me not
38 though you will not b. me, b. the works
12 39 could not believe because Isaias said
14 10 do you not b. that I am in the. 11
20 25 hand into his side, I will not believe
Acts 13 41 a work which you will not believe
Rom 11 30 you also in times past did not b. God
1 C 10 27 any of them that b. not invite you
2 Tim 2 13 if we believe not he continueth faithful
1 P 2 7 he is honor: but to them that b. not
3 1 if any b. not the word, they may be won
4 17 them that b. not the gospel of God
1 J 4 1 b. not every spirit, but try the spirits
I believe Tob 5 27 I b. that the good angel of
Tob 7 14 I b. he hath therefore made you come
Ps 26 13 I believe to see the good things of the
Mark 9 23 I do believe, Lord: help my unbelief
John 9 38 I believe, Lord. And falling down, he
Acts 8 37 I b. that Jesus Christ is the Son of
27 25 I believe God that it shall be so
1 C 11 18 among you; and in part I believe
them that believe Wisd 16 26 thy word preserveth
them that believe in thee
Mark 16 17 and these signs shall follow t. . . .
John 1 12 to them that believe in his name, who
Rom 3 22 unto all and upon all t. . . . in him
4 11 he might be the father of all t. . . .
1 C 1 21 of our preaching, to save t. . . .
Gal 3 22 might be given to them that believe
we believe John 4 42 we now b., not for thy
John 16 30 we b. that thou camest forth from God
Acts 15 11 we b. to be saved in like manner as
Rom 4 24 it shall be reputed if we b. in him
6 8 we b. that we shall live also with
10 10 with the heart we believe unto justice
1 C 4 13 we also b., for which cause we speak
Gal 2 16 we also believe in Christ Jesus, that
1 Th 4 13 if we b. that Jesus died and rose again
you believe Mat 9 28 do you b. that I can do
John 5 44 how can you b., who receive glory one
6 29 that you b. in him whom he hath sent
14 1 you b. in God, b. also in me. In my
16 31 Jesus answered them: Do you not believe
1 P 1 8 though you see him not, you believe
believed Gen 15 6 Abram believed God, and it was
Gen 27 33 wondering beyond what can be believed
Exod 4 31 and the people believed. And they
14 31 and they believed the Lord, and Moses
1 K 27 12 Achis b. David, saying: He hath done
3 K 20 25 he believed their counsel and did so
Jdth 14 6 Achior . . . believed Gad and circumcised
Ps 105 12 they b. his words: and they sang his
115 10 I have believed, therefore have I spoken
118 66 for I have believed thy commandments
Isa 53 1 who hath believed our report? And to
Dan 3 95 his servants that believed in him
6 23 because he believed in his God. And by
8 24 and do more than can be believed. And
13 41 the multitude believed them as being
Jon 3 5 the men of Ninive believed in God: and
1 Ma 1 31 in deceit: and they believed him. And
7 16 they b. him. And he took threescore
12 46 Jonathan b. him and did as he said
2 Ma 15 11 a dream worthy to be believed whereby
Mat 8 13 as thou hast b., so be it done to the
21 32 publicans and the harlots believed him
Luke 1 45 blessed art thou that hast believed
John 2 11 and his disciples believed in him
22 and they believed the scripture, and
4 50 the man b. the word which Jesus said
53 himself believed and his whole house
6 70 we have believed . . . thou art the Christ
7 39 which they should receive, who b. in him
48 hath any one of the rulers b. in him
8 31 Jesus said to those Jews who b. in him
11 27 I have believed that thou art Christ
12 38 who hath believed our hearing? And to
16 27 because you have . . . b. that I came
17 8 they have b. that thou didst send me
20 8 and he [John] saw and believed. For
29 hast seen me, Thomas, thou hast b.
29 that have not seen and have believed
Acts 2 44 all they that believed were together
5 14 who b. in the Lord, was more increased
36 all that b. in him were scattered
8 12 when they had believed Philip preaching
13 then Simon himself believed also; and
11 17 same grace as to us also who believed
13 12 then the proconsul . . . believed
48 were ordained to life everlasting, b.
14 22 to the Lord, in whom they believed
15 5 there arose some . . . Pharisees that b.
16 1 son of a Jewish woman that believed
17 4 some of them b. and were associated to
18 8 Crispus . . . believed in the Lord, with
27 [Apollo] helped them much who had b.
19 2 received the Holy Ghost since you b.
18 that believed, came confessing and
21 20 among the Jews that have believed
22 19 beat . . . them that believed in thee
27 11 but the centurion believed the pilot
28 24 some believed the things that were said
Rom 4 3 Abraham b. God. Gal 3:6; James 2:23
17 before God, whom he [Abraham] believed
18 who against hope believed in hope
10 16 Lord, who hath believed our report
13 11 salvation is nearer than when we b.
1 C 3 5 ministers of him whom you have b.
15 2 unless you have believed in vain. For
11 so we preach and so you have believed
23 who have believed in his coming
2 C 4 13 I b., for which cause I have spoken
1 Th 2 10 we have been to you that have believed
13 God who worketh in you that have b.
2 Th 1 10 wonderful in all them who have believed
10 our testimony was b. upon you in that
1 Tim 3 16 the mystery . . . which is b. in the world
2 Tim 1 12 I know whom I have believed, and I am
Heb 4 3 we who have b. shall enter into rest
11 11 [Sara] believed that he was faithful
1 J 4 16 we have b. the charity which God hath
believed not (not believed) Num 20 12 because you
have not believed me
Job 29 24 I laughed on them, they believed not
Ps 77 22 because they believed not in God
32 they b. not for his wondrous works
105 24 they b. not his word, and they murmured
Jer 40 14 and Godolias . . . believed them not
Lam 4 12 would not have believed that the
Bar 1 17 have not believed him nor put our
Luke 1 20 thou [Zachary] hast not b. my words
24 41 while they yet believed not and
John 12 37 they believed not in him: that the
16 9 of sin . . . because they b. not in him

Acts 19 9 some were hardened and believed not
28 24 but some believed not. And when they
Rom 3 3 what if some of them have not believed
10 14 call on him in whom they have not b.
11 31 so these also now have not believed
2 Th 2 11 judged who have not believed the truth
Jude 5 did . . . destroy them that believed not
many believed John 2 23 many b. in his name
John 4 39 many of the Samaritans believed in him
41 many more believed in him because of
7 31 of the people many believed in him
8 30 when he spoke these things, many b.
10 42 and many believed in him. Now there
11 45 many of the Jews . . . believed in him
12 11 many of the Jews . . . b. in Jesus
42 many of the chief men also b. in him
Acts 4 4 many of them who had heard the word b.
9 42 throughout all Joppe; and many believed
17 12 many indeed of them believed, and of
18 8 many of the Corinthians hearing, b.
believers Acts 4 32 of b. had but one heart
1 C 14 22 tongues are for a sign, not to b.
22 not to unbelievers, but to believers
believest John 1 50 because I said . . . thou b.
John 11 26 not die forever. Believest thou this
Acts 8 37 if thou believest . . . thou mayest
26 27 b. thou the prophets, O king Agrippa
27 I know that thou believest. And Agrippa
James 2 19 thou believest that there is one God
believeth Prov 14 15 the innocent b. every word
Prov 14 21 he that b. in the Lord, loveth mercy
Eccu 32 28 he that b. God, taketh heed to the
Isa 28 16 he that believeth, let him not hasten
Mark 9 22 are possible to him that believeth
16 16 that b. and is baptized shall be saved
John 3 15 believeth in him, may not perish. 16
18 he that b. in him is not judged. But
36 that b. in the Son, hath life everlasting
5 24 and b. him that sent me, hath life
6 40 b. in him, may have life everlasting
Acts 13 39 every one that believeth is justified
Rom 1 16 salvation to every one that believeth
4 5 to him that worketh not, yet believeth
9 33 b. in him, shall not be confounded
10 4 unto justice to every one that b.
14 2 one b. that he may eat all things
1 C 13 7 charity . . . believeth all things
1 J 5 1 whosoever b. that Jesus is the Christ
5 that b. that Jesus is the Son of God
10 he that b. in the Son of God, hath
believeth in me John 6 35 b. . . . shall never thirst
John 6 47 he that b. . . . hath everlasting life
7 38 he that b. . . . Out of his belly shall
11 25 that b. . . . although he be dead, shall
26 b. . . . shall not die forever. Believest
12 44 he that b. . . . doth not b. in me, but in
46 whosoever b. . . . may not remain in
14 12 b. . . . the works that I do, he also
believeth not Job 15 22 b. not that he may return
Mark 16 16 b. not, shall be condemned. And these
John 3 18 because he believeth not in the name
36 he that b. not the Son, shall not see
Rom 10 21 my hands to a people that b. not
1 C 7 12 any brother hath a wife that b. not
13 woman hath a husband that b. not
14 24 if there come in one that believeth not
1 J 5 10 that b. not the Son, maketh him a liar
10 because he b. not in the testimony
believing Tob 13 8 b. that he will show mercy to
1 Ma 2 59 Misael by believing were delivered
Mat 21 22 in prayer, believing you shall receive
Luke 8 12 lest believing they should be saved
John 20 27 be not faithless, but believing
31 that b., you may have life in his name
Acts 9 26 not b. that he [Paul] was a disciple
11 21 a great number b., were converted
16 34 rejoiced with all his house, b. God
24 14 b. all things which are written in the
Rom 15 13 fill you with joy and peace in b.
1 C 7 14 is sanctified by the believing wife
14 is sanctified by the believing husband
Eph 1 13 in whom also b., you were signed with
1 Tim 6 2 they that have believing masters
1 P 1 8 you believe, and believing shall rejoice
bell Exod 28 34 a golden bell and a pomegranate and again another golden bell and a
Exod 39 24 a bell of gold and a pomegranate
bellies Eze 7 19 their b. shall not be filled
Titus 1 12 the Cretians are . . . slothful bellies
bellowed Jer 50 11 and have bellowed as bulls
bellowing Mala 2 13 tears, with weeping and b.
bellows Jer 6 29 the bellows have failed, the
bells Exod 28 33 pomegranates . . . with little b.
Exod 39 23 little bells of the purest gold which
Eccu 45 10 compassed him with many little bells
belly Gen 38 24 she appeareth to have a big belly
Lev 3 10 the fat that covereth the belly. 14
Num 5 21 may thy belly swell and burst asunder
22 let the cursed waters enter into thy b.
27 her belly swelling, her thigh shall rot
Judg 3 21 and thrust it into his belly with such
22 the excrements of the belly came out
2 Pa 4 3 cubits encompassed the belly of the sea
Job 3 11 perish when I came out of the belly
20 14 his bread in his belly shall be turned
15 God shall draw them out of his belly
20 and yet his belly was not filled: and
23 may his belly be filled, that God may
32 19 my belly is as new wine which wanteth
40 11 his force in the navel of his belly
Ps 16 14 their belly is filled from thy hidden
30 10 is troubled . . . my soul and my belly
43 25 dust: our belly cleaveth to the earth
Prov 13 25 b. of the wicked is never to be filled
18 20 man's mouth shall his belly be satisfied
20 30 in the more inward parts of the belly
26 22 reach to innermost parts of the belly
Cant 5 14 his b. as of ivory set with sapphires
7 2 thy belly is like a heap of wheat set
Eccu 23 6 take from me the greediness of the belly
36 20 the belly will devour all meat yet one
40 32 in his belly there shall burn a fire
51 7 from the depth of the belly of hell and
Jer 51 34 filled his belly with my delicate meats
Eze 3 3 son of man, thy belly shall eat and thy
Dan 2 32 the belly and the thighs of brass: and
Job 2 1 Jonas was in the belly of the fish three
2 prayed . . . out of the belly of the fish
3 I cried out of the belly of hell and
Mat 12 40 as Jonas was in the whale's belly three
15 17 goeth into the belly. Mark 7:19
Luke 15 16 fain have filled his belly with the
John 7 38 out of his belly shall flow rivers of
Rom 16 18 not Christ our Lord but their own belly
1 C 6 13 meat for the b., and the b. for the
Phil 3 19 whose God is their b.; and whose glory
Apoc 10 9 it shall make thy belly bitter but in
10 when I had eaten it, my b. was bitter
belly's Eccu 37 5 condoleth . . . for his b. sake
Belma Jdth 7 3 from the place which is called Belma
belong Gen 33 5 and do they belong to thee? He
Gen 38 25 the man to whom these things belong
40 8 doth not interpretation belong to God
47 23 you and your lands belong to Pharao
Exod 9 4 that belong to the children of Israel
12 16 except those things that b. to eating

38 30 vessels that belong to the use thereof
Lev 7 7 it shall b. to the priest that offereth
10 15 they belong to thee and to thy sons
27 26 the firstborn, which belong to the Lord
Num 5 9 the firstfruits . . . belong to the priest
6 20 being sanctified shall b. to the priest
16 5 Lord will make known who b. to him and
30 and all things that belong to them and
18 15 men or of beasts shall belong to thee
1 K 25 22 if I leave of all that belong to him
30 13 to whom dost thou belong? or whence
2 Pa 19 11 matters which b. to the king's office
26 18 it doth not belong to thee, Ozias, to
Eze 48 22 Benjamin shall also b. to the prince
1 Ma 10 42 shall also belong to the priests that
2 Ma 3 6 did not b. to the account of sacrifices
14 4 which seemed to belong to the temple
Mark 9 40 my name because you b. to Christ
Rom 7 4 that you may belong to another who is
1 C 7 32 for things that belong to the Lord, how
belonged Gen 31 21 together with all that b. to him
Gen 32 23 were brought over that belonged to him
Josu 14 14 from that time Hebron belonged to Caleb
Judg 6 11 belonged to Joas the father of the family
Ruth 4 3 that belonged to our brother Elimelech
2 K 9 9 all that b. to Saul and all his house
16 4 I give thee all that b. to Miphiboseth
3 K 4 11 to whom belonged all Nephath-Dor, he had
9 19 all the towns that belonged to himself
4 K 24 7 all that had b. to the king of Egypt
Wisd 11 22 great power belonged to thee alone: and
1 Ma 11 35 as for other things that belonged to us
2 Ma 3 11 belonged to Hircanus son of Tobias, a
Acts 27 44 those things that b. to the ship. And so
belongeth Exod 30 28 that b. to the service of them
Num 3 26 whatsoever b. to the rite of the altar
Deut 25 7 who by law belongeth to him, the woman
Josu 24 33 Gabaath that belongeth to Phinees his
1 K 27 6 Siceleg belongeth to the kings of Juda
2 K 19 43 David b. to me more than to thee: why
2 Pa 25 8 for it b. to God both to help and to put
1 Es 7 23 all that b. to the rites of the God of
Ps 61 12 I heard, that power belongeth to God
93 1 is the God to whom revenge belongeth
Bar 1 15 to Lord our God b. justice. 2:6
Eze 21 27 till he came to whom judgment belongeth
Dan 9 8 to us belongeth confusion of face, to our
Luke 9 10 place apart, which b. to Bethsaida
Rom 9 4 Israelites, to whom b. the adoption
Heb 10 30 vengeance b. to me, and I will repay
belonging 2 Ma 3 3 charges b. to the ministry
belongs Josu 17 8 b. to the children of Ephraim
1 Ma 10 40 king's accounts, of what belongs to me
beloved Deut 21 15 wives, one b. and other hated
Deut 21 16 not make the son of the b. the firstborn
32 15 beloved grew fat and kicked: he grew
33 12 the best b. of the Lord shall dwell
2 Es 13 26 he [Solomon] was beloved of his God
Ps 28 5 and as the beloved son of unicorns
44 1 a canticle for the Beloved. My heart
59 6 that thy b. may be delivered. 107:7
67 13 king of powers is of the b., of the b.
126 2 when he shall give sleep to his beloved
Prov 15 9 that followeth justice is b. by him
31 2 the b. of my womb, what, O the b. of my
Cant 2 7 nor make the beloved wake till she
5 9 what manner of one is thy b. of the b.
17 whither is thy beloved gone, O thou
17 whither is thy beloved turned aside
8 5 with delights leaning upon her beloved
Wisd 4 10 he pleased God and was b. and living
Eccu 3 19 shalt be b. above the glory of men
20 13 shall make himself beloved: but the
45 1 Moses was beloved of God and men whose
46 16 Lord, the beloved of the Lord his God
47 17 and thou wast beloved in thy peace
Isa 44 9 their best beloved things shall not
Bar 3 37 to Jacob his servant and to Israel his b.
4 16 carried away the beloved of the widow
Dan 3 35 for the sake of Abraham thy beloved
Osee 3 1 love a woman beloved of her friend
9 6 shall inherit their beloved silver
16 I will slay the best beloved fruit
1 Ma 6 11 I that was pleasant and beloved in
Acts 15 25 with our well b. Barnabas and Paul
Rom 1 7 the beloved of God, called to be saints
9 25 I will call . . . her that was not b., b.
16 8 salute Ampliatus, most beloved to me
Eph 1 6 he hath graced us in his beloved Son
Col 3 12 as the elect of God, holy and beloved
4 9 Onesimus, a most b. and faithful brother
1 Th 1 4 brethren, beloved of God. 2 Th 2:12
1 Tim 1 2 to Timothy, his beloved son in faith
6 2 because they are faithful and beloved
Philem 1 Philemon, our beloved and fellow laborer
Jude 1 to them that are b. in God the Father
Apoc 20 8 camp of the saints and the beloved city
dearly beloved Cant 5 1 be inebriated, my d. b.
Rom 12 19 revenge not yourselves, my dearly b.
16 12 salute Persis, the dearly beloved who
1 C 10 14 my d. b., fly from the service of idols
2 C 7 1 d. b., let us cleanse ourselves from all
12 19 things, my d. b., for your edification
Phil 2 12 my d. b., as you have always obeyed
4 1 my d. b. brethren and most desired, my
1 so stand fast in the Lord, my d. b.
2 Tim 1 2 to Timothy, my d. b. son, grace, mercy
Heb 6 9 my d. b., we trust better things of you
1 P 2 11 d. b. . . . refrain yourselves from carnal
4 12 d. b., think not strange the burning
2 P 3 1 I write to you, my d. b., in which I
14 wherefore d. b. waiting for these
1 J 2 7 d. b., I write not a new commandment to
3 2 d. b., we are now the sons of God; and
21 d. b., if our heart do not reprehend
4 1 d. b., believe not every spirit but try
7 d. b., let us love one another, for
3 J 1 the ancient to the d. b. Gaius whom
2 d. b., concerning all things I make
5 d. b., thou dost faithfully whatever
11 d. b., follow not that which is evil
Jude 3 d. b., taking all care to write unto
17 my d. b., be mindful of the words which
my beloved Prov 31 2 what, O my beloved, O the
Cant 1 12 a bundle of myrrh is my beloved to me
2 3 so is my beloved among the sons. I sat
8 the voice of my b., behold he cometh
9 my beloved is like a roe or a young
10 my beloved speaketh to me: Arise, make
16 my b. to me, and I to him who feedeth
17 be like, my beloved, to a roe or to a
3 5 nor awake my beloved till she please
5 1 let my beloved come into his garden
2 the voice of my beloved knocking: Open
4 my b. put his hand through the key hole
5 I arose up to open to my beloved: my
6 opened bolt of my door to my beloved
8 if you find my beloved, that you tell
10 my beloved is white and ruddy, chosen
16 such is my beloved and he is my friend
6 1 my beloved is gone down into his garden
2 I to my beloved, and my beloved to me
7 9 worthy for my beloved to drink and for
10 I to my beloved and his turning is
11 come, my beloved, let us go forth into
13 the new and the old, my beloved, I have

8 14 flee away, O my beloved, and be like
Isa 5 1 I will sing to my beloved the canticle
1 my beloved had a vineyard on a hill
21 4 Babylon my beloved is become a wonder
Jer 11 15 my b. hath wrought much wickedness
Mat 3 17 this is my beloved Son. 17:5; Mark 9:6; Luke 9:35; 2 P 1:17
12 18 my b. in whom my soul hath been well
Mark 1 11 thou art my beloved Son. Luke 3:22
Luke 20 13 I will send my beloved son: it may be
Rom 16 5 salute Epenetus, my beloved: who is the
9 salute . . . Stachys, my beloved. Salute
1 C 15 58 my beloved brethren, be ye steadfast
Titus 1 4 to Titus my beloved son, according
2 P 3 8 of this one thing be not ignorant my b.
Jude 20 my beloved, building yourselves upon
below 3 K 17 23 him down . . . to the house below
Eccu 48 5 raisedst up a dead man from below, from
Isa 14 9 hell below was in an uproar to meet
2 Ma 9 25 to him what I have joined here below
Mark 14 66 when Peter was in the court below, there
Belsam 2 Es 7 7 who came with . . . Belsam, Mespharath
Belsan 1 Es 2 2 who came with . . . Belsan, Mesphar
belt 2 K 18 11 ten sicles of silver and a belt
4 K 3 21 all that were girded with a belt upon
Job 12 18 he looseth the b. of kings and girdeth
bemoan Jer 15 5 who shall bemoan thee? Or who
Jer 22 10 nor bemoan him with your tears: lament
Nah 3 7 who shall bemoan thee? Whence shall I
bemoaned Job 42 11 b. him and comforted him upon
Ben 1 Pa 15 18 second rank, Zacharias and Ben
Benabinadab 3 K 4 11 B., to whom belonged all
Benadad 3 K 15 18 sent them to B. son of Tabremon
3 K 15 20 Benadad hearkening to king Asa, sent
20 1 B., king of Syria, gathered. 4 K 6:24
3 thus saith Benadad: Thy silver and thy
5 thus saith Benadad, who sent us unto
9 he answered the messengers of Benadad
12 when Benadad heard this word that he
16 Benadad was drinking himself drunk in
17 Benadad sent. And they told him, saying
20 and Benadad king of Syria fled away on
26 Benadad mustered the Syrians and went
30 Benadad fleeing went into the city
32 thy servant Benadad saith: I beseech
33 and said: Thy brother Benadad. And he
33 Benadad came out to him and he lifted
4 K 8 7 and Benadad king of Syria was sick
9 Benadad the king of Syria hath sent me
13 3 and into the hand of Benadad the son of
24 Benadad his son reigned in his stead
25 took the cities out of hand of Benadad
2 Pa 16 2 and sent to Benadad king of Syria, who
4 when Benadad heard this, he sent captains
Jer 49 27 it shall devour the strongholds of B.
Amos 1 4 it shall devour the houses of Benadad
benches Eze 27 6 made thee benches of Indian ivory
bend Ps 68 24 their back bend thou down always
Ps 77 9 who bend and shoot with the bow: they
Eccu 33 27 yoke and the thong bend a stiff neck
Jer 27 8 whosoever will not bend his neck under
11 that shall bend down their neck under
12 bend down your necks under the yoke
50 14 all you that bend the bow: fight against
29 to all that bend the bow: stand together
51 3 him that bendeth, bend his bow and let
Bendecar 3 K 4 9 B., in Macces and in Salebim
bendeth Josu 15 9 it bendeth towards Baala which
Josu 15 11 bendeth to Sechrona and passeth mount
18 14 it bendeth thence going round towards
Isa 9 14 him that bendeth down, and him that
19 15 him that bendeth down or that holdeth
Jer 51 3 let not him that bendeth, bend his
bending 1 Pa 5 18 bearing . . . swords and b. the bow
1 Pa 12 2 bending the bow and using either hand
2 Es 3 24 from the house of Azarias unto the b.
25 over against the bending and the tower
Eze 17 7 this vine, bending as it were her roots
40 2 city, bending towards the south. And he
46 19 there was a place bending to the west
2 Ma 7 27 so bending herself towards him, mocking
beneath Gen 49 25 of the deep that lieth beneath. Deut 33:13
Exod 20 4 heaven above, or in the earth beneath
26 24 shall be joined together from beneath
28 27 set on each side of the ephod beneath
33 beneath at the feet of the same tunick
36 29 also joined from beneath unto the top
39 22 beneath at the feet pomegranates of
Deut 4 39 in heaven above and in the earth beneath. Josu 2:11
5 8 or that are in the earth beneath, or
28 13 shalt be always above, and not beneath
Josu 3 13 waters that are beneath shall run down
16 those that were beneath, ran down into
3 K 8 23 like thee in heaven above or on earth b.
Jdth 14 2 not as going down beneath, but as making
Job 18 16 let his roots be dried up beneath and
Prov 25 3 and the earth beneath and the heart of
Ecce 10 6 in high dignity, and the rich sitting b.
Eccu 51 9 my life was drawing near to hell beneath
Isa 51 6 and look down to the earth beneath
Jer 31 37 foundations of the earth searched b.
Amos 2 9 fruit from above, and his roots beneath
John 8 23 you are from beneath, I am from above
benediction Eccu 45 1 Moses . . . memory is in b.
1 C 10 16 chalice of benediction which we bless
Heb 12 17 when he desired to inherit the b.
Apoc 4 9 b. to him that sitteth on the throne
5 12 is worthy to receive . . . glory and b.
13 to the Lamb, benediction and honor
7 12 benediction and glory and wisdom and
beneficent Wisd 7 22 which nothing hindereth, b.
Luke 22 25 that have power over them are called b.
benefit Esth 16 16 by whose b. the kingdom was given
Wisd 16 24 for the b. of them that trust in thee
1 Tim 6 2 who are partakers of the benefit. These
benefited Wisd 11 6 they in their need were b.
Wisd 11 14 by their punishments the others were b.
benefits Judg 9 16 suitable return for the benefits
1 Pa 17 26 promised to thy servant such great b.
2 Pa 32 25 according to b. which he had received
Tob 11 19 told his parents all the b. of God
12 2 what can be worthy of his benefits
Esth 16 4 not to return thanks for benefits
Ps 77 11 and they forgot his benefits and his
1 Ma 11 53 according to the b. he had received
Benejaacan Num 33 31 they camped in Benejaacan
Num 33 32 departing from Benejaacan they came to
Benennom 2 Pa 28 3 burnt incense in valley of B.
2 Pa 33 6 through the fire in valley of Benennom
benevolent Wisd 1 6 the spirit of wisdom is b. And
Bengaber 3 K 4 13 Bengaber in Ramoth Galaad: he
Benhail 2 Pa 17 7 he sent of his princes Benhail
Benhesed 3 K 4 10 Benhesed in Aruboth: his was
Benhur 3 K 4 8 Benhur, in mount Ephraim, Bethanan
benignity Rom 2 4 benignity of God leadeth thee to
Gal 5 22 the fruit of the Spirit . . . is benignity
Col 3 12 b., humility, modesty, patience: bearing
Benjamin Gen 35 18 his father called him Benjamin
Gen 35 24 sons of Rachel: Joseph and B. 46:19
42 4 whilst B. was kept at home by Jacob
36 Benjamin you will take away: all these
43 14 whom he keepeth and this Benjamin
15 took presents and double money and B.
16 when he had seen them and Benjamin

29 Joseph lifting up his eyes, saw Benjamin
34 the greater mess came to Benjamin, so
45 14 upon the neck of his brother Benjamin
14 Benjamin in like manner wept also on his
22 to Benjamin he gave 300 pieces of silver
49 27 Benjamin a ravenous wolf in the morning
Exod 1 3 Issachar, Zabulon, and Benjamin
Num 1 11 of Benjamin, Abidan the son of Gedeon
Deut 27 12 Juda, Issachar, Joseph, and Benjamin
33 12 to Benjamin he said: The best beloved
Josu 21 4 Simeon and of Benjamin, thirteen cities
Judg 5 14 him out of Benjamin into thy people
10 9 wasted Juda and Benjamin and Ephraim
20 15 there were found of Benjamin five and
20 out from thence to fight against B.
30 they drew up their army against Benjamin
37 whilst Benjamin turned their backs
40 Benjamin looking back, saw them at the
45 when they that remained of B. saw this
46 all that were slain of Benjamin in divers
47 remained of all the number of Benjamin
48 cities and villages of B. were consumed
21 6 with repentance for their brother B.
16 all the women in Benjamin are dead
18 shall give B. any of his daughters
1 K 4 12 there ran a man of Benjamin out of the
9 1 a man of Benjamin whose name was Cis
10 2 sepulcher of Rachel in borders of B.
13 15 from Galgal to Gabaa in hill of Benjamin
2 K 2 9 and over Benjamin and over all Israel
15 went over 12 in number of Benjamin
31 the servants of David had killed of B.
3 19 and Abner spoke also to Benjamin. And he
19 that seemed good to Israel and to all B.
4 2 Beroth also was reckoned in Benjamin
19 17 with a thousand men of Benjamin and Siba
3 K 4 18 Semei the son of Ela in Benjamin. Gaber
12 23 to all the house of Juda, and Benjamin
1 Pa 2 2 sons of Israel . . . Benjamin, Nephtali
7 10 sons of Balan . . . Benjamin and Aod and
8 1 Benjamin begot Bale his firstborn, Asbel
12 2 of the brethren of Saul of Benjamin
16 came also of the men of Benjamin and of
21 6 Levi and Benjamin he did not number
27 21 over Benjamin, Jasiel the son of Abner
2 Pa 11 1 together all the house of Juda and of B.
3 to all Israel, in Juda and Benjamin
10 which are in Juda and Benjamin, well
12 he reigned over Juda and Benjamin and
23 all the countries of Juda and of B.
14 8 of Benjamin that bore shields and drew
15 2 hear ye me, Asa, and all Juda and B.
8 out of all land of Juda and out of B.
9 he gathered together all Juda and B.
25 5 of hundreds in all Juda and Benjamin
31 1 not only out of all Juda and Benjamin
15 under his charge were Eden and Benjamin
34 9 Israel and from all Juda and Benjamin
32 all that were found in Jerusalem and B.
1 Es 1 5 the chief of the fathers of Juda and B.
4 1 the enemies of Juda and Benjamin heard
10 9 the men of Juda and Benjamin gathered
32 of the sons of Herem . . . Benjamin, Maloch
2 Es 3 23 after him built Benjamin and Hasub
11 36 were portions of Juda and Benjamin
12 33 after them went . . . Benjamin and Semeia
Ps 67 28 there is Benjamin a youth, in ecstasy
79 3 shine forth before Ephraim, Benjamin
Jer 20 2 that were in the upper gate of Benjamin
37 12 he was come to the gate of Benjamin
38 7 king was sitting in the gate of Benjamin
Eze 48 22 to the border of B., shall also belong
23 the west side one portion for Benjamin
24 over against the border of Benjamin
32 the gate of Benjamin one, the gate of
Osee 5 8 in Bethaven, behind thy back, O Benjamin
Abdi 19 and Benjamin shall possess Galaad
Zach 14 10 from the gate of Benjamin even to the

children of Benjamin Josu 18 11 lot of c. . . .
Josu 18 20 this is the possession of the c. . . . 28
21 17 out of the tribe of the c. . . . Gabaon
Judg 20 3 nor were the c. . . . ignorant that the
17 of men of Israel also beside the c. . . .
18 first to go to battle against the c. . . .
21 the c. . . . coming out of Gabaa, slew of
23 out any more to fight against c. . . . 28
24 the next day to fight against the c. . . .
25 the c. . . . sallied forth out of the gates
31 the c. . . . boldly issued out of the city
34 the battle grew hot against the c. . . .
36 c. . . . when they saw themselves to be
39 for the c. . . . thought they fled and
41 the c. . . . seeing, turned their backs
21 1 shall give of his daughters to c. . . .
13 they sent messengers to the c. . . . that
14 c. . . . came at that time, and wives were
20 they commanded the c. . . . and said: Go
23 the c. . . . did as they had been commanded
2 K 2 25 the c. . . . gathered themselves together
4 2 Remmon a Berothite of the c. . . . : for
23 29 Ithai son of Ribai of Ganaath of c. . . .
1 Pa 8 40 all these were children of Benjamin
9 3 dwelt of children of Juda and of c. . . .
2 Es 11 4 dwelt . . . some of the children of B.
7 these are the children of Benjamin
31 the children of Benjamin, from Geba

Gabaa of Benjamin Judg 20 4 I came into G. . . .
Judg 20 10 that we might fight against G. . . . and
1 K 13 2 a thousand with Jonathan in G. . . . and
15 arose and went up from Galgal to G. . . .
16 were present with them, were in G. . . .
14 16 watchmen of Saul, who were in G. . . .
3 K 15 22 and with them king Asa built G. . . . and

land of Benjamin Judg 21 21 go into the l. . . .
1 K 9 16 will send thee a man of the l. . . . and
2 K 21 14 of Jonathan his son in the land of B.
Jer 1 1 Anathoth in the land of Benjamin. 32:8
17 26 from the land of B. and from the plains
32 44 shall be taken in the land of Benjamin
33 13 in the land of Benjamin and round about
37 11 out of Jerusalem to go into the l. . . .

sons of Benjamin Gen 46 21 s. . . . Bela and Bechor
Num 1 36 of the s. . . . by their generations and
2 22 in tribe of s. . . . the prince was Abidan
7 60 prince of the sons of Benjamin, Abidan
26 38 the s. . . . in their kindreds: Bela, of
41 these are the s. . . . by their kindreds
Judg 1 21 the s. . . . did not destroy the Jebusites
21 the Jebusite hath dwelt with the s. . . .
1 Pa 6 65 out of the tribe of the s. . . . , these
7 6 the s. . . . were Bela and Bechor and
9 7 of the sons of Benjamin: Salo the son of
11 31 of the s. . . . Banai a Pharathonite, Hurai
12 29 and of the sons of Benjamin . . . 3,000
Jer 6 1 strengthen yourselves, ye s. . . . in the

tribe of Benjamin Num 10 24 in t. . . . the prince
Num 13 10 of the t. . . . Phalti the son of Raphu
34 21 of the tribe of Benjamin, Elidad the
Judg 19 14 were by Gabaa, which is in the t. . . .
20 12 they sent messengers to all the t. . . .
1 K 9 21 last among all the families of t. . . .
10 20 the lot fell on the tribe of Benjamin
21 he [Samuel] brought the tribe of B.
3 K 12 21 all the house of Juda and the t. . . .
1 Pa 6 60 out of the tribe of Benjamin: Gabee and
Esth 11 2 Mardochai . . . of the tribe of Benjamin

2 Ma 3 4 one Simon of the tribe of Benjamin
Acts 13 21 Saul the son of Cis, a man of the t. . . .
Rom 11 1 of the seed of Abraham, of the t. . . .
Phil 3 5 of the stock of Israel, of the t. . . .
Apoc 7 8 of the tribe of Benjamin, 12,000 signed
Benjamin's Gen 44 12 he found the cup in B. sack
Benni 2 Es 3 17 Rehum the son of Benni. After him
Benno 1 Pa 24 26 and Musi: the son of Oziau: Benno
Bennoi 1 Es 8 33 Noadaia the son of Bennoi, Levites
Bennui 1 Es 10 30 of the sons of Phahath . . . Bennui
1 Es 10 38 of the sons of Bani . . . Bennui, Semei
2 Es 3 24 after him built Bennui son of Hanadad
10 9 Bennui of sons of Henadad, Admihel
12 8 and the Levites, Jesua, Bennui, Admihel
Benoni Gen 35 18 called the name of her son Benoni
bent Gen 6 5 heart was bent upon evil at all times
3 K 22 34 a certain man bent his bow, shooting
4 K 9 24 Jehu bent his bow with his hand and
Ps 7 13 he hath bent his bow and made it ready
10 3 the wicked have bent their bow: they
36 14 the sword: they have bent their bow
57 8 down; he hath bent his bow till they be
63 4 they have bent their bow a bitter thing
Wisd 5 22 from the clouds as from a bow well bent
Isa 5 28 sharp, and all their bows are bent
21 15 from the bent bow, from the face of a
Jer 9 3 and they have bent their tongue as a bow
Lam 2 4 he hath bent his bow as an enemy, he
3 12 he hath bent his bow and set me as mark
Zach 9 13 I have bent Juda for me as a bow, I have
Benzoheth 1 Pa 4 20 sons of Jesi Zoheth and B.
Beon Num 32 3 Eleale and Saban and Nebo and Beon
Beor Num 22 5 Balaam the son of Beor. 24:3, 15; 31:8; 36:32; Deut 23:4; Josu 13:22; 24:9; Mich 6:5
1 Pa 1 43 Bale the son of Beor: and the name of
Bera Judg 9 21 he fled and went into Bera: and dwelt
1 Pa 7 37 Salusa and Jethran and Bera. The sons of
Bercos 1 Es 2 53 the children of Bercos. 2 Es 7:55
Berea 1 Ma 9 4 they arose and went to Berea with
Acts 17 10 away Paul and Silas by night unto Berea
13 of God was also preached by Paul at B.
20 4 Sopater, the son of Pyrrhus, of Berea
bereaved Jer 18 21 let their wives be bereaved of
Beri 1 Pa 7 36 the sons of Supha . . . Beri and Jamra
Beria Gen 46 17 the sons of Aser . . . Jessuri and B.
Gen 46 17 the sons of Beria: Heber and Melchiel
1 Pa 7 23 and he called his name Beria because
Berith Judg 9 46 went into temple of their god B.
Bernice Acts 25 13 Agrippa and Bernice came down to
Acts 25 23 when Agrippa and Bernice were come with
26 30 king rose up and the governor and B.
Berodach 4 K 20 12 B. Baladan, the son of Baladan
Beromi 2 K 23 31 Azmaveth of Beromi, Eliaba of
Beroth Deut 10 6 removed their camp from Beroth
Josu 9 17 names of which . . . Caphira and Beroth
18 25 Gabaon and Rama and Beroth, and Mesphe
2 K 4 2 Beroth also was reckoned in Benjamin
8 8 out of Beroth cities of Adarezer, king
1 Es 2 25 children of Cariathiarim Cephira and
2 Es 7 29 the men of Cariathiarim, Cephira and B.
Berotha Eze 47 16 as the men go to Sedada, Emath, B.
Berothite 2 K 4 2 the sons of Remmon a Berothite
2 K 4 5 sons of Remmon the Berothite. 9
23 37 Naharai the Berothite, armorbearer of
1 Pa 11 39 Naharai a Berothite, the armorbearer of
Berothites 2 K 4 3 Berothites fled into Gethaim
berries Isa 17 6 two or three berries in the top of
Bersa Gen 14 2 and against Bersa king of Gomorrha
Bersabee Gen 21 14 wandered in the wilderness of B.
Gen 21 31 that place was called Bersabee: because
33 Abraham planted a grove in Bersabee
22 19 they went to Bersabee together and he
26 23 he went up from that place to Bersabee
28 10 Jacob being departed from Bersabee, went
Josu 15 28 Hasersual and Bersabee and Baziothia
19 2 Juda Bersabee and Sabee and Molada
Judg 20 1 from Dan to Bersabee. 1 K 3:20; 2 K 3:10; 17:11; 24:2, 15; 3 K 4:25
1 K 8 2 second was Abia, judges in Bersabee
2 K 24 7 came to the south of Juda into Bersabee
3 K 19 3 he [Elias] came to Bersabee of Juda
4 K 12 1 his mother was Sebia of B. 2 Pa 24:1
23 8 offered sacrifice, from Gabaa to B.
1 Pa 4 28 they dwelt in Bersabee and Molada and
21 2 number Israel from Bersabee even to Dan
2 Pa 19 4 out again to the people from Bersabee
30 5 to all Israel from Bersabee even to Dan
2 Es 11 27 at Bersabee and in the villages thereof
30 they dwelt from Bersabee unto the valley
Amos 5 5 neither shall you pass over to Bersabee
8 14 and the way of Bersabee liveth: and they
beryl Exod 28 20 a chrysolite, an onyx and a beryl
Eze 28 13 the onyx and the beryl and the sapphire
Apoc 21 20 the eighth, beryl: the ninth a topaz
Berzellai 2 K 17 27 Berzellai the Galaadite of
2 K 19 31 Berzellai . . . coming down from Rogelim
32 B. the Galaadite was of a great age
33 king said to Berzellai: Come with me
34 B. said to the king: How many are the
39 the king kissed Berzellai and blessed
21 8 Hadriel the son of Berzellai, that was
3 K 2 7 show kindness to the sons of Berzellai
1 Es 2 61 a wife of the daughters of B. 2 Es 7:63
61 the children of Berzellai. 2 Es 7:63
Besai 1 Es 2 17 the children of Besai, 323. The
2 Es 7 23 children of Besai, 324. The children of
52 the children of Besai, the children of
10 18 Odaia, Hasum, Besai, Hareph, Anathoth
Besecath 4 K 22 1 daughter of Hadaia of Besecath
Besee 1 Es 2 49 the children of Besee, the children
beseech Num 20 17 we b. thee that we may have leave
4 K 3 11 that we may beseech the Lord by him
2 Pa 34 26 that sent you to beseech the Lord
Jdth 12 5 to prayer, and to beseech the Lord
Job 8 5 to God, and wilt beseech the Almighty
Eccu 38 14 they shall beseech the Lord, that he
Isa 11 10 him the Gentiles shall beseech, and his
Jer 26 19 and b. the face of the Lord: and the
Mala 1 9 now beseech ye the face of God, that he
2 Ma 6 12 I b. those that shall read this book
Mark 5 18 to beseech him that he might be with him
1 C 4 16 I beseech you, be ye followers of me
2 C 2 8 I b. you, you would confirm your charity
5 20 we b. you, be reconciled to God. Him who
10 1 I Paul myself b. you by the mildness
2 I b. you that I may not be bold when I
Eph 4 1 I b. you that you walk worthy of the
Phil 4 2 I beseech Syntyche to be of one mind
2 Th 3 12 charge them that are such and b. them
Philem 9 for charity sake I rather b., whereas
Heb 13 19 I b. you the more to do this, that I may
1 P 2 11 I beseech you as strangers and pilgrims
5 1 I b., who am myself also an ancient
Jude 3 to b. you to contend earnestly for the
beseech you brethren Rom 12 1 I b. . . . present your bodies a living sacrifice
Rom 15 30 I b. . . . that you help me in your prayers
16 17 I b. . . . to mark them who make
1 C 1 10 I b. . . . that you all speak the same
16 15 I b. . . . you know the house of Stephanas
Gal 4 12 brethren, I b. you: you have not injured
1 Th 4 1 brethren, we pray and b. you in the Lord
5 12 we b. . . . to know them who labor among
14 we b. . . . rebuke the unquiet, comfort the
2 Th 2 1 we b. . . . that you be not easily moved

Heb 13 22 I b. . . . that you suffer this word of
I beseech thee Luke 8 28 I. . . . do not torment
Luke 9 38 I. . . . look upon my son because he is my
16 27 I. . . . send him to my father's house, for
Acts 8 34 I. . . . of whom doth the prophet speak
21 39 I. . . . suffer me to speak to the people
26 3 I. . . . to hear me patiently. And my life
Philem 10 I. . . . for my son whom I have begotten
2 J 5 now I. . . . , lady, not as writing a new
beseeching 2 K 14 32 beseeching thee to come to me
1 Es 10 1 when Esdras was thus praying and b.
1 Ma 13 45 beseeching Simon to grant them peace
2 Ma 10 16 beseeching the Lord by prayers to be
Mat 8 5 there came to him a centurion beseeching
Mark 1 40 there came a leper to him, beseeching
Luke 8 41 b. him that he would come into his house
Acts 16 9 man of Macedonia standing and beseeching
1 P 5 12 b. and testifying that this is the
beseeming Gen 18 25 this is not beseeming thee
Beselam 1 Es 4 7 in the days of Artaxerxes, Beselam
Beseleel Exod 31 2 I have called by name Beseleel
Exod 35 30 the Lord hath called by name Beseleel
36 1 Beseleel . . . made the things that are
37 1 Beseleel made also the ark of setim wood
38 22 which Beseleel the son of Uri the son of
2 Pa 1 5 altar of brass which Beseleel the son
1 Es 10 30 of the sons of Phahath . . . Beseleel and
beset Gen 19 4 the men of the city beset the house
Judg 19 22 came and beset the old man's house that
20 5 beset the house wherein I was, intending
3 K 20 12 beset the city. And they beset it. And
4 K 3 25 and the city was beset by the slingers
6 14 they came by night and beset the city
Eccu 46 19 enemies who beset him on every side
Osee 7 2 own devices now have beset them about
1 Ma 5 3 because they beset the Israelites round
besetteth Jdth 5 3 people that b. the mountains
besetting Acts 17 5 b. Jason's house, sought to
besiege Deut 20 12 thee, thou shalt besiege it
1 K 23 8 against Ceila and to besiege David
2 K 12 28 besiege the city and take it: lest
2 Pa 6 28 waste the country and b. the cities
Isa 21 2 go up, O Elam, besiege, O Mede: I have
29 3 and raise up bulwarks to besiege thee
Jer 21 4 that besiege you round about the walls
9 to the Chaldeans, that besiege you
1 Ma 6 19 together all the people to b. them
11 22 that he should not besiege the castle
23 he bade them besiege it still: and he
2 Ma 10 19 in sufficient number to besiege them
besieged Deut 20 19 hast b. a city a long time
Deut 28 52 shalt be besieged within thy gates
Josu 10 6 city of Gabaon which was besieged, sent
31 investing it with his army, besieged it
Judg 9 50 which he surrounded and b. with his
2 K 11 1 besieged Rabba: but David remained in
20 15 came and besieged him [Seba] in Abela
15 works round the city and the city was b.
3 K 15 27 Nadab and all Israel b. Gebbethon. So
16 17 him from Gebbethon and they b. Thersa
20 1 he fought against Samaria and b. it
4 K 6 24 army and went up and besieged Samaria
9 14 Joram had besieged Ramoth Galaas, he and
16 5 they b. Achaz, but were not able to
17 4 he b. him, bound him, and cast him into
5 to Samaria, he besieged it three years
18 9 came up to Samaria and besieged it
25 2 the city was shut up and besieged till
4 the Chaldees b. the city round about
1 Pa 20 1 Ammon: and went and besieged Rabba. But
2 Pa 32 1 into Juda and besieged the fenced cities
10 that you sit still besieged in Jerusalem
Job 19 12 have besieged my tabernacle round about
Ps 21 13 surrounded me: fat bulls have b. me
17 council of the malignant hath b. me
Isa 29 7 all that have fought and besieged and
Jer 32 2 of the king of Babylon b. Jerusalem
37 4 the Chaldeans that besieged Jerusalem
39 1 to Jerusalem, and they besieged it
52 4 they b. it and built forts against it
5 and the city was b. until the eleventh
Eze 4 3 against it, and it shall be besieged
6 12 that remaineth and is b., shall die
Dan 1 1 came to Jerusalem and besieged it. And
1 Ma 6 20 besieged them in the year 150 and they
21 some of the besieged got out; and some
11 61 he b. it and burnt all the suburbs
13 43 Simon besieged Gaza and camped round
2 Ma 11 6 that the strongholds were besieged
besieging Judg 1 8 of Israel b. Jerusalem, took
Judg 1 23 when they were besieging the city which
9 44 [Abimelech] assaulting and b. the city
2 K 11 16 as Joab was b. the city, he put Urias
3 K 8 37 enemy afflict them besieging the gates
16 15 the army was b. Gebbethon a city of
4 K 19 8 king of the Assyrians b. Lobna. Isa 37:8
2 Pa 32 9 for he with all his army was b. Lachis
Jer 52 7 Chaldeans besieging the city round about
1 Ma 11 21 that Jonathan was besieging the castle
Besloth 2 Es 7 54 children of B., the children of
Besluth 1 Es 2 52 the children of B., the children
Besodia 2 Es 3 6 Mosollam the son of Besodia built
besom Isa 14 23 sweep it and wear it out with a b.
Besor 1 K 30 9 they came to the torrent Besor
1 K 30 10 could not go over the torrent Besor
21 ordered them to abide at torrent Besor
besought Gen 25 21 Isaac b. the Lord for his wife
Gen 42 21 when he besought us, and we would not
Exod 32 11 Moses besought the Lord his God, saying
Deut 3 23 and I besought the Lord at that time
9 25 I humbly besought him that he would not
2 K 12 16 David besought the Lord for the child
3 K 13 6 the man of God b. the face of the Lord
4 K 1 13 b. him and said: Man of God, despise not
13 4 Joachaz besought the face of the Lord
2 Pa 33 13 and he entreated him and besought him
1 Es 8 23 we fasted and besought our God for this
Tob 3 11 continuing in prayer with tears b. God
Wisd 8 21 I went to the Lord and besought him and
Eccu 50 21 the people in prayer besought the Lord
2 Ma 8 14 besought the Lord that he would deliver
29 they besought the merciful Lord to be
10 4 besought the Lord, lying prostrate on
26 besought him to be merciful to them and
11 6 besought the Lord with lamentations and
12 11 being overcome besought Judas for peace
24 he besought them to let him go with his
42 they besought him that the sin which had
13 3 besought Antiochus, not for the welfare
Mat 8 31 devils besought him . . . send us. Mark 5:12
34 b. him that he would depart. Luke 8:37
14 36 b. him that they might touch. Mark 6:56
15 23 besought him, saying: Send her away, for
18 26 b. him, saying: Have patience with. 29
Mark 5 10 b. him that he would not drive him away
23 and he besought him much, saying: My
7 26 she b. him that he would cast forth the
32 b. him that he would lay his hand upon
8 22 they b. him that he would touch him
Luke 4 38 they besought him for her. And standing
5 12 a man full of leprosy besought him
7 4 when they came to Jesus, they b. him
8 31 b. him that he would not command them to
32 b. him that he would suffer them to
38 besought him that he might be with him
John 19 31 besought Pilate that their legs might be

38 besought Pilate that he might take away
Acts 16 15 b. us, saying: If you have judged me to
39 they b. them; and bringing them out
27 33 Paul besought them all to take meat
2 C 12 8 for which thing thrice I b. the Lord
besoughtest Mat 18 32 because thou besoughtest me
Bessur Josu 15 58 Halhul and Bessur and Gedor
best Gen 27 9 bring me two kids of the best that I
Gen 43 11 take of the best fruits of the land
45 22 of silver with five robes of the best
47 6 make them dwell in the best places and
11 in Egypt, in the best place of the land
Exod 22 5 shall restore the best of whatsoever
Num 10 32 thee what is the best of the riches
18 12 all the best of the oil and of the wine
29 shall be the best and choicest things
Deut 33 12 best beloved of the Lord shall dwell
Josu 22 25 we therefore thought it best and said
Ruth 3 3 put on thy best garments and go down
1 K 8 14 your best oliveyards and give them to
9 20 for whom shall be all the best things
15 9 spared Agag and the best of the flocks
15 the people spared the best of the sheep
4 K 10 3 choose the best and him that shall
1 Es 8 27 two vessels of the best shining brass
Jdth 10 3 anointed herself with the best ointment
12 14 all that shall be good and best before
14 shall be best to me all the days of my
Esth 1 7 wine also in abundance and of the best
Job 22 21 thereby thou shalt have the best fruits
34 4 see among ourselves what is the best
Prov 15 23 and a word in due time is best. The path
Cant 1 2 smelling sweet of the best ointments
7 9 thy throat like the best wine, worthy
Wisd 14 19 the resemblance in the best manner
Eccu 24 20 a sweet odor like the best myrrh: and
Isa 44 9 their best beloved things shall not
Lam 4 2 that were clothed with the best gold
Eze 20 15 milk and honey, the best of all lands
27 17 thy merchants with the best corn: they
18 rich wine, in wool of the best color
22 with all the best spices and precious
31 16 the choice and best in Libanus, all
Dan 11 15 shall take the best fenced cities: and
24 devices against the best fenced places
Osee 9 16 I will slay the best beloved fruit
Amos 6 2 to all the best kingdoms of these: if
6 themselves with the best ointments
Mich 7 4 he that is best among them, is as
1 Ma 4 1 a thousand of the best horsemen: and
8 8 some of their best provinces: and those
2 Ma 4 15 the Grecian glories for the best: for
Luke 10 42 Mary hath chosen the best part, which
Heb 13 9 best that heart be established with
James 1 17 every best gift and every perfect gift
bestow Tob 4 9 even so to b. willingly a little
Bar 6 9 silver, and bestow it on themselves
Luke 12 17 no room where to bestow my fruits? And
Acts 21 24 bestow on them that they may shave
bestowed 3 K 10 26 and he b. them in fenced cities
4 K 12 15 but they bestowed it faithfully. But
Isa 63 7 that the Lord hath bestowed upon me
2 Ma 4 19 might not be bestowed on the sacrifices
Luke 8 43 bestowed all her substance on physicians
1 J 3 1 charity the Father hath bestowed on us
betaking 2 Ma 12 42 b. themselves to prayers, they
Bete 2 K 8 8 out of Bete and out of Beroth, cities
Beten Josu 19 25 Chali and Beten and Azaph and
beth Ps 118 9 beth. Lam 1:2; 2:2; 3:4, 5, 6; 4:2
Bethacarem Jer 6 1 set up the standard over B.
Bethacharam 2 Es 3 14 lord of the street of B.
Bethanan 3 K 4 9 Bethsames and in Elon and in B.
Bethanath Josu 19 38 Magdalel Horem and Bethanath
Bethania Mat 21 17 he went out of the city into B.
Mat 26 6 when Jesus was in Bethania. Mark 14:3
Mark 11 1 when they were drawing near . . . to B.
11 he went out to Bethania with the twelve
12 when they were come out from Bethania
Luke 19 29 was come nigh to Bethphage and Bethania
24 50 he led them out as far as Bethania
John 1 28 these things were done in Bethania
11 1 man sick, named Lazarus, of Bethania
18 Bethania was near Jerusalem, and about
12 1 six days before the pasch, came to B.
Bethanites Judg 1 33 B. were tributaries to him
Bethanoth Josu 15 59 Gedor Mareth and Bethanoth
Betharaba Josu 15 6 passeth by the north into B.
Josu 15 61 in the desert Betharaba, Meddin and
18 22 Betharaba and Samaraim and Bethel and
Betharan Num 32 36 Bethnemra and B., fenced cities
Josu 13 27 in the valley of Betharan and Bethnemra
Bethaven Josu 7 2 Hai, which is beside Bethaven
Josu 18 12 reaching to the wilderness of Bethaven
1 K 13 5 in Machmas at the east of Bethaven
14 23 the fight went on as far as Bethaven
Osee 4 15 come not up into Bethaven and do not
5 8 howl ye in Bethaven behind thy back
10 5 have worshipped the kine of Bethaven
Bethazmoth 2 Es 7 28 the men of Bethazmoth, 42
Bethbera Judg 7 24 take the waters before them to B.
Judg 7 24 them and the Jordan as far as Bethbera
Bethberai 1 Pa 4 31 in Hasarsusim and in Bethberai
Bethbessen 1 Ma 9 62 retired into Bethbessen
1 Ma 9 64 he came and camped above Bethbessen
Bethchar 1 K 7 11 till they came under Bethchar
Bethdagon Josu 15 41 Gideroth and Bethdagon and
Josu 19 27 returneth towards the east to Bethdagon
1 Ma 10 83 and went into Bethdagon, their idol's
Bethel Gen 12 8 that was on east side of Bethel
Gen 12 8 his tent, having Bethel on the west
13 3 that he came from the south to Bethel
3 pitched his tent between Bethel and Hai
28 19 he called the name of the city Bethel
31 13 I am the God of Bethel, where thou didst
35 1 go up to Bethel and dwell there and
3 arise and let us go up to Bethel that
6 Jacob came to Luza . . . surnamed Bethel
8 died and was buried at the foot of B.
15 calling the name of that place Bethel
Josu 7 2 the east side of the town of Bethel
8 9 and abode between Bethel and Hai on the
12 lie in ambush between Bethel and Hai
17 one remained in city of Hai and of B.
12 9 Hai, which is on the side of Bethel
16 the king of Bethel one, the king of
16 1 from Jericho to mountain of Bethel
2 goeth out from Bethel to Luza: and
18 13 by Luza, the same is Bethel: and it
22 Betharaba and Samaraim and Bethel
Judg 1 22 of Joseph also went up against Bethel
4 5 between Rama and B. in mount Ephraim
20 31 highways whereof one goeth up to Bethel
21 19 on the north of the city of Bethel
19 way that goeth from Bethel to Sichem
1 K 7 16 he went every year about to Bethel
10 3 three men going up to God to Bethel
13 2 with Saul in Machmas and in mount B.
30 27 to them that were in Bethel and that
3 K 12 29 and he set the one in Bethel and the
32 altar he did in like manner in Bethel
32 he placed in Bethel priests of the
33 the altar which he had built in Bethel
13 1 there came a man of God . . . to Bethel
4 had cried out against the altar in B.
10 not by the way that he came into Bethel
11 a certain old prophet dwelt in Bethel

11 man of God had done that day in Bethel
32 against the altar that is in Bethel
16 34 Hiel of Bethel built Jericho: in Abiram
4 K 2 2 the Lord hath sent me as far as Bethel
2 when they were come down to Bethel
3 sons of the prophets that were at B.
23 he went up from thence to Bethel: and
10 29 the golden calves that were in Bethel
17 28 came and dwelt in Bethel and taught them
23 4 he carried the ashes of them to Bethel
15 the altar also that was at Bethel and
17 thou hast done upon the altar of B.
19 the acts that he had done in Bethel
1 Pa 7 28 habitations were B. with her daughters
2 Pa 13 19 took cities from him, Bethel and her
1 Es 2 28 the men of Bethel and Hai. 2 Es 7:32
2 Es 11 31 Mechmas and at Hai and at Bethel
Jer 48 13 house of Israel was ashamed of Bethel
Osee 10 15 so hath Bethel done to you, because
12 4 he found him in Bethel, and there he
Amos 3 14 visit upon him and upon the altars of B.
4 4 come ye to Bethel, and do wickedly
5 5 seek not B., and go not into Galgal
5 Bethel shall be unprofitable. Seek ye
6 there shall be none to quench Bethel
7 10 Amasias the priest of Bethel sent to
13 prophesy not again any more in Bethel
1 Ma 9 50 Ammaus and in Bethoron and in Bethel
Bethemec Josu 19 27 towards the north to Bethemec
Bether Cant 2 17 hart upon the mountains of Bether
Bethgader 1 Pa 2 51 Hariph the father of Bethgader
Bethgamul Jer 48 23 judgment is come . . . upon B.
Bethhagla Josu 15 6 border goeth up into Bethhagla
Josu 18 19 it passeth by Bethhagla northward: and
21 their cities were Jericho and Bethhagla
Beth-horon Josu 10 10 by way of the ascent to B.
Josu 10 11 and were in the descent of Beth-horon
16 3 unto the borders of Beth-horon nether
5 Ataroth-addar unto Beth-horon the upper
18 13 on the south of the nether Beth-horon
14 mountain that looketh towards Beth-horon
21 22 and Cibsaim and Beth-horon with their
1 K 13 18 another went by the way of Beth-horon
2 K 2 29 having gone through all Beth-horon
3 K 9 17 Solomon built Gazer and Beth-horon the
1 Pa 6 68 suburbs, and Beth-horon in like manner
2 Pa 8 5 he built B. the upper and B. the nether
25 13 cities of Juda, from Samaria to B.
Bethia 1 Pa 4 18 these are the sons of Bethia
Bethiesimoth Josu 13 20 Phasga and Bethiesimoth
Eze 25 9 cities of the land of Bethiesimoth
Bethlebaoth Josu 19 6 Bethlebaoth and Sarohen
Bethlehem Gen 35 19 Ephrata, this is Bethlehem
Gen 48 7 by another name is called Bethlehem
Josu 19 15 and Jedala and Bethlehem: twelve cities
Judg 12 8 Abesan of Bethlehem judged Israel: he
10 he died and was buried in Bethlehem
17 8 he went out from the city of B. and
19 2 returned to her father's house in B.
18 from whence we went to Bethlehem: and
Ruth 1 19 they went together and came to B. And
22 her sojournment: and returned into B.
2 4 came out of B. and said to the reapers
4 11 may become a famous name in Bethlehem
1 K 16 4 and he [Samuel] came to Bethlehem
17 15 to feed his father's flock at B. Now
20 6 that he might run to Bethlehem his
28 asked leave of me earnestly to go to B.
2 K 2 32 in sepulcher of his father in B. and
21 19 son of the Forrest an embroiderer of B.
23 14 garrison of the Philistines then in B.
15 cistern that is in B. by the gate. And
16 drew water out of cistern of Bethlehem
24 Elehanan the son of Dodo of Bethlehem
1 Pa 2 51 Salma the father of Bethlehem, Hariph
54 sons of Salma, Bethlehem, Netophathi
4 4 of Ephrata the father of Bethlehem
11 16 garrison of the Philistines in B.
17 me water of the cistern of Bethlehem
18 water out of the cistern of Bethlehem
26 Elchanan the son of his uncle of B.
2 Pa 11 6 and he [Roboam] built Bethlehem and
1 Es 2 21 the children of Bethlehem, 123. The
2 Es 7 26 children of Bethlehem and Netupha, 188
Jer 41 17 Chamaam, which is near Bethlehem: in
Mich 5 2 and thou, B. Ephrata, art a little one
Mat 2 1 when Jesus was born in Bethlehem of
5 they said to him [Herod]: In Bethlehem
6 thou B. the land of Juda art not the
8 sending them into B., said: Go and
16 killed all men children that were in B.
Luke 2 4 the city of David which is called B.
15 let us go over to B. and let us see
John 7 42 cometh of seed of David and from B.
Bethlehem Juda Judg 17 7 young man of B. J.
Judg 17 9 I am a Levite of Bethlehem Juda and I
19 1 who took a wife of Bethlehem Juda: and
18 we came out from Bethlehem Juda and we
Ruth 1 1 certain man of B. J. went to sojourn
2 other Chelion, Ephrathites of B. J.
1 K 17 12 was the son of the Ephrathite of B. J.
Bethlehemite 1 K 16 1 may send thee to Isai the B.
1 K 16 18 behold I have seen a son of Isai the B.
17 58 am the son of thy servant Isai the B.
1 Pa 20 5 the son of Saltus a Bethlehemite slew
Bethmaacha 2 K 20 14 of Israel unto Abela and B.
2 K 20 15 besieged him in Abela and in B. and
Bethmaon Jer 48 23 upon Bethgamul and upon Bethmaon
Bethmarchaboth Josu 19 5 Haima and Siceleg and B.
1 Pa 4 31 they dwelt . . . in Bethmarchaboth and in
Bethnemra Num 32 36 B. and Betharan, fenced cities
Josu 13 27 in the valley of Betharan and Bethnemra
Bethoron 1 Pa 7 24 Sara, who built Bethoron the
1 Ma 3 16 they approached even as far as Bethoron
24 he pursued him by the descent of B.
4 29 and pitched their tents in Bethoron
7 39 and encamped near to Bethoron: and an
Bethphage Mat 21 1 Jerusalem and were come to B.
Luke 19 29 when he was come nigh to Bethphage
Bethphaleth 2 Es 11 26 and at Molada and at B.
Bethphelet Josu 15 27 Hassemon and Bethphelet
Bethpheses Josu 19 21 Engannim and Enhadda and B.
Bethphogor Josu 13 20 B. and Asedoth, Phasga and
Bethrapha 1 Pa 4 12 Esthon begot Bethrapha and
Bethsabee 2 K 11 3 was told him that she was B.
2 K 12 24 David comforted Bethsabee his wife and
3 K 1 11 Nathan said to Bethsabee the mother of
15 so Bethsabee went in to the king into
16 Bethsabee bowed herself and worshipped
28 call to me Bethsabee. And when she was
31 Bethsabee bowing with her face to the
2 13 the son of Haggith came to Bethsabee
18 Bethsabee said: Well, I will speak
19 Bethsabee came to king Solomon to speak
1 Pa 3 5 four of Bethsabee the daughter of Ammiel
Ps 50 2 after he had sinned with Bethsabee
Bethsaida Mat 11 21 woe to thee B. Luke 10:13
Mark 6 45 go before him over the water to Bethsaida
8 22 they came to Bethsaida; and they bring
Luke 9 10 desert place apart which belongeth to B.
John 1 44 Philip was of Bethsaida. 12:21
5 2 Probatica which in Hebrew is named B.
Bethsames Josu 15 10 and goeth down into Bethsames
Josu 19 22 Sehesima and Bethsames: and outgoings
38 Bethanath and Bethsames: 19 cities and
21 16 Ain and Jeta and Bethsames with their

Judg 1 33 destroyed not the inhabitants of B.
1 K 6 9 way of his own coasts towards Bethsames
12 the straight way that leadeth to B.
12 followed them as far as borders of B.
15 the men also of B. offered holocausts
19 he slew of the men of Bethsames because
20 men of Bethsames said: Who shall be
3 K 4 9 in Bethsames and in Elon and in Bethanan
4 K 14 11 saw one another in Bethsames a town
13 took Amasias . . . in Bethsames. 2 Pa 25:23
1 Pa 6 59 Asan also and B., with their suburbs
2 Pa 25 21 king of Juda was in Bethsames of Juda
28 18 and they took Bethsames and Aialon
Bethsamite 1 K 6 14 into the field of Josue a B.
1 K 6 18 day the field of Josue the Bethsamite
Bethsamites Judg 1 33 the B. and Bethanites were
1 K 6 13 the Bethsamites were reaping wheat
Bethsan Josu 17 11 Bethsan and its villages, and
Josu 17 16 wherein are situate Bethsan with its
Judg 1 27 Manasses also did not destroy Bethsan
1 K 31 10 his body they hung on the wall of B.
12 bodies of his sons from the wall of B.
2 K 21 12 stolen them from the street of Bethsan
3 K 4 12 governed Thanac and Mageddo and all B.
12 from B. unto Abelmehula over against
1 Pa 7 29 borders of the sons of Manasses, Bethsan
1 Ma 5 52 great plain that is over against B.
12 40 so he rose up and came to Bethsan. And
41 chosen for battle came to Bethsan
Bethsetta Judg 7 23 fleeing as far as Bethsetta
Bethsimoth Num 33 49 camped from B. even to
Josu 12 3 by the way that leadeth to Bethsimoth
Bethsur 1 Pa 2 45 Maon the father of Bethsur. And
2 Pa 11 7 he [Roboam] built . . . Bethsur, Socho
2 Es 3 16 lord of half the street of Bethsur
Bethsura 1 Ma 4 61 he fortified it to secure B.
1 Ma 6 7 walls as before, and B. also his city
26 have fortified the stronghold of B.
31 through Idumea and approached to B.
49 made peace with them that were in B.
50 the king took Bethsura: and he placed
9 52 he fortified the city of Bethsura and
10 14 in B. there remained some of them that
14 7 had the dominion of Gazara and of B.
33 fortified the cities of Judea and B.
2 Ma 11 5 approaching to Bethsura which was in
13 19 he marched with his army to Bethsura
22 king treated with them that were in B.
Beththaphua Josu 15 53 Janum and Beththaphua
Bethul Josu 19 4 Eltholad, Bethul, and Harma
Bethulia Jdth 6 7 and to lead him [Achior] to B.
Jdth 6 10 children of Israel coming down from B.
10 loosing him they brought him to Bethulia
7 1 to his army, to go up against Bethulia
11 failed among all the inhabitants of B.
8 3 and he died in Bethulia his own city
12 7 into the valley of Bethulia and washed
15 7 the rest that were in Bethulia went
8 that returned conquerors to Bethulia
9 high priest came from Jerulsalem to B.
16 25 Judith was made great in Bethulia and
28 was buried with her husband in Bethulia
Bethzacharam 1 Ma 6 32 removed the camp to B. over
1 Ma 6 33 march on fiercely towards the way of B.
Bethzecha 1 Ma 7 19 and pitched in Bethzecha: and
betimes Judg 9 33 b. in the morning at sun rising
Prov 13 24 he that loveth him correcteth him b.
Mat 5 25 at agreement with thy adversary betimes
Betonim Josu 13 26 unto Ramoth, Masphe, and Betonim
betook 2 Pa 20 3 with fear b. himself wholly to
betray Josu 2 20 if thou wilt b. us and utter this
Isa 16 3 and betray not them that wander about
Mat 24 10 many shall betray one another: and shall
26 16 opportunity to betray him. Mark 13:11; Luke 22:6
21 is about to b. me. Mark 14:18; John 13:21
23 with me in the dish, he shall b. me
46 he is at hand that will b. me. Mark 14:42
Mark 13 12 the brother shall betray his brother
14 10 went to the chief priests to betray him
11 how he might conveniently betray him
Luke 22 4 how he might betray him to them. And
48 dost thou b. the Son of man with a kiss
John 6 65 who he was that would b. him. 13:11
72 the same was about to betray him. 12:4
13 2 Iscariot, the son of Simon, to betray him
21 20 Lord, who is he that shall betray thee
betrayed Mat 10 4 who also betrayed him. Mark 3:19
Mat 17 21 shall be b. into the hands. Mark 9:30
20 18 be b. to the chief priests. Mark 10:33
26 24 by whom the Son of man shall be betrayed. Mark 14:21; Luke 22:22
25 Judas that betrayed him said: Is it I
45 b. into the hands of sinners. Mark 14:41
48 that b. him, gave them a sign. Mark 14:44
27 3 Judas, who betrayed him, seeing that he
Luke 21 16 you shall be betrayed by your parents
John 18 2 Judas who betrayed him, knew the place
5 Judas also who b. him, stood with them
1 C 11 23 night in which he was b., took bread
betrayer 2 Ma 4 1 who was the b. of the money and
betrayers Acts 7 52 of whom you have been the b.
betrayeth Luke 22 21 hand of him that b. me is
betraying 2 Ma 4 50 in malice to the b. of the
Mat 27 4 I have sinned in b. innocent blood
betrays 4 K 6 11 who it is that b. me to the king
betrothed Exod 21 9 if he have b. her to his son
Deut 22 25 if a man find a damsel that is b. in
1 Ma 3 56 building houses or had betrothed wives
better Gen 29 19 it is b. that I give her to thee
Gen 37 27 it is better that he be sold to the
Exod 14 12 it was much better to serve them than
Lev 27 10 neither a better for a worse, nor a worse for a better
Num 14 3 is it not better to return into Egypt
18 30 offer all the goodly and better things
Judg 8 2 better than the vintages of Abiezer
9 2 whether is better for you that 70 men
11 25 unless perhaps thou art b. than Balac
18 19 whether is b. for thee, to be a priest
Ruth 2 22 it is better for thee, my daughter, to
4 15 and is much better to thee than if thou
1 K 1 8 am not I b. to thee than ten children
15 22 obedience is better than sacrifices
28 to thy neighbor who is b. than thee
16 23 Saul was refreshed and was better for
27 1 is it not better for me to flee and to
2 K 14 32 it had been better for me to be there
17 14 is better than the counsel of Achitophel
18 3 it is better . . . that thou shouldst be
19 28 were no better than worthy of death
24 14 it is better that I should fall into
3 K 2 32 two men, just and better than himself
19 4 for I am no better than my fathers. And
20 23 it is b. that we should fight against
21 2 will give thee for it a better vineyard
6 I will give thee a better vineyard for
4 K 5 12 better than all the waters of Israel
23 it is better that thou take two talents
1 Pa 21 13 better for me to fall into the hands of
2 Pa 21 13 thy brethren . . . b. men than thyself
Tob 3 6 it is better for me to die than to live
Jdth 3 2 it is better for us to live and serve
7 16 for it is better, that being captives
Job 34 33 if thou know anything better, speak
Ps 36 16 better is a little to the just, than

62 4 for thy mercy is better than lives
68 32 please God better than a young calf
83 11 better is one day in thy courts above
Prov 3 14 is better than the merchandise of silver
8 11 for wisdom is better than all the most
19 my fruit is better than gold and the
12 9 b. is the poor man that provideth for
15 16 b. is a little with the fear of the
17 better to be invited to herbs with love
16 8 better is a little with justice, than
16 wisdom, because it is better than gold
19 it is b. to be humbled with the meek
32 patient man is better than the valiant
17 1 better is a dry morsel with joy than
12 it is better to meet a bear robbed of
19 1 better is the poor man that walketh
22 better is the poor man than the lying
21 9 it is better to sit in a corner of the
19 it is better to dwell in a wilderness
22 1 good name is better than great riches
25 7 b. that it should be said to thee: Come
24 b. to sit in a corner of the housetop
27 5 open rebuke is better than hidden love
6 better are the wounds of a friend than
10 better is a neighbor that is near then
28 6 better is the poor man walking in his
Ecce 2 24 is it not better to eat and drink and
3 12 there was no b. than for a man to rejoice
22 nothing is b. than for a man to rejoice
4 6 better is a handful with rest, than both
9 better . . . that two should be together
13 better is a child that is poor and wise
17 for much better is obedience than the
5 4 it is much better not to vow than after
6 3 the untimely born is better than he
9 b. it is to see what thou mayst desire
7 2 good name is b. than precious ointments
3 it is b. to go to the house of mourning
4 anger is better than laughter: because
6 it is b. to be rebuked by a wise man
9 better is the end of a speech than the
9 better is the patient man than the
11 that former times were b. than they are
9 4 living dog is better than a dead lion
16 I said that wisdom is b. than strength
18 better is wisdom than weapons of war
10 11 he is nothing better that backbiteth
11 6 if both together, it shall be the better
Cant 1 1 for thy breasts are better than wine
Wisd 6 1 wisdom is better than strength, and a
1 a wise man is better than a strong man
15 6 to have no better things to trust in
17 he is b. than they whom he worshippeth
18 6 they might be of better courage. So
Eccu 10 30 distress: better is he that laboreth
16 3 better is one that feareth God than a
18 16 the good word is better than the gift
17 is not a word better than a gift? But
19 21 better is man that hath less wisdom
20 1 how much better is it to reprove than
27 a thief is better than a man that is
33 better is he that hideth his folly than
23 37 nothing better than the fear of God
29 16 better than the shield of the mighty, and better than the spear
28 better is the poor man's fare under
30 14 better is a poor man who is sound and
15 is better than all gold and silver: and
17 better is death than a bitter life
33 22 it is better that thy children should
36 20 meat, yet one is better than another
23 one daughter is better than another
40 29 for it is better to die than to want
41 18 better is the man that hideth his folly
42 14 better is the iniquity of a man than
Isa 56 5 name better than sons and daughters
Lam 4 9 it was better with them that were slain
Bar 6 58 it is better to be a king that showeth
67 beasts are better than they, which
70 they are no better than a white thorn
72 better therefore is the just man that
Dan 1 20 times better than all the diviners and
13 23 it is better for me to fall into you
Osee 2 7 it was better with me then than now
Jon 4 3 it is better for me to die than to. 8
Nah 3 8 art thou better than the populous
1 Ma 3 59 is better for us to die in battle than
13 5 for I am not better than my brethren
2 Ma 7 14 it is better, being put to death by men
Mat 10 31 better are you than many sparrows. Every
12 12 how much better is a man than a sheep
18 6 better for him that a millstone. Mark 9:41; Luke 17:2
8 better for thee to go into life maimed
9 b. for him if that man had not been born. Mark 14:21
Mark 5 26 and was nothing the better but rather
9 44 better for thee to enter lame into life
10 49 be of better comfort; arise, he calleth
Luke 5 39 to new: for he saith: The old is better
John 4 52 of them the hour wherein he grew better
Acts 27 36 then were they all of better cheer and
1 C 7 9 better to marry than to be burnt. But
38 he that giveth her not, doth better
11 17 you come together not for the better
12 31 be zealous for the better gifts. And I
Phil 1 10 that you may approve the better things
23 to be with Christ, a thing by far the b.
2 3 esteem others better than themselves
Heb 1 4 so much better than the angels as he hath
6 9 beloved, we trust better things of you
7 7 which is less is blessed by the better
19 a bringing in of a better hope, by which
22 Jesus made a surety of a better testament
8 6 he hath obtained a better ministry, by
6 he is a mediator of a better testament
6 which is established on better promises
9 23 things themselves with b. sacrifices than
10 34 you have a better and a lasting substance
11 16 now they desire a better that is to say
35 that they might find a b. resurrection
40 God providing some better thing for us
12 24 which speaketh better than that of Abel
1 P 3 17 it is better doing well, if such be the
2 P 2 21 b. for them not to have known the way
bewail Lev 10 6 bewail the burning which the Lord
Judg 11 37 two months and may bewail my virginity
Dan 14 39 the king came to bewail Daniel: and he
Apoc 1 7 and all tribes of earth shall bewail
18 9 shall weep and b. themselves over her
bewailed Wisd 18 10 for the children that were b.
Eccu 51 26 high, and I bewailed my ignorance of her
1 Ma 9 20 all the people of Israel bewailed him
12 52 they b. Jonathan and them that had been
13 26 all Israel b. him with great lamentation
Luke 23 27 women, who bewailed and lamented him
bewailing Mat 2 18 Rachel bewailing her children
beware Gen 24 6 b. thou never bring my son back
Exod 10 28 beware thou see not my face any more
34 12 beware thou never join in friendship
Lev 18 28 beware then lest . . . it vomit you also
22 2 b. of those things that are consecrated
Deut 4 23 b. lest thou ever forget the covenant
8 11 b. lest at any time thou forget the
11 16 b. lest perhaps your heart be deceived
12 13 beware lest thou offer thy holocausts

23 beware of this, that thou eat not the
30 beware lest thou imitate them after they
14 27 beware thou forsake him [Levite] not
15 9 beware lest perhaps a wicked thought
18 9 b. lest thou have a mind to imitate
Josu 6 18 beware ye lest you touch ought of those
Judg 13 4 beware and drink no wine nor strong
Ruth 3 14 beware lest any man know that thou
1 K 18 15 prudent, and began to beware of him
4 K 6 9 b. that thou pass not to such a place
Job 36 21 beware thou turn not aside to iniquity
Ecce 7 15 and beware beforehand of the evil day
Eccu 9 21 beware of thy neighbor and treat with
12 11 take good heed and beware of him. Set
13 10 beware that thou be not deceived into
17 11 said to them: Beware of all iniquity
18 27 in the days of sin will b. of sloth
22 32 shall hear it, will beware of him. Who
32 26 beware of thy own children, and take
37 9 beware of a counsellor. And know before
Bar 6 4 beware therefore that you imitate not
Mat 7 15 beware of false prophets who come to
10 17 b. of men. For they will deliver you
16 6 beware of the leaven of the Pharisees.
11; Mark 8:15; Luke 12:1
12 not that they should b. of the leaven
Mark 12 38 beware of the scribes. Luke 20:46
Luke 12 15 beware of all covetousness; for a man's
Acts 13 40 beware lest that come upon you which
Phil 3 2 b. of dogs, b. of evil workers, b. of the
concision
Col 2 8 lest any man cheat you by philosophy
bewitched Acts 8 11 he [Simon] had bewitched them
Gal 3 1 senseless Galatians, who hath b. you
bewitching Wisd 4 12 the b. of vanity obscureth
beyond 2 C 10 13 not glory beyond your measure
2 C 10 14 stretch not yourselves b. our measure
15 not glorying beyond measure in other
16 unto those places that are beyond you
Gal 1 13 beyond measure I persecuted the church
Bezec Judg 1 4 they slew of them in B. 10,000 men
Judg 1 5 they found Adonibezec in B. and fought
1 K 11 8 he [Saul] numbered them in Bezec: and
Bezeleel 1 Pa 2 20 Uri begot Bezeleel. Afterwards
bid Gen 45 21 sons of Israel did as they were bid
Ruth 3 6 all that her mother-in-law had bid her
2 K 2 26 to bid the people cease from pursuing
16 10 for the Lord hath bid him curse David
4 K 4 15 [Eliseus] bid him call her: and when
24 and do that which I bid thee. So she
5 13 if the prophet had bid thee do some
Tob 6 7 which thou hast bid me keep of the
Jon 3 2 in it the preaching that I bid thee
Mat 14 28 bid me come to thee upon the waters
Luke 8 55 he bid them give her to eat. And her
Acts 21 6 had bid one another farewell, we took
bidden 2 K 16 11 may curse as the Lord hath b. him
bidding 1 K 22 14 and goeth forth at thy bidding
2 C 2 13 but bidding them farewell, I went into
bier 2 K 3 31 king David himself followed the bier
Luke 7 14 came near and touched the bier. And they
big Gen 38 24 she appeareth to have a big belly
1 K 4 19 wife of Phinees was big with child
bigness Exod 9 24 hail . . . of so great bigness as
bill Deut 24 1 he shall write a bill of divorce
Deut 24 3 and hath given her a bill of divorce
Isa 50 1 this bill of the divorce of your mother
Jer 3 8 away and given her a bill of divorce
Mat 5 31 a bill of divorce. 19:7; Mark 10:4
Luke 16 6 he said to him: Take thy bill. 7
billows Ps 41 8 thy b. have passed over me. Jon 2:4
bind Num 30 3 the Lord or bind himself by an oath
Num 30 4 vow anything and bind herself by an oath
7 shall bind her soul by an oath: the day
14 if she vow and bind herself by oath
Deut 6 8 shalt bind them as a sign on thy hand
Judg 15 10 we are come to bind Samson and to pay
12 we are come to bind you and to deliver
16 5 to bind and afflict him [Samson]: which
2 Pa 6 22 bind himself with a curse before the
Job 39 10 canst thou bind the rhinoceros with thy
149 8 to bind their kings with fetters and
Prov 6 21 bind them in thy heart continually and
7 3 bind it upon thy fingers, write it upon
Eccu 7 8 nor bind sin to sin: for even in one
30 7 he shall b. up his wounds and at every
Isa 8 16 bind up the testimony, seal the law
30 26 Lord shall bind up the wound of his
Jer 30 13 to judge thy judgment to bind it up
Eze 3 25 and they shall bind thee with them
5 3 shalt b. them in the skirt of thy cloak
34 16 I will bind up that which was broken
Dan 3 20 to bind the feet of Sidrach, Misach and
Mat 12 29 first bind the strong. Mark 3:27
13 30 and bind it into bundles to burn, but the
16 19 whatsoever thou shalt bind upon earth
18 18 whatsoever you shall bind upon earth
22 13 king said to waiters: Bind his hands
23 4 they b. heavy and insupportable burdens
Mark 5 3 no man could bind him not even with
Acts 9 14 priests to bind all that invoke thy name
21 11 the Jews shall bind in this manner in
bindeth Lev 5 4 bindeth the same with an oath and
Job 26 8 he bindeth up the waters in his clouds
Ps 146 3 of heart, and bindeth up their bruises
Prov 13 13 bindeth himself for the time to come
binding Gen 37 7 I thought we were b. sheaves in
Gen 42 25 taking Simeon and binding him in their
Lev 8 8 binding it with the girdle, he fitted
Num 19 15 vessel that hath no cover nor binding
21 2 Israel binding himself by vow to the
Eccu 6 31 her bands are a healthful binding. Thou
Mark 15 1 council binding Jesus, led him away
Acts 21 11 binding his own feet and hands, he said
22 4 binding and delivering into prisons
bird Lev 17 13 if he take a wild beast or a bird
Job 5 7 is born to labor and the bird to fly
28 7 bird hath not known the path, neither
40 24 shalt thou play with him as with a bird
Prov 6 5 as a bird from the hand of the fowler
7 23 as if bird should make haste to snare
26 2 as a bird flying to other places and a
27 8 as bird that wandereth from her nest
Ecce 12 4 shall rise up at the voice of the bird
Wisd 5 11 as when a bird flieth through the air
Eccu 27 21 that letteth a bird go out of his hand
Isa 14 29 his seed shall swallow the bird. And the
16 2 as a bird fleeing away and as young ones
46 11 who call a bird from the east and from
Jer 12 9 is my inheritance to me as a speckled
bird? Is it as a bird dyed throughout
Lam 3 52 and caught me like a bird without cause
Bar 6 70 garden upon which every bird sitteth
Osee 9 11 flown away like a bird from the birth
11 11 shall fly away like a bird out of Egypt
Amos 3 5 will the bird fall into the snare upon
Soph 2 14 voice of the singing bird in the window
Luke 13 34 as bird doth her brood under her wings
Apoc 18 2 hold of every unclean and hateful bird
bird's Deut 22 6 if thou find . . . a bird's nest in
birds Gen 1 22 let the birds be multiplied upon
Gen 7 14 according to its kind, all birds and all
9 10 that is with you as well in all birds
15 10 the other; but the birds he divided not
40 17 baking, and that the birds ate out of
19 and the birds shall tear thy flesh

Lev 1 14 a holocaust to the Lord be of birds
7 26 whatsoever, whether of birds or beasts
11 13 of birds . . . they which you must not eat
20 25 defile not your souls with beasts or b.
Deut 4 17 earth or of birds that fly under heaven
14 11 all birds that are clean you shall eat
32 24 and birds shall devour them with a most
2 K 21 10 suffered neither the birds to tear them
Prov 10 4 runneth after birds that fly away. He
Ecce 9 12 as birds are caught with the snare, so
Wisd 17 17 or the melodious voice of birds among
19 11 they saw a new generation of birds when
Eccu 22 25 he that flingeth a stone at birds shall
27 10 birds resort unto their like: so truth
43 15 opened, and the clouds fly out like birds
19 as the birds lighting upon the earth
Isa 18 6 shall be left together to the birds
31 5 as birds flying, so will the Lord of
Jer 5 27 as a net is full of b., so their houses
12 4 the beasts and the birds are consumed
Bar 6 21 and other birds fly upon their bodies
Eze 17 23 and all birds shall dwell under it
39 4 given thee to the wild beasts, to the b.
17 say to every fowl and to all the birds
Dan 4 11 under it, and the b. from its branches
2 Ma 9 15 to be devoured by the birds and wild
15 33 be cut out and given by pieces to birds
Rom 1 23 image of a corruptible man and of birds
1 C 15 39 is the flesh of men . . . another of b.
James 3 7 every nature of beasts and of birds
Apoc 19 17 a loud voice, saying to all the birds
21 all the birds were filled with their
birds of the air 1 K 17 44 I will give thy flesh to the birds of the air
1 K 17 46 the Philistines this day to the b. . . .
3 K 14 11 in the field, the b. . . . shall devour
21 24 in the field, the b. . . . shall eat him
Job 12 7 and the b. . . . and they shall tell thee
Ps 8 9 the b. . . . and the fishes of the sea that
Ecce 10 20 even the b. . . . will carry thy voice and
Jer 4 25 and all the birds of the air were gone
Mat 6 26 behold the birds of the air, for they
8 20 the birds of the air nests. Luke 9:58
13 4 b. . . . came and ate them up. Mark 4:4
32 the b. . . . come and dwell. Mark 4:32
Luke 13 19 the b. . . . lodged in the branches thereof
birth Gen 5 10 after whose birth he [Enos] lived
Gen 32 9 to thy land and to the place of thy b.
38 5 after whose birth, she ceased to bear
Exod 28 10 according to the order of their birth
3 K 1 6 the next in birth after Absalom. And he
4 K 19 3 the children are come to the b. Isa 37:3
Job 3 16 as a hidden untimely b. I should not
38 12 since thy birth command the morning
Ps 106 37 and they yielded fruit of birth. And he
Ecce 7 2 day of death than day of one's birth
Wisd 6 24 her out from the beginning of her birth
7 5 kings had any other beginning of birth
Osee 9 11 flown away like a bird from the birth
2 Ma 5 22 Philip, a Phrygian by birth, but in
14 42 abuses unbecoming his noble birth. But
John 9 1 man who was blind from his birth: and
Apoc 12 2 she cried travailing in birth and was in
birthday Gen 40 20 after this was the b. of Pharao
2 Ma 6 7 by bitter constraint on the king's b.
Mat 14 6 but on Herod's birthday the daughter of
Mark 6 21 Herod made a supper for his birthday
birthright Gen 25 31 sell me thy first birthright
Gen 25 32 what will the first birthright avail me
33 Esau swore to him and sold his first b.
34 account of having sold his first b.
27 36 my first birthright he took away before
1 Pa 5 1 birthright was given to sons of Joseph
2 first birthright was accounted to Joseph
Heb 12 16 who for one mess sold his first birthright
birthrights Deut 21 17 to him are due the first b.
bishop 1 Tim 3 1 desire the office of a bishop
1 Tim 3 2 it behoveth a bishop to be blameless
Titus 1 7 for a bishop must be without crime as the
1 P 2 25 to the shepherd and bishop of your souls
bishopric Ps 108 8 his b. let another take. Acts 1:20
bishops Acts 20 28 Holy Ghost hath placed you b.
Phil 1 1 at Philippi, with the b. and deacons
bit Num 21 6 fiery serpents, which bit them and
4 K 19 28 and a bit between thy lips, and I will
Ps 31 9 with bit and bridle bind fast their
Isa 37 29 I will put . . . a bit between thy lips
Eze 38 4 I will put a bit in thy jaws: and I will
bite Deut 32 24 devour them with a most bitter b.
Prov 23 32 in the end it will bite like a snake
Ecce 10 8 a hedge, a serpent shall bite him. He
11 if a serpent b. in silence he is nothing
Jer 8 17 and they shall bite you, saith the Lord
Osee 13 14 O hell, I will be thy bite: comfort is
Amos 5 19 the wall, and a serpent should bite
9 3 the serpent, and he shall bite them
Mich 3 5 that bite with their teeth and preach
Haba 2 7 up suddenly that shall bite thee: and
Gal 5 15 if you bite and devour one another
biteth Gen 49 17 that biteth the horse's heels
Bithynia Acts 16 7 attempted to go into Bithynia
1 P 1 1 dispersed through . . . Asia and Bithynia
biting Prov 16 30 b. his lips, bringeth evil to
bitings Wisd 16 5 were destroyed with the b. of
Wisd 16 9 b. of locusts and of flies killed them
bits James 3 3 if we put bits into the mouths of
bitten Num 21 9 they that were bitten looked upon
bitter Exod 1 14 made their life b. with hard works
Exod 15 23 waters of Mara, because they were bitter
Num 5 18 himself shall hold the most b. waters
19 these most bitter waters on which I
23 wash them out with the most b. waters
26 and so give the most bitter waters to
Deut 32 24 shall devour them with a most b. bite
32 of gall, and their clusters most bitter
Ruth 1 20 but call me Mara, that is, bitter, for
1 K 15 32 doth b. death separate in this manner
2 K 17 8 that they are . . . bitter in their mind
19 35 senses quick to discern sweet and bitter
4 K 14 26 of Israel that it was exceeding bitter
Jdth 5 15 there bitter fountains were made sweet
Job 13 26 thou writest bitter things against me
Ps 63 4 they have bent their bow a bitter thing
Prov 5 4 but her end is bitter as wormwood and
27 7 hungry shall take even bitter for sweet
Ecce 7 27 found a woman more bitter than death
Wisd 14 15 father being afflicted with b. grief
Eccu 29 31 moreover he shall hear bitter words
30 17 better is death than a bitter life
38 5 was not b. water made sweet with wood
41 1 death, how bitter is the remembrance of
Isa 5 20 put b. for sweet, and sweet for bitter
24 9 drink shall be bitter to them that
38 17 in peace is my bitterness most bitter
Jer 2 19 it is an evil and a bitter thing for
4 18 thy wickedness, because it is bitter
6 26 only son, a bitter lamentation, because
Eze 27 31 of soul, with most bitter weeping. And
Amos 8 10 latter end thereof as a bitter day
Haba 1 6 Chaldeans, a bitter and swift nation
Soph 1 14 voice of the day of the Lord is bitter
2 Ma 6 7 they were led by bitter constraint
9 5 bitter torments of the inner parts
Col 3 19 love your wives and be not b. towards
James 3 11 the same hole sweet and bitter water
14 if you have bitter zeal and there be

Apoc 8 11 waters, because they were made bitter
10 9 it shall make thy belly bitter, but in
10 I had eaten it, my belly was bitter
bitterly 1 K 30 6 of every man was bitterly grieved
Eccu 18 18 a fool will upbraid bitterly: and a gift
38 17 weep b. for a day, and then comfort
Isa 21 4 depart from me. I will weep bitterly
33 7 angels of peace shall weep bitterly
Eze 27 30 loud voice, and shall cry bitterly: and
30 24 they shall groan bitterly being slain
Mat 26 75 he wept bitterly. Luke 22:62
bittern Lev 11 18 you must not eat . . . the bittern
Deut 14 18 the bittern and the charadrion, every
Isa 34 11 the b. and ericius shall possess it
Soph 2 14 the bittern and the urchin shall lodge
bitterness Exod 15 23 calling it Mara, that is, b.
Deut 29 18 a root bring forth gall and bitterness
Ruth 1 20 Almighty hath quite filled me with b.
4 K 4 41 there was now no bitterness in the pot
Job 3 5 and let it be wrapped up in bitterness
20 to them that are in bitterness of soul
7 11 I will talk with the b. of my soul
9 18 rest, and he filleth me with bitterness
10 1 I will speak in the b. of my soul. I
17 2 sinned and my eye abideth in bitterness
20 25 and glittereth in his bitterness: the
21 25 another dieth in bitterness of soul
23 2 now also my words are in bitterness
27 2 who hath brought my soul to bitterness
Ps 9 7 his mouth is full of cursing and of b.
13 3 their mouth is full of cursing and b.
Prov 14 10 that knoweth the b. of his own soul
Wisd 8 16 her conversation hath no bitterness
Eccu 4 6 curseth thee in bitterness of his soul
7 12 laugh no man to scorn in the b. of his
21 15 is no understanding where there is b.
31 39 with excess is bitterness of the soul
Isa 38 15 thee all my years in the b. of my soul
17 in peace is my bitterness most bitter
Jer 31 21 a watchtower, make to thee bitterness
Lam 1 4 and she is oppressed with bitterness
20 within me, for I am full of bitterness
3 15 he hath filled me with bitterness, he
Eze 3 14 and I went away in bitterness in the
21 6 with bitterness sigh before them. And
27 31 shall weep for thee with b. of soul
28 24 no more a stumblingblock of bitterness
Osee 10 4 judgment shall spring up as bitterness
12 14 hath provoked me to wrath with his b.
14 1 she hath stirred up her God to b.: let
Amos 6 13 you have turned judgment into b. and
Mich 1 12 unto good that dwelleth in bitterness
Acts 8 23 thou art in the gall of bitterness
Rom 3 14 whose mouth is full of cursing and b.
Eph 12 15 lest any root of b. springing up do
black Gen 30 35 that is, of white and black fleece
Gen 30 40 the white and the black were Laban's
Lev 13 31 flesh that is near it and the hair b.
37 if . . . the hair be black, let him know
Job 30 30 my skin is become black upon me and my
Cant 1 4 I am b. but beautiful, O ye daughters
5 11 branches of palm trees, black as a raven
Bar 6 20 their faces are black with the smoke
Zach 6 2 in the second chariot black horses
6 that in which were the black horses
Mat 5 36 canst not make one hair white or black
Apoc 6 5 and behold a black horse and he that
12 the sun became black as sackcloth
blacker Lam 4 8 their face is now made blacker than
blackness Nah 2 10 the faces . . . are as the b. of
blade Judg 3 22 the haft went in after the blade
Judg 6 4 wasted all things as they were in the b.
Mat 13 26 when the blade was sprung up and had
Mark 4 28 first the b., then the ear, afterwards
blains Exod 9 9 swelling blains both in man and
Exod 9 10 there came boils with swelling blains
blame Ps 30 14 I have heard the blame of many
Wisd 10 5 preserved him without blame to God
Eccu 8 10 to serve great men without blame. Let
11 7 before thou inquire, blame no man: and
Mat 12 5 break the sabbath and are without blame
Luke 1 6 both just before God . . . without blame
2 C 8 20 should blame us in this abundance which
Phil 3 6 is in the law, conversing without blame
1 Th 2 10 how . . . without b. we have been to you
3 13 confirm your hearts without blame, in
blamed Tob 2 8 his neighbors blamed him, saying
Wisd 13 6 they are less to be blamed. For they
2 Ma 2 7 Jeremias perceived it, he blamed them
2 C 6 3 that our ministry be not blamed: but
Gal 2 11 because he [Cephas] was to be blamed
Titus 2 8 the sound word that cannot be blamed
blameless Gen 44 10 and you shall be blameless
Num 5 31 the husband shall be blameless and she
32 22 then shall you be b. before the Lord
Josu 2 17 we shall be blameless of this oath
Judg 15 3 I shall be b. in what I do against
Ps 17 33 me with strength: and made my way b.
Wisd 10 15 delivered the just people and b. seed
18 21 a b. man made haste to pray for the
Eccu 40 19 a blameless wife shall be counted above
Phil 2 15 that you may be blameless and sincere
Col 1 22 present you holy and unspotted and b.
1 Th 5 23 preserved b. in the coming of our Lord
1 Tim 3 2 it behoveth a bishop to be blameless
5 7 in charge that they may be blameless
6 14 blameless, unto the coming of our Lord
2 P 3 14 found before him unspotted and b. in
blanket 4 K 8 15 on the next day he took a blanket
blaspheme 2 K 12 14 occasion to enemies . . . to b.
Tob 13 16 shall be condemned that shall b. thee
Isa 37 4 sent to blaspheme the living God. 17
Jer 23 17 they say to them that blaspheme me
Mark 3 28 wherewith they shall blaspheme: and
1 Tim 1 20 that they may learn not to blaspheme
James 2 7 do not they b. the good name that is
Jude 8 and despise dominion and b. majesty
10 b. whatever things they know not: and
Apoc 13 6 not b. his name and his tabernacle and
blasphemed Lev 24 11 when he had b. the name and
Lev 24 23 and they brought forth him that had b.
Num 16 30 you shall know that they have b. the
3 K 21 10 that he hath b. God and the king: and
13 Naboth hath blasphemed God and the king
4 K 19 6 of the Assyrians have b. me. Isa 37:6
22 whom hast thou blasphemed. Isa 37:23
Isa 1 4 they have b. the Holy One of Israel
5 24 have b. the word of the Holy One of
48 11 will I do it, that I may not be b.: and
52 5 my name is continually b. all the day
Eze 20 27 in this also your fathers blasphemed me
Dan 14 8 because he hath blasphemed against Bel
Soph 2 10 because they have b. and have been
1 Ma 7 41 were sent by king Sennacherib b. thee
2 Ma 10 34 blasphemed exceedingly, and cast forth
Mat 26 65 he hath blasphemed; what further need
27 39 that passed by, b. him. Mark 15:29
Luke 23 39 robbers who were hanged, b. him saying
Rom 2 24 God through you is b. among the Gentiles
1 C 4 13 we are blasphemed and we entreat; we are
1 Tim 6 1 name of the Lord and his doctrine be b.
Titus 2 5 that the word of God be not blasphemed
Apoc 2 9 thou art b. by them that say they are
16 9 they blasphemed the name of God who
11 and they blasphemed the God of heaven
21 men b. God for the plague of the hail

blasphemer Lev 24 14 bring forth the blasphemer
2 Ma 9 28 murderer and b. being grievously struck
1 Tim 1 13 was a blasphemer and a persecutor and
blasphemers Job 15 5 imitatest the tongue of b.
2 Ma 10 36 and to burn the blasphemers alive. And
2 Tim 3 2 covetous, haughty, proud, blasphemers
blasphemest John 10 36 thou b. because I said
blasphemeth Lev 24 16 he that b. the name of the
Mat 9 3 scribes said within themselves: He b.
Mark 2 7 he b. Who can forgive sins but God only
blasphemies 2 Es 9 18 and had committed great b.
2 Es 9 26 they were guilty of great blasphemies
Isa 51 7 be not afraid of their blasphemies
Soph 2 8 and the b. of the children of Ammon
1 Ma 7 38 remember their blasphemies and suffer
2 Ma 8 4 the blasphemies offered to his name
Mat 15 19 thefts, false testimonies, blasphemies
Mark 3 28 and the b. wherewith they shall blaspheme
Luke 5 21 who is this who speaketh blasphemies
1 Tim 6 4 from which arise envies . . . blasphemies
Apoc 13 5 a mouth speaking great things and b.
6 he opened his mouth unto b. against God
blaspheming 2 Ma 12 14 Judas with railing and b.
Luke 22 65 b., many other things they said against
Acts 13 45 contradicted those things . . . b. Then
18 6 they gainsaying and b., he shook his
2 P 2 10 they fear not to bring in sects, b.
12 b. those things which they know not
blasphemous 2 Ma 10 4 delivered up to . . . b. men
2 Ma 13 11 again in subjection to b. nations. So
blasphemy 4 K 19 3 is a day of tribulation and of rebuke and blasphemy. Isa 37:3
2 Pa 32 17 wrote also letters full of blasphemy
20 prayed against this blasphemy and cried
Tob 1 21 God had made about him for his b. and
Job 34 37 he addeth blasphemy upon his sins, let
Dan 3 96 which shall speak b. against the God of
2 Ma 10 35 inflamed in their minds because of the b.
15 24 come with b. against thy holy people
Mat 12 31 sin and blasphemy shall be forgiven
31 b. of the Spirit shall not be forgiven
26 65 you have heard the blasphemy. Mark 14:64
Mark 7 22 evil eye, blasphemy, pride, foolishness
John 10 33 we stone thee not, but for blasphemy
Acts 6 11 had heard him speak words of blasphemy
19 37 neither guilty of sacrilege nor of b.
Eph 4 31 and b. be put away from you, with all
Col 3 8 now put you also all away . . . blasphemy
Apoc 13 1 and upon his heads names of blasphemy
blast Exod 15 8 with the blast of thy anger the
Deut 28 42 blast shall consume all the trees and
2 K 22 16 at the blast of the spirit of his wrath
Job 4 9 them, perishing by the blast of God
Ps 17 16 at the blast of the spirit of thy wrath
77 46 he gave up their fruits to the blast
Wisd 11 21 might have been slain with one blast
Isa 25 4 blast of the mighty is like a whirlwind
blasted Gen 41 6 ears sprung up thin and blasted
Gen 41 23 other seven also thin and b., sprung
27 the seven thin ears that were blasted
Job 15 33 he shall be blasted as a vine when its
blasting Deut 28 22 with corrupted air and with b.
3 K 8 37 corrupt air or blasting or locust or
2 Pa 6 28 a pestilence or blasting or mildew or
Agge 2 18 I struck you with a blasting wind and
Blastus Acts 12 20 having gained Blastus who was
blaze Mark 1 45 publish and to b. abroad the word
blear-eyed Gen 29 17 Lia was blear-eyed: Rachel
Lev 21 20 if he be crookbacked or blear-eyed
bleating 1 K 15 14 what meaneth then this bleating
Tob 2 21 and when her husband heard it bleating
beatings Judg 5 16 that thou mayest hear the b.
bleed Eccu 42 5 side of a wicked slave to bleed

blemish Lev 13 26 nor the b. lower than the other
Lev 13 32 place of the b. be even with the other
39 not the leprosy, but a white blemish
21 17 throughout their families, hath a b.
21 seed of Aaron the priest hath a blemish
23 because he hath a blemish and he must
22 20 if it have a b. you shall not offer
21 there shall be no blemish in it. If it
24 19 giveth a blemish to any of his neighbors
20 what blemish he gave, the like shall be
Num 19 2 red cow . . . in which there is no b.
Deut 12 15 having blemish or defect: or clean, that
15 21 if it have a blemish or be lame or blind
17 1 ox wherein there is b. or any fault: or
2 K 14 25 there was no blemish in him [Absalom]
Dan 1 4 children in whom there was no blemish
without blemish Exod 12 5 a lamb without blemish. Lev 9:3; 23:12
Exod 29 1 herd, and two rams without blemish
Lev 1 3 a male without blemish. 10; 22:19
3 1 he shall offer them without blemish
6 female, they shall be without blemish
4 3 for his sin a calf without blemish
23 shall offer a buck goat without blemish
28 he shall offer a she goat without b.
32 for his sin, to wit, an ewe without b.
5 15 a ram without b. 18; 6:6; 9:2
14 10 he shall take two lambs without blemish
10 and an ewe of a year old without blemish
22 21 shall offer it without blemish that it
23 18 seven lambs without blemish of first
Num 6 14 he lamb of a year old without blemish
14 ewe lamb of a year old without blemish
14 one ram without blemish for a victim
28 3 lambs of a year old without b. 9; 29:2, 8, 11, 13, 17, 19, 20, 23, 26, 27, 29, 32, 36
31 you shall offer them all without blemish
Deut 12 15 or clean . . . sound and without blemish
Ps 14 2 he that walketh without b. and worketh
Eccu 31 8 rich man that is found without blemish
46 19 when he offered a lamb without blemish
Eze 43 22 shalt offer a he goat without blemish
23 calf of the herd without b. 45:18; 46:6
23 ram of the flock without blemish. 25
45 23 he shall offer . . . 7 rams without b.
46 4 shall be six lambs without blemish and
6 and the lambs shall be without blemish
13 a lamb of the same year without blemish
1 Ma 4 42 he chose priests without blemish whose
Eph 5 27 should be holy and without blemish
bless Gen 12 2 I will bless them that bless thee and
Gen 17 16 I will bless her [Sara] and of her I
16 thee a son, whom I will bless and he
20 I will bless him [Ismael] and increase
22 17 I will bless thee [Abraham] and I will
26 3 I will bless thee [Isaac]. 24
27 4 my soul may bless thee. 25
7 that I may eat and bless thee in sight
10 he may bless thee before he die. And he
19 that thy soul may bless me. 31
34 bless me, also, my father. And he said
38 I beseech thee bless me also. And when
32 26 not let thee go except thou bless me
48 9 bring them to me that I may bless them
16 bless these boys: and let my name
49 25 the Almighty shall bless thee with the
Exod 12 32 and departing, bless me [Pharao]. And
20 24 I will come to thee and will bless thee
23 25 that I may bless your bread and your
Num 6 23 thus shall you bless the children of
24 the Lord bless thee and keep thee. The
27 children of Israel and I will bless them
22 6 he whom thou shalt bless is blessed

23 20 fulfil? I [Balaam] was brought to bless
25 Balaam: Neither curse nor bless him
24 1 that he [Balaam] should bless Israel
Deut 1 11 and bless you as he hath spoken. I
7 13 and will bless the fruit of thy womb
8 10 thou mayst bless the Lord thy God for
10 8 to bless in his name until this present
14 29 that the Lord thy God may bless thee. 15:4, 10, 18; 23:20; 24:19
15 5 he will b. thee as he hath promised
14 wherewith the Lord . . . shall bless thee
16 15 the Lord thy God will bless thee in all
21 5 minister to him and to bless in his name
24 13 in his own raiment and bless thee and
26 15 and bless thy people Israel and the land
27 12 upon mount Garizim to bless the people
28 8 bless thee in the land. 30:16
12 he will bless all the works of thy hands
29 19 he should bless himself in his heart
33 11 bless, O Lord, his strength and receive
Judg 5 2 bless the Lord. 9; 2 Es 9:5; Ps 102:1, 20, 21, 22; 134:19, 20; Dan 3:57 (and so to verse 88)
Ruth 2 4 him: the Lord bless thee [Booz]. And
2 K 6 20 David returned to bless his own house
7 29 begin and bless the inheritance of the
1 Pa 4 10 if blessing thou wilt bless me [Jabes]
16 43 and David to bless also his own house
17 27 thou hast begun to bless the house of
23 13 and to bless his name forever. The
29 20 bless ye the Lord. Tob 13:10; Ps 133:1, 2
Tob 4 20 bless God at all times: and desire of
8 7 creatures that are in them, bless thee
17 we bless thee, O Lord God of Israel
19 make them, O Lord, bless thee more fully
9 9 the God of Israel bless thee, because
11 17 I bless thee, O Lord God of Israel
12 6 bless ye the God of heaven, give glory
18 bless ye him, and sing praises to him
20 bless ye God. Ps 67:27
13 12 and bless the God eternal, that he may
19 bless thou the Lord. Ps 102:22; 103:35
14 11 that they be mindful of God and b. him
Jdth 7 16 we should live and bless the Lord
Job 2 5 that he will bless thee to thy face
9 in thy simplicity? Bless God and die
Ps 5 13 for thou wilt bless the just. O Lord
15 7 I will bless the Lord, who hath given
25 12 way, in the churches I will bless thee
27 9 thy people, and bless thy inheritance
28 10 the Lord will bless his people with
33 2 I will bless the Lord at all times, his
36 22 such as bless him shall inherit the
62 5 thus will I bless thee all my life long
64 12 thou shalt bless the crown of the year
65 8 bless our God, ye Gentiles: and make
66 2 may God have mercy on us and bless us
7 may God, our God b. us, may God b. us
71 15 adore: they shall bless him all the day
95 2 sing ye to the Lord and bless his name
102 1 that is within me bless his holy name
108 28 they will curse and thou wilt bless
113 18 but we that live bless the Lord: from
127 5 may the Lord bless thee out of Sion
131 15 blessing I will bless her widow: I will
133 3 may the Lord out of Sion bless thee
144 1 I will bless thy name forever: yea
2 every day will I bless thee. They shall
21 and let all flesh bless his holy name
Prov 30 11 father and doth not bless their mother
Wisd 16 28 to prevent the sun to bless thee and
Eccu 31 28 the lips of many shall bless him that
32 17 for all these things bless the Lord
39 19 bless the Lord in his works. Magnify
41 bless the name of the Lord. 51:17
43 12 and bless him that made it: it is very
Isa 66 3 incense, as if he should b. an idol
Jer 4 2 and the Gentiles shall bless him and
31 23 the Lord bless thee, the beauty of
Bar 6 65 can they curse kings nor bless them
Dan 3 74 let the earth b. the Lord: let it praise
Agge 2 20 from this day I will bless you. And the
Luke 6 26 woe to you when men shall bless you
28 bless them that curse you and pray for
Acts 3 26 hath sent him to bless you; that every
Rom 12 14 bless them that persecute you: bless
14 bless, and curse not. Rejoice with them
1 C 4 12 we are reviled and we bless; we are
10 16 chalice of benediction which we bless
14 16 if thou shalt bless with the spirit
Heb 6 14 unless blessing I shall bless thee
James 3 9 by it we bless God and the Father: and

blessed Gen 1 22 b. them, saying: Increase. 28
Gen 2 3 blessed the seventh day. Exod 20:11
5 2 male and female; and blessed them: and
9 1 God blessed Noe and his sons. And he
14 19 Melchisedech . . . blessed him and said
24 1 the Lord had blessed him in all things
31 come in, thou blessed of the Lord: why
35 the Lord hath b. my master wonderfully
25 11 God blessed Isaac his son, who dwelt
26 12 the Lord blessed him [Isaac]. And the
27 27 field, which the Lord hath blessed, he
33 I have b. him, and he shall be blessed
41 blessing wherewith his father had b. him
28 1 Isaac called Jacob and blessed him and
6 seeing that his father had b. Jacob
30 13 for women will call me [Lia] blessed
27 that God hath blessed me for thy sake
30 Lord hath blessed thee at my coming
31 55 blessed them: and returned to his place
32 29 he blessed him [Jacob]. 35:9
39 5 Lord blessed the house of the Egyptian
47 7 he [Jacob] blessed him [Pharao]. And
48 3 he bessed me [Jacob] and he said: I
15 Jacob blessed the sons of Joseph and
20 he blessed them at that time, saying
49 28 he blessed every one with their proper
Exod 39 43 saw all things finished he blessed them
Lev 9 22 hands to the people, he blessed them
23 came forth and blessed the people. And
Num 22 6 he whom thou shalt bless is blessed
12 thou curse the people: because it is b.
24 10 thou on the contrary hast blessed them
Deut 2 7 hath blessed thee in every work of thy
7 14 blessed shalt thou be among all people
12 7 wherein the Lord . . . hath blessed you
14 24 he hath blessed thee and thou canst not
28 3 b. shalt thou be in the city, and b. in
4 blessed shall be the fruit of thy womb
5 b. shall be thy barns and b. thy stores
6 b. shalt thou be coming in and going
35 1 Moses blessed the children of Israel
Josu 8 33 first he blessed the people of Israel
14 13 Josue blessed him and gave him Hebron
17 14 the Lord hath blessed me. And Josue
22 6 Josue blessed them and sent them away
7 when he [Josue] . . . had blessed them
24 10 on the contrary I blessed you by him
Judg 13 24 the child grew and the Lord blessed him
1 K 2 20 Heli blessed Elcana and his wife: and
2 K 6 11 the Lord blessed Obededom and all his
12 that the Lord had blessed Obededom and
18 he b. the people in the name of the
13 25 and he would not go, he blessed him
14 22 his face adored, and blessed the king

19 39 king blessed Berzellai and blessed him
22 47 the Lord liveth, and my God is blessed
3 K 1 47 have blessed our Lord king David saying
8 14 and b. all the assembly of Israel. 55
66 they b. the king, and went to their
4 K 10 15 he [Jehu] blessed him [Jonadab]. And he
1 Pa 13 14 Lord b. his house and all that he had
16 2 b. the people in the name of the Lord
26 5 for the Lord had blessed him [Obededom]
29 10 and he blessed the Lord before all the
20 and all the assembly blessed the Lord
2 Pa 6 3 king turned his face and blessed all
20 26 of Blessing: for there they b. the Lord
30 27 the Levites rose up and b. the people
31 8 they blessed the Lord and the people
10 because the Lord hath b. his people
2 Es 8 6 Esdras blessed the Lord the great God
11 2 the people blessed all the men that
Tob 8 16 and Raguel and Anna . . . b. the Lord
9 8 and Gabelus wept and blessed God, and
12 22 for three hours upon their face, b. God
13 1 opening his mouth blessed the Lord
16 b. shall they be that shall build thee
Jdth 13 22 the Lord hath blessed thee by his power
15 10 they all blessed her with one voice
Job 1 5 lest perhaps my sons . . . have b. God
10 blessed the works of his hands and his
29 11 the ear that heard me blessed me and the
31 20 if his sides have not blessed me and if
42 12 Lord blessed the latter end of Job more
Ps 9 3 his soul: and the unjust man is blessed
40 3 and make him blessed upon the earth
44 3 therefore hath God blessed thee forever
61 5 they blessed with their mouth, but
84 2 Lord, thou hast blessed thy land: thou
106 38 he b. them, and they were multiplied
113 12 been mindful of us and hath blessed us
12 he hath blessed the house of Aaron. He
13 he hath blessed all that fear the Lord
117 26 we have blessed you out of the house
128 8 we have b. you in the name of the Lord
136 8 blessed shall he be who shall repay thee
147 13 he hath b. thy children within thee
Prov 3 18 he that shall retain her is blessed
16 20 he that trusteth in the Lord is blessed
20 7 shall leave behind his blessed children
29 18 but he that keepeth the law is blessed
31 28 her children rose up and called her b.
Cant 6 8 saw her and declared her most blessed
Eccu 33 12 them hath he blessed and exalted: and
34 17 of him that feareth the Lord is b. To
45 8 made him [Aaron] blessed in glory, and
46 14 that their memory might be blessed
Isa 3 12 they that call thee blessed, the same
9 16 they that call this people blessed
19 25 which the Lord of hosts hath blessed
51 2 I called him alone and blessed him
61 9 the seed which the Lord hath blessed
65 16 he that is b. upon the earth, shall be blessed in God
23 are the seed of the blessed of the Lord
Dan 2 19 Daniel blessed the God of heaven, and
3 51 praised and glorified and blessed God
4 31 I blessed the most High and I praised
13 60 they blessed God, who saveth them that
Mala 3 12 all nations shall call you blessed
1 Ma 2 69 [Mathathias] b. them and was joined
3 7 and his memory is blessed forever. And
4 24 home they sung a hymn and blessed God
55 and blessed up to heaven him that had
2 Ma 10 38 done, they blessed the Lord with hymns
11 9 all together blessed the merciful Lord
12 41 blessed the just judgment of the Lord
15 29 they blessed the Almighty Lord in their
34 all blessed the Lord of heaven, saying
Mat 14 19 he b. and brake and gave the loaves
25 34 come, ye blessed of my Father, possess
26 26 blessed and broke . . . This is my body
Mark 6 41 he blessed and broke the loaves and
8 7 little fishes: and he blessed them
10 16 laying hands upon them, he blessed them
14 61 the Christ the Son of the Blessed God
Luke 1 48 all generations shall call me blessed
2 28 [Simeon] blessed God and said: Now thou
34 Simeon blessed them and said to Mary
6 22 b. shall you be when men shall hate
9 16 heaven and b. them; and he broke and
24 30 took bread and blessed and brake and
50 lifting up his hands, he blessed them
51 whilst he blessed them, he departed
Acts 20 35 it is a more blessed thing to give
Rom 1 25 the Creator who is blessed forever
9 5 is over all things, God blessed forever
1 C 7 40 more b. shall she be if she so remain
2 C 11 31 Jesus Christ, who is blessed forever
Eph 1 3 who hath b. us with spiritual blessings
Heb 7 1 slaughter of the kings and blessed him
6 he blessed him that had the promises
7 that which is less is b. by the better
11 20 by faith . . . Isaac b. Jacob and Esau
21 Jacob dying blessed each of the sons
1 Tim 1 11 gospel of glory of the blessed God
6 15 who is the Blessed and only Mighty
Titus 2 13 looking for the b. hope and coming of
James 5 11 we account them b. who have endured

be blessed Gen 12 2 and thou shalt be blessed
Gen 12 3 all the kindred of the earth be blessed
18 18 the nations of the earth shall be b.
22 18 the nations of the earth be b. 26:4
28 14 tribes of the earth shall be blessed
48 20 in thee shall Israel be blessed and it
Num 24 9 blesseth thee, shall also himself be b.
Deut 33 24 let Aser be blessed with children, let
2 K 7 29 house of thy servant be b. forever
3 K 2 45 and king Solomon shall be blessed and
1 Pa 17 27 O Lord, it shall be blessed forever
Tob 3 23 be thy name, O God . . . blessed forever
8 9 in which thy name may be blessed forever
13 17 children, because they shall all be b.
Jdth 15 11 therefore thou shalt be blessed forever
Ps 48 19 in his lifetime his soul will be blessed
71 17 let his name be blessed forevermore
17 shall all the tribes of the earth be b.
111 2 generation of the righteous shall be b.
127 4 thus shall the man be b. that feareth
Prov 3 33 habitations of the just shall be blessed
5 18 let thy vein be blessed, and rejoice
14 21 showeth mercy to the poor, shall be b.
22 9 that is inclined to mercy shall be b.
Eccu 1 13 in the day of his death he shall be b.
19 in days of his end he shall be blessed
24 4 among the blessed she shall be blessed
34 14 and by his regard shall be blessed. For
Jer 20 14 which my mother bore me, be blessed
Luke 14 14 thou shalt be blessed because they have
John 13 17 you shall be blessed if you do them
Acts 3 25 shall all kindreds of the earth be b.
Gal 3 8 in thee shall all nations be blessed
9 shall be blessed with faithful Abraham
James 1 25 this man shall be blessed in his deed
1 P 4 14 if you be reproached . . . you shall be b.

blessed are 3 K 10 8 blessed are thy men and blessed are thy servants
Tob 13 18 blessed are all they that love thee
Ps 2 13 blessed are all they that trust in him
31 1 blessed are they whose iniquities are

83 5 b. are they that dwell in thy house
105 3 blessed are they that keep judgment
118 1 blessed are the undefiled in the way
2 b. are they that search his testimonies
127 1 blessed are all they that fear the Lord
Prov 8 32 blessed are they that keep my ways. Hear
Eccu 48 11 blessed are they that saw thee and were
Isa 30 18 blessed are all they that wait for him
32 20 blessed are ye that sow upon all waters
Mat 5 3 blessed are the poor in spirit: for
4 blessed are the meek: for they shall
5 blessed are they that mourn: for they
6 blessed are they that hunger and thirst
7 blessed are the merciful: for they shall
8 blessed are the clean of heart: for
9 blessed are the peacemakers: for they
10 b. are they that suffer persecution
11 b. are ye when they shall revile you
13 16 blessed are your eyes because they see
Luke 6 20 blessed are ye poor, for yours is the
21 blessed are ye that hunger now: for
10 23 b. are the eyes that see the things
11 28 b. are they who hear the word of God
12 37 blessed are those servants whom the
23 29 they will say: Blessed are the barren
John 20 29 blessed are they that have not seen
Rom 4 7 blessed are they whose iniquities are
1 P 3 14 if you suffer anything . . . b. are ye
Apoc 14 13 b. are the dead who die in the Lord
19 19 blessed are they that are called to the
22 14 b. are they that wash their robes in

blessed art thou Deut 33 29 b. art thou, Israel
Ruth 3 10 blessed art thou of the Lord my daughter
1 K 26 25 blessed art thou, my son David: and
Jdth 13 23 b. art thou, O daughter, by the Lord
31 blessed art thou by thy God in every
Ps 118 12 blessed art thou, O Lord: teach me thy
127 2 b. art thou, and it shall be well with
Dan 3 26 b. art thou, O Lord God. 52; 1 Pa 29:10
53 blessed art thou, in the holy temple
54 blessed art thou on the throne of thy
55 blessed art thou, that beholdest the
56 blessed art thou in the firmament of
1 Ma 4 30 blessed art thou, O Savior of Israel who
Mat 16 17 him: Blessed art thou, Simon Bar-Jona
Luke 1 28 blessed art thou among women. 42
45 blessed art thou that hast believed

blessed be Gen 9 26 b. be the Lord God of Sem
Gen 14 19 blessed be Abram by the most high God
20 blessed be the most high God by whose
24 27 blessed be the Lord God of my master
Deut 33 20 blessed be Gad in his breadth: he hath
Judg 5 24 blessed among women be Jahel the wife
24 and blessed be she in her tent. He asked
17 2 to him: Blessed be my son by the Lord
Ruth 2 19 b. be he that hath had pity on thee
20 blessed be he of the Lord: because the
4 14 blessed be the Lord. 1 K 25:39; 2 K 18: 28; 3 K 1:48; 5:7; 8:56; 10:9; 2 Pa 9:8; 1 Es 7:27; Tob 12:23; Jdth 13:24; Ps 27:6; 30:22; 67:20; 88:53; 123:6; 134:21; 143:1; Zach 11:5
1 K 15 13 blessed be thou [Samuel] of the Lord
23 21 Saul said: Blessed be ye of the Lord
25 32 blessed be the Lord the God of Israel. 3 K 8:15; 1 Pa 16:36; 2 Pa 2:12; 6:4; Ps 40:14; 71:18; 105:48
32 blessed be thy speech; and b. be thou
33 blessed be thou who hast kept me today
2 K 2 5 b. be you to the Lord, who have shown
2 Es 9 5 blessed be the high name of thy glory
Tob 9 11 may your seed be blessed by the God of
Job 1 21 blessed be the name of the Lord. Ps 112:2; Dan 2:20
Ps 17 47 the Lord liveth, and blessed be my God
65 20 b. be God who hath not turned away my
67 36 strength to his people. Blessed be God
71 19 b. be the name of his majesty forever
113 15 blessed be you of the Lord, who made
117 26 blessed be he that cometh in the name
136 9 b. be he that shall take and dash thy
Isa 19 25 blessed be my people of Egypt and the
Jer 17 7 blessed be the man that trusteth in the
Eze 3 12 blessed be the glory of the Lord from
Dan 3 95 blessed be the God of them, to wit
2 Ma 1 17 blessed be God in all things, who hath
15 34 blessed be he that hath kept his own
Mark 11 10 blessed be the kingdom of our father
Luke 1 68 b. be the Lord God of Israel; because
19 38 b. be the king who cometh in the name
2 C 1 3 blessed be the God and Father. Eph 1:3; 1 P 1:3

blessed is Exod 18:10 blessed is the Lord, who
Tob 3 13 blessed is thy name, O God of our fathers
Job 5 17 blessed is the man whom God correcteth
Ps 1 1 b. is the man who hath not walked in
31 2 blessed is the man to whom the Lord
32 12 blessed is the nation whose God is the
33 9 blessed is the man that hopeth in him
39 5 b. is the man whose trust is in the
40 2 b. is he that understandeth concerning
64 5 blessed is he whom thou hast chosen
83 6 b. is the man whose help is from thee
13 blessed is the man that trusteth in
88 16 b. is the people that knoweth jubilation
93 12 b. is the man whom thou shalt instruct
111 1 blessed is the man that feareth the
126 5 b. is the man that hath filled the
145 5 b. is he who hath the God of Jacob for
Prov 3 13 blessed is the man that findeth wisdom
8 34 blessed is the man that heareth me and
28 14 b. is the man that is always fearful
Ecce 10 17 blessed is the land whose king is noble
Wisd 14 7 blessed is the wood by which justice
Eccu 14 1 b. is the man that hath not slipped
22 b. is the man that shall continue in
25 11 blessed is he that dwelleth with a wise
12 b. is he that findeth a true friend
15 blessed is the man to whom it is given
28 23 blessed is he that is defended from a
31 8 blessed is the rich man that is found
50 30 blessed is he that is conversant in
Isa 56 2 blessed is the man that doth this and
Dan 3 52 blessed is the holy name of thy glory
12 12 blessed is he that waiteth and cometh
Mat 11 6 blessed is he that shall not be scandalized in me. Luke 7:23
21 9 blessed is he that cometh. 23:39; Mark 11: 9; Luke 13:35; John 12:13
24 46 blessed is that servant. Luke 12:43
Luke 11 27 blessed is the womb that bore thee and
14 15 blessed is he that shall eat bread in
Rom 4 8 b. is the man to whom the Lord hath not
14 22 b. is he that condemneth not himself
James 1 12 b. is the man that endureth temptation
Apoc 1 3 blessed is he that readeth and heareth
16 15 blessed is he that watcheth and keepeth
20 6 blessed and holy is he that hath part
22 7 blessed is he that keepeth the words

blessedness Rom 4 6 David termeth the b. of a man
Rom 4 9 this b. doth it remain in circumcision
Gal 4 15 where is then your blessedness? For I

blessest Num 23 11 thou contrariwise blessest them
1 Pa 17 27 for seeing thou blessest it, O Lord

blesseth Gen 27 29 that b. thee be filled with
Num 24 9 he that b. thee, shall also himself
1 K 9 13 come: because he blesseth the victim
Job 1 11 see if he blesseth thee not to thy face
Prov 11 25 the soul which b., shall be made fat
27 14 he that b. his neighbor with a loud
blessing Gen 24 48 b. the Lord God of my master
Gen 26 29 increased with the blessing of the Lord
27 12 bring upon me a curse instead of a b.
23 then blessing him, he said: Art thou my
27 blessing him [Jacob], he said: Behold
35 came deceitfully and got thy blessing
36 time he hath stolen away my blessing
36 hast thou not reserved me also a b.
38 hast thou only one blessing, father
40 in the dew of heaven . . . shall thy b.
41 hated Jacob for the blessing wherewith
28 6 after the blessing he had charged him
33 11 take the blessing which I have brought
47 10 and blessing the king, he went out. But
Exod 32 29 that a blessing may be given to you
Lev 25 21 I will give you my b. the sixth year
Num 23 20 the blessing I am not able to hinder
Deut 11 26 I set forth . . . a blessing and a curse
27 blessing, if you obey the commandments
29 shalt put the b. upon mount Garizim
12 15 eat according to the b. of the Lord
16 10 shalt offer according to the b. of the
17 according to the b. of the Lord his God
23 5 he turned his cursing into thy blessing
28 8 Lord will send forth a blessing upon
30 1 come upon thee, the blessing or the
5 blessing thee, he will make thee more
19 have set before you . . . b. and cursing
33 1 the blessing wherewith the man of God
7 this is the blessing of Juda. Hear, O
13 of the blessing of the Lord be his land
16 blessing of him that appeared in the
Josu 8 34 he read all the words of the blessing
15 19 she answered: Give me a b. Judg 1:15
1 K 25 27 wherefore receive this blessing which
30 26 receive a blessing of the prey to the
2 K 7 29 with thy blessing let the house of thy
4 K 5 15 therefore take a blessing of thy servant
1 Pa 4 10 if blessing thou wilt bless me and
2 Pa 20 26 were assembled in valley of Blessing
26 called that place the valley of B.
2 Es 9 5 they glory with all blessing and praise
13 2 our God turned the curse into blessing
Tob 3 12 blessing the Lord, she said: Blessed is
6 21 b. that sound children may be born of
22 thou mayst obtain a b. in children. And
7 7 a blessing be upon thee, my son, because
15 together and fulfil his blessing in you
17 afterwards they made merry, b. God
9 10 may a blessing come upon thy wife and
Job 29 13 b. of him that was ready to perish
Ps 3 9 thy blessing is upon thy people. When
20 7 thou shalt give him to be a blessing
23 5 shall receive a blessing from the Lord
36 26 his seed shall be in blessing. Decline
83 8 the lawgiver shall give a blessing
108 18 and he would not have a blessing and
128 8 the blessing of the Lord be upon you
131 15 blessing I will bless her widow: I will
132 3 there the Lord hath commanded blessing
144 16 fillest with b. every living creature
Prov 10 6 b. of Lord is upon the head of the just
22 blessing of the Lord maketh men rich
11 11 by the blessing of the just the city
26 a b. upon the head of them that sell
20 21 in the end shall be without a blessing
24 25 a blessing shall come upon them. He
Wisd 15 19 they have fled . . . from his blessing
Eccu 3 10 that a blessing may come upon thee
10 his b. may remain in the latter end
11 father's b. establisheth the houses
4 14 she entereth, God will give a blessing
7 36 and thy blessing may be perfected. A
11 24 blessing of God maketh haste to reward
24 in a swift hour his b. beareth fruit
32 18 seek him early, shall find a blessing
33 17 in the b. of God I also have hoped
34 20 giveth health and life and blessing
36 19 according to the blessing of Aaron
39 27 his b. hath overflowed like a river
40 28 fear of the Lord is like paradise of b.
43 33 b. the Lord, exalt him as much as
44 25 gave him the blessing of all nations
Isa 19 24 a blessing in the midst of the land
44 3 and my blessing upon thy stock. And they
65 8 destroy it not, because it is a blessing
Eze 34 26 I will make them a blessing round about
26 there shall be showers of blessing. And
44 30 that he may return a b. upon thy house
Dan 3 24 praising God and blessing the Lord. Then
Joel 2 14 will return and forgive and leave a b.
Zach 8 13 and you shall be a blessing: fear not
Mala 3 10 pour you out a b. even to abundance
1 Ma 13 47 into it with hymns, blessing the Lord
2 Ma 8 27 b. the Lord who had delivered them that
Mark 14 22 Jesus took bread; and blessing, broke
Luke 1 64 he [Zachary] spoke, blessing God. And
24 53 in the temple, praising and b. God
Rom 15 29 abundance of the blessing of the gospel
1 C 14 16 how shall he . . . say Amen to thy b.
2 C 9 5 prepare this blessing before promised
5 so as a blessing, not as covetousness
Gal 3 14 that the blessing of Abraham might come
Heb 6 7 the earth . . . receiveth blessing from
14 unless blessing I shall bless thee and
James 3 10 out of same mouth proceedeth b. and
1 P 3 9 that you may inherit a blessing: for
9 railing for railing, but contrariwise b.
blessings Gen 27 29 blesseth thee be filled with b.
Gen 28 4 give the blessings of Abraham to thee
49 25 bless thee with the b. of heaven above, with the blessings of the deep
25 with the blessings of the breasts and of
26 blessings of thy father are strengthened with the blessings of his fathers
28 blessed every one with their proper b.
Deut 28 2 and all these blessings shall come upon
33 23 shall be full of blessings of the Lord
Ps 20 4 prevented him with b. of sweetness: thou
113 14 may the Lord add blessings upon you
Eccu 37 27 wise man shall be filled with blessings
40 17 grace is like a paradise in blessings
44 26 he acknowledged him in his blessings
47 7 praised him in the b. of the Lord in
Mala 2 2 and will curse your blessings, yea I
2 C 9 6 soweth in b. shall also reap blessings
Eph 1 3 who hath blessed us with spiritual b.
blew Exod 15 10 wind blew and the sea covered them
Josu 6 8 seven priests blew the seven trumpets
13 the ark, and they blew the trumpets
Judg 7 20 the trumpets which they blew and they
Mat 7 25 the winds blew and they beat upon that
John 6 18 by reason of a great wind that blew
blind Exod 4 11 the deaf, the seeing and the blind
Exod 23 8 bribes, which even blind the wise and
Lev 19 14 nor put a stumblingblock before the b.
21 18 if he be blind, if he be lame, if he
22 22 if it be blind or broken or have a scar

Deut 15 21 lame or blind or in any part disfigured
16 19 gifts blind the eyes of the wise and
27 18 that maketh the blind to wander out of
28 29 as the b. is wont to grope in the dark
2 K 5 6 unless thou take away the blind and
8 and take away the blind and the lame
8 blind and the lame shall not come into
Tob 2 11 upon his eyes and he was made blind
11 10 and his father that was blind, rising
Job 29 15 I was an eye to the blind and a foot to
Ps 145 8 the Lord enlighteneth the blind. The
Eccu 20 31 and gifts blind the eyes of judges
Isa 6 10 blind the heart of this people and
29 18 the eyes of the blind shall see. And the
35 5 shall the eyes of the blind be opened
42 7 mightest open the eyes of the blind
16 I will lead the blind into the way
18 ye blind, behold that you may see. Who
19 who is blind, but my servant? Or deaf
19 who is blind, but he that is sold? Or
19 who is blind, but the servant of the
43 8 bring forth the people that are blind
56 10 his watchmen are all blind, they are
59 10 like the blind we have groped as if
Jer 31 8 among them shall be the blind and the
Lam 4 14 they have wandered as blind men in the
Bar 6 36 they cannot restore the blind man to
Soph 1 17 they shall walk like blind men because
Mala 1 8 if you offer the blind for sacrifice
Mat 9 27 there followed him two blind men crying
28 the blind men came to him. And Jesus
11 5 the b. see, the lame walk. Luke 7:22
12 22 possessed with a devil, blind and dumb
15 14 they are blind and leaders of the b.
14 if b. lead the b., both fall into the
30 having with them the dumb, the blind
31 seeing the dumb speak . . . the blind see
20 30 two blind men sitting by the wayside
21 14 came to him the blind and the lame
23 16 woe to you blind guides, that say
17 foolish and blind; for whether is. 19
24 blind guides who strain out a gnat
26 blind Pharisee, first make clean the
Mark 8 22 they bring to him a blind man and they
23 taking the blind man by the hand he led
10 46 Bartimeus, the blind man, sat by the
49 they call the blind man saying to him
51 blind man said to him: Rabboni, that I
Luke 4 19 sight to the blind, to set at liberty
6 39 can the blind lead the blind? Do they
7 21 to many that were blind he gave sight
14 13 call the poor . . . the lame and the blind
21 bring in . . . the blind and the lame. And
18 35 blind man sat by the wayside begging
John 5 3 lay great multitude of sick, of blind
9 1 a man who was blind from his birth
2 parents, that he should be born blind
13 they bring him that had been blind
17 they say to the blind man: What sayest
18 concerning him, that he had been blind
19 your son who you say was born blind
20 is our son, and that he was born blind
24 called the man again that had been b.
25 whereas I was blind, now I see. They
32 hath opened the eyes of one born blind
39 they who see, may become blind. And
40 Pharisees said unto him: Are we also b.
41 if you were blind you would not have
10 21 can a devil open the eyes of the blind
11 37 opened the eyes of the man born blind
Acts 13 11 thou shalt be blind not seeing the sun
Rom 2 19 thou thyself art a guide of the blind
2 P 1 9 hath not these things with him is blind
Apoc 3 17 thou art . . . poor and blind and naked

blinded Num 14 44 being blinded went up to the top
Wisd 2 21 for their own malice blinded them. And
Mark 6 52 for their heart was blinded. And when
8 17 have you still your heart blinded
John 12 40 he hath blinded their eyes and hardened
Rom 11 7 it; and the rest have been blinded
2 C 4 4 hath blinded the minds of unbelievers
1 J 2 11 the darkness hath blinded his eyes. I

blindeth Eccu 43 4 with his beams, he b. the eyes

blindfolded Luke 22 64 they blindfolded him and

blindness Gen 19 11 were without they struck with b.
Deut 28 28 strike thee with madness and blindness
4 K 6 18 the Lord this people with blindness
18 the Lord struck them with blindness
Tob 2 13 because evil of blindness had befallen
Wisd 19 16 but they were struck with blindness: as
Zach 12 4 every horse of the nations with b.
2 Ma 10 30 confounded with b. and filled with
Mark 3 5 blindness of their hearts. Eph 4:18
Rom 11 25 blindness in part has happened in Israel

blister Lev 13 2 arise a different color or a b.

blisters Lev 14 56 of a scar and of b. breaking
Lev 22 22 have a scar or blisters or a scab or

blood Gen 4 10 voice of thy brother's b. crieth
Gen 4 11 received the blood of thy brother at thy
9 4 flesh with blood you shall not eat. For
5 I will require the blood of your lives
6 whosoever shall shed man's blood, his
blood shall be shed
37 22 take away his life, nor shed his blood
26 to kill our brother and conceal his b.
31 his coat, and dipped it in the b. of a
42 22 behold his blood is required. And they
49 11 and his garment in the b. of the grape
Exod 4 9 shall be turned into blood. 7:17
7 19 that they may be turned into blood
19 let blood be in all the land of Egypt
20 servants: and it was turned into blood
21 there was b. in all the land of Egypt
12 7 they shall take the blood thereof and
13 the blood shall be unto you for a sign
13 I shall see the blood and shall pass
22 dip a bunch of hyssop in the blood
23 shall see the blood on the transom
22 2 that slew him shall not be guilty of b.
23 18 not sacrifice the b. of my victim upon
24 6 Moses took half of the blood and put it
8 he took the blood and sprinkled it
8 this is the blood of the covenant which
29 12 taking some of the blood of the calf
12 rest of the blood thou shalt pour at
16 thou shalt take of the blood thereof
20 thou shalt take of his blood and put
20 thou shalt pour the b. upon the altar
21 when thou hast taken of the blood that
30 10 blood of that which was offered for sin
34 25 shalt not offer the b. of my sacrifice
Lev 1 11 sons of Aaron shall pour the blood.
3:2, 8, 13
15 blood run down upon the brim of the
3 17 neither blood nor fat shall you eat at
4 5 he shall take also of the blood. 16:14
6 having dipped his finger in the blood
7 some of the same blood upon the horns
7 he shall pour all the rest of the b.
16 the priest . . . shall carry of the blood
18 shall put of same blood on the horns
18 rest of the blood he shall pour at the
25 priest shall dip his finger in the b.
30 priest shall take of the blood. 34
5 9 of its blood he shall sprinkle the side
6 27 if a garment be sprinkled with the b.

30 the blood of which is carried into the
7 2 the blood thereof shall be poured round
14 that shall pour out the blood of the
26 shall not eat the blood of any creature
27 that eateth blood, shall perish from
33 offereth the blood and the fat, he shall
8 15 he immolated it; and took the blood
15 he poured the rest of the blood at the
19 he immolated it and poured the blood
23 he took of the b. thereof and touched
24 blood of the ram that was immolated
30 the blood that was upon the altar
9 9 his sons brought him the blood. 12, 18
10 18 none of the blood hath been carried
12 4 in the blood of her purification. 5
7 be cleansed from the issue of her blood
14 6 shall dip . . . in the b. of the sparrow
14 priest taking of the blood of the victim
17 upon the b. that was shed for trespass
25 blood thereof upon the tip of the right
28 the blood that was shed for trespass
51 dip all in the blood of the sparrow
52 purify it . . . with the b. of the sparrow
15 19 the mouth, hath her issue of blood, shall
25 the woman that hath an issue of blood
28 if the blood stop and cease run, she
33 that hath a continual issue of blood
16 15 he shall carry in the blood thereof
15 with the blood of the calf, that he may
18 taking the blood of the calf and of the
27 and whose blood was carried into the
17 4 shall be guilty of blood: as if he had shed blood
6 the priest shall pour the blood upon
10 if any man . . . eat blood, I will set my
11 life of the flesh is in the blood. 14
11 the blood may be for an expiation of
12 that sojourn among you, shall eat blood
13 let him pour out its blood and cover it
14 for life of all flesh is in the blood
14 you shall not eat the blood of any flesh
19 16 not stand against the b. of thy neighbor
26 you shall not eat with blood. You shall
20 9 and mother, let his blood be upon him
11 their blood be upon them. 12, 13, 16, 27
18 and she open the fountain of her blood
21 2 for his kin, such as are near in blood
25 49 his kinsman by blood or by affinity
Num 18 17 their blood only thou shalt pour upon
19 4 dipping his finger in her blood, shall
5 and her flesh and her blood and her dung
23 24 prey, and drink the blood of the slain
26 1 after the blood of the guilty was shed
35 6 who hath shed blood may flee to them
11 who have shed blood against their will
15 who hath shed blood against his will
18 revenged by the blood of him that struck
27 struck by him that is the avenger of b.
31 money of him that is guilty of blood
33 stained with the blood of the innocent
33 by his blood that hath shed the b. of
Deut 12 16 only the blood thou shalt not eat but
23 beware of this, that thou eat not the b.
23 blood, for the blood is for the soul
27 shalt offer . . . the flesh and the blood
27 the blood of thy victims thou shalt pour
15 23 take heed not to eat their blood, but
17 8 matter in judgment between b. and b.
19 6 kinsman of him whose blood was shed. 12
10 to possess, lest thou be guilty of blood
21 7 our hands did not shed this blood
8 guilt of blood shall be taken from them
9 shalt be free from the innocent's blood

22 8 lest blood be shed in thy house and
32 14 drink the purest blood of the grape
42 I will make my arrows drunk with blood
42 of blood of the slain and of captives
43 will revenge the b. of his servants
Josu 2 19 his blood shall be upon his own head
19 blood of all that shall be with thee
20 3 kinsman, who is the avenger of blood
5 when avenger of blood shall pursue
9 kinsman, coveting to revenge the blood
Judg 9 24 and the shedding of their blood upon
1 K 14 32 the people ate them with the blood
33 against the Lord, eating with the blood
34 shall not sin . . . eating with the blood
25 26 withholden thee from coming to blood
26 20 let not my blood be shed upon the earth
2 K 1 16 thy blood be upon thy own head: for the
22 from the blood of the slain, from the
3 27 in revenge of the blood of Asael his
28 even of the blood of Abner the son of
4 11 shall I not require his blood at your
16 7 come out, come out, thou man of blood
8 for all the b. of the house of Saul
8 thee, because thou art a man of blood
20 12 Amasa imbrued with blood, lay in midst
23 17 shall I drink the blood of these men
3 K 2 5 and shed the blood of war in peace
5 put the blood of war on his girdle
9 down his gray hairs with blood to hell
32 shall return his b. upon his own head
33 blood shall return upon head of Joab
37 thy blood shall be upon thy own head
18 28 till they were all covered with blood
21 19 dogs have licked the blood of Naboth
19 Naboth, they shall lick thy blood also
22 35 and the blood ran out of the wound
38 and the dogs licked up his blood and
4 K 3 22 waters over against them red, like b.
23 said: It is the blood of the sword
9 7 I will revenge the blood of my servants
7 blood of all the servants of the Lord
26 b. of Naboth and for the blood of his
33 the wall was sprinkled with her blood
16 13 poured the b. of the peace offerings
15 blood of the holocaust and all the blood of the victim thou shalt
1 Pa 11 19 should drink the blood of these men
22 8 thou hast shed much blood and fought
8 after shedding so much blood before me
28 3 art a man of war, and hast shed blood
2 Pa 29 22 the priests took the blood and poured
22 rams, and their blood they poured also
22 lambs, and poured the blood upon the
24 sprinkled their blood before the altar
30 16 the priests received the blood which
Jdth 8 20 Lord our God will require our blood
11 11 and to drink the blood of them. And the
14 4 without his head wallowing in his b.
14 without the head, weltering in his b.
Esth 9 1 their enemies were greedy after their b.
16 10 having nothing of the Persian blood
Job 16 19 O earth, cover not thou my blood neither
39 30 her young ones shall suck up blood
Ps 9 13 requiring their blood he hath remembered
13 3 their feet are swift to shed blood
15 4 their meetings for blood offerings
29 10 what profit is there in my blood, whilst
49 13 or shall I drink the blood of goats
50 16 deliver me from blood, O God, thou God
57 11 wash his hands in blood of the sinner
67 24 may be dipped in the b. of thy enemies
77 44 he turned their rivers into blood and
78 3 they have poured out their blood as

10 revenging the blood of thy servants
104 29 he turned their waters into blood and
105 38 b. of their sons and of their daughters
38 and the land was polluted with blood
138 19 ye men of blood, depart from me: because
Prov 1 11 let us lie in wait for blood, let us
16 their feet . . . make haste to shed blood
18 lie in wait for their own blood and
12 6 words of the wicked lie in wait for b.
28 17 doth violence to the b. of a person
30 33 bloweth his nose, bringeth out blood
Wisd 7 2 ten months I was compacted in blood
11 7 thou gavest human blood to the unjust
12 5 and devourers of blood from the midst
14 25 are mingled together, blood, murder
Eccu 8 19 blood is as nothing in his sight and
9 13 by thy b. thou fall into destruction
11 34 of one deceitful man much blood: and a
34 a sinful man lieth in wait for blood
12 16 he will not be satisfied with blood
17 30 which flesh and blood hath invented
22 30 reproaches and threats, before blood
27 16 quarrels of the proud is shedding of b.
28 13 a hasty quarrel sheddeth blood and a
33 31 in b. of thy soul thou hast gotten him
34 25 defraudeth them . . . is a man of blood
27 sheddeth blood and he that defraudeth
50 16 offered of the blood of the grape. He
Isa 1 11 fat of fatlings and blood of calves and
15 hear: for your hands are full of blood
4 4 shall wash away the blood of Jerusalem
9 5 and garment mingled with blood, shall
15 9 waters of Dibon are filled with blood
26 21 the earth shall disclose her blood
33 15 stoppeth his ears lest he hear blood
34 3 mountains shall be melted with their b.
6 sword of the Lord is filled with blood
6 is made thick with the blood of lambs
6 with the blood of rams full of marrow
7 their land shall be soaked with blood
49 26 shall be made drunk with their own b.
59 3 your hands are defiled with blood and
63 3 their b. is sprinkled upon my garments
3 as if he should offer swine's blood
Jer 2 34 the blood of the souls of the poor
41 1 the son of Elisama of the royal blood
46 10 sword . . . shall be drunk with their b.
48 10 that withholdeth his sword from blood
51 35 my b. upon the inhabitants of Chaldea
Lam 4 13 that have shed the blood of the just
14 they were defiled with blood: and when
Eze 3 18 I will require his blood at thy hand. 20; 33:8
5 17 and blood shall pass through thee and
7 23 the land is full of the judgment of b.
9 9 and the land is filled with blood and
14 19 out my indignation upon it in blood
16 6 wast trodden under foot in thy own b.
6 said to thee when thou wast in thy b.
9 and cleansed away thy blood from thee
22 trodden under foot in thy own blood
36 by the blood of thy children whom thou
38 and they that shed blood are judged
38 I will give thee blood in fury and
18 10 a son that is . . . a shedder of blood
13 surely die, his blood shall be upon him
19 10 thy mother is like a vine in thy blood
21 32 thy b. shall be in midst of the land
22 2 dost thou not judge the city of blood
3 this is the city that sheddeth blood
4 thou art become guilty in thy blood
6 employed his arm in thee to shed blood
9 slanderers have been in thee to shed b.
12 have taken gifts in thee to shed blood
13 b. that hath been shed in midst of thee
27 wolves ravening the prey to shed blood
23 37 and blood is in their hands. 45
45 as shedders of blood are judged: because
24 7 her blood is in the midst of her, she
8 I have shed her blood upon the smooth
28 23 pestilence and blood in her streets
32 6 water the earth with thy stinking b.
33 4 him off: his blood be upon his own head
5 his blood shall be upon him: but if he
6 I will require his blood at the hand
25 you that eat with the blood and lift up
25 that shed blood: shall you possess
35 6 I will deliver thee up to blood, and blood shall pursue thee
6 whereas thou hast hated blood, blood shall pursue thee
36 18 for the blood which they had shed upon
38 22 judge him with pestilence and with blood
39 17 of Israel: to eat flesh and drink blood
18 shall drink the blood of the princes
19 shall drink blood till you be drunk
43 18 offered upon it, and blood poured out
20 thou shalt take of his blood and shalt
44 7 offer my bread the fat and the blood
15 to offer me the fat and the blood, saith
45 19 the priest shall take of the blood of
Osee 1 4 I will visit the blood of Jezrahel upon
4 2 overflowed, and blood hath touched blood
6 8 workers of idols, supplanted with blood
12 14 his blood shall come upon him and his
Joel 2 30 and in earth, blood and fire and vapor
31 the moon into blood: before the great
3 21 and I will cleanse their blood which
Mich 3 10 you that build up Sion with blood and
7 2 they all lie in wait for blood, every
Nah 3 1 woe to thee, O city of blood, all full
Haba 2 8 shall spoil thee: because of men's b.
12 to him that buildeth a town with blood
17 terrify them because of the b. of men
Soph 1 17 their b. shall be poured out as earth
Zach 9 7 I will take away his blood out of his
11 by the b. of thy testament thou hast
1 Ma 3 32 Lysias, a nobleman of the blood royal
6 34 showed the elephants the b. of grapes
7 17 and the blood of them they have shed
9 38 remembered the b. of John their brother
42 revenge for the blood of their brother
10 89 given to such as are of the royal b.
2 Ma 8 3 would hear the voice of the blood that
12 16 to run with the blood of the slain
14 45 while his blood ran down with a great
46 when he was now almost without blood
Mat 9 20 with an issue of b. Mark 5:25; Luke 8:43
16 17 flesh and blood hath not revealed it
23 30 partakers with them in b. of prophets
35 upon you may come all the just blood
35 from the b. of Abel . . . unto the b. of Zacharias. Luke 11:51
26 28 this is my blood. Mark 14:24
27 6 corbona, because it is the price of blood
8 that is, The field of blood. Acts 1:19
24 I am innocent of the blood of this just
25 said: His blood be upon us and upon our
Mark 5 29 fountain of her blood was dried up
Luke 8 44 the issue of her blood stopped. And
11 50 b. of all the prophets which was shed
13 1 whose blood Pilate had mingled with
22 20 new testament in my blood. 1 C 11:25
44 his sweat became as drops of blood
John 1 13 who are born, not of blood nor of the
6 54 of the Son of man and drink his blood

55 drinketh my blood, hath everlasting
56 my blood is drink indeed. He that eateth
57 drinketh my blood, abideth in me and
19 34 there came out blood and water. And he
Acts 2 19 blood and fire and vapor of smoke. The
20 the moon into blood before the great and
5 28 to bring the blood of this man upon us
15 20 that they refrain . . . from b. 21:25
29 things sanctified to idols and from b.
18 6 your blood be upon your own heads; I
20 26 I am clear from the blood of all men
28 he hath purchased with his own blood
22 20 when the blood of Stephen thy witness
Rom 3 15 bitterness: Their feet swift to shed b.
25 propitiation through faith in his b.
5 9 being now justified by his blood shall
1 C 10 16 the communion of the blood of Christ
11 27 of the body and of the b. of the Lord
15 50 flesh and blood cannot possess the
Gal 1 16 I condescended not to flesh and blood
Eph 1 7 have redemption through his b. Col 1:14
2 13 are made nigh by the blood of Christ
6 12 our westling is not against flesh and b.
Col 1 20 peace through the blood of his cross
Heb 2 14 children are partakers of flesh and b.
9 7 not without blood, which he offereth
12 neither by the blood of goats or of
12 by his own blood entered once into the
13 if the blood of goats and of oxen and
14 how much more shall the blood of Christ
18 was the first dedicated without blood
19 he took the blood of calves and goats
20 this is the blood of the testament
21 in like manner, he sprinkled with blood
22 all things . . . are cleansed with blood
22 without shedding of blood there is no
25 holies, every year with b. of others
10 4 impossible that with the blood of oxen
19 entering into the holies by b. of Christ
29 esteemed the b. of the testament unclean
11 28 celebrated . . . the shedding of the b.
12 4 you have not yet resisted unto blood
24 and to the sprinkling of blood which
13 11 whose blood is brought into the holies
12 sanctify the people by his own blood
20 Christ in the blood of the everlasting
1 P 1 2 sprinkling of the b. of Jesus Christ
19 but with the precious blood of Christ
1 J 1 7 the b. of Jesus Christ his Son cleanseth
5 6 this is he that came by water and blood
8 the spirit and the water and the blood
Apoc 1 5 from our sins in his own blood and hath
5 9 hast redeemed us to God in thy blood
12 11 overcame him by the blood of the Lamb
innocent blood Deut 19 10 that i. b. may not be
Deut 19 13 shalt take away the guilt of i. blood
1 K 19 5 therefore wilt thou sin against i. b.
25 31 that thou hast shed innocent blood or
3 K 2 31 thou shalt remove the innocent blood
4 K 21 16 Manasses shed also very much i. blood
24 4 i. b. that he shed, filling Jerusalem with i. b.
Ps 93 21 the just and will condemn innocent b.
105 38 and they shed innocent blood: the blood
Prov 6 17 lying tongue, hands that shed i. blood
Isa 59 7 their feet . . . make haste to shed i. b.
Jer 7 6 shed not i. blood in this place. 22:3
17 and upon shedding innocent blood and
26 15 me to death, you will shed i. b. against
Dan 13 62 them to death, and i. blood was saved
Joel 3 19 have shed innocent blood in their land
Jon 1 14 lay not upon us innocent blood: for
1 Ma 1 39 shed innocent blood about the sanctuary
2 Ma 1 8 they burnt the gate and shed i. blood

Mat 27 4 in betraying innocent blood. But they
bloodshed Eccu 40 9 bloodshed . . . for the wicked
bloodthirsty Prov 29 10 b. men hate the upright
bloody Exod 4 25 a b. spouse art thou to me. 26
2 K 21 1 it is for Saul and his bloody house
Ps 5 7 b. and the deceitful man the Lord will
25 9 wicked: nor my life with bloody men
54 24 bloody and deceitful men shall not live
58 3 iniquity, and save me from bloody men
Eze 24 6 woe to the boody city, to the pot whose
9 woe to the bloody city, of which I will
Acts 28 8 sick of a fever and of a bloody flux
bloomed Num 17 8 it had bloomed blossoms which
blossom Num 17 5 choose, his rod shall blossom
Job 8 16 at his rising his blossom shall shoot
Prov 8 19 and my blossom than choice silver. I
Isa 27 6 Israel shall blossom and bud, and they
35 2 it shall bud forth and blossom and
Osee 14 8 and they shall blossom as a vine: his
Haba 3 17 the fig tree shall not blossom: and
blossomed Eze 7 10 the rod hath blossomed, pride
Heb 9 4 the rod of Aaron that had blossomed
blossoms Gen 40 10 after the b. brought forth ripe
Num 17 8 the buds swelling it had bloomed b.
blot Deut 25 19 thou shalt blot out his name from
Deut 29 20 the Lord should blot out his name from
4 K 14 27 did not say that he would blot out the
Ps 50 11 my sins, and blot out all my iniquities
Prov 9 7 that rebuketh . . . getteth himself a b.
Eccu 11 33 and on the elect he will lay a blot of
20 26 a lie is a foul blot in a man and yet
46 23 to blot out the wickedness of the nation
Isa 43 25 I am he that blot out thy iniquities
Apoc 3 5 I will not blot out his name out of the
blotted 2 Es 4 5 let not their sin be blotted out. Jer 18:23
Ps 9 6 thou hast blotted out their name forever
68 29 let them be blotted out of the book of
108 13 generation may his name be blotted out
14 let not the sin of his mother be b. out
Prov 6 33 his reproach shall not be blotted out
Eccu 23 36 her infamy shall not be blotted out
40 12 and injustice shall be blotted out and
41 14 name of the ungodly shall be b. out
Isa 44 22 I have blotted out thy iniquities as
Acts 3 19 that your sins may be blotted out. That
blotting Col 2 14 blotting out the handwriting
blow Exod 10 19 made a very strong wind to blow
Judg 7 18 do you also blow the trumpets on every
Ps 80 4 blow up the trumpet on the new moon
147 18 his wind shall blow, and the waters
Cant 4 16 south wind, blow through my garden
Eccu 28 14 if thou blow the spark, it shall burn
43 17 at his will the south wind shall blow
Eze 7 14 blow the trumpet, let all be made ready
21 31 of my rage will I blow upon thee and
37 9 blow upon these slain, and let them
Osee 5 8 blow ye the cornet in Gabaa, the trumpet
Joel 2 1 blow ye the trumpet in Sion. 15
Luke 12 55 when ye see the south wind blow, you
John 18 22 gave Jesus a blow, saying: Answerest
Apoc 7 1 they should not blow upon the earth
blowed Agge 1 9 it home, and I blowed it away
bloweth Job 37 10 when God b. there cometh frost
Prov 30 33 he that violently bloweth his nose
Eccu 43 22 the cold north wind bloweth and the
Isa 54 16 that bloweth the coals in the fire
Bar 6 60 the wind bloweth in every country. And
blowing Exod 14 21 burning wind b. all the night
Dan 3 50 like the blowing of a wind bringing dew
Acts 27 13 the south wind gently blowing, thinking
28 13 south wind b., we came the second day
blown Wisd 5 15 as dust, which is b. away with the
Isa 40 7 spirit of the Lord hath blown upon it

24 suddenly he hath blown upon them and
blows Job 37 17 when the south wind blows upon
John 19 3 they gave him blows. Pilate therefore
blue Exod 35 35 embroidery in blue and purple
Num 15 38 putting in them ribands of blue: that
Ecce 23 11 is never without a blue mark, so every
28 21 stroke of a whip maketh a blue mark
45 12 holy robe of gold and blue and purple
Eze 23 6 who were clothed with blue, princes
27 7 blue and purple from the islands of
24 manners, with bales of blue cloth and
1 Ma 4 23 much gold and silver and blue silk and
blueness Prov 20 30 b. of wound shall wipe away
blunt 1 K 13 21 forks and their axes were blunt
Ecce 10 10 if the iron be blunt and be not as
before, but be made blunt
blush 4 K 8 11 and was troubled so far as to blush
Ps 34 26 let them blush: and be ashamed together
69 4 blush for shame that desire evils to
Isa 24 23 moon shall blush, and the sun shall
Jer 3 3 harlot's forehead, thou wouldst not b.
6 15 and they knew not how to b.: wherefore
8 12 and they have not known how to blush
blushing Ps 69 4 b. for shame that say to me: Let
Boanerges Mark 3 17 he named them Boanerges which
boar Ps 79 14 boar out of the wood hath laid it
board Exod 26 17 one b. may be joined to another b.
Exod 26 19 under every b. may be put two sockets
21 two sockets shall be put under each b.
25 reckoning two sockets for each board
35 11 board work with the oars, the pillars
36 22 two mortises throughout every board
24 two sockets were put under one board
26 of silver, two sockets for every board
30 to wit, two sockets under every board
34 the board works . . . overlaid with gold
Acts 27 2 going on board a ship of Adrumentum
boards Exod 26 15 make also the b. of tabernacle
Exod 26 17 in sides of the boards shall be made
17 after this manner shall all the boards
20 in the second side . . . shall be 20 b.
22 tabernacle thou shalt make six boards
24 shall be observed for the two boards
25 they shall be in all eight boards and
26 setim wood to hold together the boards
28 put along by the midst of the boards
29 boards also themselves thou shalt overlay
36 20 he made also the b. of the tabernacle
22 in this manner he made for all the b.
25 toward the north he made twenty boards
27 looketh to the sea, he made six boards
30 there were in all eight boards and they
31 to hold together the boards. 32
33 by midst of boards from corner to corner
38 7 but hollow, of boards and empty within
39 32 they offered . . . the rings, the boards
40 16 up and placed the boards and the sockets
Num 3 36 under their custody shall be the boards
4 31 burdens: they shall carry the boards of
3 K 6 15 built the walls . . . with boards of cedar
15 he covered it with boards of cedar
16 with boards of cedar at the hinder part
18 all was covered with boards of cedar
7 3 covered the whole vault with boards
2 Pa 3 5 greater house he ceiled with deal b.
Cant 8 9 join it together with boards of cedar
Eccu 29 28 poor man's fare under a roof of boards
Acts 27 44 some they carried on boards and some
board-work Exod 26 29 for the bars to hold the b.
boast 3 K 20 11 let not the girded boast himself
Prov 20 14 when he is gone away, then he will b.
27 1 b. not for tomorrow, for thou knowest
Isa 10 15 shall the axe boast itself against him
Jer 15 17 nor did I make a boast of the presence
Zach 12 7 may not boast and magnify themselves
Rom 2 17 in the law and makest thy boast of God
23 thou that makest thy boast of the law
11 18 boast not against the branches. But if
18 if thou boast, thou bearest not the root
2 C 9 2 I boast of you to the Macedonians. That
3 the thing which we boast of concerning
10 8 if also I should boast somewhat more
boasted Jer 11 15 crimes, in which thou hast b.
2 C 7 14 if I have boasted anything to him of
boasters Soph 3 11 I will take away . . . thy proud b.
boasteth Prov 25 14 that b. and doth not fulfil his
Prov 28 25 he that boasteth and puffeth himself
Wisd 2 13 he b. that he hath the knowledge of God
Eccu 10 30 things, than he that boasteth himself
James 3 5 a little member, and b. great things
boasting 1 K 2 3 to speak lofty things, boasting
Esth 1 4 and boasting of his power for a long
Wisd 5 8 what advantage hath the b. of riches
17 7 art were put down and their boasting of
Eccu 47 5 he beat down the boasting of Goliath
Jer 48 30 I know, saith the Lord, his boasting
Rom 3 27 where is then thy boasting? It is
2 C 7 14 so also our boasting that was made to
8 24 charity, and of our b. on your behalf
boasts Ps 73 4 that hate thee have made their b.
2 Ma 15 32 which he had stretched out with proud b.
boat Mat 8 23 entered into the boat, his disciples
Mat 8 24 the boat was covered with the waves
9 1 entering into a boat . . . came into his
13 2 he went up into a boat and sat: and all
14 13 he retired from thence by a boat into
22 obliged his disciples to go up into b.
24 boat in the midst of the sea was tossed
29 Peter going down out of the boat, walked
32 come up into the boat, the wind ceased
33 that were in the boat came and adored
Acts 27 16 we had much work to come by the boat
30 having let down the boat into the sea
32 the soldiers cut off ropes of the boat
boats 2 Ma 12 3 their wives and children into b.
2 Ma 12 6 in the night, burnt the boats and slew
Bocci Num 34 22 of tribe of children of Dan, Bocci
1 Pa 6 5 Abisue begot B., and Bocci begot Ozi
51 Abisue his son, Bocci his son, Azi his
1 Es 7 4 Ozi the son of Bocci, the son of Abisue
Bocciau 1 Pa 25 4 sons of Heman, Bocciau, Mathaniau
1 Pa 25 13 the sixth to Bocciau, to his sons
Bochri 2 K 20 1 Seba the son of B. 2, 6, 7, 10, 13. 22
Bochru 1 Pa 8 38 Asel had six sons . . . B. 9:44
bodies Gen 41 4 whose bodies were very beautiful
Gen 47 18 have nothing now left but our bodies
50 3 manner with bodies that were embalmed
Judg 19 22 refreshing their bodies with meat and
1 K 31 12 the bodies of his sons from the wall of
4 K 19 35 he saw all the bodies of the dead. And
1 Pa 10 12 took the bodies of Saul and of his sons
2 Pa 20 24 for a great space, full of dead bodies
25 they found among the dead bodies stuff
2 Es 9 37 they have dominion over our bodies
Tob 1 21 Tobias buried their bodies. But when it
2 9 carried off the bodies of them that
Ps 78 2 dead bodies of thy servants to be meat
Prov 19 29 striking hammers for the b. of fools
Eccu 44 14 their bodies are buried in peace and
Jer 31 40 and the whole valley of dead bodies
33 5 to fill them with the dead bodies of
34 20 their dead bodies shall be for meat
41 9 into which Ismahel cast all the dead b.
Bar 6 21 other birds fly upon their bodies and
Eze 1 11 and two [wings] covered their bodies
16 26 Egyptians . . . men of large bodies and

Dan 3 94 that the fire had no power on their b.
95 delivered up their b. that they might
Nah 3 3 they shall fall down on their dead b.
Soph 1 17 out as earth, and their bodies as dung
1 Ma 11 4 and the bodies that were cast abroad
2 Ma 12 39 to take away the bodies of them that
Mat 27 52 many bodies of the saints that had slept
John 19 31 that the b. might not remain upon the
Rom 1 24 to dishonor their own bodies among
8 11 he shall quicken also your mortal bodies
12 1 that you present your bodies a living
1 C 6 15 that your b. are the members of Christ
15 40 are b. celestial and bodies terrestrial
2 C 4 10 may be made manifest in our bodies
Eph 5 28 to love their wives as their own bodies
Heb 10 22 having our b. washed with clean water
13 11 the bodies of those beasts whose blood
Apoc 11 8 their bodies shall lie in the streets
9 see their b. for three days and a half
9 their bodies to be laid in sepulchers

bodily Luke 3 22 descended in a bodily shape as
2 C 10 10 but his bodily presence is weak and
1 Tim 4 8 b. exercise is profitable to little

bodkins Isa 3 20 bodkins and ornaments of the legs

body Lev 4 12 rest of the body he shall carry
Deut 21 2 measure from place where the b. lieth
28 27 part of thy body by which the dung
Judg 14 9 taken the honey from body of the lion
19 29 divided the dead body of his wife with
1 K 31 12 took the body of Saul and the bodies
2 K 20 11 stopping at the dead body of Amasa
3 K 13 22 thy dead body shall not be brought
24 and the lion stood by the dead body
25 men passing by saw the dead body cast
25 and the lion standing by the body. And
28 lion had not eaten of the dead body
29 took up the body of the man of God
4 K 13 21 cast the body into sepulcher of Eliseus
Tob 2 3 dinner and came fasting to the body
5 when he had hide the body, he ate bread
Jdth 10 3 washed her body and anointed herself
14 14 seeing the body of Holofernes lying
Esth 14 2 and she humbled her body with fasts
15 6 as if . . . not able to bear up her own b.
Prov 5 11 shalt have spent thy flesh and thy b.
Wisd 1 4 nor dwell in a body subject to sins
2 3 our body shall be ashes and our spirit
8 20 more good, I came to a body undefiled
9 15 corruptible b. is a load upon the soul
18 22 not by strength of body nor with force
Eccu 7 26 have a care of their body and show not
19 27 attire of the body and the laughter of
30 15 a sound body, than immense revenues
16 the riches of the health of the body
31 25 shalt not bring sickness upon thy body
37 sober drinking is health to soul and b.
41 14 mourning of men is about their body
47 21 by thy body thou wast brought under
Isa 51 23 thou hast laid thy body as the ground
Bar 6 70 like to a dead body cast forth in dark
Dan 7 11 and the body thereof was destroyed
Haba 3 10 the great body of waters passed away
2 Ma 3 17 with sadness and horror of the body
6 30 I suffer grievous pains in body: but in
9 7 by a grievous bruising of the body. Thus
9 worms swarmed out of the body of this
15 30 ready in body and mind to die for his
Mat 6 22 light of thy body is thy. Luke 11:34
25 be not solicitous . . . for your body. Luke 12:22
25 body more than the raiment. Luke 12:23
10 28 not them that kill the body. Luke 12:2
28 that can destroy both soul and body
14 12 came and took the body. Mark 6:29
24 28 wheresoever the b. shall be. Luke 17:37
27 58 commanded the body should be delivered
59 Joseph taking the body wrapped it up
Mark 5 29 felt in her body that she was healed
15 45 centurion, he gave the body to Joseph
Acts 9 40 turning to the body he said: Tabitha
Rom 6 6 that the body of sin may be destroyed
12 let not sin reign in your mortal body
7 24 deliver me from the body of this death
8 10 the body indeed is dead because of sin
23 sons of God, the redemption of our body
1 C 5 3 absent in body but present in spirit
6 13 the body is not for fornication, but for the Lord, and the Lord for the body
18 sin that a man doth is without the body
20 glorify and bear God in your body. Now
7 4 wife hath not power of her own body
34 be holy both in body and in spirit. But
10 16 is it not partaking of the body of the
11 27 guilty of the b. and of the blood of the
29 not discerning the body of the Lord
12 12 as the b. is one and hath many members
14 the body also is not one member, but
15 I am not of the b., is it therefore. 16
15 is it therefore not of the body. 16
18 every one of them in the body as it hath
19 were one member, where would be the body
22 the more feeble members of the body
23 less honorable members of the body
24 God hath tempered the body together
25 might be no schism in the body; but the
15 35 what manner of body shall they come
37 thou sowest not the body that shall be
38 God giveth it a body as he will: and to
38 will: and to every seed its proper body
44 it is sown a natural body, it shall rise a spiritual body
44 if there be a natural body, there is also a spiritual body
2 C 4 10 always bearing about in our body the
5 6 while we are in the body, we are absent
8 to be absent rather from the body and
10 may receive the proper things of the b.
12 2 whether in the body . . . or out of the b.
Eph 3 6 of the same body and copartners of
4 16 maketh increase of the body unto the
Phil 3 21 will reform the b. of our lowness, made like to the body of his glory
Col 1 18 he is head of the body, the church
22 hath reconciled in the body of his
2 5 though I be absent in body, yet in
11 in despoiling of the body of the flesh
17 things to come, the body is of Christ
23 not sparing the body; not in any honor
1 Th 5 23 body may be preserved blameless in the
Heb 10 5 not: but a body thou hast fitted to me
13 3 as being yourselves also in the body
James 2 16 things that are necessary for the body
26 as the body without the spirit is dead
Jude 9 Michael . . . contended about the body of

body of Jesus (Christ) Mat 27 58 to Pilate, and asked the body of Jesus
Mark 15 43 and begged the body of Jesus. Luke 23:52
Luke 24 3 they found not the b. of the Lord Jesus
John 19 38 he might take away the body of Jesus
38 and took away the body of Jesus. And
40 they took the body of Jesus and bound
20 12 where the body of Jesus had been laid
Rom 7 4 are become dead to the law by the b. . . .
1 C 12 27 now you are the body of Christ and
Eph 4 12 the edifying of the body of Christ
Heb 10 10 oblation of the body of Jesus Christ

his body Exod 22 27 the clothing of his body
Lev 14 8 he shall shave all the hair of his b.
9 eyebrows, and the hair of all his body
9 washed again his clothes and his body
15 13 washed his clothes and all his body
16 shall wash all his body with water: and
16 26 shall wash his clothes and his body
17 16 not wash his clothes and his body, he
21 20 if he have . . . a dry scurf in his body
Num 19 7 after washing his garments and body
8 shall wash his garments and his body
Deut 21 23 his body shall not remain upon the tree
Judg 3 22 the dagger, but left it in his body
16 31 took his body and buried it between
1 K 31 10 but his body they hung on the wall of
3 K 13 24 and his body was cast in the way: and
30 laid his dead body in his own sepulcher
17 21 soul of this child . . . return into his b.
Jdth 13 10 and rolled away his headless body. And
Job 41 6 his body is like molten shields, shut
Eccu 38 16 cover his body and neglect not his
48 14 after death his body prophesied. In his
Jer 26 23 cast his dead body into the graves of
36 30 his dead body shall be cast out to the
Eze 1 23 with two wings covered his body and
Dan 4 30 his body was wet with the dew. 5:21
10 6 his body was like the chrysolite and
2 Ma 9 29 carried away his body: and out of fear
14 38 ready to expose his body and life that
Mark 14 51 cloth cast about his naked body; and
Luke 23 55 sepulcher, and how his body was laid
24 23 certain women . . . not finding his body
John 2 21 he spoke of the temple of his body
Acts 19 12 were brought from his body to the sick
Rom 4 19 consider his own body now dead, whereas
1 C 6 18 sinneth against his own body. Or know
7 4 hath not power of his own body but the
Eph 1 23 the church, which is his body and the
5 23 church. He is the savior of his body
30 because we are members of his body, of
Col 1 24 flesh, for his body, which is the church
1 P 2 24 own self bore our sins in his body
my body Tob 4 3 thou shalt bury my body and
Eccu 51 3 preserved my body from destruction
Isa 50 6 I have given my body to the strikers
2 Ma 7 37 offer up my life and my body for the
Mat 26 12 pouring this ointment upon my body
26 this is my body. Mark 14:22; Luke 22:19; 1 C 11:24
Mark 14 8 to anoint my body for the burial. Amen
1 C 9 27 I chastise my body and bring it into
13 3 and if I should deliver my body to be
Gal 6 17 the marks of the Lord Jesus in my body
Phil 1 20 so shall Christ be magnified in my b.
one body 2 K 2 25 being joined in one body
Jdth 15 4 children of Israel pursuing in one b.
Rom 12 4 as in one body we have many members
5 many, are one body in Christ and every
1 C 6 16 joined to a harlot, is made one body
10 17 being many, are one bread, one body
12 12 they are many, yet are one body, so
13 were we all baptized into one body
20 there are many members, yet one body
Eph 2 16 reconcile both to God in one body by
4 4 one body and one Spirit; as you are
Col 3 15 also you are called in one body: and
whole body Eze 1 18 the w. b. was full of eyes
Eze 10 12 their whole body and their necks and
2 Ma 7 7 punished throughout the whole body
Mat 5 29 that thy whole body be cast into hell
30 that thy whole body go into hell
6 22 w. b. shall be lightsome. Luke 11:34
23 w. b. shall be darksome. Luke 11:35
Luke 11 36 if then thy whole body be lightsome
1 C 12 17 if the whole body were the eye, where
Eph 4 16 the whole body being compacted and
Col 2 19 the whole body . . . groweth unto increase
James 3 2 bridle to lead about the whole body
3 we turn about their whole body. Behold
6 tongue . . . which defileth the whole body
Boen Josu 15 6 to stone of Boen the son of Ruben
Josu 18 18 Abenboen, that is, the stone of Boen
boil Exod 23 19 not boil a kid in the milk of its dam. 34:26; Deut 14:21
Exod 29 31 boil the flesh thereof in the holy
Lev 8 31 boil the flesh before the door of the
1 K 2 15 give me flesh to boil for the priest
4 K 4 38 and boil pottage for the sons of the
20 7 laid it upon his boil, he was healed
Job 41 22 he shall make the deep sea to boil
Eze 46 20 where the priests shall boil the sin
24 ministers . . . shall boil the victims
boiled Gen 18 7 made haste and boiled it. He took
Gen 18 8 and the calf which he had boiled and
25 29 Jacob boiled pottage: to whom Esau
Exod 12 9 anything raw, nor boiled in water, but
Num 6 19 shall take the boiled shoulder of the
11 8 and boiled it in a pot and made cakes
Judg 6 19 Gedeon went in and boiled a kid, and
2 K 13 9 taking what she had boiled, she poured
3 K 19 21 killed them and boiled the flesh with
4 K 6 29 so we boiled my son and ate him. And
2 Pa 35 13 peace offerings they boiled in caldrons
Job 30 27 my inner parts have boiled without any
Isa 44 16 he boiled pottage and was filled and
Dan 14 26 and hair and boiled them together: and
32 Habacuc, and he had boiled pottage
boiling 1 K 2 13 while the flesh was in boiling
Job 41 11 smoke, like that of a pot heated and b.
Jer 1 13 and I said: I see a boiling caldron
Eze 24 5 the seething thereof is boiling hot
Amos 4 2 what shall remain of you in b. pots
boils Exod 9 9 shall be boils . . . in men and beasts
Exod 9 10 there came boils with swelling blains
11 for the boils that were upon them and
bold Prov 28 1 the just, bold as a lion, shall be
Eccu 8 18 go not on the way with a bold man
19 not into the desert with a bold man
20 5 is hateful, that is bold in speech
21 8 he that is mighty by a bold tongue
22 5 she that is bold shameth both her
1 Ma 4 35 Lysias saw . . . how bold the Jews were
Rom 10 20 Isaias is bold and saith: I was found
2 C 10 1 being absent, am bold toward you. But
2 I may not be bold when I am present
2 I am thought to be bold, against some
Eph 6 20 that therein I may be bold to speak
Phil 1 14 are much more bold to speak the word
boldly Gen 34 25 entered b. into the city and slew
Gen 34 30 when they had boldly perpetrated these
44 18 then Juda coming nearer, said boldly: I
Judg 20 31 boldly issued out of the city and seeing
2 K 18 13 if I should have acted boldly against
Job 12 6 abound, and they provoke God boldly
39 21 he pranceth boldly, he goeth forward
1 Ma 6 45 he ran up to it boldly in the midst
2 Ma 14 43 he ran boldly to the wall and manfully
Mark 15 43 went in boldly to Pilate and begged the
Acts 13 46 then Paul and Barnabas said boldly: To
18 26 began to speak boldly in the synagogue
19 8 [Paul] spoke boldly for the space of
Rom 15 15 I have written to you, brethren, more b.
boldness Jdth 16 12 and the Medes at her boldness
Esth 14 12 and give me boldness, O Lord, king of
Wisd 12 17 thou convincest the boldness of them
1 Ma 4 32 cause the boldness of their strength to

2 Ma 4 12 he had the boldness to set up, under the
8 18 trust in their weapons and in their b.
Eph 3 12 in whom we have boldness and access
bolled Exod 9 31 and the flax was now bolled: but
bolt Judg 16 3 with the posts thereof and the bolt
Cant 5 6 I opened the b. of my door to my beloved
bolts 3 K 4 13 cities with walls and brazen bolts
Ps 147 13 strengthened the bolts of thy gates
bond Tob 3 15 loose me from bond of this reproach
Isa 10 4 be not bowed down under the bond and
25 7 bond with which all people were tied
Luke 13 16 be loosed from this bond on sabbath
1 C 12 13 into one body . . . whether bond or free
Gal 3 28 there is neither b. nor free. Col 3:11
Eph 4 3 unity of the Spirit in the b. of peace
6 8 the Lord, whether he be bond or free
Col 3 14 charity which is the bond of perfection
bondage Gen 15 13 they shall bring them under b.
Exod 6 6 and will deliver you from bondage: and
13 3 out of the house of bondage. 14; 20:2; Deut 5:6; 6:13; 8:14; Josu 24:17; Judg 6:8; Jer 34:13
Deut 7 8 from the house of bondage. 13:5, 10
1 Es 9 8 give us a little life in our bondage
9 in our b. our God hath not forsaken
2 Es 5 5 we bring into bondage our sons and our
9 17 gave the head to return to their b.
Esth 14 8 to oppress us with most hard bondage
Wisd 19 13 brought their guests into bondage that
Isa 14 3 the vexation and from the hard bondage
Lam 1 3 affliction and the greatness of her b.
Acts 7 6 that they should bring them under b.
Rom 8 15 have not received the spirit of bondage
2 C 11 20 you suffer if a man bring you into b.
Gal 4 24 from mount Sina engendering unto b.
25 is, and is in bondage with her children
5 1 not held again under the yoke of b.
bondman Gen 44 17 stole the cup, he shall be my b.
Exod 21 20 he that striketh his b. or bondwoman
32 if he assault a bondman or bondwoman
Deut 24 22 thou also wast a bondman in Egypt and
Jer 2 14 is Israel a bondman or a homeborn slave
1 C 7 21 wast thou called, being a bondman, is
22 that is called in the Lord, being a b.
22 being free, is the bondman of Christ
Apoc 6 15 every bondman and every freeman hid
bondmen Gen 44 9 we will be the bondmen of my lord
Gen 44 16 we are all bondmen to my lord, both we
Lev 25 42 let them not be sold as bondmen: afflict
44 let your bondmen . . . be of the nations
Deut 6 21 we were bondmen of Pharao in Egypt
28 68 set to sale to thy enemies for bondmen
3 K 9 22 Solomon made not any to be bondmen
2 Pa 28 10 for your bondmen and bondwomen, which
1 Es 9 9 we are bondmen and in our bondage our
2 Es 9 36 we ourselves this day are bondmen: and
Esth 7 4 would God we were sold for bondmen
Apoc 13 16 freemen and bondmen to have a character
19 18 may eat the flesh of all . . . bondmen
bonds Gen 42 36 not living, Simeon is kept in bonds
Job 39 5 ass free, and who hath loosed his bonds
Ps 2 3 let us break their bonds asunder: and
106 14 and broke their bonds in sunder. Let
115 16 thy handmaid. Thou hast broken my bonds
124 5 such as turn aside into bonds, the Lord
Prov 7 22 he is drawn like a fool to bonds, till
Wisd 17 2 fettered with the bonds of darkness
Isa 28 22 not mock, lest your bonds be tied strait
52 2 loose the bonds from off thy neck, O
Jer 5 5 yoke more, and have burst the bonds
Eze 34 27 when I shall have broken the bonds
Nah 1 13 I will burst thy bonds asunder. And the
Luke 8 29 breaking the bonds, he was driven by
bondservant Lev 19 20 with a woman that is a b.
Deut 15 15 wast a bondservant in the land of Egypt
bondservants Lev 25 39 with the service of b.
bondslaves 1 C 7 23 be not made the b. of men
bondwoman Gen 21 10 cast out this b. and her son
Gen 21 10 son of the bondwoman shall not be heir
12 to thee for the boy, and for thy b.: in
13 son of the bondwoman a great nation
Exod 21 20 that striketh his bondman or bondwoman
32 if he assault a bondman or a bondwoman
Prov 30 23 a b. when she is heir to her mistress
Gal 4 22 the one by a bondwoman, and the other by
23 he who was of the bondwoman, was born
30 cast out the bondwoman and her son; for
30 son of the bondwoman shall not be heir
31 we are not the children of the b., but
bondwomen Exod 21 7 not go out as b. are wont to
Lev 25 44 let your . . . bondwomen be of the nations
Deut 28 68 to sale to thy enemies for . . . bondwomen
2 Pa 28 10 for your bondmen and bondwomen, which
2 Es 5 5 some of our daughters are bondwomen
Esth 7 4 would God we were sold for . . . b.
Nah 2 7 her b. were led away mourning as doves
bone Gen 2 23 this now is bone of my bone and flesh
Gen 29 14 thou art my bone and my flesh. And after
Exod 12 46 neither shall you break a bone thereof
Num 9 12 nor break a bone thereof, they shall
19 16 or that died of himself, or his bone
Judg 9 2 consider that I am your bone and your
2 K 5 1 we are thy bone and thy flesh. 1 Pa 11:1
19 12 you are my bone and my flesh, why are
13 art not thou my bone and my flesh? So
Job 2 5 and touch his bone and his flesh, and
19 20 my bone hath cleaved to my skin, and
30 17 my bone is pierced with sorrows: and
Ps 101 6 my bone hath cleaved to my flesh. I am
138 15 my bone is not hidden from thee, which
Eze 39 15 when they shall see the bone of a man
John 19 36 you shall not break a bone of him. And
bones Exod 13 19 Moses took Joseph's bones with
Josu 24 32 the bones of Joseph which the children
Judg 19 29 dead body of his wife with her bones
2 K 21 12 b. of Saul and the b. of Jonathan. 13
13 the bones of them that were crucified
14 buried them with the bones of Saul and
3 K 13 2 he shall burn men's bones upon thee
4 K 13 21 when it had touched the b. of Eliseus
23 14 their places with the bones of dead men
16 took the bones out of the sepulchers
18 with the bones of the prophet that came
20 and he burnt men's bones upon them
2 Pa 34 5 he burnt the bones of the priests on
Job 10 11 put me together with bones and sinews
31 22 let my arm with its bones be broken
Ps 50 10 the bones that have been humbled shall
52 6 God hath scattered the bones of them
140 7 our bones are scattered by side of hell
Prov 3 8 to thy navel moistening to thy bones
14 30 envy is the rottenness of the bones
15 30 a good name maketh the bones fat. The
16 24 sweet to the soul, and health to the b.
17 22 a sorrowful spirit drieth up the bones
Ecce 11 5 nor how the bones are joined together
Eccu 28 21 stroke of the tongue will break the b.
49 12 may the bones of the twelve prophets
Isa 58 11 with brightness, and deliver thy bones
66 14 your bones shall flourish like an herb
Jer 8 1 they shall cast out the b. of the kings of Juda and the b. of the princess thereof and the b. of the priests and the b. of the prophets and the b. of the inhabitants
Bar 2 24 b. of our kings and b. of our fathers
Eze 6 5 I will scatter your bones round about

24 4 choice pieces and full of bones. Take
5 lay together piles of bones under it
5 bones thereof are thoroughly sodden
10 heap together the bones, which I will
10 and the bones shall be consumed. Then
37 1 midst of a plain that was full of bones
3 dost thou think these bones shall live
4 prophesy concerning these bones; and
4 ye dry bones, hear the word of the Lord
5 thus saith the Lord God to these bones
7 b. came together, each one to its joint
11 all these bones are the house of Israel
11 they say: Our bones are dried up and
Amos 2 1 burnt the bones of the king of Edom
6 10 he may carry the bones out of the house
1 Ma 13 25 took the bones of Jonathan his brother
Mat 23 27 within are full of dead men's bones
Luke 24 39 a spirit hath not flesh and bones, as
his bones 3 K 13 31 lay my bones beside his b.
4 K 23 18 let him alone, let no man move his bones
18 so his bones were left untouched with
Job 20 11 his b. shall be filled with the vices
31 24 his bones are moistened with marrow
33 19 and he maketh all his bones to wither
21 and his bones that were covered shall be
40 13 his bones are like pipes of brass, his
Ps 108 18 into his entrails and like oil in his b.
Prov 12 4 confusion is a rottenness in his bones
Eccu 26 16 delight her husband and shall fat his b.
49 18 his bones were visited, and after death
Jer 50 17 king of Babylon hath broken his bones
Eph 5 30 of his body, of his flesh and of his b.
Heb 11 22 gave commandment concerning his bones
my bones Gen 2 23 this now is bone of my bones
Gen 50 24 carry my bones with you out of this
Exod 13 19 carry out my bones from hence with you
3 K 13 31 buried: lay my bones beside his bones
Job 4 14 and all my bones were affrighted: and
7 15 chooseth hanging, and my bones death
30 30 and my bones are dried up with heat
Ps 6 3 for my bones are troubled. And my soul
21 15 and all my bones are scattered. My heart
18 they have numbered all my bones. And
30 11 poverty and my bones are disturbed
31 3 because I was silent my bones grew old
34 10 my bones shall say: Lord, who is like
37 4 there is no peace for my bones, because
41 11 whilst my bones are broken, my enemies
101 4 my bones are grown dry like fuel for
Isa 38 13 as a lion so hath he broken all my b.
Jer 20 9 as a burning fire, shut up in my bones
23 9 all my bones tremble: I am become as
Lam 1 13 he hath sent fire into my bones and
3 4 he hath broken my bones. He hath built
Haba 3 16 let rottenness enter into my bones
their bones Num 24 8 they shall . . . break their b.
1 K 31 13 they took their bones and buried them
1 Pa 10 12 buried their bones under the oak that
Ps 33 21 the Lord keepeth all their bones, not
Eccu 46 14 their b. spring up out of their place
Lam 4 8 their skin hath stuck to their bones
Eze 32 27 their iniquities were in their bones
Dan 6 24 lions caught them and broke all their b.
Mich 3 2 and their flesh from their bones? Who
3 chopped their bones as for the kettle
bonfire Eze 24 9 of which I will make a great b.
Boni 1 Pa 6 46 Amasai the son of Boni, the son of
2 Es 11 15 Hasabia the son of Boni, and Sabathai
bonnet Jdth 10 3 put a bonnet upon her head and
bonnets Isa 3 19 bracelets and b. and bodkins and
Bonni 2 K 23 36 Bonni of Gadi, Selec of Ammoni
1 Pa 9 4 Omrai the son of Bonni, of the sons of
2 Es 9 4 the Levites . . . Sabania, Bonni, Sarebias
5 Bonni, Hasebnia . . . said: Arise, bless
10 15 Bonni, Azgad, Bebai, Adonia, Begoai
book Gen 5 1 book of the generation of Adam. In
Exod 17 14 write this for a memorial in a book
24 7 taking the book of the covenant, he
32 32 strike me out of the book that thou hast
33 him will I strike out of my book: but
Num 5 23 shall write these curses in a book
21 14 in the book of the wars of the Lord
Deut 29 21 that are contained in book of this law
31 26 take this book and put it in the side
Josu 1 8 let not the book of this law depart
8 31 written in the book of the law of Moses. 23:6; 4 K 14:6; 2 Pa 25:4
34 were written in the book of the law
10 13 written in the b. of the just. 2 K 1:18
18 9 parts, writing them down in a book. And
1 K 10 25 wrote it in a book and laid it up before
3 K 11 41 book of the words of days of Solomon
14 19 book of the words of the days of the kings of Israel. 15:31; 16:5, 14, 20, 27; 22:39; 4 K 1:18; 10:34; 13:8, 12; 14:15, 28; 15:11, 15, 21, 26, 31
29 book of the words of the days of the kings of Juda. 15:7, 23; 22:46; 4 K 8:23; 12:19; 14:18; 15:6, 36; 16:19; 20:20; 21:17, 25; 23:28; 24:5
4 K 22 8 I have found the book of the law in the
8 and Helcias gave the book to Saphan
10 the priest hath delivered to me a book
13 concerning the words of this book which
13 not hearkened to the words of this book
18 thou hast heard the words of the book
23 2 he read all the words of the book of
3 which were written in that book: and the
21 written in the book of this covenant
24 written in the book which Helcias the
1 Pa 9 1 b. of kings of Israel and Juda. 2 Pa 27:7
29 29 written in the book of Samuel the seer and in the book of Nathan the prophet and in the book of Gad the seer
2 Pa 13 22 in the book of Addo the prophet. And
16 11 book of the kings of Juda and Israel. 25:26; 28:26; 32:32; 35:27; 36:8
17 9 having with them the book of the law
24 27 more diligently in the book of kings
34 14 Helcias . . . found the book of the law
15 I have found the book of the law in the
16 he carried the book to the king and told
18 Helcias the priest gave me this book
21 concerning all the words of this book
21 that are written in this book. 24
26 hast heard the words of this book, and
30 of the Lord, all the words of the book
31 written in that book which he had read
35 12 written in the book of Moses. 1 Es 6:18; Dan 9:11
1 Es 6 2 book in which this record was written
2 Es 7 5 I found a book of the number of them
8 1 to bring the book of the law of Moses
3 all the people were attentive to the book
5 and Esdras opened the book before all the
8 they read in the book of the law. 9:3
18 he read in the book of the law of God
12 23 were written in the book of Chronicles
13 1 they read in the book of Moses in the
Esth 9 26 of this epistle, that is, of this book
32 contained in the history of this book
Job 19 23 they may be marked down in a book? With
31 35 himself that judgeth would write a book
Ps 39 8 in the head of the book it is written
68 29 be blotted out of book of the living
138 16 in thy book all shall be written: days

Eccu 50 29 hath written in this book the doctrine
Isa 8 1 said to me: Take thee a great book
29 11 as the words of a book that is sealed
12 the book shall be given to one that
18 deaf shall hear the words of the book
30 8 and note it diligently in a book and
34 4 heavens shall be folded together as a b.
16 diligently in the book of the Lord
Jer 25 13 all that is written in this book, all
30 2 write thee all the words . . . in a book
32 10 and I wrote it in a book and sealed it
12 subscribed the book of the purchase
36 2 take thee a roll of a book and thou
4 spoke to him, upon the roll of a book
11 son of Saphan had heard out of the book
25 spoke to the king, not to burn the book
32 the book which Joakim the king of Juda
45 1 he had written these words in a book
51 60 Jeremias wrote in one book all the evil
63 have made an end of reading this book
Bar 1 1 the book which Baruch the son of Nerias
3 Baruch read the words of this book
3 the people that came to hear the book
14 read ye this book which we have sent
4 1 this is the book of the commandments
Eze 2 9 wherein was a book rolled up: and he
3 1 eat this book, and go speak to the
2 and he caused me to eat that book: and
3 thy bowels shall be filled with this b.
Dan 1 17 understanding in every book and wisdom
12 1 that shall be found written in the book
4 shut up the words and seal the book
Nah 1 1 book of the vision of Nahum the Elcesite
Mala 3 16 a book of remembrance was written before
1 Ma 16 24 the book of the days of his priesthood
2 Ma 2 24 have attempted to abridge in one book
6 12 I beseech those that shall read this b.
8 23 after the holy Book had been read to
Mat 1 1 book of the generation of Jesus Christ
Mark 12 26 in the book of Moses, how in the bush
Luke 3 4 in b. of sayings of Isaias the prophet
4 17 book of Isaias the prophet was delivered
17 as he unfolded the book he found the
20 when he had folded the book he restored
20 42 in book of Psalms: The Lord said to my
John 20 30 which are not written in this book
Acts 1 20 in book of Psalms: Let their habitation
Gal 3 10 which are written in book of the law
Heb 9 19 he sprinkled both the book itself and
10 7 in the head of the book it is written
Apoc 1 11 what thou seest, write in a book and
5 1 a book written within and without
2 who is worthy to open the book and to
3 earth, to open the book nor to look on
4 was found worthy to open the book nor
5 hath prevailed to open the book and to
7 he came and took the book out of the
8 when he had opened the book, the four
9 art worthy, O Lord, to take the book
6 14 heaven departed as a book folded up
10 2 he had in his hand a little book open
8 go and take the book that is open, from
9 him, that he should give me the book
9 take the b. and eat it up: and it shall
10 I took the book from the hand of the
20 12 another book was opened, which is the
22 7 words of prophecy of this book. 9, 10, 18
18 the plagues written in this book. And
19 words of the book of this prophecy
19 these things that are written in this b.
book of life Eccu 24 32 these things are b. . . .
Phil 4 3 whose names are in the book of life
Apoc 3 5 not blot out his name out of the b. . . .
13 8 not written in the b. . . . 17:8; 20:15
20 12 was opened, which is the book of life
21 27 they that are written in the b. . . .
22 19 shall take away his part out of b. . . .
books 2 Pa 9 29 in the books of Ahias the Silonite
2 Pa 12 15 are written in the books of Semeias
20 34 into the books of the kings of Israel
1 Es 4 15 books of the histories of thy fathers
6 1 books that were laid up in Babylon
Esth 10 2 are written in the books of the Medes
Ecce 12 12 of making many books there is no end
Dan 7 10 and the books were opened. I beheld
9 2 I Daniel understood by books the number
1 Ma 1 59 burnt . . . the books of the law of God
60 books of the testament of the Lord were
3 48 they laid open the books of the law
12 9 having for our comfort the holy books
2 Ma 2 13 books both of the prophets and of David
24 in five books by Jason of Cyrene, we
25 considering the multitude of books
John 21 25 not be able to contain the books that
Acts 7 42 in the books of the prophets: Did you
19 19 together their books and burnt them
2 Tim 4 13 bring with thee, and the b., especially
Apoc 20 12 and the books were opened; and another
12 things which were written in the books
booth Job 27 18 as a keeper he hath made a booth
Jon 4 5 he made himself a booth there and he
booty Num 31 11 they carried away the booty, and
Num 31 50 every one of us could find in the booty
53 which every one had taken in the booty
2 K 3 22 came . . . with an exceeding great booty
2 Pa 14 14 the cities and carried off much booty
20 25 away the spoils, the booty was so great
28 5 took a great booty out of his kingdom
8 boys and girls and an immense booty: and
17 slew many of Juda and took a great booty
Jer 49 32 multitude of their cattle for a booty
Eze 29 19 take the booty thereof for a prey and
Soph 1 13 their strength shall become a booty
1 Ma 7 47 took the spoils of them for a booty
Booz Ruth 2 1 very rich, whose name was Booz. And
Ruth 2 3 the owner of that field was Booz, who
5 Booz said to the young man that was
8 Booz said to Ruth: Hear me, daughter
14 Booz said to her: At mealtime come thou
15 Booz commanded his servants, saying
19 man's name, that he was called Booz
23 she kept close to the maids of Booz
3 2 this Booz, with whose maids thou wast
7 when Booz had eaten and drunk and was
14 Booz said: Beware lest any man know that
4 1 Booz went up to the gate and sat there
2 Booz taking ten men of the ancients
5 Booz said to him: When thou shalt buy
8 Booz said to his kinsman: Put off thy
13 Booz therefore took Ruth and married
21 Salmon begot Booz, Booz begot Obed
3 K 7 21 pillar and called the name thereof Booz
1 Pa 2 11 Salma the father of Booz. And Booz begot
2 Pa 3 17 Jachin: and that on the left hand, Booz
Mat 1 5 Salmon begot Booz. Booz begot Obed
Luke 3 32 Obed, who was of Booz, who was of Salmon
borderers 2 Ma 9 25 and b. wait for opportunities
bordereth 1 Ma 14 34 Gazara, which b. upon Azotus
bore Exod 21 6 he shall bore his ear through with
Deut 15 17 bore through his ear in the door of thy
Judg 8 31 concubine . . . bore him a son [Abimelech]
13 24 bore a son and called his name Samson
1 K 1 20 about, Anna conceived and bore a son
2 21 she bore three sons and two daughters
14 1 young man that bore his armor. 6
2 K 11 27 she bore him [David] a son: and this

12 24 [Bethsabee] bore a son and he called
3 K 3 21 that it was not mine which I bore. And
11 20 bore him his son Genubath and Taphnes
21 13 bore witness against him [Naboth] before
4 K 3 25 cut down all the trees that bore fruit
1 Pa 4 9 saying: Because I bore him with sorrow
7 16 Maacha the wife of Machir bore a son
18 his sister named Queen bore Goodlyman
23 she conceived and bore a son. Osee 1:8
2 Pa 11 19 they bore him sons Jehus and Solorias
14 8 of men that bore shields and spears
8 of Benjamin that bore shields and drew
Job 3 10 doors of the womb that bore me, nor
40 19 bore through his nostrils with stakes
21 bore through his jaw with a buckle
Prov 17 25 sorrow of the mother that bore him
23 25 let her rejoice that bore thee. My son
Cant 3 4 into the chamber of her that bore me
6 8 the chosen of her that bore her. The
8 5 she was deflowered that bore thee. Put
Isa 8 3 and she conceived and bore a son. And
51 2 father, and to Sara that bore you: for
Jer 16 3 concerning their mothers that b. them
20 14 not the day in which my mother bore me
22 26 thee and thy mother that bore thee
50 12 that bore you is made even with the
Eze 23 4 and they bore sons and daughters. Now
37 children, whom they bore to me, they have
41 6 they bore outwards, that they might
42 5 because they bore up the galleries
Osee 1 3 she conceived and bore him a son. And
6 again, and bore a daughter and the
2 Ma 5 23 Menelaus who bore a more heavy hand
7 20 and bore it with a good courage, for
27 me, that bore thee nine months in my
14 39 the hatred that he bore the Jews, sent
Mat 8 17 he took our infirmities and bore our
Mark 14 56 bore false witness against him. 57
Luke 11 27 blessed is the womb that bore thee and
1 P 2 24 bore our sins in his body upon the tree
bored 4 K 12 9 chest and bored a hole in the top
borith Jer 2 22 multiply to myself the herb borith
born Gen 14 14 of the servants born in his house
Gen 15 3 my servant, born in my house, shall be
17 17 shall a son . . . be born to him that is
38 9 lest children should be born in his
41 50 Joseph had two sons born: whom Aseneth
42 32 twelve brethren born of one father: one
Exod 1 22 born of the male sex, ye shall cast
12 19 whether . . . stranger or born in the land
Lev 18 9 mother, whether born at home or abroad
22 11 his servant, born in his house, these
Num 15 13 they that are born in the land and the
30 whether he be born in the land or a
Deut 23 2 one born of a prostitute shall not enter
8 they that are born of them in the third
28 57 children that are born the same hour
29 22 children that shall be born hereafter
Judg 11 2 thou art born of another mother. Then
13 8 concerning the child that shall be born
Ruth 2 11 and the land wherein thou wast born
4 17 there is a son born to Noemi: called his
3 K 13 2 a child shall be born to the house of
1 Pa 7 21 men of Geth born in the land slew them
22 9 the son that shall be born to thee
1 Es 10 3 the wives and such as are born of them
Tob 6 21 that sound children may be born of you
Job 11 12 thinketh himself born free like a wild
14 1 man born of a woman, living for a short
38 21 know then that thou shouldst be born
Ps 21 32 a people that shall be born, which the
44 17 sons are born to thee: thou shalt make
77 6 the children that should be born and
Ecce 3 2 a time to be born and a time to die
4 14 and another born king is consumed with
6 3 that the untimely born is better than
Wisd 2 2 we are born of nothing, and after this
4 6 that are born of unlawful beds are
5 13 we also being born, forthwith ceased to
7 3 and being born I drew in the common air
Eccu 7 30 thou hadst not been born but through
23 19 wish that thou hadst not been born
41 12 if you be born, you shall be born in malediction
44 9 become as if they had never been born
49 17 Joseph, who was a man born prince of his
Jer 16 3 daughters, that are born in this place
Eze 16 4 when thou wast born, in the day of thy
5 thy soul in the day that thou wast born
47 22 born among the children of Israel: they
Mat 2 4 of them where Christ should be born
11 11 risen among them that are born of women
26 24 if he had not been born. Mark 14:21
Mark 7 26 was a Gentile, a Syrophenician born
Luke 1 35 the Holy which shall be born of thee
7 28 amongst those that are born of women
John 1 13 who are born, not of blood nor of the
3 3 unless a man be born again, he cannot
4 how can a man be born when he is old
4 his mother's womb and be born again
5 unless a man be born again of water and
7 I said to thee, you must be born again
8 41 we are not born of fornication: we have
9 34 thou wast wholly born in sins, and dost
Acts 4 36 Barnabas . . . a Levite, a Cyprian born
18 24 Apollo, born at Alexandria, an eloquent
22 3 I am a Jew, born at Tarsus in Cilicia
1 C 15 8 as by one born out of due time. For I
1 P 1 23 being born again not of corruptible seed
born blind; *see* **blind**
born of God John 1 13 b. not of blood, but of God
1 J 3 9 whosoever is born of God, committeth not
9 cannot sin because he is born of God
4 7 every one that loveth, is born of God
5 1 whosoever believeth . . . is born of God
4 whatsoever is born of God, overcometh
18 whosoever is born of God, sinneth not
is born Gen 17 12 he that is born in the house
Exod 12 48 shall be as he that is born in the land
49 shall be to him that is born in the land
Ruth 4 15 he is born of thy daughter-in-law: who
2 K 12 14 that is born to thee, shall surely die
Job 5 7 man is born to labor and the bird to fly
15 14 and he that is born of a woman that he
25 4 that is born of a woman appear clean
Ps 86 5 this man and that man is born in her
Prov 17 21 a fool is born to his own disgrace: and
Ecce 4 3 than them both, that is not yet born
Eccu 14 19 cometh to an end, and another is born
Isa 9 6 a child is born to us, and a son is
Jer 20 15 saying: A man child is born to thee
Mat 2 2 where is he that is born king of the
Luke 2 11 this day is born to you a Savior, who
John 3 6 that which is born of the flesh is flesh
6 which is born of the Spirit is spirit
8 is every one that is born of the Spirit
16 21 joy that a man is born into the world
1 J 2 29 one who doth justice, is born of him
5 1 loveth him also who is born of him. In
was born Gen 21 5 age of his father was Isaac b.
Gen 30 25 when Joseph was born, Jacob said to his
44 20 boy, that was born in his old age; whose
Num 9 14 and for him that was born in the land
10 30 to my country wherein I was born. And
26 59 who was born to him in Egypt. She bore
Josu 8 33 and he that was born among them, half

1 Pa 7 23 because he was born when it went evil
20 6 who also was born of the stock of Rapha
Job 3 3 let the day perish wherein I was born
15 7 art thou the first man that was born
Eccu 49 16 no man was born upon earth like Henoch
Jer 20 14 cursed be the day wherein I was born
Osee 2 3 as in the day that she was born: and I
1 Ma 2 7 wherefore was I born to see the ruin of
Mat 1 16 of whom was born Jesus, who is called
2 1 when Jesus was born in Bethlehem of
John 18 37 for this was I born, and for this came
Acts 7 20 at the same time was Moses born and
22 28 sum. And Paul said: But I was born so
Gal 4 23 was born according to the flesh. 29
Heb 11 23 Moses when he was born was hid three
were born Gen 6 1 daughters were born to them
Gen 10 1 unto them sons were born after the flood
17 23 all that were born in his house. 27
25 26 children were born unto him [Isaac]
35 26 that were born to him in Mesopotamia
36 5 were born to him in the land of Chanaan
46 20 and sons were born to Joseph in the land
27 the sons of Joseph, that were born to
48 5 who were born to thee in land of Egypt
50 22 were born on Joseph's knees. After which
Lev 25 45 that were born of them in your land
Josu 5 5 the people that were born in the desert
7 uncircumcised even as they were born
2 K 3 2 and sons were born to David in Hebron
5 these were born to David in Hebron
5 13 were born to David other sons also
14 were born to him in Jerusalem. 1 Pa 14:4
14 27 there were born to Absalom three sons
21 22 these four were born of Arapha in Geth
1 Pa 1 19 and to Heber were born two sons, the
2 3 these three were born to him [Juda]
9 the sons of Hesron that were born to him
3 1 of David that were born to him in Hebron
4 so six sons were born to him in Hebron
5 these sons were born to him in Jerusalem
26 6 and to Semei his son were born sons
Job 1 2 there were born to him seven sons and
Eccu 44 8 they that were born of them have left
Jer 16 3 their fathers, of whom they were born
22 26 country in which you were not born
Eze 23 15 the Chaldeans wherein they were born
Mat 19 12 are eunuchs who were born so from their
Acts 2 8 our own tongue wherein we were born
Rom 9 11 when the children were not yet born
borne Gen 22 20 Melcha also had borne children
Gen 24 36 Sara my master's wife hath borne my
29 34 because I have borne him three sons
30 20 because I have born him six sons: and
Exod 21 4 if . . . she hath borne sons and daughters
1 K 2 5 so that the barren hath borne many
4 20 fear not, for thou hast borne a son
2 K 12 15 which the wife of Urias had borne to
1 Es 10 44 among them women that had borne children
Ps 54 13 I would verily have borne with it. And
68 8 for thy sake I have borne reproach
Ecce 8 12 and by patience is borne withal, I know
Eccu 44 3 such as have b. rule in their dominions
Isa 46 3 by my bowels, are borne up by my womb
53 4 surely he hath borne our infirmities
12 and he hath borne the sins of many
Jer 15 9 she that hath borne seven is become
10 why hast thou borne me a man of strife
31 19 I have borne the reproach of my youth
Lam 3 27 when he hath borne the yoke from his
5 7 not: and we have borne their iniquities
Bar 6 3 gods . . . of wood borne upon shoulders
Eze 16 20 daughters, whom thou hast borne to me
58 thou hast borne thy wickedness, and thy
18 19 why hath not the son borne the iniquity
32 24 borne their shame with them. 25, 30
36 6 you have borne the shame of the Gentiles
44 10 and have borne their iniquity: they
Dan 13 43 have borne false witness against. 49
1 Ma 8 5 that had borne arms against them and
Mat 20 12 have borne the burden of the day and
Luke 23 29 barren, and the wombs that have not b.
1 C 15 49 we have borne the image of the earthly
borrow Exod 22 14 if a man b. of his neighbor any
Deut 15 6 thou shalt borrow of no man. Thou shalt
28 12 nations, and shalt not borrow of any one
4 K 4 3 b. of all thy neighbors empty vessels
2 Es 5 4 let us b. money for the king's tribute
Ps 36 21 the sinner shall borrow, and not pay
Mat 5 42 from him that would borrow of thee turn
borrowed 4 K 6 5 my lord, for this same was borrowed
borrower Prov 22 7 b. is servant to him that
Isa 24 2 as with the lender, so with the b.: as
borroweth Wisd 15 16 and he that b. his own breath
borrowing Eccu 18 33 make not thyself poor by b.
Boses 1 K 14 4 name of the one was Boses, and the
bosom Gen 16 5 I gave my handmaid into thy bosom
Exod 4 6 when he had put it into his bosom. And
7 put back thy hand into thy bosom. He
Num 11 12 carry them in thy bosom as the nurse
Deut 13 6 thy wife that is in thy bosom, or thy
28 54 and his wife, that lieth in his bosom
56 her husband who lieth in her bosom
Judg 16 19 her knees and lay his head in her bosom
Ruth 4 16 taking the child laid it in her bosom
2 K 12 3 ewe lamb . . . sleeping in his bosom: and
8 thy master's wives into thy bosom and
3 K 1 2 and sleep in his bosom, and warm our
3 20 was asleep and laid it in her bosom
20 and laid her dead child in my bosom
17 19 he [Elias] took him out of her bosom
Job 19 27 this my hope is laid up in my bosom
23 12 words of his mouth I have hid in my b.
31 33 have concealed my iniquity in my bosom
Ps 34 13 my prayer shall be turned into my b.
73 11 right hand out of midst of thy bosom
78 12 to our neighbors sevenfold in their b.
88 51 which I have held in my bosom, of many
128 7 that gathereth sheaves [filleth] his b.
Prov 5 20 art cherished in the bosom of another
6 27 can a man hide fire in his bosom and
21 14 gift in bosom [quencheth] greatest wrath
Ecce 7 10 anger resteth in the bosom of a fool
Eccu 9 1 be not jealous over wife of thy bosom
Isa 40 11 and shall take them up in his bosom
65 6 will render and repay into their bosom
7 back their first work in their bosom
Jer 32 18 into the bosom of their children after
Mich 7 5 from her that sleepeth in thy bosom
Luke 6 38 over shall they give into your bosom
16 22 was carried by angels into Abraham's b.
23 afar off, and Lazarus in his bosom: and
John 1 18 who is in the bosom of the Father, he
13 23 there was leaning on Jesus' bosom one
bosoms Lam 2 12 souls in the b. of their mothers
Bosor Deut 4 43 Bosor in the wilderness, which is
Josu 20 8 they appointed Bosor, which is upon the
21 36 Bosor in the wilderness, one of the
1 Pa 6 78 out of the tribe of Ruben, Bosor in the
7 37 sons of Supha . . . Bosor and Hod and
1 Ma 5 26 were shut up in Barasa and in Bosor
28 their march into the desert, to Bosor
36 took Casbon and Mageth and Bosor and
2 P 2 15 followed the way of Balaam of Bosor
Bosphorus Abdi 20 the captivity . . . that is in B.
Bosra Gen 36 33 Jobab son of Zara of B. reigned
Josu 21 27 one of the cities of refuge, and Bosra

1 Pa 1 44 Jobab the son of Zare of B. reigned
Isa 34 6 there is a victim of the Lord in Bosra
63 1 from Edom, with dyed garments from Bosra
Jer 48 24 and upon Carioth, and upon Bosra: and
49 13 that Bosra shall become a desolation
22 he shall spread his wings over Bosra
Amos 1 12 it shall devour the houses of Bosra
bosses Judg 8 21 he took the ornaments and bosses
both Mat 9 17 both are preserved. Luke 5:38
Mat 13 30 suffer both to grow until the harvest
15 14 both fall into the pit. Luke 6:39
Luke 7 42 he forgave them both. Which therefore
Acts 23 8 spirit: but the Pharisees confess both
Eph 2 14 he is our peace who hath made both one
16 and might reconcile both to God in one
18 we have access both in one Spirit to the
Apoc 22 2 on both sides of river was tree of life
bottle Gen 21 14 taking bread and a bottle of water
Gen 21 15 when the water in the bottle was spent
19 of water, and went and filled the bottle
Judg 4 19 she opened a bottle of milk and gave
1 K 1 24 bushels of flour and a bottle of wine
10 3 another carrying a bottle of wine. And
16 20 laden with bread and a bottle of wine
4 K 9 1 this little bottle of oil in thy hand
3 taking the little bottle of oil, thou
Jdth 10 5 she gave to her maid a bottle of wine
Ps 118 83 I am become like a bottle in the frost
Jer 13 12 every bottle shall be filled with wine
19 1 go and take a potter's earthen bottle
10 thou shalt break the bottle in the sight
bottles Josu 9 4 wine b. rent and sewed up again
Josu 9 13 these bottles of wine when we filled
Jer 48 12 that shall order and overturn his b.
12 break their bottles one against another
Mat 9 17 into old bottles. Mark 2:22; Luke 5:37
17 otherwise the bottles break and the wine
17 and the bottles perish. But new wine
17 they put into new b. Mark 2:22; Luke 5:38
Mark 2 22 the wine will burst the b. Luke 5:37
22 the bottles will be lost. Luke 5:37
bottom Exod 15 5 they are sunk to the bottom like
Exod 19 17 they stood at the bottom of the mount
29 12 blood thou shalt pour at the bottom
39 23 bells . . . at the bottom of the tunick
Lev 5 9 he shall let it drop at the bottom
8 15 rest of the blood at the bottom thereof
Jdth 5 12 walked through the bottom of the sea
Eccu 23 28 of men, and the bottom of the deep
24 8 penetrated into the bottom of the deep
Isa 14 19 art gone down to the bottom of the pit
51 17 drunk even to the bottom of the cup
Eze 27 34 thy riches are in the b. of the waters
43 13 the bottom thereof was a cubit and the
14 from the bottom of the ground to the
17 the bottom of it one cubit round about
Dan 6 24 did not reach the b. of the den, before
Mich 7 19 all our sins into the bottom of the sea
Zach 1 8 myrtle trees, that were in the bottom
Mat 27 51 rent . . . from top even to b. Mark 15:38
bottomless Apoc 9 1 b. pit. 2, 11; 17:8; 20:1, 3
bough Gen 8 11 carrying a bough of an olive tree
Judg 9 48 an axe, he cut down the bough of a tree
Isa 17 6 three berries in the top of a bough
boughs Lev 23 40 boughs of thick trees and willows
Judg 9 49 they cut down boughs from the trees
Job 14 7 green again and the boughs thereof sprout
Ps 79 12 the sea, and its boughs unto the river
117 27 a solemn day, with shady boughs, even
Eze 31 3 top was elevated among the thick boughs
5 and his boughs were elevated because
6 made their nests in his boughs and all
12 his boughs shall fall in every valley

2 Ma 10 7 they now carried b. and green branches
14 4 b. which seemed to belong to the temple
Mat 21 8 others cut boughs. Mark 11:8
bought Gen 17 12 as the bought servant shall be
Gen 17 23 and all whom he had bought, every male
27 as the bought servants and strangers
25 10 which he had bought of the children of
33 19 he bought that part of the field in
39 1 Egyptian, bought him of the Ismaelites
42 19 carry the corn that you have bought
43 21 when we had bought, and come to the inn
47 14 money for the corn which they bought
20 Joseph bought all the land of Egypt
49 30 which Abraham bought together with the
50 13 double cave which Abraham had bought
Exod 12 44 bought servant shall be circumcised
Lev 5 15 flocks, that may be b. for two sicles
22 11 he whom the priest had bought, and he
25 28 the buyer shall have what he bought
27 22 if a field that was bought, and not of
Josu 24 32 part of the field which Jacob had b.
Ruth 4 9 I have bought all that was Elimelech's
2 K 12 3 ewe lamb which he had b. and nourished
24 24 so David bought the floor and the oxen
3 K 10 28 b. them at a set price. And a chariot
16 24 he bought the hill of Samaria of Semer
4 K 22 6 that timber may be bought, and stones
2 Pa 1 16 merchants who went and bought at a price
2 Es 5 16 I bought no land, and all my servants
Prov 31 16 she hath considered a field and b. it
Isa 43 24 thou hast bought me no sweet cane with
Jer 32 9 I b. the field of Hanameel my uncle's
44 fields shall be bought for money and
Lam 5 4 for money: we have bought our wood
Osee 3 2 I bought her to me for fifteen pieces
Mat 13 46 sold all that he had and bought it
21 12 that sold and bought in the temple.
Mark 11:15; Luke 19:45
27 7 they bought with them the potter's field
Mark 16 1 bought sweet spices, that coming, they
Luke 14 18 I have bought a farm and I must needs
19 I have bought five yoke of oxen and I
17 28 in days of Lot . . . they bought and sold
Acts 7 16 in the sepulcher that Abraham bought
1 C 6 20 for you are bought with a great price
7 23 you are bought with a price; be not made
2 P 2 1 deny the Lord who bought them: bringing
bound Gen 22 9 when he had bound Isaac his son
Gen 24 8 thou shalt not be bound by the oath
41 47 the corn being bound up in sheaves
42 19 one of your brethren be bound in prison
Exod 39 18 and the rational were bound together
Num 30 4 wherewith she hath bound her soul and
4 peace, she shall be bound by the vow
6 neither shall she be bound to what
9 wherewith she had bound her soul of no
11 hath bound herself by vow and by oath
13 she shall not be bound by the promise
Judg 15 13 but we will deliver thee up bound. And
13 they bound him with two new cords and
14 the bands with which he was bound were
16 6 it is wherewith if thou wert bound thou
7 if I shall be bound with seven cords
8 with which she bound him [Samson]; men
10 wherewith thou mayest be bound. 13
11 if I shall be bound with new ropes
12 Dalila bound him again with these and
21 led him bound in chains to Gaza and
21 5 had bound themselves with a great oath
18 being bound with an oath and a curse
1 K 14 28 thy father hath bound the people with
2 K 3 34 thy hands were not bound nor thy feet
3 K 8 31 an oath . . . wherewith he is bound: and

4 K 5 23 bound two talents of silver in two bags
17 4 bound him and cast him into prison
23 33 Pharao Nechao bound him at Rebla which
25 7 bound him [Sedecias] with chains and
2 Pa 33 11 Manasses and carried him bound with
36 6 led him bound in chains to Babylon. And
Tob 8 3 the devil and bound him in the desert
Jdth 6 9 and so left him bound with ropes and
10 that the Assyrians had left him bound
8 3 over them that b. sheaves in the field
16 10 and bound up her locks with a crown
Job 3 18 they sometime bound together without
36 8 and be bound with the cords of poverty
13 neither shall they cry when they are b.
Ps 19 9 they are bound and have fallen: but we
67 7 out them that were bound in strength
103 9 hast set a bound which they shall not
106 10 of death: bound in want and in iron
Prov 5 22 he is fast bound with the ropes of his
22 15 folly is b. up in the heart of a child
30 4 who hath bound up the waters together
Cant 7 5 purple of the king bound in the channels
Wisd 17 17 were all bound together with one chain
Eccu 22 19 a frame of wood bound together in the
28 23 hath not been bound in its bands. For
Isa 1 6 they are not bound up nor dressed nor
22 3 are fled together and are bound hard
3 all that were bound, are bound hard
45 14 they shall go bound with manacles: and
49 9 mightest say to them that are bound
Jer 5 22 I have set the sand a bound for the sea
39 7 bound him with fetters, to be carried
40 1 taken him, being bound with chains
52 11 bound him [Sedecias] with fetters and
Bar 1 9 and brought them bound to Babylon. And
Eze 27 24 were wrapped up and bound with cords
30 21 it is not bound up, to be healed, to be
34 4 was broken you have not bound up and
45 16 shall be bound to these firstfruits
47 18 Jordan making the bound to the east sea
Dan 3 21 there men were bound and were cast
23 fell down bound in the midst of the
91 did we not cast three men bound into
4 20 let it be bound with iron and brass
Osee 4 19 the wind hath bound them up in its
5 10 as they that take up the bound: I will
13 12 iniquity of Ephraim is bound up, his
Nah 3 10 her great men were bound in fetters
Mat 14 3 apprehended John and b. him. Mark 6:17
16 19 shall be bound also in heaven. 18:18
27 2 they brought him bound and delivered him
Mark 5 4 having been often bound with fetters
Luke 8 29 was b. with chains and kept in fetters
10 34 bound up his wounds, pouring in oil and
13 16 of Abraham, whom Satan hath bound
John 11 44 came forth, bound feet and hands with
44 his face was abound about with a napkin
18 12 took Jesus and bound him: and they led
24 Annas sent him bound to Caiphas the high
19 40 bound it in linen cloths with the spices
Acts 9 2 he might bring them bound to Jerusalem
21 might carry them bound to the chief
12 6 bound with two chains: and the keepers
20 22 bound in the spirit, I go to Jerusalem
21 13 I am ready not only to be bound, but to
33 commanded him to be bound with two
22 5 that I might bring them b. from thence
25 when they had bound him [Paul] with
29 because he had bound him [Paul]. But on
23 12 bound themselves under a curse, saying
14 we have b. ourselves under great curse
21 have bound themselves by oath neither
24 27 Felix . . . left Paul bound. Now when
28 20 for the hope of Israel I am bound with
1 C 7 27 art thou bound to a wife? Seek not to
39 a woman is bound by the law as long as
Col 4 3 for which also I am bound; that I may
2 Th 1 3 we are bound to give thanks always to
2 Tim 2 9 the word of God is not bound. Therefore
Heb 13 3 bands, as if you were bound with them
Apoc 9 14 loose the four angels who are bound
20 2 bound him for a thousand years. And he

bounded Num 34 2 it shall be b. by these limits
Num 35 5 north side shall be b. with the like
Josu 15 11 is bounded westward with the great sea

bounds Exod 23 31 thy bounds from the Red Sea to
Num 34 10 thence they shall mark out the bounds
11 the bounds shall go down to Rebla over
Deut 32 8 he appointed the bounds of people
Judg 11 18 would not enter the bounds of Moab and
Josu 15 4 bounds thereof shall be the great sea
18 5 let Juda be in his bounds on the south
Job 14 5 thou hast appointed his bounds which
26 10 he hath set bounds about the waters
38 10 I set my bounds around it and made it
20 mayst bring everything to its own bounds
Prov 8 29 when he compassed the sea with its b.
17 27 he that setteth bounds to his words
22 28 pass not beyond the ancient bounds which
23 4 set bounds to thy prudence. Lift not up
10 touch not the bounds of little ones
Isa 5 14 opened her mouth without any bounds
10 13 I have removed the bounds of the people
28 25 and millet and vetches in their bounds
1 Ma 14 6 he enlarged the bounds of his nation
Mat 24 31 heavens to the utmost bounds of them

bountiful Ps 114 7 the Lord hath been b. to thee
Prov 28 8 him that will be bountiful to the poor
Isa 55 7 our God: for he is bountiful to forgive

bounty 3 K 10 13 offered her . . . of his royal b.
Eph 2 7 riches of his grace in his b. towards

bow (noun) Gen 9 13 I will set my bow in the clouds
Gen 9 14 my bow shall appear in the clouds, my
16 and the bow shall be in the clouds, and
21 16 great way off as far as a bow can carry
27 3 take thy arms, thy quiver and bow and
48 22 which I took . . . with my sword and bow
49 24 his bow rested upon the strong and the
Josu 24 12 not with thy sword nor with thy bow
1 K 2 4 the bow of the mighty is overcome and
18 4 even to his sword and to his bow and to
2 K 1 18 the children of Juda the use of the bow
22 35 and maketh my arms like a bow of brass
3 K 22 34 a certain man bent his bow shooting
4 K 6 22 not take them with thy sword or thy bow
9 24 but Jehu bent his bow with his hand
13 15 said to him: Bring a bow and arrows
15 had brought him a bow and arrows, he
16 put thy hand upon the bow. And when he
1 Pa 5 18 and bending the bow and trained up to
12 2 bending the bow, and using either hand
2 Pa 17 17 armed with bow and shield. And after him
Jdth 5 16 they went in without bow and arrow
Job 20 24 and shall fall upon a bow of brass
29 20 my bow in my hand shall be repaired
Ps 7 13 he hath bent his bow and made it ready
10 3 the wicked have bent their bow; they
17 35 hast made my arms like a brazen bow
36 14 they have bent their bow. 63:4
15 own hearts, and let their bow be broken
43 7 I will not trust in my bow: neither shall
45 10 he shall destroy the bow and break the
57 8 hath bent his bow till they be weakened
59 6 that they may flee from before the bow
77 9 who bend and shoot with the bow: they
57 were turned aside as a crooked bow

Wisd 5 22 as from a bow well bent, they shall be
Isa 21 15 that hung over them, from the bent bow
41 2 as stubble driven by the wind, to his bow
66 19 and Lydia them that draw the bow: into
Jer 9 3 they have bent their tongue, as a bow
49 35 I will break the bow of Elam and their
50 14 round about all you that bend the bow
29 declare . . . to all that bend the bow
42 they shall take the bow and the shield
51 3 let not him that bendeth, bend his bow
56 and their bow is weakened, because the
Lam 2 4 he hath bent his bow. 3:12
Eze 39 3 I will break thy bow in thy left hand
Osee 1 5 I will break in pieces the bow of Israel
7 I will not save them by bow nor by sword
2 18 I will destroy the bow and the sword
7 16 they became like a deceitful bow: their
Amos 2 15 that holdeth the bow shall not stand
Haba 3 9 thou wilt surely take up thy bow
Zach 9 10 the bow for war shall be broken: and he
13 I have bent Juda for me as a bow, I have
10 4 out of him the bow of battle, out of him
Apoc 6 2 he that sat on him had a bow, and there
bow (verb) Gen 27 29 children bow down before thee
Gen 41 43 all should bow their knee before him
49 8 sons of thy father shall bow down to thee
2 K 22 40 hast made them . . . to bow under me. My
4 K 5 18 if I bow down in the temple of Remmon
Job 22 29 he that shall bow down his eyes, he shall
39 3 they bow themselves to bring forth, and
Ps 30 3 bow down thy ear to me: make haste to
143 5 bow down thy heavens and descend: touch
Eccu 4 7 bow thy head to a great man. Bow down
8 bow down thy ear cheerfully to the poor
6 26 bow down thy shoulder and hear her
7 25 bow down their neck from their childhood
30 12 bow down his neck while he is young
33 27 continual labors bow a slave. Torture
47 21 thou didst bow thyself to women: and by
Isa 17 7 man shall bow down himself to his Maker
51 23 bow down, that we may go over: and thou
Bar 2 21 bow down your shoulder and your neck
Rom 11 10 bow down their back always. I say then
Eph 3 14 I bow my knees to the Father of our
Phil 2 10 in name of Jesus every knee should bow
bowed Gen 23 7 bowed down to the people of the land
Gen 23 12 Abraham bowed down before the people
24 26 the man bowed himself down and adored
33 3 [Jacob] went forward and bowed down
6 the handmaids . . . bowed themselves
7 Lia . . . came near and bowed down in like
7 last of all Joseph and Rachel bowed down
37 7 bowed down before my sheaf. His brethren
42 6 when his brethren had bowed down to him
43 26 they bowed down with their face to the
48 12 he bowed down with his face to the
49 15 he bowed his shoulder to carry, and
Exod 34 8 Moses making haste, bowed down prostrate
Num 21 15 rocks of the torrents were bowed down
1 K 4 19 she bowed herself and fell in labor
25 41 [Abigail] bowed herself down with her
28 14 he [Saul] bowed himself with his face
2 K 9 8 [Mephiboseth] bowed down to him and
18 21 Chusai bowed down to Joab, and ran
22 10 he bowed the heavens and came. Ps 17:10
3 K 1 16 Bethsabee bowed herself and worshipped
2 19 bowed to her and sat down upon his throne
19 18 whose knees have not been bowed before
4 K 4 34 he [Eliseus] bowed himself upon him
9 32 two or three eunuchs bowed down to him
1 Pa 21 21 bowed down to him with his face to the
29 20 bowed themselves and worshipped God
29 bowed down and adored. 2 Es 8:6
Jdth 10 20 Judith . . . bowed down to him, prostrating
Ps 37 7 and am bowed down even to the end
45 7 troubled, and kingdoms were bowed down
56 7 and they bowed down my soul. They dug
Eccu 51 21 I bowed down my ear a little and
Isa 2 9 man hath bowed himself down, and man
17 loftiness of men shall be bowed down
10 4 that you be not bowed down under the
44 15 graven thing and bowed down before it
45 24 every knee shall be bowed to me, and
Jer 48 39 how hath Moab bowed down the neck
Bar 2 18 goeth bowed down and feeble and the
Haba 3 6 hills of the world were bowed down
Luke 13 11 she was bowed together, neither could she
24 5 as they . . . bowed down their countenance
Rom 11 4 that have not bowed their knees to Baal
bowels Gen 15 4 that shall come out of thy bowels
Lev 4 11 bowels and the dung . . . he shall carry
2 K 7 12 which shall proceed out of thy bowels
16 11 my son, who came forth from my bowels
20 10 struck him in side and shed out his b.
3 K 3 26 her bowels were moved upon her child
2 Pa 21 15 a very grievous disease of thy bowels
18 with an incurable disease in his b.
19 so as to void his very bowels, his
32 21 his sons that came out of his bowels
Job 16 14 hath poured out my bowels on the earth
21 24 his bowels are full of fat, and his bones
32 18 the spirit of my bowels straiteneth me
Ps 21 15 like wax melting in midst of my bowels
24 6 remember . . . thy bowels of compassion
50 12 renew a right spirit within my bowels
Prov 12 10 the bowels of the wicked are cruel
18 8 even to the inner parts of the bowels
20 27 searcheth all the hidden things of the b.
22 18 if thou keep it in thy bowels, and it
Cant 5 4 my bowels were moved at his touch
Wisd 12 5 eaters of men's bowels, and devourers
Eccu 10 10 he hath cast away his bowels. All power
11 32 as corrupted bowels send forth stinking
17 19 them down into the bowels of the earth
30 7 at every cry his b. shall be troubled
Isa 16 11 my bowels shall sound like a harp
19 3 shall be broken in the b. thereof
46 3 who are carried by my bowels, are borne
48 19 offspring of thy bowels like the gravel
49 1 from the bowels of my mother he hath
63 15 where is . . . the multitude of thy bowels
Jer 1 5 formed thee in the bowels of thy mother
4 19 my bowels are in pain, the senses of my
31 20 therefore are my b. troubled for him
33 I will give my law in their bowels
Lam 1 20 my bowels are troubled. 2:11
Bar 2 17 whose spirit is taken away from their b.
Eze 3 3 thy b. shall be filled with this book
11 19 will put a new spirit in their bowels
Haba 2 19 there is no spirit in the bowels thereof
3 16 I have heard and my b. were troubled
2 Ma 9 5 dreadful pain in his bowels came upon
6 seeing he had tormented the b. of others
14 46 grasping his bowels with both hands
Luke 1 78 the bowels of the mercy of our God
Acts 1 18 all his bowels gushed out. And it became
2 C 6 12 in your own bowels you are straitened
7 15 his b. are more abundantly towards you
Phil 1 8 I long after you in the b. of Jesus
2 1 if any bowels of commiseration: fulfill
Col 3 12 the bowels of mercy, benignity, humility
Philem 7 bowels of the saints have been refreshed
12 do thou receive him as my own bowels
20 refreshed my bowels in the Lord. Refresh
1 J 3 17 and shall shut up his bowels from him
bowers Lev 23 42 you shall dwell in b. seven days

boweth 4 K 5 18 when he b. down in the same place
Eccu 38 19 sorrow of the heart boweth down the
33 b. down his strength before his feet
Isa 44 17 he b. down before it and adoreth it
bowing Gen 43 28 b. themselves they made obeisance
Exod 12 27 the people bowing themselves, adored
Judg 7 5 that shall drink bowing down their knees
1 K 24 9 David b. himself down to the ground
2 K 24 21 bowing with his face to the earth and
3 K 1 23 had worshipped, b. down to the ground
31 Bethsabee bowing with her face to the
2 Pa 29 30 great joy, and bowing the knee adored
Ps 16 11 set their eyes bowing down to the earth
Isa 60 14 shall come bowing down to thee, and all
Mat 27 29 bowing the knee before him, they mocked
Mark 15 19 bowing their knees, they adored him
John 8 6 Jesus bowing himself down, wrote with
19 30 bowing his head, he gave up the ghost
bowl Exod 25 33 and a bowl withal and a lily. Such
Num 7 13 a silver bowl of seventy sicles. 19, 25, 31, 37, 43, 49, 55, 61, 67, 73, 79
85 each b. seventy sicles: that is, putting
Cant 7 2 thy navel is like a round bowl never
Dan 14 32 and had broken bread in a bowl: and
bowls Exod 24 6 blood, and put it into bowls: and
Exod 25 29 shalt prepare also dishes and bowls
31 the bowls and the lilies going forth
34 at every one, bowls and lilies. Bowls
35 bowls under two branches. 37:21
36 bowls and the branches shall be of same
37 16 the divers uses of the table, dishes, b.
17 its cups and bowls and lilies came out
19 each branch and bowls withal and lilies
20 and bowls withal at every one, and lilies
22 bowls and branches were of the same
Num 4 7 mortars, the cups and bowls to pour out
7 84 dishes of silver: twelve silver bowls
3 K 7 50 and bowls . . . of most pure gold: and the
4 K 12 13 temple of the Lord, bowls or fleshhooks
25 15 also the censers and the bowls, such as
1 Pa 28 17 fleshhooks also and bowls and censers
2 Pa 4 8 also a hundred bowls of gold. He made
11 made caldrons and fleshpots and bowls
16 sea; and caldrons and fleshhooks and b.
22 the bowls and the mortars of pure gold
24 14 ministry and for holocausts and bowls
1 Es 1 9 thirty b. of gold, 1,000 b. of silver
2 Es 7 70 a thousand drams of gold, fifty bowls
Jer 52 18 and the psalteries and the bowls and the
Amos 6 6 that drink wine in bowls, and anoint
Zach 9 15 they shall be filled as bowls and as
bows 2 Pa 14 8 bore shields and drew bows, two
2 Es 4 13 with their swords and spears and bows
16 fight, with spears and shields and bows
Ps 75 4 hath he broken the powers of bows the
Isa 5 28 and all their bows are bent. The hoofs
7 24 and with bows they shall go in thither
Eze 39 9 and burn . . . the bows and the arrows
box 1 K 6 8 you shall put into a little box at the
1 K 6 11 box that had in it the golden mice and
15 little box that was at the side of it
Isa 30 8 go in and write for them upon box and
41 19 the elm and the box tree together
60 13 to thee, the fir tree and the box tree
Mat 26 7 alabaster box. Mark 14:3; Luke 7:37
boy Gen 21 12 not seem grievous to thee for the boy
Gen 21 14 and delivered the boy and sent her away
15 she cast the boy under one of the trees
16 she said: I will not see the boy die
17 God heard the voice of the boy, from the
17 God hath heard the voice of the boy
18 arise, take up the boy and hold him by
19 filled the bottle and gave the boy to
22 5 I and the boy will go with speed as far
12 lay not thy hand upon the boy, neither
37 2 flock with his brethren being but a boy
29 returning to the pit, found not the boy
30 the boy doth not appear and whither
42 22 do not sin against the boy: and you
43 8 send the boy with me, that we may set
9 I take the boy upon me, require him at
44 20 have a father an old man and a young boy
22 the boy cannot leave his father: for if
30 the boy be wanting, whereas his life
33 thy servant will stay instead of the boy
33 let the boy go up with his brethren
34 not return to my father without the boy
Judg 8 14 he took a boy of the men of Soccoth
20 he was afraid, being but yet a boy
1 K 17 33 art but a boy, but he is a warrior
20 21 I will send a boy, saying to him: Go
22 if I shall say to the boy: Behold the
22 but if I shall speak thus to the boy
35 with David, and a little boy with him
36 he said to his boy: Go and fetch me the
36 when the boy ran, he shot another arrow beyond the boy
37 the boy therefore came to the place
37 Jonathan cried after the boy. 38
38 Jonathan's boy gathered up the arrows
40 Jonathan gave his arms to the boy and
41 when the boy was gone, David rose out
2 K 14 21 and fetch back the boy Absalom. Joab
17 18 certain boy saw them and told Absalom
18 5 saying: Save me the boy Absalom. 12
3 K 11 17 Adad was then a little boy. And they
2 Pa 34 3 he [Josias] was yet a boy, he began
Tob 1 8 things did he observe when but a boy
Dan 13 45 raised up the holy spirit of a young boy
Joel 3 3 the boy they have put in the stews
1 Ma 11 54 with him Antiochus the young boy, who
Mark 9 23 father of the boy crying out with tears
Luke 9 43 Jesus . . . cured the boy and restored him
John 6 9 boy here that hath five barley loaves
boys Gen 48 16 bless these boys: and let my name
4 K 2 23 little boys come out of the city and
24 and tore of them two and forty boys
2 Pa 28 8 carried away . . . women, boys, and girls
Zach 8 5 streets of the city shall be full of b.
bracelet Gen 38 18 answered: Thy ring and bracelet
Gen 38 25 see whose ring and bracelet and staff
2 K 1 10 and the bracelet that was on his arm
Eccu 21 24 like a bracelet upon his right arm
bracelets Gen 24 22 many b. of ten sicles weight
Gen 24 30 when he had seen the earrings and b.
47 face, and I put bracelets on her hands
Exod 35 22 both men and women gave bracelets and
Num 31 50 rings and bracelets and chains that thou
Jdth 10 3 and took her bracelets and lilies and
Isa 3 19 chains and necklaces and bracelets
Eze 16 11 and put bracelets on thy hands and a
23 42 they put bracelets on their hands and
bragged Jdth 16 6 b. that he would set my borders
brain Judg 4 21 drove it through his brain fast
brake (*see also* **broke**) Mat 14 19 b. and gave the loaves. 15:36; Mark 6:41; 8:6; Luke 9:16
Luke 22 19 b. and gave to them, saying: This. Mat 26:26; Mark 14:22; 1 C 11:24
24 30 brake and gave to them. And their eyes
bramble Judg 9 14 all the trees said to the b.
Judg 9 15 let fire come out from the bramble
Luke 6 44 from b. bush do they gather the grape
branch Exod 25 33 cups as it were nuts to every b.
Exod 25 33 the fashion of nuts in the other branch
37 19 cups in manner of a nut on each branch
19 the fashion of a nut in another branch

Num 13 24 they cut off a branch with its cluster
Isa 14 19 as an unprofitable branch defiled and
25 5 shalt make b. of the mighty to wither
60 21 the branch of my planting, the work of
Jer 23 5 I will raise up to David a just branch
Eze 8 17 behold they put a branch to their nose
Mala 4 1 it shall not leave them root nor branch
Mat 24 32 b. thereof is now tender. Mark 13:28
John 15 2 every b. in me that beareth not fruit
4 as branch cannot bear fruit of itself
6 he shall be cast forth as a branch
branches Gen 40 10 vine on which were three b.
Gen 40 12 the three branches are yet three days
Exod 25 31 make a candlestick . . . and the branches
32 six branches shall come out of the sides
33 such shall be the work of the six b.
35 bowls under two b. in three places. 37:21
36 b. shall be of the same beaten work
37 17 from the shaft whereof its branches
18 three branches on one side and three on
19 the work of the six branches that went
21 six branches going out from one shaft
22 bowls and branches were of the same
Lev 23 40 and branches of palm trees and boughs
2 Es 8 15 fetch b. of olive and b. of beautiful
wood, b. of myrtle and b. of palm and
b. of thick trees
Job 15 30 the flame shall dry up his branches
Ps 79 11 b. thereof [covered] the cedars of God
12 it stretched forth its branches unto
Cant 5 11 his locks as branches of palm trees
Wisd 4 4 if they flourish in branches for a time
5 b. not being perfect, shall be broken
17 17 among the spreading branches of trees
Eccu 1 25 the branches thereof are long-lived
14 26 and shall lodge under her branches
23 35 her branches shall bring forth no fruit
24 22 I have stretched out my branches as the
22 my branches are of honor and grace
40 15 shall not bring forth many branches
50 14 as branches of palm trees, they stood
Isa 6 13 as an oak that spreadeth its branches
16 8 the branches thereof have reached even
8 the branches thereof are left, they
27 10 down and shall consume its branches
Jer 5 10 take away the branches thereof, because
11 16 it, and the branches thereof are burnt
48 32 thy branches are gone over the sea
Eze 17 6 the branches thereof looked towards him
6 it became a vine, and grew into branches
7 stretched forth her branches to him
8 that it might bring forth branches
9 dry up all the b. it hath shot forth
22 tender twig from top of the branches
23 it shall shoot forth into branches
23 its nest under shadow of the branches
19 10 her b. have grown out of many waters
11 her stature was exalted among the b.
11 her height in the multitude of her b.
14 fire is gone out from a rod of her b.
31 3 like a cedar in Libanus, with fair b.
5 and his branches were multiplied and
6 brought forth their young under his b.
7 and for the spreading of his branches
8 to be compared with him for branches
9 and thick set with many branches: and
12 his branches shall be broken on every
13 beasts of the field were among his b.
14 up their tops among the thick branches
36 8 shoot ye forth your branches and yield
Dan 4 9 in the b. thereof the fowls of the air
11 cut down the tree and chop off the b.
11 under it, and birds from its branches
18 branches thereof were most beautiful
18 had their abode in its branches. It is
Osee 10 1 Israel a vine full of branches, fruit
14 7 his branches shall spread and his glory
Joel 1 7 the branches thereof are made white
Nah 2 2 and have marred their vine branches
Zach 4 12 what are the two olive branches, that
1 Ma 13 51 with thanksgiving and b. of palm trees
2 Ma 10 7 they now carried boughs and green b.
Mat 13 32 come and dwell in the branches thereof
Mark 4 32 shooteth out great b. so that the birds
Luke 13 19 birds of the air lodged in the branches
John 12 13 took b. of palm trees and went forth
15 5 I am the vine; you the branches: he
Rom 11 16 if the root be holy, so are the branches
17 if some of the branches be broken and
18 boast not against the branches. But if
19 the branches were broken off, that I
21 if God hath not spared the natural b.
24 they that are the natural branches, be
brand Zach 3 2 this is a brand plucked out of the
brandish Ps 7 13 he will brandish his sword: he
brass Gen 4 22 artificer in every work of b. and
Exod 25 3 you must take gold, silver, and brass
26 11 fifty buckles of brass. 36:18
37 shall be of gold, and the sockets of b.
27 2 thou shalt cover it with brass. And thou
3 all its vessels thou shalt make of brass
4 a grate of brass in manner of a net
4 at the four corners . . . four rings of b.
6 thou shalt cover with plates of brass
10 with as many sockets of brass. 11
17 silver, silver heads and sockets of b.
18 linen, and shall have sockets of brass
19 of the court, thou shalt make of brass
31 4 made of gold and silver and brass, of
35 5 offer them to the Lord: gold . . . and b.
16 and its grate of brass, with the bars
24 metal of silver and b. they offered to
32 to work in gold and silver and brass
36 38 gold, and their sockets he cast of brass
38 2 he overlaid it with plates of brass
3 he prepared divers vessels of brass
4 he made the grate thereof of brass
6 overlaid them with plates of brass
8 he made also the laver of brass with
10 twenty pillars of brass with their
12 ten pillars of brass with their sockets
17 sockets of the pillars were of brass
19 entry were four with sockets of brass
20 the court round about he made of brass
29 were offered of brass 72,000 talents
30 altar of brass with the grate thereof
39 39 the altar of brass, the grate, the bars
Lev 6 28 vessels be of brass, it shall be scoured
26 19 heaven above as iron and the earth as b.
Num 31 22 brass . . . shall be purified by fire
Deut 8 9 out of its hills are dug mines of brass
28 23 be the heaven that is over thee of b.
33 25 his shoe shall be iron and brass. As
Josu 6 19 vessels of brass and iron. 24
22 8 with silver and gold, brass and iron
1 K 17 5 he had a helmet of brass upon his head
5 coat of mail was 5,000 sickles of brass
6 he had greaves of brass on his legs
6 buckler of brass covered his shoulders
38 put a helmet of brass upon his head
2 K 8 8 king David took . . . quantity of brass
10 in his hand were . . . vessels of brass
22 35 maketh my arms like a bow of brass
3 K 7 14 artificer in brass, and full of wisdom
14 and skill to work all work in brass
15 and he cast two pillars in brass, each

16 made also two chapiters of molten b.
27 he made ten bases of brass, every base
29 as it were bands of brass hanging down
30 had four wheels and axletrees of brass
36 in those plates which were of brass
38 he made also ten lavers of brass: one
45 all the vessels . . . were of fine brass
47 multitude the b. could not be weighed
14 27 Roboam made shields of brass instead
4 K 16 14 altar of brass that was before the Lord
15 but the altar of brass shall be ready
25 13 pillars of b. that were in the temple
13 and the bases and the sea of b. which
13 all the b. of them to Babylon. Jer 52:17
14 the mortars and all the vessels of b.
14 they took away also the pots of brass
16 brass of all these vessels was without
17 the chapiter of brass which was upon it
17 the pomegranates . . . were all of brass
1 Pa 15 19 Ethan, sounded with cymbals of brass
18 8 he [David] brought very much brass
8 Solomon made . . . the vessels of brass
11 the vessels of gold and silver and brass
22 3 joinings: of brass an immense weight
14 of brass and of iron there is no weight
16 in brass and in iron, whereof there is
29 2 brass for things of b., iron for things
7 of brass eighteen thousand talents
2 Pa 1 5 the altar of brass which Beseleel the
2 7 knoweth how to work . . . in brass. 14
4 1 he made also an altar of brass twenty
9 in the hall, which he covered with b.
16 the house of the Lord of the finest b.
18 the weight of the brass was not known
24 12 and such as wrought in iron and brass
1 Es 8 27 two vessels of the best shining brass
Job 6 12 strength of stones nor is my flesh of b.
20 24 and shall fall upon a bow of brass. The
28 2 stone melted with heat is turned into b.
37 18 strong, as if they were of molten brass
40 13 his bones are like pipes of brass, his
41 18 iron as straw, and brass as rotten wood
Ps 106 16 because he hath broken gates of brass
Wisd 15 9 like the workers in brass and counteth
Eccu 12 10 as a brass pot his wickedness rusteth
28 24 iron: and its bands are bands of brass
Isa 45 2 in pieces the gates of brass and will
48 4 an iron sinew and thy forehead as brass
60 17 for brass I will bring gold and for iron
17 for wood brass, and for stones iron
Jer 1 18 and a pillar of iron, and a wall of b.
6 28 they are brass and iron: they are all
15 12 iron from the north, and the brass? Thy
20 to this people as a strong wall of brass
46 22 her voice shall sound like brass for
52 17 the sea of brass that was in the house
20 twelve oxen of brass that were under
20 no weight of the b. of these vessels
22 chapiters of brass were upon both: and
22 the chapiters round about, all of brass
Eze 1 7 like the appearance of glowing brass
22 18 all these are brass and tin and iron
20 as they gather silver and brass and
24 11 and the brass thereof may be melted
27 13 to thy people slaves and vessels of b.
40 3 was like the appearance of brass with
Dan 2 32 the belly and the thighs of brass: and
35 the clay, the brass . . . broken to pieces
39 another, third kingdom of brass which
45 broke in pieces . . . the iron and the b.
4 12 tied with a band of iron and of brass
20 let it be bound with iron and brass
5 4 their gods of gold and of silver, of b.
23 hast praised the gods . . . of brass, of
10 6 like in appearance to glittering brass
14 6 is but clay within, and brass without
Mich 4 13 thy hoofs I will make brass: and thou
Zach 6 1 the mountains were mountains of brass
1 Ma 6 35 with helmets of brass on their heads
39 upon the shields of gold and of brass
8 22 graven in tables of brass and sent to
14 18 they wrote to him in tables of brass
26 and registered it in tables of brass
48 should be put in tables of brass
Luke 21 2 widow casting in two brass mites. And
1 C 13 1 I am become as sounding brass, or a
Apoc 1 15 his feet like unto fine brass. 18
9 20 not adore devils and idols of . . . brass
18 12 vessels of precious stone and of brass
brave Judg 5 11 clemency towards the brave men of
Eze 32 27 they shall not sleep with the brave
bravely Judg 20 41 turning their faces stood b.
1 Ma 16 23 deeds which he bravely achieved and the
2 Ma 7 21 she bravely exhorted every one of them
bravest 2 K 11 16 where he knew the b. men were
1 Pa 19 10 chose out the bravest men of all Israel
28 1 all the bravest of the army at Jerusalem
Jdth 5 28 when the bravest of them shall be taken
brawling Prov 21 9 housetop than with a b. woman
Prov 25 24 than with a b. woman and in a common
bray Prov 27 22 though thou shouldst bray a fool in
brazen Exod 30 18 shalt make also a brazen laver
Num 16 39 Eleazar took the brazen censers wherein
21 8 make a brazen serpent and set it up
9 Moses therefore made a brazen serpent
3 K 4 13 great cities with walls and brazen bolts
8 64 the brazen altar that was before the Lord
4 K 16 17 from the brazen oxen that held it up
18 4 broke the brazen serpent, which Moses
1 Pa 18 8 of which Solomon made the brazen sea
2 Pa 1 6 Solomon went up thither to the b. altar
6 13 for Solomon had made a brazen scaffold
7 7 the brazen altar, which he had made
12 10 instead of which the king made b. ones
Ps 17 35 hast made my arms like a brazen bow
Jer 52 18 brazen vessels that had been used in
Eze 9 2 went in, and stood by the brazen altar
2 Ma 7 3 brazen caldrons to be made hot: which
Mark 7 4 pots, and of brazen vessels and of beds
breach Lev 24 20 breach for breach, eye for eye
3 K 11 27 filled up the b. of the city of David
4 K 25 4 breach was made into the city: and all
1 Pa 13 11 he called that place the Breach of Oza
2 Pa 24 13 the breach of the walls was closed up
2 Es 6 1 and that there was no breach left in it
Ps 105 23 stood before him in the breach: to turn
143 14 there is no breach of wall nor passage
Isa 30 13 be to you as a breach that falleth
Jer 6 14 healed the breach of the daughter. 8:11
Osee 13 13 he shall not stand in the breach of
2 Ma 15 10 of the Gentiles, and their b. of oaths
breaches 4 K 22 6 and to such as mend breaches
2 Es 4 7 and the breaches began to be closed
Ps 59 4 heal thou the breaches thereof, for it
Isa 22 9 shall see the b. of the city of David
Osee 14 5 I will heal their breaches, I will love
Amos 4 3 you shall go out at the breaches one
6 12 will strike the greater house with b.
9 11 I will close up the breaches of the
1 Ma 9 62 he repaired the breaches thereof and
bread Gen 3 19 of thy face shalt thou eat bread
Gen 14 18 Salem, bringing forth bread and wine
21 14 taking bread and a bottle of water, put
24 33 and bread was set before him. But he
25 34 taking bread and the pottage of lentils
27 17 delivered him bread that she had baked

28 20 shall give me bread to eat and raiment
31 54 called his brethren to eat bread. And
37 25 sitting down to eat bread they saw some
39 6 knew he any other thing but the bread
41 54 there was bread in all the land of Egypt
43 25 heard that they should eat bread there
31 set bread on the table. And when it
45 23 carrying wheat and bread for the journey
47 13 in whole world there was want of bread
15 came to Joseph saying: Give us bread
49 20 Aser, his b. shall be fat and he shall
Exod 2 20 man go? Call him that he may eat bread
12 19 he that shall eat leavened bread, his
16 3 the flesh pots, and ate bread to the
4 I will rain bread from heaven for you
12 you shall have your fill of bread: and
15 Moses said to them: This is the bread
32 that they may know the b. wherewith
18 12 came to eat bread with them before God
23 25 that I may bless your bread and your
29 23 one roll of bread, a cake tempered with
34 the consecrated flesh or of the bread
34 28 he neither ate bread nor drank water
Lev 7 13 loaves of leavened b. with the sacrifice
21 6 of the Lord and the bread of their God
17 he shall not offer bread to his God
21 sacrifices to the Lord nor b. to his God
22 25 not offer bread to your God from the
23 14 you shall not eat either b. or parched
24 7 that the bread may be for a memorial
26 5 you shall eat your bread to the full
26 have broken the staff of your bread
26 ten women shall bake your bread in one
Num 11 8 cakes thereof of the taste of bread
14 9 we are able to eat them up as bread
15 19 shall eat of the bread of that country
28 2 offer ye my oblation and my bread and
Deut 8 3 not in bread alone doth man live, but
9 without any want thou shalt eat thy b.
9 9 neither eating b. nor drinking water. 18
16 3 shalt not eat with it leavened bread
3 shalt thou eat . . . the b. of affliction
23 4 would not meet you with bread and water
29 6 not eaten bread nor have you drunk wine
Judg 7 13 as if a hearth cake of barley bread
8 5 bread to the people that is with me
6 that we should give bread to thy army
15 that we should give bread to the men
13 16 press me, I will not eat of thy bread
19 5 taste first a little b. and strengthen
19 bread and wine for the use of myself
Ruth 2 4 come thou hither and eat of the bread
1 K 2 5 have hired out themselves for bread
36 a piece of silver and a roll of bread
36 that I may eat a morsel of bread. Now
9 7 the bread is spent in our bags: and we
10 3 three loaves of bread and another
16 20 Isai took an ass laden with bread and
20 24 and the king sat down to eat bread
34 did not eat bread on the second day
21 4 no common bread at hand, but only holy b.
6 priest therefore gave him hallowed bread
22 13 hast given him bread and a sword and
25 11 shall I then take my bread and my water
22 let me set before thee a morsel of b.
30 11 and they gave him b. to eat and water
12 he had not eaten bread nor drunk water
2 K 3 29 by the sword, or that wanteth bread
35 taste bread or anything before sunset
6 19 to every one a cake of bread and a piece
9 7 thou shalt eat bread at my table always
10 shall always eat bread at my table
12 3 eating of his bread and drinking of

20 house and he called for bread and ate
21 dead, thou didst rise up and eat bread
16 1 laden with two hundred loaves of bread
3 K 13 8 nor eat bread nor drink water in this
9 thou shalt not eat bread. 17
15 come home with me to eat bread. But he
16 neither will I eat bread nor drink water
18 that he may eat bread and drink water
19 so he ate bread and drank water in his
22 and hast returned and eaten bread and
22 shouldst not eat bread nor drink water
17 6 the ravens brought him [Elias] bread
11 bring . . . a morsel of bread in thy hand
18 4 and fed them with bread and water. 13
7 arise and eat bread and be of good cheer
22 27 and feed him with bread of affliction
4 K 4 8 detained him [Eliseus] to eat bread
8 he turned into her house to eat bread
42 bringing . . . bread of the firstfruits
6 22 but set bread and water before them
18 32 a land of bread and vineyards, a land
29 and he ate bread always before him
1 Pa 16 3 both men and women, a loaf of bread
2 Pa 2 4 the continual setting forth of bread
18 26 give him bread and water in a small
2 Es 5 15 took of them in bread and wine and in
9 15 thou gavest them bread from heaven
36 gavest our fathers to eat the bread
13 2 met not children of Israel with bread
Tob 2 5 he ate bread with mourning and fear
4 17 eat thy bread with the hungry and the
18 lay out thy bread and thy wine upon the
Jdth 10 5 and bread and cheese, and went out
Job 15 23 when he moveth himself to seek bread
20 14 his bread in his belly shall be turned
22 7 hast withdrawn bread from the hungry
24 5 prey they get bread for their children
27 14 grandsons shall not be filled with b.
28 5 the land out of which bread grew in
33 20 bread becometh abominable in him
42 11 they ate bread with him in his house
Ps 13 4 who devour my people as they eat bread
40 10 whom I trusted, who ate my bread, hath
41 4 my tears have been my bread day and
52 5 who eat up my people as they eat bread
77 20 can he also give bread, or provide
24 had given them the bread of heaven
25 man ate the bread of angels: he sent
79 6 wilt thou feed us with bread of tears
101 5 because I forgot to eat my b. Through
10 I did eat ashes like bread and mingled
103 14 mayst bring bread out of the earth
15 that bread may strengthen man's heart
104 16 broke in pieces all the support of bread
40 he filled them with the bread of heaven
126 2 you that eat the bread of sorrow. When
131 15 I will satisfy her poor with bread
Prov 9 5 eat my bread, and drink the wine which
17 hidden bread is more pleasant. And he
12 9 he that is glorious and wanteth bread
11 his land shall be satisfied with bread
20 13 open thy eyes and be filled with bread
17 the bread of lying is sweet to a man
22 9 of his bread he hath given to the poor
23 3 meats, in which is the bread of deceit
28 19 tilleth . . . shall be filled with bread
21 for morsel of bread forsaketh the truth
31 14 she bringeth her bread from afar. And
27 house and hath not eaten her bread idle
Ecce 9 7 go then and eat thy bread with joy
11 nor bread to the wise, nor riches to
10 19 for laughter they make bread and wine
11 1 cast thy bread upon the running waters

Wisd 16 20 gavest them bread from heaven prepared
Eccu 10 30 that boasteth himself and wanteth bread
12 6 hold back thy bread and give it not
14 10 he shall not have his fill of bread
15 3 with the bread of life and understanding
20 18 that eat his bread are of a false tongue
23 24 that is a fornicator all bread is sweet
29 27 for man's life is water and bread and
31 28 bless him that is liberal of his bread
29 against him that is niggardly of his b.
33 25 b. and correction and work for a slave
34 25 b. of the needy is the life of the poor
26 taketh away the bread gotten by sweat
39 31 things necessary . . . bread of flour and
45 26 prepared them bread in the first place
Isa 3 1 whole strength of bread and the whole
4 1 we will eat our own bread and wear our
21 14 south, meet with bread him that fleeth
28 28 bread corn shall be broken small: but
30 20 the Lord will give you spare bread
23 the bread of the corn of the land shall
33 16 bread is given him, his waters are sure
36 17 of wine, a land of bread and vineyards
44 15 he kindled it and baked bread: but of
19 and I have baked bread upon the coals
51 14 neither shall his bread fail. But I am
55 2 money for that which is not bread and
10 seed to the sower, and b. to the eater
58 7 deal thy bread to the hungry and bring
Jer 5 17 they shall eat up thy corn and thy bread
11 19 saying: Let us put wood on his bread
16 7 they shall not break bread among them
37 20 daily a piece of bread beside broth till
all the bread in the city were spent
44 17 and we were filled with bread and it
52 33 he ate bread before him always all the
Lam 1 11 all her people sigh, they seek bread
4 4 the little ones have asked for bread
5 6 that we might be satisfied with bread
9 fetched our bread at peril of our lives
Eze 4 9 and made thee bread thereof according
12 as barley bread baked under the ashes
13 eat their bread all filthy among the
15 thou shalt make thy bread therewith
16 will break in pieces the staff of bread
16 they shall eat bread by weight and with
17 so that when bread and water fail every
5 16 will break among you the staff of bread
12 18 eat thy bread in trouble and drink thy
19 they shall eat their bread in care
13 19 violated me . . . for a piece of bread
14 13 will break the staff of the b. thereof
16 19 my b. which I gave thee, the fine flour
49 Sodom thy sister, prise, fulness of b.
18 7 given his bread to the hungry. 16
44 3 to eat bread before the Lord: he shall
7 you offer my bread, the fat, and the
48 18 for bread to them that serve the city
Dan 11 26 that eat bread with him, shall destroy
14 32 and had broken bread in a bowl: and
Osee 2 5 my lovers, that give me my bread and
7 8 become as bread baked under the ashes
9 4 shall be like the bread of mourners
4 their bread is life for their soul
Amos 4 6 want of bread in all your places: yet
7 12 land of Juda: and eat bread there and
8 11 not a famine of bread, nor a thirst
Agge 2 13 and touch with his skirt, bread or
Mala 1 7 you offer polluted bread upon my altar
Mat 4 3 that these stones be made bread. Who
4 not in bread alone doth man. Luke 4:4
6 11 this day our supersubstantial bread
7 9 if his son shall ask bread, will he
15 2 wash not their hands when they eat b.
26 take the b. of the children. Mark 7:27
16 5 had forgotten to take bread. Mark 8:14
11 not concerning bread I said to you
12 not . . . should beware of the leaven of b.
26 26 Jesus took bread and blessed and broke
Mark 3 20 they could not so much as eat bread
6 37 let us go and buy bread for 200 pence
7 2 disciples eat b. with common hands. 5
8 4 fill them here with b. in wilderness
14 22 Jesus took bread and blessing broke and
Luke 4 3 say to this stone that it be made bread
6 4 took and ate the bread of proposition
7 33 John the Baptist came neither eating b.
9 33 take . . . nor scrip nor bread nor money
11 3 give us this day our daily bread. And
11 if he ask his father bread, will he
14 1 went into the house . . . to eat bread
15 that shall eat bread in the kingdom of
15 17 hired servants . . . abound with bread
22 19 taking bread, he gave thanks and brake
24 30 he took bread and blessed and brake
35 they knew him in the breaking of bread
John 6 5 whence shall we buy bread that they may
7 two hundred pennyworth of bread is not
23 the place where they had eaten the bread
31 he gave them bread from heaven to eat
32 Moses gave you not bread from heaven
32 my Father giveth you the true bread
33 bread of God is that which cometh down
34 Lord, give us always this bread. And
35 I am the bread of life. 48
41 I am the living bread which came. 51
50 this is the bread which cometh down
52 if any man eat of this bread, he shall
52 the bread that I will give is my flesh
59 this is the bread that came down from
59 he that eateth this bread shall live
13 18 he that eateth bread with me shall lift
26 it is to whom I shall reach b. dipped
26 when he had dipped the bread, he gave it
21 9 and a fish laid thereon and bread
13 Jesus cometh and taketh b. and giveth
Acts 2 42 communication of the breaking of bread
46 breaking bread from house to house
20 7 when we were assembled to break bread
11 [Paul] going up and breaking bread and
27 35 taking bread, he gave thanks to God
1 C 10 16 the bread which we break, is it not the
17 we being many, are one bread, one body,
all that partake of one bread
11 16 as often as you shall eat this bread
23 took bread and giving thanks, broke
27 whosoever shall eat this bread or drink
28 so let him eat of that bread and drink
2 C 9 10 will both give you bread to eat, and
2 Th 3 8 neither did we eat any man's bread for
12 that they would eat their own bread

no bread Exod 13 3 that you eat no leavened b.
Num 21 5 there is no bread, nor have we any
1 K 21 4 no common bread at hand, but only holy
6 no bread there, but only the loaves
28 20 for he had eaten no bread all that day
3 K 17 12 I have no bread, but only a handful of
21 4 face to the wall and would eat no bread
5 grieved? And why eatest thou no bread
4 K 25 3 was no bread for the people of the land
1 Es 10 6 he ate no bread and drank no water
Isa 3 7 in my house there is no b. nor clothing
Jer 38 9 for there is no more bread in the city
Dan 10 3 I ate no desirable bread, and neither
Mat 16 7 because we have taken no b. Mark 8:16
Mark 6 8 no bread nor money in their purse

unleavened bread Gen 19 3 [Lot] baked u. bread
Exod 12 8 unleavened bread with wild lettuce
15 seven days shall you eat u. b. Lev 23:6
17 feast of the u. b. 23:15; 34:18; Deut 16:16; 2 Pa 8:13; 30:21; 35:17; 1 Es 6:22
18 you shall eat unleavened bread. 20
13 6 thou eat u. b. 23:15; 34:18; Deut 16:8
7 unleavened b. shall you eat seven days
29 2 take . . . unleavened bread and a cake
23 out of the basket of u. b. Lev 8:26
Lev 8 2 take . . . a basket with unleavened bread
23 6 the solemnity of the u. b. 2 Pa 30:13
Num 6 15 a basket also of unleavened bread. 17
9 11 they shall eat it with unleavened bread
28 17 seven days shall they eat unleavened b.
Josu 5 11 ate on the next day unleavened bread
Judg 6 19 Gedeon . . . made u. bread of a measure
1 K 28 24 baked some unleavened bread and set it
4 K 23 9 ate of the u. b. among their brethren
Eze 45 21 seven days u. b. shall be eaten. And
Mark 14 12 on the first day of the u. b., when they
Luke 22 1 feast of unleavened bread . . . was at
7 the day of the unleavened bread came
1 C 5 8 with the u. b. of sincerity and truth
break Gen 32 26 let me go, for it is break of day
Exod 12 46 neither shall you break a bone thereof
14 27 it returned at the first break of day
23 24 destroy them and break their statues
34 13 break their altars and cut down their
Lev 1 17 he shall break the pinions thereof
2 14 break it small like meal and so shalt
13 29 if the leprosy break out in the head
26 19 break the pride of your stubbornness
30 your high places and break your idols
Num 9 12 nor break a bone thereof, they shall
21 at break of day left the tabernacle
24 8 break their bones and pierce them with
33 52 break in pieces their statues and waste
Deut 7 5 and break their statues and cut down
8 7 in . . . the hills deep rivers break out
12 3 and break down their statues, burn their
3 break their idols in pieces: destroy
23 25 mayst break the ears and rub them
Judg 16 6 wert bound thou couldst not break loose
9 as a man would break a thread of tow
2 K 2 22 they came to Hebron at break of day
22 39 consume them and break them in pieces
3 K 15 19 thee to come and break thy league with
4 K 3 26 to break in upon the king of Edom: but
18 21 it will break and go into his hand
2 Pa 16 3 thou mayst break thy league with Baasa
1 Es 9 14 we should . . . nor break thy commandments
Jdth 10 11 down the hill, about break of day that
14 7 at break of day, they hung up the head
9 endeavoring by art to break his rest
Job 19 2 soul and b. me in pieces with words
24 14 murderer riseth at the very break of day
26 8 so that they break not out and fall
34 24 break in pieces many and innumerable
38 11 thou shalt break thy swelling waves
39 10 will he break the clods of the valleys
15 the beasts of the field may break them
Ps 2 3 let us break their bonds asunder: and
9 and shalt break them in pieces like a
9 15 break thou the arm of the sinner and of
17 39 I will break them, and they shall not be
28 5 Lord shall break the cedars of Libanus
45 10 shall destroy the bow and b. the weapons
47 8 thou shalt break in pieces the ships of
55 8 thou shalt break the people in pieces
57 7 Lord shall b. the grinders of the lions
62 2 to thee do I watch at break of day
67 22 God shall break the heads of his enemies
74 11 I will break all the horns of sinners
Prov 25 15 a soft tongue shall break hardness
Cant 2 17 till the day break, and the shadows. 4:6
Eccu 28 21 of the tongue will break the bones
Isa 5 5 I will break down the wall thereof
10 33 shall break the earthen vessel with
28 28 hurt it, nor break it with its teeth
41 15 mountains, and break them in pieces
42 3 the bruised reed he shall not break
45 2 I will break in pieces the gates of
58 6 free, and break asunder every burden
8 then shall thy light break forth as
Jer 1 14 the north shall an evil break forth
4 3 break up anew your fallow ground and
14 21 break not thy covenant with us. Are
16 7 they shall not break bread among them
19 10 shalt break the bottle in the sight
11 even so will I break this people and
23 19 a tempest shall break out and come
28 4 I will break the yoke of the king of
11 Lord: even so will I break the yoke of
30 8 that I will break his yoke from off
43 13 he shall break the statues of the
48 12 break their bottles one against another
49 35 I will break the bow of Elam and their
Lam 4 4 there was none to break it unto them
Eze 5 16 I will break among you the staff of
13 13 cause a stormy wind to break forth
14 I will break down the wall that you
14 13 will break the staff of the bread
25 7 break thee in pieces, and thou shalt
26 4 they shall break down the walls of
29 7 thou didst break and rent all their
30 18 when I shall b. there the scepters
22 will break into pieces his strong
24 I will break the arms of Pharao and
39 3 I will break thy bow in thy left hand
Dan 2 40 so shall that break and destroy all
Osee 10 2 he shall break down their idols, he
11 Jacob shall break the furrows for
12 break up your fallow ground: but the
Joel 3 11 break forth and come, all ye nations
Amos 1 5 I will break the bar of Damascus: and
Zach 11 14 that I might break the brotherhood
16 the fat ones, and break their hoofs
1 Ma 1 66 would not break the holy law of God
4 30 who didst break the violence of
2 Ma 11 9 ready to break through not only men
13 17 this was done at the break of day
25 fear they should break the covenant
14 41 and to break open the door and to
Mat 5 19 that shall break one of these least
6 19 where thieves break through and steal
20 where thieves do not b. through nor
9 17 bottles break and the wine runneth out
12 5 priests in the temple break the sabbath
20 the bruised reed he shall not break
Luke 5 37 the new wine will break the bottles
John 5 18 because he did not only b. the sabbath
19 33 they did not break his legs. But one of
36 you shall not break a bone of him. And
Acts 20 7 when we were assembled to break bread
1 C 10 16 the bread which we break, is it not the
Gal 4 27 not: break forth and cry, thou that
breaketh Job 39 21 he b. up the earth with his
Ps 28 5 voice of the Lord breaketh the cedars
Prov 15 1 a mild answer breaketh wrath: but harsh
27 4 no mercy, nor fury when it b. forth
Ecce 10 8 he that breaketh a hedge, a serpent
Eccu 22 25 upbraideth his friend, b. friendship
Jer 23 29 as a hammer that breaketh the rock in
Bar 6 60 lightning, when it breaketh forth
Dan 2 40 as iron b. into pieces and subdueth

2 Ma 12 28 breaketh the strength of the enemies
breaking Gen 19 9 at the point of b. open the
Exod 22 2 a thief be found breaking open a house
6 if a fire breaking out light upon thorns
Lev 1 15 and breaking the place of the wound
14 56 of a scar and of blisters breaking out
Deut 9 21 breaking it [calf] into pieces, until
3 K 19 11 mountains and b. the rocks in pieces
2 Pa 15 16 breaking it into pieces, burnt it
Isa 24 19 with breaking shall the earth be broken
30 14 all to pieces with mighty breaking
Eze 16 59 despised the oath in b. the covenant
17 18 despised the oath, b. his covenant
21 6 mourn with the breaking of thy loins
Dan 3 95 Nabuchodonosor breaking forth, said
7 7 teeth, eating and breaking in pieces
2 Ma 14 43 crowd was breaking into the doors, he
Mark 14 3 breaking the alabaster box, she poured
Luke 8 29 b. the bonds, he was driven by the
24 35 they knew him in the breaking of bread
Acts 2 42 in the communication of the b. of bread
46 breaking bread from house to house
20 11 [Paul] going up and breaking bread
Eph 2 14 b. down the middle wall of partition
breast Gen 3 14 upon thy breast shalt thou go
Exod 28 29 the rational of judgment upon his b.
30 which shall be on Aaron's breast when
30 [Aaron] shall bear . . . on his breast
29 26 shalt take also the breast of the ram
27 sanctify both the consecrated breast
Lev 7 30 the fat of the victim and the breast
31 the breast shall be Aaron's and his
34 for the breast that is elevated and the
8 29 he took . . . the breast for his portion
10 14 the breast also that is offered and the
15 elevated . . . the shoulder and the breast
11 42 whatsoever goeth upon the breast on
Num 6 20 shall belong to the priest, as the b.
18 18 the consecrated breast and the right
Deut 18 3 to the priest the shoulder and the b.
Lam 4 3 sea monsters have drawn out the breast
Dan 2 32 but the breast and the arms of silver
Luke 18 13 publican . . . struck his breast, saying
John 13 25 leaning on the b. of Jesus, saith to
21 20 who also leaned on his breast at supper
breastplate Job 41 17 to hold nor spear nor a b.
Wisd 5 19 he will put on justice as a breastplate
Eccu 43 22 shall clothe the waters as a breastplate
Isa 59 17 he put on justice as a breastplate
Eze 23 24 with b. and buckler and helmet: and I
1 Ma 3 3 put on a breastplate as a giant and
Eph 6 14 having on the breastplate of justice
1 Th 5 8 having on the b. of faith and charity
breastplates 1 Ma 4 7 they saw . . . the men in b.
1 Ma 6 2 b. and shields which king Alexander
Apoc 9 9 they had b. as b. of iron, and the
17 they that sat on them had b. of fire
breasts Gen 49 25 with the blessings of the b.
Lev 9 20 the fat . . . they put upon the breasts
21 Aaron separated their breasts, and the
Job 3 12 why suckled at the breasts? For now
Ps 21 10 my hope from the breasts of my mother
Prov 5 19 let her breasts inebriate thee at all
7 18 let us be inebriated with the breasts
Cant 1 1 thy breasts are better than wine
3 remembering thy b. more than wine
12 he shall abide between my breasts
4 5 the two breasts like two young roes
10 how beautiful are thy breasts, my
10 thy b. are more beautiful than wine
7 3 breasts are like two young roes that
7 thy b. [like] to clusters of grapes
8 thy breasts shall be as the clusters
12 there will I give thee my breasts
8 1 sucking the breasts of my mother, that
8 our sister is little and hath no b.
10 my breasts are as a tower since I am
Isa 28 9 that are drawn away from the breasts
32 12 mourn for your breasts, for the
60 16 shalt be nursed with the b. of kings
66 11 filled with the b. of her consolations
12 you shall be carried at the breasts
Eze 16 7 thy b. were fashioned, and thy hair
23 3 there were their breasts pressed down
8 bruised the breasts of her virginity
21 when thy b. were pressed in Egypt
34 thou shalt rend thy breasts: because I
Osee 2 2 her adulteries from between her breasts
9 14 womb without children and dry breasts
Joel 2 16 gather . . . them that suck at the breasts
2 Ma 3 19 girded with haircloth about their b.
6 10 with the infants hanging at their b.
Luke 23 48 returned striking their breasts. And all
Apoc 15 6 girt about the b. with golden girdles
breath Gen 2 7 breathed into his face the b. of
Gen 6 17 wherein is the breath of life. 7:22
7 15 all flesh, wherein was the breath of
Deut 8 15 was the serpent burning with his breath
3 K 17 17 so that there was no b. left in him
Job 19 17 my wife hath abhorred my breath, and I
27 3 as long as breath remaineth in me
33 4 breath of the Almighty gave me life
34 14 he shall draw his spirit and breath
41 12 his breath kindleth coals, and a flame
Ps 103 29 thou shalt take away their breath and
134 17 is there any breath in their mouths
Wisd 2 2 the breath in our nostrils is smoke
11 21 scattered by the breath of thy power
15 15 nor noses to draw breath, nor ears to
16 and he that borroweth his own breath
Eccu 11 32 bowels send forth stinking breath
33 21 as thou livest and hast b. in thee
Isa 2 22 man, whose breath is in his nostrils
11 4 with the breath of his lips he shall
30 28 his breath as a torrent overflowing
33 b. of the Lord as torrent of brimstone
33 11 your breath as fire shall devour you
42 5 giveth breath to the people upon it
Jer 51 17 there is no breath in them. Bar 6:24
Lam 4 20 the breath of our mouth, Christ the
Dan 5 23 who hath thy breath in his hand, and all
10 17 in me, moreover my breath is stopped
2 Ma 7 22 I neither gave you breath nor soul
23 will restore . . . both breath and life
13 11 had of late taken b. for a little while
14 45 as he had yet breath in him, being
Acts 17 25 giveth to all life and breath and all
breathe Jdth 6 4 thou shalt breathe no more till
Ecce 3 19 all things breathe alike, and man hath
breathed Gen 2 7 b. into his face the breath of
Josu 10 40 slew all that breathed as the Lord the
Wisd 15 11 that breathed into him a living spirit
Lam 2 12 when they b. out their souls in the
John 20 22 he b. on them; and he said to them
breatheth John 3 8 Spirit breatheth where he will
breathing Wisd 11 19 b. out a fiery vapor or
Eccu 43 4 breathing out fiery vapors and shining
2 Ma 9 7 breathing out fire in his rage against
Acts 9 1 Saul . . . breathing out threatenings and
breathings Isa 57 16 and breathings I will make
breeches Exod 28 42 shalt make also linen breeches
Exod 39 27 and linen breeches of fine linen: and a
Lev 6 10 shall be vested with the . . . linen b.
16 4 cover his nakedness with linen breeches
Eccu 45 10 breeches and an ephod and he compassed
Eze 44 18 and linen breeches on their loins

breed Lev 11 9 things that breed in the waters
Deut 32 14 of the rams of the breed of Basan
breeze Ps 106 29 he turned the storm into a b.
Isa 57 13 a breeze shall take them away, but he
brethren Mat 1 2 Jacob begot Judas and his b.
Mat 1 11 Josias begot Jechonias and his b.
4 18 saw two brethren, Simon who is called
21 he saw other two brethren, James the
5 47 if you salute your brethren only
12 46 his mother and his b. stood without
47 and thy b. stand without. Luke 8:20
48 my mother, and who are my brethren
49 my mother and my b. Mark 3:33, 34
13 55 his b. James and Joseph and Simon
19 29 left house or b. Mark 10:29; Luke 18:29
20 24 with indignation against the two b.
22 25 were seven b. Mark 12:20; Luke 20:29
23 8 your master; and all you are brethren
25 40 to one of these my least brethren
28 10 tell my b. that they go into Galilee
Mark 3 31 mother and his b. came. Luke 8:19
32 thy mother and thy b. without seek
10 30 in this time: houses and b. and
Luke 8 21 my b. are they who hear the word of
14 12 call not thy friends nor thy b.
26 b. and sisters, yea and his own life
16 27 father's house, for I have five b.
21 16 be betrayed by your parents and b.
22 32 once converted, confirm thy brethren
John 2 12 and his brethren, and his disciples
7 3 his b. said to him: Pass from hence
5 neither did his brethren believe in
10 after his brethren were gone up, then
20 17 go to my brethren and say to them
21 23 went abroad among the brethren, that
Acts 1 14 the mother of Jesus and with his b.
15 Peter rising up in midst of the b.
3 22 raise up unto you of your b. 7:37
7 13 Joseph was known by his brethren
23 into his heart to visit his brethren
25 thought that his b. understood that
26 ye are brethren; why hurt you one
9 30 when the brethren had known, they
10 23 the b. from Joppe accompanied him
11 1 and b. who were in Judea heard that
12 these six brethren went with me also
29 purposed to send relief to the b.
12 17 these things to James and to the b.
14 2 minds of the Gentiles against the b.
15 1 taught the brethren: That except you
3 they caused great joy to all the b.
22 and Silas, chief men among the b.
23 to the brethren of the Gentiles that
32 with many words comforted the b.
33 were let go with peace by the b.
36 let us return and visit our b. in all
40 being delivered by the b. to the
16 2 b. that were in Lystra and Iconium
40 having seen the b., they comforted
17 6 drew Jason and certain brethren to
10 the b. immediately sent away Paul
14 the b. sent away Paul to go unto the
18 18 taking his leave of the b., sailed
27 the brethren exhorting, wrote to the
21 7 saluting the b., we abode one day
17 Jerusalem, the b. received us gladly
22 5 receiving letters to the b., I went
28 14 finding b., we were desired to tarry
15 when the b. had heard of us, they
21 any of the b. that came hither relate
Rom 8 29 might be the firstborn amongst many b.
9 3 anathema from Christ for my brethren
16 14 salute . . . the b. that are with
1 C 6 5 that is able to judge between his b.
8 and defraud, and that to your b.
8 12 when you sin thus against the b.
9 5 the apostles and the b. of the Lord
15 6 then was he seen by more than 500 b.
16 11 for I look for him with the brethren
12 him to come unto you with the b.
20 all the brethren salute you. Salute
2 C 8 23 our b., the apostles of the churches
9 3 now I have sent the brethren, that
5 to desire the b. that they would go
11 9 wanting to me, the brethren supplied
26 in the sea, in perils from false b.
Gal 1 2 brethren who are with me. Phil. 4:22
Eph 6 23 peace be to the b. and charity with
Phil 1 14 many of the b. in the Lord, growing
Col 1 2 to the saints and faithful b. in
4 15 salute the b. who are at Laodicea
1 Th 4 10 towards all the b. in all Macedonia
5 26 salute all the brethren with a holy
27 epistle be read to all the holy b.
1 Tim 4 6 these things proposing to the b.
5 1 as a father: young men, as brethren
6 2 not despise them, because they are b.
2 Tim 4 21 and all the brethren salute thee
Heb 2 11 he is not ashamed to call them b.
12 I will declare thy name to my b.
17 to be made like unto his brethren
3 1 holy b., partakers of the heavenly
7 5 to take tithes . . . of their b.
13 24 the brethren from Italy salute you
1 P 5 9 the same affliction befalls your b.
1 J 3 14 to life, because we love the brethren
16 to lay down our lives for the brethren
3 J 3 glad when the b. came and gave
5 whatever thou dost for the brethren
10 neither doth he himself receive the b.
Apoc 6 11 their brethren, who are to be slain
12 10 the accuser of our b. is cast forth
19 10 fellow servant and of thy b. 22:9
beseech you, brethren; *see* **beseech**
brevity 2 Ma 2 32 to pursue brevity of speech
briars Heb 6 8 bringeth forth thorns and briars
bribe 1 K 12 3 if I have taken a bribe at any
bribery Eccu 40 12 all b. and injustice shall be
bribes Exod 23 8 neither shalt thou take bribes
Deut 10 17 accepteth no person nor taketh bribes
1 K 8 3 took bribes and perverted judgment
Job 15 34 who love to take bribes. He hath
Ps 14 5 nor taken bribes against the innocent
Prov 15 27 he that hateth bribes shall live. By
Isa 1 23 all love b., they run after rewards
33 15 shaketh his hands from all bribes that
Amos 5 12 enemies of the just, taking bribes
Mich 3 11 her princes have judged for bribes
brick Gen 11 3 come, let us make brick and bake
Gen 11 3 and they had brick instead of stones
Exod 1 14 with hard works in clay and brick and
5 7 straw no more to the people to make b.
4 K 3 25 so that brick walls only remained: and
Jdth 5 10 them to labor in clay and brick in the
Isa 16 7 that rejoice upon the brick walls
11 parts [shall sound] for the brick wall
Jer 43 9 vault that is under the brick wall
48 31 for the men of the brick wall. 36
Nah 3 14 clay and tread, work it and make brick
brickkilns 2 K 12 31 made them pass through b.
bricks Exod 5 8 shall lay upon them the task of b.
Exod 5 14 why have you not made up the task of b.
16 and bricks are required of us as before
18 shall deliver the accustomed number of b.
19 not a whit be diminished of the bricks
Isa 9 10 the bricks are fallen down, but we will

65 3 in gardens, and sacrifice upon bricks
bridal Judg 14 20 took one of his . . . b. companions
bride Deut 33 12 as in a b. chamber shall he abide
Isa 49 18 as a b. thou shalt put them about thee
61 10 as a bride adorned with her jewels
62 5 bridegroom shall rejoice over the bride
Jer 2 32 a bride [forget] her stomacher? But my
7 34 to cease . . . the voice of the bride: for
16 9 take away . . . the voice of the bride. 25:10; Bar 2:23
33 11 shall be heard . . . the voice of the b.
Joel 2 16 and the bride out of her bride chamber
1 Ma 1 28 the bride that sat in the marriage bed
9 37 were bringing the bride out of Madaba
Mat 25 1 to meet the bridegroom and the bride
John 3 29 that hath the bride is the bridegroom
Apoc 18 23 voice of . . . b. shall be heard no more
21 2 as a bride adorned for her husband
9 I will show thee the bride, the wife of
22 17 the spirit and the bride say: Come
bridechamber Ps 18 6 as bridegroom coming out of b.
bridegroom Ps 18 6 b. coming out of bridechamber
Isa 61 10 as a bridegroom decked with a crown
62 5 the b. shall rejoice over the bride
Jer 7 34 to cease . . . voice of the bridegroom
16 9 I will take away . . . voice of the bridegroom. 25:10; Bar 2:23
33 11 shall be heard . . . the voice of the b.
Joel 2 16 let the b. go forth from his bed and
1 Ma 1 28 every b. took up lamentation: and the
9 39 the b. came forth and his friends and
Mat 9 15 can the children of the b. mourn, as
15 as long as the bridegroom is with them. Mark 2:19; Luke 5:34
15 when the bridegroom shall be taken away. Mark 2:20; Luke 5:35
25 1 their lamps went out to meet the b. and
5 the b. tarrying, they all slumbered
6 behold the b. cometh, go ye forth to
10 whilst they went to buy, the b. came
Mark 2 19 as long as they have the b. with them
Luke 5 34 can you make the children of b. fast
John 2 9 chief steward calleth the bridegroom
3 29 he that hath the bride is the b.: but
29 the friend of the b. who standeth and
Apoc 18 23 voice of b. . . . shall be heard no more
bridegroom's John 3 29 because of the b. voice
bridges 2 Ma 12 13 encompassed with b. and walls
bridle 2 K 8 1 David took the bridle of tribute
Job 30 11 and hath put a bridle into my mouth
Ps 31 9 with bit and bridle bind fast their
Eccu 28 29 words, and a just bridle for thy mouth
Isa 30 28 the bridle of error that was in the jaws
48 9 for my praise I will bridle thee, lest
Eze 29 4 I will put a bridle in thy jaws: and I
Zach 14 20 upon bridle of the horse shall be holy
James 3 2 with a b. to lead about the whole body
bridles 2 Ma 10 29 horses, comely with golden b.
Apoc 14 20 out of the press, up to the horses' b.
bridling James 1 26 not bridling his tongue but
Brie Num 26 44 Brie of whom is family of the
Num 26 45 the sons of Brie: Heber of whom is the
brief 2 Ma 2 29 ourselves . . . studying to be brief
briefly 1 P 5 12 you, as I have written briefly
Brieites Num 26 44 of whom is the family of the B.
brier Ps 57 10 before your thorns could know the b.
Isa 9 18 it shall devour the brier and the thorn
27 4 who shall make me a thorn and a brier
Mich 7 4 that is best among them, is as a brier
briers Gen 22 13 a ram amongst the briers sticking
Judg 8 7 thorns and briers of the desert. 16
Job 30 7 counted it delightful to be under the b.
Isa 5 6 briers and thorns shall come up: and I
7 23 silver, shall become thorns and briers
24 briers and thorns shall be in all the
25 fear of thorns and briers shall not come
10 17 and his briers shall be set on fire
32 13 shall thorns and briers come up: how
bright Prov 25 12 earring of gold and a b. pearl
Cant 6 9 fair as the moon, bright as the sun
Wisd 17 5 neither could the bright flames of the
Eccu 50 8 rainbow giving light in the b. clouds
9 as a bright fire, and frankincense
Bar 6 59 the moon and the stars being bright and
Eze 1 13 a bright fire, and lightning going
2 Ma 3 26 b. and glorious and in comely apparel
Mat 17 5 bright cloud overshadowed them. And lo
Luke 11 36 as a bright lamp, shall enlighten thee
Apoc 22 16 of David, the bright and morning star
brighter Eccu 17 30 what is b. than the sun; yet
Eccu 23 28 eyes of the Lord are far brighter than
brightness 2 K 22 13 by the b. before him, coals
Job 11 17 brightness like that of the noonday
31 26 and the moon going in brightness: and
Ps 17 13 at the brightness that was before him
89 17 let the b. of the Lord our God be upon
109 3 in the brightness of the saints: from
Wisd 7 26 she is the brightness of eternal light
Eccu 43 12 it is very beautiful in its brightness
Bar 4 2 walk in the way by its brightness, in the
5 3 God will show his brightness in thee
Isa 4 5 the b. of a flaming fire in the night
13 10 stars of heaven and their brightness
58 11 and will fill thy soul with brightness
59 9 we looked for . . . brightness, and we
60 3 kings in the brightness of thy rising
19 day, neither shall the b. of the moon
62 1 till her just one come forth as b.
Eze 1 4 and brightness was about it: and out
28 the appearance of the b. round about
8 2 as the appearance of brightness, as the
10 4 filled with the b. of the glory of
Dan 12 3 shall shine as the b. of the firmament
Amos 5 20 obscurity, and no brightness in it
Haba 3 4 his brightness shall be as the light
11 go in the b. of thy glittering spear
Luke 2 9 brightness of God shone round them and
Acts 22 11 I did not see for the brightness of
26 13 above the brightness of the sun shining
2 Th 2 8 destroy with the b. of his coming, him
Heb 1 3 being the brightness of his glory and
brim Lev 1 15 blood run down upon brim of the altar
3 K 7 23 sea of ten cubits from b. to b. 2 Pa 4:2
24 a graven work under the brim of it
26 brim . . . like the b. of a cup. 2 Pa 4:5
Eze 43 14 to the lowest brim two cubits and the
14 from the lesser brim to the greater brim
17 the brim was fourteen cubits long and
20 and upon the four corners of the brim
45 19 on four corners of the brim of the altar
John 2 7 they filled them up to the brim. And
brimstone Gen 19 24 b. and fire from the Lord out
Deut 29 23 burning it with b. and the heat of salt
Job 18 15 let brimstone be sprinkled in his tent
Ps 10 7 fire and brimstone and storms of winds
Isa 30 33 breath of the Lord as a torrent of b.
34 9 the ground thereof into brimstone: and
Eze 38 22 I will rain fire and brimstone upon him
Dan 3 46 to heat the furnace with b. and tow
Luke 17 29 rained fire and b. from heaven and
Apoc 9 17 breastplates of fire and . . . of brimstone
17 proceeded fire and smoke and brimstone
18 was slain the third part . . . by the b.
14 10 shall be tormented with fire and b.
19 20 into the pool of fire burning with b.
20 9 into the pool of fire and brimstone

21 8 in the pool burning with fire and b.
brink Exod 2 3 in the sedges by the river's brink
Exod 2 5 her maids walked by the river's brink
Eccu 50 8 as the lilies that are on the brink
brittle Wisd 15 13 maketh b. vessels and graven
broader Job 11 9 than the earth and b. than the sea
Eze 41 7 temple broader in the higher parts
broidered Eze 26 16 cast away their b. garments
Eze 27 7 fine broidered linen from Egypt was
16 and broidered works and fine linen
broiled Isa 44 19 I have b. fish and have eaten
Jon 4 8 Jonas: and he broiled with the heat
Luke 24 42 they offered him a piece of b. fish
broke Exod 9 25 it b. every tree of the country
Exod 32 19 broke them at the foot of the mount
Num 16 31 earth broke asunder under their feet
Deut 9 17 my hands and broke them in your sight
Judg 9 53 head of Abimelech and broke his skull
16 9 he [Samson] broke the bands as a man
12 broke the bands like threads of webs
1 K 4 18 by the door and b. his neck and died
2 K 23 16 b. through the camp of the Philistines
3 K 15 13 broke in pieces the filthy idol and
4 K 3 5 he broke the league which he had made
10 27 burnt it and broke it in pieces. They
11 18 temple of Baal and b. down his altars
18 and his images they broke in pieces
14 13 b. down the wall of Jerusalem. 2 Pa 36:19
18 4 broke the statues in pieces and cut
4 broke the brazen serpent, which Moses
16 Ezechias broke the doors of the temple
23 8 he broke down the altars of the gates
12 the king broke down: and he ran from
15 altar and the high place he broke down
25 10 broke down the walls of Jerusalem round
1 Pa 11 18 these three broke through the midst of
2 Pa 14 3 broke the statues and cut down the
22 1 Arabians who had broke in upon the camp
23 17 broke down his altars and his idols
25 23 to Jerusalem: and broke down the walls
26 6 and broke down the wall of Geth and
31 1 they broke the idols and cut down the
34 4 they broke down before him the altars
Job 20 19 because he broke in and stripped the
29 17 I broke the jaws of the wicked man and
30 26 I waited for light, and darkness b. out
38 8 the sea with doors, when it broke forth
Ps 106 14 and broke their bonds in sunder. Let
Eccu 47 8 he broke their horn forever. In all his
Isa 37 19 stone: and they broke them in pieces
Jer 28 10 of Jeremias the prophet and broke it
52 14 broke down all the wall of Jerusalem
Eze 17 16 void, and whose covenant he broke even
Dan 3 48 it broke forth and burnt such of the
Mat 26 26 broke and gave to his disciples. Mark 8:6
Mark 6 41 he blessed and broke the loaves and
8 19 when I broke the five loaves among
14 22 broke and gave to them and said: Take
Luke 5 6 and their net broke. And they beckoned
9 16 broke and distributed to his disciples
John 19 32 they broke the legs of the first and
1 C 11 24 broke and said: Take ye and eat: this
broken Gen 7 11 of the great deep were broken up
Gen 17 14 because he hath broken my covenant
Exod 28 32 that it may not easily be broken. And
Lev 2 16 part of the corn broken small and of
5 8 and be not altogether broken off. And
6 28 wherein it was sodden, shall be broken
11 33 be defiled and therefore is to be b.
13 20 the plague of leprosy is broken out
25 evil of leprosy is broken out in the
15 12 a vessel of earth, it shall be broken
21 19 if his foot or if his hand be broken
22 22 if it be blind or broken or have a scar
26 13 have broken the chains of your necks
26 after I shall have broken the staff of
Num 10 7 they shall not make a broken sound
Deut 23 1 whose testicles are b. or cut away
Josu 6 5 shall give a longer and broken tune
9 5 way, were hard, and broken in pieces
12 are become dry and broken in pieces
Judg 5 22 the hoofs of the horses were broken
7 20 and had broken their pitchers, they
15 14 the bands . . . were broken and loosed
3 K 18 30 altar of the Lord that was broken down
22 49 the ships were broken in Asiongaber
4 K 18 21 Egypt a staff of a broken reed, upon
2 Pa 20 37 destroyed thy works and the ships are b.
25 12 and they were all broken to pieces
28 24 vessels of house of God and b. them
32 5 all the wall that had been broken down
34 7 and had broken the idols in pieces
2 Es 1 3 the wall of Jerusalem is broken down
2 13 wall of Jerusalem which was broken down
Jdth 6 19 Ozias, after the assembly was broken up
Job 4 10 teeth of the whelps of lions are broken
14 12 till the heavens be broken, he shall not
16 13 am all on a sudden broken to pieces
13 he hath broken me and hath set me up
22 9 of the fatherless thou hast b. in pieces
24 20 be broken in pieces as an unfruitful
24 ears of corn they shall be broken
30 14 in upon me, as when a wall is broken
31 22 let my arm with its bones be broken
38 15 and the high arm shall be broken. Hast
Ps 3 8 thou hast broken the teeth of sinners
33 21 bones, not one of them shall be broken
36 15 own hearts, and let their bow be broken
17 the arms of the wicked shall be broken
41 11 whilst my bones are broken, my enemies
73 14 hast broken the heads of the dragon
15 thou hast broken up the fountains and
75 4 there hath he broken the powers of bows
79 13 why hast thou broken down the hedge
88 41 thou hast broken down all his hedges
106 16 he hath broken gates of brass and burst
108 17 the broken in heart, to put him to death
109 5 Lord at thy right hand hath broken kings
115 116 thou hast broken my bonds: I will
123 7 snare is broken and we are delivered
140 7 when the thickness of the earth is b. up
146 3 who healeth the broken of heart and
Prov 3 20 by his wisdom the depths have b. out
24 31 and the stone wall was broken down
Ecce 4 12 a threefold cord is not easily broken
12 6 before the silver cord be broken and
6 the wheel is broken upon the cistern
Wisd 4 5 branches not being perfect, shall be b.
Eccu 13 3 against the other, it shall be broken
21 17 heart of a fool is like a b. vessel
30 8 a horse not broken becometh stubborn
35 23 and broken the scepters of the unjust
43 16 clouds, and the hailstones are broken
Isa 5 27 nor lachet of their shoes be broken
8 15 fall, and shall be broken in pieces
13 8 shall melt and shall be broken. Gripings
14 5 Lord hath b. the staff of the wicked
29 rod of him that struck thee is broken
19 3 the spirit of Egypt shall be broken
21 9 all the graven gods thereof are broken
22 10 broken down houses to fortify the wall
25 and it shall be broken and shall fall
24 5 have broken the everlasting covenant
10 the city of vanity is broken down
19 with breaking shall the earth be b.
25 10 as straw is broken in pieces with the
27 9 as burnt stones broken in pieces, the
28 13 go and fall backward and be broken

28 but bread corn shall be broken small
30 14 it shall be broken small, as the
14 as the potter's vessel is broken all
33 20 any of the cords thereof be broken
35 6 waters are broken out in the desert
6 thou trustest upon this broken staff
38 13 as a lion so hath he b. all my bones
43 17 they are b. as flax and are extinct
46 1 Bel is broken, Nebo is destroyed: their
2 they are consumed and are broken
58 6 let them that are broken go free and
59 5 they have broken the eggs of asps
Jer 2 13 broken cisterns, that can hold no
20 thou hast broken my yoke, thou hast
5 5 have altogether broken the yoke more
10 20 laid waste, all my cords are broken
18 4 the vessel was broken which he was
19 11 as the potter's vessel is broken which
22 28 Jechonias an earthen and a b. vessel
23 9 my heart is broken within me, all my
28 2 I have broken the yoke of the king
12 had broken the chain from off the
13 thou hast broken chains of wood and thou
48 17 how is the strong staff broken, the
25 is cut off, and his arm is broken
38 I have b. Moab as an useless vessel
50 17 Nabuchodonosor . . . hath broken his bones
23 hammer of the whole earth broken and
51 30 are burnt, her bars are broken. One
58 shall be utterly broken down and her
52 7 the city was broken up, and the men
Lam 1 4 all her gates are broken down: her
2 3 he hath broken in his fierce anger
9 he hath destroyed and b. her bars
3 4 made old, he hath broken my bones
11 and hath broken me in pieces, he hath
16 he hath broken my teeth one by one
Bar 6 15 when it is broken becometh useless
43 as herself, nor her cord broken. But
Eze 6 4 your idols shall be broken in pieces
6 altars . . . shall be broken in pieces
9 because I have broken their heart
17 15 escape that hath b. the covenant? As I
19 despised, and the covenant he hath b.
23 21 and the paps of thy virginity broken
26 2 the gates of the people are broken
27 26 broken thee in the heart of the sea
30 21 I have broken the arm of Pharao king of
22 strong arm, which is already broken
31 12 his branches shall be broken on every
32 28 shalt be broken in the midst of the
34 4 which was broken you have not bound
16 I will bind up that which was broken
27 when I shall have broken the bonds
44 7 you have broken my covenant by all
Dan 2 35 and the gold broken to pieces together
42 be partly strong, and partly broken
3 44 and let their strength be broken. And
7 26 taken away and be broken in pieces
8 8 grown, the great horn was broken and
22 when that was broken, there arose up
25 and shall be broken without hand. And
11 4 his kingdom shall be broken, and it
22 before his face and shall be broken
14 32 and had broken bread in a bowl: and was
Osee 5 11 under oppression and broken in judgment
Joel 1 17 the storehouses are b. down: because
Jon 1 4 and the ship was in danger to be broken
Mich 3 3 have broken and chopped their bones
Zach 9 10 the bow for war shall be broken: and be
11 16 nor heal what is broken nor nourish
1 Ma 2 31 who had b. the king's commandment were
7 18 they have broken the covenant and the
12 37 wall . . . towards the east was broken
Mat 21 44 fall on this stone, shall be broken
24 43 suffer his house to be b. Luke 12:39
Mark 5 4 burst the chains and b. the fetters
John 7 23 that the law of Moses may not be broken
10 35 and the scripture cannot be broken
19 31 Pilate that their legs might be broken
21 11 the net was not broken. Jesus saith to
Acts 13 43 when the synagogue was broken up, many
27 35 when he had broken it, he began to eat
41 the hinder part was b. with the violence
Rom 11 17 if some of the branches be broken and
19 the branches were broken off, that I
20 because of unbelief they were broken off
2 C 11 10 this glorying shall not be broken off
Apoc 2 27 as vessel of a potter they shall be b.
brokest Exod 34 1 were in the tables which thou b.
Deut 10 2 were in them which thou b. before
Eccu 48 6 brokest easily their power in pieces
Eze 29 7 thou b. and weakenest all their loins
brood Wisd 4 3 brood of the wicked shall not thrive
Mat 3 7 ye brood of vipers, who hath showed you
Luke 13 34 as bird doth her brood under her wings
brook Lev 23 40 willows of the brook and you shall
1 K 17 40 five smooth stones out of the brook
2 K 15 23 went over the brook Cedron and all the
3 K 2 37 and shalt pass over the brook Cedron
2 Pa 32 4 stopped up all the springs and the b.
Job 40 17 willows of the brook shall compass him
Ps 82 10 as to Jabin at the brook of Cisson
Eccu 24 41 like a brook out of a river of a mighty
43 my brook became a great river and my
1 Ma 12 37 the wall that was upon the b. towards
John 18 1 with his disciples over the brook Cedron
brooks Deut 8 7 into a good land of b. and waters
Job 20 17 the brooks of honey and of butter. He
Prov 30 17 let the ravens of the brooks pick it out
Cant 5 12 his eyes as doves upon brooks of waters
Eccu 39 17 rose planted by the brooks of waters
Eze 36 4 saith the Lord God . . . to the brooks
broth Judg 6 19 broth of the flesh into a pot
Judg 6 20 that rock and pour out the broth thereon
Isa 65 4 profane broth is in their vessels. That
Jer 37 20 daily a piece of bread, beside broth
brothel Num 25 8 after the Israelite into b. house
Eze 16 24 madest thee a brothel house in every
31 hast built thy b. house at the head of
39 they shall destroy thy brothel house
2 Ma 4 12 the choicest youths in brothel houses
brother Gen 10 21 Heber, the elder b. of Japheth
Gen 13 11 were separated one brother from the
14 12 took, Lot also, the son of Abram's b.
13 Amorrhite, b. of Escol and the b. of Aner
22 23 did Melcha bear to Nachor, Abraham's b.
24 15 wife of Nachor the brother of Abraham
27 into the house of my master's brother
29 Rebecca had a brother named Laban
48 to take the daughter of my master's b.
55 her b. and mother answered: Let the maid
28 5 Syrian, brother to Rebecca his mother
29 12 told her that he was her father's b.
37 26 what will it profit us to kill our b.
27 for he is our brother and our flesh
42 15 until your youngest brother come. Send
20 bring your youngest brother. 34
21 we have sinned against our brother
43 3 unless you bring your youngest brother
5 not see my face without your youngest b.
6 told him you had also another brother
7 our father lived: if we had a brother
7 bring hither your brother with you
13 and take also your brother and go to the
14 send back with you your brother whom

29 is this your young brother of whom
44 19 have you a father or a brother? And we
20 whose brother by the mother is dead
23 except your youngest b. come with you
26 if our youngest brother go down with us
45 4 I am Joseph, your brother whom you sold
48 14 upon head of Ephraim the younger brother
19 this younger brother shall be greater
Lev 18 14 not uncover nakedness of thy father's b.
Num 36 2 to the daughters of Salphaad our brother
Deut 25 7 my husband's brother refuseth to raise
Josu 15 17 the younger b. of Caleb. Judg 1:13; 3:9
Judg 9 3 saying: He [Abimelech] is our brother
18 Abimelech . . . because he is your brother
24 their blood upon Abimelech their brother
21 6 with repentance for their b. Benjamin
Ruth 4 3 that belonged to our brother Elimelech
1 K 14 3 Achitob brother to Ichabod the son of
26 6 Sarvia the brother of Joab, saying: Who
2 K 3 30 because he had killed their brother
13 3 son of Semaa the brother of David
8 came to house of Amnon her brother
10 brought them in to her brother Amnon
20 Absalom her brother said to her: Hath
20 in the house of Absalom her brother
32 Jonadab son of Semaa David's brother
18 2 Abisai the son of Sarvia Joab's brother
23 18 Abisai also the b. of Joab. 1 Pa 11:20
24 Asael the brother of Joab was one of
3 K 9 13 which thou hast given me, brother? And
1 Pa 2 32 Jada the brother of Semei: Jether and
42 Caleb the brother of Jerameel were
4 11 Caleb the brother of Sua begot Mahir
9 17 their brother Sellum was the prince
11 26 Asahel brother of Joab. 27:7
38 Joel the brother of Nathan, Mibahar the
20 5 Adeodatus . . . slew brother of Goliath
7 son of Samaa the brother of David slew
24 25 the brother of Micha, Jesia: and the
27 18 over Juda, Eliu the brother of David
Tob 5 8 I have abode with Gabelus our brother
6 7 I beseech thee, brother Azarias, tell
9 1 brother Azarias, I pray thee hearken
11 2 brother Tobias, thou knowest how thou
Esth 2 15 Abihail the brother of Mardochai whom
Job 1 13 in the house of their eldest brother
18 in the house of their elder brother
30 29 I was b. of dragons and companion of
Ps 34 14 as a neighbor and as an own brother
48 8 no brother can redeem, nor shall man
Prov 17 17 and a brother is proved in distress
18 9 b. of him that wasteth his own works
19 a brother that is helped by his brother
24 shall be more friendly than a brother
27 10 neighbor that is near, than b. afar off
Ecce 4 8 no child, no brother and yet he ceaseth
Eccu 33 20 give not to son or wife, brother or
31 faithful servant . . . treat him as a b.
Isa 19 2 they shall fight brother against b.
Jer 9 4 let him not trust in any b. of his: for every b. will utterly supplant
Eze 22 11 the brother hath oppressed his sister
44 25 only their father . . . and b. and sister
Mala 1 2 was not Essau brother to Jacob, saith
1 Ma 2 65 your brother Simon is a man of counsel
9 19 took Judas their brother and buried him
38 remembered the blood of John their b.
42 revenge for the blood of their brother
16 9 Judas John's brother was wounded: but
2 Ma 4 7 Jason the brother of Onias ambitiously
23 Menelaus brother of the aforesaid Simon
14 17 Simon the brother of Judas had joined
Mat 10 21 brother shall deliver up brother to
Mark 12 19 if any man's b. die. Luke 20:28
Luke 6 42 brother, let me pull the mote out of
John 1 40 Andrew, brother of Simon Peter, was one
6 8 Andrew b. of Simon Peter, saith to him
11 2 hair: whose brother Lazarus was sick
19 to comfort them concerning their b.
Acts 9 17 b. Saul, the Lord Jesus hath sent me
12 2 he killed James, the brother of John
13 1 Manahen, who was foster b. of Herod
21 20 thou seest, brother, how many thousands
22 13 Ananias . . . said to me: B. Saul, look
Rom 16 23 saluteth you, and Quartus, a brother
1 C 1 1 Paul . . . and Sosthenes a brother. To
5 11 that is named a b. be a fornicator
6 6 brother goeth to law with brother and
7 12 hath any b. a wife that believeth not
15 a b. or sister is not under servitude
8 11 through thy knowledge shall weak b.
11 shall the weak brother perish, for whom
16 12 touching our brother Apollo, I give
2 C 1 1 Paul . . . and Timothy our brother: to the
8 18 brother whose praise is in the gospel
22 we have sent with them our brother also
12 18 I sent with him [Titus] a brother. Did
Gal 1 19 I saw none saving James, b. of the Lord
Col 1 1 by the will of God, and Timothy, a b.
4 7 Tychicus, our dearest b. and faithful
9 Onesimus, a most beloved and faithful b.
1 Th 3 2 and we sent Timothy, our brother, and
2 Th 3 6 from every brother walking disorderly
15 an enemy admonish him as a brother
Philem 1 prisoner of Christ Jesus and Timothy a b.
7 have been refreshed by thee, brother
16 instead of a servant, a most dear b.
20 yea, b. May I enjoy thee in the Lord
Heb 13 23 our b. Timothy is set at liberty: with
James 1 9 let the brother of low condition glory
2 15 if a brother or sister be naked and
1 P 5 12 by Sylvanus, a faithful b. unto you
2 P 3 15 as our most dear b. Paul, according
Apoc 1 9 I John, your brother and your partner

brother of James: ***see*** **James**

his brother Gen 4 2 brought forth his b. Abel
Gen 4 8 Cain said to Abel his brother: Let us
8 Cain rose up against his brother Abel
9 5 man and of his b. will I require the
14 14 to wit, that his brother Lot was taken
16 all the substance and Lot his brother
22 20 borne children to Nachor his brother
21 Hus the firstborn, and Buz his brother
32 3 messengers before him to Esau his b.
13 he had presents for his brother Esau
33 3 until his brother came near. Then Esau
4 then Esau ran to meet his brother and
35 7 to him when he fled from his brother
36 6 Esau . . . departed from his brother Jacob
38 30 afterwards his brother came out on whose
42 38 his brother is dead, and he is left
43 29 saw Benjamin his brother, by the same
30 his heart was moved upon his brother
45 14 upon the neck of his brother Benjamin
Exod 10 23 no man saw his brother, nor moved
32 27 let every man kill his brother and
29 every man in his son and in his brother
Lev 21 2 for his daughter, for his brother also
Num 6 7 make himself unclean . . . even for his b.
Deut 15 2 from his friend or neighbor or brother
19 18 hath told a lie against his brother
19 to him as he meant to do to his brother
22 26 as a robber riseth against his brother
24 7 if any man be found soliciting his b.
25 5 his brother shall take her and raise up seed for his brother

28 54 shall envy his own brother and his wife
Judg 1 3 Juda said to Simeon his brother: Come
17 Juda went with Simeon his brother and
9 21 for fear of Abimelech his brother. So
1 K 17 28 when Eliab his eldest brother heard this
2 K 3 27 in revenge of blood of Asael his b.
30 Joab and Abisai his brother slew Abner
4 9 answered Rechab and Baana his brother
10 10 he delivered to Abisai his brother
14 7 deliver him that hath slain his brother
7 we may kill him for life of his brother
20 10 Joab and Abisai his brother pursued
3 K 1 10 Solomon his brother he invited not
4 K 1 17 Joram his brother reigned in his stead
1 Pa 6 39 his brother Asaph, who stood on his
7 16 the name of his brother was Sares: and
35 the sons of Helem his brother: Supha
8 39 thee sons of Esec, his brother, were Ulam
11 45 Joha his brother a Thosaite, Eliel a
13 7 Oza and his brother drove the cart
19 11 into the hand of Abisai his brother
15 likewise fled from Abisai his brother
2 Pa 31 12 and Semei his brother was the second
13 hand of Chonenias and Semei his brother
36 4 he made Eliakim his brother king in
Prov 18 19 a brother that is helped by his brother
Wisd 10 3 fury wherewith he murdered his brother
Eccu 45 7 he exalted Aaron his brother and like
Isa 3 6 a man shall take hold of his brother
9 19 no man shall spare his brother. And he
41 6 shall say to his b.: Be of good courage
Jer 9 5 a man shall mock his brother and they
13 14 scatter them every man from his brother
23 35 every one to his neighbor and to his b.
25 26 every one against his brother: and all
31 34 teach no more . . . every man his brother
34 14 let ye go every man his brother being
15 liberty every one to his brother. 17
Eze 4 17 every man may fall against his brother
18 18 and offered violence to his brother
24 23 every one shall sigh with his brother
38 21 sword shall be pointed against his b.
47 14 every man in like manner as his brother
Osee 12 3 in the womb he supplanted his brother
Joel 2 8 no one shall press upon his brother
Amos 1 11 hath pursued his brother with the sword
Mich 7 2 every one hunteth his brother to death
Agge 2 23 every one by the sword of his brother
Zach 7 9 and compassion every man to his brother
10 a man not devise . . . against his brother
Mala 2 10 why . . . every one of us despise his b.
1 Ma 5 17 Judas said to Simon his brother: Choose
24 and Jonathan his b. passed over Jordan
55 and Simon his brother in Galilee before
9 31 rose up in the place of Judas his b.
33 Jonathan and Simon his brother knew it
35 sent his brother a captain of the people
37 was told Jonathan and Simon his brother
65 Jonathan left his b. Simon in the city
10 5 done against him and against his brother
18 king Alexander to his brother Jonathan
74 Simon his brother met him to help him
11 30 king Demetrius to his brother Jonathan
59 he made his brother Simon governor
64 left his brother Simon in the country
13 14 in the place of his brother Jonathan
25 took the bones of Jonathan his brother
14 17 that Simon his b. was made high priest
2 Ma 4 26 Jason, who had undermined his own b.
29 Lysimachus his brother succeeding: and
10 37 they slew also his brother Chereas
11 22 king Antiochus to Lysias his brother
Mat 4 21 he saw . . . and John his b. Mark 1:19
5 22 whosoever is angry with his brother
22 shall say to his brother, Raca, shall
10 2 is called Peter, and Andrew his brother
3 the son of Zebedee and John his brother
17 1 taketh Peter and James and John his b.
18 35 if you forgive not every one his b.
22 24 his brother shall marry his wife and
24 and raise up issue to his brother. Now
25 not having issue, left his wife to his b.
Mark 1 16 saw Simon and Andrew his b. 4:18
6 17 Herodias the wife of Philip his brother
12 19 his b. should take his wife. Luke 20:28
19 raise up seed to his b. Luke 20:28
13 12 brother shall betray his brother unto
Luke 3 1 Philip his brother tetrarch of Iturea
6 14 Peter and Andrew his brother, James
John 1 41 he findeth first his brother Simon
1 Th 4 6 nor circumvent his brother in business
Heb 8 11 every man his b., saying, Know the Lord
James 4 11 he that detracteth his brother or he that judgeth his brother
1 J 2 9 hateth his brother is in darkness. 11
10 loveth his b., abideth in the light
3 10 nor he that loveth not his brother
12 not as Cain who . . . killed his brother
15 whosoever hateth his b. is a murderer
17 he that shall see his brother in need
4 20 man say, I love God, and hateth his b.
20 that loveth not his b. whom he seeth
21 who loveth God, love also his brother
5 16 he that knoweth his brother to sin

my brother Gen 20 5 and she say, He is my b.
Gen 27 11 Esau my brother is a hairy man and
41 father and I will kill my brother Jacob
43 flee to Laban my brother to Haran
29 15 because thou [Jacob] art my brother
32 11 deliver me from the hand of my b. Esau
17 if thou meet my brother Esau and he
33 9 I have plenty, my brother, keep what
45 12 the eyes of my brother Benjamin see
2 K 1 26 I grieve for thee, my brother Jonathan
13 4 Thamar the sister of my brother Absalom
12 do not so, my brother, do not force me
26 let my brother Amnon . . . come with us
20 9 to Amasa: God save thee, my brother
3 K 13 30 saying: Alas! alas! my brother. For
20 32 if he be yet alive he is my brother
2 Es 7 2 I commanded Hanani my brother, and
Tob 7 5 do you know Tobias my brother? And they
Cant 8 1 who shall give thee to me for my b.
Eccu 29 33 my brother being to be lodged with me
Jer 22 18 alas, my brother, and alas, sister
1 Ma 5 17 I and my brother Jonathan will go into
Mat 12 50 he is my brother. Mark 3:35
18 21 Lord, how often shall my brother offend
Luke 12 13 Master, speak to my b. that he divide
John 11 21 my brother had not died. 32
1 C 8 13 if meat scandalize my brother, I will
13 less I should scandalize my brother
2 C 2 13 because I found not Titus my brother
Eph 6 21 doing, Tychicus, our dearest brother
Phil 2 25 to send to you Epaphroditus, my brother

thy brother Gen 4 9 where is thy brother Abel
Gen 4 11 received the blood of thy brother
20 13 thou shalt say that I am thy brother
16 given thy b. a thousand pieces of silver
27 6 thy father talking with Esau thy brother
40 shalt serve thy brother: and the time
42 Esau thy b. threateneth to kill thee
44 till the wrath of thy b. be assuaged
32 4 thus saith thy brother Jacob: I have
6 we came to Esau thy brother and behold
38 8 that thou mayst raise seed to thy b.

Exod 4 14 Aaron the Levite is thy brother, I know
7 1 Aaron thy brother shall be thy prophet
28 1 take unto thee also Aaron thy brother
2 a holy vesture for Aaron thy brother
4 holy vestments for thy brother Aaron
41 thou shalt vest Aaron thy brother and
Lev 16 2 speak to Aaron thy brother, that he
18 16 it is the nakedness of thy brother
19 17 thou shalt not hate thy brother in thy
25 14 grieve not thy brother: but thou shalt
25 if thy b. being impoverished sell. 47
35 if thy brother be impoverished and sell
36 that thy brother may live with thee
39 if thy brother constrained by poverty
Num 20 14 thus saith thy brother Israel: Thou
27 13 people, as thy brother Aaron is gone
Deut 13 6 if thy brother the son of thy mother
15 9 turn away thy eyes from thy poor brother
11 open thy hand to thy needy and poor b.
12 when thy brother . . . is sold to thee
17 15 of another nation king that is not thy b.
22 1 thou shalt bring them back to thy b.
2 if thy brother be not nigh or thou know
2 with thee until thy brother seek them
23 7 the Edomite, because he is thy brother
19 not lend to thy brother money to usury
20 to thy b. thou shalt lend that which he
24 14 whether he be thy brother or a stranger
25 31 lest thy brother depart shamefully torn
32 50 as Aaron thy brother died in mount Hor
2 K 2 22 to hold up my face to Joab thy brother
13 7 come to house of thy brother Amnon
20 hath thy brother Amnon with thee
20 sister, hold thy peace, he is thy b.
3 K 2 7 from the face of Absalom thy brother
21 Abisag . . . be given to Adonias thy b.
20 33 and said: Thy brother Benadad. And he
Esth 15 12 I am thy brother, fear not. Thou shalt
Ps 49 20 sitting thou didst speak against thy b.
Eccu 7 13 devise not a lie against thy brother
20 nor despise thy dear brother for the
29 13 lose thy money for thy brother and thy
Abdi 10 the iniquity against thy brother Jacob
12 shalt not look on in the day of thy b.
1 Ma 9 29 since thy brother Judas died, there is
13 8 the place of Judas and Jonathan thy b.
15 we have detained thy brother Jonathan
Mat 5 23 thy b. hath anything against thee
24 go first to be reconciled to thy brother
7 4 how sayest thou to thy brother: Let
18 15 if thy brother shall offend against thee
15 hear thee, thou shalt gain thy brother
Luke 6 42 say to thy brother: Brother, let me pull
15 27 he said to him: Thy brother is come
32 thy b. was dead and is come to life
17 3 if thy b. sin against thee, reprove him
John 11 23 Jesus saith to her: Thy b. shall rise
Rom 14 10 why judgest thou thy brother? Or thou
10 why dost thou despise thy brother? For
15 because of thy meat thy b. be grieved
21 thing whereby thy brother is offended
brotherhood Zach 11 14 might break the b. between
1 Ma 12 10 to send to you to renew the brotherhood
17 concerning the renewing of our b. and
Rom 12 10 with the charity of brotherhood with
1 Th 4 9 as touching the charity of brotherhood
Heb 13 1 let the charity of the b. abide in you
1 P 2 17 love the brotherhood. Fear God. Honor
3 8 being lovers of the b., merciful
2 P 1 7 in godliness, love of b.; and in love
of b., charity
brotherly 1 P 1 22 with a brotherly love, from a
brother's Gen 4 9 am I my brother's keeper? And he

Gen 4 10 the voice of thy brother's blood crieth
21 his brother's name was Jubal; he was
10 25 divided: and his brother's name Jectan
12 5 Sarai his wife and Lot his brother's son
25 25 held his brother's foot in his hand
33 11 at his brother's earnest pressing him
38 8 go in to thy brother's wife and marry
9 when he went in to his brother's wife
9 children should be born in his b. name
Lev 18 16 not uncover nakedness of thy b. wife
20 17 and she behold her brother's shame
21 hath uncovered this brother's nakedness
Deut 22 3 with every thing that is thy brother's
4 if thou see thy brother's ass or his ox
25 7 if he will not take his brother's wife
7 refuseth to raise up his brother's name
3 K 2 15 transferred and is become my brother's
Esth 2 7 brought up his b. daughter Edissa who
Prov 27 10 go not into thy brother's house in
Wisd 10 10 when he fled from his brother's wrath
Mat 7 3 mote . . . in thy brother's eye. Luke 6:41
5 mote out of thy b. eye. Luke 6:42
14 3 because of Herodias, his brother's wife
Mark 6 18 lawful for thee to have thy b. wife
Luke 3 19 reproved by him for Herodias his b. wife
Rom 14 13 put not . . . a scandal in your b. way
1 J 3 12 works were wicked; and his b. just
brothers Gen 24 53 offered gifts also to her b.
Gen 34 25 brothers of Dina, taking their swords
Eccu 34 27 defraudeth laborer of his hire, are b.
2 Pa 22 1 killed all that were his elder brothers
Osee 13 15 he shall make a separation between b.
brow Luke 4 29 brought him to the brow of the hill
brown Gen 30 32 all that is b. and spotted and
Gen 30 33 that is not . . . spotted and brown, as well
Cant 1 5 do not consider me that I am brown
bruchus Lev 11 22 you shall eat, as the bruchus
Ps 104 34 the locust came, and the bruchus, of
Joel 1 4 the bruchus hath eaten; and that which the
bruchus hath left
2 25 locust and the bruchus and the mildew
Nah 3 15 it shall devour thee like the bruchus
15 assemble together like the bruchus
16 the b. hath spread himself and flown
bruise Isa 53 10 Lord was pleased to b. him in
Jer 30 12 thy bruise is incurable, thy wound is
Amos 2 7 they bruise the heads of the poor upon
bruised Lev 22 24 that hath the testicles bruised
Num 22 25 and bruised the foot of the rider. But
1 Pa 20 3 they were cut and bruised to pieces
Ps 36 24 when he shall fall he shall not be b.
Isa 42 3 the bruised reed he shall not break
53 5 he was bruised for our sins: the
Jer 5 3 thou hast bruised them and they have
Eze 23 3 teats of their virginity were bruised
8 they b. the breasts of her virginity
Mat 12 20 the bruised reed he shall not break
Luke 4 19 to set at liberty them that are b.
20 18 fall upon that stone, shall be bruised
bruises Ps 146 3 and bindeth up their bruises
Isa 1 6 wounds and bruises and swelling sores
53 5 by his bruises we are healed. All we
bruising Gen 4 23 and a stripling to my own b.
2 Ma 9 7 by a grievous bruising of the body
Luke 9 39 a spirit seizeth him . . . bruising him
brutish Eze 21 31 hands of men that are brutish
Bubastus Eze 30 17 of B. shall fall by the sword
bubbleth Prov 15 2 mouth of fools b. out folly
buck goat: *see* goat
buck goats: *see* goats
bucket Num 24 7 water shall flow out of his bucket
Isa 40 15 Gentiles are as a drop of a bucket
buckets 3 K 18 34 fill four buckets with water

buckle Job 40 21 bore through his jaw with a b.
1 Ma 10 89 he sent him a buckle of gold as the
11 58 gave him leave . . . to wear a golden b.
14 44 or to wear a buckle of gold. Whosoever
buckler 1 K 17 6 b. of brass covered his shoulders
Prov 30 5 a buckler to them that hope in him
Jer 46 3 prepare ye the shield and buckler and
Lam 3 65 shalt give them a buckler of heart
Eze 23 24 be armed . . . with breastplate and b.
26 8 he shall lift up the b. against thee
27 10 they hung up the buckler and the helmet
bucklers Cant 4 4 a thousand b. hang upon it, all
buckles Exod 26 11 fifty b. of brass. 36:18
bud Eccu 39 17 bud forth as the rose planted by
Isa 4 2 bud of the Lord shall be in magnificence
5 24 their bud shall go up as dust: for they
14 22 Babylon and the remains and the bud
18 5 it shall bud without perfect ripeness
27 6 Israel shall blossom and bud, and they
35 2 it shall bud forth and blossom and
45 8 be opened, and bud forth a savior: and
61 11 as the earth bringeth forth her bud
Jer 33 15 will make the bud of justice to spring
Eze 16 7 to multiply as the bud of the field
29 21 a horn shall bud forth to the house
34 29 I will raise up for them a bud of renown
Dan 11 7 a plant of the bud of her roots shall
Osee 8 7 the bud shall yield no meal: and if it
budded Num 17 8 the rod of Aaron . . . was budded
Cant 6 10 flourished and the pomegranates budded
Eze 7 10 blossomed, pride hath budded. Iniquity
budding Eccu 50 11 as an olive tree budding forth
buds Gen 40 10 little by little sent out buds
Num 17 8 the buds swelling it had bloomed: and
buffet Mark 14 65 some began . . . to buffet him and
2 C 12 7 an angel of Satan to buffet me. For
buffeted Mat 26 67 spit in his face and b. him
1 C 4 11 we are naked and are buffeted and have
1 P 2 20 being buffeted for it, you endure? But
buffle Deut 14 5 the hart and the roe, the buffle
buffles 3 K 4 23 venison of harts, roes, and b.
Amos 6 13 can any one plow with buffles? For you
buffoons 2 K 6 20 as if one of the b. should be
Bugite Esth 12 6 Aman the son of Amadathi the B.
builder 2 Ma 2 30 as the master b. of a new house
Heb 11 10 whose builder and maker is God. By faith
builders 4 K 12 11 over the b. of the house of the
2 Es 4 18 every one of the builders was girded
Ps 117 22 stone which the builders rejected
Isa 49 17 thy builders are come: they that destroy
Mat 21 42 the stone which the builders rejected. Mark 12:10; Luke 20:17; 1 P 2:7
Acts 4 11 which was rejected by you the builders
building Gen 11 5 which children of Adam were b.
Josu 22 16 building a sacrilegious altar and
19 by building an altar beside the altar
29 by b. an altar to offer holocausts
3 K 3 1 made an end of b. his own house and the
6 7 the house when it was in building. The
38 and he was seven years in building it
8 13 b. I have built a house for thy dwelling
9 1 when Solomon had finished the b. of the
15 21 [Baasa] left off b. Rama and returned
22 timber . . . wherewith Baasa had been b.
1 Pa 26 27 they had consecrated to the building
28 2 I prepared all things for the building
2 Pa 14 7 there was no hinderance in building
16 5 he left off the building of Rama and
6 that Baasa had prepared for the b.
34 11 timber for the couplings of the b.
1 Es 4 1 were building a temple to the Lord
4 and troubled them in building. And they
12 city which they are building, setting
5 4 who were the promoters of that building
8 which they are b. with unpolished stones
11 we are building a temple that was built
16 that time until now it is in building
2 Es 4 1 Sanaballat heard that we were building
Jdth 5 10 in the building of his cities, they
Ecce 10 18 by slothfulness a b. shall be brought
Eccu 22 19 bound together in foundation of a b.
40 19 children, and the building of a city
50 2 the double building and the high walls
Eze 40 2 there was as the building of a city
5 he measured the breadth of the building
41 12 the building that was separate and
12 the wall of the b., five cubits thick
13 the separate building . . . 100 cubits
15 he measured the length of the building
42 1 over against the separate building. 10
5 and from the midst of the building
10 were chambers before the building. And
13 which are before the separate building
43 10 let them measure the building: and be
Haba 2 11 that is between the joints of the b.
Agge 1 2 for building the house of the Lord
Zach 1 16 the building line shall be stretched
1 Ma 3 56 to them that were building houses, or
10 44 for the b. also or repairing the works
45 for the building also of the walls of
45 also for the b. of the walls in Judea
13 27 over the sepulcher . . . a building lofty
16 23 the building of the walls which he made
2 Ma 2 30 must have care of the whole building
Luke 6 48 he is like to a man building a house
49 a man building his house upon the earth
John 2 20 years was this temple in building
1 C 3 9 you are God's building. According to
2 C 5 1 we have a building of God, a house not
Eph 2 21 all the building, being framed together
1 P 3 20 when the ark was a building: wherein
Jude 20 building yourselves upon your . . . faith
Apoc 21 18 building of the wall was of jasper
buildings Mat 24 1 to show him the b. of the temple
Mark 13 1 what buildings are here. And Jesus
2 seest thou all these great buildings
Bul 3 K 6 38 the month Bul, which is the eighth
bulk Prov 8 25 mountains with their huge bulk had
Isa 40 12 with three fingers the bulk of the earth
bull Eccu 6 2 extol not thyself . . . like a bull
bullock Lev 9 4 b. and a ram for peace offerings
Lev 9 18 he immolated also the bullock and the
19 fat also of the bullock and the rump of
22 27 when a bullock . . . is brought forth, they
27 26 bullock or sheep, they are the Lord's
Deut 15 19 not work with the firstling of a b.
33 17 his beauty as of firstling of a bullock
Judg 6 25 take a bullock of thy father's and
25 and another bullock of seven years, and
26 thou shalt take the second bullock and
28 second bullock laid upon the altar, which
3 K 18 23 and let them choose one bullock for
23 and I will dress the other bullock and
25 choose you one bullock and dress it
26 took the bullock which he gave them
33 and cut the bullock in pieces and laid
2 Pa 13 9 consecrateth his hand with a bullock
Jer 31 18 as young b. unaccustomed to the yoke
bullocks 3 K 18 23 let two b. be given us and let
1 Pa 29 21 holocausts . . . a thousand bullocks
2 Pa 29 21 they offered together seven bullocks
22 therefore they killed the bullocks
32 multitude offered, was seventy bullocks
30 24 had given . . . a thousand bullocks and
Ps 49 13 shall I eat the flesh of bullocks
65 15 I will offer to thee bullocks with goats

Eze 39 18 shall drink the blood of . . . bullocks
Dan 3 40 as in holocausts of rams and bullocks
Osee 12 11 in Galgal offering sacrifices with b.
bulls Gen 32 15 for his brother Esau . . . 20 bulls
Ps 21 13 fat bulls have besieged me. They have
67 31 the congregation of bulls with the kine
Eccu 38 26 talk is about the offspring of bulls
Isa 34 7 bulls [shall go down] with the mighty
Jer 50 11 and have bellowed as bulls. Your mother
bulrush Isa 19 6 reed and the b. shall wither
Isa 35 7 rise up the verdure of the reed and b.
bulrushes Exod 2 3 she took a basket made of b.
Isa 18 2 in vessels of bulrushes upon the waters
bulwark Isa 26 1 and a b. shall be set therein
Lam 2 8 the bulwark hath mourned, and the wall
bulwarks Deut 20 19 hast compassed it with bulwarks
Ecce 9 14 built bulwarks round about it, and the
Cant 4 4 tower of David, which is built with b.
8 9 let us build upon it bulwarks of silver
Isa 25 12 bulwarks of thy high walls shall fall
29 3 and raise up bulwarks to besiege thee
54 12 I will make thy bulwarks of jasper
Jer 33 4 saith the Lord . . . to the bulwarks and
48 7 because thou hast trusted in thy b.
18 he hath destroyed thy bulwarks. Stand
Nah 3 14 water for the siege, build up thy b.
Soph 1 16 fenced cities, and against the high b.
Buna 1 Pa 2 25 sons of Jerameel . . . Buna and Aram
bunch Exod 12 22 dip a bunch of hyssop in the blood
Judg 8 2 one bunch of grapes of Ephraim better
Jer 49 9 would they not have left a bunch? If
bunches Lev 19 10 neither shalt thou gather the b.
1 K 30 12 and two bunches of raisins. And when
2 K 16 1 and a hundred bunches of raisins, a
Isa 30 6 their treasures upon the b. of camels
bundle 1 K 25 29 kept, as in the b. of the living
Cant 1 12 a bundle of myrrh is my beloved to me
Isa 24 22 as in the gathering of one bundle
33 12 as bundle of thorns they shall be burnt
Amos 9 6 hath founded his bundle upon the earth
Acts 28 3 Paul had gathered a bundle of sticks
bundles Judg 19 17 saw the man sitting with his b.
Isa 58 6 undo the bundles that oppress, let them
Mat 13 30 bind it into bundles to burn, but the
bur Osee 9 6 bur shall be in their tabernacles
Osee 10 8 the bur and the thistle shall grow up
burden Exod 18 22 the b. being shared out unto
Exod 23 5 see the ass . . . lie underneath his burden
Num 4 27 know to what burden he must be assigned
11 17 may bear with thee the b. of the people
2 K 15 33 thou [Chusai] wilt be a burden to me
19 35 why should thy servant be a burden
4 K 5 17 from hence two mules' burden of earth
9 25 the Lord laid this burden upon him
2 Pa 10 4 and ease something of the burden, that
Ps 37 5 as a heavy burden are become heavy
Eccu 8 18 lest he burden thee with his evils
13 2 he shall take a burden upon him that
21 19 talking of a fool is like b. in the way
33 25 a wand and a burden are for an ass
Isa 9 4 the yoke of their burden . . . thou hast
10 27 his burden shall be taken away from off
13 1 burden of Babylon which Isaias . . . saw
14 25 his b. shall be taken off their shoulder
28 year that king Achaz died, was this b.
15 1 the burden of Moab. Because in the night
17 1 the burden of Damascus. Behold Damascus
19 1 the burden of Egypt. Behold the Lord will
21 1 the burden of the desert of the sea
11 the burden of Duma calleth to me out of
13 the burden in Arabia. In the forest at
22 1 the burden of the valley of vision
23 1 the burden of Tyre. Howl, ye ships of
30 6 the burden of the beasts of the south
58 6 and break asunder every burden. Deal
Jer 23 33 what is the burden of the Lord? Thou shalt say to them: You are the burden
34 that shall say: The burden of the Lord
36 b. of the Lord shall be mentioned no more, for every man's word shall be his b.
38 if you shall say: The burden of the Lord
38 this word: The burden of the Lord: and I
38 say not, The burden of the Lord
Eze 12 10 this burden concerneth my prince that is
Osee 8 10 a while from the burden of the king
Nah 1 1 the burden of Ninive. The book of the
Haba 1 1 the burden that Habacuc the prophet saw
7 shall their judgment and their b. proceed
Zach 9 1 b. of word of the Lord. 12:1; Mala 1:1
Mat 11 30 my yoke is sweet and my burden light
20 12 that have borne the burden of the day
Acts 15 28 to lay no further burden upon you than
21 3 there the ship was to unlade her burden
2 C 2 5 that I may not burden you all. To him
Gal 6 5 every one shall bear his own burden
burdened Mat 11 28 you that labor and are burdened
burdens Exod 1 11 to afflict them with burdens
Exod 5 4 get you gone to your burdens. And
Num 4 15 these are the burdens of sons of Caath
19 divide the b. that every man is to carry
31 these are their burdens. They shall carry
47 and to carry the burdens, were in all
49 according to their office and burdens
7 9 carry the b. upon their own shoulders
Deut 26 6 laying on us most grievous burdens
3 K 5 15 Solomon had 70,000 to carry burdens
4 K 8 9 taking . . . the burdens of forty camels
2 Pa 2 2 seventy thousand men to bear burdens
18 set 70,000 of them to carry burdens
34 13 over them that carried burdens for
2 Es 4 10 the strength of the bearer of burdens
17 built on the wall and that carried b.
13 15 and figs and all manner of burdens
19 none should bring in burdens on sabbath
Ps 80 7 he removed his back from the burdens
Isa 46 1 your burdens of heavy weight even unto
Jer 17 21 carry no burdens on the sabbath day
22 do not bring burdens out of your houses
24 to bring in no burdens by the gates
27 sabbath day, and not to carry burdens
Mat 23 4 they bind heavy . . . burdens and lay them
Luke 11 46 because you load men with burdens which
Gal 6 2 bear ye one another's burdens; and so
burdensome 2 K 14 26 because his hair was b. to him
Job 7 20 and I am become burdensome to myself
33 7 let not my eloquence be burdensome to
Zach 12 3 I will make Jerusalem a b. stone to all
1 Th 2 7 we might have been burdensome to you
burial Tob 4 18 wine upon the b. of a just man
Ecce 6 3 and he be without burial; of this man
Eccu 38 16 cover his body and neglect not his b.
40 1 until the day of their burial into the
Isa 14 20 not keep company with them even in b.
53 9 he shall give the ungodly for his b.
Jer 22 19 shall be buried with the b. of an ass
2 Ma 4 49 were liberal towards their burial. And
5 10 neither having foreign burial nor being
Mat 26 12 hath done it for my burial. Amen I say
Mark 14 8 to anoint my body for the burial. Amen
John 12 7 against the day of my burial. For the
buried Gen 15 15 be b. in a good old age. But
Gen 25 9 buried him in the double cave which was
10 there was he [Abraham] buried, and
35 4 buried them under the turpentine tree
8 was buried at the foot of Bethel under
19 Rachel . . . was buried in the highway

29 his sons Esau and Jacob buried him
48 7 I buried her near the way of Ephrata
49 31 there they buried him [Jacob] and
31 there was Isaac buried with Rebecca
31 there also Lia doth lie buried with
50 13 buried him [Jacob] in the double cave
14 after he [Joseph] had buried his father
Num 11 34 they buried the people that had lusted
20 1 Mary . . . was buried in the same place
Deut 10 6 where Aaron died and was buried, and
21 23 shall be buried the same day; for he
34 6 he buried him [Moses] in the valley
Josu 24 30 they buried him [Josue] in the border
32 taken out of Egypt, they b. in Sichem
33 they buried him [Eleazar] in Gabaath
Judg 2 9 they buried him [Josue] in the borders
8 32 was b. in the sepulcher of his father
10 2 he died and was buried in Samir. To
5 Jair died and was buried in the place
12 7 [Jephte] was b. in his city of Galaad
10 [Abesan] was buried in Bethlehem. To
12 [Ahialon] was buried in Zabulon. After
15 [Abdon] was buried in Pharathon in the
16 31 buried it between Saraa and Esthaol
Ruth 1 17 and there will I be buried. The Lord
1 K 25 1 buried him in his house in Ramatha
28 3 buried him [Samuel] in Ramatha his city
31 13 buried them in the wood of Jabes: and
2 K 2 4 the men of Jabes Galaad had b. Saul
5 to your master Saul, and have b. him
32 buried him [Asael] in the sepulcher of
3 32 when they had buried Abner in Hebron
4 12 b. in the sepulcher of Abner in Hebron
17 23 Achitophel . . . was b. in the sepulcher
19 37 and be b. by the sepulcher of my father
21 14 they buried them with the bones of Saul
3 K 2 10 was buried in the city of David. 11:43
34 [Joab] was buried in his house in the
13 31 wherein the man of God is buried: lay
14 18 the child died: and they buried him
31 was buried with them in the city of David. 15:24; 22:51; 4 K 8:24; 15:38; 16:20
15 8 buried him [Abiam] in the city of David
16 6 Baasa . . . was buried in Thersa: and Ela
28 was buried in Samaria. 4 K 13:13; 14:16
22 37 and they buried the king in Samaria
4 K 9 28 they b. him in his sepulcher with his
10 35 they buried him [Jehu] in Samaria: and
12 21 they b. him [Joas] with his fathers
13 9 they buried him [Joachaz] in Samaria
20 Eliseus died, and they buried him. And
14 20 he was buried in Jerusalem with his
15 7 they buried him [Azarias] with his
21 18 Manasses . . . was buried in the garden of
26 they buried him [Amon] in his sepulcher
23 30 b. him in his own sepulcher. 2 Pa 16:14
1 Pa 10 12 brought them to Jabes and b. their bones
2 Pa 22 9 and they buried him [Ochozias]; because
26 23 buried him in the field of the royal
28 27 buried him [Achaz] in city of Jerusalem
32 33 they buried him above the sepulcher
33 20 and they b. him [Manasses] in his house
35 24 they buried him in the monument of his
Tob 1 21 Tobias buried their bodies. But when
2 7 sun was down, he went and buried him
9 and at midnight buried them. Now it
14 2 he was buried honorably in Ninive. For
16 fear of the Lord, with joy they b. him
Jdth 8 3 and was buried there with his fathers
16 28 she died and was b. with her husband
Job 11 18 being buried thou shalt sleep secure
27 15 remain of him, shall be b. in death
Ecce 8 10 I saw the wicked buried: who also when
Eccu 44 14 their bodies are buried in peace and
Jer 8 2 they shall not be buried. 16:4, 6
19 11 and they shall be buried in Topheth
20 6 and there thou shalt be buried, thou and
22 19 shall be b. with the burial of an ass
25 33 shall not be gathered up nor buried
Nah 3 18 thy princes shall be buried: thy people
1 Ma 2 70 and he was buried by his sons in the
9 19 buried him in the sepulcher of their
13 25 brother, and buried them in Modin, in
2 Ma 9 15 worthy to be so much as buried, but
Mat 14 12 took the body and buried it and came
Luke 16 22 he was buried in hell. And lifting up
Acts 2 29 David . . . died and was buried; and his
5 6 carrying him [Ananias] out, buried him
9 feet of them who have b. thy husband
10 b. her [Saphira] by her husband. And
Rom 6 4 we are buried together with him by
1 C 15 4 that he was buried and that he rose
Col 2 12 buried him in baptism, in whom
buriedst Tob 2 16 gavest alms and b. the dead
buriers Eze 39 15 till the b. bury it in the valley
burn Exod 27 20 that a lamp may burn always, in
Exod 29 14 and the dung, thou shalt burn abroad
25 and shalt burn them upon the altar
30 1 shalt make also an altar to b. incense
7 shall burn sweet smelling incense upon
7 dress the lamps, he shall burn it: and
8 he shall burn an everlasting incense
Lev 1 9 shall burn them upon the altar. 3:5, 11, 16; 4:10; 7:5
13 priest shall offer it all and burn it
17 shall burn it upon the altar. 2:9; 4:19, 31, 35; 5:12; 6:15
2 16 whereof the priest shall burn for a
4 12 he shall burn them upon a pile of wood
21 shall burn it as he did the former calf
26 the fat he shall burn upon it, as is
5 10 the other he shall burn for a holocaust
6 12 the fire on the altar shall always burn
12 shall burn thereupon the fat of the
7 31 shall burn the fat upon the altar but
16 25 fat . . . he shall burn upon the altar
17 6 shall burn the fat for a sweet odor
22 22 you shall not . . . burn anything of them
Num 5 26 and burn it upon the altar: and so
18 17 their fat thou shalt burn for a most
19 5 shall burn her in the sight of all
Deut 5 23 saw the mountain burn, came to me
7 5 and burn their graven things. Because
13 16 shalt burn them with the city itself
32 22 shall burn even to the lowest hell
22 shall burn foundations of the mountains
Judg 12 1 therefore we will burn thy house. And
14 15 wilt not do it, we will burn thee and
1 K 2 28 to go up to my altar and burn incense
3 K 12 33 went upon the altar to burn incense
13 2 and he shall burn men's bones upon thee
1 Pa 23 13 and to burn incense before the Lord
2 Pa 2 4 dedicate it, to burn incense before him
26 16 he had a mind to burn incense upon the
18 Ozias, to burn incense to the Lord
19 holding . . . the censer to burn incense
28 25 he built altars to burn frankincense
2 Es 10 34 to burn upon the altar of the Lord
Jdth 16 21 that they may burn and may feel forever
Job 18 9 and thirst shall burn against him. A
20 22 he shall be straitened, he shall burn
Ps 7 14 ready his arrows for them that burn
25 2 try me: burn my reins and my heart
45 10 and the shield he shall burn in the fire
49 3 a fire shall burn before him: and a
88 47 the end? Shall thy anger burn like fire

96 3 shall burn his enemies round about
120 6 the sun shall not burn thee by day
Prov 6 27 in his bosom, and his garments not burn
Eccu 28 14 spark, it shall burn as a fire: and if
27 into it, and it shall burn in them
40 32 in his belly there shall burn a fire
43 23 it shall . . . burn the wilderness and
Isa 40 16 Libanus shall not be enough to burn
43 2 the flames shall not burn in thee: for
Jer 4 4 come forth like fire and burn and
7 20 it shall burn and shall not be quenched
31 to burn their sons and their daughters
15 14 in my rage, it shall burn upon you
17 4 in my wrath, it shall burn forever
21 10 Babylon, and he shall burn it with
32 29 shall . . . set it on fire and burn it
33 18 to burn sacrifices and to kill victims
34 5 so shall they burn thee: and they shall
36 25 to the king, not to burn the book: and
43 12 gods of Egypt, and he shall burn them
Eze 20 47 will burn in thee every green tree
22 21 will burn you in the fire of my wrath
39 9 on fire and burn the weapons, the
43 21 thou shalt burn him in a separate
Amos 6 10 shall take him up and shall burn him
Nah 2 13 I will burn thy chariots even to smoke
1 Ma 2 15 to sacrifice and to burn incense and
7 35 I will burn this house. And he went
2 Ma 10 36 and to burn the blasphemers alive. And
Mat 3 12 the chaff he will burn. Luke 3:17
13 30 bind it into bundles to burn, but the
1 C 3 15 if any man's work burn, he shall suffer
burn with fire Exod 12 10 anything left, you shall burn it with fire
Exod 29 34 thou shalt burn the remainder with fire
Lev 13 55 unclean, and shall burn it with fire
16 27 without the camp, and shall burn with f.
19 6 the third day, you shall burn with fire
Deut 7 25 graven things thou shalt burn with fire
12 3 burn their groves with fire and break
Josu 11 6 shalt burn their chariots with fire
4 K 8 12 strong cities thou wilt burn with fire
Isa 64 2 the waters would burn with fire, that
Jer 19 5 to burn their children with fire for
21 10 he shall burn it with fire. 34:2
34 22 they shall . . . burn it with fire. 38:18
37 7 city, take it and burn it with fire
9 burn this city with fire. 38:23
43 13 the temples . . . he shall b. with fire
Eze 5 2 a third part thou shalt burn with fire
4 and shalt burn them with fire: and out
16 41 they shall burn thy houses with fire
23 47 their houses they shall burn with fire
24 10 the bones, which I will burn with fire
39 9 shall burn them with fire seven years
10 they shall burn the weapons with fire
Apoc 17 16 shall burn her with fire. For God hath
burned Num 11 4 burned with desire, sitting and
Num 19 8 he also that hath burned her, shall
26 10 when the fire burned 250 men. And
31 10 their villages and castles they burned
Deut 4 11 foot of the mount, which burned even
9 21 calf, I took and burned it with fire
Josu 6 24 they burned the city [Jericho] and all
8 28 he [Josue] burned the city and made
11 9 their horses and burned their chariots
11 destroyed all and burned the city itself
13 the rest Israel burned: only Asor that
Ps 105 18 the flame burned the wicked. They made
117 12 they burned like fire among thorns
Wisd 16 18 that the beasts . . . might not be burned
19 burned in the midst of water, to destroy
Eze 20 47 every face shall be burned in it, from
Rom 1 27 have burned in their lusts one towards
1 C 13 3 if I should deliver my body to be b.
Heb 13 11 for sin, are burned without the camp
burneth Lev 16 28 whosoever b. them shall wash
Ps 82 15 as fire which burneth the wood: and as
Isa 30 27 his wrath burneth and is heavy to
Eccu 9 11 for her conversation burneth as fire
28 12 forest is, so the fire burneth: and as
43 3 at noon he burneth the earth, and who
4 b. the mountains, breathing out fiery
John 15 6 cast him into the fire and he burneth
burning Exod 21 25 b. for b., wound for wound
Lev 9 17 and burning them upon the altar, besides
10 6 the burning which the Lord has kindled
13 28 it is the sore of a burning, and
28 it is only the scar of a burning and
Num 11 3 called name of that place, The burning
15 3 burning a sweet savor unto the Lord
16 37 the censers that lie in the burning
19 17 they shall take of the ashes of the b.
Deut 8 15 the serpent burning with his breath
9 15 when I came down from the burning mount
22 at the burning also and at the place
12 31 sons and daughters and b. them with fire
28 22 with cold, with burning and with heat
29 23 burning it with brimstone and the heat
3 K 13 1 when Jeroboam was . . . burning incense
2 Pa 21 19 according to the manner of burning
Jdth 12 16 was burning with the desire of her
Ps 82 15 and as a flame burning mountains: so
Ecce 7 7 crackling of thorns b. under a pot
Wisd 16 22 fire burning in the hail and flashing
18 3 burning pillar of fire for a guide
Eccu 43 3 who can abide his burning heat? As
50 9 as . . . frankincense burning in the fire
Isa 4 4 and by the spirit of burning. And the
10 16 a b., as it were the b. of a fire. And
25 5 as with heat under a burning cloud
34 9 land thereof shall become burning pitch
64 2 would melt as at the burning of fire
65 5 my anger, a fire burning all the day
Bar 6 42 in the ways, burning olive stones. And
Dan 3 88 of the midst of the burning flame and
93 door of the burning fiery furnace and
10 6 and his eyes as a burning lamp: and his
Joel 2 3 and behind it a burning flame: the
Amos 4 11 as a firebrand plucked out of the b.
1 Ma 12 29 for they saw the lights burning. And
Luke 12 35 lamps burning in your hands. And you
24 32 was not our heart burning within us
John 5 35 he was a burning and shining light
Apoc 1 15 fine brass, as in a burning furnace
4 5 seven lamps, burning before the throne
8 8 as it were a great mountain, b. with fire
10 burning as it were a torch, and it fell
18 9 they shall see the smoke of her burning
18 seeing the place of her burning, saying
19 20 into the pool of fire b. with brimstone
21 8 in the pool b. with fire and brimstone
burning coals; *see* **coals**
burning fire; *see* **fire**
burning heat; *see* **heat**
burning wind; *see* **wind**
burnings Isa 33 14 shall dwell with everlasting b.
Jer 34 5 according to the b. of thy fathers
burnt Gen 38 24 her out that she may be burnt
Exod 3 2 bush was on fire and was not burnt
3 why the bush is not burnt. And when
32 20 laying hold of the calf . . . he burnt it
40 5 whereon the incense is burnt, before the
25 burnt upon it the incense of spices
Lev 2 11 any leaven or honey be burnt in the
4 12 they shall be burnt in the place where

6 9 it shall be burnt upon the altar all
10 which the devouring fire hath burnt
22 it shall be wholly burnt on the altar
8 16 the fat . . . he b. upon the altar. 9:10
17 the dung he burnt without the camp
20 the fat he burnt in the fire, having
21 the whole ram together he burnt upon
28 burnt them upon the altar of holocaust
9 20 after the fat was burnt upon the altar
10 15 the fat that is burnt on the altar
16 buck goat . . . he found it burnt: and being
13 24 and skin that hath been burnt, and after
20 14 he shall be burnt alive with them
Num 19 9 because the cow was burnt for sin
Judg 15 5 the corn . . . was all burnt, insomuch
6 burnt both the woman and her father
1 K 2 15 before they burnt the fat, the servant
16 let the fat first be b. today according
31 12 to Jabes Galaad and burnt them there
2 K 23 7 he set on fire and burnt to nothing
3 K 3 3 in the high places: and burnt incense
9 25 and he burnt incense before the Lord
11 8 who burnt incense and offered sacrifice
15 13 in pieces the filthy idol and burnt it
16 18 burnt himself with the king's house
22 44 and burnt incense in the high places
4 K 10 26 statue out of Baal's temple and b. it
12 3 sacrificed and burnt incense. 15:4, 35; 16:4
17 11 they burnt incense there upon altars
31 b. their children in fire to Adramelech
18 4 children of Israel burnt incense to it
23 4 and he burnt them without Jerusalem
6 he burnt it there and reduced it to dust
15 the high place he broke down and burnt
15 and burnt the grove. And as Josias
16 burnt them upon the altar and defiled it
20 he burnt men's bones upon them: and
25 9 he burnt the house of the Lord and the
1 Pa 14 12 David commanded that they should be b.
2 Pa 2 6 that incense may be burnt before him
15 16 and breaking it into pieces burnt it
16 14 b. them over him with very great pomp
30 14 in which incense was burnt to idols
34 5 and he burnt the bones of the priests
36 19 of Jerusalem, burnt all the towers
2 Es 4 2 heaps of the rubbish which are burnt
Tob 14 7 the house of God which is burnt in it
Prov 6 28 upon hot coals, and his feet not be b.
Eccu 8 13 lest thou be burnt with the flame of
28 26 the just shall not be burnt with its
48 1 and his word burnt like a torch. He
49 8 they burnt the chosen city of holiness
51 6 in midst of the fire I was not burnt
Isa 9 5 and garment . . . shall be burnt and be
13 8 countenances shall be as faces burnt
27 9 as burnt stones broken in pieces, the
42 25 and hath burnt him round about, and he
43 2 the fire, thou shalt not be burnt and
44 19 I have burnt part of it in the fire
47 14 are as stubble, fire hath burnt them
Jer 2 15 his cities are burnt down and there
9 10 because they are burnt up, for that
12 and is burnt up like a wilderness which
11 16 and the branches thereof are burnt
36 27 after that the king had burnt the volume
28 volume which Joakim . . . hath burnt. And
29 thou hast burnt that volume, saying
51 25 will make thee a burnt mountain. And
30 her dwelling places are burnt, her bars
52 13 he burnt the house of the Lord and the
Lam 5 10 our skin was burnt as an oven, by
Bar 6 54 they themselves shall be burnt in the
Eze 6 13 they burnt sweet smelling frankincense
Dan 3 48 burnt such of the Chaldeans as it found
7 11 and given to the fire to be burnt: and
Osee 2 13 Baalim, to whom she burnt incense
4 13 and burnt incense upon the hills: under
Joel 1 19 the flame hath burnt all the trees
Amos 2 1 he hath burnt the bones of the king
1 Ma 1 58 burnt incense and sacrificed at the
4 38 altar profaned and the gates burnt
5 65 he burnt the walls thereof and the
9 67 out of the city and burnt the engines
10 85 with them that were burnt, were almost
11 61 and burnt all the suburbs round about
2 Ma 1 8 they burnt the gate and shed innocent
8 33 they burnt Callisthenes, that had set
12 6 in the night, burnt the boats and slew
Mat 13 40 as cockle is gathered up and burnt
22 7 and burnt their city. Then he saith to
Acts 19 19 brought together their books and b. them
1 C 7 9 it is better to marry than to be burnt
Heb 6 8 unto a curse, whose end is to be burnt
2 P 3 10 the earth . . . shall be burnt up. Seeing
Apoc 8 7 the third part of the earth was b. up
7 the third part of the trees was b. up
7 all green grass was burnt up. And the
18 8 and she shall be burnt with the fire

burnt offering; ***see*** **offering**
burnt offerings; ***see*** **offerings**
burnt sacrifice; ***see*** **sacrifice**
burnt with fire Lev 6 30 not be eaten, but shall be burnt with fire. 7:19
Lev 9 11 the skins thereof be burnt with fire
13 the members, all which he b. . . . upon
13 52 it shall be b. . . . But if he see that
57 wandering leprosy; it must be b. . . .
21 9 name of her father, she shall be b. . . .
Josu 7 15 guilty of this fact, he shall be b. . . .
Judg 18 27 of the sword; and the city was b. . . .
1 K 30 1 smitten Siceleg and burnt it with fire
3 men came to the city and found it b. . . .
14 and we burnt Siceleg with fire. And
3 K 9 16 took Gazer and burnt it with fire: and
4 K 23 11 burnt the chariots of the sun with fire
25 9 Jerusalem, and every house he b. . . .
2 Es 1 3 gates thereof are burnt with fire. 2:3
Isa 1 7 is desolate and your cities are b. . . .
33 12 bundle of thorns, they shall be b. . . .
44 16 down before it. Part of it he b. . . .
64 11 where our fathers praised thee is b. . . .
Jer 36 32 book which Joakim . . . had b. with fire
38 17 live, and this city shall not be b. . . .
39 8 burnt . . . houses of the people with fire
49 2 heap, and her daughters shall be b. . . .
51 32 are taken, and the marshes are b. . . .
58 and her high gates shall be b. . . . and
52 13 and every great house he b. with fire
Bar 1 2 took Jerusalem and burnt it with fire
Amos 5 6 lest the house of Joseph be b. . . . and
Mich 1 7 pieces, and all her wages shall be b. . . .
1 Ma 1 33 the city, and burnt it with fire and
59 b. . . . the books of the law of God: and
3 5 them that troubled his people he b. . . .
5 5 and burnt their towers with fire and
28 took all their spoils and b. it with f.
35 to Maspha . . . and burnt it with fire
44 took the city, and the temple he b. . . .
68 b. the statues of their gods with fire
6 31 sallied forth and burnt them with fire
10 84 them that were fled into it, he b. . . .
11 4 the temple of Dagon that was b. . . .
16 10 of Azotus and he burnt them with fire
2 Ma 6 11 being discovered by Philip, were b. . . .

burst Num 5 21 may thy belly . . . burst asunder
Josu 9 13 now they are rent and burst. These

Ps 106 16 gates of brass, and burst iron bars
Wisd 4 19 shall b. them puffed up and speechless
Eccu 19 10 trusting that it will not burst thee
Isa 45 2 and will burst the bars of iron. And I
Jer 2 20 my yoke, thou hast burst my bands and
5 5 and have burst the bonds. Wherefore a
30 8 off thy neck, and will burst his bands
Dan 14 26 mouth, and the dragon burst asunder
Nah 1 13 and I will burst thy bonds asunder
Mark 2 22 the wine will burst the bottles and
5 4 he had burst the chains and broken
Acts 1 18 being hanged, burst asunder in the midst
bursteth Job 32 19 which bursteth the new vessels
burthen 2 C 12 16 I did not burthen you: but being
Apoc 2 24 I will not put upon you any other b.
burthened Num 11 17 mayest not be burthened alone
2 C 5 4 we also . . . do groan, being burthened
8 13 others should be eased and you b. but
burthensome 2 C 11 9 myself from being b. to you
2 C 12 13 I myself was not b. to you? Pardon me
14 I will not be burthensome to you. For
bury Gen 23 4 with you, that I may bury my dead
Gen 23 6 bury thy dead in our principal sepulchers
8 that I should bury my dead, hear me
11 bury thy dead. Abraham bowed down
13 and so I will bury my dead in it. And
15 thee: but what is this? Bury thy dead
20 for a possession to bury in. 49:30
47 29 not to bury me in Egypt: but I will
30 and bury me in the buryingplace of my
49 29 bury me with my fathers in the double
50 5 thou shalt bury me in my sepulcher which
5 I will go up and bury my father and
6 go up and bury thy father according
3 K 2 31 kill him and bury him [Joab], and thou
11 15 gone up to bury them that were slain
13 31 bury me in the sepulcher wherein the
14 13 shall mourn for him and shall bury him
4 K 9 10 there shall be no one to bury her. And
34 after that cursed woman and bury her
35 when they went to bury her [Jezabel]
Tob 1 20 and was careful to bury the dead and
2 4 he might bury him cautiously. And when
8 and dost thou again bury the dead? But
4 3 my soul, thou shalt bury my body: and
5 ended the time of her life, bury her
8 14 that I may bury him before it be day
12 12 pray with tears and didst bury the dead
12 hide the dead . . . and b. them by night
14 12 as soon as you shall bury your mother
Ps 78 3 there was none to bury them. 1 Ma 7:17
Wisd 18 12 were the living sufficient to bury them
Jer 7 32 and they shall bury in Topheth, because
14 16 there shall be none to bury them: they
19 11 there is no other place to bury in
Eze 39 11 there shall they bury Gog and all
12 house of Israel shall bury them for
13 people of the land shall bury him and
14 to bury and to seek out them that were
15 till the buriers bury it in the valley
Osee 9 6 Memphis shall bury them: nettles shall
2 Ma 12 39 to bury them with their kinsmen in the
Mat 8 21 first to go and b. my father. Luke 9:59
22 let the dead bury their dead. Luke 9:60
John 19 40 as the manner of the Jews is to bury
burying Gen 23 6 hinder thee from b. thy dead
Num 33 4 who were burying their firstborn, whom
4 K 13 21 some that were burying a man, saw the
Tob 2 10 being wearied with burying, he came to
buryingplace Gen 23 4 give me the right of a b.
Gen 23 9 me before you, for a possession of a b.
47 30 bury me in the b. of my ancestors. And
50 13 with the field for a possession of a b.
Judg 16 31 in the b. of his father Manue: and he
2 Ma 9 4 a common buryingplace of the Jews. But
14 to make it a common buryingplace, he
Mat 27 7 to be a buryingplace for strangers
bush Exod 3 2 flame of a fire out of midst of bush
Exod 3 2 bush was on fire and was not burnt
3 why the bush is not burnt. And when
4 called to him out of the midst of the b.
Deut 33 16 blessing of him that appeared in the b.
Mark 12 26 how in the bush God spoke to him saying
Luke 6 44 from bramble bush do men gather the
20 37 Moses also showed at the bush, when he
Acts 7 30 an angel in a flame of fire in a bush
35 angel who appeared to him in the bush
bushel Lev 19 36 the weights equal, the b. just
Deut 25 14 in thy house a greater bushel and a less
15 thy bushel shall be equal and true
4 K 7 1 bushel of fine flour shall be sold
16 a bushel of fine flour was sold for
18 a bushel of fine flour for a stater
Mat 5 13 under a bushel. Mark 4:21; Luke 11:33
bushels Lev 27 16 if the ground be sowed with 30 b.
Ruth 2 17 an ephi of barley, that is, three b.
1 K 1 24 three calves and three b. of flour
4 K 7 1 two b. of barley for a stater. 16
18 two b. of barley shall be for a stater
Isa 5 10 thirty b. of seed shall yield three b.
Agge 2 17 when you went to a heap of twenty b.
busied 2 Pa 35 14 the priests were b. in offering
Phil 4 10 but you were busied. I speak not as
business Gen 39 11 some b. without any man with
Exod 18 18 the business is above thy strength
Deut 1 12 am not able to bear your business
24 5 neither shall any public b. be enjoined
Judg 18 28 had no society or business with any man
1 K 18 5 to whatsoever business Saul sent him
21 2 the king hath commanded me a business
8 the king's business required haste
23 20 it shall be our b. to deliver him
2 K 15 2 business to come to the king's judgment
4 all that have business might come to me
4 K 4 13 hast thou any business, and wilt thou
1 Pa 26 29 for the business abroad over Israel
2 Es 11 16 the outward business of the house of God
Ps 90 6 b. that walketh about in the dark
106 23 doing business in the great waters
Ecce 8 6 and opportunity for every business
Wisd 15 12 the business of life to be gain and
Eccu 37 14 nor with an idle servant of much b.
Dan 8 27 I did the king's business, and I was
Jon 1 8 what is thy business? Of what country
2 Ma 2 27 a business full of watching and sweat
15 5 to take arms and to do the king's b.
Luke 2 49 I must be about my father's business
Acts 6 3 whom we may appoint over this business
Rom 16 2 assist her [Phebe] in whatever b. she
1 Th 4 6 nor circumvent his brother in business
11 that you do your own b. and work with
businesses 2 Tim 2 4 being a soldier to God, entangleth himself with secular b.
busy Luke 10 40 Martha was b. about much serving
busybodies 1 Tim 5 13 are tattlers also and b.
butchered 2 Pa 28 9 you have b. them cruelly
butler Gen 40 1 b. and the baker . . . offended their
Gen 40 2 the one was chief butler, the other
9 the chief butler first told his dream
20 at the banquet remembered the chief b.
23 chief butler . . . forgot his interpreter
41 9 the chief butler remembering, said
butter Gen 18 8 he took also butter and milk and
Deut 32 14 b. of the herd, and milk of the sheep
Judg 5 25 and offered him butter in a dish fit for
2 K 17 29 brought him . . . honey and butter and

Job 20 17 the brooks of honey and of butter. He
29 6 when I washed my feet with butter and
Prov 30 33 bring out milk, straineth out butter
Isa 7 15 he shall eat butter and honey, that he
22 he shall eat butter for butter and honey shall every one eat
buttocks 2 K 10 4 of their garments even to the b.
1 Pa 19 4 cut away their garments from the b.
Isa 20 4 with their buttocks uncovered to the
buy Gen 41 57 came into Egypt to buy food and to
Gen 42 2 go ye down and buy us necessaries, that
3 went down to buy corn in Egypt: whilst
5 with others that went to buy. For the
7 to buy necessaries of life. And though
10 thy servants are come to buy food. We
34 may have leave to buy what you will
43 2 go again and buy us a little food. Juda
4 and will buy necessaries for thee. But
20 we came down once before to buy food
22 money besides, to buy what we want: we
44 25 go again, and buy us a little wheat
47 19 buy us to be king's servants and
Exod 21 2 if thou buy a Hebrew servant, six years
Lev 25 14 to thy neighbor, or shalt buy of him
14 thou shalt buy of him according to the
Deut 2 6 you shall buy meats of them for money
14 26 thou shalt buy with the same money
28 68 bondwomen and no man shall buy you
Ruth 4 4 buy it and possess it; but if it
4 he answered: I will buy the field. And
5 when thou shalt buy the field at the
2 K 24 21 to buy the thrashingfloor of thee and
24 but I will buy it of thee at a price
4 K 5 26 buy oliveyards and vineyards and sheep
12 12 to buy timber and stones, to be hewed
2 Pa 34 11 to buy stones out of the quarries and
1 Es 7 17 buy diligently with this money calves
2 Es 10 31 that we would not buy them of them
Prov 17 16 riches, seeing he cannot buy wisdom
23 23 buy truth, and do not sell wisdom and
Eccu 51 33 buy her for yourselves without silver
Isa 55 1 no money, make haste, buy and eat; come
1 buy wine and milk without money and
Jer 32 7 buy my field, which is in Anathoth. 8
7 for it is thy right to buy it, being
25 buy a field for money and take witnesses
Bar 1 10 you money: buy with it holocausts and
6 24 men buy them at a high price, whereas
1 Ma 3 41 to buy the children of Israel for slaves
12 36 that they might neither buy nor sell
2 Ma 8 11 to buy up the Jewish slaves, promising
25 of them that came to buy them, and they
Mat 14 15 they may buy themselves victuals. But
25 9 and buy for yourselves. Now whilst they
10 whilst they went to buy, the bridegroom
Mark 6 36 they may buy themselves meat to eat
37 let us go and buy bread for 200 pence
Luke 9 13 perhaps we should go and buy food
22 36 let him sell his coat and buy a sword
John 4 8 were gone into the city to buy meats
6 5 whence shall we buy bread that these
13 29 buy those things which we have need of
1 C 7 30 that buy, as though they possessed not
Apoc 3 18 I counsel thee to buy of me gold
13 17 that no man might buy or sell, but he
18 11 no man shall buy their merchandise
buyer Lev 25 27 overplus he shall restore to the b.
Lev 25 28 the buyer shall have what he bought
30 the buyer shall possess it and his
52 shall repay to the b. of what remaineth
Prov 20 14 it is nought, saith every buyer: and
Eccu 37 12 treat not . . . with a buyer of selling
Isa 24 2 as with the buyer, so with the seller
Eze 7 12 let not the buyer rejoice: nor the
buyers Gen 47 15 when the buyers wanted money
buyeth Eccu 20 12 that b. much for a small price
Mat 13 44 selleth all . . . and buyeth that field
buying Eccu 27 2 in the midst of selling and b.
Eccu 42 5 of the corruption of buying and of
1 Ma 13 49 and from buying and selling; and they
Mark 15 46 Joseph buying fine linen and taking
Buz Gen 22 21 Hus the firstborn, and Buz his
1 Pa 5 14 Jeddo the son of Buz. And their brethren
Jer 25 23 Dedan and Thema and Buz and all that
Buzi Eze 1 3 Ezechiel the priest the son of Buzi
Buzite Job 32 2 Eliu son of Barachel the B. 6
byway 2 K 13 34 there came much people by a b.
Prov 12 28 the byway leadeth to death. A wise
byways Judg 5 6 went by them, walked through b.
byword Deut 28 37 be lost, as a proverb and a b.
3 K 9 7 Israel shall be a proverb and a byword
2 Pa 7 20 and will make it a byword and an example
Job 17 6 he hath made me as it were a byword
30 9 and am become their byword. They abhor
Ps 43 15 hast made us a b. among the Gentiles
68 12 I became a byword to them. They that
Eccu 42 11 thee become . . . a byword in the city
Jer 24 9 to be a reproach and a byword and a

C

Caath Gen 46 11 sons of Levi . . . Caath. Exod 6:16; Num 3:17; 26:57; 1 Pa 6:1, 16; 23:6
Exod 6 18 sons of Caath. Num 3:19; 4:2, 4, 15, 34; 9:32; 23:12; 2 Pa 20:19; 29:12; 34:12
Num 3 27 of the kindred of Caath . . . Amramites
4 18 destroy not the people of Caath from
37 the number of the people of Caath
16 1 Isaar the son of Caath. 1 Pa 6:38
26 58 Caath begot Amram: who had to wife
Josu 21 4 the lot came out for family of Caath
5 children of C. 10, 20, 26; 1 Pa 15:5
Caathites Num 3 27 families of the Caathites. 26:57; 1 Pa 6:54
Caath's Exod 6 18 the years of C. life were 133
cabe 4 K 6 25 part of a cabe of pigeon's dung
cabin 4 K 10 12 was come to the shepherd's cabin
4 K 10 14 killed them at the pit by the cabin
cabins Job 40 26 the c. of fishes with his head
Eze 27 6 cabins with things brought from the
Cabseel Josu 15 21 Cabseel and Eder and Jagur
2 K 23 20 valiant man of great deeds, of Cabseel
1 Pa 11 22 valiant man of C., who had done many
2 Es 11 25 and at C. and in the villages thereof
Cabul Josu 19 27 goeth out to the left side of C.
Cademoth Deut 2 26 messengers from wilderness of C.
1 Pa 6 79 Cademoth also and its suburbs and
Cades Gen 14 7 fountain of Misphat, the same is C.
Gen 16 14 the same is between Cades and Barad
20 1 Abraham . . . dwelt between Cades and Sur
Num 13 27 the desert of Pharan, which is in Cades
20 1 the people abode in Cades. And Mary
14 Moses sent messengers from Cades to
16 we are now in the city of Cades, which
22 they had removed the camp from Cades
27 14 water of contradiction in Cades. Deut 32:51; Eze 47:19; 48:28
33 36 into the desert of Sin, which is Cades
37 departing from Cades, they camped in
Josu 12 22 the king of Cades one, the king of
15 23 and Cades and Asor and Jethnam, Ziph
Judg 11 16 to the Red Sea, and came into Cades
17 he abode therefore in Cades and went
Ps 28 8 Lord shall shake the desert of Cades
Eccu 24 18 I was exalted like a palm tree in Cades
1 Ma 11 63 were come treacherously to Cades, which

73 pursued the enemies even to Cades to
Cadesbarne Num 32 8 when I sent them from C.
Num 34 4 reach toward the south as far as C.
Deut 1 2 Horeb by the way of mount Seir to C.
19 when we were come into C., I said
46 you abode in Cadesbarne a long time
2 14 time that we journeyed from C. till we
9 23 and when he sent you from Cadesbarne
Josu 10 41 slew . . . from Cadesbarne even to Gaza
14 6 concerning me and thee in Cadesbarne
7 sent me from C. to view the land
15 3 ascendeth into C. and reacheth into
Cadumim Judg 5 21 the torrent of Cadumim, the
Caesar Mat 22 17 is it lawful to give tribute to Caesar. Mark 12:14; Luke 20:22
Mat 22 21 render to C. Mark 12:17; Luke 20:25
Luke 2 1 went out a decree from Caesar Augustus
3 1 fifteenth year of reign of Tiberius C.
23 2 forbidding to give tribute to Caesar
John 19 12 himself king, speaketh against Caesar
15 answered: We have no king but Caesar
Acts 17 7 all do contrary to the decrees of C.
25 8 nor against Caesar have I offended
11 I appeal to Caesar. Then Festus having
12 hast thou appealed to Caesar? To Caesar shalt thou go
21 be kept till I might send him to Caesar
26 32 at liberty if he had not appealed to C.
27 24 thou must be brought before Caesar
28 19 I was constrained to appeal to Caesar
Caesarea Mat 16 13 into quarters of C. Philippi
Mark 8 27 into the towns of C. Philippi. And
Acts 8 40 till he [Philip] came to Caesarea
9 30 they brought him [Paul] down to C.
10 1 certain man in Caesarea named Cornelius
24 morrow after he [Peter] entered into C.
11 11 three men . . . sent to me from Caesarea
12 19 going down from Judea to Caesarea
18 22 [Paul] going down to Caesarea, he went
21 8 the next day departing, we came to C.
16 with us some of the disciples from C.
23 23 two hundred soldiers to go as far as C.
33 when they were come to Caesarea and had
25 1 Festus . . . went up to Jerusalem from C.
4 Festus answered: That Paul was kept in C.
6 [Festus] went down to Caesarea, and the
13 Agrippa and Bernice came down to C.
Caesar's Mat 22 21 they say to him: Caesar's. Mark 12:16; Luke 20:24
Mat 22 21 things that are C. Mark 12:17; Luke 20:25
John 19 12 thou art not Caesar's friend. For
Acts 25 10 I stand at Caesar's judgment seat
Phil 4 22 they that are of Caesar's household
cage Eccu 11 32 partridge is brought into the c.
Eze 19 9 they put him into a cage, they brought
Cain Gen 4 1 conceived and brought forth Cain
Gen 4 2 was a shepherd, and Cain a husbandman
3 Cain offered, of the fruits of the earth
5 to Cain and his offerings he had no respect: and Cain was exceedingly angry
8 Cain said to Abel his brother: Let us
8 Cain rose up against his brother Abel
9 Lord said to Cain: Where is thy brother
13 Cain said to the Lord: My iniquity is
15 whosoever shall kill Cain, shall be
16 Cain went out from the face of the Lord
17 Cain knew his wife and she conceived
24 sevenfold vengeance shall be taken for C.
25 another seed, for Abel whom Cain slew
Heb 11 4 a sacrifice exceeding that of Cain
1 J 3 12 as Cain who was of the wicked one
Jude 11 they have gone in the way of Cain
Cainan Gen 5 9 lived 90 years and begot Cainan
Gen 5 12 C. lived 70 years and begot Malaleel
13 Cainan lived after he begot Malaleel
14 the days of Cainan were 910 years
1 Pa 1 2 Adam, Seth, Cainan, Malaleel, Jared
Luke 3 36 who was of Sale, who was of Cainan
37 Malaleel, who was of Cainan, who was of
Caiphas Mat 26 3 high priest who was called Caiphas
Mat 26 57 they holding Jesus, led him to Caiphas
Luke 3 2 under the high priests Annas and C.
John 11 49 Caiphas said to them: You know nothing
18 13 for he was father-in-law to Caiphas
14 C. was he who had given the counsel
24 Annas sent him bound to Caiphas the
28 led Jesus from C. to the governor's
Acts 4 6 Annas the high priest and Caiphas and
Caius Rom 16 23 Caius, my host, and the whole
1 C 1 14 baptized none of you but Crispus and C.
cake Exod 29 2 a cake without leaven, tempered with
Exod 29 23 a cake tempered with oil. Lev 8:26
Num 6 19 one unleavened cake out of the basket
Judg 7 13 as if a hearth cake of barley bread
1 K 30 12 as also a piece of a cake of figs
2 K 6 19 to every one a cake of bread and a
3 K 17 13 of the same meal a little hearth cake
19 6 there was at his head a hearth cake
cakes Gen 18 6 make cakes upon the hearth. And he
Exod 12 39 and they made earth cakes unleavened
Lev 7 12 cakes tempered and mingled with oil
Num 11 8 and made cakes thereof of the taste of
1 K 25 18 and two hundred cakes of dry figs
2 K 16 1 a hundred cakes of figs, and a vessel
1 Pa 23 29 fine flour and of the unleavened cakes
Jer 7 18 to make cakes to the queen of heaven
44 19 did we make cakes to worship her, to
calamities Job 30 12 my c. forthwith arose: they
2 Ma 6 12 that they be not shocked at these c.
14 14 thinking the miseries and c. of the Jews
calamity Gen 44 34 lest I be a witness of the c.
Job 5 21 shalt not fear calamity when it cometh
30 3 disfigured with calamity and misery
Prov 1 27 when sudden calamity shall fall on you
Wisd 18 21 put an end to the calamity, showing
Eccu 5 10 not profit thee in the day of calamity
Isa 10 3 the calamity which cometh from afar
24 12 and calamity shall oppress the gates
47 11 and c. shall fall violently upon thee
Jer 48 16 c. thereof shall come on exceeding
Abdi 13 his evils in the day of his calamity
Soph 1 15 distress, a day of calamity and misery
calamus Exod 30 23 of c. in like manner 250
Eze 27 19 stacte and calamus were in thy market
Calano Isa 10 9 is not Calano as Charcamis: and
caldron 1 K 2 14 or into the c. or into the pot
Jer 1 13 I see a boiling caldron, and the face
Eze 11 3 city is the caldron, and we the flesh
7 they are the flesh, and this is the c.
11 this shall not be as a caldron to you
Zach 14 21 every caldron in Jerusalem and Juda
caldrons 3 K 7 40 Hiram made c. 45; 2 Pa 4:11, 16
2 Pa 35 13 they boiled in caldrons and kettles
Jer 52 18 they took the c. and the fleshhooks
Zach 14 20 the caldrons in the house of the Lord
2 Ma 7 3 and brazen caldrons to be made hot
Caleb Num 13 7 of Juda, Caleb the son of. 34:19
Num 13 31 Caleb, to still the murmuring of the
14 6 and Caleb . . . rent their garments and
24 my servant Caleb, who being full of
30 except C. the son of Jephone. Deut 1:36
38 and Caleb . . . lived of all them that
26 65 none remained of them but Caleb the
32 12 would not follow me, except Caleb the
Josu 14 6 Caleb . . . spoke to him: Thou knowest
14 from that time Hebron belonged to Caleb

15 13 to Caleb . . . he gave a portion in the
14 C. destroyed out of it the three sons
16 and Caleb said: He that shall smite
17 Othoniel . . . the younger brother of Caleb. Judg 1:13; 3:9
18 C. said to her: What aileth. Judg 1:14
19 C. gave her the upper and. Judg 1:15
21 12 villages thereof he had given to Caleb
Judg 1 12 and Caleb said: He that shall take
20 he gave Hebron to Caleb, as Moses had
1 K 25 3 he [Nabal] was of the house of Caleb
30 14 invasion . . . and upon the south of Caleb
1 Pa 2 18 Caleb the son of Hesron took a wife
19 Caleb took to wife Ephrata: who bore
24 Caleb went in to Ephrata. Hesron also
42 the sons of Caleb. 50; 4:15
46 Epha the concubine of Caleb bore Haran
48 Maacha the concubine of Caleb bore
49 the daughter of Caleb was Achsa. These
4 11 Caleb . . . begot Mahir, who was the
6 56 and the villages to Caleb son of
Eccu 46 9 did a work of mercy, he and Caleb
11 the Lord gave strength also to Caleb
1 Ma 2 56 Caleb, for bearing witness before the
calf Gen 18 7 took from thence a calf very tender
Gen 18 8 the calf which he had boiled, and set
Exod 29 1 take a calf from the herd, and two
3 offer them: and the calf and the two
10 shalt present also the calf before the
12 taking some of the blood of the calf
14 the flesh of the calf and the hide and
36 thou shalt offer a calf for sin every
32 4 made of them a molten calf. And they
8 made to themselves a molten calf and
19 he saw the calf and the dances; and
20 [Moses] laying hold of the calf which
24 I cast it into the fire, and this calf
35 for the guilt on occasion of the calf
Lev 1 5 he shall immolate the calf before the
4 3 shall offer for his sin a calf without
5 take also of the blood of the c. 16:14
8 he shall take off the fat of the calf
10 as it is taken off from the calf of
14 they shall offer for their sin a calf
15 the calf being immolated in the sight
20 with this calf, as he did also with
21 the calf itself he shall carry forth
21 shall burn it as he did the former calf
8 2 a calf for sin, two rams, a basket with
14 he offered also the calf for sin: and
17 the calf with the skin, and the flesh
9 2 take of the herd a calf for sin and a
3 a calf and a lamb, both of a year old
8 immolated the calf for his sin. And his
16 3 he shall offer a calf for sin, and a
6 and when he hath offered the calf and
11 he shall offer the calf, and praying
15 to do with the blood of the calf, that
27 the calf and the buck goat that were
23 18 one calf from the herd, and two rams
Num 15 24 they shall offer a calf out of the herd
23 2 a calf and a ram upon every altar. And
4 on every one a calf and a ram. 14
30 he laid on every altar a calf and a ram
28 12 with oil in sacrifice for every calf
14 half a hin for every calf, a third for
20 three tenths of flour . . . to every calf. 28; 29:3, 9, 14
29 2 to the Lord one calf. 8, 36
Deut 9 16 had made to yourselves a molten calf
21 the calf, I took and burned it with
Judg 15 8 laid the calf of the leg upon the thigh
1 K 1 25 they immolated a calf and offered
16 2 shalt take with thee a calf of the herd
28 24 woman had a fatted calf in the house
3 K 12 30 for the people went to adore the calf
2 Es 9 18 made also to themselves a molten calf
Ps 28 6 them to pieces, as a calf of Libanus
68 32 shall please God better than a young c.
105 19 they made also a calf in Horeb: and
20 their glory into the likeness of a calf
Prov 15 17 than to a fatted calf with hatred
Isa 11 6 the calf and the lion . . . shall abide
7 the calf and the bear shall feed
27 10 there the calf shall feed, and there
Jer 34 18 when they cut the calf in two and
19 that passed between the parts of the c.
Eze 43 19 to offer to me a calf of the herd for
21 thou shalt take the calf that is offered
22 as they expiated it with the calf. And
23 thou shalt offer a calf of the herd
25 they shall offer also a calf of the herd
45 18 thou shalt take a calf of the herd
22 shall offer . . . a calf for sin. And in
24 the sacrifice of an ephi for every calf
46 6 on the day of the new moon a calf of
7 ephi for a calf, an ephi also for a ram
11 sacrifice of an ephi to a calf, and an
Osee 8 5 thy calf, O Samaria, is cast off, my
6 the calf of Samaria shall be turned to
Luke 15 23 bring hither the fatted calf, and kill
27 thy father hath killed the fatted calf
30 hast killed for him the fatted calf
Acts 7 41 they made a calf in those days, and
Apoc 4 7 the second living creature like a calf
calf's Eze 1 7 like the sole of a calf's foot
Calita 1 Es 10 23 Celaia, the same is Calita
callings Gen 36 40 dukes of Esau in their . . . c.
Eccu 26 28 two sorts of callings have appeared
Callisthenes 2 Ma 8 33 they burnt Callisthenes
calm Tob 3 22 after a storm thou makest a calm
Jon 1 11 thee, that the sea may be calm to us
12 and the sea shall be calm to you: for
Mat 8 26 came a great calm. Mark 4:30; Luke 8:24
Calor 1 Pa 2 55 the Cinites, who came of Calor
Calphi 1 Ma 11 70 Judas son of Calphi, chief
Calubi 1 Pa 2 9 Jerameel and Ram and Calubi
calumniate Lev 19 13 shalt not c. thy neighbor
Job 10 3 that thou shouldst c. me and oppress
Ps 118 122 good: let not the proud calumniate me
Mat 5 44 for them that persecute and c. you
Luke 3 14 neither calumniate any man; and be
6 28 and pray for them that calumniate you
calumnies Ps 118 134 redeem me from the c. of men
calumny Gen 26 20 the name of the well . . . C.
Prov 28 16 shall oppress many by calumny: but he
Eccu 26 6 false calumny, all are more grievous
Isa 59 13 but spoke calumny and transgression
Eze 22 29 they oppressed the stranger by calumny
Calvary Mat 27 33 which is the place of Calvary. Mark 15:22
Luke 23 33 place which is called C. John 19:17
calved 1 K 6 7 and two kine that have calved
Job 21 10 their cow has c. and is not deprived
calves Exod 24 5 sacrificed pacific victims of c.
Num 23 1 seven altars, and prepare as many c. 29
28 11 to the Lord two c. of the herd. 19, 27
29 13 to the Lord thirteen calves of the herd
14 being in all thirteen calves: and two
17 second day you shall offer twelve calves
18 libations for every one, for the calves. 21, 24, 27, 30, 33, 37
20 third day you shall offer eleven calves
23 fourth day you shall offer ten calves
26 fifth day you shall offer nine calves
29 sixth day you shall offer seven calves

32 32 seventh day you shall offer seven c.
1 K 1 24 carried him with her, with three c.
6 7 shut up their calves at home. 10
10 taking two kine that had sucking calves
14 32 they took sheep and oxen and calves
2 K 6 12 seven choirs, calves for victims
17 29 sheep and fat calves, and they gave
3 K 1 9 Adonias having slain rams and calves
12 28 he [Jeroboam] made two golden calves
32 in Bethel, to sacrifice to the calves
4 K 10 29 nor did he forsake the golden calves
17 16 made to themselves two molten calves
2 Pa 11 15 and for the calves which he had made
13 8 golden c. which Jeroboam hath made
1 Es 6 9 let calves also and lambs and kids
17 the house of God, a hundred calves
7 17 with this money, calves, rams, lambs
8 35 twelve calves for all the people of
Tob 1 5 when all went to the golden calves
Ps 21 13 many calves have surrounded me: fat
49 9 I will not take calves out of thy house
50 21 shall they lay calves upon thy altar
Isa 1 11 and fat of fatlings and blood of c.
22 13 killing calves and slaying rams, eating
Jer 46 21 like fatted calves are turned back and
50 11 you are spread abroad as calves upon
Eze 45 23 a holocaust to the Lord, seven calves
Osee 13 2 sacrifice men, ye that adore calves
14 3 we will render the calves of our lips
Amos 6 4 the calves out of the midst of the herd
Mich 6 6 unto him, and calves of a year old
Mala 4 2 and shall leap like calves of the Lord
Heb 9 12 by the blood of goats or of calves
19 he took the blood of calves and goats
camel Gen 24 64 Rebecca . . . lighted off the camel
Lev 11 4 hoof but divideth it not, as the camel
Deut 14 7 not eat, such as the camel, the hare
1 K 15 3 suckling, ox and sheep, camel and ass
Isa 21 7 a rider upon a camel: and he beheld
Zach 14 15 mule and of the camel and of the ass
Mat 19 24 easier for a c. Mark 10:25; Luke 18:25
23 24 strain out a gnat and swallow a camel
camelopardalus Deut 14 5 the wild goat, the c.
camel's Gen 31 34 idols under the c. furniture
Mark 1 6 John was clothed with camel's hair
camels Gen 12 16 [Abraham] had . . . she asses and c.
Gen 24 10 he took ten camels of his master's herd
11 when he had made the camels lie down
14 and I will give thy camels drink also
19 I will draw water for thy camels also
20 having drawn she gave to all the camels
22 and after that the camels had drunk
30 came to the man who stood by the camels
31 the house and a place for the camels
32 he unharnassed the camels and gave
35 womenservants, camels and asses
44 and I will also draw for thy camels
46 and to thy camels I will give drink
46 I drank, and she watered the camels
61 being set upon camels, followed the
63 eyes, he saw camels coming afar off
30 43 and menservants, camels, and asses
31 17 his children and wives upon camels
32 7 and the camels into two companies
15 thirty milch camels with their colts
37 25 with their camels, carrying spices and
Exod 9 3 upon thy horses and asses and camels
Judg 6 5 multitude of men and of camels, wasting
7 12 their camels also were innumerable
8 21 with which the necks of camels of kings
1 K 27 9 oxen and the asses and the camels
30 17 who had gotten upon camels and fled
3 K 10 2 camels that carried spices. 2 Pa 9:1
4 K 8 9 the burdens of forty camels. And when
1 Pa 5 21 of camels 50,000, and of sheep 250,000
12 40 brought loaves on asses and on camels
27 30 over the camels, Ubil an Ishmahelite
2 Pa 14 15 infinite number of cattle and of camels
1 Es 2 67 their camels 435, their asses. 2 Es 7:69
Tob 9 6 and two camels and went to Rages
10 10 in cattle, in camels, and in kine
11 18 arrived safe, and the cattle and the c.
Jdth 2 8 with a multitude of innumerable camels
3 3 camels and all our goods and families
Job 1 3 was 7,000 sheep and 3,000 camels
17 have fallen upon the camels and taken
42 12 he had 14,000 sheep and 6,000 camels
Isa 30 6 treasures upon the bunches of camels
60 6 multitude of camels shall cover thee
Jer 49 29 and all their vessels and their camels
32 and their camels shall be for a spoil
Eze 25 5 I will make Rabbath a stable for camels
camels' Judg 8 26 that were about the c. necks
Mat 3 4 John had his garment of camels' hair
Camon Judg 10 5 in place which was called Camon
camp Gen 32 21 lodged that night in the camp. And
Exod 14 19 angel of God, who went before the camp
20 between Egyptians' c. and c. of Israel
16 13 quails coming up, covered the camp
13 morning a dew lay round about the camp
19 16 the people that was in the camp feared
17 to meet God from the place of the camp
32 17 the noise of battle is heard in the c.
19 when he [Moses] came nigh to the camp
26 standing in the gate of the camp he
27 through the midst of the camp, and let
33 11 when he [Moses] returned into the camp
Lev 14 3 out of the camp, when he shall find
8 purified, he shall enter into the camp
16 26 and so shall enter into the camp. 28
24 10 fell at words in the camp with a man of
Num 1 51 when you are to camp, they shall set
52 shall camp every man by his troops
2 2 shall camp by their troops, ensigns
9 all that were numbered in the camp of
10 in the camp of the sons of Ruben, on
16 were reckoned up in the camp of Ruben
18 shall be the c. of the sons of Ephraim
24 were numbered in the camp of Ephraim
31 that were numbered in the camp of Dan
3 29 shall camp on the south side. And their
35 they shall c. on the north side. Under
38 east side shall Moses and Aaron camp
4 5 when the camp is to set forward, Aaron
15 at the removing of the camp, then
5 2 they cast out of the camp every leper
3 cast ye them out of the camp, lest they
9 22 soon as it departed, they removed the c.
10 2 when the camp is to be removed. And when
22 sons of Ephraim also moved their camp
25 the last of all the camp marched the
33 providing a place for the camp. The
11 1 that were at uttermost part of the camp
9 dew fell in the night upon the camp
26 remained in the camp two of the men
27 when they prophesied in the camp, there
27 Eldad and Medad prophesy in the camp
30 Moses returned . . . into the camp. And a
31 cast them into the camp for the space
32 they dried them round about the camp
12 15 Mary therefore was put out of the camp
14 25 tomorrow remove the camp and return
44 and Moses departed not from the camp
19 7 he shall enter into the camp and shall
20 22 they had removed the camp from Cades
31 12 things for use they carried to the c.

24 you shall afterwards enter into the c.
Deut 2 14 fit for war was consumed out of the c.
15 should perish from the midst of the c.
10 6 removed their camp from Beroth of the
23 10 he shall go forth out of the camp; and
11 after sunset he shall return into the c.
14 God walketh in the midst of thy camp
14 and let thy camp be holy, and let no
29 11 that abideth with thee in the camp
Josu 1 10 pass through the midst of the camp and
3 1 before daylight, and removed the camp
2 heralds went through the midst of the c.
4 3 you shall set in the place of the camp
5 8 remained in the same place of the camp
6 11 returning into the camp, abode there
14 returned into the camp. So they did six
18 all the camp of Israel be under sin
9 6 then abode in the camp of Galgal. 10:6
17 children of Israel removed the camp
10 15 with all Israel into the camp of Galgal
21 in Maceda, where the camp then was
43 to the place of the camp in Galgal
18 9 returned to Josue, to the camp in Silo
Judg 7 1 the camp of Madian was in the valley
8 the camp of Madian was beneath him
9 arise and go down into the camp
11 down more secure to the enemies' camp
11 into part of the camp where was the
13 and came down into the camp of Madian
14 hath delivered Madian and all their c.
15 and returned to the camp of Israel
15 Lord hath delivered the camp of Madian
17 I will go into one part of the camp
18 the trumpets on every side of the camp
19 with him went into part of the camp
20 in three places round about the camp
21 place round about the enemies' camp
21 so all the camp was troubled, and
22 Lord sent the sword into all the camp
8 11 and smote the camp of the enemies, who
13 25 began to be with him in the c. of Dan
18 12 that time is called the camp of Dan
21 12 brought them to the camp in Silo
1 K 4 3 and the people returned to the camp
5 of the Lord was come into the camp
6 great shout in camp of the Hebrews
6 ark of the Lord was come into the camp
11 11 [Saul]came into the midst of the camp
13 17 went out of the camp of the Philistines
14 15 and there was a miracle in the camp
19 there arose a great uproar in the camp
21 and went up with them into the camp
17 4 went out a man baseborn from the camp
17 and run to the camp to thy brethren
23 coming up from camp of the Philistines
53 fell upon their camp. And David taking
26 6 go down with me to Saul into the camp
2 K 1 2 a man who came out of Saul's camp with
3 I am fled out of the camp of Israel
2 8 and led him about through the camp
12 went out from the camp to Gabaon. And
29 through all Beth-horon, came to the c.
17 24 David came to the camp, and Absalom
27 when David was come to the camp, Sobi
19 32 sustenance when he abode in the camp
23 13 camp of the Philistines was in valley
16 broke through camp of the Philistines
3 K 2 8 grievous curse, when I went to the c.
16 16 who was general over Israel in the c.
4 K 3 24 and they went into the camp of Israel
7 4 let us run over to camp of the Syrians
5 the evening to go to the Syrian camp
5 were come to the first part of the c.
6 in camp of Syria the noise of chariots
7 horses and asses in the camp, and fled
8 were come to the beginning of the camp
10 we went to the camp of the Syrians
12 therefore they are gone out of the camp
16 pillaged the camp of the Syrians: and
19 35 slew in camp of the Assyrians 185,000
1 Pa 9 19 keepers of the entrance of the camp
11 18 broke through the midst of the camp
2 Pa 22 1 Arabians who had broke in upon the c.
31 2 and to sing in the gates of the camp
Jdth 9 6 look upon the camp of the Assyrians now
6 to look upon the camp of the Egyptians
7 but thou lookedst over their camp, and
13 12 to prayer, and they passed the camp
15 7 went into the camp of the Assyrians
16 4 set his camp in the midst of his people
13 then the camp of the Assyrians howled
Ps 26 3 if armies in camp should stand together
77 28 they fell in the midst of their camp
105 16 and they provoked Moses in the camp
Wisd 19 7 a cloud overshadowed their camp, and
Isa 37 36 slew in camp of the Assyrians 185,000
Eze 4 2 cast up a mount and set a camp against
Amos 4 10 I made the stench of your camp to come
1 Ma 3 3 and protected the camp with his sword
41 came into the camp to buy the children
57 they removed the camp, and pitched on
4 1 they removed out of the camp by night
2 might come upon the camp of the Jews
4 the army was dispersed from the camp
5 Gorgias came by night into the camp of
7 and they saw the camp of the Gentiles
13 they went out of the camp to battle
20 and that they had set fire to the camp
23 returned to take the spoils of the camp
30 didst deliver up camp of the strangers
5 41 camp on the other side of the river, we
49 proclamation to be made in the camp
66 he removed his camp to go into the
6 32 removed the camp to Bethzacharam, over
against the king's camp
7 19 Bacchides removed the c. from Jerusalem
9 6 many withdrew themselves out of the camp
11 the army removed out of the camp, and
10 48 and moved his camp near to Demetrius
79 left privately in the c. 1,000 horsemen
11 18 destroyed by them that were within the c.
73 enemies even to Cades to their own camp
12 26 he sent spies into their camp and they
27 he set sentinels round about the camp
28 and they kindled fires in their camp
15 25 king Antiochus moved his camp to Dora
16 6 he and his people pitched their camp
2 Ma 13 15 slew four thousand men in the camp
16 having filled the camp of the enemies
Apoc 20 8 they encompassed the camp of the saints

without the camp Exod 29 14 the dung thou shalt
burn abroad without the camp
Exod 33 7 pitched it without the camp afar off
7 the tabernacle of the covenant w. . . .
Lev 4 12 he shall carry forth without the c. 21
6 11 shall carry them forth without the camp
8 17 and the dung, he burnt without the camp
9 11 skins thereof he burnt with fire w. . . .
10 4 sanctuary and carry them w. . . . And they
13 46 unclean, he shall dwell alone w. . . .
16 27 shall carry forth w. . . . and shall burn
17 3 sheep or a goat in the camp or w. . . .
24 14 forth the blasphemer w. . . . and let all
23 forth him that had blasphemed w. . . .
Num 5 4 they cast them forth without the camp
15 35 let all the multitude stone him w. . . .

19 3 priest who shall bring her forth w. . . .
9 shall pour them forth w. . . . in a most
31 13 went forth to meet them w. . . . And Moses
19 and stay without the camp seven days
Deut 23 12 shalt have a place w. . . . to which thou
Josu 6 23 kindred and made them to stay w. . . .
Heb 13 11 for sin, are burned without the camp
13 let us go forth to him without the camp
camped Exod 18 5 he was camped by the mountain
Exod 19 2 Sinai, they camped in the same place
Num 2 12 camped they of the tribe of Simeon
25 on north side camped the sons of Dan
34 camped by their troops, and marched
9 17 cloud stood still, there they camped
21 10 camped in *N.* 33:5, 8, 13, 17, 19, 21, 25, 27, 29, 31, 33, 35, 41, 43, 46; Deut 10:7; Josu 4:19; Judg 10:17; 1 K 13:5; 28:4; 1 Ma 9:2
33 9 there they camped. But departing from
11 they camped in the desert of Sin. And
15 they camped in the desert of Sinai
23 they . . . camped in the mountain Sepher
37 from Cades, they camped in mount Hor
49 they camped from Bethsimoth even to
Josu 4 8 unto the place wherein they camped
10 5 c. about Gabaon, laying siege to it
Judg 6 33 camped in the valley of Jezrael. But
11 18 camped on the other side of the Arnon
15 9 camped in the place which afterwards
20 19 rising in the morning camped by Gabaa
1 K 4 1 camped by the Stone of help. And the
17 1 camped between Socho and Azeca in the
29 1 Israel also camped by the fountain
2 K 17 26 Israel camped with Absalom in the land
3 K 20 27 camped over against them like two little
1 Pa 19 7 they came and camped over against Medaba
1 Ma 5 37 and camped over against Raphon beyond
64 he came and camped above Bethbessen
10 86 thence and camped against Ascalon
13 43 Gaza, and camped round about it, and
15 13 and Antiochus camped above Dora with
camps Gen 32 2 said: These are the camps of God
Gen 32 2 name of that place Mahanaim, that is, C.
Num 10 28 the order of the camps and marches
Cant 7 1 see . . . but the companies of camps
1 Ma 6 6 which they had gotten out of the camps
Camuel Gen 22 21 Camuel the father of the Syrians
Num 34 24 of the tribe of Ephraim, Camuel the
1 Pa 27 17 Levites, Hasabias the son of Camuel
Cana Josu 19 28 Cana, as far as the great Sidon
John 2 1 was a marriage in Cana of Galilee
11 beginning of miracles did Jesus in C.
4 46 he came again into Cana of Galilee
21 2 Nathanael who was of Cana of Galilee
Canaan Mat 15 22 behold a woman of C. who came
Cananean Mat 10 4 Simon the Cananean. Mark 3:18
Canath Num 32 42 Nobe also went and took Canath
1 Pa 2 23 and Canath and the villages thereof
Candace Acts 8 27 C. the queen of the Ethiopians
candle Mat 5 15 do men light a candle and put it
Mark 4 21 doth a candle come in to be put under a
Luke 8 16 no man lighting a candle covereth it
11 33 no man lighteth a candle and putteth
15 8 doth not light a candle and sweep the
candles Bar 6 18 they light candles to them, and
candlestick Exod 25 31 thou shalt make also a c.
Exod 25 34 in the c. itself shall be four cups
37 shalt set them upon the candlestick
39 whole weight of the c. with all the
26 35 over against the table the candlestick
30 27 the c. and furniture thereof, the altars
31 8 pure c. with the vessels thereof, and
35 14 the candlestick to bear up the lights
37 17 c. of beaten work of the finest gold
19 out from the shaft of the candlestick
24 the c. with all the vessels thereof
39 36 the c., the lamps, and the furniture of
40 4 the candlestick shall stand with its
22 he set the c. also in the tabernacle
Lev 24 4 set upon the most pure candlestick
Num 3 31 keep the ark and the table and the c.
4 9 wherewith they shall cover the c. with
8 2 let the c. be set up on the south side
2 towards which the candlestick looketh
3 he put the lamps upon the candlestick
4 this was the work of the candlestick
4 so he made the candlestick. And the
4 K 4 10 a table and a stool and a candlestick
1 Pa 28 15 to the dimensions of every candlestick
2 Pa 13 11 there is with us the golden candlestick
Eccu 26 22 as the lamp shining upon the holy c.
Dan 5 5 writing over against the candlestick
Zach 4 2 behold a c. all of gold, and its lamp
11 trees upon the right side of the c.
1 Ma 1 23 c. of light and all the vessels thereof
4 49 new holy vessels, and brought in the c.
50 up the lamps that were upon the c.
Mat 5 15 upon a c. Mark 4:21; Luke 8:16; 11:33
Apoc 2 5 I will move thy c. out of its place
candlesticks 3 K 7 49 golden c., five on the right
1 Pa 28 15 also gold for the golden candlesticks
15 silver by weight for the silver c.
2 Pa 4 7 and he made ten golden candlesticks
20 candlesticks also of most pure gold
Jer 52 19 c. and the mortars and the cups: as many
Heb 9 2 wherein were the candlesticks and the
Apoc 1 12 seven golden candlesticks. 13, 20; 2:1
20 the seven c. are the seven churches
11 4 the two c. that stand before the Lord
cane Cant 4 14 saffron, sweet cane and cinnamon
Isa 43 24 thou hast brought me no sweet cane with
Jer 6 20 sweet smelling cane from a far country
canker 2 Tim 2 17 their speech spreadeth like a c.
cankered James 5 3 your gold and silver is cankered
canopy Jdth 10 19 Holofernes sitting under a c.
Jdth 13 10 took off his canopy from the pillars
19 and behold his canopy wherein he lay
16 23 the canopy that she had taken away
canticle Exod 15 1 sung this c. to the Lord: and
Deut 31 19 write you this canticle and teach the
21 this canticle shall answer them for a
30 words of this canticle and finished it
32 44 spoke all the words of this canticle
Judg 5 12 arise, arise, and utter a canticle
2 K 22 1 the words of this canticle. Ps 17:1
Jdth 16 1 Judith sung this canticle to the Lord
Ps 29 1 a psalm of a canticle. 47:1; 66:1; 67:1; 74:1; 86:1; 91:1
32 3 sing to him a new canticle, sing well
38 1 a canticle of David. I said: I will
39 4 he put a new canticle into my mouth
41 9 and a canticle to him in the night
44 1 a canticle for the Beloved. My heart
64 1 the canticle of Jeremias and Ezechiel
65 1 canticle of a psalm of the resurrection
68 31 I will praise the name of God with a c.
75 1 a canticle to the Assyrians. In Judea
82 1 a canticle of a psalm for Asaph. O God
87 1 for the sons of Core, a psalm of a c.
90 1 a canticle for David. 94:1; 95:1
91 4 the psaltery: with a c. upon the harp
92 1 praise in the way of a canticle, for
95 1 sing ye to the Lord a new c. 97:1; 149:1
107 1 a canticle of a psalm for David himself
119 1 a gradual canticle (So the beginning of the next 14 psalms)

26 11 Henanias who was one of king's captains
32 6 he appointed captains. 33:14
21 captains of the army of the king of the Assyrians. 33:11
2 Es 2 9 the king had sent with me captains
Jdth 2 7 then Holofernes called the captains
14 4 when the captains of them shall run
11 when his c. and tribunes were come
Job 39 25 the encouraging of the captains and
Jer 40 7 captains of army that were scattered
13 c. of the army that had been scattered
41 11 the c. of the fighting men. 13; 42:8
16 all the captains of the soldiers that
42 1 captains of the warriors and Johanan
43 4 c. of the soldiers and all the people
5 c. of the soldiers took all the remnant
51 23 I will break in pieces c. and rulers
28 kings of Media, their captains, and
57 drunk, and her wise men and her c.
Eze 23 15 the resemblance of all the captains
23 young men, all the c. and rulers
Dan 3 2 the judges, the captains, the rulers. 3
1 Ma 3 55 Judas appointed captains over the people
5 18 and Azarias c. of the people with
40 Timotheus said to the c. of his army
6 28 all his friends and the c. of his army
57 to the king and to the c. of the army
2 Ma 8 22 he appointed his brethren captains
12 19 who were captains with Machabeus

Capthorim Gen 10 14 the Philistines and the C.

captivating Rom 7 23 c. me in the law of sin

captive Gen 34 29 children and wives they took c.
Exod 12 29 unto the firstborn of the c. woman
Num 24 22 for Assur shall take thee captive. And
4 K 5 2 away captive out of the land of Israel
17 27 whom you brought from thence captive
28 been carried away captive from Samaria
1 Pa 5 6 king of the Assyrians carried away c.
2 Pa 6 36 and they lead them away captive to a
37 in land to which they were led captive
30 9 that have led them away captive, and
Tob 1 2 when he [Tobias] was made captive in
Jdth 5 22 many of them were led away captive
16 11 her beauty made his soul her captive
Ps 67 19 thou hast led captivity captive; thou
Isa 5 13 therefore is my people led away captive
49 21 brought not forth, led away and c.
52 2 thy neck, O captive daughter of Sion
Jer 1 3 unto the carrying away of Jerusalem c.
13 17 flock of the Lord is carried away c.
19 all Juda is carried away captive with
29 14 caused you to be carried away captive
39 9 carried away captive to Babylon the
40 7 not been carried away captive to Babylon
41 10 Ismahel carried away captive all the
48 27 thou shalt be led away captive. Leave
52 27 Juda was carried away captive out of
28 whom Nabuchodonosor carried away c.
Dan 11 8 he shall also carry away captive into
Amos 6 7 wherefore now they shall go captive
7 11 Israel shall be carried away captive
Abdi 11 strangers carried away his army captive
Nah 2 7 and the soldier is led away captive
1 Ma 1 34 they took the women captive, and the
2 9 vessels of her glory are carried away c.
10 33 that hath been carried captive from
2 Ma 8 10 making so much money of the captive Jews
Eph 4 8 ascending on high, he led captivity c.
2 Tim 2 26 by whom they are held c. at his will
3 6 lead c. silly women laden with sins

captives Gen 31 26 my daughters are c. taken
Num 14 3 our wives and children be led away c.
31 9 took their women and their children c.
Deut 1 39 that they should be led away captives
21 10 thou lead them away captives, and seest
11 in number of captives a beautiful woman
32 42 of blood of the slain and of captives
Judg 5 12 and take hold of thy captives, O son
1 K 30 2 and had taken the women captives that
3 and their daughters were taken captives
5 wives also of David were taken captives
3 K 8 46 so that they be led away captives into
46 to which they had been led captives
50 before them that have made them c.
4 K 15 29 and carried them captives into Assyria
24 16 led them captives into Babylon. And he
2 Pa 28 11 release the captives that you have
13 you shall not bring in the captives
15 rose up and took the captives, and
29 9 led away captives for this wickedness
Tob 1 3 to his brethren his fellow captives
13 12 may call back all the captives to thee
Jdth 7 16 that being captives we should live
16 6 and my virgins captives. But the
Esth 11 4 he was of the number of the captives
Ps 70 1 the sons of Jonadab and the former c.
105 46 all those that had made them captives
Isa 14 2 they shall make them captives that had
45 13 let go my captives, not for ransom
61 1 to preach a release to the captives
Jer 24 5 so will I regard the captives of Juda
28 4 c. of Juda that are gone to Babylon
6 all the c. may return out of Babylon
29 4 to all that are carried away captives
7 have caused you to be carried away c.
43 3 us to be carried away c. to Babylon
12 he shall carry them away captives
48 46 and thy daughters are taken captives
49 6 c. of the children of Ammon to return
39 I will cause the c. of Elam to return
50 33 that have taken them c., hold them fast
52 15 carried away c. some of the poor people
Bar 6 1 to them that were to be led away c.
1 you shall be carried away captives
Eze 1 1 when I was in the midst of the captives
6 9 nations to which they are carried c.
39 23 were made captives for their iniquity
Haba 1 9 shall gather together c. as the sand
1 Ma 5 13 their wives and their children captives
8 10 away their wives and their children c.
14 7 gathered together a great number of c.
2 Ma 8 36 by the means of the c. of Jerusalem
Luke 4 19 to preach deliverance to the captives
21 24 shall be led away c. into all nations

captivity Num 21 29 and his daughters into c.
Deut 28 41 because they shall be led into captivity
30 3 will bring back again thy captivity
Judg 18 30 tribe of Dan until the day of their c.
3 K 8 47 in their heart in the place of captivity
47 make supplication to thee in their c.
4 K 24 14 to the number of 10,000 into captivity
15 judges of the land he carried into c.
25 27 seven and thirtieth year of the c.
1 Pa 5 22 dwelt in their stead till the captivity
2 Pa 6 37 pray to thee in the land of their c.
38 land of their c. to which they were led
1 Es 1 11 that came up from the c. of Babylon
2 1 that went out of the captivity which
3 8 all that were come from the captivity
4 1 that children of the c. were building
6 16 rest of the children of the c. kept
19 children of Israel of the c. kept phase
20 for all the children of the captivity
21 that were returned from captivity, and
8 35 that were come out of the c. 10:6
9 4 those that were come from the captivity

7 to the sword and to captivity and
10 7 to all the children of the captivity
8 of them that were returned from c.
16 the children of the captivity did so
2 Es 1 2 that remained and were left of the c.
3 have remained and are left of the c.
4 4 to be despised in a land of captivity
7 6 who came up from the captivity of
8 17 that were returned from the captivity
Tob 1 2 even in his captivity, forsook not the
11 when by the captivity he with his wife
15 went to all that were in captivity
3 4 are we delivered to spoil and to c.
7 4 tribe of Nephtali of the c. of Ninive
13 7 I will praise him in the land of my c.
Jdth 9 3 and their daughters into captivity
Ps 13 7 turned away the captivity of his people
52 7 shall bring back the c. of his people
64 1 and Ezechiel to the people of the c.
67 19 thou hast led captivity captive; thou
77 61 delivered their strength into captivity
84 2 turned away the captivity of Jacob
95 1 when the house was built after the c.
125 1 brought back the captivity of Sion
4 turn again our captivity, O Lord, as a
136 3 they that led us into captivity required
Isa 20 4 the c. of Ethiopia, young and old
23 13 the strong ones thereof into captivity
46 2 themselves shall go into captivity
49 25 even the captivity shall be taken away
Jer 13 19 carried away captive with an entire c.
15 2 such as are for c., to c. 43:11
20 6 dwell in thy house shall go into c.
22 22 thy lovers shall go into captivity
29 1 the ancients that were carried into c.
14 I will bring back your captivity, and
16 not gone forth with you into captivity
20 ye of the c., whom I have sent out
22 a curse by all the captivity of Juda
31 send to all them of the captivity
30 3 I will bring again the c. of my people
10 seed from the land of their captivity
16 thy enemies shall be carried into c.
18 will bring back to c. of the pavilions
31 18 I heard Ephraim when he went into c.
23 when I shall bring back their captivity
32 44 I will bring back their captivity. 33:26
33 7 I will bring back the captivity of Juda and
the captivity of Jerusalem
11 I will bring back the c. of the land
46 19 furnish thyself to go into captivity
27 thy seed out of the land of thy c.
48 7 and Chamos shall go into captivity
11 to vessel nor hath gone into captivity
47 I will bring back the captivity of Moab
49 3 Melchom shall be carried into captivity
52 31 year of the captivity of Joachin king
Lam 1 5 her children are led into captivity
18 my young men are gone into captivity
4 22 will no more carry thee away into c.
Bar 2 30 to their heart in the land of their c.
32 shall praise me in the land of their c.
3 7 praise thee in our captivity, for we
8 we are at this day in our captivity
4 10 I have seen the captivity of my people
14 and remember the captivity of my sons
24 have now seen your captivity from God
Eze 1 2 fifth year of the c. of king Joachin
3 11 get thee in to them of the captivity
15 I came to them of the captivity to the
11 24 brought me . . . to them of the captivity
25 I spoke to them of the captivity all
12 11 from their dwellings and go into c.
25 3 because they are led into captivity
29 14 I will bring back the captivity of Egypt
30 17 they themselves shall go into captivity
18 her daughters shall be led into c.
33 21 in the twelfth year of our captivity
39 25 now will I bring back the c. of Jacob
40 1 the five and twentieth year of our c.
Dan 2 25 children of the c. of Juda. 5:13; 6:13
11 33 they shall fall . . . by captivity and
Osee 6 11 shall bring back the c. of my people
Joel 3 1 when I shall bring back the c. of Juda
Amos 1 6 they have carried away a perfect c.
9 have shut up an entire c. in Edom and
15 Melchom shall go into captivity, both
4 10 even to the captivity of your horses
5 5 Galgal shall go into captivity, and
27 I will cause you to go into captivity
6 7 at the head of them that go into c.
7 17 Israel shall go into captivity out of
9 4 if they go into c. before their enemies
14 I will bring back the c. of my people
Abdi 1 20 c. of this host of the children of
20 c. of Jerusalem that is in Bosphorus
Mich 1 16 they are carried into c. from thee
Nah 3 10 she also was removed and carried into c.
Soph 2 7 will visit them and bring back their c.
3 20 when I shall have brought back your c.
Zach 6 10 take of them of the c. of Holdai and
14 2 half of the city shall go forth into c.
2 Ma 2 1 commanded them that went into captivity
to them that were carried away into c.
2 C 10 5 bringing into c. every understanding
Eph 4 8 ascending on high, he led c. captive
Apoc 13 10 that shall lead into c. shall go into c.
carbuncle Exod 28 18 in the second a c. 39:11
Eccu 32 7 is as a carbuncle set in gold. As a
Eze 28 13 thy covering . . . sapphire and the c.
Carcaa Josu 15 3 up to Addar, and compassing C.
carcass Exod 21 35 the carcass . . . they shall part
Exod 21 36 ox, and shall take the whole carcass
Lev 7 24 a carcass that hath died of itself
11 39 he that toucheth the carcass thereof
Deut 28 26 thy carcass meat for all the fowls
Josu 8 29 took down his carcass from the gibbet
Judg 14 8 he went aside to see the c. of the lion
3 K 13 28 and the lion standing by the carcass
Job 39 30 wheresoever the carcass shall be, she
Isa 14 11 to hell, thy carcass is fallen down
19 to bottom of the pit, as a rotten c.
Jer 9 22 the carcass of man shall fall as dung
carcasses Gen 15 11 fowls came down upon the c.
Lev 11 8 nor shall you touch their carcasses
11 and their carcasses you shall avoid
24 whatsoever shall touch the c. of them
27 touch their c. shall be defiled until
28 he that shall carry such carcasses
31 toucheth their c. shall be unclean
32 upon what thing . . . carcasses shall fall
36 toucheth their c. shall be defiled
38 afterwards it be touched by the c.
Num 14 29 in the wilderness shall your c. lie
32 your c. shall lie in the wilderness
33 until c. of their fathers be consumed
Deut 14 8 their carcasses you shall not touch
Judg 5 21 the torrent of Cison dragged their c.
1 K 17 46 I will give the carcasses of the army
Isa 5 25 their carcasses became as dung in the
34 3 out of their c. shall arise a stink
66 24 shall go out and see the carcasses
Jer 7 33 carcasses of this people shall be meat
16 4 their c. shall be meat for the. 19:7
18 defiled my land with c. of their idols
Eze 6 5 I will lay the dead c. of the children

43 7 and by the carcasses of their kings
9 the c. of their kings far from me
Dan 14 31 had given to them two c. every day
Nah 3 3 there is no end of carcasses, and they
Heb 3 17 whose carcasses were overthrown in the
care Num 8 26 that are committed to their care
Judg 21 17 we must use all care and provide with
1 K 17 22 under care of the keeper of the baggage
2 K 6 4 Ahio having care of the ark of God
18 3 should fall, they will not greatly care
3 K 4 27 furnished . . . with great care in their
2 Pa 24 6 not taken care to oblige the Levites
28 15 their labor and had taken care of them
Tob 9 2 not make a worthy return for thy care
14 15 he took care of them, and he closed
Esth 1 5 which was planted by the care and
2 11 having a care for Esther's welfare
Ps 54 23 cast thy care upon the Lord, and he
Ecce 2 26 to the sinner . . . superfluous care
4 4 there is vanity and fruitless care
10 4 care will make the greatest sin to
Wisd 5 16 the care of them with the most High
6 8 he hath equally care of all. But a
19 the care of discipline is love, and
12 13 who hast care of all, that thou shouldst
15 9 his care is, not that he shall labor
19 2 had sent them away with great care
Eccu 7 26 have a care of their body and show
32 2 have care of them, and so sit down
38 27 his care is to give the kine fodder
41 4 that is in care about all things and
42 9 the care for her taketh away his sleep
50 4 he took care of his nation and
Jer 49 23 through care they could not rest
Eze 4 16 shall eat bread by weight and with care
12 19 they shall eat their bread in care
1 Ma 14 43 he should have care of the holy places
16 14 taking care for the good ordering of
2 Ma 2 26 we have taken care for those indeed that
30 must have care of the whole building
30 he that taketh care to paint it, must
4 6 he saw that, except the king took care
27 as for the money . . . he took no care
Mat 13 22 care of this world . . . choketh. Mark 4:19
Luke 10 34 him to an inn and took care of him
40 no c. that my sister hath left me alone
John 10 13 he hath no care for the sheep. I am
1 C 7 21 called, being a bondman? Care not for
Col 2 1 what manner of care I have for you
1 Tim 5 8 if any man have not care of his own
Titus 2 5 having a care of the house, gentle
3 13 send forward Zenas . . . with care, that
1 P 5 2 feed the flock . . . taking care of it
7 casting all your care upon him, for he hath care of you
2 P 1 5 employing all care, minister in your
Jude 3 taking all care to write unto you
take care Deut 8 1 take great care to observe
Josu 3 4 take care you come not near the ark
23 11 this only take care of with all
Tob 10 13 to take care of the family, to govern
Eccu 41 15 take care of a good name: for this shall
2 Ma 9 21 to take care for the common good: not
14 9 take care . . . both of the country and of
Luke 10 35 take care of him; and whatsoever thou
Acts 27 3 permitted him . . . to take care of himself
1 C 9 9 doth God take care for oxen? Or doth
1 Tim 3 5 how shall he take care of the church
cared John 12 6 not because he cared for the poor
Acts 18 17 Gallio cared for none of those things
Caree 4 K 25 23 Johanan the son of C. Jer 40:13, 15, 16; 41:11, 13, 14, 16; 42:1, 8; 43:2, 4, 5
Jer 40 8 Johanan and Jonathan the sons of Caree

careful Gen 31 35 so his careful search was in vain
Josu 10 18 set careful men to keep them shut up
23 6 be careful to observe all things that
Tob 1 20 and was careful to bury the dead and
Ps 39 18 and poor: the Lord is careful for me
Eccu 32 5 the first word with careful knowledge
Luke 10 41 thou art careful . . . about many things
1 C 12 25 members might be mutually careful
2 C 8 17 being more careful of his own will
Gal 2 10 which same thing also I was c. to do
Eph 4 3 c. to keep the unity of the Spirit
Titus 3 8 many be c. to excel in good works
carefully Deut 4 9 and thy soul c. Forget not
Deut 4 15 keep therefore your souls carefully
13 14 inquire carefully and diligently the
24 8 fulfil thou it carefully. Remember what
Judg 3 23 Aod c. shutting the doors of the parlor
Ecce 9 1 that I might carefully understand them
Eccu 38 32 who is always c. set to his work and
Isa 22 16 hewed out a monument c. in a high place
Dan 6 11 those men carefully watching him, found
13 12 they watched carefully every day to
2 Ma 8 31 and when they had carefully gathered
Mark 14 44 lead him away carefully. And when
2 Tim 1 17 he [Onesiphorus] carefully sought me
2 15 c. study to present thyself approved
carefulness Ecce 2 21 laboreth in wisdom . . . and c.
Rom 12 8 he that ruleth, with carefulness; he
11 in carefulness not slothful. In spirit
2 C 7 11 how great c. it worketh in you; yea
12 to manifest our c. that we have for you
8 7 and word and knowledge and all c.
8 by the c. of others, approving the good
16 who hath given the same c. for you
1 Th 2 2 unto you the gospel of God in much c.
Heb 6 11 every one of you show forth the same c.
Carehim 1 Pa 12 6 Jesbaam of Carehim: and Joela
careless Gen 42 1 said to his sons: Why are ye c.
cares Ecce 5 2 dreams follow many cares: and in
Ecce 5 16 in many cares and in misery and
Wisd 7 4 swaddling clothes and with great cares
8 9 will be a comfort in my cares and grief
Mark 4 19 c. of the world . . . choke the word
Luke 8 14 choke with the cares and riches and
21 34 cares of this life, and that day come
caress Isa 66 12 upon the knees they shall c. you
caresseth Isa 66 13 as one whom the mother c.
carest 2 K 19 6 that thou c. not for thy nobles
Mat 22 16 carest thou for any man. Mark 12:14
Caria 1 Ma 15 23 Caria and Samus and Pamphylia
Cariath Josu 18 28 Gabaath and Cariath: 14 cities
Cariathaim Gen 14 5 smote . . . the Emim in Save of C.
Num 32 37 built Hesebon and Eleale and C. and
Josu 13 19 Cariathaim and Sabama and Sarathasar
1 Pa 6 76 its suburbs, and C. and its suburbs
Jer 48 1 Cariathaim is taken: the strong city is
23 upon C. and upon Bethgamul and upon
Eze 25 9 Beelmeon and Cariathaim, to the people
Cariath-Arbe Josu 14 15 Hebron before was called C.
Josu 15 13 Cariath-Arbe the father of Enac, which
54 Athmatha and Cariath-Arbe, this is
20 7 in mount Ephraim and Cariath-Arbe
Judg 1 10 name whereof was in former times C.
2 Es 11 25 some dwelt at Cariath-Arbe and in the
Cariathbaal Josu 15 60 C., the same is Cariathiarim
Josu 18 14 the outgoings thereof are into C.
Cariathiarim Josu 9 17 Caphira and Beroth and C.
Josu 15 9 towards Baala, which is Cariathiarim
60 Cariathbaal, the same is Cariathiarim
18 14 Cariathbaal, which is called also C.
15 the border goeth out from part of C.
Judg 18 12 they lodged in Cariathiarim of Juda
12 the camp of Dan, and is behind C. From

1 K 6 21 messengers to the inhabitants of C.
7 1 men of C. came and fetched up the ark
2 day the ark of the Lord abode in C.
1 Pa 2 50 Sobal the father of Cariathiarim. 52
53 of the kindred of C., the Jethrites
13 5 Emath, to bring the ark of God from C.
6 all the men of Israel to the hill of C.
2 Pa 1 4 had brought the ark of God from C.
1 Es 2 25 the children of Cariathiarim . . . 743
2 Es 7 29 the men of Cariathiarim . . . 743. The men
Jer 26 20 Urias the son of Semei of Cariathiarim
Cariath-senna Josu 15 49 Danna and Cariath-senna
Cariath-Sepher Josu 15 15 before was called C.
Josu 15 16 he that shall smite Cariath-Sepher
Judg 1 11 the ancient name of which was C.
12 he that shall take C. and lay it waste
Carioth Josu 15 25 New Asor and Carioth, Hesron
Jer 48 24 upon Carioth and upon Bosra: and
41 Carioth is taken, and the strongholds
Amos 2 2 it shall devour the houses of Carioth
Carith 3 K 17 3 hide thyself by torrent of Carith
3 K 17 5 he [Elias] dwelt by the torrent Carith
Carmel Josu 12 22 king of Jachanan of Carmel one
Josu 15 55 Maon and Carmel and Ziph and Jota
19 26 and it reacheth to Carmel by the sea
1 K 15 12 that Saul was come to Carmel, and had
25 2 and his possessions were in Carmel
2 he was shearing his sheep in Carmel
5 go up to Carmel, and go to Nabal and
7 the while they were with us in Carmel
40 came to Abigail to Carmel and spoke
27 3 Abigail the wife of Nabal of Carmel. 30:5; 2 K 2:2; 3:3
2 K 23 35 Hesrai of Carmel, Pharai of Arbi, Izaal
3 K 18 19 unto me all Israel, unto mount Carmel
20 together the prophets unto mount Carmel
42 Elias went up to the top of Carmel
4 K 2 25 from thence he went to mount Carmel
4 25 came to the man of God to mount Carmel
19 23 the forest of its Carmel. I have cut down
2 Pa 26 10 vines in the mountains and in Carmel
Cant 7 5 thy head is like Carmel: and the hairs
Isa 16 10 joy shall be taken away from Carmel
33 9 desert: and Basan and Carmel are shaken
35 2 the beauty of Carmel and Saron, they
37 24 its height, to the forest of its Carmel
Jer 2 7 I brought you into the land of Carmel
4 26 and behold Carmel was a wilderness
46 18 as Carmel by the sea, so shall he come
48 33 joy and gladness is taken away from C.
50 19 he shall feed on Carmel and Bason
Amos 1 2 the top of Carmel is withered. Thus
9 3 though they be hid in the top of Carmel
Mich 7 14 alone in the forest, in the midst of C.
Nah 1 4 Basan languisheth and Carmel: and the
Carmelite 1 Pa 11 37 Hesro a Carmelite, Naarai the
Carmelitess 1 Pa 3 1 Daniel of Abigail the C.
Carmelus Jdth 1 8 the nations that are in Carmelus
Carnaim 1 Ma 5 26 and in C.: all these strong and
1 Ma 5 43 fled to the temple that was in Carnaim
44 C. was subdued and could not stand
carnal Rom 7 14 but I am carnal, sold under sin
Rom 15 27 in carnal things to minister to them
1 C 3 1 as unto spiritual, but as unto carnal
2 you now able; for you are yet carnal
3 are you not c. and walk according to
9 11 matter if we reap your carnal things
2 C 1 12 not in c. wisdom but in the grace of
10 4 the weapons of our warfare are not c.
Heb 7 16 according to law of a c. commandment
1 P 2 11 refrain yourselves from carnal desires
Jude 23 hating the spotted garment which is c.
carnally Lev 19 20 if a man c. lie with a woman
Num 31 17 women that have carnally known men
Carnion 2 Ma 12 21 into a fortress called Carnion
2 Ma 12 26 then Judas went away to Carnion, where
carpenter 1 Pa 9 15 Bacbacar the carpenter and
Wisd 13 11 a carpenter, hath cut down a tree
Isa 44 13 carpenter hath stretched out his rule
Mark 6 3 is not this the carpenter, the son of
carpenter's Mat 13 55 is not this the c. son
carpenters 2 K 5 11 c., and masons for walls
4 K 12 11 and they laid it out to the carpenters
22 6 that is, to carpenters and masons and
1 Pa 14 1 masons and c. to build him a house
22 15 hewers of stones and masons and c.
carpenters' Exod 35 33 and to work . . . in c. work
Exod 35 35 to do carpenters' work and tapestry
Carpus 2 Tim 4 13 that I left at Troas with Carpus
carriage Gen 45 19 for the c. of their children
carriages Isa 10 28 he shall lay up his carriages
carriers Josu 9 23 hewers of wood and c. of water
cart 1 K 6 7 take and make a new cart: and two kine . . . tie to the cart
1 K 6 8 ark of the Lord, and lay it on the cart
10 they yoked them to the cart, and shut
11 they laid the ark of God upon the cart
14 the cart came into the field of Josue
14 they cut in pieces the wood of the cart
2 K 6 3 laid the ark of God upon a new cart
3 sons of Abinadab drove the new cart
1 Pa 13 7 carried the ark of God upon a new cart
7 Oza and his brother drove the cart
Eccu 33 5 heart of a fool is as wheel of a cart
Isa 5 18 vanity, and sin as the rope of a cart
28 27 neither shall the cart wheel turn about
28 neither shall the cart wheel hurt it
Cartha Josu 21 34 Jecnam and Cartha and Damna
Carthaginians Eze 27 12 the C. thy merchants
Carthan Josu 21 32 Hammoth Dor and Carthan with
carved 3 K 6 29 he carved with divers figures
3 K 6 32 he c. upon them figures of cherubims
35 he carved cherubims and palm trees
35 carved work standing very much out
1 Ma 13 29 by the arms ships carved, which might
carveth Wisd 13 13 c. it diligently when he hath
carvings 3 K 6 18 and carvings projecting out
3 K 6 29 carved with divers figures and carvings
32 and carvings very much projecting
Casaia 1 Pa 15 17 Ethan the son of Casaia. And
Casaloth Josu 19 18 Jezrael and C. and Sunem
Casbon 1 Ma 5 36 he marched and took C. and Mageth
case Gen 45 5 let it not seem to you a hard case
Exod 5 19 saw that they were in evil case because
1 K 22 8 not one of you that pitieth my case
23 21 the Lord, for you have pitied my case
Esth 9 1 the case being altered, the Jews began
Mat 19 10 case of a man with his wife be so
Cased Gen 22 22 Cased and Azau and Pheldas
cases Exod 18 26 they judged the easier c. only
Eccu 22 27 in all these cases a friend will flee
1 C 7 15 is not under servitude in such cases
Casis; *see* **Vale-Casis**
Casleu 2 Es 1 1 the month of Casleu. 1 Ma 1:57; 4:52, 59; 2 Ma 1:9, 18; 10:5
Zach 7 1 of the ninth month, which is Casleu
Casluim 1 Pa 1 12 Phetrusim also and C. from
Casphin 2 Ma 12 13 the name of which is Casphin
Casphor 1 Ma 5 26 of them were shut up in Casphor
cassia Exod 30 24 of cassia 500 sicles by the
Ps 44 9 myrrh and stacte and cassia perfume
Cassia Job 42 14 and the name of the second Cassia
cast Gen 2 21 God cast a deep sleep upon Adam
Gen 21 15 cast the boy under one of the trees
39 7 his mistress cast her eyes on Joseph
Exod 22 31 not eat, but shall cast it to the dogs

Book	Ch	V	Text
	26	19	thou shalt cast forty sockets of silver
		29	shall cast rings of gold to be set upon
	36	13	also he cast fifty rings of gold that
		38	and their sockets he cast of brass
	37	13	he cast four rings of gold which he put
	38	26	whereof were cast the sockets of the
		30	of which were cast the sockets in the
Lev	1	16	he shall cast beside the altar at the
	14	40	cast without the city into an unclean
		45	shall c. the stones and timber thereof
	15	8	if such a man cast his spittle upon
Num	5	17	he shall cast a little earth of the
Deut	3	27	cast thy eyes round about to the west
Judg	8	25	they cast upon it the earlets of the
1 K	17	49	took a stone and cast it with the sling
2 K	11	21	did not a woman cast a piece of a
	17	13	all Israel shall cast ropes round about
3 K	7	15	he cast two pillars in brass, each
		17	the chapiters of the pillars were cast
		24	two rows cast of chamfered sculptures
		33	and strakes and naves were all cast
		34	were of the base itself cast and joined
	14	9	and hast cast me behind thy back
	19	19	he [Elias] cast his mantle upon him
4 K	2	16	cast him upon some mountain or into
	19	32	with shield nor cast a trench about it
	23	6	cast the dust upon the graves of the
2 Pa	4	4	the oxen were cast: and the sea itself
		17	near the Jordan did the king cast them
	26	14	and bows, and slings to cast stones
	28	2	moreover also he cast statues for Baalim
Job	27	22	he shall cast upon him, and shall not
	39	3	they cast them and send forth roarings
Ps	21	11	I was cast upon thee from the womb
	49	17	and hast cast my words behind thee
	54	4	for they have cast iniquities upon me
		23	cast thy care upon the Lord, and he
Prov	16	33	lots are cast into the lap, but they
Ecce	11	1	cast thy bread upon the running waters
Wisd	5	23	thick hail shall be cast upon them from
Eccu	6	22	and they will cast her from them before
	21	18	and he will cast it behind his back
Isa	34	17	he hath cast the lot for them, and his
	37	33	with shield, nor cast a trench about it
	38	17	hast cast all my sins behind my back
	40	19	hath the workman cast a graven statue
Jer	10	14	what he hath cast is false, and there
	15	8	I have cast a terror on a sudden upon
	41	9	pit into which Ismalhel cast all the
	51	17	what he hath cast is a lie, and there
Eze	19	12	up in wrath and cast on the ground
	28	17	I have cast thee to the ground: I have
Mich	2	5	that shall cast the cord of a lot in
Nah	3	6	I will cast abominations upon thee and
Zach	5	8	cast the weight of lead upon the mouth
	11	13	cast it to the statuary, a handsome
Mala	2	3	I will cast the shoulder to you, and
1 Ma	2	36	neither did they cast a stone at them
	6	51	engines and instruments to cast fire
		51	engines to cast stones and javelins
	10	40	cast darts at the people from morning
	11	4	the bodies that were cast abroad and
		71	cast earth upon his head and prayed
2 Ma	1	16	they cast stones and slew the leader
	10	30	cast darts and fireballs against the
	14	15	they cast earth upon their heads and
		46	he cast them upon the throng, calling
Mat	5	29	and cast it from thee. 30; 18:8, 9
	7	6	neither cast ye your pearls before
	15	26	to cast it to the dogs. Mark 7:27
Mark	14	51	a linen cloth cast about his naked body
Luke	12	49	I am come to cast fire on the earth
	19	43	thy enemies shall cast a trench about
	22	41	withdrawn from them a stone's cast
John	8	7	let him first cast a stone at her
		59	they took up stones to cast at him
	21	6	cast the net on the right side of the
		6	you shall find. They cast therefore
Acts	12	8	cast thy garment about thee and follow
	27	30	as though they would have cast anchors
1 C	7	35	profit, not to cast a snare upon you
Apoc	2	14	taught Balac to cast a stumblingblock
	4	10	cast their crowns before the throne
	8	5	and cast it on the earth, and there
		7	it was cast on the earth, and the third
	12	4	of heaven and cast them to the earth
		9	was cast unto the earth, and his angels
	18	19	they cast dust upon their heads and
cast away			Gen 35 2 cast away the strange gods
Lev	26	10	coming on, you shall cast away the old
Judg	10	16	they cast away out of their coasts all
2 K	1	21	was cast away the shield of the valiant
4 K	7	15	which the Syrians had c. away in their
	13	23	nor utterly cast them away, unto this
	17	20	till he cast them away from his face
2 Pa	7	20	I will cast away from before my face
Job	8	20	God will not cast away the simple nor
	36	5	God doth not cast away the mighty
Ps	2	3	let us cast away their yoke from us
	30	23	I am cast away from before thy eyes
	50	13	cast me not away from thy face; and
	61	5	they have thought to cast away my price
Ecce	3	6	time to keep and a time to cast away
Eccu	6	24	counsel, and cast not away my advice
	10	10	he liveth he hath cast away his bowels
Isa	2	20	a man shall cast away his idols. 31:7
	5	24	have cast away the law of the Lord
	8	6	hath cast away the waters of Siloe
	30	22	shalt cast them away as the uncleanness
	41	9	and have not cast thee away. Fear not
Jer	6	19	words, and they have cast away my law
	7	15	I will cast you away from before my
		15	as I have cast away all your brethren
		29	cut off thy hair and cast it away: and
	8	9	they have cast away the word of the
	10	18	I will c. away far off the inhabitants
	14	19	hast thou utterly cast away Juda, or
	23	33	I will cast you away, saith the Lord
	31	37	I also will cast away all the seed of
Eze	18	31	your ruin. Cast away from you all your
	20	7	let every man cast away the scandals
		8	they did not every man cast away the
		13	and they cast away my judgments, which
	26	16	cast away their broidered garments
	31	12	and cast him away upon the mountains
	32	4	I will cast thee away into the open
Osee	9	17	my God will cast them away because they
Joel	1	7	stripped it bare and cast it away
Amos	2	4	he hath cast away the law of the Lord
Jon	2	5	I am cast away out of the sight of thy
	3	6	cast away his robe from him and was
Luke	9	25	lose himself and cast away himself
Rom	11	1	hath God cast away his people? God
		2	God hath not cast away his people
Gal	2	21	I cast not away the grace of God. For
cast down			Exod 4 3 cast it down upon the ground
Exod	4	3	he cast it down, and it was turned into
	7	9	thy rod and cast it down before Pharao
		12	they every one cast down their rods
Josu	10	11	Lord cast down upon them great stones
Judg	6	31	on him that hath cast down his altar. 32
3 K	19	5	he cast himself down and slept in the
	21	27	[Achab] walked with his head cast down
2 Pa	25	12	cast them down headlong from the top
2 Es	6	16	and were cast down within themselves
Tob	2	10	and cast himself down by the wall and

Jdth 7 14 we are cast down before their eyes in
Job 10 8 dost thou thus cast me down headlong
32 13 God hath cast him down, not man. He
40 28 sight of all he shall be cast down
Ps 36 14 to c. down the poor and needy, to kill
41 12 why art thou cast down, O my soul? And
54 10 cast down, O Lord, and divide their
72 18 were lifted up thou hast cast them down
88 45 hast cast his throne down to the ground
105 27 and to cast down their seed among the
139 11 thou wilt cast them down into the fire
144 14 and setteth up all that are cast down
145 8 Lord lifteth up them that are cast down
Prov 7 26 she hath cast down many wounded, and
15 13 by grief of mind the spirit is cast down
21 22 hath cast down the strength of the
Eccu 1 39 cast thee down in the midst of the
47 14 sake he cast down all the power of the
49 15 for us our walls that were cast down
Isa 19 3 and I will cast down their counsel
25 8 he shall cast death down headlong
Jer 9 19 because our dwellings are cast down
48 12 and they shall cast him down and shall
15 and they have cast down her cities
49 20 ones of the flock shall cast them down
Lam 1 9 she is wonderfully cast down, not
2 1 how hath he cast down from heaven to
2 the Lord hath cast down headlong and
5 he hath cast down Israel headlong, he
Eze 6 4 I will cast down your slain before your
32 18 and cast her down, both her and the
Dan 8 7 when he had cast him down on the ground
11 cast down the place of his sanctuary
12 truth shall be cast down on the ground
10 15 I cast down my countenance to the
11 12 and he shall cast down many thousands
Amos 5 2 virgin of Israel is cast down upon
Zach 1 21 to cast down the horns of the nations
1 Ma 4 33 cast them down with the sword of them
6 10 my heart is cast down from anxiety
9 7 his heart was cast down: because he
2 Ma 9 8 now being cast down to the ground
Mat 4 6 Son of God, cast thyself down. Luke 4:9
15 30 they cast them down at his feet, and he
Luke 4 29 they might cast him down headlong
2 C 4 9 we are cast down, but we perish not
cast forth Lev 10 5 took them and c. them forth
Num 5 4 they cast them forth without the camp
12 12 as an abortive that is cast forth from
2 Es 13 8 I cast forth the vessels of the house
Ps 16 11 they have cast me forth and now they
Wisd 18 5 one child being cast forth and saved
Isa 34 3 their slain shall be cast forth and
51 20 thy children are cast forth, they have
Jer 16 13 I will cast you forth out of this land
22 19 c. forth without the gates of Jerusalem
23 8 lands, to which I had cast them forth
Bar 6 70 a dead body cast forth in the dark
Eze 7 19 their silver shall be cast forth, and
29 5 I will cast thee forth into the desert
Osee 9 15 I will cast them forth out of my house
Amos 4 3 and you shall be cast forth into Armon
Jon 1 5 they cast forth the wares that were in
2 4 thou hast cast me forth into the deep
2 Ma 5 10 was himself cast forth both unlamented
10 34 and cast forth abominable words. But
Mat 13 48 vessels, but the bad they cast forth
John 15 6 he shall be cast forth as a branch and
Apoc 12 10 the accuser of our brethren is c. forth
cast in 3 K 7 46 king cast them in a clay ground
3 K 13 24 him, and his body was cast in the way
25 the dead body cast in the way. 28
4 K 6 6 a piece of wood and cast it in thither

Prov 1 14 cast in thy lot with us, let us all
Eccu 7 7 neither cast thyself in upon the people
Eze 5 4 shalt cast them in the midst of the
Dan 3 22 those men that had cast in Sidrach
46 king's servants that had cast them in
Amos 8 3 silence shall be cast in every place
Mat 17 26 cast in a hook: and that fish which
Mark 12 41 and many that were rich cast in much
42 she cast in two mites, which make a
43 widow hath cast in more than. Luke 21:3
44 cast in of their abundance. Luke 21:4
44 she of her want cast in all she had
Luke 21 4 hath c. in all the living that she had
cast into Gen 37 20 cast him into some old pit
Gen 37 22 cast him into this pit that is in the
24 and cast him into an old pit, where
40 15 was cast into the dungeon. The chief
Exod 1 22 male sex, ye shall cast into the river
10 19 and cast them into the Red Sea: there
15 4 his army he hath cast into the sea
25 which when he had cast into the waters
Num 11 31 cast them into the camp for the space
19 16 cast it into the flame with which
Deut 28 38 shalt cast much seed into the ground
Josu 10 27 they cast them into the cave where
2 K 18 17 cast him [Absalom] into a great pit
4 K 2 21 the waters, and cast the salt into it
4 41 he cast it into the pot and said: Pour
9 25 cast him into the field of Naboth
26 take him and cast him into the field
13 21 cast the body into the sepulcher of
23 12 cast the ashes of them into the torrent
2 Pa 24 10 and cast so much into the chest of the
30 14 and cast them into the torrent Cedron
Isa 19 8 all that cast a hook into the river
Jer 22 28 cast into a land which they know not
26 23 he cast his dead body into the graves
38 6 cast him into the dungeon of Melchias
41 7 cast them into the midst of the pit
Dan 3 6 he shall the same hour be cast into
11 he should be cast into a furnace of
15 you shall be cast the same hour into
20 and to cast them into the furnace of
21 and were cast into the furnace of
91 did we not cast three men bound into
6 7 shall be cast into the den of lions. 12
16 cast him into den of the lions. 14:30
24 they were cast into the lions' den
14 41 he cast into the den, and they were
Jon 1 12 take me up and cast me into the sea
15 took Jonas and cast him into the sea
Mich 7 19 and he will cast all our sins into the
Zach 5 8 and he cast her into the midst of the
11 13 I cast them into the house of the
Mat 5 29 that thy whole body be cast into hell
6 30 tomorrow is cast into oven. Luke 12:28
18 8 feet, to be cast into everlasting fire
9 having two eyes, to be c. into hell fire
13 42 cast them into the furnace of fire. 50
22 13 cast him into exterior darkness. 25:30
Mark 4 26 as if a man should cast seed into the
9 44 to be cast into the hell of. 46
12 41 the people cast money into the treasury
43 than all they who have cast into the
Luke 12 5 hath killed hath power to cast into hell
13 19 which a man took and cast into his
21 1 cast their gifts into the treasury
Acts 22 23 garments, and cast dust into the air
Apoc 2 22 I will cast her into a bed: and they
11 13 the rest were cast into a fear and gave
14 19 cast it into the great press of the
19 20 these two were cast alive into the pool
20 3 he cast him into the bottomless pit

9 was cast into the pool of fire. 14, 15
cast into the fire Exod 32 24 I c. . . . and this
4 K 19 18 cast their gods into the fire. Isa 37:19
Jer 22 7 shall cast them headlong into the fire
36 23 and he cast it into the fire that was
Eze 15 4 it is cast into the fire for fuel: the
Mat 3 10 be cut down and c. . . . 7:19; Luke 3:9
Mark 9 21 hath he cast him into the fire and
John 15 6 cast him into the fire and he burneth
cast into prison Gen 39 20 c. Joseph into prison
Gen 41 10 to be cast into the prison of the
4 K 17 4 c. him into prison. Jer 37:4, 14; Eze 19:9
Eccu 13 15 hurt, and to cast thee into prison
Jer 37 17 that thou hast cast me into prison
Mat 5 25 officer, and thou be cast into prison
18 30 cast him into prison till he paid the
Luke 12 58 and the exacter cast thee into prison
23 19 and for a murder was cast into prison
25 and sedition, had been cast into prison
John 3 24 for John was not yet cast into prison
Acts 12 4 [Herod] cast him [Peter] into prison
16 23 they cast them into prison, charging the
37 Romans, and have cast us into prison
22 19 they know that I cast into prison and
Apoc 2 10 devil will cast some of you into prison
cast lots Josu 18 6 I may cast lots for you. 8
Josu 18 10 he cast lots before the Lord in Silo
Ps 21 19 and upon my vesture they cast lots
Joel 3 3 they have cast lots upon my people
Abdi 11 gates, and cast lots upon Jerusalem
Jon 1 7 let us cast lots, that we may know why
7 they cast lots, and the lot fell
Nah 3 10 and they cast lots upon her nobles
Mat 27 35 they cast lots. Luke 23:34; John 19:24
John 19 24 let us cast lots for it, whose it shall
cast off Lev 26 11 my soul shall not c. you off
Lev 26 44 I did not cast them off altogether
Num 11 20 because you have cast off the Lord
2 K 14 14 that is cast off should not altogether
3 K 8 57 not leave us nor cast us off: but may
4 K 17 20 Lord cast off all the seed of Israel
23 27 I will cast off this city Jerusalem
1 Pa 28 9 thou forsake him he will cast thee off
2 Pa 11 14 Jeroboam and his sons had c. them off
Ps 42 2 why hast thou cast me off? And why do
43 10 hast cast us off and put us to shame
23 arise, and cast us not off to the end
59 3 hast cast us off and hast destroyed
12 not thou, O God, who hast cast us off
70 9 cast me not off in the time of old age
73 1 why hast thou cast off unto the end
76 8 will God then cast off forever? Or
87 6 and they are cast off from thy hand
93 14 the Lord will not cast off his people
107 12 not thou, O God, who hast cast us off
Wisd 9 4 cast me not off from among thy children
Eccu 7 28 according to thy soul, cast her not off
27 25 and no man will cast him off: in the
Isa 2 6 thou hast cast off thy people, the
27 8 when it shall be cast off, thou shalt
54 6 and as a wife cast off from her youth
Jer 33 24 which the Lord had chosen, are cast off
26 I will also cast off the seed of Jacob
Lam 2 7 the Lord hath cast off his altar, he
3 31 for the Lord will not cast off forever
32 if he hath cast off, he will also have
33 nor cast off the children of men
Eze 5 6 they have cast off my judgments and
16 45 daughter, that cast off her husband
45 sisters, that cast off their husbands
20 16 because they cast off my judgments
24 and had cast off my statutes and had
23 35 hast cast off behind thy back, bear

Osee 8 3 Israel hath cast off the thing that
5 thy calf, O Samaria, is cast off, my
Amos 1 11 hath cast off all pity and hath carried
Zach 10 6 as they were when I had cast them off
Rom 13 12 let us cast off the works of darkness
cast out Gen 3 24 he cast out Adam; and placed
Gen 4 14 thou dost cast me out this day from
21 10 cast out this bondwoman and her son
Exod 6 1 shall he cast them out of his land. And
10 11 were cast out from Pharao's presence
23 29 I will not cast them out from thy face
33 2 that I may cast out the Chanaanite
Lev 18 24 I will cast out before you. 20:23
Num 5 2 they cast out of the camp every leper
3 cast ye them out of the camp lest they
Deut 9 17 I cast the tables out of my hands and
22 21 they shall cast her out of the doors
28 27 by which the dung is cast out, with
29 28 he hath cast them out of their land
33 27 he shall cast out the enemy from before
Josu 24 18 and he hath cast out all the nations
Judg 6 9 I cast them out at your coming in and
11 7 and cast me out of my father's house
1 K 26 19 who have cast me out this day, that I
2 K 20 22 son of Bochri and cast it out to Joab
3 K 2 27 Solomon cast out Abiathar from being
9 7 I will cast out of my sight: and Israel
4 K 10 25 edge of the sword and cast them out
23 4 to cast out of the temple of the Lord
24 20 till he cast them out from his face
1 Pa 17 21 cast out nations before their face
2 Pa 13 9 you have cast out the priests of the
20 11 endeavor to c. us out of the possession
26 21 for which he had been cast out of the
33 2 nations, which the Lord cast out before
15 and he cast them all out of the city
1 Es 2 62 were c. out of the priesthood. 2 Es 7:64
10 8 he should be cast out of the company
Jdth 5 11 when the Egyptians had cast them out
Ps 5 11 cast them out: for they have provoked
35 13 they are cast out and could not stand
43 3 afflict the people and cast them out
77 54 he cast out the Gentiles before them
79 9 thou hast cast out the Gentiles and
108 10 let them be cast out of their dwellings
Prov 22 10 cast out the scoffer, and contention
Eccu 28 19 hath c. out valiant women and deprived
48 16 till they were cast out of their land
Isa 14 19 thou art cast out of thy grave as an
66 5 and cast you out for my name's sake
Jer 8 1 they shall cast out the bones of the
3 to which I have cast them out, saith
14 16 shall be cast out in the streets of
15 1 cast them out from my sight, and let
16 15 lands to which I cast them out: and
22 28 why are they cast out, he and his seed
23 3 into which I have cast them out: and I
24 9 places to which I have cast them out
27 10 cast you out and to make you perish
32 37 lands to which I have cast them out
36 30 his dead body shall be cast out to
46 28 nations to which I have cast thee out
51 34 delicate meats, and he hath cast me out
52 3 till he cast them out from his presence
Bar 2 25 they are cast out to the heat of the
Eze 4 13 nations whither I will cast them out
11 9 and I will cast you out of the midst
16 5 thou wast cast out upon the face of the
24 6 cast it out piece by piece, there hath
28 16 I cast thee out from the mountain of
31 11 I have cast him out according to his
36 5 and have cast it out to lay it waste
Dan 4 22 they shall cast thee out from. 29

Amos 2 9 I cast out the Amorrhite before their
8 8 be cast out and run down as the river
Mich 2 9 you have cast out the women of my
4 6 that I had cast out, I will gather
Soph 2 4 they shall cast out Azotus at noonday
3 19 and will gather her that was cast out
1 Ma 11 41 that he would cast out them that were
66 he cast them out from thence and took
13 11 and he cast out them that were in it
47 yet he cast them out of the city and
48 having cast out of it all uncleanness
50 cast them out from thence and cleansed
2 Ma 5 10 but he that had cast out many unburied
Mat 5 13 good for nothing any more but to be cast out. Luke 14:35
7 4 let me cast the mote out of thy eye
5 cast out first the beam. Luke 6:42
5 shalt thou see to cast out the mote
8 12 children of the kingdom shall be c. out
16 he cast out the spirits with his word
31 if thou cast us out hence, send us
9 33 after the devil was cast out, the dumb
10 1 over unclean spirits, to cast them out
12 26 if Satan cast out Satan, he is divided
27 do your children c. them out. Luke 11:19
15 17 goeth into the belly and is cast out
17 18 why could not we cast him out. Mark 9:27
20 is not cast out but by prayer. Mark 9:28
21 12 cast out all them that sold. Mark 11:15; Luke 19:45
39 they cast him forth out of the vineyard. Mark 12:8; Luke 20:15
Mark 3 23 how can Satan cast out Satan? And if a
7 26 would cast forth the devil out of her
9 17 thy disciples to cast him out. Luke 9:40
Luke 6 22 they shall cast out your name as evil
11 14 when he had cast out the devil, the dumb
20 12 they wounded him also and cast him out
John 6 37 that cometh to me, I will not cast out
9 34 thou teach out? And they cast him out
35 Jesus heard that they had cast him out
12 31 shall prince of this world be cast out
42 that they might not be cast out of the
Acts 13 50 cast them out of their coasts. But they
27 19 they cast out with their own hands the
29 they cast four anchors out of the stern
Gal 4 50 cast out the bondwoman and her son
Apoc 11 2 cast out and measure it not; because
12 9 that great dragon was cast out, that
15 serpent cast out of his mouth after the
16 river which the dragon cast out of his

cast out devils Mat 7 22 and c. . . . in thy name
Mat 10 8 the dead, cleanse the lepers, c. . . .
12 27 if I by Beelzebub cast out devils, by
28 but if I by the Spirit of God c. . . .
Mark 1 34 cast out many devils, and he suffered
3 15 power to heal sicknesses and to c. . . .
6 13 they cast out many devils and anointed
16 9 out of whom he had cast seven devils
17 in my name they shall cast out devils
Luke 11 18 you say that through Beelzebub I c. . . .
19 if I c. . . . by Beelzebub, by whom do
20 but if I by the finger of God c. . . .
13 32 I c. . . . and do cures today and tomorrow

cast up 2 K 20 15 they cast up works around
Wisd 19 10 the river cast up a multitude of frogs
Isa 29 3 and will cast up a rampart against thee
57 20 the waves thereof cast up dirt and mire
Jer 6 6 cast up a trench about Jerusalem: this
Eze 4 2 build forts and cast up a mount and
17 17 when he shall cast up mounts and build
21 22 to cast up a mount, to build forts. And
26 8 and shall cast up a mount round about
27 30 shall cast up dust upon their heads
Dan 11 15 and shall cast up a mount. Haba 1:10

castaway 1 C 9 27 myself should become a castaway

casteth Job 15 33 olive tree that c. its flower
Ps 32 10 and casteth away the counsels of princes
87 15 Lord, why casteth thou off my prayer
Prov 11 17 cruel casteth off even his own kindred
18 8 fear casteth down the slothful: and the
19 15 slothfulness casteth into a deep sleep
26 8 he that c. a stone into the heap of
Eccu 19 24 one that casteth down his countenance
Isa 33 15 that c. away avarice by oppression
Mat 9 34 by the prince of devils he casteth out devils. Mark 3:22
12 24 c. not out devils but by Beelzebub
Luke 11 14 he casteth out devils by Beelzebub
1 J 4 18 but perfect charity casteth out fear
3 J 10 he forbiddeth and c. out of the church
Apoc 6 13 as the fig tree casteth its green figs

casting Exod 36 34 c. for them sockets of silver
Exod 37 3 casting four rings of gold at the four
38 5 casting four rings at the four ends
Lev 16 8 casting lots upon them both, one to be
Judg 7 6 c. it with the hand to their mouth
9 53 c. a piece of a millstone from above
2 K 8 2 casting them down to the earth: and he
16 13 c. stones at him and scattering earth
3 K 7 37 ten bases, of one casting and measure
18 42 c. himself down upon the earth put his
21 4 c. himself upon his bed, he turned away
4 K 3 25 goodly field, every man c. his stone
Ps 125 6 went and wept, casting their seeds
Wisd 5 23 upon them from the stone casting wrath
Jer 38 9 casting him into the dungeon to die
2 Ma 5 3 with drawn swords and casting of darts
Mat 4 18 his brother, casting a net into the sea
27 5 casting down the pieces of silver in
35 casting lots. Mark 15:24; Luke 23:34
Mark 1 16 his brother, casting nets into the sea
39 in all Galilee, and casting out devils
9 37 we saw one c. out devils in thy name
10 50 c. off his garments, leaped up and came
14 52 he c. off the linen cloth, fled from
Luke 9 49 we saw a certain man casting out devils
11 14 he was casting out a devil, and the same
19 35 casting their garment on the colt, they
20 15 casting him out of the vineyard, they
21 2 poor widow casting in two brass mites
Acts 7 57 c. him [Stephen] forth without the city
27 38 casting the wheat into the sea. And
James 1 21 casting away all uncleanness and
1 P 5 7 casting all your care upon him, for he

castle 2 K 5 7 David took the c. of Sion. 1 Pa 11:5
2 K 5 9 David dwelt in the castle. 1 Pa 11:7
1 Es 6 2 is a castle in the province of Media
2 Es 1 1 I was in the castle of Susa. Dan 8:2
1 Ma 3 45 children of strangers were in the c.
4 41 that were in the castle. 6:18; 10:6, 7; 11:41; 13:21, 49; 2 Ma 15:31
6 26 have approached this day to the castle
32 Judas departed from the castle and
9 52 Gazara and the c., and set garrisons
53 put them in the castle in Jerusalem
10 32 I yield up also the power of the castle
11 20 to take the castle that was in Jerusalem
21 that Jonathan was besieging the castle
22 that he should not besiege the castle
12 36 a mount between the castle and the city
13 15 cleansed the castle from uncleannesses
53 of the temple that was near the castle
14 7 and had the dominion . . . of the castle
36 city of David in Jerusalem in the c.
15 28 and the castle that is in Jerusalem

2 Ma 4 12 under the very c., a place of exercise
27 Sostratus the governor of the castle
5 5 Menelaus fled into the c. But Jason
15 35 Nicanor's head in the top of the castle
Acts 21 34 him to be carried into the castle. And
37 about to be brought into the castle, he
22 24 him to be brought into the castle, and
23 10 to bring him into the castle. And the
16 entered into the castle and told Paul
32 next day . . . they returned to the c.
castles Gen 25 16 these are their names by their c.
Num 31 10 their villages and castles they burned
1 Pa 27 25 and in the villages and in the castles
2 Pa 27 4 and castles and towers in the forests
Jdth 2 12 and he went up to all their castles
Castors Acts 28 11 whose sign was the Castors
catch Exod 22 6 upon thorns and c. stacks of corn
Exod 36 13 might catch the loops of the curtains
Judg 21 21 c. you every man his wife among them
Ps 9 9 that he may catch the poor man: to catch the poor whilst he draweth him
34 8 net which he hath hidden catch him
139 12 evil shall catch the unjust man unto
Prov 5 22 his own iniquities catch the wicked
Cant 2 15 catch us the little foxes that destroy
Jer 5 26 snares and traps to catch men. As a
Eze 13 18 of persons of every age to catch souls
20 cushions wherewith you c. flying souls
20 will let go the souls that you catch
19 3 and he learned to catch the prey and. 6
Osee 5 14 I will catch and go: I will take away
Mark 12 13 they should catch him in his words
Luke 5 10 from henceforth thou shalt catch men
11 54 seeking to c. something from his mouth
1 C 3 19 will c. the wise in their own craftiness
catcheth Job 5 13 c. the wise in their craftiness
Prov 6 26 the woman c. the precious soul of a man
Eze 22 25 a lion that roareth and c. the prey
Mat 13 19 cometh the wicked one and catcheth away
John 10 12 wolf catcheth and scattereth the sheep
catching Gen 39 12 c. the skirt of his garment
Judg 15 15 c. it up, he slew therewith 1,000 men
2 K 2 16 every one c. his fellow by the head
Prov 7 13 catching the young man, she kisseth him
caterpillars 2 Pa 6 28 mildew or locusts or c.
Cateth Josu 19 15 Cateth and Naalol and Semeron
cats Bar 6 21 upon their heads, and cats in like
cattle Gen 1 24 the living creature in its kind, c.
Gen 1 25 according to their kinds, and cattle
2 20 the cattle of the field: but for Adam
3 14 thou art cursed among all cattle and
7 14 all the cattle in their kind, and every
21 upon the earth, both of fowl and of c.
8 1 and all the cattle which were with him
19 and all living things and cattle and
20 taking of all cattle and fowls that were
9 10 as well in all birds as in c. and beasts
29 8 till all the cattle be gathered together
34 5 and employed in feeding the cattle
23 cattle and all that they possess shall
36 6 his substance and cattle and all that
37 14 well with thy brethren and the cattle
46 32 their occupation is to feed cattle: their
47 6 make them rulers over my cattle. After
16 answered them: Bring me your cattle
17 that year for the exchange of their c.
18 and our cattle also are gone: neither
Exod 9 19 gather together thy cattle and all that
20 servants and his c. flee into houses
21 his servants and his cattle in the fields
12 29 all the firstborn of cattle. And Pharao
13 12 that is first brought forth of thy c.
Lev 1 2 offer to the Lord a sacrifice of the c.
19 19 not make thy c. to gender with beasts
20 15 shall copulate with any beast or cattle
25 7 be meat to thy beasts and to thy cattle
26 22 to destroy you and your cattle and make
Num 3 41 their c. for all the firstborn of the c.
45 cattle of the Levites for their cattle
20 4 that both we and our cattle should die
8 multitude and their cattle should die
8 multitude and their cattle shall drink
11 so that the people and their c. drink
19 if we and our c. drink of thy waters
31 9 all their cattle and all their goods
32 1 had many flocks of cattle, and their
1 Jazer and Galaad fit for feeding cattle
4 we thy servants have very much cattle
16 sheepfolds and stalls for our cattle
36 fenced cities and folds for their cattle
35 3 suburbs may be for their cattle and
Deut 2 35 left nothing of them except the cattle
3 7 the cattle and the spoils of the cities
19 wives and children and c. Josu 1:14
19 I know you have much cattle, and they
7 14 either sex, neither of men nor of cattle
11 15 hay out of the fields to feed your cattle
12 17 the firstborn of thy herds and thy cattle
13 15 all things that are in it, even the c.
20 14 excepting women and children, cattle
28 4 fruit of thy cattle, the droves of thy
11 fruit of thy cattle, with the fruit of
51 will devour the fruit of thy cattle and
30 9 womb, and in the fruit of thy cattle
Josu 8 2 all the c. you shall take for a prey
27 divided among them the cattle and the
11 14 the spoil of these cities and the cattle
21 2 and their suburbs to feed our cattle
Judg 18 21 put before them the children and the c.
1 K 23 5 Philistines and brought away their c.
25 11 my water and the flesh of my cattle
3 K 1 9 all fat cattle by the stone of Zoheleth
19 he hath killed oxen and all fat cattle
1 Pa 5 9 they possessed a great number of cattle
2 Pa 14 15 and took an infinite number of cattle
17 11 Arabians brought him cattle, 7,700 rams
26 10 he had much cattle both in the plains
32 28 for all beasts and folds for cattle
35 7 and of other small cattle 30,000
8 keep the phase 2,600 small cattle and
9 to celebrate the phase 5,000 small c.
1 Es 1 4 with silver and gold and goods and c.
2 Es 10 36 firstborn of our sons and of our cattle
Tob 10 10 in cattle, in camels, and in kine, and
11 18 arrived safe, and the cattle and the
Jdth 11 11 have a design even to kill their cattle
15 8 there was no numbering of their cattle
Job 21 10 their c. have conceived and failed not
Ps 49 10 are mine: the cattle on the hills and
77 48 he gave up their cattle to the hail
50 and their cattle he shut up in death
103 14 bringing forth grass for cattle and
106 38 their c. he suffered not to decrease
148 10 beasts and all cattle: serpents and
Prov 27 23 to know the countenance of thy cattle
Wisd 19 10 brought forth flies instead of cattle
Eccu 7 24 hast thou cattle? Have an eye to them
Isa 7 25 and the lesser cattle to tread upon
46 1 idols are put upon beasts and cattle
Jer 13 20 that is given thee, thy beautiful c.
31 12 and the increase of cattle and herds
49 32 multitude of their cattle for a booty
Bar 3 32 filled it with c. and fourfooted beasts
Eze 34 17 I judge between c. and c., of rams and
20 will judge between the fat c. and the
21 struck all the weak c. with your horns

22 I will judge between c. and c. And I
44 31 by a beast, whether it be fowl or cattle
Dan 3 81 ye beasts and cattle, bless the Lord
4 9 under it dwelt cattle and beasts, and
22 thy dwelling shall be with cattle. 29
Joel 1 18 why did the herds of c. low? Because
Soph 2 6 place of shepherds and folds for cattle
1 Ma 1 34 children and the cattle they possessed
2 30 children and their wives and their c.
38 wives and their children and their c.
10 33 from tributes even of their cattle
12 23 our c. and our possessions are yours
Luke 17 7 a servant plowing or feeding cattle
John 4 12 himself and his children and his cattle
Cauda Acts 27 16 certain island that is called C.
caught Gen 8 9 put forth his hand and caught her
Lev 7 24 beast that was caught by another beast
17 15 itself or has been caught by a beast
Deut 22 7 keeping the young which thou hast caught
Judg 15 4 he [Samson] went and caught 300 foxes
1 K 17 35 I caught them by the throat and I
20 33 Saul caught up a spear to strike him
3 K 20 33 caught the word out of his mouth and
4 K 4 27 she caught hold on his feet: and Giezi
Jdth 9 13 let him be caught in the net of his own
10 17 Holofernes was caught by his eyes. And
Ps 9 2 they are caught in the counsels which
17 sinner hath been caught in the works
58 4 behold they have caught my soul: the
Prov 6 2 mouth and caught with thy own words
25 be not caught with her winks: for the
11 6 unjust shall be c. in their own snares
Ecce 23 8 a sinner is caught in his own vanity
Jer 50 24 thou art found and caught, because
Lam 3 52 chased me and caught me like a bird
Eze 13 18 when they caught the souls of my people
14 5 the house of Israel may be caught
44 31 dead of itself or caught by a beast
Dan 6 24 before the lions caught them and broke
Nah 2 12 the lion caught enough for his whelps
2 Ma 4 41 some caught up stones, some strong
John 21 3 that night they caught nothing. But
10 the fishes which you have now caught
Acts 19 29 having caught Gaius and Aristarchus
27 15 when the ship was caught and could
2 C 12 2 such a one c. up to the third heaven
4 he was c. up into paradise and heard
16 being crafty, I caught you by guile
caul Exod 29 13 take the caul of the liver. 22
Lev 3 4 offer . . . the caul of the liver. 10; 7:4
15 the two little kidneys with the caul
4 9 kidneys and the caul that is upon them
8 16 the caul of the liver . . . he burnt. 9:10
25 the caul of the liver . . . he separated
9 19 caul of the liver, they put upon the
cauldrons Exod 38 3 vessels of brass, c., tongs
cautious Prov 12 23 a c. man concealeth knowledge
cautiously Tob 2 4 he might bury him cautiously
cavalry 2 Pa 18 30 commanded the captains of his c.
2 Pa 18 31 when the captains of the c. saw. 32
21 9 princes and all his cavalry with him
9 and all the captains of his cavalry
cave Gen 19 30 he dwelt in a cave, he and his two
Gen 23 9 that he may give me the double cave
11 to thee and the cave that is therein
17 Ephron's wherein was the double cave
17 the cave and all the trees thereof in
19 buried Sara his wife in a double cave
20 and the cave that was in it, for a
25 9 buried him in the double cave. 50:13
49 29 me with my fathers in the double cave
Josu 10 16 had hidden themselves in a cave of the
17 were found hidden in a cave of the city
18 roll great stones to mouth of the cave
22 open mouth of the cave, and bring forth
23 to him the five kings out of the cave
27 they cast them into the cave where
Judg 15 11 went down to the cave of the rock Etam
1 K 22 1 thence and fled to the cave of Odollam
24 4 there was a cave, into which Saul went
4 lay hid in the lower part of the cave
8 Saul rising up out of the cave, went
9 going out of the cave cried after Saul
11 delivered thee into my hand in the cave
2 K 23 13 harvest time into the cave of Odollam
3 K 19 9 was come thither, he abode in a cave
13 stood in the entering in of the cave
1 Pa 11 15 to the cave of Odollam, when the
Ps 56 1 when he fled from Saul into the cave
141 1 a prayer when he was in the cave. I
2 Ma 2 5 came thither, he found a hollow cave
John 11 38 was a cave; and a stone was laid over
cavern Judg 15 8 dwelt in a c. of the rock Etam
caves Judg 6 2 made themselves dens and caves
1 K 13 6 they hid themselves in caves and in
3 K 18 4 by fifty and fifty in caves. 13
Job 30 6 in caves of earth or upon the gravel
Isa 2 19 rocks and into the caves of the earth
Eze 33 27 they that are in holds and caves shall
2 Ma 6 11 others that had met together in caves
Heb 11 38 and in dens and in caves of the earth
cease Gen 8 22 night and day, shall not cease
Gen 27 45 his indignation cease, and he forget
Exod 9 28 hail may cease: that I may let you go
29 the thunders shall cease, and the hail
23 12 work: the seventh day thou shalt cease
32 12 let thy anger cease, and be appeased
34 21 seventh day thou shalt cease to plow
Lev 13 58 if it cease, he shall wash with water
15 28 if the blood stop and cease to run
Num 8 25 they shall cease to serve: and they
11 25 prophesied, nor did they c. afterwards
17 5 I will make to cease from me the
10 that their complaints may cease from
20 6 satisfied, they may cease to murmur
Deut 32 26 I will make the memory of them to cease
Judg 19 23 and cease I pray you from this folly
20 28 or shall we cease? And the Lord said
1 K 7 8 to Samuel: Cease not to cry to the Lord
12 23 that I should cease to pray for you
27 1 despair of me and cease to seek me
2 K 2 26 to bid the people cease from pursuing
24 21 which rageth among the people, may cease
1 Pa 21 22 that the plague may c. from the people
2 Es 4 11 kill them and cause the work to cease
6 9 that our hands would c. from the work
Jdth 3 2 let thy indignation towards us cease
Job 3 17 there the wicked cease from tumult and
34 36 cease not from the man of iniquity
Ps 36 8 cease from anger, and leave rage: have
45 10 making wars to cease even to the end
88 45 thou hast made his purification to cease
Prov 19 27 cease not, O my son, to hear instruction
21 26 that is just will give and will not c.
22 10 and quarrels and reproaches shall cease
25 10 heard it and cease not to upbraid thee
26 20 is taken away, contentions shall cease
Ecce 10 4 care will make the greatest sins to c.
11 6 in the evening let not thy hand cease
Eccu 10 20 memory of them to c. from the earth
24 14 world to come I shall not cease to be
46 and will not cease to instruct their
28 6 thy last things, and let enmity cease
45 2 he made prodigies to c. He glorified
Isa 1 16 from my eyes: cease to do perversely
2 22 cease ye therefore from the man whose

7 8 Ephraim shall cease to be a people
10 25 and my indignation shall cease and
13 11 make the pride of infidels to cease
17 1 Damascus shall cease to be a city and
3 aid shall cease from Ephraim, and the
21 2 made all the mourning thereof to cease
30 11 Holy One of Israel c. from before us
33 1 wearied thou shalt cease to despise
58 1 cry, cease not, lift up thy voice like
9 and cease to stretch out the finger
Jer 3 19 shalt not cease to walk after me. But
7 34 to cease out of the cities of Juda and
14 17 and let them not cease, because the
17 8 shall it cease at any time to bring
31 16 let thy voice cease from weeping, and
32 40 and will not cease to do them good
36 29 to cease from thence man and beast
48 42 and Moab shall cease to be a people
Lam 2 18 let not the apple of thy eye cease
Eze 7 24 make the pride of the mighty to cease
12 23 I will make this proverb to cease
16 41 and thou shalt cease from fornication
42 I will cease and be angry no more
26 13 the multitude of thy songs to cease
30 10 the multitude of Egypt to cease by the
18 pride of her power shall cease in her
34 10 to cease from feeding the flock any
25 evil beasts to cease out of the land
45 9 cease from iniquity and robberies and
Dan 11 18 prince of his reproach to cease and
Osee 1 4 I will cause to cease the kingdom of
2 11 I will cause all her mirth to cease
Amos 7 5 O Lord God, cease, I beseech thee, who
1 Ma 11 50 let the Jews cease from assaulting
2 Ma 4 6 that Simon would cease from his folly
7 38 brought upon all our nation, shall c.
1 C 13 8 or tongues shall cease or knowledge
Eph 1 16 I cease not to give thanks for you
Col 1 9 cease not to pray for you and to beg
ceased Gen 8 8 to see if the waters had now ceased
Gen 8 11 understood that the waters were ceased
11 8 and they ceased to build the city. And
18 11 it had ceased to be with Sara after
38 5 she ceased to bear any more. And Juda
Exod 9 33 and the thunders and the hail ceased
34 the hail and the thunders were ceased
31 17 in the seventh he ceased from work
36 6 so they ceased from offering gifts
Num 16 48 for the people, and the plague ceased
25 8 scourge c. from the children of Israel
Josu 5 12 the manna ceased after they ate of the
Judg 5 7 valiant men ceased, and rested in Israel
2 K 13 38 David ceased to pursue after Absalom
1 Es 4 24 c. till second year of reign of Adrius
Tob 5 28 at these words his mother c. weeping
Jdth 5 26 when Achior had ceased to speak these
10 1 when she had ceased to cry to the Lord
Job 29 9 the princes ceased to speak, and laid
32 1 these three men ceased to answer Job
Ps 72 19 they have suddenly ceased to be: they
105 30 pacified him: and the slaughter ceased
Wisd 5 13 also being born, forthwith ceased to be
Eccu 16 27 they have not ceased from their works
Isa 14 4 to nothing, the tribute hath ceased
24 8 the mirth of timbrels hath ceased, the
Lam 5 14 ancients have ceased from the gates
15 the joy of our heart is ceased, our
Dan 3 46 ceased not to heat the furnace with
Osee 4 10 committed fornication, and have not c.
Jon 1 15 and the sea ceased from raging. And the
1 Ma 3 45 the pipe and the harp ceased there. And
7 24 they ceased to go forth any more into
9 73 so the sword ceased from Israel: and
2 Ma 9 6 by no means ceased from his malice
Mat 14 32 the wind ceased: and. Mark 4:39; 6:51
Luke 5 4 when he had c. to speak, he said to
7 45 she hath not ceased to kiss my feet
8 24 and it ceased and there was a calm
11 1 when he c., one of his disciples said
Acts 5 42 every day they c. not in the temple
20 1 after the tumult was c., Paul calling
31 I ceased not with tears to admonish
21 14 could not persuade him [Paul], we c.
Heb 10 2 they would have ceased to be offered
1 P 4 1 suffered in the flesh, hath c. from sins
ceasest Acts 13 10 c. not to pervert the right ways
ceaseth Lev 15 25 that c. not to flow after the
Ecce 4 8 yet he ceaseth not to labor, neither
Acts 6 13 this man [Stephen] c. not to speak
2 P 2 14 adultery and of sin that ceaseth not
ceasing Eccu 15 19 seeing all men without ceasing
Eccu 20 28 confusion is with them without ceasing
1 Ma 12 11 without ceasing both in our festivals
2 Ma 3 26 scourged him without ceasing with many
9 18 his pains not ceasing, for the just
Acts 12 5 prayer was made without c. by the church
Rom 1 9 without c., I make a commemoration of
1 Th 1 2 of you in our prayers without ceasing
2 13 we also give thanks to God without c.
5 17 pray without ceasing. In all things
2 Tim 1 3 without c. I have a remembrance of thee
cedar Lev 14 4 c. wood and scarlet and hyssop
Lev 14 6 he shall dip, with the cedar wood and
49 take two sparrows and cedar wood and
51 he shall take the cedar wood and the
52 with the cedar wood and the hyssop
Num 19 6 the priest shall also take cedar wood
2 K 7 2 I dwell in a house of cedar. 1 Pa 17:1
7 not built me a house of cedar. 1 Pa 17:6
3 K 4 33 from the cedar that is in Libanus
6 9 covered the house with roofs of cedar
10 covered the house with timber of cedar
15 with boards of c., from the floor of the
15 he covered it with boards of cedar on
16 with boards of cedar at the hinder part
18 all was covered with boards of cedar
20 the altar also he covered with cedar
36 stones, and one row of beams of cedar
7 2 four galleries between pillars of cedar
3 covered whole vault with boards of c.
7 covered it with cedar wood from the
11 and, in like manner, planks of cedar
12 stones, and one row of planks of cedar
4 K 14 9 thistle of Libanus sent to a cedar tree
2 Pa 25 18 sent to the cedar in Libanus, saying
Job 40 12 he setteth up his tail like a cedar
Ps 91 13 shall grow up like the cedar of Libanus
Cant 1 16 the beams of our houses are of cedar
8 9 join it together with boards of cedar
Eccu 24 17 I was exalted like a cedar in Libanus
50 13 as the cedar planted in mount Libanus
Isa 41 19 I will plant in the wilderness the c.
Jer 22 14 and maketh roofs of cedar and painteth
15 thou comparest thyself to the cedar
Eze 17 3 and took away the marrow of the cedar
22 will take of the marrow of the high c.
23 and it shall become a great cedar: and
31 3 the Assyrian was like a c. in Libanus
Zach 11 2 for the cedar is fallen, for the mighty
cedar trees 2 K 5 11 c. t. and carpenters and
3 K 5 6 thy servants cut me down cedar trees
8 all thy desire concerning cedar trees
10 so Hiram gave Solomon cedar trees and
7 2 for he had cut cedar trees into pillars
9 11 furnishing Solomon with cedar trees
1 Pa 14 1 c. trees and masons and carpenters

22 4 the cedar trees were without number
2 Pa 1 15 cedar trees as sycamores, which grow
1 Es 3 7 to bring cedar trees from Libanus
Cedar Gen 25 13 Cedar and Abdeel. 1 Pa 1:29
Jdth 1 8 nations that are in Carmelus and Cedar
Ps 119 5 have dwelt with the inhabitants of C.
Cant 1 4 as the tents of Cedar, as the curtains
Isa 21 16 glory of Cedar shall be taken away
17 strong archers of the children of Cedar
42 11 exalted: Cedar shall dwell in houses
60 7 the flocks of Cedar shall be gathered
Jer 2 10 send into Cedar and consider diligently
49 28 against Cedar and against the kingdoms
28 arise, and go ye up to Cedar and waste
Eze 27 21 Arabia and all the princes of Cedar
cedars Num 24 6 as cedars by the waterside. Water
Judg 9 15 and devour the cedars of Libanus. Now
3 K 10 27 cedars, to be as common as. 2 Pa 9:27
4 K 19 23 and have cut down its tall cedars and
2 Pa 2 3 and didst send him cedars to build
8 send me also cedars and fir trees
Ps 28 5 voice of the Lord breaketh the cedars
5 Lord shall break the cedars of Libanus
36 35 lifted up like the cedars of Libanus
79 11 branches thereof the cedars of God
103 16 cedars of Libanus which he hath planted
148 9 hills, fruitful trees and all cedars
Cant 5 15 form as of Libanus, excellent as the c.
Isa 2 13 all the tall and lofty c. of Libanus
9 10 but we will change them for cedars
14 8 over thee, and the cedars of Libanus
37 24 I will cut down its tall cedars and
44 14 he hath cut down cedars, taken the holm
Jer 22 7 they shall cut down thy chosen cedars
23 and makest thy nest in the cedars
Eze 27 5 they have taken cedars from Libanus
24 they had cedars also in thy merchandise
31 8 the cedars in the paradise of God
Amos 2 9 whose height was like the height of c.
Zach 11 1 let fire devour thy cedars. Howl, thou
Cedes Josu 19 37 Arama, Asor and Cedes and Edri
Josu 20 7 and they appointed Cedes in Galilee
21 32 of the tribe also of Nephtali, Cedes
Judg 4 6 son of Abinoem out of Cedes in Nephtali
9 arose and went with Barac to Cedes
11 is called Sennim and was near Cedes
4 K 15 29 and Janoe and Cedes and Asor and
1 Pa 6 72 out of the tribe of Issachar, Cedes
76 out of the tribe of Nephtali, Cedes
Cedma Gen 25 15 and Naphis and Cedma. 1 Pa 1:31
Cedmihel 1 Es 2 40 children of Josue and of Cedmihel. 2 Es 7:43
2 Es 9 4 Levites, Josue and Bani and Cedmihel
5 Josue and Cedmihel, Bonni, Hasebnia
10 9 and the Levites . . . Cedmihel. 12:8
12 24 Sarebia, and Josue the son of Cedmihel
Cedmonites Gen 15 19 C. and the Hethites and
Cedron 2 K 15 23 went over the brook Cedron and
3 K 2 37 and shalt pass over the brook Cedron
15 13 and burnt it by the torrent Cedron
4 K 23 4 without Jerusalem in the valley of C.
6 without Jerusalem to the valley of C.
12 ashes of them into the torrent Cedron
2 Pa 15 16 pieces, burnt it at the torrent Cedron
29 16 carried it out abroad to the torrent C.
30 14 and cast them into the torrent Cedron
Jer 31 40 even to the torrent Cedron and to the
1 Ma 16 9 after them till he came to Cedron
John 18 1 with his disciples over the brook Cedron
Ceelatha Num 33 22 from Ressa, they came to C.
Ceila Josu 15 44 Ceila and Achzib and Maresa
1 K 23 1 the Philistines fight against Ceila
2 smite the Philistines and shalt save C.
3 how much more if we go to Ceila against
4 go to Ceila; for I will deliver the
5 David therefore and his men went to C.
5 David saved the inhabitants of Ceila
6 son of Achimelech fled to David to Ceila
7 told Saul that David was come to Ceila
8 to fight against C. and to besiege David
10 that Saul designeth to come to Ceila
11 will the men of Ceila deliver me. 12
13 David and his men . . . departing from C.
13 told Saul that David was fled from Ceila
2 Es 3 17 lord of half the street of Ceila in his
18 the son of Enadad, lord of half Ceila
ceiled 2 Pa 3 5 greater house he ceiled with deal
Agge 1 4 for you to dwell in ceiled houses
Celai 2 Es 12 20 of Sellai, Celai: of Amoc, Heber
Celaia 1 Es 10 23 and Celaia, the same is Calita
celebrate Exod 12 48 then shall he c. it according
Exod 13 5 thou shalt celebrate this manner of
23 14 year you shall celebrate feasts to me
31 16 keep the sabbath and celebrate it in
Lev 23 4 which you must c. in their seasons
32 you shall celebrate your sabbaths
39 shall c. the feast of the Lord seven
41 seventh month shall you c. this feast
Num 29 12 c. a solemnity to the Lord seven days
18 and for the lambs you shall duly c.
24 you shall celebrate in right manner
27 for the lamps you shall celebrate according to the rite. 30, 33, 37
Deut 16 1 that thou mayst celebrate the phase
10 thou shalt celebrate the festival of
13 c. the solemnity also of tabernacles
15 seven days shalt thou celebrate feasts
2 Pa 30 13 to c. the solemnity of the unleavened
35 9 of the Levites to celebrate the phase
2 Ma 1 9 celebrate ye the days of Scenopegia in
2 16 about to celebrate the purification
15 37 to celebrate the thirteenth day of the
celebrated Lev 16 11 after these things are duly c.
Deut 15 2 which shall be celebrated in this order
3 K 12 32 manner of the feast that was c. in Juda
2 Pa 7 9 had celebrated the solemnity seven days
31 1 when these things had been duly c.
32 33 all Juda . . . celebrated his funeral
35 19 the reign of Josias was this phase c.
Tob 9 12 marriage feast they c. also with the
Jdth 16 24 the joy of this victory was celebrated
Eccu 33 9 they c. festivals at an hour. Some
1 Ma 1 48 sabbath and the festival days to be c.
10 58 he celebrated her marriage at Ptolemais
2 Ma 2 12 Solomon also celebrated the dedication
Heb 11 28 by faith he celebrated the pasch and
celebrating Gen 50 10 c. the exequies with a great
celestial 1 C 15 40 there are bodies celestial
1 C 15 40 one is the glory of the celestial
Celesyria 1 Ma 10 69 governor of C. 2 Ma 3:5; 4:4
2 Ma 3 8 under color of visiting the cities of C.
8 8 wrote to Prolemee the governor of C.
Celia 1 Pa 4 19 sister of Naham the father of C.
Celita 2 Es 10 10 Sebenia, Oduia, Celita, Phelaia
cell 1 Pa 26 18 in the way: and two at every cell
cellar Cant 2 4 brought me into the cellar of wine
cellars 1 Pa 27 27 over the wine cellars, Zabdias
1 Pa 27 28 over the oil cellars, Joas. And over
Cellon Jdth 2 13 on the south of the land of C.
cells 1 Pa 26 18 in the cells also of the porters
Celtia 2 Es 8 7 Celtia, Azarias, Joazabed, Hanan
Cenchrae Acts 18 18 having shorn his head in C.
Rom 16 1 of the church that is in Cenchrae
Cendebeus 1 Ma 15 38 king appointed C. captain
1 Ma 15 40 C. came to Jamnia and began to provoke
16 1 what C. had done against their people

4 they went forth against Cendebeus
8 C. and his army were put to flight
Cenereth Num 34 11 eastward to the sea of C.
Deut 3 17 borders of Cenereth unto the sea of the
Josu 13 27 uttermost part of the sea of Cenereth
19 35 Ser and Emath and Reccath and Cenereth
Ceneroth Josu 11 2 over against south side of C.
Josu 12 3 from the wilderness to the sea of C.
Cenez Gen 36 11 Sepho and Gatham and Cenez
Gen 36 15 duke Cenez, duke Core, duke Gatham
42 duke Cenez, duke Theman. 1 Pa 1:53
Josu 15 17 Othoniel the son of C. Judg 1:13; 3:9, 11
1 Pa 1 36 Theman, Omar, Sephi, Gathan, Cenez
4 13 the sons of Cenez were Othoniel and
15 the sons of Ela: Cenez. The sons also
Cenezite Num 32 12 Jephone the C. Josu 14:6, 14
Cenezites Gen 15 19 the C., the Cedmonites, and the
Ceni 1 K 27 10 and against the south of Ceni
1 K 30 29 and that were in the cities of Ceni
Cenneroth 3 K 15 20 Maacha and all C., that is
censer Lev 16 12 taking the censer which he hath
Num 16 17 let Aaron also hold his censer. When
46 Moses said to Aaron: Take the censer
2 Pa 26 19 and holding in his hand the censer
Eze 8 11 every one had a censer in his hand
Haba 9 4 having a golden censer. Apoc 8:3
Apoc 8 5 angel took the censer and filled it
censers Exod 25 29 and bowls, censers and cups
Exod 37 16 censers of pure gold, wherein the
Lev 10 1 sons of Aaron, taking their censers
Num 4 7 and shall put with it the censers and
16 6 take every man of you your censers
17 take every one of you censers, and
17 offering to the Lord 250 censers: let
37 to take up the censers that lie in the
39 Eleazar the priest took the brazen c.
3 K 7 50 mortars and censers of most pure gold
4 K 12 13 censers or trumpets or any vessel
25 15 the censers and the bowls. 2 Pa 4:22
1 Pa 28 17 and bowls and censers of fine gold
Jer 52 19 took away the pitchers and the censers
censured Eccu 19 5 in iniquity, shall be c., and
censurer Wisd 2 14 is become a c. of our thoughts
centurion Mat 8 5 there came to him a centurion
Mat 8 8 the c. making answer, said: Lord, I am
13 Jesus said to the centurion: Go, and
27 54 the c. and they that were with him
Mark 15 39 centurion who stood over against him
44 [Pilate] sending for the centurion
45 when he understood it by the centurion
Luke 7 2 servant of certain centurion, who was
6 the centurion sent his friends to him
23 47 the c. seeing what was done, glorified
Acts 10 1 Cornelius, a c. of the Italian band
22 Cornelius, a centurion, a just man
22 25 Paul saith to the centurion that stood
26 the c. hearing, went to the tribune
24 23 [Felix] commanded a c. to keep him
27 1 should be delivered to a c., named
6 the c. finding a ship of Alexandria
11 c. believed the pilot and the master
31 Paul said to the centurion and to the
43 the c. willing to save Paul, forbade it
centurions Num 31 14 the c. that were come from the
Num 31 48 tribunes and c. were come to Moses
52 from the tribunes and from the c.
Deut 1 15 appointed them rulers, tribunes and c.
1 K 8 12 to be his tribunes and centurions
22 7 make you all tribunes and centurions
4 K 11 4 taking the centurions and the soldiers
9 the centurions did according to all
15 Joiada commanded the centurions that
19 he took the centurions and the bands
Acts 21 32 taking with him soldiers and centurions
23 17 calling to him one of the centurions
23 [tribune] having called two centurions
Cephas John 1 42 thou shalt be called Cephas
1 C 1 12 I am of Apollo; and I of Cephas; and
3 22 whether it be Paul or Apollo or Cephas
9 5 and the brethren of the Lord and Cephas
15 5 he was seen by Cephas: and after that
Gal 2 9 James and Cephas and John, who seemed
11 but when Cephas was come to Antioch
14 I said to Cephas before them all: If
Cephira 1 Es 2 25 children of Cariathiarim, C.
2 Es 7 29 men of Cariathiarim, Cephira, and
ceremonies Gen 26 5 and observed my c. and laws
Exod 12 25 you shall observe these ceremonies
18 20 to show the people the ceremonies
27 19 for all uses and ceremonies, and the
38 21 in the ceremonies of the Levites, by
Lev 5 15 transgressing the ceremonies in those
7 35 and his sons, in the c. of the Lord
9 17 besides the c. of the morning holocaust
10 19 please the Lord in the c., having a
Num 1 50 and whatsoever pertaineth to the c.
9 3 according to all the ceremonies and
12 shall observe all the c. of the phase
14 phase to the Lord according to the c.
15 24 libations thereof as the c. require
18 4 tabernacle and in all the ceremonies
29 6 with the same c. you shall offer a
Deut 4 8 that hath ceremonies and just judgments
14 that I should teach you the ceremonies
45 these are the testimonies and c. and
5 1 hear, O Israel, the ceremonies and
31 to thee all my commandments and c.
6 1 these are the precepts and ceremonies
17 the testimonies and c. which he hath
20 what mean these testimonies and c.
7 11 keep therefore the precepts and c. and
8 11 c. which I command thee this day
10 13 commandments of the Lord and his c.
11 1 observe his precepts and ceremonies
32 that you fulfil the ceremonies and
12 30 lest thou seek after their ceremonies
17 19 and keep his words and c. that are
26 17 and keep his ceremonies and precepts
28 15 and to do all his commandments and c.
45 keep his commandments and c. 30:16
30 10 and keep his precepts and c. which are
3 K 2 3 and observe his ceremonies and his
8 58 keep his commandments and his c.
9 6 not keep my commandments and my c.
4 K 17 13 and keep my precepts and ceremonies
34 neither do they keep his ceremonies
37 the c. and judgments and law, and
23 3 testimonies and his c. with all their
1 Pa 23 13 before the Lord according to his c.
31 according to the number and ceremonies
32 c. of the sanctuary and the charge
29 19 thy testimonies and thy ceremonies
2 Pa 19 10 the law, the commandment, the c.
31 21 according to the law and the ceremonies
33 8 all the law and the ceremonies and
1 Es 7 11 commandments of the Lord and his c.
2 Es 1 7 have not kept thy commandments and c.
9 13 law of truth, c. and good precepts
14 commandments and c. and the law by
10 29 our God, and his judgments and his c.
13 14 the house of my God and his ceremonies
Jdth 5 8 forsaking the c. of their fathers
Esth 3 8 that use new laws and ceremonies and
8 17 themselves to their worship and c.
9 28 which is bound to these ceremonies
Eze 43 18 these are the ceremonies of the altar

44 5 I saw to thee concerning all the c.
15 who kept the c. of my sanctuary when
16 minister unto me and to keep my c.
48 11 of the sons of Sadoc, who kept my c.
Cerethi 1 K 30 14 invasion on the south side of C.
2 K 8 18 the Cerethi and the Phelethi. 15:18; 20:7; 3 K 1:38, 44; 4 K 11:19; 1 Pa 18:17
Cerethites 2 K 20 23 Banaias . . . was over the C.
Ceros 1 Es 2 44 the children of Ceros. 2 Es 7:48
certainty Gen 41 32 it is a token of the certainty
1 K 23 23 return to me with the c. of the thing
Prov 22 21 that I might show thee the certainty
Acts 21 34 when he could not know the certainty
certified 1 Es 4 14 therefore sent and c. the king
certify 2 K 15 28 there come word from you to c. me
1 Es 4 16 we certify the king, that if this city
Ceseleththabor Josu 19 12 to the borders of C.
Cesil Josu 15 30 Eltholad and Cesil and Horma
Cesion Josu 19 20 Rabboth and Cesion, Abes, and
Josu 21 28 of the tribe of Issachar, Cesion
cession Ruth 4 7 was a testimony of c. of right
Ceteans 1 Ma 8 5 Perses the king of the Ceteans
Cethim 1 Pa 1 7 sons of Javan . . . C. and Dodanim
Isa 23 1 from the land of Cethim it is revealed
12 arise and sail over to Cethim, there
Jer 2 10 pass over to the isles of Cethim and
1 Ma 1 1 coming out of the land of Cethim, had
Cethite Eze 16 3 and thy mother a Cethite. And
Eze 16 45 your mother was a Cethite, and your
Cethlis Josu 15 40 Leheman and Cethlis and
Cetron Judg 1 30 destroyed not inhabitants of C.
Cetthim Gen 10 4 sons of Javan . . . Cetthim and
Cetura Gen 25 1 another wife named Cetura
Gen 25 4 all these were the children of Cetura
1 Pa 1 32 sons of Cetura, Abraham's concubine
33 all these are the sons of Cetura
Chabri Jdth 8 9 sent to the ancients C. and
Chabul 3 K 9 13 he called them the land of Chabul
chaff Job 21 18 shall be as c. before the face of
Isa 41 15 and shalt make the hills as chaff
Jer 23 28 what hath the c. to do with the wheat
Dan 2 35 became like the chaff of a summer's
Mat 3 12 the chaff he will burn. Luke 3:17
chain Gen 41 42 put a c. of gold about his neck
3 K 7 17 a kind of network and chain work
Prov 1 9 and a chain of gold to thy neck
Wisd 17 17 together with one chain of darkness
Eccu 6 30 her chain a robe of glory: for in her
Isa 58 9 if thou wilt take away the chain
Jer 28 10 took the chain from neck of Jeremias
12 had broken the chain from off the
Eze 16 11 a chain about thy neck. And I put a
Dan 5 7 shall have a golden chain on his neck
16 a chain of gold about thy neck and
29 a chain of gold was put about his neck
Acts 28 20 I am bound with this chain. But they
Eph 6 20 for which I am an ambassador in a chain
2 Tim 1 16 he hath not been ashamed of my chain
Apoc 20 1 a great chain, in his hand. And he
chains Exod 28 14 two little c. of the purest gold
Exod 28 22 thou shalt make on the rational chains
24 golden chains thou shalt join to the
25 ends of the chains themselves thou
39 15 in the rational little chains linked
17 on which rings the two golden chains
Lev 26 13 have broken the chains of your necks
Num 31 50 bracelets and chains, that thou mayst
Judg 8 26 golden c. that were about the camels'
16 21 led him bound in chains. 2 Pa 36:6
4 K 25 7 and bound him with chains and brought
2 Pa 3 5 like little chains interlaced with one
16 as it were little chains in the oracle
16 which he put between the little chains
33 11 and carried him bound with chains and
Job 36 8 if they shall be in chains and be bound
Ecce 4 14 out of prison and c. sometimes a man
Cant 1 10 we will make thee chains of gold
Eccu 6 25 fetters and thy neck into her chains
Isa 3 19 chains and necklaces and bracelets
Jer 27 2 make thee bands and chains: and thou
28 13 hast broken c. of wood, and thou shalt make for them chains of iron
40 1 taken him, being bound with chains
4 loosed thee this day from the chains
Eze 19 4 brought him in c. into land of Egypt
9 brought him in chains to the king of
Mark 5 3 could bind him not even with chains
4 bound with fetters and chains, he had burst the chains
Luke 8 29 was bound with c. and kept in fetters
Acts 12 6 bound with two c.: and the keepers
7 and the chains fell off from his hands
21 33 commanded him to be bound with two c.
Jude 6 in everlasting c. unto the judgment of
chair 1 K 20 25 when king sat down upon his chair
2 K 23 8 Jesbaham sitting in the c. was wisest
Job 29 7 in the street they prepared me a chair
Ps 1 1 nor sat in the chair of pestilence
106 32 praise him in the chair of the ancients
Eze 28 2 and I sit in the chair of God in the
Mat 23 2 have sitten on the chair of Moses. All
chairs Mat 21 12 c. of them that sold. Mark 11:15
Mat 23 6 the first chairs in the synagogues. Mark 12:39; Luke 20:46
Chalal 1 Es 10 30 of the sons of Phahath . . . C.
Chalane Amos 6 2 pass ye over to Chalane and see
Chalanne Gen 10 10 and C. in the land of Sennaar
chalcedony Apoc 21 19 the third, a chalcedony
Chalchal 1 Pa 2 6 Eman and Chalchal and Dara
Chalcol 3 K 4 31 Heman and Chalcol and Dorda
Chaldea Jer 50 10 Chaldea shall be made a prey
Jer 51 24 and to all the inhabitants of Chaldea
35 my blood upon the inhabitants of C.
Eze 11 24 and brought me into Chaldea, to them
23 16 she sent messengers to them into Chaldea
Chaldean 1 Es 5 12 the king of Babylon the C.
Dan 2 10 of any diviner or wise man or C.
Chaldeans 2 Pa 36 6 Nabuchodonosor king of the C.
2 Pa 36 17 brought upon them the king of the C.
2 Es 9 7 him forth out of the fire of the C.
Jdth 5 6 people is of the offspring of the C.
Job 1 17 the Chaldeans made three troops, and
Isa 13 19 the famous pride of the Chaldeans
43 14 the Chaldeans glorying in their ships
47 1 no throne for daughter of the Chaldeans
5 into darkness, O daughter of the C.
48 14 and his arm shall be on the Chaldeans
20 flee ye from the Chaldeans, declare it
Jer 21 4 the C. that besiege you round about
9 shall go out and flee over to the C.
22 25 Babylon and into the hand of the C.
32 4 not escape out of the hand of the C.
5 if you will fight against the Chaldeans
24 is given into the hands of the C. 25, 43
28 this city into the hands of the C.
29 Chaldeans that fight against this city
33 5 that come to fight with the Chaldeans
35 11 from the face of the army of the C.
37 4 the Chaldeans that besieged Jerusalem
7 the Chaldeans shall come again and fight
8 the Chaldeans shall surely depart
9 should even beat all the army of the C.
10 when the army of the C. was gone away
12 thou art fleeing to the Chaldeans
13 I am not fleeing to the Chaldeans
38 2 that shall go forth to the Chaldeans

18 be delivered into the hands of the C.
19 the Jews that are fled over to the C.
23 shall be brought out to the Chaldeans
39 5 army of the Chaldeans pursued. 52:8
8 the Chaldeans burnt the king's house
40 9 fear not to serve the Chaldeans
10 may answer the commandment of the C.
41 3 and the C. that were found there
18 into Egypt, from face of the Chaldeans
43 3 to deliver us into the hands of the C.
50 35 a sword is upon the Chaldeans, saith
52 7 the C. besieged the city round about
14 army of the Chaldeans that were with
17 C. also broke in pieces the brazen
Bar 1 2 at the time that the C. took Jerusalem
6 40 even the C. themselves dishonor them
Eze 16 29 in the land of Chanaan with the C.
23 14 images of the C. set forth in colors
23 all the C., the nobles and the kings
Dan 1 4 the learning and the tongue of the C.
2 2 and the magicians and the Chaldeans
4 the C. answered the king in Syriac
5 king answering said to the Chaldeans
10 the Chaldeans answered before the king
3 8 some C. came and accused the Jews and
48 burnt such of the C. as it found near
4 4 C. and the soothsayers, and I told the
5 7 to bring in the wise men, the C., and
11 enchanters, Chaldeans, and soothsayers
9 1 reigned over the kingdom of the C.
Haba 1 6 I will raise up the Chaldeans, a bitter
land of the Chaldeans Jdth 5 7 gods of their fathers, who were in the l. . . .
Isa 23 13 behold the l. . . . , there was not
Jer 25 12 for their iniquity, and the l. . . .
50 1 against Babylon and against the l. . . .
8 and go forth out of the land of the C.
25 hath a work to be done in the l. . . .
45 he hath thought against the l. . . .
51 4 and the slain shall fall in the l. . . .
54 and great destruction from the l. . . .
Eze 1 3 the priest the son of Buzi in l. . . .
12 13 him into Babylon, into the l. . . .
23 15 the l. . . . wherein they were born
Acts 7 4 he went out of the l. . . . and dwelt
Chaldees Gen 11 28 in Ur of the C. And Abram
Gen 11 31 brought them out of Ur of the Chaldees
15 7 brought thee out from Ur of the C.
4 K 24 2 against him the rovers of the Chaldees
25 4 Chaldees besieged the city round about
5 the army of the Chaldees pursued after
10 army of the Chaldees which was with
13 the C. broke in pieces and carried
24 be not afraid to serve the Chaldees
25 Jews and Chaldees that were with him
26 went to Egypt, fearing the Chaldees
Chale Gen 10 11 the streets of the city and Chale
Gen 10 12 Resen also between Ninive and Chale
Chali Josu 19 25 their border was Halcath and C.
chalice Ps 22 5 my chalice which inebriateth me
Ps 115 13 I will take the chalice of salvation
Mat 20 22 can you drink the chalice. Mark 10:38
23 my chalice indeed you shall drink
26 27 taking the chalice he gave thanks and
39 let this chalice pass from me
42 if this chalice may not pass away, but
Mark 10 39 you shall indeed drink of the chalice
14 23 having taken the chalice, giving
36 remove this chalice from me. Luke 22:42
Luke 22 17 having taken the c., he gave thanks
20 in like manner the c. also. 1 C 11:25
20 this is the chalice, the new testament
John 18 11 c. which my Father hath given me
1 C 10 16 the c. of benediction, which we bless
21 you cannot drink the chalice of the Lord and the chalice of devils
11 25 this c. is the new testament in my
26 eat the bread and drink this chalice
27 drink the c. of the Lord unworthily
28 of that bread and drink of the chalice
challenge Num 16 10 you should c. to yourselves
Jdth 14 12 have presumed to challenge us to fight
Eccu 31 30 challenge not them that love wine
1 Ma 15 3 my purpose is to c. the kingdom and
challenging 1 Pa 12 36 to fight and c. in battle
Cham Gen 5 31 old, begot Sem, Cham, and Japheth
Gen 7 13 Noe and Sem and Cham and. 1 Pa 1:4
9 18 out of the ark were Sem, Cham, and
18 Cham is the father of Chanaan. These
22 Cham the father of Chanaan had seen
10 1 sons of Noe: Sem, Cham, and Japheth
6 the sons of Cham: Chus and. 1 Pa 1:8
20 these are the children of Cham in
1 Pa 4 40 some of the race of Cham had dwelt before
Ps 77 51 their labor in the tabernacles of C.
104 23 was a sojourner in the land of Cham
27 and his wonders in the land of Cham
105 22 wondrous works in the land of Cham
Chamaal 1 Pa 7 33 Phosech and C. and Asoth
Chamaam 2 K 19 37 thy servant C., let him go with
2 K 19 38 let Chamaam go over with me, and I
40 on to Galgal, and Chamaam with him
Jer 41 17 sat as sojourners in Chamaam, which is
Chamath 1 Pa 2 55 who came of Calor, Chamath
chamber Gen 43 30 going into his c., he wept
Deut 33 12 as in a bride chamber shall he abide
Judg 15 1 when he would have gone into her chamber
16 9 in the chamber expecting the event
12 ambush prepared for him in the chamber
2 K 13 10 bring the mess into the chamber, that
10 to her brother Amnon in the chamber
18 33 went up to the high chamber over the gate
3 K 1 15 went in to the king into the chamber
3 17 delivered of a child with her in the c.
17 19 carried him into the upper chamber
23 brought him down from the upper chamber
20 30 into a c. that was within a chamber
22 25 shalt go into a c. within a chamber
4 K 1 2 through the lattices of his upper c.
4 10 let us therefore make him a little c.
11 turned in to the chamber and rested
6 12 that thou speakest in thy privy c.
9 2 and carry him into an inner chamber
5 he arose and went into the chamber
23 11 near the chamber of Nathanmelech
12 the top of the upper chamber of Achaz
2 Pa 18 24 when thou shalt go in from c. to c.
1 Es 10 6 went to the chamber of Johanan the son
2 Es 3 30 and unto the chamber of the corner
31 and within the chamber of the corner
Tob 3 10 she went into an upper chamber of her
6 18 go into the chamber, and for three days
7 18 bade her prepare another chamber. And
8 15 went into the chamber and found them
Jdth 8 5 she made herself a private chamber
13 1 and Vagao shut the chamber doors
3 and Judith was alone in the chamber
5 maid to stand without before the c.
14 9 noise before the door of the chamber
10 or go into the chamber of the general
13 Vagao going into his chamber, stood
16 23 she had taken away out of his chamber
Esth 2 13 from c. of the women to the king's c.
16 she was brought to the c. of the king
Ps 18 6 bridegroom coming out of his bride c.
Ecce 10 20 speak not evil . . . in thy private c.

Cant 3 4 into the chamber of her that bore me
Jer 36 12 the king's house to the secretary's c.
20 the volume in the chamber of Elisama
21 bringing it out of the c. of Elisama
Eze 8 12 every one in private in his chamber
40 7 every little chamber was one reed long
13 from the roof of one little chamber to
29 little c. thereof and the front. 33, 36
38 at every chamber was a door in the
41 5 breadth of every side c. four cubits
9 thickness of wall for the side chamber
42 1 he brought me into the chamber that
44 19 lay them up in the store chamber of
Dan 6 10 opening the windows in his upper c.
Joel 2 16 and the bride out of her bride chamber
Mat 6 6 enter into thy chamber and having
Luke 22 11 where is the guest c. where I may eat
Acts 9 37 they laid her in an upper chamber
39 they brought him into the upper c.
20 8 number of lamps in the upper chamber
chambering Rom 13 13 not in c. and impurities
chamberlains Jdth 12 6 he commanded his c. that
Jdth 14 11 they said to the chamberlains: Go in
chambers Gen 6 16 the ark . . . with lower, middle c.
1 Pa 9 26 and they were over the chambers and
33 Levites, who dwelt in the chambers
23 28 in the porches and in the chambers
28 11 a description . . . of the inner chambers
12 and of the chambers round about, for
2 Pa 3 9 upper c. also he overlaid with gold
Ps 104 30 in the inner chambers of their kings
Prov 7 27 even to the inner chambers of death
Isa 26 20 and enter into thy chambers, shut thy
Jer 22 13 buildeth . . . his c. not in judgment
14 will build me a wide house and large c.
35 2 into one of the c. of the treasures
Eze 40 7 between the little c. were five cubits
10 the little chambers of the gate that
12 border before the little c. one cubit
12 the little chambers were six cubits
16 slanting windows in the little c.
17 there were chambers and a pavement
17 thirty c. encompassed the pavement
21 little c. thereof three on this side
44 were the chambers of the singing men
41 6 side chambers . . . twice thirty-three
8 the foundations of the side chambers
9 within the side chambers of the house
10 between the chambers was the breadth
11 door of the side chambers was turned
42 4 before the chambers was a walk ten
5 where were the store chambers lower
7 wall that went about by the chambers
7 on the forepart of the chambers, was
8 length of the c. of the outward court
9 was under these chambers, an entrance
10 there were chambers before the building
11 the c. which were toward the north
12 according to the doors of the chambers
13 c. of the north and the c. of the south
45 5 they shall possess 20 store chambers
46 19 into the chambers of the sanctuary
1 Ma 4 38 c. joining to the temple thrown down
57 they renewed the gates and the c.
Luke 12 3 spoken in the ear in the chambers
chameleon Lev 11 30 the chameleon and the stello
chamfered 3 K 7 24 two rows cast of c. sculptures
chamois Deut 14 5 the c., the pygarg, the wild
Chamos Num 21 29 thou art undone, O people of C.
Judg 11 24 things which thy god Chamos possesseth
3 K 11 7 Solomon built a temple for Chamos
33 Chamos the god of Moab, and Moloch
4 K 23 13 and to Chamos the scandal of Moab
Jer 48 7 Chamos shall go into captivity, his
13 Moab shall be ashamed of Chamos, as
46 thou hast perished, O people of Chamos
champaign Josu 12 8 plains and the c. countries
Josu 18 18 on the north side to the c. countries
champion 1 K 17 51 seeing that their c. was dead
Chanaan Gen 9 18 Cham is the father of Chanaan
Gen 9 22 when Cham the father of C. had seen
25 he [Noe] said: Cursed be Chanaan
26 God of Sem, be Chanaan his servant
27 of Sem, and Chanaan be his servant
10 6 sons of Cham . . . Chanaan. 1 Pa 1:8
15 and Chanaan begot Sidon. 1 Pa 1:13
19 limits of Chanaan were from Sidon
28 1 take not a wife of the stock of C.
6 not take a wife of daughters of C.
8 not well pleased with daughters of C.
36 2 Esau took wives of the daughters of C.
38 2 daughter of a man of C., called Sue
46 10 Saul the son of a woman of Chanaan
50 11 when the inhabitants of C. saw this
Exod 15 15 the inhabitants of Chanaan became stiff
Lev 18 3 the manner of the country of Chanaan
Josu 5 1 the kings of Chanaan who possessed
22 9 in Silo, which is in Chanaan, to go
Judg 4 2 Jabin king of Chanaan. 23, 24
5 19 the kings of Chanaan fought in Thanach
10 12 Chanaan oppress you, and you cried
Ps 105 38 they sacrificed to the idols of Chanaan
134 11 all the kingdom of Chanaan. And gave
Isa 19 18 speaking the language of Chanaan and
23 11 hath given a charge against Chanaan
Dan 13 56 thou seed of Chanaan, and not of Juda
Osee 12 7 he is like C., there is a deceitful
Soph 1 11 all the people of Chanaan is hushed
2 5 the word of the Lord upon you, O C.
1 Ma 9 37 daughter of one of great princes of C.
Acts 7 11 famine upon all Egypt and Chanaan
land of Chanaan Gen 11 31 to go into the l. . . .
Gen 12 5 they went out to go into the l. . . .
13 12 Abram dwelt in the land of Chanaan
16 3 after they first dwelt in the l. . . .
17 8 the land of Chanaan for a perpetual
23 19 this is Hebron in the land of Chanaan
31 18 to Isaac his father to the l. . . .
33 18 Salem . . . which is in the land of C.
35 6 Luza, which is in the land of C. 48:3
36 5 born to him [Esau] in the land of C.
6 that he was able to acquire in l. . . .
37 1 Jacob dwelt in the land of Chanaan
42 5 famine was in the land of Chanaan
7 they answered: From the land of C.
13 the sons of one man in the land of C.
29 came to Jacob their father in the l. . . .
32 youngest is with our father in l. . . .
44 8 we brought back to thee from the l. . . .
45 17 load your beasts and go into the l. . . .
25 out of Egypt and came into the l. . . .
46 6 all that he had in the land of Chanaan
12 Her and Onan died in the land of C.
31 that were in the l. . . . are come to me
47 1 are come out of the land of Chanaan
4 famine being very grievous in the l. . . .
13 had oppressed the land . . . of Chanaan
48 7 Rachel died from me in the land of C.
49 30 over against Mambre in the land of C.
50 5 which I have digged for myself in l. . . .
13 carrying him [Jacob] into the l. . . .
Exod 6 4 to give them the land of Chanaan, the
16 35 until they reached the borders of l. . . .
Lev 14 34 when you shall be come into the l. . . .
25 38 that I might give you the land of C.
Num 13 3 send men to view the land of Chanaan

18 Moses sent them to view the land of C.
26 19 Her and Onan, who both died in l. . . .
32 30 will not pass armed with you into l. . . .
32 we will go . . . into the land of Chanaan
33 40 children of Israel were come into l. . . .
51 entering into the l. . . . destroy all
34 2 when you are entered into the l. . . .
29 Lord hath commanded to divide the l. . . .
35 10 over the Jordan into the land of C.
14 three [cities] in the land of Chanaan
Deut 32 49 and see the l. . . . which I will deliver
Josu 5 12 corn of the present year of the l. . . .
13 3 l. . . . which is divided among the lords
4 all the land of Chanaan, and Maara
14 1 children of Israel possessed in l. . . .
21 2 spoke to them in Silo in the land of C.
22 10 in the l. . . . they built an altar
11 had built an altar in the land of C.
32 out of the land of Galaad into l. . . .
24 3 brought him into the land of Chanaan
1 Pa 16 18 to thee will I give l. . . . Ps 104:11
Bar 3 22 it hath not been heard of in the l. . . .
Eze 16 3 thy nativity is of the land of Chanaan
29 multiplied thy fornications in l. . . .
17 4 and carried it away into the land of C.
Acts 13 19 seven nations in the land of Chanaan
Chanaana 3 K 22 11 the son of Chanaana. 24; 2 Pa 18:10, 23
Chanaanite Gen 12 6 the C. was at that time in
Gen 13 7 the Chanaanite and the Pherezite. Deut 7:1; 20:17; Josu 9:1; 12:8
Exod 3 8 to the places of the C. and Hethite
17 into the land of the C. 13:5, 11
23 23 C. and the Hevite and the Jebusite
28 Hevite and the C. and the Hethite
33 2 that I may cast out the Chanaanite
34 11 the Chanaanite and the Hethite and the. Josu 3:10; 24:11
Num 13 30 the Chanaanite abideth by the sea
14 25 and the Chanaanite dwell in the valleys
43 the Chanaanite are before you, and by
45 the C. that dwelt in the mountain
21 1 king Arad the C., who dwelt. 33:40
3 delivered up the C., and they cut
Deut 11 30 C. who dwelleth in the plain country
Josu 16 10 children of Ephraim slew not the C.
10 the C. dwelt in the midst of Ephraim
17 12 but the C. began to dwell in his land
Judg 1 1 shall go up before us against the C.
3 into my lot, and fight against the C.
4 and the Lord delivered the Chanaanite
5 and they defeated the Chanaanite and
9 went down and fought against the C.
10 Juda going forward against the C.
27 the Chanaanite began to dwell with them
29 Ephraim also did not slay the C. that
30 but the Chanaanite dwelt among them
3 5 dwelt in the midst of the Chanaanite
2 K 24 7 land of the Hevite and the Chanaanite
3 K 9 16 slew the C. that dwelt in the city
2 Es 9 8 to give him the land of the Chanaanite
Prov 31 24 delivered a girdle to the Chanaanite
Chanaanites Gen 10 18 families of the C. were
24 3 not wife for my son, of daughters of C.
37 not take a wife for my son of the C.
34 30 made me hateful to the Chanaanites
Deut 1 7 by the seashore, the land of the C.
Josu 7 9 the C. and all the inhabitants of
11 3 to the Chanaanites also on the east
17 13 they subdued the Chanaanites and made
16 for the C. that dwell in the low lands
18 when thou hast destroyed the C., who
Judg 1 17 they together defeated the Chanaanites
32 he dwelt in the midst of the C. 33
3 1 that had not known the wars of the C.
3 all the C. and the Sidonians and the
1 Es 9 1 abominations, namely, of the C. and
2 Es 9 24 the inhabitants of the land, the C.
Jdth 5 20 overthrew the king of the Chanaanites
Abdi 20 the places of the C. even to Sarepta
Chanaanitess Exod 6 15 and Saul the son of a C.
1 Pa 2 3 were born to him of the Chanaanitess
Chanana 1 Pa 7 10 C. and Zethan and Tharsis
Chanani 2 Es 9 4 Bonni, Serebias, Bani, and C.
chance Num 35 22 if by chance medley, and without
1 K 6 9 but it hath happened by chance. They
2 K 1 6 I came by chance upon mount Gelboe
Ecce 9 11 skilful: but time and chance in all
chanced 3 K 22 34 c. to strike the king of Israel
Luke 10 11 chanced that a certain priest went down
change Gen 35 2 be cleansed and c. your garments
Exod 13 13 an ass thou shalt change for a sheep
Lev 27 10 if he shall change it, both that which
33 if any man change it, both that which
Deut 16 19 wise, and change the words of the just
3 K 14 2 change thy dress that thou be not known
2 Pa 18 29 I will change my dress and so I will go
Tob 2 18 to those that never change their faith
Job 9 27 I change my face and am tormented with
14 14 I expect until my change come. Thou
20 thou shalt change his face and shalt
Ps 54 20 there is no change with them, and they
76 11 this is the change of the right hand
88 52 reproached the change of thy anointed
101 27 as a vesture thou shalt change them
Ecce 8 1 the most mighty will change his face
Eccu 12 19 whisper much, and c. his countenance
33 21 let no man c. thee. For it is better
37 21 a wicked word shall change the heart
Isa 9 10 but we will change them for cedars
Jer 13 23 if the Ethiopian can change his skin
Dan 7 25 think himself able to change times
Osee 4 7 I will change their glory into shame
Zach 3 4 have clothed thee with c. of garments
Mala 3 6 I am the Lord and I change not: and
1 Ma 1 51 should change all the justifications
Acts 6 14 shall change the traditions which Moses
Gal 4 20 with you now change my voice
Heb 1 12 as a vesture shalt thou change them
James 1 17 with whom there is no change nor
changed Gen 31 7 hath changed my wages ten times
Gen 31 41 hast changed also my wages ten times
Exod 14 5 the heart of Pharao . . . was changed
Lev 13 10 shall have changed the look of the hair
26 if the color of the hair be not changed
14 56 when the colors are diversely changed
24 8 every sabbath day they shall be changed
27 10 shall be holy, and cannot be changed
10 that which was changed and that for which it was changed. 33
33 neither shall it be changed for another
Num 23 19 as the son of man, that he should be c.
32 38 Nabo and Baalmeon, their names being c.
33 2 their encamping, which they changed
1 K 1 18 her countenance was no more changed
10 6 and shalt be changed into another man
2 K 12 20 when he [David] had c. his apparel, he
3 K 22 30 the king of Israel changed his dress
4 K 25 29 he changed his garments which he had
2 Pa 18 29 the king of Israel having c. his dress
Job 28 17 any vessels of gold be changed for it
30 21 thou art changed to be cruel toward me
Ps 33 1 David, when he changed his countenance
44 1 them that shall be c. 59:1; 68:1; 79:1

72 21 inflamed, and my reins have been c.
101 27 shalt change them, and they shall be c.
105 20 they c. their glory into the likeness
108 24 and my flesh is changed for oil. And I
Wisd 12 10 their thought could never be changed
20 might be c. from their wickedness
19 17 while the elements are changed in
17 the sound of the quality is changed
Eccu 18 26 the time shall be changed, and all
27 12 but a fool is changed as the moon
Isa 24 5 they have changed the ordinance, they
Jer 2 11 if a nation hath changed their gods
11 my people have c. their glory into
12 10 they changed my delightful portion
48 11 in him, and his scent is not changed
52 33 he changed his prison garments and he
Lam 4 1 dim, the finest color is changed, the
Eze 27 35 have changed their countenance. The
Dan 3 19 his face was changed against Sidrach
95 they changed the king's word and
4 13 let his heart be changed from man's
5 6 was the king's countenance changed
9 and his countenance was changed: and
10 neither let thy countenance be changed
7 28 my countenance was changed. 10:8
Mich 2 4 the portion of my people is changed
Haba 1 11 then shall his spirit be changed
Zach 7 14 they c. the delightful land into a
1 Ma 1 27 the beauty of the women was changed
2 Ma 6 29 were changed to wrath for the words
Rom 1 23 c. the glory of the incorruptible God
25 who c. the truth of God into a lie
26 their women have c. the natural use
1 C 15 51 but we shall not all be changed. In a
52 and we shall be changed. For this
Heb 1 12 thou change them and they shall be c.
changers Mat 21 12 tables of the money c. Mark 11:15
John 2 14 and the changers of money sitting
15 the money of the changers he poured out
changes 4 K 5 5 of gold and ten c. of raiment
4 K 5 22 of silver and two changes of garments
23 two changes of garments, and laid them
Wisd 7 18 courses and the changes of seasons
Isa 3 22 changes of apparel and short cloaks
changeth Job 12 20 he c. the speech of the true
Job 12 24 he changeth the heart of the princes
Eccu 13 31 heart of a man c. his countenance
25 24 the wickedness of a woman c. her face
40 5 sleep of the night c. his knowledge
Dan 2 21 he changeth times and ages: taketh
Amos 5 8 that changeth day into night: that
changing Gen 38 14 c. her dress, sat in the cross
Gen 41 14 shaved him, and changing his apparel
48 14 changing his hands. And Jacob blessed
1 Pa 17 5 I have been always changing places in
Wisd 14 26 defiling of souls, changing of nature
2 Ma 3 16 the changing of his color declared the
Acts 28 6 changing their minds, they said that
channel Josu 3 15 filled the banks of its channel
Josu 3 17 through the channel that was dried up
4 8 carrying out of the c. of the Jordan
9 stones in midst of c. of the Jordan
18 the waters returned into the channel
20 which they had taken out of the c.
22 over this Jordan through the dry c.
4 K 3 16 channel of this torrent full of ditches
17 this c. shall be filled with waters
Eccu 24 41 like a channel of a river and like an
Isa 19 7 channel of the river shall be laid bare
27 12 will strike from the c. of the river
channels Cant 7 5 of the king bound in the c.
Isa 8 7 he shall come up over all his channels

Eze 30 12 will make the c. of the rivers dry
chaos Luke 15 26 there is fixed a great chaos
chapiter 3 K 7 16 height of one chapiter was five cubits. Jer 52:22
3 K 7 16 height of other chapiter was 5 cubits
17 seven rows of nets were on one chapiter
17 and seven nets on the other chapiter
18 in like manner did he to other chapiter
20 rows round about the other chapiter
31 was in the top of the chapiter: and
4 K 25 17 chapiter of brass which was upon it
17 pomegranates that were upon the c.
chapiters 3 K 7 6 and chapiters upon the pillars
3 K 7 16 he made also two c. of molten brass
17 the chapiters of the pillars were cast
18 about each network to cover the c.
19 the chapiters that were upon the top
20 other chapiters in top of the pillars
41 two cords of the c., upon the c. of the
42 to cover the cords of the chapiters
2 Pa 3 15 and their chapiters were five cubits
4 12 the pommels and the c. and the network to cover the chapiters
13 to cover the pommels and the chapiters
Jer 52 22 chapiters of brass were upon both
22 pomegranates were upon the chapiters
Characa 2 Ma 12 17 came to C. to the Jews that
character Apoc 13 16 to have a c. in their right
Apoc 13 17 buy or sell, but he that hath the c.
14 9 receive his character in his forehead
11 whoever receiveth the c. of his name
16 2 the character of the beast. 19:20
20 4 nor received his c. on their foreheads
characters Esth 1 22 in divers languages and c.
Esth 8 9 according to their languages and c.
charadrion Lev 11 19 heron and the charadrion
Deut 14 18 the bittern and the charadrion, every
Charan Gen 36 26 sons of Dison . . . C. 1 Pa 1:41
Tob 11 1 returning, they came to Charan which
Jdth 5 9 from thence, and to dwell in Charan
Acts 7 2 before he [Abraham] dwelt in Charan
4 dwelt in Charan. And from thence
Charcamis 2 Pa 35 20 to fight in C. by the
Isa 10 9 is not Celano as Charamis: and Emath
Jer 46 2 by the river Euphrates in Charcamis
Charcas Esth 1 10 and C., the seven eunuchs
charge Gen 38 23 she cannot charge us with a lie
Exod 6 13 gave them a c. unto the children of
19 21 go down, and charge the people: lest
23 for thou didst charge and command
Num 3 25 their charge shall be in the tabernacle
4 16 to whose charge pertaineth the oil
8 26 order the Levites touching their charge
18 4 watch in the charge of the tabernacle
5 watch ye in the charge of the sanctuary
8 given thee the charge of my firstfruits
Deut 1 12 the charge of you and your differences
22 14 laying to her charge a very ill name
17 layeth to her charge a very ill name
31 14 that I may give him [Josue] a charge
1 K 17 20 gave the charge of the flock to the
2 K 3 8 to c. me with a matter concerning a
14 8 I will give charge concerning thee
18 5 king giving charge to all the princes
3 K 2 3 keep the charge of the Lord thy God
9 23 had charge over the appointed works
4 K 20 1 give charge concerning thy house
1 Pa 9 28 had the charge of the vessels for the
29 and the charge of the fine flour and
23 29 priests have the charge of the loaves
32 the charge of the sons of Aaron their
26 30 charge over Israel beyond the Jordan

28 1 who had the charge over the substance
2 Pa 31 15 and under his charge were Eden and
Esth 2 14 the charge over the king's concubines
Ps 10 6 I will give him a charge against the
13 4 hath given charge to the troops of war
23 11 hath given a charge against Chanaan
45 11 give ye charge to me. I made the earth
Jer 39 11 given charge to Nabuzardan the general
47 7 hath given it a charge against Ascalon
Eze 44 8 you have set keepers of my charge
Zach 1 6 which I gave in charge to my servants
3 7 wilt walk in my ways and keep my charge
1 Ma 3 34 he gave him charge concerning all that
5 58 gave charge to them that were in his
12 45 the army and all that have any charge
14 42 should have the charge of the sanctuary
2 Ma 2 1 gave charge to them that were carried
3 7 who had the charge over his affairs
11 1 had chief charge over all the affairs
13 2 had charge over the affairs of the realm
14 13 giving him in charge to take Judas
Mat 4 6 his angels c. over thee. Luke 4:10
Mark 14 60 the things that are laid to thy charge
Acts 7 59 Lord, lay not this sin to their charge
8 27 who had charge over all her treasures
16 24 having received such a c., thrust them
23 29 nothing laid to his c. worthy of death
25 16 himself of the things laid to his c.
27 not to signify the things laid to his c.
1 C 9 18 I may deliver the gospel without charge
1 Th 5 27 charge you . . . that this epistle be read
2 Th 3 6 we charge you, brethren, in the name of
12 we charge them that are such, and
1 Tim 1 3 mightest c. some not to teach otherwise
5 7 this give in charge, that they may
21 I charge thee before God. 6:13; 2 Tim 4:1
6 17 c. the rich of this world not to be
2 Tim 4 16 may it not be laid to their charge
chargeable 2 K 13 25 all come and be c. to thee
2 Es 5 15 were c. to the people and took of
2 C 11 9 I was chargeable to no man: and that
1 Th 2 9 lest we should be c. to any. 2 Th 3:8
charged Gen 28 1 c. him, saying: Take not a wife
Gen 28 6 after the blessing he had charged him
49 29 he charged them, saying: I am now
Exod 1 22 Pharao therefore charged all the people
Num 5 14 or is charged with false suspicion
Deut 22 20 if what he charged her with be true
Ruth 2 9 I have charged my young men not to
21 he also charged me that I should keep
2 K 11 19 he [Joab] c. the messenger, saying
23 we vigorously c. and pursued them even
18 12 the king charged thee and Abisai and
3 K 2 1 charged his son Solomon, saying: I am
4 K 7 9 we shall be charged with a crime: come
17 35 c. them, saying: You shall not fear
1 Pa 17 6 whom I c. to feed my people, saying
22 17 David also c. all the princes of Israel
2 Pa 19 9 he c. them, saying: Thus shall you do
36 23 c. me to build him a house. 1 Es 1:2
2 Es 13 15 I charged them that they should sell on
21 I charged them and I said to them
Jer 32 13 I charged Baruch before them, saying
Mat 9 30 Jesus strictly charged them, saying
12 16 charged them that they should not make him known. Mark 3:12
17 9 c. them, saying: Tell the vision to no
Mark 1 43 c. him and forthwith sent him away
5 43 he charged them strictly that no man
7 36 he c. them that they should tell no
36 the more he c. them, so much the more
8 15 he c. them, saying: Take heed and
30 c. them that they should not tell any
9 8 he charged them not to tell any man
Luke 5 14 he c. him that he should tell no man
8 56 whom he charged to tell no man what
Acts 4 18 c. them not to speak at all. 5:40
Rom 3 9 we have charged both Jews and Greeks
1 Tim 5 16 let not the church be charged: that
charges 1 Pa 22 5 [David] prepared all the charges
1 Pa 22 14 have prepared the charges of the house
14 stones I have prepared for all the c.
29 19 for which I have provided the charges
2 Pa 8 16 Solomon had all charges prepared, from
1 Es 6 4 c. shall be given out of king's house
8 the charges be diligently given to
Eccu 21 9 buildeth his house at other men's c.
1 Ma 3 30 formerly enough for c. and gifts
10 28 we will remit to you many charges
39 for the necessary c. of the holy things
44 the c. shall be given out of the. 45
2 Ma 3 3 all the c. belonging to the ministry
4 19 but might be deputed for other charges
9 16 the c. pertaining to the sacrifices
Luke 14 28 reckon the charges that are necessary
1 C 9 7 at any time, at his own charges
chargest Gen 31 32 thou chargest me with theft
charging 2 Pa 19 6 and c. the judges, he said
Luke 9 21 he strictly charging them, commanded
Acts 16 23 c. the gaoler to keep them diligently
23 22 c. him that he should tell no man
2 Tim 2 14 charging them before the Lord. Contend
chariot Gen 41 43 him go up into his second c.
Gen 46 29 Joseph made ready his chariot and went
Exod 14 6 [Pharao] made ready his chariot and
Judg 4 15 Sisara leaping down from off his c.
5 28 why is his chariot so long in coming
2 K 8 4 houghed all the c. horses. 1 Pa 18:4
3 K 4 26 had 40,000 stalls of chariot horses
7 33 wheels as are used to be made in a c.
10 29 a c. of four horses came out of Egypt
12 18 made haste to get him up into his c.
18 44 prepare thy chariot and go down, lest
20 33 and he lifted him up into his chariot
22 34 he said to the driver of his chariot
35 king of Israel stood in his c. 2 Pa 18:34
35 out of wound into midst of the chariot
38 washed his c. in the pool of Samaria
4 K 2 11 fiery chariot and fiery horses parted
12 the chariot of Israel and the driver
5 21 he leapt down from his chariot to meet
26 when the man turned back from his c.
9 17 take a chariot and send to meet them
18 went one in a chariot to meet him
19 and he sent a second chariot of horses
21 they made ready his chariot, and Joram
21 went out, each in his chariot, and
24 he fell in his chariot. And Jehu
25 when I and thou sitting in a chariot
27 strike him [Ochozias] also in his c.
28 laid him [Ochozias] upon his chariot
10 15 he lifted him up to him in his chariot
16 so he made him ride in his chariot
13 14 the chariot of Israel and the guider
1 Pa 28 18 to make the likeness of the chariot
2 Pa 1 17 a c. of four horses for 600 pieces
18 made haste to get up into his chariot
18 33 and he said to his chariot man: Turn
35 24 they removed him from the chariot into
Ps 67 18 c. of God is attended by ten thousands
103 3 who makest the clouds thy chariot
Eccu 48 9 in a chariot of fiery horses. Who art
49 10 shown him upon the chariot of cherubims
Isa 21 7 he saw a chariot with two horsemen
9 the rider upon the chariot, with two
22 6 the chariot of the horsemen, and the

18 there shall the chariot of thy glory be
43 17 who brought forth the chariot and the
Jer 51 21 I will break in pieces the chariot
Eze 23 24 well appointed with chariot and wheel
Nah 2 3 the reins of the chariot are flaming
3 2 of the running chariot and of the
Agge 2 23 and I will overthrow the chariot
Zach 6 2 in the first chariot were red horses
2 in the second chariot black horses
3 in the third chariot white horses
3 in the fourth chariot grisled horses
2 Ma 9 4 he commanded his chariot to be driven
7 violence that he fell from the chariot
10 I will destroy the c. out of Ephraim
Acts 8 28 sitting in his chariot and reading
29 go near and join thyself to this c.
38 he commanded the c. to stand still
chariots Gen 50 9 also in his train chariots
Exod 14 7 he took 600 chosen chariots and all the chariots that were in Egypt
9 all Pharao's horse and chariots and
17 in his chariots and in his horsemen. 18
23 his chariots and horsemen through the
25 overthrew the wheels of the chariots
26 upon their c. and horsemen. And when
28 covered the c. and the horsemen of
15 4 Pharao's c. he hath cast into the sea
19 with his c. and horsemen into the sea
Deut 11 4 Egyptians and to their horses and c.
20 1 enemies, and see horsemen and c.
Josu 11 4 their horses also and chariots a very
6 thou shalt burn their chariots with
9 their horses and burned their chariots
17 16 of the valley have chariots of iron
18 who as thou sayest have iron chariots
24 6 pursued your fathers with chariots
Judg 1 19 because they had many chariots armed
4 3 he had 900 chariots set with scythes
7 his chariots and all his multitude
13 gathered together his 900 chariots
15 terror into Sisara and all his chariots
16 Barac pursued after the fleeing c.
5 11 where the chariots were dashed together
1 K 8 11 your sons, and put them in his chariots
11 footmen to run before his chariots
12 and to make him arms and chariots
13 5 to fight against Israel 30,000 chariots
2 K 1 6 the chariots and horsemen drew nigh
8 4 only reserved of them for 100 chariots
10 18 Syrians the men of 700 chariots
12 31 drove over them chariots armed with
15 1 Absalom made himself chariots and
3 K 1 5 he made himself chariots and horsemen
9 19 the cities also of the chariots, and
22 overseers of the chariots and horses
10 26 Solomon gathered together chariots
26 and he had 1,400 chariots and 12,000
20 1 with him, and horses and chariots
21 overthrew the horses and chariots and
25 and chariots according to the chariots
22 31 the 2 and 30 captains of the chariots
32 when captains of the c. saw Josaphat
33 the captains of the chariots. 4 K 8:21
4 K 5 9 Naaman came with his horses and c.
6 14 he sent thither horses and chariots
15 about the city, and horses and chariots
17 mountain was full of horses and c.
7 6 in camp of Syria the noise of chariots
8 21 and all the chariots with him [Joram]
10 2 that have your master's sons and c.
13 7 than fifty horsemen and ten chariots
18 24 dost thou trust in Egypt for chariots
19 23 with multitude of my c. I have gone up
23 11 and he burnt the chariots of the sun
1 Pa 18 4 David took from him 1,000 chariots
4 hundred chariots, which he reserved for
19 6 to hire them chariots and horsemen
7 hired two and thirty thousand chariots
18 slew of the Syrians 7,000 chariots
20 3 and chariots of iron to go over them
2 Pa 1 14 he gathered to himself chariots and
14 and he had 1,400 chariots and 12,000
14 placed them in cities of the c. 9:25
8 6 and all the cities of the chariots
9 rulers of his chariots and horsemen
9 25 in the stables, and 12,000 chariots
12 3 with 1,200 chariots and threescore
14 9 with 300 chariots: and he came as far
16 8 Libyans much more numberous in chariots
Jdth 1 4 army and in the glory of his chariots
2 11 all the army, with the chariots and
4 12 and in his shields and in his chariots
9 6 trusting in their chariots and in
9 trust in their multitude and in their c.
Ps 19 8 some trust in chariots, and some in
Cant 1 8 company of horsemen, in Pharao's c.
6 11 troubled me for the c. of Aminadab
Isa 2 8 and their chariots are innumerable
22 7 thy choice valleys shall be full of c.
31 1 putting their confidence in chariots
36 24 with the multitude of my c. I have gone
66 15 his chariots are like a whirlwind
20 in chariots and in litters and on
Jer 4 13 a cloud, and his chariots as a tempest
17 25 riding in c. and on horses. 22:4
46 9 up on horses, and glory in chariots
47 3 at the rushing of his chariots and the
50 37 upon their horses and upon their c.
Eze 26 7 with horses and c. and horsemen and
10 of the horsemen and wheels and c.
Dan 11 40 like a tempest with chariots and with
Joel 2 5 shall leap like the noise of chariots
Mich 1 13 a tumult of chariots hath astonished
5 10 of thee and will destroy thy chariots
Nah 2 4 the chariots jostle one against another
13 I will burn thy chariots even to smoke
Haba 3 8 horses: and thy chariots even to smoke
Zach 6 1 four chariots came out from the midst
1 Ma 1 18 with c. and elephants and horsemen
8 6 elephants, with horsemen and chariots
2 Ma 13 2 and 300 chariots armed with hooks
Apoc 9 9 wings was as the noise of chariots
18 13 horses and chariots and slaves and
charity Prov 10 12 and charity covereth all sins
Cant 2 4 of wine, he set in order charity in me
8 7 many waters cannot quench charity
Mat 24 12 charity of many shall grow cold
Rom 5 8 God commendeth his charity towards us
12 10 one another with the c. of brotherhood
14 15 thou walkest not now according to c.
15 30 and by the charity of the Holy Ghost
1 C 8 1 knowledge puffeth up; but c. edifieth
13 1 if I . . . have not charity. 2, 3
4 charity is patient . . . c. envieth not
8 charity never falleth away: whether
13 there remaineth faith, hope, and charity
13 but the greatest of these is charity
14 1 follow after charity, be zealous for
16 24 my charity be with you all in Christ
2 C 2 4 the charity I have more abundantly
5 14 the charity of Christ presseth us
Gal 5 6 but faith that worketh by charity
13 by c. of the spirit serve one another
22 fruit of the Spirit is c., joy, peace
Eph 2 4 his exceeding c. wherewith he loved
3 19 to know also the charity of Christ

6 23 peace be to the brethren and c. with
Phil 1 16 out of c. knowing that I am set for
2 1 if there be . . . any comfort of c., if
2 be of one mind, having the same charity
Col 3 14 above all these things have charity
1 Th 4 9 as touching the charity of brotherhood
5 8 having on breastplate of faith and c.
2 Th 1 3 the c. of every one of you towards
1 Tim 1 5 the end of the commandment is charity
6 11 pursue justice, godliness, faith, c.
Philem 5 hearing of thy charity and faith
7 great joy and consolation in thy c.
9 for charity sake I rather beseech
Heb 10 24 to provoke unto c. and to good works
13 1 let the c. of the brotherhood abide
1 P 1 22 purifying your souls in obedience of c.
4 8 have a constant mutual charity among
8 charity covereth a multitude of sins
2 P 1 7 and in love of brotherhood charity
1 J 2 15 the c. of the Father is not in him
3 1 behold what manner of charity the Father
4 7 love one another, for c. is of God
10 in this is c.: not as though we had
12 and his charity is perfected in us
16 c. which God hath to us. God is c.
18 but perfect charity casteth out fear
2 J 6 this is c., that we walk according to
3 J 6 who have given testimony to thy charity
Jude 2 mercy unto you and peace and charity
Apoc 2 4 because thou hast left thy first c.
19 know thy works and thy faith and thy c.
charity of God Luke 11 42 you pass over judgment and the charity of God
Rom 5 5 the c. . . . is poured forth in our hearts
2 C 13 13 c. of God and the communication of
2 Th 3 5 Lord direct your hearts in the c. . . .
1 J 2 5 in very deed the c. . . . is perfected
3 16 in this we have known the c. of God
17 how doth the c. of God abide in him
4 9 by this hath the charity of God appeared
17 is the charity of God perfected. 5:3
in charity 1 C 4 21 shall I come to you with a rod; or in charity
1 C 16 14 let all your things be done in charity
2 C 6 6 in charity unfeigned, in the word of
Eph 1 4 and unspotted in his sight in charity
3 17 being rooted and founded in charity
4 2 supporting one another in charity
15 doing the truth in charity, we may in
16 unto the edifying of itself in charity
Col 2 2 be comforted, being instructed in c.
1 Th 3 12 make you abound in c. towards one
5 13 esteem them more abundantly in charity
1 Tim 4 12 in conversation, in charity, in faith
1 J 4 16 that abideth in charity, abideth in God
18 fear is not in c.; but perfect charity
18 he that feareth is not perfeceted in c.
2 J 3 Son of the Father, in truth and c.
your charity 2 C 2 8 confirm your c. towards
2 C 8 7 in your c. towards us . . . you may abound
8 approving good disposition of your c.
24 the evidence of your c. and of our
Phil 1 9 your c. may more and more abound in
1 Th 1 3 work of your faith and labor and c.
3 6 related to us your faith and charity
charm Jer 8 17 against which there is no charm
charmel Isa 29 17 Libanus shall be turned into c., and c. shall be esteemed as a forest
Isa 32 15 desert shall be as a c., and c. shall be counted for a forest
16 wilderness, and justice shall sit in c.
charmer Deut 18 11 be any wizard, nor charmer
charmers Ps 57 6 will not hear the voice of the c.
charmeth Ps 57 6 nor of the wizard that c. wisely
Charmi Gen 46 9 sons of Ruben . . . Charmi. Exod 6:14; 1 Pa 5:3
Num 26 6 Charmi of whom is the family of the
Josu 7 1 Charmi the son of Zabdi, the son of. 18
1 Pa 2 7 the sons of Charmi: Achar, who troubled
4 1 and Charmi and Hur and Sobal. And
Jdth 6 11 and Charmi, called also Gothoniel
8 9 sent to the ancients Chabri and Charmi
Charmites Num 26 6 of whom is the family of the C.
charms Eccu 9 4 thou perish by force of her charms
Charsena Esth 1 14 nearest him were Charsena and
chase Deut 32 30 how should . . . two c. ten thousand
Josu 23 10 one of you shall chase a thousand men
chased Deut 1 44 meeting you, c. you, as bees do
Josu 11 8 chased them as far as the great Sidon
Judg 9 40 who chased and put him to flight
44 two other companies chased the enemies
Tob 12 3 he chased from her the evil spirit
Eccu 23 30 and he shall be chased as a colt, and
Isa 49 19 thee up shall be chased far away. The
Lam 3 52 my enemies have chased me and caught
Chaselon Num 34 21 Elidad the son of Chaselon
chaseth Prov 19 26 c. away his mother, is infamous
chasing Job 39 24 c. and raging he swalloweth the
Chasluim Gen 10 14 and Chasluim, of whom came
Chasphia 1 Es 8 17 is chief in the place of C.
chaste Wisd 4 1 how beautiful is the c. generation
2 C 11 2 present you as a c. virgin to Christ
1 Tim 3 2 prudent, of good behavior, chaste
8 deacons in like manner chaste, not
11 the women in like manner chaste, not
5 22 other men's sins. Keep thyself chaste
Titus 2 2 that the aged men be sober, chaste
5 to be discreet, chaste, sober, having
James 3 17 is from above, first indeed is chaste
1 P 3 2 considering your chaste conversation
chastise Lev 26 18 I will c. you seven times more
Lev 26 28 I will chastise you with seven plagues
1 K 3 13 wickedly, and did not chastise them
Ps 6 2 nor chastise me in thy wrath. Have
37 2 indignation: nor chastise me in thy
Prov 19 18 chastise thy son, despair not: but to
Jer 30 11 but I will chastise thee in judgment
Osee 10 10 to my desire, I will chastise them
2 Ma 6 16 though he chastise his people with
Luke 23 16 I will chastise him therefore. 22
1 C 9 27 I chastise my body and bring it into
Apoc 3 19 such as I love, I rebuke and chastise
chastised Tob 11 17 because thou hast c. me and
Tob 13 5 he hath chastised us for our iniquities
11 the Lord hath chastised thee for the
Jdth 8 27 with which like servants we are c.
Ps 117 18 the Lord chastising hath chastised me
Prov 3 11 do not faint when thou art c. by him
Wisd 11 10 they were tried and c. with mercy
Jer 31 18 thou hast c. me, and I was instructed
Lam 1 13 fire into my bones, and hath c. me
Osee 7 15 I have c. them and strengthened their
10 10 when they shall be c. for their two
2 Ma 10 4 that they might be chastised by him
1 C 11 32 we are chastised by the Lord, that we
2 C 6 9 we live, as chastised and not killed
chastisement Ps 72 14 my c. hath been in the
Eccu 19 5 that hateth c., shall have less life
Isa 53 5 chastisement of our peace was upon him
Jer 30 14 wound of an enemy, with a cruel c.
1 Ma 2 49 now hath pride and c. gotten strength
2 Ma 7 33 angry with us a little while for our c.
Heb 12 8 if you be without chastisement, whereof
11 all c. for the present indeed seemeth
chastisements Deut 11 2 who saw not the c. of the
Ps 149 7 upon the nations, c. among the people

chastisest Wisd 12 22 whereas thou c. us, thou
chastiseth Ps 93 10 he that c. nations, shall be
Prov 3 12 whom the Lord loveth, he chastiseth
Wisd 12 2 thou chastiseth them that err, by
Eccu 30 1 his son, frequently chastiseth him
Heb 12 6 whom the Lord loveth, he chastiseth
chastising Jdth 7 20 our iniquities by c. us
Jdth 11 5 for chastising of all straying souls
Job 5 17 refuse not therefore the c. of the Lord
Ps 117 18 the Lord chastising hath chastised me
Wisd 1 8 neither shall the c. judgment pass him
9 to the chastising of his iniquities
chastity Exod 21 10 he refuse the price of her c.
Jdth 15 11 because thou hast loved chastity, and
16 26 and chastity was joined to her virtue
Acts 24 25 as he treated of justice and chastity
2 C 6 6 in c. in knowledge, in longsuffering
Gal 5 23 mildness, faith, modesty, continency, c.
1 Tim 2 2 a peaceable life in all piety and c.
3 4 his children in subjection with all c.
4 12 conversation, in charity, in faith, in c.
5 2 young women, as sisters, in all chastity
cheat Col 2 8 lest any man cheat you by philosophy
Chebbon Josu 15 40 Chebbon and Leheman and Cethles
Chebron 1 Ma 5 65 he took Chebron and her towns
check 2 P 2 16 had a check of his madness, the
cheek 3 K 22 24 struck Micheas on the c. 2 Pa 18:23
Job 16 11 they have struck me on the cheek, they
Eccu 35 18 the widow's tears run down the cheek
19 from the c. they go up even to heaven
Lam 3 30 he shall give his cheek to him that
Mich 5 1 shall they strike the cheek of the judge
Joel 1 6 his cheek teeth as of a lion's whelp
Mat 5 39 if one strike thee on thy right cheek
Luke 6 29 to him that striketh thee on the one c.
cheeks Exod 12 22 therewith and both the door c.
Cant 1 9 thy cheeks are beautiful as the
4 3 thy c. are as a piece of a pomegranate
5 13 his cheeks are as beds of aromatical
6 6 cheeks are as the bark of a pomegranate
Isa 50 6 my cheeks to them that plucked them
Lam 1 2 night and her tears are on her cheeks
cheer Judg 16 25 had now taken their good cheer
3 K 21 7 arise and eat bread and be of good c.
Tob 7 20 be of good cheer, my daughter: the
Prov 21 17 he that loveth good cheer, shall be in
Eccu 29 28 than sumptuous cheer abroad in another
Ps 103 15 that wine may cheer the heart of man
Luke 12 19 thy rest; eat, drink, make good cheer
Acts 27 22 I exhort you to be of good cheer. For
25 sirs, be of good cheer; for I believe
36 then were they all of better cheer
cheered 2 Ma 15 27 cheered with the presence of
cheereth Judg 9 13 my wine, that c. God and men
Eccu 36 24 beauty of a woman c. the countenance
cheerful Ps 103 15 may make the face c. with oil
Prov 15 13 a glad heart maketh a c. countenance
Eccu 26 4 his countenance shall be cheerful at
30 27 c. and good heart is always feasting
35 11 in every gift show a c. countenance
Jer 48 33 shall not sing the accustomed c. tune
2 Ma 15 9 before, he made them more cheerful
2 C 9 7 God loveth a cheerful giver. And God
James 5 13 is he cheerful in mind? Let him sing
cheerfully Wisd 6 17 showeth herself to them c.
Eccu 4 8 bow down thy ear c. to the poor, and
2 Ma 10 33 c. laid siege to the fortress four
cheerfulness Prov 16 15 in the c. of the king's
Prov 19 12 and his c. as the dew upon the grass
Bar 3 35 with c. they have shined forth to him
1 Ma 3 2 fought with c. the battle of Israel
Rom 12 8 he that showeth mercy, with c. Let
cheese Jdth 10 5 and dry figs and bread and c.
Job 10 10 as milk, and curdled me like cheese
cheeses 1 K 17 18 carry these ten little cheeses
Cheleab 2 K 3 3 his second Cheleab of Abigail
Cheliau 1 Es 10 35 Baneas and Badaias, C., Vania
Chelion Ruth 1 2 one Mahalon, and the other C.
Ruth 1 5 both died, to wit, Mahalon and Chelion
Chelion's Ruth 4 9 have bought all that was . . . C.
Chelmad Eze 27 23 Saba, Assur, and C. sold to thee
Chelmon Jdth 7 3 Chelmon, which is over against
Chelub 1 Pa 27 26 Ezri the son of Chelub; and over
Chene Eze 27 23 Haran and Chene and Eden were thy
Chereas 2 Ma 10 32 Gazara . . . where C. was governor
2 Ma 10 37 they slew also his brother Chereas and
cherish Ruth 4 15 thy soul, and c. thy old age
3 K 1 2 her stand before the king and c. him
cherished Prov 5 20 art c. in the bosom of another
Isa 34 15 cherished them in the shadow thereof
cherisheth Eph 5 29 but nourisheth and c. it
cherogril Deut 14 7 camel, the hare, and the c.
cherogrillus Lev 11 5 the c. which cheweth the
cherub Exod 25 19 let one cherub be on one side
Exod 37 8 one cherub in the top of one side and
8 other c. in the top of the other side
3 K 6 24 wing of the cherub was five cubits. 24
25 the second cherub also was ten cubits
26 one cherub was ten cubits high, and in like manner the other cherub
27 the wing of the other cherub touched
2 Pa 3 11 reached the wing of the other cherub
12 wing of the other cherub was five cubits
12 touched the wing of the other cherub
Eze 9 3 the glory . . . went up from the cherub
10 4 was lifted up from above the cherub
7 one cherub stretched out his arm from
9 one wheel by one cherub, and another wheel by another cherub
14 one face was the face of a cherub, and
28 14 thou a c. stretched out and protecting
16 and destroyed thee, O covering cherub
41 18 palm tree was between a c. and a c.
18 every cherub had two faces. The face
Cherub 1 Es 2 59 came up from . . . Cherub. 2 Es 7:61
cherubims Gen 3 24 c., and a flaming sword
Exod 25 18 thou shalt make also two cherubims
22 from the midst of the two cherubims
37 7 two c. also of beaten gold, which he
8 two cherubims at the two ends of the
Num 7 89 was over the ark between the two c.
1 K 4 4 the Lord of hosts sitting upon the c.
2 K 6 2 sitteth over it upon the cherubims
22 11 he rode upon the cherubims and flew
3 K 6 23 he made in the oracle two cherubims
25 the work was the same in both the c.
27 he set the c. in the midst of the
27 the c. stretched forth their wings and
28 he overlaid the cherubims with gold
29 made in them cherubims and palm trees
32 and he carved upon them figures of c.
32 he covered both the c. and the palm
35 he carved cherubims and palm trees
7 29 were lions and oxen and cherubims
36 cherubims and lions and palm trees
8 6 under the wings of the cherubims. For
7 the cherubims spread forth their wings
4 K 19 15 sitteth upon the cherubims. Ps 98:1
1 Pa 13 6 Lord God sitting upon the cherubims
28 18 the likeness of the chariot of the c.
2 Pa 3 7 and he graved cherubims on the walls
10 holy of holies two c. of image work
11 wings of the cherubims were extended
13 wings of the two cherubims were spread
14 a veil . . . and wrought in it cherubims
5 7 ark . . . under the wings of the cherubims

8 so that the c. spread their wings
Ps 17 11 he ascended upon the cherubims, and he
79 2 sittest upon the c. Isa 37:16; Dan 3:55
Eccu 49 10 was shown him upon the chariot of c.
Eze 10 1 that was over the heads of the c.
2 the wheels that are under the cherubims
2 coals of fire that are between the c.
3 the cherubims stood on the right side
5 the sound of the wings of the cherubims
6 the wheels that are between the c.
7 from the midst of the c. to the fire that was between the c.
8 there appeared in the c. the likeness
9 there were four wheels by the cherubims
15 and the cherubims were lifted up: this
16 when the c. went, the wheels also went
16 the c. lifted up their wings. 11:22
18 temple: and stood over the cherubims
19 the cherubims lifting up their wings
20 I understood that they were cherubims
41 18 were c. and palm trees wrought. 20
25 cherubims also wrought in the doors
Heb 9 5 over it were the cherubims of glory
Cheslon Josu 15 10 to the north into Cheslon
chest 4 K 12 9 Joiada the high priest took a chest
4 K 12 10 there was very much money in the chest
2 Pa 24 8 made a chest; and set it by the gate
10 cast so much into the chest of the Lord
11 when it was time to bring the chest
11 poured out the money that was in the c.
11 they carried back the c. to its place
1 Es 6 8 the king's chest, that is, of the tribute
7 21 to all the keepers of the public chest
chew Deut 14 7 chew the cud but divide not the
cheweth Lev 11 3 hoof divided and cheweth the cud
Lev 11 4 whatsoever cheweth indeed the cud and
5 cheweth the cud, but divideth not the
6 hare also: for that too cheweth the cud
7 the swine . . . c. not the cud. Deut 14:8
26 divideth it not, nor cheweth the cud
Deut 14 6 in two parts cheweth the cud you shall
chickens Mat 23 37 as the hen doth gather her c.
chid Judg 8 1 they chid him [Gedeon] sharply
2 Es 13 25 I chid them and laid my curse upon them
chide Exod 17 2 why chide you with me? Wherefore do
Judg 21 22 to complain against you and to chide
chiding Gen 31 36 angry said in a chiding manner
Exod 17 7 Temptation, because of the chiding
Chidon 1 Pa 13 9 they came to the floor of Chidon
chief Gen 39 21 in the sight of the chief keeper
Gen 40 2 was chief butler, the other chief baker
9 the chief butler first told his dream
16 the chief baker seeing that he had
20 remembered c. butler and the c. baker
23 chief butler, when things prospered
41 9 the chief butler remembering, said
10 me and the chief baker to be cast into
Num 31 14 being angry with the chief officers
1 K 22 9 the chief among the servants of Saul
2 K 19 13 if thou be not the chief captain of the
23 8 was the wisest chief among the three
18 was chief among three: and he lifted
19 noblest of three, and was their chief
3 K 4 13 was chief in all the country of Argob
14 the son of Addo was chief in Manaim
9 23 there were 550 chief officers set over
11 28 made him chief over the tributes of all
21 9 Naboth sit among c. of the people. 12
1 Pa 5 12 Johel the chief, and Saphan the second
15 the son of Guni, chief of the house
9 33 these are the chief of the singing men
11 6 shall be the head and chief captain
10 these are the chief of the valiant men
11 chief among the thirty: he lifted up
20 was chief of three, and he lifted up
12 3 the chief was Ahiezer, and Joas, the
9 Ezer the chief, Obdias the second, Eliab
18 upon Amasai the chief among thirty
15 5 children of Caath, Uriel was the chief
6 of the sons of Merari, Asaia the chief
7 of the sons of Gersom, Joel the chief
8 of the sons of Elisaphan, Semeias the c.
9 of the sons of Oziel, Aminadab the c.
22 and Chonenias chief of the Levites
16 5 Asaph the chief, and next after him
7 made Asaph the chief to give praise
18 17 sons of David were chief about the king
23 8 sons of Leedan: the chief Jahiel and
24 21 of the sons of Rohobia the c. Jesias
25 1 David and the chief officers of the army
26 10 of the sons of Merari: Semri the chief
10 and therefore his father made him chief
24 was chief over the treasures. His
31 the chief of the Hebronites was Jeria
27 1 under every c. were 4 and 20 thousand
2 Jesboam the son of Zabdiel was chief
3 chief of all the captains in the host
2 Pa 8 9 they were men of war and chief captains
10 chief captains of king Solomon's army
11 22 the chief ruler over all his brethren
17 14 captains of the army, Ednas the chief
19 11 shall be chief in the things which
24 6 and the king called Joiada the chief
36 14 chief of the priests and the people
1 Es 1 5 then rose up the chief of the fathers
2 68 some of the chief of the fathers, when
4 2 to Zorobabel and the c. of the fathers
5 10 the men that are the chief among them
8 17 who is chief in the place of Chasphia
24 I separated 12 of the c. of the priests
29 by weight before the c. of the priests
2 Es 12 7 these were the chief of the priests
24 the chief of the Levites were Hasebia
45 there were chief singers appointed to
Esth 3 3 that were chief at the doors of palace
13 6 who is chief over all the provinces
Cant 4 14 and aloes, with all the chief perfumes
Eccu 10 24 midst of brethren their c. is honorable
24 10 I have had the chief rule: and by my
29 27 the chief thing for man's life is water
Jer 20 1 appointed chief in the house of the Lord
37 14 he [Jonathan] was chief over the prison
49 35 bow of Elam and their chief strength
51 59 Saraias was chief over the prophecy
52 25 that was chief over the men of war
Eze 20 40 firstfruits and the chief of your tithes
27 25 sea, were thy chief in thy merchandise
27 goods, and were chief over thy people
38 2 the chief prince of Mosoch and Thubal
3 Gog, the chief prince of Mosoch. 39:1
Dan 2 48 chief of the magistrates over all the
Zach 4 7 he shall bring out the chief stone
1 Ma 1 30 the king sent the chief collector of
3 37 Antioch the chief city of his kingdom
7 21 could to maintain his chief priesthood
10 47 had been the chief promoter of peace
65 him among his chief friends, and made
11 27 he made him the chief of his friends
70 son of Calphi, c. captain of the army
13 37 write to the king's chief officers to
14 42 and that he should be chief over them
47 of the priests, and to be chief over
2 Ma 11 1 had chief charge over all the affairs
Luke 14 1 of one of the chief of the Pharisees

19 2 Zacheus who was c. of the publicans
20 46 the chief rooms at feasts: who devour
John 2 8 carry to the chief steward of the feast
9 when the chief steward had tasted the
9 chief steward calleth the bridegroom
Acts 14 11 because he [Paul] was the chief speaker
16 12 the chief city of part of Macedonia
28 7 possessions of the chief man of the
17 called together the chief of the Jews
Eph 2 20 Jesus Christ being the c. corner stone
1 Tim 1 15 to save sinners, of whom I am the chief
1 P 2 6 I lay in Sion a chief corner stone
chief men 3 K 21 8 c. men that were in his city
4 K 10 1 to Samaria to the chief men of the city
6 brought up with the c. men of the city
11 and all his chief men and his friends
1 Pa 28 1 David assembled all the chief men of
1 Es 7 28 out of Israel chief men to go up with
8 16 Zacharias and Mosollam, chief men
2 Es 4 14 and I said to the chief men and the
Mark 6 21 and tribunes chief men of Galilee
John 12 42 many of the chief men also believed in
Acts 13 50 women and the chief men of the city
15 22 and Silas, c. men among the brethren
chief priest 4 K 25 18 took Seraias the c. p.
Jer 52 24 general took Saraias the chief priest
2 Ma 14 3 Alcimus, who had been chief priest
Acts 19 14 sons of Sceva, a Jew, a chief priest
26 12 authority and permission of the c. p.
chief priests Mat 26 14 then went one of the twelve . . . to the chief priests
Mat 26 59 c. p. and the whole council sought
27 6 c. p. having taken the pieces of silver
28 11 told the c. p. all things that had been
Mark 14 10 went to the chief priests to betray
55 the c. p. and all the council sought
15 3 the c. p. accused him in many things
10 c. p. had delivered him up out of envy
11 c. p. moved the people that he should
Luke 23 4 Pilate said to the c. p. and to the
24 20 how our c. p. and princes delivered him
John 12 10 the c. p. thought to kill Lazarus also
18 35 the c. p. have delivered thee up to me
19 6 when the c. p. and servants had seen
15 c. p. answered: We have no king but
21 c. p. of the Jews said to Pilate: Write
Acts 5 24 and the c. p. heard these words, they
9 14 he hath authority from the c. priests
21 might carry them bound to the c. p.
25 2 c. p. and principal men of the Jews
26 10 having received authority of the c. p.
chief priests and ancients Mat 21 23 c. . . . saying: By what authority dost thou
Mat 26 3 then were gathered together the c. . . .
47 swords and clubs, sent from the c. . . .
27 1 the c. . . . took counsel against Jesus
3 the 30 pieces of silver to the c. . . .
12 when he was accused by the c. . . . , he
20 the c. . . . persuaded the people, that
Luke 22 52 Jesus said to c. p. . . . and ancients
Acts 4 23 all that the c. . . . had said to them
23 14 came to c. . . . and said: We have bound
25 15 the c. . . . of the Jews came unto me
chief priests and magistrates Luke 22 4 went and discoursed with the c. . . . , how
Luke 22 52 Jesus said to the c. . . . Are ye come
23 13 Pilate calling together the c. . . .
chief priests and Pharisees Mat 21 45 when the c. . . . had heard his parables
Mat 27 62 c. . . . came together to Pilate, saying
John 7 45 ministers therefore came to the c. . . .
11 47 the c. . . . gathered a council and said
56 c. . . . had given a commandment that if
18 3 of soldiers and servants from c. . . .
chief priests and scribes Mat 2 4 assembling together all the c. . . . of the people
Mat 20 18 be betrayed to the c. . . . Mark 10:33
21 15 the c. . . . were moved with indignation
Mark 11 18 when c. . . . had heard, they sought how
14 1 c. . . . sought how they might. Luke 22:2
15 31 c. p. mocking said with the scribes
Luke 19 47 c. . . . and the rulers of the people
20 19 c. . . . sought to lay hands on him the
23 10 c. . . . stood by, earnestly accusing him
chief priests and scribes and ancients Mat 16 21 many things from the a. and s. and c. p.
Mat 27 41 c. p. with the s. and ancients mocking
Mark 10 33 of man shall be betrayed to the c. . . .
11 27 there come to him the c. . . . , and they
14 43 swords and staves from the c. . . .
15 1 c. p. holding a consultation with the ancients and the scribes
Luke 9 22 rejected by the a. and c. p. and s.
20 1 c. p. and the s. with the a. met
22 66 ancients and c. p. and scribes came
chiefest 1 K 21 7 Doeg . . . c. of Saul's herdsmen
Prov 3 14 fruit than the c. and purest gold
Eccu 11 3 her fruit hath the chiefest sweetness
chiefs Gen 17 20 he shall beget twelve chiefs
Num 1 16 and the c. of the army of Israel
21 18 dug, and the c. of the people prepared
24 17 and shall strike the chiefs of Moab
Josu 10 24 [Josue] said to the chiefs of the army
Judg 20 2 chiefs of the people and all the tribes
1 Pa 5 24 and famous chiefs in their families
7 2 chiefs of the houses of their kindreds
7 and Urai, five chiefs of their families
12 23 chiefs of the army who came to David
15 16 David spoke to the c. of the Levites
26 12 the c. of the wards as well as their
32 stronger age, 2,700 c. of families
27 16 chiefs over the tribes of Israel were
2 Pa 19 8 c. of the families of Israel. 23:2
23 14 to the captains and the c. of the army
20 valiant men and the c. of the people
26 12 and the whole number of the chiefs
1 Es 3 12 the c. of the fathers and the ancients
4 3 chiefs of the fathers of Israel said to
8 1 these are the chiefs of families and
10 5 made the chiefs of the priests and of
2 Es 8 13 c. of the families of all the people
11 13 his brethren the chiefs of the fathers
12 22 the Levites the chiefs of the families
Jdth 14 11 were come, and all the c. of the army
17 the chiefs of the army of the Assyrians
Mich 3 1 hear ye chiefs of the house of Israel
child Gen 17 12 every man c. in your generations
Gen 18 13 shall I who am an old woman bear a c.
21 8 and the child grew and was weaned: and
Exod 1 16 if it be a man child, kill it: if a
2 2 and seeing him a goodly child, hid him
9 take this child and nurse him for me
9 the woman took and nursed the child
Lev 12 2 shall bear a man child, she shall be
5 if she shall bear a maid child, she
7 that beareth a man c. or a maid c.
Deut 32 25 sucking child with the man in years
Judg 13 7 the child shall be a Nazarite of God
8 concerning the c. that shall be born
12 what wilt thou that the c. should do
24 the c. grew and the Lord blessed him
Ruth 4 16 Noemi taking the child laid it in her
1 K 1 11 wilt give to thy servant a man child
22 I will not go till the child be weaned

24 the child was as yet very young: and
25 and offered the child to Heli. And Anna
27 for this child did I pray, and the Lord
2 11 the child ministered in sight of the
18 being a c. girded with a linen ephod
21 the c. Samuel became great before the
26 the child Samuel advanced and grew
3 1 child Samuel ministered to the Lord
9 understood that the Lord called the c.
4 21 she called the child Ichabod, saying
13 1 Saul was a child of one year when he
15 3 slay both man and woman, child and
2 K 6 23 Michol the daughter of Saul had no c.
12 5 that hath done this is a child of death
14 child that is born to thee shall surely
15 the Lord also struck the child which
16 David besought the Lord for the child
18 on the seventh day that the child died
18 feared to tell him that the c. was dead
18 when the child was yet alive, we spoke
18 if we tell him that the child is dead
19 he understood that the child was dead
19 said to his servants: Is the child dead
21 thou didst fast and weep for the child
21 when the c. was dead, thou didst rise
22 while the child was yet alive, I fasted
22 and the child may live? But now that
3 K 3 7 I am but a child and know not how to
17 I was delivered of a child with her in
19 this woman's child died in the night
20 she took my child from my side while
20 and laid her dead child in my bosom
21 in the morning to give my child suck
22 thy child is dead, and mine is alive
22 my child liveth, and thy child is dead
23 my child is alive and thy child is dead
23 thy child is dead, and mine liveth
25 divide, said he, the living child in
26 the woman whose child was alive, said
26 her bowels were moved upon her child
26 give her the child alive, and do not
27 give the living child to this woman
13 2 c. shall be born to the house of David
14 3 tell thee what shall become of this c.
12 the child shall die, and all Israel
17 threshold of the house, the child died
17 21 measured himself upon the child three
21 let the soul of this child, I beseech
22 the soul of the child returned into him
23 Elias took the child and brought him
4 K 4 18 the child grew. And on a certain
29 lay my staff upon the face of the child
31 laid the staff upon the face of the c.
30 mother of the child said: As the Lord
31 told him, saying: The child is not risen
32 behold the child lay dead on his bed
33 shut door upon him and upon the child
34 he went up and lay upon the child
35 the child gaped seven times and opened
Tob 4 21 while thou wast yet a child, to Gabelus
6 15 I am the only child of my parents
Job 3 3 a man child is conceived. Let that day
Ps 130 2 as a child that is weaned is towards
Prov 20 11 by his inclinations a child is known
22 15 folly is bound up in heart of a child
23 13 withhold not correction from a child
29 15 the child that is left to his own will
Ecce 4 8 he hath not a second, no child, no
13 better is a child that is poor and wise
10 16 to thee, O land, when thy king is a c.
Wisd 8 19 I was a witty child and had received
18 5 one child being cast forth and saved
Eccu 19 11 groaning in the bringing forth a child
30 8 a child left to himself will become
12 beat his sides while he is a child
Isa 3 5 the child shall make a tumult against
7 16 before the child know to refuse the evil
8 4 before the child know to call his father
9 6 a child is born to us, and a son is
10 19 and a child shall write them down. And
11 8 the sucking child shall play on the
8 the weaned child shall thrust his hand
65 20 the child shall die a hundred years old
66 7 she brought forth a man child. Who
Jer 1 6 I cannot speak, for I am a child. And
7 Lord said to me: Say not: I am a child
4 31 as of a woman in labor of a child
6 11 pour it out upon the child abroad
20 15 saying: A man child is born to thee
31 20 surely he is a tender child: for since
44 7 should die of you man and woman, child
51 22 in pieces the old man and the child
Lam 2 21 the child and the old man lie without
4 4 tongue of the sucking child hath stuck
Osee 11 1 Israel was a child, and I loved him
2 Ma 6 23 good life and conversation from a child
15 12 from a child was exercised in virtues
Mat 2 8 and diligently inquire after the child
9 and stood over where the child was
11 they found the child with Mary his
13 take the child and his mother. 20
13 Herod will seek the child to destroy
14 took the child and his mother. 21
20 are dead that sought the life of the c.
17 17 the child was cured from that hour
23 15 you make him the child of hell twofold
Mark 9 35 taking a child, he set him. Luke 9:47
36 whosoever shall receive one such child
Luke 1 59 they came to circumcise the child, and
66 what an one, think ye, shall this c. be
76 thou, child, shalt be called the prophet
80 the child grew and was strengthened
2 17 spoken to them concerning this child
21 that the child should be circumcised
27 his parents brought in the child Jesus
34 this child is set for the fall and
40 the child grew and waxed strong, full
43 the child Jesus remained in Jerusalem
9 48 shall receive this child in my name
18 17 not receive the kingdom of God as a c.
John 16 21 when she hath brought forth the child
Acts 4 27 against thy holy child Jesus, whom
7 5 when as yet he [Abraham] had no child
13 10 [Elymas] child of the devil, enemy of
1 C 13 11 when I was a c., I spoke as a child
11 I understood as a c., I thought as a c.
11 man, I put away the things of a child
Gal 4 1 as long as the heir is a child, he
Apoc 12 5 she brought forth a man child who was
13 woman who brought forth the man child

little child 4 K 5 14 like the flesh of a l. c.
Isa 11 6 and a little child shall lead them
Mat 18 2 calling unto him a l. c., set him
4 shall humble himself as this little c.
5 that shall receive one such little c.
Mark 10 15 not receive kingdom of God as a l. c.
Heb 5 13 for he is a little c. But strong meat

with child Gen 16 4 perceiving that she was w. c.
Gen 16 11 behold, said he, thou art with child
19 36 daughters of Lot were with c. by their
38 25 these things belong, I am with child
Exod 21 22 and one strike a woman with child
1 K 4 19 the wife of Phinees was big with child
4 K 15 16 the women thereof that were with child
Ecce 11 5 in the womb of her that is with child
Eccu 42 10 be found with child in her father's

Isa 26 17 as a woman with child, when she draweth
54 1 thou that didst not travail with child
Jer 31 8 the woman with child and she that is
Osee 14 1 let the women with child be ripped up
Amos 1 13 he hath ripped up the women with child
Mat 1 18 she was found with child of the Holy
23 behold a virgin shall be with child
24 19 woe to them that are with child. Mark 13:17; Luke 21:23
Luke 2 5 his espoused wife, who was with child
1 Th 5 3 as the pains upon her that is with c.
Apoc 12 2 being with child, she cried travailing
childbearing Bar 6 28 c. and menstruous women touch
1 Tim 2 15 shall be saved through childbearing
childhood Prov 29 21 servant delicately from his c.
Eccu 7 25 bow down their neck from their childhood
childishness Prov 1 22 how long will you love c.
Prov 9 6 forsake childishness and live, and
childless 1 K 15 33 thy sword hath made women c.
1 K 15 33 so shall thy mother be c. among women
Luke 20 30 to wife, and he also died childless
children Mat 2 16 killed all the men c. that
Mat 3 9 to raise up c., to Abraham. Luke 3:8
5 45 may be the children of your Father who
8 12 the c. of the kingdom shall be cast out
9 15 can the children of the bridegroom mourn
10 21 the children shall rise up against their parents. Mark 13:12
11 16 like to c. sitting in market. Luke 7:32
13 38 the good seed are the c. of the kingdom
38 the cockle are the c. of the wicked one
14 21 besides women and children. 15:38
15 26 to take the bread of the c. Mark 7:27
17 25 Jesus said to him: Then the c. are free
19 29 that have left . . . children. Mark 10:29; Luke 18:29
21 15 the children crying in the temple and
23 37 would I have gathered together thy children. Luke 13:34
Mark 2 19 can the children of the marriage fast
7 27 suffer first the children to be filled
28 under the table of the crumbs of the c.
10 13 and they brought to him young children
24 children, how hard it is for them that
30 and mothers and children and lands
12 19 and leave no chlidren. Luke 20:28
Luke 1 17 turn the hearts of fathers unto the c.
5 34 can you make the c. of bridegroom fast
16 8 the children of this world are wiser
18 16 suffer children to come to me, and
20 29 took a wife and died without children
31 all the seven, and they left no children
34 the children of this world marry and
36 being the children of the resurrection
John 8 37 that you are the children of Abraham
39 if you be the c. of Abraham, do the
21 5 children, have you any meat? They
Acts 3 25 you are the children of the prophets
13 26 children of the stock of Abraham
Rom 9 4 belongeth the adoption as of children
7 that are the seed of Abraham, children
8 not they that are the c. of the flesh
8 they that are the c. of the promise
11 when the children were not yet born
1 C 14 20 do not become children in sense; but in malice be children
2 C 12 14 neither ought the c. to lay up for the parents, but parents for the children
Gal 3 7 the same are the children of Abraham
4 3 when we were children, were serving
27 many are the children of the desolate
28 are the children of promise. But as
31 we are not the c. of the bondwoman
Eph 1 5 us unto the adoption of children
2 2 that now worketh on the c. of unbelief
3 we were by nature children of wrath
4 14 that henceforth we be no more children
5 1 be ye followers of God, as most dear c.
6 anger of God upon c. of unbelief. Col 3:6
6 1 children, obey your parents. Col 3:20
1 Th 5 5 you are c. of light and c. of the day
1 Tim 5 4 if any widow have c. or grandchildren
10 if she have brought up children, if
14 the younger should marry, bear children
Titus 1 6 husband of one wife, having faithful c.
Heb 2 10 had brought many children into glory
14 the c. are partakers of flesh and blood
10 39 we are not children of withdrawing
12 5 which speaketh to you as unto children
1 P 1 14 as c. of obedience, not fashioned
2 P 2 14 c. of malediction: leaving the right way
1 J 3 10 are manifest and the c. of the devil
2 J 13 the c. of my sister Elect salute thee
children of God Ps 28 1 to the Lord, O ye c. . . .
Wisd 5 5 are numbered among the children of God
12 7 a worthy colony of the children of God
Mat 5 9 shall be called the children of God
Luke 20 36 equal to the angels and are c. of God
John 11 52 to gather together in one the c. of God
Rom 8 21 of the glory of the children of God
9 8 are the c. . . . ; but they that are the
Gal 3 26 you are all the c. . . . by faith in
Phil 2 15 may be blameless and sincere c. of God
1 J 3 10 in this the c. of God are manifest
5 2 we know that we love the c. of God
his children Mat 18 25 should be sold and his wife and c.
Luke 14 26 and hate not . . . his wife and children
John 4 12 drank thereof himself and his children
1 Th 2 11 comforting you as a father doth his c.
1 Tim 3 4 having his children in subjection with
little children Jdth 4 8 caused the l. c. to lie prostrate
Esth 3 13 little children and women, in one day
Lam 2 19 to him for the life of thy little c.
Mat 18 3 you be converted and become as l. c.
19 13 then were little children presented to
14 suffer the little children. Mark 10:14
John 13 33 little c., yet a little while I am with
Gal 4 19 my little c., of whom I am in labor
1 J 2 1 my little c., these things I write to
12 I write to you, little children
18 little children, it is the last hour
28 little children, abide in him, that
3 7 little c., let no man deceive you
18 my little c., let us not love in word
4 4 you are of God, little children, and
5 21 little c., keep yourselves from idols
my children Luke 11 7 my c. are with me in bed
1 C 4 14 I admonish you as my dearest children
2 C 6 13 I speak as to my children, be you also
Heb 2 13 I and my c. whom God hath given me
3 J 4 this, to hear that my c. walk in truth
our children Jdth 3 5 and o. c. are thy servants
1 Ma 3 20 to destroy us and our wives and our c.
13 6 the sanctuary and our c. and wives
Mat 27 25 his blood be upon us and upon our c.
Acts 13 33 this same God hath fulfilled to our c.
their children Mat 17 24 receive of their own c. or of
Acts 7 19 that they should expose their children
21 5 us on our way, with their wives and c.
21 they ought not to circumcise their c.
1 Tim 3 12 of one wife: who rule well their c.
Titus 2 4 love their husbands, to love their c.
your children Mat 7 11 to give good gifts to your c. Luke 11:13
Mat 12 27 by whom do y. c. cast them. Luke 11:19
Luke 23 28 weep for yourselves and for your c.

Acts 2 39 the promise is to you and to your c.
1 C 7 14 otherwise your c. should be unclean
Eph 5 4 provoke not your children to anger
Col 3 21 provoke not your c. to indignation
children's Josu 14 9 be thy possession and thy c.
Tob 9 11 your c. children, unto the third and
14 14 his wife and children and c. children
15 and he saw his children's children
Job 21 8 multitude of kinsmen and of c. children
Ps 102 17 his justice unto children's children
127 6 mayst thou see thy children's children
Prov 17 6 c. children are the crown of old men
Eze 37 25 and their children's children forever
child's Exod 2 7 the child's sister said to her
4 K 4 34 and the child's flesh grew warm. Then
chimney Exod 9 8 handfuls of ashes out of the c.
Exod 9 10 they took ashes out of the chimney and
Eccu 22 30 as the vapor of a chimney and the smoke
Osee 13 3 and as the smoke out of the chimney
chin 2 K 20 9 [Joab] took Amasa by the chin with
Chios Acts 20 15 we came over against Chios; and
chips Wisd 13 12 c. of his work to dress his meat
Chloe 1 C 1 11 by them that are of the house of C.
Chobar Eze 1 1 by the river C., the heavens
Eze 1 3 land of the Chaldeans by the river C.
3 15 to them that dwelt by the river Chobar
23 which I saw by the river Chobar. 10:20
10 15 that I had seen by the river C. 22; 45:3
chodchod Eze 27 16 silk and c. in thy market
chode Exod 17 2 they chode with Moses, and said
Chodorlahomor Gen 14 1 C. king of the Elamites. 9
Gen 14 4 for they had served C. twelve years
5 in the fourteenth year came C. and the
17 he returned from the slaughter of C.
choice Josu 24 15 serve the Lord, you have your c.
1 K 9 2 name was Saul, a choice and goodly man
2 K 10 9 chose of all the choice men of Israel
24 12 I give thee thy choice of three things
4 K 3 19 every fenced city and every choice city
19 23 cedars and its c. fir trees. Isa 37:24
1 Pa 7 40 choice and most valiant captains of
21 10 I give thee the choice of three things
2 Es 5 18 one ox and six choice rams besides
Prov 8 19 and my blossoms than choice silver
10 20 tongue of the just is as choice silver
Cant 5 13 lips are as lilies dropping c. myrrh
Isa 22 7 thy choice valleys shall be full of
Jer 48 15 her choice young men are gone down
Eze 24 4 choice pieces and full of bones. Take
31 16 the choice and best in Libanus, all that
Amos 5 11 and took the choice prey from him
Acts 15 7 God made choice among us that by my
choicest Exod 29 28 because they are the choicest
Num 18 29 shall be the best and choicest things
32 by reserving the c. and fat things
Deut 12 11 whatsoever is the choicest in the gifts
1 K 15 12 out of the c. of the spoils which he
Ps 140 4 I will not communicate with the c. of
Cant 5 5 my fingers were full of the c. myrrh
Isa 5 2 planted it with the choicest vines
2 Ma 4 12 all the choicest youths in brothel
choir 2 Es 12 37 second c. of them that gave thanks
Ps 149 3 let them praise his name in choir: let
150 4 praise him with timbrel and choir
Lam 5 14 young men from the c. of the singers
choirs 2 K 6 12 there were with David seven choirs
2 Es 12 31 I appointed two great choirs to give
39 the two c. of them that gave praise
choke Mark 4 19 c. the word, and it is made
choked Judg 5 11 army of the enemies was choked
Mat 13 7 thorns grew up and choked. Mark 4:7
Luke 8 7 the thorns growing up with it, c. it
14 are choked with the cares and riches
choketh Mat 13 22 c. up the word and he becometh
choler Eccu 31 23 watching and c. and gripes
Eccu 37 33 and greediness will turn to choler
Cholhoza 2 Es 3 15 Sellum the son of Cholhoza
2 Es 11 5 Baruch the son of Cholhoza, the son of
Chonenias 1 Pa 15 22 and C. chief of the Levites
1 Pa 15 27 Chonenias the ruler of the prophecy
26 29 Chonenias and his sons were over the
2 Pa 31 12 the overseer of them was Chonenias
13 overseers under the hand of Chonenias
35 9 C. and Semeias and Nathanael his
choose Gen 13 9 if thou choose the right hand, I
Gen 27 46 stock of this land, I choose not to
Exod 17 9 choose out men, and go out and fight
Num 16 5 whom he shall c., they shall approach
7 whomsoever he shall choose, the same
17 5 whomsoever of these I shall c., his rod
Deut 12 5 place which Lord your God shall c. 11
14 place which the Lord shall choose. 26;
14:25; 15:20; 16:15; 17:10; 18:6; 31:11
18 place which the Lord thy God shall c. 21;
14:24; 16:2, 7, 11; 17:8; 26:2
14 23 the place which he shall choose. 16:16
17 15 whom the Lord thy God shall choose
30 19 choose therefore life, that both thou
Josu 4 2 choose 12 men, one of every tribe: and
18 4 choose of every tribe three men, that
24 15 choose this day that which pleaseth you
1 K 17 8 choose out a man of you, and let him
2 K 17 1 I will choose me 12,000 men and I will
24 12 choose one of them which thou wilt
3 K 18 23 let them c. one bullock for themselves
25 choose you one bullock and dress it
4 K 10 3 choose the best, and him that shall
1 Pa 21 10 choose one which thou wilt and I will do
28 4 it pleased him to c. me king over all
Job 34 4 let us choose to us judgment, and let
Prov 8 10 choose knowledge rather than gold. For
Eccu 15 18 which he shall c. shall be given him
25 18 a man will choose any plague but the
Isa 7 15 refuse the evil and to c. the good. 16
14 1 and will yet choose out of Israel and
56 4 and shall choose the things that please
66 4 I also will choose their mockeries
Jer 40 4 is before thee, as thou shalt choose
Zach 1 17 Sion, and he will yet choose Jerusalem
2 12 land, and he shall yet choose Jerusalem
1 Ma 5 17 choose thee men and go and deliver thy
10 32 such men as he shall choose to keep it
12 45 choose thee a few men that may be with
2 Ma 1 25 who didst choose the fathers and didst
5 19 God did not choose the people for the
Acts 15 22 to c. men of their own company and to
25 to choose out men and to send them
Phil 1 22 what I shall choose I know not. But I
chooser Wisd 8 4 and is the chooser of his works
chooseth Job 7 15 my soul rather chooseth hanging
Eccu 4 18 and at the first she chooseth him
choosing Exod 18 25 c. able men out of all Israel
2 Ma 6 19 c. rather to meet a most glorious death
14 42 choosing to die nobly rather than to
Acts 15 40 Paul choosing Silas, departed, being
Heb 11 25 rather choosing to be afflicted with
chop Dan 4 11 and chop off the branches thereof
2 Ma 7 4 to chop off also the extremities of
chopped Mich 3 3 have broken and c. their bones
Chorreans Gen 14 6 and the C. in the mountains
chose Gen 6 2 wives of all which they chose. And
Gen 13 11 Lot chose to himself the country about
Deut 4 37 and chose their seed after them. 10:15
14 2 he chose thee to be his peculiar people
Judg 5 8 the Lord chose new wars, and he
1 K 2 28 I chose him out of all the tribes of

13 2 Saul chose him 3,000 men of Israel
17 40 and chose him five smooth stones out
2 K 6 21 who chose me rather than thy father
10 9 chose of all the choice men of Israel
3 K 5 13 king Solomon chose workmen out of all
8 16 but I chose David to be over my people
11 34 David my servant's sake, whom I chose
14 21 city which the Lord chose out of all
4 K 23 27 this city Jerusalem, which I chose
1 Pa 19 10 chose out the bravest men of all Israel
28 4 but the Lord God of Israel chose me
4 for of Juda he chose the princes: and
2 Pa 6 5 I chose no city among all the tribes of
5 neither c. I any other man to be ruler
6 I chose Jerusalem that my name might
6 I chose David to set him over my people
12 13 Jerusalem, the city which the Lord c.
Ps 77 67 and chose not the tribe of Ephraim
68 but he chose the tribe of Juda, mount
70 he chose his servant David and took him
Wisd 7 10 and chose to have her instead of light
Eccu 45 4 chose him [Moses] out of all flesh
20 he chose him out of all men living
Bar 3 27 the Lord chose not them, neither did
Eze 20 5 in the day when I chose Israel and
Zach 3 2 the Lord that c. Jerusalem rebuke thee
1 Ma 1 65 they chose rather to die than to be
3 38 then Lysias chose Ptolemee the son of
4 35 he went to Antioch and chose soldiers
42 he chose priests without blemish, whose
7 8 the king chose Bacchides, one of his
8 17 Judas chose Eupolemus the son of John
9 25 Bacchides chose the wicked men and
10 74 he chose 10,000 men and went out of
11 23 he chose some of the ancients of Israel
12 1 he chose certain men and sent them
10 chose rather to send to you to renew
13 34 and Simon chose men and sent to king
16 4 he chose out of the country 20,000
2 Ma 14 15 who chose his people to keep them
Mat 13 48 they chose out the good into vessels
Luke 6 13 he chose twelve of them, whom also he
14 7 marking how they chose the first seats
Acts 6 5 they chose Stephen, a man full of
13 17 God of people of Israel c. our fathers
Eph 1 4 he c. us in him before the foundation
chosen Exod 14 7 he took 600 chosen chariots and
Exod 15 4 his chosen captains are drowned in the
30 23 spices, of principal and chosen myrrh
Lev 27 33 it shall not be chosen neither good
Num 11 28 minister of Moses and c. out of many
24 22 thou be chosen of the stock of Cin
31 4 let 1,000 men be chosen out of every
Deut 7 6 the Lord thy God hath chosen thee to be
7 joined unto you, and hath chosen you
18 5 hath chosen him of all thy tribes to
21 5 thy God hath chosen to minister to him
26 17 thou hast chosen the Lord this day
18 the Lord hath chosen thee this day
Josu 4 4 twelve men whom he [Josue] had chosen
8 3 he sent 30,000 chosen valiant men in
12 he had chosen 5,000 men and set them
9 27 in the place which the Lord hath chosen
24 22 have chosen you the Lord to serve him
Judg 5 30 fairest of the women is chosen out for
10 14 call upon the gods which you have c.
20 34 men chosen out of all Israel attacked
1 K 8 18 face of the king whom you have chosen
10 24 you see him whom the Lord hath chosen
12 13 your king is here, whom you have chosen
16 8 neither hath the Lord chosen this. 9
10 Lord hath not chosen any one of these
24 3 took 3,000 chosen men out of all Israel
26 2 having with him 3,000 c. men of Israel
2 K 6 1 all the chosen men of Israel, 30,000
16 18 I will be his whom the Lord hath chosen
20 14 the chosen men were gathered together
21 6 of Saul, once the chosen of the Lord
3 K 3 8 midst of the people which thou hast c.
8 44 city which thou hast c. 48; 2 Pa 6:34, 38
11 13 Jerusalem which I have chosen. 4 K 21:7; 2 Pa 33:7
32 the city which I have chosen. 36
12 21 hundred fourscore thousand chosen men
1 Pa 9 22 all these that were chosen to be porters
15 2 but the Levites whom the Lord hath c.
16 13 ye children of Jacob his chosen. He is
41 and Idithun and rest that were c.
23 4 of these 24,000 were c. and distributed
28 5 he hath chosen Solomon my son to sit
6 for I have chosen him to be my son
10 therefore seeing the Lord hath c. thee
29 1 Solomon . . . whom alone God hath chosen
2 Pa 7 12 and I have chosen this place to myself
16 I have chosen and have sanctified this
11 1 c. men and warriors to fight against
13 3 him 400,000 most valiant and c. men
3 who were also c. and most valiant for
29 11 Lord hath chosen you to stand before
2 Es 1 9 I have c. for my name to dwell there
Jdth 3 8 valiant men, and chosen for war. And
15 6 every city sent their chosen young men
Ps 24 12 him a law in the way he hath chosen
32 12 whom he hath chosen for his inheritance
46 5 he hath chosen for us his inheritance
64 5 blessed is he whom thou hast chosen
77 31 brought down the chosen men of Israel
83 11 I have c. to be an abject in the house
88 20 have exalted one chosen out of my people
104 6 ye sons of Jacob his chosen. He is the
26 Aaron the man whom he had chosen. He
43 joy, and his chosen with gladness
105 5 that we may see the good of thy chosen
23 had not Moses his chosen stood before
118 30 I have chosen the way of truth: thy
173 to save me: for I have c. thy precepts
131 13 the Lord hath chosen Sion: he hath chosen it for his dwelling
14 here will I dwell, for I have chosen it
134 4 the Lord hath chosen Jacob unto himself
Cant 5 10 white and ruddy and c. out of thousands
6 8 mother, the chosen of her that bore her
Wisd 4 15 and that he hath respect to his chosen
9 7 thou hast chosen me to be king of thy
Eccu 47 2 so was David chosen from among the
49 8 they burnt the chosen city of holiness
Isa 1 29 of the gardens which you have chosen
40 20 he hath chosen strong wood and that
41 8 art my servant Jacob whom I have chosen
9 I have chosen thee and have not cast
24 that hath chosen you is an abomination
43 10 and my servant whom I have chosen
20 to give drink to my people, to my chosen
44 1 and Israel whom I have chosen. Thus
2 thou most righteous whom I have chosen
48 10 I have chosen thee in the furnace of
49 2 and hath made me as a chosen arrow
7 Holy One of Israel, who hath c. thee
58 5 is this such a fast as I have chosen
6 this rather the fast that I have chosen
65 12 you have c. the things that displease
66 3 all these things have they chosen in
4 have c. the things that displease me
Jer 2 21 yet I planted thee a chosen vineyard
8 3 death shall be chosen rather than life
33 24 families which the Lord hath chosen

49 19 who shall be the c. one whom I. 50:44
Lam 1 15 the time to destroy my chosen men
Bar 3 30 brought her preferably to chosen gold
Eze 23 7 fornications with those chosen men
Dan 11 15 his chosen ones shall rise up to resist
35 may be chosen and made white even to
12 10 many shall be chosen and made white
Osee 11 6 it shall consume his chosen men and
Soph 3 9 will restore to the people a c. lip
Agge 2 24 as a signet, for I have chosen thee
1 Ma 4 28 together threescore thousand chosen men
6 35 in order were chosen for every beast
7 37 hast chosen this house for thy name
9 5 in Laisa, and 3,000 chosen men with
30 we have chosen thee this day to be our
12 16 we have chosen therefore Numenius the
41 with 40,000 men chosen for battle, and
15 3 I have chosen a great army and have
26 Simon sent to him 2,000 chosen men
2 Ma 13 15 with most valiant chosen young men
Mat 12 18 behold my servant whom I have chosen
20 16 many are called but few chosen. 22:14
Mark 13 20 sake of the elect which he hath chosen
Luke 10 42 Mary hath chosen the best part, which
John 6 71 have not I chosen you twelve; and one
13 18 of you all: I know whom I have chosen
15 16 you have not c. me: but I have c. you
19 I have chosen you out of the world
Acts 1 2 to the apostles whom he had chosen
24 whether of these two thou hast chosen
1 C 1 27 foolish things of the world hath God c.
28 things that are contemptible hath God c.
2 Th 2 12 God hath chosen you firstfruits unto
1 Tim 5 9 let a widow be chosen of no less than
James 2 5 hath not God c. the poor in this world
1 P 2 4 but chosen and made honorable by God
9 you are a chosen generation, a kingly

chosest 2 Es 9 7 art he that chosest Abram and

Christ 1 K 2 10 shall exalt the horn of his Christ
Ps 2 2 against the Lord and against his Christ
83 10 and look on the face of thy Christ
Lam 4 20 breath of our mouth, Christ the Lord
Dan 9 25 unto Christ the prince, there shall
26 after 62 weeks Christ shall be slain
Haba 3 13 people: for salvation with thy Christ
Mat 1 16 who is called C. 27:17, 22; John 4:25
2 4 of them where Christ should be born
16 16 thou art Christ, the son of the living
23 10 masters; for one is your master, Christ
24 5 will come in my name saying: I am C.
26 68 prophesy unto us, O Christ, who is he
Mark 15 32 let C. the king of Israel come down
Luke 4 41 speak, for they knew that he was Christ
23 35 let him save himself if he be Christ
39 if thou be Christ, save thyself and us
24 26 ought not Christ to have suffered these
46 thus it behoved Christ to suffer and
John 1 25 if thou be not Christ nor Elias nor
3 28 witness that I said, I am not Christ
7 42 that C. cometh of the seed of David
9 22 if any man should confess him to be C.
11 27 I have believed that thou art Christ
12 34 that C. abideth forever; and how sayest
Acts 2 36 made both Lord and Christ this same Jesus
3 18 that his Christ should suffer, he hath
4 26 together against the Lord and his Christ
8 5 Samaria, preached Christ unto them
26 23 that Christ should suffer and that he
Rom 5 6 did Christ, when as yet we were weak
6 9 knowing that Christ rising again from
8 10 if Christ be in you, the body indeed
9 3 to be an anathema from Christ, for my
10 6 into heaven? that is, to bring C. down
7 to bring up Christ again from the dead
14 18 that in this serveth Christ, pleaseth
15 3 Christ did not please himself, but as
7 as Christ also hath received you unto
18 things which Christ worketh not by me
20 this gospel, not where Christ was named
16 18 that are such, serve not Christ our Lord
1 C 1 17 Christ sent me not to baptize, but to
23 we preach Christ crucified, unto the
24 Christ the power of God, and the wisdom
8 12 weak conscience, you sin against Christ
10 4 followed them, and the rock was Christ
9 neither let us tempt Christ: as some
15 12 if Christ be preached, that he arose
14 if Christ be not risen again. 17
15 that he hath raised up Christ; whom he
23 firstfruits C., then they that are of C.
2 C 1 5 also by Christ doth our comfort abound
4 4 such confidence we have, through Christ
5 16 if we have known C., according to the
6 15 what concord hath Christ with Belial
11 4 if he that cometh preacheth another C.
Gal 2 20 I live, now not I; but C. liveth in me
3 13 C. hath redeemed us from the curse of
27 been baptized in Christ, have put on C.
4 19 again, until Christ be formed in you
31 freedom wherewith C. has made us free
5 2 circumcised, C. shall profit you nothing
Eph 2 12 you were at that time without Christ
3 17 C. may dwell by faith in your hearts
4 15 in him who is the head, even Christ
20 but you have not so learned Christ
5 2 as Christ also hath loved us and hath
14 dead and Christ shall enlighten thee
25 love your wives as C. loved the church
29 cherish it as also C. doth the church
Phil 1 15 some also for good will preach Christ
17 contention preach Christ not sincerely
18 C. be preached: in this also I rejoice
20 shall Christ be magnified in my body
3 8 them but as dung that I may gain C.
Col 3 4 when C. shall appear who is your life
24 inheritance. Serve ye the Lord Christ
1 Th 4 16 with them in the clouds to meet Christ
Heb 3 6 but Christ as the Son in his own house
5 5 Christ also did not glorify himself
9 11 but Christ being come an high priest
28 C. was offered once to exhaust the sins
1 P 2 21 because Christ also suffered for us
3 15 sanctify the Lord Christ in your hearts
4 1 Christ having suffered in the flesh
Apoc 12 10 of our God and the power of his C.

blood of Christ; *see* **blood**

body of Christ; *see* **body**

Christ died Rom 5 9 Christ died for us. 1 Th 5:10
Rom 14 9 to this end Christ died and rose again
15 destroy not him . . . for whom Christ died
1 C 8 11 brother perish, for whom Christ hath d.
15 3 how that Christ died for our sins
2 C 5 15 Christ died for all; that they also
Gal 2 21 by the law, then Christ died in vain
1 P 3 18 Christ also died once for our sins

Christ is Mark 12 35 that Christ is the son of David. Luke 20:41
Rom 6 4 as Christ is risen from the dead by the
1 C 3 23 you are Christ's, and Christ is God's
5 7 for Christ our pasch is sacrificed
15 13 then Christ is not risen again. 16
20 now Christ is risen from the dead, the
Eph 5 23 as Christ is the head of the church
Col 3 1 where Christ is sitting at the right
11 nor free. But Christ is all and in all
1 J 5 6 testifieth that Christ is the truth

Christ Jesus; *see* **Jesus**
cross of Christ; *see* **cross**
for Christ 2 C 5 20 for Christ therefore we are ambassadors
2 C 5 20 for Christ . . . be reconciled to God
12 10 in persecutions, in distresses, for C.
Phil 1 29 for unto you it is given for Christ
3 7 the same I have counted loss for Christ
gospel of Christ; *see* **gospel**
in Christ Rom 3 24 redemption that is in Christ
Rom 9 1 I speak the truth in Christ, I lie not
12 5 we being many, are one body in Christ
16 5 who is the first fruits of Asia in C.
7 who also were in Christ before me
10 salute Apelles, approved in Christ
1 C 3 1 as unto little ones in Christ. I gave
4 10 you are wise in Christ; we are weak
15 if you have 10,000 instructors in C.
15 18 also that are fallen asleep in Christ
19 if in this life only we have hope in C.
22 also in Christ all shall be made alive
2 C 1 21 that confirmeth us with you in Christ
2 17 from God, before God, in C. we speak
3 14 in Christ it is made void. But even
5 17 if any be in Christ a new creature
19 God indeed was in Christ, reconciling
11 3 fall from the simplicity that is in C.
12 2 I know a man in Christ above 14 years
19 we speak before God in Christ; but
Gal 1 22 churches of Judea which were in Christ
2 17 while we seek to be justified in Christ
3 24 the law was our pedagogue in Christ
27 many of you as have been baptized in C.
Eph 1 3 blessings in heavenly places, in Christ
10 to re-establish all things in Christ
12 glory, we who before hoped in Christ
20 which he wrought in Christ, raising him
2 5 hath quickened us together in Christ
4 32 even as God hath forgiven you in Christ
5 32 I speak in Christ and in the church
Phil 1 13 my bands are made manifest in Christ
2 1 if there be any consolation in Christ
Col 2 5 of your faith which is in Christ. As
1 Th 4 15 the dead who are in Christ, shall rise
1 Tim 5 11 when they have grown wanton in Christ
1 P 1 11 foretold those sufferings that are in C.
3 16 accuse your good conversation in Christ
is Christ Mat 24 23 lo here is C. Mark 13:21
Luke 2 11 a Savior who is Christ the Lord in the
23 2 and saying that he is Christ the king
Rom 9 5 of whom is C., according to the flesh
10 4 end of the law is Christ, unto justice
1 C 1 13 is Christ divided? Was Paul then
11 3 the head of every man is Christ; and the
12 12 yet are one body, so also is Christ
Gal 2 17 is Christ then the minister of sin? God
3 16 of one, And to thy seed, which is Christ
Phil 1 21 for to me, to live is Christ: and to
Col 1 27 among the Gentiles, which is Christ
of Christ Mat 1 18 the generation of Christ
Mat 11 2 heard in prison the works of Christ
22 42 what think you of Christ? Whose son is
Acts 2 31 he spoke of the resurrection of Christ
Rom 8 9 if any man have not the Spirit of C.
35 shall separate us from the love of C.
10 17 and hearing by the word of Christ. But
14 10 all stand before the judgment seat of C.
16 16 all the churches of Christ salute you
1 C 1 6 testimony of C. was confirmed in you
12 Apollo; and I of Cephas; and I of C.
2 1 declaring unto you the testimony of C.
16 him? But we have the mind of Christ
4 1 account of us as of the ministers of C.
16 followers of me as I also am of C. 11:1
6 15 your bodies are the members of Christ
15 shall I take the members of Christ and
7 22 being free, is the bondman of Christ
9 21 of God, but was in the law of Christ
11 3 man; and the head of Christ is God
15 23 Christ, then they that are of Christ
2 C 2 10 have I done it in the person of Christ
15 we are the good odor of Christ unto God
3 3 that you are the epistle of Christ
4 4 light of the gospel of the glory of C.
5 10 before the judgment seat of Christ
14 the charity of Christ presseth us
8 23 the churches, the glory of Christ
10 1 by the mildness and modesty of Christ
3 understanding unto the obedience of C.
11 10 the truth of Christ is in me, that
13 themselves into the apostles of Christ
23 am I. They are the ministers of Christ
12 9 that the power of Christ may dwell in me
13 3 do you seek a proof of Christ that
Gal 1 6 that called you into the grace of C.
10 I should not be the servant of Christ
2 16 we may be justified by the faith of C.
5 4 you are made void of Christ, you who
6 2 so you shall fulfil the law of Christ
Eph 3 4 my knowledge in the mystery of Christ
8 the unsearchable riches of Christ, and
19 to know also the charity of Christ
4 7 according to measure of the giving of C.
13 measure of the age of the fulness of C.
5 5 hath inheritance in the kingdom of C.
21 subject one to another in the fear of C.
6 6 as the servants of C. doing the will
Phil 1 10 without offence unto the day of Christ
2 16 life to my glory in the day of Christ
30 for the work of C. he came to the point
Col 2 11 in the circumcision of Christ: buried
17 to come, but the body is of Christ
3 15 let the peace of Christ rejoice in your
16 let the word of Christ dwell in you
4 3 speech to speak the mystery of Christ
1 Th 2 7 to you, as the apostles of Christ
2 Th 3 5 your hearts . . . in the patience of C.
Heb 3 14 we are made partakers of Christ: yet so
6 1 the word of the beginning of Christ
11 26 esteeming the reproach of Christ
1 P 1 11 Spirit of Christ in them did signify
4 14 if you be reproached for the name of C.
2 J 9 continueth not in the doctrine of C.
Apoc 20 6 they shall be priests of God and of C.
sufferings of Christ; *see* **sufferings**
the Christ 2 K 23 1 the C. of the God of Jacob
Mat 16 20 no one that he was Jesus the Christ
26 63 thou tell us if thou be the Christ
Mark 8 29 said to him: Thou art the Christ. And
14 61 art thou the Christ the Son of the
Luke 2 26 before he had seen the C. of the Lord
3 15 that perhaps he might be the Christ
9 20 Peter answering said: The Christ of God
22 66 if thou be the C., tell us. John 10:24
John 1 20 and he confessed: I am not the Christ
41 which is, being interpreted, the Christ
4 29 I have done. Is not he the Christ
6 70 have known that thou art the Christ
7 26 for a truth, that this is the Christ
27 when the Christ cometh, no man knoweth
31 when the Christ cometh, shall he do more
41 others said: This is the Christ. But
41 doth the Christ come out of Galilee
20 31 you may believe that Jesus is the C.
Acts 9 22 affirming that this is the Christ. And
17 3 insinuating that the C. was to suffer

18 5 to the Jews, that Jesus is the Christ
28 scriptures, that Jesus is the Christ
1 J 2 22 he who denieth that Jesus is the Christ
5 1 whosoever believeth that Jesus is the C.
to Christ Mat 1 17 transmigration of Babylon to C.
Mark 9 40 my name, because you belong to Christ
2 C 11 2 present you as a chaste virgin to C.
Eph 5 24 as the church is subject to Christ
6 5 simplicity of your heart, as to Christ
Col 2 8 of the world and not according to C.
with Christ Rom 6 8 if we be dead with Christ
Rom 6 8 we shall live also together with C.
8 17 heirs of God and joint heirs with C.
Gal 2 19 with Christ I am nailed to the cross
Phil 1 23 to be dissolved and to be with Christ
Col 2 20 if then you be dead with Christ from
3 1 if you be risen with Christ, seek the
3 your life is hid with Christ in God
Apoc 20 4 they lived and reigned with Christ
Christian Acts 26 28 persuadest me to become a C.
1 P 4 16 but if as a Christian, let him not be
Christians Acts 11 26 disciples were first named C.
Christ's 1 C 3 23 you are Christ's; and Christ is
1 C 4 10 we are fools for Christ's sake, but
2 C 10 7 trust to himself that he is Christ's
7 that as he is Christ's, so are we also
Gal 3 29 if you be Christ's, then are you the
5 24 that are Christ's, have crucified their
Phil 2 21 not the things that are Jesus Christ's
Apoc 11 15 is become our Lord's and his Christ's
Christs Mat 24 24 false Christs. Mark 13:22
chronicles 1 Pa 27 24 in the c. of king David
Esth 2 23 in the chronicles before the king
6 1 histories and chronicles of former times
Chronicles 2 Es 12 23 written in the book of C.
chrysolite Exod 28 20 in the fourth a c. 39:13
Eze 10 9 to the sight like the chrysolite stone
28 13 jasper, the chrysolite, and the onyx
Dan 10 6 his body was like the chrysolite, and
Apoc 21 20 the seventh, chrysolite: the eighth
chrysoprasus Apoc 21 20 the tenth, a c.: the
Chub Eze 30 5 Chub and the children of the land
Chun 1 Pa 18 8 and Chun, cities of Adarezer
church Num 20 4 you brought out the c. of the Lord
Deut 23 1 shall not enter into the church. 2, 3
8 in the third generation shall enter into c.
Jdth 6 21 prayed all the night long within the c.
Ps 21 26 with thee is my praise in a great church
34 18 will give thanks to thee in a great c.
39 10 declared thy justice in a great church
Eccu 3 1 sons of wisdom are the c. of the just
31 11 c. of the saints shall declare his alms
39 14 the church shall show forth his praise
44 15 and the church declare their praise
Lam 1 10 that they should not enter into the c.
Joel 2 16 sanctify the church, assemble the
1 Ma 4 59 and all the church of Israel decreed
Mat 16 18 upon this rock I will build my church
18 17 if he will not hear them, tell the c.
17 if he will not hear the church, let him
Acts 8 1 a great persecution against the church
9 31 the c. had peace throughout all Judea
12 5 was made without ceasing by the church
14 22 ordained to them priests in every c.
26 had assembled the church they related
15 3 being brought on their way by the church
4 they were received by the church
18 22 up to Jerusalem and saluted the church
Rom 16 5 the church which is in their house
1 C 4 17 as I teach everywhere in every church
14 4 he that prophesieth, edifieth the church
5 that the church may receive edification
16 19 with the church that is in their house
Eph 1 22 made him head over all the church
3 10 in heavenly places through the church
5 24 as the church is subject to Christ
25 wives, as Christ also loved the church
27 present it to himself a glorious church
29 cherisheth it as also Christ doth the c.
Phil 4 15 no church communicated with me as
Col 1 18 he is the head of the body, the church
24 for his body, which is the church
4 15 and the church that is in his house
1 Tim 3 15 which is the church of the living God
5 16 and let not the church be charged: that
1 P 5 13 the Church that is in Babylon, elected
3 J 9 I had written perhaps to the church
church of God 2 Es 13 1 not come into c. . . .
Acts 20 28 bishops, to rule the church of God
1 C 1 2 to c. . . . that is at Corinth. 2 C 1:1
10 32 without offence . . . to the church of God
11 16 no such custom, nor the church of God
22 or despise ye the church of God; and
15 9 I persecuted the c. of God. Gal 1:13
Phil 3 6 according to zeal, persecuting the c. . . .
1 Tim 3 5 how shall he take care of the c. . . .
15 which the church of the living God
in the church Ps 88 6 truth i. . . . of the saints
Ps 106 32 exalt him in the church of the people
149 1 his praise be in the c. of the saints
Eccu 21 20 mouth of prudent is sought after i. . . .
Acts 7 38 was in the church in the wilderness
11 26 they conversed there in the church
13 1 in the church which was at Antioch
1 C 6 4 who are the most despised in the church
11 18 when you come together in the church
12 28 God indeed hath set some in the church
14 19 in the church I had rather speak five
28 let him hold his peace in the church
35 is a shame for a woman to speak i. . . .
Eph 3 21 to him be glory in the church and in
5 32 I speak in Christ and in the church
Col 4 16 be read also i. . . . of the Laodiceans
of the church Num 19 20 out of the midst o. . . .
Ps 21 23 in midst of the c. will I praise thee
Eccu 15 5 in midst of the church she shall open
33 19 hearken . . . ye rulers of the church
Acts 8 3 but Saul made havoc of the church
11 12 the tidings came to the ears of the c.
12 1 to afflict some of the church. And he
20 17 he called the ancients of the church
Rom 16 1 ministry of the church . . . in Cenchrae
1 C 14 12 seek to abound unto edifying of the c.
Eph 5 23 as Christ is the head of the church
Heb 2 12 in midst of the church will I praise
James 5 14 let him bring in the priests of the c.
3 J 6 to thy charity in sight of the church
10 he forbiddeth and casteth out of the c.
Apoc 2 1 unto angel of the c. 8, 12, 18; 3:1, 7, 14
to the church 1 C 1 2 to the church of God that is at Corinth
1 Th 1 1 to the c. of the Thessalonians. 2 Th 1:1
Philem 2 to the church which is in thy house
Heb 12 23 to the church of the firstborn, who are
whole church Acts 5 11 great fear upon the w. c.
Acts 15 22 and ancients, with the whole church, to
Rom 16 23 host and the whole church saluteth you
1 C 14 23 if therefore the whole c. come together
churches Ps 25 12 in the c. I will bless thee
Ps 67 27 in the churches bless ye God the Lord
Eccu 24 2 shall open her mouth in the churches
Acts 15 41 and Cilicia, confirming the churches
16 5 the churches were confirmed in faith
1 C 14 34 let women keep silence in the churches
16 1 I have given order to the c. of Galatia
19 the churches of Asia salute you. Aquila

2 C 8 1 hath been given in the c. of Macedonia
19 he was also ordained by the churches
23 our brethren, the apostles of the c.
24 show ye to them in the sight of the c.
11 8 I have taken from other churches
12 13 that you have had less than the other c.
Gal 1 2 are with me, to the churches of Galatia
22 unknown by face to the c. of Judea
1 Th 2 14 are become followers of the c. of God
2 Th 1 4 we glory in you in the churches of God
Apoc 1 4 John to the seven c. which are in Asia
11 send to the seven churches which are
20 the seven candlesticks are the seven c.
20 seven stars are angels of the seven c.
2 7 the Spirit saith to the churches. 11, 17, 29; 3:6, 13, 22
22 16 to testify to you these things in the c.
all the churches Rom 16 4 a. . . . of the Gentiles
Rom 16 16 all the churches of Christ salute you
1 C 7 17 walk: and so in all churches I teach
14 33 as also I teach in all the churches
2 C 8 18 is in the gospel through all the c.
11 28 instance, the solicitude for all the c.
Apoc 2 23 all the c. shall know that I am he that
churlish 1 K 25 3 but her husband was churlish
Chus Gen 10 6 sons of Cham: Chus and. 1 Pa 1:8
Gen 10 7 sons of Chus: Saba and Hevila. 1 Pa 1:9
8 Chus begot Nemrod: he began. 1 Pa 1:10
Chusa Luke 8 3 Joanna, wife of C. Herod's steward
Chusai 2 K 15 32 Chusai the Arachite came to meet
2 K 15 37 Chusai the friend of David went into
16 16 Chusai . . . was come to Absalom. 17:6
18 Chusai answered Absalom: Nay, for I
17 5 Absalom said: Call Chusai the Arachite
7 Chusai said to Absalom: The counsel
8 Chusai said: Thou knowest thy father
14 counsel of C. the Arachite is better
15 Chusai said to Sadoc and Abiathar the
18 21 Joab said to Chusai: Go and tell the
21 Chusai bowed down to Joab and ran. Then
22 why might not I also run after Chusai
23 running by a nearer way passed Chusai
31 Chusai appeared; and coming up he said
32 king said to Chusai: Is the young man
32 Chusai answering him, said: Let the
1 Pa 27 33 and C. the Arachite the king's friend
Chusan Judg 3 8 into the hands of C. Rasathaim
Judg 3 10 delivered into his hands C. Rasathaim
Chusi Ps 7 1 for the words of Chusi the son of
Jer 36 14 the son of Selemias, the son of Chusi
Soph 1 1 Sophonias the son of Chusi, the son of
Cibsaim Josu 21 22 and Gazer and Cibsaim and
Cidimoth Josu 13 18 Jassa and C. and Mephaath
Cilicia Jdth 1 7 sent to all that dwelt in Cilicia
Jdth 2 12 of Ange, which are on the left of C.
15 from Cilicia to the coasts of Japheth
3 1 Libya and C. sent their ambassadors
1 Ma 11 14 king Alexander was in Cilicia at that
2 Ma 4 36 king was come back from the places of C.
Acts 6 9 of them that were of Cilicia and Asia
15 23 and in Syria and Cilicia, greeting
41 and he went through Syria and Cilicia
21 39 I am a Jew of Tarsus in C., a citizen
22 3 I am a Jew, born at Tarsus in Cilicia
23 34 and understood that he was of Cilicia
27 5 sailing over the sea of Cilicia and
Gal 1 21 I came into the regions of Syria and C.
Cin Num 24 22 thou be chosen of the stock of Cin
Cina Josu 15 22 Cina and Dimona and Adada and Cades
Cineans Gen 15 19 the C. and Cenezites, the
Cinite Num 24 21 he saw also the Cinite: and took
Judg 1 16 children of the Cinite, the kinsman of
4 11 Haber the Cinite had some time before
17 Jahel the wife of Haber the Cinite. 5:24
17 and the house of Haber the Cinite. And
1 K 15 6 Saul said to the Cinite: Go, depart
6 the C. departed from midst of Amalec
Cinites Judg 4 11 departed from rest of the C.
1 Pa 2 55 these are the Cinites, who came of
cinnamon Exod 30 23 of c. half so much, that is
Prov 7 17 my bed with myrrh, aloes and cinnamon
Cant 4 14 and saffron, sweet cane and cinnamon
Eccu 24 20 I gave a sweet smell like cinnamon
Apoc 18 13 cinnamon and odors and ointment and
circle Wisd 13 2 or the c. of the stars, or the
Eccu 43 13 with the circle of its glory, the hands
Isa 29 3 I will make a circle round about thee
58 5 to wind his head about like a circle
circles Eze 10 12 the circles were full of eyes
circuit Ps 18 7 his c. even to the end thereof
Eccu 24 8 have compassed the circuit of heaven
circuits Ecce 1 6 and returneth to his circuits
circumcise Gen 17 11 you shall c. the flesh of
Gen 34 22 must circumcise every male among us
Deut 10 16 c. therefore the foreskin of your heart
30 6 Lord thy God will circumcise thy heart
Josu 5 2 and c. the second time the children
Luke 1 59 they came to circumcise the child
John 7 22 and on the sabbath day you c. a man
Acts 21 21 that they ought not to c. their children
circumcised Gen 17 10 male kind of you shall be c.
Gen 17 12 infant of eight days old shall be c.
12 bought servant shall be c. Exod 12:44
14 flesh of his foreskin shall not be c.
23 when he c. the flesh of his foreskin
23 he c. the flesh of their foreskin
26 selfsame day was Abraham c. and Ismael
27 bought servants and strangers were c.
34 15 and all the male sex among you be c.
17 if you will not be circumcised, we will
24 they all agreed, and c. all the males
Exod 4 25 stone, and c. the foreskin of her son
Lev 12 3 the eighth day the infant shall be c.
Josu 5 3 he [Josue] c. the children of Israel
5 these were all circumcised. But the
7 and no one had c. them in the way
8 now after they were all circumcised
Jdth 14 6 circumcised the flesh of his foreskin
Jer 4 4 be c. to the Lord, and take away the
9 25 every one that hath the foreskin c.
1 Ma 1 63 the women that c. their children, were
64 those that had c. them, they put to
2 46 c. all the children whom they found
2 Ma 6 10 were accused to have c. their children
Luke 2 21 that the child should be c., his name
Acts 7 8 and c. him [Isaac] the eighth day
15 1 except you be c. after the manner of
5 saying: They must be circumcised and
16 3 taking him, he c. him [Timothy] because
1 C 7 18 is any man called, being circumcised
18 in uncircumcision? Let him not be c.
Gal 2 3 neither Titus . . . was compelled to be c.
5 2 be c., Christ shall profit you nothing
6 12 they constrain you to be circumcised
13 neither . . . who are c., keep the law
13 they will have you to be circumcised
Phil 3 5 being circumcised the eighth day, of
Col 2 11 in whom also you are circumcised with
circumcising Gal 5 3 to every man c. himself, that
circumcision Gen 17 25 Ismael . . . at time of his c.
Exod 4 26 art thou to me, because of the c.
Josu 5 4 now this is the cause of the second c.
John 7 22 Moses gave you circumcision, not because
23 if a man receive c. on the sabbath day
Acts 7 8 gave him the covenant of circumcision
10 45 the faithful of the c. who came with

11 2 that were of the c. contended with him
Rom 2 25 c. profiteth indeed if thou keep the law
25 the law, thy c. is made uncircumcision
26 this uncircumcision be counted for c.
27 by the letter and c. art a transgressor
28 nor is that c. which is outwardly in
29 the c. is that of the heart, in the
3 1 or what is the profit of circumcision
30 is one God that justifieth c. by faith
4 9 doth it remain in the c. only, or in
10 when he [Abraham] was in c. or in uncircumcision? Not in c., but in
11 he received the sign of c., a seal of
12 that he might be the father of c.; not to them only who are of the c.
15 8 Christ Jesus was minister of the c.
1 C 7 19 c. is nothing, and uncircumcision is
Gal 2 7 as to Peter was that of the c. For he
8 in Peter to the apostleship of the c.
9 the Gentiles, and they unto the c.: only
12 fearing them who were of the c. And
5 6 neither c. availeth anything. 6:15
11 if I yet preach circumcision, why do I
Eph 2 11 by that which is called c. in the flesh
Phil 3 3 we are the c. who in spirit serve God
Col 2 11 with c. not made by hand . . . but in the c. of Christ
3 11 c. nor uncircumcision, Barbarian nor
4 11 who are of the c.: these only are
Titus 1 10 especially they who are of the c.: who
circumference Eze 48 35 its c. was 18,000: and the
circumspection Wisd 12 21 with what c. hast thou
circumspectly Eph 5 15 see brethren, how you walk c.
circumvent 1 Th 4 6 nor c. his brother in business
Cis 1 K 9 1 a man of Benjamin whose name was Cis
1 K 9 3 asses of Cis, Saul's father, were lost
3 Cis said to his son Saul: Take one of
10 11 that hath happened to the son of Cis
21 Saul the son of Cis. 1 Pa 12:1; 26:28; Esth 2:5
14 51 Cis was the father of Saul, and Ner the
2 K 21 14 in the sepulcher of Cis his father: and
1 Pa 8 30 Abdon and Sur and Cis and Baal. 9:36
33 Ner begot Cis, and Cis begot Saul. 9:39
23 21 the sons of Moholi: Eleazar and Cis
22 sons of Cis their brethren took them
24 29 the son of Cis, Jeramael. The sons of
2 Pa 29 12 sons of Merari, Cis the son of Abdi
Esth 11 2 Semei the son of Cis, of the tribe of
Acts 13 21 and God gave them Saul the son of Cis
Cison Judg 4 7 in the place of the torrent Cison
Judg 4 13 of the Gentiles to the torrent Cison
5 21 torrent of C. dragged their carcasses
21 torrent of Cadumim, the torrent of C.
3 K 18 40 brought them down to the torrent Cison
Cisson Ps 82 10 as to Jabin at the brook of Cisson
cistern 1 K 19 22 came as far as the great cistern
2 K 3 26 brought him back from cistern of Sira
23 15 drink of the water out of the cistern
16 water out of c. of Bethlehem. 1 Pa 11:18
1 Pa 11 17 me water of the cistern of Bethlehem
Prov 5 15 drink water out of thy own cistern
Ecce 12 6 the wheel be broken upon the cistern
Isa 36 16 every one the water of his own cistern
Jer 6 7 as a cistern maketh its water cold
cisterns Lev 11 36 but fountains and c. and all
Deut 6 11 cisterns which thou didst not dig
4 K 18 31 shall drink water of your own cisterns
2 Pa 26 10 in the wilderness, and dug many c.
2 Es 9 25 cisterns made by others, vineyards
Jdth 7 11 the c. and the reserve of waters failed
Jer 2 13 have digged to themselves c., broken c.
39 10 he gave them vineyards and cisterns

cities Mat 9 35 Jesus went about all the cities
Mat 10 23 you shall not finish all the c. of
11 1 to teach and preach in their cities
20 began he to upbraid the c. wherein
14 13 followed him on foot out of the cities
Mark 1 38 us go into the neighboring towns and c.
6 33 flocking thither on foot from all the c.
56 into towns or into villages or cities
Luke 4 43 to other c. also I must preach the
8 1 he travelled through the c. and towns
4 hastened out of the cities unto him
13 22 he went through the cities and towns
19 17 thou shalt have power over ten cities
19 to him: Be thou also over five cities
Acts 5 16 multitude out of the neighboring c.
8 40 preached the gospel to all the cities
14 6 to Lystra and Derbe, c. of Lycaonia
15 36 and visit our brethren in all the c.
16 4 and as they passed through the cities
26 11 I persecuted them even unto foreign c.
2 P 2 6 reducing the cities of the Sodomites
Jude 7 and Gomorrha and the neighboring c.
Apoc 16 19 the cities of the Gentiles fell. And
fenced cities Num 32 36 fenced cities and folds for their cattle
Josu 10 20 escape from Israel, entered into f. c.
1 K 20 6 lest he find fenced cities and escape
3 K 10 26 he bestowed them in f. c. and with
4 K 10 2 horses and fenced cities and armor
19 25 fenced cities of fighting men should
2 Pa 11 10 are in Juda and Benjamin, well f. c.
32 1 into Juda and besieged the fenced c.
Isa 37 26 and fenced cities should be destroyed
Jer 34 7 remained of the c. of Juda, fenced c.
Dan 11 15 and shall take the best fenced cities
Osee 8 14 Juda hath built many fenced cities
Soph 1 16 and alarm against the fenced cities
strong cities Num 32 16 s. c. for our children
Josu 19 35 the strong cities are Assedim, Ser
4 K 8 12 their strong cities thou wilt burn
2 Pa 8 4 he built other strong cities in Emath
6 the strong cities that were Solomon's
14 6 he built also strong cities in Juda
21 3 and pensions, with s. c. in Juda
2 Es 9 25 they took strong cities and a fat land
Jdth 2 6 all the strong cities thou shalt bring
Eccu 28 17 destroyed the strong cities of the rich
Isa 17 9 his strong cities shall be forsaken
Jer 4 5 let us go into strong cities. Set up
5 17 they shall destroy thy strong cities
1 Ma 1 20 he took the strong cities in the land
5 26 all these strong and great cities
9 50 and they built strong cities in Judea
citizen Acts 21 39 a citizen of no mean city
citizens Lev 19 18 mindful of injury of thy c.
Judg 14 11 when the c. of that place saw him, they
Jer 37 11 there in the presence of the citizens
2 Ma 4 11 disannulled lawful ordinances of the c.
50 in malice to the betraying of the c.
5 5 though the c. ran together to the wall
6 they had been enemies, and not c.
23 bore a more heavy hand upon the c. than
13 14 temple, the city, their country and c.
Luke 15 15 cleaved to one of the citizens of that
19 14 his citizens hated him: and they sent
Eph 2 19 but you are fellow c. with the saints
citterns 3 K 10 12 and c. and harps for singers
city Mat 2 23 dwelt in a city called Nazareth
Mat 4 13 leaving the city of Nazareth, he came
5 14 city seated on a mountain cannot be hid
35 for it is the city of the great king
8 33 coming into the city, told everything
34 the whole city went out to meet Jesus

9 1 the water and came into his own city
10 5 into city of the Samaritans enter ye not
11 whatsoever city or town you shall enter
14 going forth out of that house or city
15 tolerable . . . than for that c. Luke 10:12
23 when they shall persecute you in this c.
12 25 every city or house divided against itself
21 10 the whole city was moved, saying: Who
17 he went out of the city into Bethania
18 in the morning, returning into the city
22 7 those murderers, and burnt their city
23 34 and persecute from city to city: that
26 18 go ye into the city to a certain man
28 11 some of the guards came into the city
Mark 1 33 all the city was gathered together
45 he could not openly go into the city
5 14 and told it in the city. Luke 8:34
11 19 he went forth out of the city. And when
14 13 go ye into the city; and there shall
16 came into the city; and they found as
Luke 1 26 into a city of Galilee, called Nazareth
39 with haste into a city of Juda. And
2 3 be enrolled, every one into his own city
4 out of the city of Nazareth into Judea
39 into Galilee, to their city Nazareth
4 29 rose up and thrust him out of the city
29 the hill, whereon their city was built
31 into Capharnaum, a city of Galilee
5 12 when he was in a certain city, behold
7 11 went into a city that is called Naim
12 he came nigh to the gate of the city
12 multitude of the city was with her
37 woman that was in the city, a sinner
8 39 and he went through the whole city
9 5 when ye go out of that city, shake off
52 entered into a city of the Samaritans
10 1 before his face into every city and
8 into what city soever you enter, and
10 into whatsoever city you enter, and they
11 even the very dust of your city that
14 21 into the streets and lanes of the city
18 2 there was a judge in a certain city
3 there was a certain widow in that city
19 41 seeing the city, he wept over it, saying
22 10 as you go into the city, there shall
23 19 for a certain sedition made in the city
51 of Arimathea, a city of Judea; who
24 49 but stay you in the city, till you be
John 1 44 Bethsaida, the city of Andrew and Peter
4 5 city of Samaria which is called Sichar
8 his disciples were gone into the city
28 went her way into the city and saith
30 they went therefore out of the city
39 of that city many of the Samaritans
11 54 unto a city that is called Ephrem
19 20 was crucified was nigh to the city
Acts 4 27 there assembled together in this city
7 57 casting him forth without the city
8 5 Philip going down to city of Samaria
9 there was therefore great joy in that c.
9 before had been a magician in that city
9 7 arise and go into the city, and there
10 9 drawing nigh to the city, Peter went
11 5 I was in the city of Joppe praying
12 10 iron gate that leadeth to the city
13 44 of Jupiter that was before the c. 14:12
50 women and the chief men of the city
14 4 the multitude of the city was divided
18 stoning Paul, drew him out of the city
19 he rose up and entered into the city
20 had preached the gospel to that city
15 21 in every city them that preach him
16 12 is the chief city of part of Macedonia
12 and we were in this city some days
14 seller of purple, of city of Thyatira
20 these men disturb our city, being Jews
39 desired them to depart out of the city
17 5 a tumult, set the city in an uproar
6 brethren to the rulers of the city
6 they that set the city in an uproar
8 rulers of the city hearing these things
16 the city wholly given to idolatry. He
18 10 for I have much people in the city
19 29 whole city was filled with confusion
35 that the city of the Ephesians is a
20 23 in every city witnesseth to me, saying
21 5 till we were out of the city: and we
29 Trophimus . . . in the city with him
30 and the whole city was in an uproar
39 in Cilicia, a citizen of no mean city
22 3 brought up in this city at the feet of
28 I obtained the being free of this city
24 12 neither in the synagogues nor in the c.
25 23 tribunes and principal men of the city
27 8 nigh to which was the city of Thalassa
Rom 16 23 Erastus the treasurer of the city
2 C 11 36 in perils in the city, in perils in the
32 guarded the city of the Damascenes
Titus 1 5 shouldest ordain priests in every city
Heb 11 10 looked for a city that hath foundations
16 for he hath prepared for them a city
12 22 and to the city of the living God
13 14 we have not here a lasting city, but
James 4 13 tomorrow we will go into such a city
Apoc 3 12 and the name of the city of my God
11 8 shall lie in the streets of the great c.
13 and the tenth part of the city fell
14 20 the press was trodden without the city
16 19 the great city was divided into three
17 18 which thou sawest is the great city
18 10 great city Babylon, that mighty city
18 what city is like to this great city
21 Babylon, that great city, be thrown
20 8 camp of the saints and the beloved city
21 14 wall of the city had twelve foundations
15 to measure the city and the gates
16 and the city lieth in a foursquare
16 he measured the city with the golden
18 the city itself pure gold, like to
19 the foundations of the wall of the city
21 the street of the city was pure gold
23 the city hath no need of the sun nor
22 14 enter in by the gates into the city

city of David 2 K 5 7 the castle of Sion, the same is the city of David
2 K 5 9 the castle, and called it, The c. . . .
6 10 brought in to himself into the c. . . .
12 the house of Obededom into the c. . . .
16 ark of the Lord was come into c. . . .
3 K 2 10 was buried in the city of David. 11:43; 12:16; 2 Pa 12:16
3 1 daughter, and brought her into c. . . .
8 1 out of the c. . . . , that is, out of Sion
9 24 of Pharao came up out of the c. . . .
11 27 filled up the breach of the c. of David
14 31 buried with them in the c. . . . 15:24; 22:51; 4 K 8:24; 15:38; 16:20; 2 Pa 21:1
15 8 they buried him in the c. . . . 2 Pa 9:31; 14:1; 21:20; 24:16, 25; 27:9
4 K 9 28 they buried him . . . in the city of David. 12:21; 15:7; 2 Pa 25:28
14 20 buried . . . with his fathers in c. . . .
1 Pa 11 5 castle of Sion, which is the c. of David
7 therefore it was called the c. of David
13 13 home to himself, that is, into c. . . .
15 1 also houses for himself in the c. . . .

29 of the Lord was come to the c. . . .
2 Pa 5 2 out of the c. . . . , which is Sion
8 11 removed daughter of Pharao from c. . . .
16 14 he had made for himself in the c. . . .
32 5 he repaired Mello in the city of David
30 toward the west of the city of David
33 14 he built a wall without the c. . . . , on
2 Es 3 15 the steps that go down from the c. . . .
12 36 against them by the stairs of the c. . . .
Isa 22 9 shall see the breaches of the c. . . .
1 Ma 1 35 they built the c. . . . with a great and
2 31 army that was in Jerusalem in c. . . .
7 32 and they fled into the city of David
14 36 that were in the c. . . . in Jerusalem
Luke 2 4 to the city of David, which is called
11 Christ the Lord, in the city of David
gate of the city Gen 19 1 Lot was sitting in the gate of the city
Gen 23 10 that went in at the gate of the city
34 20 going into the g. . . . , they spoke to
Deut 25 7 woman shall go to the g. . . . and call
Josu 20 4 he shall stand before the g. . . . , and
Judg 9 35 stood in the entrance of the g. . . .
40 slain of his people, even to the g. . . .
16 2 setting guards at the g. . . . , and
2 K 11 23 and pursued them even to the g. . . .
3 K 17 10 when he [Elias] was come to the g. . . .
4 K 7 10 they came to the g. . . . and told them
23 8 which was on the left hand of g. . . .
1 Pa 19 9 their army in array before the g. . . .
2 Pa 32 6 together in the street of the g. . . .
Jdth 10 6 came to the g. . . . , they found Ozias
13 12 they came to the g. . . . And Judith
Job 29 7 when I went out to the g. . . . , and in
holy city 2 Es 11 1 one part in ten to dwell in Jerusalem the holy city
2 Es 11 18 the Levites in the holy city were 284
Eccu 24 15 in the holy city likewise I rested
Isa 48 2 they are called of the holy city, and
Dan 3 28 Jerusalem the holy city of our fathers
9 24 upon thy people and upon thy h. c.
1 Ma 2 7 people and the ruin of the holy city
2 Ma 1 12 fought against us and the holy city
3 1 when the holy city was inhabited with
15 14 for the people and for all the h. c.
17 holy city and the temple were in danger
Mat 4 5 devil took him up into the holy city
27 53 came into the holy city and appeared to
Apoc 11 2 the holy city they shall tread under
21 2 and I John saw the holy city, the new
10 he showed me the holy city Jerusalem
22 19 book of life and out of the holy city
clad 3 K 11 29 clad with a new garment, found him
3 K 11 30 new garment wherewith he was clad
Job 29 14 I was clad with justice: and I clothed
Isa 59 17 was clad with zeal as with a cloak
Nah 2 3 men of the army are clad in scarlet
Zach 13 4 neither shall they be clad with a
claim Judg 11 26 attempted nothing about this c.
1 Ma 15 34 claim the inheritance of our fathers
clamor Isa 22 2 full of clamor, a populous city
Eph 4 31 clamor and blasphemy be put away from
clamorous Prov 9 13 a foolish woman and c. and
clap Judg 7 19 to clap the pitchers one against
Ps 46 2 O clap your hands, all ye nations
97 8 the rivers shall clap their hands, the
Prov 17 18 a foolish man will clap hands when he
Eccu 12 19 will shake his head and clap his hands
Isa 55 12 of the country shall clap their hands
Eze 21 17 I will clap my hands together and will
clapped Num 24 10 c. his hands together and said
Jer 5 31 and the priests clapped their hands
Lam 2 15 have clapped their hands at thee: they
Eze 22 13 clapped my hands at thy covetousness
25 6 because thou hast clapped thy hands
Nah 3 19 have clapped their hands over thee
clapping 4 K 11 12 c. their hands, they said: God
Jdth 14 13 and made a clapping with his hands
clasp Job 27 23 he shall clasp his hands upon him
clasped Zach 14 13 his hand shall be c. upon his
clasping Gen 33 4 c. him fast about the neck and
classes 2 Pa 31 17 by their classes and companies
Claudia 2 Tim 4 21 C. and all the brethren salute
Claudius Acts 11 28 which came to pass under C.
Acts 18 2 C. commanded all Jews to depart from
23 26 Claudius Lysias to the most excellent
claws Dan 4 30 and his nails like birds' claws
Dan 7 19 his teeth and claws were of iron: he
clay Exod 1 14 life bitter with hard works in c.
2 Pa 4 17 in a clay ground between Sochot and
Jdth 5 10 to labor in clay and brick in the
Job 4 19 they that dwell in houses of clay
10 9 that thou hast made me as the clay
13 12 your necks shall be brought to clay
27 16 as earth, and prepare raiment as clay
33 6 of the same clay I also was formed
38 14 the seal shall be restored as clay
Wisd 7 9 in respect to her shall be counted as c.
15 7 of the same clay he maketh both vessels
8 of the same clay by a vain labor he
10 and his life more base than clay
Eccu 33 13 as the potter's clay is in his hand
38 33 he fashioneth the clay with his arm
Isa 29 16 as if the clay should think against the
41 25 dirt, and as the potter treading clay
45 9 pots: shall the clay say to him that
64 8 thou art our father, and we are clay
Jer 18 4 which he was making of clay with his
Dan 2 33 part of iron and part of clay. 42
34 feet thereof that were of iron and of c.
35 then was the iron, the clay, the brass
41 feet and the toes, part of potter's clay
41 the iron mixed with the miry c. 43
43 as iron cannot be mixed with clay
45 broke in pieces the clay and the iron
14 6 this is but clay within, and brass
Nah 3 14 go into the clay, and tread, work it
Haba 2 6 doth he load himself with thick clay
John 9 6 he made clay of the spittle and spread the clay upon his eyes
11 that man that is called Jesus made clay
14 was the sabbath when Jesus made the c.
15 he put clay upon my eyes, and I washed
Rom 9 21 hath not the potter power over the clay
clean Gen 7 2 of all clean beasts take seven and
Gen 7 8 of beasts clean and unclean, and of
8 20 of all cattle and fowls that were clean
Lev 4 12 into a clean place where the ashes are
6 11 consumed to dust in a very clean place
7 19 he that is clean shall eat of it. If
10 10 and unholy, between unclean and clean
14 you shall eat in a most clean place
11 32 and so afterwards shall be clean. But
36 together of waters shall be clean
47 differences of the clean and unclean
13 6 he shall declare him clean, because it
6 shall wash his clothes and shall be c.
13 the leprosy which he has is very clean
13 and therefore the man shall be clean
17 him, and shall judge him to be clean
23 an ulcer, and the man shall be clean
34 clothes being washed he shall be clean
37 let him confidently pronounce him clean
39 white blemish and that the man is c.
40 off from his head, he is bald and c.
41 forehead, he is bald before and clean

58 second time, and they shall be clean
14 57 may be known when a thing is clean or
15 8 cast his spittle upon him that is clean
13 body in living water, he shall be clean
17 15 in this manner he shall be made clean
20 25 do you also separate the clean beast
25 and the clean fowl from the unclean
24 6 upon the most clean table before the
Num 9 13 if any man was clean and was not on a
18 11 that is c. in thy house, shall eat. 13
19 9 a man that is clean shall gather up
9 without the camp in a most clean place
18 a man that is clean shall dip hyssop
19 that is clean shall purify the unclean
Deut 12 15 or clean, that is to say, sound and
22 both the clean and unclean shall eat
14 11 all birds that are clean you shall eat
20 all that is clean, you shall eat. But
15 22 the clean and the unclean shall eat them
21 5 is clean or unclean should be judged
1 K 20 26 that he was not clean nor purified
21 4 if the young men be clean, especially
3 K 14 10 as dung is swept away till all be clean
4 K 5 10 recover health, and thou shalt be clean
12 may wash in them and be made clean
13 thee: Wash, and thou shalt be clean
14 and he was made clean. And returning
2 Pa 13 11 loaves are set forth on a most c. table
1 Es 6 20 all were clean to kill the phase for
Tob 3 16 have kept my soul clean from all lust
13 22 shall be paved with white and c. stones
Job 8 6 if thou wilt walk clean and upright
9 30 and my hands shall shine ever so clean
10 14 why dost thou not suffer me to be clean
11 4 is pure, and I am clean in thy sight
14 4 who can make him c. that is conceived
17 9 that hath clean hands shall be stronger
25 4 that is born of a woman appear clean
33 9 I am clean and without sin: I am
Ps 23 4 the innocent in hands, and c. of heart
50 12 create a clean heart in me, O God: and
Prov 6 29 not be clean when he shall touch her
20 9 who can say: My heart is clean, I am
11 known, if this works be clean and right
Ecce 9 2 to the clean and to the unclean, to him
Wisd 15 7 both vessels that are for clean uses
Eccu 34 4 what can be made clean by the unclean
38 34 to make clean the furnace. All these
Isa 1 16 wash yourselves, be clean, take away
25 I will clean purge away thy dross and
52 11 be ye clean, you that carry the vessels
66 17 sanctified and thought themselves clean
20 bring an offering in a clean vessel
Jer 13 27 wilt thou not be made clean after me
Eze 22 26 between the polluted and the clean: and
36 25 and I will pour upon you clean water
44 23 to discern between clean and unclean
Dan 7 9 the hair of his head like clean wool
Zach 3 5 they put a clean miter upon his head
Mala 1 11 is offered to my name a clean oblation
Mat 5 8 blessed are the clean of heart: for
8 2 canst make me c. Mark 1:40; Luke 5:12
3 be thou made clean. Mark 1:41
23 25 you make clean the outside. Luke 11:39
26 first make clean the inside of the cup
26 that the outside may become clean
27 59 wrapped it up in a clean linen cloth
Mark 1 42 from him, and he was made clean
Luke 7 22 the lepers are made clean, the deaf hear
11 41 behold, all things are clean unto you
17 14 as they went, they were made clean. And
15 when he saw that he was made clean
17 were not ten made clean? And where are
John 13 10 to wash his feet, but is clean wholly
10 wholly. And you are clean, but not all
11 therefore he said: You are not all clean
15 3 now you are clean by reason of the word
Acts 11 9 what God hath made clean, do not thou
18 6 be upon your own heads; I am clean
Rom 14 20 all things indeed are clean; but it is
Titus 1 15 all things are clean to the clean
15 and to unbelievers, nothing is clean
Heb 10 22 our bodies washed with clean water
James 1 27 religion clean and undefiled before God
Apoc 15 6 clothed with clean and white linen
19 14 clothed in fine linen, white and clean
cleanest Job 28 19 be compared to the c. dyeing
cleanness Gen 20 5 c. of my hands have I done this
Lev 13 7 seen by the priest and restored to c.
2 K 22 21 according to the cleanness of my hands.
25; Ps 17:21, 25
Job 22 30 shall be saved by the c. of his hands
Prov 22 11 he that loveth cleanness of heart, for
cleanse Exod 29 36 thou shalt c. the altar when
Lev 13 34 the other flesh, he shall cleanse him
Num 4 13 they shall cleanse the altar also from
2 Pa 29 17 they began to cleanse on the first day
Ps 18 13 from my secret ones cleanse me, O Lord
50 4 iniquity, and cleanse me from my sin
Eccu 38 10 and cleanse thy heart from all offence
Jer 4 11 not to fan nor to cleanse. A full wind
33 8 I will c. them from all their iniquity
Eze 16 30 wherein shall I cleanse thy heart
36 25 I will cleanse you from all your idols
33 day that I shall c. you from all your
37 23 have sinned: and I will cleanse them
39 12 for seven months to cleanse the land
14 that they may cleanse it: and after
16 Amona, and they shall cleanse the land
43 20 and thou shalt cleanse and expiate it
26 expiate the altar and shall cleanse it
Joel 3 21 and I will cleanse their blood which I
Nah 1 3 will not cleanse and acquit the guilty
1 Ma 4 36 now to cleanse the holy places and to
Mat 3 12 he will thoroughly cleanse his floor
10 8 cleanse the lepers, cast out devils
2 C 7 1 let us c. ourselves from all defilement
2 Tim 2 21 if any man shall c. himself from these
Titus 2 14 might c. to himself a people acceptable
Heb 9 14 cleanse our conscience from dead works
James 4 8 c. your hands, ye sinners: and purify
1 J 1 9 our sins and to c. us from all iniquity
cleansed Gen 35 2 be c. and change your garments
Lev 12 7 she shall be cleansed from the issue
8 for her, and so she shall be cleansed
13 28 he shall be cleansed, because it is
59 of skins, how it ought to be cleansed
14 2 of a leper, when he is to be cleansed
3 shall find that the leprosy is cleansed
7 he shall sprinkle him that is to be c.
14 ear of him that is cleansed. 17, 25, 28
20 and the man shall be rightly cleansed
53 house, and it shall be rightly cleansed
15 15 that he may be cleansed of the issue
16 20 after he hath cleansed the sanctuary
30 you shall be cleansed before the Lord
Num 8 7 and are cleansed, they shall take an ox
19 12 the seventh, and so shall be cleansed
12 he cannot be cleansed on the seventh
35 34 thus shall your possession be cleansed
2 Pa 34 3 he cleansed Juda and Jerusalem. 5
8 when he had cleansed the land and the
2 Es 13 9 they c. the storehouses: and I brought
Ps 18 14 and I shall be c. from the greatest sin
50 9 with hyssop, and I shall be cleansed
Isa 6 7 away, and thy sin shall be cleansed

Jer 44 10 they are not cleansed even to this day
Eze 16 9 and cleansed away thy blood from thee
24 13 thou art not c. from thy filthiness
13 neither shalt thou be cleansed before
36 25 you shall be cleansed from all your
44 26 and after one is cleansed, they shall
Dan 8 14 and the sanctuary shall be cleansed
Osee 8 5 they be incapable of being cleansed
Joel 3 21 their blood, which I have not cleansed
1 Ma 4 41 till they had cleansed the holy places
43 they cleansed the holy places and took
13 47 cleansed the houses wherein there had
50 cleansed the castle from uncleanness
2 Ma 2 19 perils, and hath cleansed the place
10 5 very same day it was cleansed again
14 36 undefiled which was lately cleansed
Mat 8 3 and forthwith his leprosy was cleansed
11 5 the lepers are cleansed, the deaf hear
Luke 4 27 none of them was cleansed but Naaman
5 13 him, saying: I will. Be thou cleansed
Acts 10 15 which God hath c., do not thou call
Heb 9 22 according to the law are c. with blood
23 patterns of heavenly things should be c.
10 2 the worshippers once c. should have no
cleanseth 1 J 1 7 cleanseth us from all sin
cleansing Lev 13 35 if after his c. the spot spread
Lev 14 32 things that appertain to his cleansing
15 13 number seven days after his cleansing
16 30 and the cleansing from all your sins
Num 33 53 cleansing the land and dwelling in it
Judg 6 11 and cleansing wheat by the winepress
2 K 4 5 who was cleansing wheat, was fallen
Mala 3 3 he shall sit refining and cleansing
2 Ma 10 7 good success in cleansing his place
Mark 1 44 offer for thy cleansing. Luke 5:14
Eph 5 26 cleansing it by the laver of water
Heb 9 13 defiled, to the cleansing of the flesh
clear Gen 24 41 thou shalt be clear from my curse
Exod 24 10 stone, and as the heaven, when clear
Lev 13 28 in its place and be not very clear
Num 14 18 and leaving no man clear, who visitest
3 K 3 21 more diligently when it was clear day
2 Pa 9 2 not anything that he did not make clear
Isa 18 4 as the noon light is clear, and as a
Eze 32 14 then will I make their waters clear
Dan 13 46 I am clear from the blood of this woman
Wisd 17 19 world was enlightened with a c. light
Acts 20 26 I am clear from the blood of all men
25 16 to c. himself of the things laid to his
Apoc 21 18 city itself pure gold like to c. glass
22 1 river of water of life, clear as crystal
clearest Exod 30 34 the c. frankincense. Lev 24:7
Lev 24 2 unto thee the finest and clearest oil
Eze 34 18 when you drank the clearest water, you
cleareth Eccu 33 4 he that cleareth up a question
clearly Gen 48 10 and he could not see clearly
Deut 27 8 words of this law plainly and clearly
1 K 14 19 degrees and was heard more clearly
Wisd 19 17 may c. be perceived by the very sight
Mark 8 25 so that he saw all things clearly
Luke 6 42 shalt thou see c. to take out the mote
Rom 1 20 are c. seen, being understood by the
cleave Gen 2 24 and shall cleave to his wife: and
Lev 1 8 all things that cleave to the liver
12 head and all that cleave to the liver
Deut 13 4 serve, and to him you shall cleave
Josu 22 5 cleave to him and serve him with all
23 8 but cleave ye unto the Lord your God
Job 41 14 members of his flesh c. one to another
Ps 100 4 the perverse heart did not cleave to me
136 6 let my tongue cleave to my jaws, if I
Jer 42 16 shall cleave to you in Egypt and there
Mat 19 5 c. to his wife. Mark 10:7; Eph 5:31
cleaved Job 19 20 my bone hath cleaved to my skin
Job 29 10 and their tongue cleaved to their throat
31 7 if a spot hath cleaved to my hands
Ps 21 16 and my tongue hath cleaved to my jaws
101 6 my bone hath cleaved to my flesh. I am
118 25 my soul hath cleaved to the pavement
Bar 1 20 many evils have cleaved to us, and the
3 4 wherefore evils have cleaved fast to us
Luke 15 15 cleaved to one of the citizens of that
cleaveth Lev 15 3 c. to his flesh and gathereth
Ps 43 25 dust: our belly cleaveth to the earth
Zach 13 7 against the man that cleaveth to me
Luke 10 11 dust of your city that cleaveth to us
cleaving Deut 11 22 in all his ways, c. unto him
Rom 12 9 is evil, cleaving to that which is good
cleft Mich 1 4 and the valleys shall be cleft as
clefts Cant 2 14 my dove in the c. of the rock
Isa 2 21 he shall go into the clefts of rocks
Jer 49 16 dwellest in the clefts of the. Abdi 3
Amos 6 12 and the lesser house with clefts. Can
clemency Josu 11 20 should not deserve any c.
Judg 5 11 his clemency towards the brave men
Esth 4 11 scepter to him in token of clemency
8 4 hand, which was the sign of clemency
13 2 to govern my subjects with clemency
Prov 11 19 clemency prepareth life: and the
16 15 his clemency is like the latter rain
20 28 his throne is strengthened by clemency
31 26 the law of clemency is on her tongue
2 Ma 2 23 with all c. showing mercy to them
Acts 24 4 I desire thee of thy c. to hear us in
Clement Phil 4 3 with C. and the rest of my
Cleopatra Esth 11 1 reign of Ptolemy and Cleopatra
1 Ma 10 57 of Egypt with Cleopatra his daughter
58 and he gave him his daughter Cleopatra
Cleophas Luke 24 18 C. answering, said to him: Art
John 19 25 his mother's sister, Mary of Cleophas
clergy 1 P 5 3 neither as lording it over the c.
clerk Acts 19 35 when the town clerk had appeased
cliffs 1 K 14 4 steep c. like teeth on the one
climb Joel 2 9 they shall climb up the houses
Amos 9 2 though they climb up to heaven, thence
climbed Jer 4 29 and have climbed up the rocks
Luke 19 4 he climbed up into a sycamore tree
climbeth John 10 1 c. up another way, the same is
climbing Eccu 25 27 as the c. of a sandy way is
cloak Gen 9 23 Sem and Japheth put a cloak upon
Deut 22 12 hem at four corners of thy cloak
Judg 4 18 and being covered by her with a cloak
Esth 8 15 clothed with a cloak of silk and purple
Ps 108 29 their confusion as with a double cloak
Isa 59 17 and was clad with zeal as with a cloak
Eze 5 3 bind them in the skirt of thy cloak
Mich 2 8 you have taken away the cloak off from
Mat 5 40 coat, let go thy cloak also unto him
27 28 they put a scarlet cloak about him
31 they took off the cloak from him and
Luke 9 29 that taketh away from thee thy cloak
2 Tim 4 13 the cloak that I left at Troas with
1 P 2 16 not as making liberty a c. for malice
cloaks Exod 12 34 tying it in their c., put it on
Isa 3 22 changes of apparel and short cloaks
clods Job 28 6 and the clods of it are gold. The
Job 38 38 and the clods fastened together
39 10 will he break the clods of the valleys
close Num 22 25 thrust herself close to the wall
Deut 15 7 harden thy heart nor close thy hand
Josu 2 15 for her house joined close to the wall
6 1 Jericho was close shut up and fenced
Ruth 1 14 Ruth stuck close to her mother-in-law
2 21 I should keep close to his reapers
23 she kept close to the maids of Booz
2 K 12 26 and laid close siege to the royal city

20 8 Joab had on a close coat of equal length
Job 41 6 shut close up with scales pressing upon
Ps 62 9 my soul hath stuck close to thee: thy
Prov 17 28 and if he close his lips, a man of
Jer 13 11 the girdle sticketh close to the loins
11 so have I brought close to me all the
30 17 I will close up thy scars and will heal
33 6 I will close their wounds and give them
Dan 10 9 and my face was close to the ground
Amos 9 11 I will close up the breaches of the
1 Ma 10 49 pursued after him and pressed them c.
Acts 27 13 from Asson, they sailed close by Crete
closed Gen 20 18 Lord had closed up every womb
Gen 29 2 mouth thereof was closed with a great
10 stone wherewith the well was closed
Exod 28 7 sides, that they may be closed together
39 6 stones, fast set and closed in gold
Num 34 12 shall be closed in by the most salt sea
Judg 3 22 was closed up with the abundance of fat
2 Pa 24 13 and the breach of the walls was closed
2 Es 4 7 and the breaches began to be closed
Tob 14 15 care of them and he closed their eyes
Jer 8 22 why then is not the wound . . . closed
Jon 2 6 the deep hath closed me round about
closely Deut 10 15 Lord hath been c. joined to
closets Mat 24 26 he is in the c., believe it not
closing Num 16 33 the ground closing upon them
closures 1 Pa 22 3 for the closures and joinings
cloth Lev 13 45 his mouth covered with a cloth
Num 4 6 spread over it a cloth all of violet
7 table of proposition in a c. of violet
8 shall spread over it a cloth of scarlet
9 they shall take also a cloth of violet
11 golden altar also in a cloth of violet
12 they shall wrap it up in a purple cloth
Deut 22 17 shall spread the c. before the ancients
1 K 21 9 wrapped up in a cloth behind the ephod
Eze 27 24 bales of blue cloth and of embroidered
Mat 9 16 raw cloth unto an old garment. Mark 2:21
27 29 wrapped it up in a clean linen cloth
Mark 14 51 a linen cloth cast about his naked body
52 casting off the linen cloth, fled from
clothe Exod 29 5 shalt c. Aaron with his vestments
Job 39 19 horse, or clothe his neck with neighing
40 5 clothe thyself with beauty, and set
Ps 131 16 I will c. her priests with salvation
18 his enemies I will c. with confusion
Eccu 15 5 shall clothe him with a robe of glory
43 22 shall c. the waters as a breastplate
Isa 22 21 I will clothe him with thy robe and
50 3 I will clothe the heavens with darkness
Bar 5 2 God will clothe thee with the double
6 32 clothe their wives and their children
Eze 44 19 they shall clothe themselves with other
Mat 6 30 God doth so clothe: how much more
Mark 15 17 they c. him with purple, and platting
Luke 12 28 if God clothe in this manner the grass
Apoc 19 8 she should c. herself with fine linen
clothed Gen 3 21 garment of skins, and c. them
Lev 6 11 being clothed with others, shall carry
Deut 22 5 shall not be clothed with man's apparel
1 K 17 5 he was clothed with a coat of mail
38 Saul clothed David with his garments
18 4 of the coat with which he was clothed
2 K 1 24 who clothed you with scarlet in delights
13 18 and she was clothed with a long robe
3 K 22 10 on his throne clothed with royal robes
1 Pa 15 27 David was clothed with a robe of fine
21 16 he and the ancients clothed in haircloth
2 Pa 5 12 their brethren, clothed with fine linen
18 9 sat on their thrones, c. in royal robes
28 15 with the spoils clothed all them that
15 when they had clothed and shod them
Jdth 10 3 and clothed herself with the garments of
Job 7 5 my flesh is clothed with rottenness
8 22 hate thee, shall be c. with confusion
10 11 thou hast clothed me with skin and flesh
19 26 I shall be clothed again with my skin
27 17 the just man shall be clothed with it
29 14 and I clothed myself with my judgment
Ps 34 13 I was clothed with haircloth. I humbled
26 let them be clothed with confusion and
44 15 clothed round about with varieties
64 14 the rams of the flock are clothed, and
92 1 he is clothed with beauty: the Lord is clothed with strength
103 2 art clothed with light as with a garment
108 29 that detract me be clothed with shame
131 9 let thy priests be clothed with justice
Prov 23 21 drowsiness shall be clothed with rags
31 21 domestics are c. with double garments
Eccu 17 2 clothed him with strength according to
45 9 clothed him with a robe of glory and
16 no stranger was ever c. with them, but
50 11 clothed with the perfection of power
Isa 23 18 and be clothed for a continuance
49 18 thou shalt be clothed with all these
61 10 he hath clothed me with the garments
Lam 4 2 that were clothed with the best gold
Bar 6 57 raiment wherewith they are clothed
Eze 7 27 prince shall be clothed with sorrow
9 2 clothed with linen. 3, 11; 10:2, 6, 7, 11
16 10 I clothed thee with embroidery, and
10 and clothed thee with fine garments
13 and wast clothed with fine linen, and
23 6 who were clothed with blue, princes
12 to her, clothed with divers colors
26 16 and be clothed with astonishment: they
34 3 you clothed yourselves with the wool
44 17 shall be clothed with linen garments
Dan 5 7 shall be clothed with purple and shall
16 thou shalt be clothed with purple and
29 Daniel was clothed with purple, and a
10 5 a man clothed in linen, and his loins
12 6 the man that was clothed in linen. 7
Jon 3 6 was clothed with sackcloth and sat in
Soph 1 8 such as are c. with strange apparel
Agge 1 6 you have clothed yourselves, but have
Zach 3 3 Jesus was c. with filthy garments; and
4 have c. thee with change of garments
5 and clothed him with garments, and the
1 Ma 8 14 wore a crown, or was clothed in purple
10 62 he should be c. with purple. 14:43
64 him clothed with purple, they all fled
11 58 to be c. in purple and to wear a golden
14 44 to be clothed with purple or to wear
Mat 6 31 or wherewith shall we be clothed? For
11 8 clothed in soft garments. Luke 7:25
Mark 1 6 John was clothed with camel's hair
5 15 sitting, clothed, and well in his wits
16 5 right side, clothed with a white robe
Luke 8 35 sitting at his feet, c. and in his
12 27 in all his glory was c. like one of
16 19 rich man who was clothed in purple and
2 C 5 2 desiring to be clothed upon with our
3 so that we be found clothed, not naked
4 we would not be unclothed, but c. upon
James 2 3 that is clothed with the fine apparel
Apoc 1 13 c. with a garment down to the feet
3 5 clothed in white garments. 18; 4:4
7 9 clothed with white robes, and palms in
13 clothed in white robes, who are they
10 1 from heaven, clothed with a cloud
11 3 prophesy 1,260 days, c. in sackcloth
12 1 a woman clothed with the sun, and the
15 6 c. with clean and white. 18:16; 19:14

17 4 c. round about with purple and scarlet
18 16 which was clothed with fine linen and
19 13 c. with a garment sprinkled with blood
14 clothed in fine linen, white and clean
clothes Lev 11 25 shall wash his clothes. 28, 40; 14:47; 15:5, 7, 8, 10, 11, 22, 23, 27; 16:26, 28; 17:15
Lev 13 34 his clothes being washed he shall be
45 shall have his clothes hanging loose
14 8 when the man hath washed his clothes
9 having washed again his clothes and his
15 13 having washed his clothes and all his
17 16 if he do not wash his clothes and his
Ruth 3 4 lift up the clothes wherewith he is
1 K 4 12 with his clothes rent, and his head
19 13 head of it, and covered it with c.
28 8 disguised himself; and put on other c.
3 K 1 1 covered with clothes, he was not warm
2 Es 4 23 followed me, did not put off our c.
Tob 1 20 and gave clothes to the naked, and was
Job 24 7 taking away their clothes who have no
Wisd 7 4 I was nursed in swaddling clothes and
Jer 41 5 and their clothes rent, and mourning
Eze 30 21 to be healed, to be tied up with c.
Luke 2 7 wrapped him up in swaddling clothes
12 find the infant wrapped in swaddling c.
8 27 he wore no c., neither did he abide in
19 36 they spread their clothes underneath
Acts 14 13 rending their clothes, they leaped out
16 22 the magistrates rending off their c.
clothest Jer 4 30 though thou c. thyself with
clothing Exod 22 27 covered, the c. of his body
Job 24 10 and them that go without clothing
31 19 that was perishing for want of clothing
Ps 44 10 in gilded clothing; surrounded with
103 6 the deep like a garment is its clothing
Prov 27 26 lambs are for thy clothing: and kids
31 22 made for herself clothing of tapestry
25 strength and beauty are her clothing
Eccu 29 27 water and bread and clothing, and a
39 31 cluster of the grape, and oil and c.
Isa 3 7 house there is no bread nor clothing
59 6 their webs shall not be for clothing
Jer 10 9 violet and purple is their clothing
2 Ma 3 33 in the same c. stood by Heliodorus
11 8 horseman going before them in white c.
Mat 7 15 come to you in the clothing of sheep
cloths Luke 24 12 saw the linen c. John 20:5, 6
John 19 40 body of Jesus and bound it in linen c.
20 7 not lying with the linen c. but apart
cloud Exod 13 21 way by day in a pillar of a c.
Exod 13 22 there never failed the pillar of the c.
14 19 together with him the pillar of the c.
20 it was a dark cloud and enlightening
24 through the pillar of fire and of the c.
16 10 the glory of the Lord appeared in a c.
19 9 come to thee in the darkness of a cloud
16 a very thick cloud to cover the mount
20 21 Moses went to the dark cloud wherein
24 15 was gone up, a cloud covered the mount
16 Sinai, covering it with a c. six days
16 called him out of the midst of the c.
18 entering into the midst of the cloud
33 9 the pillar of the cloud came down and
10 pillar of the cloud stood at the door
34 5 when the Lord was come down in a cloud
40 32 the cloud covered the tabernacle of the
33 the cloud covering all things and the
33 shining, for the cloud had covered all
34 if at any time the cloud removed from
36 c. of the Lord hung over the tabernacle
Lev 16 2 I will appear in a cloud over the oracle
13 cloud and vapor thereof may cover the
Num 9 15 was reared up, a cloud covered it
16 by day the cloud covered it, and by
17 the cloud that covered the tabernacle
17 where the cloud stood still, there they
18 all the days that the cloud abode over
20 as the cloud stayed over the tabernacle
21 if the cloud tarried from evening
10 11 the cloud was taken up from the
34 cloud also of the Lord was over them
11 25 Lord came down in a cloud and spoke
12 5 Lord came down in a pillar of the cloud
10 c. also that was over the tabernacle
14 14 and thy cloud protecteth them and thou
14 goest before them in a pillar of a c.
16 43 were gone into it, the cloud covered it
Deut 1 33 in the day by the pillar of a cloud
4 11 and there was darkness and a cloud and
5 22 out of the midst of the fire and the c.
31 15 appeared there in the pillar of a cloud
3 K 8 10 a cloud filled the house of the Lord
11 not stand to minister because of the c.
12 Lord said that he would dwell in a c.
18 44 a little cloud arose out of the sea
2 Pa 5 13 house of God was filled with a cloud
14 and minister, by reason of the cloud
6 1 promised that he would dwell in a cloud
2 Es 9 12 in a pillar of a cloud thou wast their
19 the pillar of the cloud departed not
Job 7 9 as a cloud is consumed and passeth
26 9 throne and spreadeth his cloud over it
30 15 my prosperity hath passed away like a c.
38 9 when I made a cloud the garment thereof
Ps 77 14 he conducted them with a cloud by day
98 7 spoke to them in the pillar of the cloud
104 39 he spread a cloud for their protection
Wisd 2 3 shall pass away as the trace of a cloud
19 7 a cloud overshadowed their camp, and
Eccu 24 6 and as a cloud I covered all the earth
7 my throne is in a pillar of a cloud
35 26 as cloud of rain in the time of drought
43 24 speedy coming of a cloud, and a dew
45 5 his voice, and brought him into a c.
50 6 as morning star in the midst of a cloud
Isa 4 5 where he is called upon, a c. by day
18 4 as a cloud of dew in the day of harvest
19 1 Lord will ascend upon a swift cloud
25 5 and as with heat under a burning cloud
44 22 blotted out thy iniquities as a cloud
Jer 4 13 behold he shall come up as a cloud
Lam 3 44 thou hast set a cloud before thee, that
Eze 1 4 came out of the north: and a great cloud
28 when it is in a cloud on a rainy day
8 11 cloud of smoke went up from the incense
10 3 and a cloud filled the inner court, and
4 the house was filled with the cloud
30 18 c. shall cover her, and her daughters
32 7 I will cover the sun with a cloud, and
38 9 and like a cloud to cover the land
16 upon my people of Israel like a cloud
Osee 6 4 your mercy is as a morning cloud, and
13 3 they shall be as a morning cloud and as
2 Ma 1 22 sun shone out, which before was in a c.
2 8 there shall be a cloud as it was also
Mat 17 5 a bright cloud overshadowed them. And
5 voice out of the c. Mark 9:6; Luke 9:35
Mark 9 6 there was a cloud overshadowing them
Luke 9 34 came a cloud and overshadowed them
34 afraid when they entered into the cloud
12 54 when you see a cloud rising from the
21 27 shall see the Son of man coming in a c.
Acts 1 9 a c. received him out of their sight
1 C 10 1 our fathers were all under the cloud
2 all in Moses were baptized in the cloud

Heb 12 1 having so great a cloud of witnesses
Apoc 10 1 down from heaven clothed with a cloud
11 12 and they went up to heaven in a cloud
14 14 I saw and behold a white cloud; and
14 upon the cloud one sitting like to the
15 to him that sat upon the cloud: Thrust
16 that sat on the cloud thrust his sickle
clouds Gen 9 13 I will set my bow in the clouds
Gen 9 14 when I shall cover the sky with clouds, my bow shall appear in the clouds
16 the bow shall be in the clouds, and I
Deut 33 26 the clouds run hither and thither. His
2 K 22 12 dropping waters out of the clouds of
23 4 shineth in the morning without clouds
3 K 18 45 the heavens grew dark with clouds and
Job 20 6 heaven, and his head touch the clouds
22 14 the clouds are his covert, and he doth
26 8 he bindeth up the waters in his clouds
36 28 which flow from the clouds that cover
29 if he will spread out clouds as his
37 11 corn desireth clouds, and the clouds spread their light
15 rains, to show his light of his clouds
16 knowest thou the great paths of the c.
21 sudden shall be thickened into clouds
38 34 canst thou lift up thy voice to the c.
Ps 17 12 dark waters in the clouds of the air
13 the clouds passed, hail and coals of
35 6 thy truth reacheth even to the clouds
56 11 heavens: and thy truth unto the clouds
67 35 magnificence, and his power is in the c.
76 18 waters: the clouds sent out a sound
77 23 he had commanded the clouds from above
88 7 who in the clouds can be compared to
96 2 c. and darkness are round about him
103 3 who makest the clouds thy chariot: who
107 5 and thy truth even unto the clouds
134 7 he bringeth up clouds from the end of
146 8 who covereth the heaven with clouds
Prov 3 20 and the clouds grow thick with dew
25 14 as clouds and wind, when no rain
Ecce 11 3 if the clouds be full, they will pour
4 considereth the c., shall never reap
12 2 and the clouds return after the rain
Wisd 5 22 lightning shall go directly from the c.
Eccu 2 2 make not haste in the time of clouds
13 28 what he said they extol even to the c.
35 20 prayer shall approach even to the c.
21 humbleth himself shall pierce the c.
43 15 and the clouds fly out like birds. By
16 by his greatness he hath fixed the c.
50 8 rainbow giving light in the bright c.
Isa 5 6 I will command the c. to rain no rain
14 14 I will ascend above the height of the c.
45 8 above, and let the clouds rain the just
60 8 who are these, that fly as clouds, and
Jer 10 13 lifteth up the clouds from the. 51:16
51 9 heavens and is lifted up to the clouds
Bar 3 29 and brought her down from the clouds
6 61 clouds when God commandeth them to go
Dan 3 73 ye lightnings and clouds, bless the
7 13 came with the clouds of heaven, and he
Joel 2 2 a day of c. and whirlwinds. Soph 1:15
Nah 1 3 and clouds are the dust of his feet
Mat 24 30 coming in the clouds of heaven. 26:64; Mark 14:62
Mark 13 26 the Son of man coming in the clouds
1 Th 4 16 in the clouds to meet Christ into the
2 P 2 17 and clouds tossed with whirlwinds, to
Jude 12 clouds without water, which are carried
Apoc 1 7 he cometh with the clouds, and every
cloudy Eze 30 3 a cloudy day, it shall be the time
Eze 34 12 scattered in the cloudy and dark day
Mich 4 8 and thou, O cloudy tower of the flock
clouted Josu 9 5 were c. with patches, and old
clouts Eze 16 4 with salt, nor swaddled with c.
clove Isa 48 21 he clove the rock, and the waters
club Prov 23 21 club together shall be consumed
Dan 14 25 kill this dragon without sword or club
clubs 2 Ma 4 41 caught up stones, some strong clubs
Mat 26 47 with swords and clubs. 55; Luke 22:52
cluster Num 13 24 torrent of the c. of grapes. 25
Num 13 24 cut off a branch with its c. of grapes
25 had carried a cluster of grapes. And
32 9 as far as the valley of the c. Deut 1:24
Cant 1 13 a cluster of cypress my love is to me
Eccu 39 31 the cluster of the grape and oil and
Isa 17 6 shall be as one cluster of grapes and
65 8 as if a grain be found in a cluster
Jer 6 9 as in a vine, even to one cluster
Abdi 5 have left thee at the least a cluster
Mich 7 1 the vintage: there is no cluster to eat
clusters Deut 24 21 not gather the c. that remain
Deut 32 32 of gall, and their clusters most bitter
1 K 25 18 corn and a hundred clusters of raisins
Cant 7 7 and thy breasts to clusters of grapes
8 shall be as the clusters of the vine
Apoc 14 18 gather the clusters of the vineyard
Coa 3 K 10 28 and horses . . . out of Egypt and Coa
3 K 10 28 merchants brought them out of Coa and
2 Pa 1 16 there were horses brought . . . from Coa
coaches Isa 66 20 in litters and on mules and in c.
coadjutors 1 C 3 9 we are God's coadjutors: you
coal Isa 6 6 in his hand was a live coal which he
coals 2 K 22 9 coals were kindled by it. Ps 17:9
2 K 22 13 before him the c. of fire were kindled
Tob 6 8 a little piece of its heart upon coals
Job 41 12 his breath kindleth coals, and a flame
Ps 17 13 hail and coals of fire. 14
119 4 the mighty, with coals that lay waste
Prov 6 28 can he walk upon hot coals, and his feet
25 22 thou shalt heap hot coals upon his head
Eccu 8 13 kindle not the coals of sinners by
Isa 44 12 hath wrought with his file, with coals
19 I have baked bread upon the coals
47 14 no coals wherewith they may be warmed
54 16 smith that bloweth the c. in the fire
Lam 4 8 their face is now made blacker than c.
Eze 10 2 fill thy hand with the coals of fire
John 18 18 and ministers stood at a fire of coals
21 9 they saw hot coals lying, and a fish
Rom 12 20 thou shalt heap coals of fire upon his
burning coals Lev 16 12 filled with the b. c.
Tob 8 2 part of the liver and laid it upon b. c.
Ps 139 11 b. c. shall fall upon them; thou wilt
Jer 36 22 was a hearth before him full of b. c.
Eze 1 13 appearance was like that of b. c. of
coast Josu 15 1 to uttermost of the south coast
Josu 18 14 this is their coast towards the sea
Judg 11 18 over against the east coast of land of
2 Pa 8 17 to Ailath, on the coast of the Red Sea
Joel 3 4 and all the coast of the Philistines
coasts Exod 8 2 I will strike all thy coasts with
Exod 10 4 will bring in . . . locust into thy c.
19 not so much as one in all the c. of
13 7 anything leavened . . . in all thy coasts
20 in the utmost coasts of the wilderness
Lev 26 6 I will give peace in your coasts: you
Num 32 9 that they should not enter into the c.
Deut 16 4 no leaven shall be seen in all thy c.
Josu 9 1 and on the coasts of the great sea
Judg 10 16 out of their coasts all the idols of
11 22 coasts thereof from the Arnon to the
1 K 5 6 afflicted Azotus and the c. thereof
6 9 if it go up by way of his own coasts
11 3 may send messengers to all the coasts

7 sent them into all the coasts of Israel
27 1 cease to seek me in all the coasts
2 K 21 5 left of his stock in all c. of Israel
3 K 1 3 young woman in all the coasts of Israel
4 K 10 32 ravaged them in all the c. of Israel
1 Pa 21 12 destroying in all the coasts of Israel
Jdth 2 15 from Cilicia to the coasts of Japheth
Ps 104 31 flies and sciniphs in all their coasts
33 broke in pieces the trees of their c.
Prov 31 10 from uttermost c. is the price of her
1 Ma 3 36 strangers to dwell in all their coasts
7 24 he went out into all the c. of Judea
Mat 8 34 he would depart from their c. Mark 5:17
15 21 retired into the c. of Tyre and Sidon
22 woman of Canaan who came out of those c.
39 he came into the coasts of Magedan
19 1 came into the c. of Judea. Mark 10:1
Mark 7 24 he went into the c. of Tyre and Sidon
31 again going out of the coasts of Tyre
31 through the midst of the c. of Decapolis
Acts 13 50 Jews . . . cast them out of their coasts
19 1 Paul having passed through the upper c.
27 2 meaning to sail by the coasts of Asia
coat Gen 37 3 made him a coat of divers colors
Gen 37 23 stript him of his outside coat, that
31 they took his coat and dipped it in the
32 whether it be thy son's coat, or not
33 it is my son's coat, an evil wild beast
1 K 2 19 his mother made him a little coat which
17 5 he was clothed with a coat of mail with
5 the weight of his coat of mail was 500
38 and armed him with a coat of mail. And
18 4 Jonathan stripped himself of the coat
2 K 20 8 close coat of equal length with his
1 Es 9 3 I rent my mantle and my coat, and
Job 30 18 about as with the collar of my coat
Jer 51 3 that is armed with a coat of mail
Mich 2 8 taken away the cloak off from the coat
Mat 5 40 take away thy coat, let go thy cloak
24 18 let him not go back to take his coat
Luke 6 29 cloak, forbid not to take thy coat also
22 36 let him sell his coat and buy a sword
John 19 23 the soldiers took . . . also his coat
23 the coat was without seam, woven from
21 7 girt his coat about him, for he was
coats Judg 14 12 thirty shirts, and as many coats
Judg 14 13 thirty shirts and same number of coats
2 Pa 26 14 helmets and coats of mail and bows
2 Es 4 16 shields and bows and coats of mail
Jer 46 4 furbish the spears, put on coats of mail
Eze 38 4 horsemen all clothed with coats of mail
Dan 3 21 burning fire with their coats and their
1 Ma 6 35 by every elephant 1,000 men in coats of
2 Ma 12 40 they found under the coats of the slain
Mat 10 10 scrip for your journey nor two coats
Mark 6 9 that they should not put on two coats
Luke 3 11 he that hath two coats, let him give
9 3 nor money, neither have two coats. And
Acts 9 39 showing him the coats and garments
cock Job 38 36 who gave the cock understanding
Prov 30 31 a cock girded about the loins: and a
Isa 22 17 as a cock is carried away, and he will
Mat 26 34 before the cock crow. 75; Mark 14:30, 72; Luke 22:61
74 the cock crew. Mark 14:68, 72; Luke 22: 60; John 18:27
Luke 22 34 the cock shall not crow. John 13:38
cockcrowing Tob 8 11 about the c., Raguel ordered
Mark 13 35 midnight or at the cockcrowing, or in
cockle Mat 13 25 oversowed cockle among the wheat
Mat 13 26 fruit, then appeared also the cockle
27 thy field, whence then hath it cockle
29 lest perhaps gathering up the c., you
30 gather up first the c. and bind it into
36 expound to us the parable of the cockle
38 c. are the children of the wicked one
40 c. therefore is gathered up and burnt
Cocytus Job 21 33 acceptable to the gravel of C.
coffin Gen 50 25 he was laid in a coffin in Egypt
co-heirs Heb 11 9 co-heirs of the same promise
1 P 3 7 as to the co-heirs of the grace of life
coin 1 Ma 15 6 I give thee leave to coin thy own
Mat 22 19 show me the coin of the tribute. And
coition Gen 30 39 in the very heat of c., the sheep
Colaia 2 Es 11 7 Phadaia the son of Colaia, the
cold Gen 8 22 cold and heat, summer and winter
Deut 28 22 with cold, with burning, and with heat
Job 24 7 who have no covering in the cold: who
37 9 tempest come, and cold out of the north
22 cold cometh out of the north, and to
Ps 147 17 who shall stand before face of his cold
Prov 20 4 because of the cold the sluggard would
25 13 as the cold of snow in time of harvest
20 looseth his garment in cold weather
27 15 roofs dropping through in a cold day
31 21 not fear for her house in cold of snow
Eccu 43 22 the cold north wind bloweth and the
Jer 6 7 as a cistern maketh its water cold, so
7 so hath she made her wickedness cold
18 14 can the cold waters that gush out and
Dan 3 67 ye cold and heat, bless the Lord
69 ye frost and cold, bless the Lord
Nah 3 17 swarm on the hedges in the day of cold
Zach 14 6 shall be no light, but cold and frost
Mat 10 42 a cup of cold water only in the name
24 12 the charity of many shall grow cold
John 18 18 at a fire of coals because it was cold
Acts 28 2 because of present rain and of the cold
2 C 11 27 in cold and nakedness; besides those
Apoc 3 15 thou art neither cold nor hot. 16
15 I would thou wert cold or hot. But
Colias Jer 29 21 Achab the son of Colias, and to
collar Job 30 18 as with the collar of my coat
colleague Dan 4 5 till their c. Daniel came in
collect 2 Ma 2 31 to c. all that is to be known
collection Bar 1 6 and they made a c. of money
collections 1 C 16 1 c. that are made for the
1 C 16 2 I come, the c. be not then to be made
collector 1 Ma 1 30 sent chief c. of his tributes
colony Wisd 12 7 might receive a worthy colony of
Acts 16 12 city of part of Macedonia, a colony
color Gen 30 35 and all the flock of one color
Lev 13 2 or flesh shall arise a different color
4 and the hair be of the former color
10 shall be a white color in the skin
21 but if the hair be of the former color
26 if the color of the hair be not changed
32 and the hair keep its color, and the
42 there be risen a white or reddish color
55 that the former color is not returned
Num 11 7 coriander seed, of the c. of bdellium
Esth 8 15 apparel, to wit, of violet and sky c.
15 8 she with a rosy color in her face and
10 sunk down, and her color turned pale
Prov 23 31 when the color thereof shineth in glass
Cant 1 5 because the sun hath altered my color
Lam 4 1 the finest color is changed, the stones
Eze 27 18 in rich wine, in wool of the best c.
2 Ma 3 8 under a color of visiting the cities
16 changing of his c. declared the inward
Acts 27 30 under c. as though they would have cast
colored Exod 26 14 another cover of violet c. skins
Exod 35 7 dyed red, and violet colored skins. 23
Eze 16 10 shod thee with violet colored shoes
Apoc 17 3 sitting upon a scarlet colored beast
colors Gen 30 32 all the sheep of divers colors

Gen 30 32 brown and spotted and of divers c.
33 all that is not of divers colors and
35 rams of divers colors and spotted
39 brought forth spotted and of divers c.
31 10 were of divers colors and spotted and
12 are of divers colors, spotted and
37 3 he made him a coat of divers colors
23 outside coat, that was of divers c.
Exod 28 6 linen, embroidered with divers colors
15 with embroidered work of divers c.
39 3 with the woof of the aforesaid colors
5 and a girdle of the same colors, as
Lev 14 56 when the colors are diversely changed
Judg 5 30 garments of divers colors are given to
1 Pa 29 2 stones like alabaster, and of divers c.
Job 28 16 not be compared with the dyed colors
Wisd 15 4 a graven figure with divers colors
Eze 16 13 embroidered work and many colors
18 tookest thy garments of divers colors
23 12 came to her, clothed with divers colors
14 images of the Chaldeans set forth in c.
Colossa Col 1 2 to the saints . . . who are at C.
colt Judg 15 16 with the jaw of the colt of asses
Job 11 12 himself free like a wild ass's colt
Eccu 23 30 he shall be chased as a colt: and where
Zach 9 9 and upon a colt the foal of an ass
Mat 21 5 sitting upon an ass and a colt the
7 they brought the ass and the colt and
Mark 11 2 you shall find a colt tied, upon which
4 they found the colt tied before the
5 what do you loosing the colt? Who said
7 and they brought the colt to Jesus
Luke 19 30 you shall find the colt of an ass tied
32 found the colt standing as he had said
33 as they were loosing the colt the
33 why loose you the colt? But they said
35 casting their garments on the colt
John 12 15 the king cometh, sitting on an ass's c.
colts Gen 32 15 milch camels with their colts
Judg 10 4 sons that rode on thirty ass colts
12 14 grandsons, mounted upon 70 ass colts
Isa 30 24 the ass colts that till the ground
combats 2 C 7 5 combats without, fears within
combing Isa 19 9 flax, c. and weaving fine linen
comeliness Ps 44 5 with thy c. and thy beauty set
Isa 53 2 is no beauty in him, nor comeliness
1 C 12 23 parts have more abundant comeliness
comely Gen 24 16 Rebecca . . . exceeding comely maid
Gen 39 6 Joseph saw . . . comely to behold. 49:22
1 K 16 12 beautiful to behold and of a comely face
18 prudent in his words and a c. person
17 42 ruddy, and of a comely countenance
25 3 was a prudent and very comely woman
2 K 1 23 Saul and Jonathan lovely and comely in
14 25 in all Israel there was not a man so c.
Ps 146 1 to our God be joyful and comely praise
Cant 1 15 thou art fair, my beloved, and comely
2 14 thy voice is sweet and thy face comely
6 3 sweet and comely as Jerusalem: terrible
7 6 and how comely, my dearest, in delights
Eccu 14 3 riches are not comely for a covetous
25 6 how comely is judgment for a gray head
7 how comely is wisdom for the aged, and
2 Ma 3 26 in comely apparel: who stood by him
6 18 years, and of a comely countenance
10 29 upon horses, c. with golden bridles
1 C 12 24 our comely parts have no need: but God
Heb 11 23 because they saw he was a comely babe
comers Heb 10 1 never make c. thereunto perfect
comfort Gen 5 29 this same shall comfort us from
Gen 37 35 to comfort their father in his sorrow
38 12 had taken comfort after his mourning
Ruth 4 15 shouldst have one to comfort thy soul
2 K 10 2 David sent his servants to comfort him
1 Pa 7 22 and his brethren came to comfort him
19 2 to comfort him upon the death of his
2 they were come . . . to comfort Hanon
Tob 10 4 the comfort of our life, the hope of
Jdth 8 21 comfort their hearts by your speech
11 1 be of good comfort, and fear not in
Job 2 11 together and visit him and c. him
6 10 this may be my comfort, that afflicting
7 13 if I say: My bed shall comfort me, and
15 11 great matter that God should c. thee
16 5 I would comfort you also with words
21 34 how then do ye comfort me in vain
Ps 68 21 for one that would c. me, and I found
118 76 let thy mercy be for my comfort
82 saying: When wilt thou comfort me? For
Wisd 3 18 nor speech of comfort in day of trial
8 9 will be a c. in my cares and grief
Eccu 3 7 shall be a comfort to his mother. He
38 17 then comfort thyself in thy sadness
24 c. him in the departing of his spirit
Isa 1 24 I will c. myself over my adversaries
22 4 labor not to comfort me, for the
51 3 Lord therefore will c. Sion and will c. all the ruins thereof
12 I myself will comfort you: who art
19 and thy sword, who shall comfort thee
54 11 tossed with tempest, without all c.
57 5 who seek your comfort in idols under
61 2 to comfort all that mourn: to appoint
66 13 so will I comfort you, and you shall
Jer 16 5 to mourn nor to comfort them: because
7 mourneth, to comfort him for the dead
7 to comfort them for their father and
31 13 into joy, and will comfort them and
48 17 comfort him, all you that are round
Lam 1 2 there is none to comfort her among all
17 there is none to comfort her: the Lord
21 and there is none to comfort me: all
2 13 that I may comfort thee, O virgin
Bar 4 5 be of good comfort, O people of God
21 be of good comfort, my children. 27
Eze 14 23 they shall comfort you when you shall
Osee 13 14 bite: comfort is hidden from my eyes
Zach 1 17 and the Lord will yet comfort Sion
1 Ma 12 9 having for our comfort the holy books
2 Ma 11 26 they may be of good comfort, and look
Mark 10 49 be of better comfort; arise, he calleth
John 11 19 to c. them concerning their brother
Rom 15 4 patience and comfort of the scriptures
5 the God of patience and of comfort
1 C 14 3 edification and exhortation and comfort
2 C 1 3 Father of mercies and God of all c.
4 to comfort them who are in all distress
5 also by Christ doth our comfort abound
2 7 rather forgive him and comfort him
7 4 I am filled with comfort: I exceedingly
Eph 6 22 that he may c. your hearts. Col 4:8
Phil 2 1 if any c. of charity, if any society of
19 that I also may be of good comfort when
Col 4 11 of God: who have been a comfort to me
1 Th 4 17 comfort ye one another with these words
5 11 comfort one another, and edify one
14 comfort the feeble minded, support the
Heb 6 18 we may have the strongest comfort, who
comfortable Zach 1 13 good words, c. words. And the
comforted Gen 34 3 sad, he c. her with sweet words
Gen 50 21 he comforted them and spoke gently and
Ruth 2 13 who hast comforted me and hast spoken
2 K 12 24 David c. Bethsabee his wife, and went
13 38 he was c. concerning the death of Amnon
Tob 1 19 among all his kindred and comforted them
10 7 but she could by no means be comforted

Jdth 6 16 was concluded, they comforted Achior
Job 29 13 and I comforted the heart of the widow
42 11 c. him upon all the evil that God had
Ps 22 4 thy rod and thy staff, they have c. me
70 21 turning to me thou hast comforted me
76 3 soul refused to be c.: I remembered
85 17 hast helped me and hast comforted me
118 50 this hath c. me in my humiliation
52 judgments of old: and I was comforted
125 1 of Sion, we became like men comforted
Eccu 35 21 till it come nigh he will not be c.
48 27 and comforted the mourners in Sion
Isa 12 1 turned away, and thou hast comforted me
40 1 be comforted, my people, saith your
49 13 the Lord hath c. his people. 52:9
66 13 you shall be comforted in Jerusalem
Jer 31 15 and refusing to be comforted for them
Eze 5 13 rest upon them, and I will be comforted
14 22 you shall be c. concerning the evil
31 16 were c. in the lowest parts of the
32 31 Pharao saw them and he was comforted
Zach 10 2 spoken vanity: they comforted in vain
Mat 2 18 would not be c., because they are not
5 5 that mourn: for they shall be comforted
Luke 16 25 he is comforted: and thou are tormented
John 11 31 comforted her, when they saw Mary
Acts 15 32 with many words comforted the brethren
16 40 they comforted them and departed. And
20 12 alive, they were not a little comforted
27 9 fast was now past, Paul comforted them
Rom 1 12 that I may be c. together in you, by
2 C 1 6 or whether we be c., it is for your
7 6 comforted us by the coming of Titus
7 wherewith he [Titus] was c. in you
13 therefore we were comforted. 1 Th 3:7
Col 2 2 that their hearts may be comforted
comforter Job 29 25 was a c. of them that mourned
Ecce 4 1 the innocent, and they had no comforter
Lam 1 9 cast down, not having a comforter
16 the comforter, the relief of my soul
Nah 3 7 whence shall I seek a c. for thee? Art
comforters 2 K 10 3 David hath sent c. 1 Pa 19:3
Job 16 2 you are all troublesome comforters
comforteth Job 5 11 c. with health those that mourn
2 C 1 4 c. us in all our tribulation; that we
7 6 God who comforteth the humble, comforted
comforting Eccu 7 38 not wanting in c. them that
Eze 16 54 in all that thou hast done, c. them
1 Th 2 11 manner, entreating and comforting you
Heb 10 25 comforting one another, and so much
comforts Ps 93 19 thy c. have given joy to my soul
Isa 57 18 and restored comforts to him and to
coming (noun) Mat 24 3 the sign of thy coming
Mat 24 27 the coming of the Son of man be. 37:39
25 27 at my coming I should have received
Mark 11 2 at your c. in thither, you shall find
Luke 19 23 at my coming I might have exacted it
Acts 7 52 who foretold of the c. of the Just One
13 24 John first preaching before his coming
1 C 15 23 Christ who have believed in his coming
2 C 7 6 comforted us by the coming of Titus. And not by his coming only
Phil 1 26 by my coming to you again. Only let
1 Th 2 19 our Lord Jesus Christ at his coming
4 14 who remain unto the coming of the Lord
2 Th 2 8 shall destroy with brightness of his c.
9 whose c. is according to the working of
2 Tim 4 1 dead, by his coming and his kingdom
8 but to them also that love his coming
Titus 2 13 coming of the glory of the great God
James 5 7 be patient until the coming of the Lord
8 for the coming of the Lord is at hand
2 P 3 4 where is his promise or his coming
12 unto the coming of the day of the Lord
1 J 2 28 not be comfounded by him at his coming
coming of our Lord 1 C 1 8 in day of the c. . . .
1 Th 3 13 at the c. . . . Jesus Christ with all
5 23 may be preserved blameless in c. . . .
2 Th 2 1 we beseech you, brethren, by the c. . . .
1 Tim 6 14 blameless, unto the c. . . . Jesus Christ
Jude 24 with exceeding joy, in the c. . . .
comings Eze 43 11 the goings out and the c. in
commander Gen 40 3 to prison of c. of the soldiers
4 K 25 8 Nabuzardan the c. of the army. 11
10 which was with the c. of the troops
Eze 38 7 and be thou commander over them
2 Ma 14 12 Nicanor, the c. over the elephants
commanders Num 31 48 when the c. of the army and
1 Pa 13 1 and of hundreds and with all the c.
commemoration Luke 22 19 do this for a c. of me
Rom 1 9 without ceasing I make a c. of you
1 C 11 24 this do for the c. of me. In like
25 as you shall drink, for the c. of me
Eph 1 16 making c. of you in my prayers, that
Heb 10 3 there is made a c. of sins every year
commend Ps 30 6 into thy hands I c. my spirit
Luke 23 46 Father, into thy hands I c. my spirit
Acts 20 32 now I commend you to God and to the
Rom 3 5 if our injustice c. the justice of God
16 1 I c. to you Phebe, our sister, who is
1 C 8 8 but meat doth not commend us to God
2 C 3 1 do we being again to commend ourselves
5 12 we commend not ourselves again to you
10 12 ourselves with some that c. themselves
1 Tim 1 18 this precept I commend to thee, O son
2 Tim 2 2 the same commend to faithful men, who
1 P 4 19 c. their souls in good deeds to the
commendable Eccu 37 25 fruit of understanding is c.
commendation 2 C 3 1 do we need epistles of c.
commended Ecce 8 15 therefore I commended mirth
Wisd 7 14 being c. for the gift of discipline
1 Ma 12 43 and commended him to all his friends
Luke 16 8 the lord commended the unjust steward
Acts 14 22 they commended them to the Lord, in
2 C 12 11 I ought to have been commended by you
commendeth Rom 5 8 God c. his charity towards us
2 C 10 18 not he who c. himself is approved, but he whom God commendeth
commending 2 C 4 2 c. ourselves to every man's
commentaries 2 Ma 2 13 memoirs and c. of Nehemias
commiseration Phil 2 1 if any bowels of c.: fulfill
commiserations Jer 16 5 Lord, my mercy and c.
Lam 3 22 his commiserations have not failed
Osee 2 19 judgment and in mercy and in c. And I
commission 2 Ma 3 7 sent him with c. to bring
commit Gen 19 7 brethren, do not commit this evil
Lev 6 2 extort anything or commit oppression
18 29 that shall c. any of these abominations
Num 5 6 the sins that men are wont to commit
18 22 to the tabernacle nor c. deadly sin
Judg 19 24 commit not this crime against nature
2 K 7 14 if he c. any iniquity, I will correct
4 K 17 21 and made them commit a great sin
Tob 12 10 but they that commit sin and iniquity
Ps 36 5 commit thy way to the Lord, and trust
Ecce 8 11 of men commit evils without any fear
Eccu 9 19 commit no fault, lest he take away
Jer 9 5 they have labored to commit iniquity
44 4 do not commit this abominable thing
7 why do you commit this great evil
Eze 3 20 from his justice and shall c. iniquity
8 9 abominations which they commit here
13 greater abominations which these commit
17 that they should c. these abominations
33 13 trusting in his justice, c. iniquity
2 Ma 2 26 may more easily commit to memory

13 13 to c. the event of the thing to the
2 C 11 7 did I c. a fault, humbling myself
James 2 9 you have respect to persons, you c. sin
commit adultery; *see* **adultery**
commit fornication; *see* **fornication**
committed Gen 34 7 c. an unlawful act, in ravishing
Gen 39 4 he governed the house committed to him
23 having committed all things to him
44 7 had committed so heinous a fact? The
Exod 22 3 sun is risen, he hath committed murder
Lev 6 2 which was committed to his trust; or
20 13 both have committed an abomination
17 they have committed a crime: they shall
Num 5 6 shall have c. any of all the sins that
8 26 things that are committed to their care
12 11 sin, which we have foolishly committed
Deut 9 18 all your sins, which you had committed
21 and your sin that you had committed
13 14 abomination hath been really committed
17 4 that the abomination is c. in Israel
5 who have c. that most wicked thing
21 22 when a man hath c. a crime for which
Judg 9 25 they c. robberies, taking spoils of
20 3 how so great a wickedness had been c.
6 so great an abomination c. in Israel
13 that have committed this heinous crime
21 22 the fault was committed on your part
3 K 8 47 unjustly, we have committed wickedness
14 22 had done, in their sins which they c.
1 Pa 9 26 to these four Levites were committed
29 instruments of the sanctuary c. unto
2 Pa 33 23 but [Amon] committed far greater sins
34 16 all that thou hast c. to thy servants
2 Es 9 18 and had committed great blasphemies
13 13 to them were c. the portions of their
Jdth 7 19 unjustly, we have committed iniquity
Prov 11 13 the thing c. to him by his friend
Eccu 19 15 for there is often a fault committed
48 18 but others c. many sins. Ezechias
49 5 all c. sin. For the kings of Juda
Jer 5 7 they c. adultery and rioted in the
6 15 confounded because they c. abomination
8 12 because they have c. abomination: yea
29 23 have c. adultery with the wives of
37 20 be c. into the entry of the prison
39 14 c. him [Jeremias] to Godolias the son
40 7 had c. unto him men and women and
41 10 had c. to Godolias the son of Ahicam
44 3 of the wickedness which they have c.
22 the abominations which you have c.
Bar 6 1 for the sins that you have c. before
Eze 6 9 the evils which they have c. in all
8 17 abominations which they have c. 33:29
9 4 abominations that are c. in the midst
16 50 lifted up and c. abominations before
51 Samaria committed not half thy sins
18 21 for all his sins which he hath c.
24 in his sin, which he hath committed
20 43 all your wicked deeds which you c.
22 9 have c. wickedness in the midst of
11 hath committed abomination with his
29 have used oppression and c. robbery
23 7 she c. her fornications with those
8 fornications which she had c. in Egypt
37 because they have committed adultery
33 13 his iniquity which he hath committed
16 none of his sins, which he hath c.
26 you have committed abominations, and
43 8 the abominations which they committed
44 13 wickednesses which they have committed
Dan 3 29 for we have sinned and c. iniquity
9 5 have sinned, we have c. iniquity. 15
13 52 which thou hast committed before: in
Osee 7 1 for they have committed falsehood, and
12 8 me the iniquity that I have committed
Mala 2 11 abomination hath been c. in Israel and
1 Ma 1 55 and they committed evils in the land
7 20 then he c. the country to Alcimus and
8 16 they c. their government to one man
13 39 or fault committed unto this day, we
16 17 he c. a great treachery in Israel and
2 Ma 3 22 things that had been c. to them, safe
22 sure for those that had committed them
4 3 murders also were c. by some of Simon's
38 place wherein he had c. the impiety
39 when many sacrileges had been committed
10 13 Cyprus which Philometor had c. to him
12 42 that the sin which had been c. might be
13 8 c. many sins against the altar of God
Mat 5 28 hath already committed adultery with
25 27 to have c. my money to the bankers and
Mark 15 7 in the sedition had committed murder
Luke 12 48 to whom they have committed much, of
Acts 8 3 but Saul . . . committed them to prison
25 11 or have c. anything worthy of death
27 40 they committed themselves to the sea
Rom 3 2 the words of God were committed to them
1 C 9 17 a dispensation is committed to me
2 C 12 21 lasciviousness that they have committed
Gal 2 7 me was c. gospel of the uncircumcision
1 Th 2 4 that the gospel should be c. to us
1 Tim 1 11 which hath been committed to my trust
6 20 that which is committed to thy trust
2 Tim 1 12 that which I have committed unto him
14 keep the good thing c. to thy trust
3 14 which have been c. to thee: knowing
Titus 1 3 which is committed to me according to
committed fornication; *see* **fornication**
committest Rom 2 22 that sayest, men should not commit adultery, committest adultery
Rom 2 22 thou that abhorrest idols, c. sacrilege
committeth Num 15 30 c. anything through pride
Eze 8 6 that the house of Israel c. here, that
18 12 his eyes to idols, that c. abomination
26 away from his justice and c. iniquity
Mat 5 32 marry her that is put away, committeth adultery. 19:9; Luke 16:18
19 9 marry another, committeth adultery. Mark 10:11; Luke 16:18
Mark 10 12 married to another, she c. adultery
John 8 34 whosoever c. sin is the servant of sin
1 C 6 18 that c. fornication, sinneth against his
1 J 3 4 whosoever c. sin, c. also iniquity
8 he that c. sin is of the devil: for
9 whosoever is born of God, c. not sin
committing Deut 4 25 c. evil before the Lord your
Judg 2 17 c. fornication with strange gods and
2 Ma 13 14 c. all to God, the creator of the world
1 P 2 20 if c. sin and being buffeted for it
commodious 2 Ma 8 6 possession of most c. places
2 Ma 10 15 Jews that occupy the most c. hold
Acts 27 12 it was not a commodious haven to winter
common Gen 23 16 silver of common current money
Lev 19 29 make not thy daughter a common strumpet
21 15 stock of his kindred with the c. people
Num 1 17 all the multitude of the common people
16 29 if these men die the c. death of men
20 17 but we will go by the common highway
Deut 20 6 hath not as yet made it to be common
Josu 6 9 the rest of the c. people followed. 13
9 18 then all the common people murmured
Judg 19 30 decree in common what ought to be done
1 K 6 19 slew . . . 50,000 of the common people
14 25 all the c. people came into a forest
15 8 all the common people he [Saul] slew
21 4 I have no common bread at hand, but

2 K 14 26 at 200 sicles, according to c. weight
3 K 10 27 and cedars to be as c. as sycamores
2 Pa 9 27 and cedars as common as the sycamores
Prov 21 9 brawling woman, and in a c. house. 25:24
Wisd 7 3 being born I drew in the common air
13 11 profitable for the common uses of life
18 11 a common man suffered in like manner
Jer 26 23 into the graves of the common people
52 15 and of the rest of the common sort who
Eze 12 23 shall it be any more a common saying
16 24 didst also build thee a common stew
44 that useth a common proverb, shall use
2 Ma 3 6 the common store was infinite, which
4 5 with a view to the common good of all
8 29 they had all made a common supplication
9 4 and make it a common buryingplace. 14
21 to take care for the common good: not
10 8 they ordained by a common statute and
11 15 providing for the common good in all
12 4 according to the c. decree of the city
14 25 lived quietly, and they lived in common
15 36 they all ordained by a common decree
Mark 7 2 disciples eat bread with common, that
5 but they eat bread with common hands
Acts 2 44 together and had all things in common
4 32 but all things were common unto them
5 18 apostles, and put them in the c. prison
10 14 I never did eat anything that is common
15 God hath cleansed, do not thou call c.
28 showed to me to call no man common or
11 8 nothing common or unclean hath ever
9 hath made clean, do not thou call c.
19 11 hand of Paul more than c. miracles
Rom 1 12 in you by that which is common to us
Titus 1 4 according to the common faith, grace
Jude 3 unto you concerning your c. salvation
commonly Jer 3 1 it is c. said: If a man put away
commonwealth Esth 16 9 profit of the c. requireth
commotion Jer 10 22 great c. out of land of the
Jer 51 29 the land shall be in a commotion and
Eze 3 12 behind me the voice of a great commotion
13 and the noise of a great commotion. The
37 7 was a noise, and behold a commotion
38 19 be a great c. upon the land of Israel
commune 2 Ma 11 20 are sent by me, to c. with you
2 Ma 14 21 day upon which they might c. together
communicate Ps 140 4 will not c. with the choicest
Wisd 7 13 without guile, and c. without envy and
8 9 she will c. to me of her good things
Eccu 8 5 c. not with an ignorant man, lest he
2 Ma 5 20 shall c. in the good things thereof
John 4 9 the Jews do not c. with the Samaritans
Gal 6 6 c. to him that instructeth him, in all
1 Tim 6 18 to give easily, to communicate to others
communicated Jdth 2 2 c. to them the secret of his
Gal 2 2 c. to them the gospel, which I preach
Phil 4 15 no church communicated with me, as
communicateth Eccu 26 9 scourge of tongue which c.
2 J 11 communicateth with his wicked works
communicating Rom 12 13 c. to the necessities of
2 C 9 13 the simplicity of your c. unto them
Phil 4 14 have done well in c. to my tribulation
communication Prov 3 32 his c. is with the simple
Wisd 8 18 glory in the communication of her words
Eccu 9 20 know it to be a c. with death: for thou
1 Ma 12 36 that so it might have no communication
Acts 2 42 in the c. of the breaking of bread and
2 C 8 4 the grace and c. of the ministry that
13 13 the c. of the Holy Ghost be with you
Phil 1 5 for your communication in the gospel
Philem 6 c. of thy faith may be made evident
communications 1 C 15 33 evil c. corrupt good
communion 1 C 10 16 is it not the c. of the blood

compact Ps 121 3 as a city, which is c. together
compacted Wisd 7 2 time of ten months I was c.
Eph 4 16 the whole body, being compacted and
Col 2 19 being supplied with nourishment and c.
companied Acts 1 21 who have companied with us
companies Gen 32 7 and the camels, into two c.
Gen 32 10 and now I return with two companies
Exod 6 26 out of land of Egypt by their c. 12:51
Judg 9 43 divided it into three companies, and
44 the two other c. chased the enemies
1 K 11 11 Saul put the people in three companies
13 17 out of camp of the Philistines three c.
1 Pa 27 1 served the king according to their c.
28 1 captains of the c. who waited on
2 Pa 20 21 to praise him by their companies and to
23 8 permitted not the companies to depart
13 princes and the companies about him
31 2 appointed companies of the priests and
17 and upward, by their classes and c.
35 5 by the families and companies of Levi
10 the Levites also in their companies
Cant 7 1 but the c. of camps? How beautiful
Isa 57 13 cry, let thy companies deliver thee
Eze 26 7 from the north, with horses . . . and c.
1 Ma 5 33 he came with three c. behind them
Mark 6 39 make them all sit down by companies
companion Gen 3 12 whom thou gavest me to be my c.
Exod 38 23 having for his companion Ooliab the son
2 K 20 11 have been in Joab's stead the c. of
3 K 20 35 his companion in the word of the Lord
Job 16 22 as the son of man is judged with his c.
30 29 of dragons and companion of ostriches
Eccu 6 10 is a friend a companion at the table
37 2 companion and a friend shall be turned
4 there is a companion who rejoiceth with
5 there is a companion who condoleth with
40 23 friend and companion meeting together
41 23 injustice before a companion and friend
2 C 8 19 the churches c. of our travels, for
23 for Titus, who is my companion and
Phil 4 3 my sincere c., help those women who
companions Judg 3 18 he followed his c. that came
Judg 9 41 Zebul drove Gaal and his companions
48 [Abimelech] said to his companions
11 37 may bewail my virginity with my c.
38 she was gone with her comrades and c.
14 11 brought him thirty c. to be with him
20 friends and bridal c. for her husband
4 K 4 40 they poured it out for the c. to eat
Job 17 5 he promiseth a prey to his companions
18 15 let the companions of him that is not
Cant 1 6 after the flocks of thy companions
Eccu 42 3 of the affair of c. and travellers and
Isa 1 23 are faithless, companions of thieves
Jer 40 7 they and their companions, had heard
9 swore to them and to their companions
52 8 all his c. were scattered from him
Dan 2 13 Daniel and his c. were sought for, to
17 told the matter to . . . Azarias his c.
18 and his companions might not perish
3 49 went down with Azarias and his c. into
2 Ma 8 20 Macedonians their c. were at a stand
12 22 were often thrown down by their own c.
14 18 hearing of the valor of Judas' c. and
Mat 11 17 crying to their c., say: We have piped
Acts 19 29 Gaius and Aristarchus . . . Paul's c.
22 11 being led by the hand by my companions
Heb 10 33 c. of them that were used in such sort
company Gen 14 15 Abram . . . dividing his c., he
Gen 24 59 nurse, and Abraham's servant and his c.
32 8 if Esau come to one c. and destroy it
8 the other c. that is left shall escape
38 16 wilt thou give me to enjoy my company

50 9 horsemen: and it was a great company
14 all that were in his c., after he had
Num 16 6 censers, thou Core and all thy company
11 thy c. should stand against the Lord
Judg 4 10 fighting men, having Debbora in his c.
9 44 set upon them, with his own company
1 K 10 5 thou shalt meet a company of prophets
10 behold a company of prophets met him
13 17 one c. went towards the way of Ephra
19 20 when they saw a company of prophets
30 15 canst thou bring to this company
15 and I will bring thee to this company
2 K 20 11 some men of Joab's company stopping
1 Pa 27 2 over the first company the first month
4 the company of the second month was
5 the captain of the third company for
7 in his c. were 4 and 20 thousand. 8–15
1 Es 10 8 he should be cast out of the company
Tob 1 5 [Tobias] alone fled the company of all
Job 34 8 in company with them that work iniquity
Prov 21 16 shall abide in company of the giants
Cant 1 8 to my c. of horsemen, in Pharao's
Wisd 8 16 nor her company any tediousness, but
Eccu 9 4 use not much the c. of her that is a
12 13 that keepeth company with a wicked man
32 13 in the c. of great men take not upon
Isa 14 20 thou shalt not keep company with them
Jer 31 8 great company of them returning hither
Eze 38 15 a great company and a mighty army. And
1 Ma 3 13 heard that Judas had assembled a c. of
16 went forth to meet him with a small c.
18 a great multitude or with a small c.
6 41 the marching of the c. and the rattling
7 12 a company of the scribes to require
9 44 Jonathan said to his c.: Let us arise
12 49 plain to destroy all Jonathan's company
2 Ma 1 15 he with a small c. had entered into
5 27 beasts in the mountains with his c.
12 39 Judas came with his company to take
13 15 having given his c. for a watchword
Luke 2 44 thinking that he was in the company
5 29 there was a great company of publicans
6 17 c. of his disciples and a very great
9 14 make them sit down by fifties in a c.
24 22 women also of our company affrighted us
Acts 4 23 came to their own company and related
9 7 the men who went in c. with him stood
10 28 keep c. or to come unto one of another
15 22 to choose men of their own company and
26 13 and them that were in company with me
1 C 5 9 not to keep company with fornicators
11 not to keep c. if any man that is named
2 Th 3 14 do not keep company with him, that he
Heb 12 22 to the c. of many thousands of angels
compare Wisd 7 9 neither did I c. unto her any
Lam 2 13 to what shall I compare thee? Or to
Mark 4 30 or to what parable shall we compare it
2 C 10 12 we dare not . . . c. ourselves with some
12 we compare ourselves with ourselves
compared Gen 30 8 God hath c. me with my sister
Deut 3 24 or to be compared to thy strength. I
Job 9 2 men cannot be justified c. with God
13 12 your remembrance shall be c. to ashes
22 2 can man be c. with God, even though he
25 4 can man be justified c. with God, or
28 16 it shall not be c. with the dyed colors
19 shall it be c. to the cleanest dyeing
30 19 I am compared to dirt, and am likened
41 24 power upon earth that can be c. with him
Ps 48 13 he is compared to senseless beasts, and
21 he hath been c. to senseless beasts and
88 7 can be compared to the Lord, or who
Prov 3 15 are desired, are not to be c. with her
8 11 may be desired cannot be compared to it
Wisd 7 29 c. with the light, she is found before
15 18 things without sense compared to these
Eccu 6 15 can be compared to a faithful friend
18 8 sand, so are a few years c. to eternity
Isa 46 5 and made me equal and compared me and
Eze 31 8 plane trees to be compared with him
James 1 23 compared to a man beholding his own
comparest Jer 22 15 c. thyself to the cedar? Did
comparing 1 C 2 13 comparing spiritual things with
comparison Num 13 34 in c. of whom, we seemed like
Job 4 17 man be justified in comparison of God
28 18 not be mentioned in comparison of it
Wisd 7 8 riches as nothing in comparison of her
9 gold in c. of her is as a little sand
Jer 3 11 in comparison of the treacherous Juda
Bar 3 36 no other be accounted of in c. of him
Agge 2 4 is it not in c. to that as nothing
compass Num 21 4 to c. the land of Edom. And the
Num 34 5 limits shall fetch a c. from Asemona
Josu 6 7 compass the city, armed, marching
18 4 and they may go and compass the land
2 K 5 23 but fetch a compass behind them, and
3 K 7 35 was a round compass of half a cubit
4 K 3 9 fetched a c. of seven days' journey
11 8 you shall c. him round about, having
2 Pa 4 2 from brim to brim, round in compass
14 7 cities, and compass them with walls
Job 40 17 willows of the brook shall c. him about
Ps 25 6 and will compass thy altar, O Lord
90 5 his truth shall c. thee with a shield
Prov 8 27 when with a certain law and compass
Cant 2 5 flowers, compass me about with apples
Isa 44 13 fashioned it round with the compass
Jer 31 22 the earth: a woman shall compass a man
39 Goreb: and it shall compass Goatha
Eze 26 8 he shall compass thee with forts and
Haba 2 16 shall c. thee, and shameful vomiting
1 Ma 14 48 set up with the c. of the sanctuary
2 Ma 1 15 had entered into the c. of the temple
Luke 19 43 compass thee round and straiten thee
compassed Exod 28 11 set in gold and c. about
Deut 2 1 we compassed mount Seir a long time
3 you have c. this mountain long enough
20 19 and hast compassed it with bulwarks
2 K 22 6 the cords of hell c. me: the snares of
3 K 7 15 line of 12 cubits c. both the pillars
23 line of 30 cubits c. it round. 2 Pa 4:2
24 graven work under the brim of it c. it
2 Pa 4 3 ten cubits c. the belly of the sea
9 16 armory, which was compassed with a wood
Jdth 4 4 they compassed their towns with walls
13 12 having compassed the valley, they came
Job 16 14 hath c. me round about with his lances
19 6 and compassed me with his scourges
Ps 29 12 and hast compassed me with gladness
87 18 they have compassed me about together
108 3 have c. me about with words of hatred
114 3 the sorrows of death have compassed me
117 10 all nations compassed me about; and
11 surrounding me they compassed me about
Prov 8 29 when he c. the sea with its bounds and
25 28 that lieth open and is not c. with walls
Eccu 24 8 I alone have compassed the circuit of
45 10 c. him with many little bells of gold
22 compassed him about in the wilderness
51 5 gates of afflictions, which c. me about
10 they compassed me on every side, and
Jer 52 21 a cord of 12 cubits compassed it about
23 in all, were compassed with network
Lam 3 5 and he hath c. me with gall and labor
Osee 11 12 hath compassed me about with denials
Amos 3 11 in tribulation shall be c. about

Jon 2 4 the sea, and a flood hath compassed me
6 the waters c. me about even to the soul
1 Ma 6 7 they had c. about the sanctuary with
2 Ma 3 17 for the man was so c. with sadness and
Luke 21 20 when you shall see Jerusalem c. about
Heb 5 2 he himself also is c. with infirmity
compasseth Gen 2 11 c. all the land of Hevilath
Gen 2 13 compasseth all the land of Ethiopia
Josu 15 10 it compasseth from Baala westward unto
Eccu 23 26 darkness c. me about, and the walls
compassing Josu 15 3 up to Addar and c. Carcaa
Ps 139 10 the head of them compassing me about
Prov 18 11 as a strong wall compassing him about
Eze 46 23 c. the four little courts, and there
Acts 28 13 c. by the shore, we came to Rhegium
compassion Exod 2 6 infant crying, having c. on it
Exod 34 6 patient and of much c., and true, who
3 K 8 50 that they may have compassion on them
2 Pa 36 17 no compassion on young man or maiden
2 Es 9 17 longsuffering and full of compassion
Job 30 25 my soul had compassion on the poor
Ps 24 6 remember, O Lord, thy bowels of c.
85 15 art a God of compassion and merciful
102 4 who crowneth thee with mercy and c.
13 the Lord hath c. on them that fear him
13 as a father hath c. on his children
Wisd 10 5 him strong against the c. for his son
Eccu 18 12 the c. of man is toward his neighbor
Eze 16 5 these things for thee, out of c. to
Jon 4 2 merciful God, patient and of much c.
Zach 7 9 show ye mercy and c. every man to his
1 Ma 3 44 might pray and ask mercy and compassion
Mat 9 36 he had c. on them. 14:14; Mark 6:34
15 32 I have c. on the multitudes. Mark 8:2
18 33 have had c. also on thy fellow servant even as I had c. on thee
20 34 having c. on them, touched their eyes
Mark 1 41 Jesus having c. on him, stretched forth
9 21 help us, having compassion on us. And
Luke 10 33 seeing him, was moved with c. And going
15 20 father saw him and was moved with c.
Heb 4 15 who cannot have c. on our infirmities
5 2 can have c. on them that are ignorant
10 34 you had c. on them that were in bands
1 P 3 8 of one mind, having c. one of another
compassionate Exod 22 27 will hear because I am c.
Ps 102 8 the Lord is compassionate and merciful
111 4 he is merciful and compassionate and
Eccu 2 13 for God is c. and merciful, and will
James 5 11 the Lord is merciful and campassionate
compel 1 Ma 2 15 to c. them . . . to sacrifice and
2 Ma 6 1 to compel the Jews to depart from the
Luke 14 23 compel them to come in, that my house
Gal 2 14 c. the Gentiles to live as do the Jews
compelled Exod 22 11 not be c. to make restitution
Lev 24 20 the like shall he be compelled to suffer
Josu 9 24 compelled by the dread we had of you
Prov 30 9 or being c. by poverty, I should steal
1 Ma 2 25 sent, who compelled them to sacrifice
2 Ma 6 7 were c. to go about crowned with ivy
7 1 c. by the king to eat swine's flesh
Acts 26 11 I compelled them to blaspheme: and
2 C 12 11 I am become foolish: you have c. me
Gal 2 3 neither Titus . . . c. to be circumcised
compelling Exod 32 18 nor shout of men c. to flee
complain Judg 21 22 shall begin to c. against you
Eccu 29 6 words and will complain of the time
41 10 children will complain of an ungodly
1 Ma 10 63 that no man complain of an ungodly
complained Judg 14 16 she wept before Samson and c.
complaining 1 Ma 8 32 again to us complaining of
2 Ma 4 36 him: c. of the unjust murder of Onias
complaint 2 K 19 28 what just c. therefore have I
1 Es 6 9 that there be no complaint in anything
Ecce 7 15 not find against him any just complaint
Eccu 18 15 in thy good deeds, make no complaint
35 17 the widow, when she poureth out her c.
Col 3 13 if any have a c. against another: even
complaints Num 17 10 that their c. may cease from
Job 23 4 would fill my mouth with complaints
33 10 he hath found complaints against me
1 Ma 11 25 men of his nation made c. against him
15 35 as to thy complaints concerning Joppe
Jude 16 are murmurers, full of c., walking
completed 2 Pa 29 35 house of the Lord was c.
James 1 15 sin, when it is completed, begetteth
completely 4 K 12 12 might be c. finished, and
complied 1 Es 6 12 which I will have diligently c.
comply 2 Ma 14 29 opportunity to c. with the orders
composition Exod 30 9 incense of another c. nor
Exod 30 32 make none other of the same composition
37 such a composition for your own uses
Eccu 49 1 is like the c. of a sweet smell made by
Eze 24 10 the whole composition shall be sodden
compound Exod 30 33 what man soever shall compound
compounded Exod 30 25 ointment c. after the art of
Exod 30 35 incense c. by the work of the perfumer
37 29 he compounded also the oil for the
Lev 16 12 the c. perfume for incense, he shall
comprehend Job 11 7 thou wilt c. the steps of God
John 1 5 and the darkness did not comprehend it
Eph 3 18 may be able to c. with all the saints
comprehended Dan 7 1 dream, he c. it in few words
comprised 2 Ma 2 24 been c. in five books by Jason
Rom 13 9 is comprised in this word, Thou shalt
compunction Acts 2 37 they had c. in their heart
computation Lev 25 15 according to the c. of the
comrades Judg 11 38 when she was gone with her c.
conceal Gen 37 26 our brother, and c. his blood
Deut 13 8 thy eye spare him to pity and c. him
Job 10 13 although thou c. these things in thy
27 11 Almighty hath, and I will not conceal
Prov 25 2 it is the glory of God to c. the word
Jer 50 2 proclaim, and conceal it not: say
concealed Tob 1 23 lay c., for many loved him
Job 13 9 him from whom nothing can be concealed
31 33 and have c. my iniquity in my bosom
Ps 31 5 and my injustice I have not concealed
39 11 I have not c. thy mercy and thy truth
Isa 45 3 the concealed riches of secret places
concealeth Prov 11 13 c. the thing committed to
Prov 12 23 a cautious man concealeth knowledge
17 9 he that c. a transgression, seeketh
conceit Prov 3 7 be not wise in thy own conceit
Prov 26 12 seen a man wise in his own conceit
16 sluggard is wiser in his own conceit
Wisd 8 11 I shall be found of a quick conceit
Luke 1 51 scattered the proud in c. of their heart
conceits Isa 5 21 and prudent in your own conceits
Rom 11 25 should be wise in your own conceits
12 16 humble. Be not wise in your own c.
conceive Gen 25 21 and made Rebecca to conceive
Gen 25 22 what need was there to conceive? And
30 38 in the sight of them might conceive
41 that they might conceive while they
Judg 13 3 shalt conceive and bear a son. 5, 7
Ruth 1 12 although I might conceive this night
4 13 the Lord gave her to conceive and to
Ps 50 7 and in sins did my mother conceive me
Wisd 7 15 to c. thoughts worthy of those things
Isa 7 14 a virgin shall conceive and bear a son
33 11 you shall conceive heat, you shall
Eze 38 10 thou shalt c. a mischievous design
Luke 1 31 behold thou shalt conceive in thy womb
Heb 11 11 received strength to c. seed, even
conceived Gen 4 1 who c. and brought forth Cain

Gen 4 17 she conceived and brought forth Henoch
21 2 she conceived and bore a son. 29:32, 33, 35; 30:23; 38:3; Exod 2:2; 1 Pa 7:23; Isa 8:3; Osee 1:3, 8
29 34 she conceived the third time and bore
30 5 [Bala] conceived and bore a son. And
7 again Bala conceived and bore another
10 when she [Zelpha] had conceived and
17 she conceived and bore the fifth son
19 Lia conceived again and bore the sixth
38 18 therefore at one copulation conceived
Num 11 12 have I conceived all this multitude
1 K 1 20 Anna c. and bore a son and called his
2 21 [Anna] conceived and bore three sons
2 K 11 5 she returned to her house having c.
5 told David and said: I have conceived
4 K 4 17 the woman c. and brought forth a son
Job 3 3 it was said: A man child is conceived
16 that being c. have not seen the light
4 2 who can withhold the words he hath c.
14 4 clean that is conceived of unclean seed
15 35 hath c. sorrow and hath brought. Ps 7:15
21 10 their cattle have c. and failed not
Ps 50 7 I was c. in iniquity: and in sins did
Prov 8 24 as yet, and I was already conceived
Isa 26 18 we have c. and been as it were in labor
59 4 they have c. labor and brought forth
13 we have c. and uttered from the heart
Jer 49 30 and hath conceived designs against you
Osee 1 6 she c. again and bore a daughter, and
2 5 she that c. them is covered with shame
1 Ma 12 39 Tryphon had c. a design to make himself
2 Ma 4 35 also the other nations c. indignation
Mat 1 20 that which is c. in her, is of the Holy
Luke 1 24 Elizabeth his wife conceived, and hid
36 she also hath c. a son in her old age
2 21 called by the angel before he was c.
Acts 5 4 why hast thou c. this thing in thy
Rom 9 10 when Rebecca also had conceived at once
James 1 15 when concupiscence hath conceived, it
conceiving Gen 30 42 coming was, and the last c.
Gen 31 10 time came of the ewes conceiving, I
38 4 and c. again, she bore a son [Onan]
conception Jer 20 17 her womb an everlasting c.
Osee 9 11 and from the womb and from the c.
conceptions Gen 3 16 thy sorrows and thy c.
concern Eccu 11 9 matter which doth not c. thee
2 Ma 15 18 their concern was less for their wives
19 had no little c. for them that were
Mark 4 38 doth it not c. thee that we perish
Acts 28 31 teaching the things which c. the Lord
2 C 11 30 the things that concern my infirmity
Eph 6 21 may know the things that concern me
Col 4 7 all the things that c. me, Tychicus
8 he may know the things that concern you
concerned 1 K 9 5 the asses, be concerned for us
1 K 10 2 no more of the asses, is c. for you
Amos 6 6 they are not c. for the affliction of
concerneth 1 K 21 5 as to what c. women, we have
Eze 12 10 this burden concerneth my prince that
concerns 2 Ma 11 23 diligently to their own c.
concert Eccu 32 7 c. of music in a banquet of
concertation Eccu 18 32 their c. is continual
concision Phil 3 2 beware of the concision. For we
concluded Jdth 6 16 people's prayer . . . was c.
2 Ma 15 24 and thus he concluded his prayer. But
Rom 11 32 God hath c. all in unbelief, that he
Gal 3 22 the scripture hath c. all under sin
conclusion Ecce 12 13 all hear together the c.
concord Esth 13 4 violated . . . c. of all nations
Esth 13 5 disturbing the peace and concord of the
Eccu 25 2 the concord of brethren, and the love of
2 C 6 15 and what c. hath Christ with Belial
concourse Acts 19 40 no man guilty . . . of this c.
Acts 24 12 causing any concourse of the people
concubine Gen 22 24 his c., naked Roma, bore Tabee
Gen 35 22 with Bala, the concubine of his father
36 12 Thamna was the concubine of Eliphaz
Judg 8 31 his concubine, that he had in Sichem
19 10 with him two asses laden, and his c.
24 and this man hath a concubine, I will
25 the man seeing, brought out his c.
27 his concubine lay before the door
2 K 3 7 Saul had a concubine named Respha, the
8 why didst thou go in to my father's c.
21 11 daughter of Aia, the concubine of Saul
1 Pa 1 32 sons of Cetura, Abraham's concubine
2 46 and Epha the c. of Caleb bore Haran
48 Maacha the c. of Caleb bore Saber
7 14 his concubine the Syrian bore Machir
2 Ma 4 30 for a gift to Antiochis, the king's c.
concubines Gen 25 6 to the children of the c. he
2 K 5 13 David took more concubines and wives
15 16 the king left ten women his concubines
16 21 go in to the concubines of thy father
22 he went in to his father's concubines
19 5 wives and the lives of thy concubines
20 3 he took the ten women his concubines
3 K 11 3 he had 700 wives as queens, and 300 c.
1 Pa 3 9 beside the sons of the concubines: and
2 Pa 11 21 above all his wives and concubines
21 married eighteen wives and threescore c.
Esth 2 14 the charge over the king's concubines
Cant 6 7 are threescore queens and fourscore c.
8 the queens and c., and they praised her
Dan 5 2 wives and his c. might drink in them
3 wives and his concubines drank in them
23 and thy c. have drunk wine in them
concupiscence Wisd 4 12 wandering of c. overturneth
Rom 7 7 I had not known concupiscence if the
8 wrought in me all manner of c. For
Col 3 5 evil c. and covetousness, which is the
James 1 14 but every man is tempted by his own c.
15 when c. hath conceived, it bringeth
2 P 1 4 flying the corruption of that c. which
1 J 2 16 c. of the flesh and the c. of the eyes
17 world passeth away and the c. thereof
concupiscences Rom 13 14 for the flesh in its c.
Gal 5 24 their flesh with the vices and c. If
James 4 1 are they not hence, from your c. which
3 that you may consume it on your c.
concurring Wisd 7 2 and the pleasure of sleep c.
condemn Lev 13 43 he shall c. him undoubtedly of
Deut 25 1 they shall condemn of wickedness. And if
Job 9 20 my own mouth shall condemn me: if I
10 2 I will say to God: Do not condemn me
15 6 thy own mouth shall condemn thee, and
34 12 God will not condemn without cause
17 dost thou so far c. him that is just
29 peace, who is there that can condemn
40 3 c. me, that thou mayst be justified
Ps 36 33 nor condemn him when he shall be judged
72 15 should c. the generation of thy children
93 21 just, and will condemn innocent blood
Wisd 2 20 let us c. him to a most shameful death
11 11 severe king, thou didst examine and c.
12 15 to c. him who deserveth not to be
Isa 50 9 helper: who is he that shall condemn me
54 17 thee in judgment, thou shalt condemn
Jer 26 19 and all Juda, condemn him to death
Mat 12 41 in judgment with this generation and shall c. it. 42; Luke 11:32
20 18 they shall c. him to death. Mark 10:33
Luke 6 37 c. not, and you shall not be condemned
11 31 this generation, and shall c. them
John 8 11 neither will I condemn thee. Go, and

Acts 25 16 not custom of the Romans to c. any man
Rom 8 34 who is he that shall condemn? Christ
condemnation Wisd 12 27 end also of their c. came
Wisd 17 10 it beareth witness of its condemnation
Luke 23 40 thou art under the same condemnation
Acts 25 15 came unto me, desiring c. against him
Rom 5 16 judgment indeed was by one unto c.
18 the offence of one, unto all men to c.
8 1 no c. of them that are in Christ Jesus
2 C 3 9 if the ministration of c. be glory
7 3 I speak not this to your condemnation
Apoc 17 1 I will show thee c. of the great harlot
condemned Lev 13 8 shall be c. of uncleanness
Num 35 30 none shall be c. upon evidence of one
Deut 21 22 being c. to die is hanged on a gibbet
2 Pa 36 3 c. the land in 100 talents of silver
Tob 13 16 they shall be c. that shall blaspheme
Job 32 3 answer, but only had condemned Job
Ps 108 7 when he is judged, may he go out c.
Eccu 19 6 delighted with wickedness, shall be c.
Dan 13 41 and they condemned her to death. Then
48 have c. a daughter of Israel? Return
Amos 2 8 and drank the wine of the condemned
2 Ma 4 47 judged innocent, were c. to death
13 8 he was condemned to die in ashes. But
Mat 12 7 you would never have c. the innocent
37 by thy words thou shalt be condemned
Mark 14 64 who all c. him to be guilty of death
16 16 but he that believeth not shall be c.
Luke 6 37 condemn not and you shall not be c.
24 20 delivered him to be c. to death and
John 8 10 hath no man condemned thee? Who said
Rom 8 3 hath c. sin in the flesh; that the
14 23 he that discerneth, if he eat, is c.
1 C 11 32 that we be not c. with this world
Titus 3 11 sinneth, being c. by his own judgment
Heb 11 7 by the which he condemned the world
James 5 6 you have condemned and put to death
2 P 2 6 condemned them to be overthrown, making
condemnest Rom 2 1 thou condemnest thyself. For
condemneth Prov 17 15 he that c. the just, both
Wisd 4 16 dead, c. the wicked that are living
Rom 14 22 blessed is he that c. not himself
condemning Deut 22 19 c. him besides in a hundred
3 K 8 32 c. the wicked and bringing his way upon
condescend Gen 34 23 only in this let us c., and
Num 20 21 neither would he c. to their desire
Judg 11 17 would not condescend to his request
3 K 12 7 if thou wilt yield . . . and c. to them
condescended 3 K 12 15 king c. not to the people
2 Pa 10 15 and he c. not to the people's requests
Gal 1 16 I condescended not to flesh and blood
condition Lev 25 24 be under the c. of redemption
Judg 2 2 on condition that you should not make
1 K 11 2 on this c. will I make a covenant with
Jdth 6 15 look on our low condition and have
Ecce 3 19 the condition of them both is equal
Isa 33 23 thy mast shall be in such condition
1 Ma 3 43 let us raise up the low c. of our
2 Ma 9 8 being proud above the condition of man
James 1 9 let the brother of low condition glory
conditioned Gen 41 4 very beautiful and well c.
conditions Dan 11 17 he shall make upright c. with
2 Ma 13 25 displeased with the c. of the peace
Luke 14 32 an embassy, he desireth c. of peace
condoleth Eccu 37 5 who c. with his friend for
conduct Num 33 1 under the c. of Moses and Aaron
Tob 5 14 canst thou conduct my son to Gabelus
15 I will conduct him thither and bring
Ps 5 9 conduct me, O Lord, in thy justice
44 5 right hand shall c. thee wonderfully
85 11 conduct me, O Lord, in thy way, and
1 Ma 12 4 to conduct them into the land of Juda
2 Ma 11 30 we grant therefore a safe conduct to
1 C 16 11 conduct ye him [Timothy] on his way
conducted Tob 11 19 to him by the man that c. him
Tob 12 3 he conducted me and brought me safe
Ps 42 3 they have c. me, and brought me unto
60 3 thou hast c. me; for thou hast been my
72 24 and by thy will thou hast conducted me
76 21 thou hast c. thy people like sheep, by
77 14 he conducted them with a cloud by day
72 c. them by the skilfulness of his hands
Wisd 10 10 she c. the just when he fled from his
17 and conducted them in a wonderful way
Acts 17 15 they that c. Paul, brought him as far
conducting 2 Ma 10 29 golden bridles, c. the Jews
conduit 4 K 18 17 the c. of the upper pool. Isa 7:3; 36:2
4 K 20 20 how he made a pool and a conduit and
confections Eccu 38 7 shall make sweet confections
confederacy Abdi 7 men of thy c. have deceived
1 Ma 8 17 to make a league of amity and c. with
confederate 1 Ma 10 6 that he should be his c.
1 Ma 10 16 will make him our friend and our c.
confederates Josu 10 1 to Israel and were their c.
1 Ma 8 20 we may be registered your confederates
24 war upon the Romans or any of their c.
14 40 called the Jews their friends and c.
conference Wisd 8 18 in exercise of c. with her
2 Ma 14 22 so they made an agreeable conference
conferred 3 K 1 7 he c. with Joab the son of
2 Ma 11 36 after you have diligently conferred
Acts 4 15 they conferred among themselves, saying
25 12 then Festus having c. with the council
conferring Acts 16 12 city some days c. together
confess Gen 26 7 afraid to c. that she was his
Gen 31 20 and Jacob would not confess to his
41 9 remembering, said: I confess my sin
Lev 16 21 let him confess all the iniquities of
26 40 until they confess their iniquities and
Num 5 7 they shall c. their sin and restore
32 32 we c. that we have already received
Josu 2 4 I confess they came to me, but I knew
7 19 confess and tell me what thou hast done
2 Pa 6 26 confess to thy name and be converted
2 Es 1 6 I c. the sins of the children of Israel
Tob 12 7 to reveal and confess the works of God
Job 15 18 wise men confess and hide not their
40 9 then I will confess that thy right hand
Ps 6 6 and who shall confess to thee in hell
29 10 shall dust confess to thee, or declare
31 5 I will c. against myself my injustice
66 4 let people confess to thee, O God: let
6 let the people, O God, confess to thee
70 22 I will also confess to thee thy truth
73 19 to beasts the souls that confess to thee
88 6 the heavens shall confess thy wonders
Prov 28 13 he that shall confess and forsake them
Eccu 4 31 be not ashamed to confess thy sins
39 9 in his prayer he will c. to the Lord
Isa 38 18 hell shall not confess to thee, neither
2 Ma 7 37 mayst confess that he alone is God
Mat 10 32 that shall c. me before men. Luke 12:8
32 I will also c. him before my Father
11 25 I confess to thee Father. Luke 10:21
Luke 12 8 him shall the Son of man also confess
John 9 22 if any man should c. him to be Christ
12 42 because of Pharisees they did not c. him
Acts 23 8 nor spirit: but the Pharisees c. both
24 14 this I confess to thee, that according
Rom 10 9 if thou confess with thy mouth the Lord
14 11 and every tongue shall confess to God
15 9 will I confess to thee, O Lord, among
Phil 2 11 tongue should c. that the Lord Jesus
James 5 16 c. therefore your sins one to another
1 J 1 9 if we c. our sins, he is faithful and

4 15 shall c. that Jesus is the Son of God
2 J 7 who c. not that Jesus Christ is come
Apoc 3 5 I will c. his name before my Father
confessed 2 Es 9 2 they stood and c. their sins
2 Es 9 3 four times they c. and adored the Lord
Luke 2 38 [Anna] coming in, confessed to the Lord
John 1 20 he confessed, and did not deny: and he confessed: I am not the Christ
1 Tim 6 12 hast confessed a good confession before
confesseth Eccu 20 1 hinder him that c. in prayer
1 J 2 23 that c. the Son, hath the Father also
4 2 which c. that Jesus Christ is come in
confessing 3 K 8 33 penance and c. to thy name
Dan 9 20 c. my sins and the sins of my people
Mat 3 6 Jordan, confessing their sins. Mark 1:5
Acts 19 18 came c. and declaring their deeds. And
Heb 11 13 and confessing that they are pilgrims
13 15 the fruit of lips c. to his name. And
confession 1 Es 10 11 now make c. to the Lord the
Dan 9 4 I made my c. and said: I beseech thee
Rom 10 10 confession is made unto salvation. For
2 C 9 13 for the obedience of your confession
1 Tim 6 12 hast confessed a good confession before
13 under Pontius Pilate, a good confession
Heb 3 1 high priest of our confession, Jesus
4 14 let us hold fast our confession. For
10 23 let us hold fast the c. of our hope
confide Ps 117 8 it is good to c. in the Lord
confided Ps 27 7 in him hath my heart confided
confidence 4 K 18 19 what is this c., wherein thou
1 Pa 17 25 thy servant hath found confidence to
2 Pa 14 11 with confidence in thee and in thy name
16 7 hast confidence in the king of Syria
20 17 but only stand with confidence, and you
Tob 4 12 alms shall be a great confidence before
Job 11 18 and thou shalt have confidence, hope
18 14 let his confidence be rooted out of
31 24 have said to fine gold: My confidence
39 11 wilt thou save c. in his great strength
Ps 117 8 rather than to have confidence in man
Prov 3 5 have confidence in the Lord with all
29 thy friend, when he hath c. in thee
14 26 in fear of the Lord is c. of strength
21 22 hath cast down the strength of the c.
Eccu 6 11 shall act with confidence among them
Isa 14 30 the poor shall rest with confidence
30 3 c. of the shadow of Egypt to your shame
31 1 putting their confidence in chariots
32 18 and in the tabernacles of confidence
36 4 what is this c. wherein thou trustest
Jer 17 7 and the Lord shall be his confidence
Eze 28 26 and shall dwell with confidence, when
29 16 they shall be no more a confidence to
30 9 to destroy the confidence of Ethiopia
Dan 13 35 her heart had confidence in the Lord
Amos 6 1 that have c. in the mountain of Samaria
2 Ma 7 11 said with c.: These I have from heaven
John 16 33 have confidence, I have overcome the
Acts 4 29 that with all c. they may speak thy
31 and they spoke the word of God with c.
26 26 to whom also I speak with confidence
28 31 Christ, with all c., without prohibition
2 C 1 15 in this c. I had a mind to come to you
2 3 having confidence in you all, that my
3 4 such confidence we have through Christ
12 having such hope, we use much confidence
5 6 having always confidence, knowing that
7 4 great is my confidence for you, great
16 I have confidence in you. Gal 5:10
8 22 diligent, with much confidence in you
10 2 that c. wherewith I am thought to be
Eph 3 12 we have boldness and access with c.
6 19 that I may open my mouth with c. to
Phil 1 20 with all c., as always, so now also
25 having this c., I know that I shall
3 3 not having confidence in the flesh
4 though I might have confidence in the
4 other thinketh he may have c. in the
1 Th 2 2 we had confidence in our God, to speak
2 Th 3 4 we have confidence concerning you in
1 Tim 3 13 good degree and much c. in the faith
Philem 8 I have much confidence in Christ Jesus
Heb 3 6 if we hold fast the c. and glory of
4 16 let us go with c. to the throne of
10 19 a c. in the entering into the holies
35 do not therefore lose your confidence
1 J 2 28 when he shall appear, we may have c.
3 21 we have confidence towards God: and
4 17 that we may have c. in the day of
5 14 this is the c. which we have towards
confident Ps 26 3 in this will I be confident
Prov 14 16 the fool leapeth over and is confident
Isa 32 9 ye c. daughters, give ear to my speech
10 that are confident shall be troubled
11 be troubled, ye confident ones: strip
Rom 2 19 art confident that thou art a guide
14 14 c. in the Lord Jesus, that nothing
2 C 5 8 we are c. and have a good will to be
Phil 1 6 being confident of this very thing
14 growing confident by my bands, are
confidently Lev 13 37 let him c. pronounce him
Deut 33 12 shall dwell confidently in him: as in
Ps 11 6 I will deal confidently in his regard
Prov 3 23 then shalt thou walk c. in thy way and
10 9 he that walketh sincerely, walketh c.
Eccu 29 30 stranger, he shall not deal c. nor
Isa 12 2 I will deal c. and will not fear
47 8 thou that art delicate and dwellest c.
Jer 23 6 and Israel shall dwell confidently
Eze 39 6 them that dwell c. in the islands
Acts 9 27 in Damascus he had dealt confidently
28 dealing c. in the name of the Lord
14 3 abode there, dealing c. in the Lord
Col 2 15 he hath exposed them c. in open show
Heb 13 6 we may c. say: The Lord is my helper
confines Num 21 24 the c. of the children of Ammon
Deut 3 16 confines even unto the torrent Jeboc
Josu 13 5 borders of the Amorrhite and his c.
16 6 the confines go out unto the sea: but
Judg 1 18 Juda took Gaza with its confines, and
18 and Ascalon and Accaron with their c.
11 13 from the confines of the Arnon unto
1 Pa 6 54 dwelling places by the towns and c.
Jdth 15 6 came to the extremities of their c.
Jer 49 32 destruction upon them from all their c.
Eze 45 9 separate your confines from my people
Mich 1 11 went not forth that dwelleth in the c.
1 Ma 2 46 whom they found in the c. of Israel
9 23 forth their heads in all the c. of
10 39 Ptolemais and the confines thereof
11 28 and Samaria and the confines thereof
34 out of Samaria and all their confines
59 borders of Tyre even to the c. of Egypt
confirm Deut 29 14 covenant, and c. these oaths
3 K 2 4 that the Lord may confirm his words
2 Pa 15 12 went in to c. as usual the covenant
Ps 19 5 own heart: and confirm all thy counsels
67 29 c., O God, what thou hast wrought in
Isa 35 3 hands, and confirm the weak knees. Say
Eze 13 6 persisted to c. what they have said
Dan 6 8 c. the sentence and sign the decree
9 27 he shall confirm the covenant with many
1 Ma 11 57 I confirm thee in the high priesthood
12 1 to confirm and to renew the amity with
14 24 to confirm the league with them. And
15 5 I confirm unto thee all the oblations

Luke 22 32 once converted, confirm thy brethren
Rom 15 8 to c. the promises made unto the fathers
1 C 1 8 will c. you unto the end without crime
2 C 2 8 you would c. your charity towards him
1 Th 3 2 to confirm you and exhort you concerning
13 to confirm your hearts without blame
2 Th 2 16 c. you in every good work and word
1 P 5 10 will himself perfect you and c. you
confirmation Phil 1 7 defence and c. of the gospel
Heb 6 16 an oath for confirmation if the end
confirmed 2 K 5 12 that the Lord had c. him king
2 K 7 24 thou hast c. to thyself thy people
1 Pa 14 2 the Lord had c. him king over Israel
Job 4 4 hands: thy words have c. them that were
Ps 70 6 by thee have I been c. from the womb
79 16 whom thou hast confirmed for thyself. 18
110 8 are faithful: c. forever and ever
116 2 for his mercy is confirmed upon us
Prov 15 26 words most beautiful shall be c. by him
Eccu 3 3 hath confirmed it upon the children
44 25 c. his covenant upon the head of Jacob
51 25 and in doing it I have been confirmed
Dan 9 12 he hath confirmed his words which he
11 1 that he might be strengthened and c.
1 Ma 11 27 c. him in the high priesthood. 14:38
Acts 15 32 comforted the brethren and c. them
16 5 the churches were confirmed in faith
19 20 grew the word of God and was confirmed
1 C 1 6 the testimony of Christ was c. in you
Gal 3 15 a man's testament, if it be confirmed
17 testament which was confirmed by God
Col 2 7 built up in him and c. in the faith
Heb 2 3 was c. unto us by them that heard him
2 P 1 12 and are confirmed in the present truth
confirmeth 2 C 1 21 he that c. us with you in
confirming Mark 16 20 c. the word with signs that
Acts 14 21 confirming the souls of the disciples
15 41 and Cilicia, confirming the churches
18 23 in order, confirming all the disciples
confiscated 1 Es 6 11 upon it, and his house be c.
Dan 2 5 and your houses shall be confiscated
confiscation 1 Es 7 26 or to the c. of goods or
conflict Wisd 10 12 and gave him a strong conflict
Phil 1 30 having the same conflict as that which
conflicts Wisd 4 2 winning reward of undefiled c.
1 Tim 6 5 conflicts of men corrupted in mind and
conform 2 Ma 6 9 whosoever would not c. themselves
conformable Rom 8 29 c. to the image of his Son
Phil 3 10 being made conformable to his death
conformed Rom 12 2 be not c. to this world; but be
confound Gen 11 7 and there c. their tongue that
Job 19 3 behold, these ten times you confound me
40 7 look on all that are proud and c. them
Eccu 25 35 she will confound thee in the sight of
1 C 1 27 that he may confound the wise . . . that he may confound the strong
4 14 I write not these things to confound
confounded Gen 11 9 language of whole earth was c.
Num 36 4 made by the lots shall be confounded
4 K 19 26 they trembled and were confounded, they
1 Es 9 6 my God, I am confounded and ashamed
Job 6 20 they are confounded because I have hoped
Ps 13 6 you have c. the counsel of the poor man
21 6 they trusted in thee, and were not c.
24 3 of them that wait on thee shall be c.
4 all them be c. that act unjust things
30 1 have I hoped, let me never be confounded
18 let me not be c., O Lord, for I have
33 6 and your faces shall not be confounded
34 4 let them be c. and ashamed. 39:15; 69:3
4 let them be turned back and be c. that
36 19 they shall not be c. in the evil time
52 6 they have been c. because God hath
68 7 let them not be confounded on my account
70 13 let them be c. and come to nothing that
24 when they shall be c. and put to shame
82 18 and let them be confounded and perish
85 17 they who hate me may see, and be c.
96 7 let them be all c. that adore graven
108 28 let them that rise up against me be c.
118 6 shall I not be c., when I shall look
80 justifications, that I may not be c.
116 let me not be c. in my expectation
126 5 he shall not be c. when he shall speak
128 5 let them all be confounded and turned
Prov 13 5 the wicked confoundeth, and shall be c.
Eccu 2 11 hath hoped in the Lord and hath been c.
5 14 in an unskilful word, and be c. Honor
16 and be not taken in thy tongue and c.
9 2 enter upon thy strength and thou be c.
15 4 him fast, and he shall not be confounded
24 30 that hearkeneth to me, shall not be c.
30 5 neither was he c. before his enemies
51 24 a zeal for good, and shall not be c.
37 and you shall not be c. in his praise
Isa 1 29 they shall be c. for the idols to which
19 9 they shall be c. that wrought in flax
26 11 envious people see and be confounded
29 22 Jacob shall not now be confounded
30 5 were all c. at a people that could not
31 3 they shall all be confounded together
32 11 strip you, and be confounded, gird
33 9 Libanus is confounded and become foul
37 27 they trembled and were confounded, they
41 11 that fight against thee shall be c.
42 17 let them be greatly c., that trust in
44 11 all the partakers thereof shall be c.
11 fear, and shall be confounded together
45 16 they are all confounded and ashamed
17 you shall not be confounded, and you
25 and all that resist him shall be c.
49 23 they shall not be c. that wait for him
50 7 is my helper, therefore am I not c.
54 4 fear not, for thou shalt not be c. nor
65 14 rejoice, and you shall be confounded
66 5 see in your joy: but they shall be c.
Jer 2 26 as the thief is c. when he is taken
26 so is the house of Israel confounded
6 15 they were c. because they committed
15 they were not c. with confusion, and
8 9 the wise men are confounded, they are
12 are c., because they have committed
12 they are not c. with confusion, and
9 19 we are wasted and greatly c.? Because
10 14 artist is confounded in his graven idol
14 3 they were confounded and afflicted and
4 the husbandmen were confounded, they
15 9 she is confounded and ashamed: and the
17 13 all that forsake thee shall be c.: they
18 let them be c. that persecute me, and let not me be confounded
20 11 they shall be greatly c. because they
31 19 I am confounded and ashamed because I
46 24 the daughter of Egypt is confounded and
48 1 to Nabo, it is laid waste and c.
1 the strong city is c. and hath trembled
20 Moab is confounded, because he is
39 bowed down the neck, and is confounded
49 23 Emath is confounded and Arphad: for
50 2 Babylon is taken, Bel is confounded
2 their graven things are confounded
12 your mother is c. exceedingly, and she
51 17 every founder is c. by his idol, for
47 her whole land shall be confounded and
51 are c. because we have heard reproach
Bar 6 25 be they c. also that worship them

38 and they that worship them shall be c.
Eze 16 52 be thou also confounded and bear thy
54 mayest be c. in all that thou hast done
63 that thou mayest remember and be c.
32 30 slain, fearing and c. in their strength
36 32 be c. and ashamed at your own ways
Dan 3 44 them be confounded that show evils to
44 let them be c. in all thy might, and
Osee 4 19 and they shall be c. because of their
10 6 and Israel shall be c. in his own will
Joel 1 10 the wine is c., the oil hath languished
12 vineyard is c., and the fig tree hath
17 broken down: because the corn is c.
2 26 my people shall not be c. forever. 27
Mich 3 7 they shall be c. that see visions, and
7 and the diviners shall be confounded
7 16 and shall be c. at all their strength
Zach 9 5 Accaron, because her hope is c.: and
10 5 riders of horses shall be confounded
11 all the depths of the river shall be c.
13 4 that the prophets shall be confounded
1 Ma 4 31 let them be confounded in their host
2 Ma 10 30 being both c. with blindness and filled
Acts 2 6 together and were c. in mind, because
9 22 c. the Jews who dwelt at Damascus
Rom 9 33 believeth in him, shall not be confounded. 10:11; 1 P 2:6
Phil 1 20 that in nothing I shall be confounded
1 J 2 28 not be c. by him at his coming. If you
confoundeth Prov 13 5 the wicked c., and shall be
Eccu 22 4 she that c., becometh a disgrace to her
Rom 5 5 hope c. not: because the charity of
confused Acts 19 32 the assembly was c., and the
confusion Judg 3 26 Aod, while they were in c.
Judg 8 12 all their host being put in confusion
1 K 5 6 was the confusion of a great mortality
20 30 to thy own c. and to the c. of thy
34 his father had put him to confusion
2 K 10 5 the men were sadly put to confusion
3 K 2 20 do not put me to confusion. And the
1 Es 9 7 and to spoil and to confusion of face
Jdth 8 19 the sword and to pillage and to c.
9 2 and uncovered the virgin unto confusion
14 16 one Hebrew woman hath made confusion
Job 8 22 that hate thee, shall be clothed with c.
Ps 34 26 let them be clothed with confusion and
39 16 let them immediately bear their c. that
43 16 confusion of my face hath covered me
68 20 knowest my reproach and my confusion
70 1 hoped, let me never be put to confusion
13 let them be covered with c. and shame
73 21 let not humble be turned away with c.
88 46 thou hast covered him with confusion
108 29 let them be covered with their c. as
131 18 his enemes I will clothe with c.: but
Prov 10 5 snorteth in the summer, is son of c.
14 mouth of the fool is next to confusion
12 4 that doth things worthy of confusion
18 13 himself to be a fool and worthy of c.
Eccu 5 17 for c. and repentance is upon a thief
20 28 their c. is with them without ceasing
22 3 son ill taught is the c. of the father
25 29 and impudence and confusion is great
31 16 disgraced with envy thou be put to c.
42 1 shalt thou be truly without confusion
Isa 30 3 strength of Pharao shall be to your c.
5 any profit, but to c. and to reproach
45 16 of errors are gone together into c.
Jer 3 24 confusion hath devoured the labor of
25 we shall sleep in our confusion, and
6 15 rather they were not confounded with c.
7 19 to the c. of their own countenance
8 12 they are not confounded with confusion
11 13 thou hast set up altars of confusion
20 18 and that my days should be spent in c.
Bar 1 15 justice but to us confusion of our face
2 6 to us and to our fathers c. of face
Eze 16 7 wast naked and full of confusion. 22
52 do thou also bear thy confusion, thou
63 thy mouth, because of thy confusion
39 26 they shall bear their confusion and all
Dan 3 40 is no c. to them that trust in thee
42 put us not to confusion, but deal with
9 7 to us confusion of face, as at this day
8 to us belongeth confusion of face, to
Osee 9 10 alienated themselves to that confusion
Abdi 10 confusion shall cover thee, and thou
Mich 2 6 these, confusion shall not take them
Nah 2 4 they are in confusion in the ways, the
Haba 2 10 thou hast devised c. to thy house, thou
Soph 3 19 the land where they had been put to c.
1 Ma 1 29 the house of Jacob was covered with c.
2 Ma 5 7 but received confusion at the end, for
Luke 21 25 confusion of the roaring of the sea and
Acts 19 29 the whole city was filled with confusion
21 31 told that all Jerusalem was in confusion
1 P 4 4 with them into the same confusion of
Jude 13 of the sea, foaming out their own c.
confute Job 11 3 others, shall no man confute thee
congealed Job 38 30 the surface of the deep is c.
Eccu 43 22 the water is congealed into crystal
congratulate 2 K 8 10 to c. with him and to return
1 Pa 18 10 and to c. him that he had defeated and
Phil 2 17 faith, I rejoice and c. with you all
18 do you also rejoice and c. with me
congratulated Luke 1 58 c. with her [Elizabeth]
congratulating Ruth 4 17 her neighbors c. with her
Tob 11 20 congratulating with him for all the good
congregation Exod 16 2 c. of the children of Israel murmured against Moses
Exod 16 9 said to Aaron: Say to the whole c. of
34 31 both Aaron and the rulers of the c.
Lev 8 3 gather together all the c. to the door
10 6 and indignation come upon all the c.
16 17 and his house and for the whole c.
19 2 Moses, saying: Speak to all the c.
23 36 it is the day of assembly and c.: you
Num 1 2 take the sum of all the congregation
16 9 should stand before the congregation
16 thou and thy c. stand apart before the
21 separate yourselves from among this c.
40 suffer as Core suffered and all his c.
27 20 c. of children of Israel may hear him
2 Pa 7 8 and a c. of people shall surround thee
61 9 trust in him, all ye c. of people
67 31 the c. of bulls with the kine of the
73 2 remember thy congregation, which thou
81 1 God hath stood in the c. of gods: and
105 17 and covered the congregation of Abiron
18 and a fire was kindled in their c.: the
110 1 the council of the just and in the c.
Prov 5 14 in midst of the church and of the c.
Eccu 1 39 thee down in midst of the congregation
3 30 c. of the proud shall not be healed
4 7 thyself affable to the c. of the poor
16 7 in the c. of sinners a fire shall be
21 10 the c. of sinners is like tow heaped
41 22 of iniquity before a c. and a people
45 22 the congregation of Core in their wrath
46 17 by law of the Lord he judged the c.
50 15 was in their hands before all the c.
22 he lifted up his hands over all the c.
Isa 56 8 I will still gather unto him his c.
Jer 6 18 hear, ye nations, and know, O. c., what
Osee 7 12 will strike them as their c. hath heard
1 Ma 2 42 assembled to them c. of the Assideans

56 Caleb for bearing witness before the c.
3 13 company of the faithful and a c. with
2 Ma 2 7 till God gather together the c. of the
conjecturers Gen 41 24 I told this dream to the c.
conjure Acts 19 13 I c. you by Jesus, whom Paul
conjured Jer 11 7 protesting I c. your fathers in
Jer 11 7 rising early I conjured them and said
conjuring Jdth 7 17 c. you to deliver now the city
conquer Num 13 31 we shall be able to conquer it
Apoc 6 2 forth conquering that he might conquer
conquered Num 21 32 and conquered the inhabitants
Num 32 4 the land which the Lord hath c. in the
Deut 26 1 hast conquered it and dwellest in it
Josu 10 40 Josue c. all the country of the hills
1 Ma 8 2 how they had conquered them and brought
4 had c. places that were very far off
5 arms against them, and had c. them
12 and had c. kingdoms that were near and
2 Ma 5 6 and not citizens, whom he conquered
Heb 11 33 by faith c. kingdoms, wrought justice
conquering Apoc 6 2 he went forth c. that he
conqueror Judg 8 9 when I shall return a c. in
Wisd 18 15 as a fierce conqueror into the midst
Haba 3 19 he the conqueror will lead me upon my
conquerors Jdth 15 8 that returned c. to Bathulia
Isa 9 3 as conquerors rejoice after taking a
conquest Judg 11 24 our God hath obtained by c.
Judg 21 22 not away as by the right of war or c.
conscience Job 16 20 knoweth my c. is on high
Prov 12 18 pricked as it were with a sword of c.
Ecce 7 23 thy c. knoweth that thou also hast
Wisd 17 10 troubled conscience always forecasteth
Eccu 13 30 him that hath no sin in his conscience
2 Ma 6 11 they made a c. to help themselves with
Acts 24 16 I endeavor to have always a conscience
Rom 2 15 their c. bearing witness to them and
9 1 my c. bearing me witness in the Holy
1 C 8 7 with c. of the idol: eat as a thing
7 their c. being weak, is defiled. But
10 shall not his c., being weak, be
12 wound their weak c., you sin against
10 29 c. I say, not thy own, but the other's
29 my liberty judged by another man's c.
2 C 1 12 glory is this, the testimony of our c.
4 2 commending ourselves to every man's c.
1 Tim 3 9 holding the mystery of faith in pure c.
4 2 hypocrisy, and having their c. seared
2 Tim 1 3 with a pure conscience, that without
Titus 1 15 their mind and their c. are defiled
Heb 9 9 cannot, as to the c., make him perfect
14 cleanse our c. from dead works, to serve
10 2 should have no c. of sin any longer
22 our hearts sprinkled from an evil c.
1 P 2 19 for c. towards God, a man endure sorrows
good conscience Acts 23 1 conversed with a g. c.
1 Tim 1 5 and a good c. and an unfeigned faith
19 having faith and a good conscience
Heb 13 18 we trust we have a good conscience
1 P 3 16 with modesty and fear, having a g. c.
21 the examination of a good c. towards
conscience's Rom 13 5 subject . . . also for c. sake
1 C 10 25 asking no questions for c. sake. 27
28 do not eat of it . . . and for c. sake
consciences 2 C 5 11 in your c. we are manifest
conscious 3 K 2 44 evil of which thy heart is c.
1 C 4 4 I am not c. to myself of anything, yet
consecrate Exod 13 12 thou shalt c. to the Lord
Exod 28 41 shalt consecrate the hands of them all
29 35 seven days shalt thou c. their hands
40 11 shalt c. all with the oil of unction
Lev 27 16 possession and c. it to the Lord, the
Num 6 2 will consecrate themselves to the Lord
12 shall c. to the Lord the days of his
8 13 and shalt c. them being offered to the
15 thus shalt thou purify and c. them for
4 K 23 10 no man should c. there his son or his
Jer 32 35 to c. their sons and their daughters
Eze 43 26 shall cleanse it: and they shall c. it
consecrated Exod 28 3 in which he being c. may
Exod 29 1 this, that they may be c. to me in the
7 by this rite shall he be consecrated
9 after thou shalt have c. their hands
21 after they and their vestments are c.
26 wherewith Aaron was consecrated. 28
27 shalt sanctify both the c. breast and
29 be anointed, and their hands c. in it
34 and if there remain of the c. flesh
32 29 you have c. your hands this day to the
Lev 7 30 when he hath offered and c. both to
8 9 plate of gold, c. with sanctification
12 anointed and consecrated him [Aaron]
16 32 whose hands are consecrated to do the
18 21 to be consecrated to the idol Moloch
21 7 because they are c. to their God. And
10 whose hands have been consecrated for
22 2 they beware of those things that are c.
3 approacheth to those things that are c.
23 12 on the same day that the sheaf is c.
27 10 was changed shall be c. to the Lord
21 as a possession c., pertaineth to the
28 whatsoever is once c., shall be holy
Num 3 3 whose hands were filled and consecrated
6 4 all the days that they are consecrated
7 84 in the day wherein it was consecrated
18 10 because it is a consecrated thing to
18 to thy use, as the c. breast and the
Josu 6 19 let it be consecrated to the Lord, laid
24 which they c. into the treasury of the
Judg 16 17 a Nazarite, that is to say, c. to God
17 3 I have c. and vowed this silver to the
3 K 15 13 in the grove which she had c. to him
4 K 16 3 he c. also his son, making him pass
17 17 and c. their sons and their daughters
1 Pa 18 11 and brass king David c. to the Lord
22 19 and the vessels consecrated to the Lord
26 27 which they had c. to the building and
28 12 and for the treasures of the c. things
2 Pa 17 16 son of Zechri, consecrated to the Lord
26 18 sons of Aaron, who are c. for this
28 3 and consecrated his sons in the fire
29 33 they consecrated to the Lord 600 oxen
1 Es 3 5 solemnities of the Lord, that were c.
8 25 vessels c. for the house of our God
Jdth 11 12 and the consecrated things of the Lord
Eccu 49 9 who was c. a prophet from his mother's
consecrateth 2 Pa 13 9 cometh and c. his hand with
consecrating Eze 16 21 to them, c. them by fire
consecration Exod 29 22 because it is ram of c.
Exod 29 31 thou shalt take the ram of the c. and
Lev 7 37 for sin and for trespass and for c.
8 22 the second ram, in the c. of priests
28 because it was the oblation of c., for
29 and he took of the ram of consecration
31 eat ye also the loaves of c. that are
33 the time of your c. shall be expired
33 for in seven days the c. is finished
27 29 any consecration that is offered by man
Num 6 5 until the day be fulfilled of his c.
6 time of his c. he shall not go in to
7 the c. of his God is upon his head. All
9 the head of his c. shall be defiled
13 this is the law of consecration. When
18 the hair of the c. of the Nazarite
21 in the time of his c., besides those
Wisd 12 5 from the midst of thy consecration
consent Num 14 43 you would not c. to the Lord

Deut 13 8 c. not to him, hear him not, neither
Judg 13 15 I beseech thee to consent to my request
19 10 his son-in-law would not consent to
3 K 20 8 hearken not to him nor consent to him
Tob 4 6 take heed thou never consent to sin
Jdth 12 10 to c. of her own account to dwell with
Ps 54 15 in the house of God we walked with c.
82 6 they have contrived with one consent
Prov 1 10 shall entice thee, consent not to them
Wisd 10 5 conspired together to c. to wickedness
Dan 13 20 consent to us to lie with us. But if
1 Ma 2 19 fathers, and c. to his commandments
2 Ma 11 24 would not consent to my father to turn
14 20 of one mind to consent to covenants
Mat 18 19 that if two of you shall c. upon earth
Luke 11 48 you c. to the doings of your fathers
Rom 1 32 they that consent to them that do them
7 16 I consent to the law, that it is good
1 C 7 5 not one another except perhaps by c.
12 she c. to dwell with him, let him not
13 he c. to dwell with her, let her not
1 Tim 6 3 and consent not to the sound words of
consented Lev 20 5 him and all that c. with him
4 K 2 17 but they pressed him till he consented
Tob 3 18 a husband I consented to take, with thy
Jdth 8 10 Ozias hath consented to give up the
Prov 1 30 nor c. to my counsel, but despised all
5 12 and my heart consented not to reproof
1 Ma 1 44 all nations c. according to the word
45 and many of Israel c. to his service
2 16 many of the people of Israel consented
11 29 king consented: and he wrote letters
14 41 had c. that he should be their prince
2 Ma 11 15 Machabeus consented to the request of
12 4 which when they had c. to, according to
Luke 23 51 same had not consented to their counsel
Acts 5 37 as many as c. to him were dispersed
39 and they consented to him [Gamaliel]
18 20 tarry a longer time he consented not
22 20 I stood by and consented, and kept the
Gal 2 13 dissimulation the rest of the Jews c.
2 Th 2 11 the truth, but have c. to iniquity. But
consenting Gen 39 8 no wise c. to that wicked act
Acts 7 59 and Saul was consenting to his death
Rom 12 16 high things, but c. to the humble. Be
James 3 17 c. to the good, full of mercy and
consequently 2 Pa 32 15 c. neither shall your God
consider Gen 42 12 you are come to c. the unfenced
Lev 27 14 the priest shall consider it, whether
Num 23 9 and shall consider him from the hills
Deut 8 5 that thou mayst consider in thy heart
30 15 consider that I have set before thee
32 20 will c. what their last end shall be
Judg 9 2 c. that I am your bone and your flesh
19 9 consider that the day is declining
1 K 23 22 consider the place where his foot is
23 consider and see all his lurking holes
25 17 consider and think what thou hast to do
2 K 1 18 c., O Israel, for them that are dead
1 Pa 19 3 to consider and search and spy out thy
Job 5 27 consider it thoroughly in thy mind
6 19 consider the paths of Thema, the ways
11 11 seeth iniquity, doth he not consider it
22 14 and he doth not consider our things
23 15 when I c. him I am made pensive with
31 4 doth not he consider my ways, and
37 14 consider the wondrous works of God
Ps 12 4 consider and hear me, O Lord my God
24 19 c. my enemies for they are multiplied
90 8 but thou shalt consider with thy eyes
93 9 he that formed the eye, doth he not c.
118 15 and I will consider thy ways. I will
18 I will c. the wondrous things of thy
Prov 6 6 to the ant, O sluggard, and c. her ways
10 32 lips of the just c. what is acceptable
23 1 c. diligently what is set before thy
27 23 cattle, and consider thy own flocks
Ecce 7 14 consider the works of God, that no man
26 know and consider and seek out wisdom
Cant 1 5 do not consider me that I am brown
Isa 5 12 nor do you consider the works of his
18 4 I will take my rest and c. in my place
41 20 that they may see and know and consider
44 19 they do not consider in their mind nor
Jer 2 10 and send into Cedar and c. diligently
5 1 consider and seek in the broad places
9 17 consider ye, and call for the mourning
Lam 1 11 see, O Lord, and consider, for I am
2 20 and c. whom thou hast thus dealt with
5 1 consider and behold our reproach. Our
Agge 1 5 set your hearts to consider your ways
2 16 now c. in your hearts, from this day
1 Ma 2 61 thus consider through all generations
5 16 to c. what they should do for their
2 Ma 5 17 did not consider that God was angry
6 12 that they c. the things that happened
23 he began to c. the dignity of his age
7 28 c. that God made them out of nothing
Mat 6 28 consider the lilies. Luke 12:27
Luke 12 24 consider the ravens, for they sow not
John 11 50 neither do you c. that it is expedient
Acts 15 6 assembled to consider of this matter
Rom 4 19 neither did he c. his own body now dead
Heb 3 1 c. the apostle and high priest of our
7 4 c. how great this man is, to whom also
10 24 let us consider one another, to provoke
consideration Ecce 3 11 delivered world to their c.
considered Gen 37 11 but his father c. the thing
Job 1 8 hast thou considered my servant. 2:3
13 27 hast considered the steps of my feet
32 12 as I thought you said something, I c.
38 18 hast thou c. the breadth of the earth
Ps 89 9 our years shall be c. as a spider: the
Prov 31 16 she hath c. a field and bought it: with
Ecce 4 4 again I considered all the labors of men
8 9 all these things I have considered in my
Eccu 42 18 and considered their crafty devices
Jer 23 18 who hath c. his word and heard it
Dan 3 94 considered these men, that the fire
7 8 I c. the horns, and behold another
1 Ma 4 44 he c. about the altar of holocausts
2 Ma 12 45 he c. that they who had fallen asleep
Acts 11 6 I c. and saw fourfooted creatures of
considerest Ps 9 14 for thou c. labor and sorrow
Luke 6 41 beam that is in thy own eye thou c. not
considereth Job 17 15 and who c. my patience
Job 28 3 the end of all things he considereth
34 21 ways of men, and he c. all their steps
35 14 he c. not: be judged before him and
Prov 5 21 c. the ways of man and all his steps
14 15 the discreet man considereth his steps
21 12 the just c. seriously the house of the
Ecce 11 4 he that c. the clouds, shall never reap
Eccu 14 23 he that c. her ways in his heart and
Jer 12 11 there is none that c. in the heart. The
Eze 18 28 because he c. and turneth away himself
considering 3 K 3 21 c. him more diligently when
Ecce 4 7 considering I found also another vanity
Eccu 38 29 by the anvil and c. the iron work. The
2 Ma 1 34 the king c. and diligently examining
2 25 considering the multitude of books and
3 32 c. that the king might perhaps suspect
4 4 Onias c. the danger of this contention
5 6 not c. that prosperity against one's
6 20 c. in what manner he was come to it
9 23 c. that my father also at what time

25 c. that neighboring princes and borderers
11 4 never considering the power of God, but
13 c. with himself the loss he had suffered
15 21 c. the coming of the multitude and the
Luke 20 23 considering their guile, said to them
Acts 12 12 c., he came to the house of Mary the
Gal 6 1 c. thyself, lest thou also be tempted
Phil 2 4 not c. the things that are his own
Heb 13 7 follow c. the end of their conversation
1 P 3 2 c. your chaste conversation with fear
consigned Rom 15 28 c. to them this fruit, I will
consist 2 Pa 25 8 battles c. in the strength of
Luke 12 15 a man's life doth not consist in the
Col 1 17 is before all, and by him all things c.
consisted Jdth 5 8 which c. in the worship of many
consisteth Num 16 3 the multitude c. of holy ones
consisting 2 P 3 5 through water, c. by the word
consolation Jdth 8 20 us humbly wait for his c.
Lam 1 21 thou hast brought a day of consolation
Luke 2 25 waiting for the consolation of Israel
6 24 that are rich, for you have your c.
Acts 4 36 Barnabas . . . The son of consolation
9 31 was filled with the c. of the Holy
15 31 had read, they rejoiced for the c.
2 C 1 6 we be comforted, it is for your c.
7 so shall you be also of the consolation
7 7 by the c. wherewith he was comforted
13 in our c. we did the more abundantly
Phil 2 1 if there be any consolation in Christ
2 Th 2 15 hath given us everlasting c. and good
Philem 7 I have had great joy and c. in thy
Heb 12 5 and you have forgotten the c., which
13 22 you suffer this word of c. For I have
consolations Isa 66 11 with the breasts of her c.
consort Eccu 13 20 all flesh shall c. with the
conspicuous 1 Ma 11 37 holy mountain in a c. place
1 Ma 14 48 of the sanctuary in a conspicuous place
conspiracies Acts 20 19 befell me by c. of the Jews
conspiracy 2 K 15 12 there was a strong c. and the
2 K 15 31 that Achitophel also was in the c. with
3 K 16 20 acts of Zambri and of his conspiracy
4 K 11 14 [Athalia] cried: A conspiracy, a c.
14 19 a c. against him [Amasias]. 2 Pa 25:27
15 15 the acts of Sellum and his conspiracy
Isa 8 12 say ye not: A conspiracy: for all that
12 all that his people speaketh, is a c.
Jer 11 9 a c. is found among the men of Juda
Eze 22 25 there is a conspiracy of prophets in
Acts 23 13 than forty men that had made this c.
conspire Osee 6 9 they c. with the priests who
conspired 1 K 22 8 all of you have c. against me
1 K 22 13 why have you c. against me [Saul]
3 K 15 27 Baasa . . . conspired against him [Nadab]
4 K 9 14 so Jehu . . . conspired against Joram
10 9 if I c. against my master and slew him
12 20 servants arose and c. among themselves
15 10 Sellum the son of Jabes c. against
25 Phacee . . . c. against him and smote him
30 Osee son of Ela c. and formed a plot
21 24 that had conspired against king Amon
2 Pa 24 26 men that conspired against him [Joas]
33 24 and his servants conspired against him
Wisd 10 5 when the nations had c. together to
constancy Jdth 9 14 give me c. in my mind, that I
Jdth 16 12 the Persians quaked at her constancy
Wisd 5 1 then shall the just stand with great c.
2 Ma 6 28 if with a ready mind and c. I suffer
Acts 4 13 seeing the c. of Peter and John
constant Acts 23 11 standing by him, said: Be c.
1 P 4 8 a c. mutual charity among yourselves
constantly Jer 35 16 have c. kept the commandment
Titus 3 8 these things I will have thee affirm c.
consternation Gen 27 34 in a great c., said: Bless
2 Pa 12 6 king, being in a consternation, said
Esth 4 4 heard it, she was in a consternation
Dan 10 9 when I heard, I lay in a consternation
2 Ma 13 23 he was in a consternation of mind, and
14 28 known, Nicanor was in a consternation
constitution Eccu 30 14 sound and strong of c.
constrain Gal 6 12 they c. you to be circumcised
constrained Exod 36 4 workmen being c. to come
Lev 25 39 if thy brother constrained by poverty
Judg 11 7 now you are come to me c. by necessity
Dan 14 29 c. by necessity he delivered Daniel to
2 Ma 15 2 the Jews that were c. to follow him
Luke 24 29 they constrained him, saying: Stay with
Acts 16 15 and abide there. And she [Lydia] c. us
28 19 I was constrained to appeal to Caesar
constraining Job 39 16 in vain, no fear c. her
constraint 2 Ma 6 7 they were led by bitter c.
1 P 5 2 care of it, not by c., but willingly
consul 1 Ma 15 16 Lucius the consul of the Romans
consuls Job 3 14 with kings and c. of the earth
consult Gen 25 22 she went to consult the Lord
Num 7 89 to c. the oracle, he heard the voice
9 8 stay that I may consult the Lord what
27 21 Eleazar the priest shall c. the Lord
Judg 18 5 they desired him to consult the Lord
1 K 9 9 when a man went to consult God he
22 15 did I begin today to consult the Lord
2 K 16 20 to Achitophel: Consult what we are to
23 was as if a man should consult God
3 K 14 5 wife of Jeroboam cometh in to c. thee
4 K 1 2 c. Beelzebub god of Accaron. 3, 16
8 8 and c. the Lord by him, saying: Can I
22 13 go and consult the Lord for me and for
18 who sent you to consult the Lord, thus
2 Es 6 10 let us c. together in the house of God
Eccu 37 7 c. not with him that layeth a snare
Isa 19 3 and they shall consult their idols and
41 28 no one even among them to consult or
45 21 tell ye and come and consult together
Bar 6 48 the priests consult with themselves
Eze 21 19 he shall c. at the head of the way of
consultation 2 Ma 14 20 when there had been a c.
Mat 12 14 made a c. against him, how they might
Mark 3 6 made a c. with the Herodians against
15 1 the chief priests holding a c. with the
consulted Josu 9 14 c. not the mouth of the Lord
Judg 1 1 children of Israel consulted the Lord
20 18 they c. God and said: Who shall be in
23 and c. him and said: Shall I go out
28 they c. the Lord and said: Shall we go
1 K 5 9 the Gethrites consulted together and
10 22 they c. the Lord whether he would come
14 37 Saul c. the Lord: Shall I pursue after
22 10 he consulted the Lord for him and gave
13 and hast consulted the Lord for him
23 2 David consulted the Lord. 4; 30:8; 2 K 2:1; 5:19, 23; 1 Pa 14:10
28 6 c. the Lord, and he answered him not
2 K 21 1 David consulted the oracle of the Lord
3 K 12 8 and consulted with the young men that
1 Pa 10 13 and moreover consulted also a witch
13 1 and David consulted with the captains
14 14 David consulted God again, and God
Ps 30 14 they consulted to take away my life
70 10 that watched my soul have c. together
82 4 and have consulted against thy saints
Isa 40 14 with whom hath he consulted and who
Eze 21 21 inquired of the idols and c. entrails
Dan 6 7 and judges have consulted together
Osee 4 12 my people have c. their stocks, and
1 Ma 8 15 consulted daily 320 men, that sat in
Mat 22 15 consulted . . . how to insnare him in his
26 4 they c. together that by subtilty they

27 7 after they had c. together, they bought
Acts 9 23 the Jews c. together, to kill him [Paul]
consulteth Deut 18 10 or that c. soothsayers or
Deut 18 11 any one that consulteth pythonic
consulting Eze 21 23 as one c. the oracle in vain
2 Ma 4 21 c. his own interest, he departed thence
consume Gen 41 30 famine shall c. all the land
Lev 26 16 waste your eyes and c. your lives
38 and an enemy's land shall consume you
Num 14 12 with pestilence, and will consume them
Deut 5 25 this exceeding great fire consume us
7 16 thou shalt consume all the people which
20 until he destroy and consume all that
22 he will consume these nations in thy
13 16 so as to consume all for the Lord thy
28 20 until he c. and destroy thee quickly
21 until he consume thee out of the land
38 because the locusts shall consume all
42 the blast shall consume all the trees
48 upon thy neck, till he consume thee
52 until he destroy thee and consume thee
61 volume of this law till he consume thee
29 19 the drunken may consume the thirsty
Judg 9 20 c. inhabitants of Sichem and the town
2 K 22 38 will not return again till I c. them
39 I will c. them and break them in pieces
4 K 1 10 and consume thee and thy fifty. 12
13 17 Syrians in Aphec till thou c. them
2 Es 9 31 thou didst not utterly consume them
Jdth 11 12 they design to consume the things which
Job 13 26 wilt c. me for the sins of my youth
18 13 let the firstborn death c. his arms
Eccu 14 9 be satisfied till he c. his own soul
27 32 sorrow shall c. them before they die
43 23 consume all that is green as with fire
Isa 3 15 why do you consume my people and grind
27 10 lie down, and shall c. its branches
51 8 the moth shall consume them as wool
Jer 14 12 I will consume them by the sword and
27 8 Lord: till I consume them by his hand
30 11 I will utterly consume all the nations
11 but I will not utterly consume thee
46 28 I will consume all the nations to which
28 but thee I will not consume, but I will
49 37 the sword after them, till I c. them
Bar 6 62 above, to consume mountains and woods
Eze 13 13 great hailstones in my wrath to consume
15 7 out from fire, and fire shall c. them
20 13 in the desert, and would consume them
17 neither did I c. them in the desert
35 12 desolate, they are given to us to c.
Dan 2 44 and shall consume all these kingdoms
Osee 11 6 it shall consume his chosen men, and
Soph 2 11 and shall c. all the gods of the earth
14 post, for I will consume her strength
Zach 5 4 midst of his house and shall consume it
14 12 of every one shall consume away while
12 their eyes shall c. away in their holes
12 their tongue shall c. away in their
1 Ma 5 15 with strangers, in order to consume us
Mat 6 19 where the rust and moth consume, and
20 where neither the rust nor moth c.
Luke 9 54 come down from heaven and c. them
Heb 10 27 which shall consume the adversaries
James 4 3 you may c. it on your concupiscences
consumed Gen 6 17 in the earth shall be consumed
Gen 19 17 mountain, lest thou be also consumed
41 36 the land shall not be c. with scarcity
42 2 we may live and not be c. with want
Lev 6 11 shall cause them to be consumed to dust
23 sacrifice . . . shall be c. with fire
7 17 on the third day shall be c. with fire
8 32 and the loaves, shall be c. with fire
26 44 that they should be quite consumed and
Num 12 12 of her flesh is c. with the leprosy
14 33 of their fathers be c. in the desert
17 12 behold we are consumed, we all perish
19 6 flame, with which the cow is consumed
21 28 and hath consumed Ar of the Moabites
32 13 had done evil in his sight, was c.
Deut 2 14 men that were fit for war was consumed
28 24 heaven upon thee, till thou be c.
65 and a soul consumed with pensiveness
29 5 neither are the shoes of your feet c.
32 24 shall be consumed with famine. Eze 5:12
36 and they that remained are consumed
Josu 5 6 till all they were c. that had not
7 25 things that were his were c. with fire
9 13 journey are worn out and almost c.
10 20 great slaughter and almost utterly c.
11 13 that was very strong he c. with fire
Judg 6 21 c. the flesh and the unleavened loaves
15 5 the flame consumed also the vineyards
14 as the flax is wont to be consumed at
20 48 were consumed with devouring flames
2 K 11 25 sometimes another is c. by the sword
18 8 of the people whom the forest c. thou
22 15 scattered them: lightning, and c. them
3 K 18 38 fire of Lord fell and c. the holocaust
4 K 1 10 fire from heaven and c. him and. 12
14 c. the two first captains of fifty men
7 13 of Israel, for the rest are consumed
14 26 were c. even to them that were shut
2 Pa 7 1 consumed the holocausts and the victims
2 Es 2 13 gates thereof which were c. with fire
17 gates thereof are consumed with fire
Job 1 16 hath consumed them, and I alone have
4 9 and consumed by the spirit of his wrath
19 foundation, be c. as with the moth
7 6 weaver, and are c. without any hope
9 as a cloud is consumed and passeth away
10 18 that I had been c. that eye might not
11 17 when thou shalt think thyself consumed
13 19 why am I consumed holding my peace
28 who am to be c. as rottenness and as
14 10 he shall be dead and stripped and c.
19 20 the flesh being consumed, my bone hath
20 18 that he did, and yet shall not be c.
30 18 my garment is consumed, and they have
33 21 his flesh shall be consumed away, and
25 his flesh is consumed with punishments
36 12 sword, and shall be consumed in folly
Ps 17 38 I will not turn again till they are c.
58 14 when they are c.: when they are c. by
77 33 and their days were consumed in vanity
63 fire consumed their young men: and their
103 35 let sinners be consumed out of the earth
104 35 consumed all the fruit of their ground
Prov 22 8 with the rod of his anger he shall be c.
23 21 that club together shall be consumed
Ecce 4 14 another born king is c. with poverty
Wisd 5 13 but are consumed in our wickedness
16 16 hail and rain, and consumed by fire
Eccu 36 11 let him that escapeth be consumed by
45 17 his sacrifices were c. with fire every
23 were c. in his wrathful indignation
24 and consumed them with a flame of fire
Isa 1 28 forsaken the Lord, shall be consumed
10 18 shall be c. from the soul even to the
16 4 dust is at an end, the wretch is c.
29 20 the scorner is c., and they are all
41 12 as a thing c. the men that war against
46 2 are consumed and are broken together
66 17 they shall be c. together, saith the
Jer 6 29 the lead is consumed in the fire, the
29 their wicked deeds are not consumed

9 16 sword after them till they be consumed
10 25 c. him and have destroyed his glory
12 4 the beasts and the birds are consumed
14 15 and famine shall those prophets be c.
18 behold them that are c. with famine
16 4 and they shall be c. with the sword
24 10 till they be consumed out of the land
36 23 till all the volume was consumed with
44 12 be all consumed in the land of Egypt
12 they shall be c. from the least even
18 and have been consumed by the sword
27 in the land of Egypt, shall be c. by
Lam 2 22 nourished, my enemy hath consumed them
3 22 of the Lord that we are not consumed
4 9 being c. for want of the fruits of
Bar 6 71 they themselves at last are consumed
Eze 13 14 it shall fall and shall be consumed
15 4 the fire hath c. both ends thereof, and
5 when the fire hath devoured and c. it
6 have given to the fire to be consumed
22 31 in the fire of my wrath I consumed them
24 10 the flesh shall be consumed, and the
10 be sodden, and the bones shall be c.
11 thereof and let the rust of it be c.
34 29 shall be no more c. with famine in the
43 8 which reason I consumed them in my wrath
Dan 11 16 and it shall be consumed by his hand
14 12 came in by it and consumed those things
20 c. the things that were on the table
Osee 5 15 until you are c. and seek my face. In
Nah 1 10 they shall be consumed as stubble that
Mala 3 6 you the sons of Jacob are not consumed
2 Ma 1 30 sung hymns till the sacrifice was c.
31 when the sacrifice was c., Nehemias
32 but it was consumed by the light that
2 10 from heaven and consumed the holocaust
11 sin offering was not eaten, it was c.
7 41 after the sons the mother also was c.
Gal 5 15 take heed you be not c. one of another
consumeth Job 9 22 innocent and the wicked he c.
Prov 25 20 so the sadness of a man c. the heart
Eccu 18 18 a gist of one ill taught c. the eyes
31 1 watching for riches c. the flesh, and
Isa 5 24 and the heat of the flame consumeth it
consuming Deut 4 24 the Lord thy God is a c. fire
Deut 9 3 thee, a devouring and consuming fire
Wisd 6 25 neither will I go with consuming envy
2 Ma 1 23 while the sacrifice was c., Jonathan
Heb 12 29 and reverence. For our God is a c. fire
consummate Acts 20 24 that I may c. my course
consummated Luke 13 32 and the third day I am c.
John 19 30 said: It is c. And bowing his head, he
Heb 5 9 being c., he became to all that obey
consummation Dan 9 27 shall continue even to the c.
Mat 24 3 of thy coming and of the c. of the world
14 all nations, and then shall the c. come
28 20 I am with you all days, even to the c.
consumption 2 Pa 21 19 being wasted with a long c.
Job 30 24 not forth thy hand to their c.: and if
Isa 10 22 the c. abridged shall overflow with
23 God of hosts shall make a consumption
28 22 a consumption and a cutting short upon
contain Gen 41 26 both contain the same meaning
Num 17 3 one rod shall c. all their families
3 K 8 27 heavens of heavens cannot contain thee
2 Pa 2 6 heaven of heavens connot contain him
6 18 heaven of heavens do not contain thee
Eccu 30 24 soul, pleasing God, and contain thyself
Eze 45 11 the bate may contain the tenth part of
John 21 25 would not be able to contain the books
1 C 7 9 if they do not c. themselves let them
contained Deut 29 21 curses that are c. in the
3 K 7 26 crisped lily: it contained 2,000 bates
38 one laver contained four bases and was
2 Pa 33 18 are c. in the words of the kings of
36 8 are contained in the book of the kings
2 Ma 2 4 was also c. in the same writing, how
11 22 the king's letter contained these words
Eph 2 15 the law of commandments c. in decrees
containeth Wisd 1 7 that which c. all things, hath
Eze 23 32 and scorn, which containeth very much
containing Deut 9 10 c. all the words that he
Wisd 7 23 containing all spirits, intelligible
John 2 6 pots . . . c. two or three measures
contemn Lev 26 15 my laws and c. my judgments
contemned Exod 23 21 not think him one to be c.
Num 15 31 he hath c. the word of the Lord and
2 Pa 28 19 and [Achaz] had contemned the Lord
Eze 20 27 when they had despised and c. me. And
contemneth Prov 18 3 into the depths of sins, c.
Eccu 19 1 he that c. small things, shall fall by
contemning Num 5 12 c. her husband, shall have
contemplated Ecce 1 16 my mind hath c. many things
contempt 2 Pa 28 22 he increased c. against the
2 Pa 33 19 all his sins and contempt and places
Esth 13 12 it was not out of pride and contempt
16 24 an example of c. and disobedience
Jdth 13 28 in the contempt of his pride despised
Job 12 21 he poureth contempt upon princes, and
31 34 the c. of kinsmen hath terrified me
Ps 106 40 c. was poured forth upon their princes
118 22 remove from me reproach and contempt
122 3 we are greatly filled with contempt
4 to the rich, and contempt to the proud
Prov 12 8 foolish, shall be exposed to contempt
Ecce 9 3 are filled with evil and with contempt
2 Ma 3 18 the place was like to come into c. And
5 17 this contempt had happened to the place
contemptible Wisd 10 4 course of the just by c. wood
Abdi 2 among the nations: thou art exceeding c.
Mala 1 7 the table of the Lord is contemptible
12 which is laid thereupon is contemptible
2 9 therefore have I also made you c. and
1 C 1 28 the things that are c., hath God chosen
2 C 10 10 presence is weak and his speech c., let
contend Job 9 3 if he will c. with him, he cannot
Job 23 6 I would not that he should c. with me
Prov 24 19 contend not with the wicked, nor seek
29 9 if a wise man c. with a fool, whether
Ecce 6 10 and cannot contend in judgment with
Eccu 8 2 c. not with a rich man, lest he bring
Isa 50 8 who will contend with me? Let us stand
57 16 I will not contend forever, neither
Jer 2 9 will I yet contend in judgment with
29 why will you c. with me in judgment
35 I will c. with thee in judgment because
12 5 how canst thou contend with horses? And
Mich 6 1 arise, contend thou in judgment against
Mat 5 40 if a man will c. with thee in judgment
12 19 he shall not c. nor cry out, neither
2 Tim 2 14 c. not in words, for it is to no profit
James 4 2 you contend and war, and you have not
Jude 3 to c. earnestly for the faith once
contended Gen 26 22 well, for which they c. not
Job 34 19 when he contended against the poor man
Acts 11 2 of the circumcision c. with him [Peter]
Jude 9 contended about the body of Moses, he
contendeth Job 39 32 that c. with God be so easily
content Num 18 24 c. with the oblation or tithes
Judg 17 11 he was content and abode with the man
4 K 14 10 be c. with the glory and sit at home
Esth 8 13 and this was the content of the letter
Prov 15 16 than great treasures without content
Eccu 40 18 a laborer that is c. with what he hath
2 Ma 6 30 am well content to suffer these things
Luke 3 14 any man; and be content with your pay

Phil 4 11 in whatsoever state I am, to be content
1 Tim 6 8 be covered, with these we are content
contented 1 K 30 22 be c. with them and go his way
Eccu 29 29 be c. with little instead of much, and
Eze 16 28 even so thou wast not contented. Thou
Heb 13 5 contented with such things as you have
contention 2 Es 9 17 bondage, as it were by c.
Job 6 29 answer, I beseech you, without c.: and
Prov 22 10 and contention shall go out with him
Eccu 28 13 a hasty contention kindleth a fire
Jer 15 10 a man of contention to all the earth
2 Ma 4 4 Onias considering the danger of this c.
16 they incurred a dangerous contention
Rom 1 29 full of envy, murder, contention, deceit
13 13 not in c. and envy: but put ye on
1 C 3 3 there is among you envying and c., are
Phil 1 15 some indeed, even out of envy and c.
17 some out of contention preach Christ
2 3 let nothing be done through contention
1 Tim 2 8 pure hands without anger and contention
James 3 16 where envying and contention is, there
contentions Prov 13 10 proud there are always c.
Prov 18 18 the lot suppresseth contentions, and
23 29 who hath contentions? Who falls into
26 20 talebearer is taken away, c. shall cease
1 C 1 11 that there are contentions among you
Gal 5 20 c., emulations, wraths, quarrels
1 Tim 6 4 from which arise envies, contentions
Titus 3 9 genealogies and c. and strivings about
James 3 14 if there be contentions in your hearts
4 1 from whence are wars and c. among you
contentious Prov 27 15 and a c. woman are alike
Rom 2 8 to them that are contentious and who
1 C 11 16 but if any man seem to be contentious
contentment 1 Tim 6 6 godliness with c. is great
contents Esth 3 14 c. of the letters were to this
1 Ma 15 2 contents were these: King Antiochus to
15 the contents whereof were these: Lucius
contest 2 K 21 4 we have no c. about silver and
Acts 15 2 Barnabas had no small c. with them
continency Gal 5 23 fruit of the Spirit is . . . c.
continent Tob 6 18 keep thyself continent from her
Wisd 8 21 that I could not otherwise be continent
Eccu 26 20 no price is worthy of a continent soul
Titus 1 8 a bishop must be . . . holy, continent
continual Lev 15 33 that hath a c. issue of blood
Lev 21 20 a continual scab or a dry scurf in his
Num 28 6 it is the c. holocaust which you offered
4 K 25 30 he appointed him a c. allowance, which
2 Pa 2 4 for the continual setting forth of bread
1 Es 3 5 the c. holocaust, both on the new moons
2 Es 10 33 the c. sacrifice and for a c. holocaust
Prov 15 15 a secure mind is like a continual feast
Eccu 18 32 for their concertation is continual
30 17 and everlasting rest, than c. sickness
33 27 neck, and continual labors bow a slave
38 28 by his c. diligence varieth the figure
40 4 the fear of death, c. anger, and strife
Jer 52 34 a continual provision was allowed by
Eze 46 14 Lord by ordinance c. and everlasting
Dan 8 11 it took away from him the c. sacrifice
12 was given him against the c. sacrifice
13 the vision, concerning the c. sacrifice
11 31 and shall take away the c. sacrifice
12 11 the c. sacrifice shall be taken away
Rom 9 2 sadness and c. sorrow in my heart
James 5 16 c. prayer of a just man availeth much
continually Exod 29 38 of a year old every day c.
Lev 24 2 olives to furnish the lamps continually
4 pure candlestick before the Lord c.
Judg 16 16 and continually hung upon him [Samson]
1 K 18 29 Saul became David's enemy continually
1 Pa 9 33 they might serve continually day and
16 6 to sound the trumpet c. before the ark
37 minister in the presence of the ark c.
40 upon the altar of holocausts continually
23 31 [Levites] continually before the Lord
2 Pa 24 14 offered in the house of the Lord c.
Ps 37 18 and my sorrow is continually before me
70 6 of thee shall I continually sing: I am
73 23 of them that hate thee ascendeth c.
108 15 may they be before the Lord c., and let
19 like a girdle with which he is girded c.
118 109 my soul is continually in my hands: and
Prov 5 19 be thou delighted c. with her love
6 21 bind them in thy heart continually and
19 13 wife is like a roof c. dropping through
Eccu 6 37 meditate c. in his commandments: and
17 16 his eyes are c. upon their ways. Their
20 21 it shall be c. in the mouth of the
26 yet it will be c. in the mouth of men
27 13 time: but be c. among men that think
37 15 be c. with a holy man, whomsoever
21 and the tongue is c. the ruler of them
51 15 I will praise thy name continually and
Isa 21 8 standing c. by day: and I am upon my
51 13 thou hast been afraid c. all the day
52 5 my name is continually blasphemed all
58 11 Lord will give thee rest continually
60 11 thy gates shall be open continually
65 3 a people that c. provoke me to anger
Jer 6 7 infirmity and stripes are c. before me
32 30 have continually done evil in my eyes
33 18 and to kill victims continually. And
Eze 38 8 which have been continually waste: but
39 14 men to go c. about the land, to bury
Abdi 16 all nations shall drink continually
Nah 3 19 whom hath not thy wickedness passed c.
Haba 1 17 will not spare c. to slay the nations
1 Ma 6 18 they were c. seeking their hurt and to
15 25 second time, assaulting it continually
2 Ma 13 12 on the ground for three days c., Judas
Luke 18 5 lest continually coming, she weary me
Acts 6 4 we will give ourselves c. to prayer
Heb 10 1 selfsame sacrifices which they offer c.
continuance Eccu 28 26 its c. shall not be for a
Isa 23 18 unto fulness and be clothed for a c.
65 22 works of their hands shall be of long c.
Bar 6 46 that make them, are of no long c. Can
continue Exod 28 28 that the joining . . . may c.
Num 24 22 how long shalt thou be able to c.
Deut 32 47 you may c. a long time in the land
1 K 13 14 but thy kingdom shall not continue
20 13 if my father shall continue in malice
4 K 6 25 so long did the siege continue till
1 Pa 28 7 if he continue to keep my commandments
Jdth 4 11 if you continue with perseverance in
9 18 that thy house may c. in thy holiness
Job 2 9 thou still continue in thy simplicity
15 29 neither shall his substance continue
20 21 nothing shall continue of his goods
29 19 and dew shall continue in my harvest
32 22 I know not how long I shall continue
Ps 71 5 he shall c. with the sun and before the
101 29 the children of thy servants shall c.
Prov 2 21 and the simple shall continue in it
Ecce 3 14 that all the works . . . continue forever
8 3 and do not continue in an evil work
Wisd 18 20 but thy wrath did not long continue
Eccu 6 11 a friend if he continue steadfast
21 the unwise will not continue with her
14 22 blessed is the man that shall c. in
22 29 time of his trouble c. faithful to him
39 15 if he c., he shall leave a name above
41 15 this shall continue with thee, more
16 a good name shall continue forever

44 11 good things continue with their seed
46 15 and their name continue forever, the
Isa 7 9 you will not believe, you shall not c.
Jer 3 5 or wilt thou continue unto the end
32 14 that they may continue many days. For
Eze 23 43 the woman still c. in her fornication
Dan 9 27 the desolation shall continue even to
1 Ma 7 38 suffer them not to c. any longer. Then
10 27 continue still to keep fidelity towards
2 Ma 8 26 they did not continue the pursuit
9 26 continue to be faithful to me and to
Mat 15 32 they continue with me now three days
Luke 11 8 yet if he shall c. knocking, I say to
John 8 31 if you c. in my word, you shall be my
Acts 11 23 he exhorted them . . . to c. in the Lord
13 43 persuaded them to c. in the grace of
14 21 exhorting them to continue in the faith
Rom 6 1 shall we c. in sin that grace may
1 C 7 8 it is good for them if they so c.
Gal 2 5 that truth of the gospel might continue
Phil 1 25 I know that I shall . . . c. with you all
3 16 let us also continue in the same rule
Col 1 23 if so ye continue in the faith, grounded
1 Tim 2 15 if she continue in faith and love and
5 5 let her . . . continue in supplications
2 Tim 3 14 continue thou in those things which
Heb 1 11 they shall perish but thou shalt c.
7 23 they were not suffered to continue
2 P 3 4 all things continue as they were from
continued Gen 37 35 whilst he [Jacob] c. weeping
Num 9 19 that it continued over it a long time
Deut 9 9 I continued in the mount forty days
Ruth 2 23 and continued to glean with them till
4 K 21 15 and have continued to provoke me from
Tob 2 14 but c. immoveable in the fear of God
14 17 all his kindred . . . c. in good life and
Jdth 4 14 and continued in the sight of the Lord
6 16 prayer in which they c. all the day
Job 34 1 Eliu continued his discourse and said
Eccu 2 12 who hath c. in his commandment and
46 11 his strength c. even to his old age
Jer 20 10 familiars, and continued at my side
Dan 1 21 Daniel c. even to the first year of
6 28 Daniel c. unto the reign of Darius
1 Ma 10 26 have continued in our friendship and
2 Ma 4 50 Menelaus continued in authority
5 27 they continued feeding on herbs, that
8 1 such as c. in the Jews' religion, they
Luke 22 28 who have c. with me in my temptations
John 8 7 when they c. asking him, he lifted up
Acts 12 16 Peter c. knocking. And when they had
15 35 and Paul and Barnabas c. at Antioch
19 10 this c. for the space of two years
20 7 he c. his speech until midnight. And
27 33 fourteenth day you have . . . c. fasting
Heb 8 9 they c. not in my testament: and I
James 1 25 law of liberty and hath c. therein
continueth Josu 14 11 strength of that time c. in
Job 14 2 and never continueth in the same state
21 8 their seed continueth before them
Ps 71 17 his name continueth before the sun
110 3 his justice continueth forever and
10 his praise continueth forever and ever
118 90 thou hast founded the earth, and it c.
Ecce 3 15 that which hath been made, the same c.
Eccu 6 23 she c. even to the sight of God. Give
18 22 the reward of God continueth forever
21 16 his counsel c. like a fountain of life
22 23 that c. always in the commandments
27 12 a holy man c. in wisdom as the sun
2 Tim 2 13 he c. faithful, he cannot deny himself
Heb 7 3 c. a priest forever. Now consider how
24 he c. forever, hath an everlasting

2 J 9 c. not in the doctrine of Christ, hath
9 he that c. in the doctrine, the same
continuing 1 K 22 13 c. a traitor to this day
Tob 3 11 c. in prayer with tears besought
Jdth 8 16 continuing in an humble spirit in his
Acts 2 46 c. daily with one accord in the temple
27 2 Aristarchus . . . c. with us. And the day
contract Gen 34 9 let us c. marriages one with
contradict Job 6 10 nor I c. the words of the
Job 11 10 who shall c. him? For he knoweth
Osee 4 4 as they that contradict the priest
contradicted Luke 2 34 sign which shall be c.
Acts 13 45 c. those things which were said by
19 36 as these things cannot be c., you
28 22 we know that it is everywhere c. And
contradicteth Rom 10 21 believeth not and c. me
contradicting Job 16 9 up against my face, c. me
Acts 28 19 the Jews c. it, I was constrained to
contradiction Num 20 13 this is the Water of c.
Num 27 14 offended me . . . in c. of the multitude
Ps 30 21 from the contradiction of tongues
54 10 I have seen iniquity and contradiction
79 7 made us to be a c. to our neighbors
Heb 7 7 without all c. that which is less is
Jude 11 and have perished in the c. of Core
waters of contradiction Num 20 24 incredulous . . . at the w. . . .
Num 27 14 these are the w. . . . in Cades of the
Deut 32 51 at the w. . . . in Cades of the desert
33 8 temptation and judged at the w. . . .
Ps 80 8 tempest: I proved thee at the w. . . .
105 32 they provoked him also at the w. . . .
Eze 47 19 even to the w. . . . of Cades. 48:28
contradictions 2 K 22 44 save me from the c.
Ps 17 44 thou wilt deliver me from the c. of
contrariwise Num 23 11 thou c. blessest them
Gal 2 7 c. when they had seen that to me was
1 P 3 9 not rendering evil . . . but c., blessing
contrary Gen 31 8 said on the c.: Thou shalt
Lev 26 21 if you walk c. to me and will not
23 not amend but will walk c. to me: I
24 I also will walk contrary to you and
40 against me and walked contrary unto me
Num 22 32 thy way is perverse and contrary to
24 10 thou on the c. hast blessed them three
Josu 8 5 will approach on the contrary side
24 10 on the contrary I blessed you by him
Judg 2 17 of the Lord, they did all things c.
3 K 3 22 on the contrary she said: Thou liest
13 33 on the contrary he made of the meanest
2 Pa 20 11 do the contrary and endeavor to cast
28 23 on the contrary they were the ruin
Job 4 8 on the c. I have seen those who work
Wisd 2 12 and he is contrary to our doings and
15 7 such as serve to the contrary: but
Eccu 25 30 have superiority, is c. to her husband
Eze 16 34 contrary to the custom of women in thy
34 the contrary hath been done in thee
Mich 2 8 my people, on the contrary, are risen
Mat 14 24 with the waves, for the wind was c.
Acts 17 7 these all do c. to the decrees of
23 3 c. to the law, commandest me to be
26 9 to do many things c. to the name of
27 4 Cyprus, because the winds were c.
Rom 11 24 c. to nature, were grafted into the
16 17 c. to doctrine which you have learned
2 C 2 7 on the c. you should rather forgive
Gal 5 17 these are contrary one to another
Col 2 14 the decree . . . which was contrary to
1 Tim 1 10 whatever . . . is c. to sound doctrine
Titus 2 8 who is on the c. part may be afraid
contribute 4 K 23 35 to c. according to the
Prov 23 20 revellings, who contribute flesh to

Eccu 18 33 by borrowing to c. to feasts when
Isa 46 6 you that c. gold out of the bag, and
contributed Exod 30 16 was c. by the children
2 Pa 24 10 and going in they contributed and cast
contribution Eccu 32 3 get the honor of the c.
Rom 15 26 to make a contribution for the poor
contrite Ps 33 19 them that are of a c. heart
Ps 50 19 a c. and humbled heart . . . thou wilt
Isa 57 15 with a c. and humble spirit, to revive the heart of the c.
61 1 to heal the contrite of heart and to
66 2 of a c. spirit and that trembleth at
Dan 3 39 in a c. heart and humble spirit let us
Luke 4 18 to heal the c. of heart, to preach the
contrive Job 27 4 neither shall my tongue c. lying
Eze 21 31 brutish and contrive thy destruction
contrived Ps 82 6 they have c. with one consent
contriving Nah 1 11 c. treachery in his mind
controlled Eccu 32 23 shall be c. by the things of
controversy Exod 18 16 when any c. falleth out
Deut 19 17 between whom the controversy is, shall
25 1 if there be a controversy between men
Job 31 13 when they had any c. against me: for
Eze 44 24 when there shall be a controversy
Heb 6 16 an oath . . . is the end of all their c.
contumelious Rom 1 30 c., proud, haughty, inventors
1 Tim 1 13 blasphemer and a persecutor and c.
contumeliously Mat 22 6 having treated them c.
Acts 14 5 to use them c. and to stone them: they
convenient Judg 17 8 he should find it c. for him
3 K 21 2 if thou think it more c. for thee, I
Wisd 13 15 maketh a c. dwelling place for it, and
1 Ma 4 46 mountain of the temple in a c. place
12 11 and other days, wherein it is c.
14 34 furnished them with all things c.
2 Ma 4 32 that he had found a convenient time
8 31 they laid them all up in c. places
11 36 we may decree as it is c. for you
14 5 gotten a c. time to further his madness
22 men to be ready in convenient places
15 20 and the horsemen ranged in c. places
Mark 6 21 when a c. day was come, Herod made a
Acts 24 25 when I have a c. time I will send for
Rom 1 28 to do those things which are not c.
conveniently Mark 14 11 sought how he might c.
conversant Wisd 8 3 nobility by being c. with
Wisd 13 7 being c. among his works, they search
Eccu 11 21 covenant, be c. therein and grow old
39 3 will be c. in the secrets of parables
50 30 that is c. in these good things: and
conversation Exod 34 29 horned from the c. of the
Deut 1 13 whose conversation is approved among
Tob 14 17 continued in good life and in holy c.
Wisd 8 16 her conversation hath no bitterness
Eccu 9 11 for her conversation burneth as fire
18 21 in the time of sickness show thy c.
38 14 give for ease and remedy, for their c.
50 5 obtained glory in his c. with the
Dan 2 11 the gods, whose c. is not with men
2 Ma 6 23 his good life and c. from a child
Gal 1 13 you have heard of my conversation
Eph 2 12 being aliens from the c. of Israel
4 22 put off, according to former c., the
Phil 1 27 let your c. be worthy of the gospel
3 20 our c. is in heaven; from whence also
1 Tim 4 12 be thou an example . . . in conversation
Heb 13 7 follow considering the end of their c.
James 3 13 let him show, by a good conversation
1 P 1 15 be you also in all manner of c. holy
18 from your vain c. of the tradition
2 12 having your c. good among the Gentiles
3 1 they may be won . . . by the c. of the
2 considering your chaste c. with fear
16 who falsely accuse your good c. in
2 P 2 7 oppressed by . . . lewd c. of the wicked
3 11 ought you to be in holy c. and godliness
converse Jdth 6 18 with all thine mayst c. with
Eccu 41 8 that c. near the houses of the ungodly
1 P 1 17 c. in fear during the time of your
2 P 2 18 they allure . . . such as c. in error
conversed 1 K 12 2 having then c. with you from
1 K 25 15 we conversed with them in the desert
Bar 3 38 was seen upon earth, and c. with men
Dan 13 57 they for fear conversed with you: but
Osee 4 14 because themselves c. with harlots and
Acts 11 26 they conversed there in the church a
23 1 I have c. with all good conscience
2 C 1 12 in the grace of God we have conversed
Eph 2 3 in which we all conversed in time past
conversing Dan 13 54 tree thou sawest them c.
Dan 13 58 didst thou take them conversing together
Phil 3 6 that is in the law, c. without blame
conversion Acts 15 3 relating c. of the Gentiles
convert Ps 79 4 convert us. 8, 20; 84:5; Lam 5:21
Prov 16 7 he will c. even his enemies to peace
Isa 49 6 and to convert the dregs of Israel
52 8 when the Lord shall convert Sion. Rejoice
Jer 15 19 wilt be converted, I will convert thee
31 18 convert me, and I shall be converted
19 after thou didst convert me, I did
Amos 1 3 for four I will not convert it. 6, 9
11 for four I will not c. him. 13; 2:1, 4, 6
Luke 1 16 he shall convert many of the children
Acts 3 26 that every one may convert himself
James 5 19 err from the truth and one convert him
converted 3 K 8 35 and shall be c. from their sins
3 K 8 47 and being c. make supplication to thee
2 Pa 6 24 and being converted shall do penance
26 and confess to thy name and be converted
37 and if they be converted in their heart
7 14 being c. shall make supplication to
Tob 13 8 be converted, therefore, ye sinners
Job 17 10 be you all converted and come, and I
Ps 7 13 except you will be converted, he will
21 28 and shall be converted to the Lord
22 3 he hath converted my soul. He hath led
50 15 the wicked shall be converted to thee
84 9 unto them that are c. to the heart
89 3 hast said: Be converted, O ye sons of
Eccu 5 8 delay not to be c. to the Lord, and
Isa 6 10 lest they . . . be c. and I heal them
10 21 the remnant shall be converted, the
22 a remnant of them shall be converted
45 22 be c. to me and you shall be saved
60 5 the multitude of the sea shall be c.
Jer 15 19 if thou wilt be c., I will convert thee
26 3 if so be they will hearken and be c.
31 18 convert me, and I shall be converted
Lam 5 21 to thee, and we shall be converted
Bar 3 7 we are c. from the iniquity of our
Eze 3 18 that he may be c. from his wicked way
19 and he be not c. from his wickedness
14 6 be converted and depart from your
18 23 that he should be c. from his ways and
30 be converted and do penance for all
33 9 that he may be c. from his ways, and he be not c. from his way
Osee 11 5 because they would not be converted
14 8 they shall be c. that sit under his
Joel 2 12 be c. to me with all your heart, in
Mich 5 3 remnant of his brethren shall be c. to
4 they shall be c., for now shall he be
Mat 13 15 lest they should be converted. Mark 4:12
18 3 unless you be c. and become as little
Luke 17 4 seven times in a day be c. unto thee
22 32 being once c., confirm thy brethren

6 22 Aminadab his son, Core his son, Asir
37 son of Abiasaph the son of Core. 9:19
9 19 but Sellum the son of Core the son of
26 1 Meselemia, the son of Core, of the sons
19 of the sons of Core and of Merari. Now
2 Pa 20 19 of the sons of Core praised the Lord
31 14 Core . . . was overseer of the things which
Ps 41 1 for the sons of Core. 43:1; 44:1; 45:1; 46:1; 47:1; 48:1; 83:1; 84:1; 86:1; 87:1
Eccu 45 22 congregation of Core in their wrath
Jude 11 perished in the contradiction of Core
cores Num 11 32 quails, he that did least, ten c.
2 Pa 2 10 for their food 20,000 cores of wheat and as many cores of barley
1 Es 7 22 and unto a hundred cores of wheat and
coriander Num 11 7 was like coriander seed. 16:31
Corinth Acts 18 1 from Athens, he came to Corinth
Acts 19 1 while Apollo was at Corinth, that Paul
1 C 1 2 to the church . . . at Corinth. 2 C 1:1
2 C 1 23 I came not any more to Corinth: not
2 Tim 4 20 Erastus remained at C. And Trophimus
Corinthians Acts 18 8 many of C. hearing, believed
2 C 6 11 ye Corinthians, our heart is enlarged
Corite 1 Pa 9 31 firstborn of Sellum the Corite
Corites Exod 6 24 these are the kindreds of the C.
1 Pa 9 19 the Corites were over the works of the
26 1 of the Corites Meselemia, the son of
cormorant Lev 11 17 owl and the c. and the ibis
Deut 14 17 the swan and the stork and the c.
corn Gen 27 28 abundance of corn and wine. And
Gen 27 37 established him with corn and wine
41 5 seven ears of corn came up upon one
22 seven ears of corn grew upon one stalk
35 let all the corn be laid up under
47 the corn being bound up into sheaves
42 3 went down to buy corn in Egypt: whilst
6 corn was sold by his direction to the
19 carry the corn that you have bought
26 having loaded their asses with the c.
35 they poured out their corn, and every
43 2 when they had eaten up all the corn
44 1 fill their sacks with corn, as much as
47 14 gathered up all the money for the corn
24 sow the fields, that you may have corn
Exod 9 32 and other winter corn were not hurt
13 4 you go forth in the month of new corn
22 6 and catch stacks of corn or corn standing in
23 10 and shalt gather the corn thereof. But
15 time of the month of new corn. 34:18
16 when thou hast gathered in all thy corn
19 shalt carry the firstfruits of the corn
34 22 with the firstfruits of the corn of
Lev 2 14 gift of the firstfruits of thy corn
16 part of the corn broken small and of
11 37 if it fall upon seed corn, it shall not
19 9 when thou reapest the corn of thy
23 10 shall reap your corn and shall bring
14 not eat either bread or parched corn
22 when you reap the corn of your land
27 30 all tithes of the land, whether of corn
Num 18 12 oil and of the wine and of the corn
Deut 7 13 thy corn and thy vintage, thy oil
11 14 that you may gather in your corn and
12 17 the tithes of thy corn and thy wine
14 23 the tithe of thy corn and thy wine
16 1 observe the month of new corn, which
9 thou didst put the sickle to the corn
18 4 firstfruits also of corn, of wine, and
23 19 thy brother money to usury, nor corn
25 if thou go into thy friend's corn, thou
24 19 when thou hast reaped the corn in thy
25 4 ox that treadeth out thy corn on the
33 28 eye of Jacob in land of corn and wine
Josu 5 11 unleavened bread of corn of the land
12 after they ate of the corn of the land
12 ate of the corn of the present year
12 6 which is interpreted, An ear of corn
6 to express ear of corn by same letter
15 5 presently went into the standing corn
5 both the corn that was already carried
Ruth 2 2 glean the ears of corn that escape
3 gleaned the ears of corn after the
7 to glean the ears of corn that remain
15 to glean the ears of corn as before
21 till all the corn should be reaped
1 K 8 12 plow his fields and to reap his corn
15 he will take the tenth of your corn
25 18 and five measures of parched corn and
2 K 4 6 taking ears of corn, and Rechab and
14 30 servants of Absalom set the corn on fire
31 why have thy servants set my c. on fire
17 28 parched corn and beans and lentils
4 K 4 42 of barley and new corn in his scrip
2 Pa 31 5 firstfruits of corn, wine, and oil and
32 28 storehouses also of corn, of wine, and
2 Es 5 2 let us take up corn for the price of
3 let us take corn because of the famine
10 have lent money and corn to many: let
11 and of the corn, the wine, and the oil
10 39 to the treasury the firstfruits of c.
13 5 the tithes of the corn, of the wine, and
12 all Juda brought the tithe of the corn
Jdth 2 9 he appointed corn to be prepared out of
17 harvest, and he set all the c. on fire
4 4 together corn for provision for war
10 5 parched corn and dry figs and bread
11 12 forbade them to touch, in corn, wine
Job 24 10 they have taken away the ears of corn
24 as the tops of the ears of corn they
37 11 corn desireth clouds, and the clouds
Ps 4 8 by the fruit of their corn, their wine
64 14 and the vales shall abound with corn
147 14 and filleth thee with the fat of corn
Prov 11 26 that hideth up corn, shall be cursed
14 4 where there is much corn, shall be cursed
Eccu 20 30 shall make a high heap of corn: and he
Isa 17 5 his arm shall gather the ears of corn
9 the plows and the corn that were left
28 28 but bread corn shall be broken small
30 23 the bread of the corn of the land shall
36 17 a land of corn and of wine, a land of
62 8 will no more give thy corn to be meat
Jer 5 17 they shall eat up thy corn and thy
31 12 for the corn and wine and oil and the
Lam 2 12 where is corn and wine? When they
Eze 3 15 captivity, to the heap of new corn
27 17 were thy merchants with the best corn
36 29 I will call for corn and will multiply
Osee 2 8 did not know that I gave her corn and
9 will I return and take away my corn
22 the earth shall hear the corn and the
10 11 heifer taught to love to tread out corn
Joel 1 10 hath mourned, for the corn is wasted
17 because the corn is confounded. Why
2 19 I will send you corn and wine and oil
Amos 8 5 we shall open the corn that we may
6 and may sell the refuse of the corn
9 9 nations, as corn is sifted in a sieve
Agge 1 11 upon the corn and upon the wine and
Zach 9 17 but the corn of the elect, and wine
Mat 12 1 Jesus went through the corn on the
Mark 2 23 the Lord walked through the c. fields
23 forward and to pluck the ears of corn
4 28 afterwards the full corn in the ear
Luke 6 1 as he went through the corn fields
Acts 7 12 heard that there was corn in Egypt

1 C 9 9 that treadeth out the corn. 1 Tim 5:18
Cornelius Acts 10 1 man in Caesarea named C., a
Acts 10 3 in unto him, saying to him: Cornelius
17 the men who were sent from Cornelius
22 Cornelius, a centurion, a just man
24 C. waited for them, having called
25 was come in, C. came to meet him
30 C. said: Four days ago unto this hour
31 C., thy prayer is heard and thy alms
corner Exod 36 28 others at each c. of tabernacle
Exod 36 33 by midst of the boards from c. to c.
3 K 7 34 that were at every corner of each base
4 K 14 13 to the gate of the corner. 2 Pa 25:23; Jer 31:38
2 Pa 26 9 over the gate of the corner and over
2 Es 3 19 against the going up of the strong c.
20 from the c. to the door of the house
24 unto the bending and unto the corner
30 and unto the chamber of the corner
31 and within the chamber of the corner
Job 38 6 or who laid the corner stone thereof
Ps 117 22 same is become the head of the corner
Prov 7 8 passeth through the street by the c.
21 9 to sit in a c. of the housetop. 25:24
Isa 28 16 of Sion, a tried stone, a corner stone
Jer 31 40 to the corner of the horse gate towards
51 26 not take of thee a stone for the c.
Eze 46 21 a little court in the c. of the court
21 to every c. of the court there was a
Dan 13 38 we that were in a c. of the orchard
Zach 10 4 out of him shall come forth the corner
Mat 21 42 is become the head of the corner. Mark 12:10; Luke 20:17; Acts 4:11; 1 Pa 2:7
Acts 26 26 was any of these things done in a c.
Eph 2 20 Jesus Christ being chief corner stone
1 P 2 6 I lay in Sion a chief corner stone
corners Exod 25 12 at the four corners of the ark
Exod 25 26 shalt put them in the four corners
26 19 be put two sockets at the two corners
23 in the c. at back of the tabernacle
24 also that are to be put in the corners
27 2 shall be horns at the four corners
4 at the four corners of which shall be
36 24 board on the two sides of the corners
24 mortises of the sides end in the c.
29 he did on both sides at the corners
37 3 four rings of gold at the four corners
13 which he put in the four corners at
25 from corners of which went out horns
38 2 horns whereof went out from the corners
39 17 stood out in the corners of the ephod
Num 15 38 fringes in the c. of their garments
Deut 22 12 hem at the four corners of thy cloak
1 K 14 38 bring hither all the c. of the people
3 K 6 31 posts of five corners, and two doors
7 31 and in the corners of the pillars were
32 wheels which were at the four corners
36 in the corners, cherubims and lions
2 Pa 26 15 the towers, and in the c. of the walls
28 24 altars in all the corners of Jerusalem
Job 1 19 and shook the four corners of the house
Prov 7 12 now lying in wait near the corners
Isa 44 13 he hath made it with corners and hath
Eze 41 22 the corners thereof and the length
43 17 fourteen cubits broad in the four c.
20 upon the four c. of the brim. 45:19
46 21 the four corners of the court. 22
Zach 14 10 even to the gate of the corners: and
Mat 6 5 synagogues and corners of the streets
Acts 10 11 sheet let down by the four c. 11:5
Apoc 7 1 standing on the four corners of the
cornet 1 Pa 15 28 with the sound of the cornet
Ps 97 6 with long trumpets and sound of cornet
Osee 5 8 blow ye the c. in Gabaa, the trumpet
cornets 1 K 18 6 with timbrels of joy and cornets
2 K 6 5 timbrels and cornets and cymbals
2 Pa 15 14 sound of trumpet and sound of cornets
cornfloor Osee 9 1 loved a reward upon every c.
Cornustibii Job 42 14 and the name of the third C.
Corozain Mat 11 21 woe to thee C. Luke 10:13
corporeally Col 2 9 the fulness of the Godhead c.
corpse Num 19 11 that toucheth the c. of a man. 13
Num 19 16 if any man in the field touch the c.
Deut 21 1 corpse of a man slain, and it is not
corpses Isa 37 36 behold they were all dead c.
correct 2 K 7 14 I will c. him with the rod of
Job 36 10 shall open their ear, to correct them
Ps 118 9 by what doth a young man c. his way
140 5 the just man shall correct me in mercy
Ecce 7 14 no man can c. whom he hath despised
Eccu 20 31 the mouth, so that they cannot correct
Isa 38 16 thou shalt correct me and make me to
Jer 10 24 c. me, O Lord, but yet with judgment
46 28 but I will correct them in judgment
2 Tim 3 16 profitable to teach, to reprove, to c.
Heb 12 7 son is there whom the father doth not c.
corrected Deut 21 18 being c., slighteth obedience
Ps 15 7 my reins also have c. me even till
17 36 thy discipline hath c. me unto the end
38 12 thou hast corrected man for iniquity
89 10 is come upon us: and we shall be c.
95 10 he hath c. the world, which shall not
Prov 29 19 slave will not be corrected by words
Ecce 1 15 the perverse are hard to be corrected
7 4 the mind of the offender is corrected
Wisd 9 18 of them that are upon earth may be c.
Eccu 23 20 will never be corrected all the days
correcteth Job 5 17 blessed is the man whom God c.
Prov 13 24 but he that loveth him c. him betimes
21 29 he that is righteous correcteth his way
Eccu 18 13 hath mercy and teacheth and correcteth
correction Tob 3 21 if it be under c., it shall be
Prov 3 11 reject not the correction of the Lord
10 17 way of life, to him that observeth c.
12 1 he that loveth c., loveth knowledge
22 15 rod of correction shall drive it away
23 13 withhold not correction from a child
Wisd 16 6 for a short time for their correction
Eccu 16 13 his correction judgeth a man according
33 25 and correction and work for a slave
26 he worketh under c. and seeketh to
42 5 of much correction of children and to
Jer 2 30 they have not received correction: your
5 3 they have refused to receive correction
Haba 1 12 and made him strong for correction
Soph 3 7 fear me, thou wilt receive correction
2 Ma 6 12 but for the correction of our nation
7 33 for our chastisement and correction
1 C 10 11 they are written for our correction
Eph 6 4 up in the discipline and c. of the Lord
Heb 9 10 laid on them until the time of c. But
corrupt 3 K 8 37 or c. air or blasting or locust
Job 2 8 potsherd and scraped the corrupt matter
Ps 13 1 are corrupt, and are become abominable
74 1 unto the end, corrupt not, a psalm of
Prov 15 12 a c. man loveth not one that reproveth
26 23 swelling lips joined with a c. heart
29 8 corrupt men bring a city to ruin: but
1 C 15 23 evil communications c. good manners
corrupted Gen 6 11 the earth was c. before God
Gen 6 12 had seen that the earth was corrupted
12 all flesh had corrupted its way upon
Exod 7 18 the waters shall be corrupted, and the
21 the river c., and the Egyptians could
8 14 immense heaps, and the land was c.
24 the land was c. by this kind of flies

Lev 22 25 they are all corrupted and defiled
Deut 18 20 being corrupted with pride, shall speak
28 22 with corrupted air and with blasting
Ps 37 6 my sores are putrified and corrupted
52 2 they are c. and become abominable in
Prov 25 26 with the foot, and a corrupted spring
Cant 8 5 there thy mother was corrupted, there
Eccu 11 32 as c. bowels send forth stinking breath
42 10 her virginity, lest she should be c.
46 13 by name, whose heart was not corrupted
Mich 2 10 shall be c. with a grievous corruption
Soph 3 7 rose early and c. all their thoughts
2 C 4 16 though our outward man is corrupted
7 2 we have corrupted no man, we have
11 3 so your minds should be corrupted and
Eph 4 22 who is c. according to the desire of
1 Tim 6 5 men corrupted in mind. 2 Tim 3:8
James 5 2 your riches are corrupted: and your
Jude 10 like dumb beasts, in these they are c.
Apoc 11 18 destroy them who have c. the earth
19 2 great harlot which corrupted the earth
corruptest Jer 51 25 which c. the whole earth
corrupteth Luke 12 33 approacheth nor moth c.
1 C 5 6 little leaven c. the whole lump. Gal 5:9
corruptible Wisd 9 15 the c. body is a load upon
Wisd 19 20 wasted not the flesh of c. animals
Eccu 14 20 every work that is c. shall fail in
2 Ma 6 25 and for a little time of a c. life
7 16 though thou art corruptible, thou dost
Rom 1 23 the likeness of the image of a c. man
1 C 9 25 that they may receive a c. crown; but
15 33 for this c. must put on incorruption
1 P 1 18 you were not redeemed with c. things
23 being born again not of c. seed, but
corruption Job 33 18 rescuing his soul from c.
Job 33 22 his soul hath drawn near to corruption
24 that he may not go down to corruption
30 he may withdraw their souls from c.
Ps 15 10 wilt thou give thy holy one to see c.
29 10 whilst I go down to corruption? Shall
Wisd 14 12 invention of them is the c. of life
25 c. and unfaithfulness, tumults and
Eccu 28 7 corruption and death hang over in his
31 5 and he that followeth after corruption
42 5 of the corruption of buying and of
Jer 23 15 c. is gone forth into all the land
Eze 32 5 and will fill thy hills with thy c.
Jon 2 7 and thou wilt bring up my life from c.
Mich 2 10 shall be corrupted with a grievous c.
Acts 2 27 nor suffer thy Holy One to see c. 13:35
31 neither did his flesh see corruption
13 34 dead, not to return now any more to c.
36 was laid unto his fathers and saw c.
37 God hath raised from the dead, saw no c.
Rom 8 21 shall be delivered from servitude of c.
1 C 15 42 it is sown in c., it shall rise in
50 neither shall c. possess incorruption
Gal 6 8 of the flesh also shall reap c. But
2 P 1 4 flying the c. of that concupiscence
2 12 they know not, shall perish in their c.
19 they themselves are the slaves of c.
Cos 1 Pa 4 8 Cos begot Anob and Sobaba and
1 Ma 15 23 Lycia and Alicarnassus and Cos and Side
Cosan Luke 3 28 Addi who was of Cosan who was of
Cost Lev 25 16 the less shall the purchase cost
Num 11 5 fish that we ate in Egypt free cost
2 K 24 24 the Lord my God holocausts free cost
1 Pa 21 24 offer to the Lord holocausts free cost
Eccu 22 21 and plasterings made without cost
costly 3 K 5 17 bring great stones, c. stones
3 K 7 9 all of costly stones, which were sawed
10 the foundations were of costly stones
11 and above there were costly stones of
Wisd 2 7 let us fill ourselves with costly wine
Luke 7 25 they that are in costly apparel and
1 Tim 2 9 or gold or pearls or costly attire
cottages Heb 11 9 dwelling in c., with Isaac and
couch Gen 49 4 bed and didst defile his couch
2 K 11 13 slept on his couch with the servants
Job 7 13 speaking with myself on my couch: thou
38 40 when they couch in the dens and lie in
Ps 6 7 I will water my couch with my tears
40 4 turned all his couch in his sickness
Amos 3 12 of a bed and in the couch of Damascus
couched Gen 49 9 resting thou hast c. as a lion
couches Amos 6 4 and are wanton on your couches
Acts 5 15 laid them on beds and couches that when
couching Eze 25 5 a couching place for flocks
council 2 K 23 23 David made him of his privy c.
1 Pa 11 25 and David made him of his council
26 15 house was the council of the ancients
17 and where the council was, two and two
Ps 1 5 nor sinners in the council of the just
21 17 c. of the malignant hath besieged me
25 4 I have not sat with the c. of vanity
39 11 mercy and thy truth from a great c.
110 1 c. of the just and in the congregation
Isa 16 3 take counsel, gather a council: make
Jer 6 11 and upon the council of the young men
Eze 13 9 shall not be in the c. of my people
1 Ma 8 15 that sat in council for the people
9 58 all the wicked held a council, saying
Mat 5 22 Raca, shall be in danger of the council
26 59 the whole council sought false witness
Mark 14 55 c. sought for evidence against Jesus
15 1 and the whole c., binding Jesus, led
Luke 22 66 they brought him into their council
John 11 47 and the Pharisees gathered a council
Acts 4 15 them to go aside out of the council
5 21 called together the c. and all the
27 they set them before the council. And
34 one in the c., rising up, a Pharisee
38 if this council or this work be of men
41 went from the presence of the council
6 12 brought him [Stephen] to the council
15 that sat in the council looking on him
22 30 to come together, and all the council
23 1 Paul looking upon the council, said
6 cried out in the council: Men, brethren
15 you with the c. signify to the tribune
20 bring forth Paul tomorrow into the c.
28 I brought him forth into their council
24 20 iniquity, when standing before the c.
25 12 Festus having conferred with the c.
councils 1 Ma 14 22 by them in the c. of the people
Mat 10 17 will deliver you up in c. Mark 13:9
counsel Gen 27 8 my son, follow my counsel: and
Gen 41 37 the counsel pleased Pharao and all his
45 8 not by your counsel was I sent hither
49 6 let not my soul go into their counsel
Num 24 14 I will give thee counsel, what this
31 16 by the counsel of Balaam, and made you
Deut 32 28 they are a nation without counsel and
Josu 9 24 had of you, and we took this counsel
Judg 20 11 as one man with one mind and one c.
21 19 they took counsel and said: Behold
2 K 15 31 infatuate . . . the c. of Achitophel
34 shalt defeat the counsel of Achitophel
16 23 the counsel of Achitophel, which he
23 so was all the counsel of Achitophel
17 6 what counsel dost thou [Chusai] give
7 the counsel that Achitophel hath given
11 this seemeth to me to be good counsel
14 c. of Chusai the Arachite is better
14 counsel of Achitophel was defeated
15 thus and thus did Achitophel counsel

15 and thus and thus did I counsel them
21 this manner of counsel has Achitophel
23 seeing that his c. was not followed
3 K 1 12 take my counsel and save thy life and
12 6 Roboam took counsel with the old men
6 what counsel do you give me that I. 9
8 but he left the counsel of the old men
13 leaving the counsel of the old men
14 according to the c. of the young men
20 25 he believed their counsel and did so
4 K 6 8 and took counsel with his servants
18 20 perhaps thou hast taken c. to prepare
1 Pa 12 32 rest of the tribe followed their c.
19 the lords of the Philistines taking c.
2 Pa 10 6 he took counsel with the ancients, who
6 what counsel give you to me, that I
8 but he forsook the c. of the ancients
13 leaving the counsel of the ancients
20 21 and he gave counsel to the people and
25 16 hast not hearkened to my counsel. Then
17 king of Juda, taking very bad c., sent
28 11 but hear ye my counsel and release the
30 2 king, taking counsel, and the princes
11 yielding to the c., came to Jerusalem
32 3 he took counsel with the princes and
1 Es 5 3 given you counesl to build this house
10 8 according to the counsel of the princes
2 Es 4 15 that God defeated their counsel. And
6 7 now that we may take counsel together
Tob 3 20 for thy counsel is not in man's power
4 19 seek counsel always of a wise man
Jdth 2 2 to them the secret of his counsel: and
10 8 strengthen all the counsel of thy heart
15 1 courage and counsel fled from them
Esth 1 13 all he did was by their counsel, who
21 his counsel pleased the king and the
21 did according to the c. of Mamuchan
6 13 the wise men whom he had in counsel
14 11 but turn their counsel upon themselves
Job 5 13 disappointeth the c. of the wicked
10 3 and help the counsel of the wicked
12 13 he hath counsel and understanding
15 8 hast thou heard God's counsel, and
18 7 his own counsel shall cast him down
21 16 counsel of the wicked be far from me
26 3 to whom hast thou given c.? Perhaps
29 21 held their peace at my counsel. To my
42 3 that hideth counsel without knowledge
Ps 1 1 walked in the counsel of the ungodly
13 6 confounded the counsel of the poor man
32 11 counsel of the Lord standeth forever
82 4 they have taken a malicious counsel
105 13 and they waited not for his counsel
43 they provoked him with their counsel
106 11 provoked the counsel of the most High
Prov 1 25 you have despised all my counsel and
30 nor consented to my c., but despised
2 11 counsel shall keep thee, and prudence
3 21 keep the law and counsel: and there
8 12 I wisdom dwell in counsel and am
14 counsel and equity is mine, prudence
11 14 is safety where there is much counsel
13 10 they that do all things with counsel
16 prudent man doth all things with c.
15 22 where there is no counsel: but where
19 20 hear counsel and receive instruction
20 5 counsel in the heart of a man is like
21 30 there is no counsel against the Lord
31 13 wrought by the counsel of her hands
Ecce 12 11 by the counsel of masters are given
Wisd 9 13 that can know the counsel of God? Or
Eccu 6 24 give ear, my son, and take wise c.
8 21 before a stranger do no matter of c.
15 14 left him in the hand of his own c.
17 5 he gave them counsel and a tongue and
21 16 his counsel continueth like a fountain
22 19 heart that is established by advised c.
23 1 leave me not to their counsel: nor
25 6 for ancients to know counsel! O how
7 c. to men of honor! Much experience
27 30 mischievous c. shall be rolled back
30 22 afflict not thyself in thy own counsel
32 22 a man of counsel will not neglect
23 hath done with fear without counsel
24 do thou nothing without counsel, and
37 7 hide thy c. from them that envy thee
8 every counsellor giveth out counsel
14 no heed to these in any matter of c.
17 within thyself a heart of good counsel
20 steady counsel before every action
39 10 he shall direct his counsel and his
40 25 but wise counsel is above them both
47 28 turned away the people through his c.
Isa 5 19 let the counsel of the Holy One of
7 5 Syria hath taken counsel against thee
8 10 take counsel together, and it shall be
11 2 the spirit of counsel and of fortitude
14 26 this is the counsel, that I have
16 3 take counsel, gather a council: make
19 3 I will cast down their counsel: and
11 of Pharao have given foolish counsel
17 because of the c. of the Lord of hosts
23 8 who hath taken this c. against Tyre
28 29 to make his counsel wonderful, and
29 15 to hide your counsel from the Lord
30 1 you should take c., and not of me
36 5 with what counsel or strength dost thou
44 26 perform the counsel of my messengers
46 10 my counsel shall stand, and all my will
Jer 18 18 nor counsel [perish] from the wise
23 knowest all their counsel against me
19 7 I will defeat the counsel of Juda
23 18 who hath stood in the c. of the Lord
20 latter days you shall understand his c.
22 if they had stood in my counsel, and
32 19 great in c., and incomprehensible
38 15 if I give thee counsel, thou wilt not
49 7 counsel is perished from her children
20 hear ye the c. of the Lord. 50:45
Eze 7 26 c. [shall perish] from the ancients
11 2 frame a wicked counsel in this city
Dan 4 24 let my counsel be acceptable to thee
Mich 4 12 and have not understood his counsel
Zach 6 13 c. of peace shall be between them both
1 Ma 2 65 your brother Simon is a man of counsel
4 45 a good counsel came into their minds
7 31 knew that his counsel was discovered
8 3 all their place by their c. and patience
9 59 so they went and gave him counsel. And
68 his c. and his enterprise was in vain
69 given him c. to come into their country
2 Ma 1 13 deceived by c. of the priests of Nanea
4 39 sacrileges . . . by the c. of Menelaus
7 26 promised that she would c. her son
14 5 being called to counsel by Demetrius
Mat 27 1 took counsel against Jesus, that they
28 12 taking counsel, gave a great sum of
Luke 7 30 despised c. of God against themselves
23 51 the same had not consented to their c.
John 18 14 who had given the counsel to the Jews
Acts 2 23 by the determinate counsel . . . of God
4 28 hand and thy c. decreed to be done
20 27 to declare unto you all the c. of God
27 12 the greatest part gave counsel to sail
42 the soldiers' c. was that they should
1 C 7 25 I give counsel as having obtained mercy

40 if she so remain, according to my c.
Eph 1 11 according to the counsel of his will
Philem 14 without thy counsel I would do nothing
Heb 6 17 to show . . . immutability of his counsel
Apoc 3 18 I counsel thee to buy of me gold
counselled 2 Ma 7 25 c. her to deal with the young
counsellor 2 K 15 12 Achitophel . . . David's c.
1 Pa 27 32 Jonathan, David's uncle, a counsellor
33 Achitophel was the king's counsellor
2 Pa 25 16 art thou the king's c.? Be quiet
Eccu 6 6 one of a thousand be thy counsellor
37 8 every counsellor giveth out counsel
8 one that is a counsellor for himself
9 beware of a counsellor. And know
42 22 he hath no need of any counsellor
Isa 3 3 the counsellor and the architect and
9 6 shall be called Wonderful, Counsellor
40 13 or who hath been his counsellor and
Mich 4 9 is thy counsellor perished, because
Mark 15 43 Joseph of Arimathea, a noble c., who
Luke 23 50 a man named Joseph, who was a c., a
Rom 11 34 who hath been his counsellor? Or who
counsellors 2 Pa 22 4 they were his c. after the
1 Es 4 5 they hired counsellors against them
9 and the rest of their counsellors
23 was read before . . . their counsellors
5 3 and their c.: and said thus to them
6 his c. the Arphasachites, who dwelt
6 6 your counsellors the Apharsachites
13 his counsellors diligently executed
7 14 from before the king and his seven c.
15 which the king and his c. have freely
28 before the king and his counsellors
8 25 king and his counsellors and his
Esth 13 3 when I asked my counsellors how this
Job 12 17 he bringeth c. to a foolish end, and
19 19 they that were sometime my counsellors
Prov 15 22 where there are many counsellors, they
Isa 1 26 I will restore . . . thy counsellors as
19 11 wise c. of Pharao have given foolish
counsels Exod 18 19 hear my words and counsels
2 Pa 22 5 and he walked after their counsels
Ps 9 2 caught in the c. which they devise
12 2 how long shall I take c. in my soul
19 5 own heart; and confirm all thy counsels
20 12 they have devised counsels which they
32 9 bringeth to nought the c. of nations
10 casteth away the counsels of princes
65 5 who is terrible in his counsels over
Prov 12 5 and the c. of the wicked are deceitful
15 that is wise hearkeneth unto counsels
20 followeth them that take c. of peace
20 18 designs are strengthened by counsels
24 6 safety where there are many counsels
27 9 the good counsels of a friend are sweet
Wisd 9 14 are fearful, and our counsels uncertain
Eccu 1 6 and who hath known her wise counsels
24 39 her c. more deep than the great ocean
Isa 47 13 hast failed in the multitude of thy c.
Jer 11 19 that they had devised c. against me
2 Ma 14 5 upon and what were their counsels, he
1 C 4 5 make manifest the c. of the hearts
2 C 10 4 destroying c., and every height that
count Lev 15 28 shall count seven days of her
Lev 23 15 you shall count therefore from the
Num 23 10 who can count the dust of Jacob, and
1 K 1 16 count not thy handmaid for one of the
1 Es 4 14 we count it a crime to see the king
Tob 10 9 my father and mother now count the days
Wisd 17 12 it count the ignorance of that cause
Eccu 8 15 and if thou lendest, count it as lost
29 7 and will count it as if he had found it
Acts 20 24 neither do I c. my life more precious

Phil 3 8 I count all things to be but loss for
8 count them but as dung that I may gain
13 not count myself to have apprehended
1 Tim 6 1 count their masters worthy of all honor
Philem 17 if therefore thou count me a partner
James 1 2 count it all joy when you shall fall
Apoc 13 18 let him count the number of the beast
counted Gen 31 15 hath he not c. us as strangers
Exod 30 14 he that is counted in the number from
38 21 which were counted according to the
Lev 25 16 the less time is counted, so much the
27 value of the fruits shall be counted
Num 14 34 a year shall be counted for a day. And
3 K 1 21 my son Solomon shall be c. offenders
3 8 be numbered nor counted for multitude
8 5 sheep and oxen that could not be c.
4 K 12 10 counted the money that was found in
Jdth 11 10 they are already to be c. among the
Job 3 6 let it not be counted in the days of
18 3 as beasts and counted vile before you
19 11 and he hath counted me as his enemy
15 have counted me as a stranger, and I
30 7 c. it delightful to be under the briers
33 10 he hath counted me for his enemy. He
Ps 43 22 we are c. as sheep for the slaughter
77 37 nor were they counted faithful in his
87 5 I am counted among them that go down
89 5 things that are counted nothing, shall
Prov 17 28 hold his peace, will be counted wise
Ecce 2 2 laughter I counted error: and to mirth
Wisd 4 8 nor counted by the number of years
7 9 and silver . . . shall be counted as clay
15 2 we know that we are c. with thee. For
12 they have counted our life a pastime
Eccu 40 19 blameless wife shall be counted above
30 man's table is not to be counted a
Isa 32 15 charmel shall be counted for a forest
40 15 are counted as the smallest grain of a
17 and are counted to him as nothing and
47 13 at the stars, and counted the months
Jer 46 23 her forest . . . which cannot be counted
Bar 3 11 art counted with them that go down into
Mark 11 32 counted John that he was a prophet
Rom 2 26 uncircumcision be c. for circumcision
Phil 3 7 the same I have counted loss for Christ
2 Th 1 5 that you may be counted worthy of the
1 Tim 1 12 for that he hath counted me faithful
Heb 3 3 was c. worthy of greater glory than
countenance Gen 29 17 Rachel . . . of a beautiful c.
Gen 31 2 Laban's countenance was not towards him
5 I see your father's countenance is not
33 10 as if I should have seen the c. of God
39 6 Joseph was of a beautiful countenance
40 7 why is your countenance sadder today
Lev 19 15 nor honor the c. of the mighty. But
Judg 13 6 having the countenance of an angel
1 K 1 18 her countenance was no more changed
17 42 a young man, ruddy, and of a comely c.
2 Es 2 3 why should not my c. be sorrowful
Esth 7 6 not being able to bear the countenance
Job 4 16 stood one whose countenance I knew not
29 24 the light of my c. fell not on earth
41 1 who can resist my countenance? Who
Ps 33 17 c. of the Lord is against them that
41 6 the salvation of my c. and my. 12; 42:6
Prov 15 13 a glad heart maketh a cheerful c.: but
16 15 in cheerfulness of king's c. is life
25 23 as doth a sad c. a backbiting tongue
27 17 man sharpeneth the c. of his friend
23 diligent to know the c. of thy cattle
Ecce 7 4 by the sadness of the c. the mind of
Eccu 13 32 token of a good heart and a good c.
25 24 darkeneth her countenance as a bear

31 and maketh a heavy countenance, and
35 11 in every gift show a cheerful c., and
36 24 cheereth the countenance of her husband
Isa 3 3 the honorable in countenance and the
9 the show of their c. hath answered them
Jer 1 17 I will make thee not to fear their c.
7 19 to the confusion of their own c.
49 19 shepherd that can withstand my c. 50:44
Eze 27 35 with the storm have changed their c.
Dan 3 19 and the c. of his face was changed
5 6 then was the king's countenance changed
7 28 my countenance was changed in me. 10:8
15 I cast down my c. to the ground, and
2 Ma 3 16 saw the countenance of the high priest
6 18 in years and of a comely countenance
Luke 24 5 afraid and bowed down their countenance
1 P 3 12 c. of the Lord upon them that do evil
his countenance Gen 4 5 angry and his c. fell
Num 6 26 Lord turn his countenance to thee and
1 K 16 7 look not on his countenance, nor on
21 13 changed his countenance before them
Esth 15 10 when he had lifted up his countenance
Job 34 29 when he hideth his c., who is there
Ps 10 8 his c. hath beheld righteousness
33 1 when he changed his countenance before
54 22 are divided by the wrath of his c.
66 2 the light of his c. to shine upon us
Ecce 8 1 wisdom of a man shineth in his c., and
Eccu 12 19 he will . . . change his countenance
13 31 heart of a man changeth his c., either
19 24 there is one that casteth down his c.
26 a wise man . . . is known by his c. The
26 4 his c. shall be cheerful at all times
Isa 29 22 neither shall his c. now be ashamed
Dan 5 9 and his countenance was changed: and
Mat 28 3 his countenance was as lightning, and
Luke 9 29 shape of his c. was altered, and his
2 C 3 7 for the glory of his countenance, which
James 1 23 a man beholding his own c. in a glass
thy countenance Gen 4 5 why is thy c. fallen
2 Es 2 2 why is thy countenance sad, seeing
Jdth 6 5 let not thy countenance sink, and let
Ps 4 7 light of thy c., O Lord, is signed
15 11 thou shalt fill me with joy with thy c.
16 2 let my judgment come forth from thy c.
20 7 him joyful in gladness with thy c.
43 4 thy arm and the light of thy c.: because
44 13 among the people shall entreat thy c.
79 17 shall perish at the rebuke of thy c.
88 16 walk, O Lord, in the light of thy c.
89 8 our life in the light of thy c. For
139 14 the upright shall dwell with thy c.
Eccu 7 26 and show not thy c. gay towards them
Dan 5 10 neither let thy countenance be changed
Acts 2 28 shalt make me full of joy with thy c.
countenances Isa 13 8 their c. shall be as faces
counter Apoc 2 17 I will give him a white counter
Apoc 2 17 in the counter a new name written
counterfeited Josu 8 20 they that had c. flight
countervail Eccu 6 15 able to c. the goodness
counteth Wisd 15 9 c. it a glory to make vain
counting Lev 25 50 c. only the years from the time
Lev 25 50 c. the money that he was sold for
Acts 19 19 c. the price of them, they found the
2 P 2 13 c. for a pleasure the delights of a day
countries Gen 10 31 Sem according to their . . . c.
Gen 11 9 abroad upon the face of all countries
26 3 to thy seed I will give all these c.
4 give to thy posterity all these c.
41 34 appoint overseers over all the c.
46 he went round all the c. of Egypt. And
45 5 that you sold me into these countries
Exod 34 15 with the men of those countries lest
Lev 26 36 in the countries of their enemies the
Num 32 22 shall obtain the c. that you desire
Josu 11 2 in the levels and countries of Dor
12 8 in the plains and the champaign c.
16 3 the c. of it are ended by the great sea
18 18 on the north side to the champaign c.
1 K 27 8 were of old the inhabitants of the c.
3 K 4 24 and all the kings of those countries
18 6 divided the countries between them
4 K 19 11 have done to all the countries, how
1 Pa 13 2 into all the countries of Israel and
14 17 name of David became famous in all c.
22 5 must be such as to be renowned in all c.
29 30 or in all the kingdoms of the countries
2 Pa 9 28 to him out of Egypt and out of all c.
11 23 all the c. of Juda and of Benjamin
34 33 out of all the c. of the children of
1 Es 4 10 in rest of the countries of this side
2 Es 11 25 in the houses through all their c. Of
12 29 from the countries of Geba and Azmaveth
13 26 women of other countries brought even
Jdth 1 12 would revenge himself of all those c.
15 5 through all the cities and countries
Ps 105 27 to scatter them in the countries. They
106 2 and gathered out of the countries. From
Eccu 29 24 have wandered in strange countries
39 5 he shall pass into strange countries
47 18 the countries wondered at thee for thy
Isa 37 11 kings of Assyrians have done to all c.
18 have laid waste lands and their c.
Jer 28 8 have prophesied concerning many c.
40 7 that were scattered through the c.
11 in Edom and in all the countries
13 been scattered about in the countries
47 7 against Ascalon and against the c.
Bar 6 53 nor deliver countries from oppression
Eze 5 5 nations and the c. round about her
6 more than the c. that are round about
6 8 shall have scattered you through the c.
11 16 I have scattered thee among the c.
16 in the countries whither they are come
17 and assemble you out of the countries
12 15 and scattered them in the countries
20 23 scatter them through the c. 30:23, 26
34 I will gather you out of the countries
22 4 to the Gentiles and a mockery to all c.
15 and will scatter thee among the c. and
29 12 and will disperse them through the c.
34 13 and will gather them out of the c. and
36 19 and they are dispersed through the c.
24 gather you together out of all the c.
39 10 they shall not bring wood out of the c.
Dan 9 7 in all the c. whither thou hast driven
11 40 he shall enter into the countries and
1 Ma 1 5 he subdued c. of nations and princes
3 31 to take tributes of the countries and
37 and went through the higher countries
41 the merchants of the c. heard the fame
6 1 was going through the higher countries
15 15 letters written to the kings and c.
19 to us to write to the kings and c.
19 fight against them, their cities or c.
23 to Arsaces and to all the countries
2 Ma 2 13 together out of the c. the books both
9 23 led an army into the higher countries
24 that were in the c., knowing to whom
14 2 made himself master of the countries
Luke 21 21 who are in the countries, not enter
John 4 35 see the countries, for they are white
Acts 8 1 all dispersed through the c. of Judea
25 the gospel to many c. of the Samaritans
12 20 their countries were nourished by him
Rom 15 23 having no more place in these countries

country Gen 12 1 go forth out of thy country and
Gen 12 6 Abram passed through the country into
10 and there came a famine in the country
13 7 the Pherezite dwelled in that country
11 Lot chose to himself the c. about the
19 28 Gomorrha and the whole land of that c.
29 God destroyed the cities of that c.
20 1 to the south c. and dwelt between
24 4 but that thou go to my own country and
7 house and out of my native country
62 he [Isaac] dwelt in the south country
25 6 while he yet lived to the east country
29 1 his journey and came into the east c.
30 25 away that I may return into my country
31 13 return into thy native c. And Rachel
32 3 to the land of Seir to the c. of Edom
34 1 out to see the women of that country
35 22 when he dwelt in that country, Ruben
36 6 went into another c. and departed from
35 defeated the Madianites in c. of Moab
42 30 and took us to be spies of the country
Exod 2 22 a stranger in a foreign country. 18:3
9 25 and it broke every tree of the country
18 27 returned and went into his own country
Lev 16 29 be one of your own country or. 17:15; Deut 1:16
18 3 the manner of the country of Chanaan
19 34 among you as one of the same country
Num 10 30 I will return to my country wherein I
15 19 shall eat of the bread of that country
20 17 have leave to pass through thy country
21 20 is a valley in the country of Moab, to
34 his people and his c. into thy hand
22 13 to the princes: Go into your country
35 28 the manslayer return to his own country
Deut 11 30 Chanaanite who dwelleth in the plain c.
20 19 neither shalt thou spoil the country
Josu 7 2 to them: Go up and view the country
9 11 inhabitants of our country said to us
10 37 all the towns of that c. and all the
11 16 and the plains and the west country
12 1 and all the east country that looketh
13 1 and there is a very large country left
5 the country also of Libanus towards the
Judg 1 19 and he possessed the hill country: but
11 21 the Amorrhite the inhabitant of that c.
16 24 that destroyed our country and killed
18 10 that is secure, into a spacious country
19 16 of that c. were the children of Jemini
Ruth 1 2 entering into the country of Moab, they
6 from land of Moab to her own country
2 10 take notice of me a woman of another c.
4 3 who is returned from the c. of Moab
1 K 5 6 fields in the midst of that country
27 5 in one of the cities of this country
7 dwelt in the c. of the Philistines. 11
3 K 10 6 true, which I heard in my own country
13 returned and went to her own country
15 Arabia and the governors of the country
11 21 depart that I may go to my own country
22 thou seekest to go to thy own country
16 4 him that dieth of his in the country
22 36 to his own city and to his own country
4 K 3 20 and the country was filled with water
27 from him and returned into their own c.
18 35 delivered their country out of my hand
19 7 and shall return into his own country
7 fall by the sword in his own c. Isa 37:7
24 7 again any more out of his own country
1 Pa 5 10 country that looketh to east of Galaad
11 13 the field of that c. was full of barley
2 Pa 4 17 in the country near the Jordan did the
6 28 or if their enemies waste the country
9 5 is true which I heard in my country
12 and went to her own country with her
25 10 against Juda, returned to their own c.
32 13 been able to deliver their country out
21 returned with disgrace into his own c.
1 Es 5 6 governor of c. beyond the river. 6:6, 13
6 8 out of the country beyond the river
2 Es 2 7 governors of c. beyond the river. 9
3 7 that was in the c. beyond the river
12 28 out of the plain c. about Jerusalem
13 10 fled away every man to his own country
Tob 5 7 leadeth to the country of the Medes
10 4 did we send thee to go to a strange c.
Jdth 15 6 every country and every city sent their
Esth 2 10 not tell him her people nor her c.
20 as yet declared her country and people
15 1 petition for her people and for her c.
16 10 a Macedonian both in mind and country
Job 18 19 people nor any remnants in his country
Eccu 16 5 that is wise a c. shall be inhabited
Isa 1 7 your country strangers devour before
13 5 them that come from a country afar off
22 18 a ball into a large and spacious c.
32 12 for the delightful c., for the fruitful
36 20 that hath delivered his c. out of my
37 7 and shall return to his own country
49 12 sea, and these from the south country
55 12 the trees of the country shall clap
Jer 9 22 as dung upon the face of the country
22 10 return no more nor see his native c.
26 into a strange c. in which you were not
27 10 to remove you far from your country and
30 10 I will save thee from a c. afar off and
31 8 I will bring them from the north c. and
40 7 made Godolias . . . governor of the c.
46 10 the north c., by the river Euphrates
48 21 judgment is come upon the plain country
Bar 3 11 thou art grown old in a strange country
6 13 scepter as a man, as a judge of the c.
60 manner the wind bloweth in every c.
71 and shall be a reproach in the country
Eze 17 24 all the trees of the c. shall know that
31 4 its rivulets to all the trees of the c.
5 exalted above the trees of the country
12 shall be broken on every rock of the c.
47 22 be unto you as men of the same country
Osee 12 12 Jacob fled into the country of Syria
Joel 1 10 the country is destroyed, the ground
19 hath burnt all the trees of the country
3 6 them far off from their own country
Abdi 12 in the day of his leaving his country
19 possess c. of Ephraim and c. of Samaria
Jon 1 8 of what country art thou? And whither
4 2 I said when I was yet in my own country
Mich 4 10 out of city and shalt dwell in the c.
1 Ma • 1 24 departed into his own country. 10:13
3 29 that the tributes of the c. were small
40 and pitched near Emmaus in the plain c.
5 17 will go into the c. of Galaad. And he
48 through your land, to go into our c.
7 20 he committed the country to Alcimus
24 ceased to go forth any more into the c.
8 8 the c. of the Indians and of the Medes
16 every year to rule over all their c.
9 24 all their country yielded to Bacchides
25 and made them lords of the country: and
53 took sons of the chief men of the c.
61 apprehended of the men of the country
65 the city, and went forth into the c.
69 given him counsel to come into their c.
69 to return with the rest into their c.
72 returned and went away into his own c.
10 38 to Judea out of the country of Samaria

52 Demetrius, and possessed our country
11 62 went through the c. as far as Damascus
64 left his brother Simon in the country
12 25 gave them no time to enter into his c.
13 20 this Tryphon entered within the country
22 and he came not into the c. of Galaad
24 returned, and went into his own country
49 from going out and coming into the c.
14 6 and made himself master of the country
28 the nation, and the ancients of the c.
28 have often been wars in our country
31 to tread down and destroy their country
36 were taken away out of their country
37 therein Jews for the defence of the c.
42 over the c. and over the armor and
43 all the writings in the c. should be
44 to call together an assembly in the c.
15 4 I design to go through the country that
4 them that have destroyed our country
6 leave to coin thy own money in thy c.
21 are fled out of their country to you
35 harm to the people and to our country
16 4 he chose out of the c. 20,000 fighting
13 to make himself master of the country
14 cities that were in the c. of Judea
18 and he would deliver him the country
2 Ma 2 22 made themselves masters of the whole c.
4 26 fugitive into the c. of the Ammonites
5 7 fled again into c. of the Ammonites
8 execrable, as an enemy of his country
9 that had driven many out of their c.
15 traitor to the laws and to his country
8 21 even to die for the laws and their c.
35 fleeing through the midland country
9 28 miserable death in a strange country
13 3 not for the welfare of his country, but
11 deprived of the law and of their c.
14 even to death, for . . . their country
14 9 both of the c. and of our nation
18 with which they fought for their c.
Mat 2 12 back another way into their country
8 28 c. of the Gerasens. Mark 5:1; Luke 8:26
13 54 coming into his own country, he taught
57 save in his own country. Mark 6:4
14 34 they came into the country of Genesar
21 33 householder . . . went into a strange c.
26 36 a c. place which is called Gethsemani
Mark 5 10 not drive him away out of the country
6 1 he went into his own country; and his
55 running through that whole country
15 21 coming out of the country. Luke 23:26
16 12 as they were going into the country
Luke 1 39 went into the hill country with haste
2 8 there were in the same c. shepherds
3 1 Iturea and the c. of Trachonitis, and
4 14 fame of him went out through whole c.
23 do also here in thy own country. And
24 no prophet is accepted in his own c.
37 published into every place of the c.
8 37 multitude of the c. of the Gerasens
15 14 there came a mighty famine in that c.
15 to one of the citizens of that country
John 4 44 a prophet hath no honor in his own c.
11 54 he went into a c. near the desert unto
55 many from the c. went up to Jerusalem
Acts 7 3 go forth out of thy country and from
6 his seed should sojourn in a strange c.
13 49 was published throughout the whole c.
14 6 to the whole c. round about and were
16 6 passed through . . . c. of Galatia. 18:23
27 27 deemed that they discovered some country
Heb 11 14 do signify that they seek a country
16 a better, that is to say, a heavenly c.

all the (that) country Gen 13 10 saw all the country about the Jordan, which was
Gen 14 7 smote all the country of the Amalecites
19 17 neither stay thou in all the c. about
25 these cities and all the c. about
Lev 25 24 all the c. of your possession shall be
Num 13 26 having gone round all the c., and came
32 9 viewed all the c., they overturned the
Deut 3 4 all the c. of Argob. 13, 14; 3 K 4:13
Josu 10 40 so Josue conquered all the country of
11 16 Josue took all the c. of the hills and
2 K 18 8 scattered over the face of all the c.
3 K 4 24 had all the c. which was beyond the
2 Pa 20 24 they saw afar off all the country, for
1 Es 4 20 had dominion over all the country that
Jer 31 40 and all the country of death, even to
1 Ma 12 32 and passed through all that country
14 17 and was possessed of all the country
Mat 3 5 Judea and all the c. about Jordan
9 26 fame hereof went abroad into all that c.
31 spread his fame abroad in all that c.
14 35 they sent into all that c. and brought
Mark 1 5 went out to him all the c. of Judea
28 spread forthwith into all the c. of
Luke 1 65 noised abroad over all the hill c. of
3 3 came into all the c. about the Jordan
7 17 and throughout all the c. round about
Acts 26 20 unto all the c. of Judea and to the
far country Josu 9 6 we are come from a far c.
Josu 9 9 from very far c. thy servants are come
3 K 8 41 when he shall come out of a far c. for
4 K 20 14 from a far country they came to me out
2 Pa 6 32 come from a far country for the sake
Prov 25 25 so is good tidings from a far country
Isa 39 3 from a far country they came to me
46 11 from a far c. the man of my own will
Jer 4 16 guards are coming from a far country
6 20 sweet smelling cane from a far country
8 19 daughter of my people from a far c.
Mat 25 14 a man going into a far c. Mark 13:34
Mark 12 1 to husbandmen; and went into a far c.
Luke 15 13 all together went abroad into a far c.
19 12 a certain nobleman went into a far c.
countryman Deut 15 3 of thy c. . . . shalt not have
countrymen Lev 25 17 do not afflict your countrymen
Judg 14 17 she immediately told her countrymen
1 K 14 22 joined themselves with their countrymen
2 Ma 4 5 not to be an accuser of his countrymen
10 he began to bring over his countrymen
5 6 Jason slew his countrymen without mercy
8 as an enemy of his country and c., he
11 29 desired to come down to your countrymen
12 5 heard of this cruelty done to his c.
14 8 to provide for the good of my c.: for
15 30 ready . . . to die for his countrymen
31 having called together his countrymen
1 Th 2 14 suffered . . . from your own countrymen
couple Exod 26 9 five of which thou shalt couple
Exod 26 9 thou shalt couple one to another so as
coupled Exod 26 3 other five shall be c. together
Exod 26 10 that it may be coupled with its fellow
36 10 other five he coupled one to another
39 4 two borders coupled one to the other
19 and strongly coupled with rings, which
Judg 15 4 foxes, and coupled them tail to tail
couplings 2 Pa 34 11 timber for the c. of the
courage Num 13 21 be of good courage and bring us
Judg 9 26 inhabitants of Sichem taking courage
1 K 13 4 Israel took c. against the Philistines
30 6 but David took courage and let us fight
2 K 10 12 be of good courage and let us fight
1 Pa 19 13 be of good courage and let us behave
2 Pa 15 8 he [Asa] took courage and took away

48 1 court of Enan the border of Damascus
2 Ma 4 46 went to the king in a certain court
Mat 26 3 into the court of the high priest, who
58 Peter followed . . . to the c. Mark 14:54
69 Peter sat without in the court: and
Mark 14 66 when Peter was in the court below there
68 he went forth before the court: and
15 16 the soldiers led him away into the c.
Luke 11 21 strong man armed keepeth his court
John 18 15 went in with Jesus into the court of
Phil 1 13 manifest in Christ, in all the court
Apoc 11 2 the court which is without the temple
inner court 3 K 6 36 he built the inner court
3 K 7 12 in the inner c. of house of the Lord
Esth 4 11 cometh into the king's inner court
5 1 stood in inner c. of the king's house
6 4 Aman was coming in to the inner court
Eze 8 16 brought me into the inner court. 40:28, 32; 43:5
10 3 and a cloud filled the inner court
40 19 to the front of the inner court without
23 gate of the inner court was over against
27 there was a gate of the inner court
44 chambers of singing men in the inner c.
42 3 the twenty cubits of the inner court
44 17 in at the gates of the inner court
17 in the gates of the inner court and
21 when he is to go into the inner court
27 into the sanctuary, to the inner court
45 19 on the posts of the gate of the i. c.
46 1 gate of inner court that looketh
1 Ma 9 54 walls of inner c. of the sanctuary
outward court Eze 10 5 heard even to the o. c.
Eze 40 17 brought me into the outward c. 46:21
20 breadth of the gate of the outward c.
31 porch thereof to the outward court
34 porch thereof, that is, of the outward court
37 porch thereof looked to the outward c.
42 1 brought me forth into the outward c.
3 the pavement of the outward court that
7 which were towards the outward court
8 length of chambers of the outward c.
9 into them out of the outward court
14 out of the holy places into the o. c.
44 19 when they shall go forth to the o. c.
46 20 not bring it out into the outward c.
courteously Gen 43 27 he c. saluting them again
2 Ma 3 9 had been c. received in the city by
Acts 27 3 and Julius treating Paul courteously
28 7 for three days entertained us c. And
courtesy 2 Ma 6 22 they did him this courtesy
Acts 28 1 barbarians showed us no small courtesy
courts 4 K 21 5 in the two courts of the temple. 4 K 23:12
4 K 23 12 made in the two courts of the temple
1 Pa 28 6 shall build my house and my courts
12 a description . . . of all the courts
2 Pa 23 5 in c. of house of the Lord. Ps 115:19
33 5 in the two courts of the house of the
2 Es 8 16 tabernacles . . . in their courts and in the courts of the house of God
13 7 storehouse in courts of the house of
Ps 64 5 he shall dwell in thy courts. We shall
83 3 fainteth for the courts of the Lord
11 better is one day in thy courts above
91 14 shall flourish in c. of house of our
95 8 and come into his courts: adore ye
99 4 into his courts with hymns: and give
121 2 our feet were standing in thy courts
134 2 in the courts of the house of our God
Isa 1 12 that you should walk in my courts? Offer
62 9 shall drink it in my holy courts. Go
Eze 9 7 and fill the courts with the slain
42 6 not pillars, as the pillars of the c.
46 22 corners of the court were little courts
23 compassing the four little c., and
Zach 3 7 shalt keep my courts, and I will give
1 Ma 4 38 shrubs growing up in the courts as in
48 they sanctified the temple and the c.
Acts 19 38 the courts of justice are open, and
cousin Gen 29 10 knew her to be his cousin german
1 K 14 50 son of Ner, the cousin german of Saul
Tob 7 2 how like is this young man to my c.
Isa 5 1 I will sing . . . canticle of my cousin
Jer 32 7 Hanameel the son of Sellum thy cousin
2 Ma 11 1 Lysias the king's lieutenant and c.
35 Lysias the king's cousin hath granted
Luke 1 36 thy cousin Elizabeth . . . hath conceived
Col 4 10 Mark, the cousin german of Barnabas
covenant Gen 6 18 I will establish my c. with thee. Eze 16:62
Gen 9 9 establish my c. with you. 11; Lev 26:9
12 this is the sign of the covenant which
13 it shall be the sign of a covenant
15 will remember my c. with you. Lev 26:42
16 shall remember the everlasting c. that
17 this shall be the sign of the c. which
17 2 I will make my c. between me and thee
4 my covenant is with thee [Abram], and
7 I will establish my c. between me and thee . . . by a perpetual covenant
9 shalt keep my covenant, and thy seed
10 this is my c. which you shall observe
11 for a sign of the covenant between me
13 my c. shall be in your flesh for a perpetual c.
14 because he hath broken my covenant
19 I will establish my c. with him [Isaac] for a perpetual c.
21 but my c. I will establish with Isaac
26 28 and let us make a covenant, that thou
47 26 land of priests . . . free from this c.
Exod 2 24 covenant which he made with Abraham. 4 K 13:23; 1 Pa 16:16
5 and I have remembered my covenant
19 5 will hear my voice and keep my c.
24 7 taking the book of the c., he read it
8 this is the blood of the c. which the
31 16 it is an everlasting c. between me and
34 10 I will make a covenant in sight of all
15 make no c. with the men of those
28 tables the ten words of the covenant
39 40 tabernacle and for the roof of the c.
Lev 2 13 neither . . . take away salt of the c.
24 8 children of Israel by an everlasting c.
26 15 by me and to make void my covenant
25 sword that shall avenge my covenant
44 and I should make void my c. with them
45 I will remember my former covenant
Num 4 25 tabernacle and the roof of the c.
30 the service of the c. of the testimony
6 10 in the entry of the c. of the testimony
18 19 it is a covenant of salt forever before
25 12 I give him the peace of my covenant
13 c. of the priesthood forever shall
Deut 4 13 he showed you his covenant which he
23 beware lest thou ever forget the c.
31 he will not . . . forget the covenant
5 3 made not the covenant with our fathers
7 9 keeping his c. and mercy to them that
12 will also keep his covenant with thee
8 18 that he might fulfil his covenant
9 9 tables of the c. which the Lord made
11 tables of stone, the tables of the c.
15 held the two tables of the covenant
17 2 Lord thy God and transgress his c.
29 1 these are the words of the covenant
1 c. which he made with them in Horeb

9 keep therefore words of this covenant
12 mayst pass in the covenant of the Lord
14 neither with you only do I make this c.
21 contained in book of this law and c.
25 because they forsook the covenant of
31 16 and will make void the c. which I have
20 will despise me and make void my c.
33 9 have kept thy word and observed thy c.
Josu 7 11 hath sinned and transgressed my c.
15 because he hath transgressed the c.
23 16 you shall have transgressed the c.
Judg 2 1 that I would not make void my c. with
20 this nation hath made void my c. which
1 K 11 1 make a c. with us and we will serve
2 on this condition will I make a c. with
20 8 hast brought me thy servant into a c.
2 K 23 5 he should make with me an eternal c.
3 K 8 21 the ark, wherein is the c. of the Lord. 2 Pa 6:11
23 who keepest c. and mercy. 2 Pa 6:14; 2 Es 1:5; 9:32; Dan 9:9
11 11 done this and hast not kept my covenant
19 10 have forsaken thy covenant. 14
4 K 13 23 and returned to them because of his c.
17 15 they rejected his ordinances and the c.
38 and the covenant that he made with you
18 12 but transgressed his c.: all that Moses
23 2 the words of the book of the covenant
3 to perform the words of this covenant
3 and the people agreed to the covenant
21 written in the book of this covenant
1 Pa 16 15 remember forever his c.: the word
17 to Israel for an everlasting covenant
2 Pa 13 5 to him and to his sons by a c. of salt
15 12 he went in to confirm as usual the c.
21 7 because of the c. which he had made
29 10 I have a mind that we make a c. with
34 32 did according to the c. of the Lord
1 Es 10 3 let us make a c. with the Lord our God
2 Es 9 8 thou madest a c. with him, to give him
38 we ourselves make a c. and write it
Jdth 9 18 remember, O Lord, thy c., and put them
Job 5 23 have a c. with the stones of the lands
40 23 will he make a c. with thee, and wilt
Ps 24 10 to them that seek after his c. and his
14 his c. shall be made manifest to them
43 18 we have not done wickedly in thy c.
49 5 who set his covenant before sacrifices
16 justices and take my c. in thy mouth
54 21 they have defiled his c., they are
73 20 have regard to thy c.: for they that
77 10 they kept not the c. of God: and in
37 nor were they counted faithful in his c.
57 they turned away and kept not the c.
88 29 forever: and my c. faithful to him
35 neither will I profane my covenant
40 thou hast overthrown the c. of thy
102 18 to such as keep his c. and are mindful
104 8 hath remembered his covenant forever
105 45 he was mindful of his c.: and repented
110 5 he will be mindful forever of his c.
9 he hath commanded his c. forever
131 12 if thy children will keep my covenant
Prov 2 18 hath forgotten the covenant of her God
Wisd 18 22 alleging the oaths and c. made with
Eccu 11 21 be steadfast in thy covenant, and be
14 12 c. of hell hath been shown to thee: for c. of this world shall surely die
24 32 and the covenant of the most High
28 9 remember the covenant of the most High
39 11 shall glory in the law of the covenant
41 24 of the truth of God and the covenant
42 2 of his c., and of judgment to justify
44 20 the most High, and was in c. with him
21 in his flesh he established the c. and
25 confirmed his c. upon the head of Jacob
45 6 that he might teach Jacob his covenant
31 and a covenant to David the king, the
47 13 he gave him a covenant of the kingdom
Isa 14 13 I will sit in the mountain of the c.
24 5 they have broken the everlasting c.
28 18 your covenant with hell shall not stand
33 8 the c. is made void, he hath rejected
42 6 I have given thee for a c. of the people
49 8 and given thee to be a c. of the people
54 10 the c. of my peace shall not be moved
55 3 I will make an everlasting c. with you
56 4 and shall hold fast my covenant: I will
6 and that holdeth fast my c.: I will
59 21 this is my c. with them, saith the Lord
61 8 I will make a perpetual c. with them
Jer 11 2 hear ye the words of this covenant
3 not hearken to the words of this c.
6 hear ye the words of the c. and do them
8 upon them all the words of this c.
10 house of Juda have made void my c.
14 21 remember break not thy c. with us
22 9 have forsaken the covenant of the Lord
31 31 I will make a new covenant with the
32 the c. which I made with their fathers
32 the covenant which they made void
33 shall be the covenant that I will make
32 40 I will make an everlasting covenant
33 20 if my c. with the day can be made void, and my c. with the night
21 my c. with David my servant may be
25 set my covenant with your fathers
34 10 all the people who entered into the c.
18 that have transgressed my c. and have not performed the words of the c.
50 5 joined to the Lord by an everlasting c.
Bar 2 35 I will make with them another covenant
Eze 2 3 have transgressed my c. even unto this
16 8 I entered into a covenant with thee
59 despised the oath, in breaking the c.
60 I will remember my covenant with thee
60 establish with thee an everlasting c.
61 for daughters, but not by thy covenant
17 13 he shall . . . make a covenant with him
14 but keep his covenant and observe it
15 shall he escape that hath broken the c.
16 hath made void and whose c. he broke
18 despised the oath, breaking his c.
19 despised, and the c. he hath broken
20 37 bring you into the bands of the c.
30 5 children of land of the c. shall fall
34 25 I will make a c. of peace. 37:26
37 26 it shall be an everlasting c. with them
44 7 you have broken my c. by all your
Dan 3 34 name's sake and abolish not thy c.
9 27 he shall confirm the c. with many
11 22 yea also the prince of the covenant
28 his heart shall be against the holy c.
30 indignation against c. of the sanctuary
30 that have forsaken c. of the sanctuary
32 such as deal wickedly against the c.
Osee 6 7 like Adam, have transgressed the c.
8 1 because they have transgressed my c.
10 4 you shall make a c.: and judgment
Amos 1 9 not remembered the c. of brethren
Zach 11 10 I cut it asunder to make void my c.
Mala 2 4 that my covenant might be with Levi
5 my c. was with him of life and peace
8 you have made void the c. of Levi
10 violating the covenant of our fathers
14 was thy partner and the wife of thy c.

1 Ma 1 12 let us go and make a c. with the
16 and departed from the holy covenant
2 50 your lives for the c. of your fathers
54 received the covenant of an everlasting
4 10 will remember the c. of our fathers
7 18 they have broken the c. and the oath
10 26 whereas you have kept c. with us
15 27 broke all the covenant that he had made
2 Ma 1 2 may God . . . remember his covenant that
7 36 are under the c. of eternal life: but
8 15 if not for their sakes, yet for the c.
13 25 for fear they should break the c.
14 27 displeased with the c. of friendship
Acts 7 8 gave him the c. of circumcision, and
Rom 11 27 this is to them my c.: when I shall
ark of the covenant; *see* **ark**
made a covenant Gen 15 18 God m. . . . with Abram
Exod 6 4 made a c. with them. 4 K 11:4; 1 Pa 11:3; 2 Pa 23:1; Isa 57:8
34 27 words by which I have made a covenant
Deut 5 2 Lord our God made a c. with us in Horeb
Josu 24 25 Josue therefore on that day made a c.
Judg 8 33 they made a c. with Baal, that he should
9 46 where they made a covenant with him
1 K 18 3 David and Jonathan made a c., for he
20 16 made a c. with the house of David: and
23 18 and the two made a c. before the Lord
3 K 8 9 when Lord made a c. with the children
4 K 11 17 Joiada made a c. between the Lord and
17 35 with whom he made a c. and charged them
23 3 and made a c. with the Lord, to walk
2 Pa 23 16 Joiada made a c. between himself and all
34 31 he made a c. before the Lord to walk
Job 31 1 I made a c. with my eyes, that I would
Ps 82 6 have made a c. together against thee
88 4 I have made a covenant with my elect
Wisd 1 16 fallen away and have made a c. with it
Eccu 17 10 he made an everlasting c. with them
45 8 he made an everlasting c. with him
30 he made to him a c. of peace, to be the
Isa 28 15 and we have made a covenant with hell
Jer 34 8 after that king Sedecias had made a c.
13 I made a covenant with your fathers
15 and you made a covenant in my sight
Osee 12 1 he hath made a c. with the Assyrians
tabernacle of the covenant; *see* **tabernacle**
covenanted Agge 2 6 the word that I c. with you
Luke 22 5 covenanted to give him money. And he
covenants Wisd 12 21 made c. of good promises
Eccu 17 17 their covenants were not hid by their
44 12 their seed hath stood in the covenants
19 the covenants of the world were made
45 21 in the covenants of his judgments, that
2 Ma 12 1 when these c. were made, Lysias went
14 20 all of one mind to consent to covenants
26 and the covenants came to Demetrius
cover Gen 9 14 when I shall c. the sky with clouds
Exod 10 5 to cover the face of the earth that
19 16 thick cloud [began] to cover the mount
21 33 a pit and dig one and cover it not
25 20 let them cover both sides of the
26 7 to cover the top of the tabernacle
12 thou shalt cover the back parts of the
14 make also another cover to the roof
14 another cover of violet colored skins
29 bars thou shalt cover with plates of
27 2 thou shalt cover it with brass. And
6 thou shalt cover with plates of brass
28 42 to cover the flesh of their nakedness
35 11 roof thereof and the cover, the rings
36 14 to cover the roof of the tabernacle
19 he made also a cover for the tabernacle
19 another cover over that of violet skins
39 33 c. of rams' skins dyed red, and the other c. of violet skins
40 17 tabernacle, putting over it a cover
Lev 13 12 cover all the skin from the head to
16 into whiteness and cover all the man
16 4 he shall cover his nakedness with linen
13 and vapor thereof may cover the oracle
17 13 out its blood, and cover it with earth
Num 3 26 the tabernacle itself and the cover
4 6 shall cover it again with a cover of
6 a cover of violet skins. 10, 11, 12
8 scarlet, which again they shall cover
9 they shall cover the candlestick with
14 they shall cover all the vessels of the
Deut 23 13 shalt cover that which thou art eased
31 18 I will hide and cover my face in that
2 K 17 12 we shall cover him as the dew falleth
3 K 7 18 about each network to c. the chapiters
41 the two networks to cover the two cords
42 to cover the cords of the chapiters
4 K 3 19 goodly field you shall c. with stones
2 Pa 4 12 and the network to cover the chapiters
13 to cover the pommels and the chapiters
2 Es 2 8 that I may c. the gates of the tower
4 5 cover not their iniquity, and let not
Tob 4 17 and with thy garment cover the naked
Job 3 5 and the shadow of death cover it, let
16 19 O earth, cover not thou my blood
21 26 the dust, and worms shall cover them
24 15 see me: and he will cover his face
36 28 from the clouds that cover all above
30 he shall c. also the ends of the sea
38 34 an abundance of waters may cover thee
40 17 the shades c. his shadow, the willows
Ps 61 11 in iniquity, and cover not robberies
103 9 neither shall they return to c. the
138 11 I said: Perhaps darkness shall c. me
Ecce 2 16 the times to come shall cover all
Wisd 5 17 with his right hand he will cover them
Eccu 23 26 the walls cover me and no man seeth
29 27 and a house to cover shame. Better
34 19 heat, and a cover from the sun at noon
37 3 to cover the earth with thy malice
38 16 cover his body and neglect not his
Isa 26 21 and shall cover her slain no more
28 20 a short covering cannot cover both
29 10 he will c. your prophets and princes
43 2 and the rivers shall not cover thee
58 7 shalt see one naked, cover him and
59 6 neither shall they cover themselves
60 2 behold darkness shall cover the earth
6 multitude of camels shall cover thee
Jer 3 25 and our shame shall cover us, because
46 8 will go up and will cover the earth
47 2 they shall cover the land, and all
Eze 4 12 thou shalt cover it in their sight
7 18 haircloth, and fear shall cover them
12 6 thou shalt cover thy face and shalt
24 17 on thy feet, and cover not thy face
22 you shall not cover your faces nor
26 10 horses, their dust shall cover thee
19 and many waters shall cover thee: and
30 18 a cloud shall c. her, and her daughters
32 7 I will cover the heavens when thou
7 I will cover the sun with a cloud, and
37 6 will cover you with skin: and I will
38 9 and like a cloud to cover the land
16 like a cloud, to cover the earth. Thou
Osee 10 8 say to the mountains: Cover us; and to
Abdi 10 confusion shall cover thee and thou
Jon 4 6 to cover him, for he was fatigued
Haba 2 17 iniquity of Libanus shall cover thee
Mala 2 16 but iniquity shall cover his garment

Mark 14 65 to cover his face and to buffet him and
Luke 23 30 upon us; and to the hills: Cover us
1 C 11 6 or made bald, let her cover her head
7 the man ought not to cover his head
James 5 20 and shall cover a multitude of sins
covered Gen 7 20 than the mountains which it c.
Gen 7 19 and all the high mountains . . . were c.
9 23 covered the nakedness of their father
24 65 took her cloak and covered herself
27 16 hands and covered the bare of his neck
38 15 for she had covered her face, lest she
Exod 8 6 the frogs came up and covered the land
10 15 they c. the whole face of the earth
14 28 covered the chariots and the horsemen
15 5 the depths have covered them, they are
10 thy wind blew and the sea covered them
16 13 quails coming up, covered the camp
14 when it had covered the face of the
22 27 the only thing wherewith he is covered
24 15 was gone up, a cloud covered the mount
25 20 wherewith the ark is to be covered
34 35 he [Moses] covered his face again, if
36 34 he covered the bars themselves with
40 32 the cloud covered the tabernacle of
33 for the cloud had covered all. If at
Lev 3 4 fat wherewith the flanks are covered
13 45 his mouth covered with a cloth, and he
16 2 with which the ark is covered, lest
Num 7 3 six wagons covered and twelve oxen
9 15 was reared up, a cloud covered it. But
16 by day the cloud covered it, and by
17 cloud that covered the tabernacle was
12 10 and saw her all covered with leprosy
16 43 were gone into it, the cloud covered it
22 5 covered the face of the earth. Jdth 2:11
11 hath covered the face of the land
Deut 8 4 raiment with which thou wast covered
11 4 the waters of the Red Sea covered them
22 12 cloak wherewith thou shalt be covered
Josu 2 6 covered them with the stalks of flax
7 21 the silver I covered with the earth
24 7 the sea upon them, and covered them
Judg 4 18 and being covered by her with a cloak
19 gave him to drink and covered him. And
Ruth 3 4 the clothes wherewith he is covered
15 thy mantle wherewith thou art covered
1 K 17 6 buckler of brass covered his shoulders
19 13 an image . . . and c. it with clothes
28 14 and he is covered with a mantle. And
2 K 15 30 barefoot, and with his head covered
30 went up with their heads covered
32 garment rent and his head c. with earth
19 4 king c. his head and cried with a loud
20 12 and covered him [Amasa] with a garment
3 K 1 1 when he was c. with clothes, he was not
6 9 he c. the house with roofs of cedar
10 he c. the house with timber of cedar
15 he covered it with boards of cedar on
15 c. the floor of the house with planks
18 house was covered within with cedar
18 all was covered with boards of cedar
20 he c. and overlaid it with most pure
20 the altar also he covered with cedar
22 in temple that was not c. with gold
22 altar of the oracle he c. also with gold
32 he c. both the cherubims and the palm
7 3 he c. the whole vault with boards of
7 covered it with cedar wood from the
8 7 covered the ark and the staves thereof
10 17 gold: 300 pounds of gold c. one target
18 28 till they were all covered with blood
19 13 he covered his face with his mantle
4 K 19 1 [Ezechias] c. himself with sackcloth
2 ancients of the priests covered with
2 Pa 4 9 in the hall which he c. with brass
5 8 covered the ark itself and its staves
2 Es 3 3 covered it and set up the doors. 6, 15
Jdth 4 8 altar . . . they covered with haircloth
16 5 and their horses covered the valleys
Job 6 20 unto me, and are covered with shame
10 21 dark and c. with the mist of death
15 27 fatness hath covered my flesh with ashes
22 11 shouldst not be c. with the violence
23 17 neither hath the mist covered my face
33 21 his bones that were c. shall be made
Ps 31 1 forgiven, and whose sins are covered
43 16 the confusion of my face hath c. me
20 the shadow of death hath covered us
54 6 upon me: and darkness hath covered me
67 14 as the wings of a dove c. with silver
68 8 reproach: shame hath covered my face
11 I covered my soul in fasting: and it
70 13 let them be covered with confusion
72 6 they are covered with their iniquity
79 11 the shadow of it covered the hills
84 3 thou hast covered all their sins. Thou
88 46 thou hast covered him with confusion
105 11 the water c. them that afflicted them
17 and covered the congregation of Abiron
108 29 let them be covered with their confusion
Prov 7 16 I have c. it with painted tapestry
24 31 and thorns had covered the face thereof
Cant 3 10 the midst he covered with charity for
Wisd 19 16 they were covered with sudden darkness
Eccu 24 6 as a cloud I covered all the earth
40 4 him that is covered with rough linen
28 they have covered it above all glory
47 16 wisdom, and thy soul covered the earth
48 13 was indeed covered with the whirlwind
Isa 6 2 with two they covered his face, and with
two they covered his feet
37 1 and covered himself with sackcloth and
2 of the priests covered with sackcloth
44 18 eyes are covered that they may not see
61 10 with robe of justice he hath covered me
Jer 14 3 and afflicted, and covered their heads
4 confounded, they covered their heads
51 42 she is c. with the multitude of the
51 reproach: shame hath covered our faces
Lam 2 1 how hath the Lord c. with obscurity
3 43 thou hast covered in thy wrath and
Bar 6 12 when they have covered them with a
Eze 1 11 joined, and two covered their bodies
23 every one with two wings c. his body
23 the other was covered in like manner
12 12 his face shall be covered, that he may
16 8 over thee and covered thy ignominy
18 7 covered the naked with a garment. 16
24 7 that it might be covered with dust. And
8 rock, that it should not be covered
31 15 I covered him with the deep: and I
Dan 13 32 be uncovered, for she was covered
Osee 2 5 conceived them is covered with shame
9 my flax, which covered her disgrace
Jon 2 6 the sea hath covered my head. I went
3 8 and beasts be covered with sackcloth
Mich 1 11 in the Beautiful place, c. with shame
7 10 and she shall be covered with shame
Haba 3 3 his glory covered the heavens, and the
Mala 2 13 you have covered the altar of the
1 Ma 1 29 house of Jacob was c. with confusion
2 14 they covered themselves with haircloth
6 37 towers which covered every one of them
2 Ma 3 27 him up covered with great darkness
10 30 c. him on every side with their arms
Mat 8 24 that the boat was covered with waves

10 26 nothing is c. that shall not. Luke 12:2
25 36 naked and you covered me: sick and
38 thee in? Or naked and covered thee
43 naked and you covered me not: sick and
Rom 4 7 are forgiven, and whose sins are c.
1 C 11 4 or prophesying with his head covered
5 prophesying with her head not covered
6 if a woman be not covered, let her be
1 Tim 6 8 but having food and wherewith to be c.
Heb 9 4 covered about on every side with gold
coveredst Eze 16 18 divers colors, and c. them
coverest Ps 103 3 who c. the higher rooms thereof
covereth Exod 29 13 fat that covereth the entrails. Lev 3:3; 7:3
Exod 29 22 the fat that covereth the lungs, and
Lev 3 10 and the fat that covereth the belly. 14
14 and that covereth all the vital parts
4 8 that which covereth the entrails, as
Job 9 24 he c. the face of the judges thereof
Ps 108 19 unto him like a garment which c. him
146 8 who covereth the heaven with clouds
Prov 10 6 iniquity c. the mouth of the wicked
11 mouth of the wicked covereth iniquity
12 strifes: and charity covereth all sins
26 26 he that covereth hatred deceitfully
Luke 8 16 c. it with a vessel or putteth it under
1 P 4 8 charity covereth a multitude of sins
covering Gen 8 13 Noe opening the c. of the ark
Gen 20 16 serve thee for a covering of thy eyes
Exod 24 16 covering it with a cloud six days
25 20 their wings, and covering the oracle
26 11 that of all there may be made one c.
36 18 there might be made one covering
37 9 wings, and covering all things, and the
40 33 the cloud covering all things, and the
Num 4 8 with a covering of violet skins. 14
25 the other c. and the violet c. over all
Deut 22 30 father's wife, nor remove his covering
2 K 17 19 and spread a c. over mouth of the well
22 12 he made darkness a covering round about
1 Pa 28 18 their wings, and covering the ark
2 Pa 9 16 went to the covering of every shield
Job 24 7 clothes who have no c. in the cold
8 having no covering embrace the stones
26 6 there is no covering for destruction
31 19 and the poor man that had no covering
Prov 22 27 should take the covering from thy bed
31 22 fine linen and purple is her covering
Wisd 13 14 covering every spot that is in it
Eccu 14 27 shall be protected under her covering
Isa 11 9 as the covering waters of the sea. In
14 11 be strewed, and worms shall be thy c.
22 8 covering of Juda shall be discovered
28 20 a short covering cannot cover both
50 3 and will make sackcloth their covering
Eze 27 7 and purple . . . were made thy covering
28 13 every precious stone was thy covering
16 destroyed thee, O covering cherub
Nah 2 5 and a covering shall be prepared. The
Haba 2 14 glory of the Lord, as waters c. the sea
2 Ma 3 25 adorned with a very rich covering: and
1 C 11 15 for her hair is given to her for a c.
coverlet Ruth 3 9 spread thy c. over thy servant
covert Job 22 14 the clouds are his covert, and he
Job 37 8 then the beast shall go into his covert
40 16 in the c. of the reed and in moist
Ps 17 12 made darkness his covert, his pavilion
35 8 their trust under the c. of thy wings
60 5 protected under the c. of thy wings
62 8 I will rejoice under the c. of thy wings
Wisd 10 17 she was to them for a covert by day
Isa 1 8 shall be left as a c. in a vineyard
4 6 security and c. from the whirlwind
16 4 be thou a covert to them from the face
Jer 25 38 he hath forsaken his c. as the lion
Bar 6 67 which can fly under a covert and help
1 Ma 9 38 under the covert of the mountain. And
coverts Judg 20 37 arose on a sudden out of their c.
covet Exod 20 17 shalt not c. thy neighbor's house
Deut 5 21 shalt not covet thy neighbor's wife
7 25 shalt not covet the silver and gold
1 K 15 3 nor covet anything that is his: but
Prov 1 22 fools c. those things which are hurtful
6 25 let not thy heart covet her beauty
Wisd 6 12 covet ye therefore my words and love
14 she preventeth them that covet her
Rom 7 7 if law did not say: Thou shalt not c.
13 9 bear false witness: Thou shalt not c.
1 C 10 6 that we should not covet evil things
James 4 2 you covet and have not: you kill and
5 to envy doth the spirit covet which
coveted Josu 7 21 I c. them and I took them away
Tob 3 16 that I never coveted a husband, and
Job 20 20 when he hath the things he coveted, he
Ps 105 14 they coveted their desire in the desert
118 20 my soul hath coveted to long for thy
Mich 2 2 they have coveted fields and taken
1 Ma 11 11 because he coveted his kingdom. And he
2 Ma 4 16 they coveted to be like them who were
Acts 20 33 I have not coveted any man's silver
1 C 10 6 not covet evil things as they also c.
coveter 1 P 4 15 coveter of other man's things
coveting Josu 20 9 kinsman, c. to revenge the blood
Eccu 23 5 turn away from me all coveting. Take
1 Tim 6 10 some coveting have erred from the faith
covetous Prov 1 19 way of every c. man destroy the
Prov 29 4 the land: a c. man shall destroy it
Ecce 5 9 a c. man shall not be satisfied with
Eccu 10 9 is more wicked than the covetous man
14 3 are not comely for a covetous man and
9 the eye of the c. man is insatiable
Luke 16 14 the Pharisees, who were covetous, heard
1 C 5 10 with the c. or the extortioners or the
11 be a fornicator or c. or a server of
6 10 nor c. nor drunkards nor railers nor
Eph 5 5 no fornicator or unclean or c. person
1 Tim 3 3 but modest, not quarrelsome, not c.
2 Tim 3 2 shall be lovers of themselves, covetous
covetously Eze 22 12 hast c. oppressed thy neighbors
covetousness Job 27 8 if through c. he take by
Ps 118 36 heart into thy testimonies and not to c.
Prov 28 16 that hateth c., shall prolong his days
Isa 57 17 for the iniquity of his c. I was angry
Jer 6 13 to the greatest, all are given to c.
8 10 least even to the greatest all follow c.
22 17 thy eyes and thy heart are set upon c.
Eze 22 13 I have clapped my hands at thy c.
27 to run after gains through covetousness
33 31 and their heart goeth after their c.
Amos 9 1 there is c. in the head of them all
Haba 2 9 gathereth together an evil c. to his
2 Ma 4 50 through c. of them that were in power
10 20 that were with Simon, being led with c.
Mark 7 22 murders, thefts, c., wickedness, deceit
Luke 12 15 take heed and beware of all c.: for a
2 C 9 5 so as a blessing not as covetousness
Eph 4 19 working of all uncleanness, unto c.
5 3 or c., let it not so much as be named
Col 3 5 evil concupiscence and covetousness
1 Th 2 5 nor taken an occasion of covetousness
Heb 13 5 let your manners be without c., contented
2 P 2 3 through c. shall they with feigned words
14 having their heart exercised with c.
cow Gen 15 9 take me a cow of three years old and
Lev 22 28 whether it be a cow or a sheep, they
Num 18 17 the firstling of a cow and of a sheep

19 2 that they bring unto thee a red cow
6 flame with which the cow is consumed
9 shall gather up the ashes of the cow
9 because the cow was burnt for sin. And
10 he that carried the ashes of the cow
Job 21 10 and failed not: their cow has calved
Isa 7 21 a man shall nourish a young cow and
coward Eccu 37 12 nor with a c. concerning war
cowards 2 K 3 33 not as cowards are wont to die
Cozbi Num 25 15 slain with him, was called Cozbi
Num 25 18 C. their sister, a daughter of a prince
crackling Ecce 7 7 c. of thorns burning under a pot
cracknels 3 K 14 3 with thee ten loaves and c. and
craft Eccu 38 39 shall be in the work of their c.
Dan 8 25 craft shall be successful in his hand
Acts 19 27 our craft is in danger to be set at
craftily Exod 32 12 he c. brought them out, that
Deut 15 10 neither shalt thou do anything c. in
1 K 23 22 that I lie craftily in wait for him
4 K 10 19 Jehu did this c., that he might destroy
Dan 6 6 craftily suggested to the king, and
Acts 7 19 same dealing craftily with our race
craftiness Job 5 13 catcheth the wise in their c.
1 C 3 19 I will catch the wise in their own c.
2 C 4 2 not walking in c. nor adulterating the
Eph 4 14 by cunning c. by which they lie in
craftsman Eccu 38 28 every c. and workmaster that
Bar 6 7 their tongue that is polished by the c.
Apoc 18 22 no craftsman of any art whatsoever
craftsmen 2 Es 11 35 Lod, and Ono the valley of c.
Jer 24 1 the c. and engravers of Jerusalem
29 2 c. and the engravers were departed
Osee 13 2 the whole is the work of craftsmen: to
Acts 19 24 brought no small gain to the craftsmen
38 if Demetrius and the c. that are with
crafty Job 36 13 crafty men prove the wrath of God
Prov 14 17 folly: and the crafty man is hateful
Eccu 42 18 and considered their crafty devices
2 C 12 16 being crafty, I caught you by guile
cragged Job 39 28 dwelleth among c. flints and
craggy 1 K 24 3 even upon the most craggy rocks
craved Ps 77 30 not defrauded of that which they c.
2 Ma 13 12 and had craved mercy of the Lord with
create Ps 50 12 create a clean heart in me, O God
Isa 4 5 Lord will create upon every place of
45 7 I form the light and create darkness
7 I make peace and create evil: I the
18 he did not create it in vain: he formed
65 17 I create new heavens and a new earth
18 forever in these things which I create
18 behold I create Jerusalem a rejoicing
created Gen 1 1 God created heaven and earth. And
Gen 1 21 God created the great whales and every
27 God created man to his own image, to
27 to the image of God he created him
27 male and female he created them. And
2 3 his work which God created and made
4 and the earth, when they were created
5 1 in the day that God created man, he
2 he created them male and female; and
2 in the day when they were c. And Adam
6 7 I will destroy man, whom I have c.
14 19 high God, who created heaven and earth
Deut 4 19 God created for the service of all the
26 19 than all nations which he hath created
32 6 made thee and created thee? Remember
18 hast forgotten the Lord that c. thee
Jdth 16 17 forth thy spirit, and they were created
Ps 32 9 he commanded and they were created
88 13 the north and the sea thou hast created
101 19 the people that shall be c. shall praise
103 30 forth thy spirit, and they shall be c.
148 5 he commanded, and they were created
Wisd 1 14 he created all things that they might
2 23 God created man incorruptible and to
10 1 when he was created alone. And she
Eccu 1 4 wisdom hath been c. before all things
9 he created her in the Holy Ghost, and
16 was created with the faithful in the
11 16 error and darkness are created with
17 1 God created man of the earth, and made
5 he c. of him a helpmate like to himself
6 he c. in them the science of the spirit
18 1 created all things togther. God only
23 29 to the Lord God before they were c.
24 14 before the world, was I created and
31 15 what is c. more wicked than an eye
35 wine was c. from the beginning to
33 10 earth, from whence Adam was created
38 1 for the most High hath created him
4 the most High hath created medicines
12 physician. For the Lord created him
39 30 good things were c. for the good from
33 are spirits that are c. for vengeance
35 all these were created for vengeance
40 1 great labor is created for all men and
10 all these things are c. for the wicked
Isa 40 26 and see who hath created these things
28 who hath created the ends of the earth
41 20 the Holy One of Israel hath created it
42 5 Lord God that created the heavens and
43 1 the Lord that created thee, O Jacob
7 name, I have created him for my glory
45 8 I the Lord have created him. Woe to him
12 I made the earth: and I created man
18 saith the Lord that created the heavens
46 11 I have created and I will do it. Hear
48 7 they are created now, and not of old
54 16 I have created the smith that bloweth
16 I have created the killer to destroy
57 19 I created the fruit of the lips, peace
Jer 31 22 Lord hath c. a new thing upon the earth
Eze 21 30 the place wherein thou wast created
28 13 prepared in the day that thou wast c.
Dan 14 4 that created heaven and earth and hath
Mala 2 10 hath not one God created us? Why then
Mark 13 19 beginning of creation which God created
1 C 11 9 the man was not created for the woman
Eph 2 10 c. in Christ Jesus in good works, which
3 9 in God who created all things: that the
4 24 is c. in justice and holiness of truth
Col 1 16 in him were all things c. in heaven and
16 all things were c. by him and in him
3 10 according to image of him that c. him
1 Tim 4 3 meats, which God hath c. to be received
Heb 3 4 but he that created all things is God
Apoc 4 11 because thou hast created all things
11 for thy will they were and have been c.
10 6 who c. heaven and the things which
createth Amos 4 13 the mountains and c. the wind
creation Jdth 9 17 Lord of the whole c., hear me
Eccu 16 17 my soul in such an immense creation
Eze 28 15 thy ways from the day of thy creation
Mark 10 6 from the beginning of the c. God made
13 19 as were not from the beginning of the c.
John 17 24 thou hast loved me before the creation
Rom 1 20 from the c. of the world, are clearly
Col 1 23 which is preached in all the creation
Heb 9 11 perfect tabernacle . . . not of this c.
2 P 3 4 as they were from beginning of the c.
Apoc 3 14 who is the beginning of the c. of God
Creator Jdth 9 17 God of the heavens, C. of the
Ecce 12 1 remember thy Creator in the days of
Wisd 13 5 the Creator of them may be seen so as
16 24 the creature serving thee the Creator
Eccu 1 8 is one most high Creator Almighty

24 12 the Creator of all things commanded
Isa 43 15 One, the Creator of Israel, your King
2 Ma 1 24 Lord God, C. of all things, dreadful
7 23 but the C. of the world that formed
13 14 committing all to God, the C. of the
Rom 1 25 served the creature rather than the C.
1 P 4 19 souls in good deeds to the faithful C.
creature Gen 1 20 bring forth the creeping c.
Gen 1 26 every creeping c. that moveth upon
Lev 7 26 shall not eat the blood of any creature
Wisd 5 18 he will arm the c. for the revenge of
9 2 over the c. that was made by thee
13 5 greatness of the beauty and of the c.
16 24 the creature serving thee the Creator
19 6 every creature according to its kind
Mark 16 15 preach the gospel to every creature
Rom 1 25 served the c. rather than the Creator
8 19 the expectation of the creature waiteth
20 the c. was made subject to vanity, not
21 creature also itself shall be delivered
22 every c. groaneth and travaileth in
39 any other c. shall be able to separate
2 C 5 17 if then any be in Christ a new creature
Gal 6 15 nor uncircumcision but a new creature
Col 1 15 the firstborn of every creature: for in
1 Tim 4 4 every c. of God is good, and nothing
Heb 4 13 any creature invisible in his sight
James 1 18 might be some beginning of his creature
1 P 2 13 be ye subject to every human creature
Apoc 5 13 every creature which is in heaven and
living creature Gen 1 21 God created . . . every living and moving creature
Gen 1 24 bring forth the living c. in its kind
2 19 whatsoever Adam called any living c.
6 19 of every l. c. of all flesh, thou shalt
Lev 11 46 of every l. c. that moveth in the
Ps 144 16 fillest with blessing every living c.
Eze 10 15 this is the l. c. that I had seen by
20 this is the l. c. which I saw under the
47 9 every living creature that creepeth
Apoc 4 7 the . . . living creature. 6:3, 5, 7
creatures Deut 32 24 c. that trail upon the ground
Tob 8 7 creatures that are in them, bless thee
Jdth 16 17 let all thy c. serve thee: because thou
Ps 103 25 without number: c. little and great
Wisd 2 6 let us speedily use the c. as in youth
14 11 c. of God are turned to an abomination
15 18 they worship also the vilest creatures
Eccu 24 5 the firstborn before all creatures: I
36 17 give testimony to them that are thy c.
43 27 and the monstrous creatures of whales
Acts 11 6 and saw fourfooted c. of the earth and
Apoc 8 9 the third part of those creatures died
living creatures Gen 1 28 all living creatures that move upon the earth
Gen 8 1 God remembered Noe and all the l. c.
Wisd 7 20 the nature of l. c. and rage of wild
Eze 1 5 likeness of the four l. c.: and this
13 as for the likeness of the l. c., their
13 to and fro in the midst of the l. c.
14 the l. c. ran and returned like flashes
15 as I beheld the l. c., there appeared
15 by the l. c. one wheel with four faces
19 when the l. c. went, the wheels also
19 when the l. c. were lifted up from the
22 over the heads of the l. c. was the
3 13 the noise of the wings of the l. c.
13 noise of the wheels following the l. c.
8 10 form of creeping things and of l. c.
Apoc 4 6 four living creatures. 8; 5:6; 6:1, 6; 7:11; 8:14; 14:3; 15:7; 19:4
9 when those living c. gave glory and
5 11 round about the throne, and the l. c.

credible 2 Pa 6 18 is it c. then that God should
Ps 92 5 testimonies are become exceedingly c.
credit Gen 39 19 too much c. to his wife's words
Eccu 6 7 takest him, and do not c. him easily
19 4 he that is hasty to give credit, is
27 17 loseth his c., and shall never find
1 Ma 10 46 they gave no c. to them nor received
Acts 23 21 but do not thou give credit to them
Rom 2 8 not the truth but give c. to iniquity
creditor 4 K 4 1 c. is come to take away my two
4 K 4 7 go, sell the oil and pay thy creditor
Prov 29 13 poor man and the creditor have met
Isa 50 1 who is my creditor, to whom I sold you
Luke 7 41 a certain creditor had two debtors
creek Acts 27 30 they discovered a certain creek
creep Gen 7 21 that c. upon the earth. 8:17, 19
2 Tim 3 6 they who creep into houses and lead
creepeth Gen 1 25 that creepeth on the earth. 6:20; Lev 11:41, 46
Deut 14 19 that creepeth and hath little wings
Ps 68 35 and every thing that creepeth therein
Eze 38 20 thing that creepeth upon the ground
47 9 every living creature that creepeth
creeping Gen 1 20 bring forth the c. creature
Gen 1 24 cattle and creeping things and beasts
26 every c. creature that moveth upon
6 7 from the creeping thing even to the
7 21 all c. things that creep. 8:17, 19
23 and the c. things and the fowls of the
Lev 5 2 died of itself, or any other c. thing
11 44 defile not your souls by any c. thing
22 5 he that toucheth a creeping thing
Deut 4 18 or of creeping things, that move on
1 K 14 13 Jonathan went up c. on his hands and
3 K 4 33 fowls and of c. things and of fishes
Ps 103 25 there are creeping things without number
Bar 6 19 creeping things which are of the earth
Eze 8 10 behold every form of creeping things
38 20 every c. thing that creepeth upon the
Osee 2 18 and with the c. things of the earth
Mich 7 17 as the creeping things of the earth
Haba 1 14 as the c. things that have no ruler
Acts 10 12 fourfooted beasts and c. things of the
11 6 and c. things and fowls of the air
Rom 1 23 of fourfooted beasts and of c. things
Crescens 2 Tim 4 10 Crescens into Galatia, Titus
Crete 1 Ma 10 67 son of Demetrius came from Crete
Acts 27 7 we sailed near Crete by Salmone: and
12 Phenice . . . which is a haven of Crete
13 from Asson, they sailed close by Crete
21 and not have loosed from Crete, and
Titus 1 5 for this cause I left thee in Crete
Cretes Acts 2 11 C. and Arabians: we have heard
Cretians Titus 1 12 the Cretians are always liars
crew Mat 26 74 the cock crew. Mark 14:68, 72; Luke 22:60; John 18:27
crib Job 39 9 or will he stay at thy crib? Canst
Prov 14 4 there are no oxen, the crib is empty
Isa 1 3 the ass [knoweth] his master's crib
crier Gen 41 43 c. proclaiming that all should bow
crier's Exod 32 5 made proclamation by c. voice
crime Gen 37 2 accused . . . of a most wicked crime
Exod 21 20 his hands, shall be guilty of the c.
32 30 be able to entreat him for your crime
Lev 18 23 because it is a heinous crime. Defile
20 12 because they have done a heinous crime
14 mother, he hath done a heinous crime
17 shame: they have committed a crime
Deut 21 22 when a man hath committed a crime for
Josu 22 17 stain of that crime remaineth in us
Judg 9 24 crime of the murder of the 70 sons of
19 24 commit not this crime against nature
20 6 there never was so heinous a crime and

13 that have committed this heinous crime
1 K 15 23 like the crime of idolatry, to refuse
4 K 7 9 we shall be charged with a crime: come
1 Es 4 14 count it a c. to see the king wronged
Tob 4 13 beside thy wife never endure to know a c.
Jdth 8 19 for which crime they were given up to
Esth 16 18 for which crime, both he himself that
Job 31 11 for this is a heinous crime and a most
Acts 25 5 accuse him if there by any crime in the
1 C 1 8 confirm you unto the end without crime
1 Tim 3 10 so let them minister, having no crime
Titus 1 6 if any be without crime, the husband
7 a bishop must be without crime, as the
crimes Job 13 23 make me know my c. and offenses
Prov 29 16 crimes shall be multiplied: but the
Jer 11 15 thy crimes, in which thou hast boasted
Eze 7 8 I will lay upon thee all thy crimes
16 51 thou hast surpassed them with thy c.
Amos 1 3 for three crimes . . . I will not convert. 6, 9, 11, 13; 2:1, 4, 6
5 12 I know your manifold crimes and your
Mich 1 13 in thee were found the crimes of Israel
1 Ma 7 25 to the king and accused them of many c.
crimson Isa 1 18 if they be red as crimson, they
cripple Acts 14 7 a c. from his mother's womb
crisped 3 K 7 26 or the leaf of a crisped lily
2 Pa 4 5 like the brim of a cup or of a c. lily
crisping Isa 3 22 crisping pins and looking-glasses
Crispus Acts 18 8 Crispus the ruler of the synagogue
1 C 1 14 that I baptized none of you but Crispus
crocodile Lev 11 29 and the mouse and the c. every
crookbacked Lev 21 20 if he be c. or blear eyed
crooked Lev 21 18 a little or a great or a c. nose
Ps 77 57 they were turned aside as a crooked bow
Prov 28 6 simplicity, than the rich in c. ways
Wisd 13 13 being a crooked piece of wood and full
16 5 with the bitings of crooked serpents
Eccu 2 16 have gone aside into crooked ways
Isa 27 1 and leviathan the crooked serpent
40 4 and the crooked shall become straight
42 16 before them, and c. things straight
59 8 their paths are become crooked to them
Luke 3 5 and the crooked shall be made straight
Phil 2 15 of a crooked and perverse generation
crop Lev 1 16 c. of the throat and the feathers
2 K 14 30 my field, that hath a crop of barley
Eze 17 22 I will crop off a tender twig from the
cropped Eze 17 4 he c. off the top of the twigs
cross Gen 40 19 hang thee on a cross, and the
Deut 30 13 which of us can cross the sea and bring
Mat 10 38 he that taketh not up his cross and
16 24 take up his c. and follow. Mark 8:34
27 32 forced to take up his cross. Mark 15:21
40 Son of God, come down from the cross
42 let him now come down from the cross
Mark 15 30 save thyself, coming down from the c.
32 come down now from the cross that we
Luke 9 23 take up his cross daily and follow
14 27 whosoever doth not carry his cross
23 26 they laid the cross on him to carry
John 19 17 bearing his own cross, he went forth
19 a title also and he put it upon the c.
25 there stood by the cross of Jesus his
31 bodies might not remain upon the cross
1 C 1 17 lest c. of Christ should be made void
18 the word of the cross, to them indeed
Gal 2 19 with Christ I am nailed to the cross
5 11 then is scandal of the cross made void
6 12 suffer the persecution of c. of Christ
14 glory, save in the cross of our Lord
Eph 2 16 both to God in one body by the cross
Phil 2 8 unto death, even to the death of the c.
3 18 they are enemies of the cross of Christ
Col 1 20 peace through the blood of his cross
2 14 out of the way, fastening it to the c.
Heb 12 2 endured the c., despising the shame
crossway Gen 38 14 changing her dress, sat in c.
Gen 38 21 where is the woman that sat in the c.
crossways Abdi 14 neither shalt thou stand in c.
crouch Ps 9 10 he will c. and fall, when he shall
crouching Eccu 12 11 humble himself and go c.
crow Deut 14 17 the night crow, the bittern, and
Mat 26 34 before the cock crow. 75; Luke 22:61
Mark 14 30 before the cock crow twice, thou. 72
Luke 22 34 the cock shall not crow this day till
John 13 38 the cock shall not crow till thou deny
crowd Job 30 28 I rose up and cried in the crowd
Isa 9 11 shall bring on his enemies in a crowd
Eze 30 5 the rest of the crowd and Chub and
2 Ma 14 43 the crowd was breaking into the doors
43 manfully threw himself down to the c.
45 wounded, he ran through the crowd: and
Mark 5 27 in the crowd behind him and touched
Luke 8 19 they could not come at him for the c.
9 38 a man among the crowd cried out, saying
11 27 woman from the crowd, lifting up her
19 3 he [Zacheus] could not for the crowd
crowds Isa 17 12 tumult of crowds, like the noise
crown Gen 49 26 upon the crown of the Nazarite
Exod 25 11 over it thou shalt make a golden c.
25 to the ledge itself a polished crown
25 over the same another little golden c.
27 under the crown shall the golden rings
30 3 make to it a crown of gold round about
4 two golden rings under the crown. 37:27
37 2 and he made to it a crown of gold. 27
12 he made a polished crown of gold of
12 and upon the same another golden crown
14 of the table, over against the crown
Deut 33 16 upon the crown of the Nazarite among
2 K 12 30 and he took the crown of their king
14 25 sole of foot to the crown of his head
1 Pa 20 2 David took the crown of Melchom from
2 Pa 23 11 and put the crown upon him and the
Jdth 16 10 and bound up her locks with a crown
Esth 1 11 with the crown set upon her head, to
2 17 and he set the royal crown on her head
6 8 to have the royal crown upon his head
8 15 wearing a golden crown on his head and
Job 19 9 and hath taken the crown from my head
31 36 and put it about me as a crown? At
Ps 7 17 his iniquity shall come down upon his c.
64 12 thou shalt bless the crown of the year
67 22 the hairy crown of them that walk on in
Prov 4 9 and protect thee with a noble crown
12 4 diligent woman is crown to her husband
14 24 the crown of the wise is their riches
16 31 old age is a crown of dignity, when
17 6 children's children are c. of old men
27 24 a crown shall be given to generation
Wisd 2 8 let us crown ourselves with roses
5 17 crown of beauty at the hand of the Lord
Eccu 1 11 glory and gladness and a crown of joy
22 fear of the Lord is a crown of wisdom
6 32 set her upon thee as a crown of joy
11 5 no man would think on, hath worn the c.
25 8 much experience is the crown of old men
32 3 and receive a crown as an ornament of
40 4 weareth purple and beareth the crown
45 14 a crown of gold upon his miter wherein
47 7 in offering to him a crown of glory
Isa 3 17 will make bald the crown of the head
22 18 will c. thee with a c. of tribulation
28 1 woe to the crown of pride, to the
3 the crown of pride of the drunkards of
5 Lord of hosts shall be a c. of glory

61 3 to give them a crown for ashes, the oil
10 as a bridegroom decked with a crown
62 3 thou shalt be a crown of glory in the
Jer 2 16 defloured thee, even to c. of the head
13 18 crown of your glory is come down from
48 45 crown of the head of the children of
Lam 5 16 the crown is fallen from our head: woe
Bar 5 2 c. on thy head of everlasting honor
Eze 16 12 and a beautiful crown upon thy head
21 26 remove the diadem, take off the crown
43 17 crown round about it was half a cubit
20 and upon the crown round about: and
1 Ma 6 15 he gave him the crown and his robe and
8 14 none of all these wore a crown or was
10 20 him a purple robe and a crown of gold
12 39 king of Asia, and to take the crown
13 32 [Tryphon] put on the crown of Asia
37 the golden crown and the palm which
39 we forgive it, and the crown which you
2 Ma 10 11 was come to the crown, he appointed
14 4 presenting unto him a crown of gold
Mat 27 29 c. of thorns. Mark 15:17; John 19:2, 5
1 C 9 25 they may receive a corruptible crown
Phil 4 1 most desired, my joy and my crown
1 Th 2 19 is our hope or joy or crown of glory
2 Tim 4 8 is laid up for me a crown of justice
James 1 12 he shall receive the crown of life
1 P 5 4 you shall receive a never failing c.
Apoc 2 10 I will give thee the crown of life
3 11 thou hast, that no man take thy c.
6 2 there was a crown given him, and he
12 1 on her head a crown of twelve stars
14 14 having on his head a crown of gold
crowned Tob 3 21 that his life . . . shall be c.
Ps 5 14 thou hast crowned us, as with a shield
8 6 thou hast crowned him with glory and
Cant 3 11 diadem, wherewith his mother c. him
4 8 shalt be crowned from the top of Amana
Wisd 4 2 it triumpheth c. forever, winning the
Eccu 45 9 and crowned him with majestic attire
Isa 23 8 Tyre, that was formerly crowned, whose
2 Ma 6 7 compelled to go about crowned with ivy
2 Tim 2 5 not crowned except he strive lawfully
Heb 2 7 thou hast crowned him with glory and
9 crowned with glory and honor: that
crowneth Ps 102 4 who crowneth thee with mercy
crowns Exod 39 26 miters with their little crowns
3 K 7 29 between the little c. and the ledges
1 Pa 2 54 the crowns of the house of Joab, and
Bar 6 9 their gods have golden crowns upon
Eze 23 42 and beautiful crowns on their heads
24 23 you shall have crowns on your heads
Zach 6 11 gold and silver: and shalt make crowns
14 and the crowns shall be to Helem and
1 Ma 1 10 they all put crowns upon themselves
23 the veil and the crowns and the golden
4 57 front of the temple with c. of gold
10 29 and remit the crowns and the thirds
11 13 and set two crowns upon his head, that
35 the crowns that were presented to us
Apoc 4 4 and on their heads were crowns of gold
10 cast their crowns before the throne
9 7 were, as it were, crowns like gold
crucified 2 K 21 9 they c. them on a hill before
2 K 21 13 up the bones of them that were c.
Mat 20 19 to be mocked and scourged and c. and
26 2 shall be delivered up to be crucified
27 22 they say all: Let him be crucified
23 out the more, saying: Let him be c.
26 delivered him . . . to be c. John 19:16
35 after they had c. him, they divided
38 then were c. with him two thieves
44 that were c. with him. Mark 15:32
28 5 you seek Jesus who was c. Mark 16:6
Mark 15 15 and delivered up Jesus . . . to be c.
25 it was the third hour, and they c. him
Luke 23 23 requiring that he might be crucified
33 called Calvary, they c. him there
24 7 and be c., and the third day rise again
20 to be condemned to death and c. him
John 19 18 where they c. him, and with him two
20 where Jesus was c. was nigh to the
23 the soldiers, when they had c. him
32 and of the other that was c. with him
41 in the place where he was c. a garden
Acts 2 23 have c. and slain. Whom God hath
36 Christ this same Jesus whom you have c.
4 10 whom you c., whom God hath raised
Rom 6 6 that our old man is crucified with him
1 C 1 13 was Paul then crucified for you? Or
23 we preach Christ crucified, unto the
2 2 but Jesus Christ and him c. And I was
8 would never have c. the Lord of glory
2 C 13 4 although he was c. through weakness
Gal 3 1 hath been set forth, c. among you
5 24 that are Christ's, have c. their flesh
6 14 by whom the world is crucified to me
Apoc 11 8 where their Lord also was crucified
crucify 2 K 21 6 delivered unto us that we c. them
Mat 23 34 of them you will put to death and c.
27 31 led him away to c. him. Mark 15:20
Mark 15 13 cried out: Crucify him. 14; Luke 23:21; John 19:6, 15
27 and with him they crucify two thieves
John 19 6 take him you and crucify him: for I
10 that I have power to crucify thee, and
15 saith to them: Shall I crucify your king
crucifying Mark 15 24 c. him, they divided his
Heb 6 6 c. again to themselves the Son of God
cruel Gen 49 7 their wrath because it was cruel
Job 30 21 thou art changed to be cruel toward me
41 1 not stir him up, like one that is c.
Prov 5 9 to strangers and thy years to the cruel
11 17 he that is cruel casteth off even his
12 10 but the bowels of the wicked are c.
17 11 a cruel angel shall be sent against
Wisd 12 9 by war or by cruel beasts or with one
Eccu 13 15 his cruel mind will lay up thy words
Isa 13 9 a cruel day and full of indignation
14 6 fury, that persecuted in a cruel manner
19 4 Egypt into the hand of cruel masters
Jer 6 23 they are cruel and will have no mercy
30 14 with a cruel chastisement by reason
50 42 they are cruel and unmerciful: their
Lam 4 3 daughter of my people is cruel, like
Eze 31 12 most cruel of the nations shall cut
Dan 2 15 why so cruel a sentence was gone forth
2 Ma 4 25 having the mind of a cruel tyrant and
7 27 mocking the cruel tyrant, she said
cruelly 2 Pa 28 9 you have butchered them cruelly
2 Ma 7 39 raged against him more cruelly than
cruelties 2 Ma 7 42 and of the excessive c.
cruelty 2 Pa 28 9 that your c. hath reached up to
Esth 7 4 whose cruelty redoundeth upon the king
16 10 with his cruelty staining our goodness
2 Ma 12 5 as soon as Judas heard of this cruelty
crumbs Mat 15 27 also eat of the crumbs. Mark 7:28
Luke 16 21 desiring to be filled with the crumbs
cruse 3 K 17 12 and a little oil in a cruse
3 K 17 14 nor the cruse of oil be diminished
16 and the cruse of oil was not diminished
crush Gen 3 15 she shall crush thy head, and thou
2 K 22 38 pursue after my enemies and crush them
43 I shall crush them and spread them
Jdth 9 11 and crush their power with thy power
Job 9 17 he shall crush me in a whirlwind and

40 7 and crush the wicked in their place
Ps 73 13 didst crush the heads of the dragons
109 6 he shall crush the heads in the land
Prov 15 4 is immoderate shall crush the spirit
Eccu 35 22 that he may crush their back: and
36 9 the adversary, and crush the enemy
12 crush the head of the princes of the
Isa 30 30 he shall crush to pieces with whirlwind
Lam 3 34 to c. under his feet all the prisoners
Dan 7 25 shall crush the saints of the most High
Amos 4 1 oppress the needy and crush the poor
8 4 hear this, you that crush the poor and
Mich 5 13 and will crush thy cities. And I will
Rom 16 20 the God of peace crush Satan under
crushed Lev 22 24 hath the testicles bruised or c.
Deut 28 33 oppression and be c. at all times
2 K 21 5 the man that crushed us and oppressed
Ecce 12 6 the pitcher be crushed at the fountain
Eccu 46 21 he crushed the princes of the Tyrians
Isa 24 19 with crushing shall the earth be c.
64 7 hast c. us in the hand of our iniquity
Haba 3 6 the ancient mountains were crushed to
crushing Isa 24 19 with c. shall the earth be
crystal Job 28 17 gold or crystal cannot equal it
Ps 147 17 he sendeth his crystal like morsels
Eccu 43 22 and the water is congealed into c.
Eze 1 22 appearance of c. terrible to behold
Apoc 4 6 a sea of glass like to crystal; and in
21 11 as to the jasper stone, even as crystal
22 1 river of water of life, clear as c.
cubit Gen 6 16 in a cubit shalt thou finish the
Exod 25 10 the breadth, a cubit and a half. 17
10 the height likewise a cubit and a half
23 a table . . . a cubit in breadth and a cubit and a half in height
26 13 shall hang down a cubit on the one side
30 2 it shall be a c. in length and another
37 1 a c. and a half in breadth, and the
6 propitiatory . . . cubit and a half in
10 in height it was a cubit and a half
25 altar . . . being a cubit on every side
Deut 3 11 after the measure of the c. of a man's
3 K 7 32 height of a wheel was a c. and a half
35 was a round compass of half a cubit
Eze 43 13 measures of the altar by the truest c.
13 the bottom thereof was a cubit, and the breadth a cubit
13 which is a cubit and a handbreadth
17 crown round about it was half a cubit
one cubit Exod 26 16 breadth one c. and a half
Exod 36 21 the breadth was one cubit and a half
37 1 height was of one cubit and a half
10 in breadth one cubit, and in height it
3 K 7 31 which appeared without was of one cubit
31 together it was one cubit and a half
Eze 40 12 border before the little chambers one c.
12 one cubit was the border on both sides
42 one c. and a half long, and one c. and a half broad and one c. high
42 4 the inner parts of a way of one cubit
43 14 breadth of one cubit: and from the
Mat 6 27 add to his stature one c. Luke 12:25
cubits Gen 6 15 length of ark shall be 300 c., breadth of it 50 c., and height of it 30 c.
Gen 7 20 water was 15 cubits higher than the
Exod 26 2 length of one curtain . . . 28 c. 36:9
8 length of one hair curtain . . . 30 c.
27 14 hangings of fifteen cubits. 15
36 15 curtain was 30 c. long and 4 c. broad
38 14 fifteen c. of which were on one side
15 hangings equally of fifteen cubits
Num 35 5 toward the east shall be 2,000 cubits
5 toward the south . . . shall be 2,000 c.
Josu 3 4 between you and ark space of 2,000 c.
Deut 3 11 his bed of iron . . . nine cubits long
1 K 17 4 whose height was six cubits and a span
3 K 6 2 was threescore c. in length and 20 c. in breadth and 30 c. in height
6 middle floor was six cubits in breadth
6 third floor was 7 cubits in breadth
17 temple itself . . . was 40 cubits long
7 2 height 30 cubits: and four galleries
6 porch of pillars . . . 30 c. in breadth
10 stones of ten cubits or eight cubits
15 line of 12 c. compassed both pillars
19 lily work in the porch, of four cubits
23 a line of thirty cubits compassed it
27 every base was 4 c. in length and 4 c. in breadth and 3 c. high
38 four bases and was of four cubits
4 K 14 13 to gate of corner 400 cubits. 2 Pa 25:23
2 Pa 3 3 length by the first measure 60 cubits
4 height was 120 cubits: and he overlaid
4 2 a line of thirty cubits compassed it
6 13 five cubits broad and three cubits high
1 Es 6 3 support the height of threescore cubits and the breadth of threescore cubits
2 Es 3 13 thousand c. in the wall unto the gate
Jdth 1 2 walls thereof 70 c. broad and 30 c. high
Jer 52 21 one pillar was 18 c. high: and a cord of 12 c. compassed it
Eze 40 5 reed of six cubits and a handbreadth
9 measured the porch of the gate 8 cubits
11 length of the gate thirteen cubits
12 the little chambers were six cubits
13 in breadth five and twenty cubits
14 he made also fronts of sixty cubits
21 porch . . . five and twenty cubits broad
25 and the breadth five and twenty cubits
29 porch . . . five and twenty c. in breadth
30 porch . . . five and twenty cubits long
33 porches . . . five and twenty c. broad
36 porch . . . five and twenty cubits broad
48 breadth of the gate 3 cubits on this side and 3 cubits on that side
49 porch . . . the breadth eleven cubits
41 1 six c. on this side and six c. on that
2 measured the length thereof 40 cubits
3 the gate six cubits, and the breadth of the gate seven cubits
5 the wall of the house 6 cubits: and the breadth of every side chamber 4 cubits
12 the building . . . was 70 cubits broad
12 wall of the building . . . 90 c. long
42 20 wall . . . 5,000 c. long and 500 c. broad
43 14 brim to the greater brim four cubits
15 and the Ariel itself was four cubits
16 Ariel was 12 c. long and 12 c. broad
17 brim was 14 c. long and 14 c. broad
46 22 little courts disposed, 40 cubits long
47 3 he measured a thousand cubits: and he
Dan 3 1 statue of gold, of sixty cubits high and six cubits broad
47 above the furnace nine and forty cubits
John 21 8 from the land . . . two hundred cubits
Apoc 21 17 measured the wall thereof 144 cubits
cubits high Exod 27 1 foursquare, and 3 c. high
Exod 38 18 was 20 cubits long and 5 cubits high
Num 11 31 they flew in the air two cubits high
3 K 6 26 one cherub was ten cubits high, and in
7 15 each pillar was eighteen cubits high
27 every base was . . . three cubits high
4 K 25 17 one pillar was eighteen cubits high
17 was upon it was three cubits high
2 Pa 3 15 which were five and thirty cubits high
4 1 and 20 cubits broad and 10 cubits high

2 molten sea . . . it was five cubits high
6 13 five cubits broad and three cubits high
Jdth 1 2 the walls thereof . . . thirty cubits high
2 towers . . . he made a hundred cubits high
Esth 5 14 beam to be prepared, 50 cubits high
7 9 the gibbet . . . being 50 cubits high
Eze 41 22 altar of wood was three cubits high
Dan 3 1 statue of gold of 60 cubits high
2 Ma 13 5 a tower 50 cubits high, having a
fifty cubits Gen 6 15 breadth of it 50 cubits
Exod 27 12 hangings of fifty cubits. 38:12, 13
13 breadth also of the court . . . 50 c.
3 K 7 2 the house . . . the breadth 50 cubits
6 porch of pillars of 50 c. in length
Esth 5 14 beam to be prepared, 50 cubits high
7 9 the gibbet . . . being 50 cubits high
Eze 40 15 to the face of the porch . . . 50 cubits
21 the porch . . . 50 cubits long. 36
25 length was 50 cubits, and the breadth
29 the porch . . . was 50 cubits in length
33 the porches . . . 50 cubits long, and
42 2 was . . . the breadth of 50 cubits. Over
6 places, fifty cubits from the ground
7 the outward wall . . . was 50 cubits long
8 length of the chambers . . . 50 cubits
45 2 fifty cubits for the suburbs thereof
2 Ma 13 5 in that place a tower 50 cubits high
five cubits Exod 27 1 altar . . . shall be 5 c.
Exod 27 18 the court . . . height shall be of 5 c.
38 1 altar of holocaust . . . 5 cubits square
18 embroidered hanging . . . 5 cubits high
3 K 6 6 the floor . . . was 5 cubits in breadth
10 built a floor . . . 5 cubits in height
24 one wing of the cherub was 5 cubits and the other wing of cherub was 5 c.
7 16 height of one chapiter was 5 c. Jer 52:22
16 height of the other chapiter was 5 c.
23 the height of it was 5 cubits, and a
1 Pa 11 23 whose stature was of 5 cubits, and who
2 Pa 3 11 one wing was 5 c. long . . . and the other was also 5 c. long
12 wing of other cherub was 5 cubits long
12 and his other wing was 5 cubits long
15 and their chapiters were 5 cubits
4 2 it was 5 cubits high, and a line of
6 13 scaffold . . . which was 5 cubits long and 5 cubits broad
Eze 40 7 between the little chambers were 5 c.
30 porch . . . 20 c. long and 5 c. broad
48 porch 5 c. on this side and 5 c. on
41 2 gate 5 c. on this side and 5 c. on that
9 thickness of the wall . . . 5 cubits
11 breadth of the place . . . 5 cubits
12 wall of the building, 5 cubits thick
hundred cubits Exod 27 9 hangings of a hundred cubits. 11; 38:9
Exod 27 18 in length the court . . . a h. cubits
3 K 7 2 house . . . length of it was a h. c.
2 Es 3 1 even unto the tower of a h. cubits
Jdth 1 2 towers thereof he made a h. c. high
Eze 40 19 the breadth . . . a h. c. to the east
23 measured from gate to gate a h. c. 27
47 court a h. c. long and a h. c. broad
41 13 the length of the house, a h. c.: and
13 the walls thereof, a h. c. in length
14 the breadth . . . a h. c. And he measured
15 the galleries on both sides a h. c.
42 2 was the length of a h. c., and the
8 before the face of the temple, a h. c.
ten cubits Exod 26 16 let every one of them be ten cubits in length
Exod 36 21 the length of one board was ten cubits
3 K 6 3 and it was ten cubits in breadth before
23 two cherubims . . . of ten c. in height
24 in all ten c., from the extremity of
25 the second cherub also was ten cubits
26 one cherub was ten cubits high, and in
7 10 stones of ten cubits or eight cubits
23 a molten sea of ten cubits. 2 Pa 4:2
24 for ten cubits going about the sea
2 Pa 4 1 an altar of brass . . . ten cubits high
3 engravings on the outside of ten c.
Eze 40 11 breadth of the threshold . . . ten c.
41 2 breadth of the gate was ten cubits
42 4 was a walk ten cubits broad, looking
Zach 5 2 a volume . . . breadth thereof ten c.
twenty cubits Exod 27 16 made a hanging of 20 c.
Exod 38 18 embroidered hanging . . . 20 c. long
3 K 6 2 the house . . . 20 cubits in breadth
3 a porch . . . twenty cubits in length
16 he built up 20 cubits with boards of
20 oracle was 20 c. in length and 20 c. in breadth and 20 c. in height
2 Pa 3 3 house of God . . . the breadth 20 cubits
4 and the porch . . . 20 cubits: and the
8 the length of it . . . 20 c., and breadth of it . . . 20 c.
11 wings . . . were extended 20 cubits. 13
4 1 altar of brass 20 c. long and 20 c. broad
Eze 40 49 the length of the porch was 20 cubits
41 2 he measured . . . the breadth 20 cubits
4 length thereof 20 c. and breadth 20 c.
10 breadth of 20 c. round about the house
42 3 against the 20 c. of the inner court
Zach 5 2 a volume . . . length thereof is 20 c.
two cubits Exod 25 10 length . . . two cubits and a half. 17
Exod 25 23 a table . . . two cubits in length and a
37 1 it was two cubits and a half in length
6 propitiatory . . . two c. and a half in
10 the table . . . in length two cubits
25 foursquare, and in height two cubits
Num 11 31 they flew in the air two cubits high
Eze 40 9 and the front thereof two cubits: and
41 3 the front of the gate two cubits: and
22 and the length thereof was two cubits
43 14 ground to the lowest brim two cubits
cucumbers Num 11 5 the c. come into our mind
Isa 1 8 as a lodge in a garden of cucumbers
Bar 6 69 for as a scarecrow in a garden of c.
cud Lev 11 3 hoof divided and cheweth the cud
Lev 11 4 cheweth indeed the cud and hath a hoof
5 the cherogrillus which cheweth the cud
6 cheweth the cud but divideth not the
7 divideth the hoof, cheweth not the cud
26 divideth it not nor cheweth the cud
Deut 14 6 in two parts, and cheweth the cud
7 that chew the cud, but divide not the
8 divideth hoof but cheweth not the cud
cumbereth Luke 13 7 why cumbereth it the ground
cumi Mark 5 41 he saith to her: Talitha cumi
cummin Isa 28 25 sow gith and scatter cummin
Isa 28 27 the cart wheel turn about upon cummin
27 with a rod, and cummin with a staff
Mat 23 23 you tithe mint and anise and cummin
cunning Isa 3 2 and the c. man and the ancient
Eph 4 14 wickedness of men by c. craftiness
cunningly Josu 9 4 c. devising took for themselves
cup Gen 40 11 the cup of Pharao was in my hand
Gen 40 11 grapes and pressed them into the cup
11 I held, and I gave the cup to Pharao
13 and thou shalt present him the cup
21 to his place to present him the cup
44 2 put my silver cup and the price which
5 the cup which you have stolen is that
12 he found the cup in Benjamin's sack

16 and he with whom the cup was found
17 that stole the cup, he shall be my
1 K 26 11 is at his head, and the cup of water
12 David took the spear and cup of water
16 where is king's spear and cup of water
2 K 12 3 of his bread and drinking of his cup
3 K 7 26 was like the brim of a cup. 2 Pa 4:5
Ps 10 7 shall be the portion of their cup. For
15 5 portion of my inheritance and of my cup
74 9 a cup of strong wine full of mixture
Cant 8 2 I will give thee a cup of spiced wine
Isa 51 17 cup of his wrath: thou hast drunk
17 to the bottom of the cup of dead sleep
22 out of thy hand the cup of dead sleep
22 the dregs of the cup of my indignation
Jer 16 7 shall they give them to drink of the cup
25 15 take the cup of wine of this fury at
17 I took the cup at the hand of the Lord
28 if they refuse to take the cup at thy
49 12 judgment was not to drink of the cup
51 7 Babylon hath been a golden cup in the
Lam 4 21 to thee also shall the cup come, thou
Eze 23 31 and I will give her cup into thy hand
32 thou shalt drink thy sister's cup, deep
33 with the cup of grief and sadness, with
33 with the cup of thy sister Samaria
Haba 2 16 the cup of the right hand of the Lord
Mat 10 42 these little ones a cup of cold water
23 25 you make clean the outside of the cup
26 first make clean the inside of the cup
Mark 9 40 shall give you to drink a cup of water
Luke 11 39 you Pharisees make clean outside of cup
Apoc 14 10 with pure wine in the cup of his wrath
16 19 cup of the wine of the indignation of
17 4 having a golden cup in her hand, full
18 6 in the cup wherein she hath mingled
cupbearer 2 Es 1 11 for I was the king's cupbearer
cupbearers 3 K 10 5 their apparel and the c. and
2 Pa 9 4 his cupbearers also and their garments
cups Exod 25 29 and cups, wherein libations are
Exod 25 31 the cups and the bowls and the lilies
33 three cups as it were nuts to every
33 three cups likewise of the fashion of
34 in candlestick itself shall be 4 cups
37 16 dishes, bowls and cups and censers
17 its cups and bowls and lilies came out
19 three cups in manner of a nut on each
19 three cups of the fashion of a nut in
20 and in the shaft itself were four cups
Num 4 7 the cups and bowls to pour out the
Judg 9 27 in their banquets and cups they cursed
4 K 25 14 forks and the cups and the mortars
1 Es 1 9 thirty cups of gold, silver cups of a second sort
8 27 twenty cups of gold, of a thousand
Esth 1 7 that were invited, drank in golden c.
Prov 23 30 and study to drink off their cups
Ecce 2 8 cups and vessels to serve to pour out
Cant 7 2 like a round bowl never wanting cups
Isa 22 24 from the vessels of cups even to every
Jer 35 5 Rechabites pots full of wine and cups
52 19 the cups: as many as were of gold
Mark 7 4 the washings of cups and of pots and
8 the washings of pots and of cups: and
curdled Job 10 10 as milk, and c. me like cheese
Ps 67 16 a curdled mountain, a fat mountain
17 why suspect, ye curdled mountains? A
118 70 their heart is curdled like milk: but
cure Tob 5 13 thy cure from God is at hand. And
Eccu 36 25 if she have a tongue that can cure
38 7 by these he shall cure and shall allay
Jer 33 6 give them health, and I will cure them
46 11 there shall be no cure for thee. The
Osee 6 2 he will strike, and he will cure us
Mat 17 15 disciples and they could not cure him
Luke 9 1 over all devils and to cure diseases
Acts 4 22 in whom that miraculous cure had been
cured Lev 14 48 he shall purify it, it being c.
Tob 6 9 a white speck, and they shall be cured
Job 14 17 in a bag, but hast cured my iniquity
Jer 51 9 we would have cured Babylon, but she
Mat 4 24 had the palsy, and he cured them
15 28 her daughter was cured from that hour
17 17 and the child was cured from that hour
Mark 6 5 he cured a few that were sick, laying
Luke 6 18 troubled with unclean spirits, were c.
7 21 he cured many of their diseases and
9 43 Jesus cured the boy and restored him
cures Luke 13 32 I do cures today and tomorrow
Acts 4 30 by stretching forth thy hand to cures
cureth Job 5 18 for he woundeth and cureth: he
curiosity Num 4 20 let not others by any c. see
curious Eccu 3 22 in many of his works be not c.
Eccu 3 24 be not over curious, and in many of
Acts 19 19 of them who had followed curious arts
curiously 1 K 23 22 all diligence and c. inquire
2 Ma 2 31 c. to discuss every particular point
2 Th 3 11 working not at all, but c. meddling
curled Isa 3 24 instead of c. hair, baldness and
current Gen 23 16 of silver and of common c. money
curse Gen 8 21 I will no more curse the earth
Gen 12 3 curse them that curse thee, and in
24 41 but thou shalt be clear from my curse
27 12 I shall bring upon me a curse instead
13 upon me be this curse, my son: only
Exod 22 28 prince of thy people thou shalt not c.
Num 5 21 the Lord make thee a curse and an
27 and the woman shall be a curse and an
22 6 come therefore and curse this people
6 he whom thou shalt curse is cursed
11 curse them, if by any means I may fight
12 them, nor shalt thou curse the people
17 come and curse this people. Balaam
23 7 come, said he, and curse Jacob: make
8 how shall I curse him whom God hath not
11 I sent for thee to curse my enemies
13 curse them from thence. And when he
25 to Balaam: Neither curse nor bless him
27 that thou mayest c. them from thence
24 10 I called thee to curse my enemies, and
Deut 11 26 sight this day a blessing and a curse
28 a c., if you obey not the commandments
29 Garizim, the curse upon mount Hebal
23 4 against thee Balaam . . . to curse thee
27 13 shall stand on mount Hebal to curse
30 1 the curse which I have set before thee
Josu 9 23 therefore you shall be under a curse
24 9 for Balaam son of Beor to curse you
Judg 5 23 curse ye the land of Meroz, saith the
23 curse the inhabitants thereof, because
9 57 curse of Joatham the son of Jerobaal
21 18 being bound with an oath and a curse
1 K 17 36 Philistine, who hath dared to c. the
2 K 16 9 why should this dead dog curse my lord
10 let him alone and let him curse: for
10 for the Lord hath bid him curse David
11 let him alone that he may curse as the
3 K 2 8 who cursed me with a grievous curse
8 38 whatsoever curse or imprecation shall
4 K 22 19 should become a wonder and a curse
2 Pa 6 22 and bind himself with a curse before
15 15 all that were in Juda with a curse
2 Es 13 2 hired against them Balaam to curse them
2 our God turned the curse into blessing
25 and laid my curse upon them. And I beat
Job 3 8 let them curse it who curse the day
31 30 to sin, by wishing a curse to his soul

Ps 108 28 they will curse and thou wilt bless
Prov 26 2 a curse uttered without cause shall
30 10 lest he curse thee, and thou fall
Eccu 3 11 but the mother's curse rooteth up the
4 5 of thee to curse thee behind thy back
23 19 and curse the day of thy nativity
27 23 of a curse there is reconciliation
Isa 8 21 they will be angry and curse their king
24 6 shall a curse devour the earth and
Jer 15 10 lent to me on usury: yet all curse me
24 9 proverb and to be a c. in all places
25 18 astonishment and a hissing and a c.
26 6 I will make this city a curse to all
29 18 to be a curse and an astonishment and
22 of them shall be taken up a curse by
42 18 and a curse and a reproach: and you
44 8 that you should perish and be a curse
12 and for a curse and for a reproach
22 and a curse, without an inhabitant
49 13 a reproach and a desert and a curse
Bar 3 8 to be a reproach and a curse and an
6 65 neither can they curse kings nor bless
Zach 5 3 this is the curse that goeth forth over
8 13 as you were a curse among the Gentiles
Mala 2 2 and will curse your blessings, yea I will curse them
2 Ma 6 25 a stain and a curse upon my old age
Mat 15 4 that shall curse father or. Mark 7:10
26 74 he began to c. and to swear. Mark 14:71
Mark 11 21 the fig tree which thou didst curse
Luke 6 28 bless them that curse you, and pray
Acts 23 12 bound themselves under a curse, saying
14 have bound ourselves under a great c.
Rom 12 14 that persecute you: bless, and curse not
Gal 3 10 works of the law, are under a curse
13 redeemed us from the curse of the law, being made a curse for us
Heb 6 8 is reprobate and very near unto a c.
James 3 9 by it we curse men, who are made after
Apoc 22 3 and there shall be no curse any more

cursed Gen 3 14 thou art cursed among all cattle
Gen 3 17 cursed is the earth in thy work; with
4 11 cursed shalt thou be upon the earth
5 29 on the earth, which the Lord hath c.
9 25 c. be Chanaan, a servant of servants
27 29 cursed be he that curseth thee: and
49 7 cursed be their fury because it was
Lev 20 9 he hath cursed his father and mother
24 11 blasphemed the name and had cursed it
Num 5 22 let the cursed waters enter into thy
22 6 he whom thou shalt curse is cursed
23 8 curse him whom God hath not cursed
Deut 27 15 cursed be the man that maketh a graven
16 c. be he that honoreth not his father
17 c. be he that removeth his neighbor's
18 cursed be he that maketh the blind to
19 c. be he that perverteth the judgment
20 c. be he that lieth with his. 22, 23
21 cursed be he that lieth with any beast
24 cursed be he that secretly killeth his
25 cursed be he that taketh gifts to slay
26 c. be he that abideth not in the words
28 16 cursed shalt thou be in the city, cursed in the field
17 c. shall be thy barn and c. thy stores
18 cursed shall be the fruit of thy womb
19 cursed shalt thou be coming in and cursed going out
Josu 6 26 cursed be the man before the Lord, that
Judg 9 27 in their . . . cups they c. Abimelech
21 18 cursed be he that shall give Benjamin
1 K 14 24 cursed be the man that shall eat. 28
17 43 Philistine cursed David by his gods
26 19 they are c. in the sight of the Lord
2 K 16 5 coming out he cursed as he went on
7 thus said Semei when he cursed the king
19 21 because he cursed the Lord's anointed
3 K 2 8 who cursed me with a grievous curse
4 K 2 24 he [Eliseus] saw them and cursed them
9 34 see after that c. woman and bury her
Tob 13 16 they shall be c. that shall despise thee
Job 3 1 Job opened his mouth and cursed his day
5 3 and I cursed his beauty immediately
24 18 cursed be his portion on the earth
Ps 61 2 mouth, but cursed with their heart
118 21 they are cursed who decline from thy
Prov 11 26 he that hideth up corn, shall be cursed
24 24 shall be cursed by the people, and the
Wisd 3 13 their offspring is cursed: for happy
12 11 it was a cursed seed from the beginning
14 8 idol that is made by hands, is cursed
Eccu 3 18 he is cursed of God that angereth his
23 36 shall leave her memory to be cursed
33 12 some of them hath he c. and brought
Jer 11 3 c. is the man that shall not hearken
17 5 cursed be the man that trusteth in man
20 14 cursed be the day wherein I was born
15 cursed be the man that brought the
48 10 cursed be he that doth the work of the
10 cursed be he that withholdeth his sword
Lam 2 7 he hath cursed his sanctuary: he hath
Haba 3 14 thou hast cursed his scepters, the
Mala 1 14 cursed is the deceitful man that hath
3 9 and you are cursed with want, and you
Mat 25 41 depart from me, you cursed, into
Gal 3 10 cursed is every one that abideth not
13 c. is every one that hangeth on a tree

curses Num 5 18 whereon he hath heaped curses
Num 5 19 waters on which I have heaped curses
21 these curses shall light upon thee
23 the priest shall write these curses
23 waters upon which he hath heaped the c.
Deut 28 15 these curses shall come upon thee. 45
29 20 c. that are written in this volume. 27
21 according to the c. that are contained
30 7 will turn all these c. upon thy enemies
2 Pa 34 24 the c. that are written in this book
Eccu 29 9 will pay him with reproaches and c.
Bar 1 20 curses which the Lord foretold by Moses

curseth Gen 27 29 cursed be he that curseth thee
Exod 21 17 that c. his father or mother. Lev 20:9
24 15 man that curseth his God, shall bear
Num 24 9 that c. thee shall be reckoned accursed
Prov 20 20 he that curseth his father and mother
27 14 night, shall be like to him that c.
30 11 a generation that curseth their father
Eccu 4 6 the prayer of him that curseth thee
21 30 while the ungodly curseth the devil, he curseth his own soul
34 29 when one prayeth and another curseth

cursing Deut 23 5 turned his c. into thy blessing
Deut 30 19 have set before you . . . blessing and c.
Josu 8 34 the words of the blessing and the c.
2 K 14 17 neither moved with blessing nor c.
16 12 may render me good for the cursing
13 Semei . . . cursing and casting stones
Ps 9 7 his mouth is full of cursing and of
13 3 their mouth is full of cursing and
58 13 for their cursing and lying they shall
108 18 he loved cursing, and it shall come
18 and he put on cursing, like a garment
Eccu 27 16 their cursing is a grievous hearing
Jer 23 10 land hath mourned by reason of cursing
Osee 4 2 cursing and lying and killing and theft
Rom 3 14 whose mouth is full of cursing and
James 3 10 same mouth proceedeth blessing and c.

curtain Exod 26 2 length of one curtain shall be
Exod 26 5 every curtain shall have fifty loops
8 the length of one hair curtain shall be
9 so as to double the sixth curtain in
10 in the edge of one curtain. 36:11, 17
10 in the edge of the other curtain. 36:11
12 one curtain that is over and above
36 9 length of one curtain was 28 cubits
15 one curtain was thirty cubits long
17 fifty in the edge of another curtain
Jdth 14 13 stood before the curtain and made a
14 came near to the curtain, and lifting
curtains Exod 26 1 make ten c. of fine twisted
Exod 26 2 all the c. shall be of one measure
3 five curtains shall be joined one to
4 in the sides and tops of the curtains
6 veils of the curtains are to be joined
7 eleven curtains of goats' hair. 36:14
8 measure of all the c. shall be equal
12 that which shall remain of the curtains
13 over and above in the length of the c.
35 17 the curtains of the court with the
36 8 made ten c. of twisted fine linen
9 all the curtains were of the same size
10 he joined five curtains one to another
13 might catch the loops of the curtains
15 all the curtains were of one measure
18 of all the c. there might be made one
Num 3 26 the curtains of the court: the hanging
4 25 to carry the curtains of the tabernacle
26 curtains of the court and the veil
Cant 1 4 tents of Cedar, as the c. of Solomon
Jer 10 20 tent any more and to set up my c.
49 29 shall carry off for themselves their c.
Haba 3 7 the curtains of the land of Madian
cushions Eze 13 16 that sew c. under every elbow
Eze 13 20 behold I declare against your cushions
Cusi 1 Pa 6 44 Ethan the son of Cusi the son of
custody Gen 39 22 prisoners that were kept in c.
Gen 40 4 passed, and they were kept in custody
Exod 22 10 or any beast, to his neighbor's c.
Num 3 36 under their custody shall be the boards
38 having the custody of the sanctuary
1 Ma 9 53 put them in castle in Jerusalem in c.
13 12 and Jonathan was with him in custody
14 3 he put him [Demetrius] into custody
custom Gen 29 3 c. was when all the sheep were
Gen 29 24 gone in to her according to custom
31 35 to me according to the custom of women
Exod 33 4 put on his ornaments according to c.
Lev 12 5 according to the custom of her monthly
18 3 according to c. of the land of Egypt
Num 6 17 the libations that are due by custom
Judg 11 39 custom has been kept: that from year
18 7 according to the c. of the Sidonians
21 21 come out, as the custom is, to dance
1 K 2 16 be burnt today according to the custom
20 5 according to c. am wont to sit beside
25 upon his chair, according to custom
4 K 17 33 according to the custom of the nations
40 but did according to their old custom
1 Es 6 9 according to the custom of the priests
7 24 to impose toll or tribute or custom
Jdth 13 12 two went out according to their custom
Esth 1 13 according to the custom of the kings
8 8 this was the custom, that no man durst
Wisd 14 16 wicked custom prevailing, this error
Eccu 7 14 for the custom thereof is not good
23 19 thou by thy daily custom be infatuated
Eze 16 34 contrary to the custom of women in thy
Dan 14 14 in by night, according to their custom
1 Ma 10 89 sent him a buckle of gold, as the c. is
2 Ma 11 25 according to the c. of their ancestors
12 38 purified themselves according to the c.
13 4 commanded, as the custom is with them
Mat 9 9 saw a man sitting in the custom house
17 24 of whom do they receive tribute or c.
Mark 2 14 sitting at the receipt of c. Luke 5:27
Luke 1 9 according to c. of the priestly office
2 27 to do for him according to the custom
42 according to the custom of the feast
4 16 into the synagogue, according to his c.
22 39 according to his c., to the mount of
John 18 39 you have a c. that I should release
Acts 17 2 Paul, according to his c., went in
21 21 nor walk according to the custom. What
25 16 not the c. of the Romans to condemn
28 17 against the people or the c. of our
Rom 13 7 is due: custom to whom custom: fear
1 C 11 16 we have no such custom, nor the church
Heb 5 14 who by c. have their senses exercised
customs Esth 13 4 against the c. of all nations
Eccu 34 12 by travelling, and many c. of things
1 Ma 10 29 I release you from the customs of salt
Acts 26 3 knowest all, both c. and questions
cut Gen 22 3 and when he had cut wood for the
Exod 29 17 thou shalt cut the ram in pieces, and
17 upon the flesh that is cut in pieces
39 3 he cut thin plates of gold, and drew
Lev 1 6 they shall cut the joints into pieces
8 shall lay the parts that are cut out
17 shall not cut nor divide it with knife
9 13 the victim being cut into pieces, they
19 27 nor shall you cut your hair roundwise
22 24 the testicles bruised or crushed or cut
23 22 you shall not cut it to the very ground
Deut 14 1 you shall not cut yourselves nor make
23 1 whose testicles are broken or cut away
Judg 8 16 and cut in pieces the men of Soccoth
20 6 cut her in pieces and sent the parts
1 K 6 14 they cut in pieces the wood of the cart
11 7 both the oxen, he cut them in pieces
2 K 10 4 and cut away half of their garments
3 K 7 2 for he had cut cedar trees into pillars
18 23 and cut it in pieces and lay it upon
28 and cut themselves after their manner
33 cut the bullock in pieces and laid it
4 K 12 12 and to them that cut stones, and to
24 13 he cut in pieces all the vessels of
1 Pa 19 4 and cut away their garments from the
20 3 they were cut and bruised to pieces
Job 7 6 than the web is cut by the weaver and
14 7 if it be cut, it groweth green again
28 10 in the rocks he hath cut out rivers
40 25 shall friends cut him in pieces, shall
Ps 29 12 into joy: thou hast cut my sackcloth
128 4 Lord who is just will cut the necks of
Eccu 24 21 aloes, and as the frankincense not cut
28 18 it hath cut in pieces the forces of
45 13 precious stones cut and set in gold
47 24 neither will he cut up by the roots
Isa 18 5 what is left shall be cut away and
Jer 10 3 hath cut a tree out of the forest with
16 6 men shall not cut themselves nor make
25 23 that have their hair cut round. 49:32
34 18 when they cut the calf in two and
36 23 he cut it with the penknife and he
47 5 how long shalt thou cut thyself? O
Eze 5 2 and cut it in pieces with the knife
16 4 thy navel was not cut, neither wast
27 6 they have cut thy oars out of the oaks
Dan 2 34 till a stone was cut out of a mountain
45 the stone was cut out of the mountain
13 55 the angel . . . shall cut thee in two
59 waiteth with a sword to cut thee in two
Joel 3 10 cut your plowshares into swords and

Mich 1 7 graven things shall be cut in pieces
Zach 11 10 and I cut it asunder to make void my
1 Ma 1 59 they cut in pieces and burnt with fire
2 Ma 7 4 to cut out the tongue of him that had
15 23 that the tongue . . . should be cut out
Mat 21 8 others cut boughs from the. Mark 11:8
John 19 24 let us not cut it, but let us cast
Acts 5 33 they were cut to the heart. 7:54
Rom 9 28 shall finish his word and cut it short
11 24 if thou wert cut out of the wild olive
Heb 11 37 they were stoned, they were cut asunder

cut down Exod 34 13 cut down their groves. Deut 7:5; Jdth 3:12
Lev 19 9 thou shalt not cut down all that is on
Deut 20 19 thou shalt not cut down the trees that
20 cut them down, and make engines, until
Josu 17 15 cut down room for thyself in the land
18 and shalt cut down the wood and make
Judg 6 25 cut down the grove that is about the
26 thou shalt cut down out of the grove
28 destroyed, and the grove cut down
30 of Baal, and hath cut down his grove
9 48 an axe, he cut down the bough of a tree
49 they cut down boughs from the trees
3 K 5 6 that thy servants cut me down cedar
16 3 I will cut down the posterity of Baasa
21 21 I will cut down thy posterity, and I
4 K 3 19 and shall cut down every fruitful tree
25 cut down all the trees that bore fruit
6 4 come to the Jordan, they cut down wood
18 4 cut down the groves. 23:14; 2 Pa 14:3
19 23 have cut down its tall cedars and its
24 I have cut down and I have drunk strange
2 Pa 2 10 workmen that are to cut down the trees
16 and we will cut down as many trees out
31 1 broke the idols and cut down the groves
34 4 he cut down the groves and the graven
Jdth 2 17 the trees and vineyards to be cut down
Job 4 20 till evening they shall be cut down
22 20 is not their exaltation cut down, and
Ps 73 6 they have cut down at once the gates
88 24 I will cut down his enemies before his
Wisd 13 11 hath cut down a tree proper for his
Isa 9 10 they have cut down the sycamores, but
10 33 the tall of stature shall be cut down
34 of the forest shall be cut down with
14 8 there hath none come up to cut us down
37 24 I will cut down its tall cedars and
44 14 he hath cut down cedars, taken the holm
Jer 22 7 they shall cut down thy chosen cedars
46 23 they have cut down her forest, saith
Eze 21 10 thou hast cut down every tree. And I
31 12 cruel of the nations shall cut him down
39 10 nor cut down out of the forests: for
Dan 4 11 cut down the tree and chop off the
20 cut down the tree and destroy it, but
Zach 11 2 because the fenced forest is cut down
Mat 3 10 not yield good fruit, shall be cut down
7 19 not forth good fruit, shall be cut down. Luke 3:39
Luke 13 7 I find none. Cut it down therefore
9 then after that thou shalt cut it down

cut off Exod 30 33 shall be cut off from his people. Lev 7:20, 21
Lev 17 14 whosoever eateth it, shall be cut off
20 3 cut him off from midst of. Eze 14:8, 9
5 will cut off both him and all that
22 23 that hath the ear and the tail cut off
Num 9 13 be cut off from among his people. 15:30
13 24 they cut off a branch with its cluster
21 3 they cut them off and destroyed their
Deut 23 1 or yard cut off, shall not enter into
25 12 thou shalt cut off her hand, neither
Josu 7 9 us and cut off our name from the earth
8 22 began to cut off the enemies who were
22 the enemies being cut off on both sides
10 10 cut them off all the way to Azeca and
11 11 he cut off all the souls that abode
21 Josue came and cut off the Enacims
13 6 I am he that will cut them off from
Judg 1 6 took him and cut off his fingers and
7 having their fingers and toes cut off
6 16 thou shalt cut off Madian as one man
20 32 thought to cut them off, as they did
Ruth 4 6 I must not cut off the posterity of
10 lest his name be cut off from among
1 K 2 31 I will cut off thy arm and the arm of
5 4 the palms of his hands were cut off
17 51 slew him and cut off his head. And the
24 5 secretly cut off the hem of Saul's robe
6 because he had cut off the hem of Saul's
12 when I cut off the hem of thy robe, I
31 9 they cut off Saul's head and stripped
2 K 16 9 I will go and cut off his head. And the
20 22 they cut off the head of Seba the son
3 K 13 34 house of Jeroboam . . . was cut off and
14 10 will cut off from Jeroboam him that
14 who shall cut off the house of Jeroboam
15 29 he cut off a piece of wood and cast it
32 hath sent to cut off my head? Look
4 K 9 7 thou shalt cut off the house of Achab
8 and I will cut off from Achab him that
1 Pa 10 9 cut off his head and taken away his
2 Pa 32 21 an angel, who cut off all the stout
Jdth 7 6 commanded their aqueduct to be cut off
9 12 that his pride may be cut off with his
13 10 cut off his head and took off his canopy
27 he hath cut off the head of all the
16 11 with a sword she cut off his head. The
Job 6 9 may let loose his hand and cut me off
Ps 33 17 to cut off the remembrance of them from
36 9 evildoers shall be cut off: but they
53 7 enemies: and cut them off in thy truth
76 9 or will he cut off his mercy forever
100 8 that I might cut off all the workers of
108 13 may his posterity be cut off; in one
142 12 wilt cut off all them that afflict my
Wisd 18 23 and cut off the way to the living. For
Eccu 25 36 cut her off from thy flesh, lest she
Isa 10 7 and to cut off nations not a few. For
18 5 sprigs thereof shall be cut off with
29 20 all cut off that watched for iniquity
38 12 my life is cut off as by a weaver
12 was yet but beginning, he cut me off
53 8 he is cut off out of the land of the
Jer 7 29 cut off thy hair and cast it away: and
11 19 cut him off from land of the living
33 17 not be cut off from David a man to
18 there be cut off from the priests and
48 2 let us cut it off from being a nation
25 the horn of Moab is cut off and his
Lam 3 54 over my head: I said: I am cut off
Bar 3 19 they are cut off, and are gone down
4 34 joy of her multitude shall be cut off
Eze 14 19 to cut off from it man and beast: and
17 17 and build forts, to cut off many souls
21 3 will cut off in thee the just and the
4 as I have cut off in thee the just and
23 25 they shall cut off thy nose and thy
25 7 will cut thee off from among the people
29 8 cut off man and beast out of thee
30 15 and will cut off the multitude of
33 4 if the sword come and cut him off: his
6 and cut off a soul from among them: he
37 11 our hope is lost, and we are cut off
Joel 1 5 wine: for it is cut off from your mouth

D

1 K 5 2 into temple of Dagon and set it by D.
3 Dagon lay upon his face on the ground
3 they took Dagon and set him again in
4 they found Dagon lying upon his face
4 head of Dagon and both the palms of
5 only the stump of Dagon remained in its
5 neither the priests of Dagon, nor any
5 tread on the threshold of Dagon in
7 heavy upon us and upon Dagon our god
1 Pa 10 10 fastened up in the temple of Dagon
1 Ma 10 84 the spoils of them and the temple of D.
11 4 they showed him the temple of Dagon
daily Gen 41 56 famine increased d. in all the
Exod 36 3 people d. in morning offered their
Judg 4 24 children of Israel, who grew d. stronger
2 K 3 1 but the house of Saul decaying daily
2 Pa 36 15 rising early and daily admonishing them
Tob 1 19 Tobias daily went among all his kindred
2 19 Anna his wife went daily to weaving work
10 7 daily running out looked round about
11 5 but Anna sat beside the way daily, on
Jdth 7 11 water was daily given out . . . by measure
Ps 41 4 whilst it is said to me daily: Where
Prov 8 34 that watcheth daily at my gates and
Eccu 23 11 as a slave daily put to the question
19 by thy daily custom, be infatuated
Jer 37 20 should give him daily a piece of bread
Eze 30 16 daily there shall be distresses
43 25 thou offer a he goat for sin daily
45 23 rams without blemish d. for seven days
23 and for sin a he goat daily. And he
1 Ma 6 57 we decay daily, and our provision of
8 15 consulted daily 320 men, that sat in
Mat 26 55 I sat daily with you, teaching in the
Mark 14 49 I was d. with you in the. Luke 22:53
Luke 9 23 take up his cross daily and follow
11 3 give us this day our daily bread. And
19 47 he was teaching daily in the temple
Acts 2 46 continuing daily with one accord in
47 the Lord increased daily together such
6 1 widows were neglected in the daily
16 5 the churches . . . increased in number d.
17 11 daily searching the scriptures whether
19 9 disputing daily in the school of one
1 C 15 31 I die daily, I protest by your glory
2 C 11 28 my daily instance, the solicitude for
Heb 7 27 needeth not daily, as the other priests
10 11 every priest standeth d. ministering
James 2 15 or sister be naked and want daily food
dainties Gen 49 20 he shall yield d. to kings
dainty Haba 1 16 is made fat, and his meat dainty
Dalaia 1 Pa 3 24 sons of Elioenai . . . Dalaia and
1 Es 2 60 the children of Dalaia. 2 Es 7:62
Dalaias Jer 36 12 Dalaias the son of Semeias and
Jer 36 25 Dalaias and Gamarias spoke to the king
Dalaiau 1 Pa 24 18 and twentieth to Dalaiau
daleth Ps 118 25 daleth. Lam 1:4; 2:4; 3:10, 11, 12; 4:4
Dalila Judg 16 4 and she was called Dalila. And
Judg 16 6 and Dalila said to Samson: Tell me, I
10 Dalila said to him: Behold thou hast
12 Dalila bound him again with these and
13 Dalila said to him again: How long
14 when Dalila had done this, she said
15 Dalila said to him: How dost thou say
Dalmanutha Mark 8 10 he came into the parts of D.
Dalmatia 2 Tim 4 10 Titus into Dalmatia. Only
dam Exod 22 30 seven days let it be with its dam
Exod 23 19 not boil a kid in milk of his dam. 34:26; Deut 14:21
Lev 22 27 seven days under the udder of their dam
Deut 22 6 dam sitting upon the young or upon the
damage Gen 31 39 torn, I made good all the damage
Exod 21 22 answerable for so much d. as the woman's
22 5 according to the estimation of the d.
9 or anything that may bring damage: the
Lev 5 16 he shall make good the damage itself
Prov 19 19 that is impatient, shall suffer damage
Acts 27 10 beginneth to be with injury and much d.
2 C 7 9 that you might suffer damage by us in
Damaris Acts 17 34 and a woman named Damaris and
Damascenes 2 C 11 32 guarded the city of the D.
Damascus Gen 14 15 which is on left hand of D.
Gen 15 2 son of steward . . . is this D. Eliezer
2 K 8 5 Syrians of Damascus came to succor
6 David put garrisons in Syria of D.
3 K 11 24 of Soba; and they went to Damascus
24 and they made him king in Damascus
15 18 king of Syria, who dwelt in D. 2 Pa 16:2
19 15 thy way through the desert to Damascus
20 34 do thou make thee streets in Damascus
4 K 5 12 Abana and the Pharphar, rivers of D.
8 7 Eliseus also came to D. and Benadad
9 presents and all the good things of D.
14 28 how he restored Damascus and Emath
16 9 against Damascus and laid it waste
10 king Achaz went to Damascus to meet
10 when he had seen the altar of D., king
11 Achaz had commanded from Damascus
11 until king Achaz was come from Damascus
12 when the king was come from Damascus
1 Pa 18 5 the Syrians of Damascus came also
6 [David] put a garrison in Damascus
2 Pa 24 23 all the spoils to the king of D. And
28 5 booty . . . and carried it to Damascus
23 sacrificed victims to the gods of D.
Jdth 1 7 to all that dwelt in Cilicia and D.
2 17 went down into the plains of Damascus
Cant 7 4 tower of Libanus that looketh toward D.
Isa 7 8 the head of Syria is Damascus and the
8 the head of Damascus is Rasin: and
8 4 strength of Damascus and the spoils of
10 9 is not Samaria as Damascus? As my hand
17 1 the burden of Damascus. Behold Damascus shall cease to be a city
3 and the kingdom from Damascus: and the
Jer 49 23 against Damascus. Emath is confounded
24 D. is undone, she is put to flight
27 I will kindle a fire in wall of D.
Eze 27 18 the men of Damascus were thy merchants
47 16 between border of D. and border of
17 shall be the border of Damascus and
48 1 the border of Damascus northward, by
Amos 1 3 for three crimes of Damascus and for
5 I will break the bar of Damascus: and
3 12 that dwell . . . in the couch of Damascus
5 27 to go into captivity beyond Damascus
Zach 9 1 and of Damascus the rest thereof: for
1 Ma 11 62 went through the country as far as D.
12 32 he went forward and came to Damascus
Acts 9 2 asked of him letters to Damascus, to
3 to pass that he drew nigh to Damascus
8 they brought him to Damascus. And he
10 disciple at Damascus named Ananias
19 with the disciples that were at Damascus
22 confounded the Jews who dwelt at D.
27 how in D. he had dealt confidently
22 5 I went to D. that I might bring them
6 drawing nigh to Damascus at midday
10 arise and go to Damascus; and there it
11 by my companions I came to Damascus
26 12 when I was going to Damascus with
20 to them first that are at Damascus
2 C 11 32 at D. the governor of the nation under
Gal 1 17 against I returned to Damascus. Then
Damna Josu 21 35 and Damna and Naalol, four cities
damnation Luke 20 47 shall receive greater d.

Rom 3 8 may come good? Whose damnation is just
13 2 that resist, purchase to themselves d.
1 Tim 5 12 having d. because they have made void
damsel Gen 34 4 get me this damsel to wife. But
Gen 34 12 only give me this damsel to wife. The
19 for he loved the damsel exceedingly
Deut 22 20 virginity be not found in the damsel
23 if a man have espoused a damsel that
24 the damsel, because she cried not out
25 a man find a damsel that is betrothed
26 the d. shall suffer nothing, neither
26 so also did the damsel suffer: she was
28 if a man find a d. that is a virgin
3 K 1 4 the damsel was exceeding beautiful
Mat 14 11 in a dish: and was given to the damsel
Mark 5 39 the damsel is not dead, but sleepeth
40 taketh the father and mother of the d.
40 entereth in where the damsel was lying
41 taking the damsel by the hand, he saith
41 interpreted: Damsel, I say to thee, arise
42 the damsel rose up and walked: and she
6 22 the king said to the damsel: Ask of me
28 gave it to the d., and the d. gave it
Acts 12 13 a damsel came to hearken whose name
damsel's Deut 22 19 he shall give to the d. father
damsels 1 K 25 42 five d. went with her [Abigail]
Jdth 16 14 sons of the damsels have pierced them
Ps 67 26 young damsels playing on timbrels. In
Dan Gen 14 14 appointed: and pursued them to Dan
Gen 30 6 therefore she called his name Dan
35 25 Rachel's handmaid: Dan and Nephtali
46 23 the sons of Dan: Husim. The sons of
49 16 Dan shall judge his people like another
17 let Dan be a snake in the way, a serpent
Exod 1 4 children of Israel . . . Dan and Nephtali
31 6 Achisamech of tribe of Dan. 38:23
35 34 sons of Achisamech of the tribe of Dan
Lev 24 11 Dabri, of the tribe of Dan. And they
Num 1 12 of Dan, Ahiezer the son of Amissaddai
38 of the sons of Dan . . . 62,700. Of the
2 25 on the north side camped sons of Dan
31 that were numbered in the camp of Dan
7 66 prince of the sons of Dan, Ahiezer the
10 25 marched the sons of Dan by their troops
13 13 of the tribe of Dan, Ammiel the son of
26 42 of the tribe of the children of Dan
Deut 27 13 on mount Hebal . . . Dan and Nephtali
33 22 to Dan also he said: Dan is a young
34 1 all the land of Galaas as far as Dan
Josu 19 40 lot came out to tribe of children of D.
47 the children of Dan went up and fought
47 calling the name of it Lesem Dan, by the name of Dan their father
48 possession of tribe of the sons of Dan
21 5 out of the tribes of Ephraim and of Dan
23 of tribe of Dan, Eltheco and Gabathon
Judg 1 34 Amorrhite straitened children of Dan
5 17 and Dan applied himself to ships: Aser
13 2 man of Saraa and of the race of Dan
25 began to be with him in the camp of Dan
18 1 tribe of Dan sought them an inheritance
2 children of Dan sent five most valiant
11 went therefore of the kindred of Dan
12 is called the camp of Dan and is behind
25 children of Dan said to him: See thou
29 calling the name of the city Dan after
30 his sons were priests in tribe of Dan
20 1 from Dan to Bersabee. 1 K 3:20; 2 K 3:10; 17:11; 24:2, 15; 3 K 4:25
2 K 24 6 they came into the woodlands of Dan
3 K 12 29 set the one in Bethel and other in Dan
30 went to adore the calf as far as Dan
15 20 Israel and they smote Ahion and Dan
4 K 10 29 calves that were in Bethel and Dan
1 Pa 2 2 sons of Israel . . . Dan, Joseph
12 35 of Dan also 28,600 prepared for battle
21 2 from Bersabee even to Dan. 2 Pa 30:5
27 22 over Dan, Ezrihel the son of Jeroham
2 Pa 2 14 son of a woman of daughters of Dan
16 4 they took Ahion and Dan and Abelmaim
Jer 4 15 a voice of one declaring from Dan and
8 16 snorting of his horses was heard from D.
Eze 27 19 Dan and Greece and Mosel have set forth
48 1 shall be one portion for Dan. And by
2 by the border of Dan, from the east
32 the gate of Dan one. And at the south
Amos 8 14 thy God, O Dan, liveth: and the way
dance Judg 21 21 out, as the custom is, to dance
Job 21 11 and their children dance and play. They
Ecce 3 4 a time to mourn and a time to dance
Isa 13 21 and the hairy ones shall dance there
Jer 31 13 then shall the virgin rejoice in the d.
danced 2 K 6 14 David d. with all his might before
Mat 11 17 you have not danced. Luke 7:32
14 6 daughter of Herodias danced before
Mark 6 22 had danced and pleased Herod and them
dancer Eccu 9 4 company of her that is a dancer
dances Exod 15 20 the women went forth . . . with d.
Exod 32 19 he saw the calf and the dances: and
Judg 11 34 met him with timbrels and with dances
1 K 21 11 did they not sing to him in their d.
29 5 to whom they sung in their d. saying
Jdth 3 10 him with garlands and lights and dances
Jer 31 4 shalt go forth in the dances of them
dancing Judg 9 27 d. they went into the temple
Judg 21 23 man his wife of them that were d.: and
1 K 18 6 singing and dancing to meet king Saul
2 K 6 16 [Michol] saw king David leaping and d.
1 Pa 15 29 [Michol] saw king David d. and playing
Esth 8 16 seemed to rise, joy, honor, and dancing
Lam 5 15 our dancing is turned into mourning
Luke 15 25 he heard music and dancing: he called
danger Gen 35 17 [Rachel] began to be in danger
Deut 20 4 to deliver you from danger. And the
Judg 5 2 willingly offered your lives to danger
9 offered yourselves to danger, bless
1 Pa 11 19 with the danger of their lives they
12 19 with the danger of our heads we will
Esth 4 16 expose myself to death and to danger
11 8 that was a day of darkness and danger
14 1 fearing the danger that was at hand
4 my danger is in my hands. I have heard
Prov 7 23 knoweth not that his life is in danger
Eccu 3 27 that loveth danger shall perish in it
13 16 thou walkest in danger of thy ruin
34 13 I have been in danger of death for
46 10 were delivered out of the danger from
Jon 1 4 the ship was in danger to be broken
1 Ma 11 23 Jonathan . . . and put himself in danger
14 29 have put themselves in d. and resisted
2 Ma 4 4 considering the d. of this contention
11 7 to expose themselves . . . to the danger
Mat 5 21 shall be in d. of the judgment. 22
22 shall be in danger of the council. And
22 shall be in danger of hell fire. If
Luke 8 23 they were filled and were in danger
Acts 19 27 our craft is in d. to be set at nought
40 even in danger to be called in question
Rom 8 35 nakedness? or danger? or persecution
1 C 15 30 why also are we in danger every hour
dangerous 2 K 2 26 d. to drive people to despair
Eccu 26 28 have appeared to me hard and dangerous
2 Ma 4 16 they incurred a d. contention and
Acts 27 9 when sailing was now dangerous because
2 Tim 3 1 in the last days shall come d. times
dangers Judg 9 17 exposed his life to dangers

Eccu 43 26 that sail on the sea, tell the dangers
2 Ma 1 11 been delivered by God out of great d.
2 C 1 10 doth deliver us out of so great d.
Daniel 1 Pa 3 1 sons of David . . . Daniel of Abigail
1 Es 8 2 of the sons of Ithamar, Daniel. Of the
2 Es 10 6 the subscribers were . . . D., Genthon
Eze 14 14 if these three men, Noe, D., and Job
20 Noe and D. and Job be in the midst
28 3 behold thou art wiser than Daniel: no
Dan 1 6 Daniel, Ananias, Misael and Azarias
7 gave them names: to D., Baltassar: to
8 Daniel purposed in his heart that he
9 God gave to Daniel grace and mercy
10 prince of the eunuchs said to Daniel
11 D. said to Malasar, whom the prince
11 had appointed over Daniel, Ananias
17 to D. the understanding also of all
19 not found among them all such as D.
21 D. continued even to the first year
2 13 D. and his companions were sought for
14 Daniel inquired concerning the law
15 when Arioch had told the matter to D.
16 D. went in and desired of the king
18 that Daniel . . . might not perish with
19 then was the mystery revealed to D.
19 and Daniel blessed the God of heaven
24 after this Daniel went in to Arioch
25 Arioch in haste brought in Daniel to
26 the king answered and said to Daniel
27 Daniel made answer before the king
46 on his face, and worshipped Daniel
49 Daniel requested of the king and he
49 D. himself was in the king's palace
4 5 till their colleague Daniel came in
16 Daniel, whose name was Baltassar began
5 12 were found in him, that is, in Daniel
12 let Daniel be called for and he will tell
13 Daniel was brought in before the king
13 art thou Daniel of the children of
17 Daniel made answer and said before king
29 Daniel was clothed with purple and a
6 2 three princes . . . of whom D. was one
3 Daniel excelled all the princes and
4 sought to find occasion against Daniel
5 not find any occasion against this D.
10 when D. knew this, that is to say, that
11 D. praying and making supplication
13 D., who is of children of the captivity
14 in behalf of Daniel he set his heart
16 they brought Daniel and cast him into
16 the king said to Daniel: Thy God
17 that nothing should be done against D.
20 cried with a lamentable voice to D.
20 D., servant of the living God, hath
21 Daniel answering the king, said: O king
23 that D. should be taken out of the
23 Daniel was taken out of the den: and
24 were brought that had accused Daniel
26 dread and fear the God of Daniel. For
27 delivered Daniel out of the lions' den
28 D. continued unto the reign of Darius
7 1 Daniel saw a dream: and the vision of
15 I Daniel was affrighted at these things
28 I Daniel was much troubled with my
8 1 I Daniel . . . saw in my vision when I was
15 when I Daniel saw the vision and sought
27 I Daniel languished and was sick for
9 2 I D. understood by books the number
22 Daniel, I am now come forth to teach
10 1 a word was revealed to Daniel surnamed
2 I D. mourned the days of three weeks
7 I Daniel alone saw the vision: for the
11 D., thou man of desires, understand
12 he said to me: Fear not, Daniel: for
12 4 thou, O Daniel, shut up the words and
5 I D., looked, and behold as it were
9 go, D., because the words are shut
13 45 young boy whose name was Daniel. And
51 Daniel said to the people: Separate
55 Daniel said: Well hast thou lied against
59 D. said to him: Well hast thou also
61 Daniel had convicted them of false
64 Daniel became great in the sight of
14 1 Daniel was the king's guest and was
3 but Daniel adored his God. And the king
6 D. smiled and said: O king, be not
8 D. shall die because he hath blasphemed
8 Daniel said to the king: Be it done
9 king went with Daniel into the temple
11 or else D. that hath lied against us
13 D. commanded his servants, and they
15 in the morning, and Daniel with him
16 are the seals whole, Daniel? And he
18 Daniel laughed: and he held the king
21 delivered Bel into the power of D.
23 king said to Daniel: Behold thou canst
24 Daniel said: I adore the Lord my God
26 Daniel took pitch and fat and hair
28 deliver us D. or else we will destroy
29 he delivered Daniel to them. And they
31 that they might devour Daniel. Now there
33 to Daniel, who is in the lions' den
36 Daniel . . . take the dinner that God
37 Daniel said: Thou hast remembered me
38 Daniel arose and ate. And the angel of
39 the king came to bewail Daniel: and he
39 D. was sitting in midst of the lions
40 great art thou, O Lord the God of D.
42 let all . . . fear the God of Daniel: for
42 hath delivered D. out of the lions'
1 Ma 2 60 Daniel in his innocency was delivered
Mat 24 15 which was spoken of by D. the prophet
Danna Josu 15 49 and D. and Cariath-senna, this
Daphca Num 33 12 came to Daphca. And departing
Num 33 13 departing from Daphca, they camped in
Daphne 2 Ma 4 33 place at Antioch beside Daphne
Daphnis Num 34 11 against the fountain of D.: from
Dara 1 Pa 2 6 sons of Zare . . . Dara, five in all
Darcon 2 Es 7 58 Nathinites . . . children of Darcon
dare Gen 44 26 we dare not see the man's face
Lev 26 37 none of you shall dare to resist your
Num 24 9 whom none shall dare to rouse. He that
32 7 that they may not dare to pass into
Deut 19 20 and may not dare to do such things
2 K 16 10 who is he that shall dare say, why
Job 9 19 no man dare bear witness for me. If I
37 24 to be wise, shall not dare to behold
Rom 5 7 some one would dare to die. But God
15 18 I dare not to speak of any of those
1 C 6 1 dare any of you, having a matter against
2 C 10 12 we dare not match or compare ourselves
11 21 if any man dare . . . I dare also. They
dared 1 K 17 36 who hath d. to curse the army
darest 4 K 18 20 thou trust, that thou darest to
Darius 1 Es 4 5 even until the reign of Darius
1 Es 4 24 till the second year of reign of Darius
5 5 the matter should be referred to D.
6 sent to Darius the king. The letter
7 to Darius the king all peace. Be it
6 1 then king Darius gave orders and they
12 I Darius have made the decree, which
13 what Darius the king had commanded
14 by the commandment of Cyrus and D.
15 sixth year of the reign of king D.
2 Es 12 22 in the reign of Darius the Persian
Dan 5 31 D. the Mede succeeded to the kingdom

6 1 it seemed good to Darius, and he
6 king Darius, live forever: all princes
9 king Darius set forth the decree and
25 king Darius wrote to all people, tribes
28 Daniel continued unto the reign of D.
9 1 in the first year of Darius the son of
11 1 from the first year of Darius the Mede
Agge 1 1 in the second year of Darius. 2:1, 11; Zach 1:1, 7
Zach 7 1 in the fourth year of king Darius
1 Ma 1 1 had overthrown Darius king of the

dark Gen 15 17 there arose a dark mist and there
Exod 14 20 it was a dark cloud, and enlightening
20 21 Moses went to the dark cloud wherein
Lev 13 56 place of the leprosy be somewhat dark
Deut 28 29 is wont to grope in the dark and not
Josu 2 5 of shutting the gate in the dark, they
3 K 18 45 the heavens grew dark with clouds and
4 K 7 7 they arose and fled away in the dark
Job 10 21 no more, to a land that is dark and
12 25 they shall grope as in the dark and
18 6 light shall be dark in his tabernacle
24 16 he diggeth through houses in the dark
28 3 the stone also that is in the dark
Ps 10 3 shoot in the dark the upright of heart
17 2 dark waters in the clouds of the air
34 6 let their way become dark and slippery
87 7 in the dark places, and in the shadow
13 shall thy wonders be known in the dark
90 6 business that walketh about in the dark
138 12 but darkness shall not dark to thee
Prov 2 13 the right way, and walk by dark ways
7 9 nigh the way of her house, in the dark
Wisd 17 3 under a dark veil of forgetfulness
Eccu 37 16 when thou shalt stumble in the dark
Isa 13 2 upon the dark mountain lift ye up
29 15 and their works are in the dark and
45 19 secret, in a dark place of the earth
59 9 and we have walked in the dark. We have
10 we are in dark places as dead men. He
Jer 13 16 give ye glory . . . before it be dark
16 stumble upon the dark mountains: you
23 12 shall be as a slippery way in the dark
Lam 3 6 he hath set me in dark places as those
Bar 6 70 like to dead body cast forth in the dark
Eze 8 12 what the ancients . . . do in the dark
12 6 thou shalt be carried out in the dark
7 and I went forth in the dark and was
12 he shall go forth in the dark: they
32 7 I will make the stars thereof dark
34 12 scattered in the cloudy and dark day
Dan 8 23 king . . . understanding dark sentences
Amos 8 9 the earth dark in the day of light
Haba 2 6 and a dark speech concerning him: and
Mat 10 27 that which I tell you in the dark
John 6 17 it was now dark, and Jesus was not
20 1 cometh early when it was yet dark
1 C 13 12 through a glass in a dark manner; but
2 P 1 19 light that shineth in a dark place
Apoc 16 10 his kingdom became dark and they gnawed

darkened Job 3 9 let the stars be d. with the
Ps 68 24 their eyes be d. that they see not
Ecce 12 2 and the moon and the stars be darkened
3 that look through the holes shall be d.
Isa 5 30 the light is d. with the mist thereof
13 10 sun shall be darkened in his rising
Eze 30 18 in Taphnis the day shall be darkened
Joel 2 10 the sun and moon are darkened. 3:15
Mich 3 6 the day shall be darkened over them
Zach 11 17 his right eye shall be utterly d.
Mat 24 29 sun shall be darkened. Mark 13:24
Luke 23 45 the sun was darkened and the veil of the
Rom 1 21 their foolish heart was darkened. For
11 10 let their eyes be darkened that they
Eph 4 18 having their understanding darkened
Apoc 8 12 the third part of them was darkened
9 2 the sun and the air were darkened

darkeneth Eccu 25 24 d. her countenance as a bear

darkish Lev 13 39 if he find that a d. whiteness

darkness Gen 1 2 d. was upon the face of the deep
Gen 1 4 he divided the light from the d. And
5 called the light Day, and the d. Night
18 to divide the light and the darkness
Exod 10 21 may there be darkness upon the land
22 there came horrible darkness in all the
19 9 come to thee in the d. of a cloud that
Deut 4 11 and there was darkness and a cloud
5 22 midst of the fire and cloud and the d.
23 the voice out of midst of the d. and
Josu 24 7 he put darkness between you and the
1 K 2 9 wicked shall be silent in d., because
2 K 22 10 and darkness was under his feet. And
12 he made darkness a covering round
29 O Lord, wilt enlighten my darkness
Tob 4 11 not suffer the soul to go into d. Alms
5 12 me, who sit in darkness and see not
Jdth 9 7 and darkness wearied them. The deep held
Esth 11 8 that was a day of d. and danger, of
Job 3 4 let that day be turned into darkness
5 let d. and shadow of death cover it
23 God hath surrounded him with darkness
5 14 they shall meet with d. in the day
7 4 be filled with sorrows even till d.
10 22 a land of misery and darkness where the
12 22 discovereth deep things of darkness
15 22 he may return from darkness to light
23 that the day of darkness is ready at
30 he shall not depart out of darkness
17 12 after darkness I hope for light again
13 and I have made my bed in darkness
18 18 shall drive him out of light into d.
19 8 in my way he hath set darkness. He hath
20 26 all d. is hid in his secret places
22 11 think that thou shouldst not see d.
23 17 I have not perished because of the d.
24 15 eye of the adulterer observeth d. saying
17 they walk in d. as if it were in light
26 10 till light and darkness come to an end
28 3 he hath set a time for darkness and the
29 3 and I walked by his light in darkness
30 26 I waited for light, and d. broke out
34 22 there is no darkness and there is no
37 19 for we are wrapped up in darkness
38 19 and where is the place of darkness
Ps 17 10 and darkness was under his feet. And he
12 he made d. his covert, his pavilion
29 O my God, enlighten my darkness. For by
54 6 darkness hath covered me. And I said
81 5 they walk on in darkness: all the
96 2 clouds and d. are round about him
103 20 thou hast appointed darkness, and it is
104 28 he sent darkness and made it obscure
106 10 such as sat in darkness and in the
14 he brought them out of darkness and
111 4 a light is risen up in darkness: he
138 11 perhaps darkness shall cover me: and
12 darkness shall not be dark to thee
12 d. thereof and light thereof are alike
142 3 he hath made me to dwell in darkness
Prov 7 9 in the d. and obscurity of the night
20 20 shall be put out in the midst of d.
Ecce 2 13 much as light differeth from darkness
14 the fool walketh in darkness: and I
5 16 days of his life he eateth in d. and
6 4 he came in vain and goeth to darkness
Wisd 17 2 fettered with the bonds of darkness

17 bound together with one chain of d.
20 image of that d. which was to come
20 to themselves more grievous than the d.
18 4 worthy to be . . . imprisoned in darkness
19 16 when they were covered with sudden d.
Eccu 5 1 in the time of vengeance and darkness
11 16 error and d. are created with sinners
21 11 in their end is hell and darkness
23 26 darkness compasseth me about and the
Isa 5 20 that put d. for light, and light for d.
30 and behold darkness of tribulation
8 22 they shall . . . behold trouble and d.
9 2 the people that walked in darkness
21 4 my heart failed, darkness amazed me
29 18 out of darkness . . . eyes of the blind
32 14 darkness and obscurity are come upon
42 7 and them that sit in darkness out of
16 will make darkness light before them
45 7 I form the light and create darkness
47 5 silent, and get thee into darkness
49 9 to them that are in d.: Show yourselves
50 3 I will clothe the heavens with d. and
10 that hath walked in darkness and hath
58 10 then shall thy light rise up in d. and thy d. shall be as the noonday
59 9 we looked for light, and behold d.
10 we have stumbled at noonday as in d.
60 2 darkness shall cover the earth and a
Jer 13 16 turn it into shadow of death and into d.
Lam 3 2 led me and brought me into darkness
Eze 32 8 I will cause darkness upon thy land
Dan 2 22 and knoweth what is in darkness: and
3 72 ye light and darkness, bless the Lord
Joel 2 2 a day of darkness and of gloominess
31 the sun shall be turned into darkness
Amos 5 8 that turneth darkness into morning
18 the day of the Lord is darkness and
20 shall not the day of the Lord be d.
Mich 3 6 darkness to you instead of divination
Nah 1 8 darkness shall pursue his enemies. What
Soph 1 15 a day of darkness and obscurity, a day
2 Ma 3 27 they took him up covered with great d.
Mat 4 16 the people that sat in darkness, hath
6 23 that is in thee be d.: the d. itself how
8 12 be cast out into the exterior d.: there
22 13 cast him into the exterior darkness
25 30 cast ye out into the exterior darkness
27 45 darkness over the whole earth. Mark 15:33; Luke 23:41
Luke 1 79 to enlighten them that sit in darkness
11 35 that the light in thee . . . be not d.
36 body be lightsome, having no part of d.
12 3 spoken in d., shall be published in
22 53 this is your hour and the power of d.
John 1 5 the light shineth in d., and the d. did not comprehend it
3 19 men loved d. rather than the light
8 12 that followeth me, walketh not in d.
12 35 that the d. overtake you not. And he
35 that walketh in d. knoweth not whither
46 believeth in me, may not remain in d.
Acts 2 20 the sun shall be turned into darkness
13 11 fell mist and d. upon him [Elymas]
26 18 may be converted from d. to light
Rom 2 19 a light of them that are in darkness
13 12 let us cast off the works of d. and
1 C 4 5 to light the hidden things of d. and
2 C 4 6 commanded the light to shine out of d.
6 14 what fellowship hath light with d.
Eph 5 8 you were heretofore d., but now light
11 fellowship with unfruitful works of d.
6 12 the rulers of the world of this d.
Col 1 13 delivered us from the power of d. and
1 Th 5 4 you, brethren, are not in darkness
5 we are not of the night nor of d.
Heb 12 18 you are not come to . . . d. and storm
1 P 2 9 who hath called you out of darkness
2 P 2 17 to whom the mist of darkness is reserved
1 J 1 5 God is light and in him there is no d.
6 if we . . . walk in darkness, we lie, and do
2 8 because the darkness is passed and the
9 hateth his brother, is in d. 11
11 walketh in d. and knoweth not whither
11 the darkness hath blinded his eyes
Jude 6 he hath reserved under darkness in
13 to whom storm of darkness is reserved
darksome Gen 15 12 great and d. horror seized
Job 38 17 hast thou seen the darksome doors? Hast
Prov 4 19 the way of the wicked is darksome: they
Ecce 11 8 he must remember the darksome time
Mat 6 23 body shall be darksome. Luke 11:34
dart Prov 25 18 is like a dart and a sword and
Zach 9 14 his dart shall go forth as lightning
darts Gen 49 23 that held darts provoked him
2 K 11 20 many darts are thrown from above off
Ps 54 22 his words . . . the same are darts. Cast
1 Ma 10 80 cast d. at the people from morning
2 Ma 5 3 with drawn swords and casting of d.
10 30 cast d. and fireballs against the
12 27 engines of war and a provision of d.
Eph 6 16 fiery darts of the most wicked one
dash 4 K 8 12 thou wilt dash their children and
Ps 90 12 lest thou dash thy foot against a
136 9 shall take and dash thy little ones
Jer 48 26 Moab shall dash his hand in his own
51 20 with thee I will dash nations together
Mat 4 6 lest thou d. thy foot. Luke 4:11
dashed Judg 5 11 where the chariots were dashed
Judg 9 53 d. it against the head of Abimelech
Job 30 22 and thou hast mightily dashed me. I
Eccu 33 2 he shall not be dashed in pieces as a
Isa 13 16 their infants shall be d. in pieces
Osee 10 14 the mother being dashed in pieces
14 1 let their little ones be dashed and let
Nah 3 10 her young children were dashed in pieces
dashest Jer 51 20 thou d. together for me the
dasheth Mark 9 17 dasheth him, and he foameth and
dashing Isa 25 11 with the dashing of his hands
Dathan Num 16 1 D. and Abiron . . . rose up against
Num 16 12 Moses sent to call Dathan and Abiron
24 from tents of Core and D. and Abiron
25 Moses . . . went to Dathan and Abiron
27 Dathan and Abiron coming out stood
26 9 his sons were Namuel and D. and Abiron
9 D. and Abiron princes of the people
Deut 11 6 what he hath done . . . to D. and Abiron
Ps 105 17 earth opened and swallowed up Dathan
Eccu 45 22 men that were with Dathan and Abiron
Datheman 1 Ma 5 9 fled into the fortress of D.
daub Eze 13 11 that daub without tempering that
Eze 13 15 them that daub it without tempering
15 and they that daub it are no more
daubed Exod 2 3 d. it with slime and pitch: and
Eze 13 10 and they daubed it with dirt without
12 daubing wherewith you have daubed it
14 the wall that you have daubed with
22 28 her prophets have daubed them without
daubing Eze 13 12 where is the d. wherewith you
daughter Gen 11 29 Melcha the daughter of Aran
Gen 19 33 perceived not neither when his d. lay
35 younger d. went in and lay with him
20 12 d. of my father and not the d. of my
24 15 Rebecca came out, the d. of Bathuel
23 whose daughter art thou. 47
24 I am the daughter of Bathuel. 47
48 to take the d. of my master's brother

25 20 to wife Rebecca the d. of Bathuel the
26 34 Judith the daughter of Beeri the Hethite
34 Basemath the daughter of Elon of the
28 9 Maheleth the d. of Ismael, Abraham's
29 6 behold Rachel his daughter cometh with
18 seven years for Rachel thy younger d.
23 at night he brought in Lia his d. to
24 giving his d. a handmaid named Zelpha
30 21 she bore a daughter named Dina. The
34 1 Dina the d. of Lia went out to see
7 unlawful act, in ravishing Jacob's d.
8 Sichem has a longing for your daughter
17 we will take our daughter and depart
36 2 Ada the d. of Elon the Hethite, and
2 Oolibama the d. of Ana. 14, 18
2 Ana the daughter of Sebeon. 14
3 Basemath the daughter of Ismael, sister
25 he had a son Dison and a d. Oolibama
39 Meetabel the d. of Matred. 1 Pa 1:50
39 Matred, daughter of Mezaab. 1 Pa 1:50
38 2 saw there daughter of a man of Chanaan
12 daughter of Sue the wife of Juda died
41 45 Aseneth the d. of Putiphare. 46:20
50 d. of Putiphare priest of Heliopolis
46 15 sons of Lia . . . with Dina his daughter
18 whom Laban gave to Lia his daughter
25 whom Laban gave to Rachel his daughter
Exod 2 5 daughter of Pharao came down to wash
9 Pharao's daughter said to her: Take this
9 she delivered him to Pharao's daughter
21 he took Sephora his daughter to wife
6 23 Elizabeth the daughter of Aminadab
20 10 do no work on it . . . nor thy daughter
21 7 if any man sell his daughter to be a
31 have gored a son or a daughter he shall
Lev 12 6 for a son or for a d., she shall bring
18 10 not uncover the nakedness of thy son's d. or thy daughter's d.
17 nakedness of thy wife and her d. Thou
17 shalt not take her son's d. or her daughter's d.
19 29 make not the d. a common strumpet, lest
20 14 if any man after marrying the d., marry
17 take his sister, the d. of his father or the d. of his mother
21 2 his son or for his d., for his brother
9 if d. of a priest be taken in whoredom
22 12 if the d. of a priest be married to
24 11 Salumith the daughter of Dabri, of the
Num 25 15 Cozbi the daughter of Sur, a most noble
18 Cozbi . . . daughter of a prince of Madian
26 46 name of the daughter of Aser was Sara
59 Jochabed the daughter of Levi, who was
27 8 his inheritance shall pass to his d.
9 if he have no daughter, his brethren
30 17 between the father and the d. that is as
Deut 5 14 thou nor thy son nor thy daughter nor
7 3 nor give thy d. to his son nor take his d. for thy son
12 18 shalt eat . . . thou and thy son and thy d.
13 6 or d., or thy wife that is in thy bosom
16 11 thy daughter and thy manservant and thy
14 shalt make merry . . . and thy daughter
18 10 that shall expiate his son or daughter
22 16 I gave my daughter unto this man to
17 I found not thy daughter a virgin: and
27 22 with his sister, the d. of his father
Josu 15 16 will give him Axa my daughter to wife
17 to give him Axa his d. Judg 1:13
Judg 1 12 to him will I give my daughter Axa
11 34 his only daughter met him [Jephte]
35 my daughter, thou hast deceived me
40 and lament the daughter of Jephte
19 24 I have a maiden daughter and this man

Ruth 2 2 she answered her: Go, my daughter. She
8 hear me, d., do not go to glean in any
22 better for thee, my d., to go out to
3 1 my d., I will seek rest for thee and
10 blessed art thou of the Lord, my d.
16 what hast thou done, daughter? And she
18 wait my d., till we see what end the
1 K 14 50 Achinoam the daughter of Achimaas
17 25 and will give him his daughter and will
18 17 behold my elder daughter Merob, her
19 Merob the daughter of Saul should have
20 Michol the other daughter of Saul and
27 gave him Michol his daughter to wife
25 44 Saul gave Michol his daughter, David's
2 K 3 3 Maacha the d. of Tholmai. 1 Pa 3:2
7 Respha the d. of Aia. 21:8, 10, 11
13 Michol the d. of Saul. 6:16, 20, 23; 15:29; 18:28; 21:8
11 3 Bethsabee the daughter of Eliam, the
12 3 and it was unto him as a daughter. And
14 27 born to Absalom . . . one daughter, whose
17 25 Abigail the daughter of Naas, the sister
3 K 3 1 he took his daughter and brought her
4 11 Tapheth the daughter of Solomon to wife
15 Basemath the daughter of Solomon to wife
7 8 made also a house for the d. of Pharao
9 16 and gave it for a dowry to his daughter
24 the daughter of Pharao came up out of
11 1 women besides the daughter of Pharao
15 2 Maacha the daughter of Abessalom. 10
16 31 Jezabel daughter of Ethbaal king of the
22 42 mother was Azuba the d. of Salai. And
4 K 8 18 for the daughter of Achab was his wife
26 Athalia the daughter of Amri. 2 Pa 22:2
9 34 because she is a king's daughter. And
11 2 Josaba the d. of king Joram, sister of
14 9 thy d. to my son to wife. 2 Pa 25:18
15 33 Jerusa the daughter of Sadoc. 2 Pa 27:1
18 2 Abi the daughter of Zacharias. And he
19 21 d. of Jerusalem hath wagged her head
21 19 was Messalemeth the daughter of Harus
22 1 Idida the daughter of Hadaia of Besecath
23 10 or his d. through fire to Moloch. And
31 Amital the daughter of Jeremias. 24:19
36 Zebida the daughter of Phadaia of Rume
24 8 Nohesta the daughter of Elnathan of
1 Pa 2 3 the Chanaanitess the d. of Sue. And Her
21 Hesron went in to daughter of Machir
35 he gave his daughter to wife: and she
49 the daughter of Caleb was Achsa. These
3 5 Bethsabee the daughter of Ammiel. Jebaar
4 18 Bethia the daughter of Pharao, whom
7 24 his daughter was Sara who built Bethoron
2 Pa 8 11 he removed the daughter of Pharao from
11 18 Mahalath the daughter of Jerimoth the
18 Abihail the daughter of Eliab the son
20 Maacha the daughter of Absalom. 21
13 2 Michaia the daughter of Uriel of Gabaa
20 31 Azuba the daughter of Selahi. And he
21 6 for his wife was a daughter of Achab
22 11 Josabeth the king's d. took Joas the
11 Josabeth . . . was daughter of king Joram
29 1 Abia the daughter of Zacharias. And
2 Es 6 18 to wife the daughter of Mosollam the
Tob 3 7 Sara the daughter of Raguel, in Rages
9 never see son or daughter of thee
6 11 he hath a daughter named Sara, but he
11 nor any other daughter beside her. All
7 8 and Sara their daughter wept. And after
10 promise to give me Sara thy daughter
12 is thy daughter due to be his wife
15 taking the right hand of his daughter
19 brought Sara her daughter in thither

20 be of good cheer, my daughter: the
10 12 the parents taking their d. kissed
Jdth 8 1 Judith . . . the d. of Merari. 16:8
10 12 I am a daughter of the Hebrews and I
13 23 blessed art thou, O daughter, by the
Esth 2 7 brought up his brother's d. Edissa
7 Mardochai adopted her for his d. And
15 Esther the daughter of Abihail. 9:29
15 whom he had adopted for his daughter
Ps 44 11 hearken, O daughter, and see and incline
14 all the glory of the king's daughter
136 8 daughter of Babylon, miserable: blessed
Cant 7 1 thy steps in shoes, O prince's d.! The
4 gate of the daughter of the multitude
Eccu 7 27 marry thy daughter well and thou shalt
22 3 a foolish d. shall be to his loss. A
4 a wise d. shall bring an inheritance
26 13 a d. that turneth not away herself
42 9 the father waketh for the daughter
11 keep a sure watch over a shameless d.
Isa 10 30 lift up thy voice, O d. of Gallim
22 4 for the devastation of d. of my people
23 10 d. of the sea, thou hast a girdle no
37 22 d. of Jerusalem hath wagged her head
47 1 virgin daughter of Babylon, sit on
1 no throne for d. of the Chaldeans, for
5 into darkness, O d. of the Chaldeans
Jer 4 11 the way of the daughter of my people
6 14 breach of the d. of my people. 8:11
26 with sackcloth, O d. of my people
8 19 the voice of the daughter of my people
21 for affliction of the d. of my people
22 the wound of the d. of my people closed
9 1 for the slain of the d. of my people
7 else shall I do before d. of my people
14 17 virgin d. of my people is afflicted
31 22 in deliciousness, O wandering d.? For
46 11 take balm, O virgin d. of Egypt: in
19 thou daughter inhabitant of Egypt: for
24 the daughter of Egypt is confounded
48 18 O dwelling of the daughter of Dibon
49 4 valley hath flowed away, O delicate d.
50 42 battle against thee, O d. of Babylon
51 33 d. of Babylon is like a thrashingfloor
52 1 Amital, the d. of Jeremias of Lobna
Lam 1 15 winepress for the virgin d. of Juda
2 5 multiplied in d. of Juda the afflicted
11 destruction of the d. of my people. 3:48; 4:10
13 shall I liken thee, O d. of Jerusalem
15 wagged their heads at d. of Jerusalem
4 3 the daughter of my people is cruel
6 iniquity of d. of my people is made
21 and be glad, O daughter of Edom, that
22 visited thy iniquity, O d. of Edom
Bar 2 3 should eat . . . flesh of his own d.
Eze 14 20 they shall deliver neither son nor d.
16 44 as the mother was, so also is her d.
45 thou art thy mother's daughter, that
22 11 oppressed his sister the d. of his
44 25 their father and mother and son and d.
Dan 11 6 d. of the king of the south shall come
17 he shall give him a d. of women to
13 2 Susanna the daughter of Helcias. 29
3 instructed their d. according to the
29 Susanna daughter of Helcias the wife
48 you have condemned a d. of Israel
57 a d. of Juda would not abide your
63 praised God for their d. Susanna with
Osee 1 3 took Gomer the daughter of Debelaim
6 she conceived again and bore a d. and
Mich 4 8 the kingdom to the d. of Jerusalem
5 1 laid waste, O d. of the robber: they
7 6 daughter riseth up against her mother
Soph 3 14 be glad . . . O daughter of Jerusalem
Zach 2 7 that dwellest with the d. of Babylon
9 9 shout for joy, O daughter of Jerusalem
Mala 2 11 hath married the d. of a strange God
1 Ma 9 37 the d. of one of the great princes
10 54 give me now thy daughter to wife and
57 Ptolemee went . . . with Cleopatra his d.
58 he gave him his daughter Cleopatra
11 9 I will give thee my d. whom Alexander
10 I repent that I have given him my d.
12 he took away his d. and gave her to
Mat 9 18 my daughter is even now dead; but
22 be of good heart, daughter, thy faith
10 35 daughter against her mother, and the
37 that loveth son or d. more than me
14 6 d. of Herodias danced before them: and
15 22 my d. is grievously troubled by a devil
28 her daughter was cured from that hour
Mark 5 23 my d. is at the point of death, come
34 d., thy faith hath made. Luke 8:48
35 thy daughter is dead. Luke 8:49
6 22 d. of the same Herodias had come in
7 25 whose daughter had an unclean spirit
26 cast forth the devil out of her d. Who
29 the devil is gone out of thy daughter
Luke 2 36 Anna, a prophetess, the d. of Phanuel
8 42 [Jairus] had an only daughter, almost
12 53 mother against d., and d. against mother
13 16 ought not this d. of Abraham, whom
Acts 7 21 Pharao's d. took him up and nourished
Heb 11 24 denied himself to be son of Pharao's d.

daughter of Sion 4 K 19 21 d. . . . hath despised. Isa 37:22
Ps 9 15 in the gates of the d. of Sion. 72:28
Isa 1 8 d. . . . shall be left as a covert in a
10 32 hand against the mountain of the d. . . .
16 1 to the mount of the d. . . . And it shall
23 12 shalt glory no more, O virgin d. . . .
52 2 bonds from off thy neck, O captive d. . . .
62 11 tell the d. . . . Behold thy Savior cometh
Jer 4 31 the voice of the d. of Sion dying away
6 2 I have likened the d. . . . to a beautiful
23 as men for war, against thee, O d. . . .
Lam 1 6 and from the d. . . . all her beauty is
2 1 covered with obscurity the d. . . . in his
4 fair . . . in the tabernacle of the d. . . .
8 purposed to destroy wall of the d. . . .
10 ancients of the d. . . . sit upon the
13 that I may comfort thee, O virgin d. . . .
18 to the Lord upon the walls of the d. . . .
4 22 thy iniquity is accomplished, O d. . . .
Mich 1 13 it is the beginning of sin to the d. . . .
4 8 cloudy tower of the flock, of the d. . . .
10 be in pain and labor, O d. . . . As a
13 arise and tread, O daughter of Sion
Soph 3 14 give praise, O daughter of Sion: shout
Zach 2 10 sing praise and rejoice, O d. . . . : for
9 9 rejoice greatly, O daughter of Sion
Mat 21 5 tell ye the daughter of Sion: Behold
John 12 15 fear not, daughter of Sion: behold thy

daughter-in-law Gen 11 31 Thare took . . . Sarai his d.
Gen 38 11 Juda said to Thamar his d.: Remain a
16 knew her not to be his daughter-in-law
24 thy d. hath played the harlot and she
Lev 18 15 not uncover the nakedness of thy d.
20 12 if any man lie with his d. let both die
Ruth 1 22 came with Ruth the Moabitess her d.
4 15 he is born of thy d.: who loveth thee
1 K 4 19 his d. the wife of Phinees was big
1 Pa 2 4 Thamar his d. bore him Phares and Zara
Eze 22 11 wickedly defiled his d., the brother
Mich 7 6 the d. against her mother-in-law: and a
Mat 10 35 d. against her mother-in-law. Luke 12:53

Luke 12 53 the mother-in-law against her d. and
daughter's Deut 22 17 tokens of my d. virginity
Lev 18 10 not uncover nakedness . . . of d. daughter
17 shalt not take her . . . d. daughter to
daughters Gen 6 1 and daughters were born to them
Gen 6 2 sons of God seeing the d. of men, that
4 went in to the daughters of men and
19 8 I have two daughters who as yet have
12 hast thou here . . . sons or daughters
14 sons-in-law that were to have his d.
15 take thy wife and the two daughters
16 the hand of his wife and of his two d.
30 abode in the mountain, and his two d.
30 dwelt in a cave, he and his two d.
36 the two d. of Lot were with child by
24 3 for thy son of the d. of the Chanaanites
13 the d. of the inhabitants of this city
27 46 weary of my life because of d. of Heth
28 2 a wife thence of the d. of Laban thy
6 not take a wife of the d. of Chanaan
8 not well pleased with d. of Chanaan
29 16 he [Laban] had two daughters, the name
31 26 my d. as captives taken with the sword
31 lest thou wouldst take away thy d. by
41 twenty years, fourteen for thy d. and
43 Laban answered him: The d. are mine
50 if thou afflict my daughters and if
34 9 give us your d. and take you our d.
16 give and take your daughters and our
21 we shall take their d. for wives and
36 2 Esau took wives of the d. of Chanaan
46 7 he came into Egypt with . . . daughters
49 22 daughters run to and fro upon the wall
Exod 2 16 priest of Madian had seven daughters
6 25 took a wife of the d. of Phutiel. These
21 9 deal with her after the manner of d.
34 16 take of their d. a wife for thy son
Num 21 29 his d. into captivity to Sehon the king
25 1 fornication with the daughters of Moab
26 33 Salphaad, who had no sons, but only d.
27 1 then came the daughters of Salphaad
6 the d. of Salphaad demand a just thing
36 2 shouldst give to the d. of Salphaad
6 touching the d. of Salphaad: Let them
10 d. of Salphaad did as was commanded
Deut 23 17 be no whore among the d. of Israel
Josu 17 3 Salphaad . . . had no sons, but only d.
6 the daughters of Manasses possessed
Judg 3 6 they took their d. to wives, and they gave their own d. to their sons
11 40 the d. of Israel assemble together and
12 8 he had 30 sons and as many daughters
14 1 a woman of the d. of the Philistines
2 Thamnatha of the d. of the Philistines
3 no woman among the d. of thy brethren
21 1 none of us shall give of his d. to the
7 sworn, not to give our d. to them
14 given them of the d. of Jabes Galaad
18 as to our own d. we cannot give them
18 that shall give Benjamin any of his d.
21 when you shall see the d. of Silo come
Ruth 1 11 return, my d.: why come ye with me
12 return again, my daughters, and go
13 do not so, my daughters, I beseech you
1 K 1 16 for one of the daughters of Belial
2 21 bore three sons and two daughters
8 13 your daughters also he will take to
14 49 names of his two daughters, the name
30 3 and their d. were taken captives, David
19 of their sons or d., nor of the spoils
2 K 1 20 lest d. of the Philistines rejoice, lest d. of the uncircumcised triumph
24 ye d. of Israel, weep over Saul, who
13 18 king's daughters that were virgins
1 Pa 2 34 Sesan had no sons, but daughters and
4 27 sons of Semei were 16, and six d.: but
7 15 and Salphaad had daughters. And Maacha
28 habitations were Bethel with her d. . . . Gazer and her d., Sichem also with her d., as far as Asa with her d.
29 Bethsan and her d., Thanach and her d., Mageddo and her d., Dor and her d.
8 12 who built Ono and Lod and its daughters
18 1 took away Geth and her daughters out
23 22 Eleazar died, and had no sons but d.
25 5 gave to Heman fourteen sons and three d.
2 Pa 2 14 son of a woman of the d. of Dan whose
11 21 [Roboam] begot . . . threescore daughters
13 19 Bethel and her d., and Jesama with her d., Ephron also and her d.
21 and [Abia] begot . . . sixteen daughters
29 9 our d. and wives are led away captives
1 Es 2 61 wife of the d. of Berzellai. 2 Es 7:63
9 2 they have taken of their daughters
12 give not your d. to their sons and take not their d. for your sons
2 Es 3 12 the street of Jerusalem, he and his d.
5 5 some of our daughters are bondwomen
10 30 we would not give our d. to the people
30 nor take their d. for our sons. And if
13 25 that they would not give their d. to
25 nor take their d. for their sons, nor
Jdth 9 3 and their daughters into captivity: and
Job 1 2 born to him seven sons and three d.
42 13 he had seven sons and three daughters
15 so beautiful as the daughters of Job
Ps 44 10 the d. of kings have delighted thee
13 the daughters of Tyre with gifts, yea
47 12 daughters of Juda be glad; because of
96 8 and the daughters of Juda rejoiced
143 12 their daughters decked out, adorned
Prov 30 15 the horseleech hath two daughters that
31 29 many d. have gathered together riches
Ecce 12 4 the daughters of music shall grow deaf
Cant 1 4 but beautiful, O ye d. of Jerusalem
2 2 so is my love among the daughters. As
7 I adjure you, O ye d. of Jerusalem. 3:5; 5:8; 8:4
3 10 with charity for the d. of Jerusalem
11 go forth, ye d. of Sion, and see king
5 16 he is my friend, O ye d. of Jerusalem
6 8 the d. saw her and declared her most
Eccu 7 26 hast thou daughters? Have a care of
Isa 3 16 the daughters of Sion are haughty
17 crown of the head of the d. of Sion
4 4 wash away the filth of d. of Sion and
16 2 so shall the daughters of Moab be in
32 9 ye confident d., give ear to my speech
43 6 my d. from the ends of the earth. And
49 22 carry thy d. upon their shoulders
60 4 thy d. shall rise up at thy side. Then
Jer 9 20 teach your daughters wailing: and every
19 9 feed them . . . with flesh of their d.
29 6 give your daughters to husbands and
35 8 nor our sons nor our d.: nor to build
41 10 the king's d. and all the people that
43 6 and the king's d. and every soul which
49 2 her d. shall be burnt with fire, and
3 cry, ye daughters of Rabbath, gird
Lam 3 13 into my reins the d. of his quiver
51 because of all the d. of my city. My
Bar 4 10 I have seen the captivity of . . . my d.
Eze 13 17 thy face against the d. of thy people
14 16 shall deliver neither sons nor d. 18
16 27 to the will of the d. of Philistines
46 her d. that dwell at thy left hand

46 at thy right hand is Sodom and her d.
48 Sodom herself and her d. have not done as thou hast done, and thy d.
49 the idleness of her and of her d.: and
53 by bringing back Sodom with her d.
53 by bringing back Samaria and her d.
55 Sodom and her daughters shall return
55 Samaria and her daughters shall return
55 thou and thy d. shall return to your
57 thee a reproach of the d. of Syria
57 reproach . . . of all the d. of Palestine
61 I will give them to thee for daughters
23 2 were two women, d. of one mother. And
26 6 her d. also that are in the field
8 thy daughters that are in the field
30 18 her d. shall be led into captivity
32 16 daughters of the nations shall lament
18 and the d. of the mighty nations to
Dan 13 57 thus did you do to the d. of Israel
Osee 4 13 shall your d. commit fornication and
14 I will not visit upon your daughters
Luke 1 5 his wife was of the d. of Aaron and
23 28 d. of Jerusalem, weep not over me; but
Acts 2 17 your sons and your d. shall prophesy
21 9 he [Philip] had four daughters virgins
1 P 3 6 whose daughters you are, doing well
sons and daughters; *see* **sons**
daughters-in-law Ruth 1 6 with both her d. 7
David Mat 1 1 generation of Jesus Christ, son of D.
Mat 1 6 Jesse begot David the king. And David the king begot Solomon
17 from Abraham to David . . . and from David to the transmigration
20 Joseph, son of David, fear not to take
12 3 what D. did when he was hungry. Luke 6:3
23 is not this the son of David? But the
15 22 mercy on me, O Lord, thou son of David
22 43 how doth David in spirit call him Lord
45 if David then call him Lord, how is he
Mark 2 25 what David did when he had need and was
10 47 son of D. have mercy. 48; Luke 18:38, 39
11 10 blessed be the kingdom of our father D.
12 35 scribes say that Christ is the son of D.
36 David himself saith by the Holy Ghost
37 D. himself calleth him Lord. Luke 20:44
Luke 1 27 Joseph of the house of David and the
32 shall give unto him the throne of David
69 salvation to us in the house of David
3 31 Nathan who was of D. who was of Jesse
20 41 say they that Christ is the son of D.
42 David himself saith in the book of Psalms
John 7 42 Christ cometh of the seed of David
42 from Bethlehem, the town where D. was
Acts 1 16 Holy Ghost spoke before by mouth of D.
2 25 David saith concerning him: I foresaw
29 freely speak to you of patriarch David
34 David ascended not into heaven; but he
4 25 who by the mouth of our father David
7 45 God drove out . . . unto the days of D.
13 22 he raised them up David to be king: to
22 I have found David the son of Jesse
34 I will give you the holy things of D.
36 D., when he had served in his generation
15 16 I will rebuild the tabernacle of David
Rom 1 3 was made to him of the seed of David
4 6 as D. termeth the blessedness of a man
11 9 D. saith: Let their table be made a
2 Tim 2 8 again from the dead, of the seed of D.
Heb 4 7 saying in David, Today, after so long
11 32 time would fail me to tell of . . . David
Apoc 3 7 he that hath the key of David; he that
5 5 the root of David hath prevailed to
22 16 I am the root and stock of David, the

David's 1 K 18 29 and Saul became David's enemy
1 K 19 11 sent his guards to David's house to
11 when Michol David's wife had told him
20 15 require it at hands of David's enemies
16 required it at hands of D. enemies
25 and David's place appeared empty. And
27 David's place appeared empty again
21 1 Achimelech was astonished at D. coming
24 6 after which David's heart struck him
25 9 when David's servants came, they spoke
9 to Nabal all these words in D. name
40 David's servants came to Abigail to
44 gave Michol his daughter, David's wife
26 17 Saul knew David's voice, and said: Is
2 K 2 30 there were wanting of David's servants
3 22 David's servants and Joab came, after
12 5 David's anger being exceedingly kindled
30 and it was put upon David's head and
13 32 son of Semmaa David's brother answering
15 12 Achitophel . . . David's counsellor, from
16 16 Chusai the Arachite, David's friend
18 7 were defeated there by David's army
21 17 David's men swore unto him, saying
23 1 these are David's last words. David the
24 10 but David's heart struck him after the
3 K 1 8 strength of D. army was not with Adonias
5 1 Hiram had always been David's friend
15 4 for D. sake the Lord his God gave him
1 Pa 18 2 the Moabites were made D. servants
27 32 Jonathan, David's uncle, a counsellor
Ps 29 1 at the dedication of David's house
131 10 for thy servant David's sake, turn not
Mat 22 42 whose son is he? They say to him: D.
dawn Mat 28 1 when it began to dawn towards the
2 P 1 19 well to attend . . . until the day dawn
dawning Judg 19 26 woman, at the d. of the day
Job 3 9 nor the rising of the d. of the day
38 12 and show the d. of the day its place
Ps 118 147 I prevented the dawning of the day
Wisd 16 28 adore thee at the d. of the light. For
daws Bar 6 53 as daws between heaven and the earth
daylight Josu 3 1 Josue rose before daylight and
Acts 20 11 talked a long time to them, until d.
day's 3 K 19 4 went forward one day's journey
Jon 3 4 enter into the city one day's journey
1 Ma 7 45 pursued after them one day's journey
Luke 2 44 they came a day's journey and sought
Acts 1 12 Jerusalem, within sabbath day's journey
19 40 called in question for this day's uproar
days' Gen 30 36 set the space of three days' journey
Exod 3 18 we will go three days' journey. 8:27
5 3 to go three days' journey into the
Num 10 33 from mount of Lord three days' journey
Deut 1 2 eleven days' journey from Horeb by the
4 K 3 9 fetched a compass of 7 days' journey
Jon 3 3 a great city of three days' journey
1 Ma 5 24 went 3 d. journey through the desert
daytime Ps 41 9 in the d. the Lord hath commanded
Isa 4 6 shade in the daytime from the heat
Luke 21 37 in the daytime he was teaching in the
deacons Phil 1 1 with the bishops and deacons
1 Tim 3 8 deacons in like manner chaste, not
12 let deacons be husbands of one wife
deadly Num 18 22 nor commit deadly sin, but only
Mark 16 18 they shall drink any deadly thing, it
James 3 8 the tongue . . . full of deadly poison
deaf Exod 4 11 who made the dumb and the deaf
Lev 19 14 shalt not speak evil of the deaf, nor
Ps 37 14 I, as a deaf man, heard not: and as a
57 5 like the deaf asp that stoppeth her
Ecce 12 4 the daughters of music shall grow deaf
Isa 29 18 deaf shall hear the words of the book
35 5 ears of the deaf shall be unstopped

42 18 hear, ye deaf, and, ye blind, behold
19 or deaf, but he to whom I have sent
43 8 that are deaf, and have ears. All the
Mich 7 16 their ears shall be deaf. They shall
Mat 11 5 the deaf hear. Luke 7:22
Mark 7 32 bring to him one deaf and dumb; and
37 he hath made both the deaf to hear
9 24 deaf and dumb spirit, I command thee
deal Exod 21 9 he shall deal with her after the
Deut 7 5 thus rather shall you deal with them
Josu 9 25 deal with us as it seemeth good and
Ruth 1 8 the Lord deal mercifully with you, as
1 K 20 8 deal mercifully then with thy servant
2 Pa 3 5 house he ceiled with deal boards and
Ps 11 6 I will deal confidently in his regard
50 20 deal favorably, O Lord, in thy good
104 25 to deal deceitfully with his servants
118 124 deal with thy servant according to thy
Prov 12 22 they that deal faithfully please him
Eccu 29 3 keep thy word and deal faithfully with
30 he shall not deal confidently nor open
Isa 12 2 I will deal confidently and will not
58 7 deal thy bread to the hungry and bring
Jer 21 2 if so be the Lord will deal with us
Eze 8 18 I also will deal with them in my wrath
16 59 I will deal with thee, as thou hast
23 29 they shall deal with thee in hatred
31 11 of the nations, he shall deal with him
Dan 1 13 shalt see, deal with thy servants. And
3 42 deal with us according to thy meekness
11 23 he will deal deceitfully with him: and
32 such as deal wickedly against covenant
12 10 and the wicked shall deal wickedly
Osee 11 8 how shall I deal with thee, O Ephraim
Zach 8 11 I will not deal with the remnant of
1 Ma 1 61 did they deal with the people of Israel
13 46 deal not with us according to our evil
2 Ma 6 15 doth he also deal with us, so as to
7 25 her to deal with the young man to save
10 12 and to deal peaceably with them. But
Mark 10 48 he cried a great deal the more: Son of
2 C 13 10 I may not deal more severely, according
dealer Prov 14 25 double d. uttereth lies. In the
dealeth Eccu 32 19 that d. deceitfully, shall
1 C 13 4 charity envieth not, d. not perversely
Heb 12 7 God d. with you as with his sons; for
2 P 3 9 the Lord . . . dealeth patiently for
dealing Wisd 16 2 d. well with thy people, thou
Acts 7 19 this same dealing craftily with our
9 28 d. confidently in the name of the Lord
14 3 dealing confidently in the Lord, who
dealings Job 13 9 with your deceitful dealings
Prov 14 15 servant shall prosper in his dealings
dealt Exod 1 20 God d. well with the midwives
Exod 5 16 thy people is unjustly dealt withal
18 11 because they d. proudly against them
Judg 9 16 and have dealt well with Jerobaal and
19 if therefore you have dealt well and
Ruth 1 8 as you have dealt with the dead and
1 Pa 20 3 in this manner David dealt with all
2 Pa 6 37 done wickedly, we have dealt unjustly
2 Es 9 10 thou knewest that they dealt proudly
16 they and our fathers dealt proudly
29 they dealt proudly and hearkened not
Ps 5 11 they d. deceitfully with their tongues
102 10 he hath not dealt with us according to
Lam 2 20 whom thou hast thus dealt with: shall
Bar 2 27 thou hast dealt with us, O Lord our
Eze 39 24 I have dealt with them according to
Dan 13 61 as they had maliciously dealt against
Osee 6 7 they dealt treacherously against me
Mark 5 16 what manner he had been dealt with
Luke 1 25 hath the Lord d. with me [Elizabeth]
Acts 9 27 in Damascus he had d. confidently in
25 24 of the Jews dealt with me at Jerusalem
Rom 3 13 they have dealt deceitfully. The venom
dear Eccu 7 20 nor despise thy dear brother for
Eccu 7 23 let a wise servant be dear to thee
Jer 12 7 I have given my dear soul into the
Lam 1 2 among all them that were dear to her
2 Ma 14 24 and Judas was always dear to him from
Luke 7 2 who was dear to him, being sick, was
most dear Wisd 12 7 which of all is m. d. to
Mark 12 6 one son most dear to him; he also sent
Rom 11 28 most dear for the sake of the fathers
Eph 5 1 followers of God, as most d. children
Col 4 14 Luke the most dear physician saluteth
1 Th 2 8 you were become most dear unto us. For
Philem 16 instead of servant, a m. d. brother
2 P 3 15 our most dear brother Paul, according
dearest Prov 5 19 let her be thy dearest hind
Cant 7 6 how comely, my dearest, in delights
1 C 4 14 I admonish you as my dearest children
17 Timothy who is my dearest son and
Eph 6 21 Tychicus my d. brother . . . will make
Philem 2 to Appia, our dearest sister, and to
James 1 16 do not err, my dearest brethren. Every
19 you know, my dearest brethren. And let
2 5 hearken, my dearest brethren; hath not
1 J 4 11 my dearest, if God hath so loved us
dearly beloved; *see* **beloved**
death's Apoc 13 3 his death's wound was healed
deaths Num 16 38 sanctified in the deaths of the
2 Ma 8 4 most unjust deaths of innocent children
2 C 11 23 above measure, in deaths often. Of
Debara Josu 15 7 as far as the borders of Debara
debased Isa 2 9 down, and man hath been debased
Isa 57 9 and was debased even to hell. Thou
debate Job 21 4 my d. against man, that I should
Eccu 28 11 and bring in debate in the midst of
debated Num 35 24 the cause be d. between him and
debates Isa 58 4 you fast for debates and strife
debauchery Deut 21 20 giveth himself . . . to d.
Debbaseth Josu 19 11 from Merala and came to D.
Debbora Judg 4 4 at that time D. a prophetess
Judg 4 9 Debbora . . . went with Barac to Cedes
10 having Debbora in his company. Now
14 Debbora said to Barac: Arise, for this
5 1 D. and Barac son of Abinoem sung and
12 arise, arise, O Debbora, arise, arise
15 the captains of Issachar were with D.
Debelaim Osee 1 3 Gomer the daughter of Debelaim
Deblatha Eze 6 14 from the desert of Deblatha
Deblathaim Jer 48 22 upon the house of Deblathaim
Debora Gen 35 8 D. the nurse of Rebecca died and
debt 1 K 22 2 distress and oppressed with debt
2 Es 5 10 let us forgive the debt that is owing
Mat 18 27 let him go and forgave him the debt
30 into prison till he paid the debt. Now
32 I forgave thee all the debt because
34 the torturers until he paid all the d.
Rom 4 4 according to grace, but according to d.
1 C 7 3 let the husband render the debt to his
Philem 18 is in thy debt, put that to my account
debtor Eze 18 7 restored the pledge to the d.
Mat 23 16 swear by the gold of the temple, is a d.
18 swear by gift that is upon it, is a d.
Rom 1 14 wise and to the unwise I am a debtor
Gal 5 3 that he is a debtor to do the whole
debtors Isa 58 3 you exact of all your debtors
Mat 6 12 as we also forgive our debtors. And
Luke 7 41 a certain creditor had two debtors
13 4 that they also were d. above all the
16 5 calling every one of his lord's debtors
Rom 8 12 we are debtors, not to the flesh, to
15 27 they are their debtors. For if the

debts Prov 22 26 themselves sureties for debts
Mat 6 12 forgive us our debts as we also forgive
Decapolis Mat 4 25 followed . . . from Decapolis
Mark 5 20 began to publish in D. how great things
7 31 through the midst of the coasts of D.
decay Job 11 20 eyes of the wicked shall decay
Ps 48 15 their help shall d. in hell from their
1 Ma 6 57 we decay daily, and our provision of
decayed Deut 8 4 thy raiment . . . hath not decayed
2 Es 4 10 strength of the bearer of burdens is d.
Ps 11 2 truths are d. from among the children
decayeth Heb 8 13 that which d. and groweth old
decaying Gen 25 8 d. he [Abraham] died in a good
Gen 25 17 decaying he [Ismael] died, and was
2 K 3 1 but the house of Saul decaying daily
decease Tob 8 24 after their d. come also to Tobias
Eccu 33 24 in the time of thy decease, distribute
Luke 9 31 they spoke of his decease that he should
2 P 1 15 have after my d. whereby you may keep
deceased Deut 25 5 wife of the d. shall not marry
Ruth 4 5 Ruth . . . who was wife of the deceased
10 to raise up the name of the deceased
2 Ma 4 37 sobriety and modesty of the deceased
Acts 25 19 of one Jesus deceased whom Paul
deceit Job 31 5 foot hath made haste to deceit
Ps 9 7 his mouth is full . . . of deceit: under
14 3 who hath not used deceit in his tongue
51 4 as sharp razor, thou hast wrought d.
54 12 usury and deceit have not departed
Prov 5 2 mind not the deceit of a woman. For the
12 20 deceit is in the heart of them that
23 3 his meats, in which is the bread of d.
26 24 when in his heart he entertaineth d.
Wisd 4 11 or deceit beguile his soul. For the
10 11 deceit of them that overreached him
Eccu 1 40 thy heart is full of guile and deceit
15 7 she is far from pride and deceit. Lying
19 23 his interior is full of deceit: and
41 24 of deceit in giving and taking: of
Isa 53 9 neither was there deceit in his mouth
Jer 5 27 so their houses are full of deceit
6 13 all are guilty of deceit. And they
9 6 thy habitation is in the midst of d.: through
d. they have refused to know me
8 it hath spoken deceit: with his mouth
14 14 lying vision and divination and deceit
Dan 2 9 lying interpretation and full of deceit
14 17 there is not any deceit with thee. And
Osee 11 12 house of Israel with deceit: but Juda
Soph 1 9 house of Lord . . . with iniquity and d.
1 Ma 1 31 spoke to them peaceable words in deceit
7 30 that he was come to him with deceit
8 28 shall observe their orders without d.
11 1 to get the kingdom of Alexander by d.
Mark 7 22 deceit, lasciviousness, an evil eye
Acts 13 10 full of all guile and of all deceit
Rom 1 29 full of envy, murder, contention, d.
Col 2 8 cheat you by philosophy and vain deceit
1 Th 2 3 error, nor of uncleanness, nor in d.
deceitful Job 13 9 a man, with your d. dealings
Ps 5 7 bloody and the d. man the Lord will
11 3 with deceitful lips and with a double
4 may the Lord destroy all deceitful lips
16 1 which proceedeth not from d. lips
30 19 let deceitful lips be made dumb. Which
42 1 deliver me from the unjust and d. man
51 6 all the words of ruin, O d. tongue
54 24 d. men shall not live out half their
108 2 mouth of the d. man is opened against
3 have spoken against me with d. tongues
119 2 soul from wicked lips and a d. tongue
3 added to thee, to a deceitful tongue
Prov 6 19 a deceitful witness that uttereth lies
10 3 he will disappoint the d. practices of
11 1 a d. balance is an abomination before
12 5 counsels of the wicked are deceitful
17 he that lieth is a deceitful witness
27 the deceitful man shall not find gain
13 13 deceitful souls go astray in sins
14 5 but a deceitful witness uttereth a lie
15 no good shall come to the d. son: but
17 4 the deceitful hearkeneth to lying lips
20 23 a deceitful balance is not good. The
26 28 a deceitful tongue loveth not truth
27 6 than the deceitful kisses of an enemy
31 30 favor is deceitful, and beauty is vain
Wisd 1 5 will flee from the deceitful and will
Eccu 11 31 many are the snares of the deceitful
34 of one deceitful man much blood: and
27 28 the d. stroke will wound the deceitful
34 1 the hopes . . . are vain and deceitful
5 deceitful divinations and lying omens
Isa 10 6 I will send him to a deceitful nation
32 5 neither shall the d. be called great
7 vessels of the d. are most wicked: for
Jer 15 18 as the falsehood of deceitful waters
Osee 7 16 they became like a deceitful bow: their
12 7 there is a d. balance in his hand, he
Amos 8 5 may convey in deceitful balances that
Mich 6 11 and the deceitful weights of the bag
12 their tongue was d. in their mouth
Soph 3 13 nor shall a d. tongue be found in their
Mala 1 14 cursed is the d. man that hath in his
2 C 11 13 such false apostles are d. workmen
2 P 3 3 there shall come deceitful scoffers
deceitfully Gen 27 35 brother came d. and got
Gen 34 13 answered Sichem and his father d., being
Job 13 7 lie, that you should speak d. for him
Ps 5 11 they dealt d. with their tongues judge
13 3 with their tongues they acted d.; the
23 4 in vain, nor sworn d. to his neighbor
35 3 in his sight he hath done deceitfully
104 25 to deal deceitfully with his servants
Prov 11 13 that walked d., revealeth secrets: but
20 19 that revealeth secrets and walketh d.
26 19 man that hurteth his friend deceitfully
26 he that covereth hatred deceitfully
Eccu 32 19 that dealeth d., shall meet with a
Isa 32 6 and speak to the Lord deceitfully and
Jer 6 28 they walk d., they are brass and iron
9 4 every friend will walk deceitfully
48 10 he that doth the work of the Lord d.
Dan 11 23 he will deal deceitfully with him: and
32 the covenant shall deceitfully dissemble
34 many shall be joined to them d. And
1 Ma 7 10 his brethren with peaceable words d.
27 to Judas . . . d. with friendly words
13 17 knew that he spoke deceitfully to him
16 15 the son of Abobus received them d.
Rom 3 13 they have dealt deceitfully. The venom
deceitfulness Prov 11 3 d. of the wicked shall
Eccu 37 3 the earth with thy malice and d. There
2 Ma 13 3 with great d. besought Antiochus, not
Mat 13 22 the d. of riches choketh up the word
Mark 4 19 the d. of riches . . . choke the word
Heb 3 13 be hardened through d. of sin. For we
deceits Job 15 35 and his womb prepareth deceits
Ps 37 13 and studied deceits all the day long
49 19 and thy tongue framed deceits. Sitting
72 18 for deceits thou hast put it to them
Prov 1 18 practice d. against their own souls
24 2 their lips speak deceits to be with
Eccu 10 8 wrongs and injuries and divers deceits
Eph 6 11 to stand against d. of the devil. For
deceive Exod 8 29 but do not deceive any more
Lev 19 11 neither shall any man deceive his

Judg 16 5 deceive him [Samson] and learn of him
13 how long dost thou [Samson] d. me
2 K 3 25 he came to thee that he might d. thee
3 K 22 20 who shall d. Achab king of Israel
21 and said: I will deceive him [Achab]
22 thou shalt d. him [Achab] and shalt
4 K 4 28 did I not say to thee: Do not d. me
18 29 let not Ezechias d. you: for he shall
19 10 let not thy God deceive thee, in whom
2 Pa 18 19 who shall deceive Achab king of Israel
20 before the Lord and said: I will d. him
20 by what means wilt thou deceive him
21 thou shalt deceive and shalt prevail
32 11 doth not Ezechias deceive you, to give
15 therefore let not Ezechias deceive you
Jdth 16 10 she took a new robe to deceive him
Ps 61 10 that by vanity they may together d.
Prov 7 10 in harlot's attire prepared to d. souls
12 26 way of the wicked shall deceive them
24 28 and deceive not any man with thy lips
Eccu 13 7 need of thee, he will deceive thee
Isa 3 12 d. thee and destroy the way of thy
36 14 let not Ezechias deceive you, for he
37 10 let not thy God deceive thee, in whom
Jer 23 16 that prophesy to you and deceive you
29 8 let not your prophets . . . deceive you
37 8 deceive not your souls, saying: My
Osee 9 2 and the wind shall deceive them and
Mich 1 14 to deceive the kings of Israel. Yet
Zach 13 4 garment of sackcloth, to deceive: but
1 Ma 7 14 is a priest . . . he will not deceive us
2 Ma 3 12 to d. them who had trusted to the place
Mat 24 24 to deceive, if possible, even the elect
Mark 13 5 take heed lest any man deceive you
6 they shall deceive many. And when you
1 C 3 18 let no man deceive himself: if any man
Eph 4 14 by which they lie in wait to deceive
5 6 let no man d. you. 2 Th 2:3; 1 J 3:7
Col 2 4 that no man may d. you by loftiness
1 J 1 8 if we say that we have no sin, we d.
deceived Gen 3 13 the serpent d. me, and I did eat
Gen 26 10 why hast thou [Isaac] deceived us
Num 25 18 deceived you by the idol Phogor and
31 16 that deceived the children of Israel
Deut 4 16 being d., you might make you a graven
19 being d. by error thou adore and serve
25 being deceived, make to yourselves
11 16 lest perhaps your heart be deceived
30 17 being d. with error thou adore strange
Judg 11 35 hast d. me, and thou thyself art d.
1 K 19 17 Saul said . . . why hast thou d. me so
28 12 to Saul: Why hast thou deceived me
3 K 13 18 he d. him and brought him back with
Job 12 16 both the deceiver and him that is d.
13 9 shall he be deceived as a man, with
15 31 not believe, being vainly d. by error
21 9 if my heart hath been deceived upon
Ps 76 3 to him in the night, and I was not d.
Prov 5 23 multitude of his folly he shall be d.
7 25 neither be thou deceived with her paths
Ecce 2 2 to mirth I said: Why art thou vainly d.
7 6 than to be d. by the flattery of fools
Wisd 2 21 these things they thought, and were d.
11 16 some being deceived worshipped dumb
15 4 of mischievous men hath not deceived
Eccu 3 26 suspicion of them hath deceived many
13 10 that thou be not deceived into folly
11 humbled thou be deceived into folly
26 when a rich man hath been d., he hath
27 the poor man was deceived and he is
34 7 dreams have d. many, and they have
Isa 19 13 they have d. Egypt, the stay of the
47 10 thy knowledge, this hath deceived thee
Jer 4 10 hast thou then d. this people and
20 7 thou hast d. me, O Lord, and I am d.
10 if by any means he may be deceived
23 13 they prophesied in Baal and d. my
28 22 thy men of peace have deceived thee
42 20 you have deceived your own souls: for
49 16 thy arrogancy hath deceived thee and
Lam 1 19 my friends, but they deceived me: my
Eze 13 10 they have deceived my people, saying
14 9 I the Lord have d. that prophet: and
45 20 and hath been deceived by error and
Dan 13 56 beauty hath d. thee, and lust hath
14 6 O king, be not deceived: for this
Osee 4 12 spirit of fornication hath d. them
Abdi 7 men of thy confederacy have d. thee
2 Ma 1 13 d. by the counsel of the priests of
6 25 time of a corruptible life, should be d.
7 18 be not deceived without cause: for we
12 24 by his death might happen to be d.
Gal 6 7 be not deceived. God is not mocked
Apoc 18 23 have been deceived by thy enchantments
deceivers Job 12 16 he knoweth both the d. and
2 C 6 8 as deceivers, and yet true; as unknown
deceiveth 4 K 18 32 not to Ezechias, who d. you
Jdth 5 28 that Achior . . . may know that he d. us
Job 12 24 d. them that they walk in vain where
Ps 14 4 sweareth to his neighbor and d. not
Prov 11 9 the dissembler . . . deceiveth his friend
24 12 nothing deceiveth the keeper of thy
28 10 he that d. the just in a wicked way
23 that by a flattering tongue d. him
Haba 2 5 as wine deceiveth him that drinketh it
Gal 6 3 whereas he is nothing, he d. himself
deceiving Wisd 14 21 the occasion of d. human life
James 1 22 not hearers only, d. your ownselves
26 deceiving his own heart, this man's
decent 1 C 7 35 for that which is decent and which
1 Tim 2 9 women also in decent apparel: adorning
decently 1 C 14 40 let all things be done decently
decide Judg 11 27 Lord be judge and d. this day
2 Ma 15 17 that valor might decide the matter
decided Deut 21 5 every matter should be decided
Acts 19 39 it may be d. in a lawful assembly. For
decked Ps 143 12 their daughters d. out, adorned
Isa 61 10 a bridegroom decked with a crown and
Jer 10 4 he hath decked it with silver and gold
Eze 16 11 I decked thee also with ornaments and
23 41 and a table was decked before thee
Osee 2 13 decked herself out with her earrings
deckest Jer 4 30 though thou deckest thyself with
Decla Gen 10 27 Jectan begot . . . Uzal and Decla
1 Pa 1 21 Jectan begot . . . Decla and Adoram and
declaration Ps 118 130 d. of thy words giveth
Eccu 43 6 for a declaration of times and a sign of
1 J 1 5 the declaration which we have heard
3 11 this is the d. which you have heard
declarations 2 Ma 2 32 to avoid nice d. of things
declare Lev 13 6 he shall d. him clean, because
Lev 13 11 shall d. him unclean. 20, 25, 27
30 he shall declare them unclean, because
Num 18 26 the Levites and declare unto them
Deut 32 7 ask thy father, and he will d. to thee
Judg 14 12 which if you declare unto me within
13 if you shall not be able to declare it
3 K 22 13 declare good things to the king: let
1 Pa 16 24 declare his glory among the Gentiles
17 10 I d. to thee that the Lord will build
2 Pa 18 12 with one month d. good to the king
Tob 13 4 that you may d. his wonderful works
Job 33 23 an angel . . . to d. man's uprightness
38 37 who can d. the order of the heavens
Ps 9 12 declare his ways among the Gentiles
15 that I may declare all thy praises

21 23 I will declare thy name to my brethren
29 10 dust confess to thee, or d. thy truth
37 19 I will declare my iniquity: and I will
49 6 the heavens shall declare his justice
16 why dost thou declare my justices, and
50 17 and my mouth shall declare thy praise
54 18 and at noon I will speak and declare
70 17 till now I will d. thy wonderful works
72 28 that I may declare all thy praises
74 10 I will declare forever: I will sing to
77 6 and declare them to their children
87 12 any one in the sepulcher d. thy mercy
95 3 declare his glory among the Gentiles
101 22 that they may d. the name of the Lord
24 declare unto me the fewness of my days
104 1 declare his deeds among the Gentiles
105 2 who shall declare the powers of the Lord
106 22 and declare his works with joy. They
117 17 shall declare the works of the Lord
141 3 and before him I declare my trouble
144 4 and they shall declare thy power. They
6 acts: and shall declare thy greatness
Wisd 6 24 what wisdom is . . . I will declare: and
Eccu 1 30 lips of many shall declare his wisdom
16 22 works of his justice who shall declare
25 and will seek to declare wisdom: and
17 8 might d. the glorious things of his
18 2 who is able to declare his works? For
4 shall be able to declare his mercy
24 44 and I will declare it afar off. I will
31 11 church of the saints shall declare his
36 10 they may declare thy wonderful works
13 and may declare thy great works: and
38 38 neither shall they declare discipline
39 14 nations shall declare his wisdom and
16 I will yet meditate that I may declare
42 15 I will declare the things I have seen
17 to declare all his wonderful words
43 35 who shall see him and declare him? and
44 15 let . . . the church declare their praise
Isa 42 9 new things do I declare: before they
12 shall d. his praise in the islands
43 9 who among you can declare this, and
44 7 like to me? Let him call and declare
45 19 justice, that declare right things
48 20 declare it with the voice of joy: make
53 8 who shall d. his generation? because
57 12 I will declare thy justice, and thy
66 19 they shall d. my glory to the Gentiles
Jer 4 5 declare ye in Juda, and make it heard
5 20 declare ye this to the house of Jacob
9 12 may come that he may declare this, why
31 10 declare it in the islands that are
38 15 if I shall declare it to thee, wilt
42 4 I will declare it to you: and I will
20 declare unto us, and we will do it
46 14 declare ye to Egypt and publish it
50 2 d. ye among the nations and publish
28 to declare in Sion the revenge of his
29 declare to many against Babylon, to all
51 10 let us declare in Sion the work of
Bar 6 1 to declare to them according to what
Eze 3 18 thou declare it not to him nor speak
12 16 that they may declare all their wicked
13 20 I d. against your cushions wherewith
20 4 declare to them the abominations of
23 36 declare to them their wicked deeds
40 4 declare all that thou seest, to the
Dan 2 2 to declare to the king his dreams: so
4 we will declare the interpretation. 7
16 question and declare it to the king
27 the soothsayers can declare to the
4 15 are not able to declare the meaning
5 8 nor declare the interpretation to the
15 could not declare to me the meaning
13 11 ashamed to declare to one another their
Mich 1 10 declare ye it not in Geth, weep ye
3 8 to declare unto Jacob his wickedness
Zach 9 12 thee double as I declare today. Because
2 Ma 3 34 d. unto all men the great works and
4 17 the time following will declare
9 17 the earth and declare the power of God
14 39 to declare the hatred that he bore
Acts 8 33 his generation, who shall declare
13 32 we declare unto you that the promise
20 27 I have not spared to declare unto you
1 C 3 13 the day of the Lord shall declare it
Heb 2 12 I will declare thy name to my brethren
1 P 2 9 that you may declare his virtues, who
1 J 1 2 we declare unto you the life eternal
5 this is the declaration which we . . . d.
declared Gen 43 3 the man declared unto us with
Gen 43 5 declared . . . You shall not see my face
Exod 19 7 he [Moses] declared all the words of
Deut 20 8 after these things are declared they
Judg 14 19 gave to them that had d. the riddle
Jdth 6 14 when Achior had d. all these things
Job 28 27 he saw it and declared and prepared
Ps 21 32 there shall be declared to the Lord a
39 6 I have declared and I have spoken: they
10 I have d. thy justice in a great church
11 I have d. thy truth and thy salvation
43 2 our fathers have declared to us the work
55 9 I have declared to thee my life: thou
63 10 and they declared the works of God
96 6 the heavens declared his justice: and
118 26 I have d. my ways, and thou hast heard
Ecce 12 9 declared the things that he had done
Cant 6 8 saw her and declared her most blessed
Isa 21 10 I have declared unto you. The burden
41 26 who hath d. from the beginning, that
43 12 I have declared and have saved. I have
44 8 made thee to hear and have declared
45 21 who hath d. this from the beginning
48 3 the former things of old I have d.
6 heard: but have you declared them. I
14 who among them hath d. these things
Jer 42 21 I have declared it to you this day
Osee 4 12 their staff hath declared unto them
1 Ma 4 20 the smoke . . . declared what was done
2 Ma 3 9 d. the cause for which he was come
16 d. the inward sorrow of his mind. For
7 6 as Moses d. in the profession of the
Luke 8 47 declared before all the people for
John 1 18 in bosom of the Father, he hath d. him
Acts 11 4 declared to them the matter in order
Rom 9 17 that my name may be declared throughout
2 Th 3 10 this we declared to you: that, if any
Heb 2 3 having begun to be d. by the Lord, was
4 2 unto us also it hath been declared
1 P 1 12 things which are now declared to you
Apoc 10 7 as he hath declared by his servants
declareth Ps 18 2 firmament d. the work of his
Ps 147 19 who declareth his word to Jacob: his
Eccu 25 12 declareth justice to an ear that heareth
42 19 he d. the things that are past and
Amos 4 13 and declareth his word to man, he that
Acts 17 30 now d. unto men that all should every
declaring Num 30 15 defer the d. his mind till
Judg 11 27 wrongest me by d. an unjust war against
Ps 77 4 d. the praises of the Lord and his
Jer 4 15 a voice of one declaring from Dan and
Bar 6 25 declaring to men how vile they are
Acts 15 4 d. how great things God had done with
17 3 declaring . . . the Christ was to suffer
19 18 confessing and declaring their deeds

1 C 2 1 d. unto you the testimony of Christ
decline Deut 17 11 neither shalt thou d. to the
Deut 17 20 nor decline to the right or to the
Ps 26 9 d. not in thy wrath from thy servant
36 27 decline from evil and do good, and
118 21 who d. from thy commandments. Remove
Prov 4 5 neither d. from the words of my mouth
27 decline not to the right hand nor to
13 14 that he may d. from the ruin of death
14 27 to decline from the ruin of death. In
15 24 that he may d. from the lowest hell
18 5 to decline from the truth of judgment
Eccu 9 13 lest thy heart decline towards her
12 14 if thou begin to d., he will not endure
Luke 9 12 the day began to decline. And the 12
1 P 3 11 let him decline from evil and do good
declined 3 K 22 43 [Josaphat] d. not from it: and
2 Pa 34 2 declined not neither to the right hand
Job 23 11 kept his way and have not d. from it
Ps 101 12 my days have declined like a shadow
118 51 but I declined not from thy law. I
102 I have not declined from thy judgments
157 but I have not d. from thy testimonies
Isa 29 21 and declined in vain from the just
Jer 6 4 woe unto us, for the day is declined
declineth Ps 108 23 like the shadow when it d.
Prov 14 16 a wise man feareth and d. from evil
15 27 every one declineth from evil. The
declining Judg 19 9 consider that the day is d.
1 Tim 5 21 by declining to either side. Impose
decoyed Osee 7 11 become as a dove that is decoyed
decrease Ps 106 38 cattle he suffered not to d.
Isa 60 20 and thy moon shall not decrease: for
John 3 30 but I must decrease. He that cometh
decreaseth Eccu 43 7 that d. in her perfection
decreasing Gen 8 5 waters were going and d. until
decree Deut 17 12 d. of the judge, that man shall
Judg 19 30 decree in common what ought to be done
1 Es 5 13 king Cyrus set forth a decree, that
6 11 and I have made a decree: That if any
12 I Darius have made the decree which I
Job 22 28 thou shalt decree a thing, and it shall
Ps 148 6 made a decree, and it shall not pass
Prov 8 15 lawgivers decree just things, by me
16 by me . . . the mighty decree justice
31 9 decree that which is just and do justice
Dan 2 13 decree being gone forth, the wise men
3 10 decree that every man that shall hear
12 have slighted thy decree: they worship
96 by me therefore this decree is made
4 3 I set forth a decree, that all the
14 this is the decree by the sentence of
6 7 that imperial decree . . . be published
8 confirm the sentence and sign the d.
9 king Darius set forth the decree and
12 according to the d. of the Medes and
12 nor the decree that thou hast made
15 no decree which the king hath made
Soph 2 2 before the decree bring forth the day
2 Ma 6 8 went out a d. into the neighboring
10 8 ordained by a common statute and d.
11 36 that we may decree as it is convenient
12 4 according to the common d. of the city
15 36 they all ordained by a common decree
Luke 2 1 there went out a decree from Caesar
Col 2 14 blotting out handwriting of the decree
20 why do you yet decree as though living
decreed 3 K 20 40 judgment, which thyself hast d.
2 Pa 30 2 decreed to keep the phase the second
5 they decreed to send messengers to all
1 Es 5 17 whether it hath been decreed by Cyrus
6 3 Cyrus the king decreed that the house
7 13 it is decreed by me that all they of
21 have ordered and d. to all the keepers
Isa 14 27 the Lord of hosts hath decreed, and
Dan 6 8 what is d. by the Medes and Persians
12 hast thou not decreed that every man
26 it is decreed by me, that in all my
1 Ma 4 59 d. that the days of the dedication
13 38 we have decreed in your favor, shall
14 26 they d. him liberty and registered
2 Ma 4 11 which had been d. of special favor
11 25 d. that the temple should be restored
Acts 4 28 thy counsel d. to be done. And now
16 4 that were decreed by the apostles and
decreeing Acts 21 25 d. that they should only
decrees Acts 16 4 delivered unto them the decrees
Acts 17 7 do contrary to the decrees of Caesar
Eph 2 15 the law of commandments contained in d.
decrepit Eccu 41 4 who is in a d. age and that
Dedan Jer 25 23 Dedan and Thema and Buz, and all
Jer 49 8 into deep hole, ye inhabitants of D.
Eze 25 13 they that are in Dedan shall fall by
27 15 the men of Dedan were thy merchants. 20
38 13 Saba and Dedan and the merchants of
Dedanim Isa 21 13 shall sleep, in the paths of D.
dedicate Deut 20 5 lest . . . another man d. it
2 Pa 2 4 to dedicate it, to burn incense before
2 Ma 14 33 I will d. this temple to Bacchus. And
dedicated Exod 35 29 d. voluntary offerings to
Deut 20 5 new house and hath not dedicated it
2 K 8 11 and king David d. them to the Lord
11 and gold that he had d. of all the
3 K 7 51 the things that David his father had d.
8 63 so the king . . . d. the temple of the
15 15 the things which his father had d.
4 K 12 18 the kings of Juda had d. to holy uses
1 Pa 10 10 his armor they d. in the temple of
26 26 which king David . . . had dedicated, out
2 Pa 7 5 king and all the people d. the house
15 8 [Asa] dedicated the altar of the Lord
23 9 which he had dedicated in the house of
24 7 things that had been dedicated in the
31 14 things dedicated for the holy of holies
1 Ma 4 54 in the same was it dedicated anew with
1 C 16 15 have d. themselves to the ministry
Heb 9 18 neither was the first d. without blood
10 20 a new and living way which he hath d.
dedication Num 7 10 princes offered for d. of the
Num 7 11 their gifts for the dedication of the
84 in the dedication of the altar. 88
2 Pa 7 9 dedication of the altar seven days
1 Es 6 16 kept the dedication of the house of God
17 and they offered at the dedication
2 Es 12 27 at dedication of the wall of Jerusalem
27 to keep the dedication and to rejoice
Ps 29 1 at the dedication of David's house
Dan 3 2 come to the dedication of the statue. 3
1 Ma 4 56 they kept the d. of the altar eight
59 day of the d. of the altar should be
2 Ma 2 9 he offered the sacrifice of the d.
12 Solomon also celebrated the d. eight
20 concerning . . . the d. of the altar
John 10 22 it was the feast of the dedication
deed Gen 11 6 till they accomplish them in deed
Num 13 28 in very deed floweth with milk and
30 5 swore, she shall fulfil in deed. But
Josu 23 15 as he hath fulfilled in deed what he
2 Pa 6 4 who hath accomplished in deed that
Esth 1 17 this deed of the queen will go abroad
Job 34 12 in very deed God will not condemn
Ps 57 2 if in very deed you speak justice
Jer 3 23 in very deed the hills were liars
32 11 the deed of the purchase. 12, 14, 16
14 is sealed up and this deed that is open
Mat 12 12 lawful to do a good deed on sabbath

John 17 8 known in very deed that I came out from
Acts 4 9 the good deed to the infirm man, by
10 34 in very deed I perceive that God is not
12 11 I know in very deed that the Lord hath
18 14 an heinous deed, O Jews, I should with
Rom 15 18 obedience of Gentiles by word and deed
1 C 5 2 taken away . . . that hath done this deed
2 C 8 11 perform ye it also in deed; that as
Philem 14 that thy good deed might not be as it
James 1 25 this man shall be blessed in his deed
1 J 2 5 in him in very deed the charity of God
3 18 nor in tongue, but in deed and in truth
deeds 2 K 23 20 most valiant man, of great deeds
1 Es 9 13 upon us for our most wicked deeds and
Job 36 9 shall show them . . . their wicked deeds
Ps 104 1 declare his deeds among the Gentiles
Ecce 8 14 as though they had the d. of the just
Wisd 11 21 persecuted by their own deeds, and
Eccu 5 3 who shall bring me under for my deeds
10 6 do thou nothing by deeds of injury
12 1 shall be much thanks for thy good deeds
18 15 in thy good deeds, make no complaint
20 17 shall be no thanks for his good deeds
26 3 be given . . . to a man for his good d.
35 24 to men according to their deeds: and
44 10 whose godly deeds have not failed: good
Isa 50 1 for your wicked deeds have I put your
Jer 6 29 their wicked deeds are not consumed
25 14 I will repay them according to their d.
32 44 and deeds shall be written and sealed
Bar 2 33 stiff neck and from their wicked deeds
Eze 12 16 they may declare all their wicked deeds
16 43 not done according to thy wicked deeds
20 43 all your wicked d. which you committed
44 nor according to your wicked deeds
23 36 thou declare to them their wicked deeds
36 31 your wicked deeds shall displease you
1 Ma 13 46 not with us according to our evil deeds
16 23 worthy deeds which he bravely achieved
Luke 23 41 we receive due reward of our deeds
Acts 7 22 mighty in his words and in his deeds
19 18 confessing and declaring their deeds
Rom 8 13 if you mortify the deeds of the flesh
2 C 12 12 signs and wonders and mighty deeds
Col 3 9 of the old man with his deeds, and
1 Tim 5 25 good deeds are manifest: and they that
1 P 4 19 commend their souls in good deeds to
Apoc 2 6 thou hatest the deeds of the Nicolaites
22 except they do penance from their deeds
deemed Acts 27 27 shipmen d. that they discovered
deep Gen 1 2 darkness was upon face of the deep
Gen 2 21 cast a deep sleep upon Adam: and when
7 11 fountains of the great deep were broken
8 2 fountains also of the deep . . . were shut
15 12 a deep sleep fell upon Abram and a
45 26 as it were out of a deep sleep, yet
49 25 with the blessings of the deep that
Exod 14 25 and they were carried into the deep
Deut 8 7 in . . . the hills deep rivers break out
33 13 and of the deep that lieth beneath
Judg 4 21 passing from deep sleep to death, he
1 K 26 12 a deep sleep from the Lord was fallen
Jdth 9 8 the deep held their feet and the waters
Job 4 13 when deep sleep is wont to hold men
12 22 discovereth deep things out of darkness
33 15 night when deep sleep falleth upon men
38 16 walked in the lowest parts of the deep
30 the surface of the deep is congealed
41 22 he shall make the deep sea to boil
23 he shall esteem the deep as growing old
Ps 35 7 thy judgments are a great deep. Men
63 7 man shall come to a deep heart: and
68 3 I stick fast in the mire of the deep
15 that hate me, and out of the deep waters
16 nor the deep swallow me up: and let
77 15 to drink, as out of the great deep
91 6 thy thoughts are exceeding deep. The
103 6 the deep like a garment in its clothing
106 24 works of Lord and his wonders in the d.
Prov 13 15 in the way of scorners is a deep pit
18 4 words from the mouth . . . as deep water
19 15 slothfulness casteth into a deep sleep
20 5 in the heart of a man is like deep water
22 14 mouth of a strange woman is a deep pit
23 27 a harlot is a deep ditch: and a strange
Wisd 4 3 bastard slips shall not take deep root
16 11 lest falling into deep forgetfulness
19 7 out of the great deep a springing field
Eccu 16 18 deep and all the earth and the things
22 8 waketh a man out of a deep sleep. He
23 28 the bottom of the deep and looking into
24 8 penetrated into the bottom of the deep
39 counsels more deep than the great ocean
42 18 he hath searched out the deep and the
43 25 with his thought he appeaseth the deep
Isa 29 10 for you the spirit of a deep sleep
15 woe to you that are deep of heart, to
30 33 Topheth is prepared . . . deep and wide
44 27 who say to the deep: Be thou desolate
51 10 dried . . . the water of the mighty deep
63 13 that led them out through the deep
Jer 49 8 go down into the d. hole, ye inhabitants
30 get away speedily, sit in deep holes
Eze 23 32 drink thy sister's cup, deep and wide
26 19 and shall bring the deep upon thee
31 4 the deep set him up on high, the streams
15 I covered him with the deep: and I
47 5 so as to make a deep torrent which
Dan 2 22 revealeth deep and hidden things and
Amos 7 4 it devoured the great deep and ate up
Jon 1 5 the ship, and fell into a deep sleep
2 4 hast cast me forth into the deep in
6 the deep hath closed me round about
Haba 3 10 the deep put forth its voice: the deep lifted up its hands
2 Ma 1 19 where there was a deep pit without
12 4 when they were gone forth into the deep
Luke 5 4 launch out into the deep and let down
6 48 digged deep and laid the foundation
John 4 11 and the well is deep; from whence
Acts 20 9 oppressed with a d. sleep, as Paul was
Rom 10 7 who shall descend into the deep? that
1 C 2 10 Spirit searcheth . . . deep things of God
2 C 8 2 their very deep poverty hath abounded
deeper Job 11 8 he is d. than hell, and how wilt
deepest Job 17 16 shall go down into the d. pit
Wisd 17 13 from the lowest and deepest hell, slept
deeply Ecce 12 11 goads and as nails d. fastened
Isa 31 6 return as you had deeply revolted, O
Osee 9 9 they have sinned deeply, as in the
Mark 8 12 sighing deeply in spirit, he saith
deepness Mat 13 5 they had no d. of earth. And
deeps Ps 134 6 he hath done . . . in all the d.
Ps 148 7 the earth, ye dragons, and all ye d.
defaced Eze 6 6 your works shall be defaced. And
defamed Deut 22 19 because he hath defamed by a
defeat 2 K 15 34 shalt d. the counsel of Achitophel
2 K 17 2 I will defeat him [David]: and when
Jer 19 7 I will defeat the counsel of Juda and
defeated Gen 14 15 d. them and pursued them as far
Gen 36 35 who defeated the Madianites in the
Josu 7 5 were d. by the men of the city of Hai
11 8 they defeated them and chased them
Judg 1 5 they defeated the Chanaanite and the
17 they together d. the Chanaanites that
12 4 the men of Galaad defeated Ephraim

20 35 the Lord d. them before the children of
1 K 4 3 why hath the Lord defeated us today
14 48 [Saul] d. Amalec and delivered Israel
19 8 [David] d. them with a great slaughter
2 K 5 20 to Baal Pharisim and d. them there
8 1 David d. the Philistines. 1 Pa 18:1
2 [David] d. Moab and measured. 1 Pa 18:2
3 David defeated also Adarezer. 1 Pa 18:3
9 heard that David had d. all. 1 Pa 18:9
10 fought against Adarezer and had d. him
17 14 profitable counsel of Achitophel was d.
18 7 the people of Israel were d. there by
23 12 and defeated the Philistines: and the
4 K 3 24 but Israel rising up defeated Moab
8 21 and defeated the Edomites. 2 Pa 8:2
1 Pa 1 46 and he [Adad] defeated the Madianites
14 11 Baalpharasim, David defeated them there
16 d. the army of the Philistines, slaying
18 10 that he had d. and overthrown Adarezer
2 Pa 28 5 the king of Syria, who defeated him
2 Es 4 15 God defeated their counsel. And we
Jdth 15 4 defeated all that they could find
Isa 8 10 counsel together, and it shall be d.
Jer 46 2 defeated in the fourth year of Joakim
1 Ma 7 43 the army of Nicanor was defeated and
8 5 they had defeated in battle Philip
12 31 Zabadeans: and he defeated them and
14 3 defeated the army of Demetrius: and
defect Deut 12 15 unclean . . . having blemish or d.
defective Eccu 42 25 he hath made nothing d. He
defence Jdth 7 8 but the mountains are their d.
Ps 21 20 look towards my defence. Deliver, O
58 18 thou art God my defence: my God my
Ecce 7 13 as wisdom is a d., so money is a d.
Eccu 6 14 a faithful friend is a strong defence
30 shall her fetters be a strong defence
34 19 a defence from the heat and a cover
1 Ma 4 61 might have a defence against Idumea
14 37 therein Jews for the d. of the country
2 Ma 15 11 not with defence of shield and spear
1 C 9 3 my d. with them that do examine me
2 C 7 11 yea defence, yea indignation, yea fear
Phil 1 7 in the defence and confirmation of
16 I am set for the defence of the gospel
defend Judg 9 51 the tower to defend themselves
1 K 11 3 if there be no one to defend us, we
1 Es 8 22 to defend us from the enemy in the way
Jdth 5 25 because their God will defend them
Ps 19 3 defend thee out of Sion. May he be
58 2 d. me from them that rise up against me
Wisd 2 18 true son of God, he will defend him
5 17 with his holy arm he will defend them
Isa 1 17 for the fatherless, defend the widow
Jer 15 15 d. me from them that persecute me, do
15 do not defend me in thy patience: know
50 34 he will defend their cause in judgment
Bar 6 11 these gods cannot defend themselves
defended Judg 3 31 [Samgar] also defended Israel
2 K 23 12 midst of field and d. it. 1 Pa 11:14
Jdth 6 2 Israel is defended by their God, to
Wisd 10 12 and she defended him from seducers
Eccu 28 23 that is defended from a wicked tongue
2 Ma 4 2 from the city and defended his nation
Acts 7 24 he [Moses] defended him; and striking
defender Jdth 6 13 the God of heaven is their d.
Eccu 30 6 he left behind him a defender of his
Isa 19 20 he shall send them a Savior and a d.
63 1 I that . . . am a defender to save. Why
2 Ma 14 34 that was ever the d. of their nation
defending Exod 2 17 d. the maids, watered their
Eccu 19 9 as it were d. thy sin, he will hate
Rom 2 15 or also defending one another, in the
defer Num 30 15 defer the declaring his mind till
2 K 2 26 how long dost thou defer to bid the
Ecce 5 3 if thou hast vowed . . . d. not to pay
Eccu 4 3 defer not to give to him that is in
5 8 and defer it not from day to day. For
deferred Gen 34 22 for which so great a good is d.
Deut 32 27 for wrath of the enemies I have d. it
Prov 13 12 hope that is d. afflicteth the soul
deferreth Prov 29 11 a wise man d. and keepeth it
deferring Eccu 7 20 against thy friend d. money
defied 1 K 17 10 I have d. the bands of Israel
1 K 17 45 of armies of Israel, which thou hast d.
2 K 23 9 when they defied the Philistines and
defile Gen 49 4 and didst defile his couch. Simeon
Lev 7 18 soul shall defile itself with such meat
21 or of anything that can defile and
11 37 fall upon seed corn, it shall not d. it
43 do not defile your souls, nor touch
44 defile not your souls by any creeping
18 21 nor defile the name of thy God: I am
24 defile not yourselves. Eze 20:7
20 10 defile his neighbor's wife, let them
25 defile not your souls with beasts, or
21 12 lest he d. the sanctuary of the Lord
23 he must not defile my sanctuary. I am
22 2 d. not the name of the things sanctified
Num 5 3 out of the camp, lest they defile it
35 33 defile not the land of your habitation
Deut 21 23 thou shalt not defile thy land which
2 Es 13 29 that defile the priesthood and the law
Jdth 9 11 defile the dwelling place of thy name
Cant 5 3 washed my feet, how shall I d. them
Eccu 21 31 talebearer shall defile his own soul
Isa 30 22 thou shalt defile the plates of thy
Jer 32 34 set their idols . . . to defile it. And
Eze 7 21 a prey, and they shall defile it. And
22 shall enter into it and defile it. Make
9 7 defile the house, and fill the courts
20 31 defile yourselves with all your idols
39 defile my holy name any more with your
22 3 idols against herself, to defile herself
28 7 and they shall defile thy beauty. They
44 7 sanctuary, and to defile my house: and
Dan 11 31 and they shall defile the sanctuary
2 Ma 6 2 defile the temple that was in Jerusalem
Mat 15 18 defile a man. 20; Mark 7:15, 20, 23
20 to eat with unwashed hands doth not d.
Mark 7 15 nothing from without . . . can d. him
18 entering into a man cannot defile him
1 Tim 1 10 who defile themselves with mankind
Jude 8 these men also defile the flesh and
defiled Gen 37 27 that our hands be not defiled
Exod 20 25 a tool upon it, it shall be defiled
Lev 5 3 wherewith he is wont to be defiled
7 20 if any one that is defiled shall eat
11 24 touch the carcasses . . . shall be d.
26 he that toucheth it, shall be defiled
27 touch their carcasses shall be defiled
32 carcasses shall fall, it shall be d.
33 an earthen vessel . . . shall be defiled
36 toucheth their carcasses shall be d.
38 it shall be forthwith defiled. If any
13 15 shall be d. and shall be reckoned and
44 whosoever shall be d. with leprosy
45 he shall cry out that he is defiled
15 21 days of her separation, shall be d.
23 shall be d. until the evening. 17:15
24 on which he shall sleep shall be d.
26 on which she sitteth, shall be defiled
31 shall have defiled my tabernacle that
32 and that is defiled by copulation. And
18 20 nor be defiled with mingling of seed
23 neither shalt thou be defiled with it
24 with which all the nations have been d.

25 with which the land is defiled: the
27 of the land . . . and have defiled it
30 be not defiled therein. I am the Lord
19 8 hath d. the holy thing of the Lord
29 lest the land be defiled and filled
31 of soothsayers, to be defiled by them
20 3 hath defiled my sanctuary and profaned
21 11 father or his mother, shall be defiled
14 divorced or defiled or a harlot, he
22 8 shall not eat nor be defiled therewith
9 when they shall have defiled it. I am
25 they are all corrupted and defiled
Num 5 2 or is defiled by the dead: whether it
14 who either is defiled or is charged
19 if thou be not defiled by forsaking thy
20 if thou . . . art defiled and hast lain
27 if she be defiled and having despised
28 if she be not defiled, she shall not be
29 aside from her husband and be defiled
6 9 head of his consecration shall be d.
19 18 that are d. with touching any such
Deut 23 10 that is defiled in a dream by night
24 4 again to wife: because she is defiled
Josu 7 12 he is defiled with the anathema. I
13 that is defiled with this wickedness
1 K 21 5 this way is defiled, but it shall also
4 K 23 8 he defiled the high places, where the
10 he d. Topheth, which is in the valley
13 children of Ammon, the king defiled
16 burnt them upon the altar, and d. it
1 Pa 5 1 forasmuch as he defiled his father's
2 Pa 29 19 which king Achaz in his reign had d.
36 14 and they defiled the house of the Lord
Tob 1 12 and never was defiled with their meats
Jdth 9 2 against strangers, who had d. by their
13 20 not suffered his handmaid to be defiled
Ps 54 21 they have defiled his covenant, they
73 7 they have defiled the dwelling place
78 1 they have defiled thy holy temple: they
105 39 and was defiled with their works: and
Wisd 7 25 no defiled thing cometh into her. For
Eccu 13 1 toucheth pitch, shall be d. with it
22 15 shalt not be defiled with his sin. Turn
47 22 stained thy glory and d. thy seed so
Isa 14 19 as an unprofitable branch defiled and
59 3 your hands are defiled with blood and
Jer 2 7 entered in, you defiled my land and
3 1 that woman be polluted and defiled
9 she defiled the land and played the
13 22 the soles of thy feet are defiled. If
16 18 because they have defiled my land with
23 11 the prophet and the priest are defiled
34 16 back, and have defiled my name: and
Lam 4 14 streets, they were defiled with blood
Bar 3 11 thou art defiled with the dead: thou
Eze 4 14 my soul hath not been defiled and from
18 6 hath not d. his neighbor's wife. 15
20 18 nor be ye defiled with their idols
30 you are defiled in the way of your
43 with which you have been defiled; and
22 4 thou art defiled in thy idols which
11 wickedly defiled his daughter-in-law
26 and have defiled my sanctuaries: they
23 7 defiled herself with the uncleanness
13 I saw that she was defiled and that
17 they d. her with their fornications
30 among which thou wast defiled with
28 18 thou hast defiled thy sanctuaries by
33 26 hath defiled his neighbor's wife; and
36 17 own land, they defiled it with their
18 and with their idols they defiled it
37 23 nor shall they be defiled any more
44 25 dead person, lest they be defiled, only
Dan 1 8 not be defiled with the king's table
8 requested . . . that he might not be d.
Osee 5 3 fornication, Israel is defiled. They
6 10 of Ephraim there: Israel is defiled
9 4 all that shall eat it shall be defiled
Agge 2 14 shall it be defiled? And the priests
14 answered and said: It shall be defiled
15 have offered there, shall be defiled
Zach 14 2 and the women shall be defiled: and
Mala 1 12 the table of the Lord is defiled: and
1 Ma 1 39 and defiled the holy place. And the
51 let their souls be defiled with all
65 than to be d. with unclean meats. And
2 12 the Gentiles have defiled them. To what
4 43 away the stones that had been defiled
45 because the Gentiles had defiled it
54 wherein the heathens had defiled it
2 Ma 8 2 temple, that was defiled by the wicked
14 3 had wilfully defiled himself in the
John 18 28 that they might not be defiled, but
1 C 8 7 their conscience, being weak, is d.
1 Tim 1 9 for the wicked and d., for murderers
Titus 1 15 but to them that are defiled, and to
15 their mind and their conscience are d.
Heb 9 13 sanctify such as are defiled, to the
12 15 lest . . . by it many be defiled. Lest
Apoc 3 4 which have not defiled their garments
14 4 who were not defiled with women: for
21 27 shall not enter into it anything defiled
defilement 2 C 7 1 cleanse yourselves from all d.
defileth Eze 18 11 that d. his neighbor's wife
Mat 15 11 not that which goeth into mouth d. a
11 cometh out of the mouth, this d. a man
James 3 6 tongue . . . which d. the whole body
defiling Lev 22 5 the touching of which is d.
Wisd 14 26 defiling of souls, changing of nature
deflower Eccu 20 2 lust of an eunuch shall d. a
deflowered Cant 8 5 there she was d. that bore
Jer 2 16 and of Taphnes have deflowered her
deflowering Gen 34 13 enraged at the d. of their
defraud Ecce 4 8 and d. my soul of good things
Eccu 4 1 defraud not the poor of alms, and turn
7 23 defraud him not of liberty nor leave
14 14 defraud not thyself of the good day
29 8 he will defraud him of his money and
1 C 6 8 you do wrong and defraud and that to
7 5 defraud not one another, except perhaps
defrauded Ps 77 30 were not d. of that which
Eccu 29 10 but they were afraid to be defrauded
1 C 6 7 rather suffer yourselves to be d. But
defraudeth Eccu 34 25 poor: he that d. them thereof
Eccu 34 27 he that d. the laborer of his hire
defrauding Titus 2 10 not d., but in all things
defy 1 K 17 25 for he is come up to defy Israel
1 K 17 26 that he should defy the armies of the
degree Josu 21 26 of the inferior degree. 34
2 Pa 1 1 and magnified him to a high degree
1 Tim 3 13 purchase to themselves a good degree
degrees Exod 19 19 sound of the trumpet grew by d.
Deut 7 22 he will consume these nations . . . by d.
1 K 14 19 it increased by degrees and was heard
4 K 20 9 or that it go back so many degrees
10 but let it return back ten degrees
11 the shadow ten degrees backwards by
Wisd 12 10 executing thy judgments by degrees
Isa 38 8 ten lines by the degrees by which it
Delaia 2 Es 6 10 Samaia the son of Delaia, the
delay Gen 34 19 the young man made no delay, but
Gen 43 10 if delay had not been made, we had
Exod 22 29 thou shalt not delay to pay thy tithes
Num 22 16 thus saith Balac . . . Delay not to come
Deut 7 10 without further d. immediately rendering
23 21 thou shalt not delay to pay it: because

21 if thou delay, it shall be imputed
2 K 17 16 but without delay pass over: lest the
1 Es 7 21 you give it without delay, unto a
Tob 14 12 without delay direct your steps to
Esth 4 11 to be put to death without any delay
Ps 69 6 O Lord, make no delay. In thee, O Lord
Eccu 5 8 delay not to be converted to the Lord
29 11 delay not to show him mercy. Help the
Dan 9 19 delay not for thy own sake, O my God
Haba 2 3 if it make any delay, wait for it: for
1 Ma 6 22 how long dost thou delay to execute
2 Ma 6 23 he answered without delay, according
Acts 25 17 without any delay, on day following
Heb 10 37 he will come and will not delay. But
delayed Exod 32 1 seeing that Moses d. to come
delayeth 2 P 3 9 the Lord d. not his promise, as
Delean Josu 15 38 Delean and Masepha and Jecthel
deliberate 2 K 24 13 d. and see what answer I shall
deliberation Wisd 12 20 punish . . . with so great d.
delicacies Prov 19 10 d. are not seemly for a fool
Apoc 18 3 made rich by power of her delicacies
7 glorified herself and lived in d., so
9 lived in d. with her, shall weep and
delicate Deut 28 54 nice among you and very d.
Deut 28 56 tender and d. woman that could not
Isa 47 1 shalt no more be called d. and tender
8 hear these things, thou that art d.
Jer 6 2 to a beautiful and delicate woman. The
49 4 flowed away, O delicate daughter, that
51 34 filled his belly with my d. meats and
Bar 4 26 my d. ones have walked rough ways for
Dan 13 31 Susanna was exceeding delicate and
Mich 1 16 be polled for my delicate children
delicately Prov 29 21 nourisheth his servant d.
Lam 4 5 they that were fed d. have died in
Luke 7 25 live delicately are in the houses of
delicateness Esth 15 6 she leaned, as if for d.
delicious Judg 9 11 my sweetness and my d. fruits
Wisd 16 2 gavest them their desire of d. food
20 having in it all that is delicious
deliciousness Jer 31 22 long . . . dissolute in d.
delight Deut 12 15 if the eating of flesh d. thee
2 K 19 35 can meat or drink delight thy servant
2 Es 9 25 and abounded with delight in thy great
Job 27 10 can he delight himself in the Almighty
Ps 26 4 that I may see the delight of the Lord
36 4 delight in the Lord, and he will give
11 and shall delight in abundance of peace
48 14 afterwards they shall d. in their mouth
67 31 scatter thou the nations that d. in wars
91 5 given me . . . a delight in thy doings
103 34 I will take delight in the Lord. Let
111 1 he shall delight exceedingly in his
146 10 he shall not delight in the strength of
Prov 16 13 just lips are the delight of kings
29 17 and shall give delight to thy soul
Ecce 5 19 God entertaineth his heart with delight
Wisd 6 22 if then your delight be in thrones
8 18 there is great d. in her friendship
Eccu 1 12 fear of the Lord shall d. the heart
2 9 mercy shall come to you for your d.
26 16 diligent woman shall d. her husband
35 25 he shall d. the just with his mercy
Joel 1 5 that take delight in drinking sweet wine
Mich 2 9 their houses, in which they took d.
delighted Tob 3 22 art not d. in our being lost
Ps 34 9 and shall be delighted in his salvation
44 10 the daughters of kings have d. thee
50 18 with burnt offerings thou wilt not be d.
67 4 before God: and be d. with gladness
76 4 I remembered God and was delighted and
89 14 we have rejoiced and are delighted all
118 14 I have been delighted in the way of thy
Prov 4 14 be not d. in the paths of the wicked
5 19 be thou d. continually with her love
8 30 was d. every day, playing before him
12 11 that is d. in passing his time over
20 1 is delighted therewith shall not be wise
Wisd 13 3 being delighted, took them to be gods
Eccu 16 1 neither be d. in them, if the fear
17 29 they are d. with the vanity of evil
19 6 he that is d. with wickedness shall
27 32 delighted with the fall of the just
31 24 his soul shall be delighted with him
35 19 that heareth will not be d. with them
51 20 my heart delighted in her, my foot
Isa 55 2 your soul shall be delighted in fatness
58 14 shalt thou be delighted in the Lord
66 3 their soul is d. in their abominations
Rom 7 22 I am delighted with the law of God
delighteth Ps 21 9 save him, seeing he d. in him
Prov 13 19 desire that is accomplished, d. the
Isa 42 1 my elect, my soul delighteth in him
Mich 7 18 because he delighteth in mercy. He
delightful Gen 3 6 the tree was . . . d. to behold
Job 30 7 counted it d. to be under the briers
Ps 118 39 for thy judgments are delightful
Ecce 11 7 it is delightful for the eyes to see
Eccu 45 14 delightful to the eyes for its beauty
Isa 32 12 mourn . . . for the delightful country
58 13 and call the sabbath delightful and
Jer 12 10 they have changed my d. portion into
Amos 5 11 you shall plant most d. vineyards and
Zach 7 14 changed the d. land into a wilderness
Mala 3 12 for you shall be a delightful land
delighting Ecce 2 10 d. itself in the things which
delights 2 K 1 24 clothed you with scarlet in d.
Job 22 26 then shalt thou abound in delights
28 13 in land of them that live in delights
Ps 15 11 at thy right hand are delights even
34 27 delights in the peace of his servant
Prov 8 31 my d. were to be with the children of
Ecce 2 1 I will go and abound with delights
8 and the delights of the sons of men
25 feast and abound with delights as I
Cant 7 6 how comely, my dearest, in delights
8 5 from the desert, flowing with delights
Eccu 11 29 maketh one forget great delights and
Isa 66 11 you may milk out and flow with delights
2 P 2 13 the delights of a day: stains and spots
deliver Mat 5 25 adversary d. thee to the judge and the judge d. thee to the officer
Mat 6 13 deliver us from evil. Amen. For if
10 17 will d. you up. 19; 24:9; Mark 13:9, 11
21 brother also shall deliver up the
20 19 shall d. him to the Gentiles. Mark 10:33
25 20 thou didst deliver to me five talents
27 43 let him now deliver him if he will
49 whether Elias will come to deliver him
Luke 12 58 and the judge d. thee to the exacter
20 20 that they might deliver him up to the
Acts 7 34 I am come down to deliver them. And
21 11 shall d. him into hands of the Gentiles
25 11 no man may deliver me to them: I appeal
Rom 7 24 who shall deliver me from the body
11 26 come out of Sion, he that shall deliver
1 C 5 5 to deliver such a one to Satan for the
9 18 I may d. the gospel without charge
13 3 if I should d. my body to be burned
2 C 1 10 doth d. us out of so great dangers
10 we trust that he will yet also d. us
Gal 1 4 that he might deliver us from this
Heb 2 15 might d. them who through fear of death
James 4 12 that is able to destroy and to deliver
2 P 2 9 to deliver the godly from temptation
Apoc 17 13 their strength and power they shall d.

deliverance Judg 15 18 given this very great d.
4 K 5 1 the Lord gave deliverance to Syria
13 17 the arrow of the Lord's deliverance
17 arrow of the deliverance from Syria
1 Pa 11 14 Lord gave a great d. to his people
1 Es 9 13 and hast given us a deliverance as
Jdth 12 8 direct her way to the d. of his people
13 20 for my escape and for your deliverance
Ps 17 51 giving great deliverance to his king
Isa 61 1 deliverance to them that are shut up
1 Ma 4 25 Israel had a great d. that day. And
Luke 4 19 to preach deliverance to the captives
Heb 11 35 others were racked, not accepting d.
delivered Mat 4 12 heard that John was d. up, he
Mat 11 27 all things are d. to me. Luke 10:22
18 34 d. him to the torturers until he paid
25 14 his servants and d. to them his goods
26 2 him bound, and d. him to Pontius Pilate
27 18 knew that for envy they had d. him
26 d. him unto them to be crucified. John 19:16
58 commanded that the body should be d.
Mark 1 14 after that John was d. up, Jesus came
7 4 that have been d. to them to observe
15 1 led him away and d. him to Pilate. And
10 priests had d. him up out of envy. But
15 to them Barabbas, and d. up Jesus when
Luke 1 2 as they have d. them unto us, who from
57 Elizabeth's full time of being d. was
74 being d. from the hand of our enemies
2 6 accomplished, that she should be d.
4 6 to me they are d., and to whom I will
17 Isaias the prophet was d. unto him
9 44 shall be d. into the hands of men
12 58 endeavor to be d. from him: lest perhaps
13 12 thou art delivered from thy infirmity
18 32 he shall be delivered to the Gentiles
23 25 but Jesus he delivered up to their
24 7 be d. into the hands of sinful men
20 d. him to be condemned to death and
John 18 30 we would not have d. him up to thee
35 chief priests, have d. thee up to me
36 that I should not be d. to the Jews
19 11 he that hath d. me to thee, hath the
Acts 2 23 this same being delivered up, by the
3 13 whom you indeed d. up and denied before
5 15 they might be d. from their infirmities
6 14 the traditions which Moses d. unto us
7 10 d. him out of all his tribulations
12 11 hath d. me out of the hand of Herod
14 25 they had been d. to the grace of God
15 30 down to Antioch . . . d. the epistle. Which
40 being d. by the brethren to the grace
16 4 they delivered unto them the decrees
23 33 and had d. the letter to the governor
27 1 should be delivered to a centurion
28 17 I . . . was d. prisoner from Jerusalem
Rom 1 26 d. them up to shameful affections. For
28 d. them up to a reprobate sense, to do
8 2 hath d. me from the law of sin and
21 be d. from the servitude of corruption
32 own Son, but d. him up for us all, how
15 31 I may be d. from the unbelievers that
1 C 11 2 ordinances as I have d. them to you
23 which also I d. unto you, that the Lord
24 my body, which shall be d. for you
15 3 I d. unto you first of all, which I
24 he shall have d. up the kingdom to
2 C 1 10 hath d. and doth deliver us out of
4 11 who live are always d. unto death for
Gal 2 20 loved me and d. himself for me. I cast
Eph 5 2 loved us and hath d. himself for us
25 the church, and d. himself up for it
Col 1 13 hath d. us from the power of darkness
1 Th 1 10 hath d. us from the wrath to come. For
2 Th 3 2 that we may be d. from importunate
1 Tim 1 20 whom I have d. up to Satan, that they
2 Tim 1 9 who hath d. us and called us by his
3 11 out of them all the Lord delivered me
4 17 I was d. out of the mouth of the lion
18 hath d. me from every evil work: and
1 P 2 23 d. himself to him that judged him
2 P 2 4 the angels that sinned, but d. them
7 d. just Lot, oppressed by the injustice
21 commandment which was delivered to them
Jude 3 for the faith once d. to the saints
Apoc 12 2 and was in pain to be delivered. And
4 woman who was ready to be delivered
4 when she should be d., he might devour
deliveredst 2 Es 9 28 d. them many times in thy
2 Es 9 35 land, which thou d. before them, nor
Mat 25 22 thou deliveredst two talents to me
deliverer Ps 17 3 the Lord is . . . my deliverer
Ps 17 48 my deliverer from my enemies. And
69 6 thou art my helper and my deliverer
143 2 support and my deliverer: my protector
Dan 6 27 he is the deliverer and savior, doing
deliverest Ps 34 10 who d. the poor from the hand
Wisd 16 8 thou art he who d. from all evil. For
Eccu 51 12 how thou d. them that wait for thee
2 Ma 1 25 who deliverest Israel from all evil
delivereth Gen 48 16 angel that d. me from all
Tob 12 9 for alms delivereth from death and
Prov 14 25 a faithful witness delivereth souls
1 Ma 4 11 one that redeemeth and d. Israel. And
delivering Lev 5 16 delivering it to the priest
Lev 8 27 delivering all to Aaron and to his
Num 19 5 delivering up to the fire her skin
Deut 2 22 delivering their land to them, which
Isa 31 5 protecting and delivering, passing
Jer 39 18 delivering, I will deliver thee and
2 Ma 11 17 delivering your writings, requested
Luke 21 12 d. you up to the synagogues and into
Acts 12 4 d. him to four files of soldiers to
22 4 binding and delivering into prisons
26 17 delivering thee from the people and
Phil 2 30 d. his life that he might fulfil that
delivery Gen 38 27 in the very d. of the infants
Exod 1 16 the time of delivery is come: if it
Isa 26 17 draweth near the time of her delivery
Delphon Esth 9 7 sons of Aman . . . Delphon and
delude 2 Pa 32 15 nor d. you with a vain persuasion
deluded Mat 2 16 perceiving that he was deluded
deluge Job 21 17 and a deluge come upon them and
Delus 1 Ma 15 23 things were written to . . . Delus
delusions Wisd 17 7 d. of their magic art were
Jer 23 26 that prophesy the d. of their own heart
demand Gen 30 31 if thou wilt do what I demand
Gen 34 12 I will gladly give what you shall d.
14 we cannot do what you demand, nor give
Num 27 6 daughters of Salphaad d. a just thing
Deut 15 2 cannot demand it again, because it is
3 not have power to demand it again. And
24 10 when thou shalt demand of thy neighbor
Bar 6 6 I myself will demand an account of
Dan 4 14 the word and demand of the holy ones
Luke 12 48 of him they will demand the more. I am
demanded Gen 43 7 according to what he demanded
Exod 12 32 take along with you, as you demanded
Job 9 19 if strength be d., he is most strong
Mark 15 6 prisoners, whosoever they demanded
demandest Gen 30 34 I like well what thou d. And
Judg 8 6 d. that we should give bread to. 15
demanding Eccu 31 41 press him not in d. again
Luke 1 63 d. a writing table, he wrote, saying
Demas Col 4 14 saluteth you; and Demas. Salute
2 Tim 4 9 D. hath left me, loving this world

Philem 24 there salute thee . . . Demas and Luke
Demetrius 1 Ma 7 1 D. son of Seleucus departed
1 Ma 7 4 D. sat upon the throne of his kingdom
8 31 the evils that D. the king hath done
9 1 when D. heard that Nicanor and his army
10 3 Demetrius heard these words and was
48 moved his camp near to Demetrius. And
49 the army of Demetrius fled away, and
50 and Demetrius was slain that day. And
52 have overthrown Demetrius and possessed
67 D. the son of D. came from Crete into
11 9 ambassadors to D., saying: Come, let
12 away his daughter and gave her to D.
19 Demetrius reigned in the 167th year
39 that all the army murmured against D.
40 told him all that Demetrius had done
42 D. sent to Jonathan, saying: I will
55 all the hands which D. had sent away
55 they fought against D., who turned
63 that the generals of D. were come. 12:24
12 34 to them that took part with Demetrius
14 2 heard that D. was entered within his
3 he went and defeated the army of D.
15 1 king Antiochus the son of Demetrius
2 Ma 1 7 when D. reigned in the year 169, we
14 1 that Demetrius . . . was come up with a
5 being called to counsel by Demetrius
11 incensed Demetrius against him. And
26 and the covenants came to Demetrius
Acts 19 24 Demetrius, a silversmith, who made
38 if Demetrius and the craftsmen that are
3 J 12 to D. testimony is given by all and by
king Demetrius 1 Ma 10 2 k. D. heard of it and
1 Ma 10 25 king D. to the nation of Jews, greeting
69 king D. made Apollonius his general
11 21 went away to king D. and told him that
30 king Demetrius to his brother Jonathan
32 king Demetrius to Lasthenes his parent
38 king D. seeing that the land was quiet
41 Jonathan sent to king D. desiring that
52 so king Demetrius sat in the throne
13 34 Simon chose men and sent to king D.
35 king D. in answer to this request, wrote
36 king Demetrius to Simon the high priest
14 1 king Demetrius assembled his army and
38 king D. confirmed him in the high
15 22 same things were written to king D.
2 Ma 14 4 Alcimus . . . came to king Demetrius in
demolished Judg 8 17 he d. the tower of Phanuel
Judg 9 45 Abimelech . . . d. it, so that he sowed
2 Pa 31 1 d. the high places and destroyed the
34 4 and demolished the idols that had been
6 even to Nephtali he demolished all
7 and had demolished all profane temples
demons Isa 34 14 demons and monsters shall meet
Demophon 2 Ma 12 2 Demophon . . . would not suffer
den 3 K 15 13 and he destroyed her den and broke
Job 37 8 and shall abide in his den. Out of
Ps 9 9 wait in secret like a lion in his den
Wisd 17 4 neither did the den that held them
Isa 11 8 his hand into the den of the basilisk
Jer 4 7 the lion is come up out of his den
7 11 this house . . . become a den of robbers
Dan 6 7 shall be cast into the den of lions
12 be cast into the den of the lions? And
16 and cast him into the den of the lions
17 and laid upon the mouth of the den
19 went in haste to the lions' den. And
20 coming near to the den, cried with a
23 Daniel should be taken out of the den
23 Daniel was taken out of the den: and
24 they were cast into the den of lions
24 not reach the bottom of the den, before
27 delivered Daniel out of lions' den. 14:42
14 30 they cast him into the den of lions
31 in the den there were seven lions and
33 to Daniel, who is in the lions' den
34 nor do I know the den. And the angel
35 set him in Babylon over the den in
39 he came to the den and looked in and
40 he drew him out of the lions' den. But
41 been the cause . . . he cast into the den
Amos 3 4 will lion's whelp cry out of his den
Nah 2 12 holes with prey and his den with rapine
Mat 21 13 d. of thieves. Mark 11:17; Luke 19:46
Denaba Gen 36 32 the name of his city Denaba. And
1 Pa 1 43 name of his city was Denaba. And Bale
denial Job 31 28 a d. against the most high God
denials Osee 11 12 compassed me about with denials
denied Gen 18 15 Sara d., saying: I did not laugh
Job 31 16 if I have denied to the poor what they
Wisd 12 27 time past they denied that they knew
16 16 the wicked that denied to know thee
Jer 5 12 they have denied the Lord and said
Mat 26 70 he denied before them all, saying: I
72 again he denied with an oath: I know
Mark 14 68 but he denied, saying: I neither know
70 but he denied again. And after a while
Luke 12 9 shall be d. before the angels of God
22 57 he d. him, saying: Woman, I know him
John 18 25 he denied it and said: I am not. One
27 Peter denied; and immediately the
Acts 3 13 whom you delivered up and denied before
14 you denied the Holy One and the Just
1 Tim 5 8 he hath denied the faith and is worse
Heb 11 24 Moses . . . denied himself to be the son
Apoc 2 13 thou hast not denied my faith. Even
3 8 thou hast denied my name. Behold, I will
deniest Luke 22 34 till thou thrice deniest that
denieth 1 J 2 22 who d. the Father and the Son
1 J 2 22 he who d. that Jesus is the Christ
23 whosoever denieth the Son, the same
dens Judg 6 2 made themselves dens and caves in
Job 38 40 when they couch in the dens and lie in
Ps 103 22 they shall lie down in their dens. Man
Cant 4 8 from the dens of the lions, from the
Isa 32 14 and obscurity are come upon its dens
35 7 in the dens where dragons dwelt before
Jer 9 11 to be heaps of sand and dens of dragons
2 Ma 10 6 when they were . . . in dens like wild
Heb 11 38 and in dens and in caves of the earth
Apoc 6 15 kings . . . hid themselves in the dens
deny Lev 6 2 d. to his neighbor the thing delivered
Deut 33 29 thy enemies shall deny thee, and thou
Josu 24 27 lest perhaps hereafter you will d. it
Ruth 3 12 neither do I deny myself to be near of
2 K 13 13 and he will not deny me to thee. But
3 K 2 17 for he cannot deny thee anything, to
Job 8 18 he shall deny him and shall say: I know
Prov 30 7 deny them not to me before I die. Remove
9 being filled, I should be tempted to d.
Isa 63 8 people, children that will not deny
Jer 38 5 for the king to deny you anything. Then
Dan 9 26 the people that shall deny him shall
Mat 10 33 shall d. me before men. Luke 12:9
33 I will also d. him before my Father
16 24 let him deny himself. Mark 8:34; Luke 9:23
26 34 thou wilt deny me thrice. 75; Mark 14:30,
72; Luke 22:61
35 I will not deny thee. Mark 14:31
Luke 20 27 who deny there is any resurrection
John 1 20 he confessed and did not deny: and he
13 38 till thou deny me thrice. Let not your
Acts 4 16 it is manifest and we cannot deny it
2 Tim 2 12 if we deny him, he will also deny us
13 he cannot deny himself. Of these things

Titus 1 16 in their works they deny him; being
2 P 2 1 deny the Lord who bought them: bringing
denying Lev 6 3 find a thing lost and denying it
Deut 15 9 d. to lend him that which he asketh
Wisd 17 9 denying that they saw the air, which
Luke 8 45 all denying, Peter and they that were
2 Tim 3 5 godliness, but denying the power thereof
Titus 2 12 d. ungodliness and worldly desires
Jude 4 denying the only sovereign Ruler and
depart Gen 13 9 depart from me I pray thee: if
Gen 24 54 let me depart, that I may go to my
55 afterwards she shall depart. Stay me
26 16 depart from us, for thou art become
30 26 that I may depart: thou knowest the
34 17 we will take our daughter and depart
42 15 you shall not depart hence until your
Exod 1 10 overcome us, depart out of the land
3 21 you shall not depart empty: but every
8 11 the frogs shall depart from thee and
29 the flies shall depart from Pharao
12 39 the Egyptians pressing them to depart
14 12 depart from us that we may serve the
18 27 he let his kinsman depart: and he
Num 16 26 d. from the tents of these wicked men
Deut 11 16 depart from the Lord and serve strange
15 16 if he say: I will not depart: because
26 3 lest thy brother d. shamefully torn
Josu 1 8 let not the book of this law depart
22 19 only depart not from the Lord and
Judg 6 18 depart not hence till I return to thee
7 8 ordered . . . to depart to their tents
16 17 my strength shall depart from me and
19 5 he desired to depart. But his father
5 taste first . . . and so thou shalt d.
8 afterwards thou mayest depart. And they
9 and tomorrow thou shalt depart, that
Ruth 1 16 that I should leave thee and depart
2 8 and do not depart from this place: but
1 K 2 3 let old matters depart from your mouth
10 2 when thou shalt depart from me this
3 when thou shalt depart from thence
12 20 depart not from following the Lord
15 6 depart and get ye down from Amalec
22 5 depart and go into the land of Juda
2 K 12 10 the sword shall never d. from thy house
20 21 deliver him [Seba] only, and we will d.
3 K 11 21 said to Pharao: Let me depart, that
15 19 that he [Baasa] may depart from me
20 34 having made a league I will d. from
36 thou shalt d. from me, and a lion shall
4 K 3 3 sins . . . nor did he depart from them
18 14 I [Ezechias] have offended, d. from
2 Pa 16 3 make him [Baasa] depart from me. And
23 8 permitted not the companies to d. which
35 15 so as not to d. one moment from their
1 Es 6 6 beyond the river, depart far from them
Tob 4 23 if we fear God and depart from all sin
14 12 direct your steps to depart hence: for
Jdth 5 9 commanded them to depart from thence
6 5 the paleness that is in thy face d.
13 25 thy praise shall not depart out of the
Job 9 11 if he depart I shall not understand
14 6 depart a little from him, that he may
11 as if the waters should d. out of the
15 30 he shall not depart out of darkness
16 7 if I hold my peace, it will not depart
21 14 who have said to God: Depart from us
22 17 who said to God: Depart from us: and
27 6 I will not depart from my innocence
28 28 to depart from evil is understanding
Ps 6 9 d. from me, all ye workers of iniquity
34 22 O Lord, depart not from me. Arise, and
37 22 do not thou depart from me. Attend unto
79 19 we d. not from thee, thou shalt quicken
118 115 depart from me, ye malignant: and I
138 19 ye men of blood, depart from me: because
Prov 3 7 fear God and depart from evil: for it
21 let not these things d. from thy eyes
4 21 let them not depart from thy eyes, keep
5 7 depart not from the words of my mouth
16 6 by fear of the Lord men d. from evil
17 13 evil shall not depart from his house
18 1 hath a mind to depart from a friend
19 4 even they whom he had depart. A false
22 6 when he is old he will not d. from it
Ecce 8 3 be not hasty to depart from his face
9 8 and let not oil depart from thy head
Wisd 19 2 had given them leave to depart and
Eccu 7 2 depart from the unjust, and evils shall
depart from thee
21 d. not from a wise and good wife whom
23 12 scourge shall not d. from his house
33 33 if he rise up and depart, thou knowest
35 2 and to depart from all iniquity. And
3 to d. from injustice, is to offer a
5 to depart from iniquity is that which
5 to depart from injustice is an entreaty
21 will not d. till the most High behold
38 12 let him not depart from thee, for his
39 13 memory of him shall not depart away
48 16 neither did they depart from their sins
Isa 22 4 depart from me, I will weep bitterly
52 11 depart, depart, go ye out from thence
54 10 but my mercy shall not d. from thee
14 depart far from oppression, for thou
59 21 shall not depart out of thy mouth nor
65 5 depart from me, come not near me because
Jer 6 8 lest my soul depart from thee, lest I
9 2 and I will . . . depart from them? Because
17 13 that d. from thee shall be written in
21 2 that he may depart from us. And Jeremias
37 8 the Chaldeans shall surely depart and
Lam 4 15 depart you that are defiled, they cried
15 depart, get ye hence, touch not: for
Bar 2 22 I will cause you to depart out of the
Eze 8 6 that I should depart far off from my
14 6 be converted and d. from your idols
16 42 my jealousy shall depart from thee
31 12 shall depart from his shadow and leave
33 18 the wicked shall d. from his justice
Osee 1 2 the land by fornication shall depart
9 12 woe . . . when I shall depart from them
Mich 2 4 how shall he depart from me, whereas
10 depart, for there is no rest here for
Nah 3 1 rapine shall not depart from thee. The
Zach 7 11 they turned away the shoulder to d.
10 11 the scepter of Egypt shall depart
1 Ma 2 15 and to depart from the law of God
19 so as to depart every man from the
2 Ma 6 1 to compel the Jews to depart from
Mat 7 23 depart from me. 25:41; Luke 13:27
8 34 would d. from their coasts. Mark 5:17
Mark 6 10 there abide till you d. from that place
Luke 4 42 stayed him that he should not depart
6 8 depart from me, for I am a sinful man
8 37 besought him to depart from them; for
9 4 abide there and depart not from thence
13 31 depart and get thee hence, for Herod
21 21 who are in the midst there, depart out
Acts 1 4 they should not depart from Jerusalem
16 36 now therefore depart and go in peace
39 desired them to depart out of the city
18 2 commanded all Jews to depart from Rome
20 7 being to depart on the morrow: and he
25 4 himself would very shortly d. thither
1 C 7 10 the wife depart not from her husband

11 if she depart that she remain unmarried
15 if the unbeliever depart, let him d.
2 C 12 8 that it might depart from me. And he
1 Tim 4 1 some shall d. from the faith, giving
2 Tim 2 19 let every one depart from iniquity
Heb 3 12 unbelief, to depart from the living God

departed Gen 13 11 he [Lot] d. from the east: and
Gen 18 33 the Lord departed, after he had left
21 14 she departed and wandered in wilderness
24 10 he took ten camels . . . and departed
26 17 so he departed and came to the torrent
28 10 Jacob being departed from Bersabee
31 31 that I departed unknown to thee, it was
40 and sleep departed from my eyes. And in
35 5 when they were departed, the terror of
13 he departed from him [Jacob]. But he
36 6 and departed from his brother Jacob
37 17 they are departed from this place: for
44 4 when they were now departed out of the
Exod 33 11 Josue . . . d. not from the tabernacle
Num 9 21 if it departed after a day and a night
22 as soon as it departed, they removed
12 10 that was over the tabernacle departed
14 44 and Moses departed not from the camp
16 27 when they were d. from their tents
33 3 children of Israel d. from Ramesses
20 they d. from thence and came to Lebna
28 they departed from thence and pitched
41 they departed from mount Hor and camped
Deut 10 7 Gadgad, from which place they departed
24 2 when she is departed, and marrieth
32 15 and departed from God his savior. They
Josu 3 1 they departed from Setim and came to
Judg 4 11 Haber . . . had some time before departed
16 19 his strength departed from him. And
20 not knowing that the Lord was d. from
18 20 graven god, and departed with them
1 K 4 22 glory is departed from Israel because
6 6 then let them go, and they departed
10 26 Saul also departed to his own house
15 6 Cinite d. from the midst of Amalec
34 Samuel departed to Ramatha: but Saul
16 14 spirit of the Lord departed from Saul
23 evil spirit departed from him [Saul]
18 12 Lord . . . was d. from himself [Saul]
20 43 David arose and departed: and Jonathan
22 3 David departed from thence into Maspha
5 David d. and came into the forest of
28 15 and God is departed from me [Saul]
16 seeing the Lord has departed from
2 K 3 24 and he [Abner] is gone and departed
6 19 all the people d. every one to his
11 22 the messenger d. and came and told
20 2 and all Israel departed from David
22 and they d. from the city [Abela]
22 22 have not wickedly departed from my God
3 K 12 16 so Israel departed to their dwellings
13 10 he d. by another way and returned not
14 17 the wife of Jeroboam arose and departed
4 K 3 27 they departed from him and returned
5 5 he d. and took with him ten talents of
19 he d. from him in the springtime of the
24 sent the men away, and they departed
8 14 when he was d. from Eliseus, he came
10 15 when he [Jehu] was d. thence, he came
29 departed not from the sins of Jeroboam. 31; 13:6; 15:9, 18, 24, 28
13 2 he [Joachaz] departed not from them
11 d. not from all sins of Jeroboam. 14:24
17 22 and they departed not from them, till
18 6 [Ezechias] d. not from his steps, but
19 8 had heard that he was d. from Lachis
1 Pa 21 4 Joab departed and went through all
2 Pa 8 15 priests and Levites departed not from
12 9 departed from Jerusalem. Jer 37:4
20 32 father Asa, and departed not from it
30 7 your fathers . . . who d. from the Lord
34 33 they departed not from the Lord the
2 Es 9 19 pillar of the cloud d. not from them
26 thee to wrath and departed from thee
Tob 5 23 when they were departed, his mother
11 4 so Tobias took some of that gall and d.
14 4 of the fear of God he departed in peace
14 Tobias departed out of Ninive with his
Jdth 5 17 when they d. from the worship of the
8 34 so returning they departed. And when
Job 6 13 my familiar friends also are d. from
19 13 my acquaintance like strangers have d
23 12 I have not d. from the commandments of
Ps 54 12 and deceit have not d. from its streets
104 38 Egypt was glad when they departed: for
Ecce 7 24 and it departed farther from me, much
Eccu 10 15 his heart is d. from him that made
Isa 37 8 had heard that he was d. from Lachis
37 Sennacherib . . . went out and departed
59 15 he that departed from evil, lay open
Jer 9 10 they are gone away and departed. And
29 2 engravers were d. out of Jerusalem
38 22 and they have departed from thee. And
41 10 he departed, to go over to children of
17 they departed and sat as sojourners
Lam 1 6 all her beauty is departed: her princes
Bar 3 8 who departed from thee, O Lord our God
4 12 they departed from the law of God. And
Eze 14 5 with which they have d. from me through
Dan 6 18 and even sleep departed from him. Then
9 9 for we have departed from thee: and we
13 7 when the people d. away at noon, Susanna
13 going out they d. one from another
14 13 with the king's ring, they departed
Osee 7 13 for they have departed from me: they
14 and wine, they are departed from me
10 5 because it is departed from it. For
Soph 3 18 triflers that were d. from the law
Mala 2 8 you have departed out of the way and
3 7 you have d. from my ordinances and
1 Ma 1 12 since we d. from them, many evils
16 departed from the holy covenant and
24 he departed into his own country. And
6 4 and departed with great sadness and
32 Judas departed from the castle, and
36 and they departed not from it. And upon
63 he departed in haste and returned to
7 1 departed from the city of Rome and came
10 13 and departed into his own country: only
12 46 they d. into the land of Juda: but he
2 Ma 4 21 he d. thence and came to Joppe and
10 19 Machabeus . . . d. to those expeditions
12 7 he d. as if he would return again and
12 they departed to their tents. He also
17 they departed 750 furlongs and came
29 they d. to Scythopolis, which lieth
14 34 when he had spoken thus he departed
46 and so he departed this life. But when
Mat 2 13 after they were departed, behold an
19 1 he departed from Galilee and came into
15 he departed from thence. And behold
27 5 he d. and went and hanged himself with
28 11 when they were d., behold some of the
Mark 1 42 the leprosy d. from him. Luke 5:13
Luke 1 23 [Zachary] departed to his own house
38 the angel departed from her [Mary]
2 15 after the angels departed from them
37 [Anna] departed not from the temple
4 13 the devil departed from him for a time
7 24 when the messengers of John were d.

8 35 out of whom the devils were d. 38
24 51 he d. from them and was carried up
John 4 43 he departed thence and went into Galilee
20 10 disciples departed again to their home
Acts 10 7 angel who spoke to him was departed
12 10 the angel departed from him [Peter]
14 19 [Paul] departed with Barnabas to Derbe
15 34 Judas alone departed to Jerusalem. And
38 [Mark] as having departed from them
39 they departed one from another; and
40 Paul choosing Silas, departed, being
16 40 they comforted them and departed. And
17 15 to him with all speed, they departed
18 21 [Paul] departed from Ephesus. And
23 [Paul] d. and went through the country
19 12 the diseases departed from them and
20 11 talked . . . until midnight, so he d. And
22 29 they d. from him that were about to
28 25 when they agreed not . . . they departed
Phil 4 15 when I departed from Macedonia, no
Philem 15 perhaps he d. for a season from thee
Apoc 6 14 the heaven departed as a book folded
18 14 fruits of the desire of thy soul are d.
departeth 1 K 6 3 why his hand d. not from you
Prov 16 17 path of the just departeth from evils
22 5 keepeth his own soul d. far from them
Jer 17 5 whose heart departeth from the Lord
Luke 9 39 he hardly departeth from him. And I
departing Gen 35 18 when her soul was d. for pain
Gen 35 21 departing thence, he pitched his tent
45 24 at their departing, said to them: Be
Exod 12 32 as you demanded, and d., bless me
19 2 departing out of Raphidim and coming
Num 11 34 d. from the graves of lust. 15:17
21 11 camped in Oboth. And departing thence
33 7 d. from thence they came over against
8 and d. from Phihahiroth, they passed
9 d. from . . . they came. 22, 26, 30, 32, 47
10 d. from thence also, they pitched
10 d. from the Red Sea, they camped in
13 d. from . . . they camped. 15, 19, 35, 37, 43
14 d. from Alus, they pitched their tents
16 d. also from the desert of Sinai, they
24 departing from the mountain Sepher
45 departing from Ijeabarim, they pitched
48 d. from the mountains of Abarim, they
Deut 1 19 d. from Horeb, we passed through the
2 1 and d. from thence we came into the
Judg 1 11 departing from thence he went to the
9 50 Abimelech d. from thence came to the
19 7 he rising up began to be for departing
1 K 23 13 departing from Ceila, wandered up and
3 K 19 19 Elias d. from thence, found Eliseus
4 K 19 36 Sennacherib . . . departing went away
2 Pa 24 25 d. they left him in great diseases
25 16 the prophet departing, said: I know
Eccu 38 24 comfort him in the d. of his spirit
Dan 3 29 and committed iniquity, d. from thee
2 Ma 5 11 d. out of Egypt with a furious mind
6 27 by d. manfully out of this life, I shall
Mat 27 66 and departing made the sepulcher sure
Mark 9 29 departing . . . passed through Galilee
Luke 9 33 as they were d. from him, Peter saith
Acts 13 13 and John departing from them, returned
18 1 d. from Athens, he came to Corinth
7 d. thence, he entered into the house
19 9 d. from them, he separated the disciples
21 5 departing, we went forward, they all
8 the next day d., we came to Caesarea
departure Exod 19 1 the third month of the d. of
Wisd 3 2 their departure was taken for misery
Acts 20 29 after my departure, ravening wolves
depend Num 30 14 shall d. on will of her husband
dependencies 2 Es 11 30 at Lachis and its d.
dependeth Gen 44 30 his life d. upon the life of
Mat 22 40 d. the whole law and the prophets
deplorable Ecce 5 15 a most d. evil: as he came
depose Isa 22 19 depose thee from thy ministry
deposed 2 Pa 15 16 Maacha . . . he d. from the royal
2 Pa 36 3 king of Egypt . . . deposed him [Joachaz]
1 Ma 8 13 whom they would, they deposed from the
deposited 2 Ma 3 10 that these were sums d. and
2 Ma 3 15 safe for them that had deposited them
depraved Eccu 22 20 shall not be d. by fear. As
deprive Ps 83 13 he will not d. of good things
deprived Gen 27 45 why shall I be d. of both my
Gen 30 2 who hath deprived thee of the fruit
48 11 I am not d. of seeing thee: moreover
Num 24 11 Lord hath deprived thee of the honor
Job 21 10 their cow . . . is not d. of her fruit
39 17 for God hath deprived her of wisdom
Ps 33 11 seek the Lord shall not be d. of any
Wisd 18 4 were worthy to be deprived of light
Eccu 28 19 and deprived them of their labors. He
37 24 he is deprived of all wisdom. There
2 Ma 13 11 afraid to be deprived of the law and
14 7 being d. of my ancestors' glory, I
depriving Ps 34 12 to the d. me of my soul. But
depth 2 Es 9 11 thou threwest into the depth
Job 28 14 the depth saith: It is not in me. The
Ps 64 8 who troublest the depth of the sea
67 23 I will turn them into the depth of sea
68 3 I am come into the depth of the sea
Prov 5 5 her feet go down into the depth and
18 3 when he is come into the depth of sins
Ecce 7 25 it is a great depth, who shall find
Wisd 10 19 from the d. of hell she brought them
Eccu 1 2 who hath measured . . . d. of the abyss
51 7 from the depth of the belly of hell
Isa 7 11 either unto the d. of hell or unto
14 15 into depth of the pit. They that
51 10 who madest the depth of the sea a way
Osee 5 2 have turned aside victims into the d.
Amos 9 3 from my eyes in the depth of the sea
Mat 18 6 should be drowned in d. of the sea
Mark 4 5 because it had no depth of earth. And
Rom 8 39 height nor depth nor any other creature
11 33 the depth of the riches of the wisdom
2 C 11 25 I was in the depth of the sea. In
Eph 3 18 able to comprehend . . . height and d.
depths Exod 15 5 the depths have covered them, they
Exod 15 8 the depths were gathered together in
Job 28 11 depths also of rivers he hath searched
38 16 hast thou entered into d. of the sea
Ps 32 7 laying up the depths in storehouses
70 20 back again from the depths of the earth
76 17 and the depths were troubled. Great was
105 9 he led them through the depths, as in
106 26 and they go down to the depths; their
129 1 out of the depths I have cried to thee
Prov 3 20 by his wisdom the d. have broken out
8 24 the depths were not as yet, and was
27 he enclosed the depths: when he
9 18 her guests are in the depths of hell
Dan 3 55 thou that beholdest the depths, and
Zach 10 11 d. of the river shall be confounded
Apoc 2 24 have not known the depths of Satan
deputed 2 Ma 4 19 might be d. for other charges
deputies 2 Pa 9 14 which the d. of divers nations
Esth 8 9 to the deputies and to the judges who
deputy 2 Ma 4 31 leaving Andronicus . . . for his d.
Derbe Acts 14 6 fled to Lystra and Derbe, cities
Acts 14 19 he departed with Barnabas to Derbe
16 1 he came to Derbe and Lystra. And behold
20 4 Gaius of Derbe and Timothy; and of Asia
Dercon 1 Es 2 56 children of Dercon, the children

deride Ps 2 4 the Lord shall deride them. Then
derided Eze 36 4 d. by the rest of the nations
Luke 16 14 all these things: and they derided him
23 35 rulers with them derided him, saying
derision Ps 43 14 made us . . . scoff and derision
Ps 78 4 derision to them that are round about
Wisd 5 3 whom we had some time in derision and
Jer 20 8 word of the Lord is made . . . a derision
48 26 and he also shall be in derision. For
27 Israel hath been a derision unto thee
Lam 3 14 I am made a derision to all my people
Eze 23 32 thou shalt be had in derision and scorn
Osee 7 16 this is their d. in the land of Egypt
derogated Eze 35 13 have d. from me by your words
descend Ps 48 18 nor shall his glory d. with him
Ps 103 8 the plains descend into the place which
138 8 if I descend into hell, thou art present
143 5 bow down thy heavens and descent: touch
Ecce 3 21 if the spirit of the beasts d. downward
Eze 26 20 those that d. into pit. 31:16; 32:25
Rom 10 7 who shall descend into the deep? that
descended 1 K 17 55 family is this young man d.
Prov 30 4 hath ascended up into heaven and d.
Mat 28 2 an angel of the Lord descended from
Luke 3 22 Holy Ghost d. in a bodily shape, as a
John 3 13 but he that descended from heaven, the
5 4 angel of the Lord d. at certain times
Eph 4 9 he d. first into lower parts of the
10 he that d. is the same that ascended
descendeth Ps 132 3 which d. upon mount Sion. For
descending Gen 28 12 angels of God ascending and d.
Mat 3 16 descending as a dove. Mark 1:10
John 1 33 upon whom thou shalt see the Spirit d.
51 angels of God ascending and descending
Acts 10 11 a certain vessel d., as it were. 11:5
James 3 15 this is not wisdom d. from above: but
descent Josu 7 5 them as they fled by the descent
Josu 10 11 were in the descent of Beth-horon, the
4 K 12 20 house of Mello in the descent of Sella
Eccu 46 7 in the d. he destroyed the adversaries
Isa 32 19 hail shall be in the d. of the forest
Jer 48 5 in the d. of Oronaim the enemies have
1 Ma 3 24 he pursued him by the d. of Bethoron
Luke 19 37 near the descent of mount Olivet, the
described Judg 8 14 he d. unto him 77 men. And
Prov 22 20 I have d. it to thee three manner of
description 1 Pa 28 11 gave . . . d. of the porch
descriptions 2 Ma 2 1 found in the d. of Jeremias
desert Exod 3 1 to the inner parts of the desert
Exod 13 18 led them about by the way of the d.
14 3 the desert hath shut them in. And I
16 3 why have you brought us into this d.
17 1 from the desert of Sin. Num 13:22
19 2 coming to the d. of Sinai, they camped
23 31 from the d. to the river: I will deliver
Lev 26 33 your land shall be desert and your
Num 10 12 marched . . . from the desert of Sinai
13 4 sending from the desert of Pharan
27 and came . . . to the desert of Pharan
21 20 Phasga, which looked towards the d.
24 1 setting his face towards the desert
27 14 in Cades of the d. of Sin. Deut 32:51
32 13 led them about through the desert
33 8 three days through the desert of Etham
16 departing also from the desert of Sinai
Deut 2 8 way that leadeth to the desert of Moab
3 17 borders of Cenereth unto sea of the d.
8 2 brought thee for 40 years through d.
11 24 from the d. and from Libanus. Josu 1:4
29 5 brought you 40 years through the d.
32 10 he found him in a desert land, in a
Josu 8 14 set it in battle array toward the d.
15 1 to the desert of Sin southward and to
Judg 8 7 thorns and briers of the desert. 16
11 16 he walked through the d. to the Red
20 42 began to go towards way of the desert
1 K 13 18 above valley of Seboim towards the d.
23 14 in a mountain of the desert of Ziph
19 which is on the right hand of the d.
2 K 15 23 towards way that looketh to the desert
3 K 19 15 thy way through the desert to Damascus
4 K 3 8 he answered: By the desert of Edom
1 Pa 5 9 as far as the entrance of the desert
2 Pa 20 20 went out through the desert of Thecua
24 tower that looketh toward the desert
26 10 in the waste of the desert: he had also
Tob 14 7 all the land thereof that is desert
Jdth 2 13 were over against the face of the d.
Job 1 19 wind . . . from the side of the desert
15 28 in desolate cities and in d. houses
30 6 they dwelt in d. places of torrents
38 27 that it should fill the desert and
Ps 28 7 voice of the Lord shaketh the desert
7 Lord shall shake the desert of Cades
62 3 in a desert land, and where there is no
67 8 when thou didst pass through the desert
74 7 from the west, nor from the d. hills
135 16 who led his people through the desert
Cant 3 6 who is she that goeth up by the desert
8 5 that cometh up from the desert, flowing
Wisd 5 24 shall bring all the earth to a desert
11 2 in d. places they pitched their tents
Eccu 10 31 give it honor according to its desert
Isa 16 1 from Petra of the desert, to the mount
21 1 the burden of the desert of the sea
1 cometh from the d. from a terrible
32 2 that standeth out in a desert land
15 and the desert shall be as a charmel
33 9 and Saron is become as a desert: and
41 18 I will turn the desert into pools of
42 11 d. and the cities thereof be exalted
50 2 I will make the sea a desert, I will
51 3 will make her d. as a place of pleasure
64 10 city of thy sanctuary is become a desert,
Sion is made a desert
Jer 2 6 that led us through the desert, through
4 11 the d. of the way of the daughter of
10 22 to make the cities of Juda a desert
23 10 the fields of the desert are dried up
39 4 they went out to the way of the desert
5 took Sedecias in plain of the desert
49 13 that Bosra shall become . . . a desert
51 29 to make the land of Babylon desert
Eze 6 14 abandoned from the desert of Deblatha
23 42 of men, and that came from the desert
29 9 land of Egypt shall become a desert
33 28 I will make the land . . . a desert and
47 8 and go down to the plains of the desert
Osee 13 15 wind that shall rise from the desert
Joel 2 20 into a land unpassable and desert with
Amos 6 15 even to the torrent of the d. These
Nah 1 4 bringeth all the rivers to be a desert
Soph 1 13 their houses [shall become] as a d.
2 4 Ascalon shall be a desert, they shall
9 and a desert even forever: the remnant
13 as a place not passable and as a d.
15 how is she become a desert, a place for
3 6 I have made their ways desert, so that
Zach 14 10 the land shall return even to the d.
Mala 1 3 inheritance to the dragons of the d.
1 Ma 3 45 Jerusalem . . . was like a desert: there
5 24 went three days' journey through the d.
13 21 haste to come through the desert and
Mark 1 45 was without in desert places: and they
John 11 54 he went into a country near the desert
Acts 8 26 from Jerusalem into Gaza: this is d.

desert place 2 Ma 5 27 himself into a d. p.
Mat 14 13 into a desert place apart. Mark 1:35; 6:32; Luke 4:42; 9:10
15 this is a desert place. Mark 6:35
Mark 6 31 come apart into a d. p. and rest a
Luke 9 12 we are here in a desert place. But
in the desert Gen 16 7 way of Sur in the d.
Exod 5 1 that they may sacrifice to me in the d.
7 16 to sacrifice to me in the desert: and
Lev 7 38 oblations to the Lord i. . . . of Sinai
Num 1 1 spoke to Moses in the desert of Sinai. 3:14; 9:1
19 they were numbered in the d. of Sinai
3 4 before the Lord, in the desert of Sinai
13 1 pitched their tents i. . . . of Pharan
14 33 your children shall wander in the d.
33 their fathers be consumed in the desert
16 13 to kill us in the desert, except thou
21 13 Arnon, which is in the desert and
23 went forth to meet them in the desert
26 64 numbered before . . . in the d. of Sinai
27 3 our father died in the desert and was
14 you offended me in the desert of Sin
33 11 they camped in the desert of Sin and
15 they camped in the desert of Sinai
Josu 5 4 the men fit for war, died in the desert
5 the people that were born in the desert
15 61 in the desert Betharaba, Meddin and
1 K 4 8 Egypt with all the plagues in the d.
17 28 didst thou leave those few sheep in d.
23 14 David abode in the d. in strongholds
15 David was in the desert of Ziph, in
24 David and his men were in the desert
24 2 David is in the desert of Engaddi. Saul
25 7 thy shepherds that were with us i. . . .
15 we conversed with them in the desert
2 K 16 2 drink if any man be faint in the d.
3 K 2 34 he was buried in his house in the d.
1 Pa 21 29 which Moses made in the desert and
2 Pa 8 4 and he built Palmira in the desert
24 9 appointed for all Israel, in the d.
2 Es 9 19 didst not leave them in the desert: the
21 didst thou feed them in the desert
Tob 8 3 bound him in the desert of upper Egypt
Job 24 5 others like wild asses in the desert
Ps 62 1 when he was in the desert of Edom
77 40 did they provoke him in the desert
105 14 they coveted their desire in the d.
26 to overthrow them in the desert; and
Eccu 13 23 ass is the lion's prey in the desert
Isa 35 6 waters are broken out in the desert
40 3 the voice of one crying in the desert
41 19 I will set in the desert the fir tree
43 19 I will make . . . rivers in the desert
20 I have given . . . rivers in the desert
48 21 they thirsted not in the desert, when
Jer 2 2 when thou followedst me in the desert
9 26 hair polled round, that dwell i. . . .
13 34 is carried away by the wind in the d.
17 6 he shall be like tamaric in the desert
6 he shall dwell in dryness i. . . . in a
25 24 kings of the west, that dwell in the d.
31 2 from the sword, found grace in the d.
52 8 they overtook Sedecias in the desert
Lam 4 3 like the ostrich in the desert. The
5 9 because of the sword in the desert
Eze 20 13 house of Israel provoked me i. . . . and
13 my indignation upon them in the d.
15 lifted up my hand over them in the d.
17 neither did I consume them in the d.
21 accomplish my wrath in them in the d.
36 pleaded against your fathers in the d.
Osee 9 10 I found Israel like grapes in the d.
13 5 I knew thee in the desert, in the land
Amos 5 25 and sacrifices to me in the desert
1 Ma 8 62 Bethbessen, which is in the desert
Mat 3 1 John the Baptist preaching in the d.
3 voice of one crying i. . . . Mark 1:3
15 33 have so many loaves in the desert, as
24 26 behold he is in the d., go ye not out
Mark 1 4 John was in the desert baptizing and
13 he was in the desert forty days and
Luke 3 2 was made unto John . . . in the desert
15 4 he not leave the ninety-nine in the d.
John 3 14 Moses lifted up the serpent in the d.
6 31 fathers did eat manna in the d. 49
Acts 7 30 appeared to him in the d. of mount Sina
36 in the Red Sea and in the d. 40 years
42 sacrifices to me for 40 years in the d.
44 was with our fathers in the desert
13 18 endured their manners in the desert
1 C 10 5 were overthrown in the d. Heb 3:17
Heb 3 8 in the day of temptation in the desert
into the desert Exod 4 27 said to Aaron: Go i. . . .
Exod 16 1 came into the d. of Sin. Num 20:1; 33:36
18 5 came . . . to Moses into the desert, where
Lev 16 21 shall turn him out . . . into the desert
22 shall be let go into the desert, Aaron
3 K 19 4 one day's journey into the desert. And
Eccu 8 19 go not into the d. with a bold man
Jer 50 23 how is Babylon turned into a desert
Eze 19 13 now she is transplanted into the d.
20 10 and brought them into the desert. And
29 5 I will cast thee forth into the desert
1 Ma 2 29 went down into the desert: and they
5 28 turned their march into the desert
9 33 they fled into the desert of Thecua
Mat 4 1 led by the spirit into the d. Luke 4:1
11 7 out into the desert to see. Luke 7:24
Mark 1 12 the Spirit drove him out into the d.
Luke 5 16 he retired into the desert and prayed
Acts 21 38 didst lead forth i. . . . 4,000 men that
Apoc 12 14 that she might fly into the desert
17 3 he took me away in spirit into the d.
deserts Jdth 5 14 they abode in the d. of mount
Isa 5 17 strangers shall eat the deserts turned
49 19 thy deserts . . . shall now be too narrow
52 9 rejoice . . . ye deserts of Jerusalem: for
Eze 13 4 were like foxes in the deserts. You
Luke 1 80 was in the deserts until the day of
8 29 he was driven by the devil into the d.
Heb 11 38 wandering in deserts, in mountains
deserve Gen 4 13 than that I may d. pardon. Behold
Gen 42 21 we d. to suffer these things because
Deut 7 10 rendering to them what they deserve
Josu 11 20 should not deserve any clemency and
2 Pa 19 2 didst deserve indeed the wrath of the
Jdth 6 6 the punishment they deserve from my
8 27 to be less than our sins deserve, let
Wisd 15 6 d. to have no better things to trust
deserved Num 22 29 because thou hast deserved it
Judg 12 3 what have I d., that you should rise
1 Pa 21 17 as for this flock, what hath it d.
Job 6 2 my sins, whereby I have deserved wrath
33 27 I have not received what I have d.
Wisd 12 20 enemies . . . that deserved to die, with
19 13 that had deserved well of them. And
Jer 51 6 render unto her what she hath deserved
2 Ma 4 38 repaying him his d. punishment. Now
deservedly Ps 7 5 let me d. fall empty before my
deserveth Judg 20 10 for its wickedness what it d.
Job 11 6 much less of thee than thy iniquity d.
Wisd 12 15 him who deserveth not to be punished
Heb 10 29 he deserveth worse punishments, who
design Num 35 20 anything at him with ill d.: or
Josu 22 22 if with the design of transgression

2 Ma 2 25 that d. to undertake the narrations
11 28 if you are well, you are as we desire
Mark 9 34 if any man desire to be first, he
10 35 we desire that whatsoever we ask, thou
15 8 d. that he would do as he had ever
Luke 17 22 when you shall desire to see one day
20 46 who desire to walk in long robes and
Acts 23 20 to d. thee that thou wouldst bring
24 4 I desire thee [Felix] of thy clemency
28 22 we desire to hear of thee [Paul] what
2 C 9 5 to d. the brethren . . . would go to you
11 12 from them that desire occasion, that
Gal 4 9 which you desire to serve again? You
21 you that desire to be under the law
6 12 many as desire to please in the flesh
Eph 3 20 more abundantly than we desire or
Phil 1 12 I desire you should know that the things
1 Tim 2 1 I desire . . . that thanksgivings be made
3 1 if a man desire the office of a bishop
Heb 6 11 we desire that every one of you show
11 16 now they desire a better . . . country
1 P 1 12 on whom the angels desire to look
2 2 desire the rational milk without guile
Apoc 9 6 they shall desire to die and death
desired Exod 2 16 d. to water their father's flocks
Judg 17 8 desired to sojourn wheresoever he
18 5 they desired him to consult the Lord
19 5 arising early . . . he desired to depart
Ruth 2 7 she d. leave to glean the ears of corn
1 K 8 18 because you d. unto yourselves a king
10 to the people that had desired a king
12 13 king . . . whom you have chosen and d.
23 20 as thy soul hath d. to come down: and
3 K 9 1 all that he desired and was pleased to do
10 13 all that she desired and asked of him
24 all the earth d. to see Solomon's face
2 Pa 9 12 to the queen of Saba all that she d.
23 kings of the earth desired to see the
Tob 5 10 d. that he would come in unto him. So
19 not angry that I d. to know thy family
7 9 when he d. them to sit down to dinner
Jdth 12 5 she desired that she might have liberty
Job 23 13 whatsoever his soul hath desired, that
26 4 whom hast thou desired to teach? was
31 16 if . . . denied to the poor what they d.
33 20 the meat which before he desired. His
Ps 18 11 more to be desired than gold and many
39 9 I have desired it, and thy law in the
50 18 if thou hadst d. sacrifice, I would
118 35 for this same I have desired. Incline
Prov 3 15 all the things that are d. are not to
7 18 let us enjoy the desired embraces
8 11 whatsoever may be d. cannot be compared
21 20 there is a treasure to be desired and
Ecce 2 10 whatsoever my eyes d. I refused them not
Cant 2 3 under his shadow, whom I desired: and
Wisd 8 2 have desired to take her for my spouse
5 if riches be desired in life, what is
16 25 will of them that desired it of thee
Isa 26 9 my soul hath d. thee in the night: yea
Jer 17 16 I have not desired the day of man, thou
Eze 24 13 I desired to cleanse thee, and thou
Dan 2 16 went in and desired of the king, thou
23 shown me what we desired of thee, for
Osee 6 6 I desired mercy, and not sacrifice
Jon 4 8 he d. for his soul that he might die
Mich 7 1 my soul desired the firstripe figs
Agge 2 8 the desired of all nations shall come
1 Ma 7 5 who desired to be made high priest
11 66 they desired him to make peace and
14 31 their enemies desired to tread down
2 Ma 4 19 desired it might not be bestowed on
34 Menelaus . . . d. him to kill Onias. And
6 21 desired that flesh might be brought
11 29 that you desired to come down to your
12 3 they desired the Jews who dwelt among
14 25 he desired him to marry a wife and to
15 39 it is what I desired: but if not so
Mat 13 17 d. to see the things. Luke 10:24
Luke 5 3 he d. him [Peter] to draw back a little
7 35 one of the Pharisees d. him to eat
9 40 I desired thy disciples to cast him
22 15 I have desired to eat this pasch with
31 Satan hath d. to have you [Peter] that
23 25 [Barabbas] whom they had desired; but
John 4 40 they d. that he would tarry there
12 21 desired him, saying: Sir, we would see
Acts 3 14 you desired a murderer to be granted
7 46 [David] desired to find a tabernacle
8 31 desired Philip that he would come up
10 48 they desired him to tarry. 18:20
12 20 they d. peace, because their countries
13 7 [Paulus] desired to hear the word of
21 after that they desired a king: and
28 d. of Pilate that they might kill him
42 they desired them, that on the next
15 38 Paul d. that he [Mark] . . . might not
16 39 they d. them to depart out of the city
21 12 d. him . . . not go up to Jerusalem. Then
23 18 desired me to bring this young man
28 14 we were desired to tarry with them
20 I d. to see you and to speak to you
2 C 8 6 we desired Titus that as he had begun
12 18 I desired Titus and I sent with him
Phil 4 1 most desired, my joy and my crown; so
1 Tim 1 3 as I desired thee to remain at Ephesus
Heb 12 17 when he [Esau] desired to inherit the
desiredst Deut 18 16 as thou d. of the Lord thy
desires Ps 9 3 is praised in the d. of his soul
Ps 15 3 he hath made wonderful all my desires
77 18 by asking meat for their desires. And
80 13 according to the desires of their heart
Prov 21 25 desires kill the slothful: for his
Eccu 5 2 in the strength the desires of thy
Dan 9 23 because thou art a man of desires
10 11 Daniel, thou man of desires, understand
19 fear not, O man of desires, peace be
John 8 44 desires of your father you will do
Rom 1 24 gave them up to the d. of their heart
Eph 2 3 in the d. of our flesh, fulfilling the
1 Tim 6 9 into many unprofitable and hurtful d.
2 Tim 2 22 flee thou youthful desires and pursue
3 6 who are led away with divers desires
4 3 according to their own d. they will
Titus 2 12 denying ungodliness and worldly d.
3 3 slaves to divers desires and pleasures
1 P 1 14 not fashioned according to former d.
2 11 refrain yourselves from carnal desires
4 2 not after the d. of men, but according
2 P 2 18 allure by desires of fleshly riotousness
Jude 16 walking according to their own d. 18
desirest Gen 23 15 the ground which thou desirest
Deut 12 15 if thou desirest to eat and the eating
desireth Deut 12 20 the flesh that thy soul d.
Deut 14 26 shalt buy . . . all that thy soul d.: and
1 K 2 16 take as much as thy soul desireth. But
18 25 the king d. not any dowry but only
2 K 3 21 reign over all as thy soul desireth
3 K 11 37 reign over all that thy soul desireth
Job 37 11 corn d. clouds, and the clouds spread
Ps 33 13 who is the man that desireth life: who
Prov 21 10 the soul of the wicked desireth evil
26 he longeth and desireth all the day
Ecce 6 2 wanteth nothing of all that he d.: yet
Eccu 15 22 he d. not a multitude of faithless
36 24 and a man desireth nothing more. If she

40 22 thy eye desireth favor and beauty, but
Dan 2 27 the secret that the king d. to know
2 Ma 9 14 he now desireth to make free. And the
Luke 14 32 d. conditions of peace. So likewise
Rom 8 27 knoweth what the Spirit d.; because
1 Tim 3 1 he desireth a good work. It behoveth
desiring Josu 9 6 d. to make peace with you
Judg 6 7 d. help against the Madianites. And he
1 K 12 17 in desiring a king over you. And Samuel
4 K 7 7 and fled, desiring to save their lives
2 Pa 31 21 desiring to seek his God with all his
32 1 the fenced cities, desiring to take
Jdth 6 21 desiring help of the God of Israel
Wisd 16 3 that they indeed desiring food, by
1 Ma 5 67 while d. to do manfully they went out
11 41 d. that he would cast out them that
Luke 7 3 d. him to come and heal his servant
8 20 thy mother . . . desiring to see thee
16 21 desiring to be filled with the crumbs
23 20 Pilate . . . desiring to release Jesus
Acts 9 38 d. him that he would not be slack to
19 31 d. that he would not venture himself
25 15 desiring condemnation against him. To
2 C 5 2 we groan, desiring to be clothed upon
1 Th 3 6 d. to see us as we also to see you
1 Tim 1 7 desiring to be teachers of the law
2 Tim 1 4 d. to see thee, being mindful of thy
desirous Gen 24 21 d. to know whether the Lord
Gen 37 22 being desirous to deliver him out of
Prov 7 15 to meet thee, desirous to see thee
23 3 be not desirous of his meats, in which
Wisd 13 6 seeking God and d. to find him. For
Isa 53 2 we should be desirous of him: despised
Dan 13 11 being desirous to have to do with her
15 d. to wash herself in the orchard: for
2 Ma 11 23 we are d. that they that are in our
25 being d. that this nation also should
Mark 6 19 was desirous to put him to death and
Luke 23 8 he was d. of a long time to see him
Acts 10 10 he was desirous to taste somewhat
18 27 whereas he was d. to go to Achaia
2 C 9 14 being desirous of you, because of the
Gal 5 26 let us not be made d. of vain glory
1 Th 2 8 so d. of you, we would gladly impart
desolate Gen 43 14 I shall be d. without children
Lev 26 22 that your highways may be desolate
31 I will make your sanctuaries desolate
43 enjoy her sabbaths, being d. for them
2 Es 2 3 seeing the city . . . is d. and the gates
17 because Jerusalem is d., and the gates
Job 15 28 he hath dwelt in desolate cities and
38 27 it should fill the desert and d. land
Ps 68 26 let their habitation be made desolate
Wisd 10 7 whose land . . . is d. and smoketh to
Eccu 16 5 tribe of ungodly shall become d. Many
49 8 made the streets thereof desolate
Isa 1 7 your land is d., your cities are burnt
7 shall be d. as when wasted by enemies
3 26 she shall sit desolate on the ground
5 6 I will make it desolate; it shall not
9 fair houses shall become desolate
6 11 and the land shall be left desolate
13 9 to lay the land d. and to destroy the
15 6 waters of Nemrim shall be desolate
16 8 the suburbs of Hesebon are desolate
17 9 and thou shalt be desolate. Because
27 10 the strong city shall be desolate, the
33 8 the ways are made d., no one passeth
35 1 the land that was d. and impassable
44 27 who say to the deep: Be thou d. and
49 19 for thy deserts and thy desolate places
54 1 many are the children of the desolate
3 and shall inhabit the desolate cities
58 12 places that have been d. for ages shall
61 4 and shall repair the desolate cities
62 4 thy land shall no more be called D.
64 10 a desert, Jerusalem is desolate. The
Jer 2 12 ye gates thereof, be very desolate
4 7 to make thy land desolate: thy cities
27 the land shall be desolate. 7:34
6 8 lest I make thee desolate, a land
9 11 I will make the cities of Juda d., for
12 10 portion into a desolate wilderness
11 is all the land made desolate; because
26 9 this city shall be made desolate without
32 43 whereof you say that it is desolate
33 10 place, which you say is desolate because
10 which are desolate without man and
12 again in this place that is desolate
44 2 behold they are desolate this day and
46 19 Memphis shall be made desolate and
48 9 cities thereof shall be desolate and
49 17 Edom shall be desolate: every one
33 Asor shall be . . . desolate forever
50 3 which shall make her land desolate
13 not be inhabited, but shall be wholly d.
51 36 I will make her sea desolate and will
43 a land uninhabited and desolate, a land
62 that it should be desolate forever
Lam 1 13 he hath made me desolate, wasted with
16 my children are d. because the enemy
3 11 in pieces, he hath made me desolate
Bar 4 12 over me, a widow, and desolate: I am.
Eze 5 14 I will make thee d. and a reproach
6 14 and I will make the land desolate and
12 19 that the land may become desolate from
20 laid waste, and the land shall be d.
14 15 the land to waste it, and it be d.
16 and the land shall be made desolate
15 8 their land a wilderness and desolate
19 7 and the land became desolate and the
25 13 and will make it d. from the south
26 19 when I shall make thee a d. city like
20 of the earth, as places d. of old
29 10 the land of Egypt utterly desolate
12 will make the land of Egypt desolate
12 midst of the lands that are d. 30:7
12 they shall be d. for forty years: and
30 7 they shall be d. in the midst of the
32 15 shall have made the land of Egypt d.
33 28 mountains of Israel shall be desolate
29 have made their land waste and d., for
35 3 I will make thee desolate and waste
4 thy cities, and thou shalt be desolate
7 will make mount Seir waste and d.: and
12 they are d., they are given to us to
36 3 because you have been d. and trodden
4 to desolate places and ruinous walls
34 the desolate land shall be tilled which
35 cities that were abandoned and d. and
36 and planted what was desolate, that
Dan 9 17 face upon thy sanctuary which is d.
Joel 2 3 and behind it a desolate wilderness
Mich 7 13 the land shall be made desolate because
Nah 1 5 and the hills are made desolate: and
Soph 3 6 their cities are d., there is not a
Agge 1 4 houses, and this house lie desolate
9 my house is d., and you make haste
Zach 7 14 land was left desolate behind them
1 Ma 1 41 her sanctuary was desolate like a
4 38 they saw the sanctuary desolate and
15 4 have made many cities desolate in my
Mat 12 25 every kingdom . . . shall be made d.: and
23 38 shall be left to you d. Luke 13:35
Acts 1 20 let their habitation become desolate
Gal 4 27 many are the children of the desolate

1 Tim 5 5 she that is a widow indeed and d., let
Apoc 17 16 hate the harlot and shall make her d.
18 19 for in one hour she is made desolate
desolation Lev 26 34 all the days of her d.: when
Lev 26 35 rest in the sabbaths of her desolation
2 Pa 36 21 days of the d. she kept a sabbath
Ps 72 19 how are they brought to desolation
Isa 24 3 with d. shall the earth be laid waste
12 desolation is left in the city, and
34 11 and a plummet, unto desolation. The
51 19 desolation . . . who shall comfort thee
60 12 the Gentiles shall be wasted with d.
Jer 12 11 with d. is all the land made desolate
18 16 their land might be given up to d.
22 5 this house shall become a desolation
25 11 all this land shall be a desolation
18 to make them a desolation, and a
27 16 why should this city be given up to d.
34 22 I will make the cities of Juda a d.
44 6 they are turned to desolation and waste
22 therefore your land is become a d.
49 13 that Bosra shall become a desolation
Bar 2 4 reproach and d. among all the people
4 33 so shall she be grieved for her own d.
Eze 12 19 drink their water in d.: that the land
Dan 8 13 the sin of the desolation that is made
9 2 be accomplished of the d. of Jerusalem
18 open thy eyes, and see our desolation
26 after end of the war the appointed d.
27 in the temple the abomination of d.
27 the desolation shall continue even to
11 31 shall place there abomination unto d.
12 11 abomination unto d. shall be set up
Osee 5 9 Ephraim shall be in desolation in the
12 1 he multiplied lies and desolation: and
Joel 3 19 Egypt shall be a desolation and Edom
Abdi 13 his army in the day of his desolation
Mich 6 13 therefore began to strike thee with d.
16 that I should make thee a desolation
1 Ma 1 57 set up the abominable idol of d. upon
Mat 24 15 abomination of d. Mark 13:14
Luke 11 17 kingdom divided . . . be brought to d.
21 20 know that the d. thereof is at hand
desolations 1 Es 9 9 to rebuild the d. thereof
Jer 25 9 make them . . . perpetual desolations
12 I will make it perpetual desolations
Eze 35 9 I will make thee everlasting d. and
despair 1 K 27 1 that Saul may d. of me and cease
2 K 2 26 dangerous to drive people to despair
Prov 19 18 chastise thy son, despair not: but to
Eccu 22 26 drawn a sword at a friend, d. not: for
despaired 1 K 23 26 David d. of being able to
2 K 12 15 the child . . . and his life was d. of
despairing 2 Ma 9 18 d. of life he wrote to the
Eph 4 19 who d., have given themselves up to
desperate Jer 15 18 my wound d. so as to refuse
Mich 1 9 because her wound is desperate because
despicable Jer 49 15 among the nations, d. among
despise Exod 21 8 to sell her . . . if he d. her
Lev 26 15 if you despise my laws and contemn my
44 neither did I so despise them that
Deut 31 20 will serve them; and will despise me
Judg 9 38 the people which thou didst despise
1 K 2 30 they that d. me, shall be despised
12 3 I [Samuel] will despise it this day
4 K 1 13 man of God, despise not my life and
2 Pa 26 18 go out of the sanctuary, do not despise
Tob 9 5 Raguel . . . whose adjuring I cannot d.
13 16 they shall be cursed that shall d. thee
Jdth 9 14 in my mind, that I may despise him
10 18 who can d. the people of the Hebrews
Ps 26 9 do not thou despise me, O God my savior
43 6 we will d. them that rise up against
50 19 humbled heart, O God, thou wilt not d.
54 2 and despise not my supplication: be
137 8 despise not the works of thy hands
Prov 1 7 fools despise wisdom and instruction
23 9 they will d. the instruction of thy
22 despise not thy mother when she is old
Cant 8 1 and now no man may despise me? I will
7 for love, he shall despise it as nothing
Wisd 4 18 they shall see him and shall d. him
19 20 didst not despise them, but didst
Eccu 3 15 d. him not when thou art in thy strength
4 2 despise not the hungry soul: and provoke
7 20 nor d. thy dear brother for the sake
8 6 d. not a man that turneth away from
7 despise not a man in his old age; for
9 d. not the discourse of them that are
10 26 d. not a just man that is poor and do
11 2 neither despise a man for his look
31 26 hear me, my son, and despise me not
41 and despise him not in his mirth. Speak
35 17 he will not d. prayers of the fatherless
Isa 33 1 being wearied thou shalt cease to d.
58 7 cover him, and d. not thy own flesh
Mala 1 7 O priests, that despise my name? You
2 10 every one of us despise his brother
15 despise not the wife of thy youth
16 keep your spirit and despise not. You
2 Ma 7 11 for the laws of God I now d. them
23 as now you despise yourselves for
Mat 6 24 sustain the one, and d. Luke 16:13
18 10 see that you d. not one of these little
Rom 14 3 that eateth, despise him that eateth not
10 why dost thou despise thy brother
1 C 11 22 despise ye the church of God. You
16 11 let no man despise him [Timothy], but
1 Th 5 20 despise not prophecies. But prove all
1 Tim 4 12 let no man despise thy youth: but
6 2 let them not despise them because they
Titus 2 15 let no man despise thee. Admonish them
2 P 2 10 especially them who . . . d. government
Jude 8 despise dominion and blaspheme majesty
despised Gen 16 4 with child, d. her mistress
Gen 29 31 the Lord seeing that he despised Lia
33 the Lord heard that I was despised
Lev 26 43 rejected my judgments and d. my laws
Num 5 27 having despised her husband be guilty
14 31 the land which you have despised. Your
Judg 2 20 hath despised to hearken to my voice
1 K 2 30 they that despise me, shall be d.
10 27 they despised him [Saul] and brought
17 42 and beheld David, he despised him
2 K 6 16 she [Michol] d. him [David] in her heart. 1 Pa 15:29
12 9 why . . . hast thou d. the word of the
10 because thou [David] hast d. me and
19 26 my servant d. me: for I, thy servant
4 K 19 21 the daughter of Sion hath d. thee
2 Pa 36 16 God and despised his words and misused
2 Es 2 19 they scoffed at us and despised us
4 4 give them to be d. in land of captivity
4 hear thou our God, for we are despised
Jdth 2 5 them especially that d. my commandment
5 4 have d. us and have not come out to
10 12 prey to you, because they d. you and
11 2 if thy people had not despised me, I
13 28 Holofernes, who . . . d. the God of Israel
Job 12 5 the lamp d. in the thoughts of the rich
19 18 even fools d. me and when I was gone
31 13 if I have despised to abide judgment
19 if I have d. him that was perishing
Ps 21 25 not slighted nor d. the supplication
52 6 confounded because God hath d. them
68 34 and hath not despised his prisoners

77 59 God heard, and despised them, and he
62 the sword: and he d. his inheritance
88 39 but thou hast rejected and despised
101 18 he hath not despised their petition
118 118 thou hast d. all them that fall off
141 I am very young and despised; but I
Prov 1 25 you have despised all my counsel and
30 to my counsel, but d. all my reproof
14 2 is d. by him that goeth by an infamous
Ecce 7 14 that no man can correct whom he hath d.
Eccu 2 12 called upon him, and he despised him
19 4 against his own soul, shall be despised
26 26 and a man of sense despised: and he
49 6 and despised the fear of God. So they
Isa 1 2 exalted them: but they have d. me
33 1 shalt not thyself also be despised
1 cease to despise, thou shalt be d.
37 22 daughter of Sion hath despised thee
49 7 to the soul that is despised, to the
53 3 despised and the most abject of men
3 look was as it were hidden and d.
Jer 3 20 so hath the house of Israel d. me
4 30 thy lovers have despised thee, they
33 8 sinned against me and despised me
24 they have despised my people, so that
Lam 1 2 all her friends have despised her
8 that honored her have despised her
Eze 5 6 she hath despised my judgments, so as
16 59 as thou hast despised the oath in
17 18 had d. the oath, breaking his covenant
19 upon his head the oath he hath d.
20 by which he hath despised me. And all
20 27 when they had d. and contemned me
22 8 thou hast despised my sanctuaries
26 her priests have despised my law and
Dan 11 21 stand up in his place one despised
Nah 3 11 made drunk, and shalt be despised
Zach 4 10 who hath despised little days? and
Mala 1 7 wherein have we despised thy name
2 14 wife of thy youth whom thou hast d.
1 Ma 3 14 that have d. the edict of the king
7 34 but he mocked and despised them and
2 Ma 1 27 them that are despised and abhorred
7 24 Antiochus thinking himself despised
Mark 9 11 he must suffer . . . and be despised
Luke 7 39 Pharisees . . . despised the counsel of
18 9 trusted in themselves . . . and d. others
1 C 6 4 them to judge, who are the most d.
Gal 4 14 you despised not or rejected: but
despisers Acts 13 41 behold, ye d., and wonder
despisest Isa 33 1 thou that d., shalt not thou
Rom 2 4 d. thou riches of his goodness and
despiseth Gen 16 5 to be with child, d. me. The
Job 39 22 he d. fear, he turneth not his back
Prov 11 12 he that d. his friend, is mean of
14 21 he that despiseth his neighbor, sinneth
15 20 the foolish man despiseth his mother
32 rejecteth instruction, d. his own soul
17 5 he that d. the poor, reproacheth his
28 27 he that d. his entreaty, shall suffer
29 1 despiseth him that reproveth him shall
30 17 d. the labor of his mother in bearing
Ecce 9 2 and to him that despiseth sacrifices
Eccu 14 8 away his face and d. his own soul
Jer 3 20 as a woman that despiseth her lover
Luke 10 16 that d. you, d. me; and he that d. me, d. him that sent me.
John 12 48 he that d. me and receiveth not my
Gal 3 15 a man's testament . . . no man despiseth
1 Th 4 8 that d. these things, d. not man but
despising Lev 6 2 d. the Lord, shall deny to his
Judg 11 20 he also despising the words of Israel
Wisd 14 30 sworn unjustly, in guile d. justice
Eccu 23 25 beyond his own bed, d. his own soul
1 Ma 6 59 because of our d. their laws, they
2 Ma 4 14 d. the temple and neglecting sacrifices
7 24 d. the voice of the upbraider, when
Heb 12 2 endured the cross, despising the shame
despoiling Col 2 11 d. of the body of the flesh
Col 2 15 despoiling the principalities and
Dessau 2 Ma 14 16 and went to the town of Dessau
destitute Ecce 4 1 being d. of help from any
Eccu 37 23 he shall be destitute of everything
Isa 49 21 I was destitute and alone: and these
Eze 32 15 the land shall be d. of her fulness
2 C 4 8 we are straitened, but are not d.
1 Tim 6 5 are destitute of the truth, supposing
destroy Mat 2 13 will seek the child to d. him
Mat 5 17 that I am come to destroy the law
17 am not come to destroy, but to fulfil
10 28 that can d. both soul and body in hell
12 14 how they might d. him. Mark 3:6; 11:18
26 61 this man said, I am able to d. the
Mark 1 24 art thou come to d. us. Luke 4:34
3 4 to save life or to destroy. Luke 6:9
9 21 the fire and into waters to destroy him
12 9 will . . . d. those husbandmen. Luke 20:16
14 58 I will d. this temple made with hands
Luke 9 56 Son of man came not to destroy souls
19 47 rulers of the people sought to d. him
John 2 19 destroy this temple and in three days
10 10 thief cometh . . . to kill and to destroy
Acts 6 14 shall d. this place and shall change the
Rom 3 31 do we destroy the law through faith
14 15 destroy not him with thy meat, thy
20 destroy not the works of God for meat
1 C 1 19 I will destroy the law of the wise
3 17 him shall God destroy. For the temple
6 13 God shall destroy both it and them
2 Th 2 8 shall d. with brightness of his coming
Heb 2 14 d. him who had the empire of death
James 4 12 that is able to d. and to deliver. But
1 J 3 8 that he might d. the works of the devil
Jude 5 did afterwards destroy them that
Apoc 11 18 d. them who have corrupted the earth
destroyed Mat 22 7 he d. those murderers and burnt
Mat 24 2 be left . . . stone that shall not be d.
Luke 17 27 the flood came and destroyed them all
29 rained fire . . . and destroyed them all
Acts 3 23 shall be d. from among the people
19 27 her majesty shall begin to be d. whom
Rom 6 6 that the body of sin may be destroyed
1 C 10 10 some of them murmured and were d. by
13 8 or knowledge shall be destroyed. For
15 26 enemy death shall be destroyed last
Gal 2 18 things which I have destroyed, I made
2 Tim 1 10 who hath destroyed death, and hath
Heb 11 28 he who destroyed the firstborn, might
Apoc 8 9 third part of the ships was destroyed
destroyedst Wisd 18 5 d. them all together in a
destroyer Exod 12 23 not suffer the d. to come
Jdth 8 25 were destroyed by the destroyer and
Wisd 18 25 to these the destroyer gave place
Isa 16 4 covert to them from face of the d.
Jer 6 26 destroyer shall suddenly come upon
22 7 I will prepare against thee the d.
50 9 like those of a mighty man, a d., shall
1 C 10 10 were destroyed by the destroyer. Now
destroyers Job 33 22 and his life to the d. If
Eze 2 6 thou art among unbelievers and d. and
destroyest Jdth 9 10 who d. wars from the beginning
Job 18 4 thou that d. thy soul in thy fury, shall
2 Ma 7 9 d. us out of this present life: but the
Mat 27 40 that destroyest the temple. Mark 15:29
destroyeth Job 12 23 he multiplieth nations and d.
Eccu 27 20 that d. friendship of his neighbor

20 as a man that destroyeth his friend
Lam 1 20 abroad the sword destroyeth, and at
2 Ma 3 39 d. them that come to do evil to it
destroying Num 16 47 the burning fire was now d.
Deut 2 22 d. the Horrhites, and delivering their
3 6 d. every city, men and women and
28 63 destroying and bring you to nought
Judg 21 15 repented for the d. of one tribe out
1 Pa 21 12 angel of the Lord d. in all . . . Israel
Eccu 16 10 d. the whole nation that extolled
Isa 28 2 a d. whirlwind, as the violence of
Jer 51 25 against thee, thou d. mountain, saith
Lam 2 8 hath not withdrawn his hand from d.
Eze 9 1 every one hath a destroying weapon
25 15 destroying and satisfying old enmities
2 Ma 8 17 besides their d. the ordinances of
Acts 13 19 destroying seven nations in the land of
2 C 10 4 destroying counsels. And every height
destruction Gen 19 29 Lot out of the destruction
Num 16 50 after the destruction was over. And
32 15 you shall be the cause of the d. of all
Deut 29 23 example of the d. of Sodom and Gomorrha
32 35 the day of destruction is at hand and
2 K 2 26 shall thy sword wage unto utter d.
4 K 13 19 hadst smitten Syria even to utter d.
2 Pa 14 13 Ethiopians fell to utter destruction
22 4 his counsellors . . . to his destruction
26 16 his heart was lifted up to his d. and
29 8 delivered them to trouble and to d.
30 7 he hath given them up to destruction
1 Es 9 14 angry with us unto utter destruction
Tob 14 6 the destruction of Ninive is at hand
13 its iniquity will bring it to d. And
Jdth 6 17 thou rather shalt see their destruction
7 14 before their eyes in thirst and sad d.
8 27 for our amendment, and not for our d.
11 12 they will be given up to destruction
Esth 16 13 sought the destruction of Mardochai
Job 5 22 in d. and famine thou shalt laugh: and
18 14 destruction tread upon him like a king
21 20 his eyes shall see his own destruction
30 is reserved to the day of destruction
26 6 there is no covering for destruction
28 22 destruction and death have said: With
31 3 is not destruction to the wicked and
12 it is a fire that devoureth even to d.
33 28 delivered his soul from going into d.
Ps 9 16 in the destruction which they prepared
13 3 d. and unhappiness in their ways: and
34 7 have hidden their net for me unto d.
48 11 he shall not see destruction, when he
54 24 bring them down into the pit of d.
87 12 and thy truth in destruction? Shall
102 4 redeemeth thy life from destruction
105 29 and d. was multiplied among them. Then
139 12 shall catch the unjust man unto d.
Prov 1 26 I also will laugh in your destruction
27 d., as a tempest, shall be at hand
6 15 his destruction shall presently come
15 11 hell and d. are before the Lord: how
16 18 pride goeth before destruction: and
18 7 the mouth of a fool is his destruction
12 before d., heart of a man is exalted
24 22 their destruction shall rise suddenly
27 20 hell and destruction are never filled
28 10 shall fall in his own destruction
29 27 shall be free from destruction. The
Wisd 1 12 neither procure ye d. by the works of
13 in the destruction of the living. For
14 there is no poison of d. in them, nor
3 3 their going away from us, for utter d.
5 7 ourselves in the way of iniquity and d.
16 4 inevitable d. should come upon them
18 7 and destruction of the unjust. For as
13 upon the destruction of the firstborn
15 into midst of the land of destruction
Eccu 9 13 by thy blood thou fall into d. Forsake
20 27 both of them shall inherit destruction
23 21 bringeth wrath and destruction. A hot
39 34 in the time of d. they shall pour out
36 upon the ungodly unto destruction. In
41 13 shall from malediction to destruction
48 6 broughtest down kings to destruction
50 4 of his nation and delivered it from d.
51 3 preserved my body from destruction
Isa 13 6 it shall come as a d. from the Lord
15 5 shall lift up a cry of destruction
30 13 d. thereof shall come on a sudden
49 19 land of thy destruction shall now
51 14 he shall not kill unto utter d. neither
19 desolation and d. and the famine and the
59 7 wasting and d. are in their ways. They
60 18 no more . . . wasting nor destruction
Jer 4 6 bring evil from the north, and great d.
20 d. upon d. is called for, and all the
5 18 I will not bring you to utter d. And
6 1 out of the north, and a great d. I
21 I will bring d. upon this people, by
10 19 woe is me for my destruction, my wound
14 4 d. of the land, because there came no
17 18 with a double d. destroy them. Thus
18 17 the face, in the day of their destruction
48 3 Oronaim: waste and great destruction
5 the enemies have heard a howling of d.
16 the d. of Moab is near to come: the
49 8 I have brought the d. of Esau upon him
32 I will bring destruction upon them
50 22 noise of war in the land and a great d.
51 13 thy end is come for thy entire d. The
54 great d. from the land of the Chaldeans
Lam 2 11 for the d. of the daughter of my people
13 great as the sea is thy destruction
3 47 become to us . . . a snare and destruction
48 d. of the daughter of my people. 4:10
Bar 4 6 sold to the Gentiles, not for your d.
25 thou shalt quickly see his destruction
Eze 5 17 and evil beasts unto utter destruction
7 7 d. is come upon thee that dwellest in
10 d. is gone forth, the rod hath blossomed
9 2 each one had his season of destruction
21 31 that are brutish and contrive thy d.
22 5 thou filthy one, infamous, great in d.
32 9 when I shall have brought in thy d.
Dan 14 41 those that had been the cause of his d.
Osee 9 6 they are gone because of destruction
13 9 destruction is thy own, O Israel: thy
Joel 1 15 shall come like d. from the mighty
3 14 nations in the valley of destruction
14 is near in the valley of destruction
Amos 5 9 with a smile bringeth destruction
Abdi 12 in the day of their destruction: and
Mich 1 7 will bring to d. all her idols: for
7 4 now shall be their destruction. Believe
Nah 3 3 the noise . . . of a grievous destruction
19 thy destruction is not hidden, thy wound
Soph 1 10 and a great destruction from the hills
18 make even a speedy d. of all them that
Zach 14 15 the d. of the horse and of the mule
15 shall be like this destruction. And
18 there shall be d. wherewith the Lord
1 Ma 2 49 time of d., and the wrath of indignation
3 32 let them quake at their own destruction
5 5 and devoted them to utter destruction
2 Ma 5 8 in order for his d., flying from city
13 d. of women and children and killing
6 12 that happened, not as being for the d.

8 35 unhappy by the d. of his army. And he
Mat 7 13 the way that leadeth to destruction
Rom 3 16 d. and misery in their ways: and the way
9 22 vessels of wrath, fitted for d., that
1 C 5 5 for the destruction of the flesh, that
2 C 10 8 our power . . . not for your destruction
13 10 unto edification and unto destruction
Phil 3 19 whose end is destruction; whose God
Col 2 22 which all are unto destruction by the
1 Th 5 3 then shall sudden d. come upon them
2 Th 1 9 shall suffer eternal punishment in d.
1 Tim 6 9 which drown men into d. and perdition
Heb 9 26 he hath appeared for the d. of sin
2 P 2 1 bring upon themselves swift d. And
12 naturally tending to the snare and to d.
3 16 unstable wrest . . . to their own d. You
Apoc 17 8 the beast shall go into destruction
11 the beast goeth into destruction. And
destructions Ps 106 20 delivered them from their d.
detain Rom 1 18 that detain the truth of God in
detained 4 K 4 8 who detained him to eat bread
Tob 10 1 son tarry, or why is he d. there? Is
Eccu 3 26 hath detained their minds in vanity
1 Ma 13 15 we have detained thy brother Jonathan
Rom 7 6 law of death wherein we were detained
determinate Acts 2 23 by the d. counsel . . . of God
determination Dan 11 36 the determination is made
determine Num 35 11 d. what cities shall be for
Judg 20 7 determine what you ought to do. And all
Bar 6 53 they determine no causes nor deliver
determined Num 6 13 days which he had d. by vow
Num 24 11 I had d. indeed greatly to honor thee
Ruth 1 18 seeing that Ruth was steadfastly d.
1 K 20 9 that evil is d. by my father against
33 was d. by his father to kill David
25 17 evil is determined against thy husband
2 K 19 29 what I have said is determined: thou
2 Pa 2 1 Solomon determined to build a house to
Ps 40 9 they d. against me an unjust word
118 106 I have sworn and am determined to keep
Eccu 51 24 I have determined to follow her: I
Isa 19 17 which he hath d. concerning it. In that
1 Ma 1 14 some of the people d. to do this and
65 d. within themselves that they would
2 41 they determined in that day, saying
6 23 we determined to serve thy father and
11 32 we have d. to do good to the nation
2 Ma 6 20 he d. not to do any unlawful things
10 12 was d. to be strictly just to the Jews
13 13 determined before the king should bring
Luke 22 22 according to that which is d.: but yet
Acts 15 2 they determined that Paul and Barnabas
20 16 Paul had d. to sail by Ephesus, lest
25 25 I have d. to send him [Paul]. Of whom
27 1 was d. that he should sail unto Italy
1 C 7 37 determined being steadfast in his heart
2 C 2 1 I determined this with myself, not to
8 19 glory of the Lord and our d. will
9 7 every one as he hath d. in his heart
Titus 3 12 there I have determined to winter
determineth Prov 18 18 lot . . . d. even between the
Prov 26 10 judgment d. causes: and he that putteth
determining Acts 17 26 d. appointed times and the
detest Num 23 7 make haste and detest Israel. How
Num 23 8 by what means should I detest him whom
Deut 7 76 thou shalt detest it as dung and shalt
Judg 9 23 who began to detest him [Abimelech]
Amos 6 8 I detest the pride of Jacob, and I
detestable Gen 38 10 because he did a d. thing
Lev 11 11 an abomination to you, and detestable
18 27 all these d. things the inhabitants
Wisd 19 13 exercised a more d. inhospitality than
Eccu 19 20 wickedness, and the same is detestable
Eze 18 13 hath done all these detestable things
detested Ps 55 6 the day long they d. my words
detesteth Num 23 8 whom the Lord detesteth not
Prov 6 16 and the seventh his soul detesteth
detract Num 14 11 how long will this people d. me
Ps 70 13 let . . . come to nothing that d. my soul
108 20 the work of them who d. me before the
29 that detract me be clothed with shame
Ecce 10 20 d. not the king, no not in thy thought
James 4 11 detract not one another, my brethren
detracted Num 14 23 any one of them that hath d.
Job 6 25 why have you d. the words of truth
Ps 37 21 that render evil for good, have d. me
100 5 that in private detracted his neighbor
108 4 me a return of love, they detracted me
detracteth Ps 43 17 him that reproacheth and d. me
James 4 11 he that d. his brother . . . d. the law
detracting Prov 4 24 let d. lips be far from thee
detraction Wisd 1 11 refrain your tongue from d.
Eccu 38 18 merit for a day or two, for fear of d.
2 C 12 20 lest detraction . . . be among you. Lest
1 P 2 1 dissimulation and envies and all d.
detractor Lev 19 16 thou shalt not be a d. nor
Prov 24 9 detractor is the abomination of men
detractors Prov 24 21 have nothing to do with d.
Rom 1 30 detractors hateful to God, contumelious
Deuteronomy Deut 17 18 copy out to himself the D.
Josu 8 32 he wrote upon stones the Deuteronomy
devastation Isa 22 4 for the d. of the daughter
Jer 20 8 and I often proclaim devastation: and
device 3 K 12 28 finding out a d. he made two
Wisd 19 3 they took up another foolish device
Eccu 19 19 the device of sinners is not prudence
Jer 18 11 devise a d. against you: let every
Dan 13 28 elders also came full of wicked device
Acts 17 29 divinity to be like . . . device of man
devices 2 Es 9 35 from their most wicked devices
Esth 8 3 Aman the Agagite and his most wicked d.
16 13 with certain new and unheard of d.
Job 20 18 according to multitude of his devices
Ps 5 11 let them fall from their d.: according
32 10 he rejecteth the devices of people
Prov 1 31 shall be filled with their own devices
12 2 trusteth in his own d. doth wickedly
15 5 d. of the wicked shall be rooted out
Wisd 3 10 be punished according to their own d.
11 16 for the foolish d. of their iniquity
Eccu 23 4 leave me not to their devices. Give
30 11 and wink not at his devices. Bow down
42 18 considered their crafty devices. For
Isa 1 16 take away the evil of your devices from
3 8 and their devices are against the Lord
32 7 hath framed d. to destroy the meek
Jer 4 18 thy devices have brought these things
17 10 according to fruit of his d. 32:19
18 18 let us invent devices against Jeremias
25 5 from your wicked devices and you shall
Lam 3 62 their devices against me all the day
Eze 21 24 your sins have appeared in all your d.
36 19 judged them according to . . . their d.
Dan 11 24 shall forecast d. against the best
Osee 4 9 I will repay them their devices. And
7 2 their own devices now have beset them
9 15 for wickedness of their d. I will cast
12 2 to his ways and according to his d.
Mich 3 4 have behaved wickedly in their devices
7 13 desolate . . . for the fruit of their d.
Zach 1 6 to our ways and according to our d.
2 C 2 11 we are not ignorant of his devices
devil 3 K 21 13 two men, sons of the devil, bore
3 K 21 13 like men of the devil, bore witness
Tob 3 8 devil named Asmodeus had killed them
6 14 I have heard that a devil killed them

16 over whom the devil can prevail. For
17 over them the devil hath power. But
19 and the devil shall be driven away
8 3 then the angel Raphael took the devil
12 14 to deliver Sara thy son's wife from d.
Ps 90 6 not be afraid . . . of the noonday devil
108 6 may the devil stand at his right hand
Wisd 2 24 by the envy of the devil, death came
Eccu 21 30 while the ungodly curseth the devil
Haba 3 5 the devil shall go forth before his
1 Ma 1 38 sanctuary, and an evil devil in Israel
Mat 4 1 to be tempted by the devil. Luke 4:2
5 devil took him up into the holy city
8 devil took him up into a very high
11 then the devil left him; and behold
9 32 a dumb man possessed with a devil
33 after the devil was cast out, the dumb
11 18 they say: He hath a devil. John 10:20
12 22 one possessed with a d., blind and dumb
13 39 enemy that sowed them is the devil
15 22 daughter is grievously troubled by a d.
17 17 d. went out of him and the child was
25 41 prepared for the devil and his angels
Mark 5 15 him that was troubled with the devil
16 had been dealt with who had the devil
7 26 cast forth devil out of her daughter
29 the devil is gone out of thy daughter
30 the bed and that the devil was gone out
Luke 4 3 devil said . . . if thou be the Son of
5 the devil led him into a high mountain
13 devil departed from him for a time
33 a man who had an unclean devil and he
35 when d. had thrown him into the midst
7 33 you say: He hath a devil. The Son of
8 12 the d. cometh and taketh the word out
27 man who had a d. now a very long time
29 driven by the devil into the deserts
9 42 the devil threw him down and tore him
11 14 he was casting out a devil and the
14 when he had cast out the devil, the
John 6 71 one of you is a devil? Now he meant
7 20 thou hast a devil. 8:48, 52
8 44 you are of your father the devil and
49 I have not a devil: but I honor my
10 21 not the words of one that hath a devil
21 can a d. open the eyes of the blind
13 2 d. having put into the heart of Judas
Acts 10 38 all that were oppressed by the devil
13 10 child of the d., enemy of all justice
Eph 4 27 give not place to the devil. He that
6 11 stand against the deceits of the devil
1 Tim 3 6 fall into the judgment of the devil
7 lest he fall into . . . snare of the d.
6 9 into the snare of the d. and into many
2 Tim 2 26 recover themselves from snares of the d.
Heb 2 14 empire of death, that is to say, the d.
James 4 7 resist the d. and he will fly from you
1 P 5 8 the devil as a roaring lion goeth about
1 J 3 8 committeth sin is of the d.: for the d. sinneth from the beginning
8 that he might destroy the work of the devil
10 are manifest and the children of the d.
Jude 9 disputing with the devil, contended
Apoc 2 10 devil will cast some of you into prison
12 9 serpent who is called the d. and Satan
12 the devil is come down unto you having
20 2 old serpent which is the d. and Satan
9 the devil who seduced them, was cast
devilish James 3 15 earthly, sensual, devilish
devils Lev 17 7 more sacrifice their victims to d.
Deut 32 17 they sacrificed to d. and not to God
2 Pa 11 15 for the d. and for the calves which he
Tob 6 8 driveth away all kinds of d., either
Ps 95 5 all the gods of the Gentiles are d.
105 37 sacrificed their sons . . . to devils
Bar 4 7 offering sacrifice to devils and not
35 she shall be inhabited by devils for
Mat 4 24 as were possessed by d. 8:16; Mark 1:32
8 28 two that were possessed with d., coming
31 d. besought him, saying: If thou cast
33 that had been possessed by the devils
9 34 by prince of d. he casteth. Mark 3:22
12 24 casteth not out d. but by Beelzebub, the prince of the devils. Luke 11:15
Mark 1 39 was preaching . . . and casting out devils
9 37 casting out devils in thy name, who
Luke 4 41 devils went out from many, crying out
8 2 out of whom seven d. were gone forth
30 because many d. were entered into him
33 the devils went out of the man and
35 man out of whom the devils were. 38
9 1 authority over all devils and to cure
10 17 the devils also are subject to us
1 C 10 20 they sacrifice to d. and not to God
20 you should be made partakers with d.
21 chalice of the Lord and the chalice of d.
21 partakers . . . of the table of devils
1 Tim 4 1 to spirits of error and doctrines of d.
James 2 19 the devils also believe and tremble
Apoc 9 20 that they should not adore devils
16 14 they are the spirits of devils working
18 2 is become habitation of d. and the hold
cast out devils Mat 7 22 c. . . . in thy name
Mat 10 8 cleanse the lepers, cast out devils
12 27 if I by Beelzebub cast out devils
28 if I by Spirit of God cast out devils
Mark 1 34 he cast out many devils and he suffered
3 15 power to heal sicknesses and to c. . . .
6 13 they cast out many devils and anointed
16 9 out of whom he had cast seven devils
17 in my name they shall cast out devils
Luke 11 18 you say that through Beelzebub I c. . . .
19 if I cast out devils by Beelzebub
20 if I by finger of God cast out devils
13 32 I c. . . . and do cures today and tomorrow
devise Exod 31 4 d. whatsoever may be artificially
Exod 35 32 to d. and to work in gold and silver
2 Pa 2 14 to d. ingeniously all that there may
Ps 9 2 caught in the counsels which they d.
34 4 be confounded that d. evil against me
Eccu 7 13 devise not a lie against thy brother
17 5 gave them . . . a heart to devise: and
37 9 for he will devise to his own mind
Isa 32 8 the prince will devise such things as
Jer 18 11 and devise a device against you: let
Dan 11 30 shall devise against them that have
Mich 2 1 that d. that which is unprofitable
3 I devise an evil against this family
Nah 1 9 what do ye devise against the Lord
Zach 7 10 let not a man devise evil in his heart
devised Exod 35 33 whatsoever can be devised
3 K 12 33 which he had devised of his own heart
Jdth 9 4 hast devised one thing after another
Ps 2 1 and the people devised vain things
20 12 they have d. counsels which they have
34 20 speaking in the anger . . . they d. guile
35 5 he hath devised iniquity on his bed
40 8 against me: they devised evils to me
51 3 thy tongue hath devised injustice
139 3 who have devised iniquities in their
Wisd 14 2 for this the desire of gain devised
Jer 11 19 they had devised counsels against me
48 2 they have devised evil. Come and let
Haba 2 10 hast devised confusion to thy house
1 Ma 11 8 d. evil designs against Alexander. And
John 11 53 they devised to put him to death

deviseth Prov 6 14 with wicked heart he d. evil
Prov 6 18 a heart that deviseth wicked plots
16 30 that with fixed eyes d. wicked things
24 8 that d. to do evils, shall be called
devising Josu 9 4 cunningly d. took for themselves
Wisd 14 12 beginning of fornication is d. of idols
devoted Lev 27 28 that is devoted to the Lord
1 Ma 5 5 devoted them to utter destruction and
devour Exod 10 12 upon it and d. every herb that
Num 23 24 not lie down till it devour the prey
24 8 shall devour the nations that are his
Deut 28 51 will devour the fruit of thy cattle
32 22 shall d. the earth with her increase
24 and birds shall devour them with a
42 my sword shall devour flesh, of the
Judg 9 15 bramble, and d. the cedars of Libanus
20 town of Mello, and devour Abimelech
3 K 14 11 the birds of the air shall devour: for
16 4 the fowls of the air shall devour. But
2 Pa 7 13 command the locust to devour the land
Tob 6 2 a monstrous fish came up to devour him
Job 15 34 fire shall devour their tabernacles
18 13 let it devour the beauty of his skin
20 26 fire that is not kindled shall d. him
Ps 13 4 who devour my people as they eat bread
20 10 in his wrath, and fire shall d. them
Prov 20 25 ruin to a man to devour holy ones
30 14 to devour the needy from off the earth
Eccu 23 22 quenched, till it devour some thing
36 20 the belly will devour all meat, yet
43 23 it shall devour the mountains and
51 4 that did roar, prepared to devour
Isa 1 7 your country strangers d. before your
20 the sword shall devour you because
9 12 they shall d. Israel with open mouth
18 it shall devour the brier and the
24 6 shall a curse devour the earth and the
26 11 and let fire devour thy enemies. Lord
31 8 sword not of a man shall devour him
33 11 your breath as fire shall devour you
Jer 2 3 all they that devour him offend: evils
5 14 as wood, and it shall devour them
17 they shall devour thy sons and thy
12 9 beasts of the earth, make haste to d.
12 the sword of the Lord shall devour
15 3 beasts of the earth to devour and
21 14 shall d. all things round. 46:14
30 16 that devour thee shall be devoured
46 10 the sword shall devour and shall be
48 45 it shall devour part of Moab and the
49 27 shall d. the strong holds of Benadad
50 32 it shall devour all round about him
Eze 19 3 to catch the prey and to devour men. 6
23 34 shalt devour the fragments thereof
28 18 fire from the midst of thee to devour
34 28 shall the beasts of the earth d. them
36 14 thou shalt devour men no more, nor
Dan 7 5 said to it: Arise, devour much flesh
23 shall d. the whole earth and shall
14 31 that they might devour Daniel. Now
Osee 2 12 beasts of the field shall devour her
5 7 now shall a month devour them with
8 14 it shall devour the houses thereof. Amos 1:7, 10, 14
11 6 men, and shall devour their heads
13 8 I will devour them there as a lion
Amos 1 4 it shall devour the houses of Benadad
12 it shall devour the houses of Bosra
2 2 it shall devour the houses of Carioth
5 it shall d. the houses of Jerusalem
5 6 burnt with fire, and it shall devour
Abdi 18 kindled in them and shall devour them
Nah 2 13 sword shall devour thy young lions
3 13 the fire shall devour thy bars. Draw
15 there shall the fire devour thee: thou
15 shall devour thee like the bruchus
Zach 9 15 they shall devour and subdue with
11 1 and let fire devour thy cedars. Howl
9 let the rest every one d. the flesh
12 6 they shall devour all the people round
Mat 23 14 d. the houses of widows. Mark 12:40; Luke 20:47
2 C 11 20 you suffer . . . if a man devour you, if
Gal 5 15 if you bite and devour one another
1 P 5 8 seeking whom he may devour. Whom resist
Apoc 11 5 fire . . . shall devour their enemies
12 4 that he might devour her son. And she
devoured Gen 37 20 evil beast hath devoured him
Gen 37 33 a beast hath devoured Joseph. And
41 4 they devoured them whose bodies were
7 devoured all the beauty of the former
20 they devoured and consumed the former
24 they d. the beauty of the former: I
44 28 you said: A beast devoured him: and
Exod 7 12 but Aaron's rod devoured their rods
10 15 the grass of the earth was devoured
15 7 which hath devoured them like stubble
Lev 9 24 a fire . . . devoured the holocaust and
26 16 shall be devoured by your enemies. I
Num 11 1 d. them that were at the uttermost
16 32 devoured them with their tents and
39 whom the burning fire had devoured
Deut 31 17 and they shall be devoured: all evils
2 K 18 8 than whom the sword devoured that day
Tob 12 3 delivered from being d. by the fish
Job 22 20 hath not fire d. the remnants of them
Ps 77 45 sorts of flies, which devoured them
78 7 because they have devoured Jacob; and
79 14 a singular wild beast hath devoured it
104 35 they d. all the grass in their land
Eccu 13 23 so also the poor are d. by the rich
Isa 3 14 for you have devoured the vineyard
10 17 set on fire and shall be d. in one
Jer 2 30 your sword hath d. your prophets, your
3 24 confusion hath d. the labor of our
8 16 they came and devoured the land and
10 25 have eaten up Jacob and devoured him
30 16 that devour thee shall be devoured
50 7 that found them, have devoured them
17 the king of Assyria devoured him: and
51 34 eaten me up, he hath devoured me: he
Lam 4 11 it hath d. the foundations thereof
Eze 7 15 shall be d. by the pestilence and the
15 5 when the fire hath d. and consumed
16 20 the same to them to be devoured. Is
19 12 dried up: the fire hath devoured her
14 which hath devoured her fruit: so that
22 25 the prey, they have devoured souls
23 25 thy residue shall be devoured by fire
37 have offered to them to be devoured
33 27 shall be given to the beasts to be d.
39 4 to the beasts of the earth to be d.
Dan 7 19 he devoured and broke in pieces and
14 41 they were d. in a moment before him
Osee 7 7 have devoured their judges: all their
9 strangers have devoured his strength
Joel 1 19 fire hath d. the beautiful places. 20
Amos 7 4 it devoured the great deep and ate
Soph 1 18 the land shall be d. by the fire of
3 8 jealousy shall all the earth be d.
Zach 9 4 she shall be devoured with fire. Ascalon
2 Ma 9 15 to be d. by the birds and wild beasts
Luke 8 5 the fowls of the air devoured it. And
15 30 who hath d. his substance with harlots
Apoc 20 9 there came down fire . . . and d. them
devourer Eze 36 13 thou art a devourer of men

Mala 3 11 I will rebuke for your sakes the d.
devourers Wisd 12 5 and devourers of blood from
devoureth Num 13 33 the land . . . d. its inhabitants
Job 31 12 a fire that d. even to destruction
Prov 19 28 mouth of the wicked devoureth iniquity
Isa 5 24 tongue of the fire d. the stubble and
Haba 1 13 thy peace when the wicked devoureth
3 14 that d. the poor man in secret. Thou
Mala 1 12 with the fire that devoureth it. And
devouring Lev 6 10 when the d. fire hath burnt
Deut 9 3 d. and consuming fire to destroy and
Judg 20 48 were consumed with devouring flames
2 K 22 9 and a devouring fire out of his mouth
Isa 29 6 the flame of devouring fire. 30:30
30 27 and his tongue as a devouring fire
33 14 which of you can dwell with d. fire
Joel 2 3 before the face thereof a d. fire and
5 flame of fire devouring the stubble
Lam 2 3 flaming fire devouring round about
devout Exod 35 21 with a most ready and d. mind
Exod 35 29 with d. mind offered gifts, that works
2 Pa 29 31 offered victims and . . . with a d. mind
Luke 2 25 this man was just and devout, waiting
Acts 2 5 devout men out of every nation under
8 2 devout men took order for Stephen's
dew Gen 27 28 God give thee the dew of heaven
Gen 27 39 in the dew of heaven from above shall
Exod 16 13 a dew lay round about the camp: and
Num 11 9 when the dew fell in the night upon
Deut 32 2 let my speech distil as the dew, as a
33 13 of the fruits of heaven and of the dew
28 the heavens shall be misty with dew
Judg 6 37 if there be dew on the fleece only
38 he filled a vessel with the dew. And
39 and all the ground wet with dew. And
40 there was dew on all the ground. Then
2 K 1 21 let neither dew nor rain come upon
17 12 as the dew falleth upon the ground
3 K 17 1 shall not be dew nor rain these years
Job 29 19 and dew shall continue in my harvest
38 28 or who begot the drops of dew? Out of
Ps 132 3 as the dew of Hermon, which descendeth
Prov 3 20 the clouds grow thick with dew. My
19 12 cheerfulness as dew upon the grass
Cant 5 2 my head is full of dew and my locks of
Wisd 11 23 as a drop of the morning dew, that
Eccu 18 16 shall not the dew assuage the heat
43 24 a dew that meeteth it, by the heat that
Isa 18 4 as a cloud of dew in the day of harvest
26 19 thy dew is the dew of the light: and
45 8 drop down dew, ye heavens, from above
Dan 3 50 like the blowing of a wind bringing dew
64 every shower and dew, bless ye the Lord
4 12 wet with the dew of heaven. 22, 30; 5:21
20 be sprinkled with the dew of heaven
Osee 6 4 as the dew that goeth away in morning
13 3 as the early dew that passeth away
14 6 I will be as the dew, Israel shall
Mich 5 7 remnant of Jacob . . . as a dew from the
Agge 1 10 over you were stayed from giving dew
Zach 8 12 the heavens shall give their dew: and
dews Dan 3 68 ye dews and hoar froasts, bless the
diadem 2 K 1 10 I took the d. that was on his
4 K 11 12 and put the diadem upon him, and the
1 Pa 20 2 [David] made himself a diadem of it
Job 29 14 as with a robe and a diadem. I was
Cant 3 11 see king Solomon in the diadem, whereof
Wisd 18 24 thy majesty was written upon the d.
Isa 62 3 thou shalt be . . . a royal diadem in
Eze 21 26 remove the diadem, take off the crown
1 Ma 11 54 was made king, and put on the diadem
diadems Apoc 12 3 on his heads seven diadems
Apoc 13 1 upon his horns ten diadems and upon
19 12 on his head were many diadems and he
dial 4 K 20 11 gone down in the dial of Achaz
Isa 38 8 gone down in the sun dial of Achaz
diamond Jer 17 1 with the point of a d. it is
Diana Acts 19 24 made silver temples for Diana
Acts 19 27 temple of great D. shall be reputed
28 great is D. of the Ephesians. 34
55 is a worshipper of the great Diana
Dibon Num 21 30 is perished from Hesebon unto D.
Num 32 3 and said: Ataroth and Dibon and Jazer
34 the sons of Gad built Dibon and Ataroth
Josu 13 9 the plains of Medaba, as far as Dibon
17 Dibon also, and Bamothbaal and the
2 Es 11 25 some dwelt . . . at Dibon and in the
Isa 15 2 gone up, and Dibon to the high places
9 waters of D. are filled with blood, for I will bring more upon D.
Jer 48 18 O dwelling of the daughter of Dibon
22 judgment is come . . . upon Dibon and
Dibongab Num 33 45 they pitched their tents in D.
didrachmas 2 Ma 4 19 to carry 300 d. of silver
2 Ma 10 20 taking 70,000 d., let some of them
Mat 17 23 they that received the didrachmas, came
23 doth not your master pay the d.? He
Didymus John 11 16 Thomas who is called Didymus. 20:24; 21:2
die Mat 15 4 let him die the death. Mark 7:10
Mat 22 24 if a man die having no son, his brother
26 35 though I should die with thee. Mark 14:31
Mark 12 19 if any man's brother die. Luke 20:28
Luke 7 2 servant . . . being sick, was ready to die
20 36 neither can they die any more: for they
John 4 49 come down before that my son die. Jesus
6 50 if any man eat of it, he may not die
8 21 you shall die in your sin. Whither I go
24 you shall die in your sins. For if you
11 16 let us also go that we may die with him
26 believeth in me shall not die forever
37 caused that this man should not die
50 one man should die for the people. 18:14
51 that Jesus should die for the nation
12 24 grain of wheat falling into the ground d.
25 if it die, it bringeth forth much fruit
33 signifying what death he should d. 18:32
19 7 according to the law he ought to die
21 23 that that disciple should not die
23 did not say to him: He should not die
Acts 21 13 I am ready . . . to die also in Jerusalem
25 11 worthy of death, I refuse not to die
28 6 he would suddenly fall down and die
Rom 5 6 according to the time, die for ungodly
7 scarce for a just man will one die
8 13 according to the flesh, you shall die
14 8 whether we die, we die unto the Lord
8 whether we live or whether we die, we
1 C 7 39 if her husband die, she is at liberty
9 15 it is good for me to die rather than
15 22 as in Adam all die, so also in Christ
31 I die daily, I protest by your glory
32 for tomorrow we shall die. Be not
36 is not quickened except it die first
2 C 7 3 to die together and to live together
Phil 1 21 to live is Christ; and to die is gain
Heb 7 8 here indeed men that die receive tithes
9 27 it is appointed unto men once to die
Apoc 3 2 that remain which are ready to die
9 6 they shall desire to die and death shall
14 13 are the dead who die in the Lord. From
died Mat 22 25 the first having married a wife, died
Mat 22 27 woman died also. Mark 12:22; Luke 20:32
Mark 12 20 first took a wife, and died. Luke 20:29
21 and the second took her and died: and
Luke 16 22 the beggar died and was carried by

22 rich man also died: and he was buried
20 30 he also died childless. And the third.
31 they left no children and died. Last
John 11 21 been here, my brother had not died. 32
Acts 2 29 that he [David] died and was buried
7 15 he [Jacob] died and our fathers. And
9 37 she [Dorcas] was sick and died. Whom
Rom 5 15 if by the offence of one, many died
6 10 in that he died to sin, he died once
7 10 sin revived, and I died. And the
8 34 shall condemn? Christ Jesus that died
2 C 5 14 if one died for all, then all were
15 unto him who died for them and rose
1 Th 4 13 if we believe that Jesus died and rose
Heb 11 13 all these died according to faith, not
Apoc 8 9 third part of those creatures died
11 many men died of the waters, because
16 3 every living soul died in the sea. And
Christ died Rom 5 9 Christ died for us. 1 Th 5:10
Rom 14 9 to this end Christ died and rose again
15 destroy not him . . . for whom Christ d.
1 C 8 11 brother perish, for whom Christ hath d.
15 3 how that Christ died for our sins
2 C 5 15 Christ died for all; that they also
Gal 2 21 then Christ died in vain. O senseless
1 P 3 18 Christ also died once for our sins
Dies Job 42 14 he called the name of one Dies
diet Jer 52 34 for his diet a continual provision
dieth Lev 22 8 that which dieth of itself and
Num 17 13 to tabernacle of the Lord, he dieth
19 14 the law of a man that dieth in a tent
27 8 when a man dieth without a son, his
Deut 25 5 one of them dieth without children
3 K 16 4 him that dieth of Baasa in the city
4 him that dieth of his in the country
Job 21 23 one man dieth strong and hale, rich
25 but another dieth in bitterness of
Ecce 2 16 the learned dieth in like manner as
3 19 as man dieth, so they also die: all
Eze 18 32 I desire not the death of him that d.
Zach 11 9 that which dieth, let it die: and
Mark 9 43 where their worm dieth not. 45, 47
Rom 6 9 again from the dead, dieth now no more
14 7 no man dieth to himself. For whether
Heb 10 28 dieth without any mercy under two of
Dievites 1 Es 4 9 Reum Beelteem and . . . the D.
difference Exod 9 4 d. between the possessions of
Exod 11 7 wonderful a difference the Lord maketh
Deut 1 17 there shall be no d. of persons, you
39 know not . . . d. of good and evil, they
2 Pa 12 8 that they may know the d. between my
14 11 Lord, there is no difference with thee
Eze 22 26 put no d. between holy and profane
44 23 the difference between holy and profane
Wisd 18 2 this gift, that there might be a d.
Mala 3 18 shall see the d. between the just and
1 Ma 3 18 there is no d. in the sight of the
Acts 15 9 and put no d. between us and them
differences Lev 11 47 know the d. of the clean
Deut 1 12 to bear . . . charge of you and your d.
different Lev 13 2 shall arise a d. color or a
Lev 19 19 not sow thy field with different seeds
Judg 5 30 furniture of d. kinds is heaped together
20 45 straggling and going different ways
1 Pa 28 17 he set aside a d. weight of silver
Jdth 5 23 from the different places wherein they
Job 20 2 my mind is hurried away to d. things
Wisd 2 15 other men's, and his ways are very d.
Dan 7 3 great beasts, d. one from another, came
19 beast, which was very d. from all and
2 Ma 8 9 armed men of different nations to root
12 13 by multitudes of different nations
Rom 12 6 having different gifts according to the
differeth Ecce 2 13 as light d. from darkness
1 C 15 41 star d. from star in glory. So also is
Gal 4 1 he d. nothing from a servant, though
difficult Dan 2 11 that thou askest, O king, is d.
Dan 5 12 resolving of d. things was found in
16 resolve difficult things: now if thou
difficulty Exod 18 26 whatsoever was of greater d.
Num 20 19 there shall be no d. in the price, only
Judg 18 9 possess it, there will be no d. We
2 Ma 2 25 the d. that they find that desire to
dig Gen 26 25 his servants to dig a well. To which
Exod 21 33 if a man open a pit and dig one and
Deut 6 11 cisterns which thou didst not dig
23 13 sittest down, thou shalt dig round
28 39 shalt plant a vineyard and dig it
Tob 8 11 went with him together to dig a grave
Job 3 21 as they that dig for a treasure: and
Prov 2 4 shalt dig for her as for a treasure
Eze 8 8 son of man, dig in the wall. And he
12 5 dig thee a way through the wall before
12 they shall dig through the wall to
Luke 13 8 until I dig about it and dung it. And
16 3 to dig I am not able; to beg I am
digest 1 K 1 14 d. a little the wine of which
digested 1 K 25 37 when Nabal had d. his wine
2 Pa 20 34 of Jehu . . . which he d. into the books
digged Gen 26 15 of his father Abraham had d. 18
Gen 26 18 he digged again other wells, which the
18 servants of his father Abraham had d.
19 they digged in the torrent and found
21 they digged also another; and for that
22 he digged another well for which they
32 him of a well which they had digged
50 5 sepulcher which I have d. for myself
Eccu 48 19 he digged a rock with iron and made
Isa 5 6 be pruned, and it shall not be digged
37 25 I have digged and drunk water and have
Jer 2 13 have digged to themselves cisterns
13 7 digged and took the girdle out of
18 20 they have digged a pit for my soul
22 they have digged a pit to take me
Eze 8 8 when I had digged in the wall, behold
12 7 I digged through the wall with my
Mat 25 18 digged into the earth and hid his
Luke 6 48 who d. deep and laid the foundation
diggeth Job 24 16 he d. through houses in the
Prov 16 27 the wicked man diggeth evil and in his
26 27 he that diggeth a pit, shall fall into it.
Ecce 10:8; Eccu 27:29
dignities 1 Ma 10 24 I also will . . . offer d. and
dignity Esth 9 3 lieutenants, and every one in d.
Esth 10 2 d. and greatness wherewith he exalted
Prov 14 28 multitude of people is d. of the king
16 31 old age is a crown of dignity, when
20 29 dignity of old men, their gray hairs
Ecce 10 6 a foot set in high dignity and the
Eccu 44 3 in the prophets the d. of prophets
45 30 d. of priesthood should be to him
Bar 4 3 nor thy dignity to a strange nation
2 Ma 3 11 Hircanus . . . a man of great dignity
6 23 began to consider the d. of his age
diligence Josu 23 11 take care of with all d.
Judg 21 17 and provide with great diligence, that
1 K 23 22 use all d. and curiously inquire and
2 Pa 11 12 he fortified them with great diligence
19 7 and do all things with diligence: for
32 5 he built up also with great diligence
Esth 9 29 that with all diligence this day should
10 13 all diligence and joy of the people
Wisd 14 17 by their d. they might honor as present
18 the singular d. also of the artificer
Eccu 30 27 his banquets are prepared with d.
38 28 by his continual diligence varieth the

Acts 5 23 prison indeed we found shut with all d.
diligent Deut 19 18 after most d. inquisition
2 Pa 24 13 and the workmen were diligent, and
Prov 6 11 if thou be d., thy harvest shall come
12 4 a d. woman is a crown to her husband
27 23 be d. to know the countenance of thy
Eccu 26 16 the grace of a d. woman shall delight
1 Ma 9 26 made d. search after the friends of
2 C 8 22 whom we have often proved diligent . . . but now much more diligent
2 P 3 14 waiting for these things, be diligent
diligently Deut 6 13 heed d. lest thou forget
Deut 13 14 inquire carefully and diligently, the
17 4 thou hast inquired diligently and found
19 3 paving diligently the way: and thou
24 8 observe d. that thou incur not the
Judg 18 2 to spy out the land and to view it d.
3 K 3 21 considering him more d. when it was
4 K 4 13 thou hast d. served us in all things
10 30 hast d. executed that which was right
2 Pa 12 15 Addo the seer and diligently recorded
13 22 are written d. in the book of Addo
19 11 take courage and do diligently, and
24 27 are written more d. in the book of
1 Es 5 8 and this work is carried on diligently
6 8 the charges be d. given to those men
12 which I will have d. complied with
13 d. executed what Darius the king had
7 17 buy diligently with this money calves
23 let it be given d. in the house of
26 will not do . . . the law of the king d.
Job 8 8 search d. into the memory of fathers
29 16 I knew not, I searched out most d. I
Ps 118 4 thy commandments to be kept most d.
Prov 23 1 consider d. what is set before thy
24 27 d. till thy ground: that afterward
Wisd 13 11 d. formeth a vessel profitable for
13 carveth it d. when he hath nothing
Eccu 13 16 attend d. to what thou hearest: for
27 4 hold thyself d. in the fear of the
Isa 21 7 he beheld them d. with much heed. And
30 8 upon box, and note it d. in a book
32 3 of them that hear shall hearken d.
34 16 search ye d. in the book of the Lord
55 2 hearken d. to me and eat that which
Jer 2 10 send into Cedar and consider d.: and
Bar 5 7 that Israel may walk d. to the honor
Dan 7 19 I would d. learn concerning the fourth
2 Ma 1 34 king considering and d. examining the
11 23 apply themselves diligently to their own
36 after you have d. conferred among
Mat 2 7 learned diligently . . . the time of the
8 diligently inquire after the child
16 the time which he had d. inquired of
Luke 1 3 having d. attained to all things from
15 8 seek diligently until she find it? And
Acts 16 23 charging the gaoler to keep them d.
18 25 taught d. the things that are of Jesus
26 they expounded to him . . . more d. And
22 30 meaning to know more diligently for
1 Tim 5 10 if she have d. followed every good
Heb 2 1 ought we more diligently to observe
12 3 think d. upon him that endured such
15 looking d. lest any man be wanting
1 P 1 10 prophets have inquired and d. searched
dim Gen 27 1 Isaac . . . and his eyes were dim
Gen 48 10 Israel's eyes were dim by reason of
Deut 34 7 his eye was not dim, neither were his
1 K 3 2 and his eyes were grown dim, that he
4 15 his eyes were dim and he could not see
3 K 14 4 his eyes were dim by reason of his age
Job 16 17 with weeping, and my eyelids are dim
17 7 my eye is dim through indignation and
Isa 32 3 eyes of them that see shall not be dim
Lam 4 1 how is the gold become dim, the finest
5 17 therefore are our eyes become dim
dimensions 1 Pa 28 15 d. of every candlestick
1 Pa 28 15 diversity of the dimensions of them
diminish Exod 5 8 neither shall you d. anything
Exod 30 15 the poor man shall diminish nothing
Deut 12 32 neither add anything nor diminish
Eccu 28 10 and thou shalt diminish thy sins: for
35 10 d. not the firstfruits of thy hands
Eze 29 15 I will diminish them that they shall
diminished Exod 5 11 anything of your work be d.
Exod 5 19 there shall not a whit be diminished
3 K 17 14 nor the cruse of oil be d. until the
16 the cruse of oil was not diminished
Job 21 21 number of his months be d. by one
Prov 13 11 substance got in haste shall be d.
24 10 thy strength shall be diminished
Wisd 11 8 while they were d. for a manifest
Eccu 31 33 is his life, who is d. with wine? What
42 22 nor can he be d., and he hath no need
Isa 19 6 the streams of the banks shall be d.
21 17 of the children of Cedar shall be d.
Bar 2 34 and they shall not be diminished. And
Dan 3 37 are diminished more than any nation
diminishing Num 36 3 a d. of our inheritance. And
Eccu 39 23 there is no d. of his salvation. The
diminution Rom 11 12 riches . . . and the d. of them
Dimona Josu 15 22 Cina and Dimona and Adada and
Dina Gen 30 21 she bore a daughter named Dina
Gen 34 1 Dina the daughter of Lia went out to
25 brothers of Dina, taking their swords
26 and took away their sister Dina, out
46 15 sons of Lia . . . with Dina his daughter
dine 3 K 13 7 come home with me to dine, and I
Luke 11 37 Pharisee prayed that he would dine
John 21 12 Jesus saith to them: Come and dine
dined John 21 15 when they had d., Jesus saith
dining room Judg 5 28 she spoke from the d. r.: Why
Mark 14 15 show you a large d. r. Luke 22:12
Dinites 1 Es 4 9 D. and the Apharsathacites, the
dinner Tob 2 1 d. was prepared in Tobias's house
Tob 2 3 left his d. and came fasting to the
7 9 he desired them to sit down to dinner
12 12 didst leave thy dinner and hide the dead
Dan 13 13 us now go home, for it is dinner time
14 33 carry the dinner which thou hast into
36 take the dinner that God hath sent
Mat 22 4 behold I have prepared my dinner; my
Luke 11 38 why he was not washed before dinner
14 12 when thou makest a d. or a supper, call
dints Lev 14 37 in the walls thereof . . . little d.
Dionysius Acts 17 34 among whom was Dionysius
Dioscorus 2 Ma 11 21 of the month of Dioscorus
Diotrephes 3 J 9 D. who loveth to have pre-eminence
dip Exod 12 22 dip a bunch of hyssop in the blood
Lev 4 17 shall dip his finger in it and sprinkle
25 priest shall dip his finger in the
14 6 shall dip with the cedar wood and the
16 and shall dip his right finger in it
51 shall dip all in the blood of the
Num 19 18 a man that is clean shall dip hyssop
Deut 33 24 let him dip his foot in oil. His shoe
Ruth 2 14 and dip thy morsel in the vinegar. So
Luke 16 24 that he may dip the tip of his finger
dipped Gen 37 31 d. it in the blood of a kid
Lev 4 6 having dipped his finger in the blood
9 9 he d. his finger therein and touched
11 32 they shall be dipped in water and shall
Josu 3 15 and their feet were dipped in part of
Ps 67 24 that thy foot may be d. in the blood
John 13 26 to whom I shall reach bread dipped. And when he had dipped the bread

dippeth Mat 26 23 he that d. his hand. Mark 14:20
dipping Lev 8 15 d. his finger in it, he touched
Lev 14 27 dipping the finger of his right hand
Num 19 4 dipping his finger in her blood, shall
dipsas Deut 8 15 there was . . . the dipsas, and
dipt 1 K 14 27 rod . . . and d. it in a honeycomb
direct Gen 24 40 and will direct thy way: and thou
Josu 1 8 then shalt thou direct thy way and
2 Es 1 11 direct thy servant this day, and give
Tob 3 14 to thee, O Lord, I direct my eyes
4 20 and desire of him to direct thy ways
14 12 direct your steps to depart hence
Jdth 12 8 that he would direct her way to the
Ps 5 9 direct my way in thy sight. For there
7 10 and thou shalt direct the just: the
24 5 direct me in thy truth and teach me
25 12 my foot hath stood in the direct way
89 16 their works: and direct their children
17 direct thou the works of our hands
17 the work of our hands do thou direct
118 133 direct my steps according to thy word
Prov 3 6 think on him, and he will d. thy steps
16 9 but the Lord must direct his steps
Eccu 2 6 direct thy way, and trust in him. Keep
36 19 direct us into the way of justice
37 19 that he may direct thy way in truth
39 10 and he shall direct his counsel and
Isa 45 13 and I will direct all his ways: he
Jer 10 23 in a man to walk and to d. his steps
31 21 direct thy heart into the right way
1 Ma 8 25 according as the time shall direct
Luke 1 79 to d. our feet into the way of peace
1 Th 3 11 God himself . . . d. our way unto you
2 Th 3 5 the Lord direct your hearts, in the
directed 2 Pa 26 5 Lord, he d. him in all things
2 Pa 27 6 he had his way directed before the
Jdth 13 24 who hath d. thee to the cutting off
Ps 36 23 shall the steps of a man be directed
39 3 set my feet upon a rock, and d. me
58 5 have I run and directed my steps. Rise
101 29 their seed shall be directed forever
118 5 that my ways may be d. to keep thy
128 was I d. to all thy commandments: I
140 2 let my prayer be directed as incense
Prov 15 3 and thy thoughts shall be directed
Eccu 49 3 he was d. by God unto the repentance
4 directed his heart towards the Lord
51 27 I d. my soul to her and in knowledge
directest Ps 66 5 and d. the nations upon earth
directing Wisd 10 4 d. the course of the just by
direction Gen 42 6 corn was sold by his direction
Num 21 18 prepared by the d. of the lawgiver
directions Ps 98 4 thou hast prepared directions
directly Jdth 7 5 by a narrow pathway lead d.
Wisd 5 22 of lightning shall go d. from the clouds
director Wisd 7 15 and the director of the wise
dirt Job 30 19 I am compared to dirt and likened
Ps 17 43 like the dirt in the streets. Thou
Isa 41 25 he shall make princes to be as dirt
57 20 waves thereof cast up dirt and mire
Eze 13 10 they daubed it with dirt without straw
dirty Eccu 22 1 is pelted with a dirty stone and
disabled 2 Ma 8 24 d. the greater part of Nicanor's
disagree 2 Pa 18 12 let not thy word d. with them
disallow Num 30 12 doth not disallow the promise
Disan Gen 36 21 sons of Seir . . . Eser and Disan
Gen 36 28 Disan had sons: Hus and Aram. These
30 duke Disan: these were dukes of the
1 Pa 1 38 sons of Seir . . . Dison, Eser, Disan
42 the sons of Disan: Hus and Aran. Now
disannul Isa 14 27 decreed, and who can d. it
1 Ma 14 44 to disannul any of these things or to
Gal 3 17 doth not disannul, to make the promise
disannulled 2 Ma 4 11 he d. the lawful ordinances
disappoint Ps 16 13 arise, O Lord, d. him and
Prov 10 3 he will d. the deceitful practices
disappointeth Job 5 13 d. the counsel of the
discern Lev 10 10 to d. between holy and unholy
2 K 19 35 my senses quick to d. sweet and bitter
3 K 3 9 to judge . . . and d. between good and
11 for thyself wisdom to d. judgment
Job 12 11 doth not the ear discern words and the
Eze 44 23 how to discern between clean and unclean
discerned Eccu 4 29 by the tongue wisdom is d.
discerner Heb 4 12 us a d., if the thoughts and
discerneth Job 34 3 mouth d. meats by the taste
Rom 14 23 but he that discerneth if he eat, is
discerning 1 C 11 29 not d. the body of the Lord
1 C 12 10 to another the discerning of spirits
Heb 5 14 to the d. of good and evil. Wherefore
discharge 1 Ma 11 35 tributes . . . we d. them of
discharged Exod 39 24 when he d. his ministry
1 Ma 10 33 that all be d. from tributes even of
disciple Mat 10 24 d. is not above. Luke 6:40
Mat 10 25 enough for d. that he be as master
42 cup of cold water in name of a disciple
27 57 Joseph who also himself was a disciple
Luke 14 26 cannot be my disciple. 27, 33
John 9 28 be thou his disciple; but we are the
18 15 Peter followed Jesus, so did another d.
15 that d. was known to the high priest
16 other disciples . . . spoke to portress
19 26 had seen his mother and the d. standing
27 saith to the disciple: Behold thy
27 disciple took her to his own. Afterwards
38 because he was a disciple of Jesus
20 2 to Simon Peter and to the other d.
3 and that other d. came to the sepulcher
4 that other disciple did outrun Peter
8 when that other disciple also went in
21 7 d. whom Jesus loved said to Peter: It
20 saw that d. whom Jesus loved following
23 that that disciple should not die. And
24 this is that d. who giveth testimony
Acts 9 10 d. at Damascus, named Ananias. And the
26 not believing that he was a disciple
36 a certain disciple named Tabitha which
16 1 a certain d. there named Timothy, the
21 16 one Mnason, a Cyprian, an old d., with
disciples Mat 8 23 his d. followed him. Mark 6:1; Luke 22:39
Mat 9 10 sat down with Jesus and his d. Mark 2:15
10 1 called his twelve disciples together
11 1 end of commanding his twelve disciples
2 John . . . sending two of his disciples
12 1 his d., being hungry, began to pluck
49 stretching . . . his hand towards his d.
14 19 gave the loaves to his d., and the d. to the multitudes
22 obliged his d. to go up into the boat
15 32 Jesus called together his d. Mark 8:1
36 and the disciples gave to the people
16 5 when his d. were come over the water
13 asked his d., saying: Whom. Mark 8:27
20 commanded his d. that they should tell
17 6 d. hearing, fell upon their face and
13 d. understood he had spoken to them
19 13 the disciples rebuked them. Mark 10:13
20 17 took the twelve d. apart and said to
21 1 Jesus sent two disciples. Mark 11:1; 14:13; Luke 19:29
6 d. going, did as Jesus commanded them
22 16 [Pharisees] sent to him their d. with
26 8 d. seeing it, had indignation, saying
19 disciples did as Jesus appointed to
35 in like manner said all the disciples

56 d. all leaving him, fled. Mark 14:50
27 64 lest perhaps his d. come and steal him
28 7 tell ye his d. that he is risen: and
8 running to tell his disciples. And
16 the eleven disciples went into Galilee
Mark 2 18 the d. of John and the Pharisees used
18 the d. of John and of the Pharisees fast
23 his d. began to go forward and to pluck
7 2 d. eat bread with common . . . hands
8 4 d. answered him: From whence can any one
27 and his d. into the towns of Caesarea
33 seeing his disciples, threatened Peter
9 30 he taught his d. and said to them: The
10 24 d. were astonished at his words. But
11 14 and his disciples heard it. And they
12 43 calling his d. together, he saith to
16 7 tell his d. and Peter that he goeth
Luke 5 33 the d. of the Pharisees in like manner
6 1 disciples plucked the ears and did eat
13 called . . . his d.; and he chose twelve
17 in plain place, and company of his d.
7 11 there went with him his disciples
18 John's d. told him of all these things
19 John called to him two of his d. and
9 18 his disciples also were with him: and
54 when his d. James and John had seen
11 1 one of his d. said to him: Teach us to
1 as John also taught his disciples. And
18 15 when the d. saw, they rebuked them
19 37 d. began with joy to praise God with
John 1 35 John stood and two of his disciples
37 the two disciples heard him speak and
2 2 Jesus was invited and his disciples
11 and his disciples believed in him
12 and his brethren and his disciples
17 his d. remembered that it was written
22 his d. remembered that he had said
3 22 d. came into the land of Judea: and
25 a question between some of John's d.
4 1 heard that Jesus maketh more disciples
2 himself did not baptize, but his d.
8 his d. were gone into the city to buy
31 d. prayed him, saying: Rabbi, eat. But
6 8 one of his d. saith to him: There is
16 his d. went down to the sea. And when
22 that his disciples were gone away alone
24 Jesus was not there nor his disciples
62 knowing that his disciples murmured
67 after this many of his d. went back
9 27 will you also become his disciples
28 but we are the disciples of Moses. We
12 4 one of the d., Judas . . . said: Why was
16 his d. did not know at the first; but
13 5 began to wash the feet of the d. and
22 the disciples looked one upon another
23 on Jesus' bosom one of his disciples
18 17 thou also one of this man's disciples
19 high priest asked Jesus of his d. and
25 art not thou also one of his d.? He
20 10 the d. departed to their home. But
18 Magdalen cometh and telleth the d.
19 where the d. were gathered together
20 the d. were glad when they saw the
26 again his disciples were within and
30 other signs . . . in the sight of his d.
21 1 Jesus showed himself again to the d.
2 sons of Zebedee and two others of his d.
4 yet the d. knew not that it was Jesus
Acts 6 1 the number of the disciples increasing
2 together the multitude of the d., said
7 number of the d. was multiplied in
9 1 slaughter against the d. of the Lord
19 was with the d. that were at Damascus
25 the d. taking him in the night, conveyed
26 essayed to join himself to the d.; and
38 d. hearing that Peter was there, sent
11 26 the d. were first named Christians
29 the disciples . . . purposed to send
13 52 the disciples were filled with joy
14 19 as the d. stood round about him [Paul]
21 confirming the souls of the disciples
27 abode no small time with the d. And
15 10 a yoke upon the necks of the d. which
18 23 confirming all the disciples. Now a
27 wrote to the d. to receive him. Who
19 1 to Ephesus and found certain d. And
9 separated the d., disputing daily in
30 the disciples suffered him not. And
20 1 Paul calling to him the disciples, and
30 to draw away disciples after them
21 4 finding disciples, we tarried there
16 with us some of disciples from Caesarea

disciples asked him; *see* **asked**

disciples came Mat 5 1 his d. came unto him
Mat 9 14 then came to him the d. of John, saying
13 10 and his d. came and said to him: Why
36 his d. came to him, saying: Expound
14 12 his d. came and took the body. Mark 6:29
15 d. came . . . saying: This is a desert. Mark 6:35
15 12 came his d. and said to him: Dost thou
23 his d. came . . . saying: Send her away
17 18 then came the d. to Jesus secretly
18 1 d. came to Jesus, saying: Who thinkest
24 1 d. came to show him the buildings of
3 the d. came to him privately, saying
26 17 d. came to Jesus, saying: Where wilt
28 13 say you, His d. came by night and
Mark 14 16 d. went their way and came into the city
John 4 27 d. came and they wondered that he
21 8 the other d. came in the ship, for

disciples said Mat 8 21 another of his d. said to
Mat 17 18 d. said: Why could not we cast
Mark 5 31 d. said to him: Thou seest the multitude
13 1 one of his d. said to him: Master
John 4 33 the d. said one to another: Hath any
6 61 many of his d. hearing it, said: This
11 12 his d. said: Lord, if he sleep, he
16 17 some of his d. said one to another
29 his d. said to him: Behold, now thou
20 25 other d. said to him: We have seen

disciples say Mat 15 33 d. say unto him: Whence
Mat 19 10 d. say unto him: If the case of a man
Mark 14 12 d. say to him: Whither wilt thou that
John 11 8 d. say . . . Jews but now sought to stone

my disciples Isa 8 16 seal the law among my d.
Mat 26 18 I make the pasch with my disciples
Mark 14 14 I may eat the pasch with my d. Luke 22:11
John 8 31 you shall be my disciples indeed. And
13 35 all men know that you are my disciples
15 8 that you . . . become my disciples. As

said to his disciples Mat 16 24 s. . . . If any man will come after me
Mat 26 1 s. . . . : You know that after two days
36 s. . . . : Sit you here till I go yonder
Mark 2 16 s. . . . : Make them sit down by fifties
12 22 s. . . . : Be not solicitous for your
16 1 s. . . . : There was a certain rich man
17 1 s. . . . : It is impossible that scandals
22 s. . . . : The days will come when you
Luke 9 44 s. . . . : Lay you up in your hearts these
John 6 12 s. . . . : Let us go into Judea again
11 16 Thomas . . . said to his fellow disciples

thy disciples Mat 9 14 thy disciples do not fast. Mark 2:18
Mat 12 2 thy d. do that which is not lawful

15 2 why do thy d. transgress the tradition
17 15 I brought him to thy disciples and
Mark 7 5 why do not thy d. walk according to
9 17 I spoke to thy d. to cast him out
Luke 9 40 I desired thy d. to cast him out and
19 39 Master, rebuke thy disciples. To whom
John 7 3 that thy d. also may see thy works
to his disciples Mat 14 19 gave loaves t. . . .
Mat 15 35 he brake and gave to his disciples
16 21 began to show to his d. that he must
23 1 to his d., saying: The scribes and
26 26 broke and gave to his d. Mark 8:6
40 cometh to his d. and findeth them
45 cometh to his d. and saith to them
Mark 3 9 he spoke to his d. that a small ship
4 34 he explained all things to his d.
6 41 broke loaves and gave to his d. 8:6
9 13 coming to his d. he saw great multitude
10 23 saith to his d.: How hardly shall they
14 32 saith to his d.: Sit you here, while
Luke 9 16 he broke and distributed to his d.
22 45 come to his d. he found them sleeping
John 21 14 was manifested to his disciples, after
with his disciples Mat 9 19 followed him, w. . . .
Mat 26 20 he sat down with his twelve disciples
Mark 3 7 Jesus retired with his d. to the sea
8 10 into a ship with his d. John 6:22
34 calling multitude together with his d.
10 46 as he went out of Jericho w. . . . and
Luke 8 22 he went into a little ship w. . . . and
John 6 3 and there he sat with his disciples
11 54 there he abode with his disciples
18 1 went forth with his d. over the brook
1 garden into which he entered w. . . .
2 often resorted thither with his d.
discipline Jdth 11 6 thy d. is cried up in all
Job 34 35 and his words sound not discipline
Ps 2 12 embrace discipline, lest at any time
17 36 thy discipline, the same shall teach
36 thy discipline hath corrected me unto
49 17 seeing thou hast hated discipline
118 66 teach me goodness and discipline and
Prov 19 25 he will understand discipline. He that
Wisd 1 5 the Holy Spirit of d. will flee from
3 11 he that rejecteth wisdom and d., is
6 18 is the most true desire of discipline
19 the care of discipline is love and
7 14 commended for the gift of discipline
Eccu 1 7 to whom hath the discipline of wisdom
31 of wisdom is the signification of d.
34 fear of the Lord is wisdom and d.
4 19 him with the affliction of her d.
10 33 poor man is glorified by his d. and
11 15 wisdom and discipline . . . are with God
16 24 learn the discipline of understanding
18 14 that receiveth the discipline of mercy
20 9 success . . . to a man without d. and
26 in the mouth of men without discipline
23 2 the discipline of wisdom over my heart
7 hear . . . the discipline of the mouth
26 17 her discipline is the gift of God. Such
32 18 feareth the Lord, will receive his d.
33 4 shall be heard and shall keep d. and
18 for all that seek discipline. Hear
38 38 neither shall they declare discipline
39 11 he shall show forth the discipline
41 17 my children, keep discipline in peace
51 31 yourselves together into house of d.
34 let your soul receive discipline: for
36 receive ye discipline as a great sum
Soph 3 2 neither hath she received discipline
Eph 6 4 bring them up in d. . . . of Lord. Servants
Phil 4 8 if any praise of discipline, think on
Heb 12 5 neglect not the d. of the Lord; neither
7 persevere under discipline. God dealeth
disclose Eccu 4 21 will d. her secrets to him
Eccu 6 9 is a friend that will d. hatred and
19 8 be a sin with thee, disclose it not
27 24 to d. the secrets of a friend, leaveth
42 1 disclose not the thing that is secret
Isa 26 21 the earth shall disclose her blood
disclosed 2 Ma 13 21 d. the secrets to the enemies
discloseth Eccu 27 17 that d. the secret of a
disclosing Eccu 11 29 is the d. of his works
Eccu 22 27 disclosing of secrets or a treacherous
discomfited 1 Ma 4 36 our enemies are d.: let
1 Ma 5 7 were discomfited in their sight and
21 the heathens were d. before his face
43 all the heathens were discomfited
9 15 right wing was discomfited by them
16 saw that the right wing was d. and
68 Bacchides, and he was d. by them: and
10 82 they were d. by him and fled. And they
14 13 kings were d. in those days. And he
disconsolate Tob 10 4 mother wept and was . . . d.
discord Prov 6 14 at all times he soweth discord
Prov 6 19 that soweth discord among brethren
discords Prov 17 19 that studieth d., loveth
discourage 2 K 11 25 let not this thing d. thee
discouraged Deut 1 21 nor be any way discouraged
Josu 14 8 discouraged the heart of the people
1 Ma 4 27 he was amazed and discouraged: because
9 7 and he [Judas] was discouraged. Then
11 49 they were discouraged in their minds
Col 3 21 lest they be discouraged. Servants
discourse Job 34 1 Eliu continued his d. and
Ecce 12 13 hear together the conclusion of the d.
Eccu 6 35 mayst hear every discourse of God
8 9 despise not the d. of them that are
11 let not the d. of the ancients escape
9 23 all thy discourse on the commandments
11 8 not others in the midst of their d.
22 9 in the end of the discourse he saith
27 14 the discourse of sinners is hateful
Dan 2 23 made known to us the king's discourse
2 Ma 2 31 to put the discourse in order and
discoursed 3 K 4 33 he d. of beasts and of fowls
Luke 22 4 went and d. with the chief priests
John 11 56 d. one with another standing in temple
Acts 20 7 Paul discoursed with them, being to
discourses Luke 24 17 what are these d. that you
discover Lev 18 15 neither shalt thou d. her
Lev 18 17 not take . . . to discover her shame
18 neither shalt thou d. her nakedness
20 11 if . . . d. the nakedness of his father
Num 5 13 and her husband cannot discover it
1 K 20 12 if I shall discover my father's mind
13 I will discover it to thy ear and
Tob 12 11 I discover then the truth unto you
Job 41 4 who can d. the face of his garment
Ps 28 9 he will discover the thick woods: and
Prov 25 9 discover not the secret to a stranger
Eccu 1 39 God d. thy secrets and cast thee down
27 19 if thou discover his secrets, follow
Isa 3 17 the Lord will discover their hair
Eze 16 37 and will d. thy shame in their sight
Dan 2 47 seeing thou couldst d. this secret
Nah 3 5 I will d. thy shame to thy face and
Mat 26 73 thy speech doth discover thee. Then
discovered Exod 20 26 lest thy nakedness be d.
Lev 20 17 have d. one another's nakedness and
Judg 16 18 that he had d. to her all his mind
1 K 14 11 d. themselves to the garrison of the
Ps 17 16 the foundations of the world were d.
Isa 22 8 covering of Juda shall be discovered
47 3 thy nakedness shall be discovered

57 8 thou hast discovered thyself near me
Jer 13 22 thy nakedness is discovered, the soles
Lam 4 22 he hath discovered thy sins. Remember
Eze 16 36 thy shame d. through thy fornications
21 24 and have d. your prevarications and
22 10 they have d. the nakedness of their
23 10 they d. her disgrace, took away her
18 she d. her fornications and d. her disgrace
29 disgrace of thy fornication shall be d.
Osee 7 1 the iniquity of Ephraim was d. and
1 Ma 7 31 knew that his counsel was discovered
2 Ma 6 11 being d. by Philip, were burnt with
12 41 had d. the things that were hidden
Acts 21 3 when we had discovered Cyprus, leaving
27 27 deemed that they d. some country. Who
39 they discovered a certain creek that
discovereth Job 12 22 he d. deep things out of
Prov 29 24 putting him to his oath, and d. not
Eccu 14 7 at the last he d. his wickedness. The
37 18 soul of a holy man d. sometimes true
discreet Prov 14 8 wisdom of a d. man is to
Prov 14 15 the discreet man considereth his steps
Titus 2 5 young women . . . to be discreet, chaste
discuss 2 Ma 2 31 to d. every particular point
disdain Eze 16 31 by d. enhanceth her price, but
disease Lev 15 13 suffereth this d. be healed
Lev 15 25 long as she is subject to this d. shall
2 Pa 21 15 shalt be sick of a very grievous d.
18 with an incurable d. in his bowels
19 his disease ended with his life. And
2 Ma 9 21 being taken with a grievous disease
Mat 9 35 and healing every disease and every
Mark 5 34 be thou whole of thy disease. While he
diseased 3 K 15 23 his old age he was d. in his
Mat 14 35 and brought to him all that were diseased
John 6 2 miracles . . . on them that were d. Jesus
diseases Deut 28 61 bring upon thee all the d.
2 Pa 24 25 they left him in great diseases: and
Ps 102 3 who healeth all thy diseases. Who
Mat 4 24 that were taken with divers diseases
8 17 took our infirmities and bore our d.
10 1 power . . . to heal all manner of d. and
Mark 1 34 that were troubled with divers diseases
Luke 4 40 that had any sick with divers diseases
6 18 to be healed of their diseases. And
7 21 he cured many of their diseases and
9 1 authority over all devils and to cure d.
Acts 19 12 the diseases departed from them and
28 9 all that diseases in the island
disfigure Mat 6 16 they d. their faces that they
disfigured Lev 14 37 d. with paleness or redness
Job 30 3 disfigured with calamity and misery
disgrace 2 Pa 32 21 returned with d. into his
Jdth 8 20 he will . . . bring them to disgrace
Prov 3 35 the promotion of fools is disgrace
17 21 a fool is born to his own disgrace
Eccu 3 13 father without honor is d. of the son
5 17 mark of d. upon the double tongued
21 27 wise man will be grieved with the d.
22 11 all men will speak of his disgrace
4 becometh a disgrace to her father
23 31 he shall be in disgrace with all men
Isa 23 9 bring to disgrace all the glorious
Jer 14 21 do not d. in us the throne of thy
46 12 nations have heard of thy disgrace
Eze 16 39 leave thee naked and full of disgrace
58 hast borne thy wickedness and thy d.
23 10 they discovered her disgrace, took away
18 and she . . . discovered her disgrace
29 let thee go naked and full of disgrace
29 the d. of thy fornication shall be
Osee 2 9 my flax which covered her disgrace
Nah 3 6 will disgrace thee and will make an

2 Ma 9 2 to flight [Antiochus] returned with d.
disgraced 2 K 16 21 that thou hast d. thy father
Eccu 10 16 Lord d. the assemblies of the wicked
22 5 shall be disgraced by them both. A tale
31 16 lest being d. with envy thou be put
Nah 1 14 thy grave, for thou art disgraced
disgracefully Jer 6 14 healed the breach . . . d. 8:11
disgraceth 1 C 11 4 head covered, d. his head
1 C 11 5 head not covered, d. her head: for it
disguised 1 K 28 8 [Saul] d. himself and put on
3 K 20 38 d. himself by sprinkling dust on his
dish Num 7 13 a silver dish weighing 130 sicles. 19, 25, 31, 37, 43, 49, 55, 61, 67, 73, 79
Num 7 85 each dish weighing 130 sicles of silver
Judg 5 25 butter in a dish fit for princes. She
Mat 14 8 give me here in a dish. Mark 6:25
11 his head was brought in a dish: and it
23 25 clean outside of the cup and of the d.
26 clean inside of the cup and of the d.
26 23 hand with me in the dish. Mark 14:20
Mark 6 27 head should be brought in a dish. And
28 brought his head in a dish: and gave
dishes Exod 25 29 thou shalt prepare also dishes
Exod 37 16 for the divers uses of the table, d.
Num 7 84 the offerings . . . twelve d. of silver
dishonest Eccu 37 13 nor with the d. of honesty
dishonestly 2 K 13 2 hard to do anything d. with
dishonesty Dan 13 63 there was no d. found in her
2 C 4 2 the hidden things of dishonesty, not
dishonor Lev 21 9 d. the name of her father, she
Job 14 21 his children come to honor or dishonor
Prov 6 33 gathereth to himself shame and d. and
14 28 people the dishonor of the prince. He
Eccu 1 38 bring d. upon thy soul and God discover
3 12 glory not in the d. of thy father
Bar 6 40 the Chaldeans themselves d. them: who
1 Ma 1 42 her dishonor was increased according
2 Ma 9 1 Antiochus returned with d. out of
Rom 1 24 to d. their own bodies among themselves
9 21 to make . . . another unto dishonor
1 C 15 43 it is sown in d., it shall rise in
2 C 6 8 by honor and dishonor, by evil report
11 21 I speak according to dishonor, as if
2 Tim 2 20 unto honor, but some unto dishonor
dishonored Prov 25 8 thou hast d. thy friend. Treat
Eccu 10 23 seed shall be d., which transgresseth
John 8 49 and you have dishonored me. But I seek
1 C 7 36 man think that he seemeth dishonored
James 2 6 you have dishonored the poor man. Do
dishonorest Rom 2 23 by transgression . . . d. God
dishonoreth Eccu 10 32 that d. his own soul. The
Mich 7 6 the son dishonoreth the father, and the
disjointed Eccu 25 32 hands and d. knees, a woman
disloyal Ps 72 27 all them that are d. to thee
dismayed Deut 20 3 let not your heart be d., be
Deut 31 6 nor be ye dismayed at their sight: for
8 fear not, neither be d. Josu 10:25
Josu 1 9 fear not and be not dismayed. 1 Pa 28:20; 2 Pa 20:15
8 1 fear not, nor be thou dismayed: take
1 K 17 11 the Philistines were dismayed and greatly
32 let not any man's heart be dismayed
28 5 and his heart was very much dismayed
1 Pa 22 13 fear not, nor be dismayed. Behold I
2 Pa 20 17 fear ye not, nor be you d.: tomorrow
32 7 be not afraid nor dismayed for the
Jer 8 9 they are dismayed and taken: for they
23 4 and they shall not be dismayed: and
30 10 neither be dismayed, O Israel: for
46 5 I have seen them dismayed, and turning
27 and be not thou dismayed, O Israel
50 36 valiant ones, and they shall be d.
Eze 2 6 neither be thou d. at their. 3:9

dismiss Luke 2 29 now thou dost d. thy servant
dismissed Ps 33 1 before Achimelech, who d. him
Mat 14 22 till he dismissed the people. And
23 having dismissed the multitude. 15:39
Mark 6 45 whilst he dismissed the people. And
46 when he had d. them, he went up to
Acts 5 40 they dismissed them. And they indeed
15 30 they being d., went down to Antioch
19 40 he dismissed the assembly. And after
23 22 the tribune dismissed the young man
disobedience Esth 16 24 example of contempt and d.
Rom 5 19 by the disobedience of one man, many
2 C 10 6 in readiness to revenge all d., when
Heb 2 2 d. received a just recompense of reward
disobedient Deut 8 20 if you be d. to the voice
3 K 13 26 man of God that was d. to the mouth
2 Es 13 27 shall we also be d. and do all this
Bar 1 19 we were d. to the Lord our God: and
Rom 1 30 things disobedient to parents, foolish
1 Tim 1 9 the law is . . . for the unjust and d.
2 Tim 3 2 d. to parents, ungrateful, wicked
Titus 1 10 there are also many disobedient, vain
Dison Gen 36 21 sons of Seir . . . Dison. 1 Pa 1:38
Gen 36 25 he had a son Dison and a daughter
26 the sons of Dison. 1 Pa 1:41
30 duke Dison: these were dukes of Horrites
1 Pa 1 40 son of Ana: Dison. The sons of Dison
disorder Wisd 14 26 disorder in marriage, and the
disorderly Eccu 7 17 among the multitude of the d.
2 Th 3 6 every brother walking disorderly and
7 for we were not disorderly among you
11 some among you who walk disorderly
dispatched 2 Ma 12 18 before he had d. anything
dispensation 1 C 9 17 a d. is committed to me
Eph 1 10 in d. of the fulness of times, to
3 2 heard of the d. of the grace of God
9 what is the d. of the mystery which
Col 1 25 minister according to the d. of God
dispensers 1 C 4 1 d. of the mysteries of God
1 C 4 2 it is required among the dispensers
disperse 1 K 14 34 d. yourselves among the people
Prov 15 7 lips of the wise shall d. knowledge
Eze 20 23 to disperse them among the nations
22 15 I will disperse thee in the nations
29 12 will d. them through the countries
30 23 I will d. Egypt among the nations. 26
2 Ma 14 13 and d. all them that were with him
dispersed Ps 146 2 together the d. of Israel
Wisd 2 3 shall be d. as a mist, which is driven
5 15 thin froth which is d. by the storm
Isa 11 12 shall gather together the d. of Juda
Eze 12 15 when I shall have d. them among the
36 19 they are d. through the countries
46 18 that my people be not dispersed every
Soph 3 10 the children of my dispersed people
Zach 7 14 I d. them throughout all kingdoms
1 Ma 4 4 the army was d. from the camp. And
6 54 they were d. every man to his own
11 47 all d. themselves through the city
Mat 26 31 sheep of the flock shall be dispersed
Mark 14 27 and the sheep shall be dispersed. But
John 7 35 will he go unto the dispersed among
11 52 the children of God that were d. From
Acts 5 37 as many as consented to him were d.
8 1 they were all dispersed through the
4 they that were d. went about preaching
11 19 who had been d. by the persecution
2 C 9 9 he hath dispersed abroad, he hath given
1 P 1 1 Peter . . . to the strangers dispersed
dispersion Jer 25 34 the days of your . . . d. are
display Isa 13 10 shall not d. their light: the
displayed Eccu 43 13 of the most High have d. it
displease Exod 21 8 if she d. the eyes of her
Num 22 34 if it displease thee that I go, I
Prov 24 18 lest the Lord see, and it d. him and
Eccu 21 18 heard it and it shall displease him
Isa 65 12 chosen the things that d. me. 66:4
Eze 36 31 and your wicked deeds shall d. you
Mark 6 26 he would not displease her: but sending
displeased Gen 48 17 Joseph . . . was much displeased
1 Pa 21 7 and God was displeased with this thing
Job 34 33 it of thee, because it hath d. thee
Eze 6 9 they shall be d. with themselves because
20 43 you shall be d. with yourselves in
2 Ma 11 1 displeased with what had happened
13 25 men of that city were much displeased
14 27 d. with the covenant of friendship
Mark 10 14 he was much d. and saith to them: Suffer
41 began to be much d. at James and John
displeaseth Ecce 5 3 and foolish promise d. him
displeasing 1 K 8 6 the word was d. in the eyes
1 K 18 8 word was displeasing in his eyes and
2 K 11 27 David had done was d. to the Lord
dispose Luke 22 29 I d. to you, as my Father hath
disposed Ps 83 6 he hath d. to ascend by steps
Prov 16 33 but they are disposed of by the Lord
Eze 46 22 were little courts disposed, forty
2 Ma 8 21 disposed even to die for the laws
Luke 22 29 as my Father hath disposed to me, a
disposest Wisd 12 18 with great favor d. of us
disposeth Prov 16 9 heart of man d. his way: but
disposition 1 Pa 12 28 young man of excellent d.
2 Pa 30 16 the disposition and law of Moses the
Wisd 7 17 to know the d. of the whole world and
Eccu 19 18 d. of the law is in all wisdom. But
31 18 judge of the d. of thy neighbor by
Acts 7 53 by the disposition of angels and have
2 C 8 8 the good disposition of your charity
dispositions 2 Pa 23 18 according to d. of David
Wisd 7 19 the d. of the stars, the natures of
disputed Mark 9 33 they had d. among themselves
Acts 9 29 he disputed with the Greeks; but they
17 17 he d. therefore in the synagogue with
18 Stoics disputed with him; and some
18 19 he disputed with the Jews. And when
disputer 1 C 1 20 where is d. of this world? Hath
disputes Rom 14 1 not in d. about thoughts. For
disputing Job 32 11 long as you were d. in words
Ecce 6 11 many words that have much vanity in d.
Mark 9 13 scribes disputing with them. And
Acts 6 9 arose some . . . d. with Stephen. And
15 7 when there had been much disputing
19 8 d. and exhorting concerning the kingdom
9 d. daily in the school of one Tyrannus
24 12 neither in temple did they find me d.
disquiet Job 3 18 bound together without d., have
Ps 31 12 and why dost thou disquiet me. 42:5
Jer 50 34 to d. the inhabitants of Babylon. A
disquieted Ps 38 7 he is disquieted in vain. He
Ps 38 12 surely in vain is any man disquieted
Eccu 28 16 tongue of a third person hath d. many
Acts 15 19 are not to be disquieted. But that we
disquieting Wisd 14 25 perjury, d. of the good
disregarded Gen 39 13 saw . . . herself disregarded
dissemble Eccu 23 13 if he d. it, he offendeth
Dan 11 32 the covenant shall deceitfully dissemble
2 Ma 6 24 not become our age, said he, to d.
dissembled 1 K 10 27 he d. as though he heard not
Job 3 26 have I not dissembled? Have I not kept
dissembler Prov 11 9 d. with his mouth deceiveth
dissemblers Job 36 13 d. and crafty men prove
dissembleth Prov 12 16 he that d. injuries is
dissembling Prov 29 5 with flattering and d. words
dissension 1 Ma 3 29 small because of the d. and
John 7 43 arose a d. among the people because of
10 19 d. rose again among the Jews for these

Acts 15 39 arose a d. so that they departed one
23 7 d. between the Pharisees and Sadducees
10 there arose a great d., the tribune
1 C 14 33 is not the God of d. but of peace
dissensions Rom 16 17 mark them who make d. and
2 C 12 20 d., detractions, whisperings, swellings
Gal 5 20 works of the flesh . . . dissensions
dissimulation Wisd 14 25 theft and d., corruption
2 Ma 6 25 through my dissimulation, and for a
Rom 12 9 let love be without dissimulation
Gal 2 13 to his d. the rest of Jews consented
13 also was led by them into that d. But
James 3 17 good fruits, without judging, without d.
dissimulations 1 P 2 1 laying away all . . . d. and
dissipated Job 17 11 my thoughts are dissipated
Ps 118 126 they have dissipated thy law. Therefore
dissolute Jer 31 22 how long wilt thou be d. in
Rom 1 31 dissolute, without affection, without
dissolution 2 Tim 4 6 time of my d. is at hand
dissolved 2 C 5 1 if our earthly house . . . be d.
Phil 1 23 having a desire to be dissolved and
2 P 3 11 all these things are to be dissolved
12 the heavens being on fire shall be d.
dissolveth 1 J 4 3 every spirit that d. Jesus
dissolving 2 K 13 8 d. it in his sight she made
dissuaded 1 Ma 9 9 they d. him, saying: We shall
distaff 2 K 3 29 leper or that holdeth the d.
distance Deut 19 7 three cities at equal d. one
Deut 20 15 the cities that are at a great d. from
21 2 d. of every city round about: and the
Judg 18 7 at a d. from Sidon and from all men
22 at a distance from the house of Michas
Ps 21 20 remove not thy help to a distance
55 1 for a people that is removed at a d.
Ecce 6 5 nor known the d. of good and evil
Isa 22 11 nor regarded him even at a distance
distil Deut 32 2 let my speech d. as the dew
distilling 2 Ma 8 27 d. the beginning of mercy
distinction Rom 3 22 there is no d.: for all
Rom 10 12 there is no d. of the Jew and the
1 C 14 7 except they give a d. of sounds, how
distinctly 2 Es 8 8 d. and plainly to be understood
distinguish 1 Es 3 13 one could not d. the voice
Ps 42 1 d. my cause from the nation that is
Jon 4 11 how to d. between their right hand
distinguished Ps 105 33 he d. with his lips. They
Eccu 16 26 he d. their parts and their beginnings
33 8 they were d., the sun being made and
Eze 22 26 nor have d. between the polluted and
1 Ma 6 40 part of the king's army was d. by
distinguisheth 1 C 4 7 who distinguisheth thee
distraction Ecce 8 16 to understand the d. that
distress Deut 26 7 looked down upon our . . . d.
Deut 28 53 in distress and extremity wherewith
55 wherewith thy enemies shall d. thee
57 in the siege and distress, wherewith thy
32 38 help you and protect you in your d.
Judg 10 14 let them deliver you in the time of d.
Ruth 1 13 am grieved the more for your distress
1 K 22 2 all that were in d. and oppressed
26 24 let him deliver me from all distress
28 15 I am in great d.: for the Philistines
2 K 4 9 delivered my soul out of all distress
22 7 in my distress I will call upon the
3 K 1 29 hath delivered my soul out of all d.
22 27 feed him with . . . water of distress
4 K 13 4 for he saw the distress of Israel
2 Pa 15 4 when in their d. they shall return
6 Lord will trouble them with all d.
28 22 in the time of his d. he increased
33 12 after that he was in distress he prayed
Esth 11 8 a day . . . of tribulation and distress
Job 15 24 and distress shall surround him, as a
27 9 when distress shall come upon him
36 15 deliver the poor out of his distress
Ps 4 2 when I was in d., thou hast enlarged
Prov 1 27 and distress shall come upon you: then
11 8 the just is delivered out of distress
12 13 the just shall escape out of distress
17 17 and a brother is proved in distress
21 23 keepeth his soul from distress. The
24 10 being weary in the day of distress
Eccu 4 3 to give to him that is in distress
6 10 he will not abide in the day of d.
10 29 linger not in the time of distress
Isa 8 22 and behold . . . weakness and distress
22 cannot fly away from their distress
25 4 strength to the needy in his distress
26 16 have sought after thee in distress
30 6 in a land of trouble and distress
53 8 he was taken away from distress and
Jer 19 9 in the distress wherewith their enemies
Lam 1 20 behold, O Lord, for I am in distress
Bar 6 36 nor deliver a man from distress. They
Eze 4 16 shall drink water by measure and in d.
7 25 when distress cometh upon them, they
Abdi 12 magnify thy mouth in the day of d.
Jon 2 8 when my soul was in distress within
Soph 1 15 a day of tribulation and distress
17 I will d. men and they shall walk
1 Ma 2 53 Joseph in the time of his distress
Luke 21 23 shall be distress in the land and
25 upon the earth distress of nations
John 16 33 in the world you shall have distress
Rom 8 35 separate us . . . distress? or famine
2 C 1 4 to comfort them who are in all d., by
distressed Judg 2 15 they were greatly distressed
Judg 10 9 and Israel was distressed exceedingly
1 K 13 6 for the people were distressed, they
Mat 9 36 distressed and lying like sheep that
2 C 4 8 we suffer tribulation, but are not d.
Heb 11 37 being in want, distressed, afflicted
distresses 2 K 22 46 be straitened in their d.
Ps 30 8 hast saved my soul out of distresses
106 6 delivered them out of their d. 13, 19
28 he brought them out of their d. And
Isa 65 16 the former distresses are forgotten
Eze 30 16 in Memphis there shall be daily d.
1 Ma 13 3 and the distresses that we have seen
2 C 6 4 in distresses, in stripes, in prisons
12 10 in distresses, for Christ. For when I
distribute 4 K 12 15 money to d. it to the workmen
4 K 22 5 let them d. it to those that work in
2 Pa 31 15 to d. faithfully portions to their
19 distribute portions to all the males
Job 21 17 he shall d. the sorrows of his wrath
Ps 47 14 and d. her houses, that ye may relate
Prov 11 24 some d. their own goods, and grow
Eccu 1 24 wisdom shall distribute knowledge and
20 19 doth not d. with right understanding
33 24 thy decease, d. thy inheritance. Fodder
Isa 53 12 will I d. to him very many, and he
Luke 11 22 he will distribute his spoils. He that
1 C 13 3 if I should d. all my goods to feed
distributed Josu 19 41 d. by lot in Silo, before
Josu 21 40 their suburbs, each d. by the families
2 K 6 19 distributed . . . to every one a cake of
4 K 22 9 have given it to be d. to the workmen
1 Pa 23 4 of these 24,000 were chosen and d.
6 and David distributed them into courses
24 3 David distributed them, that is, Sadoc
25 6 all these . . . were d. to sing in the
2 Pa 23 18 whom David had distributed in the house
35 13 they distributed them speedily among
Tob 1 19 d. to every one as he was able, out
Ps 111 9 he hath d., he hath given to the poor

1 Ma 6 35 they d. the beasts by the legions: and
2 Ma 1 35 he took and d. them to them with his
Luke 9 16 broke and distributed to his disciples
John 6 11 he d. to them that were set down. In
1 C 7 17 as the Lord hath d. to every one, so
distribution Num 36 4 d. made by the lots shall
1 Pa 4 33 the distribution of their dwellings
Ps 77 54 their land by a line of distribution
Acts 4 35 d. was made to every one, according as
distributions Heb 2 4 and d. of the Holy Ghost
distrust Rom 4 20 he staggered not by distrust
distrustful Eccu 41 4 the d. that loseth patience
distrusting 2 Ma 8 13 d. the justice of God, fled
2 Ma 9 22 not d. my life, but having great hope
disturb Acts 16 20 these men d. our city, being
disturbance Esth 11 5 and a d. upon the earth
Ps 30 21 hide them . . . from the d. of men. Thou
Wisd 18 20 d. of the multitude in the wilderness
22 he overcame the disturbance, not by
Acts 19 23 there arose no small disturbance about
1 P 3 6 doing well and not fearing any d. Ye
disturbed 1 K 28 15 why hast thou d. my rest, that
2 K 7 10 they . . . shall be disturbed no more
Ps 30 11 through poverty, and my bones are d.
Prov 30 21 by three things the earth is disturbed
Mich 7 17 they shall be d. in their houses: they
1 Ma 7 22 that d. the people resorted to him
disturbest 1 K 26 14 criest and d. the king? And
ditch Prov 23 27 a harlot is a deep ditch: and a
Isa 22 11 you made a d. between the two walls
Luke 6 39 do they not both fall into the ditch
ditches 4 K 3 16 of this torrent full of d. For
Isa 33 4 as when the ditches are full of them
Jer 2 34 not in ditches have I found them, but
divers Gen 30 32 all the sheep of d. colors and
Gen 30 32 of d. colors as well among the sheep, as
33 all that is not of divers colors and
35 rams of divers colors and spotted
37 by this means the color was divers
39 brought forth spotted and of d. colors
31 10 were of divers colors and spotted
12 upon the females, are of divers colors
37 3 he made him a coat of divers colors
23 coat, that was of divers colors: and
Exod 8 21 be filled with flies of divers kinds
12 38 and herds and beasts of divers kinds
28 15 embroidered work of divers colors
35 24 and setim wood for divers uses. The
37 16 vessels for the d. uses of the table
38 3 he prepared divers vessels of brass
Lev 7 24 you shall have for divers uses. If any
Num 15 39 going astray after divers things, but
31 51 received all the gold in divers kinds
Deut 22 9 not sow thy vineyard with d. seeds
25 13 thou shalt not have divers weights
Judg 5 30 garments of divers colors are given
20 46 slain of Benjamin in divers places
3 K 6 29 he carved with d. figures and carvings
29 palm trees and divers representations
7 31 corners of pillars were d. engravings
35 having its gravings and d. sculptures
4 K 20 13 he showed . . . divers precious odors
1 Pa 29 2 stones like alabaster and of d. colors
2 Pa 5 13 with divers kind of musical instruments
9 14 sum which the deputies of d. nations
15 18 gold and silver and vessels of d. uses
23 13 playing on instruments of d. kinds
26 15 he made . . . engines of divers kinds
29 27 with trumpets and divers instruments
34 13 that carried burdens for divers uses
17 and of the workmen, for divers works
2 Es 5 18 I gave store of divers wines and many
Jdth 5 10 whole land of Egypt with d. plagues
Ps 77 45 he sent amongst them d. sorts of flies
104 31 there came divers sorts of flies and
Wisd 15 4 a graven figure with divers colors
Eccu 10 8 because of . . . and divers deceits. But
Isa 22 24 divers kinds of vessels, every little
Eze 16 18 thy garments of divers colors and
23 12 to her, clothed with divers colors
27 18 in the multitude of divers riches
24 were thy merchants in divers manners
2 Ma 1 35 many goods and divers presents and he
12 27 dwelt a multitude of d. nations: and
15 21 the divers preparations of armor and
Mat 4 24 that were taken with divers diseases
Mark 1 34 that were troubled with d. diseases
13 8 earthquakes in d. places. Luke 21:11
Luke 4 40 that had any sick with d. diseases
Acts 2 4 they began to speak with d. tongues
2 Tim 3 6 who are led away with d. desires: ever
Titus 3 3 slaves to d. desires and pleasures
Heb 1 1 in d. manners spoke in times past to
2 4 bearing them witness . . . by d. miracles
9 10 in drinks and d. washings and justices
James 1 2 you shall fall into d. temptations
1 P 1 6 made sorrowful in d. temptations: that
diverse Jdth 6 13 be put to death by d. torments
Prov 20 10 d. weights and d. measures, both are
23 d. weights are an abomination before
1 C 12 10 to another, d. kinds of tongues; to
diversely Lev 14 56 when colors are d. changed
diversified Exod 26 1 ten curtains . . . d. with
Eccu 33 11 hath divided them and d. their ways
diversion Bar 3 17 their d. with the birds of
diversities Wisd 7 20 the d. of plants and the
1 C 12 4 there are diversities of graces, but
5 there are diversities of ministries
6 there are diversities of operations
diversity 1 Pa 28 14 the d. of the vessels and
1 Pa 28 15 diversity of the dimensions of them
16 according to diversity of the tables
divide Gen 1 6 let it d. the waters from the
Gen 1 14 to divide the day and the night and
18 to divide the light and the darkness
49 7 I will divide them in Jacob and will
27 in the evening shall divide the spoil
Exod 14 16 thy hands over the sea, and divide it
15 9 I will divide the spoils, my soul shall
21 35 the live ox, and shall divide the price
Lev 1 12 they shall divide the joints, the head
17 shall not cut nor d. it with a knife
2 6 thou shalt d. it into little pieces
13 56 divide it from that which is sound
Num 4 19 and shall divide the burdens that every
31 27 thou shalt divide the spoil equally
33 54 you shall divide it among you by lot
34 17 that shall divide the land unto you
29 Lord hath commanded to d. the land
36 2 that thou shouldst divide the land
Deut 1 38 he [Josue] shall divide the land by
3 28 [Josue] shall d. unto them the land
14 7 chew the cud but divide not the hoof
19 3 thou shalt divide the whole province
20 14 thou shalt d. all the prey to the army
21 16 he meaneth to divide his substance
31 7 thou shalt divide it by lot. And the
Josu 1 6 thou shalt divide by lot to this people
13 7 d. the land in possession to the nine
18 5 d. to yourselves the land into seven
22 8 divide the prey of your enemies with
1 K 30 24 and they shall divide alike. And this
2 K 19 29 thou and Siba divide the possessions
3 K 3 25 divide, said he, the living child in
26 neither mine nor thine, but d. it
11 11 I will divide and rend thy kingdom

2 Es 9 11 thou didst divide the sea before them
22 and didst divide lots for them: and
Job 27 17 and the innocent shall d. the silver
40 25 in pieces, shall merchants divide him
Ps 16 14 divide them from the few of the earth
54 10 cast down, O Lord, and d. their tongues
59 8 rejoice, and I will d. Sichem. 107:8
67 13 beauty of the house shall divide spoils
Prov 5 16 and in the streets divide thy waters
16 19 than to divide spoils with the proud
17 2 shall d. the inheritance among the
Wisd 5 24 and as a whirlwind shall divide them
Eccu 14 15 to divide by lot thy sorrows and labors
Isa 9 3 prey, when they divide the spoils
53 12 he shall divide the spoils of the
56 3 Lord will d. and separate me from
Jer 37 11 to divide a possession there in the
Eze 5 1 to weigh in, and divide the hair: and
45 1 you shall begin to divide the land
47 21 you shall divide this land unto you
22 you shall divide it by lot for an
22 they shall d. the possession with you
48 29 which you shall divide by lot to the
Dan 11 39 and shall divide the land gratis. And
Mich 2 4 is returning that will d. our land
13 they shall divide and pass through
Haba 3 9 thou wilt d. the rivers of the earth
1 Ma 3 36 and divide their land by lot. So the
Luke 12 13 that he divide the inheritance with
22 17 said: Take and divide it among you
divided Gen 1 4 he d. the light from the darkness
Gen 1 7 divided the waters that were under
2 10 river . . . divided into four heads. The
10 5 by these were divided the islands of
25 in his days the earth was d. 1 Pa 1:19
32 by these were the nations divided on
15 10 and divided them in the midst and laid
10 the birds he divided not. And the fowls
25 23 two peoples shall be divided out of
32 7 divided the people that was with him
33 1 he divided the children of Lia and of
38 29 why is the partition divided for thee
Exod 14 21 and the water was divided. And the
26 33 holy of holies shall be d. with it
Lev 11 3 whatsoever hath the hoof divided and
Num 2 32 divided according to the houses of
26 53 to these shall the land be divided
55 yet so that by lot the land be d. to
33 54 possession shall be d. by the tribes
Deut 32 8 when the Most High d. the nations
Josu 8 27 divided among them the cattle and the
11 14 divided among themselves all the spoil
13 1 which is not yet divided by lot: to wit
3 d. among the lords of the Philistines
32 this possession Moses divided in the
14 4 children of Joseph d. into two tribes
5 and they divided the land. 19:51
18 9 surveying it d. it into seven parts
10 divided the land to the children of
23 4 since he hath divided to you by lot
Judg 5 15 Ruben being d. against himself. 16
7 16 he d. the 300 men into three parts
9 43 army and d. it into three companies
19 29 divided the dead body of his wife
2 K 1 23 even in death they were not divided
5 20 Lord hath d. my enemies before me as waters are d.
12 31 d. them with knives and made them
3 K 11 30 garment . . . d. it into twelve parts
16 21 people of Israel divided into two
18 6 they d. the countries between them
4 K 2 8 waters, and they were d. hither and
14 struck the waters . . . they were not d.
14 struck the waters, and they were d.
1 Pa 13 11 troubled because the Lord had d. Oza
14 11 divided my enemies by my hand, as
16 3 and he divided to all and every one
24 4 he divided them so that there were of
5 he divided both the families one with
31 the lot divided all equally. Moreover
2 Pa 5 11 the courses . . . were not d. among them
Jdth 9 3 spoils to be divided to thy servants
Job 38 24 spread, and heat divided upon the earth
54 22 are d. by the wrath of his countenance
77 13 he divided the sea and brought them
54 and by lot divided to their land by a
135 13 who divided the Red Sea into parts
Wisd 5 12 the d. air presently cometh together
Eccu 33 11 the Lord hath d. them and diversified
44 26 d. him his portion in twelve tribes
45 25 d. unto him the firstfruits of the
47 23 shouldst make the kingdom to be d.
Isa 33 23 shall the spoils of much prey be d.
34 17 his hand hath d. it to them by line
59 2 your iniquities have d. between you
63 12 that divided the waters before them
Lam 4 16 face of the Lord hath divided them
Eze 37 22 neither shall they be d. any more
Dan 2 41 the kingdom shall be divided, but
5 28 thy kingdom is divided and is given
11 4 it shall be d. towards the four winds
Osee 10 2 their heart is divided: now they shall
Zach 14 1 thy spoils shall be divided in the
4 mount of Olives shall be divided in
1 Ma 1 7 he d. his kingdom among them, while
9 11 horsemen were d. into two troops and
16 7 he d. the people, and set the horsemen
2 Ma 8 28 they d. the spoils to the feeble and
30 they d. amongst them many spoils giving
12 20 divided them by bands, went forth
Mat 12 26 he is divided against himself: how
27 35 they d. his garments. Mark 15:24
35 they d. my garments among them; and
Mark 3 24 if a kingdom be d. against itself that
25 if a house be d. against itself, that
26 he is divided and cannot stand, but
6 41 the two fishes be divided among them
Luke 11 17 every kingdom divided against iself
18 if Satan also be d. against himself
12 52 shall be . . . five in one house d.: three
53 father shall be d. against the son
15 12 he d. unto them his substance. And not
Acts 2 45 they sold and divided them to all
13 19 d. their land among them by lot, as it
14 4 the multitude of the city was divided
23 7 and the multitude was divided. For the
Rom 12 3 as God hath divided to every one the
1 C 1 13 is Christ d.? Was Paul then crucified
7 33 how he may please his wife: and he is d.
Heb 7 2 to whom Abraham d. the tithes of all
Apoc 16 19 great city was d. into three parts
divider Zach 9 6 the d. shall sit in Azotus, and
Luke 12 14 who hath appointed me . . . divider over
divideth Lev 11 4 hath a hoof, but d. it not. 26
Lev 11 5 cheweth the cud, but d. not the hoof. 6
7 though it d. the hoof, cheweth not the
Deut 14 6 every beast that divideth the hoof
8 it divideth the hoof, but cheweth not
Job 28 4 flood divideth from the people that
Ps 28 7 voice of the Lord d. the flame of fire
dividing Gen 14 15 d. his company, he rushed upon
Num 21 13 d. the Moabites and the Amorrhites
Josu 14 2 dividing all by lot, as the Lord had
19 49 an end of dividing the land by lot
Judg 5 30 perhaps he is now dividing the spoils
Luke 23 34 they d. his garments, cast lots. And

1 C 12 11 d. to every one according as he will
divination Num 22 7 went with the price of d.
Num 23 23 there is no . . . divination in Israel
24 1 not as he had gone before, to seek d.
4 K 21 6 used divination and observed omens
Prov 16 10 divination is in the lips of the king
Jer 14 14 lying vision and divination and deceit
Eze 12 24 nor doubtful divination in the midst of
13 7 and spoken a lying divination: and you
21 21 seeking divination, shuffling arrows
22 right hand was the d. for Jerusalem
Mich 3 6 darkness to you instead of divination
divinations 4 K 17 17 gave themselves to d. and
2 Pa 33 6 [Manasses] followed divinations gave
Eccu 34 5 deceitful divinations . . . are vanity
Eze 13 23 see vain things, nor divine d. any more
Mich 5 11 there shall be no divinations in thee
divine Gen 44 5 in which he is wont to divine
Lev 19 26 you shall not divine nor observe dreams
1 K 28 8 divine to me by thy divining spirit
Eccu 39 17 hear me, ye d. offspring, and bud forth
50 17 a divine odor to the most high Prince
Eze 13 9 see vain things and that divine lies
23 nor divine divinations any more, and I
21 29 in thy regard, and they divine lies
Rom 11 4 what saith the divine answer to him
Heb 9 1 had also justifications of d. service
2 P 1 3 as all things of his divine power which
4 be made partakers of the divine nature
divined Mich 3 11 her prophets d. for money: and
diviner Prov 23 7 like a soothsayer and d., he
Dan 2 10 ask such a thing of any diviner, or wise
diviners Deut 18 14 hearken to soothsayers and d.
1 K 6 2 called for the priests and the diviners
4 K 23 24 diviners by spirits . . . Josias took away
Isa 8 19 seek of pythons and of diviners, who
19 3 they shall consult . . . their diviners
44 25 that make void the tokens of diviners
Jer 27 9 hearken not to your prophets and d.
29 8 your d. deceive you: and give no heed
50 36 a sword upon her diviners and they shall
Dan 1 20 ten times better than all the diviners
2 2 commanded to call together the d. and
27 or the d. or soothsayers can declare
4 4 then came in the diviners, the wise men
6 Baltassar, prince of the diviners
Mich 3 7 the diviners shall be confounded: and
Zach 10 2 the diviners have seen a lie and the
divining Gen 44 15 like me in science of d. And
Lev 20 27 in whom there is a . . . d. spirit, dying
1 K 28 7 a woman that hath a divining spirit
8 divine to me by thy divining spirit
Eze 22 28 seeing vain things and divining lies
Acts 16 16 brought to her masters much gain by d.
divinity Acts 17 29 d. to be like unto gold, or
Rom 1 20 his eternal power also and divinity
Apoc 5 12 is worthy to receive power and d. and
division Exod 8 23 I will put a d. between my
Josu 13 24 a possession, of which this is the d.
1 K 23 28 called that place, the Rock of d. Then
1 Pa 27 5 in his d. were four and twenty thousand
2 Ma 8 22 captains over each d. of his army
John 9 16 there was a division among them. They
Heb 4 12 reaching unto the d. of the soul and
divisions Gen 15 17 fire passing between those d.
Josu 11 23 according to their d. and tribes. And
12 7 to every one their divisions, as well
1 Pa 24 1 the divisions of the sons of Aaron
26 1 and the divisions of the porters: of the
12 were the divisions of the porters, so
19 these are the divisions of the porters
28 13 of the divisions of the priests and of
2 Pa 8 14 and the porters in their divisions
1 Es 6 18 set aside the priests in their d. and
Prov 21 1 as the d. of waters, so the heart of
Isa 28 21 up as in the mountain of divisions
divorce Deut 24 1 he shall write a bill of d.
Deut 24 3 given her a bill of divorce. Jer 3:8
Isa 50 1 this bill of the d. of your mother
Mat 5 31 bill of d. 19:7; Mark 10:4
divorced Lev 21 14 divorced . . . he shall not take
Lev 22 13 if she be a widow or divorced and
Num 30 10 she that is divorced, shall fulfil
divulgeth Wisd 2 12 d. against us the sins of
Doch 1 Ma 16 15 fortress that is called Doch
doctor 2 Pa 26 11 Maasias the d. and under the hand
Mat 22 35 a doctor of the law asked him, tempting
Acts 5 34 Gamaliel, a doctor of the law, respected
1 Tim 2 7 a d. of the Gentiles in faith and truth. I
doctors Deut 29 10 all stand . . . ancients and d.
Deut 31 28 ancients of your tribes and your d.
Luke 2 46 sitting in the midst of the doctors
5 17 doctors of the law sitting by, that
Acts 13 1 at Antioch prophets and doctors, among
1 C 12 28 secondly prophets, thirdly doctors
29 are all doctors? Are all workers of
Eph 4 11 other some pastors and doctors, for the
doctrine Exod 28 30 put in . . . doctrine and truth
Lev 8 8 rational, on which was D. and Truth
Num 24 16 who knoweth the d. of the Highest
Deut 32 2 let my doctrine gather as the rain
33 3 shall receive of his doctrine. Moses
8 and thy doctrine be to thy holy man
Job 12 20 taketh away the doctrine of the aged
20 3 the d. with which thou reprovest me
Ps 59 1 to David himself, for doctrine, when
Prov 1 3 to receive the instruction of doctrine
13 1 wise son heareth d. of his father: but
21 16 that shall wander out of the way of d.
22 17 apply thy heart to my doctrine: which
24 14 so also is the doctrine of wisdom to
Eccu 6 23 wisdom of d. is according to her name
16 25 I will show forth good doctrine in
21 22 doctrine to a fool is as fetters on
24 44 I make doctrine to shine forth to all
46 I will yet pour out d. as prophecy
50 29 in this book the doctrine of wisdom
Jer 3 15 shall feed you with knowledge and d.
10 8 the doctrine of their vanity is wood
Mat 7 28 in admiration at this doctrine. 22:23; Mark 6:2; 11:18
16 12 beware . . . of the d. of the Pharisees
Mark 1 22 were astonished at his d. Luke 4:32
27 what is this new doctrine. Acts 17:19
4 2 said unto them in his doctrine. 12:38
John 7 16 my d. is not mine, but his that sent
17 the d. whether it be of God or whether
18 19 the high priest asked Jesus of his d.
Acts 2 42 persevering in the d. of the apostles
5 28 have filled Jerusalem with your d.
13 12 admiring at the doctrine of the Lord
Rom 6 17 unto that form of d., into which you
12 7 he that teacheth, in doctrine; he that
16 17 the d. which you have learned and avoid
1 C 2 13 but in the d. of the Spirit, comparing
14 6 unless I speak to you . . . in doctrine
26 every one of you hath a psalm, hath a d.
Eph 4 14 carried about with every wind of d.
1 Tim 1 10 other thing is contrary to sound d.
4 6 of the good doctrine which thou hast
13 to exhortation and to d. Neglect not
16 take heed to thyself and to doctrine
5 17 who labor in the word and doctrine
6 1 the Lord and his doctrine be blasphemed
3 that d. which is according to godliness
2 Tim 3 10 thou hast fully known my doctrine

4 2 rebuke in all patience and doctrine
3 when they will not endure sound d.
Titus 1 9 faithful word which is according to d.
9 he may be able to exhort in sound d.
2 1 the things that become sound doctrine
7 show thyself an example . . . in d., in
10 they may adorn the doctrine of God
Heb 6 2 of the d. of baptisms and imposition
2 J 9 continueth not in the d. of Christ
9 he that continueth in the doctrine
10 bring not this doctrine, receive him not
Apoc 2 14 that hold the doctrine of Balaam, who
15 that hold the d. of the Nicolaites
24 whosoever have not this doctrine and
doctrines Isa 29 13 commandment and d. of men
Mat 15 9 teaching d. and commandments of men
Mark 7 7 teaching doctrines and precepts of men
Col 2 22 according to the precepts and d. of men
1 Tim 4 1 giving heed to . . . doctrines of devils
Heb 13 9 led away with various and strange d.
Dodanim Gen 10 4 sons of Javan . . . D. 1 Pa 1:7
Dodau 2 Pa 20 37 Eliezer the son of Dodau of
Dodo 2 K 23 9 Eleazar the son of Dodo the Aholite
2 K 25 24 Elehanan the son of Dodo of Bethlehem
doe Prov 6 5 deliver thyself as a doe from the
Isa 13 14 they shall be as a doe fleeing away
Doeg 1 K 21 7 his name was Doeg, an Edomite, the
1 K 22 9 Doeg the Edomite who stood by and was
18 the king said to Doeg: Turn thou and
18 Doeg the Edomite turned and fell upon
22 day when Doeg the Edomite was there
Ps 51 2 when Doeg the Edomite came and told
doer James 1 23 hearer of the word and not a doer
James 1 25 forgetful hearer, but a doer of the work
4 11 thou art not a doer of the law, but a
doers Ps 25 4 with the doers of unjust things
Rom 2 13 d. of the law shall be justified. For
James 1 22 be ye doers of the word and not hearers
dog Exod 11 7 shall not a dog make the least noise
Deut 23 18 shall not offer . . . the price of a dog
1 K 17 43 am I a dog, that thou comest to me
24 15 pursue? After a dead dog, after a flea
2 K 9 8 look upon such a dead dog as I am? Then
16 9 why should this dead dog curse my lord
4 K 8 13 but what am I thy servant a dog that
Tob 6 1 the dog followed him and he lodged
11 9 the dog, which had been with them
Jdth 11 15 so much as one dog bark against thee
Ps 21 21 my only one from the hand of the dog
Prov 26 11 as a dog that returneth to his vomit
17 as he that taketh a dog by the ears
Ecce 9 4 living dog is better than a dead lion
Eccu 13 22 fellowship hath a holy man with a dog
Isa 66 3 as if he should brain a dog: he that
2 P 2 22 the dog is returned to his vomit: and
dog's 2 K 3 8 am I a dog's head against Juda
dogs Exod 22 31 eat, but shall cast it to the d.
Judg 7 5 as dogs are wont to lap, thou shalt set
3 K 14 11 that shall die . . . the dogs shall eat
16 4 of Baasa in the city, the dogs shall eat
21 19 dogs have licked the blood of Naboth
23 dogs shall eat Jezabel. 4 K 9:10
24 the dogs shall eat him [Achab]. Now
22 38 and the dogs licked up his blood and
4 K 9 36 dogs shall eat the flesh of Jezabel
Job 30 1 not have set with the dogs of my flock
Ps 21 17 many dogs have encompassed me: the
58 7 and shall suffer hunger like dogs. 15
67 24 tongue of thy dogs be red with the
Isa 56 10 dumb dogs not able to bark, seeing vain
11 impudent dogs, they never had enough
Jer 15 3 sword to kill, and the dogs to tear
Mat 7 6 give not that which is holy to dogs
15 26 and cast it to the dogs. Mark 7:27
Luke 16 21 the dogs came and licked his sores
Phil 3 2 beware of dogs, beware of evil workers
Apoc 22 15 without are dogs and sorcerers and
doing Ps 117 23 this is the Lord's doing: and it
2 K 3 37 that it was not the king's doing, that
doings Deut 11 2 his great doings and strong hand
4 K 21 11 Juda also to sin with his filthy d.
1 Pa 16 8 make known his d. among the nations
Ps 63 10 of God, and understood his doings
91 5 given me . . . a delight in thy doings
Wisd 2 12 and he is contrary to our doings and
Isa 3 10 he shall eat the fruit of his doings
58 1 show my people their wicked doings
59 12 our wicked doings are with us and we
Jer 7 3 make your ways and your doings good
5 order well your ways and your doings
11 18 then thou showedst me their doings
18 11 make ye your ways and your d. good
21 14 according to the fruit of your doings
23 2 upon you for the evil of your doings
14 no man should return from his evil d.
22 turned them . . . from their wicked d.
26 3 unto them for wickedness of their d.
13 amend your ways and your doings and
44 22 because of the evil of your doings
Bar 6 4 that you imitate not the d. of others
Eze 14 22 you shall see their way and their d.
23 you shall see their ways and their d.
20 43 shall remember . . . all your wicked d.
24 14 and according to thy doings saith the
36 17 with their ways and with their doings
31 your doings that were not good: and
44 6 let all your wicked doings suffice you
7 broken my covenant by all your wicked d.
Soph 3 11 shalt not be ashamed for all thy d.
Luke 11 48 you consent to the doings of your fathers
23 51 not consented to their counsel or d.
domestics Prov 31 21 all her d. are clothed with
Eph 2 19 with the saints and the domestics of God
dominations Col 1 16 whether thrones or d., or
dominion Gen 1 26 let him have d. over the fishes
Gen 3 16 he shall have dominion over thee. And
4 7 thou [Cain] shalt have d. over it
37 8 shall we be subject to thy dominion
Deut 15 6 shalt have d. over very many nations
6 no one shall have dominion over thee
Josu 12 2 Sehon . . . had dominion from Aroer which
4 and had dominion in mount Hermon and
21 42 but were brought under their dominion
Judg 14 4 Philistines had dominion over Israel
2 K 8 3 when he went to extend his dominion
3 K 9 19 and in all the land of his dominion
1 Pa 29 12 thou hast dominion over all, in thy
2 Pa 8 6 and in all the land of his dominion
21 10 from being under the dominion of Juda
26 2 restored it to the dominion of Juda
1 Es 4 20 had dominion over all the country that
2 Es 9 28 and they had dominion over them. Then
37 they have dominion over our bodies
Esth 4 11 provinces that are under his dominion
9 16 which were subject to the king's d.
13 2 brought all the world under my d., I
Ps 18 14 if they shall have no dominion over me
21 29 he shall have d. over the nations. All
48 15 the just shall have dominion over them
102 22 in every place of his dominion, O my
105 41 they that hated them had d. over them
113 2 Israel [was made] his dominion. The
118 133 let no iniquity have dominion over me
144 13 thy dominion endureth throughout all
Wisd 9 2 that he should have dominion over the
17 2 to have dominion over the holy nation

Eccu 1 8 is the God of dominion. He created
17 4 he had dominion over beasts and fowls
Isa 26 13 other lords besides thee have had d.
39 2 nothing in his house nor in all his d.
Jer 31 32 and I had dominion over them, saith
34 10 no more have dominion over them: and
51 28 and all the land of their dominion
Dan 11 5 his dominion shall be great. And after
1 Ma 10 52 and have gotten the dominion and have
65 him governor and partaker of his d.
11 8 king Ptolemee got the d. of the cities
14 7 and had the dominion of Gazara and of
15 29 got the dominion of many places in my
30 places whereof you have gotten the d.
Rom 6 9 death shall no more have dominion over
14 sin shall not have dominion over you
7 1 the law hath d. over a man as long
2 C 1 23 not because we exercise dominion over
Eph 1 21 above all . . . virtue and dominion and
Jude 8 these men . . . despise dominion and
dominions Num 21 26 land that had been of his d.
4 K 20 13 nor in all his dominions that Ezechias
1 Pa 18 3 he went to extend his dominions as far
Jdth 1 1 brought many nations under his d. and
Eccu 44 3 have borne rule in their dominions
1 Ma 8 24 any war . . . in all their dominions: the
Dommim 1 K 17 1 and Azeca in borders of Dommim
Domum 4 K 15 29 Abel Domum Maacha and Janoe
donaries 2 Ma 12 40 some of the d. of the idols
door Gen 4 7 sin forthwith be present at the door
Gen 6 16 door of the ark thou shalt set in the
18 1 sitting at the door of his tent, in the
2 meet them from the door of his tent
10 she laughed behind the door of the tent
19 6 Lot went out to them and shut the door
10 shut the door: and them that were
11 so that they could not find the door
43 19 to the steward of the house at the d.
Exod 12 7 on the upper door posts of the houses
22 in the blood that is at the door and
22 sprinkle transom of the door therewith
22 and both the door cheeks: let none of
22 none of you go out of the door of his
23 he will pass over the door of the house
21 6 he shall be set to the door and the
33 8 every one stood in the door of his
9 pillar of the cloud . . . stood at the d.
35 17 the hanging in the door of the entry
Lev 1 3 offer . . . at the door of the testimony
4 4 bring it to the door of the testimony
14 38 shall go out of the door of the house
Num 4 5 the veil that hangeth before the door
11 10 every one at door of his tent. And
Deut 15 17 bore through his ear in the door of thy
Josu 2 19 whosoever shall go out of the door of
Judg 3 24 went out by a postern door. And the
25 seeing that no man opened the door
4 20 stand before the door of the tent
18 16 the 600 men stood before the door
17 and the priest stood before the door
19 22 and began to knock at the door, calling
26 to door of the house where her lord
27 the man arose and opened the door
27 his concubine lay before the door
1 K 1 9 upon a stool before door of the temple
4 18 fell from his stool backwards by the d.
2 K 13 17 and shut the door after her. 18
3 K 6 8 the door for the middle side was on
34 and each door was double and so opened
14 6 sound of her feet coming in at the d.
4 K 4 4 and go in, and shut thy door when thou
5 the woman went and shut the door upon
15 was called and stood before the door
21 him upon bed . . . and shut the door: and
33 going in he shut the door upon him
5 9 stood at door of the house of Eliseus
6 32 when messenger shall come, shut door
9 3 and thou shalt open the door and flee
10 and he opened the door and fled. Then
2 Es 3 20 to the door of the house of Eliasib
21 from the door of the hours of Eliasib
Jdth 14 9 noise before the door of the chamber
Esth 5 1 over against the door of the house
Job 31 9 have laid wait at my friend's door
32 my door was open to the traveller. If
34 my peace and not gone out to the door
Ps 140 3 and a door round about my lips. Incline
Prov 9 14 sat at the door of her house, upon
17 19 that exalteth his door, seeketh ruin
26 14 as the door turneth upon its hinges
Cant 5 6 I opened the bolt of my door to my
8 9 if she be a d., let us join it together
Wisd 6 15 he shall find her sitting at his door
19 16 sought the passage of his own door
Eccu 14 24 and hearkeneth at her door. He that
21 27 folly of a man to hearken at the door
Isa 57 8 behind the door . . . hast set up thy
Bar 6 58 or a door in the house, to keep things
Eze 8 7 brought me in to the door of the court
8 I had digged in the wall, behold a door
14 brought me in by the door of the gate
16 at the door of the temple of the Lord
40 13 five and twenty cubits: d. against d.
38 at every chamber was a door in the
41 11 door of the side chambers was turned
11 one d. was toward the north, and another d. was toward the south
42 2 in the face of the north door was the
12 was a door in the head of the way
46 3 shall adore at the door of that gate
Dan 3 93 to door of the burning fiery furnace
13 18 and went out by a back door to fetch
25 ran to the door of the orchard and
26 they rushed in by the back door to see
14 10 shut the door fast, and seal it with
13 going forth they shut the door and
17 as soon as he had opened the door, the
2 Ma 2 5 cave . . . and so stopped the door. Then
14 41 break open the door and to set fire
Mat 6 6 having shut the door, pray to thy
25 10 and the door was shut. But at last
27 60 stone to door of monument. Mark 15:46
Mark 1 33 all the city was gathered at the door
2 2 was no room; no, not even at the door
16 3 roll us back the stone from the door
Luke 11 7 trouble me not, the door is now shut
13 25 be gone in and shall shut the door
25 you shall begin to knock at the door
John 10 1 he that entereth not by the door into
2 he that entereth in by the door is the
7 I am the door of the sheep. All others
9 I am the door. By me, if any man
18 16 but Peter stood at the door without
Acts 3 9 have buried thy husband are at the d.
12 6 keepers before the d. kept the prison
13 when he [Peter] knocked at the door
14 26 open the door of faith to the Gentiles
1 C 16 9 a great door and evident is opened
2 C 2 12 a door was opened unto me in the Lord
Col 4 3 God may open unto us a door of speech
James 5 9 the judge standeth before the door
Apoc 3 8 I have given thee a door opened, which
20 if any man . . . open to me the door, I
4 1 a door was opened in heaven and the
door of the tabernacle Exod 29 4 to the d. . . . of the testimony. 40:12; Lev 12:6; 15:14; 17:9

Exod 29 42 at the d. . . . of the testimony. Lev 4:18; 14:11, 23; 15:29; 17:6; 19:21; Josu 19:51
33 10 pillar of the cloud stood at d. . . .
35 15 of spices: the handing at the d. . . .
38 8 women that watched at the d. . . . He
Lev 1 5 the altar, which is before the d. . . .
4 14 calf, and shall bring it to the d. . . .
8 3 all the congregation to the d. . . .
4 gathered together before the d. . . .
31 boil the flesh before the d. . . . and
33 shall not go out of the d. . . . 10:7
9 5 before the d. . . . : where when all the
16 7 in the d. . . . of the testimony: and
17 4 offer it not at the d. . . . an oblation
5 before the d. . . . of the testimony and
Num 6 13 to the d. . . . of the covenant. 10:3; 11:16; 16:50
18 before the d. . . . of the covenant: and
16 19 against them to the d. . . . , the glory
19 4 sprinkle it over against the d. . . .
25 6 who were weeping before the d. . . .
27 2 at the d. . . . of the covenant and said
1 K 2 22 the women that waited at the d. . . .
doorkeeper 2 K 4 5 doorkeeper . . . fallen asleep
doorkeepers 4 K 22 4 which the d. of the temple
4 K 25 18 the second priest and three doorkeepers
1 Pa 15 23 were doorkeepers of the ark. Sebenias
Eze 44 11 doorkeepers of the gates of the house
14 I will make them d. of the house, for
doors Gen 19 9 point of breaking open the doors
Exod 33 10 worshipped at the doors of their tents
Num 3 26 the hanging that is drawn before the d.
Deut 6 9 the entry, and on the doors of thy house
11 20 upon the posts and doors of thy house
22 21 they shall cast her out of the doors
Judg 3 23 Aod carefully shutting the doors of
24 saw the doors of the parlor shut. And
11 31 come forth out of doors of my house
16 3 he took both the doors of the gate
1 K 3 15 opened the doors of house of the Lord
21 13 stumbled against the doors of the gate
3 K 6 17 temple itself before d. of the oracle
31 he made little doors of olive tree
32 and two doors of olive tree: and he
34 and two doors of fir tree, one of each
7 50 hinges for the doors . . . were of gold
4 K 12 9 the priests that kept the doors put
18 16 Ezechias broke the doors of the temple
2 Pa 3 7 gold of . . . doors was of the finest
15 before the doors of the temple two
4 9 a great hall, and doors in the hall
22 graved the doors of the inner temple
22 doors of temple without were of gold
28 24 shut up the doors of the temple of God
29 3 opened the doors of house of the Lord
7 they have shut up the doors that were
2 Es 3 1 sanctified it and set up the doors
3 covered it and set up the d. 6, 15
13 built it and set up the doors. 14
6 1 I had not set up the doors in the
10 let us shut the doors of the temple
7 1 I had set up the doors and numbered
11 19 and their brethren, who kept the doors
Jdth 13 1 and Vagao shut the chamber doors and
Esth 3 2 at the doors of the palace. 3
15 9 she passed through all the d. in order
Job 3 10 it shut not up the doors of the womb
38 8 who shut up the sea with doors, when
10 around it, and made it bars and doors
17 hast thou seen the darksome doors
41 5 who can open the doors of his face
Ps 77 23 and had opened the doors of heaven
Prov 5 8 come not nigh the doors of her house
8 3 in the very doors she speaketh, saying
34 waiteth at the posts of my doors. He
Ecce 12 4 they shall shut the doors in the street
Wisd 19 16 others were at the d. of the just men
Eccu 6 36 let thy foot wear the steps of his d.
28 28 make doors and bars to thy mouth. Melt
30 1 and not grope after the doors of his
Isa 6 4 the lintels of the doors were moved
26 20 shut thy doors upon thee, hide thyself
45 1 to open the doors before him and the
Bar 6 17 the priests secure the doors with bars
Eze 33 30 of thee . . . in the doors of the houses
40 26 a porch before the doors thereof: and
41 16 the windows were shut over the doors
23 there were two doors in the temple
24 in the two d. on both sides were two little d.
24 two wickets on both sides of the doors
25 cherubims also wrought in the doors
42 2 and their doors were toward the north
11 their fashions and their d. were alike
12 according to the doors of the chambers
Dan 13 17 shut the doors of the orchard. 18, 36
20 the doors of the orchard are shut
39 opening the doors he leaped out: but
14 20 they showed him the private doors by
Mich 7 5 keep the doors of thy mouth from her
Mala 1 10 that will shut the doors and will kindle
1 Ma 1 58 sacrificed at the doors of the houses
4 57 chambers, and hanged doors upon them
2 Ma 14 43 the crowd was breaking into the doors
Mat 24 33 it is nigh, even at the d. Mark 13:29
John 20 19 and the doors were shut . . . Jesus came
26 Jesus cometh, the doors being shut
Acts 5 19 opening the d. of the prison and leading
23 the keepers standing before the doors
16 26 immediately all the doors were opened
27 seeing the doors of the prison open
21 30 and immediately the doors were shut
Dor Josu 11 2 in the levels and countries of Dor
Josu 12 23 king of Dor, and of province of Dor one
17 11 inhabitants of Dor, with the towns
21 32 and Hammoth Dor, and Carthan, with their
Judg 1 27 nor the inhabitants of Dor and Jeblaam
1 Pa 7 29 Dor and her daughters: in these dwelt
Dora 1 Ma 15 11 by the seacoast and came to Dora
1 Ma 15 13 Antiochus camped above Dora with a
25 king Antiochus moved his camp to Dora
Dorcas Acts 9 36 Tabitha, which . . . is called D.
Acts 9 39 garments which Dorcas made them. And
Dorda 3 K 4 31 Chalcol and Dorda the sons of Mahol
Dorymenus 1 Ma 3 38 Ptolemee the son of Dorymenus
Dositheus Esth 11 1 D. who said he was a priest
2 Ma 12 19 D. and Sosipater, who were captains with
24 fell into the hands of the band of D.
35 Dositheus . . . took hold of Gorgias: and
doted Eze 23 5 against me and d. on her lovers
Eze 23 7 of all them on whom she doted. Moreover
9 Assyrians, upon whose lust she doted
16 she doted upon them with the lust of
Dothain Gen 37 17 heard them say: Let us go to D.
Gen 37 17 his brethren, and found them in Dothain
Jdth 4 5 faceth the great plain near Dothain
7 3 which looketh toward Dothain, from the
Dothan 4 K 6 13 saying: Behold he is in Dothan
doting Eccu 25 4 old man that is a fool and d.
double Gen 23 9 that he may give me the d. cave
Gen 23 17 wherein was the double cave, looking
19 in a double cave of the field, that
25 9 buried him in the d. cave. 50:13
43 12 take with you double money and carry
15 took the presents and double money
49 29 with my fathers in the double cave
Exod 16 5 let it be double to that they were wont

29 he giveth you a double provision: let
22 4 he shall restore double. 7, 9
26 9 so as to double the sixth curtain in
39 9 a rational . . . foursquare, double, of
Deut 19 9 shalt double the number of the three
21 17 give him a d. portion of all he hath
Judg 17 10 and a double suit of apparel and thy
3 K 6 34 each door was double, and so opened
4 K 2 9 that in me may be thy double spirit
1 Pa 12 33 50,000 to his aid, with no d. heart
Ps 11 3 with a double heart have they spoken
108 29 confusion as with a double cloak. I
Prob 8 13 I hate . . . mouth with a double tongue
14 25 and the double dealer uttereth lies
31 21 domestics are clothed with d. garments
Wisd 11 13 a double affliction came upon them
Eccu 1 36 come not to him with a double heart
2 14 to them that are of a double heart
5 11 sinner proved by a double tongue. Be
20 10 the recompense of which is double
23 13 dissemble it, he offendeth double
26 1 the number of his years is double
42 25 all things are double, one against
50 2 the double building and the high walls
Isa 40 2 received . . . double for all her sins
61 7 for your double confusion and shame
7 shall they receive double in their
Jer 16 18 repay first their double iniquities
17 18 with a d. destruction destroy them
Bar 5 2 clothe thee with the double garment
Eze 47 13 for Joseph hath a double portion. And
Nah 1 9 shall not rise a double affliction
Zach 9 12 I will render thee double as I declare
1 Tim 5 17 be esteemed worthy of double honor
James 1 8 double minded man is inconstant in
4 8 purify your hearts, ye double minded
Apoc 18 6 double unto her double according to
6 mingle ye double unto her. As much as
doubled Exod 28 16 it shall be foursquare and d.
double-tongued Prov 18 8 words of the d. are as
Eccu 5 17 mark of disgrace upon the d., but to
6 1 that is envious and double-tongued
28 15 whisperer and the d. is accursed: for
1 Tim 3 8 like manner chaste, not double-tongued
doubt Exod 10 10 who can d. but that you intend
Num 32 23 no man can d. but you sin against God
1 K 22 22 that without doubt he would tell Saul
Tob 7 13 I doubt not but God hath regarded my
14 d. not but I will give her to thee
Esth 15 1 no doubt but he was Mardochai, to go to
Mat 14 31 why didst thou doubt? And when they
Luke 9 7 he was in a doubt, because it was said
John 14 7 without d. have known my Father also
Acts 5 24 they were in doubt concerning them
10 29 making no doubt, I came when I was
25 20 in a doubt of this manner of question
1 J 2 19 they would no doubt have remained
doubted Mat 28 17 they adored; but some doubted
doubtful Deut 17 8 hard and d. matter in judgment
Eze 12 24 nor doubtful divination in the midst
doubting John 13 22 doubting of whom he spoke
Acts 10 17 whilst Peter was doubting within himself
20 go with them, doubting nothing. 11:12
doubtless Luke 11 20 d. the kingdom of God is
Heb 11 15 they had doubtless time to return. But
dough Exod 12 34 the people therefore took dough
Exod 12 39 had brought out of Egypt, in dough
Num 15 21 firstfruits of your dough to the Lord
Jer 7 18 the women knead the dough to make cakes
dove Gen 8 8 he sent forth also a dove after him
Gen 8 10 again sent forth the dove out of the
12 he sent forth the dove which returned
Ps 54 7 who will give me wings like a dove
67 14 as wings of a dove covered with silver
Cant 2 10 make haste, my love, my dove, my
14 my dove in the clefts of the rock
5 2 open to me, my sister, my love, my d.
6 8 one is my dove, my perfect one is but
Isa 38 14 I will meditate like a dove: my eyes are
Jer 25 38 because of the wrath of the dove and
46 16 us return . . . from sword of the dove
48 28 like the dove that maketh her nest
50 16 for fear of the sword of the dove
Osee 7 11 is become as a dove that is decoyed
11 11 like a dove out of land of Assyrians
Soph 3 1 provoking and redeemed city, the dove
Mat 3 16 Spirit of God descending as a dove
Mark 1 10 the Spirit as a dove descending and
Luke 3 22 the Holy Ghost descended . . . as a dove
John 1 32 I saw the Spirit coming down as a dove
doves Cant 5 12 his eyes as d. upon brooks of
Isa 59 11 and shall lament as mournful doves
60 8 that fly . . . as d. to their windows? For
Eze 7 16 shall be in the mountains like doves
Nah 2 7 were led away mourning as d., murmuring
Mat 10 16 wise as serpents and simple as doves
21 12 chairs of them that sold d. Mark 11:15
Luke 2 24 to offer a pair of turtle doves or
John 2 14 them that sold oxen and sheep and doves
16 to them that sold doves he said: Take
doves' Cant 4 1 thy eyes are doves' eyes, besides
downfall Job 31 29 if I have been glad at the d.
Ps 91 12 shall hear of the d. of the malignant
Prov 17 16 his house high, seeketh a downfall
downward 4 K 19 30 shall take root d. Isa 37:31
Ecce 3 21 if the spirit of the beasts descend d.
Eze 1 27 and from his loins downward, I saw
8 2 of his loins, and downward, fire: from
Dan 10 6 all downward even to the feet, like in
dowry Gen 30 20 hath endowed me with a good d.
Gen 34 12 raise the dowry and ask gifts and I
Exod 22 17 shall give money according to the d.
1 K 18 25 the king desireth not any dowry, but
3 K 9 16 gave it for a dowry to his daughter
2 Ma 1 14 sums of money under the title of a d.
drachms 2 Ma 12 43 sent 12,000 d. of silver to
drag Haba 1 15 he drew them in his d. and gathered
Haba 1 16 will he offer victims to his drag and
dragged Judg 5 21 the torrent of Cison d. their
Lam 5 5 we were dragged by the necks, we were
dragging Luke 21 12 dragging you before kings and
John 21 8 dragging the net with fishes. As soon
Acts 8 3 dragging away men and women committed
dragon 2 Es 2 13 before the d. fountain and to
Ps 73 14 hast broken the heads of the dragon
90 13 under foot the lion and the dragon
103 26 this sea dragon which thou hast formed
Eccu 25 23 to abide with a lion and a dragon
Isa 51 9 hast not thou . . . wounded the dragon
Jer 51 34 he hath swallowed me up like a dragon
Eze 29 3 Pharao . . . thou great dragon that liest
32 2 art like . . . the d. that is in the sea
Dan 14 22 was a great dragon in that place and
25 I will kill this dragon without sword
26 the dragon burst asunder. And he said
27 he hath killed the dragon and he hath
Apoc 12 3 behold a great red dragon having seven
4 the dragon stood before the woman who
7 his angels fought with the dragon and the d. fought with his angels
9 that great dragon was cast out that
13 when the dragon saw that he was cast
16 river which the d. cast out of his
17 the dragon was angry against the woman
13 2 the dragon gave him his own strength
4 they adored the dragon which gave power

11 he spoke as a dragon. And he executed
16 13 I saw from the mouth of the dragon
20 2 he laid hold on the dragon the old
dragon's Dan 14 26 put them into the d. mouth
dragons Deut 32 33 their wine is the gall of d.
Esth 10 7 the two dragons are I and Aman. The
11 6 two great dragons came forth ready to
Job 30 29 I was the brother of dragons, and
Ps 73 13 didst crush the heads of the dragons
148 7 the earth, ye dragons, and all ye deeps
Isa 34 13 it shall be the habitation of dragons
35 7 in the dens where dragons dwelt before
43 20 glorify me, the d. and the ostriches
Jer 9 11 to be heaps of sand and dens of dragons
10 22 Juda a desert and a dwelling for d.
14 6 they snuffed up the wind like dragons
49 33 Asor shall be a habitation for dragons
50 39 therefore shall dragons dwell there
51 37 Babylon . . . a dwelling place for d.
Mich 1 8 I will make a wailing like the dragons
Mala 1 3 his inheritance to the d. of the desert
drams 2 Es 7 70 a thousand drams of gold, fifty
2 Es 7 71 gave . . . 20,000 drams of gold. 72
drank Gen 24 46 I drank, and she watered the camels
Gen 24 54 they ate and drank together and lodged
25 34 he [Esau] ate and drank and went his
43 34 they drank and were merry with him
Exod 34 28 he neither ate bread nor drank water
Num 20 11 the people and their cattle drank and
Deut 32 38 d. the wine of their drink offerings
Judg 15 19 when he [Samson] had drank them he
19 6 sat down together and ate and drank
3 K 10 21 vessels out of which king Solomon d.
13 19 so he ate bread and drank water in his
17 6 and he [Elias] drank of the torrent
19 6 he ate and drank and he fell asleep
8 he arose and ate and drank and walked
4 K 6 23 they ate and drank and he let them go
7 8 went into one tent and ate and drank
1 Pa 29 22 and they ate and drank before the Lord
1 Es 10 6 he ate no bread and drank no water
Jdth 12 19 she took and ate and drank before him
20 and drank exceeding much wine, so much
Ps 68 13 they that drank wine made me their song
Eze 34 18 when you drank the clearest water, you
19 they d. what your feet had troubled
Dan 1 5 the wine of which he drank himself
8 nor with the wine which he drank: and
5 1 every one drank according to his age
3 wives and his concubines, drank in them
4 they drank wine and praised their gods
14 14 and they ate and drank up all. And the
Amos 2 8 drank the wine of the condemned in
Mark 14 23 they all drank of it. And he said to
John 4 12 Jacob . . . drank thereof himself and
1 C 10 4 all drank the same spiritual drink
4 they drank of the spiritual rock that
draught Luke 5 4 let down your nets for a draught
Luke 5 9 astonished . . . at the d. of the fishes
draw Gen 24 11 are wont to come out to draw water
Gen 24 13 this city will come out to draw water
19 I will draw water for thy camels also
20 she ran back to the well to draw water
43 that shall come out to draw water and
44 I will also draw for thy camels: let the
Exod 2 16 daughters, who came to draw water: and
5 4 why do you . . . draw off the people from
15 9 I will draw my sword, my hand shall
27 7 thou shalt draw them through rings
Lev 26 33 I will draw out the sword after you
Deut 2 6 you shall draw waters for money and
13 5 he spoke to draw you away from the Lord
Judg 3 22 he did not draw out the dagger but
9 54 draw thy sword and kill me [Abimelech]
20 32 designed to draw them away from the
1 K 9 11 found maids coming out to draw water
14 19 said to the priest: Draw in thy hand
36 let us draw near hither unto God. And
31 4 draw thy sword and kill me: lest these
2 K 17 13 city, and we will draw it into the river
3 K 13 4 he was not able to draw it back again
4 K 21 13 draw the pencil often over the face
1 Pa 10 4 Saul said . . . draw thy sword and kill me
Tob 6 4 by the gill and draw him to thee. And
Jdth 7 7 they were seen secretly to draw water
9 the springs that they may not d. water
8 12 not a word that may draw down mercy
Job 5 16 but iniquity shall draw in her mouth
20 15 God shall draw them out of his belly
21 33 he shall draw every man after him
34 14 he shall draw his spirit and breath
40 20 canst thou draw out the leviathan with
Ps 26 2 whilst the wicked draw near against me
27 3 draw me not away together with the
54 19 from them that draw near to me: for
68 15 draw me out of the more, that I may not
Prov 12 2 is good, shall draw grace from the
20 5 but a wise man will draw it out. Many
Ecce 4 17 house of God, and draw nigh to hear
12 1 and the years draw nigh of which thou
Eccu 51 31 draw near to me, ye unlearned and
Cant 1 3 draw me: we will run after thee to the
Wisd 15 15 eyes to see not noses to draw breath
Isa 5 18 to you that draw iniquity with cords
7 6 draw it away to us and make the son of
12 3 you shall draw waters with joy out
29 13 this people draw near me with their
45 20 draw near together, ye that are saved
57 3 draw near hither, you sons of the
66 19 will send . . . them that draw the bow
Jer 14 3 they came to draw, they found no water
38 10 draw up Jeremias the prophet out of the
Eze 4 1 draw upon it the plan of the city of
5 2 I will draw out sword. 12; 12:14
21 3 I will draw forth my sword out of its
19 with his hand he shall draw lots, he
28 7 they shall draw their swords against
29 4 I will draw thee out of the midst of
30 11 shall draw their swords upon Egypt
32 3 and I will draw thee up in my net. And
Osee 11 4 I will draw them with the cords of
Amos 8 1 a hook to draw down the fruit. 2
Nah 3 14 draw thee water for the siege, build up
2 Ma 1 21 then he bade them draw it up and bring
Luke 5 3 draw back a little from the land. And
12 58 lest perhaps he draw thee to the judge
14 5 will not immediately draw him out
John 2 8 draw out now and carry to the chief
4 7 a woman of Samaria to draw water. Jesus
11 sir, thou hast nothing wherein to draw
15 may not thirst, nor come hither to draw
6 44 except the Father . . . draw him; and I
12 32 I will draw all things to myself. Now
21 6 they were not able to draw it, for the
Acts 20 32 to draw away disciples after them
Heb 7 19 by which we draw nigh to God. Inasmuch
10 22 let us draw near with a true heart
James 2 6 they draw you before the judgment seats
4 8 nigh to God and he will draw nigh to
drawest Exod 4 9 thou d. out of the river shall
draweth Deut 15 9 seventh year of remission d. nigh
Judg 19 9 the day . . . draweth toward evening: tarry
Ps 9 9 the poor, whilst he draweth him to him
Prov 12 13 ruin draweth nigh to the evil man: but
Isa 26 17 she d. near the time of her delivery
Lam 4 18 our end draweth near: our days are

Dan 2 1 Nabuchodonosor had a dream and his
1 and his dream went out of his mind
3 the king said to them: I saw a dream
4 tell to thy servants thy dream and
5 unless you tell me the dream and the
6 if you tell the dream and the meaning
6 tell me the d. and the interpretation
9 if therefore you tell me not the dream
9 tell me therefore the dream that I may
26 canst tell me the dream that I saw
28 thy dream and the visions of thy head
36 this is the dream: we will also tell
45 the dream is true and the interpretation
4 2 I saw a dream that affrighted me: and
3 show me the interpretation of the d.
4 and I told the dream before them: but
5 gods, and I told the dream before him
15 I king Nabuchodonosor saw this dream
16 the dream be to them that hate thee
7 1 Daniel saw a dream: and the vision of
1 writing the dream, he comprehended it
Joel 2 28 your old men shall dream dreams and
2 Ma 15 11 told them a d. worthy to be believed
Mat 27 19 I have suffered . . . in a dream because
Acts 2 17 your old men shall dream dreams. And
dreamed Gen 37 5 a dream that he had dreamed
Gen 37 6 hear my dream which I dreamed. I thought
9 he dreamed also another dream, which
10 this dream that thou hast dreamed
40 5 both dreamed a dream the same night
8 have d. a dream, and there is nobody
8 tell me what you have dreamed. The
16 I also dreamed a dream, that I had thee
41 5 he slept again and d. another dream
11 both of us dreamed a dream foreboding
15 I have dreamed a dream, and there is no
17 so Pharao told what he had dreamed
22 sleep again, and dreamed a dream: Seven
42 9 which formerly he had dreamed, he said
Deut 13 1 that saith he hath dreamed a dream
Jer 23 25 and say: I have dreamed, I have d.
dreamer Gen 37 19 behold the dreamer cometh. Come
Deut 13 3 hear the words of that prophet or d.
dreamers Jer 27 9 hearken not to your . . . d. and
Zach 10 2 the dreamers have spoken vanity: they
dreameth Isa 29 8 that is hungry d. and eateth
Isa 29 8 as he that is thirsty dreameth and
dreams Gen 37 8 this matter of his d. and words
Gen 37 20 it shall appear what his d. avail him
41 12 to whom we told our dreams, and he
15 I have dreamed dreams and there is no
42 9 remembering the dreams, which formerly
Lev 19 26 you shall not divine nor observe dreams
Deut 13 5 prophet or forger of d. shall be slain
18 10 or observeth dreams and omens, neither
1 K 28 6 answered him not, neither by dreams
15 by the hand of prophets nor by dreams
2 Pa 33 6 he [Manasses] observed dreams, followed
Job 7 14 thou wilt frighten me with dreams
Ecce 5 2 dreams follow many cares: and in many
6 where there are many dreams there are
Wisd 18 17 visions of evil dreams troubled them
Eccu 34 1 dreams lift up fools. The man that
3 the vision of dreams is the resemblance
5 the dreams of evildoers are vanity
7 dreams have deceived many and they have
Isa 56 10 sleeping and loving dreams. And most
Jer 23 27 forget my name through their dreams
32 the prophets that have lying dreams
29 8 give no heed to your dreams which you
Dan 1 17 understanding also of all visions and d.
2 2 to declare to the king his dreams: so
4 6 tell me the visions of my dreams that
5 12 interpretation of dreams . . . found in
Joel 2 28 your old men shall dream dreams and
Acts 2 17 your old men shall dream dreams and
dreamt Judg 7 13 I d. a dream, and it seemed to
dregs Ps 39 3 me out of the . . . mire of dregs
Ps 74 9 the dregs thereof are not emptied: all
Isa 49 6 and to convert the dregs of Israel
51 17 and thou hast drunk even to the dregs
22 dregs of the cup of my indignation
Eze 23 34 shalt drink it up even to the dregs
dress Gen 2 15 to dress it and to keep it. And
Gen 38 14 changing her dress, sat in the cross
Exod 16 23 that are to be dressed, dress them
30 7 when he shall d. the lamps, he shall
Num 4 16 pertaineth the oil to dress the lamps
Deut 16 7 thou shalt dress, and eat it in the
Judg 13 15 let us dress a kid for thee. And the
3 K 14 2 arise and change thy dress, that thou
17 12 that I may go in and dress it, for
18 23 and I will dress the other bullock
25 choose you one bullock and dress it
22 30 the king of Israel changed his dress
2 Pa 18 29 I will change my d., and so I will go
29 king of Israel having changed his d.
Job 6 26 you dress up speeches only to rebuke
Wisd 13 12 chips of his work to dress his meat
Jer 4 30 thou shalt dress thyself out in vain
Bar 6 10 and they dress our harlots: and again
Eze 46 20 where they shall dress the sacrifice
dressed Gen 27 14 she d. meats, such as she knew
Exod 16 23 meats that are to be d., dress them
Lev 7 9 whatsoever is dressed on the gridiron
1 K 25 18 wine and five sheep ready dressed
2 K 12 4 ewe, and d. it for the man that was
3 K 18 26 took the bullock . . . and dressed it
Jdth 12 15 and she arose and dressed herself out
Isa 1 6 they are not bound up nor dressed nor
44 16 with part of it he dressed his meat
dresser Luke 13 7 said to the d. of the vineyard
dressers 4 K 25 12 he left some d. of vines and
1 Pa 27 27 over the dressers of the vineyards
2 Pa 26 10 he had also . . . dressers of vines in
Isa 61 5 shall be . . . the d. of your vines. But
dressing Num 4 9 for the d. of the lamps: and over
Jdth 10 4 this dressing up did not proceed from
Eccu 27 7 dressing of a tree showeth the fruit
drew Gen 19 10 and drew in Lot unto them and shut
Gen 24 45 down to the well and drew water. And
37 28 they drew him [Joseph] out of the pit
47 29 that the day of his death drew nigh
49 32 he drew up his feet upon the bed and
Exod 2 19 he drew water also with us and gave
14 10 when Pharao drew near, the children
38 7 he drew them through the rings that
39 3 and drew them small into threads, that
40 19 he drew the veil before it to fulfill the
Josu 8 26 Josue drew not back his hand which
Judg 8 10 and 120,000 warriors that d. the sword
20 but he drew not his sword: for he was
16 14 he drew out the nail with the hairs
20 15 men that drew the sword. 25; 2 K 24:9; 4 K 3:26; 1 Pa 21:5
17 were found 400,000 that drew swords
30 drew up their army against Benjamin
35 fighting men and that drew the sword
1 K 7 6 they drew water and poured it out before
17 41 Philistine . . . drew nigh against David
48 coming and drew nigh to meet David
51 [David] drew it out of the sheath
2 K 1 6 horsemen drew nigh unto him [Saul]
22 17 and drew me out of many waters. He
23 16 and drew water out of the cistern of
3 K 2 1 days of David drew nigh that he should

1 Pa 10 2 Philistines drew near pursuing after
11 18 drew water out of cistern of Bethlehem
2 Pa 14 8 that bore shields and drew bows, two
Tob 6 4 when he had done so, he drew him out
11 15 Tobias took hold of it and d. it from
Ps 106 18 they drew nigh even to the gates of
Prov 7 21 drew him away with the flattery of her
23 35 of pain: they drew me, and I felt not
Wisd 7 3 being born I drew in the common air
Isa 41 5 astonished, they drew near and came
Jer 38 13 they drew up Jeremias with the cords
Dan 14 40 he drew him out of the lions' den. But
Haba 1 15 he drew them in his drag and gathered
Soph 3 2 she drew not near to her God. Her
1 Ma 2 49 the days drew near that Mathathias
5 50 the men of the army drew near and
6 42 Judas and his army drew near for battle
9 12 the legion drew near on two sides
10 82 then Simon drew forth his army and
15 14 the ships drew near by sea: and they
2 Ma 10 25 when he [Timotheus] drew near, prayed
Mat 13 48 when it was filled, they drew out
21 1 when they drew nigh to Jerusalem and
34 when the time of the fruits drew nigh
26 51 drew out his sword: and striking the
Luke 15 1 publicans and sinners d. near unto him
25 his elder son . . . drew nigh to house
18 35 when he drew nigh to Jericho, that a
19 41 when he drew near, seeing the city
22 47 drew near to Jesus for to kiss him
23 54 Parasceve, and the sabbath drew on
24 28 they drew nigh to the town, whither
John 18 10 Simon Peter, having a sword, drew it
21 11 drew the net to land full of great
Acts 5 37 drew away the people after him: he also
7 17 when the time of the promise drew near
31 as he [Moses] drew near to view it
9 3 he drew nigh to Damascus; and suddenly
14 18 stoning Paul, drew him out of the city
17 6 drew Jason and certain brethren to the
19 33 they drew forth Alexander out of the
21 30 taking Paul, they drew him out of the
Apoc 12 4 his tail drew the third part of the
drewest Lam 3 57 thou d. near in the day when
dried Gen 8 7 till the waters were d. up upon the
Gen 8 13 that the face of the earth was dried
14 second month . . . the earth was dried
Exod 14 22 through the midst of the sea dried up
Num 6 3 nor . . . eat grapes either fresh or d.
11 32 they dried them round about the camp
Josu 2 10 Lord d. up the water of the Red Sea
3 17 through the channel that was dried up
4 24 Red Sea, which he dried up till we
5 1 heard that the Lord had dried up the
3 K 17 7 after some time the torrent was d. up
4 K 19 24 have dried up with the soles of my feet
Job 12 15 waters, all things shall be dried up
14 11 emptied river should be dried up; so
18 16 let his roots be dried up beneath. Let
30 30 and my bones are dried up with heat
Ps 21 16 my strength is d. up like a potsherd
73 15 thou hast dried up the Ethan rivers
105 9 rebuked the Red Sea, and it was d. up
Eccu 40 13 riches of the unjust shall be dried up
Isa 5 13 multitude were dried up with thirst
19 5 water of the sea shall be dried up
6 shall be diminished and be dried up
7 sown by the water shall be dried up
37 25 have dried up with the sole of my foot
51 10 hast not thou dried up the sea, the
Jer 23 10 the fields of the desert are dried up
50 38 waters, and they shall be dried up
Eze 17 10 shall it not be dried up when the
24 and have dried up the green tree and
19 12 the burning wind dried up her fruit
12 rods are withered and dried up: the
37 11 they say: Our bones are dried up and
Osee 9 16 their root is dried up, they shall
Joel 1 20 the springs of waters are dried up
Mark 5 29 fountain of her blood dried up and she
11 20 they saw the fig tree dried up from
Apoc 16 12 and dried up the water thereof, that
drieth Prov 17 22 sorrowful spirit d. up the bones
Nah 1 4 rebuketh the sea and drieth it up: and
drink Gen 19 33 made their father drink wine. 35
Gen 19 34 let us make him drink wine also to
21 19 and gave the boy to drink. And God was
24 14 let down thy pitcher that I may drink
14 d. and I will give thy camels drink
17 give me a little water to drink of
18 she answered: Drink, my lord. And
18 down her pitcher . . . and gave him d.
19 for thy camels also, till they all d.
43 give me a little water to drink of thy
44 both drink thou, and I will also draw
45 I said to her: Give me a little to d.
46 both drink thou, and to thy camels I will give drink
29 7 first give the sheep drink and so lead
30 38 when the flocks should come to drink
35 14 pouring drink offerings upon it and
Exod 2 19 and gave the sheep to drink. But he
7 18 when they drink the water of the river
21 the Egyptians could not d. the water
24 Egyptians dug . . . for water to drink
24 they could not drink of the water of
15 23 could not drink the waters of Mara
24 saying: What shall we d.? But he cried
17 1 was no water for the people to drink
2 give us water, that we may drink. And
6 out of it that the people may drink
24 11 they saw God, and they did eat and d.
32 6 the people sat down to eat and drink
20 to the children of Israel to drink
Lev 10 9 you shall not drink wine nor anything
Num 5 24 he shall give them her to drink. And
26 bitter waters to the woman to drink
6 3 they shall not drink vinegar of wine or of any other drink
20 after this the Nazarite may drink wine
20 5 neither is there any water to drink
8 multitude and their cattle shall drink
17 we will not drink the waters of thy
19 if we and our cattle d. of thy waters
21 22 we will not drink waters of the wells
23 24 it . . . drink the blood of the slain
33 14 where the people wanted water to drink
Deut 2 6 waters for money, and shall drink. The
28 water for money, and so we will drink
14 26 wine also and strong drink and all that
28 39 plant . . . and shalt not d. the wine
29 6 nor have you drunk wine or strong d.
32 14 might d. the purest blood of the grape
38 drank the wine of the d. offerings
Judg 4 19 gave him to drink and covered him
7 5 that shall d. bowing down their knees
13 4 drink no wine nor strong drink. 7
14 neither let her drink wine or strong d.
19 22 refreshing their bodies with meat and d.
Ruth 2 9 go to the vessels and drink of the
9 waters whereof the servants drink. She
1 K 1 15 drunk neither wine nor any strong d.
30 11 him bread to eat and water to drink
2 K 11 11 into my house to eat and to drink and
13 David called him to eat and to drink
16 2 thy servants to eat, and the wine to d.

19 35 can meat or drink delight thy servant
23 15 O that some man would get me a drink
16 but he [David] would not drink, but
17 shall I drink the blood of these men
17 therefore he [David] would not drink
3 K 13 8 I will . . . nor d. water in this place
9 shalt not eat bread nor drink water
16 neither will I eat bread nor d. water
17 thou shalt not drink water there, nor
18 he may eat bread and drink water. He
22 shouldst not eat bread nor drink water
17 4 there thou shalt drink of the torrent
10 water in a vessel that I may drink
18 41 said to Achab: Go up, eat and drink
42 Achab went up to eat and drink: and
4 K 3 17 filled with waters, and you shall d.
6 22 that they may eat and drink, and go
9 34 when he was come in to eat and to d.
18 27 that they may . . . drink their urine
31 shall drink water of your own cisterns
1 Pa 11 18 brought it to David to drink: and he would not drink of it
19 and should drink the blood of these men
19 and therefore he would not drink. These
2 Pa 28 15 refreshed them with meat and drink
1 Es 3 7 meat and drink and oil to the Sidonians
2 Es 8 10 eat fat meats and drink sweet wine
12 all the people went to eat and drink
Tob 3 10 three nights did neither eat or drink
4 18 not eat and drink . . . with the wicked
7 10 I will not eat nor drink here this day
12 19 I seemed indeed to eat and to drink
19 but I use an invisible meat and drink
Jdth 5 15 were made sweet for them to drink
7 7 little rather than to drink their fill
11 11 cattle and to drink the blood of them
12 12 she may eat with him and drink wine
17 drink now and sit down and be merry
18 Judith said: I will drink, my lord
Esth 14 17 not drunk the wine of the d. offerings
Job 1 4 three sisters to eat and drink with
5 5 the thirsty shall drink up his riches
21 20 he shall d. of the wrath of the Almighty
40 18 he will drink up a river and not wonder
Ps 35 9 shalt make them drink of the torrent
49 13 or shall I drink the blood of goats
59 5 made us drink the wine of sorrow. Thou
68 22 they gave me vinegar to drink. Let their
74 9 the sinners of the earth shall drink
77 15 gave them to drink, as out of the great
44 their showers that they might not drink
79 6 for our drink tears in measure? Thou
101 10 and mingled my drink with weeping
103 11 all the beasts of the field shall drink
109 7 he shall drink of the torrent in the
Prov 4 17 drink the wine of iniquity. But the
5 15 drink water out of thy own cistern
9 5 drink the wine which I have mingled
23 7 eat and drink, will he say to thee
30 that . . . study to d. off their cups
25 21 if he thirst, give him water to drink
31 5 lest they drink and forget judgment
6 give strong d. to them that are sad
7 let them drink and forget their want
Ecce 2 24 is it not better to eat and drink and
5 17 that a man should eat and drink and
8 15 but to eat and drink and be merry and
9 7 drink thy wine with gladness: because
Cant 5 1 eat, O friends, and drink, and be
7 9 wine, worthy for my beloved to drink
Wisd 11 5 when their drink failed them while the
Eccu 9 15 and thou shalt drink it with pleasure
15 3 water of wholesome wisdom to drink
24 29 they that drink me, shall yet thirst
26 15 will drink of every water near her
29 31 shall . . . give d. to the unthankful
31 21 be not the first to ask for drink. How
32 if thou drink it moderately, thou shalt
Isa 5 11 and to drink till the evening, to be
22 you that are mighty to drink wine
21 5 behold . . . them that eat and drink
22 13 let us eat and drink; for tomorrow
24 9 shall not d. wine with a song: the d. shall be bitter to them that d. it
27 3 I will suddenly give it to drink: lest
32 6 and take away drink from the thirsty
36 12 and drink their urine with you? Then
16 drink ye everyone the water of his
43 20 to give drink to my people, to my chosen
44 12 he shall drink no water and shall be
49 10 at the fountains . . . shall give them d.
51 22 thou shalt not drink it again any
62 8 strangers shall not drink thy wine
9 shall drink it in my holy courts. Go
65 13 my servants shall drink, and you shall
Jer 2 18 Egypt, to drink the troubled water
18 to drink the water of the river? Thy
8 14 hath given us water of gall to drink
9 15 and give them water of gall to drink
16 7 neither shall they give them to drink
8 to sit with them and to eat and drink
19 13 poured out drink offerings to. 32:29
22 15 did not thy father eat and drink and
23 15 and will give them gall to drink: for
25 15 make all the nations to drink thereof
16 they shall drink and be troubled and
17 to all the nations to drink of it, to
26 king of Sesac shall drink after them
27 drink ye, and be drunken, and vomit
28 the cup at thy hand to drink, thou
28 drinking you shall drink; for behold
35 2 thou shalt give them wine to drink
5 I said to them: Drink ye wine. And they
6 answered: We will not d. wine: because
6 you shall drink no wine, neither you
8 so as to drink no wine all our days
14 commanded his sons not to drink wine
44 17 pour out d. offerings to her. 18, 19, 25
49 12 judgment was not to drink of the cup
12 of the cup, shall certainly drink
12 but drinking, thou shalt drink. For
51 39 in their heat I will set them to drink
Eze 4 11 thou shalt drink water by measure, the
11 from time to time thou shalt drink it
16 they shall drink water by measure
12 18 drink thy water in hurry and sorrow
19 and drink their water in desolation
23 32 thou shalt drink thy sister's cup, deep
34 shalt d. it, and shalt d. it up even
25 4 and they shall drink thy milk. And I
39 17 to eat flesh and drink blood. You shall
18 shall drink the blood of the princes
19 shall drink the blood till you be drunk
44 21 no priest shall drink wine when he is
Dan 1 10 hath appointed you meat and drink: who
12 given us to eat, and water to drink
16 and the wine that they should drink
5 2 that the king . . . might drink in them
Osee 2 5 my wool and my flax, my oil and my d.
Joel 3 3 sold for wine, that they might drink
Amos 4 1 bring, and we will drink. The Lord God
8 went to one city to drink water and
5 11 shall not d. the wine of them. Because
6 6 that drink wine in bowls and anoint

Wisd 2 3 which is d. away by the beams of the
Isa 41 2 as stubble driven by the wind, to his
Jer 23 2 my flock and driven them away and have
12 they shall be d. on and fall therein
29 14 to which I have driven you out, saith
18 to which I have d. them out: because
50 17 the lions have driven him away: first
Eze 34 4 which was driven away you have not
16 and that which was driven away, I will
Dan 4 30 he was driven away from among men
5 21 he was driven out from the sons of
9 7 whither thou hast driven them for their
Osee 13 3 as the dust that is driven with a
1 Ma 3 6 his enemies were driven away for fear
7 6 he hath driven us out of our land
14 26 hath driven away in fight the enemies
2 Ma 4 26 was driven out a fugitive into the
5 9 he that had driven many out of their
9 4 commanded his chariot to be driven
10 15 that were driven out of Jerusalem
Luke 8 29 d. by the devil into the deserts. And
Acts 27 15 the ship to the winds, we were driven
17 down the sail yard and so were driven
James 3 4 ships . . . are driven by strong winds
driver 3 K 22 34 said to the d. of his chariot
4 K 2 12 the chariot of Israel and the driver
Job 39 7 he heareth not the cry of the driver
drivers Nah 2 3 and the drivers are stupefied
drives 4 K 9 20 for he drives furiously. And Joram
driveth Tob 6 8 smoke thereof d. away all kind
Ps 1 4 like the dust, which the wind driveth
Prov 18 22 d. away a good wife, d. away a good
25 23 the north wind driveth away rain, as
Eccu 1 27 the fear of the Lord driveth out sin
23 27 driveth from him the fear of God and
31 1 thought thereof driveth away sleep
38 26 goad, that d. the oxen therewith and
Isa 59 19 which the spirit of the Lord d. on
driving 2 K 13 16 thou now dost . . . in d. me away
4 K 9 20 the d. is like the d. of Jehu the son
2 Tim 3 13 erring and driving into error. But
dromedaries Isa 60 6 the d. of Madian and Epha
drop Exod 9 33 did there drop any more rain upon
Lev 5 9 he shall let it drop at the bottom
Job 26 14 hear scarce a little drop of his word
Ecce 10 18 of hands, the house shall drop through
Wisd 11 23 as a drop of the morning dew that
Eccu 18 8 as a drop of water of the sea are
Isa 40 15 Gentiles are as a drop of a bucket
45 8 drop down dew, ye heavens, from above
Eze 20 46 drop towards the south and prophesy
Joel 3 18 mountains shall drop down sweetness
Amos 7 16 shalt not drop thy word upon the house
9 13 the mountains shall drop sweetness
Mich 2 6 it shall not drop upon these, confusion
11 I will let drop to thee of wine and of
11 this people upon whom it shall drop
dropped Judg 5 4 and the heavens dropped water
1 K 14 26 the honey dropped, but no man put his
2 K 21 10 till water d. upon them out of heaven
Job 29 22 and my speech dropped upon them. They
Ps 67 9 the heavens dropped at the presence of
Cant 5 5 my hands dropped with myrrh, and my
dropping 2 K 22 12 d. waters out of the clouds of
Prov 5 3 lips . . . like a honeycomb dropping
19 13 is like a roof continually d. through
27 15 roofs dropping through in a cold day
Cant 4 11 are as a dropping honey comb, honey and
5 13 his lips are as lilies d. choice myrrh
drops Deut 32 2 and as drops upon the grass
Job 36 27 he lifteth up the drops of rain, and
38 28 or who begot the drops of dew? Out of
Cant 5 2 locks [full] of drops of the nights
Eccu 1 2 hath numbered . . . the drops of rain
Mich 5 7 as drops upon the grass which waiteth
Luke 22 44 his sweat became as drops of blood
dropsy Luke 14 2 man . . . that had the dropsy. And
dross Prov 26 23 vessel adorned with silver d.
Isa 1 22 thy silver is turned into dross: thy
25 I will clean purge away thy dross and
Eze 22 18 the house of Israel is become dross
18 they are become the dross of silver
19 because you are all turned into dross
drought Jdth 7 17 longer by the drought of thirst
Jdth 11 10 for drought of water they are already
Isa 27 11 harvest shall be destroyed with d.
32 2 as rivers of waters in drought and the
Jer 2 6 led us . . . through a land of drought
14 1 concerning the words of the drought
17 8 time of d. it shall not be solicitous
Eccu 35 26 as cloud of rain in the time of d.
Jer 50 38 a drought upon her waters and they
Osee 2 3 and will kill her with drought. And I
Agge 1 11 I called for a drought upon the land
drove Gen 15 11 and Abram drove them away. And
Gen 32 16 he sent them . . . every drove by itself
16 be a space between drove and drove
Exod 2 17 the shepherds came and drove them away
3 1 he drove the flock to the inner parts
9 24 hail and fire mixed with it drove on
Josu 24 12 I drove them out from their places
Judg 4 21 drove it through his brain fast into
9 40 drove him to the city: and many were
41 Zebul drove Gaal and his companions
2 K 6 3 sons of Abinadab, drove the new cart
12 31 drove over them chariots armed with
4 K 16 6 drove the men of Juda out of Aila
1 Pa 8 13 these drove away the inhabitants of
13 7 Oza and his brother drove the cart
2 Es 13 28 and I drove him from me. Remember
Dan 3 49 he drove the flame of the fire out
1 Ma 1 56 drove away the people of Israel into
Mark 1 12 Spirit drove him out into the desert
John 2 15 he drove them all out of the temple
Acts 7 45 the Gentiles, whom God drove out before
18 16 [Gallio] d. them from the judgment seat
droves Gen 32 19 all that followed the droves
Gen 33 8 what are the droves that I met? He
Deut 28 4 blessed shall be . . . d. of thy herds
drown Ps 68 16 not the tempest of water d. me
Cant 8 7 neither can the floods drown it: if
1 Tim 6 9 which drown men into destruction and
drowned Mat 18 6 better . . . that he should be d.
drowsiness Prov 23 21 d. shall be clothed with
drunk Gen 9 21 was made drunk and was uncovered
Gen 19 32 let us make him drunk with wine and
24 19 when he had drunk, she said: I will
22 after that the camels had drunk, the
26 30 after they had eaten and drunk: arising
27 25 wine also, which after he had drunk
Lev 10 9 nor anything that may make drunk, thou
11 34 that is drunk out of any such vessel
Num 5 24 when she hath drunk them up. 27
6 3 everything that may make a man drunk
Deut 29 6 nor have you d. wine or strong drink
32 42 I will make my arrows d. with blood
Judg 7 6 rest of the multitude had d. kneeling
Ruth 3 7 when Booz had eaten and drunk and was
1 K 1 9 after she had eaten and d. in Silo
13 Heli therefore thought her to be drunk
14 how long wilt thou be drunk? Digest a
15 and have drunk neither wine nor any
25 36 for he [Nabal] was very drunk and
30 12 nor drunk water three days and three
2 K 11 13 he [David] made him [Urias] drunk
13 28 when Amnon shall be drunk with wine

3 K 13 22 eaten bread and drunk water in the
23 when he had eaten and d., he saddled
16 9 d. in the house of Arsa the governor
20 16 Benadad was drinking himself d. in
4 K 19 24 and I have drunk strange waters and
Jdth 12 20 as he had never drunk in his life. And
13 4 Holofernes . . . being exceedingly d.
Job 12 25 them stagger like men that are drunk
Cant 5 1 I have drunk my wine with my milk
Eccu 31 31 wine drunk to excess shall rebuke
35 joyful, and not to make them drunk
Isa 29 9 be drunk, and not with wine: stagger
37 25 I have digged and drunk water and have
49 26 they shall be made drunk with their
51 17 hast drunk at the hand of the Lord
17 thou hast drunk even to the bottom
17 and thou hast drunk even to the dregs
21 thou that art drunk but not with wine
63 6 made them drunk in my indignation
Jer 35 14 they have d. none to this day because
46 10 and shall be drunk with their blood
51 7 that made all the earth drunk: the
7 the nations have drunk of her wine
39 I will make them drunk, that they
57 and I will make her princes drunk
Lam 4 21 thou shalt be made drunk and naked
5 4 we have drunk our water for money
Eze 39 19 till you be drunk of the victim which
Dan 5 2 being now drunk he commanded that
23 have drunk wine in them: and thou hast
Joel 1 5 awake, ye that are drunk, and weep
Abdi 16 as you have drunk upon my holy mountain
Nah 3 11 thou also shalt be made drunk and
Agge 1 6 you have drunk, but have not been
1 Ma 16 16 when Simon and his sons had drunk
Luke 12 45 to drink and be drunk: the lord of that
13 26 we have eaten and d. in thy presence
John 2 10 when men have well drunk, then that
Acts 2 15 these are not drunk as you suppose
1 C 11 21 one is hungry and another is drunk
Eph 5 18 be not d. with wine, wherein is luxury
1 Th 5 7 that are drunk, are drunk in the night
Apoc 17 2 drunk with the wine of her whoredom
6 woman d. with the blood of the saints
18 3 all nations have drunk of the wine
drunkard Prov 26 9 thorn should grow in hand of d.
Eccu 19 1 a workman that is a drunkard shall not
1 C 5 11 railer or a drunkard or an extortioner
drunkards Isa 28 1 woe . . . to the d. of Ephraim
Isa 28 3 crown of pride of the d. of Ephraim
Mat 24 49 eat and drink with drunkards: the lord
1 C 6 10 nor drunkards . . . shall possess the
drunken Deut 29 19 the d. may consume the thirsty
Ps 106 27 troubled, and reeled like a drunken
Eccu 26 11 a drunken woman is a great wrath: and
31 36 wine d. with moderation is the joy
38 wine d. with excess raiseth quarrels
39 wine d. with excess is bitterness
Isa 19 14 as a drunken man staggereth and vomiteth
24 20 the earth be shaken as a drunken man
Jer 23 9 I am become as a drunken man and as
25 27 drink ye and be drunken and vomit
drunkenness Jdth 13 19 wherein he lay in his d.
Prov 20 1 and drunkenness [is] riotous: whosoever
31 4 no secret where drunkenness reigneth
Eccu 31 40 heat of d. is the stumblingblock of
Isa 5 11 early in the morning to follow d. and
22 and stout men at drunkenness. That
28 7 and through drunkenness have erred
7 have been ignorant through d., they are
7 they have gone astray in drunkenness
29 9 stagger, and not in drunkenness. For
56 12 us take wine and be filled with d.

Jer 13 13 the inhabitants of Jerusalem, with d.
Eze 23 33 shalt be filled with d. and sorrow
Osee 4 11 and d. take away the understanding
Mich 2 11 let drop to thee of wine and of d.
Luke 21 34 be overcharged with surfeiting and d.
Rom 13 13 not in rioting and drunkenness
Gal 5 21 works of the flesh . . . drunkenness
Drusilla Acts 24 24 Felix coming with Drusilla
dry Lev 2 14 thou shalt dry it at the fire
Lev 7 10 whether . . . tempered with oil or dry
21 20 a dry scurf in his body or a rupture
22 22 blisters or a scab or a dry scurf: you
Num 11 6 our soul is dry, our eyes behold nothing
Josu 4 22 over this Jordan through the dry channel
9 12 loaves . . . now they are become dry
Judg 6 37 it be dry on all the ground beside
39 I pray that the fleece only may be dry
40 it was dry on the fleece only and there
16 7 cords made of sinews not yet dry but
1 K 25 18 took . . . 200 cakes of dry figs and laid
2 K 17 19 as it were to dry sodden barley: and
Jdth 5 12 of the sea, and passed it dry foot
10 5 oil and parched corn and dry figs
Job 13 25 and thou pursuest a dry staw. For thou
15 30 the flame shall dry up his branches
Ps 89 6 the evening he shall fall, grow dry
101 4 my bones are grown dry like fuel for
Prov 17 1 better is a dry morsel with joy than
Eccu 6 3 and thou be left as a dry tree in
13 8 till he have drawn thee dry twice
39 29 land, and the earth was made dry: and
Isa 19 5 the river shall be wasted and dry
10 and its watery places shall be dry
41 17 their tongue hath been dry with thirst
42 15 and will dry up the standing pools
44 27 and I will dry up thy rivers. Who say
56 3 enunch say: Behold I am a dry tree
Jer 50 12 a wilderness unpassable and dry. Because
51 36 desolate, and will dry up her spring
Eze 17 9 dry up all the branches it hath shot
24 caused the dry tree to flourish. I the
19 13 in a land not passable, and dry. And
20 47 every green tree and every dry tree
30 12 the channels of the rivers dry, and
37 2 plain, and they were exceeding dry
4 ye dry bones, hear the word of the
Dan 3 46 heat the furnace with . . . dry sticks
Osee 9 14 without children, and dry breasts
13 15 and it shall dry up his springs and
Nah 1 10 as stubble that is fully dry. Out of
Mat 12 43 through dry places seeking rest and
Luke 23 31 what shall be done in the dry? And
dry ground Exod 14 16 midst of sea on dry g.
Exod 14 21 and turned it into dry ground: and the
15 19 walked on dry ground in the midst of
Josu 3 17 stood girded upon the dry ground in
4 18 and began to tread on the dry ground
4 K 2 8 they both passed over on dry ground
Ps 106 33 the sources of waters into dry ground
dry land Gen 1 9 let the dry land appear. And
Gen 1 10 God called the dry land, Earth; and
Exod 4 9 pour it out upon the dry land and
14 29 marched through . . . upon dry land and
Josu 15 19 given me a southern and dry land, give
Judg 1 15 for thou hast given me a dry land: give
Heb 11 29 through the Red Sea, as by dry land
drying Josu 4 23 your God d. up the waters thereof
Eccu 14 9 consume his own soul, drying it up
Eze 26 5 shall be a drying place for nets in
14 thou shalt be a drying place for nets
47 10 there shall be drying of nets: there
dryness Jer 17 6 shall dwell in d. in the desert
Soph 2 9 the d. of thorns and heaps of salt

2 Es 3 13 in wall unto the gate of the dunghill
14 gate of the d. Melchias . . . built, lord
12 31 upon the wall toward the dunghill gate
Job 2 8 [Job] sitting on a dunghill. And his
20 7 he shall be destroyed like a dunghill
Ps 112 7 lifting up the poor out of the d.: that
Eze 7 19 their gold shall become a dunghill
Luke 14 35 profitable for the land nor for the d.
Dura Dan 3 1 set it up in the plain of Dura of
durst Gen 35 5 durst not pursue after them as
Exod 3 6 he durst not look at God. And the Lord
Josu 6 1 no man durst go out or come in or
10 21 no man durst move his tongue against
21 42 none of their enemies durst stand
2 Pa 17 10 they d. not make war against Josaphat
Jdth 14 10 no man durst knock or open and go into
Job 29 22 to my words they durst add nothing
1 Ma 12 42 he durst not stretch forth his hand
Mat 22 46 neither durst any man ask him any
Mark 12 34 no man after that durst ask him any
Luke 20 40 durst not ask him any more questions
John 21 12 none . . . durst ask him: Who art thou
Acts 5 13 no man durst join himself unto them
7 32 Moses being terrified durst not behold
Jude 9 he durst not bring against him the
dust Gen 3 19 dust thou art, and into dust thou
Gen 18 27 whereas I am dust and ashes. What if
Exod 9 9 be there dust upon all the land of
Lev 6 11 shall cause them to be consumed to dust
14 41 the dust of the scraping be scattered
43 the dust scraped off and it be plastered
45 dust without the town into an unclean
Num 23 10 who can count the dust of Jacob and
Deut 9 21 until it was as small as dust, I threw
28 24 Lord give thee dust for rain upon thy
Josu 7 6 and they put dust upon their heads
1 K 2 8 raiseth up the needy from the dust
4 12 and his head strewed with dust. And
2 K 1 2 and dust strewed on his head: and when
3 K 16 2 I have exalted thee out of the dust
18 38 consumed . . . the stones and the dust
20 10 if the dust of Samaria shall suffice
38 by sprinkling dust on his face and his
41 wiped off the dust from his face and
4 K 13 7 and had brought them low as dust by
23 6 burnt it there and reduced it to dust
Job 2 12 they sprinkled dust upon their heads
7 5 clothed with . . . the filth of dust
21 behold now I shall sleep in the dust
10 9 thou wilt bring me into dust again
14 8 and its stock be dead in the dust
20 11 they shall sleep with him in the dust
21 26 they shall sleep together in the dust
38 38 when was the dust poured on the earth
39 14 perhaps wilt warm them in the dust
40 8 hide them in the dust together and
42 6 do penance in dust and ashes. And after
Ps 1 4 like the dust, which the wind driveth
7 6 and bring down my glory to the dust
17 43 shall beat them as small as the dust
21 16 brought me down into the dust of death
29 10 shall dust confess to thee, or declare
34 5 them become as dust before the wind
77 27 he rained upon them flesh as dust
102 14 he remembereth that we are dust: man's
103 29 fail and shall return to their dust
Ecce 12 7 and the dust return into its earth
Wisd 5 15 the hope of the wicked is as dust
Eccu 27 5 with a sieve, the dust will remain
Isa 5 24 and their bud shall go up as dust
16 4 the dust is at an end, the wretch is
17 13 he shall be carried away as the dust
25 12 down to the ground, even to the dust
26 5 he shall pull it down even to the dust
19 give praise, ye that dwell in the dust
29 5 shall be like small dust: and as ashes
40 15 behold the islands are as a little dust
41 2 shall give them as the dust to his
47 1 come down, sit in the dust, O virgin
49 23 they shall lick up the dust of thy feet
52 2 shake thyself from the dust, arise
65 25 and dust shall be the serpent's food
Jer 50 12 bore you is made even with the dust
Lam 2 10 have sprinkled their heads with dust
3 29 he shall put his mouth in the dust
Bar 6 12 wipe their face because of the dust
16 their eyes are full of dust by the
Eze 24 7 that it might be covered with dust
26 4 I will scrape her dust from her and
10 their dust shall cover thee: thy walls
12 thy dust in the midst of the waters
27 30 shall cast up dust upon their heads
Osee 13 3 as the dust that is driven with a
Mich 1 10 in the house of Dust sprinkle yourselves with dust
7 17 they shall lick the dust like serpents
Soph 2 2 forth the day as dust passing away
Mat 10 14 shake off the dust. Mark 6:11; Luke 9:5
Luke 10 11 the very dust of your city . . . we wipe
Acts 13 51 shaking off the dust of their feet
22 23 as they . . . cast dust into the air, the
Apoc 18 19 cast dust upon their heads and cried
dust of the earth Gen 13 16 to number the d. . . .
Gen 28 14 thy seed shall be as the d. . . . : thou
Exod 8 16 strike the dust of the earth: and may
17 he struck the dust of the earth and
17 all the d. . . . was turned into sciniphs
2 K 22 43 I shall beat them as small as d. . . .
2 Pa 1 9 is as innumerable as the d. . . . Give
Eccu 44 22 should increase as the d. . . . and that
Dan 12 2 many of those that sleep in d. . . . shall
Amos 2 7 heads of the poor upon the d. . . . and
duty 2 Pa 8 14 to the duty of every day: and the
1 Es 3 4 the duty of the day in its day. And
2 Ma 2 31 the duty of the author of a history
1 Tim 5 4 make a return of duty to her parents
dwell Mat 12 45 enter and d. there. Luke 11:26
Mat 13 32 birds . . . dwell in the branches thereof
Mark 4 32 so that the birds of the air may dwell
Acts 1 20 let there be none to dwell therein
2 14 and all you that dwell in Jerusalem
7 4 into this land wherein you now dwell
17 26 to dwell upon the whole face of the
28 16 Paul was suffered to dwell by himself
Rom 8 9 so be that Spirit of God dwell in you
1 C 7 12 if she consent to dwell with him, let
13 if he consent to dwell with her, let her
2 C 6 16 I will dwell in them and walk among
12 9 that power of Christ may dwell in me
Eph 3 17 that Christ may dwell by faith in your
Col 1 19 that all fulness should dwell; and
3 16 let the word of Christ dwell in you
Apoc 3 10 that dwell upon the earth. 6:10; 11:10; 13:8, 14
7 15 on the throne shall dwell over them
12 12 rejoice, O heavens, and you that d.
13 6 blaspheme . . . them that dwell in heaven
12 caused the earth and them that dwell
21 3 he will dwell with them. And they
dwellest John 1 38 where dwellest thou? He saith
Apoc 2 13 I know where thou dwellest, where the
dwelleth Mat 23 21 by him that dwelleth in it
Acts 7 48 dwelleth not in houses made by hand
17 24 dwelleth not in temples made with hands
Rom 7 17 sin, that dwelleth in me. 20
18 for I know that there dwelleth not in me

8 11 his Spirit that d. in you. Therefore
1 C 3 16 Spirit of God dwelleth in you? But if
Col 2 9 in him dwelleth all the fulness of
2 Tim 1 14 by the Holy Ghost who dwelleth in us
James 4 5 doth the spirit covet which d. in you
2 P 3 13 a new earth . . . in which justice d.
2 J 2 for sake of the truth which d. in us
Apoc 2 13 was slain among you, where Satan d.
dwelling Mark 5 3 who had his d. in the tombs
Acts 2 5 there were dwelling at Jerusalem, Jews
Heb 11 9 he abode in the land, d. in cottages
1 P 3 7 d. with them according to knowledge
2 P 2 8 he [Lot] was just: d. among them, who
dwelling place 3 K 8 43 firmament of thy d. p.
2 Pa 6 21 this place, hear thou from thy d. p.
30 from heaven, from thy high d. p. and
39 from thy firm d. p., their prayers
30 27 came to the holy d. p. of heaven
36 15 spared his people and his d. p. And
Ps 51 7 out, and remove thee from thy d. p.
73 7 have defiled the d. p. of thy name
Wisd 9 8 and an altar in the city of thy d. p.
13 15 maketh a convenient d. p. for it and
Eccu 24 14 in the holy d. p. I have ministered
51 13 thou hast exalted my d. p. upon the
Jer 51 37 to heaps, a d. p. for dragons, an
Lam 1 3 Juda hath removed her dwelling place
dwelling places 1 Pa 6 54 these are their d. p.
2 Pa 9 4 the dwelling places for his servants
Job 21 28 where are the d. p. of the wicked? Ask
Ps 48 12 their d. p. to all generations: they
Jer 51 30 her d. p. are burnt, her bars are broken
Eze 6 6 about your altars, in all your d. p.
14 desert of Deblatha in all their d. p.
dwellings Lev 23 14 generations and all your d.
Lev 23 17 out of all your dwellings, two loaves
21 everlasting ordinance in all your d.
31 ordinance unto you in all your . . . d.
Num 35 29 for an ordinance in all your dwellings
Deut 16 7 thou shalt go into thy dwellings. Six
Josu 22 4 return, and go to your dwellings and
6 and they returned to their dwellings
7 when he sent them away to their d.
Judg 21 24 by their tribes and families to their d.
1 K 13 2 sent back every man to their dwellings
2 K 18 17 Israel fled to their own dwellings. 19:8
20 1 return to thy d., O Israel. 2 Pa 10:16
3 K 8 66 and went to their dwellings rejoicing
12 16 go home to thy dwellings, O Israel
16 so Israel departed to their dwellings
14 12 they fled every man to their dwellings
23 7 women wove as it were little dwellings
1 Pa 4 33 the distribution of their dwellings
2 Pa 7 10 sent away the people to their dwellings
10 16 Israel went away to their dwellings
25 22 and they fled to their dwellings. And
Job 39 6 and his dwellings in the barren land
Ps 54 16 there is wickedness in their dwellings
73 20 been filled with dwellings of iniquity
108 10 let them be cast out of their dwellings
Jer 9 19 because our dwellings are cast down
Eze 12 11 they shall be removed from their d.
Luke 16 9 receive you in to everlasting dwellings
dwelt Mat 2 23 dwelt in a city called Nazareth
Mat 4 13 he came and dwelt in Capharnaum on the
Luke 13 4 above all the men that d. in Jerusalem
John 1 14 was made flesh and dwelt among us, and
Acts 7 2 [Abraham] dwelt in Caran. 4
9 22 confounded the Jews who d. at Damascus
32 came to the saints who dwelt at Lydda
35 that d. at Lydda and Saron saw him
11 29 relief to the brethren who d. in Judea
19 10 all they who d. in Asia heard the word
17 known to all . . . that d. at Ephesus
22 12 of all the Jews who d. there [Damascus]
2 Tim 1 5 also dwelt first in thy grandmother
Apoc 11 10 tormented them that d. upon the earth
dyed Exod 25 5 rams' skins dyed red. 26:14; 35:7, 23; 36:19; 39:33
Job 28 16 not be compared with the dyed colors of
Isa 63 1 with dyed garments from Bosra, this
Jer 12 9 is it as a bird dyed throughout? Come
Eze 23 15 with dyed turbans on their heads, the
violet and purple and scarlet twice dyed; *see* **violet**
dyeing Job 28 19 be compared to the cleanest d.
dying Exod 19 12 toucheth the mount d. he shall
Lev 20 2 dying let him die. 9, 15; 24:16, 17
27 dying let them die: they shall stone
27 29 not be redeemed, but dying shall die
Num 26 10 swallowed up Core, many others dying
Judg 20 43 there was no rest of their men dying
Ruth 1 17 the land that shall receive thee dying
1 K 14 44 dying thou shalt die, O Jonathan. And
22 16 dying thou shalt die, Achimelech, thou
Ps 48 11 when he shall see the wise dying: the
Ecce 10 1 d. flies spoil the sweetness of the
Jer 4 31 of the daughter of Sion, dying away
Mark 7 10 curse father . . . dying let him die. But
Luke 8 42 only daughter . . . and she was dying
2 C 6 9 dying, and behold we live; as chastised
Heb 11 21 Jacob dying, blessed each of the sons
22 Joseph, when he was dying, made mention

E

each Exod 16 29 let each man stay at home, and
Exod 25 26 of the same table over each foot. Under
26 21 sockets shall be put under each board
25 reckoning two sockets for each board
28 21 each stone with the name of one
36 12 might be joined each with the other
28 two others at each corner of the
37 13 four corners at each foot of the table
19 in the manner of a nut on each branch
Num 4 27 each man shall know to what burden
6 15 with oil and the libations of each
7 11 let each of the princes one day after
85 each dish weighing 130 sicles of silver, and each bowl seventy sicles
28 24 and from the libations of each. The
29 14 two tenths [of flour] to each ram
35 8 each shall give towns to the Levites
Josu 18 4 according to number of each multitude
21 40 each distributed by the families
3 K 4 7 provided necessaries, each man his
22 the provision of Solomon for each day
6 34 each door was double, and so opened
7 15 brass, each pillar was 18 cubits high
18 and two rows round about each network
34 that were at every corner of each base
42 rows of pomegranates for each network
10 19 and two lions stood, one at each hand
22 10 sat each on his throne clothed with
4 K 9 21 of Juda went out, each in his chariot
15 20 tax . . . each man 50 sicles of silver
1 Pa 20 6 six on each hand and foot: who also
2 Pa 4 13 two rows . . . were joined to each wreath
31 19 and in the suburbs of each city, there
Eze 33 30 each man to his neighbor, saying
2 Ma 8 22 captains over each division of his army
Phil 2 3 each esteem others better than themselves
Heb 11 21 blessed each of the sons of Joseph
Apoc 4 8 creatures had each of them six wings
21 21 twelve pearls, one to each: and every
each one Gen 1 12 each one according to its
Gen 11 3 each one said to his neighbor: Come

15 10 laid the two pieces of each one against
Exod 39 14 Israel, each one with its several name
Num 7 3 one wagon and each one an ox, and they
Josu 19 49 by lot to each one by their tribes
Eze 9 2 each one had his weapon of destruction
10 21 each one had four faces, and each
21 faces, and each one had four wings
37 7 came together, each one to its joint
2 Ma 8 22 giving to each one 1,500 men. And after
14 21 brought out and set for each one. But
Phil 2 4 each one not considering . . . his own
each other 1 K 10 11 said to each other: What
2 K 14 6 and they quarrelled with each other
Tob 9 8 leaped up and they kissed each other
Jdth 5 26 to kill him, saying to each other
Ps 84 11 mercy and truth have met each other
Eze 41 24 which were folded within each other
1 Th 5 15 that which is good towards each other
2 Th 1 2 charity . . . towards each other aboundeth
each side Exod 28 27 on each side of the ephod
Exod 37 27 rings under the crown at each side
3 K 6 34 two doors of fir tree, one of each side
Jdth 1 2 each side was extended the space of
Eze 16 16 places sewed together on each side
John 19 18 with him two others, one on each side
eagerly Eccu 31 7 woe to them that e. follow
eagerness Acts 17 11 received the word with all **e.**
eagle Lev 11 13 you must not eat . . . the eagle
Deut 14 12 eat not: to wit, the eagle and the
28 49 like an eagle that flyeth swiftly
32 11 as the eagle enticing her young to fly
Job 9 26 as an eagle flying to the prey. If I
39 27 will the eagle mount up at thy command
Prov 23 5 wings like those of an eagle, and shall
30 19 the way of an eagle in the air, the way
Jer 48 20 he shall fly as an eagle and shall
49 16 shouldst make thy nest as high as an **e.**
22 he shall come up as an eagle and fly
Eze 1 10 the face of an eagle over all the four
10 14 in the fourth the face of an eagle
17 3 a large e. with great wings, long-limbed
7 another large eagle with great wings
Dan 7 4 lioness, and had the wings of an eagle
Osee 8 1 like an eagle upon the house of the
Abdi 4 thou be exalted as an eagle, and though
Mich 1 16 enlarge thy baldness as the eagle
Haba 1 8 they shall fly as an eagle that maketh
Apoc 4 7 was like an eagle flying. And the four
8 13 I beheld, and heard the voice of one **e.**
12 14 two wings of a great eagle, that she
eagle's Ps 102 5 shall be renewed like the eagle's
eagles Exod 19 4 carried you upon the wings of **e.**
2 K 1 23 they were swifter than eagles, stronger
Prov 30 17 pick it out and the young eagles eat it
Isa 40 31 they shall take wings as eagles, they
Jer 4 13 his horses are swifter than eagles
Lam 4 19 were swifter than the eagles of the air
Dan 4 30 his hairs grew like the feathers of **e.**
Mat 24 28 shall the e. also be gathered. Luke 17:37
ear Exod 21 6 he shall bore his ear through with
Exod 29 20 tip of the right ear. Lev 8:24; 14:14, 17, 25, 28
Lev 8 23 he touched the tip of Aaron's right ear
22 23 that hath the ear and the tail cut off
Deut 15 17 take an awl and bore through his ear
Judg 12 6 which is interpreted, An ear of corn
6 to express an ear of corn by the same
1 K 9 15 Lord had revealed to ear of Samuel
2 K 7 27 hast revealed to the ear of thy servant
22 45 at hearing of the ear they will obey
1 Pa 17 25 revealed to the ear of thy servant
Job 12 11 doth not the ear discern words, and
13 1 my ear hath heard them, and I have
29 11 the ear that heard me blessed me
32 11 I have given ear to your wisdom, as
34 3 the ear trieth words, and the mouth
36 10 he also shall open their ear to correct
15 and shall open his ear in affliction
42 5 with the hearing of the ear, I have
Ps 17 45 at the hearing of the ear they have
48 5 I will incline my ear to a parable
76 2 my voice, and he gave ear to me. In
91 12 my ear shall hear of the downfall of
93 9 he that planted the ear, shall he not
114 2 he hath inclined his ear unto me: and
Prov 5 13 have not inclined my ear to masters
15 31 ear that heareth the reproofs of life
18 15 ear of the wise seeketh instruction
20 12 the hearing ear and the seeing eye
21 13 that stoppeth his ear against the cry
25 12 the wise, and the obedient ear. As
Ecce 1 8 neither is the ear filled with hearing
Wisd 1 10 the ear of jealousy heareth all things
Eccu 3 31 a good ear will hear wisdom with all
16 6 greater things than these my ear hath
25 12 declareth justice to an ear that
51 21 I bowed down my ear a little, and
Isa 50 4 in the morning he wakeneth my ear
5 the Lord God hath opened my ear, and I
55 3 incline your ear and come to me: hear
59 1 neither is his ear heavy that it
Jer 7 24 nor inclined their ear. 11:8; 44:5
26 they have not . . . inclined their ear
17 23 did not hear, nor incline their ear
34 14 nor did they incline their ear. And you
35 15 you have not inclined your ear nor
Amos 3 12 two legs or the tip of the ear
Mich 5 14 the nations that have not given ear
Mala 3 16 the Lord gave ear and heard it: and a
Mat 10 27 which you hear in the ear, preach
26 51 cut off his ear. Mark 14:47
Mark 4 28 first the blade, then the ear, afterwards the full corn in the ear
Luke 12 3 which you have spoken in the ear
22 50 cut off his right ear. John 18:10
51 he had touched his ear, he healed him
John 18 26 kinsman to him whose ear Peter cut off
Acts 8 10 to whom they all gave ear, from the
28 26 with the ear you shall hear, and shall
1 C 2 9 eye hath not seen nor ear heard neither
12 16 if the ear should say, because I am not
Apoc 2 11 he that hath an ear, let him hear. 17, 29; 3:6, 13, 22
13 9 if any man have an ear, let him hear
give ear Num 23 18 stand, O Balac, and give ear
Deut 32 1 let the earth give ear to the words
Judg 5 3 hear, O ye kings, give ear, ye princes
2 Pa 24 19 would not give ear when they testified
Job 6 28 give ear, and see whether I lie. Answer
Ps 16 1 supplication. Give ear unto my prayer
38 13 supplication: give ear to my tears
48 2 give ear, all ye inhabitants. Joel 1:2
53 4 give ear to the words of my mouth. For
79 2 give ear, O thou that rulest Israel
83 9 my prayer: give ear, O God of Jacob
85 6 give ear, O Lord, to my prayer: and
142 1 give ear to my supplication in thy
Wisd 6 3 give ear, you that rule the people
Eccu 6 24 give ear, my son, and take wise counsel
Isa 1 2 hear, O ye heavens, and give ear, O
10 give ear to the law of our God, ye
8 9 and give ear, all ye lands afar off
28 23 give ear, and hear my voice, hearken
32 9 daughters, give ear to my speech. For
42 23 among you that will give ear to this
49 1 give ear, ye islands, and hearken, ye

51 1 give ear to me, you that follow that
4 and give ear to me, O my tribes: for
Jer 13 15 hear ye, and give ear: Be not proud
26 5 to give ear to the words of my servants
Bar 3 9 give ear, that thou mayst learn wisdom
4 9 give ear, all you that dwell near Sion
Zach 1 4 thoughts: but they did not give ear
1 Ma 2 65 give ear to him always, and he shall
Acts 13 16 and you that fear God, give ear. The
thy ear 1 K 20 13 I will discover it to thy ear
4 K 19 16 incline thy ear. Ps 16:6; 44:11; 70:2; 85:1; 87:3; 101:3; Prov 4:20; 5:1; 22:17; Eccu 2:2; 6:34; Isa 37:17; Bar 2:16
2 Es 1 11 let thy ear be attentive to the prayer
Ps 9 17 thy ear hath heard the preparation
30 3 bow down thy ear to me: make haste
Prov 2 2 that thy ear may hearken to wisdom
Eccu 4 8 bow down thy ear cheerfully to the poor
Isa 48 8 neither was thy ear opened of old. For
Lam 3 56 turn not away thy ear from my sighs
Dan 9 18 incline, O my God, thy ear, and hear
earlets Judg 8 24 accustomed to wear golden e.
Judg 8 24 give me the earlets of your spoils
25 they cast upon it the earlets of the
26 weight of the earlets that he requested
Jdth 10 3 took her bracelets and lilies and e.
early Gen 19 27 Abraham got up e. in the morning
Gen 32 22 rising early he took his two wives
Exod 8 20 arise early and stand before Pharao
34 4 rising very early he went up into the
Num 14 40 rising up very early in the morning
Deut 11 14 will give to your land the early rain
Josu 6 15 seventh day, rising up early they went
8 10 [Josue] rising early in the morning
Judg 7 1 rising up early and all people with him
19 5 arising early in the morning, he desired
21 4 rising early the next day, they built
1 K 5 3 when the Azotians arose early the next
15 12 when Samuel rose early, to go to Saul
25 37 early in the morning when Nabal had
4 K 3 22 they rose early in the morning. 2 Pa 20:20
6 15 servant of the man of God rising early
19 35 when he arose early in the morning
2 Pa 29 20 Ezechias rising early assembled all the
36 15 rising early and daily admonishing them
Job 1 5 rising up early offered holocausts
8 5 yet if thou wilt arise early to God
Ps 45 6 God will help it in the morning early
107 3 I will arise in the morning early. I
Prov 8 17 that in the morning early watch for me
11 27 well doth he rise early who seeketh
Cant 7 12 let us get up early to the vineyards
Wisd 6 15 he that awaketh early to seek her shall
Eccu 6 36 go to him early in the morning and
32 18 they that will seek him early, shall
39 6 his heart to resort early to the Lord
Isa 5 11 woe to you that rise up early in the
26 9 in the morning early I will watch to
28 19 in the morning early it shall pass
Jer 5 24 who giveth us the early and latter rain
7 13 I have spoken to you rising up early
25 rising up early and sending. And they
11 7 rising early I conjured them and said
25 4 rising early and sending. 15
26 5 whom I sent to you rising up early
32 33 I taught them early in the morning
35 14 I have spoken to you, rising early
44 4 I sent to you . . . rising early and
Dan 6 19 rising very early in the morning
Osee 6 1 they will rise early to me: Come and
3 the early and the latter rain. Joel 2:23
13 3 as the early dew that passeth away
Soph 3 7 they rose early and corrupted all their
1 Ma 5 30 early in the morning, when they lifted
Mat 20 1 went out early . . . to hire laborers
Mark 1 35 rising very early, going out, he went
16 2 very early in the morning, the first day
9 he rising early the first day of the
Luke 21 38 all the people came early in morning
24 1 early in the morning they came to the
John 8 2 early in the morning he came again
20 1 Magdalen cometh early when it was yet
Acts 5 21 early in the morning entered into the
James 5 7 till he receive the early and latter
earned Agge 1 6 that hath e. wages put them into
earnest Gen 33 11 at his brother's e. pressing him
Exod 36 3 while they were earnest about the work
2 Ma 12 23 earnest in punishing the profane, of
Luke 23 5 were more earnest, saying: He stirreth
Acts 18 5 Paul was e. in preaching, testifying
1 Tim 4 16 be earnest in them. For in doing this
earnestly Judg 19 7 father-in-law e. pressed him
1 K 20 28 he asked leave of me earnestly to go
2 Pa 33 13 he entreated him and besought him e.
2 Es 9 26 admonished them e. to return to thee
Tob 8 6 so they both arose and prayed earnestly
Ecce 2 18 wherewith I had earnestly labored under
9 10 thy hand is able to do, do it earnestly
2 Ma 4 16 followed earnestly their ordinances
Luke 7 4 they besought him e., saying to him
22 56 servant maid . . . had earnestly beheld
23 10 scribes stood by earnestly accusing him
Acts 3 5 he looked e. upon them, hoping that he
1 P 1 22 love one another earnestly: being born
Jude 3 beseech you to contend e. for the faith
earnestness Jdth 4 7 to the Lord with great e.
earring Job 42 11 one ewe and one earring of gold
Prov 25 12 as an e. of gold and a bright pearl
earrings Gen 24 22 man took out golden earrings
Gen 24 30 when he had seen the earrings and
47 so I put earrings on her to adorn her
35 4 and the earrings which were in their
Exod 32 2 take the golden earrings from the ears
3 bringing the earrings to Aaron. And
35 22 both men and women gave . . . earrings
Isa 3 20 tablets and sweet balls and earrings
Eze 16 12 e. in thy ears and a beautiful crown
Osee 2 13 decked herself out with her earrings
ears Gen 41 5 seven ears of corn. 22
Gen 35 4 the earrings which were in their ears
41 6 then seven other ears sprung up thin
26 seven full ears are seven years of
27 seven thin ears . . . are seven years of
44 18 speak a word in thy ears and be not
50 4 speak in the ears of Pharao: for my
Exod 10 2 thou mayest tell in the ears of thy
17 14 deliver it to the ears of Josue: for
32 2 take the golden earrings from the ears
Lev 2 14 of the ears yet green, thou shalt dry
19 9 nor . . . gather the e. that remain. 23:22
23 10 you shall bring sheaves of ears, the
Deut 5 1 judgments, which I speak in your ears
23 25 mayst break the ears and rub them in
29 4 eyes to see and ears that may hear
32 44 of this canticle in ears of the people
Josu 6 5 and shall sound in your ears, all the
20 thundered in the ears of the multitude
Ruth 2 2 and glean the ears of corn that escape
2 gleaned the ears of corn after the
7 she desired leave to glean the ears
15 to glean the ears of corn as before
1 K 3 11 his ears shall tingle. 4 K 21:12; Jer 19:3
8 21 rehearsed them in the ears of the Lord
15 14 which soundeth in my ears and the lowing
18 23 spoke all these words in ears of David
25 24 thy handmaid speak . . . in thy ears

2 K 4 6 entered . . . taking ears of corn and
7 22 things that we have heard with our e.
22 7 and my cry shall come to his ears
4 K 19 28 thy pride hath come up to my ears
1 Pa 17 20 whom we have heard of with our ears
2 Pa 6 40 thy ears be attentive. 2 Es 1:6; Ps 129:2
7 15 and my ears attentive to the prayer
31 5 noised abroad in the ears of the people
2 Es 8 3 ears of all the people were attentive
Esth 16 6 they deceive the ears of princes that
Job 4 12 my ears by stealth as it were received
13 17 receive with your ears hidden truths
15 21 sound of dread is always in his ears
24 10 they have taken away the ears of corn
24 as the tops of the ears of corn they
28 22 with our ears we have heard the fame
33 16 then he openeth the ears of men and
Ps 17 7 my cry before him came into his ears
33 16 and his ears unto their prayers. But
39 7 but thou hast pierced ears for me
43 2 we have heard, O God, with our ears
57 5 like the deaf asp that stoppeth her e.
77 1 incline your ears to the words of my
113 6 they have ears and hear not: they have
134 17 they have ears, but they hear not
Prov 23 9 speak not in the ears of fools: because
12 thy ears to words of knowledge. Withhold
26 17 as he that taketh a dog by the ears
28 9 he that turneth away his ears from
Cant 2 14 let thy voice sound in my ears: for
Wisd 15 15 nor ears to hear, nor fingers of hands
Eccu 17 5 he gave them . . . eyes and ears and a
11 their ears heard his glorious voice
21 6 poor shall reach the ears of God and
27 15 irreverence shall make one stop his e.
28 28 hedge in thy ears with thorns, hear
33 19 hearken with your ears, ye rulers of
38 30 noise of hammer is always in his ears
43 26 when we hear with our ears, we shall
Isa 5 9 these things are in my ears, saith
6 10 and make their ears heavy, and shut
10 their eyes, and hear with their ears
11 3 according to the hearing of the ears
17 5 his arm shall gather the ears of corn
5 seeketh ears in the vale of Raphaim
22 14 Lord of hosts was revealed in my ears
30 21 thy ears shall hear the word of one
32 3 ears of them that hear shall hearken
33 15 stoppeth his ears lest he hear blood
35 5 the ears of the deaf shall be unstopped
37 29 thy pride came up to my ears: therefore
42 20 thou that hast ears open, wilt thou
43 8 that are deal, and have ears. All the
49 20 shall still say in thy ears: The place
64 4 not heard, nor perceived with the ears
Jer 2 2 go and cry in the ears of Jerusalem
5 21 and see not: and ears, and hear not
6 10 behold, their ears are uncircumcised
9 20 let your ears receive the word of his
25 4 nor inclined your ears to hear. When
26 11 as you have heard with your ears. Then
28 7 that I speak in thy ears and in the ears of all the people
Bar 2 31 and ears, and they shall hear. And
Eze 3 10 and hear with thy ears. 20:4; 44:5
8 18 when they shall cry to my ears with
9 1 he cried in my ears with a loud voice
12 2 ears to hear, and hear not: for they
16 12 forehead, and earrings in thy ears
23 25 they shall cut off thy nose and thy e.
Joel 2 25 I will restore to you the ears which
Mich 7 16 the mouth, their ears shall be deaf
Zach 7 11 they stopped their ears, not to hear
Mat 11 15 that hath ears to hear. 13:9, 43; Mark 4:9, 23; Luke 8:8; 14:35
12 1 began to pluck the ears. Mark 2:23; Luke 6:1
13 15 with their ears they have been dull
15 lest they should . . . hear with their ears. Acts 28:27
16 blessed are . . . your ears because they
Mark 7 33 he put his fingers into his ears and
35 immediately his ears were opened and
8 18 having ears, hear you not? neither do
Luke 1 44 thy salutation sounded in my ears
4 21 fulfilled this scripture in your ears
Acts 2 14 with your ears receive my words. For
7 51 uncircumcised in heart and ears, you
56 they stopped their ears and with one
11 22 tidings came to the ears of the church
17 20 bringest in certain new things to our e.
28 27 with their ears they have heard heavily
Rom 11 8 ears that they should not hear, until
2 Tim 4 3 teachers, having itching ears: and
James 5 4 entered into the ears of the Lord of
1 P 3 12 and his ears unto their prayers: but
earthborn Ps 48 3 you that are e., and you sons
earthen Lev 6 28 e. vessel, wherein it was sodden
Lev 11 33 an earthen vessel, into which any of
14 5 to be immolated in an earthen vessel
50 one sparrow in an earthen vessel over
Num 5 17 shall take holy water in an e. vessel
2 K 17 28 brought him beds . . . and e. vessels
Prov 26 23 e. vessel adorned with silver dross
Eccu 13 3 what agreement shall the earthen pot
Isa 45 9 a sherd of the earthen pots: shall
Jer 19 1 and take a potter's earthen bottle
2 by the entry of the earthen gate: and
22 28 Jechonias an e. and a broken vessel
32 14 and put them in an earthen vessel, that
Lam 4 2 they esteemed as earthen vessels, the
2 C 4 7 we have this treasure in e. vessels
earthly Job 4 19 who have an earthly foundation
Wisd 9 15 the e. habitation presseth down the
15 13 of e. matter maketh brittle vessels
John 3 12 I have spoken to you earthly things
1 C 15 47 the first man was of the earth, earthly
48 as is the earth, such also are the e.
49 as we have borne the image of the e.
2 C 5 1 if our e. house . . . be dissolved, that
Phil 3 19 their shame; who mind earthly things
James 3 15 earthly, sensual, devilish. For where
earthquake 3 K 19 11 Lord is not in the e. And
3 K 19 12 and after the earthquake a fire: the
Isa 29 6 and with e. and with a great noise
Amos 1 1 two years before the earthquake. And
Zach 14 5 as you fled from the face of the e.
Mat 27 54 having seen the earthquake and things
28 2 was a great earthquake. Acts 16:26; Apoc 6:12; 8:5; 11:13; 16:18
Apoc 11 13 that were slain in the earthquake
19 lightnings and voices and an e. and
16 18 such an earthquake, so great. And the
earthquakes Esth 11 5 behold there were . . . e.
Mat 24 7 there shall be . . . e. Mark 13:8; Luke 21:11
ease 1 K 24 4 Saul went to ease nature: now David
3 K 12 10 made our yoke heavy, do thou ease us
2 Pa 10 4 and ease something of the burden that
9 ease the yoke which thy father laid
10 made our yoke heavy, do thou ease it
Eccu 38 14 what they give for ease and remedy
Jer 49 31 and go up to a nation that is at ease
eased Deut 23 14 cover that which thou art e. of
2 C 8 13 not that others should be eased and
easier Exod 18 26 they judged the e. cases only
2 Pa 29 34 Levites are sanctified with e. rite
Eccu 22 18 a mass of iron is easier to bear than

Mat 9 5 whether is easier to say. Mark 2:9; Luke 5:23
19 24 e. for a camel. Mark 10:25; Luke 18:25
Luke 16 17 easier for heaven and earth to pass
easily Exod 28 32 that it may not e. be broken
1 K 16 16 and thou mayest bear it more easily
Job 39 32 contendeth with God be so e. silenced
Prov 18 14 a spirit that is e. angered, who can
29 22 he that is easily stirred up to wrath
Ecce 4 12 a threefold cord is not easily broken
Wisd 6 13 is easily seen by them that love her
13 9 how did they not more easily find
14 28 or easily forswear themselves. For
Eccu 6 7 and do not credit him easily. For there
Isa 10 19 that they shall easily be numbered
2 Ma 2 26 may more easily commit to memory: and
2 Th 2 2 not e. moved from your sense, nor be
1 Tim 6 18 charge the rich . . . to give easily
easing Judg 3 24 e. nature in his summer parlor
east Gen 10 30 Sephar, a mountain in the east
Gen 11 2 when they removed from the east, they
12 8 Bethel on the west, and Hai on the e.
13 11 [Lot] departed from the east: and they
14 look . . . to the east and to the west
25 6 separated them . . . to the east country
28 14 abroad to the west and to the east
29 1 and came into the east country. And he
Exod 27 13 of the court, which looketh to the east
38 13 towards the east he prepared hangings
Lev 15 14 towards the propitiatory to the east
Num 2 3 on the east Juda shall pitch his tents
21 11 that faceth Moab toward the east. And
23 7 from the mountains of the east: Come
35 5 toward the east shall be 2,000 cubits
Deut 3 27 cast thy eyes round . . . to the east
Josu 11 3 Chanaanites also on the east and on
12 1 all the e. country that looketh towards
3 sea of Ceneroth towards the east and
13 5 country also of Libanus towards the e.
16 1 Jericho and waters thereof, on the east
5 their possession towards the east was
17 10 the tribe of Issachar on the east. And
19 27 returneth towards the e. to Bethdagon
20 8 beyond the Jordan on the east of Jericho
23 4 the land, from the east of the Jordan
Judg 8 11 on the east of Nobe and Jegbaa, and
11 18 came over against the east coast of
1 K 13 5 in Machmas at the east of Bethaven
3 K 7 25 three looked . . . towards the east and
39 temple over against the e. southward
17 3 go towards the east and hide thyself
4 K 13 17 and said: Open the window to the east
1 Pa 5 10 country that looketh to east of Galaad
12 15 toward the east and toward the west
26 14 lot of the east fell to Selemias. But
17 towards the east were six Levites
2 Pa 4 4 other three that remained toward the e.
10 sea on right side over against the e.
29 4 and assembled them in the east street
31 14 porter of the east gate, was overseer
2 Es 3 26 against the water gate toward the east
29 son of Sechenias, keeper of the e. gate
Job 1 3 great among all the people of the east
23 8 if I go to the east, he appeareth not
Ps 67 34 above the heaven of heavens, to the e.
74 7 neither from the east nor from the
102 13 as far as the east is from the west
Isa 9 12 the Syrians from the east and the
11 14 shall spoil the children of the east
41 2 raised up the just one from the east
43 5 I will bring thy seed from the east
46 11 who call a bird from the east and from
Jer 31 40 corner of horse gate towards the east
49 28 and waste the children of the east
Bar 4 36 about thee, O Jerusalem, towards the e.
37 gathered together from the east even
5 5 and look about towards the east and
Eze 8 16 and their faces to the east: and they
10 19 it stood in the entry of the e. gate
11 1 and brought me into the east gate
25 4 will I deliver thee to men of the e.
10 to the people of the east with the
39 11 the valley . . . on the east of the sea
40 6 that looked toward the east. 42:15
19 breadth . . . hundred cubits to the east
22 the gate that looked to the e. 43:4
23 gate of the north and that of the east
32 the inner court by way of the east
44 one at the side of the east gate which
41 14 the separate place toward the east
42 9 an entrance from the east, for them
10 of the court that was toward the east
12 separated towards the east as one
16 he measured toward the east with the
43 1 gate that looked towards the e. 46:12
2 came in by the way of the east: and
17 and its steps turned toward the east
44 1 which looked towards the east: and it
45 7 from side of the east even to the east
46 1 inner court that looketh toward the east
47 1 threshold of the house toward the east
1 of the house looked toward the east
2 the way that looked toward the east
3 went out towards the east, he measured
8 toward the hillocks of sand to the east
18 making the bound to the east sea and
48 10 toward the east also 10,000 in breadth
17 suburbs . . . to the east 250 and to
18 residue . . . 10,000 toward the east
21 the firstfruits unto the east border
Dan 8 9 became great . . . against the east
11 44 tidings out of the east and out of
Joel 2 20 with his face towards the east sea
Amos 8 12 from the north to the east: they shall
Zach 8 7 save my people from the land of the e.
14 4 over against Jerusalem toward the e.
4 divided in the midst thereof to the e.
8 half of them to the east sea and half
1 Ma 12 37 towards the east was broken down and
Mat 2 1 there came wise men from the east to
2 we have seen his star in the east and
9 star which they had seen in the east
8 11 many shall come from the east and the
24 27 as lightning cometh out of the east
Luke 13 29 there shall come from the east and the
Apoc 21 13 on the east three gates. And the wall
east side Gen 4 15 at the east side of Eden
Gen 12 8 that was on the east side of Bethel
Deut 4 41 beyond the Jordan at the east side. 49
Josu 4 19 against the east side of the city
7 2 on the east side of the town of Bethel
11 8 Masphe, which is on the east side
12 3 on the east side by the way that leadeth
13 8 beyond river Jordan on the e. side. 27
32 over against Jericho on the east side
15 5 on the east side the beginning shall
16 6 along on the east side of Janoe. And
18 20 is the border of it on the east side
19 13 then to the east side of Gethhepher
Judg 20 43 down on the east side of the city Gabaa
21 19 on the east side of the way that goeth
1 Pa 4 39 Gador as far as to the east side of
6 78 Jericho, on east side of the Jordan
2 Pa 5 12 standing on the east side of the altar
Eze 11 23 that is on the east side of the city
47 18 the east side is from the midst of
18 thus you shall measure the east side

48 1 the east side thereof to the sea shall
2 from the east side even to the side of the sea. 3, 4, 5, 6, 7, 8
16 on the east side, 4,500. 32
23 from the east side to the west side
Jon 4 5 sat toward the east side of the city
eastern Judg 6 3 rest of the e. nations came up
Judg 6 33 the e. people were gathered together
7 12 all the eastern people lay scattered
8 10 left of all the troops of e. people
eastward Num 34 3 sea for its furthest limits e.
Num 34 11 they shall come eastward to the sea of
Deut 3 17 to the foot of mount Phasga eastward
Josu 16 6 it goeth round the borders eastward
18 7 possessions beyond the Jordan e.: which
19 12 it returneth from Sarid eastward to
4 K 10 33 from the Jordan e., all the land of
1 Pa 5 9 eastward he had his habitations as far
7 28 and eastward Noran and westward Gazer
9 18 until that time, in the king's gate e.
2 Es 12 36 and to the water gate eastward: and
Eze 40 10 of the gate that looked eastward were
easy Judg 18 7 dwelt therein . . . secure and easy
1 K 14 6 it is easy for the Lord to save either
4 K 20 10 it is an easy matter for the shadow
Prov 14 6 the learning of the wise is easy. Go
Eccu 11 23 it is easy in the eyes of God on a
28 it is easy before God in the day of
46 8 it is not easy to fight against God
Bar 6 60 when it breaketh forth, is easy to be seen
Jon 4 2 and easy to forgive evil. And now, O
1 Ma 3 18 it is an easy matter for many to be
2 Ma 2 27 we have taken in hand no easy task
Acts 24 23 keep him and that he should be easy
James 3 17 easy to be persuaded, consenting to
eat Mat 6 25 for your life, what you shall eat. Luke 12:22
Mat 6 31 what shall we eat: or what shall we
9 11 your master eat with publicans and
12 1 to pluck the ears and to eat. Luke 6:1
4 eat the loaves of proposition. Mark 2:26
4 not lawful for him to eat. Mark 2:26; Luke 6:4
14 16 give you them to e. Mark 6:37; Luke 9:13
20 they did all eat. 15:37; Mark 6:42; Luke 9:17
21 that did eat was 5,000. Mark 6:44
15 2 wash not their hands when they eat
20 to eat with unwashed hands doth not
27 the whelps also eat of the crumbs
32 because they . . . have not what to eat
38 they that did eat were 4,000 men beside
24 49 shall eat and drink with drunkards
25 35 I was hungry and you gave me to eat
42 was hungry and you gave me not to eat
26 17 for thee to eat the pasch. Mark 14:12
26 take ye and eat. This is. 1 C 11:24
Mark 2 16 why doth your master eat and drink
3 20 they could not so much as eat bread
5 43 something should be given her to eat
6 31 they had not so much as time to eat
36 they may buy themselves to eat. And he
37 and we will give them to eat. And he
7 2 his disciples eat bread with common
3 the Jews eat not without often washing
4 unless they be washed, they eat not
5 but they eat bread with common hands
8 1 great multitude, and had nothing to eat
2 three days and have nothing to eat
8 they did eat and were filled; and they
11 14 no man hereafter eat fruit of thee
14 14 where I may eat the pasch. Luke 22:11
Luke 5 30 why do you eat and drink with publicans
33 but thine eat and drink? To whom he
7 36 of the Pharisees desired him to eat
8 55 he bid them give her to eat. And her
10 8 eat such things as are set before you
11 37 he going in, sat down to eat. And the
12 19 eat, drink, make good cheer. But God
29 what you shall eat or what you shall
45 to eat and to drink, and be drunk
14 1 went into the house . . . to eat bread
15 that shall eat bread in the kingdom
15 16 with the husks the swine did eat; and
23 kill it and let us eat and make merry
17 8 whilst I eat and drink, and afterwards
27 in days of Noe . . . they did eat and
28 in days of Lot: they did eat and drink
22 8 for us the pasch, that we may eat
15 I have desired to eat this pasch with
16 I will not eat it till it be fulfilled
30 you may eat and drink at my table
24 41 he said: Have you here anything to eat
John 4 31 disciples prayed him, saying: Rabbi, e.
32 I have meat to eat which you know not
33 hath any man brought him to eat? Jesus
6 5 we buy bread that these may eat? And
26 but because you did eat of the loaves
31 our fathers did eat manna in the desert
31 gave them bread from heaven to eat
49 your fathers did eat manna. 59
50 if any man eat of it, he may not die
52 any man eat of this bread he shall live
53 this man give us his flesh to eat
54 except you eat the flesh of the Son of
18 28 but that they might eat the pasch
Acts 9 9 [Paul] did neither eat nor drink. Now
10 13 arise, Peter: kill and eat. 11:7
14 never did eat anything that is common
41 did eat and drink with him after he
11 3 uncircumcised and didst eat with him
23 12 neither eat nor drink till they killed
14 will eat nothing till we have slain
21 neither to eat nor to drink till they
27 35 taking bread . . . he [Paul] began to eat
Rom 12 20 thy enemy be hungry, give him to eat
14 2 believeth that he may eat all things
2 he that is weak, let him eat herbs
21 it is good not to eat flesh and not
23 discerneth, if he eat, is condemned
1 C 5 11 with such a one, not so much as to eat
8 7 eat as a thing sacrificed to an idol
8 if we eat shall we have the more; nor if we eat not, shall we have
10 eat those things which are sacrificed
13 I will never eat flesh lest I should
9 4 have not we power to eat and to drink
13 eat the things that are of the holy
10 3 did all eat the same spiritual food
7 the people sat down to eat and drink
18 are not they that eat of the sacrifices
25 whatsoever is sold in the shambles, eat
27 eat of anything that is set before you
28 sacrificed to idols, do not eat of it
31 whether you eat or drink or whatsoever
11 20 it is not now to eat the Lord's supper
21 taketh before his own supper to eat
22 not houses to eat and to drink in
26 as often as you shall eat this bread
27 whosoever shall eat this bread or
28 so let him eat of that bread and drink
33 when you come together to eat, wait
34 any man be hungry, let him eat at home
15 32 let us eat and drink for tomorrow
2 C 9 10 will both give you bread to eat and will
Gal 2 12 [Peter] did eat with the Gentiles
2 Th 3 8 neither did we eat any man's bread
10 will not work, neither let him eat

12 that they would eat their own bread
Heb 13 10 altar whereof they have no power to e.
James 5 3 rust . . . shall eat your flesh like fire
Apoc 2 7 I will give to eat of the tree of life
14 to eat and to commit fornication: so
20 to eat of things sacrificed to idols
10 9 take the book and eat it up: and it
17 16 shall eat her flesh and shall burn her
19 18 you may eat the flesh of kings and
eaten Mark 8 9 that had eaten were about 4,000
Luke 13 26 we have eaten and drunk in thy presence
24 43 when he had eaten before them, taking
John 2 17 zeal of thy house hath eaten me up
6 13 which remained . . . to them that had e.
23 place where they had eaten the bread
Acts 12 23 [Herod] being eaten up by worms, he gave
27 38 and when they had eaten enough, they
Apoc 10 10 when I had eaten it, my belly was
eater Judg 14 14 out of the eater came forth meat
Isa 55 10 seed to the sower, and bread to the e.
Nah 3 12 shall fall into the mouth of the eater
eaters Wisd 12 5 and eaters of men's bowels and
eateth Mark 14 18 one of you that eateth with me
Luke 15 2 receiveth sinners and eateth with them
John 6 55 he that eateth my flesh. 57
58 that eateth me, the same also shall
59 he that eateth this bread, shall live
13 18 he that e. bread with me, shall lift
Rom 14 3 not him that e. despise him that e. not
3 e. not, let him not judge him that e.
6 he that eateth, eateth to the Lord
6 he that e. not, to the Lord he e. not
20 evil for that man who e. with offence
1 C 9 7 and eateth not of the fruit thereof
7 and e. not of the milk of the flock
11 29 that e. and drinketh unworthily, e. and drinketh judgment
eating Mat 11 18 John came neither e. Luke 7:34
Mat 11 19 the Son of man came eating. Luke 7:34
24 38 they were e. and drinking, marrying
26 21 whilst they were eating, Mark 14:22
Mark 14 18 when they were at table and eating
Luke 10 7 e. and drinking such things as they
Acts 1 4 [Jesus] eating together with them
Ebal Gen 10 28 Jectan begot . . . Ebal and Abimael
Gen 36 23 the sons of Sobal . . . Ebal. 1 Pa 1:40
ebony Eze 27 15 teeth of ivory and ebony. The
Ecbatana 1 Es 6 2 there was found in Ecbatana
Tob 5 8 is situate in the mount of Ecbatana
Jdth 1 1 strong city which he called Ecbatana
2 Ma 9 3 when he was come about Ecbatana, he
Eccetan 1 Es 8 12 Joanan the son of Eccetan and
Ecclesiastes Ecce 1 1 the words of Ecclesiastes
Ecce 1 2 vanity of vanities, said E. 12:8
12 I Ecclesiastes was king over Israel
7 28 this have I found, said Ecclesiastes
12 9 whereas Ecclesiastes was very wise
Echaia 2 Es 10 26 Echaia, Hanan, Anan, Melluch
Echi Gen 46 21 sons of Benjamin . . . Naaman and E.
echo Wisd 17 18 echo from the highest mountains
eclipsed Eccu 17 30 sun; yet it shall be eclipsed
ecstasy Ps 30 1 a psalm for David, in an ecstasy
Ps 67 28 Benjamin a youth, in ecstasy of mind
Acts 10 10 came upon him [Peter] an ecstasy of
11 5 and I saw in an e. of mind a vision
Eddo 1 Es 8 17 I sent them to E., who is chief
1 Es 8 17 words that they should speak to Eddo
Edema Josu 19 36 and Edema and Arama, Asor and
Eden Gen 4 16 the earth, at the east side of Eden
4 K 19 12 children of Eden that were in Thelassar
2 Pa 29 12 son of Zemma and Eden the son of Joah
31 15 under his charge were Eden and Benjamin
Isa 37 12 children of Eden, that were in Thalassar
Eze 27 23 Chene and Eden were thy merchants
Eder Josu 15 21 Gabseel and Eder and Jagur and
1 Pa 23 23 sons of Musi: Moholi and Eder. 24:30
edge Exod 26 10 fifty loops in the edge of one curtain. 36:17
Exod 36 11 loops of violet in edge of one curtain
11 in edge of other curtain in like manner
17 fifty in the edge of another curtain
1 K 22 19 he smote with the edge of his sword
Eccu 30 10 lest . . . thy teeth be set on edge. Give
Jer 31 29 the teeth . . . are set on edge. Eze 18:2
30 his teeth shall be set on edge. Behold
Eze 43 13 the border thereof unto its edge and
edge of the sword Exod 17 13 Amalec and his people to flight by the e. . . .
Num 21 24 he was slain by them with the e. . . .
Deut 13 15 in habitants of that city with the e. . . .
20 13 therein of the male sex with the e. . . .
17 but shalt kill them with the e. . . .
Josu 6 21 and the asses, they slew with e. . . .
10 28 Maceda and destroyed it with the e. . . .
30 they destroyed the city with the e. . . .
37 took it and destroyed it with e. . . .
39 round about he destroyed with e. . . .
Judg 1 25 they smote the city with the e. . . .
4 15 with e. . . . at sight of Barac, in so
18 27 secure, and smote them with the e. . . .
20 37 into the city and smote it with e. . . .
1 K 15 8 common people he slew with the e. . . .
2 K 15 14 and smote the city with the e. . . . And
4 K 10 25 and captains slew them with the e. . . .
Jdth 2 16 that resisted him he slew with e. . . .
7 17 our end may be short by the e. . . . which
15 6 they pursued them with the e. . . . until
Eccu 28 22 many have fallen by the e. . . . but not
Jer 21 7 he shall strike them with the e. . . .
1 Ma 5 28 slew every male by the e. . . . and took
51 they slew every male with the e. . . .
Luke 21 24 shall fall by the e. . . . ; and shall be
Heb 11 34 escaped the e. . . . , recovered strength
edged sword; *see* **sword**
edges Exod 28 7 [ephod] shall have two edges
edict 1 Es 4 23 copy of e. of king Artaxerxes
1 Es 7 11 the edict, which king Artaxerxes gave
Esth 1 19 let an edict go out from thy presence
3 15 edict was hung up in Susan. 8:14; 9:14
4 3 to which the king's cruel edict was come
8 he gave him also a copy of the edict
16 19 this edict, which we now send, shall be
Dan 6 7 an edict be published: That whosoever
12 spoke to the king concerning the edict
1 Ma 1 60 according to the edict of the king. 2:33
2 34 neither will we obey the king's edict
3 14 they have despised the e. of the king
Heb 11 23 they feared not the king's edict. By
edicts 1 Es 8 36 they gave the king's e. to the
1 Ma 6 23 according to his orders and obey his e.
edification Rom 14 18 keep things that are of e.
Rom 15 2 please his neighbor unto good, to e.
1 C 14 3 speaketh to men unto edification and
5 that the church may receive edification
26 let all things be done to edification
2 C 10 8 the Lord has given us unto edification
12 19 but all things . . . for your edification
13 10 the Lord hath given me unto edification
Eph 4 29 that which is good, to the e. of faith
1 Tim 1 4 rather than the edification of God
edified Acts 9 31 Galilee and Samaria; and was e.
1 C 14 17 but the other is not edified. I thank
edifieth 1 C 8 1 but charity edifieth. And if any
1 C 14 4 speaketh in a tongue, edifieth himself
4 he that prophesieth, e. the church
edify 1 C 10 23 but all things do not edify. Let

1 Th 5 11 edify one another, as you also do
edifying 1 C 14 12 abound unto the e. of the church
Eph 4 12 for the edifying of the body of Christ
16 unto the edifying of itself in charity
Edissa Esth 2 7 up his brother's daughter E. who
Edna 1 Es 10 30 of the sons of Phahath . . . Edna
2 Es 12 15 of Haram, Edna: of Maraioth, Helci
Ednas 1 Pa 12 20 there fled to him of Manasses, E.
2 Pa 17 14 captains of the army, Ednas the chief
Edom Gen 25 30 his name was called Edom. And Jacob
Gen 32 3 sent messengers . . . to country of Edom
36 1 generations of Esau, the same is Edom
8 Esau dwelt in mount Seir: he is Edom
9 generations of Esau the father of Edom
19 the dukes of them: the same is Edom
43 these are the dukes of Edom. 1 Pa 1:54
Exod 15 15 then were the princes of Edom troubled
Num 20 14 messengers from Cades to king of Edom
18 Edom answered them: Thou shalt not pass
34 3 wilderness of Sin, which is by Edom
Josu 15 1 from frontier of Edom, to the desert
21 by the borders of Edom to the south
Judg 5 4 and passedst by the regions of Edom
11 17 he sent messengers to the king of Edom
1 K 14 47 the children of Ammon and Edom and the
2 K 8 14 and he put guards in Edom and placed
14 and all Edom was made to serve David
3 K 11 1 women . . . of Edom and of Sidon and of
14 the Edomite of the king's seed, in Edom
15 when David was in Edom and Joab the
15 and had killed every male in Edom
16 till he had slain every male in Edom
22 48 was then no king appointed in Edom
4 K 3 8 he answered: By the desert of Edom
9 of Juda and the king of Edom went
12 and the king of Edom went down to him
20 water came by the way of Edom and the
26 to break in upon the king of Edom: but
8 20 Edom revolted from being under Juda. 22
14 7 he slew of E. in the valley of Saltpits
10 hast beaten and prevailed over Edom
1 Pa 1 51 there began to be dukes in Edom instead
18 11 as well from Edom and from Moab and
13 he put a garrison in Edom, that Edom should serve David
2 Pa 21 8 Edom revolted from being subject to Juda
10 Edom revolted from being under the
25 19 hast said: I have overthrown Edom
20 because of the gods of Edom. So Joas
Ps 59 2 and Joab returned and slew of Edom
10 into Edom will I stretch out my shoe
11 who will lead me into Edom? 107:11
62 1 when he was in the desert of Edom
107 10 over Edom I will stretch out my shoe
136 7 remember, O Lord, the children of Edom
Isa 11 14 Edom and Moab shall be under the rule
63 1 who is this that cometh from Edom
Jer 9 26 upon Juda and upon Edom and upon the
25 21 and Edom and Moab and the children
27 3 thou shalt send them to the king of E.
40 11 among the children of Ammon and in Edom
49 7 against Edom. Thus saith the Lord
17 Edom shall be desolate: every one that
20 which he hath taken concerning Edom
22 the heart of the valiant ones of Edom
Lam 4 21 and be glad, O daughter of Edom, that
22 visited thy iniquity, O daughter of E.
Eze 25 12 because Edom hath taken vengeance
13 I will stretch forth my hand upon E.
14 I will lay my vengeance upon Edom
14 shall do in Edom according to my wrath
32 29 there is Edom and her kings and all her
36 5 the rest of the nations and of all E.
Dan 11 41 saved out of his hand, Edom and Moab
Joel 3 19 and Edom a wilderness destroyed: because
Amos 1 6 to shut them up in Edom. And I will
9 have shut up an entire captivity in E.
11 for three crimes of Edom and for four
2 1 burnt the bones of the king of Edom
9 12 they may possess the remnant of Edom
Abdi 1 thus saith the Lord God to Edom: We
8 destroy the wise out of Edom, and
Mala 1 4 if Edom shall say: We are destroyed
land of Edom Gen 36 16 sons of Eliphaz in l. . . .
Gen 36 17 dukes of Rahuel, in the land of Edom
21 sons of Seir in the land of Edom. And
31 kings that ruled in the land of Edom
Num 20 22 which is in the borders of the l. . . .
21 4 to compass the land of Edom. And the
33 37 uttermost borders of the land of Edom
Judg 11 18 and went round the land of Edom at
3 K 9 26 shore of Red Sea in the land of Edom
1 Pa 1 43 king that reigned in the land of Edom
2 Pa 8 17 which is in the land of Edom. And
Isa 34 6 a great slaughter in the land of Edom
Edomite Deut 23 7 thou shalt not abhor the E.
1 K 21 7 his name was Doeg, an Edomite, the
22 9 Doeg the Edomite who stood by and was
18 Doeg the Edomite turned and fell upon
22 day when Doeg the Edomite was there
3 K 11 14 adversary to Solomon, Adad the E. of
Ps 51 2 when Doeg the Edomite came and told
Edomites Gen 36 43 Esau the father of the E. And
3 K 11 17 Adad fled, he and certain Edomites
4 K 8 21 in the night and defeated the Edomites
16 6 and the Edomites came into Aila: and
2 Pa 21 9 rose in the night and defeated the E.
25 14 Amasias after he had slain the E., set
28 17 Edomites came and slew many of Juda
Ps 82 7 the tabernacles of the Edomites and
Edrai Num 21 33 all his people, to fight in Edrai
Deut 1 4 who abode in Astaroth and in Edrai
3 1 us with his people to fight in Edrai
10 as far as Selcha and Edrai, cities of
Josu 12 4 who dwelt in Astaroth and in Edrai
13 12 who reigned in Astaroth and Edrai
31 half Galaad and Astaroth and Edrai
Edri Josu 19 37 Asor and Cedes and Edri, Enhasor
efface 4 K 21 13 I will e. Jerusalem, as tables
effaced 4 K 21 13 as tables are wont to be effaced
Jer 20 11 reproach, which never shall be effaced
effect Gen 18 19 Lord may bring to e. all the
Lev 7 18 the oblation shall be of no effect
Num 30 9 she had bound her soul of no effect
Judg 18 5 and the things should have effect
4 K 19 25 and now I have brought it to effect
Esth 3 14 of the letters were to this effect
8 3 against the Jews, should be of no e.
16 17 in our name are void and of no effect
Isa 37 26 and now I have brought it to effect
Eze 12 23 at hand, and the effect of every vision
1 Ma 10 51 Egypt, with words to this effect, saying
11 29 to this effect. King Demetrius to his
2 Ma 11 16 to this effect: Lysias to the people
34 Romans also sent them a letter to this e.
14 11 when this man had spoken to this e.
Rom 3 3 make the faith of God without effect
4 14 the promise is made of no effect. For
Gal 3 17 to make the promise of no effect. For
effects Wisd 13 4 their power and their effects
effectual Heb 4 12 word of God is living and e.
effeminate 3 K 14 24 also the e. in the land
3 K 15 12 he took away the e. out of the land
22 47 the remnant also of the effeminate
4 K 23 7 destroyed also the pavilions of the e.
Job 36 14 and their life among the effeminate

Prov 18 8 souls of the effeminate shall be hungry
Isa 3 4 the effeminate shall rule over them
Osee 4 14 offered sacrifice with the effeminate
1 C 6 10 nor the e. nor liers with mankind nor
Egeus Esth 2 3 under the hand of E. the eunuch
Esth 2 8 were delivered to Egeus the eunuch
15 Egeus the eunuch the keeper of the
egg Tob 11 14 like the skin of an egg. And Tobias
Luke 11 12 if he shall ask an egg will he reach
eggs Deut 22 6 sitting upon the young or upon the e.
Job 39 14 when she leaveth her eggs on the earth
Isa 10 14 as eggs are gathered, that are left
59 5 they have broken the eggs of asps
5 that shall eat of their eggs, shall die
Jer 17 11 as the partridge hath hatched eggs
Egla 2 K 3 5 sixth Jethraam of Egla the wife of
Eglon Josu 10 3 to Dabir king of Eglon, saying
Josu 10 5 king of Lachis, the king of Eglon. 23
34 he passed from Lachis to Eglon and
36 went up also with all Israel from Eglon
37 as he had done to Eglon, so did he
12 12 the king of Eglon one, the king of
15 39 Lachis and Bascath and Eglon, Chebbon
Judg 3 12 strengthened against them Eglon king
14 served Eglon king of Moab 18 years
15 sent presents to Eglon king of Moab
17 he presented the gifts to Eglon king
17 now Eglon was exceeding fat. And when
Egyptian Gen 16 1 having a handmaid an Egyptian
Gen 16 3 she took Agar the Egyptian her handmaid
21 9 son of Agar the E. playing with Isaac
25 12 whom Agar the Egyptian, Sara's servant
39 1 an E., bought him of the Ismaelites
5 Lord blessed the house of the Egyptian
45 called him in the Egyptian tongue
Exod 1 19 Hebrew women are not as the E. women
2 11 an Egyptian striking one of the Hebrews
12 he slew the Egyptian and hid him in
14 as thou didst yesterday kill the E.
7 11 by E. enchantments and certain secrets
14 24 the Lord looking upon the E. army
Lev 24 10 whom she had of an Egyptian, among
Deut 23 7 thou shalt not abhor . . . the Egyptian
1 K 30 11 they found an Egyptian in the field
2 K 23 21 he also slew an Egyptian, a man worthy
21 spear out of the hand of the Egyptian
1 Pa 2 34 a servant an Egyptian, named Jeraa
11 23 he slew an Egyptian whose stature was
Isa 19 23 and the Egyptian to the Assyrians and
24 third to the E. and the Assyrian: a
Acts 7 24 [Moses] striking the E., he avenged him
28 as thou didst yesterday kill the E.
21 38 art not thou [Paul] that Egyptian
Egyptians Gen 12 12 when the E. shall see thee
Gen 12 14 the Egyptians saw the woman that she
41 56 all the barns and sold to the Egyptians
43 32 unlawful for the Egyptians to eat with
32 for the Egyptians also that ate with
45 2 weeping, which the Egyptians . . . heard
46 34 E. have all shepherds in abomination
50 11 this is a great mourning to the E.
Exod 1 13 the Egyptians hated the children of
3 8 out of the hands of the Egyptians. 14:30; 18:9; Judg 6:9
9 they are oppressed by the Egyptians
21 to this people, in the sight of the E.
6 5 wherewith the E. have oppressed them
6 out from the work prison of the E. 7
7 5 Egyptians shall know that I am the Lord. 14:4, 18
18 E. shall be afflicted when they drink
21 the Egyptians could not drink the water
22 magicians of the Egyptians with their
24 Egyptians dug round about the river
8 21 houses of E. shall be filled with flies
26 sacrifice the abominations of the E.
26 things which the Egyptians worship
9 4 and the possessions of the Egyptians
6 the beasts of the Egyptians died but
10 2 how often I have plagued the Egyptians
6 thy servants and of all the Egyptians
14 rested in all the coasts of the E.
11 3 favor to his people in the sight of the E.
5 every firstborn in land of the E. shall
7 Lord maketh between the E. and Israel
12 23 will pass through striking the E.: and
27 striking the E. and saving our houses
33 the Egyptians pressed the people to go
35 they asked of the Egyptians vessels
36 favor to the people in sight of the E.
36 and they stripped the Egyptians. And
39 the Egyptians pressing them to depart
14 5 it was told the king of the Egyptians
9 when the Egyptians followed the steps
10 lifting up their eyes, saw the E. behind
12 that we may serve the Egyptians? For it
13 for the Egyptians, whom you see now
17 I will harden the heart of the E. to
23 the Egyptians pursuing went in after
25 Egyptians said: Let us flee from Israel
26 waters may come again upon the E. upon
27 as the Egyptians were fleeing away
31 the Egyptians dead upon the seashore
18 8 had done to Pharao and the Egyptians
10 and out of the hand of the Egyptians
19 4 seen what I have done to the E., how
32 12 let not the Egyptians say, I beseech
Lev 26 13 brought you out of land of the Egyptians
Num 14 13 Moses said to the Lord: That the E. from
20 15 and the Egyptians afflicted us and
33 3 in sight of all the E. who were burying
Deut 7 18 thy God did to Pharao and to all the E.
11 4 to all the host of the E. and to their
26 6 Egyptians afflicted us and persecuted
Josu 24 6 the Egyptians pursued your fathers
7 put darkness between you and the E.
Judg 10 11 did not the Egyptians and Amorrhites
1 K 10 18 delivered you from hand of the E.
3 K 4 30 all the Orientals and of the Egyptians
4 K 7 6 kings of the Hethites and of the E.
1 Es 9 1 and the Egyptians and the Amorrhites
Jdth 5 11 when the Egyptians had cast them out
13 when an innumerable army of the E.
9 6 pleased to look upon the camp of the E.
Isa 19 2 will set the E. to fight against the E.
21 the Egyptians shall know the Lord
23 the Egyptians shall serve the Assyrian
Eze 16 26 hast committed fornication with the E.
29 12 I will scatter the Egyptians among the
13 I will gather the Egyptians from the
Acts 7 22 all the wisdom of the Egyptians; and he
Heb 11 26 than the treasure of the Egyptians
28 the E. attempting, were swallowed up
Egyptians' Exod 14 20 between E. camp and the camp
either Exod 30 4 under the crown on either side
Exod 39 4 one to the other in the top on e. side
16 they set the rings on either side
Deut 7 14 shall be barren among you of either sex
16 19 and not go aside to either part. Thou
Judg 20 16 by the stone's going on either side
3 K 10 19 two hands on e. side holding the seat
1 Pa 12 2 bending the bow and using either hand
2 Pa 9 18 and two arms one on either side and
Jdth 5 12 stand firm as a wall on either side
2 Ma 3 26 who stood by him on either side and
Ela Gen 36 41 duke Ela, duke Phinon. 1 Pa 1:52

3 K 4 18 Semei the son of Ela in Benjamin. Semei
16 6 and Ela his son reigned in his stead
8 Ela the son of Baasa reigned over Israel
9 Ela was drinking in Thersa, and drunk
13 and the sins of Ela his son, who sinned
14 the rest of the acts of Ela and all that
4 K 15 30 Osee son of Ela. 17:1; 18:1, 9
1 Pa 4 15 the son of Jephone, were Hir and Ela
15 the sons of Ela: Cenez. The sons also
9 8 Ela the son of Ozi, the son of Mochori
Elad 1 Pa 7 21 his son Ezer, and Elad: and the
Elada 1 Pa 7 20 Elada his son, Thahath his son
Elai Jdth 8 1 Ozias the son of Elai, the son of
Elam Gen 10 22 sons of Sem: Elam and. 1 Pa 1:17
1 Pa 8 24 Hanania and Elam . . . sons of Sesac
26 3 sons of Meselemia . . . Elam the fifth
1 Es 2 7 the children of Elam, 1,254. 2 Es 7:12
31 the children of the other Elam, 1,254
10 2 the son of Jehiel of the sons of Elam
2 Es 7 34 the men of the other Elam, 1,254
10 14 Elam, Zethu, Bani, Bonni, Azgad, Bebai
12 41 Melchia and Elam and Ezer. And singers
Isa 11 11 from Elam and from Sennaar and from
21 2 go up, O Elam, besiege, O Mede: I have
22 6 Elam took the quiver, the chariot
Jer 25 25 all the kings of Elam and all the kings
49 34 came to Jeremias the prophet against E.
35 I will break the bow of Elam and their
36 I will bring upon Elam the four winds
36 no nation to which the fugitives of E.
37 I will cause Elam to be afraid before
38 I will set my throne in Elam and destroy
39 will cause captives of Elam to return
Eze 32 24 there is Elam and all his multitude
Dan 8 2 Susa, which is in the province of Elam
Elamites Gen 14 1 king of the Elamites . . . made
1 Es 4 9 Susanechites, the Dievites and the E.
Acts 2 9 Parthians and Medes and Elamites and
Elasa 1 Pa 2 39 Helles begot E. E. begot Sisamoi
1 Pa 8 37 Rapha, of whom was born Elasa, who
9 43 Raphaia begot Elasa: of whom was born
1 Es 10 22 of the sons of Pheshur . . . Elasa. And
Jer 29 3 by the hand of Elasa the son of Saphan
Elath Deut 2 8 by the way of the plain from Elath
4 K 14 22 [Azarias] built Elath and restored it
elbow Eccu 41 24 leaning with thy elbow over meat
Eze 13 18 that sew cushions under every elbow
Elcana Exod 6 24 sons also of Core: Aser and E.
1 K 1 1 and his name was Elcana, the son of
4 and Elcana offered sacrifice and gave
8 Elcana her husband said to her. 23
19 and Elcana knew Anna his wife: and the
21 Elcana her husband went up and all his
2 11 Elcana went to Ramatha, to his house
20 Heli blessed Elcana and his wife: and
1 Pa 6 23 Aser his son, Elcana his son, Abiasaph
25 the sons of Elcana. 26
27 Jeroham his son, Elcana his son. The
34 Samuel the son of Elcana, the son of
35 Suph the son of Elcana, son of Mahath
36 Amasai the son of Elcana, the son of
9 16 son of Asa, the son of Elcana, who
12 6 Elcana and Jesia and Azareel and Joezer
15 23 Barachias and Elcana were doorkeepers
2 Pa 28 7 Elcana who was next to the king. And
Elcesite Nah 1 1 the vision of Nahum the Elcesite
Elchanan 1 Pa 11 26 Asahel brother of Joab, and E.
Eldaa Gen 25 4 Henoch and Abida and E. 1 Pa 1:33
Eldad Num 11 26 of whom one was called Eldad
elder Gen 10 21 elder brother of Japheth, sons
Gen 19 31 the elder said to the younger. 34
33 the elder went in and lay with her
37 the elder bore a son and she called
24 2 said to the elder servant of his house
25 23 the elder shall serve the younger. And
27 1 he called Esau, his elder son, and said
23 hairy hands made him like to the elder
29 16 the name of the elder was Lia: and the
48 14 head of Manasses who was the elder
1 K 18 17 my e. daughter Merob, her will I give
3 K 2 22 [Adonias] is my elder brother and
1 Pa 24 31 both the e. and the younger. The lot
25 8 the elder equally with the younger
2 Pa 22 1 killed all that were his e. brothers
Tob 13 1 Tobias the elder opening his mouth
Job 1 18 wine in the house of their e. brother
15 10 men, much elder than thy fathers. Is
Eccu 32 4 speak, thou that art elder: for it
Eze 16 46 thy elder sister is Samaria, she and
61 thy sisters, thy elder and thy younger
23 4 their names were Oolla the elder and
Luke 15 25 his elder son was in the field and
Rom 9 12 the elder shall serve the younger
elders Gen 50 7 e. of the land of Egypt and the
Exod 19 7 calling together the e. of the people
Num 22 4 he said to the elders of Madian: So
7 the elders of Madian went with the
Deut 5 23 all the princes of the tribes and the e.
32 7 thee: thy elders, and they will tell
Josu 23 2 for the elders and for the princes and
Job 32 4 they were his elders that were speaking
Dan 13 18 knew not that the elders were hid
19 the two elders arose and ran to her
24 the elders also cried out against her
28 the two elders also came full of wicked
34 the two elders rising up in the midst
36 the elders said: As we walked in the
41 believed them as being the elders
61 they arose up against the two elders
eldest Gen 44 12 searched, beginning at the e.
Num 1 20 Ruben the eldest son of Israel by their
Judg 8 20 he said to Jether his eldest son: Arise
1 K 17 13 three eldest sons followed Saul to the
14 the three eldest having followed Saul
28 when Eliab his eldest brother heard
4 K 3 27 he took his eldest son that should have
2 Pa 21 3 to Joram, because he was the eldest
Job 1 13 in the house of their eldest brother
1 Ma 16 2 Simon called his two eldest sons, Judas
2 Ma 7 2 one of them, who was the eldest, said
John 8 9 went out one by one beginning at the e.
Eleale Num 32 3 Eleale . . . is a very fertile soil
Num 32 37 children of Ruben built Hesebon and E.
Isa 15 4 Hesebon shall cry, and Eleale, their
16 9 with my tears, O Hesebon and Eleale
Jer 48 34 from the cry of Hesebon even to Eleale
Eleazar Exod 6 23 bore him Nadab and Abiu and E.
Exod 6 25 Eleazar the son of Aaron took a wife
28 1 Nadab and Abiu, Eleazar and Ithamar
Lev 10 6 said to Aaron and to Eleazar and Ithamar
12 Moses spoke to Aaron and to Eleazar
16 [Moses] being angry with Eleazar and
Num 3 2 Abiu and Eleazar and Ithamar. 26:60
4 E. and Ithamar performed the priestly
32 E. the son of Aaron the priest. 4:16; 16:37; 25:7, 11; 26:1
20 26 shalt vest therewith Eleazar his son
28 he vested Eleazar his son with them
29 he [Moses] came down with Eleazar. And
31 31 and Moses and E. did as the Lord had
Deut 10 6 Eleazar his son succeeded him in the
Josu 22 31 Phinees the son of Eleazar. 1 Pa 9:20; 1 Es 7:5; Eccu 45:28
1 K 7 1 and they sanctified Eleazar his son
2 K 23 9 after him was Eleazar the son of Dodo
1 Pa 6 3 sons of Aaron: Nadab and Abiu, E. 24:1

4 Eleazar begot Phinees and Phinees begot
50 sons of Aaron: Eleazar his son, Phinees
11 12 after him was Eleazar his uncle's son
23 21 sons of Moholi: Eleazar and Cis. And
22 and Eleazar died, and had no sons
24 2 Eleazar and Ithamar did the office
3 the sons of Eleazar. 4, 5
6 house which was over the rest, of E.
28 the son of Moholi: Eleazar, who had no
1 Es 8 33 with him [Meremoth] was Eleazar the
2 Es 12 41 Maasia and Semeia and Eleazar and Azzi
1 Ma 2 5 Eleazar who was surnamed Abaron: and
6 43 Eleazar the son of Saura saw one of the
8 17 Jason the son of Eleazar and he sent
2 Ma 6 24 might think that Eleazar at the age of
18 E. one of the chief of the scribes
Mat 1 15 Elius begot E. E. begot Mathan. And
Eleazar the priest Num 16 39 E. . . . took the brazen censers
Num 19 3 you shall deliver her to E. the priest
26 3 E. the priest being in the plains of
63 that were enrolled by Moses and E. . . .
27 2 they stood before Moses and E. . . .
19 he shall stand before E. the priest
21 Eleazar the priest shall consult the
22 set him [Josue] before E. the priest
31 6 Phinees the son of E. . . . Josu 22:13
12 brought them to Moses and E. . . . and
13 Moses and E. the priest and all princes
21 E. . . . spoke to the men of the army
26 E. . . . and the princes of the multitude
29 thou shalt give it to E. the priest
41 to E. . . . , as had been commanded him
51 Moses and E. . . . received all the gold
32 2 they came to Moses and E. the priest
28 Moses therefore commanded E. . . . and
34 17 shall divide the land unto you: E. . . .
Josu 14 1 which E. . . . and Josue the son. 19:51
17 4 they came in the presence of E. . . .
21 1 came to E. the priest and to Josue
elect 2 K 22 27 with the e. thou wilt be e. Ps 17:27
Tob 13 10 bless ye the Lord, all his elect, keep
Ps 88 4 I have made a covenant with my elect
Wisd 3 9 grace and peace is to his elect. But
Eccu 11 33 on the elect he will lay a blot. Of
24 4 in the multitude of the e. she shall
13 and take root in my elect. From the
46 2 great for the saving the elect of God
47 24 by the roots the offspring of his elect
Isa 42 1 my elect, my soul delighteth in him
45 4 Israel my elect, I have even called thee
65 9 my e. shall inherit it and my servants
15 your name for an execration to my e.
23 my elect shall not labor in vain nor
Zach 9 17 corn of the elect, and wine springing
Mat 24 22 for sake of the elect those days shall
24 to deceive, if possible, even the e.
31 shall gather together his e. Mark 13:27
Mark 13 20 for sake of the elect which he hath
22 seduce, as it were possible, even the e.
Luke 18 7 will not God revenge his elect who
Rom 16 13 salute Rufus, elect in the Lord, and
1 Tim 5 21 I charge thee before . . . the e. angels
2 Tim 2 10 endure all things for sake of the elect
1 P 1 1 e. according to the foreknowledge of
2 6 I lay in Sion a chief corner stone, e.
2 J 1 the ancient to the lady Elect and her
13 the children of thy sister Elect salute
Apoc 17 14 are called and elect and faithful. And
elect of God Luke 23 25 if he be Christ, e. . . .
Rom 8 33 who shall accuse against the e. . . .
Col 3 12 put ye on as the elect of God, holy
Titus 1 1 according to the faith of the e. . . .

elected 1 P 5 13 in Babylon, e. together with you
election Acts 9 15 this man is to me a vessel of e.
Rom 9 11 that the purpose of God, according to e.
11 5 according to the election of grace
7 the election hath obtained it; and
28 touching the e. they are most dear
1 Th 1 4 brethren beloved of God, your election
2 P 1 10 may make sure your calling and election
Elehanan 2 K 23 24 E. the son of Dodo of Bethlehem
elements Wisd 7 17 to know . . . virtues of the e.
Wisd 19 17 while the elements are changed in
Gal 4 3 serving under the e. of the world
9 you again to weak and needy elements
Col 2 8 according to the elements of the world
20 dead with Christ from the e. of this
Heb 5 12 the first elements of the words of God
2 P 3 10 the elements shall be melted with heat
12 the e. shall melt with the burning
Eleoenai 1 Es 8 4 of the sons of Phahath Moab, E.
Eleph Josu 18 28 Sela, Eleph, and Jebus, which is
elephant 1 Ma 6 35 stood by every e. 1,000 men
1 Ma 6 46 went between the feet of the elephant
elephants 1 Ma 1 18 multitude with chariots and e.
1 Ma 3 34 to him half the army and the elephants
6 30 thirty-two elephants, trained to battle
34 showed the e. the blood of grapes
8 6 having 120 elephants, with horsemen
11 56 Tryphon took the elephants and made
2 Ma 11 4 horsemen and his fourscore elephants
13 2 footmen, 5,000 horsemen, 22 elephants
15 the greatest of the e. with them that
14 12 Nicanor, the commander over the e.
elephants' 3 K 10 22 gold and silver and e. teeth
Eleutherus 1 Ma 11 7 far as the river, called E.
1 Ma 12 30 they had passed the river Eleutherus
elevate Lev 14 24 shall e. them together. And the
Num 5 25 and shall elevate it before the Lord
6 20 he shall elevate them in the sight of
Job 15 12 why doth thy heart elevate thee and
elevated Lev 7 34 the breast that is elevated
Lev 10 15 they have elevated before the Lord
Jdth 1 7 his heart was e. and he sent to all
22 12 elevated above the height of the stars
Ps 8 2 thy magnificence is e. above the heavens
Isa 2 14 and upon all the elevated hills, and
6 1 upon a throne high and elevated: and
30 25 upon every elevated hill rivers of
Eze 31 3 his top was e. among the thick boughs
5 his boughs were e. because of many
elevating Exod 29 24 sanctify them e. before the
Exod 29 26 e. it, thou shalt sanctify it before
Lev 8 29 elevating it before the Lord, as the
9 21 elevating them before the Lord, as Moses
Eli Mat 27 46 Eli, Eli, lamma sabachthani. Mark 15:34
Elia 1 Pa 8 27 Elia and Zechri the sons of Jeroham
1 Es 10 21 of the sons of Harim, Maasia and Elia
26 and Abdi and Jerimoth and Elia. And of the
Eliab Num 1 9 Eliab the son of Helon. And of the
Num 2 7 the prince was Eliab. 10:16
7 24 Eliab the son of Helon offered a silver
29 this is the oblation of Eliab the son
16 1 Dathan and Abiron the sons of Eliab. 12; Deut 11:6
26 8 the son of Phallu was Eliab. His sons
1 K 16 6 when they were come in, he saw Eliab
17 13 Eliab the first born and the second
28 when E. his eldest brother heard this
1 Pa 2 13 Isai begot Eliab his firstborn, the
6 27 Nahath his son, Eliab his son, Jeroham
12 9 Eliab the third, Masmana the fourth
15 18 Eliab and Banaias and Maasias and
20 Eliab and Maasias and Banaias sung
16 5 Eliab and Banaias and Obededom: and

2 Pa 11 18 Abihail the daughter of Eliab the son
Eliaba 2 K 23 32 Eliaba of Salaboni. The sons of
1 Pa 11 32 Azmoth a Bauramite, Eliaba a Salabonite
Eliachim 2 Es 12 40 priests, Eliachim, Maasia
Jdth 4 5 Eliachim the priest wrote to all that
6 Eliachim had appointed them. And all
10 Eliachim the high priest of the Lord
Eliacim 4 K 18 18 there went out to them Eliacim
4 K 18 26 then Eliacim the son of Helcias and
37 Eliacim the son of Helcias who was over
19 2 he sent Eliacim who was over the house
23 34 Pharao Nechao made Eliacim the son of
Isa 22 20 I will call my servant Eliacim the
36 3 there went out to him Eliacim the son
11 E. and Sobna and Joahe said to Rabsaces
22 Eliacim the son of Helcias that was over
37 2 he [Ezechias] sent Eliacim who was
Mat 1 13 Abiud begot E. E. begot Azor. And Azor
Eliada 3 K 11 23 adversary, Razon the son of E.
1 Pa 3 8 Elisama and Eliada and Elipheleth
2 Pa 17 17 after him was E. valiant in battle
Eliakim 2 Pa 36 4 he made E. his brother king
Elial 1 Pa 8 20 and Elial and Adaia and Baraia
Eliam 2 K 11 3 Bethsabee the daughter of Eliam
2 K 23 24 Eliam the son of Achitophel the Gelonite
Elias 3 K 17 1 Elias the Thesbite of inhabitants
3 K 17 13 Elias said to her: Fear not, but go
15 did according to the word of Elias
16 which he spoke in the hand of Elias
18 she said to Elias: What have I to do
19 Elias said to her: Give me thy son
22 the Lord heard the voice of Elias
23 Elias took the child and brought him
24 the woman said to Elias: Now, by this
18 1 word of the Lord came to Elias. 21:28
2 Elias went to show himself to Achab
7 and said: Art thou my lord Elias? And
8 tell thy master: Elias is here. 11, 14
15 Elias said: As the Lord of hosts liveth
16 and Achab came to meet Elias. And when
21 and Elias coming to all the people
22 and Elias said again to the people
25 then Elias said to the prophets of Baal
27 Elias jested at them, saying: Cry out
30 Elias said to all the people: Come ye
36 Elias the prophet came near and said
40 Elias said to them: Take the prophets
40 Elias brought them down to the torrent
41 Elias said to Achab: Go up, eat and
42 Elias went up to the top of Carmel
46 the hand of the Lord was upon Elias
19 1 told Jezabel all that Elias had done
2 Jezabel sent a messenger to Elias saying
3 then Elias was afraid, and rising up
9 what dost thou here, Elias. 13
13 when Elias heard it, he covered his face
19 Elias departing . . . found Eliseus
19 when Elias came up to him he cast
20 left the oxen and ran after Elias
21 followed Elias and ministered to him
21 20 Achab said to Elias: Hast thou found
4 K 1 3 angel of the Lord spoke to Elias. 15
4 shalt surely die. And Elias went away
8 and he said: It is Elias the Thesbite
10 Elias answering, said to the captain
12 Elias answering, said: If I be a man
13 he fell upon his knees before Elias
17 word of the Lord which Elias spoke
2 1 when the Lord would take up Elias
1 Elias and Eliseus were going from Galgal
2 Elias said to Eliseus: Stay thou here
4 Elias said to Eliseus: Stay here because
6 Elias said to him: Stay here because the
8 Elias took his mantle and folded it
9 Elias said to Eliseus: Ask what thou
11 Elias went up by a whirlwind into
13 and he took up the mantle of Elias
14 struck the waters with mantle of Elias
14 he said: Where is now the God of Elias
15 spirit of E. hath rested upon Eliseus
3 11 who poured water on the hands of Elias
9 36 which he spoke by his servant Elias
10 10 spoke in the hand of his servant Elias
17 word of Lord, which he spoke by Elias
2 Pa 21 12 was a letter brought him from Elias
Eccu 48 1 Elias the prophet stood up as a fire
4 was Elias magnified in his wondrous
13 Elias was indeed covered with the
Mala 4 5 I will send you Elias the prophet
1 Ma 2 58 Elias . . . was taken up into heaven
Mat 11 14 he is Elias that is to come. He that
16 14 some John the Baptist and other some E.
17 3 appeared . . . Moses and Elias. Mark 9:3
4 and one for Elias. Mark 9:4; Luke 9:33
10 that Elias must come first. Mark 9:10
11 Elias indeed shall come and restore all
12 Elias is already come and they know
27 47 heard, said: This man calleth Elias
49 let us see whether Elias will come to
Mark 6 15 others said: It is Elias. But others
8 28 John the Baptist; but some E. Luke 9:19
9 11 Elias, when he shall come first, shall
12 I say to you that Elias also is come
15 35 hearing, said: Behold he calleth Elias
36 let us see if Elias come to take him
Luke 1 17 before him in spirit and power of Elias
4 25 were many widows in the days of Elias
26 to none of them was Elias sent, but to
9 8 by other some, that Elias had appeared
30 they were Moses and Elias, appearing in
John 1 21 art thou Elias? And he said: I am not
25 if thou be not Christ nor Elias nor
Rom 11 2 what the scripture saith of Elias
James 5 17 Elias was a man passible like unto us
Eliasaph Num 1 14 Eliasaph the son of Duel. Of
Num 2 14 in the tribe of Gad the prince was E.
3 24 Eliasaph the son of Lael. And their
7 42 Eliasaph the son of Duel offered a
10 20 the prince was Eliasaph the son of Duel
Eliasib 1 Pa 24 12 the eleventh to Eliasib, the
1 Es 10 6 chamber of Johanan the son of Eliasib
24 of the singing men, Eliasib: and of
27 of the sons of Zethua, Elioenai, E.
36 of the sons of Bani, Maaddi . . . E.
2 Es 3 1 then Eliasib the high priest arose
20 the door of the house of Eliasib. 21
21 to the end of the house of Eliasib
12 10 Joacim begot E., and E. begot Joiada
22 in the days of Eliasib and Joiada
23 unto days of Jonathan the son of E.
13 4 over this thing was Eliasib the priest
7 evil that Eliasib had done for Tobias
28 Joiada the son of Eliasib the high
Eliasub 1 Pa 3 24 sons of Elioenai, Oduia and E.
Eliatha 1 Pa 25 4 the sons of Heman . . . Eliatha
1 Pa 25 27 the twentieth [lot] to Eliatha, to his
Elica 2 K 23 25 Elica of Harodi, Heles of Phalti
Elicians Jdth 1 6 Erioch king of the Elicians
Elidad Num 34 21 of the tribe of Benjamin, E.
Eliel 1 Pa 5 24 Eliel and Esriel and Jeremia and
1 Pa 6 34 Jeroham the son of Eliel, the son of
8 22 Eliel and Abdon and . . . sons of Sesac
11 46 Eliel a Mahumite and Jeribai and Josaia
46 Eliel and Obed and Jasiel of Masobia
12 11 Eliel the seventh, Johanan the eighth
15 9 of the sons of Hebron, Eliel the chief

11 Semeia, Eliel and Aminadab: and he said
2 Pa 31 13 Jozabad and Eliel and Jesmachias
Eliezer Gen 15 2 of my house is this Damascus E.
Exod 2 22 whom he called Eliezer, saying: For
18 4 the other Eliezer: For the God of my
1 Pa 7 8 sons of Bechor . . . Eliezer and Elioenai
15 24 Banaias and Eliezer the priests, sounded
23 15 sons of Moses were Gersom and Eliezer
17 the sons of Eliezer were: Rohobia the
17 and Eliezer had no more sons. But the
26 25 Eliezer, whose son Rohobia, and his son
27 16 over the Rubenites, Eliezer the son of
2 Pa 20 37 Eliezer the son of Dodau of Maresa
1 Es 8 16 so I sent Eliezer and Ariel and Semeias
10 18 his brethren Maasia and Eliezer and
23 the sons of the Levites . . . Eliezer
31 of the sons of Herem, Eliezer, Josue
Luke 3 29 Eliezer who was of Jorim, who was of
Elihoreph 3 K 4 3 E. and Ahia, the sons of Sisa
Elim Exod 15 27 children of Israel came into Elim
Exod 16 1 they set forward from Elim and all the
1 desert of Sin, which is between E. and
Num 33 9 they came into Elim where there were
Isa 15 8 unto the well of Elim the cry thereof
Elimelech Ruth 1 2 he was named E., and his wife
Ruth 1 3 Elimelech the husband of Noemi died
2 1 her husband Elimelech had a kinsman
3 Booz, who was of the kindred of E.
4 3 that belonged to our brother Elimelech
Elimelech's Ruth 4 9 I have bought all that was E.
Elioda 2 K 5 16 Elisama and Elioda and Eliphaleth
Elioenai 1 Pa 3 23 the sons of Naaria, Elioenai
1 Pa 3 24 the sons of Elioenai, Oduia and Eliasub
7 8 Elioenai and Amai and Jerimoth and
8 20 Elioenai and Selethai and Eliel and
26 3 Johanan the sixth, Elioenai the seventh
1 Es 10 22 of the sons of Pheshur, Elioenai, Maasia
27 of the sons of Zethua, Elioenai, Eliasib
2 Es 12 40 E., Zacharia, Hanania with trumpets and
Eliphal 1 Pa 11 35 Eliphal the son of Ur, Hepher
Eliphalet 1 Pa 8 39 the second and E. the third
1 Pa 14 5 born to him [David] . . . Eliphalet. 7
Eliphaleth 2 K 5 16 and Elioda and Eliphaleth
1 Pa 3 7 Jebaar also and Elisama and Eliphaleth
Eliphalu 1 Pa 15 18 Mathathias and Eliphalu. 21
Eliphaz Gen 36 4 Ada bore Eliphaz: Basemath bore
Gen 36 10 Eliphaz the son of Ada the wife of
11 and Eliphaz had sons: Theman, Omar
12 concubine of Eliphaz the son of Esau
15 sons of Eliphaz the firstborn of Esau
16 these are the sons of Eliphaz in the
1 Pa 1 35 sons of Esau: Eliphaz, Rahuel, Jehus
36 sons of Eliphaz: Theman, Omar, Sephi
Job 2 11 Eliphaz the Themanite and Baldad. 42:9
4 1 E. the Themanite answered. 15:1; 22:1
42 7 he said to Eliphaz the Themanite: My
Eliphelet 2 K 23 34 Eliphelet the son of Aasbai
1 Es 8 13 these are their names: Eliphelet and
10 33 Eliphelet, Jermai, Manasse, Semei
Elipheleth 1 Pa 3 8 and Eliada and E., nine: all
Elisa Gen 10 4 sons of Javan: Elisa and Tharsis
1 Pa 1 7 sons of Javan: E. and Tharsis, Cethim
Eze 27 7 blue and purple from the islands of E.
Elisama Num 1 10 E. the son of Ammiud. 2:10; Num 7:48, 53
Num 10 22 in whose army the prince was Elisama
2 K 5 16 Japhia and Elisama and Elioda and
4 K 25 25 Nathanias the son of Elisama of the
1 Pa 2 41 Icamia begot Elisama. Now the sons of
3 6 daughter of Ammiel. Jebaar also and E.
8 Elisama and Eliada and Elipheleth, nine
7 26 Ammiud, who begot Elisama, of whom was
14 7 born to him [David] . . . Elisama and
2 Pa 17 8 with them Elisama and Joram priests
Jer 36 12 princes sat there, Elisama the scribe
20 in the chamber of Elisama the scribe
21 bringing it out of the chamber of E.
41 1 Nathanias the son of Elisama of the
Elisaphan Lev 10 4 Moses called Misael and E.
Num 3 30 their prince shall be Elisaphan the
34 25 of the tribe of Zabulon, Elisaphan
1 Pa 15 8 of the sons of Elisaphan. 2 Pa 29:13
Elisaphat 2 Pa 23 1 captains of hundreds . . . E.
Eliseus 3 K 19 16 E. son of Saphat, of Abelmeula
3 K 19 17 shall be slain by Eliseus. And I will
4 K 2 1 Elias and Eliseus were going from Galgal
2 Elias said to Eliseus: Stay thou here
2 Eliseus said to him: As the Lord liveth
3 came forth to Eliseus and said to him
4 Elias said to Eliseus: Stay here because
5 that were at Jericho, came to Eliseus
9 Elias said to Eliseus: Ask what thou
9 Eliseus said: I beseech thee that in
12 Eliseus saw him and cried: My father
14 and Eliseus passed over. And the sons
15 spirit of Elias hath rested upon E.
19 the men of the city said to Eliseus
22 according to the word of Eliseus, which
3 11 here is Eliseus the son of Saphat, who
13 and Eliseus said to the king of Israel
14 Eliseus said to him: As the Lord of
4 1 cried to Eliseus, saying: Thy servant
2 Eliseus said to her: What wilt thou
8 a day when Eliseus passed by Sunam
17 at the same hour that Eliseus had said
32 Eliseus therefore went into the house
38 and Eliseus returned to Galgal and
5 8 Eliseus the man of God had heard this
9 stood at door of the house of Eliseus
10 and Eliseus sent a messenger to him
25 Eliseus said: Whence comest thou, Giezi
6 1 the sons of the prophets said to E.
12 Eliseus the prophet, that is in Israel
17 Eliseus prayed and said: Lord, open
17 chariots of fire round about Eliseus
18 according to the word of Eliseus. And
18 Eliseus prayed to the Lord, saying
19 E. said to them: This is not the way
20 Eliseus said: Lord, open the eyes
21 king of Israel said to Eliseus when he
31 if the head of Eliseus son of Saphat
32 but Eliseus sat in his house and the
7 1 Eliseus said: Hear ye the word of the
8 1 Eliseus spoke to the woman whose son
4 the great things that Eliseus hath done
5 her son whom Eliseus raised to life
7 Eliseus also came to Damascus and
10 Eliseus said to him: Go tell him: Thou
13 Eliseus said: The Lord hath shown me
14 when he was departed from Eliseus
14 what saith Eliseus to thee? And he
9 1 Eliseus the prophet called one of the
13 14 Eliseus was sick of the illness whereof
15 Eliseus said to him: Bring a bow and
16 Eliseus put his hands over the king's
17 Eliseus said: Shoot an arrow. And he
17 Eliseus said: The arrow of the Lord's
20 and Eliseus died and they buried him
21 cast the body into the sepulcher of E.
21 when it had touched the bones of E.
Eccu 48 13 his spirit was filled up in Eliseus
Luke 4 27 many lepers . . . in the time of Eliseus
Elisua 2 K 5 15 Jebahar and Elisua and Nepheg
1 Pa 14 5 Elisua and Eliphalet and Noga and
Elisur Num 1 5 Elisur the son of Sedeur. Of Simeon
Num 2 10 prince shall be Elisur the son of Sedeur

38 23 worker in tapestry and embroidery in
39 28 and a girdle . . . of embroidery work
Eze 16 10 and I clothed thee with embroidery
Emer 1 Es 2 59 Cherub and Adon and Emer. And they
emerald Exod 28 17 sardius stone, a topaz and an e.
39 10 row was a sardius, a topaz, an emerald
Tob 13 21 shall be built of sapphire and of e.
Eccu 32 8 as a signet of an emerald in a work of
Eze 28 13 thy covering . . . carbuncle and the e.
Apoc 4 3 in sight like unto an emerald. And
21 19 the fourth an e.: the fifth, sardonyx
emeralds Jdth 10 19 with e. and precious stones
emerods 1 K 5 6 Azotus and the coasts there with e.
1 K 5 9 they had emerods in their secret parts
12 were afflicted with the emerods: and
6 5 you shall make five golden emerods and
5 make the likeness of your emerods and
11 the likeness of the emerods. And the kine
17 these are the golden emerods which the
Emim Gen 14 5 the Emim in Save of Cariathaim
Emims Deut 2 10 the E. first were the inhabitants
Deut 2 11 but the Moabites call them Emims. The
eminent Job 28 18 e. things shall not be mentioned
Isa 57 15 thus saith the High and the Eminent
Eze 17 22 it on a mountain high and eminent. On the
emissary Lev 16 8 to be the emissary goat. 10
Lev 16 26 that hath let go the emissary goat
Emmanuel Isa 7 14 his name shall be called E.
Isa 8 8 fill breadth of thy land, O Emmanuel
Mat 1 23 they shall call his name Emmanuel
Emmaus 1 Ma 3 40 pitched near E. in the plain
1 Ma 3 57 pitched on the south side of Emmaus
4 3 the king's forces that were in Emmaus
Luke 24 13 to a town . . . named Emmaus. And they
Emmer 1 Pa 9 12 Mosollamith the son of Emmer
1 Pa 24 14 the sixteenth to Emmer, the seventeenth
1 Es 2 37 the children of Emmer, 1,052. 2 Es 7:40
10 20 of the sons of Emmer, Hanani and Zebedia
2 Es 3 29 Sadoc the son of Emmer over against
7 61 that came up from . . . Emmer: and could
11 13 Mosollamoth the son of Emmer, and their
Jer 20 1 Phassur the son of Emmer, the priest
Emona Josu 18 24 town Emona and Ophini and Gabee
Emor Judg 9 28 ruler over the men of Emor the
emperor Esth 3 2 so the e. had commanded them
empire 1 K 2 10 he shall give empire to his king
1 Pa 16 28 bring ye to the Lord glory and empire
29 12 the empire of all things. Now therefore
Jdth 2 3 to bring all the earth under his empire
Esth 1 20 though all the provinces of thy empire
8 13 subject to the empire of king Assuerus
10 2 his empire and the dignity and greatness
13 1 provinces that are subject to his e.
7 may restore to our empire the peace
Isa 9 7 his empire shall be multiplied and there
45 25 in the Lord are my justices and empire
Eze 30 6 pride of her e. shall be brought down
Dan 6 26 in all my empire and my kingdom all
11 19 shall turn his face to e. of his own
1 Tim 6 16 to whom be honor and empire everlasting
Heb 2 14 destroy him who had the e. of death
1 P 4 11 to whom is glory and empire forever
5 11 to him be glory and empire. Apoc 1:6
Jude 25 empire and power before all ages, and
employed Gen 34 5 and e. in feeding the cattle
Ps 76 13 and will be employed in thy inventions
118 23 thy servant was e. in thy justifications
78 but I will be e. in thy commandments
Wisd 14 19 willing to please him that employed him
Eze 22 6 hath employed his arm in thee to shed
2 Ma 4 20 was employed for the making of galleys
Acts 17 21 employed themselves in nothing else
employing 2 P 1 5 employing all care, minister in

emptied Job 14 11 an e. river should be dried up
Ps 74 9 but the dregs thereof are not emptied
Phil 2 7 emptied himself, taking the form of a
empty Gen 1 2 the earth was void and empty, and
Exod 3 21 you shall not depart empty: but every
27 8 empty and hollow in the inside, as it
34 20 shalt thou appear before me empty
38 7 hollow, of boards, and empty within
Deut 15 13 thou shalt not let him go away empty
16 16 no one shall appear with his hands empty
Judg 7 16 empty pitchers and lamps within the
Ruth 1 21 the Lord hath brought me back empty
3 17 I will not have thee return empty to
1 K 6 3 send it not away empty, but render
20 19 for thy seat will be empty till after
25 David's place appeared empty. 27
2 K 1 22 the sword of Saul did not return empty
4 K 4 3 neighbors empty vessels not a few
2 Es 5 13 may he be shaken out and become empty
Jdth 1 11 sent them back empty and rejected them
Job 7 3 so I also have had empty months, and
22 9 thou hast sent widows away empty, and
26 7 out of the north over the empty space
Ps 7 5 let me deservedly fall empty before my
106 9 he hath satisfied the empty soul and
Prov 14 4 there are no oxen, the crib is empty
Eccu 29 12 and send him not away empty handed
35 6 not appear empty in the sight of the
Isa 29 8 when he is awake, his soul is empty
8 faint with thirst and his soul is empty
32 6 to make empty the soul of the hungry
Jer 14 3 they carried back their vessels empty
48 12 shall empty his vessels and break their
51 34 he hath made me as an empty vessel: he
Eze 24 11 set it empty upon burning coals, that it
Mat 12 44 findeth it empty, swept and garnished
Mark 12 3 sent him away empty. Luke 20:10, 11
Luke 1 53 and the rich he hath sent empty away
2 P 1 8 they will make you to be neither empty
emulation Num 11 29 why hast thou e. for me? O
Ps 36 8 leave rage; have no e. to do evil
Rom 11 14 I may provoke to emulation them who
2 C 9 2 and your e. hath provoked very many
emulations Gal 5 20 e., wraths, quarrels
emulous Ps 36 1 be not emulous of evildoers: nor
Rom 11 11 Gentiles, that they may be e. of them
Enac Num 13 23 Sisai and Tholmai the sons of Enac
Num 13 29 walled. We saw there the race of Enac
34 certain monsters of the sons of Enac
Josu 15 13 Cariath-Arbe the father of Enac, which
14 Ahiman and Tholmai of the race of E.
21 11 the city of Arbe the father of Enac
Judg 1 20 destroyed out of it the three sons of E.
Enacims Deut 1 28 we have seen the sons of the E.
Deut 2 10 like the race of the Enacims they were
11 were like the sons of the Enacims. But
21 and of tall stature, like the Enacims
9 2 great and tall, the sons of the Enacims
Josu 11 21 Josue came and cut off the Enacims from
22 he left not any of the stock of the E.
14 12 wherein are the Enacims, and cities
15 Adam the greatest among the Enacims
Enadad 2 Es 3 18 Bavai the son of Enadad, lord of
Enaim Josu 15 34 Taphua and Enaim and Jerimoth
Enan Num 1 15 Ahira the son of Enan. 2:29; 7:78, 83; 10:27
Num 34 9 as Zephrona and the village of Enan
10 from village of Enan unto Sephama
Jdth 8 1 Melchias the son of Enan the son of
Eze 47 17 from the sea even to the court of Enan
48 1 court of Enan the border of Damascus
encamp Exod 14 2 encamp over against Phihahiroth
Exod 14 2 Beelsephon: you shall encamp before it

Num 1 50 shall encamp round about the tabernacle
10 31 knowest in what places we should encamp
Ps 33 8 angel of the Lord shall e. round about
encamped Exod 13 20 Socoth they encamped in Etham
Exod 14 9 found them encamped at the seaside: all
15 27 trees: and they encamped by the waters
17 1 encamped in Raphidim, where there was
Num 2 5 the tribe of Issachar encamped, whose
21 13 left and encamped over against Arnon
22 1 and encamped in the plains of Moab
1 K 13 16 the Philistines encamped in Machmas
26 3 Saul encamped in Gabaa Hachila, which
1 Pa 11 15 Philistines e. in the valley of Raphaim
1 Ma 7 39 and encamped near to Bethoron: and an
11 65 Simon encamped against Bethsura, and
67 army encamped by the water of Genesar
encamping Num 33 2 according to places of their e.
enchanter Eccu 12 13 who will pity an e. struck by
enchanters 2 Pa 33 6 with him magicians and e.
Isa 47 9 for the great hardness of thy enchanters
12 stand now with thy enchanters and with
Dan 5 11 him prince of the wise men, enchanters
enchantments Exod 7 11 they also by Egyptian e.
Exod 7 22 with their e. did in like manner. 8:7
8 18 magicians with their e. practiced in
Wisd 18 13 anything before by reason of the e.
Isa 8 19 of diviners, who mutter in their e.
Apoc 18 23 deceived by thy enchantments. And in
enclosed Exod 39 13 set and e. in gold by their
Num 22 24 wherewith the vineyards were enclosed
2 Pa 11 11 when he had enclosed them with walls
Job 7 12 thou hast enclosed me in a prison
Prov 8 27 and compass he enclosed the depths
Cant 4 12 my sister, my spouse, is a garden e.
Luke 5 6 enclosed a very great multitude of
encompass Exod 40 8 e. the court with hangings
Ps 31 10 mercy shall e. him that hopeth in the
47 13 surround Sion and encompass her: tell
48 6 the iniquity of my heel shall e. me
Eze 16 57 that encompass thee on all sides. Thou
Zach 9 8 I will e. my house with them that serve
encompassed 1 K 23 26 Saul and his men e. David
2 Pa 13 13 he e. Juda, who perceived it not, with
Ps 17 6 the sorrows of hell encompassed me: and
21 17 many dogs have e. me: the council of
31 7 refuge from the trouble which hath e. me
118 61 the cords of the wicked have e. me: but
Isa 50 11 e. with flames, walk in the light of
Eze 4 8 I have encompassed thee with bands: and
40 17 thirty chambers e. the pavement. And
2 Ma 12 13 strong city, e. with bridges and walls
Apoc 20 8 and encompassed the camp of the saints
encompasseth Eccu 43 13 it e. the heaven about with
encountered 2 Ma 15 26 e. them, calling upon God
encourage Deut 1 38 exhort and encourage him, and
Deut 3 28 command Josue and e. and strengthen him
2 K 11 25 encourage thy warriors against the city
Wisd 18 8 so thou didst also e. and glorify us
encouraged 2 Pa 23 1 Joiada being e., took the
2 Pa 32 8 the people were encouraged with these
Isa 41 7 encouraged him that forged at that
1 Ma 12 50 e. one another and went out ready for
2 Ma 8 21 were greatly e. and disposed even to
15 10 after he had encouraged them, he showed
encouraging Exod 32 18 not cry of men e. to fight
Josu 8 16 encouraging one another, pursued them
Job 39 25 the encouraging of the captains, and
end Gen 6 13 the end of all flesh is come before
Gen 23 9 which he hath in the end of his field
47 21 to the other end thereof. Deut 4:32; Jer 12:12
Exod 23 16 the feast also in the end of the year
36 24 where the mortises of the sides end
Num 23 10 just, and my last end be like to them
34 5 shall end in the shore of the great sea
6 and the same shall be the end thereof
Deut 31 30 canticle, and finished it even to end
32 20 consider what their last end shall be
29 and would provide for their last end
Josu 15 5 salt sea even to the end of the Jordan
8 in the end of the valley of Raphaim
18 19 salt sea at the south end of the Jordan
Judg 19 27 that he might end the journey he had
Ruth 3 18 will we see what end the thing will
1 K 3 12 I will begin, and I will make an end
9 27 were going down in the end of the city
14 27 and he put forth the end of the rod
43 a little honey with the end of the rod
2 K 3 25 to this end he [Abner] came to thee
3 K 1 41 and now the feast was at an end: Joab
2 Pa 2 6 to this end only, that incense may be
6 19 to this end only it is made, that thou
8 1 at the end of 20 years after Solomon
2 Es 3 21 to the end of the house of Eliasib
4 2 sacrifice and make an end in a day
6 6 for which end thou hast also set up
Tob 3 12 when she was making an end of her prayer
Jdth 7 17 that our end may be short by the edge
16 3 Lord putteth an end to wars, the Lord
Job 6 11 or what is my end that I should keep
7 2 hireling looketh for the end of his
12 17 bringeth counsellors to a foolish end
20 7 in the end he shall be destroyed like
26 10 till light and darkness come to an end
28 3 the end of all things he considereth
34 36 let Job be tried even to the end: cease
Ps 9 11 away his face not to see to the end
19 man shall not be forgotten to the end
15 11 right hand are delights even to the end
18 7 his going out is from the end of heaven
7 his circuit even to the end thereof
29 13 to the end that my glory may sing to
37 7 and am bowed down even to the end: I
38 5 O Lord, make me know my end. And what
43 23 arise, and cast us not off to the end
45 10 wars to cease even to end of the earth
64 1 to the end, a psalm of David. The
73 19 forget not to the end the souls of
118 96 I have seen an end of all perfection
134 7 up clouds from the end of the earth
Prov 5 4 but her end is bitter as wormwood, and
14 13 mourning taketh hold of the end of joy
20 21 in the end shall be without a blessing
23 32 in the end, it will bite like a snake
24 14 thou shalt have hope in the end, and
Ecce 3 11 God hath made from beginning to the end
7 3 we are put in mind of the end of all
9 better is the end of a speech than the
9 12 man knoweth not his own end: but as
10 13 end of his talk is a mischievous error
Wisd 2 1 in the end of a man there is no remedy
5 there is no going back of our end: for
17 we shall know what his end shall be
4 17 they shall see the end of the wise man
5 4 esteemed . . . their end without honor
8 1 reacheth therefore from end to end
11 14 wondering at the end of what was come
15 him they admired in the end when they
12 22 to the end that when we judge we may
27 end also of their condemnation came
14 14 shall be found to come shortly to an e.
27 the beginning and end of all evil. For
16 3 to the end that they indeed desiring
18 21 and put an end to the calamity, showing
19 1 even to the end there came upon them
4 a necessity . . . brought them to this end

Eccu 1 19 in days of his end he shall be blessed
7 40 in all thy works remember thy last end
10 15 and it shall ruin him in the end
11 29 in the end of a man is the disclosing
14 19 one cometh to an end, and another is
20 that is corruptible shall fall in end
16 22 the examination of all is in the end
18 10 hath known their end that it is evil
21 10 the end of them is a flame of fire
11 in their end is hell and darkness and
22 9 in the end of the discourse he saith
31 4 in the end he is still poor. He that
26 in the end thou shalt find my words
33 24 when thou shalt end the days of thy
36 10 hasten the time, and remember the end
40 2 and the day of their end: from him
14 transgressors shall pine away in the end
43 28 is established the end of their journey
46 22 the end of his life. 23; 47:12
47 26 Solomon had an end with his fathers
31 them, and put an end to all their sins
51 19 unto the very end I will seek after her
Isa 5 8 even to the end of the place: shall you
13 5 afar off, from the end of heaven: the
16 4 the dust is at an end, the wretch is
22 1 to year: the solemnities are at an end
32 10 the vintage is at an end, the gathering
38 12 my generation is at an end, and it is
12 thou wilt make an end of me. 13
40 2 for her evil is come to an end, her
Jer 1 3 end of the eleventh year of Sedecias
5 31 what then shall be done in the end
12 4 said: He shall not see our last end
25 33 of the earth even to the other end
29 11 to give you an end and patience. And
31 17 there is hope for thy last end, saith
34 14 at the end of seven years, let ye go
44 27 famine, till there be an end of them
51 13 end is come for thy entire destruction
Lam 1 9 and she hath not remembered her end
3 18 my end and my hope is perished from
4 18 our end draweth near: our days are fulfilled, for our end is come
Bar 3 7 for this end thou hast put thy fear in
Eze 3 16 at the end of seven days the word of
7 2 the end is come upon the four quarters
3 now is an end come upon thee, and I
6 an end is come, the end is come, it
11 13 an end of all the remnant of Israel
22 15 I will put an end to thy uncleanness
23 27 I will put an end to thy wickedness
29 13 at the end of forty years I will gather
30 13 I will make an end of the idols of
38 8 at the end of years thou shalt come to
Dan 2 18 to the end that they should ask mercy
4 26 at the end of twelve months he was
31 at the end of the days I Nabuchodonosor
7 26 in pieces and perish even to the end
28 hitherto is the end of the word. I
8 17 in the time of the end the vision shall
19 to pass in the end of the malediction: for the time hath its end
9 24 and sin may have an end, and iniquity
26 the end thereof shall be waste, and
26 after the end of the war the appointed
27 even to the consummation and to the end
11 6 after the end of years they shall be
13 in the end of times and years, he shall
27 as yet the end is unto another time
12 6 shall it be to the end of these wonders
Amos 1 11 and hath kept his wrath to the end
5 18 to what end is it for you? The day of
6 11 he shall answer: There is an end. And
8 2 the end is come upon my people Israel
Nah 1 8 will make an utter end of the place
9 he will make an utter end: these shall
Haba 1 4 and judgment cometh not to the end
2 3 it shall appear at the end and shall
Zach 9 10 even to the end of the earth. 1 Ma 14:10
1 Ma 1 51 to the end that they should forget the
2 13 to what end then should we live any
13 34 to the end that he should grant an
2 Ma 5 7 but received confusion at the end, for
7 1 for which end they were tormented with
9 24 to the end that if anything contrary
10 9 this was the end of Antiochus that was
13 he put an end to his life by poison
15 38 will here make an end of my narration
Mat 13 39 the harvest is the end of the world
40 so shall it be at end of the world. 49
21 41 bring those evil men to an evil end
24 6 the end is not yet. Mark 13:7; Luke 21:9
13 he that shall persevere to the end, he
26 58 that he [Peter] might see the end. And
28 1 in the end of the sabbath, when it
Mark 3 26 and cannot stand, but hath an end
Luke 1 33 of his kingdom there shall be no end
22 37 the things concerning me have an end
Acts 7 19 to the end that they might not be kept
21 27 the seven days were drawing to an end
26 16 to this end have I appeared to thee
Rom 6 6 to the end that we may serve sin no
21 ashamed? For the end of them is death
22 and the end life everlasting. For the
10 4 end of the law is Christ unto justice
14 9 to this end Christ died and rose again
1 C 15 24 afterwards the end, when he shall have
Phil 3 19 whose end is destruction; whose God is
1 Th 2 16 wrath of God is come upon them to the e.
1 Tim 1 5 the end of the commandment is charity
Heb 6 8 unto a curse, whose end is to be burnt
16 is the end of all their controversy
7 3 beginning of days nor end of life, but
8 13 and groweth old, is near its end
9 26 at the end of ages, he hath appeared
13 7 considering end of their conversation
James 5 11 and you have seen the end of the Lord
1 P 1 9 receiving the end of your faith, even
4 7 the end of all is at hand. Be prudent
17 end of them that believe not the gospel
Apoc 1 8 the beginning and the end. 21:6; 22:13

latter end Job 42 12 blessed the l. e. of Job
Prov 19 20 thou mayst be wise in thy latter end
23 18 thou shalt have hope in the latter end
Ecce 1 11 with them that shall be in the l. e.
Wisd 2 16 preferreth the latter end of the just
Eccu 1 13 it shall go well in the latter end and
2 3 thy life may be increased in the l. e.
3 10 his blessing may remain in the l. e.
6 29 in latter end thou shalt find rest in
30 1 that he may rejoice in his latter end
38 21 and remember the latter end. Forget
Isa 41 22 shall know the latter end of them and
47 7 hast thou remembered thy latter end
Jer 17 11 in his latter end he shall be a fool
Amos 8 10 the latter end thereof as a bitter day

made an end Num 16 31 made an end of speaking. Deut 20:9; 1 K 18:1; 24:17; 2 K 13:36; Jer 26:8; 43:1; 1 Ma 3:23
Deut 26 12 when thou hast made an end of tithing
Josu 19 49 had made an end of dividing the land
1 K 10 13 when he had made an end of prophesying
13 10 had made an end of offering. 2 K 6:18; 1 Pa 16:2
2 K 20 18 in Abela: and so they made an end
3 K 3 1 until he had made an end of building

8 54 when Solomon had made an end of praying
2 Pa 7 1 Solomon had made an end of his prayer
20 23 and when they had made an end of them
1 Es 10 17 they made an end with all the men that
Ps 118 87 they had almost made an end of me upon
Isa 33 1 thou shalt have made an end of spoiling
Jer 51 63 have made an end of reading this book
Eze 42 15 when he had made an end of measuring
43 23 shalt have made an end of the expiation
Amos 7 2 had made an end of eating the grass
Mat 11 1 Jesus had made an end of commanding
no end Job 16 3 shall windy words have no end
Ps 144 3 and of his greatness there is no end
Ecce 12 12 of making many books there is no end
Eccu 38 7 and of his works there shall be no end
Isa 2 7 and there is no end of their treasures
9 7 and there shall be no end of peace
Bar 3 18 and there is no end of their getting
25 it is great, and hath no end: it is
Nah 2 9 there is no end of the riches of all
3 3 there is no end of carcasses, and they
9 strength thereof, and there is no end
Luke 1 33 of his kingdom there shall be no end
one end Gen 47 21 from one end of the borders
Exod 26 28 the boards from one end to the other
Deut 4 32 from one end of heaven to the other **e.**
13 7 from one end of the earth to the other
4 K 10 21 was filled, from one end to the other
Jer 12 12 shall devour from one end of the land
25 33 from one end of the earth even to the
51 31 city is taken from one end to the other
unto the end Deut 11 12 beginning of year u. . . .
Ps 4 1 unto the end (and so at the beginning of many psalms)
9 7 words of enemy have failed unto the end
12 1 wilt thou forget me unto the end? How
17 36 hath corrected me unto the end: and thy
48 10 and shall still live unto the end. He
67 17 there the Lord shall dwell unto the end
73 1 why hast thou cast us off unto the end
3 hands against their pride unto the end
88 47 turnest thou away unto the end? Shall
Eccu 23 24 not be weary of sinning unto the end
Isa 57 16 neither will I be angry unto the end
Jer 3 5 or wilt thou continue unto the end
Dan 12 13 stand in thy lot unto end of the days
2 Ma 8 29 reconciled to his servants unto the end
Mat 10 22 he that shall persevere unto the end
Mark 13 13 he that shall endure unto the end, he
John 13 1 the world, he loved them unto the end
1 C 1 8 who also will confirm you unto the end
2 C 1 13 I hope that you shall know unto the end
Heb 3 6 confidence and glory of hope unto the end
14 beginning of his substance firm u. . . .
6 11 the accomplishing of hope unto the end
Apoc 2 26 keep my works unto the end, I will
endanger Dan 1 10 you shall e. my head to the king
endeavor 2 Pa 20 11 endeavor to cast us out of the
Job 6 27 you endeavor to overthrow your friend
13 8 do you endeavor to judge for God? Or
Jer 2 33 why dost thou endeavor to show thy way
2 Ma 11 19 I will endeavor to be a means of your
Luke 12 58 way, endeavor to be delivered from him
Acts 24 16 I endeavor to have always a conscience
2 P 1 15 I will e. that you frequently have
endeavored Gen 37 21 e. to deliver him out of
Judg 9 52 the gate, endeavored to set fire to it
1 K 19 10 Saul e. to nail David to the wall with
Jer 48 30 neither hath it e. to do according as
endeavorest Jer 49 16 e. to lay hold on the height
endeavoreth Judg 9 31 e. to set the city against
Wisd 15 9 he e. to do like the workers in brass
endeavoring 4 K 17 4 Osee e. to rebel had sent
Jdth 14 9 endeavoring by art to break his rest
endeavors Esth 9 25 that his e. might be made void
ended Gen 2 2 the seventh day God ended his work
Gen 24 15 he had not yet ended these words within
27 30 Isaac had scarce ended his words, when
49 32 when he had ended the commandments
Exod 7 25 and seven days were fully ended, after
31 18 he had ended these words. Judg 15:17; 2 Ma 9:5
Deut 32 45 [Moses] ended all these words, speaking
34 8 they mourned for Moses were ended
Josu 6 8 when Josue had ended his words, and the
16 3 countries of it are ended by the great
3 K 9 10 when 20 years were ended after Solomon
4 K 8 3 when the 7 years were ended, the woman
10 25 when the burnt offering was ended, that
1 Pa 17 11 when thou shalt have ended thy days
2 Pa 18 34 and the fight was ended that day: but
21 19 bowels, his disease ended with his life
29 29 when the oblation was ended, the king
34 helped them till the work was ended
Tob 4 5 when she also shall have ended the time
14 1 and the words of Tobias were ended
Jdth 6 16 so when their weeping was ended, and
Job 10 20 fewness of my days be ended shortly
Ps 71 20 praises of David the son of Jesse are **e.**
Wisd 4 16 youth soon ended, the long life of the
Isa 24 8 noise of them that rejoice is ended
13 or grapes, when the vintage is ended
60 20 the days of thy mourning shall be ended
Jer 8 20 harvest is past, the summer is ended
Eze 4 8 thou hast ended the days of thy siege
9 8 the slaughter being ended I was left
Dan 1 18 when the days were ended, after which
2 Ma 15 40 the readers. But here it shall be ended
Mat 7 28 when Jesus had fully ended. 19:1; 26:1
Luke 4 2 and when they were ended he was hungry
13 all the temptations being ended, the
Acts 19 21 these things were ended, Paul purposed
24 27 when two years were ended, Felix had
ending Gen 44 12 eldest and e. at the youngest
Wisd 7 18 beginning and e. and midst of the times
endless 1 Tim 1 4 to fables and e. genealogies
Endor Josu 17 11 inhabitants of Endor with the
1 K 28 7 that hath a divining spirit at Endor
Ps 82 11 who perished at Endor: and became as
endow Exod 22 16 shall e. her and have her to wife
endowed Gen 30 20 hath e. me with a good dowry
ends Exod 28 23 two ends at top of the rational
Exod 28 24 the rings that are in the ends thereof
25 ends of the chains themselves thou
37 8 two cherubims at the two ends of the
38 5 casting four rings at the four ends
Num 24 20 whose latter ends shall be destroyed
Deut 28 64 parts of the earth to the ends thereof
3 K 8 8 the ends of them were seen without in
2 Pa 5 9 ends of the staves wherewith the ark
Job 28 24 for he beholdeth the ends of the world
36 30 he shall cover also the ends of the sea
Ps 18 5 their words unto the ends of the world
72 17 understand concerning their last ends
Prov 14 12 the ends thereof lead to death. 16:25
Wisd 3 19 dreadful are the ends of a wicked race
Eze 15 4 fire hath consumed both ends thereof
Dan 4 8 the sight thereof was even to the ends
Rom 10 18 their words unto ends of whole world
1 C 10 11 upon whom the e. of the world are come
ends of the earth Deut 28 49 a nation from afar and from the uttermost e. . . .
Deut 33 17 push the nations even to the e. . . .
1 K 2 10 Lord shall judge the ends of the earth
Tob 13 13 ends of the earth shall worship thee
Job 37 3 his light is upon the ends of the earth

Ps 21 28 all the ends of the earth shall remember
47 11 thy praise unto the ends of the earth
58 14 will rule Jacob and all the e. . . .
60 3 to thee have I cried from ends of earth
64 6 art the hope of all the e. . . . and in
66 8 and all the ends of the earth fear him
71 8 from the river unto e. . . . Eccu 44:23
94 4 for in his hands are all the e. . . .
97 3 the ends of the earth have seen the
Prov 17 24 wise: the eyes of fools are in e. . . .
Wisd 6 2 learn ye that are judges of the e. . . .
Isa 5 26 will whistle to them from the e. . . .
24 16 from the e. . . . we have heard praises
26 15 thou hast removed all the e. . . . far
40 28 who hath created the ends of the earth
41 5 the ends of the earth were astonished
9 I have taken thee from the e. . . . and
42 10 new song, his praise is from the e. . . .
43 6 my daughters from the ends of the earth
44 23 shout with joy, ye ends of the earth
45 22 and you shall be saved, all ye e. . . .
48 20 and speak it out even to the e. . . .
52 10 e. . . . shall see the salvation of our
62 11 hath made it to be heard in the e. . . .
Jer 6 22 great nation shall rise from e. . . .
10 13 up the clouds from the e. . . . 51:16
16 19 Gentiles shall come from the e. . . .
25 31 the noise is come even to the e. . . .
32 whirlwind shall go forth from e. . . .
31 8 and will gather them from the e. . . .
50 41 many kings shall rise from the e. . . .
Dan 4 19 thy power unto the ends of the earth
Mich 5 4 he be magnified even to the e. . . .
1 Ma 1 3 he went through even to the e. . . .
8 4 that came against them from the e. . . .
Mat 12 42 forth from ends of the earth. Luke 11:31
endued 2 Pa 2 12 endued with understanding and
Eccu 44 3 power and endued with their wisdom
45 12 man, endued with judgment and truth
Luke 24 49 till you be endued with power from on
James 3 13 a wise man and endued with knowledge
endure Exod 10 7 how long shall we e. this scandal
2 K 7 29 house of thy servant, that it may e.
Tob 4 13 thy wife never e. to know a crime
Ps 88 30 I will make his seed to e. for evermore
37 David: his seed shall endure forever
103 31 may the glory of the Lord e. forever
Eccu 2 2 humble thy heart and endure: incline
3 join thyself to God and endure, that
4 and in thy sorrow endure, and in thy
12 14 begin to decline, he will not endure it
16 22 who shall declare? Or who shall endure
48 2 could not e. the commandments of the
Wisd 11 26 and how could anything endure, if thou
Bar 4 35 her from the Eternal, long to endure
Eze 22 14 shall thy heart endure or shall thy
2 Ma 9 10 no man could endure to carry, for the
Mark 13 13 he that shall endure unto the end, he
1 Th 1 4 in all tribulations which you endure
2 Tim 2 10 I endure all things for the sake of
4 3 they will not endure sound doctrine
Heb 12 20 they did not e. that which was said
1 P 2 19 if a man endure sorrows, suffering
20 and being buffeted for it, you endure
endured 3 K 2 26 and hast endured trouble in all the
troubles my father endured
Wisd 16 6 but thy wrath endured not forever, but
22 snow and ice endured the force of fire
17 16 he endured a necessity from which he
1 Ma 10 15 and the labors that they had endured
Acts 13 18 endured their manners in the desert
Rom 9 22 endured with much patience vessels of
2 Tim 3 11 what persecutions I endured, and out
Heb 10 32 you e. a great fight of afflictions
11 27 endured seeing him that is invisible
12 2 endured the cross, despising the shame
3 endured such opposition from sinners
James 5 11 we account them blessed who have e.
Apoc 2 3 patience, and hast e. for my name
endurest Ps 101 13 but thou, O Lord, e. forever
endureth 1 Pa 16 34 for his mercy endureth forever. 41;
2 Pa 5:13; 7:3, 6; 20:21; 1 Es 3:11; Jdth
13:21; Ps 99:5; 105:1; 106:1; 117:1, 2, 3,
4, 29; 135 *passim;* Jer 33:11; Dan 3:89;
1 Ma 4:24
Ps 137 8 thy mercy, O Lord, endureth forever
144 13 thy dominion endureth throughout all
Isa 40 8 the word of our Lord endureth forever
John 6 27 which perisheth, but for that which e.
1 C 13 7 hopeth all things, endureth all things
James 1 12 blessed is the man that e. temptation
1 P 1 25 the word of the Lord endureth forever
enduring Ps 18 10 fear of Lord is holy, e. forever
2 C 1 6 worketh the e. of the same sufferings
1 Th 1 3 enduring of the hope of our Lord Jesus
Heb 6 15 patiently e. he obtained the promise
Eneas Acts 9 33 named Eneas, who had kept his bed
Acts 9 33 E., the Lord Jesus Christ healeth thee
enemies' Lev 26 41 them into their e. land
Judg 7 11 go down more secure to the e. camp
21 round about the enemies' camp. So all
Bar 3 10 that thou art in thy enemies' land
enemy Mat 5 43 hate thy enemy. But I say to you
Mat 13 25 his e. came and oversowed cockle among
28 an enemy hath done this. And the
39 enemy that sowed them is the devil
Luke 10 19 tread . . . upon all the power of the e.
Acts 13 10 [Elymas] enemy of all justice, thou
Rom 8 7 wisdom of the flesh is an e. to God
12 20 if thy enemy be hungry, give him to eat
1 C 15 26 the e. death shall be destroyed last
Gal 4 16 am I then become your enemy, because
2 Th 3 15 yet do not esteem him as an enemy
James 4 4 friendship of this world is e. of God
4 becometh an enemy of God. O, do you
enemy's Exod 23 4 if thou meet thy e. ox or ass
Lev 26 35 when you shall be in the enemy's land
38 an enemy's land shall consume you
Deut 20 1 numbers of enemy's army greater than
Lam 1 7 when her people fell in the e. hand
Engaddi Josu 15 62 the city of salt and Engaddi
1 K 24 1 and dwelt in strongholds of Engaddi
2 David is in the desert of Engaddi
2 Pa 20 2 in Asasonthamar, which is Engaddi
Cant 1 13 in the vineyards of Engaddi. Behold
Eze 47 10 from Engaddi even to Engallim there
engaged Prov 6 1 e. fast thy hand to a stranger
2 Ma 15 19 that were to be engaged in battle
2 Tim 2 4 to whom he hath engaged himself. For he
engagement 2 Ma 10 29 were in the heat of the e.
Engallim Eze 47 10 from Engaddi even to Engallim
Engannim Josu 15 34 and Zanoe and Engannim and
Josu 19 21 Rameth and Engannim and Enhadda and
21 29 and Jaramoth and Engannim, with their
engendering Gal 4 24 e. unto bondage; which is
engine 1 Ma 13 44 that were within the e. leaped
engines Deut 20 20 cut them down and make engines
2 Pa 26 15 he made . . . engines of diverse kinds
Eze 21 22 to set engines against the gates, to
26 9 and he shall set engines of war and
1 Ma 5 30 carrying ladders and engines to take
6 20 they made battering slings and engines
31 they made engines: but they sallied
37 wooden towers . . . and e. upon them

51 set up there battering slings and e.
51 engines to cast stones and javelins
52 they also made e. against their e.
9 64 against it many days, and made engines
67 sallied out of the city and burnt the e.
11 20 made many engines of war against it
13 43 he made e. and set them to the city
15 25 assaulting it continually and making e.
2 Ma 12 15 who without any rams or e. of war threw
engrave Exod 28 11 shalt e. them with the names
engraved Exod 28 21 with 12 names shall they be e.
Exod 39 14 were engraved with the names of the
3 K 7 36 he engraved also in those plates, which
Eccu 45 14 wherein was e. Holiness, an ornament
engraven 3 K 7 36 that they seemed not to be e.
2 C 3 7 engraven with letters upon stones
engraver Exod 28 11 with the work of an engraver
engraver's Exod 28 36 shalt grave with e. work
engravers Jer 24 1 away . . . and e. of Jerusalem
Jer 29 2 and the engravers were departed out
engraving Exod 27 10 heads of which with their e.
Exod 27 11 their heads with their e. of silver
35 33 in e. stones and in carpenters' work
39 29 wrote on it with the e. of a lapidary
2 Pa 2 7 and that hath skill in engraving with
engravings 3 K 7 31 in corners . . . were divers e.
2 Pa 4 3 certain engravings on the outside
Enhadda Josu 19 21 Engannim and Enhadda and
enhanceth Eze 16 31 by disdain e. her price, but
Enhasor Josu 19 37 Enhasor and Jeron and Magdalel
enjoined Deut 24 5 public business be e. him
3 K 13 9 it was e. me by the word of the Lord
Heb 9 20 which God hath enjoined unto you. The
enjoy Gen 38 16 thou give me to enjoy my company
Exod 30 38 the like, to enjoy the smell thereof
Lev 26 34 then shall the land enjoy her sabbaths
43 shall enjoy her sabbaths, being desolate
Deut 8 9 and enjoy abundance of all things
28 41 shalt beget . . . and shalt not e. them
33 23 Nephtali shall enjoy abundance, and
Prov 1 33 shall enjoy abundance without fear of
7 18 let us enjoy the desired embraces till
Ecce 2 1 abound with delights and e. good things
5 17 drink and enjoy the fruit of his labor
18 to eat thereof, and to enjoy his portion
7 15 in the good day enjoy good things, and
Wisd 2 6 let us enjoy the good things that are
Eccu 3 7 honoreth his father shall enjoy a long
1 Tim 6 17 giveth us . . . all things to enjoy
Philem 20 may I enjoy thee in the Lord. Refresh
enjoyed Ecce 6 6 and hath not enjoyed good things
Rom 15 24 if . . . I shall have enjoyed you: but
enjoying Ecce 2 10 my heart from e. every pleasure
enkindle Jdth 8 12 stir up wrath and e. indignation
enkindled Exod 32 11 Lord, is thy indignation e.
Exod 22 24 my rage shall be enkindled and I will
Num 11 10 wrath of the Lord was exceedingly e.
Deut 29 20 his wrath . . . should be exceedingly e.
2 K 6 7 indignation of Lord was e. against Oza
2 Pa 32 25 and wrath was enkindled against him
1 Es 7 23 lest his wrath should be e. against the
Ps 73 1 why is thy wrath e. against the sheep
123 3 when their fury was enkindled against
Jer 7 20 my indignation is e. against this
1 Ma 13 7 spirit of the people was enkindled
enlarge Gen 9 27 may God enlarge Japheth, and may
2 K 22 37 thou shalt enlarge my steps under me
1 Pa 4 10 thou wilt bless me and wilt enlarge my
Ps 118 32 when thou didst enlarge my heart
Eccu 50 5 he prevailed to enlarge the city, and
Isa 54 2 enlarge the place of thy tent and
Amos 1 13 of Galaad to enlarge his border. And I
Mich 1 16 enlarge thy baldness as the eagle
Mat 23 5 they . . . enlarge their fringes. And
enlarged Exod 34 24 and shall have e. thy borders. Deut 12:20; 19:8
1 K 2 1 my mouth is enlarged over my enemies
Ps 4 2 was in distress, thou hast enlarged me
17 37 thou hast enlarged my steps under me
117 5 the Lord heard me and enlarged me
Eccu 50 5 enlarged the entrance of the house
Isa 5 14 therefore hath hell enlarged her soul
57 8 thou hast enlarged thy bed and made
60 5 and thy heart shall wonder and be e.
Haba 2 5 hath enlarged his desire like hell
1 Ma 14 6 he e. the bounds of his nation and made
2 C 6 11 our heart is enlarged. You are not
13 be you also enlarged. Bear not the
enlargeth Prov 18 16 a man's gift e. his way
enlarging Prov 21 4 is the e. of the heart: the
enlighten 2 K 22 29 O Lord, wilt e. my darkness
1 Es 9 8 that our Lord would e. our eyes and
Job 33 30 and e. them with the light of the living
Ps 12 4 e. my eyes that I never sleep in death
17 29 O my God, enlighten my darkness. For by
Wisd 17 5 neither . . . stars e. that horrible
Eccu 24 45 will e. all that hope in the Lord
Isa 60 19 brightness of the moon enlighten thee
Bar 1 12 strength, and enlighten our eyes, that
Luke 1 79 to e. them that sit in darkness and
11 36 as a bright lamp, shall enlighten thee
Eph 3 9 to enlighten all men that they may
5 14 and Christ shall enlighten thee. See
Apoc 22 5 because the Lord God shall e. them
enlightened 1 K 14 27 and his eyes were e. And
1 K 14 29 that my eyes are e. because I tasted
Ps 33 6 come ye to him and be enlightened
76 19 thy enlightenings e. the world: the
Wisd 17 19 the whole world was e. with a clear
Eccu 2 10 love him, and your hearts shall be e.
Isa 60 1 arise, be enlightened, O Jerusalem
Eph 1 18 the eyes of your heart enlightened
Apoc 18 1 the earth was e. with his glory. And he
21 23 the glory of God hath enlightened it
enlightener Prov 29 13 Lord is the e. of them both
enlightenest Ps 75 5 e. wonderfully from the
enlighteneth Ps 145 8 the Lord e. the blind. The
Eccu 34 20 and e. the eyes and giveth health and
43 10 the Lord e. the world on high. By the
John 1 9 which e. every man that cometh into
enlightening Exod 14 20 cloud, and e. the night
Ps 18 9 of the Lord is lightsome, e. the eyes
enliven Ps 118 17 bountifully to thy servant, e. me
enlivened Ps 118 50 because thy word hath e. me
1 P 3 18 in the flesh, but enlivened in the spirit
enmities Gen 3 15 I will put e. between thee and
Eze 25 15 destroying and satisfying old enmities
1 Ma 11 12 and his enmities were made manifest
2 Ma 4 3 when the enmities proceeded so far
Gal 5 20 works of the flesh . . . enmities
Eph 2 14 the enmities in his flesh: making void
16 killing the enmities in himself. And
enmity Gen 26 21 called the name of it, Enmity
Num 35 23 without hatred and e., he do any of
Eccu 5 17 to the whisperer hatred and enmity
6 9 there is a friend that turneth to enmity
28 6 thy last things, and let enmity cease
2 Ma 12 3 as though they had no enmity to them
Ennom Josu 15 8 valley of the son of Ennom. 4 K 23:10; Jer 7:31, 32; 19:2, 6; 32:35
Josu 18 16 the valley of the children of Ennom
16 Geennom, that is the valley of Ennom
2 Es 11 30 from Bersabee unto the valley of Ennom
Ennon John 3 23 John was baptizing in Ennon near

Enoch 1 Pa 5 3 Enoch and Phallu, Esron and
Jude 14 of these Enoch . . . prophesied, saying
Enos Gen 4 26 born a son, whom he called Enos
Gen 5 6 Seth . . . begot Enos. And Seth lived after he begot Enos
9 Enos lived ninety years, and begot
11 all the days of Enos were 905 years
1 Pa 1 1 Adam, Seth, Enos, Cainan, Malaleel
enough Gen 45 28 enough for me if Joseph my son
Exod 12 4 which may be enough to eat the lamb
16 16 of it as much as is enough to eat
Num 16 3 let it be enough for you that all
Deut 1 6 stayed long enough in this mountain
2 3 have compassed this mountain long enough
3 26 it is enough: speak no more to me of
2 K 24 16 said to the angel . . . It is enough
3 K 16 31 enough for him to walk in the sins of
19 4 it is enough for me, Lord, take away
1 Pa 21 15 it is enough, now stop thy hand. And
2 Pa 20 12 as for us we have not strength enough
25 9 the Lord is rich enough to be able to
29 34 the priests were few and were not e.
30 3 there were not priests e. sanctified
Jdth 7 11 there was not . . . enough to satisfy them
Prov 24 12 if thou say: I have not strength enough
27 27 milk of the goats be e. for thy food
30 15 the fourth never saith: It is enough
16 and the fire never saith: It is enough
Wisd 14 22 it was not enough for them to err
18 25 the proof only of wrath was enough
Eccu 5 1 say not: I have enough to live on
43 34 for you can never go far enough. Who
Isa 10 32 it is yet day enough to remain in
40 16 Libanus shall not be enough to burn
56 11 impudent dogs, they never had enough
Jer 49 9 have taken what was enough for them
Eze 34 18 was it not enough for you to feed
Abdi 5 have stolen till they had enough? If
Nah 2 12 lion caught enough for his whelps and
Agge 1 6 have eaten, but have not had enough
1 Ma 3 30 should not have as formerly enough
2 Ma 2 33 this be enough by way of a preface
5 15 this was not enough: he presumed also
7 42 now there is enough said of the
Mat 10 25 enough for the disciple that he be
25 9 lest perhaps there be not enough for
Mark 14 41 it is enough: the hour is come: behold
Luke 22 38 he said to them, It is enough. And
John 14 8 show us the Father, and it is enough
Acts 27 38 when they had eaten enough, they
3 J 10 as if these things were not enough
enraged Gen 34 13 e. at the deflowering of their
Judg 18 25 lest men enraged come upon thee, and
2 Pa 16 10 he was greatly enraged because of this
25 10 but they being much enraged against Juda
Dan 8 7 near the ram, he was e. against him
enrich 1 K 17 25 the king will e. with great riches
Prov 8 21 that I may enrich them that love me
Eze 27 33 didst enrich the kings of the earth
enriched Gen 14 23 lest thou say I have e. Abram
Gen 26 13 and the man was enriched. 30:43
31 1 Jacob . . . being e. by his substance
Job 15 29 he shall not be enriched, neither shall
Ps 64 10 thou hast many ways e. it. The river
Eccu 11 18 that is enriched by living sparingly
27 1 that seeketh to be e., turneth away
Jer 5 27 are they become great and enriched
Lam 1 5 her lords, her enemies are enriched
Dan 11 2 fourth shall be enriched exceedingly
1 Ma 2 18 the king's friends and e. with gold
2 C 9 11 being enriched in all things, you may
enriching 2 C 6 10 as needy yet enriching many
enrolled Num 11 26 they also had been enrolled
Num 26 63 that were e. by Moses and Eleazar
1 Ma 10 36 let there be e. in the king's army
65 enrolled him amongst his chief friends
13 40 fit to be e. among ours, let them be e.
Luke 2 1 that the whole world should be enrolled
3 all went to be e., every one into his
5 to be e. with Mary his espoused wife
enrolling Luke 2 2 this e. was first made by
Acts 5 37 Judas of Galilee in the days of the e.
Ensemes Josu 18 17 north, and going out to Ensemes
ensign Isa 11 10 standeth for an e. of the people
Isa 30 17 a mountain, and as an e. upon a hill
ensigns Num 2 2 shall camp by their troops, e.
Ps 73 4 have set up their ensigns for signs
ensnared Prov 6 2 who art e. with the words of thy
ensue Gen 41 35 years, that shall now presently e.
Exod 21 23 if her death ensue thereupon, he shall
entangle Job 18 11 fears . . . shall entangle his
Prov 29 6 a snare shall entangle the wicked man
entangled Job 6 18 paths of their steps are e.
Prov 7 21 she entangled him with many words
Ecce 7 30 and he hath entangled himself with an
1 Tim 6 10 entangled themselves in many sorrows
2 P 2 20 if . . . they be again entangled in them
entangleth 2 Tim 2 4 e. himself with secular
enter Gen 6 18 thou shalt enter into the ark
Gen 10 19 until thou enter Sodom and Gomorrha
12 11 when he was near to enter into Egypt
31 44 let us enter into a league: that it
Exod 8 3 which shall . . . enter into thy house
11 4 at midnight I will enter into Egypt
23 32 shalt not enter into league with them
28 29 when he shall enter into the sanctuary
29 30 that shall enter into the tabernacle
33 3 that thou mayst enter into the land. Deut 27:3
Lev 10 9 when you enter into the tabernacle
12 4 neither shall she enter into sanctuary
14 8 he shall enter into the camp. Num 19:7
16 2 that he enter not at all into the
26 and so shall enter into the camp. 28
20 22 the land into which you are to enter
21 23 yet so that he e. not within the veil
Num 4 15 shall the sons of Caath enter in to
5 22 cursed waters enter into thy belly
8 15 they shall enter into the tabernacle
13 22 unto Rohob as you enter into Emath
14 30 shall not enter into the land, over
31 24 shall afterwards enter into the camp
32 9 that they should not e. into the coasts
Deut 4 21 nor enter into the excellent land which
10 11 that they may enter and possess the
23 1 shall not enter into the church. 2, 3
8 shall enter into the church of the Lord
32 52 but thou shalt not enter into it
Josu 6 5 they shall enter in every one at the
Judg 11 18 he would not enter the bounds of Moab
2 K 3 21 and may enter into a league with thee
17 13 and if he shall enter into any city
17 not be seen nor enter into the city
4 K 7 4 if we enter into the city, we shall die
11 8 if any man shall enter the precinct of
1 Pa 4 39 they went forth to enter into Gador
2 Pa 7 2 neither could the priests enter into
23 19 that none who was unclean . . . should e.
2-Es 2 8 and the house that I shall enter into
Job 5 26 shalt enter into the grave in abundance
34 23 of man to enter into judgment with God
Ps 23 7 and the king of glory shall enter in. 9
36 15 let their sword enter into their own
70 16 I will enter into the powers of the Lord
94 11 that they shall not enter into my rest
117 20 the just shall enter into it. I will

131 3 if I shall enter into the tabernacle
142 2 e. not into judgment with thy servant
Prov 2 10 if wisdom shall enter into thy heart
23 10 e. not into the field of the fatherless
Wisd 1 4 wisdom will not enter into a malicious
Eccu 9 2 lest she enter upon thy strength and
39 2 will enter withal into the subtilties
Isa 2 10 enter thou into the rock and hide thee
3 14 Lord will enter into judgment. Mich 6:2
19 1 will enter into Egypt, and the idols
23 the Assyrian shall enter into Egypt
26 2 and let the just nation . . . enter in
20 go, my people, e. into thy chambers
37 24 will enter to the top of its height
Jer 7 2 that enter in at these gates, to adore
8 14 let us enter into the fenced city
14 18 if I enter into the city, behold them
16 5 enter not into the house of feasting
17 20 that enter in by these gates. Thus
25 then shall there enter in by the gates
21 13 who shall enter into our houses? But
22 2 people, who enter in by these gates
4 shall there enter in by the gates
41 17 to go forward and enter into Egypt
42 15 if you . . . enter in to dwell there
18 when you shall enter into Egypt, and
Lam 1 10 Gentiles enter into her sanctuary, of
10 they should not e. into thy church
4 12 should e. in by the gates of Jerusalem
Eze 7 22 robbers shall enter into it and defile
13 9 neither shall they enter into the land
20 38 shall not enter into the land of Israel
38 10 projects shall enter into thy heart
41 6 that they might enter in through the
44 3 he shall enter in by the way of the
9 shall enter into my sanctuary, no
16 they shall enter into my sanctuary
17 when they shall enter in at the gates
46 2 the prince shall enter by the way of
Dan 11 7 shall enter into the province of the
24 he shall enter into rich and plentiful
40 he shall enter into the countries and
41 shall enter into the glorious land
Osee 4 1 Lord shall enter into judgment with
9 4 it shall not enter into the house of
11 9 and I will not enter into the city
Joel 2 9 they shall enter into the city: they
Amos 5 19 or enter into the house and lean with
Abdi 13 neither shalt thou enter into the gate
Jon 3 4 Jonas began to enter into the city
Haba 3 16 let rottenness enter into my bones
1 Ma 12 25 them no time to enter into his country
2 Ma 5 15 also to enter into the temple, the most
Mat 6 6 thou shalt pray, e. into thy chamber
7 13 enter ye in at the narrow gate: for
8 8 shouldst enter under my roof. Luke 7:6
10 5 into city of the Samaritans e. ye not
11 whatsoever city or town you shall e.
12 29 e. into house of the strong. Mark 3:27
45 they enter in and dwell there: and the
18 9 better for thee having one eye, to e.
19 17 if thou wilt enter into life, keep the
23 13 you yourselves do not enter in; and
13 are going in, you suffer not to enter
25 21 e. thou into the joy of thy lord. 23
26 41 enter not into temptation. Mark 14:38
Mark 5 12 swine, that we may enter into them
6 10 wheresoever you shall enter an house
8 26 if thou enter into the town, tell nobody
9 24 enter not any more into him. And crying
42 better for thee to e. into life maimed
44 better for thee to enter lame into life
10 15 as a little child, shall not e. into it
13 15 nor enter therein to take anything out
Luke 8 32 he would suffer them to enter into them
9 4 whatsoever house you shall enter. 10:5
10 8 into what city soever you enter. 10
13 24 strive to enter by the narrow gate
24 shall seek to enter, and shall not be
21 21 who are in the countries, not enter
22 40 lest ye enter into temptation. 46
24 26 and so to enter into his glory? And
John 3 4 can he enter a second time into his
10 9 by me, if any man enter in, he shall be
Acts 20 29 ravening wolves will enter in among you
Heb 3 11 if they shall enter into my rest. 4:3, 5
18 they should not enter into his rest
19 could not enter in because of unbelief
4 3 have believed, shall enter into rest
6 that some are to enter into it, and they
6 did not enter because of unbelief
11 let us hasten to enter into that rest
Apoc 15 8 no man was able to enter into the temple
21 27 shall not enter into it anything defiled
22 14 may e. in by the gates into the city
enter into the kingdom Dan 11 9 king . . . shall enter into the kingdom
Mat 5 20 you shall not e. . . . You have heard
7 21 to me Lord, Lord, shall e. . . . of heaven
21 he shall e. . . . of heaven. Many will say
18 3 as little children, you shall not e. . . .
19 23 a rich man shall hardly e. . . . of heaven
24 than for a rich man to enter into the kingdom. Mark 10:25; Luke 18:25
Mark 5 46 with one eye to e. into the kingdom of
10 23 that have riches e. . . . of heaven
24 for them that trust in riches to e. . . .
John 3 5 the Holy Ghost, he cannot e. . . . of God
Acts 14 21 through many tribulations we must e. . . .
entered Gen 19 23 and the Lord entered into Segor
Gen 31 33 when he had entered into Rachel's tent
34 25 entered boldly into the city and slew
42 5 they entered into the land of Egypt
46 8 Israel that entered into Egypt. 27
Exod 12 25 when you have entered into the land
Lev 16 23 when he entered into the sanctuary
23 10 when you shall have entered into the land. 25:2; Num 34:2
Num 7 89 when Moses entered into the tabernacle
Josu 2 1 entered into the house of a woman
3 to thee and are entered into thy house
3 8 when you shall have e. into part of the
10 20 from Israel, entered into fenced cities
1 K 22 8 hath e. into league with son of Isai
2 K 4 6 they entered into the house secretly
10 14 before Abisai, and e. into the city
4 K 19 23 I have entered into the furthest parts
2 Pa 12 11 the king e. into the house of the Lord
27 2 only that he entered not into the temple
32 1 Sennacherib . . . came and e. into Juda
1 Es 10 6 Esdras . . . e. in thither: he ate no
Job 38 16 hast thou e. into the depths of the
22 hast thou e. into the storehouses of
Prov 4 12 which when thou shalt have entered
Wisd 10 16 she entered into the soul of the
Isa 20 1 that Tharthan entered into Azotus when
28 15 have entered into a league with death
Jer 2 7 when ye entered in, you defiled my
4 29 they have entered into thickets and
9 21 is entered into our houses to destroy
32 35 neither entered it into my heart that
34 10 who entered into the covenant, heard
44 21 hath it not entered into his heart
Bar 4 13 neither have they e. by the paths of
Eze 2 2 the spirit entered into me. 3:24
4 14 no unclean flesh hath entered into my

16 8 I entered into a covenant with thee
36 20 when they entered among the nations
42 14 when the priests shall have entered in
44 2 God of Israel hath entered in by it
Dan 10 3 flesh nor wine entered into my mouth
Abdi 11 foreigners entered into his gates
1 Ma 1 18 he entered into Egypt with a great
23 he proudly entered into the sanctuary
6 62 the king entered into mount Sion and
7 2 as he entered into the house of the
8 19 they entered into the senate house and
11 3 when Ptolemee entered into the cities
13 Ptolemee entered into Antioch and set
12 3 and entered into the senate house and
48 as soon as Jonathan e. into Ptolemais
13 20 Tryphon entered within the country
47 he e. into it with hymns, blessing
51 they entered into it the three and
14 2 that Demetrius was entered within his
15 10 Antiochus entered into the land of his
16 16 entered into the banqueting place and
2 Ma 1 15 had e. into the compass of the temple
3 14 Heliodorus entered in to order this
9 2 e. into the city called Persepolis
Mat 8 5 when he had entered into Capharnaum
23 when he e. into the boat, his disciples
12 4 he [David] entered into the house of
24 38 Noe entered into the ark. Luke 17:27
Mark 1 21 they entered into Capharnaum, and
2 1 he entered into Capharnaum. Luke 7:1
3 1 he e. again into the synagogue. Luke 6:6
5 13 entered into the swine. Luke 8:33
6 56 whithersoever he entered, into towns
11 11 he entered . . . into the temple. 15
Luke 1 40 she entered into the house of Zachary
7 44 I entered into thy house, thou gavest
8 30 because many devils were e. into him
9 34 when they entered into the cloud. And
46 there entered a thought into them
52 they e. into a city of the Samaritans
10 38 he entered into a certain town. 17:12
11 52 you yourselves have not entered in
22 3 Satan entered into Judas, who was
John 4 38 and you have entered into their labors
6 22 that Jesus had not entered into ship
13 27 after the morsel, Satan entered into
18 1 there was a garden into which he e.
19 9 he entered into the hall again, and he
21 3 they went forth and entered the ship
Acts 5 21 entered into the temple and taught
9 17 entered into the house. And laying
10 24 he [Peter] entered into Caesarea. And
11 8 common or unclean hath ever entered
12 we entered into the man's house. And he
20 when they were entered into Antioch
14 1 they entered together into the synagogue
19 [Paul] rose up and e. into the city
16 40 entered into house of Lydia; and having
18 7 entered into house of a certain man
19 30 Paul would have e. in unto the people
21 26 entered into the temple, giving notice
23 16 entered into the castle and told Paul
25 23 entered into the hall of audience with
28 8 to whom Paul entered in; and when he
Rom 5 12 by one man sin entered into this world
20 the law e. in that sin might abound
1 C 2 9 neither hath it e. into the heart of
Heb 4 10 he that is entered into his rest, the
6 20 the forerunner Jesus is entered for us
9 6 the priests indeed always entered
12 entered once into the holies, having
24 Jesus is not entered into the holies
James 5 4 cry of them hath e. into the ears of the
Jude 4 certain men are secretly entered in
Apoc 11 11 spirit of life from God e. into them
entereth Lev 14 46 he that e. into the house when
Deut 11 30 valley that reacheth and entereth far
Eccu 4 14 whithersoever she e., God will give
Jer 25 31 the Lord entereth into judgment with
Eze 42 12 towards the east as one entereth in
Soph 1 9 every one that entereth arrogantly
Mat 15 17 whatsoever entereth into the mouth
Mark 5 40 e. in where the damsel was lying. And
7 19 because it entereth not into his heart
Luke 22 10 follow him into the house where he e.
John 10 1 he that entereth not by the door into
2 that e. in by the door is the shepherd
Heb 6 19 which entereth in even within the veil
9 25 as the high priest e. into the holies
entering Exod 24 18 e. into the midst of the cloud
Num 33 51 e. into the land of Chanaan, destroy
Deut 4 1 entering in mayst possess the land
11 8 the land, to which you are entering
Josu 9 15 e. into a league promised that they
13 5 to the entering into Emath. Judg 3:3; 1 Pa 13:5
Ruth 1 2 e. into the country of Moab, they abode
2 K 10 8 men in array at the e. in of the gate
3 K 10 2 e. into Jerusalem with a great train
14 12 when thy feet shall be e. into the city
19 13 stood in the entering in of the cave
4 K 7 3 four lepers at entering in of the gate
10 8 by the entering in of the gate until
23 8 in the entering in of the gate of Josue
11 at the entering in of the temple of the
2 Pa 33 14 from the entering in of the fish gate
Mat 2 11 e. into the house, they found the child
9 1 entering into a boat, he passed over
Mark 4 19 lusts after other things entering in
7 15 e. into him can defile him. But the
18 from without e. into a man cannot defile
24 e. into a house, he would that no man
16 5 entering into the sepulcher, they saw
Luke 11 26 entering in they dwell there. And the
52 that were e. in, you have hindered
19 1 e. in, he walked through Jericho. And
30 at your e. into which you shall find
45 e. into the temple, he began to cast out
Acts 8 3 entering in from house to house, and
13 14 e. into synagogue on the sabbath
18 19 entering into the synagogue, disputed
19 8 entering into the synagogue, he spoke
21 8 entering into the house of Philip the
1 Th 1 9 what manner of e. in we had unto you
Heb 4 1 the promise . . . of e. into his rest
10 19 e. into the holies by blood of Christ
enterprise 1 Ma 9 68 counsel and his e. was in vain
enterprises 2 K 8 6 preserved David in all his e.
2 K 8 14 preserved David in all enterprises
entertain Eccu 29 31 he shall e. and feed and
entertained Judg 19 21 he e. them with a feast
Acts 28 7 named Publius . . . e. us courteously
Heb 13 2 being not aware of it, have e. angels
entertaineth Prov 26 24 in his heart he e. deceit
Ecce 5 19 because God e. his heart with delight
entertainment Wisd 18 3 harmless sun of a good e.
entice Prov 1 10 if sinners shall e. thee, consent
enticed 2 K 15 6 he e. the hearts of the men of
enticeth Wisd 15 5 e. the fool to lust after it
enticing Deut 32 11 the eagle e. her young to fly
entire Jer 13 19 captive with an e. captivity
Jer 51 13 is come for thy entire destruction
Amos 1 9 have shut up an entire captivity in
James 1 4 that you may be perfect and entire
entirely 2 Pa 15 16 Priapus: and he e. destroyed
entitle 2 Ma 4 9 e. them that were at Jerusalem

entrails Exod 12 9 the head, with the feet and e.
Exod 29 13 the fat that covereth the entrails. Lev 3:3; 4:8; 7:3; 8:25
17 having washed his entrails and feet
Lev 1 9 the entrails and feet being washed
13 entrails and the feet they shall wash
8 16 the fat that was upon the entrails
21 having first washed the entrails. 9:14
Tob 6 5 take out the entrails of this fish
Ps 108 18 it went in like water into his entrails
Eze 21 21 inquired of the idols and consulted e.
Eccu 51 29 my e. were troubled in seeking her
entrance Exod 26 36 hanging in e. of the tabernacle
Exod 27 16 in the entrance of the court there
Deut 8 20 which the Lord destroyed at thy e.
Josu 8 29 threw it in the very e. of the city
Judg 1 24 show us the entrance into the city
6 4 even to the entrance of Gaza: and they
9 35 in the e. of gate of the city. Prov 1:21
2 K 15 2 stood by the entrance of the gate, and
3 K 6 31 in the entrance of the oracle he made
33 he made in the entrance of the temple
8 65 multitude from the entrance of Emath
22 10 by the entrance of the gate of Samaria
4 K 7 17 trod upon him in the e. of the gate
14 25 from the e. of Emath. 2 Pa 7:8; Amos 6:15
1 Pa 5 9 as far as the entrance of the desert
9 19 keepers of the entrance of the camp
2 Pa 3 17 pillars he put at the e. of the temple
12 10 who guarded the entrance of the palace
23 13 standing upon the step in the entrance
26 8 even to the entrance of Egypt for his
29 16 to the entrance of house of the Lord
Wisd 7 6 all men have one entrance into life
Eccu 50 5 enlarged the entrance of the house
Jer 1 15 in the e. of the gates of Jerusalem
Eze 26 10 as by the entrance of a city that is
42 9 an entrance from the east, for them
Dan 14 12 made under the table a secret entrance
1 Ma 14 5 made an e. to the isles of the sea
2 Ma 1 16 opening a secret entrance of the temple
1 Th 2 1 our entrance in unto you, that it was
2 P 1 11 so an e. shall be ministered to you
entrances 2 Es 12 25 of the e. before the gates
entrap Eccu 8 14 to entrap thee in thy words
entreat Exod 32 30 I may be able to e. him for your
3 K 13 6 e. face of the Lord. Zach 7:2; 8:21, 22
4 K 5 18 thou shalt e. the Lord for thy servant
Job 11 19 and many shall entreat thy face. But
Ps 44 13 the rich among the people shall e. thy
Eccu 28 4 and doth he entreat for his own sins
33 20 repent and thou entreat for the same
Lam 3 8 when I cry and entreat, he hath shut
Luke 15 28 his father . . . began to entreat him
1 C 4 13 we are blasphemed, and we entreat; we
Phil 4 3 and I entreat thee also, my sincere
1 Th 4 10 we entreat you that you abound more
1 Tim 5 1 rebuke not, but e. him as a father
2 Tim 4 2 reprove, entreat, rebuke in all patience
entreated 2 Pa 33 13 he e. him and besought him
Job 19 16 I entreated him with my own mouth. My
17 I entreated the children of my womb
Ps 89 13 and be e. in favor of thy servants. We
118 58 I entreated thy face with all my heart
134 14 and will be e. in favor of his servants
Bar 2 8 we have not e. the face of the Lord
Dan 9 13 and we entreated not thy face, O Lord
1 C 16 12 I much e. him [Apollo] to come unto
entreating Jer 15 6 I am weary of entreating thee
Bar 6 40 entreating him, that he may speak, as
2 Ma 13 23 e. the Jews and yielding to them, he
1 Th 2 11 entreating and comforting you, as a
entreaty Prov 28 27 that despiseth his e., shall
Eccu 35 5 from injustice, is an entreaty for sins
2 C 8 4 with much entreaty begging of us the
entry Exod 29 32 they shall eat in e. of tabernacle
Exod 36 37 a hanging in the entry of the tabernacle. 39:38; 40:5, 26
38 15 he made the entry of the tabernacle
18 in the entry thereof an embroidered
19 the pillars in the entry were four
26 of the entry where the veil hangeth
30 the sockets in entry of the tabernacle
39 40 the hanging in the entry of the court
40 8 with hangings, and the entry thereof
27 altar of holocausts in entry of the
31 drawing the hanging in the entry
Lev 3 2 slain in the entry of the tabernacle. 8
13 shall immolate it in the entry of the
4 7 altar of holocaust in e. of tabernacle
Num 3 26 that is hanged in the e. of the court
4 25 that hangeth in entry of the tabernacle
26 the veil in the entry that is before
6 10 to the priest in entry of the covenant
12 5 stood in e. of the tabernacle. Deut 31:15
16 27 stood in the entry of their pavilions
Deut 6 9 thou shalt write them in the entry and
4 K 16 18 the king's entry from without he turned
Esth 2 21 presided in first entry of the palace
Jer 19 2 is by the entry of the earthen gate
26 10 in the entry of the new gate. 36:10
32 8 to the entry of the prison, and said
35 4 who was keeper of the entry. And I
37 20 Jeremias remained in the entry of the prison. 38:13, 28
20 committed into the entry of the prison
38 6 which was in the entry of the prison
52 24 and the three keepers of the entry
Eze 8 5 the idol of jealousy in the very entry
10 19 stood in the entry of the east gate
11 1 in e. of the gate five and twenty men
27 3 that dwelleth at the entry of the sea
40 40 which goeth up to the e. of the gate
46 19 by entry that was at side of the gate
envied Gen 30 1 without children, e. her sister
Gen 37 11 his brethren therefore envied him: but
49 23 and quarrelled with him and envied him
Eze 31 9 were in the paradise of God, e. him
envies Gal 5 21 envies, murders, drunkenness
1 Tim 6 4 from which arise envies, contentions
1 P 2 1 all guile and dissimulations and e.
envieth Prov 28 22 to be rich and envieth others
Eccu 14 6 is none worse than he that e. himself
1 C 13 4 charity e. not, dealeth not perversely
envious Prov 23 6 eat not with an envious man
Eccu 6 1 shall every sinner that is envious
14 3 what should an e. man do with gold
8 the eye of the envious is wicked, and
37 12 nor with an e. man of giving thanks
Isa 26 11 let the envious people see and be
environed Josu 8 10 e. with the aid of the fighting
2 Ma 15 13 and environed with great beauty and
envy Gen 37 8 ministered nourishment to their e.
Deut 28 54 shall envy his own brother and his
56 will envy her husband who lieth in her
Job 5 2 and envy slayeth the little one. I have
Ps 36 1 nor envy them that work iniquity. For
7 envy not the man who prospereth in his
Prov 3 31 envy not the unjust man, and do not
14 30 envy is the rottenness of the bones
23 17 let not thy heart envy sinners: but
Ecce 4 4 their industries are exposed to the e.
9 6 hatred, and their envy are all perished
Wisd 2 24 by the envy of the devil, death came
6 25 neither will I go with consuming envy
7 13 communicate without envy, and her

14 24 one killeth another through envy, or
Eccu 9 16 envy not the glory and riches of a
30 26 envy and anger shorten a man's days
31 16 lest being disgraced with envy thou be
37 7 thy counsel from them that envy thee
40 4 wrath, envy, trouble, unquietness, and
45 22 through e. the men that were with Dathan
48 2 they that provoked him in their envy
Isa 11 13 envy of Ephraim shall be taken away
13 perish: Ephraim shall not envy Juda
Eze 35 11 thy wrath and according to thy envy
1 Ma 8 16 there is no envy nor jealousy amongst
Mat 27 18 that for envy they had delivered him
Mark 15 10 had delivered him up out of envy. But
Acts 5 17 were filled with envy. And they laid
7 9 the patriarchs through envy sold Joseph
13 45 were filled with envy and contradicted
17 5 the Jews, moved with envy, and taking
Rom 1 29 full of envy, murder, contention, deceit
13 13 not in contention and envy: but put ye
Phil 1 15 some indeed, even out of envy and
Titus 3 3 living in malice and envy, hateful and
James 4 2 you kill and envy and cannot obtain
5 to envy doth the spirit covet which
envying Gen 26 14 Palestines e. him, stopped up
1 C 3 3 is among you envying and contention
Gal 5 26 provoking one another, e. one another
James 3 16 where envying and contention is, there
envyings 2 C 12 20 lest perhaps contentions, e.
Epaphras Col 1 7 as you learned of Epaphras, our
Col 4 12 Epaphras saluteth you, who is one of
Philem 23 there salute thee Epaphras, my fellow
Epaphroditus Phil 2 23 to send to you Epaphroditus
Phil 4 18 received from E. the things you sent
Epenetus Rom 16 5 salute Epenetus my beloved: who
Epha Gen 25 4 of Madian was born Epha and Opher
1 Pa 1 33 sons of Madian: Epha and Epher and
2 46 Epha the concubine of Caleb bore Haran
47 Gesan and Phalet and Epha and Saaph
Isa 60 6 the dromedaries of Madian and Epha
Epher 3 K 4 10 his was Socho and all land of E.
1 Pa 1 33 sons of Madian: Epha and Epher and
4 17 sons of Esra, Jether and Mered and E.
5 24 Epher and Jesi and Eliel and Esriel
Ephesian Acts 21 29 had seen Trophimus the E.
Ephesians Acts 19 28 great is Diana of the E. 34
Acts 19 35 city of the Ephesians is a worshipper
Ephesus Acts 18 19 [Paul] came to Ephesus. 19:1
Acts 18 21 he departed from Ephesus. And going
24 came to Ephesus, one mighty in the
19 17 and Gentiles that dwelt at Ephesus
26 a great multitude not only of Ephesus
35 ye men of Ephesus, what man is there
20 16 Paul had determined to sail by Ephesus
17 sending from Miletus to Ephesus, he
1 C 15 32 I fought with beasts at Ephesus, what
16 8 I will tarry at Ephesus until Pentecost
Eph 1 1 to all the saints who are at Ephesus
1 Tim 1 3 as I desired thee to remain at Ephesus
2 Tim 1 18 he ministered unto me at Ephesus, thou
4 12 but Tychicus I have sent to Ephesus
Apoc 1 11 to Ephesus and to Smyrna and to Pergamus
2 1 unto angel of the church of E. write
ephi Exod 16 36 gomor is the tenth part of an ephi
Num 15 4 fine flour, the tenth part of an ephi
Ruth 2 17 about the measure of an ephi of barley
1 K 17 17 for thy brethren an ephi of frumenty
Eze 45 10 shall have just balances and a just e.
11 the ephi and the bate shall be equal
11 and the ephi the tenth part of a core
13 sixth part of an ephi of a core of
24 sacrifice of an ephi for every calf
24 every calf, and an ephi for every ram
24 hin of oil for every ephi. 46:5, 7, 11
46 5 the sacrifice of an ephi for a ram
7 ephi for a calf, an ephi also for a ram
11 ephi to a calf, and an ephi to a ram
14 by morning the sixth part of an ephi
ephod Exod 25 7 precious stones to adorn the ephod
Exod 28 4 a rational and an ephod, a tunick
6 they shall make the ephod of gold and
12 put them in both sides of the ephod
15 according to workmanship of the ephod
26 borders that are over against the ephod
27 to be set on each side of the ephod
27 rational may be fitted with the ephod
28 unto the rings of the e. with a violet
28 rational and ephod may not be loosed
31 the tunick of the ephod all of violet
29 5 the ephod and the rational, which thou
35 9 stones, for the adorning of the ephod
27 precious stones for the ephod and the
39 2 he made an ephod of gold, violet, and
7 he set them in the sides of the ephod
8 according to the work of the ephod
17 stood out in the corners of the ephod
18 the ephod and the rational were bound
20 made also the tunick of the ephod all
Lev 8 7 over it he put the ephod, and binding
Judg 8 27 Gedeon made an ephod thereof and put
17 5 and made an ephod and theraphim, that
18 14 in these houses there is an ephod and
17 to take away graven god and the ephod
18 took away . . . the ephod and the idols
20 agreed to their words and took the e.
1 K 2 18 being a child girded with a linen e.
28 and to wear the ephod before me: and I
14 3 wore the ephod. And the people knew
21 9 wrapped up in a cloth behind the ephod
22 18 men that wore the linen ephod. And
23 6 he came down having an ephod with him
9 the priest: Bring hither the ephod
30 7 bring me hither the e. And Abiathar brought the ephod to David
2 K 6 14 David was girded with a linen ephod
1 Pa 15 27 David also had on him an e. of linen
Eccu 45 10 an ephod, and he compassed him with
Osee 3 4 shall sit many days . . . without ephod
Ephod Num 34 23 Hanniel the son of Ephod. Of the
ephpheta Mark 7 34 said to him: Ephpheta, which
Ephra Judg 6 11 under an oak that was in Ephra
Judg 6 24 when he [Gedeon] was yet in Ephra
8 27 put it in his city Ephra. And all
32 in sepulcher of his father in Ephra
9 5 came to his father's house in Ephra
1 K 13 17 one company went towards way of Ephra
Ephraim Gen 41 52 he named the second Ephraim
Gen 46 20 bore him: Manasses and Ephraim. The sons
48 1 taking his two sons Manasses and E.
5 Ephraim and Manasses shall be reputed
13 he set Ephraim on his right hand, that
14 put it upon the head of Ephraim the
17 put right hand upon the head of Ephraim
20 God do to thee as to Ephraim and as
20 and he set Ephraim before Manasses
50 22 he saw the children of Ephraim to the
Num 1 10 of Ephraim, Elisama the son of Ammiud
32 of the sons of E., by the generations
2 18 shall be the camp of the sons of E.
24 were numbered in the camp of Ephraim
7 48 the prince of the sons of Ephraim
10 22 the sons of Ephraim also moved their
13 9 of the tribe of E. 34:24; Josu 21:21; 1 Pa 6:66
26 28 sons of Joseph . . . Manasses and Ephraim
35 the sons of Ephraim by their kindreds
37 the kindreds of the sons of Ephraim

Deut 33 17 these are the multitudes of Ephraim
34 2 and the land of Ephraim and Manasses
Josu 14 4 into two tribes, of Manasses and E.
16 4 Manasses and Ephraim . . . possessed it
5 the border of the children of Ephraim
8 of the tribe of the children of E.
9 separated for the children of Ephraim
10 children of E. slew not the Chanaanite
10 Chanaanite dwelt in midst of Ephraim
17 8 belongs to the children of Ephraim
10 possession of Ephraim is on the south
17 Josue said . . . to E. and Manasses
21 5 out of the tribes of E. and of Dan
Judg 1 29 E. also did not slay the Chanaanite
5 14 out of Ephraim he destroyed them
7 24 all E. shouted and took the waters
8 1 the men of Ephraim said to him: What
2 one bunch of grapes of Ephraim better
10 9 wasted Juda and Benjamin and Ephraim
12 1 there arose a sedition in Ephraim
4 he [Jephte] fought against Ephraim
4 the men of Galaad defeated Ephraim
4 had said: Galaad is a fugitive of E.
4 dwelleth in midst of E. and Manasses
5 by which Ephraim was to return. And when any one of the number of E. came
6 there fell at that time of Ephraim
15 buried in Pharathon in land of Ephraim
2 K 2 9 made him king . . . and over Ephraim
13 23 Baalhasor, which is near Ephraim
18 6 battle was fought in forest of Ephraim
4 K 14 13 from the gate of Ephraim to the gate
1 Pa 7 20 the sons of Ephraim were Suthala
22 Ephraim their father mourned many
9 3 in Jerusalem dwelt . . . of children of E.
12 30 of the sons of Ephraim 20,800, men of
27 10 a Phallonite of the sons of Ephraim
14 a Pharathonite of the sons of Ephraim
20 over the sons of Ephraim, Osee the
2 Pa 13 4 mount Semeron, which was in Ephraim
15 9 the strangers with them of Ephraim
17 2 in the cities of Ephraim, which Asa
25 7 with Israel and all the children of E.
10 army that came to him out of Ephraim
23 gate of Ephraim to gate of the corner
28 7 Zechri a powerful man of Ephraim slew
12 of the chief men of the sons of Ephraim
30 1 wrote letters to Ephraim and Manasses
10 through the land of Ephraim and of
18 great part of the people from Ephraim
31 1 out of Ephraim also and Manasses, till
34 6 in cities of Manasses and of Ephraim
9 gathered together from Manasses and E.
2 Es 8 16 in the street of the gate of Ephraim
12 38 above the gate of Ephraim and above
Ps 59 9 Ephraim is the strength of my head
77 9 sons of Ephraim who bend and shoot
67 chose not the tribe of Ephraim: but he
79 3 shine forth before Ephraim, Benjamin
107 9 Ephraim the protection of my head
Eccu 47 23 out of Ephraim a rebellious kingdom
29 showed Ephraim the way of sin, and
Isa 7 2 Syria hath rested upon Ephraim and his
5 unto the evil of Ephraim and the son
8 Ephraim shall cease to be a people
9 the head of Ephraim is Samaria, and the
17 time of separation of E. from Juda
9 9 all the people of Ephraim shall know
20 shall eat . . . Manasses E., and E. Manasses
11 13 envy of Ephraim shall be taken away
13 E. shall not envy Juda, and Juda shall not fight against Ephraim
17 3 and aid shall cease from Ephraim, and
28 1 to the drunkards of Ephraim, and to
3 crown of pride of the drunkards of E.
Jer 7 15 your brethren, the whole seed of E.
31 9 to Israel, and Ephraim is my firstborn
18 I heard Ephraim when he went into
20 Ephraim is an honorable son to me
Eze 37 16 for Joseph the stick of Ephraim, and
19 which is in the hand of Ephraim, and
48 5 one portion for Ephraim. And by the border of Ephraim
Osee 4 17 Ephraim is a partaker with idols, let
5 3 I know Ephraim, and Israel is not hid
3 Ephraim hath committed fornication
5 Israel and Ephraim shall fall in their
9 Ephraim shall be in desolation in the
11 E. is under oppression, and broken
12 I will be like a moth to Ephraim: and
13 Ephraim saw his sickness, and Juda his
13 Ephraim went to the Assyrian and sent
14 I will be like a lioness to Ephraim
6 4 what shall I do to thee, O Ephraim
10 the fornications of Ephraim there
7 1 the iniquity of Ephraim was discovered
8 E. himself is mixed among the nations
8 Ephraim is become as bread baked under
11 E. is become as a dove that is decoyed
8 9 Ephraim hath given gifts to his lovers
11 Ephraim hath made many altars to sin
9 3 Ephraim is returned to Egypt and hath
8 the watchman of E. was with my God
11 as for Ephraim, their glory hath flown
13 Ephraim, as I saw, was a Tyre founded
13 Ephraim shall bring out his children
16 Ephraim is struck, their root is dried
10 6 shame shall fall upon Ephraim, and
11 E. is a heifer taught to love to tread
11 I will ride upon Ephraim, Juda shall
11 3 I was like a foster father to Ephraim
8 how shall I deal with thee, O Ephraim
9 I will not return to destroy Ephraim
12 E. hath compassed me about with denials
12 1 Ephraim feedeth on the wind, and
8 Ephraim said: But yet I am become rich
14 Ephraim hath provoked me to wrath with
13 1 when E. spoke, a horror seized Israel
12 the iniquity of Ephraim is bound up
14 9 Ephraim shall say, What have I to do
Abdi 19 they shall possess the country of E.
Zach 9 10 I will destroy the chariot out of E.
13 I have filled Ephraim: and I will raise
10 7 shall be as the valliant men of Ephraim

mount Ephraim Josu 17 15 possession of m. E. is
Josu 19 50 Thamnath Saraa, in mount Ephraim: and
20 7 Nephtali, and Sichem in mount Ephraim
21 21 with suburbs thereof in mount Ephraim
24 30 Thamnathsare . . . in m. E. Judg 2:9
33 which was given him in mount Ephraim
Judg 3 27 sounded the trumpet in mount Ephraim
4 5 between Rama and Bethel in mount E.
7 24 sent messengers into all mount Ephraim
10 1 who dwelt in Samir of mount Ephraim
17 1 a man of mount Ephraim whose name
8 when he was come to mount Ephraim, as
18 2 when they came to mount Ephraim, they
13 thence they passed into mount Ephraim
19 1 who dwelt on the side of mount Ephraim
16 he also was of mount Ephraim and dwelt
18 which is on the side of mount Ephraim
1 K 1 1 there was a man . . . of mount Ephraim
9 3 they had passed through mount Ephraim
14 22 that had hid themselves in mount E.
2 K 20 21 a man of mount Ephraim, Seba the son of
3 K 4 8 Benhur, in mount Ephraim, Bendecar in

erect Lev 26 1 neither shall you erect pillars nor
erected Gen 35 20 Jacob erected a pillar over her
Exod 26 23 which shall be erected in the corners
Num 23 4 I have erected seven altars and have
Josu 22 29 which is erected before his tabernacle
1 K 15 12 had e. for himself a triumphant arch
ericius Isa 14 23 a possession for the ericius
Isa 34 11 bittern and ericius shall possess it
15 there hath the ericius had its hole
Erioch Jdth 1 6 in plain of Erioch king of the
err Ps 94 10 I said: These always err in heart
Prov 14 22 they err that work evil: but mercy
16 10 his mouth shall not err in judgment
Wisd 12 2 thou chastiseth them that err, by
13 6 for they perhaps err, seeking God and
14 22 it was not enough for them to err
Eccu 15 12 say not: He hath caused me to err
Isa 19 14 they have caused Egypt to err in all
35 8 so that fools shall not err therein
63 17 why hast thou made us to err, O Lord
Jer 23 32 cause my people to err by their lying
Eze 14 9 when the prophet shall err and speak
Amos 2 4 their idols have caused them to err
Mich 3 5 prophets that make my people err: that
2 Ma 2 2 they should not err in their minds
Mat 22 29 you err, not knowing the Scriptures
Mark 12 24 do ye not therefore err, because you
27 the living. You therefore do greatly e.
1 C 6 9 do not err: neither fornicators nor
Heb 3 10 I said: They always err in heart. And
5 2 them that are ignorant and that err
James 1 16 do not err, therefore, my dearest
5 19 if any of you err from the truth, and
erred Job 34 32 if I have erred, teach thou me
Ps 118 110 I have not erred from thy precepts
Wisd 5 6 we have erred from the way of truth
17 1 undisciplined souls have erred. For
Isa 28 7 and through drunkenness have erred
29 24 they that erred in spirit, shall know
47 15 every one hath erred in his own way
1 Tim 6 10 have erred concerning the faith. 21
2 Tim 2 18 who have erred from the truth, saying
erreth Prov 14 8 and the imprudence of fools erreth
erring Eccu 16 23 foolish and e. man thinketh
2 Tim 3 13 erring and driving into error. But
Titus 3 3 we also were some time . . . erring
error Deut 4 19 being deceived by e., thou adore
Deut 30 17 deceived with error thou adore strange
Job 15 31 being vainly deceived by error, that
Ecce 2 2 laughter I counted error: and to mirth
7 26 fool, and the error of the imprudent
10 5 e. proceeding from face of the prince
13 end of his talk is a mischievous error
12 14 will bring into judgment for every e.
Wisd 1 12 seek not death in the e. of your life
12 24 for a long time in the ways of error
14 16 this error was kept as a law, and
Eccu 11 16 e. and darkness are created with sinners
15 13 Lord hateth all abomination of error
17 26 tarry not in the error of the ungodly
Isa 26 3 the old error is passed away: thou wilt
30 28 the bridle of error that was in the jaws
Eze 45 20 ignorant and hath been deceived by e.
Mat 27 64 last error shall be worse than the first
Rom 1 27 recompense which was due to their error
Eph 4 22 according to the desire of error. And
1 Th 2 3 our exhortation was not of error nor
2 Th 2 10 shall send them the operation of error
1 Tim 4 1 giving heed to spirits of error, and
2 Tim 3 13 erring and driving into error. But
James 5 20 be converted from the error of his way
2 P 2 18 such as converse in error: promising
3 17 led aside by the error of the unwise
1 J 4 6 by this we know . . . the spirit of error
Jude 11 after the error of Balaam they have
errors Josu 23 12 if you will embrace the e. of
4 K 17 19 they walked in the errors of Israel
Ecce 1 17 to know prudence and learning and e.
2 12 to behold wisdom and errors and folly
Isa 30 10 see errors for us. Take away from
45 16 the forgers of errors are gone together
Esaan Josu 15 52 Arab and Ruma and Esaan and
Esau Gen 25 25 his name was called E. Immediately
Gen 25 27 Esau became a skilful hunter and a
28 Isaac loved Esau because he ate of
29 Esau, coming faint out of the field
33 Esau swore to him, and sold his first
26 34 Esau . . . married wives, Judith the
27 1 he [Isaac] called Esau, his elder son
6 I heard thy father talking with Esau
11 Esau my brother is a hairy man, and I
15 put on him very good garments of Esau
19 Jacob said: I am Esau thy firstborn
21 whether thou be my son Esau, or not
22 but the hands are the hands of Esau
24 art thou my son Esau? He answered
30 Jacob being now gone out abroad, E. came
32 I am thy firstborn son Esau. Isaac was
34 Esau having heard his father's words
38 Esau said to him: Hast thou only one
41 Esau therefore always hated Jacob
42 Esau thy brother threateneth to kill
28 6 Esau seeing that his father had blessed
32 3 sent messengers before him to Esau
4 thus shall ye speak to my lord Esau
6 we came to Esau thy brother, and behold
8 if Esau come to one company and destroy
11 deliver me from hand of my brother Esau
13 presents for his brother Esau, 200 she
17 if thou meet my brother Esau, and he
18 sent them as a present to my lord Esau
19 speak ye the same words to Esau when
33 1 Jacob lifting up his eyes, saw Esau
4 Esau ran to meet his brother and
8 Esau said: What are the droves that I
15 Esau answered: I beseech thee, that
16 so Esau returned that day . . . to Seir
35 1 when thou didst flee from Esau thy
29 his sons Esau and Jacob buried him
36 1 these are the generations of Esau. 9
2 Esau took wives of the daughters of
5 are the sons of Esau. 15, 19; 1 Pa 1:35
6 Esau took his wives and his sons and
8 Esau dwelt in mount Seir: he is Edom
10 the son of Ada the wife of Esau: and
12 concubine of Eliphaz the son of Esau
12 are the sons of Adad the wife of Esau
13 sons of Basemath the wife of Esau. 17
14 Oolibama . . . the wife of Esau. 18
15 sons of Eliphaz the firstborn of Esau
17 the sons of Rahuel, the son of Esau
43 same is Esau the father of the Edomites
Deut 2 4 of your brethren the children of Esau
5 I have given mount Seir to Esau for a
8 by our brethren the children of Esau
12 the children of Esau dwelt there, as
22 done in favor of the children of Esau
29 as the children of Esau have done that
Josu 24 4 to him again I gave Jacob and Esau
4 I gave to Esau mount Seir for his
1 Pa 1 34 his sons were Esau and Israel. The sons
Jer 49 8 brought the destruction of Esau upon
10 I have made Esau bare, I have revealed
Abdi 6 how have they searched Esau, how have
8 understanding out of the mount of Esau
9 may be cut off from the mount of Esau

18 18 the house of Esau [shall be] stubble
18 shall be no remains of the house of E.
19 shall inherit the mount of Esau, and
21 to judge the mount of Esau: and the
Mala 1 2 was not Esau brother to Jacob, saith
3 loved Jacob, but have hated Esau? And
1 Ma 5 3 Judas fought against children of Esau
65 and attacked the children of Esau
Rom 9 13 Esau I have hated. What shall we say
Heb 11 20 Isaac blessed Jacob and Esau. By faith
12 16 as Esau; who for one mess, sold his
Esbaal 1 Pa 8 33 Saul begot . . . Esbaal. 9:39
Esbon 1 Pa 7 7 the sons of Bela: Esbon and Ozi
escape Gen 19 19 I cannot e. to the mountain, lest
Gen 32 8 other company that is left shall e.
Num 21 35 not letting any one escape, and they
Deut 4 42 might e. to some one of these cities
19 3 may have near at hand whither to escape
Josu 10 20 that were able to escape from Israel
20 3 may escape the wrath of the kinsman
Judg 3 29 none of them could escape. And Moab
20 47 only 600 men that were able to escape
Ruth 2 2 that escape the hands of the reapers
1 K 23 26 David despaired of being able to e.
2 K 15 14 flee: for we shall not escape else
20 6 lest he find fenced cities and e. us
3 K 18 40 and let not one of them escape. And
19 17 whosoever shall e. the sword of Hazael
17 whosoever shall e. the sword of Jehu
4 K 10 24 if any of the men escape, whom I have
25 go in and kill them, let none escape
1 Pa 4 43 Amalecites, who had been able to e.
21 12 and not to be able to escape their sword
2 Pa 20 24 no one was left that could e. death
Tob 2 8 thou didst scarce escape the sentence
13 2 there is none that can escape thy hand
Jdth 13 20 for my escape and for your deliverance
15 2 they made haste to e. from the Hebrews
Job 11 20 the way to escape shall fail them
Prov 12 13 the just shall escape out of distress
19 5 he that speaketh lies shall not escape
Ecce 7 27 that pleaseth God, shall e. from her
Wisd 2 8 withered: let no meadow e. our riot
16 15 it is impossible to escape thy hand
Eccu 6 35 sayings of praise may not e. thee
8 11 discourse of the ancients escape thee
11 10 thou run before, thou shalt not escape
16 14 sinner shall not e. in his rapines
20 4 so thou shalt escape wilful sin. There
30 pleaseth great men shall e. iniquity
23 10 thou shalt not escape free from them
Isa 10 20 that shall escape of the house of
14 31 is none that shall escape his troop
20 6 and how shall we be able to escape
Jer 11 11 they shall not be able to escape: and
25 29 and shall you . . . escape free? You shall
not escape free: for I will
32 4 Sedecias . . . shall not escape out of
34 3 shalt not escape out of his hand
38 18 shalt not escape out of their hands
23 thou shalt not escape their hands
42 17 nor escape from the face of the evil
44 14 there shall be none that shall escape
46 6 nor the strong think to escape: they
48 8 every city, and no city shall escape
50 29 round about, and let none escape; pay
Eze 6 8 some that shall escape the sword
7 16 of them as shall flee shall escape
17 15 shall he escape that hath broken the
18 all these things, he shall not escape
Dan 11 42 the land of Egypt shall not escape
13 22 do it not, I shall not e. your hands
Joel 2 3 is there any one that can escape it
2 Ma 3 38 scourged, if so be he escaped: for
6 26 yet should I not escape the hand of
7 19 that thou shalt escape unpunished, for
31 shalt not escape the hand of God. For
9 22 great hope to escape the sickness. But
10 20 let some of them escape. But when it
21 having let their adversaries escape
Luke 21 36 worthy to escape all these things
Acts 27 42 any of them swimming out, should escape
Rom 2 3 that thou shalt e. the judgment of God
1 Th 5 3 and they shall not escape. But you
Heb 2 3 how shall we escape if we neglect
2 P 2 18 those who for a little while escape
escaped Gen 14 13 one that had escaped told Abram
Deut 2 36 not a . . . city that escaped our hands
3 4 there was not a town that escaped us
7 20 all that have escaped thee, and could
Judg 3 26 escaped and passed by the place of the
1 K 14 41 were taken, and the people escaped
19 10 David fled and escaped that night
12 he [David] went and fled away and e.
18 David fled and e. and came to Samuel
22 20 Abiathar, escaped and fled to David
23 13 that David was fled from Ceila and had e.
30 17 there escaped not a man of them, but
2 Pa 16 7 king of Syria escaped out of thy hand
30 6 the remnant of you that have escaped
36 20 whosoever escaped the sword, was led
Job 1 15 I alone have e. to tell thee. 16, 17, 19
Eccu 16 11 wonder if he had escaped unpunished
27 22 as a roe escaped out of the snare
40 7 as if he had e. in the day of battle
Isa 4 2 that shall have escaped of Israel
Jer 31 2 that were left and e. from the sword
48 19 say to him that hath escaped: What
50 28 that have escaped out of the land of
51 50 you that have escaped the sword, come
Lam 2 22 that escaped and was left: those that I
Eze 24 27 mouth be opened to him that hath escaped
1 Ma 4 26 such of the strangers as escaped, went
2 Ma 7 35 hast not yet escaped the judgment of
11 12 many . . . wounded, escaped naked: yea
12 fled away shamefully and escaped. And
12 6 slew . . . them that e. from the fire
35 and so Gorgias escaped to Maresa. But
John 10 39 he escaped out of their hands. And he
Acts 28 1 when we had escaped, then we knew that
4 who though he hath escaped the sea
2 C 11 33 by the wall, and so escaped his hands
Heb 11 34 of fire, escaped the edge of the sword
12 25 if they escaped not who refused him
escapeth Eccu 36 11 let him that e. be consumed
Eccu 42 20 no thought e. him, and no word can
Eze 24 26 when he that e. shall come to thee
Escol Gen 14 13 Amorrhite the brother of Escol
Gen 14 24 that came with me, Aner, Escol, and
escutcheons 1 Ma 4 57 front of temple with . . . e.
Esdras 1 Es 7 1 Esdras the son of Saraias the son
1 Es 7 6 this Esdras went up from Babylon, and
10 for Esdras had prepared his heart to
11 which king Artaxerxes gave to Esdras
12 Artaxerxes king of kings to Esdras
21 whatsoever Esdras the priest, the scribe
25 thou Esdras according to the wisdom
10 1 when Esdras was thus praying and
2 and said to Esdras: We have sinned
5 so Esdras arose and made the chiefs
6 Esdras rose up from before the house
10 Esdras the priest stood up and said
16 Esdras the priest, and the men heads
2 Es 8 1 they spoke to Esdras the scribe, to
2 Esdras the priest brought the law
4 Esdras the scribe stood upon a step

5 and Esdras opened the book before all
6 Esdras blessed the Lord the great God
9 Esdras . . . said: This is a holy day
13 gathered together to Esdras the scribe
12 1 Esdras, Amaria, Melluch, Hattus, Sebenias
13 of Esdras, Mosollam: and of Amaria
26 days . . . of E. the priest and scribe
33 E. and Mosollam, Judas and Benjamin
35 and Esdras the scribe before them at
2 Ma 8 23 holy Book had been read to them by E.
Esdrelon Jdth 1 8 in the great plain of Esdrelon
Jdth 4 5 to all that were over against Esdrelon
7 3 Chelmon, which is over against Esdrelon
Esdrin 2 Ma 12 36 that were with E. had fought
Eseban Gen 36 26 sons of Dison: Hamdan and Eseban
1 Pa 1 41 sons of Dison: Hamram and Eseban and
Esebon Gen 46 16 Esebon and Heri and Arodi and
Esec 1 Pa 8 39 the sons of Esec, his brother, were
Eselias 2 Pa 34 8 Saphan the son of Eselias, and
Esem Josu 15 29 and Baala and Jim and Esem and
Eser Gen 36 21 sons of Seir . . . Eser. 1 Pa 1:38
Gen 36 27 the sons of Eser. 1 Pa 1:42
30 duke Dison, duke Eser, duke Disan
Esna Josu 15 43 Jephtha and Esna and Nesib
especially Gen 31 3 e. the Lord saying to him
Gen 47 13 more especially of Egypt and Chanaan
Exod 6 12 especially as I am of uncircumcised lips
10 26 especially as we know not what must
22 15 especially if it were hired and came
33 12 especially whereas thou hast said
Lev 10 18 especially whereas none of the blood
Deut 17 16 e. since the Lord hath commanded you
31 2 e. as the Lord also hath said to me
Josu 8 20 e. as they that had counterfeited flight
1 K 18 5 e. in the eyes of Saul's servants. Now
21 4 men be clean, especially from women
22 8 e. when even my son hath entered into
Jdth 2 5 them e. that despised my commandment
Osee 13 10 now especially let him save thee in
2 Ma 8 7 e. in the nights he went upon these
10 12 especially by reason of the wrong that
Acts 26 3 e. as thou [Agrippa] knowest all, both
Gal 6 10 e. to those who are of the household
Phil 4 22 e. they that are of Caesar's household
1 Tim 4 10 Savior of all men, e. of the faithful
5 8 his own, and e. of those of his house
17 e. they who labor in the word and
2 Tim 4 13 the books, especially the parchments
Titus 1 10 e. they who are of the circumcision
Philem 16 most dear brother, especially to me
2 P 2 10 e. them who walk after the flesh in
Esphatha Esth 9 7 and Delphon and Esphatha and
espousals Cant 3 11 him in the day of his espousals
Jer 2 2 remembered . . . the love of thy espousals
espouse Osee 2 19 I will e. thee to me. 20
espoused Exod 22 16 seduce a virgin not yet e.
Deut 20 7 that hath e. a wife, and not taken
22 23 if a man have espoused a damsel that
28 that is a virgin, who is not espoused
2 K 3 14 whom I e. to me for 100 foreskins of
Mat 1 18 Mary was espoused to Joseph, before
Luke 1 27 to a virgin espoused to a man whose
2 5 to be enrolled with Mary his e. wife
2 C 11 2 I have espoused you to one husband
Esra 1 Pa 4 17 sons of Esra, Jether and Mered
Esriel Josu 17 2 to the children of Esriel and to
1 Pa 5 24 Eliel and Esriel and Jeremia and Odoia
Esron Josu 15 3 reacheth into E., going up to Addar
Ruth 4 18 Phares begot E., E. begot Aram, Aram
1 Pa 5 3 Enoch and Phallu, Esron and Charmi
Mat 1 3 Phares begot E. And E. begot Aram. And
Luke 3 33 Esron who was of Phares who was of
essayed Acts 9 26 essayed to join himself to the

establish Gen 6 18 I will e. my covenant with thee. Eze 16:62
Gen 9 9 will e. my covenant with you. 11; 26:9
17 7 I will establish my covenant between
19 I will establish my covenant with him
21 my covenant I will e. with Isaac, whom
2 K 7 12 I will establish his kingdom. 1 Pa 28:7
13 I will e. the throne of his. 1 Pa 22:10
3 K 9 5 I will e. the throne of thy kingdom
15 4 his son after him and to e. Jerusalem
4 K 15 19 and to establish him in the kingdom
1 Pa 17 11 and I will establish his kingdom. He
12 and I will establish his throne forever
2 Pa 12 13 Lord chose . . . to establish his name
Ps 20 12 which they have not been able to e.
118 38 e. thy word to thy servant in thy fear
Eccu 37 17 e. within thyself a heart of good
40 19 building of a city shall e. a name
Isa 9 7 kingdom; to establish it and strengthen
44 24 the heavens, that establish the earth
62 7 give him no silence till he e. and
Jer 51 53 and establish her strength on high
Eze 16 60 I will e. with thee an everlasting
37 26 I will e. them and will multiply them
Amos 5 15 and establish judgment in the gate
1 Ma 14 46 pleased all the people to e. Simon
2 Ma 1 29 e. thy people in thy holy place, as
Rom 3 31 God forbid: but we establish the law
10 3 of God, and seeking to establish their
16 25 to him that is able to establish you
Heb 10 9 that he may e. that which followeth
1 P 5 10 will perfect you . . . and establish you
established Gen 9 17 covenant which I have e.
Gen 27 37 I have established him with corn and
Exod 15 17 which thy hands have established. The
1 K 13 13 the Lord would now have e. thy kingdom
14 47 Saul having his kingdom established
20 31 thou shalt not be e. nor thy kingdom
2 K 7 26 house of thy servant David shall be e.
3 K 2 24 who hath e. me and placed me upon the
45 throne of David shall be e. before the
3 1 kingdom was e. in the hand of Solomon
8 26 let thy words be e., which thou hast
1 Pa 17 23 concerning his house be e. forever
2 Pa 6 17 let thy word be established which thou
11 17 established Roboam the son of Solomon
17 5 and the Lord established the kingdom in
21 4 and he [Joram] had established himself
Ps 32 6 by word of the Lord the heavens were e.
40 13 and hast e. me in thy sight forever
74 4 I have established the pillars thereof
92 1 he hath e. the world which shall not
135 6 who e. the earth above the waters: for
139 12 a man full of tongue shall not be e.
148 6 he hath established them forever, and
Prov 3 19 hath established the heavens by prudence
4 26 and all thy ways shall be established
8 25 mountains . . . had not as yet been e.
28 when he established the sky above and
15 22 are many counsellors, they are e. A
16 12 the throne is established by justice
25 5 and his throne shall be e. with justice
29 14 his throne shall be established forever
Eccu 22 19 that is e. by advised counsel. The
24 15 and so was I established in Sion, and
31 11 are his goods established in the Lord
42 17 settled to be established for his glory
26 he hath e. the good things of every
43 28 is e. the end of their journey, and by
44 21 in his flesh he e. the covenant, and
46 16 Samuel . . . established a new government
Isa 42 5 that e. the earth and the things that
48 2 and are e. upon the God of Israel: the

Dan 6 9 Darius set forth the decree and e. it
Zach 5 11 that it may be e. and set there upon
1 Ma 1 17 the kingdom was e. before Antiochus
Heb 8 6 which is established on better promises
13 9 that the heart be established with grace
establisheth Eccu 3 11 father's blessing e. the houses
Dan 2 21 away kingdoms and establisheth them
establishment Ps 96 2 are the e. of his throne
Estaol Josu 15 33 in the plains: Estaol and Sarea
estate Ruth 1 13 grown up and come to man's estate
1 K 2 33 shall die when they come to man's e.
Esth 15 2 remember . . . days of thy low estate
Eccu 11 13 lifted him up from his low estate
20 11 shall lift up his head from a low e.
29 23 hath undone many of good estate and
33 20 give not thy estate to another, lest
1 Ma 15 3 to restore it to its former estate
esteem Tob 13 14 and shall esteem thy land as holy
Job 41 18 for he shall esteem iron as straw
20 as stubble will he esteem the hammer
23 he shall esteem the deep as growing old
Mat 11 16 whereunto shall I e. this generation
Luke 13 20 e. the kingdom of God to be like
Phil 2 3 each e. others better than themselves
1 Th 5 13 that you e. them more abundantly in
2 Th 3 15 yet do not e. him as an enemy, but
esteemed Deut 2 11 they were esteemed as giants
Ecce 2 10 esteemed this my portion, to make use
Wisd 2 16 we are esteemed by him as triflers
22 nor esteemed the honor of holy souls
5 4 we fools esteemed their life madness
7 8 e. riches nothing in comparison of her
15 15 they have esteemed all the idols of
18 8 as a drop of water . . . are they e.
Isa 29 17 charmel shall be esteemed as a forest
53 3 and despised, whereupon we e. him not
Lam 4 2 how are they e. as earthen vessels, the
2 Ma 3 2 princes e. the place worthy of the
4 15 they e. the Grecian glories for the
7 12 he esteemed the torments as nothing
Mat 14 5 because they esteemed him as a prophet
1 Tim 5 17 let the priests that rule well be e.
Heb 10 29 e. blood of the testament unclean
esteemeth Ecce 10 3 the fool . . . e. all men fools
Rom 14 14 that e. anything to be unclean, to him
esteeming Jdth 8 27 e. these very punishments to
Wisd 1 16 esteeming it a friend have fallen away
Heb 11 26 e. the reproach of Christ greater
Estemo Josu 21 14 and Jether and Estemo and Holon
Esthamo 1 K 30 28 and that were in Esthamo, and
1 Pa 4 17 and Sammai and Jesba the father of E.
19 and Esthamo, who was of Machathi. The
Esthaol Josu 19 41 Saraa and E. and Hirsemes, that
Judg 13 25 camp of Dan, between Saraa and Esthaol
16 31 buried it between Saraa and Esthaol
18 2 sent five . . . from Saraa and Esthaol
8 returned to their brethren in Saraa
8 to their brethren in Saraa and Esthaol
11 from Saraa and E., 600 men furnished
Esthaolites 1 Pa 2 53 came the Saraites and E.
Esthemo 1 Pa 6 58 and Jether and E. with their
Esther Esth 2 7 by another name was called Esther
Esth 2 15 Esther the daughter of Abihail the
18 for the marriage and wedding of Esther
20 neither had Esther as yet declared her
20 he commanded, Esther observed: and she
22 immediately he told it to queen Esther
4 9 and Atach went back and told Esther
13 he sent word to Esther again, saying
15 again Esther sent to Mardochai in these
17 did all that Esther had commanded him
5 1 Esther put on her royal apparel, and
2 when he saw Esther the queen standing
3 what wilt thou, queen Esther? What is
7 Esther answered: My petition and request
12 queen Esther also hath invited no other
7 2 what is thy petition, Esther, that is
6 Esther said: It is this Aman that is
7 Aman also rose up to entreat Esther
8 upon the bed on which Esther lay, and
8 1 gave the house of Aman . . . to queen E.
1 Esther had confessed to him that he
2 Esther set Mardochai over her house
7 Assuerus answered Esther the queen
7 I have given Aman's house to Esther
9 25 afterwards Esther went in to the king
29 Esther . . . wrote also a second epistle
31 as Mardochai and Esther had appointed
32 of this book, which is called Esther
10 6 E. whom the king married and made
14 1 queen Esther also, fearing the danger
15 12 what is the matter, Esther? I am thy
16 13 of Esther the partner of our kingdom
Esther's Esth 2 11 having a care for E. welfare
Esth 4 4 Esther's maids and her eunuchs went in
5 5 quickly, that he may obey Esther's will
Esthon 1 Pa 4 11 who was the father of Esthon
estimated Lev 27 27 how much soever it was e. by
estimation Exod 22 5 according to e. of the damage
Lev 5 18 the measure and estimation of the sin
6 6 the e. and measure of the offence
27 2 shall give the price according to e.
8 and not able to pay the estimation, he
13 shall add above the e. the fifth part
15 shall give the fifth part of the e.
19 the fifth part of the money of the e.
25 all estimation shall be made according
27 shall redeem it according to thy e.
Etam Judg 15 8 dwelt in a cavern of the rock Etam
Judg 15 11 went down to the cave of the rock Etam
13 brought him [Samson] from the rock E.
1 Pa 4 3 this is the posterity of Etam. Jezrahel
32 their towns also were Etam and Aen
2 Pa 11 6 he [Roboam] built Bethlehem and Etam
eternal Gen 21 33 upon name of the Lord God e.
2 K 23 5 he should make with me an e. covenant
Tob 13 6 and extol the eternal King of worlds
12 bless the God eternal, that he may
Ps 23 7 be ye lifted up, O eternal gates. 9
54 20 and the Eternal shall humble them. For
76 6 I had in my mind the eternal years
138 24 of iniquity and lead me in the e. way
Wisd 7 26 she is the brightness of eternal light
17 2 exiled from the eternal providence
Isa 45 17 Israel is saved . . . with an e. salvation
Bar 4 7 provoked him who made you, the e. God
10 which the E. hath brought upon them. 14
22 my hope is in the Eternal that he will
35 fire shall come upon her from the E.
Dan 6 26 he is the living and e. God forever
13 42 eternal God, who knowest hidden things
2 Ma 1 25 art just and almighty and eternal, who
Rom 1 20 his eternal power also and divinity
16 26 according to the precept of the e. God
2 C 4 17 exceedingly an eternal weight of glory
18 the things which are not seen, are e.
5 1 house not made with hands, e. in heaven
Eph 3 11 according to the eternal purpose, which
2 Th 1 9 who shall suffer eternal punishments
Heb 5 9 obey him, the cause of e. salvation
6 2 of the dead and of eternal judgment
9 12 having obtained eternal redemption
15 receive the promise of e. inheritance
1 P 5 10 who hath called us unto his e. glory
Jude 7 suffering the punishment of e. fire
Apoc 14 6 having the e. gospel, to preach unto

eternal life; *see* **life**
eternity 1 Pa 16 36 blessed be . . . from e. to e.
1 Pa 29 10 God of Israel, our father from e. to e.
2 Es 9 5 bless the Lord your God from e. to e.
Ps 9 16 the Lord shall reign to e., yea for
40 14 Lord the God of Israel from e. to e.
47 15 this is God, our God unto e. and for
89 2 from e. and to e. thou art God. Turn
102 17 mercy of Lord is from e. and unto e.
Prov 8 23 I was set up from e., and of old before
Ecce 12 5 man shall go into house of his eternity
Eccu 18 8 so are a few years compared to eternity
39 25 he seeth from e. to e., and there is
42 21 he is from e. to e., and to him nothing
Isa 57 15 and the Eminent that inhabiteth eternity
Dan 12 3 many to justice, as stars for all e.
Mich 5 2 the beginning, from the days of eternity
Haba 3 6 bowed down by the journeys of his e.
Rom 16 25 was kept secret from eternity, which
Eph 3 9 hath been hidden from eternity in God
2 P 3 18 to him be glory . . . unto the day of e.
Ethai 2 K 15 19 the king said to E. the Gethite
2 K 15 21 Ethai answered the king, saying: As
22 David said to Ethai: Come and pass over
22 Ethai the Gethite passed, and all the
18 2 third part under the hand of Ethai
5 king commanded Joab and Abisai and E.
12 king charged thee and Abisai and Ethai
1 Pa 11 31 valiant men . . . Ethai the son of Ribai
2 Pa 11 20 and Ethai and Ziza and Salomith
Etham Exod 13 20 they encamped in Etham in the
Num 33 6 from Soccoth they came into Etham
8 marched three days through desert of E.
Ethan 3 K 4 31 wiser than Ethan the Ezrahite
1 Pa 2 6 sons of Zare: Zamri and Ethan and Eman
8 the sons of Ethan: Azarias, and the
6 42 the son of Adaia, the son of Ethan
44 on the left hand Ethan the son of Cusi
15 17 their brethren: Ethan the son of Casaia
19 the singers, Heman, Asaph, and Ethan
Ps 73 15 thou hast dried up the Ethan rivers
88 1 of understanding, for Ethan the Ezrahite
Ethanim 3 K 8 2 festival day in the month of E.
Ethbaal 3 K 16 31 to wife Jezabel daughter of E.
Etheel 2 Es 11 7 Masia the son of Etheel, the son
Ethei 1 Pa 2 35 bore him E. And E. begot Nathan
Ether Josu 15 42 Labana and Ether and Asan
Ethi 1 Pa 12 11 Ethi the sixth, Eliel the seventh
Ethiopia Gen 2 13 compasseth all the land of E.
4 K 19 9 he heard of Theraca king of Ethiopia
Jdth 1 9 till you come to the borders of Ethiopia
Esth 1 1 who reigned from India to Ethiopia
8 9 provinces, from India even to Ethiopia
13 1 who reigneth from India to Ethiopia
16 1 Artaxerxes, from India to Ethiopia
Job 28 19 topaz of Ethiopia shall not be equal
Ps 67 32 E. shall stretch out her hands to God
Isa 11 11 from Phetros and from Ethiopia and
18 1 which is beyond the rivers of Ethiopia
20 3 three years upon Egypt and upon E.
4 the captivity of E., young and old
5 and ashamed of Ethiopia their hope
37 9 about Tharaca the king of Ethiopia
43 3 thy atonement, E. and Saba for thee
45 14 the merchandise of E. and of Sabaim
Eze 29 10 of Syene, even to the borders of E.
30 4 and there shall be dread in Ethiopia
5 E. and Libya and Lydia and all the
9 to destroy the confidence of Ethiopia
Dan 11 43 he shall pass through Libya and E.
Nah 3 9 E. and Egypt were the strength thereof
Haba 3 7 I saw the tents of Ethiopia, for their
Soph 3 10 from beyond the rivers of Ethiopia
Acts 8 27 a man of Ethiopia, an eunuch, of great
Ethiopian Num 12 1 because of his wife the E.
2 Pa 14 9 Zara the Ethiopian came out against
Jer 13 23 if the Ethiopian can change his skin
38 7 Abdemelech the Ethiopian, an eunuch
10 the king commanded Abdemelech the E.
12 Abdemelech the E. said to Jeremias
39 15 go and tell Abdemelech the Ethiopian
Ethiopians 2 Pa 12 3 and Troglodites and E. And
2 Pa 14 12 and the Lord terrified the Ethiopians
12 the E. fled. And Asa and the people
13 the E. fell even to utter destruction
16 8 were not the E. and the Libyans much
21 16 Arabians, who border on the Ethiopians
Ps 71 9 before the E. shall fall down: and his
73 14 to be meat for the people of the E.
86 4 the people of the Ethiopians, these
Jer 46 9 let the valiant men come forth, the E.
Eze 38 5 Persians, E., and Libyans with them
Amos 9 7 are not you as the children of the E.
Soph 2 12 you E. also shall be slain with my
Acts 8 27 Candace the queen of the Ethiopians
Ethnan 1 Pa 4 7 of Halaa, Sereth, Isaar, and E.
Etroth Num 32 35 E. and Sophan and Jazer and
Eubulus 2 Tim 4 21 E. and Pudens and Linus and
Eumenes 1 Ma 8 8 from them they gave to king E.
Eunice 2 Tim 1 5 Lois and in thy mother Eunice
eunuch Gen 37 36 Putiphar, an e. of Pharao. 39:1
Deut 23 1 eunuch who testicles are broken or cut
3 K 22 9 the king of Israel called an eunuch
4 K 8 6 and the king appointed her an eunuch
23 11 near chamber of Nathanmelech the eunuch
25 19 out of the city one e. Jer 52:25
Jdth 12 10 said to Vagao his e.: Go and persuade
Esth 2 3 under the hand of Egeus the eunuch
8 and were delivered to Egeus the eunuch
9 eunuch to fasten the women's ornaments
14 under the hand of Susagaz the eunuch
15 Egeus the eunuch the keeper of the
4 5 she called for Atach the eunuch, whom
Wisd 3 14 the eunuch, that hath not wrought
Eccu 20 2 the lust of an eunuch shall deflower
30 21 as an eunuch embracing a virgin and
Isa 56 3 let not the eunuch say: Behold I am
Jer 38 7 Abdemelech the Ethiopian, an eunuch
Acts 8 27 an eunuch of great authority under
34 the e., answering Philip, said: I
36 the eunuch said: See, here is water
38 into the water, both Philip and the e.
39 and the eunuch saw him no more. And he
eunuchs Gen 40 1 two eunuchs, the butler and the
1 K 8 15 to give his eunuchs and servants. Your
4 K 9 32 two or three eunuchs bowed down to him
20 18 they shall be e. in the palace. Isa 39:7
24 12 [Joachin] and his eunuchs: and the
15 and the king's wives and his eunuchs
2 Pa 18 8 king of Israel called one of the e.
Esth 1 10 seven e. that served in his presence
12 he had signified to her by the eunuchs
15 which he had sent to her by the eunuchs
2 21 and Thares, two of the king's eunuchs
4 4 Esther's maids and her eunuchs went in
6 2 Bagathan and Thares the eunuchs, who
7 9 Harbona, one of the eunuchs that stood
12 1 with Bagatha and Thara the king's e.
6 because of the two eunuchs of the king
Isa 56 4 thus saith the Lord to the eunuchs
Jer 29 2 the eunuchs and the princes of Juda
34 19 the eunuchs and the priests and all
41 16 the children and the eunuchs, whom
Dan 1 3 to Asphenez the master of the eunuchs
7 master of the eunuchs gave them names
8 he requested the master of the eunuchs

9 in the sight of the prince of the e.
10 prince of the eunuchs said to Daniel
11 prince of the e. had appointed over
18 the prince of the eunuchs brought them
Mat 19 12 e. who were born so . . . e. who were made so by men . . . e. who have made themselves e.

Eupator 1 Ma 6 17 and he called his name Eupator
2 Ma 2 21 Antiochus the Illustrious and his son E.
10 10 now we will relate the acts of Eupator
13 being accused for this to Eupator by
13 1 that Antiochus Eupator was coming with

Euphrates Gen 2 14 the fourth river is Euphrates
2 Pa 35 20 to fight in Charcamis by the Euphrates
Jdth 1 6 about the Euphrates and the Tigris
2 14 he passed over the Euphrates and came
Eccu 24 36 maketh understanding to abound as the E.
Jer 13 4 go to the Euphrates, and hide it there
5 I went, and hid it by the Euphrates
6 go to the E., and take from thence the
7 I went to the Euphrates, and digged
51 63 shalt throw it into the midst of the E.

river Euphrates Gen 15 18 to the great river E.
Deut 1 7 as far as the great river Euphrates
11 24 from the great r. E. unto the western
Josu 1 4 Libanus unto the great river Euphrates
2 K 8 3 extend his dominion over the river E.
4 K 23 29 the king of Assyria to the river E.
24 7 from the river of Egypt unto the r. E.
1 Pa 5 9 entrance of the desert and the river E.
18 3 his dominions as far as the river E.
2 Pa 9 26 the kings from the river Euphrates
Jer 46 2 which was by the river E. in Charcamis
6 towards the north by the r. Euphrates
10 in the north country, by the river E.
1 Ma 3 32 from the river E. to the river of Egypt
37 he passed over the river Euphrates and
Apoc 9 14 are bound in the great river Euphrates
16 12 vial upon that great river Euphrates

Eupolemus 1 Ma 8 17 Judas chose Eupolemus the son
2 Ma 4 11 Eupolemus who went ambassador to Rome

Euroaquilo Acts 27 14 wind called Euroaquilo

Eutychus Acts 20 9 named E. sitting on the window

evangelist Isa 41 27 to Jerusalem I will give an e.
Acts 21 8 into the house of Philip the evangelist
2 Tim 4 5 do the work of an evangelist, fulfil

evangelists Eph 4 11 prophets, and other some e.

evangelizing Luke 8 1 evangelizing the kingdom

Eve Gen 3 20 Adam called the name of his wife Eve
Gen 4 1 and Adam knew Eve his wife, who conceived
Tob 8 8 and gavest him Eve for a helper. And
2 C 11 3 the serpent seduced Eve by his subtilty
1 Tim 2 13 for Adam was first formed; then Eve

even Gen 30 16 when Jacob returned at even from
Exod 27 5 the grate shall be even to the midst
Lev 13 32 blemish be even with the other flesh
Mark 13 35 cometh at even or at midnight or at the

evening Gen 1 5 there was e. and morning one day
Gen 1 8 evening and morning were the . . . day. 13, 19, 23, 31
8 11 she came to him in the e., carrying a
19 1 two angels came to Sodom in the evening
24 11 in the e. at the time when the women are
49 27 in the evening shall divide the spoil
Exod 12 6 shall sacrifice it in the evening. And
18 day of the month in the evening you
18 day of the same month in the evening
16 6 in the e. you shall know that the Lord
12 in the evening you shall eat flesh, and
13 so it came to pass in the evening that
29 39 in the morning and another in the e.
41 other lamb thou shalt offer in the e.
30 8 shall place them [lamps] in the evening
Lev 6 20 in the morning and half of it in the e.
11 24 shall be unclean until the e. 28, 31, 32, 39, 40; 14:46; 15:5, 7, 8, 10, 11, 16, 17, 18, 20, 22, 27; 22:6; Num 19:7, 8, 10, 19, 21, 22
27 shall be defiled until e. 15:23; 17:15
23 32 from e. until e. you shall celebrate
24 3 shall set them from e. until morning
Num 9 5 fourteenth day of month at e. Josu 5:10
11 fourteenth day of the month in the e.
15 from e. there was over the tabernacle
21 if the cloud tarried from evening until
28 4 in the morning and the other in the e.
8 other lamb in like manner in the e.
Deut 16 4 was sacrificed the first day in the e.
6 shalt immolate the phase in the evening
23 11 before he be washed with water in the e.
28 67 shalt say: Who will grant me evening
67 at evening: Who will grant me morning
Josu 7 6 before the ark of the Lord until the e.
8 29 king thereof on a gibbet until the e.
10 26 gibbets and they hung until the evening
Judg 19 9 day is declining, and draweth toward e.
16 the field and from his work in the e.
20 26 they fasted that day till the evening
21 2 abiding before him till the evening
Ruth 2 17 gleaned therefore in the field till e.
1 K 14 24 man that shall eat food till evening
17 16 the Philistine came out morning and e.
20 5 in the field till e. of the third day
30 17 from the e. unto the e. of the next day
2 K 1 12 and fasted until evening for Saul and
11 13 he went out in the evening and slept on
3 K 17 6 bread and flesh in the evening, and he
22 35 king of Israel . . . died in the evening
4 K 5 24 now it was the evening, he took them
7 5 they arose in the evening, to go to
16 15 holocaust and the evening sacrifice
1 Pa 16 40 holocausts continually, morning and e.
23 30 and in like manner in the evening, as
2 Pa 2 4 and for the holocausts, morning and e.
13 11 to the Lord every day morning and e.
11 to be lighted always in the evening
18 34 against the Syrians until the evening
31 3 be offered always morning and evening
1 Es 3 3 holocaust to the Lord morning and e.
9 4 sorrowful until the evening sacrifice
5 and at the evening sacrifice I rose up
Jdth 12 9 she took her own meat in the evening
Esth 2 14 she that went in at evening, came out
Job 4 20 morning till e. they shall be cut down
7 4 and again I shall look for the evening
11 17 noonday shall arise to thee at evening
38 32 and make the evening star to rise upon
Ps 29 6 in the evening weeping shall have place
54 18 evening and morning and at noon I
58 7 they shall return at evening and. 15
64 9 outgoings of the morning and of the e.
89 6 in the evening he shall fall, grow dry
103 23 his work, and to his labor until the e.
140 2 lifting up of my hands, as e. sacrifice
Ecce 11 6 in the evening let not thy hand cease
Eccu 18 26 morning until the e. the time shall be
Isa 5 11 and to drink till the evening, to be
17 14 the time of the evening, behold there
21 13 in the forest at evening you shall sleep
Jer 5 6 wolf in the evening hath spoiled them
6 4 shadows of the evening are grown longer
Eze 12 4 and thou shalt go forth in the evening
7 and in the e. I digged through the wall
24 18 my wife died in the evening: and I did
33 22 had been upon me in the evening, before
46 2 gate shall not be shut till the evening
Dan 8 14 unto evening and morning 2,300 days

26 vision of the evening and the morning
9 21 at the time of the evening sacrifice
Haba 1 8 leopards, and swifter than e. wolves
Soph 2 7 they shall rest in the evening: because
3 3 her judges are evening wolves, they
Zach 14 7 the time of the e. there shall be light
1 Ma 9 13 fought from morning even unto the e.
10 80 darts at the people from morning till e.
Mat 14 15 when it was e. his disciples came to
23 and when it was e. he was there alone
16 2 when it is e. you say: It will be fair
26 20 when it was evening he sat down with
27 57 when it was e. there came a certain
Mark 1 32 e. after sunset, they brought to him
Luke 24 29 stay with us because it is towards e.
Acts 4 3 till the next day; for it was now e.
28 23 from morning until e. And some believed
when evening was come Mat 8 16 w. . . . they brought to him many that were possessed
Mat 20 8 w. . . . the lord of the vineyard saith
Mark 4 35 w. . . . : Let us pass over to the other
11 19 w. . . . he went forth out of the city
14 17 w. . . . he cometh with the twelve. And
15 42 when e. was now come, because it was
John 6 16 w. . . . his disciples went down to the
event Gen 41 13 the event of the things proved to
Judg 16 9 expecting the event of the thing, and
2 K 11 25 for various is the event of war: and
Wisd 11 15 in the end, when they saw the event
13 19 for the event of all things he asketh
2 Ma 9 25 and expect what shall be the event, I
13 13 to commit the event of the thing to
eventide Wisd 8 8 and the events of times and ages
everlasting Gen 9 16 remember the e. covenant
Gen 48 4 seed after thee for an e. possession
49 26 until the desire of the e. hills should
Exod 12 14 with an e. observance. Seven days shall
30 8 he shall burn an everlasting incense
21 it shall be an everlasting law to him
31 16 it is an everlasting covenant between
40 13 of them may prosper to an e. priesthood
Lev 6 18 it shall be an ordinance everlasting in
10 9 because it is an everlasting precept
16 29 this shall be to you an e. ordinance
23 21 it shall be an everlasting ordinance. 31, 41; Num 18:23
24 8 children of Israel by an e. covenant
Num 18 8 the priestly office by e. ordinances
Deut 33 15 of the fruits of the everlasting hills
27 underneath are the everlasting arms
2 K 7 24 thy people Israel to be an e. people
1 Pa 16 17 to Israel for an everlasting covenant
Job 10 22 and no order, but e. horror dwelleth
Ps 75 5 enlightenest wonderfully from e. hills
77 66 he put them to an everlasting reproach
92 2 from of old: thou art from everlasting
104 10 to Israel for an everlasting testament
105 48 Lord the God of Israel from e. to e.
111 7 the just shall be in e. remembrance
Prov 10 25 but the just is as an e. foundation. As
Wisd 6 21 desire of wisdom bringeth to e. kingdom
8 13 and shall leave behind me an e. memory
10 14 accused him and gave him e. glory. She
Eccu 1 4 the understanding of prudence from e.
5 and her ways are e. commandments. To
15 6 shall cause him to inherit an e. name
17 10 he made an e. covenant with them, and
24 28 my memory is unto e. generations. They
26 24 as e. foundations upon a solid rock
30 17 and e. rest, than continual sickness
31 10 made perfect, he shall have glory e.
45 8 made an e. covenant with him and gave
19 was made to him for an e. testament
31 made their glory in their nation e.
49 14 to the Lord, prepared for e. glory
Isa 24 5 have broken the everlasting covenant
33 14 of you shall dwell with e. burnings
35 10 e. joy shall be upon their heads: they
40 28 the Lord is the everlasting God, who
51 11 joy e. shall be upon their heads, they
54 8 with e. kindness have had mercy on
55 3 I will make an e. covenant. Jer 32:40
13 the Lord shall be named for an e. sign
56 5 I will give them an e. name which shall
60 15 I will make thee to be an e. glory, a
19 shall be unto thee for an e. light. 20
61 7 everlasting joy shall be unto them
63 12 to make himself an everlasting name
16 redeemer, from everlasting is thy name
Jer 5 22 a bound for the sea, an e. ordinance
10 10 he is the living God and the e. king
20 11 have not understood the e. reproach
17 my grave, and her womb an e. conception
23 40 I will bring an e. reproach upon you
31 3 yea I have loved thee with an e. love
49 13 and all her cities shall be e. wastes
50 5 be joined to the Lord by an e. covenant
51 39 slumber and sleep an everlasting sleep
57 they shall sleep an everlasting sleep
Bar 2 35 them another covenant that shall be e.
4 22 shall come to you from our e. Savior
24 upon you with great honor and e. glory
29 shall bring you everlasting joy again
5 1 the beauty and honor of that e. glory
2 set a crown on thy head of e. honor
7 every high mountain and the e. rocks
Eze 16 60 will establish with thee an e. covenant
22 20 into the pit to the everlasting people
35 5 thou hast been an everlasting enemy and
9 I will make thee e. desolation and thy
36 2 aha, the e. heights are given to us for
37 26 it shall be an e. covenant with them
46 14 Lord by ordinance continual and e.
15 by morning: an everlasting holocaust
Dan 3 100 his kingdom is an e. kingdom, and his
4 31 his power is an everlasting power. 7:14
7 27 whose kingdom is an e. kingdom, and all
9 24 and everlasting justice may be brought
1 Ma 2 51 receive great glory and an e. name. Was
54 the covenant of an e. priesthood. Jesus
57 obtained the throne of an e. kingdom
6 44 and to get himself an everlasting name
Mat 18 8 feet, to be cast into everlasting fire
25 41 depart from me, you cursed, into e. fire
46 and these shall go into e. punishment
Mark 3 29 shall be guilty of an everlasting sin
Luke 16 9 they may receive you into e. dwellings
2 Th 2 15 hath given us everlasting consolation
3 16 Lord of peace himself give you e. peace
1 Tim 6 16 to whom be honor and empire everlasting
everlasting life; *see* **life**
everlastingly Bar 3 3 and shall we perish e.
every one's 1 P 1 17 judgeth according to e. work
everybody's Eccu 42 12 behold not e. beauty: and
everywhere 3 K 8 41 shall hear e. thy great name
Wisd 2 9 let us everywhere leave tokens of joy
7 24 reacheth e. by reason of her purity
Jer 50 15 against her, she hath e. given her hand
2 Ma 8 7 fame of his valor was spread abroad e.
Mark 16 20 they going forth preached everywhere
Acts 17 30 that all should everywhere do penance
21 28 teacheth all men e. against the people
28 22 that it is everywhere contradicted
1 C 4 17 as I teach everywhere in every church
Phil 4 12 e. and in all things I am instructed
Evi Num 31 8 their kings Evi and Recem and Hur

evidence Num 35 30 condemned upon the e. of one
2 Ma 3 24 gave a great evidence of his presence
Mark 14 55 the council sought for evidence against
2 C 8 24 the evidence of your charity and of our
Heb 11 1 the evidence of things that appear not
evidences Mark 14 56 their e. were not agreeing
evident Gen 26 9 it is evident she is thy wife
Tob 2 22 is evident thy hope is come to nothing
2 Ma 14 15 protected his portion by evident signs
15 35 an evident and manifest sign of God
1 C 16 9 great door and evident is opened unto
Philem 6 of thy faith may be made evident in
Heb 7 14 it is e. that our Lord sprung out of
15 is yet far more evident: if according
evidently Lev 13 11 he is evidently unclean. 36
1 Tim 3 16 e. great is the mystery of godliness
evil Mat 5 11 speak all that is evil against you
Mat 5 37 that which is . . . above these is of e.
39 I say to you not to resist evil: but if
6 23 if thy eye be evil, thy whole body will
34 sufficient for the day is the e. thereof
7 11 if you being evil know how. Luke 11:13
18 good tree cannot bring forth evil fruit
9 4 why do you think evil in your hearts
12 33 or make the tree evil and its fruit evil
34 whereas you are evil? For out of the
35 e. man out of e. treasure . . . e. things
39 an evil . . . generation seeketh a sign
15 19 from the heart come forth evil thoughts
20 15 is thy eye evil because I am good? So
21 41 will bring those evil men to an e. end
24 48 if that evil servant shall say in his
27 23 what evil hath he done. Mark 15:14; Luke 23:22
Mark 5 29 body that she was healed of the evil
7 21 from within . . . proceed evil thoughts
22 evil eye, blasphemy, pride, foolishness
Luke 6 9 to do good or to do evil. Mark 3:4
22 cast out your name as e. for the Son
35 kind to the unthankful and to the evil
43 good tree that bringeth forth e. fruit
45 e. man out of e. treasure bringeth forth that which is e.
7 21 he cured many of their . . . evil spirits
8 2 who had been healed of evil spirits
11 34 if it be evil, thy body also will be
John 3 19 than the light: for their works were e.
20 every one that doth evil hateth the
5 29 but they that have done evil, unto the
7 7 of it, that the works thereof are evil
18 23 if I have spoken evil, give testimony of e.
Acts 7 6 and treat them evil four hundred years
9 13 how much evil he hath done to thy
19 9 speaking evil of the way of the Lord
13 to invoke over them that had e. spirits
23 5 shalt not speak evil of the prince of
28 21 relate or speak any evil of thee. But
Rom 2 9 every soul of man that worketh evil
3 8 let us do evil that there may come good
7 15 but the evil which I hate, that I do
19 the evil which I will not, that I do
21 to do good, evil is present with me
9 11 yet born nor had done any good or evil
12 9 hating that which is evil cleaving to
17 to no man rendering evil for evil
21 be not overcome by e., but overcome e.
13 3 terror to the good work but to the e.
4 if thou do that which is evil, fear
8 to execute wrath upon him that doth e.
14 16 let not our good be evil spoken of
20 is evil for that man who eateth with
16 19 to be wise in good and simple in evil
1 C 5 13 put away the evil one from among
10 30 why am I evil spoken of, for that for
15 33 e. communications corrupt good manners
2 C 5 10 he hath done, whether it be good or e.
6 8 by evil report and good report; as
Eph 5 16 the time, because the days are evil
6 13 may be able to resist in the evil day
Phil 3 2 beware of dogs, beware of evil workers
Col 1 21 enemies in mind in evil works: yet now
3 5 evil concupiscence and covetousness
1 Th 5 14 see that none render evil for evil
22 from all appearance of evil refrain
2 Th 3 2 delivered from importunate and e. men
1 Tim 5 14 no occasion to the adversary to speak e.
6 4 blasphemies, evil suspicions, conflicts
2 Tim 3 13 evil men and seducers shall grow
4 14 Alexander . . . hath done me much evil
18 delivered me from every evil work
Titus 1 12 always liars, evil beasts, slothful
3 2 to speak evil of no man, not to be
Heb 3 12 there be in any of you an evil heart
5 14 to the discerning of good and evil
10 22 sprinkled from an evil conscience
James 3 8 an unquiet evil, full of deadly poison
16 there is inconstancy and every e. work
5 10 take for an example of suffering evil
1 P 3 9 not rendering evil for evil, nor railing
16 whereas they speak evil of you, they may
4 4 of riotousness speaking evil of you
2 P 2 2 way of truth shall be evil spoken of
3 J 11 follow not that which is evil, but that
11 he that doth evil hath not seen God
Apoc 2 2 thou canst not bear them that are evil
evil things Mat 12 35 e. treasure bringeth forth e. things
Mark 7 23 all these evil things come from within
Luke 16 25 likewise Lazarus evil things, but now
Rom 1 30 proud, haughty, inventors of evil things
1 C 10 6 that we should not covet evil things
1 P 3 12 the Lord upon them that do evil things
from evil Mat 6 13 temptation. But deliver us from evil
John 17 15 that thou shouldst keep them from evil
2 Th 3 3 will strengthen and keep you from evil
1 P 3 10 let him refrain his tongue from evil
11 let him decline from evil and do good
no evil Luke 23 41 but this man hath done no evil
Acts 23 9 we find no evil in this man. What if
Rom 13 10 love of our neighbor worketh no evil
1 C 13 5 not provoked to anger, thinketh no e.
2 C 13 7 now we pray God that you may do no evil
Eph 4 29 let no evil speech proceed from you
Titus 2 8 be afraid, having no evil to say of us
evildoer Job 8 20 nor reach out his hand to the e.
2 Tim 2 9 labor even unto bands, as an evildoer
evildoers Ps 36 1 be not emulous of evildoers; nor
Ps 36 9 evildoers shall be cut off: but they
93 16 who shall rise up for me against the e.
Eccu 34 5 and the dreams of evildoers are vanity
1 P 2 12 they speak against you as evildoers
14 by him for the punishment of evildoers
Evilmerodach 4 K 25 27 E. king of Babylon. Jer 52:31
evils Gen 42 36 all these evils are fallen upon me
Gen 48 16 angel that delivereth me from all e.
Exod 15 26 none of the e. that I laid upon Egypt
Num 11 15 that I be not afflicted with so great e.
Deut 29 22 evils wherewith Lord hath afflicted it
31 17 all evils and afflictions shall find
17 that these evils have found me. But I
18 for all the evils which they have done
21 after many evils and afflictions shall
29 evils shall come upon you in the latter
32 23 I will heap evils upon them and will
Josu 23 15 upon you all the e. he hath threatened
Judg 6 13 why have these evils fallen upon us
15 3 for I [Samson] will do you evils. And

1 K 10 19 hath saved you out of all your evils
2 K 16 8 and behold thy evils press upon thee
19 7 than all the evils that have befallen
3 K 14 10 I will bring evils upon. 4 K 21:12; 22:16; 2 Pa 34:24; Jer 6:19; 11:11
4 K 22 20 that thy eyes may not see all the evils
2 Pa 7 22 therefore all these evils are come upon
20 9 if evils fall upon us, the sword of
33 6 he wrought many evils before the Lord
Esth 10 9 and he delivered us from all evils and
11 9 was troubled, fearing their own evils
Job 3 10 nor took away evils from my eyes. Why
30 26 and evils are come upon me: I waited
Ps 7 5 rendered to them that repaid me evils
20 12 they have intended evils against thee
22 4 I will fear no evils, for thou art with
26 5 in the day of evils he hath protected
27 3 but evils are in their hearts. Give
34 26 who rejoice at my evils. Let them be
37 13 that sought evils to me spoke vain
39 13 evils without number have surrounded me
15 be ashamed that desire evils to me
40 6 my enemies have spoken evils against me
8 against me: they devised evils to me
53 7 turn back the evils upon my enemies
69 4 blush for shame that desire evils to me
70 24 and put to shame that seek evils to me
87 4 my soul is filled with evils: and my
89 15 the years in which we have seen evils
106 26 depths: their soul pined away with evils
39 afflicted through the trouble of evils
108 20 and who speak evils against my soul
Prov 1 33 enjoy abundance without fear of evils
13 3 guard on his speech shall meet with e.
15 28 mouth of wicked overfloweth with evils
16 17 path of the just departeth from evils
17 16 refuseth to learn, shall fall into evils
20 30 blueness of wound shall wipe away evils
22 8 that soweth iniquity shall reap evils
24 8 he that deviseth to do evils, shall be
27 21 heart of the wicked seeketh after evils
Ecce 4 3 not yet born, nor hath seen the evils
8 11 of men commit evils without any fear
14 they are just men to whom evils happen
Wisd 14 22 call so many and so great evils peace
18 19 not know why they suffered these evils
Eccu 7 1 do no evils, and no evils shall lay hold
2 and evils shall depart from thee. My
3 sow not e. in the furrows of injustice
8 18 lest he burden thee with his evils
11 27 be not unmindful of evils: and in the day of evils be not unmindful
35 mischievous man, for he worketh evils
12 3 for him that is always occupied in e.
17 if evils come upon thee, thou shalt
30 14 who is weak and afflicted with evils
33 1 no e. shall happen to him that feareth
1 will keep him and deliver him from e.
Isa 3 9 souls, for evils are rendered to them
13 11 I will visit the evils of the world
Jer 2 3 evils shall come upon them, saith the
13 my people have done two evils. They
11 17 for the evils of the house of Israel
19 15 all the e. that I have spoken against
23 12 I will bring evils upon them, the year
32 23 all these evils are come upon them
36 3 shall hear all the evils that I purpose
44 9 you forgotten the e. of your fathers and the e. of the kings of Juda and the e. of their wives and your e. and the e. of your wives
23 therefore are these evils come upon you
Bar 1 20 many evils have cleaved to us and the
2 2 Lord would bring upon us great evils
7 pronounced against us all these evils
3 4 wherefore evils have cleaved fast to us
4 18 that hath brought the evils upon you
29 he that hath brought evils upon you
6 48 when war cometh upon them or evils
49 from war nor save themselves from evils
Eze 6 9 the evils which they have committed
11 of the evils of the house of Israel
Dan 3 44 that show evils to thy servants, let
Amos 9 10 who say: The evils shall not approach
Abdi 13 neither shalt thou also look on in his e.
1 Ma 1 10 evils were multiplied in the earth
12 from them, many evils have befallen us
55 and they committed evils in the land
2 6 these saw the evils that were done in
43 all they that fled from the evils
3 42 saw that evils were multiplied and that
59 than to see the evils of our nation
6 12 I remember the evils that I have done
13 for this cause these e. have found me
7 23 Judas saw all the evils that Alcimus
8 31 concerning the evils that Demetrius
10 5 he will remember all the evils that we
13 32 and brought great evils upon the land
15 12 he perceived that evils were gathered
2 Ma 4 1 and had been the promoter of evils
5 20 partaker of the evils of the people
6 3 very bad was this invasion of evils
10 4 they might no more fall into such evils
10 the evils that happened in the wars
13 4 that he was the cause of all the evils
Mark 3 10 to touch him, as many as had evils
Luke 3 19 for all the evils which Herod had done
1 Tim 6 10 desire of money is the root of all e.
James 1 13 God is not a tempter of evils, and he
Evodia Phil 4 2 I beg of Evodia, and I beseech
ewe Gen 21 28 Abraham set apart seven ewe lambs
Gen 21 29 what mean these seven ewe lambs which
30 thou shalt take seven ewe lambs at my
Lev 4 32 if he offer . . . an ewe without blemish
5 6 offer of the flocks an ewe lamb, or a
14 10 he shall take . . . an ewe of a year old
Num 6 14 one ewe lamb of a year old without
2 K 12 3 nothing at all but one little ewe lamb
4 took the poor man's ewe and dressed it
6 he shall restore the ewe fourfold
Job 42 11 and every man gave him one ewe and one
ewes Gen 30 41 when the ewes went first to ram
Gen 30 41 the eyes of the rams and of the ewes
31 10 time came of the ewes conceiving, I
38 thy ewes and goats were not barren, the
32 14 for his brother Esau . . . 200 ewes and
Josu 24 32 field . . . for a hundred young ewes
Ps 77 70 brought him from following the ewes
exact Gen 31 39 lost by theft, thou didst e. it of
Lev 25 37 nor exact of him any increase of fruits
Deut 15 3 foreigner or stranger thou mayst e. it
2 Es 5 7 do you every one exact usury of your
11 which you were wont to exact of them
Eccu 19 23 one that uttereth an exact word telling
Isa 58 3 and you exact of all your debtors
2 Ma 2 29 the e. handling of every particular
exacted 4 K 23 35 he e. both the silver and the
Luke 19 23 might have exacted it with usury? And
exacter Zach 10 4 out of him every e. together
Luke 12 58 judge deliver thee to the e. and the e. cast thee into prison
exacteth Job 11 6 that he e. much less of thee
exaction 2 Es 10 31 would leave . . . e. of every
exactness Eccu 42 4 of e. of balance and weights
exalt Gen 50 20 he might e. me, as at present
Exod 15 2 and I will exalt him. The Lord is as
Josu 3 7 will I begin to exalt thee [Josue]

1 K 2 10 and shall exalt the horn of his Christ
Ps 27 9 and rule them and exalt them forever
36 34 he will exalt thee to inherit the land
98 5 exalt ye the Lord our God. 9
106 32 let them exalt him in the church of
117 28 thou art my God, and I will exalt thee
149 4 he will exalt the meek unto salvation
Prov 4 8 take hold on her, and she shall e. thee
Wisd 11 9 how thou didst exalt thine and didst
Eccu 11 1 wisdom of the humble shall exalt his
15 4 she shall exalt him among his neighbors
43 33 exalt him as much as you can: for he
34 when you exalt him put forth all your
44 23 that he would exalt his seed as the
Isa 10 15 shall the saw exalt itself against
15 a staff exalt itself, which is but
13 2 exalt the voice, lift up the hand, and
14 13 I will exalt my throne above the stars
25 1 I will exalt thee and give glory to
42 21 to magnify the law and exalt it. But
Eze 31 14 of the trees . . . shall exalt themselves
Dan 3 57 praise and exalt him (and so to verse 88)
Mat 23 12 exalt himself shall be humbled: and he
2 C 12 7 lest the greatness . . . should exalt me
James 4 10 sight of the Lord, and he will e. you
1 P 5 6 that he may exalt you in the time of
exaltation Exod 17 15 name thereof, The Lord my e.
Job 22 20 is not their exaltation cut down, and
James 1 9 brother of low condition glory in his e.
exalted 1 K 2 1 my horn is exalted in my God
2 K 5 12 he had e. his kingdom over his people
22 47 strong God of my salvation shall be e.
47 13 away his sins and exalted his horn
51 13 thou hast exalted my dwelling place
3 K 1 5 Adonias . . . e. himself, saying: I will
14 7 as I exalted thee from among the people
16 2 as I have exalted thee out of the dust
4 K 19 22 against whom hast thou e. thy voice
1 Pa 14 2 his kingdom was e. over his people
Tob 13 23 blessed be the Lord, who hath e. it
Jdth 1 7 then was kingdom of Nabuchodonosor e.
Job 17 4 therefore they shall not be exalted
36 7 on the throne forever, and they are e.
Ps 7 7 be thou e. in the borders of my enemies
9 12 let thy hand be exalted: forget not
12 3 how long shall my enemy be e. over me
17 47 let the God of my salvation be exalted
19 6 in the name of our God we shall be e.
20 14 be thou e., O Lord, in thy own strength
26 6 exalted me upon a rock. 60:3
36 20 after they shall be honored and exalted
35 I have seen the wicked highly exalted
45 11 I will be e. among the nations and I will be e. in the earth
46 10 gods of the earth are exceedingly e.
56 6 be thou e., O God, above the. 12; 107:6
63 8 a deep heart: and God shall be exalted
65 7 let not them that provoke him be e.
71 16 above Libanus shall fruit thereof be e.
74 11 the horns of the just shall be exalted
87 16 and being e. have been humbled and
88 14 strengthened, and thy right hand e.
17 and in thy justice they shall be exalted
18 in thy good pleasure shall our horn be e.
20 have exalted one chosen out of my people
25 in my name shall his horn be exalted
91 11 my horn shall be exalted like that of
96 9 art exalted exceedingly above all gods
111 9 ever: his horn shall be e. in glory
117 16 right hand of the Lord hath exalted me
130 1 my heart is not exalted: nor are my eyes
2 e. my soul: as a child that is weaned
148 13 the Lord: for his name alone is exalted
14 he hath exalted the horn of his people
Prov 11 11 of the just city shall be exalted
18 10 the just runneth to it and shall be e.
12 heart of a man is exalted: and before
Eccu 11 4 be not e. in the day of thy honor
13 estate, and hath exalted his head
20 30 that worketh justice shall be exalted
24 3 her own people she shall be exalted
17 I was exalted like a cedar in Libanus
18 I was exalted like a palm tree in
19 as a plane tree . . . was I exalted
33 12 them hath he blessed and exalted: and
45 7 he exalted Aaron his brother and like
Isa 1 2 brought up children and exalted them
2 2 it shall be exalted above the hills
11 Lord alone shall be e. in that day. 17
5 16 Lord of hosts shall be e. in judgment
26 11 Lord, let thy hand be exalted and let
30 18 shall he be exalted sparing you: because
33 10 now will I be exalted: now will I
37 23 against whom hast thou exalted thy voice
40 4 every valley shall be exalted, and
42 11 desert and the cities thereof be e.
49 11 a way, and my paths shall be exalted
52 13 he shall be exalted and extolled and
55 9 as the heavens are e. above the earth
9 are my ways exalted above your ways
Bar 5 6 bring them to thee exalted with honor
Eze 17 24 high tree, and exalted the low tree
19 11 her stature was exalted among the
21 26 this that hath exalted the low one
29 15 it shall no more be exalted over the
31 5 his height exalted above all the trees
10 because he was exalted in height, and
Dan 3 52 and exalted above all forever. 54, 55
52 and exalted above all in all ages
Abdi 4 though thou be exalted as an eagle
Zach 14 10 she shall be exalted and shall dwell
1 Ma 1 4 his heart was exalted and lifted up
8 13 and they were greatly exalted. And
11 16 king Ptolemee was exalted. And Zabdiel
26 he e. him in the sight of all his
2 Ma 5 20 shall be e. again with great glory
Mat 11 23 Capharnaum, shalt thou be . . . exalted
23 12 humble himself shall be e. Luke 14:11; 18:14
Luke 1 52 and hath exalted the humble. He hath
10 15 thou, Capharnaum, which art exalted
Acts 2 33 being exalted by the right hand of God
5 31 him hath God exalted. Phil 2:9
13 17 e. the people when they were sojourners
2 C 11 7 that you might be exalted? Because
exalteth 1 K 2 7 he humbleth and he exalteth
Prov 14 29 he that is impatient, e. his folly
34 justice exalteth a nation: but sin
17 19 he that exalteth his door, seeketh ruin
Eccu 1 24 and e. the glory of them that hold her
7 12 there is one that humbleth and exalteth
Luke 14 11 that exalteth himself. 18:14
2 C 10 5 every height that exalteth itself
James 2 13 mercy exalteth itself above judgment
examination Eccu 16 22 the e. of all is in the end
Dan 13 48 without e. or knowledge of the truth
Acts 24 8 of whom thou mayest by e. have knowledge
25 26 e. being made, I may have what to write
1 P 3 21 the examination of a good conscience
examine 1 Es 10 16 tenth month to e. the matter
Job 9 12 if he e. on a sudden, who shall answer
31 14 when he shall e., what shall I answer
Ps 10 5 his eyelids examine the sons of men
138 23 heart: examine me, and know my paths
Wisd 2 19 let us e. him by outrages and tortures
6 4 most High, who will e. your works and
11 11 others . . . thou didst e. and condemn

Eccu 2 17 when the Lord shall begin to examine
13 14 will e. thee concerning thy secrets
18 20 before judgment examine thyself, and
Dan 13 51 one another, and I will examine them
1 C 9 3 with them that do examine me in this
examined Wisd 16 11 were e. for the remembrance
Luke 23 14 having examined him before you, find
Acts 4 9 if we this day are examined concerning
12 19 Herod . . . having examined the keepers
28 18 who when they had examined me, would
1 C 2 14 because it is spiritually examined
examining 2 Ma 1 34 considering and diligently e.
example Num 5 21 Lord make thee a curse and an e.
Num 5 27 shall be a curse and an e. to all the
Deut 29 23 after example of destruction of Sodom
Ruth 4 11 that she may be an example of virtue
3 K 9 8 this house shall be made an example of
2 Pa 7 20 will make it a byword and an example
Tob 2 12 that an example might be given to
Esth 1 18 by this example all the wives of the
16 24 for an e. of contempt and disobedience
Job 17 6 and I am an example before them. My
Prov 24 32 by the example I received instruction
Eccu 19 3 shall be lifted up for a greater e.
Jer 48 39 an example to all round about him
Eze 5 15 an e. and an astonishment amongst the
14 8 will make him an e. and a proverb and
Nah 3 6 thee, and will make an example of thee
Zach 13 5 for Adam is my example from my youth
2 Ma 6 28 I shall leave an example of fortitude
31 the memory of his death for an example
John 13 15 I have given you an example, that as
1 C 14 10 there are, for example, so many kinds
2 Th 1 5 for an example of the just judgment of
1 Tim 4 12 be thou an example of the faithful
Titus 2 7 show thyself an example of good works
Heb 4 11 fall into the same example of unbelief
8 5 the e. and shadow of heavenly things
James 5 10 take for an example of suffering evil
1 P 2 1 suffered for us, leaving you an e.
2 P 2 6 making them an e. to those that should
Jude 7 were made an example, suffering the
exasperated Ps 105 33 because they e. his spirit
Ps 106 11 because they had e. the words of God
exasperating Ps 77 8 a perverse and e. generation
exceed Num 3 46 that e. the number of the Levites
Deut 25 3 that they exceed not the number of forty
3 K 10 7 thy works exceed the fame which I heard
Eccu 31 20 and exceed not, lest thou offend. And
43 32 for he will yet far exceed and his
exceeded Gen 41 49 the plenty exceeded measure
Gen 43 34 so that it exceeded by five parts
3 K 10 23 king Solomon e. all the kings of the
2 Pa 9 6 thou hast e. the same with thy virtues
Job 42 3 that above measure e. my knowledge
excel Ecce 7 13 learning and wisdom excel in this
Eccu 33 7 why doth one day excel another, and one
Eze 32 19 whom dost thou excel in beauty? Go
Rom 3 9 do we excel them? No, not so. For we
Titus 3 8 be careful to excel in good works
14 men also learn to excel in good works
excelled Dan 6 3 Daniel e. all the princes and
excellence Dan 4 27 in the glory of my excellence
excellency 1 Ma 1 42 e. was turned into mourning
2 C 4 7 e. may be of the power of God, and not
excellent Gen 49 15 the land that it was excellent
Exod 38 23 was an excellent artificer in wood and
Deut 3 25 will see this excellent land beyond the
4 21 not enter into the excellent land which
8 10 for the e. land which he hath given thee
9 6 giveth thee not this excellent land in
11 17 you perish quickly from the e. land
28 12 Lord will open his excellent treasure
Josu 23 13 you from off this excellent land. 15
16 shall be taken away from this e. land
2 K 23 1 the e. psalmist of Israel said: The
1 Pa 12 1 most valiant and excellent warriors. 8
28 Sadoc also a young man of e. disposition
Jdth 11 6 thou only art excellent and mighty
Cant 5 15 his form as of Libanus, e. as the cedars
Eccu 14 21 every excellent work shall be justified
Dan 5 14 e. knowledge and understanding and
Luke 1 3 to thee . . . most excellent Theophilus
Acts 23 26 to the most excellent governor, Felix
24 3 we accept it . . . most excellent Felix
26 25 I am not mad, most excellent Felix
1 C 12 31 I show unto you yet a more e. way
2 C 9 14 because of the e. grace of God in you
Phil 3 8 for the e. knowledge of Jesus Christ
Heb 1 4 as he hath inherited a more e. name
2 P 1 17 coming down to him from the e. glory
excelleth Eze 20 6 which e. amongst all lands
2 C 3 10 by reason of the glory that excelleth
excelling Gen 49 3 Ruben . . . excelling in gifts
1 P 2 13 whether . . . to the king as excelling
except Wisd 6 8 will not except any man's person
excepted 1 C 15 27 he is e. who put all things
excepting Deut 20 14 sword, e. women and children
Mat 5 32 excepting for the cause of fornication
excess Ps 30 23 I said in the excess of my mind
Ps 115 11 I said in my excess: Every man is a liar
Eccu 31 31 wine drunk to excess shall rebuke the
38 wine drunken with excess is bitterness
Jer 18 13 the virgin of Israel hath done to e.
1 P 4 3 e. of wine, revellings, banquetings
2 P 2 13 sporting themselves to excess, rioting
excessive Job 24 19 from the snow waters to e. heat
Eccu 33 30 be not excessive towards any one: and
2 Ma 7 42 the sacrifices, and of the e. cruelties
exchange Gen 47 17 he gave them food in exchange
Gen 47 17 maintained them . . . for e. of their
Job 28 15 neither shall silver be weighed in e.
Ps 43 13 there was no reckoning in the exchange
Eze 48 14 shall not sell thereof nor exchange
Mat 16 26 what exchange shall a man give for his
Mark 8 37 a man give in exchange for his soul
exchanged Eze 27 15 e. for thy price teeth of ivory
exchequer 1 Es 7 20 treasury and the king's e.
excite Lam 2 14 iniquity, to e. thee to penance
excited 2 Es 4 6 heart of the people was e. to work
exclude Ps 67 31 who seek to e. them that are tried
Gal 4 17 they would exclude you, that you might
excluded 2 Ma 4 21 that he was wholly e. from
Rom 3 27 where is then thy boasting? It is e.
excrements Judg 3 22 the e. of the belly came out
excuse Deut 30 13 thou mayst e. thyself and say
Eccu 32 21 will find an e. according to his will
Luke 14 18 they began all at once to make excuse
John 15 22 now they have no excuse for their sin
2 C 12 19 think you that we excuse ourselves to
excused 3 K 15 22 let no man be e.: and they took
Luke 14 18 I pray thee, hold me excused. 19
Heb 12 19 they that heard, excused themselves
excuses Ps 140 4 to evil words: to make e. in sins
execrable Eccu 10 7 all iniquity of nations is e.
Eze 24 13 thy uncleanness is execrable: because
2 Ma 5 8 as a forsaker of the laws and execrable
execration Num 5 18 he hath heaped curses with e.
Isa 65 15 you shall leave your name for an e.
Jer 42 18 shall be an e. and an astonishment
44 12 they shall be for an execration and
execute Exod 12 12 of Egypt I will e. judgments
Exod 31 10 that they may execute their office
Deut 20 5 lest . . . another man execute his office
1 K 28 18 neither didst thou execute the wrath
2 K 15 15 we thy servants will willingly execute

3 K 6 12 and e. my judgments and keep all my
1 Pa 28 21 how to execute all thy commandments
Jdth 9 2 who gavest him a sword to e. vengeance
Ps 102 20 are mighty in strength and e. his word
118 84 when wilt thou e. judgment on them that
149 7 to execute vengeance upon the nations
9 to e. upon them the judgment that is
Wisd 9 3 and e. justice with an upright heart
Eccu 45 19 to e. the office of the priesthood and
Jer 7 5 if you will execute the judgment between
22 3 e. judgment and justice. 23:5; Eze 45:9
23 20 not return till he execute it and till
Eze 5 8 I myself will execute judgments in the
10 will e. judgments. 11:9; 25:11; 30:14, 19
16 41 shall execute judgments upon thee in
23 25 which they shall execute upon thee with
25 17 and I will execute great vengeance upon
28 22 when I shall execute judgments in her
Osee 11 9 I will not execute the fierceness of
Joel 2 11 they are strong and execute his word
Mich 2 1 in the morning light they execute it
5 14 I will execute vengeance in wrath and
7 9 until he . . . execute judgment for me
1 Ma 6 22 dost thou delay to execute the judgment
10 42 the priests that execute the ministry
14 47 was well pleased to execute the office
Rom 13 4 an avenger to execute wrath upon him
Jude 15 to execute judgment upon all and to
executed Num 18 7 shall be executed by the priests
Num 33 4 upon their gods also he had e. vengeance
1 K 15 11 and hath not executed my commandments
4 K 10 30 hast diligently e. that which was right
1 Pa 6 10 this is he that e. the priestly office
18 14 reigned over all Israel and e. judgment
21 6 Joab unwillingly e. the king's orders
2 Pa 24 24 and on Joas they e. shameful judgments
1 Es 6 13 executed what Darius the king had
7 26 judgment shall be executed upon him
Jer 30 24 till he have executed and performed the
Eze 5 15 when I shall have e. judgments in thee
18 8 hath e. true judgment between man and
17 but hath executed my judgments, and
23 10 and they executed judgments in her
28 26 when I shall have e. judgments upon
39 21 shall see my judgment that I have e.
Dan 3 28 thou hast e. true judgments in all the
2 Ma 3 23 Heliodorus executed that which he had
Luke 1 8 when he executed the priestly function
Apoc 13 12 he e. all the power of the former beast
executeth Ps 9 17 be known when he e. judgments
Ps 145 7 who e. judgment for them that suffer
Eccu 20 3 that by violence e. unjust judgment
Jer 5 1 can find a man that executeth judgment
Rom 3 5 is God unjust, who executeth wrath
executing 2 Pa 11 14 from e. the priestly office
1 Es 4 22 that you be not negligent in e. this
Wisd 12 10 e. thy judgments by degrees thou gavest
execution Gen 38 25 when she was led to execution
2 Ma 6 28 he was forthwith carried to execution
executioner Mark 6 27 sending an e. he commanded
exequies Gen 50 10 celebrating the e. with a
exercise 2 Pa 19 6 you e. not the judgment of man
Ps 54 3 I am grieved in my exercise; and am
Wisd 8 18 in e. of conference with her, wisdom
Jer 9 24 I am the Lord that exercise mercy and
1 Ma 1 15 they built a place of e. in Jerusalem
2 Ma 4 9 license to set him up a place for e.
12 under the very castle, a place for e.
14 partakers . . . of the e. of the discus
Mat 20 25 the greater exercise power upon them
2 C 1 23 not because we exercise dominion over
1 Tim 4 7 and exercise thyself unto godliness
8 bodily exercise is profitable to little
exercised 4 K 25 19 army who exercised the young soldiers. Jer 52:25
2 Pa 9 26 exercised authority over all the kings
Ps 76 4 and was e. and my spirit swooned away
7 I was exercised and I swept my spirit
118 27 I shall be e. in thy wondrous works
48 I was exercised in thy justifications
Ecce 1 13 painful occupation . . . to be e. therein
3 10 the sons of men to be exercised in it
Wisd 16 4 come upon them that exercised tyranny
19 13 they e. a more detestable inhospitality
Isa 2 4 neither shall they be e. any more to war
Eze 22 13 covetousness, which thou hast exercised
35 11 which thou hast e. in hatred to them
2 Ma 15 12 and who from a child was e. in virtues
Heb 5 14 by custom have their senses exercised
12 11 to them that are exercised by it, the
2 P 2 14 having their heart e. with covetousness
exercising 1 K 20 20 as if I were e. myself at a
exhaust Heb 9 28 once to exhaust the sins of many
exhibit 2 C 6 4 exhibit ourselves as the ministers
exhort Deut 1 38 exhort and encourage him [Josue]
2 K 11 25 e. them that thou mayest overthrow it
2 Ma 7 24 did not only exhort him by words, but
Acts 2 40 did he testify and exhort them, saying
27 22 now I exhort you to be of good cheer
2 C 6 1 we helping do exhort you that you
1 Th 3 2 and exhort you concerning your faith
2 Th 2 16 e. your hearts and confirm you in
1 Tim 6 2 these things teach and e. If any man
Titus 1 9 may be able to exhort in sound doctrine
2 6 in like manner, e. that they be sober
9 exhort servants to be obedient to their
15 exhort and rebuke with all authority
Heb 3 13 e. one another every day, whilst it is
exhortation Jdth 4 14 moved by this exhortation
Acts 13 15 if you have any word of exhortation to
1 C 14 3 speaketh to men unto edification and e.
2 C 1 4 the e. wherewith we also are exhorted
6 we be in tribulation, it is for your e.
8 17 he [Titus] accepted the e.; but being
13 11 rejoice, be perfect, take exhortation
1 Th 2 3 our exhortation was not of error, nor
1 Tim 4 13 attend unto reading, to exhortation
exhorted 2 Pa 35 2 e. them to minister in the
Tob 8 4 Tobias e. the virgin and said to her
1 Ma 5 53 he exhorted the people all the way
13 3 e. them, saying: You know what great
2 Ma 2 3 he e. them that they would not remove
7 5 exhorted one another to die manfully
21 she bravely e. every one of them in
26 and when he had e. her with many words
8 16 e. them not to be reconciled to the
11 7 arms, e. the rest to expose themselves
12 42 e. the people to keep themselves from
13 12 Judas e. them to make themselves ready
14 having e. his people to fight manfully
15 8 he e. his people not to fear the coming
17 thus being e. with the words of Judas
Acts 11 23 he exhorted them all with purpose of
20 2 and had exhorted them with many words
1 C 14 31 that all may learn and all may be e.
2 C 1 4 wherewith we also are exhorted by God
6 or whether we be e., it is for your
exhorteth Bar 4 30 he e. thee, that named thee
Rom 12 8 he that exhorteth, in exhorting; he
exhorting 2 Ma 12 31 e. them to be still friendly
Luke 3 18 many other things e., did he preach to
Acts 14 21 e. them to continue in the faith; and
18 27 the brethren e., wrote to the disciples
19 8 and e. concerning the kingdom of God
20 1 e. them, took his leave and set forward
Rom 12 8 he that exhorteth, in exhorting; he

2 C 5 20 God as it were exhorting by us. For
exile 2 K 14 13 not bring home again his own exile
exiled Wisd 17 2 lay there e. from the eternal
exorcists Acts 19 13 Jewish e. who went about
expect Job 3 9 let it expect light and not see it
Job 14 14 warfare, I expect until my change come
35 14 be judged before him and expect him
Ps 26 14 expect the Lord, do manfully, and let
36 34 expect the Lord and keep his way: and
103 11 the wild asses shall e. in their thirst
27 all expect of thee that thou give them
Isa 28 10 e. again; a little there, a little. 13
Soph 3 8 expect me, saith the Lord, in the day
2 Ma 9 25 expect what shall be the event, I have
Heb 9 28 to them that expect him unto salvation
expectation Gen 49 10 shall be the e. of nations
Job 17 15 where is now then my expectation, and
Ps 39 2 with expectation, I have waited for
118 116 and let me not be confounded in my e.
Prov 10 28 the expectation of the just is joy; but
11 7 the e. of the solicitous shall perish
23 the e. of the wicked is indignation
17 8 the e. of him that expecteth, is a most
23 18 thy expectation shall not be taken away
Wisd 17 12 and while there is less e. from within
Jer 14 8 O expectation of Israel, the Savior
2 Ma 3 21 the expectation of the mixed multitude
9 24 anything contrary to e. shall fall out
Luke 21 26 men withering away from fear and e. of
Acts 12 11 from all the e. of the people of the
Rom 8 19 the expectation of the creature waiteth
Phil 1 20 according to my expectation and hope
Heb 10 27 a certain dreadful e. of judgment and
expected Job 30 26 I e. good things, and evils are
Ps 68 21 my heart hath expected reproach and
2 Ma 15 20 all e. what judgment would be given
expecteth Prov 17 8 expectation of him that e. is
2 Ma 6 14 whom the Lord patiently expecteth, that
expecting Deut 11 11 plains, e. rain from heaven
Judg 16 9 and in the chamber e. the event of the
Isa 18 2 to a nation e. and trodden under foot
7 from a nation e., e. and trodden under
Lam 4 17 expecting help for us in vain, when we
Acts 28 6 e. long and seeing that there came no
Heb 10 13 expecting until his enemies be made
expedient Esth 3 8 it is not e. for thy kingdom
Eccu 37 31 all things are not expedient for all
Mat 5 29 it is e. for thee that one of thy. 30
19 10 be so, it is not expedient to marry
John 11 50 is e. that one man should die. 18:14
16 7 it is expedient to you that I go: for
1 C 6 12 all things are not expedient. 10:22
2 C 12 1 if I must glory, it is not e. indeed
Heb 13 17 for this is not expedient for you
expedition Jdth 2 7 he mustered men for the e.
expeditions 2 Ma 8 7 nights he went upon these e.
2 Ma 10 19 departed to those e. which urged more
expelled Deut 2 23 were e. by the Cappadocians
expenses Exod 21 19 his e. upon the physicians
3 K 9 15 this is the sum of the expenses, which
4 K 12 12 need of expenses to uphold the house
1 Pa 29 2 prepared the expenses for the house of
1 Es 2 69 gave towards the expenses of the work
Dan 14 7 who it is that eateth up these expenses
experience Gen 30 27 I have learned by experience
Jdth 6 6 that thou shalt experience these things
Esth 3 5 proved by experience that Mardochai did
Eccu 21 25 a man of experience will be abashed at
25 8 much e. is the crown of old men, and
34 9 a man that hath much experience shall
10 that hath no experience, knoweth little
36 22 and a man of experience will resist it
2 Ma 8 9 of great experience in matters of war
2 C 8 2 in much experience of tribulation they
experienced Wisd 12 26 e. the worthy judgment of
Eccu 34 10 he that hath been experienced in many
experiencing Gen 28 8 e. also that his father was
experiment 2 C 2 9 that I may know the experiment
expert Cant 3 8 holding swords and most e. in war
Bar 3 26 of great stature, expert in war. The
expiate Lev 16 16 may expiate the sanctuary from
Lev 16 19 let him expiate and sanctify it from
33 he shall expiate the sanctuary and the
Deut 18 10 any one that shall expiate his son or
Eze 43 20 and thou shalt cleanse and expiate it
22 they shall expiate the altar as they
26 seven days shall they e. the altar and
45 18 and thou shalt expiate the sanctuary
expiated Lev 8 15 which being e. and sanctified
Num 19 19 being e. the seventh day, he shall wash
20 if any man be not e. after this rite
35 33 neither can it otherwise be expiated
1 K 3 14 iniquity of his house shall not be e.
Eze 43 22 the altar, as they e. it with the calf
expiating Lev 9 15 e. the altar, he offered the
expiation Exod 28 36 hast offered the victim of e.
Exod 29 36 a calf for sin every day for expiation
Lev 1 4 acceptable and help to its expiation
16 30 upon this day shall be the expiation
17 11 and the blood may be for an expiation
25 9 in time of expiation in all your land
Num 5 8 the ram that is offered for expiation
19 13 was not sprinkled with the water of e.
21 one that shall touch the waters of e.
28 30 buck goat also which is slain for e.
29 5 offered for the expiation of the people
11 are wont to be offered for sin, for e.
31 23 sanctified with the water of expiation
2 Pa 29 24 altar for an expiation of all Israel
2 Es 12 44 their God and the observance of e.
Eccu 7 36 that thy expiation and thy blessing
Eze 43 23 shalt have made an end of the expiation
45 17 to make e. for the house of Israel
20 and thou shalt make e. for the house
expired Gen 29 14 days of one month were expired
Gen 50 4 the time of the mourning being expired
Exod 12 41 was 430 years. Which being expired, the
Lev 8 33 time of your consecration shall be e.
12 6 when days of her purification are e.
23 16 morrow after the seventh week be e.
25 29 to redeem it, until one year be expired
Num 6 13 determined by vow shall be expired
Judg 11 39 two months being expired, she returned
2 Pa 36 21 till the seventy years were expired
Jer 25 12 when the seventy years shall be expired
Eze 43 27 the days being expired, departing we
explain Ecce 1 8 man cannot explain them by word
Eccu 24 31 they that explain me shall have life
explained 2 Pa 9 2 Solomon e. to her all that she
Mark 4 34 apart he explained all things to his
expose 2 Ma 11 7 exhorted rest to e. themselves
2 Ma 14 38 was ready to expose his body and life
Mat 1 19 not willing publicly to expose her, was
Acts 7 19 that they should expose their children
exposed Judg 5 15 Barac who e. himself to danger
Judg 9 17 exposed his life to dangers to deliver
2 Es 5 9 that we be not e. to the reproaches of
Job 20 28 the offspring of his house shall be e.
Prov 12 8 foolish, shall be exposed to contempt
Ecce 4 4 are e. to the envy of their neighbor
Wisd 11 15 his being wickedly exposed to perish
1 Ma 6 44 he e. himself to deliver his people and
Acts 7 21 when he [Moses] was exposed, Pharao's
Col 2 15 he hath exposed them confidently in
expostulated Gen 20 10 he expostulated with him
expound Gen 41 15 is no one that can expound them

Gen 41 24 there is no man that can expound it
Deut 1 5 Moses began to expound the law and to
Judg 14 14 could not in three days e. the riddle
16 thou wilt not expound to me the riddle
Mat 13 36 expound to us the parable of. 15:15
expounded Judg 14 17 troublesome to him, he e. it
Luke 24 27 he e. to them in all the scriptures
Acts 18 26 and e. to him the way of the Lord more
28 23 he e., testifying the kingdom of God
express Judg 12 6 not being able to e. an ear of
Wisd 14 17 made an express image of the king whom
expressed Wisd 17 1 thy words cannot be expressed
exquisite Ecce 19 22 there is an e. subtilty and
extend 1 K 26 11 that I e. not my hand upon the
2 K 8 3 to extend his dominion over the river
1 Pa 18 3 when he went to extend his dominions
Ps 35 11 extend thy mercy to them that know thee
84 6 wilt thou e. thy wrath from generation
extended 2 Pa 3 4 porch in the front, which was e.
2 Pa 3 11 wings of the cherubims were e. twenty
13 spread forth and were e. twenty cubits
1 Es 9 9 hath e. mercy upon us before the king
Jdth 1 2 each side was e. the space of twenty
extent Num 35 5 toward the sea . . . the same extent
Num 35 8 according to e. of their inheritance
exterior Mat 8 12 out into the e. darkness. 25:30
Mat 22 13 cast him into the exterior darkness
Exterminans Apoc 9 11 Apollyon; in Latin E. One
extinct Isa 43 17 are broken as flax and are e.
extinguish Mat 12 20 flax he shall not extinguish
Eph 6 16 to extinguish all the fiery darts of
1 Th 5 19 extinguish not the spirit. Despise not
extinguished Job 18 5 light of the wicked be e.
Mark 9 43 the fire is not extinguished. 45, 47
extinguisheth Wisd 16 17 water, which e. all things
Eccu 19 5 and he that hateth babbling, e. evil
extirpate Deut 9 3 to destroy and e. and bring
Eccu 7 6 have strength enough to e. iniquities
extirpated Eccu 47 8 and e. the Philistines the
extol Tob 13 6 extol the eternal King of worlds
Jdth 16 2 psalm, extol and call upon his name
Ps 29 2 I will extol thee, O Lord, for thou
33 4 and let us extol his name together
50 16 and my tongue shall extol thy justice
58 17 and will extol thy mercy in the morning
144 1 I will extol thee, O God my king: and
Eccu 6 2 extol not thyself in the thoughts of
10 29 extol not thyself in doing thy work
13 28 what he said they extol even to the
extolled Ps 65 17 and I extolled him with my tongue
Eccu 16 10 that extolled themselves in their sins
Isa 52 13 he shall be exalted and extolled and
extort Lev 6 2 or shall by force extort anything
extortioner Exod 22 25 not be hard upon them as e.
1 C 5 11 or a railer or a drunkard or an e.
extortioners Luke 18 11 as the rest of men, e.
1 C 5 10 the covetous or the e. or the servers
6 10 nor e., shall possess the kingdom of
extremities 4 K 9 35 feet and the e. of her hands
Jdth 15 6 they came to the e. of their confines
Job 38 13 didst thou hold the e. of the earth
2 Ma 7 4 to chop off also the e. of his hands
extremity Deut 28 53 e. wherewith thy enemy shall
3 K 6 24 from e. of one wing to e. of the other
Ecce 6 13 son, who shall be in extremity of want
eyebrows Lev 14 9 he shall shave . . . his eyebrows
eyelids Job 16 17 weeping, and my eyelids are dim
Job 41 9 eyes like the eyelids of the morning
Ps 10 5 his eyelids examine the sons of men
131 4 sleep to my eyes or slumber to my e.
Prov 4 25 let thy eyelids go before thy steps
6 4 eyes, neither let thy eyelids slumber
30 13 and their eyelids lifted up on high
Eccu 26 12 haughtiness of her eyes and by her e.
Jer 9 18 and our eyelids run down with waters
eyesalve Apoc 3 18 anoint thy eyes with eyesalve
eyewitnesses Luke 1 2 from the beginning were e.
2 P 1 16 we were eyewitnesses of his greatness
Ezar 1 Pa 4 4 Ezar the father of Hosa, these are
Ezechias 4 K 16 20 E. his son reigned. 2 Pa 28:27
4 K 18 1 reigned E. the son of Achaz the king of
10 in the sixth year of Ezechias, that is
15 E. gave all the silver that was found
16 E. broke the doors of the temple of the
19 speak to Ezechias: Thus saith the great
29 let not Ezechias deceive you. Isa 36:14
31 do not hearken to Ezechias. Isa 36:16
32 hearken not to E., who deceiveth you
37 came to E. with their garments rent
19 3 thus saith E. This day is a. Isa 37:3
9 he sent messengers to E. Isa 37:9
14 when E. had received the letter of the
20 Isaias the son of Amos sent to E.
29 to thee, O Ezechias, this shall be a
20 1 E. was sick unto death: and Isaias the
3 E. wept with much weeping. And before
5 go back and tell E. the captain of my
8 E. had said to Isaias: What shall be
10 E. said: It is an easy matter for the
12 letters and presents to E. Isa 39:1
12 for he had heard that E. had been sick
13 E. rejoiced at their coming. Isa 39:2
13 that Ezechias showed them not. Isa 39:2
14 E. said to him: From a far country they
15 E. said: They saw all the things that
16 said to E.: Hear the word of. Isa 39:5
19 E. said to Isaias: The word of the Lord
20 the rest of the acts of E. 2 Pa 32:32
21 E. slept with his fathers. 2 Pa 32:33
21 3 E. his father had destroyed. 2 Pa 33:3
1 Pa 3 13 begot Achaz, the father of E., of whom
23 sons of Naaria, Elioenai and Ezechias
2 Pa 28 12 E. the son of Sellum and Amasa the son
29 1 E. began to reign when he was five and
27 E. commanded that they should offer
30 E. and the princes commanded the Levites
31 E. added and said: You have filled your
36 E. and all the people rejoiced because
30 1 Ezechias sent to all Israel and Juda
18 E. prayed for them, saying: The Lord
22 E. spoke to the heart of all the Levites
31 2 E. appointed companies of the priests
8 when E. and his princes came in, they
9 E. asked the priests and the Levites
11 E. commanded to prepare storehouses in
13 by the commandment of E. the king and
20 E. did all things which we have said
32 2 when E. saw that Sennacherib was come
11 doth not E. deceive you, to give you up
12 is it not this same E. that hath
15 let not E. deceive you nor delude you
16 and against E. his servant. He wrote
17 so neither can the God of E. deliver
20 E. the king and Isaias the prophet the
22 the Lord saved E. and the inhabitants
24 E. was sick even to death. Isa 38:1
26 came not upon them in the days of E.
27 Ezechias was rich and very glorious and
30 this same E. was he that stopped the
1 Es 2 16 children of Ather, who were of E. 98
Eccu 48 19 E. fortified his city and brought in
25 Ezechias did that which pleased God
49 5 except David and E. and Josias, all
Isa 1 1 in the days of Ozias, Joathan, Achaz, and
Ezechias. Osee 1:1; Mich 1:1
36 4 tell Ezechias: Thus saith the great king

15 let not E. make you trust in the Lord
18 neither let E. trouble you, saying: The
22 went in to E. with their garments rent
37 5 the servants of Ezechias came to Isaias
14 E. took the letter from the hand of
14 E. spread it before the Lord, saying
15 and Ezechias prayed to the Lord, saying
21 Isaias the son of Amos sent to E.
38 2 E. turned his face toward the wall and
3 and Ezechias wept with great weeping
5 say to Ezechias: Thus saith the Lord
22 E. had said: What shall be the sign
39 3 E. said: From a far country they came
4 E. said: All things that are in my house
8 E. said to Isaias: The word of the Lord
Mat 1 9 Achaz begot E. E. begot Manasses. And
Ezechias king of Juda 4 K 18 14 E. . . . sent messengers to the king of the
4 K 18 14 the Assyrians put a tax upon E. . . .
19 10 thus shall you say to E. . . . : Let not
1 Pa 4 41 came in the days of E. . . . and they beat
2 Pa 30 24 E. . . . had given to the multitude a
32 8 encouraged with these words of E. . . .
9 to E. . . . and to all the people that
Prov 25 1 which the men of E. . . . copied out. It
Isa 37 10 thus shall you speak to E. . . . , saying
38 9 the writing of E. . . . when he had been
Jer 15 4 because of Manasses the son of E. . . .
26 18 was a prophet in the days of E. . . .
19 did E. . . . and all Juda condemn him to
2 Ma 15 22 didst send thy angel in time of E. . . .
king Ezechias 4 K 18 9 in fourth year of king E.
4 K 18 13 fourteenth year of king E. Isa 36:1
17 to king Ezechias with a strong army
19 1 when king E. heard these words, he rent
5 the servants of king E. came to Isaias
20 14 Isaias the prophet came to k. E. Isa 39:3
2 Pa 29 18 they went in to king E. and said to him
20 king E. rising early, assembled all the
Isa 36 2 to king E. with a great army, and he
37 1 when king E. had heard it, that he rent
Ezechiel 1 Es 8 5 sons of Sechenias, the son of E.
Ps 64 1 the canticle of Jeremias and Ezechiel
Eccu 49 10 Ezechiel that saw the glorious vision
Eze 1 3 the word of the Lord came to Ezechiel
24 24 E. shall be unto you for a sign of
Ezecias Soph 1 1 Amraias the son of Ezecias, in
Ezel 1 K 20 19 beside the stone, which is called E.
Ezer 1 Pa 7 21 Suthala, and his son E. and Elad
1 Pa 12 9 Ezer the chief, Obdias the second
2 Es 12 41 and Elam and Ezer. And the singers
Eziel 2 Es 3 8 and next to him built Eziel the
Ezrahite 3 K 4 31 wiser than Ethan the Ezrahite
Ps 87 1 understanding of Eman the Ezrahite
88 1 of understanding, for Ethan the E.
Ezrel 1 Es 10 41 of the sons of Bani . . . Ezrel
Ezri Judg 6 11 the father of the family of Ezri
Judg 6 24 Ephra, which is of the family of Ezri
8 32 father in Ephra of the family of Ezri
1 Pa 27 26 the ground, was Ezri the son of Chelub
Ezricam 1 Pa 3 23 the sons of Naaria . . . Ezricam
1 Pa 8 38 Asel had six sons . . . Ezricam. 9:44
9 14 Ezricam the son of Hasebia of the sons
2 Pa 28 7 and Ezricam the governor of his house
Ezriel 1 Pa 7 14 the son of Manasses, Ezriel: and
Jer 36 26 Saraias the son of Ezriel, and Selemias
Ezrihel 1 Pa 27 22 over Dan, Ezrihel the son of

F

fable Tob 3 4 are made a fable and a reproach
Eccu 20 21 a man without grace is as a vain fable
fables Ps 118 85 the wicked have told me fables
Bar 3 23 the tellers of fables and searchers of
1 Tim 1 4 not to give heed to fables and endless
4 7 avoid foolish and old wives' fables
2 Tim 4 4 they . . . will be turned unto fables
Titus 1 14 not giving heed to Jewish fables and
2 P 1 16 we have not by following artificial f.
faceth Num 21 11 that f. Moab toward the east
Jdth 4 5 Esdrelon, which faceth the great plain
facility Jer 3 9 by the f. of her fornication
facing 2 Pa 13 13 and while he stood f. his enemies
fact Gen 44 7 had committed so heinous a fact
Josu 7 15 that shall be found guilty of this fact
20 6 to give an account of his fact, and
Judg 6 29 inquired for the author of the fact
2 Pa 6 15 accomplished in fact what thou hast
faction Amos 6 7 f. of the luxurious ones shall be
factors Eze 27 9 their mariners were thy factors
fade Eccu 14 18 all flesh shall fade as grass
James 1 11 so also shall the rich man fade away
1 P 1 4 unto an inheritance . . . that cannot f.
faded Ps 17 46 strange children have faded away
Isa 15 6 withered away, the spring is faded
24 4 the earth mourned and faded away, and
4 the world faded away, the height of
fadeth Job 30 16 my soul fadeth within myself
Wisd 6 13 wisdom is glorious and never fadeth
Nah 1 4 the flower of Libanus fadeth away
fading Isa 28 1 the fading flower the glory of. 4
1 P 5 4 shall receive a never fading crown
fail 2 K 3 29 there not fail from the house of Joab
2 K 22 37 under me, and my ankles shall not fail
3 K 9 5 there shall not fail a man of thy race
2 Pa 6 16 there shall not fail thee a man. 7:18
Jdth 12 3 thou hast brought with thee fail thee
Job 11 20 and the way to escape shall fail them
17 5 and the eyes of his children shall fail
40 28 his hope shall fail him, and in the
Ps 70 9 when my strength shall fail, do not thou
88 34 him: nor will I suffer my truth to f.
101 28 selfsame, and thy years shall not fail
103 29 they shall fail and shall return to
Prov 29 18 when prophecy shall fail, the people
Eccu 3 15 if his understanding fail, have patience
14 20 is corruptible shall fail in the end
26 15 against every arrow, until she fail
Isa 19 6 the rivers shall fail: the streams
51 6 forever, and my justice shall not fail
14 neither shall his bread fail. But I
58 11 of water whose waters shall not fail
Jer 2 24 all that seek her shall not fail: in
18 14 shall the snow of Libanus fail from
31 36 if these ordinances shall fail before
36 then also the seed of Israel shall fail
Bar 2 18 eyes that fail, and the hungry soul
Eze 4 17 when bread and water fail, every man
12 22 be prolonged, and every vision shall f.
33 28 the proud strength thereof shall fail
47 12 their fruit shall not fail: every month
Dan 9 27 the victim and the sacrifice shall fail
Amos 8 4 and make the needy of the land to fail
Nah 2 10 the heart melteth, and the knees fail
Haba 3 17 labor of the olive tree shall fail
1 Ma 2 61 that trust in him fail in strength
Luke 16 9 that when you shall fail, they may
22 32 prayed for thee that thy faith fail not
Gal 6 9 in doing good let us not fail. For in
Heb 1 12 selfsame and thy years shall not fail
11 32 time would fail me to tell of Gedeon
failed Exod 13 22 never f. the pillar of the cloud
Num 11 33 neither had that kind of meat failed
Deut 32 36 they who were shut up have also failed
Josu 3 16 the Dead Sea, until they wholly failed
5 1 passed over their heart failed them

23 14 of all the words . . . not one hath f.
3 K 8 56 hath not failed so much as one word
Jdth 7 11 the reserve of waters failed among all
Job 21 10 their cattle have conceived and f. not
Ps 9 7 the swords of the enemy have f. unto
63 7 they have failed in their search. Man
68 4 my eyes have failed, whilst I hope in
118 82 my eyes have failed for thy word, saying
141 4 when my spirit failed me, then thou
5 flight hath failed me: and there is no
Wisd 11 5 when their drink failed them, while the
Eccu 22 10 for the dead, for his light hath failed
34 7 have failed that put their trust in
44 10 mercy, whose godly deeds have not failed
Isa 16 4 he hath failed, that trod the earth
21 4 my heart failed, darkness amazed me
29 20 that did prevail hath failed, the
47 13 hast failed in the multitude of thy
Jer 6 29 the bellows have failed, the lead is
14 6 their eyes f. because there was no
51 30 dwelt in holds: their strength hath f.
Lam 2 11 my eyes have failed with weeping, my
3 22 because his commiserations have not f.
4 17 we were yet standing, our eyes failed
1 Ma 3 29 that the money of his treasures failed
2 Ma 13 19 repulsed, he failed, he lost his men
faileth Prov 26 20 when the wood f., the fire shall
Wisd 3 15 and the root of wisdom never faileth
Eccu 22 10 fool, for his understanding faileth
24 6 should rise light that never faileth
41 3 need and to him whose strength faileth
Luke 12 33 treasure in heaven which faileth not
failing Wisd 17 14 fainted away, their soul f. them
Eccu 30 23 a never failing treasure of holiness
John 2 3 wine failing, the mother of Jesus
Gal 6 9 we shall reap, not failing. Therefore
James 1 4 you may be perfect . . . f. in nothing
fain Luke 15 16 he would fain have filled his belly
faint Gen 25 29 Esau, coming f. out of the field
Gen 25 30 red pottage, for I am exceeding faint
Num 14 35 in this wilderness shall it faint away
Judg 8 5 bread to the people . . . for they are f.
15 to the men that are weary and faint
1 K 2 33 that thy eyes may faint and thy soul
14 28 this day. And the people were faint
2 K 16 2 drink if any man be faint in the desert
17 29 that the people were faint with hunger
21 15 David growing faint, Jesbibenob, who
Ps 38 11 strength of thy hand hath made me faint
Prov 3 11 do not faint when thou art chastised
Isa 5 27 there is none that shall faint nor labor
13 7 therefore shall all hands be faint and
29 8 he is awake, is yet faint with thirst
40 28 he shall not faint nor labor, neither
30 youths shall faint and labor, and young
31 weary, they shall walk and not faint
44 12 he shall hunger and faint, he shall
Jer 51 46 lest your hearts faint, and ye fear
Eze 21 7 feeble, and every spirit shall faint
Amos 8 13 and the young men shall faint for thirst
Haba 2 13 the nations in vain, and they shall f.
1 Ma 3 17 and we are ready to faint with fasting
Mat 15 32 fasting, lest they faint in the way
Mark 8 3 they will faint in the way: for some of
Luke 18 1 ought always to pray and not to faint
2 C 4 1 as we have obtained mercy we faint not
16 for which cause we faint not; but
Eph 3 13 not to faint at my tribulations for you
fainted Josu 2 11 and our heart fainted away
Judg 4 21 he [Sisara] fainted away and died. And
5 27 he [Sisara] fainted, and he died: he
16 16 his soul fainted away and was wearied
Ps 72 26 my flesh and my heart hath fainted away
89 7 in thy wrath we have fainted away. 9
106 5 and thirsty: their soul fainted in them
118 81 my soul hath fainted after thy salvation
123 my eyes have fainted after thy salvation
142 7 my spirit hath fainted away. Turn not
Wisd 17 14 fainted away, their soul failing them
Jer 4 31 my soul hath fainted because of them
15 9 her soul hath fainted away: her sun
Lam 2 11 fainted away in the streets of the city
12 when they fainted away as the wounded
19 that have fainted for hunger at the top
Dan 10 8 I fainted away and retained no strength
Apoc 2 3 hast endured . . . and hast not fainted
faintest Job 4 5 is come upon thee, and thou f.
fainteth Ps 83 3 f. for the courts of the Lord
fainthearted Deut 20 8 that is fearful and f.
Eccu 2 15 woe to them that are f., who believe
4 9 and be not fainthearted in thy soul
7 9 be not f. in thy mind: neglect not to
Isa 35 4 say to the f.: Take courage and fear not
fainting Ps 118 53 a f. hath taken hold of me
Eccu 17 20 hath strengthened them that were f.
26 26 a man of war fainting through poverty
2 Ma 3 24 were struck with f. and dread. For there
Heb 12 3 not wearied fainting in your minds
fair Gen 2 9 fair to behold, and pleasant to eat
Gen 3 6 was good to eat and fair to the eyes
6 2 daughters of men, that they were fair
41 5 came up upon one stalk full and fair
22 grew upon one stalk, full and very fair
Judg 5 10 speak, you that ride upon fair asses
Prov 11 22 swine's snout, a woman fair and foolish
26 7 as a lame man hath fair legs in vain
Cant 1 14 behold thou art fair. 15
4 7 thou art all fair, O my love, and there
6 9 fair as the moon, bright as the sun
Eccu 3 17 as the ice in the fair warm weather
13 7 he will speak thee fair and will say
24 19 as a fair olive tree in the plains and
24 I am the mother of fair love and of
Isa 2 16 and upon all that is fair to behold
5 9 unless many great and fair houses shall
Jer 11 16 plentiful olive tree, fair, fruitful
46 20 is like a fair and beautiful heifer
Lam 2 4 killed all that was fair to behold
Eze 31 3 cedar in Libanus with fair branches
Amos 8 13 the fair virgins and the young men shall
Mat 16 2 you say, It will be fair weather, for
fairer Judg 15 2 sister, who is younger and fairer
Lam 4 7 old ivory, fairer than the sapphire
Dan 1 15 their faces appeared fairer and fatter
fairest Lev 23 40 the fruits of the fairest tree
Judg 5 30 f. of the women is chosen out for him
Cant 1 7 fairest among women, go forth and follow
Isa 3 25 thy fairest men also shall fall by the
fairs Eze 27 12 supplied thy f. with a multitude
Eze 27 17 they set forth . . . rosin in thy fairs
46 11 in the fairs and in the solemnities
faith 1 Pa 5 20 they had put their faith in him
Tob 2 18 that never change their faith from him
Wisd 1 2 himself to them that have faith in him
3 14 gift of faith shall be given to him
Eccu 1 35 agreeable to him, is faith and meekness
25 16 beginning of faith is to be fast joined
45 4 he sanctified him in his faith and
49 12 and redeemed themselves by strong faith
Isa 11 5 loins: and faith the girdle of his reins
33 6 there shall be faith in thy times
Jer 5 1 executeth judgment and seeketh faith
7 28 faith is lost, and is taken away out
Haba 2 4 but the just shall live in his faith
Soph 3 4 prophets are senseless men without f.
1 Ma 14 35 and faith, which he kept to his nation

Book	Ch	V	Text
2 Ma	12	25	given his faith that he would restore
Mat	8	10	not found so great faith. Luke 7:9
	9	2	Jesus seeing their faith, said to the man sick of the palsy. Mark 2:5
	17	19	if you have faith as a grain. Luke 17:6
	21	21	if you have faith and stagger not
	23	23	justice and mercy and faith. These things
Mark	4	40	you fearful? Have you not faith yet
	11	22	saith to them: Have the faith of God
Luke	5	20	whose faith when he saw, he said: Man
	17	5	said to the Lord: Increase our faith
	18	8	shall he find, think you, f. on earth
Acts	3	16	the faith which is by him hath given
	6	7	also of the priests obeyed the faith
	13	8	turn away the proconsul from the faith
	14	8	seeing that he had faith to be healed
	17	31	giving faith to all, by raising him up
	20	21	God, and faith in our Lord Jesus Christ
	24	24	Felix . . . heard of him the faith that
Rom	1	5	apostleship for obedience to the faith
		17	revealed therein from faith unto faith
	3	3	make the faith of God without effect
	4	5	his f. is reputed to justice according
		9	unto Abraham f. was reputed to justice
		14	be heirs, faith is made void, the promise
	10	17	faith then cometh by hearing; and
	14	22	hast thou faith? Have it to thyself
1 C	12	9	to another, faith in the same Spirit
	13	2	if I should have all faith, so that I
		13	there remain faith, hope, and charity
Gal	1	23	doth now preach the faith which once
	3	23	before the faith came, we were kept
		23	unto that faith which was to be revealed
		25	after the faith is come, we are no
	5	6	but faith that worketh by charity. You
		23	the fruit of the Spirit is . . . faith
Eph	4	5	one Lord, one faith, one baptism. One
	6	23	to the brethren and charity with faith
Phil	1	27	laboring together for the faith of the
Col	2	12	by the faith of the operation of God
2 Th	3	2	evil men; for all men have not faith
1 Tim	1	5	good conscience and an unfeigned faith
		14	abounded exceedingly with faith and
		19	having faith and a good conscience
		19	made shipwreck concerning the faith
	4	1	times some shall depart from the faith
	5	8	he hath denied the faith and is worse
		12	they have made void their first faith
	6	10	some coveting have erred from the faith
		11	pursue justice, godliness, f., charity
		21	promising, have erred concerning the f.
2 Tim	1	5	that faith which is in thee unfeigned
	2	18	and have subverted the faith of some
		22	pursue justice, faith, charity, and peace
	3	8	in mind, reprobate concerning the faith
		10	my doctrine, manner of life, purpose, f.
	4	7	I have kept the faith. As to the rest
Titus	1	1	according to the faith of the elect of
		4	according to the common faith, grace
Heb	4	2	being mixed with faith of those things
	11	1	faith is the substance of things to be
		6	without faith it is impossible to please
		13	these died according to faith, not
	13	7	whose faith follow, considering the end
James	2	1	have not the faith of our Lord Jesus
		14	man say he hath faith but hath not works
		14	works? Shall faith be able to save him
		17	faith also if it have not works, is dead
		18	thou hast faith and I have works: show
		20	faith without works is dead. 26
		22	faith did cooperate with his works; and
		22	and by works faith was made perfect
2 P	1	1	that have obtained equal faith with us
1 J	5	4	which overcometh the world, our faith
Jude		3	you to contend earnestly for the faith
Apoc	2	13	my name, and hast not denied my faith
	13	10	the patience and the faith of the saints
	14	12	who keep . . . the faith of Jesus. And I
by (the) faith Prov	15	27	by mercy and faith sins
Acts	15	9	purifying their hearts by faith. Now
	26	18	the saints by the faith that is in me
Rom	1	17	the just man liveth by faith. Gal 3:11
	3	22	justice of God, by faith of Jesus Christ
		28	account a man to be justified by faith
		30	that justifieth circumcision by faith
	5	1	being justified therefore by faith, let
	9	32	because they sought it not by faith
	11	20	broken off. But thou standest by faith
2 C	5	7	for we walk by faith and not by sight
Gal	2	16	the law, but by the f. of Jesus Christ
		16	we may be justified by the faith of
	3	8	God justifieth the Gentiles by faith
		14	may receive promise of the Spirit by f.
		22	the promise by the faith of Jesus Christ
		24	that we might be justified by faith
		26	you are all children of God by faith
	5	5	we in spirit, by faith, wait for the
Eph	3	12	with confidence by the faith of him
		17	that Christ may dwell by faith in your
2 Tim	3	15	by the faith which is in Christ Jesus
Heb	10	38	my just man liveth by faith but if he
	11	3	by faith we understand that the world
		4	by faith Abel offered to God a sacrifice
		5	by faith Henoch was translated, that
		7	by faith Noe, having received an answer
		7	heir of the justice which is by faith
		8	by faith he that is called Abraham
		9	by faith he abode in the land, dwelling
		11	by faith also Sara herself, being barren
		17	by faith Abraham, when he was tried
		20	by faith . . . Isaac blessed Jacob and
		21	by faith Jacob dying blessed each of
		22	by faith Joseph, when he was dying
		23	by faith Moses . . . was hid three months
		24	by faith Moses, when he was grown up
		27	by faith he left Egypt, not fearing the
		28	by faith he celebrated the pasch, and
		29	by faith they passed through the Red
		30	by faith the walls of Jericho fell down
		31	by faith Rahab the harlot perished not
		33	who by faith conquered kingdoms, wrought
James	2	24	is justified; and not by faith only
1 P	1	5	are kept by faith unto salvation, ready
in (the) faith Eccu	32	27	regard thy soul in faith
Osee	2	20	and I will espouse thee to me in faith
Acts	3	16	in the faith of his name, this man
	14	21	exhorting them to continue in the faith
	16	5	the churches were confirmed in faith
Rom	4	19	[Abraham] was not weak in faith; neither
		20	[Abraham] was strengthened in faith
	14	1	him that is weak in faith take unto
1 C	16	13	stand fast in the faith, do manfully
2 C	1	23	helpers of your joy: for in f. you stand
	8	7	in all things you abound in faith and
	13	5	try your own selves if you be in the f.
Gal	2	20	I live in the faith of the Son of God
Phil	3	9	Jesus, which is of God, justice in f.
Col	1	23	if so ye continue in the faith grounded
	2	7	in him and confirmed in the faith
2 Th	2	12	in . . . the spirit and faith of the truth
1 Tim	1	2	to Timothy, his beloved son in faith
		4	the edification of God, which is in f.
	2	7	doctor of the Gentiles in faith and
		15	if she continue in faith and love and
	3	13	much confidence in faith which is
	4	12	be thou an example . . . in faith, in

2 Tim 1 13 which thou hast heard of me in faith
Titus 1 13 that they may be sound in the faith
2 2 that the aged men be . . . sound in faith
3 15 salute them that love us in the faith
James 1 6 let him ask in faith, nothing wavering
2 5 the poor in this world, rich in faith
1 P 5 9 whom resist ye, strong in faith: knowing
of (the) faith Mat 6 30 ye of little faith. 8:26; 16:8; Luke 12:28
Mat 14 31 of little faith, why didst thou doubt
Acts 6 5 they chose Stephen, a man full of faith
11 24 full of the Holy Ghost and of faith
14 26 had opened the door of faith to Gentiles
Rom 3 26 who is of the faith of Jesus Christ
27 of works? No, but by the law of faith
4 11 circumcision, seal of the justice of f.
13 but through the justice of faith. For
16 which is of the faith of Abraham, who
9 30 justice that is of faith. 10:6
10 8 this is the world of faith which we
12 3 divided to every one the measure of f.
6 to be used according to the rule of f.
14 23 he eat, is condemned; because not of f.
23 for all that is not of faith is sin
16 26 eternal God, for the obedience of faith
2 C 4 13 having the same spirit of faith, as it
Gal 3 2 law, or by the hearing of faith. 5
7 they who are of faith, the same are the
9 they that are of faith shall be blessed
12 the law is not of faith: but, He that
6 10 who are of the household of the faith
Eph 4 13 until we all meet in the unity of faith
29 which is good, to the edification of f.
6 16 taking the shield of faith wherewith
Phil 1 25 for your furtherance and joy of faith
3 9 my justice . . . which is of the faith of
1 Th 5 8 having on the breastplate of faith and
2 Th 1 11 and the work of faith in power; that
1 Tim 3 9 holding the mystery of faith in a sure
4 6 nourished up in the words of faith and
6 12 fight the good fight of faith: lay
Heb 6 1 dead work, and of faith towards God
10 22 with a true heart in fulness of faith
39 but of faith to the saving of the soul
11 39 being approved by the testimony of faith
12 2 Jesus the author and finisher of faith
James 5 15 the prayer of faith shall save the sick
through faith Rom 3 25 through f. in his blood
Rom 3 30 and uncircumcision through faith. Do
31 do we, then, destroy the law through f.
5 2 access through faith into this grace
Eph 2 8 by grace you are saved through faith
Heb 6 12 through faith and patience shall inherit
thy faith Mat 9 22 thy faith hath made thee whole. Mark 5:34; 10:52; Luke 8:48; 17:9; 18:42
Mat 15 28 woman, great is thy faith: be it done
Luke 7 50 thy faith hath made thee safe, go in
22 32 prayed for thee that thy faith fail not
Philem 5 hearing of thy charity and faith
6 communication of thy faith may be made
James 2 18 show me thy faith without works; and I
your faith Mat 9 29 according to your faith, be
Luke 8 25 where is your faith? Who being afraid
Rom 1 8 your faith is spoken of in the whole
12 common to us both, your faith and mine
1 C 2 5 that your faith might not stand on
15 17 not risen again, your faith is vain. 14
2 C 1 23 exercise dominion over your faith
10 15 having hope of your increasing faith
Eph 1 15 hearing of your faith that is in the
Phil 2 17 the sacrifice and service of your faith
Col 1 4 hearing your faith in Christ Jesus
2 5 steadfastness of your faith which is in
1 Th 1 3 mindful of the work of your faith and
3 2 and exhort you concerning your faith
5 sent to know your faith: lest perhaps
6 related to us your faith and charity
7 we were comforted . . . by your faith
10 things that are wanting to your faith
2 Th 1 3 your faith groweth exceedingly, and
4 for your patience and faith and in
James 1 3 trying of your faith worketh patience
1 P 1 7 that the trial of your faith, much more
9 receiving the end of your faith, even
21 your faith and hope might be in God
2 P 1 5 all care, minister in your faith, virtue
Jude 20 yourselves upon your most holy faith
faithful Num 12 7 is most f. in all my house
Deut 7 9 he is a strong and faithful God, keeping
32 4 God is f. and without any iniquity
1 K 2 35 I will raise me up a faithful priest
35 I will build him a faithful house and
3 20 knew that Samuel was a faithful prophet
22 14 all thy servants is so faithful as David
25 28 surely make for my lord a faithful house
2 K 7 16 thy house shall be f., and thy kingdom
3 K 11 38 will build thee up a faithful house
2 Es 9 8 thou didst find his heart faithful
13 13 they were approved as faithful, and to
Tob 5 4 go now and seek thee out some f. man
Jdth 8 23 through many tribulations, remaining f.
Ps 18 8 testimony of the Lord is f., giving
77 8 whose spirit was not faithful to God
37 nor were they counted f. in his covenant
88 29 forever: and my covenant faithful to him
38 forever and a faithful witness in heaven
100 6 my eyes were upon the f. of the earth
110 8 all his commandments are f.: confirmed
144 13 the Lord is faithful in all his words
Prov 11 13 he that is f., concealeth the thing
18 soweth justice, there is a f. reward
13 17 but a faithful ambassador is health
14 5 a faithful witness will not lie: but a
25 a faithful witness delivereth souls: and
20 6 merciful: but who shall find a f. man
25 13 so is a faithful messenger to him that
28 20 a f. man shall be much praised: but he
Wisd 3 9 that are f. in love shall rest in him
Eccu 1 16 was created with the f. in the womb
16 and is known with the just and faithful
6 14 a faithful friend is a strong defence
15 nothing can be compared to a f. friend
16 a f. friend is the medicine of life
15 10 God, and shall abound in a f. mouth
22 29 time of his trouble continue f. to him
31 28 and the testimony of his truth is f.
33 3 a man of understanding is f. to the
3 the law of God, and the law is f. to
31 if thou have a f. servant, let him
34 8 be made plain in the mouth of the f.
36 18 that thy prophets may be found faithful
37 26 the fruits of his understanding are f.
44 21 in temptation he was found faithful
46 18 and he was known to be f. in his words
48 25 great prophet and f. in the sight of
Isa 1 21 how is the faithful city, that was full
26 called the city of the just, a f. city
8 2 and I took unto me faithful witnesses
25 1 thy designs of old faithful, amen
49 7 for the Lord's sake, because he is f.
55 3 with you: the f. mercies of David
Dan 2 45 the interpretation thereof is faithful
6 4 because he was f. and no fault nor
Osee 11 12 with God and is faithful with the saints
1 Ma 2 52 was not Abraham found f. in temptation
3 13 Judas had assembled a company of the f.

7 8 Bacchides . . . was faithful to the king
14 41 till there should arise a f. prophet
2 Ma 1 2 that he made with . . . his f. servants
9 26 to be faithful to me and to my son
Mat 24 45 is a faithful and wise servant, whom
25 21 well done, good and f. servant. 23
21 hast been f. over a few things. 23
Luke 12 42 is the faithful and wise steward
16 10 f. in that which is least, is f. also
11 not been f. in the unjust mammon
12 not been f. in that which is another's
19 17 thou hast been faithful in a little
Acts 10 45 f. of circumcision, who came with Peter
13 34 give you the holy things of David f.
16 15 if you have judged me to be faithful
Rom 4 12 that follow the steps of the faithful
1 C 1 9 God is f. 10:13; 2 C 1:18; 2 Th 3:3
4 17 my dearest son and faithful in the Lord
7 25 obtained mercy of Lord, to be faithful
2 C 6 15 what part hath the f. with unbeliever
Gal 3 9 shall be blessed with faithful Abraham
Eph 1 1 and to the faithful in Christ Jesus
6 21 Tychicus, my . . . f. minister. Col 4:7
Col 1 2 to the saints and faithful brethren in
1 7 who is for you a f. minister of Christ
4 9 a most beloved and faithful brother, who
1 Th 5 24 he is faithful who hath called you, who
1 Tim 1 12 Lord, for that he hath counted me f.
15 a faithful saying. 3:1; 4:9; 2 Tim 2:11; Titus 3:8
3 11 but sober, faithful in all things. Let
4 3 received with thanksgiving by the f.
10 of all men, especially of the faithful
12 be thou an example of the faithful in
5 16 if any of the faithful have widows, let
6 2 because they are faithful and beloved
2 Tim 2 2 the same command to faithful men, who
13 if we believe not, he continueth f., he
Titus 1 6 having f. children, not accused of riot
9 embracing that faithful word which is
Heb 2 17 become a merciful and f. high priest
3 2 who is faithful to him that made him
5 Moses indeed was f. in all his house
10 23 for he is faithful that hath promised
11 11 that he was faithful who had promised
1 P 1 21 who through him are faithful in God
4 19 in good deeds to the faithful Creator
5 12 by Sylvanus, a f. brother unto you
1 J 1 9 he is faithful and just, to forgive
Apoc 1 5 Jesus Christ, who is the f. witness
2 10 be thou f. until death: and I will give
13 when Antipas was my faithful witness
3 14 Amen, the faithful and true witness
17 14 are called and elect and faithful. And
19 11 sat upon him was called f. and true
21 5 for these words are most faithful. 22:6
faithfully 4 K 12 15 but they bestowed it f. But
2 Pa 19 9 you do in the fear of the Lord f., and
31 12 they brought in f. both the firstfruits
15 to distribute f. portions to their brethren
18 victuals were given faithfully out of the
34 12 and they did all faithfully. Now the
Tob 1 6 offering faithfully all his firstfruits
Prov 12 22 they that deal faithfully please him
Eccu 7 22 hurt not the servant that worketh f.
29 3 thy word and deal f. with him: and
3 J 5 thou dost f. whatever thou dost for
faithfulness 1 K 26 23 his justice and his f.
Ps 32 4 all his works are done with faithfulness
Jer 42 5 witness between us of truth and f.
Lam 3 23 are new every morning, great is thy f.
faithless Eccu 15 22 of f. and unprofitable children
Isa 1 23 thy princes are f., companions of thieves
Eze 6 9 I have broken their heart that was f.
Luke 9 41 f. and perverse generation, how long
John 20 27 and be not faithless, but believing
fall Mat 7 27 fell, and great was the fall thereof
Mat 10 29 not one of them shall fall on the
12 11 if the same fall into a pit on the
15 14 lead the blind, both fall into the pit
27 the crumbs that fall from the table of
21 44 shall fall on this stone. Luke 20:18
44 on whomsoever it shall f. Luke 20:18
24 29 the stars shall fall from heaven and
Luke 2 34 this child is set for the fall and
6 39 do they not both fall into the ditch
8 13 in time of temptation they fall away
11 17 and house upon house shall fall. And
14 5 have an ass or an ox fall into a pit
16 17 than one tittle of the law to fall
21 24 shall fall by the edge of the sword
23 30 say to the mountains: Fall upon us
Acts 27 17 lest they should fall into quicksands
29 fearing lest we should fall upon rough
32 ropes of the boat, and let her fall off
28 6 he would suddenly fall down and die. But
Rom 11 11 they so stumbled, that they should fall
1 C 10 12 to stand, let him take heed lest he fall
2 C 11 3 fall from simplicity that is in Christ
Phil 1 19 I know that this shall fall out to me
1 Tim 3 6 he fall into the judgment of the devil
7 lest he fall into reproach and the snare
6 9 fall into temptation and into the snare
Heb 4 11 lest any man fall into the same example
10 31 to fall into the hands of the living God
James 1 2 joy, when you shall fall into divers
5 12 that you fall not under judgment. Is
2 P 3 17 you fall from your own steadfastness
Apoc 6 16 fall upon us and hide us from the face
7 16 neither shall the sun fall on them nor
9 1 I saw a star fall from heaven upon the
fallen Acts 1 25 Judas hath by transgression fallen
Acts 15 16 tabernacle of David, which is f. down
26 14 when we were all f. down on the ground
27 41 when we were fallen into a place where
Rom 11 22 towards them indeed that are fallen
1 C 15 6 present, and some are fallen asleep
18 they also that are fallen asleep in
Gal 5 4 in the law: you are fallen from grace
Phil 1 12 have f. out rather to the furtherance of
Heb 6 6 are fallen away: to be renewed again
1 P 1 24 and the flower thereof is fallen away
Apoc 2 5 from whence thou art fallen: and do
14 8 that great Babylon is fallen, is fallen
17 10 five are fallen, one is, and the other
18 2 Babylon the great is fallen, is fallen
falleth Mat 17 14 he falleth often into the fire and
Mark 5 22 seeing him, falleth down at his feet
Luke 15 12 portion of substance that f. to me
Rom 14 4 to his own lord he standeth or falleth
1 C 13 8 charity never falleth away: whether
falling Mat 2 11 and falling down they adored him; **and**
Mat 4 9 if falling down thou wilt adore me
18 26 servant falling down besought. 29
Mark 13 25 the stars of heaven shall be f. down
Luke 5 12 falling on his face, besought him
10 18 I saw Satan like lightning f. from
John 9 38 and falling down, he adored him. And
12 24 the grain of wheat f. into the ground
Acts 7 59 falling on his knees, he cried with
9 4 falling on the ground, he heard a voice
10 25 meet him, and falling at his feet adored
20 37 f. on the neck of Paul, they kissed him
22 7 falling on the ground, I heard a voice
1 C 14 25 falling down on his face, he will adore
fallow Jer 4 3 break up anew your fallow ground

Osee 10 12 break up your fallow ground: but the
falls Josu 9 7 the land which falls to our lot
Prov 23 29 who falls into pits? Who hath wounds
Eccu 23 9 swearing, for in it there are many f.
false Gen 42 16 whether it be true or false
Gen 43 18 may bring upon us a false accusation
Num 5 14 or is charged with false suspicion
Judg 16 10 hast told me [Dalila] a false thing
4 K 9 12 it is false, but rather do thou tell
Jdth 5 5 shall not a false word come out of my
Job 16 9 a false speaker riseth up against my
Ps 57 4 they have spoken false things. Their
Eccu 20 18 eat his bread are of a false tongue
20 the slipping of a false tongue is
26 7 false calumny, all are more grievous
34 4 can come from that which is false
36 21 and the wise heart false speeches
Isa 57 4 you wicked children, a false seed
Jer 10 14 what he hath cast is false, and
40 16 what thou sayst of Ismahel is false
Lam 2 14 have seen false and foolish things
14 have seen for thee false revelations
Bar 6 7 false things and they cannot speak
44 that are done about them, are false
47 they have left false things and
50 hereafter that they are false things
58 better to be . . . than such false gods
Haba 2 18 graven it, a molten and a false image
Zach 8 17 love not a false oath: for all these
13 2 I will take away the false prophets
Mala 3 5 witness against . . . false swearers
2 Ma 5 5 there was gone forth a false rumor
Mat 7 15 beware of false prophets, who come to
15 19 from heart come . . . false testimonies
24 11 many false prophets shall rise and
24 shall arise f. Christs and f. prophets
26 60 many false witnesses had come in. And
60 there came two false witnesses. And
Mark 13 22 rise up f. Christs and f. prophets
Luke 6 26 did their fathers to the f. prophets
Acts 6 13 they set up false witnesses, who said
13 6 certain man, a magician, a f. prophet
21 24 which they have heard of thee, are false
1 C 15 15 yea, and we are found false witnesses
2 C 11 13 such f. apostles are deceitful workmen
26 in sea, in perils from false brethren
Gal 2 4 because of false brethren unawares
Titus 2 3 in holy attire, not false accusers, not
2 P 2 1 there were also false prophets among
1 J 4 1 many false prophets are gone out into
Apoc 16 13 from the mouth of the false prophet
19 20 taken, and with him the false prophet
20 10 the false prophet shall be tormented
false witness Exod 20 16 thou shalt not bear f. w.
Exod 23 1 to bear false witness for a wicked
Deut 5 20 neither shalt thou bear false witness
19 18 that the false witness hath told a lie
3 K 21 10 let them bear false witness: that he
Prov 19 5 f. witness shall not be unpunished. 9
25 18 a man that beareth false witness against
Dan 13 43 have borne false witness against me
49 have borne f. witness against her
61 had convicted them of false witness
Mat 19 18 thou shalt not bear false witness. Luke 18:20; Rom 13:9
26 59 the whole council sought false witness
Mark 10 19 bear not false witness, do no fraud
14 56 many bore false witness against him
57 some rising up, bore false witness
falsehood Isa 28 15 by f. we are protected
Isa 28 17 hail shall overturn the hope of f.
59 13 uttered from the heart words of f.
Jer 3 10 not returned . . . but with falsehood
5 31 the prophets prophesied falsehood
8 8 lying pen of scribes hath wrought f.
13 25 forgotten me and hast trusted in f.
15 18 as the falsehood of deceitful waters
Osee 7 1 they have committed falsehood and the
2 Ma 15 10 showed withal the f. of the Gentiles
falsely Lev 6 3 denying it, shall also swear falsely
Lev 19 12 thou shalt not swear falsely by my name
Jer 5 2 this also they will swear falsely
7 9 to swear falsely, to offer to Baalim
14 14 prophets prophesy f. in my name: I sent
27 15 they prophesy in my name falsely: to
29 9 they prophesy f. to you in my name
21 prophesy unto you in my name falsely
Zach 5 4 that sweareth falsely by my name: and it
1 Tim 6 20 oppositions of knowledge f. so called
1 P 3 16 ashamed who falsely accuse your good
falsified 1 Ma 11 53 f. all whatsoever he had said
fame Gen 45 16 the fame was abroad in the king's
Josu 9 9 we have heard the fame of his power
3 K 10 1 having heard of the fame of Solomon
7 thy wisdom and thy works exceed the f.
2 Pa 9 1 Saba heard of the fame of Solomon
Esth 9 4 the fame of his name increased daily
Job 28 22 with our ears we have heard the fame
Eccu 3 18 evil f. is he that forsaketh his father
Jer 6 24 we have heard the fame thereof, our
Nah 3 19 all that have heard the fame of thee
1 Ma 3 26 his fame came to the king, and all
41 merchants . . . heard the fame of them
8 1 Judas heard of the fame of the Romans
14 10 the fame of his glory was renowned
2 Ma 8 7 and the fame of his valor was spread
Mat 4 24 his fame went throughout all Syria
9 26 the fame hereof went abroad into all
31 spread his fame abroad in all that
14 1 Herod . . . heard the fame of Jesus. And
Mark 1 28 the fame of him was spread forthwith
Luke 4 14 fame of him went out through the whole
37 the fame of him was published into
5 15 the fame of him went abroad the more
Phil 4 8 whatsoever of good fame, if there be
familiar Job 6 13 my f. friends also are departed
Ps 54 14 one mind, my guide and my familiar
familiarly Judg 19 4 with him and drinking f.
familiars Jer 20 10 the men that were my f. and
families Gen 10 18 f. of the Chanaanites were spread
Gen 10 32 these are the families of. Exod 6:15; Num 3:27; 26:7, 14, 18, 22, 34, 58; 1 Pa 4:2
47 24 for food for your families and children
Exod 6 25 heads of the Levitical f. 1 Pa 15:12
12 21 go take a lamb by your families, and
Num 1 18 reckoning them up by the . . . families
30 by the generations and families. 32, 34
2 34 marched by families and houses of their
3 21 of Gerson were two families, the
27 come the families of the Amramites
33 of Merari are families of the Moholites
4 29 sons of Merari by the families and
7 2 heads of the families. 3 K 8:1; 1 Pa 23:9; 26:21; 29:6; 2 Pa 1:2; 5:2; 1 Es 8:29; 10:16; 2 Es 7:70; 12:12, 23
18 31 eat them . . . you and your families
26 55 the land be divided to the tribe and f.
32 28 Moses commanded . . . the princes of the f.
33 54 be divided by the tribes and the f.
36 1 princes of the families of Galaad
8 the inheritance may remain in the f.
Josu 7 17 which being brought by its families
14 1 princes of the families . . . gave to them
19 51 princes of the families . . . distributed
21 1 princes of the families of Levi came
10 sons of Aaron, of the families of Caath

20 to rest of families of children of Caath
33 all the cities of families of Gerson
40 each distributed by the families. And
Judg 9 6 all the families of the city of Mello
1 K 9 21 my kindred the last among all the f.
10 19 by your tribes and by your families
4 K 3 17 you shall drink, you and your families
1 Pa 2 55 the families of the scribes that dwell
4 21 families of the house of them that
6 54 the families of the Caathites: for they
7 9 they were numbered by the families
8 6 heads of families. 26:26; 27:1; 2 Es 7:71
9 33 singing men of families of the Levites
16 28 O ye families of the nations: bring ye
23 6 by the families of the sons of Levi
24 5 he [David] divided both the families
6 of the priestly and Levitical f. 31
26 32 chiefs of families. 1 Es 8:1
2 Pa 17 14 the number of the houses and families
19 8 chiefs of the f. 23:2; 2 Es 8:13; 12:22
25 5 and appointed them by families and
26 12 number of the chiefs by the families
35 4 prepare yourselves by your . . . f.
5 by the families and companies of Levi
12 to give them by the houses and families
Jdth 3 3 our goods and families are in thy sight
Ps 106 41 made him families like a flock of sheep
Jer 1 15 I will call together all the families
2 4 all ye families of the house of Israel
31 1 will be the God of all the f. of Israel
33 24 two families which the Lord had chosen
Eze 20 32 we . . . as the families of the earth
Amos 3 2 have I known of all the f. of the earth
Nah 3 4 that sold . . . f. through her witchcrafts
Zach 12 12 the land shall mourn: f. and f. apart
12 the f. of the house of David apart
13 families of the house of Nathan apart
13 families of the house of Levi apart
13 the families of Semei apart, and their
14 the rest of the f., f. and f. apart
14 17 that shall not go up of the families
1 Tim 5 14 be mistresses of f., give no occasion
their families Gen 10 5 t. f. in their nations
Exod 6 14 the heads of their houses by their f.
19 kindreds of Levi by their families
12 3 take a lamb by their families and
Lev 21 17 of thy seed throughout their families
Num 1 2 take the sum . . . by their families
20 by their generations and families. 22, 24, 26, 28, 36, 38, 40, 42
45 by their houses and families. 4:2, 22
47 Levites in the tribes of their families
3 15 number sons of Levi by . . . their f.
39 and Aaron numbered . . . by their families
11 10 the people weeping by their families
17 3 one rod shall contain all their families
20 30 thirty days throughout all their f.
26 38 the sons of . . . by their families. 50, 57; Josu 19:32; 1 Pa 6:62, 63
42 the kindreds of Dan by their families
34 14 children of . . . by their f. Josu 13:28; 16:8; 18:11, 28; 19:40
Josu 17 2 of Manasses according to their families
18 20 children of Benjamin . . . and their f.
Judg 21 24 returned by their tribes and families
1 Pa 4 38 and in the houses of their families
5 7 they were numbered by their families
15 chief of the house in their families
24 and famous chiefs in their families
6 19 kindreds of Levi according to their f.
60 all their cities throughout their f.
7 4 with them by their families and peoples
7 five chiefs of their families and most
40 heads of their f. 8:10, 28; 9:9; 26:6
9 9 brethren by their families, 956. All
13 their brethren heads in their families
19 their families in turns were keepers
34 of the Levites, princes in their f.
23 24 sons of Levi in their kindreds and f.
24 4 sixteen chief men by their families: and
4 of Ithamar eight by their families and
30 according to the houses of their f.
26 13 they cast lots . . . by their families
31 Hebronites . . . according to their f.
2 Pa 31 17 to the priests by their families
family Gen 26 14 herds and a very great family
Gen 45 16 Pharao with all his family was glad
50 4 Joseph spoke to the family of Pharao
Lev 25 10 every one shall go back to his former f.
Num 4 24 the office of the f. of the Gersonites
28 the service of the f. of the Gersonites
33 the office of the f. of the Merarites
26 5 of whom is the family of the. So chap. 26 passim
12 of him is the f. of the. 13, 15, 16, 17
40 of Hered is the f. of the Heredites
58 families of Levi: the family of Lobni, the f. of Hebroni, the f. of Moholi, the f. of Musi, the f. of Core
27 3 why is his name taken away out of his f.
36 12 their uncle . . . of the f. of Manasses
12 remained in the . . . f. of their father
Deut 29 18 family or a tribe whose heart is turned
Josu 7 17 it was found to be the family of Zare
21 4 the lot came out for family of Caath
Judg 6 11 Joas the father of the family of Ezri
15 my family is the meanest in Manasses
24 Ephra, which is of the family of Ezri
8 32 in Ephra of the family of Ezri. But
18 2 valiant men of their stock and family
19 priests . . . in a tribe and f. in Israel
Ruth 4 6 not cut off the posterity of my own f.
10 name be cut off from among his family
14 not suffered thy f. to want a successor
1 K 17 55 of what f. is this young man descended
58 young man, of what family art thou
18 18 what is my life, or my father's family
2 K 21 18 race of Arapha of family of the giants
1 Pa 6 70 left of the family of the sons of Caath
23 11 they were counted in one family and in
2 Pa 22 10 Athalia . . . killed all the royal family
Tob 5 16 of what family or what tribe art thou
17 dost thou seek the f. of him thou hirest
19 Tobias answered: Thou art of a great f.
19 not angry that I desired to know thy f.
10 13 to take care of the family, to govern
11 3 let the family follow softly after us
18 wife and all the family arrived safe
Job 1 3 and a family exceeding great: and this
Ecce 2 7 and had a great family: and herds of
Eccu 8 5 lest he speak ill of thy family
49 17 Joseph . . . the support of his family
Amos 3 1 concerning the whole family that I
Mich 2 3 I devise an evil against this family
Zach 14 18 if the family of Egypt go not up nor
Mat 24 45 lord hath appointed over his family
Luke 2 4 he was of the house and f. of David
12 42 whom his lord setteth over his family
famine Gen 12 10 came a f. in the country; and
Gen 12 10 the famine was very grievous in the
26 1 when a famine came in the land, after
41 27 are seven years of famine to come
30 the famine shall consume all the land
36 let it be in readiness against the f.
50 before the famine came, Joseph had
54 famine prevailed in the whole world

56 the famine increased daily in all the
56 for the famine had oppressed them also
42 5 the famine was in the land of Chanaan
43 1 famine was heavy upon all the land
45 6 since the f. began to be upon the land
11 for there are yet five years of famine
47 4 the famine being very grievous in the
13 and a famine had oppressed the land
Exod 16 3 might destroy all the multitude with f.
Deut 28 20 the Lord shall send upon thee famine
32 24 they shall be consumed with famine
Ruth 1 1 there came a famine in the land. And
2 K 21 1 was a famine in the days of David
24 13 either seven years of famine shall come
3 K 8 37 if a famine arise in the land, or a
18 2 there was a grievous famine in Samaria
4 K 4 38 and there was a famine in the land
6 25 there was a great famine in Samaria
7 4 the city, we shall die with the famine
12 they know that we suffer great famine
8 1 for the Lord hath called a famine, and
25 3 and a famine prevailed in the city
1 Pa 21 12 either three years' famine: or three
2 Pa 6 28 if a famine arise in the land, or a
20 9 if evils fall upon us . . . famine, we
2 Es 5 3 let us take corn because of the famine
Jdth 5 9 there was a famine over all the land
11 10 also a famine hath come upon them
Job 5 20 in famine he shall deliver thee from
22 in destruction and f. thou shalt laugh
18 12 let his strength be wasted with famine
Ps 32 19 from death, and feed them in famine
36 19 in the days of f. they shall be filled
104 16 he called a famine upon the land: and
Prov 10 3 not afflict the soul of the just with f.
28 3 violent shower which bringeth a famine
Eccu 39 35 hail, famine . . . created for vengeance
40 9 famine and affliction and scourges
48 2 he brought a famine upon them, and they
Isa 5 13 their nobles have perished with famine
14 30 I will make thy root perish with famine
51 19 f. and the sword, who shall comfort thee
Jer 5 12 we shall not see the sword and famine
11 22 sons and their daughters shall die by f.
14 12 and by famine and by the pestilence
13 there shall be no famine among you
15 sword and f. shall not be in this land
15 by sword and f. shall those prophets
16 because of the famine and the sword
18 behold them that are consumed with f.
15 2 such as are for famine, to famine
16 4 with the sword and with famine: and
18 21 deliver up their children to famine
21 7 pestilence and the sword and the f.
9 shall die by sword and by f. 42:17, 22
24 10 among them the sword and the famine
27 8 that nation with the sword and with f.
13 thy people by the sword and by famine
28 8 of war and of affliction and of famine
29 17 send upon them the sword and the famine
18 them with the sword and with famine
32 24 by the sword and the famine and the
36 the sword and by f. and by pestilence
34 17 to the pestilence and to the famine
38 2 shall die by the sword and by famine
42 16 famine . . . shall cleave to you in
44 12 shall fall by the sword and by the f.
12 and by the famine shall they die: and
13 Jerusalem by the sword and by famine
18 consumed by the sword and by f. 27
52 6 a famine overpowered the city: and
Lam 5 10 by reason of the violence of the f.
Bar 2 25 have died in grievous pains, by famine
Eze 5 12 and shall be consumed with famine
16 upon them the grievous arrows of famine
16 I will gather together f. against you
17 I will send in upon you famine and
6 11 they shall fall by the sword, by the f.
12 and is besieged, shall die by the f.
7 15 the pestilence and the famine within
15 devoured by the pestilence and the f.
12 16 from the sword and from the famine
14 13 I will send famine upon it and will
21 judgments, the sword and the famine and
34 29 shall be no more consumed with famine
36 29 and will lay no famine upon you. And
30 you bear no more the reproach of f.
Amos 8 11 I will send forth a f. into the land
11 not a famine of bread, nor a thirst
1 Ma 6 54 the famine had prevailed over them
9 24 in those days there was a very great f.
13 49 many of them perished through famine
Luke 4 25 there was a great famine throughout
15 14 came a mighty famine in that country
Acts 7 11 there came a famine upon all Egypt
11 28 a great famine over the whole world
Rom 8 35 or distress? or famine? or nakedness?
Apoc 6 8 to kill with sword, with famine, and
18 8 death and mourning and famine, and she
famines Mat 24 7 shall be pestilences and f. and
Mark 13 8 earthquakes in divers places, and f.
Luke 21 11 and famines and terrors from heaven
famished Gen 41 55 also they began to be f., the
famous Gen 11 4 let us make our name famous before
Ruth 4 11 may have a famous name in Bethlehem
1 K 9 6 man of God in this city, a famous man
18 30 and his name became very famous. And
1 Pa 5 24 and powerful men and famous chiefs
14 17 the name of David became famous in all
Isa 13 19 the famous pride of the Chaldeans
Eze 26 11 thy famous statues shall fall to the
31 18 thou that art famous and lofty among
fan Isa 29 5 multitude of them that fan thee
Isa 41 16 thou shalt fan them, and the wind shall
Jer 4 11 not to fan nor to cleanse. A full wind
15 7 I will scatter them with a fan in the
51 2 fanners, and they shall fan her and
Mat 3 12 whose fan is in his hand. Luke 3:17
fancieth Eccu 34 6 the heart f. as that of a
fanners Jer 51 2 I will send to Babylon fanners
far Gen 18 11 far advanced in years. Josu 13:1; 23:1, 2; 1 K 4:18
Gen 18 25 far be it from thee to do this thing
Deut 11 30 valley that reacheth and entereth far
Josu 8 4 the city; and go not very far from it
Judg 18 28 because they dwelt far from Sidon
19 11 near Jebus, and the day was far spent
1 K 2 30 saith the Lord: Far be this from me
7 12 thus far the Lord hath helped us
12 23 far from me be this sin against the
20 9 Jonathan said: Far be this from thee
22 15 far be this from me; let not the king
2 K 7 18 that thou hast brought me thus far
12 8 I shall add far greater things unto
3 K 8 46 the land of their enemies far or near
4 K 8 11 and was troubled so far as to blush
2 Pa 26 15 and his name went forth far abroad
33 23 but [Amon] committed far greater sins
1 Es 6 6 beyond the river, depart far from them
2 Es 4 19 on the wall one far from another
Jdth 7 7 there were springs not far from the
Job 5 4 his children shall be far from safety
13 21 withdraw thy hand far from me, and let
17 4 set their heart far from understanding
19 13 he hath put my brethren far from me
21 16 counsel of the wicked be far from me

22 18 whose way of thinking be far from me
23 away iniquity far from thy tabernacle
30 10 they abhor me and flee far from me
34 10 far from God be wickedness, and iniquity
17 how dost thou so far condemn him that
Ps 70 12 O God, be not thou far from me: O my
72 27 they that go far from thee shall perish
87 9 hast put away my acquaintance far from
19 and neighbor thou hast put far from me
102 12 so far hath he removed our iniquities
108 18 blessing, and it shall be far from him
118 155 salvation is far from sinners: because
Prov 4 24 let detracting lips be far from thee
5 8 remove thy way far from her, and come
6 11 and want shall flee far from thee
15 29 the Lord is far from the wicked: and he
19 7 his friends have departed far from him
22 5 own soul, departeth far from them
30 8 remove far from me vanity and lying
31 10 far and from the uttermost coasts is
Ecce 3 5 and a time to be far from embraces
Eccu 9 18 far from the man that hath power to
13 13 keep not far from him, lest thou be
15 7 for she is far from pride and deceit
16 22 the testament is far from some and
23 28 eyes of the Lord are far brighter than
30 24 drive away sadness far from thee. For
43 32 for he will yet far exceed and his
34 for you can never go far enough. Who
47 30 removed them far away from their land
Isa 6 12 the Lord shall remove men far away
29 13 their heart is far from me and they
46 11 hardhearted, who are far from justice
49 19 thee up shall be chased far away. The
54 14 depart far from oppression, for thou
59 9 therefore is judgment far from us
11 for salvation, and it is far from us
Jer 2 5 that they are gone far from me and
12 2 thou . . . and far from their reins. And
25 26 kings of the north far and near, every
27 10 to remove you far from your country
48 24 cities of land of Moab, far or near
51 64 thus far are the words of Jeremias
Lam 1 16 the relief of my soul is far from me
Bar 3 21 received it, it is far from their face
6 72 for he shall be far from reproach
Eze 11 15 have said: Get ye far from the Lord
22 5 that are far from thee shall triumph
43 9 their fornications . . . far from me
44 10 Levites that went away far from me
Dan 13 51 these two far from one another, and I
Mich 7 11 that day shall the law be far removed
1 Ma 8 23 far be the sword and enemy from them
13 5 far be it from me to spare my life in
2 Ma 4 3 when the enmities proceeded so far
40 a man far gone both in age and in
Mat 8 30 there was, not far from them, an herd
15 8 their heart is far from me. Mark 7:6
16 22 Lord, be it far from thee, this shall
Mark 6 35 when the day was now far spent, the
51 they were far more astonished within
12 34 thou art not far from the kingdom of
Luke 2 36 she was far advanced in years, and
7 6 when he was now not far from the house
22 51 suffer ye thus far. And when he had
24 29 and the day is now far spent. And he
John 21 8 for they were not far from the land
Acts 10 14 Peter said: Far be it from me; for I
17 27 he be not far from every one of us
Phil 1 23 with Christ, a thing by far the better
Heb 7 15 is yet far more evident: if according

as far as Gen 10 30 we go on as far as Sephar
Gen 11 31 they came as far as Haran, and dwelt
12 6 place of Sichem as far as the noble vale
14 15 pursued them as far as Hoba, which is
21 16 way off as far as a bow can carry
22 5 will go with speed as far as yonder
25 18 he dwelt from Hevila as far as Sur
49 13 road of ships, reaching as far as Sidon
Num 13 24 going forward as far as the torrent
14 45 pursued them as far as Horma. And the
21 26 of his dominions, as far as the Arnon
32 9 they were come as far as the valley of
34 4 toward the south as far as Cadesbarne
4 and shall reach as far as Asemona. And
8 Emath, as far as the borders of Sedada
9 limits shall go as far as Zephrona
12 and shall reach as far as the Jordan
Deut 1 7 as far as the great river Euphrates
24 as far as the valley of the cluster
44 slaughter of you from Seir a. . . . Horma
2 23 dwelt in Haserim as far as Gaza
36 situate in a valley, as far as Galaad
3 10 and Basan, as far as Selcha and Edrai
16 of Galaad as far as the torrent Arnon
30 4 if thou be driven as far as the poles
34 1 all the land of Galaad as far as Dan
3 the city of palm trees as far as Segor
Josu 7 5 them from the gate as far as Sabarim
10 11 stones from heaven as far as Azeca
11 8 as far as the great Sidon. 19:28
17 that goeth up to Seir as far as Baalgad
12 2 half Galaad, as far as the torrent
13 4 of the Sidonians as far as Apheca
9 plains of Medaba, as far as Dibon
11 and all Basan as far as Salecha, all
25 as far as Aroer which is over against
27 as far as the uttermost part of the sea
15 7 reaching as far as borders of Debara
19 11 to Dabbaseth: as far as the torrent
24 6 and horsemen, as far as the Red Sea
Judg 7 23 fleeing as far as Bethsetta and the
11 33 twenty cities, and as far as Abel
1 K 6 12 as far as the borders of Bethsames
14 23 the fight went on as far as Bethaven
17 52 as far as Geth and as far as Accaron
19 22 and came as far as the great cistern
4 K 2 2 the Lord hath sent me as far as Bethel
6 Lord hath sent me as far as the Jordan
6 2 let us go as far as the Jordan and take
7 15 went after them as far as the Jordan
18 8 smote the Philistines as far as Gaza
Luke 24 50 he led them out as far as Bethania
Acts 11 22 they sent Barnabas as far as Antioch
13 6 through whole island, as far as Paphos
17 15 Paul, brought him as far as Athens
23 23 soldiers to go as far as Caesarea and
28 15 came to meet us as far as Appii Forum
Rom 15 19 Jerusalem round about as far as unto
2 C 10 14 for we are come as far as to you in

far country Josu 9 6 we are come from a far c.
Josu 9 9 they answered: From a very far country
3 K 8 41 when he shall come out of a far country
4 K 20 14 from a far c. they came to me. Isa 39:3
2 Pa 6 32 come from a far country for the sake
Prov 25 25 so is good tidings from a far country
Isa 46 11 from a far country the man of my own
Jer 4 16 guards are coming from a far country
6 20 sweet smelling cane from a far country
8 19 of my people from a far country: Is
Mat 25 14 even as a man going into a far country
Mark 12 1 husbandmen; and went into a far c.
13 34 as a man going into a far country
Luke 15 13 went abroad into a far country: and
19 12 nobleman went into a far country to

far off Deut 12 21 if the place . . . be far off

Deut 14 24 Lord thy God shall choose, are far off
30 11 not above thee nor far off from thee
Josu 9 22 saying: We dwell far off from you
Judg 18 17 the 600 valiant men waiting not far off
Ps 54 8 I have gone far off flying away: and
118 150 but they are gone far off from thy law
Wisd 14 17 because they dwelt far off, they
Eccu 47 17 went abroad to the islands far off
Isa 17 13 rebuke him, and he shall flee far off
22 3 bound together, they are fled far off
26 15 all the ends of the earth far off. Lord
33 13 hear, you that are far off, what I
17 they shall see the land far off. Thy
48 9 I will remove my wrath far off: and for
57 9 hast sent thy messengers far off, and
19 peace to him that is far off and to
59 14 and justice hath stood far off: because
Jer 10 18 will cast away far off the inhabitants
Lam 3 17 soul is removed far off from peace
Eze 6 12 he that is far off shall die of the
8 6 that I should depart far off from my
11 16 I have removed them far off among the
Dan 9 7 and to them that are far off in all
Joel 2 20 I will remove far off from you the
3 6 you might remove them far off from
8 the Sabeans, a nation far off, for the
Haba 2 3 as yet the vision is far off and it
Zach 6 15 that are far off, shall come and
1 Ma 8 4 places that were very far off from
12 that were near and that were far off
Acts 2 39 and to all that are far off, whomsoever
fare Eccu 19 7 thou shalt not fare the worse
Eccu 29 28 better is the poor man's fare under
32 28 in him, shall fare never the worse
Jon 1 3 he paid the fare thereof, and went down
2 Ma 11 21 fare ye well. In the year 148. 33, 38
Acts 15 29 you shall do well. Fare ye well. They
3 J 2 fare well as thy soul doth prosperously
farewell Tob 5 22 his father and his mother f.
Acts 21 6 when we had bid one another f., we took
23 30 accusers to plead before thee. Farewell
2 C 2 13 bidding them f., I went into Macedonia
farm Mat 22 5 one to his farm, and another to his
Mark 14 32 they came to a farm called Gethsemani
Luke 14 18 I have bought a farm, and I must needs
farther Exod 8 28 go no farther: pray for me
Lev 13 5 if the leprosy be grown no farther
27 if the leprosy be grown farther in the
Josu 8 6 till they pursuing us be drawn farther
17 18 and mayst proceed f., when thou hast
Judg 19 8 till the day be f. advanced, afterwards
20 45 they went farther, they still pursued
1 K 10 3 and go farther on and shall come to the
2 K 2 28 did not pursue after Israel any farther
3 K 8 8 but were not seen farther out, and
Ecce 7 24 and it departed farther from me, much
Jer 31 39 line shall go out farther in his sight
Mark 1 19 going on from thence a little farther
Luke 24 28 he made as though he would go farther
Acts 4 17 that it may be no farther spread among
2 Tim 3 9 they shall proceed no farther: for
farthest Deut 28 64 from the f. parts of the earth
Isa 49 6 even to the f. part of the earth. Thus
Mat 24 31 from the f. parts of the heavens to
farthing Mat 5 26 till thou repay the last farthing
Mat 10 29 two sparrows sold for a farthing? And
Mark 12 42 in two mites, which make a farthing
farthings Luke 12 6 five sparrows sold for two f.
fashion Exod 37 19 three cups of the f. of a nut
Judg 11 38 from thence came a fashion in Israel
Eccu 33 13 in his hand, to fashion and order it
Eze 43 11 form of the house and of the fashion
2 Ma 4 10 countrymen to the f. of the heathens
Acts 16 21 preach a f. which it is not lawful for
1 C 7 31 the fashion of this world passeth away
fashioned Exod 32 4 f. them by founders' work
Deut 27 6 of stones not fashioned nor polished
Job 10 8 and fashioned me wholly round about
Wisd 7 1 in the womb of my mother I was f.
15 16 fashioned them. For no man can make
19 6 every creature . . . was fashioned again
Isa 29 16 should say to him that f. it: Thou
44 13 hath f. it round with the compass
Eze 16 7 thy breasts were fashioned and thy
1 P 1 14 not f. according to the former desires
fashioneth Wisd 13 13 f. it and maketh it like
Wisd 15 7 f. every vessel for our service and
Eccu 38 33 he fashioneth the clay with his arm
Isa 45 9 shall the clay say to him that f. it
fashions Eze 42 11 their f. and their doors were
2 Ma 4 11 brought in fashions that were perverse
fast Gen 2 21 when he was fast asleep, he took
Gen 33 4 clasping him fast about the neck, and
34 3 his soul was fast knit unto her, and
Exod 39 6 stones, fast set and closed in gold
Deut 28 60 they shall stick fast to thee. Moreover
Judg 4 21 through his brain fast into the ground
9 49 every man as fast as he could, and
2 K 12 16 David kept a fast, and going in by
21 thou didst fast and weep for the child
23 now that he is dead, why should I fast
3 K 21 9 proclaim a fast and make Naboth sit
12 proclaimed a fast and made Naboth sit
2 Pa 20 3 and he proclaimed a fast for all Juda
1 Es 8 21 I proclaimed there a fast by the river
Jdth 6 20 together after their fast was over
13 4 Holofernes lay on his bed, fast asleep
Job 34 37 let him be tied fast in the mean time
41 8 they hold one another fast and shall
Ps 9 16 the Gentiles have stuck fast in the
31 9 with bit and bridle bind fast their jaws
68 3 I stick fast in the mire of the deep
15 of the mire, that I may not stick fast
72 6 therefore pride hath held them fast
Prov 5 22 he is fast bound with the ropes of his
6 1 hast engaged fast thy hand to a stranger
23 34 as a pilot fast asleep, when the stern
Wisd 2 5 it is fast sealed, and no man returneth
4 3 deep root, nor any fast foundations
4 standing not fast, they shall be shaken
Eccu 4 14 that hold her fast, shall inherit life
15 4 she shall hold him fast, and he shall
25 16 of faith is to be fast joined unto it
27 2 as a stake sticketh fast in the midst
2 and buying, sin shall stick fast. Sin
Isa 5 29 and they shall keep fast hold of it
56 4 and shall hold fast my covenant: I will
6 and that holdeth fast my covenant: I
58 3 in the day of your fast your own will
4 you fast for debates and strife, and
4 do not fast as you have done until
5 is this such a fast as I have chosen
5 wilt thou call this a fast, and a day
6 this rather the fast that I have chosen
Jer 14 12 when they fast I will not hear their
36 9 they proclaimed a fast before the Lord
50 33 taken them captives, hold them fast
Bar 3 4 evils have cleaved fast to us. Remember
Eze 3 26 thy tongue stick fast to the roof of
Dan 2 43 they shall not stick fast one to another
14 10 shut the door fast, and seal it with
Joel 1 14 sanctify ye a fast, call an assembly
2 15 sanctify a fast, call a solemn assembly
Jon 1 6 why art thou fast asleep? Rise up, call
3 5 they proclaimed a fast and put on
Zach 7 5 did you keep a fast unto me? And when

8 19 the fast of the fourth month and the fast of the fifth and the fast of the seventh and the fast of the tenth
23 shall hold fast the skirt of one that
2 Ma 14 38 held his fast purpose of keeping himself
Mat 6 16 when you fast, be not as the hypocrites
16 that they may appear unto men to fast
18 that thou appear not to men to fast
9 14 why do we and the Pharisees fast often
14 thy disciples do not fast. Mark 2:18
15 then they shall fast. Mark 2:20; Luke 5:35
26 48 shall kiss, that is he, hold him fast
Mark 2 18 John and of the Pharisees used to fast
18 of John and of the Pharisees fast; but
19 can the children of the marriage fast
19 bridegroom with them, they cannot fast
Luke 5 33 the disciples of John fast often and
34 children of the bridegroom fast whilst
18 12 I fast twice in a week: I give tithes
Acts 16 24 and made their feet fast in the stocks
27 9 because the fast was now past, Paul
41 forepart indeed, sticking fast, remained
1 C 15 2 if you hold fast after what manner I
16 13 watch ye, stand fast in the faith, do
Gal 5 1 stand f. and be not held again under
Phil 1 27 that you stand fast in one spirit, with
4 1 so stand fast in the Lord, my dearly
1 Th 5 21 all things; hold fast that which is good
2 Th 2 14 stand fast; and hold the traditions
Heb 3 6 if we hold fast the confidence and glory
4 14 of God: let us hold fast our confession
6 18 fled for refuge to hold fast the hope
10 23 let us hold fast the confession of our
Apoc 2 13 thou holdest fast my name and hast not
25 which you have, hold fast till I come
3 11 hold fast that which thou hast, that
fasted Judg 20 26 they fasted that day till the
1 K 7 6 they fasted on that day and they said
31 13 wood of Jabes: and fasted seven days
2 K 1 12 and fasted until evening for Saul and
12 22 while the child was yet alive, I fasted
3 K 21 27 [Achab] fasted and slept in sackcloth
1 Pa 10 12 in Jabes, and they fasted seven days
1 Es 8 23 we fasted and besought our God for this
2 Es 1 4 I fasted and prayed before the face of
Jdth 8 6 and fasted all the days of her life
Isa 58 3 why have we fasted, and thou hast not
Bar 1 5 heard it they wept and fasted and
Zach 7 5 when you fasted and mourned in the
1 Ma 3 47 they f. that day and put on haircloth
Mat 4 2 when he had fasted forty days and forty
Acts 27 21 after they had fasted a long time, Paul
fasten Num 16 38 and fasten them to the altar
Prov 22 26 them that fasten down their hands, and
Isa 22 23 I will fasten him as a peg in a sure
fastened Exod 28 28 may be f. by the rings thereof
Exod 39 19 being f. to the girdle and strongly
30 they f. it to the miter with a violet
Judg 4 22 and the nail fastened in his temples
15 4 and fastened torches between the tails
1 K 19 10 missed him and was f. in the wall, and
3 K 6 6 that they might not be f. in the walls
21 fastened on the plates with nails of
4 K 18 16 plates of gold which he had f. on them
1 Pa 10 10 his head they f. up in the temple of
Job 38 38 when . . . the clods fastened together
Ps 31 4 in my anguish, whilst the thorn is f.
37 3 for thy arrows are fastened in me
Ecce 12 11 as goads and as nails deeply f. in
Isa 22 25 that was fastened in the sure place
Acts 28 3 viper . . . fastened on his hand. And
fastenest Judg 16 13 about a nail f. it in the
fastening Num 16 39 f. them to the altar: that the
Wisd 13 15 in a wall and fastening it with iron
Eccu 14 25 f. a pin in her walls shall set up
Acts 3 4 Peter with John f. his eyes upon him
Col 2 14 of the way, fastening it to the cross
fastest Mat 6 17 when thou f. anoint thy head and
fasteth Eccu 34 31 so a man that f. for his sins
fasting Num 30 14 to afflict her soul by fasting
2 Es 9 1 came together with fasting and with
Tob 2 3 left his dinner and came fasting to
12 8 prayer is good with fasting and alms
Esth 4 3 with fasting, wailing, and weeping
Ps 34 13 I humbled my soul with fasting; and my
68 11 I covered my soul in fasting: and it
108 24 my knees are weakened through fasting
Jer 36 6 house of the Lord on the fasting day
Dan 9 3 to pray and make supplication with f.
Joel 2 12 your heart in fasting and in weeping
1 Ma 3 17 we are ready to faint with fasting
2 Ma 13 12 with weeping and f., lying prostrate
Mat 15 32 send them away fasting. Mark 8:3
17 20 not cast out but by prayer and fasting
Mark 9 28 by nothing but by prayer and fasting
Acts 13 2 they were ministering to the Lord and f.
3 they f. and praying, and imposing their
14 22 when they . . . had prayed with fasting
27 33 and continued fasting, taking nothing
fastings Jdth 4 7 humbled their souls in fastings
Jdth 4 11 you continue with perseverance in f.
Luke 2 37 by f. and prayers serving night and
2 C 6 5 in labors, in watchings, in fastings
11 27 in fastings often, in cold and nakedness
fasts Esth 9 31 fasts and cries and the days of
Esth 14 2 and she humbled her body with fasts
fat Gen 4 4 of his flock and of their fat: and
Gen 27 39 in the fat of the earth and in the dew
41 2 seven kine very beautiful and fat
49 20 Aser, his bread shall be fat, and he
Exod 23 18 fat of my solemnity remain until the
29 13 the fat that covereth the entrails. Lev 3:3; 7:3; 8:25
13 kidneys and the fat that is upon them. 22
22 thou shalt take the fat of the ram
22 and the fat that covereth the lungs
Lev 3 3 entrails and all the fat that is within
4 fat wherewith the flanks are covered
9 offer . . . the fat and the whole rump
10 the fat that covereth the belly. 14
10 with the fat that is about the flanks
15 fat of the liver with the little. 4:9
16 savor. All the fat shall be the Lord's
17 neither blood nor fat shall you eat at
4 8 he shall take off the fat of the calf
19 all the fat thereof he shall take off
26 but the fat he shall burn upon it
31 taking off all the fat, as is wont to
35 all the fat also he shall take off, as
35 as the fat of the ram that is offered
6 12 fat of the peace offerings. 3 K 8:64; 2 Pa 7:7; 29:35
7 4 the fat which is by the flanks, and
23 the fat of a sheep and of an ox and of
24 fat of a carcass that hath died of
25 the fat that should be offered for the
30 hold in his hands the fat of the victim
31 who shall burn the fat upon the altar
33 that offereth the blood and the fat, he
8 16 the fat that was upon the entrails
16 two little kidneys with their fat. 9:19
20 joints, and the fat he burnt in the
25 and the rump and all the fat that
25 and the two kidneys with their fat he
26 a wafer, he put them upon the fat and
9 10 the fat and the little kidneys and the

19 the fat also of the bullock and the
20 after the fat was burnt upon the altar
24 and the fat that was upon the altar
10 15 the fat that is burnt on the altar
16 25 the fat that is offered for sins, he
17 6 shall burn the fat for a sweet odor to
Num 13 21 the ground, fat or barren, woody or
18 17 their fat thou shalt burn for a most
32 by reserving the choicest and fat things
Deut 31 20 have eaten and are full and fat, they
32 14 milk of the sheep with fat of lambs
15 the beloved grew fat and kicked: he
15 he grew fat and thick and gross, he
38 of whose victims they ate the fat
Judg 3 17 Eglon was exceeding fat. And when he
22 was closed up with abundance of fat
1 K 2 15 before they burnt the fat, the servant
16 let the fat first be burnt today
15 22 rather than to offer the fat of rams
32 Agag was presented to him very fat
2 K 1 22 from the fat of the valiant, the arrow
17 29 brought him [David] . . . fat calves
3 K 1 9 having slain . . . and all fat cattle
19 he hath killed oxen and all fat cattle
4 23 ten fat oxen and 20 out of the pastures
1 Pa 4 40 they found fat pastures and very good
41 because they found there fat pastures
2 Pa 7 7 holocausts and the sacrifices and the fat
35 14 in offering of holocausts and the fat
2 Es 8 10 eat fat meats, and drink sweet wine
9 25 they took strong cities and a fat land
25 they ate and were filled and became fat
35 in the large and fat land which thou
Tob 8 22 he caused also two fat kine and four
Job 15 26 raised up, and is armed with a fat neck
27 and the fat hangeth down on his sides
21 24 his bowels are full of fat, and his
Ps 16 10 they have shut up their fat: their
19 4 thy whole burnt offering be made fat
21 13 fat bulls have besieged me. They have
30 all the fat ones of the earth have
64 13 the beautiful places . . . shall grow fat
67 16 the mountain of God is a fat mountain, a curdled mountain, a fat mountain
77 31 and he slew the fat ones amongst them
80 17 he fed them with the fat of wheat
143 14 sheep fruitful . . . their oxen fat
147 14 filleth thee with the fat of corn
Prov 11 25 which blesseth, shall be made fat
13 4 of them that work, shall be made fat
15 30 a good name maketh the bones fat. The
21 17 he that loveth wine and fat things
Ecce 12 5 the locust shall be made fat, and the
Eccu 26 16 her husband, and shall fat his bones
35 8 of the just maketh the altar fat and
38 11 fine flour, and make a fat offering
47 2 as the fat taken away from the flesh
Isa 1 11 I desire not . . . fat of fatlings and
10 16 shall send leanness among his fat ones
25 6 a feast of fat things, a feast of wine
6 of fat things full of marrow, of wine
28 1 on the head of the fat valley. 4
30 23 land shall be most plentiful and fat
34 7 their ground with the fat of fat ones
43 24 filled me with the fat of thy victims
Jer 5 28 they are grown gross and fat; and have
Eze 34 3 and you killed that which was fat: but
14 and be fed in fat pastures upon the
16 that which was fat and strong I will
20 will judge between the fat cattle and
39 18 and of all that are well fed and fat
19 you shall eat the fat till you be full
44 7 you offer my bread, the fat, and the
15 to offer me the fat and the blood
Dan 3 40 and as in thousands of fat lambs: so
14 26 Daniel took pitch and fat and hair
Amos 4 1 ye fat kine that are in the mountains
5 22 I regard the vows of your fat beasts
Mich 6 7 with many thousands of fat he goats
Haba 1 16 through them his portion is made fat
Zach 11 16 shall eat the flesh of the fat ones
Apoc 18 14 all fat and goodly things are perished

father Mat 4 21 in a ship with Zebedee their father
Mat 8 21 first to go and bury my f. Luke 9:59
10 21 brother to death, and the f. the son
37 he that loveth father or mother more
15 4 honor thy father and mother. 19:19; Mark 7:10; 10:19; Luke 18:20; Eph 6:2
4 he that shall curse father. Mark 7:10
5 whosoever shall say to father or mother
19 5 shall a man leave father and mother
29 hath left . . . f. or mother. Mark 10:29
Mark 1 20 leaving their father Zebedee in the
5 40 father and the mother of the damsel
9 23 the father of the boy crying out with
13 12 shall betray . . . and the f. his son
15 21 Simon . . . father of Alexander and of
Luke 8 50 answered the father of the maid: Fear
51 and the f. and mother of the maiden
12 53 the father shall be divided against
15 12 father, give me the portion of the
18 I will arise and will go to my father
18 f., I have sinned against heaven. 21
22 the father said to his servants: Bring
16 24 said: Father Abraham, have mercy on me
27 father, I beseech thee, that thou
30 no, father Abraham, but if one went
John 4 53 the father therefore knew that it was
6 42 whose father and mother we know? How
8 44 he is a liar and the father thereof
Acts 28 8 it happened that f. of Publius lay sick
Rom 4 11 that he might be the father of all them
12 might be the father of circumcision; not
16 of Abraham, who is the father of us all
17 I have made thee father of many nations
18 be made the father of many nations
Gal 4 2 until the time appointed by the father
Phil 2 22 as a son with the father, so hath he
1 Th 2 11 comforting you, as f. doth his children
1 Tim 5 1 not, but entreat him as a father: young
Heb 7 3 without f., without mother, without
12 7 whom the father doth not correct? But

his father Mat 2 22 in the room of Herod his father, he
Mat 10 35 a man at variance against his father
15 6 he shall not honor his father or his
Mark 7 11 if a man shall say to his father or
12 to do anything for his father or mother
9 20 he asked his father: How long time
10 7 a man shall leave his father and
Luke 1 62 they made signs to his father, how he
67 Zachary his father was filled with the
2 33 his father and mother were wondering
9 43 boy, and restored him to his father
11 11 if he ask his father bread, will he
12 53 and the son against his father, the
14 26 and hate not his father and mother
15 12 the younger of them said to his father
20 rising up he came to his father. And
20 a great way off, his father saw him
28 his father therefore coming out began
29 said to his father: Behold, for so
Acts 7 4 after his father was dead, he removed
14 called thither Jacob, his father, and
13 36 and was laid unto his fathers, and saw
16 1 his father was a Gentile. 3
Eph 5 31 this cause shall a man leave his father

Heb 7 10 he was yet in the loins of his father
our father Mat 3 9 we have Abraham for our f. Luke 3:8
Mark 11 10 blessed be the kingdom of our father
Luke 1 73 which he swore to Abraham our father
John 4 12 art thou greater than our father Jacob
8 39 said to him: Abraham is our father
53 art thou greater than our f. Abraham
Acts 4 25 by the mouth of our father David, thy
7 2 God of glory appeared to our father
Rom 4 1 who is our father according to the flesh
12 uncircumcision of our father Abraham
9 10 conceived at once, of Isaac our father
James 2 21 was not Abraham our father justified
thy father Dan 5 11 in the days of thy f. knowledge
11 thy father appointed him prince of the
11 soothsayers, thy father, I say, O king
18 gave to . . . thy father a kingdom and
1 Ma 6 23 we determined to serve thy father
11 9 shalt reign in the kingdom of thy f.
Mat 15 4 honor thy father and mother. 19:19; Mark 7:10; 10:19; Luke 18:20; Eph 6:2
Luke 2 48 thy father and I have sought thee
15 27 thy father hath killed the fatted calf
your father Mat 23 9 call none your father upon earth
John 8 38 that you have seen with your father
41 you do the works of your father. They
44 you are of your father the devil, and
44 the desires of your father you will do
56 Abraham your father rejoiced that he
Father Wisd 14 3 but thy providence, O Father
Eccu 23 1 O Lord, Father, and sovereign ruler
4 Lord, Father, and God of my life, leave
51 14 upon the Lord, the Father of my Lord
Isa 9 6 the Father of the world to come, the
Mat 6 4 thy Father who seeth in secret. 6, 18
6 the door, pray to thy Father in secret
18 but to thy Father who is in secret
11 25 I confess to thee, O Father. Luke 10:21
26 yea, Father; for so hath it seemed good
27 no one knoweth . . . but the Father. 24:36; Mark 13:32
27 neither doth any one know the Father
13 43 sun, in the kingdom of their Father
16 27 shall come in the glory of his Father. Mark 8:38
Mark 14 36 Abba, Father, all things are possible
Luke 9 26 his majesty and that of his Father
10 22 who the Son is, but the Father; and
22 and who the Father is, but the Son
11 2 Father, hallowed be thy name. Thy
22 42 Father, if thou wilt, remove this
23 34 Father, forgive them, for they know not
46 Father, into thy hands I commend my
John 3 35 the Father loveth the Son and. 5:20
4 21 nor in Jerusalem, adore the Father
23 shall adore the Father in spirit and
23 Father also seeketh such to adore him
5 18 also said God was his Father, making
19 but what he seeth the Father doing
21 as the Father raiseth up the dead and
22 neither doth the Father judge any man
23 thy Son, as they honor the Father. He
23 honoreth not the Father, who hath sent
26 as the Father hath life in himself
36 which the Father hath given me to
36 of me, that the Father hath sent me
37 the Father himself who hath sent me
45 that I will accuse you to the Father
6 37 all that the Father giveth to me shall
39 this is the will of the Father who
44 except the Father . . . draw him; and
46 not that any man hath seen the Father
46 is of God, he hath seen the Father
58 as the living Father hath sent me
58 sent me, and I live by the Father
8 16 but I and the Father that sent me. And
18 F. that sent me giveth testimony of me
19 where is thy Father? Jesus answered
27 that he called God his Father. Jesus
28 but as the Father hath taught me, these
41 we have one Father, even God. Jesus
10 15 the F. knoweth me, and I know the F.
17 therefore doth the Father love me
30 I and the Father are one. The Jews
36 him whom the Father hath sanctified
38 Father is in me, and I in the Father
11 41 Father, I give thee thanks that thou
12 27 say? Father, save me from this hour
28 Father, glorify thy name. A voice
49 the Father who sent me, he gave me
50 as the Father said unto me, so do I
13 1 pass out of this world to the Father
3 knowing that the Father had given him
14 6 no man cometh to the Father but by me
8 Lord, show us the Father. 9
9 that seeth me seeth the Father also
10 I am in the F., and the F. in me. 11
10 the Father who abideth in me, he doth
13 I go to the Father: and whatsoever
13 shall ask the Father in my name. 15:16
13 the Father may be glorified in the Son
16 I will ask the Father. 16:26
26 whom the Father will send in my name
28 be glad, because I go to the Father
28 for the Father is greater than I. And
31 may know that I love the Father; and
31 Father hath given me commandment, so
15 9 as the Father hath loved me, I also
26 whom I will send you from the Father
26 who proceedeth from the Father, he
16 3 they have not known the Father nor me
10 of justice: because I go to the Father
15 whatsoever the Father hath, are mine
16 see me: because I go to the Father. 17
23 if you ask the Father anything in my
27 the Father himself loveth you because
28 I came forth from the Father, and am
28 leave the world, and I go to the Father
32 alone, because the Father is with me
17 1 Father, the hour is come, glorify thy
5 and now glorify thou me, O Father
11 holy Father, keep them in thy name
21 as thou, Father, in me, and I in thee
24 Father, I will that where I am, they
25 just Father, the world hath not known
20 21 as the Father hath sent me, I also
Acts 1 7 the Father hath put in his own power
24 14 so do I serve the Father and my God
Rom 8 15 sons, whereby we cry: Abba, Father. For
2 C 1 3 blessed be the God and Father of our. Eph 1:3; 1 P 1:3
3 F. of mercies, and God of all comfort
6 18 I will be a Father to you; and you shall
11 31 Father of our Lord Jesus Christ, who is
Gal 4 6 into your hearts, crying: Abba, Father
Eph 1 17 Father of glory, may give unto you the
2 18 access both in one Spirit to the Father
3 14 I bow my knees to the Father of our
4 6 one God and Father of all, who is above
Col 1 19 in him, it hath well pleased the Father
Heb 1 5 I will be to him a Father, and he shall
12 9 obey the Father of spirits and live
James 1 17 coming down from the Father of lights
1 P 1 17 and if you invoke as Father him who
1 J 1 2 life eternal, which was with the F.
3 our fellowship may be with the Father

2 1 we have an advocate with the Father
14 because you have known the Father. I
22 who denieth the Father and the Son
23 the same hath not the Father. He that
23 confesseth the Son, hath the F. also
24 shall abide in the Son and in the F.
3 1 the Father hath bestowed upon us, that
4 14 that the Father hath sent his Son to
5 7 the F., the Word, and the Holy Ghost
2 J 4 received a commandment from the Father
9 same hath both the Father and the Son
Apoc 1 6 and priests to God and his Father, to
14 1 his name and the name of his Father

Father who is in heaven Mat 5 16 glorify your F. . . .
Mat 6 1 shall not have a reward of your F. . . .
7 11 how much more will your F. . . . give
21 he that doth the will of my F. . . .
10 32 also confess him before my F. . . .
33 will also deny him before my F. . . .
12 50 will of my Father, that is in heaven
16 17 not revealed it to thee, but my F. . . .
18 10 always see the face of my F. . . . For
14 it is not the will of your F. . . . that
19 shall be done to them by my F. . . .
23 9 one is your Father, who is in heaven
Mark 11 25 that your Father also who is in heaven
26 neither will your F. . . . forgive you

God and the Father Rom 15 6 you may glorify God and the Father of
1 C 15 24 have delivered up the kingdom of G. . . .
Eph 5 20 giving thanks to G. . . . Col 3:17
Col 1 13 we give thanks to God and the Father
James 1 27 clean and undefiled before G. . . . is
3 9 by it we bless G. . . . and by it we

God the Father John 6 27 for him hath God the Father sealed
1 C 8 6 to us there is but one God the Father
Gal 1 1 by Jesus Christ, and G. . . . who raised
3 peace from G. . . . Eph 1:2; 6:23; 1 Tim 1:2; 2 Tim 1:2; Titus 1:4; 2 J 3
Col 1 12 giving thanks to God the Father, who
2 2 of the mystery of God the Father and of
1 Th 1 1 in G. . . . and in the Lord Jesus Christ
Phil 2 11 Jesus Christ is in the glory of G. . . .
1 P 1 2 according to foreknowledge of G. . . .
2 P 1 17 he received from G. . . . honor and
2 J 3 mercy and peace from God the Father
Jude 1 to them that are beloved in G. . . .

my Father Mat 7 21 that doth the will of my F.
Mat 10 32 I will also confess him before my F.
33 I will also deny him before my Father
11 27 are delivered to me by my F. Luke 10:22
12 50 shall do the will of my Father, that
15 13 my heavenly Father hath not planted
16 17 but my Father who is in heaven. And I
18 10 always see the face of my Father who
19 it shall be done to them by my Father
35 my heavenly Father do to you if you
20 23 for whom it is prepared by my Father
25 34 come, ye blessed of my Father, possess
26 29 with you new in the kingdom of my F.
39 my Father, if it be possible, let this
42 my Father, if this chalice may not pass
53 thinkest thou that I cannot ask my F.
Luke 22 29 as my Father hath disposed to me, a
24 49 I send the promise of my Father upon
John 2 16 make not the house of my Father a house
5 17 my Father worketh until now; and I
43 I am come in the name of my Father
6 32 my Father giveth you the true bread
40 the will of my Father that sent me
66 unless it be given him by my Father
8 19 neither me do you know nor my Father
19 perhaps you would know my Father also
38 that which I have seen with my Father
49 but I honor my Father, and you have
54 it is my Father that glorifieth me
10 18 have I received from my Father. A
25 that I do in the name of my Father
29 that which my Father hath given me is
29 them out of the hand of my Father
32 I have showed you from my Father; for
37 if I do not the works of my Father
12 26 to me, him will my Father honor. Now
14 7 have known my Father also; and from
20 you shall know that I am in my Father
21 loveth me, shall be loved of my Father
23 my Father will love him, and we will
15 1 vine; and my Father is the husbandman
8 in this is my Father glorified; that
15 whatsoever I have heard of my Father
23 that hateth me, hateth my Father also
24 and hated both me and my Father. But
18 11 chalice which my Father hath given me
20 17 for I am not yet ascended to my Father
17 I ascend to my F. and to your F., to
Apoc 2 28 as I also have received of my Father
3 5 I will confess his name before my F.
21 set down with my Father in his throne

of the Father Mat 28 19 in the name of the F.
John 1 14 of the only begotten of the Father
18 who is in the bosom of the Father, he
6 45 that hath heard of the Father and hath
15 16 shall ask of the Father in my name
16 25 will show you plainly of the Father
Acts 1 4 should wait for the promise of the F.
2 33 having received of the F. the promise
Rom 6 4 risen from dead by glory of the Father
1 J 2 15 the charity of the Father is not in
16 not of the Father, but is of the world

our Father Mat 6 9 our F. who art in heaven
Rom 1 7 peace from God our Father. 1 C 1:3; 2 C 1:2; Phil 1:2; Col 1:3; 2 Th 1:2; Philem 3
Gal 1 4 according to will of God and our Father
Phil 4 20 now to God and our Father be glory
1 Th 1 3 Jesus Christ before God and our Father
3 11 God himself and our Father, and our Lord
13 in holiness, before God and our Father
2 Th 1 1 in God our Father, and the Lord Jesus
2 15 Christ himself, and God and our Father

your Father Mat 5 16 glorify your F. who is in
Mat 5 45 you may be the children of your Father
48 also your heavenly Father is perfect
6 1 not have a reward of your Father who
8 your Father knoweth what is needful
14 your heavenly Father will forgive you
15 will your Father forgive you. Mark 11:26
26 and your heavenly Father feedeth them
62 your F. knoweth that you have. Luke 12:30
7 11 how much more will your Father who is
10 20 Spirit of your Father that speaketh
29 fall on the ground without your Father
18 14 it is not the will of your Father who
Mark 11 25 that your Father . . . may forgive you
26 neither will your Father . . . forgive
Luke 6 36 as your Father also is merciful. Judge
11 13 how much more will your Father from
12 32 hath pleased your Father to give you
John 8 42 if God were your Father, you would
20 17 I ascend to my F. and to your F., to

father-in-law Gen 29 25 said to his f. 30:25
Gen 31 20 Jacob would not confess to his f.
38 13 was told Thamar that her father-in-law
25 she sent to her father-in-law, saying
Exod 3 1 fed the sheep of Jethro his f., the
4 18 Moses . . . returned to Jethro his f.

Judg 19 3 when his father-in-law had heard this
4 tarried in the house of his f. three
5 but his f. kept him and said to him
7 his f. earnestly pressed him and made
8 his f. said to him again: I beseech
9 his f. spoke to him again: Consider
1 K 4 19 her f. and her husband were dead, she
21 for her father-in-law and her husband
Tob 10 13 to honor her father- and mother-in-law
14 14 returned to his father- and mother-in-law
Eze 22 11 and the f. hath wickedly defiled his
1 Ma 11 2 because he was his father-in-law. Now
John 18 13 for he was father-in-law to Caiphas
fatherless Exod 22 24 your chlidren fatherless
Deut 10 18 he doth judgment to the fatherless
14 29 stranger and the f. and the widow. 16:11, 14; 24:19, 21
24 17 judgment of the stranger nor of the f.
20 stranger, for the f. and the widow
26 12 stranger and to the f. and to the. 13
27 19 stranger, of the f., and the widow
Job 6 27 you rush in upon the fatherless, and
22 9 arms of the fatherless thou hast broken
24 3 driven away the ass of the fatherless
9 have violently robbed the fatherless
29 12 and the fatherless, that had no helper
31 17 if . . . f. hath not eaten thereof: for
21 if I have lifted up my hand against f.
Ps 9 18 to judge for the fatherless and for
81 3 judge for the needy and fatherless
93 6 they have murdered the fatherless
108 9 may his children be f., and his wife a
12 none to pity his fatherless offspring
145 9 he will support the fatherless and the
Prov 23 10 enter not into field of the fatherless
Eccu 4 10 be merciful to the f. as a father and
35 17 will not despise the prayers of the f.
Isa 1 17 judge for the f., defend the widow
23 they judge not for the fatherless: and
9 17 neither shall he have mercy on their f.
10 2 that they might rob the fatherless
Jer 5 28 not managed the cause of the f., and
7 6 if you oppress not the stranger, the f.
22 3 afflict not the stranger, the f., and
49 11 leave thy f. children: I will make
Bar 6 37 nor do good to the fatherless. Their
Eze 22 7 they have grieved the f. and widow
Osee 14 4 thou wilt have mercy on the fatherless
Zach 7 10 oppress not the widow and the f. and
Mala 3 5 that oppress . . . the widows and the f.
2 Ma 3 10 subsistence of the widows and the f.
8 30 equal portions to the feeble, the f.
James 1 27 to visit the f. and widows in their
father's Gen 9 22 his f. nakedness was uncovered
Gen 9 23 they saw not their father's nakedness
27 5 to fulfil his father's commandment
34 Esau having heard his father's words
29 9 Rachel came with her father's sheep
12 told her that he was her f. brother
31 1 hath taken away all that was our f.
5 I see your father's countenance is not
9 God hath taken your father's substance
16 God hath taken our father's riches
19 Rachel stole away her father's idols
37 2 of Bala and of Zelpha his father's wives
12 brethren . . . feeding their f. flocks
48 12 taken them from his father's lap, he
13 towards his father's right hand, and
17 taking his father's hand, he tried to
49 4 thou wentest up to thy father's bed
50 1 [Joseph] fell upon his father's face
Exod 2 16 desired to water their father's flocks
6 20 Jochabed his aunt by the father's side
Lev 16 32 office of priesthood in his f. stead
18 8 not uncover nakedness of thy f. wife
11 nakedness of thy f. wife's daughter
12 not uncover nakedness of thy f. sister
14 not uncover nakedness of thy f. brother
22 13 she shall eat of her father's meats
Num 27 6 a possession among their f. kindred
10 give the inheritance to his f. brethren
Deut 22 30 no man shall take his father's wife
27 20 that lieth with his father's wife
Judg 6 25 take a bullock of thy father's and
25 the altar of Baal, which is thy father's
1 K 17 15 David . . . to feed his father's flock
34 thy servant kept his father's sheep
18 18 what is my life, or my father's family
20 12 if I shall discover my father's mind
2 K 3 8 why didst thou go in to my f. concubine
9 7 mercy for Jonathan thy father's sake
15 34 as I have been thy father's servant
16 22 he went in to his father's concubines
3 K 11 12 not do it, for David thy father's sake
17 certain Edomites of his f. servants
4 K 10 3 and set him on his father's throne
23 30 made him king in his father's stead
1 Pa 5 1 as he defiled his father's bed, his
25 6 all these under their father's hand
Tob 3 7 from one of her father's servant maids
11 13 Tobias . . . anointed his father's eyes
Prov 4 3 I also was my father's son, tender and
27 10 and thy father's friend forsake not
Eccu 3 11 f. blessing establisheth the houses
Eze 18 14 son who, seeing all his father's sins
1 Ma 11 40 that he might be king in his f. place
Mat 21 31 which of the two did the father's will
Luke 1 59 they called him by his father's name
2 49 I must be about my Father's business
1 C 5 1 that one should have his father's wife
father's house Gen 12 1 go forth . . . out of thy father's house
Gen 20 13 after God brought me out of my f. h.
24 7 who took me out of my father's house
23 any place in thy f. h. to lodge? And
38 thou shalt go to my father's house
40 a wife for my son . . . of my f. h. But
28 21 I shall return prosperously to my f. h.
31 14 goods and inheritance of our f. h.
30 hadst a longing after thy f. h.: why
34 19 the greatest man in all his f. h. And
38 11 remain a widow in thy f. h. till Sela
11 [Thamar] dwelt in her father's house
41 51 made me to forget . . . my f. h. And he
46 31 to his brethren and to all his f. h.
31 and my father's house . . . are come
47 12 he nourished them and all his f. h.
50 22 dwelt in Egypt with all his f. h.: and
Lev 22 13 having no children, return to her f. h.
Num 18 1 and thy f. h. with thee shall bear
30 4 in her father's house and but yet a girl
17 that abideth in her father's house
Deut 22 21 cast her out of the doors of her f. h.
21 to play the whore in her father's house
Josu 2 12 will show mercy to my father's house
6 25 saved Rahab the harlot and her f. h.
Judg 6 15 I am the least in my father's house
27 [Gedeon] fearing his father's house
9 5 he came to his father's house in Ephra
18 now risen up against my father's house
11 7 and cast me out of my father's house
14 15 we will burn thee and thy father's house
19 he [Samson] went up to his f. h.: but
19 2 left him and returned to her f. h. in
3 brought him into her father's house
1 K 2 27 plainly appear to thy father's house

28 I gave to thy father's house of all
31 and the arm of thy father's house, that
9 20 for thee and for all thy father's house
17 25 his father's house free from tribute
18 2 not let him return to his father's house
22 1 his father's house had heard of it
11 Achimelech . . . and all his father's house
15 or any one in all my father's house
16 shalt die . . . and all thy father's house
22 death of all the souls of thy f. h.
2 K 3 29 of Joab and upon all his father's house
19 28 all of my father's house were no better
24 17 against me and against my f. h. And
3 K 18 18 thou and thy father's house, who have
1 Pa 9 19 with his brethren and his f. h., the
21 17 upon me and upon my father's house
28 4 the house of Juda, my father's house
2 Es 1 6 I and my father's house have sinned
Esth 4 14 thou and thy f. h. shall perish. And
Ps 44 11 forget thy people and thy f. h. And the
Eccu 42 10 found with child in her father's house
Isa 22 24 upon him all the glory of his f. h.
1 Ma 16 2 and my f. house have fought against
Luke 15 17 hired servants in my father's house
16 27 send him to my father's house, for
Acts 7 20 three months in his father's house
Father's John 14 2 in my F. house there are many
John 14 24 not mine; but the Father's who sent me
15 10 have kept my Father's commandments
fathers Luke 1 17 he may turn the hearts of the fathers
Luke 6 23 did their fathers to the prophets. But
26 did their f. to the false prophets
John 7 22 it is of Moses, but of the fathers
Acts 7 2 men, brethren, and fathers, hear. 22:1
32 I am the God of thy fathers, the God
22 3 truth of the law of the fathers
26 6 promise that was made by God to the f.
Rom 9 5 whose are the f., and of whom is Christ
11 28 they are most dear for sake of the f.
15 8 to confirm the promises made unto the f.
1 C 4 15 in Christ, yet not many fathers. For
Gal 1 14 zealous for the traditions of my fathers
Eph 6 4 f., provoke not your children. Col 3:21
1 Tim 1 9 for murderers of fathers and murders
Heb 1 1 spoke in times past to the fathers by
8 9 testament which I made to their fathers
12 9 we have had fathers of our flesh, for
2 P 3 4 since the time that the fathers slept
1 J 2 13 I write unto you, fathers, because you
our fathers Mat 23 30 had been in the days of our fathers
Luke 1 55 as he spoke to our fathers, to Abraham
72 to perform mercy to our fathers and
John 4 20 our fathers adored on this mountain
6 31 our fathers did eat manna in the
Acts 3 13 the God of our fathers hath glorified
25 testament which God made to our fathers
5 30 God of our fathers hath raised up
7 11 and our fathers found no food. But
12 in Egypt, he sent our fathers first
15 and he [Jacob] died, and our fathers
19 afflicted our fathers, that they
38 on mount Sina, and with our fathers
39 whom our fathers would not obey; but
44 was with our fathers in the desert as
45 our fathers receiving, brought in
45 drove out before the face of our f.
13 17 God . . . chose our fathers, and exalted
32 promise which was made to our fathers
15 10 neither our fathers nor we have been
22 14 God of our fathers hath preordained thee
28 17 against . . . the custom of our fathers
25 well did the Holy Ghost speak to our f.
1 C 10 1 our fathers were all under the cloud

your fathers Mat 23 32 fill ye up then the measure of your f.
Luke 11 47 the prophets: and your f. killed them
48 consent to the doings of your fathers
John 6 49 your f. did eat manna in the desert. 59
Acts 7 51 as your fathers did, so do you also
52 prophets have not your f. persecuted
Heb 3 9 where your fathers tempted me, proved
1 P 1 18 of the tradition of your fathers. But
fathers' Dan 11 24 never did, nor his f. fathers
fathoms Acts 27 28 who also sounding, found 20 f.
Acts 27 28 a little further, they found 15 fathoms
fatigue Num 11 1 repining at their fatigue. And
fatigued Jon 4 6 to cover him, for he was f.
1 Ma 10 81 and so their horses were fatigued
fatlings 3 K 1 25 and hath killed oxen and f.
Isa 1 11 I desire not . . . fat of fatlings and
Mat 22 4 my beeves and fatlings are killed and
fatness Gen 27 28 give thee . . . f. of the earth
Judg 9 9 can I leave my fatness, which both
Job 15 27 fatness hath covered his face, and the
36 16 rest of thy table shall be full of f.
Ps 62 6 soul be filled as with marrow and f.
72 7 iniquity . . . as it were from fatness
Isa 17 4 the fatness of his flesh shall grow
55 2 your soul shall be delighted in fatness
Jer 31 14 fill the soul of the priests with f.
Rom 11 17 and of the fatness of the olive tree
fats Joel 3 13 press is full, the fats run over
fatted 1 K 28 24 the woman had a fatted calf in
3 K 4 23 besides . . . buffles and fatted fowls
Prov 15 17 than to a fatted calf with hatred. A
Jer 46 21 like fatted calves are turned back
Luke 15 23 bring hither the fatted calf and kill
27 thy father hath killed the fatted calf
30 hast killed for him the fatted calf
fatten Ps 140 5 not the oil of the sinner f. my
fatter Dan 1 15 faces appeared fairer and fatter
fattest Eze 24 5 take the f. of the flock and
fault Gen 31 36 for what fault of mine and for
Gen 40 15 without any fault was cast into dungeon
Num 15 26 f. of all the people through ignorance
Deut 17 1 wherein there is blemish or any fault
24 5 he shall be free at home without fault
Judg 9 19 dealt . . . without fault with Jerobaal
21 22 the fault was committed on your part
1 K 19 5 by killing David, who is without fault
29 3 and I have found no fault in him since
Tob 3 9 she reproved the maid for her fault
Esth 16 15 the Jews . . . are in no fault at all
Prov 6 30 fault is not so great when a man hath
Eccu 9 19 commit no fault, lest he take away
19 15 for there is often a fault committed
Dan 6 4 no f. nor suspicion was found in him
1 Ma 13 39 as for any oversight or fault committed
Mark 7 2 with unwashed hands, they found fault
Rom 9 19 why doth he then find fault? For who
1 C 6 7 there is plainly a fault among you
2 C 11 7 did I commit a fault, humbling myself
Gal 6 1 if a man be overtaken in any fault, you
Heb 8 8 for finding fault with them, he saith
faultless Heb 8 7 if that former had been faultless
fauns Jer 50 39 dwell there with the fig fauns
favor Gen 18 3 found favor in thy sight. 47:29; Exod 33:13; Num 32:5; 1 K 27:5; 2 Es 2:5; Esth 7:3
Gen 30 27 find favor in thy sight. 32:5
33 8 that I might find favor before my lord
10 have found favor in thy eyes. 1 K 20:29
15 only to find favor . . . in thy sight
34 11 let me find favor in your sight: and
39 4 Joseph found f. in sight of his master
21 favor in the sight of the chief keeper

50 4 if I have found favor in your sight
Exod 3 21 I will give favor to this people in the
11 3 the Lord will give favor to his people
12 36 the Lord gave favor to the people in
18 8 Lord had done . . . in favor of Israel
23 3 neither shalt thou favor a poor man
33 12 thou hast found favor in my sight. If
Num 11 11 wherefore do I not find favor before
Deut 2 22 done in favor of the children of Esau
24 1 and she find not favor in his eyes
1 K 16 22 [David] hath found favor in my sight
3 K 11 19 Adad found great favor before Pharao
1 Pa 19 2 for his father did a favor to me. And
Tob 1 13 favor in the sight of Salmanasar the
Jdth 12 17 for thou hast found favor before me
Esth 2 9 and found favor in his sight. And he
17 she had favor and kindness before him
5 8 if I have found favor in the king's
8 5 if I have found favor in his sight
Ps 29 8 in thy favor, thou gavest strength
89 13 be entreated in favor of thy servants
105 4 us, O Lord, in the favor of thy people
134 14 will be entreated in f. of his servants
Prov 22 1 good favor is above silver and gold
28 23 shall afterward find favor with him
31 30 favor is deceitful, and beauty is vain
Ecce 9 11 to the learned, nor favor to the skilful
Wisd 12 18 with great favor disposest of us: for
Eccu 3 34 provideth for him that showeth favor
18 11 he filled up his mercy in their favor
32 14 before shamefacedness goeth favor: and
39 23 at his commandment favor is shown, and
40 22 thy eye desireth favor and beauty and
42 1 and shalt find favor before all men
Jer 29 10 will perform my good word in your favor
Bar 1 12 and may find favor in their sight. And
2 14 that we may find favor in the sight of
Eze 22 30 before me in favor of the land, that I
1 Ma 10 60 he found favor in their sight. 11:24
13 38 all that we have decreed in your favor
2 Ma 4 11 which had been decreed of special favor
45 to persuade the king to favor him. So
Acts 2 47 and having favor with all the people
7 10 he gave him favor and wisdom in the
25 3 requesting f. against him, that he would
Heb 13 16 by such sacrifices God's f. is obtained
favorable Gen 43 14 God make him favorable to you
Lev 1 3 to make the Lord favorable to him: and
19 5 the Lord, that he may be f. 22:29
Num 14 8 if the Lord be f., he will bring us
Ruth 2 2 householder that will be f. to me
Ps 76 8 will he never be more favorable again
Isa 26 15 thou hast been f. to the nation, O Lord
favorably Gen 47 25 let my lord look f. upon us
Ps 50 20 deal favorably, O Lord, in thy good will
favored Gen 29 17 Rachel was well favored and of
Gen 41 3 other seven . . . ill f. and leanfleshed
19 other seven kine, so very ill favored
21 were as lean and ill favored as before
Dan 1 4 was no blemish, well favored, and
favors 2 Ma 8 20 for this they received many f.
2 Ma 9 26 remembering f. both public and private
fawn Job 39 1 observed the hinds when they fawn
Prov 5 19 let her be thy most agreeable fawn
fawning Tob 11 9 by his f. and wagging his tail
fear of God Gen 20 11 there is not the f. . . .
2 K 23 3 the just ruler in the fear of God
2 Es 5 15 but I did not so for the fear of God
Tob 2 14 immoveable in the fear of God, giving
14 4 with great increase of the fear of God
Ps 13 3 is no fear of God before their eyes
35 2 there is no fear of God before his eyes
Eccu 9 22 let thy glory be in the fear of God
10 25 fear of God is the glory of the rich
16 1 if the fear of God be not with them
19 18 the fear of God is all wisdom and
21 better is a man . . . with the f. of God
21 13 perfection of the f. of God is wisdom
23 27 driveth from him the fear of God, and
37 is nothing better than the fear of God
25 8 and the fear of God is their glory
14 fear of God hath set itself above all
15 it is given to have the fear of God
16 f. of God is the beginning of his love
28 8 remember the fear of God, and be not
37 15 thou shalt know to observe f. . . . , whose
49 6 High, and despised the fear of God
Rom 3 18 there is no f. of God before their eyes
fear of the Lord Josu 22 25 children from f. . . .
1 K 11 7 fear of the Lord fell upon the people
2 Pa 17 10 the fear of the Lord came upon all
19 7 let the fear of the Lord be with you
9 shall you do in the fear of the Lord
20 29 the fear of the Lord fell upon all
Tob 6 22 the virgin with the fear of the Lord
9 12 celebrated also with the f. . . . But
14 16 lived ninety-nine years in the f. . . .
Jdth 8 24 not receive the trials with the f. . . .
Job 6 14 from his friend forsaketh the f. . . .
28 28 the fear of the Lord, that is wisdom
Ps 18 10 the fear of the Lord is holy, enduring
33 12 I will teach you the fear of the Lord
110 10 fear of the Lord is the beginning of wisdom. Prov 1:7; 9:10; Eccu 1:16
Prov 1 29 and received not the fear of the Lord
2 5 shalt thou understand fear of the Lord
8 13 the fear of the Lord hateth evil: I
10 27 fear of the Lord shall prolong days
14 26 in the fear of the Lord is confidence
27 fear of the Lord is a fountain of life
15 16 better is a little with f. of the Lord
27 by fear of the Lord every one declineth
33 the f. . . . is the lesson of wisdom
16 6 by f. . . . men depart from evil. When
19 23 the fear of the Lord is unto life
22 4 fruit of humility is fear of the Lord
23 17 be thou in the f. . . . all the day long
Eccu 1 11 the f. . . . is honor and glory and
12 the f. . . . shall delight the heart
17 fear of the Lord is the religiousness
22 fear of the Lord is a crown of wisdom
27 the fear of the Lord driveth out sin
34 f. . . . is wisdom and discipline: and
36 be not incredulous of the f. . . . : and
7 21 wife whom thou hast gotten in f. . . .
23 31 because he understood not the f. . . .
27 4 hold thyself diligently in the f. . . .
40 26 above these is the fear of the Lord
27 there is no want in the f. . . . , and
28 f. . . . is like a paradise of blessing
45 28 in glory, by imitating him in f. . . .
Isa 2 10 from the face of the f. . . . 19, 21
11 3 be filled with the spirit of the f. . . .
33 6 the fear of the Lord is his treasure
Acts 9 31 edified, walking in the f. . . . , and
2 C 5 11 knowing therefore the fear of the Lord
fearful Deut 20 8 what man is there that is f.
Deut 28 65 the Lord will give thee a fearful heart
Judg 7 3 whosoever is fearful and timorous, let
1 K 4 13 his heart was f. for the ark of God
2 Pa 13 7 was unexperienced and of a f. heart
Prov 28 14 blessed is the man that is always f.
Wisd 9 14 thoughts of mortal men are fearful
17 10 whereas wickedness is fearful, it
Eccu 22 22 a fearful heart in the imagination
23 as a fearful heart in the thought of

1 Ma 3 56 planting vineyards or were fearful
Mat 8 26 why are you fearful. Mark 4:40
Heb 10 31 it is a f. thing to fall into the hands
Apoc 21 8 the fearful and unbelieving and the
fearfully Ps 138 14 for thou art f. magnified
fearfulness Deut 28 67 for the f. of thy heart
fearing Lev 25 19 your fill, f. no man's invasion
Josu 5 1 f. the coming in of the children of
Judg 6 27 fearing his father's house and the men
1 K 15 24 f. the people and obeying their voice
17 24 fearing him [Goliath] exceedingly. And
3 K 1 50 Adonias f. Solomon, arose and went and
51 Adonias, f. king Solomon, hath taken
4 K 25 26 went to Egypt, fearing the Chaldees
Tob 2 9 Tobias fearing God more than the king
Jdth 8 29 are a holy woman and one fearing God
Job 1 1 was simple and upright, and fearing God
8 simple and upright man and fearing God
2 3 a man simple and upright and f. God
Eccu 23 27 and the eyes of men fearing him: and
Eze 32 30 f., and confounded in their strength
39 26 their land securely fearing no man
1 Ma 12 40 f. lest Jonathan would not suffer him
Mark 5 33 but the woman fearing and trembling
Acts 10 2 fearing God with all his house, giving
23 10 f. lest Paul should be pulled in pieces
27 17 f. lest they should fall into quicksands
29 f. lest we should fall upon rough
Gal 2 12 f. them who were of the circumcision
Col 3 22 but in simplicity of heart, fearing God
Heb 11 27 not fearing the fierceness of the king
1 P 3 6 well, and not fearing any disturbance
fears Job 18 11 f. shall terrify him on every side
Cant 3 8 his thigh, because of fears in the night
Wisd 17 8 they who promised to drive away fears
18 17 fears unlooked for came upon them. And
Eccu 40 2 their thoughts and fears of the heart
2 C 7 5 combats without, fears within. But God
feast Gen 29 22 number of his friends to the f.
Gen 43 16 and kill victims and prepare a feast
32 and they think such a feast profane
Exod 12 14 you shall keep it for a f. to the Lord
17 the f. of unleavened bread. 23:15; 34:18; Deut 16:16; 2 Pa 8:13; 30:21; 35:17; 1 Es 6:22
23 16 feast of the harvest of the firstfruits
16 the feast also in the end of the year
34 22 the feast of weeks. Deut 16:16; 2 Pa 8:13; 2 Ma 12:31
22 feast when the time of year returneth
Lev 23 34 the feast of tabernacles. Deut 16:16; 31:10; 2 Pa 8:13; 1 Es 3:4; Zach 14:16, 18, 19; 2 Ma 10:6
39 celebrate the feast of the Lord seven
41 seventh month shall you celebrate this f.
Num 28 17 on the fifteenth day the solemn feast
Deut 12 12 there shall you feast before the Lord
14 26 before the Lord thy God, and shalt f.
16 11 thou shalt feast before the Lord thy
26 11 thou shalt feast in all the good things
27 7 eat there and feast before the Lord
Judg 14 12 within the seven days of the feast
17 wept before him seven days of the feast
19 21 he entertained them with a feast. While
1 K 25 36 he [Nabal] had a feast in his house
36 in his house, like the feast of a king
2 K 12 4 to make a feast for that stranger, who
13 27 a feast as it were the feast of a king
3 K 1 41 and now the feast was at an end: Joab
12 32 appointed a feast in the eighth month
32 the feast that was celebrated in Juda
33 ordained a f. to the children of Israel
2 Es 8 14 should dwell in tabernacles, on the f.
Tob 2 2 some of our tribe . . . to feast with us
7 9 be killed, and a feast to be prepared
8 21 spoke to his wife to make ready a feast
9 12 had said, Amen, they went to the feast
12 the marriage feast they celebrated
Esth 1 5 when the days of the feast were expired
5 commanded a feast to be made seven days
2 18 he commanded a magnificent feast to be
Ps 67 4 let the just feast and rejoice before
Prov 15 15 secure mind is like a continual feast
Ecce 2 25 who shall so feast and abound . . . as I
10 19 and wine that the living may feast
Eccu 31 17 be not hasty in a feast. Judge of the
39 37 in his commandments they shall feast
Isa 25 6 a f. of fat things, a f. of wine, of
Lam 1 4 are none that come to the solemn feast
2 7 as in the day of a solemn feast
Bar 6 31 as men do at the f. when one is dead
Eze 45 25 seventh month . . . in the solemn feast
Osee 9 5 in the day of the feast of the Lord
12 9 tabernacles, as in the days of the f.
1 Ma 10 21 at the feast day of the tabernacles
2 Ma 2 28 as they that prepare a feast and seek
6 7 when the feast of Bacchus was kept
8 33 when they kept the feast of the victory
Mark 14 1 the feast of the pasch and of the
Luke 2 42 according to the custom of the feast
5 29 Levi made him a great feast in his
14 13 when thou makest a feast, call the
22 1 feast of the unleavened bread, which
23 17 unto them one upon the feast day. But
John 2 8 carry to the chief steward of the f.
7 2 Jews' f. of tabernacles was at hand
10 then he also went up to the feast, not
14 about the midst of the feast, Jesus
10 22 it was the feast of the dedication
1 C 5 8 let us feast, not with the old leaven
made a feast Gen 19 3 made them a feast. 26:30
Gen 21 8 Abraham made a great feast on the day
40 20 [Pharao] made a great feast for his
Judg 14 10 and made a feast for his son Samson
2 K 3 20 David made feast for Abner and his men
13 27 made a feast as it were feast of a king
3 K 3 15 made a great feast for all his servants
8 65 and Solomon made . . . a solemn feast
Esth 1 3 made a great f. for all the princes
9 also Vasthi the queen made a feast
Job 1 4 his sons went and made a feast by
Dan 5 1 Baltasar the king made a great feast
1 Ma 16 15 he made them a great feast and hid men
feasted Tob 11 21 they feasted and rejoiced all
Luke 16 19 and feasted sumptuously every day
James 5 5 you have feasted upon earth: and in
feasting Esth 9 17 should celebrate it with f.
Esth 9 18 to be a holy day of f. and gladness
22 should be days of feasting and gladness
Job 1 5 days of their feasting were gone about
Ps 41 5 and praise: the noise of one feasting
Ecce 7 3 mourning than to the house of feasting
Eccu 30 27 a cheerful and good heart is always f.
37 32 be not greedy in any feasting, and pour
Jer 16 5 enter not into the house of feasting
8 do not thou go into the house of f.
Nah 1 10 while they are f. and drinking together
Jude 12 feasting together without fear, feeding
feasts Exod 23 14 you shall celebrate feasts
Lev 23 2 these are the feasts of the Lord. 37
44 Moses spoke concerning the feasts
Deut 16 15 seven days shalt thou celebrate feasts
Judg 16 25 rejoicing in their feasts, when they
2 Es 10 33 on the new moons, on the set feasts
Jdth 8 6 the feasts of the house of Israel
Esth 8 17 there was wonderful rejoicing, feasts

Prov 23 20 be not in the feasts of great drinkers
Eccu 18 33 by borrowing to contribute to feasts
Isa 5 12 the pipe and wine are in your feasts
Lam 2 6 caused f. and sabbaths to be forgotten
Bar 1 14 to be read . . . on f. and proper days
Eze 36 38 as flock of Jerusalem in her solemn f.
45 17 shall give . . . the libations on the f.
46 9 before the Lord in the solemn feasts
Amos 8 10 I will turn your feasts into mourning
1 Ma 10 34 I will that all the f. and the sabbaths
Mat 23 6 they love the first places at feasts
Luke 20 46 and the chief rooms at feasts: who
2 P 2 13 rioting in their feasts with you
feathered Job 39 26 doth the hawk wax f. by thy
Ps 77 27 f. fowls like as the sand of the sea
148 10 cattle: serpents and feathered fowls
feathers Lev 1 16 the feathers he shall cast
Eze 17 3 a large eagle . . . full of feathers
7 eagle with great wings and many f.
Dan 4 30 his hairs grew like the f. of eagles
fed Gen 29 9 for she [Rachel] fed the flock. And
Gen 30 36 son-in-law who fed the rest of his flock
31 4 into the field, where he fed the flocks
36 24 when he fed the asses of Sebeon his
41 2 and fat: and they fed in marshy places
3 they fed on the very bank of the river
Exod 3 1 now Moses fed the sheep of Jethro his
16 32 the bread, wherewith I fed you in the
35 with this meat were they fed, until
Deut 8 16 fed thee in the wilderness with manna
3 K 4 27 foresaid governors of the king fed them
18 4 caves, and fed them with bread. 13
1 Pa 27 29 and over the herds that fed in Saron
Tob 1 20 he fed the hungry and gave clothes to
Job 24 2 taken away flocks by force and fed them
21 he hath fed the barren that beareth not
Ps 36 3 and thou shalt be fed with its riches
77 72 he fed them in the innocence of his
80 17 he fed them with the fat of wheat
Wisd 19 9 they fed on their food like horses
Isa 14 30 firstborn of the poor shall be fed
Jer 5 7 I fed them to the full, and they
Lam 3 16 one by one, he hath fed me with ashes
4 5 they that were fed delicately have
Eze 16 19 and honey, wherewith I fed thee
34 2 should not the flocks be fed by the
2 the shepherds . . . that fed themselves
8 fed themselves and fed not my flocks
14 and be fed in fat pastures upon the
19 my sheep were fed with that which you
39 18 and of all that are well fed and fat
Zach 11 7 and I fed the flock. And I cut off
Mat 25 37 did we see thee hungry, and fed thee
Mark 5 14 they that fed them fled and told it
Luke 8 34 which when they that fed them saw done
feeble Deut 15 21 or in any part disfigured or f.
2 Pa 28 15 of them as could not walk and were f.
Ps 104 37 not among their tribes one that was f.
Prov 30 25 ants, a feeble people, which provide
Wisd 2 11 is f., is found to be nothing worth
Eccu 25 32 feeble hands and disjointed knees
Isa 16 14 it shall be left small and feeble
33 24 he that is near, say: I am feeble
35 3 strengthen ye the feeble hands and
Jer 6 24 our hands grow feeble: anguish hath
50 43 his hands are grown feeble: anguish
Bar 2 18 goeth bowed down and feeble and the
Eze 7 17 all hands shall be made feeble. 21:7
Mala 1 14 in sacrifice that which is feeble
1 Ma 1 27 and the young men were made feeble
2 Ma 8 28 they divided the spoils to the feeble
30 giving equal portions to the feeble
Luke 14 21 bring in hither the poor and the f.
1 C 12 22 those that seem to be the more feeble
1 Th 5 14 comfort the feeble minded, support the
Heb 12 12 which hang down, and the feeble knees
feebleness Jer 47 3 the children, for f. of hands
feed Gen 1 30 that they may have to feed upon
Gen 29 7 drink, and so lead them back to feed
30 31 I will feed and keep thy sheep again
37 13 thy brethren feed the sheep in Sichem
16 tell me where they feed the flocks
45 11 there I will feed thee, for there are
46 32 their occupation is to feed cattle
50 21 I will feed you and your children. And
Exod 10 5 they shall feed upon all the trees
22 5 to feed upon that which is other men's
34 3 nor the sheep feed over against it
Lev 6 12 priest shall feed it, putting wood on
Deut 11 15 out of the fields to feed your cattle
Josu 14 4 suburbs to feed their beasts and flocks
21 2 and their suburbs to feed our cattle
1 K 17 15 David . . . to feed his father's flock
2 K 5 2 thou shalt feed my people Israel, and
7 7 whom I commanded to feed my people
3 K 17 4 have commanded the ravens to feed thee
9 a widow woman there to feed thee. He
22 27 feed him with bread of affliction and
1 Pa 11 2 God said . . . thou shalt feed my people
17 6 judges . . . whom I charged to feed my
2 Pa 10 16 do thou, O David, feed thy own house
2 Es 9 21 didst thou feed them in the desert
Job 30 17 they that feed upon me do not sleep
39 4 their young are weaned and go to feed
Ps 32 19 from death: and feed them in famine
48 15 like sheep, death shall feed upon them
77 71 to feed Jacob his servant, and Israel
79 6 how long wilt thou feed us with the
Cant 1 7 feed thy kids beside the tents of the
4 5 are twins, which feed among the lilies
6 1 to feed in the gardens and to gather
Wisd 16 20 thou didst feed thy people with the
Eccu 15 3 bread of life . . . she shall feed him
29 31 he shall entertain and feed and give
Isa 5 17 the lambs shall feed according to their
7 25 they shall be for the ox to feed on
11 7 the calf and the bear shall feed: their
27 10 there the calf shall feed and there
30 23 lamb in that day shall feed at large
40 11 he shall feed his flock like a shepherd
49 9 they shall feed in the ways and their
26 I will feed thy enemies with their own
58 14 will feed thee with the inheritance of
61 5 shall stand and shall feed your flocks
65 25 wolf and the lamb shall feed together
Jer 3 15 they shall feed you with knowledge
6 3 every one shall feed them that are
9 15 I will feed this people with wormwood
19 9 I will feed them with the flesh of
22 22 the wind shall feed all thy pastors
23 2 to the pastors that feed my people
4 over them, and they shall feed them
15 behold I will feed them with wormwood
50 19 he shall feed on Carmel and Bason
Eze 34 3 was fat: but my flock you did not feed
10 neither shall the shepherds feed
13 I will feed them in the mountains of
14 I will feed them in the most fruitful
15 I will feed my sheep: and I will cause
16 I will feed them in judgment. And as
18 for you to feed upon good pastures? But
23 over them, and he shall feed them, even
Osee 4 16 now will the Lord feed them, as a lamb
9 2 the winepress shall not feed them, and
Jon 3 7 let them not feed nor drink water. And
Mich 5 4 he shall stand and feed in the strength

6 shall feed the land of Assyria with
7 14 feed thy people with thy rod, the flock
14 they shall feed in Basan and Galaad
Soph 2 7 house of Juda, there they shall feed
3 13 they shall feed and shall lie down
Zach 11 4 my God: feed the flock of the slaughter
9 and I said: I will not feed you: that
7 I will feed the flock of slaughter
Luke 15 15 sent him into his farm to feed swine
John 21 15 he saith to him: Feed my lambs. 16
17 he said to him: Feed my sheep. Amen
1 C 13 3 distribute all my goods to feed the poor
1 P 5 2 feed the flock of God which is among
Apoc 12 6 there they should feed 1,260 days
feedest Cant 1 6 where thou f., where
feedeth Gen 48 15 God that f. me from my youth
Prov 10 4 he that trusteth to lies f. the winds
15 14 the mouth of fools f. on foolishness
28 7 he that f. gluttons, shameth his father
Cant 2 16 who feedeth among the lilies. 6:2
Eccu 40 30 he feedeth his soul with another man's
Eze 45 15 those that Israel feedeth for sacrifice
Osee 12 1 Ephraim f. on the wind and followeth
Mat 6 26 your heavenly Father feedeth them
Luke 12 24 nor barn, and God feedeth them. How
1 C 9 7 who feedeth the flock, and eateth not
feeding Gen 34 5 employed in feeding the cattle
Gen 37 2 Joseph . . . was feeding the flock with
12 in Sichem feeding their father's flocks
Num 32 1 saw the lands . . . fit for f. cattle
4 fertile soil for the feeding of beasts
Job 1 14 and the asses feeding beside them, and
Eze 34 10 to cease from feeding the flock any
Dan 4 20 let his feeding be with the wild beasts
Nah 2 11 feeding place of the young lions, to
2 Ma 5 27 they continued feeding on herbs, that
Mat 8 30 herd of many swine feeding. Luke 8:32
Mark 5 11 a great herd of swine, feeding. And
Luke 17 7 a servant plowing or feeding cattle
Jude 12 together without fear, f. themselves
feel Gen 27 12 if my father shall feel me, and
Gen 27 21 come hither, that I may feel thee
Jdth 16 21 that they may burn and may feel forever
Ps 113 7 they have hands and feel not: they have
Prov 14 35 good for nothing shall feel his anger
Eccu 31 22 with it, and thou shalt feel no pain
Bar 6 19 their garments, and they feel it not
23 they were molten, did they feel it
Dan 5 23 that neither see nor hear nor feel
Acts 17 27 they may feel after him or find him
feet Gen 24 32 his feet and the feet of the men
Exod 12 9 you shall eat the head with the feet
28 33 beneath at the feet of the same tunick
39 22 at the feet pomegranates of violet
Lev 1 9 the entrails and feet being washed with
13 entrails and the feet they shall wash
4 11 the flesh with the head and the feet
8 21 washed the entrails and the feet. 9:14
11 20 whatsoever goeth upon four feet shall
21 whatsoever walketh upon four feet but
35 whether it be oven, or pots with feet
42 goeth upon the breast on four feet or hath many feet
13 12 cover all the skin from head to feet
Num 22 27 she fell under the feet of the rider
Josu 9 13 and the shoes we have on our feet
4 3 where the feet of the priests stood
Judg 5 28 why are the feet of his horses so slow
1 K 2 9 he will keep the feet of his saints
25 41 to wash the feet of servants of my lord
2 K 9 13 [Miphiboseth] was lame of both feet
22 34 my feet like the feet of harts. Ps 17:34; Haba 3:19
4 K 6 32 sound of his master's feet is behind
9 35 found nothing but the skull and the f.
21 8 feet of Israel to be moved out of the
1 Pa 19 4 garments from the buttocks to the feet
Jdth 1 2 side was extended the space of 20 feet
Esth 8 3 she fell down at the king's feet and
Job 2 7 from the sole of the feet even to the
Ps 113 7 feel not: they have feet and walk not
121 2 our feet were standing in thy courts
Prov 6 18 f. that are swift to run into mischief
26 6 is lame of feet and drinketh iniquity
Wisd 14 11 a snare to the feet of the unwise
Eccu 21 22 to a fool is as fetters on the feet
25 27 sandy way is to the feet of the aged
26 23 so are the firm feet upon the soles of
40 25 gold and silver make the f. stand sure
45 10 he put upon him a garment to the feet
Isa 7 20 shall shave . . . the hairs of the feet
26 6 shall tread it down, the f. of the poor
28 3 of Ephraim shall be trodden under feet
52 7 f. of him that bringeth good. Nah 1:15
Bar 6 16 dust by the feet of them that go in
Eze 1 7 their feet were straight feet, and the
Dan 2 33 the feet part of iron and part of clay
34 it struck the statue upon the feet
41 whereas thou sawest the feet and the
42 the toes of the feet were part of iron
3 20 to bind the feet of Sidrach, Misach
7 7 treading down the rest with its feet
10 6 all downward even to the feet, like
1 Ma 6 46 went between the feet of the elephant
Mat 18 8 than having two hands or two feet to
Mark 9 44 than having two feet, to be cast into
Luke 1 79 to direct our f. into the way of peace
8 41 and he fell down at the feet of Jesus
10 39 sitting also at the Lord's feet, heard
John 11 44 came forth, bound feet and hands with
12 3 anointed the feet of Jesus and wiped
13 5 began to wash the f. of the disciples
14 also ought to wash one another's feet
20 12 one at the head and one at the feet
Acts 4 35 down before the feet of the apostles
37 laid it at f. of the apostles. 5:2
5 9 the feet of them who have buried thy
7 57 their garments at the feet of a young
16 29 fell down at the feet of Paul and Silas
22 3 brought up . . . at the feet of Gamaliel
Rom 10 15 beautiful are feet of them that preach
1 C 12 21 nor again the head to the feet: I have
1 Tim 5 10 if she have washed the saints' feet, if
Apoc 1 13 clothed with a garment down to the feet
22 8 to adore before the feet of the angel
her feet Judg 5 27 at her feet he [Sisara] fell
Judg 5 27 he rolled before her feet and he lay
3 K 14 6 Ahias heard the sound of her feet
Jdth 10 3 put sandals on her feet and took her
13 30 he [Achior] fell down at her feet
Prov 5 5 her feet go down into depth, and her
Isa 23 7 her feet shall carry her afar off to
Dan 7 4 stood upon her feet as a man, and the
Apoc 12 1 and the moon under her feet, and on
his feet Gen 24 32 to wash his feet and the feet of
Gen 49 32 he drew up his feet upon the bed
Exod 4 25 Sephora . . . touched his feet, and said
24 10 under his feet . . . a work of sapphire
29 17 having washed his entrails and feet
Ruth 3 4 lift up the clothes . . . towards his f.
7 uncovering his feet, laid herself down
8 he saw a woman lying at his feet. And
14 she slept at his feet till the night
1 K 25 24 she [Abigail] fell at his feet and said
2 K 4 4 had a son that was lame of his feet
9 3 who is lame of his feet. Where is he

19 24 he had neither washed his feet nor
22 10 down: and darkness was under his feet
3 K 2 5 in his shoes that were on his feet
5 3 put them under the soles of his feet
15 23 old age he was diseased in his feet
4 K 4 27 she caught hold on his feet: and Giezi
37 she came and fell at his feet, and
9 13 his garment laid it under his feet
13 21 came to life and stood upon his feet
2 Pa 16 12 of a most violent pain in his feet
Tob 6 2 he went out to wash his feet, and
4 and he began to pant before his feet
11 10 began to run stumbling with his feet
Esth 13 13 have kissed even the steps of his feet
Job 18 8 he hath thrust his feet into a net
11 on every side shall entangle his feet
Ps 8 8 hast subjected all things under his f.
17 10 down: and darkness was under his feet
104 18 they humbled his feet in fetters: the
131 7 will adore in place where his feet
Prov 6 28 hot coals, and his feet not be burnt
19 2 that is hasty with his f. shall stumble
29 5 words, spreadeth a net for his feet
Eccu 38 32 turning the wheel about with his feet
33 boweth down his strength before his f.
Isa 6 2 with two they covered his feet, and
41 3 no path shall appear after his feet
Lam 3 34 to crush under his f. all the prisoners
Dan 7 19 the rest he stamped upon with his feet
Nah 1 3 clouds are the dust of his feet. He
Haba 3 5 the devil shall go forth before his f.
Zach 14 4 his feet shall stand . . . upon the mount
2 Ma 3 25 struck Heliodorus with his fore feet
7 4 the extremities of his hands and feet
Mat 15 30 they cast them down at his feet, and
22 13 bind his hands and feet and cast him
28 9 took hold of his feet and adored him
Mark 5 22 seeing him, falleth down at his feet
7 25 came in and fell down at his feet. For
Luke 7 38 standing behind at his feet, she began
38 began to wash his feet with tears and
38 kissed his feet and anointed them with
8 35 sitting at his feet, clothed, and in
47 fell down before his feet and declared
15 22 on his hand, and shoes on his feet
17 16 he fell on his face before his feet
24 40 he showed them his hands and feet
John 11 2 and wiped his feet with her hair. 13:3
32 she fell down at his feet, and saith
13 10 needeth not but to wash his feet, but
Acts 3 7 his feet and soles received strength
5 10 she fell down before his feet and gave
13 25 shoes of his feet I am not worthy to
14 7 man at Lystra, impotent in his feet, a
21 11 binding his own feet and hands, he said
1 C 15 25 hath put all his enemies under his feet
26 all things under his feet. Eph 1:22; Heb 2:8
Apoc 1 15 his feet like unto fine brass. 2:18
17 seen him, I fell at his feet as dead
10 1 and his feet as pillars of fire. And
13 2 his feet were as the feet of a bear
19 10 I fell down before his feet to adore

my feet 2 K 22 34 my feet like the feet of harts. Ps 17:34; Haba 3:19
2 K 22 39 they shall fall under my feet. Ps 17:39
Job 13 27 put my feet in the stocks. 33:11
27 and hast considered the steps of my f.
29 6 when I washed my feet with butter
30 12 they have overthrown my feet and have
Ps 17 37 under me: and my feet are not weakened
21 17 they have dug my hands and feet. They
24 15 he shall pluck my f. out of the snare
30 9 hast set my feet in a spacious place
37 17 whilst my feet are moved, they speak
39 3 he set my feet upon a rock and directed
55 13 delivered . . . my feet from falling
56 7 they prepared a snare for my feet
65 9 hath not suffered my feet to be moved
72 2 my feet were almost moved: my steps
114 8 hath delivered . . . my f. from falling
118 59 turned my feet unto thy testimonies
101 I have restrained my feet from every
105 thy word is a lamp to my feet and a
Cant 5 3 I have washed my feet, how shall I
Eccu 24 11 trodden under my f. the hearts of all
Isa 60 13 I will glorify the place of my feet
Jer 18 22 take me, and have hid snares for my f.
Lam 1 13 he hath spread a net for my feet, he
Eze 2 2 spoke to me, and he set me upon my feet
3 24 the spirit . . . set me upon my feet
43 7 the place of the soles of my feet where
Luke 7 44 thou gavest me no water for my feet
44 she with tears hath washed my feet
45 hath not ceased to kiss my feet. My
46 she with ointment hath anointed my f.
24 39 see my hands and feet, that it is I
John 13 6 to him: Lord, doth thou wash my feet
8 thou shalt never wash my feet. Jesus
9 not only my feet, but also my hands

their feet Gen 43 24 and they washed their feet
Exod 30 19 shall wash their hands and feet in it
40 29 and his sons washed their hands and f.
Lev 8 24 touched . . . great toes of their right f.
Num 16 31 earth broke asunder under their feet
Josu 3 13 set soles of their feet in the waters
15 as soon as . . . their feet were dipped
10 24 put their feet upon the necks of them
Judg 19 21 after they had washed their feet, he
2 K 4 12 cutting off their hands and f., hanged
2 Pa 3 13 and they stood upright on their feet
2 Es 9 21 grow old, and their feet were not worn
Jdth 9 8 the deep held their feet, and the
Ps 13 3 their feet are swift to shed blood
Prov 1 16 their feet run to evil. Isa 59:7
Wisd 15 15 as for their feet, they are slow to
Isa 3 16 a noise as they walked with their feet
Jer 14 10 that have loved to move their feet
Eze 1 7 their feet were straight feet, and the
37 10 and they stood up upon their feet
Zach 14 12 while they stand upon their feet, and
Mat 7 6 they trample them under their feet and
John 13 12 then after he had washed their feet
Acts 13 51 shaking off the dust of their feet
16 24 and made their feet fast in the stocks
Rom 3 15 t. f. swift to shed blood. Destruction
Apoc 11 11 they stood upon their feet, and great

thy feet Exod 3 5 the shoes from thy f. Josu 5:16
2 K 3 34 nor thy feet laden with fetters: but
11 8 go into thy house and wash thy feet
3 K 14 12 thy f. shall be entering into the city
Prov 4 26 make straight the path for thy feet
Eccu 6 25 put thy feet into her fetters, and thy
12 18 an enemy . . . will undermine thy feet
Isa 20 2 take off thy shoes from thy feet. And
49 23 they shall lick up the dust of thy feet
60 14 shall worship the steps of thy feet
Jer 13 22 the soles of thy feet are defiled. If
38 22 they have plunged thy feet in the mire
Eze 2 1 son of man, stand upon thy feet, and
24 17 thy shoes on thy feet, and cover not
32 2 didst trouble the waters with thy feet
Acts 7 33 loose the shoes from thy feet, for the
14 9 stand upright on thy feet. And he
26 16 rise up, and stand upon thy feet: for
Apoc 3 9 to come and adore before thy feet

your feet Gen 18 4 wash ye your feet and rest

Gen 19 2 wash your feet, and in the morning you
Exod 12 11 and you shall have shoes on your feet
Deut 29 5 neither are shoes of your feet consumed
Josu 10 24 set your feet on necks of these kings
Jdth 14 5 Lord will destroy them under your feet
Jer 13 16 before your feet stumble upon the dark
Eze 24 23 you shall have . . . shoes on your feet
34 18 must also tread down with your feet
18 you troubled the rest with your feet
19 which you had trodden with your feet
19 they drank what your feet had troubled
Mala 4 3 be ashes under the sole of your feet
Mat 10 14 shake off the dust from your feet. Mark 6:11; Luke 9:5
John 13 14 have washed your feet; you also ought
Rom 16 20 crush Satan under your feet speedily
Eph 6 15 your feet shod with the preparation of
Heb 12 13 make straight steps with your feet
feign Gen 26 9 why didst thou f. her to be thy
2 K 13 5 upon thy bed, and feign thyself sick
14 2 feign thyself to be a mourner and put
3 K 14 6 why dost thou f. thyself to be another
Luke 20 20 spies who should feign themselves just
feigned 2 P 2 3 with f. words make merchandise of
feignest 2 Es 6 8 f. these things out of thy
feigning Judg 20 32 they artfully f. a flight
Luke 20 47 house of widows, feigning long prayer
Felix Acts 23 24 bring him safe to F. the governor
Acts 23 26 to the most excellent governor, Felix
24 3 places, most excellent Felix, with all
22 Felix put them off, having most certain
24 Felix, coming with Drusillas his wife
25 Felix being terrified, answered: For
27 Felix had for successor Portius Festus
27 F. being willing to show the Jews a
25 14 a certain man was left prisoner by F.
fell Mat 7 25 the rain fell, and the floods came. 27
Mat 7 25 it fell not, for it was founded on
27 it fell, and great was the fall thereof
13 4 some f. by wayside. Mark 4:4; Luke 8:5
5 some fell upon stony ground. Mark 4:5
7 f. among thorns. Mark 4:7; Luke 8:7, 14
8 f. upon good ground. Mark 4:8; Luke 8:8
17 6 the disciples hearing, fell upon their
26 39 he fell upon his face, praying and
Mark 3 11 fell down before him: and they cried
5 33 fell down before him and told him all
7 25 came in and fell down at his feet
14 35 he fell flat on the ground; and he
Luke 1 12 was troubled, and fear fell upon him
5 8 he fell down at Jesus' knees, saying
6 49 it fell, and the ruin of that house
8 6 other some fell upon a rock: and as
28 saw Jesus, he fell down before him
41 and he fell down at the feet of Jesus
47 fell down before his feet and declared
10 30 to Jericho, and fell among robbers
36 to him that fell among the robbers
13 4 upon whom the tower fell in Siloe
15 20 running to him fell upon his neck
16 21 that fell from the rich man's table
17 16 he fell on his face before his feet
John 11 32 she fell down at his feet, and saith
18 6 went backward and fell to the ground
Acts 1 26 the lot fell upon Matthias, and he was
5 5 Ananias hearing these words, fell down
10 she fell down before his feet and gave
7 59 said this, he fell asleep in the Lord
9 18 immediately there fell from his eyes
10 44 Holy Ghost fell on all them that heard
11 15 Holy Ghost fell upon them, as upon us
12 7 and the chains fell off from his hands
13 11 there fell a mist and darkness upon him
16 29 he went in and trembling, fell down
19 17 at Ephesus; and fear fell on them all
20 9 occasion of his sleep fell from third
21 35 it fell out that he was carried by the
Rom 15 3 them that reproached thee, fell upon me
1 C 10 8 there fell in one day 23,000. Neither
Heb 11 30 by faith the walls of Jericho fell down
James 1 11 the flower thereof fell off, and the
Apoc 1 17 had seen him, I feel at his feet as
4 10 the 4 and 20 ancients fell down. 5:14
5 8 ancients fell down before the Lamb
6 13 the stars from heaven fell upon the
7 11 they fell down before the throne upon
8 10 a great star fell from heaven, burning
10 it fell on the third part of the rivers
11 11 great fear fell upon them that saw them
13 and the tenth part of the city fell
16 fell on their faces and adored God
16 2 there fell a sore and grievous wound
19 and the cities of the Gentiles fell
19 4 the four living creatures fell down
10 I fell down before his feet to adore
22 8 I fell down to adore before the feet
felling 4 K 6 5 as one was f. some timber, that
fellow Exod 26 10 it may be coupled with its f.
1 K 10 27 shall this fellow be able to save us
21 15 that you have brought in this fellow
15 shall this fellow come into my house
2 K 2 16 every one catching his f. by the head
2 Pa 18 26 put this fellow in prison and give him
Tob 1 3 to his brethren his fellow captives
Jon 1 7 they said every one to his fellow
2 Ma 4 42 as for the sacrilegious fellow himself
Mat 18 28 he found one of his fellow servants
29 his f. servant falling down besought
31 his f. servants seeing what was done
33 compassion also on thy fellow servant
24 49 begin to strike his fellow servants
John 11 16 said to his fellow disciples: Let us
Rom 16 7 my kinsmen and fellow prisoners: who
21 Timothy, my fellow laborer, saluteth
2 C 8 23 Titus . . . my companion and f. laborer
Eph 2 19 you are fellow citizens with the saints
3 6 the Gentiles should be fellow heirs
Phil 2 25 Epaphroditus, my brother and f. laborer
4 3 Clement and the rest of my f. laborers
Col 1 7 Epaphras, our most beloved f. servant
4 7 minister and fellow servant in the Lord
10 you. Aristarchus, my fellow prisoner
Philem 1 to Philemon, our beloved and f. laborer
2 to Archippus, our fellow soldier, and
23 Epaphras, my fellow prisoner in Christ
24 Demas and Luke my fellow laborers. The
3 J 8 that we may be f. helpers of the truth
Apoc 6 11 till their fellow servants and their
19 10 I am thy f. servant, and of thy. 22:9
fellows Ps 44 8 anointed thee . . . above thy fellows
Heb 1 9 with the oil of gladness above thy f.
fellowship Eccu 13 1 that hath f. with the proud
Eccu 13 2 hath f. with one more honorable than
2 have no f. with one that is richer
21 if the wolf shall at any time have f.
22 what f. hath a holy man with a dog
1 C 1 9 called unto the fellowship of his Son
2 C 6 14 what f. hath light with darkness
Gal 2 9 Barnabas the right hands of fellowship
Eph 5 11 have no f. with the unfruitful works
Phil 3 10 fellowship of his suffering, being made
1 J 1 3 you also may have fellowship with us
3 our f. may be with the Father and with
6 if we say that we have f. with him
7 we have fellowship one with another
felt Gen 27 22 when he had felt him, Isaac said

Exod 10 21 so thick that it may be felt. And Moses
2 Pa 26 20 because he had quickly f. the stroke of
Prov 23 35 of pain: they drew me, and I felt not
Mark 5 29 she felt in her body that she was healed
female Gen 1 27 male and female he created them
Gen 5 2 he created them male and female; and
6 19 two . . . of the male sex and the female
7 2 take 7 and 7, the male and the female
3 beasts . . . the male and the female
3 fowls . . . the male and the female: that
9 in to Noe into the ark, male and female
16 went in male and female of all flesh
Exod 1 22 of the female, ye shall save alive
Lev 3 1 male or female . . . without blemish
6 whether he offer male or female, they
27 6 for a female three [sicles]. A man that
Num 31 35 spoil . . . 32,000 persons of the f. sex
Deut 4 16 might make . . . image of male or female
Mark 10 6 God made them male and female. For
Gal 3 28 there is neither male nor female. For
1 P 3 7 giving honor to the female as to the
females Gen 31 10 males which leaped upon the f.
Gen 31 12 all the males leaping upon the females
fence 1 Es 9 9 and to give us a fence in Juda
Job 1 10 hast not thou made a fence for him
Ps 61 4 thrusting down . . . a tottering fence
fenced Deut 3 5 cities were f. with very high walls
Josu 6 1 Jericho was close shut up and fenced
1 K 6 18 from the fenced city to the village
4 K 3 19 you shall destroy every fenced city
17 9 of the watchmen to the f. city. 18:8
Isa 2 15 high tower and every fenced wall. And
5 2 he fenced it in and picked the stones
Jer 8 14 let us enter into the fenced city, and
Eze 36 35 the cities . . . are peopled and fenced
Dan 11 24 devices against the best fenced places
Zach 11 2 because the f. forest is cut down
fenced cities Num 32 36 sons of Gad built . . . f. c.
Josu 10 20 they . . . entered into fenced cities
1 K 20 6 lest he find fenced cities and escape
3 K 10 26 he bestowed them in fenced cities
4 K 10 2 your master's fenced cities and
19 25 fenced cities of fighting men should
2 Pa 11 10 and Hebron . . . well fenced cities
32 1 Sennacherib . . . besieged the fenced c.
Isa 37 26 and fenced cities should be destroyed
Jer 34 7 remained of the c. of Juda, fenced c.
Dan 11 15 and shall take the best fenced cities
Osee 8 14 Juda hath built many fenced cities
Soph 1 16 and alarm against the fenced cities
fences Isa 58 12 be called the repairer of the f.
fencing Exod 26 13 f. both sides of the tabernacle
fenny Eze 47 11 in the f. places they shall not
fertile Num 32 4 a very f. soil for the feeding
fertility Deut 1 25 to show its f., they brought
fervent 1 Ma 2 54 being f. in the zeal of God
Acts 18 25 being f. in spirit, spoke and taught
Rom 12 11 in spirit fervent, serving the Lord
festival Num 10 10 banquet, and on your f. days
Deut 16 10 thou shalt celebrate the f. of weeks
14 thou shalt make merry in thy f. time
4 K 10 20 he said: Proclaim a festival for Baal
2 Pa 8 13 on the festival days three times a year
Tom 2 1 when there was a festival of the Lord
6 your festival days shall be turned into
Jdth 16 27 on festival days she came forth with
Esth 9 29 this day should be established a f.
Ps 73 8 let us abolish all the festival days
Lam 2 22 thou hast called as to a festival
Osee 2 11 her sabbaths and all her festival times
1 Ma 1 48 should prohibit . . . the festival days
festival day 1 K 30 16 as it were keeping a f. day
3 K 8 2 festival day in the month of Ethanim
Eccu 43 7 moon is the sign of the festival day
Mat 26 5 not on the f. day, lest. Mark 14:2
Mark 15 6 on the f. day he was wont to release
John 2 23 at the pasch, upon the festival day
4 45 had done at Jerusalem on the f. day
45 for they also went to the festival day
5 1 was a festival day of the Jews, and
6 4 the pasch, the f. day of the Jews, was
7 8 go you up to this f. day, but I go not up to this f. day
11 sought him on the festival day and
11 56 that he is not come to the f. day? And
12 12 that was come to the festival day when
20 came up to adore on the festival day
13 1 before the festival day of the pasch
29 which we have need of for the f. day
Col 2 16 drink, or in respect of a festival day
festivals Eccu 33 9 celebrated f. at an hour
Eccu 47 12 to the festivals he added beauty, and
Isa 1 13 and other festivals I will not abide
1 Ma 12 11 in our festivals . . . remember you
festivities Amos 5 21 and have rejected your f.
festivity Jdth 16 31 the day of the f. of this
John 7 37 on the last and great day of the f.
Festus Acts 24 27 had for successor Portius F.
Acts 25 1 when Festus was come into the province
4 Festus answered: That Paul was kept in
9 Festus, willing to show the Jews a
12 Festus having conferred with the council
13 came down to Caesarea to salute Festus
14 Festus told the king of Paul, saying
22 Agrippa said to Festus: I would also
24 Festus saith: King Agrippa, and all ye
26 24 Festus said with a loud voice: Paul
25 I am not mad, most excellent Festus
32 Agrippa said to Festus: This man might
Festus' Acts 25 23 at F. commandment, Paul was
fetch Gen 18 4 I will fetch a little water and
Gen 27 13 fetch me the things which I have said
42 16 send one of you to fetch him: and you
Num 34 5 the limits shall fetch a compass from
Deut 30 4 the Lord thy God will fetch thee back
Judg 11 5 ancients of Galaad went to fetch Jephte
1 K 4 3 let us fetch unto us the ark of the
6 21 come ye down and fetch it up to you
16 11 Samuel said to Isai: Send and fetch him
20 21 saying to him: Go and f. me the arrows
31 send and fetch him [David] to me: for
36 fetch me the arrows which I shoot. And
26 22 let one . . . come over and fetch it
2 K 5 23 but fetch a compass behind them, and
6 2 David arose and went . . . to f. the ark
14 21 and fetch back the boy Absalom. And
3 K 17 11 when she was going to fetch it, he
2 Es 8 15 fetch branches of olive and branches
Dan 13 18 to fetch what she had commanded them
2 Ma 2 15 send some that may fetch them to you
fetched Gen 43 24 he f. water, and they washed
1 K 7 1 came and fetched up the ark of the
10 23 they ran and fetched him [Saul] thence
2 K 10 16 Adarezer sent and fetched the Syrians
14 2 fetched from thence a wise woman: and
4 K 3 9 they fetched a compass of seven days'
Lam 5 9 we fetched our bread at the peril of
fetching 1 K 17 49 fetching it about struck the
fettered Ps 145 7 Lord looseth them that are f.
Wisd 17 2 being f. with the bonds of darkness
fetters 2 K 3 34 nor thy feet laden with fetters
2 Pa 33 11 carried him bound with chains and f.
Ps 101 21 the groans of them that are in fetters
104 18 they humbled his feet in fetters: the
149 8 to bind their kings with fetters and
Eccu 6 25 put thy feet into her fetters and thy

50 shall her fetters be a strong defence
21 22 doctrine to a fool is as fetters on
33 28 and fetters are for a malicious slave
30 obedient, bring him down with fetters
Jer 39 7 bound him [Sedecias] with f. 52:11
Lam 3 7 get out: he hath made my fetters heavy
Nah 3 10 all her great men were bound in fetters
Mark 5 4 having been often bound with fetters
4 and broken the fetters in pieces and
Luke 8 29 bound with chains and kept in fetters
fever Deut 28 22 afflict thee . . . with the fever
Mat 8 14 wife's mother lying and sick of a fever
15 the fever left her and. Mark 1:31
Mark 1 30 wife's mother lay in a fit of a fever
Luke 4 38 mother was taken with a great fever
39 commanded the fever, and it left her
John 4 52 at the seventh hour the fever left him
Acts 28 8 father of Publius lay sick of a fever
few Gen 27 44 shalt dwell with him a few days
Gen 29 20 they seemed but a few days because
34 30 we are few: they will gather themselves
47 9 days of my pilgrimage . . . few and evil
Lev 25 52 if few, he shall make the reckoning
26 22 your cattle, and make you few in number
Num 13 19 whether they be . . . few in number or
Deut 4 27 shall remain a few among the nations
28 62 you shall remain few in number, who
Josu 7 3 against enemies that are very few
1 K 14 6 Lord to save either by many or by few
17 28 why didst thou leave those few sheep
18 27 after a few days David rose up and
4 K 4 3 go, borrow . . . empty vessels not a few
1 Pa 16 19 small number: very few and sojourners
2 Pa 14 11 whether thou help with few or with many
29 34 priests were few and were not enough
2 Es 2 12 arose in the night, I and some few men
7 4 the people few in the midst thereof
Ps 16 14 divide them from the few of the earth
104 12 were but a small number: yea very few
106 39 then they were brought to be few: and
108 8 may his days be few: and his bishopric
Ecce 5 1 earth: therefore let thy words be few
9 14 a little city and few men in it: there
Eccu 7 34 purify thyself with a few. Offer to
18 8 so are a few years compared to eternity
20 15 he will give a few things and upbraid
43 36 we have seen but a few of his works
Isa 10 7 and to cut off nations not a few. For
19 trees of his forest shall be so few
24 6 be mad, and few men shall be left
13 as if a few olives, that remain, should
Jer 29 6 and be not few in number. And seek
30 19 they shall not be made few: and I will
42 2 for we are left but a few of many, as
44 28 a few men that shall flee from the
Bar 2 13 are left but a few among the nations
Eze 12 16 I will leave a few men of them from
Dan 7 1 he comprehended it in few words: and
11 20 in a few days he shall be destroyed
1 Ma 3 17 how shall we, being few, be able to
18 to be shut up in the hands of a few
6 54 remained in the holy places but a few
7 1 came up with a few men into a city
28 I will come with a few men to see
9 9 fight against them: for we are but few
12 45 choose thee a few men that may be
15 10 so that few were left with Tryphon
2 Ma 2 22 being but a few, they made themselves
6 17 let this suffice in a few words for a
12 34 that a few of the Jews were slain. But
14 30 together a few of his men and hid
Mat 7 14 to life: and few there are that find it
9 37 great, but laborers are few. Luke 10:2
15 34 a few little fishes. And he. Mark 8:7
20 16 many are called, but few chosen. 22:14
25 21 been faithful over a few things. 23
Mark 6 5 that he cured a few that were sick
Luke 12 48 shall be beaten with few stripes. And
13 23 Lord, are they few that are saved
Acts 17 4 of noble women not a few. But the Jews
12 of men not a few. And when the Jews of
24 4 thy clemency to hear us in few words
Eph 3 3 as I have written above in a few words
Heb 12 10 they indeed for a few days according
13 22 I have written to you in a few words
1 P 3 20 wherein a few, that is, eight souls
Apoc 2 14 but I have against thee a few things. 20
3 4 but thou hast a few names in Sardis
fewer Num 26 54 to the fewer a less [portion]
Num 26 56 shall be taken by the more or the fewer
33 54 larger part, and to the fewer a lesser
35 8 from them that have less, fewer. Each
2 Ma 5 5 taking with him no fewer than 1,000 men
8 9 giving him no fewer than 20,000 armed
10 17 slew . . . no fewer than 20,000. And
12 4 drowned no fewer than 200 of them
fewest Deut 7 7 you are the fewest of any people
fewness Job 10 20 f. of my days be ended shortly
Ps 101 24 declare unto me the fewness of my days
fidelity Gen 39 16 a proof therefore of her f.
2 K 15 20 thou hast shown grace and fidelity
Esth 6 3 hath Mardochai received for his f.
13 3 excelled the rest in wisdom and f.
13 by whose fidelity and good services
16 23 receive a worthy reward for their f.
Eccu 6 15 to countervail the goodness of his f.
15 16 if thou . . . perform acceptable f.
22 28 keep fidelity with a friend in his
27 18 and be joined to him with fidelity
40 12 and fidelity shall stand forever. The
46 17 by his f. he was proved a prophet. And
1 Ma 10 27 continue still to keep f. towards us
2 Ma 14 8 out of fidelity to the king's interest
Rom 1 31 without fidelity, without mercy. Who
Titus 2 10 in all things showing good fidelity
field Gen 2 5 every plant of the field before it
Gen 2 20 Adam called . . . all the cattle of the f.
4 8 when they were in the field, Cain rose
23 9 cave which he hath in the end of his f.
11 the field I deliver to thee, and the
13 I will give money for the field: take
17 the field that before was Ephron's
19 buried Sara . . . in double cave of the f.
20 the field was made sure to Abraham
24 63 gone forth to meditate in the field
65 who cometh towards us along the field
25 9 which was situated in f. of Ephron
29 Esau, coming faint out of the field
27 5 he [Esau] was gone into the field to
27 is as the smell of a plentiful field
29 2 he [Jacob] saw a well in the field
30 14 Ruben, going out . . . into the field
16 when Jacob returned at even from the f.
31 4 called Rachel and Lia into the field
33 19 he [Jacob] bought that part of the field
34 7 behold his sons came from the field
37 7 we were binding sheaves in the field
15 found him there wandering in the f.
49 29 cave which is in the field of Ephron
30 Abraham bought . . . with the f. of Ephron
50 13 bought together with the field for a
Exod 9 19 all that thou hast in the field: for
22 hail . . . upon every herb of the field
25 the hail smote every herb of the field
16 25 today it shall not be found in the f.
22 5 restore the best . . . in his own field

5 if any man hurt a field or a vineyard
23 16 whatsoever thou hast sown in the field
16 gathered in all the corn out of the f.
Lev 14 7 sparrow that it may fly into the field
53 to fly freely away into the field
17 5 victims which they kill in the field
19 19 not sow thy field with different seeds
25 3 six years thou shalt sow thy field
4 thou shalt not sow thy field nor prune
11 the things that grow in the f. of their
27 16 if he vow the field of his possession
17 if he vow his field immediately from
19 he that vowed will redeem his field
22 if a field that was bought, and not of
28 to the Lord, whether it be . . . field
Num 19 16 if any man in the field touch the corpse
22 23 out of the way and went into the field
Deut 5 21 thou shalt not covet . . . his field
22 25 if a man find a damsel . . . in the f.
27 she was alone in the field: she cried
24 19 thou hast reaped the corn in thy field
28 3 be in the city, and blessed in the field
16 thou be in the city, cursed in the field
Josu 5 13 when Josue was in the field of the city
11 8 as far as . . . the field of Masphe
12 7 from Baalgad in the field of Libanus
15 18 her husband to ask a field of her father
24 32 the field which Jacob had bought of the
Judg 1 14 husband admonished her to ask a field
9 32 that is with thee and lie hid in the f.
42 people went out into the field. 2 K 18:6
44 enemies that were scattered about the f.
13 9 to his wife as she was sitting in field
19 16 an old man returning out of the field
Ruth 2 2 I will go into the field and glean
3 the owner of that field was Booz, who
7 she hath been in the field from morning
8 do not go to glean in any other field
17 she gleaned therefore in the field till
22 lest in another man's field some one
3 2 with whose maids . . . in the field is
4 4 he answered: I will buy the field. And
5 when thou shalt buy the field at the
1 K 4 16 and have fled out of the field this day
6 14 the cart came into the field of Josue
18 was till that day in the field of Josue
11 5 Saul came, following oxen out of the f.
19 3 and stand beside my father in the field
20 5 that I may be hid in the field till
11 and let us go out into the field. And
11 were both of them gone out into the f.
24 so David was hid in the field, and the
35 Jonathan went into the field, according
30 11 they found an Egyptian in the field
2 K 2 16 was called: The field of the valiant
10 8 were by themselves in the field. Then
11 23 and they came out to us into the field
14 6 quarrelled with each other in the field
30 you know field of Joab near my field
30 have set part of the field on fire
20 12 Amasa out of the highway into the field
23 11 there was a field full of lentils. And
12 he stood in the midst of the field and
3 K 11 29 and they two were alone in the field
14 11 them that shall die in the field, the
21 23 shall eat Jezabel in field. 4 K 9:10
24 if he [Achab] die in field, the birds
4 K 3 19 goodly field you shall cover with stones
25 and they filled every goodly field
4 39 out into the field to gather wild herbs
39 gathered of it wild gourds of the field
21 and met him in the field of Naboth
25 and cast him into the field of Naboth
26 if I do not requite thee in this field
26 take him and cast him into the field
36 in the field of Jezrahel the dogs shall
37 flesh of Jezabel . . . in f. of Jezrahel
18 17 which is in the way of the fuller's f.
19 26 they became like the grass of the field
1 Pa 11 13 field of that country was full of barley
14 these men stood in midst of the field
19 9 the kings . . . stood apart in the field
2 Pa 26 23 buried him in field of royal sepulchers
35 22 went to fight in the field of Mageddo
Jdth 8 2 them that bound sheaves in the field
Job 24 6 they reap the field that is not their
Ps 49 11 with me is the beauty of the field
77 12 did he do . . . in the field of Tanis
43 his wonders in the field of Tanis. And
102 15 as flower of the f. so shall he flourish
103 16 the trees of the field shall be filled
Prov 23 10 enter not into field of the fatherless
24 30 I passed by the field of the slothful
27 26 and kids for the price of the field
31 16 she hath considered a field and bought
Cant 2 1 I am the flower of the field and the
7 11 beloved, let us go forth into the field
Wisd 17 16 if any one . . . a laborer in the field
19 7 out of the great deep a springing field
Eccu 37 13 nor with the field laborer of every work
Isa 5 8 lay field to field, even to the end of
7 3 in the way of the fuller's field. 36:2
37 27 they became like the grass of the field
40 6 glory thereof as the flower of the field
43 20 the beast of the field shall glorify me
63 14 as a beast that goeth down in the field
Jer 7 20 my wrath . . . upon the trees of the field
12 4 long . . . herb of every field wither
13 27 abominations upon the hills in the field
14 5 the hind also brought forth in the field
17 2 children . . . sacrificing in the field
18 14 fail from the rock of the field? Or can
26 18 Sion shall be plowed like a field, and
32 7 thee my field which is in Anathoth. 8
9 I bought the f. of Hanameel my uncle's
25 buy a field for money and take witnesses
35 9 nor to have vineyard or field or seed
41 8 we have stores in the field, of wheat
Eze 7 15 that is in the field shall die by sword
16 7 to multiply as the bud of the field
20 46 prophesy against forest of the south f.
26 6 her daughters also that are in the field
8 thy daughters that are in the field
31 15 all the trees of the field trembled
32 4 I will cast thee away into the open f.
33 27 that is in the field, shall be given to
34 27 tree of the field shall yield its fruit
36 30 will multiply . . . increase of the field
39 5 shalt fall upon the face of the field
Dan 14 32 was going into the field, to carry it
Osee 10 4 as bitterness in the furrows of the f.
12 11 are as heaps in the furrows of the field
13 8 the beast of the field shall tear them
Joel 1 11 the harvest of the field is perished
12 all the trees of the field are withered
Mich 1 6 as a heap of stones in the field when
3 12 Sion shall be plowed as a field, and
Zach 10 1 to every one grass in the field. For
Mala 3 11 neither shall vine in the f. be barren
Mat 6 28 consider the lilies of the field, how
30 if the grass of the field, which is
13 24 man that sowed good seed in his field
27 thou not sow good seed in thy field
31 a man took and sowed in his field. Which
36 the parable of the cockle of the field
38 the field is the world. And the good

44 like unto a treasure hidden in a field
44 all that he hath and buyeth that field
24 18 he that is in the field, let him not
40 two shall be in the field. Luke 17:35
27 7 bought with them the potter's field
8 that field was called Haceldama, that
8 Haceldama, that is, The field of blood
10 they gave them unto the potter's field
Mark 31 16 that shall be in the field. Luke 17:31
Luke 12 28 the grass that is today in the field
15 25 now his elder son was in the field
17 7 him, when he is come from the field
Acts 1 18 hath possessed a field of the reward
19 same field was called in their tongue
19 that is to say, The field of blood
fields Gen 34 28 their houses and in the fields
Gen 39 5 substance both at home and in the fields
47 23 to Pharao: Take seed and sow the fields
Exod 8 13 out of the villages and out of the f.
9 3 my hand shall be upon thy fields: and
19 not gathered together out of the fields
21 his servants and his cattle in the f.
25 all that were in the f., both men and
10 5 all the trees that spring in the fields
22 6 or corn standing in the fields, he that
Lev 25 31 sold acccording to the same law as the f.
Num 16 14 hast given us possessions of fields
20 17 we will not go through the fields
21 22 we will not go aside into the fields
Deut 11 15 your hay out of the fields to feed your
32 13 that he might eat the fruits of the f.
Josu 4 13 marched through the plains and fields
21 12 the fields and the villages thereof he
Judg 9 27 went out into the fields, wasting
43 laid ambushes in the fields. And seeing
1 K 4 2 here and there in the fields about 4,000
5 6 in the villages and fields in the midst
8 12 to plow his fields and to reap his
14 he will take your fields and your
14 15 miracle in the camp through the fields
22 7 son of Isai give every one of you f.
2 K 1 21 neither be they fields of firstfruits
4 K 7 12 out of camp and lie hid in the fields
1 Pa 6 56 the fields of the city . . . to Caleb
16 32 let the fields rejoice, and all things
2 Pa 31 19 sons of Aaron who were in the fields
2 Es 5 4 let us give up our fields and vineyards
5 our fields and our vineyards other men
11 restore ye to them this day their f.
Jdth 3 3 all mountains and hills and fields
15 2 and fled by the ways of the fields
Ps 64 12 thy fields shall be filled with plenty
95 12 the fields and all things that are in
106 37 they sowed f. and planted vineyards
131 6 have found it in the fields of the wood
Cant 2 7 roes and the harts of the fields. 3:5
Eccu 40 22 more than these green sown fields
Jer 4 17 round about her as keepers of fields
6 25 go not out into the fields nor walk
8 10 their f. to others for an inheritance
14 18 if I go forth into the fields, behold
23 3 will make them return to their own f.
10 the fields of the desert are dried up
25 37 the fields of peace have been silent
32 15 fields and vineyards shall be possessed
43 fields shall be purchased in this land
44 fields shall be bought for money and
Mich 2 2 they have coveted fields, and taken
Haba 3 17 and the fields shall yield no food: the
1 Ma 14 8 and the trees of the fields their fruit
16 10 towers that were in the f. of Azotus
Mark 2 23 Lord walked through the corn fields on
5 14 told it in the city and in the fields
Luke 6 1 as he went through the corn fields
James 5 4 who have reaped down your fields, which
fierce 2 K 2 17 was a very fierce battle that day
2 Pa 28 13 the fierce anger of the Lord. Jer 4:8; 25:37, 38; Soph 2:2
Wisd 11 18 a multitude of bears or fierce lions
16 5 when the fierce rage of beasts came
24 is made fierce against the unjust for
18 15 as a fierce conqueror into the midst
Isa 13 13 and for the day of his fierce wrath
Jer 12 13 the fierce wrath of the Lord. 51:45
49 37 will bring evil upon them, my f. wrath
Lam 1 12 spoke in the day of his fierce anger
2 3 he hath broken in his fierce anger
4 11 he hath poured out his fierce anger
Jon 3 9 will turn away from his fierce anger
Soph 3 8 indignation, all my fierce anger
2 Ma 10 35 pushing forward with fierce courage
Mat 8 28 exceeding fierce, so that none could
fiercely 1 Ma 6 33 made his troops march on f.
2 Ma 3 25 he ran f. and struck Heliodorus with
15 2 do not act so f. and barbarously, but
12 15 time of Josue, f. assaulted the walls
fierceness Jdth 3 11 mitigate the f. of his heart
Osee 11 9 I will not execute the f. of my wrath
Nah 1 6 shall resist in the f. of his anger
1 Ma 6 47 of the king and the f. of his army
2 Ma 15 21 of armor, and the f. of the beasts
Heb 11 27 not fearing the fierceness of the king
Apoc 19 15 the fierceness of the wrath of God
fiercest 2 Ma 11 9 but also the f. beasts and
fiery Num 21 6 among the people fiery serpents
Deut 33 2 saints. In his right hand a fiery law
4 K 2 11 behold a fiery chariot and fiery horses
Wisd 11 19 breathing out a fiery vapor or sending
Eccu 43 4 breathing out fiery vapors and who
48 9 of fire, in a chariot of fiery horses
Dan 3 93 door of the burning fiery furnace, and
2 Ma 10 3 taking fire out of the fiery stones
Eph 6 16 be able to extinguish all the f. darts
fifties Exod 18 21 of hundreds and of fifties and
Exod 18 25 over fifties and over tens. Deut 1:15
4 K 1 14 and the fifties that were with them
1 Ma 3 55 appointed captains . . . over fifties
Mark 6 40 in ranks, by hundreds and by fifties
Luke 9 14 make them sit down by fifties in a
fig Gen 3 7 they sewed together fig leaves, and
Deut 8 8 wherein fig trees and pomegranates and
1 Pa 27 28 over the oliveyards and the fig groves
Ps 104 33 vineyards and their fig trees: and he
Jer 50 39 dragons dwell there with the fig fauns
Osee 2 12 will destroy her vines and her fig trees
Amos 4 9 your olive groves and fig groves: yet
Nah 3 12 thy strongholds shall be like fig trees
fig tree Judg 9 10 trees said to the fir tree
3 K 4 25 under his vine and under his fig tree. Mich 4:4; 1 Ma 14:12
4 K 18 31 own vineyard and of his own fig tree
Prov 27 18 he that keepeth the fig tree shall eat
Cant 2 13 fig tree hath put forth her green figs
Isa 34 4 falleth from the vine and from the f. t.
36 16 his vine and every one of his fig tree
Jer 8 13 there are no figs on the fig tree, the
Osee 9 10 like the firstfruits of the fig tree
Joel 1 7 hath pilled off the bark of my fig tree
12 and the fig tree hath languished: the
2 22 fig tree and the vine have yielded
Haba 3 17 fig tree shall not blossom: and there
Agge 2 20 hath the vine and the fig tree and the
Zach 3 10 under the vine and under the fig tree
Mat 21 19 fig tree by the wayside, he came to it
19 immediately the fig tree withered away
21 not only this of the fig tree shall you

24 32 from fig t. learn a parable. Mark 13:28
Mark 11 13 when he had seen afar off a fig tree
20 they saw the fig tree dried up from
21 behold the fig tree which thou didst
Luke 13 6 a certain man had a fig tree planted
7 I come seeking fruit on this fig tree
21 29 see the fig tree and all the trees
John 1 48 when thou wast under the fig tree, I
50 I saw thee under the fig tree, thou
James 3 12 can the fig tree, my brethren, bear
Apoc 6 13 as the fig tree casteth its green figs
fight Gen 49 19 Gad, being girded, shall fight
Exod 14 14 the Lord will fight for you, and you
17 9 go out and fight against Amalec
32 18 not the cry of men encouraging to fight
Num 10 9 against the enemies that fight against
21 33 with all his people to fight in Edrai. Deut 3:1
22 11 if by any means I may fight with them
31 3 arm of you men to fight, who may take
32 6 shall your brethren go to fight and
Deut 1 30 himself will fight for you, as he did
41 we will go up and fight, as the Lord
42 go not up, and fight not, for I am not
2 9 fight not against the Moabites, neither
19 take heed thou fight not against them
32 with all his people to fight at Jasa
3 22 the Lord your God will fight for you
4 34 wonders by fight and a strong hand
20 4 will fight for you against your enemies
9 shall prepare their bands to fight
10 thou come to fight against a city, thou
19 number of them that fight against thee
21 10 if thou go out to fight against thy
25 11 one begin to fight against the other
29 7 Og . . . came out against us to fight
33 7 his hands shall fight for him, and he
Josu 1 14 are strong of hand and fight for them
9 2 to fight against Josue and Israel with
10 25 your enemies, against whom you fight
11 5 waters of Merom, to fight against Israel
19 in Gabaon, for he took all by fight
20 and they should fight against Israel
14 11 this day, as well to fight as to march
22 12 in Silo, to go up and fight against them
33 would go up against them and fight
23 10 Lord your God himself will fight for you
Judg 1 3 and fight against the Chanaanite that
3 2 might learn to fight with their enemies
10 he [Othoniel] went out to fight, and
5 14 they that led the army to fight. The
6 31 avengers of Baal, that you fight for him
8 1 when thou wentest to fight against Madian
9 38 go out and fight against him [Abimelech]
10 18 whosoever . . . shall first begin to fight
11 6 fight against children of Ammon. 8; 12:1
9 that I should fight for you against
32 Jephte passed . . . to fight against them
12 3 you should rise up to fight against me
20 10 that we might fight against Gabaa of
14 to fight against whole people of Israel
17 were found 400,000 . . . prepared to fight
20 from thence to fight against Benjamin
23 shall I go out any more to f. against
24 went out the next day to fight against
28 shall we go out any more to fight
1 K 4 1 gathered themselves together to fight
2 was slain in that fight . . . about 4000
9 have served you: take courage and fight
8 20 before us, and fight our battles for us
11 1 began to fight against Jabes Galaad
13 5 were assembled to fight against Israel
14 20 and they came to the place of the fight
22 with their countrymen in the fight
23 the fight went on as far as Bethaven
15 18 thou [Saul] shalt fight against them
17 2 they set the army in array to fight
8 why are you come out prepared to fight
8 let him come down and fight hand to hand
9 if he be able to fight with me, and
10 let him fight with me hand to hand
20 the army, which was going out to fight
32 go and will fight against the Philistine
33 this Philistine nor to fight against him
48 David made haste and ran to the fight
18 17 and fight the battles of the Lord. Now
23 1 the Philistines fight against Ceila
8 to go down to fight against Ceila
28 15 the Philistines fight against me, and
29 4 when we shall begin to fight: for how
8 that I may not go and fight against
2 K 2 28 Israel any farther nor fight any more
10 12 courage, and let us fight for our people
13 began to fight against the Syrians
11 15 front of battle, where fight is strongest
20 approach so near to the wall to fight
3 K 12 21 to fight against the house of Israel
24 go up nor fight against your brethren
20 14 who shall begin to fight? And he said
18 or whether they come to fight, take them
23 better that we should fight against them
25 we will fight against them in the plains
26 up to Aphee to fight against Israel
39 thy servant went out to fight hand to
22 6 shall I go to Ramoth Galaad to fight
31 you shall not fight against any, small
4 K 3 21 kings were come up to fight against them
8 28 to fight against Hazael king. 2 Pa 22:5
10 3 and fight for the house of your master
16 5 Rasin . . . came up to Jerusalem to fight
19 9 he is come out to fight with thee: and
1 Pa 12 19 with the Philistines against Saul to f.
19 but he [David] did not fight with them
36 and of Aser 40,000 going forth to fight
38 men of war well appointed to fight
2 Pa 11 1 and warriors to fight against Israel
4 not go up nor f. against your brethren
13 12 fight not against the Lord the God of
15 6 for nation shall fight against nation
18 5 shall we go to Ramoth Galaad to f. 14
30 fight ye not with small or great, but
34 and the fight was ended that day: but
20 1 gathered together to f. against Josaphat
17 it shall not be you that shall fight
22 who were come out to fight against Juda
35 20 Mechao king of Egypt came up to fight
21 but I fight against another house
22 would not return but prepared to fight
22 went to fight in the field of Mageddo
2 Es 4 8 to come and to fight against Jerusalem
14 fight for your brethren, your sons and
16 and half were ready for to fight, with
20 unto us: our God will fight for us
Jdth 7 3 to fight against the children of Israel
10 18 for their sakes to fight against them
14 12 have presumed to challenge us to fight
Job 17 3 let any man's hand fight against me
Ps 34 1 overthrow them that fight against me
143 1 who teacheth my hands to fight, and my
Wisd 5 21 the whole world shall fight with him
Eccu 4 33 even unto death fight for justice, and
29 17 it shall fight for thee against thy
46 8 it is not easy to fight against God
Isa 7 1 up to Jerusalem to fight against it
11 13 Juda shall not fight against Ephraim
19 2 Egyptians to f. against the Egyptians
2 they shall f. brother against brother

31 4 Lord of hosts come down to fight upon
37 9 he is come forth to f. against thee
41 11 all that fight against thee shall be
51 22 thy God, who will fight for his people
Jer 1 19 they shall fight against thee. 15:20
21 4 with which you fight against the king
5 I myself will fight against you with
32 5 if you will f. against the Chaldeans
24 the Chaldeans, who fight against it
29 Chaldeans that fight against this
34 22 city, and they shall fight against it
37 7 again and fight against this city
9 the Chaldeans that fight against you
50 14 fight against her, spare not arrows
51 30 of Babylon have forborne to fight
Eze 17 17 shall Pharao fight against him: when
Dan 10 20 to fight against the prince of the
11 11 shall fight against the king of the
40 the king of the south shall fight
Zach 10 5 they shall fight, because the Lord
14 3 shall fight against those nations
14 Juda shall fight against Jerusalem
1 Ma 2 40 and not fight against the heathens
41 against us to fight on the sabbath
41 we will fight against him: and we will
3 17 be able to fight against so great a
21 but we will fight for our lives and our
43 let us fight for our people and our
58 that you may fight with these nations
4 21 his army in the plain ready to fight
41 Judas appointed men to fight against
5 31 Judas saw that the fight was begun
32 fight ye today for your brethren. And
39 ready to come to fight against thee
57 let us go f. against the Gentiles
67 they went out unadvisedly to fight
6 34 mulberries to provoke them to fight
7 31 he went out to fight against Judas
9 8 if we may be able to fight against
9 then we will fight against them: for
30 in his stead to fight our battles
44 let us arise and fight against our
10 2 and went forth against him to fight
11 46 kept the passages . . . and began to f.
12 24 than before to fight against him
27 in arms all night long ready to fight
40 but would fight against him: he sought
13 9 fight thou our battles, and we will
14 1 succors to fight against Tryphon. And
13 none left in the land to fight against
26 hath driven away in fight the enemies
15 19 them no harm nor fight against them
19 no aid to them that fight against them
31 we will come and fight against you
16 3 and go out and fight for our nation
2 Ma 7 19 hast attempted to fight against God
8 16 against them, but to fight manfully
12 11 after a hard fight, in which by the help
13 14 exhorted his people to fight manfully
15 17 they resolved to fight and to set upon
Acts 5 39 you be found even to fight against God
1 C 9 26 I so fight, not as one beating the air
1 Tim 6 12 fight the good fight of faith: lay hold
2 Tim 4 7 I have fought a good fight, I have
Heb 10 32 you endured a great f. of affliction
12 1 let us run by patience to the fight
Apoc 2 16 will fight against them with the sword
13 4 who shall be able to fight with him
17 14 these shall fight with the Lamb, and
19 11 with justice doth he judge and fight
fighter Dan 11 22 arms of f. shall be overcome
fightest 1 K 25 28 fightest the battles of the Lord
fighteth Exod 14 25 Lord f. for them against us
Deut 20 20 take the city which f. against thee
2 Pa 32 8 the Lord our God . . . fighteth for us
Wisd 16 17 for the world fighteth for the just
Eccu 38 29 he f. with the heat of the furnace
fighting Num 32 21 let every f. man pass over the
Josu 10 14 voice of a man and fighting for Israel
Judg 11 23 his people of Israel f. against him
20 16 f. with the left hand as well as with
1 K 17 19 of Terebinth f. against Philistines
2 K 12 29 and after fighting he [David] took it
4 K 9 14 he and all Israel f. with Hazael king
Jdth 4 12 not by fighting with the sword but by
Ps 55 2 hath afflicted me fighting against me
Eccu 46 19 in f. against the enemies who beset
Isa 37 26 hills f. together, and fenced cities
1 Ma 7 28 there be no fighting between me and
8 26 give them, whilst they are fighting
2 Ma 15 27 f. with their hands, but praying
Rom 7 23 fighting against the law of my mind
fighting men Num 2 4 whole sum of the f. men
Num 2 6 the whole number of his fighting men
8 the army of fighting men of his stock
11 the whole army of his fighting men. 13, 15, 19, 21, 23, 26, 28, 30
31 49 have reckoned the number of the f. men
Deut 2 16 after all the fighting men were dead
Josu 4 13 and 40,000 f. men by their troops and
6 3 round about the city, all ye f. men
7 4 there went up therefore 3,000 f. men
8 1 all the multitude of fighting men
3 all the army of fighting men with him
10 with the aid of the fighting men. And
10 2 all its fighting men were most valiant
Judg 4 6 thou shalt take with thee 10,000 f. men
14 and 10,000 fighting men with him. And
20 46 and 20,000 f. men, most valiant for
2 K 24 9 and of Juda 500,000 fighting men. But
4 K 19 25 fenced cities of f. men should be turned
1 Pa 5 18 fighting men, bearing shields and swords
21 5 and of Juda 470,000 fighting men. But
figs Num 13 24 the pomegranates and of the figs
Num 20 5 nor bringeth forth figs nor vines nor
1 K 25 18 and two hundred cakes of dry figs, and
30 12 as also a piece of a cake of figs and
2 K 16 1 a hundred cakes of figs and a vessel
2 loaves and the figs for thy servants
4 K 20 7 Isaias said: Bring me a lump of figs
1 Pa 12 40 to eat: meal, figs, raisins, wine, oil
2 Es 13 15 lading asses with wine and grapes and f.
Jdth 10 5 and parched corn and dry figs and
Cant 2 13 fig tree hath put forth her green figs
Isa 38 21 that they should take a lump of figs
Jer 5 17 shall eat thy vineyards and thy figs
8 13 there are no figs on the fig tree
24 1 behold two baskets full of figs, set
2 the other basket had very bad figs
2 good f. like f. of the first season
3 and I said: Figs, the good figs very good; and the bad figs very bad
5 like these good figs, so will I regard
8 as the very bad figs, that cannot be
29 17 I will make them like bad figs that
Amos 7 14 I am a herdsman plucking wild figs
Mich 7 1 my soul desired the firstripe figs
Nah 3 12 like fig trees with their green figs
Mat 7 16 grapes of thorns, or figs of thistles
Mark 11 13 for it was not the time for figs. And
Luke 6 44 men do not gather figs from thorns
James 3 12 bear grapes; or the vine, figs? So
Apoc 6 13 as the fig tree casteth its green figs
figure Wisd 15 4 a graven f. with divers colors
Wisd 15 5 loveth the lifeless f. of a dead image
Eccu 38 28 graven seals . . . and varieth the f.

49 11 the enemies, under the figure of rain
Eze 24 3 thou shalt speak by a figure a parable
Rom 5 14 Adam, who is a f. of him who was to come
1 C 4 6 a f. transferred to myself and to Apollo
10 6 these things were done in a f. of us
11 these things happened to them in figure
Heb 1 3 glory, and the figure of his substance
figures Lev 19 28 in yourselves any f. or marks
Num 12 8 not by riddles and f. doth he see the
3 K 6 29 he carved with divers f. and carvings
32 f. of cherubims and f. of palm trees
4 K 23 24 figures of idols . . . Josias took away
Eze 41 25 temple, and the figures of palm trees
Acts 7 43 figures which you made to adore them
file Isa 44 12 smith hath wrought with his file
files Acts 12 4 delivering him to four files of
fillet Exod 28 28 a violet fillet. 37; 39:19, 30
Ecce 12 6 before . . . the golden fillet shrink
filleth Job 9 18 he filleth me with bitterness
Ps 128 7 wherewith the mower f. not his hand
147 14 and filleth thee with the fat of corn
Prov 13 25 the just eateth and filleth his soul
Eccu 24 35 who filleth up wisdom as the Phison
filling Gen 26 15 filling them up with earth
Exod 40 28 the laver . . . filling it with water
4 K 24 4 filling Jerusalem with innocent blood
Eccu 1 22 crown of wisdom, filling up peace and
Mark 15 36 one running and filling a sponge with
Acts 14 16 f. our hearts with food and gladness
Col 2 23 in any honor to the filling of the flesh
filth Exod 32 25 by occasion of the shame of the f.
Lev 15 31 that they may not die in their filth
16 16 in midst of the f. of their habitation
Deut 7 26 abhor it as uncleanness and filth
28 57 the filth of the afterbirths, that come
29 17 have seen their abominations and filth
32 5 are none of his children in their filth
3 K 15 12 he removed all the filth of the idols
2 Pa 29 5 take away all f. out of the sanctuary
1 Es 9 11 who have filled it . . . with their f.
Job 7 5 clothed with rottenness and f. of dust
9 31 yet thou shalt plunge me in filth
Isa 4 4 if the Lord shall wash away the filth
28 8 all tables were full of vomit and f.
Jer 2 24 in her monthly f. they shall find her
Eze 24 11 let the filth of it be melted in the
1 P 3 21 putting away of the filth of the flesh
filthiness 1 Es 6 21 from the f. of the nations
Prov 30 12 are not washed from their filthiness
Wisd 2 16 he abstaineth from our ways as from f.
Lam 1 9 her f. is on her feet, and she hath
Eze 24 13 art not cleansed from thy filthiness
36 25 you shall be cleansed from all your f.
Osee 5 11 because he began to go after f. And
2 Ma 9 9 the f. of his smell was noisome to the
Mat 23 27 dead men's bones and of all filthiness
Apoc 17 4 full of the abomination and filthiness
filthy Lev 15 3 when a f. humor at every moment
3 K 15 13 broke in pieces the filthy idol and
4 K 21 11 Juda also to sin with his f. doings
Ps 9 5 his ways are filthy at all times. Thy
Eze 4 13 eat their bread all filthy among the
22 5 thou filthy one, infamous, great in
Zach 3 3 Jesus was clothed with f. garments
4 take away the filthy garments from
Rom 1 27 men with men working that which is f.
Col 3 8 filthy speech out of your mouth. Lie
1 Tim 3 8 to much wine, not greedy of f. lucre
Titus 1 7 no striker, not greedy of f. lucre
11 not for filthy lucre's sake. 1 P 5:2
Apoc 22 11 he that is filthy, let him be filthy
finally Eph 6 10 f., brethren, be strengthened in
find Mat 7 7 seek and you shall find. Luke 11:9
Mat 7 14 to life: and few there are that find it
10 39 lose his life . . . shall find it. 16:25
11 29 you shall find rest to your souls
17 26 thou shalt find a stater: take that
18 13 if it so be that he find it: Amen
21 2 you shall find an ass tied and a colt
22 9 as many as you shall find, call to the
24 46 lord shall come he shall find so doing
Mark 11 2 you shall find a colt tied, upon which
13 perhaps he might find anything on it
13 36 on a sudden, he find you sleeping. And
Luke 2 12 you shall find the infant wrapped in
5 19 they could not find by what way they
6 7 that they might find an accusation
12 37 when he cometh, shall find watching
38 the third watch, and find them so
43 lord shall come, he shall find so doing
13 7 on this fig tree, and I find none. Cut
15 4 that which was lost until he find it
8 and seek diligently until she find it
18 8 shall he find, think you, faith on
19 30 you shall find the colt of an ass tied
23 4 find no cause in this man. 14
22 I find no cause of death in him. I
John 7 34 shall seek me and shall not f. me. 36
35 will he go, that we shall not find him
10 9 and go out and shall find pastures
18 38 I find no cause in him. 19:4, 6
21 6 right side of the ship and you shall f.
Acts 7 46 desired to find a tabernacle for the
17 27 they may feel after him or find him
23 9 we find no evil in this man [Paul]
24 12 they find me disputing with any man, or
Rom 7 18 accomplish that which is good, I f. not
21 I find a law, that when I have a will
9 19 why doth he then find fault? For who
2 C 9 4 with me, and find you unprepared, we
12 20 I shall not find you such as I would
2 Tim 1 18 Lord grant unto him to find mercy of
Heb 4 16 mercy, and find grace in seasonable aid
11 35 they might find a better resurrection
Apoc 3 2 I find not thy works full before my
9 6 shall seek death, and shall not find it
18 14 they shall find them no more at all
findeth Mat 7 8 he that seeketh, f. Luke 11:10
Mat 10 39 he that f. his life, shall lose it
12 43 places seeking rest, and findeth none
44 findeth it empty, swept, and garnished
26 40 disciples, and findeth them asleep
43 and findeth them sleeping. Mark 14:37
Luke 11 25 he findeth it swept and garnished
John 1 41 he findeth first his brother Simon
43 he findeth Philip. And Jesus saith to
45 Philip findeth Nathanael, and saith to
5 14 Jesus findeth him in the temple, and
finding Luke 2 45 not f. him, they returned
Luke 11 24 seeking rest; and not finding, he
24 23 not finding his body, came, saying
Acts 4 21 not finding how they might punish them
13 28 finding no cause of death in him, they
17 6 not finding them, they drew Jason and
18 2 finding a certain Jew, named Aquila
21 4 f. disciples, we tarried there 7 days
27 6 there centurion f. ship of Alexandria
28 14 f. brethren, we were desired to tarry
Heb 8 8 for finding fault with them, he saith
fine 3 K 7 45 the vessels . . . were of fine brass
3 K 10 17 shield. And 300 targets of fine gold
4 K 23 33 and he set a fine upon the land, of a
1 Pa 28 17 censers of f. gold and for little lions
2 Pa 3 5 with plates of fine gold throughout
Job 31 24 if I . . . have said to fine gold: My
Isa 3 23 lawns and headbands and fine veils and

Eze 16 10 and clothed thee with fine garments
23 41 thou sattest on a very fine bed, and a
26 12 and pull down thy fine houses: and
Dan 2 32 head of this statue was of fine gold
James 2 2 having a golden ring, in fine apparel
3 that is clothed with the fine apparel
1 P 3 8 and in fine, be ye all of one mind
Apoc 1 15 his feet like unto fine brass, as in
2 18 fire, and his feet like to fine brass
fine flour; *see* **flour**
fine linen; *see* **linen**
fine twisted linen; *see* **linen**
finest Exod 25 31 candlestick . . . of the f. gold
Exod 37 11 overlaid it with the f. gold. 3 K 10:18
17 of beaten work of the finest gold
Lev 24 2 unto thee the finest and clearest oil
2 Pa 3 7 and the gold . . . was of the finest
4 16 make for Solomon . . . of the finest brass
Isa 13 12 yea a man than the finest of gold
Lam 4 1 dim, the finest color is changed, the
finger Exod 8 19 this is the finger of God. And
Exod 29 12 upon horns of the altar with thy finger
31 18 written with the finger of God. And the
Lev 4 6 having dipped his finger in the blood
17 priest . . . shall dip his finger in it
30 shall take of the blood with his finger
8 15 dipping his finger in it, he touched
9 9 he dipped his f. therein and touched
14 16 shall dip his right finger in it, and
27 dipping the finger of his right hand in
16 14 sprinkle with his finger seven times
19 sprinkling with his finger seven times
Num 19 4 dipping his finger in her blood, shall
Deut 9 10 tables of stone written with f. of God
Judg 18 19 and put thy finger on thy mouth and
3 K 12 10 my little f. is thicker than. 2 Pa 10:10
Job 21 5 and lay your finger on your mouth
29 9 princes . . . laid the f. on their mouth
Prov 6 13 with the foot, speaketh with the finger
Isa 58 9 and cease to stretch out the finger
Mat 23 4 but with a finger of their own they
Luke 11 20 if I by the finger of God cast out
16 24 that he may dip the tip of his finger
John 8 6 wrote with his finger on the ground
20 25 except I . . . put my finger into the
27 put in thy finger hither, and see my
fingers Judg 1 6 and cut off his fingers and toes
Judg 1 7 having their fingers and toes cut off
2 K 21 20 that had six fingers on each hand
1 Pa 20 6 fingers and toes were four and twenty
Ps 8 4 thy heavens, the works of thy fingers
143 1 who teacheth . . . my fingers to war
Prov 7 3 bind it upon thy fingers, write it
31 19 her f. have taken hold of the spindle
Cant 5 5 my fingers were full of choicest myrrh
Wisd 15 15 hear, not fingers of hands to handle
Isa 2 8 which their own fingers have made
17 8 the things that his fingers wrought
40 12 with three f. the bulk of the earth
59 3 your f. [are defiled] with iniquity
Jer 52 21 thickness thereof was four fingers
Dan 5 5 appeared fingers, as it were of the
Mark 7 33 he put his fingers into his ears and
Luke 11 46 the packs with one of your fingers
fingers' Exod 37 12 crown of gold, of 4 f. breadth
fining-pot Prov 27 21 silver is tried in the f.
finish Gen 6 16 a cubit shalt thou f. the top
Job 6 28 finish what you have begun: give ear
Eccu 38 28 by his watching shall f. the work
31 he setteth his mind to f. his work
34 shall give his mind to f. the glazing
Zach 4 9 house, and his hands shall finish it
1 Ma 13 10 made haste to finish all the walls of
Mat 10 23 you shall not finish all the cities of
Luke 14 28 whether he have wherewithal to f. it
29 and is not able to finish it, all that
30 began to build and was not able to f.
Rom 9 28 for he shall finish his word, and cut
2 C 8 6 he would f. among you this same grace
Heb 8 5 when he was to finish the tabernacle
finished Gen 2 1 heavens and the earth were f.
Exod 39 31 work of the tabernacle . . . was f.
43 when Moses saw all things finished
Lev 8 33 in seven days the consecration is f.
9 22 and the peace offerings being finished
Num 7 1 Moses had finished the tabernacle, and
Deut 31 24 this law in a volume, and finished it
30 Moses . . . finished it even to the end
3 K 6 9 built the house and finished it. 14
38 house was f. in all the works thereof
7 22 so the work of the pillars was finished
40 finished all the work of king Solomon
51 Solomon finished all the work that he
9 1 when Solomon had f. the building of the
25 the temple was finished. And king
4 K 12 12 the repairs . . . might be completely f.
1 Pa 27 24 Joab . . . began to number but he f. not
28 20 till thou hast finished all the work
2 Pa 4 11 and finished all the king's work in the
22 and thus all the work was finished
7 11 Solomon finished the house of the Lord
8 16 until the day wherein he finished it
24 14 when they had finished all the works
29 17 they finished what they had begun
28 their office till the holocaust was f.
31 7 in the seventh month they finished them
1 Es 5 16 in building and is not yet finished
6 14 built and f. by the commandment of
2 Es 6 15 the wall was f. the five and twentieth
Eccu 50 21 and they had finished their office
Dan 5 26 numbered thy kingdom and hath f. it
9 24 that transgression may be finished
12 7 all these things shall be finished
1 Ma 4 51 f. all the works that they had begun
Mat 13 53 when Jesus had finished these parables
Luke 7 1 when he had finished all his words
John 17 4 I have f. the work which thou gavest
Acts 21 7 we having finished the voyage by sea
2 Tim 4 7 fight, I have finished my course, I
Heb 4 3 foundation of the world were finished
Apoc 10 7 the mystery of God shall be finished
11 7 when they shall have finished their
20 3 till the thousand years be finished
5 till the thousand years were finished
7 when the thousand years shall be f.
finisher Heb 12 2 Jesus, the author and f. of faith
finishing 1 Es 6 15 were f. this house of God
Ps 28 1 at the finishing of the tabernacle
Eccu 37 14 of the finishing of the year nor
2 Ma 2 9 and of the finishing of the temple
fins Lev 11 9 lawful to eat. All that hath fins
Lev 11 10 whatsoever hath not fins and scales
Deut 14 9 all that have fins and scales, you shall
10 without fins and scales, you shall not
fir 3 K 5 8 cedar trees and fir trees. 10; 9:11
3 K 6 15 floor of the house with planks of fir
34 two doors of fir tree, one of each
4 K 19 23 tall cedars and its choice fir trees
2 Pa 2 8 send me also cedars and fir trees
Isa 14 8 the fir trees also have rejoiced over
37 24 tall cedars and its choice fir trees
41 19 I will set in the desert the fir tree
55 13 the shrub, shall come up the fir tree
60 13 to thee, the fir tree and the box tree
Eze 27 5 with fir trees of Sanir they have built
31 8 the fir trees did not equal his top

Osee 14 9 make him flourish like a green fir tree
Zach 11 2 howl, thou fir tree, for the cedar is
fire Gen 11 3 make brick and bake them with fire
Gen 15 17 a lamp of fire passing between those
19 24 brimstone and fire from the Lord out
22 6 carried in his hands fire and a sword
7 behold, saith he, fire and wood: where
Exod 3 2 Lord appeared to him in a flame of fire
9 24 hail and fire mixed with it drove on
12 8 flesh that night roasted at the fire
9 in water, but only roasted at the fire
13 21 cloud, and by night in a pillar of fire
22 pillar of fire by night. Num 14:14; 2 Es 9:12, 19
14 24 the pillar of fire and of the cloud
19 18 Lord was come down upon it in fire
22 6 if a fire breaking out light upon
6 that kindled the fire shall make good
35 3 you shall kindle no fire in any of
40 36 and a fire by night in the sight of
Lev 1 7 shall put fire on the altar, having
12 under which the fire is to be put: but
17 putting fire under the wood. 3:5
2 14 thou shalt dry it at the fire and break
3 11 altar, for the food of the fire. 16
14 it for the food of the Lord's fire
6 9 the fire shall be of the same altar
10 which the devouring fire hath burnt
12 the fire on the altar shall always burn
13 this is the perpetual fire which shall
23 sacrifice . . . be consumed with fire
7 17 on third day shall be consumed with fire
8 20 the fat he burnt in the fire, having
32 the loaves, shall be consumed with fire
9 24 a fire, coming forth from the Lord
10 1 taking their censers, put fire therein
1 offering before the Lord strange fire
2 fire coming out from the Lord. Num 16:35
16 1 upon their offering strange fire: and
13 the perfumes are put upon the fire
23 8 you shall offer sacrifice in fire to
Num 3 4 when they offered strange fire before
6 18 take his hair and lay it upon the fire
9 15 appearance of fire until the morning
16 by night as it were the appearance of f.
11 1 the fire of the Lord being kindled
2 and the fire was swallowed up. And he
3 the fire of the Lord had been kindled
16 7 putting fire in them tomorrow, put
37 take up censers and to scatter the fire
46 putting fire in it from the altar, put
19 5 delivering up to the fire her skin
21 28 a fire is gone out of Hesebon, a flame
26 10 when the fire burned 250 men. And there
61 when they had offered the strange fire
28 6 sweet odor of a sacrifice by fire to
13 sweet odor and an offering by fire
24 seven days for the food of the fire
31 23 all that may pass through the fire shall be purified by fire
23 whatsoever cannot abide the fire, shall
Deut 1 33 showing you the way by fire, and in the
4 24 Lord thy God is a consuming fire, a
36 he showed thee his exceeding great fire
5 5 you feared the fire and went not up
9 3 a devouring and consuming fire to
21 the calf, I took and burned it with f.
12 31 daughters, and burning them with fire
18 10 making them to pass through the fire
16 any more this exceeding great fire
32 22 a fire is kindled in my wrath, and
Josu 7 25 that were his, were consumed with fire
11 11 and burned the city itself with fire
13 very strong he consumed with fire
Judg 6 21 and there arose a fire from the rock
9 15 let fire come out from the bramble
20 let fire come out from him and consume
20 let fire come out from men of Sichem
49 with the smoke and with the fire a
15 5 setting them on fire he let the foxes go
14 to be consumed at the approach of fire
16 9 tow . . . when it smelleth the fire: so
20 38 taken the city, they should make a fire
2 K 22 9 and a devouring fire out of his mouth
13 the coals of fire were kindled. The
31 the word of the Lord is tried by fire
3 K 18 23 and put no fire under it. 25
24 the God that shall answer by fire, let
38 then the fire of the Lord fell, and
19 12 after the earthquake a fire: the Lord is not in the fire
12 after the fire a whistling of a gentle
4 K 1 10 let fire come down from heaven. 12
10 there came down fire from heaven, and
12 fire came down from heaven. 14; 2 Pa 7:1; 2 Ma 2:10
6 17 and chariots of fire round about Eliseus
16 3 son, making him pass through the fire
17 17 sons and their daughters through fire
31 burnt their children in fire to Adramelech
19 18 they have cast their gods into the fire
21 6 he made his son pass through fire
23 10 or his daughter through fire to Moloch
11 burnt the chariots of the sun with fire
1 Pa 21 26 he heard him [David] by sending fire
2 Pa 7 3 saw the fire coming down, and the glory
28 3 and consecrated his sons in the fire
33 6 made his sons to pass through the fire
35 13 and they roasted the phase with fire
2 Es 2 13 thereof which were consumed with fire
17 the gates thereof are consumed with f.
9 7 out of the fire of the Chaldeans, and
Tob 6 19 lay the liver of the fish on the fire
Jdth 16 21 he will give fire and worms into their
Esth 16 24 perish by the sword and by fire, and
Job 1 16 the fire of God fell from heaven, and
15 34 fire shall devour their tabernacles
18 5 and the flame of his fire not shine
20 26 a fire that is not kindled shall devour
22 20 hath not fire devoured the remnants
23 10 as gold that passeth through the fire
28 5 place hath been overturned with fire
31 12 it is a fire that devoureth even to
41 9 his sneezing is like the shining of f.
10 lamps, like torches of lighted fire
Ps 10 7 fire and brimstone and storms of winds
11 7 as silver tried by the fire, purged
16 3 by night, thou hast tried me by fire
17 9 and a fire flamed from his face: coals
13 clouds passed, hail and coals of fire
14 gave his voice: hail and coals of fire
31 the words of the Lord are fire tried
20 10 shalt make them as an oven of fire
10 his wrath, and fire shall devour them
28 7 voice of Lord divideth the flame of f.
38 4 in my meditation a fire shall flame out
45 10 the shield he shall burn in the fire
49 3 a fire shall burn before him: and a
57 9 fire hath fallen on them, and they
65 10 hast tried us by f., as silver is tried
12 we have passed through fire and water
67 3 as wax melteth before the fire, so let
77 14 all the night with a light of fire
21 and a fire was kindled against Jacob
48 to the hail, and their stock to the f.
63 fire consumed their young men: and

78 5 shall thy zeal be kindled like a fire
82 15 as fire which burneth the wood: and
88 47 end? Shall thy anger burn like fire
96 3 a fire shall go before him and shall
101 4 are grown dry like fuel for the fire
104 39 fire to give them light in the night
105 18 fire was kindled in their congregation
117 12 they burned like fire among thorns
139 11 thou wilt cast them down into the fire
148 8 fire, hail, snow, ice, stormy winds
Prov 6 27 can a man hide fire in his bosom, and
17 3 as silver is tried by fire, and gold
26 20 wood faileth, the fire shall go out
21 as . . . wood to fire, so an angry man
30 5 every word of God is fire tried
16 the fire never saith: It is enough
Cant 8 6 the lamps thereof are fire and flames
Wisd 10 6 the fire come down upon Pentapolis
13 2 imagined either the fire or the wind
16 16 hail and rain, and consumed by fire
17 in water . . . the fire had more force
18 at one time the fire was mitigated
19 the fire, above its own power, burned
22 snow and ice endured the force of fire
22 fire burning in the hail and flashing
27 which could not be destroyed by fire
17 5 no power of fire could give them light
6 there appeared to them a sudden fire
18 3 a burning pillar of fire for a guide
19 19 the fire had power in water above its
Eccu 2 5 gold and silver are tried in the fire
3 33 water quencheth a flaming fire, and
7 19 the vengeance . . . is fire and worms
8 4 and heap not wood upon his fire
13 the flame of the fire of their sins
9 9 hereby lust is enkindled as a fire
11 her conversation burneth as fire. Sit
11 34 of one spark cometh a great fire, and
15 17 he hath set water and fire before thee
16 7 of sinners a fire shall be kindled and
20 15 opening of his mouth is kindling of a f.
21 10 the end of them is a flame of fire
22 30 smoke of the fire goeth up before the fire
23 23 not leave off till he hath kindled fire
28 12 wood of forest is, so the fire burneth
13 a hasty contention kindleth a fire
14 blow the spark, it shall burn as a fire
31 31 fire trieth hard iron: so wine drunk
36 11 be consumed by the rage of the fire
38 29 vapor of the fire wasteth his flesh
39 31 for the life of men are water, fire
35 fire, hail, famine, and death, all
40 32 in his belly there shall burn a fire
43 23 consume all that is green as with fire
45 17 his sacrifices were consumed with fire
24 consumed them with a flame of fire
48 1 Elias the prophet stood up as a fire
3 he brought down fire from heaven thrice
9 wast taken up in a whirlwind of fire
50 9 as a bright fire, and frankincense burning in the fire
Isa 4 5 brightness of a flaming f. in the night
5 24 tongue of the f. devoureth the stubble
9 5 shall be burnt, and be fuel for the f.
18 wickedness is kindled as a fire, it
19 the people shall be as fuel for the f.
10 16 as it were the burning of a fire. And
17 the light of Israel shall be as a fire
26 11 let fire devour thy enemies. Lord, thou
29 6 the flame of devouring fire. 30:30
30 14 wherein a little fire may be carried
27 and his tongue as a devouring fire
33 the nourishment thereof is fire and
31 9 hath said it, whose fire is in Sion
33 11 your breath as fire shall devour you
12 shall be as ashes after a fire, as a
14 of you can dwell with devouring fire
43 2 when thou shalt walk in the fire, thou
44 16 I am warm, I have seen the fire. But
19 I have burnt part of it in the fire
47 14 are as stubble, fire hath burnt them
14 nor fire, that they may sit thereat
50 11 all you that kindle a fire . . . walk in the light of your fire
54 16 that bloweth the coals in the fire
64 2 would melt as at the burning of fire
65 5 in my anger, a fire burning all the day
66 15 the Lord will come with fire, and his
15 and his rebuke with flames of fire
16 the Lord shall judge by fire and by
24 and their fire shall not be quenched
Jer 4 4 lest my indignation come forth like fire
5 14 will make my words in thy mouth as fire
6 29 the lead is consumed in the fire, the
7 18 wood, and the fathers kindle the fire
31 sons and their daughters in the fire
11 16 a great fire was kindled in it and the
15 14 a fire is kindled in my rage, it shall
17 4 thou hast kindled a fire in my wrath
27 I will kindle a fire in the gates
21 12 lest my indignation go forth like a fire
14 I will kindle a fire in the forest
22 7 shall cast them headlong into the fire
23 29 are not my words as a fire, saith the
29 22 whom king of Babylon fried in the fire
36 23 consumed with the fire that was on the
43 12 he shall kindle a fire in the temples
48 45 there came a fire out of Hesebon and a
49 27 I will kindle a fire in the wall of. Amos 1:14
50 32 I will kindle a fire in his cities
51 58 of the nations shall go to the fire
Lam 1 13 he hath sent fire into my bones, and
3 in Jacob as it were a flaming fire
4 poured out his indignation like fire
4 11 he hath kindled a fire in Sion, and it
Bar 4 35 f. shall come upon her from the Eternal
6 54 when fire shall fall upon the house of
62 the fire also being sent from above
Eze 1 4 a great cloud, and a fire infolding it
13 was like that of burning coals of fire
13 a bright fire and lightning going forth from the fire
27 as the appearance of fire within it
27 as it were the resemblance of fire
5 4 out of it shall come forth a fire
8 2 a likeness as the appearance of fire
2 of his loins and downward, fire: and
10 2 fill thy hand with the coals of fire
6 take fire from the midst of the wheels
7 stretched out his arm . . . to the fire
15 4 it is cast into the fire for fuel: the
4 fire hath consumed both ends thereof
5 when the fire hath devoured and consumed
6 which I have given to the fire to be
7 they shall go out from fire, and fire shall consume them
16 21 to them, consecrating them by fire
19 12 dried up: the fire hath devoured her
14 a fire is gone out from a rod of her
20 31 your children pass through the fire
47 I will kindle a fire in thee and will
47 flame of the fire shall not be quenched
21 31 in the fire of my rage will I blow upon
32 thou shalt be fuel for the fire, thy
22 20 that I may kindle a fire in it to melt
21 will burn you in the fire of my wrath

31 in the fire of my wrath I consumed them
23 25 thy residue shall be devoured by fire
24 12 thereof is not gone out, not even by f.
28 14 walked in the midst of the stones of f.
16 out of the midst of the stones of fire
18 I will bring forth a fire from the midst
30 8 when I shall have set a fire in Egypt
14 and will make a fire in Taphnis, and
16 I will make a fire in Egypt: Pelusium
36 5 in the fire of my zeal I have spoken
38 19 in my zeal and in the fire of my anger
22 I will rain fire and brimstone upon him
39 6 I will send a fire on Magog and on
Dan 3 22 the flame of the fire slew those men
49 he drove the flame of the fire out of
50 the fire touched them not at all, nor
66 fire and heat, bless the Lord: praise
94 that the fire had no power of their
94 nor the smell of the fire had passed
7 9 his throne like flames of fire: the
10 a swift stream of fire issued forth
11 body . . . given to the fire to be burnt
11 33 shall fall by the sword and by fire
12 10 made white, and shall be tried as fire
Osee 7 6 himself was heated as a flaming fire
8 14 I will send a fire upon his cities
Joel 1 19 fire hath devoured the beautiful. 20
2 3 before the face thereof a devouring f.
5 like the noise of a flame of fire
30 and in earth, blood and fire and vapor
Amos 1 4 I will send a fire into house of Azael
7 will send a fire on the wall of Gaza
10 will send a fire upon the wall of Tyre
12 I will send fire into Theman, and it
2 2 I will send a fire into Moab, and it
5 I will send a fire into Juda, and it
7 4 the Lord called for judgment unto fire
Abdi 18 the house of Jacob shall be a fire
Mich 1 4 shall be cleft, as wax before the fire
6 10 is a fire in the house of the wicked
Nah 1 6 his indignation is poured out like fire
2 3 shield of his mighty men is like fire
3 13 enemies, the fire shall devour thy bars
15 there shall the fire devour thee: thou
Haba 2 13 the people shall labor in a great fire
Soph 1 18 the land shall be devoured by the fire
3 8 with the fire of my jealousy shall all
Zach 2 5 I will be to it . . . a wall of fire
3 2 this a brand plucked out of the fire
9 4 and she shall be devoured with fire
11 1 Libanus, and let fire devour thy cedars
12 6 like a furnace of fire amongst wood
13 9 bring the third part through the fire
Mala 1 10 will kindle the fire on my altar gratis
12 with the fire that devoureth it. And
3 2 he is like a refining fire and like
4 1 day that cometh shall set them on fire
1 Ma 6 39 and they shone like lamps of fire. And
51 engines and instruments to cast fire
2 Ma 1 18 Scenopegia and the day of the fire
19 took privately the fire from the altar
20 they found no fire, but thick water
20 that had hid it, to seek for the fire
22 there was a great fire kindled, so that
33 that were led away, had hid the fire
2 1 commanded them . . . to take the fire
7 5 yet alive, to be brought to the fire
9 7 breathing out fire in his rage against
10 3 taking fire out of the fiery stones
12 6 sword them that escaped from the fire
9 light of the fire was seen at Jerusalem
13 8 the fire and ashes of which were holy
Mat 3 11 baptize you in the Holy Ghost and fire
12 burn with unquenchable fire. Luke 3:17
5 22 fool, shall be in danger of hell fire
13 42 cast them into the furnace of fire. 50
17 14 for he falleth often into the fire and
18 8 feet, to be cast into everlasting fire
9 two eyes, to be cast into hell fire
25 41 you cursed, into everlasting fire
Mark 9 21 hath he cast him into the fire and
42 go into hell, into unquenchable fire
43 the fire is not extinguished. 45, 47
44 into the hell of unquenchable fire
46 to be cast into the hell of fire
48 every one shall be salted with fire
14 54 he sat with the servants at the fire
Luke 3 16 with the Holy Ghost and with fire
9 54 that we command fire to come down
12 49 I am come to cast fire on the earth
17 29 it rained fire and brimstone from
22 55 and when they had kindled a fire in
John 18 18 stood at a fire of coals, because it
Acts 2 3 parted tongues as it were of fire, and
19 blood and fire, and vapor of smoke
7 30 an angel in a flame of fire in a bush
28 2 kindling a fire, they refreshed us all
3 of sticks, and had laid them on the fire
5 he . . . shaking off the beast into the f.
Rom 12 20 shalt heap coals of fire upon his head
1 C 3 13 because it shall be revealed in fire
13 and the fire shall try every man's work
15 himself shall be saved, yet so as by f.
2 C 11 29 who is scandalized, and I am not on f.
2 Th 1 8 in a flame of fire, giving vengeance
Heb 1 7 and his ministers a flame of fire. But
10 27 the rage of a fire which shall consume
11 34 quenched the violence of fire, escaped
12 29 for our God is a consuming fire
James 3 5 how small a fire kindleth a great wood
6 and the tongue is a fire, a world of
5 3 and shall eat your flesh like fire
1 P 1 7 than gold which is tried by the fire
2 P 3 7 reserved unto fire against the day of
12 heavens being on f. shall be dissolved
Jude 7 suffering the punishment of eternal f.
23 save, pulling them out of the fire
Apoc 1 14 and his eyes were as a flame of fire
2 18 hath his eyes like to a flame of fire
3 18 buy of me gold fire tried, that thou
8 5 and filled it with the f. of the altar
7 there followed hail and fire, mingled
8 mountain, burning with fire, was cast
9 17 breastplates of fire and of hyacinth
17 from their mouths proceeded fire and
18 by the fire and by the smoke and by
10 1 his feet as pillars of fire. And he
11 5 fire shall come out of their mouths
13 13 also fire to come down from heaven
14 10 and shall be tormented with fire and
18 who had power over fire; and he cried
15 2 a sea of glass mingled with fire, and
16 8 to afflict men with heat and fire. And
17 16 her flesh and shall burn her with fire
19 12 his eyes were as a flame of fire, and
20 were cast alive into the pool of fire
20 9 came down fire from God out of heaven
9 cast into the pool of fire. 14, 15
21 8 portion in the pool burning with fire

burn with fire; *see* **burn**

burning fire Exod 24 17 the glory of the Lord was like a burning fire
Num 16 39 whom the burning fire had devoured
47 which the burning fire was now destroying
Ps 103 4 makest . . . thy ministers a burning f.

104 32 hail for rain, a b. f. in the land
Prov 16 27 evil, and in his lips is a burning fire
Eccu 23 22 a hot soul is a burning fire, it will
Jer 20 9 came in my heart as a burning fire
Dan 3 6 into furnace of burning fire. 11, 20, 21
17 to save us from the furnace of b. f.
23 midst of the furnace of burning fire
7 9 the wheels of it like a burning fire
Heb 12 18 a burning fire and a whirlwind and
burnt with fire; *see* **burnt**
cast into the fire; *see* **cast**
midst of the fire Deut 4 12 spoke . . . from the midst of the fire. 15; 9:10; 10:4
Deut 4 33 voice of God speaking out of m. . . .
36 didst hear his words out of the m. . . .
5 4 to face in the mount out of the m. . . .
22 out of the m. . . . and the cloud and
24 have heard his voice out of the m. . . .
26 who speaketh out of the m. . . . , as we
Eccu 51 6 and in the m. . . . I was not burnt. From
Eze 1 4 is, out of the m. . . . as it were the
5 4 cast them in the midst of the fire
Dan 3 25 and opening his mouth in the m. . . .
88 flame and saved us out of the m. . . .
91 cast three men bound into the m. . . .
92 men loose and walking in the m. . . .
93 Abdenago went out from the m. . . .
set fire Judg 9 52 endeavored to set fire to it
2 Pa 36 19 enemies set fire to the house of God
Ps 59 2 when he set fire to Mesopotamia of
73 7 they have set fire to thy sanctuary
Eze 30 8 when I shall have set a fire in Egypt
1 Ma 4 20 that they had set fire to the camp
10 84 Jonathan set fire to Azotus and the
11 48 they set fire to the city and got many
2 Ma 8 33 that had set fire to the holy gates
10 36 to set f. to the towers and the gates
14 41 open the door and to set fire to it
set on fire Josu 8 8 taken it, set it on fire
Josu 8 19 to the city, took it and set it on fire
22 that had taken and set the city on fire
Judg 1 8 set the whole city [Jerusalem] on fire
9 49 surrounding the fort they set it on f.
15 5 which being set on fire, both the corn
2 K 14 30 of barley: go now and set it on fire
30 servants of Absalom set the corn on f.
30 have set part of the field on fire
23 7 they shall be set on fire and burnt
Jdth 2 17 and he set all the corn on fire and he
16 6 that he would set my borders on fire
Ps 9 2 man is proud, the poor is set on fire
79 17 things set on fire and dug down shall
Isa 10 17 and his briers shall be set on fire
27 4 shall I set it on fire together? Or
42 25 set him on fire, and he understood not
Jer 32 29 shall come and set it on fire and burn
Eze 39 9 shall set on fire and burn the weapons
Mala 4 1 that cometh shall set them on fire
2 Ma 8 6 towns and cities, he set them on fire
12 6 set the haven on fire. 9
James 3 6 our nativity, being s. . . . by hell. For
fireballs 2 Ma 10 30 cast darts and f. against
firebrand Amos 4 11 were as a f. plucked out of
Zach 12 6 and as a firebrand amongst hay: and
firebrands Isa 7 4 the two tails of these firebrands
fired Judg 20 42 they that fired the city came
firepans Exod 27 3 thou shalt make . . . firepans
Exod 38 3 he prepared . . . pot-hooks and firepans
Num 4 14 say, firepans, fleshhooks, and forks
fires Exod 35 14 oil for the nourishing of fires
1 Ma 12 28 they kindled fires in their camp. But
firm Exod 15 17 in thy most firm habitation which
2 K 7 16 and thy throne shall be firm forever
23 5 firm in all things and assured. For
3 K 8 13 to be thy most firm throne forever
1 Pa 17 14 his throne shall be most firm forever
2 Pa 6 33 from heaven thy firm dwelling place
39 that is, from thy firm dwelling place
24 13 its former state and made it stand firm
Jdth 5 12 that the waters were made to stand firm
Job 41 15 heart . . . as firm as a smith's anvil
Ps 73 13 by thy strength didst make the sea firm
118 89 thy word standeth firm in heaven. Thy
Prov 12 7 the house of the just shall stand firm
19 21 the will of the Lord shall stand firm
Wisd 6 19 keeping of her laws is f. foundation
Eccu 6 30 her fetters . . . a firm foundation, and
17 24 stand firm in the lot set before thee
26 23 firm feet upon the soles of a steady
Eze 17 5 that it might take a firm root over
1 Ma 2 16 Mathathias and his sons stood firm
13 37 we are ready to make a firm peace with
Rom 4 16 the promise might be firm to all seed
2 Tim 2 19 the sure foundation of God standeth f.
Heb 3 14 hold the beginning of his substance f.
6 19 as an anchor of the soul, sure and firm
2 P 1 19 we have the more firm prophetical word
firmament Gen 1 6 let there be a firmament made
Gen 1 7 God made a firmament and divided the
7 waters that were under the f. from those that were above the f.
8 God called the firmament Heaven; and
15 to shine in the firmament of heaven
17 he set them in the firmament of heaven
20 may fly . . . under the f. of heaven
3 K 8 43 in the firmament of thy dwelling place
49 in heaven, in the f. of thy throne
Ps 17 3 the Lord is my firmament, my refuge
18 2 the f. declareth the work of his hands
24 14 the Lord is a firmament to them that
70 3 thou art my firmament and my refuge
71 16 there shall be a f. on the earth on
150 1 praise ye him in the f. of his power
Eccu 43 1 the firmament on high is his beauty
9 shining gloriously in the firmament
Eze 1 22 was the likeness of the firmament, as
23 under the f. were their wings straight
25 when a voice came from above the f.
26 above the f. that was over their heads
10 1 in the f. that was over the heads of
Dan 3 56 blessed art thou in the f. of heaven
12 3 shall shine as the brightness of the f.
firmly Eccu 42 17 Lord Almighty hath f. settled
first Gen 16 3 after they first dwelt in the land
Gen 25 25 he that came forth first was red and
31 to him: Sell me thy first birthright
32 what will the first birthright avail me
33 to him, and sold his first birthright
34 of having sold his first birthright
27 36 my first birthright he took away before
29 7 f. give the sheep drink, and so lead
26 to give the younger in marriage first
30 41 so when the ewes went first to ram
42 and they of the first time, Jacob's
32 17 he commanded the first, saying: If thou
38 28 saying: This shall come forth the first
40 9 the chief butler first told his dream
43 18 which we carried back the first time
44 19 didst ask thy servants the first time
Exod 10 6 from the time they were first upon the
12 2 it shall be the first in the months
48 his males shall first be circumcised
13 12 all that is first brought forth of
14 27 it returned at the first break of day
28 17 in the first row shall be a sardius
34 26 the first of the fruits of thy ground

39 10 the first row was a sardius, a topaz
Lev 5 8 who shall offer the first for sin
8 21 having first washed the entrails. 9:14
16 3 unless he first do these things: he
Num 2 9 they by their troops shall march first
5 25 yet so as first to take a handful of
10 5 on the east side, shall f. go forward
10 on the first days of your months you
13 first went forward according to the
31 2 revenge first the children of Israel
Deut 2 10 the Emims first were the inhabitants
13 9 let thy hand be first upon him, and
16 1 which is the first [month] of the spring
17 7 hands of the witnesses shall be first
20 10 a city, thou shalt first offer it peace
21 17 this is the first of his children, and
17 to him are due the first birthrights
25 6 and the first son he shall have of her
26 2 shalt take the first of all thy fruits
Josu 8 33 first he blessed the people of Israel
18 11 first came up the lot of the children
21 10 for the first lot came out for them
Judg 10 18 shall first begin to fight against the
11 31 whosoever shall first come forth out
19 5 said to him: taste first a little bread
20 18 the first to go to the battle against
23 so that they first went up and wept
30 as they had done the first and second
Ruth 4 4 besides thee, who art first, and me
1 K 2 16 let the fat first be burnt today
14 14 the first slaughter which Jonathan and
35 [Saul] first began to build an altar
20 2 great or little, without first telling
2 K 17 9 when any one shall fall at the first
19 20 the first of all the house of Joseph
43 why was it not told me first, that I
21 9 died together in the first days of the
23 19 but to the three first he attained not
23 but he attained not to the first three
3 K 17 13 but first make for me of the same meal
18 25 one bullock and dress it first because
20 9 didst send for to me thy servant at f.
17 of the provinces went out first. And
4 K 1 14 and consumed the two first captains
7 5 were come to the f. part of the camp
1 Pa 5 1 his first birthright was given to the
2 the first birthright was accounted to
9 2 first that dwelt in their possession
11 6 shall first strike the Jebusites
6 Joab the son of Sarvia went up first
21 yet he attained not to the first three
25 and the first among the thirty, but
15 13 lest as the Lord at first struck us
23 16 the sons of Gersom: Subuel the first
17 sons of Eliezer were: Rohobia the first
18 the sons of Isaar: Salomith the first
19 the sons of Hebron: Jeriau the first
20 the sons of Oziel: Micha the first
24 7 the first lot came forth to Joiarib
23 Jeriau the first, Amarias the second
25 9 and the first lot came forth to Joseph
27 2 over the first company . . . Jesboam
29 29 the acts of . . . first and last. 2 Pa 9:29; 12:15; 20:34; 25:26; 26:22
2 Pa 16 11 the works of Asa first and last are
17 3 he walked in the first ways of David
28 26 his works first and last are. 35:27
1 Es 9 2 hath been first in his transgression
2 Es 7 5 number of them who came up at first
Tob 3 8 killed them at their first going in to
6 1 he lodged the first night by the river
7 10 unless thou first grant me my petition
Jdth 5 7 they dwelt first in Mesopotamia because
Job 13 4 having first shown that you are forgers
14 9 leaves, as when it was first planted
15 7 art thou the first man that was born
33 when its grapes are in the first flower
18 2 understand f., and so let us speak
Prov 3 9 give him of the f. of all thy fruits
18 17 the just is first accuser of himself
Wisd 6 14 she first showeth herself unto them
7 1 of him that was f. made of the earth
3 the first voice which I uttered was
10 1 preserved him, that was first formed
13 3 the first author of beauty made all
Eccu 4 18 and at the first she chooseth him
12 17 thee, thou shalt find him there first
23 33 first she hath been unfaithful to the
24 38 who first hath perfect knowledge of
31 12 be not the first to open thy mouth
16 stretch not out thy hand first, lest
20 leave off first, for manners' sake
21 reach not out thy hand first of all
21 and be not the first to ask for drink
32 5 to speak the first word with careful
15 but be first to run home to thy house
45 26 prepared them bread in the f. place
Isa 9 1 at the first time the land of Zabulon
41 4 the Lord, I am the first and the last
27 the first shall say to Sion: Behold
42 9 the things that were first, behold
43 27 thy f. father sinned, and thy teachers
44 6 I am the f. and I am the last. 48:12
56 11 gain, from the first even to the last
65 7 I will measure back their first work
Jer 16 18 and I will repay first their double
24 2 figs like the figs of the first season
33 11 captivity of the land as at the first
36 28 words that were in the first volume
50 17 first the king of Assyria devoured
Eze 10 11 the place whither they first turned
29 17 f. month, the f. of the month. 45:18
Dan 7 4 the first was like a lioness, and had
8 three of the first horns were plucked
8 21 horn . . . the same is the first king
Osee 2 7 I will . . . return to my first husband
Mich 4 8 yea the first power shall come, the
Agge 2 4 that saw this house in its first glory
10 this last house more than of the first
Zach 6 2 in the first chariot were red horses
1 Ma 1 1 who first reigned in Greece, coming
2 18 come thou first and obey the king's
5 40 if he pass over unto us first, we
43 he passed over to them first, and all
6 2 that reigned first in Greece, had
7 13 first the Assideans that were among
43 himself was first slain in the battle
8 24 if there come first any war upon the
27 also if war shall come first upon the
10 4 let us first make a peace with him
16 6 so he went over first: then the men
2 Ma 7 4 tongue of him that had spoken first
7 when the first was dead after this
8 received the torments of the first
8 23 himself leading the first band, he
11 7 Machabeus . . . first taking his arms
12 22 when the first hand of Judas came
Mat 5 24 go first to be reconciled to thy
6 33 seek . . . f. kingdom of God. Luke 12:31
7 5 cast out f. the beam out. Luke 6:42
8 21 suffer me f. to go and bury. Luke 9:59
10 2 the first, Simon who is called Peter
12 29 unless he f. bind the strong. Mark 3:27
45 that man is made worse than the first
13 30 gather up first the cockle and bind
17 10 that Elias must come first. Mark 9:10

26 that fish which shall first come up
19 30 that are first, shall be last: and the last shall be first. Mark 10:31
20 8 beginning from the last even to the f.
10 when the first also came, they thought
16 the last be first, and the first last
27 he that will be first among you, shall
21 28 coming to the first, he said: Son, go
31 they say to him: The first. Jesus saith
22 25 the first having married a wife, died
38 greatest and the first commandment
23 6 they love the first places at feasts
6 f. chairs in the synagogues. Luke 20:46
26 first make clean the inside of the cup
27 64 last error shall be worse than the f.
Mark 4 28 fruit first the blade, then the ear
9 11 Elias, when he shall come first, shall
34 if any man desire to be first, he shall
10 44 whosoever will be first among you shall
12 20 the f. took a wife and died. Luke 20:29
28 asked him which was the f. commandment
29 the first commandment of all is, Hear
30 this is the first commandment. And the
39 and to sit in the first chairs in the
13 10 the gospel must first be preached. And
16 9 appeared first to Mary Magdalen, out
Luke 2 2 this enrolling was f. made by Cyrinus
6 1 to pass on the second first sabbath
9 61 let me first take my leave of them
10 5 first say: Peace be to this house. And
11 26 of that man becomes worse than the f.
13 30 they are last that shall be first
30 and they are first that shall be last
14 7 marking how they chose the f. seats
8 sit not down in the first place, lest
18 the first said to him: I have bought
28 doth not first sit down and reckon
31 doth not first sit down and think
15 22 bring forth quickly the first robe
16 5 he said to the first: How much dost
17 25 but first he must suffer many things
19 16 the first came, saying: Lord, thy pound
21 9 these things must first come to pass
John 1 41 he findeth first his brother Simon
2 10 every man at first setteth forth good
5 4 he that went down first into the pond
7 51 any man, unless it first hear him and
8 7 let him first cast a stone at her
12 16 disciples did not know at the first
18 13 they led him away to Annas first, for
19 32 they broke the legs of the first and
39 at the first came to Jesus by night
20 4 came first to the sepulcher. 8
19 that same day, the first of the week
Acts 3 26 to you first God, raising up his Son
7 12 in Egypt, he sent our fathers first
11 26 the disciples were f. named Christians
12 10 passing through the f. and second ward
13 24 John f. preaching, before his coming
46 behoved us f. to speak the word of God
15 14 Simon hath related how God f. visited
26 20 to them first that are at Damascus, and
23 he should be the first that should rise
27 43 cast themselves first into the sea, and
Rom 1 16 to the Jew f., and to the Greek. 2:10
2 9 of the Jew first, and also of the Greek
3 2 much every way. First indeed, because
10 19 first, Moses saith: I will provoke you
11 35 or who hath first given to him, and
15 24 if first, in part, I shall have enjoyed
1 C 11 18 for first of all I hear that when you
12 28 first apostles, secondly prophets
14 30 sitting, let the first hold his peace
15 3 for I delivered unto you first of all
36 is not quickened, except it die first
45 the first man Adam was made into living
46 that was not first which is spiritual
47 first man of the earth, earthly: the
2 C 8 5 they gave their ownselves first to Lord
Eph 4 9 also descended f. into the lower parts
6 2 is the first commandment with a promise
1 Th 4 15 dead who are in Christ, shall rise f.
2 Th 2 3 unless there come a revolt first and
1 Tim 1 16 that in me f. Christ Jesus might show
2 1 I desire therefore, first of all, that
13 for Adam was first formed; then Eve
3 10 let these also first be proved; and so
5 4 let her learn first to govern her own
12 they have made void their first faith
2 Tim 1 5 dwelt first in thy grandmother Lois
2 6 laboreth, must f. partake of the fruits
4 16 at my first answer no man stood with me
Titus 3 10 after the first and second admonition
Heb 1 6 when he bringeth in the first begotten
4 6 they, to whom it was f. preached, did
5 12 the first elements of the words of God
7 2 who first indeed by interpretation, is
27 to offer sacrifices f. for his own sins
9 2 there was a tabernacle made the first
6 into the first tabernacle the priests
18 first indeed dedicated without blood
10 9 he taketh away the first, that he may
12 16 for one mess sold his first birthright
James 3 17 is from above, first indeed is chaste
1 P 4 17 if first at us, what shall be the end
2 P 1 20 understanding this first, that no
3 3 knowing this first, that in the last
1 J 4 10 but because he hath first loved us
19 because God first hath loved us. If
Apoc 1 5 the first begotten of the dead, and the
17 I am the First and the Last. 22:13
2 4 because thou hast left thy f. charity
5 and do penance, and do the first works
8 saith the First and the Last, who was
4 1 the first voice which I heard, as it
7 first living creature was like a lion
8 7 the first angel sounded the trumpet
13 12 to adore the first beast, whose wound
16 2 the first went and poured out his vial
20 5 finished. This is the f. resurrection
6 that hath part in the f. resurrection
21 1 the f. heaven and the f. earth was gone
19 the first foundation was jasper: the

first day Gen 8 5 f. day of the month, the tops
Gen 8 13 first day of the month, the waters were
Exod 12 15 in the first day there shall be no
15 leavened, from first day until seventh
16 the first day shall be holy and solemn
40 2 first day of month, thou shalt set up
15 second year, first day of the month
Lev 23 7 the first day shall be most solemn
24 first day of the month, you shall keep
35 first day shall be called most solemn
39 first day and eighth day shall be a
40 take to you on first day the fruits
Num 1 1 first day of second month. 18
7 12 the first day Nahasson the son of
28 11 first day of month you shall offer
18 first day of them shall be venerable
29 1 f. day of seventh month. 1 Es 3:6; 2 Es 8:2
6 the holocaust of first day of the month
33 38 he died . . . first day of the month when
Deut 1 3 first day of the month, Moses spoke
16 4 of that which was sacrificed the f. day
Judg 20 31 as they had done first and second day
2 Pa 29 17 they began to cleanse on the first day

1 Es 7 8 first day of the first month. 10:17
9 on the first day of the fifth month
10 16 in the first day of the tenth month
2 Es 8 18 he read . . . from the first day till
Esth 9 17 f. day with them all of the slaughter
11 2 in the first day of the month Nisan
Ps 23 1 on the first day of the week, a psalm
Eze 26 1 f. day of the month, that the word. 32:1
31 1 third month, first day of the month
Dan 10 12 from first day that thou didst set thy
Agge 1 1 in f. day of the month the word of the
Mat 26 17 on f. day of the Azymes, the disciples
28 1 towards first day of the week came Mary
Mark 14 12 first day of unleavened bread, when
16 2 first day of the week they come to the
9 he rising early the first day of the
Luke 24 1 first day of the week very early they
John 20 1 first day of the week Mary Magdalen
Acts 20 7 first day of the week when we were
18 from first day that I came into Asia
1 C 16 2 on first day of the week let every one
Phil 1 5 from the first day until now. Being
first month; *see* **month**
first year; *see* **year**
firstborn Gen 10 15 Chanaan begot Sidon his f.
Gen 22 21 Hus the firstborn, and Buz his brother
25 13 the firstborn of Ismael was Nabajoth
27 19 Jacob said: I am Esau thy firstborn
32 answered: I am thy firstborn son Esau
35 23 the sons of Lia: Ruben the firstborn
36 15 sons of Eliphaz the firstborn of Esau
38 6 Juda took a wife for Her his firstborn
7 Her, the firstborn of Juda, was wicked
41 51 called the name of the f. Manasses
43 33 firstborn according to his birthright
46 8 his children . . . his firstborn Ruben
48 18 this is the f., put thy right hand
49 3 Ruben, my firstborn . . . my strength
Exod 4 22 Israel is my son, my firstborn. I have
23 I will kill thy son, thy firstborn
6 14 the sons of Ruben the f. of Israel
11 5 every f. in land of the Egyptians
5 from the firstborn of Pharao. 12:29
5 to the f. of the handmaid . . . and all the f. of beasts
12 12 I . . . will kill every firstborn in the
29 the Lord slew every firstborn. 13:15
29 unto the firstborn of the captive woman
29 slew . . . all the firstborn of cattle
13 2 sanctify unto me every firstborn that
13 f. of an ass thou shalt change for a
13 f. of men thou shalt redeem with a
15 from the f. of man to the f. of beasts
15 all the firstborn of my sons I redeem
22 29 shalt give the f. of thy sons to me
30 same with the firstborn of thy oxen
34 20 firstborn of thy sons thou shalt redeem
Lev 27 26 the firstborn . . . no man may sanctify
Num 3 2 sons of Aaron: his firstborn Nadab
12 the Levites . . . for every firstborn
13 every f. is mine: since I struck the f. in the land of Egypt
13 sanctified to myself whatsoever is f.
40 number the firstborn of the male sex
41 take the Levites . . . for all the f.
41 for all the firstborn of the cattle
42 Moses reckoned up . . . the firstborn
45 take the Levites for the firstborn
46 price of the 273 of the firstborn
50 for the f. of the children of Israel
8 16 I have taken them instead of the f.
17 from the day that I slew every f. in
18 I have taken the Levites for all the f.
18 15 firstborn of all flesh . . . belong to
15 for f. of man thou shalt take a price
26 5 Ruben the firstborn of Israel. 1 Pa 5:3
33 4 who were burying their firstborn whom
Deut 12 6 shall offer . . . firstborn of your herds
17 not eat . . . firstborn of thy herds
14 23 shalt eat . . . firstborn of thy herds
21 15 son of the hated be the firstborn, and
16 not make son of the beloved the f.
17 the son of the hated for the firstborn
Josu 6 26 in his f. may he lay the foundation
17 1 for he is the firstborn of Joseph
1 to Machir the firstborn of Manasses
1 K 8 2 the name of his firstborn was Joel
14 49 the name of the firstborn was Merob
17 13 three sons . . . Eliab the firstborn
2 K 3 2 f. was Ammon of Achinoam. 1 Pa 3:1
13 21 loved him because he was his firstborn
3 K 16 34 in Abiram his f. he laid its foundations
1 Pa 1 13 Chanaan begot Sidon his firstborn
29 firstborn of Ismahel, Nabajoth, then
2 3 Her the firstborn of Juda was wicked
13 and Isai begot Eliab his firstborn
25 Jerameel the firstborn of Hesron were
25 sons of Jerameel . . . Ram his firstborn
27 sons of Ram the firstborn of Jerameel
42 sons of Caleb . . . Mesa his firstborn
50 Hur the firstborn of Ephrata, Sobal
3 1 the firstborn Ammon of Achinoam, the
15 sons of Josias were, firstborn Johanan
4 4 Hur the firstborn of Ephratha the
5 1 for he [Ruben] was his firstborn: but
1 he was not accounted for the firstborn
6 28 sons of Samuel: the firstborn Vasseni
8 1 Benjamin begot Bale his firstborn
30 his firstborn son Abdon, and Sur and
39 sons of Esec . . . Ulam the firstborn
9 5 of Siloni: Asaia the firstborn, and his
31 Mathathias . . . firstborn of Sellum
36 his firstborn son Abdon and Sur and
26 2 sons of Meselemia: Zacharias the f.
4 the sons of Obededom, Semeias the f.
10 Semri the chief, for he had not a f.
2 Es 10 36 firstborn of our sons . . . to be offered
Job 18 13 the firstborn death consume his arms
Ps 77 51 he killed all the firstborn in the
88 28 I will make him my f. high above the
104 36 he slew all the firstborn in their land
134 8 he slew the f. of Egypt from man even
135 10 who smote Egypt with their firstborn
Wisd 18 13 upon the destruction of the firstborn
Eccu 24 5 the firstborn before all creatures
36 14 hast raised up to be thy firstborn
Isa 14 30 the firstborn of the poor shall be fed
Jer 31 9 father to Israel, and Ephraim is my f.
Eze 44 30 the firstfruits of all the firstborn
Mich 6 7 shall I give my f. for my wickedness
Zach 12 10 to grieve for death of the firstborn
Mat 1 25 brought forth her f. son. Luke 2:7
Rom 8 29 he might be the f. amongst many brethren
Col 1 15 God, the firstborn of every creature
18 the firstborn from the dead; that in
Heb 11 28 who destroyed the firstborn, might not
12 23 to the church of the firstborn, who
firstfruit Rom 11 16 if the f. be holy, so is the
firstfruits Exod 22 29 not delay to pay . . . thy f.
Exod 23 16 feast of the harvest of the f. of thy
19 shalt carry the firstfruits of the corn
25 2 that they bring f. to me: of every
34 22 keep the feast of weeks with the f. of
35 5 set aside with you f. to the Lord. Let
21 offered f. to the Lord with a most
Lev 2 12 you shall offer only the f. of them

14 gift of f. of thy corn to the Lord
14 so shalt thou offer thy f. to the Lord
7 14 shall be offered to the Lord for f. and
32 offerings shall fall to the priest for f.
19 23 you shall take away the f. of them
22 12 things that are sanctified, nor of the f.
23 10 the f. of your harvest to the priest
15 wherein you offered the sheaf of the f.
17 two loaves of the f. of two tenths
17 which you shall bake for the f. of the
20 lifted them up with the loaves of the f.
25 5 shalt thou gather the grapes of the f.
11 shall you gather the f. of the vines
Num 15 19 shall separate firstfruits to the Lord
20 as you separate f. of your barnfloors
21 shall you give f. of your dough to the
18 8 have given thee the charge of my f.
11 firstfruits . . . I have given to. 12, 19
26 offer the firstfruits of them to the
27 reckoned to you as an oblation of f.
28 receive tithes, offer the f. to the
30 you had given the f. of the barnfloor
28 26 day also of f. when after the weeks
31 29 because they are the f. of the Lord
41 Moses delivered the number of the f. of
Deut 12 6 tithes and firstfruits of your hands. 11
17 voluntarily and the f. of thy hands
18 4 f. also of corn, of wine, and of oil
26 10 I offer the f. of the land which the
1 K 2 29 to eat the f. of every sacrifice of my
15 21 the f. of those things that were slain
2 K 1 21 upon you, neither be they fields of f.
4 K 4 42 to the man of God bread of the f.
2 Pa 31 5 offered in abundance the f. of corn
10 since the f. began to be offered in the
12 brought in faithfully both the f. and
14 of the f. and the things dedicated for
2 Es 10 35 that we would bring the f. of our
35 firstfruits of all fruit of every tree
37 we would bring the f. of our meats
39 carry to the treasury the f. of corn
12 43 for the libations and for the f. and
13 5 the porters, and the f. of the priests
31 at times appointed, and for the f.
Tob 1 6 offering faithfully all his f. and his
Ps 77 51 the f. of all their labor. 104:36
Eccu 7 34 their portion . . . of the f. and of
35 offer . . . the f. of the holy things
35 10 and diminish not the f. of thy hands
45 25 divided unto him the f. of the increase
Jer 2 3 Israel . . . the f. of his increase: all
Eze 20 40 there will I require your f. and the
44 30 the f. of all the firstborn and all
30 the f. of your meats to the priest
45 1 separate ye f. to the Lord, a portion
13 these are the f., which you shall take
16 bound to these f. for the prince in
47 12 every month they shall bring forth f.
48 8 the f. which you shall set apart. 9
10 these shall be the f. of the sanctuary
12 for them shall be the f. of the f.
14 neither . . . f. of the land be alienated
18 the residue in length by the f. of the
18 shall be as the f. of the sanctuary
20 the f. . . . shall be set apart for the f. of the sanctuary
21 every side of the f. of the sanctuary
21 of the firstfruits unto the east border
21 f. of the sanctuary . . . in the midst
Dan 3 38 or incense or place of f. before the
Osee 9 10 fathers like the f. of the fig tree
Mala 3 8 afflict thee? in tithes and in f.
1 Ma 3 49 they brought . . . the f. and tithes
Rom 8 23 who have the firstfruits of the Spirit
16 5 who is the firstfruits of Asia in Christ
1 C 15 20 dead, the firstfruits of them that sleep
23 the f. Christ, then they that are of
16 15 that they are the firstfruits of Achaia
2 Th 2 12 for that God hath chosen you firstfruits
Apoc 14 4 the firstfruits to God and to the Lamb

firstling Exod 34 20 f. of an ass thou shalt redeem
Num 18 17 f. of a cow and of a sheep and of a
Deut 33 17 his beauty as of f. of a bullock, his

firstlings Gen 4 4 offered of the f. of his flock
Deut 15 19 of the f. that come of thy herds and
19 shalt not shear the f. of thy sheep
2 Es 10 36 the f. of our oxen and of our sheep

firstripe Num 13 21 when the f. grapes are fit to
Num 18 13 all the f. of the fruits that the
Mich 7 1 my soul desired the firstripe figs

fish Num 11 5 we remember the fish that we ate
2 Pa 33 14 from the entering in of the fish gate
2 Es 3 3 the fish gate the sons of Asnaa built
12 38 above the fish gate and the tower of
13 16 brought fish and all manner of wares
Tob 6 2 monstrous fish came up to devour him
5 take out the entrails of this fish
7 which thou hast bid me keep of the fish
19 lay the liver of the fish on the fire
11 4 take with thee of the gall of the fish
8 his eyes with this gall of the fish
13 Tobias taking of the gall of the fish
12 3 from being devoured by the fish, thee
Ps 104 29 into blood, and destroyed their fish
Jer 16 16 and they shall fish them: and after
Eze 29 4 fish of thy rivers to stick to thy
4 all thy fish shall stick to thy scales
5 desert, and all the fish of thy river
Jon 2 1 the Lord prepared a great fish to
1 Jonas was in the belly of the fish
2 prayed . . . out of the belly of the f.
11 the Lord spoke to the fish: and it
Soph 1 10 the noise of a cry from the fish gate
Mat 7 10 if he shall ask him a fish, will he
17 26 that fish which shall first come up
Luke 11 11 or a fish, will he for a fish give
24 42 offered him a piece of a broiled fish
John 21 9 and a fish laid thereon, and bread
13 giveth them, and fish in like manner

fishermen Mark 1 16 into the sea, for they were f.
Luke 5 2 the fishermen were gone out of them

fishers Isa 19 8 the fishers also shall mourn
Jer 16 16 I will send many fishers, saith the
Eze 47 10 the f. shall stand over these waters
Mat 4 18 net into the sea, for they were fishers
19 I will make you to be fishers of men
Mark 1 17 make you to become fishers of men

fishes Gen 1 26 dominion over the fishes of the
Gen 1 28 rule over the fishes of the sea and
9 2 fishes of the sea are delivered into
Exod 7 18 fishes that are in the river shall die
21 the fishes that were in the river died
Num 11 22 shall the fishes of the sea be gathered
Deut 4 18 fishes, that abide in the waters under
3 K 4 33 and of creeping things and of fishes
Job 12 8 and the fishes of the sea shall tell
40 26 and the cabins of fishes with his head
Ps 8 9 fishes of the sea, that pass through
Ecce 9 12 as fishes are taken with the hook
Wisd 19 10 a multitude of frogs instead of fishes
Isa 19 10 mourn that made pools to take fishes
50 2 the fishes shall rot for want of water
Eze 38 20 fishes of the sea . . . shall be moved
47 9 there shall be fishes in abundance
10 there shall be many sorts of the f.
10 as the fishes of the great sea, a very

Osee 4 3 f. of the sea also shall be gathered
Haba 1 14 wilt make men as the fishes of the sea
Soph 1 3 I will gather . . . the f. of the sea
Mat 13 47 gathering together of all kind of f.
14 17 have . . . five loaves and two f. Luke 9:13
19 took the five loaves and the two fishes. Mark 6:41
15 34 said: Seven, and a few little fishes
36 taking the seven loaves and the fishes
Mark 6 38 they say: Five, and two fishes. And he
41 taken the 5 loaves and the 2 fishes
43 baskets of fragments, and of the fishes
8 7 and they had a few little fishes; and
Luke 5 6 a very great multitude of fishes, and
9 at the draught of the fishes which they
9 16 taking the 5 loaves and the 2 fishes
John 6 9 hath five barley loaves and two fishes
11 in like manner also of the fishes, as
21 6 to draw it for the multitude of fishes
8 dragging the net with fishes. As soon
10 bring hither of the fishes which you
11 full of great fishes, 153. And although
1 C 15 39 another of birds, another of fishes
fishing John 21 3 Peter saith to them: I go a f.
fishpools Cant 7 4 thy eyes like the fishpools
fist Exod 21 18 or with his fist, and he die not
Isa 58 4 and strike with the fist wickedly
fit Num 1 3 the men of Israel fit for war, and you
Num 13 21 when . . . grapes are fit to be eaten
32 1 Jazer and Galaad fit for feeding cattle
Deut 2 14 of the men that were fit for war
20 20 fit for other uses, cut them down
Josu 5 4 all the men fit for war, died in the
Judg 5 25 him butter in a dish fit for princes
20 2 God, 400,000 footmen fit for war. Nor
Ruth 1 12 spent with age and not fit for wedlock
1 K 14 52 a valiant man and fit for war, he took
16 18 great strength and a man fit for war
1 Pa 7 11 men, 17,200 fit to go out to war
40 were of the age that was fit for war
2 Pa 26 13 who were fit for war and fought for
Wisd 4 5 and sour to eat, and fit for nothing
Eccu 33 30 him to work: for so it is fit for him
Jer 13 7 rotten, so that it was fit for no use
10 this girdle which is fit for no use
Eze 15 5 was whole it was not fit for work
Dan 13 15 as they watched a fit day, she went in
1 Ma 10 19 great power, and fit to be our friend
13 40 you be fit to be enrolled among ours
2 Ma 2 30 fit things for the adorning of it
3 37 who might be a fit man to be sent
Mark 1 30 wife's mother lay in a fit of a fever
Luke 9 62 back, is fit for the kingdom of God
15 32 it was fit that we should make merry
Acts 22 22 for it is not fit that he should live
2 C 3 6 who also hath made us fit ministers of
2 Tim 2 2 who shall be fit to teach others also
Heb 13 21 fit you in all goodness, that you may
fitches Eze 4 9 take to thee . . . millet and f.
fitly Eph 4 16 being compacted and fitly joined
fitted Exod 26 5 and one may be fitted to the other
Exod 28 27 the rational may be f. with the ephod
Lev 8 8 girdle, he fitted it to the rational
Rom 9 22 vessels of wrath, fitted for destruction
Heb 10 5 not: but a body thou hast fitted to me
fitting 2 Th 1 3 for you, brethren, as it is f.
Heb 7 26 it was fitting that we should have such
fix Ps 31 8 I will fix my eyes upon thee. Do not
Dan 11 45 he shall fix his tabernacle Apadno
Haba 2 1 and fix my foot upon the tower: and I
fixed Lev 13 51 grown, it is a fixed leprosy: he
Lev 16 16 which is fixed among them in the midst
Deut 2 30 hardened his spirit and fixed his heart
1 K 17 49 the stone was fixed in his forehead
26 7 his spear fixed in the ground at his
3 K 8 54 he had fixed both knees on the ground
2 Es 2 6 he sent me: and I fixed him a time
Prov 16 30 that with fixed eyes deviseth wicked
Eccu 43 16 he hath fixed the clouds and the
Lam 2 4 he hath fixed his right hand as an
Luke 4 20 in the synagogue were fixed on him
16 26 us and you there is f. a great chaos
1 C 4 11 are buffeted, and have no fixed abode
flag Exod 39 19 lest they should flag loose
Isa 33 23 shalt not be able to spread the flag
flagitious 2 Ma 7 34 and of all men most f.
flame Exod 3 2 Lord appeared to him in f. of fire
Num 19 6 twice dyed, and cast it into the flame
21 28 a flame from the city of Sehon, and
Judg 13 20 when the flame from the altar went up
20 angel of Lord ascended also in the f.
15 5 the flame consumed also the vineyards
Job 15 30 the flame shall dry up his branches
18 5 and the flame of his fire not shine
41 12 a flame cometh forth out of his mouth
Ps 28 7 voice of the Lord divideth the f. of
38 4 in my meditation a fire shall flame out
82 15 and as a flame burning mountains: so
105 18 the flame burned the wicked. They made
Eccu 8 13 lest thou be burnt with the flame of
16 7 unbelieving nation wrath shall flame
21 10 the end of them is a flame of fire
28 26 just shall not be burnt with its flame
45 24 consumed them with a flame of fire
51 6 from the oppression of the flame which
Isa 5 24 the heat of the flame consumeth it
10 17 and the Holy One thereof as a flame
29 6 the flame of devouring fire. 30:30
Jer 48 45 a flame out of the midst of Sion, and
Eze 20 47 flame of the fire shall not be quenched
Dan 3 22 the flame of the fire slew those men
24 they walked in the midst of the flame
47 the flame mounted up above the furnace
49 he drove the flame of the fire out of
88 us out of the midst of the burning f.
Joel 1 19 the flame hath burnt all the trees
2 3 fire, and behind it a burning flame
5 like the noise of a flame of fire
Abdi 18 house of Joseph [shall be] a flame
1 Ma 2 59 were delivered out of the flame. Daniel
2 Ma 1 32 there was kindled a flame from them
Luke 16 24 for I am tormented in this flame
Acts 7 30 an angel in a flame of fire in a bush
2 Th 1 8 in a flame of fire, giving vengeance to
Heb 1 7 and his ministers a flame of fire. But
Apoc 1 14 his eyes were as a f. of fire. 19:12
2 18 who hath his eyes like to a f. of fire
flamed Ps 17 9 a fire flamed from his face: coals
flames Exod 20 18 saw the voices and the flames
Judg 20 40 and that the flames ascended on high
48 were consumed with devouring flames
Cant 8 6 the lamps thereof are fire and flames
Wisd 17 5 neither could the bright flames of
19 20 the flames wasted not the flesh of
Isa 43 2 the flames shall not burn in thee
47 14 themselves from the power of the f.
50 11 encompassed with f., walk in the light
11 in the flames which you have kindled
66 15 and his rebuke with flames of fire
Dan 7 9 his throne like flames of fire: the
flaming Gen 3 24 cherubims and a flaming sword
Eccu 3 33 water quencheth a flaming fire, and
Isa 4 5 brightness of a f. fire in the night
Dan 2 3 a flaming fire devouring round about
Osee 7 6 himself was heated as a flaming fire
Nah 2 3 reins of his chariot are flaming in the

flank 2 K 20 8 a sword hanging down to his flank
flanks Lev 3 4 fat wherewith the f. are covered
Lev 3 10 with the fat that is about the flanks
15 the caul . . . which is by the f. 4:9
7 4 the fat which is by the flanks, and the
flash Exod 19 16 lightning [began] to flash, and
flashes Eze 1 14 returned like f. of lightning
flashing Wisd 16 22 the hail and f. in the rain
flat Gen 17 3 fell flat on his face. Num 16:4
Num 14 5 fell down flat upon the ground. 20:6
16 22 they fell flat on their face, and said
22 31 [Balaam] falling flat on the ground
Josu 7 6 fell flat on the ground. Judg 13:20; 2 Pa 20:18; Dan 8:18
10 why liest thou flat on the ground
Judg 7 13 and beat it down flat to the ground
1 Pa 21 16 he and the ancients . . . fell down f. on
Mark 14 35 he fell flat on the ground; and he
Luke 19 44 and beat thee flat to the ground and
flattereth Prov 7 13 and with an impudent face, f.
flattering Prov 6 24 the f. tongue of the stranger
Prov 23 23 that by a f. tongue deceiveth him
29 5 to his friend with f. and dissembling
flattery Prov 7 21 away with the f. of her lips
Ecce 7 6 to be deceived by the flattery of fools
1 Th 2 5 time, the speech of flattery, as you
flax Exod 9 31 flax and the barley were hurt
Exod 9 31 green, and the flax was now boiled
Josu 2 6 covered them with the stalks of flax
Judg 15 14 as the flax is wont to be consumed
Prov 31 13 she hath sought wool and flax and
Isa 19 9 shall be confounded that wrought in f.
42 3 smoking flax he shall not quench: he
43 17 they are broken as flax and are extinct
Eze 40 3 with a line of flax in his hand and a
Osee 2 5 that give me my bread . . . and my flax
9 will set at liberty my wool and my f.
Mat 12 20 smoking flax he shall not extinguish
flay 2 Pa 29 34 not enough to f. the holocausts
flayed Lev 1 6 when they have flayed the victim
2 Pa 35 11 and the Levites flayed the holocausts
Mich 3 3 have flayed their skin from off them
flea 1 K 24 15 after a dead dog, after a flea
1 K 26 20 of Israel is come out to seek a flea
fled Gen 14 10 remained fled to the mountain
Gen 31 22 it was told Laban . . . that Jacob fled
35 7 to him when he fled from his brother
39 12 leaving the garment in her hand, fled
18 garment which I held, and fled out
Exod 2 15 he [Moses] fled from his sight, and
4 3 a serpent: so that Moses fled from it
14 5 told . . . that the people was fled
Num 16 34 all Israel . . . fled at the cry of them
43 Moses and Aaron fled to the tabernacle
35 25 into the city, to which he had fled
Deut 23 15 master the servant that is fled to thee
Josu 7 5 slew them as they fled by the descent
10 16 the five kings were fled and had hidden
20 6 city and house from whence he fled
Judg 1 6 Adonibezec fled: and they pursued after
4 15 off his chariot and fled away on foot
5 22 the stoutest of the enemies fled amain
7 21 crying out and howling they fled away
8 4 could not pursue after them that fled
12 Zebee and Salmana fled, and Gedeon
9 21 when he had said thus he fled and
51 men and the women were fled together
11 3 he [Jephte] fled and avoided them not
20 31 whilst they fled by two highways
39 children of Benjamin thought they fled
41 that before had made as if they fled
45 they fled into the wilderness and
Ruth 2 12 under whose wings thou art fled. And
1 K 4 10 every man fled to his own dwelling
16 have fled out of the field this day
17 Israel has fled before the Philistines
14 22 hearing that the Philistines fled
17 24 when they saw the man, f. from his face
51 that their champion was dead, fled away
19 8 and they fled from his [David's] face
10 David fled and escaped that night. Saul
12 [David] went and fled away and escaped
18 fled and escaped and came to Samuel
20 1 David fled from Najoth, which is in
21 10 fled that day from the face of Saul
22 1 and fled to the cave of Odollam. And
17 they knew that he [David] was fled
20 Abiathar, escaped and fled to David
23 6 when Abiathar . . . fled to David to
13 that David was fled from Ceila and had
27 4 told Saul that David was fled to Geth
29 3 since the day that he fled over to me
30 17 who had gotten upon camels and fled
31 1 men of Israel fled from before the
7 seeing that the Israelites were fled
7 forsook their cities and fled: and
2 K 1 3 I am fled out of the camp of Israel
4 the people are fled from the battle
4 3 and the Berothites fled into Gethaim
4 and his nurse took him up and fled
6 stabbed him in the groin and fled away
10 13 they immediately fled before him [Joab]
14 seeing that the Syrians were fled, they fled also. 1 Pa 19:15
18 Syrians fled before Israel, and David
19 the kings . . . were afraid and fled away
13 29 every man upon his mule, and fled. And
34 but Absalom fled away: and the young
37 but Absalom fled and went to Tholomai
38 Absalom after he was fled and come into
18 17 Israel f. to their own dwellings. 19:8
19 3 backs, and fled away from the battle
9 he is fled out of the land for Absalom
23 10 the people that were f. away, returned
11 when the people were fled from the face
3 K 2 7 when I fled from the face of Absalom
28 Joab fled into the tabernacle of the
29 that Joab was fled into the tabernacle
11 17 then Adad fled, he and certain Edomites
23 Razon . . . who had fled from his master
40 he [Jeroboam] arose and fled into Egypt
12 18 and he [Roboam] fled to Jerusalem. And
20 20 the Syrians fled, and Israel pursued
20 Benadad king of Syria fled away on
30 they that remained fled to Aphec, into
4 K 3 24 defeated Moab, who fled before them
7 7 they arose and fled away in the dark
7 and fled, desiring to save their lives
8 21 but the people fled into their tents
9 10 he opened the door and fled. Then Jehu
27 Ochozias . . . fled by the way of the
27 he [Ochozias] f. into Mageddo and died
14 12 they fled every man to their dwellings
19 in Jerusalem: and he fled to Lachis
19 37 they fled into the land of the Armenians
25 4 all the men of war fled in the night
4 Sedecias fled by the way that leadeth
1 Pa 10 1 and the men of Israel fled from before
7 in the plains, saw this, they fled
11 13 people fled from before the Philistines
12 1 while he yet fled from Saul the son
20 there fled to him [David] of Manasses
19 18 but the Syrian fled before Israel: and
2 Pa 10 2 for he was fled thither from Solomon
18 his chariot, and fled into Jerusalem
13 16 the children of Israel fled before Juda

14 12 Asa and Juda: and the Ethiopians fled
25 22 Juda fell before Israel and they fled
27 and he [Amasias] fled into Lachis, and
2 Es 13 10 they that ministered were fled away
Tob 1 5 he alone fled the company of all, and
Jdth 10 12 of the Hebrews, and I am fled from them
11 13 knowing this, am fled from them, and
15 1 courage and counsel fled from them
2 and fled by the ways of the fields and
Job 9 25 they have fled away and have not seen
Ps 3 1 when he fled from the face of his son
30 12 they that saw me without fled from me
56 1 when he fled from Saul into the cave
113 3 the sea saw and fled: Jordan was turned
142 9 O Lord, to thee have I fled: teach me
Wisd 10 6 just man who fled from the wicked that
10 when he fled from his brother's wrath
15 19 they have fled from the praise of God
Eccu 27 22 he is gone afar off, he is fled, as a
Isa 10 29 astonished, Gabaath of Saul fled away
20 6 our hope, to whom we fled for help
21 15 they are fled from before the swords
22 3 all the princes are fled together and
3 bound together, they are fled far off
33 3 voice of the angel the people fled
37 38 and they fled into the land of Ararat
Jer 4 29 the archers, all the city is fled away
26 21 Urias . . . fled and went into Egypt. And
38 19 the Jews that are fled over to the
39 4 the men of war saw them, they fled: and
40 12 all the places to which they had fled
41 15 fled with eight men from the face of
46 5 they fled apace, and they looked not
21 back, and are fled away together, and
48 45 that fled from the snare stood in the
52 7 the men of war fled, and went out of
15 that were fled over to the king of
Eze 21 12 the princes of Israel, that are fled
33 21 there came to me one that was fled
22 evening, before he that was fled came
Dan 10 7 they fled away and hid themselves. And
Osee 12 12 Jacob fled into the country of Syria
Jon 1 10 that he fled from the face of the Lord
Zach 14 5 as you fled from the face of the
1 Ma 1 19 Ptolemee was afraid . . . and fled
40 inhabitants of Jerusalem fled away
2 15 were fled into the city of Modin to
28 and his sons fled into the mountains
43 all they that fled from the evils
44 the rest fled to the nations for safety
3 11 down slain, and the rest fled away
24 fled into the Land of the Philistines
4 14 the Gentiles were routed, and fled
22 all fled away into the land of the
5 9 they fled into the fortress of Datheman
11 the fortress into which we are fled
34 they fled away before his face: and
43 fled to the temple that was in Carnaim
6 4 he fled away from thence and departed
7 19 took many of them that were fled away
32 and they fled into the city of David
44 they threw away their weapons and fled
9 18 Judas was slain, and the rest fled away
33 they fled into the desert of Thecua and
40 the rest fled into the mountains, and
10 12 and the strangers . . . fled away. And
49 and the army of Demetrius fled away and
64 clothed with purple, they all fled away
82 they were discomfited by him and fled
83 f. into Azotus and went into Bethdagon
84 all them that were fled into it, he
11 16 and Alexander fled into Arabia, there
46 the king fled into the palace, and they
55 Demetrius, who turned his back and fled
70 all that were on Jonathan's side fled
73 they of his part that fled saw this
15 11 he fled along by the seacoast and came
21 are fled out of their country to you
37 Tryphon fled away by ship to Orthosias
16 8 and the rest fled into the stronghold
10 they fled even to the towers that were
2 Ma 5 5 and Menelaus fled into the castle. But
7 and fled again into the country of the
8 13 some of them . . . fled away: others sold
10 32 Timotheus f. into Gazara a stronghold
11 12 Lysias himself fled away shamefully
14 14 Gentiles who had fled out of Judea from
Mat 8 33 they that kept them fled: and coming
26 56 the disciples all leaving him, fled
Mark 5 14 they that fed them fled and told it in
14 50 disciples leaving him, all fled away
52 the linen cloth, fled from them naked
16 8 they going out, fled from the sepulcher
Luke 8 34 that fed them saw done, they fled away
John 6 15 fled again into the mountain himself
Acts 7 29 Moses fled upon this word and was a
14 6 they understanding it, fled to Lystra
16 27 supposing that prisoners had been fled
19 16 they fled out of that house naked and
Heb 6 18 who have fled for refuge to hold fast
Apoc 12 6 and the woman fled into the wilderness
16 20 and every island fled away, and the
20 11 earth and heaven fled away, and there

flee Gen 16 8 I flee from the face of Sarai, my
Gen 19 20 here at hand, to which I may flee, it
27 43 arise and flee to Laban my brother
35 1 when thou didst flee from Esau thy
Exod 9 20 made his servants . . . flee into houses
14 25 Egyptians said: Let us flee from Israel
21 13 thee a place to which he must flee
32 18 the shout of men compelling to flee
Lev 26 17 you shall flee when no man pursueth
25 when you shall flee into the cities
36 they shall flee as it were from the
Num 10 35 hate thee, flee from before thy face
35 6 who hath shed blood may flee to them
15 that he may f. to them, who hath shed
Deut 4 42 that any one might flee to them who
19 3 who is forced to flee for manslaughter
5 he shall flee to one of the cities
11 if . . . he flee to one of the cities
28 7 seven ways shall they flee before thee
25 and flee seven ways, and be scattered
Josu 7 12 enemies, but he shall f. from them
8 5 we will flee and turn our backs as we
6 they will think that we flee as before
20 had no more power to flee this way or
10 19 hindermost of them as they flee, and do
20 3 may flee to them: and may escape the
4 he shall flee to one of these cities
9 might flee to them, and not die by the
Judg 6 11 by the winepress, to flee from Madian
20 31 seeing their enemies flee, pursued
32 by their seeming to flee to bring them
36 children of Benjamin . . . began to flee
36 gave them place to flee, that they
47 to escape and flee to the wilderness
1 K 19 17 and let my enemy go and flee away? And
25 10 servants . . . who flee from their masters
27 1 is it not better for me [David] to flee
1 I will flee then out of his hands. And
2 K 4 4 as she made haste to flee, he fell
15 14 let us flee: for we shall not escape
18 3 we flee away, they will not much mind
24 13 or thou shalt flee three months before
4 K 9 3 thou shalt open the door and flee and

15 no man go forth or f. out of the city
1 Pa 21 12 three months to flee from thy enemies
2 Es 6 11 I said: Should such a man as I flee
Job 19 29 flee then from the face of the sword
20 24 he shall flee from weapons of iron
27 22 out of his hand he would willingly flee
30 10 they abhor me and flee far from me
Ps 59 6 that they may flee from before the bow
67 2 that hate him f. from before his face
103 7 at thy rebuke they shall flee: at the
113 5 O thou sea, that thou didst flee: and
138 7 whither shall I flee from thy face
Prov 4 15 flee from it, pass not by it: go aside
6 11 and want shall flee far from thee
13 19 hate them that flee from evil things
28 17 if he f. even to the pit, no man will
Cant 6 4 for they have made me flee away. Thy
8 14 flee away, O my beloved, and be like
Wisd 1 5 spirit of discipline will flee from the
Eccu 21 2 flee from sins as from the face of
22 27 these cases a friend will flee away
32 21 a sinful man will flee reproof and
Isa 10 3 to whom will ye flee for help? And
13 14 everyone shall flee to his own land
15 5 bars thereof shall flee unto Segor
9 lion upon them that shall flee of Moab
16 3 hide them that flee, and betray not
17 13 rebuke him, and he shall flee far off
24 18 that shall flee from the noise of the
30 16 will f. to horses: therefore shall you f.
17 a thousand men shall flee for fear
17 and for fear of five shall you flee
20 will not cause thy teacher to f. away
31 8 he shall flee not at the face of the
35 10 sorrow and mourning shall flee. 51:11
48 20 flee ye from the Chaldeans, declare
Jer 21 9 flee over to the Chaldeans that besiege
25 35 shepherds shall have no way to flee
44 14 none return but they that shall flee
28 that shall flee from the sword, shall
46 6 let not the swift flee away nor the
48 6 flee, save your lives: and be as heath
44 he that shall flee from the fear, shall
49 5 any to gather together them that flee
8 flee and turn your backs, go down into
30 flee ye, get away speedily, sit in
50 16 every one shall flee to his own land
28 the voice of them that flee and of
51 6 flee ye from the midst of Babylon and
Bar 6 54 their priests indeed will flee away
Eze 7 16 such of them as shall f. shall escape
29 16 that they may flee and follow them
Amos 2 16 shall flee away naked in that day
5 19 a man should flee from the face of a
7 12 go, flee away into the land of Juda
9 1 they shall flee, and he that shall flee
Abdi 14 to kill them that flee: and thou shalt
Jon 1 3 Jonas rose up to flee into Tharsis
4 2 I went before to flee into Tharsis
Nah 2 8 the men flee away. They cry: Stand
3 7 shall see thee, shall flee from thee
Zach 2 6 flee ye out of the land of the north
7 flee, thou that dwellest with the
14 5 you shall flee to the valley of those
5 you shall flee as you fled from the
1 Ma 4 5 for he said: These men flee from us
9 10 God forbid . . . we should flee away
10 43 whosoever shall flee into the temple
73 no stone nor rock nor place to flee to
Mat 3 7 showed you to f. from wrath. Luke 3:7
10 23 you in this city, flee into another
23 33 how will you flee from the judgment of
24 16 let them flee to the mountains. Mark 13:14; Luke 21:21
2 Tim 2 22 but flee thou youthful desires, and
fleece Gen 30 35 of white and black fleece, he
Judg 6 37 I will put this f. of wool on the floor
37 if there be dew on the fleece only
38 wringing the fleece, he filled a vessel
39 once more, seeking a sign in the fleece
39 that the fleece only may be dry, and
40 and it was dry on the fleece only, and
Job 31 20 not warmed with the fleece of my sheep
Ps 71 6 down like rain upon the fleece; and as
fleeces 4 K 3 4 and 100,000 rams with their fleeces
fleeing Exod 14 27 as the Egyptians were f. away
Lev 26 37 upon their brethren as f. from wars
Josu 8 7 whilst we are fleeing, and they
15 fleeing by the way of the wilderness
10 11 when they were f. from the children of
Judg 4 16 Barac pursued after the f. chariots
17 Sisara f. came to the tent of Jahel
7 23 fleeing as far as Bethsetta and the
1 K 14 16 multitude . . . fleeing this way and that
3 K 20 30 Benadad fleeing, went into the city
4 K 9 23 Joram turned his hand, and f. said to
2 Pa 12 5 together in Jerusalem, f. from Sesac
Tob 1 21 fleeing from Judea by reason of the
23 Tobias fleeing naked away with his son
Jdth 14 5 when you shall know that they are f.
15 3 children of Israel seeing them fleeing
16 14 killed them like children fleeing away
Wisd 14 6 hope of the world fleeing to a vessel
Isa 13 14 they shall be as a doe fleeing away
16 2 as a bird fleeing away, and as young
31 9 his princes fleeing shall be afraid
Jer 4 21 how long shall I see men fleeing away
37 12 thou art fleeing to the Chaldeans. And
13 I am not fleeing to the Chaldeans. But
2 Ma 8 35 fleeing through the midland country
fleet 3 K 9 26 Solomon made a f. in Asiongaber
3 K 9 27 Hiram sent his servants in the fleet
fleeth Deut 19 4 the law of the slayer that fleeth
Job 14 2 is destroyed and fleeth as a shadow
20 8 as a dream that fleeth away he shall
Prov 28 1 the wicked man fleeth when no man
Eccu 29 20 the unclean fleeth from his surety
Isa 21 14 meet with bread him that fleeth. For
Jer 48 19 inquire of him that fleeth: and say to
fleets Eze 27 28 thy fleets shall be troubled
flesh Gen 2 21 ribs, and filled flesh for it
Gen 2 23 of my bones, and flesh of my flesh
24 they shall be two in one flesh. And
6 3 in man forever, because he is flesh
9 4 flesh with blood you shall not eat
15 every living soul that beareth flesh
17 11 circumcise the flesh of your foreskin
13 my covenant shall be in your flesh
14 flesh of his foreskin shall not be
23 he circumcised the f. of their foreskin
24 circumcised f. of his foreskin. Jdth 14:6
37 27 for he is our brother and our flesh
41 18 exceeding beautiful and full of flesh
Exod 4 7 and it was like the other flesh. If
12 8 they shall eat the flesh that night
16 3 when we sat over the flesh pots and
8 the Lord will give you flesh to eat
12 in the evening you shall eat flesh
22 31 flesh that beasts have tasted of before
28 42 to cover the flesh of their nakedness
29 14 the flesh of the calf and the hide and
17 upon the flesh that is cut in pieces
31 shalt boil the f. thereof in the holy
34 if there remain of the consecrated f.

	30	32	the flesh of man shall not be anointed
Lev	4	11	the flesh with the head and the feet
	6	27	whatsoever shall touch the f. thereof
	7	6	shall eat this flesh in a holy place
		15	flesh of it shall be eaten the same day
		19	the flesh that hath touched any unclean
		21	and shall eat of such kind of flesh
	8	17	the calf with the skin and the flesh
		31	boil the flesh before the door of the
	9	11	the flesh and skins thereof he burnt
	11	8	the flesh of these you shall not eat
		11	their flesh you shall not eat, and
	13	2	in whose skin or flesh shall arise a
		4	lower than the other flesh. 20, 26, 30, 34
		10	and the living f. itself shall appear
		14	when the live flesh shall appear in him
		15	live f., if it be spotted with leprosy
		21	and be not lower than the flesh that
		24	the f. also and the skin that hath been
		31	place of the spot is equal with the f.
		32	the blemish be even with the other f.
	16	27	with fire, their skins and their flesh
	17	14	not eat the blood of any flesh at all
	18	12	because she is the flesh of thy father
		13	because she is thy mother's flesh. Thou
		17	shame: because they are her flesh
	19	28	not make any cuttings in your flesh
	21	5	nor make incisions in their flesh. They
	26	29	you shall eat the flesh of your sons
Num	8	7	let them shave all the hairs of their f.
	11	4	who shall give us flesh to eat. 18
		13	whence should I have flesh to give
		13	give us flesh that we may eat. I am
		18	tomorrow you shall eat flesh: for I
		18	that the Lord may give you flesh
		21	I will give them flesh to eat a whole
		33	as yet the f. was between their teeth
	12	12	one half of her flesh is consumed with
	18	18	but the flesh shall fall to thy use
	19	5	up to the fire her skin and her flesh
Deut	12	20	wilt eat the f. that thy soul desireth
		23	must not eat the soul with the flesh
		27	thy oblations the flesh and the blood
		27	and the flesh thou thyself shalt eat
	14	8	be unclean, their flesh you shall not
	28	53	flesh of thy sons and of thy daughters
		56	the f. of her son and of her daughter
	32	42	and my sword shall devour flesh, of the
Judg	6	19	and putting the flesh in a basket, and
		20	take the f. and the unleavened loaves
		21	touched the flesh and the unleavened
		21	consumed the flesh and the unleavened
	8	7	will thresh your flesh with the thorns
	9	2	consider that I am your bone and your f.
1 K	2	13	came, while the flesh was in boiling
		15	give me flesh to boil for the priest
		15	I will not take of thee sodden flesh
	25	11	shall I then take . . . f. of my cattle
3 K	17	6	the ravens brought him bread and f.
	19	21	and boiled the flesh with the plow
4 K	4	34	and the child's flesh grew warm. Then
	5	14	his flesh was restored, like the flesh of a little child
	9	36	the dogs shall eat the flesh of Jezabel
		37	the flesh of Jezabel shall be as dung
2 Pa	32	8	with him is an arm of flesh; with us
2 Es	5	5	our f. is as the f. of our brethren
Tob	6	6	he roasted the flesh thereof, and they
Jdth	16	21	will give fire, and worms into their f.
Job	10	4	hast thou eyes of flesh: or shalt thou
		11	hast clothed me with skin and flesh
	19	20	the flesh being consumed, my bone hath

Ps	49	13	shall I eat the flesh of bullocks? Or
	55	5	I will not fear what f. can do against
	77	27	he rained upon them flesh as dust: and
		39	and he remembered that they are flesh
	78	2	the flesh of thy saints for the beasts
Prov	23	20	revellings, who contribute flesh to eat
Wisd	7	1	of my mother I was fashioned to be f.
	19	20	wasted not the flesh of corruptible
Eccu	7	19	vengeance on the flesh of the ungodly
	14	19	so is the generation of flesh and blood
	17	30	that which f. and blood hath invented
	28	5	he that is but flesh, nourisheth anger
	31	1	watching for riches consumeth the f.
	47	2	as the fat taken away from the flesh
Isa	9	20	shall eat the flesh of his own arm
	10	18	from the soul even to the flesh, and
	22	13	eating flesh and drinking wine: let
	31	3	their horses, flesh, and not spirit
	44	19	I have broiled flesh and have eaten
	49	26	will feed thy enemies with their own f.
	65	4	that eat swine's flesh, and profane
	66	17	they that did eat swine's flesh, and
Jer	7	21	your sacrifices, and eat ye the flesh
	11	15	shall the holy f. take away from thee
	17	5	maketh flesh his arm and whose heart
	19	9	with the flesh of their sons and with the flesh of their daughters
		9	shall eat every one the f. of his friend
Bar	2	3	should eat the flesh of his own son and the flesh of his own daughter
Eze	4	14	no unclean flesh hath entered into my
	11	3	city is the caldron, and we the flesh
		7	are the f. and this is the caldron
		11	you shall not be as flesh in the midst
		19	away the stony heart out of their f.
		19	and will give them a heart of flesh
	23	20	whose flesh is as the flesh of asses
	24	10	the flesh shall be consumed, and the
	36	26	the stony heart out of your flesh, and will give you a heart of flesh
	37	6	will cause flesh to grow over you and
		8	sinews and the flesh came up upon them
	39	17	to eat flesh and drink blood. You shall
		18	you shall eat the flesh of the mighty
	40	43	upon the tables was f. of the offering
	44	7	in heart, and uncircumcised in f. 9
Dan	7	5	said to it: Arise, devour much flesh
	10	3	neither flesh nor wine entered into my
Osee	8	13	they shall sacrifice f. and shall eat
Mich	3	2	and their flesh from their bones? Who
		3	who have eaten the flesh of my people
		3	as flesh in the midst of the pot. Then
Agge	2	13	if a man carry sanctified flesh in the
Zach	11	9	every one the flesh of his neighbor
		16	he shall eat the flesh of the fat ones
	14	12	flesh of every one shall consume away
1 Ma	1	50	and swine's flesh to be immolated, and
	7	17	the flesh of thy saints and the blood
2 Ma	6	18	to open his mouth to eat swine's flesh
		21	desired that flesh might be brought
	7	1	compelled by the king to eat swine's f.
Mat	16	17	flesh and blood hath not revealed it
	19	5	two shall be in one flesh. Mark 10:8
		6	they are not two, but one f. Mark 10:8
	24	22	no flesh should be saved. Mark 13:20
	26	41	willing, but the flesh weak. Mark 14:38
Luke	24	39	a spirit hath not flesh and bones, as
John	1	14	and the Word was made flesh and dwelt
	6	54	except you eat the flesh of the Son
		64	the flesh profiteth nothing. The words
Rom	3	20	no flesh shall be justified. Gal 2:16
	6	19	because of the infirmity of your flesh

7 25 God; but with the flesh, the law of sin
8 3 in that it was weak through the flesh
3 in likeness of sinful flesh and of sin
12 we are debtors, not to the flesh, to
13 14 and make not provision for the flesh in
14 21 it is good not to eat flesh, and not to
1 C 1 29 that no flesh should glory in his sight
6 16 shall be . . . two in one flesh. Eph 5:31
8 13 I will never eat flesh, lest I should
15 39 all flesh is not the same flesh: but one
39 one is the f. of men, another of beasts
50 flesh and blood cannot possess kingdom
2 C 4 11 may be made manifest in our mortal flesh
7 5 our flesh had no rest, but we suffered
Gal 1 16 I condescended not to flesh and blood
3 3 you would now be made perfect by flesh
5 13 make not liberty occasion to the flesh
17 the flesh lusteth against the spirit
17 spirit: and the spirit against the flesh
24 are Christ's have crucified their flesh
6 13 that they may glory in your flesh. But
Eph 2 3 in the desires of our flesh, fulfilling
6 12 wrestling is not against flesh and blood
Col 2 13 dead in . . . uncircumcision of your f.
Heb 2 14 children are partakers of f. and blood
12 9 we have had fathers of our flesh, for
James 5 3 shall eat your flesh like fire. You
2 P 2 10 who walk after the flesh in the lust
Jude 7 going after other flesh, were made an
8 these men also defile the flesh, and
Apoc 17 16 shall eat her flesh and shall burn her
19 18 the f. of kings and the f. of tribunes and
the f. of mighty men and the f. of horses
. . . and the f. of all freemen
21 all the birds were filled with their f.

according to the flesh John 8 15 you judge a. . . .
Rom 1 3 seed of David, according to the flesh
4 1 who is our father according to the f.
8 1 who walk not according to the flesh. 4
5 they that are according to the flesh
12 live according to the flesh. For it
13 for if you live according to the flesh
9 3 are my kinsmen according to the flesh
5 of whom is Christ according to the f.
1 C 1 26 that there are not many wise a. . . . , not
10 18 behold Israel according to the flesh
2 C 1 17 do I purpose according to the flesh
5 16 we know no man according to the flesh
16 known Christ according to the flesh
10 2 as if we walked according to the flesh
3 we do not war acccording to the flesh
11 18 many glory according to the flesh, I
Gal 4 23 was born according to the flesh. 29
Eph 6 5 are your lords according to the flesh
Col 3 22 your masters according to the flesh

all flesh Gen 6 12 all f. had corrupted its way
Gen 6 13 the end of all flesh is come before me
17 flood upon the earth to destroy all f.
19 of every living creature of all flesh
7 15 into the ark, two and two of all flesh
16 went in male and female of all flesh
21 all flesh was destroyed that moved upon
8 17 things that are with thee of all flesh
9 11 all flesh shall be no more destroyed
15 waters of a flood to destroy all flesh
16 God and every living soul of all flesh
17 established between me and all flesh
Num 16 22 God of the spirits of all f. 27:16
18 15 whatsoever is firstborn of all flesh
Deut 5 26 what is all flesh, that it should hear
3 K 2 2 I am going the way of all flesh: take
Jdth 7 16 should die and be a reproach to all f.
Job 12 10 and the spirit of all flesh of man
34 15 all flesh shall perish together, and
Ps 64 3 my prayer: all flesh shall come to thee
135 25 who giveth food to all flesh: for his
144 21 let all f. bless his holy name forever
Prov 4 22 that find them, and health to all flesh
Eccu 1 10 upon all flesh according to his gift
13 20 all flesh shall consort with the like
14 18 all flesh shall fade as grass, and as
17 4 he put the fear of him upon all flesh
18 12 the mercy of God is upon all flesh
39 24 the works of all flesh are before him
40 8 such things happen to all flesh from
41 5 this sentence is from Lord upon all f.
44 19 all flesh should no more be destroyed
27 found grace in the eyes of all flesh
45 4 meekness, and chose him out of all f.
Isa 40 5 all flesh together shall see that the
6 all flesh is grass, and all the glory
49 26 all flesh shall know that I am the Lord
66 16 by fire and by his sword unto all flesh
23 all flesh shall come to adore before my
24 shall be a loathsome sight to all flesh
Jer 12 12 there is no peace for all flesh. They
25 31 he entereth into judgment with all f.
32 27 I am the Lord the God of all flesh
45 5 I will bring evil upon all flesh, saith
Eze 20 48 all flesh shall see that I the Lord
21 4 forth out of its sheath against all f.
5 that all flesh may know that I the Lord
Dan 4 9 their abode and all flesh did eat of it
14 4 earth, and hath power over all flesh
Joel 2 28 I will pour out my spirit upon all f.
Zach 2 13 let all flesh be silent at the presence
Luke 3 6 all flesh shall see the salvation of
John 17 2 hast given him power over all flesh
Acts 2 17 pour out of my Spirit upon all flesh
1 C 15 39 all flesh is not the same flesh: but one
1 P 1 24 all flesh is as grass; and all the

his flesh Exod 21 28 his f. shall not be eaten
Lev 15 3 cleaveth to his f. and gathereth there
7 he that toucheth his flesh, shall wash
16 24 shall wash his flesh in the holy place
28 shall wash his clothes and flesh with
20 19 uncovered the shame of his own flesh
22 6 when he hath washed his flesh with
3 K 21 27 and put haircloth upon his flesh, and
4 K 6 30 which he wore within next to his flesh
Job 2 5 touch his bone and his flesh, and then
14 22 his flesh, while he shall live, shall
31 31 who will give us of his flesh that we
33 21 his flesh shall be consumed away and
25 his flesh is consumed with punishments
41 14 members of his f. cleave one to another
Ecce 4 5 hands together and eateth his own flesh
Eccu 23 23 that is wicked in the mouth of his f.
38 29 vapor of the fire wasteth his flesh
44 21 in his f. he established the covenant
Isa 17 4 the fatness of his f. shall grow lean
2 Ma 9 9 his flesh fell off, and the filthiness
John 6 53 how can this man give us his flesh to
Acts 2 31 neither did his flesh see corruption
Gal 6 8 he that soweth in his flesh, of flesh
Eph 2 14 of partition, the enmities in his flesh
6 29 for no man ever hated his own flesh
30 we are members of his body, of his f.
Col 1 22 he hath reconciled in the body of his f.
2 18 puffed up by the sense of his flesh
Heb 5 7 who in the days of his flesh, with a
10 20 through the veil, that is to say, his f.

in the flesh Lev 13 18 has been an ulcer i. . . .
Jer 9 26 nations are uncircumcised in the flesh
Rom 2 28 circumcision which is outwardly i. . . .
7 5 when we were in the f., the passions of

8 3 of sin, hath condemned sin in the flesh
8 they who are in the flesh, cannot please
9 you are not in the flesh, but in spirit
2 C 10 3 though we walk in the flesh, we do not
Gal 2 20 I live now in the flesh: I live in faith
6 12 as many as desire to please in the f.
Eph 2 11 being heretofore Gentiles in the flesh
11 which is called circumcision in the f.
Phil 1 22 if to live in the flesh, this is to me
24 to abide still in the flesh, is needful
3 3 Jesus, not having confidence in the f.
4 might also have confidence in the flesh
4 thinketh he may have confidence in the f.
Col 2 1 have not seen my face in the flesh: that
1 Tim 3 16 which was manifested in the flesh, was
Philem 16 how much more to thee both in the flesh
1 P 3 18 being put to death indeed in the flesh
4 1 Christ therefore having suffered i. . . .
1 that hath suffered i. . . . hath ceased
2 he may live the rest of his time i. . . .
6 indeed according to men, in the flesh
1 J 4 2 Jesus Christ is come i. . . . 2 J 7
my flesh Gen 2 23 this now is bone . . . f. of my f.
2 K 19 13 art not thou my bone and my flesh
Job 4 15 before me, the hair of my flesh stood up
6 12 of stones, nor is my flesh of brass
7 5 my flesh is clothed with rottenness
13 14 why do I tear my flesh with my teeth
16 16 and have covered my flesh with ashes
19 22 and glut yourselves with my flesh? Who
26 and in my flesh I shall see my God
21 6 and trembling taketh hold on my flesh
Ps 15 9 my flesh also shall rest in hope
26 2 draw near against me, to eat my flesh
27 7 and my flesh hath flourished again
37 4 there is no health in my flesh. 8
62 2 for thee my flesh, O how many ways
72 26 for thee my flesh and my heart hath
83 3 my heart and my flesh have rejoiced
101 6 my bone hath cleaved to my flesh. I am
108 24 fasting: and my flesh is changed for
118 120 pierce thou my flesh with thy fear
Ecce 2 3 to withdraw my flesh from wine, that
Jer 51 35 the wrong done to me and my flesh be
Lam 3 4 my skin and my flesh he hath made old
John 6 52 bread that I will give is my flesh
55 he that eateth my f. and drinketh. 57
56 my flesh is meat indeed: and my blood
Acts 2 26 moreover my flesh also shall rest in
Rom 7 18 not in me, that is to say, in my flesh
11 14 them who are my flesh, and may save
2 C 12 7 there was given me a sting of my flesh
Gal 4 13 and your temptation in my flesh, you
Col 1 24 of the sufferings of Christ, in my f.
of the flesh Exod 12 46 you carry forth o. . . .
Lev 6 29 of the priestly race shall eat o. . . .
7 18 any man eat of the flesh of the victim
20 one that is defiled shall eat of the f.
8 32 whatsoever shall be left of the flesh
13 3 than the skin and the rest of the flesh
17 11 life of the flesh is in the blood. 14
Deut 12 15 eating of the f. delight thee, kill and
16 4 neither shall any of the flesh of that
28 55 not give them of the f. of his children
Judg 6 19 the broth of the flesh into a pot, he
Prov 14 30 soundness of heart is life of the flesh
Ecce 12 12 much study is an affliction of the flesh
Eccu 23 6 let not the lusts of the f. take hold
2 Ma 6 21 of the flesh of the sacrifice: that
John 1 13 of blood or of the will of the flesh
3 6 which is born of the flesh is flesh
Rom 8 5 mind the things that are of the flesh
6 for the wisdom of the flesh is death
7 wisdom of the flesh is an enemy to God
13 you mortify the deeds of the flesh, you
9 8 not they that are children of the flesh
1 C 5 5 to Satan for the destruction of the f.
7 28 shall have tribulation of the flesh
2 C 7 1 cleanse . . . from all defilement of f.
Gal 4 13 know, how through infirmity of the f.
5 16 you shall not fulfil lusts of the flesh
19 now the works of the flesh are manifest
6 8 of the flesh also shall reap corruption
Eph 2 3 fulfilling the will of the flesh and of
Col 2 11 in despoiling of the body of the flesh
23 in any honor to the filling of the f.
Heb 9 10 justices of the flesh laid on them
13 defiled, to the cleansing of the flesh
1 P 3 21 putting away of the filth of the flesh
1 J 2 16 concupiscence of the flesh, and the
thy flesh Gen 40 19 the birds shall tear thy f.
1 K 17 44 I will give thy flesh to the birds
2 K 5 1 we are thy bone and thy flesh. 1 Pa 11:1
4 K 5 10 and thy flesh shall recover health
Prov 5 11 shalt have spent thy f. and thy body
Ecce 5 5 not thy mouth to cause thy flesh to sin
11 10 heart, and put away evil from thy flesh
Eccu 25 36 cut her off from thy flesh lest she
Isa 58 7 cover him and despise not thy own flesh
Eze 32 5 I will lay thy f. upon the mountains
fleshhook 1 K 2 13 with a f. of three teeth in his
1 K 2 14 all that the fleshhook brought up, the
fleshhooks Exod 27 3 tongs and f. and firepans
Exod 38 3 caldrons, tongs, fleshhooks, pothooks
Num 4 14 firepans, f. and forks, pothooks, and
3 K 7 50 pots and f. and bowls and mortars
4 K 12 13 bowls or f. or censers or trumpets
1 Pa 28 17 for f. also and bowls and censers of
2 Pa 4 11 Hiram made caldrons and fleshhooks
16 the caldrons and fleshhooks and bowls
Jer 52 18 they took the caldrons and the f. and
fleshly Tob 8 9 not for f. lust do I take my
2 C 3 3 but in the fleshly tables of the heart
2 P 2 18 allure by the desires of f. riotousness
flew Num 11 31 they f. in the air two cubits high
2 K 22 11 he rode upon the cherubims, and flew
Ps 17 11 he flew: he flew upon the wings of the
Isa 6 2 covered his feet, and with two they f.
6 and one of the seraphims flew to me
Nah 3 17 the sun arose, and they flew away, and
flies Exod 8 21 shall be filled with flies of
Exod 8 22 so that flies shall not be there: and
24 came a very grievous swarm of flies
24 land was corrupted by this kind of flies
29 the flies shall depart from Pharao
31 he took away the flies from Pharao
Ps 77 45 amongst them divers sorts of flies
104 31 there came divers sorts of flies and
Ecce 10 1 dying f. spoil sweetness of ointment
Wisd 16 9 bitings of locusts and of flies killed
19 10 how the ground brought forth flies
flieth Ps 90 6 arrow that flieth in the day, of the
Wisd 5 11 as when a bird flieth through the air
John 10 12 and leaveth the sheep and flieth: and
13 the hireling flieth because he is a
flight Num 21 29 hath given his sons to flight
Josu 8 20 as they that had counterfeited flight
24 had pursued after Israel in his flight
Judg 12 5 of Ephraim came thither in the flight
20 32 but they artfully feigning a flight
45 in that flight . . . they slew of them
2 K 18 16 from pursuing after Israel in their f.
Jdth 5 12 opened the sea to them in their flight
15 1 only to save themselves by flight: so
4 they went without order in their flight
7 in their flight had left behind them

Ps 141 5 flight hath failed me: and there is no
Wisd 5 11 parting it by the force of her flight
Isa 52 12 neither shall you make haste by flight
Amos 2 14 flight shall perish from the swift
9 1 there shall be no flight for them: they
Mat 24 20 pray that your flight be not in the
Heb 11 34 put to flight the armies of foreigners
fling Num 35 20 or fling anything at him with ill
flingeth Eccu 22 25 he that f. a stone at birds
flint Job 19 24 graven with an instrument in flint
Job 22 24 he shall give for earth flint, and for flint torrents of gold
28 9 stretched forth his hand to the flint
Isa 5 28 of their horses shall be like the f.
Eze 3 9 thy face like an adamant and like f.
flints Job 39 28 and dwelleth among cragged flints
floats 3 K 5 9 I will put them together in floats
2 Pa 2 16 will convey them in floats by sea
flock Gen 4 4 offered the firstlings of his flock
Gen 21 28 apart seven ewe lambs of the flock
27 9 go thy way to the flock, bring me
29 6 Rachel his daughter cometh with his f.
9 father's sheep for she fed the flock
11 having watered the flock, he kissed her
30 35 all the flock of one color, that is
36 son-in-law, who fed the rest of his f.
40 Jacob separated the flock and put the
35 21 pitched his tent beyond the Flock tower
37 2 was feeding the flock with his brethren
38 12 the Odollamite the shepherd of his f.
17 I will send thee a kid out of the flock
Exod 3 1 he drove the flock to the inner parts
Lev 3 6 sacrifice of peace offering be of the f.
4 32 if he offer of the flock a victim for
6 6 a ram without blemish out of the flock
Judg 15 1 and he brought her a kid of the flock
1 K 16 20 a bottle of wine and a kid of the flock
17 15 to feed his father's flock at Bethlehem
20 the charge of the flock to the keeper
34 took a ram out of midst of the flock
25 7 ought missing to them of the flock
1 Pa 17 7 the pastures, from following the flock
21 17 as for this flock, what hath it deserved
1 Es 10 19 offer for their offence a ram of the f.
2 Es 3 1 they built the f. gate: they sanctified
31 chamber of the corner of the flock gate
12 38 of Emath, and even to the flock gate
Job 21 11 their little ones go out like a flock
30 1 not have set with the dogs of my flock
Ps 64 14 the rams of the flock are clothed and
77 52 guided them in wilderness like a flock
106 41 made him families like a f. of sheep
113 4 hills like the lambs of the flock. 6
Cant 6 4 thy hair is as a flock of goats that
5 thy teeth as a flock of sheep which
Eccu 18 13 correcteth, as shepherd doth his flock
47 3 as with the lambs of flock in his
Isa 40 11 he shall feed his flock like a shepherd
63 11 the sea with the shepherds of his flock
Jer 10 21 and all their flock is scattered. Behold
13 17 f. of the Lord is carried away captive
20 where is the flock that is given thee
23 2 you have scattered my f. and driven
3 gather together the remnant of my flock
25 34 with ashes, ye leaders of the flock
35 leaders of the flock [no way] to save
36 howling of the principal of the flock
31 10 will keep him as shepherd doth his f.
49 20 little ones of f. shall cast them down
50 6 my people have been a lost flock, their
8 be ye as kids at the head of the flock
17 Israel is a scattered flock, the lions
51 23 in pieces the shepherd and his flock
Bar 4 26 for they were taken away as a flock
Eze 24 5 take the fattest of the flock and lay
34 3 was fat: but my flock you did not feed
8 my shepherds did not seek after my f.
10 I will require my flock at their hand
10 cause them to cease from feeding the f.
10 I will deliver my flock from their mouth
12 as the shepherd visiteth his flock
22 I will save my flock, and it shall be
36 37 I will multiply them as a flock of men
38 as a holy f., as the f. of Jerusalem
43 23 shalt offer . . . a ram of the flock. 25
45 15 one ram out of a flock of two hundred
Amos 6 4 that eat the lambs out of the flock
7 15 Lord took me when I followed the flock
Mich 2 12 I will put them together as a flock
4 8 thou, O cloudy tower of the flock
7 14 the flock of thy inheritance, them that
Haba 3 17 the f. shall be cut off from the fold
Zach 9 16 will save . . . as the f. of his people
10 2 they were led away as a flock: they
3 the Lord of hosts hath visited his f.
11 4 feed the flock of the slaughter, which
7 I will feed the flock of slaughter for this, O ye poor of the flock
7 I called a Cord, and I fed the flock
11 the poor of the flock that keep for me
17 shepherd . . . that forsaketh the flock
Mala 1 14 man that hath in his flock a male and
Mat 26 31 sheep of the flock shall be dispersed
Mark 10 1 and the multitudes flock to him again
Luke 2 8 keeping the night watches over their f.
12 32 fear not, little flock, for it hath
Acts 20 28 heed to yourselves, and to the whole f.
29 will enter in among you, not sparing f.
1 C 9 7 who feedeth the flock, and eateth not
7 and eateth not of the milk of the flock
1 P 5 2 feed the flock of God which is among
3 a pattern of the flock from the heart
flocked Mark 1 45 they f. to him from all sides
flocking 2 Ma 3 18 others also came f. together
Mark 6 33 they ran flocking thither on foot from
flocks Gen 29 7 the flocks into the folds again
Gen 29 8 mouth, then we may water the flocks
30 32 go round through all thy flocks and
38 when the flocks should come to drink
40 when the flocks were separated one
43 and he [Jacob] had many f., maidservants
31 4 field, where he [Jacob] fed the flocks
8 all the flocks brought forth white ones
18 he took all his substance and flocks
38 the rams of thy flocks I did not eat
41 for thy daughters, and six for thy f.
43 are mine, and the children and thy f.
32 7 flocks and the sheep and the oxen
33 13 in one day all the flocks will die
36 7 bear them, for the multitude of their f.
37 12 in Sichem feeding their father's f.
16 tell me where they feed the flocks
46 32 flocks and herds and all they have
47 4 because there is no grass for the f.
50 8 flocks and herds they left in the land
Exod 2 16 desired to water their father's flocks
10 26 all the flocks shall go with us: there
Lev 1 10 and if the offering be of the flocks
5 6 offer of the flocks an ewe lamb or a
15 ram without blemish out of the flocks
18 he shall offer of the flocks a ram
Num 32 1 sons of Ruben and Gad had many flocks
Deut 7 13 the flocks of thy sheep upon the land
12 21 shalt kill of thy herds and of thy f.
15 14 give him for his way out of thy flocks
Josu 14 4 suburbs to feed their beasts and flocks

Judg 5 16 mayest hear the bleatings of the flocks
6 5 all their flocks came with their tents
13 19 Manue took a kid of the flocks and the
1 K 8 17 your flocks also he will tithe and
15 9 spared Agag and the best of the flocks
14 meaneth then this bleating of the f.
30 20 he took all the flocks and the herds
3 K 20 27 like two little flocks of goats: but
1 Pa 4 39 valley to seek pastures for their f.
2 Pa 35 7 of lambs and of kids of the flocks
Job 24 2 have taken away flocks by force, and
Ps 49 9 house: nor he goats out of thy flocks
Prov 27 23 cattle, and consider thy own flocks
Cant 1 6 wander after the f. of thy companions
7 follow after the steps of the flocks
4 1 thy hair is as flocks of goats which
Isa 17 2 cities of Aroer shall be left for f.
32 14 joy of wild asses, the pastures of f.
60 7 the flocks of Cedar shall be gathered
61 5 strangers . . . shall feed your flocks
65 10 plains shall be turned to folds of f.
Jer 3 24 hath devoured . . . their flocks and
5 17 they shall eat up thy flocks and thy
6 3 shall come to her with their flocks
31 24 husbandmen and they that drive the f.
33 12 shepherds causing their f. to lie down
13 the flocks pass again under the hand
49 29 they shall take their tents and their f.
50 45 little ones of the f. shall pull them
Eze 25 5 of Ammon a couching place for flocks
34 2 should not the flocks be fed by the
6 my flocks were scattered upon the face
8 as my flocks have been made a spoil
8 fed themselves, and fed not my flocks
17 as for you, O my flocks, thus saith
31 you my flocks, the flocks of my pasture
36 38 waste cities be full of flocks of men
Osee 5 6 with their flocks . . . they shall go to
Joel 1 18 and the flocks of sheep are perished
Soph 2 14 flocks shall lie down in the midst
2 Ma 14 14 Gentiles . . . came to Nicanor by flocks
23 sent away the flocks of the multitudes
flocks of sheep Gen 13 5 had f . . . and herds
Gen 29 2 well in the field and three f. . . .
Deut 7 13 will bless . . . the flocks of thy sheep
8 13 shalt have herds of oxen and f. . . .
28 18 cursed . . . the flocks of thy sheep
51 nor oil nor herds of oxen nor f. . . .
1 K 15 9 spared Agag and the best of the f. . . .
2 Pa 32 29 he had f. . . . and herds without number
Jdth 2 8 herds of oxen and f. . . . 3:3; 8:7
Ps 77 70 David, and took him from the f. . . .
Ecce 2 7 and herds of oxen and great f. . . .
Cant 4 2 thy teeth as f. . . . that are shorn
Mich 5 8 as a young lion among the f. . . . : who
flood Gen 6 17 bring the waters of a great flood
Gen 7 7 ark because of the waters of the flood
10 waters of the f. overflowed the earth
17 flood was forty days upon the earth
9 11 neither . . . a flood to waste the earth
15 shall no more be waters of a flood
28 Noe lived after the flood 350 years
10 1 unto them sons were born after the f.
32 nations divided on earth after the f.
11 10 begot Arphaxad two years after the f.
Job 22 16 flood hath overthrown their foundation
28 4 the flood divideth from the people
Ps 28 10 the Lord maketh the flood to dwell
31 6 in a flood of many waters, they shall
Eccu 21 16 of wise man shall abound like a flood
39 28 as a flood hath watered the earth
40 10 for their sakes came the flood. All
44 18 remnant left . . . when the flood came
19 should no more be destroyed with the f.
Jer 46 7 who is this that cometh up as a flood
8 Egypt riseth up like a flood, and the
Dan 11 10 he shall come with haste like a flood
Jon 2 4 the sea, and a flood hath compassed me
Nah 1 8 with a flood that passeth by, he will
Mat 24 38 as in the days before the flood, they
39 they knew not till the flood came and
Luke 6 48 when a flood came, the stream beat
17 27 the flood came and destroyed them all
2 P 2 5 bringing in the flood upon the world
flood-gates Gen 7 11 f. of heaven were opened
Gen 8 2 flood-gates of heaven were shut up
4 K 7 2 Lord should make flood-gates. 19
Ps 41 8 at the noise of thy flood-gates. All
Isa 24 18 the flood-gates from on high are opened
Mala 3 10 if I open not unto you the f. of heaven
floods 2 K 22 5 f. of Belial have made me afraid
Job 36 27 and poureth out showers like floods
Ps 92 3 the f. have lifted up, O Lord: the f. have
lifted up their voice
3 the floods have lifted up their waves
Cant 8 7 neither can the floods drown it: if a
1 Ma 6 11 and into what floods of sorrow wherein
Mat 7 25 the rain fell and the floods came. 27
floor Deut 25 4 treadeth out thy corn on the floor
Judg 6 37 this fleece of wool on the floor; if
2 K 6 6 when they came to the floor of Nachon
24 24 David bought the floor and the oxen
3 K 6 6 the floor that was underneath was
6 third floor was seven cubits in breadth
6 middle floor was six cubits in breadth
10 and he built a floor over all the house
15 from the floor of the house to the top
15 covered floor of the house with planks
16 of the temple, from floor to the top
30 floor of the house he also overlaid
7 7 cedar wood from the floor to the top
1 Pa 13 9 they came to the floor of Chidon, Oza
21 20 he was thrashing wheat in the floor
28 11 a description . . . of the upper floor
2 Pa 3 6 he paved also the floor of the temple
Esth 1 6 upon a floor paved with porphyry and
Isa 21 10 my thrashing, and the children of my f.
30 24 as it was winnowed in the floor. And
Osee 9 2 the floor and the winepress shall not
13 3 driven with a whirlwind out of the f.
Mich 4 12 them together as the hay on the floor
Mat 3 12 he will thoroughly cleanse his floor
Luke 3 17 he will purge his floor, and will
floored Eze 41 16 f. with wood all round about
floors 3 K 6 5 of the temple he built floors
Joel 2 24 the floors shall be filled with wheat
flour Gen 18 6 together three measures of flour
Exod 16 31 taste thereof like to flour with honey
29 2 shalt make them all of wheaten flour
40 a tenth part of flour. Lev 14:21
Lev 2 2 shall take a handful of the flour. 6:15
4 a sacrifice baked in the oven of flour
5 flour tempered with oil. 9:4; 14:10; 23:13;
Num 7:19, 25, 31, 37, 43, 49, 55, 61, 67,
73, 79; 15:9; 28:9, 12, 13, 20, 28; 29:3,
9, 14
7 the flour shall be tempered with oil
5 11 tenth part of ephi of f. 6:20; Num 28:5
6 15 frankincense that is put upon the flour
7 9 every sacrifice of flour that is baked
23 17 two tenths of flour leavened, which
Num 15 6 there shall be a sacrifice of flour
Judg 6 19 unleavened loaves of a measure of flour
1 K 1 24 three calves and three bushels of flour
1 Pa 16 3 roasted beef, and flour fried with oil
Eccu 39 31 things necessary . . . bread of flour

fine flour Lev 2 1 offering shall be of f. f.
Lev 7 12 fine flour fried, and caked tempered
24 5 thou shalt take also fine flour and
Num 8 8 take . . . fine flour tempered with oil
15 4 shall offer a sacrifice of fine flour
2 K 6 19 beef, and fine flour fried with oil
3 K 4 22 provision . . . 30 measures of fine f.
4 K 7 1 a bushel of fine flour shall be sold
16 a bushel of fine flour was sold for
18 a bushel of fine flour for a stater
1 Pa 9 29 the charge of the fine flour and wine
23 29 the sacrifice of fine flour and of
Eccu 35 4 thanks, that offereth fine flour
38 11 savor, and a memorial of fine flour
Eze 16 13 thou didst eat fine flour and honey
19 which I gave thee, the fine flour
46 14 of oil to be mingled with the fine f.
Dan 14 2 twelve great measures of fine flour
2 Ma 1 8 we offered sacrifices and fine flour
Apoc 18 13 wine and oil and fine flour and wheat
flourish Ps 71 16 shall flourish like the grass
Ps 89 6 he shall flourish and pass away: in
91 13 the just shall flourish like the palm
14 shall f. in the courts of the house of
102 15 as flower of the field so shall he f.
131 18 upon him shall my sanctification f.
Prov 14 11 the tabernacles of the just shall f.
Ecce 12 5 way, the almond trees shall flourish
Cant 7 12 let us see if the vineyard flourish . . . if the pomegranates flourish
Wisd 4 4 if they f. in branches for a time, yet
Isa 17 11 in the morning thy seed shall flourish
35 1 rejoice, and shall f. like the lily
66 14 your bones shall flourish like an herb
Eze 17 24 have caused the dry tree to flourish
Osee 14 9 make him f. like a green fir tree
flourished Ps 27 7 my flesh hath f. again, and
Cant 2 15 for our vineyard hath flourished. My
6 10 to look if the vineyard had flourished
Eccu 51 19 she flourished as a grape soon ripe
Agge 2 20 the olive tree as yet flourished? From
Phil 4 10 your thought for me hath f. again, as
flourishing Prov 17 22 a joyful mind maketh age f.
Cant 1 15 and comely. Our bed is flourishing
Isa 18 5 before the harvest it was all f., and
Dan 4 1 in my house and f. in my palace: I saw
flow Lev 15 25 that ceaseth not to flow after the
Num 24 7 water shall flow out of his bucket
Deut 33 22 he shall flow plentifully from Basan
1 Pa 12 15 when it is used to flow over its banks
Job 36 28 which flow from the clouds that cover
Prov 22 18 it shall flow in thy lips: that thy
Ecce 1 7 rivers . . . they return, to flow again
Cant 4 16 let the aromatical spices thereof flow
Isa 2 2 and all nations shall flow unto it
66 11 milk out and flow with delights, from
Jer 31 12 shall flow together to the good things
51 44 shall no more flow together to him
Eze 21 2 let thy speech flow towards the holy
Joel 3 18 and the hills shall flow with milk
18 waters shall flow through all the
Mich 4 1 hills: and people shall flow to it
Zach 1 17 shall yet flow with good things: and
John 7 38 out of his belly shall flow rivers of
flowed Num 16 13 that f. with milk and honey, to
Ps 104 41 he opened the rock, and waters flowed
Eccu 50 3 the wells of water flowed out and they
Jer 49 4 thy valley hath flowed away, O delicate
Lam 3 54 waters have flowed over my head: I said
Jon 1 11 for the sea flowed and swelled. And he
flower Job 8 12 when it is yet in flower and is not
Job 14 2 who cometh forth like a flower and is
15 33 when its grapes are in the first flower
33 as an olive tree that casteth its f.
Ps 102 15 as f. of the field so shall he flourish
Cant 2 1 I am the flower of the field and the
13 the vines in flower yield their sweet
Wisd 2 7 let not the flower of the time pass
Eccu 42 9 lest she pass away the f. of her age
50 8 as the flower of roses in the days
Isa 11 1 a flower shall rise up out of his root
28 1 fading f. the glory of his joy. 4
40 6 glory thereof as the f. of the field
7 is withered, and the f. is fallen. 8
Jer 28 9 give a flower to Moab, for in its flower it shall go out
Nah 1 4 the flower of Libanus fadeth away. The
James 1 10 as the flower of the grass shall be
11 the flower thereof fell off, and the
1 P 1 24 glory thereof as the flower of grass
24 and the flower thereof is fallen away
flowers Lev 12 2 the separation of her flowers
Lev 15 24 with her in the time of her flowers
25 manner as if she were in her flowers
18 19 not approach a woman having her f.
20 18 lie with a woman in her flowers, and
3 K 7 49 the flowers like lilies, and the lamps
2 Pa 4 21 and certain flowers and lamps and
Cant 2 5 stay me up with flowers, compass me
12 the flowers have appeared in our land
7 12 if the f. be ready to bring forth
Eccu 24 23 my flowers are the fruit of honor and
39 19 send forth flowers, as the lily, and
floweth Exod 3 8 floweth with milk and honey. 17; 13:5; 33:3; Num 13:28; Deut 11:9; 31:20; Eccu 46:10
Num 16 14 floweth with rivers of milk and honey
flowing Exod 15 8 as the flowing water stood
Lev 20 24 flowing with milk and honey. Num 14:8; Deut 6:3; 26:9, 15; 27:3; Josu 5:6; Jer 11:5; 32:22; Bar 1:20; Eze 20:6, 15
Ps 143 13 full, flowing out of this into that
Cant 8 5 from the desert, flowing with delights
flown Wisd 5 11 moved her wings and hath f. through
Osee 9 11 their glory hath flown away like a
Nah 3 16 hath spread himself and flown away
flute Eccu 40 21 f. and the psaltery make a sweet
Dan 3 5 the trumpet and of the flute. 7, 10
15 hear sound of the trumpet, flute, harp
flutes Jdth 3 10 dances and timbrels and flutes
flux Acts 28 8 sick of a fever, and of a bloody f.
fly Gen 1 20 fowl that may fly over the earth
Gen 7 14 all birds and all that fly went in
Exod 23 7 thou shalt fly lying. The innocent
Lev 11 20 of things that fly, whatsoever goeth
14 7 that it may fly into the field. And
53 let go the sparrow to fly freely away
Deut 4 17 or of birds, that fly under heaven
32 11 as the eagle enticing her young to fly
3 K 8 33 if thy people shall fly before their
Job 5 7 is born to labor and the bird to fly
Ps 54 7 dove, and I will fly and be at rest
Prov 10 4 same runneth after birds that fly away
23 5 or eagle, and shall fly towards heaven
Wisd 5 22 be shot out and shall fly to the mark
17 16 necessity from which he could not fly
Eccu 4 23 observe the time, and fly from evil
43 15 and the clouds fly out like birds
Isa 7 18 that the Lord shall hiss for the fly
8 22 cannot fly away from their distress
11 14 they shall fly from the shoulders of
60 8 who are these, that fly as clouds
Jer 48 20 he shall fly as an eagle and shall
49 22 he shall come up as an eagle and fly
Bar 6 21 other birds fly upon their bodies
67 which can fly under a covert and help

Eze 13 20 you catch, the souls that should fly
32 10 my sword shall begin to fly upon their
Dan 4 11 let the beasts fly away that are under
Osee 11 11 they shall fly away like a bird out of
Haba 1 8 they shall fly as an eagle that maketh
2 Ma 8 24 army, they obliged them to fly. And
Mat 2 13 and his mother, and fly into Egypt
John 10 5 they follow not, but fly from him
Acts 27 30 shipmen sought to fly out of the ship
1 C 6 18 fly fornication. Every sin that a man
10 14 fly from the service of idols. I speak
1 Tim 6 11 thou, O man of God, fly these things
James 4 7 the devil, and he will fly from you
Apoc 9 6 to die, and death shall fly from them
12 14 that she might fly into the desert
19 17 did fly through the midst of heaven
flyeth Deut 28 49 like an eagle that f. swiftly
flying Gen 31 20 that he was flying away. And when
Lev 11 23 of flying things whatsoever hath four
13 57 a flying and wandering leprosy: it must
26 36 sound of a flying leaf shall terrify
Job 9 26 as an eagle flying to the prey. If I
Ps 54 8 lo, I have gone far off flying away
Prov 26 2 as a bird flying to other places and
Eccu 11 3 the bee is small among flying things
Isa 16 2 as young ones flying out of the nest
30 6 the viper and the flying basilisk
31 5 as birds flying, so will the Lord of
Eze 13 20 wherewith you catch flying souls: and
Dan 9 21 flying swiftly touched me at the time
Zach 6 1 I saw, and behold a volume flying. And
2 I said: I see a volume flying: the
2 Ma 5 8 flying from the city, hated by all men
2 P 1 4 f. the corruption of that concupiscence
2 20 f. from the pollutions of the world
Apoc 4 7 living creature was like an eagle f.
8 13 eagle f. through the midst of heaven
14 6 angel f. through the midst of heaven
foal Gen 49 11 tying his foal to the vineyard, and
Zach 9 9 upon a colt the foal of an ass. And I
Mat 21 5 foal of her that is used to the yoke
foals Gen 32 15 she asses and ten of their foals
foameth Mark 9 17 and he foameth and gnasheth with
Luke 9 39 and teareth him, so that he foameth
foaming Mark 9 19 the ground, he rolled about f.
Jude 13 the sea, foaming out their own confusion
fodder Eccu 33 25 f. and a wand and a burden are
Eccu 38 27 his care is to give the kine fodder
foe Eccu 19 8 tell not thy mind to friend or foe
foes I K 25 22 and add more to the foes of David
fold Prov 6 10 wilt f. thy hands a little. 24:33
Mich 2 12 them together as a flock in the fold
Haba 3 17 flock shall be cut off from the fold
John 10 16 sheep I have that are not of this fold
16 shall be one fold and one shepherd
folded 4 K 2 8 Elias took his mantle and folded it
Isa 34 4 heavens shall be folded together as a
Lam 1 14 they are folded together in his hand
Eze 41 24 doors, which were folded within each
Luke 4 20 and when he had folded the book, he
Apoc 6 14 the heavens departed as a book folded up
foldeth Ecce 4 5 the fool f. his hands together
folding 3 K 6 34 and so opened with folding leaves
folds Gen 29 7 to bring the flocks into the folds
Num 32 24 folds and stalls for your sheep and
36 fenced cities, and folds for their
Deut 28 4 of thy herds and the folds of thy sheep
2 Pa 32 28 for all beasts and folds for cattle
Isa 65 10 plains shall be turned to f. of flocks
Soph 2 6 place of shepherds and f. for cattle
follies Ps 39 5 regard to vanities and lying f.
Amos 3 9 behold the many follies in the midst
folly Judg 19 23 cease I pray you from this folly
1 K 25 25 he is a fool, and folly is with him
2 K 13 12 done in Israel. Do not thou this folly
Job 6 30 neither shall folly sound in my mouth
8 14 his folly shall not please him, and
36 12 sword, and shall be consumed in folly
42 8 that folly be not imputed to you: for
Ps 21 3 it shall not be reputed as folly in me
Prov 5 23 in the multitude of his f. he shall be
6 32 for the f. of his heart shall destroy
12 23 the heart of fools publisheth folly
13 16 he that is a fool, layeth open his f.
14 17 the impatient man shall work folly
18 the childish shall possess folly, and
24 the folly of fools, imprudence. A
29 that is impatient, exalteth his folly
15 2 the mouth of fools bubbleth out folly
21 folly is joy to the fool: and the wise
17 12 than a fool trusting in his own folly
19 3 folly of a man supplanteth his steps
22 15 f. is bound up in the heart of a child
26 4 answer not a fool according to his folly
5 answer a fool according to his folly
11 so is the fool that repeateth his folly
27 22 his folly would not be taken from him
29 20 folly is rather to be looked for than
Ecce 1 17 and learning and errors and folly: and
2 3 to wisdom, and might avoid folly, till
12 to behold wisdom and errors and folly
13 I saw that wisdom excelled folly, till
5 2 in many words shall be found folly
10 1 than a small and short-lived folly
13 the beginning of his words is folly
Wisd 10 8 left also unto men memorial of their f.
Eccu 6 2 lest thy strength be quashed by folly
8 18 shalt perish together with his folly
13 10 that thou be not deceived into folly
11 humbled thou be deceived into folly
20 33 better is he that hideth his folly
21 27 folly of a man to hearken at the door
22 16 shalt not be wearied out with his folly
41 18 better is the man that hideth his folly
47 22 to have thy folly kindled, that thou
27 of his seed, the folly of the nation
Isa 9 17 and every mouth hath spoken folly
Jer 23 13 have seen f. in the prophets of Samaria
29 23 because they have acted folly in Israel
Bar 3 28 they perished through their folly. Who
Osee 2 10 I will lay open her folly in the eyes
2 Ma 4 6 that Simon would cease from his folly
2 C 11 1 bear with some little of my folly: but
2 Tim 3 9 their folly shall be manifest to all men
2 P 2 16 voice, forbade the folly of the prophet
fomented Isa 1 6 nor dressed nor f. with oil. Your
fond 2 K 13 2 was exceedingly fond of her, so that
food Gen 6 21 shalt take unto thee of all food
Gen 6 21 and it shall be food for thee and them
41 55 the people cried to Pharao for food
57 came into Egypt to buy food and to
42 1 hearing that food was sold in Egypt
10 but thy servants are come to buy food
43 2 go again and buy us a little food
20 we came down once before to buy food
45 7 the earth, and may have food to live
47 12 father's house, allowing food to every
16 for them I will give you food if you
17 he gave them food in exchange for their
22 a certain allowance of food was given
24 shall have for seed and for food for
Lev 3 11 burn them . . . for the food of the. 16
14 take of it for food of the Lord's fire
Num 11 22 that it may suffice for their food? Or
21 5 our soul now loatheth this very light f.
28 24 seven days for the food of the fire

Deut 8 3 and gave thee manna for thy food
10 18 and giveth him food and raiment. And
18 8 shall receive the same portion of food
Josu 5 12 use that food any more, but they ate
Ruth 1 6 his people, and had given them food
1 K 14 24 cursed be the man that shall eat food
24 so none of the people tasted any food
28 man that shall eat any food this day
2 K 9 10 shalt bring in f. for thy master's son
3 K 5 9 to furnish food for my household. So
19 6 and walked in the strength of that food
2 Pa 2 10 for their food 20,000 cores of wheat
Jdth 5 15 years they received food from heaven
Job 28 4 food of the needy man hath forgotten
30 4 the root of junipers was their food
36 31 and giveth food to many mortals. In his
38 41 who provideth food for the raven when
Ps 64 10 thou hast prepared their food: for so
68 22 they gave me gall for my food: and in
103 27 that thou give them food in season
110 5 hath given food to them that fear him
135 25 who giveth food to all flesh: for his
145 7 wrong: who giveth food to the hungry
146 9 who giveth to beasts their food: and
Prov 6 8 gathereth her food in the harvest
13 23 much food is in the tillage of fathers
27 27 milk of the goats be enough for thy f.
30 25 provide themselves food in the harvest
Wisd 16 2 them their desire of delicious food
3 they indeed desiring food, by means of
20 thy people with the food of angels
19 9 they fed on their food like horses
20 neither did they melt that good food
Eccu 14 17 in hell there is no finding food. All
Isa 65 25 and dust shall be the serpent's food
Jer 52 6 there was no food for the people of
Lam 1 11 given all their precious things for f.
19 while they sought their f. to relieve
Eze 47 12 the fruits thereof shall be for food
Dan 4 9 and in it was food for all. 18
Joel 1 16 is not your food cut off before your
Haba 3 17 the fields shall yield no food: the
Luke 9 13 and buy food for all this multitude
Acts 7 11 and our fathers found no food. But
14 16 filling our hearts with f. and gladness
1 C 10 3 and did all eat the same spiritual food
1 Tim 6 8 but having food, and wherewith to be
James 2 15 and want daily food: and one of you
fool 1 K 25 25 according to his name, he is a fool
Job 5 3 I have seen a fool with a strong root
Ps 13 1 the fool hath said in his heart: There
38 9 hast made me a reproach to the fool
48 11 the senseless and the fool shall perish
52 1 fool said in his heart: There is no God
91 6 nor will the f. understand these things
Prov 7 22 he is drawn like a fool to bonds, till
9 16 to the fool she said: Stolen waters are
10 8 precepts: a fool is beaten with lips
14 mouth of the fool is next to confusion
23 fool worketh mischief as it were for
11 29 winds: and the f. shall serve the wise
12 15 way of a fool is right in his own eyes
16 a fool immediately showeth his anger
13 16 that is a fool, layeth open his folly
14 3 in mouth of a fool is the rod of pride
9 a fool will laugh at sin, but among
14 fool shall be filled with his own ways
16 the fool leapeth over and is confident
15 5 a fool laugheth at the instruction
21 folly is joy to the fool: and the wise
17 7 eloquent words do not become a fool
10 than a hundred stripes with a fool
12 than a fool trusting in his own folly
16 what doth it avail a f. to have riches
21 a fool is born to his own disgrace
21 his father shall not rejoice in a fool
28 even a fool, if he will hold his peace
18 2 f. receiveth not the words of prudence
6 lips of a fool intermeddle with strife
7 the mouth of a fool is his destruction
13 showeth himself to be a fool and worthy
19 10 delicacies are not seemly for a fool
25 the fool shall be wiser: but if thou
24 7 wisdom is too high for a fool, in the
8 deviseth to do evils, shall be called f.
9 the thought of a fool is sin: and the
26 1 so glory is not seemly for a fool. As
4 answer not a f. according to his folly
5 answer a fool according to his folly
8 so is he that giveth honor to a fool
10 he that putteth a fool to silence
11 so is the fool that repeateth his folly
12 shall be more hope of a f. than of him
27 3 the anger of a fool is heavier than
22 shouldst bray a fool in the mortar
28 26 trusteth in his own heart, is a fool
29 9 if a wise man contend with a fool
11 a fool uttereth all his mind: a wise
30 22 by a fool when he is filled with meat
32 there is that hath appeared a fool
Ecce 2 14 his head: the fool walketh in darkness
16 of the wise no more than of the fool
19 whether he will be a wise man or a fool
4 5 the fool foldeth his hands together
6 8 what hath wise man more than the fool
7 7 under a pot, so is the laughter of a f.
10 anger resteth in the bosom of a fool
26 to know the wickedness of the fool
10 2 the heart of a fool is in his left hand
3 the fool when he walketh in the way
3 whereas he himself is a fool, esteemeth
6 a fool set in high dignity, and the rich
12 lips of a fool shall throw him down
14 a fool multiplieth words. A man cannot
Wisd 15 5 enticeth the fool to lust after it
Eccu 5 15 the tongue of the fool is his ruin
18 18 a fool will upbraid bitterly: and a
19 11 hearing of a word, the f. is in travail
12 so is a word in the heart of a fool
20 7 babbler and a fool will regard no time
14 gift of the fool shall do thee no good
17 a fool shall have no friend, and there
21 17 heart of a fool is like a broken vessel
19 the talking of a fool is like a burden
21 is destroyed, so is wisdom to a fool
22 doctrine to a fool is as fetters on
23 a fool lifteth up his voice in laughter
25 foot of a f. is soon in his neighbor's
26 a fool will peep through the window
22 7 that teacheth a fool is like one that
9 who uttereth wisdom to a fool: and in
10 weep for the f., for his understanding
12 wicked life of a wicked fool is worse
13 mourning . . . for a fool and an ungodly
14 talk not much with a fool, and go not
17 what other name hath he but fool? Sand
22 fearful heart in imagination of a fool
23 fearful heart in the thought of a fool
25 4 an old man that is a fool and doting
27 12 but a fool is changed as the moon. In
31 7 every fool shall perish by it. Blessed
40 is the stumblingblock of the fool
33 5 heart of a fool is as a wheel of a cart
Isa 32 5 the fool shall no more be called prince
6 the fool will speak foolish things
Jer 10 14 every man is become a f. for knowledge

10 3 is a fool, esteemeth all men fools
15 the labor of fools shall afflict them
Wisd 5 4 we fools esteemed their life madness
Eccu 8 20 advise not with fools, for they cannot
20 13 the graces of fools shall be poured out
21 29 the heart of fools is in their mouth
34 1 deceitful: and dreams lift up fools
Isa 19 11 princes of Tanis are become fools. 13
32 4 the heart of fools shall understand
35 8 so that fools shall not err therein
Luke 11 40 ye fools, did not he that made that
Rom 1 22 themselves to be wise, they became f.
1 C 4 10 we are fools for Christ's sake, but
foot Gen 8 9 where her foot might rest, returned
Gen 25 25 held his brother's foot in his hand
32 31 but he [Jacob] halted on his foot
35 8 and was buried at the foot of Bethel
41 44 no man shall move hand or foot in all
Exod 12 37 being about 600,000 men on foot, beside
21 24 hand for hand, foot for foot. Deut 19:21
24 4 built an altar at the foot of the mount
25 26 four golden rings . . . over each foot
29 20 great toes of their right hand and foot
30 18 laver with its foot. 31:9; 40:11
32 19 broke them at the foot of the mount
35 16 vessels thereof: the laver and its foot
37 13 four corners at each foot of the table
38 8 the laver of brass with the foot thereof
39 39 laver with the foot thereof. Lev 8:11
Lev 4 7 rest of the blood at the foot of the
18 he shall pour at the foot of the altar
25 and pouring out the rest at the foot
30 and shall pour out the rest at the foot
34 the rest he shall pour out at the foot
8 23 great toe of his right foot. 14:14, 17, 25, 28
9 9 poured the rest at the foot thereof
21 19 if his foot or if his hand be broken
Num 22 25 wall, and bruised the foot of the rider
Deut 2 5 as the step of one foot can tread upon
3 17 to the foot of mount Phasga eastward
4 11 you came to the foot of the mount which
49 and unto the foot of mount Phasga. And
8 4 for age, and thy foot is not worn, lo
11 24 place that your foot shall tread upon
25 9 shall take off his shoe from his foot
28 35 incurable from sole of the foot to
56 nor set down her foot for over much
65 be any rest for the sole of thy foot
32 35 in due time, that their foot may slide
33 24 and let him dip his foot in oil. His
Josu 1 3 place that the sole of your foot shall
11 3 also who dwelt at the foot of Hermon
14 9 the land which thy foot hath trodden
Judg 4 15 from off his chariot, fled away on foot
Ruth 4 8 he took it off from his foot. And he
1 K 23 22 consider the place where his foot is
25 20 down to the foot of the mountain, David
2 K 14 25 from the sole of the foot to the crown
15 16 forth, and all his household on foot
17 king going forth and all Israel on foot
18 who had followed him from Geth on foot
21 20 each hand, and six toes on each foot
3 K 18 44 cloud arose out of sea like man's foot
1 Pa 20 6 six on each hand and foot: who also
2 Pa 33 8 make the foot of Israel to be removed
Jdth 2 7 and 120,000 fighting men on foot, and
5 12 of the sea and passed it dry foot
6 9 tied Achior to a tree hand and foot
Job 18 9 sole of his foot shall be held in a
23 11 my foot hath followed his steps, I
29 15 to the blind, and a foot to the lame
31 5 and my foot hath made haste to deceit
39 15 she forgetteth that the foot may tread
Ps 9 16 their foot hath been taken in the very
25 12 my foot hath stood in the direct way
35 12 let not the foot of pride come to me
55 2 for man hath trodden me under foot
65 6 in the river they shall pass on foot
67 24 thy foot may be dipped in the blood
90 12 lest thou dash thy f. against a stone
13 shalt trample under foot the lion
93 18 if I said: My foot is moved: thy mercy
120 3 may he not suffer thy f. to be moved
Prov 1 15 restrain thy foot from their paths
3 23 way, and thy foot shall not stumble
26 will keep thy foot that thou be not
4 27 the left: turn away thy foot from evil
6 13 presseth with the foot, speaketh with
25 17 withdraw thy f. from the house of thy
19 is like a rotten tooth and weary foot
26 as a fountain troubled with the foot
Ecce 4 17 keep thy f. when thou goest into the
Eccu 6 36 thy foot wear the steps of his doors
21 25 foot of a fool is soon in his neighbor's
46 10 the number of 600,000 men on foot
50 17 poured out at the foot of the altar
51 20 my foot walked in the right way and
Isa 1 6 from the sole of the foot unto the top
14 25 upon my mountains tread him under foot
16 4 failed, that trod the earth under foot
18 7 from a nation . . . trodden under foot
26 6 the foot shall tread it down, the feet
32 20 sending thither the foot of the ox
37 25 have dried up with the sole of my foot
58 13 if thou turn away thy foot from the
Jer 2 25 keep thy foot from being bare and thy
12 10 have trodden my portion under foot
Bar 5 6 they went out from thee on foot, led
Eze 1 7 the sole of their foot was like the sole of a calf's foot
6 11 and stamp with thy foot and say: Alas
16 6 that thou wast trodden under foot
22 trodden under foot in thy own blood
25 6 thy hands and stamped with thy foot
29 11 foot of man shall not pass through it
11 neither shall the foot of beasts go
32 13 foot of man shall trouble them no more
36 3 been desolate and trodden under foot
Dan 8 13 the strength be trodden under foot
Amos 2 15 the swift of foot shall not escape
Mich 5 5 when he shall set his foot in our houses
7 10 now shall she be trodden under foot
Haba 2 1 I will . . . fix my foot upon the tower
3 12 thou wilt tread the earth under foot
Zach 10 5 treading under foot the mire of the ways
1 Ma 5 48 we will only pass through on foot. But
10 72 your foot cannot stand before our face
2 Ma 5 21 and the sea passable on foot: such was
10 26 lying prostrate at the foot of the altar
11 4 in the multitude of his foot soldiers
Mat 4 6 lest perhaps thou dash thy f. Luke 4:11
14 13 followed him on foot out of the cities
18 8 if . . . thy f. scandalize. Mark 9:44
Mark 6 33 they ran flocking thither on foot from
Acts 7 5 in it; no, not the pace of a foot: but
1 C 12 15 if the foot should say, because I am not
Heb 10 29 hath trodden under foot the Son of God
Apoc 10 2 and he set his right foot upon the sea
2 sea, and his left foot upon the earth
11 2 holy city they shall treat under foot
footmen Num 11 21 there are 600,000 f. of this
Judg 20 2 people of God, 400,000 f. fit for war
1 K 4 10 there fell of Israel 30,000 footmen
8 11 and his running f. to run before his
15 4 them as lambs: 200,000 footmen and
2 K 8 4 from him, 1,700 horsemen and 20,000 f.

10 6 and the Syrians of Soba, 20,000 f.
3 K 20 29 slew of the Syrians 100,000 footmen
4 K 13 7 and ten chariots and 10,000 footmen
1 Pa 18 4 and 7,000 horsemen and 20,000 footmen
19 18 slew of the Syrians . . . 40,000 footmen
Jdth 7 2 in his troops 120,000 footmen and
Eccu 16 11 so did he with the 600,000 footmen
Jer 12 5 been wearied with running with footmen
1 Ma 6 30 number of his army was 100,000 footmen
15 38 gave him army of footmen and horsemen
16 5 army of f. and horsemen came against
7 set the horsemen in the midst of the f.
2 Ma 11 11 they slew of them 11,000 footmen and
12 10 five thousand footmen . . . set upon
20 who had with him 120,000 footmen and
33 he came out with 3,000 footmen and
13 2 having with him 110,000 footmen, 5,000
footstep Bar 2 23 land shall be without any f.
footsteps Ps 16 5 that my f. be not moved. I have
Ps 76 20 and thy footsteps shall not be known
Dan 14 18 pavement, mark whose f. these are
19 I see the f. of men and women and
footstool 1 Pa 28 2 the f. of our God might rest
2 Pa 9 18 king made . . . a footstool of gold
Ps 98 5 adore his footstool, for it is holy
109 1 until I make thy enemies thy footstool
Isa 66 1 my throne, and the earth my footstool
Lam 2 1 hath not remembered his footstool
Mat 5 35 by the earth, for it is his footstool
22 44 until I make thy enemies thy f. Mark 12:36; Luke 20:43; Acts 2:35; Heb 1:13
Acts 7 49 is my throne, and the earth my f.
Heb 10 13 until his enemies be made his footstool
James 2 3 thou there, or sit under my footstool
forbade Deut 2 37 places which Lord our God f.
Jdth 11 12 which God f. them to touch, in corn
Mark 9 37 who followeth not us, and we forbade him
Luke 9 49 in thy name, and we forbade him because
Acts 27 43 f. it to be done; and he commanded that
2 P 2 16 voice, forbade the folly of the prophet
forbear 3 K 22 6 Galaad to fight, or shall I f.
3 K 22 15 Galaad to battle, or shall we forbear
2 Pa 18 5 Galaad to fight or shall we forbear
14 to Ramoth Galaad to fight, or forbear
35 21 forbear to do against God, who is with
2 Es 9 30 thou didst f. with them for many years
Prov 24 11 drawn to death forbear not to deliver
Eze 2 5 will hear and if so be they will f.
7 if perhaps they will hear and forbear
3 11 if so be they will hear and will f.
27 he that forbeareth, let him forbear
2 C 12 6 I f., lest any man should think of me
forbearance Rom 3 26 through f. of God, for the
forbeareth Eze 3 27 that f., let him forbear
forbearing Eph 6 9 to them f. threatenings, knowing
1 Th 3 1 f. no longer, we thought it good to
5 I, forbearing no longer, sent to know
forbid Num 11 28 said: My lord Moses forbid them
Num 22 13 Lord hath f. me to come with you
Deut 4 23 which the Lord hath forbid to be made
Judg 7 4 whom I shall forbid to go, let him
1 Ma 1 47 should f. holocausts and sacrifices
Mat 19 14 forbid them not to come to me. Mark 10: 14; Luke 18:16
Mark 9 38 but Jesus said: Do not forbid him
Luke 6 29 forbid not to take thy coat also. Give
9 50 forbid him not; for he that is not
Acts 10 47 can any man forbid water, that these
1 C 14 39 and forbid not to speak with tongues
God forbid Gen 44 17 God f. that I should do so
Josu 24 16 God forbid we should leave the Lord
1 K 20 2 God forbid, thou [David] shalt not die
2 K 20 20 God forbid that I should, I do not
1 Pa 11 19 saying: God f. that I should do this
Job 27 5 God f. that I should judge you to be
1 Ma 9 10 God forbid we should do this thing
Luke 20 16 they hearing, said to him: God forbid
Rom 3 3 faith of God without effect? God f.
6 I speak according to man. God forbid
31 God forbid: but we establish the law
6 2 God forbid. For we that are dead to sin
15 the law, but under grace? God forbid
7 7 is the law sin? God forbid. But I do
13 made death unto me? God forbid. But sin
9 14 is there injustice with God? God forbid
11 1 hath God cast away his people? God f.
11 stumbled, that they should fall? God f.
1 C 6 15 the members of an harlot? God forbid
Gal 2 17 then the minister of sin? God forbid
3 21 against the promises of God? God forbid
6 14 God forbid that I should glory, save in
forbidden Lev 4 27 by law of Lord are f. 5:17
Josu 6 18 ought of those things that are f.
4 K 12 8 the priests were f. to take any more
2 Ma 6 5 things which were forbidden by the laws
Acts 16 6 they were f. by the Holy Ghost to
forbiddeth Lev 4 22 that the law of the Lord f.
2 Ma 12 40 which the law forbiddeth to the Jews
3 J 10 them that do receive them he f. and
forbidding Luke 23 2 f. to give tribute to Caesar
1 Tim 4 3 f. to marry, to abstain from meats
forbore 1 K 23 13 wherefore he [Saul] f. to go out
Jer 41 8 he forbore, and slew them not with
forborne Jer 51 30 of Babylon have f. to fight
force Gen 21 25 servants had taken away by force
Gen 31 31 wouldst take away thy daughters by f.
Lev 6 2 shall by force extort anything, or
Judg 3 22 with such force that the haft went in
1 K 2 16 me now or else I will take it by force
2 K 13 12 do not so, my brother, do not force me
2 Pa 32 2 whole force of the war was turning
Jdth 1 4 he gloried . . . in the f. of his army
5 27 his armies, men unarmed and without f.
Job 24 2 have taken away flocks by force and
40 11 his force in the navel of his belly
Wisd 4 4 through the force of winds they shall
5 11 parting it by the force of her flight
7 20 rage of wild beasts, the force of winds
16 17 in water . . . the fire had more force
22 snow and ice endured the force of fire
18 22 overcame . . . nor with force of arms
19 12 foregoing signs by the f. of thunders
Eccu 9 4 thou perish by the force of her charms
39 34 they shall pour out their force: and
46 6 by hailstones of exceeding great force
Isa 40 29 he that . . . increaseth force and might
Dan 8 6 towards him in the f. of his strength
24 strengthened, but not by his own force
14 35 over the den in the f. of his spirit
1 Ma 1 53 that should force them to do these
7 29 prepared to take away Judas by force
13 38 in your favor, shall stand in force
2 Ma 10 17 assaulting them with great force, won
24 would take Judea by force of arms
Mat 5 41 will force thee one mile, go with him
John 6 15 to take him by force and make him king
Acts 23 10 to take him by force from among them
25 Jews might take him away by f. and kill
Heb 9 17 testament is of f., after men are dead
James 3 4 the force of the governor willeth
forced Gen 47 22 not f. to sell their possesions
Deut 19 3 who is forced to flee for manslaughter
1 K 13 12 forced by necessity, I [Saul] offered
28 23 his servants and the woman forced him
2 K 15 20 shalt thou be f. to go forth with us
23 21 forced the spear out of the hand of

4 K 5 23 he forced him, and bound two talents
Jdth 2 14 and he forced all the stately cities
Eccu 31 25 if thou hast been forced to eat much
Mat 27 32 him they forced to take up his cross
Mark 15 21 they forced one Simon a Cyrenian who
forces 2 K 8 9 defeated all the f. of Adarezer
Eccu 28 18 hath cut in pieces the forces of people
Dan 11 10 shall assemble multitude of great f.
10 he shall join battle with his forces
1 Ma 3 27 gathered the forces of all his kingdom
41 were joined to them the forces of Syria
4 3 to attack the king's forces that were
9 66 he began to slay and to increase in f.
10 36 as is due to all the king's forces
71 if thou trustest in thy forces, come
11 38 sent away all his forces, every man
60 and all the forces of Syria gathered
13 54 he made him captain of all the forces
15 10 and all the forces assembled to him
forcibly Mich 2 2 houses they have f. taken them
ford Gen 32 22 passed over the ford of Jaboc
fords Josu 2 7 that leadeth to the f. of the Jordan
Judg 3 28 seized upon the fords of the Jordan
12 5 the Galaadites secured the fords of the
2 K 19 18 they passed the fords before the king
Jer 51 32 the fords are taken, and the marshes
fore 2 Ma 3 25 struck Heliodorus with his f. feet
foreboding Gen 41 11 dream f. things to come
forecast Dan 11 24 f. devices against the best
2 C 8 21 for we forecast what may be good not
forecasteth Wisd 17 10 always f. grievous things
forefathers Esth 1 13 and judgments of their f.
2 Tim 1 3 whom I serve from my forefathers with
forefront Eze 47 1 f. of the house looked toward
forefronts Eze 40 38 door in the f. of the gates
forego Ruth 4 6 which I profess I do willingly f.
foregoing Wisd 19 12 not without f. signs by the
forehead Exod 28 38 over f. of the high priest
Exod 28 38 the plate shall be always on his f.
Lev 8 9 upon the miter over the f., he put
13 41 if the hair fall from his forehead
42 if in the bald head or in the bald f.
1 K 17 49 struck the Philistine in the forehead
49 and the stone was fixed in his forehead
2 Pa 26 19 there arose a leprosy in his forehead
20 and saw the leprosy in his forehead
Isa 3 21 rings, and jewels hanging on the f.
48 4 as an iron sinew, and thy f. as brass
Jer 3 3 thou hadst a harlot's forehead, thou
Eze 3 7 the house of Israel are of a hard f.
8 thy f. harder than their foreheads
16 12 and I put a jewel upon thy forehead
Apoc 14 9 receive his character in his f. or in
17 5 on her forehead a name was written
foreheads Eze 3 8 forehead harder than their f.
Eze 9 4 mark Thau upon the foreheads of the men
Apoc 7 3 the servants of our God in their f.
9 4 not the sign of God on their foreheads
13 16 in their right hand or on their f.
14 1 name of his Father written on their f.
20 4 nor received his character on their f.
22 4 his name shall be on their foreheads
foreign Exod 2 22 stranger in a f. country. 18:3
Exod 21 8 no power to sell her to a f. nation
2 Pa 14 2 he destroyed the altars of f. worship
Osee 8 12 laws, which have been accounted as f.
1 Ma 11 38 except the foreign army, which he had
2 Ma 4 13 progress of heathenish and f. manners
5 10 neither having foreign burial nor
10 24 together a multitude of foreign troops
14 26 Nicanor assented to the f. interest
Acts 26 11 I persecuted them even unto f. cities
foreigner Exod 12 43 no f. shall eat of it. But
Deut 15 3 of the f. or stranger thou mayst exact
foreigners Ps 59 10 the f. are made subject. Who
Ps 86 4 behold the foreigners, and Tyre and the
Abdi 11 and foreigners entered into his gates
Eph 2 19 you are no more strangers and f.; but
Heb 11 34 put to flight the armies of f.: women
foreknew Rom 8 29 whom he f., he also predestinated
Rom 11 2 not cast away his people, which he f.
foreknowledge Acts 2 23 counsel and f. of God, you
1 P 1 2 according to the f. of God the Father
foreknown 1 P 1 20 f. indeed before the foundation
foremost Gen 33 2 handmaids and their children f.
2 K 18 27 running of the f. seemeth to me like
forepart Exod 14 19 of the cloud, leaving the f.
Eze 42 7 on the forepart of the chambers, was
Acts 27 41 forepart indeed, sticking fast, remained
29 30 cast anchors out of the f. of the ship
forerunner Heb 6 20 where the f. Jesus is entered
forerunners Wisd 12 8 wasps, f. of thy host, to
foresaid 1 K 10 10 they came to the f. hill, and
3 K 4 27 the f. governors of the king fed them
2 Pa 22 6 received many wounds in the f. battle
Tob 4 22 and receive of him the foresaid sum of
2 Ma 3 7 to bring him the foresaid money. So
foresaw Acts 2 25 I f. the Lord before my face
foresee Ecce 4 13 knoweth not to f. for hereafter
foreseeing Acts 2 31 f. this, he spoke of the
Gal 3 8 the scripture, f., that God justifieth
foreseen Ps 138 4 and thou hast f. all my ways
Wisd 7 21 such things as are hid, and not foreseen
foreseeth Ps 36 13 f. that his day shall come
foreshowed Wisd 18 19 that troubled them f. these
foreskin Gen 17 11 circumcise flesh of your f.
Gen 17 14 flesh of his f. shall not be circumcised
23 circumcised the flesh of their foreskin
24 circumcised the flesh of his f. Jdth 14:6
Exod 4 25 circumcised the foreskin of her son
Deut 10 16 circumcise the foreskin of your heart
Jer 9 25 every one that hath the f. circumcised
foreskins Josu 5 3 in the hill of the foreskins
1 K 18 25 only 100 foreskins of the Philistines
27 two hundred men, and brought their f.
2 K 3 14 for a hundred f. of the Philistines
Jer 4 4 take away the f. of your hearts, ye
forest 1 K 14 25 common people came into a forest
1 K 14 26 when the people came into the forest
22 5 and came into the forest of Haret
2 K 18 6 battle was fought in the f. of Ephraim
8 more of people whom the forest consumed
17 cast him into a great pit in the f.
3 K 7 2 house of forest of Libanus. 10:17, 21
4 K 2 24 came forth two bears out of the forest
14 9 beasts of the f. that are in Libanus
19 23 thereof and the forest of its Carmel
2 Es 2 8 Asaph the keeper of the king's forest
Eccu 28 12 wood of the f. is, so the fire burneth
Isa 9 18 shall kindle in the thicket of the f.
10 18 glory of his forest and of his beautiful
19 that remain of the trees of his forest
34 thickets of the forest shall be cut
21 13 in the f. at evening you shall sleep
22 8 the armory of the house of the forest
29 17 charmel shall be esteemed as a forest
32 15 charmel shall be counted for a forest
19 hail shall be in the descent of the f.
37 24 its height, to the forest of its Carmel
44 14 that stood among the trees of the f.
23 sound with praise, thou, O forest
56 9 to devour, all ye beasts of the forest
Jer 10 3 hath cut a tree out of the forest
21 14 and I will kindle a fire in the forest
46 23 they have cut down her forest, saith
Eze 20 46 prophesy against f. of the south field

47 say to the south forest: Hear the word
31 6 beasts of the f. brought forth their
Osee 2 12 I will make her as a forest, and the
Amos 3 4 will a lion roar in the forest if he
Mich 7 14 them that dwell alone in the forest
Zach 11 2 because the fenced forest is cut down
1 Ma 4 38 growing up in the courts as in a f.
forests 2 Pa 27 4 castles and towers in the f.
Eze 15 2 that are among the trees of the forests
6 vine tree among the trees of the f.
34 25 shall sleep secure in the forests. And
39 10 nor cut down out of the forests: for
Mich 3 12 as the high places of the forests
5 8 as a lion among the beasts of the f.
foretell Deut 8 19 now I f. thee that thou shalt
Deut 13 1 and he foretell a sign and a wonder
30 18 I foretell thee this day that thou
1 K 8 9 foretell them the right of the king
Eze 13 6 and they foretell lies, saying: The
2 C 13 2 I have told before, and f., as present
Gal 5 21 of the which I foretell you, as I have
foretelleth Deut 18 22 that same prophet f. in
2 K 7 11 Lord f. to thee, that the Lord will
Isa 41 26 that showeth nor that foretelleth
foretold Gen 21 2 time that God had foretold her
Gen 41 54 of scarcity, which Joseph had foretold
Num 26 65 Lord had foretold that they should die
1 K 3 13 I have f. unto him that I will judge
3 K 13 32 which he hath f. in word of the Lord
4 K 7 20 it fell out to him as it was foretold
23 16 spoke, who had foretold these things
17 came from Juda and f. these things
Isa 45 21 who hath foretold this from that time
48 5 I foretold thee of old, before they
Bar 1 20 curses which the Lord foretold by
Eze 33 33 when that which was f. shall come
Mat 28 7 I have foretold it to you. And they
Mark 13 23 behold I have foretold you all things
Acts 7 52 who f. of the coming of the Just One
Rom 9 29 as Isaias foretold: Unless the Lord of
Gal 5 21 as I have foretold to you, that day
1 Th 3 4 we foretold you that we should suffer
1 P 1 11 when it f. those sufferings that are
forgave Mat 18 27 let him go and f. him the debt
Mat 18 32 I forgave thee all the debt because
Luke 7 42 to pay, he forgave them both. Which
43 I suppose that he to whom he f. most
forge Ps 57 3 your hands forge injustice in the
Eccu 51 3 from the lips of them that forge lies
forged Num 16 28 I have not f. them out of my own
Deut 18 22 prophet hath forged it by the pride
Isa 41 7 encouraged him that f. at that time
Dan 13 43 have maliciously forged against me
forger Deut 13 5 forger of dreams shall be slain
Haba 2 18 the forger thereof hath trusted in a
forgers Job 13 4 shown that you are forgers of lies
Isa 45 16 the forgers of errors are gone together
forget Gen 27 45 he f. the things thou hast done
Gen 41 51 God hath made me to f. all my labors
50 17 to f. the wickedness of thy brethren
Deut 4 9 forget not the words that thy eyes have
23 lest thou ever forget the covenant of
31 nor forget the covenant by which he
6 13 lest thou forget the Lord, who brought
8 11 thou forget the Lord thy God. 19
9 7 forget not how thou provokedst the Lord
25 19 under heaven. See thou forget it not
1 K 1 11 not forget thy handmaid, and wilt give
9 5 lest perhaps my father forget the asses
4 K 17 38 the covenant . . . you shall not forget
Job 8 13 are the ways of all that forget God
11 16 shalt also forget misery, and remember
24 20 let mercy forget him: may worms be his
Ps 9 12 thy hand be exalted: forget not the poor
18 into hell, all the nations that f. God
12 1 how long, O Lord, wilt thou forget me
44 11 f. thy people and thy father's house
49 22 these things, you that forget God
58 12 lest at any time my people forget
73 19 f. not to the end the souls of thy poor
23 forget not the voices of thy enemies
76 10 or will God forget to show mercy? Or
77 7 and may not forget the works of God
102 2 never forget all he hath done for thee
118 16 justifications: I will not f. thy words
93 thy justifications I will never forget
141 but I forget not thy justifications
136 5 if I forget thee, O Jerusalem, let my
Prov 3 1 my son, forget not my law, and let thy
4 5 forget not, neither decline from the
31 5 lest they drink and forget judgment
7 let them drink, and forget their want
Wisd 16 23 did even forget its own strength. For
Eccu 7 29 forget not the groanings of thy mother
11 29 an hour maketh one f. great delights
23 19 lest God forget thee in their sight
29 19 forget not the kindness of thy surety
35 9 the Lord will not f. the memorial
37 6 forget not thy friend in thy mind, and
38 22 the latter end. Forget it not: for
Isa 44 21 my servant, O Israel, forget me not
49 15 can a woman forget her infant, so as
15 she should f., yet will not I f. thee
54 4 shalt forget the shame of thy youth
Jer 2 32 will a virgin forget her ornament or
23 27 seek to make my people forget my name
Lam 5 20 why wilt thou forget us forever? Why
Osee 1 6 Israel: but I will utterly forget them
4 6 God, I also will forget thy children
Amos 8 7 I will never forget all their works
1 Ma 1 51 that they should forget the law and
2 Ma 2 2 not forget the commandments of the
Heb 6 10 that he should forget your work, and
13 2 hospitality do not forget; for by
16 not forget to do good and to impart
forgetful James 1 25 not becoming a f. hearer
forgetfulness Ps 87 13 thy justice in land of f.
Wisd 14 26 forgetfulness of God, defiling of souls
16 11 lest falling into deep forgetfulness
17 3 were scattered under a dark veil of f.
forgeth Eccu 27 25 winketh with the eye f. wicked
forgettest Ps 43 24 f. our want and our trouble
forgetteth Lev 5 2 f. his uncleanness, he is
Job 39 15 she f. that the foot may tread upon
forgetting Phil 3 13 f. the things that are behind
forging Haba 2 18 trusted in a thing of his own f.
forgive Gen 50 17 to f. the servants of the God of
Exod 10 17 forgive me my sin this time also
23 21 he will not f. when thou hast sinned
32 31 either forgive them this trespass
Num 14 19 forgive . . . the sins of this people
30 9 of no effect: the Lord will forgive her
Deut 29 20 and the Lord would not forgive him
Josu 24 19 and will not forgive your wickedness
1 K 25 28 forgive the iniquity of thy handmaid
3 K 8 34 f. the sin of thy people Israel and
36 forgive the sins of thy servants and
39 and forgive, and do so as to give to
50 forgive thy people that have sinned
2 Pa 6 25 forgive the sin of thy people Israel
27 and forgive the sins of thy servants
30 and forgive and render to every one
39 and do judgment and forgive thy people
7 14 then will I hear from heaven and will f.
2 Es 5 10 let us f. the debt that is owing to us
Ps 24 18 my labor: and forgive me all my sins

39 14 forgive me, that I may be refreshed
77 39 he is merciful and will f. their sins
78 9 forgive us our sins for thy name's sake
Eccu 2 13 will f. sins in the day of tribulation
16 12 he is mighty to forgive and to pour
28 2 f. thy neighbor if he hath hurt thee
Isa 2 9 debased: therefore forgive them not
55 7 our God: for he is bountiful to forgive
Jer 18 23 forgive not their iniquity, and let not
31 34 I will forgive their iniquity. 36:3
33 8 I will forgive all their iniquities
Dan 4 24 perhaps he will forgive thy offences
Joel 2 14 he will return and forgive, and leave
Jon 3 9 can tell if God will turn and forgive
4 2 compassion, and easy to forgive evil
1 Ma 13 39 committed unto this day, we forgive it
Mat 6 12 f. us our debts, as we also f. our
14 if you will f. men their offences, your
14 will forgive you also your offences
15 but if you will not forgive. Mark 11:26
15 neither will your Father f. Mark 11:26
9 6 hath power on earth to forgive sins. Mark 2:10; Luke 5:24
18 21 offend against me, and I forgive him
35 if you f. not every one his brother
Mark 2 7 who can forgive sins but God. Luke 5:21
11 25 f. if you have aught against any man
25 that your Father . . . may forgive you
Luke 6 37 forgive, and you shall be forgiven
11 4 f. us our sins, for we also f. every
17 3 and if he do penance, forgive him
4 saying, I repent: forgive him. And
23 34 Father, f. them, for they know not
John 20 23 whose sins you shall forgive, they are
2 C 2 7 you should rather f. him and comfort
1 J 1 9 to f. us our sins, and to cleanse us
forgiven Lev 4 26 it shall be forgiven him. 31, 35; 5:10, 16, 18; Num 15:28
Lev 19 22 on him, and the sin shall be forgiven
Num 14 20 I have forgiven according to thy word
15 25 it shall be forgiven them because they
26 it shall be forgiven all the people
Ps 31 1 are they whose iniquities are forgiven
5 thou hast f. the wickedness of my sin
84 3 thou hast f. the iniquity of thy people
Eccu 5 5 be not without fear about sin forgiven
21 1 pray that they may be forgiven thee
28 2 then shall thy sins be forgiven to thee
Isa 22 14 this iniquity shall not be forgiven
27 9 iniquity of the house of Jacob be f.
40 2 to an end, her iniquity is forgiven
1 Ma 15 8 due to the king . . . is forgiven thee
Mat 9 2 thy sins are f. thee. 5; Mark 2:5, 9; Luke 5:20, 23; 7:48
12 31 and blasphemy shall be f. men, but
31 of the Spirit shall not be forgiven
32 against the Son of man, it shall be f.
32 Ghost, it shall not be f. Luke 12:10
Mark 3 28 all sins shall be forgiven unto the
4 12 and their sins should be forgiven them
Luke 6 37 forgive, and you shall be forgiven
7 47 many sins are forgiven her, because
47 to whom less is forgiven, he loveth
12 10 it shall be forgiven him: but to him
John 20 23 shall forgive, they are forgiven them
Acts 8 22 thought of thy heart may be f. thee
Rom 4 7 blessed are they whose iniquities are f.
Eph 4 32 even as God hath forgiven you in Christ
Col 3 13 Lord hath forgiven you, so do you also
James 5 15 if he be in sins, they shall be f. him
1 J 2 12 because your sins are forgiven you
forgiveness Lev 6 7 he shall have forgiveness
Ps 129 4 with thee there is merciful forgiveness
Eccu 17 28 his f. to them that turn to him! For
28 5 doth he ask forgiveness of God? Who
Dan 9 9 to thee . . . mercy and forgiveness
Mark 3 29 shall never have f., but shall be
Acts 13 38 through him f. of sins is preached to
26 18 that they may receive f. of sins, and
forgivest Tob 3 13 time of tribulation f. the sins
forgiveth Ps 102 3 who f. all thy iniquities: who
Luke 7 49 who is this that forgiveth sins also
forgiving 2 Es 9 17 thou, a f. God, gracious and
Eph 4 32 forgiving one another. Col 3:13
Col 2 13 together with him, f. you all offences
forgot Gen 40 23 butler . . . f. his interpreter
Deut 24 19 field, and hast forgot and left a sheaf
Judg 3 7 they f. their God and served Baalim
1 K 12 9 they forgot the Lord their God, and he
Ps 77 11 they f. his benefits and his wonders
101 5 withered: because I f. to eat my bread
105 13 had quickly done, they forgot his works
21 they f. God, who saved them, who had
118 139 because my enemies forgot thy words
Wisd 19 19 the water forgot its quenching nature
Jer 23 27 as their fathers forgot my name for
Osee 2 13 went after her lovers and forgot me
Mark 8 14 they forgot to take bread; and they
James 1 24 presently f. what manner of man he was
forgotten Gen 41 30 abundance before shall be f.
Lev 5 3 having forgotten it, come afterwards
4 sweareth . . . and having forgotten it
Num 15 24 the multitude have forgotten to do it
Deut 26 13 I have . . . forgotten thy precepts
32 18 forgotten the Lord that created thee
Job 19 14 they that knew me, have forgotten me
28 4 whom the food of the needy man hath f.
Ps 9 11 said in his heart: God hath forgotten
13 hath not forgotten the cry of the poor
19 the poor man shall not be forgotten
30 13 am forgotten as one dead from the heart
41 10 why hast thou f. me? And why go I
43 18 yet we have not forgotten thee: and we
21 if we have f. the name of our God, and
118 30 thy judgments I have not forgotten
61 I have not f. thy law. 109, 153
83 I have not forgotten thy justifications
176 I have not forgotten thy commandments
136 5 let my right hand be forgotten. Let my
Prov 2 18 hath forgotten the covenant of her God
Ecce 6 4 and his name shall be wholly forgotten
9 5 for the memory of them is forgotten
Wisd 2 4 and our name in time shall be forgotten
Eccu 3 15 relieving of father shall not be f.
13 13 not far from him, lest thou be f.
39 12 wisdom, and it shall never be forgotten
Isa 17 10 because thou hast f. God thy savior
23 15 that thou, O Tyre, shalt be forgotten
16 thou harlot, that hast been forgotten
49 14 me, and the Lord hath forgotten me
51 13 thou hast f. the Lord thy maker, who
57 11 thou hast forgotten me. Eze 22:12; 23:35
59 15 truth hath been forgotten; and he that
65 11 that have forgotten my holy mount
16 the former distresses are forgotten
Jer 2 32 my people have forgotten me. 18:15
3 21 they have f. the Lord their God
13 25 because thou hast forgotten me and
23 40 shame which shall never be forgotten
30 14 all thy lovers have forgotten thee
44 9 have you f. the evils of your fathers
50 5 covenant, which shall never be f.
6 they have f. their resting place
Lam 2 6 caused feasts and sabbaths to be f.
3 17 peace, I have forgotten good things
Bar 4 8 you have f. God, who brought you up

Eze 21 32 thou shalt be forgotten: for I the
33 13 all his justices shall be forgotten
Dan 14 37 hast not forgotten them that love thee
Osee 4 6 and thou hast f. the law of thy God
8 14 Israel hath forgotten his Maker and
13 6 lifted up their heart and have f. me
2 Ma 12 42 been committed might be forgotten
Mat 16 5 they had forgotten to take bread. Who
Luke 12 6 and not one of them is f. before God
Heb 12 5 you have forgotten the consolation
2 P 1 9 having f. that he was purged from his
forks Num 4 14 forks, pothooks, and shovels
1 K 13 21 their forks and their axes were blunt
4 K 25 14 took away . . . the forks and the cups
form Deut 4 12 but you saw not any form at all
1 K 28 14 he said to her: What form is he of
2 K 14 20 I should come about with this form
2 Pa 4 7 the form which they were commanded
Job 31 15 did not one and the same form me in
Cant 5 15 his form as of Libanus, excellent as
Wisd 11 18 made the world of matter without form
Isa 45 7 I form the light and create darkness
52 14 and his form among the sons of men
Jer 33 2 Lord, who will do and will form it
Eze 8 10 behold every form of creeping things
43 11 show them the form of the house
11 that they may keep the whole form
Dan 3 92 form of the fourth is like Son of God
11 25 they shall form designs against him
1 Ma 12 2 letters . . . according to the same form
Acts 7 44 according to the form which he had
Rom 2 20 having form of knowledge and of truth
6 17 unto that form of doctrine, into which
Phil 2 6 who being in the form of God, thought
7 taking the form of a servant, being made
2 Tim 1 13 hold the form of sound words, which thou
1 P 3 21 baptism being of the like form, now
formed Gen 2 7 formed man of the slime of the
Gen 2 8 wherein he placed man whom he had formed
19 having formed out of the ground all
Num 17 8 blossoms were formed into almonds
4 K 15 30 and formed a plot against Phacee, the
19 25 from the days of old I have formed it
Job 33 6 and of the same clay I also was formed
Ps 73 17 and the spring were formed by thee
89 2 or the earth and the world was formed
93 9 that f. the eye, doth he not consider
94 5 and his hands formed the dry land
103 26 this sea dragon which thou hast formed
118 73 thy hands have made me and formed me
138 5 thou hast formed me, and hast laid thy
16 days shall be formed, and no one in
Wisd 10 1 that was first formed by God the father
Isa 27 11 he that formed it shall not spare it
37 26 from the days of old I have formed it
40 19 hath the goldsmith formed it with gold
43 1 Lord that . . . formed thee, O Israel
7 glory I have formed him and made him
10 before me there was no God formed
21 this people have I formed for myself
44 2 the Lord that made and formed thee
10 who hath formed a god and made a graven
12 with hammers he hath formed it and
13 rule: he hath formed it with a plane
21 I have formed thee, thou art my servant
45 18 that formed the earth and made it, the
18 he formed it to be inhabited. I am
49 5 the Lord that formed me from the womb
54 17 no weapon that is formed against thee
Jer 1 5 before I formed thee in the bowels of
10 16 for it is he who formed all things
Amos 7 1 behold the locust was formed in the
2 Ma 7 22 I know not how you were formed in
23 that formed the nativity of man and
Rom 9 20 shall thing f. say to him that formed it
Gal 4 19 again, until Christ be formed in you
1 Tim 2 13 for Adam was first formed; then Eve
former Gen 29 30 love of the latter before the f.
Gen 40 13 will restore thee to thy former place
41 7 devoured all the beauty of the f. 24
20 they devoured and consumed the former
Exod 4 8 nor hear the voice of the former sign
14 27 break of day to the former place
34 1 tables of stone like unto the former
Lev 4 21 shall burn it as he did the former calf
6 11 shall put off his former vestments
13 4 the hair be of the former color. 21
55 that the former color is not returned
25 10 shall go back to his former family
26 45 I will remember my former covenant
27 24 it shall return to the former owner
Num 6 12 yet so that the f. days be made void
Deut 10 1 two tables of stone like the former. 3
24 4 the former husband cannot take her
Judg 1 10 was in former times Cariath-Arbe
16 28 restore to me now my former strength
Ruth 3 10 thy latter kindness has surpassed the f.
4 7 this in former times was the manner
3 K 20 25 horses according to the former horses
2 Pa 24 13 house of the Lord in its former state
28 13 and heap up upon our former offenses
1 Es 3 12 that had seen the former temple; when
2 Es 5 15 f. governors that had been before me
6 5 fifth time according to the f. word
Job 8 7 if thy former things were small, thy
8 inquire of the former generation and
Ps 70 1 sons of Jonadab and the former captives
78 8 remember not our former iniquities
Ecce 1 11 there is no remembrance of f. things
7 11 cause that f. times were better than
Eccu 21 1 for thy former sins also pray that
36 17 which the former prophets spoke in
Isa 41 22 tell us the former things what they
43 9 shall make us hear the former things
18 remember not f. things, and look not
46 9 remember the former age, and I am God
48 3 the f. things of old I have declared
65 16 the former distresses are forgotten
17 f. things shall not be in remembrance
Jer 11 10 are returned to the former iniquities
34 5 the former kings that were before thee
36 28 write in it all the former words that
Eze 40 21 according to measure of the former gate
24 thereof according to their f. measures
28 according to the former measures. 32, 35
Dan 7 24 he shall be mightier than the former
11 29 latter time shall not be like the f.
Zach 1 4 to whom the f. prophets have cried
7 7 by the hand of the former prophets
12 by the hand of his former prophets
8 11 people according to the former days
14 10 to the place of the former gate
1 Ma 4 47 a new altar according to the former
12 16 to renew with them the former amity
14 22 to renew the f. friendship. 17
15 3 to restore it to its former estate
Mat 21 36 other servants more than the former
Luke 9 19 that one of the f. prophets is risen
Acts 1 1 former treatise, I made, O Theophilus
15 7 in f. days God made choice among us
Rom 3 25 justice, for remission of former sins
Eph 4 22 to put off, according to f. conversation
Heb 7 18 is indeed a setting aside of the former
8 7 if that former had been faultless, there
13 a new, he hath made the former old. And
9 1 the f. indeed had also justifications

8 the former tabernacle was yet standing
15 which were under the former testament
10 32 but call to mind the f. days, wherein
1 P 1 14 the former desires of your ignorance
2 P 2 20 become unto them worse than the former
Apoc 2 19 last works which are more than the f.
13 12 executed all the power of the f. beast
21 4 for the former things are passed away
formerly Gen 42 9 which f. he had dreamed, he
Deut 2 12 Horrhites also formerly dwelt in Seir
20 giants formerly dwelt in it, whom the
Job 16 13 I that was f. so wealthy, am all on a
Isa 23 8 Tyre, that was formerly crowned, whose
1 Ma 3 30 should not have as formerly enough
Acts 26 9 I indeed did f. think, that I ought to
formeth Wisd 13 11 f. a vessel profitable for the
Wisd 15 17 he formeth a dead thing with his
Amos 4 13 he that formeth the mountains and
Zach 12 1 formeth the spirit of man in him
forming Prov 8 30 I was with him f. all things
fornicated Eccu 23 33 she hath f. in adultery
fornicating Deut 31 16 rising up will go a f.
Eze 6 9 their eyes that went a fornicating
fornication Num 14 33 and shall bear your f.
Judg 2 17 committing f. with strange gods and
2 Pa 21 13 imitating the f. of the house of Achab
Tob 4 13 to keep thyself, my son, from all f.
Prov 12 12 desire of the wicked is f. of evil men
Wisd 14 12 beginning of f. is devising of idols
Eccu 26 12 fornication of a woman shall be known
41 21 be ashamed of f. before father and
Jer 3 9 by the facility of her f. she defiled
13 27 neighing, the wickedness of thy f.
Eze 16 20 them to be devoured. Is thy f. small
34 after thee there shall be no such f.
41 and thou shalt cease from fornication
23 8 poured out their fornication upon her
11 carried her f. beyond f. of her sister
27 thy f. brought out of the land of Egypt
29 disgrace of thy f. shall be discovered
43 this woman still continue in her f.
Osee 1 2 the land by f. shall depart from the
4 11 f. and wine and drunkenness take away
12 the spirit of f. hath deceived them
18 they have gone astray by fornication
5 4 spirit of f. is in the midst of them
Mat 5 32 excepting for the cause of fornication
19 9 his wife, except it be for fornication
John 8 41 we are not born of fornication: we
Acts 15 20 refrain . . . from f., and from things
29 from things strangled, and from f. 21:25
Rom 1 29 being filled with all . . . fornication
1 C 5 1 heard, that there is f. among you, and
1 such f. as the like is not among the
6 13 but the body is not for fornication, but
18 fly fornication. Every sin that a man
18 he that committeth fornication, sinneth
7 2 for fear of f., let every man have his
2 C 12 21 f. and lasciviousness, that they have
Gal 5 19 which are f., uncleanness, immodesty
Eph 5 3 f. and all uncleanness, or covetousness
Col 3 5 upon the earth; f., uncleanness, lust
1 Th 4 3 that you should abstain from fornication
Jude 7 having given themselves to f., and
Apoc 2 21 she will not repent of her fornication
9 21 from their sorceries nor from their f.
14 8 the wine of the wrath of her f. 18:3
17 4 abomination and filthiness of her f.
19 2 which corrupted the earth with her f.
commit fornication Exod 34 16 thy sons also to c. f. with their gods
Lev 20 5 with him, to c. f. with Moloch, out
6 shall c. f. with them, I will set my
2 Pa 21 11 inhabitants of Jerusalem to c. f. 13
Isa 23 17 she shall c. f. again with all the
Eze 16 33 come to thee from every side to c. f.
20 30 and you c. f. with their abominations
Osee 4 13 therefore shall your daughters c. f.
14 your daughters, when they shall c. f.
1 C 10 8 neither let us c. f., as some of them
Apoc 2 14 children of Israel to eat and to c. f.
committed fornication Exod 34 15 c. f. with their
Exod 34 16 after they themselves have c. f., they
Lev 17 7 to devils, with whom they have c. f.
Num 25 1 c. f. with the daughters of Moab, who
Judg 8 27 all Israel c. f. with it, and it became
Eze 16 17 of men, and hast c. f. with them. And
26 and thou hast c. f. with the Egyptians
28 thou hast also c. f. with the Assyrians
23 3 they c. f. in Egypt, in their youth they c. f.
5 Oolla c. f. against me and doted on her
37 and they have c. f. with their idols
Osee 2 5 their mother hath c. f., she that
4 10 have c. f. and have not ceased: because
12 and they have c. f. against their God
5 3 Ephraim hath c. f., Israel is defiled
9 1 for thou hast c. f. against thy God
1 C 10 8 as some of them c. f., and there fell
Apoc 17 2 kings of the earth have c. f. 18:3
18 9 kings of the earth who have c. f. and
fornications 4 K 9 22 long as the f. of Jezabel
Jer 3 2 hast polluted the land with thy f.
Eze 16 22 after all thy abominations and f.
25 hast multiplied thy fornications. 26
29 multiplied thy f. in land of Chanaan
34 to the custom of women in thy f. and
36 thy fornications with thy lovers and
23 7 committed her f. with those chosen men
8 f. which she had committed in Egypt
14 and she increased her fornications
17 they defiled her with their f. and she
18 with them. And she discovered her f.
19 she multiplied her f., remembering
29 shall be discovered . . . and thy f.
35 bear thou also . . . thy fornications
43 7 they and their kings by their f. and
9 let them put away their fornications
Osee 1 2 take thee a wife of fornications and
2 have of her children of fornications
2 2 let her put away her fornications from
4 they are the children of fornications
6 10 the house of Israel: the f. of Ephraim
Nah 3 4 because of the multitude of the f.
4 that sold nations through her f. and
Mat 15 19 come forth . . . adulteries, f., thefts
Mark 7 21 proceed evil thoughts, adulteries, f.
Apoc 17 5 mother of the f. and the abominations
fornicator Eccu 23 24 to a man that is a f. all
1 C 5 11 brother, be a f. or covetous or server
Eph 5 5 understand, that no f. or unclean or
Heb 12 16 lest there be any f. or profane person
fornicators 1 C 5 9 not to keep company with f.
1 C 5 10 I mean not with f. of this world, or
6 9 do not err: neither f. nor idolaters
1 Tim 1 10 for f., for them who defile themselves
Heb 13 4 for f. and adulterers God will judge
Forrest 2 K 21 19 Adeodatus the son of the F.
forsake Deut 12 19 heed thou f. not the Levite
Deut 14 27 beware thou f. him not, because
31 6 not leave thee nor forsake thee. 8
16 there will they forsake me and will
17 I will forsake them and will hide my
Josu 1 5 leave thee nor forsake thee [Josue]
Judg 9 13 can I forsake my wine, that cheereth
1 K 12 22 the Lord will not forsake his people
3 K 6 13 and will not forsake my people Israel

4 K 10 29 nor did he forsake the golden calves
1 Pa 28 9 if thou f. him, he will cast thee off
20 and will not leave thee nor f. thee
2 Pa 7 19 but if thou turn away and forsake my
13 10 the Lord is our God whom we forsake not
15 2 but if you f. him, he will f. you
24 20 forsaken the Lord, to make him f. you
1 Es 8 22 wrath upon all them that forsake him
2 Es 9 17 full of compassion, didst not f. them
31 utterly consume them nor f. them
10 39 will not forsake the house of our God
Job 27 6 I have begun to hold, I will not f.
Ps 26 9 be thou my helper, forsake me not; do
36 28 and will not forsake his saints: they
37 22 forsake me not, O Lord my God: do not
70 9 shall fail, do not thou forsake me
18 and gray hairs: O Lord, forsake me not
88 31 if his children f. my law, and walk not
93 14 neither will he f. his own inheritance
118 8 do not thou utterly forsake me. By
53 because of the wicked that f. thy law
139 9 do not thou forsake me, lest they
Prov 1 8 forsake not the law of thy mother. 6:20
4 2 you a good gift, forsake not my law
6 f. her not, and she shall keep thee
15 pass not by it: go aside and forsake it
9 6 f. childishness, and live, and walk
27 10 friend and thy father's friend f. not
28 4 they that forsake the law, praise the
13 he that shall confess and forsake them
Eccu 4 22 if he go astray, she will forsake him
7 32 made thee: and f. not his ministers
9 14 f. not an old friend, for the new will
13 5 if thou have nothing, he will f. thee
8 he will f. thee and shake his head
17 21 turn to the Lord and forsake thy sins
28 27 they that f. God shall fall into it
29 22 hath lost all shame, he shall f. him
Isa 41 17 I the God of Israel will not f. them
55 7 let the wicked forsake his way and the
Jer 14 9 is called upon by us, forsake us not
17 13 that forsake thee shall be confounded
23 39 you away, carrying you, and will f. you
51 9 let us f. her, and let us go every man
Lam 5 20 why wilt thou f. us for a long time
Eze 20 8 neither did they f. the idols of Egypt
23 8 she did not forsake her fornications
Amos 5 7 wormwood, and f. justice in the land
Jon 2 9 observe vanities, f. their own mercy
1 Ma 2 21 not profitable for us to f. the law
2 Ma 1 5 and never forsake you in the evil time
5 11 that the Jews would f. the alliance
Heb 13 5 leave thee, neither will I forsake thee
forsaken Deut 9 12 have quickly f. the way that
Deut 9 16 and had quickly forsaken his way which
28 20 inventions by which thou hast f. me
32 18 hast forsaken the God that begot thee
Josu 22 16 why have you forsaken the Lord the God
18 you have forsaken the Lord today, and
Judg 6 13 the Lord hath f. us and delivered us
10 10 we have forsaken the Lord. 1 K 12:10
13 yet you have f. me and have worshipped
1 K 8 8 they have f. me and served strange gods
15 11 he hath forsaken me and hath not
3 K 11 33 he hath f. me and hath adored Astarthe
19 10 of Israel have f. thy covenant. 14
4 K 22 17 they have forsaken me and have sacrificed. 2 Pa 34:25
2 Pa 13 11 Lord our God, whom you have forsaken
21 10 for he [Joram] had forsaken the Lord
24 20 f. the Lord, to make him forsake you
24 because they had f. the Lord. 28:6
1 Es 9 9 our God hath not forsaken us, but hath
10 for we have forsaken thy commandments
2 Es 13 11 why have we forsaken the house of God
Jdth 13 17 God, who hath not forsaken them that
Job 18 4 shall the earth be forsaken for thee
19 14 my kinsmen have f. me, and they that
Ps 9 11 thou hast not f. them that seek thee
21 2 look upon me: why hast thou forsaken me
36 25 and I have not seen the just forsaken
39 13 of my head: and my heart hath f. me
70 11 saying: God hath forsaken him: pursue
118 87 I have not forsaken thy commandments
Eccu 2 12 in his commandment, and hath been f.
16 and that have forsaken the right ways
41 11 who have f. the law of the most High
44 13 and their glory shall not be forsaken
51 28 therefore I shall not be forsaken
Isa 1 4 they have forsaken the Lord. Jer 17:13
7 16 land which thou abhorrest shall be f.
17 9 his strong cities shall be forsaken
24 11 all mirth is forsaken: the joy of the
27 10 the beautiful city shall be forsaken
32 14 the house is f., the multitude of the
42 16 to them, and have not forsaken them
49 14 Sion said: The Lord hath forsaken me
54 6 as a woman forsaken and mourning in
7 for a small moment have I f. thee, but
58 2 hath not f. the judgments of their
60 15 because thou wast forsaken and hated
62 4 thou shalt no more be called Forsaken
12 a city sought after, and not forsaken
65 11 and you, that have forsaken the Lord
Jer 1 16 who have f. me and have sacrificed to
2 13 they have forsaken me, the fountain
17 because thou hast forsaken the Lord
29 you have all forsaken me, saith the
4 29 all the cities are forsaken, and there
5 7 thy children have f. me and swear by
19 as you have forsaken me and served a
7 29 forsaken the generation of his wrath
9 13 they have f. my law which I gave
12 7 I have forsaken my house, I have left
15 6 thou hast forsaken me, saith the Lord
19 4 because they have forsaken me and have
22 9 they have f. the covenant of the Lord
25 38 he hath forsaken his covert as the lion
46 19 and shall be forsaken and uninhabited
51 5 and Juda have not been forsaken by
Bar 3 12 hast forsaken the fountain of wisdom
4 1 they that have forsaken it, to death
12 I am forsaken of many for the sins of
Eze 8 12 the Lord hath forsaken the earth. 9:9
36 4 and to the cities that are forsaken
Dan 11 30 that have forsaken the covenant of the
Osee 4 10 forsaken the Lord in not observing his
Zach 11 16 who shall not visit what is forsaken
1 Ma 1 55 them that had f. the law of the Lord
10 14 some of them that had f. the law and
15 12 upon him, and his troops had f. him
2 Ma 5 20 as it was f. in the wrath of Almighty
7 16 that our nation is forsaken by God
Mat 27 46 my God, my God, why hast thou forsaken me. Mark 15:34
2 C 4 9 we suffer persecution, but are not f.
forsaker 2 Ma 5 8 as a forsaker of the laws and
forsakest Jdth 6 15 f. not them that trust on
forsaketh Job 6 14 f. the fear of the Lord. My
Prov 2 17 and forsaketh the guide of her youth
10 17 that forsaketh reproofs goeth astray
15 10 grievous to him that f. the way of life
17 14 he suffereth reproach, he f. judgment
28 21 for a morsel of bread f. the truth
Eccu 3 18 evil fame is he that f. his father
Zach 11 17 shepherd . . . that forsaketh the flock

2 Ma 6 16 with adversity, he forsaketh them not
forsaking Num 5 19 by f. thy husband's bed, these
Judg 2 13 f. him and serving Baal and Astaroth
2 Pa 29 6 in the sight of the Lord God, f. him
Jdth 6 8 wherefore forsaking the ceremonies of
Heb 10 25 not forsaking our assembly, as some are
forsook Deut 29 25 because they f. the covenant
Deut 32 15 he f. God who made him and departed
Judg 2 17 f. the way in which their fathers had
1 K 31 7 forsook their cities and fled: and the
3 K 9 9 because they forsook the Lord their God
4 K 17 16 forsook all the precepts of the Lord
21 22 forsook the Lord the God of. 2 Pa 7:22
1 Pa 5 25 they forsook the God of their fathers
10 7 forsook their cities and were scattered
2 Pa 10 8 he forsook the counsel of the ancients
12 1 [Roboam] forsook the law of the Lord
24 18 they forsook the temple of the Lord
Tob 1 2 even in his captivity, forsook not the
Jdth 8 18 of our fathers, who forsook their God
Wisd 10 13 she f. not the just when he was sold
Eccu 49 6 kings of Juda forsook the law of the
Jer 16 11 because your fathers forsook me, saith
11 they forsook me and kept not my law
Eze 39 23 captives . . . because they forsook me
1 Ma 1 40 own seed, and her children forsook her
2 Tim 4 16 no man stood with me, but all f. me
Jude 6 but forsook their own habitation, he
forswear Prov 30 9 forswear the name of my God
Wisd 14 28 unjustly or easily f. themselves
Mat 5 33 thou shalt not forswear thyself: but
forsworn Josu 9 20 if we should be forsworn
fort Judg 9 49 surrounding the fort they set it
forthwith Gen 4 7 shall not sin f. be present
Gen 17 23 f. the very same day, as God had
20 8 Abimelech f. rising up in the night
32 25 sinew of his thigh, and f. it shrank
34 19 forthwith fulfilled what was required
37 23 they f. stript him of his outside coat
41 14 f. at the king's command, Joseph
Exod 34 2 that thou mayst f. go up into mount
Lev 9 8 f. Aaron, approaching to the altar
10 5 went f. and took them as they lay
11 38 by the carcasses, it shall be f. defiled
14 38 house, and f. shut it up seven days
45 they shall destroy it f. and shall cast
Num 6 9 be defiled: and he shall shave it f.
11 28 f. Josue . . . said: My Lord Moses forbid
22 31 f. the Lord opened the eyes of Balaam
30 13 if f. he gainsay it, she shall not be
31 3 Moses f. said: Arm of you men to fight
35 31 guilty of blood, but he shall die f.
Deut 7 10 repaying forthwith them that hate him
13 15 shalt forthwith kill the inhabitants
25 8 they shall cause him to be sent for f.
Josu 6 20 the walls f. fell down: and every man
Judg 3 20 he forthwith rose up from his throne
22 and f. by the secret parts of nature
27 f. he sounded the trumpet in mount
13 21 f. Manue understood that it was an
16 21 f. pulled out his eyes and led him
19 10 f. went forward and came over against
20 19 f. the children of Israel rising in
1 K 23 25 f. he went down to the rock and abode
28 20 f. Saul fell all along on the ground
3 K 19 20 he [Eliseus] f. left the oxen and ran
20 41 he f. wiped off the dust from his face
1 Pa 21 28 David . . . f. offered victims there
2 Pa 10 2 Jeroboam . . . heard it, f. he returned
Tob 2 3 he forthwith leaped up from his place
11 7 forthwith adore the Lord thy God: and
Jdth 10 17 f. Holofernes was caught by his eyes
Job 30 12 my calamities f. arose: they have
Wisd 5 13 so we also being born, f. ceased to be
1 Ma 2 32 f. they went out towards them and
11 22 f. he came to Ptolemais and wrote to
2 Ma 3 8 so Heliodorus f. began his journey
31 f. begged of Onias that he would
4 10 forthwith he began to bring over his
5 18 had been f. scourged and put back
6 28 he was forthwith carried to execution
7 3 caldrons . . . which f. being heated
10 22 and forthwith took the two towers
11 36 send some one forthwith, that we
14 12 f. he sent Nicanor . . . into Judea
16 they f. removed from the place where
Mat 3 16 forthwith came out of the water: and
4 22 they f. left their nets and father and
8 3 and forthwith his leprosy was cleansed
14 22 forthwith Jesus obliged his disciples
21 3 and forthwith he will let them go. Now
26 49 f. coming to Jesus, he said: Hail
Mark 1 10 f. coming out of the water, he saw the
20 f. he called them. And leaving their
21 f. upon the sabbath days going into
28 the fame of him was spread f. into all
30 of a fever: and f. they tell him of her
43 charged him and f. sent him away
5 29 f. the fountain of her blood was dried
6 25 I will that forthwith thou give me in
Acts 3 7 f. his feet and soles received strength
12 23 f. an angel of the Lord struck him
21 32 who, f. taking with him soldiers and
fortification 1 Ma 10 11 with square stones for f.
fortifications Isa 33 16 f. of rocks shall be his
2 C 10 4 unto the pulling down of fortifications
fortified 3 K 9 19 and were not walled, he f.
2 Pa 11 12 he fortified them with great diligence
12 1 when the kingdom of Roboam was . . . f.
17 2 soldiers in all the fortified cities
26 9 Ozias built towers . . . and fortified
Ps 30 22 wonderful mercy to me in a f. city
Eccu 48 19 Ezechias f. his city and brought in
50 1 in his days fortified the temple
Jer 1 18 I have made thee this day a f. city
Mich 7 12 to thee, and to the fortified cities
12 from the f. cities even to the river
1 Ma 1 36 and they fortified themselves therein
4 61 he fortified it to secure Bethsura
5 46 Ephron . . . strongly fortified and
6 26 have f. the stronghold of Bethsura
9 52 he fortified the city of Bethsura
62 breaches thereof and they fortified it
12 38 built Adiada . . . and fortified it
13 10 and he fortified it round about. And
48 f. it and made it his habitation. But
53 he f. the mountain of the temple that
14 33 he fortified the cities of Judea and
34 he fortified Joppe which lieth by the
fortify 2 Pa 14 7 f. them with towers and gates
Isa 22 10 broken down houses to fortify the wall
Dan 11 39 he shall do this to fortify Moazim
Nah 2 1 watch the way, fortify thy loins
1 Ma 15 39 and to fortify the gates of the city
fortifying 1 Ma 10 45 walls of Jerusalem, and the f.
1 Ma 13 33 fortifying them with high towers and
fortitude Jdth 9 14 f. that I may overthrow him
Job 4 6 where is thy fear, thy fortitude, thy
Wisd 8 7 she teacheth . . . justice and fortitude
Isa 11 2 the spirit of counsel and of fortitude
Dan 2 20 wisdom and fortitude are his. And he
2 Ma 6 28 I shall leave an example of fortitude
31 for an example of virtue and fortitude
Acts 6 8 Stephen, full of grace and fortitude
fortress 1 Ma 1 35 made it a fortress for them
1 Ma 5 9 they fled into the fortress of Datheman

11 they are preparing . . . to take the f.
29 went till they came to the fortress
30 ladders and engines to take the f.
9 50 the fortress that was in Jericho, and
16 15 them deceitfully into a little fortress
2 Ma 10 33 laid siege to the fortress four days
37 having . . . pillaged and sacked the f.
11 5 to Bethsura . . . he laid siege to that f.
12 21 the other baggage before him into a f.
fortresses Isa 34 13 thistle in the f. thereof
Osee 10 14 all thy fortresses shall be destroyed
1 Ma 10 36 to be in the f. of the great king
12 33 far as Ascalon and the neighboring f.
35 resolution with them to build f. in
13 33 he stored up victuals in the fortresses
15 7 and the fortresses which thou hast
forts 4 K 24 10 city was surrounded with their f.
Jer 52 4 built forts against it round about
Eze 4 2 lay siege against it and build forts
17 17 shall cast up mounts and build forts
21 22 to cast up a mount, to build forts
26 8 he shall compass thee with forts
Fortunatus 1 C 16 15 house of Stephanas and of F.
1 C 16 17 rejoice in presence of Stephanas and F.
fortune Deut 18 11 pythonic spirits or f. tellers
Isa 65 11 that set a table for fortune and offer
Forum Acts 28 15 to meet us as far as Appii Forum
forward Gen 26 22 going f. from thence, he digged
Gen 44 4 and had gone forward a little way
Exod 14 15 to the children of Israel to go forward
17 1 setting forward from the desert of Sin
Num 1 51 when you are to go forward the Levites
9 17 then the children of Israel marched f.
21 they marched f.: and if it departed
10 5 on the east side, shall first go f.
13 24 going forward as far as the torrent
21 10 Israel setting f. camped in Oboth. And
Judg 1 10 Juda going f. against the Chanaanite
18 21 when they were going f. and had put
1 K 16 13 came upon David from that day forward
18 9 with a good eye from that day and f.
30 25 this hath been done from that day f.
4 K 20 9 wilt thou that the shadow go forward
1 Es 3 8 to hasten forward the work of the Lord
2 Es 4 16 it came to pass from that day forward
Job 39 21 he goeth forward to meet armed men
Prov 4 18 the path of the just . . . goeth forward
27 he will bring forward thy ways in peace
Ecce 1 6 the spirit goeth forward surveying all
Jer 41 17 to go forward and enter into Egypt
Eze 10 22 of every one to go straight forward
39 22 their God from that day and forward
Zach 1 15 a little, but they helped f. the evil
1 Ma 6 38 to hasten them forward that stood
10 30 I leave to you from this day forward
2 Ma 6 19 forward voluntarily to the torment
9 4 judgment of heaven urging him forward
10 35 pushing forward with fierce courage
13 6 all men thrusting him f. unto death
15 25 but Nicanor . . . came forward with
Mark 2 23 began to go forward and to pluck the
14 35 when he was gone forward a little
Acts 19 33 the Jews thrusting him forward. And
2 C 8 11 as your mind is forward to be willing
12 if the will be forward, it is accepted
9 2 for I know your forward mind: for which
Titus 3 13 send forward Zenas, the lawyer, and
3 J 6 do well to bring forward on their way
set forward Gen 24 10 set forward and went on
Gen 43 8 that we may set f. and may live: lest
Exod 16 1 they set forward from Elim, and all the
Num 4 5 when the camp is to set forward, Aaron
10 17 sons of Gerson and Merari set forward
28 by their troops, when they set forward
Deut 1 24 when they had set forward and had gone
Judg 19 9 arose to set forward with his wife and
1 Es 8 31 we set forward from the river Ahava
Wisd 14 18 helped to set forward the ignorant
Acts 20 1 set forward to go into Macedonia. And
went forward Gen 12 9 Abram went forward, going
Gen 31 18 and went forward to Isaac his father
33 3 he [Jacob] went forward and bowed down
37 17 and Joseph went f. after his brethren
Exod 3 4 Lord saw that he went forward to see
40 34 the children of Israel went forward
Num 10 13 the first went forward according to the
22 1 they went forward and encamped in the
Judg 19 10 went f. and came over against Jebus
2 K 17 17 they went forward to carry the message
3 K 19 4 he went forward one day's journey into
4 K 4 25 she went f. and came to the man of God
Jer 7 24 and went backward and not forward from
Eze 1 9 but every one went straight forward
12 every one of them went straight forward
1 Ma 12 32 he went f. and came to Damascus and
forwarded Isa 40 13 who hath f. the spirit of the
foster Osee 11 3 was like a f. father to Ephraim
Acts 13 1 Manahen . . . f. brother of Herod the
fought Exod 17 8 came and fought against Israel
Exod 17 10 he [Josue] fought against Amalec; but
Num 21 1 he [king Arad] fought against them
23 came to Jasa and fought against them
26 who fought against the king of Moab
31 7 and when they had fought against the
21 the men of the army, that had fought
27 between them that fought and went out
28 that fought and were in the battle
Josu 10 29 Israel to Lebna, and fought against it
36 to Hebron and fought against it
42 Lord the God of Israel fought for him
19 47 went up and fought against Lesem and
23 3 how he himself hath fought for you
24 8 and when they fought against you, I
9 and Balac . . . fought against Israel
11 men of that city fought against you
Judg 1 5 and fought against him [Adonibezec]
9 and fought against the Chanaanite
5 13 Lord hath f. among the valiant ones
19 the kings came and fought, the kings
19 kings of Chanaan fought in Thanach
20 the stars . . . fought against Sisara
9 16 for the benefits of him who f. for you
39 Gaal . . . fought against Abimelech
52 coming near the tower, fought stoutly
11 25 against Israel and fought against him
12 4 of Galaad he fought against Ephraim
20 22 place where they had fought before
1 K 4 10 the Philistines fought, and Israel was
12 9 of Moab, and they fought against them
13 15 to meet the people who f. against them
14 47 f. against all his enemies round about
19 8 fought against the Philistines. 23:5; 2 K 21:15; 2 Pa 26:6
31 1 Philistines f. against Israel. 1 Pa 10:1
2 K 8 10 because he had fought against Adarezer
10 17 array against David and f. against him
11 17 out of the city, fought against Joab
12 26 and Joab fought against Rabbath of the
27 I [Joab] have fought against Rabbath
18 6 the battle was fought in the forest of
3 K 14 19 acts of Jeroboam, how he fought and how
16 27 acts of Amri and the battles he fought
20 1 he f. against Samaria and besieged it
29 the seventh day the battle was fought
22 32 violent assault, they f. against him
35 and the battle was fought that day

4 K	3	23	the kings have fought among themselves
	8	29	when he [Joram] fought against Hazael
	9	15	wounded him, when he f. with Hazael
	12	17	Hazael . . . fought against Geth and took
	13	12	valor wherewith he f. against. 14:15, 28
1 Pa	5	10	they fought against the Agarites. 19
	19	17	against them and they fought with him
	20	5	another battle also was f. against the
	22	8	hast shed much blood and fought many
2 Pa	14	13	his army fought against them, and they
	20	29	the Lord had f. against the enemies of
	26	13	were fit for war and f. for the king
	27	5	he fought against the king of the
Jdth	1	5	f. against Arphaxad and overcame him
	5	16	their God fought for them and overcame
Ps	108	3	fought against me without cause. 119:7
	128	1	often have they fought against me. 2
Cant	1	5	sons of my mother have f. against me
Isa	20	1	fought against Azotus and had taken it
	29	7	nations that have fought against Ariel
		7	all that have fought and besieged and
		8	that have fought against mount Sion
	63	10	enemy, and he fought against them
Jer	12	6	even they have fought against thee
	34	1	all the people f. against Jerusalem
		7	of Babylon fought against Jerusalem
Zach	14	3	as when he fought in the day of battle
		12	that have fought against Jerusalem
1 Ma	1	2	he fought many battles and took the
	3	2	and they fought with cheerfulness the
		12	sword of Apollonius and fought with it
	5	3	fought against the children of Esau
		7	and he fought many battles with them
		21	fought many battles with the heathens
		56	heard . . . of the battles that were f.
	6	31	to Bethsura and fought many days and
		31	burnt them with fire and f. manfully
		37	valiant men who fought from above
		52	engines and they fought for many days
		63	fought against him and took the city
	8	10	against them and fought with them and
	9	13	the battle was fought from morning
		17	the battle was hard fought and there
		64	fought against it many days and made
		68	they fought against Bacchides and he
	10	50	the battle was hard fought till the
	11	41	because they fought against Israel
		55	and they fought against Demetrius, who
		72	put them to flight, and they fought
	12	13	the kings . . . have fought against us
	13	3	what great battles I . . . have fought
	14	32	resisted and fought for his nation and
	16	2	have fought against the enemies of
2 Ma	1	12	fought against us and the holy city
	8	20	they had fought against the Galatians
		30	and Bacchides who fought against them
	10	14	Gorgias . . . fought against the Jews
	12	36	that were with Esdrin had fought long
	13	23	fought with Judas, and was overcome
	14	18	courage with which they fought for
	15	9	the battles they had fought before
1 C	15	32	I fought with beasts at Ephesus, what
2 Tim	4	7	I have fought a good fight, I have
Apoc	12	7	Michael and his angels fought with the
		7	and the dragon fought and his angels
foul Gen	34	7	had done a foul thing in Israel
Eccu	20	26	a lie is a foul blot in a man and
Isa	33	9	Libanus is confounded and become foul
found Mat	1	18	she was found with child of the
Mat	2	8	when you have found him, bring me word
		11	they found the child with Mary his
	8	10	I have not f. so great faith. Luke 7:9
	13	44	which a man having found, hid it, and
		46	when he had found one pearl of great
	18	28	he found one of his fellow servants
	20	6	went out and found others standing
	21	19	f. nothing on it but leaves. Mark 11:13
	22	10	gathered together all that they found
	26	60	they found not, whereas many false
	27	32	they found a man of Cyrene, named
Mark	1	37	when they had found him, they said to
	7	2	with unwashed hands, they found fault
		30	she found the girl lying upon the bed
	11	4	they found the colt tied before the
	14	16	they found as he had told them and
		40	returned, he found them again asleep
		55	put him to death, and found none
Luke	1	30	for thou hast found grace with God
	2	16	they found Mary and Joseph, and the
		46	they found him in the temple, sitting
	4	17	he found the place where it was
	7	10	found the servant whole who had been
	8	35	they came to Jesus and found the man
	9	36	was uttered, Jesus was found alone
	13	6	seeking fruit on it, and found none
	15	5	when he hath found it, lay it upon
		6	I have found my sheep that was lost
		9	when she hath found it, call together
		9	I have f. the groat which I had lost
		24	to life again: was lost, and is found
		32	life again; he was lost, and is found
	17	18	no one found to return and give glory
	19	32	found the colt standing as he had said
		48	they found not what to do to him
	22	13	going, found as he had said to them
		45	he found them sleeping for sorrow
	23	2	we have found this man perverting our
	24	2	and they found the stone rolled back
		3	going in, they found not the body of
		24	found it so as the women had said, but
		24	had said, but him they found not. Then
		33	they f. the eleven gathered together
John	1	41	we have found the Messias, which is
		45	we have found him of whom Moses in the
	2	14	he found in the temple them that sold
	6	25	when they had found him on the other
	9	35	when he found him, he said to him
	11	17	found that he had been four days
	12	14	Jesus found a young ass, and sat upon
Acts	5	10	young men coming in, found her dead
		23	the prison indeed we found shut with
		23	but opening it, we found no man within
		39	you be found even to fight against God
	7	11	and our fathers found no food. But
		46	David, who found grace before God
	8	40	but Philip was found in Azotus; and
	9	2	he found any men and women of this way
		33	he found there a certain man named
	10	27	and found many that were come together
	11	25	when he had f., he brought to Antioch
	12	19	sought for him, and found him not
	13	6	they found a certain man, a magician
		22	I have found David, the son of Jesse
	17	23	I found an altar also, on which was
	19	1	found certain disciples. And he said
		19	the price of them, they found the money
	21	2	when we had found a ship sailing over to
	23	29	I f. to be accused concerning questions
	24	5	we have f. this to be a pestilent man
		17	I was found purified in the temple
		20	these men themselves say, if they f.
	25	25	yet have I found nothing that he hath
	27	28	who also sounding, found 20 fathoms
		28	a little further, they found 15 fathoms
Rom	4	1	say then that Abraham hath found, who
	7	10	same was found to be unto death to me

fountain Gen 14 7 and came to the f. of Misphat
Gen 16 7 having found her by a fountain of water
Lev 20 18 and she open the fountain of her blood
Num 20 6 treasure, a fountain of living water
34 11 over against the fountain of Daphnis
Josu 15 7 waters that are called f. of the sun
7 shall be at the fountain Rogel. And
9 fountain of the water of Nephtoa. 18:15
17 7 inhabitants of the fountain of Taphua
17 Ensemes . . . the fountain of the sun
Judg 7 1 came to fountain that is called Harad
1 K 29 1 camped by fountain which is in Jezrahel
2 K 17 17 Achimaas stayed by the f. Rogel: and
3 K 1 9 which was near the fountain Rogel
2 Es 2 13 before the dragon fountain and to the
14 I passed to the gate of the fountain
3 15 gate of the fountain Sellum . . . built
12 35 scribe before them at the fountain gate
Jdth 7 6 that the fountain which supplied them
12 7 washed herself in a fountain of water
Esth 10 6 little fountain which grew into a river
11 10 little f. grew into a very great river
Ps 35 10 for with thee is the fountain of life
Prov 6 11 thy harvest shall come as a fountain
13 14 law of the wise is a fountain of life
14 27 fear of the Lord is a fountain of life
16 22 knowledge is a fountain of life to him
18 4 f. of wisdom as an overflowing stream
25 26 as a fountain troubled with the foot
Ecce 12 6 the pitcher be crushed at the fountain
Cant 4 12 my spouse . . . a fountain sealed up
15 the fountain of gardens: the well of
Wisd 11 7 instead of a f. of an ever running
Eccu 1 5 word of God . . . the fountain of wisdom
21 16 his counsel continueth like f. of life
26 15 as a thirsty traveller to the fountain
Isa 19 7 shall be laid bare from its fountain
58 11 shalt be . . . like a fountain of water
Jer 2 13 forsaken me, the f. of living water
9 1 and a fountain of tears to my eyes
Bar 3 12 hast forsaken the fountain of wisdom
Osee 13 15 and shall make his fountain desolate
Joel 3 18 fountain shall come forth of the house
Zach 13 1 a fountain open to the house of David
Mark 5 29 the fountain of her blood was dried up
John 4 14 shall become in him a fountain of water
James 3 11 doth a f. send forth out of the same
Apoc 21 6 of the fountain of the water of life
fountains Gen 7 11 all the f. of the great deep
Gen 8 2 f. also of the deep . . . were shut up
Exod 15 27 Elim, where there were twelve f. 33:9
Lev 11 36 f. and cisterns and all gatherings of
Deut 8 7 of brooks and of waters and of f.
Tob 8 7 fountains and the rivers and all thy
Jdth 5 15 there bitter fountains were made sweet
41 2 panteth after the fountains of water
67 27 the Lord, from the fountains of Israel
73 15 thou hast broken up the fountains and
113 8 stony hill into fountains of waters
Ps 17 16 then the fountains of waters appeared
Prov 5 16 let thy fountains be conveyed abroad
8 24 neither had the f. of waters as yet
28 and poised the fountains of waters
Isa 12 3 with joy out of the savior's fountains
41 18 fountains in the midst of the plains
49 10 at f. of waters he shall give them
Dan 3 77 ye fountains, bless the Lord: praise
2 P 2 17 these are fountains without water and
Apoc 7 17 to the fountains of the waters of life
8 10 rivers and upon the fountains of waters
14 7 the sea and the fountains of waters
16 4 upon the rivers and the f. of waters
fourfold 2 K 12 6 he shall restore the ewe f.
Luke 19 8 of a thing, I restore him fourfold
fourfooted Bar 3 32 with cattle and f. beasts
Acts 10 12 were all manner of fourfooted beasts
11 6 saw f. creatures of the earth, and
Rom 1 23 of f. beasts, and of creeping things
fourscore Gen 16 16 Abram was f. and six years old
2 K 19 32 Berzellai . . . fourscore years old. 35
3 K 12 21 house of Juda . . . hundred f. thousand
4 K 6 25 was sold for f. pieces of silver and
10 24 Jehu had prepared him f. men without
2 Pa 26 17 Azarias . . . and with him f. priests
Ps 89 10 in the strong they be fourscore years
Cant 6 7 are threescore queens and f. concubines
Jer 41 5 f. men, with their beards shaven, and
Luke 2 37 a widow until fourscore and four years
foursquare Exod 27 1 make also an altar . . . f.
Exod 28 16 it shall be foursquare. 30:2
37 25 being a cubit on every side foursquare
39 8 he made also a rational . . . foursquare
3 K 6 33 temple posts of olive tree foursquare
Eze 40 47 a hundred cubits broad foursquare
41 21 the threshold was foursquare, and the
43 16 Ariel . . . foursquare, with equal sides
45 2 sanctuary on every side 500 by 500 f.
48 20 by 5 and 20 thousand foursquare, shall be
Apoc 21 16 the city lieth in a foursquare, and the
fowl Gen 1 20 let the waters bring forth . . . fowl
Gen 1 21 God created . . . every winged fowl
30 to every fowl of the air, and to all
7 14 and every fowl according to its kind
21 of fowl and of cattle and of beasts
Lev 20 25 and the clean fowl from the unclean
Jer 9 10 from the fowl of the air to the beasts
Eze 17 23 every fowl shall make its nest under
39 4 I have given thee . . . to every fowl
17 say to every fowl and to all the birds
44 31 by a beast, whether it be f. or cattle
Dan 7 6 had upon it four wings as of a fowl
Osee 7 12 bring them down as the fowl of the air
fowler Prov 6 5 a bird from the hand of the f.
Amos 3 5 bird fall . . . if there be no fowler
fowlers Ps 123 7 out of the snare of the fowlers
Jer 5 26 wicked men, that lie in wait as fowlers
fowling Lev 17 13 if by hunting or fowling he take
fowls Gen 6 20 of fowls according to their kind
Gen 7 8 beasts clean and unclean, and of fowls
8 17 all flesh as well in fowls as in beasts
20 taking of all cattle and f. that were
15 11 the fowls came down upon the carcasses
Lev 11 46 this is the law of beasts and fowls
3 K 4 23 harts, roes, and buffles, and fatted f.
33 he discoursed of beasts and of fowls
2 Es 5 18 and six choice rams, besides fowls
Ps 77 27 feathered fowls like as the sand of
148 10 all cattle: serpents and feathered fowls
Eccu 17 4 he had dominion over beasts and fowls
Isa 18 6 the fowls shall be upon them all the
fowls of the air Luke 8 5 f. . . . devoured it
Acts 10 12 creeping things of the earth, and f. . . .
11 6 beasts and creeping things and f. . . .
fox 2 Es 4 3 if a fox go up, he will leap over
Luke 13 32 go and tell that fox, Behold I cast
foxes Judg 15 4 he went and caught 300 foxes
Judg 15 5 setting them on fire he let the foxes go
Ps 62 11 they shall be the portions of foxes
Cant 2 15 catch us the little foxes that destroy
Lam 5 18 destroyed, foxes have walked upon it
Eze 13 4 were like foxes in the deserts. You
Mat 8 20 f. have holes, and the birds. Luke 9:58
fragments 2 Pa 34 4 strewed the f. upon the graves
Eze 23 34 shalt devour the fragments thereof
Mat 14 20 twelve full baskets of f. Mark 6:43
15 37 of what remained of the fragments. And

Mark 8 8 that which was left of the fragments
19 many baskets full of fragments. 20
Luke 9 17 of fragments that remained to them
John 6 12 gather up the fragments that remain
13 filled 12 baskets with the fragments
fragrant Gen 27 27 the f. smell of his garments
frail Wisd 14 1 piece of wood more f. than the
Wisd 14 8 because being frail it is called a god
frame Exod 25 10 frame an ark of setim wood, the
Ps 102 14 fear him: for he knoweth our frame
Eccu 22 19 a frame of wood bound together in the
Jer 18 11 behold I frame evil against you and
Eze 11 2 and frame a wicked counsel in this
2 Ma 7 22 neither did I frame the limbs of
framed Deut 4 28 that were f. with men's hands
Job 41 3 words, and framed to make supplication
Ps 49 19 with evil, and thy tongue f. deceits
Isa 29 16 or the thing framed should say to him
32 7 he hath framed devices to destroy the
Jer 10 5 they are framed after the likeness
Dan 2 9 have also f. a lying interpretation
2 Ma 15 40 the speech be always nicely framed
Eph 2 21 all the building, being framed together
Heb 11 3 world was framed by the word of God
7 framed the ark for the saving of his
framest Ps 93 20 who framest labor in commandment
frameth Prov 12 19 hasty witness, f. a lying tongue
frankincense Exod 30 34 savor and the clearest f.
Lev 2 1 pour oil upon it, and put frankincense
2 f., and shall put it a memorial upon
15 pouring oil upon it and putting on f.
16 small and of the oil and all the f.
5 11 not put oil upon it nor put any f.
6 15 all the f. that is put upon the flour
24 7 shalt put upon them the clearest f.
Num 5 15 not pour oil thereon nor put f. upon it
1 Pa 9 29 fine flour and wine and oil and f.
2 Pa 28 25 he built altars to burn frankincense
2 Es 13 5 they laid up gifts and f. and vessels
9 house of God, the sacrifice and the f.
Cant 3 6 aromatical spices, of myrrh and f.
4 6 mountain of myrrh and the hill of f.
11 smell of thy garments as smell of f.
Eccu 24 21 and aloes and as the f. not cut and
39 18 give ye a sweet odor as frankincense
50 8 as the sweet smelling f. in the time
9 as a bright fire, and f. burning in the
Isa 60 6 shall come bringing gold and f.: and
Jer 6 20 to what purpose do you bring me f.
17 26 and victims and sacrifices and f. and
Bar 1 10 money, buy with it holocausts and f.
Eze 6 13 where they burnt sweet smelling f.
Mat 2 11 gifts; gold, frankincense, and myrrh
Apoc 18 13 ointment and f. and wine and oil and
fraud Exod 22 9 to do any fraud, either in ox
Lev 6 5 all that he would have gotten by fraud
Esth 16 6 with crafty fraud they deceive the ears
Dan 11 21 shall obtain the kingdom by fraud
Mark 10 19 bear not false witness, do no fraud
Acts 5 2 by f. kept back part of the price. 3
James 5 4 by fraud has been kept back by you
fray Zach 1 21 and these are come to fray them
free Gen 44 17 go you away free to your father
Gen 47 26 which was free from this covenant
Exod 21 2 in the seventh he shall go out free
5 and children, I will not go out free
11 she shall go out free without money
26 he shall let them go free for the eye
27 he shall in like manner make them free
Lev 19 20 not redeemed with a price nor made f.
20 because she was not a free woman. And
Num 11 5 fish that we ate in Egypt free cost
Deut 15 12 seventh year thou shalt let him go f.
13 when thou sendest him out free, thou
15 and the Lord thy God made thee free
18 from them when thou makest them free
21 9 shalt be f. from the innocent's blood
14 please thee not, thou shalt let her go f.
24 5 he shall be free at home without fault
1 K 17 25 his father's house free from tribute
2 K 24 24 will not offer . . . holocausts free cost
4 K 12 4 of their own f. heart they bring into
15 5 and he dwelt in a free house apart
1 Pa 21 24 offer to the Lord holocausts free cost
Jdth 12 11 by doing so as to pass free from him
16 28 made her handmaid free, and she died
Job 3 19 and the servant is free from his master
11 12 thinketh himself born free like a wild
39 5 who hath sent out the wild ass free
Ps 67 10 for thy inheritance a free rain, O God
87 6 man without help, free among the dead
118 108 the free offerings of my mouth make
Prov 29 27 the word, shall be free from destruction
Eccu 10 28 that are free shall serve a servant
11 10 rich, thou shalt not be free from sin
23 10 thou shalt not escape free from them
26 28 merchant is hardly free from negligence
Isa 35 6 the tongue of the dumb shall be free
57 14 give free passage, turn out of the path
58 6 let them that are broken go free and
Jer 25 29 you be as innocent and escape free? You shall not escape free
34 9 let his manservant . . . go free. 10
10 and they obeyed and let them go free
11 handmaids whom they had let go free
14 thou shalt let him go free from thee
16 whom you had let go free and set at
Dan 13 53 and letting the guilty to go free
Amos 4 5 call free offerings and proclaim it
1 Ma 2 11 she that was free is made a slave
10 29 I free you and all the Jews from
31 and let Jerusalem be holy and free
39 as a free gift to the holy places
43 in my kingdom, let them have it free
11 28 would make Judea free from tribute
15 7 let Jerusalem be holy and free, and
2 Ma 9 14 he now desireth to make free. And the
Mat 17 25 to him: Then the children are free
John 8 32 and the truth shall make you free
33 how sayest thou: You shall be free
36 if . . . the son shall make you free, you shall be free indeed
Acts 22 28 I obtained the being free of this city
Rom 6 20 of sin, you were free men to justice
22 but now being made free from sin, and
1 C 7 21 if thou mayest be made f., use it rather
22 being free, is the bondman of Christ
9 1 am not I free? Am not I an apostle
19 whereas I was free as to all, I made
12 13 Jews or Gentiles, whether bond or free
Gal 3 28 there is neither bond nor free: there
4 22 bondwoman, and the other by a f. woman
23 but he of the free woman, was by promise
26 that Jerusalem, which is above, is free
30 not be heir with son of the free woman
31 of the bondwoman, but of the free: by
31 freedom wherewith Christ has made us f.
Eph 6 8 the Lord, whether he be bond or free
Col 3 11 barbarian nor Scythian, bond nor free
1 P 2 16 as free, and not as making liberty a
freed Rom 6 18 being then f. from sin, we have
freedom 1 Ma 10 34 be all days of immunity and f.
Gal 4 31 by f. wherewith Christ has made us free
freely Lev 14 53 go the sparrow to fly f. away
2 Pa 31 14 which were freely offered to the Lord
1 Es 1 4 besides that which they offer freely

2 68 offered freely to the house of the Lord
7 15 have f. offered to the God of Israel
17 take freely, and buy diligently with
25 yea and the ignorant teach ye freely
8 28 that is freely offered to the Lord the
Ps 53 8 I will f. sacrifice to thee, and will
93 1 the God of revenge hath acted freely
Jer 37 4 Jeremias walked freely in the midst
Osee 14 5 I will love them freely: for my wrath
1 Ma 10 33 I set at liberty freely, that all be
Mat 10 8 freely have you received, freely give
Acts 2 29 let me freely speak to you of the
Rom 3 24 being justified freely by his grace
2 C 11 7 preached unto you gospel of God freely
Apoc 21 6 fountain of the water of life, freely
22 17 let him take the water of life freely
freeman 1 C 7 22 a bondman, is the f. of the Lord
Apoc 6 15 every bondman and every freeman, hid
freemen Apoc 13 16 rich and poor, f. and bondmen
Apoc 19 18 the flesh of all freemen and bondmen
free-will 1 Es 3 5 a f. offering was made to the
freezeth Eccu 43 21 when it f., it shall become
frequent 2 Pa 26 8 of Egypt for his f. victories
Ecce 6 1 another evil . . . frequent among men
1 Tim 5 23 stomach's sake, and thy f. infirmities
frequented Dan 13 6 men f. the house of Joakim
frequently Eccu 30 1 his son, f. chastiseth him
2 C 11 23 in many more labors, in prisons more f.
2 P 1 15 that you f. have after my decease
fresh Num 6 3 eat grapes either fresh or dried
fretteth Prov 19 3 he f. in his mind against God
fretting 3 K 21 4 into his house angry and f.
fried Lev 6 21 and shall be fried in a fryingpan
Lev 7 12 anointed with oil, and fine flour fried
2 K 6 19 beef, and fine flour fried with oil
17 28 and beans and lentils and fried pulse
1 Pa 9 31 such things as were f. in the fryingpan
16 3 of roasted beef and flour f. with oil
Jer 29 22 whom king of Babylon fried in the fire
2 Ma 7 5 and to be fried in the fryingpan
friend Gen 26 26 and Ochozath his friend and
Exod 11 2 that every man ask of his friend
22 7 or any vessel unto his friend to keep
32 27 every man kill his brother and friend
33 11 as a man is wont to speak to his friend
Lev 19 18 thou shalt love thy friend as thyself
Deut 13 6 thy friend, whom thou lovest as thy
15 2 to whom anything is owing from his f.
19 5 slipping from the handle struck his f.
Judg 15 2 therefore I gave to thy friend: but
2 K 13 3 Amnon had a friend, named Jonadab
15 37 Chusai the friend of David went into
16 16 Chusai the Arachite, David's friend
17 is this thy kindness to thy friend
17 why wentest thou not with thy friend
3 K 4 5 Zabud . . . the king's friend: and
5 1 Hiram had always been David's friend
1 Pa 27 33 Chusai the Arachite, the king's friend
2 Pa 20 7 gavest it to seed of Abraham thy friend
Jdth 8 22 Abraham . . . was made the friend of God
Job 6 14 that taketh away mercy from his friend
27 you endeavor to overthrow your friend
36 33 he showeth his friend concerning it
Ps 87 19 friend and neighbor thou hast put far
Prov 3 28 say not to thy friend: Go, and come
29 practise not evil against thy friend
6 1 son, if thou be surety for thy friend
3 run about, make haste, stir up thy f.
7 4 call prudence thy friend, that she
11 9 dissembler . . . deceiveth his friend
12 he that despiseth his friend, is mean
13 thing committed to him by his friend
12 26 neglecteth loss for sake of a friend
13 20 f. of fools shall become like to them
16 29 an unjust man allureth his friend: and
17 17 that is a friend loveth at all times
18 hands, when he is surety for his friend
18 1 that hath a mind to depart from a f.
17 his friend cometh and shall search him
22 11 shall have the king for his friend
24 be not a friend to an angry man, and
25 8 when thou hast dishonored thy friend
9 treat thy cause with thy friend, and
26 19 so is the man that hurteth his friend
27 6 better are the wounds of a friend than
9 the good counsels of a friend are sweet
10 thy own friend and thy father's friend
17 sharpeneth the countenance of his friend
29 5 speaketh to his friend with flattering
Cant 5 16 such is my beloved, and he is my friend
Wisd 1 16 esteeming it a friend have fallen away
Eccu 6 1 instead of a f. become not an enemy
7 if thou wouldst get a friend, try him
8 there is a friend for his own occasion
9 there is a f. that turneth to enmity
9 is a friend that will disclose hatred
10 is a friend a companion at the table
11 a friend if he continue steadfast
14 a faithful friend is a strong defence
15 nothing can be compared to faithful f.
16 a faithful f. is the medicine of life
17 according to him shall his friend be
7 13 neither do the like against thy friend
20 do not transgress against thy friend
9 14 forsake not an old friend, for the
15 a new friend is as new wine: it shall
12 8 f. shall not be known in prosperity
9 a friend is known in his adversity
14 13 do good to thy friend before thou die
19 8 tell not thy mind to friend or foe
13 reprove a friend, lest he may not have
15 admonish thy friend: for there is often
20 17 a fool shall have no friend, and there
25 for bashfulness promiseth to his friend
22 25 that upbraideth his friend, breaketh
26 thou hast drawn a sword at a friend
26 to a friend, if thou hast opened a sad
27 in all these cases a friend will flee
28 keep fidelity with a friend in his
31 will not be ashamed to salute a friend
25 12 blessed . . . that findeth a true friend
27 17 that discloseth the secret of a friend
17 shall never find a friend to his mind
20 as a man that destroyeth his friend
24 to disclose the secrets of a friend
28 20 neither shall he have a friend in whom
29 13 lose thy money for . . . thy friend
33 6 a friend that is a mocker is like a
20 give not to . . . friend, power over thee
37 1 every f. will say: I also am his friend
1 is a friend that is only a f. in name
2 a friend shall be turned to an enemy
4 rejoiceth with his friend in his joys
5 who condoleth with his friend for his
6 forget not thy friend in thy mind and
40 23 friend and companion meeting together
41 23 injustice before a companion and friend
Isa 19 2 shall fight . . . friend against friend
41 8 chosen, the seed of Abraham, my friend
Jer 9 4 every friend will walk deceitfully
8 one speaketh peace with his friend
19 9 shall eat every one the flesh of his f.
22 13 that will oppress his f. without cause
34 17 liberty . . . every man to his friend
Osee 3 1 love a woman beloved of her friend
Mich 7 5 believe not a friend, and trust not in

Haba 2 15 to him that giveth drink to his friend
Zach 3 10 every man shall call his friend under
8 17 in your hearts against his friend
1 Ma 10 16 we will make him our friend and our
19 art a man . . . fit to be our friend
20 that thou be called the king's friend
13 36 Simon the high priest and f. of kings
14 39 he made him his friend and glorified
15 32 Athenobius the king's friend came to
2 Ma 7 24 would take him for a f. and furnish
11 14 would persuade the king to be their f.
Mat 11 19 a friend of publicans. Luke 7:34
20 13 friend, I do thee no wrong: didst thou
22 12 friend, how camest thou in hither not
26 50 friend, whereto art thou come? Then
Luke 11 5 which of you shall have a friend and
5 to him: Friend, lend me three loaves
6 a friend of mine is come off his
8 give him because he is his friend
14 10 may say to thee: Friend, go up higher
John 3 29 friend of the bridegroom . . . rejoiceth
11 11 Lazarus our friend sleepeth; but I go
19 12 this man, thou art not Caesar's friend
James 2 23 he [Abraham] was called the f. of God
4 4 will be a f. of this world, becometh
friendly Prov 18 24 shall be more f. than a brother
1 Ma 7 27 his brethren deceitfully with f. words
2 Ma 12 31 to be still friendly to their nation
friend's Deut 23 25 if thou go into thy f. corn
Job 31 9 if I have laid wait at my friend's door
friends Gen 29 22 number of his f. to the feast
Gen 31 30 didst desire to go to thy friends, and
Judg 14 20 but his wife took one of his friends
Ruth 1 18 her any more to return to her friends
2 K 3 8 mercy . . . to his brethren and friends
3 K 16 11 slew . . . all his kinsfolks and friends
4 K 10 11 Jehu slew . . . and his friends and his
Tob 8 22 for all his neighbors and all his f.
Esth 5 10 he called together to him his friends
14 the rest of his friends answered him
6 13 he told Zares his wife and his friends
16 14 against us left alone without friends
Job 2 11 when Job's three friends heard all the
6 13 my familiar friends also are departed
12 4 he that is mocked by his friends as I
16 21 my friends are full of words: my eye
19 21 have pity on me, at least you my friends
32 3 he [Eliu] was angry with his friends
35 4 thy words and thy friends with thee
40 25 shall friends cut him in pieces, shall
42 7 against thee and against thy two f.
10 Job, when he prayed for his friends
Ps 37 12 my f. and neighbors have drawn near
107 10 the aliens are become my friends. Who
138 17 to me thy friends, O God, are made
Prov 14 20 but the friends of the rich are many
17 9 repeateth it again, separateth friends
19 4 riches make many friends: but from
6 are friends of him that giveth gifts
7 his friends have departed far from him
Cant 5 1 eat, O friends, and drink, and be
8 13 in the gardens, the friends hearken
Wisd 7 14 that use, become the friends of God
27 maketh the friends of God and prophets
Eccu 6 5 a sweet word multiplieth friends and
13 enemies, take heed of thy friends
13 25 shaken, he is kept by his friends
28 11 a sinful man will trouble his friends
29 33 the honorable presence of my friends
30 3 in midst of his friends he shall glory
6 will requite kindness to his friends
41 28 of upbraiding speeches before friends
42 3 of the gift of inheritance of friends
Jer 20 4 up to fear, thee and all thy friends
6 be buried, thou and all thy friends
29 23 adultery with the wives of their f.
Lam 1 2 all her friends have despised her and
19 I called for my friends, but they
Dan 13 33 her f. and all her acquaintance wept
14 1 and was honored above all his friends
Zach 3 8 and thy friends that dwell before thee
1 Ma 2 18 be in the number of the king's friends
39 Mathathias and his friends heard of it
45 Mathathias and his friends went round
3 38 mighty men of the king's friends. And
6 10 he called for all his friends and said
14 he called Philip, one of his friends
28 and he called together all his friends
7 6 brethren have destroyed all thy f.
7 let him punish all his friends and
8 king chose Bacchides, one of his f.
15 we will do you no harm nor your f.
8 12 with their friends and such as relied
20 be registered your confederates and f.
31 made thy yoke heavy upon our friends
9 26 diligent search after the f. of Judas
28 all the friends of Judas came together
35 to desire the Nabutheans his f. that
39 bridegroom came forth, and his friends
10 65 enrolled him amongst his chief friends
11 26 exalted him in the sight of all his f.
27 he made him the chief of his friends
33 nation of the Jews who are our friends
57 and to be one of the king's friends
12 14 nor to the rest of our allies and f.
43 commended him to all his friends and
15 17 ambassadors of the Jews our f. came to
28 sent to him Athenobius one of his f.
2 Ma 1 14 Antiochus with his f. came to the place
3 31 f. of Heliodorus forthwith begged of
4 3 committed by some of Simon's friends
8 1 calling together their kinsmen and f.
9 Nicanor . . . one of his special friends
10 13 accused for this to Eupator by his f.
14 11 the rest also of the king's friends
Mark 3 21 when his friends had heard of it, they
5 19 go into thy house to thy friends and
Luke 7 6 the centurion sent his friends to him
12 4 I say to you, my friends: Be not
14 12 call not thy friends nor thy brethren
15 6 call together his f. and neighbors
9 call together her f. and neighbors
29 a kid to make merry with my friends
16 9 make unto you friends of the mammon of
21 16 and brethren and kinsmen and friends
23 12 Herod and Pilate were made friends
John 15 13 a man lay down his life for his friends
14 you are my friends if you do the
15 I have called you friends: because all
Acts 10 24 called . . . his kinsmen and special f.
19 31 the rulers of Asia, who were his f.
24 23 not prohibit any of his f. to minister
27 3 permitted him to go to his friends, and
3 J 14 peace be to thee. Our f. salute thee
14 salute the friends by name. Jude, the
friendship Exod 34 12 thou never join in f. with
2 Pa 19 2 in f. with them that hate the Lord
20 35 king of Juda made f. with Ochozias
Prov 25 10 grace and friendship deliver a man
Wisd 8 18 that there is great delight in her f.
Eccu 6 12 thou shalt have unanimous friendship
17 feareth God, shall likewise have good f.
22 25 that upbraideth his friend, breaketh f.
27 20 that destroyeth the f. of his neighbor
48 11 and were honored with thy friendship
Dan 11 6 to the king of the north to make f.

1 Ma 10 20 affairs, and keep friendship with us
23 prevented us to gain the f. of the Jews
26 and have continued in our friendship
54 let us make f. one with another: and
12 10 to renew the brotherhood and f., lest
14 18 to renew the friendship and alliance
22 to renew the former friendship. 15:17
2 Ma 6 21 for the old f. they had with the man
22 for the sake of their old friendship
14 27 displeased with the covenant of f.
James 4 4 f. of this world is the enemy of God
friendships Josu 23 12 if you . . . join f., know ye
Prov 17 9 concealeth a transgression, seeketh f.
Dan 11 23 after f., he will deal deceitfully
fright 4 K 7 15 Syrians had cast away in their f.
frighted Luke 24 37 they being troubled and f.
Heb 12 21 Moses said: I am frighted, and tremble
frighten 2 Pa 32 18 that he might f. them and
2 Es 6 9 all these men thought to frighten us
Job 7 14 thou wilt frighten me with dreams and
frightened 1 K 28 20 f. with the words of Samuel
2 Pa 26 20 yea, himself also being frightened
2 Ma 14 17 was f. with the sudden coming of the
fringes Num 15 38 to make to themselves fringes
Mat 23 5 broad, and enlarge their fringes. And
fro Gen 49 22 daughters run to and fro upon the
Eccu 26 10 of oxen that is moved to and fro
frogs Exod 8 2 strike all thy coasts with frogs
Exod 8 3 river shall bring forth abundance of f.
4 the frogs shall come in to thee and
5 bring forth frogs upon the land of
6 the frogs came up and covered the land
7 they brought forth frogs upon the land
8 to take away the frogs from me and
9 that the frogs may be driven away
11 the frogs shall depart from thee and
12 made to Pharao concerning the frogs
13 the frogs died out of the houses and
Ps 77 45 and frogs which destroyed them. And
104 30 their land brought forth frogs in
Wisd 19 10 the river cast up a multitude of frogs
Apoc 16 13 three unclean spirits like frogs. For
front Exod 26 9 sixth curtain in the f. of the
Josu 8 10 with ancients in the front of the army
Judg 3 27 he himself [Aod] going in the front
2 K 11 15 set ye Urias in the front of the battle
2 Pa 3 4 and the porch in the front, which was
Eze 40 9 the front thereof two cubits: and the
14 to the front the court of the gate
18 the pavement in the front of the gates
19 to the f. of the inner court without
21 and the front thereof and the porch
24 he measured the front thereof and the
26 and another on that side in the front
29 little chamber thereof and the f. 33, 36
31 the palm trees thereof in the front
34 the graven palm trees in the front
37 the graving of palm trees in the front
41 3 he measured the front of the gate two
25 the planks were thicker in the front of
1 Ma 4 57 they adorned the front of the temple
9 11 in the front were all men of valor
frontier Josu 15 1 from f. of Edom, to the desert
frontiers Num 34 4 f. shall go out to the town
Deut 2 19 nigh the f. of the children of Ammon
fronts Eze 40 10 and the fronts of one measure
Eze 40 14 he made also fronts of sixty cubits
16 slanting windows . . . in their fronts
16 before the f. the representation of palm
49 and there were pillars in the fronts
41 1 measured the fronts six cubits broad
frost Gen 31 40 I parched with heat and with frost
Exod 16 14 like unto the hoar frost on the ground
Job 6 16 they that fear the hoary frost, the
37 10 when God bloweth there cometh frost
38 29 frost from heaven who hath gendered it
Ps 118 83 I am become like a bottle in the frost
Eccu 43 21 shall pour frost as salt upon the earth
Jer 36 30 heat by day and to the frost by night
Bar 2 25 the sun, and to the frost of the night
Dan 3 69 ye frost and cold, bless the Lord
Zach 14 6 shall be no light, but cold and frost
frosts Dan 3 68 dews and hoar frosts, bless the
froth Wisd 5 15 as a thin f. which is dispersed
Osee 10 7 hath made her king to pass as froth
froward Prov 4 24 remove from thee a f. mouth
1 P 2 18 and gentle, but also to the froward
frugal Eccu 31 19 use as a f. man the things that
fruit Gen 1 11 the fruit tree yielding fruit after
Gen 3 2 of the fruit of the trees that are in
3 fruit of the tree which is in the midst
6 took of the fruit thereof and did eat
4 12 it shall not yield to thee its fruit
30 2 fruit of thy womb. Deut 7:13; 28:4, 11, 18, 53; 30:9; Ps 131:11
Lev 19 23 shall have planted in it fruit trees
23 fruit that comes forth shall be unclean
24 all their fruit shall be sanctified to
26 4 and the trees shall be filled with fruit
20 nor the trees yield their fruit. If you
Deut 7 13 fruit of thy land. 28:11
11 17 nor the earth yield her fruit, and you
16 13 when thou hast gathered in thy fruit
22 9 and fruit of the vineyard be sanctified
24 20 have gathered the fruit of thy olive trees
28 4 fruit of thy ground. 18
51 and will devour the fruit of thy cattle
4 K 3 25 cut down all the trees that bore fruit
19 29 plant vineyards and eat the fruit of
30 root downward, and bear fruit upward
2 Es 9 25 fruit trees in abundance: and they ate
10 35 firstfruits of all fruit of every tree
37 would bring . . . the f. of every tree
Job 21 10 calved and is not deprived of her fruit
Ps 1 3 shall bring forth its fruit in due
4 8 by the fruit of their corn, their wine
20 11 their fruit shalt thou destroy from
57 12 if indeed there be fruit to the just
66 7 the earth hath yielded her fruit. May
71 16 shall the fruit thereof be exalted
78 1 made Jerusalem as a place to keep fruit
84 13 and our earth shall yield her fruit
103 13 shall be filled with f. of thy works
104 35 consumed all the fruit of their ground
106 37 and they yielded fruit of birth. And
126 3 children: the reward, the f. of the womb
Prov 1 31 shall eat the fruit of their own way
3 14 her fruit than the chiefest and purest
8 19 my fruit is better than gold and
10 16 but the fruit of the wicked, unto sin
11 30 f. of the just man is a tree of life
12 14 the fruit of his own mouth. 13:2
18 20 of the fruit of a man's mouth shall
22 4 fruit of humility is fear of the Lord
27 18 fig tree, shall eat the fruit thereof
31 16 with the fruit of her hands she hath
31 give her of the fruit of her hands
Ecce 5 9 that loveth riches shall reap no fruit
17 drink and enjoy the fruit of his labor
Cant 2 3 and his fruit was sweet to my palate
5 1 and eat the fruit of his apple trees
7 8 will take hold of the fruit thereof
8 11 for the f. thereof a thousand pieces
12 for them that keep the fruit thereof
Wisd 3 11 is vain and their labors without fruit
13 she shall have fruit in the visitation

15 the fruit of good labors is glorious
Eccu 1 22 filling up peace and fruit of salvation
6 3 eat up thy leaves and destroy thy fruit
11 3 her fruit hath the chiefest sweetness
24 in swift hour his blessing beareth fruit
23 35 her branches shall bring forth no fruit
24 23 and my flowers are the fruit of honor
27 7 dressing of a tree showeth the fruit
37 25 f. of his understanding is commendable
Isa 3 10 he shall eat the fruit of his doings
4 2 the fruit of the earth shall be high
10 12 I will visit the f. of the proud heart
17 6 f. thereof that shall be left upon it
27 9 this is all the fruit, that the sin
28 4 shall be as a hasty fruit before the
37 30 plant vineyards and eat the fruit of
31 downward, and shall bear fruit upward
57 19 I created the fruit of the lips, peace
Jer 2 7 land of Carmel, to eat the f. thereof
12 2 they prosper and bring forth fruit
17 8 cease at any time to bring forth fruit
10 according to f. of his devices. 32:19
21 14 according to the fruit of your doings
29 5 plant orchards and eat the f. of them
Lam 2 20 shall women then eat their own fruit
Eze 17 8 might bring forth branches and bear f.
9 shall he not . . . strip off its fruit
23 into branches, and shall bear fruit
19 10 her fruit and her branches have grown
12 the burning wind dried up her fruit
14 fire . . . which hath devoured her fruit
34 27 tree of the field shall yield its fruit
36 8 and yield your fruit to my people
30 I will multiply the fruit of the tree
47 12 shall grow all trees that bear fruit
12 not fall off and their f. shall not fail
Dan 4 9 and its fruit exceeding much. 18
Osee 9 16 is dried up, they shall yield no fruit
16 I will slay the best beloved fruit of
10 1 branches, the fruit is agreeable to it
1 according to the multitude of his fruit
13 you have eaten the fruit of lying
14 9 fir tree: from me is thy fruit found
Joel 2 22 the tree hath brought forth its fruit
Amos 2 9 and I destroyed his fruit from above
6 13 and the fruit of justice into wormwood
8 1 a hook to draw down the fruit. 2
Mich 6 7 f. of my body for the sin of my soul
7 13 and for the fruit of their devices
Zach 8 12 the vine shall yield her fruit and the
Mala 3 11 he shall not spoil the f. of your land
1 Ma 10 30 and the half of the fruit of trees
14 8 and the trees of the fields their fruit
Mat 3 8 fruit worthy of penance. Luke 3:8
7 17 evil tree bringeth forth evil fruit
18 good tree cannot bring forth evil fruit
12 33 make the tree good and its fruit good
33 make the tree evil and its fruit evil
33 by the f. the tree is known. Luke 6:44
13 8 they brought forth fruit. Mark 4:8
23 understandeth and beareth fruit and
26 sprung up and had brought forth fruit
21 19 may no fruit grow on thee henceforward
41 shall render him the f. in due season
26 29 I will not drink of the f. of the vine. Mark 14:25; Luke 22:18
Mark 4 7 choked it, and it yielded no fruit
20 yield fruit, the one thirty, another
28 the earth of itself bringeth forth fruit
29 and when the fruit is brought forth
11 14 may no man hereafter eat fruit of thee
12 2 to receive . . . the f. of the vineyard
Luke 1 42 and blessed is the fruit of thy womb
6 43 tree that bringeth forth evil fruit
8 8 yielded fruit a hundredfold. Saying
14 of this life, and yield no fruit. But
15 and bring forth fruit in patience. Now
13 6 he came seeking fruit on it, and found
7 I come seeking fruit on this fig tree
9 if happily it bear fruit: but if not
20 10 they should give him of the fruit of
21 30 when they now shoot forth their fruit
John 12 25 if it die, it bringeth forth much fruit
15 2 branch in me that beareth not fruit
2 every one that beareth fruit, he will
2 that it may bring forth more fruit
4 the branch cannot bear fruit of itself
5 same beareth much fruit: for without me
8 that you bring forth very much fruit
16 should go and should bring forth fruit
16 and your fruit should remain: that
Acts 2 30 of the fruit of his loins one should
Rom 1 13 that I might have some f. among you also
6 21 what fruit therefore had you then in
22 you have your fruit unto sanctification
7 4 that we may bring forth fruit to God
5 members, to bring forth fruit unto death
15 28 consigned to them this fruit, I will
1 C 9 7 vineyard, and eateth not of the fruit
10 that thrasheth, in hope to receive f.
14 14 but my understanding is without fruit
Gal 5 22 but the fruit of the Spirit is, charity
Eph 5 9 the f. of the light is in all goodness
Phil 1 11 Christ, filled with the fruit of justice
22 flesh, this is to me the fruit of labor
4 17 I seek the gift, but I seek the fruit
Col 1 6 bringeth forth fruit and groweth, even
Heb 12 11 the most peaceable fruit of justice
13 15 fruit of lips confessing to his name
James 3 18 the fruit of justice is sown in peace
5 7 waiteth for the precious fruit of the
18 and the earth brought forth her fruit
good fruit Mat 3 10 that doth not yield g. f.
Mat 7 17 good tree bringeth forth good fruit
18 can an evil tree bring forth good f.
19 bringeth not forth good fruit. Luke 3:9
Luke 6 43 tree that bringeth forth good fruit
fruitful Gen 41 34 during the seven f. years
Deut 20 20 if there be any trees that are not f.
Judg 18 9 land which is exceeding rich and f.
4 K 3 19 and shall cut down every fruitful tree
18 32 you away to a land . . . a fruitful land
1 Pa 4 40 country spacious and quiet and fruitful
Ps 51 10 I, as a f. olive tree in the house of
91 15 shall still increase in a f. old age
106 34 a fruitful land into barrenness, for
127 3 thy wife as a f. vine, on the sides of
143 13 their sheep f. in young, abounding in
148 9 all hills, fruitful trees and all cedars
Isa 5 1 vineyard on a hill in a fruitful place
32 12 delightful country, for the f. vineyard
Jer 11 16 olive tree, fair, f., and beautiful
48 11 Moab hath been f. from his youth and
Eze 34 14 feed them in the most f. pastures
Acts 14 16 giving rains and f. seasons, filling
Col 1 10 being fruitful in every good work, and
fruitfulness Gen 41 47 f. of the seven years came
Deut 30 9 abound . . . in the fruitfulness of thy
Isa 5 17 shall eat the deserts turned into f.
fruitless Exod 23 26 shall not be one f. nor barren
Ecce 2 26 and a fruitless solicitude of mind
4 4 also there is vanity and fruitless care
Wisd 15 4 shadow of a picture, a fruitless labor
Mat 13 22 the word, and he becometh fruitless
Mark 4 19 choke the word, and it is made f.
fruits Gen 4 3 Cain offered, of the f. of the

Gen 41 34 into barns the fifth part of the fruits
Exod 10 15 what fruits soever were on the trees
34 26 the first of the fruits of thy ground
Lev 19 25 in fifth year you shall eat the fruits
23 39 shall have gathered in all the fruits
40 first day fruits of the fairest tree
25 3 vineyard and shalt gather the fruits
15 according to the computation of the f.
16 shall sell to thee the time of the f.
19 the ground may yield you its fruits
20 if we sow not nor gather our fruits
21 it shall yield the fruits of three years
22 and shall eat of the old fruits, until
27 the value of the f. shall be counted
27 nor exact of him any increase of f.
27 30 whether of corn or of the f. of trees
Num 13 21 bring us of the fruits of the land
27 they showed them the f. of the land
28 as may be known by these fruits: but
18 13 firstripe of the fruits, that the
28 26 you shall offer new fruits to the Lord
Deut 1 25 taking of the fruits thereof, to show
14 22 set aside the tithes of all thy fruits
16 15 will bless thee in all thy fruits
26 2 shalt take the first of all thy fruits
12 made an end of tithing all thy fruits
28 33 knowest not, eat the fruits of thy land
42 shall consume all the trees and the f.
51 will devour . . . the fruits of thy land
32 13 that he might eat the f. of the fields
33 13 of the fruits of heaven and of the dew
14 of the fruits brought forth by the sun
15 of the f. of the everlasting hills
16 the f. of the earth and the fulness
Judg 9 11 my sweetness and my delicious fruits
2 Es 9 37 the f. thereof grow up for the kings
Job 9 26 passed by as ships carrying fruits
22 21 thereby thou shalt have the best fruits
31 39 if I have eaten the fruits thereof
Ps 64 11 multiply its fruits: it shall spring up
77 46 he gave up their fruits to the blast
Prov 3 9 give him of the first of all thy fruits
15 6 in the fruits of the wicked is trouble
18 21 that love it, shall eat the fruits
Cant 4 13 with the f. of the orchard. Cyprus
6 10 to see the fruits of the valleys and
7 12 the flowers be ready to bring forth f.
13 in our gates are all fruits: the new
Wisd 4 5 their fruits shall be unprofitable
10 7 the trees bear fruits that ripen not
16 19 to destroy the fruits of a wicked land
22 destroyed the fruits of the enemies
26 not the growing of f. that nourisheth
Eccu 1 20 and fulness is from the fruits thereof
6 19 and soweth and wait for her good fruits
20 and shalt quickly eat of her fruits
24 26 desire me, and be filled with my fruits
35 the Tigris in the days of the new f.
42 water abundantly the f. of my meadow
37 26 f. of his understanding are faithful
Isa 37 30 in the second year eat fruits: but in
65 21 vineyards, and eat the fruits of them
Jer 6 19 the f. of their own thoughts because
7 20 wrath . . . upon the fruits of the land
12 13 you shall be ashamed of your fruits
29 28 plant gardens and eat the f. of them
Lam 4 9 for want of the fruits of the earth
Eze 25 4 they shall eat thy fruits: and they
47 12 the fruits thereof shall be for food
48 18 the fruits thereof shall be for bread
Dan 4 11 shake off its leaves and scatter its f.
Amos 9 14 shall make gardens, and eat the fruits
Agge 1 10 earth was hindered from yielding her f.

1 Ma 11 34 for the fruits of the land and of
Mat 7 16 by their fruits you shall know them. 20
21 34 when the time of the fruits drew nigh
34 that they might receive the fruits
43 to a nation yielding the fruits thereof
Luke 3 8 bring forth therefore fruits worthy of
12 16 brought forth plenty of fruits. And
17 I have no room to bestow my fruits
2 C 9 10 increase growth of f. of your justice
2 Tim 2 6 laboreth, must first partake of the f.
James 3 17 full of mercy and good fruits, without
Apoc 18 14 the fruits of the desire of thy soul
22 2 the tree of life, bearing twelve fruits
2 yielding its fruits every month, and
frumenty Lev 23 14 corn or f. of the harvest
Josu 5 11 of the land and f. of the same year
Ruth 2 14 and she heaped to herself frumenty
1 K 17 17 for thy brethren an ephi of frumenty
frustrate 1 Es 4 5 f. their design all the days
fryingpan Lev 2 5 if thy oblation be from the f.
Lev 6 21 with oil and shall be fried in a f.
7 9 is dressed on the gridiron or in the f.
1 Pa 9 31 such things as were fried in the f.
23 29 of the fryingpan and of the roasting
2 Ma 7 5 to the fire and to be fried in the f.
fryingpans 2 Ma 7 3 f. and brazen caldrons to be
fuel Ps 101 4 my bones are grown dry like fuel
Isa 9 5 be burnt, and be fuel for the fire
19 the people shall be as f. for the fire
44 15 it hath served men for fuel: he took
Eze 15 4 it is cast into the fire for fuel
21 32 thou shalt be fuel for the fire, thy
fugitive Gen 4 12 f. and a vagabond shalt thou be
Gen 4 14 I shall be a vagabond and a fugitive
16 Cain . . . dwelt as a fugitive on the
Num 35 12 when the fugitive shall be in them
28 the f. ought to have stayed in the city
Judg 12 4 had said: Galaad is a f. of Ephraim
3 K 12 2 fugitive from the face of king Solomon
2 Ma 4 26 was driven out a f. into the country of
fugitives Num 35 6 be separated for refuge to f.
Num 35 11 cities . . . for the refuge of f. 13
32 fugitives . . . may by no means return
4 K 25 11 the f. that had gone over to the king
Wisd 19 3 pursued them as f. whom they had pressed
Isa 11 12 shall assemble the fugitives of Israel
16 4 my fugitives shall dwell with thee
Jer 39 9 and the f. that had gone over to him
49 36 to which the f. of Elam shall not come
52 15 captives some . . . of the fugitives
Eze 17 21 his f. with all his bands shall fall
1 Ma 1 56 into the secret places of fugitives
fulfil Gen 26 3 to f. the oath which I swore to
Gen 27 5 to fulfil his father's commandment
Exod 5 9 with works, and let them fulfil them
13 fulfil your work every day as before
18 23 thou shalt f. the commandment of God
40 19 to fulfil the commandment of the Lord
Lev 25 18 keep my judgments and fulfil them
Num 4 43 all that go in to fulfil the rites
15 8 sacrifice of oxen, to fulfil thy vow
23 19 hath he spoken, and will he not fulfil
30 3 but shall fulfil all that he promised
5 and swore, she shall fulfil in deed
10 shall fulfil whatsoever they vow
15 vowed or promised, she shall fulfil
Deut 4 6 shall observe and f. them in practice
5 1 learn them and fulfil them in work
8 18 that he might fulfil his covenant
11 32 that you fulfil the ceremonies and
24 8 fulfil thou it carefully. Remember
26 16 and fulfil them with all thy heart
28 58 if thou wilt not keep and fulfil all

29 9 words of this covenant, and fulfil them
30 12 we may hear and fulfil it in work
31 12 and keep and fulfil all the words of
32 46 to f. all that is written in this law
Josu 22 5 in work fulfil the commandment and
Judg 13 14 commanded her, let her f. and observe
1 K 1 23 I pray that the Lord may f. his word
3 K 6 12 I will fulfil my word to thee which I
2 Pa 6 16 fulfil to thy servant David my father
36 22 to f. the word of the Lord, which he
Tob 7 15 together, and f. his blessing in you
Ps 19 7 the Lord fulfil all thy petitions
148 8 ice, stormy winds, which f. his word
Prov 25 14 boasteth and doth not f. his promises
Eccu 26 2 shall fulfil the years of his life in
Dan 11 14 up themselves to fulfil the vision
13 62 to fulfil the law of Moses: and they
2 Ma 3 8 indeed to fulfil the king's purpose
Mat 3 15 so it becometh us to fulfil all justice
5 17 I am not come to destroy, but to fulfil
Rom 2 27 uncircumcision, if it fulfil the law
Gal 5 16 you shall not fulfil the lusts of flesh
6 2 so you shall fulfil the law of Christ
Phil 2 2 f. ye my joy, that you be of one mind
30 that he might fulfil that which on your
Col 1 25 you, that I may fulfil the word of God
4 17 received in the Lord, that thou fulfil
2 Th 1 11 f. all the good pleasure of his goodness
2 Tim 4 5 evangelist, fulfil thy ministry. Be
James 2 8 if then you fulfil the royal law
fulfilled Gen 21 1 fulfilled what he had spoken
Gen 29 21 the time is f., that I may go in unto
32 10 which thou hast f. to thy servant
34 19 forthwith fulfilled what was required
41 28 which shall be fulfilled in this order
32 cometh to pass and is f. speedily
Lev 12 4 until the days of her purification be f.
Num 6 5 until the day be f. of his consecration
32 12 of Nun: these have fulfilled my will
Josu 7 2 they f. his command and viewed Hai
23 15 as he hath fulfilled in deed, what he
1 K 15 13 I have fulfilled the word of the Lord
2 K 7 12 when thy days shall be f. and thou
14 22 thou hast f. the request of thy servant
3 K 2 27 that the word of the Lord might be fulfilled. 2 Pa 36:21; 1 Es 1:1
2 Pa 1 9 O Lord God, let thy word be fulfilled
10 15 will of God, that his word might be f.
23 8 with those who had fulfilled the sabbath
2 Es 9 8 and thou hast fulfilled thy words
Tob 14 6 the word of the Lord must be fulfilled
Jdth 13 18 by me . . . he hath fulfilled his mercy
Job 23 14 when he shall have f. his will in me
Wisd 4 13 a short space, he fulfilled a long time
Eccu 34 8 word of the law shall be f. without
Jer 44 25 and fulfilled with your hands, saying
25 you have fulfilled your vows and
Lam 2 17 purposed, he hath fulfilled his word
4 18 our days are fulfilled, for our end
Dan 4 30 the same hour the word was f. upon
8 17 the end the vision shall be fulfilled
9 24 vision and prophecy may be fulfilled
1 Ma 2 55 Jesus, whilst he fulfilled the word
3 49 the Nazarites that had f. their days
Mat 2 17 was f. that which was sopken by. 27:9
13 14 the prophecy of Isaias is f. in them
26 54 how then shall the scriptures be f.
Mark 13 4 these things shall begin to be f.
15 28 the scripture was f., which saith
Luke 1 20 which shall be fulfilled in their time
2 43 having f. the days, when they returned
4 21 this day is f. this scripture in your
21 22 that all things may be fulfilled that
24 till the times of the nations be f.
32 not pass away till all things be f.
22 16 till it be f. in the kingdom of God
37 that is written must yet be fulfilled
24 44 that all things must needs be f.
John 3 29 this my joy therefore is fulfilled
12 38 of Isaias the prophet might be f.
15 25 that the word may be f. which is
18 9 that the word might be fulfilled which
32 that the word of Jesus might be f.
Acts 1 16 the scripture must needs be fulfilled
3 18 Christ should suffer, he hath so f.
12 25 having fulfilled their ministry, taking
13 27 sabbath, judging him have f. them
29 when they had fulfilled all things
33 this same God hath f. to our children
Rom 8 4 that justification of law might be f.
13 8 loveth his neighbor, hath f. the law
2 C 10 6 when your obedience shall be fulfilled
Gal 5 14 all the law is fulfilled in one word
James 2 23 scripture was f., saying: Abraham
Jude 2 and peace, and charity be fulfilled
Apoc 15 8 till the seven plagues . . . were f.
17 17 till the words of God be fulfilled
that it might be fulfilled Mat 1 22 t. . . . which the Lord spoke by the. 2:15
Mat 2 23 t. . . . which was said by the prophets
4 14 t. . . . which was said by Isaias the
8 17 t. . . . He took our infirmities and bore
12 17 t. . . . which was spoken by Isaias
13 35 t. . . . which was spoken by the. 21:4
27 35 t. . . . They divided my garments among
that the scripture (scriptures) may (might) be fulfilled
Mat 26 56 now all this was done t. . . . Then the
Mark 14 49 did not lay hands on me. But t. . . .
John 13 18 t. . . . He that eateth bread with me
17 12 but the son of perdition, t. . . . And
24 t. . . . saying: They have parted my
28 t. . . . , said: I thirst. Now there was
36 t. . . . You shall not break a bone of
fulfilleth Deut 27 26 and f. them not in work
fulfilling Gen 50 3 while they were f. his commands
Num 6 21 for the f. of his sanctification. And
Eze 5 2 to the f. of the days of the siege
Acts 13 25 when John was fulfilling his course
Rom 13 10 love therefore is fulfilling of the law
Eph 2 3 fulfilling the will of the flesh and
fuller Mark 9 2 as no f. upon earth can make white
fuller's 4 K 18 17 in way of the f. field. Isa 7:3; 36:2
Mala 3 2 he is . . . like the fuller's herb
fully Exod 7 25 and seven days were fully ended
Lev 25 30 and the whole year be fully out, the
3 K 11 6 and did not fully follow the Lord
Tob 8 19 make them, O Lord, bless thee more f.
Nah 1 10 consumed as stubble that is fully dry
Mat 7 28 when Jesus had fully ended these words
Rom 4 21 most fully knowing, that whatsoever he
2 Tim 3 10 but thou hast fully known my doctrine
fulness Deut 33 16 fruits of earth and of the f.
1 Pa 16 32 the sea roar, and the fulness thereof
Ps 23 1 earth is the Lord's and the fulness
49 12 world is mine and the fulness thereof
88 12 the world and the fulness thereof thou
95 11 sea be moved, and the f. thereof. 97:7
105 15 and sent fulness into their souls
Prov 19 23 he shall abide in f. without being
Ecce 5 11 f. of the rich will not suffer him to
Eccu 1 20 to fear God is the fulness of wisdom
20 and fulness is from the fruits thereof
45 26 prepared them bread . . . unto fulness
Isa 23 18 that they may eat unto fulness and be
Jer 5 24 for us the f. of the yearly harvest
Eze 16 49 iniquity of Sodom . . . fulness of bread

19 7 f. thereof by the noise of his roaring
32 15 the land shall be destitute of her f.
2 Ma 6 14 may punish them in the f. of their sins
Mat 9 16 taketh away the fulness thereof from
John 1 16 of his f. we all have received, and
Rom 11 12 how much more the fulness of them? For
25 until the fulness of the Gentiles should
1 C 10 26 earth is the Lord's, and the f. thereof
Gal 4 4 when the fulness of the time was come
Eph 1 10 dispensation of the fulness of times, to
23 fulness of him who is filled all in all
3 19 may be filled unto all the f. of God
4 13 measure of the age of the f. of Christ
Col 1 19 Father, that all fulness should dwell
2 2 riches of fulness of understanding, unto
9 for in him dwelleth all the fulness of
1 Th 1 5 in the Holy Ghost, and in much fulness
Heb 10 22 with a true heart in fulness of faith
fume Eccu 13 4 done wrong, and yet he will fume
function Luke 1 8 when he exercised the priestly f.
functions Num 3 3 to do the f. of the priesthood
funeral Gen 23 3 rose up from the f. obsequies
2 K 3 31 and mourn before the funeral of Abner
2 Pa 21 19 people did not make a funeral for him
Acts 8 2 took order for Stephen's funeral and
funnels Zach 4 2 seven f. for the lights that were
Zach 4 12 beaks in which are the funnels of gold
furbish Jer 46 4 furbish the spears, put on coats
furbished Eze 21 9 the sword is sharpened and f.
Eze 21 10 it is furbished that it may glitter
11 and I have given it to be furbished
11 this sword is sharpened and it is f.
15 the sword that is furbished to glitter
28 be furbished to destroy and to glitter
furious Prov 22 24 do not walk with a furious man
2 Ma 5 11 out of Egypt with a furious mind, he
15 33 hand of the f. man to be hanged up
furiously 4 K 9 20 of Namsi, for he drives f.
furlongs 2 Ma 11 5 space of five f. from Jerusalem
2 Ma 12 9 seen at Jerusalem 240 furlongs off
10 were gone from thence nine furlongs
16 a pool adjoining of two furlongs broad
17 from thence they departed 750 furlongs
29 which lieth 600 f. from Jerusalem
Luke 24 13 which was 60 furlongs from Jerusalem
John 6 19 about five and twenty or thirty f.
11 18 near Jerusalem, about 15 furlongs off
Apoc 14 20 horses' bridles, for 1,600 furlongs
21 16 with the golden reed for 12,000 f.
furnace Gen 15 17 there appeared a smoking f.
Gen 19 28 up from the earth as the smoke of a f.
Exod 19 18 smoke arose from it as out of a furnace
Deut 4 20 brought you out of the iron f. of Egypt
3 K 8 51 from the midst of the furnace of iron
Prov 17 3 tried by fire, and gold in the furnace
27 21 and gold [is tried] in the furnace
Wisd 3 6 as gold in the furnace he hath proved
Eccu 2 5 acceptable men in the f. of humiliation
27 6 the furnace trieth the potter's vessels
38 29 he fighteth with the heat of the f.
34 his watching to make clean the furnace
43 3 as one keeping a f. in the works
Isa 31 9 in Sion, and his furnace in Jerusalem
48 10 chosen thee in the furnace of poverty
Jer 11 4 land of Egypt, from the iron furnace
Eze 22 18 and lead in the midst of the f. 20
22 as silver is melted in midst of the f.
Dan 3 6 be cast into a f. of burning fire. 11
15 into the f. of burning fire. 20, 21
17 is able to save us from the furnace
19 the f. should be heated seven times
22 the furnace was heated exceedingly
23 in the midst of the f. of burning fire
46 to heat the furnace with brimstone and
47 the flame mounted up above the furnace
48 the Chaldeans as it found near the f.
49 down with Azarias . . . into the furnace
49 drove flame of the fire out of the f.
50 made the midst of the furnace like the
51 and blessed God in the furnace, saying
93 came to door of the burning fiery f.
Zach 12 6 the governors of Juda like a furnace
Mala 4 1 day shall come kindled as a furnace
Mat 13 42 shall cast them into the f. of fire. 50
Apoc 1 15 unto fine brass, as in a burning f.
9 2 arose, as the smoke of a great furnace
furnaces 2 Es 3 11 the tower of the furnaces. 12:37
furnish Lev 24 2 to furnish the lamps continually
Judg 19 20 will f. all things that are necessary
3 K 5 9 to furnish food for my household. So
Ps 77 19 can God f. a table in the wilderness
Eccu 29 32 go, stranger, and furnish the table
39 39 he will f. every work in due time
Jer 46 19 furnish thyself to go into captivity
1 Ma 8 26 or furnish them with wheat or arms
2 Ma 7 24 and f. him with things necessary
1 Tim 1 4 which furnish questions rather than the
furnished Judg 18 11 Esthaol 600 men, f. with arms
3 K 4 27 they f. the necessaries also for king
1 Pa 12 34 them 37,000 f. with shield and spear
37 Manasses 120,000 f. with arms for war
Eccu 38 26 with what wisdom shall he be furnished
Eze 27 9 furnished mariners for the service of
1 Ma 14 10 that they should be f. with ammunition
34 f. them with all things convenient for
Mark 14 15 show you large dining room f. Luke 22:12
Acts 20 34 with me, these hands have furnished. I
2 Tim 3 17 be perfect, furnished to every good
furnishing 3 K 9 11 f. Solomon with cedar trees
furniture Gen 2 1 finished, and all the f. of them
Gen 31 34 the idols under the camel's furniture
Exod 25 39 weight of candlestick with all the f.
30 27 candlestick and f. thereof, the altars
28 f. that belongeth to the service of
39 32 the roof and the whole f., the rings
36 lamps and the furniture of them with
Lev 8 10 anointed the tabernacle with all the f.
Num 1 50 shall carry the tabernacle and all the f.
3 26 cords of the tabernacle and all the f.
31 the veil and all the f. of this kind
4 32 by account all the vessels and f.
19 18 all the tent and all the f. and the
Judg 5 30 furniture of different kinds is heaped
3 K 10 21 furniture of the house of the forest of
1 Pa 26 27 building and furniture of the temple
2 Pa 5 5 with all the f. of the tabernacle. And
29 19 and all the furniture of the temple
1 Es 1 6 with goods and with beasts and with f.
Isa 39 2 all the storehouses of his furniture
Eze 12 4 shalt bring forth thy f. as the f. of one that
27 9 for the service of thy various f.
27 thy treasures and thy manifold f.
Nah 2 9 of the riches of all the precious f.
1 Ma 15 26 and gold and abundance of furniture
furrows 3 K 18 32 of the breadth of two furrows
Job 31 38 with it the furrows thereof mourn
Eccu 7 3 sow not evils in the f. of injustice
38 27 shall give his mind to turn up furrows
Eze 17 7 that he might water it by the furrows
10 shall it not wither in the furrows
Osee 10 4 up as bitterness in the f. of the field
11 Jacob shall break the f. for himself
12 11 are as heaps in the f. of the field
further Deut 7 10 without f. delay immediately

1 K 13 23 in order to advance further in Machmas
20 37 the arrow is there further beyond thee
1 Es 4 21 till further orders be given by me
Job 38 11 shalt come, and shalt go no further
Ecce 2 12 I passed further to behold wisdom and
2 Ma 10 27 they went forth further from the city
14 5 a convenient time to f. his madness
Mat 26 39 going a little further, he fell upon
65 what further need have we of witnesses
Mark 5 35 thou trouble the master any further
7 12 and further you suffer him not to do
14 63 what need we any further witnesses
Luke 22 71 what need we any further testimony
Acts 15 28 to lay no further burden upon you than
24 4 that I be no further tedious to thee
27 28 and going on little further, they found
Heb 7 11 what further need was there that another
furtherance Phil 1 12 rather to f. of the gospel
Phil 1 25 you all, for your f. and joy of faith
furthered 3 K 1 7 priest, who f. Adonias's side
1 Es 8 36 they f. the people and the house of God
furthermost Deut 34 2 land of Juda unto the f. sea
Josu 18 16 f. part of the valley of Raphaim
furthest Num 34 3 sea for its f. limits eastward
4 K 19 23 I have entered into the furthest parts
fury Gen 49 6 in their fury they slew a man
Gen 49 7 cursed be their fury, because it was
Lev 26 28 go against you with opposite fury
Num 25 4 my fury may be turned away from Israel
32 14 to augment the fury of the Lord against
Deut 13 17 Lord may turn from wrath of his fury
28 28 madness and blindness and fury of mind
32 24 with the fury of creatures that trail
Judg 20 5 my wife with an incredible fury of lust
Jdth 5 2 transported with exceeding great fury
Esth 1 12 and inflamed with a very great fury
Job 16 10 he hath gathered together his fury
18 4 that destroyest thy soul in thy fury
35 15 he doth not now bring on his fury
Ps 123 3 their fury was enkindled against us
Prov 15 1 but a harsh word stirreth up fury
27 4 anger hath no mercy, nor fury when
Wisd 10 3 fury wherewith he murdered his brother
Eccu 27 33 and fury are both of them abominable
39 33 in their fury they lay on grievous
Isa 7 4 with the wrath of the fury of Rasin
13 9 of indignation and of wrath and fury
14 6 that brought nations under in fury
34 2 and his fury upon all their armies
42 25 out upon him the indignation of his f.
51 13 at the presence of his f. who afflicted
13 where is now the fury of the oppressor
Jer 6 11 am I full of the fury of the Lord
10 24 with judgment: and not in thy fury
21 5 with a strong arm and in fury and
25 15 take the cup of wine of this fury
30 23 his fury going forth, a violent storm
44 6 my fury was poured forth and was
Lam 3 60 thou hast seen all their fury and all
Eze 5 13 I will accomplish my fury and will
9 8 by pouring out thy fury upon Jerusalem
16 38 I will give thee blood in fury and
20 33 will reign . . . with f. poured out. 34
22 20 will I gather you together in my fury
23 25 they shall execute upon thee with fury
25 14 according to my wrath and my fury
17 upon them, rebuking them in fury
Dan 2 12 the king in fury and in great wrath
3 13 in fury and in wrath commanded that
19 then was Nabuchodonosor filled with f.
Amos 1 11 all pity, and hath carried on his fury
Mich 7 18 he will send his fury in no more

G

Gaal Judg 9 26 Gaal the son of Obed came with his
Judg 9 28 Gaal . . . cried: Who is Abimelech, and
30 Zebul . . . hearing the words of Gaal
31 G. the son of Obed is come into Sichem
35 G. the son of Obed went out and stood
36 when Gaal saw the people, he said
37 Gaal said: Behold there cometh people
39 Gaal went out in sight of the people
41 Zebul drove Gaal and his companions
Gaas Josu 24 30 north side of mount Gaas. Judg 2:9
2 K 23 30 Heddai of the torrent Gaas, Abialbon
1 Pa 11 32 Hurai of the torrent Gaas, Abiel an
Gaba Isa 10 29 passed in haste, Gaba is our lodging
Gabaa Josu 15 57 Accain, Gabaa and Thamna: ten
Judg 19 12 but I will pass over to Gabaa: and
14 when they were by Gabaa, which is in
16 and dwelt as a stranger in Gabaa: but
20 9 this we will do in common against G.
13 deliver up the men of Gabaa that have
14 gathered themselves together into G.
15 besides the inhabitants of Gabaa, who
19 rising in the morning, camped by Gabaa
21 children of Benjamin coming out of G.
25 sallied forth out of the gates of G.
29 ambushes round about the city of Gabaa
31 up to Bethel and the other to Gabaa
43 on the east side of the city Gabaa
1 K 7 1 into the house of Abinadab in Gabaa
10 26 departed to his own house in Gabaa
11 4 messengers therefore came to G. of Saul
13 3 garrison of Philistines which was in G.
15 from Galgal to G. in hill of Benjamin
14 2 Saul abode in uttermost part of Gabaa
5 other to the south over against Gabaa
15 34 but Saul went up to his house in Gabaa
22 6 whilst Saul abode in Gabaa and was
23 19 the Ziphites went up to Saul in Gabaa
26 1 the men of Ziph came to Saul in Gabaa
3 and Saul encamped in Gabaa Hachila
2 K 5 25 he smote the Philistines from Gabaa
6 3 house of Abinadab, who was in G. 4
21 6 may crucify them to the Lord in Gabaa
4 K 23 8 high places . . . from Gabaa to Bersabee
1 Pa 2 49 of Machbena and the father of Gabaa
8 6 heads of families that dwelt in Gabaa
2 Pa 13 2 Michaia the daughter of Uriel of G.
16 6 he built with them Gabaa and Maspha
1 Es 2 26 the children of Rama and Gabaa, 621
Jdth 3 14 to the Idumeans into the land of Gabaa
Osee 5 8 blow ye the cornet in G., the trumpet
9 9 sinned deeply, as in the days of Gabaa
10 9 from the days of Gabaa, Israel hath
9 battle in Gabaa against the children
Gabaa of Benjamin; *see* **Benjamin**
Gabaath Josu 18 28 Gabaath and Cariath: 14 cities
Josu 24 33 they buried him Eleazar in Gabaath
2 K 23 29 Ithai the son of Ribai of Gabaath
1 Pa 11 31 Ethai the son of Ribai of Gabaath
12 3 the sons of Samaa of Gabaath, and
Isa 10 29 astonished, Gabaath of Saul fled away
Gabae Josu 21 17 Gabaon and Gabae and Anathoth
Gabaon Josu 9 3 they that dwelt in Gabaon, hearing
Josu 9 17 names of which are Gabaon and Caphira
10 2 Gabaon was a great city, and one of the
4 bring help, that we may take Gabaon
5 camped about Gabaon, laying siege
6 city of Gabaon which was besieged
10 them with a great slaughter in Gabaon
12 move not, O sun, toward Gabaon, nor
41 all the land of Gosen even to Gabaon

11 19 except the Hevite, who dwelt in Gabaon
18 25 Gabaon and Rama and Beroth and Mesphe
21 17 Gabaon and Gabae and Anathoth
2 K 2 12 went out from the camp to Gabaon. And
13 and met them by the pool of Gabaon
16 the field of the valiant, in Gabaon
24 by the way of the wilderness in Gabaon
3 30 he had killed their brother Asael at G.
20 8 at the great stone which is in Gabaon
3 K 9 2 as he had appeared to him in Gabaon
3 4 he went therefore to G. to sacrifice
4 did Solomon offer upon that altar in G.
1 Pa 8 29 at Gabaon dwelt Abigabaon and the
9 35 in G. dwelt Jehiel the father of G.
12 4 and Samaias of Gabaon, the stoutest
14 16 slaying them from Gabaon to Gazera
16 39 in the high place, which was in Gabaon
21 29 at that time in high place of Gabaon
2 Pa 1 3 multitude to the high place of Gabaon
13 came from the high place of Gabaon
2 Es 7 25 children of Gabaon, 95. The children
Isa 28 21 as in the valley which is in Gabaon
Jer 28 1 son of Azur, a prophet of Gabaon
41 12 by the great waters that are in Gabaon
16 whom he had brought back from Gabaon
Gabaonite 2 Es 3 7 to them built Meltias the G.
Gabaonites Josu 9 22 Josue called the G. and said
Josu 10 1 that the G. were gone over to Israel
2 K 21 1 because he [Saul] slew the Gabaonites
2 the king, calling for the Gabaonites
2 G. were not of the children of Israel
3 David therefore said to the Gabaonites
4 G. said to him: We have no contest
9 gave them into hands of the Gabaonites
Gabathon Josu 21 23 of tribe of Dan, Eltheco and G.
Gabbatha John 19 13 called . . . in Hebrew G. And
Gabee Josu 18 24 the town Emona and Ophini and G.
1 Pa 6 60 out of the tribe of Benjamin: Gabee
Gabelus Tob 1 17 he saw Gabelus in want, who was
Tob 4 21 I lent ten talents . . . to Gabelus in
5 8 I have abode with Gabelus our brother
14 canst thou conduct my son to Gabelus
9 3 to go to Gabelus to Rages the city of
6 finding Gabelus, gave him his note of
8 and Gabelus wept, and blessed God and
10 2 is Gabelus dead, thinkest thou, and no
11 18 also which he had received of Gabelus
12 3 he received the money of Gabelus, he
Gaber 3 K 4 19 Gaber . . . in the land of Galaad
Gabim Isa 10 31 inhabitants of G., take courage
Gabriel Dan 8 16 G., make this man to understand
Dan 9 21 the man Gabriel . . . touched me at the
Luke 1 19 I am Gabriel, who stand before God
26 the angel G. was sent from God into a
gad Eccu 25 34 wicked woman liberty to gad abroad
Gad Gen 30 11 and therefore called his name Gad
Gen 35 26 the sons of Zelpha . . . Gad and Aser
46 16 the sons of Gad: Sephian and Haggi
49 19 Gad, being girded, shall fight before
Exod 1 4 children of Israel . . . Gad and Aser
Num 1 14 of Gad, Eliasaph the son of Duel. Of
24 of the sons of Gad . . . 45,650. Of the
7 42 prince of the sons of Gad . . . offered
26 15 the sons of Gad by their kindreds
18 these are the families of Gad, of which
32 1 sons of Ruben and Gad had many flocks
Deut 3 12 gave the cities thereof to Ruben and G.
16 to the tribes of Ruben and Gad I gave
27 13 on mount Hebal . . . Ruben, Gad, and Aser
29 8 delivered it . . . to Ruben and Gad and
33 20 to Gad he said: Blessed be Gad in his
Josu 13 8 with whom Ruben and Gad have possessed
18 7 Gad and Ruben . . . have already received
21 7 of the tribes of Ruben and of Gad and
1 K 13 7 over the Jordan into the land of Gad
22 5 Gad the prophet said to David: Abide
2 K 24 5 city, which is in the vale of Gad. And
11 and the word of the Lord came to Gad
13 when Gad was come to David. 1 Pa 21:11
14 David said to Gad: I am. 1 Pa 21:13
18 and Gad came to David that day and said
19 up according to word of Gad. 1 Pa 21:19
4 K 10 33 all the land of Galaad and Gad and
1 Pa 2 2 sons of Israel . . . Gad and Aser. The
5 18 the sons of Ruben and of Gad. 12:37
26 he carried away Ruben and Gad and the
12 14 were of the sons of Gad, captains
21 9 Lord spoke to Gad the seer of David
18 commanded Gad to tell David to go up
29 29 and in the book of Gad the seer
2 Pa 29 25 the regulation . . . of Gad the seer
Jer 49 1 why then hath Melchom inherited Gad
Eze 48 27 side of the sea, one portion for Gad
28 by the border of Gad, the south side
34 the gate of Gad one, the gate of Aser
children of Gad Num 32 25 the children of Gad and Ruben said to Moses
Num 32 29 if the c. of G. . . . pass with you over
31 the c. of G. . . . answered: As the Lord
33 Moses therefore gave to the c. of G.
34 14 tribe of the c. of G. . . . have received
Josu 4 12 children of Ruben also and Gad . . . went
13 28 this is the possession of the c. of G.
22 9 the c. of G. . . . returned, and parted
11 children of Ruben and of Gad . . . had
15 came to children of Ruben and of Gad
21 c. of Ruben and of Gad . . . answered
25 between us and you . . . ye c. of G.
30 words of the children of Ruben and Gad
32 from the children of Ruben and Gad
34 the c. of G. called the altar which
1 Pa 5 11 the c. of G. dwelt over against them
tribe of Gad Num 2 14 in the tribe of Gad the prince was Eliasaph. 10:20
Num 13 16 of the tribe of Gad, Guel the son of
Deut 4 43 Ramoth . . . in the tribe of Gad
Josu 13 24 Moses gave to the tribe of Gad and to
20 8 Ramoth in Galaad of the tribe of Gad
21 37 of the tribe of Gad, Ramoth in Galaad
1 Pa 6 63 out of the tribe of Gad and out of
80 out of the tribe of Gad, Ramoth in
Apoc 7 5 of the tribe of Gad, 12,000 signed
Gaddel 1 Es 2 47 the children of Gaddel, the
Gaddi Num 13 12 Gaddi the son of Susi
1 Pa 12 8 from Gaddi also there went over to
Gaddis 1 Ma 2 2 John who was surnamed Gaddis
Gader Josu 12 13 Dabir one, the king of Gader one
Gaderoth 1 Pa 12 4 Johanan, and Jezabad of G.
2 Pa 28 18 and they took . . . Gaderoth and Socho
Gadgad Num 33 32 they came to mount Gadgad
Deut 10 7 from thence they came to Gadgad
Gadi 2 K 23 36 Nathan of Soba, Bonni of Gadi
4 K 15 14 Manahem the son of Gadi went up from
17 reigned Manahem son of Gadi over
Gadites Josu 1 12 to the Rubenites and the G.
Josu 12 6 in possession to the Rubenites and G.
22 1 called the Rubenites and the Gadites
1 Pa 26 32 made them rulers over . . . the Gadites
Gador 1 Pa 4 39 they went forth to enter into G.
Gaham Gen 22 24 Roma bore Tabee and Gaham
Gaher 1 Es 2 47 the children of Gaher. 2 Es 7:49
gain Prov 12 27 deceitful man shall not find gain
Prov 15 27 greedy of gain troubleth his own house
Wisd 14 2 for this the desire of gain devised
15 12 and the business of life to be gain
Eccu 46 3 how great glory did he gain when he

56 11 every one after his own gain, from the
Dan 2 8 that you seek to gain time, since
1 Ma 10 23 to gain the friendship of the Jews
2 Ma 11 3 and to make a gain of the temple
Mat 16 26 if he gain the whole world. Mark 8:36; Luke 9:25
18 15 hear thee, thou shalt gain thy brother
Acts 16 16 to her masters much gain by divining
19 seeing that the hope of their gain
19 25 you know that our gain is by this trade
24 brought no small gain to the craftsmen
1 C 9 19 of all, that I might gain the more. And
20 Jews, a Jew, that I might gain the Jews
21 might gain them that were under the law
21 I might g. them that were without the law
22 I became weak, that I might g. the weak
Phil 1 21 to live is Christ: and to die is gain
3 7 the things that were gain to me, the
8 them but as dung, that I may gain Christ
1 Tim 6 5 truth, supposing gain to be godliness
6 godliness with contentment is great gain
James 4 13 and will traffic and make our gain
gained Eccu 44 7 all these have g. glory in their
2 Ma 8 8 seeing that the man gained ground
Mat 25 16 traded with the same and g. other five
17 received the two, gained other two
20 I have gained other five over and above
22 to me: behold I have gained other two
Luke 19 15 much every man had gained by trading
16 Lord, thy pound hath gained ten pounds
18 thy pound hath gained five pounds
Acts 12 20 having g. Blastus, who was the king's
27 21 Crete, and have gained this harm and loss
gaineth Prov 11 30 and he that g. souls, is wise
gain's Jude 16 admiring persons for g. sake. But
gains Eze 22 27 to run after g. through covetousness
gainsaid Num 30 6 if her father . . . gainsaid it
Num 30 6 because her father hath gainsaid it
13 because her husband gainsaid it
1 K 14 39 none of the people gainsaid him [Saul]
gainsay Num 30 8 shall hear it and not gainsay it
Num 30 9 if as soon as he heareth he gainsay it
13 if forthwith he g. it, she shall not
16 if he gainsay it after that he knew it
Josu 1 18 he that shall gainsay thy mouth and
Jdth 12 13 who am I that I should gainsay my lord
1 Ma 14 44 to gainsay his words or to call
Luke 21 15 shall not be able to resist and g.
gainsayers Titus 1 9 and to convince the gainsayers
gainsayeth Isa 45 9 woe to him that g. his maker
gainsaying Acts 18 6 they g. and blaspheming, he
Titus 2 9 in all things pleasing, not gainsaying
gait Eccu 19 27 gait of the man, show what he is
Gaius Acts 19 29 having caught Caius and Aristarchus
Acts 20 4 Secundus, and G. of Derbe, and Timothy
3 J 1 to the dearly beloved Gaius whom
Galaad Gen 31 21 going on towards mount Galaad
Gen 31 23 overtook him in the mount of Galaad
25 pitched his tent in the same mount of G.
48 name thereof was called Galaad
37 25 some Ismaelites . . . coming from Galaad
Num 26 29 Machir begot Galaad, of whom is the
30 Galaad had sons: Jezer, of whom is
27 1 Hepher the son of Galaad. Josu 17:3
32 1 saw the lands of Jazer and Galaad
26 sheep and cattle in the cities of Galaad
29 give them Galaad in possession. But if
39 went into G. and wasted it, cutting
36 1 the princes of the families of Galaad
Deut 2 36 situate in a valley, as far as Galaad
3 12 Arnon, unto the half of mount Galaad
13 I delivered the other part of Galaad
15 to Machir also I gave Galaad. And to
4 43 Ramoth in Galaad, which is in the
Josu 12 2 half Galaad, as far as the torrent
5 Gessuri and Machati and of half Galaad
13 11 Galaad, and the borders of Gessuri
25 border of Jazer and all the cities of G.
31 and half Galaad, and Astaroth, and Edrai
17 1 father of Galaad, who was a warlike man
1 had for possession Galaad and Basan
20 8 Ramoth in Galaad of the tribe of Gad
21 37 of tribe of Gad, Ramoth in G. 1 Pa 6:80
22 9 to go into Galaad the land of their
Judg 5 17 Galaad rested beyond the Jordan, and
7 3 went away from mount G. and returned
17 pitched their tents in Galaad: against
18 princes of Galaad said one to another
18 shall be the leader of people of Galaad
11 1 was a harlot, and his father was Galaad
2 Galaad had a wife of whom he had sons
5 the ancients of G. went to fetch Jephte
8 the princes of Galaad said to Jephte
11 went with the princes of Galaad and
29 round G. and Manasses and Maspha of G.
12 4 calling to him all the men of Galaad
4 the men of Galaad defeated Ephraim
4 he had said: G. is a fugitive of Ephraim
7 and was buried in his city of Galaad
2 K 2 9 made him [Isboseth] king over Galaad
24 6 and by Jazer they passed into Galaad
3 K 4 13 of Jair the son of Manasses in Galaad
17 1 the Thesbite of the inhabitants of G.
4 K 10 33 from Aroer . . . and Galaad and Basan
15 29 Janoe and Cedes and Asor and Galaad
1 Pa 2 21 Machir the father of Galaad. 23; 7:14
5 14 Jara, the son of Galaad, the son of
16 they dwelt in Galaad and in Basan
7 17 these are the sons of Galaad, the son
26 31 most valiant men in Jazer Galaad
27 21 over half tribe of Manasses in Galaad
Ps 59 9 Galaad is mine and Manasses is. 107:9
Cant 4 1 goats, which come up from mount Galaad
6 4 a flock of goats, that appear from G.
Jer 8 22 is there no balm in Galaad? Or is
22 6 thou art to me G. the head of Libanus
46 11 go up into Galaad, and take balm
50 19 be satisfied in mount Ephraim and G.
Eze 47 18 from the midst of Galaad and from
Osee 6 8 Galaad is a city of workers of idols
12 11 if Galaad be an idol, then in vain
Amos 1 3 have thrashed Galaad with iron wains
13 ripped up the women with child of G.
Abdi 19 and Benjamin shall possess Galaad
Mich 7 14 they shall feed in Basan and Galaad
Zach 10 10 will bring them to the land of Galaad
1 Ma 5 9 the Gentiles that were in G. assembled
17 will go into the country of Galaad
27 the rest of the cities of Galaad. 36
13 22 he came not into the country of Galaad
Jabes Galaad Judg 21 8 inhabitants of J. G. were
Judg 21 10 inhabitants of Jabes Galaad to the sword
12 found of Jabes Galaad 400 virgins
14 of the daughters of Jabes Galaad
1 K 11 1 began to fight against Jabes Galaad
9 shall you say to men of Jabes Galaad
31 11 inhabitants of Jabes Galaad had heard
12 came to Jabes Galaad and burnt them
2 K 2 4 that the men of Jabes Galaad had buried
5 messengers to the men of Jabes Galaad
21 12 from the men of Jabez Galaad, who had
1 Pa 10 11 when the men of Jabez Galaad had heard
land of Galaad Num 32 40 gave l. . . . to Machir
Deut 3 10 all the l. . . . and Basan as far as
16 I gave of the l. . . . as far as the
34 1 the Lord showed him all the l. . . .

Josu 17 5 beside the l. . . . and Basan beyond the
6 the l. . . . fell to the lot of the rest
22 13 sent to them into the l. . . . Phinees
15 into the l. . . . and said to them
32 out of l. . . . into land of Chanaan
Judg 10 4 until this present day in the l. . . .
20 1 Dan to Bersabee, with the l. . . . to the
1 K 13 7 over Jordan into land of Gad and Galaad
2 K 17 26 camped with Absalom in the l. . . .
3 K 4 19 Gaber the son of Uri, in the l. . . .
4 K 10 33 all the land of Galaad and Gad and
1 Pa 2 22 three and twenty cities in the l. . . .
5 9 great number of cattle in the l. . . .
1 Ma 5 20 8,000 to Judas to go into the l. . . .
25 happened to their brethren in the l. . . .
45 all the Israelites that were in l. . . .
55 Judas and Jonathan were in the l. . . .
Ramoth Galaad 3 K 4 13 Bengaber in R. G.: he had
3 K 22 3 know ye not that R. G. is ours, and we
4 come with me to battle to Ramoth Galaad
6 shall I go to R. G. to fight, or shall
12 go up to R. G. and prosper, for the
15 Micheas, shall we go to R. G. to battle
20 that he may go up and fall at R. G.
29 king of Juda went up to Ramoth Galaad
4 K 8 28 against Hazael king of Syria in R. G.
9 1 of oil in thy hand and go to R. G.
4 of the prophet went away to R. G.
14 Joram had besieged R. G., he and all
2 Pa 18 2 he persuaded him to go up to R. G.
3 king of Juda: Come with me to R. G.
5 shall we go to R. G. to fight. 14
11 go up to R. G., and thou shalt prosper
19 that he may go up and fall in R. G.
28 king of Juda went up to Ramoth Galaad
22 5 against Hazael king of Syria, at R. G.
Galaadite Judg 10 3 to him succeeded Jair the G.
Judg 11 1 was at that time Jephte the Galaadite
40 lament the daughter of Jephte the G.
12 7 Jephte the Galaadite judged Israel
2 K 17 27 Berzellai the Galaadite of Rogelim
19 31 Berzellai also the G. coming down
32 Berzellai the G. was of a great age
3 K 2 7 kindness to sons of Berzellai the G.
1 Es 2 61 daughters of Berzellai, the G. 2 Es 7:63
Galaadites Num 26 29 of whom is family of the G.
Judg 12 5 the Galaadites secured the fords of the
5 the G. said to him: Art thou not an
4 K 15 25 fifty men of sons of the Galaadites
Galal 1 Pa 9 15 of the Levites . . . Galal and
1 Pa 9 16 the son of Galal the son of Idithum
2 Es 11 17 Samua the son of Galal the son of
Galalai 2 Es 12 35 his brethren . . . Malalai, G.
Galatia 1 Ma 8 2 acts, which they had done in G.
Acts 16 6 through Phrygia, and the country of G.
18 23 went through the country of Galatia
1 C 16 1 I have given order to the churches of G.
Gal 1 2 are with mę, to the churches of Galatia
2 Tim 4 10 Crescens into G., Titus into Dalmatia
1 Pa 1 1 strangers dispersed through Pontus, G.
Galatians 2 Ma 8 20 had fought against the Galatians
Gal 3 1 O senseless G., who hath bewitched you
galbanum Exod 30 34 g. of sweet savor and the
Eccu 24 21 perfumed my dwelling as . . . galbanum
Galgal Josu 4 19 camped in Galgal, over against
Josu 4 20 Josue pitched in Galgal and said to
5 9 name of that place was called Galgal
10 the children of Israel abode in Galgal
9 6 then abode in the camp at Galgal. 10:6
10 7 Josue went up from G., and all the army
9 Josue going up from Galgal all the night
15 with all Israel into the camp of Galgal
43 to the place of the camp in Galgal
12 23 the king of the nations of Galgal one
14 6 came to Josue in Galgal, and Caleb
15 7 and so northward looking towards Galgal
Judg 2 1 angel of the Lord went up from Galgal
3 19 returning from Galgal, where the idols
1 K 7 16 he went every year . . . to Galgal
10 8 thou shalt go down before me to Galgal
11 14 let us go to Galgal and let us renew
15 and all the people went to Galgal
15 made Saul king before the Lord in Galgal
13 4 were called together after Saul to Galgal
7 when Saul was yet in Galgal, all the
8 Samuel came not to G., and the people
12 Philistines come down upon me to Galgal
15 Samuel arose and went up from Galgal
15 from Galgal to Gabaa in hill of Benjamin
15 12 had passed on and gone down to Galgal
21 sacrifice to the Lord their God in Galgal
33 him in pieces before the Lord in Galgal
2 K 19 15 and all Juda came as far as Galgal
40 so the king went on to Galgal, and
4 K 2 1 Elias and Eliseus were going from Galgal
4 38 Eliseus returned to G., and there was
2 Es 12 29 from the house of Galgal and from the
Osee 4 15 go ye not into Galgal, and come not up
9 15 all their wickedness is in Galgal
12 11 were they in G. offering sacrifices
Amos 4 4 to Galgal, and multiply transgressions
5 5 seek not Bethel, and go not into Galgal
5 G. shall go into captivity, and Bethel
Mich 6 5 answered him from Setim to Galgal
1 Ma 9 2 they took the road that leadeth to G.
Galgala Deut 11 30 dwelleth . . . over against Galgala
Galilean Mat 26 69 also wast with Jesus the Galilean
Mark 14 70 of them; for thou art also a Galilean
Luke 22 59 was also with him; for he is also a G.
John 7 52 art thou also a Galilean? Search the
Galileans Luke 13 1 some that told him of the G.
Luke 13 2 think you that these G. were sinners
John 4 45 the G. received him, having seen all
Acts 2 7 are not all these that speak Galileans
Galilee Josu 13 2 all G., Philistia, and all
Josu 20 7 they appointed Cedes in Galilee
21 32 Cedes in Galilee, one of the cities
3 K 9 11 gave Hiram 20 cities in land of Galilee
4 K 15 29 took Aion . . . and Galaad and Galilee
1 Pa 6 76 of the tribe of Nephtali, Cedes in G.
Jdth 1 8 he sent . . . to the inhabitants of G.
Tob 1 1 which is in the upper parts of Galilee
Isa 9 1 Jordan of the Galilee of the Gentiles
1 Ma 5 14 there came other messengers out of G.
15 all Galilee is filled with strangers
17 and deliver thy brethren in Galilee
23 he took with him those that were in G.
55 and Simon his brother in Galilee
10 30 cities . . . out of Samaria and G.
11 63 treacherously to Cades, which is in G.
Mat 2 22 retired into the quarters of Galilee
4 15 the Jordan, Galilee of the Gentiles
23 Jesus went about all Galilee, teaching
17 21 when they abode together in Galilee
21 11 Jesus the prophet from Nazareth of G.
Mark 1 9 Jesus came from Nazareth of Galilee
28 forthwith into all the country of G.
39 in their synagogues and in all Galilee
6 21 and tribunes and chief men of Galilee
9 29 they passed through Galilee, and he
15 41 when he was in Galilee followed him
Luke 1 26 into a city of Galilee called Nazareth
3 1 and Herod being tetrarch of Galilee
4 31 into Capharnaum, a city of Galilee
44 was preaching in the synagogues of G.
5 17 were come out of every town of Galilee

8 26 Gerasens, which is over against G.
13 2 sinners above all the men of Galilee
17 11 through the midst of Samaria and G.
23 6 hearing G., asked if the man were of G.
24 6 spoke unto you when he was yet in G.
John 2 1 was a marriage in Cana of Galilee
11 miracles did Jesus in Cana of Galilee
4 46 again therefore into Cana of Galilee
7 1 Jesus walked in Galilee; for he would
9 he himself stayed in Galilee. But
41 doth the Christ come out of Galilee
52 out of Galilee a prophet riseth not
12 21 Philip, who was of Bethsaida of G.
21 2 and Nathanael, who was of Cana of G.
Acts 1 11 ye men of Galilee, why stand you
5 37 rose up Judas of Galilee in the days
9 31 had peace throughout . . . all Galilee
from Galilee Mat 3 13 cometh Jesus from Galilee
Mat 4 25 followed him from Galilee. Mark 3:7; Luke 23:49
19 1 he departed from Galilee and came into
27 55 who had followed Jesus from Galilee
Luke 2 5 Joseph also went up from Galilee out
23 5 beginning from Galilee to this place
55 that were come with him from Galilee
Acts 10 37 it began from G., after the baptism
13 31 by them who came up with him from G.
into Galilee 1 Ma 5 20 allotted to Simon to go into G.
1 Ma 5 21 Simon went into Galilee and fought
12 47 of whom he sent 2,000 into Galilee
49 sent an army and horsemen into Galilee
Mat 4 12 delivered up, he retired into Galilee
26 32 I will go before you into G. Mark 14:28
28 7 he will go before you into G. Mark 16:7
10 that they go into Galilee, there they
16 the eleven disciples went into Galilee
Mark 1 14 Jesus came into Galilee, preaching the
Luke 2 39 they returned into G. to their city
4 14 in the power of the spirit into G.
John 1 43 he would go forth into Galilee, and
4 3 he left Judea and went again into G.
43 departed thence and went into Galilee
45 when he was come into Galilee, the
47 that Jesus was come from Judea into G.
54 when he was come out of Judea into G.
sea of Galilee Mat 4 18 Jesus walking by the sea of Galilee
Mat 15 29 he came nigh the sea of Galilee. And
Mark 1 16 passing by the sea of Galilee, he saw
7 31 he came by Sidon to the sea of Galilee
John 6 1 Jesus went over the sea of Galilee
gall Deut 29 18 bringing forth g. and bitterness
Deut 32 32 their grapes are grapes of gall
33 their wine is the gall of dragons
Tob 6 5 and lay up his heart and his gall
9 the gall is good for anointing the eyes
11 4 take with thee of the gall of the fish
4 so Tobias took some of that gall
8 anoint his eyes with this gall of the
13 Tobias taking of the gall of the fish
Job 20 14 turned into the gall of asps within him
Ps 68 22 they gave me gall for my food, and in
Jer 8 14 hath given us water of gall to drink
9 15 and give them water of gall to drink
23 15 and will give them gall to drink
Lam 3 5 hath compassed me with gall and labor
19 remember . . . the wormwood and the g.
Haba 2 15 to him that . . . presenteth his gall
Mat 27 34 him wine to drink mingled with gall
Acts 8 23 thou art in the gall of bitterness and
galleries 3 K 7 2 four g. between pillars of
Eze 41 15 the galleries on both sides 100 cubits
16 galleries round about on three sides
42 5 because they bore up the galleries
gallery Eze 42 3 a g. joined to a triple g.
galley Isa 33 21 neither shall the great g. pass
galleys Num 24 24 shall come in g. from Italy
Dan 11 30 the galleys . . . shall come upon him
2 Ma 4 20 was employed for the making of galleys
Gallim 1 K 25 44 son of Laid, who was of Gallim
Isa 10 30 lift up thy voice, O daughter of Gallim
15 8 the howling thereof unto Gallim
Gallio Acts 18 12 when Gallio was proconsul of Achaia
Acts 18 14 Gallio said to Jews: If it were some
17 Gallio cared for none of these things
Gamaliel Num 1 10 G. the son of Phadassur. 2:20
Num 7 54 Gamaliel . . . offered a silver dish
59 this was the offering of Gamaliel
10 23 the prince was Gamaliel the son of
Acts 5 34 rising up, a Pharisee, named Gamaliel
22 3 brought up . . . at the feet of Gamaliel
Gamarias Jer 29 3 Gamarias the son of Helcias
Jer 36 10 Baruch read . . . in the treasury of G.
11 Micheas the son of Gamarias the son of
12 the princes sat there . . . Gamarias
25 Gamarias spoke to the king, not to burn
game 2 Ma 4 18 g. that was used every fifth year
games 2 Ma 4 14 to be partakers of the games
Gamul 1 Pa 24 17 two and twentieth [lot] to Gamul
Gamzo 2 Pa 28 18 and they took . . . Gamzo, with their
gaoler Acts 16 23 charging the g. to keep them
gap Eze 22 30 and stand in the gap before me
gaped 4 K 4 35 the child g. seven times and opened
garden 3 K 21 2 I may make me a g. of herbs
4 K 9 27 fled by the way of the garden house
21 18 buried in the garden of his own house, in the garden of Oza
26 buried him . . . in the garden of Oza
25 4 the two walls by the king's garden
Esth 1 5 a feast . . . in the court of the garden
7 7 banquet into the g. set with trees
8 the king came back out of the garden
Cant 4 16 south wind, blow through my garden
5 1 let my beloved come into his garden
1 I am come into my garden, O my sister
6 1 my beloved is gone down into his g.
10 I went down into the garden of nuts
Eccu 24 42 I will water my garden of plants
Isa 1 8 as a lodge in a garden of cucumbers
30 off, and as a garden without water
51 3 her wilderness as the g. of the Lord
58 11 thou shalt be like a watered garden
61 11 as the g. causeth her seed to shoot
Jer 31 12 their soul shall be as a watered garden
39 4 by the way of the king's garden and
52 7 and leadeth to the king's garden
Lam 2 6 he hath destroyed his tent as a garden
Bar 6 69 as a scarecrow in a g. of cucumbers
70 no better than a white thorn in a garden
Eze 36 35 is become as a garden of pleasure
Joel 1 20 as a garden bed that thirsteth after
2 3 the land is like a garden of pleasure
Luke 13 19 a man took and cast into his garden
John 18 1 where there was a garden, into which
26 did not I see thee in the garden with
19 41 place where he was crucified, a garden and in the garden a new sepulcher
gardener John 20 15 she thinking that it was the g.
gardens Num 24 6 as watered g. near the rivers
Ecce 2 5 I made gardens and orchards and set
Cant 4 15 the fountain of gardens: the well of
6 1 to feed in the gardens, and to gather
8 13 thou that dwellest in the gardens
Isa 1 29 you shall be ashamed of the gardens
65 3 that immolate in gardens, and sacrifice
66 17 thought themselves clean in the gardens

Jer 29 28 plant gardens and eat the fruits of
Amos 4 9 hath eaten up your many gardens and
9 14 shall make gardens, and eat the fruits
Gareb 2 K 23 38 Gareb also a Jethrite; Urias
1 Pa 11 40 Gareb a Jethrite, Urias a Hethite
Jer 31 39 measuring line . . . upon the hill G.
Garizim Deut 11 29 put the blessing upon mount G.
Deut 27 12 these shall stand upon mount Garizim
Josu 8 33 half of them by mount Garizim, and half
Judg 9 7 stood on the top of mount Garizim
garland Isa 28 5 garland of joy to the residue
garlands Jdth 3 10 received him with g. and
Acts 14 12 bringing oxen and g. before the gate
garlic Num 11 5 the onions and the garlic
garment Gen 39 12 catching the skirt of g.
Gen 39 12 leaving the garment in her hand
13 woman saw the garment in her hands
15 he left the g. that I held. 18
16 for a proof . . . she kept the garment
49 11 his garment in the blood of the grape
Exod 28 4 tunick and a strait linen garment
29 5 with the linen garment and the tunick
Lev 6 27 if a garment be sprinkled with the blood
8 7 with the strait linen garment, girding
11 32 or a garment or skins or haircloths
13 47 garment that shall have the leprosy
51 he shall judge the garment unclean
55 taken hold of the outside of the garment
56 after the garment is washed, he shall
59 leprosy of any garment woollen or linen
15 17 the garment or skin that he weareth
19 19 a garment that is woven of two sorts
Num 31 20 every garment or vessel or anything
Deut 22 11 g. that is woven of woolen and linen
Josu 7 21 I saw among the spoils a scarlet garment
Judg 3 16 girded therewith under his garment
17 5 a priestly garment, and idols: and he
2 K 20 12 covered him with a garment, that they
3 K 11 29 prophet Ahias . . . clad with new garment
30 and Ahias taking his new garment
4 K 9 13 taking every man his garment laid it
1 Es 9 5 having rent my mantle and my garment
Esth 4 4 and she sent a garment, to clothe him
Job 13 28 and as a garment that is moth-eaten
30 18 my g. is consumed, and they have
38 9 when I made a cloud the garment thereof
14 as clay, and shall stand as a garment
41 4 who can discover the face of his g.
Ps 68 12 I made haircloth my garment: and I
101 27 all of them shall grow old like a g.
103 2 art clothed with light as with a g.
6 the deep like a garment is its clothing
108 18 and he put on cursing, like a garment
19 may it be unto him like a garment
132 2 ran down to the skirt of his garment
Prov 20 16 take away the g. of him that is surety
25 20 one that looseth his g. in cold weather
20 as a moth doth by a g. and a worm
27 13 take away his g. that hath been surety
30 4 the waters together as in a garment
Cant 5 3 I have put off my garment, how shall I
Eccu 45 10 he put upon him a garment to the feet
Isa 3 6 thou hast a garment, be thou our ruler
9 5 and garment mingled with blood, shall
22 17 he will lift thee up as a garment
30 22 garment of thy molten things of gold
50 9 shall all be destroyed as a garment
51 6 the earth shall be worn away like a g.
8 the worm shall eat them up as a g.
Isa 61 3 a g. of praise for the spirit of grief
Jer 43 12 as a shepherd putteth on his garment
Bar 5 1 off, O Jerusalem, the g. of thy mourning
2 thee with the double garment of justice
6 12 have covered them with a purple garment
Eze 16 8 and I spread my garment over thee
18 7 covered the naked with a garment. 16
Dan 7 9 his garment was white as snow, and the
Agge 2 13 sanctified flesh in the skirt of his g.
Zach 13 4 they be clad with a g. of sackcloth
Mala 2 16 but iniquity shall cover his garment
2 Ma 8 35 laying aside his garment of glory
Mat 3 4 had his garment of camels' hair and a
9 16 raw cloth unto an old g. Mark 2:21
16 the fulness thereof from the garment
20 touched the hem of his g. Luke 8:44
21 if I shall touch only his g. Mark 5:28
14 36 touch but the hem of his g. Mark 6:56
22 11 man who had not on a wedding garment
12 not having on a wedding garment? But he
Mark 5 27 behind him and touched his garment
10 50 casting off his garment leaped up and
13 16 not turn back to take up his garment
Luke 5 36 piece from a new g. upon an old g.
23 11 garment, and sent him back to Pilate
John 19 2 and they put on him a purple garment
5 the crown of thorns and the purple g.
Acts 12 8 cast thy g. about thee, and follow me
Heb 1 11 and they shall all grow old as a garment
Jude 23 hating also the spotted garment which
Apoc 1 13 clothed with a garment down to the feet
19 13 clothed with a g. sprinkled with blood
16 on his garment and on his thigh written
garments Gen 3 21 made for Adam and his wife, g.
Gen 24 53 forth vessels of silver and gold and g.
27 15 put on him very good garments of Esau
38 14 put off the garments of her widowhood
19 put on the garments of her widowhood
Exod 28 32 to be made in the outmost parts of g.
Lev 14 55 of the leprosy of garments and houses
Josu 7 24 silver and the g. and the golden rule
9 5 with patches, and old g. upon them
13 these g. we have on, and the shoes we
Judg 5 30 g. of divers colors are given to Sisara
14 19 thirty men, whose g. he took away and
1 K 15 9 herds and the garments and the rams
2 K 13 18 that were virgins used such kind of g.
3 K 10 25 presents . . . garments and armor. 2 Pa 9:24
4 K 5 22 talent of silver and two changes of g.
23 two changes of g., and laid them upon
26 hast received money and received g.
10 22 forth g. for all the servants of Baal
22 and they brought them forth garments
11 14 Athalia rent her garments. 2 Pa 23:13
2 Pa 20 25 stuff of various kinds, and garments
1 Es 2 69 and a hundred garments for the priests
2 Es 7 70 bowls and 530 garments for priests
72 of silver, and 67 garments for priests
Jdth 10 2 and put away the g. of her widowhood
3 herself with the g. of her gladness
12 15 and dressed herself out with her g.
15 14 to Judith in gold and silver and g.
16 9 put off her the garments of widowhood
9 and put on her the garments of joy
Esth 14 2 she put on g. suitable for weeping and
15 4 she laid away the garments she wore
Job 9 31 in filth, and my g. shall abhor me
40 5 and be glorious and put on goodly g.
Ps 21 19 they parted my garments amongst them
Prov 31 21 domestics are clothed with double g.
Eccu 42 13 from garments cometh a moth, and from
Isa 52 1 O Sion, put on the g. of thy glory
59 17 he put on the garments of vengeance
61 10 clothed me with the g. of salvation
63 1 from Edom, with dyed g. from Bosra
3 their blood is sprinkled upon my g.
Eze 16 10 and clothed thee with fine garments

1 Ma 9 51 he placed g. in them, that they might
52 set g. in them and provisions of
11 3 he put g. of soldiers in every city
garters Num 31 50 in g. and tablets, rings and
gasp 2 Ma 7 9 when he was at the last gasp
Gaspha 2 Es 11 21 dwelt in Ophel and Siaha and G.
gate Gen 23 18 that went in at the gate of his
Gen 28 17 house of God and the gate of heaven
Exod 32 26 standing in the gate of the camp, he
27 return from gate to gate through the
Deut 21 19 his city to the gate of judgment
22 15 ancients of the city that are in the g.
24 shalt bring them both out to the gate
Josu 2 5 at the time of shutting the gate
7 gone out, the gate was presently shut
7 5 the enemies pursued them from the gate
Judg 9 51 having shut and strongly barred the g.
52 [Abimelech] approaching to the gate
16 3 he took both the doors of the gate
Ruth 4 1 Booz went up to the gate and sat there
11 all the people that were in the gate
1 K 9 18 came to Samuel in midst of the gate
21 13 stumbled against the doors of the gate
2 K 3 27 took him aside to middle of the gate
10 8 men in array at entering in of the gate
11 9 Urias slept before gate of the king's
15 2 stood by the entrance of the gate
18 4 the king stood by the gate, and all the
24 watchman that was on the top of gate
33 to the high chamber over the gate
19 8 the king arose and sat in the gate
8 that the king sat in the gate: and all
23 15 cistern that is in Bethlehem by the gate
16 cistern of Bethlehem that was by the g.
3 K 14 27 before the gate of the king's house
22 10 by the entrance of the gate of Samaria
4 K 7 1 for a stater, in the gate of Samaria
3 four lepers at entering in of the gate
11 then the guards of the gate went and
17 hand he leaned, to stand at gate
17 trod upon him in entrance of the gate
18 at this very time tomorrow in the gate
20 the people trod upon him in the gate
9 31 at Jehu coming in at the gate, and
10 8 heaps by the entering in of the gate
11 6 let a third part be at the gate of Sur
6 be at the gate behind the dwelling
19 way of the gate of the shieldbearers
14 13 g. of Ephraim to g. of corner. 2 Pa 25:23
15 35 he built the highest gate of the house
23 8 in the entering in of the gate of Josue
1 Pa 9 18 in the king's gate eastward, the sons
21 porter of the gate of the tabernacle
11 17 of Bethlehem, which is in the gate
18 of Bethlehem, which was in the gate
26 14 learned man, the north gate fell by lot
16 gate which leadeth to the way of the
2 Pa 8 14 in their divisions by gate and gate
18 9 in the open court by gate of Samaria
23 5 the gate that is called the Foundation
15 she was come within the horse gate
20 brought him through the upper gate
24 8 by the gate of the house of the Lord
26 9 over the gate of the corner and over the gate of the valley
27 3 the high gate of house of the Lord
31 14 Levite, the porter of the east gate
32 6 all together in the street of the gate
33 14 from the entering in of the fish gate
35 15 the porters kept guard at every gate
2 Es 2 13 out by night by the gate of the valley
13 dragon fountain and to the dung gate
14 I passed to the gate of the fountain
15 I came to the gate of the valley and
3 1 priests, and they built the flock gate
3 the fish gate the sons of Asnaa built
6 built the old gate: they covered it and
13 the gate of the valley Hanun built
13 in wall unto the gate of the dunghill
14 gate of the dunghill Melchias . . . built
15 gate of the fountain Sellum . . . built
26 as far as over against the water gate
28 upward from the horse gate the priests
29 Sechenias, keeper of the east gate
30 over against the judgment gate and
31 chamber of the corner of the flock gate
8 1 street which is before the water gate
3 street that was before the water gate
16 and in the street of the water gate
16 in the street of the gate of Ephraim
12 31 upon the wall toward the dunghill gate
35 scribe before them at the fountain gate
36 David, and to the water gate eastward
38 above the g. of Ephraim and above the old g. and above the fish g.
38 of Emath, and even to the flock gate
38 and they stood still in the watch gate
Jdth 8 32 you shall stand at the gate this night
Esth 3 19 Mardochai stayed at the king's gate
21 when Mardochai abode at the king's gate
4 2 even to the gate of the palace: for no
6 Mardochai . . . before the palace gate
5 9 sitting before the gate of the palace
13 the Jew sitting before the king's gate
6 12 Mardochai returned to the palace gate
Job 5 4 and shall be destroyed in the gate
30 14 a wall is broken and a gate opened
31 21 when I saw myself superior in the gate
Ps 68 13 that sat in the gate spoke against me
117 20 this is the gate of the Lord, the just
126 5 shall speak to his enemies in the gate
Prov 22 22 do not oppress the needy in the gate
24 7 in the gate he shall not open his mouth
Cant 7 4 which are in the gate of the daughter
Isa 14 31 howl, O gate; cry, O city: all Philistia
22 7 shall place themselves in the gate
28 6 return out of the battle to the gate
29 21 him that reproved them in the gate
66 17 in the gardens behind the gate within
Jer 7 2 stand in the gate of the house of the
17 19 the gate of the children of the people
19 2 is by the entry of the earthen gate
20 2 were in the upper gate of Benjamin
26 10 in the entry of the new gate. 36:10
31 38 even to the gate of the corner. And
40 and to the corner of the horse gate
37 12 he was come to the gate of Benjamin
12 the captain of the gate who was there
38 14 to the third gate, that was in the house
39 4 by gate that was between the two walls
43 9 brick wall at gate of Pharao's house
52 7 the gate that is between the two walls
Eze 8 3 into Jerusalem, near the inner gate
5 on north side of the gate of the altar
14 brought me in by the door of the gate
9 2 came from the way of the upper gate
10 19 it stood in the entry of the east gate
11 1 and brought me into the east gate
1 in entry of the g. five and twenty men
40 3 in his hand, and he stood in the gate
6 to the gate that looked toward the east
6 breadth of the threshold of the gate
8 the threshold of the gate. 11; 46:2
8 the porch of the gate. 9, 39, 40; 44:3; 46:2, 8
10 the little chambers of the gate that
11 the length of the gate thirteen cubits

13 13 he measured the gate. 28, 32
14 to the front the court of the gate
15 before the face of the gate which
15 to the face of the porch of inner gate
16 which were within the gate on every side
19 from the face of the lower gate
20 the breadth of the gate. 48; 41:2, 3
21 according to measure of the former gate
22 measure of gate that looked to the east
23 gate of the inner court was over against the gate of the north
23 he measured from gate to gate. 27
24 the gate that looked to the south
27 there was a gate of the inner court
28 into the inner court at the south gate
35 the gate that looked to the north. 44
40 which goeth up to the entry of the gate
41 at sides of the gate were eight tables
44 without inner gate were the chambers
44 one at the side of the east gate
41 3 the front of the gate two cubits
3 and the gate six cubits, and the breadth
20 even to the upper parts of the gate
42 15 brought me out by the way of the gate
43 1 he brought me to the gate that looked
4 the gate that looked to the east
44 1 brought me back to the way of the gate
2 this gate shall be shut, it shall not
4 brought me by the way of the north gate
45 19 the gate of the inner court. 46:1
46 2 gate shall not be shut till the evening
3 shall adore at the door of that gate
9 goeth in by the north gate to adore
9 out by the way of the south gate: and
9 that goeth in by the way of south gate
9 out by the way of the north gate: he
9 of the gate whereby he came in, but
12 gate that looketh towards the east
12 gate shall be shut after he is gone
19 by entry that was at side of the gate
47 1 brought me again to gate of the house
2 led me out by the way of the north gate
2 the way without the outward gate to
48 31 the gate *N.* one. 32, 33, 34
Dan 8 2 vision that I was over the gate of Ulai
6 I had seen standing before the gate
Amos 5 10 hated him that rebuketh in the gate
12 oppressing the poor in the gate
15 and establish judgment in the gate
Abdi 13 neither shalt thou enter into the gate
Mich 1 9 it hath touched the gate of my people
12 evil is come . . . into gate of Jerusalem
2 13 they shall . . . pass through the gate
Soph 1 10 the noise of a cry from the fish gate
Zach 14 10 from the gate of Benjamin even to the
10 even to the place of the former gate
10 even to the gate of the corners
1 Ma 5 21 pursued them even to the gate of Ptolemais
2 Ma 1 8 they burnt the gate and shed innocent
Mat 7 13 enter ye in at the narrow gate; for
13 wide is the gate, and broad is the way
14 how narrow is the gate, and strait the
26 71 as he [Peter] went out of the gate
Mark 11 4 found the colt tied before the gate
Luke 13 24 strive to enter by the narrow gate
16 20 Lazarus, who lay at his gate, full of
Acts 3 2 at the gate of the temple which is
10 sat begging alms at the Beautiful gate
10 17 for Simon's house, stood at the gate
12 10 they came to the iron g. that leadeth
13 he knocked at the door of the gate, a
14 she told that Peter stood before the g.
14 voice, she opened not the gate for joy
14 12 bringing oxen and garlands before the g.
16 13 forth without the gate by a river side
Heb 13 12 Jesus . . . suffered without the gate
Apoc 3 20 I stand at the gate and knock. If any
21 21 every several gate was of one several

gate of the city Gen 19 1 Lot was sitting in g. . . .
Gen 23 10 that went in at the gate of the city
34 20 going into the g. . . . , they spoke to
Deut 25 7 woman shall go to the g. . . . and call
Josu 20 4 he shall stand before the g. . . . , and
Judg 9 35 stood in the entrance of the g. . . .
40 slain of his people, even to the g. . . .
16 2 setting guards at the g. . . . , and
2 K 11 23 and pursued them even to the g. . . .
3 K 17 10 when he [Elias] was come to the g. . . .
4 K 7 10 they came to the g. . . . and told them
23 8 which was on the left hand of g. . . .
1 Pa 19 9 their army in array before the g. . . .
2 Pa 32 6 together in the street of the g. . . .
Jdth 10 6 came to the g. . . . , they found Ozias
13 12 they came to the g. . . . And Judith
Job 29 7 when I went out to the g. . . . , and in

gates Gen 8 2 the flood gates of heaven were shut
Gen 22 17 possess the g. of their enemies. 24:60
Exod 20 10 stranger . . . within thy gates. Deut 5:14; 14:21, 29; 24:14
Deut 3 5 high walls and with gates and bars
14 27 the Levite that is within thy gates
28 and shalt lay it up within thy gates
15 7 dwelleth within the gates of thy city
22 shalt eat it within the g. of thy city
16 11 and the Levite that is within thy gates
14 and the widow that are within thy gates
18 judges and magistrates in all thy gates
17 2 found among you within any of thy gates
5 wicked thing, to the gates of thy city
8 words of the judges within thy gates
20 11 receive it and open the gates to thee
26 12 that they may eat within the gates and
28 52 thou shalt be besieged within thy gates
55 distress thee within all thy gates
57 shall oppress thee within thy gates
31 12 strangers that are within thy gates
Josu 6 26 last of his children set up its gates
Judg 5 8 overthrew the gates of the enemies
11 people of Lord went down to the gates
20 25 sallied forth out of the gates of Gabaa
Ruth 3 11 that dwell within the gates of my city
1 K 17 52 the valley and to the gates of Accaron
23 7 into a city, that hath gates and bars
2 K 18 24 and David sat between the two gates
3 K 8 37 enemy afflict them besieging the gates
16 34 son Segub he set up the gates thereof
4 K 23 8 he broke down the altars of the gates
1 Pa 9 19 keepers of the gates of the tabernacle
22 chosen to be porters at the gates
23 to keep the gates of house of the Lord
27 might open the gates in the morning
22 3 iron for the nails of the gates
26 13 lots . . . for every one of the gates
2 Pa 8 5 walled cities with gates and bars
14 7 and fortify them with towers and gates
23 5 third part . . . shall be at the gates
19 he appointed also porters in the gates
31 2 to sing in the gates of the camp
2 Es 1 3 gates thereof are burnt with fire. 2:3
2 8 that I may cover the gates of the tower
13 the gates . . . consumed with fire. 17
6 1 I had not set up the doors in the gates
7 3 let not the gates of Jerusalem be opened
3 the gates were shut and barred
12 25 were keepers of the gates and of the entrances before the gates

30 they purified the people and the gates
13 19 the gates of Jerusalem were at rest
19 they shut the gates, and I commanded
19 I set some of my servants at the gates
22 and should come to keep the gates
Tob 13 21 the gates of Jerusalem shall be built
Jdth 1 3 he made the gates thereof according
10 10 Judith . . . passed through the gates
13 13 open the gates for God is with us
Esth 6 10 sitteth before the gates of the palace
16 18 before the gates of this city Susan
Job 38 17 have the gates of death been opened
Ps 9 15 liftest me up from the gates of death
15 may declare all thy praises in the g.
23 7 lift up your gates, O ye princes. 9
7 be ye lifted up, O eternal gates. 9
72 28 in the gates of the daughter of Sion
73 6 they have cut down at once the gates
86 2 the Lord loveth the gates of Sion
99 4 go ye into his gates with praise, into
106 16 because he hath broken gates of brass
18 drew nigh even to the gates of death
117 19 open ye to me the gates of justice
147 13 strengthened the bolts of thy gates
Prov 1 21 in the entrance of the gates of the city
8 3 beside the gates of the city: in the
34 that watcheth daily at my gates and
14 19 the wicked before the gates of the just
31 23 her husband is honorable in the gates
31 let her works praise her in the gates
Cant 7 13 in our gates are all fruits: the new
Wisd 16 13 leadest down to the gates of death
Eccu 49 15 and set up the gates and the bars
51 5 life, and from the gates of afflictions
Isa 3 26 and her gates shall lament and mourn
13 2 and let the rulers go into the gates
24 12 and calamity shall oppress the gates
26 2 open ye the gates and let the just
38 10 days I shall go to the gates of hell
45 1 him, and the gates shall not be shut
2 will break in pieces the gates of brass
54 12 and thy gates of graven stones, and all
60 11 thy gates shall be open continually
18 praise [shall possess] thy gates
62 10 go through the gates, prepare the way
Jer 1 15 the entrance of the gates of Jerusalem
2 12 ye gates thereof, be very desolate
7 2 men of Juda, that enter in at these g.
14 2 and the gates thereof are fallen
15 7 will scatter them with a fan in the g.
17 19 out, and in all the gates of Jerusalem
20 Jerusalem, that enter in by these gates
21 them not in by gates of Jerusalem
24 to bring in no burdens by the gates
25 shall there enter in by the gates of
27 them in by the gates of Jerusalem
27 I will kindle a fire in the gates
22 2 thy people, who enter in by these gates
4 enter in by the gates of this house
19 forth without the gates of Jerusalem
49 31 they have neither gates nor bars
51 58 her high gates shall be burnt with fire
Lam 1 4 all her gates are broken down: her
2 9 her gates are sunk into the ground
4 12 enter in by the gates of Jerusalem
5 14 the ancients have ceased from the gates
Bar 6 17 the gates are made sure on every side
Eze 21 15 in all their gates I have set the dread
22 to set engines against the gates
26 2 the gates of the people are broken
10 when they shall go in at thy gates
38 11 a wall, they have no bars nor gates
40 18 pavement in the front of the gates according to the length of the gates
38 a door in the forefronts of the gates
44 11 doorkeepers of the gates of the house
17 in at the gates of the inner court
17 when they minister in the gates of the
48 31 gates of the city according to the names
31 three gates. 32, 33, 34
Abdi 11 and foreigners entered into his gates
Nah 2 6 the gates of the rivers are opened
3 13 gates of thy land shall be set wide
Zach 8 16 and judgment of peace in your gates
11 1 open thy gates, O Libanus, and let
1 Ma 4 38 altar profaned and the gates burnt
57 renewed the gates and the chambers
5 47 and stopped up the gates with stones
9 50 with high walls and gates and bars
10 76 opened the gates to him [Jonathan]
12 38 Simon . . . set up gates and bars
48 shut the gates of the city and took him
13 33 high towers and great walls and gates
15 39 and to fortify the gates of the city
2 Ma 8 33 that had set fire to the holy gates
10 36 to set fire to the towers and the gates
Mat 16 18 the gates of hell shall not prevail
Acts 9 24 they watched the g. also day and night
Apoc 21 12 great and high, having twelve gates
12 in the gates twelve angels, and names
13 on the . . . three gates: and on the
15 to measure the city and the gates
21 the twelve gates are twelve pearls
25 the gates thereof shall not be shut
22 14 may enter in by the g. into the city
Gatham Gen 36 11 Eliphaz had sons: . . . G. and Cenez
Gen 36 16 sons of Eliphaz . . . duke Gatham
Gathan 1 Pa 1 36 sons of Eliphaz . . . Gathan
Gatherer Prov 30 1 G. the son of Vomiter
gatherings Lev 11 36 all g. together of waters
Gaulon Josu 20 8 G. in Basan of the tribe of
Josu 21 27 Gaulon in Basan, one of the cities of
1 Pa 6 71 to the sons of Gersom . . . Gaulon
Gaver 4 K 9 27 struck him in the going up to G.
gay Eccu 7 26 show not thy countenance gay
Bar 6 8 for a maiden that loveth to go gay
Gaza Gen 10 19 comes to Gerara even to Gaza
Deut 2 23 that dwelt in Haserim as far as Gaza
Josu 10 41 from Cadesbarne even to Gaza
11 22 except the cities of Gaza and Geth and
15 47 Gaza with its towns and villages
Judg 1 18 Juda took Gaza with its confines
6 4 blade even to the entrance of Gaza
16 1 he [Samson] went also into Gaza and
21 and led him bound in chains to Gaza
1 K 6 17 emerods . . . for Gaza one, for Ascalon
4 K 18 8 smote the Philistines as far as Gaza
Jer 25 20 Ascalon and Gaza and Accaron and
47 1 of Palestine before Pharao took Gaza
5 baldness is come upon Gaza: Ascalon
Amos 1 6 for three crimes of Gaza and for four
7 I will send a fire on the wall of Gaza
Soph 2 4 Gaza shall be destroyed, and Ascalon
Zach 9 5 and Gaza, and shall be very sorrowful
5 and the king shall perish from Gaza
1 Ma 11 61 and he went from thence to Gaza
61 they that were in Gaza shut him out
62 the men of Gaza made supplication to
13 43 Simon besieged Gaza and camped round
Acts 8 26 goeth down from Jerusalem into Gaza
Gazabar 1 Esd 1 8 Mithridates the son of Gazabar
Gazam 1 Es 2 48 Necoda, the children of Gazam
Gazan 3 K 4 24 the river, from Thaphsa to G.
Gazara 1 Ma 7 45 even till ye come to Gazara

1 Ma 9 52 fortified the city of Bethsura and G.
13 54 all the forces: and he dwelt in G.
14 7 had the dominion of G. and of Bethsura
34 Gazara, which bordereth upon Azotus
15 28 you hold Joppe and Gazara and the
35 thy complaints concerning Joppe and G.
16 1 John came up from Gazara and told
19 he sent others to Gazara to kill John
21 one running before, told John in Gazara
2 Ma 10 32 Timotheus fled into G. a stronghold
Gazarim 2 Ma 5 23 in G., Andronicus and Menelaus
2 Ma 6 2 that in Gazarim of Jupiter Hospitalis
gaze Eccu 9 5 gaze not upon a maiden lest her
Eccu 9 8 gaze not about upon another's beauty
41 27 gaze not upon another man's wife
gazed Isa 47 13 they that gazed at the stars
Gazer Josu 10 33 Horam king of Gazer came up to
Josu 12 12 of Eglon one, the king of Gazer one
16 3 Beth-horon the nether, and to Gazer
10 slew not the Chanaanite who dwelt in G.
21 21 Gazer and Cibsaim and Beth-horon
Judg 1 29 the Chanaanite that dwelt in Gazer
3 K 9 15 and Heser and Mageddo and Gazer
16 king of Egypt came up and took G.
17 Solomon built Gazer and Beth-horon
1 Pa 6 67 Ephraim and Gazer with its suburbs
7 28 and westward Gazer and her daughters
20 4 after this there arose a war at Gazer
1 Ma 5 8 he took the city of G. and her towns
Gazera 1 Pa 14 16 slaying them from Gabaon to G.
gazingstock Heb 10 33 tribulations, were made a g.
Gazites Josu 13 3 the Gazites, the Azotians
Geba 2 Es 7 30 the men of Rama and Geba, 621
2 Es 11 31 the children of Benjamin, from Geba
12 29 from the countries of Geba and
Gebal Ps 82 8 Gebal and Ammon and Amalec
Eze 27 9 ancients of Gebal and the wise men
Gebbai 2 Es 11 8 after him Gebbai, Sellai
Gebbar 1 Es 2 20 the children of Gebbar, 95
Gebbethon Josu 19 44 Elthece and G. and Balaath and
3 K 15 27 slew him in G. which is a city of
27 Nadab and all Israel besieged Gebbethon
16 15 the army was besieging Gebbethon
17 all Israel with him from Gebbethon
Geddel 1 Es 2 56 of Dercon, the children of G.
2 Es 7 49 of Hanan, the children of Geddel
Geddelthi 1 Pa 25 4 sons of Heman . . . G.
1 Pa 25 29 two and twentieth to G.
Geddiel Num 13 11 Geddiel the son of Sodi
Gedelias Jer 38 1 Gedelias the son of Phassur
Gedeon Num 1 11 Abidan the son of G. 2:22; 7:60, 65; 10:24
Judg 6 11 when Gedeon his son was threshing and
6 13 Gedeon said to him: I beseech thee
6 19 so Gedeon went in and boiled a kid
6 22 Gedeon seeing that it was the angel
6 24 Gedeon built there an altar to the Lord
6 27 Gedeon taking ten men of his servants
6 29 Gedeon the son of Joas did all this
6 34 spirit of the Lord came upon Gedeon
6 36 Gedeon said to God: If thou wilt save
7 1 Jerobaal, who is the same as Gedeon
7 2 the Lord said to Gedeon. 4, 5, 7
7 13 when Gedeon was come, one told his
7 14 nothing else but the sword of Gedeon
7 15 when Gedeon had heard the dream and
7 19 Gedeon and the 300 men that were with him
7 20 the sword of the Lord and of Gedeon
7 24 Gedeon sent messengers into all mount
7 25 carrying heads of Oreb and Zeb to Gedeon
8 4 when Gedeon was come to the Jordan
8 11 Gedeon went up by the way of them that
8 12 and Gedeon pursued and took them
8 21 Gedeon rose up and slew Zebee and
8 22 all the men of Israel said to Gedeon
8 27 Gedeon made an ephod thereof and put
8 27 it became a ruin to Gedeon and to all
8 28 forty years, while Gedeon presided
8 32 and Gedeon the son of Joas died
8 33 after Gedeon was dead, the children
8 35 mercy to house of Jerobaal Gedeon
Jdth 8 1 Jamnor the son of Gedeon, the son of
Heb 11 32 would fail me to tell of Gedeon, Barac
Gedera Josu 15 36 Adithaim and Gedera and
Gederite 1 Pa 27 28 was Balanam a Gederite
Gederothaim Josu 15 36 Gedera and Gederothaim
Gedor Josu 15 58 Halhul and Bessur and Gedor
1 Pa 4 4 Phanuel the father of Gedor, and Ezar
18 Judaia bore Jared the father of Gedor
8 31 and Gedor and Ahio and Zacher and
9 37 Gedor also and Ahio and Zacharias
12 7 Zabadia the sons of Jeroham of Gedor
1 Ma 15 39 he commanded him to build up Gedor
40 prisoners, and to kill, and to build G.
Geennom Josu 15 8 which is over against Geennom
Josu 18 16 Raphaim, and it goeth down into G.
Gehon Gen 2 13 name of the second river is G.
Eccu 24 37 and riseth up as Gehon in the time of
Gelboe 1 K 28 4 all Israel and came to Gelboe
1 K 31 1 and fell down slain in mount Gelboe
8 and his three sons lying in mount Gelboe
2 K 1 6 I came by chance upon mount Gelboe
21 ye mountains of Gelboe, let neither
21 12 when they had slain Saul in Gelboe
1 Pa 10 1 and fell down wounded in mount Gelboe
8 Saul and his sons lying on mount Gelboe
Gelonite 2 K 23 34 son of Achitophel the G.
Gemalli Num 13 13 Ammiel the son of Gemalli
gender Lev 19 19 not make thy cattle to g. with
gendered Job 38 29 the frost . . . who hath g. it
genealogies 1 Tim 1 4 to give heed to . . . endless g.
Titus 3 9 avoid foolish questions and genealogies
genealogy 1 Es 2 62 sought the writing of their g.
1 Es 8 1 and the genealogy of them, who came
Heb 7 3 without mother, without g., having
general Gen 21 22 Phicol the g. of his army. 33
Judg 4 2 had general of his army named Sisara
7 Sisara the general of Jabin's army
21 7 we have all in general sworn, not to
2 K 2 8 Abner . . . general of Saul's army
10 16 and Sobach . . . was their general
24 2 said to Joab the general of his army
3 K 1 19 Joab the general of the army. 11:15, 21
2 32 Abner . . . general of the army of Israel
32 Amasa . . . general of the army of Juda
16 16 Amri . . . who was general over Israel
4 K 4 13 the king or to the general of the army
5 1 Naaman, general of the army of the king
25 15 the general of the army took away. 20
18 the general of the army took Seraias
1 Pa 11 6 and Joab . . . was made the general
19 16 Sophach, general of the army. 18
27 34 general of the king's army was Joab
Jdth 2 4 Holofernes the general of his armies
5 1 Holofernes the g. of the army. 13:19
14 10 into chamber of the g. of the Assyrians
Jer 25 20 all his people, and all in general
39 9 g. of the army carried away captive
10 Nabuzardan the g. left some of the poor
11 had given charge to Nabuzardan the g.
13 therefore Nabuzardan the general sent
40 1 Nabuzardan the g. had let him go from
2 the general of the army taking Jeremias
5 general of the army gave him victuals

41 10 g. of the army had committed to Godolias
43 6 which Nabuzardan the g. had left with
48 38 in the streets thereof g. mourning
52 12 came Nabuzardan the g. of the army
14 that were with the general broke down
15 Nabuzardan the g. carried away captives
16 Nabuzardan the g. left some for
19 the general took away the pitchers
24 the g. took Saraias the chief priest
26 Nabuzardan the general took them
30 Nabuzardan the g. carried away of the
Dan 2 14 Arioch the general of the king's army
1 Ma 8 10 they sent a general against them
10 69 king Demetrius made Apollonius his g.
2 Ma 10 11 g. of the army of Phenicia and Syria
14 2 against Antiochus, and his g. Lysias
generals 1 Ma 11 63 heard that the g. of Demetrius were come. 12:24
generation Gen 5 1 the book of the g. of Adam
Gen 7 1 I have seen just before me in this g.
15 16 in the fourth g. they shall return
50 22 children of Ephraim to the third g.
Exod 1 6 and all his brethren and all that g.
17 16 be against Amalec, from g. to g.
20 5 unto the third and fourth g. 34:7; Num 14:18; Deut 5:9; Tob 9:11
Lev 22 4 seed goeth from him as in generation
Num 32 13 until the whole g. that had done evil
Deut 1 35 not one of the men of this wicked g.
2 14 g. of men that were fit for war was
23 2 of the Lord, until the tenth g.
3 even after the tenth g. shall not enter
8 that are born of them, in the third g.
29 22 and the following generation shall say
32 5 they are a wicked and perverse g.
7 think upon every g.: ask thy father
20 it is a perverse g., and unfaithful
Judg 2 10 that g. was gathered to their fathers
4 K 10 30 the throne of Israel to the fourth g.
15 12 thy children to fourth g. shall sit
Tob 14 15 his children's children to the fifth g.
17 all his g. continued in good life
Job 8 8 inquire of the former g. and search
42 16 children's children unto the fourth g.
Ps 9 6 I shall not be moved from g. to g.
11 8 keep us from this generation forever
13 6 the Lord is in the just generation
21 32 be declared to the Lord a g. to come
23 6 the generation of them that seek him
47 14 that ye may relate it in another g.
60 7 the king: his years even to g. and g.
70 18 to all the generation that is to come
72 15 I should condemn the g. of thy children
76 9 off his mercy forever from g. to g.
77 4 from their children, in another g.
6 that another g. might know them. The
8 fathers, a perverse and exasperating g.
8 a g. that set not their heart aright
78 13 show forth thy praise unto g. and g.
84 6 thou extend thy wrath from g. to g.
88 2 thy truth with my mouth to g. and g.
5 will build up thy throne unto g. and g.
89 1 hast been our refuge from g. to g.
94 10 was I offended with that generation
99 5 his truth [endureth] to g. and g.
101 19 things be written unto another g.
25 thy years are unto generation and g.
105 31 to him unto justice, to g. and g.
108 13 in one g. may his name be blotted out
111 2 g. of the righteous shall be blessed
144 4 g. and g. shall praise thy works
145 10 thy God, O Sion, unto g. and g.
Prov 27 24 a crown shall be given to g. and g.
30 11 a generation that curseth their father
12 a g. that are pure in their own eyes
13 a generation whose eyes are lofty
14 a g. that for teeth hath swords
Ecce 1 4 g. passeth away and another g. cometh
Wisd 4 1 how beautiful is the chaste generation
12 10 that they were a wicked generation
14 6 left to the world seed of generation
19 11 they saw a new generation of birds
Eccu 3 1 their generation, obedience and love
4 17 his generation shall be in assurance
14 19 so is the generation of flesh and blood
39 13 shall be in request from g. to g.
44 1 renown, and our fathers in their g.
14 their name liveth unto g. and g.
Isa 13 20 it shall not be founded unto g. and g.
34 10 from g. to g. it shall lie waste
17 from g. to g. they shall dwell therein
38 12 my g. is at an end and it is rolled
51 8 my justice shall be from g. to g.
53 8 who shall declare his generation
58 12 shalt raise up foundations of g. and g.
60 15 a joy unto g. and g. And thou shalt
61 4 that were destroyed for g. and g.
66 9 I that give generation to others
Jer 2 30 your generation is like a ravaging lion
7 29 forsaken the generation of his wrath
50 39 shall it be built up from g. to g.
Lam 5 19 forever, thy throne from g. to g.
Joel 1 3 and their children to another g.
2 2 even to the years of g. and g.
3 20 forever, and Jerusalem to g. and g.
1 Ma 5 2 thought to destroy the g. of Jacob
Mat 1 1 book of the generation of Jesus Christ
18 now the g. of Christ was in this wise
11 16 whereunto shall I esteem this g.
12 34 g. of vipers, how can you speak good
39 adulterous g. seeketh a sign. 16:4
41 shall rise in judgment with this g. 42; Luke 11:31, 32
45 so shall it be also to this wicked g.
17 16 perverse generation, how long shall I
23 33 you serpents, g. of vipers, how will
36 these things shall come upon this g.
24 34 this g. shall not pass. Mark 13:30; Luke 21:32
Mark 8 12 why doth this generation seek a sign
12 a sign shall not be given to this g.
38 this adulterous and sinful generation
9 18 incredulous g., how long shall I be
Luke 1 50 his mercy is from g. unto generations
7 31 shall I liken the men of this g.? And
9 41 faithless and perverse g., how long
11 29 this g. is a wicked g.: it asketh a
30 the Son of man also be to this g.
50 may be required of this generation
51 it shall be required of this generation
16 8 of this world are wiser in their g.
17 25 and be rejected by this generation
Acts 2 40 save yourselves from this perverse g.
8 33 his g. who shall declare, for his life
13 36 David, when he had served in his g.
Phil 2 15 of a crooked and perverse generation
Heb 3 10 I was offended with this generation, and
1 P 2 9 but you are a chosen g., a kingly
1 J 5 18 the generation of God preserveth him
generations Gen 2 4 the g. of the heaven and
Gen 6 9 these are the g. of. 10:1; 11:10, 27; 25:12, 19; 36:1, 9; Num 3:1; 1 Pa 1:29; Ruth 4:18
9 Noe was a just . . . man in his g.
9 12 soul that is with you, for perpetual g.
10 20 in their kindreds and tongues and g.
17 7 thy seed after thee in their g. 9
12 every man child in your g.: he that is

25 13 according to their calling and g.
37 2 these are his [Jacob's] generations
Exod 3 15 and this is my memorial unto all g.
12 14 keep it a feast to the Lord in your g.
17 you shall keep this day in your g.
42 of Israel must observe in their g.
16 32 let it be kept unto g. to come
33 before the Lord to keep unto your g.
29 42 by perpetual oblation unto your g.
30 8 before the Lord throughout your g.
10 make atonement upon it in your g.
31 be holy unto me throughout your g.
31 13 a sign between me and you in your g.
16 sabbath and celebrate it in their g.
Lev 3 17 by a perpetual law for your g. and in
6 18 be an ordinance everlasting in your g.
7 36 by a perpetual observance in their g.
10 9 an everlasting precept through your g.
23 14 a precept forever throughout your g.
21 in all your dwellings and g. 31
41 an everlasting ordinance in your g. Num 18:23
24 3 a perpetual service and rite in your g.
Num 1 20 by their g. and families. 22, 24, 26, 28, 36, 38, 40, 42
30 by the g. and families. 32, 34
10 8 shall be an ordinance forever in your g.
Deut 7 9 his commandments, unto a thousand g.
1 Pa 16 15 which he commanded to a thousand g.
Esth 9 28 shall celebrate throughout all g.
10 13 throughout all the g. hereafter of the
Ps 32 11 the thoughts of his heart to all g.
44 18 remember thy name throughout all g.
48 12 their dwelling places to all g.
20 shall go into the g. of his fathers
71 5 before the moon, throughout all g.
101 13 forever: and thy memorial to all g.
104 8 which he commanded to a thousand g.
118 90 thy truth unto all g.: thou hast
134 13 thy memorial, O Lord, unto all g.
144 13 thy dominion endureth throughout all g.
Eccu 2 11 my children, behold the g. of men
16 26 parts, and their beginnings in their g.
24 28 my memory is unto everlasting g.
44 7 these have gained glory in their g.
Isa 41 4 calling the g. from the beginning
51 9 as in days of old, in the ancient g.
Bar 6 2 for a long time, even to seven g.
Dan 3 100 kingdom, and his power to all g.
4 31 power, and his kingdom is to all g.
1 Ma 2 51 which they have done in their g.
61 and thus consider through all g.
Mat 1 17 g. from Abraham to David are 14 g.
Luke 1 48 henceforth all g. shall call me blessed
50 his mercy is from generation unto g.
Eph 3 5 which in other g. was not known to sons
21 unto all generations, world without end
Col 1 26 been hidden from ages and generations
Genesar 1 Ma 11 67 encamped by the water of G.
Mat 14 34 they came into the country of Genesar
Genesareth Mark 6 53 they came into the land of G.
Luke 5 1 he stood by the lake of Genesareth
genital Num 25 8 and the woman in the g. parts
Genneus 2 Ma 12 2 Apollonius the son of Genneus
Genthon 2 Es 10 6 Daniel, Genthon, Baruch
2 Es 12 4 went up with Zorobabel . . . Genthon
16 of Genthon, Mosollam: of Abia, Zechri
Gentile Mark 7 26 was a Gentile, a Syrophenician
Acts 16 1 believed; but his father was a Gentile
3 they all knew that his father was a G.
Gal 2 3 Titus, who was with me, being a Gentile
Col 3 11 where there is neither Gentile nor Jew
Gentiles Gen 10 5 divided the islands of the Gentiles
Lev 26 33 I will scatter you among the Gentiles
38 you shall perish among the Gentiles
45 of Egypt, in the sight of the Gentiles
Josu 23 7 that you are come in among the Gentiles
Judg 4 2 Haroseth of the Gentiles. 3, 16
2 K 22 44 keep me to be the head of the Gentiles
50 thanks to thee, O Lord, among the G.
1 Pa 16 24 declare his glory among the Gentiles
2 Pa 36 14 all the abominations of the Gentiles
2 Es 4 2 will the Gentiles let them alone
5 8 Jews that were sold to the Gentiles
9 not exposed to reproaches of the G.
6 6 it is reported amongst the Gentiles
Tob 1 12 all ate of the meats of the Gentiles
13 3 praise him in sight of the Gentiles
4 scattered you among the Gentiles, who
14 8 the Gentiles shall leave their idols
Jdth 4 9 not be made a reproach to the Gentiles
7 21 they may not say among the Gentiles
14 6 leaving the religion of the Gentiles
Esth 14 10 that they may open the mouths of Gentiles
Ps 2 1 why have the Gentiles raged, and the
8 I will give thee the Gentiles for thy
9 6 thou hast rebuked the Gentiles and the
12 declare his ways among the Gentiles
16 G. have stuck fast in the destruction
16 ye Gentiles shall perish from his land
20 the Gentiles be judged in thy sight
21 G. may know themselves to be but men
17 44 thou wilt make me head of the Gentiles
21 28 kindreds of the Gentiles shall adore
43 3 thy hand destroyed the Gentiles, and
15 hast made us a byword among the Gentiles
64 8 the Gentiles shall be troubled, and
65 8 bless our God, ye Gentiles: and make
77 54 he cast out the Gentiles before them
78 10 lest they should say among the Gentiles
79 9 thou hast cast out the Gentiles and
95 3 declare his glory among the Gentiles
7 to the Lord, O ye kindreds of the G.
10 say ye among the Gentiles: The Lord
97 2 his justice in the sight of the Gentiles
101 16 and the Gentiles shall fear thy name
104 1 declare his deeds among the Gentiles
44 gave them the lands of the Gentiles
110 7 them the inheritance of the Gentiles
113 2 lest the G. should say: Where is their
125 2 then shall they say among the Gentiles
134 15 idols of the Gentiles are silver and
Wisd 14 11 even to the idols of the Gentiles
Eccu 10 19 overthrown the lands of the Gentiles
35 23 he will repay vengeance to the Gentiles
Isa 2 4 he shall judge the G. and rebuke
9 1 Jordan of the Galilee of the Gentiles
11 10 him the Gentiles shall beseech, and his
29 8 shall be the multitude of all the G.
34 1 come near, ye Gentiles, and hear and
40 15 the Gentiles are as a drop of a bucket
42 1 shall bring forth judgment to the G.
6 for a light of the Gentiles: that thou
45 20 ye that are saved of the Gentiles
49 6 thee to be the light of the Gentiles
22 I will lift up my hand to the Gentiles
52 10 arm in the sight of all the Gentiles
54 3 thy seed shall inherit the Gentiles
55 4 a leader and a master to the Gentiles
60 3 the Gentiles shall walk in thy light
5 strength of the G. shall come to thee
11 that strength of the G. may be brought
12 the G. shall be wasted with desolation
16 thou shalt suck the milk of the Gentiles
61 6 you shall eat the riches of the Gentiles
9 shall know their seed among the Gentiles •

62 2 the Gentiles shall see thy just one
63 3 of the G. there is not a man with me
66 12 glory of the Gentiles, which you shall
19 of them that shall be saved, to the G.
19 they shall declare my glory to the G.
Jer 3 19 inheritance of the armies of the Gentiles
4 2 the Gentiles shall bless him and shall
10 2 learn not according to ways of the G.
14 22 among the graven things of the Gentiles
16 19 to thee the Gentiles shall come from
31 7 neigh before the head of the Gentiles
46 1 word of the Lord . . . against the G.
Lam 1 1 mistress of the G. become as a widow
10 seen the G. enter into her sanctuary
2 9 and her princes are among the Gentiles
4 15 said among the Gentiles: He will no more
20 we shall live among the Gentiles
Bar 4 6 you have been sold to the Gentiles
6 3 gods . . . causing fear to the Gentiles
Eze 5 6 so as to be more wicked than the G.
7 because you have surpassed the Gentiles
8 midst of thee in the sight of the G.
11 16 removed them far off among the Gentiles
20 32 we will be as the Gentiles, and as
22 4 have I made thee a reproach to the G.
16 will possess thee in sight of the G.
28 25 be sanctified in them before the G.
34 29 bear any more the reproach of the G.
36 6 have borne the shame of the Gentiles
7 that the Gentiles . . . bear their shame
23 name which was profaned among the G.
23 the G. may know that I am the Lord
24 I will take you from among the Gentiles
39 7 Gentiles shall know that I am the Lord
Mich 5 8 remnant of Jacob shall be among the G.
Soph 2 11 place, all the islands of the Gentiles
3 8 my judgment is to assemble the Gentiles
Agge 2 23 the strength of the kingdom of the G.
Zach 8 13 as you were a curse among the Gentiles
23 ten men of all languages of the Gentiles
9 10 he shall speak peace to the Gentiles
Mala 1 11 my name is great among the Gentiles
14 my name is dreadful among the Gentiles
1 Ma 2 12 and the Gentiles have defiled them
68 render to the Gentiles their reward
3 10 Apollonius gathered together the G.
45 there was the habitation of the Gentiles
48 the G. searched for the likeness of
4 7 and they saw the camp of the Gentiles
14 the Gentiles were routed, and fled
45 because the Gentiles had defiled it
58 the reproach of the G. was turned away
60 lest the G. should at any time come and
5 9 the G. that were in Galaad assembled
57 let us go fight against the Gentiles
6 18 seeking . . . to strengthen the Gentiles
7 23 the evils . . . much more than the G.
13 41 yoke of the Gentiles was taken off
2 Ma 1 27 deliver them that are slaves to the G.
27 that the G. may know that thou art our
6 4 the riot and revellings of the Gentiles
8 into the neighboring cities of the G.
9 themselves to the ways of the Gentiles
11 2 make it a habitation of the Gentiles
3 as of the other temples of the Gentiles
14 14 the Gentiles who had fled out of Judea
15 10 showed withal the falsehood of the G.
Mat 4 15 the Jordan, Galilee of the Gentiles
10 5 ye not into the way of the Gentiles
18 a testimony to them and to the Gentiles
12 18 he shall show judgment to the Gentiles
21 in his name the Gentiles shall hope
20 19 shall deliver him to the G. Mark 10:33
25 princes of the Gentiles lord it over
Mark 10 42 who seem to rule over the Gentiles
Luke 2 32 a light to the revelation of the Gentiles
18 32 he shall be delivered to the Gentiles
21 24 shall be trodden down by the Gentiles
22 25 the kings of the Gentiles lord it over
John 7 35 go unto the dispersed among the Gentiles and teach the Gentiles
12 20 were certain Gentiles among them who
Acts 4 25 why did the Gentiles rage, and the
27 with the Gentiles and the people of
7 45 into the possession of the Gentiles
9 15 to carry my name before the Gentiles
29 he spoke also to the Gentiles, and
10 45 grace . . . poured out upon the Gentiles
11 1 heard that the G. also had received
18 to the G. given repentance unto life
13 46 life, behold we turn to the Gentiles
47 I have set thee to be light of the G.
48 Gentiles hearing it, were glad, and
14 2 minds of the G. against the brethren
5 there was an assault made by the G.
26 had opened the door of faith to the G.
15 3 relating the conversion of the Gentiles
7 by my mouth the G. should hear the word
12 wonders God had wrought among the G.
14 to take of the G. a people to his name
19 they, who from among G. are converted
23 brethren of the G. that are at Antioch
17 4 of the Gentiles a great multitude, and
12 of honorable women that were G., and
18 6 from henceforth I will go unto the G.
19 10 both Jews and Gentiles. And God wrought
17 became known to all the Jews and G. that
20 21 testifying both to Jews and Gentiles
21 11 deliver him into the hands of the G.
19 things God had wrought among the G. by
21 teachest those Jews, who are among the G.
25 as touching the G. that believe, we
28 hath brought in G. into the temple, and
22 21 go, for unto the Gentiles afar off, will
26 20 Judea, and to the Gentiles did I preach
23 show light to the people and to the G.
28 28 salvation of God is sent to the Gentiles
Rom 1 13 you also, even as among other Gentiles
2 24 blasphemed among G., as it is written
14 when the Gentiles, who have not the law
3 29 is he not also of the G.? Yes, of the G.
9 30 Gentiles, who followed not after justice
11 11 by their offence, salvation is come to G.
12 riches of the Gentiles; how much more
13 for I say to you, Gentiles: as long
13 as long . . . as I am apostle of the G.
25 until fulness of the G. should come in
15 9 the G. are to glorify God for his mercy
9 O Lord, among the Gentiles, and will
10 rejoice, ye Gentiles, with his people
11 and again: Praise the Lord, all ye G.
12 he that shall rise up to rule the G., in him the G. shall hope
16 minister of Christ Jesus among the G.
16 that the oblation of the G. may be made
18 for obedience of the G., by word and
27 if Gentiles have been made partakers of
16 4 also all the churches of the Gentiles
1 C 1 23 and unto the Gentiles foolishness: but
10 32 without offence to Jews and to Gentiles
12 13 into one body, whether Jews or Gentiles
2 C 11 26 in perils from the Gentiles, in perils
Gal 1 16 I might preach him among the Gentiles
2 2 which I preach among the Gentiles, but
8 wrought in me also among the Gentiles
9 that we should go unto the Gentiles, and

12 James, he did eat with the Gentiles: but
14 livest after the manner of the Gentiles
14 how dost thou compel the G. to live as
15 Jews, and not of the Gentiles sinners
3 8 that God justifieth the G. by faith
14 blessing of Abraham might come on the G.
Eph 2 11 being heretofore Gentiles in the flesh
3 1 prisoner of Jesus Christ, for you G.
6 the Gentiles should be fellow heirs, and
8 this grace, to preach among the Gentiles
4 7 you walk not as also the Gentiles walk
Col 1 27 this mystery among the Gentiles, which
1 Th 2 16 prohibiting us to speak to the Gentiles
4 5 not in the passion of lust, like the G.
1 Tim 2 7 doctor of the Gentiles in faith and
3 16 hath been preached unto the Gentiles
2 Tim 1 11 an apostle and teacher of the Gentiles
4 17 that all the Gentiles may hear: and I
1 P 2 12 your conversation good among the G.
4 3 to have fulfilled the will of the G.
3 J 7 out, taking nothing of the Gentiles
Apoc 11 2 because it is given unto the Gentiles
16 19 and the cities of the Gentiles fell
gentle 3 K 12 7 wilt speak gentle words to them
3 K 19 12 after the fire a whistling of a g. air
Job 4 16 the voice as it were of a gentle wind
Wisd 7 23 gentle, kind, steadfast, assured, secure
2 Ma 15 12 gentle in his manners and graceful in
Titus 1 8 given to hospitality, gentle, sober
2 5 gentle, obedient to their husbands
3 2• not to be litigious, but g.: showing
1 P 2 18 not only to the good and gentle, but
gently Gen 50 21 and spoke gently and mildly
Ps 71 6 showers falling gently upon the earth
2 Ma 10 4 be chastised by him more gently and
Acts 27 13 south wind gently blowing, thinking that
Genubath 3 K 11 20 bore him [Adad] his son G.
3 K 11 20 and Genubath dwelt with Pharao among
Gera Gen 46 21 sons of Benjamin . . . Asbel and Gera
Judg 3 15 a savior called Aod, the son of Gera
2 K 16 5 Semei the son of Gera. 19:16, 18; 3 K 2:8
1 Pa 8 3 sons of Bale were Addar and Gera and Abiud . . . and Gera
7 and Achia and Gera he removed them
Gerara Gen 10 19 from Sidon as one comes to G.
Gen 20 1 Abraham . . . sojourned in Gerara
2 the king of Gerara sent and took her
26 1 Isaac went to Abimelech . . . to G.
6 Isaac abode in Gerara. And when he was
17 came to the torrent of G. to dwell
20 herdsmen of Gerara strove against
26 when Abimelech . . . came from Gerara
2 Pa 14 13 were with him pursued them to G.
14 took all the cities round about Gerara
Gerasens Mat 8 28 into the country of G. Mark 5:1; Luke 8:26
Luke 8 37 multitude of the country of the G.
Gergesite Gen 10 16 and the Amorrhite and the G.
Deut 7 1 Hethite and the G. and the Amorrhite
2 Es 9 8 and of the Jebusite and of the G.
Josu 3 10 the Hevite and the Pherezite, the G.
24 11 Hethite and the G. and the Hevite
1 Pa 1 14 and the Amorrhite and the Gergesite
Gergesites Gen 15 21 the G. and the Jebusites
german 1 K 14 50 Abner . . . the cousin g. of Saul
Col 4 10 Mark, the cousin german of Barnabas
Gerrenians 2 Ma 13 24 from Ptolemais unto the G.
Gersam Exod 2 22 a son, whom he called Gersam
Exod 18 3 sons of whom one was called Gersam
Judg 18 30 the son of Gersam the son of Moses
Gersom 1 Pa 6 71 to the sons of Gersom, out of
1 Pa 15 7 of the sons of Gersom, Joel the chief
23 15 the sons of Moses were Gersom and
16 the sons of Gersom: Subuel the first
26 24 Subael the son of Phinees, Gersom
1 Es 8 2 of the sons of Phinees, Gersom
Gerson Gen 46 11 the sons of Levi: Gerson. Exod 6:16; Num 3:17; 26:57; 1 Pa 6:1, 16; 23:6
Exod 6 17 the sons of Gerson. Num 3:18; 1 Pa 6:17; 23:7
Num 3 21 of Gerson were two families, the
4 22 take the sum of the sons of Gerson
27 the sons of Gerson shall carry, by the
38 the sons of G. also were numbered
7 7 oxen he gave to the sons of Gerson
10 17 sons of Gerson and Merari set forward
Josu 21 6 the lot came out to the children of G.
27 to children of Gerson . . . two cities
33 all the cities of the families of G.
1 Pa 6 20 of Gerson: Lobni his son, Jahath
43 Jeth the son of G., the son of Levi
62 to the sons of Gerson by their families
2 Pa 29 12 of the sons of Gerson, Joah the son
Gersonite 1 Pa 29 8 by the hand of Jahiel the G.
Gersonites Num 4 24 office of the family of the G.
Num 4 28 the service of the family of the G.
41 this is the people of the Gersonites
26 57 Gerson, of whom is the family of the G.
Gersonni 1 Pa 26 21 sons of Ledan, the sons of G.
1 Pa 26 21 families, of Ledan, and G., Jehieli
Gerzi 1 K 27 8 and pillaged Gessuri and Gerzi
Gesan 1 Pa 2 47 sons of Jahaddai . . . Gesan
Gessen Gen 45 10 thou shalt dwell in the land of Gessen
Gen 46 28 that he should meet him in G.
34 that you may dwell in the land of G.
47 1 behold they stay in the land of Gessen
4 thy servants may be in the land of G.
6 and give them the land of Gessen
27 Israel dwelt . . . in the land of Gessen
50 8 which they left in the land of Gessen
Exod 8 22 I will make the land of Gessen wherein
9 26 only in the land of Gessen where
Gessur 2 K 3 3 of Tholmai king of G. 1 Pa 3:2
2 K 13 37 the son of Ammiud the king of Gessur
38 after he was fled and come into Gessur
14 23 went to Gessur and brought Absalom
32 wherefore am I come from Gessur
15 8 made a vow when he was in Gessur
1 Pa 2 23 he took Gessur and Aram the towns of
Gessuri Deut 3 14 the borders of Gessuri and Machati. Josu 12:5; 13:11
Josu 13 2 Galilee, Philistia, and all Gessuri
13 would not destroy Gessuri and Machati
1 K 27 8 and pillaged Gessuri and Gerzi
2 K 2 9 king over Galaad and over Gessuri
get Gen 19 9 they said: Get thee back thither
Gen 34 4 he said: Get me this damsel to wife
Exod 5 4 works? Get you gone to your burdens
10 28 get thee from me, and beware thou see
19 24 get thee down; and thou shalt come up
32 7 get thee down: thy people, which thou
33 1 get thee up from this place, thou and
Num 16 45 get you out from the midst of this
Josu 2 16 get ye up to the mountains, lest
1 K 15 6 depart and get thee down from Amalec
2 K 5 8 and get up to the gutters of the tops
13 15 said to her: Arise and get thee gone
19 26 I might get on and go with the king
23 15 that some man would get me a drink
3 K 1 13 get thee in to king David and say to
12 18 made haste to get him up into. 2 Pa 10:18
17 3 get thee hence, and go towards the east
4 K 7 12 and then we may get into the city. And
Tob 1 3 every day gave all he could get to his
2 19 what she could get for their living by
5 2 how I shall get this money, I cannot

Job 24 5 prey they get bread for their children
Ps 10 2 to my soul: Get thee away from hence
Prov 4 5 get wisdom, get prudence: forget not
7 get wisdom, and with all thy
16 16 get wisdom, because it is better than
Ecce 3 6 a time to get and a time to lose. A
Cant 7 12 let us get up early to the vineyards
Eccu 6 7 if thou wouldst get a friend, try him
21 12 shall get the understanding thereof
27 21 go, and thou shalt not get him again
29 8 he shall get him for an enemy without
32 3 and get the honor of the contribution
46 2 might get the inheritance for Israel
Isa 22 15 get thee in to him that dwelleth in
30 22 thou shalt say to it: Get thee hence
40 9 get thee up upon a high mountain, thou
47 5 silent, and get thee into darkness
Jer 46 4 harness the horses, and get up, ye
9 get ye up on horses and glory in
48 44 he that shall get up out of the pit
49 30 get away speedily, sit in deep holes
Lam 3 7 round about, that I may not get out
4 15 depart, get ye hence, touch not: for
Bar 4 25 and thou shalt get up upon his neck
Eze 3 11 get thee in to them of the captivity
11 15 have said: Get ye far from the Lord
Amos 3 12 as if a shepherd should get out of
Nah 2 5 they shall quickly get upon the walls
Soph 3 19 and I will get them praise and a name
1 Ma 3 14 said: I will get me a name and will be
5 57 let us also get us a name and let us
6 44 and to get himself an everlasting name
11 1 to get the kingdom of Alexander by
14 1 to get him succors to fight against
2 Ma 5 7 yet he did not get the principality
Luke 9 12 they may lodge and get victuals; for
13 31 get thee hence, for Herod hath a mind
Acts 10 20 get thee down and go with them, doubting
22 18 and get thee quickly out of Jerusalem
27 43 and save themselves, and get to land
Geth Josu 11 22 except the cities of Gaza and Geth
1 K 6 17 emerods . . . for Geth one, for Accaron
7 14 restored to Israel, from Accaron to Geth
17 4 Goliath, of Geth, whose height was
23 Goliath, the Philistine, of Geth, showed
52 as far as Geth and as far as Accaron
21 10 and came to Achis the king of Geth
12 afraid at face of Achis king of Geth
27 2 Achis the son of Maoch, king of Geth
3 David dwelt with Achis at Geth, he and
4 told Saul that David was fled to Geth
11 neither brought he any of them to Geth
2 K 1 20 tell it not in Geth, publish it not
15 18 men who had followed him from Geth
18 2 under hand of Ethai, who was of Geth
21 20 fourth battle was in Geth: where there
22 these four were born of Arapha in Geth
3 K 2 39 Achis son of Maacha the king of Geth
39 that his servants were gone to Geth
40 and went to Achis to Geth to seek his
40 he brought them out of Geth. And it was
41 Semei had gone from Jerusalem to Geth
4 K 12 17 fought against Geth and took it and set
14 25 who was of Geth, which is in Opher
1 Pa 7 21 men of Geth born in the land slew
8 13 these drove away the inhabitants of G.
18 1 and took away Geth and her daughters
20 6 there was another battle also in Geth
7 these were the sons of Rapha in Geth
2 Pa 11 8 Geth and Maresa and Ziph and Aduram
26 6 broke down the wall of Geth and the
Ps 55 1 when the Philistines held him in Geth
Amos 6 2 go down into Geth of the Philistines
Mich 1 10 declare ye it not in Geth, weep ye not
14 messengers to the inheritance of Geth
Gethaim 2 K 4 3 the Berothites fled into G.
2 Es 11 33 Asor, Rama, Gethaim, Hadid, Seboim
Gether Gen 10 23 Aram: Us and Hull and G.
1 Pa 1 17 Hus and Hul and Gether and Mosoch
Gethhepher Josu 19 13 to the east side of G.
Gethite 2 K 6 10 house of Obededom the G. 11
2 K 15 19 the king said to Ethai the Gethite
22 Ethai the Gethite passed, and all the
21 19 slew Goliath the G., the shaft of whose
1 Pa 20 5 slew the brother of Goliath the G.
Gethites Josu 13 3 the G. and the Accronites
1 K 5 8 the Gethites answered: Let the ark
9 the Gethites consulted together
2 K 15 18 and all the Gethites, valiant warriors
Gethremmon Josu 19 45 Bane and Barach and G.
Josu 21 24 and G., with their suburbs. 25
1 Pa 6 69 with its suburbs, and Gethremmon
Gethsemani Mat 26 36 country place which is called G.
Mark 14 32 they came to a farm called Gethsemani
getteth Prov 9 7 g. himself a blot. Rebuke not
Prov 10 4 hand of the industrious getteth riches
Jer 51 21 chariot, and him that g. up into it
getting 3 K 18 45 Achab getting up went away to
Wisd 13 19 for getting and for working and for
15 12 that we must be getting every way
Eccu 42 4 weights, of getting much or little
Bar 3 18 there is no end of their getting
2 Ma 10 36 others also getting up after them
Gezem 2 Es 7 51 Nathinites . . . children of Gezem
Gezer 2 K 5 25 from Gabaa until thou come to G.
Gezeron 1 Ma 4 15 they pursued them as far as G.
Gezez 1 Pa 2 46 bore Haran and Mosa and Gezez. And
Haran begot Gezez
Gezonite 1 Pa 11 33 the sons of Assem a Gezonite
ghimel Lam 1 3 ghimel. 2:3; 3:7, 8, 9; 4:3; *see also* **gimel**
ghost 2 Ma 3 31 was ready to give up the ghost
Mat 27 50 with a loud voice yielded up the ghost
Mark 15 37 gave up the ghost. Luke 23:46; Acts 5:5, 10;
12:23; John 19:30
39 manner he had given up the ghost
Ghost; *see* **Holy Ghost**
giant Num 13 34 sons of Enac of the g. kind
Job 16 15 he hath rushed in upon me like a giant
Ps 18 6 rejoiced as a giant to run the way
32 16 nor shall the giant be saved by his own
Eccu 47 4 did not he kill the giant, and take
1 Ma 3 3 put on a breastplate as a giant, and
giants Gen 6 4 giants were upon the earth
Deut 2 11 they were esteemed as giants and were
20 it was accounted a land of giants: and giants
formerly dwelt in it
3 11 remained of the race of the giants. His
13 all Basan is called the Land of giants
2 K 21 18 race of Arapha of family of the giants
23 13 in the valley of the giants. And David
Jdth 16 8 nor tall g. oppose themselves to him
Job 26 5 the giants groan under the waters and
Prov 9 18 he did not know that giants are there
21 16 shall abide in company of the giants
Wisd 14 6 when the proud g. perished, the hope
Eccu 16 8 the ancient g. did not obtain pardon
Isa 14 9 it stirred up the giants for thee. All
26 14 dead live, let not the g. rise again
19 land of the giants thou shalt pull down
Bar 3 26 there were the giants, those renowned
gibbet Gen 40 22 the other he hanged on a gibbet
Gen 41 13 and he was hanged upon a gibbet
Deut 21 22 condemned to die, is hanged on a gibbet
Josu 8 29 he hung the king thereof on a gibbet
29 took down his carcass from the gibbet
Esth 2 23 and they were both hanged on a gibbet

Osee 8 9 Ephraim hath given gifts to his lovers
Amos 5 22 if you offer me holocausts and your g.
1 Ma 3 30 formerly enough for charges and gifts
10 24 request, and offer dignities and gifts
28 many charges, and will give you gifts
54 I will give thee and her gifts worthy
15 5 other g. soever they remitted to thee
16 19 would give them silver and gold and g.
2 Ma 2 13 the kings, and concerning the holy gifts
3 2 glorified the temple with very great g.
9 16 promiseth to adorn with goodly gifts
13 23 honored the temple and left gifts. He
Mat 2 11 offered him gifts: gold, frankincense
7 11 know how to give good g. Luke 11:13
Luke 21 1 cast their gifts into the treasury
5 adorned with goodly stones and gifts
Rom 11 29 for the gifts and the calling of God are
12 6 and having different gifts, according to
1 C 12 31 but be zealous for the better gifts. And
14 1 charity, be zealous for spiritual gifts
Eph 4 8 captivity captive; he gave gifts to men
Heb 5 1 may offer up gifts and sacrifices for
8 3 appointed to offer gifts and sacrifices
4 there would be others to offer gifts
9 9 to which g. and sacrifices are offered
11 4 God giving testimony to his gifts; and
Apoc 11 10 and shall send gifts one to another
Gihon 3 K 1 33 and bring him [Solomon] to Gihon
3 K 1 38 and brought him [Solomon] to Gihon
45 have anointed him king in Gihon: and
2 Pa 32 30 upper source of the waters of Gihon
33 14 on the west side of G. in the valley
gilded Ps 44 10 in gilded clothing; surrounded
2 Ma 5 2 in g. raiment and armed with spears
gill Tob 6 4 him by the gill and draw him to
Gilo Josu 15 51 Gosen and Olon and Gilo: eleven
2 K 15 12 David's counsellor, from his city Gilo
Gilonite 2 K 15 12 also sent for Achitophel the G.
gilt Apoc 17 4 g. with gold and precious stones. 18:16
gimel Ps 118 17 gimel. Give bountifully to thy
gin Job 18 10 a gin is hidden for him in the
Gineth 3 K 16 21 followed Thebni the son of G. 22
gird Exod 12 11 eat it: you shall gird your reins
Exod 28 39 shalt gird the tunick with fine linen
29 5 which thou shalt gird with the girdle
8 tunicks, and gird them with a girdle
1 K 25 13 let every man gird on his sword. And
2 K 3 31 and gird yourselves with sackcloths
4 K 4 29 gird up thy loins and take my staff in
9 1 gird up thy loins and take this little
Job 38 3 gird up thy loins like a man. 40:2
Ps 44 4 gird thy sword upon thy thigh, O thou
Isa 8 9 and be overcome, gird yourselves and
32 11 be confounded, gird your loins. Mourn
Jer 1 17 gird up thy loins and arise and speak
4 8 gird yourselves with haircloth. 49:3
6 26 gird thee with sackcloth, O daughter
Eze 7 18 and they shall gird themselves with
Joel 1 13 gird yourselves and lament, O ye
1 Ma 3 58 gird yourselves and be valiant men and
Luke 12 37 he will gird himself and make them
17 8 gird thyself and serve me whilst I eat
John 21 18 younger, thou didst gird thyself and
18 another shall gird thee and lead thee
Acts 12 8 gird thyself and put on thy sandals
girded Gen 49 19 Gad, being girded, shall fight
Gen 49 19 he himself shall be girded backward
Lev 8 13 g. them with girdles and put miters on
16 4 he shall be girded with a linen girdle
Josu 3 17 stood girded upon the dry ground in the
Judg 3 16 was girded therewith under his garment
1 K 2 18 being a child girded with a linen ephod
17 39 David having girded his sword upon his
25 13 and they girded on every man his sword
13 and David also girded on his sword
2 K 6 14 David was girded with a linen ephod
20 8 was girded with a sword hanging down
21 16 g. with a new sword, attempted to kill
22 30 in thee I will run girded: in my God I
33 God who hath girded me with strength
40 thou hast girded me with strength to
3 K 18 46 g. up his loins and ran before Achab
20 11 let not the girded boast himself as the
32 they girded sackcloth on their loins
4 K 3 21 all that were girded with a belt upon
2 Es 4 18 was girded with a sword about his reins
Tob 5 5 a beautiful young man, standing girded
Jdth 4 15 offered the sacrifices girded with
Job 30 18 they have girded me about, as with the
Ps 17 40 thou hast girded me with strength unto
64 7 thy strength, being girded with power
13 the hills shall be girded about with
92 1 with strength, and hath girded himself
108 19 like a girdle with which he is girded
Prov 30 31 a cock girded about the loins: and a
31 17 she hath girded her loins with strength
Eccu 45 9 g. him about with a glorious girdle
Isa 15 3 they are girded with sackcloth: on the
45 5 I g. thee, and thou hast not known me
Lam 2 10 dust, they are girded with haircloth
Eze 16 10 I girded thee about with fine linen
23 15 girded with girdles about their reins
27 31 and shall be girded with haircloth
44 18 not be g. with anything that causeth
Dan 10 5 his loins were g. with the finest gold
Joel 1 8 like a virgin girded with sackcloth
Haba 3 16 may go up to our people that are g.
2 Ma 3 19 the women, girded with haircloth about
John 13 4 having taken a towel, girded himself
5 with the towel wherewith he was girded
girdeth Job 12 18 kings, and g. their loins with
girding Lev 8 7 g. him with the girdle and
Isa 22 12 baldness, and to g. with sackcloth
2 Ma 10 25 and girding their loins with haircloth
girdle Exod 28 4 linen garment, a miter and a g.
Exod 28 39 miter and a g. of embroidered work
29 5 which thou shalt gird with the girdle
8 tunicks, and gird them with a girdle
39 5 a girdle of the same colors, as the Lord
19 being fastened to the g. and strongly
28 a girdle of fine twisted linen, violet
Lev 8 7 girding him with the g. and putting on
8 binding it with the girdle, he fitted it
16 4 he shall be girded with a linen girdle and
Deut 23 13 carrying a paddle at thy girdle. And
1 K 18 4 sword and to his bow and to his girdle
3 K 2 5 and put the blood of war on his girdle
4 K 1 8 a hairy man with a girdle of leather
Ps 108 19 like a girdle with which he is girded
Prov 31 24 delivered a girdle to the Chanaanite
Eccu 45 9 girded him about with a glorious g.
Isa 3 24 instead of a girdle, a cord, and instead
5 27 neither shall girdle of their loins be
11 5 justice shall be the g. of his loins: and faith the g. of his reins
22 21 will strengthen him with thy girdle
23 10 of the sea, thou hast a girdle no more
Jer 13 1 go, and get thee a linen girdle and
2 I got a girdle according to the word
4 take the girdle which thou hast got
6 take from thence the girdle which I
7 and took the girdle out of the place
7 behold the girdle was rotten so that it
10 shall be as this girdle which is fit for
11 as the g. sticketh close to the loins
Mat 3 4 a leather g. about his loins. Mark 1:6

Acts 21 11 when he was come to us, took Paul's g.
11 man whose g. this is, Jews shall bind
Apoc 1 13 girt about the paps with a golden girdle
girdles Exod 28 40 tunicks and g. and miters for
Lev 8 13 girded them with g. and put miters on
Eze 23 15 girded with girdles about their reins
Apoc 15 6 girt about the breasts with golden g.
girl Num 30 4 house, and but yet a girl in age
Num 30 17 daughter that is as yet but a girl in age
4 K 5 4 said the girl from the land of Israel
Joel 3 3 and the girl they have sold for wine
Mat 9 24 the girl is not dead, but sleepeth
Mark 7 30 she found the girl lying upon the bed
Acts 16 16 girl having a pythonical spirit met us
girls Num 31 18 the g. and all the women that are
2 Pa 28 8 boys and girls and an immense booty
Zach 8 5 the city shall be full of boys and g.
girt 1 K 2 4 the weak are girt with strength
Ps 17 33 God who hath girt me with strength and
1 Ma 3 3 girt his warlike armor about him in
Luke 12 35 let your loins be girt, and lamps
John 21 7 girt his coat about him, for he was
Eph 6 14 stand therefore, having your loins girt
1 P 1 13 having the loins of your mind girt up
Apoc 1 13 girt about the paps with a golden
15 6 girt about the breasts with golden
gith Isa 28 25 sow gith and scatter cummin and
Isa 28 27 gith shall not be thrashed with saws
27 gith shall be beaten out with a rod
giver 2 C 9 7 for God loveth a cheerful giver. And
glad Gen 45 16 Pharao with all his family was g.
Exod 4 14 and seeing thee shall be glad at heart
1 K 11 9 the men of Jabes; and they were glad
3 K 8 66 glad in heart for all the good things
1 Pa 16 31 heavens rejoice and the earth be glad
2 Pa 7 10 and glad for the good that the Lord
Job 31 29 if I have been glad at the downfall of
Ps 5 12 let all them be glad that hope in thee
9 3 I will be glad and rejoice in thee: I
13 7 shall rejoice and Israel shall be glad
15 9 my heart hath been glad, and my tongue
30 8 I will be glad and rejoice in thy mercy
31 11 be glad in the Lord, and rejoice, ye
34 27 let them rejoice and be glad, who are
39 17 rejoice and be glad in thee. 69:5
47 12 and the daughters of Juda be glad
52 7 shall rejoice, and Israel shall be glad
66 5 let the nations be glad and rejoice
95 11 heavens rejoice and let the earth be g.
96 1 earth rejoice: let many islands be glad
8 Sion heard, and was glad. And the
104 38 Egypt was glad when they departed: for
118 74 see me and shall be glad: because
Prov 2 14 who are glad when they have done evil
10 1 a wise son maketh the father glad: but
12 25 with a good word he shall be made glad
15 13 glad heart maketh cheerful countenance
24 17 when thy enemy shall fall, be not glad
Cant 1 3 we will be glad and rejoice in thee
Isa 14 7 still, it is glad and hath rejoiced
35 1 the land . . . shall be glad, and the
65 18 you shall be glad and rejoice forever
66 10 with Jerusalem and be glad with her
Lam 4 21 and be glad, O daughters of Edom, that
Bar 4 33 at thy ruin, and was glad of thy fall
Dan 6 23 then was the king exceeding glad for
Osee 7 3 they have made the king g. with their
Joel 2 21 fear not, O land, be glad and rejoice
Jon 4 6 Jonas was exceeding glad of the ivy
Haba 1 15 for this he will be glad and rejoice
Soph 3 14 O Israel: be glad and rejoice with
1 Ma 3 7 and made Jacob glad with his works
10 26 we have heard of it and are glad
11 44 the king was very glad of their coming
Mat 5 12 be glad and rejoice, for your reward
Mark 14 11 who hearing it were glad; and they
Luke 6 23 be glad in that day and rejoice; for
15 32 that we should make merry and be glad
22 5 they were glad and covenanted to
23 8 Herod seeing Jesus, was very glad
John 8 56 see my day: he saw it, and was glad
11 15 I am glad for your sakes that I was
14 28 loved me, you would indeed be glad
20 20 the disciples therefore were glad when
Acts 2 26 for this my heart hath been glad, and
13 48 Gentiles hearing it were glad, and
Rom 10 15 that bring glad tidings of good things
2 C 2 2 who is he then that can make me glad
7 9 now I am glad: not because you were made
1 P 4 13 you may also be glad with exceeding
2 J 4 I was exceeding glad. 3 J 3
Apoc 19 7 let us be glad and rejoice and give
gladly Gen 27 9 thy father, such as he g. eateth
Gen 34 12 I will g. give what you shall demand
47 25 upon us, and we will g. serve the king
Prov 29 12 prince that gladly heareth lying words
Mark 12 37 and a great multitude heard him gladly
Acts 21 17 the brethren received us gladly. And the
2 C 11 19 also. For you gladly suffer the foolish
12 9 in infirmity. Gladly therefore will I
15 I most gladly will spend and be spent
1 Th 2 8 we would gladly impart unto you not only
gladness Deut 28 47 not serve . . . with joy and g.
Jdth 10 3 herself with the garments of her g.
Esth 9 18 to be a holy day of feasting and g.
19 for banquets and g. so as to rejoice on
22 should be days of feasting and gladness
Ps 4 7 thou hast given gladness in my heart
20 7 thou shalt make him joyful in gladness
29 6 shall have place, and in the morning g.
12 and hast compassed me with gladness
44 8 anointed thee with the oil of gladness
16 they shall be brought with gladness
50 10 thou shalt give joy and gladness: and
67 4 be delighted with gladness. Sing ye to
99 2 serve ye the Lord with gladness. Come
104 43 with joy, and his chosen with gladness
125 2 was our mouth filled with gladness
Ecce 9 7 joy, and drink thy wine with gladness
Wisd 8 16 any tediousness, but joy and gladness
Eccu 1 11 is honor and glory and gladness
12 shall give joy and g. and length of days
18 heart, it shall give joy and gladness
15 6 heap upon him a treasure of joy and g.
Isa 16 10 gladness and joy shall be taken away
22 13 behold joy and gladness, killing calves
35 10 they shall obtain joy and gladness and
51 3 joy and gladness shall be found therein
11 they shall obtain joy and gladness
Jer 7 34 voice of joy and the voice of g. 33:11
15 16 thy word was to me a joy and gladness
16 9 of mirth and the voice of gladness. 25:10
33 9 a g. before all the nations of the earth
48 33 joy and g. is taken away from Carmel
Bar 4 23 you back to me with joy and gladness
34 her g. shall be turned to mourning
Joel 1 16 joy and g. from the house of our God
Soph 3 17 he will rejoice over thee with gladness
Zach 8 19 to the house of Juda, joy and gladness
1 Ma 4 59 the month of Casleu with joy and g.
5 54 went up to mount Sion with joy and g.
13 52 should be kept every year with gladness
2 Ma 3 30 appeared, was filled with joy and g.
Luke 1 14 thou shalt have joy and gladness and
Acts 2 46 they took their meat with gladness
14 16 filling our hearts with food and g.

Heb 1 9 anointed thee with the oil of gladness
glances Isa 3 16 wanton g. of their eyes, and made
glass Prov 23 31 color thereof shineth in the g.
1 C 13 12 see now through a glass in a dark manner
James 1 23 beholding his own countenance in a g.
Apoc 15 2 and I saw as it were a sea of glass
21 18 itself pure gold, like to clear glass
21 gold, as it were transparent glass
glasses Isa 3 23 pins and looking-glasses and
glazing Eccu 38 34 give his mind to finish the g.
glean Ruth 2 2 I will . . . glean the ears of corn
Ruth 2 7 she desired leave to glean the ears
8 do not go to glean in any other field
15 to glean the ears of corn as before
23 and continued to glean with them till
gleaned Ruth 2 3 g. the ears of corn after the
Ruth 2 17 she gleaned therefore in the field
17 threshing what she had gleaned, she
19 where hast thou gleaned today and where
gleaneth Mich 7 1 for I am become as one that g.
glitter Job 39 23 the spear and shield shall g.
Eze 21 10 it is furbished that it may glitter
15 the sword that is furbished to glitter
28 be furbished to destroy and to g.
glittered 1 Ma 6 39 the mountains g. therewith
glittereth Job 20 25 glittereth in his bitterness
glittering Dan 10 6 in appearance to g. brass
Nah 3 3 the shining sword and of the g. spear
Haba 3 11 go in the brightness of thy g. spear
2 Ma 5 3 casting of darts and g. of golden armor
Luke 9 29 raiment became white and glittering
Apoc 19 8 with fine linen, glittering and white
globe Isa 40 22 sitteth upon the g. of the earth
gloominess Joel 2 2 a day of darkness and of g.
gloried Jdth 1 4 g. as a mighty one in the force
Isa 23 7 city, which gloried from of old in her
Jer 48 42 because he hath g. against the Lord
glories 2 Ma 4 15 esteemed the Grecian g. for the
1 P 1 11 and the glories that should follow
gloriest Jer 49 4 why g. thou in the valleys
glorieth Wisd 2 16 g. that he hath God for his
Eccu 38 26 and that glorieth in the goad, that
Jer 9 24 let him that glorieth glory in this
1 C 1 31 that g. may glory in the Lord. 2 C 10:11
glorified Exod 14 4 I shall be g. in Pharao. 18
Exod 14 17 I will be glorified in Pharao and in
33 16 that we may be glorified by all people
Lev 10 3 I will be g. in the sight of all the
1 Pa 17 18 thou hast thus glorified thy servant
Tob 11 16 and they glorified God, both he and his
Ps 88 8 who is g. in the assembly of the saints
Prov 4 8 thou shalt be glorified by her when
13 18 that yieldeth to reproof, shall be g.
18 12 before he be glorified, it is humbled
27 18 the keeper of his master, shall be g.
Wisd 18 1 the same things, they glorified thee
Eccu 10 33 the poor man is g. by his discipline
34 he that is g. in poverty, how much more
34 he that is g. in wealth, let him fear
11 13 have wondered at him and have g. God
45 3 he g. him in the sight of kings and
Isa 24 14 when the Lord shall be g., they shall
26 15 art thou glorified? Thou hast removed
43 23 nor hast thou g. me with thy victims
44 23 redeemed Jacob, and Israel shall be g.
49 5 I am glorified in the eyes of the Lord
55 5 Holy One of Israel, for he hath g. thee
60 9 Israel, because he hath glorified thee
66 5 said: Let the Lord be glorified, and
Eze 27 25 thou wast replenished and glorified
28 22 and I will be g. in the midst of thee
39 13 a noted day, wherein I was glorified
Dan 3 51 praised and g. and blessed God in the
52 and worthy to be praised and glorified
4 31 I praised and g. him that liveth forever
5 23 all thy ways, thou hast not glorified
Agge 1 8 acceptable to me, and I shall be g.
1 Ma 3 14 and will be glorified in the kingdom
11 51 Jews were g. in the sight of the king
14 15 he g. the sanctuary and multiplied
39 friend, and g. him with great glory
2 Ma 3 2 g. the temple with very great gifts
30 because he had glorified his place
Mat 9 8 g. God that gave such power to men
15 31 and they glorified the God of Israel
Mark 2 12 all wondered and glorified God, saying
Luke 5 26 they glorified God. 7:16
13 13 she was made straight, and g. God
23 47 the centurion . . . glorified God, saying
John 7 39 because Jesus was not yet glorified
11 4 the Son of God may be glorified by it
12 16 when Jesus was glorified, then they
23 that the Son of man should be g. Amen
28 I have both g. it, and will glorify it
13 31 now is the Son of man glorified, and God is glorified in him
32 if God be glorified in him, God also
14 13 the Father may be glorified in the Son
15 8 in this is my Father glorified; that
17 4 I have glorified thee on the earth
10 mine; and I am glorified in them
Acts 3 13 hath g. his Son Jesus, whom you indeed
4 21 all men glorified what had been done
11 18 they held their peace and g. God, saying
13 48 glad, and glorified the word of Lord
21 20 they hearing it, glorified God, and said
Rom 1 21 they have not glorified him as God, or
8 17 that we may be also glorified with him
30 and whom he justified, them he also g.
2 C 3 10 was glorious in this part was not g., by
Gal 1 24 and they glorified God in me. Then after
2 Th 1 10 he shall come to be glorified in his
12 the name of our Lord Jesus may be g.
3 1 may be glorified, even as among you; and
1 P 1 8 rejoice with joy unspeakable and g.
Apoc 18 7 as much as she hath glorified herself
glorifieth Ps 14 4 he g. them that fear the Lord
Wisd 8 3 she glorifieth her nobility by being
John 8 54 it is my Father that glorifieth me
glorify Exod 15 2 he is my God and I will g. him
1 K 2 30 whosoever shall g. me, him will I g.
1 Pa 16 4 to glorify and praise the Lord God of
1 Es 7 27 to g. the house of the Lord which is in
Jdth 8 17 so also we may glorify in our humility
Ps 21 24 all ye the seed of Jacob, glorify him
49 15 will deliver thee, and thou shalt g. me
23 sacrifice of praise shall glorify me
85 9 O Lord, and they shall glorify thy name
12 and I will glorify thy name forever
90 15 I will deliver him and I will g. him
Wisd 18 8 thou didst also encourage and g. us
Eccu 24 2 shall g. herself in the sight of his
36 7 glorify thy hand, and thy right arm
43 30 shall we be able to do to glorify him
32 g. the Lord as much as ever you can
45 19 and to glorify his people in his name
47 7 so in ten thousand did he glorify him
Isa 24 15 g. ye the Lord in instruction: the name
29 13 with their lips g. me, but their heart is
23 and shall glorify the God of Israel
43 20 beast of the field shall glorify me
58 13 g. him, while thou dost not thy own
60 7 I will glorify the house of my majesty
13 and I will glorify the place of my feet
21 planting, the work of my hand to g. me
61 3 the planting of the Lord to glorify him

Jer 30 19 I will g. them, and they shall not be
Dan 4 34 magnify and glorify the King of heaven
1 Ma 15 9 we will glorify thee and thy nation
Mat 5 16 good works and glorify your Father who
John 8 54 if I glorify myself, my glory is
12 28 Father, glorify thy name. A voice
28 glorified it, and will g. it again
13 32 God also will glorify him in himself
32 and immediately will he glorify him
16 14 he shall glorify me; because he shall
17 1 g. thy Son, that thy Son may g. thee
5 and now glorify thou me, O Father
21 19 by what death he should glorify God
Rom 15 6 you may glorify God and the Father of
9 Gentiles are to g. God for his mercy
1 C 6 20 glorify and bear God in your body. Now
Heb 5 5 so Christ also did not glorify himself
1 P 2 12 glorify God in the day of visitation
4 16 but let him glorify God in that name

glorifying Luke 2 20 the shepherds returned, g. and
Luke 5 25 went away to his own house, g. God
17 15 with a loud voice glorifying God
18 43 he saw, and followed him, g. God
2 C 9 13 glorifying God for obedience of your

glorious Exod 15 11 g. in holiness, terrible and
Deut 28 58 fear his glorious and terrible name
2 K 6 20 how g. was the king of Israel today
22 I [David] shall appear more glorious
1 Pa 29 13 to thee, and we praise thy g. name
2 Pa 2 9 build, is to be exceeding great and g.
18 1 was rich and very glorious. 32:27
1 Es 4 10 the great and g. Asenaphar brought over
Tob 13 13 thou shalt shine with a glorious light
Jdth 9 15 for this will be a glorious monument
16 16 great art thou and g. in thy power
Esth 11 11 were exalted, and they devoured the g.
Job 40 5 set thyself up on high and be glorious
Ps 86 3 g. things are said of thee, O city of
Prov 8 18 riches and glory, g. riches and justice
12 9 than he that is g. and wanteth bread
25 6 appear not glorious before the king
Wisd 3 15 for the fruit of good labors is glorious
6 13 wisdom is g. and never fadeth away and
Eccu 11 4 his works are glorious and secret and
6 the glorious have been delivered into
17 8 they might declare the g. things of his
11 their ears heard his glorious voice
18 3 for who shall search out his g. acts
5 to find out the g. works of God: when
40 3 from him that sitteth on a glorious throne
42 21 he hath beautified the g. works of his
43 1 the beauty of heaven with its g. show
45 9 he girded him about with a g. girdle
48 6 in pieces, and the g. from their bed
49 10 Ezechiel that saw the glorious vision
Isa 5 14 high and g. ones shall go down into it
11 10 and his sepulcher shall be glorious
13 19 that Babylon, glorious among kingdoms
23 9 bring to disgrace all the g. ones of the
43 4 honorable in my eyes, thou art g.: I
58 13 and the holy of the Lord glorious, and
62 2 thy just one, and all kings thy g. one
63 14 thy people to make thyself a g. name
Jer 17 12 high and g. throne from the beginning
Lam 2 1 to the earth the g. one of Israel and
Dan 3 26 is worthy of praise and glorious. 56
45 God, and glorious over all the world
53 to be praised and exceeding g. forever
11 16 he shall stand in the glorious land
41 he shall enter into the glorious land
45 the seas, upon a g. and holy mountain
Soph 2 15 is the g. city that dwelt in security
1 Ma 2 64 in the law: for by it you shall be g.
2 Ma 3 26 bright and g. and in comely apparel
6 19 a most g. death than a hateful life
8 15 for the sake of his holy and g. name
2 C 3 7 with letters upon stones, was glorious
10 even that which was g. in this part was
11 if that which is done away was glorious
Eph 5 27 a glorious church, not having spot or

gloriously Exod 15 1 for he is g. magnified. 21
Eccu 43 9 shining g. in the firmament of heaven
Luke 13 17 the things that were g. done by him

glory Exod 28 2 Aaron thy brother for glory and
Exod 28 40 girdles and miters for glory and beauty
Deut 26 19 to his own praise and name and glory
Josu 7 19 give glory to the Lord. 1 Pa 16:34; 2 Pa 5:13; 20:21; Tob 13:3, 12; Ps 104:1; 105:1; 106:1
Judg 7 2 lest Israel should glory against me
1 K 2 8 princes, and hold the throne of glory
4 21 the glory is gone from Israel because
22 the glory is departed from Israel
6 5 give glory to the God of Israel
3 K 3 13 given thee: to wit, riches and glory
4 K 14 10 be content with the glory, and sit at
1 Pa 16 28 bring ye to the Lord glory and empire
29 give to the Lord glory to his name
35 we may give glory to thy holy name
29 11 magnificence and power and glory
12 thine are riches and thine is glory
25 and gave him the glory of a reign
28 age, full of days and riches and glory
2 Pa 1 11 not asked riches and wealth and g. 12
9 22 was magnified . . . for riches and glory
17 5 acquired immense riches and much glory
2 Es 11 17 to praise, and to give glory in prayer
Tob 3 24 sight of the g. of the most high God
12 6 give glory to him in the sight of all
13 6 with fear and trembling give ye glory
10 keep days of joy and give glory to him
20 my seed, to see the glory of Jerusalem
Jdth 1 4 army and in the glory of his chariots
6 15 and glory in their own strength. So
7 24 and will give glory to his own name
9 9 their arrows and glory in their spears
10 8 that Jerusalem may glory in thee and
13 21 give all of you glory to him, because
15 10 thou art the glory of Jerusalem, thou
16 27 days she came forth with great glory
Esth 1 4 the riches of the glory of his kingdom
5 11 and with how great glory the king had
13 12 or any desire of glory, that I refused
14 9 and extinguished the glory of thy temple
15 that I hate the glory of the wicked
16 the sign of my pride and glory, which
16 3 not bearing the glory that is given them
Job 12 19 he leadeth away priests without glory
22 29 hath been humbled, shall be in glory
36 11 days in good and their years in glory
39 20 the glory of his nostrils is terror
Ps 5 12 that love thy name shall glory in thee
7 18 I will give g. to the Lord according
8 6 hast crowned him with glory and honor
17 50 therefore will I give glory to thee
20 6 glory and great beauty shalt thou lay
23 7 the King of Glory shall enter in. 9
8 who is this King of Glory? The Lord. 10
10 Lord of hosts, he is the King of Glory
28 2 bring to the Lord glory. 95:8
31 11 just, and glory, all ye right of heart
43 9 in God shall we glory all the day long
44 14 all the glory of the king's daughter
48 7 glory in the multitude of their riches
15 shall decay in hell from their glory
17 glory of his house shall be increased

51 3 why dost thou g. in malice, thou that
65 2 to his name: give glory to his praise
67 35 give ye glory to God for Israel, his
78 9 and for the glory of thy name, O Lord
83 12 the Lord will give grace and glory. He
84 10 him: that glory may dwell in our land
88 18 thou art the glory of their strength
93 3 O Lord: how long shall sinners glory
95 7 bring ye to the Lord glory and honor
96 7 things, and that glory in their idols
99 4 with hymns: and give glory to him
104 3 g. ye in his holy name: let the heart
105 20 changed their glory into the likeness
47 holy name, and may glory in thy praise
106 8 let mercies of the Lord give glory to him. 15, 21, 31
111 3 glory and wealth shall be in his house
9 his horn shall be exalted in glory
113 1 not to us; but to thy name give glory
117 21 I will give glory to thee because
135 26 give glory to the God of heaven: for
27 give glory to the Lord of lords: for
137 2 and I will give glory to thy name. For
4 may all kings of the earth give glory
139 14 they shall give glory to thy name: and
144 5 magnificence of the g. of thy holiness
11 shall speak of the g. of thy kingdom
12 g. of the magnificence of thy kingdom
149 5 the saints shall rejoice in glory: they
9 written: this glory is to all his saints
Prov 3 16 and in her left hand riches and glory
35 the wise shall possess glory: the
8 18 with me are riches and glory, glorious
11 16 a gracious woman shall find glory: and
15 33 and humility goeth before glory
17 6 the glory of children are their fathers
21 21 shall find life, justice, and glory. The
22 4 fear of the Lord, riches and glory and
25 2 g. of kings to search out the speech
27 majesty, shall be overwhelmed by glory
26 1 so glory is not seemly for a fool. As
28 12 in joy of the just there is great glory
29 23 g. shall uphold the humble of spirit
Ecce 10 1 wisdom and g. is more precious than
Wisd 4 1 is the chaste generation with glory
5 17 shall they receive a kingdom of glory
7 25 emanation of glory of the almighty God
8 10 I shall have glory among the multitude
18 g. in the communication of her words
10 14 him, and gave him everlasting glory
15 9 counteth it a glory to make vain things
18 24 the glory of the fathers was graven
Eccu 1 11 fear of the Lord is honor and glory
24 exalteth the g. of them that hold her
3 12 g. not in the dishonor of thy father
12 his shame is no glory to thee. For the
13 the glory of a man is from the honor
19 shalt be beloved above the g. of men
4 25 a shame that bringeth glory and grace
5 15 and g. is in the word of the wise, but
6 30 her chain a robe of glory: for in her
32 shalt put her on as a robe of glory
9 16 envy not glory and riches of a sinner
10 25 fear of God is the glory of the rich
11 4 glory not in apparel at any time, and
16 they that glory in evil things, grow
14 27 the heat, and shall rest in her glory
15 5 shall clothe him with a robe of glory
17 8 glory in his wondrous acts, that they
26 give g. before death. Praise perisheth
27 and shalt glory in his mercies. How
20 11 there is an abasement because of glory
23 38 it is great glory to follow the Lord
24 1 shall glory in the midst of her people
34 sitting on the throne of glory forever
25 8 and the fear of God is their glory
30 3 of his friends he shall glory in him
31 10 he shall have glory everlasting. He
35 10 give glory to God with a good heart
39 11 shall glory in the law of the covenant
20 give glory to him with the voice
40 28 they have covered it above all glory
43 10 the glory of the stars is the beauty
13 heaven about with the circle of its g.
44 2 Lord hath wrought great glory through
7 all these have gained glory in their
13 and their glory shall not be forsaken
20 was not found the like to him in glory
22 he gave him glory in his posterity
45 2 he made him like the saints in glory
8 nation, and made him blessed in glory
9 and clothed him with a robe of glory
25 he added glory to Aaron and gave him an
28 the son of Eleazar is the third in glory
31 their g. in their nation everlasting
46 3 how great glory did he gain when he
15 the glory of the holy men remaining
47 7 in offering to him a crown of glory
9 to the most High, with words of glory
13 kingdom and a throne of g. in Israel
48 4 and who can glory like to thee? Who
49 7 and their glory to a strange nation
14 the Lord, prepared for everlasting g.
19 Seth and Sem obtained glory among men
50 5 and obtained glory in his conversation
11 when he put on the robe of glory and
14 all the sons of Aaron in their glory
22 to give glory to God with his lips and to glory in his name
51 1 I will give glory to thee, O Lord, O
2 I will give glory to thy name: for
23 that giveth me wisdom, will I give g.
Isa 2 10 from the glory of his majesty. 19, 21
4 2 Lord shall be in magnificence and glory
5 over all the g. shall be a protection
10 3 and where will ye leave your glory
12 glory of the haughtiness of his eyes
18 the glory of his forest and of his
14 18 have all of them slept in glory, every
16 14 the glory of Moab shall be taken away
17 3 as the glory of the children of Israel
4 the glory of Jacob shall be made thin
20 5 their hope, and of Egypt their glory
21 16 all the glory of Cedar shall be taken
22 23 he shall be for a throne of glory to
24 all the glory of his father's house
23 9 to pull down the pride of all glory
12 thou shalt glory no more, O virgin
24 16 heard praises, the g. of the just one
25 1 I will . . . give glory to thy name
28 1 fading flower the glory of his joy. 4
5 Lord of hosts shall be a crown of glory
30 30 make glory of his voice to be heard
35 2 the glory of Libanus is given to it
40 6 the glory thereof as the flower of the
42 12 they shall give glory to the Lord and
49 3 servant Israel, for in thee will I glory
60 13 glory of Libanus shall come to thee
15 make thee to be an everlasting glory
61 6 you shall pride yourselves in their g.
62 3 thou shalt be a crown of glory in the
66 11 from the abundance of her glory. For
12 torrent the glory of the Gentiles
Jer 2 11 have changed their glory into an idol
9 23 let not the wise man glory in his
23 let not the strong man glory in his

23 let not the rich man g. in his riches
24 let him that glorieth glory in this
10 7 king of nations? for thine is the glory
13 11 for a glory: but they would not hear
16 give ye glory to the Lord. 33:11
18 crown of your glory is come down from
46 9 ye up on horses, and glory in chariots
50 38 idols, and they g. in monstrous things
Bar 2 17 shall not give glory and justice to
18 hungry soul giveth glory and justice
4 24 with great honor and everlasting glory
5 1 beauty and honor of that everlasting g.
Eze 3 23 the glory which I saw by the river
8 4 g. of the God of Israel. 10:19; 11:22
24 21 my sanctuary, the glory of your realm
25 their strength and the joy of their glory
26 20 shall give glory in the land of the
43 2 glory of the God of Israel came in by
Dan 2 37 hath given thee . . . power and glory
3 43 and give glory to thy name, O Lord
4 27 and in the glory of my excellence
33 came to the honor and g. of my kingdom
5 18 and greatness and glory and honor
7 14 and he gave him power and glory and a
11 39 he shall increase glory and shall give
Osee 4 7 I will change their glory into shame
9 11 as for Ephraim, their glory hath flown
10 5 that rejoiced over it in its glory
Mich 1 15 to Odollam shall the glory of Israel
Haba 2 16 art filled with shame instead of glory
Agge 2 4 that saw this house in its first glory
8 and I will fill this house with glory
10 shall be the glory of this last house
Zach 2 5 I will be in g. in the midst thereof
8 after the glory he hath sent me to the
6 13 he shall bear the glory and shall sit
11 3 because their glory is laid waste: the
12 7 glory of the inhabitants of Jerusalem
Mala 2 2 it to heart, to give glory to my name
1 Ma 1 42 was increased according to her glory
2 9 vessels of her glory are carried away
12 our beauty, and our glory is laid waste
51 you shall receive great glory and an
9 10 brethren, and let us not stain our g.
10 58 marriage at Ptolemais with great glory
11 6 to meet the king at Joppe with glory
12 12 and we rejoice at your glory. But we
14 9 the young men put on them glory and
21 have told us of your glory and honor
29 have raised their nation to great glory
35 what glory he meant to bring his nation
39 glorified him with great glory. For he
15 9 temple with great glory so that your glory shall be made manifest
32 and saw the glory of Simon and his
36 made report . . . of the glory of Simon
2 Ma 5 16 the ornament and the glory of the place
20 shall be exalted again with great glory
8 35 laying aside his garment of glory
14 7 being deprived of my ancestors' glory
15 13 another man, admirable for age and glory
Mat 4 8 of the world and the glory of them
16 27 come in the g. of his Father. Mark 8:38
Mark 13 26 in the clouds, with great power and g.
Luke 2 14 g. to God in the highest; and on earth
32 and the glory of thy people Israel
4 6 this power, and the glory of them
14 10 then shalt thou have glory before them
17 18 no one found to return and give glory
19 38 peace in heaven, and glory on high
John 5 41 I receive not glory from men. But I
44 who receive glory one from another
44 the glory which is from God alone you
7 18 he that seeketh the glory of him that
8 50 I seek not my own glory: there is one
54 if I glorify myself, my g. is nothing
9 24 and said to him: Give glory to God
12 43 they loved the glory of men more than
17 5 with the glory which I had, before the
22 the glory which thou hast given me
24 that they may see my glory which thou
Acts 7 2 the God of glory appeared to our
Rom 2 7 seek glory and honor and incorruption
10 glory and honor and peace to every one
4 2 he hath whereof to g., but not before
20 strengthened in faith, giving g. to God
5 2 we stand and glory in the hope of the glory of the sons of God
3 we glory also in tribulations, knowing
11 we glory in God, through our Lord Jesus
6 4 risen from the dead by the g. of the
8 18 to be compared with the glory to come
21 corruption, into the liberty of glory
9 4 to whom belongeth . . . the glory, and the
23 mercy, which he hath prepared unto glory
11 36 are all things: to him be glory forever
15 17 I have therefore glory in Christ Jesus
16 27 Jesus Christ, to whom be honor and glory
1 C 1 29 that no flesh should glory in his sight
31 he that glorieth, may glory in the Lord
2 7 God ordained before world, unto our g.
8 never have crucified the Lord of glory
3 21 let no man therefore glory in men. For
4 7 why dost thou glory, as if thou hadst
9 15 that any man should make my glory void
16 preach the gospel, it is no glory to me
11 7 the woman is the glory of the man. For
15 nourish her hair, it is a glory to her
12 26 if one member glory, all the members
15 31 I die daily, I protest by your glory
40 but, one is the glory of the celestial
41 one is the g. of the sun, another g. of the moon, and another g. of the stars
41 for star differeth from star in glory
43 sown in dishonor, it shall rise in glory
2 C 1 12 for our glory is this, the testimony
14 that we are your glory, as you also are
20 also by him, amen to God, unto our glory
3 7 behold the face of Moses, for the glory
8 ministration of spirit be rather in g.
9 if ministration of condemnation be glory
9 ministration of justice aboundeth in g.
10 by reason of the glory that excelleth
11 much more that which remaineth is in g.
18 into the same image from glory to glory
4 4 the light of gospel of glory of Christ
17 exceedingly an eternal weight of glory
5 12 give you occasion to glory in our behalf
12 them who glory in face, and not in heart
8 23 apostles of churches, glory of Christ
10 13 we will not glory beyond our measure
16 not to glory in another man's rule, in
17 that glorieth, let him glory in the Lord
11 12 desire occasion, that wherein they glory
16 foolish, that I also may glory a little
18 seeing that many g. according to flesh
18 according to flesh, I will glory also
30 if I must needs glory, I will glory of
12 1 if I must glory, it is not expedient
5 for such an one I will glory; but for
5 for myself I will glory nothing, but in
6 though I should have a mind to glory
9 therefore will I glory in my infirmities
Gal 1 5 to whom is glory forever and ever. Amen
5 26 let us not be made desirous of vain g.
6 4 so he shall have glory in himself only

13 that they may glory in your flesh. But
14 God forbid that I should glory, save in
Eph 1 6 unto the praise and glory of his grace
17 Father of glory, may give unto you the
18 glory of his inheritance in the saints
2 9 not of works, that no man may glory. For
3 13 tribulations for you, which is your g.
21 to him be glory in the church, and in
Phil 2 3 through contention, neither by vain g.
16 forth the word of life to my glory in
3 3 serve God; and glory in Christ Jesus
19 and whose glory is in their shame; who
4 19 to his riches in glory in Christ Jesus
20 now to God and our Father be glory
Col 1 27 the riches of the glory of this mystery
27 which is Christ, in you the hope of g.
3 4 you shall appear with him in glory
1 Th 2 6 nor sought we glory of men, neither of
12 called you unto his kingdom of glory
19 what is our hope or joy or crown of g.
20 for you are our glory and joy. For
2 Th 1 4 also glory in you in the churches of God
9 Lord, and from the glory of his power
2 13 unto the purchasing of the glory of our
1 Tim 1 17 be honor and glory forever and ever
3 16 in the world, is taken up in glory. Now
2 Tim 2 10 is in Christ Jesus, with heavenly glory
4 18 to whom be glory forever and ever. Amen
Heb 2 7 crowned him with glory and honor, and
9 crowned with glory and honor: that
10 who had brought many children into glory
3 3 counted worthy of greater g. than Moses
6 if we hold fast the confidence and glory
9 5 the cherubims of glory overshadowing the
13 21 to whom is glory forever and ever
James 1 9 of low condition g. in his exaltation
2 1 faith of our Lord Jesus Christ of glory
3 14 glory not, and be not liars against
1 P 1 7 may be found unto praise and glory and
21 from the dead, and hath given him glory
24 the glory thereof as the flower of
2 20 what glory is it if, committing sin
4 11 to whom is glory and empire forever
5 1 as also a partaker of that glory which
4 receive a never fading crown of glory
11 to him be glory and empire forever and
2 P 1 17 from God the Father honor and glory
17 down to him from the excellent glory
3 18 to him be glory both now and unto the
Jude 25 be glory and magnificence, empire and
Apoc 1 6 to him be glory and empire forever and
4 9 creatures gave glory and honor and
11 to receive glory and honor and power
5 12 and strength and honor and glory and
13 honor and glory and power forever and
7 12 and glory and wisdom and thanksgiving
11 13 and gave glory to the God of heaven
16 9 did they penance to give him glory
19 1 and glory and power is to our God. For
7 and rejoice and give glory to him: for
21 24 shall bring their glory and honor into
26 they shall bring the glory and honor of

glory of God Ps 18 2 heavens show forth g. . . .
Prov 25 2 it is glory of God to conceal the word
John 11 4 unto death, but for the glory of God
40 thou shalt see the glory of God? They
12 43 the glory of men more than the g. . . .
Acts 7 55 saw the g. . . . and Jesus standing on
Rom 1 23 changed the g. of the incorruptible God
3 23 have sinned, and do need glory of God
1 C 10 31 else you do, do all to the glory of God
11 7 he is the image and glory of God; but
2 C 4 6 light of knowledge of the glory of God
15 in thanksgiving unto the glory of God
Phil 1 11 Christ, unto the glory and praise of God
2 11 Christ is in the glory of God the Father
1 Tim 1 11 gospel of the glory of the blessed God
Titus 2 13 coming of the glory of the great God
1 P 4 14 of the honor, glory, and power of God
Apoc 21 11 having the glory of God, and the light
23 the glory of God hath enlightened it

glory of the Lord Exod 16 7 the morning you shall see the g. . . .
Exod 16 10 the g. . . . appeared. Lev 9:23; Num 14:10; 16:19, 43; 20:6
24 16 g. . . . dwelt upon Sinai, covering it
17 sight of the g. . . . was like a burning
40 32 testimony and the g. . . . filled it
Num 14 21 whole earth shall be filled with g. . . .
3 K 8 11 g. . . . had filled the house. 2 Pa 5:14
2 Pa 7 3 g. . . . upon the house: and falling
Ps 103 31 may the g. . . . endure forever: the Lord
137 5 great is the g. . . . For the Lord is
Eccu 42 16 and full of the g. . . . is his work
Isa 26 10 and he shall not see the g. . . . Lord
35 2 they shall see the g. . . . and the
40 5 g. . . . shall be revealed, and all flesh
60 1 is come, and g. . . . is risen upon thee
Eze 2 1 vision of the likeness of the g. . . .
3 12 blessed be the g. . . . from his place
23 behold the g. . . . stood there, like
9 3 g. . . . of Israel went up from the
10 4 g. . . . was lifted up from above the
4 filled with brightness of the g. . . .
18 g. . . . went forth from the threshold
11 23 g. . . . went up from midst of the city
43 5 the house was filled with the g. . . .
44 4 g. . . . filled the house of the Lord
Isa 58 8 and the g. . . . shall gather thee up
Haba 2 14 filled, that men may know the g. . . .
2 C 3 18 we all beholding the glory of the Lord
8 19 administered by us, to the g. . . . , and

his glory Lev 9 6 do it, and his glory will appear to you
1 Pa 16 24 declare his glory among the Gentiles
Ps 20 6 his glory is great in thy salvation
28 9 in his temple all shall speak his glory
48 18 nor shall his glory descend with him
95 3 declare his glory among the Gentiles
96 6 justice: and all people saw his glory
101 17 Sion: and he shall be seen in his glory
112 4 and his glory above the heavens. Who
Prov 19 11 and his glory is to pass over wrongs
Eccu 17 11 their eye saw the majesty of his glory
42 17 settled to be established for his g.
26 shall be filled with beholding his g.
45 3 his people, and showed him his glory
Isa 6 3 all the earth is full of his glory
8 7 king of the Assyrians and all his g.
10 16 and under his glory shall be kindled a
25 11 he shall bring down his glory with
59 19 from the rising of the sun his g.
60 2 and his glory shall be seen upon thee
Jer 10 25 him, and have destroyed his glory
Dan 5 20 kingdom, and his g. was taken away
Osee 14 7 his glory shall be as the olive tree
Haba 3 3 his glory covered the heavens, and the
Zach 10 3 made them as the horse of his glory
1 Ma 2 62 sinful man, for his glory is dung and
10 64 his accusers saw his glory proclaimed
14 4 his power and his glory pleased them
5 with all his glory he took Joppe for a
10 fame of his glory was renowned even to
Mat 6 29 not even Solomon in all his glory was. Luke 12:27

Luke 9 32 they saw his glory, and the two men
24 26 and so to enter into his glory? And
John 1 14 we saw his glory, the glory as it were
2 11 manifested his g., and his disciples
7 18 of himself, seeketh his own glory
12 41 when he saw his glory and spoke of him
Rom 3 7 abounded through my lie, unto his glory
9 23 he might show the riches of his glory
Eph 1 12 unto the praise of his glory. 14
3 16 according to the riches of his glory, to
Phil 3 21 made like to the body of his glory
Col 1 11 according to the power of his glory
1 Th 2 12 called you unto his kingdom and glory
Heb 1 3 who being the brightness of his glory
1 P 4 13 when his glory shall be revealed, you
5 10 hath called us unto his eternal glory
2 P 1 3 by his own proper glory and virtue
Jude 24 spotless before the presence of his g.
Apoc 18 1 earth was enlightened with his glory
my glory Gen 45 13 my father of all my glory
Gen 49 6 nor my glory be in their assembly
Exod 29 43 the altar shall be sanctified by my g.
33 22 when my glory shall pass, I will set
Job 19 9 he hath stripped me of my glory and
29 20 my glory shall always be renewed, and
Ps 3 4 O Lord, art my protector, my glory
7 6 and bring down my glory to the dust
29 13 the end that my glory may sing to thee
56 9 arise, O my glory, arise psaltery. 107:3
61 8 in God is my salvation and my glory
107 2 sing, and will give praise with my g.
Isa 13 3 wrath, them that rejoice in my glory
42 8 not give my glory to another. 48:11
43 7 name, I have created him for my glory
46 12 salvation in Sion, and my g. in Israel
66 18 they shall come and shall see my glory
19 of me, and have not seen my glory
19 shall declare my glory to the Gentiles
Eze 39 21 I will set my glory among the nations
thy glory Exod 15 7 in the multitude of thy glory
Exod 33 18 said: Show me thy glory. He answered
Num 27 20 in sight of all, and part of thy glory
Deut 33 29 thy help, and the sword of thy glory
2 Pa 26 18 shall not be accounted to thy glory
2 Es 9 5 blessed be the high name of thy glory
Ps 16 15 satisfied when thy glory shall appear
25 8 and the place where thy glory dwelleth
44 10 of kings have delighted thee in thy g.
56 6 and thy glory above all the earth. 12
62 3 to see thy power and thy glory. For
70 8 with praise, that I may sing thy glory
72 24 with thy glory thou hast received me
101 16 and all the kings of the earth thy glory
107 6 heavens, and thy g. over all the earth
Eccu 9 22 let thy glory be in the fear of God
33 24 let no stain sully thy glory. In the
36 16 words, and thy people with thy glory
47 22 hast stained thy glory and defiled thy
Isa 22 18 there shall the chariot of thy g. be
52 1 Sion, put on the garments of thy g.
60 19 light, and thy God for thy glory. Thy
63 15 habitation and the place of thy glory
Jer 14 21 not disgrace in us the throne of thy g.
48 18 come down from thy glory, and sit in
Eze 23 26 take away the instruments of thy glory
Dan 3 52 blessed is the holy name of thy glory
53 thou in the holy temple of thy g.
Haba 2 16 shameful vomiting shall be on thy g.
Mark 10 37 other on thy left hand in thy glory
glorying Isa 43 14 Chaldeans g. in their ships
1 C 5 6 your glorying is not good. Know you
2 C 7 4 great is my glorying for you. I am
10 15 not g. beond measure in other men's
11 10 this g. shall not be broken off in me
17 foolishness, in this matter of glorying
glowing Eze 1 7 like the appearance of g. brass
glueth Eccu 22 7 is like one that g. a potsherd
glut Job 19 22 glut yourselves with my flesh
glutted Prov 25 16 g. therewith, thou vomit it
Eze 23 17 and her soul was glutted with them
22 with whom thy soul hath been g. 28
glutton Mat 11 19 man that is a g. Luke 7:34
gluttons Prov 28 7 that feedeth g., shameth his
gnash Ps 36 12 shall g. upon him with his teeth
Ps 111 10 he shall gnash with his teeth and pine
gnashed Job 16 10 hath g. with his teeth upon me
Ps 34 16 they gnashed upon me with their teeth
Lam 2 16 hissed, and gnashed with the teeth
Acts 7 54 they gnashed with the teeth at him
gnasheth Mark 9 17 foameth and g. with the teeth
gnashing Mat 8 12 shall be weeping and g. of teeth.
13:42, 50; 22:13; 24:51; 25:30; Luke 13:28
gnat Mat 23 24 strain out a gnat, and swallow
gnaw Bar 6 19 of the earth, gnaw their hearts
gnawed Job 30 3 who gnawed in the wilderness
Apoc 16 10 and they gnawed their tongues for pain
Gnidus 1 Ma 15 23 Gnidus and Cyprus and Cyrene
Acts 27 7 and were scarce come over against Gnidus
goad 1 K 13 21 were blunt, even to the goad
Eccu 38 26 glorieth in the goad, that driveth the
Jer 46 20 from the north one that shall g. her
Acts 9 5 for thee to kick against the g. 26:14
goads Ecce 12 11 the words of the wise are as g.
goat Gen 15 9 and a she goat of three years
Lev 3 12 if his offering be a goat, and he offer it
4 28 he shall offer a she goat. Num 15:27
5 6 an ewe lamb or a she goat, and the
7 23 an ox and of a goat you shall not eat
9 3 take ye a he goat for sin, and a calf
15 he slew the he goat: and expiating the
16 8 and the other to be the emissary goat
10 whose lot was to be the emissary goat
20 then let him offer the living goat: and
22 when the goat hath carried all their
26 he that hath let go the emissary goat
17 3 if he kill an ox or a sheep or a goat in
22 27 or a goat is brought forth, they shall
Num 18 17 and of a goat thou shalt not cause to be
Deut 14 4 beasts that you shall eat . . . the goat
5 the wild goat, the camelopardalus
Eze 43 22 shalt offer a he goat without blemish
25 seven days shalt thou offer a he goat
45 23 seven days: and for sin, a he goat daily
Dan 8 5 behold a he goat came from the west
5 the he goat had a notable horn between
8 and the he goat became exceeding great
21 the he goat is the king of the Greeks
buck goat Lev 4 23 he shall offer a buck goat
Lev 10 16 when Moses sought for the buck goat
16 15 when he hath killed the buck goat
18 blood of the calf and of the buck goat
27 the calf and the buck goat that were
23 19 a buck goat for sin. Num 7:16, 22, 28, 34,
40, 46, 52, 58, 64, 70, 76, 82; 15:24; 29:5,
11, 16, 22, 25, 28, 31, 34, 38
Num 28 15 a buck goat also shall be offered to. 29:19
22 and one buck goat for sin to make
29 a buck goat also, which is slain for
29 19 and a buck goat for a sin offering
Goatha Jer 31 39 and it shall compass Goatha
goat's Exod 25 4 and fine linen and goat's hair
1 K 19 13 put a goat's skin with the hair at the
16 the bed, and a goat's skin at its head
goats Gen 30 32 the sheep, as among the g. 33

Gen 30 35 separated the same day the she goats and the sheep and the he goats
31 38 thy ewes and goats were not barren, the
32 14 for his brother Esau, 200 she goats, 20 he goats
Lev 1 10 a holocaust of goats, be of sheep or
22 19 beeves or of the sheep or of the goats
27 32 the tithes of oxen and sheep and goats
Num 7 17 two oxen, five rams, five he goats
31 20 of the skins or hair of goats, or of
Deut 32 14 and goats with the marrow of wheat
1 K 24 3 which are accessible only to wild goats
25 2 had 3,000 sheep and a thousand goats
3 K 20 27 like two little flocks of goats: but the
2 Pa 17 11 cattle, 7,700 rams and as many he g.
29 21 lambs and seven he goats for sin
23 and they brought the he goats for sin
1 Es 6 17 sin offering for all Israel 12 he g.
8 35 lambs and twelve he goats for sin
Jdth 3 3 flocks of sheep and goats and horses
Job 39 1 when the wild goats bring forth among
Ps 49 9 house: nor he goats out of thy flocks
13 or shall I drink the blood of goats
65 15 I will offer to thee bullocks with g.
Prov 27 27 let the milk of the goats be enough
Cant 4 1 thy hair is as flocks of goats, which
6 4 thy hair is as a flock of goats that
Eze 34 17 and cattle, of rams and of he goats
39 18 rams and of lambs and of he goats
Mich 6 7 with many thousands of fat he goats
Mat 25 32 separateth the sheep from the goats
33 right hand, but the goats on his left
Heb 9 12 neither by the blood of goats, or of
13 if the blood of goats and of oxen, and
19 he took the blood of calves and goats
10 4 with the blood of oxen and goats sin
buck goats Lev 16 5 two buck goats for sin
Lev 16 7 shall make the two b. g. to stand
Num 7 23 five rams, five buck goats, five lambs. 29, 35, 41, 47, 53, 59, 65, 71, 77, 83
87 libations: twelve buck goats for sin
88 rams sixty, buck goats sixty, lambs
Isa 1 11 of calves and lambs and buck goats
34 6 with the blood of lambs and buck goats
Zach 10 3 and I will visit upon the buck goats
goats' Exod 26 7 eleven curtains of g. hair. 36:14
Exod 35 6 and fine linen, g. hair. 23, 26
goatskins Heb 11 37 about in sheepskins, in g.
Gob 2 K 21 18 was also a second battle in Gob
2 K 21 19 and there was a third battle in Gob
god Num 23 21 neither is there an image god to be
Judg 6 31 if he be a god, let him revenge himself
8 3 with Baal, that he should be their god
9 27 they went into the temple of their god
46 went into temple of their god Berith
11 24 things which thy god Chamos possesseth
16 23 great sacrifices to Dagon their god and
23 our god hath delivered our enemy
24 also seeing this, praised their god
24 our god hath delivered our adversary
17 3 a graven and a molten god. 4; 18:14
5 also therein a little temple for the god
18 17 to take away the graven god and the molten god
18 and the idols and the molten god
20 and the idols and the graven god and
1 K 5 7 heavy upon us and upon Dagon our god
3 K 11 33 Chamos the god of Moab, and Moloch the god of the children of Ammon
18 27 he is a god and perhaps he is talking
4 K 1 2 Beelzebub, the god of Accaron. 3, 6, 16
18 34 god of Emath and of Arphad. Isa 36:19
34 where is the god of Sepharvaim. Isa 36:19
19 37 in temple of Nesroch his god. Isa 37:38
1 Pa 10 10 dedicated in the temple of their god
2 Pa 32 21 he was come into the house of his god
1 Es 1 7 had put them in the temple of his god
Jdth 5 29 that Nabuchodonosor is god of the earth
Wisd 14 8 because being frail it is called a god
15 he began now to worship as a god and
20 took him now for a god that a little
15 8 clay by a vain labor he maketh a god
16 no man can make a god like to himself
Isa 42 17 say to a molten thing: You are our god
44 10 who hath formed a god and made a
17 but the residue thereof he made a god
45 20 and pray to a god that cannot save
46 6 and hire a goldsmith to make a god
Dan 1 2 of Sennaar, to the house of his god
2 brought into treasure house of his god
3 95 nor adore any god, except their own god
4 5 according to the name of my god, who
6 7 shall ask any petition of any god or
11 36 shall magnify himself against every god
38 but he shall worship the god Maozim
38 a god whom his fathers knew not, he
14 5 not Bel seem to thee to be a living god
23 say now, that this is not a living god
Amos 5 26 the star of your god, which you made
Jon 1 5 the men cried to their god: and they
Mich 4 5 walk every one in the name of his god
Haba 1 11 and fall: this is his strength of his god
Acts 7 43 and the star of your god Rempham
12 22 it is the voice of a god, and not of
28 6 their minds, they said, that he was god
2 C 4 4 the god of this world hath blinded the
no god (no God) Deut 32 21 me with that which was no god
3 K 8 23 there is no God like thee. 2 Pa 6:14
4 K 1 6 it because there was no God in Israel
2 Pa 32 15 for if no god of all the nations and
Jdth 6 2 there is no God but Nabuchodonosor
Ps 13 1 in his heart: There is no God. 52:1
80 10 there shall be no new god in thee
Wisd 12 13 for there is no other God but thou
Eccu 36 2 is no God beside thee. 5, 13; Isa 45:14
Isa 43 10 before me there was no God formed, and
44 6 last, and besides me there is no God
45 5 there is no God besides me. 21
46 9 I am God, and there is no God beside
Dan 14 24 living God: but that is no living god
Osee 8 6 a workman made it, and it is no god
13 4 and thou shalt know no God but me
strange god Exod 34 14 adore not any strange god
Deut 32 12 and there was no strange god with him
Ps 43 21 spread forth our hands to a strange god
80 10 neither shalt thou adore a strange god
Jer 5 19 served a strange god in your own land
Dan 11 39 to fortify Maozim with a strange god
Mala 2 11 married the daughter of a strange god
God Gen 17 8 and I will be their God. Exod 29:45
Gen 28 21 the Lord shall be my God: and this
30 2 am I as God, who hath deprived thee
48 21 behold I die, and God will be with you
Exod 6 7 for my people, I will be your God
Lev 22 33 that I might be your God. 25:38; Num 15:41
26 12 walk among you, and will be your God
Ruth 1 16 shall be my people, and thy God my God
4 K 1 3 is there not a God in Israel, that ye go
16 though there were not a God in Israel
1 Pa 17 22 and thou, O Lord, art become their God
2 Pa 6 40 for thou art my God: let thy eyes
goddess 3 K 11 5 Astarthe g. of the Sidonians. 33
Acts 19 37 nor of blasphemy against your goddess
Godhead Col 2 9 fulness of the G. corporeally
godliness Eccu 49 4 sinners he strengthened g.

Isa 11 2 the spirit of knowledge and of g.
2 Ma 3 1 because of the g. of Onias the high
12 45 who had fallen asleep with godliness
1 Tim 2 10 but as it becometh women professing g.
3 16 evidently great is the mystery of g.
4 7 and exercise thyself unto godliness. For
8 godliness is profitable to all things
6 3 that doctrine which is according to g.
5 truth, supposing gain to be godliness
6 godliness with contentment is great gain
11 and pursue justice, godliness, faith
2 Tim 3 5 having an appearance indeed of g., but
Titus 1 1 truth, which is according to godliness
2 P 1 3 which appertain to life and godliness
6 in patience, g.; and in g., love of
3 11 be in holy conversation and godliness
godly Eccu 43 37 to the g. he hath given wisdom
Eccu 44 10 whose godly deeds have not failed
2 Tim 3 12 all that will live godly in Christ Jesus
Titus 2 12 soberly and justly and godly in this
2 P 2 9 how to deliver the g. from temptation
Godolia 1 Es 10 18 his brethren Maasia . . . and G.
Godolias 4 K 25 22 he gave the government to G.
4 K 25 23 of Babylon had made G. governor
23 came to Godolias to Masphath. Jer 40:8, 12, 13
24 Godolias swore to them and to their men
25 and smote Godolias so that he died
1 Pa 25 3 the sons of Idithun, Godolias, Sori
9 the second to G., to him and his sons
Jer 39 14 the prison and committed him to G.
40 5 not with me: but dwell with Godolias
9 Godolias . . . swore to them and to
11 had made Godolias . . . ruler over them
14 G. son of Ahicam believed them not
15 spoke to G. privately in Masphath
16 G. the son of Ahicam said to Johanan
41 1 ten men with him, came to Godolias
2 were with him, and they struck G.
3 all the Jews that were with Godolias
4 second day after he had killed Godolias
6 he said to them: Come to Godolias
9 the men whom he slew because of G.
10 of the army had committed to G.
16 after that he had slain G. the son of
18 son of Nathanias had slain Godolias
43 6 the general had left with G.
Soph 1 1 Chusi the son of G. the son of Amarias
God's Job 36 2 somewhat to speak in G. behalf
Wisd 7 26 the unspotted mirror of God's majesty
Rom 13 4 for he is God's minister to thee, for
4 for he is God's minister: an avenger to
1 C 3 9 for we are God's coadjutors: you are
9 God's husbandry; you are God's building
23 you are Christ's; and Christ is God's
Heb 13 16 by such sacrifices God's favor is
gods Gen 3 5 you shall be as gods, knowing
Gen 31 30 why hast thou stolen away my gods
32 with whomsoever thou shalt find thy g.
Exod 12 12 against all the gods of Egypt I will
18 11 Lord is great above all g. 2 Pa 2:5
20 23 you shall not make gods of silver nor
23 you make to yourselves gods of gold
21 6 his master shall bring him to the gods
22 8 of house shall be brought to the gods
9 of both parties shall come to the gods
20 he that sacrificeth to gods shall be put
28 thou shalt not speak ill of the gods
32 1 make us gods that may go before. 23
4 these are thy gods, O Israel, that. 8
31 have made to themselves gods of gold
34 17 not make to thyself any molten gods
Deut 4 7 that hath gods so nigh them, as our
28 there you shall serve gods that were
10 17 he is the God of gods, and the Lord of
29 18 to go and serve gods of those nations
32 17 to gods whom they knew not, that were
Josu 24 14 put away the gods which your fathers
15 the gods which your fathers served
15 the gods of the Amorrhites. Judg 6:10
Judg 2 12 the gods of the people that dwelt round
9 9 which both gods and men make use of
10 6 the gods of Syria and of Sidon and of
14 go and call upon the gods which you
18 24 you have taken away my gods which I
Ruth 1 15 returned to her people and to her gods
1 K 4 8 us from the hand of these high gods
8 these are the gods that struck Egypt
6 5 his hand from you and from your gods
17 43 the Philistine cursed David by his g.
28 13 I saw gods ascending out of the earth
3 K 12 28 behold thy gods, O Israel, who brought
14 9 made thee strange gods and molten gods
18 24 call ye on the names of your gods. 25
19 2 things may the gods do to me. 20:10
20 23 their gods are gods of the hills
4 K 5 17 holocaust or victim to other gods
17 29 every nation made gods of their own
31 and Anamelech the gods of Sepharvaim
18 33 have any of the gods of the nations
35 among all the gods of the nations
19 12 have the gods of the nations delivered
18 they were not gods, but the works of
1 Pa 5 25 the gods of the people of the land
16 25 and he is to be feared above all gods
26 all the gods of the nations are idols
2 Pa 13 8 which Jeroboam hath made you for gods
9 made a priest of those who are no gods
25 14 set up the g. of the children of Seir
14 he had brought thence to be his gods
15 why hast thou adored g. that have not
20 of enemies, because of the gods of Edom
28 23 victims to the gods of Damascus that
23 the g. of the kings of Syria help them
32 13 have the gods of any nations and lands
14 who is there among all the gods of the
17 as the gods of other nations could not
19 against the gods of the people of the
Jdth 3 13 to destroy all the gods of the earth
5 7 would not follow gods of their fathers
8 consisted in the worship of many gods
Esth 14 12 give me boldness, O Lord, king of gods
Ps 46 10 for the strong gods of the earth are
49 1 the God of gods, the Lord hath spoken
81 1 hath stood in the congregation of gods
1 in the midst of them he judgeth gods
6 I have said: you are gods and all of
83 8 the God of gods shall be seen in Sion
85 8 is none among the gods like unto thee
94 3 God, and a great King above all gods
95 4 he is to be feared above all gods. For
5 all the g. of the Gentiles are devils
96 9 art exalted exceedingly above all gods
134 5 is great, and our God is above all gods
135 2 praise ye the God of gods: for his
Wisd 12 24 holding those things for gods which are
27 very things which they took for gods
13 2 to be the gods that rule the world
3 being delighted, took them to be gods
10 called gods the works of hands of men
15 13 maketh brittle vessels and graven gods
15 all the idols of the heathens for gods
Isa 21 9 all the graven gods thereof are broken
36 18 have any of the gods of the nations
20 who is there among all the g. of these
37 12 have the gods of the nations delivered

19 into the fire, for they were not gods
41 23 and we shall know that ye are gods. Do
Jer 2 11 they are not gods: but my people have
28 where are the g. whom thou hast made
28 to the number of thy cities were thy g.
5 7 and swear by them that are not gods
10 11 the g. that have not made heaven and
11 12 shall go and cry to the gods to whom
13 the number of thy cities were thy gods
16 20 unto himself, and they are no gods
43 12 fire in the temples of the g. of Egypt
13 temples of the gods of Egypt he shall
44 3 offer sacrifice and worship other gods
8 by sacrificing to other gods in the land
15 their wives sacrificed to other gods
46 25 Egypt and upon her gods and upon her
48 35 places and that sacrificeth to his g.
Bar 6 3 you shall see in Babylon gods of gold
11 these gods cannot defend themselves
14 it known to you that they are not g.
22 you may know that they are no gods
28 they are not gods, fear them not. 64
29 how can they be called gods? Because
29 women set offerings before the gods
39 to be said, that they are gods. 44, 63
46 that are made by them be gods? But
49 how then can they be thought to be g.
50 shall be manifest that they are no g.
51 known that they are not gods, but the
54 upon the house of these gods of wood
55 supposed or admitted that they are g.
56 neither are these gods of wood and of
58 that are therein, than such false gods
68 manner of appearance that they are g.
71 you shall know that they are not gods
Dan 2 11 except the gods, whose conversation is
47 your God is the God of gods and Lord
3 12 they worship not thy gods nor do they
14 that you do not worship my gods nor
18 that we will not worship thy gods nor
90 bless the Lord the God of gods: praise
4 5 hath in him the spirit of the holy g.
6 hast in thee the spirit of the holy g.
15 the spirit of the holy gods is in thee
5 11 that hath the spirit of the holy gods
14 that thou hast the spirit of the gods
23 hast praised the gods of silver and of
6 12 a request to any of the gods or men
11 36 great things against the God of gods
37 he shall not regard any gods: for he
Osee 14 4 the works of our hands are our gods
Soph 2 11 shall consume all the gods of the earth
2 Ma 11 23 father being translated amongst the g.
John 10 34 in your law: I said you are gods
35 if he called them gods, to whom the
Acts 7 40 make us gods to go before us. For as
14 10 gods are come down to us in likeness
17 18 a setter forth of new gods because
19 26 are not gods which are made by hands
1 C 8 5 for there be gods many, and lords many
5 although there be that are called gods
Gal 4 8 served them, who, by nature, are not g.

strange gods Gen 35 2 cast away the s. g. that
Gen 35 4 they gave him all the s. g. they had
Exod 20 3 thou shalt not have s. g. Deut 5:7
23 13 by name of s. g. you shall not swear
Deut 6 14 you shall not go after the s. g. of
7 4 that he may rather serve strange gods
8 19 and follow s. g. and serve and adore
11 16 Lord, and serve s. g. and adore them
28 walk after s. g. which you know not
13 2 let us go and follow s. g. which thou
6 go and serve s. g. 13; 17:3; 1 K 26:19; 2 Pa 7:19
18 20 him to say, or in the name of s. g.
28 14 nor follow s. g. nor worship them
36 there thou shalt serve s. g. 64
29 26 have served s. g. and adored them
30 17 thou adore strange gods and serve them
31 16 will go a fornicating after s. g. in the
18 done because they have followed s. g.
20 they will turn away after strange gods
32 16 they provoked him by strange gods
Josu 23 16 and shall have served strange gods
24 2 and they served strange gods. And I
16 leave the Lord, and serve strange gods
20 if you . . serve strange gods, he will
23 put away strange gods from among you
Judg 2 12 they followed s. g. and the gods of
17 committing fornication with s. g. and
19 following s. g., serving them, and
10 13 and have worshipped s. g.: therefore
16 cast away of their coasts all the idols of s. g.
1 K 7 3 put away the s. g. from among you
8 8 have forsaken me and served s. g.
3 K 9 6 but will go and worship strange gods
9 followed strange gods and adored them
11 4 turned away by women to follow s. g.
10 that he should not follow s. g.: but he
14 9 hast made thee s. g. and molten gods
4 K 17 7 of Egypt, and they worshipped s. g.
35 you shall not fear s. g. nor. 37
38 neither shall ye worship s. g., but fear
22 17 have sacrificed to s. g., provoking me
2 Pa 7 22 land of Egypt, and laid hold on s. g.
33 15 he took away the s. g. and the idol
34 25 have sacrificed to s. g. to provoke me
Jdth 8 18 worshipped s. g. For which crime
Jer 1 16 sacrificed to s. g. and have adored
7 6 walk not after s. g. to your own hurt
9 to go after s. g. which you know not
18 to offer libations to strange gods and
11 10 have gone after strange gods. 13:10
16 11 went after strange gods and served them
13 there you shall serve s. g. day and
19 4 have sacrificed therein to s. g. whom
13 out drink offerings to s. g. 32:29
22 9 have adored s. g. and served them
25 6 go not after strange g. to serve them
35 15 follow not s. g. nor worship them
44 5 and not to sacrifice to strange gods
Bar 1 22 to serve strange gods and to do evil
Osee 3 1 they look to s. g. and love the husks

their gods Exod 23 24 thou shalt not adore t. g.
Exod 23 32 league with them nor with their gods
33 sin against me, if thou serve their gods
34 16 to commit fornication with their gods
Num 25 2 they ate of them and adored their g.
33 4 upon their gods also he had executed
Deut 7 16 neither shalt thou serve their gods lest
12 2 worshipped their gods upon high
30 these nations have worshipped their g.
31 done to their g. all the abominations
20 18 which they have done to their gods
32 31 for our God is not as their gods: our
37 where are t. g. in whom they trusted
Josu 23 7 should swear by the name of their g.
Judg 2 3 their gods may be your ruin. And when
3 6 their sons, and they served their gods
2 K 7 23 Egypt, from the nations and their gods
3 K 11 2 away your heart to follow their gods
8 and offered sacrifice to their gods
20 23 their gods are gods of the hills
4 K 17 33 served also their own gods according

19 18 cast their g. into the fire. Isa 37:19
1 Pa 14 12 they left there their gods, and David
Esth 14 7 for we have worshipped their gods
Jer 2 11 if a nation hath changed their gods
Bar 6 9 their g. have golden crowns upon their
10 of the harlots, they adorn their gods
15 becometh useless, even so are their g.
31 they roar and cry before their gods
38 their gods, of wood and of stone
41 their gods themselves have no sense
69 so are their gods of wood and of silver
70 their gods of wood, and laid over with
Dan 5 4 and praised their gods of gold and of
11 8 away captive into Egypt their gods
1 Ma 5 68 he burnt the statues of their gods
Gog 1 Pa 5 4 Gog his son, Semei his son
Eze 38 3 I come against thee, O Gog. 39:1
14 say to Gog: Thus saith the Lord God
16 I shall be sanctified in thee, O Gog
18 in the day of the coming of Gog upon
39 1 prophesy against Gog, and say: Thus
11 I will give Gog a noted place for a
11 there shall they bury Gog and all his
11 valley of the multitude of Gog. 15
Apoc 20 7 of the earth, Gog and Magog, and shall
goings Josu 15 7 the g. out thereof shall be at
Josu 16 8 g. out thereof are at most salt sea
Ps 16 5 perfect thou my goings in thy paths
67 25 seen thy g., O God, the g. of my God
143 13 young, abounding in their g. forth
Eze 43 11 the goings out and the comings in and
44 5 with all the g. out of the sanctuary
48 30 these are the goings out of the city
Golan Deut 4 43 Golan in Basan, which is in
gold Gen 2 11 Hevilath, where gold groweth
Gen 2 12 the gold of that land is very good
13 2 [Abram] rich in possession of gold
24 35 him sheep and oxen, silver and gold
41 42 put a chain of gold about his neck
44 8 out of thy lord's house gold or silver
Exod 20 23 nor . . . make to yourselves gods of gold
25 3 things you must take: gold and silver
11 overlay it with the purest gold. 24; 30:3
13 shalt overlay them with gold. 28; 30:5
17 make a propitiatory of the purest gold
18 make also two cherubims of beaten gold
29 prepare also dishes . . . of the purest g.
31 candlestick . . . of the finest gold
36 bowls and the branches . . . of purest gold
38 the snuffers also . . . of the purest gold
39 shall be a talent of purest gold
26 29 thou shalt overlay with gold and shalt
32 pillars shall have heads of gold
32 four pillars . . . be overlaid with gold
37 overlay with gold five pillars of setim
37 their heads shall be of gold and the
28 5 they shall take gold and violet and
6 they shall make the ephod of gold
8 variety of the work shall be of gold
11 with the names . . . set in gold and
13 thou shalt make also hooks of gold
14 two little chains of the purest gold
15 make the rational . . . of gold
20 they shall be set in gold by their rows
22 on the rational chains . . . purest gold
36 make also a plate of the purest gold
30 3 thou shalt make to it a crown of gold
31 4 artificially made of gold and silver
32 24 which of you hath any gold? And
31 have made to themselves gods of gold
35 5 offer them to the Lord: gold and silver
22 every vessel of gold was set aside
32 to devise and to work in gold and
36 34 the board works . . . overlaid with gold
36 pillars . . . he overlaid with gold
38 five pillars . . . covered with gold
37 1 he overlaid it with the purest gold. 26
2 he made to it a crown of gold. 27
4 bars . . . which he overlaid with gold
6 made the propitiatory . . . of the purest g.
7 two cherubims also of beaten gold
11 overlaid it with the finest g. 3 K 10:18
12 he made a polished crown of gold
15 overlaid them with gold. 2 Pa 3:10
16 and cups and censers of pure gold
17 made the candlestick of the finest gold
22 all beaten work of the purest gold
23 the seven lamps . . . of the purest gold
24 thereof weighed a talent of gold
38 24 all the gold that was spent in the
39 2 he made an ephod of gold, violet, and
6 onyx stones, fast set and closed in gold
8 he made a rational . . . of gold, violet
13 set and enclosed in gold by their rows
15 little chains . . . of the purest gold
23 little bells of the purest gold
24 a bell of gold and a pomegranate
29 sacred veneration of the purest gold
37 the altar of gold and the ointment
40 5 the altar of gold whereon the incense
24 altar of gold under the roof of the
Lev 8 9 forehead he put the plate of gold
Num 7 14 mortar of ten sicles of gold
20 a little mortar of gold. 26, 32, 38, 44, 50, 56, 62, 68, 74, 80
84 twelve little mortars of gold. 86
86 that is, in all 120 sicles of gold
8 4 candlestick . . . was of beaten gold
24 13 me his house full of silver and gold. 18
31 22 gold . . . shall be purified by fire
50 what gold every one of us could find
51 received all the gold in divers kinds
Deut 1 1 where there is very much gold
7 25 shalt not covet the silver and gold
8 13 shalt have . . . plenty of gold and of
17 17 not have . . . immense sums of silver and g.
29 17 idols, wood and stone, silver and gold
Josu 6 19 whatsoever gold or silver there shall
24 except the gold and silver, and vessels
22 8 to your settlements, with silver and gold
Judg 8 26 earlets . . . was 1,700 sicles of gold
2 K 1 24 gave ornaments of gold for your attire
8 7 and David took the arms of gold which
11 silver and gold that he had dedicated
12 30 weight of which was a talent of gold
21 4 have no contest about silver and gold
3 K 6 20 and overlaid it with most pure gold
21 overlaid with most pure gold and fastened on the plates with nails of gold
22 that was not covered with gold
22 of the oracle he covered also with gold
28 he overlaid the cherubims with gold
30 floor . . . he also overlaid with gold
32 and he overlaid them with gold: and he
32 trees and the other things with gold
7 48 altar of gold and the table of gold
49 golden candlesticks . . . of pure gold
49 and the lamps over them of gold: and
50 mortars and censers of most pure gold
50 hinges for the doors . . . were of gold
51 brought in . . . the silver and the gold
9 11 furnishing Solomon with . . . gold
10 2 immense quantity of gold and precious
11 Hiram, which brought gold from Ophir
14 weight of the gold that was brought
16 made 200 shields of the purest gold

16 allowed 600 sicles of gold for the
17 and three hundred targets of fine gold
17 three hundred pounds of gold covering
21 all the vessels . . . were of gold: and
21 furniture . . . was of most pure gold
22 brought from thence gold and silver
14 26 shields of gold which Solomon had made
15 15 he brought in . . . silver and gold and
18 then Asa took all the silver and gold
19 sent thee presents of silver and gold
20 3 thy silver and thy gold is mine: and
5 silver and thy gold . . . thou shalt
7 he sent . . . for my silver and gold: and
22 49 on the sea to sail into Ophir for gold
4 K 5 5 took . . . six thousand pieces of gold
7 8 they took from thence silver and gold
12 13 not made . . . any vessel of gold and
14 14 took all the gold and silver. 2 Pa 25:24
16 8 gathered together the silver and gold
20 13 showed them . . . the gold and the silver
23 33 set a fine of . . . a talent of gold
35 Joakim gave the silver and the gold
35 exacted both the silver and the gold
25 15 such as were of gold in gold, and such
1 Pa 18 11 and gold which he had taken from all
20 2 found in it a talent weight of gold
21 25 so David gave . . . 600 sicles of gold
22 14 the charges . . . of gold 100,000 talents
16 skilful in their work, in gold and in
28 14 gold by weight for every vessel for
15 also gold for the golden candlesticks
16 also g. for the tables of proposition
17 and bowls and censers of fine gold, and for little lions of gold
18 altar of incense, he gave purest g.
29 2 gold for vessels of gold, and silver
3 gold and silver for the temple of my
4 talents of gold of the gold of Ophir
5 gold for wheresoever . . . need of gold
7 they gave . . . of gold 5,000 talents
2 Pa 1 15 the king made silver and gold to be
2 7 that knoweth how to work in gold. 14
3 4 he overlaid it within with pure gold
5 overlaid them with plates of fine gold
7 gold of the plates . . . of the finest
9 he made also nails of gold, and the
9 chambers also he overlaid with gold
4 8 also a hundred bowls of gold. He made
20 candlesticks also of most pure gold
21 all were made of the finest gold
22 bowls and the mortars, of pure gold
22 doors of temple without were of gold
5 1 had vowed, the silver and the gold
9 1 carried spices and abundance of gold
10 brought gold from Ophir, and thyine
13 weight of the gold that was brought
14 who brought gold and silver to Solomon
15 the sum of six hundred pieces of gold
16 golden shields of 300 pieces of gold
17 ivory and overlaid it with pure gold
18 to the throne, and a footstool of gold
20 vessels of king's table were of gold
20 of Libanus were of the purest gold
21 they brought thence gold and silver
15 18 into house of the Lord, g. and silver
16 2 then Asa brought out silver and gold
3 I have sent thee silver and gold that
21 3 them great gifts of silver and of gold
32 27 great treasures of silver and of gold
36 3 condemned the land . . . talent of gold
1 Es 1 4 help him . . . with silver and gold and
6 hands with vessels of silver and gold
9 number of them: thirty bowls of gold
9 and twenty knives, thirty cups of gold
2 69 they gave . . . 61,000 solids of gold
7 15 to carry the silver and gold which the
16 silver and gold that thou shalt find
18 with the rest of the silver and gold
8 25 I weighed unto them the silver and gold
27 I weighed . . . twenty cups of gold of a
27 best shining brass, beautiful as gold
28 and the silver and gold that is freely
30 received weight of the silver and gold
33 silver and the gold . . . were weighed
2 Es 7 70 treasure a thousand drams of gold
71 gave . . . 20,000 drams of gold and
72 people gave, was 20,000 drams of gold
Tob 12 8 more than to lay up treasures of gold
Jdth 2 10 but gold and silver he took out of the
10 19 which was woven of purple and gold
15 14 they gave to Judith in gold and silver
Esth 1 6 the beds also were of gold and silver
15 9 he sat . . . glittering with gold and
Job 3 15 or with princes, that possess gold
22 24 give . . . for flint torrents of gold
23 10 as gold that passeth through the fire
28 1 gold hath a place wherein it is melted
6 sapphires, and the clods of it are gold
15 the finest gold shall not purchase it
17 gold or crystal cannot equal it
31 24 if I have thought gold my strength
24 have said to fine gold: My confidence
41 21 shall strew gold under him like mire
42 11 man gave him . . . one earring of gold
Ps 18 11 more to be desired than gold and
67 14 of her back with the paleness of gold
71 15 shall be given of the gold of Arabia
104 37 brought them out with silver and gold
113 4 idols of Gentiles are silver and gold
118 72 above thousands of gold and silver
127 I loved thy commandments above gold
134 15 idols of the Gentiles are silver and g.
Prov 1 9 head, and a chain of gold to thy neck
3 14 fruit than the chiefest and purest gold
8 10 choose knowledge rather than gold
19 my fruit is better than gold and the
12 27 of a just man shall be precious gold
16 16 wisdom, because it is better than gold
17 3 tried by fire, and gold in the furnace
20 15 is gold and a multitude of jewels
22 1 good favor is above silver and gold
25 11 like apples of gold on beds of silver
27 21 firing-pot and gold in the furnace
Ecce 2 8 together for myself silver and gold
Cant 1 10 we will make thee chains of gold
3 10 the seat of gold, the going up of purple
5 11 his head is as the finest gold: his
14 his hands are turned and as of gold
15 marble that are set upon bases of gold
Wisd 3 6 as gold in the furnace he hath proved
7 9 all gold in comparison of her is as a
13 10 of the hands of men, gold and silver
Eccu 2 5 gold and silver are tried in the fire
6 15 no weight of gold and silver is able
7 20 thy dear brother for the sake of gold
21 the grace of her modesty is above gold
8 3 gold and silver hath destroyed many
14 3 what should an envious man do with gold
21 24 learning . . . is as an ornament of gold
28 29 melt down thy gold and silver and
29 14 shall bring thee more profit than gold
30 15 is better than all gold and silver
31 5 that loveth g. shall not be justified
6 many have been brought to fall for gold
7 gold is a stumblingblock to them that
8 that hath not gone after gold nor put

32 7 of wine is as a carbuncle set in gold
8 signet of an emerald in a work of gold
40 25 gold and silver make the feet stand
45 10 with many little bells of gold all
12 he gave him a holy robe of gold and
13 precious stones cut and set in gold
14 and a crown of gold upon his miter
47 20 thou didst gather gold as copper and
50 10 as a massy vessel of gold, adorned
51 36 and possess abundance of gold by her
Isa 2 7 land is filled with silver and gold
20 shall cast away . . . his idols of gold
13 12 a man shall be more precious than gold, yea a man than the finest of gold
17 shall not seek silver nor desire gold
30 22 garment of thy molten things of gold
31 7 shall cast away . . . his idols of gold
39 2 the storehouses . . . of the gold and of
40 19 hath the goldsmithy formed it with gold
46 6 that contribute gold out of the bag
60 6 come, bringing gold and frankincense
9 their silver and their gold with them
17 for brass I will bring gold, and for
Jer 4 30 deckest thyself with ornaments of gold
10 4 he hath decked it with silver and gold
9 from Tharsis, and gold from Ophaz
52 19 and as many as were of gold, in gold
Lam 4 1 how is the gold become dim, the finest
2 that were clothed with the best gold
Bar 3 18 that hoard up silver and gold wherein
30 brought her preferable to chosen gold
6 3 you shall see in Babylon gods of gold
7 laid over with gold and silver
8 so do they take gold and make them up
9 convey away from them gold and silver
23 the gold also which they have, is for
29 offerings before the gods . . . of gold
38 their gods . . . of gold and of silver
50 but of wood, and laid over with gold
54 the house of these gods . . . of gold
56 gods of wood . . . laid over with gold
57 take from them the gold and silver
69 gods of wood . . . laid over with gold. 70
Eze 7 19 and their gold shall become a dunghill
19 their gold shall not be able to deliver
16 13 thou wast adorned with gold and silver
17 thy beautiful vessels, of my gold and
27 22 spices and precious stones and gold
28 4 gold and silver into thy treasures
13 emerald: gold the work of thy beauty
38 13 to take a prey, to take silver and gold
Dan 2 32 head of this statue was of fine gold
35 silver and the gold broken to pieces
38 thou therefore art the head of gold
45 broke in pieces . . . silver and the gold
3 1 Nabuchodonosor made a statue of gold
5 4 praised their gods of g. and of silver
16 have a chain of gold about thy neck
23 praised the gods of silver and of gold
29 chain of gold was put about his neck
10 5 loins were girded with the finest gold
11 38 he shall worship with gold and silver
43 have power over the treasures of gold
Osee 2 8 and multiplied her silver and gold
8 4 and their gold they have made idols
Joel 3 5 have taken away my silver and my gold
Nah 2 9 the silver, take the spoil of the gold
Haba 2 19 it is laid over with gold and silver
Soph 1 18 and their gold be able to deliver
Agge 2 9 silver is mine, and the gold is mine
Zach 4 2 behold a candlestick all of gold and
12 beaks in which are the funnels of gold
6 11 thou shalt take gold and silver: and
9 3 and gold as the mire of the streets
13 9 and I will try them as gold is tried
14 14 be gathered together, gold and silver
Mala 3 3 refine them as gold and as silver
1 Ma 1 23 the vials and the little mortars of gold
24 he took the silver and gold and the
2 18 enriched with gold and silver and many
3 41 they took silver and gold in abundance
4 23 and they got much gold and silver
57 front of the temple with crowns of gold
6 1 and abounding in silver and gold
2 coverings of gold, and breastplates
12 away all the spoils of gold and of silver
39 when sun shone upon the shields of gold
8 3 mines of silver and of gold that are
10 20 and he sent him . . . a crown of gold
60 and he gave them much silver and gold
89 he sent him a buckle of gold, as the
11 24 he took gold and silver and raiment
58 sent him vessels of g. for his service
58 and he gave him leave to drink in gold
14 24 to Rome with a great shield of gold
43 should be clothed with purple and gold
44 purple, or to wear a buckle of gold
15 18 and they brought also a shield of gold
26 Simon sent . . . silver also and gold
32 his magnificence in gold and silver
16 11 he had abundance of silver and gold
19 that he would give them silver and gold
2 Ma 2 2 seeing the idols of gold and silver
3 11 400 talents of silver and 200 of gold
25 upon him seemed to have armor of gold
4 39 quantity of gold being already carried
14 4 presenting unto him a crown of gold
15 15 gave to Judas a sword of gold, saying
Mat 2 11 gifts; gold, frankincense, and myrrh
10 9 do not possess gold nor silver nor
23 16 shall swear by the gold of the temple
17 whether is greater, the gold or the
17 the temple that sanctifieth the gold
Acts 3 6 silver and gold I have none; but what
17 29 suppose the divinity to be like unto g.
20 33 I have not coveted any man's silver, g.
1 C 3 12 build upon this foundation, gold, silver
1 Tim 2 9 not with plaited hair, or g., or pearls
2 Tim 2 20 not only vessels of gold and of silver
Heb 9 4 covered about on every part with gold
James 5 3 your gold and silver is cankered: and
1 P 1 7 faith, much more precious than gold
18 with corruptible things as gold or
3 3 or the wearing of gold or the putting
Apoc 3 18 to buy of me gold fire tried, that thou
4 4 and on their heads were crowns of gold
9 7 on their heads . . . crowns like gold
20 not adore devils and idols of gold
14 14 having on his head a crown of gold
17 4 gilt with gold and precious stones. 18:16
18 12 merchandise of gold and silver and
21 15 had a measure of a reed of gold to
18 city itself pure gold, like to clear
21 the street of the city was pure gold

plates of gold; ***see*** **plates**
rings of gold; ***see*** **rings**
talents of gold; ***see*** **talents**
vessels of gold; ***see*** **vessels**
vessels of silver and gold; ***see*** **vessels**

golden Gen 24 22 the man took out g. earrings
Exod 25 11 over it thou shalt make a golden crown
12 four g. rings, which thou shalt put
24 thou shalt make to it a golden ledge
25 over the same another little g. crown
26 shalt prepare also four golden rings
27 under the crown shall the golden rings

28 24 the golden chains thou shalt join to
34 shall be a g. bell and a pomegranate
34 another golden bell and a pomegranate
32 2 take the golden earrings from the ears
37 11 he made to it a golden ledge round
12 and upon the same another golden crown
27 two golden rings under the crown at
39 17 the two golden chains should hang
Num 4 11 they shall wrap up the golden altar
Josu 7 21 a g. rule of fifty sicles: and I coveted
24 and the garments and the golden rule
Judg 8 24 were accustomed to wear golden earlets
26 besides the golden chains that were
1 K 6 5 make five g. emerods and five g. mice
11 box that had in it the golden mice
17 these are the golden emerods which
18 the g. mice according to the number
3 K 6 35 and he overlaid all with golden plates
7 49 the g. candlesticks, five on the right
49 over them of gold: and golden snuffers
12 28 he [Jeroboam] made two golden calves
4 K 10 29 nor did he forsake the golden calves
1 Pa 18 7 David took the golden quivers which the
28 15 gave also gold for the g. candlesticks
2 Pa 4 7 and he made ten golden candlesticks
19 the golden altar and the tables, upon
21 flowers and lamps and golden tongs: all
9 15 king Solomon made 200 golden spears
16 300 g. shields of 300 pieces of gold
12 9 the g. shields that Solomon had made
13 8 golden calves, which Jeroboam hath made
11 there is with us the golden candlestick
1 Es 6 5 let the g. and silver vessels of the
Tob 1 5 when all went to the g. calves which
Ps 44 14 is within in golden borders, clothed
Prov 11 22 a g. ring in a swine's snout, a woman
Ecce 12 6 the golden fillet shrink back and the
Eccu 26 23 golden pillars upon bases of silver
Jer 51 7 Babylon hath been a golden cup in the
Bar 6 9 their gods have g. crowns upon their
Dan 3 7 adored the golden statue which king
10 adore the golden statue. 12, 14, 18
5 3 the golden and silver vessels brought
7 shall have a golden chain on his neck
Zach 4 12 that are by the two golden beaks in
1 Ma 1 23 took away the golden altar and the
23 golden ornament that was before the
11 58 purple, and to wear a golden buckle
13 37 the golden crown and the palm which
2 Ma 10 29 upon horses, comely with g. bridles
11 8 them in white clothing, with g. armor
Heb 9 4 having a golden censer, and the ark of
4 was a golden pot that had manna, and the
James 2 2 a man having a golden ring, in fine
Apoc 1 12 I saw seven golden candlesticks: and
13 midst of the seven golden candlesticks
13 girt about the paps with a g. girdle
20 and the seven golden candlesticks. The
2 1 the midst of the 7 golden candlesticks
5 8 golden vials full of odors, which are
8 3 before the altar, having a g. censer
3 prayers of all saints upon g. altar
9 13 from the four horns of the golden altar
15 6 girt about the breasts with g. girdles
7 golden vials full of the wrath of God
17 4 having a golden cup in her hand, full
21 16 he measured the city with the g. reed
goldsmith 2 Es 3 8 the son of Araia the goldsmith
Isa 40 19 hath the goldsmith formed it with gold
46 6 and hire a goldsmith to make a god
goldsmith's 2 Es 3 30 Melcias the g. son built
goldsmiths 2 Es 3 31 g. and the merchants built
Wisd 15 9 he striveth with the goldsmiths and

Bar 6 45 they are made by workmen and by g.
Golgotha Mat 27 33 the place that is called G.
Mark 15 22 him into the place called Golgotha
John 19 17 Calvary, but in Hebrew Golgotha
Goliath 1 K 17 4 of the Philistines, named G.
1 K 17 23 baseborn man whose name was Goliath
21 9 here is the sword of Goliath the
22 10 and gave him the sword of Goliath the
2 K 21 19 an embroiderer of Bethlehem slew G.
1 Pa 20 5 slew the brother of G. the Gethite
Ps 143 1 a psalm of David against Goliath
Eccu 47 5 he beat down the boasting of Goliath
Gomer Gen 10 2 sons of Japheth: Gomer. 1 Pa 1:5
Gen 10 3 the sons of Gomer: Ascenez. 1 Pa 1:6
Eze 38 6 Gomer and all his bands, the house of
Osee 1 3 took Gomer the daughter of Debelaim
gomor Exod 16 16 eat: a gomor for every man
Exod 16 18 they measured by the measure of a g.
32 fill a gomor of it and let it be kept
33 into it, as much as a gomor can hold
36 a gomor is the tenth part of an ephi
Gomorrha Gen 10 19 until thou enter Sodom and G.
Gen 13 10 before the Lord destroyed Sodom and G.
14 2 and against Bersa king of Gomorrha
8 king of Sodom and the king of G.
10 and the king of G. turned their backs
18 20 the cry of Sodom and G. is multiplied
19 24 Lord rained upon Sodom and Gomorrha
28 he looked towards Sodom and Gomorrha
Deut 29 23 example of destruction of Sodom and G.
32 32 of Sodom and of the suburbs of G.
Isa 1 9 we should have been like to Gomorrha
10 law of our God, ye people of Gomorrha
13 19 as the Lord destroyed Sodom and G.
Jer 23 14 the inhabitants thereof as Gomorrha
49 18 as Sodom was overthrown and Gomorrha
50 40 as the Lord overthrew Sodom and G.
Amos 4 11 as God destroyed Sodom and Gomorrha
Soph 2 9 the children of Ammon [shall be] as G.
Mat 10 15 for the land of Sodom and Gomorrha in
Rom 9 29 and we had been like unto Gomorrha. What
Jude 7 as Sodom and G. and the neighboring
Gomorrhites Gen 14 11 the substance of the . . . G.
2 P 2 6 cities of the Sodomites and of the G.
gomors Exod 16 22 that is, two gomors every man
good Mat 5 13 it is good for nothing any more
Mat 5 45 his sun to rise upon the good and bad
7 11 know how to give good gifts to your
17 every g. tree bringeth forth g. fruit
18 a good tree cannot bring forth evil
9 2 be of good heart, son, thy sins are
22 be of good heart, daughter, thy faith
11 26 so hath it seemed good in thy sight
12 12 it is lawful to do a good deed on the
33 make the tree good and its fruit good
35 a good man out of a good treasure
13 24 man that sowed good seed in his field
27 didst thou not sow good seed in thy
37 he that soweth the good seed, is the
38 the good seed are the children of the
45 like to a merchant seeking good pearls
48 they chose out the good into vessels
14 27 good heart: it is I. Mark 6:50
15 26 it is not good to take the bread of
17 4 it is good for us to be here. Mark 9:4; Luke 9:33
19 16 good master, what good shall I do that
17 why askest thou me concerning good
17 one is good, God. But if thou wilt
20 15 is thy eye evil, because I am good
22 10 all that they found, both bad and good
25 21 well done, good and faithful servant. 23
Mark 7 27 it is not good to take the bread of

9 49 salt is good. But if the salt become
10 17 good Master, what shall I do that I
18 why callest thou me good? None is good but one, that is God
Luke 1 3 it seemed good to me also, having
19 and to bring thee these good tidings
2 10 I bring you good tidings of great joy
14 on earth peace to men of good will
6 38 good measure and pressed down and
45 bringeth forth that which is good
8 15 they who in a good and perfect heart
10 21 so it hath seemed good in thy sight
11 13 know how to give good gifts to your
13 give the good Spirit to them that ask
12 19 rest; eat, drink, make good cheer
14 34 salt is good. But if the salt shall
18 18 good master, what shall I do to
19 why dost thou call me good? None is good but God alone
19 17 well done, thou good servant, because
John 1 46 can anything of good come from Nazareth
2 10 at first setteth forth good wine, and
10 thou hast kept the good wine until now
10 11 I am the good shepherd. The good shepherd giveth his life
14 I am the good shepherd; and I know
Acts 4 9 the good deed done to the infirm man
6 3 seven men of good reputation, full of
10 22 having good testimony from all nation
38 who went about doing good, and healing
14 16 doing good from heaven, giving rains
15 25 hath seemed g. to us, being assembled
28 it hath seemed good to the Holy Ghost
34 it seemed good unto Silas to remain
16 2 and Iconium, gave a good testimony. Him
24 10 I will with g. courage answer for myself
27 22 now I exhort you to be of good cheer
25 sirs, be of good cheer; for I believe
Rom 2 10 peace to every one that worketh good
3 8 do evil, that there may come good? whose
12 there is none that doth good, there is
7 12 the commandment holy and just and good
13 which is good, made death unto me? God
13 that which is good, wrought death in me
15 for I do not that good which I will; but
16 I consent to the law, that it is good
18 to say, in my flesh, that which is good
18 accomplish that which is g., I find not
19 for the good which I will, I do not; but
8 28 all things work together unto good, to
9 11 yet born, nor had done any good or evil
11 24 were grafted into the good olive tree
12 2 that you may prove what is the good and
9 is evil, cleaving to that which is good
21 by evil, but overcome evil by good. Let
13 3 do that which is good: and thou shalt
4 he is God's minister to thee, for good
14 16 let not then our g. be evil spoken of
21 it is good not to eat flesh, and not to
15 2 of you please his neighbor unto good, to
16 18 and by pleasing speeches and good words
19 but I would have you to be wise in good
1 C 5 6 your glorying is not good. Know you
7 1 it is good for a man not to touch woman
8 it is good for them if they so continue
26 that this is good for present necessity
26 that it is good for a man so to be. Art
9 15 it is good for me to die, rather than
15 33 evil communications corrupt g. manners
2 C 2 15 we are the good odor of Christ unto God
5 8 have a good will to be absent rather
10 he hath done, whether it be good or evil
6 8 dishonor, by evil report and good report
8 8 approving also the good disposition of
21 for we forecast what may be good not
13 7 but that you may do that which is good
Gal 4 18 but be zealous for that which is good
18 that which is good in good thing always
6 9 and in doing good, let us not fail. For
10 time, let us work good to all men, but
Eph 1 9 according to his good pleasure, which he
4 28 with his hands the thing which is good
29 that which is good, to the edification
6 7 with a good will serving, as to the Lord
8 whatsoever good thing any man shall do
Phil 1 15 some also for good will preach Christ
2 13 to accomplish, according to his g. will
19 that I also may be of good comfort, when
4 8 whatsoever of good fame, if there be
1 Th 3 1 we thought it good to remain at Athens
6 you have a good remembrance of us always
5 15 ever follow that which is good towards
21 all things; hold fast that which is good
2 Th 1 11 all the good pleasure of his goodness
2 15 consolation, and good hope in grace
1 Tim 1 8 we know that the law is good, if a man
18 that thou war in them a good warfare
2 3 this is good and acceptable in the sight
3 2 prudent, of good behavior, chaste, given
7 he must have a good testimony of them
13 purchase to themselves a good degree
4 4 for every creature of God is good, and
6 thou shalt be a good minister of Christ
6 of faith, and of the good doctrine which
5 25 also good deeds are manifest: and they
6 12 fight the good fight of faith: lay hold
12 hast confessed a good confession before
13 under Pontius Pilate, a good confession
19 good foundation against the time to come
2 Tim 1 14 keep the g. thing committed to thy trust
2 3 labor as a good soldier of Christ Jesus
4 7 I have fought a good fight, I have
Titus 2 10 in all things showing good fidelity
3 8 these things are good and profitable
Philem 14 that thy good deed might not be as it
Heb 6 5 have moreover tasted the good word of
11 12 from one, and him as good as dead, as
James 2 7 do not they blaspheme the good name
3 13 let him show by a good conversation
17 consenting to the good, full of mercy
17 full of mercy and good fruits, without
1 P 2 12 your conversation g. among the Gentiles
14 and for the praise of the good: for so
18 not only to the good and gentle, but
3 10 that will love life and see good days
13 hurt you if you be zealous of good
16 falsely accuse your good conversation
4 10 as good stewards of the manifold grace
19 commend their souls in good deeds to
3 J 11 which is evil, but that which is good
11 he that doth good, is of God: he that

do good Mat 5 44 do good to them that hate you. Luke 6:27
Mark 3 4 is it lawful to do good on the sabbath
14 7 you will, you may do them good: but
Luke 6 9 on the sabbath days, to do good or to
33 if you do good to them who do good to
35 do good, and lend, hoping for nothing
Rom 7 21 that when I have a will to do good, evil
Heb 13 16 not forget to do good and to impart
James 4 17 knoweth to do good, and doth it not
1 P 3 11 let him decline from evil and do good

good conscience; *see* **conscience**
good fruit; *see* **fruit**
good ground; *see* **ground**
good man 2 K 18 27 he is a g m. and cometh with

3 K 1 52 if he be a good man, there shall not so
Prov 13 22 the good man leaveth heirs, sons and
14 14 and the good man shall be above him
Mat 12 35 a good man out of a good treasure
Luke 6 45 a good man out of the good treasure
23 50 a counsellor, a good and a just man
John 7 12 some said: He is a good man. And
Acts 11 24 for he was a good man, and full of
Rom 5 7 yet perhaps for a good man some one
good things Gen 45 18 you all the g. t. of Egypt
Exod 18 9 Jethro rejoiced for all the g. things
Num 10 29 Lord hath promised g. things to Israel
Deut 26 11 shalt feast in all the good things
30 9 to rejoice over thee in all good things
Judg 8 35 according to all the g. things he had
1 K 19 4 Jonathan spoke good things of David
24 19 what good things thou hast done to me
2 K 7 28 spoken to thy servant these good things
3 K 8 56 all the good things that he promised
66 good things that the Lord had done
22 13 mouth declare good things to the king
4 K 8 9 and all the good things of Damascus
2 Pa 6 41 and thy saints rejoice in good things
19 11 Lord will be with you in good things
1 Es 9 12 may eat the good things of the land
2 Es 9 36 the bread thereof and the good things
Tob 4 23 we shall have many good things if we
7 6 was speaking many good things of him
11 20 good things that God had done for him
12 3 filled with all g. things through him
13 12 give glory to the Lord for thy good t.
Job 2 10 if we have received good things at the
21 16 their g. things are not in their hand
22 18 had filled their houses with g. things
30 26 I expected good things, and evils are
Ps 4 6 many say, Who showeth us good things
12 6 to the Lord, who giveth me good things
24 13 his soul shall dwell in good things
26 13 I believe to see the good things of
38 3 kept silence from good things: and my
64 5 filled with the g. things of thy house
83 13 he will not deprive of good things
102 5 satisfieth thy desire with good things
106 9 filled the hungry soul with g. things
127 5 thou see the good things of Jerusalem
Prov 11 27 he rise early who seeketh good things
12 14 a man be filled with good things. 13:2
14 22 mercy and truth prepare good things
16 20 learned in word shall find good things
19 8 keepeth prudence shall find g. things
Ecce 2 1 I will go . . . and enjoy good things
24 to show his soul good things of his
4 8 and defraud my soul of good things
6 6 hath not enjoyed good things: do not
7 15 in the good day enjoy good things and
9 18 offend in one, shall lose many g. t.
Wisd 2 6 let us enjoy the good things that are
4 12 bewitching of vanity obscureth good t.
8 9 will communicate to me of her good t.
10 8 that they were ignorant of good things
13 1 by these good things that are seen
Eccu 11 14 good things and evil, life and death
15 the ways of good things are with him
27 in the day of good things be not
27 be not unmindful of good things
30 18 good things that are hidden in a mouth
32 17 replenisheth thee with all his good t.
39 30 good things were created for the good
30 for the wicked, good and evil things
42 26 he hath established the good things
44 11 good things continue with their seed
45 31 their good t. might not be abolished
50 30 that is conversant in these g. things
Isa 1 19 shall eat the good things of the land
63 7 for the multitude of his good things
Jer 5 25 your sins have withholden good things
12 6 when they speak good things to thee
30 10 Jacob . . . abound with all good things
31 12 together to the g. things of the Lord
14 shall be filled with my good things
33 9 that shall hear of all the good things
9 and be troubled for all the g. things
Lam 3 17 peace, I have forgotten good things
Zach 1 17 my cities shall yet flow with g. t.
1 Ma 10 27 we will reward you with good things
14 9 treated together of the good things
2 Ma 5 20 shall communicate in the good things
Mat 7 11 give good things to them that ask him
12 34 how can you speak good things, whereas
35 bringeth forth good things: and an evil
Luke 1 53 hath filled the hungry with good things
16 25 receive good things in thy lifetime
John 5 29 they that have done good things shall
Rom 10 15 that bring glad tidings of good things
12 17 providing good things, not only in the
Gal 6 6 that instructeth him, in all good things
Heb 9 11 come an high priest of the good things
10 1 law having a shadow of the good things
good work; *see* **work**
good works; *see* **works**
no good 1 K 2 24 no good report that I hear
3 K 22 18 that he prophesieth no good to me
Job 24 21 to the widow he hath done no good
Prov 14 15 no good shall come to deceitful son
17 26 no good thing to do hurt to the just
19 2 no knowledge of soul, there is no good
Ecce 8 15 was no good for a man under the sun
Eccu 12 3 no good for him that is always occupied
20 14 gift of the fool shall do thee no good
38 22 and thou shalt do him no good, and
Jer 8 15 we looked for peace and no good came
14 19 looked for peace, and there is no good
Luke 6 43 no good tree that bringeth forth evil
Good-havens Acts 27 8 place, which is called G.
goodlier 1 K 9 2 a goodlier person than he
goodliest 1 K 8 16 your g. young men . . . he will
3 K 20 3 wives and thy g. children are mine
goodly Exod 2 2 seeing him a g. child, hid him
Exod 26 31 embroidered work and goodly variety
Num 18 30 if you offer all the g. and the better
Deut 3 25 and this goodly mountain and Libanus
4 22 shall pass and possess the goodly land
6 10 given thee great and goodly cities
18 thou mayst possess the goodly land
8 12 hast built goodly houses and dwelt in
1 K 9 2 was Saul, a choice and goodly man, and
4 K 3 19 every g. field you shall cover with
25 and they filled every goodly field
Job 40 5 glorious, and put on goodly garments
Ps 15 6 are fallen unto me in goodly places; for my inheritance is goodly to me
22 5 which inebriateth me, how goodly is it
Jer 3 19 the goodly inheritance of the armies
2 Ma 9 16 promiseth to adorn with goodly gifts
Luke 21 5 it was adorned with goodly stones and
Apoc 18 14 all fat and goodly things are perished
Goodlyman 1 Pa 7 18 sister named Queen bore G.
goodman Mat 10 25 if they have called the g. of the
Mat 13 27 servants of the goodman of the house
24 43 if the g. of the house knew at what
Luke 22 11 shall say to the goodman of the house
goodness 1 Es 8 22 all them that seek him in g.
2 Es 9 25 abounded with delight in thy great g.
35 their kingdoms, and in thy manifold g.
Esth 16 2 abused unto pride the g. of princes
10 with his cruelty staining our goodness

Ps 37 21 detracted me because I followed g.
51 5 hast loved malice more than goodness
64 12 the crown of the year of thy goodness
84 13 the Lord will give g.: and our earth
118 66 teach me goodness and discipline and
68 in thy g. teach me thy justifications
Wisd 1 1 think of the Lord in g. and seek
7 26 majesty, and the image of his g.
12 22 we judge we may think on thy g.
Eccu 6 15 to countervail the g. of his fidelity
45 29 in goodness and readiness of his soul
Bar 2 27 hast dealt . . . according to all thy g.
Osee 3 5 they shall fear the Lord, and his g.
2 Ma 6 13 it is a token of great goodness when
Rom 2 4 or despisest thou the riches of his g.
11 22 see then the g. and the severity of God
22 but towards thee, the goodness of God
22 if thou abide in goodness, otherwise
Gal 5 22 the fruit of the Spirit is . . . goodness
Eph 5 9 fruit of the light is in all goodness
2 Th 1 11 fulfil all the good pleasure of his g.
Titus 3 4 when the goodness and kindness of God
Heb 13 21 fit you in all goodness, that you may
goodness' Ps 24 7 thou me: for thy g. sake, O Lord
goods Gen 24 10 carrying something of all his g.
Gen 31 14 have we anything left among the goods
Exod 22 8 lay his hand upon his neighbor's goods
11 forth his hand to his neighbor's goods
Num 31 9 and all their cattle and all their goods
Deut 13 16 all the household goods that are there
28 11 will make thee abound with all goods
Josu 6 23 her brethren also and all her goods
7 11 and have hidden it among their goods
24 sheep, the tent also and all the goods
1 Pa 29 3 I give of my own proper goods, gold
1 Es 1 4 with silver and gold and goods and cattle
6 and gold, with goods and with beasts
7 26 confiscation of g. or at least to prison
2 Es 9 25 and possessed houses full of all goods
Tob 1 19 as he was able, out of his goods: he
Jdth 3 3 horses and camels and all our goods
15 14 the peculiar goods of Holofernes, they
Esth 3 13 and to make a spoil of their goods
9 10 not touch the spoils of their goods
16 and no man took any of their goods
Job 20 21 nothing shall continue of his goods
Ps 15 2 God, for thou hast no need of my g.
Prov 11 24 some distribute their own goods and
28 10 the upright shall possess his goods
Ecce 6 3 and his soul make no use of the goods
Eccu 5 10 be not anxious for g. unjustly gotten
11 19 and now I will eat of my goods alone
14 4 another will squander away his goods
5 he shall not take pleasure in his g.
16 30 the earth, and filled it with his goods
29 21 attributeth to himself g. of his surety
31 3 he shall be filled with his goods
11 therefore are his goods established
34 24 sacrifice of the goods of the poor
Eze 12 7 I brought forth my goods by day
7 as the goods of one that removeth
27 27 and thy pilots, who kept thy goods
38 13 and to carry away goods and substance
2 Ma 1 35 he gave the priests many g. and divers
Mat 12 29 house of the strong and rifle his goods
24 47 he shall place him over all his goods
25 14 servants and delivered to them his g.
Mark 3 27 and rob him of his goods, unless he
Luke 6 30 of him that taketh away thy goods
12 18 that are grown to me, and my goods
19 soul, thou hast much goods laid up
16 1 that he had wasted his goods. And he
17 31 and his goods in the house, let him
19 8 the half of my goods I give to the
Acts 2 45 their possessions and goods they sold
1 C 13 3 if I should distribute all my goods to
Heb 10 34 joy the being stripped of your own goods
gore Exod 21 28 if an ox gore a man or a woman
Exod 21 35 if one man's ox gore another man's ox
gored Exod 21 31 if he have gored a son or a
Gorgias 1 Ma 3 38 Nicanor and G., mighty men
1 Ma 4 1 then Gorgias took 5,000 men and
5 G. came by night into the camp of Judas
18 Gorgias and his army are near us in
20 G. saw that his men were put to flight
5 59 G. and his men went out of the city
2 Ma 8 9 also with him Gorgias, a good soldier
10 14 Gorgias, who was governor of the holds
12 32 after Pentecost they marched against G.
35 a valiant man, took hold of Gorgias
35 and so Gorgias escaped to Maresa. But
Gorgias' 2 Ma 12 37 he put G. soldiers to flight
Gortyna 1 Ma 15 23 were written to . . . Gortyna
Gosen Josu 10 41 land of Gosen even to Gabaon
Josu 11 16 land of Gosen and the plains and the
15 51 Gosen and Olon and Gilo: eleven
gospel Mat 4 23 preaching the gospel of the kingdom. 9:35; Mark 1:14
Mat 11 5 the poor have the gospel preached to
24 14 this gospel of the kingdom shall be
26 13 wheresoever this g. shall be preached
Mark 1 1 beginning of the gospel of Jesus Christ
15 at hand: repent and believe the gospel
8 35 for my sake and the gospel. 10:29
13 10 unto all nations the g. must first be
14 9 wheresoever this g. shall be preached
16 15 preach the gospel to every creature
Luke 4 18 to preach the gospel to the poor, he
7 22 to the poor the gospel is preached
9 6 preaching the gospel and healing
20 1 in the temple, and preaching the g.
Acts 8 25 preached the gospel to many countries
40 he preached the g. to all the cities
14 6 and were there preaching the gospel
20 when they had preached the g. to that
15 7 Gentiles should hear the word of the g.
16 10 God had called us to preach the gospel
20 24 to testify gospel of the grace of God
Rom 1 1 separated unto the gospel of God. Which
9 I serve . . . in the gospel of his Son
15 I am ready to preach the gospel to you
16 for I am not ashamed of the gospel. For
2 16 by Jesus Christ, according to my gospel
10 15 them that preach the gospel of peace
16 but all do not obey the gospel. For
11 28 as concerning the gospel, indeed, they
15 16 sanctifying the gospel of God, that the
20 and I have so preached this gospel, not
16 25 establish you, according to my gospel
1 C 1 17 not to baptize, but to preach the gospel
4 15 for in Christ Jesus, by the gospel, I
9 14 that they who preach the gospel, should
14 the gospel, should live by the gospel
16 if I preach the gospel, it is no glory
16 woe is unto me if I preach not gospel
18 preaching g., I may deliver the gospel
18 that I abuse not my power in the gospel
15 1 gospel which I preached to you, which
2 C 4 3 if our gospel be also hid, it is hid to
4 the light of gospel of glory of Christ
8 18 brother, whose praise is in the gospel
10 16 beyond you, to preach the gospel, not
11 4 another g. which you have not received
7 preached unto you gospel of God freely
Gal 1 6 the grace of Christ, unto another gospel
7 and would pervert the gospel of Christ

8 preach gospel to you besides that which
9 if anyone preach to you gospel, besides
11 the g. which was preached by me is not
2 2 and communicated to them the gospel
5 that truth of the gospel might continue
7 that to me was committed the gospel of
14 uprightly unto the truth of the gospel
4 13 I preached the gospel to you heretofore
Eph 1 13 of truth, the gospel of your salvation
3 6 promise in Christ Jesus, by the gospel
6 15 the preparation of the gospel of peace
19 to make known the mystery of the gospel
Phil 1 7 in defence and confirmation of the g.
12 rather to the furtherance of the gospel
16 I am set for the defence of the gospel
27 laboring together for faith of the g.
2 22 so hath he served with me in the gospel
4 3 who have labored with me in the gospel
15 that in the beginning of the gospel
Col 1 5 in the word of the truth of the gospel
23 immoveable from the hope of the gospel
1 Th 1 5 for our gospel hath not been unto you
2 2 to speak unto you the gospel of God in
4 the gospel should be committed to us
8 not only the gospel of God, but also our
9 we preached among you the gospel of God
2 Th 1 8 who obey not the gospel of our Lord
2 13 also he hath called you by our gospel
1 Tim 1 11 is according to the gospel of the glory
2 Tim 1 8 but labor with the gospel, according to
10 light life and incorruption by the g.
2 8 of the seed of David, according to my g.
Philem 13 ministered to me in the bands of the g.
1 P 1 12 them that have preached the g. to you
25 which by the g. hath been preached
4 6 for this cause was the gospel preached
17 that believe not the gospel of God
Apoc 14 6 having the eternal gospel to preach to
gospel of Christ Rom 15 19 replenished the g. . . .
Rom 15 29 of the blessing of the gospel of Christ
1 C 9 12 give any hindrance to the g. . . . Know
2 C 2 12 come to Troas for the gospel of Christ
9 13 obedience of your confession unto g. . . .
10 14 as far as to you in the gospel of Christ
Phil 1 5 your communication in the g. of Christ
27 conversation be worthy of the g. . . .
1 Th 3 2 minister of God in the gospel of Christ
gospel's 1 C 9 23 I do all things for the g. sake
Gossem 2 Es 2 19 and G. the Arabian heard of it
2 Es 6 1 and Gossem . . . heard that I had built
2 Sanaballat and G. sent to me, saying
6 G. hath said it, that thou and the Jews
got Gen 19 27 Abraham got up early in the
Gen 27 35 came deceitfully and got thy blessing
39 15 left the garment . . . and got him out
1 K 25 42 got upon an ass and five damsels went
2 K 13 29 all the king's sons arose and got up
3 K 13 13 when they had saddled him, he got up
4 K 9 16 he got up and went into Jezrahel
Ps 43 4 they got not the possession of the land
Prov 13 11 substance got in haste shall be
Ecce 2 7 I got me menservants and maidservants
Jer 13 2 I got a girdle according to the word
4 take the girdle which thou hast got
1 Ma 3 3 he got his people great honor and put
4 23 they got much gold and silver and blue
6 21 and some of the besieged got out
7 22 they got the land of Juda into their
11 8 king Ptolemee got the dominion of the
48 the city, and got many spoils that day
49 saw that the Jews had got the city
15 29 got the dominion of many places in
2 Ma 4 24 got the high priesthood for himself
27 so Menelaus got the principality: but
10 35 with fierce courage got up upon it
12 11 the help of God they got the victory
Acts 27 44 pass, that every soul got safe to land
Gothoniel 1 Pa 27 15 Netophathite of the race of G.
Jdth 6 11 Simeon, and Charmi, called also G.
gotten Gen 4 1 I have g. a man through God
Gen 12 5 souls which they had gotten in Haran
31 18 whatsoever he had gotten in Mesopotamia
Lev 6 5 all that he would have gotten by fraud
1 K 25 20 when she had gotten upon an ass and
30 17 who had gotten upon camels and fled
Job 31 25 and because my hand had gotten much
Prov 20 21 the inheritance gotten hastily in the
Ecce 2 21 he leaveth what he hath g. to an idle
Eccu 5 10 not anxious for goods unjustly gotten
6 28 when thou hast gotten her, let her
7 21 wife, whom thou hast g. in the fear
23 33 hath g. her children of another man
30 31 blood of thy soul thou hast g. him
34 21 sacrificeth of a thing wrongfully g.
26 taketh away the bread gotten by sweat
Eze 28 4 hast gotten gold and silver into thy
1 Ma 2 10 her kingdom, and gotten of her spoils
49 pride and chastisement gotten strength
6 6 which they had gotten out of the camps
8 3 had gotten possession of all the place
10 52 g. the dominion and have overthrown
15 30 whereof you have gotten the dominion
2 Ma 4 10 had gotten the rule into his hands
14 5 having gotten a convenient time to
gourds 4 K 4 39 gathered of it wild gourds of the
govern 2 Pa 10 4 thou g. us with a lighter hand
Tob 10 13 to g. the house and to behave herself
Prov 16 1 and of the Lord to govern the tongue
Wisd 9 12 I shall govern thy people justly and
10 2 gave him power to govern all things
Isa 48 17 that govern thee in the way that thou
Dan 13 5 judges that seemed to g. the people
1 Tim 5 4 her learn first to govern her own house
governed Gen 39 4 g. the house committed to him
3 K 4 12 Bana . . . who g. Thanac and Mageddo
4 K 15 5 Joatham the king's son g. the palace
2 Pa 26 21 Joatham his son g. the king's house
Prov 14 29 patient is governed with much wisdom
Wisd 14 6 a vessel, which was g. by thy hand
governest 3 K 21 7 g. well the kingdom of Israel
governeth Job 37 12 will of him that g. them
Wisd 14 3 but thy providence, O Father, g. it
government Gen 36 43 in the land of their g.
4 K 25 22 he gave the government to Godolias the
Eccu 10 1 g. of a prudent man shall be steady
46 16 established a new g. and anointed
Isa 9 6 the government is upon his shoulder
1 Ma 8 16 committed their g. to one man every
9 31 Jonathan took upon him the g. at that
2 Ma 9 24 knowing to whom the whole g. was left
2 P 2 10 despise government, audacious, self
governments Prov 1 5 shall possess g. He shall
Prov 20 18 wars are to be managed by governments
1 Ma 11 28 free from tribute, and the three g.
1 C 12 28 helps, governments, kinds of tongues
governor Gen 41 43 g. over the whole land of
Gen 42 6 Joseph was g. in the land of Egypt
45 8 and governor in all the land of Egypt
3 K 4 6 Ahisar g. of the house: and Adoniram
16 9 in house of Arsa the g. of Thersa
18 3 called Abdias the governor of his house
22 26 with Ammon the governor of the city
4 K 23 8 the gate of Josue governor of the city
25 23 of Babylon had made Godolias g.
2 Pa 18 25 to Amon the governor of the city
28 7 Ezricam the governor of his house

34 8 Maasias the governor of the city
1 Es 5 3 who was governor beyond the river
6 Thathanai g. of the country beyond
14 Sassabasar, whom also he appointed g.
6 6 g. of the country beyond the river
7 be built by the governor of the Jews
13 Thathanai, g. of the country beyond
2 Es 3 7 governor that was in the country beyond
5 14 me to be governor in the land of Juda
18 require my yearly allowance as g.
12 26 in the days of Nehemias the governor
Prov 11 14 where there is no governor, the people
Eccu 39 4 great men and appear before the g.
41 21 and of a lie before a g. and a man in
Jer 40 5 hath made g. over the cities of Juda
7 made Godolias . . . governor of the
41 2 Babylon had made g. over the land
18 had made governor in the land of Juda
Dan 2 48 made him g. over all the provinces
Agge 1 1 Zorobabel . . . governor of Juda. 14; 2:3, 22
Zach 9 7 he shall be as a governor in Juda
1 Ma 10 65 made him g. and partaker of his
69 was g. of Celesyria. 2 Ma 3:5; 4:4
11 59 he made his brother Simon governor
2 Ma 4 27 Sostratus the governor of the castle
29 Sostratus was made g. of the Cyprians
8 8 wrote to Ptolemee the g. of Celesyria
10 14 Gorgias, who was governor of the holds
32 Gazara . . . where Chereas was governor
12 2 Nicanor the governor of Cyprus, would
32 against Gorgias the g. of Idumea
13 24 made him g. and prince from Ptolemais
14 12 he sent Nicanor . . . g. into Judea
Mat 27 2 delivered him to Pontius Pilate the g.
11 stood before the g., and the g. asked
14 so that the g. wondered exceedingly
15 the g. was accustomed to release to
21 the governor answering, said to them
23 the g. said to them: Why, what evil
27 soldiers of the g. taking Jesus into
28 14 if the g. shall hear of this, we will
Luke 2 2 made by Cyrinus the governor of Syria
3 1 Pontius Pilate being governor of Judea
20 20 authority and power of the governor
Acts 7 10 appointed him governor over Egypt and
23 24 bring him safe to Felix the governor
26 to the most excellent governor, Felix
33 and had delivered the letter to the g.
24 1 who went to the governor against Paul
10 governor making a sign to him to speak
26 30 king rose up, and the g., and Bernice
2 C 11 32 at Damascus, the governor of the nation
James 3 4 the force of the governor willeth
governor's John 18 28 from Caiphas to the g. hall
governors 3 K 4 7 Solomon had twelve g. over
3 K 4 27 the foresaid g. of the king fed them
10 15 Arabia, and the g. of the country
2 Pa 11 11 he put in them g. and storehouses
1 Es 8 36 court, and the g. beyond the river
2 Es 2 7 let him give me letters to the g.
9 I came to the governors of the country
5 14 allowance that was due to the governors
15 g. that had been before me were
Jdth 2 2 called all the ancients and all the g.
Esth 1 3 and the g. of the provinces in his sight
8 9 to the governors and to the deputies
9 3 the judges of the provinces and the g.
13 1 to the governors and princes of. 16:1
Dan 3 2 captains, the rulers, and g., and all
6 1 appointed over the kingdom 120 g.
2 that the g. might give an acount to
3 Daniel excelled all the princes and g.
4 the g. sought to find occasion against
6 the g. craftily suggested to the king
7 and governors, the senators, and judges have
Zach 12 5 g. of Juda shall say in their heart
6 I will make the g. of Juda like a
1 Ma 10 37 let the governors be taken from among
12 4 they gave them letters to their g.
2 Ma 5 22 he left also g. to afflict the people
Mat 10 18 you shall be brought before governors
Mark 13 9 you shall stand before g. and kings
Luke 21 12 dragging you before kings and g. for
Gal 4 2 but is under tutors and governors until
1 P 2 14 or to governors as sent by him for the
Gozam Isa 37 12 whom my fathers have destroyed, G.
Gozan 4 K 17 6 and Habor by the river of G.
4 K 18 11 and in Habor by the rivers of Gozan
19 12 destroyed, to wit, Gozan and Haran and
1 Pa 5 26 brought them . . . to the river of Gozan
grace Gen 6 8 Noe found g. before the Lord
Gen 19 19 thy servant hath found g. before thee
Exod 33 13 and may find grace before thy eyes
16 that we have found grace in thy sight
17 for thou hast found grace before me
34 9 if I have found grace in thy sight
Num 11 15 and let me find grace in thy eyes
Judg 6 17 if I have found g. before thee, give
Ruth 2 2 wheresoever I shall find grace with a
10 that I should find g. before thy eyes
13 I have found g. in thy. 1 K 20:3; 2 K 14:22
1 K 1 18 thy handmaid may find g. in thy eyes
2 K 15 20 thou hast shown grace and fidelity
25 if I shall find grace in the sight of
16 4 let me find grace before thee, my lord
Jdth 10 8 the God of our fathers give thee grace
Ps 44 3 grace is poured abroad in thy lips
83 12 the Lord will give grace and glory
Prov 1 9 that grace may be added to thy head
3 4 shalt find g. and good understanding
22 life to thy soul and g. to thy mouth
34 and to the meek he will give grace
12 2 good, shall draw grace from the Lord
13 15 good instruction shall give grace: in
14 9 but among the just grace shall abide
16 23 mouth: and shall add grace to his lips
22 11 grace of his lips shall have the king
25 10 grace and friendship deliver a man
Ecce 10 12 of the mouth of a wise man are grace
Wisd 3 9 grace and peace is to his elect. But
4 15 grace of God and his mercy is with
16 25 obedient to thy grace that nourisheth
Eccu 3 20 and thou shalt find grace before God
4 25 a shame that bringeth glory and grace
7 21 the grace of her modesty is above gold
37 a gift hath grace in the sight of all
37 and restrain not grace from the dead
17 18 shall preserve the grace of a man
18 7 what is man and what is his grace
20 21 a man without grace is as a vain fable
21 19 in lips of wise, grace shall be found
24 22 my branches are of honor and grace
25 in me is all grace of the way and of
26 16 grace of a diligent woman shall delight
19 shamefaced woman is grace upon grace
32 3 receive a crown as an ornament of g.
9 good grace shall come to thee. 14
37 24 grace is not given him from the Lord
39 19 smell, and bring forth leaves in grace
40 17 grace is like a paradise in blessings
44 27 found grace in the eyes of all flesh
Jer 31 2 from the sword, found g. in the desert
Dan 1 9 and God gave to Daniel grace and mercy
Zach 4 7 shall give equal g. to the g. thereof
12 10 will pour out . . . the spirit of grace
2 Ma 12 45 had great grace laid up for them

Luke 1 28 hail, full of grace, the Lord is with
30 for thou hast found grace with God
2 52 and age and grace with God and men
4 22 they wondered at the words of grace
John 1 14 among us . . . full of grace and truth
16 have received, and grace for grace
17 grace and truth came by Jesus Christ
Acts 4 33 and great grace was in them all. For
6 8 Stephen, full of grace and fortitude
7 46 David. Who found grace before God and
10 45 grace of the Holy Ghost was poured out
11 17 God gave them the same g., as to us
14 3 testimony to the word of his grace
15 11 by the grace of the Lord Jesus Christ
20 32 to God, and to the word of his grace, who
Rom 1 5 by whom we have received grace and
7 grace be unto you, and peace from God. 1 C 1:3; 2 C 1:2; Gal 1:3; Eph 1:2; Phil 1:2; Col 1:3; 1 Th 1:2; 2 Th 1:2; Philem 3
11 I may impart unto you some spiritual g.
3 24 being justified freely by his grace
4 4 reward is not reckoned acccording to g.
16 according to g. the promise might be firm
5 2 have access through faith into this g.
15 by the grace of one man, Jesus Christ
16 condemnation; but g. is of many offences
17 they who receive abundance of grace, and
20 where sin abounded, g. did more abound
21 so also grace might reign by justice
6 1 continue in sin, that grace may abound
14 you are not under law, but under grace
15 not under the law, but under grace? God
11 5 saved according to the election of g.
6 and if by grace, it is not now by works
6 works: otherwise grace is no more grace
12 3 I say, by the grace that is given me, to
6 according to the grace that is given us
15 15 because of the grace which is given me
1 C 1 7 nothing is wanting to you in any grace
12 9 another, grace of healing in one Spirit
30 have all the grace of healing? Do all
15 10 his grace in me hath not been void, but
16 3 I send to carry your grace to Jerusalem
2 C 1 12 carnal wisdom, but in the grace of God
15 that you might have a second grace: and
4 15 that the grace abounding through many
8 4 with much entreaty begging of us grace
6 he would finish among you this same g.
7 us, so in this g. also you may abound
19 companion of our travels, for this grace
9 8 God is able to make all grace abound in
12 9 to me: My grace is sufficient for thee
Gal 1 6 him that called you into grace of Christ
15 womb, and called me by his grace, to
2 9 when they had known the grace that was
5 4 in the law: you are fallen from grace
Eph 1 6 unto the praise and glory of his grace
7 according to the riches of his grace
2 5 Christ, by whose grace you are saved
7 come the abundant riches of his grace
8 for by grace you are saved through faith
3 8 is given this grace, to preach among the
4 7 but to every one of us is given grace
29 it may administer grace to the hearers
6 24 grace be with all them that love our
Col 3 16 singing in grace in your hearts to God
4 6 let your speech be always in grace
18 mindful of my bands. Grace be with you
2 Th 1 12 according to the grace of our God, and
2 15 consolation, and good hope in grace
1 Tim 1 2 g., mercy and peace from God the Father
4 14 neglect not the grace that is in thee
6 21 concerning the faith. Grace be with thee
2 Tim 1 2 grace, mercy, and peace, from God the
9 according to his own purpose and grace
2 1 in the grace which is in Christ Jesus
4 22 be with thy spirit. Grace be with you
Titus 1 4 grace and peace from God the Father
3 7 that, being justified by his grace, we
Heb 4 16 with confidence to the throne of grace
16 mercy, and find grace in seasonable aid
10 29 offered an affront to the Spirit of g.
12 28 an immoveable kingdom, we have grace
13 9 that the heart be established with g.
25 grace be with you all
James 4 6 he giveth greater grace. Wherefore
6 proud, and giveth grace to the humble
1 P 1 2 grace unto you and peace be multiplied
10 prophesied of the grace to come in you
13 trust perfectly in the grace which is
3 7 to the co-heirs of the grace of life
4 10 as every man hath received grace
10 as good stewards of the manifold grace
5 5 but to the humble he giveth grace
10 the God of all grace, who hath called
14 grace be to all you who are in Christ
2 P 1 2 grace to you and peace be accomplished
3 18 grow in grace and in the knowledge of
2 J 3 grace be with you, mercy and peace
3 J 4 I have no greater grace than this, to
Apoc 1 4 grace be unto you and peace from him

grace of God Eccu 34 13 delivered by the g. . . .
Luke 2 40 and the grace of God was in him. And
Acts 11 23 and had seen the grace of God, rejoiced
13 43 persuaded them to continue in the g. . . .
14 25 they had been delivered to the g. . . .
15 40 delivered by the brethren to g. . . .
20 24 to testify gospel of the grace of God
Rom 4 5 to the purpose of the grace of God. As
5 15 much more the grace of God, and the gift
6 23 the grace of God, life everlasting, in
7 25 grace of God, by Jesus Christ our Lord
1 C 1 4 for grace of God that is given you in
3 10 according to the grace of God that is
15 10 by the grace of God, I am what I am; and
10 yet not I, but the grace of God with me
2 C 6 1 you receive not the grace of God in vain
8 1 make known . . . the grace of God, that
9 14 because of excellent grace of God in you
Gal 2 21 I cast not away the grace of God. For if
Eph 3 2 dispensation of the grace of God which
7 according to the gift of the g. of God
Col 1 6 heard and knew the grace of God in truth
2 Tim 1 6 that thou stir up the grace of God which
2 11 grace of God our Savior hath appeared
3 15 faith. The grace of God be with you all
Heb 2 9 through the grace of God, he might taste
12 15 lest any man be wanting to the g. . . .
1 P 5 12 that this is the true grace of God

grace of our Lord Rom 16 20 the g. . . . Jesus Christ be with. 24; 1 C 16:23; Gal 6:18; Phil 4:23; 1 Th 5:28; 2 Th 3:18; Philem 25; Apoc 22:21
2 C 8 9 for you know the grace of our Lord Jesus
13 13 g. . . . Jesus Christ, and the charity of
1 Tim 1 14 now the grace of our Lord hath abounded
Jude 4 turning the g. . . . God into riotousness

graced Eph 1 6 his grace, in which he hath g. us

graceful 2 Ma 15 12 Onias . . . g. in his speech

graces Jdth 9 13 by the g. of the words of my
Esth 15 17 admirable, and thy face is full of g.
Prov 4 9 shall give to thy head increase of g.
Eccu 20 13 graces of fools shall be poured out
1 C 12 4 now there are diversities of graces, but
28 miracles; then the graces of healings

gracious Gen 32 20 perhaps he will be g. to me

Gen 33 10 be g. to me and take the blessing
43 29 said: God be gracious to thee, my son
Exod 34 6 the Lord God, merciful and gracious
2 Es 9 17 a forgiving God, gracious and merciful
31 thou art a merciful and gracious God
Job 33 26 to God, and he will be gracious to him
Ps 110 4 being a merciful and gracious Lord
144 8 the Lord is gracious and merciful
Prov 11 16 a gracious woman shall find glory
Wisd 15 1 thou, our God, art gracious and true
Eccu 6 5 a g. tongue in a good man aboundeth
Joel 2 13 he is gracious and merciful, patient
Jon 4 2 that thou art a g. and merciful God
2 Ma 1 2 may God be gracious to you and
25 alone art g., who alone art just
9 27 my intentions, will be g. unto you
gradual Ps 119 1 a gradual canticle (so at the beginning of the next 14 psalms)
graft Rom 11 23 God is able to graft them
grafted Rom 11 19 that I might be grafted in
Rom 11 23 shall be grafted in: for God is able to
24 be grafted into their own olive tree
24 were grafted into the good olive tree
grain Gen 41 48 the abundance of g. was laid up
Wisd 11 23 is as the least grain of the balance
Isa 40 15 as the smallest g. of a balance
65 8 as if a grain be found in a cluster
Mat 13 31 like to a grain of mustard seed. Luke 13:19; 17:6
17 19 if you have faith as a grain of mustard
Mark 4 31 it is as a grain of mustard seed
John 12 24 unless the grain of wheat falling into
1 C 15 37 but bare grain, as of wheat, or of some
grandchildren Gen 31 43 to my children and g.
Exod 34 7 to the g. unto the third and fourth
4 K 17 41 and g., as their fathers did, so do
Tob 14 1 saw the children of his grandchildren
Eccu 45 16 only his children alone, and his g.
1 Tim 5 4 but if any widow have children, or g.
grandfather Gen 28 4 which he promised to thy g.
grandfathers Exod 10 6 have not seen, nor thy g.
grandmother 2 Tim 1 5 first in thy g. Lois
grandsons Gen 46 7 into Egypt with . . . his g.
Exod 10 2 the ears of thy sons and of thy g.
Deut 4 9 teach them to thy sons and to thy g.
25 if you shall beget sons and grandsons
6 2 thy sons and thy g. all the days of
Judg 12 14 he had 40 sons, and of them 30 g.
1 Pa 8 40 and they had many sons and grandsons
Tob 14 5 seven young men, his g., and said
Job 27 14 his g. shall not be filled with bread
Prov 13 22 good man leaveth heirs, sons and g.
grant Num 20 21 to g. them passage through his
Num 21 23 he would not grant that Israel should
Deut 28 67 who will grant me evening? And at
67 who will grant me morning? For the
Judg 11 37 grant me only this which I desire: Let
Ruth 1 9 may he grant you to find rest in the
4 7 that the grant might be sure, the man
1 K 1 17 God of Israel grant thee thy petition.
3 K 12 7 grant their petition and wilt speak
4 K 5 17 grant to me thy servant, to take
Tob 7 10 unless thou first grant me my petition
Job 6 8 who will grant that my request may come
14 13 who will grant me this, that thou mayst
19 23 who will grant me that my words may be
23 who will grant me that they may be
23 3 who will grant me that I might know
29 2 who will grant me, that I might be
31 35 who would grant me a hearer, that the
Ps 84 8 thy mercy: and grant us thy salvation
107 13 grant us help from trouble: for vain is
Eccu 50 25 may he grant us joyfulness of heart
Bar 2 14 grant that we may find favor in the
1 Ma 11 50 grant us peace, and let the Jews cease
13 34 should grant an immunity to the land
45 beseeching Simon to grant them peace
2 Ma 3 31 the most High to grant him his life
11 26 to send to them and grant them peace
30 we grant therefore a safe conduct to
Mark 10 37 grant to us, that we may sit, one on
Luke 1 73 our father, that he would grant to us
Acts 4 29 grant unto thy servants that with all
Rom 15 5 grant you to be of one mind one towards
Eph 3 16 that he would grant you, according to
granted Josu 14 10 Lord therefore hath g. me life
Judg 11 36 the victory hath been granted to thee
1 K 1 27 the Lord hath granted me my petition
2 K 14 21 I am appeased and have g. thy request
1 Pa 4 10 God granted him the things he prayed
2 Pa 1 12 wisdom and knowledge are granted to thee
1 Es 7 6 the king granted him all his request
Job 10 12 thou hast granted me life and mercy
Wisd 6 7 to him that is little, mercy is granted
1 Ma 11 66 to make peace, and he granted it them
13 50 for peace, and he granted it to them
2 Ma 2 32 is to be granted to him that maketh
3 33 sake the Lord hath granted thee life
35 vows to him that had granted him life
4 10 which when the king had granted and
11 18 he hath granted as much as the matter
35 whatsoever Lysias . . . hath g. you, we also have granted
Acts 3 13 desired a murderer to be g. to you
2 C 12 4 which it is not granted to man to utter
Apoc 19 8 it is g. to her that she should clothe
granteth Job 34 29 when he g. peace, who is there
granting Acts 14 3 g. signs and wonders to be
grape Gen 49 11 garment in the blood of the g.
Num 6 3 anything that is pressed out of the g.
Deut 32 14 might drink the purest blood of the g.
Eccu 39 31 and honey and the cluster of the grape
50 16 and offered of the blood of the grape
51 19 she flourished as a grape soon ripe
Isa 17 11 of thy planting shall be the wild g.
Jer 8 13 there is no grape on the vines, and
31 29 the fathers have eaten a sour grape
30 every man that shall eat the sour g.
Luke 6 44 bramble bush do they gather the grape
grapegatherer Jer 6 9 back thy hand, as a g.
grapegatherers Eccu 33 16 gathereth after the g.
Jer 49 9 if grapegatherers had come to thee
Abdi 5 if the grapegatherers had come into
grapes Gen 40 10 brought forth ripe g.: and the
Gen 40 11 I took the grapes and pressed them
Lev 19 10 g. that fall down in thy vineyard
25 5 neither shalt thou gather the grapes
Num 6 3 nor shall they eat grapes either fresh
13 21 when the firstripe grapes are fit to be
24 the torrent of the cluster of g. 25
24 off a branch with its cluster of grapes
25 of Israel had carried a cluster of g.
Deut 23 24 mayst eat as many g. as thou pleasest
32 32 their grapes are grapes of gall
Judg 8 2 one bunch of grapes of Ephraim better
9 27 treading down the grapes: and singing
2 Es 13 15 lading asses with wine and grapes
Job 15 33 when its grapes are in the first flower
Cant 7 7 thy breasts to clusters of grapes
Eccu 33 17 as one that gathereth grapes, have I
Isa 5 2 that it should bring forth grapes, and it brought forth wild grapes. 4
17 6 shall be as one cluster of grapes, and
24 13 or grapes, when the vintage is ended
Jer 25 30 shout as it were of them that tread g.
48 33 the treader of the g. shall not sing

Eze 18 2 the fathers have eaten sour grapes and
Osee 3 1 gods, and love the husks of the g.
9 10 found Israel like grapes in the desert
Amos 9 13 the treader of g. [shall overtake] him
Mich 7 1 gleaneth in autumn the g. of the vintage
1 Ma 6 34 showed the elephants the blood of g.
Mat 7 16 do men gather grapes of thorns, or figs
James 3 12 can the fig tree . . . bear grapes; or
Apoc 14 18 because the grapes thereof are ripe
grasping 2 Ma 14 46 g. his bowels with both
grass Gen 47 4 there is no g. for the flocks of
Exod 10 15 the grass of the earth was devoured
Num 22 4 as the ox is wont to eat the grass
Deut 32 2 herb, and as drops upon the grass
2 K 23 4 as the grass springeth out of the earth
3 K 18 5 to see if we can find grass, and save
4 K 19 26 they became like the grass of the field
Job 5 25 thy offspring like the g. of the earth
6 5 will the wild ass bray when he hath g.
30 4 and they ate grass and barks of trees
38 27 and should bring forth green grass
40 10 with thee, he eateth grass like an ox
15 to him the mountains bring forth grass
Ps 36 2 they shall shortly wither away as g.
71 16 shall flourish like the grass of the
89 6 morning man shall grow up like grass
91 8 when the wicked shall spring up as g.
101 5 I am smitten as grass, and my heart
12 shadow, and I am withered like grass
102 15 man's days are as grass, as the flower
103 14 bringing forth grass for cattle, and
104 35 they devoured all the grass in their
105 20 into likeness of a calf that eateth g.
128 6 be as grass upon the tops of houses
146 8 who maketh grass to grow on the
Prov 19 12 his cheerfulness as dew upon the grass
Eccu 14 18 all flesh shall fade as grass, and as
40 16 shall be pulled up before all grass
Isa 15 6 the grass is withered away, the spring
37 27 they became like the grass of the field
27 and like the grass of the housetops
40 6 all flesh is grass, and all the glory
7 the g. is withered, and the flower. 8
7 upon it. Indeed the people is grass
42 15 will make all their grass to wither
51 12 who shall wither away like grass
Jer 9 22 as grass behind the back of the mower
14 5 because there was no grass. 6
50 11 spread abroad as calves upon the grass
Eze 34 14 there shall they rest on the green grass
Dan 4 12 the stump . . . among the grass. 20
12 with the wild beasts in the g. of earth
22 thou shalt eat grass as an ox. 29
30 did eat grass like an ox. 5:21
Amos 7 2 had made an end of eating the grass
Mich 5 7 and as drops upon the grass, which
Zach 10 1 of rain, to every one g. in the field
Mat 6 30 if the grass of the field, which is
14 19 multitudes to sit down upon the grass
Mark 6 39 by companies upon the green grass
Luke 12 28 if God clothe in this manner the g.
John 6 10 now there was much grass in the place
James 1 10 as the flower of the grass shall he
11 burning heat and parched the grass and
1 P 1 24 all flesh is as grass; and all the
24 glory thereof as the flower of grass
24 the grass is withered, and the flower
Apoc 8 7 and all green grass was burnt up. And
9 4 should not hurt the grass of the earth
grate Exod 27 4 a grate of brass in manner of a
Exod 30 3 gold, as well as the grate thereof
35 16 altar of holocaust, and its g. of brass
37 26 the purest gold, with its grate and
38 4 he made the grate thereof of brass
30 altar of brass with the grate thereof
39 39 altar of brass, the grate, the bars
grateful 2 Ma 15 40 not be g. to the readers
gratis Isa 52 3 you were sold g., and you shall
Isa 52 5 my people is taken away gratis. They
Dan 11 39 and shall divide the land gratis
Mala 1 10 kindle the fire on my altar gratis
grave Exod 28 9 shalt g. on them the names of
Exod 28 36 wherein thou shalt g. with engraver's
Num 19 16 or his grave, he shall be unclean
2 K 3 32 voice, and wept at the grave of Abner
2 Pa 2 14 knoweth how to g. all sort of graving
Tob 8 11 went with him together to dig a grave
Job 3 22 when they have found the grave
5 26 shalt enter into the grave in abundance
10 19 carried from the womb to the grave
17 1 and only the grave remaineth for me
Eccu 30 18 as messes of meat set about a grave
Isa 14 19 thou art cast out of thy grave as an
Jer 20 17 that my mother might have been my grave
Bar 6 17 like a dead man carried to the grave
Eze 32 23 his multitude lay round about his grave
24 all his multitude round about his grave
Nah 1 14 I will make it thy grave, for thou
Zach 3 9 I will grave the graving thereof
John 11 17 been four days already in the grave
31 she goeth to the grave to weep there
12 17 when he called Lazarus out of the g.
graved 2 Pa 3 5 he graved in them palm trees
2 Pa 3 7 and he graved cherubims on the walls
4 22 he graved the doors of the inner temple
gravel Job 21 33 acceptable to the g. of Cocytus
Job 30 6 in caves of earth or upon the gravel
Prov 20 17 his mouth shall be filled with gravel
Isa 48 19 offspring of thy bowels like the gravel
graven Exod 32 16 writing also of God was graven
Exod 39 6 g. by the art of a lapidary, with the
Deut 4 16 you might make you a graven similitude
23 and make to thyself a graven likeness
Judg 17 3 a graven and a molten god. 4; 18:14
18 17 went about to take away the graven god
20 and the idols and the graven god
30 they set up to themselves the g. idol
3 K 7 24 a graven work under the brim of it
4 K 16 17 king Achaz took away the graven bases
2 Pa 33 7 he set also a g. and a molten statue
Job 19 24 be graven with an instrument in flint
Wisd 15 4 a graven figure with divers colors
13 maketh brittle vessels and g. gods
18 24 the glory of the fathers was graven
Eccu 38 28 he who maketh graven seals and by
45 13 graven by the work of a lapidary
Isa 21 9 the graven gods thereof are broken
40 19 hath the workman cast a graven statue
45 20 that set up the wood of their g. work
49 16 I have graven thee in my hands: thy
54 12 and thy gates of graven stones and all
Jer 10 14 is confounded in his graven idol
17 1 it is graven upon the table of their
Eze 40 26 and there were graven palm trees
34 the graven palm trees in the front
Nah 1 14 will destroy the graven and molten
Haba 2 18 the maker thereof hath graven it
1 Ma 8 22 graven in tables of brass and sent
graven thing Exod 20 4 to thyself a g. t. Deut 5:8
Lev 26 1 make to yourselves any idol or g. t.
Deut 27 15 that maketh a graven and molten thing
Judg 18 18 that were gone in took away the g. t.
Ps 105 19 in Horeb: and they adored the g. t.
Isa 42 17 confounded, that trust in a g. t.
44 10 hath formed a god made a g. t.
15 he made a g. t. and bowed down before it

17 made a god, and a g. t. for himself
Haba 2 18 what doth the g. t. avail, because
graven things Deut 7 5 and burn their g. t.
Deut 7 25 their graven things thou shalt burn
2 Pa 34 3 groves and the idols and the g. t.
4 he cut down the groves and the g. t.
Ps 77 58 moved him to jealousy with their g. t.
96 7 be all confounded, that adore g. t.
Isa 30 22 shalt defile the plates of thy g. t.
42 8 to another nor my praise to g. t.
48 5 my g. and molten things have commanded
Jer 14 22 any among the g. t. of the Gentiles
50 2 their graven things are confounded
51 52 I will visit her graven things, and in
Dan 11 8 into Egypt their gods and their g. t.
Mich 1 7 her g. things shall be cut in pieces
5 12 I will destroy thy g. t. and thy
graves Exod 14 11 perhaps there were no g. in
Num 11 34 place was called, The graves of lust
34 departing from the g. of lust. 33:17
33 16 they came to the graves of lust. And
Deut 9 22 at the graves of lust you provoked the
4 K 23 6 upon the graves of the common people
2 Pa 34 4 strewed the fragments upon the graves
Job 21 32 he shall be brought to the graves and
Wisd 19 3 lamenting at the graves of the dead
Jer 8 1 they shall cast . . . out of their g.
26 23 into the graves of the common people
Eze 32 22 their g. are round about him. 25, 26
23 whose g. are set in the lowest parts
37 12 I will open your graves, and will bring
13 shall have brought you out of your g.
1 Ma 11 4 graves of them that were slain in the
Mat 27 52 the graves were opened: and many bodies
John 5 28 all that are in the graves shall hear
graving Exod 28 11 the graving of a jeweller
Exod 38 10 whole graving of the work, of silver
12 all the graving of the work, of silver
3 K 7 37 casting and measure and the like g.
2 Pa 2 14 knoweth to grave all sort of graving
Eze 40 37 the graving of palm trees in the front
Zach 3 9 I will grave the graving thereof
Acts 17 29 the graving of art, and device of men
gravings Exod 38 17 with all their g. of silver
Exod 38 19 and their heads and gravings of silver
3 K 7 28 were gravings between the joinings
35 having its g. and divers sculptures
Eze 40 22 g. according to the measure of the gate
gravity Titus 2 7 doctrine, in integrity, in gravity
gray Gen 42 38 bring down my g. hairs. 44:29
Gen 44 31 shall bring down his gray hairs with
Ps 70 18 and unto old age and gray hairs: O
Prov 20 29 dignity of old men, their gray hairs
Wisd 2 10 nor honor the ancient g. hairs of the
4 8 the understanding of a man is g. hairs
Eccu 6 18 even to thy gray hairs thou shalt
25 6 comely is judgment for a gray head
Isa 46 4 to your gray hairs I will carry you
Osee 7 9 gray hairs also are spread about
2 Ma 6 23 the inbred honor of his gray head
grayheaded 1 K 12 2 I am old and g.: and my
grazed Gen 41 18 g. on green places in a marshy
greater Gen 1 16 a g. light to rule the day
Gen 4 13 my iniquity is greater than that I
43 34 the greater mess came to Benjamin
48 19 this younger brother shall be greater
49 3 excelling in gifts, g. in command
Exod 18 26 whatsoever was of greater difficulty
19 19 was drawn out to a greater length
Num 26 54 to g. number thou shalt give g. portion
Deut 9 14 over a nation that is greater and
11 23 which are g. and stronger than you
20 1 the enemy's army greater than thine
25 13 weights in thy bag, a g. and a less
14 in thy house a g. bushel and a less
Josu 10 2 and greater than the town of Hai
1 K 14 30 had there not been made a g. slaughter
2 K 12 8 shall add far greater things unto thee
13 15 he hated her was greater than the love
16 g. than that which thou didst before
3 K 1 47 the name of Solomon g. than thy name
47 make his throne greater than thy throne
7 6 another porch before the greater porch
12 the greater court was made round with
2 Pa 3 5 the g. house he ceiled with deal boards
33 23 but [Amon] committed far greater sins
Job 32 7 I hoped that greater age would speak
33 12 answer thee, that God is g. than man
Prov 16 21 sweet in words shall attain to g. things
Wisd 6 9 a greater punishment is ready for the
17 12 the g. doth it count the ignorance
Eccu 3 20 the greater thou art, the more humble
10 27 is none g. than he that feareth God
16 6 greater things than these my ear hath
19 3 shall be lifted up for a g. example
43 36 from us that are greater than these
Lam 4 6 made greater than the sin of Sodom
Eze 8 6 thou shalt see g. abominations. 13, 15
36 11 and will give you greater gifts than
43 14 from the lesser brim to the g. brim
Dan 4 33 and greater majesty was added to me
5 12 a greater spirit and knowledge
6 3 a greater spirit of God was in him
7 20 things, and was greater than the rest
32 shall be greater than all the kingdoms
11 13 a multitude much greater than before
Amos 6 12 he will strike the greater houses
1 Ma 4 35 again into Judea with greater numbers
6 27 they will do greater things than these
12 24 were come again with a g. army than
2 Ma 8 24 disabled the greater part of Nicanor's
Mat 9 16 there is made a g. rent. Mark 2:21
11 11 a greater than John the Baptist: yet
11 kingdom of heaven is greater than he
12 6 is here a greater than the temple
41 and behold a greater than Jonas here
42 behold a greater than Solomon here
13 32 grown up, it is g. than all herbs
18 1 is the g. in the kingdom of heaven. 4
20 25 that are the g., exercise power upon
26 whosoever will be the g. among you
23 14 you shall receive the g. judgment
17 whether is greater, the gold or the
19 whether is greater, the gift or the
Mark 4 32 and becometh greater than all herbs
10 43 will be g., shall be your minister
12 31 no other commandment g. than these
33 is a g. thing than all holocausts and
40 these shall receive greater judgment
Luke 9 46 which of them should be greater. But
48 the lesser among you all, he is the g.
12 18 down my barns and will build greater
16 10 faithful also in that which is greater
10 unjust also in that which is greater
20 47 these shall receive greater damnation
22 24 of them should seem to be the greater
26 he that is the greater among you, let
27 which is greater, he that sitteth at
John 1 50 greater things than these shalt thou
4 12 art thou g. than our father Jacob
5 20 g. works than these will he show him
36 I have a greater testimony than that
8 53 art thou g. than our father Abraham
10 29 hath given me is greater than all
13 16 servant is not greater than his Lord
16 apostle greater than he that sent him

14 12 and greater than these shall he do
28 for the Father is greater than I
15 13 greater love than this no man hath
20 servant is not greater than his master
19 11 me to thee, hath the greater sin
Acts 19 32 the greater part knew not for what cause
1 C 14 5 g. is he that prophesieth, than he that
Heb 3 3 this man was counted worthy of g. glory
3 hath greater honor than the house. For
6 13 he had no one greater by whom he might
16 men swear by one greater than themselves
9 11 by a g. and more perfect tabernacle not
11 26 esteeming the reproach of Christ greater
James 3 1 that you receive the greater judgment
4 6 he giveth greater grace. Wherefore
2 P 2 11 angels who are greater in strength and
1 J 3 20 God is greater than our heart and
4 4 g. is he that is in you than he that
5 9 the testimony of God is greater. For
9 testimony of God, which is greater
3 J 4 I have no greater grace than this, to
greatest Gen 19 11 from the least to the g. 2 Pa 34:30; Jdth 13:15; 15:8; Jer 6:13; 8:10; 31:34; 42:1, 8; 44:12; Bar 1:4; 1 Ma 5:45
Gen 34 19 greatest man in all his father's house
25 when pain of the wound was greatest
Lev 21 10 is the greatest among his brethren
Josu 14 15 Adam the greatest among the Enacims
Judg 16 6 wherein thy greatest strength lieth
1 Pa 12 14 soldiers, and the g. over a thousand
Ps 18 14 I shall be cleansed from the g. sin
Prov 15 5 abundant justice . . . the g. strength
21 14 and a gift [quencheth] the g. wrath
Ecce 10 4 care will make the g. sins to cease
Jon 3 5 sackcloth from the g. to the least
2 Ma 13 15 slew . . . greatest of the elephants
15 18 their g. and principal fear was for
Mat 22 38 this is the greatest and the first
23 11 he that is the greatest among you shall
Mark 9 33 which of them should be the greatest
Acts 8 10 gave ear, from the least to the g.
27 12 the g. part gave counsel to sail thence
1 C 13 13 but the greatest of these is charity
Heb 8 11 from the least to the greatest of them
greatly Gen 32 7 Jacob was greatly afraid; and in
Gen 32 11 for I am greatly afraid of him [Esau]
Num 24 11 determined indeed g. to honor thee
Deut 6 3 and thou mayst be greatly multiplied
Judg 2 15 to them: and they were g. distressed
1 K 12 19 all the people greatly feared the Lord
13 7 that followed him were greatly afraid
17 11 [Saul] . . . dismayed and greatly afraid
30 6 David was g. afflicted: for the people
2 K 18 3 should fall, they will not greatly care
2 Pa 16 10 he was greatly enraged because of this
Jdth 8 8 and she was greatly renowned among all
Ps 40 10 ate my bread, hath g. supplanted me
44 12 the king shall greatly desire thy beauty
70 23 my lips shall greatly rejoice, when I
118 74 because I have g. hoped in thy words
114 and in thy word I have greatly hoped
122 3 for we are greatly filled with contempt
4 our soul is greatly filled: we are a
144 3 great is the Lord, and g. to be praised
Prov 23 24 the father of the just rejoiceth greatly
Wisd 12 23 thou hast also greatly tormented them
Eccu 1 8 a powerful king and g. to be feared
11 6 mighty men have been g. brought down
17 23 injustice, and g. hate abomination
25 3 I am greatly grieved at their life
Isa 42 17 let them be greatly confounded, that
61 10 I will greatly rejoice in the Lord
Jer 5 11 have greatly transgressed against me
9 19 how are we wasted and g. confounded
20 11 they shall be g. confounded because
42 11 of Babylon, of whom you are g. afraid
Eze 25 12 hath greatly offended and hath sought
Dan 13 27 the servants were greatly ashamed: for
Jon 1 10 the men were greatly afraid and they
Zach 9 9 rejoice greatly, O daughter of Sion
1 Ma 3 31 and he was greatly perplexed in mind
6 1 city of Elymais . . . greatly renowned
8 13 kingdom: and they were g. exalted
11 42 I will g. honor thee and thy nation
2 Ma 8 21 words they were greatly encouraged and
11 1 being greatly displeased with what had
14 27 was g. displeased with the covenant
15 27 g. cheered with the presence of God
Mark 9 25 greatly tearing him, he went out of
12 27 living. You therefore do greatly err
Acts 3 11 called Solomon's, greatly wondering
2 Tim 4 15 he hath greatly withstood our words
1 P 1 6 wherein you shall g. rejoice if now
greatness Gen 29 20 because of the g. of his love
Gen 41 31 greatness of the scarcity shall destroy the greatness of the plenty
47 20 because of the greatness of the famine
Exod 15 16 upon them, in the greatness of thy arm
Num 14 19 according to greatness of thy mercy
Deut 3 24 begun to show unto thy servant thy g.
5 24 hath shown us his majesty and his g.
9 26 which thou hast redeemed in thy g.
1 Pa 17 21 by his g. and terrors cast out nations
21 15 took pity for the greatness of the evil
29 12 in thy hand g. and the empire of all
Esth 1 4 the g. and boasting of his power
5 11 declared to them the g. of his riches
10 2 and g. wherewith he exalted Mardochai
13 2 to abuse the greatness of my power but
Job 23 6 overwhelm me with the weight of his g.
26 14 to behold the thunder of his greatness
36 19 lay down thy g. without tribulation
Ps 70 8 that I may sing thy glory; thy g. all
78 11 according to the g. of thy arm, take
144 3 and of his greatness there is no end
6 and shall declare thy greatness. They
150 2 according to the multitude of his g.
Wisd 6 8 stand in awe of any man's greatness
13 5 g. of the beauty and of the creature
15 2 we are thine, knowing thy greatness
Eccu 2 23 according to his g., so also is his
17 7 to show them the greatness of his works
43 16 by his g. he hath fixed the clouds
Isa 15 7 according to the g. of their work, is
40 26 by the g. of his might and strength and
63 1 walking in the g. of his strength, I
Jer 13 22 the g. of thy iniquity, thy nakedness
Lam 1 3 affliction and the g. of her bondage
Bar 2 18 for the greatness of evil she hath done
Eze 28 5 by the g. of thy wisdom . . . thou hast
31 2 to whom art thou like in thy greatness
7 he was most beautiful for his g. and
Dan 4 19 thy g. hath grown and hath reached to
5 18 thy father a kingdom and greatness
19 for the greatness that he gave to him
7 27 g. of the kingdom . . . may be given to
1 Ma 9 22 noble acts that he did, and of his g.
2 Ma 14 18 g. of courage with which they fought
15 23 fear and dread of the g. of thy arm
2 C 12 7 lest the g. of the revelations should
Eph 1 19 is the exceeding greatness of his power
2 P 1 16 but we were eyewitnesses of his g.
greaves 1 K 17 6 he had g. of brass on his legs
Grecian 2 Ma 4 15 esteemed the G. glories for
Grecians 1 Ma 8 18 from them the yoke of the G.
Greece Isa 66 19 Italy and G., to the islands

Eze 27 13 Greece, Thubal, and Mosoch, they
19 Greece and Mosel have set forth in thy
Dan 11 2 shall stir up all against kingdom of G.
Zach 9 13 above thy sons, O Greece, and I will
1 Ma 1 1 Alexander . . . who first reigned in G.
6 2 that reigned first in Greece, had
8 9 who were in Greece had a mind to go
Acts 20 2 he came into Greece; where, when he had
greediness Eccu 23 6 from me the g. of the belly
Eccu 37 33 and greediness will turn to choler
greedy Prov 15 27 that is g. of gain troubleth
Eccu 37 32 be not greedy in any feasting and
1 Ma 4 17 be not greedy of the spoils: for there
1 Tim 3 8 to much wine, not greedy of filthy lucre
Titus 1 7 no striker, not greedy of filthy lucre
Greek Luke 23 38 in letters of Greek and Latin
John 19 20 written in Hebrew, in G., and in Latin
Acts 21 37 who said: Canst thou speak Greek? Art
Rom 1 16 to the Jew first, and to the Greek. For
2 10 to the Jew first, and also to the Greek
10 12 there is no distinction of Jew and Greek
Gal 3 28 there is neither Jew nor Greek: there is
Apoc 9 11 is Abaddon, and in Greek Apollyon
Greeks Dan 8 21 he goat is the king of the Greeks
Dan 10 20 there appeared the prince of the G.
Joel 3 6 have sold to the children of the G.
1 Ma 1 11 137th year of the kingdom of the G.
2 Ma 4 36 Antioch, and also the G. went to him
11 24 to turn to the rites of the Greeks
Acts 6 1 murmuring of the Greeks against the
9 29 disputed with the Greeks: but they
11 20 spoke also to G., preaching the Lord
14 1 the Jews and of the Greeks did believe
18 4 he persuaded the Jews and the Greeks
Rom 1 14 to the Greeks and to the barbarians, to
3 9 we have charged both Jews and Greeks
1 C 1 22 and the Greeks seek after wisdom: but
24 that are called, both Jews and Greeks
green Gen 1 11 let earth bring forth the green herb
Gen 1 12 the earth brought forth the green herb
8 11 of an olive tree, with green leaves
9 3 even as the g. herbs have I delivered
30 37 Jacob took green rods of poplar and
37 parts that were whole remained green
41 3 very bank of the river in g. places
18 they grazed on g. places in a marshy
Exod 9 31 the barley was green, and the flax
10 15 remained not anything that was green
Lev 2 14 to the Lord, of the ears yet green
Deut 29 23 more, nor any green thing grow therein
3 K 14 23 under every green tree. 4 K 16:4; 2 Pa 28:4; Isa 57:5; Jer 2:20; 3:6, 13
4 K 19 26 the green herb on the tops of houses
Job 8 11 can the rush be green without moisture
14 7 if it be cut, it groweth green again
38 27 and should bring forth green grass
39 8 and seeketh for every green thing
Ps 36 2 as the green herbs shall quickly fall
Prov 11 28 just shall spring up as a green leaf
27 25 the green herbs have appeared, and the
Cant 2 13 fig tree hath put forth her green figs
Eccu 14 18 leaf that springeth out on a g. tree
40 22 but more than these green sown fields
43 23 consume all that is green as with fire
Jer 17 2 and their groves and their green trees
8 and the leaf thereof shall be green
Eze 17 24 dried up the green tree and have caused
20 47 will burn in thee every green tree
31 10 shot up his top green and thick, and
34 14 shall they rest on the green grass and
Osee 14 9 make him flourish like a g. fir tree
Nah 3 12 like fig trees with their green figs
2 Ma 10 7 carried boughs and green branches and
Mark 6 39 by companies upon the green grass
Luke 23 31 if in the green wood they do these
Apoc 6 13 as the fig tree casteth its green figs
8 7 and all green grass was burnt up. And
9 4 nor any green thing nor any tree: but
greenness Isa 15 6 faded, all the g. is perished
greeting 1 Es 4 11 thy servants . . . send g.
1 Es 4 17 king sending greeting and peace
7 12 to Esdras the priest . . . greeting
Esth 13 1 that are subject to his empire . . . g.
16 1 king Artaxerxes . . . sendeth greeting
1 Ma 10 18 to his brother Jonathan, greeting
25 to the nation of the Jews, greeting. 11:30; 13:36; 15:2
11 32 to Lasthenes his parent, greeting
12 6 to the Spartans, their brethren, greeting
20 Arius . . . to Onias the high priest, g.
14 20 the Spartans to Simon . . . greeting
15 16 Lucius . . . to king Ptolemee, greeting
2 Ma 11 16 to the people of the Jews, g. 34
22 Antiochus to Lysias his brother, g.
27 and to the rest of the Jews, greeting
Acts 15 23 writing by their hands . . . greeting
23 26 to most excellent governor, Felix, g.
James 1 1 which are scattered abroad, greeting
grew Gen 2 5 herb of the ground before it g.
Gen 21 8 and the child grew and was weaned
20 he grew and dwelt in the wilderness
41 22 seven ears of corn g. upon one stalk
47 27 g. and was multiplied exceedingly
Exod 1 20 multiplied and grew exceedingly strong
16 21 and after the sun grew hot, it melted
19 19 sound of the trumpet grew by degrees
Deut 26 5 grew into a nation great and strong
32 15 the beloved grew fat and kicked: he
15 he grew fat and thick and gross, he
Judg 4 24 of Israel, who grew daily stronger
13 24 the child g. and the Lord blessed him
20 34 and the battle grew hot against the
1 K 2 26 the child Samuel advanced and grew on
3 19 Samuel grew, and the Lord was with him
11 11 he slew . . . until the day grew hot
2 K 17 22 over the Jordan until it grew light
23 10 till his hand was weary and grew stiff
3 K 18 45 the heavens grew dark with clouds and
4 K 4 18 the child grew. And on a certain day
34 him, and the child's flesh grew warm
1 Pa 10 3 and the battle grew hard against Saul
19 5 till their beards grew and then to
2 Pa 17 1 Josaphat . . . g. strong against Israel
12 Josaphat g. and became exceeding great
24 15 Joiada grew old and was full of days
Job 28 5 out of which bread grew in its place
31 18 from my infancy mercy grew up with me
Ps 31 3 because I was silent, my bones g. old
38 4 my heart grew hot within me: and in my
Eze 16 7 were fashioned, and thy hair grew
17 6 grew into a spreading vine and shot
6 became a vine and grew into branches
10 wither in the furrows where it grew
Dan 4 30 till his hairs grew like the feathers
10 19 when he spoke to me, I grew strong
Mat 13 7 thorns grew up and choked. Mark 4:7
Mark 4 8 brought forth fruit that grew up and
Luke 1 80 the child grew and was strengthened
2 40 and the child grew, and waxed strong
13 19 and it grew and became a great tree
John 4 52 the hour wherein he grew better. And
Acts 19 20 mightily grew the word of God, and was
gridiron Lev 2 7 sacrifice be from the gridiron
Lev 7 9 whatsoever is dressed on the gridiron
grief Deut 19 6 pushed on by his g. should pursue
1 K 1 10 as Anna had her heart full of grief

16 out of abundance of my sorrow and grief
25 31 this shall not be an occasion of grief
Job 2 13 they saw that his grief was very great
Ps 30 11 my life is wasted with grief: and my
68 27 have added to the grief of my wounds
Prov 12 25 grief in the heart of a man shall bring
15 13 by grief of mind the spirit is cast down
19 13 foolish son is the grief of his father
Wisd 8 9 will be a comfort in my cares and grief
14 15 father being afflicted with bitter grief
Eccu 18 15 thing, add not grief by an evil word
26 8 jealous woman is the g. and mourning
36 22 a perverse heart will cause grief
37 1 is not this a grief even to death
Isa 61 3 garment of praise for the spirit of g.
65 14 you . . . shall howl for grief of spirit
Eze 23 33 with the cup of grief and sadness
Dan 13 10 not make known their grief one to the
Mich 4 9 why art thou drawn together with grief
1 Ma 6 8 upon his bed, and fell sick for grief
9 grief came more and more upon him
13 I perish with great grief in a strange
2 C 2 5 if anyone have caused grief, he hath
Heb 13 17 may do this with joy, and not with g.
grievance Haba 1 3 shown me iniquity and g.
grieve Lev 25 14 buy of him; g. not thy brother
2 K 1 26 I grieve for thee, my brother Jonathan
Ps 68 21 for one that would g. together with me
Eccu 3 14 father, and grieve him not in his life
Isa 17 11 inheritance, and shall g. thee much
Zach 12 10 son, and they shall grieve over him
10 manner is to grieve for the death of
Eph 4 30 and grieve not the holy Spirit of God
grieved Ruth 1 13 am g. the more for your distress
1 K 15 11 Samuel was grieved and he cried unto
20 3 not Jonathan know this, lest he be g.
34 he [Jonathan] was grieved for David
30 6 soul of every man was bitterly grieved
2 K 6 8 David was g. because Lord had struck
13 21 he [David] was exceedingly grieved
3 K 21 5 the matter that thy soul is so grieved
2 Es 2 10 heard it, and it g. them exceedingly
Ps 54 3 I am grieved in my exercise; and am
77 41 and grieved the holy one of Israel
104 28 obscure: and grieved not his words
Prov 31 6 and wine to them that are g. in mind
Eccu 6 26 bear her and be not g. with her bands
9 20 upon the arms of them that are grieved
12 9 of a man, his enemies are grieved: and
21 27 wise man will be g. with the disgrace
25 3 I am greatly grieved at their life
26 25 at two things my heart is grieved, and
Jer 5 3 struck them, and they have not g.
Bar 4 8 you have g. Jerusalem that nursed you
33 so shall she be grieved for her own
Eze 18 16 and hath not grieved any man nor
22 7 they have g. the fatherless and widow
31 15 Libanus grieved for him, and all the
Dan 6 14 heard these words, he was very much g.
Jon 4 10 thou art grieved for the ivy, for which
Haba 3 10 the mountains saw thee and were g.
1 Ma 2 24 Mathathias saw and was grieved and his
3 7 he grieved many kings, and made Jacob
2 Ma 4 35 were much g. for the unjust murder of
37 Antiochus therefore was g. in his
Mat 18 31 were very much grieved, and they came
Mark 3 5 being g. for the blindness of their
John 21 17 Peter was grieved because he had said
Acts 4 2 being grieved that they taught the
16 18 Paul being g., turned, and said to the
20 38 being g. most of all for the word which
Rom 14 15 because of thy meat, thy brother be g.
2 C 2 5 caused grief, he hath not grieved me

grieveth 2 K 19 2 king grieveth for his son
Prov 26 15 it grieveth him to turn it to his mouth
Wisd 14 24 envy or grieveth him by adultery: and
Eze 18 12 that grieveth the needy and the poor
grievous Gen 12 10 famine was very g. in the land
Gen 12 17 Pharao . . . with most grievous stripes
18 20 their sin is become exceedingly g.
21 12 let it not seem grievous to thee for
47 4 the famine being very g. in the land
Exod 8 24 came a very grievous swarm of flies
9 3 very grievous murrain upon thy horses
Deut 6 22 wonders great and very g. in Egypt
7 15 the g. infirmities of Egypt which thou
26 6 laying on us most g. burdens: and we
28 59 lasting, infirmities g. and perpetual
3 K 2 8 who cursed me with a g. curse when
12 4 thy father laid a grievous yoke upon us
4 take off a little of the g. service
17 17 fell sick, and the sickness was very g.
18 2 there was a grievous famine in Samaria
2 Pa 10 4 oppressed us with a most grievous yoke
21 15 thou shalt be sick of a very g. disease
Job 2 7 struck Job with a very grievous ulcer
23 2 hand of my scourge is more g. than my
31 11 crime, and a most grievous iniquity
Ps 70 20 great troubles . . . many and grievous
Prov 15 10 instruction is g. to him that forsaketh
Ecce 4 8 also is vanity and a grievous vexation
5 12 there is also another grievous evil
Wisd 2 15 he is grievous unto us, even to behold
17 10 always forecasteth g. things. For
20 themselves more g. than the darkness
Eccu 26 7 calumny, all are more g. than death
27 16 their cursing is a grievous hearing
29 34 these things are grievous to a man of
31 2 a g. sickness maketh the soul sober
33 30 and do no g. thing without judgment
39 33 in their fury they lay on g. torments
Isa 7 13 small thing for you to be g. to men that
are g. to my God also
21 2 a g. vision is told me: he that is
15 bent bow, from the face of a g. battle
Jer 10 19 my wound is very grievous. But I said
14 17 affliction, with an exceeding g. evil
16 4 shall die by the death of g. illnesses
30 12 incurable, thy wound is very grievous
Bar 2 25 and they have died in grievous pains
Eze 5 16 upon them the g. arrows of famine
14 21 my four g. judgments, the sword and
Joel 2 6 the people shall be in grievous pains
Amos 5 12 manifold crimes and your g. sins
Mich 2 10 shall be corrupted with a g. corruption
Nah 3 3 multitude slain and of a g. destruction
19 not hidden, thy wound is grievous: all
2 Ma 6 3 this evasion of evils and g. to all
30 I suffer g. pains in body: but in soul
9 7 by a grievous bruising of the body
21 being taken with a grievous disease
Acts 25 7 objecting many and g. causes, which
Apoc 16 2 there fell a sore and grievous wound
grievously Gen 21 11 Abraham took this g. for
Judg 4 3 for twenty years had g. oppressed them
6 2 and they were g. oppressed by them
10 8 they were afflicted and g. oppressed
1 K 31 3 and he was g. wounded by the archers
3 K 22 34 out of the army, for I am g. wounded
2 Pa 35 23 out of the battle for I am g. wounded
1 Es 9 7 we ourselves also have sinned g. unto
Tob 10 9 their spirit is grievously afflicted
Wisd 19 15 these grievously afflicted them whom
Lam 1 8 Jerusalem hath g. sinned, therefore
Eze 14 13 against me, so as to transgress g.
20 13 they grievously violated my sabbaths

2 Ma 7 39 taking it g. that he was mocked. So
9 28 and blasphemer, being g. struck, as
14 28 took it g. that he should make void
45 he was g. wounded, he ran through
Mat 8 6 palsy, and is grievously tormented
15 22 my daughter is g. troubled by a devil
griffon Lev 11 13 not eat . . . the griffon
grind Judg 16 21 shutting him up in prison made him g.
Isa 3 15 people and grind the faces of the poor
47 2 take a millstone and g. meal: uncover
21 44 it shall g. him to powder. Luke 20:18
grinder's Ecce 12 4 when g. voice shall be low
grinders Ps 57 7 break the grinders of the lions
Ecce 12 3 grinders shall be idle in small number
grindeth Prov 30 14 and g. with their jaw teeth
grinding Mat 24 41 two women shall be g. Luke 17:35
gripes Eccu 31 23 g. are with an intemperate man
gripings Isa 13 8 g. and pains shall take hold
grisled Zach 6 3 in the fourth chariot g. horses
6 6 the g. went forth to land of the south
gristle Job 40 13 his g. like plates of iron
groan Job 24 12 they have made men to groan
Job 26 5 the giants groan under the waters and
Jer 51 52 in all her land the wounded shall g.
Eze 30 24 they shall groan bitterly being slain
Joel 1 18 why did the beast groan, why did the
Rom 8 23 we ourselves groan within ourselves
2 C 5 2 for in this also we groan, desiring to
4 who are in this tabernacle, do groan
groaned Eccu 25 25 her husband g., and hearing
2 Ma 6 30 he groaned and said: O Lord, who
Mark 7 34 he groaned and said to him: Ephpheta
John 7 33 g. in the spirit, and troubled himself
groaneth Eccu 30 21 seeth with his eyes and g.
Rom 8 22 we know that every creature groaneth
groaning Exod 2 23 children of Israel g., cried
Exod 2 24 he heard their g. and remembered
6 5 I have heard the groaning of the
Ps 37 9 I roared with the groaning of my heart
10 my groaning is not hidden from thee
101 6 through the voice of my groaning, my
Wisd 5 3 and groaning for anguish of spirit
11 13 a g. for the remembrance of things
Eccu 19 11 as a woman g. in the bringing forth
John 11 38 Jesus therefore again g. in himself
Acts 7 34 I have heard their groaning and am
groanings Judg 2 18 heard the g. of the afflicted
Ps 6 7 I have labored in my g., every night
Eccu 7 29 forget not the groanings of thy mother
Rom 8 26 asketh for us with unspeakable g. And
groans Ps 11 6 needy, and the g. of the poor
Ps 101 21 that he might hear the groans of them
Jer 45 3 I am wearied with my groans, and I
Eze 26 15 g. of thy slain when they shall be
groat Luke 15 8 if she lose one groat, doth not
Luke 15 9 I have found the g. which I had lost
groats Luke 15 8 what woman having ten groats
groin 2 K 2 23 with a back stroke in the groin
2 K 3 27 and he stabbed him there in the groin
4 6 stabbed him [Isboseth] in the groin
grope Deut 28 29 mayst thou grope at midday as the blind is wont to grope
Job 5 14 and grope at noonday as in the night
12 25 they shall grope as in the dark and
Eccu 30 1 and not grope after the doors of his
groped Isa 59 10 we have groped for the wall
Isa 59 10 we have groped as if we had no eyes
groping 2 P 1 9 blind and g., having forgotten
gross Deut 32 15 he grew fat and thick and g.
Jer 5 28 they are grown gross and fat; and
Mat 13 15 of this people is grown g. Acts 28:27
ground Gen 2 5 every herb of the g. before it grew
Gen 2 9 forth of the ground all manner of trees
19 formed out of the g. all the beasts
9 20 began to till the g. and planted
23 15 ground which thou desirest is worth
Exod 3 5 whereon thou standest is holy ground
9 23 and lightning running along the g.
23 10 six years thou shalt sow thy ground
19 carry firstfruits of the corn of thy g.
34 26 the first of the fruits of thy ground
Lev 25 5 what the g. shall bring forth of itself
19 the ground may yield you its fruits
26 4 ground shall bring forth its increase
20 g. shall not bring forth her increase
27 16 if g. be sowed with thirty bushels
Num 11 8 ground it in a mill or beat it in a
31 in air two cubits high above the g.
13 21 the ground, fat or barren, woody or
16 33 into hell, the g. closing upon them
18 13 fruits that the ground bringeth forth
Deut 21 3 drawn in the yoke nor plowed the g.
28 4 of thy womb and the fruit of thy g. 18
23 the ground thou treadest on, of iron
38 shalt cast much seed into the ground
42 consume all trees and fruits of thy g.
Josu 7 21 hid them in the ground in the midst
15 19 the upper and the nether watery g. Judg 1:15
Judg 4 21 through his brain fast into the ground
6 39 dry, and all the ground wet with dew
16 13 fastenest it in g., I shall be weak
1 K 26 7 spear fixed in the ground at his head
28 23 he [Saul] arose from the g. and sat
2 K 12 17 came to make him rise from the ground
20 then David arose from the ground and
3 K 7 46 the king cast them in a clay ground
19 waters are very bad, and the g. barren
1 Pa 27 26 the husbandmen who tilled the ground
2 Pa 4 17 in a clay ground between Sochot and
31 5 things which the ground bringeth forth
2 Es 10 37 tithes of our ground to the Levites
Job 5 6 sorrow doth not spring out of the g.
14 19 the g. by little and little is washed
39 24 and raging he swalloweth the ground
Ps 71 9 and his enemies shall lick the ground
104 35 consumed all the fruit of their ground
Prov 24 27 without, and diligently till thy ground
28 19 tilleth his g., shall be filled with bread
Wisd 19 10 how the ground brought forth flies
Eccu 33 10 all men are from the ground and out
37 10 lest he thrust a stake into the ground
Isa 14 1 will make them rest upon their own g.
21 9 gods thereof are broken unto the ground
28 24 shall he open and harrow his ground
29 4 thy speech shall be heard out of the g.
4 out of the g. thy speech shall mutter
30 24 and the ass colts that till the ground
34 7 their ground with the fat of fat ones
9 the ground thereof into brimstone
51 23 thou hast laid thy body as the ground
53 2 as a root out of a thirsty ground
Jer 4 3 break up anew your fallow ground and
Lam 2 9 her gates are sunk into the ground
Bar 5 7 valleys to make them even with the g.
Eze 12 6 thy face and shalt not see the ground
12 that he may not see the ground with
13 14 I will make it even with the ground
17 5 and put it in the ground for seed that
41 16 and the ground was up to the windows
20 from the ground even to the upper parts
42 6 places fifty cubits from the ground
43 14 from the bottom of the ground to the
Dan 8 5 whole earth, and he touched not the g.
Osee 10 12 of mercy, break up your fallow ground
Joel 1 10 the g. hath mourned, for the corn is
Agge 1 11 upon all that the ground bringeth forth

2 Ma 8 3 ready to be made even with the ground
8 seeing that the man gained ground by
9 14 haste to lay it even with the ground
14 33 this temple of God even with the ground
Mat 13 5 some fell upon stony ground. Mark 4:5
20 received the seed upon stony ground
Luke 13 7 why cumbereth it the ground? But
24 5 their countenance towards the ground
John 12 24 the grain of wheat falling into the g.
Acts 7 33 wherein thou standest is holy ground
9 8 Saul arose from the ground; and when
1 Tim 3 15 God, the pillar and ground of the truth

dry ground; *see* **dry**

good ground Eze 17 8 was planted in a g. g. upon
Mat 13 8 others fell upon good ground: and they
23 received the seed upon good ground is
Mark 4 8 fell upon good ground; and brought
20 who are sown upon good ground, who
Luke 8 8 other some fell upon good ground; and
15 that on the good ground are they who

on the ground Gen 44 14 down before them o. . . .
Gen 50 18 prostrate on the ground they said
Exod 16 14 like unto the hoar frost on the ground
Num 16 45 as they were lying on the g., Moses said
22 31 worshipped him falling flat on the g.
Deut 22 6 bird's nest in a tree or on the ground
Josu 7 6 fell flat on the ground before the ark
10 why liest thou flat on the ground
Judg 3 25 found their lord lying dead on the g.
6 37 and it be dry on all the ground beside
40 and there was dew on all the ground
8 25 spreading a mantle on the ground, they
13 20 saw this, they fell flat on the ground
1 K 5 3 Dagon lay upon his face on the ground
14 32 and calves and slew them on the g.
28 20 Saul fell all along on the g., for he
3 K 8 54 he had fixed both knees on the ground
1 Pa 21 16 [David] fell down flat on the ground
2 Pa 20 18 Josaphat . . . fell flat on the ground
Esth 15 7 bearing up her train flowing on the g.
Job 2 13 they sat with him on the ground seven
Ecce 10 7 princes walking on the g. as servants
Isa 3 26 she shall sit desolate on the ground
47 1 daughter of Babylon, sit on the ground
Jer 14 2 gates . . . become obscure on the ground
Lam 2 21 and old man lie without on the ground
Eze 19 12 plucked up in wrath, and cast on the g.
26 16 they shall sit on the ground, and
Dan 8 7 when he had cast him down on the ground
12 truth shall be cast down on the ground
18 spoke to me I fell flat on the ground
2 Ma 10 4 lying prostrate on the g., that they
13 12 prostrate on the ground for three days
Mat 10 29 not one of them shall fall on the g.
Mark 4 16 that are sown on the stony ground: who
14 35 he fell flat on the ground; and he
John 8 6 wrote with his finger on the ground
8 stooping down, he wrote on the ground
9 6 he spat on the ground and made clay
Acts 9 4 falling on the ground, he heard a voice
22 7 falling on the ground, I heard a voice
26 13 we were all fallen down on the ground

to the ground Gen 18 2 adored down to the g.
Gen 19 1 worshipped prostrate to the ground
24 52 servant . . . falling down to the ground
33 3 [Jacob] with his face to the g.
43 26 bowed down with their face to the g.
44 11 took down their sacks to the ground
48 12 [Joseph] with his face to the ground
Lev 19 9 face of the earth to the very ground
23 22 you shall not cut it to the very g.
Josu 5 15 Josue fell on his face to the ground
6 5 walls of city shall fall to the ground
Judg 7 13 and beat it down flat to the ground
1 K 3 19 not one of his words fell to the g.
14 45 hair of his head fall to the g. 3 K 1:52
20 41 David . . . on his face to the g.
24 9 David bowing himself down to the g.
28 14 bowed himself with his face to the g.
2 K 2 22 I be obliged to stab thee to the g.
14 22 Joab falling down to the ground
18 11 why didst thou not stab him to the g.
28 [Achimaas] with his face to the g.
20 10 and shed out his bowels to the ground
3 K 1 23 bowing down to the ground, Nathan said
4 K 2 15 worshipped him, falling to the ground
10 10 not fallen to the g. any of the words
1 Pa 21 21 Ornan . . . with his face to the g.
2 Pa 7 3 with their faces to the g. 2 Es 8:6
Jdth 10 20 prostrating herself to the ground
Ps 88 45 hast cast his throne down to the g.
146 6 bringeth wicked down even to the ground
Isa 25 12 shall be pulled down to the ground
26 5 he shall bring it down even to the g.
Lam 2 2 and brought them down to the ground
10 hang down their heads to the ground
Bar 6 26 if they fall to the g., they rise not
Eze 26 11 famous statues shall fall to the g.
28 17 beauty, I have cast thee to the g.
38 20 every wall shall fall to the ground
Dan 10 9 and my face was close to the ground
15 I cast down my countenance to the g.
Amos 3 14 cut off, and shall fall to the ground
9 9 not a little stone fall to the ground
Abdi 3 who shall bring me down to the ground
Nah 2 6 the temple is thrown down to the g.
1 Ma 4 40 they fell down to the ground on their
6 46 and it fell to the ground upon him
2 Ma 3 27 Heliodorus suddenly fell to the ground
4 42 and some struck down to the ground
9 8 now being cast down to the ground
Luke 19 44 and beat thee flat to the ground and
John 18 6 went backward and fell to the ground

upon the ground Gen 38 9 his seed upon the g.
Exod 4 3 Lord said: Cast it down upon the g.
Num 14 5 they fell down flat upon the ground
20 6 and Aaron . . . fell flat upon the g.
Deut 28 56 woman, that could not go upon the g.
32 24 creatures that trail upon the ground
Ruth 2 10 worshipping upon the g. said to him
1 K 14 25 in which there was honey upon the g.
25 23 Abigail . . . and adored upon the g.
30 16 were lying spread upon all the ground
2 K 12 16 going in by himself lay upon the g.
13 31 the king . . . fell upon the ground
14 4 she fell before him upon the ground
17 12 as the dew falleth upon the ground
4 K 4 37 she . . . worshipped upon the ground
13 18 strike with an arrow upon the ground
Tob 12 16 they fell upon the ground on their face
Jdth 7 4 prostrated themselves upon the ground
14 14 body of Holofernes lying upon the ground
16 Holofernes lieth upon the ground and
Job 1 20 down upon the ground and worshipped
Ps 140 7 the earth is broken up upon the ground
Isa 44 3 out waters upon the thirsty ground
Lam 2 10 the ancients . . . sit upon the ground
Eze 24 7 she hath not shed it upon the ground
38 20 thing that creepeth upon the ground
Mat 15 35 multitude to sit down upon the ground
Mark 9 19 being thrown down upon the ground, he
Luke 22 44 blood, trickling down upon the ground

grounded Job 38 6 upon what are its bases g.
Isa 30 32 of the rod shall be strongly grounded
Col 1 23 continue in the faith, g. and settled

grove Gen 21 33 Abraham planted a g. in Bersabee
Deut 16 21 thou shalt plant no grove nor any
Judg 6 25 cut down the g. that is about the altar
26 shalt cut down out of the grove
28 destroyed and the grove cut down
30 of Baal and hath cut down his grove
3 K 15 13 grove which she had consecrated to him
16 33 he planted a g.: and Achab did more
4 K 13 6 still remained a grove also in Samaria
21 7 he set also an idol of the grove which
23 4 been made for Baal and for the grove
6 he caused the grove to be carried out
7 as it were little dwellings for the g.
15 reduced to powder and burnt the g.
2 Pa 15 16 because she had made in a grove an idol
groves Exod 34 13 cut down their g. Deut 7:5
3 K 14 15 made to themselves groves. 4 K 17:16
Deut 12 3 burn their groves with fire, and break
14 23 groves upon every high hill and under
18 19 and the prophets of the groves 400
4 K 17 10 they made them statues and groves
16 and made to themselves . . . groves
18 4 cut down the groves. 23:14; 2 Pa 14:3; 31:1
21 3 up altars to Baal, and made groves
1 Pa 27 28 over the oliveyards and the fig groves
2 Pa 17 6 high places and the groves out of Juda
19 3 thou hast taken away the groves out
24 18 served groves and idols, and wrath came
33 3 built altars to Baalim and made groves
19 places and set up groves and statues
34 3 from the high places and the groves
4 he cut down the g. and the graven
7 had destroyed the altars and the g.
Jdth 3 12 their cities, and cut down their groves
Isa 17 8 wrought such as groves and temples
27 9 the groves and temples shall not stand
Jer 17 2 remember their altar and their groves
Amos 4 9 your olive groves and fig groves
Mich 5 13 I will pluck up thy groves out of the
grow Gen 38 11 till Sela my son grow up: for he
Gen 41 52 God hath made me to grow in the land
48 16 may they grow into a multitude upon
19 and his seed shall grow into nations
49 4 poured out as water, grow thou not
Lev 13 7 but if the leprosy grow again, after
25 7 all things that grow shall be meat to
11 the things that grow in the field
12 as they grow you shall presently eat
22 till new g. up, you shall eat the old
47 sojourner grow strong among you
Num 6 5 shall let the hair of his head grow
Deut 8 8 pomegranates and oliveyards grow
14 28 tithe of all things that grow to thee
29 23 nor any green thing grow therein
Judg 16 22 and now his hair began to grow again
2 K 13 4 why dost thou grow so lean from day to
3 K 10 27 sycamores, which grow in the plains. 2 Pa 1:15; 9:27
1 Es 4 22 lest by little and little the evil grow
2 Es 9 21 their garments did not grow old, and
37 the fruits thereof g. up for the king
Tob 8 10 let us grow old both together in health
Job 8 11 or a sedge-bush grow without water
Ps 64 13 places of the wilderness shall g. fat
89 6 in the morning man shall grow up like
6 in the evening he shall fall, grow dry
91 13 he shall grow up like the cedar of
101 27 all of them shall g. old like a garment
146 8 who maketh grass to grow on the
Prov 3 20 and the clouds grow thick with dew
11 24 their own goods, and grow richer
26 9 as if a thorn should grow in the hand
Ecce 12 4 the daughters of music shall grow deaf
Eccu 2 6 keep his fear, and grow old therein
9 15 as new wine: it shall grow old and
11 16 glory in evil things, grow old in evil
21 and grow old in the work of thy
14 19 some grow and some fall off: so is
30 12 a child, lest he grow stubborn and
Isa 17 4 fatness of his flesh shall grow lean
34 13 nettles shall grow up in its houses
53 2 he shall grow up as a tender plant
Jer 6 24 our hands grow feeble: anguish hath
Eze 16 7 thou didst increase and grow great
37 6 and will cause flesh to grow over you
Osee 10 8 thistle shall g. up over their altars
47 12 shall grow all trees that bear fruit
Jon 4 10 hast not labored nor made it to grow
Mat 6 28 the lilies of the field, how they grow
13 30 suffer both to grow until the harvest
21 19 may no fruit grow on thee henceforward
24 12 the charity of many shall grow cold
26 37 began to grow sorrowful and to be sad
Mark 4 27 the seed should spring, and grow up
Luke 12 27 consider the lilies, how they grow
33 yourselves bags which grow not old
Eph 4 15 grow up in him who is the head, even
2 Tim 2 16 they grow much towards ungodliness
3 13 evil men and seducers shall grow worse
Heb 1 11 and they shall all grow old as a garment
1 P 2 2 thereby you may grow unto salvation
2 P 3 18 grow in grace and in the knowledge of
groweth Gen 2 11 land of Hevilath, where gold g.
Judg 18 10 anything that groweth on the earth
Job 6 17 after it g. hot they shall be melted
14 7 if it be cut, it groweth green again
Mark 4 32 it groweth up and becometh greater than
Eph 2 21 groweth up into an holy temple in Lord
Col 1 6 bringeth forth fruit and groweth, even
2 19 groweth unto the increase of God. If
2 Th 1 3 because your faith groweth exceedingly
Heb 8 13 decayeth and groweth old, is near its
growing Gen 49 22 Joseph is a growing son
Exod 1 7 growing exceedingly strong they filled
2 K 3 1 David . . . g. always stronger and
5 10 he went on prospering and growing up
21 15 David g. faint, Jesbibenob, who was
1 Pa 11 9 David went on growing and increasing
Job 41 23 shall esteem the deep as growing old
Wisd 16 26 not the g. of fruits that nourisheth
Eccu 40 16 the weed growing over every water
Dan 8 3 higher than the other and growing up
1 Ma 4 38 and shrubs growing up in the courts
Luke 8 7 the thorns growing up with it, choked
Phil 1 14 growing confident by my bands are much
grown Gen 18 12 saying: After I am grown old
Gen 19 13 their cry is grown loud before the Lord
25 27 when they were grown up, Esau became
38 14 Sela was grown up and she had not been
Exod 2 9 when he was grown up, she delivered him
11 after Moses was grown up, he went out
Lev 13 5 if the leprosy be grown no farther and
11 leprosy, and grown into the skin. The
27 if the leprosy be grown farther in the
32 if the spot be not grown, and the hair
51 if he find that it is grown, it is a
53 if he see that it is not grown, he
Josu 13 1 thou art grown old and advanced in age
17 13 children of Israel were grown strong
Judg 1 28 after Israel was grown strong he made
11 2 after they were grown up, thrust out
Ruth 1 13 would wait till they were grown up
1 K 3 2 and his eyes were grown dim, that he
2 K 10 5 at Jericho till your beards be grown
12 3 lamb . . . which had grown up in his
1 Es 9 6 our sins are grown up even unto heaven

Jdth 13 1 when it was grown late, his servants
Ps 6 8 I have g. old amongst all my enemies
68 5 my enemies are grown strong who have
101 4 my bones are grown dry like fuel for
Jer 5 28 they are grown gross and fat; and have
6 4 shadows of the evening are g. longer
50 43 his hands are g. feeble: anguish hath
Bar 3 11 thou art g. old in a strange country
Eze 19 10 branches have grown out of many waters
Dan 4 19 O king, who art grown great and become
19 thy greatness hath grown and hath
8 8 when he was grown, the great horn
23 when iniquities shall be grown up
11 2 when he shall be grown mighty by his
13 52 that art grown old in evil days, now
1 Ma 6 6 that they were grown strong by the
Mat 13 15 of this people is g. gross. Acts 28:27
32 but when it is grown up, it is greater
Luke 12 18 all things that are grown to me and
1 Tim 5 11 when they have grown wanton in Christ
Heb 11 24 by faith Moses, when he was grown up
grows Prov 7 9 in the dark, when it grows late
growth 2 C 9 10 increase g. of fruits of your
grudge James 5 9 g. not, brethren, one against
grype Deut 14 12 eat not . . . eagle and the grype
guard Num 1 53 watch, and guard the tabernacle
Num 3 28 shall have the guard of the sanctuary
32 that watch for the g. of the sanctuary
1 K 28 2 I will appoint thee to guard my life
2 Pa 35 15 the porters kept guard at every gate
2 Es 3 15 pool of Siloe unto the king's guard
Jdth 7 8 the steep hills and precipices g. them
Ps 38 2 I have set a guard to my mouth when
Prov 13 3 he that hath no guard on his speech
Eccu 22 33 who will set a guard before my mouth
2 Ma 3 23 with his guard about the treasury
28 came with many servants and all his g.
Mat 27 65 you have a guard; go, guard it as you
guarded 2 Pa 12 10 g. the entrance of the palace
2 Pa 7 5 they guarded them all day and night
Mat 27 64 the sepulcher to be guarded until the
2 C 11 32 guarded the city of the Damascenes, to
guarding Prov 2 8 guarding the ways of saints
guards Judg 16 2 setting g. at gate of the city
1 K 19 11 Saul therefore sent his g. to David's
2 K 8 14 he put guards in Edom and placed
4 K 7 11 then the guards of the gate went and
11 18 priest set guards in house of the Lord
Jdth 7 9 set guards at the springs that they
Jer 4 16 guards are coming from a far country
Eze 12 14 his g. and his troops I will scatter
Nah 3 17 thy guards are like the locusts: and
Mat 27 66 sealing the stone and setting guards
28 4 the guards were struck with terror
11 some of the guards came into the city
Guel Num 13 16 Guel the son of Machi. These
guess Wisd 9 16 hardly do we g. aright at things
guest Wisd 5 15 remembrance of a g. of one day
Eccu 29 30 to go as a guest from house to house
Dan 14 1 Daniel was the king's guest and was
Luke 19 7 a guest with a man that was a sinner
22 11 where is the guest chamber, where I
guests 2 K 19 28 me thy servant among the g.
3 K 1 49 all the guests of Adonias were afraid
Prov 9 18 her guests are in the depths of hell
Wisd 19 13 brought their guests into bondage that
Eccu 9 22 let just men be thy guests, and let
Soph 1 7 a victim, he hath sanctified his guests
Mat 22 10 the marriage was filled with guests
11 the king went in to see the guests: and
guide Exod 13 21 might be g. of their journey
Num 10 31 wilderness, and thou shalt be our guide
Ps 24 9 he wili guide the mild in judgment
26 11 guide me in the right path, because
54 14 but thou a man of one mind, my guide
79 10 thou wast the guide of its journey
Prov 2 17 forsaketh the guide of her youth
6 7 ant . . . although she hath no guide
11 3 simplicity of the just shall guide them
23 19 wise: and guide thy mind in the way
Wisd 7 15 because he is the guide of wisdom
18 3 a burning pillar of fire for a guide
Jer 3 4 my father, the guide of my virginity
2 Ma 5 15 that traitor . . . being his guide
Rom 2 19 that thou thyself art guide of the blind
guided Judg 16 26 to the lad that guided his steps
Ps 77 52 g. them in the wilderness like a flock
Prov 20 24 steps of a man are guided by the Lord
guider 4 K 13 14 chariot of Israel and the guider
guides 1 Ma 4 2 of the castle were their guides
Mat 23 24 blind guides, who strain out a gnat
guideth Eccu 50 31 the light of God g. his steps
guile Ps 31 2 in whose spirit there is no guile
Ps 33 14 evil, and thy lips from speaking guile
34 20 anger of the earth they devised guile
35 4 words of his mouth are iniquity and g.
Wisd 7 13 which I have learned without guile
14 30 sworn unjustly, in g. despising justice
Eccu 1 40 thy heart is full of guile and deceit
Luke 20 23 he, considering their guile, said to
John 1 47 indeed, in whom there is no guile
Acts 13 10 O full of all guile and of all deceit
2 C 12 16 but being crafty, I caught you by guile
1 P 2 1 laying away all malice and all guile
2 desire the rational milk without guile
22 neither was guile found in his mouth
3 10 and his lips that they speak no guile
guilefully Num 25 18 have g. deceived you by the
guilt Exod 21 16 being convicted of the g., shall
Exod 32 35 for the guilt on occasion of the calf
Deut 19 13 take away the guilt of innocent blood
21 8 g. of blood shall be taken from them
guiltless Exod 20 7 Lord will not hold him g.
1 K 26 9 against Lord's anointed, and shall be g.
2 K 14 9 but may the king and his throne be g.
3 K 2 9 do not thou hold him [Semei] guiltless
guilty Gen 43 9 I will be g. of sin against thee
Gen 44 32 will be g. of sin against my father
Exod 21 20 his hands, shall be guilty of the crime
22 2 slew him shall not be guilty of blood
28 43 lest being guilty of iniquity they die
Lev 5 2 forgetteth his uncleanness, he is g.
3 know it, he shall be g. of an offence
17 and being guilty of sin, understand
7 18 meat, shall be guilty of transgression
17 4 to the Lord, shall be guilty of blood
19 7 shall be profane and g. of impiety
Num 5 27 despised her husband be g. of adultery
26 1 after the blood of the guilty was shed
16 he shall be guilty of murder. 21
27 he shall not be guilty that killed him
31 money of him that is guilty of blood
Deut 19 6 life of him who is not guilty of death
10 possess, lest thou be guilty of blood
21 1 not known who is guilty of the murder
22 8 thou be guilty, if any one slip and fall
26 neither is she guilty of death: for as
Josu 6 18 you be guilty of transgression, and all
7 12 him that is guilty of this wickedness
15 that shall be found guilty of this fact
22 31 because you are not g. of this revolt
2 Es 9 26 they were guilty of great blasphemies
Ps 33 22 they that hate the just shall be guilty
Prov 26 18 as he is guilty that shooteth arrows
Jer 6 13 all are guilty of deceit. And they
Eze 22 4 thou art become guilty in thy blood

Dan 13 53 letting the guilty to go free, whereas
Nah 1 3 will not cleanse and acquit the guilty
2 Ma 4 47 Menelaus who was g. of all the evil
12 3 men of Joppe also were guilty of this
Mat 26 66 answering, said: He is guilty of death
Mark 3 29 shall be guilty of an everlasting sin
14 64 all condemned him to be guilty of death
Acts 19 37 men, who are neither guilty of sacrilege
40 there being no man guilty, of whom we
1 C 11 27 shall be guilty of the body and of the
James 2 10 in one point, is become guilty of all
Guni Gen 46 24 sons of Nephtali . . . Guni. Num 26:48; 1 Pa 7:13
1 Pa 5 15 Abdiel the son of Guni, chief of the
Gunites Num 26 48 of whom is family of the Gunites
Gurbaal 2 Pa 26 7 Arabians that dwelt in Gurbaal
gush Jer 18 14 the cold waters that gush out
gushed Gen 43 30 upon his brother, and tears g. out
Isa 48 21 the rock, and the waters gushed out
Acts 1 18 midst: and all his bowels gushed out
gutters 2 K 5 8 get up to gutters of the tops of

H

ha Job 39 25 heareth the trumpet, he saith: Ha, ha
Eze 25 3 because thou hast said: Ha, ha, upon
Haba 1 Pa 7 34 sons of Somer . . . Haba and Aram
Habacuc Dan 14 32 in Judea a prophet called H.
Dan 14 33 the angel of the Lord said to Habacuc
34 H. said: Lord, I never saw Babylon
36 Habacuc cried, saying: O Daniel, thou
38 set Habacuc again in his own place
Haba 1 1 burden that Habacuc the prophet saw
3 1 a prayer of Habacuc the prophet for
Haber Judg 4 11 H. the Cinite had some time
Judg 4 17 Jahel the wife of H. the Cinite. 5:24
17 king of Asor and the house of Haber
1 Pa 7 31 the sons of Baria: Haber and Melchiel
Haber's Judg 4 21 so Jahel H. wife took a nail
Habia 2 Es 7 63 of the priests the children of H.
habit 2 K 20 8 of equal length with his habit
Phil 2 7 of men, and in habit found as a man. He
habitable Exod 16 35 till they came to a h. land
Jer 22 6 a wilderness and cities not habitable
habitation Exod 15 13 carried them to thy holy h.
Exod 15 17 thy inheritance, in thy most firm h.
Lev 16 16 in midst of the filth of their h.
Num 15 2 shall be come into the land of your h.
24 21 thy habitation indeed is strong: but
33 55 adversaries in the land of your h.
35 33 defile not the land of your habitation
Deut 15 11 wanting poor in the land of thy h.
26 15 thy high h. of heaven, and bless
1 Pa 4 33 this was their h. and the distribution
5 9 eastward he had his h. as far as the
23 25 people, and a h. in Jerusalem forever
Ps 32 14 from his h. which he hath prepared
68 26 let their habitation be made desolate
106 4 not the way of a city for their h.
7 that they might go to a city of h.
36 they made a city for their habitation
Wisd 9 15 the earthly h. presseth down the mind
Isa 12 6 and praise, O thou habitation of Sion
33 20 thy eyes shall see Jerusalem, a rich h.
34 13 it shall be the habitation of dragons
63 15 behold thy holy h. and the place
Jer 9 6 thy h. is in the midst of deceit
25 30 shall utter his voice from his holy h.
33 12 h. of shepherds causing their flocks
48 19 and look out, O habitation of Aroer
49 20 they shall destroy them with their h.
33 Asor shall be a habitation for dragons
50 19 I will bring Israel again to his h.
45 their habitation shall be destroyed
51 35 be upon Babylon, saith the h. of Sion
Haba 3 11 and the moon stood still in their h.
Zach 2 13 for he is risen up out of his holy h.
1 Ma 1 40 the city was made the h. of strangers
3 45 there was the h. of the Gentiles: and
13 48 and he fortified it and made it his h.
2 Ma 11 2 city and make it a h. of the Gentiles
14 35 that the temple of thy h. should be
Acts 1 20 let their h. become desolate, and let
17 26 times, and limits of their habitation
2 C 5 1 know, if our earthly house of this h.
2 to be clothed upon with our h. that is
Eph 2 22 into an habitation of God in the Spirit
Jude 6 but forsook their own habitation, he
Apoc 18 2 and is become the habitation of devils
habitations Exod 12 20 in all your h. you shall
Exod 35 3 shall kindle no fire in any of your h.
Lev 3 17 a perpetual law . . . in all your h.
23 3 the sabbath of the Lord in all your h.
1 Pa 7 28 their possessions and h. were Bethel
Prov 3 33 but the h. of the just shall be blessed
Eze 34 13 I will feed them . . . in all the h.
Habor 4 K 17 6 placed them in Hala and H. 18:11
1 Pa 5 26 brought them to Lahela and to Habor
Habsanias Jer 35 3 Jeremias the son of Habsanias
Haccus 2 Es 3 21 Urias the son of Haccus, built
Haceldama Mat 27 8 field was called H. Acts 1:19
Hachamoni 1 Pa 11 11 Jesbaam the son of H.
1 Pa 27 32 Jahiel the son of Hachamoni were with
Hachelai 2 Es 10 1 Athersatha the son of H.
Hachila 1 K 23 19 holds of the wood in mount H.
1 K 26 1 David is hid in the hill of Hachila
3 Saul encamped in Gabaa Hachila
Hacupha 1 Es 2 51 the children of H. 2 Es 7:53
Hadad 1 Pa 1 30 of Ismahel . . . Massa, Hadad
Hadaia 4 K 22 1 Idida the daughter of Hadaia
Hadar Gen 25 15 Ismael's children . . . Hadar
Hadassa Josu 15 37 Sanan and Hadassa and
Haddan 1 Es 4 2 since the days of Asor Haddan
Hadid 1 Es 2 33 the children of Lod, Hadid
2 Es 7 37 children . . . of Hadid . . . 721
11 34 Hadid, Seboim, and Neballat, Lod
Hadrach Zach 9 1 word of Lord in the land of H.
Hadriel 1 K 18 19 she was given to Hadriel
2 K 21 8 whom she [Michol] bore to Hadriel
haft Judg 3 16 sword with a haft in the midst
Judg 3 22 with such force that the haft went in
Hagab 1 Es 2 46 the children of Hagab, the
Hagaba 1 Es 2 45 the children of H. 2 Es 7:48
Haggi Gen 46 16 sons of Gad: Sephian and H.
Haggia 1 Pa 6 30 Sammaa his son, Haggia his son
Haggith 2 K 3 4 Adonias, son of H. 3 K 1:5, 11; 2:13
Hai Gen 12 8 west, and Hai on the east: he built
Gen 13 3 pitched his tent between Bethel and Hai
Josu 7 2 Josue sent men from Jericho against Hai
2 fulfilled his command, and viewed Hai
5 defeated by the men of the city of Hai
8 1 arise and go up to the town of Hai
2 and thou shalt do to the city of Hai
3 men with him, to go up against Hai: and
9 abode between Bethel and Hai, on the west side of the city of Hai
12 to lie in ambush between Bethel and Hai
14 when king of Hai saw this, he made haste
17 not one remained in the city of Hai and
18 the shield . . . towards the city of Hai
21 returned and slew the men of Hai. And
23 took the king of the city of Hai alive
25 12,000 persons all of city of Hai
26 till all inhabitants of Hai were slain
9 3 that Josue had done to Jericho and Hai
10 1 that Josue had taken Hai and had

1 thereof so did he to Hai and its king
2 and greater than the town of Hai
12 9 the king of Hai, which is on the side
1 Es 2 28 the men of Bethel and Hai. 2 Es 7:32
2 Es 11 31 the children of Benjamin . . . at Hai
Jer 49 3 howl, O Hesebon, for Hai is wasted
hail Exod 9 18 an exceeding great hail: such as
Exod 9 19 the hail shall fall upon, shall die
22 there may be hail in the whole land of
23 and the Lord sent thunder and hail
23 the Lord rained hail upon the land of
24 hail and fire mixed with it drove on
25 the hail destroyed through all the land
25 the hail smote every herb of the field
26 land of Gessen . . . the hail fell not
28 and the hail may cease: that I may
29 cease, and the hail shall be no more
33 and the thunders and the hail ceased
34 the hail and the thunders were ceased
10 5 which the hail hath left may be eaten
12 every herb that is left after the hail
15 on the trees, which the hail had left
Job 38 22 thou beheld the treasures of the hail
Ps 17 13 hail and coals of fire. 14
77 47 he destroyed their vineyards with hail
48 he gave up their cattle to the hail
104 32 gave them hail for rain, a burning
148 8 fire, hail, snow, ice, stormy winds
Wisd 5 23 and thick hail shall be cast upon them
16 16 persecuted by strange waters and hail
22 first burning in the hail . . . destroyed
Eccu 39 35 fire, hail . . . created for vengeance
Isa 28 2 mighty and strong, as a storm of hail
17 h. shall overturn the hope of falsehood
32 19 hail shall be in the descent of forest
Agge 2 18 with the mildew and with hail, yet
Mat 26 49 hail Rabbi. And he kissed. Mark 14:45
27 29 hail, king of the Jews. Mark 15:18; John 19:3
28 9 Jesus met them, saying: All hail. But
Luke 1 28 hail, full of grace, the Lord is with
Apoc 8 7 there followed hail and fire, mingled
11 19 and an earthquake and great hail
16 21 great hail, like a talent, came down
21 for the plague of the hail: because it
hailstones Josu 10 11 more were killed with h.
Eccu 43 16 fixed the clouds, and the h. are broken
46 6 heard him by h. of exceeding great
Isa 30 30 he shall crush to pieces with . . . h.
Eze 13 11 I will cause great hailstones to fall
13 and great h. in my wrath to consume
38 22 blood and with violent rain, and vast h.
hair Exod 25 4 and fine linen and goat's hair
Exod 26 7 eleven curtains of goats' hair. 36:14
8 length of one hair curtain shall be
35 6 fine linen and goat's hair. 23, 26
Lev 13 3 in his skin, and the hair turned white
4 the hair be of the former color. 21
10 shall have changed the look of the h.
20 flesh, and the hair turned white
26 if the color of the hair be not changed
30 the hair yellow and thinner than
31 that is near it, and the hair black
32 not grown, and the hair keep its color
36 whether the hair be turned yellow
37 spot be stayed, and the hair be black
40 the man whose hair falleth off from
41 if the hair fall from his forehead, he is
14 8 shall shave all the hair of his body
9 he shall shave the hair of his head
9 eyebrows and the hair of all his body
19 27 nor shall you cut your hair roundwise
Num 6 5 shall let the hair of his head grow
18 the hair of the consecration of the
18 take his hair and lay it upon the fire
31 20 for use, of the skins or hair of goats
Deut 21 12 she shall shave her hair and pare her
Judg 16 22 and now his hair began to grow again
20 16 so sure that they could hit even a hair
1 K 14 45 shall not one hair of his head fall
19 13 and put a goat's skin with the hair
2 K 14 11 shall not one hair of thy son fall to
26 and when he [Absalom] polled his hair
26 because his hair was burdensome to him
26 he weighed the hair of his head at
3 K 1 52 so much as one hair of his head fall
2 Es 13 25 and shaved off their hair and made them
Jdth 10 3 plaited the hair of her head and put a
13 9 she took him by the hair of his head
Esth 14 2 to rejoice, she filled with her torn hair
Job 4 15 before me, the hair of my flesh stood up
Cant 4 1 thy hair is as flocks of goats, which
9 eyes, and with one hair of thy neck
6 4 thy hair is as a flock of goats, that
Eccu 27 15 shall make the hair of the head stand
Isa 3 17 and the Lord will discover their hair
24 and instead of curled hair, baldness
Jer 7 29 cut off thy hair and cast it away: and
9 26 all that have their hair polled round
25 23 that have their hair cut round. 49:32
Eze 5 1 a sharp knife that shaveth the hair
1 thee a balance . . . and divide the hair
16 7 were fashioned, and thy hair grew
44 20 shave their heads nor wear long hair
Dan 3 94 not a hair of their head had been
7 9 the hair of his head like clean wool
14 26 Daniel took pitch and fat and hair
35 carried him by the hair of his head
2 Ma 7 7 off the skin of his head with the hair
Mat 3 4 had his garment of camels' hair and a
5 36 not make one hair white or black
Mark 1 6 John was clothed with camel's hair; and
Luke 21 18 a hair of your head shall not perish
11 2 wiped his feet with her hair. 12:3
Acts 27 34 for there shall not an hair of the head
1 C 11 14 if he nourish his hair, it is a shame
15 if a woman nourish her hair, it is glory
15 her hair is given to her for a covering
1 Tim 2 9 not with plated h., or gold, or pearls
1 P 3 3 the outward plaiting of the hair or
Apoc 6 12 sun became black as sackcloth of hair
9 8 and they had hair as the hair of women
haircloth 2 K 21 10 daughter of Aia took h.
3 K 21 27 put h. upon his flesh and fasted and
4 K 6 30 the people saw the h. which he wore
1 Pa 21 16 the ancients clothed in h., fell down
Jdth 4 8 altar of the Lord they covered with h.
8 6 she wore h. upon her loins and fasted
9 1 putting on h., laid ashes on her head
10 2 she took off her h. and put away the
Ps 34 13 I was clothed with h. I humbled
68 12 I made h. my garment: and I became
Isa 3 24 and instead of a stomacher, haircloth
Jer 4 8 gird yourselves with h., lament and
48 37 and upon every back there shall be h.
49 3 gird yourselves with h.: mourn and
Lam 2 10 with dust, they are girded with h.
Eze 7 18 and they shall gird themselves with h.
27 31 shall be girded with h.: and they
1 Ma 2 14 they covered themselves with haircloth
3 47 they fasted that day and put on h.
2 Ma 3 19 the women, girded with h. about their
10 25 heads and girding their loins with h.
haircloths Lev 11 32 a garment or skins or h.
Jdth 4 8 the priests put on h. and they caused
15 sacrifices to the Lord girded with h.
hairs Gen 42 38 will bring down my gray h. 44:29

Gen 44 31 his gray hairs with sorrow unto hell
Num 8 7 let them shave all the hairs of their
Judg 16 14 he drew out the nail with the hairs
3 K 2 9 down his gray hairs with blood to hell
1 Es 9 3 and plucked off the hairs of my head
Ps 39 13 multiplied above the h. of my. 68:5
70 18 unto old age and gray hairs: O God
Prov 20 29 dignity of old men, their gray hairs
Cant 7 5 hairs of thy head as the purple of the
Wisd 2 10 nor honor the ancient gray h. of the
4 8 understanding of a man is gray hairs
Eccu 6 18 to thy gray h. thou shalt find wisdom
Isa 7 20 shall shave . . . the hairs of the feet
46 4 to your gray hairs I will carry you
Dan 4 30 till his hairs grew like the feathers
Osee 7 9 gray hairs also are spread about
Mat 10 30 hairs of your head are all. Luke 12:7
Luke 7 38 and wiped them with the hairs of her
44 and with her hairs hath wiped them
Apoc 1 14 his head and his hairs were white as
hairy Gen 25 25 came forth first was red, and h.
Gen 27 11 knowest that Esau . . . is a hairy man
23 his hairy hands made him like to the
4 K 1 8 a hairy man with a girdle of leather
Ps 67 22 the h. crown of them that walk on in
Isa 13 21 and the hairy ones shall dance there
34 14 and the hairy ones shall cry out one
Hala 4 K 17 6 he placed them in Hala and. 18:11
Halaa 1 Pa 4 5 had two wives, Halaa and Maara
1 Pa 4 7 the sons of Halaa, Sereth, Isaar, and
Halcath Josu 19 25 their border was H. and Chali
hale Job 21 23 one man dieth strong and hale
half Exod 24 6 Moses took half of the blood
Exod 25 10 be of two cubits and a half. 17
10 the breadth, a cubit and a half. 17
10 the height likewise a cubit and a half
23 table . . . a cubit and a half in height
26 12 with the half thereof thou shalt cover
16 in breadth one cubit and a half
30 13 every one give . . . half a sicle
13 half a sicle shall be offered to the
15 rich man shall not add to half a sicle
23 and of cinnamon half so much
36 21 the breadth was one cubit and a half
37 1 two cubits and a half in length. 6
1 and a cubit and a half in breadth. 6
1 the height was of one cubit and a half
10 in height it was a cubit and a half
Lev 6 20 half of it in the morning, and half of it in the evening
Num 15 9 flour tempered with half a hin of oil
28 14 half a hin for every calf, a third for
31 42 out of the half of the children of
43 out of the half that fell to the rest
34 13 to the nine tribes and to the half tribe
15 two tribes and a half, have received
Deut 3 12 unto the half of mount Galaad: and I
16 half the torrent and the confines
Josu 8 33 half of them by mount Garizim and half by
12 2 had dominion . . . of half Galaad as far as
5 unto borders . . . of half Galaad: the
13 25 half the land of the children of Ammon
31 half Galaad and Astaroth and Edrai
14 2 to the nine tribes and the half tribe
3 to two tribes and a half Moses had given
22 7 to the half that remained Josue gave
1 K 14 14 slaughter . . . within half an acre of land
2 K 10 4 cut away half of their garments even to
19 40 half of people of Israel were there
3 K 3 25 give half to the one, and half to the
10 7 found that the half hath not been told
13 8 if thou wouldst give me half thy house
16 9 who was captain of half the horsemen
1 Pa 2 52 he that saw half of the places of rest
54 half of the place of rest of Sarai
2 Es 3 11 Melchias . . . built half the street and
12 lord of half the street of. 16, 17
18 the son of Enadad, lord of half Ceila
4 6 joined it all together unto the half
16 half of their young men did the work and half were ready for to fight
12 32 Osias, and half of the princes of Juda
37 the half of the people upon the wall
39 the half of the magistrates with me
13 24 spoke half in the speech of Azotus
Tob 8 24 the half that remained should after
10 10 Sara unto him and half of all his
11 14 and he stayed about half an hour
12 5 half of all things that they had brought
Esth 5 6 shouldst ask the half of my kingdom
7 2 although thou ask the half of my kingdom
Ps 54 24 shall not live out half their days
Wisd 18 18 thrown here, another there, half dead
Eze 16 51 Samaria committed not half thy sins
40 42 one cubit and a half long, and one cubit and a half broad
43 17 round about it was half a cubit
Dan 7 25 a time and times and half a time. 12:7
9 27 in the half of the week the victim
Osee 3 2 and for half a core of barley
Zach 14 2 half of the city shall go forth into
4 half of the mountain shall be separated
4 the north and half thereof to the south
8 half of them to the east sea, and half of them to the last sea
1 Ma 3 34 he delivered to him half the army
37 the king took half of the army that
10 30 and the half of the fruit of trees
Mark 6 23 though it be the half of my kingdom
Luke 10 30 went away, leaving him half dead
19 8 the half of my goods I give to the
Apoc 8 1 silence . . . as it were for half an hour
11 9 their bodies for three days and a half
11 after three days and a half, the spirit
12 14 for a time and times, and half a time
one half Num 12 12 one half of her flesh is
Num 31 36 one h. was given to them that had been
Josu 13 31 to one half of the children of Machir
2 K 10 4 shaved off the one h. of their beards
3 K 16 21 one half of the people followed Thebni . . . and one half followed Amri
2 Pa 9 6 scarce one half of thy wisdom had been
2 Es 4 21 let one half of us hold our spears
Tob 8 24 he gave one half to Tobias, and made
12 4 to accept of one half of all things
Esth 5 3 if thou shouldst even ask one half of
Job 21 21 of his months be diminished by one h.
Eccu 29 7 he will scarce pay one half and will
half tribe of Manasses; *see* **Manasses**
Halhul Josu 15 58 Halhul and Bessur and Gedor
hall 2 Pa 4 9 great h., and doors in the h.
Esth 5 1 house, over against the king's hall
1 his throne in the hall of the palace
Mat 27 27 taking Jesus into the hall, gathered
Luke 22 55 kindled a fire in the midst of the h.
John 18 28 from Caiphas to the governor's hall
28 and they went not into the hall, that
33 Pilate therefore went into the h. 19:9
Acts 23 35 him to be kept in Herod's judgment hall
25 23 had entered into hall of audience, with
hallowed 1 K 21 6 priest . . . gave him h. bread
Mat 6 9 hallowed be thy name. Luke 11:2
halt 3 K 18 21 how long do you halt between two
halted Gen 32 31 but he halted on his foot
Ps 17 46 and have halted from their paths
halter Mat 27 5 hanged himself with an halter

halteth Mich 4 6 I will gather up her that h.
Mich 4 7 I will make her that halteth, a
Soph 3 19 I will save her that halteth, and will
halting Heb 12 13 no one, h., may go out of the
Hamathite Gen 10 18 Chanaan begot . . . the H. 1 Pa 1:16
Hamdan Gen 36 26 the sons of Dison: H. and Eseban
hammer Judg 4 21 taking also a h.: and going in
Judg 4 21 striking it with the hammer, drove it
5 26 her right hand to the workman's h.
3 K 6 7 there was neither hammer nor axe nor
Job 41 20 as stubble will he esteem the hammer
Eccu 38 30 noise of the hammer is always in his
Isa 41 7 coppersmith striking with the hammer
Jer 23 29 as a hammer that breaketh the rock
50 23 the hammer of the whole earth broken
hammerer Gen 4 22 Tubalcain, who was a h.
hammers Prov 19 29 hammers for the bodies of fools
Isa 44 12 and with hammers he hath formed it
Jer 10 4 put it together with nails and hammers
Hammoth Josu 21 32 Hammoth Dor, and Carthan
Hamon Josu 19 28 Rohob and Hamon and Cana
1 Pa 6 76 out of the tribe of Nephtali . . . Hamon
Hamram 1 Pa 1 41 sons of Dison: Hamram
hamstring Josu 11 6 thou shalt h. their horses
hamstringed Josu 11 9 he h. their horses and
Hamuel 1 Pa 4 26 sons of Masma: Hamuel
Hamul Gen 46 12 sons were born to Phares: . . . H.
Num 26 21 sons of Phares were Hesron . . . and H.
1 Pa 2 5 sons of Phares were Hesron and Hamul
Hamulites Num 26 21 of whom is family of the H.
Hanadad 2 Es 3 24 Bennui the son of Hanadad
Hanameel Jer 31 38 from the tower of H. even
Jer 32 7 H. the son of Sellum thy cousin
8 Hanameel my uncle's son came to me
9 and I bought the field of Hanameel
Hanan 1 Pa 4 20 Rinna the son of Hanan and Thilon
1 Pa 8 23 and Abdon and Zechri and Hanan and
38 Ismahel, Saria, Obdia, and Hanan. 9:44
11 43 Hanan the son of Maacha, and Josaphat
1 Es 2 46 the children of Hanan, the. 2 Es 7:49
2 Es 8 7 Jozabed, Hanan, Phalaia, the Levites
10 10 Celita, Phalaia, Hanan, Micha, Rohob
22 Pheltia, Hanan, Anaia, Osee, Hanania
13 13 and next to them Hanan, the son of
Jer 35 4 to treasure house of the sons of Hanan
Hananeel 2 Es 3 1 the tower of H. 12:38; Zach 14:10
Hanani 3 K 16 1 Jehu the son of H. 7; 2 Pa 19:2; 20:34
1 Pa 25 4 Hananias, Hanani, Eliatha, Geddelthi
25 the eighteenth lot to Hanani, the
2 Pa 16 7 at that time Hanani the prophet came
2 Es 1 2 that Hanani one of my brethren came
7 2 I commanded Hanani my brother, and
12 35 Judas and Hanani, with the musical
Hanania 1 Pa 8 24 and Hanania . . . sons of Sesac
1 Es 10 28 of the sons of Babai . . . Hanania
2 Es 3 30 after him built Hanania the son of
10 23 Osee, Hanania, Hasub, Alohes, Phalea
12 12 Saraia, Maraia: of Jeremias, Hanania
40 Zacharia, Hanania with trumpets. And
Hananias 1 Pa 3 19 Zorobabel begot . . . Hananias
1 Pa 3 21 the son of Hananias was Phaltias
25 4 Jerimoth, Hananias, Hanani
23 the sixteenth [lot] to Hananias
2 Es 7 2 I commanded . . . Hananias ruler of the
Jer 28 1 Hananias the son of Azur, a prophet
5 Jeremias the prophet said to H. 15
10 Hananias the prophet took the chain
11 H. spoke in presence of all the people
12 after that H. the prophet had broken
13 and tell Hananias: Thus saith the Lord
15 hear now, Hananias: The Lord hath
17 Hananias the prophet died in that year
36 12 Sedecias the son of Hananias, and
37 12 Selemias the son of Hananias: and he
Hanathon Josu 19 14 to the north of Hanathon
handbreadth 3 K 7 26 the laver was a h. thick
2 Pa 4 5 thickness of it was a handbreadth
Eze 40 5 reed of six cubits and a handbreadth
43 the borders of them were of one h.
43 13 truest cubit, which is a cubit and a h.
13 the border thereof one handbreadth
handed 2 K 17 2 he is now weary and weak handed
Eccu 29 12 send him not away empty handed because
handful Lev 2 2 shall take a h. of the flour. 6:15
Lev 5 12 priest; who shall take a handful thereof
Num 5 26 to take a handful of the sacrifice of
3 K 17 12 but only a handful of meal in a pot
Ecce 4 6 better is a handful with rest, than
13 19 violated me . . . for a handful of barley
handfuls Exod 9 8 take to you handfuls of ashes
Ruth 2 16 let fall some of your h. of purpose
3 K 20 10 dust of Samaria shall suffice for h.
handkerchiefs Acts 19 12 his body to the sick, h.
handle Deut 19 5 the iron slipping from the h.
Wisd 15 15 nor fingers of hands to handle, and
Luke 24 39 it is I myself; handle and see
Col 2 21 touch not, taste not, handle not; which
handled Eze 21 11 furbished, that it may be h.
Eze 27 29 all that handled the oar shall come
2 Ma 5 16 unworthily handled and profaned them
1 J 1 1 upon, and our hands have handled
handling 2 Ma 2 49 the exact h. of every particluar
2 Tim 2 15 rightly handling the word of truth. But
handmaid Gen 16 1 Sarai . . . having a handmaid
Gen 16 2 me from bearing: go in unto my h.
3 [Sarai] took Agar the Egyptian her h.
5 I gave my handmaid into thy bosom
6 thy h. is in thy own hand, use her as
8 Agar, handmaid of Sarai, whence comest
29 24 giving his daughter a h. named Zelpha
30 9 gave Zelpha her handmaid to her husband
18 because I gave my h. to my husband
35 25 the sons of Bala, Rachel's handmaid
26 the sons of Zelpha, Lia's handmaid
Exod 11 5 firstborn of the h. that is at the
20 17 neither shalt thou desire . . . his h.
23 12 son of thy h. and the stranger may be
Judg 9 18 Abimelech the son of his handmaid
19 19 for the use of myself and of thy h.
Ruth 2 13 and hast spoken to the heart of thy h.
3 9 I am Ruth thy handmaid: spread thy
1 K 1 11 not forget thy h. and wilt give to
16 count not thy h. for one of daughters
18 thy h. may find grace in thy eyes. So
25 24 let thy handmaid speak, I beseech
25 but I thy h. did not see thy servants
27 which thy h. hath brought to thee
28 forgive the iniquity of thy handmaid
31 thou shalt remember thy handmaid. And
41 thy servant be a h. to wash the feet
28 21 thy handmaid hath obeyed thy voice
22 hear thou also the voice of thy h.
2 K 14 6 thy handmaid had two sons: and they
7 whole kindred rising against thy h.
12 let thy handmaid speak one word to my
15 thy h. said: I will speak to the king
15 king will perform request of his h.
16 to deliver his handmaid out of the hand
17 let thy h. say, that the word of the
19 these words into the mouth of thy h.
20 17 hear the words of thy handmaid. He
3 K 1 13 didst not thou . . . swear to me thy h.
17 thou didst swear to thy h. by the Lord
3 20 while I thy h. was asleep, and laid
4 K 4 2 I thy handmaid have nothing in my house

16 man of God, do not lie to thy handmaid
Jdth 11 4 receive the words of thy handmaid, for
4 if thou wilt follow the words of thy h.
13 I thy h. knowing this, am fled from
14 I thy handmaid worship God even now
14 thy h. will go out, and I will pray
12 4 thy h. shall not spend all these things
13 18 by me his h. he hath fulfilled his
20 not suffered me his h. to be defiled
16 28 made her handmaid free, and she died
Esth 14 18 thy handmaid hath never rejoiced, since
15 10 she rested her weary head upon her h.
Ps 85 16 and save the son of thy handmaid
115 16 I am . . . the son of thy handmaid
122 2 as the eyes of the handmaid are on the
Wisd 9 5 I am thy servant and son of thy h.
Eccu 41 27 be not inquisitive after his handmaid
Isa 24 2 as with the h., so with her mistress
Luke 1 38 behold the h. of the Lord; be it done
48 hath regarded the humility of his h.
handmaids Gen 20 14 oxen and servants and h.
Gen 20 17 Abimelech and his wife and his h.
31 33 went into the tent . . . of both the h.
32 22 he took his two wives and his two h.
33 1 divided the children . . . of the two h.
2 put both the handmaids . . . foremost
6 handmaids and their children came near
1 K 8 16 servants also and h. . . . he will take
2 K 6 20 uncovering himself before the h. of
22 with the handmaids . . . I shall appear
Esth 4 16 I with my handmaids will fast in like
Job 40 24 with a bird, or tie him up for thy h.
Prov 27 27 house and for maintenance for thy h.
Isa 14 2 possess them . . . for servants and h.
Jer 34 11 back again their servants and their h.
16 subjection to be your servants and h.
Joel 2 29 upon my servants and h. in those days
Acts 2 18 and upon my h. will I pour out in
handsome Zach 11 13 a h. price, that I was prized
handstaves Eze 39 9 and burn . . . the handstaves
handwriting Col 2 14 blotting out the h. of the
Hanes Isa 30 4 thy messengers came even to Hanes
hang Gen 40 19 and hang thee on a cross
Exod 26 13 there shall hang down a cubit on the
32 shalt hang it up before four pillars
39 17 the two golden chains should hang
Num 25 4 hang them up on gibbets against the sun
Deut 11 18 hang them for a sign on your hands
Jdth 14 1 hang ye up this head upon our walls
Cant 4 4 a thousand bucklers hang upon it, all
Eccu 28 7 corruption and death hang over in his
Isa 22 24 they shall hang upon him all the glory
Lam 2 10 virgins of Jerusalem hang down their
Eze 15 3 of it for any vessel to hang thereon
Heb 12 12 lift up the hands which hang down
hanged Gen 40 22 the other he h. on a gibbet
Gen 41 13 office: and he was hanged upon a gibbet
Exod 26 33 the veils shall be hanged on with rings
Num 3 26 that is h. in the entry of the court
Deut 21 22 condemned to die is hanged on a gibbet
Josu 10 26 and hanged them upon five gibbets
2 K 4 12 hanged them over the pool in Hebron
17 23 Achitophel . . . hanged himself, and was
21 12 where the Philistines had hanged them
Lam 5 12 the princes were hanged up by their
1 Ma 1 64 they hanged the children about their
4 57 chambers, and hanged doors upon them
2 Ma 15 33 hand of the furious man to be h. up
Mat 18 6 millstone should be hanged about his neck. Mark 9:41; Luke 17:2
27 5 and hanged himself with an halter
Luke 23 39 one of those robbers who were hanged
Acts 1 18 being hanged, burst asunder in the
hangeth Exod 30 6 veil, that h. before the ark
Exod 38 26 of the entry where the veil hangeth
Num 4 5 shall take down the veil that hangeth
25 the hanging that hangeth in the entry
Deut 11 21 long as the heaven h. over the earth
21 23 accursed of God that hangeth on a tree
2 Pa 28 11 indignation of the Lord h. over you
13 fierce anger of the Lord h. over Israel
Job 15 27 and the fat hangeth down on his sides
26 7 space, and h. the earth upon nothing
Gal 3 13 cursed is every one that hangeth on tree
hanging Exod 26 36 make also a h. in the entrance
Exod 26 37 before which the hanging shall be drawn
27 16 be made a hanging of twenty cubits of
28 38 h. over forehead of the high priest
35 15 the h. at the door of the tabernacle
17 the hanging in the door of the entry
36 37 he made also a hanging in the entry
38 18 an embroidered hanging of violet
39 38 h. in the entry of the tabernacle. 40:5, 26
40 the hanging in the entry of the court
40 31 drawing the h. in the entry thereof
Lev 13 45 shall have his clothes hanging loose
Num 3 26 h. also that is hanged in the entry of
26 the h. that is drawn before the doors
4 25 the hanging that hangeth in the entry
Deut 28 66 shall be as it were h. before thee
2 K 18 10 saying: I saw Absalom h. upon an oak
20 8 with a sword h. down to his flank in a
3 K 7 29 as it were bands of brass hanging down
Jdth 15 2 but hanging down the head, leaving all
Job 7 15 that my soul rather chooseth hanging
32 6 h. down my head, I was afraid to show
Isa 3 21 and jewels hanging on the forehead and
Jer 52 23 were 96 pomegranates hanging down: and
2 Ma 6 10 the infants hanging at their breasts
Acts 5 30 hanging him upon a tree. 10:39
28 4 saw the beast h. on his hand, they said
hangings Exod 27 9 shall be h. of fine twisted
Exod 27 11 shall be hangings of 100 cubits long
12 hangings of fifty cubits. 38:12, 13
14 hangings of fifteen cubits. 15
38 9 were hangings of fine twisted linen
11 at the north side the hangings, the
15 were hangings equally of fifteen cubits
16 the hangings of the court were woven
39 39 the hangings of the court, and the
40 8 shalt encompass the court with hangings
Esth 1 6 hangings fastened with cords of silk
hangs Exod 27 21 that hangs before the testimony
Job 23 17 the darkness that hangs over me
Haniel 1 Pa 7 39 sons of Olla: Aree and Haniel
Hanni 2 Es 12 9 Becbecia and Hanni and their
Hanniel Num 34 23 of the tribe of Manasses, H.
Hanon 2 K 10 1 Hanon his son reigned in his
2 K 10 2 I will show kindness to H. 1 Pa 19:2
3 said to Hanon their lord: Thinkest
4 Hanon took the servants of David and
1 Pa 19 2 they were come . . . to comfort Hanon
3 said to Hanon: Thou thinkest perhaps
4 Hanon shaved the heads and beards of
6 Hanon and the rest of the people sent
Hanun 2 Es 3 13 gate of the valley H. built
2 Es 3 30 after him built . . . Hanun the sixth
Hapham 1 Pa 7 12 Sepham and H. the sons of Hir
Hapharaim Josu 19 19 Hapharaim and Seon
Haphsiba 2 K 21 2 the name of his mother was H.
happen 1 K 10 7 these signs shall h. to thee
1 K 28 10 there shall no evil happen to thee
3 K 8 38 whatsoever curse . . . shall happen to
Tob 2 12 permitted to happen to him that an
6 15 lest the same thing should happen to me
7 11 fear lest it might happen to him also

Ecce 8 14 there are just men to whom evils happen
9 2 all things equally happen to the just
3 that the same things happen to all men
Wisd 2 17 let us prove what shall happen to him
Eccu 22 31 if any evil happen to me by him, I
33 1 no evils shall h. to him that feareth
40 8 such things happen to all flesh, from
Joel 1 2 did this ever happen in your days or
2 Ma 12 24 by his death might h. to be deceived
Mark 13 18 that these things happen not in winter
Luke 21 13 it shall h. unto you for a testimony
John 5 14 lest some worse thing happen to thee
happened Gen 26 1 barrenness which had h. in the
Gen 26 20 on occasion of that which had happened
31 35 it has now happened to me according to
39 11 happened on a certain day that Joseph
Lev 10 19 and to me what thou seest has happened
Ruth 2 3 happened that the owner of that field
1 K 6 9 touched us, but it hath h. by chance
10 11 that hath happened to the son of Cis
14 15 and it happened as a miracle from God
38 see by whom this sin hath happened
20 26 thought it might have happened to him
25 2 it happened that he was shearing his
2 K 11 2 it h. that David arose from his bed
18 9 it h. that Absalom met the servants of
20 1 there h. to be there a man of Belial
4 K 6 5 it h. as one was felling some timber
2 Pa 18 33 it happened that one of the people shot
32 31 to inquire of the wonder that had h.
Tob 2 10 it happened one day that being wearied
3 7 it happened on the same day that Sara
7 11 knowing what had h. to those seven
8 12 lest perhaps it may have happened to
17 it hath not happened as we suspected
Jdth 5 13 to tell what had happened to posterity
8 27 have happened for our amendment and not
Ps 118 56 this h. to me: because I sought after
Wisd 19 4 of those things which had happened
Isa 51 19 two things that have happened to thee
Bar 2 2 such as never happened under heaven
Eze 16 34 it hath h. in thee contrary to the
Dan 5 10 what had happened to the king and his
1 Ma 4 26 and told Lysias all that had happened
5 25 all that happened to their brethren
2 Ma 1 34 that he might prove what had happened
5 17 this contempt had h. to the place
6 12 they consider the things that h., not
9 3 the news of what had h. to Nicanor
7 it h. as he was going with violence
10 10 the evils that happened in the wars
11 1 greatly displeased with what had h.
12 34 h. that a few of the Jews were slain
42 they saw before their eyes what had h.
13 7 it happened that Menelaus . . . was put
Mark 9 20 time is it since this hath h. unto him
Luke 8 42 it h. as he went, that he was thronged
24 14 of all these things which had happened
Acts 3 10 at that which had happened to him
5 7 wife, not knowing what had happened
28 8 it h. that the father of Publius lay
Rom 11 25 that blindness in part has h. in Israel
1 C 10 11 all these things h. to them in figure
Phil 1 12 the things which have happened to me
1 P 4 12 as if some new thing happened to you
2 P 2 22 that of the true proverb has happened
happeneth Bar 3 10 how h. it, O Israel, that
Luke 12 54 shower is coming: and so it happeneth
Happhim 1 Pa 7 15 took wives for his sons H. and
happier Ecce 4 3 him h. than them both, that
happily Gen 30 11 she said: Happily. And
Prov 30 29 and the fourth that walketh happily
Luke 13 9 if happily it bear fruit: but if not
Acts 17 27 if h. they may feel after him or find
happiness Gen 30 13 Lia said: This is for my h.
2 Ma 9 19 wisheth much health and welfare and h.
happy 2 Pa 9 7 h. are thy men and happy are thy
Tob 13 20 happy shall I be if there shall remain
Job 21 23 dieth strong and hale, rich and happy
Ps 143 15 they have called the people happy that
15 happy is that people whose God is the
Wisd 3 13 is cursed: for happy is the barren: and
Eccu 14 2 happy is he that hath no sadness of
25 32 that doth not make her husband happy
26 1 happy is the husband of a good wife
Bar 4 4 we are happy, O Israel: because the
Mala 3 15 now we call the proud people happy
1 Ma 10 55 happy is the day wherein thou didst
2 Ma 7 24 would make him a rich and a happy man
Acts 26 2 I think myself happy, O king Agrippa
Harad Judg 7 1 fountain that is called Harad
Haram 2 Es 12 15 of Haram, Edna: of Maraioth
Isa 37 12 have destroyed, Gozam and Haram and
Haran Gen 11 31 they came as far as Haran
Gen 11 32 and he [Thare] died in Haran. And the
12 4 when he [Abram] went forth from Haran
5 souls which they had gotten in Haran
27 43 and flee to Laban my brother in Haran
28 10 Jacob . . . went on to Haran. And when
29 4 whence are you? They answered: Of H.
4 K 19 12 destroyed, to wit, Gozan and Haran and
1 Pa 2 46 the concubine of Caleb bore Haran
46 and Gezez. And Haran begot Gezez
2 Es 10 26 Echaia, Hanan, Anan, Melluch, Haran
27 Hanan, Anan, Melluch, Haran, Baana
Eze 27 23 H. and Chene . . . were thy merchants
Harbona Esth 1 10 he commanded . . . Harbona and
Esth 7 9 Harbona . . . said: Behold the gibbet
harbor 1 Tim 5 10 if she have received to harbor
harborless Isa 58 7 bring the needy and the h.
hard Gen 18 14 is there anything hard to God
Gen 35 17 by reason of her hard labor she began
45 5 let it not seem to you a hard case
Exod 1 14 life better with hard works in clay
9 35 it was made exceeding hard: neither did
22 25 thou shalt not be hard upon them as
Deut 1 17 if anything seem hard to you, refer
17 8 a hard and doubtful matter in judgment
Josu 4 3 to take . . . twelve very hard stones
9 5 the loaves . . . were hard and broken
Judg 11 5 and as they pressed hard upon them
2 K 3 39 the sons of Sarvia are too hard for me
13 2 he thought it hard to do anything
3 K 10 1 came to try him with hard questions
4 K 2 10 thou [Eliseus] hast asked a hard thing
1 Pa 10 3 and the battle grew hard against Saul
2 Pa 9 1 came to try him with hard questions
Job 41 15 his heart shall be as hard as a stone
Ps 16 4 words of thy lips, I have kept h. ways
59 5 thou hast shown thy people hard things
Prov 30 18 three things are hard to me, and the
Ecce 1 8 things are hard: man cannot explain
15 the perverse are hard to be corrected
Cant 8 6 as death, jealousy as hard as hell
Wisd 5 7 and have walked through hard ways, but
11 4 of their thirst out of the hard stone
Eccu 3 27 a hard heart shall fear evil at the
26 28 appeared to me hard and dangerous
31 31 fire trieth hard iron: so wine drunk
Isa 14 3 thee rest . . . from the hard bondage
22 3 are fled together and are bound hard
27 1 Lord with his hard and great . . . sword
50 7 set my face as a hard rock, and
Jer 5 23 heart of this people is become hard
32 17 arm: no word shall be hard to thee
27 flesh: shall anything be hard for me

Eze 2 4 are children of a hard face and of an
3 7 of a hard forehead and an obstinate
29 18 made his army to undergo hard service
Jon 1 13 the men rowed hard to return to land
Zach 8 6 if it seem hard in the eyes of the
6 shall it be hard in my eyes, saith the
1 Ma 9 17 the battle was hard fought. 10:50
2 Ma 12 11 after a hard fight, in which by the
21 it was . . . hard to come at by reason
Mat 25 24 I know that thou art a hard man; thou
Mark 10 24 how hard is it for them that trust in
John 6 61 saying is hard, and who can hear it
Acts 9 5 it is hard for thee to kick. 26:14
Heb 5 11 and hard to be intelligibly uttered
2 P 3 16 certain things hard to be understood
Jude 15 hard things which ungodly sinners have
harden Exod 4 21 I shall h. his heart. 7:3; 14:4
Exod 14 17 I will h. the heart of the Egyptians
Deut 15 7 thou shalt not harden thy heart nor
1 K 6 6 why do you harden your hearts, as
2 Pa 30 8 harden not your necks, as your fathers
Ps 94 8 hear his voice: harden not your hearts
Heb 3 8 harden not your hearts. 15; 4:7
hardened Exod 7 13 Pharao's heart was hardened. 22; 8:19, 32; 9:7
Exod 7 14 Pharao's heart is h. he will not
8 15 h. his own heart and did not hear
9 12 the Lord h. Pharao's heart. 10:20, 27; 11:10
35 his heart was h., and the heart of
10 1 I have h. his heart and the heart of
13 15 when Pharao was hardened and would not
14 8 the Lord hardened the heart of Pharao
Deut 2 30 Lord thy God had hardened his spirit
Josu 11 20 that their hearts should be hardened
1 K 6 6 as Egypt and Pharao h. their hearts
4 K 17 14 h. their necks like to the neck of
2 Pa 36 13 and he hardened his neck and his heart
2 Es 9 16 dealt proudly and hardened their necks
17 they hardened their necks and gave
29 and h. their neck and would not hear
Job 11 13 thou hast h. thy heart, and hast spread
38 30 the waters are hardened like a stone
39 16 she is h. against her young ones, as
Prov 28 14 he that is h. in mind, shall fall into
Isa 63 17 why hast thou hardened our heart, that
Jer 7 26 but have hardened their neck and have
17 23 h. their neck, that they might not
19 15 because they have h. their necks, that
30 14 thy iniquities, thy sins are hardened
15 for thy h. sins I have done these
Dan 5 20 and his spirit hardened unto pride
John 12 40 their eyes, and hardened their heart
Acts 19 9 some were hardened, and believed not
Heb 3 13 that none of you be hardened through
hardeneth Prov 21 29 wicked man impudently h. his
Rom 9 18 he will; and whom he will, he hardeneth
harder Jer 5 2 their faces h. than the rock
Eze 3 8 and thy forehead harder than their
hardest Deut 8 15 streams out of the h. rock
Deut 32 13 and oil out of the hardest stone
hardhearted Isa 46 11 hear me, O ye h., who are
hardiness 2 Ma 13 18 taste of the h. of the Jews
hardly Wisd 9 16 h. do we guess aright at things
Eccu 13 32 token . . . thou shalt hardly find
26 28 a merchant is h. free from negligence
Mat 19 23 a rich man shall hardly enter into the
Mark 10 23 h. shall they that have. Luke 18:24
Luke 9 39 him, he hardly departeth from him
hardness Job 30 21 in the h. of thy hand thou
Prov 25 15 and a soft tongue shall break hardness
Eccu 16 11 together in the hardness of their heart
Isa 47 9 for the great h. of thy enchanters
Mat 19 8 by reason of the h. of your. Mark 10:5
Mark 16 14 their incredulity and h. of heart
Rom 2 5 according to thy h. and impenitent heart
hare Lev 11 6 is unclean. The hare also: for that
Deut 14 7 not eat, such as the camel, the hare
Harem 2 Es 7 35 children of Harem, 320. The
2 Es 10 5 Harem, Merimuth, Obdias, Daniel
Hareph 2 Es 7 24 children of Hareph, 112
2 Es 10 19 Hareph, Anathoth, Nebai, Megphias
Hares Judg 1 35 he dwelt in the mountain Hares
Haret 1 K 22 5 and came into the forest of Haret
Harhur 1 Es 2 51 the children of H. 2 Es 7:53
Harim 1 Pa 24 8 the third [lot] to Harim
1 Es 2 32 the children of Harim. 39
10 21 of the sons of Harim, Maasia and Elia
Hariph 1 Pa 2 51 H. the father of Bethgader
harlot Gen 38 15 thought she was harlot: for she
Gen 38 21 there was no harlot in this place
22 that there never sat a harlot there
24 saying: Thamar . . . hath played the h.
Lev 18 18 not take thy wife's sister for a h.
21 7 they shall not take to wife a harlot
14 defiled or a harlot he shall not take
Num 25 6 went in . . . to a harlot of Madian
Josu 2 1 woman that was a harlot named Rahab
6 17 let only Rahab the harlot live, with
25 Josue saved Rahab the harlot and her
Judg 11 1 the son of a woman that was a harlot
16 1 saw there a woman a harlot, and went
Job 31 10 let my wife be the harlot of another
Prov 5 3 lips of a harlot are like a honeycomb
6 26 price of a harlot is scarce one loaf
23 27 a harlot is a deep ditch: and a strange
Eccu 9 10 that is a harlot, shall be trodden upon
41 25 of looking upon a harlot: and of
Isa 1 21 was full of judgment, become a harlot
23 15 be unto Tyre as the song of a harlot
16 thou harlot that hast been forgotten
57 3 seed of the adulterer and of the harlot
Jer 3 6 tree, and hath played the harlot there
8 rebellious Israel had played the h.
8 but went and played the harlot also
9 played the harlot with stones and with
Eze 16 15 thou playedst the harlot because of
16 and hast played the harlot upon them
28 after thou hadst played the harlot with
31 wast not as a harlot that by disdain
35 O harlot, hear the word of the Lord
23 19 played the harlot in the land of Egypt
30 hast played the h. with the nations
44 and they went in to her as to a harlot
Osee 3 3 thou shalt not play the harlot, and
4 15 if thou play the harlot, O Israel, at
Amos 7 17 thy wife shall play the harlot in the
Mich 1 7 gathered together of the hire of a h.
7 unto the hire of a h. they shall return
Nah 3 4 of the harlot that was beautiful and
1 C 6 15 make them the members of an harlot? God
16 joined to a harlot, is made one body
Heb 11 31 by faith Rahab the harlot perished not
James 2 25 Rahab the h., was not she justified
Apoc 17 1 the condemnation of the great harlot
15 thou sawest, where the harlot sitteth
16 these shall hate the harlot and shall
19 2 who hath judged the great harlot which
harlot's Josu 6 22 go into the harlot's house
Prov 7 10 woman meeteth him in harlot's attire
Jer 3 3 thou hadst a harlot's forehead, thou
5 7 adultery, and rioted in the h. house
harlots 3 K 3 16 came two women that were harlots
Prov 29 3 he that maintaineth harlots, shall
Eccu 9 6 give not thy soul to harlots in any
19 3 and he that joineth himself to harlots
Bar 6 10 prostitutes, and they dress out h.

10 when they receive it of the harlots
16 33 gifts are given to all harlots: but
Osee 4 14 because themselves conversed with h.
21 31 the publicans and the h. shall go into
32 the publicans and the h. believed him
Luke 15 30 hath devoured his substance with h.
harm Gen 26 29 that thou do us no harm, as we
Gen 31 52 pass beyond it, thinking harm to me
42 4 lest perhaps he take any harm in the
1 K 26 21 David, I will no more do thee harm
27 12 done much harm to his people Israel
2 K 20 6 now will Seba . . . do us more harm than
Eccu 5 4 sinned, and what harm hath befallen me
38 16 if thou hadst suffered some great harm
Jer 39 12 upon him and do him [Jeremias] no harm
Dan 3 50 troubled them nor did them any harm
Joel 2 8 the windows, and shall take no harm
1 Ma 7 15 we will do you no h. nor your friends
9 71 swore that he would do him no harm
15 19 that they should do them no harm nor
35 they did great harm to the people and
Acts 16 28 do thyself no harm, for we all are here
27 21 not . . . have gained this harm and loss
28 5 beast into the fire, suffered no harm
6 seeing that there came no harm to him
Harma Josu 15 30 and Cesil and Harma and Siceleg
Josu 19 4 Eltholad, Bethul, and Harma, and
harmless Prov 18 8 are as if they were harmless
Wisd 18 3 thou gavest them a harmless sun of
Mich 2 8 that passed h. you have turned to
harmony Job 38 37 make the h. of heaven to sleep
harness Jer 46 4 h. the horses, and get up, ye
1 Ma 6 43 harnessed with the king's harness
harnessed 1 Ma 6 43 h. with the king's harness
harnesses 2 Ma 5 3 glittering . . . of h. of all
Harodi 2 K 23 25 Semma of H., Elica of H.
Haromaph 2 Es 3 10 Jedaia the son of Haromaph
Haroseth Judg 4 2 dwelt in H. of the Gentiles
Judg 4 13 from H. of the Gentiles to the torrent
16 pursued . . . unto H. of the Gentiles
harp Gen 4 21 of them that play upon the harp
1 K 10 5 a timbrel and a pipe and a harp
16 16 a man skilful in playing on the harp
23 David took his harp and played with
1 Pa 25 3 who prophesied with a harp to give
Job 21 12 they take the timbrel and the harp and
30 31 my harp is turned to mourning and my
Ps 32 2 give praise to the Lord on the harp
42 5 I will give praise upon the harp: why
56 9 arise psaltery and harp. 107:3
70 22 I will sing to thee with the harp
80 3 the pleasant psaltery with the harp
91 4 psaltery: with a canticle upon the h.
97 5 sing praise to the Lord on the harp
146 7 praise: sing to our God upon the harp
150 3 praise him with psaltery and harp
Isa 5 12 the harp and . . . are in your feasts
16 11 my bowels shall sound like a harp for
23 16 take a harp, go about the city, thou
24 8 the melody of the harp is silent. They
Dan 3 5 hear the sound . . . of the harp. 7, 10, 15
Amos 5 23 I will not hear the canticles of thy h.
1 Ma 3 45 and the pipe and harp ceased there
1 C 14 7 that give sound, whether pipe or harp
harped 1 C 14 7 be known what is piped or h.
harpers Apoc 14 2 as the voice of h. harping on
Apoc 18 22 the voice of harpers and of musicians
harping Apoc 14 2 as the voice of harpers h. on
harps Gen 31 27 with timbrels and with harps
2 K 6 5 on harps and lutes and timbrels and
10 12 and citterns and harps for singers
1 Pa 15 16 on psalteries and harps and cymbals
21 sung a song of victory . . . upon harps
21 cymbals and psalteries and harps. 25:6; 2 Pa 5:12; 29:25; 2 Es 12:27
16 5 the instruments of psaltery, and harps
25 1 prophesy with h. and with psalteries
2 Pa 9 11 harps and psalteries for the singing
20 28 with psalteries and h. and trumpets
Jdth 15 15 men, playing on instruments and harps
Eccu 39 20 and with harps, and in praising him
Isa 30 32 to rest upon him with timbrels and h.
Eze 26 13 sound of thy h. shall be heard no more
1 Ma 4 54 with canticles and harps and lutes
13 51 harps and cymbals and psalteries
Apoc 5 8 having every one of them harps and
14 2 of harpers harping on their harps
15 2 sea of glass, having the harps of God
harrow Isa 28 24 shall he open and h. his ground
harrows 1 Pa 20 3 and made harrows and sleds
Harsa 1 Es 2 52 children of Harsa. 2 Es 7:54
harsh Prov 15 1 but a h. word stirreth up fury
Eccu 19 7 rehearse not again a wicked and h. word
harshly Gen 31 24 anything h. against Jacob. 29
1 K 20 10 if thy father should answer thee h.
2 K 19 43 men of Juda answered more harshly than
hart Gen 49 21 Nephtali, a hart let loose, and
Deut 12 15 the roe and the hart, shalt thou eat it
22 even as the roe and the hart is eaten
14 5 that you shall eat . . . the hart and
15 22 eat them . . . as the roe and as the hart
Ps 41 2 as the h. panteth after the fountains
Cant 2 9 beloved is like a roe or a young hart
17 to a young hart upon the mountains
8 14 like to the roe and to the young hart
35 6 then shall the lame man leap as a hart
harts 2 K 22 34 like the feet of harts. Ps 17:34
3 K 4 23 besides venison of harts, roes, and
Ps 103 18 high hills are a refuge for the harts
Cant 2 7 roes and the harts of the fields. 3:5
Haba 3 19 will make my feet like the feet of h.
Haruphite 1 Pa 12 5 and Saphatia the Haruphite
Harus 4 K 21 19 Messalemeth the daughter of Harus
harvest Gen 8 22 seedtime and harvest, cold and
Gen 30 14 going out in the time of the wheat h.
Exod 23 16 feast of the harvest of the firstfruits
34 22 firstfruits of corn of thy wheat h.
Lev 23 10 firstfruits of your harvest to the priest
14 parched corn or frumenty of the h.
26 5 the threshing of your h. shall reach
Josu 3 15 the Jordan, it being harvest time, had
Judg 15 1 days of the wheat harvest were at hand
Ruth 1 22 in the beginning of the barley harvest
1 K 12 17 is it not wheat harvest today? I will
2 K 21 9 died together in first days of the h.
10 from the beginning of the harvest, till
23 13 and came to David in the harvest time
Jdth 2 17 in the days of the harvest, and he set
8 2 died in the time of the barley harvest
Job 5 5 whose harvest the hungry shall eat and
18 16 and his harvest destroyed above. Let
29 19 and dew shall continue in my harvest
Prov 6 8 and gathereth her food in the harvest
11 thy harvest shall come as a fountain
10 5 gathered in the harvest, is a wise son
25 13 as the cold of snow in time of harvest
26 1 as snow in summer, and rain in harvest
30 25 provide themselves food in the harvest
Eccu 24 36 as the Jordan in the time of harvest
Isa 9 3 as they that rejoice in the harvest
16 9 hath rushed in upon . . . thy harvest
17 5 as when one gathereth in the harvest
11 the harvest is taken away in the day of
18 4 as a cloud of dew in the day of h.
5 before the h. it was all flourishing
23 3 the harvest of the river is her revenue

27 11 its harvest shall be destroyed with
Jer 5 24 for us the fulness of the yearly h.
8 20 the harvest is past, the summer is
40 10 gather ye the vintage and the harvest
12 gathered wine and a very great harvest
48 32 robber hath rushed in upon thy harvest
50 16 holdeth the sickle in the time of h.
51 33 the time of her harvest shall come
Osee 6 11 thou also, O Juda, set thee a harvest
Joel 1 11 the harvest of the field is perished
3 13 put ye in the sickles, for the h. is
Amos 4 7 were yet three months to the harvest
Mat 9 37 the harvest indeed is great. Luke 10:2
38 pray ye therefore the Lord of the harvest. Luke 10:2
38 forth laborers into his h. Luke 10:2
13 30 suffer both to grow until the harvest
30 in the time of the harvest I will say
39 the harvest is the end of the world
Mark 4 29 sickle, because the harvest is come
John 4 35 months, and then the harvest cometh
35 for they are white already to harvest
Apoc 14 15 for the harvest of the earth is ripe
Hasaba 1 Pa 3 20 of Phadaia were born . . . Hasaba
Hasabia 1 Pa 6 45 Meloch the son of Hasabia the
1 Pa 25 19 the twelfth [lot] to Hasabia, to his
2 Es 11 15 Azaricam the son of Hasabia the son
22 Bani the son of Hasabia the son of
Hasabias 1 Pa 25 3 sons of Idithun . . . Hasabias
1 Pa 26 30 of the Hebronites Hasabias and his
27 17 over the Levites, Hasabias the son of
2 Pa 35 9 and Hasabias . . . princes of the Levites
1 Es 8 19 and Hasabias and with him Isaias
24 of the priests, Sarabias and Hasabias
Hasadias 1 Pa 3 20 of Phadaia were born . . . H.
Hasarsuhal 1 Pa 4 28 they dwelt in . . . Hasarsuhal
Hasarsusim 1 Pa 4 31 they dwelt in . . . H. and in
Hasbadana 2 Es 8 4 there stood by him . . . H.
Hasebia 1 Pa 9 14 Hasebia of the sons of Merari
2 Es 10 11 Micha, Rohob, Hasebia, Zachur, Sarebia
12 21 of Helcias, Hasebia: of Idaia
24 the chief of the Levites was Hasebia
Hasebias 2 Es 3 17 after him built Hasebias, lord
Hasebna 2 Es 10 25 Rehum, Hasebna, Maasia, Echaia
Hasebnia 2 Es 9 5 Hasebnia, Serebia . . . said
Hasebonia 2 Es 3 10 built Hattus the son of H.
Hasem 2 Es 7 22 children of Hasem, 328. The
Haserim Deut 2 23 Hevites, that dwelt in Haserim
Haseroth Num 11 34 they came unto Haseroth and
Num 13 1 the people marched from Haseroth and
33 17 graves of lust, they camped in Haseroth
18 from Haseroth they came to Rethma
Deut 1 1 wilderness . . . between Laban and H.
Hasersual Josu 15 28 H. and Bersabee. 2 Es 11:27
Josu 19 3 Hasersual, Bala, and Asem and
Hasersusa Josu 19 5 Hasersusa and Bethlebaoth
Hasim 1 Pa 7 12 Hasim the sons of Aher. And the
Hasom 1 Es 10 33 of the sons of Hasom, Mathanai
Hasor 1 K 12 9 Sisara, captain of the army of H.
Hasra 2 Pa 34 22 son of H. keeper of the wardrobe
Hassemon Josu 15 27 Asergadda and Hassemon and
Hassub 1 Pa 9 14 Hassub the son of Ezricam the
Hasub 2 Es 3 11 Hasub . . . built half the street
2 Es 3 23 after him built Benjamin and Hasub
10 23 Osee, Hanania, Hasub, Alohes, Phalea
11 15 of the Levites Semeia the son of Hasub
Hasum 1 Es 2 19 the children of Hasum, 223. The
2 Es 8 4 Misael and Melchia and Hasum and
10 18 Odaia, Hasum, Besai, Hareph, Anathoth
Hasupha 1 Es 2 43 the children of H. 2 Es 7:47
hasted Josu 10 13 sun . . . hasted not to go down
2 Pa 26 20 himself [Ozias] . . . hasted to go out
Acts 20 16 he hasted, if it were possible for him

hasten 1 Es 3 8 h. forward the work of the Lord
1 Es 3 9 stood to hasten them that did the work
Eccu 36 10 hasten the time and remember the end
Isa 8 3 his name, Hasten to take away the
28 16 he that believeth, let him not hasten
Jer 9 18 let them h. and take up a lamentation
46 22 for they shall hasten with an army
1 Ma 6 38 to h. them forward that stood thick
Heb 4 11 hasten therefore to enter into that rest
hastened 2 Pa 34 12 the sons of Caath, who h. the work
Wisd 4 14 he h. to bring him out of the midst of
2 Ma 4 14 h. to be partakers of the games and
Eccu 43 5 and at his words he hath h. his course
9 7 and commanding the matter to be h., it
Luke 8 4 hastened out of the cities unto him
1 Th 2 16 have h. the more abundantly to see your
hastening Ecce 9 10 in hell, whither thou art h.
hastily Judg 9 54 called h. to his armorbearer
Prov 20 21 inheritance gotten h. in the beginning
25 8 seen, utter not hastily in a quarrel
hasting 2 P 3 12 h. unto the coming of the day
hasty Prov 12 19 he that is a h. witness, frameth
Prov 19 2 that is h. with his feet shall stumble
29 20 hast thou seen a man hasty to speak
Ecce 5 1 let not thy heart be hasty to utter a
8 3 be not hasty to depart from his face
Eccu 4 34 be not hasty in thy tongue; and slack
19 4 he that is hasty to give credit, is
28 13 hasty contention kindleth a fire: and
13 a hasty quarrel sheddeth blood and
31 17 be not hasty in a feast. Judge of the
Isa 28 4 shall be as a hasty fruit before the
hatched Isa 59 5 shall be h. into a basilisk
Jer 17 11 as the partridge hath hatched eggs
hatchet Ps 73 6 with axe and h. they have
hate Mat 5 43 thy neighbor, and hate thy enemy
Mat 5 44 good to them that hate you. Luke 6:27
6 24 either he will hate the one. Luke 16:13
24 10 and shall hate one another. And many
Luke 1 71 and from the hand of all that hate us
6 22 shall you be when men shall hate you
14 26 and hate not his father and mother
John 7 7 the world cannot hate you; but me it
15 18 if the world hate you, know ye that
Rom 7 15 but the evil which I hate, that I do
1 J 3 13 wonder not . . . if the world hate you
Apoc 2 6 of the Nicolaites, which I also hate
17 16 these shall hate the harlot and shall
hated Mat 10 22 you shall be hated by all men. Mark 13:13; Luke 21:17
Mat 24 9 you shall be hated by all nations for
Luke 19 14 his citizens hated him: and they sent
John 15 18 that it hath hated me before you
24 and hated both me and my Father. But
25 their law: They hated me without cause
17 14 and the world hath hated them, because
Rom 9 13 Jacob I have loved, but Esau I have h.
Eph 5 29 for no man ever hated his own flesh; but
Heb 1 9 hast loved justice, and hated iniquity
hateful Gen 34 30 made me h. to the Chanaanites
Prov 14 17 folly: and the crafty man is hateful
20 the poor man shall be h. even to his
Wisd 12 4 they did works hateful to thee by
14 9 wicked and his wickedness are hateful
Eccu 7 28 to her that is h., trust not thyself
9 25 that is rash in his word shall be h.
10 7 pride is hateful before God and men
20 5 and there is another that is hateful
16 again: such a man as this is hateful
21 31 that shall abide with him shall be h.
27 14 the discourse of sinners is hateful
37 23 that speaketh sophistically is hateful
42 9 married, lest she should be hateful

2 Ma 5 24 sent that hateful prince Apollonius
6 19 a most glorious death than a h. life
Rom 1 30 detractors, h. to God, contumelious
Titus 3 3 envy, hateful and hating one another
Apoc 18 2 the hold of every unclean and h. bird
hatest Judg 14 16 thou h. me and dost not love me
2 K 19 6 and thou hatest them that love thee
Ps 5 7 thou hatest all the workers of iniquity
Wisd 11 25 hatest none of the things which thou
Eze 23 28 into the hands of them whom thou h.
Apoc 2 6 thou hatest the deeds of the Nicolaites
hateth Exod 23 5 the ass of him that hateth thee
Deut 1 27 Lord hateth us and therefore he hath
16 22 which things the Lord thy God hateth
22 16 because he h. her, he layeth to her
24 3 another husband, and he also hateth her
25 16 these things, and he h. all injustice
Jdth 5 21 with them: for their God h. iniquity
Ps 10 6 that loveth iniquity h. his own soul
Prov 6 16 six things there are which the Lord h.
8 13 the fear of the Lord hateth evil: I
12 1 but he that hateth reproof is foolish
13 24 he that spareth the rod hateth his son
15 10 he that hateth reproof shall die
27 but he that hateth bribes shall live
28 16 that h. covetousness, shall prolong his
29 24 with a thief, hateth his own soul
Eccu 12 3 the Highest hateth sinners and hath
7 the Highest also h. sinners and will
15 11 do not thou the things that he hateth
13 the Lord h. all abomination of error
19 5 h. chastisement, shall have less life
5 he that h. babbling, extinguisheth
21 7 he that hateth to be reproved walketh
25 3 three sorts my soul hateth, and I am
33 2 a wise man hateth not the commandments
Isa 1 14 my soul h. your new moons and your
John 3 20 every one that doth evil h. the light
7 7 cannot hate you; but me it hateth
12 25 he that hateth his life in this world
15 23 he that h. me, h. my Father also
1 J 2 9 and hateth his brother, is in darkness
11 he that hateth his brother. 3:15
4 20 and hateth his brother, he is a liar
Hathath 1 Pa 4 13 sons of Othoniel, Hathath
Hatil 1 Es 2 57 children of Hatil. 2 Es 7:59
hating Deut 19 11 if any man h. his neighbor, lie
Wisd 11 25 didst not . . . make anything hating it
Rom 12 9 hating that which is evil, cleaving to
Titus 3 3 envy, hateful and hating one another
Jude 23 hating also the spotted garment which
Hatipha 1 Es 2 54 children of Hatipha. 2 Es 7:56
Hatita 1 Es 2 42 children of Hatita. 2 Es 7:46
hatred Gen 37 8 nourishment to their envy and h.
Num 35 20 if through hatred any one push a man
22 if by chance medley and without hatred
Deut 19 4 is proved to have had no hatred. 6
2 K 13 15 hated her with an exceeding great h.
15 the hatred wherewith he hated her was
Tob 1 18 had a hatred for the children of Israel
Esth 14 13 turn his heart to the h. of our enemy
Ps 24 19 have hated me with an unjust hatred
35 3 his iniquity may be found unto hatred
108 3 compassed me about with words of h.
5 evil for good: and hatred for my love
138 22 I have hated them with a perfect h.
Prov 10 12 h. stirreth up strifes: and charity
18 lying lips hide h.: he that uttereth
15 17 love than to a fatted calf with hatred
26 26 he that covereth hatred deceitfully
Ecce 3 8 a time of love and a time of hatred
9 1 whether he be worthy of love or hatred
6 h. and their envy are all perished
Eccu 5 17 to the whisperer hatred and enmity
6 9 that will disclose hatred and strife
Eze 23 29 they shall deal with thee in hatred
35 11 which thou hast exercised in h. to them
1 Ma 13 17 should bring upon himself a great h.
2 Ma 3 1 and the hatred his soul had of evil
14 39 declare the h. that he bore the Jews
Hattus 1 Pa 3 22 Semeia, whose sons were Hattus
1 Es 8 2 Daniel. Of the sons of David, Hattus
2 Es 3 10 next to him built Hattus the son of
10 4 Hattus, Sebenia, Melluch, Harem
12 2 Hattus, Sebenias, Rheum, Marimuth
haughtily Mich 2 3 and you shall not walk h.
haughtiness Prov 21 4 h. of the eyes is the
Eccu 23 5 give me not haughtiness of my eyes
26 12 shall be known by the h. of her eyes
Isa 2 11 the h. of men shall be made to stoop
17 the h. of men shall be humbled, and
9 9 in the pride and h. of their heart
10 12 glory of the haughtiness of his eyes
Jer 48 29 his h. and his arrogancy and his pride
2 Ma 5 21 such was the h. of his mind. He left
haughty 2 K 22 28 thou wilt humble the haughty
Prov 6 17 h. eyes, a lying tongue, hands that
Isa 3 16 because the daughters of Sion are h.
Rom 1 30 hateful to God, contumelious, proud, **h.**
2 Tim 3 2 men shall be . . . haughty, proud
haven Ps 106 30 he brought them to the haven
1 Ma 14 5 he took Joppe for a haven and made
2 Ma 12 6 and set the haven on fire in the night
9 set the haven on fire with the ships
14 1 by the haven of Tripolis to places
Acts 27 12 it was not a commodious h. to winter in
12 winter there, which is a haven of Crete
havens Judg 5 17 and abode in the havens
Acts 27 8 which is called Good-havens, nigh
havock 1 Ma 7 7 let him go and see all the h.
1 Ma 7 9 to see the havock that Judas had made
15 29 you have made great havock in the land
31 for the havock that you have made
Acts 8 3 but Saul made havock of the church
Havoth Num 32 41 he called them Havoth Jair
Deut 3 14 he called Basan Havoth Jair
Judg 10 4 from his name were called Havoth Jair
hawk Deut 14 15 the owl and the larus and the hawk
Lev 11 16 you must not eat . . . the hawk
Job 39 13 is like the wings . . . of the hawk
hay Gen 24 25 good store of both straw and hay
Gen 24 32 the camels and gave straw and hay
Deut 11 15 your hay out of the fields to feed
Judg 19 19 we have straw and hay for provender
Prov 27 25 hay is gathered out of the mountains
Amos 2 13 wain screaketh that is laden with hay
Mich 4 12 them together as the hay of the floor
Zach 12 6 wood, and as a firebrand amongst hay
1 C 3 12 precious stones, wood, hay, stubble
Hazael 3 K 19 15 anoint Hazael to be king over
3 K 19 17 whosoever shall escape sword of Hazael
4 K 8 8 the king said to Hazael: Take with
9 Hazael went to meet him [Eliseus]
12 Hazael said to him: Why doth my lord
13 Hazael said: But what am I thy servant
15 died, and Hazael reigned in his stead
28 to fight against Hazael king of Syria
29 he fought against Hazael king of Syria
9 14 fighting with Hazael king of Syria
15 when he fought with H. king of Syria
10 32 Hazael ravaged them in all the coasts
12 17 Hazael king of Syria went up and fought
18 and sent it to Hazael king of Syria
13 3 delivered them into the hand of Hazael
3 into the hand of Benadad the son of H.
22 Hazael king of Syria afflicted Israel

24 H. king of Syria died, and Benadad
25 the hand of Benadad the son of Hazael
2 Pa 22 5 to fight against Hazael king of Syria
Hazia 2 Es 11 5 Cholhoza the son of Hazia
Hazir 2 Es 10 20 Megphias, Mosollam, Hazir
he Lev 9 3 take ye a he goat for sin, and a
Lev 9 15 he slew the he goat; and expiating
Num 6 14 one he lamb of a year old without
7 17 two oxen, five rams, five he goats
17 11 7,700 rams and as many he goats
29 21 they offered . . . and seven he goats
23 and they brought the he goats for a sin
1 Es 6 17 sin offering for all Israel 12 he goats
8 35 lambs, and twelve he goats for sin
Ps 49 9 house: nor he goats out of thy flocks
118 33 he. Lam 1:5; 2:5; 3:13, 14, 15; 4:5
headbands Isa 3 23 lawns and h. and fine veils
headless Jdth 13 10 and rolled away his h. body
headlong Deut 22 8 any one slip and fall down h.
Judg 5 15 as one going headlong and into a pit
22 the stoutest . . . fell headlong down
4 K 9 33 throw her [Jezabel] down headlong
2 Pa 25 12 cast them down headlong from the top
Job 10 8 dost thou thus cast me down headlong
18 7 his own counsel shall cast him down h.
Ecce 10 12 lips of a fool shall throw him down h.
Isa 9 16 blessed, shall be thrown down h.
25 8 he shall cast death down h. forever
22 7 and shall cast them h. into the fire
Lam 2 2 the Lord hath cast down headlong and
5 he hath cast down Israel headlong
2 Ma 6 10 threw down headlong from the walls
Mark 5 13 was carried headlong into the sea
Luke 4 29 they might cast him down headlong
headstrong Eccu 30 8 to himself will become h.
heal Num 12 13 O God, I beseech thee heal her
Deut 32 39 I will strike and I will heal, and
4 K 5 6 that thou mayest h. him of his leprosy
7 sent to me to h. a man of his leprosy
20 8 the sign that the Lord will heal me
2 Pa 7 14 forgive their sins and will h. the land
Tob 3 25 Raphael was sent to heal them both
12 14 now the Lord hath sent me to heal thee
Job 5 18 he striketh, and his hands shall heal
Ps 6 3 heal me, O Lord, for my bones are
40 5 heal my soul, for I have sinned against
59 4 heal thou the breaches thereof, for it
Ecce 3 3 a time to kill and a time to heal. A
Eccu 38 9 to the Lord and he shall heal thee
Isa 6 10 lest . . . be converted, and I heal them
19 22 Egypt with a scourge, and shall h. it
22 pacified towards them and heal them
30 26 shall heal the stroke of their wound
61 1 to heal the contrite of heart and to
Jer 3 22 and I will h. your rebellions. Behold
17 14 heal me, O Lord, and I shall be healed
30 17 scar, and will heal thee of thy wounds
Lam 2 13 thy destruction: who shall heal thee
Osee 5 13 and he shall not be able to heal you
6 2 he hath taken us, and he will heal us
14 5 I will heal their breaches, I will
Zach 11 16 nor heal what is broken nor nourish
Mat 8 7 saith to him: I will come and heal him
10 1 and to heal all manner of diseases
8 heal the sick, raise the dead, cleanse
12 10 lawful to h. on the sabbath. Luke 14:3
13 15 be converted and I should heal them. John 12:40; Acts 28:27
Mark 3 2 he would h. on the sabbath. Luke 6:7
15 he gave them power to heal sicknesses
Luke 4 18 sent me to heal the contrite of heart
23 physician, heal thyself: as great
5 17 power of the Lord was to heal them
7 3 him to come and heal his servant
10 9 heal the sick that are therein and
John 4 47 him to come down and heal his son
healed Gen 20 17 God h. Abimelech and his wife
Lev 13 18 an ulcer . . . and it has been healed
24 after it is healed hath a white or
37 let him know that the man is healed
15 13 if he who suffereth this disease be h.
22 4 shall not eat . . . until he be healed
Num 21 9 bitten looked upon, they were healed
Deut 28 27 itch: so that thou canst not be healed
Josu 5 8 place of the camp until they were h.
1 K 6 3 for sin, and then you shall be healed
4 K 2 21 I have healed these waters, and there
22 the waters were healed unto this
5 3 he would certainly have healed him
11 I thought he would have . . . healed me
8 29 he [Joram] went back to be healed in
9 15 to be healed in Jezrahel of his wounds
20 5 behold I have healed thee [Ezechias]
7 laid it upon his boil, he was healed
2 Pa 22 6 he returned to be healed in Jezrahel
Job 34 17 can he be h. that loveth not judgment
Ps 29 3 cried to thee, and thou hast healed me
106 20 he sent his word and healed them: and
Prov 28 25 that trusteth in the Lord, shall be h.
Wisd 9 19 for by wisdom they were healed
10 4 destroyed the earth, wisdom healed it
16 7 was not healed by that which he saw
10 for thy mercy came and healed them
11 and were quickly healed, lest falling
12 nor mollifying plaster that h. them
Eccu 3 30 of the proud shall not be healed
38 21 wound, and that he should be healed
Isa 53 5 and by his bruises we are healed. All
57 18 I healed him and brought him back
19 near, said the Lord, and I healed him
Jer 6 14 h. the breach of the daughter. 8:11
15 18 desperate so as to refuse to be healed
17 14 heal me, O Lord, and I shall be h.
51 8 for her pain, if so she may be healed
9 cured Babylon, but she is not healed
Eze 30 21 it is not bound up, to be healed
34 4 which was sick you have not healed
47 8 go out, and the waters shall be healed
9 waters . . . and they shall be healed
11 fenny places they shall not be healed
Osee 7 1 when I would have healed Israel, the
11 3 and they knew not that I healed them
Mat 8 8 servant shall be healed. Luke 7:7
13 servant was healed at the same hour
16 and all that were sick he healed
9 21 only his garment, I shall be healed
12 15 he healed them. 15:30; 19:2; 21:14; Luke 4:40
22 he healed him. Luke 14:1; 22:51; Acts 28:8
14 14 compassion on them and h. their sick
Mark 1 34 he healed many that were troubled with
3 10 he healed many, so that they pressed
5 29 she felt in her body that she was h.
6 13 many that were sick, and healed them
Luke 5 15 to hear and to be healed by him of
6 18 and to be healed of their diseases
19 virtue went out from him and h. all
8 2 who had been healed of evil spirits
36 told them how he had been healed
43 and could not be healed by any. She
47 and how she was immediately healed
9 11 healed them who had need of healing
13 14 in them therefore come and be healed
14 that Jesus had healed on the sabbath
John 5 10 said to him that was healed: It is the
13 he who was healed knew not who it was

7 23 because I have healed the whole man on
Acts 4 14 the man also that had been healed
5 16 with unclean spirits; who were all h.
8 8 and that were lame, were healed. They
14 8 seeing that he had faith to be healed
9 in the island, came and were healed: who
Heb 12 13 out of the way; but rather be healed
1 P 2 24 by whose stripes you were healed. For
Apoc 13 3 and his death's wound was healed. And
12 beast, whose wound to death was healed
healer Exod 15 26 for I am the Lord thy healer
Isa 3 7 shall answer, saying: I am no healer
healeth Ps 102 3 who healeth all thy diseases
Ps 146 3 who healeth the broken of heart and
Wisd 16 12 thy word, O Lord, which h. all things
Acts 9 34 Lord Jesus Christ healeth thee: arise
healing Jer 8 15 for a time of healing, and behold fear
Jer 14 19 so that there is no healing for us
19 we have looked . . . for the time of h.
30 13 bind it up: thou hast no h. medicines
Mat 4 23 and healing all manner of sickness and
9 35 h. every disease and every infirmity
Luke 9 6 preaching the gospel and h. everywhere
11 healed them who had need of healing
Acts 10 38 who went about doing good, and healing
1 C 12 9 to another, grace of h. in one spirit
30 have all the grace of healing? Do all
Apoc 22 2 were for the healing of the nations
healings 1 C 12 28 then the graces of healings
health Gen 29 6 is he [Laban] in health? He is in health
Gen 42 15 by the health of Pharao you shall not
16 by the health of Pharao you are spies
43 27 is the old man your father in health
28 thy servant our father is in health
Josu 10 21 the army returned . . . in good health
2 K 14 19 by the health of thy soul, my lord
4 K 5 10 and thy flesh shall recover health
Tob 8 6 that health might be given them. And
10 let us grow old both together in h.
19 sacrifice of thy praise and of their h.
10 8 Tobias thy father, that thou art in h.
14 15 found them in h. in a good old age
Job 5 11 comforteth with health those that mourn
Ps 37 4 there is no health in my flesh. 8
Prov 3 8 for it shall be health to thy navel
4 22 that find them, and health to all flesh
12 18 but the tongue of the wise is health
13 17 but a faithful ambassador is health
16 24 sweet to the soul, and h. to the bones
29 1 health shall not follow him. When just
Wisd 1 14 made the nations of the earth for h.
7 10 I loved her above health and beauty
13 18 for health he maketh supplication to
Eccu 17 27 and in health thou shalt give thanks
30 15 health of the soul in holiness of
16 the riches of the health of the body
31 37 sober drinking is health to soul and
34 20 giveth health and life and blessing
38 7 and shall make up ointments of health
58 8 and thy health shall speedily arise
Jer 33 6 I will . . . give them health and I
Eze 16 4 thou washed with water for thy health
Mala 4 2 shall arise, and health in his wings
2 Ma 1 1 of Judea, send health and good peace
10 to the Jews that are in Egypt, health
3 32 a sacrifice of health for the recovery
9 19 wisheth much health and welfare and
Mat 9 12 they that are in health need not a
12 13 it was restored to health even as the
healthful Eccu 6 31 her bands are a h. binding
health's Acts 27 34 some meat for your h. sake
heap Gen 31 46 stones together, made a heap
Gen 31 47 and Laban called it The witness heap
48 this h. shall be a witness between me
48 called Galaad, that is, The witness h.
51 this heap and the stone which I have
52 this heap I say, and the stone, be they
Deut 13 16 that it be a heap forever: it shall be
32 23 I will heap evils upon them and will
Josu 3 13 shall stand together upon a heap
7 26 upon him [Achan] a great h. of stones
8 28 burned the city and made it a heap
29 heaping upon it a great heap of stones
Ruth 3 7 he went to sleep by the heap of sheaves
2 K 18 17 laid an exceeding great heap of stones
2 Pa 28 13 and heap up upon our former offenses
Job 5 26 heap of wheat is brought in its season
8 17 shall be thick upon a heap of stones
21 32 shall watch in the heap of the dead
27 16 if he shall heap together silver as
Prov 25 22 shalt heap hot coals upon his head
26 8 a stone into the heap of Mercury: so
Ecce 2 26 to heap up and to gather together
Cant 7 2 thy belly is like a heap of wheat, set
Eccu 4 21 and will heap upon him treasures of
8 4 tongue, and h. not wood upon his fire
15 6 she shall heap upon him a treasure
20 30 land shall make a high heap of corn
39 22 at his word the waters stood as a heap
Isa 17 1 shall be as a ruinous heap of stones
25 2 thou hast reduced the city to a heap
Jer 26 18 Jerusalem shall be a heap of stones
49 2 and it shall be destroyed into a heap
Eze 3 15 to the heap of new corn, to them
24 4 heap together into it the pieces
10 heap together the bones, which I will
Mich 1 6 will make Samaria as a heap of stones
3 12 Jerusalem shall be as a heap of stones
Haba 2 5 and heap together unto him all people
Agge 2 17 when you went to a heap of 20 bushels
2 Ma 13 5 having a heap of ashes on every side
Rom 12 20 thou shalt heap coals of fire upon his
2 Tim 4 3 they will heap to themselves teachers
heaped Num 5 18 whereon he hath heaped curses
Num 5 19 waters, on which I have heaped curses
23 upon which he hath heaped the curses
Judg 5 30 is heaped together to adorn the necks
Ruth 2 14 she heaped to herself frumenty and ate
Job 22 25 silver shall be h. together for thee
Ecce 2 8 I heaped together for myself silver and
Eccu 21 10 of sinners is like tow heaped together
Zach 9 3 and heaped together silver as earth
heapeth Prov 28 8 he that h. together riches by
Haba 2 6 that heapeth together that which is
heaping Josu 8 29 h. upon it great heap of stones
heaps Exod 8 14 them together into immense heaps
4 K 10 8 lay ye them in two h. by the entering
19 25 should be turned to heaps of ruin
2 Pa 31 6 carrying them all, made many heaps
7 to lay the foundations of the heaps
8 they saw the heaps and they blessed
9 Ezechias asked . . . why the h. lay so
2 Es 4 2 stones out of the heaps of the rubbish
Job 15 28 desert houses that are reduced into h.
Wisd 18 23 down dead by heaps one upon another
Jer 9 11 will make Jerusalem to be heaps of sand
50 26 stones out of the way, and make heaps
51 37 and Babylon shall be reduced to heaps
Osee 12 11 their altars also are as heaps in the
Soph 2 9 dryness of thorns and heaps of salt
hearken Gen 4 23 of Lamech, h. to my speech
Gen 21 12 hearken to her voice: for in Isaac
23 11 do thou rather hearken to what I say
49 2 hearken to Israel your father: Ruben
Exod 6 9 they did not hearken to him [Moses]
12 children of Israel do not h. to me

7 13 and he did not hearken to them, as the
Lev 26 21 if you will not hearken to me. 27
Deut 9 23 neither would you h. to his voice
18 14 hearken to soothsayers and diviners
Judg 2 16 but they would not hearken to them
20 hath despised to hearken to my voice
11 28 would not h. to the words of Jephte
20 13 they would not h. to the proposition
1 K 8 7 hearken to the voice of the people
9 h. to their voice; but yet testify
22 to Samuel: Hearken to their voice
12 14 if you will . . . hearken to his voice
15 if you will not hearken to the voice
15 1 h. thou unto the voice of the Lord
19 then didst thou not h. to the voice
22 to h. rather than to offer the fat of
30 24 no man shall h. to you in this matter
2 K 2 23 Asael refused to h. to him [Abner]
12 18 he [David] would not h. to our voice
13 14 he would not hearken to her prayers
16 he [Amnon] would not hearken to her
3 K 8 29 that thou mayest hearken to the prayer
30 thou mayest h. to the supplication of
11 38 if then thou wilt h. to all that I shall
12 16 seeing that the king would not hearken
20 8 hearken not to him nor consent to him
36 because thou wouldst not h. to the word
4 K 17 40 they did not hearken, but did according
18 31 do not hearken to Ezechias. Isa 36:16
32 hearken not to Ezechias, who deceiveth
2 Pa 6 21 h. then to the prayers of thy servant
25 20 Amasias would not h. to him, because
33 10 the Lord spoke . . . and they would not h.
Tob 9 1 brother Azarias, I pray thee hearken to
10 10 he by no means would hearken to him
14 10 hearken therefore, my children, to your
Job 21 5 hearken to me and be astonished and
32 10 hearken to me, I also will show you
33 1 my speeches, and hearken to all my words
31 attend, Job, and hearken to me: and
34 2 words, and ye learned, hearken to me
16 and hearken to the voice of my words
34 to me, and let a wise man hearken to me
37 14 hearken to these things, Job: Stand
Ps 5 3 hearken to the voice of my prayer
33 12 children, hearken to me: I will teach
44 11 h., O daughter, and see and incline
80 9 if thou wilt h. to me, there shall be
140 1 hearken to my voice, when I cry to thee
Prov 2 2 that thy ear may hearken to wisdom
4 20 hearken to my words and incline thy
23 22 h. to thy father, that begot thee
Cant 8 13 the friends hearken: make me hear thy
Eccu 9 4 h. not to her lest thou perish by
16 24 hearken to me, my son, and learn the
19 9 he will h. to thee, and will watch
21 27 folly of a man to hearken at the door
33 19 h. with your ears, ye rulers of the
Isa 1 19 if you be willing and will h. to me
28 23 give ear, and hear my voice, hearken
32 3 that hear shall hearken diligently
34 1 hearken, ye people; let the earth
42 23 that will . . . hearken for times to come
46 3 hearken unto me, O house of Jacob
48 12 h. to me, O Jacob, and thou Israel
49 1 and hearken, ye people from afar. The
51 4 hearken unto me, O my people, and
7 h. to me, you that know what is just
55 2 h. diligently to me and eat that which
Jer 6 17 h. ye to the sound of the trumpet. And
17 and they said: we will not hearken
7 23 h. to my voice, and I will be your
27 but they will not hearken to thee
11 3 that shall not h. to the words of this
7 and said: Hearken ye to my voice: and
11 to me, and I will not hearken to them
16 12 so as not to hearken to me. So I
17 24 if you will hearken to me, saith the
27 if you will not hearken to me. 26:4
22 5 if you will not hearken to these words
23 16 h. not to the words of the prophets
26 3 if so be they will hearken and be
13 and hearken to the voice of the Lord
27 9 hearken not to your prophets and
14 h. not to the words of the prophets
16 h. not to the words of your prophets
17 h. not to them, but serve the king
32 33 and they would not hearken to receive
34 14 and your fathers did not hearken to me
38 15 counsel, thou wilt not hearken to me
20 hearken . . . to the word of the Lord
42 6 when we shall hearken to the voice of
13 neither will we h. to the voice of the
44 16 we will not hearken to thee: but we
Bar 2 22 if you will not hearken to the voice
Eze 3 6 to them, they would hearken to thee
7 of Israel will not hearken to thee
7 because they will not hearken to me
20 8 provoked me and would not h. to me
Dan 9 19 O Lord, be appeased, hearken and do
Osee 5 1 and hearken, O ye house of Israel
Zach 1 4 neither did they hearken to me, saith
7 11 but they would not hearken and they
1 Ma 2 22 we will not h. to the words of king
5 61 because they did not hearken to Judas
Acts 12 13 damsel came to h. whose name was Rhode
James 2 5 hearken, my dearest brethren: hath not
hearkened Gen 3 17 because thou hast h. to the
Exod 8 19 he hearkened not unto them. 9:12
16 20 they hearkened not to him, but some
Deut 1 43 I spoke, and you hearkened not: but
1 K 2 25 h. not to the voice of their father
12 1 I have hearkened to your voice in all
15 20 I have h. to the voice of the Lord
28 21 I h. unto the words which thou spokest
2 K 14 16 the king hath h. to me to deliver his
3 K 12 24 they h. to the word of the Lord and
4 K 3 14 I would not have hearkened to thee
17 14 they h. not, but hardened their necks
18 12 because they h. not to the voice of the
21 9 they h. not: but were seduced by
22 13 our fathers have not h. to the words
2 Pa 24 17 by their services and hearkened to them
25 16 and moreover hast not h. to my counsel
35 22 hearkened not to the words of Nechao
2 Es 9 16 and h. not to thy commandments. 29
Ps 80 12 not my voice: and Israel h. not to me
105 25 they h. not to the voice of the Lord
Isa 42 24 they have not hearkened to his law
48 18 O that thou hadst hearkened to my
Jer 3 25 have not h. to the voice of the Lord. Bar **1:18**, 21; 3:4; Dan 9:10
7 24 they h. not nor inclined their ear
26 and they have not hearkened to me
28 hath not h. to the voice of the Lord
8 6 I attended and h.; no man speaketh
25 3 speaking, and you have not hearkened
4 you have not h. nor inclined your ears
26 5 sending, and you have not hearkened
29 19 they have not h. to my words, saith
34 17 you have not hearkened to me, in
35 15 not inclined your ear nor h. to me
37 13 but he hearkened not to him: so Jerias
40 3 have not h. to his voice. Dan 9:14
Bar 2 10 we have not hearkened to his voice
24 they h. not to thy voice, to serve the

Dan 3 30 we have not h. to thy commandments
9 6 we have not h. to thy servants the
Osee 9 17 because they hearkened not to him
Soph 3 2 she hath not hearkened to the voice
Agge 1 12 all the remnant of the people h.
Acts 27 21 O ye men, have h. unto me, and not have
hearkeneth Prov 12 15 that is wise h. unto counsels
Prov 17 4 the deceitful hearkeneth to lying lips
Eccu 4 16 he that h. to her, shall judge nations
14 24 in at her windows and h. at her door
24 30 he that h. to me, shall not be
28 20 he that h. to it shall never have
hearkening 1 K 28 23 h. to their voice, he arose
3 K 15 20 Benadad h. to king Asa, sent the
Jdth 14 14 when with h., he perceived no motion
Ps 102 20 hearkening to the voice of his orders
heart Mat 5 8 blessed are the clean of heart
Mat 9 2 be of good heart. 22; 14:27
11 29 because I am meek and humble of heart
12 34 out of abundance of the h. Luke 6:45
40 be in the heart of the earth 3 days and
13 15 h. of this people is grown. Acts 28:27
15 18 mouth, come forth from the heart, and
19 from the heart come forth evil thoughts
22 37 Lord thy God with thy whole heart. Mark 12:30; Luke 10:27
Mark 6 50 have a good heart, it is I, fear ye not
7 21 out of the heart of men proceed evil
12 33 should be loved with the whole heart
16 14 their incredulity and hardness of h.
Luke 2 19 words, pondering them in her heart
51 kept all these words in her heart
4 18 sent me to heal the contrite of heart
8 15 they who in a good and perfect heart
24 25 O foolish and slow of heart to believe
32 was not our heart burning within us
John 13 2 having now put into the heart of Judas
Acts 2 46 with gladness and simplicity of heart
4 32 multitude of believers had but one h.
5 33 they were cut to the heart. 7:54
7 51 and uncircumcised in heart and ears
11 23 exhorted them all with purpose of heart
16 14 whose heart the Lord opened to attend
Rom 1 21 and their foolish heart was darkened
2 29 the circumcision is that of the heart
6 17 but have obeyed from the h., unto that
10 10 for with the h. we believe unto justice
1 C 2 9 neither hath it entered into h. of man
2 C 1 12 in simplicity of h. and sincerity of
2 4 of much affliction and anguish of heart
3 3 but in the fleshly tables of the heart
5 12 them who glory in face, and not in heart
6 11 O ye Corinthians, our heart is enlarged
8 16 carefulness for you in the h. of Titus
Eph 6 6 doing the will of God from the heart
Col 3 22 but in simplicity of heart, fearing God
23 whatsoever you do, do it from the heart
1 Th 2 16 in sight, not in heart, have hastened
1 Tim 1 5 from a pure heart, and a good conscience
2 Tim 2 22 that call on the Lord out of a pure h.
Heb 3 10 they always err in heart. And they have
12 in any of you an evil heart of unbelief
4 12 the thoughts and intents of the heart
10 22 let us draw near with a true heart in
13 9 that the h. be established with grace
1 P 1 22 from a sincere heart love one another
3 4 but the hidden man of the heart in the
5 3 a pattern of the flock from the heart
1 J 3 20 if our heart reprehend us, God is
20 God is greater than our heart and
21 if our heart do not reprehend us, we
Apoc 18 7 she saith in her heart: I sit a queen
his heart Mat 5 28 adultery with her in his heart. And
Mat 13 19 that which was sown in his heart: this
24 48 say in his heart: My lord is long
Mark 7 19 because it entereth not into his heart
11 23 not stagger in his heart, but believe
Luke 6 45 out of the good treasure of his heart
12 45 if that servant shall say in his h.
Acts 7 23 it came into his heart to visit his
1 C 7 37 being steadfast in his heart, having no
37 and hath judged this in his heart, to
14 25 secrets of his heart are made manifest
2 C 9 7 as he hath determined in his heart, not
James 1 26 deceiving his own heart, this man's
my heart Acts 2 26 for this my heart hath been glad, and
Acts 13 22 a man according to my own heart, who
21 13 weeping and afflicting my heart? For I
Rom 9 2 continual sorrow in my heart. For I
10 1 will of my heart . . . if for them unto
Phil 1 7 you all, for that I have you in my heart
their heart Mat 13 15 understand with their h. Acts 28:27
Mat 15 8 their h. is far from me. Mark 7:6
Mark 6 52 the loaves: for their heart was blinded
Luke 1 51 proud in the conceit of their heart
66 laid them up in their heart, saying
8 12 taketh the word out of their heart
9 47 seeing the thoughts of their heart
John 12 40 their eyes, and hardened their heart
40 eyes, nor understand with their heart
Acts 2 37 they had compunction in their heart
Rom 1 24 gave them up to desires of their heart
2 C 3 15 Moses is read, the veil is upon their h.
Heb 8 10 in their heart will I write them: and I
2 P 2 14 their heart exercised with covetousness
thy heart Mat 6 21 treaure is, there is thy heart
Acts 5 3 why hath Satan tempted thy heart, that
4 thou conceived this thing in thy heart
8 21 thy heart is not right in the sight of
22 perhaps this thought of thy heart may
37 if thou believest with all thy heart
Rom 2 5 according to thy . . . and impenitent h.
10 6 say not in thy heart, Who shall ascend
8 word is nigh thee, even . . . in thy heart
9 believe in thy heart that God hath
your heart Mat 19 8 reason of hardness of your h.
Mark 8 17 have you still your heart blinded
10 5 because of the hardness of your heart
Luke 12 34 treasure is, there will your heart be
16 15 before men, but God knoweth your h.
John 14 1 let not your heart be troubled. 27
16 6 to you, sorrow hath filled your heart
22 you again, and your heart shall rejoice
Eph 1 18 eyes of your heart enlightened, that you
hearth Gen 18 6 make cakes upon the hearth. And
Exod 27 5 shalt put under the hearth of the altar
38 4 under it in the the midst of the altar a h.
Judg 7 13 as if a hearth cake of barley bread
3 K 17 13 make for me . . . a little hearth cake
19 6 there was at his head a hearth cake
Isa 30 14 fire may be carried from the hearth
Jer 36 22 h. before him full of burning coals
23 into the fire that was upon the hearth
23 with the fire that was on the hearth
heartily Gen 29 13 h. kissing him, brought him
heart's Ps 20 3 hast given him his h. desire
hearts Exod 23 9 you know the h. of strangers
Lev 26 36 I will send fear in their hearts in
Num 32 9 overturned the h. of the children of
Deut 1 28 the messengers have terrified our h.
11 18 lay up these my words in your hearts
20 8 he make the h. of his brethren to fear
32 46 set your hearts on all the words which
Josu 11 20 that their hearts should be hardened
24 23 and incline your hearts to the Lord

Judg 9 3 inclined their hearts after Abimelech
1 K 6 6 why do you harden your hearts as Egypt
and Pharao hardened their hearts
7 3 and prepare your hearts unto the Lord
10 26 the army, whose hearts God had touched
2 K 15 6 enticed the hearts of the men of Israel
3 K 8 58 may he incline our hearts to himself
61 let our hearts also be perfect with the
1 Pa 22 19 give therefore your hearts and your
28 9 for the Lord searcheth all hearts and
29 17 know my God that thou provest hearts
2 Pa 6 14 walk before thee with all their hearts
30 thou only knowest the hearts of the
Jdth 8 21 comfort their h. by your speech, that
Job 1 5 and have blessed God in their hearts
8 10 and utter words out of their hearts
Ps 4 5 the things you say in your hearts, be
7 10 the searcher of hearts and reins is God
18 9 of the Lord are right, rejoicing hearts
21 27 their hearts shall live forever and ever
27 3 neighbor, but evils are in their hearts
32 15 who hath made the hearts of every one
34 25 let them not say in their hearts: It
36 15 let their sword enter into their own h.
44 6 into the hearts of the king's enemies
47 14 set your hearts on her strength: and
61 9 pour out your hearts before him. God
77 18 and they tempted God in their hearts
94 8 hear his voice, harden not your hearts
139 3 have devised iniquities in their hearts
Prov 15 11 more the hearts of the children of men
17 3 furnace: so the Lord trieth the hearts
21 2 himself: but the Lord weigheth the h.
27 19 h. of men are laid open to the wise
Ecce 9 3 h. of the children of men are filled
Wisd 4 14 nor lay up such things in their hearts
Eccu 2 10 and your hearts shall be enlightened
20 fear the Lord, will prepare their h.
17 7 he set his eye upon their hearts to
21 20 will think upon his words in their h.
23 28 and looking into the hearts of men
24 11 trodden under my feet the hearts of all
31 31 shall rebuke the hearts of the proud
48 21 then their hearts and hands trembled
Jer 4 4 take away the foreskins of your hearts
11 20 and triest the reins and the hearts
51 46 lest your hearts faint, and ye fear
Lam 3 41 let us lift up our h. with our hands
Bar 3 7 thou hast put thy fear in our hearts
6 5 say you in your hearts: Thou oughtest
19 which are of the earth, gnaw their h.
Eze 14 3 placed their uncleannesses in their h.
Osee 7 2 and lest they may say in their hearts
Joel 2 13 rend your hearts and not your garments
Nah 2 7 as doves, murmuring in their hearts
Soph 1 12 say in their hearts: The Lord will not
Agge 1 5 set your hearts to consider your ways
7 set your hearts upon your ways: go up
2 16 consider in your hearts, from this day
19 set your hearts from this day, and
19 were laid, and lay it up in your hearts
Zach 8 17 none of you imagine evil in your h.
2 Ma 15 17 strengthen the hearts of the young men
27 but praying to the Lord with their h.
Mat 9 4 why do you think evil in your hearts
18 35 every one his brother from your hearts
Mark 2 6 sitting there and thinking in their h.
8 why think you these things in your h.
3 5 grieved for the blindness of their h.
4 15 the word that was sown in their hearts
Luke 1 17 he may turn the hearts of the fathers
2 35 that out of many hearts thoughts may
3 15 were thinking in their hearts of John
5 22 what is it you think in your hearts
9 44 lay you up in your hearts these words
16 15 God knoweth your hearts: for that
21 14 lay it up therefore in your hearts
34 lest your hearts be overcharged with
24 38 why do thoughts arise in your hearts
Acts 1 24 who knowest the hearts of all men
7 39 in their hearts turned back into Egypt
14 16 filling our h. with food and gladness
15 8 God, who knoweth the h., gave testimony
9 them, purifying their hearts by faith
Rom 2 15 show work of law written in their hearts
5 5 charity of God is poured forth in our h.
8 27 he that searcheth the h., knoweth what
16 18 seduce the hearts of the innocent. For
1 C 4 5 will make manifest counsels of hearts
2 C 1 22 given pledge of the Spirit in our hearts
3 2 are our epistle, written in our hearts
4 6 hath shined in our hearts, to give light
7 3 you are in our hearts, to die together
Gal 4 6 sent Spirit of his Son into your hearts
Eph 3 17 Christ may dwell by faith in your hearts
4 18 because of the blindness of their hearts
5 19 making melody in your hearts to the Lord
6 22 and that he may comfort your hearts
Phil 4 7 keep your hearts and minds in Christ
Col 2 2 that their hearts may be comforted
3 15 peace of Christ rejoice in your hearts
16 singing in grace in your hearts to God
4 8 concern you, and comfort your hearts
1 Th 2 4 men, but God, who proveth our hearts
3 13 confirm your hearts without blame, in
2 Th 2 16 exhort your hearts, and confirm you in
3 5 and the Lord direct your hearts, in the
8 harden not your hearts. 15; 4:7
Heb 10 16 I will give my laws in their hearts
22 having our hearts sprinkled from an evil
James 3 14 there be contentions in your hearts
4 8 purify your hearts, ye double-minded
5 5 riotousness you have nourished your h.
8 patient, and strengthen your hearts
1 P 3 15 sanctify the Lord Christ in your hearts
2 P 1 19 and the day star arise in your hearts
1 J 3 19 in his sight shall persuade our hearts
Apoc 2 23 he that searcheth the reins and hearts
17 17 God hath given into their hearts to do
hearty Eccu 29 11 towards poor be thou more h.
heat Gen 8 22 cold and heat, summer and winter
Gen 18 1 his tent, in the very heat of the day
30 39 in the very heat of coition, the sheep
31 40 day and night was I parched with heat
Deut 28 22 with cold, with burning and with heat
29 23 it with brimstone and the heat of salt
24 this exceeding great heat of his wrath
2 K 4 5 house of Isboseth in the h. of the day
Jdth 8 3 the heat came upon his head and he died
Job 24 19 from the snow waters to excessive heat
28 2 stone melted with heat is turned into
30 30 and my bones are dried up with heat
38 24 spread and heat divided upon the earth
Ps 18 7 that can hide himself from his heat
Wisd 2 3 was overpowered with the heat thereof
Eccu 14 27 under her covering from the heat
18 16 shall not the dew assuage the heat
31 40 the heat of drunkenness is the
34 19 a defence from the heat and a cover
38 29 fighteth with the heat of the furnace
43 3 keeping a furnace in the works of heat
24 meeteth it, by the heat that cometh
Isa 4 6 a shade in the daytime from the heat
5 24 and the heat of the flame consumeth it
25 4 the whirlwind, a shadow from the heat
5 tumult of strangers, as heat in thirst

5 and as with heat under a burning cloud
27 8 with his severe spirit in day of heat
33 11 you shall conceive heat, you shall
49 10 neither shall heat nor the sun strike
Jer 17 8 it shall not fear when the heat cometh
36 30 shall be cast out to the heat by day
51 39 in their heat I will set them drink
Bar 2 25 they are cast out to the h. of the sun
Dan 3 46 ceased not to heat the furnace with
66 O ye fire and heat, bless the Lord
67 O ye cold and heat, bless the Lord
Jon 4 8 he broiled with the heat: and he desired
2 Ma 10 29 but when they were in the heat of the
Luke 12 55 you say: There will be heat: and it
Acts 28 3 viper coming out of the heat, fastened
2 P 3 10 the elements shall be melted with heat
Apoc 7 16 shall the sun fall on them nor any heat
16 8 to afflict men with heat and fire. And
9 and men were scorched with great heat
burning heat Lev 26 16 you with poverty and b. h.
Job 15 2 and fill his stomach with burning heat
43 3 and who can abide his burning heat
Osee 12 1 wind, and followeth the burning heat
James 1 11 the sun rose with a burning heat and
1 P 4 12 think not strange the burning heat
2 P 3 12 elements shall melt with the burning h.
heated Job 41 11 smoke, like that of a pot heated
Dan 3 19 should be h. seven times more than it had been accustomed to be h.
22 the furnace was heated exceedingly
Osee 7 4 like an oven heated by the baker: the
6 in the morning he himself was heated
7 they were all heated like an oven
2 Ma 7 3 be made hot: which forthwith being h.
heath Jer 48 6 be as heath in the wilderness
heathen Joel 2 17 the h. should rule over them
Mat 18 17 let him be to thee as the heathen and
heathenish 2 Ma 4 13 of h. and foreign manners
heathens Tob 8 5 not be joined together like h.
Ps 78 1 the h. are come into thy inheritance
105 35 they were mingled among the heathens
Wisd 15 15 all the idols of the heathens for gods
Jer 10 2 signs of heaven which the h. fear
1 Ma 1 12 and make a covenant with the heathens
14 to do after the ordinances of the h.
16 and joined themselves to the heathens
2 40 not fight against the heathens for our
4 54 wherein the heathens had defiled it
5 10 the heathens . . . are gathered together
19 make no war against the h. till we
21 fought many battles with the heathens
21 the h. were discomforted before his face
22 fell of the heathens almost 3,000 men
43 the h. were discomfited before them
12 53 the heathens . . . sought to destroy them
13 6 all the heathens are gathered together
14 36 the h. were taken away out of their
2 Ma 4 10 countrymen to the fashion of the h.
6 24 was gone over to the life of the h.
8 5 he could not be withstood by the h.
10 2 altars which the h. had set up in the
14 3 in the time of mingling with the h.
Mat 5 47 do not also the heathens this? Be
6 7 speak not much, as the heathens. For
32 these things do the heathens seek
1 C 5 1 as the like is not among the heathens
10 20 but the things which the h. sacrifice
12 2 you know that when you were heathens
heats Mat 20 12 burden of the day and the heats
heaven Mat 5 12 your reward is very great in h.
Mat 5 34 neither by heaven, for it is the throne
6 9 our Father who art in heaven, hallowed
10 be done on earth as it is in heaven
20 lay up to yourselves treasures in h.
11 23 shalt thou be exalted up to heaven
14 19 looking up to heaven. Mark 6:41; 7:34
16 19 shall be bound also in heaven. 18:18
19 shall be loosed also in heaven. 18:18
18 10 their angels in heaven always see the
19 21 thou shalt have treasure in heaven. Mark 10:21; Luke 18:22
22 30 shall be as the angels of God in heaven
23 22 he that sweareth by heaven, sweareth
24 29 powers of h. shall be moved. Luke 21:26
30 sign of the Son of man in heaven
30 coming in the clouds of heaven. 26:64; Mark 14:62
36 knoweth, no not the angels of heaven
Mark 12 25 but are as the angels in heaven. And
13 25 powers that are in h. shall be moved
27 earth to the uttermost part of heaven
32 neither the angels in heaven nor the
16 19 was taken up into h., and sitteth on
Luke 2 15 angels departed from them into heaven
3 21 heaven was opened; and the Holy Ghost
4 25 when h. was shut up three years and
6 23 your reward is great in heaven. For
9 16 he looked up to h. and blessed them
10 15 Capharnaum which art exalted unto h.
20 that your names are written in heaven
12 33 a treasure in heaven which faileth not
15 7 there shall be joy in heaven upon one
18 I have sinned against h. and before. 21
18 13 as lift up his eyes towards heaven
19 38 peace in heaven, and glory on high
24 51 from them, and was carried up to h.
John 1 51 you shall see the heaven opened and
3 13 no man hath ascended into heaven but
13 the Son of man who is in heaven. And
17 1 lifting up his eyes to heaven, he said
Acts 1 10 were beholding him going up to heaven
11 why stand you looking up to heaven
11 who is taken up from you into heaven
11 as you have seen him going into h.
2 19 I will show wonders in the heaven
34 David ascended not into heaven; but
3 21 whom heaven indeed must receive unto
7 42 gave them up to serve the host of h.
49 heaven is my throne, and the earth my
55 looking up steadfastly to heaven, saw
10 11 he saw the heaven opened, and a certain
16 the vessel was taken up into heaven
11 10 and all were taken up again into heaven
Rom 10 6 thy heart, Who shall ascend into heaven
2 C 5 1 not made with hands, eternal in heaven
12 2 such a one caught up to the third heaven
Eph 6 9 Lord both of them and you is in heaven
Phil 3 20 but our conversation is in heaven; from
Col 1 5 hope that is laid up for you in heaven
20 earth, and the things that are in heaven
4 1 that you also have a master in heaven
Heb 9 24 the true: but into heaven itself, that
12 26 will move not only the earth, but h.
James 5 18 prayed again: and the heaven gave rain
1 P 1 4 cannot fade, reserved in h. for you
3 22 being gone into heaven, the angels and
1 J 5 7 three who give testimony in heaven, the
Apoc 3 12 which cometh down out of heaven from
4 1 a door was opened in heaven, and the
6 14 the heaven departed as a book folded up
8 1 silence in heaven . . . for half an hour
13 eagle flying through the midst of h.
10 5 lifted up his hand to heaven. And he
11 6 these have power to shut heaven, that
12 and they went up to heaven in a cloud
13 and gave glory to the God of heaven

15 and there were great voices in heaven
19 the temple of God was opened in heaven
12 1 great sign appeared in heaven: a woman
3 there was seen another sign in heaven
7 there was a great battle in heaven
8 was their place found any more in h.
10 I heard a loud voice in heaven, saying
13 6 and them that dwell in heaven. And it
14 6 angel flying through the midst of h.
17 out of the temple which is in heaven
15 1 I saw another sign in heaven, great
5 the temple . . . in heaven was opened
16 11 they blasphemed the God of heaven
18 5 her sins have reached unto heaven, and
20 rejoice over her, thou heaven, and
19 1 the voice of much people in heaven
11 I saw heaven opened, and behold a white
14 the armies that are in h. followed him
17 that did fly through the midst of h.
20 9 came down fire from God out of heaven
11 earth and heaven fled away, and there
21 2 coming down out of heaven from God. 10

Father who is in heaven; *see* **Father**

from heaven Mat 2 17 a voice from heaven. Mark 1:11; Luke 3:22; John 12:28; Acts 11:9; Apoc 10:8; 11:12; 14:2, 13; 8:4
Mat 16 1 a sign from heaven. Mark 8:11; Luke 11:16
21 25 was it from h. or from men. Luke 20:4
26 if we say, From heaven. Mark 11:31; Luke 20:5
24 29 the stars shall fall from heaven and
28 2 angel of the Lord descended from h.
Mark 11 30 baptism of John, was it from heaven
Luke 9 54 fire to come down from h. and consume
10 18 Satan like lightning falling from h.
11 13 how much more will your Father from h.
17 29 it rained fire and brimstone from h.
21 11 and famines and terrors from heaven
22 43 appeared to him an angel from heaven
John 1 32 coming down, as a dove from heaven
3 13 but he that descended from heaven, the
27 unless it be given him from heaven
31 he that cometh from h., is above all
6 31 he gave them bread from heaven to eat
32 Moses gave you not bread from heaven
32 giveth you the true bread from heaven
33 that which cometh down from heaven
38 I came down from heaven, not to do
41 bread which came down from heaven. 51, 59
42 saith he, I came down from heaven
50 bread which cometh down from heaven
Acts 2 2 there came a sound from heaven, as of
9 3 and suddenly a light from heaven shined
10 11 down by the four corners from h. 11:5
14 16 doing good from heaven, giving rains
22 6 from heaven there shone round about me
26 13 I saw in the way light from heaven above
Rom 1 18 wrath of God is revealed from heaven
1 C 15 47 the second man, from heaven, heavenly
2 C 5 2 with our habitation that is from heaven
Gal 1 8 we, or an angel from heaven, preach a
1 Th 1 10 to wait for his Son from heaven, whom
4 15 Lord himself shall come down from h.
2 Th 1 7 Jesus shall be revealed from heaven
Heb 12 25 from him that speaketh to us from h.
1 P 1 12 Holy Ghost being sent down from heaven
2 P 1 18 voice we heard brought down from h.
Apoc 6 13 the stars from heaven fell upon the
8 10 a great star fell from heaven, burning
9 1 I saw a star fall from heaven upon the
10 1 angel come down from heaven. 18:1
4 I heard a voice from h., saying to me
13 13 also fire to come down from heaven
16 21 great hail . . . came down from heaven
20 1 I saw an angel coming down from heaven

heaven . . . earth Mat 5 18 till h. and e. pass, one jot
Mat 5 35 swear not, neither by h. nor by e. James 5:12
11 25 O Father, Lord of h. and e. Luke 10:21; Acts 17:24
24 35 h. and e. shall pass. Mark 13:31; Luke 21:33
28 18 is given to me in heaven and in earth
Luke 12 56 discern face of the h. and of the e.
16 17 is easier for heaven and earth to pass
Acts 4 24 he that didst make h. and e. Apoc 14:7
10 11 let down . . . from heaven to the earth
17 24 Lord of h. and e. dwelleth not in temples
1 C 8 5 gods, either in heaven or on earth
Eph 1 10 that are in heaven and on earth, in him
3 15 paternity in heaven and earth is named
Phil 2 10 in heaven, on earth, and under the earth
Col 1 16 created in heaven and on earth, visible
Apoc 5 3 able, neither in heaven nor on earth
13 which is in heaven and on the earth
9 1 star fell from heaven upon the earth
10 6 who created heaven . . . and the earth
13 13 fire from heaven . . . unto the earth
21 1 I saw a new heaven and a new earth
1 first h. and the first earth was gone

kingdom of heaven; *see* **kingdom**

stars of heaven; *see* **stars**

under heaven Luke 17 24 that lighteneth from under heaven
Luke 17 24 unto the parts that are under heaven
Acts 2 5 men, out of every nation under heaven
4 12 there is no other name under heaven
Col 1 23 in all the creation that is under heaven

heavenly Mat 5 48 as also your h. Father is perfect
Mat 6 26 and your heavenly Father feedeth them
48 your h. Father will forgive you also
15 13 which my h. Father hath not planted
18 35 my heavenly Father do to you if you
Luke 2 13 a multitude of the h. army, praising
John 3 12 if I shall speak to you h. things
Acts 26 19 I was not incredulous to the h. vision
1 C 15 47 the second man, from heaven, heavenly
48 the earthly: and such as is the heavenly
48 such also are they that are heavenly
49 let us bear also image of the heavenly
Eph 1 3 blessings in heavenly places, in Christ
20 on his right hand in the heavenly places
2 6 made us sit together in heavenly places
3 10 in heavenly places through the church
2 Tim 2 10 is in Christ Jesus, with heavenly glory
4 18 will preserve me unto his h. kingdom
Heb 6 4 have tasted also the heavenly gift, and
8 5 the example and shadow of h. things
9 23 patterns of h. things should be cleansed
23 the h. things themselves with better
11 16 better, that is to say, a h. country
12 22 of the living God, the h. Jerusalem

heavens Mat 3 16 lo, the heavens were opened to
Mat 24 31 from the farthest parts of the heavens
Mark 1 10 he saw the heavens opened and the
Acts 7 55 I see the heavens opened, and the Son
Eph 4 10 also that ascended above all the heavens
Heb 1 10 the works of thy hands are the heavens
4 14 priest that passed into the heavens
7 26 and made higher than the heavens; who
8 1 the throne of majesty in the heavens
12 23 firstborn, who are written in the h.
2 P 3 5 that the h. were before, and the earth
7 heavens and the earth, which are now
10 the heavens shall pass away with great
12 h. being on fire shall be dissolved
13 we look for new heavens and a new earth
Apoc 12 12 rejoice, O heavens, and you that dwell

heavier 2 Pa 10 14 yoke, which I will make h.
Job 6 3 sand of the sea this would appear h.
Prov 27 3 anger of a fool is h. than them both
Eccu 22 17 what is heavier than lead? And what
heavily Isa 9 1 way of the sea . . . was h. loaded
Acts 28 27 with their ears have they heard heavily
heaviness Ps 118 28 hath slumbered through h.
heavy Gen 43 1 the famine was heavy upon all the
Exod 17 12 Moses' hands were heavy: so they took
Num 11 14 people, because it is too heavy for me
Judg 1 35 house of Joseph was heavy upon him
1 K 5 6 hand of Lord was h. upon the Azotians
7 his hand is heavy upon us and upon
12 the hand of God was exceeding heavy
3 K 12 4 thy father, and of his most heavy yoke
10 thy father made our yoke h. 2 Pa 10:10
11 my father put a heavy yoke upon you
14 my father made your yoke heavy, but I
14 5 I am sent to thee with heavy tidings
2 Pa 10 4 who laid upon us a heavy servitude
11 my father laid upon you a h. yoke. 14
Ps 31 4 day and night thy hand was h. upon me
37 5 as a h. burden are become h. upon me
Prov 27 3 a stone is heavy, and sand weighty
Wisd 17 20 over them only was spread a h. night
Eccu 25 31 and maketh a heavy countenance and a
40 1 h. yoke is upon the children of Adam
Isa 6 10 and make their ears heavy, and shut
24 20 iniquity thereof shall be heavy upon
30 27 his wrath burneth and is heavy to bear
46 1 your burdens of heavy weight even unto
47 6 thou hast laid thy yoke exceeding h.
59 1 neither is his ear h. that it cannot
Lam 3 7 get out: he hath made my fetters heavy
1 Ma 8 31 thy yoke heavy upon our friends and
2 Ma 5 23 Menelaus who bore a more heavy hand
Mat 23 4 they bind heavy and insupportable
26 43 for their eyes were heavy. Mark 14:40
Mark 14 33 and he began to fear and to be heavy
Luke 9 32 were with him were heavy with sleep
1 J 5 3 and his commandments are not heavy
Hebal Deut 11 29 the curse upon mount Hebal
Deut 27 4 set up the stones . . . in mount Hebal
13 shall stand on mount Hebal to curse
Josu 8 30 Josue built altar . . . in mount Hebal
33 by mount Garizim, and half by mount H.
1 Pa 1 22 Hebal and Abimael and Saba and Ophir
Heber Gen 10 21 H. the elder brother of Japheth
Gen 10 24 begot Sale, of whom was born Heber
25 to Heber were born two sons. 1 Pa 1:19
11 14 Sale . . . begot Heber. 1 Pa 1:18
15 Sale lived after he begot Heber
16 Heber lived 34 years, and begot
17 Heber lived after he begot Phaleg
46 17 sons of Beria: Heber and Melchiel
Num 26 45 the sons of Brie: Heber, of whom is
1 Pa 1 25 Heber, Phaleg, Ragau, Serug, Nachor
4 18 his wife Judaia bore . . . Heber
5 13 their brethren . . . Zie and Heber
7 32 Heber begot Jephlat and Somer and
8 12 sons of Elphaal were Heber and
17 and Heber . . . sons of Elphaal
22 and Heber . . . sons of Sesac
2 Es 12 20 of Sellai, Celai: of Amoc, Heber
Luke 3 35 Phaleg, who was of Heber, who was of
Heberites Num 26 45 of whom is family of the H.
Hebrew Gen 14 13 had escaped told Abram the H.
Gen 39 14 he hath brought in a H. to abuse us
17 the H. servant whom thou hast brought
41 12 was there a young man a Hebrew
Exod 1 16 office of midwives to the Hebrew women
19 the H. women are not as the Egyptian
2 7 a Hebrew woman to nurse the babe
21 2 if thou buy a H. servant, six years
Deut 15 12 when thy brother a H. man or H. woman is sold to thee
Jdth 12 10 persuade that Hebrew woman to consent
14 16 one Hebrew woman hath made confusion
Esth 3 7 which in Hebrew is called Phur
Jer 34 9 being a H. man or a H. woman, go free
14 every man his brother being a Hebrew
Jon 1 9 he said to them: I am a Hebrew
Luke 23 38 letters of Greek and Latin and Hebrew
John 5 2 which in Hebrew is named Bethsaida
19 13 Lithostrotos, and in Hebrew Gabbatha
17 Calvary, but in Hebrew Golgotha
20 written in H., in Greek, and in Latin
Acts 21 40 spoke unto them in the H. tongue. 22:2
26 13 voice speaking to me in the H. tongue
Phil 3 5 Benjamin, and Hebrew of the Hebrews
Apoc 9 11 whose name in Hebrew is Abaddon, and
16 16 which in Hebrew is called Armagedon
Hebrews Gen 40 15 away out of the land of the H.
Gen 43 32 for Egyptians to eat with the Hebrews
Exod 1 15 spoke to the midwives of the Hebrews
2 6 this is one of the babes of the Hebrews
11 Egyptian striking one of the Hebrews
13 next day he saw two H. quarrelling
3 18 God of the H. hath called us. 5:3
7 16 God of the Hebrews sent me to thee
9 1 saith the Lord God of the H. 13; 10:3
Num 24 24 the Assyrians, and shall waste the H.
1 K 4 6 great shout in the camp of the Hebrews
9 you come to be servants to the Hebrews
13 3 Saul . . . saying: Let the Hebrews hear
7 some of the H. passed over the Jordan
19 lest the H. should make them swords
14 11 the Hebrews come forth out of the holes
21 H. that had been with the Philistines
29 3 to Achis: what mean these Hebrews
Jdth 10 12 I am a daughter of the H., and I am
18 who can despise the people of the H.
15 2 they made haste to escape from the H.
16 31 by the H. in the number of holy days
2 Ma 7 31 author of all mischief against the H.
11 13 that the H. could not be overcome
15 38 city being possessed by the Hebrews
Acts 6 1 murmuring of the Greeks against the H.
2 C 11 22 they are Hebrews: so am I. They are
Phil 3 5 Benjamin, an Hebrew of the Hebrews
Hebri 1 Pa 24 27 Soam and Zacchur and Hebri
Hebron Gen 13 18 vale of Mambre, which is in H.
Gen 23 2 died in the city of Arbee which is H.
19 Mambre, this is Hebron in the land of
35 27 Mambre, the city of Arbee, this is H.
37 14 being sent from the vale of Hebron, he
Exod 6 18 the sons of Caath: . . . Hebron. Num 3:19; 1 Pa 6:2, 18; 23:12
Num 13 23 up at the south side and came to H.
23 H. was built seven years before Tanis
Josu 10 3 sent to Oham king of Hebron and to
5 king of H., the king of Jerimoth. 23
36 he went up . . . from Eglon to Hebron
39 as he had done to Hebron and Lebna
11 21 and cut off the Enacims . . . from Hebron
12 10 the king of Hebron one, the king of
14 13 Josue blessed him and gave him Hebron
14 from that time Hebron belonged to Caleb
15 the name of Hebron before was called
15 13 the father of Enac, which is Hebron
54 Cariath-Arbe, this is Hebron and Sior
20 7 and Cariath-Arbe, the same is Hebron
21 11 father of Enac, which is called Hebron
13 Hebron a city of refuge, and the suburbs
Judg 1 10 the Chanaanite, that dwelt in Hebron
20 they gave Hebron to Caleb, as Moses

10 11 Ephraim is a h. taught to love to tread
Heb 9 13 the ashes of an heifer being sprinkled
height Gen 6 15 the height of it thirty cubits
Exod 25 10 the height likewise cubit and a half
23 table . . . a cubit and a half in height
27 18 court . . . height shall be of 5 cubits
30 2 shall be . . . two [cubits] in height
37 1 the height was of one cubit and a half
10 in height it was a cubit and a half
25 altar . . . and in height two cubits
38 1 the altar . . . three [cubits] in height
1 K 16 7 look not . . . on the h. of his stature
17 9 whose height was six cubits and a span
20 7 that his malice is come to its height
3 K 6 2 the house . . . thirty cubits in height
10 built a floor . . . 5 cubits in height
20 the oracle . . . twenty cubits in height
23 cherubims . . . of ten cubits in height
7 2 house . . . the height thirty cubits
16 h. of one chapiter was 5 cubits. Jer 52:22
23 the height of it was five cubits, and
32 height of a wheel was a cubit and half
4 K 19 23 gone up to the height of the mountains
2 Pa 3 4 height was a hundred and twenty cubits
33 14 and raised it up to a great height
1 Es 6 3 support the height of threescore cubits
Jdth 1 3 according to the height of the towers
Job 22 12 elevated above the height of the stars
Ps 55 4 from the height of the day I shall fear
102 11 according to the height of the heaven
Eccu 1 2 who hath measured the height of heaven
17 31 beholdeth power of the h. of heaven
50 2 the height of the temple was founded
Isa 7 11 depth of hell, or unto the height above
14 14 will ascend above the h. of the clouds
24 4 the height of the people of the earth
37 24 gone up to the height of the mountains
24 and will enter to the top of its h.
Jer 49 16 to lay hold on the height of the hill
Eze 1 18 the wheels had also a size and a h.
19 11 she saw her height in the multitude
31 5 therefore was his height exalted above
10 because he was exalted in height and
10 his heart was lifted up in his height
14 shall exalt themselves for their height
14 that are watered stand up in their h.
40 5 building one reed, and the h. one reed
41 8 I saw in the house the height round
Dan 4 7 the height thereof was exceeding great
8 the height thereof reached unto heaven
17 whose height reached to the skies, and
11 4 when he shall come to his height, his
Amos 2 9 whose h. was like the h. of cedars
Mich 5 4 in the height of the name of the Lord
2 Ma 6 15 to suffer our sins to come to their h.
Rom 8 39 nor height, nor depth, nor any other
2 C 10 5 every h. that exalteth itself against
Eph 3 18 what is the breadth and length and h.
Apoc 21 16 the length and the h. and the breadth
heights Ps 41 8 all thy heights and thy billows
Ps 94 4 the heights of the mountains are his
Eze 36 2 everlasting heights are given to us
2 Ma 9 8 to weigh the heights of the mountains
heinous Gen 44 7 had committed so h. a fact
Exod 32 21 bring upon them a most heinous sin
31 this people hath sinned a heinous sin
Lev 18 23 with it, because it is a heinous crime
20 12 because they have done a heinous crime
14 mother, he hath done a heinous crime
Judg 20 6 there never was so heinous a crime
13 that have committed this heinous
Job 31 11 this is a heinous crime, and a most
Acts 18 14 some matter of injustice, or h. deed

heir Gen 15 3 my servant . . . shall be my heir
Gen 15 4 he shall not be thy heir: but he that
4 him shalt thou have for thy heir. And
21 10 son of the bondwoman shall not be heir
2 K 14 7 and that we may destroy the heir
Prov 30 23 bondwoman when she is heir to her
Ecce 2 18 being like to have an heir after me
Eccu 22 29 that thou mayst also be heir with him
23 32 and bringeth in an heir by another
Jer 49 1 hath Israel no son: or hath he no heir
Mich 1 15 yet will I bring an heir to thee
Mat 21 38 this is the h. Mark 12:7; Luke 20:14
Rom 4 13 that he should be heir of the world; but
Gal 4 1 say, as long as the heir is a child, he
7 and if a son, an heir also through God
30 son of the bondwoman shall not be heir
Heb 1 2 he hath appointed heir of all things
11 7 heir of the justice which is by faith
heirs 1 Es 9 12 may have your children your h.
Prov 13 22 the good man leaveth heirs, sons
Rom 4 14 for if they who are of the law be heirs
8 17 if sons, heirs also; heirs indeed of God, and joint heirs with Christ
Gal 3 29 heirs according to the promise. Now I
Eph 3 6 the Gentiles should be fellow heirs, and
Titus 3 7 we may be heirs, according to hope of
Heb 6 17 to show to the heirs of the promise the
James 2 5 rich in faith and heirs of the kingdom
1 P 3 22 that we might be made heirs of life
Helam 2 K 10 17 over the Jordan and came to Helam
Helba Judg 1 31 of Helba and of Aphec and of
Helcath Josu 21 31 and Helcath and Rohob with
Helchias 2 Es 1 1 Nehemias the son of Helchias
Helci 2 Es 12 15 of Maraioth, Helci: of Adaia
Helcia 2 Es 8 4 Helcia and Maasia on his
Helcias 4 K 18 18 Eliacim the son of Helcias. 26, 37; Isa 22:20; 36:3, 22
4 K 22 4 go to Helcias the high priest, that
8 Helcias the high priest said to Saphan
8 and Helcias gave the book to Saphan
10 H. the priest hath delivered to me
12 and he commanded Helcias the priest
14 Helcias the priest . . . went to Holda
23 4 the king commanded Helcias the high
23 which Helcias the priest had found
1 Pa 6 13 Sellum begot H., and H. begot Azarias
45 the son of Amasai the son of Helcias
9 11 Azarias the son of Helcias, the son of
26 11 of Hosa . . . Helcias the second
2 Pa 34 9 they came to Helcias the high priest
14 Helcias the priest found the book
18 Helcias the priest gave me this book
20 he commanded Helcias and Ahicam
22 Helcias and they that were sent with
35 8 Helcias . . . gave to the priests
1 Es 7 1 Azarias the son of Helcias the son
2 Es 11 11 Saraia the son of Helcias the son of
12 6 Helcias, Idaia. These were the
21 of Helcias, Hasebia: of Idaia
Jer 1 1 Jeremias the son of Helcias, of the
29 3 Gamarias the son of Helcias, whom
Bar 1 1 son of Sedei the son of Helcias
7 Joakim the priest the son of Helcias
Dan 13 2 Susanna the daughter of Helcias. 29
63 Helcias and his wife praised God
Helec Num 26 30 Galaad had sons: Jezer . . . and H.
Josu 17 2 to the children of Helec and to the
Helecites Num 26 30 of whom is the family of the H.
Heled 2 K 23 29 Heled the son of Baana. 1 Pa 11:30
Helem 1 Pa 7 35 the sons of Helem his brother
Zach 6 14 the crowns shall be to H. and Tobias
Heleph Josu 19 33 the border began from Heleph
Heles 2 K 23 26 Heles of Phalti, Hira the son

Heli 1 K 1 3 sons of H., Ophni and Phinees. 4:4, 11
1 K 1 9 Heli the priest sitting upon a stool
12 Heli observed her mouth. Now Anna
13 Heli therefore thought her to be drunk
17 then Heli said to her: Go in peace
25 offered the child to Heli. And Anna
2 11 before the face of Heli the priest
12 sons of Heli were children of Belial
20 Heli blessed Elcana and his wife
22 Heli was very old and he heard all
27 there came a man of God to Heli
3 1 ministered to the Lord before Heli
2 one day when Heli lay in his place
5 he ran to Heli and said: Here am I
6 arose and went to Heli and said. 8
9 Heli understood that the Lord called
12 I will raise up against Heli all the
14 have I sworn to the house of Heli
15 feared to tell the vision to Heli
16 Heli called Samuel and said: Samuel
4 13 Heli sat upon a stool over against
14 Heli heard the noise of the cry and
14 made haste and came and told Heli
15 Heli was ninety and eight years old
16 said to Heli: I am he that came from
14 3 Phinees the son of Heli the priest
3 K 2 27 he spoke concerning the house of Heli
Luke 3 23 Joseph, who was of Heli, who was of
Heliodorus 2 Ma 3 7 he called for Heliodorus
2 Ma 3 8 Heliodorus forthwith began his journey
14 H. entered in to order this matter
23 H. executed that which he had resolved
25 struck Heliodorus with his fore feet
27 Heliodorus suddenly fell to the ground
31 friends of H. forthwith begged of Onias
32 that some mischief had been done to H.
33 the same young men . . . stood by H.
35 H. after he had offered a sacrifice
37 when the king asked H., who might be
40 the things concerning Heliodorus
4 1 as though he had incited H. to do
5 18 as H. who was sent by king Seleucus
Heliopolis Gen 41 45 Putiphare priest of H. 50; 46:20
Eze 30 17 the young men of H. . . . shall fall
Helisur Num 10 18 whose prince was Helisur
hell Gen 37 35 I will go down to my son into hell
Gen 42 38 gray hairs with sorrow to h. 44:29, 31
Num 16 30 and they go down alive into hell, you
33 and they went down alive into hell
Deut 32 22 and shall burn even to the lowest hell
1 K 2 6 he bringeth down to hell and bringeth
2 K 22 6 cords of hell compassed me: the snares
3 K 2 6 let not his hoary head go down to hell
9 down his gray hairs with blood to hell
Tob 6 15 down their old age with sorrow to hell
13 2 thou leadest down to hell, and bringest
Esth 13 7 that these wicked men going down to h.
Job 7 9 that shall go down to hell, shall not
11 8 he is deeper than hell, and how wilt
14 13 that thou mayst protect me in hell and
17 13 if I wait hell is my house, and I have
21 13 and in a moment they go down to hell
24 19 and his sin even to hell. Let mercy
26 6 hell is naked before him, and there is
Ps 6 6 and who shall confess to thee in hell
9 18 the wicked shall be turned into hell
15 10 thou wilt not leave my soul in hell
17 6 the sorrows of hell encompassed me
29 4 brought forth, O Lord, my soul from h.
30 18 the wicked . . . be brought down to hell
48 15 they are laid in hell like sheep; death
15 their help shall decay in hell from
16 will redeem my soul from hand of hell
54 16 and let them go down alive into hell
85 13 delivered my soul out of the lower h.
87 4 and my life hath drawn nigh to hell
88 49 deliver his soul from the hand of hell
93 17 helper, my soul had almost dwelt in h.
113 17 nor any of them that go down to hell
114 3 and the perils of hell have found me
138 8 I descend into hell, thou art present
140 7 our bones are scattered by side of hell
Prov 1 12 let us swallow him up alive like hell
2 18 unto death, and her paths to hell. None
5 5 depth, and her steps go in as far as h.
7 27 her house is the way to hell, reaching
9 18 her guests are in the depths of hell
15 11 hell and destruction are before the
24 he may decline from the lowest hell
23 14 shalt . . . deliver his soul from hell
27 20 hell and destruction are never filled
30 16 hell, and the mouth of the womb, and
Ecce 9 3 they shall be brought down to hell
10 wisdom nor knowledge shall be in hell
Cant 8 6 as death, jealousy as hard as hell
Wisd 1 14 nor kingdom of hell upon the earth
2 1 been known to have returned from hell
5 14 things as these the sinners said in hell
10 19 from depth of h. she brought them out
17 13 them from the lowest and deepest hell
Eccu 9 17 even to h. the wicked shall not please
14 12 covenant of h. hath been shown to thee
17 for in hell there is no finding food
21 11 in their end is hell and darkness
28 25 evil death: and hell is preferable to it
51 7 from the depth of the belly of hell
9 my life was drawing near to h. beneath
Isa 5 14 therefore hath hell enlarged her soul
7 11 sign . . . either unto the depth of hell
14 9 hell below was in an uproar to meet
11 thy pride is brought down to hell, thy
15 yet thou shalt be brought down to hell
28 15 and we have made a covenant with hell
18 your covenant with h. shall not stand
38 10 days I shall go to the gates of hell
18 hell shall not confess to thee neither
57 9 far off, and wast debased even to hell
Bar 2 17 are in hell . . . shall not give glory
3 11 counted with them that go down into h.
19 are cut off and are gone down to hell
Eze 31 15 in the day when he went down to hell
16 when I brought him down to hell with
17 also shall go down with him to hell
32 27 went down to hell with their weapons
Dan 3 88 hath delivered us from hell and saved
Osee 13 14 be thy death; O hell, I will be thy bite
Amos 9 2 though they go down even to hell
Jon 2 3 I cried out of the belly of hell, and
Haba 2 5 who hath enlarged his desire like hell
Mat 5 22 fool, shall be in danger of hell fire
29 that thy whole body be cast into hell
30 than that thy whole body go into hell
10 28 can destroy both soul and body in hell
11 23 thou shalt go down even unto hell. For
16 18 the gates of hell shall not prevail
18 9 two eyes, to be cast into hell fire
23 15 you make him the child of hell twofold
33 will you flee from the judgment of hell
Mark 9 42 than having two hands to go into hell
44 into the hell of unquenchable fire
46 to be cast into the hell of fire
Luke 10 15 thou shalt be thrust down to hell. He
12 5 killed, hath power to cast into hell
16 22 also died: and he was buried in hell
Acts 2 24 having loosed the sorrows of hell, as
27 thou wilt not leave my soul in hell

31 neither was he left in hell, neither
James 3 6 our nativity, being set on fire by hell
2 P 2 4 by infernal ropes to the lower hell
Apoc 1 18 and have the keys of death and of hell
6 8 name was Death, and hell followed him
20 13 death and hell gave up their dead that
14 hell and death were cast into the pool
Helles 1 Pa 2 39 begot H., and H. begot Elasa
1 Pa 11 27 valiant men . . . Helles a Phalonite
27 10 for the seventh month, was Helles
helm James 3 4 they turned about with a small helm
Helmadan Luke 3 28 Cosan, who was of Helmadan, who
helmet 1 K 17 5 h. of brass upon his head. 38
Wisd 5 19 will take true judgment instead of a h.
Isa 59 17 a helmet of salvation upon his head
Eze 23 24 with breastplate and buckler and helmet
27 10 they hung up the buckler and the helmet
Eph 6 17 take unto you the helmet of salvation
1 Th 5 8 and for a helmet the hope of salvation
helmets 2 Pa 26 14 shields and spears and helmets
Jer 46 4 stand forth with helmets, furbish the
Eze 38 5 with them, all with shields and helmets
1 Ma 6 35 with helmets of brass on their heads
Helmondeblathaim Num 33 46 camped in H., and departing from H.
Helon Num 1 9 Eliab the son of Helon. 2:7; 7:24, 29; 10:16
1 Pa 6 58 cities for refuge . . . Helon. 69
Jer 48 21 judgment is come . . . upon Helon
help Gen 2 18 let us make him a help like unto
Lev 1 4 acceptable, and help to its expiation
Deut 22 27 cried, and there was no man to h. her
28 31 and may there be none to help thee
32 38 let them arise and h. you and protect
33 29 the shield of thy help and the sword
Josu 10 4 come up to me and bring help that we
Judg 5 23 they came not to the help of the Lord, to help his most valiant men
11 5 out of the land of Tob to help them
1 K 4 1 camped by the Stone of help. And the
5 1 carried it from the Stone of help into
7 12 called the place, the Stone of help
2 K 10 11 then thou shalt help me. 1 Pa 19:12
11 thee, then I will help thee. 1 Pa 19:12
19 all the Syrians were afraid to h. the
19 18 that they might help over the king's
3 K 20 16 with him, who were come to help him
4 K 14 26 that there was no one to help Israel
1 Pa 5 20 Naphis and Nodab gave them help. And
12 17 if you are come peaceably to me to help
22 there came some to David to help him
18 5 Syrians . . . came also to help Adarezer
19 19 Syria would not help . . . Ammon any
22 17 princes of Israel to help Solomon his
2 Pa 12 7 I will give them a little help, and my
14 11 whether thou h. with few or with many
11 help us, O Lord our God, for with
20 17 and you shall see the help of the Lord
25 8 to God both to h. and to put to flight
28 16 to king of the Assyrians asking help
19 he [Achaz] had stripped it of help
23 gods of the kings of Syria help them
23 with victims, and they will help me
1 Es 1 4 help him every man from his place with
6 22 that he should help their hands in the
Jdth 6 21 desiring help of the God of Israel
7 14 therefore there is no one to help us
Job 6 13 there is no help for me in myself, and
10 3 and help the counsel of the wicked
30 13 prevailed, and there was none to help
35 8 thy justice may help the son of man
Ps 7 11 just is my help from the Lord: who
19 3 may he send thee h. from the sanctuary
21 12 very near: for there is none to h. me
20 remove not thy help to a distance from
34 2 arms and shield: and rise up to h. me
36 40 Lord will help them and destroy them
37 23 attend unto my help, O Lord, the God
39 14 look down, O Lord, to help me. Let
40 4 the Lord help him on his bed of sorrow
43 26 help us and redeem us for thy name's
45 6 God will help it in the morning early
48 15 their help shall decay in hell from
59 13 give us help from trouble: for vain
61 8 he is the God of my help, and my hope
69 2 O Lord, make haste to help me. Let
6 I am needy and poor: O God, help me
70 12 O my God, make haste to my help
78 9 help us, O God, our savior: and for
83 6 blessed . . . whose help is from thee
87 5 I am become as a man without help
88 20 I have laid h. upon one that is mighty
22 my hand shall help him: and my arm
44 hast turned away the help of his sword
93 22 refuge: and my God the help of my hope
106 12 and there was none to help them. Then
107 13 grant us help from trouble: for vain is the help of man
108 12 may there be none to help him: nor
26 help me, O Lord my God: save me
118 86 persecuted me unjustly, do thou h. me
117 help me, and I shall be saved: and I
175 thee; and thy judgments shall help me
120 1 from whence help shall come to me. My
2 my help is from the Lord, who made
123 8 our help is in the name of the Lord
Ecce 4 1 being destitute of help from any. And
Wisd 13 16 knowing that it is unable to h. itself
16 it is an image and hath need of help
18 for help calleth upon that which is
16 11 they might not be able to use thy help
Eccu 8 19 is no help, he will overthrow thee
11 12 is an inactive man that wanteth help
12 18 while he pretendeth to help thee, will
29 12 mercy. Help the poor because of the
15 obtain help for thee against all evil
34 20 and a help from falling: he raiseth
36 26 is a help like to himself, and a pillar
40 24 brethren are a help in the time of
27 and it needeth not to seek for help
51 10 there was no one that would help me
14 in the time of the proud without help
Isa 10 3 afar? To whom will ye flee for help
20 6 to whom we fled for help, to deliver
30 2 hoping for help in strength of Pharao
5 they were no help nor to any profit
7 Egypt shall help in vain, and to no
31 1 them that go down to Egypt for help
41 6 everyone shall help his neighbor and
63 5 looked about, and there was none to h.
Jer 15 11 I shall help thee in the time of
37 6 which is come forth to help you
Lam 4 14 when they could not help walking in it
17 failed, expecting help for us in vain
Bar 4 17 as for me, what help can I give you
6 57 neither shall they help themselves
67 fly under a covert and help themselves
Dan 10 13 of the chief princes came to help me
11 34 shall be relieved with a small help
45 top thereof, and none shall help him
Osee 13 9 own, O Israel: thy help is only in me
Nah 3 11 thou shalt seek help from the enemy
1 Ma 3 53 their face unless thou, O God, h. us
5 39 have hired the Arabians to help them
7 20 and left with him troops to help him
8 13 they had a mind to help to a kingdom

4 of Heman also: the sons of Heman
5 all these were the sons of Heman the
5 God gave to Heman fourteen sons and
6 to sing . . . Asaph and Idithun and H.
2 Pa 5 12 and they that were under Heman, and
29 14 of the sons of Heman, Jahiel and
35 15 H. and Idithun the prophets of the
Hemath 1 Pa 18 3 king of Soba of the land of H.
1 Pa 18 9 when Thou king of Hemath heard that
Hemor Gen 33 19 Hemor, the father of Sichem
Gen 34 2 Sichem the son of Hemor . . . saw her
4 going to Hemor his father, he said
6 when Hemor . . . come out to speak to
8 Hemor spoke to them: The soul of my son
18 their offer pleased Hemor and Sichem
26 they killed also Hemor and Sichem
Josu 24 32 Jacob had bought of sons of Hemor
Acts 7 16 bought . . . of the sons of Hemor, the
hen Mat 23 37 as the hen doth gather her chickens
Henadad 1 Es 3 9 the sons of H. and their sons
2 Es 10 9 Bennui of the sons of Henadad
Henanias 2 Pa 26 11 army . . . under the hand of H.
henceforth Mat 23 39 you shall not see me h. till
Luke 1 48 from h. all generations shall call me
12 52 from h. five in one house divided
John 14 7 from henceforth you shall know him
19 12 henceforth Pilate sought to release
Acts 18 6 h. I will go unto the Gentiles. And
2 C 5 16 henceforth we know no man according to
Gal 6 17 h. let no man be troublesome to me
Eph 4 14 henceforth we be no more children
Heb 10 13 henceforth expecting until his enemies
henceforward Mat 21 19 may no fruit grow on thee h.
Eph 4 17 h. you walk not as also the Gentiles
Henoc 1 Pa 1 3 Henoc, Mathusale, Lamech
Henoch Gen 4 17 conceived and brought forth H.
Gen 4 17 called . . . by the name of his son H.
18 Henoch begot Irad, and Irad begot
5 18 Jared lived 162 years and begot Henoch
19 and Jared lived after he begot Henoch
21 and Henoch lived 65 years and begot
22 Henoch walked with God: and lived
23 all the days of Henoch were 365 years
25 4 was born Epha and Opher and Henoch
46 9 the sons of Ruben: Henoch and Phallu
Exod 6 14 the sons of Ruben . . . H. and Phallu
Num 26 5 Henoch, of whom is the family of the
1 Pa 1 33 sons of Madian . . . Henoch and Abida
Eccu 44 16 Henoch pleased God, and was translated
49 16 no man was born upon earth like Henoch
Luke 3 37 Mathusale, who was of Henoch, who was
Heb 11 5 by faith Henoch was translated, that he
Henochites Num 26 5 of whom is family of the H.
Henos Luke 3 38 Cainan, who was of Henos, who was of
Hepher Num 26 32 Galaad had sons: Jezer . . . and H.
Num 26 33 Hepher was the father of Salphaad
27 1 Salphaad the son of Hepher. Josu 17:3
Josu 17 2 to the children of Hepher and to the
1 Pa 4 6 Naara bore him Ozam and Hepher and
11 36 Hepher a Mecherathite, Ahia a
Hepherites Num 26 32 is the family of the H.
Her Gen 38 3 a son and called his name Her
Gen 38 6 Juda took a wife for Her his firstborn
7 Her, the firstborn of Juda, was wicked
46 12 Her and Onan died in land of Chanaan
Num 26 16 Her, of him is family of the Herites
19 the sons of Juda, Her and Onan, who
1 Pa 2 3 sons of Juda: Her, Onan, and Sela
3 Her the firstborn of Juda was wicked
4 21 Her the father of Lecha, and Laada the
Luke 3 28 Helmadan, who was of Her, who was of
herald 3 K 22 36 h. proclaimed through all the
Dan 3 4 a herald cried with a strong voice
heralds Josu 3 2 h. went through midst of the
Heran Num 26 36 the son of Suthala was Heran
Heranites Num 26 36 is the family of the H.
herb Gen 1 11 earth bring forth the green herb
Gen 1 12 earth brought forth the green herb
29 I have given you every herb bearing
2 5 every h. of the ground before it grew
Exod 9 22 and upon every herb of the field
25 the hail smote every herb of the field
10 12 devour every herb that is left after
Deut 32 2 the dew, as a shower upon the herb
4 K 19 26 the green herb on the tops of houses
Ps 103 14 and herb for the service of men
Wisd 16 12 neither herb nor mollifying plaster
Isa 37 27 became like . . . the h. of the pasture
66 14 your bones shall flourish like an herb
Jer 2 22 multiply to thyself the herb borith
12 4 and the herb of every field wither
Mala 3 2 refining fire, and like the fuller's h.
Luke 11 42 tithe mint and rue and every herb
herbs Gen 3 18 shalt eat the herbs of the earth
Gen 9 3 as the green herbs have I delivered
Exod 10 15 in the herbs of the earth in all Egypt
3 K 21 2 that I may make me a garden of herbs
4 K 4 39 out into the field to gather wild h.
Job 8 12 it withereth before all herbs. Even
Ps 36 2 as the green herbs shall quickly fall
146 8 and herbs for the service of men
Prov 15 17 better to be invited to herbs with love
27 25 and the green herbs have appeared
Isa 44 4 they shall spring up among the herbs
2 Ma 5 27 and they continued feeding on herbs
Mat 13 32 greater than all herbs. Mark 4:32
Mark 4 32 and becometh greater than all herbs
Rom 14 2 but he that is weak, let him eat herbs
Heb 6 7 herbs meet for them by whom it is tilled
Hercules 2 Ma 4 19 silver for the sacrifice of Hercules
2 Ma 4 20 money . . . to the sacrifice of Hercules
herd Gen 18 7 he himself ran to the herd and
Gen 24 10 took ten camels of his master's herd
Exod 29 1 take a calf from the herd. Eze 45:18
Lev 1 3 offering be a holocaust and of the herd
3 1 he will offer of the herd, whether
9 2 take of the herd a calf for sin, and a
23 18 one calf from the herd and two rams
Num 7 15 an ox of the herd, and a ram. 21, 27, 33, 39, 45, 51, 57, 63, 69, 75, 81
87 twelve oxen out of the herd for a
8 8 they shall take an ox of the herd
8 another ox of the h. for a sin offering
15 24 they shall offer a calf out of the herd
28 11 offer . . . two calves of the herd. 19, 27
29 2 offer . . . one calf of the herd. 8
13 offer . . . thirteen calves of the herd
17 offer 12 calves of the herd, 2 rams
Deut 21 3 shall take a heifer of the herd, that
32 14 butter of the herd, and milk of the
1 K 16 2 shalt take with thee a calf of the h.
2 Pa 13 9 his hand with a bullock of the herd
Eze 43 19 offer to me a calf of the herd for sin
23 thou shalt offer a calf of the herd
25 they shall offer also a calf of the h.
46 6 of the new moon a calf of the herd
Amos 6 4 the calves out of the midst of the h.
Haba 3 17 there shall be no herd in the stalls
Mat 8 30 herd of many swine. Mark 5:11; Luke 8:32
31 send us into the herd of swine. And
32 h. ran violently down. Luke 8:33
Mark 5 13 herd with great violence was carried
herds Gen 13 5 of sheep and herds of beasts
Gen 26 14 had possessions of sheep and of herds
34 28 they took their sheep and their herds
45 10 sons' sons, thy sheep, and thy herds

46 32 flocks and herds and all they have
47 1 brethren, their sheep and their herds
50 8 herds, which they left in the land of
Exod 10 9 with our sheep and herds: for it is
24 let your sheep only and herds remain
12 32 your sheep and herds take along with
38 also with them sheep and herds and
Deut 7 13 will bless . . . thy herds and the flocks
8 13 shalt have herds of oxen and flocks
12 6 firstborn of your herds and your sheep
17 not eat . . . the firstborn of thy herds
21 thou shalt kill of thy herds and of
14 23 shalt eat . . . firstborn of thy herds
26 shalt buy . . . either of the herds or
15 19 of the firstlings that come of thy h.
28 4 the droves of thy herds and the folds
18 the herds of thy oxen and the flocks
51 nor herds of oxen nor flocks of sheep
1 K 15 9 of the herds and the garments and
14 the lowing of the herds, which I hear
15 the best of the sheep and of the herds
30 20 he took all the flocks and the herds
1 Pa 27 29 over the herds that fed in Saron
2 Pa 32 29 [Ezechias] had . . . herds without number
Jdth 2 8 herds of oxen and flocks of sheep. 3:3
8 7 large possessions of herds of oxen and
Ecce 2 7 had a great family: and herds of oxen
Jer 3 24 their flocks and their herds, their sons
5 17 shall eat up thy flocks and thy herds
31 12 and the increase of cattle and herds
Osee 5 6 with their h., they shall go to seek
Joel 1 18 why did the herds of cattle low
herdsman Amos 7 14 I am a h. plucking wild figs
herdsmen Gen 4 20 as dwell in tents and of h.
Gen 13 7 strife between the herdsmen of Abram
8 no quarrel . . . between my h. and thy h.
26 20 h. of Gerara strove against h. of Isaac
1 K 21 7 the chiefest of Saul's herdsmen
Amos 1 1 who was among the herdsmen of Thecua
hereafter Exod 10 14 nor shall be hereafter. 11:6
Exod 16 32 unto generations to come hereafter
Deut 29 22 the children that shall be born h.
Josu 24 27 lest perhaps hereafter you will deny it
Ecce 1 11 nor indeed of those things which h. are
4 13 who knoweth not to foresee for h.
Isa 41 23 the things that are to come hereafter
44 7 to come and that shall be hereafter
Bar 6 50 it shall be known hereafter that they
Eze 16 16 not been done before nor shall be h.
Dan 2 29 thy bed, what should come to pass h.
45 the king what shall come to pass h.
1 Ma 15 8 and what should be the king's h.
2 Ma 11 19 h. also I will endeavor to be a means
Mat 26 64 h. you shall see the Son of man sitting
Mark 11 14 may no man hereafter eat fruit of thee
Luke 22 69 h. the Son of man shall be sitting on
John 13 7 now; but thou shalt know hereafter
36 now; but thou shalt follow hereafter
Apoc 1 19 things which must be done h. 4:1
9 12 come yet two woes more hereafter. And
hereby Gen 42 33 h. shall I know that you are
Eccu 9 9 and hereby lust is kindled as a fire
Hered Num 26 40 the sons of Bela: H. and Noeman
Num 26 40 of H. is family of the Heredites
Josu 12 14 of Herma one, the king of Hered one
Heredites Num 26 40 of Hered is family of the H.
herein John 9 30 herein is a wonderful thing, that
Herem 1 Es 10 31 of the sons of Herem, Eliezer
2 Es 3 11 Melchias the son of Herem, and Hasub
heresies 1 C 11 19 for there must be also heresies
heresy Acts 5 17 which is heresy of the Sadducees
Acts 24 14 to the way, which they call a heresy
heretic Titus 3 10 a man that is a heretic, after

Heri Gen 46 16 sons of Gad: . . . Esebon and Heri
Herites Num 26 16 of him is the family of the H.
Herma Josu 12 14 the king of Herma one
Hermas Rom 16 14 salute Asyncritus, Phlegon, Hermas
Hermes Rom 16 14 salute . . . Hermas, Patrobas, H.
Hermogenes 2 Tim 1 15 of whom are Phigellus and H.
Hermon Deut 3 8 from the torrent Arnon unto the mount Hermon. Josu 12:1
Deut 4 48 mount Sion, which is also called Hermon
Josu 11 3 who dwelt at the foot of Hermon in
17 by plain of Libanus under mount H.
12 4 had dominion in mount Hermon and in
13 11 all mount Hermon and all Basan as far
Judg 3 3 from mount Baal Hermon to the entering
1 Pa 5 23 unto Baal, H., and Sanir, and mount H.
Ps 88 13 Thabor and Hermon shall rejoice in
132 3 as the dew of Hermon, which descendeth
Cant 4 8 from the top of Sanir and Hermon, from
Hermoniim Ps 41 7 the land of Jordan and H.
Hernapher 1 Pa 7 36 sons of Supha . . . Hernapher
Herod Mat 2 1 of Juda in the days of king Herod
Mat 2 3 king Herod hearing this, was troubled
7 Herod, privately calling the wise men
12 that they should not return to Herod
13 H. will seek the child to destroy him
14 he was there until the death of Herod
16 Herod perceiving that he was deluded
19 when Herod was dead, behold an angel
22 in the room of Herod his father, he
14 1 Herod the tetrarch heard the fame of
3 for Herod had apprehended John and
6 danced . . . and pleased H. Mark 6:22
Mark 6 14 king Herod heard, for his name was
16 Herod hearing said: John whom I
17 Herod himself had sent and apprehended
18 John said to Herod: It is not lawful
20 Herod feared John, knowing him to be
21 Herod made a supper for his birthday
8 15 Pharisees, and of the leaven of Herod
Luke 1 5 there was in the days of Herod, the
3 1 and Herod being tetrarch of Galilee
19 for all the evils which Herod had done
19 Herod the tetrarch, when he was
9 7 Herod the tetrarch heard of all
9 Herod said: John I have beheaded; but
13 31 for Herod hath a mind to kill thee
23 7 he sent him away to Herod, who was
8 Herod seeing Jesus, was very glad
11 Herod with his army set him at nought
12 Herod and Pilate were made friends
15 nor Herod neither. For I sent you to
Acts 4 27 Herod and Pontius Pilate, with the
12 1 H. the king stretched forth his hands
6 when H. would have brought him forth
11 delivered me out of the hand of Herod
19 when Herod had sought for him, and
21 Herod being arrayed in kingly apparel
13 1 foster brother of Herod the tetrarch
Herodian Rom 16 11 salute Herodian, my kinsman
Herodians Mat 22 16 their disciples with the H.
Mark 3 6 made a consultation with the Herodians
12 13 some of the Pharisees and of the H.
Herodias Mat 14 3 because of H., his brother's wife
Mat 14 6 the daughter of Herodias danced before
Mark 6 17 H. the wife of Philip his brother
19 now Herodias laid snares for him: and
22 the daughter of the same Herodias had
Luke 3 19 was reproved by him for Herodias
Herod's Mat 14 6 on Herod's birthday, the daughter
Luke 8 3 the wife of Chusa, Herod's steward
23 7 that he was of Herod's jurisdiction
Acts 23 35 him to be kept in H. judgment hall. And
heroes 1 Pa 11 11 number of the heroes of David

heron Lev 11 19 you must not eat . . . the heron
Deut 14 16 the heron and the swan and the stork
Job 39 13 ostrich is like the wings of the heron
Ps 103 17 highest of them is house of the heron
Hesebon Num 21 25 H. and in the villages thereof
Num 21 26 Hesebon was the city of Sehon the
27 come into H., let the city of Sehon be
28 a fire is gone out of Hesebon, a flame
30 their yoke is perished from Hesebon
34 Amorrhites, the inhabitant of Hesebon
32 3 H. and Eleale and Saban and Nebo
37 the children of Ruben built Hesebon
Deut 1 4 Sehon . . . who dwelt in Hesebon. 3:2; 4:46; Josu 12:2; Judg 11:19
Josu 13 10 Sehon . . . who reigned in Hesebon. 21
17 Hesebon and all their villages, which
26 from Hesebon unto Ramoth, Masphe and
21 37 H. and Jaser, four cities with their
Judg 11 26 whereas he hath dwelt in Hesebon
1 Pa 6 81 H. also with its suburbs, and Jazer
2 Es 9 22 possessed . . . land of the king of H.
Jdth 5 20 and all the mighty ones in Hesebon
Cant 7 4 thy eyes like the fishpools in Hesebon
Isa 15 4 Hesebon shall cry, and Eleale, their
16 8 the suburbs of Hesebon are desolate
9 I will water thee with my tears, O H.
Jer 48 2 no more rejoicing in Moab over Hesebon
34 from the cry of Hesebon even to Eleale
45 the snare stood in the shadow of H.
45 but there came a fire out of Hesebon
49 3 howl, O Hesebon, for Hai is wasted
Sehon king of Hesebon Deut 2 24 into thy hand S. . . .
Deut 2 26 to S. . . . with peaceable words, saying
30 S. . . . would not let us pass: because
3 6 them, as we had done to S. . . .
29 7 S. . . . and Og king of Basan came out
Josu 9 10 that were beyond the Jordan, S. . . .
12 5 of half Galaad: the borders of S. . . .
13 27 other part of the kingdom of S. . . .
Heser 3 K 9 15 to build . . . Heser and Mageddo
hesitations Phil 2 14 without murmurings and h.
Hesli Luke 3 25 Nahum, who was of Hesli, who was of
Hesmona Num 33 29 they camped in Hesmona
Num 33 30 and departing from H., they came to
Hesrai 2 K 23 35 Hesrai of Carmel, Pharai of Arbi
Hesro 1 Pa 11 37 Hesro a Carmelite, Naari the son
Hesron Gen 46 9 sons of Ruben: . . . Hesron. Exod 6:14
Gen 46 12 sons were born to Phares: Hesron and
Num 26 6 Hesron, of whom is the family of the
21 sons of Phares were Hesron. 1 Pa 2:5
Josu 15 25 and Carioth, Hesron, which is Asor
1 Pa 2 9 sons of Hesron that were born to him
18 Caleb the son of Hesron took a wife
21 H. went in to the daughter of Machir
24 when Hesron was dead, Caleb went in
24 Hesron also had to wife Abia who bore
25 of Jerameel the firstborn of Hesron
4 1 the sons of Juda: Phares, Hesron, and
Hesronites Num 26 6 of whom is family of the H. 21
heth Ps 118 57 heth. Lam 1:8; 2:8; 3:22, 23, 24; 4:8
Heth Gen 23 3 he spoke to the children of Heth
Gen 23 5 the children of Heth answered, saying
7 bowed down to the . . . children of H.
10 dwelt in midst of the children of Heth
16 in the hearing of the children of Heth
18 in the sight of the children of Heth
20 to bury in, by the children of Heth
25 10 he had bought of the children of Heth
27 46 life because of the daughters of Heth
Hethalon Eze 47 15 by the way of Hethalon. 48:1
Hethim Judg 1 26 went into the land of Hethim
Hethite Gen 10 15 Chanaan begot Sidon . . . the H.
Gen 25 9 Ephron the son of Seor the Hethite
26 34 Judith the daughter of Beeri the H.
36 2 Ada the daughter of Elon the Hethite
49 29 the field of Ephron the Hethite. 30
50 13 buryingplace, of Ephron the Hethite
Exod 3 8 the H. and the Amorrhite. 17; 13:5; Deut 20:17; Josu 9:1; 12:8; Judg 3:5; 2 Es 9:8
23 23 Amorrhite and the H. 33:2; Josu 11:3
34 11 the Chanaanite and the H. and the
Num 13 30 Hethite and the Jebusite and the
Deut 7 1 the H. and the Gergezite and the
Josu 3 10 H., the Hevite, and the Pherezite
12 8 and in the south was the Hethite
24 11 H. and the Gergezite and the Hevite
1 K 26 6 David spoke to Achimelech the Hethite
2 K 11 3 Urias the Hethite. 6, 17, 24; 12:9, 10; 23:39; 3 K 15:5
1 Pa 1 13 and Chanaan begot . . . the Hethite
11 41 Urias a Hethite, Zabad the son of
2 Es 9 8 land of the Chanaanite, of the Hethite
Hethites Gen 15 20 the H. and the Pherezites
Josu 1 4 all the land of the Hethites unto the
3 K 9 20 that were left of the . . . Hethites. 2 Pa 8:7
10 29 did all the kings of the Hethites
11 1 Edom and of Sidon and of the H.
4 K 7 6 hath hired . . . the kings of the H.
2 Pa 1 17 in all the kingdoms of the Hethites
1 Es 9 1 abominations . . . of the Hethites and
Jdth 5 20 overthrew the king . . . of the Hethites
Hevi Josu 13 21 princes of Madian: Hevi and
Hevila Gen 10 7 sons of Chus: Saba and H. 1 Pa 1:9
Gen 10 29 Jectan begot . . . Hevila. 1 Pa 1:23
25 18 he dwelt from Hevila as far as Sur
1 K 15 7 and Saul smote Amalec from Hevila
Hevilath Gen 2 11 land of H. where gold groweth
Hevite Gen 10 17 Chanaan begot . . . the H. 1 Pa 1:15
Gen 34 2 Sichem the son of Hemor the Hevite
36 2 the daughter of Sebeon the Hevite
Exod 3 8 Hevite and Jebusite. 17; 13:5; 23:23; 33:2; 34:11; Deut 7:1; 20:17; Josu 9:1; 12:8; 24:11; Judg 3:5
23 28 the Hevite and the Chanaanite. 2 K 24:7
Josu 3 10 the Hevite and the Pherezite
11 3 the H. also who dwelt at the foot of
19 delivered itself . . . except the H.
Hevites Deut 2 23 H. also that dwelt in Haserim
Josu 13 4 on the south side are the Hevites
Judg 3 3 Hevites that dwelt in mount Libanus
3 K 9 20 that were left of the . . . H. 2 Pa 8:7
4 K 17 31 the Hevites made Nebahaz and Tharthac
Jdth 5 20 overthrew the king . . . of the Hevites
hew Exod 34 1 hew thee two tables of stone. Deut 10:1
Deut 19 5 gone with him to the wood to hew wood
3 K 5 6 a man that has skill to hew wood
15 80,000 to hew stones in the. 2 Pa 2:2, 18
1 Pa 22 2 stonecutters to hew stones and polish
Jer 6 6 hew down her trees and cast up a
hewed 1 K 15 33 Samuel h. him [Agag] in pieces
3 K 5 18 and the masons of Hiram hewed them
6 7 house . . . was built of stones hewed
7 11 costly stones, of equal measure, hewed
12 with three rows of hewed stones
4 K 12 12 to buy timber and stones, to be hewed
Jdth 1 2 city . . . of stones squared and hewed
Isa 22 16 thou hast hewed thee out a sepulcher
16 here, thou hast hewed out a monument
Osee 6 5 have I hewed them by the prophets, I
2 Ma 1 16 hewed them in pieces and cutting off
Mat 27 60 which he had hewed out in a rock. And
Mark 15 46 which was hewed out of a rock. And he
Luke 23 53 in a sepulcher that was hewed in stone
hewers Deut 29 11 hewers of wood and them that
Josu 9 23 your race shall always be h. of wood
1 Pa 22 15 hewers of stones and masons and

1 Es 3 7 they gave money to hewers of stones
Jer 46 22 come against her, as hewers of wood
hewing Josu 9 21 to serve . . . in hewing wood and
Josu 9 27 hewing wood and carrying water, until
hewn Exod 20 25 shalt not build it of h. stones
Deut 10 3 when I had hewn two tables of stone
Prov 9 1 she hath hewn her out seven pillars
Isa 51 1 look unto the rock whence you are hewn
Bar 6 38 that are hewn out of the mountains
Hezechiel 1 Pa 24 16 the twentieth [lot] to H.
Hezeci 1 Pa 8 17 and Hezeci . . . sons of Elphaal
Hezecia 2 Es 10 17 Ater, Hezecia, Azur, Odaia
Hezecias 2 Es 7 21 of Ater, children of H.
Hezion 3 K 15 18 Tabremon the son of Hezion
Hezir 1 Pa 24 15 the seventeenth [lot] to Hezir
hid Mat 5 14 seated on a mountain cannot be hid
Mat 10 26 nor hid, that shall not be known
11 25 because thou hast hid these things
13 33 hid in three measures of meal. Luke 13:21
44 which a man having found, hid it, and
25 18 the earth, and hid his lord's money
25 went and hid thy talent in the earth
Mark 4 22 nothing hid which shall not be made
7 24 know it, and he could not be hid
Luke 1 24 and hid herself five months, saying
8 47 the woman seeing that she was not hid
9 45 this word, and it was hid from them
18 34 this word was hid from them, and they
John 8 59 but Jesus hid himself and went out of
12 36 went away, and hid himself from them
2 C 4 3 if our gospel be also hid, it is hid to them
Col 3 3 and your life is hid with Christ in God
1 Tim 5 25 they that are otherwise cannot be hid
Heb 11 23 was hid three months by his parents
Apoc 6 15 hid themselves in the dens and in the
hidden Mat 13 35 I will utter things hidden from
Mat 13 44 like unto a treasure hidden in a field
Luke 8 17 h., that shall not be known. 12:2
10 21 because thou hast hidden these things
11 33 and putteth it in a hidden place nor
19 42 but now they are hidden from thy eyes
Acts 26 26 none of these things are hidden from him
1 C 2 7 a wisdom which is hidden, which God
4 5 will bring to light the hidden things of
2 C 4 2 we renounce the h. things of dishonesty
Eph 3 9 which hath been hidden from eternity in
Col 1 26 mystery which hath been h. from ages and
1 P 3 4 but the hidden man of the heart in the
Apoc 2 17 I will give the hidden manna, and will
Hiel 3 K 16 34 Hiel of Bethel built Jericho
Hieronymus 2 Ma 12 2 also H. and Demophon
Hierapolis Col 4 13 are at Laodicea, and them at H.
high Mat 4 8 him up into a very high mountain
Mat 17 1 them up into a h. mountain. Mark 9:1
Mark 8 31 by the ancients and by the high priests
Luke 3 2 under the high priests Annas and
4 5 devil led him into a high mountain
16 15 is high to men, is an abomination
22 54 led him to the high priest's house
Acts 13 17 with an h. arm brought them out from
Rom 12 16 not minding high things, but consenting
1 Tim 2 2 for all that are in high station: that
Apoc 21 10 in spirit to a great and high mountain
12 it had a wall great and high, having
cubits high; *see* **cubits**
high mountains; *see* **mountains**
high place Num 23 14 he had brought him to a h. p.
1 K 9 12 of the people today in the high place
13 before he go up to the h. p. to eat
14 Samuel . . . to go up to the high place
19 go up before me to the high place that
25 and they went down from the high place
10 5 prophets coming down from the h. p.
13 he [Saul] came to the high place. And
3 K 3 4 for that was the great high place
4 K 23 15 high place which Jeroboam . . . had made
15 altar and the high place he broke down
1 Pa 16 39 before the tabernacle . . . in the h. p.
21 29 at that time in the h. p. of Gabaon
2 Pa 1 3 to the high place of Gabaon, where was
13 came from the high place of Gabaon to
Prov 9 14 sat . . . in a high place of the city
Eccu 37 18 that sit in a high place to watch. But
Isa 22 16 a monument carefully in a high place
57 15 dwelleth in the high and holy place
Jer 30 18 city shall be built in her high place
Eze 16 31 hast made thy h. p. in every street
20 29 what meaneth the high place to which
29 the name thereof was called High-place
high places Lev 26 30 I will destroy your h. p.
Num 21 28 inhabitants of the h. p. of the Arnon
22 41 he brought him to the h. p. of Baal
33 52 statues and waste all their high places
Josu 11 13 cities that were on hills and h. p.
2 K 1 18 that are dead, wounded on thy h. p.
25 Jonathan slain in the high places? I
22 34 and setting me upon my high places
3 K 3 2 people sacrificed in the high places
3 only he sacrificed in the high places
12 31 he made temples in the high places
32 in Bethel priests of the high places
13 2 upon thee the priests of the h. p.
32 against all the temples of the h. p.
33 of the people priests of the h. p.
33 was made a priest of the high places
15 14 the high places he did not take away
22 44 he took not away the high places: for
44 burnt incense in the h. p. 4 K 12:3; 14:4; 15:4, 35; 16:4; 2 Pa 28:4
4 K 12 3 he took not away the h. p. 14:4
15 4 but the high places he did not destroy
35 but the high places he took not away
17 9 built them high places in all their
29 temples of the high places. 17:32; 23:19
32 made . . . priests of the high places
18 4 he destroyed the high places and
22 is it not he, whose high places and
21 3 he turned and built up the high places
23 5 appointed to sacrifice in the h. p.
8 and he defiled the high places where
9 the priests of the high places came not
13 high places also that were at Jerusalem
20 slew all the priests of the high places
2 Pa 11 15 to himself priests for the high places
14 2 and he destroyed . . . the high places
15 17 but high places were left in Israel
17 6 he took away also the high places and
20 33 yet he took not away the high places
21 11 he built also high places in the cities
31 1 demolished the h. p. and destroyed
32 12 that hath destroyed his high places
33 3 [Manasses] built again the high places
17 still sacrificed in the high places
19 places wherein he built high places
34 3 cleansed Juda . . . from the high places
Job 25 2 who maketh peace in his high places
39 27 and make her nest in high places? She
Ps 17 34 and who setteth me upon high places
148 1 praise ye him in the high places
Eccu 22 21 as pales set in high places, and
26 21 the sun . . . in the high places of God
46 11 he went up to the high places of the
Isa 15 2 to the high places to mourn over Nabo
16 12 that Moab is wearied on his high places
36 7 is it not he whose high places and
58 14 I will lift thee up above the high p.

Jer 7 31 have built the high places of Topheth
17 3 thy high p. for sin in all thy borders
19 5 have built the high places of Baalim
26 18 of the house the high places of woods
32 35 they have built the high places of Baal
48 35 him that offereth in the high places
Eze 6 3 and I will destroy your high places
6 the high places shall be thrown down
16 16 made thee high places sewed together
43 7 of their kings, and by the high places
Osee 10 8 the h. p. of the idol, the sin of Israel
Amos 4 13 walketh upon the high p. of the earth
7 9 high places of the idol shall be thrown
Mich 1 3 will tread upon the h. p. of the earth
5 and what are the high places of Juda
3 12 mountain of the temple as the h. p.
Haba 3 19 will lead me upon my high p., singing
Eph 6 12 spirits of wickedness in the high places
high priest Exod 28 38 over forehead of the h. p.
Exod 29 30 be appointed high priest in his stead
35 19 the vesture of Aaron the high priest
39 24 wherewith the high priest went adorned
Lev 8 7 he vested the high priest with the
16 17 when the h. p. goeth into the sanctuary
21 10 the high priest . . . is the greatest
Num 35 25 until death of the h. p. 28; Josu 20:6
32 before the death of the high priest
1 Pa 29 22 prince, and Sadoc to be high priest
Mat 26 3 into the court of the high priest, who
51 striking the servant of the h. p., cut
57 led him to Caiphas the high priest
58 even to court of the h. p. Mark 14:54
62 the high priest rising up. Mark 14:60; Acts 5:17
63 the high priest said to him: I adjure
65 the high priest rent his garments
Mark 1 44 go show thyself to the high priest
2 26 under Abiathar the high priest and did
14 53 they brought Jesus to the high priest
61 again the high priest asked him and
63 the high priest rending his garments
66 of the maidservants of the h. p.
Luke 22 50 struck the servant of h. p. John 18:10
John 11 4 Caiphas, h. p. of that year. 51; 18:13
18 15 that disciple was known to the h. p.
15 went in with Jesus into court of h. p.
16 disciple, who was known to the h. p.
19 the h. p. asked Jesus of his disciples
22 answerest thou the high priest so
24 sent him bound to Caiphas the h. p.
26 servants of the h. p. saith to him: Did
Acts 4 6 Annas the high priest, and Caiphas
6 were of the kindred of the high priest
5 21 the h. p. coming, and they that were
27 the high priest asked them, saying
7 1 high priest said: Are these things so
9 1 went to the high priest and asked of
22 5 the high priest doth bear me witness, and
23 2 the high priest Ananias commanded them
4 dost thou revile the high priest of God
5 I knew not . . . that he is high priest
24 1 after 5 days high priest Ananias came
Heb 2 17 become a merciful and faithful h. priest
3 1 consider the apostle and high priest of
4 14 having therefore a great high priest
15 for we have not a high priest, who
5 1 every high priest taken from among men
5 that he might be made a high priest: but
10 called by God a high priest according to
6 20 made a high priest forever according
7 26 that we should have such a high priest
8 1 we have such an high priest, who is set
3 every high priest is appointed to offer
9 7 the high priest alone, once a year: not
11 come an high priest of the good things
25 as high priest entereth into the holies
10 21 a high priest over the house of God. Let
13 11 brought into the holies by the h. p.
most high Mark 5 7 Jesus, Son of the m. h. God. Luke 8:28
Luke 1 32 be called the Son of the most High
35 power of the m. H. shall overshadow
Acts 7 48 the most High dwelleth not in houses
16 17 servants of the most high God, who
Heb 7 1 priest of the most high God, who met
on high Luke 1 78 Orient from on h. hath visited
Luke 12 29 drink: and be not lifted up on high
19 38 peace in heaven, and glory on high
24 49 you be endued with power from on high
Eph 4 8 ascending on high, he led captivity
Heb 1 3 on the right hand of the majesty on high
higher Gen 7 20 cubits h. than the mountains
Deut 26 19 thee higher than all nations. 28:1
28 43 rise up over thee and shall be higher
Judg 1 36 the rock, and the higher places
16 27 roof and the higher part of the house
1 K 10 23 he [Saul] was higher than any of the
3 K 1 37 make his throne higher than the throne
Jdth 13 16 and she went up to a higher place
Job 11 8 he is higher than heaven, and what
22 12 think that God is higher than heaven
35 5 the sky, that it is higher than thee
Ps 103 3 coverest the higher rooms thereof with
Ecce 5 7 he that is high, hath another higher
7 there are others still h. than these
Eze 31 8 the cedars . . . were not higher than he
41 7 temple broader in the higher parts
7 they went to the higher by the midst
Dan 8 3 horns, and one higher than the other
1 Ma 3 37 and went through the higher countries
6 1 was going through the higher countries
43 it was higher than the other beasts
2 Ma 9 23 led an army into the higher countries
25 when I went into the higher provinces
Luke 14 10 may say to thee: Friend, go up higher
Acts 10 9 the higher parts of the house to pray
Rom 13 1 let every soul be subject to h. powers
Heb 7 26 and made higher than the heavens; who
highest Num 24 16 knoweth the doctrine of the H.
4 K 15 36 he [Joatham] built the highest gate
Ps 17 14 from heaven, and the h. gave his voice
70 19 the h. great things thou hast done
73 5 in the going out and on the highest top
86 5 the Highest himself hath founded her
103 17 h. of them is the house of the heron
Prov 8 2 standing in the top of the h. places
Wisd 17 18 bounding echo from the h. mountains
Eccu 9 23 discourse on commandments of the H.
11 4 works of the Highest only are wonderful
12 3 the Highest hateth sinners, and hath
7 Highest also hateth sinners and will
24 7 I dwelt in the highest places, and my
Jer 48 28 mouth of the hole in the highest place
Lam 3 38 proceed out of the mouth of the H.
2 Ma 3 2 place worthy of the highest honor
Mat 21 9 Hosanna in the highest. Mark 11:10
Mark 12 39 to have the highest places at suppers
Luke 1 76 shalt be called the prophet of the H.
2 14 glory to God in the highest; and on
6 35 you shall be the sons of the Highest
highly Ps 36 35 have seen the wicked h. exalted
highminded Isa 2 12 that is proud and h.
Rom 11 20 thou standest by faith: be not h., but
1 Tim 6 17 not to be highminded, nor to trust in
highness Ps 11 9 according to thy h. thou hast
Isa 33 16 fortifications of rocks shall be his h.

highway Gen 35 19 Rachel . . . was buried in the h.
Num 20 17 but we will go by the common highway
21 22 we will go the king's highway, till
Deut 2 27 land, we will go along by the highway
2 K 20 12 he removed Amasa out of the highway
Isa 11 16 shall be a highway for the remnant of
Jer 6 25 into the fields, nor walk in the highway
Eze 21 21 king of Babylon stood in the highway
Osee 6 9 like the jaws of highway robbers, they
highways Lev 26 22 that your h. may be desolate
Judg 20 31 whilst they fled by two highways
32 seeming to flee to bring them to the h.
Jer 3 21 a voice was heard in the highways
Mat 22 9 go ye therefore into the h. Luke 14:23
hill Exod 17 9 I will stand on the top of the hill
Exod 17 10 Hur went up upon the top of the hill
Josu 5 3 of Israel in the hill of the foreskins
Judg 1 19 Juda, and he possessed the hill country
7 1 in valley on north side of the high hill
16 3 carried them up to the top of the hill
1 K 10 5 thou shalt come to the hill of God where
10 and they came to the foresaid hill
13 15 Galgal to Gabaa in the hill of Benjamin
23 14 the desert of Ziph, in a woody hill
26 1 David is hid in the hill of Hachila
13 stood on the top of the hill afar off
2 K 2 24 came as far as the h. of the aqueduct
25 body, they stood on the top of a hill
16 1 David was a little past top of the hill
21 9 and they crucified them on a hill before
3 K 11 7 on hill that is over against Jerusalem
14 23 groves on every high hill. 4 K 17:10
16 24 the name of Semer the owner of the h.
24 he bought the hill of Samaria of Semer
4 K 1 9 as he was sitting on the top of a hill
1 Pa 13 6 David . . . to the hill of Cariathiarim
Tob 11 5 the way daily, on the top of a hill
Jdth 10 11 when she went down the hill, about the
Ps 3 5 he hath heard me from his holy hill
14 1 who shall rest in thy holy hill? He
41 7 land of Jordan . . . from the little hill
42 3 brought me unto thy holy hill and into
113 8 the stony h. into fountains of waters
Cant 4 6 will go . . . to the h. of frankincense
Isa 5 1 my beloved had a vineyard on a hill
10 18 of his forest and of his beautiful hill
32 daughter of Sion, the h. of Jerusalem
30 17 mountain, and as an ensign upon a hill
25 upon every elevated hill rivers of
31 4 mount Sion, and upon the hill thereof
40 4 mountain and hill shall be made low
Jer 2 20 on every high hill . . . didst prostitute
16 16 shall hunt them . . . from every hill
31 39 measuring line . . . upon the hill Gareb
49 16 to lay hold on the height of the hill
50 6 they have gone from mountain to hill
Eze 6 13 in every high hill and on all the tops
20 28 they saw every high h. and every shady
34 6 have wandered . . . in every high hill
26 them a blessing round about my hill
Amos 9 13 sweetness, and every hill shall be tilled
Zach 14 10 from the hill to Remmon to the south
Luke 1 39 Mary went into the hill country
65 over all the hill country of Judea
3 5 mountain and hill shall be brought low
4 29 brought him to the brow of the hill
hillock Gen 31 47 the hillock of testimony
hillocks Eze 47 8 forth toward the h. of sand
hill's 2 K 16 13 Semei by the h. side went over
hills Gen 49 26 the desire of the everlasting h.
Num 23 9 and shall consider him from the hills
Deut 1 7 come to . . . the plains and the hills
8 7 and the hills deep rivers break out: a
9 out of its hills are dug mines of brass
11 11 it is a land of hills and plains
12 2 gods upon high mountains and hills
33 15 of the fruits of the everlasting hills
Josu 10 40 conquered all the country of the hills
11 13 except the cities that were on hills
16 Josue took all the country of the hills
18 18 it passeth along to the hills that are
3 K 20 23 their gods are gods of the hills
28 have said: The Lord is God of the h.
22 17 I saw all Israel scattered upon the h.
4 K 16 4 high places and on the h. 2 Pa 28:4
Jdth 3 3 all mountains and hills and fields
7 8 steep hills and precipices guard them
15 2 of the fields and the paths of the hills
Job 15 7 or wast thou made before the hills
39 28 among cragged flints and stony hills
Ps 49 10 are mine: the cattle on the hills
64 13 the h. shall be girded about with joy
71 3 for the people: and the hills justice
74 7 from the west nor from the desert hills
75 5 wonderfully from the everlasting hills
77 58 provoked him to anger on their hills
79 11 the shadow of it covered the hills
103 10 between the midst of the h. the waters
13 thou waterest the hills from thy
18 high hills are a refuge for the harts
113 4 the hills like the lambs of the flock
6 and ye hills, like lambs of the flock
148 9 mountains and all hills, fruitful trees
Prov 8 25 before the hills I was brought forth
Cant 2 8 he cometh . . . skipping over the hills
Eccu 16 19 the mountains also and the hills and
Isa 2 2 it shall be exalted above the hills
14 and upon all the elevated hills
7 25 all the hills that shall be raked with
37 26 hills fighting together, and fenced
40 12 weighed . . . the hills in a balance
41 15 and shalt make the hills as chaff
18 I will open rivers in the high hills
42 15 will lay waste the mountains and hills
54 10 be moved, and the hills shall tremble
55 12 and the hills shall sing praise before
65 7 and have reproached me upon the hills
Jer 3 23 in very deed the hills were liars and
4 24 trembled: and all the h. were troubled
13 27 abominations upon the h. in the field
Eze 6 3 saith the Lord . . . and to the hills
32 5 will fill thy hills with thy corruption
35 8 slain: in thy hills and in thy valleys
36 4 saith the Lord God . . . to the hills
6 say to the mountains and to the hills
Dan 3 75 ye mountains and hills, bless the Lord
Osee 4 13 and burnt incense upon the hills
10 8 cover us; and to the h.: Fall upon us
Joel 3 18 hills shall flow with milk: and waters
Mich 4 1 be prepared . . . high above the hills
6 1 and let the hills hear thy voice. Let
Nah 1 5 the hills are made desolate: and the
Haba 3 6 the hills of the world were bowed down
Soph 1 10 and a great destruction from the hills
Luke 23 30 upon us; and to the hills: Cover us
hillside Jdth 7 3 they came by the h. to the top
hin Exod 29 40 fourth part of a hin. Lev 23:13; Num 15:4; 28:5, 7
Exod 30 24 of oil of olives the measure hin
Num 15 6 third part of a hin of oil. Eze 46:14
9 of flour tempered with half a hin of oil
28 14 half a hin for every calf, a third for
Eze 4 11 drink . . . the sixth part of a hin
45 24 a hin of oil for every ephi. 46:5, 7
46 11 find: and a hin of oil to every ephi
hind Prov 5 19 let her be thy dearest hind

Jer 14 5 hind also brought forth in the field
hinder Gen 16 13 here have I seen the h. parts of
Gen 23 6 no man shall have power to hinder thee
Num 23 20 the blessing I am not able to hinder
Ruth 2 15 would even reap with you, h. her
3 K 6 16 at the hinder part of the temple, from
7 25 their hinder parts were all hid within
2 Pa 4 4 h. parts of the oxen were inward under
1 Es 4 21 h. those men, that this city be not
5 5 Jews, and they could not hinder them
Job 15 11 but thy wicked words hinder this. Why
34 31 I will not hinder thee in thy turn
Ps 67 14 h. parts of her back with the paleness
77 66 smote his enemies on the hinder parts
Eccu 18 22 let nothing hinder thee from praying
20 1 not to hinder him that confesseth in
32 5 knowledge, and hinder not music
Joel 2 20 hinder part towards the utmost sea
Mark 4 38 he was in the hinder part of the ship
Acts 8 36 what doth h. me from being baptized
27 41 h. part was broken with the violence of
Heb 12 15 root of bitterness springing up do h.
hindered 1 Es 4 4 people of the land h. the hands
1 Es 4 23 and hindered them with arm and power
6 8 those men, lest the work be hindered
Wisd 17 19 none were hindered in their labors
Eccu 19 25 and if he be hindered from sinning
20 23 that is h. from sinning through want
Agge 1 10 earth was h. from yielding her fruits
1 Ma 9 55 his works were h. and his mouth was
13 49 were h. from going out and coming into
Luke 11 52 were entering in, you have hindered
Rom 1 13 unto you, and have been h. hitherto
15 22 I was h. very much from coming to you
Gal 5 7 you did run well, who hath hindered you
1 Th 2 18 and again: but Satan hath hindered us
1 P 3 7 that your prayers be not hindered
hindereth Wisd 7 22 which nothing h. beneficent
hindermost Josu 10 19 kill all the h. of them
hindmost Deut 25 18 and slew the h. of the army
1 Ma 4 15 the hindmost of them fell by the sword
5 53 Judas gathered together the hindmost
hindrance 2 Pa 14 7 there was no h. in building
Wisd 19 7 in the Red Sea a way without hindrance
1 C 9 12 lest we should give any hindrance to
hinds Job 39 1 hast thou observed the hinds
hinges 3 K 7 50 h. for the doors . . . of gold
Prov 26 14 as the door turneth upon its hinges
Amos 8 3 the hinges of the temple shall screak
9 1 strike the hinges and let the lintels be
Hir 1 Pa 4 15 sons of Caleb . . . Hir and Ela
1 Pa 7 12 Sepham and Hapham the sons of Hir
Hira 2 K 23 26 Hira the son of Acces. 1 Pa 27:9
Hiram Gen 36 43 dukes of Esau . . . duke Hiram
2 K 5 11 Hiram . . . sent messengers. 1 Pa 14:1
3 K 5 1 Hiram had always been David's friend
1 Hiram king of Tyre sent his servants
2 Solomon sent to Hiram, saying: Thou
7 when Hiram had heard the words of
8 Hiram sent to Solomon, saying: I have
10 so Hiram gave Solomon cedar trees and
11 Solomon allowed Hiram 20,000 measures
11 thus gave Solomon to Hiram every year
12 was peace between Hiram and Solomon
18 masons of Solomon and masons of Hiram
7 13 sent, and brought Hiram from Tyre
40 and Hiram made caldrons. 2 Pa 4:11
45 all the vessels that Hiram made for
9 11 H. the king of Tyre furnishing Solomon
11 Solomon gave Hiram twenty cities in
12 H. came out of Tyre to see the towns
14 H. sent to king Solomon 120 talents
27 Hiram sent his servants in the fleet
10 11 navy also of Hiram which brought gold
22 went with the navy of Hiram by sea
1 Pa 1 54 duke Magdiel, duke Hiram. These are
2 Pa 2 3 he sent also to Hiram king of Tyre
11 Hiram king of Tyre sent a letter to
13 have sent thee my father Hiram, a wise
4 16 did Hiram his father make for Solomon
8 2 cities which H. had given to Solomon
18 Hiram sent him ships by the hands
9 10 servants of Hiram . . . brought gold
21 to Tharsis with the servants of Hiram
Hiras Gen 38 1 a certain Odollamite, named Hiras
Gen 38 12 went up to Thamnas . . . he and Hiras
Hircanus 2 Ma 3 11 some part . . . belonged to H.
hire Exod 22 15 and came for the hire of his work
Deut 23 18 shalt not offer the hire of a strumpet
24 14 shalt not refuse the hire of the needy
3 K 5 6 I will give thee the h. of thy servants
1 Pa 19 6 to hire them chariots and horsemen out
Tob 4 15 immediately pay him his hire and let
5 4 faithful man to go with thee for his h.
14 shalt return, I will pay thee thy hire
Eccu 34 27 that defraudeth the laborer of his h.
Isa 23 18 her h. shall be sanctified to the Lord
46 6 and hire a goldsmith to make a god
Eze 16 33 thou hast given hire to all thy lovers
41 shalt give no hire any more. And my
22 25 they have taken riches and hire, they
Mich 1 7 gathered together of the h. of a harlot
7 unto h. of a harlot they shall return
3 11 and her priests have taught for hire
Zach 8 10 there was no hire for men, neither was there hire for beasts
Mat 20 1 to hire laborers into his vineyard
8 pay them their hire, beginning from
Luke 10 7 for the laborer is worthy of his hire
James 5 4 the hire of the laborers, who have
hired Gen 30 16 h. thee for my son's mandrakes
Exod 22 15 especially if it were hired and came
Lev 19 13 the wages of him that hath been hired
22 10 or a h. servant, shall not eat of them
25 50 and the reckoning of a hired servant
Deut 23 4 because they hired against thee Balaam
Judg 9 4 he h. to himself men that were needy
18 4 and hath hired me to be his priest
1 K 2 5 have hired out themselves for bread
2 K 10 6 children of Ammon . . . h. the Syrians
4 K 7 6 king of Israel hath hired against us
1 Pa 19 7 they hired 2 and 30 thousand chariots
2 Pa 24 12 they hired with it stonecutters and
25 6 he hired also of Israel 100,000 valiant
1 Es 4 5 they hired counsellors against them
2 Es 6 12 Tobias and Sanaballat had hired him
13 2 they h. against them Balaam, to curse
Tob 4 15 let not the wages of thy hired servant
5 17 or the h. servant himself to go with
Eccu 7 22 h. man that giveth thee his life
Isa 7 20 with a razor that is hired by them
Osee 8 10 though they shall have h. the nations
1 Ma 5 39 they have hired the Arabians to help
6 29 came to him also . . . hired troops
Mat 20 7 to him: Because no man hath hired us
Mark 1 20 in the ship with his hired men, they
Luke 15 17 how many hired servants in my father's
19 make me as one of thy hired servants
Acts 28 30 two whole years in his own hired lodging
hireling Exod 12 45 the h. shall not eat thereof
Lev 25 6 to thy maidservant and thy hireling
40 he shall be as a h. and a sojourner
Deut 15 18 years according to wages of a h.
Job 7 1 his days are like the days of a h.
2 h. looketh for the end of his work
14 6 wished for day come, as that of the h.

Isa 16 14 three years, as the years of a h.
21 16 according to the years of a hireling
Mala 3 5 that oppress the hireling in his wages
John 10 12 the hireling, and he that is not the
13 the h. flieth because he is a h.
hirelings Jer 46 21 her h. also that lived in
hirest Tob 5 17 the family of him thou h.
Hirsemes Josu 19 41 and Esthaol and Hirsemes
hiss 3 K 9 8 astonished and shall hiss. Jer 19:8
Job 27 23 shall hiss at him, beholding his place
Isa 7 18 that the Lord shall hiss for the fly
Jer 49 17 and shall hiss at all its plagues
50 13 and shall hiss at all her plagues
Soph 2 15 every one that passeth by her shall h.
hissed 2 Pa 29 8 to be h. at, as you see with
Lam 2 15 they have h. and wagged their heads
16 they have hissed, and gnashed with
Eze 27 36 the merchants . . . have hissed at thee
hissing Mich 6 16 and the inhabitants thereof a h.
Jer 19 8 an astonishment and a h. 25:9, 18; 29:18; 51:37
18 16 to desolation and to a perpetual h.
Wisd 17 9 h. of serpents, they died for fear
histories 1 Es 4 15 of the h. of thy fathers
Esth 2 23 it was put in the h. and recorded
6 1 he commanded the h. and chronicles
16 7 this is proved both from ancient h.
2 Ma 2 25 to undertake the narrations of h.
history Esth 9 32 contained in the h. of this book
2 Ma 2 31 is the duty of the author of a history
15 39 done well and as it becometh the h.
hit Judg 20 16 that they could hit even a hair
hitherto Gen 44 28 hitherto he appeareth not
Exod 7 16 and hitherto thou wouldst not hear
1 Pa 12 29 h. great part of them followed . . . Saul
Job 38 11 hitherto thou shalt come, and shalt
Jer 48 47 the Lord h. the judgments of Moab
Dan 7 28 hitherto is the end of the word. I
John 16 24 hitherto you have not asked anything
Rom 1 13 unto you, and have been hindered h.
hitherward Jer 50 5 to Sion, their faces are h.
hoard Bar 3 18 that hoard up silver and gold
hoarfrost Exod 16 14 like unto the hoarfrost on
Ps 77 47 destroyed . . . mulberry trees with h.
hoarfrosts Dan 3 68 ye dews and h., bless the
hoarse Ps 68 4 my jaws are become hoarse: my
hoary Lev 19 32 rise up before the hoary head
3 K 2 6 let not his hoary head go down to hell
Job 6 16 they that fear the h. frost, the snow
Hoba Gen 14 15, pursued them as far as Hoba
Hobab Num 10 29 Moses said to Hobab the son of
Judg 4 11 Cinites his brethren the sons of H.
Hobia 1 Es 2 61 the children of Hobia
Hod 1 Pa 7 37 sons of Supha . . . Hod
Hodes 1 Pa 8 9 he begot of H. his wife Jobab
Hodsi 2 K 24 6 and to the lower land of Hodsi
hoisting Acts 27 40 h. up the mainsail to the
Holda 4 K 22 14 went to Holda the prophetess
Holdai 1 Pa 27 15 for the twelfth month, was H.
Zach 6 10 Holdai and of Tobias and of Idaias
holden Acts 2 24 that he should be holden by it. For
holds Jer 51 30 they have dwelt in holds: their
Eze 33 27 they that are in holds and caves shall
2 Ma 10 14 Gorgias, who was governor of the holds
17 won the holds, killed them that came
23 slew more than 20,000 in the two holds
strong holds; *see* **strongholds**
hole Exod 28 32 shall be a hole for the head
Exod 33 22 I will set thee in a hole of the rock
39 21 a hole for the head in the upper part
21 a woven border round about the hole
4 K 12 9 took a chest and bored a h. in the top
Ps 7 16 he is fallen into the hole he made
Cant 5 4 put his hand through the key hole and
Isa 11 8 child shall play on the h. of the asp
34 15 there hath the ericius had its hole
51 1 hole of the pit from which you are dug
Jer 13 4 hide it there in a hole of the rock
48 28 maketh her nest in mouth of the hole
49 8 down into the deep h., ye inhabitants
Eze 8 7 I saw, and behold a hole in the wall
James 3 11 out of the same hole, sweet and bitter
holes 1 K 14 11 Hebrews come forth out of the h.
1 K 23 23 see all his lurking holes, wherein he
Jdth 14 12 the mice, coming out of their holes
Job 38 40 when they . . . lie in wait in holes
Ecce 12 3 look through the h. shall be darkened
Isa 2 19 they shall go into the holes of rocks
21 of rocks and into the holes of stones
7 19 valleys and in the holes of the rocks
Jer 16 16 hill and out of the holes of the rocks
49 30 get away speedily, sit in deep holes
Nah 2 12 filled his holes with prey, and his den
Agge 1 6 wages, put them into a bag with holes
Zach 14 12 eyes shall consume away in their holes
1 Ma 1 56 the people of Israel into lurking holes
Mat 8 20 the foxes have holes. Luke 9:58
holiday Ps 75 11 shall keep holiday to thee
2 Ma 5 25 the Jews keeping h., he commanded his
holidays Eccu 33 9 he ordered the seasons and h.
holies Num 4 19 by touching the h. of h.
2 Es 7 65 should not eat of the holies of holies
Jdth 5 23 Jerusalem again, where their holies are
1 Ma 3 51 for thy holies are trodden down
59 the evils of our nation and of the h.
2 Ma 14 36 Lord the holy of all holies, keep this
Heb 8 2 a minister of the holies, and of the
9 8 the way into the holies was not yet made
12 entered once into the holies, having
24 holies made with hands, the patterns of
25 as high priest entereth into the holies
10 19 confidence in the entering into the h.
13 11 brought into the h. by the high priest
holy of holies; *see* **holy**
holily 1 Th 2 10 how holily and justly and without
holiness Exod 15 11 like to thee, glorious in h.
1 K 14 41 this iniquity be in thy people, give h.
Jdth 9 18 thy house may continue in thy holiness
Ps 29 5 praise to the memory of his holiness
88 36 once have I sworn by my h.: I will
92 5 holiness becometh thy house, O Lord
95 6 holiness and majesty in his sanctuary
96 12 praise to the remembrance of his h.
107 8 hear me: God hath spoken in his h.
144 5 magnificence of the glory of thy h.
Eccu 30 15 health of the soul in h. of justice
23 a never failing treasure of holiness
24 gather up thy heart in his holiness
37 12 man without religion concerning h.
45 14 miter wherein was engraved Holiness
47 12 magnify the h. of God in the morning
49 8 they burnt the chosen city of holiness
50 12 he honored the vesture of holiness
Isa 64 11 the house of our holiness . . . is burnt
Amos 4 2 Lord God hath sworn by his holiness
Mala 2 11 Juda hath profaned the h. of the Lord
2 Ma 3 12 for the reverence and holiness of it
15 18 fear was for the holiness of the temple
Luke 1 75 in h. and justice before him all our
Eph 4 24 created in justice and holiness of truth
1 Th 3 13 in holiness, before God and our Father
Heb 12 14 follow peace with all men, and h.
hollow Exod 27 8 empty and hollow in the inside
Exod 38 7 altar itself was not solid, but hollow
Cant 2 14 rock, in the hollow place of the wall
Isa 7 19 with shrubs and in all hollow places

40 12 the waters in the hollow of his hand
Jer 52 21 four fingers, and it was h. within
2 Ma 2 5 Jeremias . . . he found a hollow cave
holm Isa 44 14 he hath . . . taken the holm and
Dan 13 58 he answered: Under a holm tree. And
Holofernes Jdth 2 4 called H. the general of
Jdth 2 7 then Holofernes called the captains
3 1 coming to Holofernes, said: Let thy
13 under him by the power of Holofernes
5 1 and it was told Holofernes the general
26 the great men of Holofernes were angry
6 1 Holofernes being in a violent passion
7 H. commanded his servants to take
8 the servants of H. taking him [Achior]
12 all that he had said being asked by H.
12 the people of H. would have killed him
13 how Holofernes himself being angry had
7 1 H. on the next day gave orders to his
6 H., in going round about, found that
8 came to H., saying: The children of
10 and these words pleased Holofernes
15 ourselves all up to the people of H.
17 city into the hand of the army of H.
10 13 I will go to presence of the prince H.
16 brought her to the tent of Holofernes
17 Holofernes was caught by his eyes
19 Judith seeing Holofernes sitting under
20 servants of Holofernes lifted her up
11 1 Holofernes said to her: Be of good
18 all these words pleased H. and his
20 H. said to her: God hath done well
12 3 H. said to her: If these things which
10 H. made a supper for his servants and
16 the heart of Holofernes was smitten
17 H. said to her: Drink now, and sit down
20 H. was made merry on her occasion and
13 4 Holofernes lay on his bed, fast asleep
11 delivered the head of H. to her maid
19 then she brought forth the head of H.
19 behold the head of Holofernes. 28
29 Achior seeing the head of Holofernes
14 4 shall run to the tent of Holofernes
7 they hung up the head of Holofernes
9 break his rest, that H. might have
14 and seeing the body of H., lying upon
16 H. lieth upon the ground, and his head
15 1 the army heard that H. was beheaded
14 the peculiar goods of H., they gave to
16 23 offered . . . all the arms of Holofernes
Holon Josu 21 15 and Holon and Dabir and Ain and
holy Mat 7 6 give not that which is holy to
Mark 8 38 of his Father with the holy angels
Luke 1 35 the Holy which shall be born of thee
49 things to me; and holy is his name
70 by mouth of his h. prophets. Acts 3:21
72 and to remember his holy testament
2 23 the womb, shall be called holy to the
9 26 of his Father and of the holy angels
John 17 11 holy Father, keep them in thy name
Acts 4 27 in this city against thy holy child
30 by the name of thy holy Son Jesus
7 33 wherein thou standest is holy ground
10 22 received an answer of an holy angel, to
Rom 1 2 promised before . . . in holy scripture
7 12 wherefore the law indeed is holy, and
12 and the commandment holy, and just and
11 16 if the root be holy, so are the branches
16 the firstfruit be holy, so is the lump
12 1 your bodies living sacrifices, holy
16 16 salute . . . with an holy kiss. 1 C 16:20;
2 C 13:12; 1 Th 5:26; 1 P 5:13
1 C 3 17 the temple of God is holy, which you are
7 14 be unclean; but now they are holy. But
34 may be holy both in body and in spirit
Eph 1 4 that we should be holy and unspotted in
13 signed with the holy Spirit of promise
3 5 it is now revealed to his holy apostles
4 30 and grieve not the holy Spirit of God
5 18 but be ye filled with the holy Spirit
27 it should be holy, and without blemish
Phil 4 8 whatsoever holy, whatsoever lovely
Col 1 22 to present you holy and unspotted, and
3 12 as the elect of God, holy and beloved
1 Th 4 8 who also hath given his holy Spirit in
5 27 epistle be read to all the holy brethren
2 Tim 1 9 delivered us and called us by his holy
3 15 thou hast known the holy scriptures
Titus 1 8 gentle, sober, just, holy, continent
2 3 in holy attire, not false accusers, not
Heb 3 1 wherefore, holy brethren, partakers of
7 26 have such a high priest, holy, innocent
9 2 forth of loaves, which is called the h.
1 P 1 15 him that hath called you, who is holy
15 in all manner of conversation holy
16 you shall be holy, for I am holy
2 5 a spiritual house, a holy priesthood
9 a holy nation, a purchased people
3 5 holy women also, who trusted in God
2 P 1 18 we were with him in the holy mount
21 the holy men of God spoke, inspired
2 21 turn back from that holy commandment
3 2 told you before from the holy prophets
11 be in holy conversation and godliness
1 J 3 3 sanctifieth himself, as he also is h.
Apoc 4 8 holy, holy, holy, Lord God Almighty
6 10 how long, O Lord, holy and true, dost
14 10 in the sight of the holy angels and in
15 4 thou only art holy: for all nations
18 20 and ye holy apostles and prophets; for
20 6 blessed and holy is he that hath part
22 11 that is holy, let him be sanctified
holy city 2 Es 11 1 one part in ten to dwell in Jerusalem
the holy city
2 Es 11 18 the Levites in the holy city were 284
Eccu 24 15 in the holy city likewise I rested
Isa 48 2 they are called of the holy city, and
Dan 3 28 Jerusalem the holy city of our fathers
9 24 upon thy people and upon thy h. c.
1 Ma 2 7 people and the ruin of the holy city
2 Ma 1 12 fought against us and the holy city
3 1 when the holy city was inhabited with
15 14 for the people and for all the h. c.
17 holy city and the temple were in danger
Mat 4 5 devil took him up into the holy city
27 53 came into the holy city and appeared to
Apoc 11 2 the holy city they shall tread under
21 2 and I John saw the holy city, the new
10 he showed me the holy city Jerusalem
22 19 book of life and out of the holy city
holy day 2 Es 8 9 this is a h. d. to the Lord
2 Es 8 10 it is the holy day of the Lord
10 31 not buy them . . . or on the holy day
Esth 8 17 and banquets, and keeping holy day
9 17 they ordained to be kept holy day
Isa 58 13 from doing thy own will in my holy day
1 Ma 5 25 rested till the holy day of the sabbath
Holy Ghost Eccu 1 9 he created her in the H. G.
Mat 1 18 was found with child of the Holy Ghost
20 conceived in her is of the Holy Ghost
3 11 baptize you in the H. G. Mark 1:8; Luke
3:16
12 32 that shall speak against the Holy Ghost
28 19 and of the Son and of the Holy Ghost
Mark 3 29 blaspheme against the H. G. Luke 12:10
12 36 David himself saith by the Holy Ghost
13 11 you that speak, but the Holy Ghost

Luke 1 15 filled with the Holy Ghost. 41; Acts 2:4; 4:8, 31; 9:17; 13:9
35 the Holy Ghost shall come upon thee
2 25 the Holy Ghost was in him [Simeon]
26 had received an answer from the H. G.
3 21 the H. G. descended in a bodily shape
4 1 full of the H. G. Acts 6:3; 7:55; 11:24
10 21 he rejoiced in the Holy Ghost and said
12 12 the Holy Ghost shall teach you in the
John 1 33 that baptizeth with the Holy Ghost
3 5 again of water and the Holy Ghost, he
14 26 the Paraclete, the Holy Ghost, whom
20 22 receive ye the Holy Ghost. Whose sins
Acts 1 2 giving commandments by the H. G. to the
5 shall be baptized with the H. G. 11:16
8 shall receive the power of the H. G.
16 which the H. G. spoke before by the
2 4 as the Holy Ghost gave them to speak
33 Father the promise of the Holy Ghost
38 shall receive the gift of the H. G.
4 25 by the Holy Ghost . . . hast said: Why
5 3 that thou shouldst lie to the H. G.
32 witnesses of these things and the H. G.
6 5 a man full of faith and of the H. G.
7 51 you always resist the Holy Ghost: as
8 15 that they might receive the H. G. For
17 received the Holy Ghost. 10:47; 19:2
18 of the apostles, the H. G. was given
19 he may receive the Holy Ghost. But
9 31 filled with consolation of Holy Ghost
10 38 God anointed him with the Holy Ghost
44 Holy Ghost fell on all them. 11:15
45 grace of the Holy Ghost was poured out
13 2 fasting, the Holy Ghost said to them
4 they being sent by the H. G., went to
52 disciples were filled with . . . H. G.
15 8 giving unto them the Holy Ghost, as
28 it hath seemed good to the Holy Ghost
16 6 forbidden by Holy Ghost to preach the
19 2 as heard whether there be a Holy Ghost
6 Holy Ghost came upon them, and they
20 23 Holy Ghost in every city witnesseth to
28 the Holy Ghost hath placed you bishops
21 11 saith the Holy Ghost: The man whose
28 25 well did the H. G. speak to our fathers
Rom 5 5 charity of God is poured . . . by the H. G.
9 1 bearing me witness in the Holy Ghost
14 17 peace and joy in the Holy Ghost. For
15 13 and in the power of the Holy Ghost. 19
16 and sanctified in the Holy Ghost. I have
30 by the charity of the H. G., that you
1 C 6 19 members are the temple of the Holy Ghost
12 3 say Lord Jesus, but by the Holy Ghost
2 C 6 6 in sweetness, in the Holy Ghost, in
13 13 communication of the H. G. be with you
1 Th 1 5 but in power also, and in the Holy Ghost
6 tribulation, with joy of the Holy Ghost
2 Tim 1 14 committed to thy trust by the Holy Ghost
Titus 3 5 renovation of the Holy Ghost; whom he
Heb 2 4 and distributions of the Holy Ghost
3 7 wherefore, as the Holy Ghost saith
6 4 were made partakers of the Holy Ghost
9 8 the Holy Ghost signifying this, that
14 Christ, who by the Holy Ghost offered
10 15 the Holy Ghost also doth testify this
1 P 1 12 the H. G. being sent down from heaven
2 P 1 21 spoke, inspired by the Holy Ghost
1 J 5 7 Father, the Word, and the Holy Ghost
Jude 20 holy faith, praying in the Holy Ghost

holy of holies Exod 26 33 h. . . . shall be divided
Exod 26 34 ark of the testimony in the h. . . .
Lev 2 3 h. . . . of the offerings of the Lord. 10
6 25 it is holy of holies. 29; 10:12; 14:13
27 28 shall be holy of holies to the Lord
Num 4 5 shall go into . . . the holy of holies
18 9 offering . . . becometh holy of holies
3 K 6 16 house of the oracle to be h. . . .
7 50 doors of inner house of the h. . . .
8 6 into the h. . . . under the. 2 Pa 5:7
1 Pa 6 49 for every work of the holy of holies
23 13 to minister in the holy of holies
2 Pa 3 8 the house of the holy of holies. 10
4 22 the doors . . . for the holy of holies
31 14 things dedicated for the holy of holies
1 Es 2 63 should not eat of the holy of holies
Eze 41 4 said to me: This is the holy of holies
42 13 approach to the Lord into the h. . . .
44 13 holy things that are by the h. . . .
45 3 it shall be the temple and the h. . . .
48 12 the firstfruits of the land h. . . .
Heb 9 3 which is called the holy of holies

Homam 1 P 1 39 sons of Lotan: Hori, Homam

home Gen 26 31 Isaac sent them . . . to their own h.
Gen 27 15 garments of Esau, which she had at h.
39 5 multiplied all his substance both at h.
16 to her husband when he returned home
42 4 whilst Benjamin was kept at home by
Exod 16 29 let each man stay at home and let none
Deut 24 5 he shall be free at home without fault
Judg 7 3 from mount Galaad and returned home
19 18 we are going to our home, which is on
29 when he was come home he took a sword
Ruth 1 8 said to them: Go ye h. to your mothers
2 7 and hath not gone home for one moment
1 K 1 23 stayed at home and gave her son suck
2 20 they went to their own home. And the
6 7 shut up their calves at home. 10
10 22 behold he is hidden at home. And they
24 23 David swore to Saul. So Saul went home
2 K 13 7 David sent home to Thamar, saying
14 13 and not bring home again his own exile
17 23 Achitophel . . . went home to his house
20 22 from the city, every one to their home
3 K 5 14 so that two months they were at home
12 16 go home to thy dwellings, O Israel
13 7 come home with me to dine, and I will
15 come home with me to eat bread. But
4 K 14 10 content with the glory and sit at home
1 Pa 13 13 therefore he brought it not home to
2 Pa 25 10 to him out of Ephraim, to go h. again
19 stay at home, why dost thou provoke
Tob 2 19 she brought home what she could get
20 a young kid and brought it home
Prov 7 11 not able to abide still at home, now
19 my husband is not at home, he is gone
20 will return home the day of the full
Eccu 32 15 but be first to run home to thy house
Jer 39 14 that he might go home and dwell among
Lam 1 20 and at home there is death alike
Dan 13 13 let us now go home, for it is dinner
Agge 1 9 you brought it home, and I blowed it
1 Ma 4 24 returning home they sung a hymn and
Mat 8 6 my servant lieth at home sick of the
Mark 8 3 send them away fasting to their home
Luke 15 6 and coming home, call together his
John 11 20 went to meet him: but Mary sat at home
20 10 departed again to their home. But
Acts 21 6 we took ship; and they returned home
1 C 4 35 let them ask their husbands at home. For
11 34 if any man be hungry, let him eat at h.

homeborn Jer 2 14 a bondman or a h. slave? Why

homes Judg 9 55 returned to their homes. And God

Hon Num 16 1 and Hon . . . rose up against Moses

honestly Rom 13 13 let us walk honestly, as in the
1 Th 4 11 walk h. towards them that are without

honesty Eccu 37 13 nor with the dishonest of h.

honey Gen 43 11 carry . . . a little balm and honey
Exod 3 8 floweth with milk and honey. 17; 13:5; 33:3; Num 13:28; Deut 11:9; 31:20; Eccu 46:10
Lev 2 11 neither shall any . . . honey be burnt
20 24 flowing with milk and honey. Num 14:8; Deut 6:3; 26:9, 15; 27:3; Josu 5:6; Jer 11:5; 32:22; Bar 1:20; Eze 20:6, 15
Num 16 13 land that flowed with milk and honey
14 floweth with rivers of milk and honey
Deut 8 8 grow: a land of oil and honey. Where
32 13 that he might suck honey out of the
Judg 14 9 taken the h. from the body of the lion
18 said to him: What is sweeter than h.
1 K 14 25 in which there was h. upon the ground
26 behold the honey dropped, but no man
29 because I tasted a little of this honey
43 I did but taste a little honey with
17 29 fried pulse and honey and butter
3 K 14 3 and cracknels and a pot of honey
4 K 18 32 a land of olives and oil and honey
2 Pa 31 5 firstfruits of corn, wine, and oil and h.
Job 20 17 the brooks of honey and of butter
Ps 18 11 sweeter than honey and the honeycomb
80 17 filled them with honey out of the rock
118 103 palate. More than honey to my mouth
Prov 24 13 eat honey, my son, because it is good
25 16 hast found h., eat what is sufficient
27 not good for a man to eat much honey
Cant 4 11 honey and milk are under thy tongue
5 1 have eaten the honeycomb with my honey
Eccu 24 27 for my spirit is sweet above honey
27 my inheritance above honey and the
39 31 salt, milk, and bread of flour and h.
49 2 his remembrance shall be sweet as h.
Isa 7 15 he shall eat butter and honey, that he
22 butter and honey shall every one eat
Jer 41 8 of wheat and barley and oil and honey
Eze 3 4 it was sweet as honey in my mouth
16 13 thou didst eat fine flour and honey
19 and oil and honey wherewith I fed thee
27 17 they set forth balm and honey and oil
Mat 3 4 his meat was locusts and wild honey
Apoc 10 9 in thy mouth it shall be sweet as h.
10 it was in my mouth sweet as honey: and

honeycomb Judg 14 8 in mouth of lion and a h.
1 K 14 27 his hand, and dipt it in a honeycomb
Ps 18 11 sweeter than honey and the honeycomb
Prov 5 3 lips of a harlot are like a honeycomb
16 24 well ordered words are as a honeycomb
24 13 and the h. most sweet to thy throat
27 7 soul that is full shall tread upon h.
Cant 4 11 lips, my spouse, are as a dropping h.
5 1 I have eaten the h. with my honey
Eccu 24 27 my inheritance above honey and the h.
Luke 24 42 of a broiled fish and a honeycomb

honor (noun) Num 24 11 deprived thee of the honor
2 K 10 3 that for the honor of thy father, David
1 Pa 19 3 that David to do honor to thy father
2 Es 12 43 might bring . . . in h. of thanksgiving
Jdth 1 11 empty, and rejected them without h.
15 10 thou art the honor of our people: for
Esth 1 20 lesser, give honor to their husbands
6 3 what honor and reward hath Mardochai
11 this honor is he worthy of, whom the
8 16 to rise, joy, honor, and dancing. And
9 21 should celebrate them with solemn h.
12 6 was in great honor with the king
13 14 should transfer the honor of my God
16 2 and the honor that hath been bestowed
Job 14 21 his children come to honor or dishonor
Ps 8 6 hast crowned him with glory and honor
28 2 bring to the Lord glory and honor
48 13 and man when he was in honor did. 21
95 7 bring ye to the Lord glory and honor
98 4 the king's honor loveth judgment
Prov 5 9 give not thy honor to strangers and
20 3 it is an honor for a man to separate
22 9 shall purchase victory and honor: but
26 8 so is he that giveth honor to a fool
Ecce 6 2 given riches and substance and honor
Wisd 2 22 nor esteemed the honor of holy souls
3 17 last old age shall be without honor
4 19 they shall fall after this without h.
5 4 esteemed . . . their end without honor
8 10 honor with the ancients though I be
Eccu 1 11 the fear of the Lord is honor and
3 13 glory of a man is from the honor of
13 father without honor is the disgrace
5 15 honor and glory is in the word of the
7 4 seek not . . . of the king the seat of h.
33 soul and give honor to the priests
10 5 of the scribe he shall lay his honor
27 the judge and the mighty is in honor
31 give it honor according to its desert
11 4 be not exalted in the day of thy honor
20 28 manners of lying men are without honor
24 22 my branches are of honor and grace
23 my flowers are the fruit of honor and
27 7 how comely . . . counsel to men of honor
9 shalt put her on as a long robe of h.
29 9 instead of honor and good turn will
32 3 and get the honor of the contribution
37 29 a wise man shall inherit honor among
45 14 Holiness, an ornament of honor: a
Bar 4 3 give not thy honor to another nor
24 shall come upon you with great honor
37 Holy One, rejoicing for the h. of God
5 1 put on the beauty and honor of that
2 crown on thy head of everlasting honor
4 the peace of justice and honor of piety
6 will bring them to thee exalted with h.
7 may walk diligently to the h. of God
Dan 2 6 shall receive of me . . . great honor
4 33 came to the h. and glory of my kingdom
5 18 and greatness and glory and honor
11 20 most vile and unworthy of kingly honor
21 the kingly h. shall not be given him
13 50 hath given thee the honor of old age
Mala 1 6 if then I be a father, where is my h.
1 Ma 2 8 temple is become as a man without h.
3 3 he got his people great honor and put
10 86 of the city to meet him with great h.
12 8 Onias received the ambassador with h.
43 received him with h. and commended
14 21 have told us of your glory and honor
40 received Simon's ambassadors with h.
2 Ma 3 2 the place worthy of the highest honor
6 7 crowned with ivy in honor of Bacchus
23 the inbred honor of his gray head
15 2 give h. to the day that is sanctified
Mat 13 57 prophet is not without h. Mark 6:4
John 4 44 a prophet hath no honor in his own
Acts 12 23 he had not given the honor to God
Rom 2 7 seek glory and honor and incorruption
10 glory and honor and peace to everyone
9 21 lump, to make one vessel unto honor, and
12 10 with honor preventing one another. In
13 7 to whom fear: honor, to whom honor. Owe
15 7 Christ also hath received you unto honor
16 27 Jesus Christ, to whom be h. and glory
1 C 4 10 you are honorable, but we without honor
12 23 about these we put more abundant honor
24 which wanted the more abundant honor
2 C 6 8 by h. and dishonor, by evil report and
Phil 2 29 Lord; and treat with honor such as he is
Col 2 23 not in any honor to the filling of the

1 Th 4 4 his vessel in sanctification and honor
1 Tim 1 17 be honor and glory forever and ever
5 17 be esteemed worthy of double honor
6 1 count their masters worthy of all honor
16 to whom be honor and empire everlasting
2 20 some indeed unto honor, but some unto
21 these, he shall be a vessel unto honor
Heb 2 7 crowned him with glory and honor, and
9 crowned with glory and honor: that
3 3 hath greater honor than the house. For
5 4 neither doth any man take the honor to
1 P 1 7 found unto praise and glory and honor
2 7 to you therefore that believe, he is h.
3 7 giving honor to the female as to the
4 14 which is of the honor, glory, and power
2 P 1 17 from God the Father honor and glory
Apoc 4 9 creatures gave glory and honor and
11 to receive glory and honor and power
5 12 and strength and honor and glory and
13 to the Lamb benediction and honor and
7 12 honor and power and strength to our
14 7 give him honor, because the hour of
21 24 shall bring their glory and h. into it
26 the glory and honor of the nations into
honor (verb) Exod 20 12 h. thy father and thy. Deut 5:16
Lev 19 15 nor h. the countenance of the mighty
32 and honor the person of the aged man
Num 22 17 I am ready to honor thee [Balaam] and
24 11 I had determined . . . to honor thee
Judg 13 17 shall come to pass, we may honor thee
1 K 15 30 yet honor me now before the ancients
Tob 4 3 thou shalt honor thy mother all the
10 13 to honor her father and mother-in-law
Prov 3 9 honor the Lord with thy substance and
19 6 many honor the person of him that is
Wisd 2 10 nor honor the ancient gray hairs of the
14 17 whom men could not honor in presence
17 king whom they had a mind to honor
17 they might honor as present, him that
19 20 people, O Lord, and didst honor them
Eccu 3 9 honor thy father in work and word
7 29 honor thy father, and forget not the
33 honor God with all thy soul and give
10 32 who will honor him that dishonoreth
38 1 honor the physician for the need thou
50 15 to honor the offering of the most high
1 Ma 11 42 I will greatly honor thee and thy
Mat 15 4 honor thy father and thy mother. 19:19; Mark 7:10; 10:19; Luke 18:20; Eph 6:2
6 he shall not honor his father or his
John 5 23 may h. the Son as they h. the Father
8 49 but I honor my Father, and you have
12 26 to me, him will my Father honor. Now
Rom 11 13 Gentiles, I will honor my ministry, if
1 Tim 5 3 honor widows, that are widows indeed
1 P 2 17 honor all men. Love the brotherhood
17 fear God. Honor the king. Servants, be
honorable Deut 1 15 your tribes men wise and h.
1 K 22 14 at thy bidding and is h. in thy house
2 K 23 23 who were the most h. among the thirty
4 K 5 1 was a great man with his master, and h.
1 Pa 4 9 Jabes was more h. than any of his
Tob 12 7 but h. to reveal and confess the works
Ps 71 14 their names shall be h. in his sight
138 17 thy friends . . . are made exceedingly h.
Prov 31 23 her husband is honorable in the gates
Wisd 10 10 made him honorable in his labors and
11 she stood by him and made him honorable
Eccu 1 14 the love of God is honorable wisdom
3 3 made the father h. to the children
10 24 midst of brethren their chief is h.
25 is the glory of the rich and of the h.
13 2 with one more honorable than himself
15 2 will meet him as an honorable mother
24 16 I took root in an honorable people
29 33 give place to the h. presence of my
Isa 3 3 h. in countenance and the counsellor
5 and the base against the honorable
9 15 the aged and h., he is the head: and
43 4 since thou became h. in my eyes, thou
Jer 31 20 Ephraim is an honorable son to me
Dan 13 4 he was the most honorable of them all
1 Ma 2 17 an h. and great man in this city and
2 Ma 6 28 if . . . I suffer an honorable death
Luke 14 8 lest perhaps one more h. than thou be
Acts 13 50 Jews stirred up religious and h. women
17 12 believed, and of h. women that were
1 C 4 10 you are honorable, but we without honor
12 23 such as we think to be less honorable
Heb 13 4 marriage honorable in all, and the
1 P 2 4 but chosen and made honorable by God
honorably Tob 14 2 he was buried h. in Ninive
1 Ma 10 60 he went honorably to Ptolemais and he
11 60 and they met him h. out of the city
14 23 the people to receive the men h. and
honored 1 K 2 29 rather h. thy sons than me
1 K 25 35 thy voice, and have honored thy face
Tob 1 16 with which he had been h. by the king
Jdth 12 12 that she may be honored before his face
Ps 36 20 after they shall be h. and exalted
Wisd 14 20 little before was but honored as a man
Eccu 3 21 God alone, and he is h. by the humble
10 23 that seed of men shall be h., which
28 and he that is ignorant shall not be h.
33 is a man that is h. for his wealth
14 21 and the worker thereof shall be h.
21 31 silent and wise man shall be honored
24 1 wisdom . . . shall be honored in God
38 6 men, that he may be h. in his wonders
48 11 and were honored with thy friendship
50 12 he honored the vesture of holiness
Lam 1 8 that honored her have despised her
Dan 14 1 and was h. above all his friends
Haba 2 5 proud man be, and he shall not be h.
1 Ma 10 88 words, that he h. Jonathan yet more
2 Ma 3 12 which is h. throughout the whole world
13 23 honored the temple and left gifts. He
Mat 6 2 that they may be honored by men. Amen
Acts 28 10 who also h. us with many honors, and
1 P 4 11 that in all things God may be honored
honoreth Deut 27 16 he that h. not his father
Prov 14 31 he that hath pity on the poor, h. him
Eccu 3 5 he that h. his mother is as one that
6 he that h. his father shall have joy
7 that h. his father shall enjoy a long
8 that feareth the Lord, h. his parents
Mala 1 6 the son honoreth the father, and the
Mat 15 8 people h. me with their lips. Mark 7:6
John 5 23 who h. not the Son, h. not the Father
honors 1 Ma 1 41 her h. were brought to nothing
1 Ma 11 27 and all the honors he had before
2 Ma 4 15 nought by the honors of their fathers
Acts 28 10 also honored us with many honors, and
hoof Exod 10 26 shall not a hoof remain of them
Lev 11 3 whatsoever hath the hoof divided and
4 cheweth indeed the cud and hath a hoof
5 the cud but divideth not the hoof. 6
7 divideth the hoof, cheweth not. 14:8
26 every beast that hath a hoof, but
Deut 14 6 every beast that divideth the hoof in
7 chew the cud but divide not the hoof
Job 39 21 he breaketh up the earth with his hoof
Eze 32 13 neither shall the h. of beasts trouble
hoofs Judg 5 22 the h. of the horses were broken
4 K 9 33 the hoofs of the horses trod upon her
Ps 68 32 that bringeth forth horns and hoofs

Isa 5 28 hoofs of their horses shall be like
26 11 with hoofs of his horses he shall tread
Mich 4 13 thy hoofs I will make brass: and thou
Zach 11 16 of the fat ones, and break their hoofs
hook Job 40 20 draw out the leviathan with a h.
Ecce 9 12 as fishes are taken with the hook
Isa 19 8 all that cast a hook into the river
Amos 8 1 behold a hook to draw down the fruit
2 I said: A hook to draw down fruit
Haba 1 15 he lifted up all them with his hook
Mat 17 26 go to the sea and cast in a hook
hooks Exod 28 13 thou shalt make also h. of gold
Exod 28 14 which thou shalt put into the hooks
25 thou shalt join together with two hooks
39 16 two hooks and as many rings of gold
17 which they put into the hooks that
Isa 18 5 shall be cut off with pruning hooks
2 Ma 13 2 and 300 chariots armed with hooks
hoop Deut 14 18 the hoop also and the bat
hope (noun) Acts 2 26 my flesh also shall rest in h.
Acts 16 19 seeing that the hope of their gain
23 6 concerning the hope and resurrection of
24 15 having hope in God, which these also
26 6 for hope of the promise that was made
7 for which hope, O king, I am accused by
27 20 h. of our being saved was now taken away
28 20 that for the hope of Israel, I am bound
Rom 4 18 who against hope believed in hope; that
5 2 we stand, and glory in hope of the glory
4 and patience trial; and trial hope; and
5 and hope confoundeth not: because the
8 20 of him that made it subject, in hope
24 saved by h. But h. that is seen is not h.
12 12 rejoicing in h. Patient in tribulation
15 4 of the scriptures, we might have hope
13 the God of hope fill you with all joy
13 that you may abound in hope, and in the
1 C 9 10 he that ploweth should plow in hope
10 that thrasheth, in hope to receive fruit
13 13 there remain faith, hope, and charity
15 19 if in this life only we have h. in Christ
2 C 1 7 that our hope for you may be steadfast
3 12 having therefore such hope, we use much
10 15 but having hope of your increasing faith
Gal 5 5 by faith, wait for the hope of justice
Eph 1 18 know what the hope is of his calling
2 12 having no hope of the promise, and
4 4 you are called in one h. of your calling
Phil 1 20 according to my expectation and hope
Col 1 5 hope that is laid up for you in heaven
23 immoveable from the hope of the gospel
27 which is Christ, in you the h. of glory
1 Th 1 3 of the enduring of the hope of our Lord
2 19 what is our hope, or joy, or crown of
4 12 even as others who have no hope. For
5 8 and for a helmet the hope of salvation
2 Th 2 15 consolation, and good hope in grace
1 Tim 1 1 our Savior, and of Christ Jesus our hope
Titus 1 2 unto the hope of life everlasting, which
13 looking for the blessed hope and coming
3 7 according to hope of life everlasting
Heb 3 6 confidence and glory of h. unto the end
6 11 the accomplishing of hope unto the end
18 fled for refuge to hold fast the hope
7 19 but a bringing in of a better hope, by
10 23 hold fast the confession of our hope
1 P 1 3 hath regenerated us unto a lively hope
21 that your faith and hope might be in
3 15 a reason of that hope which is in you
1 J 3 3 every one that hath this hope in him
hope (verb) Mat 12 21 in his name the Gentiles shall hope
Luke 6 34 to them of whom you hope to receive
Acts 26 7 unto which, our 12 tribes . . . hope to
Rom 8 24 what a man seeth, why doth he hope for
25 if we hope for that which we see not
15 12 Gentiles, in him the Gentiles shall hope
24 I hope that as I pass, I shall see you
2 C 1 13 I hope that you shall know unto the end
Phil 2 19 and I hope in the Lord Jesus to send
23 him therefore I hope to send unto you
1 Tim 4 10 because we hope in the living God, who
Philem 22 I hope that through your prayers I shall
2 J 12 I hope that I shall be with you and
3 J 14 I hope speedily to see thee, and we
hoped Luke 23 8 he hoped to see some sign
Luke 24 21 we hoped that it was he that should
2 C 8 5 not as we hoped, but they gave their own
Eph 1 12 we who before hoped in Christ: in whom
Heb 11 1 substance of things to be hoped for, the
hopes Jdth 13 15 now had no hopes that she would
Eccu 34 1 the hopes of a man that is void of
Jer 18 12 they said: We have no hopes: for we
2 Ma 7 34 be not lifted up . . . with vain hopes
13 3 in hopes that he should be appointed
hopeth Ps 20 8 king h. in the Lord: and through
Ps 31 10 encompass him that h. in the Lord
33 9 blessed is the man that hopeth in him
Ecce 9 4 liveth always or that hopeth for this
Mat 24 50 in a day that he h. not. Luke 12:46
1 C 13 7 hopeth all things, endureth all things
hoping Isa 30 2 h. for help in the strength of
Luke 6 35 do good, and lend, hoping for nothing
Acts 3 5 hoping that he should receive something
24 26 hoping also withal, that money should
1 Tim 3 14 hoping that I shall come to thee shortly
hoppeth Lev 11 21 wherewith it h. upon the earth
Hoppha 1 Pa 24 13 the thirteenth [lot] to Hoppha
Hor Num 20 22 they came to mount Hor, which
Num 20 25 and bring them up into mount Hor
27 they went up into mount Hor before all
21 4 they marched from mount Hor by the
33 37 from Cades, they camped in mount Hor
38 Aaron the priest went up into mount Hor
41 they departed from mount Hor and
Deut 32 50 Aaron thy brother died in mount Hor
Horam Josu 10 33 Horam king of Gazer came up
Horeb Exod 3 1 came to the mountain of God, Horeb
Exod 17 6 there before thee upon the rock Horeb
33 6 laid aside their ornaments by mount H.
Deut 1 2 eleven days' journey from Horeb by
6 the Lord our God spoke to us in Horeb
19 departing from Horeb we passed through
4 10 stand before the Lord thy God in H.
15 the Lord God spoke to you in Horeb
5 2 our God made a covenant with us in H.
9 8 in Horeb also thou didst provoke him
18 16 desiredst of the Lord thy God in Horeb
29 1 covenant which he made with them in H.
3 K 8 9 stone which Moses put there at Horeb
19 8 nights, unto the mount of God, Horeb
2 Pa 5 10 tables which Moses put there at Horeb
Ps 105 19 they made also a calf in Horeb: and
Eccu 48 7 in Horeb the judgments of vengeance
Mala 4 4 which I commanded him in Horeb for
Horem Josu 19 38 Horem and Bethanath and
Hori Gen 36 22 Lotan had sons: Hori and Heman
1 Pa 1 39 the sons of Lotan: Hori, Homam. And
Horma Num 14 45 pursued them as far as Horma
Num 21 3 called the name of that place Horma
Deut 1 44 slaughter of you from Seir as far as H.
Josu 19 29 it returneth to Horma to the strong
Judg 1 17 the name of the city was called Horma
1 Pa 4 30 Bathuel and in Horma and in Siceleg
horn Exod 21 29 ox was wont to push with his horn
1 K 2 1 my horn is exalted in my God: my mouth
10 and shall exalt the horn of his Christ

16 1 fill thy horn with oil, and come, that
13 then Samuel took the horn of oil and
2 K 22 3 my shield and the horn of my salvation
3 K 1 39 Sadoc the priest took a horn of oil
50 and took hold on the horn of the altar
51 hath taken hold of the h. of the altar
2 28 and laid hold on the horn of the altar
1 Pa 25 5 to lift up the horn: and God gave to
Jdth 9 11 to beat down . . . the horn of thy altar
Ps 17 3 horn of my salvation and my support
43 6 push down our enemies with the horn
74 5 to the sinners: Lift not up the horn
6 lift not up your horn on high: speak
88 18 good pleasure shall our h. be exalted
25 in my name shall his horn be exalted
91 11 my horn shall be exalted like that of
111 9 his horn shall be exalted in glory
117 27 boughs, even to the horn of the altar
131 17 there will I bring forth a h. to David
148 14 he hath exalted the horn of his people
Eccu 47 6 and to set up the horn of his nation
8 this day: he broke their horn forever
13 exalted his horn forever: and he gave
Jer 48 25 the horn of Moab is cut off, and his
Lam 2 3 hath broken . . . all the horn of Israel
17 set up the horn of thy adversaries
Eze 29 21 horn shall bud forth to the house of
32 2 didst push with the horn in thy rivers
Dan 7 8 another little horn sprung out of the
8 like the eyes of a man were in this h.
11 the great words which that horn spoke
20 and of that horn that had eyes and a
21 that horn made war against the saints
8 5 had a notable horn between his eyes
8 was grown, the great horn was broken
9 of one of them came forth a little h.
21 great horn that was between his eyes
Mich 4 13 I will make thy horn iron, and thy
Zach 1 21 lifted up the h. upon the land of Juda
1 Ma 2 48 they yielded not the horn to the sinner
Luke 1 69 hath raised up an horn of salvation
horned Exod 34 29 knew not that his face was h.
Exod 34 30 seeing the face of Moses horned, were
35 when he came out was horned, but he
hornets Exod 23 28 sending out hornets before
Deut 7 20 will send also hornets among them
Josu 24 12 I sent before you hornets and I drove
horns Gen 22 13 sticking fast by the horns, which
Exod 27 2 shall be horns at the four corners
29 12 put it upon the horns of the altar
30 2 height. Horns shall go out of the same
3 the walls round about and the horns
10 and Aaron shall pray upon the horns
37 25 from the corners of which went out horns
26 its grate and the sides and the horns
38 2 h. whereof went out from the corners
Lev 4 7 blood upon the h. of the altar. 18
25 touching therewith the h. of the altar
30 shall touch the horns of the altar. 34
8 15 touched the horns of the altar. 9:9
16 18 let him pour it upon the horns thereof
Deut 33 17 his horns as the horns of a rhinoceros
3 K 22 11 made himself horns of iron. 2 Pa 18:10
Ps 21 22 my lowness from horns of the unicorns
68 32 that bringeth forth horns and hoofs
74 11 I will break all the horns of sinners
11 the horns of the just shall be exalted
Jer 17 1 graven . . . upon the h. of their altars
Eze 34 21 struck all the weak cattle with your h.
43 15 from the Ariel upward were four horns
20 shalt put it upon the four h. thereof
Dan 7 7 had seen before it, and had ten horns
8 I considered the horns, and behold
8 three of the first horns were plucked
20 concerning the ten horns that he had
20 came up, before which three horns fell
24 and the ten horns of the same kingdom
8 3 before the water, having two high h.
4 I saw the ram pushing with his horns
6 went up to the ram that had the horns
7 struck the ram: and broke his two h.
8 there came up four horns under it
20 the ram which thou sawest with horns
Amos 3 14 horns of the altars shall be cut off
6 14 taken unto us horns by our own strength
Haba 3 4 as the light: horns are in his hands
Zach 1 18 eyes and saw: and behold four horns
19 are the horns that have scattered Juda
21 the four horns which have scattered Juda
21 to cast down the horns of the nations
9 15 as bowls and as the horns of the altar
1 Ma 7 46 and they pushed them with the horns
Apoc 5 6 having seven horns and seven eyes
9 13 from the four horns of the golden altar
12 3 having 7 heads and ten h. 13:1; 17:3, 7
13 1 upon his horns ten diadems, and upon
11 he had two horns, like a lamb, and he
17 12 the ten horns . . . are ten kings, who
16 the ten horns which thou sawest in the
Horonite 2 Es 2 10 Sanaballat the H. 19; 13:28
Horrhites Deut 2 12 H. also formerly dwelt in Seir
Deut 2 22 destroying the H. and delivering
horrible Exod 10 22 there came horrible darkness
Deut 4 34 stretched out arm and horrible visions
Wisd 11 19 shooting h. sparks out of their eyes
17 5 stars enlighten that horrible night
Jer 18 13 who hath heard such horrible things
Osee 6 10 I have seen a horrible thing in the
horribly Wisd 6 6 h. and speedily will he appear
Wisd 17 3 being h. afraid and troubled with
Eze 32 10 their kings shall be h. afraid for
Horrite Gen 36 20 the sons of Seir the Horrite
Horrites Gen 36 21 dukes of the Horrites. 29, 30
horror Gen 15 12 darksome h. seized upon him
Deut 32 10 in a desert land, in a place of horror
Jdth 4 2 dread and h. seized upon their minds
Job 4 13 in the horror of a vision by night
10 22 where . . . everlasting horror dwelleth
18 20 horror shall fall upon them that went
Osee 13 1 when Ephraim spoke, a h. seized Israel
2 Ma 3 17 with sadness and horror of the body
horse Exod 14 9 all Pharao's horse and chariots
Exod 15 1 the horse and the rider he hath thrown
21 the horse and his rider he hath thrown
3 K 10 29 and a horse for 150. 2 Pa 1:17
2 Pa 23 15 she was come within the horse gate
2 Es 3 28 upward from the horse gate the priests
Tob 6 17 to their lust, as the horse and mule
Esth 6 8 upon the horse that the king rideth
9 and let the first . . . hold his horse
10 take the robe and the horse, and do as
11 so Aman took the robe and the horse
11 setting him on the horse, went before
Job 39 18 she scorneth the horse and his rider
19 wilt thou give strength to the horse
Ps 31 9 not become like the horse and the mule
32 17 vain is the horse for safety: neither
146 10 not delight in the strength of the h.
Prov 21 31 horse is prepared for the day of battle
26 3 a whip for a horse, and a snaffle for
Eccu 30 8 a horse not broken becometh stubborn
33 6 is a mocker, is like a stallion horse
Isa 43 17 brought forth the chariot and the horse
63 13 as a horse in the wilderness that
Jer 8 6 as a horse rushing to the battle. The
51 21 in pieces the horse and his rider, and

29 of the Hethites and of Syria sell h.
18 5 find grass and save the h. and mules
20 1 two and thirty kings with him, and h.
21 overthrew the horses and chariots and
25 horses according to the former horses
4 K 2 11 fiery chariots and fiery horses parted
3 7 thy people: and my horses, thy horses
5 9 Naaman came with his h. and chariots
6 14 he sent thither horses and chariots
15 saw an army . . . and h. and chariots
17 mountain was full of h. and chariots
7 6 the noise of chariots and of horses
7 left their tents and their h. and asses
10 no man there, but h. and asses tied
13 let us take the five horses that are
14 they brought therefore two horses, and
9 19 and he sent a second chariot of horses
33 the hoofs of the horses trod upon her
10 2 master's sons and chariots and horses
11 16 by the way by which the horses go in
14 20 brought him [Amasias] away upon horses
18 23 I will give you 2,000 horses, and see
23 11 and he took away the horses which the
2 Pa 1 16 there were h. brought him from Egypt
17 a chariot of four h. for 600 pieces
9 25 Solomon had 40,000 horses in the
28 horses were brought to him out of Egypt
25 28 brought him [Amasias] back on horses
1 Es 2 66 their horses 736, their mules. 2 Es 7:68
Jdth 3 3 goats and horses . . . are in thy sight
9 16 nor is thy pleasure in strength of h.
16 5 and their horses covered the valleys
Ps 19 8 trust in chariots, and some in horses
Ecce 10 7 I have seen servants upon horses: and
Wisd 19 9 for they fed on their food like horses
Eccu 48 9 taken up . . . in a chariot of fiery h.
Isa 2 8 their land is filled with horses and
5 28 hoofs of their horses shall be like
30 16 said: No, but we will flee to horses
31 1 woe to them . . . trusting in horses
3 their horses, flesh, and not spirit
36 8 I will give thee 2,000 horses, and thou
66 20 all your brethren . . . upon horses and
Jer 4 13 his horses are swifter than eagles
5 8 they are become as amorous horses and
6 23 they shall mount upon horses, prepared
8 16 the snorting of his horses was heard
12 5 how canst thou contend with horses
17 25 riding in chariots and on horses. 22:4
46 4 harness the horses, and get up, ye
9 get ye up on horses, and glory in
50 37 a sword upon their horses and upon
42 they shall ride upon horses: like a
Eze 17 15 that it might give him h. and much
23 6 all horsemen, mounted upon horses. And
12 to the horsemen that rode upon horses
20 and whose issue as the issue of horses
26 7 king of Babylon . . . with horses and
10 by reason of the multitude of his h.
11 with hoofs of his horses he shall tread
27 14 they brought horses and horsemen and
38 4 h. and horsemen all clothed with coats
15 with thee, all of them riding upon h.
39 20 shall be filled at my table with h.
Osee 1 7 I will not save them . . . nor by horses
14 4 save us, we will not ride upon horses
Joel 2 4 of them is as the appearance of horses
Amos 4 10 even to the captivity of your horses
6 13 can horses run upon the rocks or can
Mich 5 10 I will take away thy horses out of the
Haba 1 8 their horses are lighter than leopards
3 8 who will ride upon thy horses: and thy
15 madest a way in the sea for thy horses
Agge 2 23 horses and their riders shall come down
Zach 1 8 behind him were horses, red, speckled
6 2 in the first chariot were red horses
2 and in the second chariot black horses
3 and in the third chariot white horses
3 in the fourth chariot grisled horses
6 that in which were the black horses
10 5 riders of horses shall be confounded
1 Ma 10 81 their horses were fatigued. Then Simon
2 Ma 5 3 horses set in order by ranks, running
10 29 there appeared . . . five men upon h.
James 3 3 we put bits into the mouths of horses
Apoc 9 7 like unto horses prepared unto battle
9 and many horses running to battle. And
17 thus I saw the horses in the vision
17 the heads of the horses were as the
19 power of the horses is in their mouths
18 13 and horses and chariots and slaves and
19 14 followed him on white horses, clothed
18 mighty men, and the flesh of horses
horses' Apoc 14 20 the press up to the h. bridles
Hosa Josu 19 29 to strong city of Tyre and to H.
1 Pa 4 4 Gedor, and Ezar the father of Hosa
16 38 and Hosa he appointed to be porters
26 10 of H., that is, of the sons of Merari
11 the brethren of Hosa, were thirteen
16 to Sephim and Hosa towards the west
Hosanna Mat 21 9 saying: H. to the son of David. 15
Mat 21 9 Hosanna in the highest. Mark 11:10
Mark 11 9 H., blessed is he that. John 12:13
Hosiel 1 Pa 23 9 sons of Semei . . . Hosiel
Hospitalis 2 Ma 6 2 in Gazarim of Jupiter H.
hospitality Rom 12 13 pursuing hospitality. Bless
1 Tim 3 2 given to hospitality. Titus 1:8
Heb 13 2 and hospitality do not forget; for
hostage 1 Ma 1 11 who had been a hostage at Rome
hostages 4 K 14 14 the king's treasures and h.
2 Pa 25 24 sons of the hostages he brought back
1 Ma 8 7 tribute, and that he should give h.
9 53 and he took the sons . . . for hostages
10 6 the hostages that were in the castle
9 and the h. were delivered to Jonathan
11 62 he took their sons for hostages and
13 16 and his two sons for hostages, that
hot Gen 36 24 the hot waters in the wilderness
Exod 16 21 and after the sun grew hot, it melted
Lev 6 22 shall offer it hot for a most sweet
Josu 9 12 these loaves we took hot when we set
Judg 20 34 battle grew hot against the children
1 K 11 9 tomorrow, when the sun shall be hot
11 he slew . . . until the day grew hot
21 6 Lord, that hot loaves might be set up
2 Es 7 3 not . . . be opened till the sun be hot
Tob 2 11 hot dung out of a swallow's nest fell
Job 6 17 after it groweth hot they shall be
37 17 are not the garments hot, when the
Ps 38 4 my heart grew hot within me: and in my
Prov 6 28 can he walk upon hot coals, and his
25 22 shalt heap hot coals upon his head
Eccu 23 22 a hot soul is a burning fire, it will
Eze 24 5 the seething thereof is boiling hot
11 burning coals, that it may be hot
Dan 13 15 in the orchard: for it was hot weather
Jon 4 8 commanded a hot and burning wind: and
2 Ma 7 3 and brazen caldrons to be made hot
John 21 9 they saw hot coals lying, and a fish
Apoc 3 15 neither cold nor hot. 16
15 I would thou wert cold or hot. But
Hotham 1 Pa 7 32 Heber begot . . . Hotham
1 Pa 11 44 Samma and Jehiel the sons of Hotham
hotly Gen 31 36 hast thou so hotly pursued me
houghed 2 K 8 4 h. all the chariot horses. 1 Pa 18:4
houp Lev 11 19 you must not eat . . . the houp

hour 3 K 19 2 if by this hour tomorrow I
Tob 11 14 he stayed about half an hour: and a
14 5 at the hour of his death he called
Jdth 6 6 from this h. thou shalt be associated
13 7 in this hour look on the works of my
9 strengthen me, O Lord God, at this h.
Job 10 14 and thou hast spared me for an hour
Eccu 11 24 in a swift hour his blessing beareth
29 affliction of an h. maketh one forget
12 14 for an hour he will abide with thee
33 9 they celebrated festivals at an hour
Dan 3 5 in the hour that you shall hear the
15 at what hour soever you shall hear
4 16 think within himself for about one h.
Mat 9 22 woman was made whole from that hour
10 19 it shall be given you in that hour
14 15 the hour is now past. Mark 6:35
15 28 her daughter was cured from that hour
17 17 and the child was cured from that hour
18 1 at that hour the disciples came to
20 3 going out about the third hour, he saw
5 out about the sixth and the ninth hour
6 about the eleventh hour he went out
9 that came about the eleventh hour, they
12 these last have worked but one hour
24 36 day and hour no one knoweth. Mark 13:32
42 not what hour your Lord will come
43 what hour thief would come. Luke 12:39
44 at what hour you know not the Son of
50 and at an hour that he knoweth not
25 13 you know not the day nor the hour
26 40 could you not watch one h. Mark 14:37
45 the hour is at hand, and the Son of man
27 45 from the sixth hour there was darkness
45 darkness . . . until the ninth hour. Mark 15:33; Luke 23:44
46 about ninth hour Jesus cried. Mark 15:34
Mark 13 11 shall be given you in that hour, that
14 35 the hour might pass from him. And he
41 the hour is come: behold the Son of man
15 25 and it was the third hour, and they
33 when the sixth hour was come, there
Luke 1 10 without, at the hour of incense. And
12 40 at what hour you think not, the Son of
46 and at the hour that he knoweth not
14 17 sent his servant at the hour of supper
17 31 in that hour, he that shall be on the
22 14 when the hour was come, he sat down
53 this is your hour, and the power of
23 44 and it was almost the sixth hour; and
John 1 39 day: now it was about the tenth hour
2 4 my hour is not yet come. His mother
4 6 the well. It was about the sixth hour
21 the hour cometh when you shall neither
23 the hour cometh and now is, when the
52 the hour wherein he grew better. And
52 at the seventh hour the fever left him
5 25 the hour cometh and now is, when the
28 the hour cometh, wherein all that are
7 30 his hour was not yet come. 8:20
12 23 the hour is come that the Son of man
27 say? Father, save me from this hour
27 for this cause I came unto this hour
13 1 Jesus knowing that his hour was come
16 2 the hour cometh, that whosoever
4 that when the hour shall come, you may
21 sorrow, because her hour is come; but
25 the hour cometh, when I will no more
32 the hour cometh, and it is now come
17 1 the hour is come, glorify thy Son
19 14 of the pasch, about the sixth hour
27 from that hour, the disciple took her
Acts 2 15 seeing it is but the third hour of the
3 1 temple at the ninth hour of prayer
10 3 the ninth hour of the day, an angel
9 the house to pray, about the sixth hour
30 four days ago, unto this hour, I was
30 praying in my house, at the ninth hour
23 23 spearmen for third hour of the night
Rom 13 11 is now hour for us to rise from sleep
1 C 4 11 even unto this hour we both hunger and
15 30 why also are we in danger every hour
Gal 2 5 by subjection, no not for an hour, that
1 J 2 18 little children, it is the last hour
18 we know that it is the last hour
Apoc 3 3 know at what hour I will come to thee
10 keep thee from the hour of temptation
8 1 silence in heaven . . . for half an hour
9 15 were prepared for an hour and a day and
11 13 at that hour there was made a great
14 7 the hour of his judgment is come; and
15 the hour is come to reap: for the
17 12 power as kings one hour after the beast
18 10 for in one hour is thy judgment come
17 in one hour are so great riches come
19 for in one hour she is made desolate

same hour Exod 9 18 rain tomorrow at this s. h.
Deut 28 57 children that are born the same hour
Josu 11 6 at this same hour I will deliver all
1 K 9 16 tomorrow about this same hour I will
3 K 20 6 this same h. I will send my servants
4 K 4 16 at this time and this same hour, if
17 at the same hour that Eliseus had said
Dan 3 6 he shall the same hour be cast into a
15 shall be cast the same hour into
4 30 the same hour the word was fulfilled
5 5 the same hour there appeared fingers
Mat 8 13 servant was healed at the same hour
26 55 in that same hour Jesus said to the
Luke 2 38 she, at the same hour, coming in
7 21 in that same hour he cured many of
10 21 in that same hour, he rejoiced in the
12 12 shall teach you in the same hour what
20 19 to lay hands on him the same hour
John 4 53 the same hour that Jesus said to him
Acts 16 18 her. And he went out the same hour
33 taking them the same hour of the night
22 13 and I the same hour looked upon him. But

hours Tob 12 22 lying prostrate for three hours
Jdth 7 18 for many hours . . . they cried to God
John 11 9 are there not twelve hours of the day
Acts 5 7 about the space of three hours after
19 34 for space of about two hours, cried out

household Gen 18 19 he will command . . . his h.
Gen 31 37 and searched all my household stuff
35 2 Jacob having called . . . his household
45 20 leave nothing of your household stuff
Exod 1 1 went in, every man with his household
1 K 27 3 every man with his household, and David
2 K 2 3 David brought up every man with his h.
6 11 blessed Obededom and all his household
15 16 king went forth and all his household
16 2 the asses are for the king's household
19 18 might help over the king's household
41 brought the king and his household over
3 K 4 7 victuals for the king and for his h.
5 9 necessaries, to furnish food for my h.
4 K 8 1 go thou and thy household and sojourn
2 going with her h., she sojourned in the
Jdth 15 14 precious stones and all household stuff
Prov 31 15 given a prey to her h., and victuals
Eccu 4 35 thy house, terrifying them of thy h.
6 11 with confidence among them of thy h.
30 2 in the midst of them of his household
32 26 take heed of them of thy household
Mich 7 6 a man's enemies are they of his own h.

Mat 10 25 how much more them of his household
36 enemies shall be they of his own h.
Acts 10 7 he called two of his household servants
16 15 when she was baptized, and her h., she
Rom 16 11 salute them that are of Aristobulus' h.
11 salute them that are of Narcissus' h.
1 C 1 16 and I baptized also the h. of Stephanus
Gal 6 10 to those who are of the h. of the faith
Phil 4 22 they that are of Caesar's household
2 Tim 4 19 and Aquila, and the h. of Onesiphorus
householder Ruth 2 2 shall find grace with a h.
Mat 13 52 is like to a man that is a householder
20 1 is like to an householder who went out
21 33 h. who planted a vineyard and made a
Luke 12 39 if the householder did know at what
households Deut 11 6 swallowed up with their h.
houseroom Eccu 29 34 the upbraiding of houseroom
housetop Ps 101 8 a sparrow all alone on the h.
Prov 21 9 to sit in a corner of the h. 25:24
Mat 24 17 he that is on the h. Mark 13:15
Luke 17 31 he that shall be on the h., and his
housetops Isa 22 1 art wholly gone up to the h.
Isa 37 27 and like the grass of the housetops
Jer 48 38 upon all the housetops of Moab and in
Mat 10 27 the ear, preach ye upon the housetops
Luke 12 3 shall be preached on the housetops
howl Isa 13 6 howl ye, for the day of the Lord
Isa 14 31 howl, O gate; cry, O city: all
15 4 the well appointed men of Moab howl, his soul shall howl to itself
16 7 therefore shall Moab howl to Moab, everyone shall howl
23 1 howl, ye ships of the sea. 14
6 howl, ye inhabitants of the island
65 14 and shall howl for grief of spirit
Jer 4 8 with haircloth, lament and howl: for
25 34 howl, ye shepherds, and cry: and
47 2 the inhabitants of the land shall howl
48 20 howl ye, and cry, tell ye it in Arnon
49 3 howl, O Hesebon, for Hai is wasted
51 8 howl for her, take balm for her pain
Eze 21 12 cry and howl, O son of man, for this
30 2 howl ye: Woe, woe to the day: for the
Osee 5 8 howl ye in Bethaven, behind thy back
Joel 1 13 howl, ye ministers of the altars: go
Mich 1 8 therefore will I lament and howl: I
Soph 1 11 howl, ye inhabitants of the Morter
Zach 11 2 howl, thou fir tree, for the cedar
2 howl, ye oaks of Basan, because the
James 5 1 weep and howl in your miseries, which
howled Judg 5 28 his mother looked out . . . and h.
Jdth 16 13 then the camp of the Assyrians howled
Isa 15 2 and over Medaba, Moab hath howled: on
Jer 48 39 is it overthrown, and they have howled
Osee 7 14 heart, but they howled in their beds
Joel 1 11 the vinedressers have howled for the
howling Judg 7 21 crying out and h. they fled away
Isa 15 8 the howling thereof unto Gallim, and
Jer 3 21 and howling of the children of Israel
20 16 let him hear . . . howling at noontide
25 36 howling of the principal of the flock
46 12 and thy howling hath filled the land
48 5 enemies have heard a h. of destruction
Eze 21 22 to lift up the voice in howling, to
Soph 1 10 the fish gate, and a h. from the Second
Zach 11 3 voice of the howling of the shepherds
Hozai 2 Pa 33 19 are written in the words of Hozai
Hucac 1 Pa 6 75 of the tribe of Aser . . . Hucac
huckster Eccu 26 28 a h. shall not be justified
Hucuca Josu 19 34 goeth out from thence to Hucuca
huge Prov 8 25 mountains with their huge bulk
Hul 1 Pa 1 17 sons of Sem . . . Hus and Hul
Hull Gen 10 23 the sons of Aram: Us and Hull
human Wisd 11 7 gavest human blood to the unjust
Wisd 14 21 the occasion of deceiving human life
Rom 6 19 I speak an human thing, because of the
1 C 2 4 in persuasive words of human wisdom, but
13 not in learned words of human wisdom
10 13 take hold on you, but such as is human
1 P 2 13 subject therefore to every h. creature
humane Wisd 12 19 that they must be just and h.
humanity Esth 16 4 in themselves the laws of h.
Esth 16 11 found our humanity so great towards him
2 Ma 9 27 he will behave with moderation and h.
12 30 they had treated them with humanity
14 9 according to thy h. which is known to
humble Gen 16 9 and h. thyself under her hand
Judg 19 24 and you may humble them and satisfy
2 K 22 28 with thy eyes thou wilt h. the haughty
2 Pa 33 23 he did not h. himself before the Lord
2 Es 9 24 didst h. before them the inhabitants of
Jdth 8 16 let us humble our souls before him
16 continuing in an humble spirit in his
20 and he will humble all the nations that
9 16 the prayer of the humble and the meek
Esth 11 11 and the humble were exalted and they
Job 5 11 who setteth up the humble on high and
40 6 behold every arrogant man and h. him
Ps 9 18 to judge for fatherless and for the h.
17 28 for thou wilt save the humble people
33 19 and he will save the humble of spirit
54 20 hear, and the Eternal shall h. them
71 4 poor: and he shall h. the oppressor
73 21 let not the humble be turned away with
101 18 had regard to the prayer of the humble
Prov 29 23 glory shall uphold the humble of spirit
Eccu 2 2 humble thy heart and endure: incline
3 20 the more humble thyself in all things
21 alone, and he is honored by the humble
4 7 humble thy soul to the ancient and bow
6 12 if he humble himself before thee and
7 19 humble thy spirit very much: for the
10 18 planted the humble of these nations
21 memory of them that are humble in mind
11 1 wisdom of the h. shall exalt his head
12 6 do good to the humble, and give not
11 though he humble himself and go
13 9 humble thyself to God and wait for
18 21 humble thyself before thou art sick
29 5 in promises they humble their voice
Isa 10 2 violence to the cause of the humble
45 2 will h. the great ones of the earth
57 15 with a contrite and h. spirit, to revive the spirit of the h.
Jer 13 18 humble yourselves, sit down: for the
Dan 3 39 in a contrite heart and h. spirit let
87 ye holy and humble of heart, bless the
Amos 2 7 and turn aside the way of the humble
Mat 11 29 because I am meek and humble of heart
18 4 shall h. himself as this little child
23 12 that shall h. himself shall be exalted
Luke 1 52 seat, and hath exalted the humble
Rom 12 16 high things, but consenting to the h.
2 C 7 6 but God, who comforteth the humble
12 21 when I come, God h. me among you: and I
James 4 6 proud, and giveth grace to the humble
1 P 3 8 modest, humble: not rendering evil for
5 5 but to the humble he giveth grace
humbled Deut 21 14 because thou hast humbled her
Deut 22 24 he hath humbled his neighbor's wife
29 to wife, because he hath humbled her
Judg 3 30 Moab was humbled that day under the
4 23 God that day humbled Jabin the king
6 6 Israel was humbled exceedingly in the
8 28 Madian was h. before the children of
11 33 the children of Ammon were humbled by

Ruth 1 21 Noemi, whom the Lord hath humbled
1 K 7 13 the Philistines were humbled, and they
3 K 21 29 hast thou not seen Achab h. before me
29 because he hath h. himself . . . I will
4 K 22 19 thou hast h. thyself before the Lord
1 Pa 17 10 have humbled all thy enemies. And I
18 1 defeated the Philistines and h. them
20 4 of the race of Raphaim and humbled them
2 Pa 12 7 when the Lord saw that they were h.
7 because they are h., I will not destroy
12 but yet because they were humbled, the
28 19 the Lord had h. Juda because of Achaz
32 26 and he humbled himself afterwards
33 23 as Manasses his father had h. himself
34 27 and thou hast humbled thyself in the
Jdth 4 7 they humbled their souls in fastings
Job 22 29 he that hath been h., shall be in glory
Ps 34 13 I humbled my soul with fasting; and my
14 as one mourning . . . so was I humbled
37 9 I am afflicted and humbled exceedingly
39 3 I was dumb and was h. and kept silence
43 20 thou hast humbled us in the place of
25 our soul is humbled down to the dust
50 10 bones that have been h. shall rejoice
19 a contrite and humbled heart . . . thou
80 15 should soon have humbled their enemies
87 16 being exalted have been h. and troubled
88 11 thou hast humbled the proud one, as one
89 15 the days in which thou hast humbled us
104 18 they humbled his feet in fetters: the
105 42 they were humbled under their hands
106 12 their heart was humbled with labors
114 6 I was humbled, and he delivered me
115 10 but I have been humbled exceedingly
118 67 before I was humbled I offended
71 it is good for me that thou hast h. me
75 and in thy truth thou hast humbled me
107 I have been h., O Lord, exceedingly
Prov 16 19 it is better to be h. with the meek
18 12 before he be glorified, it is humbled
25 7 shouldst be humbled before the prince
Eccu 13 10 not deceived into folly and be humbled
11 lest being humbled thou be deceived
40 2 unto him that is humbled in earth and
Isa 2 11 the lofty eyes of men are humbled and
12 is arrogant, and he shall be humbled
17 the haughtiness of men shall be humbled
5 15 man shall be humbled, and the eyes of
58 3 have we humbled our souls, and thou
Eze 22 10 they have h. the uncleanness of the
Dan 5 22 Baltasar, hast not humbled thy heart
Osee 7 10 the pride of Israel shall be humbled
Zach 10 11 the pride of Assyria shall be humbled
1 Ma 12 15 delivered, and our enemies are h.
Mat 23 12 exalt himself shall be h. Luke 14:11; 18:14
Phil 2 8 he h. himself, becoming obedient unto
James 4 10 be humbled in the sight of the Lord
1 P 5 6 be you humbled therefore under the
humblest Jdth 6 15 thou h. them that presume of
humbleth 1 K 2 7 he humbleth and he exalteth
Eccu 7 12 there is one that h. and exalteth
19 23 is one that humbleth himself wickedly
35 21 prayer of him that h. himself shall
Luke 14 11 h. himself, shall be exalted. 18:14
humbling Eccu 34 31 doth his h. himself profit
2 C 11 7 did I commit a fault, humbling myself
humbly Deut 9 25 h. besought him that he would not
Jdth 8 20 let us humbly wait for his consolation
Ps 130 2 if I was not humbly minded, but exalted
humiliation Ps 9 14 see my h. which I suffer
Ps 118 50 this hath comforted me in my h.
153 see my h. and deliver me: for I have
Prov 29 23 humiliation followeth the proud
Eccu 2 4 endure, and in thy h. keep patience
5 acceptable men in the furnace of h.
Mich 6 14 thy h. shall be in the midst of thee
humility Jdth 8 17 also we may glorify in our h.
Ps 30 8 thou hast regarded my humility: thou
Prov 11 2 but where h. is, there also is wisdom
15 33 wisdom: and h. goeth before glory
22 4 fruit of humility is fear of the Lord
Eccu 13 24 as h. is an abomination to the proud
Luke 1 48 hath regarded the h. of his handmaid
Acts 8 33 in humility his judgment was taken
20 19 serving the Lord with all humility, and
Eph 4 2 with all h. and mildness, with patience
Phil 2 3 but in humility, let each esteem others
Col 2 18 willing in humility, and religion of
23 show of wisdom is superstition and h.
3 12 the bowels of mercy, benignity, humility
1 P 5 5 you all insinuate h. one to another
humor Lev 15 3 a filthy h. . . . cleaveth to his
hundred; *see* p. 1244.
hundredfold Gen 26 12 found that same year a h.
Mat 13 8 forth fruit, some an hundredfold
23 yieldeth the one an h. and another
19 29 shall receive an h. and shall possess
Luke 8 8 yielded fruit a hundredfold. Saying
hundreds Exod 18 21 rulers of thousands and of h.
Exod 18 25 rulers over thousands and over h.
1 K 29 2 marched with their hundreds and their
2 K 18 1 captains of thousands and of hundreds. 1 Pa 27:1; 29:6; 2 Pa 1:2; 25:5
4 went forth . . . by h. and by thousands
1 Pa 13 1 the captains of thousands and of h.
26 26 captains over thousands and over h. 28:1
1 Ma 3 55 appointed captains . . . over hundreds
Mark 6 40 they sat down in ranks, by hundreds
hundredth 2 Es 5 11 the h. part of the money
hung Exod 13 16 as a thing hung between thy eyes
Exod 40 35 if it hung over, they remained in the
36 the cloud of the Lord hung over the
Josu 2 21 she h. the scarlet cord in the window
8 29 he hung the king thereof on a gibbet
10 26 gibbets and they h. until the evening
Judg 16 16 continually hung upon him [Samson]
1 K 31 10 his body they hung on the wall of
2 K 18 9 while he [Absalom] hung between the
Jdth 13 8 loosed his sword that hung tied upon it
14 7 they hung up the head of Holofernes
Ps 136 2 we hung up our instruments. For there
Isa 21 15 from the sword that hung over them
22 25 that which hung thereon shall perish
Eze 27 10 they h. up the buckler and the helmet
11 hung up their quivers on thy walls
1 Ma 4 51 upon the table and hung up the veils
7 47 hung it up over against Jerusalem
2 Ma 15 35 he hung up Nicanor's head in the
hunger Deut 25 18 when thou wast spent with h.
Deut 28 20 shall send upon thee famine and hunger
48 shalt serve thy enemy . . . in h. and
2 K 17 29 that the people were faint with hunger
2 Pa 32 11 to give you up to die by hunger and
2 Es 9 15 them bread from heaven in their hunger
Job 18 12 famine, and let hunger invade his ribs
30 3 barren with want and hunger, who
Ps 33 11 rich have wanted and have suffered h.
58 7 and shall suffer hunger like dogs. 15
Prov 19 15 and an idle soul shall suffer hunger
Eccu 24 29 they that eat me, shall yet hunger
Isa 44 12 he shall hunger and faint, he shall
49 10 they shall not hunger nor thirst
Jer 38 9 into the dungeon to die there with h.
42 14 where we shall . . . nor suffer hunger
Lam 2 19 children, that have fainted for hunger
4 9 than with them that died with hunger

1 Ma 13 49 they were straitened with hunger and
Mat 5 6 blessed are they that hunger and thirst
Luke 6 21 blessed are ye that hunger now: for
25 that are filled: for you shall hunger
15 17 bread, and I here perish with hunger
John 6 35 he that cometh to me shall not hunger
1 C 4 11 unto this hour we both hunger and thirst
2 C 11 27 in much watchings, in hunger and thirst
Apoc 7 16 they shall no more hunger nor thirst
hungered Eccu 16 27 have neither h. nor labored
hungry 1 K 2 5 and the hungry are filled, so
Tob 1 20 he fed the hungry and gave clothes to
4 17 eat thy bread with the hungry and the
Job 5 5 whose harvest the hungry shall eat and
22 7 hast withdrawn bread from the hungry
24 10 and from the hungry they have taken
Ps 49 12 if I should be hungry, I would not tell
106 5 they were h. and thirsty: their soul
9 hath filled the hungry soul with good
36 hath placed there the hungry: and they
145 7 wrong; who giveth food to the hungry
Prov 6 30 for he stealeth to fill his hungry soul
18 8 souls of the effeminate shall be hungry
25 21 if thy enemy be hungry, give him to eat
27 7 a soul that is hungry shall take even
28 15 as a roaring lion and a hungry bear
Eccu 4 2 despise not the h. soul: and provoke
Isa 8 21 pass by it, they shall fall and be h.
21 when they shall be h., they will be
9 20 to the right hand, and shall be hungry
29 8 as he that is h. dreameth and eateth
32 6 to make empty the soul of the hungry
58 7 deal thy bread to the hungry and bring
10 shalt pour out thy soul to the hungry
65 13 shall eat, and you shall be hungry
Jer 31 12 garden, and they shall be h. no more
25 and I have filled every hungry soul
Bar 2 18 the h. soul giveth glory and justice
Eze 18 7 hath given his bread to the h. 16
Mat 4 2 nights, afterwards he was hungry
12 1 his disciples being hungry, began to
3 David did when he was hungry. Mark 2:25; Luke 6:3
21 18 returning into the city, he was hungry
25 35 I was hungry, and you gave me to eat
37 when did we see thee hungry. 44
42 I was hungry, and you gave me not to
Mark 11 12 came out from Bethania, he was hungry
Luke 1 53 he hath filled the hungry with good
4 2 when they were ended, he was hungry
Acts 10 10 being hungry, he was desirous to taste
Rom 12 20 if thy enemy be hungry, give him to eat
1 C 11 21 one . . . is hungry and another is drunk
34 if any man be h., let him eat at home
Phil 4 12 both to be full, and to be hungry; both
hunt Ps 93 21 will h. after the soul of the just
Jer 16 16 and they shall hunt them from every
hunted 1 K 26 20 as the partridge is hunted in the
hunter Gen 10 9 stout hunter before the Lord
Gen 25 27 Esau became a skilful hunter and a
hunter's Ecce 7 27 woman . . . who is the h. snare
hunters Ps 90 3 me from the snare of the hunters
Jer 16 16 I will send them many hunters, and
Eze 32 30 princes of the north, and all the h.
hunteth Mich 7 2 every one h. his brother to
hunting Gen 25 28 because he ate of his hunting
Gen 27 3 thou hast taken something by hunting
7 bring me of thy hunting and make
25 bring me the meats of thy hunting, my
31 made of what he had taken in hunting
Lev 17 13 if by hunting or fowling, he take a
Hupham Num 26 39 sons of Benjamin . . . Hupham
Huphamites Num 26 39 family of the Huphamites

Hur Exod 17 10 Aaron and Hur went up upon
Exod 17 12 Aaron and Hur stayed up his hands on
24 14 you have Aaron and Hur with you: if
31 2 Uri the son of Hur. 35:30; 38:22; 2 Pa 1:5
Num 31 8 and Hur and Rebe, five princes of
Josu 13 21 and Hur and Rebe, dukes of Sehon
1 Pa 2 19 to wife Ephrata; who bore him Hur
20 Hur begot Uri: and Uri begot Bezeleel
50 Hur the firstborn of Ephrata. 4:4
4 1 sons of Juda . . . Charmi and Hur and
2 Es 3 9 Raphaia the son of Hur, lord of the
Hurai 1 Pa 11 32 Hurai of the torrent Gaas
Huram 1 Pa 8 5 Gera and Sephuphan and H.
Huri Num 13 6 of Simeon, Saphat the son of H.
1 Pa 5 14 the sons of Abihail the son of Huri
hurling 1 Pa 12 2 using either hand in h. stones
hurried Job 20 2 my mind is h. away to different
hurry Eze 12 18 drink thy water in h. and sorrow
hurt Gen 21 23 that thou wilt not hurt me nor
Gen 26 29 nor have done anything to hurt thee
31 7 God hath not suffered him to hurt me
Exod 9 31 flax therefore and the barley were h.
32 and other winter corn were not hurt
12 23 not suffer the destroyer . . . to h. you
22 5 if any man hurt a field or a vineyard
10 and it die or be hurt or be taken
14 if a man borrow . . . and it be hurt or
22 you shall not hurt a widow or an orphan
23 if you hurt them they will cry out to
Num 5 19 bitter waters . . . shall not hurt thee
28 be not defiled, she shall not be hurt
Judg 8 11 who were secure and suspected no hurt
1 K 24 10 men that say: David seeketh thy hurt
3 K 13 28 eaten of the dead body nor h. the ass
1 Es 4 22 the evil grow to the hurt of the kings
Jdth 11 1 I have never h. a man that was willing
Job 35 6 if thou sin, what shalt thou hurt him
8 thy wickedness may hurt a man that is
Ps 70 13 confusion and shame that seek my hurt
88 23 son of iniquity have power to hurt him
104 14 he suffered no man to hurt them: and
Prov 8 36 sin against me, shall hurt his own soul
17 26 no good thing to do hurt to the just
Ecce 5 12 riches kept to the hurt of the owner
8 9 ruleth over another to his own hurt
10 9 removeth stones, shall be hurt by them
Wisd 11 20 the hurt might be able to destroy them
14 29 swear amiss, they look not to be hurt
18 2 because they were not hurt now: and
19 6 thy children might be kept without h.
Eccu 7 22 hurt not the servant that worketh
13 15 and he will not spare to do thee hurt
20 8 many words, shall hurt his own soul
28 2 thy neighbor if he hath hurt thee
30 32 if thou hurt him unjustly, he will
38 22 him no good, and shalt hurt thyself
Isa 11 9 they shall not hurt nor shall they
27 3 lest any hurt come to it, I keep it
28 28 neither shall the cart wheel hurt it
65 25 they shall not hurt nor kill in all
Jer 7 6 after strange gods to your own hurt
25 7 might provoke me . . . to your own hurt
Eze 33 12 of the wicked shall not hurt him
Dan 3 92 the fire, and there is no hurt in them
6 22 the lions, and they have not hurt me
23 the den, and no hurt was found in him
1 Ma 5 48 and no man shall hurt you: we will
6 18 were continually seeking their hurt
7 22 power, and did much hurt in Israel
2 Ma 8 36 and therefore they could not be hurt
12 25 they let him go without hurt, for the
14 40 by insnaring him to hurt the Jews very
Mark 16 18 deadly thing, it shall not hurt them

Luke 4 35 out of him, and hurt him not at all
10 19 enemy: and nothing shall hurt you
Acts 7 26 brethren; why hurt you one another
18 10 shall set upon thee, to hurt thee; for
1 P 3 13 who is he that can hurt you if you be
Apoc 2 11 shall not be hurt by the second death
6 6 see thou hurt not the wine and the oil
7 2 to whom it was given to hurt the earth
3 hurt not the earth nor the sea nor the
9 4 should not hurt the grass of the earth
10 their power was to hurt men five months
19 have heads: and with them they hurt
11 5 if any man will hurt them, fire shall
22 11 he that hurteth, let him hurt still
hurteth Prov 26 19 man that hurteth his friend
Apoc 22 11 he that hurteth, let him hurt still
hurtful 1 Es 4 15 h. to the kings and provinces
Prov 1 22 fools covet those things which are h.
Jer 4 14 shall hurtful thoughts abide in thee
2 Ma 15 40 it is hurtful always to drink wine
1 Tim 6 9 into many unprofitable and h. desires
hurts Luke 7 21 cured many of their diseases and hurts
Hus Gen 22 21 Hus the firstborn, and Buz
Gen 36 28 Disan had sons: Hus and Aram. These
1 Pa 1 17 sons of Sem . . . Aram and Hus and Hul
42 sons of Disan: Hus. Now these are
Job 1 1 there was a man in the land of Hus
Lam 4 21 Edom that swellest in the land of Hus
Husam Gen 36 34 Husam . . . reigned in his stead. 1 Pa 1:45
1 Pa 1 46 Husam also died, and Adad . . . reigned
Husathi 2 K 21 18 then Sobochai of H. slew Saph
Husathite 1 Pa 11 29 valiant . . . Sobbochai a H.
1 Pa 20 4 Sabachai the Husathite slew Saphai
27 11 eighth . . . Sobochai a Husathite
Husati 2 K 23 27 Mobonnai of Husati, Selmon the
husband Gen 3 6 gave to her h. who did eat
Gen 16 2 [Sarai] said to her husband: Behold
3 and gave her to her husband to wife
20 3 thou hast taken; for she hath a h.
29 32 affliction: now my h. will love me
34 now also my h. will be joined to me
30 1 said to her husband: Give me children
5 her husband had gone in unto her [Bala]
9 gave Zelpha her handmaid to her husband
15 that thou hast taken my h. from me
39 16 kept the garment and showed it to her h.
Exod 21 22 as the woman's husband shall require
Lev 21 3 a maiden sister, who hath had no h.
7 one that has been put away from her h.
Num 5 12 gone astray, and contemning her husband
13 and her husband cannot discover it, but
14 if the spirit of jealousy stir up the h.
20 if thou hast gone aside from thy h.
27 having despised her h., be guilty of
29 if a woman hath gone aside from her h.
30 h. stirred up by spirit of jealousy
31 the husband shall be blameless, and
26 59 she bore to her husband Amram sons
30 7 if she have a husband and shall vow
8 the day that her husband shall hear it
11 if the wife in the house of her h.
12 if her husband hear, and hold his peace
13 because her husband gainsaid it and
14 it shall depend on the will of her h.
15 if the h. hearing it hold his peace
17 laws . . . between the h. and the wife
Deut 24 2 is departed and marrieth another h.
4 the former h. cannot take her again
25 11 other's wife willing to deliver her h.
28 56 will envy her husband who lieth in her
Josu 15 18 she was moved by her husband to ask
Judg 1 14 her h. admonished her to ask a field
13 6 when she was come to her husband
9 Manue her husband was not with her
10 she made haste and ran to her husband
14 15 soothe thy husband and persuade him
20 and bridal companions for her husband
19 3 her h. followed her, willing to be
20 3 husband of the woman that was killed
Ruth 1 3 Elimelech the husband of Noemi died
5 having lost both her sons and her h.
2 1 her husband Elimelech had a kinsman
1 K 1 8 Elcana her husband said to her. 23
21 Elcana her h. went up, and all his
22 said to her husband: I will not go
2 19 when she went up with her husband
4 19 father-in-law and her h. were dead
21 and for her father-in-law and her h.
25 3 her h. was churlish and very bad and
17 evil is determined against thy husband
19 but she told not her husband Nabal
2 K 3 15 and took her from her h. Phaltiel
16 her husband followed her, weeping
11 26 heard that Urias her husband was dead
14 5 widow woman; for my husband is dead
7 and will leave my husband no name nor
4 K 4 1 thy servant my husband is dead, and
9 she said to her husband: I perceive
14 she hath no son, and her husband is old
22 she called her h. and said: Send with
26 all well with thee and with thy h.
Tob 2 21 when her husband heard it bleating
3 16 I never coveted a h. and have kept
18 but a husband I consented to take
10 13 to love her husband, to take care of
11 6 returning she told her husband, saying
Jdth 8 2 her husband was Manasses, who died in
7 her husband left her great riches and
15 11 after thy h. hast not known any other
16 26 after the death of Manasses her h.
28 was buried with her h. in Bethulia
Prov 6 34 the jealousy and rage of the husband
7 19 my husband is not at home: he is gone
12 4 diligent woman is a crown to her husband
31 11 heart of her husband trusteth in her
23 her husband is honorable in the gates
28 her husband, and he praised her. Many
Eccu 4 10 merciful . . . as a h. to their mother
22 4 shall bring an inheritance to her h.
5 shameth both her father and husband
23 32 every woman also that leaveth her h.
33 she hath offended against her husband
25 25 her h. groaned, and hearing he sighed
30 have superiority, is contrary to her h.
32 that doth not make her husband happy
26 1 happy is the husband of a good wife
2 a virtuous woman rejoiceth her husband
16 of diligent woman shall delight her h.
36 24 cheereth the countenance of her husband
25 mercy, her h. is not like other men
40 23 above them both is a wife with her h.
42 10 having a h., lest she should misbehave
Isa 54 1 more than of her that hath a husband
Jer 3 14 saith the Lord: for I am your husband
Eze 16 32 that bringeth in strangers over her h.
45 that cast off her h. and her children
44 25 sister, that hath not had another h.
Dan 13 28 people were come to Joakim her husband
63 Susanna, with Joakim her husband, and
Osee 2 2 not my wife, and I am not her husband
7 I will go and return to my first h.
16 that she shall call me: My husband
Joel 1 8 sackcloth for the husband of her youth
Mat 1 16 begot Joseph the husband of Mary
19 Joseph her husband being a just man

Mark 10 12 the wife shall put away her husband
Luke 2 36 had lived with her h. seven years
16 18 that is put away from her husband
John 4 16 go, call thy husband, and come hither
17 I have no husband. Jesus said to her
18 thou now hast, is not thy husband
Acts 5 9 of them who have buried thy husband
10 out, and buried her by her husband
Rom 7 2 the woman that hath an husband, whilst
2 whilst her h. liveth is bound to the law
2 if her h. be dead, she is loosed from the law of her h.
3 whilst her h. liveth, she shall be called
3 if her husband be dead, she is delivered from the law of her h.
1 C 7 2 let every woman have her own husband
3 wife also in like manner to the husband
3 let the h. render the debt to his wife
4 power of her own body, but the husband
4 h. also hath not power of his own body
10 the wife depart not from her husband
11 or be reconciled to her husband. And let
11 let not the husband put away his wife
13 if any woman hath a h. that believeth
13 her, let her not put away her husband
14 the unbelieving husband is sanctified
14 wife is sanctified by the believing h.
16 whether thou shalt save thy husband? Or
34 world, how she may please her husband
39 by law as long as her husband liveth
39 if her husband die, she is at liberty
2 C 11 2 I have espoused you to one husband that
Gal 4 27 more than of her that hath a husband
Eph 5 23 the husband is the head of the wife, as
33 and let the wife fear her husband
1 Tim 3 2 blameless, the husband of one wife
5 9 who hath been the wife of one husband
Titus 1 6 husband of one wife, having faithful
Apoc 21 2 prepared as a bride adorned for her h.
husbandman Gen 4 2 a shepherd, and Cain a h.
Gen 9 20 Noe, a husbandman, began to till
25 27 Esau became skilful hunter and a h.
Wisd 17 16 if any one were a h. or a shepherd
Jer 51 23 I will break in pieces the husbandman
Amos 5 16 they shall call the h. to mourning and
Zach 13 5 I am no prophet, I am a h.: for Adam
John 15 1 vine; and my Father is the husbandman
2 Tim 2 6 the husbandman, that laboreth, must
James 5 7 the h. waiteth for the precious fruit
husbandmen 4 K 25 12 dressers of vines and h.
1 Pa 27 26 over the tillage and the husbandmen
Isa 61 5 the sons of strangers shall be your h.
Jer 14 4 the h. were confounded, they covered
31 24 the h. and they that drive the flocks
52 16 left some for vinedressers and for h.
Joel 1 11 the husbandmen are ashamed, the
Mat 21 33 let it out to h. Mark 12:1; Luke 20:9
34 he sent his servants to the husbandmen
35 the h. laying hands on his servants
38 the h. seeing the son, said among
40 what will he do to those husbandmen
41 will let out his vineyard to other h.
Mark 12 2 and at the season he sent to the h.
2 to receive of the h. of the fruit of
7 but the h. said one to another: This
9 come and destroy those h. Luke 20:16
Luke 20 10 he sent a servant to the h., that they
14 when the h. saw, they thought within
husbandry 2 Pa 26 10 he was a man that loved h.
Eccu 7 16 hate not laborious works nor husbandry
2 Ma 12 1 the Jews gave themselves to husbandry
1 C 3 9 you are God's husbandry; you are God's
husband's Gen 3 16 shalt be under thy h. power
Num 5 19 not defiled by forsaking thy h. bed
Deut 25 7 my husband's brother refuseth to raise
Jdth 16 28 and she abode in her husband's house
Dan 13 7 and walked in her husband's orchard
husbands Num 36 8 shall take h. of the same tribe
Judg 12 9 whom he sent abroad and gave to h.
Ruth 1 9 find rest in houses of the husbands
11 that you may hope for husbands of me
Tob 3 8 she had been given to seven husbands
9 thou murderer of thy h. Wilt thou
10 as thou hast already killed seven h.
6 14 that she hath been given to seven h.
7 11 what had happened to those seven h.
8 12 as it did to the other seven husbands
Esth 1 17 that they will despise their husbands
18 will slight commandments of their h.
20 all wives . . . give honor to their h.
22 that the husbands should be rulers
Jer 18 21 let their husbands be slain by death
29 6 give your daughters to h. and let them
44 19 offerings to her, without our husbands
Eze 16 45 sisters, who cast off their husbands
John 4 18 for thou hast had five husbands: and
1 C 14 35 let them ask their husbands at home. For
Eph 5 22 let women be subject to their husbands
24 also let the wives be to their husbands
25 husbands, love your wives. Col 3:19
Col 3 18 wives, be subject to your husbands
1 Tim 3 12 let deacons be the h. of one wife
Titus 2 4 to love their husbands, to love their
5 gentle, obedient to their husbands
1 P 3 1 let wives be subject to their husbands
5 being in subjection to their own h.: as
7 ye husbands, likewise dwelling with
hushed Soph 1 11 all the people of Chanaan is h.
Husi 3 K 4 16 Baana the son of Husi, in Aser and
Husim Gen 46 23 the sons of Dan: Husim. The sons
1 Pa 8 8 after he sent away Husim and Bara his
husks Osee 3 1 love the husks of the grapes. And I
Luke 15 16 with the husks the swine did eat; and
hyacinth Apoc 9 17 breastplates of fire and of h.
hyacinths Cant 5 14 and as of gold, full of h.
Hyades Job 9 9 maketh Arcturus and Orion and H.
Hymeneus 1 Tim 1 20 of whom is H. and Alexander
2 Tim 2 17 of whom are Hymeneus and Philetus: who
hymn 3 K 8 28 hear the hymn and the prayer which
1 Pa 16 36 the people say Amen, and a hymn to God
Jdth 16 15 let us sing a hymn to the Lord, let us sing a new hymn to our God
Ps 64 2 a hymn, O God, becometh thee in Sion
14 shall shout, yea they shall sing a h.
118 171 my lips shall utter a hymn, when thou
136 3 sing . . . a hymn of the songs of Sion
148 14 a hymn to all his saints: to the
1 Ma 4 24 returning home they sung a hymn and
Mat 26 30 a hymn being said, they went out unto
Mark 14 26 when they had said a hymn, they went
hymns 1 Pa 13 8 played . . . with h. and with harps
2 Pa 7 6 singing the hymns of David by their
1 Es 3 11 they sung together hymns and praise
2 Es 12 8 and their brethren were over the hymns
Ps 60 1 unto the end, in hymns. 66:1
99 4 go ye . . . into his courts with hymns
1 Ma 4 33 let all . . . praise thee with hymns
13 47 and then he entered into it with hymns
51 psalteries and hymns and canticles
2 Ma 1 30 the priests sung h. till the sacrifice
10 38 blessed the Lord with hymns and
12 37 singing hymns with a loud voice, he
Eph 5 19 speaking to yourselves in psalms, and h.
Col 3 16 admonishing one another in psalms, hymns
hypocrisy Isa 32 6 work iniquity, to practice h.
Mat 23 28 you are full of hypocrisy and iniquity

Luke 12 1 leaven of the Pharisees, which is h.
1 Tim 4 2 speaking lies in hypocrisy, and having
hypocrite Job 8 13 hope of the h. shall perish
Job 13 16 no h. shall come before his presence
15 34 the congregation of the h. is barren
17 8 shall be raised up against the h. and
20 5 joy of the hypocrite but for a moment
27 8 what is the hope of the hypocrite if
34 30 maketh a man that is a h. to reign
Eccu 1 37 be not a hypocrite in the sight of men
Isa 9 17 for every one is a hypocrite and wicked
Mat 7 5 h., cast out first the beam. Luke 6:42
hypocrites Isa 33 14 trembling hath seized upon the h.
Mat 6 2 as the hypocrites do in the synagogue
5 you shall not be as the h., that love
16 be not as the hypocrites, sad. For
15 7 h., well hath Isaias prophesied of you
22 18 why do you tempt me, ye hypocrites
23 13 woe to you scribes and Pharisees, hypocrites. 14, 15, 23, 25, 27, 29
24 51 appoint his portion with the hypocrites
Mark 7 6 well did Isaias prophesy of you h.
Luke 12 56 you h., you know how to discern the
13 15 ye h., doth not every one of you on
hyssop Exod 12 22 dip a bunch of h. in the blood
Lev 14 4 offer for himself . . . scarlet and h.
6 he shall dip with . . . the hyssop
49 cedar wood and scarlet and hyssop
51 shall take the cedar wood and the h.
52 with the cedar wood and the hyssop
Num 19 6 shall also take cedar wood and hyssop
3 K 4 33 unto the hyssop that cometh out of wall
Ps 50 9 thou shalt sprinkle me with hyssop and
John 19 29 a sponge full of vinegar about hyssop
Heb 9 19 with water and scarlet wool and hyssop

I

I am: *see* **am**
ibis Lev 11 17 you must not eat . . . the ibis
Isa 34 11 ibis and the raven shall dwell in it
Icamia 1 Pa 2 41 Sellum begot I., and I. begot
ice Job 38 29 out of whose womb came the ice
Ps 148 8 fire, hail, snow, ice, stormy winds
Wisd 16 22 snow and ice endured the force of fire
29 shall melt away as the winter's ice
19 20 food, which was apt to melt as ice
Eccu 3 17 as the ice in the fair warm weather
Dan 3 70 ye ice and snow, bless the Lord
Ichabod 1 K 4 21 she called the child Ichabod
1 K 14 3 Achitob brother to Ichabod the son of
Iconium Acts 13 51 feet against them, came to I.
Acts 14 1 it came to pass in Iconium, that they
18 certain Jews from Antioch and Iconium
20 returned again to Lystra and to Iconium
16 2 brethren that were in Lystra and I.
2 Tim 3 11 came upon me at Antioch, at Iconium and
Icuthiel 1 Pa 4 18 wife Judaia bore . . . Icuthiel
Idaia 1 Pa 4 37 Idaia the son of Semri the son
2 Es 7 39 priests: the children of Idaia . . . 973
11 10 of the priests Idaia the son of Joarib
12 6 went up with Zorobabel . . . Idaia. 7
Idaias Zach 6 10 take of them . . . and of Idaias
Zach 6 14 the crowns shall be to . . . Idaias
Idida 4 K 22 1 the name of his mother was Idida
Idithun 1 Pa 9 16 Galal the son of I. 2 Es 11:17
1 Pa 16 38 Obededom the son of Idithun, and Hosa
41 after him Heman and Idithun and the
42 Heman and Idithun sounded the trumpet
42 the sons of Idithun he made porters
25 1 the ministry the sons of . . . Idithun
3 and of Idithun: the sons of Idithun
3 under the hand of their father Idithun
6 to sing . . . Asaph and Idithun and
2 Pa 5 12 and they that were under Idithun with
29 14 of the sons of Idithun, Semeias and
35 15 Heman and I. the prophets of the king
Ps 38 1 unto the end, for Idithun. 61:1; 76:1
idle Exod 5 8 they are i. and therefore they cry
Exod 5 17 you are idle, and therefore you say
Prov 19 15 and an idle soul shall suffer hunger
31 27 and hath not eaten her bread idle
Ecce 2 21 what he hath gotten to an i. man
12 3 the grinders shall be idle in a small
Wisd 14 5 works of thy wisdom might not be idle
Eccu 33 26 let his hands be idle, and he seeketh
28 send him to work, that he be not idle
37 14 nor with idle servant of much
Mat 12 36 every idle word that men shall speak
20 3 standing in the market place idle. And
6 why stand you here all the day idle
Luke 24 11 these words seemed as idle tales; and they
1 Tim 5 13 being idle they learn to go about from
13 are not only idle, but tattlers also
idleness Prov 12 11 pursueth i. is very foolish
Prov 28 19 he that followeth idleness shall be
Eccu 33 29 for idleness hath taught much evil
Eze 16 49 iniquity of Sodom . . . idleness of her
idol Lev 18 21 to be consecrated to the i. Moloch
Lev 20 2 give of his seed to the idol Moloch
26 1 shall not make to yourselves any idol
Num 23 21 there is no idol in Jacob, neither is
25 18 deceived you by the idol Phogor and
Deut 7 26 anything of the idol into thy house
9 12 have made to themselves a molten idol
Judg 18 30 set up to themselves the graven idol
31 the idol of Michas remained with them
3 K 11 5 and Moloch the idol of the Ammonites
7 a temple for Chamos the idol of Moab
7 Moloch the i. of the children of Ammon
15 13 and broke in pieces the filthy idol
4 K 21 7 he set also an idol of the grove which
23 13 Astaroth the idol of the Sidonians
2 Pa 15 16 had made in a grove an idol of Priapus
33 15 the idol out of the house of the Lord
Wisd 14 8 idol that is made by hands, is cursed
Eccu 30 19 what good . . . an offering do to an i.
Isa 10 10 hath found the kingdoms of the idol
40 20 set up an idol that may not be moved
44 19 of residue thereof shall I make an i.
66 3 incense, as if he should bless an idol
Jer 2 11 have changed their glory into an idol
4 15 notice of the idol from mount Ephraim
10 14 artist is confounded in his graven i.
51 17 every founder is confounded by his i.
Eze 8 3 where was set the idol of jealousy to
5 the idol of jealousy in the very entry
Dan 14 2 the Babylonians had an idol called Bel
Osee 10 8 the high places of the idol, the sin
12 8 become rich, I have found me an idol
11 if Galaad be an idol, then in vain
Amos 1 5 inhabitants from the plain of the idol
7 9 high places of the i. shall be thrown
16 not drop thy word upon house of the i.
Zach 11 17 shepherd and idol, that forsaketh the
1 Ma 1 57 set up the abominable i. of desolation
62 they sacrificed upon altar of the idol
1 C 8 4 we know that an idol is nothing in the
7 with the conscience of the idol: eat as
7 eat as a thing sacrificed to an idol
10 19 anything? Or, that the idol is anything
idolaters 1 C 6 9 not err: neither fornicators nor i.
1 C 10 7 neither become ye idolaters, as some of
Apoc 21 8 sorcerers and idolaters and all liars
idolatry 1 K 15 23 like the crime of i. to refuse
Acts 17 16 seeing city wholly given to idolatry

Gal 5 19 immodesty, luxury, idolatry, witchcrafts
idol's 1 Ma 10 83 Bethdagon, their idol's temple
1 C 8 10 sit at meat in the idol's temple, shall
idols Gen 31 19 Rachel stole away her father's i.
Gen 31 34 she in haste hid the idols under the
Exod 34 15 gods, and have adored their idols
Lev 26 30 your high places and break your idols
30 shall fall among ruins of your idols
Deut 12 3 with fire and break their i. in pieces
29 17 their idols, wood and stone, silver and
Judg 3 19 from Galgal, where the idols were
26 and passed by the place of the idols
10 6 and served idols, Baalim and Astaroth
16 away out of their coasts all the idols
17 5 a priestly garment and idols: and he
18 18 ephod and the idols and the molten god
20 took the ephod and the idols and the
1 K 31 9 publish it in the temples of their idols
2 K 5 21 they left there their idols: which David
3 K 15 12 he removed all the filth of the idols
21 26 followed the i. which the Amorrhites
4 K 16 3 according to the idols of the nations
17 41 nevertheless served also their idols
21 2 according to the idols of the nations
23 24 figures of idols . . . Josias took away
1 Pa 10 9 and shown in the temples of the idols
16 26 all the gods of the nations are idols
2 Pa 15 8 took away the i. out of all the land
23 17 they broke down his altars and his i.
24 18 served groves and idols, and wrath came
30 14 in which incense was burnt to idols
31 1 they broke the idols and cut down the
33 22 he sacrificed to all the idols which
34 3 high places and the groves and the i.
4 demolished the idols that had been set
5 burnt . . . on the altars of the idols
7 and had broken the idols in pieces.
Tob 14 8 the Gentiles shall leave their idols
Esth 14 8 their hands to the power of their idols
10 may . . . praise the strength of idols
Ps 96 7 graven things, and that glory in their i.
105 36 and served their idols: and it became
38 they sacrificed to the idols of Chanaan
113 4 i. of Gentiles are silver and. 134:15
Wisd 14 11 had even to the idols of the Gentiles
12 of fornication is the devising of idols
27 worship of abominable i. is the cause
29 whilst they trust in idols, which are
30 giving heed to idols, and have sworn
15 15 esteemed all the idols of the heathens
Isa 1 29 they shall be confounded for the idols
2 8 their land also is full of idols: they
18 and idols shall be utterly destroyed
20 shall cast away his idols of silver and his idols of gold. 31:7
10 10 their idols of Jerusalem and of Samaria
11 as I have done to Samaria and her i.
11 so do to Jerusalem and her idols? And
19 1 the idols of Egypt shall be moved at
3 and they shall consult their idols
41 29 vain: their idols are wind and vanity
44 9 makers of i. are all of them nothing
46 1 their idols are put upon beasts and
48 5 shouldst say: My idols have done these
57 5 your comfort in idols under every green
65 4 and sleep in the temple of idols: that
Jer 2 8 prophesied in Baal, and followed idols
8 19 provoked me to wrath with their idols
16 18 my land with the carcasses of their i.
32 34 they have set their idols in the house
44 23 because you have sacrificed to idols
50 2 confounded, their idols are overthrown
38 because it is a land of idols, and they
51 47 and I will visit the idols of Babylon
Bar 6 72 is the just man that hath no idols
Eze 6 4 your idols shall be broken in pieces
4 cast down your slain before your idols
5 dead carcasses . . . before your idols
6 your idols shall be no more, and your
9 that went a fornicating after their i.
13 your slain shall be amongst your i.
13 frankincense to all their idols. And
7 20 images of their abominations and idols
8 10 the idols of the house of Israel. 18:6, 15
14 5 departed from me through all their i.
6 converted, and depart from your idols
7 and place his idols in his heart and
16 36 with the idols of thy abominations
18 12 and that lifteth up his eyes to idols
20 7 defile not yourselves with i. of Egypt
8 did they forsake the idols of Egypt
16 their heart went after idols. Yet my
18 nor be ye defiled with their idols
24 been after the idols of their fathers
31 defile yourselves with all your idols
39 walk ye every one after your idols
39 defile my holy name . . . with your idols
21 21 he inquired of the idols and consulted
22 3 that hath made idols against herself
4 thou art defiled in thy idols which
23 30 thou wast defiled with their idols
37 committed fornication with their idols
39 sacrificed their children to their idols
49 you shall bear the sins of your idols
30 13 I will also destroy the idols, and I
13 I will make an end of the idols of
36 18 and with their idols they defiled it
25 I will cleanse you from all your idols
37 23 be defiled any more with their idols
44 10 have wandered from me after their idols
12 ministered to them before their idols
Dan 14 4 I do not worship idols made with hands
Osee 4 17 Ephraim is a partaker with idols, let
6 8 Galaad is a city of workers of idols
8 4 and their gold they have made idols
10 1 he hath abounded with idols. Their heart
2 he shall break down their idols, he
11 2 to Baalim and sacrificed to idols
13 2 of their silver as the likeness of idols
14 9 what have I to do any more with idols
Amos 2 4 their idols have caused them to err
5 26 Moloch, and the image of your idols
Mich 1 7 will bring to destruction all her idols
Haba 2 18 his own forging, to make dumb idols
Zach 10 2 for the idols have spoken what was
13 2 I will destroy the names of idols out
1 Ma 1 45 they sacrificed to idols, and profaned
50 to be built, and temples and idols
2 23 to sacrifice to the i. upon the altar
3 48 searched for the likeness of their idols
13 47 houses wherein there had been idols
2 Ma 2 2 seeing the idols of gold and silver
10 2 streets, as also the temples of the i.
12 40 of the donaries of the idols of Jamnia
Acts 15 20 themselves from pollutions of idols, and
29 things sacrificed to idols. Apoc 2:20
17 23 passing by, and seeing your idols, I
21 25 that which has been offered to idols
Rom 2 22 thou that abhorrest idols, committest
1 C 5 10 extortioners, or the servers of idols
11 a server of idols, or a railer, or a
8 1 things that are sacrificed to idols. 10
4 meats that are sacrificed to idols, we
10 14 fly from the service of idols. I speak
19 what is offered in sacrifice to idols

illness 4 K 1 2 shall recover of this my illness
4 K 8 8 saying: Can I recover of this my i. 9
13 14 sick of the illness whereof he died
2 Pa 16 12 in his illness he did not seek the Lord
21 19 and he died of a most wretched illness
illnesses Jer 16 4 by the death of grievous i.
illuminated Heb 6 4 who were once i., have tasted
Heb 10 32 being i., you endured a great fight of
illumination 2 Tim 1 10 manifest by i. of our Savior
illusions Ps 37 8 my loins are filled with i.
illustrious 2 K 1 19 the i. of Israel are slain
1 Pa 11 21 illustrious among the second three and
1 Ma 1 11 wicked root, Antiochus the Illustrious
10 1 Antiochus, surnamed the Illustrious
2 Ma 2 21 also the wars against Antiochus the I.
4 7 Antiochus, who was called the I. 10:9
10 13 coming over to Antiochus the I., had
Illyricum Rom 15 19 round about as far as unto I.
image Gen 1 26 let us make man to our image and
Gen 1 27 and God created man to his own image
27 to the image of God he created him
5 3 begot a son to his own i. and likeness
9 6 for man was made to the image of God
Num 23 21 neither is there an i. god to be seen
Deut 4 16 similitude or image of male or female
1 K 19 13 Michol took an image and laid it on the
16 they found an image upon the bed and
2 Pa 3 10 of holies two cherubims of image work
Job 4 16 an image before my eyes, and I heard
Ps 38 7 surely man passeth as an image: yea
72 20 thou shalt bring their i. to nothing
Wisd 2 23 to the i. of his own likeness he made
7 26 majesty and the image of his goodness
13 13 and maketh it like the image of a man
16 it is an image and hath need of help
14 15 made to himself the image of his son
17 and made an express image of the king
15 5 loveth lifeless figure of a dead image
17 20 an image of that darkness which was to
Eccu 17 1 and made him after his own image. And
Isa 40 18 what image will you make for him? Hath
44 13 and he hath made the image of a man
Jer 2 6 land of drought and the image of death
Amos 5 26 tabernacle for . . . image of your idols
Haba 2 18 graven it, a molten and a false image
Mat 22 20 whose image and inscription. Mark 12:16
Luke 20:24
Rom 1 23 God into the likeness of the image of a
8 29 conformable to the image of his Son
1 C 11 7 he is the image and glory of God; but
15 49 have borne the image of the earthly, let
49 let us bear also image of the heavenly
2 C 3 18 into the same image from glory to glory
4 4 Christ, who is the image of God, should
Col 1 15 who is the image of the invisible God
3 10 according to the image of him that
Heb 10 1 not the very image of the things; by the
Apoc 13 14 should make the image of the beast
15 to give life to the image of the beast
15 that the i. of the beast should speak
15 will not adore the image of the beast
14 9 shall adore the beast and his image
11 who have adored the beast and his i.
15 2 that had overcome the beast and his i.
16 2 them that adored the image thereof
19 20 of the beast, and who adored his image
20 4 had not adored the beast nor his image
images 4 K 11 18 his images they broke in pieces
Eze 7 20 made of it the i. of their abominations
16 17 thou madest thee images of men and
23 14 i. of the Chaldeans set forth in colors
imagination Gen 8 21 i. and thought of man's heart
Eccu 22 22 fearful heart in the i. of a fool
40 2 their imagination of things to come
imaginations Lam 3 61 all their i. against me
imagine Prov 26 5 lest he i. himself to be wise
Zach 8 17 let none of you imagine evil in your
2 P 3 9 delayeth not his promise, as some i.
imagined Wisd 13 2 have i. either the fire or
Eccu 25 9 that are not to be imagined by the
Osee 7 15 they have imagined evil against me
1 Ma 6 8 had not fallen out to him as he i.
imaginest Jdth 6 5 thou i. these my words cannot
imagineth Nah 1 11 that i. evil against the Lord
imbrued 2 K 20 12 Amasa i. with blood lay in the
imitate Deut 12 30 beware lest thou imitate them
Deut 18 9 to i. abominations of those nations
Wisd 4 2 when it is present, they imitate it
Bar 6 4 that you imitate not the doings of
2 Th 3 7 know how you ought to imitate us: for
9 ourselves a pattern unto you, to i. us
imitatest Job 15 5 i. the tongue of blasphemers
imitating 2 Pa 21 13 i. the fornication of . . . Achab
Eccu 45 28 by i. him in the fear of the Lord
Eze 21 23 and imitating the leisure of sabbaths
immaculate 2 K 22 31 his way is i., the word
immense Exod 8 14 them together into i. heaps
Deut 17 17 nor immense sums of silver and gold
3 K 3 8 an i. people which cannot be numbered
10 2 an i. quantity of gold and precious
1 Pa 22 3 joinings: and of brass an i. weight
2 Pa 17 5 he acquired i. riches and much glory
24 11 there was gathered an i. sum of money
28 8 Israel carried away . . . immense booty
Eccu 16 17 my soul in such an immense creation
30 15 a sound body, than immense revenues
Bar 3 25 hath no end: it is high and immense
2 Ma 3 6 was full of immense sums of money and
immensely Josu 22 10 they built an altar i. great
immoderate Prov 15 4 is i. shall crush the spirit
immodesty Gal 5 19 are fornication, uncleanness, i.
immolate Lev 1 5 shall i. the calf before the Lord
Lev 1 11 he shall i. it at the side of the altar
3 13 and shall immolate it in the entry
4 29 i. it in the place of the holocaust
33 shall i. it in the place where the
9 4 i. them before the Lord, offering for
14 13 he shall immolate the lamb where the
19 then shall he immolate the holocaust
16 11 for his own house, he shall immolate it
22 29 if you i. a victim for thanksgiving
Num 6 17 ram he shall i. for a sacrifice
19 3 shall immolate her in the sight of all
Deut 16 5 mayst not i. the phase in any one
6 thou shalt immolate the phase in the
27 7 shalt immolate peace victims, and eat
3 K 13 2 he shall i. upon thee the priests of
Isa 65 3 that i. in gardens, and sacrifice upon
Mich 4 13 shalt i. the spoils of them to the
immolated Lev 4 15 calf being i. in the sight
Lev 4 24 when he hath i. it in the place where
6 25 it shall be immolated before the Lord
7 2 where the holocaust is i., the victim
8 15 he i. it: and took the blood, and
19 he i. it and poured the blood thereof
23 when Moses had i. it, he took of the
24 blood of the ram that was immolated
9 8 to the altar, i. the calf for his sin
12 he i. also the victim of holocaust
18 he i. also the bullock and the ram
14 5 command one of the sparrows to be i.
6 the blood of the sparrow that is i. 51
13 where victim for sin is wont to be i.
14 the victim that was i. for trespass
25 the lamb being i., he shall put of
50 having i. one sparrow in an earthen

Josu 8 31 [Josue] i. victims of peace offerings
1 K 1 25 they i. a calf and offered the child
2 Pa 29 24 priests immolated them and sprinkled
30 15 immolated the phase on the 14th day
17 and therefore the Levites i. the phase
35 11 the phase was i.: and the priests
1 Ma 1 50 swine's flesh to be i., and unclean
immolateth Num 15 4 whosoever i. the victim
immolating 2 Pa 30 22 i. victims of peace offerings
immortal Wisd 1 15 for justice is perpetual and i.
Wisd 4 1 the memory thereof is i.: because it is
Eccu 17 29 because the son of man is not i.
1 Tim 1 17 to the king of ages, immortal, invisible
immortality Wisd 3 4 their hope is full of i.
Wisd 8 13 by the means of her I shall have i.
17 to be allied to wisdom is immortality
15 3 thy power is the root of immortality
Eccu 6 16 friend is the medicine of life and i.
1 C 15 53 and this mortal must put on immortality
54 when this mortal hath put on immortality
1 Tim 6 16 lords; who only hath immortality, and
immoveable 1 Pa 16 30 he hath founded the world i.
Tob 2 14 continued immoveable in the fear of God
Col 1 23 immoveable from the hope of the gospel
Heb 12 27 things may remain which are immoveable
28 receiving an i. kingdom, we have grace
immunity 1 Ma 10 34 be all days of i. and freedom
1 Ma 13 34 that he should grant an i. to the land
immutability Heb 6 17 promise the i. of his counsel
immutable Heb 6 18 by two immutable things, in
impart Rom 1 11 I may i. unto you some spiritual
1 Th 2 8 we would gladly impart unto you not only
Heb 13 16 not forget to do good and to impart
imparteth 2 Ma 8 12 he i. to the Jews that were
impassable Isa 35 1 land that was desolate and i.
Isa 41 18 the i. land into streams of waters
impatience Jdth 8 24 but uttered their impatience
impatient Prov 14 17 the i. man shall work folly
Prov 14 29 that is impatient, exalteth his folly
19 19 he that is i., shall suffer damage
impediment Exod 4 10 I have more i. and slowness
1 C 7 35 attend upon the Lord, without i. But
impenitent Rom 2 5 to thy hardness and i. heart
imperfect Ps 138 16 eyes did see my imperfect being
imperial Dan 6 7 an i. decree . . . be published
impieties 2 Ma 8 33 a worthy reward for his i.
impiety Lev 19 7 he shall be . . . guilty of i.
Eze 7 11 iniquity is risen up into a rod of i.
2 Ma 4 38 wherein he had committed the impiety
impious 2 Ma 4 13 that i. wretch and no priest
importunate Gen 39 10 the woman was i. with the
2 Th 3 2 and that we may be delivered from i.
importunity Luke 11 8 because of his i., he will
impose Josu 9 22 why would you impose upon us
1 Es 7 24 you have no authority to impose toll or
Mat 19 13 that he should impose hands upon them
1 Tim 5 22 impose not hands lightly upon any man
imposed Mat 19 15 when he had imposed hands upon
Acts 6 6 they praying, imposed hands upon them
19 6 when Paul had imposed his hands on
imposing Acts 13 3 i. their hands upon them, sent
imposition Acts 8 18 i. of hands of the apostles
1 Tim 4 14 with imposition of the hands of the
2 Tim 1 6 in thee, by the imposition of my hands
Heb 6 2 of baptisms, and imposition of hands
impossible Wisd 16 15 it is i. to escape thy hand
Dan 4 6 no secret is impossible to thee: tell
2 Ma 4 6 was i. that matters should be settled
Mat 17 19 and nothing shall be impossible to you
19 26 with men this is impossible. Mark 10:27
Luke 1 37 no word shall be impossible with God
17 1 it is i. that scandals should not come
18 27 the things that are i. with men, are
Acts 2 24 i. that he should be holden by it
Heb 6 4 for it is i. for those who were once
18 in which it is impossible for God to lie
10 4 it is i. that with the blood of oxen
11 6 without faith it is i. to please God
impotent Acts 14 7 man at Lystra, i. in his feet, a
impoverished Lev 25 25 if thy brother being i. 47
Lev 25 35 if thy brother be i. and weak of hand
2 Es 5 18 the people were very much impoverished
imprecation 3 K 8 38 i. shall happen to any man
Josu 6 25 Josue made an i., saying: Cursed be
impregnable Jdth 7 9 they suppose . . . to be i.
2 Ma 12 21 it was impregnable and hard to come at
imprisoned Wisd 18 4 of light and i. in darkness
imprudence Prov 14 8 and the i. of fools erreth
Prov 14 24 is their riches: the folly of fools, i.
imprudent Ecce 7 26 to know . . . the error of the i.
impudence Eccu 25 29 a woman's anger and impudence
Eccu 26 14 take heed of the impudence of her eyes
impudent Prov 7 13 and with an i. face, flattereth
Isa 56 11 impudent dogs, they never had enough
impudently Prov 21 29 wicked man i. hardeneth his
Eze 23 12 i. prostituting herself to the children
impugned Gal 1 23 now preach faith which once he i.
impunity Esth 3 8 they should grow insolent by i.
impulse Eze 1 12 whither the i. of the spirit
Eze 10 22 i. of every one to go straight forward
impurities Rom 13 13 not in chambering and i., not
impute 2 K 19 19 impute not to me, my lord, the
2 Pa 30 19 will not impute it to them that they
imputed Deut 23 21 shall be i. to thee for a sin
1 Pa 21 3 which may be imputed as a sin to Israel
Job 42 8 that folly be not imputed to you: for
Ps 31 2 to whom the Lord hath not imputed sin
Eze 33 16 he hath committed, shall be i. to him
Rom 4 8 man to whom the Lord hath not i. sin
5 13 sin was not imputed, when law was not
imputing 2 C 5 19 not imputing to them their sins
inaccessible 1 Tim 6 16 inhabiteth light i., whom no
inactive Eccu 11 12 an i. man that wanteth help
inbred 2 Ma 6 23 the i. honor of his gray head
incapable Osee 8 5 how long will they be i. of
incense Exod 25 6 and for sweet smelling incense
Exod 30 1 make also an altar to burn incense
7 Aaron shall burn sweet smelling incense
8 he shall burn an everlasting incense
9 not offer . . . i. of another composition
20 to offer on it incense to the Lord
27 anoint . . . the altars of incense and
35 thou shalt make incense compounded by
36 most holy shall this incense be unto you
31 8 they may make . . . the altars of incense
11 incense of spices . . . shall they make
35 8 make ointment and most sweet incense
15 the altar of incense and the bars
15 oil of unction and the incense of spices
28 to make the incense of most sweet
37 25 he made also the altar of incense
29 he compounded also . . . incense of the
39 37 they offered . . . the incense of spices
40 5 whereon the incense is burnt, before
Lev 4 7 upon horns of the altar of the sweet i.
10 1 put fire therein and incense on it
16 12 the compounded perfume for incense
40 25 burnt upon it the incense of spices
Num 4 16 to whose charge . . . the sweet incense
7 14 a little mortar . . . full of incense. 20, 26,
32, 38, 44, 50, 56, 62, 68, 74, 80
86 mortars of gold full of incense
16 7 put incense upon it before the Lord
17 censers, and put incense upon them
35 the 250 men that offered the incense
38 because incense hath been offered in

40 come near to offer incense to the Lord
46 put incense upon it and go quickly
47 he [Aaron] offered the incense: and
Deut 33 10 they shall put incense in thy wrath
1 K 2 28 to go up to my altar and burn incense
3 K 3 3 sacrificed in high places, and burnt i.
9 25 and he burnt incense before the Lord
11 8 who burnt incense . . . to their gods
12 33 went upon the altar to burn incense
13 1 when Jeroboam was . . . burning incense
2 who now burn incense upon thee, and
22 44 burnt incense in the high places. 4 K 12:3; 14:4; 15:4, 35; 2 Pa 28:4
4 K 16 4 he sacrificed also and burnt incense
17 11 they burnt incense there upon altars
18 4 children of Israel burnt incense to it
23 5 them also that burnt incense to Baal
1 Pa 6 49 and upon the altar of incense for
23 13 and to burn incense before the Lord
28 18 for the altar of incense, he gave
2 Pa 2 4 to burn incense before him and to
6 that incense may be burnt before him
13 11 incense made according to the ordinance
25 14 adored them and burnt incense to them
26 16 to burn incense upon the altar of incense
18 not belong to thee, Ozias, to burn i.
19 in his hand the censer to burn incense
19 house of the Lord at the altar of i.
28 3 burnt incense in the valley of Benennom
29 7 and have not burnt incense nor offered
11 to worship him and to burn i. to him
30 14 in which incense was burnt to idols
32 12 altar and upon it you shall burn i.
Ps 140 2 let my prayer be directed as incense
Wisd 18 21 prayer and by i. making supplication
Eccu 45 20 to offer sacrifice to God, incense and
Isa 1 13 vain: incense is an abomination to me
43 23 oblations nor wearied thee with i.
66 3 he that remembereth incense, as if he
Jer 41 5 they had offerings and i. in their hand
Eze 8 11 a cloud of smoke went up from the i.
16 18 settest my oil and my sweet incense
23 41 whereupon thou didst set my incense
Dan 2 46 in sacrifice to him victims and i.
3 38 neither is there . . . oblation or i.
Osee 2 13 Baalim, to whom she burnt incense and
4 13 mountains, and burnt i. upon the hills
1 Ma 1 58 they burnt incense and sacrificed at
2 15 to compel them . . . to burn incense
4 49 the candlestick and the altar of incense
50 they put i. upon the altar and lighted
2 Ma 2 5 and the ark and the altar of incense
10 3 and set forth incense and lamps and
Luke 1 9 it was his lot to offer incense, going
10 without, at the hour of incense. And
11 on the right side of the altar of i.
Apoc 8 3 there was given to him much incense
4 incense of the prayers of the saints
incensed Prov 28 4 keep it, are i. against him
2 Ma 7 39 the king being i. with anger, raged
14 11 of Judas, i. Demetrius against him
Acts 14 2 Jews stirred up and i. the minds of the
incest Lev 18 17 such copulation is incest
inches Exod 25 25 a polished crown, four i. high
incisions Lev 21 5 nor make i. in their flesh
incited 2 Ma 4 1 as though he had i. Heliodorus
inclinations Prov 20 11 by his i. a child is known
Bar 1 22 after the i. of his own wicked heart
1 Ma 10 47 and their i. were towards Alexander
incline Josu 24 23 and i. your hearts to the Lord
3 K 8 58 may he incline our hearts to himself
4 K 19 16 incline thy ear, and hear: open, O Lord
Ps 16 6 i. thy ear unto me and hear my words
44 11 daughter, and see and incline thy ear
48 5 I will incline my ear to a parable: I
70 2 incline thy ear unto me and save me
77 1 i. your ears to the words of my mouth
85 1 incline thy ear, O Lord, and hear me
87 3 before thee: i. thy ear to my petition
101 3 when I am in trouble, i. thy ear to me
118 36 incline my heart into thy testimonies
140 4 incline not my heart to evil words: to
Prov 2 2 incline thy heart to know prudence
3 thou wilt . . . i. thy heart to prudence
4 20 and incline thy ear to my sayings
5 1 and incline thy ear to my prudence
22 17 incline thy ear and hear the words of
Eccu 2 2 incline thy ear and receive the words
6 34 if thou wilt incline thy ear, thou
Isa 37 17 incline, O Lord, thy ear and hear
55 3 incline your ear and come to me: hear
Jer 17 23 did not hear nor incline their ear
34 14 to me, nor did they incline their ear
Bar 2 16 incline thy ear and hear us. Open thy
Dan 9 18 incline, O my God, thy ear and hear
inclined Judg 9 3 they inclined their hearts after
2 K 19 14 i. the heart of all the men of Juda
1 Es 7 28 and hath inclined his mercy toward me
Ps 114 2 he hath inclined his ear unto me: and
118 112 I have inclined my heart to do thy
Prov 5 13 have not inclined my ear to masters
22 9 he that is i. to mercy shall be blessed
Jer 7 24 they hearkened not nor i. their ear
26 not hearkened to me, nor i. their ear
11 8 they obeyed not nor inclined their ear
25 4 hearkened nor i. your ears to hear
35 15 you have not inclined your ear nor
44 5 they heard not nor inclined their ear
inclineth Prov 2 18 for her house i. unto death
incommunicable Wisd 14 21 gave the i. name to
incomparably Jdth 10 4 she appeared . . . i. lovely
incomprehensible Job 9 10 doth things great and i.
Jer 32 19 great in counsel and i. in thought
Rom 11 33 how incomprehensible are his judgments
inconsiderately Job 39 34 answer, who hath spoken i.
inconstancy James 3 16 there is i. and every evil
inconstant James 1 8 a double minded man is i. in
incontinency 1 C 7 5 lest Satan tempt you for your i.
incontinent 2 Tim 3 3 slanderers, i., unmerciful
incorruptible Wisd 2 23 God created man i. and to
Rom 1 23 they changed glory of the i. God into
1 C 9 25 corruptible crown; but we an i. one
15 52 the dead shall rise again incorruptible
1 P 1 4 unto an inheritance i. and undefiled
23 not of corruptible seed, but i. by
incorruptibility 1 P 3 4 the i. of a quiet and a
incorruption Wisd 6 19 the firm foundation of i.
Wisd 6 20 and incorruption bringeth near to God
Rom 2 7 seek glory and honor and i., eternal
1 C 15 42 sown in corruption, it shall rise in i.
50 neither shall corruption possess i.
53 for this corruptible must put on i.
Eph 6 24 that love our Lord Jesus Christ in i.
2 Tim 1 10 brought to light life and incorruption
increase Gen 1 22 i. and multiply. 28; 8:17; 9:1
Gen 9 7 increase you and multiply and go upon
17 6 I will make thee increase exceedingly
20 I will . . . increase and multiply him
24 60 mayst thou increase to thousands of
26 22 and made us to increase upon the earth
28 3 bless thee and make thee to increase
35 11 i. thou and be multiplied. Nations
48 4 I will cause thee to i. and multiply
Lev 19 25 eat fruits thereof, gathering the i.
25 16 jubilee, the more shall the price i.
37 nor exact of him any increase of fruits

26 4 ground shall bring forth its increase
9 I will look on you and make you i.
20 the ground shall not bring forth her i.
Num 32 14 the i. and offspring of sinful men
Deut 7 22 the beasts of the earth should increase
20 19 neither can it increase the number of
28 59 the Lord shall increase thy plagues
32 22 shall devour earth with her increase
2 K 24 3 the Lord thy God increase thy people
Tob 14 4 with great increase of the fear of God
Ps 91 15 they shall still i. in a fruitful old
Prov 4 9 she shall give to thy head i. of graces
13 11 is gathered with the hand shall i.
22 16 the poor, to increase his own riches
29 2 when just men increase, the people
Eccu 1 21 shall fill all her house with her i.
23 3 lest my ignorances increase and my
28 12 his riches he shall increase his anger
44 22 that he should i. as the dust of the
45 25 the firstfruits of the i. of the earth
Isa 1 5 you that increase transgression? The
29 19 the meek shall increase their joy in
Jer 2 3 to the Lord, the firstfruits of his i.
3 16 and increase in the land in those days
23 3 they shall increase and be multiplied
31 12 and the increase of cattle and herds
Eze 16 7 and thou didst increase and grow great
18 8 not lent upon usury nor taken any i.
13 upon usury, and that taketh an increase
17 hath not taken usury and increase, but
22 12 thou hast taken usury and increase and
34 27 and the earth shall yield her increase
36 30 will multiply . . . the i. of the field
Dan 11 39 he shall i. glory and shall give them
Amos 8 5 lessen the measure and i. the sicle
Zach 8 12 the earth shall give her increase and
1 Ma 9 66 he began to slay and to i. in forces
14 8 the land of Juda yielded her increase
2 Ma 4 13 an increase and progress of heathenish
Luke 17 5 said to the Lord: Increase our faith
John 3 30 he must i., but I must decrease. He
1 C 3 6 Apollo watered, but God gave increase
7 watereth; but God that giveth increase
2 C 9 10 and increase the growth of the fruits
Eph 4 16 part, maketh increase of the body, unto
Col 2 19 groweth unto the increase of God. If
increased Gen 7 17 the waters i. and lifted up
Gen 26 29 with peace have sent thee away i.
41 56 the famine increased daily in all the
Exod 1 7 the children of Israel increased and
12 the more they were multiplied and i.
5 5 you see that the multitude is i.: how
9 34 the thunders were ceased, i. his sin
23 30 till thou be increased and dost possess
Num 16 42 when . . . the tumult increased, Moses
1 K 14 19 uproar . . . and it increased by degrees
2 K 15 12 the people running together i. with
2 Pa 28 22 he [Achaz] i. contempt against the Lord
Jdth 10 4 the Lord increased this her beauty, so
Job 1 10 and his possession hath i. on the earth
Ps 48 17 when the glory of his house shall be i.
104 24 he increased his people exceedingly
Eccu 2 3 that thy life may be i. in the latter
50 20 house the sound of sweet melody was i.
24 who hath i. our days from our mother's
Isa 9 3 the nation, and hast not i. the joy
Eze 23 14 and she increased her fornications
28 5 thou hast increased thy strength: and
36 11 and they shall be multiplied and i.
1 Ma 1 42 her dishonor was i. according to her
2 30 because afflictions i. upon them. And
2 Ma 4 4 which increased the malice of Simon
Mark 4 8 grew up and increased and yielded
Acts 2 47 Lord i. daily together such as should
5 14 believed in the Lord, was more i.
6 7 word of the Lord increased. 12:24
7 17 the people i. and were multiplied in
9 22 Saul increased much more in strength
16 5 faith, and increased in number daily
increaseth Prov 4 18 path of the just . . . i. even
Isa 40 29 i. force and might to them that are not
increasing Gen 26 13 he went on prospering and i.
1 Pa 11 9 David went on growing and increasing
Eccu 43 8 name, i. wonderfully in her perfection
2 Ma 4 50 Menelaus . . . increasing in malice
9 11 his pains i. every moment. And when
Acts 6 1 the number of the disciples increasing
2 C 10 15 but having hope of your increasing faith
Col 1 10 and increasing in the knowledge of God
incredible Acts 26 8 should it be thought a thing i.
Judg 20 5 wife with an i. fury of lust, so that
incredulity Mark 16 14 upbraided them with their i.
incredulous Num 20 10 hear, ye rebellious and i.
Num 20 24 he was i. to my words at the waters
Deut 1 26 but being i. to the word of the Lord
Wisd 10 7 of salt is a monument of an i. soul
Eccu 1 36 be not i. to the fear of the Lord: and
2 18 that fear the Lord, will not be i.
16 29 be not thou i. to his word. After this
Mark 9 18 i. generation, how long shall I be
Luke 1 17 and the i. to the wisdom of the just
Acts 26 19 I was not i. to the heavenly vision: but
Titus 1 16 being abominable and i., and to every
3 3 were some time unwise, incredulous
Heb 3 18 but to them that were incredulous? and
1 P 3 20 which had been some time incredulous
incur Lev 19 17 lest thou incur sin through him
Lev 21 1 let not a priest incur an uncleanness
Deut 24 8 thou i. not the stroke of the leprosy
incurable Deut 28 35 be thou i. from the sole of
Deut 32 33 the venom of asps, which is incurable
2 Pa 21 18 the Lord struck him with an i. disease
Eccu 28 30 and thy fall be incurable unto death
Isa 14 6 the people in wrath with an i. wound
Jer 30 12 thy bruise is incurable, thy wound is
15 for thy affliction? thy sorrow is i.
2 Ma 9 5 with an i. and an invisible plague
incurred 2 Ma 4 16 they i. a dangerous contention
incursions 1 Ma 15 41 and make i. upon the ways of
indebted 1 Ma 10 43 shall flee, being i. to the
Luke 11 4 every one that is indebted to us. And
indecently Lam 5 13 they abused the young men i.
India Esth 1 1 reigned from India to Ethiopia
Esth 8 9 provinces, from India even to Ethiopia
13 1 who reigneth from India to Ethiopia
16 1 Artaxerxes, from India to Ethiopia
Job 28 16 compared with the dyed colors of India
Indian Eze 27 6 made thee benches of I. ivory
1 Ma 6 37 and an Indian to rule the beast
Indians 1 Ma 8 8 the country of the I. and of
indigence Prov 28 27 his entreaty, shall suffer i.
indigent Eccu 40 29 in thy lifetime be not i.
indignation Gen 27 45 and his i. cease, and he
Exod 32 11 why, O Lord, is thy i. enkindled
Lev 10 6 and i. come upon all the congregation
Num 1 53 lest there come indignation upon the
18 5 lest i. rise upon the children of
Deut 1 37 neither is his i. against the people to
9 19 I feared his indignation and anger
29 23 the Lord destroyed in his wrath and i.
28 cast them out . . . in very great i.
Josu 23 16 shall the i. of the Lord rise up
1 K 28 18 didst thou execute the wrath of his i.
2 K 6 7 indignation of the Lord was enkindled
4 K 3 27 there was great indignation in Israel
5 12 and was going away with indignation

22 17 my i. shall be kindled against this
23 26 from the wrath of his great indignation
2 Pa 28 11 indignation of Lord hangeth over you
29 10 will turn away the wrath of his i.
30 8 wrath of his i. shall be turned away
Jdth 3 2 let thy indignation towards us cease
5 2 with exceeding great fury and i., and
7 24 perhaps he will put a stop to his i.
8 12 that may stir up wrath and enkindle i.
Esth 1 18 the king's indignation is just. If
Job 3 26 and indignation is come upon me
17 7 my eye is dim through indignation
20 23 may send forth the wrath of his i.
30 28 I went mourning, without indignation
32 2 and Eliu . . . was moved to indignation
40 6 scatter the proud in thy indignation
Ps 6 2 rebuke me not in thy indignation nor
8 my eye is troubled through indignation
29 6 wrath is in his indignation; and life
37 2 rebuke me not, O Lord, in thy i.: nor
68 25 pour out thy indignation upon them
77 49 he sent upon them the wrath of his i.
49 indignation and wrath and trouble
84 4 away from the wrath of thy indignation
89 7 and are troubled in thy indignation
101 11 because of thy anger and indignation
Prov 11 23 the expectation of the wicked is i.
Ecce 1 18 much wisdom there is much indignation
Wisd 12 27 seeing with i. that they suffered by
Eccu 16 12 mighty to forgive and to pour out i.
36 8 raise up indignation and pour out wrath
45 23 they were consumed in his wrathful i.
Isa 9 12 his i. is not turned away. 17, 21
10 5 and my indignation is in their hands
25 my indignation shall cease, and my
13 9 a cruel day, and full of indignation
13 the indignation of the Lord of hosts
16 6 and his i. is more than his strength
26 20 a moment, until the i. pass away
27 4 there is no indignation in me: who
30 27 his lips are filled with indignation
34 2 the i. of the Lord is upon all nations
42 25 poured out upon him the i. of his fury
51 20 full of the indignation of the Lord
22 the dregs of the cup of my indignation
54 8 in a moment of i. have I hid my face
63 3 I have trampled on them in my i. and
5 my indignation itself hath helped me
6 and have made them drunk in my i. and
66 15 to render his wrath in indignation
Jer 4 4 lest my indignation come forth like
26 at the presence of the wrath of his i.
7 20 my i. is enkindled against this place
10 25 pour out thy i. upon the nations that
18 20 and to turn away thy i. from them
21 5 fury and in i. and in great wrath
12 my indignation go forth like a fire
23 19 whirlwind of the Lord's i. shall come
30 24 will not turn away the wrath of his i.
32 31 hath been to me a provocation and i.
37 and in my wrath and in my great i.
33 5 I have slain in my wrath and in my i.
36 7 great is the wrath and i. which the
42 18 and my indignation hath been kindled
18 so shall my i. be kindled against you
44 6 my i. and my fury was poured forth
Lam 2 4 poured out his indignation like fire
6 delivered up . . . to the i. of his wrath
3 1 see my poverty by the rod of his i.
Bar 2 20 hast sent out thy wrath and thy i.
Eze 3 14 I went away . . . in the i. of my spirit
5 13 and will cause my i. to rest upon them
13 when I shall have accomplished my i.
15 shall have executed judgments . . . in i.
6 12 I will accomplish my i. upon them
13 13 a stormy wind to break forth in my i.
14 19 and pour out my i. upon it in blood
16 42 and my indignation shall rest in thee
20 8 I would pour out my i. upon them. 13
21 threatened to pour out my i. upon them
21 17 together, and will satisfy my i: I the
31 and I will pour out upon thee my i.
22 22 when I have poured out my i. upon you
31 I poured out my i. upon them, in the
24 8 that I might bring my i. upon her
13 before I cause my i. to rest in thee
30 15 will pour out my i. upon Pelusium
36 6 I have spoken . . . in my indignation
18 I poured out my indignation upon them
38 18 indignation shall come up in my wrath
Dan 9 16 let . . . thy indignation be turned away
11 30 i. against covenant of the sanctuary
14 27 had heard this, they took great i.
Osee 13 11 will take him away in my indignation
Mich 5 14 I will execute vengeance . . . in i.
Nah 1 6 who can stand before the face of his i.
6 his indignation is poured out like fire
Haba 3 8 was thy . . . indignation in the sea
Soph 2 2 before the day of the Lord's i. come
3 may be hid in the day of the Lord's i.
3 8 and to pour upon them my indignation
Zach 7 12 a great i. came from the Lord of hosts
8 2 with a great i. have I been jealous
1 Ma 2 44 slew . . . the wicked men in their i.
49 time of destruction and the wrath of i.
2 Ma 4 35 also the other nations conceived i.
49 even the Tyrians being moved with i.
8 4 would show his i. on this occasion
Mat 20 24 with i. against the two brethren. But
21 15 son of David; were moved with i.
26 8 disciples seeing it, had indignation
Mark 14 4 there were some that had indignation
Rom 2 8 not the truth, but give credit to . . . i.
2 C 7 11 yea defence, yea indignation, yea fear
Eph 4 31 let all bitterness and anger and i.
Col 3 8 put you also all away: anger . . . i.
21 provoke not your children to i., lest
Apoc 16 19 wine of the indignation of his wrath
indiscreet Eccu 23 17 be accustomed to i. speech
indissoluble Heb 7 16 to the power of an i. life
indolent Josu 18 3 how long are you i. and slack
indulgence 1 C 7 6 I speak this by indulgence, not
industries Ecce 4 4 their i. are exposed to the
industrious Gen 41 33 provide a wise and i. man
Gen 47 6 that there are industrious men among
3 K 11 28 seeing him a young man ingenious and i.
Prov 10 4 hand of the industrious getteth riches
21 5 thoughts of the industrious always
industry Jdth 11 6 i. of thy mind is spoken of
Ecce 10 10 after industry shall follow wisdom
inebriate Prov 5 19 let her breasts i. thee at all
inebriated Ps 35 9 they shall be i. with the
Prov 7 18 let us be inebriated with the breasts
11 25 he that inebriateth, shall be i. also
Cant 5 1 and be inebriated, my dearly beloved
Isa 34 5 my sword is inebriated in heaven
Jer 31 25 I have i. the weary soul: and I have
Lam 3 15 he hath inebriated me with wormwood
Zach 9 15 they shall be i. as it were with wine
inebriateth Ps 22 5 my chalice which i. me
Prov 11 25 he that i., shall be inebriated also
ineffable Job 37 23 and in justice, and he is i.
inestimable Job 36 26 number of his years is i.
inevitable Wisd 16 4 that i. destruction should
inexcusable Rom 1 20 so that they are inexcusable
Rom 2 1 thou art i., O man, whosoever thou art

inexhaustible Wisd 8 18 i. riches in the works of
inexorable Lam 3 42 wrath: therefore thou art i.
infamous Prov 2 15 perverse, and their steps i.
Prov 14 2 despised by him that goeth by an i. way
19 26 chaseth away his mother, is i. and
Eze 22 5 thou filthy one, infamous, great in
23 10 became i. women and they executed
infamy Eccu 23 36 her i. shall not be blotted out
infancy Gen 46 34 shepherds from our i. until now
Judg 13 5 a Nazarite of God from his infancy. 7
3 K 18 12 feareth the Lord from his infancy
Tob 1 10 from his infancy he taught him to fear
2 13 always feared God from his infancy
Job 31 18 from my infancy mercy grew up with me
Eze 4 14 from my infancy even till now, I have
Mark 9 20 him? But he said: From his infancy
2 Tim 3 15 from thy infancy thou hast known the
infant Gen 17 12 i. of eight days old shall be
Exod 2 6 seeing within it an infant crying
Num 11 12 as nurse is wont to carry the little i.
Deut 28 50 ancients nor have pity on the infant
Isa 49 15 can a woman forget her infant, so as
65 20 shall no more be an i. of days there
Luke 1 41 the infant leaped in her womb. And
44 the infant in my womb leaped for joy
2 12 you shall find the infant wrapped in
16 and the infant lying in the manger
infants Gen 38 27 in the very delivery of the i.
Jdth 7 16 wives and our i. die before our eyes
16 6 to make my i. a prey, and my virgins
Ps 8 3 out of the mouth of i. and sucklings
Wisd 10 21 made the tongues of infants eloquent
Isa 13 16 their infants shall be dashed in pieces
2 Ma 5 13 and killing of virgins and infants
6 10 with the i. hanging at their breasts
Mat 21 16 out of the mouth of i. and of sucklings
Luke 18 15 they brought unto him also infants
Rom 2 20 a teacher of infants, having the form
infatuate 2 K 15 31 infatuate . . . the counsel of
infatuated Eccu 23 19 lest . . . be i. and suffer
infected Lev 13 49 if it be i. with a white or
Isa 24 5 the earth is i. by the inhabitants
inferior Josu 21 26 of Caath, of the i. degree
Josu 21 34 Levites of the i. degree, by their
Job 13 2 I also know: neither am I inferior to
15 8 shall his wisdom be inferior to thee
Dan 2 39 shall rise up another kingdom, i. to
Eccu 22 5 will not be inferior to the ungodly
inferiors Jer 14 3 sent their i. to the water
infernal 2 P 2 4 drawn down by infernal ropes to the
infidel 1 Tim 5 8 faith, and is worse than an i.
infidels Isa 13 11 make the pride of i. to cease
1 C 14 23 come in unlearned persons or infidels
infinite Num 20 20 meet them with i. multitude
Num 32 1 their substance in beasts was infinite
Deut 26 5 strong and of an infinite multitude
Judg 11 20 gathering an i. multitude, went out
2 Pa 14 15 and took an infinite number of cattle
24 24 Lord delivered into their hands an i.
Job 22 5 wickedness and thy infinite iniquities
Ecce 1 15 and the number of fools in infinite
4 16 people, of all that were before him is i.
Wisd 7 14 for she is an infinite treasure to man
2 Ma 3 6 the common store was infinite, which
infinity Ecce 7 30 entangled himself with an i. of
infirm 2 Ma 9 21 as for me, being i. but yet
John 5 7 the infirm man answered him: Sir, I
Acts 4 9 the good deed done to the infirm man
1 C 11 30 are there many infirm and weak among you
infirmities Deut 7 15 and the grievous i. of Egypt
Deut 28 59 lasting, i. grievous and perpetual
Ps 15 4 their i. were multiplied: afterwards
Isa 53 4 surely he hath borne our infirmities
Mat 8 17 he took our infirmities and bore our
10 1 diseases, and all manner of i. And
Luke 5 15 and to be healed by him of their i.
8 2 been healed of evil spirits and i.
Acts 5 15 they might be delivered from their i.
Rom 15 1 stronger, ought to bear i. of the weak
2 C 12 5 glory nothing, but in my infirmities
9 therefore will I glory in my infirmities
10 for which cause I please myself in my i.
1 Tim 5 23 thy stomach's sake, and thy frequent i.
4 15 who cannot have compassion on our i.
infirmity 3 K 8 37 whatsoever plague, whatsoever i.
2 Pa 6 28 whatsoever scourge or infirmity shall
29 knowing his own scourge and infirmity
Prov 18 14 spirit of man upholdeth his infirmity
Eccu 31 27 and no infirmity shall come to thee
Isa 40 30 and young men shall fall by infirmity
53 3 man of sorrows, and acquainted with i.
10 was pleased to bruise him in infirmity
Jer 6 7 i. and stripes are continually before
Mat 4 23 manner of sickness and every infirmity
9 35 healing every disease and every i.
Luke 13 11 woman who had a spirit of infirmity
12 woman, thou art delivered from thy i.
John 5 4 was made whole of whatsoever infirmity
5 had been 8 and 30 years under his i.
Rom 6 19 because of the infirmity of your flesh
8 26 the Spirit also helpeth our infirmity
2 C 11 30 of the things that concern my infirmity
12 9 for power is made perfect in infirmity
Gal 4 13 know, how through infirmity of the flesh
Heb 5 2 he himself also is compassed with i.
7 28 maketh men priests, who have infirmity
inflamed Jdth 8 15 nor be i. to anger like the
Ps 72 21 my heart hath been i., and my reins
104 19 the word of the Lord inflamed him. The
Isa 5 11 till the evening, to be i. with wine
Dan 13 8 and they were i. with lust towards her
2 Ma 4 38 i. to anger, he commanded Andronicus
10 35 inflamed in their minds because of
14 45 being inflamed in mind he arose: and
inflameth James 3 6 inflameth wheel of our nativity
infolding Eze 1 4 great cloud, and a fire i. it
inform 1 K 22 8 there is no one to inform me
Eccu 42 8 be not ashamed to i. the unwise and
information 1 K 22 8 or that giveth me any i.
Esth 12 5 gave him presents for the information
2 Ma 3 9 told him what i. had been given
1 Tim 1 16 for the i. of them that shall believe
informed 3 K 10 3 Solomon i. her of all the things
ingenious 3 K 11 28 seeing him a young man i. and
ingeniously 2 Pa 2 14 to devise i. all that there
inglorious Isa 52 14 his visage be i. among men
ingrafted Rom 11 17 wild olive, art i. in them
James 1 21 receive the ingrafted word, which is
inhabit Isa 21 14 that i. the land of the south
Isa 54 3 and shall inhabit the desolate cities
65 21 they shall build houses and i. them
22 they shall not build, and another i.
Jer 49 18 there shall no son of man inhabit it
30 sit in deep holes, you that i. Asor
33 abide there, nor son of man inhabit it
50 40 neither shall the son of man i. it
Amos 9 14 build the abandoned cities and i. them
Soph 2 5 woe to you that inhabit the seacoast
Apoc 17 2 who i. the earth have been made drunk
inhabited Judg 1 21 Jebusites that i. Jerusalem
Wisd 11 2 through wildernesses that were not i.
Eccu 10 3 and cities shall be i. through the
16 5 that is wise a country shall be i.
Isa 13 20 it shall no more be inhabited forever
44 26 to Jerusalem: Thou shalt be inhabited
45 18 create it in vain: he formed it to be i.

62 4 my pleasure in her, and thy land i.
4 with thee: and thy land shall be i.
Jer 17 6 the desert in a salt land, and not i.
25 this city shall be inhabited forever
46 26 it shall be i., as in the days of
50 13 it shall not be i., but shall be wholly
39 shall be no more inhabited forever
Bar 4 35 endure and she shall be i. by devils
Eze 12 20 the cities that are now i. shall be
26 19 city like the cities that are not i.
20 down into the pit, that thou be not i.
29 11 nor shall it be i. during forty years
35 9 thy cities shall not be i.: and thou
36 10 the cities shall be i., and the ruinous
33 and shall cause the cities to be i.
Joel 3 20 Judea shall be inhabited forever
Zach 1 11 all the earth is i. and is at rest
2 4 Jerusalem shall be i. without walls
7 7 when Jerusalem as yet was inhabited
9 5 and Ascalon shall not be inhabited
12 6 Jerusalem shall be inhabited again
1 Ma 3 45 Jerusalem was not i. but was like a
2 Ma 3 1 when the holy city was i. with all
6 2 as they were that i. the place and
12 13 i. by multitudes of different nations
Acts 13 27 they that i. Jerusalem, and the rulers
inhabiteth Isa 57 15 Eminent that i. eternity
1 Tim 6 16 inhabiteth light inaccessible, whom no
inheritance Mat 21 38 and we shall have his i.
Mark 12 7 us kill him; and the i. shall be ours
Luke 12 13 to my brother that he divide the i.
20 14 us kill him, that the i. may be ours
Acts 7 5 he gave him no inheritance in it; no
20 32 to give an i. among all the sanctified
Gal 3 18 for if the inheritance be of the law
Eph 1 14 who is the pledge of our inheritance
18 glory of his inheritance in the saints
5 5 hath i. in the kingdom of Christ and of
Col 3 24 receive of the Lord the reward of i.
Heb 1 14 who shall receive the i. of salvation
9 15 receive the promise of eternal i. For
11 8 which he was to receive for an i.; and
1 P 1 4 unto an i. incorruptible and undefiled
inheritances Isa 49 8 possess the i. that were
1 Ma 6 24 could find and have spoiled our i.
inherited Jer 49 1 why then hath Melchom i. Gad
Eze 33 24 Abraham was one, and he i. the land
1 Ma 2 10 what nation hath not i. her kingdom
Heb 1 4 as he hath i. a more excellent name
inhospitality Wisd 19 13 more detestable i. than
iniquity Mat 7 23 depart from me, you that work i.
Mat 13 41 scandals and them that work iniquity
23 28 you are full of hypocrisy and iniquity
24 12 because i. hath abounded, the charity
Luke 11 39 your inside is full of rapine and i.
Acts 1 18 a field of the reward of iniquity and
8 23 of bitterness and in the bonds of i.
24 20 say, if they found in me any iniquity
Rom 1 29 being filled with all iniquity, malice
2 8 not truth, but give credit to iniquity
6 13 members as instruments of i. unto sin
19 members to serve uncleanness and i.
19 uncleanness and iniquity, unto iniquity
1 C 13 6 rejoiceth not in i., but rejoiceth with
2 Th 2 7 the mystery of iniquity already worketh
10 in all seduction of iniquity to them
11 truth, but have consented to iniquity
2 Tim 2 19 let every one depart from iniquity who
Titus 2 14 he might redeem us from all iniquity
Heb 1 9 hast loved justice, and hated iniquity
James 3 6 the tongue is a fire, a world of i.
1 J 1 9 and to cleanse us from all iniquity
3 4 committeth sin, committeth also i.
4 also iniquity; and sin is iniquity
5 17 all iniquity is sin. And there is a
initiated Num 25 3 Israel was i. to Beelphegor
Num 25 5 that have been initiated to Beelphegor
Ps 105 28 they also were i. to Beelphegor: and
injured Num 16 15 nor have injured any of them
Acts 25 11 if I have i. them, or have committed
2 C 7 2 receive us. We have injured no man, we
Gal 4 12 beseech you: you have not i. me at all
injuries 2 K 19 19 nor remember the i. of thy
Prov 12 16 he that dissembleth injuries is wise
Eccu 10 8 because of . . . wrongs and injuries
21 5 injuries and wrongs will waste riches
29 9 and he . . . will repay him injuries
injuring Eze 18 17 away his hand from i. the poor
injurious Eccu 8 14 against face of an i. person
Eccu 19 28 in the anger of an injurious man
22 30 so also i. words and reproaches and
injuriously 2 Ma 1 28 that treat us i. with pride
injury Lev 19 18 nor be mindful of the injury
2 K 10 6 seeing that they had done an injury
1 Pa 19 6 that they had done an injury to David
Prov 9 7 teacheth a scorner, doth an injury to
Eccu 10 6 remember not any injury done thee by
6 do thou nothing by deeds of injury
2 Ma 8 17 setting before their eyes the injury
17 the injury they had done to the city
9 4 to revenge upon the Jews the i. done
14 28 having received no injury from the man
Acts 7 24 avenged him who suffered the injury
27 he that did the injury to his neighbor
25 10 to the Jews I have done no injury, as
27 10 voyage beginneth to be with injury and
2 C 12 13 burthensome to you? Pardon me this i.
injustice Deut 25 16 and he hateth all injustice
Job 11 14 let not i. remain in thy tabernacle
Ps 7 15 he hath been in labor with injustice
31 5 and my injustice I have not concealed
5 confess against myself my i. to the
51 4 thy tongue hath devised injustice: as
54 12 in the midst thereof are labor and i.
57 3 your hands forge i. in the earth. The
93 4 shall all speak who work injustice
106 17 were brought low for their injustice
Eccu 7 3 sow not evils in the furrows of i.
17 23 turn away from thy i. and greatly hate
35 3 to depart from injustice, is to offer
5 to depart from i., is an entreaty for
40 12 all bribery and i. shall be blotted
41 23 of i. before a companion and friend
Isa 10 1 and when they write, write injustice
Jer 22 13 that buildeth up his house by injustice
Haba 1 3 to see rapine and injustice before me
John 7 18 and there is no injustice in him
Acts 18 14 if it were some matter of injustice, or
Rom 1 18 against all ungodliness and i. of those
18 men that detain the truth of God in i.
3 5 if our injustice commend the justice of
9 14 is there injustice with God? God forbid
2 C 6 14 what . . . hath justice with injustice
2 P 2 7 Lot, oppressed by the i. and lewd
13 receiving the reward of their i.
injustices Eccu 10 8 to another because of i. and
Eccu 35 3 propitiatory sacrifice for injustices
ink Jer 36 18 and I wrote in a volume with ink
2 C 3 3 written not with ink, but with Spirit
2 J 12 I would not by paper and ink: for I
3 J 13 I would not by ink and pen write to
inkhorn Eze 9 2 had a writer's i. at his reins
Eze 9 3 had a writer's inkhorn at his loins
11 that had the inkhorn at his back
inlaid Cant 1 10 chains of gold, i. with silver
inn Gen 42 27 give his beast provender in the inn

20 27 inquired of him concerning their state
2 K 11 3 the king . . . i. who the woman was
Eccu 11 7 and when thou hast i., reprove justly
Eze 21 21 he i. of the idols and consulted
Dan 1 20 that the king i. of them, he found
2 14 Daniel i. concerning the law and the
Mat 2 4 he i. of them where Christ should be
16 time which he had diligently inquired
1 P 1 10 the prophets have i. and diligently
inquirest Tob 7 6 Tobias concerning whom thou i.
inquireth Eze 14 10 the iniquity of him that i.
inquiring Wisd 13 17 i. concerning his substance
Eze 14 4 come to the prophet i. of me by him
Acts 10 17 from Cornelius, i. for Simon's house
inquisition Deut 19 18 after most diligent i.
Wisd 1 9 i. shall be made into the thoughts
Eccu 23 34 and i. shall be made of her children
inquisitive Eccu 3 24 works thou shalt not be i.
Eccu 41 27 wife, and be not i. after his handmaid
insatiable Eccu 14 9 eye of the covetous man is i.
inscription Ps 15 1 i. of a title. 55:1; 56:1; 57:1; 58:1; 59:1
Mat 22 20 whose image and i. is this. Mark 12:16
Mark 15 26 the i. of his cause was written over
Luke 20 24 whose image and inscription hath it
insensibility Job 12 17 bringeth . . . judges to i.
Rom 11 8 God hath given them the spirit of i.
inside Exod 27 8 empty and hollow in the inside
Lev 14 41 that the house be scraped on the i.
3 K 6 15 built the walls of house on the inside
15 with boards of cedar on the inside
Mat 23 26 first make clean the inside of the cup
Luke 11 39 your i. is full of rapine and iniquity
insinuate 1 P 5 5 do you all i. humility one to
insinuating Acts 17 3 and i. that the Christ was
insnare Mat 22 15 how to insnare him in his speech
insnaring 2 Ma 14 40 thought by i. him to hurt the
insolent Deut 28 50 a most i. nation, that will
1 Ma 3 20 against us with an i. multitude
inspection Mich 7 4 day of thy i., thy visitation
inspiration Job 32 8 i. of the Almighty giveth
inspired Wisd 15 11 that i. into him the soul that
2 Tim 3 16 inspired of God, is profitable to
2 P 1 21 spoke, inspired by the Holy Ghost
inspireth Eccu 4 12 wisdom i. life into her
instance 2 C 11 28 my daily i., the solicitude for
Eph 6 18 in the same watching with all instance
instant Isa 29 6 it shall be at an i. suddenly
Luke 23 23 but they were instant with loud voices
Rom 12 12 in tribulation. Instant in prayer
Col 4 2 be instant in prayer; watching in
2 Tim 4 2 be instant in season, out of season
instituted Heb 11 7 was i. heir of the justice
instruct Judg 3 1 that by them he might i. Israel
Job 6 24 been ignorant in anything, instruct me
Ps 31 8 and I will instruct thee in this way
93 12 blessed is the man whom thou shalt i.
104 22 that he might i. his princes as himself
Prov 14 33 and it shall instruct all the ignorant
16 23 heart of the wise shall i. his mouth
29 17 i. thy son, and he shall refresh thee
Eccu 7 25 hast thou children? Instruct them
24 46 and will not cease to instruct their
30 13 i. thy son and labor about him, lest
Isa 28 26 he will instruct him in judgment: his
Dan 12 3 they that instruct many to justice
1 C 2 16 mind of the Lord, that he may i. him
14 19 that I may instruct others also; than
Gal 6 1 you, who are spiritual, i. such a one in
2 Tim 3 15 which can instruct thee to salvation
16 to correct, to instruct in justice
instructed Gen 49 32 wherewith he i. his sons
Exod 35 35 both of them hath he i. with wisdom
Deut 18 14 thou art otherwise i. by the Lord
2 Pa 17 9 the cities of Juda and i. the people
1 Es 7 11 i. in the words and commandments
Prov 31 1 the vision wherewith his mother i. him
Eccu 10 28 a man . . . well i. will not murmur when
26 18 nothing so much worth as a well i. soul
40 31 man well i. and taught, will look to
42 8 thou shalt be well i. in all things
Isa 40 14 who hath i. him and taught him the
Jer 6 8 be thou i., O Jerusalem, lest my soul
13 21 instructed them against thy own head
31 18 thou hast chastised me, and I was i.
32 33 when I taught them . . . and i. them
Dan 1 4 acute in knowledge, and i. in science
7 16 instructed me: These four great beasts
9 22 he instructed me and spoke to me and
13 3 had i. their daughter according to the
Mat 13 52 every scribe i. in the kingdom of
14 8 she being i. before by her mother
Luke 1 4 words in which thou hast been i.
Acts 7 22 Moses was i. in all the wisdom of the
18 25 this man was i. in the way of the Lord
Rom 2 18 things, being instructed by the law
Gal 6 6 let him that is instructed in the word
Phil 4 12 everywhere, and in all things I am i.
Col 2 2 being instructed in charity, and unto
Heb 12 10 to their own pleasure, instructed us
instructeth Job 33 16 i. them in what they are
Job 35 11 and i. us more than the fowls of the
Eccu 30 2 that i. his son shall be praised in
37 26 a wise man i. his own people, and the
Gal 6 6 communicate to him that i. him, in all
instructing Eccu 44 4 i. the people in most holy
Titus 2 12 i. us, that, denying ungodliness and
instruction 2 Pa 35 3 by whose i. all Israel
Ps 2 10 kings, understand: receive instruction
Prov 1 2 to know wisdom and instruction: to
3 to receive the instruction of doctrine
7 fools despise wisdom and instruction
8 hear the instruction of thy father
29 because they have hated instruction
4 1 hear . . . the instruction of a father
13 take hold on instruction, leave it not
5 2 and thy lips may preserve instruction
12 why have I hated instruction, and my
23 die, because he hath not received i.
6 23 and reproofs of i. are the way of life
8 10 receive my instruction, and not money
33 hear i. and be wise, and refuse it not
13 15 good i. shall give grace: in the way
18 shame to him that refuseth instruction
15 5 fool laugheth at the i. of his father
10 i. is grievous to him that forsaketh
14 heart of the wise seeketh instruction
32 he that rejecteth i., despiseth his own
16 22 instruction of fools is foolishness
18 15 ear of the wise seeketh instruction
19 20 hear counsel and receive instruction
27 cease not, O my son, to hear i., and
23 9 they will despise the i. of thy speech
12 thy heart apply itself to instruction
23 and do not sell wisdom and instruction
24 4 by i. the storerooms shall be filled
32 by the example I received instruction
Wisd 6 12 and love them, and you shall have i.
27 receive therefore i. by my words, and
Eccu 6 18 from thy youth up receive instruction
34 incline thy ear, thou shalt receive i.
8 10 shalt learn . . . i. of understanding
22 6 stripes and instruction of wisdom are
45 6 a law of life and i., that he might
50 29 the doctrine of wisdom and instruction
Isa 24 15 glorify the Lord in i.: the name of
26 16 thy instruction was with them. As a

2 K 12 31 over them chariots armed with iron
21 16 iron of whose spear weighed 300 ounces
23 7 touch them, he must be armed with iron
3 K 6 7 nor any tool of i. heard in the house
8 51 from the midst of the furnace of iron
22 11 made himself horns of iron and said
4 K 6 6 cast it in thither; and the iron swam
1 Pa 20 3 and chariots of iron to go over them
22 3 iron for the nails of the gates and
14 brass and of iron there is no weight
16 in brass and in iron, whereof there
29 2 iron for things of iron, wood for
7 of iron a hundred thousand talents
2 Pa 2 7 knoweth how to work . . . in iron. 14
18 10 Sedecias . . . made him horns of iron
24 12 and such as wrought in iron and brass
Job 19 24 with an iron pen and in a plate of
20 24 he shall flee from weapons of iron
28 2 iron is taken out of the earth, and
40 13 brass, his gristle like plates of iron
41 18 shall esteem iron as straw, and brass
Ps 2 9 thou shalt rule them with a rod of iron
104 18 in fetters: the iron pierced his soul
106 10 of death: bound in want and in iron
16 gates of brass and burst iron bars
149 8 their nobles with manacles of iron
Prov 27 17 iron sharpeneth iron, so a man
Ecce 10 10 if the iron be blunt, and be not as
Wisd 13 15 in a wall, and fastening it with iron
Eccu 22 18 and a mass of iron is easier to bear
28 24 its yoke is a yoke of iron: and its
31 31 fire trieth hard iron: so wine drunk
38 29 anvil and considering the iron work
39 31 life of men, are water, fire, and iron
48 19 he digged a rock with iron and made a
Isa 10 34 the forest shall be cut down with iron
45 2 brass, and will burst the bars of iron
48 4 thy neck is as an iron sinew, and thy
60 17 for iron I will bring silver . . . and for stones iron
Jer 1 18 I have made thee . . . a pillar of iron
6 28 deceitfully, they are brass and iron
11 4 land of Egypt, from the iron furnace
15 12 shall i. be allied with i. from the north
17 1 sin of Juda is written with pen of iron
28 13 shalt make for them chains of iron
14 I have put a yoke of iron upon the neck
Eze 4 3 take unto thee an iron pan and set it
3 set it for a wall of iron between thee
22 18 all these are brass and tin and iron
20 silver and brass and tin and iron
27 12 riches with silver, iron, tin, and lead
19 set forth in thy marts wrought iron
Dan 2 33 the legs of iron, the feet part of iron
34 feet thereof that were of iron and of
35 then was the iron . . . broken to pieces
40 the fourth kingdom shall be as iron. As iron breaketh into pieces
41 part of potter's clay, and part of iron
41 it shall take its origin from the iron
41 the iron mixed with the miry clay. 43
42 the toes of the feet were part of iron
43 as iron cannot be mixed with clay
45 broke in pieces the clay and the iron
4 12 let it be tied with a band of iron
20 let it be bound with iron and brass
5 4 gods of gold and . . . of iron and
23 hast praised the gods . . . of iron and
7 7 it had great iron teeth, eating and
19 his teeth and claws were of iron, he
Amos 1 3 have thrashed Galaad with iron wains
Mich 4 13 I will make thy horn iron, and thy
2 Ma 11 9 fiercest beasts and walls of iron

Acts 12 10 they came to the i. gate that leadeth
Apoc 2 27 shall rule them with a rod of i. 19:15
9 9 as breastplates of iron, and the noise
12 5 to rule all nations with an iron rod
18 12 and of brass and of iron and of marble
irons Wisd 17 15 kept shut up in prison without i.
irregularity Wisd 14 26 and the i. of adultery
irrational 2 P 2 12 but these men, as i. beasts
irreprehensibly Tob 10 13 and to behave herself i.
irreverence Eccu 27 15 its i. shall make one stop
irruption 1 Pa 14 13 the Philistines made an i.
is 2 C 1 17 should be with me, It is, and It is not
2 C 1 18 was to you, was not, It is, and It is not
19 it is and It is not, but, It is, was in
20 the promises of God are in him, It is
Apoc 1 4 that is and that was and that is to come
8 who is and who was and who is to come
4 8 who was and who is and who is to come
Isaac Gen 17 19 thou shalt call his name Isaac
Gen 17 21 covenant I will establish with Isaac
21 3 called the name of his son . . . Isaac
5 this age of his father was Isaac born
9 son of Agar . . . playing with Isaac her
10 shall not be heir with my son Isaac
12 in Isaac shall thy seed be called
22 2 take thy only begotten son Isaac whom
3 took with him two young men and I.
6 and laid it upon Isaac his son: and he
7 Isaac said to his father: My father
9 and when he had bound Isaac his son
24 4 a wife from thence for my son Isaac
14 thou hast provided for thy servant Isaac
62 Isaac was walking along the way to the
64 Rebecca also, when she saw Isaac
66 the servant told Isaac all that he had
25 5 gave all his possessions to Isaac
6 and separated them from Isaac his son
9 Isaac and Ismael his sons buried him
11 God blessed Isaac his son, who dwelt
19 these are the generations of Isaac the
19 Abraham begot Isaac. 1 Pa 1:34
21 Isaac besought the Lord for his wife
26 Isaac was threescore years old when
28 Isaac loved Esau because he ate of
26 1 Isaac went to Abimelech king of the
6 Isaac abode in Gerara. And when he was
12 Isaac sowed in that land, and he
16 Abimelech himself said to Isaac: Depart
20 strove against the herdsmen of Isaac
27 Isaac said to them: Why are ye come
31 and Isaac sent them away peaceably
32 servants of Isaac came, telling him
35 offended the mind of Isaac and Rebecca
27 1 Isaac was old, and his eyes were dim
20 Isaac said to his son: How couldst
21 Isaac said: Come hither that I may feel
22 Isaac said: The voice indeed is the
30 Isaac had scarce ended his words, when
32 Isaac said to him: Why! who art thou
33 son Esau, Isaac was struck with fear
37 Isaac answered: I have appointed him
39 Isaac being moved, said to him [Esau]
46 Rebecca said to Isaac: I am weary of
28 1 Isaac called Jacob and blessed him
5 when Isaac had sent him away, he took
31 18 went forward to Isaac his father to the
42 unless . . . fear of Isaac had stood by me
53 swore by the fear of his father Isaac
35 12 land which I gave to Abraham and Isaac
27 he came to Isaac his father in Mambre
27 wherein Abraham and Isaac sojourned
28 and the days of Isaac were 180 years
46 1 victims there to the God of his father I.

48 15 my fathers Abraham and Isaac walked
16 names of my fathers Abraham and Isaac
49 31 there was Isaac buried with Rebecca his
50 23 Abraham, Isaac, and Jacob. Exod 33:1
Exod 2 24 made with Abraham, Isaac, and Jacob. 4 K 13:23
6 3 appeared to Abraham, to Isaac, and
8 to give it to Abraham, Isaac, and Jacob
32 13 remember Abraham, Isaac, and Israel
Lev 26 42 that I made with Isaac and Jacob and
Num 32 11 promised . . . to Abraham, Isaac. Deut 9:5
Deut 1 8 swore to . . . Abraham, Isaac, and Jacob. 6:10; 29:13; 30:20; 34:4
9 27 remember thy servants Abraham, Isaac
Josu 24 4 and gave him Isaac: and to him
1 Pa 1 28 the sons of Abraham, Isaac and Ismahel
16 16 and his oath to Isaac. Ps 104:9
Jdth 8 23 so Isaac . . . passed through many
Eccu 44 24 he did in like manner with Isaac for
Jer 33 26 rulers of the seed of Abraham, Isaac
Bar 2 34 oath to their fathers, Abraham, Isaac
Dan 3 35 for the sake of . . . Isaac thy servant
2 Ma 1 2 that he made with Abraham and Isaac
Mat 1 2 Abraham begot I. And I. begot Jacob
8 11 shall sit down with, Abraham and Isaac
Luke 3 34 Jacob, who was of Isaac, who was of
13 28 when you shall see Abraham and Isaac
Acts 7 8 so he begot Isaac, and circumcised him
8 and Isaac begot Jacob; and Jacob
Rom 9 7 in Isaac shall thy seed be. Heb 11:18
10 conceived at once, of Isaac our father
Gal 4 28 as Isaac was, are children of promise
Heb 11 9 with Isaac and Jacob, the co-heirs of
17 when he was tried, offered Isaac: and
20 to come, Isaac blessed Jacob and Esau
James 2 21 offering up I. his son upon the altar
God of Isaac Gen 28 13 the God of Isaac. Exod 3:6
Gen 32 9 God of my father Isaac, O Lord, who
Exod 3 15 God of Abraham, the God of Isaac. 16; 4:5; Tob 7:15
3 K 18 36 God of Abraham and Isaac. 1 Pa 29:18; 2 Pa 30:6
Mat 22 32 God of Abraham and the God of Isaac. Mark 12:26; Acts 3:13
Luke 20 37 G. . . . and the God of Jacob. Acts 7:32
Isaar Exod 6 18 the sons of Caath: Amram and Isaar. 1 Pa 6:2, 18; 23:12
Exod 6 21 the sons also of Isaar. 1 Pa 23:18
Num 16 1 Core the son of Isaar. 1 Pa 6:38
1 Pa 4 7 the sons of Halaa, Sereth, Isaar
24 22 the son of Isaar Salemoth, and the
Isaarites 1 Pa 26 23 with the Amramites and I.
1 Pa 26 29 Chonenias . . . over the Isaarites
Isai Ruth 4 17 Obed: he is the father of Isai
Ruth 4 22 Obed begot Isai, Isai begot David
1 K 16 1 and come that I may send thee to Isai
3 thou shalt call Isai to the sacrifice
5 and he sanctified Isai and his sons and
8 Isai called Abinadab and brought him
9 Isai brought Samma and he said of
10 Isai therefore brought his seven sons
10 Samuel said to Isai. 11
19 then Saul sent messengers to Isai
20 Isai took an ass laden with bread and
22 Saul sent to Isai, saying: Let David
17 12 name was Isai, who had eight sons
17 Isai said to David his son: Take for
20 away loaded as Isai had commanded him
58 I am the son of thy servant Isai the
1 Pa 2 12 Obed begot Isai. And Isai begot Eliab
son of Isai 1 K 16 18 I have seen a son of Isai
1 K 20 27 why cometh not the son of Isai to meat
30 know that thou lovest the son of Isai
31 long as the son of Isai liveth upon
22 7 will the son of Isai give every one of
8 entered into league with the son of I.
9 I saw the son of Isai in Nobe with
13 against me, thou, and the son of Isai
25 10 is David? and what is the son of Isai
2 K 20 1 inheritance in son of Isai. 2 Pa 10:16
23 1 David the son of Isai. 1 Pa 10:14; 29:26
3 K 12 16 what inheritance in the son of Isai
1 Pa 12 18 and for thee, O son of Isai: peace
2 Pa 11 18 the daughter of Eliab the son of Isai
Isaia 2 Es 11 7 Etheel the son of Isaia. And
Isaias 4 K 19 2 [Ezechias] sent . . . to Isaias the
4 K 19 5 servants of king Ezechias came to I.
6 Isaias said to them: Thus shall you say
20 I. the son of Amos sent to Ezechias
20 1 Isaias . . . came and said to him: Thus
4 and before Isaias was gone out of the
7 Isaias said: Bring me a lump of figs
8 Ezechias had said to Isaias: What shall
9 Isaias said to him: This shall be the
11 Isaias the prophet called upon the Lord
14 I. the prophet came to king Ezechias
16 Isaias said to Ezechias: Hear the word
19 Ezechias said to Isaias: The word of
1 Pa 26 25 Rohobias, and his son Isaias, and his
2 Pa 26 22 were written by Isaias the son of Amos
32 20 and Isaias . . . prayed against this
1 Es 8 7 of the sons of Alam, Isaias the son of
19 with him Isaias of the sons of Merari
Eccu 48 23 he purified them by the hand of Isaias
25 which Isaias . . . had commanded him
Isa 1 1 the vision of Isaias the son of Amos
2 1 that Isaias the son of Amos saw. 13:1
7 3 the Lord said to Isaias: Go forth
20 2 the Lord spoke by the hand of Isaias
3 as my servant Isaias hath walked
37 2 and he sent Eliacim . . . to Isaias
5 servants of Ezechias came to Isaias
6 Isaias said to them: Thus shall you
21 Isaias . . . sent to Ezechias, saying
38 1 Isaias . . . came unto him [Ezechias]
4 the word of the Lord came to Isaias
21 Isaias had ordered that they should
39 3 I. the prophet came to king Ezechias
5 Isaias said to Ezechias: Hear the word
8 Ezechias said to Isaias: The word of
Mat 3 3 was spoken of by Isaias the prophet
4 14 which was said by Isaias the prophet
8 17 spoken by the prophet Isaias, saying
12 17 which was spoken by Isaias the prophet
13 14 the prophecy of Isaias is fulfilled
15 7 well hath I. prophesied of you. Mark 7:6
Mark 1 2 as it is written in Isaias the prophet
Luke 3 4 in the book of the sayings of Isaias
4 17 book of I. the prophet was delivered
John 1 23 as said the prophet Isaias. And they
12 38 that the saying of Isaias the prophet
39 Isaias said again: He hath blinded
41 these things said Isaias, when he saw
Acts 8 28 and reading Isaias the prophet. And
30 heard him reading the prophet Isaias
28 25 speak to our fathers by I. the prophet
Rom 9 27 Isaias crieth out concerning Israel: If
29 as Isaias foretold: Unless the Lord of
10 16 for I. saith: Lord, who hath believed
20 but Isaias is bold, and saith: I was
15 12 and again Isaias saith: There shall be
Isari 1 Pa 25 11 the fourth lot to Isari
Isbaab 1 Pa 24 13 the fourteenth [lot] to Isbaab
Isboseth 2 K 2 8 but Abner . . . took Isboseth
2 K 2 10 Isboseth the son of Saul was 40 years
12 and the servants of Isboseth . . . went

15 number of Benjamin of the part of I.
3 7 Isboseth said to Abner: Why didst thou
8 angry for the words of I., and said
14 and David sent messengers to Isboseth
15 Isboseth sent and took her from her
4 1 Isboseth . . . heard that Abner was slain
5 went into the house of Isboseth in the
8 brought the head of Isboseth to David
8 said to the king: Behold the head of I.
12 head of Isboseth they took and buried
Iscariot Mat 10 4 Iscariot, who also betrayed him. Mark 3:19
Mat 26 14 who was called Judas Iscariot, to the
Mark 14 10 Judas Iscariot, one of the twelve
43 yet speaking, cometh Judas Iscariot
Luke 6 16 Judas Iscariot, who was the traitor
22 3 Judas, who was surnamed Iscariot
John 6 72 he meant Judas Iscariot, the son of
12 4 Judas Iscariot, he that was about to
13 2 put into the heart of Judas Iscariot
26 gave it to Judas I. the son of Simon
14 22 Judas saith to him, not the Iscariot
island Isa 23 2 silent, you that dwell in the i.
Isa 23 6 howl, ye inhabitants of the island
Acts 13 6 they had gone through the whole island
27 16 under a certain i. that is called Cauda
26 and we must come unto a certain island
28 1 knew that island was called Melita. But
7 possessions of the chief man of island
9 all that had diseases in the island
11 ship . . . that had wintered in the island
Apoc 1 9 in the island which is called Patmos
16 20 and every island fled away, and the
islands Gen 10 6 by these were divided the i.
Esth 10 1 all the islands of the sea tributary
Ps 71 10 the kings of Tharsis and the islands
96 1 rejoice: let many islands be glad
Eccu 43 25 the Lord hath planted islands therein
47 17 thy name went abroad to the islands
Isa 11 11 Emath and from the islands of the sea
24 15 glorify . . . in the islands of the sea
40 15 the islands are as a little dust. And
41 1 let the islands keep silence before me
5 the islands saw it and feared, the ends
42 4 and the islands shall wait for his law
10 ye islands, and ye inhabitants of them
12 shall declare his praise in the islands
15 I will turn rivers into islands and will
49 1 give ear, ye islands, and hearken, ye
51 5 the islands shall look for me, and
59 18 he will repay the like to the islands
60 9 the islands wait for me, and the ships
66 19 and Greece, to the islands afar off
Jer 25 22 land of the i. that are beyond the sea
31 10 declare it in the islands that are afar
Eze 26 15 shall not the i. shake at the sound
18 the i. in the sea shall be troubled
27 3 mart of the people for many islands
6 things brought from the i. of Italy
7 blue and purple from the i. of Elisa
15 many i. were the traffic of thy hand
35 inhabitants of the i. are astonished
39 6 that dwell confidently in the islands
Dan 11 18 he shall turn his face to the islands
Soph 2 11 place, all the islands of the Gentiles
1 Ma 6 29 from the i. of the sea hired troops
8 11 islands that at any time had resisted
11 38 together from the i. of the nations
Apoc 6 14 every mountain and the i. were moved
isle Isa 20 6 inhabitants of this isle shall
Jer 47 4 the remnant of the isle of Cappadocia
isles Jer 2 10 pass over to the i. of Cethim and
1 Ma 14 5 made an entrance to the i. of the sea
15 1 sent letters from the isles of the sea
Ismael Gen 16 11 thou shalt call his name Ismael
Gen 16 15 to Abram: who called his name Ismael
16 old when Agar brought him forth Ismael
17 18 O that Ismael may live before thee. And
20 as for Ismael I have also heard thee
23 Abraham took Ismael his son, and all
25 Ismael his son was full 13 years old
26 was Abraham circumcised and Ismael
25 9 Isaac and Ismael his sons buried him
12 these are the generations of Ismael
13 the firstborn of Ismael was Nabajoth
16 these are the sons of Ismael: and
28 9 [Esau] went to Ismael and took a wife
9 Maheleth, the daughter of Ismael
36 3 Basemath the daughter of Ismael
4 K 25 23 captains . . . I. the son of Nathanias
25 Ismael . . . came and ten men with him
1 Es 10 22 of the sons of Pheshur . . . Ismael
Ismaelites Gen 37 25 saw some I. on their way
Gen 37 27 that he be sold to the Ismaelites
28 and sold him to the Ismaelites for
39 1 Putiphar . . . bought him of the I.
Judg 8 24 I. were accustomed to wear golden
Ismael's Gen 25 17 years of I. life were 137
Ismahel 1 Pa 1 28 sons of Abraham, Isaac and I.
1 Pa 1 29 firstborn of Ismahel, Nabajoth, then
31 Cedma: these are the sons of Ismahel
8 38 Asel had six sons . . . Ismahel. 9:44
2 Pa 19 11 Zabadias the son of Ismahel, who is
23 1 captains of hundreds . . . Ismahel the
Jdth 2 13 pillaged . . . the children of Ismahel
Jer 40 8 Masphath: and Ismahel . . . and Johanan
14 hath sent Ismahel . . . to kill thee
15 I will go and I will kill Ismahel the son
16 what thou sayst of Ismahel is false
41 1 that Ismahel . . . came to Godolias
2 Ismahel the son of Nathanias arose
3 Ismahel slew also all the Jews that were
6 Ismahel . . . went forth from Masphath
7 Ismahel . . . slew them and cast them
8 that said to Ismahel: Kill us not
9 the same did Ismahel . . . fill with them
9 the pit into which Ismahel cast all
10 Ismahel carried away captive all the
10 Ismahel . . . took them and he departed
11 the evil that Ismahel . . . had done
12 they went out to fight against Ismahel
13 all the people that were with Ismahel
14 all the people whom Ismahel had taken
15 Ismahel . . . fled with eight men
16 whom they had recovered from Ismahel
18 because Ismahel . . . had slain Godolias
Ismahelite 1 Pa 2 17 father was Jether the I.
1 Pa 27 30 over the camels, Ubil an Ismahelite
Ismahelites Ps 82 7 tabernacles of . . . the I.
Ismiel 1 Pa 4 36 Ismiel and Banaia, Ziza also
Israelite Num 25 8 after the I. into the brothel house
Num 25 14 name of the Israelite that was slain
John 1 47 behold an Israelite indeed, in whom
Rom 11 1 for I also am an Israelite of the seed
Israelites 1 K 14 21 returned to be with the I.
1 K 14 22 the Israelites that had hid themselves
17 11 Saul and all the I. hearing these words
24 the Israelites, when they saw the man
31 7 seeing that the Israelites were fled
1 Pa 9 2 the first that dwelt . . . were the I.
Jdth 6 13 be delivered for this cause to the I.
1 Ma 5 3 because they beset the I. round about
9 against I. that were in their quarters
45 Judas gathered together all the I.
6 18 had shut up the I. round about the
Rom 9 4 who are Israelites, to whom belongeth

J

10 Jabes called upon the God of Israel
10 12 bodies . . . and brought them to Jabes
12 bones under the oak that was in Jabes
Jabes Galaad; *see* **Galaad**
Jabin Josu 11 1 when Jabin king of Asor had heard
Judg 4 17 peace between Jabin the king of Asor
23 God that day humbled Jabin the king of
24 overpowered Jabin king of Chanaan
Ps 82 10 as to Jabin at the brook of Cisson
Jabin's Judg 4 7 Sisara the general of J. army
Jabnia 2 Pa 26 6 broke down . . . the wall of J.
Jaboc Gen 32 22 passed over the ford of Jaboc
Josu 12 2 the torrent Jaboc, which is the border
Judg 11 13 Arnon unto the Jaboc and the Jordan
22 from the Arnon to the Jaboc and from
Jacan Deut 10 6 from Beroth of the children of J.
1 Pa 1 42 of Eser: Balaan and Zavan and Jacan
5 13 Jacan and Zie and Heber, seven
Jachanan Josu 12 22 the king of J. of Carmel one
Jachin Gen 46 10 sons of Simeon: . . . J. Exod 6:15; Num 26:12
3 K 7 21 he called the name thereof Jachin
1 Pa 9 10 of the priests . . . Jachin. 2 Es 11:10
24 17 one and twentieth [lot] to Jachin
2 Pa 3 17 was on the right hand, he called Jachin
Jachinites Num 26 12 of him is family of the J.
Jacim 1 Pa 8 19 and Jacim . . . sons of Semei
1 Pa 24 12 the twelfth [lot] to Jacim, the
jacinth Apoc 21 20 the eleventh, a jacinth: the
Jacoba 1 Pa 4 36 Elioenai and Jacoba and Isuhaia
Jacob's Gen 30 40 and the rest were Jacob's
Gen 30 42 Laban's: and they of the first time, J.
32 18 thou shalt answer: Thy servant Jacob's
32 the sinew that shrank in Jacob's thigh
34 7 unlawful act, in ravishing J. daughter
46 19 sons of Rachel Jacob's wife: Joseph
Exod 1 5 all the souls that came out of J. thigh
John 4 6 Jacob's well was there. Jesus therefore
Jada 1 Pa 2 28 Onam had sons Semei and Jada. And
1 Pa 2 32 the sons of Jada the brother of Semei
Jadaia 1 Es 2 36 the children of Jadaia . . . 973
Jadason Jdth 1 6 and the Tigris and the Jadason
Jaddo 1 Pa 27 21 over the half tribe . . . Jaddo
Jadias 1 Pa 27 30 over the asses, Jadias a
Jadihel 1 Pa 7 6 sons of Benjamin . . . Jadihel
1 Pa 7 10 the son of Jadihel: Balan. And the sons
11 all these were sons of Jadihel, heads
26 2 sons of Meselemia . . . J. the second
Jadon 2 Es 3 7 next to them built . . . and Jadon
Jagur Josu 15 21 Cabseel and Eder and Jagur and
Jahaddai 1 Pa 2 47 the sons of Jahaddai, Rogom
Jahala 2 Es 7 57 Nathinites . . . children of J.
Jahath 1 Pa 4 2 Raia the son of Sobal begot J.
1 Pa 6 20 Lobni his son, Jahath his son, Zamma
24 22 the son of Salemoth Jahath: and his
2 Pa 34 12 overseers of the workmen were Jahath
Jahaziel 1 Pa 23 19 Jahaziel the third. 24:23
2 Pa 20 14 Jahaziel the son of Zacharias the son
Jahel Judg 4 17 Sisara fleeing came to tent of J.
Judg 4 18 J. went forth to meet Sisara and said
21 so Jahel Haber's wife took a nail of
22 Jahel went out to meet him, and said
5 6 in the days of Jahel the paths rested
24 blessed among women be Jahel the wife
Jahelel Gen 46 14 Sared and Elon and Jahelel
Jahiel 1 Pa 15 18 Jahiel and Ani and Eliab and
1 Pa 16 5 Semiramoth and J. and Mathathias
23 8 sons of Leedan: the chief Jahiel
27 32 and Jahiel the son of Hachamoni were
2 Pa 21 2 Azarias and Jahiel and Michael
29 13 of the sons of Elisaphan, Samri and J.
14 the sons of Heman, Jahiel and Semei
35 8 Zacharias and J. rulers of the house
1 Es 8 9 sons of Joab, Obedia the son of Jahiel
Jair Deut 3 14 Jair the son of Manasses possessed
Num 32 41 Jair the son of Manasses went and
41 Havoth Jair, that is to say, the villages of Jair
Deut 3 14 Havoth Jair, that is to say, the towns of Jair. Judg 10:4
Josu 13 30 and all the villages of Jair, which are
Judg 10 3 to him succeeded Jair the Galaadite
5 and Jair died: and was buried in the
3 K 4 13 he had the towns of Jair the son of
1 Pa 2 22 and Segub begot Jair, and he had
23 Gessur and Aram the towns of Jair, and
Esth 2 5 Mardochai the son of Jair. 11:2
Jairite 2 K 20 26 Ira the J. was the priest of
Jairus Mark 5 22 rulers of the synagogue named J.
Luke 8 41 there came a man whose name was Jairus
jakes 4 K 10 27 made a jakes in its place unto
Jala 1 Es 2 56 the children of Jala, the children of
Jalaleel 2 Pa 29 12 Azarias the son of Jalaleel
Jalel Num 26 26 sons of Zabulon . . . Jalel
Jaleleel 1 Pa 4 16 the sons also of Jaleleel
Jalelites Num 26 26 of whom is family of the J.
Jalon 1 Pa 4 17 Mered and Epher and Jalon
Jambri 1 Ma 9 36 children of J. came forth out
1 Ma 9 37 children of J. made a great marriage
James Mat 4 21 James the son of Zebedee. 10:3; Mark 1:19; 3:17
Mat 10 3 James the son of Alpheus, and Thaddeus
13 55 and his brethren James and Joseph and
27 56 Mary the mother of J. Mark 15:40; 10:1
Mark 1 29 and Andrew, with James and John
3 18 and Thomas and James of Alpheus and
10 35 James and John . . . come to him
41 much displeased at James and John
Luke 5 10 so were also James and John the sons
6 14 James and John, Philip and
15 James the son of Alpheus, and Simon
9 54 disciples, J. and John, had seen this
24 10 and Mary of James and the other women
Acts 1 13 where abode Peter and John, James and
13 where abode . . . James of Alpheus and
12 2 he killed James, the brother of John
17 he said: Tell these things to James
15 13 James answered, saying: Men, brethren
21 18 Paul went in with us unto James; and all
1 C 15 7 after that, he was seen by James, then
Gal 1 19 saving James the brother of the Lord
2 9 given to me, James and Cephas and John
12 before that some came from James, he
James 1 1 James the servant of God and of our
brother of James Mark 3 17 and John the b. . . . ; and he named
Mark 5 37 and John the b. . . . And they come
6 3 son of Mary, the brother of James and
Luke 6 16 Jude the b. . . . ; and Judas Iscariot
Acts 1 13 abode . . . Jude the brother of James
Jude 1 Jude . . . brother of James: to them
Jamin Gen 46 10 sons of Simeon . . . Jamin. Exod 6:15; Num 26:12; 1 Pa 4:24
1 Pa 2 27 were Moos, Jamin, and Achar. And Onam
2 Es 8 7 Jamin, Accub, Sephtai, Odia, Maasia
Jaminites Num 26 12 is the family of the J.
Jamne Gen 46 17 sons of Aser: Jamne and Jesua
Jamnia 1 Ma 4 15 even to the plains . . . of Jamnia
1 Ma 5 58 his army, and they went towards Jamnia
10 69 a great army, and came to Jamnia
15 40 Cendebeus came to Jamnia and began to
2 Ma 12 8 men of J. designed to do in like manner
40 of the donaries of the idols of Jamnia
Jamnites 2 Ma 12 9 he came upon the J. also by
Jamnor Jdth 8 1 son of Elai the son of Jamnor
Jamra 1 Pa 7 36 and Sual and Beri and Jamra, Bosor

Jamuel Gen 46 10 sons of Simeon: J. and. Exod 6:15
Janai 1 Pa 5 12 and Janai and Saphat in Basan
Janne Luke 3 24 Melchi, who was of Janne, who was
Jannes 2 Tim 3 8 Jannes and Mambres resisted Moses
Janoe Josu 16 6 along on east side to Janoe
Josu 16 7 it goeth down from Janoe into Ataroth
4 K 15 29 took Aion . . . and Janoe and Cedes
Janum Josu 15 53 Janum and Beththaphua and
Japheth Gen 5 31 Sem, Cham, and Japheth. 6:10; 7:13; 9:18; 10:1; 1 Pa 1:4
Gen 9 23 Sem and Japheth put a cloak upon
27 may God enlarge Japheth, and may
10 2 sons of Japheth: Gomer and. 1 Pa 1:5
21 Heber, the elder brother of Japheth
Jdth 2 15 from Cilicia to the coasts of Japheth
Japhia Josu 10 3 and to Japhia king of Lachis
2 K 5 16 Japhia and Elisama and Elioda and
1 Pa 3 7 and Noge and Nepheg and Japhia and
14 6 born to him [David] . . . Japhia, Elisama
Japhie Josu 19 12 and ascendeth towards Japhie
Jara 1 Pa 5 14 Huri the son of Jara the son of
1 Pa 9 42 Ahaz begot J., and J. begot Alamath
Jaramoth Josu 21 29 and Jaramoth and Engannim
Jare Gen 10 26 Jectan begot . . . Jare. 1 Pa 1:20
Jared Gen 5 15 Malaleel lived . . . and begot Jared
Gen 5 16 Malaleel lived after he begot Jared
18 Jared lived 162 years, and begot Henoch
19 Jared lived after he begot Henoch
20 all the days of Jared were 962 years
1 Pa 4 18 and his wife Judaia bore Jared the
Luke 3 37 Henoch, who was of Jared, who was of
Jarephel Josu 18 27 Recem, Jarephel, and Tharela
Jarib 1 Pa 4 24 Jamin, Jarib, Zara, Saul: Sellûm
1 Es 8 16 Semeias and Elnathan and Jarib and
10 18 and Eliezer and Jarib and Godolia
1 Ma 14 29 of Mathathias of the children of Jarib
Jarim Josu 15 10 passeth by the side of mount J.
Jasa Num 21 23 came to Jasa and fought against
Deut 2 32 us with all his people to fight at Jasa
Judg 11 20 went out against him to Jasa and made
Isa 15 4 their voice is heard even to Jasa
Jer 48 21 upon Helon and upon Jasa and upon
34 from the cry of Hesebon . . . to Jasa
Jaser Josu 13 25 border of J. and all the cities of
Josu 21 36 cities of refuge, Misor and Jaser and
37 and Hesebon and Jaser, four cities
1 Pa 2 18 her sons were Jaser and Sobab and
Jasi 1 Es 10 37 of the sons of Bani . . . Jasi
Jasiel 1 Pa 7 13 sons of Nephtali were Jasiel
1 Pa 11 46 Eliel and Obed and Jasiel of Masobia
27 21 over Benjamin, J. the son of Abner
Jason 1 Ma 8 17 Jason the son of Eleazar, and
1 Ma 12 16 Antipater the son of Jason. 14:22
2 Ma 1 7 after Jason withdrew himself from the
2 24 in five books by Jason of Cyrene
4 7 Jason the brother of Onias ambitiously
13 and unheard of wickedness of Jason
19 the wicked Jason sent from Jerusalem
22 received in a magnificent manner by J.
23 Jason sent Menelaus, brother of the
24 for himself, by offering more than J.
26 Jason, who had undermined his own
5 5 Jason taking with him no fewer than
6 Jason slew his countrymen without mercy
Acts 17 6 not finding them, they drew Jason and
7 hither also: whom Jason hath received
9 having taken satisfaction of Jason
Rom 16 21 Lucius and J. and Sosipater, my kinsmen
Jason's Acts 17 5 besetting J. house, sought to
jasper Exod 28 18 in the second . . . a jasper. 39:11
Isa 54 12 I will make thy bulwarks of jasper
Eze 28 13 thy covering . . . topaz and the jasper
Apoc 4 3 like the jasper and the sardine stone
21 11 as to the jasper stone, even as crystal
18 wall thereof was of jasper stone: but
19 the first foundation was jasper: the
Jassa Josu 13 18 and Jassa and Cedimoth and
1 Pa 6 78 out of the tribe of Ruben . . . Jassa
Jassen 2 K 23 32 the sons of Jassen, Jonathan
Jasub Num 26 24 sons of Issachar . . . Jasub. 1 Pa 7:1
1 Es 10 29 of the sons of Bani . . . Jasub and
Isa 7 3 go forth . . . thou and Jasub thy son
Jasubites Num 26 24 is the family of the J.
Jathanael 1 Pa 26 2 sons of Meselemia . . . J. the
Jaus 1 Pa 23 10 sons of Semei . . . Jaus and Baria
1 Pa 23 11 Jaus and Baria had not many children
Javan Gen 10 2 sons of Japheth: . . . J. 1 Pa 1:5
Gen 10 4 the sons of Javan: Elisa. 1 Pa 1:7
javelins 1 Ma 6 51 engines to cast stones and j.
jaw Judg 15 16 with the jaw of the colt of asses
Judg 15 19 opened a great tooth in jaw of the ass
Job 40 21 or bore through his jaw with a buckle
Prov 30 14 and grindeth with their jaw teeth
jawbone Judg 15 9 called Lechi, that is, the J.
Judg 15 14 he was come to place of the Jawbone
15 finding a j., even the j. of an ass
16 with the jawbone of an ass . . . I have
17 he threw the jawbone out of his hand
17 is interpreted the lifting up of the j.
19 Spring of him that invoked from the j.
jaws Job 29 17 I broke the j. of the wicked man
Job 33 2 let my tongue speak within my jaws
Ps 21 16 my tongue hath cleaved to my jaws
31 9 with bit and bridle bind fast their j.
68 4 my jaws are become hoarse: my eyes
136 6 let my tongue cleave to my jaws if I
Isa 30 28 that was in the jaws of the people
Eze 29 4 but I will put a bridle in thy jaws
38 4 about and I will put a bit in thy jaws
Osee 6 9 like the jaws of highway robbers, they
11 4 that taketh off the yoke on their jaws
Jazer Num 21 32 sent some to take a view of Jazer
Num 32 1 saw the lands of Jazer and Galaad
3 Ataroth and Dibon and Jazer and
35 and Etroth and Sophan and Jazer
2 K 24 6 by Jazer they passed into Galaad and
6 81 suburbs, and Jazer with its suburbs
26 31 most valiant men in Jazer Galaad
Isa 16 8 branches thereof have reached even to J.
9 I will lament with the weeping of J.
Jer 48 32 for thee with the mourning of Jazer
32 they are come even to the sea of Jazer
Jaziel Gen 46 24 sons of Nephtali: J. and Guni
1 Pa 12 3 Jaziel and Phallet the sons of Azmoth
15 18 Zacharias and Ben and Jaziel and
16 6 Banaias and Jaziel the priests to
Jaziz 1 Pa 27 31 over the sheep Jaziz an Agarene
Jeabarim Num 21 11 pitched their tents in J.
jealous Exod 20 5 the Lord thy God, mighty, j.
Exod 34 14 Lord his name is J., he is a j. God
Deut 4 24 is a consuming fire, a jealous God
5 9 I am the Lord thy God, a jealous God
6 15 the Lord thy God is a jealous God in
Josu 24 19 he is a holy God, and mighty and j.
Eccu 9 1 be not j. over the wife of thy bosom
26 8 a jealous woman is the grief and
9 with a j. woman is a scourge of the
30 3 maketh his enemy jealous and in the
37 12 touching her of whom she is jealous
Eze 39 25 I will be jealous for my holy name
Nah 1 2 the Lord is a jealous God and a
Zach 8 2 I have been jealous for Sion . . . have I been jealous for her
2 C 11 2 I am j. of you with the jealousy of God
jealousy Num 5 14 spirit of j. stir up the husband
Num 5 15 because it is a sacrifice of jealousy

18 remembrance, and the oblation of j.
25 from her hand the sacrifice of j.
29 this is the law of jealousy. If a
30 husband stirred up by the spirit of j.
Deut 29 20 his wrath and jealousy against that man
Ps 77 58 moved him to j. with their graven
Prov 6 34 the jealousy and rage of the husband
Cant 8 6 is strong as death, j. as hard as hell
Wisd 1 10 the ear of jealousy heareth all things
Eze 8 3 the idol of j. to provoke to j. And
5 the idol of jealousy in the very entry
16 38 I will give thee blood in fury and j.
42 and my jealousy shall depart from thee
23 25 I will set my jealousy against thee
Soph 1 18 shall be devoured by the fire of his j.
3 8 with the fire of my j. shall all the
Zach 8 2 been jealous for Sion with a great j.
1 Ma 8 16 is no envy nor jealousy amongst them
Rom 10 19 I will provoke you to j. by that which
1 C 10 22 do we provoke you to jealousy by
22 do we provoke the Lord to jealousy? Are
2 C 11 2 I am jealous of you with the j. of God
Jebaar 1 Pa 3 6 Jebaar also and Elisama and
Jebahar 2 K 5 15 Jebahar and Elisua. 1 Pa 14:5
Jebania 1 Pa 9 8 Rahuel the son of Jebania: and
Jeblaam Josu 17 11 and its villages, and Jeblaam
Judg 1 27 nor inhabitants of Dor and Jeblaam
4 K 9 27 going up to Gaver, which is by Jeblaam
Jebnael Josu 19 33 and Jebnael even to Lecum
Jebneel Josu 15 11 cometh into J. and is bounded
Jeboc Num 21 24 land from the Arnon unto the J.
Deut 2 37 all that border upon the torrent Jeboc
3 16 confines even unto the torrent Jeboc
Jebsem 1 Pa 7 2 sons of Thola . . . Jebsem and
Jebus Josu 18 28 Jebus, which is Jerusalem
Judg 19 10 forward and came over against Jebus
11 and now they were come near Jebus
14 so they passed by Jebus and went on
1 Pa 11 4 went to Jerusalem, which is Jebus
5 the inhabitants of Jebus said to David
Jebusite Gen 10 15 Chanaan begot . . . the J. 1 Pa 1:14
Exod 3 8 Hevite and Jebusite. 17; 13:4; 23:23; 33:2; 34:11; Deut 7:1; 20:17; Josu 9:1; 12:8; 24:11; Judg 3:5
Num 13 30 the Hethite and the Jebusite and the
Josu 3 10 he shall destroy . . . the Jebusite
11 3 Pherezite and the J. in the mountains
15 8 on side of the J. towards the south
63 could not destroy the Jebusite that
63 Jebusite dwelt with the children of Juda
18 16 by side of the Jebusite to the south
Judg 1 21 J. hath dwelt with sons of Benjamin
2 K 24 16 thrashingfloor of Areuna the J. 18
1 Pa 21 15 by the thrashingfloor of Ornan the J. 18, 28; 2 Pa 3:1
2 Es 9 8 to give him the land of . . . the J.
Zach 9 7 governor in Juda, and Accaron as a J.
Jebusites Gen 15 21 the Gergesites and the J.
Judg 1 21 of Benjamin did not destroy the J.
19 11 let us turn into the city of the J.
2 K 5 6 went to Jerusalem to the Jebusites
8 whosoever should strike the Jebusites
3 K 9 20 were left of the . . . J. 2 Pa 8:7
1 Pa 11 4 where the J. were the inhabitants
6 whosoever shall first strike the J.
1 Es 9 1 abominations of . . . the Jebusites
Jdth 5 20 overthrew the king . . . of the Jebusites
Jecemia 1 Pa 3 18 sons of Jechonias . . . Jecemia
Jechelia 4 K 15 2 of his mother was J. 2 Pa 26:3
Jechonias 1 Pa 3 16 of Joakim was born Jechonias
1 Pa 3 17 the sons of J. were Asir, Salathiel
Esth 2 6 carried away Jechonias. Jer 24:1; 27:20; Bar 1:9
11 4 from Jerusalem with J. king of Juda
Jer 22 24 if Jechonias . . . were a ring on my
28 is this man Jechonias an earthen
28 4 I will bring back to this place J.
29 2 after that Jechonias . . . were departed
37 1 Sedecias . . . reigned instead of J.
Bar 1 3 this book in the hearing of Jechonias
Mat 1 11 Josias begot J. and his brethren in the
12 Jechonias begot Salathiel. And
Jecmaam 1 Pa 23 19 sons of Hebron . . . J. the fourth
Jecmaan 3 K 4 12 unto Abelmehula over against J.
1 Pa 6 68 cities of refuge . . . Jecmaan
24 23 and his son . . . Jecmaan the fourth
Jecnam Josu 21 34 Jecnam and Cartha and Damna
Jeconam Josu 19 11 torrent which is over against J.
Jecsan Gen 25 2 who bore him Zamran and Jecsan
Gen 25 3 Jecsan also begot Saba and Dadan
1 Pa 1 32 Zamran, Jecsan, Madan, Madian
32 and the sons of Jecsan, Saba and Dadan
Jectan Gen 10 25 his brother's name Jectan
Gen 10 26 Jectan begot Elmodad. 1 Pa 1:20
29 all these were the sons of Jectan
1 Pa 1 19 the name of his brother was Jectan
23 all these are the sons of Jectan
Jectehel 4 K 14 7 called the name thereof J.
Jecthel Josu 15 38 Masepha and Jecthel, Lachis
Jedaia 1 Pa 9 10 the priests: Jedaia, Joiarib
2 Es 3 10 and next to him Jedaia the son of
Jedala Josu 19 15 and Jedala and Bethlehem
Jeddel 2 Es 7 58 Nathinites . . . children of Jeddel
Jeddo 1 Pa 5 14 Jesisi the son of Jeddo
Jeddoa 2 Es 12 11 Jonathan begot Jeddoa. And in
2 Es 12 22 and Joiada and Johanan and Jeddoa
Jeddu 1 Es 10 43 of the sons of Nebo . . . Jeddu
Jeddua 2 Es 10 21 Mesizabel, Sadoc, Jeddua
Jedebos 1 Pa 4 3 posterity of Etam . . . Jedebos
Jedei 1 Pa 24 7 the second [lot] to Jedei, the
Jediel 1 Pa 5 24 heads of the house . . . Jediel
Jedihel 1 Pa 11 45 Jedihel the son of Zamri
1 Pa 12 20 Jozabad and Jedihel and Michael
Jedlaph Gen 22 22 Azau and Pheldas and Jedlaph
Jegaal 1 Pa 3 22 Hattus and Jegaal and Baria
Jegbaa Num 32 35 Sophan and Jazer and Jegbaa
Judg 8 11 on the east of Nobe and Jegbaa, and
Jegedelias Jer 35 4 son of J. the man of God
Jehedeia 1 Pa 24 20 of the sons of Subael, J.
Jeheziel 1 Pa 12 4 Jeremias and J. and Johanan
Jehias 1 Pa 15 24 Obededom and Jehias were porters
Jehiel 1 Pa 5 7 had for princes Jehiel and
1 Pa 9 35 in Gabaon dwelt Jehiel the father of
11 44 Samma and Jehiel the sons of Hotham
15 18 Obededom and Jehiel, the porters
20 Jehiel and Ani and Eliab and Maasias
21 J. and Ozaziu sung a song of victory
16 5 Jahiel and Semiramoth and Jehiel
2 Pa 20 14 the son of Banaias the son of Jehiel
26 11 was under the hand of Jehiel the scribe
31 13 Jehiel and Azarias and Nahath and
35 9 Hasabias and Jehiel and Jozabad princes
1 Es 8 13 Eliphelet and Jehiel and Samaias and
10 2 Sechenias the son of Jehiel of the
21 and Semeia and Jehiel and Ozias. And
43 of the sons of Nebo, Jehiel, Mathathias
Jehieli 1 Pa 26 21 of Ledan, and Gersonni, Jehieli
1 Pa 26 22 the sons of Jehieli: Zathan and Joel
Jehu 3 K 16 1 word of the Lord came to Jehu
3 K 16 7 of the Lord came in the hand of Jehu
7 he slew him, that is to say, Jehu
12 had spoken to Baasa in the hand of Jehu
19 16 anoint Jehu . . . to be king over Israel
17 of Hazael, shall be slain by Jehu
4 K 9 2 thou shalt see J. the son of Josaphat
5 and Jehu said: Unto whom of us all

11 Jehu went forth to servants of his lord
13 sounded trumpet and said: Jehu is king
14 so Jehu . . . conspired against Joram
15 Jehu said: If it please you, let no man
17 saw the troop of J. coming and said
18 Jehu said: What hast thou to do. 19
20 the driving is like the driving of J.
21 they went out to meet Jehu, and met
22 he said: Is there peace, Jehu? And he
24 but Jehu bent his bow with his hand
25 Jehu said to Badacer his captain: Take
27 Jehu pursued him and said: Strike him
30 Jehu came into Jezrahel. But Jezabel
31 looked out of a window at Jehu coming
32 Jehu lifted up his face to the window
36 Jehu said: It is the word of the Lord
10 1 Jehu wrote letters and sent to Samaria
5 ancients and the tutors sent to Jehu
11 so Jehu slew all that were left of
18 Jehu gathered together all the people
19 Jehu did this craftily that he might
23 Jehu . . . went to the temple of Baal
24 Jehu had prepared him fourscore men
25 J. commanded his soldiers and captains
28 so Jehu destroyed Baal out of Israel
30 Lord said to Jehu: Because thou hast
31 Jehu took no heed to walk in the law
34 the rest of the acts of Jehu and all
35 Jehu slept with his fathers, and they
36 the time that Jehu reigned over Israel
12 1 in seventh year of Jehu, Joas began to
13 1 Joachaz the son of Jehu. 14:8; 2 Pa 25:17
15 12 word of the Lord which he spoke to J.
1 Pa 2 38 Obed begot Jehu, Jehu begot Azarias
4 35 Joel and Jehu the son of Josabia
12 3 Beracha, and Jehu an Anathothite
2 Pa 19 2 Jehu . . . the seer met him [Josaphat]
20 34 are written in the words of Jehu the
22 7 come should go out also against Jehu
8 J. was rooting out the house of Achab
Osee 1 4 blood of Jezrahel upon the house of J.
Jehuel 1 Pa 9 6 of the sons of Zara: Jehuel
Jehus Gen 36 5 Oolibama bore Jehus and Ihelon and
Gen 36 14 Jehus and Thelon and Core. 1 Pa 1:35
18 duke Jehus, duke Thelon, duke Core
1 Pa 7 10 sons of Balan: Jehus and Benjamin
8 10 Jehus and Sechia and Marma. These were
39 Jehus the second, and Eliphalet the
2 Pa 11 19 bore him sons Jehus and Somorias and
Jemai 1 Pa 7 2 sons of Thola . . . Jemai and Jebsem
Jemini Judg 3 15 the son of Gera, the son of J.
Judg 19 16 men of that country were children of J.
1 K 9 1 of Aphia the son of a man of Jemini
4 through land of J. and found them not
21 am not I a son of Jemini of the least
22 7 hear me now, ye sons of Jemini: will
2 K 16 11 how much more now a son of Jemini
19 16 Gera the son of Jemini. 3 K 2:8
20 1 the son of Bochri, a man of Jemini
1 Pa 27 12 an Anathothite of the sons of Jemini
Esth 2 5 Mardochai . . . of the race of Jemini
Ps 7 1 the words of Chusi the son of Jemini
Jemla 3 K 22 8 Micheas the son of Jemla. 22:9; 2 Pa 18:7, 8
Jemlech 1 Pa 4 34 Mosabab and Jemlech and Josa
Jemna Num 26 44 sons of Aser . . . Jemna, of whom
1 Pa 7 30 children of Aser were Jemna and Jesua
35 Supha and Jemna and Selles and Amal
2 Pa 31 14 Core the son of Jemna the Levite, the
Jemnaites Num 26 44 is the family of the J.
Jephdaia 1 Pa 8 25 J. and Phanuel the sons of
Jephlat 1 Pa 7 32 Heber begot Jephlat and Somer
1 Pa 7 33 the sons of Jephlat: Phosech and
Jephleti Josu 16 3 westward, by the border of J.
Jephone Num 13 7 Caleb the son of Jephone. 14:6, 30, 38; 26:65; 32:12; 34:19; Deut 1:36; Josu 14:6, 14; 15:13; 21:12; 1 Pa 4:15; 6:56; Eccu 46:9
1 Pa 7 38 the sons of Jether: Jephone and
Jephtahel Josu 19 14 are the valley of Jephtahel
Jephte Judg 11 1 at that time J. the Galaadite
Judg 11 2 thrust out Jephte, saying: Thou canst
5 the ancients of Galaad went to fetch J.
8 the princes of Galaad said to Jephte
9 J. also said to them: If you be come
11 Jephte therefore went with the princes
11 J. spoke all his words before the Lord
14 Jephte again sent word by them and
15 thus saith Jephte: Israel did not take
28 would not hearken to the words of J.
29 the spirit of the Lord came upon Jephte
32 J. passed over to the children of Ammon
34 when J. returned into Maspha to his
40 and lament the daughter of Jephte the
12 1 they said to Jephte: When thou wentest
7 and Jephte the Galaadite judged Israel
1 K 12 11 Lord sent Jerobaal and Badan and J.
Jephtha Josu 15 43 Jephtha and Esna and Nesib
Jephthael Josu 19 27 and to the valley of J.
Jephthe Heb 11 32 Samson, Jephthe, David, Samuel
Jeraa 1 Pa 2 34 a servant an Egyptian, named J.
Jeramael 1 Pa 24 29 the son of Cis, Jeramael
Jerameel 1 K 27 10 and against the south of J.
1 K 30 29 that were in the cities of Jerameel
1 Pa 2 9 Jerameel and Ram and Calubi. And
25 the sons of Jerameel. 33
26 and Jerameel married another wife
27 sons of Ram the firstborn of Jerameel
42 sons of Caleb the brother of Jerameel
Jercaam 1 Pa 2 44 Raham the father of Jercaam
Jeremia 1 Pa 5 24 Esriel and Jeremia and Odoia
Jeremias 4 K 23 31 Amital the daughter of J. 24:19
1 Pa 12 4 Jeremias and Jeheziel and Johanan
10 Jeremias the fifth, Ethai the sixth
13 Jeremias the tenth, Machbani the
2 Pa 35 25 mourned for him, particularly Jeremias
36 12 did not reverence the face of Jeremias
21 word of Lord by the mouth of J. 1 Es 1:1
22 which he had spoken by the mouth of J.
2 Es 10 2 Saraias, Azarias, Jeremias, Pheshur
12 1 went up with Zorobabel . . . Jeremias
12 Maraia: of Jeremias, Hanania. Of Esdras
33 Benjamin and Semeia and Jeremias. And
Ps 64 1 the canticle of Jeremias and Ezechiel
136 1 a psalm of David, for Jeremias. Upon
Eccu 49 8 according to the prediction of J. For
Jer 1 1 words of Jeremias the son of Helcias
11 what seest thou, Jeremias. 24:3
7 1 the word that came to J. 18:1; 21:1; 25:1; 30:1; 32:1; 34:1, 8; 35:1; 40:1; 44:1
11 1 word that came from the Lord to J.
14 1 word of the Lord that came to Jeremias
18 18 let us invent devices against Jeremias
19 14 Jeremias came from Topheth, whither
20 1 Phassur . . . heard Jeremias prophesying
3 Phassur brought J. out of the stocks
3 J. said to him: The Lord hath not
21 3 J. said to them: Thus shall you say
25 13 that J. hath prophesied against all
26 7 heard Jeremias speaking these words
8 J. had made an end of speaking. 43:1
9 were gathered together against Jeremias
12 Jeremias spoke to all the princes and
20 according to all the words of Jeremias
24 hand of Ahicam . . . was with Jeremias
27 1 this word came to Jeremias. 36:1

28 12 the word of the Lord came to J. 29:30; 32:26; 33:11, 19, 23; 34:12; 35:12; 39:15; 42:7; 43:8
29 27 why hast thou not rebuked Jeremias
32 6 J. said: The word of the Lord came
35 3 I took Jezonias the son of Jeremias
18 J. said to the house of the Rechabites
36 4 so Jeremias called Baruch the son of
4 Baruch wrote from the mouth of Jeremias
5 Jeremias commanded Baruch, saying
10 read out of the volume the words of J.
19 hide thee, both thou and Jeremias
27 Baruch had written from the mouth of J.
32 Jeremias took another volume and gave
32 wrote in it from the mouth of Jeremias
37 4 Jeremias walked freely in the midst of
11 Jeremias went forth out of Jerusalem
13 Jeremias answered: It is not so, I am
13 Jerias took Jeremias and brought him
14 the princes were angry with Jeremias
15 J. went into the house of the prison
15 and Jeremias remained there many days
16 word from the Lord? And J. said: There
17 J. said to king Sedecias: In what have
20 commanded that J. should be committed
20 J. remained in the entry. 38:13, 28
38 1 heard the words that Jeremias spoke
6 took J. and cast him into the dungeon
6 they let down Jeremias by ropes into
6 and Jeremias sunk into the mire. Now
7 that they had put J. in the dungeon
11 he let them down by cords to Jeremias
12 put these old rags . . . and J. did so
13 they drew up Jeremias with the cords
14 king said to Jeremias: I will ask thee
15 J. said to Sedecias: If I shall declare
16 king Sedecias swore to J., in private
17 J. said to Sedecias: Thus saith the
19 Sedecias said to Jeremias: I am afraid
20 J. answered: They shall not deliver
24 Sedecias said to J.: Let no man know
27 the princes came to J. and asked him
39 11 given charge . . . concerning Jeremias
13 took J. out of the court of the prison
40 2 the general of the army taking Jeremias
6 J. went to Godolias . . . to Masphath
42 5 they said to J.: The Lord be witness
43 2 proud men, made answer, saying to J.
44 15 answered Jeremias, saying: As for the
20 and Jeremias spoke to all the people
24 Jeremias said to all the people and
45 1 in a book, out of the mouth of J.
51 60 Jeremias wrote in one book all the evil
61 J. said to Saraias: When thou shalt
64 thus far the words of Jeremias
52 1 Amital, the daughter of J. of Lobna
Bar 6 1 a copy of the epistle that J. sent
2 Ma 2 5 when J. came thither he found a hollow
7 when J. perceived it, he blamed them
15 15 Jeremias stretched forth his right hand
Mat 16 14 and others Jeremias or one of the

Jeremias the prophet 2 Pa 36 12 not reverence the face of Jeremias the prophet
Jer 20 2 Phassur struck Jeremias the prophet and
25 2 which J. . . . spoke to all the people
28 5 J. . . . said to Hananias. 15
6 J. . . . said: Amen, the Lord do so: the
10 took the chain from the neck of J. . . .
12 Jeremias the prophet went his way. And
12 the chain from off the neck of J. . . .
29 1 of the letter which J. . . . sent from
29 this letter in the hearing of J. . . .
32 2 J. . . . was shut up in the court of the
34 6 J. . . . spoke all these words to Sedecias
36 8 all that J. . . . had commanded him
26 take up Baruch the scribe and J. . . .
27 word of the Lord came to J. . . . 37:5
37 2 that he spoke in the hand of J. . . .
3 son of Maasias the priest to J. . . .
12 he took hold of J. . . . , saying: Thou
38 9 that they have done against J. . . .
10 draw up J. . . . out of the dungeon
14 king Sedecias sent, and took J. . . .
42 2 said to J. . . . Let our supplication
4 J. . . . said to them: I have heard you
43 6 J. . . . and Baruch the son of Nerias
45 1 the word that J. . . . spoke to Baruch
46 1 the word of the Lord that came to J. . . . 47:1; 49:34
13 word that the Lord spoke to J. . . .
50 1 hath spoken . . . in the hand of J. . . .
51 59 word that J. . . . commanded Saraias
Dan 9 2 the word of the Lord came to J. . . .
2 Ma 2 1 is found in the descriptions of J. . . .
15 14 this is . . . J. the prophet of God
Mat 2 17 was spoken by Jeremias the prophet. 27:9

Jeremiel Jer 36 26 the king commanded Jeremiel

Jeria 1 Pa 26 31 chief of the Hebronites was J.

Jerias Jer 37 12 Jerias the son of Selemias
Jer 37 13 Jerias took Jeremias and brought him

Jeriau 1 Pa 23 19 sons of Hebron: J. the first
1 Pa 24 23 his son Jeriau the first, Amarias the

Jeribai 1 Pa 11 46 Jeribai and Josaia the sons of

Jericho Num 22 1 over against where J. is situate
Num 26 3 the Jordan over against J. 63; 31:12; 33:48; 34:15; 35:1; 36:13; Josu 16:1; 21:36; 1 Pa 6:78
Deut 32 49 land of Moab over against Jericho
34 1 to the top of Phasga over against J.
3 and the breadth of the plain of Jericho
Josu 2 1 view the land and the city of Jericho
2 and it was told the king of Jericho
3 king of Jericho sent to Rahab, saying
3 17 the people marched over against Jericho
4 13 through the plains . . . of city of J.
19 against east side of city of Jericho
5 10 month, at evening in the plains of J.
13 in the field of the city of Jericho
6 1 Jericho was close shut up and fenced
2 I have given into thy hands Jericho
25 whom he had sent to spy out Jericho
26 raise up and build the city of Jericho
7 2 when Josue sent men from Jericho
8 2 as thou hast done to Jericho and to
9 3 all that Josue had done to Jericho and
10 1 as he had done to Jericho and the king
28 had done to the king of Jericho. 30
12 9 king of Jericho one: the king of Hai
13 32 over against Jericho on the east side
16 1 wilderness which goeth up from Jericho
7 it cometh to Jericho, and goeth out
18 12 the side of Jericho on the north side
21 their cities were Jericho and Bethhagla
20 8 beyond the Jordan to the east of J.
Josu 24 11 the Jordan, and you came to Jericho
2 K 10 5 stay at Jericho, till your beards be
3 K 16 34 in his days Hiel of Bethel built J.
4 K 2 4 because the Lord hath sent me to J.
4 and when they were come to Jericho
5 sons of the prophets that were at J.
15 the sons of the prophets at Jericho
18 for he [Eliseus] abode at Jericho
25 5 overtook him in the plains of Jericho
1 Pa 19 5 and ordered them to stay at Jericho
2 Pa 28 15 upon beasts and brought them to J.
1 Es 2 34 the children of Jericho, 345. 2 Es 7:36

Jersia 1 Pa 8 27 and Jersia . . . sons of Jeroham
Jeruel 2 Pa 20 16 against the wilderness of J.
Jerusa 4 K 15 33 of his mother was J. 2 Pa 27:1
Jerusalem Mat 2 1 wise men from the east to J.
Mat 2 3 troubled, and all Jerusalem with him
3 5 then went out to him Jerusalem and all
4 25 from Decapolis and from Jerusalem
5 35 nor by J., for it is the city of the
15 1 came to him from J. scribes and
16 21 he must go to J. and suffer many things
20 17 Jesus going up to J., took the twelve
18 we go up to J. Mark 10:33; Luke 18:31
21 1 when they drew nigh to Jerusalem and
10 when he was come into Jerusalem, the
23 37 J., J., thou that killest the prophets. Luke 13:34
Mark 1 5 all they of J., and were baptized by
3 8 and from Jerusalem and from Idumea
22 the scribes who were come down from J.
7 1 some of the scribes, coming from J.
10 32 they were in the way going up to J.
11 1 when they were drawing near to J. and
11 he entered into J., into the temple
15 they came to Jerusalem. And when he
27 and they come again to Jerusalem
15 41 women that came up with him to J.
Luke 2 22 they carried him to J. to present him
25 was a man in Jerusalem named Simeon
41 his parents went every year to J.
42 they going up into J. according to
43 the child Jesus remained in Jerusalem
45 they returned into J., seeking him
4 9 he brought him to J. and set him on
5 17 of Galilee and Judea and Jerusalem
6 17 people from all Judea and Jerusalem
9 31 that he should accomplish in J. But
51 steadfastly set his face to go to J.
53 his face was of one going to Jerusalem
10 30 man went down from J. to Jericho, and
13 4 above all the men that dwelt in J.
22 and making his journey to Jerusalem
33 that a prophet perish out of J.
17 11 as he was going to J., he passed
19 11 parable because he was nigh to J. and
28 he went before, going up to Jerusalem
21 20 when you shall see J. compassed about
24 Jerusalem shall be trodden down by the
23 7 who was also himself at J. in those
28 daughters of Jerusalem, weep not over
24 13 which was 60 furlongs from Jerusalem
18 art thou only a stranger in Jerusalem
33 went back to Jerusalem: and they found
47 unto all nations, beginning at J.
52 went back into J. with great joy. And
John 1 19 when the Jews sent from Jerusalem
2 13 and Jesus went up to Jerusalem. 5:1
23 when he was at J. at the pasch, upon
4 20 at Jerusalem is the place where men
21 neither on this mountain nor in J.
45 seen all the things he had done at J.
5 2 is at Jerusalem a pond called Probatica
7 25 some there of J. said: Is not this he
10 22 was the feast of the dedication at J.
11 18 Bethania was near Jerusalem, about
55 many from the country went up to J.
12 12 had heard that Jesus was coming to J.
Acts 1 4 they should not depart from Jerusalem
8 you shall be witnesses unto me in J.
12 they returned to Jerusalem. 8:25
12 called Olivet, which is nigh Jerusalem
2 5 now there were dwelling at J., Jews
14 and all you that dwell in Jerusalem
43 signs were done by the apostles in J.
4 5 scribes were gathered together in J.
5 16 and there came also together to J. a
28 you have filled J. with your doctrine
6 7 of the disciples was multiplied in J.
8 1 against the church which was at J.
14 when the apostles, who were in J., had
26 that goeth down from J. into Gaza
27 had come to J. to adore. And he was
9 2 he might bring them bound to Jerusalem
13 hath done to thy saints in Jerusalem
21 persecuted in J. those that called
26 when he was come to Jerusalem, he
28 coming in and going out in Jerusalem
10 39 he did in land of the Jews and in J.
11 2 when Peter was come up to J., they
22 church that was at J., touching these
27 came prophets from J. to Antioch: and
12 25 Saul returned from Jerusalem, having
13 13 John . . . returned to Jerusalem. But
27 they that inhabited J., and the rulers
31 who came up with him from Galilee to J.
15 2 should go up . . . to J. about this
4 when they were come to Jerusalem, they
34 and Judas alone departed to Jerusalem
16 4 apostles and ancients who were at J.
18 22 going down to Caesarea, he went up to J.
19 21 to go to J., saying: After I have been
20 16 for him, to keep day of Pentecost at J.
22 I go to J.: not knowing the things which
23 afflictions wait for me at J. But I
21 4 Spirit, that he should not go up to J.
11 Jews shall bind in this manner in J.
12 desired him that he would not go up to J.
13 only to be bound, but to die also in J.
15 being prepared we went up to Jerusalem
17 when we were come to Jerusalem, the
31 that all Jerusalem was in confusion. Who
22 5 from thence to Jerusalem to be punished
17 to pass, when I was come again to J.
18 and get thee quickly out of Jerusalem
23 11 as thou hast testified of me in J., so
24 11 12 days, since I went up to adore in J.
25 1 after three days, he went up to J. from
3 he would command him to be brought to J.
7 about him, who were come down from J.
9 wilt thou go up to J., and there be
14 when I was at J., the chief priests
20 asked him whether he would go to J., and
24 multitude of Jews dealt with me at J.
26 4 among my own nation in J., all the Jews
10 which also I did at J., and many of the
20 them first that are at Damascus, and J.
28 17 was delivered prisoner from J. into the
Rom 15 19 so that from J. round about as far as
25 but now I shall go to J., to minister
26 for poor of the saints that are in J.
31 may be acceptable in J. to the saints
1 C 16 3 I send to carry your grace to Jerusalem
Gal 1 17 neither went I to J., to the apostles
18 after three years, I went to Jerusalem
2 1 I went up again to J. with Barnabas
4 25 which hath affinity to that Jerusalem
26 that Jerusalem, which is above, is free
Heb 12 22 of the living God, the heavenly J.
Apoc 3 12 the new J., which cometh down out of
21 2 I John saw the holy city, the new J.
10 he showed me the holy city Jerusalem
inhabitants of Jerusalem 4 K 23 2 all the i. . . . with him, the priests and the
2 Pa 20 18 all the i. . . . fell flat on the ground
20 ye men of Juda, and all the i. . . .

7 Jesus saith to him: I will come and
10 Jesus hearing this, marvelled; and
13 Jesus said to the centurion: Go, and
14 when Jesus was come into Peter's
20 Jesus saith to him: The foxes have
22 Jesus said to him: Follow me, and let
26 Jesus saith to them: Why are you
29 to do with thee, Jesus Son of God
34 the whole city went out to meet Jesus
9 9 when Jesus passed on from thence, he
10 sat down with Jesus and his disciples
12 Jesus hearing it, said: They that are
15 Jesus said to them: Can the children
19 Jesus rising up followed him, with his
22 Jesus turning and seeing her, said
23 when Jesus was come into the house
27 as Jesus passed from thence, there
28 Jesus saith to them, Do you believe
30 Jesus strictly charged them, saying
10 5 these twelve Jesus sent: commanding
11 1 when J. had made an end of commanding
4 Jesus making answer said to them: Go
7 Jesus began to say to the multitudes
12 15 Jesus knowing it, retired from thence
25 Jesus knowing their thoughts, said to
13 1 Jesus going out of the house, sat by
53 when Jesus had finished these parables
57 Jesus said to them: A prophet is not
14 1 Herod . . . heard the fame of Jesus. And
12 buried it, and came and told Jesus
13 when Jesus had heard, he retired from
16 Jesus said to them: They have no need
22 Jesus obliged his disciples to go up
29 walked upon the water to come to Jesus
31 Jesus stretching forth his hand took
15 28 Jesus answering, said to her: O woman
29 when Jesus had passed away from thence
32 Jesus called together his disciples
34 Jesus said to them: How many loaves
16 8 Jesus knowing it, said: Why do you
15 Jesus saith to them: But whom do you
17 Jesus answering said to him: Blessed
20 no one that he was Jesus the Christ
21 Jesus began to show to his disciples
24 Jesus said to his disciples: If any
17 1 Jesus taketh unto him Peter and James
4 Peter answering, said to Jesus: Lord
8 saw no one but only Jesus. And as they
9 Jesus charged them, saying: Tell the
17 J. rebuked him, and the devil went
18 came the disciples to Jesus secretly
19 Jesus said to them: Because of your
21 Jesus said to them: The Son of man
24 Jesus prevented him [Peter], saying
25 Jesus said to him: Then the children
18 1 disciples came to Jesus, saying: Who
2 Jesus calling unto him a little child
22 Jesus saith to him: I say not to thee
19 14 Jesus said to them: Suffer the little
21 Jesus saith to him: If thou wilt be
23 Jesus said to his disciples: Amen, I
28 Jesus said to them: Amen I say to you,
20 17 Jesus going up to Jerusalem, took the
22 Jesus answering, said: You know not
25 Jesus called them to him and said: You
30 heard that Jesus passed by, and they
32 Jesus stood and called them, and said
34 Jesus having compassion on them, touched
21 1 Jesus sent two disciples, saying to
6 going, did as Jesus had commanded them
11 this is Jesus the prophet from
16 Jesus said to them: Yea, have you
21 Jesus answering said to them: Amen
24 Jesus answering said to them: I also
27 answering Jesus, they said: We know not
31 Jesus saith to them: Amen I say to you
42 Jesus saith to them: Have you never
22 1 J. answering, spoke again in parables
18 Jesus knowing their wickedness, said
20 J. saith to them: Whose image and
29 J. answering, said to them: You err
37 Jesus said to him: Thou shalt love the
41 Jesus asked them, saying: What think
24 1 Jesus being come out of the temple
4 J. answering, said to them: Take heed
26 1 when Jesus had ended all these words
4 by subtilty they might apprehend Jesus
6 when Jesus was in Bethania in the house
10 Jesus knowing it, said to them: Why
17 disciples came to Jesus, saying: Where
18 Jesus said: Go ye into the city to a
19 the disciples did as Jesus appointed
26 Jesus took bread, and blessed, and
31 J. saith to them: All you shall be
34 J. said to him: Amen I say. Luke 23:43
49 coming to Jesus, he said: Hail, Rabbi
50 J. said to him: Friend, whereto art
50 they came up and laid hands on Jesus
51 one of them that were with Jesus
52 J. saith to him: Put up again thy
55 Jesus said to the multitudes: You are
57 they holding Jesus led him to Caiphas
59 sought false witness against Jesus
63 but Jesus held his peace. And the
64 J. saith to him: Thou hast said it
69 also wast with Jesus the Galilean
75 Peter remembered the word of Jesus
27 1 took counsel against Jesus, that they
11 and Jesus stood before the governor
11 Jesus saith to him: Thou sayest it.
17 Barabbas, or Jesus that is called
20 ask Barabbas, and make Jesus away
22 what shall I do then with Jesus that
26 having scourged Jesus, delivered him
27 soldiers . . . taking J. into the hall
37 this is Jesus the king of the Jews
46 Jesus cried with a loud voice, saying
50 Jesus again crying with a loud voice
54 that were with him watching Jesus
55 who had followed Jesus from Galilee
57 who also himself was a disciple of J.
58 to Pilate and asked the body of Jesus
28 5 that you seek Jesus who was crucified
9 Jesus met them, saying: All hail. But
10 Jesus said to them: Fear not. Go
16 mountain where J. had appointed them
18 Jesus coming, spoke to them, saying
Mark 1 17 J. said to them: Come after me, and I
25 Jesus threatened him, saying: Speak no
41 J. having compassion on him, stretched
2 5 when Jesus had seen their faith, he
8 Jesus presently knowing in his spirit
15 sat down together with Jesus and his
17 Jesus hearing this, saith to them: They
19 J. saith to them: Can the children of
3 7 Jesus retired with his disciples to
5 6 seeing Jesus afar off, he ran and
7 with thee, Jesus the Son of the most
13 Jesus immediately gave them leave. And
15 they came to Jesus, and they see him
20 how great things Jesus had done for him
21 when Jesus had passed again in the
27 when she had heard of Jesus, came in
30 Jesus knowing in himself the virtue
36 Jesus having heard the word that was
6 4 Jesus said to them: A prophet is not

30 coming together unto Jesus, related to
34 Jesus going out saw a great multitude
8 17 which Jesus knowing, saith to them
9 1 after six days Jesus taketh with him
3 and they were talking with Jesus. And
4 said to Jesus: Rabbi, it is good for
7 any more, but Jesus only with them
14 presently all the people seeing Jesus
22 Jesus saith to him: If thou canst
24 when Jesus saw the multitude running
26 but Jesus taking him by the hand
38 but Jesus said: Do not forbid him
10 14 whom when Jesus saw, he. Luke 13:12
18 Jesus said to him: Why callest thou
21 Jesus looking on him, loved him and
23 Jesus looking round about, saith to
24 Jesus again answering, saith to them
27 Jesus looking on them, saith: With men
29 Jesus answering said: Amen I say to
38 Jesus said to them: You know not what
39 Jesus saith to them: You shall indeed
42 Jesus calling them, saith to them
47 Jesus son of David, have mercy on me
49 Jesus, standing still, commanded him
51 Jesus answering, said to him: What
52 Jesus saith to him: Go thy way, thy
11 6 said to them as J. had commanded them
7 and they brought the colt to Jesus
22 Jesus answering, saith to them: Have
29 Jesus answering, said to them: I will
33 answering, say to Jesus: We know not
33 Jesus answering, saith to them: Neither
12 17 Jesus answering, said to them: Render
24 Jesus answering, saith to them: Do ye
35 Jesus answering, said, teaching in
41 J. sitting over against the treasury
13 2 J. answering said to him: Seest thou
5 Jesus answering, began to say to them
14 6 but Jesus said: Let her alone, why do
18 Jesus saith: Amen I say to you, one of
22 Jesus took bread; and blessing, broke
27 Jesus saith to them: You will all
30 Jesus saith to him: Amen I say to thee
48 J. answering said to them: Are you come
53 they brought Jesus to the high priest
55 sought for evidence against Jesus
60 asked Jesus, saying: Answerest thou
62 Jesus said to him: I am. And you shall
72 the word that Jesus had said unto him
15 1 binding Jesus, led him away and
15 and delivered up Jesus, when he had
34 Jesus cried out with a loud voice
37 Jesus having cried out with a loud
16 1 that coming, they might anoint Jesus
Luke 1 31 and thou shalt call his name Jesus
2 21 his name was called Jesus, which was
27 parents brought in the child Jesus to
43 the child Jesus remained in Jerusalem
52 J. advanced in wisdom and age and grace
3 21 that Jesus also being baptized and
23 Jesus himself was beginning about the
29 Her, who was of Jesus, who was of
4 1 Jesus being full of the Holy Ghost
8 Jesus answering said to him: It is. 12
14 Jesus returned in the power of the
35 Jesus rebuked him, saying: Hold thy
38 Jesus rising up out of the synagogue
5 10 Jesus saith to Simon: Fear not: from
12 full of leprosy, who seeing Jesus
19 his bed into the midst before Jesus
22 when Jesus knew their thoughts
31 J. answering said to them: They that
6 3 Jesus answering them, said: Have you
9 then Jesus said to them: I ask you
11 another, what they might do to Jesus
7 3 when he had heard of Jesus, he sent
4 when they came to J., they besought
9 which Jesus hearing, marvelled: and
19 and sent them to Jesus, saying: Art
40 Jesus answering said to him: Simon
8 28 when he saw Jesus, he fell down
28 Jesus, Son of the most high God
30 Jesus asked him, saying: What is thy
35 they came to Jesus and found the man
38 but Jesus sent him away, saying
39 great things Jesus had done to him
40 when Jesus was returned, the multitude
41 and he fell down at the feet of Jesus
45 Jesus said: Who is it that touched me
46 Jesus said: Somebody hath touched me
50 Jesus hearing this word, answered the
9 33 Peter saith to Jesus: Master, it is
36 was uttered, Jesus was found alone
41 Jesus answering, said: O faithless
43 and Jesus rebuked the unclean spirit
50 Jesus said to him: Forbid him not
58 J. said to him: The foxes have holes
60 Jesus said to him: Let the dead bury
62 Jesus said to him: No man putting
10 29 said to Jesus: And who is my neighbor
30 Jesus answering, said: A certain man
37 J. said to him: Go, and do thou
13 14 that Jesus had healed on the sabbath
14 3 Jesus answering, spoke to the lawyers
17 13 Jesus, master, have mercy on us
17 J. answering, said: Were not ten made
18 16 Jesus, calling them together, said
19 Jesus said to him: Why dost thou call
31 Jesus took unto him the twelve and
38 Jesus, son of David, have mercy on me
40 Jesus standing, commanded him to be
42 Jesus said to him: Receive thy sight
19 3 he sought to see Jesus who he was
5 and when Jesus was come to the place
9 J. said to him: This day is salvation
35 they brought him to Jesus. And casting
35 on the colt, they set Jesus thereon
20 3 J. answering, said to them: I will also
8 Jesus said to them: Neither do I tell
34 J. said to them: The children of this
22 2 how they might put Jesus to death
47 drew near to Jesus, for to kiss him
48 Jesus said to him: Judas, dost thou
51 Jesus answering, said: Suffer ye thus
52 Jesus said to the chief priests and
23 20 spoke to them, desiring to release Jesus
25 but Jesus he delivered up to their will
26 the cross on him to carry after Jesus
28 J. turning to them, said: Daughters of
34 Jesus said: Father, forgive them, for
42 he said to Jesus: Lord, remember me
46 Jesus crying with a loud voice, said
24 15 Jesus himself also drawing near, went
36 Jesus stood in the midst of them and
John 1 29 John saw Jesus coming to him, and he
36 beholding Jesus walking, he saith
37 him speak, and they followed Jesus
38 Jesus turning, and seeing them
42 he brought him [Simon] to Jesus. And
42 Jesus looking upon him, said: Thou art
43 Jesus saith to him: Follow me. Now
45 Jesus the son of Joseph of Nazareth
47 Jesus saw Nathanael coming to him and
2 1 and the mother of Jesus was there. And
2 and Jesus also was invited, and his
3 the wine failing, the mother of Jesus

21 1 Jesus showed himself again to the
4 Jesus stood on the shore: yet the
4 disciples knew not that it was Jesus
5 Jesus . . . said to them: Children
7 disciples therefore whom Jesus loved
10 Jesus saith to them: Bring hither of
12 Jesus saith to them: Come and dine
13 Jesus cometh and taketh bread and
14 third time that Jesus was manifested
15 Jesus saith to Simon Peter: Simon, son
20 saw that disciple whom Jesus loved
21 he saith to Jesus: Lord, and what
22 Jesus saith to him: So I will have him
23 Jesus did not say to him: He should
25 many other things which Jesus did
Acts 1 1 all things which Jesus began to do and
11 this Jesus who is taken up from you
14 the women and Mary the mother of Jesus
16 leader of them that apprehended Jesus
2 32 this Jesus hath God raised again
36 same Jesus, whom you have crucified
3 13 hath glorified his Son Jesus, whom
4 2 preached in Jesus the resurrection
13 knew them that they had been with J.
27 this city against thy holy child J.
30 by the name of thy holy Son Jesus
7 45 receiving, brought in with Jesus into
55 J. standing on the right hand of God
8 35 Philip . . . preached unto him Jesus
9 5 I am Jesus whom thou persecutest. 26:15
20 he preached Jesus in the synagogues
13 23 hath raised up to Israel a Savior, J.
33 fulfilled to our children, raising up J.
16 7 the Spirit of Jesus suffered them not
17 7 saying that there is another king, Jesus
18 preached to them J. and the resurrection
18 25 taught diligently things that are of J.
28 by the scriptures, that J. is the Christ
19 4 come after him, that is to say, in Jesus
13 conjure you by J., whom Paul preacheth
15 Jesus I know, and Paul I know; but who
25 19 and of one Jesus deceased, whom Paul
28 23 persuading them concerning Jesus, out of
Rom 8 11 if the Spirit of him that raised up J.
1 C 12 3 speaking . . . saith Anathema to Jesus
2 C 4 5 ourselves your servants through Jesus
10 in our body the mortification of Jesus
10 life also of J. may be made manifest. 11
14 knowing that he who raised up J., will
14 will raise us up also with Jesus, and
Eph 4 21 taught in him, as the truth is in Jesus
Phil 2 21 not the things that are Jesus Christ's
Col 4 11 and Jesus, that is called Justus: who
1 Th 1 10 Jesus, who hath delivered us from the
4 13 if we believe that Jesus died, and rose
13 so them who have slept through Jesus
Heb 2 9 we see Jesus, who was made a little
3 1 high priest of our confession, Jesus
4 8 if Jesus had given them rest, he would
14 Jesus the Son of God: let us hold fast
6 20 where the forerunner Jesus is entered
7 22 by so much is Jesus made a surety of
9 24 Jesus is not entered into the holies
12 2 Jesus, the author and finisher of faith
24 J. the mediator of the new testament
13 12 Jesus also, that he might sanctify the
1 J 2 22 who denieth that Jesus is the Christ
4 3 every spirit that dissolveth Jesus, is
15 confess that Jesus is the Son of God
5 1 believeth that Jesus is the Christ, is
5 believeth that Jesus is the Son of God
Jude 5 Jesus, having saved the people out of
Apoc 1 9 of God and for the testimony of Jesus
14 12 of God and the faith of Jesus. And I
17 6 with the blood of the martyrs of Jesus
19 10 who have the testimony of Jesus. Adore
10 testimony of Jesus is the spirit of
20 4 were beheaded for the testimony of J.
22 16 I Jesus have sent my angel to testify

body of Jesus; *see* **body**

Christ Jesus Acts 5 42 to teach and preach Christ Jesus
Acts 24 24 of him the faith, that is in C. J.
Rom 3 24 the redemption, that is in Christ Jesus
6 3 we, who are baptized in Christ Jesus
11 alive unto God, in Christ Jesus our Lord
23 life everlasting, in Christ Jesus our
8 1 that are in Christ Jesus, who walk not
2 the spirit of life, in Christ Jesus hath
34 Christ Jesus that died, yea that is
15 8 I say that C. J. was minister of the
16 I should be minister of Christ Jesus
17 I have therefore glory in Christ Jesus
16 3 Aquila, my helpers in Christ Jesus, who
9 salute Urbanus, our helper in C. J., and
1 C 1 2 to them that are sanctified in C. J.
4 grace of God that is given you in C. J.
30 of him are you in Christ Jesus, who of
3 11 but that which is laid; which is C. J.
4 15 for in Christ Jesus, by the gospel, I
17 of my ways, which are in Christ Jesus
9 1 have not I seen Christ Jesus our Lord
15 31 which I have in Christ Jesus our Lord
16 24 my charity be with you all in C. J. Amen
2 C 2 14 maketh us to triumph in Christ Jesus
4 6 glory of God, in face of Christ Jesus
13 5 know you not your own selves, that C. J.
Gal 2 4 liberty, which we have in Christ Jesus
16 we also believe in Christ Jesus, that we
3 14 on the Gentiles through Christ Jesus
26 children of God by faith, in C. J. For
28 for you are all one in Christ Jesus. And
4 14 as an angel of God, even as Christ Jesus
5 6 in C. J. neither circumcision. 6:15
Eph 1 1 and to the faithful in Christ Jesus
2 6 in heavenly places, through Christ Jesus
7 in his bounty towards us in Christ Jesus
10 created in Christ Jesus in good works
13 but now in Christ Jesus, you, who some
3 6 copartners of his promise in C. J., by
11 which he made, in Christ Jesus our Lord
21 glory in the church, and in Christ Jesus
Phil 1 1 to all the saints in Christ Jesus, who
6 will perfect it unto the day of C. J.
26 your rejoicing may abound in C. J. for
2 5 be in you, which was also in C. J.
3 3 serve God; and glory in Christ Jesus
9 which is of the faith of Christ Jesus
14 supernal vocation of God in Christ Jesus
4 7 keep your hearts and minds in C. J.
19 to his riches in glory in Christ Jesus
21 salute ye every saint in Christ Jesus
Col 1 2 saints and faithful brethren in C. J.
4 hearing your faith in Christ Jesus, and
7 for you a faithful minister of C. J.
28 may present every man perfect in C. J.
2 2 of God the Father and of Christ Jesus
4 12 servant of Christ Jesus, who is always
1 Th 2 14 God which are in Judea, in Christ Jesus
5 18 this is the will of God in Christ Jesus
1 Tim 1 1 God our Savior, and of Christ Jesus our
2 God the Father and from C. J. 2 Tim 1:2
12 even to Christ Jesus our Lord, for that
14 faith and love, which is in Christ Jesus
15 that Christ Jesus came into this world
16 in me first Christ Jesus might show
2 5 of God and men, the man Christ Jesus

3 13 in the faith which is in Christ Jesus
4 6 shalt be a good minister of Christ Jesus
5 21 I charge thee before God and C. J., and
6 13 all things, and before Christ Jesus, who
2 Tim 1 1 the promise of life, which is in C. J.
9 grace, which was given us in C. J.
13 and in the love which is in Christ Jesus
2 1 in the grace which is in Christ Jesus
3 labor as a good soldier of Christ Jesus
10 salvation, which is in Christ Jesus
3 12 all that will live godly in Christ Jesus
15 by the faith which is in Christ Jesus
Titus 1 4 and from Christ Jesus our Savior. For
Philem 1 Paul, a prisoner of Christ Jesus, and
6 every good work, that is in you in C. J.
8 I have much confidence in Christ Jesus
23 Epaphras, my fellow prisoner in C. J.
1 P 5 10 unto his eternal glory in Christ Jesus
14 grace be to all you, who are in C. J.
2 P 1 2 in the knowledge of God and of C. J.
2 J 3 and from C. J. the Son of the Father
Apoc 1 9 kingdom, and patience in Christ Jesus

Jesus answered Mat 11 25 J. . . . and said: I confess to thee
Mat 17 16 J. . . . and said: O unbelieving and
Mark 12 29 J. . . . him: The first commandment of all
15 5 but J. still a. nothing; so that
Luke 4 4 J. . . . him: It is written that
John 1 48 J. . . . and said to him: Before that
50 J. . . . and said to him: Because I
2 19 J. . . . and said to them: Destroy
3 3 J. . . . and said to him: Amen, amen
5 Jesus answered: Amen, amen, I say
10 J. . . . and said to him: Art thou
4 10 J. . . . and said to her: If thou
13 J. . . . and said to her: Whosoever
5 17 J. . . . them: My Father worketh
19 J. . . . and said to them: Amen, amen
6 26 J. . . . them and said: Amen, amen
29 J. . . . and said to them: This is
43 J. therefore a. and said to them: Murmur
71 Jesus answered them: Have not I chosen
7 16 J. . . . them and said: My doctrine
21 J. . . . and said to them: One work
8 14 J. . . . and said to them: Although
19 Jesus answered: Neither me do you
34 Jesus answered them: Amen, amen, I
49 Jesus answered: I have not a devil
54 Jesus answered: If I glorify myself
9 3 Jesus answered: Neither hath this
10 25 Jesus answered them: I speak to you
32 Jesus answered them: Many good works
34 Jesus answered them: Is it not written
11 9 Jesus answered: Are there not 12 hours
12 23 J. . . . them, saying: The hour is
30 J. . . . and said: This voice came
13 7 J. . . . and said to him: What I do
8 Jesus answered him: If I wash thee
26 Jesus answered: He it is to whom
36 Jesus answered: Whither I go, thou
38 Jesus answered him: Wilt thou lay
14 23 J. . . . and said to him: If anyone
16 31 Jesus answered them: Do you now
18 8 Jesus answered: I have told you
20 J. . . . him: I have spoken
23 Jesus answered him: If I have spoken
34 Jesus answered: Sayest thou this
36 Jesus answered: My kingdom is
37 Jesus answered: Thou sayest that
19 11 J. . . . : Thou shouldst not

Jesus came Mat 16 13 Jesus came into the quarters of
Mat 17 7 Jesus came and touched them: and said
26 36 Jesus came with them into a country
Mark 1 9 Jesus came from Nazareth of Galilee
14 Jesus came into Galilee, preaching the
John 11 17 Jesus therefore came and found that
19 5 Jesus therefore came forth, bearing
20 19 Jesus came and stood in the midst
24 was not with them when Jesus came
Acts 1 21 Jesus came in and went out among us
1 Tim 1 15 Jesus came into this world to save

Jesus Christ Mat 1 1 book of the generation of J. C.
Mark 1 1 the beginning of the gospel of J. C.
John 1 17 grace and truth came by Jesus Christ
17 3 God, and J. C., whom thou hast sent
Acts 2 38 in the name of J. C. 3:6; 8:12
3 20 hath been preached unto you, J. C.
4 33 testimony of the resurrection of J. C.
8 37 I believe that J. C. is the Son of God
10 36 preaching peace by Jesus Christ: he
17 3 this is J. C., whom I preach to you
Rom 1 1 Paul, a servant of Jesus Christ, called
6 among whom are you also called of J. C.
8 thanks . . . through J. C., for you all
2 16 God shall judge secrets of men by J. C.
3 22 justice of God, by faith of Jesus Christ
26 justifier of him, who is of faith of J. C.
4 24 that raised up Jesus Christ, our Lord
5 15 by the grace of one man, Jesus Christ
17 reign in life through one, Jesus Christ
21 unto life everlasting, through J. C. our
7 25 grace of God, by Jesus Christ our Lord
8 11 he that raised up Jesus Christ from dead
15 5 towards another, according to J. C.
16 25 preaching of J. C., according to the
27 through J. C., to whom be honor and glory
1 C 1 1 Paul, called to be an apostle of J. C.
9 fellowship of his Son J. C. our Lord. Now
2 2 to know anything among you, but J. C.
8 6 and one Lord Jesus Christ, by whom are
2 C 1 1 Paul, an apostle of J. C. Eph 1:1; Col 1:1; 2 Tim 1:1; Titus 1:1
19 the Son of God, J. C., who was preached
4 5 preach not ourselves, but Jesus Christ
Gal 1 1 neither by man, but by Jesus Christ, and
12 it; but by revelation of Jesus Christ
2 16 works of law, but by the faith of J. C.
3 1 before whose eyes J. C. hath been set
22 the promise, by faith of Jesus Christ
Eph 1 5 adoption of children through Jesus Christ
2 20 J. C. himself being the chief corner
3 1 I Paul, the prisoner of Jesus Christ
Phil 1 1 Paul and Timothy, the servants of J. C.
8 after you all in the bowels of J. C.
11 fruit of justice, through Jesus Christ
19 supply of the Spirit of Jesus Christ
3 8 loss for excellent knowledge of J. C.
12 wherein I am also apprehended by J. C.
Col 2 6 you have received Jesus Christ the Lord
2 Tim 1 10 by the illumination of our Savior J. C.
4 1 I charge thee, before God and J. C., who
Titus 2 13 the great God and our Savior J. C.
3 6 through Jesus Christ our Savior: that
Philem 9 now a prisoner also of Jesus Christ
Heb 13 8 J. C. yesterday and today and the same
21 through J. C. to whom is glory forever
1 P 1 1 Peter, an apostle of Jesus Christ, to
2 and sprinkling of the blood of J. C.
3 by the resurrection of J. C. from the
7 and honor at the appearing of J. C.
13 offered you in the revelation of J. C.
2 5 sacrifices, acceptable to God by J. C.
3 21 by the resurrection of Jesus Christ
4 11 God may be honored through Jesus Christ
2 P 1 1 servant and apostle of Jesus Christ
1 justice of our God and Savior J. C.

11 kingdom of our Lord and Savior J. C.
2 20 knowledge of our Lord and Savior J. C.
3 18 knowledge of our Lord and Savior J. C.
1 J 1 3 Father, and with his Son Jesus Christ
7 blood of J. C. his Son cleanseth us
2 1 with the Father, Jesus Christ the just
3 23 believe in the name of his Son J. C.
4 2 that J. C. is come in the flesh. 2 J 7
5 6 that came by water and blood, J. C.
Jude 1 Jude, the servant of Jesus Christ, and
1 preserved in Jesus Christ, and called
25 through J. C. our Lord, be glory and
Apoc 1 1 revelation of J. C., which God gave
2 the testimony of J. C. 12:17
5 from J. C., who is the faithful witness
Jesus gave Mat 8 18 Jesus . . . gave orders to pass
Mat 26 26 Jesus . . . broke; and gave to his
Mark 5 13 Jesus immediately gave them leave. And
14 22 Jesus . . . gave to them, and said: Take ye
15 37 Jesus . . . gave up the ghost. Luke 23:46; John 19:30
John 4 44 Jesus himself gave testimony that a
19 9 thou? But Jesus gave him no answer
Jesus of Nazareth Mat 26 71 this man also was with Jesus of Nazareth
Mark 1 24 have we to do with thee, J. . . . Luke 4:34
10 47 heard that it was J. of N., began to
14 67 thou also wast with Jesus of Nazareth
16 6 you seek J. . . . who was crucified: he
Luke 18 37 that Jesus of Nazareth was passing by
24 19 they said: Concerning J. . . . who was a
John 18 5 they answered him: Jesus of Nazareth
7 and they said: Jesus of Nazareth
19 19 J. . . . the King of the Jews. This title
Acts 2 22 J. . . . a man approved of God among you
6 14 that this J. . . . shall destroy this
10 38 J. . . . : how God anointed him with the
22 8 I am J. . . . , whom thou persecutest. And
26 9 contrary to name of Jesus of Nazareth
Jesus seeing Mat 8 18 J. s. great multitudes about
Mat 9 2 Jesus seeing their faith, said to the
4 Jesus seeing their thoughts, said
Mark 12 34 Jesus seeing that he had answered
Luke 9 47 Jesus seeing the thoughts of their
18 24 Jesus seeing him become sorrowful
Jesus spoke Mat 13 34 J. spoke in parables to the
Mat 14 27 Jesus spoke to them, saying: Be of
23 1 Jesus spoke to the multitudes and to
John 8 12 again therefore Jesus spoke to them
20 words Jesus spoke in the treasury
10 6 this proverb Jesus spoke to them
11 13 Jesus spoke of his death; and they
12 36 these things Jesus spoke; and. 17:1
Jesus went Mat 4 23 Jesus went about all Galilee
Mat 9 35 Jesus went about all the cities and
12 1 Jesus went through the corn on the
15 21 Jesus went from thence and retired into
21 12 Jesus went into the temple of God and
Mark 8 27 Jesus went out, and his disciples
10 32 Jesus went before them, and they were
Luke 7 6 Jesus went with them. And when he
14 1 Jesus went into the house of one of
John 2 13 and Jesus went up to Jerusalem. 5:1
5 13 Jesus went aside from the multitude
6 1 Jesus went over the sea of Galilee
3 Jesus therefore went up into a
7 14 Jesus went up into the temple and
8 1 Jesus went unto mount Olivet. And
Lord Jesus Mark 16 19 the Lord Jesus, after he had spoken
Luke 24 3 found not the body of the Lord Jesus
Acts 1 21 that the Lord Jesus came in and went
7 58 saying: Lord Jesus, receive my spirit
8 16 baptized in the name of the L. J. 19:5
9 17 Saul, the Lord Jesus hath sent me, he
11 20 preaching the Lord Jesus. And the
16 31 they said: Believe in the Lord Jesus
18 4 bring in the name of the Lord Jesus
5 bringing in name of the Lord Jesus
19 13 name of the Lord J., saying: I conjure
17 name of the Lord Jesus was magnified
20 24 which I received from the Lord Jesus, to
35 remember the word of the Lord Jesus, how
21 13 in Jerusalem, for name of the Lord J.
Rom 10 9 confess with thy mouth the Lord Jesus
14 14 am confident in the Lord Jesus, that
1 C 11 23 delivered unto you, that the Lord Jesus
12 3 no man can say the Lord Jesus, but by
Gal 6 17 the marks of the Lord Jesus in my body
Eph 1 15 your faith that is in the Lord Jesus
Phil 2 19 I hope in the Lord Jesus to send Timothy
1 Th 2 15 who both killed the Lord Jesus, and
4 1 we pray and beseech you in the Lord J.
2 I have given to you by the Lord Jesus
2 Th 1 7 rest with us when the Lord Jesus shall
12 that the name of our Lord Jesus may be
2 8 Lord Jesus shall kill with the spirit
Philem 5 faith, which thou hast in the Lord Jesus
Apoc 22 20 come, Lord Jesus. The grace of our
name of Jesus; *see* **name**
name of our Lord Jesus Christ; *see* **name**
our Lord Jesus Christ Acts 4 10 by the name of o. . . . of Nazareth, whom
Acts 15 26 given their lives for name of o. . . .
20 21 God, and faith in our Lord J. C. And
Rom 1 4 by resurrection of our Lord J. C. from
5 1 peace with God, through our Lord J. C.
11 glory in God, through our Lord J. C.
8 39 love of God, which is in C. J. our Lord
15 6 God and the Father of our Lord J. C.
30 brethren, through our Lord J. C., and by
16 20 grace of our Lord J. C. be with you. 24; 1 C 16:23; 2 C 13:13; 1 Th 5:28; 2 Th 3:18; Apoc 22:21
1 C 1 2 invoke the name of our Lord J. C., in
7 manifestation of our Lord J. C. Who
8 in day of the coming of our Lord J. C.
10 by the name of o. . . . that you
5 4 in the name of o. . . . , you being gathered
5 in the day of our Lord J. C. your
6 11 justified in name of our Lord J. C., and
15 57 given us the victory through o. . . .
16 22 any man love not our Lord J. C., let
2 C 1 3 blessed be the God and Father of o. . . . Eph 1:3; 1 P 1:3
14 are ours, in the day of our Lord J. C.
8 9 for you know the grace of our Lord J. C.
11 31 God and Father of o. . . . , who is
Gal 1 3 God the Father, and from our Lord J. C.
6 14 save in the cross of our Lord J. C.; by
18 grace of o. . . . be with your spirit. Phil 4:23; Philem 25
Eph 1 17 that the God of our Lord J. C., the
3 14 my knees to the Father of our Lord J. C.
5 20 in the name of o. . . . , to God the
6 24 be with all them that love our Lord J. C.
Phil 3 20 look for the Savior, our Lord J. C.
Col 1 3 Father of our Lord J. C., praying always
1 Th 1 3 enduring of the hope of our Lord J. C.
2 19 you, in the presence of our Lord J. C.
3 11 our Father, and our Lord J. C., direct
13 at the coming of our Lord J. C., with
5 9 purchasing of salvation by our Lord J. C.
23 blameless in coming of our Lord J. C.
2 Th 1 8 obey not the gospel of our Lord J. C.
2 1 by the coming of our Lord J. C., and of

13 purchasing of the glory of our Lord J. C.
15 our Lord J. C. himself, and God and our
3 6 in the name of o. . . . that you
1 Tim 6 3 sound words of o. . . . , and to
14 unto the coming of our Lord J. C., which
Heb 13 20 the great pastor of the sheep, o. . . .
James 1 1 James the servant of God and of o. . . .
2 1 have not the faith of o. . . . of glory
2 P 1 8 in the knowledge of our Lord J. C.
14 as o. . . . also hath signified to me
16 the power and presence of o. . . .
Jude 4 the only sovereign Ruler, and o. . . .
17 before by the apostles of o. . . .
21 waiting for the mercy of o. . . . unto
24 exceeding joy in the coming of o. . . .
the Lord Jesus Christ Acts 9 34 Eneas, t. . . . healeth thee: arise
Acts 10 48 baptized in the name of the Lord J. C.
11 17 who believed in the Lord Jesus Christ
15 11 by the grace of t. . . . we believe
28 31 teaching . . . the Lord Jesus Christ, with
Rom 1 7 peace . . . from the Lord J. C. 1 C 1:3; 2 C 1:2; Eph 1:2; 6:23; Phil 1:2; Col 1:3; 2 Th 1:2; Philem 3
13 14 but put ye on the Lord Jesus Christ, and
Phil 2 11 the Lord J. C. is in the glory of God
Col 3 17 do all in the name of the Lord J. C.
1 Th 1 1 God the Father, and in t. . . . 2 Th 1:1
2 Th 1 12 grace of our God, and of the Lord J. C.
3 12 beseech them by the Lord J. C., that
2 Tim 2 8 be mindful that the Lord J. C. is risen
4 22 the Lord J. C. be with thy spirit. Grace
Jesus' Luke 5 8 he fell down at Jesus' knees, saying
John 12 9 they came, not for Jesus' sake only
13 23 there was leaning on Jesus' bosom
2 C 4 11 delivered unto death for Jesus' sake
Jeta Josu 21 16 Ain and Jeta and Bethsames
Jeteba 4 K 21 19 daughter of Harus of Jeteba
Jetebatha Num 33 33 and camped in J. Deut 10:7
Num 33 34 from Jetebatha they came to Hebrona
Jeth 1 Pa 6 43 the son of Semei, the son of Jeth
Jethela Josu 19 42 and Aialon and Jethela
Jether Josu 15 48 in the mountain Samir and J.
Josu 21 14 and Jether and Estemo and Holon and
Judg 8 20 he said to Jether his eldest son: Arise
1 K 30 27 south, and to them that were in Jether
3 K 2 5 Amasa the son of Jether. 32
1 Pa 2 17 whose father was J. the Ismahelite
32 sons of Jada . . . Jether and Jonathan
32 and Jether also died without children
4 17 Jether and Mered and Epher and
6 58 cities for refuge . . . Jether and
7 38 the sons of Jether: Jephone and
Jetheth Gen 36 40 duke J., duke Oolibama. 1 Pa 1:51
Jethma 1 Pa 11 46 Jethma a Moabite, Eliel and
Jethnam Josu 15 23 Cades and Asor and Jethnam
Jethra 2 K 17 25 Jethra of Jezrael, who went
Jethraam 2 K 3 5 the sixth Jethraam of Egla
Jethrahem 1 Pa 3 3 sons of David . . . Jethrahem
Jethrai 1 Pa 6 21 Zara his son, Jethrai his son
Jethram Gen 36 26 sons of Dison: . . . Jethram
Jethran 1 Pa 1 41 sons of Dison . . . Jethran
1 Pa 7 37 sons of Supha . . . Jethran and Bera
Jethrite 2 K 23 38 Ira the J., Gareb also a J. 1 Pa 11:40
Jethrites 1 Pa 2 53 kindred of Cariathiarim, the J.
Jethro Exod 3 1 Moses fed the sheep of Jethro
Exod 4 18 returned to Jethro his father-in-law
18 and Jethro said to him: Go in peace
18 1 when Jethro the priest of Madian
5 Jethro the kinsman of Moses came
6 I Jethro thy kinsman come to thee
9 Jethro rejoiced for all the good things
12 Jethro the kinsman of Moses offered

Jethson Josu 21 36 Misor and Jaser and Jethson
Jethur Gen 25 15 Jethur and Naphis and Cedma
Jetur 1 Pa 1 31 Jetur, Naphis, Cedma: these are
Jew Esth 2 5 a Jew, named Mardochai, the
Esth 3 4 he had told them that he was a Jew
5 13 so long as I see Mardochai the Jew
6 10 hast spoken to Mardochai the Jew who
8 7 Assuerus answered . . . Mardochai the Jew
9 29 and Mardochai the Jew wrote also a
11 3 a Jew who dwelt in the city of Susan
Dan 14 27 they said: The king is become a Jew
Zach 8 23 fast the skirt of one that is a Jew
1 Ma 2 23 came a certain Jew . . . to sacrifice to
2 Ma 6 6 neither . . . profess himself to be a Jew
9 17 that he would become a Jew himself
John 4 9 how dost thou, being a Jew, ask of me
18 35 Pilate answered: Am I a Jew? Thy own
Acts 10 28 abominable it is for man that is a Jew
13 6 prophet, a Jew, whose name was Bar-jesu
18 2 finding a certain Jew, named Aquila
24 a certain Jew, named Apollo, born at
19 14 seven sons of Sceva, a Jew, a chief
34 soon as they perceived him to be a Jew
21 39 Paul said to him: I am a Jew of Tarsus
22 3 he saith: I am a Jew, born at Tarsus
24 24 Drusilla his wife, who was a Jew, sent
Rom 1 16 Jew first, and to the Greek. 2:10
2 9 of the Jew first, and also of the Greek
17 if thou art called a Jew and restest in
28 for it is not he is a Jew, who is so
29 but he is a Jew, that is one inwardly
3 1 what advantage then hath the Jew, or
10 12 there is no distinction of Jew and Greek
1 C 9 20 I became to the Jews, a Jew, that I
Gal 2 14 being a Jew, livest after the manner of
3 28 there is neither Jew nor Greek: there is
Col 3 11 where there is neither Gentile nor Jew
jewel Prov 17 8 is a most acceptable jewel
Eze 16 12 and I put a jewel upon thy forehead
jeweller Exod 28 11 and the graving of a jeweller
jewels Judg 8 26 besides the ornaments and jewels
Prov 20 15 there is gold and a multitude of jewels
Cant 1 9 the turtle-dove's, thy neck as jewels
7 1 joints of thy thighs are like jewels
Isa 3 21 rings, and j. hanging on the forehead
61 10 as a bride adorned with her jewels
Eze 7 20 have turned the ornament of their j.
Osee 2 13 decked herself out . . . with her jewels
Jewish 2 Ma 8 11 to buy up the Jewish slaves
Acts 16 1 Timothy, the son of a Jewish woman
19 13 some also of Jewish exorcists who went
Titus 1 14 not giving heed to Jewish fables and
Jews Mat 28 15 was spread abroad among the Jews even
Luke 7 3 sent unto him the ancients of the Jews
John 1 19 when the Jews sent from Jerusalem
2 6 manner of the purifying of the Jews
13 the pasch of the Jews was at hand. 11:55
18 the Jews therefore answered. 8:48
20 the Jews then said: Six and forty
3 1 Nicodemus, a ruler of the Jews. This
25 some of John's disciples and the Jews
4 9 the Jews do not communicate with the
22 we know; for salvation is of the Jews
5 1 was a festival day of the Jews, and
10 the Jews therefore said. 7:35; 8:22, 52, 57; 11:36; 18:31
16 therefore did the Jews persecute Jesus
18 the Jews sought the more to kill him
6 4 pasch, the festival day of the Jews
41 the Jews therefore murmured at him
53 the Jews therefore strove among
7 1 because the Jews sought to kill him
11 the Jews therefore sought him on the

13 openly of him, for fear of the Jews
15 the Jews wondered, saying: How doth
8 31 said to those Jews who believed him
9 18 Jews then did not believe concerning
22 because they feared the Jews: for the Jews had already agreed
10 19 dissension rose again among the Jews
24 the Jews therefore came round about
31 the Jews then took up stones to stone
11 8 the Jews but now sought to stone thee
19 many of the Jews were come to Martha
31 the Jews therefore, who were with her
33 and the Jews that were come with her
45 many therefore of the Jews who were
54 walked no more openly among the Jews
12 9 multitude of the Jews knew that he was
11 many of the Jews, by reason of him
13 33 as I said to the Jews: Whither I go
18 12 tribune and the servants of the Jews
14 who had given the counsel to the Jews
20 temple, whither all the Jews resort
36 I should not be delivered to the Jews
38 he went out again to the Jews and
19 7 the Jews answered him. 10:33
12 but the Jews cried out, saying: If
14 he saith to the Jews: Behold your King
20 this title therefore many of the Jews
21 chief priests of the Jews said to
31 the Jews, because it was the parasceve
38 but secretly for fear of the Jews
40 as the manner of the Jews is to bury
42 because of the parasceve of the Jews
20 19 together for fear of the Jews, Jesus
Acts 2 5 Jews, devout men, out of every nation
11 Jews also, and proselytes, Cretes and
9 22 confounded the Jews . . . at Damascus
23 the Jews consulted together to kill him
10 39 things that he did in land of the Jews
11 19 speaking the word to none, but to Jews
12 3 seeing that it pleased the Jews, he
13 5 preached . . . in the synogogues of Jews
43 synogogue was broken up, many of Jews
45 Jews seeing the multitudes, were filled
50 Jews stirred up religious . . . women and
14 1 together into the synogogue of Jews
1 the Jews and of the Greeks did believe
2 the unbelieving Jews stirred up and
4 some of them indeed held with the J.
5 assault made by Gentiles and the Jews
18 came thither certain J. from Antioch
16 3 circumcised him, because of the Jews
20 these men disturb our city, being Jews
17 1 there was a synagogue of the Jews. And
5 the Jews, moved with envy, and taking
10 went into the synagogue of the Jews
13 and when the Jews of Thessalonica had
17 disputed . . . in synagogue with the J.
18 2 commanded all J. to depart from Rome
4 he persuaded the Jews and the Greeks
5 testifying to J., that Jesus is Christ
12 J. with one accord rose up against Paul
14 Gallio said to Jews: If it were some
14 Jews, I should with reason bear with
19 the synagogue, disputed with the Jews
28 with much vigor he convinced the Jews
19 10 both Jews and Gentiles. And God wrought
17 this became known to all the Jews and
33 multitude, the J. thrusting him forward
20 3 spent 3 months, the Jews laid wait for
19 befell me by conspiracies of the Jews
21 testifying both to Jews and Gentiles
21 11 is, the Jews shall bind in this manner
20 how many thousands there are among Jews
21 that thou teachest those Jews, who are
27 J. that were of Asia, when they saw him
22 12 having testimony of all Jews who dwelt
30 for what cause he was accused by the J.
23 12 some of the Jews gathered together, and
20 he said: The Jews have agreed to desire
25 feared lest perhaps the Jews might take
27 this man, being taken by the Jews, and
24 5 raising seditions among all the Jews
9 the J. also added, and said that these
19 certain J. of Asia, who ought to be
27 being willing to show the Jews pleasure
25 2 principal men of Jews, went unto him
7 the Jews stood about him, who were come
8 neither against the law of the Jews, nor
9 Festus, willing to show Jews pleasure
10 to the Jews I have done no injury, as
14 the ancients of the Jews, came unto me
24 about whom all the multitude of the J.
26 2 things whereof I am accused by the Jews
3 and questions that are among the Jews
4 my own nation in Jerusalem, all the Jews
7 hope, O king, I am accused by the Jews
21 for this cause the Jews, when I was in
28 17 he called together the chief of the J.
19 Jews contradicting it, I was constrained
29 the Jews went out from him having much
Rom 3 9 we have charged both Jews and Greeks
29 is he the God of the Jews only? Is he
9 24 not only of Jews, but also of Gentiles
1 C 1 22 for both the Jews require signs, and the
23 unto Jews indeed a stumblingblock, and
24 that are called, both Jews and Greeks
9 20 I became to the Jews, a Jew, that I might gain the Jews
10 32 be without offence to the Jews, and to
12 13 into one body, whether Jews or Gentiles
2 C 11 24 of the Jews five times did I receive 40
Gal 2 13 the rest of the Jews consented, so that
14 the Gentiles, and not as the Jews do
14 compel Gentiles to live as do the Jews
15 we by nature are Jews, and not of the
1 Th 2 14 even as they have from the Jews, who
Apoc 2 9 say they are Jews, and are not. 3:9

king of the Jews Mat 2 2 he that is born k. . . .
Mat 27 11 art thou the k. . . . Mark 14:2; Luke 23:3; John 18:33
29 hail, k. . . . Mark 15:18; John 19:3
37 this is Jesus the king of the Jews
Mark 15 9 that I release to you the k. . . .
12 will you then that I do to the k. . . .
26 his cause was written over: The K. . . .
Luke 23 37 if thou be the k. . . . save thyself. And
38 this is the king of the Jews. And one
John 18 39 that I release unto you the k. . . .
19 19 Jesus of Nazareth the K. . . . This
21 write not, The King of the Jews; but
21 that he said, I am the King of the Jews

nation of the Jews Esth 3 6 had heard that he was of the n. . . .
Esth 3 6 destroy all the n. . . . that were in
7 month the n. . . . should be destroyed
1 Ma 8 25 the n. . . . shall help them according
27 if war shall come first upon n. . . .
10 25 to the n. . . . greeting. 11:30; 13:31; 15:2
11 33 determined to do good to the n. . . .
12 3 n. . . . have sent us to renew the
14 47 be captain and prince of the n. . . .
15 1 the priest and prince of the n. . . .
2 Ma 10 8 n. . . . should keep those days every
Acts 10 22 having good testimony from all n. . . .

people of the Jews 1 Ma 8 20 the p. . . . have sent
1 Ma 8 23 be to the Romans and to the p. . . .

30 thus saith the Lord against Joakim the
32 which J. the king of Juda had burnt
Bar 1 7 they sent it to Jerusalem to Joakim
Dan 1 1 the third year of the reign of Joakim
2 Lord delivered into his hands Joakim
13 1 in Babylon, and his name was Joakim
4 Joakim was very rich and had an orchard
6 these men frequented the house of J.
28 when the people were come to Joakim
29 send to Susanna . . . the wife of Joakim
63 Susanna, with Joakim her husband and
Joanan 1 Es 8 12 of the sons of Azgad, Joanan
Joanna Luke 3 27 Juda, who was of Joanna, who was
Luke 8 3 J. the wife of Chusa, Herod's steward
24 10 it was Mary Magdalen and Joanna and
Joarib 2 Es 11 10 Idaia the son of Joarib, Jocin
1 Ma 2 1 a priest of the sons of Joarib from
Joas Judg 6 11 and oak that . . . belonged to Joas
Judg 6 29 Gedeon the son of Joas. 7:14; 8:32
30 they said to Joas: Bring out thy son
8 29 Jerobaal the son of Joas went and dwelt
3 K 22 26 city, and with Joas the son of Amalech
4 K 11 2 took Joas the son of Ochozias and
21 Joas was 7 years old when he. 2 Pa 24:1
12 1 seventh year of Jehu, J. began to reign
2 and J. did that which was right before
4 J. said to the priests: All the money
6 three and twentieth year of king Joas
7 king Joas called Joiada the high priest
18 J. king of Juda took all the sanctified
20 and slew Joas in the house of Mello
13 1 in three and twentieth year of Joas
9 and Joas his son reigned in his stead
10 in the seven and thirtieth year of Joas
10 Joas . . . reigned over Israel in Samaria
13 and Joas slept with his fathers. 14:16
13 but Joas was buried in Samaria
14 Joas . . . went down to him [Eliseus]
25 Joas the son of Joachaz took the cities
25 three times did Joas beat him, and he
14 1 in the second year of Joas son of
1 Amasias son of Joas. 13, 17, 23; 2 Pa 25:23, 25
3 to all things that Joas his father did
8 then Amasias sent messengers to Joas
9 and Joas . . . sent again to Amasias
11 so Joas king of Israel went up, and he
13 Joas king of Israel took Amasias. 2 Pa 25:23
17 after the death of Joas son of Joachaz
23 Jeroboam the son of Joas. 27; Osee 1:1; Amos 1:1
1 Pa 3 11 Ochozias of whom was born Joas: and his
7 8 sons of Bechor . . . Joas and Eliezer
12 3 the chief was Ahiezer, and Joas, the
27 28 over the oil cellars, Joas. And over
2 Pa 18 25 and carry him [Micheas] to . . . Joas
22 11 Josabeth the king's daughter took Joas
24 4 Joas had a mind to repair the house
22 king Joas did not remember the kindness
24 on Joas they executed shameful judgments
25 17 Amasias king of Juda . . . sent to Joas
21 so Joas king of Israel went up and
Joatham Judg 9 5 there remained only Joatham
Judg 9 7 this being told to Joatham, he went
57 the curse of Joatham . . . came upon them
4 K 15 5 J. the king's son governed the palace
7 J. his son reigned in his. 2 Pa 26:23
30 in the twentieth year of Joatham the
32 reigned J. son of Ozias king of Juda
36 the rest of the acts of J. 2 Pa 27:7
38 J. slept with his fathers. 2 Pa 27:9
16 1 Achaz the son of Joatham king of Juda
2 Pa 26 21 J. his son governed the king's house
27 1 Joatham was five and twenty years old
6 and Joatham was strengthened, because
Mat 1 9 Ozias begot J., and J. begot Achaz
Joathan 1 Pa 2 47 sons of Jahaddai . . . Joathan
1 Pa 5 17 in the days of Joathan. Mich 1:1
Isa 1 1 in the days of Ozias, Joathan, Achaz
7 1 days of Achaz the son of Joathan
Osee 1 1 in the days of Ozias, Joathan, Achaz
Job Gen 46 13 the sons of Issachar: . . . Job and
Tob 2 12 of his patience, as also of holy Job
15 as the kings insulted over holy Job
Job 1 1 land of Hus, whose name was Job
5 Job sent to them and sanctified them
5 so did Job all days. Now on a certain
8 thou considered my servant Job. 2:3
9 doth Job fear God in vain? Hast not
14 there came a messenger to Job and said
20 then Job rose up, and rent his garments
22 Job sinned not by his lips, nor spoke
2 7 struck Job with a very grievous ulcer
10 Job did not sin with his lips. Now
3 1 Job opened his mouth and cursed his day
6 1 Job answered and said: O that my sins
9 1 Job answered and said: Indeed I know
12 1 Job answered and said: Are you then
16 1 Job answered and said: I have often
19 1 Job answered and said: How long do you
21 1 then Job answered and said: Hear
23 1 Job answered and said: Now also my
26 1 Job answered and said: Whose helper
27 1 Job also added, taking up his. 29:1
32 1 these three men ceased to answer Job
2 he [Eliu] was angry against Job
3 answer, but only had condemned Job
4 Eliu waited while Job was speaking
12 none of you that can convince Job
33 1 hear therefore, O Job, my speeches and
31 attend, Job, and hearken to me: and
34 5 for Job hath said: I am just, and God
7 what man is there like Job, who
35 but Job hath spoken foolishly and his
36 let Job be tried even to the end
35 16 Job openeth his mouth in vain and
37 14 hearken to these things, Job: Stand
38 1 Lord answered Job out of whirlwind
39 31 and the Lord went on and said to Job
33 Job answered the Lord, and said. 42:1
40 1 Lord answering Job out of the whirlwind
42 7 the Lord had spoken these words to Job
7 before me, as my servant Job hath. 8
8 and go to my servant Job, and offer
8 and my servant Job shall pray for you
9 and the Lord accepted the face of Job
10 Lord also was turned at penance of Job
10 the Lord gave Job twice as much as
12 the Lord blessed the latter end of Job
15 so beautiful as the daughters of Job
16 Job lived after these things 140 years
Eze 14 14 if these three men, Noe, Daniel, and Job
20 Noe and Daniel and Job be in the midst
James 5 11 you have heard of the patience of Job
Jobab Gen 10 29 Jectan begot . . . J. 1 Pa 1:23
Gen 36 33 Jobab . . . reigned in his. 1 Pa 1:44
34 when Jobab was dead, Husam. 1 Pa 1:45
Josu 11 1 he sent to Jobab king of Madon and
1 Pa 8 9 Jobab and Sebia and Mosa and Molchom
18 Jezlia and Jobab, sons of Elphaal
Jobania 1 Pa 9 8 Jobania the son of Jeroham: and
Job's Job 2 11 when Job's three friends heard
Jochabed Exod 6 20 Amram took to wife Jochabed
Num 26 59 Amram, who had to wife Jochabed the
jod Ps 118 73 jod. Lam 1:10; 2:10; 3:28, 29, 30; 4:10
Jodaia 2 Es 12 19 of J., Azzi: of Sellai, Celai

Joed 2 Es 11 7 son of Mosollam the son of Joed
Joel 1 K 8 2 name of his firstborn son was Joel
1 Pa 4 35 Joel, and Jehu the son of Josabia the
5 4 the sons of Joel: Samaia his son, Gog
8 the son of Samma the son of Joel, dwelt
6 33 the son of Joel, the son of Samuel, the
7 3 Izrahia, of whom were born . . . Joel
11 38 Joel the brother of Namthan, Mibahar
15 7 of the sons of Gersom, Joel the chief
11 the Levites, Uriel, Asaia, Joel, Semeia
17 Levites, Heman the son of Joel, and of
23 8 Jahiel and Zethan and Joel, three. The
26 22 sons of Jehieli: Zathan and Joel, his
27 20 over the half tribe of Manasses, Joel
2 Pa 29 12 Joel the son of Azarias, of the sons of
1 Es 10 43 Zabad, Zabina, Jeddu, and Joel and
2 Es 11 9 Joel the son of Zechri their ruler
Joel 1 1 the word of the Lord that came to Joel
Acts 2 16 was spoken of by the prophet Joel
Joela 1 Pa 12 7 Joela and Zabadia the sons of
Joezer 1 Pa 12 6 and Azareel and Joezer and
Jogli Num 34 22 of Dan, Bocci the son of Jogli
Joha 1 Pa 8 16 and Joha, the sons of Baria. And
1 Pa 11 45 Joha his brother a Thosaite, Eliel a
2 Pa 34 8 Joha the son of Joachaz the recorder
Johanan 4 K 25 23 Johanan the son of Caree and
1 Pa 3 15 sons of Josias were the firstborn J.
24 Pheleia and Accub and Johanan and
6 9 Azarias begot J., J. begot Azarias
12 4 Jeremias and Jeheziel and Johanan
12 Johanan the eighth, Elzebad the ninth
26 3 Elam the fifth, Johanan the sixth
2 Pa 17 15 after him Johanan the captain, and
23 1 Ismahel the son of Johanan, and
28 12 Ephraim, Azarias the son of Johanan
1 Es 10 6 and went to the chamber of Johanan
28 of the sons of Bebai, Johanan, Hanania
2 Es 6 18 Johanan his son had taken to wife
12 13 Mosollam: and of Amaria, Johanan
22 and Joiada and Johanan and Jeddoa
Jer 40 8 the sons of Caree Johanan and Jonathan
13 Johanan the son of Caree and all the captains. 41:11, 16; 42:8; 43:4, 5
15 J. the son of Caree spoke to Godolias
16 the son of Ahicam said to Johanan
41 13 were with Ismahel, had seen Johanan
14 they returned and went to Johanan the
15 with eight men, from the face of J.
42 1 the captains of the warriors and J.
43 2 J. the son of Caree and all the proud
Johel 1 Pa 5 12 Johel the chief, and Saphan
1 Pa 6 36 the son of Elcana the son of Johel
John 1 Ma 2 1 arose Mathathias the son of John
1 Ma 2 2 sons: John who was surnamed Gaddis
8 17 Judas chose Eupolemus the son of John
9 36 took John and all that he had and went
38 remembered blood of John their brother
13 54 saw that J. his son was a valiant man
16 1 then John came up from Gazara and
2 his two eldest sons, Judas and John
9 John pursued after them till he came
19 he sent others to Gazara to kill John
21 one running before, told J. in Gazara
23 rest of the acts of John and his wars
2 Ma 4 11 by means of John the father of that
11 17 John and Abesalom who were sent from
Mat 3 4 the same John had his garment of
13 unto John, to be baptized by him
14 but John stayed him, saying: I ought
4 12 John was delivered up. Mark 1:14
21 son of Zebedee, and J. his brother. 10:3; Mark 1:19
9 14 came to him the disciples of John
11 2 when John had heard in prison the
4 go and relate to John. Luke 7:22
7 began to say . . . concerning J. Luke 7:24
13 and the law prophesied until John
18 John came neither eating nor drinking
14 3 Herod had apprehended John and bound
4 J. said to him: It is not lawful for
10 he sent and beheaded John in the prison
21 25 the baptism of John, whence was it
26 for all held John as a prophet. And
32 John came to you in the way of justice
Mark 1 4 John was in the desert baptizing and
6 John was clothed with camel's hair
9 was baptized by John in the Jordan
29 and Andrew, with James and John. And
2 18 the disciples of John and the Pharisees
3 17 and John the brother of James: and he
6 16 John whom I beheaded, he is risen
17 had sent and apprehended John and
18 John said to Herod: it is not lawful
20 Herod feared John, knowing him to be
9 37 John answered him, saying. Luke 9:49
10 35 and James and John . . . come to him
41 much displeased at James and John
11 30 baptism of John, was it from. Luke 20:4
32 all men counted John that he was a
Luke 1 13 and thou shalt call his name John: and
60 not so: but he shall be called John
63 he wrote, saying: John is his name
3 2 made unto John, the son of Zachary
15 were thinking in their hearts of John
16 John answered, saying to all: I
20 above all, and shut up John in prison
5 10 so also were James and John the sons
33 why do the disciples of John fast
6 14 James and John, Philip and Bartholomew
7 19 J. called to him two of his disciples
24 the messengers of John were departed
9 8 by some, that John was risen from the
9 John I have beheaded; but who is this
54 disciples, James and John, had seen
11 1 as John also taught his disciples
16 16 law and the prophets were until John
20 6 are persuaded that John was a prophet
John 1 6 sent from God, whose name was John
15 John beareth witness of him and crieth
19 this is the testimony of John, when
26 John answered them, saying: I baptize
28 Jordan, where John was baptizing
29 next day, John saw Jesus coming to
32 John gave testimony, saying: I saw
35 the next day again John stood and two
3 23 John also was baptizing near Salim
24 John was not yet cast into prison
26 they came to John, and said to him
27 John answered and said: A man cannot
4 1 and baptizeth more than John, though
5 33 you sent to John, and he gave
36 a greater testimony than that of John
10 40 that place where John was baptizing
41 and they said: John indeed did no sign
21 15 Simon, son of J., lovest thou me. 16, 17
Acts 1 5 John indeed baptized with water. 11:16
13 where abode Peter and John, James and
22 beginning from the baptism of John
3 1 Peter and John went up into the temple
3 when he had seen Peter and John about
4 Peter with John fastening his eyes
11 as he held Peter and John, all the
4 6 Caiphas and John and Alexander and as
13 the constancy of Peter and of John
19 Peter and John answering, said to them
8 14 they sent unto them Peter and John

10 37 after the baptism which John preached
12 2 he killed James, the brother of John
12 the house of Mary the mother of John
25 taking with them J., who was surnamed
13 5 and they had John also in the ministry
13 John departing from them, returned to
24 J. first preaching, before his coming
25 John was fulfilling his course, he
15 37 taken with them John also, that was
18 25 knowing only the baptism of John
Gal 2 9 given to me, James and Cephas and John
Apoc 1 1 by his angel to his servant John, who
4 John to the seven churches which are in
9 I John, your brother and your partner
21 2 I John saw the holy city, the new
22 8 I John, who have heard and seen these
John the Baptist Mat 3 1 those days cometh J. . . .
Mat 11 11 a greater than John the Baptist: yet
12 from the days of J. the B. until now
14 2 this is J. the B.: he is risen from the
8 give me . . . head of J. the B. Mark 6:25
16 14 some J. . . . , and other some Elias. Mark 8:28; Luke 9:19
17 13 spoken to them of John the Baptist
Mark 6 14 J. the B. is risen again from the dead
24 she said: The head of John the Baptist
Luke 7 20 John the Baptist hath sent us to thee
28 is not a greater prophet than J. . . .
33 J. . . . came neither eating bread nor
John's 1 Ma 16 9 Judas J. brother was wounded
Luke 7 18 John's disciples told him of all these
29 being baptized with John's baptism
John 3 25 between some of John's disciples and
Acts 19 3 baptized? Who said: In John's baptism
Joiada 2 K 8 18 Banaias the son of Joiada. 20:23; 23:20, 22; 3 K 1:8, 26, 32, 36, 38, 44; 2:25, 29, 34, 35, 46; 4:4; 1 Pa 11:22, 24; 18:17; 27:5
4 K 11 4 Joiada sent and taking the centurions
9 that Joiada the priest had commanded
9 on the sabbath came to J. the priest
15 Joiada commanded the centurions that
17 J. made a covenant between the Lord
12 2 days that Joiada the priest taught him
7 king Joas called Joiada the high priest
9 and Joiada the high priest took a chest
1 Pa 12 27 Joiada prince of the race of Aaron and
27 34 after Achitophel was Joiada the son
2 Pa 22 11 wife of J. the high priest and sister
23 1 Joiada being encouraged took the
3 Joiada said to them: Behold the king's
8 that J. the high priest had commanded
8 Joiada the high priest permitted not
9 Joiada the priest gave to the captains
11 and Joiada . . . anointed him [Joas]
14 Joiada the high priest going out to
16 Joiada made a covenant between himself
18 J. appointed overseers in the house
24 2 all the days of Joiada. 14
3 Joiada took for him [Joas] two wives
6 and the king called Joiada the chief
12 the king and Joiada gave it to those
14 rest of money before the king and J.
15 Joiada grew old and was full of days
17 after the death of Joiada, the princes
20 Zacharias the son of Joiada the priest
22 kindness that J. his father had done
25 revenge of the blood of the son of J.
2 Es 3 6 Joiada the son of Phasea, and
12 10 Eliasib begot J., and J. begot Jonathan
22 in the days of Eliasib and Joiada
13 28 of the sons of J. the son of Eliasib
Jer 29 26 made thee priest instead of Joiada
Joiarib 1 Pa 9 10 of the priests: Jedaia, Joiarib
1 Pa 24 7 the first lot came forth to Joiarib
1 Es 8 16 Joiarib and Elnathan, wise men
2 Es 11 5 the son of Adaia the son of Joiarib
12 6 went up with Zorobabel . . . Joiarib
19 of Joiarib, Mathanai: of Jodaia, Azzi
join Exod 1 10 join with our enemies, and
Exod 23 1 neither shalt thou join thy hand to bear
28 24 chains thou shalt join to the rings
25 shalt join together with two hooks on
32 26 on the Lord's side, let him join with
34 12 beware thou never join in friendship
36 32 join together the boards of the other
Num 16 5 the holy he will join to himself
18 4 a stranger shall not join himself with
Deut 20 3 you join battle this day against your
Josu 23 12 if you . . . join friendships, know ye
Judg 20 23 go up against them and join battle
2 K 5 24 pear trees, then shalt thou join battle
1 Es 9 14 nor join in marriage with the people of
Tob 7 15 may he join you together and fulfil
Job 38 31 able to join together the shining
Eccu 2 3 join thyself to God and endure, that
6 35 join thyself from thy heart to their
Isa 5 8 woe to you that join house to house
Eze 37 17 join them one to the other into one
Dan 11 10 he shall join battle with his forces
1 Ma 11 1 deceit and join it to his own kingdom
13 14 that he meant to join battle with
Acts 5 13 no man durst join himself unto them
8 29 near, and join thyself to this chariot
9 26 essayed to join himself to the disciples
joined Gen 29 34 my husband will be j. to me
Exod 26 3 five curtains shall be joined one to
4 that they may be joined one to another
6 veils of the curtains are to be joined
10 that it may be joined with the other
11 wherewith the loops may be joined
17 one board may be j. to another board
24 shall be joined together from beneath
28 7 the two edges joined in the top on
36 10 he joined five curtains, one to another
12 might be joined each with the other
16 five of which he joined apart, and the
17 they might be joined one to another
22 mortises . . . one might be joined to the
29 also joined from beneath unto the top
39 19 rings, which a violet fillet joined
Lev 18 14 who is joined to thee by affinity
Num 11 4 also being joined with them, and said
16 9 and joined you to himself, that you
Deut 7 7 is the Lord joined unto you, and hath
10 15 Lord hath been closely joined to thy
Josu 2 15 for her house joined close to the wall
17 10 they are joined together in the tribe
Judg 3 13 he joined to him the children of Ammon
Ruth 3 2 with whose maids thou wast joined in
1 K 4 2 and when they had joined battle, Israel
13 22 j. themselves with their countrymen
24 the men of Israel were joined together
2 K 2 25 being joined in one body, they stood
3 K 7 32 wheels . . . were joined one to another
34 of the base itself cast and j. together
11 2 to these was Solomon joined with a most
1 Pa 12 17 let my heart be joined to you: but if
2 Pa 4 13 that two rows of pomegranates were j.
18 1 Josaphat . . . was joined by affinity to
19 2 thou art joined in friendship with them
2 Es 4 6 we built the wall and joined it all
Tob 3 17 never have I j. myself with them that
8 4 these three nights we are joined to God
5 we must not be joined together like heathens
Jdth 14 6 and was joined to the people of Israel
16 26 and chastity was joined to her virtue

Ps 82 9 the Assyrian also is joined with them
Prov 10 22 neither shall affliction be j. to them
16 5 though hand should be joined to hand
26 23 swelling lips j. with a corrupt heart
Ecce 11 5 how the bones are joined together
Eccu 25 16 of faith is to be fast joined unto it
27 18 and be joined to him with fidelity
Isa 14 1 the stranger shall be joined with them
54 15 to thee before, shall be joined to thee
Jer 50 5 shall be joined to the Lord by an
Eze 1 9 wings of one were joined to the wings
11 two wings of every one were joined
32 39 are joined with them that are slain
42 3 a gallery joined to a triple gallery
Zach 2 11 nations shall be joined to the Lord
14 5 valley of the mountains shall be j.
1 Ma 1 16 and joined themselves to the heathens
2 43 joined themselves to them and were
69 [Mathathias] was joined to his fathers
3 2 had joined themselves to his father
41 joined to them the forces of Syria
4 14 the trumpet. And they joined battle
34 they joined battle: and there fell
6 21 wicked men of Israel joined themselves
7 39 and an army of Syria joined him
43 the armies joined battle on the
9 46 they joined battle. And Jonathan
10 26 and have not joined with our enemies
49 the two kings joined battle, and the
53 have joined battle with him, and both
78 to Azotus, and they joined battle
11 69 in ambush rose . . . and joined battle
2 Ma 8 23 first band, he j. battle with Nicanor
9 25 to him what I have joined here below
10 28 was risen both sides joined battle
12 12 having joined hands, they departed
34 when they had j. battle, it happened
13 3 Menelaus also joined himself with
14 17 of Judas had joined battle with Nicanor
Mat 19 6 what God hath joined together. Mark 10:9
Acts 5 36 about 400, joined themselves: who was
1 C 6 16 joined to a harlot, is made one body
17 he who is joined to Lord, is one spirit
Eph 4 16 being compacted and fitly j. together
joineth Exod 12 4 neighbor that j. to his house
Eccu 19 3 he that joineth himself to harlots
joining Exod 26 24 the like j. shall be observed
Exod 28 27 that looketh towards the nether joining
28 that the j. artificially wrought may
Jdth 7 9 overcome them without joining battle
Eccu 27 2 in the midst of the joining of stones
1 Ma 4 38 the chambers joining to the temple
2 Ma 7 21 j. a man's heart to a woman's thought
8 9 joining also with him Gorgias, a good
joinings 3 K 7 28 were gravings between the j.
3 K 7 29 and in the joinings likewise above
1 Pa 22 3 and for the closures and joinings
joint Exod 26 24 one joint shall hold them all
Exod 36 29 top, and went together into one joint
Job 31 22 let my shoulder fall from its joint
Eze 37 7 bones came together, each one to its j.
Rom 8 17 joint heirs with Christ: yet so, if we
Eph 3 16 by what every joint supplieth, according
joints Lev 1 6 they shall cut the j. into pieces
Lev 1 12 they shall divide the joints, the head
8 20 joints and the fat he burnt in the fire
3 K 6 18 the joints thereof artfully wrought
Cant 7 1 joints of thy thighs are like jewels
Dan 5 5 the king beheld the joints of the hand
6 the joints of his loins were loosed
10 10 lifted me . . . upon the j. of my hands
16 at the sight of thee my j. are loosed
Haba 2 11 the timber that is between the joints
Col 2 19 whole body, by joints and bands, being
Heb 3 12 of the joints also and the marrow, and
Jona Mat 16 17 blessed art thou Simon Bar-Jona
Luke 3 40 Joseph, who was of Jona, who was of
John 1 42 thou art Simon the son of Jona: thou
Jonadab 2 K 13 3 Amnon had a friend, named J.
2 K 13 5 Jonadab said to him: Lie down upon
32 J. the son of Semmaa, David's brother
35 Jonadab said to the king: Behold
4 K 10 15 he found Jonadab the son of Rechab
15 and Jonadab said: It is. If it be
23 J. the son of Rechab went to the
Ps 70 1 of the sons of Jonadab and the former
Jer 35 6 Jonadab . . . commanded us, saying. 10
8 we have obeyed the voice of Jonadab
14 words of Jonadab the son of Rechab
16 sons of Jonadab . . . have constantly
18 you have obeyed the commandment of J.
19 be wanting a man of the race of J.
Jonas 4 K 14 25 which he spoke by his servant J.
Jon 1 1 word of the Lord came to Jonas. 3:1
3 Jonas rose up to flee into Tharsis
5 Jonas went down into the inner part
7 cast lots, and the lot fell upon Jonas
15 they took Jonas and cast him into the
2 1 a great fish to swallow up Jonas
1 Jonas was in the belly of the fish
2 Jonas prayed to the Lord his God
11 vomited out Jonas upon the dry land
3 3 and Jonas arose and went to Ninive
4 Jonas began to enter into the city one
4 1 Jonas was exceedingly troubled and
5 Jonas went out of the city and sat
6 and it came up over the head of Jonas
6 Jonas was exceeding glad of the ivy
8 the sun beat upon the head of Jonas
9 Lord said to Jonas: Dost thou think
Mat 12 39 sign of Jonas. 16:4; Luke 11:29
40 as Jonas was in the whale's belly
41 they did penance at the preaching of Jonas. Luke 11:32
41 and behold a greater than Jonas here
Luke 11 30 as Jonas was a sign to the Ninivites
32 and behold more than Jonas here. No
Joppe Josu 19 46 the border that looketh towards J.
2 Pa 2 16 convey them in floats by sea to Joppe
1 Es 3 7 trees from Libanus to the sea of Joppe
Jon 1 3 he went down to Joppe and found a ship
1 Ma 10 75 they pitched their tents near Joppe
75 a garrison of Apollonius was in Joppe
76 gates to him: so Jonathan took Joppe
11 6 Jonathan came to meet the king at J.
12 33 and he turned aside to Joppe and took
13 11 and with him a new army into Joppe
14 5 he took Joppe for a haven and made an
34 he fortified Joppe which lieth by the
15 28 you hold Joppe and Gazara and the
35 as to thy complaints concerning Joppe
2 Ma 4 21 he departed thence and came to Joppe
12 3 the men of Joppe also were guilty of
Acts 9 36 in Joppe there was a certain disciple
38 Lydda was nigh to Joppe, the disciples
42 it was made known throughout all Joppe
43 he abode many days in Joppe, with one
10 5 and now send men to Joppe, and call
8 he had related all, he sent them to J.
23 brethren from Joppe accompanied him
32 send to J. and call hither Simon. 11:13
11 5 I was in the city of Joppe praying
Joppites 2 Ma 12 7 root out all the Joppites
Jora 1 Es 2 18 the children of Jora, 112
Jorai 1 Pa 5 13 their brethern . . . Sebe and J.
Joram 2 K 8 10 Thou sent Joram his son to king

3 K 22 51 J. his son reigned in. 2 Pa 21:1
4 K 1 17 Joram his brother reigned in his stead
17 second year of J. son of Josaphat
3 1 Joram the son of Achab reigned over
6 king Joram went out that day from
8 16 in the fifth year of Joram son of Achab
16 reigned J. son of Josaphat king of Juda
21 Joram came to Seira, and all the chariots
23 the rest of the acts of Joram and all
24 Joram slept with his fathers and was
25 in twelfth year of Joram son of Achab
25 Ochozias son of Joram. 29; 2 Pa 22:1, 6
28 he went also with Joram son of Achab
28 and the Syrians wounded Joram: and
29 Ochozias . . . went down to visit Joram
9 14 so Jehu . . . conspired against Joram
14 Joram had besieged Ramoth Galaad, he
16 into Jezrahel; for J. was sick there
16 Ochozias . . . was come down to visit J.
17 Joram said: Take a chariot and send
21 and Joram said: Make ready the chariot
21 Joram king of Israel and Ochozias
22 Joram saw Jehu, he said: Is there peace
23 and Joram turned his hand and fleeing
24 and shot Joram between the shoulders
29 in the eleventh year of Joram, the son
11 2 but Josaba the daughter of king Joram
12 18 which Josaphat and Joram and Ochozias
1 Pa 3 11 father of J.: and J. begot Ochozias
26 25 and his son Isaias, and his son Joram
2 Pa 17 8 with them Elisama and Joram priests
21 3 but the kingdom he gave to Joram
4 so Joram rose up over the kingdom of
5 Joram was two and thirty years old
9 and Joram went over with his princes
16 stirred up against Joram the spirit of
22 5 went with Joram . . . to fight against
5 Galaad: and the Syrians wounded Joram
6 Ochozias . . . went down to visit Joram
7 Ochozias that he should come to Joram
10 killed all royal family of house of Joram
11 Josabeth . . . was daughter of King Joram
Mat 1 8 Josaphat begot J. and J. begot Ozias
Jorim Luke 3 29 Eliezer, who was of Jorim, who was
Josa 1 Pa 4 34 Mosabab and Jemlech and Josa
Josaba 4 K 11 2 J. the daughter of king Joram
Josabeth 2 Pa 22 11 J. the king's daughter took Joas
2 Pa 22 11 Josabeth . . . was daughter of king Joram
Josabhesed 1 Pa 3 20 and Hasadias, J., five
Josabia 1 Pa 4 35 Jehu the son of Josabia
Josachar 4 K 12 21 Josachar . . . struck him [Joas]
Josaia 1 Pa 11 46 and Josaia the sons of Elnaim
Josaphat 2 K 8 16 Josaphat was recorder. 20:24; 3 K 4:3; 1 Pa 18:15
3 K 22 49 king Josaphat made navies on the sea
50 Ochozias . . . said to Josaphat: Let my
4 17 J. the son of Pharue in Issachar
15 24 J. his son reigned in his. 2 Pa 17:1
22 2 Josaphat king of Juda came down to
4 he said to Josaphat: Wilt thou come
5 J. said to king of Israel. 2 Pa 18:4
7 Josaphat said: Is there not here. 4 K 3:11; 2 Pa 18:6
8 the king of Israel said to Josaphat. 18, 30; 2 Pa 18:7, 17, 29
8 Josaphat said: Speak not so. 2 Pa 18:7
10 king of Israel and J. king of Juda. 29; 4 K 3:12; 2 Pa 18:9, 28
32 when captains of the chariots saw J.
32 Josaphat cried out. And the captains
41 Josaphat . . . began to reign over Juda
45 J. had peace with the king of Israel
46 the rest of the acts of J. 2 Pa 20:34
50 in the ships. And Josaphat would not
51 J. slept with his fathers. 2 Pa 21:1
52 in the seventeenth year of Josaphat
4 K 1 17 Joram the son of Josaphat. 8:16
3 1 in the eighteenth year of Josaphat
7 [Joram] sent to Josaphat king of Juda
12 Josaphat said: The word of the Lord is
14 if I did not reverence the face of J.
8 16 fifth year . . . of Josaphat king of Juda
9 2 Jehu the son of Josaphat. 14
12 18 which Josaphat . . . had dedicated to
1 Pa 3 10 begot Asa. And his son was Josaphat
11 43 of Maacha, and Josaphat a Mathanite
15 24 Sebenias and Josaphat and Nathanael
2 Pa 17 3 and the Lord was with Josaphat because
5 all Juda brought presents to Josaphat
10 durst not make war against Josaphat
11 Philistines also brought presents to J.
12 and J. grew and became exceeding great
18 1 Josaphat was rich and very glorious
3 said to J. king of Juda: Come with me
31 captains of the cavalry saw Josaphat
19 1 Josaphat . . . returned to his house in
4 J. dwelt at Jerusalem: and he went out
8 in Jerusalem also J. appointed Levites
20 1 gathered together to fight against J.
2 there came messengers and told J.
3 and Josaphat being seized with fear
5 J. stood in midst of the assembly of
15 dwell in Jerusalem and thou king J.
18 Josaphat and Juda . . . fell flat on the
20 Josaphat standing in the midst of them
25 then Josaphat came, and all the people
27 Josaphat at their head, into Jerusalem
30 and the kingdom of Josaphat was quiet
31 Josaphat reigned over Juda, and he was
35 J. king of Juda made friendship with
37 and Eliezer . . . prophesied to Josaphat
21 2 he had brethren the sons of Josaphat
2 all these were the sons of Josaphat
12 thou hast not walked in the ways of J.
22 9 because he was the son of Josaphat
Joel 3 2 them down into the valley of Josaphat
12 come up into the valley of Josaphat
Mat 1 8 Asa begot J. and J. begot Joram
Josedec 1 Pa 6 14 Saraias begot Josedec and
1 Pa 6 15 J. went out, when the Lord carried away
1 Es 3 2 Josue the son of Josedec. 8; 5:2; 10:18; 2 Es 12:26
Eccu 49 14 Jesus the son of Josedec. Agge 1:12, 14; 2:3, 5; 6:11
Joseph Mat 1 16 Jacob begot Joseph the husband of Mary
Mat 1 18 his mother Mary was espoused to Joseph
19 Joseph her husband being a just man and
20 Joseph, son of David, fear not to take
24 Joseph rising up from sleep, did as the
2 13 appeared in sleep to Joseph. 19
13 55 and his brethren James and Joseph and
27 56 and Mary the mother of James and Joseph
57 rich man of Arimathea, named Joseph who
59 Joseph taking the body, wrapped it up
Mark 6 3 brother of James and Joseph and Jude
15 40 mother of James the less and of Joseph
43 Joseph of Arimathea, a noble counsellor
45 he gave the body to Joseph. And Joseph buying fine linen
47 and Mary the mother of Joseph beheld
Luke 1 27 espoused to a man whose name was Joseph
2 4 Joseph also went up from Galilee out of
16 they found Mary and Joseph, and the
3 23 as it was supposed, the son of Joseph
24 Janne, who was of Joseph, who was of
26 Semei, who was of Joseph, who was of

30 Judas, who was of Joseph, who was of
4 22 said: Is not this the son of Joseph
23 50 man named Joseph, who was a counsellor
John 1 45 Jesus the son of Joseph of Nazareth
4 5 which Jacob gave to his son Joseph
6 42 is not this Jesus the son of Joseph
19 38 Joseph of Arimathea, because he was a
Acts 1 23 J., called Barsabas, who was surnamed
4 36 J., who by the apostles was surnamed
Joseph's Gen 39 5 of the Egyptian for J. sake
Gen 50 22 were born on Joseph's knees. After which
Exod 13 19 and Moses took Joseph's bones with him
Josias 3 K 13 2 to the house of David, J. by name
4 K 21 24 and made Josias his son their king in
26 and his son Josias reigned in his stead
22 1 J. was eight years old when. 2 Pa 34:1
3 eighteenth year of king Josias. 23:23
23 16 Josias turned himself, he saw there
19 Josias took away: and he did to them
24 the diviners . . . Josias took away: that
28 the rest of the acts of Josias and all
29 king Josias went to meet him: and was
30 Joachaz the son of Josias. 2 Pa 36:1
34 made Eliacim the son of Josias king in the room of Josias his father
1 Pa 2 14 Manasses begot Amon the father of J.
15 the sons of Josias were, the firstborn
2 Pa 33 25 made Josias his son king in his stead
34 33 Josias took away all the abominations
35 1 and Josias kept a phase to the Lord
7 Josias gave to all the people that
16 according to the commandment of king J.
18 keep such a phase as Josias kept, with
19 eighteenth year of the reign of Josias
20 Josias went out to meet him [Nechao]
20 after that J. had repaired the temple
22 Josias would not return, but prepared
25 Jeremias; whose lamentations for Josias
26 the rest of the acts of Josias and of
Eccu 49 1 the memory of Josias is like the
5 except David and Ezechias and J. all
Jer 1 2 which came to him in the days of Josias
3 Joakim the son of Josias. 22:18; 25:1; 26:1; 27:1; 35:1; 36:1, 9; 45:1; 46:2
3 Sedecias the son of Josias. 37:1; Bar 1:8
3 6 said to me in the days of king Josias
22 11 saith the Lord Sellum the son of J.
25 3 from the thirteenth year of Josias the
36 2 from days of Josias even to this day
Soph 1 1 in the days of Josias . . . king of Juda
Zach 6 10 shalt go into the house of Josias
Mat 1 10 Amon begot J. and J. begot Jechonias
Josphia 1 Es 8 10 Selomith the son of Josphia
jostle Nah 2 4 the chariots jostle one against
jot Mat 5 18 one jot or one tittle shall not pass
Jota Josu 15 55 Carmel and Ziph and Jota
journey Gen 24 21 made his j. prosperous or not
Gen 28 2 take a j. to Mesopotamia of Syria
5 took his journey and went to Mesopotamia
29 1 then Jacob went on in his journey
13 when he had heard the causes of his j.
30 26 he set the space of three days' journey
32 1 Jacob also went on the journey he had
33 12 I will accompany thee in thy journey
35 3 and accompanied me in my journey
42 4 lest perhaps he take any harm in the j.
45 23 carrying wheat and bread for the j.
46 1 Israel taking his journey with all that
48 7 Rachel died . . . in the very journey
Exod 3 18 three days' journey, into the wilderness 5:3; 8:27
4 24 when he [Moses] was in his journey
13 21 that he might be the guide of their j.
18 8 which had befallen them in the j.
23 20 before thee and keep thee in thy j.
Num 9 10 dead, or shall be in a journey afar off
13 not on a j. and did not make the phase
10 33 from mount of the Lord three days' j.
11 31 for the space of one day's journey
21 4 began to be weary of their journey and
Deut 1 2 eleven days' journey from Horeb by the
2 7 the Lord . . . knoweth thy journey, how
6 7 in thy house and walking on thy j.
Josu 5 6 during the forty years of the journey
8 13 by reason of the very long journey are
Judg 17 8 as he was on his j. and had turned
18 5 whether their j. should be prosperous
6 Lord looketh on your way and the J.
26 they went on the journey they had begun
19 8 the Levite prepared to go on his j.
14 by Jebus, and went on their journey
22 drink, after the labor of the journey
27 that he might end the j. he had begun
1 K 28 22 strength and be able to go on thy j.
2 K 11 10 didst thou not come from thy journey
3 K 12 25 returned from their journey, as the
18 27 on a journey or perhaps he is asleep
19 4 he went forward one day's journey into
4 K 3 9 fetched a compass of seven days' j.
2 Es 2 6 for how long shall thy journey be and
Tob 5 21 may you have a good journey, and God be
22 that were to be carried in their journey
8 21 necessary for such as go on a journey
10 11 of the Lord be with you in your j.
Job 28 4 the people that are on their journey
Ps 67 20 will make our journey prosperous to us
79 10 thou wast the guide of its journey in
Prov 7 19 not at home, he is gone a very long j.
9 15 pass by the way and go on their j.
Wisd 13 19 for a good journey he petitioneth him
Eccu 39 29 ways were made plain for their journey
43 28 is established the end of their journey
Jon 3 3 a great city of three days' journey
4 to enter into the city one day's j.
1 Ma 5 24 went three days' j. through the desert
7 45 pursued after them one day's journey
8 19 they went to Rome, a very long journey
10 78 to Azotus as one that was making a j.
13 31 Tryphon when he was upon a journey
2 Ma 3 8 Heliodorus forthwith began his journey
5 1 Antiochus prepared for a second journey
9 4 be driven, without stopping in his j.
Mat 10 10 nor scrip for your journey, nor two
25 15 and immediately he took his journey
Luke 2 44 they came a day's journey and sought
9 3 take nothing for your journey; neither
10 33 Samaritan being on his j., came near
11 6 a friend of mine is come off his j.
13 22 and making his journey to Jerusalem
John 4 6 wearied with his journey, sat thus on
Acts 1 12 within a sabbath day's journey. And
9 3 as he went on his journey, it came to
10 9 whilst they were going on their journey
Rom 1 10 I may have a prosperous j., by the will
15 24 I shall begin to take my j. into Spain
journeyed Deut 2 14 that we j. from Cadesbarne
Josu 14 10 when Israel j. through the wilderness
24 17 in all the way by which we journeyed
journeying 2 C 11 26 in journeying often, in perils
journeys Haba 3 6 bowed down by the j. of his
joy Mat 2 10 they rejoiced with exceeding great joy
Mat 13 20 and immediately receiveth it with joy
44 for joy thereof goeth and selleth all
25 21 enter thou into the joy of thy lord. 23
28 8 with fear and great joy, running to
Luke 1 14 thou shalt have joy and gladness and

44 the infant in my womb leaped for joy
2 10 I bring you good tidings of great joy
8 13 they hear, receive the word with joy
10 17 the 72 returned with joy, saying
15 7 there shall be joy in heaven upon one
10 there shall be joy before the angels
19 6 came down; and received him with joy
37 began with joy to praise God with a
24 41 believed not, and wondered for joy, he
52 back into Jerusalem with great joy
John 3 29 with joy because of the bridegroom's
29 this my joy therefore is fulfilled
15 11 that my joy may be in you, and your joy may be filled
16 20 your sorrow shall be turned into joy
21 for joy that a man is born into the
22 your joy no man shall take from you
24 receive; that your joy may be full
17 13 may have my joy filled in themselves
Acts 2 28 thou shalt make me full of joy with
8 9 was therefore great joy in that city
12 14 voice, who opened not the gate for joy
13 52 the disciples were filled with joy and
15 3 they caused great joy to all brethren
Rom 14 17 peace and joy in the Holy Ghost. For he
15 13 the God of hope fill you with all joy
32 that I may come to you with joy, by the
2 C 1 23 faith: but we are helpers of your joy
2 3 you all, that my joy is joy of you all
7 4 I exceedingly abound with joy in all our
13 abundantly rejoice for the joy of Titus
8 2 they have had abundance of joy; and
Gal 5 22 the fruit of the Spirit is . . . joy
Phil 1 4 supplication for you all, with joy; for
7 gospel, you all are partakers of my joy
25 for your furtherance and joy of faith
2 2 fulfil ye my joy, that you be of one
29 receive him therefore with all joy in
4 1 my joy and my crown; so stand fast in
Col 1 11 patience and longsuffering with joy
1 Th 1 6 tribulation, with joy of the Holy Ghost
2 19 what is our hope, or joy, or crown of
20 for you are our glory and joy. For
3 9 in all the joy wherewith we rejoice for
2 Tim 1 4 thy tears, that I may be filled with joy
Philem 7 I have had great joy and consolation in
Heb 10 34 took with joy the being stripped of your
12 2 having joy set before him, endured the
11 seemeth not to bring with it joy, but
13 17 that they may do this with joy, and
James 1 2 count it all joy when you shall fall
4 9 mourning, and your joy into sorrow
1 P 1 8 shall rejoice with joy unspeakable
4 13 may also be glad with exceeding joy
1 J 1 4 your joy may be full. 2 J 12
Jude 24 of his glory with exceeding joy, in
joyed 1 K 2 1 because I have j. in thy salvation
joyful 2 K 6 15 brought the ark . . . with joyful shouting. 1 Pa 15:28
1 Pa 15 16 that the j. noise might resound on high
2 Pa 7 10 j. and glad for the good that the Lord
15 14 with a loud voice with joyful shouting
1 Es 6 22 for the Lord had made them joyful and
2 Es 12 42 God had made them joyful with great
43 Juda was joyful in the priests and
Tob 10 10 sent him away safe and j. from him
Jdth 16 24 and the people were joyful in the sight
Job 38 7 the sons of God made a joyful melody
Ps 20 7 thou shalt make him joyful in gladness
45 5 of the river maketh the city of God j.
62 6 my mouth shall praise thee with j. lips
64 9 shalt make the outgoings . . . to be j.
94 2 make a joyful noise to him with psalms
95 12 things that are in them shall be joyful
97 6 made a joyful noise before the Lord our
112 9 in a house, the joyful mother of children
125 3 things for us: we are become joyful
146 1 to our God be joyful and comely praise
149 2 let the children of Sion be joyful in
5 they shall be joyful in their beds
Prov 15 20 a wise son maketh a father joyful: but
17 22 a joyful mind maketh age flourishing
23 25 let thy father and thy mother be joyful
27 11 wisdom, my son, and make my heart j.
Eccu 31 55 wine . . . to make men joyful, and not
Isa 24 14 shall make a joyful noise from the sea
25 9 we shall rejoice and be joyful in his
41 16 Holy One of Israel thou shalt be j.
54 1 forth praise and make a joyful noise
56 7 will make them j. in my house of prayer
61 10 and my soul shall be joyful in my God
Jer 31 13 make them joyful after their sorrow
51 14 and they shall lift up a joyful shout
Joel 2 23 rejoice and be joyful in the Lord
Soph 3 17 he will be joyful over thee in praise
Zach 10 7 their heart shall be j. in the Lord
1 Ma 5 64 assembled to them with j. acclamations
joyfully 1 Pa 29 17 j. offered all these things
Ps 94 1 let us joyfully sing to God our savior
97 4 sing j. to God, all the earth. 99:2
Ecce 9 9 live joyfully with the wife whom thou
joyfulness Tob 3 22 weeping thou pourest in j.
Ps 125 7 they shall come with j., carrying
Eccu 30 23 j. of the heart is the life of a man
50 25 may he grant us joyfulness of heart
Isa 65 14 servants shall praise for j. of heart
joyous Isa 22 2 a populous city, a j. city: thy
joys Eccu 37 4 rejoiceth with his friend in his j.
Jozabad 4 K 12 21 J. the son of Somer his
1 Pa 12 20 J. and Jedihel and Michael
26 4 of Obededom . . . Jozabad the second
2 Pa 17 18 after him also was Jozabad, and with
24 26 J. the son of Semarith a Moabitess
31 13 Jerimoth and Jozabad and Eliel and
35 9 and Jozabad princes of the Levites
1 Es 8 33 with them Jozabad the son of Josue
Jozabed 1 Es 10 22 Nathanael, Josabed, and Elasa
1 Es 10 23 Josabed and Semei and Celaia
2 Es 8 7 Jozabed, Hanan, Phalaia, the Levites
11 16 Sabathai and Jozabed, who were over
Jubal Gen 4 21 his brother's name was Jubal
jubilation Ps 26 6 a sacrifice of jubilation
Ps 88 16 blessed is the people that knoweth j.
Isa 49 13 ye mountains, give praise with j.
jubilee Lev 25 10 for it is the year of jubilee
Lev 25 11 because it is the jubilee and the
12 because of the sanctification of the j.
13 in the year of the j. all shall return
14 the number of years from the jubilee
16 the more years remain after the j.
28 bought, until the year of the jubilee
30 be redeemed, not even in the jubilee
31 in the j. it shall return to the owner
33 in the j. they shall all return to
40 work with thee until year of the jubilee
50 of his selling unto the year of the j.
51 be many years that remain until the j.
54 in the year of the j. he shall go out
27 17 immediately from the year of jubilee
18 of years that remain until the jubilee
21 when the day of jubilee cometh, it
23 the number of years; unto the jubilee
24 in the jubilee, it shall return to the
Num 36 4 jubilee . . . is come, the distribution
Josu 6 4 trumpets, which are used in the j. 13
6 take the seven trumpets of the jubilee

Ps 46 6 God is ascended with jubilee, and the
Jucadam Josu 15 56 Jezrael and Jucadam and
Juchal Jer 37 3 J. the son of Selemias. 38:1
Jud Josu 19 45 and Jud and Bane and Barach
Judaia 1 Pa 4 18 his wife Judaia bore Jared
Judas Mat 1 2 Jacob begot Judas and his brethren
Mat 1 3 Judas begot Phares and Zara of Thamar
10 4 J. Iscariot, who also betrayed. Mark 3:19
26 14 who was called Judas Iscariot, to the
25 Judas that betrayed him, answering
47 Judas, one of the twelve, came and with
27 3 then Judas, who betrayed him, seeing
Mark 14 10 Judas Iscariot, one of the twelve went
43 yet speaking, cometh Judas Iscariot
Luke 3 30 Simeon, who was of Judas, who was of
33 Phares, who was of Judas, who was of
6 16 Judas Iscariot, who was the traitor
22 3 Satan entered into Judas, who was
47 he that was called Judas, one of the
48 Judas, dost thou betray the Son of man
John 12 4 Judas Iscariot, he that was about to
13 2 having now put into the heart of Judas
26 bread, he gave it to Judas Iscariot
29 thought, because Judas had the purse
14 22 Judas saith to him, not the Iscariot
18 2 and Judas also . . . knew the place
3 Judas therefore having received a band
5 Judas also, who betrayed him, stood
Acts 1 16 by mouth of David concerning Judas
25 from which Judas hath by transgression
5 37 rose up Judas of Galilee in the days
9 11 seek in the house of Judas, one named
15 22 Judas, who was surnamed Barsabas, and
27 we have sent therefore Judas and Silas
32 Judas and Silas, being prophets also
34 and Judas alone departed to Jerusalem
Judas' 1 Ma 9 13 that were on Judas' side, even
2 Ma 14 18 hearing of the valor of J. companions
Jude Mat 13 55 and his brethren . . . Simon and Jude
Mark 6 3 brother of James and Joseph and Jude
Luke 6 16 Jude the brother of James, and Judas
Acts 1 13 where abode . . . Jude the brother of
Jude 1 Jude, the servant of Jesus Christ, and
Judea 1 K 23 3 behold we are in fear here in J.
2 Pa 2 7 which I have with me in Judea and
36 23 Jerusalem, which is in J. 1 Es 1:2, 3
1 Es 5 1 prophesied to the Jews that were in J.
8 that we went to the province of Judea
7 14 counsellors, to visit J. and Jerusalem
2 Es 2 5 that thou wouldst send me into Judea
7 convey me over, till I come into Judea
6 7 saying: There is a king in Judea. The
18 there were many in Judea sworn to him
7 6 and who returned into Judea, every one
Tob 1 21 Sennacherib . . . fleeing from Judea
Ps 75 2 in Judea God is known: his name is
113 2 Judea was made his sanctuary, Israel
Jer 14 2 Judea hath mourned, and the gates
40 11 of Babylon had left a remnant in J.
Dan 5 13 my father the king brought out of Judea
14 32 was in Judea a prophet called Habacuc
Joel 3 20 and Judea shall be inhabited forever
1 Ma 3 34 concerning the inhabitants of Judea
4 29 they came into Judea and pitched their
35 might come again into J. with greater
5 8 city of Gazer . . . and returned into J.
23 brought them into Judea with great joy
60 were pursued unto the borders of Judea
6 48 army pitched their tents against Judea
53 such as had stayed in Judea of them
7 24 he went out into all the coasts of J.
46 forth out of all the towns of Judea
9 1 again Bacchides and Alcimus into J.
50 and they built strong cities in Judea
60 to his adherents that were in Judea
63 he sent word to them that were of J.
10 38 the three cities that are added to J.
38 Samaria, let them be accounted with J.
45 for the building of the walls in Judea
11 20 gathered together them that were in J.
28 he would make Judea free from tribute
34 ratified . . . all the borders of Judea
34 cities . . . which are added to Judea
12 35 with them to build fortresses in Judea
13 33 Simon built up the strongholds of J.
14 33 fortified the cities of J. and Bethsura that lieth in the borders of J.
15 30 dominion without the borders of Judea
39 to march with his army towards Judea
40 to ravage J. and to take the people
41 make incursions upon the ways of Judea
16 10 and he returned into Judea in peace
14 cities that were in the country of J.
2 Ma 1 1 in Jerusalem and in the land of Judea
10 people that is at Jerusalem and in J.
10 24 as though he would take Judea by force
11 5 he came into Judea, and approaching
13 1 was coming with a multitude against J.
13 king should bring his army into Judea
14 12 sent Nicanor . . . governor into Judea
14 the Gentiles who had fled out of Judea
Mat 2 22 hearing that Archelaus reigned in Judea
3 1 Baptist preaching in the desert of J.
5 out to him Jerusalem and all Judea
4 25 from Jerusalem and from Judea and
19 1 came into the coasts of Judea beyond
24 16 they that are in Judea, let them flee
Mark 1 5 out to him all the country of Judea
3 7 followed him from Galilee and Judea
10 1 into the coasts of Judea beyond the
13 14 let them that are in Judea, flee into
Luke 1 5 the days of Herod, the king of Judea
65 over all the hill country of Judea
2 4 out of the city of Nazareth into Judea
3 1 Pontius Pilate being governor of Judea
5 17 every town of Galilee and Judea and
6 17 multitude of people from all Judea
7 17 of him went forth throughout all Judea
21 21 who are in Judea flee to the mountains
23 5 teaching throughout all Judea
51 of Arimathea, a city of Judea; who
John 3 22 disciples came into the land of Judea
4 3 he left J. and went again into Galilee
47 that Jesus was come from Judea into
54 when he was come out of Judea into
7 1 for he would not walk in J., because
3 pass from hence and go into Judea
11 7 let us go into Judea again. The
Acts 1 8 and in all Judea and Samaria and even
2 9 inhabitants of Mesopotamia, Judea, and
14 men of Judea, and all you that dwell
8 1 dispersed through the countries of J.
9 31 church had peace throughout all Judea
10 37 word . . . published through all Judea
11 1 apostles and brethren, who were in J.
29 to the brethren who dwelt in Judea
12 19 and going down from Judea to Caesarea
15 1 some coming down from Judea, taught
21 10 there came from J. a certain prophet
26 20 Jerusalem, and unto all country of J.
28 21 received letters concerning thee from J.
Rom 15 31 from the unbelievers that are in Judea
2 C 1 16 to be brought on my way towards Judea
Gal 1 22 unknown by face to the churches of J.
1 Th 2 14 churches of God which are in Judea, in
judge Mat 5 25 adversary deliver thee to the judge

Mat 5 25 the judge deliver thee to the officer
7 1 judge not, that you may not be judged
2 with what judgment you judge, you
Luke 6 37 judge not, and you shall not be judged
12 14 who hath appointed me judge or divider
57 do you not judge that which is just
58 lest perhaps he draw thee to the judge
58 the judge deliver thee to the exacter
18 2 there was a judge in a certain city
6 hear what the unjust judge saith. And
19 22 out of thy own mouth I judge thee
John 3 17 into the world to judge the world, but
5 22 neither doth the Father judge any man
30 as I hear, so I judge: and my judgment
7 24 judge not according to the appearance, but judge just judgment
51 doth our law judge any man unless it
8 15 you judge according to the flesh: I judge not any man
16 if I do judge, my judgment is true
26 I have to speak and to judge of you
12 47 and keep them not, I do not judge him
47 I came not to judge the world, but to
48 same shall judge him in the last day
18 31 and judge him according to your law
Acts 4 19 to hear you rather than God, judge ye
7 7 which they shall serve will I judge
27 appointed thee prince and judge. 35
10 42 to be j. of the living and of the dead
13 46 j. yourselves unworthy of eternal life
15 19 I j. that they, who from among Gentiles
17 31 hath appointed a day wherein he will j.
18 15 I will not be judge of such things. And
23 3 for sittest thou to j. me according to
24 10 thou hast been judge over this nation
Rom 2 16 day when God shall judge the secrets of
27 fulfil law, j. thee, who by the letter
3 6 otherwise how shall God judge this world
14 3 not, let him not judge him that eateth
13 let us not therefore j. one another any
13 but judge this rather, that you put not
1 C 4 3 but neither do I judge my own self. For
5 judge not before the time; until the
5 12 I to do to judge them that are without
12 do not you judge them that are within
13 them that are without, God will judge
6 2 that the saints shall judge this world
2 are you unworthy to j. smallest matters
3 know you not that we shall j. angels
4 set them to j., who are most despised in
5 that is able to j. between his brethren
10 15 wise men: j. ye yourselves what I say
11 13 you yourselves judge: doth it become a
31 if we would judge ourselves, we should
14 29 two or three; and let the rest judge
Col 2 16 let no man therefore judge you in meat
2 Tim 4 1 who shall judge the living and the dead
8 which the Lord the just j. will render
Heb 10 30 again: The Lord shall judge his people
12 23 to God the judge of all, and to the
13 4 fornicators and adulterers God will j.
James 2 4 do you not judge within yourselves
4 11 if thou judge the law, thou art not a doer of the law, but a judge
12 there is one lawgiver and judge, that
5 9 the judge standeth before the door
1 P 4 5 who is ready to judge the living and
Apoc 6 10 dost thou not judge and revenge our
18 8 God is strong, who shall judge her
19 11 with justice doth he judge and fight

judged Mat 7 1 judge not, that you may not be j.
Mat 7 2 judgment you judge, you shall be j.
Luke 6 37 judge not, and you shall not be judged
7 43 said to him: Thou hast judged rightly
John 3 18 that believeth in him is not judged
18 that doth not believe is already j.
16 11 prince of this world is already judged
Acts 3 13 when he judged he should be released
16 15 if you have judged me to be faithful
24 6 would also have j. according to our law
21 resurrection of dead am I j. this day
25 9 there be judged of these things. 20
10 judgment seat, where I ought to be j.
Rom 2 12 in the law, shall be judged by the law
3 4 and mayest overcome when thou art j.
7 why am I also yet judged as a sinner
1 C 2 2 I judged not myself to know any thing
15 and he himself is judged of no man. For
4 3 it is a very small thing to be judged
5 3 have already judged, as though I were
6 1 go to be judged before the unjust, and
2 if the world shall be judged by you, are
7 37 and hath judged this in his heart, to
10 29 liberty j. by another man's conscience
11 31 judge ourselves, we should not be judged
32 whilst we are j., we are chastised by
14 24 convinced of all, he is judged of all
2 Th 2 11 all may be judged who have not believed
James 2 12 to be judged by the law of liberty
5 9 that you may not be judged. Behold
1 P 2 23 to him that judged him unjustly. Who
4 6 that they might be judged indeed
Apoc 11 18 the dead, that they should be judged
16 5 because thou hast judged these things
18 20 God hath judged your judgment on her
19 2 who hath judged the great harlot which
20 12 the dead were judged by those things
13 were judged every one according to

judges Num 25 5 Moses said to the j. of Israel
Deut 16 18 thou shalt appoint j. and magistrates
17 8 of the j. within thy gates do vary
19 17 in the sight of the priests and the j.
21 2 thy ancients and judges shall go out
25 1 and they call upon the judges: they
32 31 our enemies themselves are judges
Josu 8 33 princes and judges stood on both sides
23 2 and for the princes and for the judges
24 1 ancients and the princes and the j.
Judg 2 16 the Lord raised up judges to deliver
18 when the Lord raised them up judges
Ruth 1 1 in the days of one of the judges, when the judges ruled
1 K 8 1 he appointed his sons to be judges over
2 second was Abia, judges in Bersabee
2 K 7 11 from the day that I appointed judges
4 K 23 22 phase kept from the days of the judges
24 15 judges of the land he carried into
1 Pa 17 6 to any one, of all the judges of Israel
10 since the days that I gave judges
23 4 and 6,000 were overseers and judges
2 Pa 1 2 rulers and to the judges of all Israel
19 5 he set judges of the land in all the
6 charging the judges, he said: Take heed
1 Es 7 25 appoint judges and magistrates that
10 14 with them the ancients and the judges
Esth 3 12 to the judges of the provinces and of
8 9 and to the judges, who were rulers
9 3 j. of the provinces and the governors
Job 9 24 he covereth the face of the judges
12 17 bringeth . . . judges to insensibility
Ps 140 6 their judges falling upon the rock
148 11 princes and all judges of the earth
Wisd 1 1 you that are the judges of the earth
6 2 that are j. of the ends of the earth
Eccu 20 31 presents and gifts blind the eyes of j.
46 13 all the judges, every one by name

Isa 1 26 I will restore thy judges as they were
40 23 made the judges of the earth as vanity
Bar 2 1 that he spoke to us and to our judges
Dan 3 2 king sent to call together . . . the j.
3 the judges, the captains, and rulers
94 nobles and the magistrates and the j.
6 7 and judges have consulted together
13 5 of the people appointed j. that year
5 out from Babylon from the ancient j.
41 the elders and the j. of the people
Osee 7 7 oven, and have devoured their judges
13 10 thy judges, of whom thou saidst: Give
Soph 3 3 her judges are evening wolves: they
Mat 12 27 they shall be your judges. Luke 11:19
Acts 13 20 he gave unto them judges, until Samuel
James 2 4 are become judges of unjust thoughts

judges' Eccu 38 38 upon the judges' seat they

judgest Gen 18 25 thou who judgest all the earth
Job 10 2 tell me why thou judgest me so. Doth
Ps 9 5 sat on the throne, who judgest justice
66 5 thou judgest the people with justice
93 2 lift up thyself, thou that j. the earth
Wisd 12 18 master of power, j. with tranquillity
Jer 11 20 who judgest justly and triest the
Eze 20 4 if thou j. them, if thou j., O son
Rom 2 1 O man, whosoever thou art that judgest
1 for wherein thou judgest another, thou
1 thou dost same things which thou judgest
3 O man, that judgest them who do such
14 4 who art thou that judgest another man's
10 thou, why judgest thou thy brother? or
James 4 13 who art thou that judgest thy neighbor

judgeth Job 21 22 who j. those that are high
Job 22 13 he judgeth as it were through a mist
31 35 he himself that j. would write a book
36 31 by these he j. people and giveth food
Ps 7 9 the Lord judgeth the people. Judge me
57 12 a God that judgeth them on the earth
81 1 in the midst of them he judgeth gods
Prov 17 26 to strike the prince, who j. right
29 14 the king that judgeth the poor in truth
Wisd 8 8 past, and judgeth of things to come
Eccu 8 17 he j. according to that which is just
16 13 judgeth a man according to his works
Isa 59 4 is there any one that judgeth truly
John 8 50 there is one that seeketh and judgeth
12 48 not my words, hath one that j. him
Rom 14 5 for one judgeth between day and day: and another judgeth every day
1 C 2 15 the spiritual man judgeth all things
4 4 but he that judgeth me, is the Lord
James 4 11 he that j. his brother, detracteth the law and j. the law
1 P 1 17 judgeth according to every one's work

judging Lev 27 12 j. whether it be good or bad
Job 34 6 in judging me there is a lie: my arrow
Wisd 12 19 in j. thou givest place for repentance
Eccu 4 10 in j. be merciful to the fatherless
Isa 16 5 j. and seeking judgment and quickly
Dan 13 53 in judging unjust judgments, oppressing
Mat 19 28 judging the twelve tribes. Luke 22:30
Acts 13 27 sabbath, j. him have fulfilled them
2 C 5 14 us: judging this, that if one died for
James 3 17 without judging, without dissimulation

judgment Mat 5 21 be in danger of the j. 22
Mat 5 40 if a man will contend with thee in j.
7 2 with what j. you judge, you shall be
12 18 he shall show judgment to the Gentiles
20 till he send forth j. unto victory
41 Ninive shall rise in j. Luke 11:32
42 the south shall rise in j. Luke 11:31
23 14 you shall receive the greater judgment
23 judgment and mercy and faith. These
33 how will you flee from the j. of hell
27 19 was sitting in the place of judgment
Mark 12 40 these shall receive greater judgment
Luke 10 14 for Tyre and Sidon at the j. than for
11 42 and pass over j. and the charity of
John 3 19 this is the judgment: because the
5 22 but hath given all judgment to the Son
24 cometh not into j., but is passed from
27 he hath given him power to do judgment
29 done evil, unto the resurrection of j.
30 so I judge: and my judgment is just
7 24 appearance, but judge just judgment
8 16 if I do judge, my judgment is true
9 39 for judgment I am come into this world
12 31 now is the judgment of the world: now
16 8 of sin and of justice and of judgment
11 judgment: because the prince of this
19 13 and sat down in the judgment seat in
Acts 8 33 in humility his j. was taken away. His
12 21 [Herod] sat in the judgment seat, and
18 12 Paul, and brought him to the j. seat
16 he drove them from the judgment seat
17 beat him before the judgment seat; and
23 35 him to be kept in Herod's j. hall. And
24 25 chastity, and of the j. to come, Felix
25 6 Caesarea, and next day he sat in j. seat
10 I stand at Caesar's j. seat, where I
17 on day following, sitting in j. seat, I
26 6 fathers, do I stand subject at judgment
Rom 2 2 for we know that the judgment of God is
3 thou shalt escape the judgment of God
5 revelation of the just judgment of God
5 16 j. indeed was by one unto condemnation
14 10 we shall all stand before j. seat of
1 C 1 10 same mind, and in the same judgment. For
11 29 eateth and drinketh j. to himself, not
34 that you come not together unto judgment
2 C 5 10 manifested before the j. seat of Christ
Gal 5 10 he that troubleth you, shall bear the j.
2 Th 1 5 example of the just judgment of God
1 Tim 3 6 he fall into the judgment of the devil
5 24 are manifest, going before to judgment
Titus 3 11 being condemned by his own judgment
Heb 6 2 of the dead, and of eternal judgment
9 27 once to die, and after this the judgment
10 27 a certain dreadful expectation of j.
James 2 6 they draw you before the j. seats
13 j. without mercy to him that hath not
13 mercy exalteth itself above judgment
3 1 that you receive the greater judgment
5 12 that you fall not under judgment. Is
1 P 4 17 j. should begin at the house of God
2 P 2 3 whose j. now of a long time lingereth
4 unto torments to be reserved unto j.
11 not against themselves a railing j.
Jude 4 were written of long ago unto this j.
6 chains, unto the j. of the great day
9 against him the j. of railing speech
15 to execute j. upon all and to reprove
Apoc 14 7 the hour of his judgment is come; and
18 10 for in one hour is thy judgment come
20 God hath judged your judgment on her
20 4 and judgment was given unto them; and

day of judgment Jdth 16 20 in d. . . . he will visit
2 Ma 6 14 when the d. . . . shall come, he may
Mat 10 15 land of Sodom and Gomorrha in d. . . .
11 22 Sidon in the d. . . . than for you. 24
12 36 render an account for it in the d. . . .
2 P 2 9 reserve the unjust unto the day of j.
3 7 reserve unto fire against the d. . . .
1 J 4 17 may have confidence in the day of j.

Judi Jer 36 14 all the princes sent Judi the son
Jer 36 21 the king sent Judi that he should take

23 when Judi had read three or four pages
Judith Gen 26 34 Esau . . . married wives, Judith
Jdth 8 1 when Judith a widow had heard these
4 Judith his relict was a widow now
30 Judith said to them: As you know that
9 1 J. went into her oratory: and putting
10 10 Judith praying to the Lord, passed
19 Judith seeing Holofernes sitting under
11 4 Judith said to him: Receive the words
12 2 Judith answered him and said: Now I
4 J. said: As thy soul liveth, my lord
12 then Vagao went in to Judith and said
13 Judith answered him: Who am I that I
18 Judith said: I will drink my lord
13 3 and Judith was alone in the chamber
5 Judith spoke to her maid to stand
6 Judith stood before the bed praying
13 Judith from afar off cried to the
17 J. said: Praise ye the Lord our God
27 Judith said to him [Achior]: The God
14 1 Judith said to all the people: Hear me
13 thought that he was sleeping with J.
15 he went into the tent of J., and not
15 9 with all his ancients to see Judith
14 they gave to Judith in gold and silver
16 1 Judith sung this canticle to the Lord
8 Judith . . . weakened him with the beauty
23 Judith offered for an anathema of
24 this victory was celebrated with J.
25 and Judith was made great in Bethulia
Julia Rom 16 15 salute Philologus and Julia, Nereus
Julius Acts 27 1 centurion, named J., of the band
Acts 27 3 and Julius treating Paul courteously
Junias Rom 16 7 salute Andronicus and J., my kinsmen
juniper 3 K 19 4 and sat under a juniper tree
3 K 19 5 slept in the shadow of the juniper tree
junipers Job 30 4 the root of j. was their food
Jupiter 2 Ma 6 2 the temple of Jupiter Olympius
2 Ma 6 2 that in Gazarim of Jupiter Hospitalis
Acts 14 11 and they called Barnabas, Jupiter: but
12 priest also of J. that was before city
Jupiter's Acts 19 35 Diana, and of J. offspring
jurisdiction Luke 23 7 that he was of Herod's j.
just Mat 5 45 raineth upon the just and the
Mat 9 13 I am not come to call the just, but
13 43 then shall the just shine as the sun
49 separate the wicked from among the just
20 4 and I will give you what shall be just
23 28 outwardly indeed appear to men just
29 and adorn the monuments of the just
35 all the just blood that hath been shed
35 from the blood of Abel the just, even
25 37 then shall the just answer him, saying
46 but the just, into life everlasting
Mark 2 17 I came not to call the j. Luke 5:32
Luke 1 6 and they were both just before God
17 incredulous to the wisdom of the just
2 25 and this man was just and devout
12 57 do you not judge that which is just
14 14 thee at the resurrection of the just
15 7 more than upon 99 just who need not
18 9 who trusted in themselves as just and
20 20 spies who should feign themselves just
John 5 30 so I judge: and my judgment is just
7 24 appearance, but judge just judgment
17 25 just Father, the world hath not known
Acts 3 14 you denied the Holy One and the Just
4 19 if it be just in the sight of God, to
24 15 resurrection of the just and unjust. And
Rom 2 5 revelation of the just judgment of God
13 for not the hearers of the law are just
3 8 come good? whose damnation is just. What
10 is written: There is not any man just
26 he himself may be just, and justifier
5 19 obedience of one, many shall be made j.
7 12 and the commandment holy, and just and
1 C 15 34 awake, ye just, and sin not. For some
Eph 6 1 obey your parents . . . for this is just
Phil 4 8 whatsoever modest, whatsoever just
Col 4 1 do to your servants that which is just
2 Th 1 5 example of the just judgment of God
6 seeing it is a just thing with God to
2 Tim 4 8 which the Lord the j. judge will render
Titus 1 8 gentle, sober, just, holy, continent
Heb 2 2 received a just recompense of reward
11 4 obtained a testimony that he was just
12 23 to the spirits of the just made perfect
1 P 3 12 the eyes of the Lord are upon the just
18 for our sins, the just for the unjust
2 P 2 7 delivered just Lot, oppressed by the
8 for in sight and hearing he was just
8 vexed the just soul with unjust works
1 J 1 9 he is faithful and just, to forgive
2 1 with the Father, Jesus Christ the just
29 if you know that he is just, know ye
3 7 doth justice is just, even as he is j.
10 whosoever is not just, is not of God
12 works were wicked: and his brother's j.
Apoc 15 3 just and true are thy ways, O King of
16 5 thou art just, O Lord, who art and who
7 true and just are thy judgments. And
19 2 true and just are his judgments, who
22 11 he that is just, let him be justified
just man Eccu 33 15 the sinner against a just man
Isa 3 10 say to the just man that it is well
57 1 the just man is taken away from before
Bar 6 72 better . . . just man that hath no idols
Eze 3 20 if the just man shall turn away from
21 but if thou warn the just man, that
18 24 if the just man turn himself away from
Amos 2 6 he hath sold the just man for silver
Mat 1 19 Joseph her husband being a just man
10 41 receiveth a j. m. in name of a j. m. shall receive reward of a j. m.
27 19 thou nothing to do with that just man
24 innocent of the blood of this just man
Mark 6 20 knowing him to be a just and holy man
Luke 23 47 saying: Indeed this was a just man
50 a counsellor, a good and a just man
Acts 10 22 Cornelius, a centurion, a just man and
Rom 1 17 the just man liveth by faith. Gal 3:11
5 7 for scarce for a just man will one die
1 Tim 1 9 the law is not made for the just man
Heb 10 38 my just man liveth by faith; but if he
James 5 16 prayer of a just man availeth much
1 P 4 18 if the just man shall scarcely be saved
just men Prov 29 2 when just men increase, the
Ecce 8 14 are just men to whom evils happen
9 1 there are just men and wise men, and
Eccu 9 22 let just men be thy guests and let
Eze 23 45 they therefore are just men: these
Mat 13 17 prophets and just men have desired to
just one Isa 24 16 the glory of the just one
Isa 41 2 who hath raised up the just one from
10 hand of my just one hath upheld thee
51 5 my just one is near at hand, my savior
62 1 not rest till her just one come forth
2 the Gentiles shall see thy just one
Acts 7 52 foretold of coming of the Just One
22 14 shouldst know his will, and see Just One
James 5 6 and put to death the Just One, and he
juster Gen 38 26 she is juster than I: because
justice Mat 3 15 so it becometh us to fulfil all justice
Mat 5 6 that hunger and thirst after justice
20 unless your justice abound more than
6 1 you do not your justice before men

33 33 kingdom of God and his j. Luke 12:31
21 32 John came to you in the way of justice
Luke 1 75 in holiness and j. before him all our
John 16 8 convince the world of sin and of j.
10 of justice: because I go to the Father
Acts 10 35 he that feareth him, and worketh j.
13 10 enemy of all j., thou ceasest not to
19 38 courts of justice are open, and there
24 25 as he treated of justice, and chastity
Rom 1 17 for the justice of God is revealed
32 having known the justice of God, did not
3 5 if our injustice commend the justice of
21 without the law justice of God is made
22 justice of God, by faith of Jesus Christ
25 showing of his justice, for remission
26 for showing of his justice in this time
4 3 it was reputed to him unto justice. 22, 23; Gal 3:6; James 2:23
5 his faith is reputed to j., according
6 to whom God reputeth j. without works
11 a seal of justice of the faith, which
11 unto them also it may be reputed to j.
13 world; but through the justice of faith
5 17 they who receive abundance of . . . j.
18 so also by the j. of one, unto all men
21 so also grace might reign by justice
6 13 your members as instruments of justice
16 sin unto death, or of obedience unto j.
18 we have been made servants of justice
19 now yield your members to serve justice
20 of sin, you were free men to justice
9 28 finish his word, and cut it short in j.
30 Gentiles, who followed not after justice
30 have attained to j., even the justice that is of faith
31 Israel, by following after the law of j.
31 is not come unto the law of justice. Why
10 3 they, not knowing the justice of God
3 have not submitted themselves to justice
4 unto justice to every one that believeth
5 Moses wrote, that the justice which is
6 justice which is of faith, speaketh thus
10 for, with heart, we believe unto justice
14 17 not meat and drink; but j. and peace and
1 C 1 30 who of God is made unto us wisdom and j.
2 C 3 9 much more the ministration of justice
5 21 might be made the justice of God in him
6 7 by the armor of j. on the right hand and
14 what . . . hath justice with injustice
9 9 the poor: his justice remaineth forever
10 increase the growth of fruits of your j.
11 15 be transformed as ministers of justice
Gal 2 21 if justice be by the law, then Christ
3 21 verily justice should have been by law
5 5 by faith, wait for the hope of justice
Eph 4 24 created in justice and holiness of truth
5 9 is in all goodness and justice and truth
6 14 and having on the breastplate of justice
Phil 1 11 Christ, filled with the fruit of justice
3 6 according to the j. that is in the law
8 be found in him, not having my justice
9 Jesus, which is of God, justice in faith
1 Tim 6 11 and pursue justice, godliness, faith
2 Tim 2 22 pursue justice, faith, charity and peace
3 16 to correct, to instruct in justice
4 8 there is laid up for me a crown of j.
Titus 3 5 not by the works of justice, which we
Heb 1 8 a scepter of justice is the scepter of
9 thou hast loved j., and hated iniquity
5 13 is unskilful in the word of justice: for
7 2 by interpretation, is king of justice
11 7 heir of the justice which is by faith
33 wrought justice, obtained promises
12 11 the most peaceable fruit of justice
James 1 20 of man worketh not the justice of God
3 18 the fruit of justice is sown in peace
1 P 2 24 dead to sins, should live to justice
2 P 1 1 in the justice of our God and Savior
2 5 eighth person, the preacher of justice
21 not to have known the way of justice
3 13 his promises, in which justice dwelleth
1 J 2 29 who doth justice, is born of him
3 7 he that doth justice is just, even
Apoc 19 11 with justice doth he judge and fight
justice' Mat 5 10 suffer persecution for justice' sake
1 P 3 14 you suffer anything for justice' sake
justification Job 27 6 my j., which I have begun
Ps 118 62 for the judgments of thy justification
Eze 16 27 and will take away thy justification
Rom 4 25 and rose again for our justification
5 16 grace is of many offences, unto j. For
18 of one, unto all men to j. of life. For
8 4 that j. of the law might be fulfilled
10 but the spirit liveth, because of j.
justifications Num 9 3 ceremonies and j. 14; 2 Pa 19:10
2 Pa 34 31 and keep his commandments . . . and j.
Ps 104 45 that they might observe his j. and
Dan 9 18 is not for our j. that we present our
1 Ma 1 51 and should change all the j. of God
2 40 the heathens for our lives and our j.
Luke 1 6 all the commandments and j. of the
Heb 9 1 the former indeed had also j. of divine
Apoc 19 8 the fine linen are the j. of saints
thy justifications Ps 118 5 to keep thy j.
Ps 118 8 I will keep thy j.: O, do not thou
12 teach me thy j. 26, 64, 68, 94, 124, 135, 171
16 I will think of thy j.: I will not
20 my soul hath coveted to long for thy j.
23 but thy servant was employed in thy j.
24 and thy justifications my counsel
27 me to understand the way of thy j.
33 before me for a law the way of thy j.
48 I was exercised in thy justifications
54 thy j. were the subject of my song
56 because I sought thy justifications
71 humbled me, that I may learn thy j.
80 let my heart be undefiled in thy j.
83 the frost: I have not forgotten thy j.
93 thy j. I will never forget: for by them
112 I have inclined my heart to do thy j.
117 and I will meditate always on thy j.
141 and despised: but I forget not thy j.
145 hear me, O Lord: I will seek thy j.
155 they have not sought thy justifications
justified Job 4 17 shall man be j. in comparison
Job 9 2 man cannot be j. compared with God
11 2 shall a man full of talk be justified
25 4 can man be j. compared with God, or he
33 12 is the thing in which thou art not j.
40 3 and condemn me, that thou mayst be j.
Ps 18 10 of the Lord are true, j. in themselves
50 6 that thou mayst be j. in thy words, and
72 13 then have I in vain justified my heart
142 2 in thy sight no man living shall be j.
Wisd 6 11 kept just things justly, shall be j.
Eccu 1 28 he that is without fear, cannot be j.
13 26 proud things, and they have j. him
14 21 and every excellent work shall be j.
18 1 God only shall be justified, and he
17 than a gift? But both are with a j. man
22 be not afraid to be j. even to death
23 14 he swear in vain, he shall not be j.
26 28 a huckster shall not be j. from the
31 5 he that loveth gold shall not be j.
Isa 43 9 let them be justified and hear and
45 26 shall all the seed of Israel be j.

K

17 19 keep his words and ceremonies that
23 9 thou shalt keep thyself from every evil
26 16 to keep and fulfil them with all thy
17 keep his ceremonies. 4 K 17:34
27 1 keep every commandment that I command
28 13 thee this day, and keep and do them
15 to keep and to do all his commandments
58 if thou wilt not keep and fulfil all
29 9 keep . . . the words of this covenant
31 12 and keep and fulfil all the words of
Josu 10 18 set careful men to keep them shut up
22 29 God keep us from any such wickedness
Judg 13 12 or from what shall he keep himself
Ruth 2 8 this place: but keep with my maids
21 I should keep close to his reapers
1 K 2 9 he will keep the feet of his saints
7 1 sanctified Eleazar . . . to keep the ark
2 K 15 16 left ten women . . . to keep the house
20 3 whom he had left to keep the house and
22 24 and shall keep myself from my iniquity
44 thou wilt k. me to be the head of the
3 K 2 3 keep the charge of the Lord thy God
8 25 keep . . . what thou hast spoken to him
9 4 if thou . . . wilt k. my ordinances and
20 39 keep this man: and if he shall slip
4 K 11 6 and keep the watch of the king's house
6 keep the watch of the house of Messa
7 k. the watch of the house of the Lord
23 21 keep the phase to the Lord your God
1 Pa 9 23 keep the gates of the house of the Lord
22 12 and to k. the law of the Lord thy God
23 32 let them keep the observances of the
28 8 keep ye and seek all the commandments of
29 18 keep forever this will of their heart
19 keep thy commandments. 2 Es 1:5; Ps 118:60, 63, 134, 146; Dan 9:4
2 Pa 7 17 and keep my justices and my judgments
23 6 let all the rest . . . keep the watches
28 10 you have a mind to keep under the
30 1 keep the phase to the Lord the God of
2 the king . . . decreed to keep the phase
3 for they could not keep it in its time
5 they should come and keep the phase
23 to keep other seven days: which they
35 8 gave to the priests to keep the phase
18 keep such a phase as Josias kept with
36 21 and the land might keep her sabbaths
1 Es 8 29 keep them, till you deliver them by
2 Es 10 29 they would . . . keep all the commandments
12 27 to keep the dedication, and to rejoice
13 22 and should come to keep the gates and
Tob 4 13 to k. thyself . . . from all fornication
6 7 which thou hast bid me k. of the fish
18 days keep thyself continent from her
13 10 keep days of joy and give glory to him
Jdth 4 5 should keep watch where the way was
Job 6 11 my end that I should keep patience
22 15 thou desire to keep the path of ages
Ps 11 8 keep us from this generation forever
16 8 hand keep me, as the apple of thy eye
17 24 and shall keep myself from my iniquity
24 20 keep thou my soul, and deliver me: I
33 14 k. thy tongue from evil, and thy lips
36 34 expect the Lord and keep his way: and
37 k. innocence, and behold justice: for
49 3 shall come, and shall not keep silence
58 10 I will keep my strength to thee: for
75 11 of the thought shall keep holiday to
78 1 made Jerusalem as a place to k. fruit
88 29 I will keep my mercy for him forever
32 if they . . . keep not my commandments
90 11 over thee: to keep thee in all thy ways
102 18 keep his covenant. Eze 17:14
105 3 blessed are they that keep judgment
106 43 who is wise and will keep these things
118 5 be directed to keep thy justifications
8 I will keep thy justifications: O! do
17 enliven me: and I shall keep thy words
34 and I will keep it with my whole heart
44 so shall I always k. thy law, forever
57 I have said, I would keep thy law. I
88 I shall k. the testimonies of thy mouth
101 evil way: that I may keep thy words
106 to keep the judgments of thy justice
120 7 all evil: may the Lord keep thy soul
8 may the Lord k. thy coming in and thy
126 1 unless the Lord keep the city, he
139 5 keep me, O Lord, from the hand of the
140 9 keep me from the snare, which they
Prov 2 7 he will keep the salvation of the
11 counsel shall keep thee, and prudence
20 and mayst keep the paths of the just
3 21 thy eyes: keep the law and counsel: and
26 will keep thy foot that thou be not
4 6 forsake her not, and she shall k. thee
13 keep it, because it is thy life. Be
21 keep them in the midst of thy heart
23 with all watchfulness keep thy heart
5 2 that thou mayst keep thoughts, and thy
17 keep them to thyself alone, neither let
6 22 when thou sleepest, let them keep thee
24 may keep thee from the evil woman and
7 1 my son, keep my words, and lay up my
5 she may keep thee from the woman that
8 32 blessed are they that keep my ways
22 18 for thee if thou keep it in thy bowels
23 26 heart: and let thy eyes keep my ways
25 10 keep these for thyself, lest thou fall
28 4 that keep it, are incensed against him
Ecce 3 6 a time to keep and a time to cast away
7 a time to keep silence and a time to
4 17 k. thy foot, when thou goest into the
Cant 3 3 the watchmen who keep the city, found
8 12 and 200 for them that keep the fruit
Wisd 1 11 keep yourselves . . . from murmuring
14 23 or keep watches full of madness, so
24 they neither keep life, nor marriage
17 4 did the den . . . keep them from fear
Eccu 1 18 religiousness shall keep and justify
33 if thou desire wisdom, keep justice
2 4 and in thy humiliation keep patience
6 keep his fear and grow old therein. Ye
5 12 word of peace and justice k. with thee
6 27 and keep her ways with all thy power
7 24 for thy profit, keep them with thee
9 18 keep thee far from the man that hath
10 31 keep thy soul in meekness and give
12 4 keep them against the day of vengeance
13 13 keep not far from him, lest thou be
22 15 keep thyself from him, that thou mayst
28 keep fidelity with a friend in his
23 7 he that will keep it shall not perish
27 13 keep in the word till its time: but
28 1 surely keep his sins in remembrance
29 3 k. thy word and deal faithfully with
33 1 but in temptation God will keep him
4 be heard and shall keep discipline
23 in all thy works keep the pre-eminence
39 2 he will keep the sayings of renowned
41 17 keep discipline in peace: for wisdom
20 not good to keep all shamefacedness
42 11 keep a sure watch over a shameless
Isa 5 29 and they shall keep fast hold of it
14 20 thou shalt not keep company with them
26 3 thou wilt keep peace: peace, because
27 3 I am the Lord that keep it, I will

3 come to it, I keep it night and day
41 1 let the islands keep silence before
43 6 to the south: Keep not back: bring
47 11 which thou canst not keep off: misery
56 1 keep ye judgment and do justice: for
4 they that shall keep my sabbaths and
Jer 2 25 keep thy foot from being bare, and
31 10 he will keep him as the shepherd doth
Bar 4 1 they that keep it, shall come to life
6 58 door in the house to keep things safe
Eze 43 11 they may keep the whole form thereof
44 16 unto me, and to keep my ceremonies
24 shall keep my laws and my ordinances
Osee 12 6 keep mercy and judgment and hope in
Amos 5 13 the prudent shall keep silence at that
Mich 7 5 keep the doors of thy mouth from her
Nah 1 15 keep festivals and pay thy vows: for
2 1 is come . . . that shall keep the siege
Haba 2 20 let all the earth keep silence before
Zach 3 7 if thou wilt . . .. keep my charge, thou
7 shalt keep my courts, and I will give
7 5 years: did you keep a fast unto me
11 11 poor of the flock that keep for me
14 16 to keep the feast of tabernacles. 18, 19
Mala 2 7 of the priest shall keep knowledge
15 keep your spirit and despise not. 16
1 Ma 4 61 garrison there to keep it. 6:50; 12:34
5 18 of the army in Judea to keep it: and
10 20 that thou . . . keep friendship with us
27 now continue still to keep fidelity
11 32 keep the things that are just with
2 Ma 1 18 to keep the purification of the temple
18 that you also may keep the day of
2 16 do well if you keep the same days
10 8 Jews should keep those days every year
11 19 will keep yourselves loyal in affairs
24 they would keep to their own manner of
12 42 the people to keep themselves from sin
14 15 chose his people to keep them forever
36 keep this house forever undefiled
Mat 19 17 into life, keep the commandments
Mark 7 9 that you may keep your own tradition
Luke 4 10 charge over thee, that they keep thee
8 15 hearing the word, keep it and bring
11 28 who hear the word of God and keep it
John 8 51 if any man keep my word, he shall. 52
55 I do know him and do keep his word
12 7 that she may keep it against the day
47 man hear my words and keep them not
14 15 if you love me, keep my commandments
23 love me, he will keep my word, and
15 10 if you keep my commandments, you
20 my word, they will keep yours also
17 11 keep them in thy name whom thou hast
15 thou shouldst keep them from evil
Acts 5 3 by fraud keep part of the price of the
8 20 keep thy money to thyself to perish
10 28 that is Jew, to keep company or to come
15 41 commanding them to k. the precepts
16 4 unto them the decrees for to keep, that
23 charging gaoler to keep them diligently
20 16 possible for him, to k. day of Pentecost
24 23 he commanded a centurion to keep him
Rom 2 25 profiteth indeed, if thou keep the law
26 uncircumcised keep justices of the law
14 19 keep the things that are of edification
1 C 5 9 not to keep company with fornicators
11 written to you, not to keep company, if
7 37 his heart, to keep his virgin, doth well
11 2 keep my ordinances as I have delivered
14 34 let women keep silence in the churches
2 C 11 9 to you, and so I will keep myself. The
Gal 6 13 who are circumcised, keep the law; but
Eph 4 3 careful to keep the unity of the Spirit
Phil 4 7 keep your hearts and minds in Christ
2 Th 3 3 will strengthen and keep you from evil
14 do not keep company with him, that he
1 Tim 5 22 other men's sins. Keep thyself chaste
6 14 that thou keep the commandment without
20 O Timothy, keep that which is committed
2 Tim 1 12 that he is able to keep that which I
14 keep the good thing committed to thy
James 1 27 to keep one's self unspotted from
2 10 whosoever shall keep the whole law
2 P 1 15 you may keep a memory of these things
1 J 2 3 keep his commandments. 3:22; 5:2, 3
21 children, keep yourselves from idols
Jude 21 keep yourselves in the love of God
Apoc 2 26 and keep my works unto the end, I will
3 10 I will also keep thee from the hour of
12 17 who keep the commandments of God. 14:12
22 9 that keep the words of the prophecy
keeper Gen 4 9 am I my brother's keeper? And he
Gen 28 15 I will be thy keeper whithersoever
39 21 favor in the sight of the chief keeper
40 4 k. of the prison delivered them to Joseph
1 K 17 20 gave charge of the flock to the keeper
22 under care of keeper of the baggage
4 K 22 14 son of Araas keeper of the wardrobe
2 Pa 34 22 son of Hasra keeper of the wardrobe
2 Es 2 8 Asaph the keeper of the king's forest
3 29 Sechenias, keeper of the east gate
Jdth 13 20 his angel hath been my keeper, both
Esth 2 3 overseer and keeper of the king's women
15 Egeus . . . the keeper of the virgins
Job 7 20 shall I do to thee, O keeper of men
27 18 and as a keeper he hath made a booth
Ps 114 6 the Lord is the keeper of little ones
120 5 the Lord is thy keeper, the Lord is
Prov 24 12 nothing deceiveth the k. of thy soul
27 18 he that is the keeper of his master
Cant 1 5 made me the keeper in the vineyards
Jer 35 4 Maasias . . . who was keeper of the entry
Osee 12 12 Israel . . . was a keeper for a wife
Acts 16 27 the keeper of the prison, awaking out
36 the k. of the prison told these words
keepers 1 Pa 9 19 k. of gates of the tabernacle
1 Pa 9 19 their families in turns were keepers
1 Es 7 21 to all the keepers of the public chest
2 Es 12 25 were keepers of the gates and of the
Eccu 12 3 when the k. of the house shall tremble
Cant 5 7 the keepers that go about the city
7 k. of the walls took away my veil
8 11 he let out the same to keepers, every
Jer 4 17 round about her as keepers of fields
52 24 priest, and the three k. of the entry
Eze 44 8 you have set keepers of my charge in
Acts 5 23 the keepers standing before the doors
12 6 the k. before the door kept the prison
19 having examined the k., he commanded
keepest Exod 34 7 who keepest mercy unto thousands
3 K 8 23 who keepest covenant and mercy with. 2 Pa 6:14; 2 Es 1:5
2 Es 9 32 who keepest covenant and mercy, turn not
Dan 9 4 who keepest the covenant and mercy
1 Ma 15 7 which thou keepest in thy hands
keepeth Gen 43 14 your brother, whom he keepeth
Exod 21 18 if . . . he die not, but keepeth his bed
1 K 16 11 a young one, who keepeth the sheep
Ps 18 12 for thy servant keepeth them, and in
120 4 slumber nor sleep, that keepeth Israel
7 the Lord keepeth thee from all evil
126 1 he watcheth in vain that keepeth it
144 20 the Lord keepeth all them that love him
145 7 who k. truth forever: who executeth
9 the Lord keepeth the strangers: he

Prov 13 3 he that k. his mouth, k. his soul: but
6 justice k. the way of the innocent
16 17 evils: he that k. his soul k. his way
18 22 he that k. an adulteress, is foolish
19 8 he that k. prudence shall find good
16 k. the commandment, k. his own soul
21 23 he that k. his mouth and his tongue
23 keepeth his soul from distress. The
22 5 he that k. his own soul departeth far
27 18 he that k. the fig tree, shall eat the
28 7 he that keepeth the law is a wise son
29 11 deferreth, and k. it till afterwards
18 but he that keepeth the law is blessed
27 the son that keepeth the word, shall be
Ecce 8 5 he that k. the commandment, shall find
Eccu 12 13 that keepeth company with a wicked man
21 12 he that keepeth justice shall get the
29 1 in hand, keepeth the commandments
35 1 he that k. the law, multiplieth
Isa 26 2 just nation, that keepeth the truth
56 2 that k. the sabbath from profaning it
2 keepeth his hands from doing any evil
Bar 6 69 as a scarecrow . . . keepeth nothing
Luke 11 21 when a strong man armed keepeth his
John 7 19 yet none of you keepeth the law
9 16 not of God, who k. not the sabbath
12 25 in this world, k. it unto life eternal
14 21 hath my commandments and keepeth them
24 loveth me not, keepeth not my words
1 J 2 4 and keepeth not his commandments
5 he that k. his word, in him in very
3 24 he that k. his commandments, abideth
Apoc 1 3 and k. those things which are written
16 15 watcheth, and keepeth his garments
22 7 that k. the words of the prophecy of
keeping Lev 6 2 the thing delivered to his k.
Deut 7 9 keeping his covenant and mercy to
13 18 thy God, keeping all his precepts
22 7 k. the young which thou hast caught
Josu 22 3 keeping the commandment of the Lord
1 K 25 16 we were with them keeping the sheep
30 16 as it were keeping a festival day
3 K 11 38 k. my commandments and my precepts
2 Pa 8 15 and as to the keeping of the treasures
35 16 k. the phase and offering holocausts
Job 2 3 evil, and still keeping his innocence
Ps 18 12 keeping them there is a great reward
Prov 2 8 k. the paths of justice and guarding
Wisd 6 19 and love is the keeping of her laws
19 k. of her laws is the firm foundation
Eccu 32 27 for this is the k. of the commandments
33 8 and keeping his commandment. And he
40 6 sleep, as in the day of keeping watch
42 6 sure k. is good over a wicked wife
43 3 as one k. a furnace in the works of
2 Ma 3 40 the keeping of the treasury fell out
4 33 keeping himself in a safe place at
5 25 the Jews k. holiday, he commanded his
6 11 were keeping the sabbath day privately
14 38 k. himself pure in the Jews' religion
Luke 2 8 k. the night watches over their flock
Acts 15 29 from which things keeping yourselves
20 31 watch, k. in memory, that for 3 years
21 24 that thou thyself also walkest k. law
kept Gen 26 5 kept my precepts and commandments
Gen 39 16 she kept the garment and showed it to
20 where the king's prisoners were kept
22 prisoners that were kept in custody
40 4 passed, and they were kept in custody
42 4 whilst Benjamin was kept at home by
34 this man again, that is kept in prison
36 is not living, Simeon is kept in bonds
Exod 12 16 shall be kept with the like solemnity
16 30 the people kept the sabbath on the
32 let it be kept unto generations to
34 put it in the tabernacle to be kept
Lev 23 34 shall be kept the feast of tabernacles
Num 9 7 why are we kept back that we may not
19 kept the watches of the Lord and. 23
17 10 that it [rod] may be kept there for
21 24 were kept with a strong garrison. So
Deut 7 8 kept his oath which he swore to your
32 10 he kept him as the apple of his eye
33 9 these have kept thy word and observed
Josu 5 10 they kept the phase on the fourteenth
Judg 2 22 walk in it, as their fathers kept it
11 39 in Israel, and a custom has been kept
19 5 his father-in-law kept him and said
Ruth 2 20 living, he hath kept also to the dead
23 she kept close to the maids of Booz
1 K 9 24 it was kept of purpose for thee when
13 13 hast not kept the commandments of
17 34 thy servant kept his father's sheep
25 21 have I kept all that belonged to this
29 the soul of my lord shall be kept as
33 kept me today from coming to blood
39 and hath kept his servant from evil
26 15 why then hast thou not kept thy lord
16 who have not kept your master, the
30 23 who hath kept us and hath delivered
2 K 12 16 for the child: and David kept a fast
13 34 young man that kept the watch, lifted
18 16 k. back the people from pursuing after
22 22 because I have kept the ways of the Lord
3 K 2 43 why then hast thou not kept the oath
3 6 thou hast kept thy great mercy for him
8 24 hast kept with thy servant David my
11 10 he kept not the things which the Lord
11 and hast not kept my covenant and my
34 David . . . who kept my commandments and
13 21 hast not kept the commandment which
14 8 David, who kept my commandments, doing
27 that kept watch before the gate of the
4 K 12 9 the priests that kept the doors put
18 6 but [Ezechias] kept his commandments
23 22 there was no such a phase kept from the
23 this phase that was kept to the Lord
1 Pa 10 13 he had commanded, and kept it not
2 Pa 7 8 Solomon k. the solemnity at that time
9 he had k. the dedication of the altar
30 21 k. the feast of unleavened. 1 Es 6:22
34 21 our fathers have not kept the words
35 1 Josias kept a phase to the Lord in
15 the porters kept guard at every gate
17 children of Israel . . . kept the phase
18 keep such a phase as Josias kept, with
36 21 she kept a sabbath, till the 70 years
1 Es 3 4 and they kept the feast of tabernacles
6 16 k. the dedication of the house of God
19 kept the phase on the fourteenth day
2 Es 1 7 we . . . have not kept thy commandments
8 18 and they kept the solemnity seven days
9 34 and our fathers have not kept thy law
11 19 and the porters . . . who kept the doors
12 44 they kept watch of their God, and the
Tob 1 12 he kept his soul and never was defiled
2 13 feared God . . . and k. his commandments
3 16 have kept my soul clean from all lust
19 perhaps thou hast kept me for another
Jdth 7 11 and when they had kept this watch for
Job 3 26 not dissembled? have I not k. silence
23 11 I have kept his way, and have not
29 2 the days in which God kept me? When
Ps 16 4 words of thy lips, I have k. hard ways
17 22 because I have k. the ways of the Lord
39 3 and kept silence from good things

77 10 they kept not the covenant of God: and
56 and they kept not his testimonies
57 turned away and kept not the covenant
98 7 they kept his testimonies and the
118 4 thy commandments to be kept most
55 name, O Lord: and have kept thy law
67 therefore have I kept thy word. Thou
136 because they have not kept thy law
158 away; because they kept not thy word
167 my soul hath kept thy testimonies: and
168 I have kept thy commandments and thy
Prov 13 22 substance of the sinner is k. for the
Ecce 5 12 riches kept to the hurt of the owner
9 2 all things are kept uncertain for the
Cant 1 5 my vineyard I have not kept. Show me
7 13 old, my beloved, I have kept for thee
Wisd 6 5 rightly nor kept the law of justice
11 they that have kept just things justly
10 12 she kept him safe from his enemies and
14 16 this error was kept as a law, and
17 15 he was kept shut up in prison without
18 4 who kept thy children shut up, by whom
19 6 children might be kept without hurt
Eccu 13 25 is shaken, he is kept up by his friends
44 20 who kept the law of the most High and
Isa 23 18 they shall not be kept in store nor
42 14 I have kept silence, I have been
48 6 things are kept which thou knowest not
Jer 16 11 they forsook me and kept not my law
35 18 have kept all his precepts and have
Eze 5 7 have not kept my judgments and have
18 9 and kept my judgments, to do truth: he
19 kept all my commandments and done
27 27 thy pilots, who kept thy goods and were
44 8 you have not kept the ordinances of my
15 kept the ceremonies of my sanctuary
48 11 kept my ceremonies and went not
Dan 7 28 in me: but I kept the word in my heart
Amos 1 11 and hath kept his wrath to the end
2 4 and hath not kept his commandments
Mich 6 16 thou hast kept the statutes of Amri
Mala 2 9 you have not kept my ways, and have
3 7 ordinances, and have not kept them
14 that we have kept his ordinances and
1 Ma 2 53 Joseph . . . kept the commandment and
4 56 kept the dedication of the altar
59 dedication of the altar should be kept
5 27 they were kept shut up in the rest
7 49 this day should be kept every year
8 12 as relied upon them, they kept amity
10 26 you have kept covenant with us and
11 46 kept the passages of the city and
12 47 but he kept with him 3,000 men
13 52 be kept every year with gladness
14 35 faith which he kept to his nation
2 Ma 1 19 there they kept it safe, so that the
3 1 the laws as yet were very well kept
15 concerning things given to be kept
4 18 when the game . . . was kept at Tyre
6 6 and neither were the sabbaths kept
7 when the feast of Bacchus was kept
8 27 their spoils, they kept the sabbath
33 they kept the feast of victory at
10 6 and they kept eight days with joy
6 had kept the feast of the tabernacles
30 with their arms, and kept him safe
12 38 kept the sabbath in the same place
15 3 commanded the sabbath day to be kept
4 commanded the seventh day to be kept
34 hath kept his own place undefiled
Mat 8 33 they that kept them fled: and coming
19 20 have I kept from my youth. Luke 18:21
Mark 6 20 kept him, and when he heard him, did
9 9 and they kept the word to themselves
Luke 2 19 Mary kept all these words, pondering
51 kept all these words in her heart
8 29 bound with chains and kept in fetters
19 20 which I have kept laid up in a napkin
John 2 10 thou hast kept the good wine until
15 10 have kept my Father's commandments
20 if they have kept my word, they will
17 6 them; and they have kept thy word
12 with them, I kept them in thy name
12 those whom thou gavest me have I kept
Acts 5 2 by fraud kept back part of the price
7 19 to the end they might not be k. alive
53 the law . . . and have not kept it. Now
9 33 man named Eneas, who had kept his bed
12 4 to four files of soldiers to be kept
5 Peter therefore was kept in prison
6 keepers before the door k. the prison
20 20 now I have kept back nothing that was
22 2 tongue, they kept the more silence. And
20 I . . . kept the garments of them that
23 35 him to be k. in Herod's judgment hall
25 4 that Paul was kept in Caesarea, and that
21 I commanded him to be k., until I might
28 16 by himself, with a soldier that kept him
Rom 15 22 you, and have been kept away till now
16 25 which was kept secret from eternity
2 C 11 9 kept myself from being burthensome to
Gal 3 23 we were kept under the law shut up, unto
2 Tim 4 7 my course, I have kept the faith. As to
James 5 4 by fraud has been kept back by you
2 P 3 7 by the same word are kept in store
Jude 6 angels who kept not their principality
Apoc 3 8 hast kept my word, and hast not denied
10 thou hast kept the word of my patience
kernel Num 6 4 from the raisin even to the kernel
kettle 1 K 2 14 and thrust it into the kettle
Joel 2 6 all faces shall be made like a kettle
Eccu 13 3 the earthen pot have with the kettle
Mich 3 3 chopped their bones as for the kettle
Nah 2 10 all are as the blackness of a kettle
kettles 2 Pa 35 13 they boiled in caldrons and k.
key Judge 3 25 they took a key: and opening, they
Cant 5 4 put his hand through the key hole, and
Isa 22 22 will lay the key of the house of David
Luke 11 52 have taken away the key of knowledge
Apoc 3 7 he that hath the key of David; he that
9 1 key of the bottomless pit. 20:1
keys Mat 16 19 I will give to thee the keys of the
Apoc 1 18 and have the keys of death and of hell
kick Acts 9 5 hard for thee to k. against. 26:14
kicked Deut 32 15 the beloved grew fat and kicked
1 K 2 29 why have you kicked away my victims
2 K 6 6 the oxen kicked and made it lean aside
kid Gen 37 31 dipped it in the blood of a kid
Gen 38 17 will send thee a kid out of the flock
20 and Juda sent a kid by his shepherd
23 I sent the kid which I promised: and
Exod 12 5 which rite also you shall take a kid
23 19 not boil a kid in the milk of his dam. 34:26; Deut 14:21
Num 15 12 for every ox and ram and lamb and kid
Judg 6 19 so Gedeon went in and boiled a kid
13 15 and let us dress a kid for thee. And
19 then Manue took a kid of the flocks
14 6 tore the lion as he would have torn a kid
15 1 he [Samson] brought her a kid of the
1 K 16 20 a bottle of wine and a kid of the flock
Tob 2 20 a young kid, and brought it home. And
Isa 11 6 leopard shall lie down with the kid
Luke 15 29 thou hast never given me a kid to
kidneys Lev 3 4 the two kidneys with the fat
Lev 3 4 liver with the two little kidneys

10 with the kidneys and the fat that
10 the vitals and both the little kidneys
10 the liver with the little kidneys. 15; 4:9; 7:4
15 the two little kidneys with the caul
4 9 little kidneys and the caul. 9:10
7 4 the two little kidneys and the fat
8 16 the liver and the two little kidneys
25 and the two kidneys with their fat
9 19 the two little kidneys with their fat
29 13 take . . . the two kidneys. 22

kids Gen 27 9 bring me two kids of the best
Gen 27 16 skins of the k. she put about his hands
2 Pa 35 7 of lambs and of kids of the flocks
1 K 10 3 one carrying three kids, and another
1 Es 6 9 let calves also, and lambs, and kids
Prov 27 26 and kids for the price of the field
Cant 1 7 feed thy kids beside the tents of the
Jer 50 8 be ye as kids at the head of the flock
51 40 the slaughter, and like rams with kids
Eze 27 21 to thee with lambs and rams and kids

kill Gen 4 14 findeth me, shall kill me. And the
Gen 4 15 whosoever shall kill Cain, shall be
15 whosoever found him should not k. him
12 12 and they will kill me, and keep thee
20 11 will kill me for the sake of my wife
26 7 lest perhaps they would k. him because
27 41 I will kill my brother Jacob. These
42 thy brother threateneth to kill thee
32 11 perhaps he come and kill the mother
34 30 they will gather . . . and kill me; and
37 18 they thought to kill him [Joseph]. And
20 let us k. him and cast him into some
26 will it profit us to kill our brother
42 37 kill my two sons, if I bring him not
43 16 and kill victims and prepare a feast
Exod 1 16 if it be a man child, kill it: if a
2 14 wilt thou kill me as thou didst yesterday kill the Egyptian
15 Pharao . . . sought to kill Moses: but
4 23 I will kill thy son, thy firstborn. And
5 21 you have given him a sword to kill us
8 26 now if we kill those things which the
12 12 and will kill every firstborn in the
13 13 do not redeem it, thou shalt kill it
17 3 forth out of Egypt, to kill us and our
19 24 come up to the Lord, lest he kill them
20 13 thou shalt not kill. Thou shalt not
21 12 striketh a man with a will to kill him
14 if a man kill his neighbor on set
29 if the ox . . . shall kill a man or
22 1 any man steal an ox . . . and kill or
29 11 shalt kill him in the sight of the
32 12 that he might k. them in the mountains
27 let every man kill his brother and
Lev 17 3 if he kill an ox or a sheep or a goat
5 victims, which they kill in the field
20 4 and if the people . . . will not kill him
15 him die: the beast also ye shall kill
Num 11 15 otherwise, I beseech thee to kill me
14 16 therefore did he kill them in the
16 13 and honey, to kill us in the desert
22 29 I had a sword that I might kill thee
25 5 let every man kill his neighbors that
31 17 kill all that are of the male sex
33 55 if you will not kill the inhabitants
35 12 may not have power to kill him, until
19 kinsman . . . shall kill the murderer
19 apprehendeth him, he shall kill him
21 soon as he findeth him, shall kill him
Deut 4 42 should kill his neighbor unwillingly
5 17 thou shalt not kill. Neither shalt thou
9 28 he might kill them in the wilderness
12 15 kill, and eat according to the blessing
21 thou shalt kill of thy herds and of
13 15 shalt forthwith kill the inhabitants
17 7 shall be first upon him to kill him
20 17 shalt kill them with the edge of the
32 39 I will kill and I will make to live
Josu 10 19 and kill all the hindermost of them as
17 13 tributaries and they did not kill them
20 3 whosoever shall kill a person unawares
Judg 8 19 had saved them, I would not kill you
9 54 draw thy sword and kill me [Abimelech]
13 23 if the Lord had a mind to kill us
15 12 promise me that you will not kill me
13 they said: We will not kill thee: but
16 2 they might k. him [Samson] as he went
20 25 as to kill 18,000 men that drew the
31 so as to wound and kill some of them
21 11 you shall kill, but the virgins you shall
1 K 5 10 have brought the ark . . . to kill us
11 let it return . . . and not kill us and
11 12 bring the men and we will kill them
15 18 go and kill the sinners of Amalec and
16 2 will hear of it and he will kill me
17 9 be able to fight with me and kill me
9 if I prevail against him and kill him
26 man that shall kill this Philistine
19 1 spoke . . . that they should kill David
2 Saul my father seeketh to kill thee
17 let me go, or else I will kill thee
20 8 any iniquity in me, do thou kill me
33 determined by his father to kill David
22 17 turn, and kill the priests of the Lord
24 11 I had a thought to kill thee [Saul]
26 9 kill him not; for who shall put forth
15 one of the people in to kill the king
30 15 swear . . . that thou wilt not kill me
31 4 draw thy sword and kill me [Saul]
2 K 1 9 stand over me and kill me [Saul]: for
14 to put out thy hand to kill the Lord's
13 28 say to you: Strike him and kill him
14 7 that we may kill him for the life of
11 and that they may not kill my son
32 mindful of my iniquity, let him k. me
17 2 I will kill the king who will be left
21 16 Jesbibenob . . . attempted to kill David
3 K 1 51 swear . . . that he will not kill his
2 8 swore to him . . . I will not kill thee
29 sent Banaias . . . saying: Go, kill him
31 do as he hath said: and k. him [Joab]
3 26 the child alive, and do not kill it
11 40 Solomon . . . sought to kill Jeroboam
12 27 they will k. me [Jeroboam] and return
17 18 and that thou shouldst kill my son
20 maintained, so as to kill her son
18 9 hand of Achab, that he should kill me
12 he not finding thee, will kill me
14 that he [Achab] may kill me [Abdias]
21 21 and I will kill of Achab him that
4 K 5 7 am I God, to be able to kill and give
6 21 my father, shall I kill them? And he
22 thou shalt not kill them, for thou
22 that thou mayst kill them: but set
7 4 but if they kill us, we shall but die
8 12 their young men thou wilt k. with the
10 25 go in and kill them, let none escape
17 26 sent lions . . . and behold they k. them
1 Pa 10 4 Saul said . . . draw thy sword and k. me
2 Pa 20 7 didst not thou our God kill all the
23 of mount Seir, to k. and destroy them
22 11 and therefore Athalia did not kill him
25 16 counsellor? Be quiet, lest I kill thee
16 I know that God is minded to kill thee
35 6 and being sanctified kill the phase
21 God, who is with me, lest he kill thee

1 Es 6 20 all were clean to kill the phase for
2 Es 4 11 and kill them and cause the work to
6 10 they will come to k. thee, and in the
Tob 3 10 wilt thou kill me also as thou hast
Jdth 5 26 and they had a mind to kill him, saying
11 11 have a design even to k. their cattle
16 6 and kill my young men with the sword
Job 9 23 let him kill at once, and not laugh at
13 15 although he should k. me, I will trust
20 16 and the viper's tongue shall kill him
Ps 9 8 places, that he may kill the innocent
36 14 and needy, to k. the upright of heart
58 1 sent and watched his house to kill him
61 4 you all kill as if you were thrusting
138 19 if thou wilt kill the wicked, O God
Prov 1 32 away of little ones shall kill them
21 25 desires kill the slothful: for his
23 28 whom she shall see unwary, she will k.
Ecce 3 3 a time to kill and a time to heal. A
Wisd 11 9 thine, and didst kill their adversaries
20 very sight might kill them through fear
18 5 thought to kill the babes of the just
Eccu 9 18 from the man that hath power to kill
47 4 kill the giant and take away reproach
Isa 11 9 shall not hurt nor shall they kill in
13 18 arrows they shall kill the children
14 30 famine, and I will kill thy remnant
51 14 shall not kill unto utter destruction
65 25 they shall not hurt nor kill in all
Jer 15 3 the sword to kill, and the dogs to
29 21 he shall kill them before your eyes
33 18 and to kill victims continually. And
38 25 from us, and we will not kill thee
40 14 hath sent Ismahel . . . to kill thee
15 I will go and I will kill Ismahel the
15 no man shall know it, lest he k. thee
41 8 kill us not, for we have stores in
43 3 to kill us and to cause us to be
Eze 9 6 you shall see Thau, kill him not
13 19 to kill souls which should not die
21 10 it is sharpened to kill victims: it is
28 come out of the scabbard to kill, be
23 47 they shall kill their sons and daughters
25 16 will kill the killers and will destroy
26 8 daughters . . . he shall kill with the
11 thy people he shall kill with the
28 8 they shall kill thee and bring thee
Dan 8 25 he shall kill many: and he shall rise
13 53 and the just thou shalt not kill
14 25 I will kill this dragon without sword
Osee 2 3 through, and will kill her with drought
Amos 9 4 the sword, and it shall kill them. And
Abdi 14 to kill them that flee: and thou shalt
1 Ma 5 2 they began to kill some of the people
9 32 and Bacchides . . . sought to kill him
11 10 for he hath sought to kill me. And
12 40 sought to seize upon him and to k. him
15 40 take the people prisoners and to kill
16 19 he sent others to Gazara to kill John
21 he hath sent men to kill thee also
22 the men that came to kill him, and he
2 Ma 4 34 desired him to kill Onias. And he went
5 12 commanded the soldiers to kill and not
24 to kill all that were of perfect age
15 22 didst kill 185,000 of the army of
Mat 5 21 thou shalt not kill. Luke 18:20; Rom 13:9; James 2:11
21 whosoever shall kill shall be in danger
10 28 fear ye not them that kill the body
28 and are not able to kill the soul: but
17 22 they shall kill him, and the third day
21 38 is the heir: come, let us kill him. Mark 12:7; Luke 20:14
Mark 9 30 hands of men, and they shall kill him
10 19 do not kill, do not steal, bear not
34 on him and scourge him and kill him
14 1 will lay hold on him and kill him. But
Luke 11 49 and some of them they will kill and
12 4 be not afraid of them who kill the
13 31 for Herod hath a mind to kill thee
15 23 hither the fatted calf and kill it
19 27 them hither and kill them before me
John 5 18 the Jews sought the more to kill him
7 1 because the Jews sought to kill him
20 why seek you to kill me? The multitude
20 hast a devil; who seeketh to kill thee
25 is not this he whom they seek to kill
8 22 will he kill himself, because he said
37 you seek to kill me. 40
10 10 but for to steal and to kill and to
12 10 chief priests thought to kill Lazarus
Acts 7 28 wilt thou kill me, as thou didst
28 didst yesterday kill the Egyptian
9 23 the Jews consulted together to kill him
24 day and night, that they might kill him
29 Greeks; but they sought to kill him
10 13 arise, Peter; kill and eat. 11:7
13 28 of Pilate, that they might kill him
21 31 as they went about to kill him, it was
23 15 he come near, are ready to kill him
25 might take him away by force and k. him
25 3 laying wait to kill him in the way. But
26 21 apprehended me, went about to kill me
27 42 they should kill the prisoners, lest any
2 Th 2 8 Lord Jesus shall kill with the spirit
James 2 11 not commit adultery, but shalt kill
4 2 you kill and envy, and cannot obtain
1 J 3 12 wherefore did he kill him? Because his
Apoc 2 23 I will kill her children with death
6 4 and that they should kill one another
8 to kill with sword, with famine, and
9 5 that they should not kill them; but
15 year: for to kill the third part of men
11 7 shall overcome them and kill them. And
13 10 he that shall kill by the sword, must

killed Gen 34 26 they killed also Hemor and
Gen 37 31 blood of a kid, which they had killed
Exod 4 24 Lord met him and would have killed him
29 16 when thou hast killed him [ram], thou
Lev 5 2 that which hath been killed by a beast
16 15 when he hath killed the buck goat for
20 16 the woman . . . shall be killed together
23 12 shall be killed for a holocaust of
Num 11 22 multitude of sheep and oxen killed
14 15 thou hast killed so great a multitude
16 41 you have killed the people of the Lord
21 6 which bit them and killed many of them
22 40 when Balac had killed oxen and sheep
31 8 Balaam . . . they killed with the sword
19 k. a man or touched one that is k.
35 27 he shall not be guilty that killed him
Deut 19 5 struck his friend and killed him: he
21 6 heifer that was killed in the valley
Josu 6 21 killed all that were in it, man and
10 11 more were killed with the hailstones
28 took Maceda . . . and killed the king
20 9 whosoever had killed a person unawares
Judg 7 22 the camp and they killed one another
9 18 have killed his sons 70 men upon
45 Abimelech . . . killed the inhabitants
49 with the fire 1,000 persons were killed
12 6 presently they took him and killed him
16 24 destroyed our country and k. very many
30 he k. many more at his death than he had k. before in his life
20 3 husband of the woman that was killed

1 K 11 13 no man shall be k. this day because
17 35 and I strangled and killed them. For
36 have killed both a lion and a bear
19 11 that he [David] might be killed in the
24 19 into thy hand and thou hast not k. me
25 11 which I have killed for my shearers
28 24 had a fatted calf . . . and killed it
30 2 they had not killed any person, but
2 K 1 10 standing over him, I killed him [Saul]
2 31 servants of David had k. of Benjamin
3 30 because he had k. their brother Asael
4 7 they struck him and k. him [Isboseth]
11 17 and Urias the Hethite was killed also
21 who k. Abimelech the son of Jerobaal
12 9 thou hast k. Urias . . . with the sword
19 22 shall there any man be killed this day
21 17 striking the Philistine, killed him
23 8 who killed 800 men at one onset. After
3 K 1 19 he hath killed oxen and all fat cattle
25 and hath killed oxen and fatlings and
3 27 let it not be killed, for she is the
11 15 slain, and had k. every male in Edom
13 24 lion found him in the way and k. him
26 lion, and he hath torn him and k. him
18 4 when Jezabel killed the prophets. 13
40 to the torrent of Cison and k. them
19 21 he took a yoke of oxen and killed them
4 K 3 23 they have killed one another: go now
9 31 for Zambri that hath killed his master
10 14 killed them at the pit by the cabin
14 19 after him to Lachis and k. him there
15 10 struck him publicly and killed him
17 25 sent lions among them, which k. them
1 Pa 10 2 and they killed Jonathan and Abinadab
11 22 [Banaias] went down and killed a lion
2 Pa 18 2 Achaz at his command k. sheep and oxen
21 13 hast killed thy brethren, the house
22 1 had k. all that were his elder brothers
9 when he was brought to him, he k. him
10 Athalia . . . k. all the royal family
23 14 when she is without, let her be killed
14 not be killed in the house of the Lord
15 gate of the palace, they k. her there
24 22 father had done to him, but k. his son
23 killed all the princes of the people
25 13 having k. three thousand, took away
27 they sent and k. him [Amasias] there
29 22 therefore they killed the bullocks, and
22 they k. also the rams, and their blood
22 they killed the lambs and poured the
33 25 the people slew them that had k. Amon
2 Es 9 26 they k. the prophets who admonished
Tob 1 24 after forty-five days, the king was k.
3 8 a devil named Asmodeus had killed them
10 as thou hast already k. seven husbands
6 14 I have heard that a devil killed them
7 9 Raguel commanded a sheep to be killed
8 22 two fat kine and four wethers to be k.
Jdth 6 12 people of Holofernes would have k. him
13 18 he hath killed the enemy of his people
16 14 they have killed them like children
Ps 43 22 for thy sake we are killed all the day
77 51 killed all the firstborn in the land
Wisd 16 9 the bitings . . . of flies killed them
Eccu 30 35 sadness hath killed many, and there
Isa 27 7 as he k. them that were slain by him
34 2 hath killed them, and delivered them
Jer 15 7 I have killed and destroyed my people
41 4 second day after he had k. Godolias
Lam 2 4 he hath killed all that was fair to
21 hast killed, and shown them no pity
3 43 thou hast killed and hast not spared
Eze 11 6 you have killed a great many in this
26 15 when they shall be k. in the midst
34 3 and you killed that which was fat: but
Dan 14 27 destroyed Bel, he hath k. the dragon
Nah 2 12 whelps, and killed for his lionesses
1 Ma 3 11 and he overthrew him and killed him
5 13 were in the places of Tubin are killed
11 45 men, and would have killed the king
2 Ma 10 17 killed them that came in the way and
37 they killed Timotheus, who was found
Mat 21 35 beat one and killed another and stoned
39 out of the vineyard and killed him
22 4 my beeves and fatlings are killed and
23 31 sons of them that killed the prophets
35 you killed between the temple and the
Mark 8 31 and be rejected . . . and be killed
9 30 after that he is killed, he shall rise
12 5 he sent another, and him they killed
5 some they beat, and others they killed
8 laying hold on him, they killed him
Luke 9 22 and be killed, and the third day rise
11 47 prophets: and your fathers killed them
48 they indeed killed them, and you build
12 5 fear ye him, who after he hath killed
15 27 thy father hath killed the fatted calf
30 hast killed for him the fatted calf
20 15 out of the vineyard, they killed him
22 7 necessary that the pasch should be k.
Acts 3 15 the author of life you killed, whom
10 39 they killed, hanging him upon a tree
12 2 he killed James, the brother of John
16 27 drawing his sword, would have killed
22 20 I . . . kept garments of them that k. him
23 12 eat, nor drink, till they killed Paul
21 eat nor to drink, till they have k. him
27 and ready to be k. by them, I rescued
Rom 7 11 seduced me, and by it k. me. Wherefore
2 C 6 9 we live; as chastised, and not killed
1 Th 2 15 who both killed the Lord Jesus, and
1 J 3 12 as Cain, who . . . killed his brother
Apoc 13 10 must be killed by the sword. Here is
killer Isa 54 16 I have created the k. to destroy
killers Eze 25 16 and will kill the killers
killest Mat 23 37 that k. the prophets. Luke 13:34
killeth Lev 24 17 he that striketh and k. a man
Lev 24 18 he that killeth a beast, shall make
Deut 19 4 that killeth his neighbor ignorantly
27 24 he that secretly killeth his neighbor
1 K 2 6 the Lord killeth and maketh alive
Job 5 2 anger indeed killeth the foolish and
24 14 he killeth the needy and the poor man
Wisd 1 11 mouth that belieth, killeth the soul
14 24 but one killeth another through envy
16 14 a man indeed killeth through malice
Eccu 34 26 is like him that killeth his neighbor
Isa 66 3 he that killeth a sheep in sacrifice
John 16 2 whosoever k. you, will think that he
2 C 3 6 the letter k., but the spirit quickeneth
killing Gen 46 1 k. victims there to the God of
Deut 2 34 k. the inhabitants of them, men and
Josu 11 14 cities, and the cattle, k. all the men
Judg 9 56 killing his seventy brethren. The
20 39 killing thirty men of their army. And
1 K 19 5 by killing David, who is without fault
2 K 8 13 valley of the saltpits, killing 18,000
Prov 19 18 to the killing of him set not thy soul
Eccu 21 3 of a lion, killing the souls of men
Isa 22 13 killing calves and slaying rams, eating
Osee 4 2 cursing and lying and killing and
1 Ma 6 45 killing on the right hand and on the
2 Ma 5 13 and killing of virgins and infants
Eph 2 16 cross, killing the enmities in himself
kin Lev 18 6 approach to her that is near of kin
Lev 21 2 of his citizens; but only for his kin

Num 35 24 between him that struck and next of kin
Ruth 3 12 do I deny myself to be near of kin
2 K 14 11 that the next of kin be not multiplied
Jer 32 8 thou art next of kin to possess it
kind Gen 1 11 yielding fruit after its kind
Gen 1 12 as yieldeth seed according to its kind
12 seed each one according to its kind
21 every winged fowl according to its kind
24 forth the living creature in its kind
25 that creepeth on the earth after its k.
29 have in themselves seed of their own k.
6 20 of fowls according to their kind, and of beasts in their kind
20 creepeth on the earth according to its k.
7 14 every beast according to its kind and all the cattle in their kind
14 upon the earth according to its kind
17 10 male kind of you shall be circumcised
Exod 8 21 and upon thy houses all kind of flies
24 land was corrupted by this k. of flies
34 19 all of the male kind, that openeth the
Lev 7 21 and shall eat of such kind of flesh
11 14 the vulture, according to their kind
15 and all that is of the raven kind
16 hawk according to its k. Deut 14:15
19 the charadrion according to its kind
22 shall eat, as the bruchus in its kind
11 22 every one according to their k. 29
14 54 is the law of every kind of leprosy
19 19 to gender with beasts of any other k.
Num 3 31 veil and all the furniture of this kind
34 of the male kind from one month. 39
36 that pertain to this kind of service
11 33 neither had that kind of meat failed
13 34 of the sons of Enac, of the giant kind
Deut 14 13 and the kite according to their kind
14 and all of the raven's kind: and the
18 the charadrion, every one in their kind
1 K 5 7 of Azotus seeing this kind of plague
2 K 1 17 David made this kind of lamentation
13 18 virgins, used such kind of garments
24 3 lord the king by this kind of thing
3 K 7 17 a kind of network and chain work
2 Pa 5 13 with divers kind of musical instruments
10 7 and soothe them with kind words, they
24 12 and artificers of every kind of work
2 Es 6 14 according to their works of this kind
13 26 king of Israel sin in this kind of thing
Tob 6 8 driveth away all kind of devils
8 21 and prepare all kind of provisions that
Job 30 7 pleased themselves among these kind
Ps 68 17 heâr me, O Lord, for thy mercy is kind
Wisd 7 23 gentle, kind, steadfast, assured
11 19 unknown beasts of a new kind full of
18 12 innumerable dead, with one k. of death
19 6 every creature according to its kind
Eccu 37 31 every kind pleaseth not every soul
Dan 3 5 and of all kind of music. 3:7, 10, 15
2 Ma 11 31 Jews may use their own kind of meats
12 3 were guilty of this kind of wickedness
Mat 13 47 together of all kind of fishes
17 20 this kind is not cast out but by
Mark 9 28 this kind can go out by nothing but
Luke 6 35 he is kind to the unthankful, and to
1 C 13 4 charity is patient, is kind: charity
Eph 4 32 be ye kind one to another; merciful
kindle Exod 35 3 you shall k. no fire in any of
Ps 77 38 and did not kindle all his wrath
Eccu 8 13 kindle not the coals of sinners by
32 20 and shall kindle justice as a light
Isa 9 18 shall k. in the thicket of the forest
50 11 behold all you that kindle a fire
Jer 7 18 wood, and the fathers kindle the fire
17 27 I will kindle a fire in the gates of
21 14 I will kindle a fire in the forest
43 12 he shall kindle a fire in the temple
49 27 I will k. a fire in the wall. Amos 1:14
50 32 I will kindle a fire in his cities
Eze 20 47 I will kindle a fire in thee and will
22 20 that I may kindle a fire in it to
Mala 1 10 will kindle the fire on my altar
kindled Exod 22 6 he that k. the fire shall make
Exod 32 10 that my wrath may be kindled against
Lev 10 6 the buring which the Lord has kindled
Num 11 1 the fire of the Lord being kindled
3 fire of the Lord had been k. against
Deut 6 15 Lord thy God be kindled against thee
7 4 the wrath of the Lord will be kindled
29 27 wrath of the Lord was kindled against
31 17 my wrath shall be kindled against
32 22 a fire is kindled in my wrath and
Judg 2 20 wrath of Lord was k. against Israel
6 39 let not thy wrath be kindled against me
1 K 11 6 his anger was exceedingly kindled
2 K 12 5 David's anger being exceedingly k.
22 9 of his mouth: coals were kindled by it
13 before him, the coals of fire were k.
24 1 anger of the Lord was again k. against
4 K 13 3 wrath of Lord was k. against Israel
22 13 the great wrath of the Lord is kindled
17 indignation shall be k. against this
23 26 his anger was kindled against Juda
Job 19 11 his wrath is kindled against me, and
20 26 a fire that is not k. shall devour him
42 7 my wrath is kindled against thee and
Ps 2 13 when his wrath shall be kindled in a
17 9 from his face: coals were kindled by
77 21 and a fire was kindled against Jacob
78 5 shall thy zeal be kindled like a fire
105 18 fire was kindled in their congregation
Eccu 9 9 and hereby lust is kindled as a fire
16 7 of sinners a fire shall be kindled
23 23 not leave off till he hath k. a fire
47 22 and to have thy folly kindled, that
Isa 5 25 wrath of the Lord kindled against his
9 18 wickedness is kindled as a fire, it
10 16 under his glory shall be k. a burning
44 15 and he kindled it and baked bread: but
50 11 in the flames which you have kindled
Jer 11 16 a great fire was kindled in it, and
15 14 a fire is kindled in my rage, it shall
17 4 thou hast kindled a fire in my wrath
21 12 lest my indignation . . . be kindled
42 18 and my indignation hath been kindled
18 so shall my indignation be k. against
44 6 was kindled in the cities of Juda
Lam 2 3 he hath kindled in Jacob as it were
4 11 he hath kindled a fire in Sion, and it
Eze 20 48 see, that I the Lord have kindled it
Osee 8 5 my wrath is kindled against them. How
Abdi 18 they shall be kindled in them and
Zach 10 3 my wrath is k. against the shepherds
Mala 4 1 day shall come kindled as a furnace
1 Ma 2 24 his wrath was kindled according to
12 28 and they kindled fires in their camp
2 Ma 1 22 there was a great fire kindled, so
32 there was kindled a flame from them
Luke 12 49 what will I, but that it be kindled
22 55 and when they had kindled a fire in
kindleth Job 41 12 his breath kindleth coals
Eccu 28 11 for a passionate man kindleth strife
13 a hasty contention kindleth a fire
James 3 5 how small of a fire k. a great wood
kindling Eccu 20 15 opening of his mouth is k.
Isa 30 33 as a torrent of brimstone kindling it
Acts 28 2 kindling a fire, they refreshed us all

kindly Judg 19 3 to speak k. to her and to bring
Jer 52 32 he spoke kindly to him Joachin
2 Ma 9 21 but yet kindly remembering you
12 30 that they were used kindly by them
kindness Gen 20 13 shalt do me this kindness
Gen 21 23 according to the k. that I have done
24 12 show kindness to my master Abraham
14 that thou hast shown k. to my master
40 14 do me this k., to put Pharao in mind
47 29 and thou shalt show me this kindness
Ruth 2 20 kindness which he showed to the living
3 10 thy latter kindness has surpassed the
1 K 12 7 concerning all the kindness of the Lord
15 6 shown kindness to all the children of
20 14 shalt show me the kindness of the Lord
15 thou shalt not take away thy kindness
2 K 9 1 that I may show kindness to him for
10 2 I will show k. to Hanon. 1 Pa 19:2
2 as his father showed kindness to me
16 17 is this thy kindness to thy friend
3 K 2 7 show kindness to the sons of Berzellai
2 Pa 1 8 hast shown great kindness to my father
24 22 king Joas did not remember the kindness
Esth 2 17 she had favor and kindness before him
Eccu 29 19 forget not the kindness of thy surety
30 6 will requite kindness to his friends
Isa 54 8 with everlasting k. have I had mercy
63 7 given them according to his kindness
2 Tim 3 3 incontinent, unmerciful, without k.
Titus 3 4 when the goodness and kindness of God
kindnesses 2 Es 13 14 and wipe not out my k. which
kindred Gen 12 1 thy country and from thy k.
Gen 12 3 shall all the k. of the earth be blessed
24 4 go to my own country and kindred
38 shalt take a wife of my own kindred
40 take a wife for my son of my own k.
41 when thou shalt come to my kindred
31 3 land of thy fathers and to thy kindred
43 7 asked us in order concerning our k.
45 18 from thence your father and kindred
Exod 2 1 took a wife of his own kindred
Lev 20 5 my face against that man and his k.
21 15 he shall not mingle the stock of his k.
25 41 shall return to his kindred and to the
Num 3 27 of the kindred of Caath come the
25 14 a prince of the k. and tribe of Simeon
27 6 them a possession among their father's k.
36 7 wives of their own tribe and kindred
Josu 2 18 brethren and all thy kindred into thy
6 23 all her goods and her kindred, and
7 14 its kindreds and the k. by its houses
Judg 1 25 that man and all his k. they let go
9 1 to all the k. of his mother's father
16 31 all his k. going down took his body
17 7 of Bethlehem Juda, of the k. thereof
18 11 there went therefore of the k. of Dan
Ruth 2 3 who was of the kindred of Elimelech
3 13 if he will take thee by the right of k.
4 4 posession of it by the right of k.
1 K 9 21 my k. the last among all the families
10 21 the lot fell upon the kindred of Metri
2 K 9 12 kindred of the house of Siba served
14 7 whole k. rising against thy handmaid
16 5 a man of kindred of the house of Saul
1 Pa 2 53 of the kindred of Cariathiarim
4 8 Soboba and the kindred of Aharehel
27 whole k. could not reach to the sum of
5 7 his kindred when they were numbered
24 heads of the house of their kindred
6 61 sons of Caath that remained of their k.
66 of the kindred of the sons of Caath
71 of the k. of half tribe of Manasses
2 Pa 19 10 every cause . . . between k. and k.
Tob 1 3 fellow captives that were of his k.
17 a great multitude of his kindred
19 Tobias daily went among all his kindred
7 14 be married to one of her own kindred
14 17 his kindred . . . continued in good life
Jdth 14 6 with all the succession of his kindred
Esth 16 18 and all his kindred hang on gibbets
Job 32 2 Eliu . . . of the kindred of Ram, was
Ps 73 8 whole k. of them together: Let us
Prov 11 17 casteth off even his own kindred
Jer 3 14 one of a city, and two of a kindred
8 3 that shall remain of this wicked k.
Dan 13 30 parents and children and all her k.
63 with Joakim her husband and all her k.
2 Ma 5 6 prosperity against one's own k. is a
9 if for k. sake he should have refuge
Mark 6 4 own house and among his own kindred
Luke 1 61 there is none of thy k. that is called
Acts 4 6 were of the kindred of the high priest
7 3 and from thy kindred, and come into
13 his kindred was made known to Pharao
14 and all his kindred, 75 souls. So
kindreds Gen 10 20 children of Cham in their k.
Gen 10 31 children of . . . according to their kindreds. Josu 13:15, 31; 19:8
36 40 the dukes of Esau in their kindreds
Exod 6 15 these are the kindreds of. 19, 24
16 sons of . . . by their kindreds. 17; Num 4:22, 34; 26:12, 15, 20, 23, 26, 35, 41, 42, 44, 48; Josu 19:23, 48; 21:7
25 of the Levitical families by their k.
Num 1 4 and of the houses in their kindreds
16 by their tribes and kindreds
18 reckoning them up by the kindreds
30 houses of their kindreds. 24, 26, 28, 34, 36, 38, 40, 42, 44; 2:2, 32; 1 Pa 5:13; 7:2
4 38 k. and houses of their fathers. 42, 46
17 2 of every one of them a rod by their k.
26 2 upward, by their houses and kindreds
25 these are the kindreds of. 27, 37, 42, 47, 50; 1 Pa 6:19
38 sons of . . . in their k. 1 Pa 23:24
34 14 according to the number of their k.
Josu 7 14 it shall come by its kindreds and the
13 23 of the Rubenites, by their kindreds
24 Gad and to his children by their k.
29 possession according to their kindreds
15 1 children of . . . by their kindreds. 20; 17:2; 19:1, 10, 16, 24, 31, 39
12 of children of Juda in their kindreds
16 5 was according to their kindreds
19 17 lot came out to Issachar by their k.
21 1 came to the princes of the kindreds
38 by their families and kindreds
1 K 10 21 tribe of Benjamin and the k. thereof
1 Pa 4 38 were named princes in their kindreds
7 9 heads of their kindreds. 11; 8:13
12 30 great valor renowned in their kindreds
26 31 according to their families and k.
Ps 21 28 kindreds of the Gentiles shall adore
95 7 to the Lord, O ye k. of the Gentiles
Jer 25 9 will take . . . all the k. of the north
Acts 3 25 in thy seed shall the k. of the earth
kine Gen 32 15 camels with their colts, forty k.
Gen 33 13 sheep, and kine with young: which
41 2 out of which came up seven kine, very
18 and seven kine came up out of the river
19 there followed these, other seven kine
26 the seven beautiful kine and the seven
27 the seven lean and thin kin that came
1 K 6 7 cart: and two kine that have calved
10 taking two k. that had suckling calves
12 the kine took the straight way that

14 laid the kine upon it a holocaust to
Tob 8 22 he caused also two fat kine and four
10 10 half of all his substance . . . in kine
Ps 67 31 the congregation of bulls with the kine
Eccu 38 27 his care is to give the kine fodder
Osee 10 5 have worshipped the kine of Bethaven
Amos 4 1 ye fat kine that are in the mountains
king Mat 1 6 and Jesse begot David the king. And
Mat 1 6 David the king begot Solomon of her
2 1 of Juda in the days of king Herod
3 king Herod hearing this, was troubled
9 who having heard the king, went their
5 35 for it is the city of the great king
14 9 the king was struck sad. Mark 6:26
18 23 likened to a king who would take an
21 5 behold thy king cometh to thee, meek
22 2 likened to a king who made a marriage
7 when the king had heard of it, he was
11 the king went in to see the guests: and
13 then the king said to the waiters; bind
25 34 then shall the king say to them that
40 the king answering, shall say to them
Mark 6 14 king Herod heard, for his name was
22 the king said to the damsel: Ask of me
25 with haste to the king, she asked
Luke 1 5 the days of Herod, the king of Judea
14 31 what king, about to go to make war
31 to make war against another king
19 38 blessed be the king who cometh in the
23 2 and saying that he is Christ the king
John 6 15 to take him by force and make him king
12 15 thy king cometh, sitting on an ass's
18 37 said to him: Art thou a king then
37 thou sayest that I am a king. For this
19 12 for whosoever maketh himself a king
14 he saith to the Jews: Behold your king
15 to them: Shall I crucify your king
15 answered: We have no king but Caesar
Acts 7 18 till another king arose in Egypt, who
12 1 Herod the k. stretched forth his hands
13 21 and after that they desired a king
22 he raised them up David to be king
17 7 saying that there is another king, Jesus
25 13 and after some days, king Agrippa and
14 Festus told the king of Paul, saying: A
24 Festus saith: King Agrippa, and all ye
26 especially before thee, O king Agrippa
26 2 I think myself happy, O king Agrippa
7 for which hope, O king, I am accused by
13 at midday, O king, I saw in the way a
19 O king Agrippa, I was not incredulous to
26 the king knoweth of these things, to
27 believest thou the prophets, O king
30 the king rose up, and the governor, and
2 C 11 32 nation under Aretas the king, guarded
1 Tim 1 17 to the k. of ages, immortal, invisible
6 15 King of kings, and Lord of lords. Apoc 17:14; 19:16
Heb 7 1 this Melchisedech was king of Salem
2 by interpretation, is king of justice
2 king of Salem, that is, king of peace
11 27 not fearing the fierceness of the king
1 P 2 13 whether it be to the king as excelling
17 fear God. Honor the king. Servants, be
Apoc 9 11 they had over them a king, the angel
15 3 and true are thy ways, O King of ages
kingdom of God Wisd 10 10 showed him the k. of God
Mat 6 33 ye therefore first the k. . . . Luke 12:31
12 28 then is the k. of G. come upon you
21 31 shall go into the k. of G. before you
43 the k. of G. shall be taken from you
Mark 1 14 preaching the gospel of the k. of God
15 the k. . . . is at hand. Luke 10:11; 21:31
4 11 know the mystery of the k. . . . Luke 8:10
26 the k. of God as if a man should cast
30 to what shall we liken the k. of God
8 39 till they see the k. . . . coming in power
9 46 with one eye to enter into the k. of G.
10 14 for of such is the k. . . . Luke 18:16
15 shall not receive the k. . . . Luke 18:17
23 have riches enter into k. . . . Luke 18:24
24 trust in riches, to enter into k. of G.
25 rich man to enter into k. . . . Luke 18:25
12 34 thou art not far from the k. of God
14 25 drink it new in the kingdom of God
15 43 himself looking for k. . . . Luke 25:51
Luke 4 43 cities also I must preach the k. . . .
6 20 poor, for yours is the kingdom of God
7 28 he that is the lesser in the k. . . .
8 1 preaching and evangelizing the k. . . .
9 2 he sent them to preach the k. . . .
11 spoke to them of the kingdom of God
27 taste death till they see the k. . . .
60 but go thou and preach the k. . . .
62 looking back, is fit for the k. . . .
10 9 the kingdom of God is come nigh unto
11 20 the kingdom of God is come upon you
13 18 to what is the kingdom of God like
20 shall I esteem the k. . . . to be like
28 and all the prophets in the k. . . .
29 shall sit down in the kingdom of God
14 15 he that shall eat bread in the k. . . .
16 16 from that time the k. . . . is preached
17 20 when the k. . . . should come, he
20 k. . . . cometh not with observation
21 lo, the kingdom of God is within you
19 11 they thought that the k. . . . should
22 16 till it be fulfilled in the k. . . .
18 of the vine till the k. . . . come
John 3 3 he cannot see the kingdom of God
5 cannot enter into the kingdom of God
Acts 1 3 to them, and speaking of the k. . . .
8 12 believed Philip preaching of the k. . . .
14 21 many tribulations we must enter k. . . .
19 8 and exhorting concerning the k. . . .
20 25 gone preaching the k. . . . , shall see my
28 23 testifying the kingdom of God, and
31 to him, preaching the kingdom of God
Rom 14 17 for the kingdom of God is not meat and
1 C 4 20 the kingdom of God is not in speech, but
6 9 unjust shall not possess kingdom of God
10 shall possess the kingdom of God. And
15 50 flesh and blood cannot possess k. . . .
Gal 5 21 shall not obtain the kingdom of God. But
Col 4 11 are my helpers in the kingdom of God
2 Th 1 5 counted worthy of the kingdom of God
kingdom of heaven Mat 3 2 the k. . . . is at hand. 4:17; 10:7
Mat 5 3 for theirs is the kingdom of heaven. 10
19 be called the least in the k. . . .
19 he shall be called great in the k. . . .
20 you shall not enter into the k. . . . 18:3
7 21 shall enter into the k. of h.: but he
8 11 and Isaac and Jacob in the k. of h.
11 11 he that is lesser in the k. of h. is
12 the k. of h. suffereth violence, and
13 11 to know the mysteries of the k. of h.
24 the k. of h. is likened to a man that
31 the k. of h. is like to a grain of
33 the k. of h. is like to leaven, which
44 k. of h. is like unto a treasure hidden
45 k. of h. is like to a merchant seeking
47 k. of h. is like to a net cast into the
52 every scribe instructed in the k. of h.
16 19 give to thee the keys of the k. of h.
18 1 who . . . is the greater in the k. of h.

4 he is the greater in the k. of h. And
23 is the k. of h. likened to a king who
19 12 made themselves eunuchs for the k. of h.
14 to me: for the k. of h. is for such
23 shall hardly enter into the k. of h.
24 a rich man to enter into the k. of h.
20 1 k. of h. is like to an householder who
22 2 k. of h. is likened to a king who made
23 13 you shut the k. of h. against men, for
25 1 the k. of h. is like to ten virgins
kingly Gen 41 40 only in the k. throne will I be
Dan 11 20 vile and unworthy of kingly honor
21 kingly honor shall not be given him
Acts 12 21 Herod being arrayed in kingly apparel
1 P 2 9 a chosen generation, a k. priesthood
king's Gen 14 17 which is the king's vale. But
Gen 39 20 where the king's prisoners were kept
41 14 at king's command, Joseph was brought
25 the king's dream is one: God hath
45 16 the fame was abroad in the king's court
47 14 and brought it unto the king's treasure
Num 21 22 we will go the king's highway till we
1 K 18 22 now therefore be the king's son-in-law
23 to be the king's son-in-law. 26
25 to be avenged of the king's enemies
20 29 he came not to the king's table. Then
21 8 for the king's business required haste
22 14 David, who is the king's son-in-law
23 20 to deliver him into the king's hands
26 16 where is the king's spear and the cup
22 behold the king's spear: let one of
2 K 3 37 that it was not the king's doing, that
9 13 he ate always of the king's table
13 18 the king's daughters that were virgins
14 1 the king's heart was turned to Absalom
24 saw not the king's face. 28
15 2 business to come to the king's judgment
16 2 the asses are for the king's household
18 18 pillar, which is in the king's valley
19 18 might help over the king's household
42 have we eaten anything of the king's
24 4 but the king's words prevailed over
3 K 1 44 they have set him upon the king's mule
4 5 of Nathan the priest, the king's friend
10 22 the king's navy, once in three years
28 the king's merchants brought them out
11 14 Adad the Edomite of the king's seed
13 6 the king's hand was restored to him
22 12 will deliver it into the k. hands. 15
4 K 7 9 us go and tell it in the king's court
11 and told it within the king's palace
9 34 her: because she is a king's daughter
12 10 king's scribe and the high priest came
18 could be found . . . in the king's palace
13 16 put his hands over the king's hands
16 15 offer . . . the king's holocaust and his
18 the king's entry from without he turned
22 12 commanded . . . Asaia the king's servant
15 carried away . . . and the king's mother
and the king's wives
25 4 the two walls by the king's garden
1 Pa 9 18 in the king's gate eastward, the sons
21 4 but the king's word rather prevailed
6 Joab unwillingly executed the king's
27 33 Achitophel was the king's counsellor
33 Chusai the Arachite, the king's friend
34 general of the king's army was Joab
29 6 overseers of the king's possessions
2 Pa 1 16 horses brought . . . by the k. merchants
4 11 finished all the king's work in the
8 9 set none to serve in the king's works
15 departed not from king's commandments
9 20 vessels of the k. table were of gold
21 the king's ships went to Tharsis with
10 16 upon the king's speaking roughly, said
18 5 God will deliver it into the k. hand
11 Lord will deliver them into k. hand
19 11 matters which belong to the k. office
22 11 Josabeth the king's daughter took Joas
24 11 the king's scribe . . . went in: and
21 stoned him at the king's commandment
25 16 art thou the k. counsellor? Be quiet
26 11 Henanias . . . one of the k. captains
30 6 proclaiming according to k. orders
31 3 the k. part was that, of his proper
34 20 commanded . . . Asaa the king's servant
35 7 all these were of the k. substance
10 according to the king's commandment
1 Es 5 17 let him search in the king's library
6 8 of the king's chest . . . the charges
7 20 be given out of . . . king's exchequer
27 who hath put this in the king's heart
8 36 gave the king's edicts to the lords that were
from the king's court
2 Es 1 11 man. For I was the king's cupbearer
2 8 Asaph the keeper of the king's forest
9 and gave them the king's letters. And
14 I passed . . . to the king's aqueduct
18 king's words, which he had spoken to me
3 15 pool of Siloe unto the king's guard
5 4 let us borrow money for king's tribute
11 23 king's commandment was concerning them
Esth 1 7 as was worthy of a king's magnificence
12 would not come at king' commandment
18 wherefore the k. indignation is just
2 3 overseer and keeper of the k. women
4 among them all shall please the k. eyes
8 when the king's ordinance was noised
13 they passed . . . to the king's chamber
14 the charge over the king's concubines
19 Mardochai stayed at the king's gate
21 when Mardochai abode at the k. gate
21 and Thares, two of the king's eunuchs
3 3 not observe the king's commandment
8 moreover despise the king's ordinances
12 the king's scribes were called in the
12 wrote . . . to all the k. lieutenants
13 were sent by the king's messengers to
15 haste to fulfil the king's commandment
4 2 no one . . . might enter the k. court
3 to which the k. cruel edict was come
7 to pay money into the king's treasures
11 cometh into the k. inner court, who
5 1 house, over against the king's hall
8 have found favor in the king's sight
13 Jew sitting before the king's gate
6 8 to be clothed with the king's apparel
9 let the first of the king's princes
7 8 not yet gone out of the king's mouth
10 Mardochai; and the king's wrath ceased
8 3 she fell down at the king's feet and
5 be destroyed in all the k. provinces
8 write ye . . . in the king's name and
8 which were sent in the king's name. 10
9 k. scribes and secretaries were called
14 the king's edict was hung up in Susan
15 Mardochai . . . from the k. presence
17 whithersoever the k. commandments came
9 16 which were subject to king's dominion
20 that abode in all the king's provinces
25 might be made void by the k. letters
11 3 among the first of the king's court
12 1 abode at that time in the k. court
1 Bagatha and Thara the king's eunuchs
14 17 nor hath the king's banquet pleased me
15 11 and God changed the king's spirit into

16 3 endeavor to oppress the k. subjects
Ps 44 6 into the hearts of the king's enemies
14 all the glory of the king's daughter
98 4 and the king's honor loveth judgment
Prov 16 15 in cheerfulness of the k. countenance
Eccu 48 26 and he lengthened the king's life
Jer 39 4 city by the way of the king's garden
41 10 away captive . . . the king's daughters
43 6 remnant of Juda . . . the k. daughters
52 7 walls and leadeth to the king's garden
25 of them that were near the k. person
Eze 17 13 he shall take one of the king's seed
Dan 1 3 bring in some . . . of the king's seed
4 as might stand in the king's palace
8 would not be defiled with the k. table
13 children that eat of the king's meat
15 children that ate of the king's meat
19 and they stood in the king's presence
2 14 Arioch the general of the king's army
23 made known to us the king's discourse
49 Daniel himself was in the k. palace
3 22 for the king's commandment was urgent
95 and they changed the king's word and
4 28 while the word was yet in the k. mouth
5 5 surface of the wall of the k. palace
6 then was the king's countenance changed
8 then came in all the king's wise men
29 by the k. command Daniel was clothed
6 15 those men perceiving the king's design
24 by the king's commandment, those men
8 27 was risen up, I did the king's business
14 1 Daniel was the king's guest and was
13 having sealed it with the king's ring
Amos 7 1 latter rain after the king's mowing
13 because it is the king's sanctuary and
Soph 1 8 I will visit . . . upon the king's sons
Zach 14 10 Hananeel even to the k. winepresses
1 Ma 2 18 and obey the king's commandment as all
18 be in number of the king's friends
23 according to the king's commandment
31 and it was told to the king's men
31 who had broken the king's commandment
34 neither will we obey the king's edict
3 38 mighty men of the king's friends. And
39 destroy it according to the k. orders
4 3 to attack the king's forces that were
6 32 Bethzacharam over against the k. camp
40 part of the k. army was distinguished
42 there fell of the king's army 600 men
43 beasts harnessed with the k. harness
48 the king's army went up against them
48 the king's army pitched their tents
7 7 all the havock . . . in the king's lands
10 20 that thou be called the king's friend
36 let there be enrolled in the k. army
36 as is due to all the king's forces
40 of silver, out of the king's accounts
44 be given out of the king's revenues
45 shall be given out of the k. account
11 57 and to be one of the king's friends
13 15 money that he owed in the k. account
37 to write to the king's chief officers
15 8 and what should be the king's hereafter
32 Athenobius the king's friend came to
32 astonished and told him the k. words
2 Ma 3 6 to bring all into the king's hands
8 but indeed to fulfil the k. purpose
4 25 having received the king's mandate, he
6 7 by bitter constraint on the k. birthday
8 8 to send aid to the king's affairs
11 1 Lysias the k. lieutenant and cousin
22 the k. letter contained these words
27 the king's letter to the Jews was in
35 Lysias the king's cousin hath granted
13 15 he set upon the k. quarter by night
26 with regard to the king's coming and
14 8 out of fidelity to the king's interest
11 the rest also of the king's friends
15 5 arms, and to do the king's business
Acts 12 20 Blastus, who was the king's chamberlain
Heb 11 23 and they feared not the king's edict

king's house 2 K 11 2 upon roof of the k. h.
2 K 11 8 Urias went out from the king's house
9 Urias slept before the gate of the k. h.
15 35 thou shalt hear out of the king's house
3 K 9 1 house of the Lord and the k. h. 2 Pa 7:11
10 12 house of the Lord and of the k. h. 2 Pa 12:9
14 27 before the gate of the king's house
15 18 treasures of the k. h. 4 K 24:13; 2 Pa 25:24
16 18 burnt himself with the king's house
4 K 11 6 and keep the watch of the king's house
20 slain with the sword in the k. h.
15 25 in the tower of the king's house near
25 9 he burnt . . . king's house. Jer 52:13
2 Pa 9 11 stairs . . . and in the king's house
21 17 that was found in the king's house
23 5 and a third part at the king's house
20 the upper gate into the king's house
26 21 Joatham his son governed the king's h.
1 Es 6 4 shall be given out of the king's house
2 Es 3 25 lieth out from the king's high house
Jdth 2 10 silver he took out of the king's house
Esth 2 9 beautiful maidens of the king's house
4 13 because thou art in the king's house
5 1 inner court of the king's h. 6:4
Jer 26 10 and they went up from the king's house
36 12 he went down into the king's house to
38 7 an eunuch that was in the king's house
8 Abdemelech went out of the king's h.
11 Abdemelech . . . went into the king's h.
39 8 the Chaldeans burnt the king's house

king's servants Gen 47 19 buy us to be the k. s.
Judg 3 24 the k. s. going in, saw the doors
1 K 22 17 k. s. would not put forth their hands
26 22 let one of the k. s. come over and
2 K 11 24 some of the king's servants are slain
15 15 the k. s. said to him: Whatsoever
3 K 1 9 and all the men of Juda, the k. s.
47 the k. s. going in have blessed our lord
Esth 2 2 the k. s. and his officers said: Let
3 2 all the k. s. that were at the doors
3 k. s. that were chief at the doors of
4 11 all the k. s. and all the provinces
Dan 3 46 k. s. that had cast them in, ceased

king's son 2 K 16 19 is it not the king's son
2 K 18 12 not lay my hands upon the king's son
20 tidings, because the king's son is dead
4 K 11 4 showed them the king's son: and he
12 and he brought forth the king's son
15 5 but Joatham the king's son governed
2 Pa 23 3 behold the king's son shall reign
11 and they brought out the king's son
28 7 Zechri . . . slew Maasias the king's son
Ps 71 2 to the king's son thy justice: to judge

king's sons 2 K 13 23 invited all the k. s. 3 K 1:19, 25
2 K 13 27 let Amnon and all the king's sons go
29 all the king's sons arose and got up
30 Absalom hath slain all the king's sons
32 think that all the k. sons are slain
33 saying: All the king's sons are slain
35 behold the king's sons are come: as
36 the king's sons also appeared: and
3 K 1 9 invited all his brethren the king's sons
4 K 10 6 the king's sons, being 70 men, were
7 they took the king's sons and slew 70
8 have brought the heads of the k. sons

11 2 stole him from among k. s. 2 Pa 22:11
1 Pa 27 32 were with the k. sons. And Achitophel
king's treasures; *see* **treasures**
kings Mat 10 18 and before kings for my sake, for a
Mat 11 8 are in the houses of kings. Luke 7:25
17 24 the kings of the earth, of whom do
Mark 13 9 shall stand before governors and k.
Luke 10 24 many prophets and kings have desired
21 12 dragging you before k. and governors
22 25 the kings of the Gentiles lord it over
Acts 4 26 the kings of the earth stood up and
9 15 my name before the Gentiles, and kings
1 Tim 2 2 for kings, and for all that are in high
6 15 King of kings. Apoc 17:14; 19:16
Heb 7 1 returning from the slaughter of the k.
Apoc 1 5 the prince of the kings of the earth
6 15 kings of the earth and the princes and
10 11 and peoples and tongues and kings
16 12 for the kings from the rising of the
14 unto the kings of the whole earth
17 9 sitteth, and they are seven kings
12 the ten horns . . . are ten kings, who
12 shall receive power as kings one hour
18 hath kingdom over the k. of the earth
18 3 k. of the earth have committed. 18:9
19 18 that you may eat the flesh of kings
19 saw the beast and the k. of the earth
21 24 k. of the earth shall bring their glory
kings' Prov 30 28 and dwelleth in kings' houses
kinsfolks 3 K 16 11 all his k. and friends
2 Ma 15 18 was less . . . for their brethren and k.
Luke 1 58 and k. heard that the Lord had showed
2 44 sought him among their kinsfolks and
kinsman Exod 18 1 Jethro . . . the k. of Moses, had
Exod 18 5 Jethro the k. of Moses came with
6 I Jethro thy kinsman come to thee
7 and he went out to meet his kinsman
8 Moses told his kinsman all that the
12 Jethro the kinsman of Moses offered
14 when his kinsman had seen all things
27 he let his k. depart: and he returned
Lev 25 25 if . . . k. will, he may redeem what
26 if he have no kinsman, and he himself
49 uncle or his uncle's son or his k.
Num 10 29 son of Raguel the Madianite, his k.
35 12 the kinsman of him that is slain may
19 the kinsman of him that was slain. 21
Deut 19 6 kinsman of him whose blood was shed
12 shall deliver him into hand of the k.
Josu 20 3 and may escape the wrath of the kinsman
9 and not die by the hand of the kinsman
Judg 1 16 the Cinite, the kinsman of Moses, went
4 11 sons of Habab, the kinsman of Moses
Ruth 2 1 her husband Elimelech had a kinsman
20 again she said: The man is our kinsman
3 2 this Booz . . . is our near kinsman
9 for thou art a near kinsman. And he
4 1 and when he had seen the k. going by
3 they sat down, and he spoke to the k.
4 there is no near kinsman besides thee
5 to raise up the name of thy kinsman in
8 Booz said to his kinsman: Put off thy
Tob 6 11 Raguel, a near kinsman of thy tribe
Prov 23 11 their near kinsman is strong: and he
Eccu 41 25 turning away thy face from thy kinsman
Jer 6 21 neighbor and kinsman shall perish
Amos 6 10 and a man's kinsman shall take him up
John 18 26 a k. to him whose ear Peter cut off
Rom 16 11 salute Herodian, my kinsman. Salute
kinsmen Num 27 3 among the k. of our father
Ruth 4 7 the manner in Israel between kinsmen
Tob 2 15 so his relations and kinsmen mocked
11 20 Achior and Nabath the kinsmen of Tobias
Job 19 14 my kinsmen have forsaken me and they
21 8 their seed . . . a multitude of kinsmen
31 34 contempt of k. hath terrified me
Eze 11 15 thy kinsmen and all the house of Israel
2 Ma 8 1 calling together their k. and friends
12 39 to bury them with their kinsmen in the
Luke 14 12 nor thy kinsmen nor thy neighbors who
21 16 and brethren and kinsmen and friends
Acts 10 24 called together his k. and . . . friends
Rom 9 3 for my brethren, who are my k. according
16 7 salute Andronicus and Junias, my k. and
21 Lucius and Jason and Sosipater, my k.
kinswoman Ruth 1 15 thy k. is returned to her
kiss Gen 27 26 give me a kiss, my son. He came
Gen 31 28 not suffered me to kiss my sons and
2 K 20 9 took Amasa by the chin . . . to kiss him
3 K 19 20 let me . . . kiss my father and my mother
Tob 11 7 to him, go to thy father and kiss him
Prov 24 26 he shall kiss the lips, who answereth
Cant 1 1 him kiss me with the kiss of his mouth
8 1 I may find thee without and kiss thee
Eccu 29 5 they kiss the hands of the lender
Mat 26 48 whomsoever I shall kiss. Mark 14:44
Luke 7 45 gavest me no kiss; but she, since she
45 hath not ceased to kiss my feet. My
22 47 drew near to Jesus, for to kiss him
48 betray the Son of man with a kiss
Rom 16 16 salute one another with an holy kiss.
1 C 16:20; 2 C 13:12; 1 P 5:14
1 Th 5 26 salute all the brethren with a holy kiss
kissed Gen 27 27 he came near, and kissed him
Gen 29 11 having watered the flock, he kissed her
31 55 Laban . . . kissed his sons and daughters
45 15 Joseph kissed all his brethren and
48 10 he [Jacob] kissed and embraced them
Exod 4 27 in the mountain of God, and k. him
18 7 worshipped and k. him: and they saluted
Ruth 1 9 and she [Noemi] kissed them. And they
14 Orpha kissed her mother-in-law and
1 K 10 1 poured it upon his head and kissed him
2 K 14 33 before him: and the king k. Absalom
15 5 he put forth his hand . . . and k. him
19 39 the king kissed Berzellai and blessed
Tob 7 7 and Raguel went to him and kissed him
9 8 leaped up and they kissed each other
10 12 parents taking their daughter k. her
11 11 receiving him kissed him, as did also
Job 31 27 if . . . I have kissed my hand with my
Ps 84 11 each other: justice and peace have k.
Mat 26 49 hail, Rabbi. And he k. him. Mark 14:45
Luke 7 38 kissed his feet and anointed them
15 20 fell upon his neck and kissed him
Acts 20 37 falling on neck of Paul, they kissed him
kisses Prov 27 6 the deceitful k. of an enemy
kisseth Prov 7 13 the young man, she k. him
kissing Gen 29 13 heartily k. him, brought him
Gen 33 4 about the neck, and kissing him, wept
50 1 Joseph . . . weeping and kissing him
1 K 20 41 kissing one another, they wept together
3 K 19 18 not worshipped him kissing the hands
kitchens Eze 46 23 there were k. built under
Eze 46 24 this is the house of the kitchens
kite Lev 11 14 you must not eat . . . the kite
Deut 14 13 ringtail and the vulture and the kite
Jer 8 7 kite in the air hath known her time
Zach 5 9 they had wings like the wings of the k.
kites Isa 34 15 thither are the kites gathered
knead Jer 7 18 the women k. the dough to make
kneaded 1 K 28 24 the woman . . . taking meal k. it
knee Gen 41 43 should bow their knee before him
2 Pa 29 30 great joy, and bowing the knee adored
Esth 3 2 Mardochai did not bend his knee. 5
Isa 45 24 every knee shall be bowed to me and

Eze 21 7 and water shall run down every knee
Mat 27 29 bowing the knee before him, they mocked
Rom 14 11 every knee shall bow to me, and every
Phil 2 10 every knee should bow, of those that are
kneel Mich 6 6 wherewith shall I k. before the
kneeled Acts 21 5 we kneeled down on the shore, and
kneeling Judg 7 6 of the multitude had drunk k.
2 Pa 6 13 kneeling down in the presence of all
Mark 1 40 k. down, said to him: If thou wilt
10 17 running up and kneeling before him
Luke 22 41 kneeling down, he prayed. Acts 20:36
Acts 9 40 Peter kneeling down prayed, and turning
knees Gen 30 3 that she may bear upon my knees
Deut 28 35 with a very sore ulcer in the knees
Judg 7 5 that shall drink bowing down their k.
16 19 but she made him sleep upon her knees
3 K 8 54 he had fixed both knees on the ground
18 42 put his face between his knees. And
19 18 knees have not been bowed before Baal
4 K 1 13 he fell upon his knees before Elias
4 20 she set him on her knees until noon
1 Es 9 5 I fell upon my knees and spread out
Esth 3 2 bent their knees and worshipped Aman
Job 3 12 why received upon the knees? Why
4 4 hast strengthened the trembling knees
Ps 108 24 my knees are weakened through fasting
Eccu 25 32 feeble hands and disjointed knees, a
Isa 35 3 hands, and confirm the weak knees
66 12 upon the knees they shall caress you
Eze 7 17 and all knees shall run with water
47 4 me through the water up to the knees
Dan 5 6 his knees struck one against the other
10 10 lifted me up upon my knees and upon
Nah 2 10 the heart melteth and the knees fail
Mat 17 14 man falling down on his knees before
Mark 15 19 bowing their knees, they adored him
Luke 5 8 he fell down at Jesus' knees, saying
Acts 7 59 falling on his knees, he cried with
Rom 11 4 that have not bowed their knees to Baal
Eph 3 14 I bow my knees to the Father of our Lord
Heb 12 12 which hang down, and the feeble knees
knelt Dan 6 10 he knelt down three times a day
knew Mat 1 25 he knew her not till she brought forth
Mat 7 23 I never knew you: depart from me, you
12 7 if you knew what this meaneth: I will
17 12 and they knew him [Elias] not, but
21 45 they knew that he spoke of them
24 39 they knew not till the flood came and
43 if the goodman of the house knew at
26 74 to swear that he knew not the man
27 18 he k. that for envy they had delivered
Mark 1 34 not to speak, because they knew him
6 33 they saw them going away, and many knew
38 when they knew, they say: Five, and
54 the ship, immediately they knew him
9 5 he knew not what he said: for they
12 12 they knew that he spoke. Luke 20:19
14 40 and they knew not what to answer him
15 10 he knew that the chief priests had
Luke 2 43 and his parents knew it not. And
4 41 for they knew that he was Christ
5 22 when Jesus knew their thoughts
6 8 but he knew their thoughts; and said
7 37 when she knew that he sat at meat in
9 11 when the people knew, they followed
12 47 servant who knew the will of his lord
48 he that knew not, and did things
20 7 that they knew not whence it was
24 31 eyes were opened and they knew him
35 how they knew him in the breaking of
John 1 10 by him, and the world knew him not
31 I knew him not. 33
2 9 wine, and knew not whence it was, but
9 but the waiters knew who had drawn the
24 unto them, for that he knew all men
25 of man; for he knew what was in man
4 53 the father therefore knew that it was
5 6 knew that he had been now a long time
13 he who was healed knew not who it was
6 6 for he himself knew what he would do
15 when he knew that they would come to
65 Jesus knew from the beginning who they
11 42 I knew that thou hearest me always
56 any man knew where he was, he should
12 9 of the Jews knew that he was there
13 11 he knew who he was that would betray
16 19 Jesus knew that they had a mind to ask
18 2 and Judas also . . . knew the place
20 9 as yet they knew not the scripture
14 and she knew not that it was Jesus
21 4 disciples knew not that it was Jesus
Acts 2 30 knew that God hath sworn to him with
3 10 they knew him, that it was he who sat
4 13 they knew them that they had been with
7 18 arose in Egypt, who knew not Joseph
12 9 he k. not that it was true which was
14 as soon as she knew Peter's voice
16 3 they all k. that his father was Gentile
19 32 the greater part knew not for what cause
23 5 Paul said: I knew not, brethren, that
27 39 day, they knew not the land; but they
28 1 knew that island was called Melita. But
Rom 1 21 they knew God, they have not glorified
1 C 1 21 the world, by wisdom, knew not God, it
2 8 which none of princes of this world k.
2 C 5 21 him, who knew no sin, he hath made sin
Col 1 6 heard and knew the grace of God in truth
1 J 3 1 knoweth not us, because it knew not him
Jude 5 though you once knew all things, that
knewest Ruth 2 11 to a people which thou k. not
2 Es 9 10 thou knewest that they dealt proudly
Ps 141 4 failed me, then thou knewest my paths
Isa 55 5 call a nation, which thou knewest not
Dan 5 22 whereas thou knewest all these things
Mat 25 26 knewest that I reap where I sow not
Luke 19 22 thou k. that I was an austere man
knife Lev 1 17 not cut nor divide it with a k.
Prov 23 2 put a knife to thy throat, if it be so
Eze 5 2 and cut it in pieces with the knife
knit Gen 34 2 his soul was fast knit unto her
Exod 36 18 wherewith the roof might be knit
1 K 18 1 soul of Jonathan was k. with the soul
knives Josu 5 2 make thee knives of stone, and
2 K 12 31 divided them with knives and made
3 K 18 28 cut themselves . . . with knives and
1 Es 1 9 nine and twenty knives, thirty cups
knock Judg 19 22 began to k. at the door, calling
Jdth 14 10 no man durst knock or open and go into
Eccu 13 3 if they knock one against the other
Mat 7 7 k. and it shall be opened. Luke 11:9
Luke 13 25 stand without and knock at the door
Apoc 3 20 I stand at the gate and knock. If any
knocked Acts 12 13 when he k. at the door of the
knocketh Mat 7 8 him that k., it shall. Luke 11:10
Luke 12 36 when he cometh and knocketh, they may
knocking Cant 5 2 voice of my beloved knocking
Luke 11 8 yet if he shall continue knocking
Acts 12 16 Peter continued knocking. And when
knots Wisd 13 13 piece of wood, and full of knots
know Mat 6 3 let not thy left hand know what thy
Mat 7 11 k. how to give good gifts. Luke 11:13
16 by their fruits you shall know them. 20
9 6 you may know that the Son of man. Mark 2:10; Luke 5:24
30 see that no man know this. But they
11 27 neither doth any one know the Father

13 11 to you it is given to know the
15 12 dost thou know that the Pharisees, when
16 3 you know then how to discern the face. Luke 12:56
20 25 you know that the princes of the
22 16 k. that thou art a true speaker. Mark 12:14
24 32 you k. that summer is nigh. Luke 21:30
33 know ye that it is nigh. Mark 13:29
43 this know ye, that if the goodman of
25 24 I know that thou art a hard man; thou
26 2 you know that after two days shall be
27 65 go, guard it as you know. And they
28 5 I know that you seek Jesus who was
Mark 1 24 I know who thou art. Luke 4:34
4 11 to know the mystery of the kingdom of. Luke 8:10
13 and how shall you know all parables
5 43 that no man should know it. 7:24
9 29 would not that any man should know it
10 42 you know that they who seem to rule
13 28 you know that summer is very near
14 68 I neither know nor understand what
Luke 1 4 that thou mayest know the verity of
18 whereby shall I know this? For I am
7 39 would know surely who and what manner
8 46 I know that virtue is gone out from me
10 11 k. that kingdom of God is at hand. 21:31
12 39 this know ye, that if the householder did know at what
16 4 I know what I will do, that when I
19 15 that he might know how much every man
20 21 we know that thou speakest and
21 20 then know that the desolation thereof
John 3 2 we know that thou art come a teacher
11 we speak what we know, and we testify
4 10 if thou didst know the gift of God
22 we adore that which we know; for
25 I know that the Messias cometh, who
42 know that this is indeed the Savior of
5 32 I know that the witness which he
42 but I know you, that you have not the
6 42 whose father and mother we know? How
7 15 how doth this man know letters, having
17 he shall know of the doctrine, whether
27 but we know this man, whence he is
28 you both know me, and you know whence
29 I know him, because I am from him, and
51 first hear him and know what he doth
8 14 I know whence I came, and whither I
19 neither me do you know, nor my Father
19 if you did know me, perhaps you would know my Father also
28 then shall you know that I am he and
32 you shall know the truth, and the
37 I know that you are the children of
52 now we know that thou hast a devil
55 but I do know him and do keep his
9 20 we know that this is our son, and that
24 we know that this man is a sinner
25 one thing I know, that whereas I was
29 we know that God spoke to Moses: but
31 we know that God doth not hear sinners
10 4 him, because they know his voice
14 and I know mine, and mine know me
15 knoweth me, and I know the Father
27 and I know them, and they follow me
38 that you may know and believe that the
11 22 I know that whatsoever thou wilt ask
24 I know that he shall rise again in the
49 said to them: You know nothing
12 50 I know that his commandment is life
13 7 now; but thou shalt know hereafter
12 know you what I have done to you? You
17 if you know these things, you shall be
18 you all: I know whom I have chosen
35 all men know that you are my disciples
14 4 whither I go you know, and the way you k.
7 from henceforth you shall know him
17 but you shall know him; because he
20 you shall know that I am in my Father
31 that the world may know that I love
15 18 know ye that it hath hated me before
16 30 we know that thou knowest all things
17 3 that they may know thee, the only true
18 21 they know what things I have said
19 4 you may know that I find no cause in
21 24 we know that his testimony is true
Acts 1 7 it is not for you to know the times or
2 22 in the midst of you, as you also know
36 house of Israel know most certainly
3 17 I k. that you did it through ignorance
10 28 he said to them: You k. how abominable
37 k. the word which hath been published
12 11 now I know in very deed, that the Lord
15 7 you know, that in former days God
17 19 may we k. what this new doctrine is
20 we would know . . . what these things
19 15 Jesus I know, and Paul I know; but who
25 you know that our gain is by this trade
20 18 you k. from first day that I came into
25 I k. that all you, among whom I have
29 I know that after my departure, ravening
34 you . . . know: for such things as were
21 24 all will know that the things which they
34 when he could not know the certainty for
22 14 that thou shouldst know his will, and
19 I said: Lord, they know that I cast into
24 to know for what cause they did so cry
30 meaning to k. more diligently for what
23 15 as if you meant to know something more
28 and meaning to know the cause which they
26 4 nation in Jerusalem, all Jews do know
27 Agrippa? I know that thou believest
28 22 k. that it is everywhere contradicted
Rom 2 2 for we know that the judgment of God is
3 19 we know, that what things soever the law
6 3 know you not that all we, who are
16 know you not, that to whom you yield
7 1 know you not, brethren, for I speak
1 for I speak to them that know the law
14 for we know that the law is spiritual
18 I know that there dwelleth not in me
8 22 we know that every creature groaneth
28 we know that to them that love God, all
11 2 know you not what the scripture saith
14 14 I know, and am confident in the Lord
15 29 I know, that when I come to you, I shall
1 C 2 2 I judged not myself to know anything
12 we may know the things that are given
3 16 know you not, that you are the temple
4 19 and will know, not the speech of them
5 6 k. you not that little leaven corrupteth
6 3 k. you not that we shall judge angels
9 know you not that the unjust shall not
15 know you not that your bodies are the
16 or know you not, that he who is joined
19 know you not, that your members are the
8 1 we know that we all have knowledge
2 he hath not yet known as he ought to k.
4 we know that an idol is nothing in the
9 13 know you not, that they who work in the
24 know you not that they that run in race
11 3 I would have you know, that the head of
12 2 you k. that when you were heathens, you
13 2 if I should have prophecy and should k.
9 we know in part, and we prophesy in part

12 I know in part; but then I shall know even as I am known
14 37 let him know things that I write to you
38 if any man know not, he shall not be
16 15 you know the house of Stephenas, and
18 know them, therefore, that are such
2 C 1 13 I hope that you shall know unto the end
2 4 that you might know the charity I have
9 that I may know the experiment of you
5 1 for we know, if our earthly house of
16 we know no man according to the flesh
16 but now we know him so no longer. If
8 9 for you know the grace of our Lord Jesus
9 2 for I know your forward mind: for which
12 2 I know a man in Christ above 14 years
3 and I know such a man, whether in the
13 5 know you not your own selves, that
6 you shall k. that we are not reprobates
Gal 3 7 know ye therefore, that they who are of
Eph 1 18 that you may know what the hope is of
3 19 to know also the charity of Christ, which
5 5 for know you this and understand, that
6 21 that you also may know the things that
22 you may know the things concerning us
Phil 1 12 brethren, I desire you should know, that
19 I know that this shall fall out to me
25 I know that I shall abide, and continue
2 19 when I know the things concerning you
22 know ye the proof of him, that as a son
3 10 that I may know him, and the power of
4 12 I know both how to be brought low, and I know how to abound
15 you also know, O Philippians, that in
Col 2 1 I would have you know, what manner of
4 6 may know how you ought to answer every
8 may know the things that concern you
1 Th 1 5 as you know what manner of men we have
2 1 yourselves know, brethren, our entrance
2 been shamefully treated, as you know
5 time, the speech of flattery, as you k.
11 you know in what manner, entreating
3 3 know, that we are appointed thereunto
4 also it is come to pass, and you know
5 sent to know your faith: lest perhaps
4 2 you know what precepts I have given
4 you should k. how to possess his vessel
5 2 yourselves know perfectly, that the day
12 to know them who labor among you, and
2 Th 2 6 now you know what withholdeth, that he
3 7 know how you ought to imitate us: for
1 Tim 1 8 we know that the law is good, if a man
3 15 thou mayest know how thou oughtest to
2 Tim 1 12 I know whom I have believed, and I am
2 25 give them repentance to know the truth
3 1 know also this, that, in the last days
Titus 1 16 they profess that they know God: but
Heb 8 11 know the Lord: for all shall know me
10 30 we know him that hath said: Vengeance
12 17 know ye that afterwards, when he
13 23 know ye that our brother Timothy is
James 1 19 you know, my dearest brethren. And
2 20 wilt thou know, O vain man, that faith
4 4 know you not that the friendship of
5 20 he must know that he who causeth a
2 P 1 12 though indeed you know them and are
1 J 2 3 we know that we have known him, if
5 by this we know that we are in him
18 we know that it is the last hour
20 the Holy One, and know all things
21 the truth, but as to them that know it
29 if you know that he is just, know ye that every one also who doth
3 2 we know that, when he shall appear
5 you know that he appeared to take away
14 we know that we have passed from death
15 you know that no murderer hath eternal
19 in this we know that we are of the
24 we know that he abideth in us, by the
4 6 by this we know the spirit of truth
13 we know that we abide in him, and he
5 2 we know that we love the children of
13 you may know that you have eternal
15 we know that he heareth us whatsoever
15 we know that we have the petitions
19 we know that we are of God, and the
20 we know that the Son of God is come
20 that we may know the true God and may
Jude 10 what things soever they naturally know
Apoc 2 2 I know thy works. 19; 3:1, 8, 15
9 I know thy tribulation and thy poverty
13 I know where thou dwellest, where the
23 all the churches shall know that I am
3 9 they shall know that I have loved thee

know not (not know) Mat 16 3 can you not know the signs of the times
Mat 20 22 you know not what you ask. Mark 10:38
21 27 they said: We know not. He also said
24 42 you know not what hour your Lord will
44 at what hour you know not the Son of
25 13 you know not the day nor the hour
26 70 I k. not what thou sayest. Luke 22:60
Mark 11 33 answering, say to Jesus: We know not
12 24 you know not the scriptures nor the
13 33 for ye know not when the time is
35 you know not when the lord of the
14 71 I know not this man of whom you speak
Luke 1 34 this be done, because I know not man
2 49 did you not know that I must be about
9 55 you know not of what spirit you are
23 34 for they know not what they do. But
24 16 held, that they should not know him
John 1 26 the midst of you, whom you know not
4 22 you adore that which you know not
32 I have meat to eat which you know not
7 28 sent me, is true, whom you know not
8 43 why do you not know my speech
9 12 where is he? He saith: I know not
21 how he now seeth, we know not; or who
21 who hath opened his eyes, we know not
25 if he be a sinner I know not: one
29 man, we know not from whence he is
30 that you know not from whence he is
10 5 they know not the voice of strangers
12 16 disciples did not know at the first
14 5 we know not whither thou goest; and
15 21 they know not him that sent me. If I
16 3 they have not known the Father nor me
18 we know not what he speaketh. And
17 25 the world hath not known thee; but I
20 2 we know not where they have laid him
13 I know not where they have laid him
Acts 7 40 we know not what is become of him
Rom 7 7 but I do not know sin, but by the law
8 26 we know not what we should pray for as
1 C 6 2 know you not that the saints shall judge
14 11 if then I k. not the power of the voice
2 C 12 2 in body, I know not, or out of the body
2 of the body, I know not; God knoweth. 3
Phil 1 22 and what I shall choose I know not. But
1 Th 4 5 like the Gentiles that know not God: and
2 Th 1 8 vengeance to them who know not God, and
1 Tim 3 5 if a man know not how to rule his own
James 4 14 know not what shall be on the morrow
2 P 2 12 those things which they know not, shall
1 J 2 21 as to them that know not the truth
Jude 10 blaspheme whatever things they k. not

Apoc 3 3 thou shalt not know at what hour I will
knowest Mark 10 19 thou k. the commandments. Luke 18:20
Luke 22 34 thrice deniest that thou knowest me
John 1 48 whence knowest thou me? Jesus answered
3 8 thou knowest not whence he cometh
10 in Israel and knowest not these things
13 7 what I do thou knowest not now; but
16 30 we know that thou knowest all things
19 10 knowest thou not that I have power to
21 15 thou knowest that I love thee. 16, 17
17 Lord, thou knowest all things; thou
Acts 1 24 who knowest the hearts of all men
25 10 no injury, as thou very well knowest
26 3 as thou knowest all, both customs and
Rom 2 4 knowest thou not, that the benignity of
18 and knowest his will, and approvest the
1 C 7 16 for how knowest thou, O wife, whether
16 how knowest thou, O man, whether thou
2 Tim 1 15 thou knowest this, that all they who are
18 me at Ephesus, thou very well knowest
3 J 12 thou knowest that our testimony is true
Apoc 3 17 and knowest not that thou art wretched
7 14 thou knowest. And he said to me: These
knoweth Mat 6 8 knoweth what is needful for you, before
Mat 6 32 knoweth that you have need. Luke 12:30
11 27 no one knoweth the Son, but the Father
24 36 that day and hour no one k. Mark 13:32
50 at an hour that he k. not. Luke 12:46
Mark 4 27 and grow up, whilst he knoweth not
Luke 10 22 no one knoweth who the Son is, but
16 15 before men, but God k. your hearts
John 7 27 cometh, no man knoweth whence he is
49 that knoweth not the law, are accursed
10 15 as the Father knoweth me, and I know
12 35 in darkness, k. not whither he goeth
14 17 because it seeth him not nor k. him
15 15 the servant k. not what his lord doth
19 35 and he knoweth that he saith true
Acts 15 8 God, who k. the hearts, gave testimony
19 35 what man is there that knoweth not that
26 26 the king knoweth of these things, to
Rom 8 27 k. what the Spirit desireth; because
1 C 2 11 what man knoweth the things of a man
11 no man knoweth, but the Spirit of God
3 20 Lord k. the thoughts of the wise, that
8 2 and if any man think that he knoweth
14 16 he knoweth not what thou sayest. For
2 C 11 11 because I love you not? God knoweth it
31 blessed forever, knoweth that I lie not
12 2 of the body, I know not; God knoweth. 3
2 Tim 2 19 the Lord knoweth who are his; and let
James 4 17 who k. to do good, and doth it not
2 P 2 9 Lord k. how to deliver the godly from
1 J 2 4 he who saith that he knoweth him, and
11 and knoweth not whither he goeth
3 1 the world knoweth not us, because it
20 than our heart, and knoweth all things
4 6 he that knoweth God, heareth us. He
7 is born of God and knoweth God. He
8 he that loveth not, knoweth not God
5 16 he that k. his brother to sin a sin
Apoc 2 17 name written, which no man knoweth but
19 12 which no man knoweth but himself. And
knowing Mat 12 15 Jesus knowing it. 16:8
Mat 12 25 Jesus knowing their thoughts, said to
22 18 Jesus knowing their wickedness, said
29 you err, not knowing the Scriptures
Mark 2 8 Jesus presently knowing in his spirit
5 30 Jesus knowing in himself the virtue
33 knowing what was done in her, came and
6 20 knowing him to be a just and holy man
8 17 which Jesus knowing, saith to them
12 15 who k. their wiliness, saith to them
Luke 8 53 to scorn, knowing that she was dead
9 33 for Elias; not knowing what he said
John 6 62 Jesus, knowing in himself, that his
13 1 Jesus knowing that his hour was come
3 knowing that the Father had given him
18 4 knowing all things that should come
19 28 k. that all things were accomplished
21 12 thou? knowing that it was the Lord
Acts 5 7 wife, not knowing what had happened
13 27 rulers thereof, not k. him, nor the
17 23 what . . . you worship, without knowing
18 25 knowing only the baptism of John. This
20 22 not k. things which shall befall me
23 6 knowing that one part were Sadducees
24 10 k. that for many years thou hast been
Rom 4 21 most fully k., that whatsoever he has
5 3 k. that tribulation worketh patience
6 6 knowing this, that our old man is
9 k. that Christ rising again from dead
10 3 they, not knowing the justice of God
13 11 and that k. the season; that it is now
1 C 15 58 knowing that your labor is not in vain
2 C 1 7 knowing that as you are partakers of
4 14 knowing that he who raised up Jesus
5 6 knowing that, while we are in the body
11 k. therefore the fear of the Lord, we
Gal 2 16 but knowing that man is not justified by
4 8 not k. God, you served them, who, by
Eph 6 8 knowing that whatsoever good thing any
9 knowing that the Lord both of them and
Phil 1 16 knowing that I am set for the defence
Col 3 24 knowing that you shall receive of Lord
4 1 k. that you also have a master in heaven
1 Th 1 4 knowing, brethren beloved of God, your
1 Tim 1 9 knowing this, that the law is not made
6 4 he is proud, knowing nothing, but sick
2 Tim 2 23 knowing that they beget strifes. But
3 14 knowing of whom thou hast learned them
Titus 3 11 knowing that he, that is such an one, is
Philem 21 knowing that thou wilt also do more than
Heb 10 34 knowing that you have a better and a
11 8 went out, not knowing whither he went
James 1 3 knowing that the trying of your faith
3 1 knowing that you receive the greater
1 P 1 18 k. that you were not redeemed with
5 9 k. that the same affliction befalls
2 P 3 3 knowing this first, that in the last
17 knowing these things before, take heed
Apoc 12 12 knowing that he hath but a short time
knowledge Gen 2 9 the tree of knowledge of good. 17
Gen 31 26 to carry away, without my knowledge
Exod 31 3 and knowledge in all manner of work
35 31 with wisdom and understanding and k.
Lev 10 10 k. to discern between holy and unholy
1 K 2 3 the Lord is a God of all knowledge
3 K 9 27 sailors that had knowledge of the sea
2 Pa 1 10 give me wisdom and k. that I may
11 but hast asked wisdom and knowledge
12 wisdom and k. are granted to thee: and
Esth 14 14 who hast the knowledge of all things
Job 13 2 according to your knowledge I also know
21 14 we desire not the k. of thy ways. Who
22 shall any one teach God knowledge, who
22 2 even though he were of perfect k.
32 17 answer my part and will show my k.
35 16 vain and multiplieth words without k.
36 3 I will repeat my k. from the beginning
4 and perfect k. shall be proved to thee
26 behold, God is great, exceeding our k.
42 3 that hideth counsel without knowledge
3 that above measure exceeded my k.
Ps 18 3 and night to night showeth knowledge

72 11 is there knowledge in the most High
93 10 not rebuke: he that teacheth man k.
118 66 teach me goodness . . . and knowledge
138 6 thy k. is become wonderful to me: it is
Prov 1 4 young man k. and understanding
22 and the unwise hate knowledge? Turn ye
2 5 and shalt find the knowledge of God
6 out of his mouth cometh prudence and k.
10 into thy heart, and k. please thy soul
8 9 and just to them that find knowledge
10 not money: choose k. rather than gold
9 10 the knowledge of the holy is prudence
10 14 wise men lay up k.: but the mouth of
11 9 but the just shall be delivered by k.
12 1 he that loveth correction, loveth k.
23 a cautious man concealeth knowledge
14 18 the prudent shall look for knowledge
15 2 tongue of the wise adorneth knowledge
7 the lips of the wise shall disperse k.
16 22 k. is a fountain of life to him that
18 15 a wise heart shall acquire knowledge
19 2 where there is no knowledge of the soul
27 and be not ignorant of the words of k.
20 15 lips of knowledge are a precious vessel
21 11 follow the wise, he will receive k.
22 12 the eyes of the Lord preserve knowledge
20 manner of ways, in thoughts and k.
23 12 and thy ears to words of knowledge
27 21 righteous heart seeketh after knowledge
28 2 knowledge of those things that are said
29 7 the poor: the wicked is void of k.
Ecce 1 18 he that addeth k., addeth also labor
2 21 a man laboreth in wisdom and knowledge
26 God hath given . . . wisdom and k. and
9 10 nor wisdom nor k. shall be in hell
Wisd 1 7 all things, hath knowledge of the voice
2 13 boasteth that he hath the k. of God
6 24 bring the knowledge of her to light
7 16 in his hand . . . k. and skill of works
17 given me the true k. of the things that
8 4 she that teacheth the k. of God
8 if a man desire much k., she knoweth
10 10 and gave him the k. of the holy things
13 1 in whom there is not the k. of God
14 22 them to err about the knowledge of God
Eccu 1 15 by the knowledge of her great works
17 of the Lord is the religiousness of k.
24 wisdom shall distribute knowledge and
26 of wisdom is . . . religiousness of k.
4 21 and will heap upon him treasures of k.
29 is discerned: and understanding and k.
5 12 in the truth of thy judgment and in k.
11 15 and the k. of the law are with God
16 25 I show forth in truth his knowledge
17 5 filled them with k. of understanding
21 16 knowledge of a wise man shall abound
21 k. of the unwise is as words without
24 24 the mother . . . of k. and of holy hope
32 of the most High and the k. of truth
37 who sendeth knowledge as the light and
38 who first hath perfect knowledge of her
25 13 he that findeth wisdom and knowledge
32 5 the first word with careful knowledge
33 8 by the knowledge of the Lord they were
11 with much k. the Lord hath divided them
38 6 is come to the knowledge of men, and
6 the most High hath given k. to men
39 10 he shall direct his counsel and his k.
40 5 the sleep of the night changeth his k.
42 19 the Lord knoweth all k. and hath
51 27 my soul to her, and in k. I found her
Isa 5 13 captive, because they had not knowledge
11 2 spirit of knowledge and of godliness
9 earth is filled with the k. of the Lord
28 9 whom shall he teach knowledge? And
32 4 the heart of fools shall understand k.
33 6 riches of salvation, wisdom and k.
40 14 path of justice and taught him k.
44 25 and that make their knowledge foolish
45 20 have no k. that set up the wood of
47 10 and thy k., this hath deceived thee
53 11 by his k. shall this my just servant
Jer 3 15 shall feed you with k. and doctrine
4 22 evil, but to do good they have no k.
10 12 stretcheth out the heavens by his k.
14 every man is become a fool for k.
51 17 every man is become foolish by his k.
Bar 3 20 way of knowledge they have not known
27 neither did they find the way of k.
37 he found out all the way of knowledge
Dan 1 4 skilful in all wisdom and acute in k.
17 to these children God gave knowledge
2 21 and k. to them that have understanding
5 11 k. and wisdom were found in him: for
12 because a greater spirit and knowledge
14 excellent k. and understanding and
12 4 pass over and k. shall be manifold
13 48 without examination or k. of the truth
Osee 4 1 and there is no k. of God in the land
6 been silent, because they had no k.
6 because thou hast rejected knowledge
6 6 and the k. of God more than holocausts
Mala 2 7 the lips of the priest shall keep k.
1 Ma 8 9 destroy them, and they had k. thereof
9 32 Bacchides had k. of it and sought to
70 and Jonathan had k. of it, and he sent
12 22 since this is come to our k., you do
2 Ma 6 30 O Lord, who hast the holy knowledge
9 11 he began to come to the k. of himself
12 21 had k. of the coming of Judas, he sent
Mat 14 35 men of that place had k. of him, they
Mark 7 18 so are you also without knowledge
Luke 1 77 to give k. of salvation to his people
11 52 you have taken away the key of k.
Acts 17 13 had k. that the word of God was also
24 8 have k. of all these things, whereof we
22 off, having most certain k. of this way
Rom 1 28 they liked not to have God in their k.
2 20 having form of knowledge and of truth
3 20 for by the law is the knowledge of sin
10 2 zeal of God, but not according to k.
11 33 O the depth of . . . the knowledge of God
15 14 replenished with all k., so that you
1 C 1 5 in all utterance, and in all knowledge
8 1 we know that we all have knowledge
1 k. puffeth up; but charity edifieth. And
7 but there is not knowledge in every one
10 if man see him that hath knowledge sit
11 through thy k. shall the weak brother
12 8 and to another, the word of knowledge
13 2 should know all mysteries, and all k.
8 cease, or k. shall be destroyed. For
14 6 to you either in revelation, or in k.
15 34 some have not the knowledge of God, I
2 C 2 14 manifesteth the odor of his knowledge
4 6 to give the light of k. of the glory of
6 6 chastity, in knowledge, in longsuffering
8 7 you abound in faith and word and k., and
10 5 exalteth itself against the k. of God
11 6 I be rude in speech, yet not in k.; but
Eph 1 17 wisdom and of revelation, in the k. of
3 4 may understand my k. in the mystery of
19 Christ, which surpasseth all k., that
4 13 and of the knowledge of the Son of God
Phil 1 9 more and more abound in knowledge, and
3 8 but loss for the excellent k. of Jesus

Col 1 9 beg that you may be filled with the k.
10 and increasing in the knowledge of God
2 2 unto the k. of the mystery of God the
3 hid all the treasures of wisdom and k.
3 10 new, him who is renewed unto knowledge
1 Tim 2 4 and to come to the k. of the truth
6 20 and oppositions of k. falsely so called
2 Tim 3 7 never attaining to the k. of the truth
Heb 10 26 if we sin wilfully after having the k.
James 3 13 who is a wise man and endued with k.
1 P 3 7 dwelling with them according to k.
2 P 1 2 in the k. of God and of Christ Jesus
3 through the k. of him who hath called
5 in virtue, k.; and in k., abstinence
8 in the k. of our Lord Jesus Christ
2 20 through the k. of our Lord and Savior
3 18 and in the k. of our Lord and Savior
knowledges Job 37 16 clouds and the perfect k.
known Mat 10 26 nor hid, that shall not be known. Luke 8:17; 12:2
12 33 for by the fruit the tree is known
Luke 6 44 for every tree is known by its fruit
19 42 if thou also hadst known, and that in
44 hast not k. the time of thy visitation
24 18 and hast not known the things that
John 6 70 we have believed and have known that
7 4 himself seeketh to be known openly
26 have the rulers known for a truth that
8 55 you have not known him, but I know
14 7 if you had known me, you would without
7 without doubt have k. my Father also
9 with you, and have you not known me
17 7 they have known that all things which
8 have known in very deed that I came
25 but I have known thee: and these have known that thou hast sent me
18 15 was known to the high priest. 16
Acts 1 19 became k. to all the inhabitants of
2 14 be this known to you, and with your
3 16 this man, whom you have seen and known
4 10 be it known to you. 13:38; 28:28
16 a known miracle hath been done by them
7 13 Joseph was known by his brethren and
9 30 when the brethren had known, they
15 18 to the Lord was his own work known from
19 17 this became known to all the Jews and
26 5 having known me from the beginning, if
Rom 1 19 that which is known of God is manifest
32 having known the justice of God, did not
3 17 the way of peace they have not known
7 7 for I had not known concupiscence, if
9 22 his wrath, and to make his power known
10 19 but I say: Hath not Israel known? First
11 34 hath k. the mind of the Lord. 1 C 2:16
16 26 mystery . . . known among all nations; to
1 C 2 8 for if they had known it, they would
8 2 he hath not yet k. as he ought to know
3 man love God, the same is known by him
13 12 but then I shall know even as I am known
14 7 how shall it be known what is piped or
9 how shall it be known what is said? For
38 if any man know not, he shall not be k.
2 C 1 13 than what you have read and known. And
14 you have known us in part, that we are
3 2 which is known and read by all men
5 16 if we have known Christ according to the
6 8 yet true; as unknown, and yet known; as
Gal 2 9 when they had known the grace that was
4 9 after that you have known God, or rather are known by God
Eph 3 5 was not known to the sons of men, as it
Phil 4 5 let your modesty be known to all men
1 Tim 4 3 and by them that have known the truth
2 Tim 3 10 but thou hast fully known my doctrine
15 thou hast known the holy scriptures
Heb 3 10 and they have not known my ways, as I
2 P 2 21 not to have known the way of justice
21 after they have known it, to turn back
1 J 2 3 we know that we have known him, if
13 fathers, because you have known him
14 because you have known the Father
3 6 hath not seen him nor known him
16 in this we have known the charity of
4 16 we have known and have believed the
2 J 1 all they that have known the truth
Apoc 2 24 who have not known the depths of Satan
made known John 15 15 my Father, I have made known to you
John 17 26 I have made known thy name to them
Acts 2 28 hast made known to me the ways of life
7 13 his kindred was made known to Pharao
9 24 their laying in wait was made known
42 it was made known throughout all Joppe
23 22 that he had made known these things unto
Eph 3 3 the mystery has been made known to me
10 wisdom of God may be made known to the
Phil 4 6 let your petitions be made known to God
2 P 1 16 made known to you the power and
make known Mat 12 16 they should not m. him k. Mark 3:12
John 17 26 to them, and will make it known; that
1 C 15 1 now I make known unto you, brethren
2 C 8 1 we make known unto you, brethren, the
Eph 1 9 might make known unto us the mystery of
6 19 to make known the mystery of the gospel
21 Lord, will make k. to you. Col 4:7
Col 1 27 to whom God would make known the riches
4 9 here, they shall make known to you
Apoc 1 1 to make known to his servants the

L

Laabim Gen 10 13 Mesraim begot . . . L. 1 Pa 1:11
Laad 1 Pa 4 2 Jahath, of whom were born . . . Laad
Laada 1 Pa 4 21 sons of Sela . . . Laada the
Laadan 1 Pa 7 26 Thaan, who begot Laadan: and his
Laban Gen 24 29 Rebecca had a brother named Laban
Gen 24 50 Laban and Bathuel answered: The word
25 20 took to wife Rebecca . . . sister to L.
27 43 arise and flee to Laban my brother
28 2 of the daughters of Laban thy uncle
5 of Syria to Laban the son of Bathuel
29 5 know you Laban the son of Nachor? They
10 and that they were the sheep of Laban
19 Laban answered: It is better that I
21 and he said to Laban: Give me my wife
26 Laban answered: It is not the custom
31 1 heard the words of the sons of Laban
27 Laban said to him: Let me find favor
31 Laban said: What shall I give thee
34 Laban said: I like well what thou
31 12 I have seen all that Laban hath done to
19 time Laban was gone to shear his sheep
22 it was told Laban . . . that Jacob fled
33 so Laban went into the tent of Jacob
43 Laban answered him: The daughters are
47 and Laban called it The witness heap
48 L. said: This heap shall be a witness
55 Laban arose in the night and kissed
32 4 I have sojourned with Laban and have
46 18 sons of Zelpha, whom L. gave to Lia
25 sons of Bala, whom L. gave to Rachel
Deut 1 1 Thophel and Laban and Haseroth, where
Labana Josu 15 42 L. and Ether and Asan, Jephtha
Labanath Josu 19 26 and Sihor and Labanath, and it
Laban's Gen 30 40 the white and the black were L.

Gen 30 42 those that were lateward, became Laban's
31 2 Laban's countenance was not towards him
labor Gen 3 17 with labor and toil shalt thou eat
Gen 31 42 my affliction and labor of my hands
35 17 by reason of her hard labor she began
Exod 18 8 all the labor which had befallen them
18 thou art spent with foolish labor
20 9 six days shalt thou labor. Deut 5:13
Lev 26 20 your labor shall be spent in vain, the
Num 20 14 all the labor that hath come upon us
21 4 to be weary of their journey and labor
Deut 24 15 shalt pay him the price of his labor
25 18 when thou wast spent with hunger and l.
26 7 looked down upon our affliction and l.
Judg 19 22 drink, after the labor of the journey
1 K 4 19 she bowed herself and fell in labor
2 Pa 28 15 anointed them because of their labor
2 Es 3 16 pool, that was built with great labor
9 32 all the labor which hath come upon us
Tob 2 19 their living by the labor of her hands
Jdth 5 10 slaves of them to labor in clay and
Job 5 7 man is born to labor and the bird to
Ps 7 15 he hath been in labor with injustice
9 7 under his tongue are labor and sorrow
14 for thou considerest labor and sorrow
24 18 see my abjection and my labor; and
47 7 were pains as of a woman in labor
48 9 shall labor forever, and shall still
72 5 they are not in the labor of men
16 this thing, it is a labor in my sight
77 51 the firstfruits of all their labor
89 10 what is more of them is labor and
93 20 thee, who framest labor in commandment
103 23 and to his labor until the evening
104 36 the firstfruits of all their labor
126 1 they labor in vain that build it
139 10 l. of their lips shall overwhelm them
Prov 23 4 labor not to be rich: but set bounds
30 17 that despiseth the labor of his mother
Ecce 1 3 what hath a man more of all his labor
17 that in these also there was labor
18 addeth knowledge, addeth also labor
2 10 my portion, to make use of my own l.
22 profit shall a man have of all his l.
3 9 what hath man more of his labor
13 drinketh and seeth good of his labor
4 6 rest, than both hands full with labor
8 yet he ceaseth not to labor, neither
8 for whom do I l. and defraud my soul
5 14 take nothing away with him of his l.
17 drink and enjoy the fruit of his labor
18 portion and to rejoice of his labor
6 7 all the labor of man is for his mouth
8 15 take nothing else with him of his labor
17 and the more he shall labor to seek
9 9 in thy labor wherewith thou laborest
10 10 with much labor it shall be sharpened
15 the labor of fools shall afflict them
Wisd 6 15 early to seek her, shall not labor
9 10 be with me and may labor with me, that
16 with labor do we find the things that
15 4 a fruitless labor, a graven figure
7 with labor fashioneth every vessel for
8 clay by a vain labor maketh a god
9 his care is, not that he shall labor
16 20 bread from heaven prepared without l.
Eccu 6 20 in working about her thou shalt labor
13 32 thou shalt hardly find, and with labor
30 13 instruct thy son and labor about him
34 28 what profit have they but the labor
40 1 great labor is created for all men
Isa 5 27 that shall faint nor labor among them
13 8 shall be in pain as a woman in labor
14 3 shall give thee rest from thy labor
21 3 as the anguish of a woman in labor
22 4 weep bitterly: labor not to comfort me
23 4 saying: I have not been in labor, nor
26 18 conceived and been as it were in labor
40 28 he shall not faint nor labor, neither
30 youths shall faint and labor and young
42 14 I will speak now as a woman in labor
45 14 the labor of Egypt . . . shall come over
55 2 your l. for that which doth not satisfy
59 4 they have conceived labor and brought
65 23 my elect shall not labor in vain nor
66 7 before she was in l., she brought forth
8 Sion hath been in labor and hath
Jer 3 24 hath devoured the labor of our fathers
4 31 as of a woman in labor of a child
6 24 taken hold of us, as a woman in labor
13 21 lay hold on thee, as a woman in labor
20 5 substance of this city and all its l.
18 out of the womb, to see l. and sorrow
22 23 thee as the pains of a woman in labor
30 6 hands on his loins, like a woman in l.
48 41 as the heart of a woman in l. 49:22
49 24 have taken her as a woman in labor
50 43 hold of him, pangs as a woman in l.
Lam 3 5 hath compassed me with gall and labor
65 give them a buckler of heart, thy l.
Eze 30 16 shall be in pain like a woman in labor
Osee 13 13 sorrows of a woman in labor shall come
Mich 4 9 sorrow hath taken thee as a woman in l.
10 in pain and labor, O daughter of Sion
Haba 2 13 people shall labor in a great fire
3 17 the labor of the olive tree shall fail
Agge 1 11 and upon all the labor of the hands
Mala 1 13 and you have said: Behold of our labor
2 Ma 2 28 of many, we willingly undergo the l.
Mat 6 28 they l. not, neither do they. Luke 12:27
11 28 all you that labor and are burdened
John 4 38 reap that in which you did not labor
6 27 l. not for the meat which perisheth
16 21 a woman when she is in labor, hath
Rom 16 12 Tryphaena and Tryphosa, who labor in
1 C 3 8 own reward, according to his own labor
4 12 we labor, working with our own hands
15 58 knowing that your labor is not in vain
2 C 5 9 we labor, whether absent or present
11 27 brethren. In labor and painfulness, in
Gal 4 19 children, of whom I am in labor again
Eph 4 28 let him labor, working with his hands
Phil 1 22 flesh, this is to me the fruit of labor
Col 1 29 also I labor, striving according to his
4 13 that he hath much labor for you, and
1 Th 1 3 of the work of your faith, and labor
2 9 our labor and toil: working night and
3 5 and our labor should be made vain
5 12 to know them who labor among you, and
2 Th 3 8 in labor and in toil we worked night
10 for therefore we labor and are reviled
5 17 they who labor in the word and doctrine
2 Tim 1 8 but labor with the gospel, according to
2 3 labor as a good soldier of Christ Jesus
9 I labor even unto bands, as an evildoer
4 5 be thou vigilant, labor in all things
Heb 13 3 them that labor, as being yourselves
James 5 10 example of suffering evil, of labor
2 P 1 10 labor the more, that by good works
Apoc 2 2 I know thy works and thy labor and thy
labored Josu 24 13 land in which you had not l.
2 K 20 15 with Joab, l. to throw down the walls
Job 9 29 wicked, why have I labored in vain
39 16 she hath labored in vain, no fear
Ps 6 7 I have labored in my groanings, every
68 4 I have labored with crying: my jaws

Ecce 2 11 to the labors wherein I had labored in
18 wherewith I had earnestly labored
19 I have labored and been solicitous
5 15 him that he hath labored for the wind
17 wherewith he hath labored under the sun
Wisd 14 19 labored with all his art to make the
Eccu 16 27 they have neither hungered nor labored
24 47 I have not l. for myself only. 33:18
31 3 the rich man hath labored in gathering
4 the poor man hath labored in his low
51 35 how I have labored a little, and have
Isa 43 22 neither hast thou l. about me, O Israel
47 12 sorceries, in which thou hast labored
15 of thee, in which thou hast labored
49 4 I have labored in vain, I have spent
53 11 because his soul hath l., he shall
62 8 thy wine, for which thou hast labored
Jer 9 5 they have labored to commit iniquity
Eze 29 20 Egypt, because he hath labored for me
Dan 6 14 till sunset he labored to save him
Jon 4 10 ivy, for which thou hast not labored
Luke 5 5 Master, we have labored all the night
John 4 38 others have l., and you have entered
Rom 16 6 salute Mary, who hath l. much among
12 who hath much labored in the Lord
1 C 15 10 I have labored more abundantly than all
Gal 4 11 lest perhaps I have labored in vain
Phil 2 16 not run in vain, nor labored in vain
4 3 help those women who have labored with
laborer Wisd 17 16 shepherd or a l. in the field
Eccu 34 27 defraudeth the laborer of his hire
37 13 nor with the field laborer of every
40 18 the life of a laborer that is content
Luke 10 7 for the laborer is worthy of his hire
Rom 16 21 Timothy, my fellow laborer, saluteth
2 C 8 23 Titus, who is my . . . fellow laborer
Phil 2 25 my brother and fellow laborer, and
1 Tim 5 18 the laborer is worthy of his reward
Philem 1 to Philemon, our . . . fellow laborer
laborers Mat 9 37 the laborers are few. Luke 10:2
Mat 9 38 that he send forth laborers. Luke 10:2
20 1 to hire laborers into his vineyard
2 having agreed with the l. for a penny
8 call the l. and pay them their hire
Phil 4 3 the rest of my fellow laborers, whose
Philem 24 Demas and Luke my fellow laborers. The
James 5 4 the hire of the laborers, who have
laborest Ecce 9 9 wherewith thou l. under the sun
laboreth Prov 16 26 him that l., l. for himself
Ecce 2 21 for when a man laboreth in wisdom and
Eccu 10 30 better is he that l. and aboundeth
11 11 there is an ungodly man that laboreth
38 28 that laboreth night and day, he who
Mala 3 14 he laboreth in vain that serveth God
1 C 16 16 that worketh with us, and laboreth. And
2 Tim 2 6 the husbandman, that laboreth, must
laboring Ecce 2 20 heart renounced l. any more
Ecce 5 11 sleep is sweet to a l. man, whether
Mark 6 48 seeing them laboring in rowing, for
Acts 20 35 so l. you ought to support the weak
Phil 1 27 laboring together for the faith of the
laborious Eccu 7 16 hate not laborious works nor
labors Gen 5 29 comfort us from the works and l.
Gen 41 51 hath made me to forget all my labors
Deut 28 33 eat fruits of thy land and all thy l.
2 Es 5 13 out of his house and out of his l.
Job 39 11 strength and leave thy labors to him
Ps 77 46 blast, and their labors to the locust
87 16 poor and in labors from my youth: and
104 44 they possessed the labors of the people
106 12 their heart was humbled with labors
108 11 and let strangers plunder his labors
127 2 thou shalt eat the labors of thy hands
Prov 5 10 thy labors be in another man's house
Ecce 2 11 labors wherein I had labored in vain
19 he shall have rule over all my labors
24 his soul good things of his labors
4 4 I considered all the labors of men
Wisd 3 11 is vain and their labors without fruit
15 the fruit of good labors is glorious
5 1 them, and taken away their labors
8 7 justice: her labors have great virtues
10 10 made him honorable in his labors and accomplished his labors
17 to the just the wages of their labors
17 19 none were hindered in their labors
Eccu 14 15 to divide by lot thy sorrows and labors
16 2 their life and respect not their labors
28 19 women, and deprived them of their l.
33 27 meek, and continual labors bow a slave
38 26 is occupied in their labors, and his
Jer 51 58 l. of the people shall come to nothing
Eze 23 29 they shall take away all thy labors
Osee 12 8 my l. shall not find me the iniquity
1 Ma 10 15 and the labors that they had endured
John 4 38 and you have entered into their labors
2 C 6 5 in labors, in watchings, in fastings
10 15 beyond measure in other men's labors
11 23 in many more labors, in prisons more
Apoc 14 13 that they may rest from their labors
lace Judg 16 13 seven locks of my head with a l.
Judg 16 14 out the nail with the hairs and the l.
Cant 4 3 thy lips are as a scarlet lace: and
Lacedemon 2 Ma 5 9 to L. as if for kindred sake
Lachis Josu 10 3 and to Japhia king of Lachis
Josu 10 5 king of Lachis, the king of Eglon. 23
31 from Lebna he passed unto Lachis
32 Lord delivered Lachis into the hands
33 of Gazer came up to succor Lachis
34 and he passed from Lachis to Eglon
35 according to all that he had done to L.
12 11 Jerimoth one, the king of Lachis one
15 39 Lachis and Bascath and Eglon, Chebbon
4 K 14 19 he fled to Lachis. And they sent after him to Lachis and killed him
18 14 to the king of the Assyrians to Lachis
17 from Lachis to king Ezechias with a
19 8 heard that he was departed from Lachis
2 Pa 11 9 and Aduram and Lachis and Azecha
25 27 and he [Amasias] fled into Lachis
32 9 with all his army was besieging Lachis
2 Es 11 30 at Lachis and its dependencies, and at
Isa 36 2 sent Rabsaces from Lachis to Jerusalem
37 8 heard that he was departed from Lachis
Jer 34 7 against Lachis and against Azecha: for
Mich 1 13 hath astonished the inhabitants of L.
lad Judg 16 26 said to lad that guided his steps
ladder Gen 28 12 he saw in his sleep a ladder
Gen 28 13 the Lord leaning upon the ladder
ladders 1 Ma 5 30 carrying ladders and engines to
laded 2 Es 4 17 that carried burdens and that l.
Acts 28 10 they laded us with such things as were
laden Judg 19 10 leading with him two asses laden
1 K 16 20 Isai took an ass laden with bread and
2 K 3 34 nor thy feet laden with fetters: but
16 1 asses, laden with 200 loaves of bread
Jdth 15 7 them and they were laden exceedingly
Eccu 3 29 wicked heart shall be l. with sorrows
Isa 1 4 nation, a people laden with iniquity
Amos 2 13 wain, screaketh that is laden with hay
2 Tim 3 6 lead captive silly women l. with sins
lading 2 Es 13 15 l. asses with wine and grapes
Acts 27 10 not only of lading and ship, but also
lady Esth 15 7 and the other maid followed her lady
Isa 47 5 no more be called the lady of kingdoms
7 hast said: I shall be a lady forever

2 J 1 the ancient to the lady Elect, and her
5 I beseech thee, lady, not as writing
Lael Num 3 24 their prince Eliasaph the son of Lael
Lahela 1 Pa 5 26 and brought them to Lahela and to
Lahem 1 Pa 4 22 and who returned into Lahem. Now
laid Gen 15 10 laid the two pieces of each one
Gen 22 6 laid it upon Isaac his son: and he
9 and laid the wood in order upon it
9 laid him on the altar upon the pile
28 18 stone which he had laid under his head
50 25 he was laid in a coffin in Egypt
Exod 2 3 laid him in the sedges by the river's
15 26 of the evils that I laid upon Egypt
21 30 for his life whatsoever is laid upon
33 6 laid aside their ornaments by mount
34 22 returneth that all things are laid in
Lev 1 7 having before laid in order a pile of
8 31 loaves . . . that are laid in the basket
14 42 that other stones be laid in the place
Num 11 11 why hast thou laid the weight of all
23 2 they laid together a calf and a ram
4 have laid on every one a calf and a ram
30 he laid on every altar a calf and a ram
Deut 34 9 Moses had laid his hands upon him
Josu 14 15 among the Enacims was laid there: and
Judg 6 28 the second bullock laid upon the altar
9 34 laid ambushes near Sichem in four places
43 laid ambushes in the fields. And seeing
15 8 laid the calf of the leg upon the thigh
19 28 took her up and laid her upon his ass
20 38 whom they had laid in ambushes, that
Ruth 3 7 uncovering his feet, laid herself down
15 measures of barley and laid it upon her
4 16 taking the child laid it in her bosom
1 K 6 11 they laid the ark of God upon the cart
14 and laid the kine upon it a holocaust
7 12 stone and laid it between Masphath and
15 5 [Saul] laid ambushes in the torrent
27 laid hold upon the skirt of his mantle
17 39 not used to it. And he laid them off
19 13 took an image and laid it on the bed
25 18 of dry figs, and laid them upon asses
2 K 6 3 laid the ark of God upon a new cart
12 26 and laid close siege to the royal city
13 8 but he [Amnon] was laid down: and she
19 laid her hands upon her head and went
18 17 they laid an exceeding great heap of
22 16 foundations of the world were laid open
3 K 2 28 and laid hold on the horn of the altar
43 the commandment that I laid upon thee
3 20 and laid it in her bosom: and laid her dead child in my bosom
12 4 thy father laid a grievous yoke upon us
13 29 laid it upon the ass, and going back
30 laid his dead body in his own sepulcher
14 13 he only . . . shall be laid in a sepulcher
16 34 in Abiram . . . he laid its foundations
17 19 abode, and laid him upon his own bed
18 33 he [Elias] laid the wood in order and
33 in pieces and laid it upon the wood
4 K 4 21 laid him upon the bed of the man of God
31 laid the staff upon face of the child
5 23 and laid them upon two of his servants
9 13 man his garment laid it under his feet
25 Lord laid this burden upon him, saying
28 his servants laid him upon his chariot
11 16 they laid hands on her: and thrust her
12 11 they laid it out to the carpenters and
15 20 Manahem laid a tax upon Israel, on all
20 7 and laid it upon his boil, he was healed
2 Pa 3 3 are the foundations which Solomon laid
7 22 laid hold on strange gods and adored
10 4 who laid upon us a heavy servitude
9 ease the yoke which thy father laid upon
11 my father laid upon you a heavy yoke. 14
16 14 they laid him on his bed full of spices
23 15 and they laid hold on her by the neck
29 23 and they laid their hand upon them
1 Es 3 10 laid the foundations of the temple. 5:16
11 foundations of the temple . . . were laid
5 8 stones; and timber is laid in the walls
2 Es 13 25 I chid them and laid my curse upon them
Tob 8 2 liver, and laid it upon burning coals
Jdth 9 1 haircloth, laid ashes on her head: and
Job 29 9 and laid the finger on their mouth
31 9 if I have laid wait at my friend's door
38 4 when I laid the foundations of the
5 who hath laid the measures thereof, if
6 or who laid the corner stone thereof
Ps 48 15 they are laid in hell like sheep: death
65 11 thou hast laid afflictions on our back
80 15 laid my hand on them that troubled them
87 7 they have laid me in the lower pits in
88 20 I have laid help upon one that is mighty
118 110 sinners have laid a snare for me: but
138 5 me, and hast laid thy hand upon me
139 6 they have laid for me a stumblingblock
140 9 the snare which they have laid for me
Prov 26 26 his malice shall be laid open in the
27 19 hearts of men are laid open to the wise
30 32 would have laid his hand upon his mouth
Isa 19 7 channel of the river shall be laid bare
44 28 temple: Thy foundations shall be laid
47 6 hast laid thy yoke exceeding heavy
7 hast not l. these things to thy heart
51 23 thou hast laid thy body as the ground
53 6 Lord hath laid on him the iniquity of
57 7 lofty mountain, thou hast laid thy bed
Jer 8 5 they have laid hold on lying and have
20 12 for to thee I have laid open my cause
26 8 and all the people laid hold on him
Lam 2 14 they have not laid open thy iniquity
3 53 pit, and they have laid a stone over me
Bar 6 7 laid over with gold. 50, 56, 69, 70
Eze 4 5 and I have laid upon thee the years of
11 7 slain, whom you have laid in the midst
13 14 foundation thereof shall be laid bare
16 57 before thy malice was laid open: as it
32 25 are laid in the midst of the slain
27 laid their swords under their heads
39 21 and my hand that I have laid upon them
Dan 6 17 and laid upon the mouth of the den
18 laid himself down without taking supper
13 34 laid their hands upon her head. And
Osee 7 6 when he laid snares for them: he slept
Amos 2 8 garments laid to pledge by every altar
Mich 5 1 they have laid siege against us, with
Haba 2 19 it is laid over with gold and silver
3 13 thou hast laid bare his foundation
Agge 2 16 before there was a stone laid upon
19 day that the foundations . . . were laid
Zach 3 9 stone that I have laid before Jesus
4 9 have laid the foundations of this house
Mala 1 12 and that which is laid thereupon is
2 2 because you have not laid it to heart
1 Ma 3 48 they laid open the books of the law
6 8 he laid himself down upon his bed and
10 75 was in Joppe, and he laid siege to it
11 68 they laid an ambush for him in the
14 30 he was laid to his people. And their
32 laid out much of his money and armed
2 Ma 1 21 the sacrifices that were laid on, to be
21 and the things that were laid upon it
4 43 accusation was laid against Menelaus
10 33 laid siege to the fortress four days
11 5 he laid siege to that fortress. But

12 13 laid siege to a certain strong city
Mat 3 10 axe is laid to the root of. Luke 3:9
21 7 and laid their garments upon them and
22 6 the rest laid hands on his servants
26 50 laid hands on Jesus and held. Mark 14:46
55 temple, and you laid not hands on me
27 60 and laid it in his own new monument
28 6 see the place where the Lord was laid
Mark 6 19 now Herodias laid snares for him: and
29 took his body and laid it in a tomb
56 they laid the sick in the streets and
8 25 he laid his hands upon his eyes, and
12 3 having laid hands on him, beat him and
14 60 things that are laid to thy charge by
15 46 laid him in a sepulcher. Luke 23:53
47 Magdalen . . . beheld where he was laid
16 6 behold the place where they laid him
Luke 1 66 laid them up in their heart, saying
2 7 clothes, and laid him in a manger
12 swaddling clothes, and laid in a manger
6 48 and laid the foundation upon a rock
13 13 he laid his hands upon her, and
14 29 after he hath laid the foundation and
19 22 taking up what I laid not down and
23 26 they laid hold of one Simon of Cyrene
26 they laid the cross on him to carry
55 sepulcher, and how his body was laid
24 12 the linen cloths laid by themselves
John 7 30 no man laid hands on him. 44; 8:20
11 34 and said: Where have you laid him
38 a cave; and a stone was laid over it
19 41 wherein no man yet had been laid
42 there . . . they laid Jesus because
20 2 we know not where they have laid him
12 where the body of Jesus had been laid
13 I know not where they have laid him
15 tell me where thou hast laid him, and
21 9 and a fish laid thereon, and bread
Acts 3 2 whom they laid every day at the gate
4 3 they laid hands upon them and put
35 laid it down before the feet of the
37 l. it at feet of the apostles. 5:2
5 15 laid them on beds and couches, that
18 they laid hands on the apostles and
7 16 and were laid in the sepulcher that
57 laid down their garments at the feet
8 17 then they laid their hands upon them
9 37 they laid her in an upper chamber
13 29 tree, they laid him in a sepulcher
36 and was laid unto his fathers, and saw
16 23 they had laid many stripes upon them
34 he laid table for them, and rejoiced
20 3 spent 3 months, the Jews laid wait for
10 down, he laid himself upon him, and
21 27 stirred up all the people, and l. hands
23 29 but having nothing laid to his charge
25 16 clear himself of things l. to his charge
27 not to signify things l. to his charge
28 3 bundle of sticks, and had laid them on
8 when he had prayed, and l. his hands on
Rom 16 4 who have for my life laid down their
1 C 3 10 I have laid the foundation and another
11 no man can lay, but that which is laid
2 Tim 4 16 me: may it not be laid to their charge
Heb 9 10 laid on them until time of correction
1 J 3 16 because he hath laid down his life for
Apoc 1 17 he laid his right hand upon me, saying
11 9 not suffer their bodies to be laid in
20 2 and he laid hold of the dragon the old
laid up Gen 41 35 let all the corn be laid up
Gen 41 48 the abundance of grain was laid up in
Num 17 7 when Moses had laid them up before
Deut 33 21 in his portion the teacher was laid up
Josu 6 19 to the Lord, laid up in his treasures
Ruth 2 23 and the wheat were laid up in the barns
1 K 10 25 book and laid it up before the Lord
21 12 David laid up these words in his heart
3 K 7 51 laid them up in the treasures of the
4 K 5 24 laid them up in the house and sent the
20 17 that thy fathers have laid up in store
1 Es 6 1 the books that were laid up in Babylon
2 Es 13 5 they laid up gifts and frankincense
Job 19 27 this my hope is laid up in my bosom
Prov 24 32 I had seen, I laid it up in my heart
Isa 23 18 shall not be kept in store nor laid up
39 6 that thy fathers have laid up in store
Jer 36 20 they laid up the volume in the chamber
1 Ma 1 37 laid them up there: and they became
4 46 they laid up the stones in the mountain
2 Ma 8 31 laid them all up in covenient places
12 45 had great grace laid up for them. It
Luke 12 19 soul, thou hast much goods laid up
19 20 which I have kept laid up in a napkin
Col 1 5 hope that is laid up for you in heaven
2 Tim 4 8 as to the rest, there is laid up for me
laid waste Josu 8 24 returned and l. w. the city
4 K 16 9 against Damascus and laid it waste
19 11 how they have laid them waste: and
Ps 78 7 Jacob: and have laid waste his place
79 14 boar out of the wood hath l. it waste
Wisd 4 19 and they shall be utterly laid waste
Isa 1 8 and as a city that is laid waste
15 1 Ar of Moab is laid waste, it is silent
23 14 sea, for your strength is laid waste
24 3 desolation shall the earth be l. w.
37 18 kings of the Assyrians have l. w.
Jer 4 7 desolate: thy cities shall be l. w.
13 woe unto us, for we are laid waste
20 and all the earth is laid waste
10 20 my tabernacle is laid waste, all my
12 11 they have laid it waste, and it hath
25 38 the land is laid waste because of the
47 4 the Philistines shall be laid waste
48 1 woe to Nabo, for it is laid waste, and
15 Moab is laid waste, and they have cast
49 10 seed is laid waste, and his brethren
51 55 the Lord hath laid Babylon waste and
Eze 6 6 the cities shall be laid waste and the
12 20 are now inhabited shall be laid waste
25 3 of Israel, because it was laid waste
26 2 shall be filled, now she is laid waste
30 16 Alexandria shall be laid waste, and in
33 21 saying: The city is laid waste. And the
35 15 of Israel, because it was laid waste
15 thou shalt be laid waste, O mount Seir
Dan 3 96 destroyed, and their houses laid waste
Joel 1 7 he hath laid my vineyard waste and
Amos 7 9 sanctuaries of Israel shall be l. w.
Mich 2 4 we are l. w. and spoiled: the portion
5 1 shalt thou be laid waste, O daughter
Nah 2 2 the spoilers have laid them waste and
3 7 shall say: Ninive is laid waste: who
Zach 11 2 the mighty are laid waste: howl ye
3 because their glory is laid waste: the
1 Ma 2 12 our beauty and our glory is laid waste
lain Gen 26 10 might have lain with thy wife
Num 5 20 and hast lain with another man: these
Josu 10 27 into the cave where they had lain hid
2 K 13 20 hath thy brother Amnon lain with thee
Job 30 13 they had lain in wait against me and
Isa 34 14 there hath the lamia lain down and
Lais Judg 18 7 the five men going on came to Lais
Judg 18 14 had been sent to view the land of Lais
27 came to L. to a people that was quiet
29 Dan . . . which before was called Lais
1 K 25 44 wife, to Phalti the son of Lais, who

2 K 3 15 her husband Phaltiel the son of Lais
Laisa Isa 10 30 attend, O Laisa, poor Anathoth
1 Ma 9 5 Judas had pitched his tents in Laisa
lake 1 K 30 30 and that were in the lake Asan
1 Ma 9 33 pitched by the water of the lake Asphar
Luke 5 1 he stood by the lake of Genesareth
2 saw two ships standing by the lake
8 22 over to the other side of the lake
23 down a storm of wind upon the lake
33 place into the lake, and were stifled
Apoc 18 17 that sail into the lake, and mariners
lamb Exod 12 3 let every man take a lamb by their
Exod 12 4 less than may suffice to eat the lamb
4 which may be enough to eat the lamb
5 it shall be a lamb without blemish
21 go take a lamb by your families and
29 39 sacrifice . . . one lamb in the morning
40 with one lamb a tenth part of flour
41 the other lamb thou shalt offer in the
Lev 3 7 if he offer a lamb before the Lord, he
5 6 offer of the flocks an ewe lamb or a
9 3 goat for sin, and a calf and a lamb
12 6 a lamb of a year old for a holocaust. Num 7:15, 21, 27, 33, 39, 45, 51, 57, 63, 69, 75, 81
8 and she is not able to offer a lamb
14 12 he shall take a lamb and offer it for
13 he shall immolate the lamb where the
21 he shall take a lamb for an offering
24 priest receiving the lamb for trespass
25 the lamb being immolated, he shall put
23 12 lamb without blemish of the first
Num 6 12 offering a lamb of one year for sin
14 one he lamb of a year old without
14 one ewe lamb of a year old without
15 5 for every lamb and for every ram
12 for every ox and ram and lamb and kid
28 7 the fourth part of a hin for every lamb
8 you shall offer the other lamb in like
13 of a tenth of flour . . . for every lamb
14 third for a ram, and a fourth for a lamb
21 of a tenth to every lamb. 29; 29:10, 15
29 4 to a ram, one tenth to a lamb, which in
2 K 12 3 nothing at all but one little ewe lamb
Prov 7 22 as a lamb playing the wanton, and not
Eccu 13 21 fellowship with the lamb, so the sinner
46 19 when he offered a lamb without blemish
Isa 11 6 the wolf shall dwell with the lamb
16 1 send forth, O Lord, the lamb, the ruler
30 23 lamb in that day shall feed at large
53 7 and shall be dumb as a lamb before his
65 25 wolf and the lamb shall feed together
Jer 11 19 I was as a meek lamb that is carried
Eze 46 13 lamb of the same year without blemish
15 shall offer the lamb . . . morning by
Osee 4 16 feed them as a lamb in a spacious place
John 1 29 behold the Lamb of God. 36
Acts 8 32 like a lamb without voice before his
1 P 1 19 as of a lamb unspotted and undefiled
Apoc 5 6 a Lamb standing as it were slain
8 ancients fell down before the Lamb
12 the Lamb that was slain is worthy to
13 to the Lamb benediction and honor and
6 1 I saw that the Lamb had opened one of
16 and from the wrath of the Lamb: for
7 9 the throne and in sight of the Lamb
10 upon the throne, and to the Lamb. And
14 them white in the blood of the Lamb
17 the Lamb, which is in the midst of the
12 11 overcame him by the blood of the Lamb
13 8 in the book of life of the Lamb, which
11 he had two horns, like a lamb, and he
14 4 they follow the Lamb whithersoever he
4 the firstfruits to God and to the Lamb
10 angels, and in the sight of the Lamb
15 3 and the canticle of the Lamb, saying
17 14 shall fight with the Lamb, and the Lamb shall overcome them
19 7 for the marriage of the Lamb is come
9 to the marriage supper of the Lamb
21 9 thee the bride, the wife of the Lamb
14 names of the 12 apostles of the Lamb
22 is the temple thereof, and the Lamb
23 and the Lamb is the lamp thereof
27 written in the book of life of the Lamb
22 1 from the throne of God and of the Lamb
3 throne of God and of the Lamb shall be
lambs Gen 21 28 Abraham set apart seven ewe lambs
Gen 21 29 what mean these seven ewe lambs which
30 thou shalt take seven ewe lambs at my
33 19 that part of the field . . . for 100 lambs
Exod 29 38 two lambs of a year old. Num 28:3, 9
Lev 14 10 he shall take two lambs without blemish
23 18 shall offer with the loaves seven lambs
19 two l. of the first year for sacrifices
Num 7 17 five lambs of a year old. 23, 29, 35, 47, 53, 65, 71, 77, 83
87 twelve lambs of a year old, and their
88 goats sixty, lambs of a year old sixty
28 11 seven l. of a year old. 19; 29:2, 8, 36
21 of a tenth . . . to all the seven lambs
29 in all are seven lambs. 29:4, 10
29 13 fourteen lambs of a year old. 17, 20, 23, 29, 32
15 being in all fourteen lambs: and a
18 libations . . . for the lambs. 21, 24, 27, 30, 33, 37
Deut 32 14 milk of the sheep with fat of lambs
1 K 15 4 Saul . . . numbered them as lambs
4 K 3 4 paid to king of Israel 100,000 lambs
1 Pa 29 21 a thousand lambs with their libations
2 Pa 29 21 seven lambs and seven he goats for
22 and they killed the lambs and poured
32 a hundred rams and 200 lambs. And they
35 7 solemnity of the phase, of lambs and of
1 Es 6 9 let calves also and lambs and kids
17 hundred calves, 200 rams, 400 lambs
7 17 with this money, calves, rams, lambs
8 35 96 rams, 77 lambs, and 12 he goats
Ps 113 4 hills like the lambs of the flock. 6
Prov 27 26 lambs are for thy clothing: and kids
Wisd 19 9 they skipped like lambs, praising thee
Eccu 47 3 he played with lions as with lambs: and
3 manner as with the lambs of the flock
Isa 1 11 blood of calves and l. and buck goats
5 17 the lambs shall feed according to their
34 6 is made thick with the blood of lambs
40 11 shall gather together the l. with his
Jer 51 40 I will bring them down like lambs to
Eze 27 21 thy merchants came to thee with lambs
39 18 of rams and of lambs and of he goats
46 4 shall be six lambs without blemish
5 for the lambs what sacrifice his hand
6 six lambs and the rams shall be without
7 for the lambs, as his hand shall find
11 to the lambs, the sacrifice shall be
Dan 3 40 and as in thousands of fat lambs: so
Amos 6 4 that eat the lambs out of the flock
Luke 10 3 I send you as lambs among wolves: carry
John 21 15 he saith to him: Feed my lambs. 16
lame Lev 21 18 if he be blind, if he be lame
Deut 15 21 if it have a blemish or be lame or
2 K 4 4 had a son that was lame of his feet
4 haste to flee, he fell and became lame
5 6 take away the blind and the lame. 8
8 blind and the lame shall not come into
9 3 son of Jonathan left, who is lame of

13 he [Miphiboseth] was lame of both feet
19 26 the king: for I thy servant am lame
Prov 26 6 is lame of feet and drinketh iniquity
7 as a lame man hath fair legs in vain
29 15 eye to the blind, and a foot to the lame
Isa 33 23 divided: the lame shall take the spoil
35 6 then shall the lame man leap as a hart
Jer 31 8 shall be the blind and the lame, the
Mala 1 8 if you offer the lame and the sick
13 you brought in of rapine the lame and
Mat 11 5 blind see, the lame walk. Luke 7:22
15 30 the blind, the lame, the maimed, and
31 seeing the dumb speak, the lame walk
18 8 thee to go into life maimed or lame
21 14 came to him the blind and the lame in
Mark 9 44 better for thee to enter lame into
14 13 call the poor, the maimed, the lame
21 feeble and the blind and the lame
John 5 3 sick, of blind, of lame, of withered
Acts 3 2 a certain man who was lame from his
8 8 with the palsy, and that were lame
Lamech Gen 4 18 Mathusael begot Lamech: who took
Gen 4 23 Lamech said to his wives . . . Hear my
voice, ye wives of Lamech
24 for Lamech seventy times sevenfold
5 25 Mathusala lived . . . and begot Lamech
26 Mathusala lived after he begot Lamech
28 Lamech lived 182 years and begot a son
30 and Lamech lived after he begot Noe
31 the days of Lamech came to 777 years
1 Pa 1 3 Henoc, Mathusale, Lamech, Noe, Sem
Luke 3 36 Noe, who was of Lamech, who was of
lamed Ps 118 89 lamed. Lam 1:12; 2:12; 3:34, 35, 36;
4:12
lament Judg 11 40 and l. the daughter of Jephte
Judg 21 2 began to lament and weep, saying
Job 10 20 that I may lament my sorrow a little
Eccu 38 16 begin to l. as if thou hadst suffered
Isa 3 26 her gates shall lament and mourn and
16 9 I will l. with the weeping of Jazer
19 8 that cast a hook into the river shall l.
59 11 and shall lament as mournful doves
Jer 4 8 with haircloth, lament and howl: for
28 the heavens shall lament from above
22 10 lament him that goeth away, for he
18 they shall not lament for him, Alas my
48 31 will I lament for Moab, and I will cry
Eze 24 16 and thou shalt not lament nor weep
27 32 song for thee and shall lament thee
32 16 and they shall lament therewith: the
16 daughters of the nations shall lament
16 they shall l. therewith: the daughters
Joel 1 8 lament like a virgin girded with
13 gird yourselves and lament, O ye
Amos 5 16 are skilful in lamentation to lament
Mich 1 8 will I l. and howl: I will go stripped
John 16 20 you shall lament and weep, but the
lamentable Wisd 18 10 a l. mourning was heard for
Dan 6 20 cried with a l. voice to Daniel and
lamentation Gen 50 10 a great and vehement l.
2 K 1 17 David made this kind of lamentation
1 Es 10 1 the people wept with much lamentation
Tob 2 6 festival days shall be turned into l.
Jdth 7 18 there was great weeping and lamentation
Jer 6 26 as for an only son, a bitter l. because
7 29 and take up a lamentation on high
9 10 I will take up weeping and lamentation
18 let them hasten and take up a l. for
31 15 voice was heard on high of lamentation
Eze 19 1 take thou up a l. for the princes of
14 there is a l., and it shall be for a l.
26 17 taking up a lamentation over thee, they
27 2 take up a lamentation for Tyre: and say
28 11 take up a l. upon the king of Tyre
32 2 take up a lamentation for Pharao the
16 this is the l., and they shall lament
Amos 5 1 I take up concerning you for a l.
16 such as are skilful in l. to lament
8 10 mourning, and all your songs into l.
Zach 12 11 there shall be a great l. in Jerusalem
11 like the lamentation of Adaremmon in
1 Ma 1 28 every bridegroom took up lamentation
2 14 with haircloth and made great l. And
4 39 rent their garments and made great l.
9 20 bewailed him with great lamentation
41 of their musical instruments into l.
12 52 Israel mourned with great lamentation
13 26 all Israel bewailed him with great l.
Mat 2 18 a voice in Rama was heard, lamentation
lamentations 2 Pa 35 25 whose l. for Josias all the
2 Pa 35 25 it is found written in the Lamentations
Eze 2 9 there were written in it lamentations
2 Ma 11 6 besought the Lord with l. and tears
lamented 1 K 6 19 the people l. because the Lord
Ps 77 63 and their maidens were not lamented
Jer 16 4 they shall not be lamented. 25:33
6 they shall not be buried nor lamented
Mat 11 17 we have l., and you have not mourned
Luke 23 27 women, who bewailed and lamented him
lamenting 2 K 3 33 king mourning and l. over Abner
Wisd 19 3 and lamenting at the graves of the dead
lamia Isa 34 14 there hath the lamia lain down
lamma Mat 27 46 Eli, Eli, lamma sabacthani? That is
Mark 15 34 Eloi, Eloi, lamma sabacthani? Which is
lamp Gen 15 17 furnace and a lamp of fire passing
Exod 27 20 that a lamp may burn always in the
1 K 3 3 before the l. of God went out, Samuel
2 K 21 17 lest thou put out the lamp of Israel
22 29 for thou art my lamp, O Lord: and
3 K 11 36 may remain a lamp for my servant David
15 4 his God gave him a lamp in Jerusalem
2 Pa 21 7 he had promised to give a lamp to him
Job 12 5 the lamp despised in the thoughts of
18 6 l. that is over him, shall be put out
21 17 how often shall the lamp of the wicked
29 3 when his lamp shined over my head and
Ps 17 29 thou lightest my lamp, O Lord: O my
118 105 thy word is a lamp to my feet and a
131 17 I have prepared a lamp for my anointed
Prov 6 23 the commandment is a lamp, and the law
13 9 l. of the wicked shall be put. 24:20
20 20 his lamp shall be put out in the midst
27 spirit of a man is the lamp of the Lord
21 4 the heart: the lamp of the wicked is sin
31 18 her lamp shall not be put out in the
Eccu 26 22 lamp shining upon the holy candlestick
Isa 62 1 and her savior be lighted as a lamp
Jer 25 10 of the mill, and the light of the lamp
Dan 10 6 his eyes as a burning lamp: and his
Zach 4 2 of gold, and its lamp upon the top of it
3 one upon the right side of the lamp
Luke 11 36 as a bright lamp, shall enlighten thee
Apoc 18 23 light of the l. shall shine no more
21 23 the Lamb is the lamp thereof. And the
22 5 shall not need the light of the lamp
lamps Exod 25 37 shalt make also seven lamps, and
Exod 30 7 when he shall dress the lamps, he shall
35 14 the vessels thereof and the lamps and
37 23 he made also the seven lamps with
39 36 the lamps and the furniture of them
40 4 candlestick shall stand with its lamps
23 placing the lamps in order according
Lev 24 2 oil of olives to furnish the lamps
Num 4 9 necessary for the dressing of the lamps
9 cover the candlestick with the lamps
16 pertaineth the oil to dress the lamps

8 2 when thou shalt place the seven lamps
2 the lamps look over against the north
3 he put the lamps upon the candlestick
Judg 7 16 pitchers, and lamps within the pitchers
20 held their lamps in their left hands
3 K 7 49 and the lamps over them of gold: and
1 Pa 28 15 golden candlesticks and their lamps
15 candlesticks and for their lamps
15 every candlestick and the lamps thereof
2 Pa 4 20 with their lamps to give light before
21 certain flowers and lamps and golden
13 11 golden candlestick and the l. thereof
29 7 put out the lamps and have not burnt
Job 41 10 out of his mouth go forth lamps, like
Cant 8 6 the lamps thereof are fire and flames
Eze 1 13 fire and like the appearance of lamps
Soph 1 12 I will search Jerusalem with lamps
1 Ma 4 50 lighted up the lamps that were upon
6 39 and they shone like lamps of fire
2 Ma 1 8 lighted the l. and set forth the loaves
10 3 and set forth incense and lamps and
Mat 25 1 taking their lamps went out to meet the
3 having taken their lamps, did not take
4 oil in their vessels with the lamps
7 virgins arose and trimmed their lamps
8 your oil for our lamps are gone out
Luke 12 35 girt, and lamps burning in your hands
Acts 20 8 there were a great number of lamps in
Apoc 4 5 seven lamps burning before the throne
Lampsacus 1 Ma 15 23 to L. and to the Spartans
Lamuel Prov 31 1 the word of king Lamuel. The
Prov 31 4 give not to kings, O Lamuel, give not
lance 2 K 23 7 iron and with the staff of a lance
lances 2 K 18 14 took three lances in his hand
Job 16 14 compassed me round about with his l.
Prov 26 18 shooteth arrows and lances unto death
lancets 3 K 18 28 with knives and lancets till
landmark Deut 19 14 nor remove thy neighbor's l.
landmarks Deut 27 17 that removeth neighbor's l.
Job 24 2 some have removed landmarks, have
lands Gen 10 5 of the Gentiles in their lands
Gen 10 20 generations and lands and nations
11 4 we be scattered abroad into all lands
8 them from that place into all lands
47 18 now left but our bodies and our lands
19 will be thine, both we and our lands
23 you and your lands belong to Pharao
Num 32 1 when they saw the lands of Jazer and
Deut 9 5 thou shalt go in to possess their lands
Josu 10 42 their kings and their lands he took
17 16 Chanaanites that dwell in the low lands
2 K 9 7 will restore the l. of Saul thy father
3 K 2 26 go to Anathoth to thy lands, for indeed
4 K 8 3 king for her house and for her lands. 5
6 hers, and all the revenues of the lands
19 17 have destroyed nations, and the lands
2 Pa 9 14 lords of the lands, who brought gold
17 10 the lands that were round about Juda
20 10 through whose l. thou didst not allow
29 fell upon all the kingdoms of the lands
32 13 have done to all the people of the l.
13 have the gods of any nations and lands
1 Es 3 3 the people of the lands round about
9 1 from the people of the lands. 2 Es 10:28
2 holy seed with the people of the lands
7 into the hands of the kings of the l.
11 the uncleanness . . . of other lands
2 Es 5 3 that said: Let us mortgage our lands
9 30 into the hand of the people of the l.
Jdth 5 20 they possessed their lands and their
Esth 8 13 be notified in all lands and peoples
Job 5 23 a covenant with the stones of the lands
Ps 48 12 have called their lands by their names
104 44 gave them the lands of the Gentiles
Eccu 10 19 overthrown the lands of the Gentiles
Isa 8 9 and give ear, all ye lands afar off
36 20 among all the gods of these lands
37 18 the Assyrians have laid waste lands
Jer 6 12 over to others, with their lands and
16 15 all the lands to which I cast them out
23 3 of my flock, out of all the lands
8 brought hither . . . out of all the l.
27 6 I have given all these lands into the
32 37 lands to which I have cast them out
Eze 20 6 which excelleth amongst all lands
15 into the land . . . the best of all lands
41 the lands into which you are scattered
25 7 and destroy thee out of the lands
29 12 midst of the l. that are desolate. 30:7
32 9 among the nations upon the lands
35 10 the two lands shall be mine and I will
39 27 out of the lands of their enemies and
Dan 11 42 he shall lay his hand upon the lands
1 Ma 7 7 all the havock . . . in the king's lands
Mat 19 29 that hath left . . . lands. Mark 10:29
Mark 10 30 mothers and children and lands with
Acts 4 34 as were owners of lands or houses
lanes Luke 14 21 into streets and lanes of the city
language Gen 11 9 language of the whole earth was
Gen 31 47 according to the propriety of his l.
4 K 18 26 speak not to us in the Jews' language
28 cried out . . . in the Jews' language
2 Es 13 24 could not speak the Jews' language
24 they spoke according to the language
Isa 19 18 speaking the language of Chanaan and
36 11 speak not to us in the Jews' language
13 with a loud voice in the Jews' language
Jer 5 15 whose language thou shalt not know
2 Ma 7 8 but he answered in his own language
21 exhorted every one of them in her own l.
27 she said in her own language: My son
12 37 beginning in his own l., and singing
15 29 blessed the Almighty Lord in their own l.
37 called, in the Syrian l., the day before
languages Esth 1 22 sent letters . . . in divers l.
Esth 3 12 according to their different l.
8 9 according to their l. and characters
Ps 18 4 there are no speeches nor languages
Dan 3 4 is commanded, O nations, tribes, and l.
7 all the . . . languages fell down and
5 19 all people, tribes, and l. trembled
6 25 to all people, tribes, and languages
Zach 8 23 ten men of all l. of the Gentiles
languish Cant 2 5 because I languish with love
Cant 5 8 that you tell him that I l. with love
Isa 19 8 spread nets . . . shall languish away
Lam 3 20 and my soul shall languish within me
Eze 21 15 languish in heart, and that multiplieth
Osee 4 3 that dwelleth in it shall languish
1 Ma 4 32 boldness of their strength to languish
languished Ps 87 10 my eyes l. through poverty
Isa 24 7 mourned, the vine hath languished away
33 9 the land hath mourned and languished
Dan 8 27 I Daniel l. and was sick for some
Joel 1 10 wine is confounded, the oil hath l.
12 and the fig tree hath languished
languisheth Nah 1 4 Basan l. and Carmel: and
languishing Deut 28 32 l. at the sight of them
Deut 28 65 Lord will give thee . . . languishing eyes
2 Es 2 1 I was as one l. away before his face
lanterns John 18 3 cometh thither with lanterns and
Laodicea Col 2 1 for them that are at L. 4:13
Col 4 15 salute the brethren who are at Laodicea
Apoc 1 11 and to Philadelphia and to Laodicea
3 14 to the angel of the church of Laodicea
Laodiceans Col 4 16 be read also in church of the L.

Col 4 16 you read that which is of the L.
Laomin 1 Pa 1 32 Assurim and Latussim and L.
lap Gen 48 12 taken them from his father's lap
Judg 7 5 that shall lap the water with their tongues, as dogs are wont to lap
2 Es 5 13 I shook my lap and said: So may God
Prov 16 33 lots are cast into the lap, but they
lapidary Exod 39 6 and graven by the art of a l.
Exod 39 29 on it with the engraving of a lapidary
Eccu 45 13 graven by the work of a lapidary for
Lapidoth Judg 4 4 Debbora a prophetess wife of L.
lapped Judg 7 6 of them that had lapped water
Judg 7 7 by the 300 men that lapped water I will
large Gen 24 25 and a large place to lodge in
Gen 34 21 large and wide wanteth men to till it
Josu 13 1 there is a very large country left
2 K 18 9 mule went under a thick and large oak
22 20 he brought me forth into a large place
2 Es 9 35 in the large and fat land which thou
Jdth 8 7 man servants and large possessions
Job 36 16 he shall set thee at large out of the
Ps 17 20 he brought me forth into a large place
118 45 walked at large: because I have sought
Isa 22 18 into a large and spacious country
30 23 lamb in that day shall feed at large
Jer 22 14 me a wide house and large chambers
Eze 16 26 thy neighbors, men of large bodies
17 3 a large eagle with great wings
7 and there was another large eagle with
8 that it might become a large vine
Mark 14 15 show you a l. dining room. Luke 22:12
largeness 3 K 4 29 l. of heart as the sand that
larger Num 33 54 you shall give a larger part
Amos 6 2 if their border be larger than your
larus Lev 11 16 you must not eat . . . the larus
Deut 14 15 the owl and the larus and the hawk
lasciviousness Mark 7 22 deceit, l., an evil eye
2 C 12 21 lasciviousness, that they have committed
Eph 4 19 given themselves up to lasciviousness
last Gen 19 34 I lay last night with my father
Gen 30 42 coming was, and the last conceiving
33 2 place: and Rachel and Joseph last
7 last of all Joseph and Rachel bowed
47 2 five men also the last of his brethren
49 1 that shall befall you in the last days
Num 2 31 they shall march last. This is the
10 25 the last . . . marched the sons of Dan
23 10 just, and my last end be like to them
24 24 at the last they themselves also shall
34 12 at the last shall be closed in by the
Deut 8 16 at the last he had mercy on thee
32 20 consider what their last end shall be
29 and would provide for their last end
Josu 6 26 in the last of his children set up
8 13 last of that multitude reached to the
Judg 20 5 fury of lust, so that at last she died
1 K 9 21 my kindred the last among all the
2 K 19 11 why are you the last to bring the king
12 you the last to bring back the king
23 1 now these are David's last words
3 K 14 10 shut up, and the last in Israel. 21:21
1 Pa 23 27 according to the last precepts of David
29 29 the acts of . . . first and last. 2 Pa 9:29; 12:15; 20:34; 25:26; 26:22
2 Pa 16 11 works of Asa first and last are written
28 26 his works first and last are. 35:27
35 14 for the priests the sons of Aaron last
1 Es 8 13 sons of Adonicam, who were the last
2 Es 8 18 read . . . from first day till the last
Ps 72 17 understand concerning their last ends
93 8 people: and, you fools, be wise at last
138 5 all things, the last and those of old
Prov 5 11 and thou mourn at the last, when thou
Wisd 3 17 last old age shall be without honor
Eccu 3 27 hard heart shall fear evil at the last
7 40 remember thy last end, and thou shalt
12 12 at the last thou acknowledge my words
13 8 and at last he will laugh at thee
14 7 at the l. he discovereth his wickedness
27 26 at the last he will writhe his mouth
28 6 remember thy last things, and let
30 10 at the last thy teeth be set on edge
33 16 I awaked last of all, and as one that
48 27 things that are to come to pass at last
Isa 2 2 in the last days the mountain of the
9 1 at the last the way of the sea beyond
41 4 the Lord, I am the first and the last
44 6 I am the first and I am the last. 48:12
46 10 the things that shall be at last and
56 11 gain, from the first even to the last
Jer 12 4 said: He shall not see our last end
31 17 and there is hope for thy last end
48 47 the captivity of Moab in the last days
50 12 she shall be the last among the nations
17 and last this Nabuchodonosor king of
Bar 6 71 they themselves at last are consumed
Eze 35 5 in the time of their last iniquity
Osee 3 5 Lord and his goodness in the last days
Amos 9 1 I will slay the last of them with the
Mich 4 1 it shall come to pass in the last days
Agge 2 10 great be the glory of this last house
Zach 14 8 half of them to the last sea: they shall
2 Ma 5 8 at the last having been shut up by
7 9 when he was at the last gasp, he said
41 last of all . . . the mother also was
Mat 5 26 till thou repay the last farthing
12 45 the last state of that man is made
19 30 that are first, shall be last: and the last shall be first
20 8 beginning from the last even to the
12 these last have worked but one hour
14 I will also give to this last even as
16 the last be first, and the first last
21 37 last of all he sent to them his son
22 27 last of all the woman died also. Mark 12:22; Luke 20:32
25 11 at last came also the other virgins
26 60 last of all there came two false
27 64 the last error shall be worse than the
Mark 9 34 to be first, he shall be the last of
10 31 first shall be l.: and the l., first
12 6 he also sent him unto them last of all
Luke 11 26 the last state of that man becomes
12 59 until thou pay the very last mite
13 30 they are last that shall be first
30 and they are first that shall be last
Acts 2 17 in the last days . . . I will pour out
1 C 4 9 God hath set forth us apostles, the last
15 8 last of all, he was seen also by me, as
26 enemy death shall be destroyed last: For
45 the last Adam into a quickening spirit
52 at the last trumpet: for the trumpet
1 Tim 4 1 in the last times some shall depart from
2 Tim 3 1 in the last days, shall come dangerous
Heb 1 1 fathers by the prophets, last of all
James 5 3 wrath against the last days. Behold
1 P 1 5 ready to be revealed in the last time
20 manifested in the last times for you
2 P 3 3 that in the last days there shall come
1 J 2 18 little children, it is the last hour
18 we know that it is the last hour
Apoc 1 17 I am the First and the Last. 22:13
2 8 saith the First and the Last, who was
19 thy last works which are more than the
15 1 seven angels having the 7 last plagues
21 9 vials full of the seven last plagues

last day Job 19 25 in last day I shall rise
Eccu 18 24 wrath that shall be at the last day
John 6 39 raise it up again in the last day
40 I will raise him up in last day. 44, 45
7 37 on last and great day of the festivity
11 24 he shall rise again . . . at last day
12 48 the same shall judge him in last day
last days Gen 49 1 befall you in the last days
Isa 2 2 in the last days the mountain of the
Jer 48 47 the captivity of Moab in the last days
Osee 3 5 and his goodness in the last days
Acts 2 17 in the last days . . . I will pour out
2 Tim 3 1 in last days shall come dangerous times
James 5 3 to yourselves wrath against last days
2 P 3 3 in last days there shall come deceitful
Lasthenes 1 Ma 11 31 which we have written to L.
1 Ma 11 32 king Demetrius to Lasthenes his parent
lasting Lev 14 44 it is a lasting leprosy, and the
Deut 28 59 shall increase . . . plagues great and l.
Ecce 2 11 that nothing was lasting under the sun
Heb 10 34 have a better and a lasting substance
13 14 we have not here a lasting city, but
latchet Gen 14 23 woof thread unto the shoe l.
Isa 5 27 nor latchet of their shoes be broken
Mark 1 7 the latchet of whose shoes I am not worthy. Luke 3:16; John 1:27
late Jdth 5 23 of late returning to the Lord their
Jdth 13 1 when it was grown late, his servants
Prov 7 9 in the dark, when it grows late, in
2 Ma 13 11 had of late taken breath for a little
Mark 6 47 when it was late, the ship was in the
John 20 19 when it was late that same day, the
lately Deut 24 5 when a man hath l. taken a wife
Eze 11 3 were not houses lately built? This city
2 Ma 14 36 undefiled which was lately cleansed
Acts 18 2 lately come from Italy with Priscilla
lateward Gen 30 42 that were l., became Laban's
Exod 9 32 not hurt, because they were lateward
Jer 2 31 to Israel, or a lateward springing land
3 3 and there was no lateward rain: thou
Latin Luke 23 38 in letters of Greek and Latin and
John 19 20 written in Hebrew, in Greek, and in L.
Apoc 9 11 Greek Apollyon; in Latin Exterminans
latitude Gen 26 22 he called the name thereof, L.
latter Gen 29 30 he preferred the love of the l.
Gen 30 42 when the latter coming was and the last
Exod 4 8 will believe the word of the l. sign
Num 24 14 do to thy people in the latter days
20 whose latter ends shall be destroyed
Deut 4 30 in the latter time thou shalt return
11 14 the early rain and the latter rain. Jer 5:24; Osee 6:3; Joel 2:23
31 29 shall come upon you in the l. times
Ruth 3 10 thy latter kindness has surpassed the
Job 8 7 thy latter things would be multiplied
29 23 opened their mouth as for a l. shower
Prov 16 15 his clemency is like the latter rain
31 25 and she shall laugh in the latter day
Isa 30 8 it shall be in the latter days for a
Jer 23 20 in the l. days you shall understand
49 39 in the latter days I will cause the
Eze 38 16 thou shalt be in the latter days
Dan 2 28 is to come to pass in the l. times
10 14 befall thy people in the latter days
11 29 the latter time shall not be like
Amos 7 1 the shooting up of the latter rain
1 it was the latter rain after the
Zach 10 1 ask . . . rain in the latter season
James 5 7 till he receive the early and l. rain
2 P 2 20 their latter state is become unto them
latter end; ***see*** **end**
lattice Prov 7 6 of my house through the lattice
lattices 4 K 1 2 Ochozias fell through the lattices
Cant 2 9 the windows, looking through the l.
Latusim Gen 25 3 children of Dadan were . . . Latusim
Latussim 1 Pa 1 32 sons of Dadan: Assurim and L.
laugh Gen 18 13 why did Sara laugh, saying: Shall
Gen 18 15 Sara denied, saying: I did not laugh
15 Lord said: Nay, but thou didst laugh
21 6 shall hear of it will laugh with me
Job 5 22 in destruction and famine thou shalt l.
9 23 not laugh at the pains of the innocent
21 3 after, if you please, laugh at my words
22 19 the innocent shall laugh them to scorn
41 20 he will laugh him to scorn who shaketh
Ps 2 4 that dwelleth in heaven shall laugh
24 3 neither let my enemies laugh at me
36 13 but the Lord shall laugh at him: for
51 8 the just . . . shall laugh at him, and
58 9 but thou, O Lord, shalt laugh at them
Prov 1 26 I also will laugh in your destruction
14 9 a fool will laugh at sin, but among
29 9 whether he be angry or laugh, he shall
31 25 and she shall laugh in the latter day
Ecce 3 4 a time to weep and a time to laugh
Wisd 4 18 but the Lord shall laugh them to scorn
Eccu 7 12 l. no man to scorn in the bitterness
13 8 and at last he will laugh at thee
20 18 and how many will laugh him to scorn
21 23 a wise man will scarce laugh low to
30 10 laugh not with him, lest thou have
Haba 1 10 he shall laugh at every stronghold
Luke 6 21 ye that weep now; for you shall laugh
25 woe to you that now laugh: for you
laughed Gen 17 17 Abraham . . . laughed, saying in
Gen 18 10 she laughed behind the door of the tent
12 she laughed secretly, saying: After I
4 K 19 21 daughter of Sion . . . l. thee to scorn
2 Pa 30 10 they laughed at them and mocked them
Job 12 4 of the just man is laughed to scorn
29 24 if at any time I laughed on them, they
Ps 21 8 that saw me have laughed me to scorn
Wisd 17 8 of a fear worthy to be laughed at. For
Isa 37 22 despised thee and l. thee to scorn
Jer 51 18 vain works, and worthy to be l. at
Dan 14 18 Daniel laughed: and he held the king
1 Ma 10 70 I am laughed at and reproached because
Mat 9 24 they laughed him to scorn. Mark 5:40; Luke 8:53
laugheth Prov 15 5 fool l. at the instruction
laughingstock Eccu 42 11 she make thee become a l.
Jer 20 7 I am become a laughingstock all the
Haba 1 10 princes shall be his laughingstock
laughter Gen 21 6 God hath made a laughter for me
Job 8 21 until thy mouth be filled with laughter
Prov 14 13 laughter shall be mingled with sorrow
Ecce 2 2 laughter I counted error: and to mirth
7 4 anger is better than laughter: because
7 under a pot, so is the l. of a fool
10 19 for laughter they make bread, and
Eccu 19 27 laughter of the teeth and the gate of
21 23 fool lifteth up his voice in laughter
27 14 their l. is at the pleasures of sin
James 4 9 your laughter be turned into mourning
launch Luke 5 4 launch out into the deep, and let
launched Luke 8 22 of the lake. And they l. forth
Acts 27 2 we l., meaning to sail by coasts of Asia
4 when we had l. from thence, we sailed
laver Exod 30 18 shalt make also a brazen laver
Exod 31 9 vessels, the laver with its foot. 40:11
35 16 vessels thereof, the laver and its foot
38 8 he made also the laver of brass with
39 39 laver with the foot thereof. Lev 8:11
40 7 the laver between the altar and the
28 set the laver between the tabernacle
3 K 7 26 and the laver was a handbreadth thick

30 were undersetters under the l. molten
31 the mouth also of the laver within
35 that the laver might be set thereon
38 one laver contained four bases and was
4 K 16 17 king Achaz took away . . . the laver
Eph 5 26 by the laver of water in word of life
Titus 3 5 saved us, by the laver of regeneration
lavers 3 K 7 38 he made also ten lavers. 2 Pa 4:6
3 K 7 38 upon every base . . . he put as many l.
43 bases, and the ten lavers on the bases
2 Pa 4 14 he made also bases and lavers, which
law Gen 47 26 it is become as a law, except the
Exod 12 24 thou shalt keep this thing as a law
49 same law shall be to him that is born
24 12 give thee tables of stone and the law
28 43 it shall be a law forever to Aaron
30 21 it shall be an everlasting law to him
Lev 3 17 a perpetual law for your generations
6 9 this is the law of a holocaust: It shall
14 this is the law of the sacrifice and
25 this is the law of the victim for sin
7 1 the law of the sacrifice for a trespass
7 same shall be the law of both these
11 law of the sacrifice of peace offerings
34 and to his sons by a law forever, from
37 this is the law of holocaust and of
10 15 and to thy sons by a perpetual law
11 46 this is the law of beasts and fowls
12 7 law for her that beareth a man child
13 59 this is the law touching the leprosy of
14 54 is the law of every kind of leprosy
15 32 law of him that hath the issue of seed
25 31 according to the same law as the fields
Num 5 29 this is the law of jealousy. If a
6 13 this is the law of consecration. When
21 this is the law of the Nazarite, when
8 24 this is the law of the Levites: from
15 15 shall be all one law and judgment
29 the same law shall be for all that sin
18 11 to thy daughters, by a perpetual law
19 14 the law of a man that dieth in a tent
27 11 of Israel sacred by a perpetual law
31 21 this is the ordinance of the law
36 6 is the law promulgated by the Lord
Deut 1 5 Moses began to expound the law and
4 8 all the law, which I will set forth this
44 this is the law that Moses set before
17 18 Deuteronomy of this law in a volume
19 that are commanded in the law; and that
19 4 shall be the law of slayer that fleeth
25 7 brother's wife, who by law belongeth to
27 3 on them all the words of this law
8 the stones all the words of this law
26 abideth not in the words of this law
28 58 fulfil all the words of this law. 31:12
61 not written in the volume of this law
29 21 are contained in the book of this law
29 we may do all the words of this law
30 10 ceremonies which are written in this law
31 9 Moses wrote this law and delivered it
11 thou shalt read the words of this law
24 wrote the words of this law in a volume
32 46 to fulfil all that is written in this l.
33 2 saints. In his right hand a fiery law
4 commanded us a law, the inheritance
Josu 1 7 thou mayst observe and do all the law
8 let not the book of this law depart
8 34 were written in the book of the law
22 5 fulfil the commandment and the law
1 K 10 25 told the people the law of the kingdom
30 25 an ordinance and as a law in Israel
2 K 7 19 this is the law of Adam, O Lord God
4 K 17 13 law which I commanded your fathers
34 his ceremonies and judgments and law
37 law and the commandments which he
21 8 law which my servant Moses commanded
22 8 found the book of the law. 2 Pa 34:15
11 king had heard the words of the law
16 the words of the law which the king
23 24 he might perform the words of the law
1 Pa 15 13 by our doing something against the law
2 Pa 5 10 when the Lord gave the law to the
13 11 made according to ordinance of the law
14 4 to do the law and all the commandments
15 3 priest a teacher and without the law
17 9 having with them the book of the law
19 10 there is question concerning the law
23 11 gave him the law to hold in his hand
30 5 kept it as it is prescribed by the law
31 21 according to the law and the ceremonies
33 8 all the law and the ceremonies and
34 14 the priest found the book of the law
19 when he had heard the words of the law
35 13 that which is written in the law: but
25 and it became like a law in Israel
1 Es 7 12 learned scribe of the law of the God
14 law of thy God, which is in thy hand
21 scribe of the law of the God of heaven
25 for them who know the law of thy God
26 whosoever will not do the law of thy God
and the law of the king
10 3 let it be done according to the law
2 Es 8 2 then Esdras the priest brought the law
7 among the people to hear the law: and
8 they read in the book of the law. 9:3
9 when they heard the words of the law
13 interpret to them the words of the law
14 they found written in the law, that
9 13 right judgments and the law of truth
14 and the law by the hand of Moses thy
10 36 our cattle, as it is written in the l.
13 3 when they had heard the law, that they
29 and the law of priests and Levites. So
Esth 1 19 law of the Persians and of the Medes
4 16 go in to the king, against the law
15 13 this law is not made for thee, but for
Job 22 22 receive the law of his mouth, and lay
28 26 when he gave a law for the rain and
Ps 24 8 will give a law to sinners in the way
12 he hath appointed him a law in the way
26 11 set me, O Lord, a law in thy way, and
36 31 the law of his God is in his heart and
70 4 out of hand of transgressor of the law
77 5 in Jacob: and made a law in Israel
104 10 appointed the same to Jacob for a law
118 33 set before me for a law the way of thy
72 the law of thy mouth is good to me
102 because thou hast set me a law. How
Prov 1 8 forsake not the law of thy mother. 6:20
3 21 thy eyes: keep the law and counsel
6 23 is a lamp, and the law a light, and
8 27 when with a certain law and compass
29 bounds, and set a law to the waters
13 14 law of the wise is a fountain of life
28 4 they that forsake the law, praise the
7 he that keepeth the law is a wise son
9 away his ears from hearing the law
29 18 but he that keepeth the law is blessed
31 26 the law of clemency is on her tongue
Wisd 2 11 let our strength be the law of justice
12 us with transgressions of the law, and
6 5 nor kept the law of justice nor walked
14 16 this error was kept as a law, and
18 4 by whom the pure light of the law was
9 unanimously ordered a law of justice
Eccu 11 15 and knowledge of the law are with God

17 9 and the law of life for an inheritance
19 18 disposition of the law is in all wisdom
21 transgresseth the law of the most High
23 33 unfaithful to the law of the most High
24 33 Moses commanded a law in the precepts
32 19 that seeketh the law, shall be filled
33 3 of God, and the law is faithful to him
34 8 the word of the law shall be fulfilled
35 1 he that keepeth the law, multiplieth
38 39 searching in the law of the most High
39 11 shall glory in the law of the covenant
41 11 forsaken the law of the most high Lord
42 2 of the law of the most High and of
44 20 who kept the law of the most High and
45 6 a law of life and instruction that he
49 6 forsook the law of the most High and
Isa 1 10 give ear to the law of our God, ye
2 3 for the law shall come forth from Sion
8 16 seal the law among my disciples. And I
20 to the law rather, and to the testimony
29 24 that murmured, shall learn the law
33 18 he that pondereth the words of the law
42 21 and to magnify the law, and exalt it
51 4 a law shall go forth from me, and my
Jer 2 8 they that held the law knew me not and
18 18 law shall not perish from the priest
Lam 2 9 the law is no more, and her prophets
Bar 4 1 the commandments of God and the law
Eze 7 26 the law shall perish from the priest
43 12 this is the law of the house upon the
12 this then is the law of the house
Dan 2 14 Daniel inquired concerning the law and
6 5 perhaps concerning the law of his God
10 Daniel knew . . . that the law was made
15 the law of the Medes and Persians is
Osee 4 6 thou hast forgotten the law of thy God
Mich 4 2 for the law shall go forth out of Sion
Haba 1 4 therefore the law is torn in pieces
Soph 3 4 have acted unjustly against the law
18 that were departed from the law, I
Agge 2 12 ask the priests the law, saying: If a
Zach 7 12 lest they should hear the law and the
Mala 2 6 the law of truth was in his mouth and
7 they shall seek the law at his mouth
8 have caused many to stumble at the law
9 and have accepted persons in the law
1 Ma 1 46 should follow the law of the nations
51 end that they should forget the law
2 19 from service of the law of his fathers
20 will obey the law of our fathers. God
21 not profitable for us to forsake the law
22 transgress the commandments of our law
24 according to the judgment of the law
26 showed zeal for the law as Phinees
27 every one that hath zeal for the law
42 one that had a good will for the law
48 recovered the law out of the hands of
50 my sons, be ye zealous for the law
58 while he was full of zeal for the law
64 and behave manfully in the law: for
67 take to you all that observe the law
68 take heed to the precepts of the law
3 48 they laid open the books of the law
56 man to his house, according to the law
4 47 took whole stones according to the law
53 offered sacrifice according to the law
10 14 that had forsaken the law and the
14 14 he sought the law, and took away every
29 of their holy places and the law: and
15 21 may punish them according to their law
2 Ma 2 2 how he gave them the law that they
3 not remove the law from their heart
18 as he promised in the law, will shortly
3 15 made the law concerning things given
6 23 the ordinances of the holy law made by
7 1 to eat swine's flesh against the law
30 commandment of the law which was
10 26 to their adversaries, as the law saith
12 40 which the law forbiddeth to the Jews
13 7 by such a law it happened that Menelaus
7 Menelaus the transgressor of the law
11 were afraid to be deprived of the law
15 9 and speaking to them out of the law
Mat 5 17 to destroy the law or the prophets
18 or one tittle shall not pass of the law
7 12 this is the law and the prophets
11 13 prophets and the law prophesied until
12 5 have ye not read in the law, that on
22 35 one of them a doctor of the law, asked
36 is the great commandment in the law
40 dependeth the whole law and the
23 23 left the weightier things of the law
Luke 2 27 according to the custóm of the law
5 17 also Pharisees and doctors of the law
10 26 what is written in the law? How readest
16 16 the law and the prophets were until
17 than one tittle of the law to fall
John 1 17 the law was given by Moses; grace and
45 of whom Moses in the law, and the
7 19 did not Moses give you the law, and
19 yet none of you keepeth the law? Why
49 that knoweth not the law, are accursed
51 doth our law judge any man unless it
8 5 Moses in the law commanded us to stone
17 in your law it is written, that the
10 34 in your law: I said you are gods? If
12 34 we have heard out of the law, that
15 25 in their law: They hated me without
18 31 and judge him according to your law
19 7 we have a law; and according to the law he ought to die
Acts 5 34 named Gamaliel, a doctor of the law
6 13 against the holy place and the law
7 53 who have received the law by the
13 15 after the reading of the law and the
18 13 men to worship God contrary to law
15 questions . . . and of your law, look
21 20 and they are all zealous for the law
24 thou thyself also walkest keeping law
28 everywhere against people, and the law
22 3 taught according to truth of the law
3 fathers, zealous for the law, as also
12 one Ananias, a man according to the law
23 3 thou to judge me according to the law
3 contrary to law commandest me to be
29 accused concerning questions of their l.
24 6 also have judged according to our law
14 are written in the law and the prophets
25 8 neither against the law of the Jews, nor
Rom 2 12 whosoever have sinned without the law, shall perish without the law
12 and whosoever have sinned in the law, shall be judged by the law
13 for not the hearers of the law are just
13 the doers of the law shall be justified
14 when the Gentiles, who have not the law
14 by nature those things that are of law
14 having not law are a law to themselves
15 who show the work of the law written in
17 art called Jew and restest in the law
18 things, being instructed by the law
20 form of knowledge and of truth in law
23 thou that makest thy boast of the law
23 by transgression of law dishonorest God
25 profiteth indeed, if thou keep the law
25 but if thou be a transgressor of the law

26 uncircumcised keep justices of the law
27 uncircumcision, if it fulfil the law
27 art a transgressor of the law? For it is
3 19 soever the law speaketh, it speaketh to
19 speaketh to them that are in the law
20 by the works of the law no flesh shall
20 for by the law is the knowledge of sin
21 without law the justice of God is made
21 witnessed by the law and the prophets
27 it is excluded. By what law? Of works
27 of works? No, but by the law of faith
28 by faith, without the works of the law
31 do we, then, destroy law through faith
31 God forbid: but we establish the law
4 13 not through the law was the promise to
14 for if they who are of the law be heirs
15 for the law worketh wrath. For where
15 where there is no law, neither is there
16 not to that only which is of the law
5 13 until the law sin was in the world; but
20 law entered in, that sin might abound
6 14 you are not under law, but under grace
15 because we are not under the law, but
7 1 for I speak to them that know the law
1 law hath dominion over man, as long as
2 her husband liveth is bound to the law
2 she is loosed from law of her husband
3 she is delivered from law of her husband
4 you also are become dead to the law, by
5 passions of sins, which were by the law
6 now we are loosed from the law of death
7 the law sin? God forbid. But I do not
7 but I do not know sin, but by the law
7 if law did not say: Thou shalt not covet
8 for without the law sin was dead. And I
9 and I lived some time without the law
12 wherefore the law indeed is holy, and
14 for we know that the law is spiritual
16 I consent to the law, that it is good
21 I find then a law, that when I have a
23 but I see another law in my members
23 fighting against the law of my mind, and
23 and captivating me in the law of sin
25 God; but with the flesh, the law of sin
8 2 flesh. For the law of the spirit of life
2 delivered me from the law of sin and of
3 for what the law could not do, in that
4 that the justification of the law might
9 4 to whom belongeth . . . giving of the law
31 but Israel, by following after the law
31 is not come unto the law of justice. Why
10 4 for the end of the law is Christ, unto
5 wrote, that the justice which is of law
13 8 his neighbor, hath fulfilled the law
10 love therefore is fulfilling of the law
1 C 6 6 but brother goeth to law with brother
7 39 woman is bound by the law as long as her
9 8 doth not the law also say these things
21 under the law, as if I were under law
21 whereas myself was not under the law
21 might gain them that were under the law
21 to them that were without the law, as if
21 the law, as if I were without the law
21 but was in the law of Christ, that I
21 gain them that were without the law
14 21 in law it is written: In other tongues
34 but to be subject, as also the law saith
15 56 is sin: and the power of sin is the law
Gal 2 16 man is not justified by works of the law
16 not by the works of the law: because
16 by the works of the law no flesh shall
19 I through the law, am dead to the law
21 if justice be by the law, then Christ
3 2 receive the Spirit by works of the law
5 doth he do it by the works of the law
9 as many as are of the works of the law
10 which are written in the book of the law
11 in the law no man is justified with God
12 but the law is not of faith: but, He
13 redeemed us from the curse of the law
17 the law which was made after 430 years
18 for if the inheritance be of the law
19 why then was the law? It was set because
21 was the law then against the promises of
21 for if there had been a law given which
21 justice should have been by the law
23 we were kept under the law shut up, unto
24 the law was our pedagogue in Christ
4 4 made of woman, made under the law: that
5 redeem them who were under the law: that
21 tell me, you that desire to be under the law, have you not read the law
5 3 that he is a debtor to do the whole law
4 Christ, you who are justified in the law
14 for all the law is fulfilled in one word
18 by the spirit, you are not under the law
23 chastity. Against such there is no law
6 2 so you shall fulfil the law of Christ
13 who are circumcised, keep the law; but
Eph 2 15 making void the law of commandments
Phil 3 5 according to the law, a Pharisee
6 justice that is in the law, conversing
8 not having my justice, which is of law
1 Tim 1 7 desiring to be teachers of the law
8 we know that the law is good, if a man
9 the law is not made for the just man
Titus 3 9 contentions and strivings about the law
Heb 7 5 tithes of the people according to law
11 under it the people received the law
12 a translation also be made of the law
16 who is made not according to the law of
19 the law brought nothing to perfection
28 the law maketh men priests, who have
28 oath, which was since the law, the Son
8 4 others to offer gifts according to law
9 19 the law had been read by Moses to all
22 almost all things, according to the law
10 1 law having a shadow of the good things
8 which are offered according to the law
James 1 25 looked into the perfect law of liberty
2 8 if then you fulfil the royal law
10 whosoever shall keep the whole law but
11 art become a transgressor of the law
12 to be judged by the law of liberty. For
4 11 detracteth the law and judgeth the law
11 if thou judge the law, thou art not a doer of the law

law of God 2 Es 8 18 in the book of the l. . . .
2 Es 10 28 separated themselves . . . to the l. . . .
29 that they would walk in the law of God
Tob 1 8 observe . . . according to the law of God
Eccu 33 3 understanding is faithful to the l. . . .
Isa 30 9 that will not hear the law of God
Bar 4 12 they departed from the law of God
1 Ma 1 59 with fire the books of the l. . . .
66 they would not break the holy l. . . .
2 15 and to depart from the law of God
4 42 whose will was set upon the law of God
2 Ma 4 2 and was zealous for the law of God
Rom 7 22 for I am delighted with the law of God
25 I myself, with mind serve the law of God
8 7 for it is not subject to the law of God
1 C 9 21 whereas I was not without law of God

law of the Lord Exod 13 9 law of the Lord be always in thy mouth
Lev 4 27 by the law of the Lord are forbidden

Josu 24 26 in the volume of the law of the Lord
4 K 10 31 no heed to walk in the law of the Lord
1 Pa 16 40 that is written in the law of the Lord
22 12 to keep the law of the Lord thy God
2 Pa 12 1 he forsook the law of the Lord and all
31 4 that they might attend to the l. . . .
35 26 was commanded by the law of the Lord
1 Es 7 10 his heart to seek the law of the Lord
2 Es 9 3 read in the book of the law of the Lord
Ps 1 2 his will is in the law of the Lord
18 8 the l. . . . is unspotted, converting
118 1 who walk in the law of the Lord
Eccu 46 17 by the law of the Lord he judged the
Isa 5 24 cast away the law of the Lord of hosts
Jer 8 8 and the law of the Lord is within us
44 10 nor walked in the law of the Lord
Amos 2 4 he hath cast away the law of the Lord
1 Ma 1 55 that had forsaken the law of the Lord
60 whosoever observed the law of the Lord
Luke 2 23 in the l. . . . : Every male opening the
24 in the l. . . . , a pair of turtledoves
39 all things according to the l. . . .
his law Deut 17 11 teach thee according to his l.
Job 11 6 wisdom, and that his law is manifold
Ps 1 2 on his law he shall meditate day and
77 10 and in his law they would not walk
104 45 that they might . . . seek after his law
Eccu 2 19 love him, shall be filled with his law
45 21 and give light to Israel in his law
Isa 42 4 the islands shall wait for his law
24 and they have not hearkened to his law
Jer 44 23 have not walked in his law and in
Dan 9 10 to walk in his law, which he set before
Osee 4 10 the Lord in not observing his law
1 Ma 1 43 and every one should leave his own law
2 Ma 1 4 may he open your heart in his law
my law Exod 16 4 whether they will walk in my law
Exod 16 28 will you refuse to keep . . . my law
2 Pa 6 16 that thy children . . . walk in my law
Ps 77 1 attend, O my people, to my law: incline
88 31 and if his children forsake my law and
Prov 3 1 my son, forget not my law, and let
4 2 you a good gift, forsake not my law
7 2 my law as the apple of thy eye: bind
Isa 51 7 people who have my law in your heart
Jer 6 19 words, and they have cast away my law
9 13 because they have forsaken my law
16 11 they forsook me and kept not my law
26 4 not hearken to me to walk in my law
31 33 I will give my law in their bowels
Eze 22 26 her priests have despised my law and
Osee 8 1 because they . . . have violated my law
thy law Deut 33 10 Jacob, and thy law, O Israel
2 Es 9 26 and threw thy law behind their backs
29 admonish them to return to thy law
34 and our fathers have not kept thy law
Jdth 3 4 let all we have be subject to thy law
Ps 39 9 and thy law in the midst of my heart
93 12 and shalt teach him out of thy law
118 18 consider the wondrous things of thy law
29 and out of thy law have mercy on me
34 I will search thy law; and I will
44 so shall I always keep thy law forever
51 but I declined not from thy law
53 because of wicked that forsake thy law
55 name, O Lord: and have kept thy law
57 I have said, I would keep thy law
61 I have not forgotten thy law. 109, 153
70 milk: but I have meditated on thy law
77 thy law is my meditation. 174
85 told me fables: but not as thy law
92 unless thy law had been my meditation
97 how have I loved thy law, O Lord! It
113 I have loved thy law. 163
126 to do: they have dissipated thy law
136 because they have not kept thy law
142 forever: and thy law is the truth
150 they are gone far off from thy law
165 much peace have they that love thy law
129 4 by reason of thy law, I have waited
Wisd 16 6 of the commandment of thy law. For he
Jer 32 23 and they walked not in thy law: and
Bar 2 28 didst command him to write thy law
Dan 6 13 Daniel . . . hath not regarded thy law
9 11 all Israel have transgressed thy law
lawful Lev 7 16 morrow, it is lawful to eat it
Lev 11 9 which it is lawful to eat. 14:4
39 of which it is lawful for you to eat
17 13 beast or a bird, which is lawful to eat
1 K 20 19 on the day when it is lawful to work
2 Es 13 15 a day on which it was lawful to sell
Tob 2 21 it is not lawful for us either to eat
Jer 38 5 not lawful for the king to deny you
Dan 6 12 which it is not lawful to violate
1 Ma 14 44 should not be lawful for any of the
2 Ma 4 11 disannuled the lawful ordinances of the
6 4 brought in things that were not lawful
21 which it was lawful for him to eat
Mat 12 2 disciples do that which is not lawful
4 which it was not lawful for him to eat
10 is it lawful to heal on the sabbath. Luke 14:3
12 it is lawful to do a good deed on the
14 4 it is not lawful for thee to have her
19 3 lawful for a man to put away. Mark 10:2
20 15 is it not lawful for me to do what I
22 17 is it lawful to give tribute to Caesar. Mark 12:14; Luke 20:22
27 6 it is not lawful to put them into the
Mark 2 24 sabbath day that which is not lawful
26 which was not lawful to eat but for
3 4 is it lawful to do good on the sabbath
12 14 John said to Herod: It is not lawful
Luke 6 2 which is not l. on the sabbath days
4 which is not lawful to eat but only
9 be l. on the sabbath days to do good
John 5 10 not lawful for thee to take up thy bed
18 31 it is not lawful for us to put any man
Acts 16 21 preach a fashion which it is not l. for
19 39 it may be decided in a l. assembly. And
22 25 is it lawful for you to scourge a man
1 C 6 12 all things are lawful to me. 10:22, 23
lawfully 1 Tim 1 8 law is good, if man use it l.
2 Tim 2 5 not crowned, except he strive lawfully
lawgiver Num 21 18 by the direction of the l.
Ps 9 21 appoint O Lord, a lawgiver over them
83 8 the lawgiver shall give a blessing
Isa 33 22 is our judge, the Lord is our lawgiver
James 4 12 there is one lawgiver and judge, that
lawgivers Job 36 22 none is like him among the l.
Prov 8 15 by me . . . lawgivers decree just things
lawns Isa 3 23 lawns and headbands and fine veils
laws Gen 26 5 observed ceremonies and my laws
Exod 18 16 show the precepts of God and his laws
Lev 18 5 keep my laws. 19:19; 20:22
20 23 walk not after the laws of the nations
26 15 if you despise my laws and contemn
43 my judgments and despised my laws
45 precepts and laws which the Lord gave
Num 30 17 the laws . . . between the husband and
Esth 1 13 who knew the laws and judgments of
3 8 that use new laws and ceremonies and
13 4 which used new laws and acted against
5 using perverse laws and going against
16 4 violate in themselves the l. of humanity
15 at all, but contrariwise use just laws

19 Jews may freely follow their own laws
Wisd 6 19 and love is the keeping of her laws
19 the keeping of her laws is the firm
9 5 the understanding of judgment and laws
19 15 joy, and who lived under the same laws
Eccu 4 19 till she try him by her laws and trust
Isa 10 1 woe to them that make wicked laws: and
24 5 because they have transgressed the laws
33 25 night, and laws to heaven and earth
Eze 43 11 all its order and all its laws, and
44 5 and concerning all the laws thereof
24 judge: they shall keep my laws and my
Dan 7 25 himself able to change times and laws
Osee 8 12 I shall write to him my manifold laws
1 Ma 1 15 according to the laws of the nations
3 21 will fight for our lives and our laws
29 that he might take away the laws of old
6 59 may live according to their own laws
59 because of our despising their laws
10 37 and let them walk in their own laws
13 3 fought for the laws and the sanctuary
2 Ma 2 23 restored the laws that were abolished
3 1 the laws as yet were very well kept
4 17 acting wickedly against the laws of God
5 15 Menelaus, that traitor to the laws
6 1 depart from the laws of their fathers
5 things which were forbidden by the laws
28 the most venerable and most holy laws
7 2 than to transgress the laws of God
9 will raise us up, who die for his laws
11 for the laws of God I now despise them
23 despise yourselves for sake of his laws
24 he would turn from laws of his fathers
37 my body for the laws of our fathers
8 21 and disposed even to die for the laws
36 they followed the laws appointed by him
11 24 them to live after their own laws
31 meats, and their own laws as before
13 14 to stand up even to death for the laws
Heb 8 10 I will give my laws. 10:16
lawsuits 1 C 6 7 that you have lawsuits one with
lawyer Luke 10 25 lawyer stood up, tempting him and
Titus 3 13 send forward Zenas, the lawyer, and
lawyers Luke 7 30 Pharisees and the l. despised
Luke 11 45 one of the lawyers, answering, saith
46 woe to you lawyers. 52
53 the lawyers began violently to urge
14 3 spoke to the lawyers and Pharisees
lay Gen 19 33 neither when his daughter lay down
Gen 19 34 behold I lay last night with my father
35 daughter went in and lay with him
35 did he perceive when she lay down nor
22 12 lay not thy hand upon the boy neither
28 11 he took of the stones that lay there
31 37 lay it here before my brethren and thy
34 2 and took her away and lay with her
Exod 5 8 you shall lay upon them the task of
7 4 I will lay my hand upon Egypt and will
12 30 house wherein there lay not one dead
16 13 a dew lay round about the camp. And
22 8 that he did not lay his hand upon his
24 11 neither did he lay his hand upon those
29 10 shall lay their hands upon his head
15 and his sons shall lay their hands. 19
33 5 now presently lay aside thy ornaments
Lev 1 8 they shall lay the parts that are cut
12 and shall lay them upon the wood, under
3 2 he shall lay his hand upon the head
10 5 forthwith and took them as they lay
Num 6 18 take his hair and lay it upon the fire
12 11 lay not upon us this sin, which we
Deut 9 25 I lay prostrate before the Lord forty
11 25 shall lay the dread and fear of you
21 8 lay not innocent blood to their charge
22 29 he that lay with her shall give to the
25 2 they shall lay him down and shall cause
Josu 6 26 his firstborn may he lay the foundation
8 2 lay an ambush for the city behind it
4 lay an ambush behind the city: and go
14 not knowing that there lay an ambush
19 city, the ambush that lay hid, rose up
20 9 before the people to lay open his cause
22 20 his wrath lay upon all the people of
23 that we might lay upon it holocausts
Judg 5 27 he [Sisara] lay lifeless and wretched
6 20 lay them upon that rock and pour out
26 whereupon thou didst lay the sacrifice
7 12 eastern people lay scattered in the
15 15 the jawbone of an ass which lay there
16 9 was not known wherein his strength lay
19 lay his head in her bosom. And she
19 27 his concubine lay before the door with
Ruth 3 4 feet and shalt lay thyself down there
1 K 2 22 they lay with the women that waited at
3 2 one day when Heli lay in his place
5 3 Dagon lay upon his face on the ground
6 8 of the Lord and lay it on the cart
19 24 lay down naked all that day and night
24 4 David and his men lay hid in the inner
7 as to lay my hand upon him, because
28 9 dost thou lay a snare for my life, to
2 K 2 21 and lay hold on one of the young men
12 16 in by himself lay upon the ground
13 6 so Amnon lay down, and made as if he
14 overpowered her and lay with her. Then
18 12 would not lay my hands upon the king's
20 12 with blood, lay in the midst of the way
3 K 13 4 lay hold on him. And his hand which he
31 buried: lay my bones beside his bones
18 23 cut it in pieces and lay it upon wood
23 lay it on wood, and put no fire under it
4 K 4 29 lay my staff upon the face of the child
32 behold the child lay dead on his bed
34 lay upon the child: and he put his
35 he went up and lay upon him: and the
6 8 and such a place let us lay ambushes
10 8 he said: Lay ye them in two heaps by
1 Pa 12 8 when he lay hid in the wilderness
2 Pa 22 6 in Jezrahel where he [Joram] lay sick
31 7 to lay the foundations of the heaps
9 and the Levites, why the heaps lay so
1 Es 6 3 and that they lay the foundations that
8 31 and of such as lay in wait by the way
Tob 1 23 lay concealed, for many loved him
2 3 of the children of Israel lay slain
4 2 lay them as a foundation in thy heart
18 lay out thy bread and thy wine upon the
6 19 that night lay the liver of the fish
Jdth 3 9 a fear lay upon all those provinces
10 1 rose from the place wherein she lay
13 4 Holofernes lay on his bed, fast asleep
19 and behold his canopy wherein he lay
Job 21 5 and lay your finger on your mouth
19 God shall lay up the sorrow of the
22 22 and lay up his words in thy heart. If
36 19 aside. Lay down thy greatness without
39 34 I will lay my hand upon my mouth. One
40 27 lay thy hand upon him: remember the
41 17 when a sword shall lay at him, it
Ps 20 6 great beauty shalt thou lay upon him
49 20 lay a scandal against thy mother's
50 21 then shall they lay calves upon thy
83 4 where she may lay her young ones
104 38 for the fear of them lay upon them
Prov 3 18 of life to them that lay hold on her
7 1 words, and lay up my precepts with thee

16 3 lay open thy works to the Lord: and
Wisd 4 14 nor lay up such things in their hearts
8 12 shall lay their hands on their mouths
17 2 lay there exiled from the eternal
Eccu 7 1 and no evils shall lay hold of thee
6 lay a stumblingblock for thy integrity
10 5 of the scribe he shall lay his honor
11 33 and on the elect he will lay a blot
15 1 justice, shall lay hold on her, and
27 26 words he will lay a stumblingblock
39 33 fury they lay on grievous torments
Isa 5 8 house to house, and lay field to field
13 9 to lay the land desolate and to destroy
22 22 will lay the key of the house of David
28 16 I will lay a stone in the foundations
38 21 and lay it as a plaster upon the wound
43 17 they lay down to sleep together, and
53 10 if he shall lay down his life for sin
54 11 behold I will lay thy stones in order and will lay thy foundations
56 2 the son of man that shall lay hold on
59 15 from evil, lay open to be a prey: and
Jer 17 11 hatched eggs which she did not lay
Lam 4 19 lay in wait for us in the wilderness
Eze 3 20 I will lay a stumblingblock before him
4 1 thee a tile, and lay it before thee
2 lay siege against it and build forts
3 and thou shalt lay siege against it
4 shalt lay the iniquities of the house
6 5 I will lay the dead carcasses of the
7 4 I will lay thy ways upon thee, and. 9
8 I will lay upon thee all thy crimes
11 21 I will lay their way upon their head
17 19 I will lay upon his head the oath he
23 8 they also lay with her in her youth
24 5 lay together piles of bones under it
25 14 I will lay my vengeance upon Edom by
17 when I shall lay my vengeance upon
26 12 shall lay thy stones and thy timber
32 5 will lay thy flesh upon the mountains
23 multitude lay round about his grave
36 29 and will lay no famine upon you. And
37 6 I will lay sinews upon you, and will
38 12 to lay thy hand upon them that had
40 42 to lay the vessels upon, in which the
42 13 they shall lay the most holy things
14 there they shall lay their vestments
Dan 10 9 I lay in a consternation upon my face
11 42 he shall lay his hand upon the lands
13 37 there hid came to her and lay with her
Osee 2 10 I will lay open her folly in the eyes
Amos 7 8 I will lay down the trowel in the
Abdi 7 eat with thee shall lay snares under
Jon 1 14 and lay not upon us innocent blood
Mich 1 6 and will lay her foundations bare
Mala 2 2 if you will not lay it to heart, to give
1 Ma 6 57 place that we lay siege to is strong
9 40 the place where they lay in ambush and
11 69 they that lay in ambush rose out of
2 Ma 3 29 by the power of God lay speechless
9 14 to lay it even with the ground and to
14 33 I will lay this temple of God even
Mat 8 20 not where to lay his head. Luke 9:58
9 18 lay thy hand upon her, and she shall
23 4 and lay them on men's shoulders; but
Mark 1 30 wife's mother lay in a fit of a fever
2 4 wherein the man sick of the palsy lay
5 23 lay thy hand upon her, that she may be
7 32 that he would lay his hand upon him
11 7 and they lay their garments on him and
Luke 5 18 him in and to lay him before him
25 he took up the bed on which he lay
15 5 found it, lay it upon his shoulders
16 20 Lazarus, who lay at his gate, full of
19 21 up what thou didst not lay down and
John 5 3 in these lay a great multitude of sick
4 of whatsoever infirmity he lay under
10 15 and I lay down my life for my sheep
17 because I lay down my life, that I may
18 but I lay it down of myself, and I
18 I have power to lay it down: and I
13 37 I will lay down my life for thee. Jesus
38 wilt thou lay down thy life for me
15 13 that a man lay down his life for his
Acts 7 59 Lord, lay not this sin to their charge
15 28 to lay no further burden upon you than
27 20 no small storm lay on us, all hope of
28 8 father of Publius lay sick of a fever
Rom 9 33 behold I lay in Sion a stumblingstone
1 C 3 11 for other foundation no man can lay, but
1 P 2 6 I lay in Sion, a chief corner stone
1 J 3 16 we ought to lay down our lives for the

lay hands 2 Es 13 21 I will lay hands on you
Esth 3 6 to lay his hands upon Mardochai alone
Mat 21 46 and seeking to lay hands on him, they
Mark 12 12 sought to lay h. on him. Luke 20:19
14 49 and you did not lay hands on me. But
16 18 they shall lay their hands upon the sick
Luke 21 12 they will lay their hands on you and
Acts 8 19 on whomsoever I shall lay my hands

lay hold 2 K 2 21 lay h. on one of the young men
3 K 13 4 lay hold on him. And his hand which
Prov 3 18 tree of life to them that lay h. on her
Eccu 7 1 and no evils shall lay hold of thee
15 1 possesseth justice, shall lay hold on
Isa 10 6 the spoils, and to lay hold on the prey
56 2 son of man that shall lay hold on this
Jer 6 23 they shall lay hold on arrow and shield
13 21 shall not sorrows lay hold on thee
49 16 endeavorest to lay hold on the height
Eze 38 12 to take spoils and lay hold on the prey
Mark 3 21 they went out to lay hold on him. For
14 1 might by some wile lay hold on him
44 that is he; lay hold on him and lead
1 Tim 6 12 fight of faith: lay hold on eternal life
19 that they may lay hold on the true life

lay up Gen 6 21 shalt lay it up with thee: and
Exod 16 23 remain, lay it up until the morning
33 lay it up before the Lord to keep
Num 17 4 shalt lay them up in the tabernacle
Deut 11 18 lay up these my words in your hearts
14 28 and shalt lay it up within thy gates
2 K 19 19 nor lay it up in thy heart, O king
Tob 6 5 and lay up his heart and his gall and
12 8 more than to lay up treasures of gold
Prov 10 14 wise men lay up knowledge: but the
Eccu 13 15 his cruel mind will lay up thy words
Isa 10 28 Machmas he shall lay up his carriages
Jer 40 10 and lay it up in your vessels and
Eze 44 19 lay them up in the store chamber of the
Agge 2 19 were laid and lay it up in your hearts
Mat 6 19 lay not up to yourselves treasures on
20 lay up to yourselves treasures in
Luke 9 44 lay you up in your hearts these words
21 14 lay it up therefore in your hearts
2 C 12 14 neither ought the children to lay up for
1 Tim 6 19 to lay up in store for themselves a good

lay waste Deut 32 25 sword shall lay them waste
Judg 1 12 take Cariath-Sepher and lay it waste
Ps 119 4 the mighty, with coals that lay waste
Isa 11 15 the Lord shall lay waste the tongue of
24 1 the Lord shall lay waste the earth
Jer 36 29 and shall lay waste this land: and
Eze 19 7 widows, and to lay waste their cities
30 12 will lay waste the land and all that
36 5 and have cast it out to lay it waste

Dan 8 24 he shall lay all things waste and
layeth Deut 22 16 l. to her charge a very ill name
3 K 20 7 and see that he layeth snares for us
Prov 13 16 that is a fool, layeth open his folly
Eccu 27 29 he that layeth a snare for another
37 7 with him that layeth a snare for thee
50 30 he that layeth them up in his heart
Isa 57 1 no man layeth it to heart, and men
Zach 12 1 layeth the foundations of the earth
Luke 12 21 so is he that layeth up treasure for
John 13 4 he riseth from supper and layeth aside
laying Exod 32 20 laying hold of the calf which
Lev 6 12 laying on the holocaust, shall burn
Num 23 14 laying on every one a calf and a ram
27 23 l. his hands on his head, he repeated
Deut 22 14 laying to her charge a very ill name
26 6 laying on us most grievous burdens
Josu 9 4 laying old sacks upon their asses and
10 5 camped about Gabaon, laying siege to it
Judg 9 48 bough of a tree and laying it on his
16 3 [Samson] laying them on his shoulders
29 laying hold on both the pillars on
Ps 32 7 laying up the depths in storehouses
Wisd 13 14 laying it over with vermillion and
2 Ma 8 35 laying aside his garment of glory
Mat 18 28 laying hold of him, he throttled him
21 35 husbandmen laying hands on his servants
Mark 6 5 laying his hands upon them. 10:16
8 23 laying his hands on him. Acts 9:17
12 8 laying hold on him, they killed him
Luke 4 40 laying his hands on every one of them
Acts 9 24 their laying in wait was made known
18 17 all laying hold on Sosthenes, the ruler
25 3 laying wait to kill him in the way. But
1 C 16 2 laying up what it shall well please him
Heb 6 1 not laying again the foundation of
12 1 laying aside every weight and sin
1 P 2 1 laying away all malice and all guile
2 P 1 14 the laying away of this my tabernacle
Lazarus Luke 16 20 a certain beggar named Lazarus
Luke 16 23 afar off, and Lazarus in his bosom
25 likewise L. evil things, but now he
John 11 1 was a certain man sick, named Lazarus
2 whose brother Lazarus was sick. His
5 Jesus loved . . . Mary and Lazarus. When
11 Lazarus our friend sleepeth; but I go
14 Jesus said to them plainly: L. is dead
43 Lazarus, come forth. And presently he
12 1 to Bethania, where L. had been dead
2 L. was one of them that were at table
9 but that they might see Lazarus, whom
10 chief priests thought to kill L. also
17 when he called L. out of the grave
lead Gen 29 7 drink and so lead them back to feed
Exod 14 11 thou do this, to lead us out of Egypt
15 10 they sunk as lead in the mighty waters
32 34 lead this people whither I have told
33 12 commandest me to lead forth this people
Num 27 17 may lead them out or bring them in
31 22 and brass and iron and lead and tin
Deut 4 27 to which the Lord shall lead you. And
17 16 nor lead back the people into Egypt
21 10 and thou lead them away captives and
Judg 4 6 go, and lead an army to mount Thabor
2 K 5 2 that did lead out and bring in Israel
2 Pa 6 36 they lead them away captive to a land
2 Es 9 19 them by day to lead them in the way
Tob 4 23 lead indeed a poor life, but we shall
5 20 I will lead thy son safe and bring him
Jdth 6 7 Achior and to lead him to Bethulia
7 5 narrow pathway lead directly between
Job 19 24 with an iron pen and in a plate of lead
37 12 that governeth them shall lead them

Ps 30 4 sake, thou wilt lead me and nourish me
59 11 who will lead me into Edom. 107:11
118 35 lead me into path of thy commandments
124 5 Lord shall lead out with the workers
138 10 even there also shall thy hand lead me
24 iniquity: and l. me in the eternal way
142 10 thy good spirit shall lead me into the
Prov 4 11 will lead thee by the paths of equity
14 12 ends thereof lead to death. 16:25
Wisd 9 11 and shall lead me soberly in my works
Eccu 6 4 lead him into the lot of the wicked
22 17 what is heavier than lead? And what
47 20 and didst multiply silver as lead, and
Isa 11 6 and a little child shall lead them
15 7 they shall lead them to the torrent of
20 4 king of the Assyrians lead away the
42 16 and I will lead the blind into the way
63 14 so didst thou lead thy people to make
Jer 6 29 the lead is consumed in the fire, the
32 5 and he shall lead Sedecias to Babylon
Eze 22 18 brass and tin and iron and lead. 20
27 12 with silver, iron, tin, and lead
39 2 I will lead thee out and will make
Osee 2 14 and will lead her into the wilderness
Joel 3 19 he the conqueror will lead me upon
Zach 5 7 behold a talent of lead was carried
8 cast the weight of lead upon the mouth
Mat 6 13 lead us not into temptation. Luke 11:4
15 14 if the blind lead the blind, both fall
Mark 13 11 when they shall lead you and deliver
14 44 on him and lead him away carefully
Luke 6 39 can the blind lead the blind? Do they
13 15 the manger, and lead them to water
John 21 18 another shall gird thee and lead thee
Acts 13 11 [Elymas] sought some one to lead him
21 38 didst lead forth into desert 4,000 men
1 Tim 2 2 we may lead a quiet and a peaceable life
2 Tim 3 6 lead captive silly women laden with sins
Heb 8 9 to lead them out of the land of Egypt
James 3 2 able also with a bridle to lead about
Apoc 7 17 shall rule them and shall lead them to
13 10 he that shall lead into captivity
leader Exod 15 13 hast been a l. to the people
Deut 1 30 Lord God, who is your leader, himself
8 15 was thy leader in the great and terrible
31 6 Lord thy God he himself is thy leader
8 Lord who is your leader, he himself
32 12 the Lord alone was his leader: and
Judg 1 1 and shall be the leader of the war
4 14 behold he is thy leader. And Barac went
9 49 as he could, and followed their leader
10 18 shall be the leader of people of Galaad
20 18 answered them: Let Juda be your leader
1 Pa 19 16 and Sophach . . . was their leader
2 Pa 13 12 God is the leader in our army, and his
2 Es 9 12 a cloud thou wast their leader by day
Isa 55 4 a leader and a master to the Gentiles
63 14 the spirit of the Lord was their leader
Jer 30 21 their leader shall be of themselves
Dan 3 38 neither is there . . . prince or leader
9 26 people with their l. that shall come
1 Ma 2 66 let him be the leader of your army
13 8 thou art our leader in the place of
2 Ma 1 13 when the leader himself was in Persia
16 they cast stones and slew the leader
10 28 making their rage their l. in battle
12 36 their helper and leader of the battle
Luke 22 26 he that is the leader, as he that
Acts 1 16 leader of them that apprehended Jesus
leaders 1 Pa 12 34 of Nephtali, a thousand leaders
Jdth 5 2 he called . . . the leaders of Ammon
Ps 67 28 the princes of Juda are their leaders
Jer 25 34 with ashes, ye leaders of the flock

35 leaders of the flock to save themselves
Mat 15 14 they are blind and leaders of the blind
leadest Tob 13 2 l. down to hell and bringest up
Ps 79 2 thou that leadest Joseph like a sheep
Wisd 16 13 leadest down to the gates of death
leadeth Gen 35 16 to the land which l. to Ephrata
Gen 35 19 in the highway that leadeth to Ephrata
38 14 the crossway that leadeth to Thamnas
Num 21 4 by the way that leadeth to the Red Sea
Deut 2 1 wilderness that leadeth to the Red Sea
8 way that leadeth to the desert of Moab
Josu 2 7 way that l. to the fords of the Jordan
12 3 by the way that leadeth to Bethsimoth
13 16 all the plain, that leadeth to Medaba
1 K 6 12 straight way that leadeth to Bethsames
4 K 25 4 way that leadeth to the plains of the
1 Pa 26 16 gate which leadeth to the way of the
Tob 1 1 beyond the way that l. to the west
5 2 nor did I ever know the way which l.
7 that l. to the country of the Medes
Job 12 19 he leadeth away priests without glory
Prov 12 28 life: but the by-way leadeth to death
16 29 l. him into a way that is not good
Jer 52 7 walls, and leadeth to the king's garden
7 the way that leadeth to the wilderness
Eze 42 1 by the way that leadeth to the north
1 Ma 9 2 took the road that leadeth to Galgal
13 20 about by the way that leadeth to Ador
Mat 7 13 the way that leadeth to destruction
14 strait is the way that leadeth to life
Mark 9 1 leadeth them up into an high mountain
John 10 3 sheep by name, and leadeth them out
Acts 12 10 came to the iron gate that leadeth to
Rom 2 4 benignity of God l. thee to penance
leading Num 16 2 leading men of the synagogue
Judg 19 10 leading with him two asses laden, and
2 Ma 8 23 himself leading the first band, he
Acts 5 19 and leading them out, said: Go and
9 8 leading him by the hands, brought him
leaf Lev 26 36 sound of a flying l. shall terrify
3 K 7 26 of a cup or the leaf of a crisped lily
Job 13 25 against a leaf, that is carried away
Ps 1 3 and his leaf shall not fall off: and
Prov 11 28 the just shall spring up as a green l.
Eccu 14 18 as the leaf that springeth out on a
Isa 34 4 down as the leaf falleth from the vine
64 6 we have all fallen as a leaf, and our
Jer 8 13 figs on the fig tree, the leaf is fallen
17 8 the leaf thereof shall be green, and
Eze 47 12 their leaf shall not fall off and their
league Gen 14 13 these had made league with Abram
Gen 21 27 both of them made a league. And Abraham
32 made a league for the well of oath
31 44 let us enter into a league: that it
Exod 23 32 shalt not enter into league with them
Deut 7 2 thou shalt make no league with them
Josu 9 7 if so, we can make no league with you
11 servants, make ye a league with us
15 entering into a league promised that
16 three days after the league was made
Judg 2 2 that you should not make a league with
1 K 22 8 even my son hath entered into league
2 K 3 12 make a league with me [Abner], and
13 I [David] will make a league with thee
21 and may enter into a league with thee
5 3 king David made a league with them in
3 K 5 12 and they two made a league together
15 19 is a l. between me and thee. 2 Pa 16:3
19 break thy league with Baasa king of
20 34 having made a league I will depart
34 made a league with him and let him go
4 K 3 5 when Achab was dead, he broke the l.
2 Pa 16 3 thou mayst break thy league with Baasa
20 37 thou hast made a league with Ochozias
2 Es 6 2 let us make a league together in the
Isa 28 15 we have entered into a l. with death
18 your l. with death shall be abolished
Dan 11 6 years they shall be in league together
1 Ma 8 17 to Rome to make a league of amity and
11 9 let us make a league between us, and
14 24 to confirm the league with them. And
lean Gen 41 19 so very ill favored and lean
Gen 41 21 were as lean and ill favored as before
27 the seven lean and thin kine that came
Judg 16 26 let me lean upon them and rest a little
2 K 6 6 the oxen kicked and made it lean aside
13 4 why dost thou grow so lean from day to
4 K 18 21 upon which if a man l., it will break
1 Pa 13 9 oxen . . . had made it lean a little to
Job 8 15 he shall lean upon his house, and it
Prov 3 5 and lean not upon thy own prudence
Isa 10 20 they shall lean no more upon him that
20 they shall lean upon the Lord the Holy
17 4 fatness of his flesh shall grow lean
36 6 upon which if a man lean, it will go
50 10 let him . . . lean upon his God. Behold
Eze 34 20 between the fat cattle and the lean
Amos 5 19 lean with his hand upon the wall, and a
leaned 2 K 1 6 and Saul leaned upon his spear
4 K 7 2 lords, upon whose hand the king leaned
17 appointed that lord on whose hand he l.
Isa 30 12 and tumult, and have leaned upon it
Eze 29 7 and when they leaned upon thee, thou
Mich 3 11 they leaned upon the Lord, saying: Is
John 21 20 also leaned on his breast at supper
leaner Dan 1 10 if he should see your faces l.
leaneth 4 K 5 18 and he leaneth upon my hand
leanfleshed Gen 41 3 river, ill favored and l.
leaning Gen 28 13 Lord leaning upon the ladder
Ps 61 4 if you were thrusting down a l. wall
Cant 8 5 with delights, l. upon her beloved
Eccu 41 24 of leaning with thy elbow over meat
John 13 23 there was leaning on Jesus' bosom
25 leaning on the breast of Jesus, saith
leanness Isa 10 16 shall send l. among his fat
leap 2 K 22 30 in my God I will l. over the wall
2 Es 4 3 fox go up, he will leap over their
Isa 35 6 then shall the lame man leap as a hart
Joel 2 5 shall leap like the noise of chariots
Mala 4 2 shall leap like calves of the herd
leaped Gen 31 10 that the males which l. upon the
3 K 18 26 they leaped over the altar that they
Tob 2 3 he forthwith leaped up from his place
9 8 leaped up and they kissed each other
Dan 13 39 and opening the doors he leaped out
1 Ma 9 48 Jonathan . . . leaped into the Jordan
13 44 within the engine leaped into the city
Mark 10 50 casting off his garment leaped up and
Luke 1 41 the infant leaped in her womb. And
44 the infant in my womb leaped for joy
Acts 14 9 feet. And he leaped up, and walked
13 they l. out among the people, crying
leapeth Prov 14 16 fool l. over and is confident
leaping Gen 31 12 all the males leaping upon the
Judg 4 15 leaping down from off his chariot
2 K 6 16 saw king David leaping and dancing
Cant 2 8 he cometh leaping upon the mountains
Acts 3 8 he leaping up, stood and walked and
8 walking and leaping and praising God
19 16 l. upon them, and mastering them both
leapt 4 K 5 21 l. down from his chariot to meet
Wisd 18 15 thy almighty word leapt down from
learn Deut 4 10 and may learn to fear me all the
Deut 5 1 learn them and fulfil them in work
14 23 that thou mayest learn to fear the Lord
17 19 that he may learn to fear the Lord

31 12 that hearing they may learn and fear
Josu 4 25 may learn the most mighty hand of the
Judg 3 2 might l. to fight with their enemies
16 5 learn of him wherein his great strength
1 K 17 18 and learn with whom they are placed
3 K 8 43 that all . . . may learn to fear thy
18 37 that this people may learn that thou
Job 33 16 instructeth them in what they are to l.
Ps 118 71 that I may learn thy justifications
73 and I will learn thy commandments
Prov 6 6 consider her ways and learn wisdom
17 16 that refuseth to learn, shall fall
22 25 lest perhaps thou learn his ways and
Wisd 6 2 learn, ye that are judges of the ends
10 my words, that you may learn wisdom
9 18 may learn the things that please thee
Eccu 6 33 wilt attend to me, thou shalt learn
8 10 for of them thou shalt learn wisdom
12 of them thou shalt learn understanding
16 24 learn the discipline of understanding
18 19 justice, and learn before thou speak
Isa 1 17 learn to do well: seek judgment
26 9 of the world shall learn justice. Let
10 wicked, but he will not learn justice
29 24 they that murmured shall learn the law
Jer 10 2 learn not according to the ways of the
12 16 and will learn the ways of my people
Bar 3 9 give ear that thou mayst learn wisdom
14 learn where is wisdom, where is
Eze 23 48 and all women shall learn not to do
Dan 7 19 I would diligently learn concerning
Mich 4 3 neither shall they learn war any more
1 Ma 10 72 ask, and learn who I am, and the rest
2 Ma 7 2 what wouldst thou ask or learn of us
Mat 9 13 learn what this meaneth, I will have
11 29 up my yoke upon you, and learn of me
24 32 from fig tree l. a parable. Mark 13:28
1 C 4 6 that in us you may learn, that one be
14 31 all may learn, and all may be exhorted
35 if they would learn anything, let them
Gal 1 12 I receive it of man, nor did I learn it
3 2 this only would I learn of you: Did you
1 Tim 1 20 that they may learn to blaspheme
2 11 let the women learn in silence, with all
5 4 let her learn first to govern her own
13 they learn to go about from house to
Titus 3 14 let our men also learn to excel in good
learned Gen 9 24 learned what his younger son
Gen 30 27 I have learned by experience that God
1 K 26 4 l. that he was most certainly come
1 Pa 25 8 the learned and the unlearned together
26 14 Zacharias, a very wise and learned man
27 32 Jonathan . . . a wise and learned man
1 Es 2 63 till there arose a priest learned and
7 12 to Esdras . . . the most learned scribe
8 18 they brought us a most learned man
2 Es 7 65 until . . . a priest learned and skilful
34 2 words, and ye learned, hearken to me
Ps 89 12 and men learned in heart, in wisdom
105 35 among the heathens and l. their works
118 7 when I shall have l. the judgments of
Prov 8 12 and am present in learned thoughts
16 20 learned in word shall find good things
30 3 I have not learned wisdom, and have
Ecce 1 16 many things wisely, and I have learned
2 14 I learned that they were to die both
16 the learned dieth in like manner as
3 14 have learned that all the works which
9 11 nor riches to the learned, nor favor
Wisd 6 11 they that have learned these things
7 13 I have learned without guile and
21 have learned: for wisdom . . . taught me
Eccu 8 11 they have learned of their fathers
34 9 and he that hath learned many things
39 11 forth the discipline he hath learned
Isa 29 11 shall deliver to one that is learned
33 18 where is the learned? Where is he that
50 4 Lord hath given me a learned tongue
Jer 13 23 do well, when you have learned evil
Eze 19 3 he learned to catch the prey and to. 6
7 he learned to make widows and to lay
Dan 11 33 they that are learned among the people
35 and some of the learned shall fall
12 3 but they that are learned shall shine
10 but the learned shall understand. And
Mat 2 7 learned diligently of them the time
John 6 45 Father, and hath learned, cometh to
7 15 know letters, having never learned
Rom 16 17 to the doctrine which you have learned
1 C 2 13 speak, not in learned words of human
Eph 4 20 but you have not so learned Christ; if
Phil 4 9 things which you have both learned, and
11 I have learned, in whatsoever state I am
Col 1 7 as you learned of Epaphras, our most
2 7 in the faith, as also you have learned
1 Th 4 9 yourselves have learned of God to love
2 Th 2 14 hold traditions which you have learned
2 Tim 3 14 things which thou hast learned, and
14 knowing of whom thou hast learned them
Heb 5 8 he learned obedience by the things which
learning Exod 35 31 and knowledge and all l.
Ps 70 15 because I have not known learning, I
Prov 12 8 a man shall be known by his learning
14 6 the learning of the wise is easy
19 11 learning of a man is known by patience
Ecce 1 17 my heart to know prudence and learning
7 13 but learning and wisdom excel in this
Eccu 4 29 learning by the word of the wise and
19 19 learning of wickedness is not wisdom
21 24 l. to the prudent is as an ornament
Dan 1 4 that he might teach them the learning
Acts 26 24 much learning doth make thee mad. And
Rom 15 4 were written for our learning: that
2 Tim 3 7 ever learning, and never attaining to
least Gen 16 2 I may have children of her at least
Gen 19 11 from the least to the greatest. 2 Pa 34:30; Jdth 13:15; 15:8; Jer 8:10; 42:1, 8; 44:12; Bar 1:4; 1 Ma 5:45
24 55 let the maid stay at least ten days
32 10 I am not worthy of the least of all thy
33 15 some of the people at least, who are
Exod 11 7 shall not a dog make the least noise
Num 11 32 of quails he that did least, ten cores
12 14 been ashamed for seven days at least
Josu 10 28 he left not in it the least remains
Judg 6 15 I am the least in my father's house
16 10 now at least tell me wherewith
19 13 there or at least in the city of Rama
1 K 9 21 son of Jemini of the least tribe of
2 K 13 26 at least let my brother Amnon . . . come
20 8 as to come out with the least motion
4 K 18 24 one lord of the least of my master's
1 Pa 12 14 the least of them was captain over a
1 Es 7 26 judgment . . . or at least to prison
Jdth 7 9 at least being wearied out they will
Job 17 16 that there at least I shall have rest
19 6 at least now understand, that God hath
21 pity on me, at least you my friends
Wisd 11 23 is as the least grain of the balance
Eccu 42 10 herself or at the least become barren
Isa 10 14 the mouth, or made the least noise
36 9 of the least of my master's servants
60 22 the least shall become a thousand, and
Jer 3 4 at the least from this time call to me
6 13 l. of them even to the greatest. 31:34
Eze 2 5 if so be they at least will hear

Dan	13	32	so at least they might be satisfied
Osee	4	15	O Israel, at least let not Juda offend
Abdi		5	have left thee at the least a cluster
Jon	3	5	from the greatest to the least
Mat	2	6	art not the least among the princes of
	5	19	break one of these least commandments
		19	shall be called the least in the
	13	32	which is the least indeed of all seeds
	25	40	to one of these my least brethren, you
		45	you did it not to one of these least
Luke	12	26	able to do so much as the least thing
	16	10	faithful in that which is least, is
Acts	5	15	his shadow at the least, might
	8	10	gave ear, from the l. to the greatest
1 C	15	9	for I am the least of the apostles, who
Eph	3	8	to me, the least of all the saints, is
Heb	8	11	from the least to the greatest of them
leather 4 K	1	8	hairy man with a girdle of leather
leathern Mat	3	4	l. girdle about his loins. Mark 1:6
leave Gen	2	24	a man shall leave father and mother
Gen	11	6	neither will they leave off from their
	28	15	neither will I leave thee, till I shall
	42	33	leave one of your brethren with me and
		34	afterwards may have leave to buy what
	44	22	the boy cannot leave his father: for if he leave him, he will die
	45	20	leave nothing of your household stuff
	46	30	seen thy face, and leave thee alive
Exod	16	19	no man leave thereof till the morning
	21	26	and leave them but one eye, he shall
Lev	19	10	shalt leave them to the poor and the
	22	13	no stranger hath leave to eat of them
	23	22	you shall leave them for the poor and
	25	46	shall leave them to your posterity and
Num	9	12	they shall not leave anything thereof
	10	31	do not leave us: for thou knowest in
	20	17	may have leave to pass through thy
	21	22	that I may have leave to pass through
	32	15	will leave the people in the wilderness
		26	will leave our children and our wives
Deut	4	31	merciful God: he will not leave thee
	24	20	but shalt leave it for the stranger
	26	10	thou shalt leave them in the sight of
	28	51	will leave thee no wheat nor wine nor
	31	6	not leave thee nor forsake. 8; Josu 1:5; 1 Pa 28:20
Josu	10	33	his people, so as to leave none alive
	11	8	all, so as to leave no remains of them
	22	29	and leave off following his steps, by
	24	16	God forbid we should leave the Lord
		20	if you l. the Lord, and serve strange
Judg	9	9	can I leave my fatness, which both
		11	can I leave my sweetness and my
		24	and to leave the crime of the murder
Ruth	1	16	to desire that I should leave thee and
	2	7	she desired leave to glean the ears of
		16	leave them, that she may gather them
1 K	14	36	and let us not leave a man of them
	17	28	why didst thou leave those few sheep
	20	28	he asked leave of me earnestly to go
	25	22	if I leave of all that belong to him
2 K	2	21	Asael would not leave off following him
	11	15	leave ye him that he may be wounded
	14	7	and will leave my husband no name nor
	17	12	we shall not leave of the men that are
3 K	8	57	not leave us nor cast us off. But may
	19	18	and I will leave me 7,000 men in Israel
4 K	2	2	I will not leave thee. 4, 6; 4:30
	21	14	I will l. the remnants of my inheritance
1 Pa	28	8	may leave it to your children after you
1 Es	9	8	to leave us a remnant and give us a pin
		14	not to leave us a remnant to be saved
2 Es	6	9	the work, and that we would leave off
	9	19	didst not leave them in the desert: the
	10	31	and that we would leave the seventh year
Tob	1	14	gave him leave to go whithersoever he
	11	2	knowest how thou didst leave thy father
	12	12	and didst leave thy dinner and hide the
	14	8	and the Gentiles shall leave their idols
Job	20	13	he will spare it and not leave it, and
	39	11	leave thy labors to him? Wilt thou
Ps	15	10	thou wilt not leave my soul in hell
	36	8	cease from anger, and leave rage: have
		33	the Lord will not leave him in his hands
	48	11	shall leave their riches to strangers
	124	3	Lord will not leave the rod of sinners
Prov	2	13	who leave the right way, and walk by
	3	3	let not mercy and truth leave thee; put
	4	13	take hold on instruction, leave it not
	20	7	shall leave behind him blessed children
Ecce	10	4	ascend upon thee, leave not thy place
Wisd	2	9	let us everywhere leave tokens of joy
	8	13	and shall leave behind me an everlasting
	19	2	they had given them leave to depart
Eccu	4	5	and leave not to them that ask of thee
	7	23	him not of liberty nor leave him needy
	11	20	and that he must leave all to others
	14	15	shalt thou not leave to others to
	23	1	leave me not to their counsel: nor
		4	leave me not to their devices. Give
		23	will not leave off till he hath kindled
		36	shall leave her memory to be cursed
	24	46	will leave it to them that seek wisdom
	29	18	lost shame, will leave him to himself
		21	will leave him that delivered him. A
	31	20	leave off first, for manners' sake
	39	15	shall leave a name above a thousand
	47	24	but God will not leave off his mercy
	51	14	that he would not leave me in the day
Isa	10	3	and where will ye leave your glory
	65	15	and you shall leave your name for an
Jer	9	2	I will leave my people and depart from
	17	11	midst of his days he shall leave them
	26	2	unto them: leave not out one word
	48	28	leave the cities, and dwell in the
	49	11	leave thy fatherless children: I will
	50	20	merciful to them whom I shall leave
Bar	6	41	shall perceive this, will leave them
Eze	6	8	I will leave in you some that shall
	12	16	and I will leave a few men of them
	16	39	leave thee naked and full of disgrace
	31	12	depart from his shadow and leave him
Dan	4	12	leave the stump of its roots in the
		20	leave the stump of the roots thereof
	14	25	give me leave, O king, and I will kill
		25	and the king said: I give thee leave
Joel	2	14	and leave a blessing behind him
Soph	3	12	I will leave in the midst of thee a
Mala	4	1	shall not leave them root nor branch
1 Ma	1	43	and every one should leave his own law
		51	leave their children uncircumcised and
	10	30	I leave to you from this day forward
	11	58	he gave him leave to drink in gold
	15	6	I give thee leave to coin thy own money
2 Ma	6	28	I shall leave an example of fortitude
Mat	5	24	leave there thy offering before the
	18	12	doth he not l. the 99. Luke 15:4
	19	5	shall a man leave father and mother. Mark 10:7; Eph 5:31
	23	23	done, and not to leave those undone
Mark	5	13	gave them leave. And the unclean
	12	19	die, and leave his wife behind him, and leave no children
		21	and neither did he leave any issue
		22	like manner; and did not leave issue
Luke	9	61	first take my leave of them that are

11 42 and not to leave the other undone
19 44 shall not leave in thee a stone upon
20 28 and he leave no children, that his
John 14 18 I will not leave you orphans, I will
27 peace I leave with you, my peace I
16 28 I leave the world, and I go to the
32 to his own, and shall leave me alone
19 38 Pilate gave leave. He came therefore
Acts 2 27 thou wilt not leave my soul in hell
6 2 that we should leave the word of God
18 18 taking his l. of the brethren, sailed
21 taking his leave, and saying: I will
20 1 and exhorting them, took his leave, and
21 40 and when he had given him leave, Paul
Heb 13 5 I will not leave thee, neither will I
leaven Exod 12 15 be no leaven in your houses
Exod 12 19 not be found any leaven in your houses
23 18 not sacrifice blood of my victim upon l.
29 2 cake without leaven tempered with oil
34 25 the blood of my sacrifice upon leaven
Lev 2 4 loaves without l., tempered with. 7:12
5 flour tempered with oil and without l.
11 shall be made without leaven, neither shall any leaven or
6 16 and his sons shall eat, without leaven
8 26 a loaf without leaven and a cake
10 12 eat it without leaven beside the altar
Num 6 15 wafers without leaven anointed with
Deut 16 3 seven days shalt thou eat without l.
4 no leaven shall be seen in all thy
Osee 7 4 from the mingling of the leaven
Amos 4 5 offer a sacrifice of praise with l.
Mat 13 33 is like to leaven, which. Luke 13:21
16 6 beware of the leaven of the Pharisees. 11; Mark 8:15; Luke 12:1
12 beware of the l. of bread, but of the
1 C 5 6 little l. corrupteth the whole. Gal 5:9
7 purge out the old leaven, that you may
8 not with the old leaven nor with the leaven of malice
leavened Exod 12 15 whosoever shall eat anything l.
Exod 12 20 you shall not eat anything leavened
34 took dough before it was leavened: and
39 for it could not be leavened, the
13 3 place: that you eat no leavened bread
7 shall not be seen anything leavened
Lev 6 17 it shall not be leavened because part
7 13 loaves of leavened bread with the
23 17 of two tenths of flour leavened, which
Deut 16 3 shalt not eat with it leavened bread
Osee 7 4 leaven, till the whole was leavened
Mat 13 33 until the whole was l. Luke 13:21
leaves Gen 3 7 they sewed together fig leaves
Gen 8 11 bough of an olive tree with green l.
Num 17 8 blossoms, which spreading the leaves
3 K 6 34 door . . . opened with folding leaves
Job 14 9 it shall spring, and bring forth l.
Eccu 6 3 and it eat up thy leaves and destroy
39 19 bring forth leaves in grace, and praise
Isa 1 30 as an oak with the leaves falling off
Eze 31 3 with fair branches, and full of leaves
14 among the thick branches and leaves
47 12 and the leaves thereof for medicine
Dan 4 9 its leaves were most beautiful and its
11 shake off its leaves and scatter its
Mat 21 19 found nothing on it but leaves only
24 32 and the leaves come forth. Mat 13:28
Mark 11 13 seen afar off a fig tree having leaves
13 to it, he found nothing but leaves
Apoc 22 2 leaves of the tree were for the healing
leaveth Job 39 14 she l. her eggs on the earth
Prov 12 11 leaveth a reproach in his strongholds
13 22 the good man leaveth heirs, sons and
27 8 so is a man that leaveth his place
Ecce 2 21 he l. what he hath gotten to an idle
Eccu 18 6 when he leaveth off, he shall be at
23 32 woman also that leaveth her husband
27 24 leaveth no hope to an unhappy soul
John 10 12 and leaveth the sheep and flieth
leaving Gen 39 12 he l. the garment in her hand
Exod 14 19 pillar of the cloud, l. the forepart
Lev 16 23 vestments . . . and leaving them there
Num 14 18 wickedness and leaving no man clear
20 6 Moses and Aaron leaving the multitude
Deut 3 19 leaving your wives and children and
Josu 8 17 l. the towns open as they had rushed
1 K 17 22 David leaving the vessels which he had
23 28 returned, leaving the pursuit of David
3 K 12 13 leaving the counsel of the old men
2 Pa 10 13 leaving the counsel of the ancients
11 14 l. their suburbs and their possessions
Jdth 14 6 leaving the religion of the Gentiles
15 2 leaving all things behind, they made
Wisd 12 2 that l. their wickedness, they may
Abdi 12 in the day of his leaving his country
2 Ma 2 29 leaving to the authors the exact
4 31 leaving Andronicus . . . for his deputy
6 31 leaving not only to young men, but
Mat 4 13 leaving the city Nazareth, he came and
20 leaving their nets, followed. Mark 1:18
21 17 leaving them, he went out of the city
22 22 and leaving him, went their ways. That
26 44 leaving them, he went again: and he
56 the disciples all leaving him, fled
Mark 1 20 leaving their father Zebedee in the
7 8 leaving the commandment of God, you
8 13 leaving them, he went up again into
12 12 and leaving him, they went their way
20 took a wife, and died leaving no issue
14 50 then his disciples leaving him, all
Luke 5 11 leaving all things, they followed him
28 leaving all things, he rose up and
10 30 went away, leaving him half dead
Acts 21 3 Cyprus, l. it on the left hand, we
23 32 next day, l. the horsemen to go with him
Rom 1 27 leaving the natural use of the women
Heb 6 1 leaving the word of the beginning of
1 P 2 21 suffered for us, leaving you an example
2 P 2 15 leaving the right way they have gone
leavings Judg 1 7 gathered up the l. of the meat
Ruth 2 14 and was filled, and took the leavings
Mark 6 43 and they took up the leavings, twelve
Lebana 1 Es 2 45 the children of L. 2 Es 7:48
Lebaoth Josu 15 32 Lebaoth and Selim and Aen
Lebna Num 33 20 thence and came to Lebna. Removing
Num 33 21 removing from L. they camped in Ressa
Josu 10 29 from Maceda with all Israel to Lebna
30 they did to the king of Lebna, as they
31 from Lebna he passed unto Lachis
32 that was in it, as he had done to L.
39 as he had done to Hebron and Lebna
12 15 the king of Lebna one, the king of
Lebni Num 3 18 sons of Gerson: Lebni and Semei
Lebnites Num 3 21 the Lebnites and the Semeites
Lebona Judg 21 19 south of the town of Lebona
Lecha 1 Pa 4 21 Her the father of Lecha, and
Lechi Judg 15 9 camped in place . . called Lechi
Leci 1 Pa 7 19 sons of Semida were . . . Leci
Lecum Josu 19 33 and Jebnael even to Lecum
led Gen 12 20 they led him away, and his wife
Gen 37 28 and they led him [Joseph] into Egypt
38 25 when she was led to execution, she sent
Exod 13 17 Lord led them not by the way of the
18 led them about by the way of the
Num 14 3 and children be led away captives
32 13 led them about through the desert 40

Deut 1 39 that they should be led away captives
28 41 they shall be led into captivity
32 10 he led him about and taught him: and
Judg 5 14 they that led the army to fight. The
16 21 led him bound in chains to Gaza and
2 K 2 8 and led him about through the camp
3 K 8 46 so that they be led away captives into
48 to which they had been led captives
4 K 5 2 led away captive . . . a little maid
6 19 he [Eliseus] led them into Samaria
24 16 the king of Babylon led them captives
2 Pa 6 37 land to which they were led captive
38 captivity, to which they were led away
25 11 taking courage led forth his people
29 9 and our wives are led away captives
30 9 masters that have led them away captive
36 6 and led him bound in chains to Babylon
20 escaped the sword, was led into Babylon
2 Es 1 9 though you should be led away to the
Jdth 5 22 many of them were led away captive
Ps 22 3 he hath led me on the paths of justice
67 19 high, thou hast led captivity captive
105 9 he led them through the depths, as in
106 7 and he led them into the right way
135 16 who led his people through the desert
136 3 that led us into captivity required
Prov 7 22 followeth her as an ox led to be a
24 11 deliver them that are led to death
Wisd 19 11 being led by their appetite they asked
Isa 5 13 is my people led away captive, because
23 13 they have led away the strong ones
48 21 in the desert, when he led them out
49 21 brought not forth, led away and captive
53 7 he shall be led as a sheep to the
55 12 with joy, and be led forth with peace
63 13 he that led them out through the deep
Jer 2 6 that led us through a desert, through
17 that time when he led thee by the way
48 27 him, thou shalt be led away captive
Lam 1 5 her children are led into captivity
3 2 he hath led me and brought me into
Bar 2 14 sight of them that have led us away
4 27 by him that hath led you away. For
5 6 from thee on foot, led by the enemies
6 1 them that were to be led away captives
Eze 25 3 because they are led into captivity
30 18 daughters shall be led into captivity
37 2 he led me about through them on every
41 7 and it led into the upper loft of the
46 21 he led me about by the four corners
47 2 he led me out by the way of the north
Dan 13 45 when she was led to be put to death
Amos 2 10 I led you forty years through the
Nah 2 7 and the soldier is led away captive
7 her bondwomen were led away mourning
Zach 10 2 they were led away as a flock: they
2 Ma 1 19 when our fathers were led into Persia
33 where the priests that were led away
4 38 to be led about through all the city
6 7 they were led by bitter constraint
10 when they had openly led about through
29 they that led him and had been a little
9 23 led an army into the higher countries
10 20 being led with covetousness, were
Mat 4 1 Jesus was led by the spirit into the
26 57 they holding Jesus led him to Caiphas
27 31 and led him away to crucify him. And
Mark 8 23 hand, he led him out of the town; and
15 1 led him away and delivered him to
16 the soldiers led him away into the
20 and they led him out to crucify him
Luke 4 1 was led by the Spirit into the desert
5 devil led him into a high mountain
21 24 shall be led away captives into all
22 54 they led him to the high priest's
23 1 rising up, led him to Pilate. And they
26 as they led him away, they laid hold
32 led with him to be put to death. And
24 50 he led them out as far as Bethania
John 18 13 they led him away to Annas first, for
28 then they led Jesus from Caiphas to
19 16 and they took Jesus and led him forth
Acts 8 32 was led as a sheep to the slaughter
22 11 being led by hand by my companions, I
Rom 8 14 whosoever are led by the Spirit of God
1 C 12 2 to dumb idols, according as you were led
Gal 2 13 so that Barnabas also was led by them
5 18 but if you are led by the spirit, you
Eph 4 8 on high, he led captivity captive; he
2 Tim 3 6 who are led away with divers desires
Heb 13 9 be not led away with various and
2 P 3 17 lest being led aside by the error of
Ledan 1 Pa 26 21 sons of Ledan . . . of Ledan were heads
of the families, of Ledan
leddest 1 Pa 11 2 thou wast he that l. out and
ledge Exod 25 24 make to it a golden l. 37:11
Exod 25 25 to the ledge itself a polished crown
37 12 to the ledge itself he made a polished
ledges 3 K 7 29 the little crowns and the ledges
Leedan 1 Pa 23 7 sons of Gerson were Leedan and
1 Pa 23 8 the sons of Leedan: the chief Jahiel
9 the heads of the families of Leedan
leeks Num 11 5 the leeks and the onions and the
lees Isa 25 6 of wine purified from the lees
Jer 48 11 his youth, and hath rested upon his l.
Soph 1 12 the men that are settled on their lees
leftest 2 Es 9 28 thou l. them in the hand of
leg Judg 15 8 calf of the leg upon the thigh
legacy Eze 46 17 if he give a legacy out of his
legion 1 Ma 6 45 boldly in the midst of the l.
1 Ma 9 12 the legion drew near on two sides
10 82 then Simon . . . attacked the legion
Mark 5 9 my name is Legion, for we are many
Luke 8 30 what is thy name? But he said: Legion
36 how he had been healed from the legion
legions 1 Ma 6 35 distributed the beasts by legions
1 Ma 6 38 stood thick together in the legions
Mat 26 53 more than twelve legions of angels
legs Lev 11 21 but hath the legs behind longer
Deut 28 35 ulcer in the knees and in the legs
1 K 17 6 he had greaves of brass on his legs
Ps 146 10 nor take pleasure in the legs of a man
Prov 26 7 as a lame man hath fair legs in vain
Cant 5 15 his legs as pillars of marble, that are
Isa 3 20 bodkins and ornaments of the legs and
47 2 strip thy shoulder, make bare thy legs
Dan 2 33 the legs of iron, the feet part of iron
Amos 3 12 get out of the lion's mouth two legs
John 19 31 that their legs might be broken and
32 they broke the legs of the first and
33 dead, they did not break his legs
Leheman Josu 15 40 Chebbon and Leheman and
Leheth 1 Pa 23 10 the sons of Semei were Leheth
1 Pa 23 11 and Leheth was the first, Zeza the
leisure Eccu 38 25 cometh by his time of leisure
Eze 21 23 and imitating the leisure of sabbaths
1 C 16 12 he will come when he shall have leisure
lend Exod 22 25 if thou lend money to any of my
Deut 15 6 thou shalt lend to many nations. 28:12
8 thou shalt lend him that which thou
9 denying to lend him that which he
23 19 not lend to thy brother money to usury
20 to thy brother thou shalt lend that
28 44 he shall lend to thee, and thou shalt not lend
to him
Eccu 8 15 lend not to a man that is mightier

29 2 lend to thy neighbor in the time of
10 many have refused to lend, not out
1 Ma 9 35 they would lend them their equipage
Luke 6 34 if you lend to them of whom you hope
34 sinners also lend to sinners, for to
35 do good, and lend, hoping for nothing
11 5 to him: Friend, lend me three loaves
lender Eccu 29 5 they kiss the hands of the l.
Eccu 29 34 and the reproaching of the lender
Isa 24 2 as with the lender, so with the borrower
lendest Eccu 8 15 if thou l., count it as lost
lendeth Ps 36 26 showeth mercy and lendeth. 111:5
Prov 19 17 mercy on the poor, lendeth to the Lord
22 7 borrower is servant to him that lendeth
Eccu 20 16 today a man lendeth, and tomorrow
29 1 showeth mercy, lendeth to his neighbor
length Gen 6 15 length of the ark shall be
Gen 13 17 walk through the land in the length
29 30 having at length obtained the marriage
41 9 at length the chief butler remembering
Exod 19 19 was drawn out to a greater length
25 10 the length . . . two cubits and a half. 17
23 make a table . . . two cubits in length
26 2 length of one curtain . . . 28 cubits. 36:9
8 l. of one hair curtain . . . 30 cubits
13 over and above in the l. of the curtains
16 of tabernacle . . . ten cubits in length
27 18 in length the court . . . 100 cubits
28 16 a span both in length and in breadth
30 2 it shall be a cubit in length and
36 21 the length of one board was ten cubits
37 1 two cubits and a half in length. 6
10 the table . . . in length two cubits
Deut 30 20 is thy life and the length of thy days
Judg 3 16 of the length of the palm of the hand
14 17 at length on the seventh day as she
1 K 28 23 at length hearkening to their voice, he
2 K 20 8 coat of equal length with his habit
3 K 6 2 was threescore cubits in length and
3 a porch . . . twenty cubits in length
20 the oracle was twenty cubits in length
7 2 the length of it was a hundred cubits
6 porch of pillars of 50 cubits in length
27 every base was four cubits in length
2 Pa 3 3 l. by the first measure sixty cubits
4 porch . . . which was extended in length
8 the length of it . . . twenty cubits
Job 12 12 wisdom, and in length of days prudence
Ps 20 5 thou hast given him length of days
22 6 in house of the Lord unto l. of days
90 16 I will fill him with length of days
92 5 thy house, O Lord, unto length of days
Prov 3 2 they shall add to thee length of days
16 length of days is in her right hand
Wisd 19 11 at length they saw a new generation of
Eccu 1 12 shall give joy . . . and length of days
23 38 l. of days shall be received from him
30 23 the joy of a man is length of life
Bar 3 14 mayst know also where is length of days
Eze 40 11 the length of the gate thirteen cubits
18 according to the length of the gates
20 the length and the breadth of the gate
25 the length was fifty cubits, and the
29 the porch . . . fifty cubits in length
49 length of the porch was twenty cubits
41 2 measured the length thereof 40 cubits
4 the length thereof twenty cubits
13 the length of the house, 100 cubits
13 walls thereof, 100 cubits in length
15 he measured the length of the building
22 the length thereof was two cubits
22 the length thereof . . . were of wood
42 2 was the length of a hundred cubits
8 l. of the chambers of the outward court
8 length before the face of the temple
45 1 the land to be holy, in length 25,000
3 the length of 5 and 20 thousand. 48:9
5 five and twenty thousand of length
7 the length according to every part
48 8 5 and 20 thousand in breadth and in l.
10 five and twenty thousand in length. 13
13 length shall be 5 and 20 thousand
18 residue in length by the firstfruits
Zach 2 2 and how great the length thereof. And
5 2 the length thereof is twenty cubits
2 Ma 5 5 the wall, the city at length was taken
Mark 16 14 at length he appeared to the eleven
Rom 1 10 if by any means now at length I may have
Eph 3 18 what is the breadth and l. and height
Phil 4 10 that now at length your thought for me
Apoc 21 16 the length thereof is as great as the
16 the length and the height and the
lengthen 3 K 3 14 I will lengthen thy days. And
Isa 54 2 lengthen thy cords and strengthen the
lengthened Ps 128 3 they have l. their iniquity
Eccu 48 26 and he lengthened the king's life
lenity Esth 13 2 my subjects with clemency and l.
lent Exod 12 36 so that they lent unto them
1 K 1 28 I also have lent him to the Lord all
28 he [Samuel] shall be lent to the Lord
2 20 for the loan thou hast lent to the Lord
2 Es 5 10 have lent money and corn to many: let
Tob 4 21 I lent ten talents of silver while thou
Wisd 15 8 when his life which was lent him shall
Eccu 29 4 many have looked upon a thing lent as a
Jer 15 10 I have not lent on usury, neither hath any man lent to me on usury
Eze 18 8 hath not lent upon usury nor taken any
lentils Gen 25 34 bread and the pottage of lentils
2 K 17 28 and beans and lentils and fried pulse
23 11 for there was a field full of lentils
Eze 4 9 beans and lentils and millet and
leopard Eccu 28 27 and as a l. it shall tear them
Isa 11 6 the leopard shall lie down with the kid
Jer 5 6 a leopard watcheth for their cities
13 23 his sin, or the leopard his spots
Dan 7 6 another like a leopard, and it had upon
Osee 13 7 as a l. in the way of the Assyrians
Apoc 13 2 beast which I saw was like to a leopard
leopards Cant 4 8 from the mountains of the l.
Haba 1 8 their horses are lighter than leopards
leper Lev 13 46 all the time that he is a leper
Lev 14 2 this is the rite of a leper, when
32 this is the sacrifice of a leper that
22 4 of the seed of Aaron, that is a leper
Num 5 2 that they cast out of the camp every l.
2 K 3 29 a leper or that holdeth the distaff
4 K 5 1 a valiant man and rich, but a leper
27 and he went out from him a leper as
15 5 struck the king, so that he was a leper
2 Pa 26 21 Ozias the king was a leper unto the day
23 sepulchers because he was a leper
Isa 53 4 we have thought him as it were a leper
Mat 8 2 a leper came and adored him, saying
26 6 in the house of Simon the l. Mark 14:3
Mark 1 40 came a leper to him, beseeching him
lepers 4 K 7 3 four lepers at entering in of the
4 K 7 8 so when these lepers were come to the
Mat 10 8 cleanse the lepers, cast out devils
11 5 the lepers are cleansed, the deaf hear
Luke 4 27 there were many lepers in Israel in
7 22 the lepers are made clean, the deaf
17 12 met him ten men that were lepers, who
leprosy Lev 13 2 the stroke of leprosy, shall
Lev 13 3 if he see the leprosy in his skin and
3 place where the leprosy appears lower

3 it is the stroke of the leprosy, and
5 and if the leprosy be grown no farther
6 if the leprosy be somewhat obscure and
7 but if the leprosy grow again, after
9 if the stroke of the leprosy be in a
11 shall be judged an inveterate leprosy
12 if the l. spring out running about in
13 shall judge that the leprosy which he
15 if it be spotted with leprosy, is unclean
20 when he shall see the place of the l.
20 the plague of leprosy is broken out in
22 he shall judge him to have the leprosy
25 evil of leprosy is broken out in the scar
26 appearance of the leprosy be somewhat
27 if the leprosy be grown farther in the
29 if the leprosy break out in the head
30 it is the leprosy of the head and the
39 him know that it is not the leprosy, but
43 shall condemn him undoubtedly of l.
44 whosoever shall be defiled with the l.
47 garment that shall have the leprosy in
49 it shall be accounted the leprosy and
51 that it is grown, it is a fixed leprosy
54 wash that part wherein the leprosy is
55 returned nor yet the leprosy spread
55 leprosy has taken hold of the outside
56 place of the leprosy be somewhat dark
57 without spot, a flying and wandering l.
59 l. of any woollen or linen garment
14 3 shall find that the leprosy is cleansed
34 be the plague of leprosy in a house
35 there is the plague of l. in my house
36 and see whether it have the leprosy
36 shall go in to view the l. of the house
39 if he find that the leprosy is spread
40 stones wherein the leprosy is, be taken
44 perceive that the leprosy is returned
44 it is a lasting leprosy, and the house
48 perceive that the leprosy is not spread
54 is the law of every kind of leprosy
55 of the leprosy of garments and houses
Num 12 10 Mary appeared white as snow with a l.
10 and saw her all covered with leprosy
12 of her flesh is consumed with the l.
Deut 17 8 cause and cause, leprosy and leprosy
24 8 thou incur not the stroke of the leprosy
4 K 5 3 certainly have healed him of the leprosy
6 that thou mayest heal him of his leprosy
7 to me to heal a man of his leprosy
11 with his hand the place of the leprosy
27 leprosy of Naaman shall also stick to
2 Pa 26 19 there arose a leprosy in his forehead
20 and saw the leprosy in his forehead
21 in a house apart being full of the l.
Mat 8 3 and forthwith his leprosy was cleansed
Mark 1 42 the l. departed from him. Luke 5:13
Luke 5 12 a man full of leprosy, who seeing
leprous Exod 4 6 he brought it forth l. as snow
Lesa Gen 10 19 and Seboim even to Lesa. These
Lesem Josu 19 47 fought against Lesem and took it
less Gen 18 28 be five less than fifty just
Exod 12 4 if the number be less than may suffice
16 17 they gathered, one more, another less
18 he find less that had provided less
Lev 25 16 the less time is counted, so much the less shall the purchase cost
Num 22 18 my God, to speak either more or less
26 54 portion, and to the fewer a less: to
35 8 and from them that have less, fewer
Deut 25 13 weights in thy bag, a greater and a less
14 house a greater bushel and a less
1 K 25 36 she told him nothing less or more
3 K 8 27 contain thee, how much less this house
2 Pa 6 18 how much less this house which I have
Jdth 8 27 to be less than our sins deserve, let
Job 11 6 that he exacteth much less of thee
25 6 how much less man that is rottenness
Ps 8 6 made him a little less than the angels
Ecce 8 17 to seek, so much the less shall he find
Wisd 13 6 as these, they are less to be blamed
17 12 there is less expectation from within
Eccu 17 22 face of the Lord, and offend less
19 5 chastisement, shall have less life
21 better is a man that hath less wisdom
38 25 that is less in action shall receive
Eze 15 5 how much less when the fire hath
16 47 hast thou done a little less than they
Agge 1 9 for more, and behold it became less
2 Ma 15 18 their concern was less for their wives
Mark 4 31 is less than all the seeds that are
15 40 and Mary the mother of James the less
Luke 7 47 to whom l. is forgiven, he loveth l.
1 C 8 8 if we eat not, shall we have the less
12 23 such as we think to be less honorable
2 C 11 5 done nothing less than great apostles
23 I speak as one less wise: I am more; in
12 13 what is there that you have had less
15 loving you more, I be loved less. But
1 Tim 5 9 of no less than threescore years of age
Heb 7 7 that which is less, is blessed by the
lessen Amos 8 5 that we may lessen the measure
lessened Gen 8 13 the waters were lessened upon
Eccu 19 4 is light of heart and shall be lessened
Jer 30 19 glorify them and they shall not be l.
lessening Eccu 31 40 l. strength and causing wounds
lesser Gen 1 16 lesser light to rule the night
Exod 18 22 let them judge the lesser matters only
Num 33 54 larger part, and to the fewer a lesser
Isa 7 25 and the lesser cattle to tread upon
Eze 43 14 from the lesser brim to the greater
Amos 6 12 and the lesser houses with clefts
Mat 11 11 he that is l. in the kingdom. Luke 7:28
Luke 9 48 he that is the lesser among you all
lesson Prov 15 33 fear of the Lord is the l. of
Eccu 9 1 in thy regard the malice of a wicked l.
let Gen 24 14 let down thy pitcher that I may
Gen 24 18 quickly she let down the pitcher
46 she speedily let down the pitcher
Exod 17 11 if he let them down a little, Amalec
23 11 seventh year thou shalt let it alone
32 10 let me alone, that my wrath may be
40 3 and shalt let down the veil before it
Lev 20 4 if the people . . . let alone the man
Deut 9 14 let me alone that I may destroy them
Josu 2 15 then she let them down with a cord
18 by which thou hast let us down: and
1 K 19 12 she let him down through a window
Cant 8 11 he let out the same to keepers
Jer 38 6 they let down Jeremias by ropes into
11 let them down by cords to Jeremias
Eze 1 24 stood, their wings were let down
25 they stood and let down their wings
Mat 5 16 so let your light shine before men
31 let him give her a bill of divorce
40 let go thy cloak also unto him
15 14 let them alone: they are blind
21 33 let it out to husbandmen. Luke 20:9
41 will let out his vineyard to other
Mark 2 4 they let down the bed wherein the man
12 1 tower, and let it out to husbandmen
14 6 let her alone, why do you molest her
Luke 4 34 let us alone, what have we to do with
5 4 and let down your nets for a draught
5 at thy word I will let down the net
19 and let him down through the tiles
13 8 let it alone this year also, until

Zach 12 13 families of the house of Levi apart
Mala 2 4 that my covenant might be with Levi
8 you have made void the covenant of Levi
Luke 3 24 Mathat, who was of Levi, who was. 29
5 27 saw a publican named Levi, sitting
29 Levi made him a great feast in his
Heb 7 9 even Levi who received tithes, paid
sons of Levi Gen 26 11 sons of Levi: Gerson and
Exod 6 16 these are the names of the sons of Levi
32 26 the sons of Levi gathered themselves
28 the sons of Levi did according to the
Num 3 15 number the sons of Levi by the houses
17 there were found sons of Levi by their
16 7 take too much upon you, ye sons of L.
8 again to Core: Hear ye sons of Levi
10 the sons of Levi to approach unto him
18 21 I have given to the sons of Levi all
23 but only the sons of Levi may serve me
26 57 the number of the sons of Levi by their
Deut 21 5 priests the sons of Levi shall come
31 9 delivered it to the priests the s. . . .
3 K 12 31 who were not of the sons of Levi
1 Pa 6 1 the sons of Levi were. 16
9 18 the sons of Levi waited by their turns
12 26 of the sons of Levi, 4,600. And Joiada
15 15 the sons of Levi took the ark of God
23 6 by the families of the sons of Levi
24 these are the sons of Levi. 24:30
27 the sons of Levi are to be numbered
24 20 of the rest of the sons of Levi there
1 Es 8 15 among the priests for the sons of Levi
2 Es 12 23 sons of Levi, heads of the families
Mala 3 3 and he shall purify the sons of Levi
Eze 40 46 who among the sons of Levi come near
Heb 7 5 they that are of the sons of Levi, who
tribe of Levi Num 1 49 number not the tribe of L.
Num 3 6 bring the tribe of Levi, and make them
17 3 name of Aaron shall be for the t. . . .
18 2 with thee thy brethren also of t. . . .
Deut 10 8 he separated the t. . . . to carry
13 14 to the t. . . . he gave no possession. 33
1 Pa 23 14 were numbered in the tribe of Levi
Eccu 45 7 like to himself of the tribe of Levi
Apoc 7 7 of the tribe of Levi, 12,000 signed
leviathan Job 3 8 are ready to raise up a l.
Job 40 20 canst thou draw out the leviathan
Isa 27 1 shall visit leviathan the bar serpent and leviathan the crooked serpent
Levite Exod 4 14 Aaron the Levite is thy brother
Deut 12 12 the Levite that dwelleth in your cities
18 the Levite that dwelleth in thy cities
19 take heed thou forsake not the Levite
14 27 L. that is within thy gates. 16:11
29 the Levite that hath no other part nor
16 14 the Levite also and the stranger and
18 6 if a L. go out of any one of the cities
26 11 L. and the stranger that is with thee
12 thou shalt give it to the Levite and
13 I have given it to the Levite and to
Judg 17 7 he was a Levite and dwelt there. Now
9 I am a Levite of Bethlehem Juda, and I
18 3 of the young man the Levite. 15
19 1 a certain Levite who dwelt on the side
8 the L. prepared to go on his journey
20 3 the Levite the husband of the woman
1 Pa 9 31 Mathathias a Levite . . . was overseer
24 6 Semeias . . . a Levite, wrote them down
2 Pa 20 14 Levite of the sons of Asaph was there
31 12 the overseer . . . Chonenias the Levite
14 Core the son of Jemna the Levite
Luke 10 32 a Levite, when he was near the place
Acts 4 36 Joseph . . . a Levite, a Cyprian born
Levites Exod 38 21 the ceremonies of the Levites
Lev 25 32 houses of Levites which are in cities
33 the houses of the cities of the Levites
Num 1 47 the Levites . . . were not numbered with
51 the L. shall take down the tabernacle
53 the Levites shall pitch their tents
2 17 shall be carried by officers of the L.
33 the Levites were not numbered among
3 9 thou shalt give the Levites for a gift
12 I have taken the Levites from the
12 the Levites shall be mine. For every
32 prince of the princes of the Levites
39 all the Levites that Moses and Aaron
41 thou shalt take the Levites to me
45 take the Levites for the firstborn of
45 cattle of the Levites for their cattle
45 Levites shall be mine. I am the Lord
46 that exceed the number of the Levites
49 whom they had redeemed from the L.
4 2 sons of Caath from midst of the L. 18
46 all that were reckoned up of the L.
7 5 thou shalt deliver them to the Levites
6 oxen, delivered them to the Levites
8 6 take the Levites out of the midst of
9 bring the L. before the tabernacle
10 when the Levites are before the Lord
11 Aaron shall offer the Levites as a
12 the Levites also shall put their hands
13 set the Levites in the sight of Aaron
18 I have taken the Levites for all the
20 did with the Levites all that the Lord
22 had commanded Moses touching the L.
24 this is the law of the Levites: From
26 order the Levites touching their charge
18 3 the L. shall watch to do thy commands
6 I have given you your brethren the L.
6 command the L. and declare unto them
31 30 thou shalt give them to the Levites
47 gave it to the Levites that watched
35 2 to the L. out of their possessions
6 cities, which you shall give to the L.
8 each shall give towns to the Levites
Deut 18 1 priests and Levites and all that are
7 as all his brethren the Levites do
27 14 the Levites shall pronounce and say
31 25 he [Moses] commanded the Levites
Josu 14 3 the Levites, who received no land among
4 neither did L. receive other portion
18 7 for the Levites have no part among you
21 5 children of Caath, that is, to the L.
8 gave to the Levites the cities and
34 of Merari, L. of the inferior degree
39 all the cities of the Levites within the
Judg 17 13 I have a priest of the race of the L.
1 K 6 15 the Levites took down the ark of God
2 K 15 24 the Levites with him carrying the ark
3 K 8 4 priests and the Levites carried them
1 Pa 6 48 their brethren also the Levites, who
64 gave to the Levites the cities and
9 2 and the Levites and the Nathineans
14 of the Levites: Semeia the son of
26 to these four Levites were committed
33 singing men of families of the Levites
34 the heads of the Levites, princes in
13 2 and to the priests and the Levites
15 2 carry the ark of God, but the Levites
4 sons of Aaron also and the Levites
11 the Levites, Uriel, Asaia, Joel
14 priests and the Levites were sanctified
16 David spoke to the chiefs of the L.
17 they appointed Levites, Heman the son
22 Chonenias chief of the L. presided
26 when God had helped the Levites who
27 all the Levites that carried the ark

16 4 [David] appointed Levites to minister
23 2 gathered . . . the priests and Levites
3 the L. were numbered from the age
26 shall not be office of the Levites
30 the Levites are to stand in the morning
26 17 towards the east were six Levites
27 17 over the Levites, Hasabias the son of
28 13 divisions of the priests and of the L.
21 courses of the priests and the Levites
2 Pa 5 4 the L. took up the ark and brought
5 the priests with the Levites carried
12 both the Levites and the singing men
7 6 and the Levites with the instruments
8 14 Levites in their order to give praise
15 the priests and Levites departed not
11 13 priests and Levites . . . came to him
13 9 the sons of Aaron and the Levites
10 and the Levites are in their order
17 8 with them the Levites, Semeias and
8 and Tobias and Thobadonias and Levites
19 8 in Jerusalem also Josaphat appointed L.
11 you have before you the L. for masters
20 19 and the Levites of the sons of Caath
23 2 gathered together the Levites out of
5 of the Levites and of the porters shall
6 and they that minister of the Levites
7 let the Levites be round about the king
8 Levites and all Juda did according
18 under hands of the priests and the L.
24 5 he assembled the priests and Levites
5 speed; but the Levites were negligent
6 to oblige the Levites to bring in
11 by hands of the Levites, for they saw
29 4 he brought the priests and the Levites
5 hear me, ye Levites, and be sanctified
12 then the Levites arose, Mahath the
16 the Levites took it away and carried
25 set the L. in the house of the Lord
26 Levites stood, with the instruments
30 commanded the Levites to praise the
34 the Levites their brethren helped them
34 Levites are sanctified with an easier
30 15 the Levites being at length sanctified
16 out, from the hands of the Levites
17 the Levites immolated the phase for
21 L. also and priests with instruments
22 spoke to the heart of all the Levites
25 with the priests and Levites and all
27 the priests and the Levites rose up
31 2 companies of the priests and the L.
2 both of the priests and of the Levites
4 to give to the priests and the Levites
9 asked the priests and the Levites why
17 to the Levites from the twentieth year
19 males, among the priests and the L.
34 9 which the L. and porters had gathered
12 all L. skilful to play on instruments
13 masters of the number of the Levites
30 the priests and the Levites and all
35 3 and he [Josias] spoke to the Levites
8 people and to the priests and the L.
9 princes of the Levites, gave to the rest of the Levites
10 the Levites also in their companies
11 and the Levites flayed the holocausts
14 the Levites prepared for themselves
15 the Levites prepared meats for them
18 with the priests and the Levites and all
1 Es 1 5 rose up . . . the priests and Levites
2 40 the Levites: the children of Josue
70 the Levites . . . dwelt in their cities
3 8 priests, and the Levites and all that
8 appointed Levites from twenty years old
9 sons, and their brethren the Levites
10 L. the sons of Asaph with cymbals
12 many of the priests and the Levites
6 16 priests and the Levites and the rest
18 and the Levites in their courses over
20 priests and the Levites were purified
7 7 and of the children of the Levites
13 Levites in my realm, that are minded
24 concerning all the priests and the L.
8 20 gave for the service of the Levites
29 before chief of priests and of the L.
30 the priests and the Levites received
33 and Noadaia the son of Bennoi, Levites
9 1 priests and Levites have not separated
10 5 chiefs of the priests and of the L.
15 Mesollam and Sebethai, Levites, helped
23 of the sons of the Levites, Jozabed
2 Es 3 17 after him built the Levites, Rehum
7 1 the porters and singing men and L.
42 the Levites: the children of Josue
73 priests and the L. and the porters
8 7 the L. made silence among the people
9 and the Levites who interpreted to all
11 the Levites stilled all the people
13 priests and the Levites were gathered
9 4 stood up upon the step of the Levites
5 and the Levites Josue and Cedmihel
38 our Levites and our priests sign it
10 9 and the Levites, Josue the son of
28 priests, Levites, porters and singing
34 lots among the priests and the Levites
37 the tithes of our ground to the Levites
37 the L. also shall receive the tithes
38 shall be with the Levites in the tithes of the Levites
38 Levites shall offer the tithe of their
11 3 priests, the Levites, the Nathinites
15 of the Levites, Semeia the son of
16 of the princes of the Levites, and
18 Levites in the holy city were 284
20 and the Levites were in all the cities
22 overseer of the Levites in Jerusalem
36 of the Levites were portions of Juda
12 1 these are the priests and the Levites
8 the Levites, Jesua, Bennui, Cedmihel
22 the Levites the chiefs of the families
24 the chief of the Levites were Hasebia
27 sought the L. out of all their places
30 priests and the Levites were purified
43 thanksgiving, for the priests and L.
43 the priests and Levites that assisted
46 they sanctified the Levites, and the Levites sanctified the sons of Aaron
13 5 the oil, the portions of the Levites
10 portions of the Levites had not been
10 the Levites and the singing men, and
13 of the Levites Phadaia, and next to
22 I spoke also to the Levites that they
29 and the law of priests and Levites
30 courses of the priests and the Levites
Isa 66 21 will take of them to be priests and L.
Jer 33 18 be cut off from the priests and Levites
21 the Levites and priests my ministers
22 servant, and the Levites my ministers
Eze 43 19 shalt give to the priests and the L.
44 10 the Levites that went away far from me
15 priests and Levites, the sons of Sadoc
45 5 shall be for the Levites, that minister
48 11 astray as the Levites also went astray
12 of holies, by the border of the Levites
13 the Levites in like manner shall have
22 from the possession of the Levites
John 1 19 from Jerusalem priests and Levites to

Levitical Deut 17 9 priests of the L. race. 24:8
Deut 17 18 the priests of the L. tribe, and he
1 Pa 15 12 that are the heads of the L. families
24 6 of the priestly and L. families. 31
Esth 11 1 he was a priest and of the L. race
Heb 7 11 perfection was by the L. priesthood, for
levity Esth 16 9 cometh the levity of our mind
levy 3 K 5 13 levy was of thirty thousand men
3 K 5 14 and Adoniram was over this levy. And
2 Ma 8 36 promised to levy the tribute for the
lewd Eccu 30 13 lest his lewd behavior be an
2 Ma 6 4 and of men lying with lewd women. And
2 P 2 7 and lewd conversation of the wicked
Lia Gen 29 16 the name of the elder was Lia: and
Gen 29 17 but Lia was blear eyed: Rachel was
24 when morning was come he saw it was Lia
31 the Lord seeing that he despised Lia
30 9 Lia, perceiving that she had left off
13 Lia said: This is for my happiness
14 which he brought to his mother Lia
16 Lia went out to meet him and said
19 Lia conceived again and bore the sixth
31 4 called Rachel and Lia into the field
14 Rachel and Lia answered; Have we any
33 went into the tent of Jacob and of Lia
33 1 he divided the children of Lia and of
2 Lia and her children in the second
7 Lia also with her children came near
34 1 Dina the daughter of Lia went out to
35 23 the sons of Lia: Ruben the firstborn
46 15 these are the sons of Lia, whom she
18 Zelpha, whom Laban gave to Lia his
49 31 wife: there also Lia doth lie buried
Ruth 4 11 like Rachel and Lia, who built up the
liar Ps 115 11 in my excess: Every man is a liar
Prov 30 6 lest thou be reproved and found a liar
Eccu 25 4 a rich man that is a liar: an old man
John 8 44 he is a liar, and the father thereof
55 I shall be like to you a liar. But
Rom 3 4 but God is true; and every man a liar
1 J 1 10 we make him a liar, and his word is
2 4 is a liar, and the truth is not in him
22 who is a liar, but he who denieth that
4 20 and hateth his brother, he is a liar
5 10 not the Son, maketh him a liar: because
liars Ps 61 10 the sons of men are liars in the
Wisd 10 14 showed them to be l. that had accused
Jer 3 23 in very deed the hills were liars
1 Tim 1 10 for menstealers, for liars, for perjured
Titus 1 12 Cretians are always liars, evil beasts
James 3 14 and be not liars against the truth
Apoc 2 2 and are not, and hast found them liars
21 8 sorcerers and idolaters and all liars
Lia's Gen 35 26 sons of Zelpha, Lia's handmaid
Libanus Deut 1 7 of the Chanaanites and of L.
Deut 3 25 and this goodly mountain and Libanus
11 24 from the desert and from L. Josu 1:4
Josu 9 1 they also that dwell by Libanus, the
11 17 as far as Baalgad, by the plain of L.
12 7 from Baalgad in the field of Libanus
13 5 the country also of Libanus towards
6 that dwell in the mountains from L.
Judg 3 3 Hevites that dwelt in mount Libanus
9 15 and devour the cedars of Libanus. Now
3 K 4 33 from the cedar that is in Libanus unto
5 6 cut me down cedar trees out of Libanus
9 shall bring them down from Libanus to
14 he sent them to Libanus, 10,000 every
7 2 house of the forest of L. 10:17, 21; 2 Pa 9:20
9 19 to build in Jerusalem and in Libanus
4 K 14 9 a thistle of Libanus sent to a cedar tree which is in Libanus
9 beasts of the forest that are in L.
19 23 the top of Libanus, and have cut down
2 Pa 2 8 send me . . . pine trees from Libanus
8 are skilful in cutting timber in L.
16 we will cut down as many trees of L.
8 6 he built in Jerusalem and in Libanus
25 18 thistle that is in Libanus sent to the cedar in Libanus
18 the beasts that were in the wood of L.
1 Es 3 7 to bring cedar trees from Libanus
Jdth 1 7 sent to all that dwelt in . . . Libanus
Ps 28 5 Lord shall break the cedars of Libanus
6 them to pieces, as a calf of Libanus
36 35 lifted up like the cedars of Libanus
71 16 above Libanus shall the fruit thereof
91 13 shall grow up like the cedar of Libanus
103 16 cedars of Libanus which he hath planted
Cant 3 9 made him a litter of the wood of L.
4 8 come from Libanus, my spouse, come
14 with all the trees of Libanus, myrrh
15 run with a strong stream from Libanus
5 15 his form as of Libanus, excellent as
7 4 thy nose is as the tower of Libanus
Eccu 24 17 I was exalted like a cedar in Libanus
50 13 as the cedar planted in mount Libanus
Isa 2 13 all the tall and lofty cedars of L.
10 34 Libanus with its high ones shall fall
14 8 the cedars of Libanus, saying: Since
29 17 Libanus shall be turned into charmel
33 9 Libanus is confounded and become foul
35 2 the glory of Libanus is given to it
37 24 I have gone up . . . to the top of L.
40 16 Libanus shall not be enough to burn
60 13 glory of Libanus shall come to thee
Jer 18 14 shall the snow of Libanus fail from
22 6 thou art to me Galaad the head of L.
20 go up to Libanus and cry: and lift up
23 thou that sittest in Libanus and
Eze 17 3 a large eagle . . . came to Libanus
27 5 they have taken cedars from Libanus
31 3 Assyrian was like a cedar in Libanus
15 Libanus grieved for him, and all the
16 the choice and best in Libanus, all that
Osee 14 6 root shall shoot forth as that of L.
7 tree: and his smell as that of Libanus
8 memorial shall be as the wine of L.
Nah 1 4 and the flower of Libanus fadeth away
Haba 2 17 iniquity of Libanus shall cover thee
Zach 10 10 bring them to land of Galaad and L.
11 1 open thy gates, O Libanus, and let fire
libation Exod 29 40 for l. of the same measure
Num 15 7 same measure of wine for the libation
28 7 for a libation you shall offer of wine
29 16 the sacrifice and the libation thereof. **19, 22, 25, 28, 31, 34, 38**
39 sacrifice, for libation, and for victims
Eccu 50 16 stretched forth his hand to make a l.
Joel 1 9 sacrifice and libation is cut off. 13
2 14 sacrifice and libation to the Lord
libations Exod 25 29 wherein the libations are to be offered. 37:16
Exod 30 9 neither shall you offer l. And Aaron
Lev 6 14 the law of the sacrifice and libations
7 29 a sacrifice also, that is, the libations
9 17 adding in the sacrifice the libations
14 20 put it on the altar with the libations
31 for a holocaust with their l. 23:18
23 13 the libations shall be offered with it
13 l. also of wine, the fourth part of a
37 holocausts and libations according to
Num 4 7 and bowls to pour out the libations
6 15 wafers . . . and the libations of each
17 the libations that are due by custom
7 87 twelve lambs . . . and their libations

15 5 same measure of wine to pour out in l.
10 wine for libations of the same measure
24 the sacrifice and libations thereof
28 8 sacrifice and of the libations thereof
9 with oil in sacrifice, and the libations
14 these shall be the libations of wine
15 perpetual holocaust with its libations
24 from the holocaust and from the l. of
30 besides perpetual holocaust and the l.
31 them all without blemish with their l.
29 6 holocaust with the accustomed l. With
11 holocaust with their sacrifice and l.
14 for their l. three tenths of flour
18 sacrifices and libations for every one
21 sacrifices and the libations of every one. 24, 27, 30, 33, 37
Judg 13 19 a kid of the flocks, and the libations
23 not have received a holocaust and l.
4 K 16 13 offered libations and poured the blood
15 their sacrifices and their libations
1 Pa 29 21 a thousand lambs, with their libations
2 Pa 29 35 offerings and the l. of holocausts: and
1 Es 7 17 the sacrifices and libations of them
2 Es 10 37 firstfruits of our meats and our l.
12 43 for the l. and for the firstfruits and
Isa 57 6 thou hast poured out libations to them
65 11 table for fortune, and offer l. upon it
Jer 7 18 and to offer libations to strange gods
Eze 20 28 odors and poured forth their libations
44 30 l. of all things that are offered
45 17 prince shall give . . . the libations
liberal Eccu 31 28 shall bless him that is l. of
1 Ma 3 30 had given before with a liberal hand
2 Ma 4 49 were liberal towards their burial
Libertines Acts 6 9 the synagogue of the Libertines
liberty Lev 25 29 shall have the l. to redeem it
Tob 1 14 with liberty to do whatever he had a
Jdth 6 18 shall give this liberty to his servants
12 5 that she might have liberty to go
Ps 104 20 he set him at liberty. He made him
Eccu 7 23 defraud him not of liberty nor leave
25 34 nor to a wicked woman liberty to gad
30 11 give him not liberty in his youth, and
33 26 his hands be idle, and he seeketh l.
Jer 34 15 liberty every one to his brother. 17
16 whom you had let go free and set at l.
17 behold I proclaim a liberty for you
Osee 2 9 I will set at liberty my wool and my
1 Ma 10 33 set at l. freely, that all be discharged
43 let them be set at liberty, and all
13 16 when he is set at liberty he may not
14 26 they decreed him [Simon] liberty
Luke 4 19 set at liberty them that are bruised
Acts 25 16 have l. to make his answer, to clear
26 32 this man might have been set at liberty
Rom 8 21 corruption, into the liberty of glory
1 C 7 39 if her husband die, she is at liberty
8 9 liberty become stumblingblock to weak
10 29 for why is my liberty judged by another
2 C 3 17 Spirit of the Lord is, there is liberty
Gal 2 4 who came in privately to spy our liberty
5 13 brethren, have been called unto liberty
13 make not liberty occasion to the flesh
Heb 13 23 our brother Timothy is set at liberty
James 1 25 looked into the perfect law of liberty
2 12 to be judged by the law of liberty
1 P 2 16 as making liberty a cloak for malice
2 P 2 19 promising them liberty, whereas they
library 1 Es 5 17 let him search in the king's l.
1 Es 6 1 and they searched in the library of
2 Ma 2 13 how he made a library and gathered
Libya Jdth 3 1 Libya and Cilicia sent their
Eze 30 5 Ethiopia and Libya and Lydia, and all
Dan 11 43 he shall pass through L. and Ethiopia
Acts 2 10 and the parts of Libya about Cyrene
Libyans 2 Pa 12 3 L. and Troglodites and Ethiopians
2 Pa 16 8 and the Libyans much more numerous
Jer 46 9 and the Libyans that hold the shield
Eze 27 10 Lydians and the L. were thy soldiers
38 5 Persians, Ethiopians and L. with them
Nah 3 9 Africa and the Libyans were thy helpers
license Eccu 15 21 he hath given no man l. to sin
1 Ma 1 14 he gave them license to do after the
2 Ma 4 9 l. to set him up a place for exercise
lick 3 K 21 19 they shall lick thy blood also
Ps 71 9 and his enemies shall lick the ground
Isa 49 23 they shall lick up the dust of thy
Mich 7 17 they shall lick the dust like serpents
licked 3 K 18 38 l. up the water that was in the
3 K 21 19 wherein the dogs have licked the blood
22 38 and the dogs licked up his blood
Luke 16 21 the dogs came and licked his sores
lie Gen 3 15 shalt lie in wait for her heel. To
Gen 19 32 drunk with wine, and let us lie with him
34 tonight, and thou shalt lie with him
24 11 when he had made the camels lie down
38 16 he said: Suffer me to lie with thee
23 surely she cannot charge us with a lie
39 7 said: Lie with me. But he. 12
14 he came in to me to lie with me: and
49 31 wife: there also Lia doth lie buried
Exod 21 13 he that did not lie in wait for him
22 16 seduce a virgin . . . and lie with her
23 1 shalt not receive the voice of a lie
5 if thou see the ass . . . lie underneath
34 24 no man shall lie in wait against thy
Lev 18 20 shalt not lie with thy neighbor's wife
22 shalt not lie with mankind as with
23 woman shall not lie down to a beast
19 11 you shall not steal. You shall not lie
20 lie with woman that is bondservant and
20 11 if a man lie with his stepmother, and
12 if any man lie with his daughter-in-law
13 if any one lie with a man as with a
16 woman that shall lie under any beast
18 man lie with a woman in her flowers
20 any man lie with the wife of his uncle
Num 10 6 who lie on the south side shall take up
14 29 in wilderness shall your carcasses lie
32 your carcasses shall lie in wilderness
16 37 the censers that lie in the burning
21 15 lie down in the borders of the Moabites
23 19 God is not a man, that he should lie
24 it shall not lie down till it devour
Deut 19 11 any man . . . lie in wait for his life
18 that the false witness hath told a lie
22 22 if a man lie with another man's wife
23 some one find her . . . and lie with her
25 and taking hold of her, lie with her
28 and taking her, lie with her, and the
Josu 2 16 there lie ye hid three days, till they
8 12 to lie in ambush between Bethel and Hai
10 22 the five kings that lie hid therein
15 46 all places that lie towards Azotus
24 27 you will deny it and lie to the Lord
Judg 9 32 is with thee and lie hid in the field
21 20 lie hid in the vineyards, and when you
1 K 23 19 doth not David lie hid with us in the
22 that I lie craftily in wait for him
2 K 12 11 shall lie with thy wives in the sight
13 5 lie down upon thy bed and feign thyself
11 and said: Come lie with me, my sister
15 28 I will lie hid in the plains of the
4 K 4 16 man of God, do not lie to thy handmaid
7 12 out of the camp and lie hid in the
Jdth 4 8 the little children to lie prostrate

Job 6 28 give ear, and see whether I lie. Answer
7 4 if I lie down to sleep, I shall say
13 7 hath God any need of your lie, that
31 10 and let other men lie with her. For
34 6 in judging me there is a lie: my arrow
36 4 for indeed my words are without a lie
38 40 in the dens and lie in wait in holes
Ps 5 7 thou wilt destroy all that speak a lie
65 3 thy enemies shall lie to thee. Let all
88 36 I will not lie unto David: his seed
103 22 and they shall lie down in their dens
131 3 shall go up into the bed wherein I lie
Prov 1 11 let us lie in wait for blood, let us
18 themselves lie in wait for their own
12 6 words of the wicked lie in wait for
14 5 a faithful witness will not lie: but
5 a deceitful witness uttereth a lie
24 15 lie not in wait nor seek after
Ecce 4 11 if two lie together, they shall warm
Wisd 2 12 let us therefore lie in wait for the
10 8 they could not so much as lie hid
17 3 while they thought to lie hid in their
Eccu 4 26 own person, nor against thy soul a lie
30 be ashamed of the lie of thy ignorance
7 13 devise not a lie against thy brother
14 not willing to make any manner of lie
20 26 a lie is a foul blot in a man, and yet
27 31 as a lion shall lie in wait for him
28 30 thy enemies who lie in wait for thee
34 8 law shall be fulfilled without a lie
41 21 a lie before a governor and a man in
Isa 11 6 the leopard shall lie down with the
27 10 there shall he lie down and shall
34 10 it shall lie waste, none shall pass
44 20 perhaps there is a lie in my right hand
65 10 a place for the herds to lie down in
Jer 5 26 wicked men, that lie in wait as fowlers
20 6 to whom thou hast prophesied a lie
25 33 they shall lie as dung upon the face
27 14 king of Babylon: they tell you a lie
28 15 hast made this people to trust in a lie
29 31 and hath caused you to trust in a lie
33 12 causing their flocks to lie down. And
43 2 saying to Jeremias: Thou tellest a lie
51 17 his idol, for what he hath cast is a lie
Lam 2 21 the old man lie without on the ground
Eze 4 9 days that thou shalt lie upon thy side
19 2 the lioness lie down among the lions
34 15 and I will cause them to lie down
Dan 13 20 wherefore consent to us and lie with us
38 and we saw them lie together. And him
Joel 1 13 lie in sackcloth, ye ministers of
Mich 2 11 spirit, and that I rather spoke a lie
7 2 they all lie in wait for blood, every
Haba 2 3 appear at the end and shall not lie
Soph 2 14 and flocks shall lie down in the midst
15 a place for beasts to lie down in
3 13 they shall feed and shall lie down
Agge 1 4 houses, and this house lie desolate
Zach 10 2 the diviners have seen a lie, and the
13 3 spoken a lie in the name of the Lord
1 Ma 1 38 and this was a place to lie in wait
John 8 44 when he speaketh a lie, he speaketh
Acts 5 3 that thou shouldst lie to the Holy
23 21 for there lie in wait for him more than
Rom 1 25 who changed the truth of God into a lie
3 7 abounded through my lie, unto his glory
9 1 I speak the truth in Christ, I lie not
2 C 11 31 blessed forever, knoweth that I lie not
Gal 1 20 to you, behold, before God, I lie not
Eph 4 14 by which they lie in wait to deceive
Col 3 9 lie not one to another: stripping
1 Tim 2 7 an apostle, I say the truth, I lie not
Heb 6 18 in which it is impossible for God to lie
1 J 1 6 we lie, and do not the truth. But if
2 21 and that no lie is of the truth. Who
27 things, and is truth and is no lie
Apoc 3 9 they are Jews, and are not, but do lie
11 8 their bodies shall lie in the streets
14 5 in their mouth there was found no lie
21 27 or maketh a lie, but they that are
22 15 every one that loveth and maketh a lie
lied Josu 7 11 have stolen and lied and have
Job 24 25 who can convince me that I have lied
Ps 17 26 that are strangers have lied to me
26 12 me: and iniquity hath lied to itself
77 36 with their tongue they lied unto him
80 16 enemies of the Lord have lied to him
Isa 57 11 and afraid, that thou hast lied and
Dan 13 55 thou lied against thy own head. 59
14 11 else Daniel that hath lied against us
1 Ma 13 19 he lied, and did not let Jonathan go
Acts 5 4 thou hast not lied to men, but to God
liers 1 C 6 10 effeminate, nor liers with mankind
lies Judg 16 13 thou deceive me and tell me lies
Judg 16 15 hast told me lies these three times
Esth 16 5 as to endeavor to undermine by lies
Job 13 4 shown that you are forgers of lies
Prov 6 19 a deceitful witness that uttereth lies
10 4 that trusteth to lies feedeth the winds
14 25 and the double dealer uttereth lies
19 5 he that speaketh lies shall not escape
9 he that speaketh lies, shall perish
Wisd 14 28 prophesy lies or they live unjustly
Eccu 51 3 from the lips of them that forge lies
Isa 28 15 we have placed our hope in lies, and
59 3 your lips have spoken lies, and your
Jer 9 3 have bent their tongues . . . for lies
5 have taught their tongue to speak lies
16 19 surely our fathers have possessed lies
23 25 that prophesy lies in my name and say
26 of the prophets that prophesy lies
27 10 they prophesy lies to you: to remove
Eze 13 6 vain things, and they foretell lies
8 spoken vain things and have seen lies
9 upon the prophets . . . that divine lies
19 lies to my people that believe lies
22 with lies you have made the heart of
21 29 they divine lies: to bring thee upon
22 28 seeing vain things and divining lies
11 27 they shall speak lies at one table
Osee 7 3 and the princes with their lies. They
13 and they have spoken lies against me
12 1 he multiplied lies and desolation
Mich 6 12 inhabitants thereof have spoken lies
Nah 3 1 city of blood, all full of lies and
Soph 3 13 shall not do iniquity nor speak lies
1 Tim 4 2 speaking lies in hypocrisy, and having
liest Deut 11 19 when thou liest down and risest
Josu 7 10 arise, why l. thou flat on the ground
1 K 24 12 but thou liest in wait for my life
3 K 3 22 thou liest: for my child liveth, and
Cant 1 6 where thou liest in the midday, lest I
Eze 29 3 that liest in the midst of thy rivers
lieth Gen 49 25 the blessing of the deep that l.
Deut 21 2 from the place where the body lieth
27 20 he that lieth with his father's wife
21 cursed be he that lieth with any beast
22 cursed be he that lieth with his sister
23 he that lieth with his mother-in-law
28 54 and his wife, that lieth in his bosom
56 her husband, who lieth in her bosom
33 13 and of the deep that lieth beneath
Josu 12 3 south side that lieth under Asedoth
Judg 7 12 the sand that lieth on the seashore
16 5 of him wherein his great strength lieth

6 wherein thy greatest strength lieth. 15
2 K 2 24 aqueduct, that lieth over against the
17 9 perhaps he now lieth hid in pits or
2 Es 3 25 which lieth out from the king's high
Jdth 14 16 behold Holofernes l. upon the ground
Ps 9 9 lieth in wait in secret like a lion
9 lieth in ambush that he may catch the
Prov 25 28 as a city that lieth open and is not
12 17 he that lieth, is a deceitful witness
23 28 she lieth in wait in the way as a
Cant 4 3 besides that which lieth hid within
Eccu 11 33 he lieth in wait and turneth good into
34 a sinful man lieth in wait for blood
12 15 in his heart he lieth in wait, to throw
27 11 the lion always lieth in wait for prey
Jer 9 8 and secretly he lieth in wait for him
Bar 6 43 by some passenger, lieth with him, she
1 Ma 6 57 it lieth upon us to take order for
11 1 like the sand that lieth upon the
14 33 Bethsura that lieth in the borders of
34 fortified Joppe which lieth by the sea
2 Ma 12 29 lieth 600 furlongs from Jerusalem
Mat 8 6 my servant lieth at home sick of the
1 C 9 16 for a necessity lieth upon me: for woe
Titus 1 2 which God, who lieth not, hath promised
Apoc 21 16 and the city lieth in a foursquare, and
lieutenant 2 Ma 11 1 Lysias the king's l. and
lieutenants Esth 3 12 to all the king's l. and to
Esth 9 3 lieutenants, and every one in dignity
life Gen 1 20 forth the creeping creature having l.
Gen 1 30 wherein there is life, that they may
2 7 into his face the breath of life, and
9 tree of life. 3:22, 24; Prov 11:30; 13:12; 15:4
6 17 wherein is the breath of life. 7:22
7 11 in the 600th year of the life of Noe
15 flesh, wherein was the breath of life
9 5 brother, will I require the life of man
18 10 at this time, life accompanying. 14
25 7 days of Abraham's life were 175 years
17 and the years of Ismael's life were 137
42 7 of Chanaan to buy necessaries of life
Exod 6 16 the years of the life of Levi were 137
18 and the years of Caath's life were 133
20 and the years of Amram's life were 137
21 23 thereupon, he shall render life for life
Lev 17 11 life of the flesh is in the blood. 14
14 the life of all flesh is in the blood
Deut 19 4 that fleeth, whose life is to be saved
6 take away the life of him who is not
21 shalt require life for life, eye for eye
30 15 set before thee this day life and good
19 I have set before you life and death
19 choose therefore life, that both thou
Josu 14 10 the Lord therefore hath granted me life
Judg 6 4 at all in Israel for sustenance of life
2 K 14 7 may kill him for the life of his brother
15 21 in death or in life, there will thy
18 14 and whilst he yet panted for life
3 K 3 11 hast not asked for thyself long life
19 2 thy life as the life of one of them
4 K 4 16 if life accompany, thou shalt have a son
5 7 am I God . . . able to kill and give life
8 1 whose son he had restored to life. 5
5 how he had raised one dead to life, the
5 is her son whom Eliseus raised to life
10 24 him go shall answer life for life. And
13 21 man came to life and stood upon his feet
2 Pa 1 11 not asked . . . nor many days of life
1 Es 6 10 and pray for the life of the king
9 8 give us a little life in our bondage
9 to give us life and to set up the house
2 Es 9 6 thou givest life to all these things
Tob 2 18 that life which God will give to those
4 3 honor thy mother all days of her life
5 shall have ended the time of her life
23 we lead indeed a poor l., but we shall
14 17 his generation continued in good life
Jdth 8 6 and fasted all the days of her life
16 30 all the time of her life there was none
Esth 16 12 to deprive us of our kingdom and life
13 and good services our life was saved
Job 3 20 and life to them that are in bitterness
7 1 life of man upon earth is a warfare
10 12 thou hast granted me life and mercy
26 4 to teach? Was it not him that made life
30 2 were thought unworthy of life itself
33 4 breath of the Almighty gave me life
36 14 and their life among the effeminate
Ps 15 11 hast made known to me the ways of life
20 5 he asked life of thee: and thou hast
29 6 his indignation: and life in his good
33 13 who is the man that desireth life: who
35 10 for with thee is the fountain of life
40 3 Lord preserve him and give him life
70 20 turning thou hast brought me to life
84 7 wilt turn, O God, and bring us to life
87 11 shall physicians raise to life and
118 93 for by them thou hast given me life
132 3 hath commanded . . . life for evermore
Prov 2 19 shall they take hold of the paths of l.
3 2 thee length of days and years of life
18 she is a tree of life to them that lay
22 there shall be life to thy soul and
4 10 years of l. may be multiplied to thee
22 they are life to those that find them
23 because life issueth out from it
5 6 they walk not by the path of life
6 23 and reproofs . . . are the way of life
8 35 he that shall find me, shall find life
9 11 years of life shall be added to thee
10 11 the mouth of the just is a vein of life
16 the work of the just is unto life
11 19 clemency prepareth life: and the
12 28 in the path of justice is life: but the
13 8 ransom of a man's life are his riches
14 law of the wise is a fountain of life
14 27 fear of the Lord is a fountain of life
30 soundness of heart is l. of the flesh
15 10 to him that forsaketh the way of life
24 the path of life is above for the wise
31 ear that heareth the reproofs of life
16 15 of the king's countenance is life
22 knowledge is a fountain of life to him
18 21 death and life are in power of tongue
19 23 the fear of the Lord is unto life
21 21 shall find life, justice, and glory
22 4 fruit of humility is . . . glory and life
28 2 life of the prince shall be prolonged
30 8 give me only the necessaries of life
31 12 and not evil, all days of her life
Ecce 3 12 to rejoice, and to do well in this life
6 8 but to go thither where there is life
7 13 give life to him that possesseth them
9 9 this is thy portion in life, and in thy
Wisd 1 12 not death in the error of your life
2 12 against us the sins of our way of life
4 9 gray hairs. And a spotless life is old
16 soon ended, the long life of the unjust
7 6 all men have one entrance into life
8 5 if riches be desired in life, what is
7 have nothing more profitable in life
13 11 profitable for the common uses of life
17 to speak to that which hath no life
18 for life prayeth to that which is dead
14 12 invention of them is corruption of life

		21	the occasion of deceiving human life
		24	so that now they neither keep life
		29	trust in idols, which are without life
	15	12	and the business of life to be gain
	16	13	that hast power of life and death
Eccu	3	7	honoreth his father shall enjoy long l.
	4	13	he that loveth her, loveth life: and
		14	that hold her fast, shall inherit life
	6	16	faithful friend is the medicine of life
		31	in her is the beauty of life, and her
	10	11	all power is of short life. A long
	11	14	good things and evil, life and death
	15	3	with the bread of l. and understanding
		18	before man is life and death, good and
	17	9	and the law of life for an inheritance
	19	5	chastisement, shall have less life
	21	16	counsel continueth like fountain of life
	22	12	wicked life of a wicked fool is worse
	24	25	in me is all hope of life and of virtue
		30	it is a miserable life to go as a guest
	29	27	chief thing for man's l. is water and
	30	17	better is death than a bitter life
		23	of the heart, is the life of a man
		23	the joy of a man is length of life
	31	4	hath labored in his low way of life
		32	wine taken with sobriety is equal life
		34	what taketh away life? Death. Wine
	33	15	set against evil, and life against death
	34	20	giveth health and life and blessing
		25	of the needy is the life of the poor
	37	21	arise, good and evil, life and death
		28	life of a man is in the number of his
		34	he that is temperate, shall prolong life
	39	31	things necessary for the life of men
	40	18	the life of a laborer that is content
		30	the life of him that looketh toward
		30	man's table is not to be counted a life
	41	7	among dead there is no accusing of life
		16	a good life hath its number of days
	45	6	a law of life, and instruction, that he
	48	26	and he lengthened the king's life
Isa	4	3	that is written in life in Jerusalem
	38	16	if man's life be such, and the life of my spirit be in such things
	57	10	rest: thou hast found life of thy hand
Jer	8	3	death shall be chosen rather than life
	21	8	behold I set before you the way of life
Lam	2	19	for the life of thy little children
Bar	1	11	pray ye for the life of Nabuchodonosor . . . and for the life of Balthasar his
	3	9	hear, O Israel, the commandments of life
		14	also where is length of days and life
	4	1	they that keep it, shall come to life
Eze	10	17	for the spirit of life was in them
	13	18	people, they gave life to their souls
	33	15	and walk in the commandments of life
Dan	7	12	times of life were appointed them for
Jon	1	14	let us not perish for this man's life
Haba	3	2	in midst of the years bring it to life
Mala	2	5	my covenant was with him of life and
1 Ma	10	61	men of a wicked life, assembled
2 Ma	3	33	sake the Lord hath granted thee life
		35	vows to him that had granted him life
	6	18	most glorious death than a hateful life
		20	any unlawful things for the love of life
		23	good life and conversation from a child
		24	gone over to the life of the heathens
		25	for a little time of a corruptible life
		27	by departing manfully out of this life
	7	9	destroyest us out of this present life
		14	shalt have no resurrection unto life
		22	I neither gave you . . . soul nor life
		23	will restore . . . both breath and life
	9	18	despairing of life he wrote to the Jews
	14	46	calling upon the Lord of l. and spirit
		46	to him again; and so he departed this l.
Mat	2	20	dead that sought the life of the child
	6	25	be not solicitous for your life, what
		25	is not the life more than the meat
	7	14	strait is the way that leadeth to life
	18	8	thee to go into life maimed or lame
		9	having one eye to enter into life than
	19	17	if thou wilt enter into life, keep
Mark	3	4	to save life or to destroy. Luke 6:9
	9	42	is better for thee to enter into life
Luke	8	14	and pleasures of this life, and yield
	12	15	a man's life doth not consist in the
		22	be not solicitous for your life, what
		23	the life is more than the meat, and
	15	24	was dead and is come to life again. 32
	21	34	drunkenness and the cares of this life
John	1	4	in him was life, and the life was the
	3	36	not the Son, shall not see life; but
	5	21	raiseth up the dead, and giveth life
		21	Son also giveth life to whom he will
		24	but is passed from death to life
		26	as the Father hath life in himself
		26	to the Son also to have live in himself
		29	forth unto the resurrection of life
		40	come to me that you may have life
	6	33	heaven, and giveth life to the world
		35	I am the bread of life. 48
		52	is my flesh, for the life of the world
		54	you shall not have life in you. He
		64	spoken to you are spirit and life
	8	12	but shall have the light of life
	10	10	I am come that they may have life and
	11	25	I am the resurrection and the life
	12	1	been dead, whom Jesus raised to life
	14	6	am the way and the truth and the life
	20	31	you may have life in his name. After
Acts	2	28	hast made known to me the ways of life
	3	15	but the author of life you killed
	5	20	the people all the words of this life
	7	38	received the words of life to give
	11	18	Gentiles given repentance unto life
	17	25	seeing it is he who giveth to all life
	27	22	there shall be no loss of any man's life
Rom	5	17	shall reign in life through one, Jesus
		18	unto all men to justification of life
	6	4	so we also may walk in newness of life
	7	10	commandment that was ordained to life
	8	2	flesh. For the law of the spirit of life
		6	wisdom of the spirit is life and peace
		38	nor life, nor angels nor principalities
	11	15	receiving of them be, but life from dead
1 C	3	22	Cephas, or the world, or life, or death
	14	7	even things without life that give sound
	15	19	in this life only we have hope in Christ
2 C	1	8	so that we were weary even of life. But
	2	16	to the others the odor of life unto life
	4	10	l. also of Jesus may be made manifest. 11
		12	death worketh in us, but life in you
	5	4	is mortal may be swallowed up by life
Gal	3	21	which could give life, verily justice
Eph	4	18	being alienated from the life of God
	5	26	by the laver of water in word of life
Phil	1	20	body, whether it be by life, or by death
	2	16	holding forth the word of life to my
	4	3	whose names are in the book of life
Col	3	3	and your life is hid with Christ in God
		4	Christ shall appear, who is your life
1 Tim	2	2	we may lead a quiet and a peaceable life
	4	8	having promise of the life that now is
	6	19	that they may lay hold on the true life
2 Tim	1	1	according to the promise of life, which

10 brought to light life and incorruption
3 10 my doctrine, manner of life, purpose
Heb 7 3 beginning of days nor end of life, but
16 to the power of an indissoluble life
11 35 received their dead raised to life
James 1 12 he shall receive the crown of life
4 15 for what is your life? It is a vapor
1 P 3 7 to the co-heirs of the grace of life
10 he that will love life and see good
2 P 1 3 which appertain to life and godliness
1 J 1 1 have handled, of the word of life
2 the life was manifested; and we have
2 16 of the eyes, and the pride of life
3 14 that we have passed from death to life
5 11 and this life is in his Son. He that
12 he that hath the Son, hath life. He
12 that hath not the Son, hath not life
16 and life shall be given to him who
Apoc 2 7 I will give to eat of the tree of life
10 and I will give thee the crown of life
7 17 to the fountains of the waters of life
8 9 died, which had life in the sea, and
11 11 spirit of life from God entered into
13 15 to give life to the image of the beast
21 6 of the fountain of the water of life
22 1 he showed me a river of water of life
2 was the tree of life, bearing twelve
17 let him take the water of life freely

book of life; *see* **book**

eternal life (life eternal) 2 Ma 7 9 in the resurrection of eternal life
2 Ma 7 36 are under the covenant of eternal life
10 25 what must I do to possess eternal life
John 6 69 thou hast the words of eternal life
12 25 in this world, keepeth it unto l. e.
17 2 that he may give eternal life to all
3 this is e. l.: That they may know thee
Rom 2 7 honor and incorruption, eternal life
Acts 13 46 judge . . . unworthy of eternal life
1 Tim 6 12 lay hold on eternal life, whereunto thou
1 J 1 2 declare unto you the life eternal which
3 15 no murderer hath eternal life abiding
5 11 God hath given to us eternal life
13 you may know that you have e. l., you
20 this is the true God and life eternal

everlasting life (life everlasting) Tob 12 9 to find mercy and life everlasting
Eccu 24 31 explain me shall have l. e. All these
Dan 12 2 shall awake: some unto life everlasting
Mat 19 16 I do that I may have life everlasting
29 and shall possess life everlasting
25 46 but the just into life everlasting
Mark 9 44 for thee to enter lame into l. e.
10 17 that I may receive life everlasting
30 in the world to come life everlasting
Luke 18 18 what shall I do to possess e. l. And
30 in the world to come life everlasting
John 3 15 but may have life everlasting. 16
36 that believeth in the Son, hath l. e.
4 14 of water, springing up into l. e.
36 gathereth fruit unto life everlasting
5 24 believeth him that sent me, hath l. e.
39 for you think in them to have l. e.
6 27 for that which endureth unto l. e.
40 believeth in him, may have l. e. and
47 believeth in me, hath everlasting life
55 my blood, hath everlasting life: and
10 28 I give them life everlasting; and they
12 50 I know that his commandment is l. e.
Acts 13 48 as many as were ordained to l. e.
Rom 5 21 reign by justice unto life everlasting
6 22 your fruit unto . . . life everlasting
23 the grace of God, life everlasting, in
Gal 6 8 of spirit shall reap life everlasting
1 Tim 1 16 believe in him unto life everlasting
Titus 1 2 unto the hope of life everlasting, which
3 7 according to hope of life everlasting
1 P 3 22 that we might be made heirs of l. e.
1 J 2 25 he hath promised us, life everlasting
Jude 21 mercy of Lord Jesus Christ unto l. e.

his life Gen 37 22 do not take away his life
Gen 44 30 his life dependeth upon the life of
47 28 the days of his life. Deut 17:19; 22:19, 29; 1 K 1:11, 28; 7:15; 3 K 4:21; 11:34; 15:5; 4 K 25:29, 30; Tob 2:14; Ecce 5:16, 17; Eccu 23:20; 52:33, 34; 1 Ma 9:71
Exod 21 30 he shall give for his life whatsoever
Deut 19 11 lie in wait for his life and rise and
22 26 his brother, and taketh away his life
24 6 for he hath pledged his life to thee
15 poor and with it maintaineth his life
Judg 9 17 exposed his life to dangers to deliver
16 30 than he had killed before in his life
1 K 19 5 he [David] put his life in his hand
23 15 that Saul was come out to seek his life
2 K 12 15 to David, and his life was despaired of
3 K 2 23 spoken this word against his own life
15 6 and Jeroboam all the time of his life
20 39 thy life shall be for his life. 42
2 Pa 21 19 bowels, his disease ended with his l.
2 Es 6 11 would go into temple to save his life
Tob 2 15 and kinsmen mocked at his life, saying
3 21 his life, if it be under trial, shall
14 4 and the rest of his life was in joy
Jdth 12 20 as he had never drunk in his life
Esth 7 7 entreat Esther the queen for his life
Job 2 6 is in thy hand, but yet save his life
4 a man hath he will give for his life
24 22 up, he shall not trust to his life
33 18 and his life from passing to the sword
20 becometh abominable to him his life
22 and his life to the destroyers. If
Prov 7 23 knoweth not that his life is in danger
Ecce 5 19 not much remember the days of his life
7 1 what is profitable for him in his life
8 15 with him of his labor in days of his l.
Wisd 2 15 for his life is not like other men's
15 8 when his life which was lent him shall
9 shall labor nor that his life is short
10 earth, and his life more base than clay
Eccu 3 14 father, and grieve him not in his life
7 22 the hired man that giveth thee his life
26 2 fulfil the years of his l. in peace
29 19 for he hath given his life for thee
31 9 hath done wonderful things in his life
33 his life, who is diminished with wine
46 22 before the time of the end of his life
23 and showed him the end of his life
47 12 times even to the end of his life
48 15 in his life he did great wonders, and
50 1 who in his life propped up the house
Isa 53 10 if he shall lay down his life for sin
Jer 21 9 his life shall be to him as a spoil
38 2 shall live, and his life shall be safe
44 30 into the hand of them that seek his l.
30 his enemy, and that sought his life
51 6 and let every one save his own life
45 that every man may save his life from
Eze 7 13 strengthened in the iniquity of his l.
32 10 every one for his own life, in the day
33 5 look to himself, he shall save his life
Amos 2 14 neither shall the strong save his life
15 shall the rider of the horse save his l.
2 Ma 3 31 upon the most High to grant him his l.
7 25 with the young man to save his life
10 13 he put an end to his life by poison

12 24 to let him [Timotheus] go with his l.
14 38 was ready to expose his body and life
Mat 10 39 he that findeth his life, shall lose
39 he that shall lose his life. 16:25; Luke 9:24
16 25 that will save his life, shall lose it
20 28 to give his life a redemption for many
Mark 8 35 whosoever will save h. l. Luke 9:24
35 whosoever shall lose his life for my
10 45 to give his life a redemption for many
14 26 yea and his own life also, he cannot
17 33 whosoever shall seek to save his life
John 10 11 shepherd giveth his life for his sheep
12 25 he that loveth his life, shall lose it
25 he that hateth his life in this world
15 13 that a man lay down his life for his
Rom 5 10 shall we be saved by his life. And not
Phil 2 30 delivering his life, that he might
1 J 3 16 he hath laid down his life for us
my life Gen 19 19, shown to me in saving my life
Gen 27 46 said to Isaac: I am weary of my life
Judg 12 3 I put my life in my own hands and
1 K 18 18 who am I, or what is my life, or my
20 1 thy father, that he seeketh my life
22 23 that seeketh my life, seeketh thy life
24 12 but thou liest in wait for my life
26 21 my life hath been precious in thy eyes
24 so let my life be much set by in the
28 2 I will appoint thee to guard my life
9 then dost thou lay a snare for my life
21 and I have put my life in my hand
2 K 1 9 and as yet my whole life is in me. So
16 11 forth from my bowels, seeketh my life
18 13 have acted boldly against my own life
19 34 are the days of the years of my life
3 K 19 10 they seek my life to take it away. 14
20 32 I beseech thee let me have my life
4 K 1 13 man of God, despise not my life
14 now I beseech thee to spare my life
Jdth 12 14 all the days of my life. Ps 22:6; 26:4
18 because my life is magnified this day
Esth 7 3 give me my life for which I ask, and
Job 7 7 remember that my life is but wind, and
9 21 and I shall be weary of my life. One
10 1 my soul is weary of my life, I will let
27 6 doth not reprehend me in all my life
Ps 7 6 and tread down my life on the earth
25 9 wicked: nor my life with bloody men
26 1 the Lord is the protector of my life
30 11 my life is wasted with grief: and my
14 they consulted to take away my life
41 9 prayer to the God of my life. I will
55 9 I have declared to thee my life: thou
62 5 thus will I bless thee all my life long
87 4 and my life hath drawn nigh to hell
142 3 hath brought down my life to the earth
145 2 in my life I will praise the Lord: I
Ecce 2 17 I was weary of my life when I saw
Eccu 23 1 father, and sovereign ruler of my life
4 O Lord, father, and God of my life
51 5 out of hands of them that sought my l.
9 and my life was drawing near to hell
Isa 38 12 my life is cut off, as by a weaver
Lam 3 53 my life is fallen into the pit, and
58 my soul, thou the Redeemer of my life
Jon 2 7 wilt bring up my life from corruption
4 3 I beseech thee take my life from me
1 Ma 13 5 far be it from me to spare my life
2 Ma 7 37 I, like my brethren, offer up my life
9 22 not distrusting my life, but having
John 10 15 and lay down my life for my sheep
17 I lay down my life, that I may take
13 37 I will lay down my life for thee

Acts 20 24 neither do I count my life more precious
26 4 my life indeed from my youth, which was
Rom 11 3 I am left alone, and they seek my life
16 4 who have for my life laid down their
our life Gen 47 25 our life is in thy hand
Deut 6 24 well with us all the days of our life
Tob 10 4 the comfort of our life, the hope of our
Ps 89 8 our l. in the light of thy countenance
Wisd 2 1 time of our life is short and tedious
3 our life shall pass away as the trace
15 12 they have counted our life a pastime
Eccu 48 12 live only in our life, but after death
Isa 38 20 our psalms all the days of our life
their life Exod 1 14 made their life bitter with
2 K 1 23 lovely and comely in their life, even in
Ps 16 14 from the few of the earth in their life
Ecce 2 3 ought to do . . . all the days of t. l.
Wisd 5 4 we fools esteemed their life madness
12 23 who in their life have lived foolishly
16 9 was found no remedy for their life
Eccu 16 2 trust not to their life, and respect not
22 13 mourning . . . all the days of their l.
25 3 I am greatly grieved at their life
Jer 21 7 of them seek their life. 34:29; 40:37
Eze 7 13 their life be yet among the living
thy life Gen 3 14 all the days of thy life. 17; Deut 4:9; 6:2; 16:3; 23:6; Josu 1:5; 1 K 25:28; Tob 4:6
Gen 19 17 spoke to him, saying: Save thy life
47 8 the days of the years of thy life
Exod 4 19 they are all dead that sought thy life
Deut 28 66 thy life shall be as it were hanging
66 day, neither shalt thou trust thy life
30 20 he is thy life and the length of thy
1 K 25 29 and persecute thee and seek thy life
26 24 as thy life hath been much set by this
2 K 4 8 thy enemy who sought thy life: and the
19 5 thy servants, that have saved thy life
3 K 1 12 save thy life and the life of thy son
Jdth 10 15 thou hast saved thy life by taking
13 25 for that thou hast not spared thy life
Esth 4 13 not that thou mayst save thy life only
Ps 102 4 who redeemeth thy life from destruction
Prov 4 13 keep it, because it is thy life. Be not
Ecce 9 9 all the days of thy unsteady life
Eccu 2 3 that thy life may be increased in the
9 19 no fault, lest he take away thy life
13 18 love God all thy life, and call upon
18 33 thou shalt be an enemy to thy own life
33 24 when thou shalt end the days of thy l.
37 30 prove thy soul in thy life: and if it be
Isa 43 4 men for thee, and people for thy life
Jer 4 30 despised thee, they will seek thy life
11 21 men of Anathoth, who seek thy life
22 25 into hand of them that seek thy life
38 16 hands of these men that seek thy life
39 18 but thy life shall be saved for thee
45 5 I will give thee thy life and save thee
John 13 38 wilt thou lay down thy life for me
lifeless Judg 5 27 he [Sisara] lay l. and wretched
Wisd 15 5 he loveth the l. figure of a dead
lifetime Ps 48 19 in his l. his soul will be
Eccu 40 29 in thy lifetime be not indigent: for
1 Ma 3 12 and fought with it all his lifetime
Luke 16 25 receive good things in thy lifetime
Heb 2 15 all their lifetime subject to servitude
lift Gen 13 14 lift up thy eyes. 31:12; Isa 49:18; 60:4; Jer 3:2; Eze 8:5; 23:27; Zach 5:5
Gen 14 22 I lift up my hand to the Lord God
48 17 he tried to lift it from Ephraim's head
Exod 14 16 lift thou up thy rod and stretch forth
20 25 if thou lift up a tool upon it, it

23 5 by, but shalt lift him up with him
Lev 23 11 who shall lift up the sheaf before the
Num 16 3 why lift you up yourselves above the
23 24 shalt lift itself up as a lion: it shall
Deut 22 4 not slight it, but shalt lift it up
32 40 I will lift up my hand to heaven and
Josu 8 18 said to Josue: Lift up the shield that
Judg 8 28 could they any more lift up their heads
Ruth 3 4 shalt go in and lift up the clothes
1 Pa 25 5 sons of Heman . . . to lift up the horn
1 Es 9 6 ashamed to lift up my face to thee
Jdth 9 11 lift up thy arms as from the beginning
Job 10 15 if just, I shall not lift up my head
11 15 thou lift up thy face without spot
22 26 and shalt lift up thy face to God
38 34 lift up thy voice. Isa 10:30; 40:9; 58:1; Jer 22:20
39 20 wilt thou lift him up like the locusts
Ps 17 49 wilt lift me up above them that rise
23 7 lift up your gates, O ye princes. 9
27 2 when I lift up my hands to thy holy
62 5 in thy name I will lift up my hands
73 3 lift up thy hands against their pride
74 5 to the sinners: Lift not up the horn
6 lift not up your horn on high: speak
93 2 lift up thyself, thou that judgest
109 7 therefore shall he lift up the head
133 2 lift up your hands to the holy places
Prov 23 5 lift not up thy eyes to riches which
Ecce 4 10 falleth, he hath none to lift him up
Eccu 20 11 that shall lift up his head from a low
34 1 deceitful, and dreams lift up fools
36 3 lift up thy hand over the strange
38 3 skill of the physician shall lift up
40 26 riches and strength lift up the heart
Isa 2 4 nation shall not lift up sword against
5 26 he will lift up a sign to the nations
10 15 as if a rod should lift itself up
24 he shall lift up his staff over thee
26 shall lift it up in the way of Egypt
11 15 shall lift up his hand over the river
13 2 lift ye up a banner, exalt the voice, lift up the hand
15 5 shall lift up a cry of destruction
22 17 he will lift thee up as a garment
24 14 these shall lift up their voice and
33 10 I be exalted, now will I lift up myself
37 4 lift up thy prayer for the remnant
40 9 lift it up, fear not. Say to the
26 lift up your eyes. 51:6; Jer 13:20; Eze 33:25
49 22 I will lift up my hand to the Gentiles
58 14 I will lift thee up above the high
62 10 lift up the standard to the people
Jer 22 27 they lift up their mind to return
50 2 and publish it, lift up a standard
32 there shall be none to lift him up
51 14 and they shall lift up a joyful shout
Lam 2 19 lift up thy hands to him for the life
3 41 let us lift up our hearts with our
Eze 17 14 a low kingdom and not lift itself up
21 22 to lift up the voice in howling, to set
26 8 shall lift up the buckler against thee
Dan 11 14 shall lift up themselves to fulfil the
Osee 4 8 and shall lift up their souls to their
Amos 4 2 when they shall lift you up on pikes
Zach 2 9 I lift up my hand upon them, and they
12 3 that shall lift it up shall be rent
Mat 12 11 he not take hold on it and lift it up
Luke 18 13 would not so much as lift up his eyes
21 28 look up and lift up your heads because
John 4 35 lift up your eyes and see the countries
13 18 shall lift up his heel against me
Heb 12 12 lift up the hands which hang down and
lifted Gen 7 17 and lifted up the ark on high
Gen 18 2 lifted up his eyes. 22:13; 24:63; Josu 5:13; 2 K 13:34; Eze 18:6, 15
21 16 she lifted up her voice and wept. And
31 10 lifted up my eyes. Ps 120:1; 122:1; Eze 8:5; Dan 4:31; 8:3; 10:5; Zach 1:18; 2:1; 5:1, 9; 6:1
45 2 lifted up his voice. 1 K 24:17; 2 K 3:32; Eccu 46:23
Exod 6 8 I lifted up my hand. Num 14:30; Job 31:21; Eze 20:5, 6, 15, 23, 28, 42; 36:7; 44:12; 47:14
17 11 when Moses lifted up his hands, Israel
Lev 8 27 having lifted them up before the Lord
23 20 when the priest hath lifted them up
Num 8 21 Aaron lifted them up in the sight of
10 35 when the ark was lifted up, Moses said
20 11 when Moses had lifted up his hand and
Deut 8 14 thy heart be lifted up, and thou
17 16 being lifted up with the number of his
20 that his heart be not lifted up with
Josu 8 19 and when he had lifted up his shield
Judg 2 4 lifted up their voice. Ruth 1:9, 14; 2 K 13:36; 2 Pa 5:13; 1 Es 3:12; Ps 92:3; Isa 52:8
21 2 lifted up their voices. Ruth 1:14; 1 K 11:4; 30:4; Eccu 50:20
2 K 18 28 have lifted up their hands against the
20 21 lifted up his hand. 3 K 11:26; Ps 105:26; Eccu 48:20
23 18 l. up his spear against. 1 Pa 11:11, 20
3 K 20 33 he lifted him [Benadad] up into his
4 K 9 32 Jehu lifted up his face to the window
10 15 he lifted him up to him into the chariot
14 10 and thy heart hath lifted thee up: be
19 22 against whom . . . lifted up thy eyes on
25 27 lifted up the head of Joachin king of
2 Pa 25 19 thy heart is lifted up. Eze 28:2, 5, 6
26 16 his heart was lifted up. 32:25; Eze 31:10; Dan 5:20
32 26 because his heart had been lifted up
2 Es 9 15 upon which thou hadst lifted up thy hand
Jdth 10 20 the servants of Holofernes lifted her up
11 2 I would never have lifted up my spear
Job 2 12 when they had lifted up their eyes afar
11 12 a vain man is lifted up into pride and
24 24 they are lifted up for a little while
30 22 thou hast lifted me up and set me as it
Ps 23 7 and be ye lifted up, O eternal gates. 9
24 1 thee, O Lord, have I lifted up my soul
26 6 now he hath lifted up my head above my
36 35 wicked . . . lifted up like the cedars
72 18 when they were lifted up thou hast cast
76 3 with my hands lifted up to him in the
82 3 that hate thee have lifted up the head
85 4 thee, O Lord, I have lifted up my soul
92 3 the floods have lifted up their waves
101 11 having lifted me up thou hast thrown me
106 25 and the waves thereof were lifted up
118 48 I lifted up my hands to thy commandments
142 8 for I have lifted up my soul to thee
Prov 16 18 the spirit is lifted up before a fall
30 13 and their eyelids lifted up on high
32 a fool after he was lifted up on high
Eccu 11 13 hath lifted him up from his low estate
19 3 he shall be lifted up for a greater
32 1 they made thee ruler? Be not lifted up
6 be not lifted up out of season with
46 3 he lifted up his hands. 50:22
48 22 their hands, they lifted them up to
Isa 18 3 when the sign shall be lifted up on

9 let it expect light and not see it nor
16 being conceived have not seen the light
20 why is light given to him that is in
12 22 bringeth up to l. the shadow of death
25 grope as in the dark, and not in the l.
15 22 he may return from darkness to light
17 12 after darkness I hope for light again
18 5 the light of the wicked be extinguished
6 light shall be dark in his tabernacle
18 he shall drive him out of light into
22 28 thee and light shall shine in thy ways
24 13 they have been rebellious to the light
16 and they have not known the light. If
17 walk in darkness as if it were in light
18 he is light upon the face of the water
25 3 upon whom shall not his light arise
26 10 till light and darkness come to an end
28 11 things he hath brought forth to light
29 3 and I walked by his light in darkness
24 light of my countenance fell not on
30 26 I waited for light, and darkness broke
33 28 that it may live and see the light
30 enlighten them with the light of the
36 30 and lighten with his light from above
32 in his hands he hideth the light and
37 3 his light is upon the ends of the earth
11 and the clouds spread their light
15 rains, to show his light of his clouds
21 but now they see not the light: the
38 15 from the wicked their light shall be
19 where is the way where light dwelleth
24 by what way is the light spread, and
Ps 4 7 l. of thy countenance. 43:4; 88:16; 89:8
26 1 the Lord is my light and my salvation
35 10 and in thy light we shall see light
36 6 bring forth thy justice as the light
37 11 light of my eyes itself is not with me
42 3 send forth thy light and thy truth
48 20 fathers: and he shall never see light
55 13 of God, in the light of the living
66 2 light of his countenance to shine upon
73 16 thou hast made the morning light and
77 14 and all the night with a light of fire
96 11 light is risen to the just, and joy to
103 2 and art clothed with light as with a
104 39 fire to give them light in the night
111 4 a light is risen up in darkness: he is
118 105 to my feet, and a light to my paths
130 declaration of thy words giveth light
126 2 is vain for you to rise before light
138 11 shall be my light in my pleasures
12 and night shall be light as the day
12 the light thereof are alike to thee
148 3 praise him, all ye stars and light
Prov 4 18 path of the just, as a shining light
6 23 is a lamp, and the law a light
13 9 the light of the just giveth joy: but
15 30 light of the eyes rejoiceth the soul
Ecce 2 13 much as light differeth from darkness
11 7 light is sweet and it is delightful
12 2 before the sun and the light and the
Wisd 5 6 light of justice hath not shined unto
11 sound of the wings beating the light air
6 23 love the light of wisdom, all ye that
24 bring the knowledge of her to light
7 10 chose to have her instead of light: for her light cannot be put out
26 she is the brightness of eternal light
29 being compared with the light, she is
10 17 and for the light of stars by night
16 28 adore thee at the dawning of the light
17 5 no power of fire could give them light
19 world was enlightened with a clear l.
18 4 were worthy to be deprived of light
4 by whom the pure light of the law was
Eccu 19 4 to give credit, is light of heart
22 10 the dead, for his light hath failed
24 6 should rise light that never faileth
37 who sendeth knowledge as the light
44 to shine forth to all as morning light
32 20 and shall kindle justice as a light
33 7 excel another, and one light another
36 1 and show us the light of thy mercies
42 16 the sun giving light hath looked upon
43 7 light that decreaseth in her perfection
45 21 and give light to Israel in his law
46 18 because he saw the God of light: and
50 8 as the rainbow giving light in the
31 the light of God guideth his steps
Isa 2 5 let us walk in the light of the Lord
5 20 that put darkness for light, and light
30 the light is darkened with the mist
8 20 they shall not have the morning light
9 2 in darkness, have seen a great light
2 of the shadow of death, light is risen
10 17 the light of Israel shall be as a fire
13 10 stars . . . shall not display their light
10 moon shall not shine with her light
18 4 as the noon light is clear, and as a
26 19 for thy dew is the dew of the light
30 26 light of the moon shall be as the light of the sun, and the light of the sun shall be sevenfold, as the light of seven
42 6 the people, for a light of the Gentiles
16 I will make darkness light before them
45 7 I form the light, and create darkness
49 6 thee to be the light of the Gentiles
50 10 walked in darkness, and hath no light
11 walk in the light of your fire and in
51 4 shall rest to be a l. of the nations
58 8 then shall thy light break forth as the
10 shall thy light rise up in darkness
59 9 looked for light, and behold darkness
60 1 thy light is come, and the glory of
3 the Gentiles shall walk in thy light
19 no more have the sun for thy light
19 unto thee for an everlasting light. 20
Jer 4 23 heavens, and there was no light in them
13 16 you shall look for light, and he will
20 3 when it was light next day, Phassur
25 10 of the will, and the light of the lamp
31 35 giveth the sun for light of the day
35 of the stars, for light of the night
Lam 3 2 me into darkness, and not into light
Bar 3 14 where is the light of the eyes and
20 young men have seen the light and
33 he that sendeth forth light, and it
34 the stars have given light in their
4 2 in the presence of the light thereof
5 9 with joy in the light of his majesty
6 18 they light candles to them, and in
66 as the sun nor give light as the moon
Eze 8 17 is this a light thing to the house
32 7 and the moon shall not give her light
Dan 2 22 in darkness: and light is with him
3 72 ye light and darkness, bless the Lord
Osee 6 3 is prepared as the morning light, and
5 judgments shall go forth as the light
Amos 5 18 of the Lord is darkness, and not light
20 day of Lord be darkness, and not light
8 9 the earth dark in the day of light
Mich 2 1 in the morning light they execute it
7 8 sit in darkness, the Lord is my light
9 he will bring me forth into the light
Haba 3 4 his brightness shall be as the light
11 in the light of thy arrows, they shall

Soph 3 5 he will bring his judgment to light
Zach 14 6 that there shall be no light, but cold
7 time of the evening there shall be l.
1 Ma 1 23 the candlestick of light and all the
4 50 and they gave light in the temple
6 33 the king rose before it was light and
11 67 before it was light they were ready
2 Ma 1 32 was consumed by the light that shined
12 9 light of the fire was seen at Jerusalem
Mat 4 16 sat in darkness, hath seen great light
16 shadow of death, light is sprung up
5 14 you are the light of the world. A city
15 neither do men light a candle and put
16 so let your light shine before men
6 22 l. of thy body is thy eye. Luke 11:34
23 if then the light that is in thee be
10 27 in the dark, speak ye in the light: and
11 30 my yoke is sweet and my burden light
24 29 moon shall not give her l. Mark 13:24
Luke 2 32 a l. to the revelation of the Gentiles
8 16 come in may see the light. 11:33
11 35 that the light which is in thee be not
12 3 shall be published in the light: and
15 8 doth not light a candle and sweep the
16 8 generation than the children of light
22 56 maid had seen sitting at the light
24 22 who before it was light, were at the
John 1 4 and the life was the light of men
5 and the light shineth in darkness and
7 to give testimony of the light. 8
8 he was not the light, but was to give
9 that was the true light, which
3 19 the light is come into the world and
19 loved darkness rather than the light
20 doth evil hateth the light, and cometh not
to the light
21 that doth truth, cometh to the light
5 35 he was a burning and a shining light
35 for a time to rejoice in his light
8 12 I am the light of the world. 9:5
12 but shall have the light of life
11 9 because he seeth the l. of this world
10 because the light is not in him
12 35 a little while, the light is among you
35 walk whilst you have the light, that
36 whilst you have the l., believe in the l.,
that you may be the children of l.
46 I am come a light into the world
Acts 9 3 and suddenly a light from heaven shined
12 7 a light shined in the room: and he
13 47 I have set thee to be the l. of Gentiles
16 29 then calling for a light, he went in
22 6 there shone round about me a great light
9 that were with me, saw indeed the light
11 did not see for the brightness of the l.
26 13 I saw in the way light from heaven above
18 be converted from darkness to light, and
23 rise from dead, and should show light to
27 33 when it began to be l. Paul besought
Rom 2 19 a light of them that are in darkness
13 12 and put on the armor of light. Let us
1 C 4 5 who both will bring to light the hidden
2 C 4 4 the light of gospel of glory of Christ
6 God, who commanded the light to shine
6 to give light of knowledge of the glory
17 momentary and light of our tribulation
6 14 what fellowship hath light with darkness
11 14 transformeth himself into angel of light
Eph 5 8 darkness, but now light in the Lord
8 walk then as children of the light. For
9 fruit of the light is in all goodness
13 are made manifest by the light; for all
13 for all that is made manifest is light
Col 1 12 of the lot of the saints in light: who
1 Th 5 5 for all you are the children of light
1 Tim 6 16 inhabiteth light inaccessible, whom no
2 Tim 1 10 brought to light life and incorruption
1 P 2 9 of darkness into his marvellous light
2 P 1 19 as to a light that shineth in a dark
1 J 1 5 God is light, and in him there is no
7 but if we walk in the light, as he
7 as he also is in the light, we have
2 8 passed, and the true light now shineth
9 he that saith he is in the light, and
10 loveth his brother, abideth in the l.
Apoc 18 23 light of the lamp shall shine no more
21 11 light thereof was like to a precious
24 nations shall walk in the light of it
22 5 shall not need the light of the lamp
5 nor the light of the sun, because the
lighted Gen 24 61 she saw Isaac, l. off the camel
1 K 25 23 lighted off the ass and fell before
2 Pa 13 11 to be lighted always in the evening
Job 41 10 lamps, like torches of lighted fire
Isa 9 8 Jacob, and it hath lighted upon Israel
62 1 and her savior be lighted as a lamp
1 Ma 4 50 lighted up the lamps that were upon
2 Ma 1 8 lighted the lamps and set forth the
lighten Job 36 30 and l. with his light from
Jon 1 5 into the sea, to lighten it of them
lightened Acts 27 18 they lightened the ship. 38
lighteneth Luke 17 24 as the lightning that l.
lighter Exod 18 22 so it may be lighter for thee
3 K 12 9 said to me: Make the yoke . . . lighter
2 Pa 10 4 do thou govern us with a lighter hand
Haba 1 8 their horses are lighter than leopards
lightest Ps 17 29 lightest my lamp, O Lord
lighteth Luke 11 33 no man lighteth a candle and
lighting Jdth 13 16 and l. up the lights they all
Eccu 43 19 as the birds lighting upon the earth
Luke 8 16 no man lighting a candle covereth it
lightly Isa 9 1 land of Nephtali was l. touched
1 Tim 5 22 impose not hands lightly upon any man
lightness Tob 3 17 with them that walk in l.
2 C 1 17 I was thus minded, did I use lightness
lightning Exod 9 23 l. running along the ground
Exod 19 16 to be heard, and lightning to flash
Deut 32 41 if I shall whet my sword as the l.
2 K 22 15 them: lightning, and consumed them
Ps 143 6 send forth lightning, and thou shalt
Wisd 5 22 shafts of lightning shall go directly
Eccu 32 14 before a storm goeth lightning: and
Jer 51 16 he hath turned lightning into rain
Bar 6 60 the lightning . . . is easy to be seen
Eze 1 13 lightning going forth from the fire
14 ran and returned like flashes of l.
Dan 10 6 his face as the appearance of lightning
Nah 2 4 like lightning running to and fro
Zach 9 14 his dart shall go forth as lightning
Mat 24 27 as lightning cometh out of the east
28 3 his countenance was as lightning
Luke 10 18 I saw Satan like l. falling from
17 24 as the l. that lighteneth from under
lightnings Job 38 35 canst thou send lightnings
Job 41 14 he shall send lightnings against him
Ps 17 15 he multiplied l. and troubled them
76 19 thy l. enlightened the world: the earth
96 4 his l. have shone forth to the world
134 7 he hath made lightnings for the rain
Eccu 43 14 sendeth forth swiftly the lightnings
Jer 10 13 he maketh l. for rain and bringeth forth
Dan 3 73 ye lightnings and clouds, bless the
Apoc 4 5 from the throne proceeded lightnings
8 5 were thunders and voices and lightnings
11 19 there were lightnings and voices. 16:18
lights Gen 1 14 let there be lights made in the

3 K 7 15 line of . . . cubits compassed. 23; 2 Pa 4:2
4 K 21 13 over Jerusalem the line of Samaria
Job 38 5 who hath stretched the line upon it
Ps 77 54 their land by a line of distribution
138 3 my path and my line thou hast searched
Isa 34 11 a line shall be stretched out upon it
17 hand hath divided it to them by line
Jer 31 39 the measuring line shall go out farther
Lam 2 8 he hath stretched out his line and
Eze 40 3 with a line of flax in his hand, and a
47 3 the man that had the line in his hand
Amos 7 17 thy land shall be measured by a line
Zach 1 16 the building line shall be stretched
2 1 man, with a measuring line in his hand
linen Exod 28 4 tunick and a strait linen garment
Exod 28 40 shalt prepare linen tunicks and girdles
42 thou shalt make also linen breeches
29 5 with the linen garment and the tunick
8 shalt put on them the linen tunicks
38 16 court were woven with twisted linen
Lev 6 10 the tunick and the linen breeches
8 7 priest with the strait linen garment
13 he vested them with linen tunicks
10 5 as they lay, vested with linen tunicks
13 47 a woolen or linen garment that shall
59 leprosy of any woolen or linen garment
16 4 he shall be vested with a linen tunick
4 cover his nakedness with l. breeches
4 he shall be girded with a linen girdle
4 shall put a linen miter upon his head
32 he shall be vested with the linen robe
Deut 22 11 woven of woolen and linen together
1 K 2 18 being a child girded with a linen ephod
22 18 day 85 men that wore the linen ephod
2 K 6 14 David was girded with a linen ephod
1 Pa 15 27 David also had on him an ephod of linen
Eccu 40 4 to him that is covered with rough linen
Jer 13 1 go, and get thee a linen girdle, and
Eze 9 2 in midst of them, clothed with linen
3 that was clothed with linen. 11; 10:2, 6, 7; Dan 12:6, 7
27 7 fine broidered linen from Egypt was
30 21 be healed . . . and swathed with linen
44 17 shall be clothed with linen garments
18 they shall have linen miters on their
18 and linen breeches on their loins
Dan 10 5 and behold a man clothed in linen
Mat 27 59 wrapped it up in a clean linen cloth
Mark 14 51 a linen cloth cast about his naked
52 casting off the linen cloth, fled from
Luke 24 12 saw the linen cloths laid by themselves
John 19 40 bound it in linen cloths, with the
20 5 saw the linen cloths lying. 6
7 not lying with the linen cloths, but
Acts 10 11 linen sheet let down by four corners
Apoc 15 6 clothed with clean and white linen
fine linen Exod 25 4 and fine linen and goat's hair
Exod 28 5 scarlet twice dyed and fine l. 35:35
39 shalt gird the tunick with fine linen
39 thou shalt make a fine linen miter
35 6 offer them to the Lord: . . . fine linen dyed, and fine linen, goats' hair. 23
25 purple and scarlet and fine linen
38 23 purple, scarlet, and fine linen. 39:1
39 25 they made also fine linen tunicks with
26 with their little crowns of fine linen
27 and linen breeches of fine linen: and
1 Pa 4 21 house of them that wrought fine linen
15 27 was clothed with robe of fine linen
2 Pa 5 12 clothed with fine linen, sounded with
Prov 31 22 fine linen and purple is her covering
24 she made fine linen and sold it and
Isa 3 22 and fine linen and crisping pins
19 9 flax, combing and weaving fine linen
Eze 16 10 and I girded thee about with fine linen
13 and wast clothed with fine linen and
27 16 they set forth . . . fine linen and silk
Mark 15 46 Joseph buying fine linen, and taking
46 wrapped him up in f. l. Luke 23:53
Luke 16 19 was clothed in purple and fine linen
Apoc 18 12 fine linen and purple and silk and
16 which was clothed in fine linen and
19 8 should clothe herself with fine linen
8 the fine linen are the justifications
14 clothed in fine linen, white and clean
fine twisted linen. Exod 26 1 ten curtains of fine twisted linen. 36:8
Exod 26 31 a veil of . . . fine twisted linen. 36:35
36 a hanging of . . . fine twisted linen. 27:16; 36:37; 38:18
27 9 hangings of fine twisted linen. 38:9
18 the court . . . made of fine twisted l.
28 6 ephod of . . . fine twisted linen. 39:2
8 scarlet twice dyed and fine twisted l.
15 rational of . . . fine twisted linen. 39:8
39 22 of violet, purple, scarlet, and f. . . .
28 a girdle of f. . . . , violet, purple, and
lines 2 K 8 2 and he measured with two lines
4 K 20 9 that the shadow go forward ten lines
10 for the shadow to go forward ten lines
11 ten degrees backwards by the lines
Ps 15 6 the lines are fallen unto me in goodly
Isa 38 8 bring again the shadow of the lines
8 in the sun dial . . . ten lines backward. And the sun returned ten lines
linger Gen 45 9 come down to me, linger not. And
Eccu 10 29 linger not in the time of distress
lingered Gen 19 16 as he l., they took his hand
lingereth 2 P 2 3 now of a long time lingereth not
linked Exod 28 14 chains . . . linked one to another. 22; 39:15
lintel Zach 12 2 I will make Jerusalem a lintel
lintels Isa 6 4 the l. of the doors were moved
Amos 9 1 the hinges, and let the lintels be shook
Linus 2 Tim 4 21 Pudens and Linus and Claudia and
lion Gen 49 9 resting thou hast couched as a lion
Num 23 24 shall lift itself up as a lion: it shall
24 9 lying down he hath slept as a lion and
Deut 33 20 he hath rested as a lion and hath
22 Dan is a young lion, he shall flow
Judg 14 5 young lion met him raging and roaring
6 tore the lion as he would have torn a
8 went aside to see carcass of the lion
8 swarm of bees in the mouth of the lion
9 the honey from the body of the lion
18 honey? And what is stronger than a lion
1 K 17 34 and there came a lion or a bear and
36 I thy servant have killed both a lion
37 delivered me out of the paw of the lion
2 K 17 10 whose heart is as the heart of a lion
23 20 and slew a lion in the midst of a pit
3 K 13 24 a lion found him in the way and killed
24 and the lion stood by the dead body
25 and the lion standing by the body
26 the Lord hath delivered him to the lion
28 and the lion standing by the carcass
28 the lion had not eaten of the dead body
20 36 from me, and a lion shall slay thee
36 a lion found him and slew him. Then
1 Pa 11 22 killed a lion in the midst of a pit
12 8 faces were like the faces of a lion
28 17 he gave by weight, for every lion
Esth 14 13 my mouth in the presence of the lion
Job 4 10 the roaring of the lion, and the voice
Ps 7 3 he seized upon my soul like a lion
9 9 in wait in secret like a lion in his

16 12 me, as a lion prepared for the prey
12 a young lion dwelling in secret places
21 14 me, as a lion ravening and roaring
90 13 thou shalt trample under foot the lion
Prov 19 12 as the roaring of a lion, so. 20:2
22 13 is a lion without, I shall be slain
26 13 is a lion in the way, and a lioness in
28 1 but the just, bold as a lion, shall be
15 as a roaring lion and a hungry bear
30 30 a lion, the strongest of beasts, who
Ecce 9 4 living dog is better than a dead lion
Eccu 4 35 not as a lion in thy house, terrifying
21 3 teeth thereof are the teeth of a lion
25 23 more agreeable to abide with a lion
27 11 the lion always lieth in wait for prey
31 vengeance as a lion shall lie in wait
28 27 it shall be sent upon them as a lion
Isa 5 29 their roaring like that of a lion
11 6 the calf and the lion . . . shall abide
7 the lion shall eat straw like the ox
15 9 lion upon them that shall flee of Moab
21 8 and a lion cried out: I am upon the
30 6 whence come the lioness and the lion
31 4 like as the lion roareth and the lion's
35 9 no lion shall be there, nor shall any
38 13 as a lion so hath he broken all my
65 25 the lion and the ox shall eat straw
Jer 2 30 your generation is like a ravaging lion
4 7 the lion is come up out of his den and
5 6 a lion out of the wood hath slain them
12 8 is become to me as a lion in the wood
25 38 he hath forsaken his covert as the lion
49 19 shall come up as a lion from. 50:44
Lam 3 10 in wait: as a lion in secret places
Eze 1 10 the face of a lion on the right side
10 14 in the third was the face of a lion
19 3 one of her whelps, and he became a lion
5 young lions, and set him up for a lion
6 among the lions, and became a lion
22 25 like a lion that roareth and catcheth
32 3 thou art like the lion of the nations
41 19 face of a lion was toward the palm tree
Osee 11 10 after the Lord, he shall roar as a lion
13 8 I will devour them there as a lion
Joel 1 6 his teeth are like the teeth of a lion
Amos 3 4 will a lion roar in the forest if he
8 the lion shall roar, who will not fear
5 19 should flee from the face of a lion
Mich 5 8 as a lion among the beasts of the
8 as a young lion among the flocks of
Nah 2 11 young lions, to which the lion went, to enter in thither, the young lion
12 the lion caught enough for his whelps
1 Ma 3 4 in his acts he was like a lion, and
2 Tim 4 17 delivered out of the mouth of the lion
1 P 5 8 adversary the devil, as a roaring lion
Apoc 4 7 first living creature was like a lion
5 5 behold the lion of the tribe of Juda
10 3 a loud voice as when a lion roareth
13 2 and his mouth as the mouth of a lion
lioness Gen 49 9 couched as a lion and as a l.
Num 24 9 hath slept as a lion and as a lioness
23 24 the people shall rise up as a lioness
Job 4 10 the voice of the lioness, and the teeth
10 16 for pride thou wilt take me as a l.
28 8 neither hath the lioness passed by it
38 39 wilt thou take the prey for the lioness
Prov 26 13 there is . . . a lioness in the roads
Isa 30 6 whence come the lioness and the lion
Eze 19 2 why did thy mother the lioness lie down
Dan 7 4 the first was like a lioness, and had
Osee 5 14 I will be like a lioness to Ephraim
13 7 and I will be to them as a lioness
lionesses Nah 2 12 and killed for his lionesses
lion's Gen 49 9 Juda is a lion's whelp: to the
Ps 21 22 save me from the lion's mouth; and
Eccu 13 23 the wild ass is the lion's prey in the
Isa 31 4 as the lion roareth, and the l. whelp
Osee 5 14 like a lion's whelp to the house of
Joel 1 6 his cheek teeth as of a lion's whelp
Amos 3 4 will the lion's whelp cry out of his
12 should get out of the lion's mouth
1 Ma 3 4 like a lion's whelp roaring for his
lions 2 K 1 23 than eagles, stronger than lions
2 K 23 20 he slew the two lions of Moab, and he
3 K 7 29 were lions and oxen and cherubims
29 under the lions and oxen . . . bands of
36 cherubims and lions and palm trees
10 19 and two lions stood, one at each hand
20 little lions stood upon the six steps
4 K 17 25 the Lord sent lions among them, which
26 the Lord hath sent lions among them
1 Pa 28 17 fine gold, and for little lions of gold
17 for lions of silver he set aside a
2 Pa 9 18 and two lions standing by the arms
19 twelve other little lions standing
Job 4 10 teeth of the whelps of lions are broken
11 the young lions are scattered abroad
Ps 34 17 malice: my only one from the lions
56 5 my soul from midst of the young lions
57 7 shall break the grinders of the lions
103 21 young lions roaring after their prey
Cant 4 8 from the dens of the lions, from the
Wisd 11 18 a multitude of bears or fierce lions
Eccu 47 3 he played with lions as with lambs
Isa 5 29 they shall roar like young lions: yea
Jer 2 15 the lions have roared upon him, and
50 17 flock, the lions have driven him away
51 38 they shall roar together like lions
38 shake their manes like young lions
Eze 19 2 the lioness lie down among the lions
2 her whelps in the midst of young lions
5 took one of her young lions, and set
6 he went up and down among the lions
38 13 all the lions thereof shall say to thee
Dan 6 7 be cast into the den of lions. 12
16 cast him into den of the lions. 14:30
20 thou, to deliver thee from the lions
22 hath shut up the mouths of the lions
34 the den, before the lions caught them
14 31 in the den there were seven lions
39 Daniel was sitting in midst of the l.
Nah 2 11 where is now the dwelling of the lions
11 the feeding place of the young lions
13 the sword shall devour thy young lions
Soph 3 3 in the midst of her as roaring lions
Zach 11 3 the voice of the roaring of the lions
1 Ma 2 60 was delivered out of mouth of the l.
2 Ma 11 11 violently upon the enemy, like lions
Heb 11 33 promises, stopped the mouths of lions
Apoc 9 8 their teeth were as lions: and they
17 of the horses were as the heads of lions
lions' Dan 6 19 went in haste to the lions' den
Dan 6 24 they were cast into the lions' den
27 delivered Daniel out of l. den. 14:42
14 33 to Daniel, who is in the lions' den
40 he drew him out of the lions' den
lip Prov 12 19 lip of truth shall be steadfast
Soph 3 9 will restore to the people a chosen lip
lips Exod 6 12 I am of uncircumcised lips. 30
1 K 1 13 and only her lips moved, but her voice
Jdth 13 6 and the motion of her lips in silence
Job 19 20 nothing but lips are left about my
Ps 11 3 with deceitful lips and with a double
4 may Lord destroy all deceitful lips
5 our lips are our own; who is Lord over

13 3 the poison of asps is under their lips
16 1 proceedeth not from deceitful lips
21 8 they have spoken with the lips, and
30 19 let deceitful lips be made dumb. Which
58 8 and a sword is in their lips: for who
31 their mouth, the word of their lips
62 6 shall praise thee with joyful lips
119 2 deliver my soul from wicked lips and a
139 4 the venom of asps is under their lips
10 labor of their lips shall overwhelm
Prov 4 24 let detracting lips be far from thee
5 3 lips of a harlot are like a honeycomb
7 21 him away with the flattery of her lips
10 8 precepts: a fool is beaten with lips
10 the foolish in lips shall be beaten
13 in the lips of the wise is wisdom found
18 lying lips hide hatred: he that
21 the lips of the just teach many: but
32 the lips of the just consider what is
12 22 lying lips are abomination of the Lord
14 3 the lips of the wise preserve them
7 he knoweth not the lips of prudence
15 7 the lips of the wise shall disperse
16 10 divination is in the lips of the king
13 just lips are the delight of kings
17 4 the deceitful hearkeneth to lying lips
7 nor lying lips [become] a prince
18 6 lips of a fool intermeddle with strife
20 15 lips of knowledge are a precious vessel
24 2 robberies, and their lips speak deceits
26 he shall kiss the lips, who answereth
26 23 swelling lips joined with corrupt heart
Ecce 10 12 lips of a fool shall throw him down
Eccu 1 30 lips of many shall declare his wisdom
2 14 of a double heart and to wicked lips
21 19 in the lips of the wise, grace shall be
28 lips of the unwise will be telling
26 28 not be justified from sins of the lips
31 28 the lips of many shall bless him that
39 20 glory to him with the voice of your l.
51 3 from the lips of them that forge lies
Isa 6 5 because I am a man of unclean lips
5 of a people that hath unclean lips
28 11 with the speech of lips, and with
29 13 with their lips glorify me, but their
57 19 I created the fruit of the lips, peace
59 3 your lips have spoken lies, and your
Lam 3 62 lips of them that rise up against me
Osee 14 3 we will render the calves of our lips
Mala 2 7 lips of the priest shall keep knowledge
Mat 15 8 honoreth me with their lips. Mark 7:6
Rom 3 13 the venom of asps is under their lips
1 C 14 21 in other tongues and other lips I will
Heb 13 15 fruit of lips confessing to his name
his lips Lev 5 4 and uttereth with his lips
Job 1 22 Job sinned not by his lips nor spoke
2 10 things Job did not sin with his lips
11 5 and would open his lips to thee, that
23 12 from the commandments of his lips
Ps 20 3 withholden from him that will of his l.
105 33 and he distinguished with his lips
Prov 10 19 that refraineth his lips is most wise
16 23 mouth: and shall add grace to his lips
27 evil, and in his lips is a burning fire
30 deviseth wicked things, biting his lips
17 28 close his lips, a man of understanding
18 7 and his lips are the ruin of his soul
20 offspring of his lips shall fill him
19 1 rich man that is perverse in his lips
20 19 him that . . . openeth wide his lips
22 11 grace of his lips shall have the king
26 24 an enemy is known by his lips, when
Cant 5 13 his lips are as lilies dropping choice
7 9 for his lips and his teeth to ruminate
Wisd 1 6 not acquit the evil speaker from his l.
Eccu 12 15 enemy speaketh sweetly with his lips
23 7 keep it, shall not perish by his lips
50 22 to give glory to God with his lips
Isa 11 4 with breath of his lips he shall slay
30 27 his lips are filled with indignation
Mala 2 6 iniquity was not found in his lips
1 P 3 10 and his lips that they speak no guile
my lips Jdth 9 13 graces of the words of my l.
Job 13 6 and attend to the judgment of my lips
16 6 and would move my lips, as sparing you
27 4 my lips shall not speak iniquity
32 20 I will open my lips, and will answer
33 3 my lips shall speak a pure sentence
Ps 15 4 mindful of their names by my lips
39 10 I will not restrain my lips: O Lord
50 17 thou wilt open my lips: and my mouth
62 4 than lives: thee my lips shall praise
65 14 my vows, which my lips have uttered
70 23 my lips shall greatly rejoice when I
118 13 with my lips I have pronounced all the
171 my lips shall utter a hymn when thou
140 3 mouth: and a door round about my lips
Prov 8 6 and my lips shall be opened to preach
7 and my lips shall hate wickedness
Eccu 22 33 mouth, and a sure seal upon my lips
Jer 17 16 that which went out of my lips hath
Dan 10 16 likeness of a son of man touched my l.
Haba 3 16 troubled: my l. trembled at the voice
thy lips Deut 23 23 is once gone out of thy lips
4 K 19 28 and a bit between thy lips, and I will
Job 8 21 and thy lips [be filled] with rejoicing
15 6 and thy own lips shall answer thee
Ps 16 4 for the sake of the words of thy lips
33 14 and thy lips from speaking guile. Turn
44 3 grace is poured abroad in thy lips
Prov 5 2 and thy lips may preserve instruction
22 18 bowels, and it shall flow in thy lips
23 16 when thy lips shall speak what is right
24 28 and deceive not any man with thy lips
27 2 mouth: a stranger, and not thy own lips
Cant 4 3 thy lips are as a scarlet lace: and
11 thy lips . . . as a dropping honeycomb
Eccu 1 37 let not thy lips be a stumblingblock
Isa 6 7 behold this hath touched thy lips, and
37 29 I will put . . . a bit between thy lips
lips' Prov 12 13 the sins of the lips' ruin
liquor Lev 11 34 every liquor that is drunk out of
list 2 K 17 9 some other place where he list
Lithostrotos John 19 13 the place that is called L.
litigious Titus 3 2 not to be litigious, but gentle
litter Cant 3 9 king Solomon hath made him a l.
2 Ma 3 27 him into a litter they carried him out
9 8 was carried in a l., bearing witness
litters Isa 66 20 in chariots and in litters and
little Gen 6 14 thou shalt make little rooms in
Gen 18 4 I will fetch a little water and wash ye
24 17 give me a little water to drink of thy
25 34 little account of having sold his first
27 16 the little skins of the kids she put
30 30 thou hadst put but little before I came
33 10 receive a little present at my hands
40 4 some little time passed, and they were
10 which by little and little sent out buds
43 2 go again and buy us a little food. Juda
11 a little balm and honey and storax
44 4 city and had gone forward a little way
25 go again, and buy us a little wheat. And
Exod 2 3 put the little babe therein and laid
12 39 which a little before they had brought
17 2 a little more and they will stone me
11 if he let them down a little, Amalec

23 30 by little and little I will drive them
28 14 two little chains of the purest gold
33 dyed, with little bells set between
35 18 the pins . . . with their little cords
39 15 made also in the rational little chains
23 and little bells of the purest gold
26 and miters with their little crowns of
40 the little cords and the pins thereof
Lev 2 6 thou shalt divide it into little pieces
3 4 of the liver with the two little kidneys
10 both the little kidneys, with the fat
10 of the liver with the little kidneys. 15
15 the two little kidneys with the caul
4 9 little kidneys and the caul. 9:10
9 fat of the liver with the little kidneys
5 8 back the head of it to the l. pinions
7 4 the two little kidneys, and the fat
4 caul of the liver with the l. kidneys
8 16 little kidneys with their fat. 9:19
14 37 as it were little dints, disfigured with
20 4 little regarding my commandment, let
21 18 if he have a little or a great . . . nose
25 25 impoverished sell his little possession
Num 4 7 with it the censers and little mortars
5 17 he shall cast a little earth of the
7 14 a little mortar of ten sicles of gold
20 a little mortar of gold. 26, 32, 38, 44, 50, 56, 62, 68, 74, 80
84 twelve little mortars of gold. 86
11 12 nurse is wont to carry the little infant
Deut 1 17 you shall hear the little as well as
31 as a man is wont to carry his little son
7 22 will consume . . . by little and little
14 19 that creepeth and hath little wings
28 38 seed into the ground, and gather little
Judg 4 19 give me, I beseech thee, a little water
16 26 let me lean upon them and rest a little
17 5 also therein a little temple for the god
8 had turned aside a little into the house
18 15 and when they had turned a little aside
19 5 to him: Taste first a little bread and
8 I beseech thee to take a little meat
20 33 began by little and little to come forth
1 K 1 14 digest a little the wine, of which thou
2 19 his mother made him a little coat which
6 8 you shall put into a little box at the
11 little box that had in it the golden
15 the little box that was at the side of
10 1 Samuel took a little vial of oil and
14 29 because I tasted a little of this honey
43 I did but taste a little honey with
17 18 carry these ten little cheeses to the
30 he [David] turned a little aside from
20 2 will do nothing great or little without
35 Jonathan . . . and a little boy with him
22 15 of this matter, either little or great
30 2 the women captives . . . little and great
2 K 6 22 I will be little in my own eyes: and
7 19 yet this hath seemed l. in thy sight
12 3 nothing at all but one little ewe lamb
8 if these things be little, I shall add
13 6 and make in my sight two little messes
8 in his sight she made little messes
10 Thamar took the little messes which she
16 1 David was a little past the top of
17 20 after they had tasted a little water
19 36 I thy servant will go on a little way
23 8 was like the most tender little worm
3 K 6 31 he made little doors of olive tree and
7 29 between the l. crowns and the ledges
8 64 was too l. to receive the holocaust
10 20 and 12 little lions stood upon the six
11 17 Egypt: and Adad was then a little boy
12 4 take off a l. of the grievous service
10 my little finger is thicker than the. 2 Pa 10:10
17 10 give me a little water in a vessel
12 I have . . . a little oil in a cruse
13 make for me . . . a little hearth cake
18 44 a little cloud arose out of the sea
20 27 like two little flocks of goats: but
36 when he was gone a little from him, a
4 K 2 23 little boys came out of the city and
4 2 nothing in my house but a little oil
10 let us . . . make him a little chamber
10 and put a little bed in it for him
5 2 had led away captive . . . a little maid
9 1 take this little bottle of oil in thy
3 taking the little bottle of oil, thou
10 18 Achab worshipped Baal a little, but I
23 2 the people both little and great. 25:26
7 as it were l. dwellings for the grove
1 Pa 17 17 this hath seemed little in thy sight
26 13 cast lots equally, both l. and great
28 17 fine gold, and for little lions of gold
2 Pa 3 5 like little chains interlaced with one
16 he made also as it were little chains
16 which he put between the little chains
5 9 but if a man were a little outward
9 19 moreover twelve other little lions
12 7 and I will give them a little help
15 13 let him die, whether little or great
21 15 vital parts come out by little and l.
31 15 to their brethren, both little and great
1 Es 4 22 lest by l. and l. the evil grow to the
9 8 and now as a little and for a moment
8 give us a little life in our bondage
Tob 4 9 if thou have little, take care even so
6 8 if thou put a little piece of its heart
Jdth 7 7 to refresh themselves a little rather
Job 1 11 but stretch forth thy hand a little
10 20 that I may lament my sorrow a little
14 6 depart a little from him, that he may
19 the ground by l. and l. is washed away
26 14 heard scarce a little drop of his word
32 20 I will speak and take breath a little
36 2 suffer me a little, and I will show
Ps 8 6 made him a little less than the angels
36 16 better is a little to the just, than
41 7 and Hermoniim, from the little hill
103 25 number: creatures little and great
113 13 fear the Lord, both little and great
Prov 6 10 thou wilt sleep a little. 24:33
10 thou wilt slumber a little. 24:33
10 wilt fold thy hands a little. 24:33
13 11 that which by l. and l. is gathered
15 16 better is a little with fear of Lord
16 8 better is a little with justice than
30 24 four very little things of the earth
Ecce 5 11 man, whether he eat little or much
9 14 a little city and few men in it: there
Cant 2 15 the little foxes that destroy the vines
3 4 when I had a little passed by them
8 8 our sister is l. and hath no breasts
Wisd 6 7 to him that is little, mercy is granted
8 he made the little and the great and
7 9 in comparison of her is as a little sand
12 2 chastisest them that err, by l. and l.
8 to destroy them by little and little
14 5 trust their lives even to a little wood
20 that a l. before was but honored as
15 8 a l. before was made of earth himself
8 a little after returneth to the same
16 27 being warmed with a little sunbeam
Eccu 6 20 shalt labor a little, and shalt quickly
19 1 things, shall fall by little and little

22 11 weep but a little for the dead, for he
25 25 groaned and hearing he sighed a little
34 issue to thy water, no, not a little
29 29 contented with little instead of much
31 22 how sufficient is a little wine for a
34 10 that hath no experience, knoweth little
40 6 a little and as nothing is his rest
42 4 and weights, of getting much or little
45 10 compassed him with many little bells
47 28 Roboam that had little wisdom, who
51 21 I bowed down my ear a little and
35 how I have labored a little and have
Isa 3 18 ornaments of shoes and little moons
5 10 vineyard shall yield one little measure
22 24 kinds of vessels, every little vessel
26 20 hide thyself a little for a moment
28 10 a little there, a little there. 13
30 14 wherein a little fire may be carried
14 or a little water be drawn out of the
40 15 the islands are as a little dust
50 2 is my hand shortened and become little
66 2 but to him that is poor and little and
Jer 16 6 the great and the little shall die in
52 18 the bowls and the little mortars and
Eze 11 16 I will be to them a little sanctuary
16 47 nor hast thou done a little less than
40 7 little chamber was one reed. 13, 49
7 between the l. chambers. 10, 12, 16, 21
41 24 two little doors, which were folded
46 21 was a little court in the corner of
22 were little courts disposed, forty
Dan 7 8 another little horn sprung out of the
8 9 came forth a little horn: and it
14 12 they little regarded it, because they
Osee 7 4 the city rested a little from the
Amos 7 2 raise up Jacob, for he is very little
9 9 shall not a little stone fall to the
Agge 1 6 have sowed much and brought in little
Zach 1 15 I was angry a little, but they helped
4 10 who hath despised little days? And
1 Ma 1 23 vials and the little mortars of gold
16 15 them deceitfully into a little fortress
2 Ma 3 30 that a little before was full of fear
6 25 a little time of a corruptible life
29 and had been a little before more mild
8 8 the man gained ground by little and l.
9 10 the man that thought a little before
15 19 had no little concern for them that
Mat 6 30 ye of l. faith. 8:26; 16:8; Luke 12:28
14 31 O thou of little faith, why didst thou
15 34 a few little fishes. Mark 8:7
26 39 going a little further, he fell upon
Mark 1 19 going on from thence a little farther
6 31 into a desert place and rest a little
14 35 when he was gone forward a little
Luke 5 3 to draw back a little from the land
8 22 he went into a little ship with his
12 32 fear not, little flock, for it hath
16 10 is unjust in that which is little, is
19 17 thou hast been faithful in a little
John 2 15 a scourge of little cords, he drove
6 7 that every one may take a little
Acts 20 12 youth alive, and were not a l. comforted
26 28 in a little thou persuadest me to become
29 that both in a little and in much, not
27 28 and going on little further, they found
1 C 5 6 little leaven corrupteth the. Gal 5:9
2 C 8 15 and he that had little, had no want. And
11 1 bear with some little of my folly: but
16 foolish, that I also may glory a little
1 Tim 4 8 bodily exercise is profitable to little
5 23 use a little wine for thy stomach's sake
Heb 2 7 a little lower than the angels. 9

James 3 5 the tongue is indeed a little member
1 P 1 6 be for a little time made sorrowful in
5 10 after you have suffered a little, will
Apoc 3 8 thou hast a little strength, and hast
6 11 that they should rest for a little time
10 2 he had in his hand a little book open
11 18 that fear thy name, little and great
13 16 both little and great, rich and poor
19 5 and you that fear him, little and great
18 bondmen, and of little and of great
20 3 that, he must be loosed a little time

little child; *see* **child**

little children Lam 2 19 to him for the life of thy little children
Mat 18 3 you be converted and become as l. c.
19 13 then were little children presented to
14 suffer the little children. Mark 10:14
John 13 33 little c., yet a little while I am with
Gal 4 19 my little c., of whom I am in labor
1 J 2 1 my little c., these things I write to
12 I write unto you, little children
18 little children, it is the last hour
28 little children, abide in him, that
3 7 little c., let no man deceive you
18 my little c., let us not love in word
4 4 you are of God, little children, and
5 21 little c., keep yourselves from idols

little one Gen 19 20 to which I may flee, it is a little one . . . is it not a little one
1 K 15 17 when thou wast a little one in thy own
Job 5 2 and envy slayeth the little one. I
Prov 9 4 whosoever is a little one, let him come
16 he that is a little one, let him turn
21 11 punished, the little one will be wiser
Isa 54 11 poor little one, tossed with tempest
69 22 and a little one a most strong nation
Jer 49 15 I have made thee a little one among
Amos 7 5 raise up Jacob, for he is a little one
Mich 5 2 thou, Bethlehem . . . art a little one

little ones Num 32 17 our l. o. and all we have
2 Pa 20 13 with their little ones and their wives
Job 21 11 their little ones go out like a flock
Ps 16 14 they have left to their l. o. the rest
18 8 is faithful, giving wisdom to l. ones
114 6 the Lord is the keeper of little ones
118 130 giveth understanding to little ones
136 9 shall take and dash thy little ones
Prov 1 4 to give subtilty to little ones, to the
32 the turning away of little ones shall
7 7 I see little ones, I behold a foolish
8 5 O little ones, understand subtilty
23 10 touch not the bounds of little ones
27 12 l. ones passing on have suffered losses
Isa 33 18 where is the teacher of little ones
Jer 48 4 proclaim a cry for her little ones
49 20 little ones of the flock shall cast
50 45 the little ones of the flocks shall
Lam 4 4 the little ones have asked for bread
Dan 14 9 besides their wives and little ones
Osee 14 1 let their little ones be dashed and
Joel 2 16 gather together the little ones and
Nah 3 17 thy little ones like the locusts of
Zach 13 7 will turn my hands to the little ones
Mat 10 42 to drink to one of these little ones
11 25 revealed them to l. ones, Luke 10:21
18 6 scandalize one of these little ones. Mark 9:41; Luke 17:2
10 despise not one of these little ones
14 one of these little ones should perish
1 C 3 1 carnal. As unto little ones in Christ
1 Th 2 7 we became little ones in midst of you

little while Gen 42 24 turned himself away a l. w.
Ruth 4 1 turn aside for a l. while and sit down

Job 6 19 ways of Saba, and wait a little while
13 13 hold your peace a little while, that I
14 20 hast strengthened him for a little while
24 24 they are lifted up for a little while
Ps 36 10 little w., and the wicked shall not be
Isa 10 25 yet a little and a very little while
29 17 is it not yet a very little while, and
54 8 have I hid my face a little while from
Jer 51 33 a l. while, and the time of her harvest
Osee 1 4 yet a little while, and I will visit
Agge 2 7 one little while, and I will move the
2 Ma 7 33 our God is angry with us a little while
13 11 had of late taken breath for a l. while
Mat 26 73 after a little while they came that
Luke 22 58 after a little while, another seeing
John 7 33 little while I am with you. 13:33
12 35 yet a little while, the light is among
14 19 a little while; and the world seeth
16 16 l. w. and now you shall not see. 17, 19
16 a l. w. and you shall see me, 17, 19
18 this that he saith: A little while
Acts 5 34 the men to be put forth a little while
Heb 10 37 for yet a little and a very little while
James 4 15 vapor which appeareth for a little while
2 P 2 18 those who for a little while escape
live Gen 3 22 and eat, and live forever. And the
Gen 6 19 ark, that they may live with thee
20 go in with thee, that they may live
12 13 and that my soul may live for thy sake
17 18 O that Ismael may live before thee
19 20 a little one, and my soul shall live
20 7 pray for thee, and thou shalt live
27 40 thou shalt live by the sword and shalt
46 stock of this land, I choose not to live
42 2 buy us necessaries, that we may live
18 do as I have said, and you shall live
43 8 that we may set forward and may live
45 7 the earth, and may have food to live
Exod 19 13 it be beast or man, he shall not live
21 22 she miscarry indeed, but live herself
35 they shall sell the live ox and shall
22 18 wizards thou shalt not suffer to live
33 20 for man shall not see me and live. And
Lev 11 10 things that move and live in the waters
13 14 when the live flesh shall appear in him
15 live flesh, if it be spotted with
18 5 which if a man do, he shall live in them
25 35 he live with thee, take not usury
36 that thy brother may live with thee
Num 4 19 but do this to them that they may live
14 21 as I live. 28; Jer 22:24; 46:18; Eze 5:11; 14:16, 18, 20; 16:48; 17:16, 19; 18:3; 20:3, 31, 33; 33:11, 27; 34:8; 35:6, 11; Soph 2:9
21 8 struck shall look on it, shall live
24 23 who shall live when God shall do these
Deut 4 1 that doing them, thou mayst live, and
10 the time that they live on the earth
5 16 that thou mayst live a long time. 22:7; 25:15
26 as we have heard, and be able to live
33 that you may live and it may be well
8 1 that you may live and be multiplied
3 not in bread alone doth man live, but
11 9 may live in it a long time: which the
16 20 that thou mayst live and possess the
19 5 to one of the cities aforesaid, and live
20 16 thou shalt suffer none at all to live
30 6 with all thy soul that thou mayst live
16 thou mayst live and he may multiply
19 that both thou and thy seed may live
31 13 all the days that they live in the land
32 39 I will kill and I will make to live
40 heaven, and I will say: I live forever
47 that every one should live in them
33 6 let Ruben live, and not die, and be he
Josu 6 17 let only Rahab the harlot live, with
9 21 so let them live as to serve the whole
1 K 20 14 if I live, thou shalt show me the
2 K 1 10 that he could not live after the fall
12 22 him to me, and the child may live
3 K 1 31 may my lord David live forever. King
8 40 fear thee all the days that they live
4 K 4 7 and thou and thy sons live of the rest
7 4 if they spare us, we shall live: but
10 19 shall be wanting shall not live. Now
18 32 honey, and you shall live, and not die
20 1 house, for thou shalt die, and not live
2 Pa 6 31 all the days that they live upon the
2 Es 2 3 O king, live forever. Dan 2:4; 3:9; 5:10; 6:21
5 2 price of them, and let us eat and live
9 29 which if a man do, he shall live in them
Tob 3 6 for me to die than to live. Jon 4:3, 8
5 4 thou mayst receive it, while I yet live
12 6 to him in the sight of all that live
Jdth 3 2 it is better for us to live and serve
7 16 that being captives we should live and
Job 7 16 with hope, I shall now live no longer
14 14 shall man that is dead . . . live again
22 while he shall live, shall have pain
21 7 why then do the wicked live, are they
28 13 the land of them that live in delights
33 28 that it may live and see the light
Ps 21 27 their hearts shall live forever and ever
31 to him my soul shall live: and my seed
37 20 my enemies live and are stronger than
48 10 and shall still live unto the end. He
54 24 men shall not live out half their days
65 9 who hath set my soul to live: and hath
68 33 seek ye God, and your soul shall live
71 15 he shall live, and to him shall be given
88 49 who is the man that shall live, and not
103 33 sing to the Lord as long as I live
113 18 but we that live bless the Lord: from
117 17 I shall not die, but live: and shall
118 77 mercies come unto me, and I shall live
116 thy word, and I shall live: and let me
144 give me understanding, and I shall live
175 my soul shall live and shall praise thee
Prov 4 4 commandments, and thou shalt live. 7:2
9 6 forsake childishness, and live, and
15 27 but he that hateth bribes shall live
Ecce 6 3 and live many years and attain to a
9 3 and with contempt while they live and
9 live joyfully with the wife whom thou
11 8 if a man live many years and have
Wisd 3 17 they live long, they shall be nothing
5 16 but the just shall live for evermore
8 9 to take her to me to live with me
14 28 prophesy lies or they live unjustly
Eccu 5 1 say not: I have enough to live on
13 6 have anything, he will live with thee
17 25 with them that live and give praise
37 29 and his name shall live forever. My
42 24 all these things live and remain
48 12 we live only in our life, but after
Isa 6 6 in his hand was a live coal, which he
26 14 let not the dead live, let not the
19 thy dead men shall live, my slain shall
38 1 house, for thou shalt die, and not live
16 shalt correct me and make me to live
49 18 I live, saith the Lord, thou shalt
55 3 hear and your soul shall live, and I
Jer 21 9 shall live, and his life shall be to him
27 17 king of Babylon, that you may live
35 7 that you may live many days upon the
38 2 forth to the Chaldeans, shall live
2 life shall be safe and he shall live

17 thy soul shall live, and this city
20 well with thee, and thy soul shall live
49 11 children: I will make them live: and
Lam 4 20 under thy shadow we shall live among
Bar 1 12 that we may live under the shadow of
Eze 3 18 converted from his wicked way and live
21 living he shall live, because thou
13 19 souls alive which should not live
22 return from his evil way, and live
16 6 I said to thee . . . Live: I have said to thee: Live in thy blood
18 9 he is just, he shall surely live
13 such a one live? he shall not live
17 of his father, but living he shall live
19 and done them, living, he shall live
21 and justice, living, he shall live
22 which he hath wrought, he shall live
23 be converted from his ways, and live
24 if the just man turn . . . shall he live
28 hath wrought, he shall surely live
32 saith the Lord God, return ye and live
20 11 a man do, he shall live in them. 13, 21
25 judgments in which they shall not live
33 10 away in them: how then can we live
11 the wicked turn from his way and live
12 not be able to live in his justice
13 the just that he shall surely live
15 he shall surely live, and shall not
16 judgment and justice, he shall surely l.
19 and justice: he shall live in them
37 3 dost thou think these bones shall live
5 spirit into you, and you shall live
6 give you spirit, and you shall live
9 these slain, and let them live again
14 my spirit in you, and you shall live
47 9 the torrent shall come, shall live
9 shall live to which the torrent shall
Dan 6 6 unto him: King Darius, live forever
Osee 6 3 us up, and we shall live in his sight
14 8 they shall live upon wheat and they
Amos 5 4 seek ye me, and you shall live. But
6 seek ye the Lord, and live: lest the
14 good and not evil, that you may live
Haba 2 4 but the just shall live in his faith
Zach 1 5 the prophets, shall they live always
10 9 they shall live with their children
13 3 shall say to him: Thou shalt not live
1 Ma 2 13 to what end then should we live any
33 come forth . . . and you shall live. And
4 35 they were ready either to live or to
6 59 that they may live according to their
2 Ma 11 23 are in our realm should live quietly
24 them to live after their own laws
25 they may live according to the custom
12 2 would not suffer them to live in peace
Mat 4 4 not in bread alone doth man live, but
9 18 thy hand upon her, and she shall live
Mark 5 23 that she may be safe and may live
Luke 7 25 in costly apparel and live delicately
10 28 right: this do and thou shalt live
20 38 but of the living: for all live to him
John 5 25 and they that hear shall live. For as
6 52 eat of this bread, he shall live
58 sent me, and I live by the Father
58 the same shall also live by me. This
59 eateth this bread, shall live forever
11 25 although he be dead, shall live
14 19 because I live, and you shall live
Acts 17 28 in him we live, and move, and are; as
22 22 for it is not fit that he should live
24 2 through thee we live in much peace, and
25 24 out that he ought not to live any longer
28 4 yet vengeance doth not suffer him to l.
Rom 6 2 how shall we live any longer therein
8 we shall live also together with Christ
8 12 are debtors, not to the flesh, to live
13 for if you live according to the flesh
13 deeds of the flesh, you shall live. For
10 5 man that shall do it, shall live by it
14 8 whether we live, we live unto the Lord
8 whether we live, or whether we die, we
11 as I live, saith the Lord, every knee
1 C 9 14 the gospel, should live by the gospel
2 C 4 11 for we who live are always delivered
5 15 that they also who live, may not now live to themselves
6 9 known; as dying, and behold we live; as
7 3 to die together, and to live together
13 4 we shall live with him by power of God
Gal 2 14 compel Gentiles to live as do the Jews
19 dead to the law, that I may live to God
20 and I live, now not I; but Christ liveth
20 I l. now in the flesh: I l. in the faith
3 12 he that doth these things, shall live in
5 25 if we live in the Spirit, let us also
Phil 1 21 to me, to live is Christ: and to die is
22 if to live in the flesh, this is to me
1 Th 3 8 now we live, if you stand in the Lord
5 10 sleep, we may live together with him
2 Tim 2 11 with him, we shall live also with him
3 12 all that will live godly in Christ Jesus
Titus 2 12 we should live soberly and justly and
Heb 12 9 obey the Father of spirits and live
James 4 15 if we shall live, we will do this or
1 P 2 24 dead to sins, should live to justice
4 2 that now he may live the rest of his
6 may live according to God in the Spirit
1 J 4 9 the world, that we may live by him

lived Gen 5 3 *N.* lived . . . years. 6, 9, 10, 12, 15, 16, 18, 19, 21, 22, 25, 26, 28, 30; 11:12; 14, 16, 18, 20, 22, 24, 26; 23:1; 50:22
Gen 5 5 all the time that Adam lived came to
7 *N.* lived after he begot *N.* 11:11, 13, 15, 17, 19, 21, 23, 25
9 28 Noe lived after the flood 250 years
21 23 land wherein thou hast l. a stranger
25 6 while he [Abraham] yet lived, to the
8 [Abraham] having lived a long time
43 7 if our father lived; if we had a
47 28 he [Israel] lived in it 17 years
Num 14 38 and Caleb the son of Jephone lived
22 33 slain thee, and she should have lived
Deut 4 33 of fire, as thou hast heard, and lived
5 24 God speaking with man, man hath lived
Josu 4 14 as they had feared Moses while he lived
24 31 that lived a long time after Josue
Judg 2 7 ancients that lived a long time after
2 K 19 6 if Absalom had lived, and all we had
3 K 12 6 Solomon his father while he yet lived
4 K 14 17 lived after death of Joas. 2 Pa 25:25
2 Pa 10 6 his father Solomon, while he yet lived
34 33 as long as he lived they departed not
Tob 14 1 his sight, he lived two and forty years
2 after he had lived 102 years, he was
16 after he had lived ninety-nine years
Job 42 16 Job lived after these things 140 years
Ecce 6 6 although he lived 2,000 years and hath
Wisd 12 23 who in their life have lived foolishly
14 22 they lived in a great war of ignorance
15 17 because he indeed hath lived, though
19 15 and who lived under the same laws
Eccu 30 5 while he lived he saw and rejoiced
Jer 46 21 also that lived in the midst of her
Eze 37 10 spirit came into them, and they lived

1 Ma 6 55 whom king Antiochus while he lived had
2 Ma 5 27 and there lived amongst wild beasts in
9 9 whilst he lived in sorrow and pain, his
14 25 he l. quietly, and they l. in common
Luke 2 36 had lived with her husband seven
John 4 51 word, saying, that his son lived
Acts 26 5 sect of our religion I lived a Pharisee
Rom 7 9 and I lived some time without the law
Eph 6 3 that thou mayest be long lived upon earth
Col 3 7 some time, when you lived in them. But
Apoc 13 14 had the wound by the sword and lived
18 7 and lived in delicacies, so much
9 and lived in delicacies with her, shall
20 4 and they lived and reigned with Christ
5 the rest of the dead lived not, till

lively 1 P 1 3 regenerated us unto a lively hope

liver Exod 29 13 the caul of the liver. 22; Lev 3:4, 10; 7:4; 8:16, 25; 9:10, 19
Lev 1 8 all things that cleave to the liver
12 divide . . . all that cleave to the liver
3 15 the liver with the little kidneys. 4:9
Tob 6 5 his heart and his gall and his liver
19 lay the liver of the fish on the fire
8 2 took out of his bag part of the liver
Prov 7 23 till the arrow pierce his liver; as if
Lam 2 11 my liver is poured out upon the earth
Osee 13 8 I will rend the inner parts of their l.

lives Gen 9 5 will require the blood of your l.
Lev 26 16 waste your eyes, and . . . consume your l.
Josu 2 14 be our lives for you unto death, only
9 20 let their lives be saved, lest the
24 and provided for our lives, compelled
Judg 5 2 willingly offered your lives to danger
18 Zabulon and Nephtali offered their l.
2 K 19 5 lives of thy sons and of thy daughters
5 lives of thy wives and the lives of thy concubines
23 17 that went, and the peril of their lives
3 K 3 11 not asked . . . the lives of thy enemies
20 31 Israel: perhaps he will save our lives
4 K 1 13 lives of thy servants that are with me
7 7 and fled, desiring to save their lives
1 Pa 11 19 with the danger of their lives they
2 Pa 1 11 nor the lives of them that hate thee
Esth 8 11 to stand for their lives, and to kill
9 16 the Jews stood for their lives, and
Ps 62 4 thy mercy is better than lives: thee my
Prov 12 10 the just regardeth the l. of his beasts
Wisd 14 5 trust their lives even to a little wood
Jer 19 7 them that seek their lives. 34:21; 46:26
9 that seek their lives, shall straiten
48 6 flee, save your lives: and be as
Lam 5 9 fetched our bread at peril of our lives
1 Ma 2 40 against the heathens for our lives
50 give your lives for the covenant of
3 21 we will fight for our l. and our laws
9 9 let us save our lives now and return
12 51 seeing that they stood for their lives
13 4 all my brethren have lost their lives
Acts 15 26 have given their lives for the name of
27 10 lading and ship, but also of our lives
1 J 3 16 we ought to lay down our lives for
Apoc 12 11 they loved not their lives unto death

livest Deut 12 19 time that thou l. in the land
Eccu 33 20 power over these while thou livest
21 as long as thou livest, and hast breath
Gal 2 14 being a Jew, livest after the manner of

liveth Gen 9 3 everything that moveth and liveth
Gen 16 14 well of him that liveth and seeth me
Deut 15 11 poor brother, that liveth in the land
28 43 the stranger that liveth with thee
Judg 8 19 as the Lord liveth. Ruth 3:13; 1 K 14:39, 45; 19:6; 20:3, 22; 25:34; 26:10, 16; 28:10; 29:6; 2 K 2:27; 4:9; 12:5; 14:11; 15:21; 3 K 1:29; 2:24; 17:1; 22:14; 4 K 2:2, 4, 6; 4:30; 5:16, 20; 2 Pa 18:13; Jer 4:2; 38:16
1 K 1 26 as thy soul l. 17:55; 4 K 2:2, 4, 6; 4:30; Jdth 12:4
20 31 as long as the son of Isai liveth
25 26 the Lord liveth. 2 K 22:47; Ps 17:47; Jer 5:2; 12:16; 16:14, 15; 23:7, 8; 44:26; Osee 4:15
26 the Lord liveth and thy soul liveth
2 K 15 21 as my Lord the king liveth: in what
3 K 3 22 my child liveth, and thy child is dead
23 thy child is dead, and mine liveth
17 12 as the Lord thy God liveth. 18:10
23 and said to her: Behold thy son liveth
18 15 as the Lord of hosts liveth. 4 K 3:14
Jdth 11 5 as . . . the king of the earth liveth
5 and his power liveth which is in thee
13 20 as the same Lord liveth, his angel
Job 19 25 for I know that my Redeemer liveth
27 2 as God liveth, who hath taken away
30 23 is appointed for every one that liveth
Ecce 7 16 a wicked man liveth a long time in his
9 4 there is no man that liveth always
Eccu 10 10 while he liveth he hath cast away his
18 1 he that liveth forever created all
25 10 he that l. and seeth the fall of his
44 14 their name liveth unto generation
Dan 4 31 glorified him that liveth forever
12 7 had sworn, by him that liveth forever
Amos 8 14 and say: Thy God, O Dan, liveth, and the way of Bersabee liveth
2 Ma 14 10 as long as Judas liveth, it is not
Luke 4 4 man liveth not by bread alone, but by
John 4 50 thy son liveth. 53
11 26 every one that liveth and believeth
Rom 1 17 the just man l. by faith. Gal 3:11
6 10 in that he liveth, he liveth unto God
7 1 dominion over man, as long as it liveth
2 whilst her husband liveth. 3
8 10 spirit liveth, because of justification
14 7 for none of us liveth to himself; and
1 C 7 39 by law as long as her husband liveth
2 C 13 4 yet he liveth by the power of God. For
Gal 2 20 now not I; but Christ liveth in me. And
1 Tim 5 6 for she that liveth in pleasures, is
Heb 7 8 there he hath witness, that he liveth
9 17 no strength, whilst the testator liveth
10 38 my just man liveth by faith; but if he
1 P 1 23 who liveth and remaineth forever
Apoc 4 9 who liveth forever and ever. Apoc 15:7
10 him that l. forever and ever. 5:14; 10:6

living Gen 1 21 every living and moving creature
Gen 1 24 earth bring forth the living creature
2 7 of life, and man became a living soul
19 Adam called any l. creature, the same
3 20 she was the mother of all the living
6 19 of every living creature of all flesh
8 17 all living things that are with thee
19 and all living things and cattle and
24 62 well which is called Of the living and
25 11 well named Of the living and seeing
26 19 in the torrent, and found living water
42 13 with our father, the other is not l.
32 one is not living, the youngest is
36 Joseph is not living, Simeon is kept
43 27 your father . . . Is he yet living
28 our father is in health, he is yet l.
45 3 I am Joseph: is my father yet living
26 Joseph thy son is living; and he is
28 if Joseph my son be yet living: I will

Lev 11 2 of all the living things of the earth
46 the law . . . of every living creature
13 10 the living flesh itself shall appear
14 4 to offer for himself two l. sparrows
5 in an earthen vessel over l. waters. 50
7 he shall let go the living sparrow
51 the living sparrow, and shall dip all
51 is immolated, and in the living water
52 shall purify . . . with the living water and with the living sparrow
15 13 having washed . . . in living water, he
16 20 then let him offer the living goat
18 18 her nakedness, while she is yet living
Num 16 48 standing between the dead and the l.
19 17 shall pour living waters upon them
20 6 open . . . a fountain of living water
Deut 5 3 us, who are now present and living
26 should hear the voice of the l. God
31 27 while I am yet living, and going in
Josu 3 10 Lord the living God is in the midst
Judg 18 7 being very rich, and living separated
Ruth 2 20 kindness which he showed to the living
1 K 17 26 should defy the armies of the l. God
36 to curse the army of the living God
25 29 be kept as in the bundle of the living
2 K 20 3 day of their death l. in widowhood
3 K 3 25 divide, said he, the living child in two
27 give the living child to this woman and
4 K 19 4 hath sent to reproach the living God
16 sent to upbraid unto us the living God
Tob 2 19 what she could get for their living
Job 12 10 is the soul of every living thing and
14 1 born of a woman, living for a short time
28 21 it is hid from the eyes of all living
33 30 enlighten them with light of the living
Ps 38 6 all things are vanity: every man living
41 3 thirsted after the strong living God
55 13 sight of God, in the light of the living
68 29 be blotted out of book of the living
83 3 my flesh have rejoiced in the living God
142 2 sight no man living shall be justified
144 16 fillest with blessing every l. creature
Ecce 4 2 I praised the dead rather than the l.
15 I saw all men living that walk under the
7 3 the living thinketh what is to come
8 10 who also when they were yet living were
9 4 a living dog is better than a dead lion
5 the living know that they shall die
10 19 and wine, that the living may feast
Cant 4 15 the well of living waters, which run
Wisd 1 13 in the destruction of the living. For
4 10 living among sinners he was translated
16 condemneth the wicked that are living
7 20 the natures of living creatures and
12 24 living after the manner of children
15 11 that breathed into him a living spirit
18 12 neither were the living sufficient to
23 and cut off the way to the living
Eccu 7 37 hath grace in sight of all the living
11 18 that is enriched by living sparingly
16 31 soul of every living thing hath shown
17 27 give thanks whilst thou art living
42 8 approved in the sight of all men living
43 27 variety of beasts and of all l. things
44 6 living at peace in their houses. All
45 20 he chose him out of all men living, to
Isa 8 19 seek . . . for the living of the dead
37 4 sent to blaspheme the living God. 17
38 11 not see the Lord God in land of the l.
19 the living, he shall give praise to thee
Jer 2 13 forsaken me, fountain of living water
10 10 the true God: he is the living God
17 13 the Lord, the vein of living waters
23 36 perverted the words of the living God
Lam 3 39 why hath a living man murmured, man
Eze 3 21 living he shall live, because thou
7 13 their life be yet among the living
10 15 the living creature that I had seen
20 this is the living creature which I saw
18 17 of his father, but living he shall live
19 and done them, living, he shall live
21 and justice, living, he shall live
47 9 every living creature that creepeth
Dan 4 14 till the living know that the most High
6 20 Daniel, servant of the living God
26 he is the living and eternal God
14 4 the living God, that created heaven
5 Bel seem to thee to be a living god
23 say now, that this is not a living god
24 Lord my God: for he is the living God: but that is no living God
Osee 1 10 ye are the sons of the living God
Zach 14 8 living waters shall go out from
2 Ma 11 24 keep to their own manner of living
15 4 there is the living God himself in
Mat 16 16 art Christ, the Son of the living God
22 32 God of the dead, but of the living. Mark 12:27; Luke 20:38
26 63 I adjure thee by the living God, that
Mark 12 44 in all she had, even her whole living
Luke 15 13 wasted his substance, l. riotously
21 4 cast in all the living that she had
24 5 why seek you the living with the dead
John 4 10 he would have given thee living water
11 from whence then hast thou living water
6 41 I am the living bread. 51
58 as the living Father hath sent me
7 38 shall flow rivers of living water
11 27 art Christ the Son of the living God
Acts 10 42 to be judge of the l. and of the dead
14 14 from these vain things, to the l. God
Rom 9 26 shall be called sons of the living God
12 1 you present your bodies a l. sacrifice
14 9 Lord both of the dead and of the living
1 C 15 45 man Adam was made into a living soul
2 C 3 3 written . . . with Spirit of living God
6 16 you are the temple of the living God; as
Col 2 20 yet decree as though living in the world
1 Th 1 9 idols, to serve the living and true God
1 Tim 3 15 which is the church of the living God
4 10 because we hope in the living God, who
5 6 pleasures, is dead while she is living
6 17 but in the living God, who giveth us
2 Tim 4 1 who shall judge the living and the dead
Titus 3 3 living in malice and envy, hateful, and
Heb 3 12 unbelief, to depart from the living God
4 12 the word of God is living and effectual
7 25 always living to make intercession for
9 14 from dead works, to serve the living God
10 20 Christ; a new and living way which he
31 to fall into the hands of the living God
12 22 Sion, and to the city of the living God
1 P 2 4 upon whom coming, as to a living stone
5 be you also as living stones built up
4 5 who is ready to judge the living and
Apoc 1 18 behold I am living forever and ever
4 7 first living creature was like a lion
7 the second living creature like a calf
7 third living creature, having the face
7 fourth living creature was like an
6 3 I heard the second living creature
5 I heard the third living creature
7 voice of the fourth living creature
7 2 having the sign of the living God; and

every living soul Gen 8 21 no more destroy e. . . .
Gen 9 10 every l. soul that is with you. 12

15 and with e. . . . that beareth flesh
16 that was made between God and e. . . .
Apoc 16 3 and every living soul died in the sea
land of the living Ps 26 13 good things of the Lord in the land of the living
Ps 51 7 place: and thy root out of the l. . . .
114 9 I will please Lord in the l. . . .
141 6 art my hope, my portion in the l. . . .
Isa 53 8 because he is cut off out of the l. . . .
Jer 11 19 bread, and cut him off from the l. . . .
Eze 26 20 when I shall give glory in the l. . . .
32 23 heretofore spread terror in the l. . . .
24 that caused their terror in the l. . . .
25 spread their terror in the l. . . . 26
27 terror of the mighty in the l. . . .
32 I have spread my terror in the l. . . .
living creatures; *see* **creatures**
lizard Lev 11 30 the lizard . . . unclean
lo Mat 3 16 and lo, the heavens were opened to
Mat 17 5 lo, a voice out of the cloud, saying
24 23 shall say to you: Lo here is Christ or
28 7 lo, I have foretold it to you. And
Mark 13 21 lo, here is Christ; lo, he is here
Luke 9 39 and lo, a spirit seizeth him, and he
13 16 hath bound, lo, these eighteen years
17 21 lo, the kingdom of God is within you
Apoc 14 1 lo a lamb stood upon mount Sion and
load Gen 45 17 load your beasts, and go into
Wisd 9 15 corruptible body is a l. upon the soul
Haba 2 6 he load himself with thick clay
Luke 11 46 you load men with burdens which they
loaded Gen 42 26 l. their asses with the corn
1 K 17 20 went away loaded as Isai had commanded
Isa 9 1 way of the sea . . . was heavily loaded
loading Gen 44 13 l. their asses again, returned
loaf Lev 8 26 taking . . . a loaf without leaven
Lev 24 5 two tenths shall be in every loaf
1 Pa 16 3 both men and women, a loaf of bread
Prov 6 26 price of a harlot is scarce one loaf
Mark 8 14 they had but one loaf with them in
loan 1 K 2 20 for the loan thou hast lent to
Prov 28 8 together riches by usury and loan
loathe Prov 29 27 wicked l. them that are in the
Wisd 16 3 might loathe even that which was
loatheth Num 21 5 now l. this very light food
loathsome Num 11 20 become l. to you because
Isa 66 24 they shall be a loathsome sight to all
loaves Exod 29 32 l. also that are in the basket
Lev 2 4 l. without leaven tempered with. 7:12
7 13 l. of leavened bread with the sacrifice
8 31 eat ye also the loaves of consecration
32 be left of the flesh and the loaves
2 22 shall eat nevertheless of the loaves
23 17 two loaves of the firstfruits, of two
18 offer with the loaves seven lambs
20 hath lifted them up with the loaves
24 5 and shalt bake twelve loaves thereof
Num 4 7 the loaves shall be always on it: and
Josu 9 5 the loaves also, which they carried for
12 these loaves we took hot when we
Judg 6 19 made unleavened loaves of a measure
20 the flesh and the unleavened l. 21
1 K 10 3 and another three loaves of bread
4 will give thee two loaves, and thou
17 17 take . . . and these ten loaves, and run
21 3 though it were but five loaves, give
6 that hot loaves might be set up. Now
25 18 Abigail made haste and took 200 loaves
2 K 16 1 laden with two hundred loaves of bread
2 the l. and the figs for thy servants
3 K 14 3 take also with thee ten loaves and
4 K 4 42 bringing . . . twenty loaves of barley
1 Pa 12 40 brought loaves on asses and on
2 Pa 13 11 loaves are set forth on a most clean
1 Ma 4 51 they set the loaves upon the table
2 Ma 1 8 lighted the lamps and set forth the l.
Mat 14 17 we have not here but five loaves and
19 he took the five loaves and the two
19 and gave the loaves to his disciples
15 33 we have so many loaves in the desert
34 how many l. have you? Mark 6:38; 8:5
36 taking the seven loaves. Mark 8:6
16 9 the 5 loaves among 5,000 men, and how
10 nor the 7 loaves among 4,000 men
Mark 6 41 when he had taken the five loaves and
41 and broke the loaves and gave to his
52 understood not concerning the loaves
8 19 when I broke the five loaves among
20 when also the 7 loaves among 4,000
Luke 9 13 we have no more than five loaves and
16 taking the five loaves and the two
11 5 to him: Friend, lend me three loaves
John 6 9 hath five barley loaves and two fishes
13 fragments of the five barley loaves
26 but because you did eat of the loaves
Heb 9 2 table, and the setting forth of loaves
loaves of proposition Exod 25 30 shalt set upon the table loaves of proposition
Exod 35 13 bars and the vessels and the l. . . .
39 35 the vessels thereof and the l. . . .
40 21 setting there in order the l. . . . , as
Lev 21 8 to their God, and offer the l. . . .
Num 8 2 north, towards the table of the l. . . .
1 K 21 6 no bread there but only the l. . . .
3 K 7 48 table of gold upon which the l. . . .
1 Pa 9 32 were over the l. . . . , to prepare
23 29 priests have the charge of the l. . . .
2 Pa 4 19 tables upon which were the l. . . .
2 Es 10 33 for the l. . . . and for the continual
2 Ma 10 3 forth incense and lamps and l. . . .
Mat 12 4 did eat the l. of proposition. Mark 2:26
Lobna 4 K 8 22 Lobna also revolted at the same
4 K 19 8 king of the Assyrians besieging Lobna
23 31 daughter of Jeremias of Lobna. 24:19
1 Pa 6 57 cities for refuge Hebron and Lobna
2 Pa 21 10 Lobna also revolted from being under
Isa 37 8 king of the Assyrians besieging Lobna
Jer 52 1 Amital, the daughter of Jeremias of L.
Lobni Exod 6 17 sons of Gerson: Lobni. 1 Pa 6:17
Num 26 58 families of Levi: the family of Lobni
1 Pa 6 20 of Gerson: Lobni his son, Jahath
29 Moholi: Lobni his son, Semei his son
lock Eze 8 3 and took me by a lock of my head
locking Judg 3 23 of the parlor, and l. them
locks Judg 16 13 if thou plattest the seven l. of
Judg 16 19 shaved his seven locks and began to
2 Pa 8 5 cities with gates and bars and locks
2 Es 3 3 the locks and the bars. 6, 13, 14, 15
Jdth 16 10 and bound up her locks with a crown
Cant 5 2 my locks [full] of the drops of
11 his locks as branches of palm trees
Bar 6 17 secure the doors with bars and locks
locust Exod 10 4 will bring in tomorrow the l.
Exod 10 12 unto the locust, that it come upon it
Lev 11 22 and ophiomachus and the locust
3 K 8 37 or corrupt air or blasting or locust
2 Pa 7 13 command the locust to devour the land
Ps 77 46 blast, and their labors to the locust
104 34 the locust came, and the bruchus
Prov 30 27 the locust hath no king, yet they all
Ecce 12 5 flourish, the locust shall be made fat
Jer 51 27 bring the horse as the stinging locust
Joel 1 4 hath left, the locust hath eaten: and
4 which the locust hath left, the bruchus
2 25 ears which the locust . . . have eaten
Amos 7 1 the locust was formed in the beginning

Nah 3 15 make thyself many like the locust
locusts Exod 10 13 the burning wind raised the l.
Exod 10 19 it took the locusts and cast them
Num 13 34 in comparison . . . we seemed like l.
Deut 28 38 because the locusts shall consume all
Judg 6 5 and like locusts filled all places
7 12 in the valley, as a multitude of l.
2 Pa 6 28 if a famine arise . . . or locusts
Jdth 2 11 covered the face of the earth like l.
Job 39 20 wilt thou lift him up like the locusts
Ps 108 23 declineth: and I am shaken off as l.
Wisd 16 9 the bitings of locusts . . . killed them
Eccu 43 19 is as the coming down of locusts. The
Isa 33 4 as the locusts are gathered, as when
40 22 the inhabitants thereof are as locusts
Jer 46 23 they are multiplied above locusts and
51 14 I will fill thee with men as with l.
Nah 3 17 thy guards are like the locusts: and
17 thy little ones like the l. of l.
Mat 3 4 his meat was locusts and wild honey
Mark 1 6 and he ate locusts and wild honey
Apoc 9 3 there came out locusts upon the earth
7 the shapes of the locusts were like
Lod 1 Pa 8 12 who built Ono and Lod and its
1 Es 2 33 the children of Lod. 2 Es 7:37
2 Es 11 34 Hadid, Seboim, and Neballat, Lod
Lodabar 2 K 9 4 Machir the son of Ammiel in L.
2 K 9 5 the son of Ammiel of Lodabar. 17:27
lodge Gen 19 2 house of your servant, and lodge
Gen 24 23 place in thy father's house to lodge
25 and hay, and a large place to lodge in
Deut 24 12 the pledge shall not lodge with thee
Judg 19 11 city of the Jebusites, and lodge there
13 we will lodge there, or at least in
15 they turned into it to lodge there
15 no man would receive them to lodge
2 K 17 8 and will not lodge with the people
Tob 6 10 where wilt thou that we lodge? And the
Isa 1 8 as a lodge in a garden of cucumbers
Jer 14 8 as a wayfaring man turning in to lodge
Soph 2 14 the urchin shall lodge in the threshold
Luke 9 12 they may lodge and get victuals; for
Acts 21 16 disciple, with whom we should lodge. And
1 C 16 19 in their house, with whom I also lodge
lodged Gen 24 54 drank together and lodged there
Gen 31 54 when they had eaten, they lodged there
32 21 himself lodged that night in the camp
Josu 2 1 harlot named Rahab, and l. with her
Judg 18 12 they lodged in Cariathiarim of Juda
19 26 door of the house where her lord lodged
20 4 with my wife, and there I lodged
2 K 7 2 the ark of God is lodged within skins
Tob 6 1 l. the first night by the river Tigris
Eccu 29 33 my brother being to be lodged with me
1 Ma 11 6 they lodged there. And Jonathan
Luke 13 19 birds of the air lodged in the branches
Acts 10 18 asked, if Simon, . . . were lodged there
23 then bringing them in, he lodged them
lodgeth Eccu 14 25 he that lodgeth near her house
Eccu 36 28 lodgeth wheresoever the night taketh
Acts 10 6 he lodgeth with one Simon a tanner
32 Peter: he lodgeth in the house of Simon
lodging Gen 24 32 he brought him in into his l.
Judg 18 3 the Levite, and lodging with him, they
19 19 is with me: we want nothing but l.
23 because this man is come into my l.
Eccu 14 25 where good things shall rest in his l.
Isa 10 29 passed in haste, Gaba is our lodging
Jer 9 2 a lodging place of wayfaring men, and
Acts 28 30 two whole years in his own hired lodging
Philem 22 but withal prepare me also a lodging
lodgings Acts 28 23 very many to him unto his l.
loft Eze 41 7 it led into the upper loft of the
Acts 20 9 fell from third loft down, and was taken
loftiness Isa 2 17 the l. of men shall be bowed
Jer 48 29 pride and the loftiness of his heart
1 C 2 1 came not in loftiness of speech or of
Col 2 4 may deceive you by loftiness of words
lofty 1 K 2 3 not multiply to speak lofty things
Ps 130 1 not exalted: nor are my eyes lofty
Prov 30 13 a generation whose eyes are lofty and
Isa 2 11 the lofty eyes of men are humbled and
13 upon all the tall and lofty cedars of
5 15 eyes of the lofty shall be brought low
10 33 down, and the lofty shall be humbled
57 7 upon a high and lofty mountain thou
Eze 31 18 and lofty among the trees of pleasure
1 Ma 13 27 a building lofty to the sight, of
loins Gen 35 11 kings shall come out of thy loins
3 K 2 5 on his girdle that was about his loins
8 19 that shall come forth out of thy loins
18 46 he [Elias] girded up his loins and ran
20 31 let us put sackcloth on our loins and
32 they girded sackcloth on their loins
4 K 1 8 a girdle of leather about his loins
4 29 gird up thy loins and take my staff
9 1 gird up thy loins and take this little
2 Pa 6 9 son, who shall come out of thy loins
10 10 is thicker than the loins of my father
Jdth 8 6 she wore haircloth upon her loins
Job 12 18 and girdeth their loins with a cord
16 14 his lances, he hath wounded my loins
38 3 gird up thy loins like a man. 40:2
40 11 his strength is in his loins, and his
Ps 37 8 for my loins are filled with illusions
Prov 30 31 a cock girded about the loins: and a
31 17 hath girded her loins with strength
Isa 5 27 neither shall girdle of their loins be
11 5 justice shall be the girdle of his l.
20 2 loose the sackcloth from off thy loins
21 3 therefore are my loins filled with pain
32 11 be confounded, gird your loins. Mourn
Jer 1 17 gird up thy loins and arise, and speak
13 1 thou shalt put it about thy loins and
2 a girdle . . . and put it about my loins
4 girdle . . . which is about thy loins
11 as the girdle sticketh close to the l.
30 6 every man with his hands on his loins
Eze 1 27 from his loins and upward, and from his loins downward
8 2 from the appearance of his loins and
2 and from his loins and upward as the
9 3 had a writer's inkhorn at his loins
21 6 mourn with the breaking of thy loins
29 7 brokest and weakenest all their loins
44 18 and linen breeches on their loins, and
47 5 me through the water up to the loins
Dan 5 6 the joints of his loins were loosed
10 5 loins were girded with the finest gold
Nah 2 1 watch the way, fortify thy loins
10 and all the loins lose their strength
2 Ma 10 25 girding their loins with haircloth and
Mat 3 4 leathern girdle about loins. Mark 1:6
Luke 12 35 let your loins be girt, and lamps
Acts 2 30 of the fruit of his loins one should
Eph 6 14 stand therefore, having your loins girt
7 5 also came out of the loins of Abraham
10 he was yet in the loins of his father
1 P 1 13 having the loins of your mind girt up
Lois 2 Tim 1 5 dwelt first in thy grandmother Lois
long Exod 27 1 five cubits long. 2 Pa 3:11, 12; 6:13
Exod 27 9 a hundred cubits long. 11; Eze 40:47
36 15 one curtain was thirty cubits long
38 18 twenty cubits long. 2 Pa 4:1
Num 10 21 so long was the tabernacle carried
Deut 1 5 stayed long enough in this mountain

2 3 have compassed this mountain long enough
3 11 his bed . . . being nine cubits long
4 26 you shall not dwell therein long, but
5 33 and your days may be long in the land
19 6 if the way be too long and take away
Josu 5 4 during the time of the long going about
9 11 take with you victuals for a long way
13 by reason of the very long journey are
10 14 was not before nor after so long a day
Judg 5 28 why is his chariot so long in coming
11 26 for so long a time attempted nothing
20 31 pursued them a long way, so as to wound
2 K 3 1 a long war between the house of Saul
13 18 and she was clothed with a long robe
19 on her head and rent her long robe
3 K 3 11 hast not asked for thyself long life
6 17 forty cubits long. Eze 46:22
4 K 6 25 so long did the siege continue till
9 22 so long as the fornications of Jezabel
2 Pa 21 19 being wasted with a long consumption
Jdth 6 21 and they prayed all the night long
Ps 62 5 thus will I bless thee all my life long
94 10 forty years long was I offended with
97 6 with long trumpets, and sound of cornet
118 20 coveted to long for thy justifications
119 6 my soul hath been long a sojourner
Prov 7 19 home, he is gone a very long journey
Wisd 3 17 they live long, they shall be nothing
4 16 soon ended, the long life of the unjust
17 2 being fettered with . . . a long night
18 20 but thy wrath did not long continue
Eccu 3 7 shall enjoy a long life: and he that
6 22 cast her from them before it be long
7 18 wrath, for it will not tarry long
10 11 a long sickness is troublesome to the
27 9 put her on as a long robe of honor
Isa 22 11 a distance, that wrought it long ago
65 22 works . . . shall be of long continuance
Lam 2 20 their children of a span long? Shall the
Bar 4 35 fire shall come . . . long to endure
6 46 make them, are of no long continuance
Eze 40 7 was one reed long and one reed broad
21 fifty cubits long. 33, 36; 42:7
30 porch . . . was 5 and 20 cubits long
42 one cubit and a half long, and one
41 12 the wall . . . ninety cubits long. And he
42 20 measured the wall . . . 500 cubits long
43 16 and the Ariel was twelve cubits long
17 the brim was fourteen cubits long and
44 20 shave their heads, nor wear long hair
45 6 of the city . . . 5 and 20 thousand long
Osee 11 7 my people shall long for my return
1 Ma 8 19 went to Rome, a very long journey
21 7 were letters sent long ago to Onias
27 in arms all night long ready to fight
2 Ma 2 33 to make a long prologue and to be
6 1 but not long after the king sent a
7 5 was suffering therein long torments
10 6 not long before they had kept the
12 36 that were with Esdrin had fought long
Mat 11 21 they had long ago done penance in
23 14 houses of widows, praying long prayers
24 38 my lord is long a coming. Luke 12:45
Mark 12 38 who love to walk in long robes and to
40 under the pretence of long prayer
Luke 1 21 that he tarried so long in the temple
10 13 they would have done penance long ago
20 46 who desire to walk in long robes and
47 houses of widows, feigning long prayer
Acts 20 9 deep sleep, as Paul was long preaching
27 14 but not long after, there arose against
28 6 expected long, and seeing that there
Rom 1 11 I long to see you, that I may impart
Phil 1 8 God is my witness, how I long after you
1 Tim 3 15 if I tarry long, that thou mayest know

all the day long Deut 33 12 shall he abide a. . . .
Ps 24 5 on thee have I waited all the day long
31 3 whilst I cried out all the day long
34 28 thy praise all the day long. The unjust
36 26 and lendeth all the day long; and his
37 7 I walked sorrowful all the day long
13 and studied deceits all the day long
43 9 in God shall we glory all the day long
16 all the day long my shame is before me
22 we are killed all the day long: we are
51 4 a. . . . thy tongue hath devised injustice
55 2 all the day long he hath afflicted me
3 have trodden on me all the day long
6 all the day long they detested my words
70 8 thy greatness all the day long. Cast
15 thy salvation all the day long. Because
101 9 all the day long my enemies reproached
139 3 all the day long they designed battles
Prov 23 17 thou in fear of the Lord a. . . . : because
Isa 52 5 my name is continually blasphemed a. . . .
Lam 1 13 wasted with sorrow all the day long
3 14 their song all the day long. He hath
Osee 12 1 a. . . . he multiplied lies and desolation
Rom 8 36 all the day long they designed battles
10 21 all the day long have I spread my hands

as long as Lev 15 25 a. . . . she is subject to this
Deut 11 21 a. . . . the heaven hangeth over the earth
1 K 20 31 a. . . . the son of Isai liveth upon earth
Ps 103 33 I will sing to the Lord a. . . . I live
145 2 will sing to my God a. . . . I shall be
Eccu 33 21 a. . . . thou livest, and hast breath in
Eze 42 11 were as long as they, and as broad
2 Ma 14 10 a. . . . Judas liveth, it is not possible
Mat 9 15 a. . . . the bridegroom is with. Mark 2:19
25 45 as long as you did it not to one of
40 as long as you did it to one of these
Mark 2 19 as long as they have the bridegroom
John 9 5 as long as I am in the world, I am
Rom 7 1 dominion over man, as long as it liveth
11 13 as long indeed as I am the apostle of
1 C 7 39 by law as long as her husband liveth
Gal 4 1 say, as long as the heir is a child, he
2 P 1 13 as long as I am in this tabernacle

how long Exod 10 3 how long refusest thou to
Exod 10 7 how long shall we endure this scandal
16 28 how long will you refuse to keep my
Num 14 11 how long will this people detract me
11 how long will they not believe me
27 how long doth this wicked multitude
24 22 how l. shalt thou be able to continue
Josu 18 3 how long are you indolent and slack
Judg 16 13 how long dost thou deceive me and tell
1 K 1 14 how long wilt thou be drunk? Digest a
16 1 how long wilt thou mourn for Saul
2 K 2 26 how long dost thou defer to bid the
19 10 how l. are you silent, and bring not
3 K 18 21 how long do you halt between two sides
2 Es 2 6 for how long shall thy journey be
Job 7 19 how long wilt thou not spare me
8 2 how long wilt thou speak these things
2 how long shall the words of thy mouth
18 2 how long will you throw out words
19 2 how long do you afflict my soul and
32 22 I know not how long I shall continue
Ps 4 3 how long will you be dull of heart
6 4 but thou, O Lord, how long? Turn to
12 1 how long, O Lord, wilt thou forget me
1 how long dost thou turn away thy face
2 how long shall I take counsels in my
3 how long shall my enemy be exalted
61 4 how long do you rush in upon a man

73 10 how long, O God, shall the enemy
78 5 how long, O Lord, wilt thou be angry
79 5 how long wilt thou be angry against
6 how long wilt thou feed us with the
81 2 how long will you judge unjustly
88 47 how long, O Lord, turnest thou away
89 13 return, O Lord, how long? and be
93 3 how long shall sinners, O Lord: how long shall sinners glory
Prov 1 22 how long will you love childishness
6 9 how long wilt thou sleep, O sluggard
Isa 6 11 and I said: How long, O Lord? And he
Jer 4 14 how long shall hurtful thoughts abide
21 how long shall I see men fleeing away
21 how long shall I hear the sound of the
12 4 how long shall the land mourn and the
13 27 be made clean after me: how long yet
23 26 how long shall this be in the heart
31 22 how long wilt thou be dissolute in
47 5 how long shalt thou cut thyself? O
6 how long wilt thou not be quiet? Go
Dan 8 13 speaking: How long shall be the vision
12 6 how long shall it be to the end of
Osee 8 5 how long will they be incapable of
Haba 1 2 how long, O Lord, shall I cry and
2 6 how long also doth he load himself
Zach 1 12 how long wilt thou not have mercy on
1 Ma 6 22 how long dost thou delay to execute
Mat 17 16 how long shall I be with you. Mark 9:18; Luke 9:41
16 how long shall I suffer you. Mark 9:18
Mark 9 20 how long time is it since this hath
John 10 24 how long dost thou hold our souls in
Apoc 6 10 how long, O Lord, holy and true, dost
long time Gen 25 8 [Abraham] having lived a l. t.
Gen 37 34 mourning for his son a long time
Num 9 19 if . . . it continued over it a long time
20 15 there we dwelt a long time, and the
Deut 1 46 you abode in Cadesbarne a long time
2 1 we compassed mount Seir a long time
4 40 mayst remain a long time upon the land
5 16 thou mayst live a long time. 22:7; 25:15
11 9 may live in it a long time: which the
17 20 sons may reign a long time over Israel
20 19 thou hast besieged a city a long time
32 47 you may continue long time in the land
Josu 11 18 Josue made war a long time against
22 3 you left your brethren this long time
23 1 when a long time was passed, after that
24 7 you dwelt in the wilderness a long time
31 that had lived a long time after Josue
Judg 2 7 ancients that lived a long time after
3 25 waiting a long time till they were
2 K 7 19 house of thy servant for long time to
14 2 that had a l. time been mourning
Tob 1 18 after a long time, Salmanasar . . . dead
Esth 1 4 he might show . . . for a long time
Ecce 7 16 a wicked man liveth a long time in his
11 1 after a long time thou shalt find it
Wisd 4 8 old age is not that of long time nor
13 short space, he fulfilled a long time
12 24 they went astray for a long time
Eccu 28 26 its continuance shall not be for l. t.
49 15 let Nehemias be a long time remembered
Jer 20 8 I am speaking now this long time
29 28 it is a long time: build ye houses
Lam 5 20 why wilt thou forsake us for a l. t.
Bar 6 2 there many years, and for a long time
1 Ma 12 10 long time passed since you sent to us
2 Ma 6 13 to go on in their ways for a long time
14 38 for a l. t. had held fast his purpose
Mat 25 19 after a long time the lord of those
Mark 9 20 how long time is it since this hath
Luke 8 27 who had a devil now a very long time
18 3 and he would not for a long time
20 9 and he was abroad for a long time
23 8 desirous for a long time to see him
John 5 6 knew that he had been now a long time
14 9 have I been so long a time with you
Acts 8 11 for a long time he had bewitched them
14 3 long time therefore they abode there
20 11 and having talked a long time to them
27 21 after they had fasted a long time, Paul
Heb 4 7 today after so long a time, as it is
2 P 2 3 now of a long time lingereth not
longanimity Gal 5 22 fruit of the Spirit is . . . l.
longed 2 K 23 15 David l. and said: O. 1 Pa 11:17
Ps 118 40 I have longed after thy precepts
131 because I longed for thy commandments
174 I have longed for thy salvation
Phil 2 26 for indeed he longed after you all: and
longer Lev 11 21 but hath the legs behind longer
Num 9 22 over the tabernacle . . . a longer time
10 5 if the sound of the trumpets be longer
Josu 6 5 shall give a longer and broken tune
2 Pa 5 9 because they were something longer
Tob 10 1 but as Tobias made longer stay upon
Jdth 7 17 which is made longer by the drought of
Job 11 9 measure of him is l. than the earth
Jer 6 4 shadows of the evening are grown l.
1 Ma 2 13 what end then should we live any longer
7 38 suffer them not to continue any longer
Luke 22 43 being in an agony, he prayed the l.
Acts 18 20 him, that he would tarry a longer time
25 24 out that he ought not to live any longer
Rom 6 2 how shall we live any longer therein
no longer Gen 45 1 Joseph could no l. refrain
Exod 2 3 when she could hide him no longer, she
9 28 and that you may stay here no longer
Deut 31 2 I can no longer go out and come in
Josu 22 23 they no longer said that they would go
3 K 10 5 she had no longer any spirit in her
2 Es 2 17 and let us be no longer a reproach
Job 7 16 with hope, I shall now live no longer
34 23 it is no longer in the power of man
Prov 6 15 and shall no longer have any remedy
Isa 64 9 and remember no longer our iniquity
Jer 44 22 so that the Lord could no longer bear
Luke 16 2 now thou canst be steward no longer
John 16 10 and you shall see me no longer. And
Rom 6 6 to end that we may serve sin no longer
2 C 5 16 but now we know him so no longer. If
Gal 3 25 we are no longer under a pedagogue. For
1 Th 3 1 forbearing no longer, we thought it
3 5 I, forbearing no longer, sent to know
Apoc 10 6 that time shall be no longer. But in
longeth Job 7 2 as a servant l. for the shade
Ps 83 2 my soul longeth and fainteth for the
Prov 21 26 he longeth and desireth all the day
longing Gen 31 30 hadst a l. after thy father's
Gen 34 8 Sichem has a longing for your daughter
Deut 18 6 a longing mind to come to the place
long-limbed Eze 17 3 large eagle . . . long-limbed
longlived Exod 20 12 that thou mayest be l. upon
Eccu 1 25 the branches thereof are longlived
Isa 53 10 he shall see a longlived seed and
Eph 6 3 and thou mayest be longlived upon earth
longsuffering 2 Es 9 17 l. and full of compassion
Ps 102 8 merciful: l. and plenteous in mercy
Rom 2 4 despisest thou the riches of his . . . l.
2 C 6 6 chastity, in knowledge, in longsuffering
Col 1 11 in all patience and longsuffering with
2 Tim 3 10 faith, longsuffering, love, patience
2 P 3 15 longsuffering of our Lord, salvation
look Gen 13 14 look from the place wherein thou
Gen 15 5 look up to heaven and number the stars

19 17 look not back, neither stay thou in
47 25 only let my lord look favorably upon us
49 18 I will look for thy salvation, O Lord
Exod 3 6 his face: for he durst not look at God
25 20 let them look one towards the other
40 look and make it according to the
28 26 borders that . . . look towards the back
33 13 look upon thy people this nation. And
Lev 13 5 the seventh day he shall look on him. 6
10 shall have changed the look of the hair
32 seventh day he shall l. upon it. 14:39
50 shall look upon it and shall shut it
26 9 will look on you and make you increase
Num 8 2 that the lamps look over against north
18 7 and thy sons look ye to the priesthood
21 8 whosoever being struck shall look on it
Deut 9 27 look not on the stubbornness of this
26 15 look from thy sanctuary and thy high
1 K 1 11 thou wilt look down on the affliction
6 9 you shall look; and if it go up by
14 17 look, and see who is gone from us
16 7 look not on his countenance nor on the
18 9 Saul did not look on David with a good
19 2 kill thee: wherefore look to thyself
20 6 if thy father look and inquire for me
2 K 9 8 thou shouldst look upon such a dead
16 12 the Lord may look upon my affliction
20 12 stood still to look upon him [Amasa]
3 K 12 16 now David look to thy own house. So
18 43 go up and look toward the sea. And he
4 K 6 32 look then, when the messenger shall
33 shall I look for more from the Lord
Tob 2 18 look for that life which God will give
Jdth 6 15 pride and look on our low condition
8 32 the Lord may look down upon his people
9 6 as thou wast pleased to look upon the
6 look upon the camp of the Assyrians
11 19 not such another woman . . . in look, in
13 7 in this hour look on the works of thy
Job 3 21 that look for death, and it cometh not
6 8 that God may give me what I look for
7 4 and again I shall look for the evening
33 27 he shall look upon men and shall say
35 5 look up to heaven and see and behold
13 the Almighty will look into the causes
40 7 look on all that are proud, and
Ps 10 5 his eyes look on the poor man: his
21 2 look upon me: why hast thou forsaken
20 from me; look towards my defence
24 16 look thou upon me, and have mercy on
34 17 Lord, when wilt thou look upon me
39 14 look down, O Lord, to help me. Let
68 7 who look for thee, O Lord, the Lord of
17 l. upon me according to the multitude
79 15 look down from heaven and see and visit
83 10 and look on the face of thy Christ
85 16 look upon me and have mercy on me
89 16 look upon thy servants and upon their
111 8 moved until he look over his enemies
117 7 and I will look over my enemies. It is
118 6 I shall look into all thy commandments
132 look thou upon me and have mercy on
Prov 4 25 let thy eyes look straight on, and
7 6 I look out of the window of my house
14 18 the prudent shall look for knowledge
20 8 scattereth away all evil with his look
23 31 look not upon the wine when it is
27 19 as the faces of them that look therein
Ecce 12 3 they that look through the holes shall
Cant 6 10 to look if the vineyard had flourished
Wisd 8 12 they shall look upon me when I speak
14 29 swear amiss, they look not to be hurt
Eccu 9 3 look not upon a woman that hath a mind
7 look not round about thee in the ways
11 2 neither despise a man for his look
16 19 when God shall look upon them, they
19 26 a man is known by his look, and a
25 28 look not upon a woman's beauty and
33 22 than that thou look toward the hands
34 18 to whom doth he look, and who is his
35 15 look not upon an unjust sacrifice
40 31 and taught, will look to himself
43 12 look upon the rainbow and bless him
Isa 5 30 we shall look towards the land and
8 17 of Jacob, and I will look for him
21 will be angry . . . and look upwards
22 and they shall look to the earth and
17 7 his eyes shall look to the Holy One of
8 he shall not look to the altars which
33 20 look upon Sion the city of our
38 18 down into the pit, look for thy truth
43 18 things, and look not on things of old
51 1 look unto the rock whence you are
2 look unto Abraham your father and
5 the islands shall look for me and shall
6 and look down to the earth beneath
53 3 his look was as it were hidden and
63 15 look down from heaven, and behold from
Jer 13 16 you shall look for light, and he will
48 19 and look out, O habitation of Aroer
Bar 2 16 look down upon us, O Lord, from thy
4 36 look about thee, O Jerusalem, towards
5 5 look about towards the east and behold
Eze 33 4 doth not look to himself, if the sword
5 and did not look to himself, his blood
5 but if he look to himself, he shall
6 and the people look not to themselves
Dan 1 13 look upon our faces and the faces of
2 31 and the look thereof was terrible. The
13 9 that they might not look unto heaven
Osee 3 1 and they look to strange gods and
Abdi 12 shalt not look on in the day of thy
13 neither shalt thou also look on in his
Mich 4 11 stoned. And let our eye look upon Sion
7 7 I will look towards the Lord, I will
10 my eyes shall look down upon her: now
Haba 1 13 and thou canst not look on iniquity
Zach 12 10 they shall look upon me whom they
2 Ma 1 27 and look upon them that are despised
7 6 the Lord God will look upon the truth
14 to look for hope from God, to be
28 look upon heaven and earth and all
8 2 that he would look upon his people
11 26 comfort, and look to their own affairs
Mat 5 28 shall look on a woman to lust after her
11 3 look we for another. Luke 7:19, 20
27 4 what is that to us? Look thou to it
24 blood of this just man; look you to it
Mark 13 9 but look to yourselves. For they shall
Luke 9 38 look upon my son, because he is my
13 11 neither could she look upwards at all
21 28 look up and lift up your heads because
John 19 37 they shall look on him whom they
Acts 3 4 said: Look upon us. But he looked
12 why look you upon us, as if by our
6 3 look ye out among you seven men of
18 15 your law, look you to it: I will not
22 13 said to me: Brother Saul, look up. And
24 15 God, which these also themselves l. for
1 C 16 11 for I look for him with the brethren
2 C 3 13 might not steadfastly look on the face
4 18 we look not at things which are seen
Phil 3 20 whence also we look for the Savior, our
1 P 1 12 on whom the angels desire to look
2 P 3 13 we look for new heavens and a new earth
2 J 8 look to yourselves, that you lose not

Apoc 5 3 to open the book nor to look on it
looked Gen 8 13 looked, and saw that the face
Gen 19 28 he looked towards Sodom and Gomorrha
23 19 field that looked towards Mambre
Exod 2 12 when he had looked about this way
25 Lord looked upon the children of Israel
4 31 he had looked upon their affliction
16 10 they looked towards the wilderness
Num 12 10 when Aaron had looked on her and saw
21 9 when they that were bitten looked upon
20 Phasga, which l. towards the desert
Deut 26 7 and looked down upon our affliction
Judg 5 28 his mother looked out at a window
6 14 the Lord looked upon him [Gedeon]
13 19 he [Manue] and his wife looked on
18 23 they looked back and said to Michas
Ruth 1 6 that the Lord had l. upon his people
1 K 9 16 I have looked down upon my people
14 16 the watchmen of Saul . . . looked, and
17 42 when the Philistine looked and beheld
24 9 Saul looked behind him; and David
2 K 2 20 Abner looked behind him and said: Art
13 34 lifted up his eyes and looked and
24 20 Areuna looked and saw the king and his
3 K 7 25 looked towards the north. 2 Pa 4:4; Eze 8:3; 46:19
18 43 he went up and looked and said: There
19 6 he looked, and behold there was at his
4 K 3 14 hearkened to thee nor looked on thee
6 10 looked well to himself there not once
9 30 adorned her head and looked out of a
1 Pa 21 20 when Ornan looked up and saw the angel
2 Pa 13 14 when Juda looked back, they saw the
26 20 looked upon him and saw the leprosy
2 Es 4 14 looked and rose up: and I said to the
Tob 10 7 daily running out looked round about
Jdth 10 20 after she had l. on his face, bowed
12 11 for it is looked upon as shameful among
Job 22 17 l. upon the Almighty as if he could do
Ps 13 2 the Lord hath looked down from heaven
21 18 they have looked and stared upon me
32 13 the Lord hath looked from heaven
14 he hath looked upon all that dwell on
52 3 God looked down from heaven on the
53 9 eye hath looked down upon my enemies
65 18 if I have looked at iniquity in my
68 21 I looked for one that would grieve
84 12 justice hath looked down from heaven
91 12 my eye also hath looked down upon my
101 20 he hath looked forth from his high
20 Lord hath looked down upon the earth
118 166 I looked for thy salvation, O Lord
141 5 I looked on my right hand, and beheld
Prov 29 20 folly is rather to be looked for than
31 27 she hath looked well to the paths of
Eccu 11 13 eye of God hath looked upon him for
16 30 God looked upon the earth and filled
42 16 the sun . . . hath looked upon all things
29 4 have looked upon a thing lent as a
51 10 I looked for the succor of men, and
Isa 5 2 he looked that it should bring forth
4 that I looked that it should bring
7 I looked that he should do judgment
22 11 you have not looked up to the maker
30 13 on a sudden, when it is not looked for
59 9 looked for light, and behold darkness
11 we have looked for judgment, and there
63 5 I looked about, and there was none
Jer 4 24 I looked upon the mountains, and behold
26 I looked, and behold Carmel was a
8 15 we looked for peace and no good came
14 19 we have looked for peace, and there
22 our God, whom we have looked for? For
36 16 they looked upon one another with
46 5 fled apace, and they looked not back
47 3 the fathers have not looked back to
Lam 2 16 this is the day which we looked for
3 50 Lord regarded and looked down from the
4 17 when we looked attentively toward a
Eze 2 9 I looked, and behold a hand was sent
8 14 which looked to the north. 40:35
17 6 branches thereof looked towards him
40 6 that looked toward the east. 42:15; 43:1; 44:1; 47:1, 2
10 of the gate that looked eastward were
20 court, which looked northward. And the
22 gate that looked to the east. 43:4
24 the gate that looked to the south
37 porch thereof looked to the outward
41 12 the way that looked toward the sea
Dan 10 18 he that looked like a man touched me
12 5 I Daniel looked, and behold as it
13 35 she weeping looked up to heaven, for
14 17 the king looked upon the table and
39 he came to the den and looked in, and
Joel 1 20 the beasts . . . have looked up to thee
Agge 1 9 you have looked for more, and behold
Zach 4 2 have looked, and behold a candlestick
5 9 I lifted up my eyes and looked: and
2 Ma 3 19 others looked out of the windows. And
Mark 5 32 he looked about to see her who had
Luke 2 38 to all that looked for the redemption
9 16 he looked up to heaven and blessed
22 61 the Lord turning, looked on Peter
23 51 himself looked for the kingdom of God
John 13 22 therefore looked one upon another
20 11 she stooped down and looked into the
Acts 1 9 while they looked on, he was raised up
3 5 he looked earnestly upon them, hoping
22 13 and I the same hour looked upon him. But
Heb 11 10 looked for a city that hath foundations
26 for he looked unto the reward. By faith
James 1 25 that hath looked into the perfect law
1 J 1 1 which we have looked upon, and our
Apoc 4 1 after these things I looked. 15:5
lookedst Jdth 9 7 but thou l. over their camp
lookest Haba 1 13 why l. thou upon them that do
looketh Gen 25 18 which looketh towards Egypt
Exod 26 20 that looketh to the north. Lev 1:11
27 12 that looketh to the west. 38:12; Num 35:5
13 which looketh to the east. 1 Pa 5:10
28 27 that looketh towards the nether joining
36 25 looketh toward north. Eze 40:40, 44, 46
27 side . . . which looketh to the sea
Lev 13 51 seventh day when he looketh on it again
Num 8 2 towards which the candlestick looketh
23 28 l. towards the wilderness. Josu 12:1
33 7 which looketh towards Beelsephon
Josu 15 2 lay thereof, that looketh to the south
16 6 but Machmethath looketh to the north
17 7 which looketh towards Sichem: and it
18 14 mountain that l. towards Beth-horon
16 l. on the valley of the children of
19 46 the border that looketh towards Joppe
Judg 9 37 by the way that looketh towards the oak
16 3 hill which looketh towards Hebron
18 6 the Lord looketh on your way, and
2 K 15 23 the way that looketh to the desert
2 Pa 20 24 tower, that looketh toward the desert
Jdth 7 3 the top, which looketh toward Dothain
Job 7 2 as the hireling l. for the end of his
28 24 l. on all things that are under heaven
39 8 he l. round about the mountains of his
29 from thence she looketh for the prey
Ps 103 32 he l. upon the earth and maketh it
112 6 l. down on the low things in heaven

137 6 Lord is high and looketh on the low
Cant 7 4 of Libanus, that l. toward Damascus
Eccu 4 16 he that looketh upon her, shall remain
5 7 and his wrath looketh upon sinners
11 32 as a spy that looketh on the fall of
14 24 he who looketh in at her windows and
40 30 that l. toward another man's table
Eze 11 1 looketh towards the rising of the sun
40 45 chamber which looketh toward the south
46 1 that looketh toward the east. 12
looking Gen 19 26 his wife looking behind her
Gen 23 17 double cave, looking towards Mambre
26 8 Abimelech . . . l. out through a window
30 41 while they were looking upon them
Exod 14 24 Lord looking upon the Egyptian army
37 9 and looking one towards the other
Deut 13 14 inquire . . . by looking well into it
28 32 thy eyes looking on and languishing
Josu 8 20 looking back and seeing the smoke of
15 7 so northward looking towards Galgal
Judg 20 40 Benjamin looking back, saw that the
2 K 1 7 l. behind him and seeing me, he called
6 16 l. out through a window, saw king
3 K 7 5 looking one upon another, with equal
30 laver molten, l. one against another
4 K 2 24 looking back, he saw them and cursed
1 Pa 15 29 l. out at a window, saw king David
Tob 7 2 Raguel looking upon Tobias, said to
Job 15 22 l. round about for the sword on every
Cant 2 9 looking through the lattices, looking through the windows
Eccu 23 28 looking into the hearts of men, into
41 25 ashamed . . . of looking upon a harlot
Isa 38 14 my eyes are weakened looking upward
Eze 42 4 looking to the inner parts of a way
1 Ma 4 19 appeared l. forth from the mountain
2 Ma 7 4 his brethren and his mother looking on
15 but he looking upon the king, said
Mat 14 19 looking up to heaven. Mark 6:41; 7:34
Mark 3 5 looking round about on them. 34
8 24 looking up, he said: I see men as it
9 7 looking about, they saw no man any
10 21 Jesus looking on him, loved him and
23 Jesus looking round about, saith to
27 Jesus looking on them, saith: With men
14 67 looking on him she saith: Thou also
15 40 there were also women looking on afar
43 also himself looking for the kingdom
16 4 looking, they saw the stone rolled
Luke 6 10 looking round about on them all, he
9 62 hand to the plow and looking back
19 5 looking up, he saw him, and said to
21 1 looking on, he saw the rich men cast
John 1 42 Jesus looking upon him, said: Thou art
Acts 1 11 why stand you looking up to heaven
6 15 looking on him, saw his face as if it
7 55 looking up steadfastly to heaven, saw
11 6 looking, I considered, and saw
13 9 filled with Holy Ghost, l. upon him
14 8 [Paul] looking upon him, and seeing that
23 1 Paul looking upon the council, said: Men
21 ready, looking for a promise from thee
27 12 looking towards the southwest and
Titus 1 13 looking for the blessed hope and coming
Heb 12 2 looking on Jesus, the author and
15 looking diligently, lest any man be
2 P 3 12 looking for and hasting unto the coming
looking-glasses Isa 3 23 crisping pins and l.
looks Eze 2 6 be thou dismayed at their looks
Eze 10 22 by the river Chobar, and their looks
Nah 2 4 their looks are like torches, like
2 Ma 15 12 Onias . . . modest in his looks, gentle
Loomim Gen 25 3 children of Dadan . . . Loomim

loop Exod 26 5 one l. may be against another l.
loops Exod 26 4 thou shalt make loops of violet
Exod 26 5 every curtain shall have fifty loops
10 fifty loops in the edge of the other
11 wherewith the loops may be joined
36 11 made also loops of violet in the edge
12 that the loops might meet one against
13 might catch the loops of the curtains
17 fifty loops in the edge of one curtain
loose Gen 27 40 shalt shake off and l. his yoke
Gen 49 21 Nephtali, a hart let loose and giving
Exod 39 19 joined lest they should flag loose and
Lev 13 45 shall have his clothes hanging loose
Josu 5 16 loose, saith he, thy shoes from off
Judg 16 6 wert bound thou couldst not break l.
Tob 3 15 that thou l. me from the bond of this
Job 6 9 that he may let loose his hand and cut
Prov 18 9 he that is loose and slack in his work
23 8 and shalt loose thy beautiful words
Isa 20 2 loose the sackcloth from off thy loins
52 2 loose the bonds from off thy neck
58 6 loose the bands of wickedness, undo
Dan 3 92 I see four men loose, and walking
Mat 16 19 whatsoever thou shalt loose on earth
18 18 whatsoever you shall loose upon earth
21 2 loose them and bring them to me. And if
Mark 1 7 am not worthy to stoop down and loose
11 2 loose him and bring him. Luke 19:30
4 of two ways: and they loose him. And
Luke 3 16 not worthy to l. John 1:27; Acts 13:25
13 15 loose his ox or his ass from the
19 31 why do you loose him? you shall say
33 said to them: Why loose you the colt
11 44 to them: Loose him and let him go
Acts 7 33 loose the shoes from thy feet, for the
Apoc 5 2 book and to loose the seals thereof
5 and to loose the seven seals thereof
9 14 loose the four angels who are bound
loosed Gen 49 24 of his arms and his hands were l.
Exod 28 28 rational and ephod may not be loosed
Judg 15 14 he was bound were broken and l.
Jdth 13 8 loosed his sword that hung tied upon
Job 39 5 free, and who hath loosed his bonds
Eccu 22 19 frame of wood . . . shall not be loosed
Isa 5 27 shall the girdle of their loins be l.
33 23 thy tacklings are loosed, and they
Jer 40 4 I have loosed thee this day from the
Dan 5 6 the joints of his loins were loosed
10 16 sight of thee my joints are loosed
2 Ma 12 46 that they may be loosed from sins
Mat 16 19 it shall be loosed also in heaven. 18:18
Mark 7 35 the string of his tongue was loosed
Luke 1 64 and his tongue loosed, and he spoke
13 16 loosed from this bond on the sabbath
Acts 2 24 having loosed the sorrows of hell, as
16 26 the bands of all were loosed. And the
22 30 he l. him, and commanded the priests to
27 13 when they had loosed from Asson, they
21 not have loosed from Crete, and have
Rom 7 2 she is loosed from law of her husband
6 now we are loosed from the law of death
1 C 7 27 bound to a wife? seek not to be loosed
27 art thou loosed from a wife? seek not
Apoc 9 15 the four angels were loosed, who were
20 3 after that he must be loosed a little
7 Satan shall be loosed out of his prison
looseth Job 12 18 he looseth the belt of kings
Ps 145 7 Lord looseth them that are fettered
Prov 25 20 that l. his garment in cold weather
loosing Jdth 6 10 l. him they brought him to
Mark 11 5 them: What do you loosing the colt
Luke 19 33 as they were loosing the colt, the
Acts 27 40 the sea, loosing withal the rudder bands

lording 1 P 5 3 as lording it over the clergy
lord's Gen 44 8 should steal out of thy l. house
Mat 25 18 into the earth and hid his lord's money
Luke 16 5 every one of his lord's debtors, he
Lord's Ps 10 5 the Lord's throne is in heaven
Ps 21 29 the kingdom is the Lord's: and he shall
23 1 earth is the Lord's and the fulness
113 16 the heaven of heaven is the Lord's
117 23 this is the Lord's doing: and it is
Isa 44 5 one shall say: I am the Lord's, and
49 7 rise up, and adore for the Lord's sake
Jer 5 10 because they are not the Lord's. For
Joel 2 17 priests the Lord's ministers shall weep
Nah 1 3 the Lord's ways are in a tempest, and
Soph 2 2 day of the Lord's indignation. 3
Zach 9 1 of all the tribes of Israel is the L.
Luke 10 39 sitting also at the Lord's feet, heard
Rom 14 8 live, or whether we die, we are the L.
1 C 10 26 the earth is the Lord's, and the fulness
11 20 it is not now to eat the Lord's supper
Apoc 1 10 I was in the spirit on the Lord's day
11 15 of this world is become our Lord's
lords Gen 19 2 my lords, turn in to the house
Deut 10 17 the Lord of lords. Ps 135:3, 27
Josu 13 3 divided among lords of the Philistines
1 K 6 5 upon you all and upon your lords. And
12 lords of the Philistines followed them
7 7 l. of the Philistines went up against
29 2 the lords of the Philistines marched
6 thou pleasest not the lords. Return
4 K 7 2 one of lords, upon whose hand the king
1 Pa 12 19 lords of the Philistines taking counsel
2 Pa 9 14 lords of the lands, who brought gold
1 Es 8 36 lords that were from the king's court
Eccu 46 21 and all the lords of the Philistines
Isa 16 8 lords of the nations have destroyed
26 13 other lords besides thee have had
Lam 1 5 her adversaries are become her lords
1 Ma 7 26 sent Nicanor one of his principal lords
9 25 and made them lords of the country
1 C 8 5 for there be gods many, and lords many
Eph 6 5 be obedient to them that are your lords
1 Tim 6 15 King of kings and Lord of l. Apoc 19:16
Apoc 17 14 he is Lord of lords and King of kings
lose Judg 18 9 lose no time; let us go and possess
1 K 25 15 neither did we ever lose any thing all
Prov 24 10 if thou lose hope being weary in the
Ecce 3 6 a time to get and a time to lose. A
9 18 offend in one, shall lose many good
Eccu 29 13 lose thy money for thy brother and
Eze 36 15 nor lose thy nation any more, saith
Nah 2 10 and all the loins lose their strength
Mat 5 13 if the salt l. its savor. Luke 14:34
10 39 that findeth his life, shall lose it
39 he that shall lose his life for me
42 he shall not l. his reward. Mark 9:40
16 25 that will save his life, shall lose it. Mark 8:35; Luke 9:24
25 shall lose his life for my sake. Mark 8:35; Luke 9:24
Luke 9 25 gain the whole world and lose himself
15 4 if he shall lose one of them, doth
8 if she lose one groat, doth not light
17 33 seek to save his life shall lose it
33 lose it, shall preserve it. I say to
John 6 39 hath given me, I should lose nothing
12 25 he that loveth his life, shall lose it
Heb 10 35 do not therefore lose your confidence
2 J 8 that you lose not the things which you
loses Eccu 27 17 secret of a friend, l. his credit
loseth Eccu 41 4 the distrustful that l. patience
loss Exod 22 6 fire, shall make good the loss
Exod 22 12 shall make the loss good to the owner
Josu 10 21 without the loss of any one: and no
Judg 16 28 for the loss of my two eyes I may take
1 Es 4 13 and this loss will fall upon the kings
Jdth 10 13 without the loss of one man of his army
Prov 12 26 that neglecteth a loss for the sake of
22 3 the simple passed on and suffered loss
Eccu 18 6 he leaveth off, he shall be at loss
20 9 there is a finding that turneth to loss
22 3 a foolish daughter shall be to his loss
2 Ma 11 13 with himself, the loss he had suffered
Mat 16 26 suffer the l. of his soul. Mark 8:36
Acts 27 21 not . . . have gained this harm and loss
22 there shall be no loss of any man's life
Rom 11 15 if loss of them be the reconciliation of
1 C 3 15 man's work burn, he shall suffer loss
Phil 3 7 the same I have counted loss for Christ
8 I count all things to be but loss for
8 I have suffered the loss of all things
losses Prov 27 12 passing on have suffered losses
lost Gen 31 39 whatsoever was lost by theft
Lev 6 3 shall find a thing lost, and denying
Deut 22 3 that is thy brother's, which is lost
28 37 thou shalt be lost, as a proverb and a
Josu 2 9 inhabitants . . . have lost all strength
Ruth 1 5 having lost both her sons and her
1 K 9 3 the asses of Cis . . . were lost: and
20 asses which were lost three days ago
25 21 nothing was lost of all that pertained
Tob 3 22 art not delighted in our being lost
14 3 old when he lost the sight of his eyes
Job 19 10 I am lost, and he hath taken away my
Ps 118 176 gone astray like a sheep that is lost
Prov 23 34 fast asleep, when the stern is lost
Ecce 5 13 are lost with very great affliction
Wisd 19 4 they lost the remembrance of those
Eccu 2 16 woe to them that have lost patience
8 15 and if thou lendest, count it as lost
29 13 hide it not under a stone to be lost
18 he that hath lost shame, will leave
22 when he hath lost all shame, he shall
Isa 27 13 they that were lost shall come from
Jer 2 25 I have lost all hope, I will not do
7 28 faith is lost and is taken away out
50 6 my people have been a lost flock
Eze 19 5 seeing . . . that her hope was lost, took
28 17 hast lost thy wisdom in thy beauty
34 4 have you sought that which was lost
16 I will seek that which was lost: and
37 11 our hope is lost, and we are cut off
1 Ma 13 4 my brethren have lost their lives
18 and the children, therefore he lost
2 Ma 2 14 as were lost by the war we had, and
13 19 was repulsed, he failed, he lost his men
Mat 10 6 go ye rather to the lost sheep of the
15 24 to the sheep that are lost of the house
18 11 to save that which was lost. Luke 19:10
Mark 2 22 and the bottles will be lost. Luke 5:37
Luke 15 4 and go after that which was lost until
6 I have found my sheep that was lost
9 have found the groat which I had lost
24 to life again: was lost, and is found
32 life again; he was lost, and is found
John 6 12 that remain, lest they be lost. They
17 12 none of them is lost but the son of
18 9 given me, I have not lost any one
2 C 4 3 hid, it is hid to them that are lost
lot Lev 16 9 that whose lot fell to be offered
Lev 27 24 had it in the lot of his possession
Num 26 55 so that by lot the land be divided
56 whatsoever shall fall by lot, that
33 54 you shall divide it among you by lot
54 to every one as the lot shall fall
34 2 be fallen into your possession by lot

13 the land which you shall possess by lot
36 2 thou shouldst divide the land by lot
Deut 1 38 and he shall divide the land by lot
31 7 fathers, and thou shalt divide it by lot
32 9 Jacob the lot of his inheritance. He
Josu 1 6 thou shalt divide by lot to this people
7 14 what tribe soever the lot shall find
9 7 in the land which falls to our lot
13 1 left, which is not yet divided by lot
14 2 dividing all by lot, as the Lord had
15 1 the lot of the children of Juda by
16 1 the lot of the sons of Joseph fell
17 1 this lot fell to the tribe of Manasses
6 lot of the rest of children of Manasses
8 the lot of Manasses took in the land
14 why hast thou given me but one lot
17 thou shalt not have one lot only: but
18 11 the lot of the children of Benjamin
19 1 the second lot came forth for the
9 possession and lot of children of Juda
10 third lot fell to children of Zabulon
17 the fourth lot came out to Issachar
24 the fifth lot fell to the tribe of the
32 sixth lot came out to the sons of
40 seventh lot came out to the tribe of
49 made an end of dividing the land by lot
51 distributed by lot in Silo, before the
21 4 the lot came out for family of Caath
6 the lot came out to children of Gerson
8 of Moses, giving to every one by lot
10 for the first lot came out for them
22 7 Josue gave a lot among the rest of
23 4 divided to you by lot all the land
Judg 1 3 come up with me into my lot and fight
3 may go along with thee into thy lot
16 into the wilderness of his lot, which
18 1 they had not received their lot among
20 14 of all cities which were of their lot
1 K 10 20 the lot fell on the tribe of Benjamin
21 the lot fell upon the kindred of Metri
1 Pa 6 54 for they fell to them by lot. And they
63 Zabulon they gave by lot twelve cities
65 and they gave them by lot out of the
16 18 Chanaan: the lot of your inheritance
24 5 divided . . . one with the other by lot
7 the first lot came forth to Joiarib
31 the younger. The lot divided all equally
25 9 the first lot came forth to Joseph
26 14 the lot of the east fell to Selemias
14 learned man, the north gate fell by lot
Esth 3 7 the lot was cast into an urn, which in
9 24 and had cast Phur, that is, the lot
26 because Phur, that is, the lot was
13 17 be merciful to thy lot and inheritance
Ps 77 54 and by lot divided to them their land
104 11 Chanaan, the lot of your inheritance
124 3 rod of sinners upon the lot of the just
Prov 1 14 cast in thy lot with us, let us all have
18 18 the lot suppresseth contentions and
Wisd 2 9 this is our portion and this our lot
3 14 acceptable lot in the temple of God
5 5 God, and their lot is among the saints
Eccu 6 4 shall lead him into lot of the wicked
14 15 to divide by lot thy sorrows and labors
17 20 hath appointed to them the lot of truth
24 stand firm in the lot set before thee
25 26 let the lot of sinners fall upon her
48 5 raisedst . . . from the lot of death
Isa 17 14 us, and the lot of them that spoiled us
34 17 he hath cast the lot for them, and his
57 6 torrent is thy portion, this is thy lot
Jer 13 25 this is thy lot, and the portion of
Eze 24 6 there hath no lot fallen upon it. For
45 1 shall begin to divide the land by lot
47 22 you shall divide it by lot for an
48 29 the land which you shall divide by lot
Dan 12 13 thou shalt rest, and stand in thy lot
Jon 1 7 cast lots, and the lot fell upon Jonas
Mich 2 5 none that shall cast the cord of a lot
1 Ma 3 36 coasts, and divide their land by lot
Luke 1 9 it was his lot to offer incense, going
John 19 24 and upon my vesture they have cast lot
Acts 1 26 the lot fell upon Matthias, and he was
8 21 thou hast no part nor lot in this
13 19 divided their land among them, by lot
26 18 a lot among saints, by faith that is in
Eph 1 11 in whom we also are called by lot, being
Col 1 12 partakers of the lot of the saints in
Lot Gen 11 27 Aran begot Lot. And Aran died before
Gen 11 31 Thare took . . . Lot the son of Aran
12 4 and Lot went with him: Abram was
5 and he took Sarai his wife, and Lot
13 1 out of Egypt . . . and Lot with him
5 Lot also . . . had flocks of sheep and
7 between the herdsmen of Abram and of Lot
8 said to Lot: Let there be no quarrel
10 Lot, lifting up his eyes, saw all the
11 Lot chose to himself the country about
12 and Lot abode in the towns that were
14 after Lot was separated from him
14 12 and they took . . . Lot also, the son of
14 that his brother Lot was taken, he
16 [Abram] brought back . . . Lot his
19 1 Lot was sitting in the gate of the city
5 they called Lot and said to him: Where
6 Lot went out to them and shut the door
9 they pressed very violently upon Lot
10 put out their hand and drew in Lot unto
12 they said to Lot: Hast thou here any of
14 so Lot went out and spoke to his
18 Lot said to them: I beseech thee, my
23 the earth, and Lot entered into Segor
29 delivered Lot out of the destruction
30 Lot went up out of Segor and abode
36 two daughters of Lot were with child
Deut 2 9 I have given Ar to the children of Lot
19 I have given it to the children of Lot
Ps 82 9 are come to the aid of the sons of Lot
Eccu 16 9 the place where Lot sojourned
Luke 17 28 as it came to pass in the days of Lot
29 Lot went out of Sodom, it rained fire
2 P 2 7 delivered just Lot, oppressed by the
Lotan Gen 36 20 sons of Seir . . . Lotan. 1 Pa 1:38
Gen 36 22 and Lotan had sons: Hori and
22 sister of Lotan was Thamna. 1 Pa 1:39
29 dukes of the Horrites. Duke Lotan
1 Pa 1 39 the sons of Lotan: Hori, Homam
Lot's Luke 17 32 not return back. Remember L. wife
lots Lev 16 8 casting lots upon them both, one to
Num 36 4 the distribution made by the lots
2 Es 9 22 didst divide lots for them: and they
Esth 9 26 Phurim, that is, of lots. 28
31 observe the days of lots and celebrate
31 fasts and cries and the days of lots
10 10 commanded that there should be two lots
11 both lots came to the day appointed
Ps 30 16 my lots are in thy hands. Deliver me
67 14 if you sleep among the midst of lots
Prov 16 33 lots are cast into the lap, but they
Eze 21 19 and with his hand he shall draw lots
Mat 27 35 divided his garments, casting lots
Mark 15 24 his garments, casting lots upon them
Acts 1 26 they gave them lots, and the lot fell
cast lots Josu 18 6 I may cast lots for you. 8
Josu 18 10 he cast lots before the Lord in Silo
1 K 14 42 cast lots between me and Jonathan

1 Pa 24 31 cast lots over against their brethren
25 8 and they cast lots by their courses
26 13 they cast lots equally, both little and
2 Es 10 34 and we cast lots among the priests
11 1 but the rest of the people cast lots
Ps 21 19 and upon my vesture they cast lots
Joel 3 3 and they have cast lots upon my people
Abdi 11 gates, and cast lots upon Jerusalem
Jon 1 7 let us cast lots that we may know why
7 they cast lots, and the lot fell upon
Nah 3 10 they cast lots upon her nobles, and all
loud Gen 19 13 their cry is grown loud before
Gen 27 38 when he [Esau] wept with a loud cry
Exod 19 16 of the trumpet sounded exceeding loud
1 Es 3 13 the people shouted with a loud shout
2 Es 12 41 the singers sung loud, and Jerzaia was
Ps 32 3 sing well unto him with a loud noise
Luke 23 23 but they were instant with loud voices
Apoc 12 10 I heard a loud voice in heaven, saying
with a loud voice Deut 5 22 w. . . . , adding nothing
Deut 27 14 and say to all the men of Israel w. . . .
1 K 28 12 she cried out w. . . . and said to Saul
2 K 15 23 all wept w. . . . , and all the people
19 4 king covered his head and cried w. . . .
3 K 8 55 all assembly of Israel w. . . .
18 28 cried w. . . . and cut themselves after
4 K 18 28 Rabsaces stood and cried out w. . . .
2 Pa 15 14 they swore to the Lord w. . . . with
20 19 praised Lord the God of Israel w. . . .
32 18 cried out w. . . . , in the Jews' tongue
1 Es 3 12 temple before their eyes, wept w. . . .
10 12 multitude answered and said w. . . .
2 Es 9 4 cried w. . . . to the Lord their God
Tob 6 3 being afraid of him, cried out w. . . .
Jdth 14 14 he cried out w. . . . , with weeping
Esth 4 1 he cried w. . . . in the street in the
Prov 27 14 he that blessed his neighbor w. . . .
Isa 36 13 cried out w. . . . in the Jews' language
Eze 8 18 when they shall cry to my ears w. . . .
9 1 he cried in my ears w. . . . , saying
11 13 down upon my face and cried w. . . .
27 30 they shall mourn over thee w. . . .
Dan 13 24 Susanna cried out w. . . . 42
46 he cried out w. . . . I am clear from
60 all the assembly cried out w. . . .
14 17 cried out w. . . . : Great art thou. 40
1 Ma 2 19 Mathathias answered and said w. . . .
27 Mathathias cried out in city w. . . .
3 50 cried w. . . . toward heaven, saying
54 with trumpets, and cried out w. . . .
13 8 they answered w. . . . saying: Thou art
45 they cried w. . . . beseeching Simon to
2 Ma 12 37 singing hymns w. . . . he put Gorgias'
Mat 27 46 Jesus cried w. . . . saying: Eli, Eli
50 Jesus again crying w. . . . yielded up
Mark 1 26 and crying out w. . . . went out of him
5 7 crying w. . . . he said: What have I to
15 34 Jesus cried out w. . . . saying: Eloi
37 Jesus having cried out w. . . . , gave up
Luke 1 42 she cried w. . . . and said: Blessed art
4 33 unclean devil, and he cried out w. . . .
8 28 w. . . . he said: What have I to do with
17 15 went back, w. . . . glorifying God
19 37 began with joy to praise God w. . . .
23 46 Jesus crying w. . . . said: Father, into
John 11 43 he cried w. . . . : Lazarus, come forth
Acts 7 56 crying out w. . . . stopped their ears
59 he cried w. . . . saying: Lord, lay not
8 7 spirits, crying w. . . . went out. And
14 9 said with loud voice: Stand upright on
16 28 Paul cried w. . . . , saying: Do thyself
26 24 Festus said w. . . . : Paul, thou
Apoc 5 2 proclaiming w. . . . : Who is worthy to
12 saying w. . . . : The Lamb that was
6 10 they cried w. . . . , saying: How long
7 2 he cried w. . . . to the four angels, to
10 they cried w. . . . , saying: Salvation
8 13 saying w. . . . : Woe, woe, woe to the
10 3 he cried w. . . . as when a lion roareth
14 7 saying w. . . . : Fear the Lord, and give
9 saying w. . . . : If any man shall adore
15 crying w. . . . to him that sat upon the
18 he cried w. . . . to him that had the
19 17 cried w. . . . , saying to all the birds
louder Exod 19 19 grew by degrees l. and l.
3 K 18 27 cry with a l. voice: for he is a god
love Gen 29 18 Jacob being in love with her, said
Gen 29 20 because of the greatness of his love
30 he preferred the love of the latter
32 now my husband will love me. And again
34 2 saw her, he was in love with her
Exod 20 6 to them that love me and. Deut 5:10
21 5 I love my master and my wife and
Lev 19 18 thou shalt love thy friend as thyself
34 and you shall love him as yourselves
Deut 6 5 love the Lord thy God. 11:1; 19:9; 30:6, 16, 20
7 9 and mercy to them that love him, and
13 he will love thee and multiply thee
10 12 and walk in his ways and love him
19 do you therefore love strangers because
11 13 love the Lord your God. 22; Josu 22:5; 23:11
13 3 whether you love him with all your heart
Judg 5 31 let them that love thee shine, as the
14 16 thou hatest me and dost not love me
1 K 18 22 all his servants love thee [David]
2 K 1 26 amiable to me above the love of women
26 loveth her only son, so did I love thee
13 2 so that he fell sick for the love of her
15 was greater than the love with which
19 6 and thou hatest them that love thee
3 K 11 2 Solomon joined with a most ardent love
2 Es 1 5 and mercy with those that love thee
Tob 6 22 moved rather for love of children than
8 9 but only for the love of posterity
10 13 to love her husband, to take care of the
13 18 blessed are all they that love thee
Job 15 34 tabernacles, who love to take bribes
Ps 4 3 why do you love vanity, and seek after
5 12 they that love thy name shall glory
17 2 I will love thee, O Lord, my strength
30 24 love the Lord, all ye his saints
39 17 let such as love thy salvation say
68 37 that love his name shall dwell therein
69 5 let such as love thy salvation say
96 10 you that love the Lord, hate evil: the
108 4 instead of making me a return of love
5 evil for good: and hatred for my love
118 132 judgment of them that love thy name
165 much peace have they that love thy law
121 6 and abundance for them that love thee
144 20 Lord keepeth all them that love him
Prov 4 6 love her, and she shall preserve thee
5 19 delighted continually with her love
8 17 I love them that love me: and they
21 that I may enrich them that love me
36 own soul. All that hate me love death
9 8 rebuke a wise man, and he will love thee
15 17 better to be invited to herbs with love
18 21 they that love it, shall eat the fruits
20 13 love not sleep, lest poverty oppress
27 5 open rebuke is better than hidden love
Ecce 3 8 a time of love and a time of hatred
9 1 whether he be worthy of love or hatred
6 their love also and their hatred and
Cant 1 3 than wine: the righteous love thee

		8	have I likened thee, O my love. Thy
		13	a cluster of cypress my love is to me
		14	behold thou art fair, O my love
	2	2	so is my love among the daughters. As
		5	apples: because I languish with love
		10	arise, make haste, my love, my dove
		13	arise, my love, my beautiful one, and
	4	1	how beautiful art thou, my love, how
		7	thou art all fair, O my love, and
	5	2	open to me, my sister, my love, my
		8	tell him that I languish with love
	6	3	thou art beautiful, O my love, sweet
	8	4	nor awake my love till she please
		6	love is strong as death, jealousy as
		7	all the substance of his house for love
Wisd	1	1	love justice, you that are the judges
	3	9	they that are faithful in love shall
	6	12	my words and love them, and you shall
		13	is easily seen by them that love her
		19	and the care of discipline is love
		19	and love is the keeping of her laws
		22	love wisdom, that you may reign forever
		23	love the light of wisdom, all ye that
	8	7	if a man love justice: her labors have
	15	6	make them and they that love them
Eccu	1	10	hath given her to them that love him
		14	the love of God is honorable wisdom
		15	show herself love her by the sight and
	2	10	love him, and your hearts shall be
		18	they that love him will keep his way
		19	that love him shall be filled with
	3	1	their generation, obedience and love
	4	15	and God loveth them that love her
	6	34	if thou love to hear, thou shalt be
	7	32	love him that made thee: and forsake
		39	things thou shalt be confirmed in love
	8	20	love but such things as please them
	10	10	more wicked thing than to love money
	11	15	love and the ways of good things are
	13	18	love God all thy life and call upon
	15	13	they that fear him shall not love it
	24	24	I am the mother of fair love and of
	25	2	brethren, and the love of neighbors
		16	fear of God is the beginning of his l.
	27	18	love thy neighbor and be joined to him
	31	30	challenge not them that love wine
	34	15	of God are upon them that love him
	40	20	the love of wisdom is above them both
Isa	1	23	they all love bribes, they run after
	56	6	to worship him and to love his name
	61	8	for I am the Lord that love judgment
	63	9	saved them: in his love and in his
	66	10	glad with her, all you that love her
Jer	2	2	youth and the love of thy espousals
		24	heart, snuffed up the wind of his love
		33	to show thy way good to seek my love
	31	3	loved thee with an everlasting love
Eze	23	17	were come to her to the bed of love
Dan	9	4	and mercy to them that love thee
	13	10	were both wounded with the love of her
		20	seeth us, and we are in love with thee
	14	37	hast not forgotten them that love thee
Osee	3	1	and love a woman beloved of her friend
		1	gods, and love the husks of the grapes
	9	15	I will love them no more, all their
	10	11	taught to love to tread out corn, but
	11	4	cords of Adam, with the bands of love
	14	5	I will love them freely: for my wrath
Amos	5	15	hate evil, and love good, and establish
Mich	3	2	you that hate good, and love evil
	6	8	to do judgment and to love mercy, and
Soph	3	17	he will be silent in his love, he will
Zach	8	17	his friend: and love not a false oath
		19	only love ye truth and peace. Thus
1 Ma	4	33	the sword of them that love thee
2 Ma	6	20	unlawful things for the love of life
	14	26	seeing the love they had one to another
Mat	5	43	thou shalt love thy neighbor and hate
		44	love your enemies. Luke 6:27, 35
		46	if you l. them that l. you. Luke 6:32
	6	5	that love to stand and pray in the
		24	will hate the one and love the other. Luke 16:13
	19	19	thou shalt love thy neighbor as thyself. 22:39; Mark 12:31; Rom 13:9; Gal 5:14; James 2:8
	22	37	shalt love the Lord thy God. Mark 12:30; Luke 10:27
	23	6	they love the first places at feasts
Mark	12	33	to love one's neighbor as one's self
		38	beware of the scribes, who love to walk
Luke	6	32	sinners also love those that love them
	11	43	you love the uppermost seats in the
	20	46	love salutations in the marketplace
John	5	42	you have not the love of God in you
	8	42	your Father, you would indeed love me
	13	34	that you love one another. 15:12, 17
		35	if you have love one for another
	14	15	if you love me, keep my commandments
		21	I will love him and will manifest
		23	if any one love me, he will keep my
		23	my Father will love him, and we will
		31	may know that I love the Father: and
	15	9	have loved you. Abide in my love
		10	you shall abide in my love; as I also
		10	and do abide in his love. These things
		13	greater love than this no man hath
		19	the world would love its own: but
	17	26	love wherewith thou hast loved me
	21	15	thou knowest that I love thee. 16, 17
Rom	8	28	we know that to them that love God, all
		35	shall separate us from love of Christ
		39	love of God, which is in Christ Jesus
	12	9	let love be without dissimulation
	13	8	owe no man anything, but to love one
		10	love of our neighbor worketh no evil
		10	love therefore is fulfilling of the law
	15	14	you also are full of love, replenished
1 C	2	9	God hath prepared for them that love him
	8	3	if any man love God, the same is known
	16	22	if any man love not our Lord Jesus
2 C	11	11	because I love you not? God knoweth it
	13	11	God of peace and of love shall be with
Eph	1	15	and of your love towards all the saints
	5	2	walk in love, as Christ also hath loved
		25	husbands, love your wives. Col 3:19
		28	so also ought men to love their wives
		33	particular love his wife as himself
Col	1	4	and the love which you have towards all
		8	manifested to us your love in the spirit
		13	into the kingdom of the Son of his love
1 Th	4	9	yourselves have learned of God to love
2 Th	2	10	receive not the love of the truth, that
1 Tim	1	14	with faith and love, which is in Christ
	2	15	if she continue in faith and love and
2 Tim	1	7	but of power and of love and of sobriety
		13	and in the love which is in Christ Jesus
	3	10	faith, longsuffering, love, patience
	4	8	to them also that love his coming. Make
Titus	2	2	sound in faith, in love, in patience
		4	wise, to love their husbands, to love
	3	15	thee: salute them that love us in faith
Heb	6	10	love which you have shown in his name
James	1	12	hath promised to them that love him. 2:5
1 P	1	8	whom having not seen, you love: in
		22	with a brotherly love, from a sincere
	2	17	honor all men. Love the brotherhood

3 10 he that will love life and see good
2 P 1 7 in godliness, love of brotherhood; and in love of brotherhood, charity
1 J 2 15 love not the world, nor the things
3 11 that you should love one another
14 to life, because we love the brethren
18 let us not love in word nor in tongue
23 love one another as he hath given
4 7 let us love one another, for charity
11 we also ought to love one another
12 we love one another. 2 J 5
19 let us therefore love God, because
20 if any man say, I love God, and hateth
20 how can he love God, whom he seeth not
21 who loveth God, love also his brother
5 2 know that we love the children of God
2 when we love God, and keep his
2 J 1 children, whom I love in the truth
3 J 1 beloved Gaius, whom I love in truth
Jude 21 keep yourselves in the love of God
Apoc 3 19 such as I love, I rebuke and chastise
loved Gen 24 67 he [Isaac] loved her so much
Gen 25 28 Isaac loved Esau because he ate of
28 his hunting: and Rebecca loved Jacob
34 19 he loved the damsel exceedingly, and
37 3 Israel loved Joseph above all his sons
4 seeing that he was loved by his father
Deut 4 37 he loved thy fathers and chose their
7 8 because the Lord hath loved you and
10 15 joined to thy fathers, and loved them
23 5 into thy blessing, because he l. thee
33 3 he hath loved the people, all the
Judg 16 4 loved a woman who dwelt in the valley
1 K 1 5 sorrow because he [Elcana] loved Anna
16 21 [Saul] loved him [David] exceedingly
18 1 loved him as his own soul. 3; 20:17
16 but all Israel and Juda loved David
20 but Michol . . . loved David. And it was
28 Michol the daughter of Saul loved him
19 1 Jonathan the son of Saul loved David
20 17 because he [Jonathan] loved him [David]
2 K 12 24 name Solomon, and the Lord loved him
25 because the Lord loved him [Solomon]
13 1 Amnon . . . loved the sister of Absalom
15 the love with which he had loved her
21 his son Amnon, for he loved him
3 K 3 3 Solomon loved the Lord, walking in
10 9 the Lord hath loved Israel forever
11 1 king Solomon loved many strange women
2 Pa 2 11 because the Lord hath loved his people
11 21 Roboam loved Maacha the daughter of
26 10 for he was a man that loved husbandry
Tob 1 23 lay concealed, for many loved him
Jdth 15 11 because thou hast loved chastity and
Job 19 19 whom I loved most is turned against
Ps 10 8 the Lord is just and hath loved justice
25 8 have loved . . . the beauty of thy house
44 8 thou hast loved justice and hated
46 5 beauty of Jacob which he hath loved
50 8 thou hast loved truth: the uncertain
51 5 thou hast loved malice more than
6 thou hast loved all the words of ruin
77 36 and they loved him with their mouth
68 tribe of Juda, mount Sion which he l.
108 18 he loved cursing, and it shall come
114 1 I have loved, because the Lord will
118 47 thy commandments, which I loved. 48
97 how have I loved thy law, O Lord
113 hated the unjust: and have l. thy law
119 therefore have I loved thy testimonies
127 have I loved thy commandments above
140 refined: and thy servant hath loved it
159 I have loved thy commandments, O Lord
163 iniquity: but I have loved thy law
166 O Lord: and I loved thy commandments
167 and hath loved them exceedingly
Prov 16 13 speaketh right things shall be loved
Cant 1 2 young maidens have loved thee. Draw
Wisd 7 10 I loved her above health and beauty
8 2 her have I loved and have sought her
3 the Lord of all things hath loved her
Eccu 47 10 and loved God that made him: and he
Isa 43 4 I have loved thee, and I will give men
48 14 the Lord hath loved him, he will do
57 8 thou hast loved their bed with open
Jer 2 25 I have loved strangers and I will walk
5 31 and my people loved such things: what
8 2 host of heaven, whom they have loved
14 10 that have loved to move their feet and
31 3 I have loved thee with an everlasting
Eze 16 37 and all whom thou hast loved, with all
Osee 4 18 have loved to bring shame upon them
9 1 thou hast loved a reward upon every
10 those things were, which they loved
11 2 Israel was a child, and I loved him
12 7 in his hand, he hath loved oppression
Soph 2 1 O nation not worthy to be loved
Zach 13 6 in the house of them that loved me
Mala 1 2 I have loved you, saith the Lord: and
2 have said: Wherein hast thou loved us
2 and I have loved Jacob, but have hated
2 11 holiness of the Lord, which he loved
Mark 10 21 Jesus looking on him, loved him and
12 33 should be loved with the whole heart
Luke 7 47 because she hath loved much. But to
10 27 thou shalt love the Lord thy God with
John 3 16 God so loved the world as to give his
19 men loved darkness rather than the
11 5 Jesus loved Martha and her sister Mary
36 behold how he loved him. But some of
12 43 they loved the glory of men more than
13 1 having loved his own who were in the
1 he loved them unto the end. And when
23 one of his disciples, whom Jesus loved
34 one another as I have loved you. 15:12
14 21 loveth me, shall be loved of my Father
28 if you loved me, you would indeed be
15 9 as the Father hath loved me, I also have loved you
16 27 because you have loved me and have
17 23 hast loved them, as thou hast also loved me
24 hast loved me before the creation of
26 love wherewith thou hast loved me
19 26 the disciple standing whom he loved
20 2 disciple whom Jesus loved. 21:20
21 7 disciple therefore whom Jesus loved
Rom 8 37 because of him that hath loved us. For
9 13 Jacob I have loved, but Esau I have
2 C 12 15 loving you more, I be loved less. But
Gal 2 20 faith of Son of God, who loved me, and
Eph 2 4 exceeding charity wherewith he loved us
5 2 walk in love, as Christ also hath loved
25 wives, as Christ also loved the church
2 Th 2 15 God and our Father, who hath loved us
Heb 1 9 thou hast loved justice, and hated
2 P 2 15 who loved the wages of iniquity, but
1 J 4 10 not as though we had loved God, but
10 but because he hath first loved us
11 if God hath so loved us, we also ought
19 because God first hath loved us
Apoc 1 5 who hath loved us and washed us from
3 9 they shall know that I have loved thee
12 11 they loved not their lives unto death
lovedst Wisd 16 26 children, O Lord, whom thou l.
loveliness Ps 49 2 out of Sion the l. of his beauty
lovely 2 K 1 23 and Jonathan l. and comely

Jdth 10 4 she appeared . . . incomparably lovely
Ps 83 2 how lovely are thy tabernacles, O Lord
Cant 5 16 most sweet, and he is all lovely
Isa 64 11 our l. things are turned into ruins
Jer 3 19 and give thee a lovely land, the
Phil 4 8 whatsoever holy, whatsoever lovely
lover Wisd 8 2 I became a lover of her beauty
Jer 3 20 as a woman that despiseth her lover
2 Ma 14 37 a man that was a lover of the city
15 14 this is a lover of his brethren and
lovers Jer 22 22 thy lovers shall go into captivity
Wisd 15 6 the l. of evil things deserve to
Jer 3 1 prostituted thyself to many lovers
4 30 thy lovers have despised thee, they
22 20 by, for all thy lovers are destroyed
30 14 all thy lovers have forgotten thee and
Eze 16 8 behold thy time was the time of lovers
33 thou hast given hire to all thy lovers
36 through thy fornications with thy l.
37 I will gather together all thy lovers
23 5 against me, doted on her lovers
9 delivered her into hands of her lovers
22 I will raise up against thee all thy l.
Osee 2 5 she said: I will go after my lovers
7 and she shall follow after her lovers
10 her folly in the eyes of her lovers
12 rewards which my lovers have given me
13 went after her lovers and forgot me
8 9 Ephraim hath given gifts to his lovers
2 Tim 3 2 men shall be lovers of themselves
4 lovers of pleasures more than of God
1 P 3 8 being lovers of the brotherhood
lovest Gen 22 2 son Isaac, whom thou lovest
Deut 13 6 whom thou lovest as thy own soul
21 11 a beautiful woman and lovest her
Judg 16 15 how dost thou say thou lovest me, when
1 K 20 30 that thou lovest the son of Isai to
2 K 19 6 thou lovest them that hate thee, and
1 Pa 29 17 provest hearts and lovest simplicity
Ecce 9 9 joyfully with the wife whom thou lovest
Wisd 11 25 thou lovest all things that are, and
27 are thine, O Lord, who lovest souls
John 11 3 behold, he whom thou lovest is sick
21 15 Simon, son of John, lovest thou me. 16, 17
17 the third time: Lovest thou me
loveth Gen 44 20 his father loveth him tenderly
Deut 10 18 l. the stranger and giveth him food
15 16 because he loveth thee and thy house
Judg 5 9 my heart loveth the princes of Israel
Ruth 4 15 thy daughter-in-law; who loveth thee
2 K 1 26 as the mother loveth her only son, so
2 Pa 9 8 because God loveth Israel and will
Job 34 17 can he be healed that l. not judgment
Ps 10 6 that l. iniquity hateth his own soul
32 5 he loveth mercy and judgment: the earth
33 13 who loveth to see good days? Keep
36 28 the Lord loveth judgment and will not
83 12 God loveth mercy and truth: the Lord
86 2 Lord loveth the gates of Sion above
98 4 and the king's honor loveth judgment
145 8 cast down: the Lord loveth the just
Prov 3 12 whom the Lord loveth, he chastiseth
12 1 that loveth correction, l. knowledge
13 24 he that loveth him correcteth him
14 21 believeth in the Lord, loveth mercy
15 12 loveth not one that reproveth him
17 17 that is a friend loveth at all times
19 that studieth discords, loveth quarrels
19 8 possesseth a mind, loveth his own soul
21 17 he that loveth good cheer, shall be
17 he that loveth wine and fat things
22 11 he that loveth cleanness of heart
26 28 a deceitful tongue loveth not truth
29 3 man that loveth wisdom, rejoiceth his
Ecce 5 9 he that loveth riches shall reap no
Cant 1 6 show me, O thou whom my soul loveth
3 1 him whom my soul loveth. 2, 3, 4
Wisd 7 28 God loveth none but him that dwelleth
15 5 loveth the lifeless figure of a dead
Eccu 3 4 that loveth God, shall obtain pardon
27 he that loveth danger shall perish
4 13 and he that loveth her, loveth life
15 and God loveth them that love her
13 19 every beast loveth its like: so also
30 1 he that loveth his son, frequently
31 5 that l. gold, shall not be justified
47 24 the seed of him that loveth the Lord
Bar 6 8 for a maiden that loveth to go gay
Osee 3 1 as the Lord loveth the children of
Mat 10 37 he that loveth father or mother more
37 he that loveth son or daughter more
Luke 7 5 he loveth our nation; and he hath
42 which . . . of the two loveth him most
47 whom less is forgiven, he loveth less
John 3 35 the Father loveth the Son. 5:20
12 25 he that loveth his life, shall lose it
14 21 he it is that loveth me. And he that loveth me, shall be loved of my
24 he that loveth me not, keepeth not my
16 27 the Father himself loveth you because
Rom 13 8 for he that loveth his neighbor, hath
2 C 9 7 for God loveth a cheerful giver. And God
Eph 5 28 he that loveth his wife, loveth himself
Heb 12 6 whom the Lord loveth, he chastiseth
1 J 2 10 he that loveth his brother, abideth
3 10 nor he that loveth not his brother
14 he that loveth not, abideth in death
4 7 every one that loveth is born of God
8 he that loveth not, knoweth not God
20 he that loveth not his brother, whom
21 who loveth God, love also his brother
5 1 loveth him who begot, loveth him also who is born of him
3 J 9 who loveth to have the pre-eminence
Apoc 22 15 every one that loveth and maketh a lie
loving Wisd 7 22 loving that which is good
Isa 56 10 dogs . . . sleeping and loving dreams
Rom 12 10 loving one another with the charity of
2 C 12 15 loving you more, I be loved less. But
2 Tim 4 9 Demas hath left me, loving this world
low Josu 17 16 that dwell in the low lands
4 K 13 7 and had brought them low as dust
Jdth 6 15 pride and look on our low condition
Job 6 5 will the ox low when he standeth before
Ps 89 3 turn not man away to be brought low
93 5 thy people . . . they have brought low
105 43 were brought low by their iniquities
106 17 were brought low for their injustices
112 6 looketh down on the low things in
137 6 Lord is high and looketh on the low
141 7 for I am brought very low. Deliver me
Prov 12 25 grief . . . shall bring him low, but
26 25 when he shall speak low, trust him not
Ecce 12 4 when the grinder's voice shall be low
Eccu 11 13 hath lifted him up from his low estate
20 11 lift up his head from a low estate
21 23 a wise man will scarce laugh low to
24 11 the hearts of all the high and low
31 4 hath labored in his low way of life
33 12 them hath he cursed and brought low
Isa 5 15 eyes of the lofty shall be brought low
25 12 walls shall fall and be brought low
26 5 on high, the high city he shall lay low
32 19 and the city shall be made very low
40 4 mountain and hill shall be made low
Eze 17 6 into a spreading vine of low stature

14 14 that it may be a low kingdom and not
24 high tree, and exalted the low tree
21 26 hath exalted the low one and brought
29 14 and they shall be there a low kingdom
Dan 3 37 and are brought low in all the earth
Joel 1 18 why did the herds of cattle low
1 Ma 3 43 up the low condition of our people
51 are in mourning and are brought low
6 40 the other part by the low places
14 14 all those . . . that were brought low
Luke 3 5 and hill shall be brought low
19 3 crowd, because he was low of stature
Phil 4 12 I know both how to be brought low, and
James 1 9 let the brother of low condition glory
10 and the rich, in his being low; because
lower Gen 6 16 with lower, middle chambers
Lev 13 3 where the leprosy appears lower than
4 not lower than the other flesh. 34
20 lower than the other flesh. 30
21 not lower than the flesh that is near
25 lower than the other skin. 26
14 37 redness, and lower than all the rest
Deut 28 43 and thou shalt go down and be lower
2 K 24 6 to the lower land of Hodsi, and they
Ps 62 10 go into the lower parts of the earth
85 13 delivered my soul out of the lower hell
87 7 they have laid me in the lower pit
138 15 my substance in the lower parts of the
Eccu 24 45 will penetrate to all the lower parts
Isa 22 9 together the waters of the lower pool
Eze 40 18 pavement in the front . . . was lower
19 from the face of the lower gate to the
41 7 from the lower parts they went to the
42 5 were the store chambers lower above
5 above out of them from the lower parts
6 appear above out of the lower places
Eph 4 9 first into the lower parts of the earth
Heb 2 7 a little lower than the angels. 9
2 P 2 4 by infernal ropes to the lower hell
lowering Mat 16 3 for the sky is red and lowering
lowest Deut 32 22 shall burn even to the l. hell
3 K 12 31 priests of the lowest of the people
4 K 14 26 up in prison, and the lowest persons
17 32 of the lowest of the people, priests
Job 38 16 walked in the lowest parts of the deep
Prov 15 24 he may decline from the lowest hell
Wisd 17 13 them, from the lowest and deepest hell
Lam 3 55 upon thy name . . . from the lowest pit
Eze 26 20 in the lowest parts of the earth. 31:16
29 15 be the lowest among other kingdoms
31 14 to the l. parts of the earth. 18; 32:24
32 23 are set in the lowest parts of the pit
43 14 ground to the lowest brim two cubits
Jon 2 7 to the lowest parts of the mountains
Luke 14 9 with shame to take the lowest place
10 sit down in the lowest place; that
lowing 1 K 6 12 along the way, l. as they went
1 K 15 14 the lowing of the herds, which I hear
lowliness Eccu 19 24 exceedingly with a great l.
lowly Jdth 16 13 howled when my l. ones appeared
Eccu 13 11 be not lowly in thy wisdom, lest
2 C 10 1 in presence indeed am lowly among you
lowness Ps 21 22 my l. from the horns of the
Phil 3 21 who will reform the body of our lowness
loyal 2 Ma 11 19 keep yourselves loyal in affairs
Lucifer Isa 14 12 thou fallen from heaven, O L.
Lucius 1 Ma 15 16 Lucius the consul of the Romans
Acts 13 1 Simon who was called Niger, and L.
Rom 16 21 L. and Jason and Sosipater, my kinsmen
lucre 1 K 8 3 they turned aside after lucre
1 Tim 3 8 not greedy of filthy lucre. Titus 1:7
Titus 1 7 no striker, not greedy of filthy lucre
lucre's Titus 1 11 not for filthy l. sake. 1 P 5:2

Lud Gen 10 22 sons of Sem: . . . Lud. 1 Pa 1:17
Ludim Gen 10 13 Mesraim begot Ludim. 1 Pa 1:11
Luith Isa 15 5 by the ascent of Luith. Jer 48:5
Luke Col 4 14 Luke, the most dear physician
2 Tim 4 11 only Luke is with me. Take Mark, and
Philem 24 Demas and Luke my fellow laborers. The
lukewarm Apoc 3 16 because thou art lukewarm, and
lump 4 K 20 7 said: Bring me a lump of figs
Isa 38 21 that they should take a lump of figs
Rom 9 21 of the same lump, to make one vessel
11 16 the firstfruit be holy, so is the lump
1 C 5 6 leaven corrupteth the whole l. Gal 5:9
lumps Dan 14 26 made lumps and put them into
lunatic Mat 17 14 pity on my son, for he is a l.
lunatics Mat 4 24 possessed by devils, and lunatics
lungs Exod 29 22 the fat that covereth the lungs
3 K 22 34 between the lungs and the stomach
lurking 1 K 23 23 his l. holes wherein he is hid
1 Ma 1 56 people of Israel into lurking holes
lust Gen 4 7 the lust thereof shall be under the
Num 11 34 the graves of lust. 33:16, 17; Deut 9:22
Judg 19 24 may humble them and satisfy your lust
20 5 wife with an incredible fury of lust
Tob 3 16 have kept my soul clean from all lust
18 take, with thy fear, not with my lust
6 17 and to give themselves to their lust
22 rather for love of children than for l.
8 9 not for fleshly lust do I take my
Wisd 15 5 enticeth the fool to lust after it
Eccu 9 9 hereby lust is enkindled as a fire
20 2 the lust of an eunuch shall deflour
Eze 23 9 Assyrians, upon whose lust she doted
11 she was mad with lust more than she
16 doted upon them with the lust of her
20 she was mad with lust after lying
Dan 11 37 and he shall follow the lust of women
13 8 were inflamed with lust towards her
11 to declare to one another their lust
14 they acknowledged their lust; and
56 and lust hath perverted thy heart
Mat 5 28 shall look on a woman to lust after her
Col 3 5 earth; fornication, uncleanness, lust
1 Th 4 5 not in the passion of lust, like the
2 P 2 10 the flesh in the lust of uncleanness
lusted Num 11 34 buried the people that had l.
lusteth Gal 5 17 flesh lusteth against the spirit
lusts Eccu 18 30 go not after thy lusts, but turn
Eccu 23 6 let not the lusts of the flesh take
Mark 4 19 the lusts after other things entering
Rom 1 27 burned in their l. one towards another
6 12 body, so as to obey the lusts thereof
Gal 5 16 you shall not fulfil the lusts of flesh
1 P 4 3 who have walked in riotousness, lusts
2 P 3 3 walking after their own lusts, saying
lutes 2 K 6 5 on harps and lutes and timbrels
1 Ma 4 54 with canticles and harps and lutes
luxurious Amos 6 7 faction of the l. ones shall be
Eccu 21 18 the l. man hath heard it and it shall
Prov 20 1 wine is a luxurious thing, and
luxury Wisd 2 9 go without his part in luxury
Gal 5 19 immodesty, luxury, idolatry, witchcrafts
Eph 5 18 not drunk with wine, wherein is luxury
Luza Gen 28 19 Bethel, which before was called L.
Gen 35 6 Jacob came to Luza, which is in the
48 3 God Almighty appeared to me at Luza
Josu 16 2 and goeth out from Bethel to Luza
18 13 along southward by Luza, the same is
Judg 1 23 the city, which before was called Luza
26 built there a city and called it Luza
Lycaonia Acts 14 6 Lystra, and Derbe, cities of L.
Lycaonian Acts 14 10 up their voices in L. tongue
Lycia 1 Ma 15 23 Samus and Pamphylia and Lycia
Acts 27 5 we came to Lystra, which is in Lycia

M

Maacha Gen 22 24 Roma bore . . . Tahas and Maacha
2 K 3 3 Absalom the son of Maacha. 1 Pa 3:2
10 6 of the king of Maacha a thousand men
8 of the Syrians . . . of Istob and of M.
3 K 2 39 Achis the son of M. the king of Geth
15 2 the name of his mother was Maacha the
10 his mother's name was Maacha, the
13 he also removed his mother Maacha from
20 they smote . . . Abeldomum Maacha and
4 K 15 29 and took Aion and Abel Domum Maacha
1 Pa 2 48 M. the concubine of Caleb bore Saber
7 15 and he had a sister named Maacha: the
16 Maacha the wife of Machir bore a son
8 29 the name of his wife was Maacha. 9:35
11 43 Hanan the son of M., and Josaphat
19 6 out of Syria Maacha and out of Soba
7 and the king of Maacha with his people
27 16 Saphatias the son of Maacha: over the
2 Pa 11 20 after her he [Roboam] married Maacha
21 Roboam loved Maacha . . . above all his
22 head of them Abia the son of Maacha
15 16 M. the mother of king Asa he deposed
Maachathi 4 K 25 23 Jezonias the son of Maachathi
Maachati Jer 40 8 Jezonias the son of Maachati
Maaddi 1 Es 10 34 of the sons of Bani, Maaddi
Maai 2 Es 12 35 Galalai, Maai, Nathanael, and
Maala Num 26 33 Maala and Noa and Hegla. 27:1; Josu 17:3
Num 36 11 Maala and Thersa and Hegla and Melcha
Maara Josu 13 4 Maara of the Sidonians as far as
Maasai 1 Pa 9 12 Maasai the son of Adiel the son
Maasia 1 Es 10 18 his brethren M. and Eliezer and
1 Es 10 22 Maasia, Ismael, Nathanael, Jozabed and
2 Es 8 4 Helcia and Maasia on his right hand
7 Maasia, Celtia, Azarias, Jozabed, Hanan
10 25 Rehum, Hasebna, Maasia, Echaia, Hanan
11 5 of the sons of Phares, Maasia the son
12 40 priests Eliachim, Maasia, Miamin
41 and Maasia and Semeia and Eleazar and
Maasias 1 Pa 15 18 Eliab and Banaias and Maasias
1 Pa 15 20 Eliab and Maasias and Banaias sung
2 Pa 23 1 and Maasias the son of Adaias, and
26 11 Jehiel the scribe and M. the doctor
28 7 Zechri . . . slew Maasias the king's son
1 Es 10 30 Edna and Chalal, Banaias, and Maasias
34 8 and Maasias the governor of the city
2 Es 3 23 built Azarias the son of Maasias the
Jer 29 21 and to Sedecias the son of Maasias
21 1 Sophonias the son of M. 29:25; 37:3
32 12 the son of Neri the son of Maasias
35 4 above the treasure of Maasias the son
51 59 Nerias the son of Maasias. Bar 1:1
Maazia 2 Es 10 8 Maazia, Belgia, Semeia: these
Maaziau 1 Pa 24 18 four and twentieth to Maaziau
Mabsam Gen 25 13 Ismael's children . . . Mabsam
1 Pa 1 29 of Ismahel . . . Abdeel and Mabsam and
Mabsar Gen 36 42 dukes of Esau . . . duke Mabsar
1 Pa 1 53 dukes in Edom . . . duke Mabsar, duke
Macces 3 K 4 9 Bendecar, in M. and in Salebim
Maceda Josu 10 10 all the way to Azeca and Maceda
Josu 10 16 in a cave of the city of Maceda. 17
21 all the army returned to Josue in M.
28 Josue took Maceda and destroyed it
28 he did to the king of M. as he had
29 he passed from Maceda with all Israel
12 16 the king of Maceda one, the king of
15 41 and Naama and Maceda: sixteen cities
Macedonia Acts 16 9 was a man of M. standing and
Acts 16 9 pass over into Macedonia, and help us
10 we sought to go into Macedonia, being
12 is chief city of part of M., a colony
18 5 Timothy were come from M., Paul was
19 21 when he had passed through Macedonia and
22 sending into Macedonia two of them that
29 Gaius and Aristarchus, men of M., Paul's
20 1 set forward to go into Macedonia. And
3 he took resolution to return through M.
Rom 15 26 it hath pleased them of Macedonia and
1 C 16 5 I shall have passed through Macedonia
5 for I shall pass through Macedonia. And
2 C 1 16 and to pass by you into Macedonia, and
16 again from Macedonia to come to you, and
2 13 bidding them farewell, I went into M.
7 5 when we were come into Macedonia, our
8 1 been given in the churches of Macedonia
11 9 the brethren supplied who came from M.
Phil 4 15 when I departed from M., no church
1 Th 1 7 to all that believe in Macedonia and in
8 not only in Macedonia, and in Achaia
4 10 do it towards all the brethren in all M.
1 Tim 1 3 when I went into Macedonia, that thou
Macedonian Esth 16 10 M. both in mind and country
1 Ma 1 1 the son of Philip the Macedonian. 6:2
Acts 27 2 Aristarchus, the M. of Thessalonica
Macedonians Esth 16 14 of the Persians to the M.
2 Ma 8 20 M. their companions were at a stand
2 C 9 2 mind: for which I boast of you to the M.
4 lest, when the M. shall come with me
Macelloth 1 Pa 8 31 and Zacher and Macelloth
1 Pa 8 32 and Macelloth begot Samaa. 9:38
9 37 Ahio and Zacharias and Macelloth
27 4 after him was another named Macelloth
Maceloth Num 33 25 went and camped in Maceloth
Num 33 26 departing from Maceloth, they came
Macenias 1 Pa 15 18 M. and Obededom and. 21
Macer 2 Ma 10 12 Ptolemee that was called Macer
Machabeus 1 Ma 2 4 and Judas who was called M.
1 Ma 2 66 Judas Machabeus who is valiant and
3 1 Judas, called Machabeus, rose up in
5 24 Judas M. and Jonathan his brother
34 understood that it was M., and they
8 20 Judas M. and his brethren and the
2 Ma 2 20 concerning Judas M. and his brethren
5 27 Judas M., who was the tenth, had
8 1 M. and they that were with him. 10:1, 25, 33; 11:6
5 when M. had gathered a multitude, he
16 M. calling together 7,000 that were
10 16 that were with M., beseeching the
19 Machabeus left Simon and Joseph and
21 was told M. what was done, he assembled
30 two of whom took M. between them and
35 young men of them that were with M.
11 7 then M. himself, first taking his arms
15 M. consented to the request of Lysias
15 whatsoever M. wrote to Lysias concerning
12 15 Machabeus calling upon the great Lord
19 who were captains with Machabeus, slew
20 M. having set in order about him
13 24 he embraced M. and made him governor
14 6 of whom Judas Machabeus is captain
27 to send Machabeus prisoner in all haste
30 when Machabeus perceived that Nicanor
15 7 M. ever trusted with all hope that God
21 M. considering the coming of the
Machathi 1 Pa 4 19 Esthamo, who was of Machathi
Machati Deut 3 14 the borders of Gessuri and Machati. Josu 12:5; 13:11
Josu 13 13 would not destroy Gessuri and Machati
2 K 23 34 the son of Aasbai the son of Machati
Machbani 1 Pa 12 13 Machbani the eleventh, these
Machbena 1 Pa 2 49 Sue the father of Machbena
Machi Num 13 16 Guel the son of Machi. These are
Machir Gen 50 22 children of M. the son of Manasses

Num 26 29 of Manasses was born Machir, of whom
29 Machir begot Galaad, of whom is the
27 1 Galaad the son of Machir. 36:1; Josu 17:3; 1 Pa 7:17
32 39 children of Machir . . . went into Galaad
40 Moses gave the land of Galaad to Machir
Deut 3 15 to Machir also I gave Galaad. And to
Josu 13 21 to children of M. the son of Manasses
31 to one half of the children of Machir
17 1 to Machir the firstborn of Manasses
Judg 5 14 out of Machir there came down princes
2 K 9 4 behold he is in the house of Machir
5 brought him out of the house of Machir
17 27 Machir the son of Ammihel of Lodabar
1 Pa 2 21 Hesron went in to daughter of Machir
23 the sons of Machir father of Galaad
7 14 his concubine the Syrian bore Machir
15 and Machir took wives for his sons
16 Maacha the wife of Machir bore a son

Machirites Num 26 29 whom is the family of the M.

Machmas 1 K 13 2 and 2,000 were with Saul in M.
1 K 13 5 going up they camped in Machmas at
11 Philistines were gathered together in M.
16 but the Philistines encamped in Machmas
23 in order to advance further in Machmas
14 5 towards the north over against Machmas
31 Philistines from Machmas to Ailon
1 Es 2 27 the men of Machmas, 122. 2 Es 7:31
Isa 10 28 at M. he shall lay up his carriages
1 Ma 9 73 and Jonathan dwelt in Machmas: and

Machmethath Josu 16 6 M. looketh to the north
Josu 17 7 M. which looketh towards Sichem: and

mad 1 K 21 14 you saw the man was mad; why have
4 K 9 11 why came this mad man to thee [Jehu]
19 28 thou hast been mad against me, and
Wisd 14 28 they are mad when they are merry: or
Isa 24 6 they that dwell therein shall be mad
37 29 when thou wast mad against me, thy
44 25 and make the soothsayers mad. That
Jer 25 16 they shall . . . be mad because of the
Eze 23 11 she was mad with lust more than she
20 and she was mad with lust after lying
Osee 7 5 the princes began to be mad with wine
9 7 foolish, the spiritual man was mad, for
Mark 3 21 for they said: He is become mad. And
John 10 20 said: He hath a devil and is mad: why
Acts 12 15 they said to her: Thou art mad. But
26 11 and being yet more mad against them, I
24 much learning doth make thee mad. And
25 I am not mad, most excellent Festus, but
1 C 14 23 will they not say that you are mad? But

Madaba 1 Ma 9 36 of Jambri came forth out of M.
1 Ma 9 37 were bringing the bride out of Madaba

Madai Gen 10 2 Madai and Javan. 1 Pa 1:5

Madan Gen 25 2 Madan and Madian and Jesboc. 1 Pa 1:32

Madia 2 Es 12 5 Madia, Belga, Semeia, and

Madian Gen 25 2 Madan and M. and Jesboc. 1 Pa 1:32
Gen 25 4 of Madian was born Epha and Opher
Exod 2 15 sight, and abode in the land of Madian
16 priest of Madian had seven daughters
3 1 father-in-law, the priest of M. 18:1
4 19 the Lord said to Moses in Madian: Go
Num 22 4 he said to the elders of Madian: So
25 6 before his brethren to a harlot of M.
14 was slain with the woman of Madian
18 a daughter of a prince of Madian, who
Josu 13 21 Moses slew with the princes of Madian
Judg 6 1 delivered them into the hand of Madian
3 Israel had sown, Madian and Amalec
6 humbled exceedingly in sight of Madian
11 the winepress, to flee from Madian
13 delivered us into the hands of Madian
14 shalt deliver Israel out of hand of M.
16 thou shalt cut off Madian as one man
33 all Madian and Amalec . . . were gathered
7 1 the camp of Madian was in the valley
2 Madian shall not be delivered into
7 will . . . deliver Madian into thy hand
8 the camp of Madian was beneath him
12 Madian and Amalec . . . lay scattered
13 and came down into the camp of Madian
14 for the Lord hath delivered Madian
15 Lord hath delivered the camp of Madian
23 from all Manasses pursued after Madian
24 come down to meet Madian, and take
25 having taken two men of Madian, Oreb and
25 they pursued Madian, carrying the heads
8 1 when thou wentest to fight against M.
3 into your hands the princes of Madian
5 Zebee and Salmana the kings of Madian
22 delivered us from the hand of Madian
26 purple raiment which the kings of M.
28 Madian was humbled before the children
9 17 to deliver you from the hands of Madian
3 K 11 18 they arose out of Madian and came
1 Pa 1 33 sons of Madian: Epha and Epher and
Jdth 2 16 carried away all the children of Madian
Ps 82 10 do to them as thou didst to Madian
Isa 9 4 hast overcome, as in the day of Madian
10 26 according to the slaughter of Madian
60 6 the dromedaries of Madian and Epha
Haba 3 7 the curtains of the land of Madian
Acts 7 29 was a stranger in the land of Madian

Madianite Gen 37 28 when the M. merchants passed
Num 10 29 Hobab son of Raguel the Madianite
25 15 Madianite woman that was slain with him

Madianites Gen 36 35 who defeated the Madianites
Gen 37 36 the Madianites sold Joseph in Egypt
Num 25 15 Sur, a most noble prince among the M.
17 let the M. find you their enemies
31 2 revenge first . . . on the Madianites
3 revenge of the Lord on the Madianites
7 when they had fought against the M.
Judg 6 7 desiring help against the Madianites
1 Pa 1 46 he defeated the M. in the land of Moab

madman 1 K 21 15 to play the m. in my presence

madmen 1 K 21 15 have we need of m., that you have

Madmena 1 Pa 2 49 Saaph the father of Madmena

madness Deut 28 28 Lord strike thee with madness
Esth 16 5 they break out into so great madness
Ps 57 5 their m. is according to the likeness
Wisd 5 4 we fools esteemed their life madness
14 23 or keep watches full of madness, so
Osee 9 7 for the . . . multitude of thy madness
8 madness is in the house of his God
Zach 12 4 I will strike . . . his rider with m.
2 Ma 4 40 far gone both in age and in madness
14 5 convenient time to further his madness
Luke 6 11 and they were filled with madness
2 P 2 16 but had a check of his madness, the

Madon Josu 11 1 he sent to Jobab king of Madon
Josu 12 19 the king of Madon one, the king of

Maeleth Ps 52 1 unto the end, for Maeleth

Magala 1 K 17 20 [David] came to the place of M.

Magdal Exod 14 2 which is between M. and the sea
Jer 44 1 dwelling in Magdal and in Taphnis
46 14 declare ye to Egypt and publish it in M.

Magdalel Josu 19 38 Jeron and Magdalel

Magdalen Luke 8 2 who is called Magdalen, out of

Mary Magdalen; *see* Mary

Magdalgad Josu 15 37 Hadassa and Magdalgad

Magdalum Num 33 7 they camped before Magdalum

Magdiel Gen 36 43 dukes of Esau . . . duke Magdiel
1 Pa 1 54 dukes in Edom . . . duke Magdiel

Magedan Mat 15 39 and came into the coasts of M.

Mageddo Josu 12 21 the king of Mageddo one

Josu 17 11 inhabitants of M. with their villages
Judg 1 27 Dor and Jeblaam and Mageddo with
5 19 in Thanach by the waters of Mageddo
3 K 4 12 who governed Thanac and Mageddo
9 15 to build . . . Heser and Mageddo
4 K 9 27 he fled into Mageddo and died there
23 29 [Josias] was slain at Mageddo.
30 servants carried him dead from Mageddo
1 Pa 7 29 Mageddo and her daughters: Dor and
2 Pa 35 22 went to fight in the field of Mageddo
Mageddon Zach 12 11 in the plain of Mageddon
Mageth 1 Ma 5 26 of them were shut up . . . in M.
1 Ma 5 36 he marched and took Casbon and Mageth
magic Wisd 17 7 the delusions of their magic art
magical Acts 8 11 them with his m. practices
magician Acts 8 9 who before had been a magician
Acts 13 6 a certain man, a m., a false prophet
8 Elymas the magician . . . withstood them
magicians Exod 7 11 called the . . . magicians
Exod 7 22 the m. of the Egyptians with their
8 7 the m. also by their enchantments
18 the m. with their enchantments
19 the magicians said to Pharao: This is
9 11 neither could the magicians stand
Lev 20 6 the soul that shall go aside after m.
1 K 28 3 Saul had put away all the magicians
9 how he hath rooted out the magicians
2 Pa 33 6 had with him magicians and enchanters
Dan 2 2 the wise men and the magicians and
5 15 the magicians have come in before me
magistrates Deut 16 18 appoint judges and magistrates. 1 Es 7:25
1 Es 9 2 hand of the princes and m. hath been
2 Es 2 16 m. knew not whither I went or what
16 priests or to the nobles or to the m.
4 14 I said to the chief men and the m.
19 I said to the nobles and to the m.
5 7 I rebuked the nobles and magistrates
17 the magistrates . . . were at my table
7 5 I assembled the princes and magistrates
12 39 the half of the magistrates with me
13 11 I pleaded the matter against the m.
Dan 2 48 chief of the m. over all the wise men
3 2 nobles, the m., and the judges. 3, 94
4 33 nobles and my m. sought for me
6 7 the magistrates . . . have consulted
Luke 12 11 you into synagogues and to m. and
Acts 16 20 presenting them to the m., they said
22 and the m. rending off their clothes
35 the m. sent the serjeants, saying, Let
36 the m. have sent to let you go; now
38 the serjeants told these words to m.
magnificence Deut 32 3 give ye m. to our God
Deut 33 26 by his m. the clouds run hither and
1 Pa 16 27 praise and magnificence are before him
17 19 thou hast shown all this magnificence
29 11 thine, O Lord, is m. and power and
Esth 1 7 as was worthy of a king's magnificence
2 18 bestowed gifts according to princely m.
Ps 8 2 thy m. is elevated above the heavens
28 4 the voice of the Lord is magnificence
67 35 his m. and his power is in the clouds
40 21 thou hast multiplied thy magnificence
110 3 his work is praise and magnificence
144 5 shall speak of the m. of the glory of
12 and the glory of the m. of thy kingdom
Eccu 43 32 yet far exceed, and his m. is wonderful
44 2 hath wrought great glory through his m.
Isa 4 2 the bud of the Lord shall be in m. and
1 Ma 15 32 saw the glory of Simon and his m. in
Jude 25 be glory and magnificence, empire and
magnificent Isa 22 5 and m. upon the mountain
Isa 33 21 because only there our Lord is m.
2 Ma 2 9 for he treated wisdom in a m. manner
4 22 he was received in a m. manner by Jason
magnified Gen 19 19 and thou hast m. thy mercy
Exod 15 1 he is gloriously m., the horse. 21
6 right hand, O Lord, is m. in strength
Num 14 17 then the strength of the Lord be m.
Josu 4 14 in that day the Lord m. Josue in the
2 K 7 22 therefore thou art magnified, O Lord
26 that thy name may be magnified forever
1 Pa 17 24 let thy name remain and be magnified
29 25 the Lord magnified Solomon over all
2 Pa 1 1 with him and m. him to a high degree
9 22 Solomon was magnified above all the
32 23 [Ezechias] was magnified thenceforth
Jdth 12 18 because my life is magnified this day
13 25 because he hath so magnified thy name
31 the God of Israel shall be magnified
Ps 34 27 let them say always: The Lord be m.
39 17 say always: The Lord be magnified. 69:5
56 11 thy mercy is m. even to the heavens
137 2 for thou hast magnified thy holy name
138 14 praise thee, for thou art fearfully m.
Eccu 25 9 to be imagined by the heart have I m.
36 4 thou shalt be magnified among them
45 2 and m. him in the fear of his enemies
48 4 thus was Elias m. in his wondrous
Isa 33 5 the Lord is m., for he hath dwelt on
Eze 38 23 will be m. and I will be sanctified
Dan 8 10 it was m. even unto the strength of
11 it was m. even to the prince of the
Mich 5 4 now shall he be m. even to the ends
Soph 2 8 have m. themselves upon their borders
10 been m. against the people of the Lord
Mala 1 5 Lord be m. upon the border of Israel
1 Ma 5 63 the men of Juda were m. exceedingly
8 14 in purple, to be magnified thereby
10 65 king m. him and enrolled him amongst
2 Ma 4 24 when he had m. the appearance of his
Luke 4 15 synagogues, and was magnified by all
Acts 5 13 but the people magnified them. And the
19 17 name of the Lord Jesus was m. And many
2 C 10 15 magnified in you according to our rule
Phil 1 20 shall Christ be magnified in my body
magnify Gen 12 2 bless thee and m. thy name
Job 7 17 is a man that thou shouldst m. him
Ps 9 18 may no more presume to magnify himself
11 5 have said: We will magnify our tongue
33 4 magnify the Lord with me: and let us
68 31 and I will magnify him with praise
71 17 be blessed: all nations shall m. him
Wisd 19 20 thou didst magnify thy people, O Lord
Eccu 10 26 do not m. a sinful man that is rich
39 20 magnify his name and give glory to
43 35 who shall m. him as he is from the
47 12 m. the holiness of God in the morning
49 13 how shall we m. Zorobabel: For he was
Isa 28 29 his counsel wonderful and m. justice
42 21 and to magnify the law and exalt it
Dan 4 34 I . . . do not praise and magnify and
11 36 and shall m. himself against every god
Abdi 12 thou shalt not m. thy mouth in the day
Zach 12 7 may not boast and m. themselves against
1 Ma 10 3 with peaceable words to magnify him
Luke 1 46 my soul doth magnify the Lord. And my
Rom 15 11 and magnify him, all ye people. And
Apoc 15 4 and magnify thy name? For thou only
magnifying Acts 10 46 with tongues, and m. God
Magog Gen 10 2 of Japheth: Gomer and M. 1 Pa 1:5
Eze 38 2 face against Gog, the land of Magog
39 6 I will send a fire on Magog, and on
Apoc 20 7 of the earth, Gog and Magog, and shall
Magron 1 K 14 2 pomegranate tree, which was in M.
Isa 10 28 into Aiath, he shall pass into Magron

Mahalath 2 Pa 11 18 Roboam took to wife Mahalath
Mahalon Ruth 1 2 his two sons, the one Mahalon
Ruth 1 5 both died, to wit, Mahalon and Chelion
4 10 Ruth the Moabitess, the wife of M.
Mahalon's Ruth 4 9 and M., of the hand of Noemi
Mahanaim Gen 32 2 the name of that place M.
Maharai 2 K 23 28 Maharai the Netophathite, Heled
1 Pa 11 30 Maharai a Netophathite, Heled the
Mahath 1 Pa 6 35 Elcana the son of Mahath the
2 Pa 29 12 then the Levites arose, Mahath the son
31 13 Jesmachias and Mahath . . . overseers
Luke 3 26 Nagge, who was of Mahath, who was of
Mahazioth 1 Pa 25 4 sons of Heman . . . Mahazioth
1 Pa 25 30 three and twentieth [lot] to Mahazioth
Maheleth Gen 28 9 M. the daughter of Ismael
Ps 87 1 for Maheleth, to answer understanding
Mahida 1 Es 2 52 the children of M. 2 Es 7:54
Mahir 1 Pa 4 11 Caleb the brother of Sua begot M.
Mahol 3 K 4 31 Chalcol and Dorda the sons of M.
Mahumite 1 Pa 11 46 Eliel a Mahumite and Jeribai
maid Gen 24 14 the maid to whom I shall say
Gen 24 16 an exceeding comely maid and a most
28 then the maid ran and told in her
55 let the maid stay at least ten days
57 let us call the maid and ask her will
Exod 2 8 the maid went and called her mother
Lev 12 5 but if she shall bear a maid child she
7 beareth a man child or a maid child
21 14 not take, but a maid of his own people
22 13 she was wont to do when she was a maid
Deut 22 29 to the father of the maid 50 sicles
Ruth 2 5 over the reapers: Whose maid is this
2 K 17 17 and there went a maid and told them
4 K 5 2 out of the land of Israel a little maid
Tob 3 9 when she reproved the maid for her
7 14 that this maid might be married to one
Jdth 10 2 she called her maid and going down into
5 she gave to her maid a bottle of wine
10 through the gates, she and her maid
12 12 let not my good maid be afraid to go
19 what her maid had prepared for her
13 5 and Judith spoke to her maid to stand
11 delivered head of Holofernes to her m.
Esth 15 7 the other maid followed her lady
Mat 9 25 her by the hand. And the maid arose
26 69 there came to him a servant maid
71 another maid saw him [Peter], and she
Luke 8 50 answered the father of the maid
52 the maid is not dead, but sleepeth
54 cried out, saying: Maid, arise. And
22 56 certain servant maid had seen sitting
John 18 17 the maid therefore that was portress
maiden Lev 21 3 a maiden sister who hath had no
Judg 19 24 I have a maiden daughter, and this
2 Pa 36 17 no compassion on young man or maiden
Eccu 9 5 gaze not upon a maiden, lest her
20 2 eunuch shall deflour a young maiden
Bar 6 8 for a maiden that loveth to go gay
Luke 8 51 the father and mother of the maiden
maidens Esth 2 3 to look for beautiful maidens
Esth 2 8 Esther also among rest of the maidens
9 seven of the most beautiful maidens
Ps 77 63 and their maidens were not lamented
148 12 young men and maidens: let the old
Prov 31 15 and given . . . victuals to her maidens
Cant 1 2 therefore young maidens have loved thee
6 7 and young maidens without number. One
Eze 9 6 utterly destroy old and young, maidens
maid's Exod 22 17 if the m. father will not give
maids Gen 24 61 Rebecca and her m. being set
Exod 2 5 she sent one of her maids for it: and
5 her maids walked by the river's brink
17 Moses arose and defending the maids
Ruth 2 8 but keep with my maids and follow
13 who am not like to one of thy maids
22 to go out to reap with his maids, lest
23 she kept close to the maids of Booz
3 2 with whose maids thou wast joined in
1 K 9 11 found maids coming out to draw water
Tob 3 7 from one of her father's servant maids
8 14 send one of thy maids, and let her see
Jdth 8 5 in which she abode shut up with her m.
Esth 2 9 deck out both her and her waiting maids
4 4 Esther's maids and her eunuchs went in
15 5 she took two maids with her, and upon
Prov 9 3 she hath sent her maids to invite
Dan 13 15 she went in . . . with two maids only
17 she said to the maids: Bring me oil
19 when the maids were gone forth, the
21 therefore thou didst send away thy m.
36 this woman came in with two maids, and
36 and sent away the maids from her. Then
maidservant Exod 20 10 do no work . . . nor thy m.
Exod 21 26 any man strike the eye of his . . . m.
27 if he strike out a tooth of his . . . m.
Lev 25 6 for meat, to thee and . . . to thy m.
Deut 5 14 any work therein, thou . . . nor thy m.
14 thy manservant and thy m. may rest
21 shalt not covet . . . his maidservant
12 18 shalt eat . . . and thy maidservant
16 11 shalt feast . . . and thy maidservant
14 shalt make merry . . . and thy m., the
Jdth 8 32 might, and I will go out with my m.
Job 31 13 to abide judgment with . . . my m., when
Jer 34 9 every man his maidservant . . . go free
10 and every man his maidservant go free
16 back again . . . every man his m. whom
Mark 14 69 again a m. seeing him, began to say
maidservants Gen 12 16 he [Abram] had . . . m. and
Gen 30 43 he [Jacob] had many . . . m. and
Deut 12 12 feast . . . your menservants and m.
4 K 5 26 to buy . . . menservants and maidservants
Tob 8 15 she sent one of her maidservants, who
Job 19 15 my m. have counted me as a stranger
Ecce 2 7 I got me menservants and m. and had a
Jer 34 11 into subjection as menservants and m.
Mark 14 66 cometh one of the m. of the high priest
Luke 12 45 to strike the menservants and m.
mail 1 K 17 5 he was clothed with a coat of mail
1 K 17 5 and the weight of his coat of mail was
38 and armed him with a coat of mail
2 Pa 26 14 helmets and coats of mail and bows
2 Es 4 16 for to fight, with . . . coats of mail
Jer 46 4 furbish the spears, put on coats of m.
51 3 that is armed with a coat of mail
Eze 38 4 horsemen all clothed with coats of mail
1 Ma 6 35 every elephant 1,000 men in coats of m.
Maiman 1 Pa 24 9 the sixth [lot] to Maiman
maimed 2 Ma 7 5 when he was now maimed in all
Mat 15 30 the blind, the lame, the maimed, and
18 8 thee to go into life maimed or lame
Mark 9 42 to enter into life maimed, than having
Luke 14 13 call the poor, the maimed, the lame
mainsail Acts 27 40 hoisting up the m. to the wind
maintain Exod 35 8 oil to m. lights and to make
1 Ma 7 21 he could to m. his chief priesthood
maintained Gen 47 17 he maintained them that year
2 K 9 10 that he [Miphiboseth] may be maintained
3 K 17 20 widow with whom I am . . . maintained
Ps 9 5 thou hast m. my judgment and my cause
maintainers Job 13 4 and m. of perverse opinions
maintaineth Deut 24 15 and with it m. his life
Prov 29 3 he that m. harlots, shall squander
1 Ma 2 27 zeal for the law, and m. the testament
maintenance Prov 27 27 for m. for thy handmaids
1 Ma 14 29 the maintenance of their holy places

majestic Eccu 45 9 crowned him with m. attire
majesty Exod 40 33 the majesty of the Lord shining
Num 14 22 all the men that have seen my majesty
Deut 5 24 our God hath shown us his majesty
2 Pa 7 1 majesty of the Lord filled the house
2 m. of the Lord had filled the temple
Tob 13 7 shown his m. toward a sinful nation
Esth 13 11 there is none that can resist thy m.
15 17 heart was troubled for fear of thy m.
Job 37 4 shall thunder with the voice of his m.
Ps 28 3 the God of majesty hath thundered, the
71 19 and blessed be the name of his majesty
19 whole earth shall be filled with his m.
95 6 holiness and majesty in his sanctuary
Prov 25 27 he that is a searcher of majesty shall
Wisd 7 26 the unspotted mirror of God's majesty
9 10 and from the throne of thy majesty
18 24 thy majesty was written upon the diadem
Eccu 17 11 their eye saw the majesty of his glory
18 4 shall show forth the power of his m.
Isa 2 10 from the glory of his majesty. 19, 21
3 8 to provoke the eyes of his majesty
60 7 I will glorify the house of my majesty
63 12 right hand, by the arm of his majesty
Bar 5 9 with joy in the light of his majesty
Eze 43 2 and the earth shone with his majesty
4 m. of the Lord went into the temple
Dan 4 33 and greater majesty was added to me
2 Ma 2 8 the majesty of the Lord shall appear
15 13 environed with great beauty and m.
Mat 19 28 shall sit on the seat of his majesty
24 30 heaven with much power and majesty
25 31 Son of man shall come in his majesty
31 shall he sit upon the seat of his m.
Luke 9 26 when he shall come in his majesty
31 Moses and Elias appearing in majesty
21 27 in a cloud with great power and m.
Acts 19 27 her majesty shall begin to be destroyed
Heb 1 3 sitteth on the right hand of the majesty
8 1 right hand of the throne of majesty in
Jude 8 despise dominion and blaspheme m.
Apoc 15 8 with smoke from the majesty of God
Malachias Mala 1 1 Israel by the hand of M.
Malalai 2 Es 12 35 Malalai, Golalai, Maai
Malaleel Gen 5 12 Cainan . . . begot Malaleel
Gen 5 13 Cainan lived after he begot Malaleel
15 Malaleel lived 65 years and begot
16 Malaleel lived after he begot Jared
17 the days of Malaleel were 895 years
1 Pa 1 2 Cainan, Malaleel, Jared, Henoc
2 Es 11 4 son of Saphatias the son of Malaleel
Luke 3 37 Jared, who was of Malaleel, who was
Malasar Dan 1 11 Daniel said to Malasar
Dan 1 16 M. took their portions and the wine
Malchus John 18 10 the name of the servant was M.
male Gen 1 27 male and female he created them
Gen 5 2 he created them male and female; and
6 19 two . . . of the male sex and the female
7 2 take 7 and 7, the male and the female
3 two and two, the male and the female
9 into the ark, male and female, as the
16 went in male and female of all flesh
17 10 male kind of you shall be circumcised
14 the male, whose flesh of his foreskin
23 every male among the men of his house
34 15 and all the male sex among you be
22 we must circumcise every male among us
Exod 1 22 born of the male sex, ye shall cast
12 5 a lamb without blemish, a male, of one
13 12 whatsoever thou shalt have of male sex
15 to the Lord all . . . of the male sex
34 19 all of the male kind that openeth the
Lev 1 3 shall offer a male without blemish. 10
3 1 male or female . . . without blemish
6 whether he offer male or female, they
6 29 every male of the priestly race. 7:6
22 19 it shall be a male without blemish
27 6 for a male shall be given five sicles
Num 1 2 as many as are of the male sex, from
20 all that were of the male sex. 22
3 15 number . . . every male from one month
22 of the male sex from one month. 28
34 of the male kind from one month. 39
40 number the firstborn of the male sex
27 3 he had no male children. Why is his
31 17 kill all that are of the male sex, even
Deut 4 16 similitude or image of male or female
15 19 thy God whatsoever is of the male sex
20 13 all that are therein of the male sex
Josu 17 2 these are the male children of Manasses
Judg 21 11 every male, and all women that have
3 K 11 15 and had killed every male in Edom
16 till he had slain every male in Edom
Mala 1 14 man that hath in his flock a male
1 Ma 5 28 he [Judas] slew every male by the edge
35 he [Judas] slew every male thereof
51 they slew every male with the edge of
Mat 19 4 made them m. and female. Mark 10:6
Luke 2 23 every male opening the womb shall be
Gal 3 28 there is neither male nor female. For
malediction Num 5 27 the m. shall go through her
Eccu 41 12 you shall be born in malediction: and
12 in malediction shall be your portion
13 ungodly shall from m. to destruction
Dan 8 19 to come to pass in the end of the m.
9 11 m. and the curse, which is written in
2 P 2 14 with covetousness, children of m.
maledictions Eccu 10 15 shall be filled with m.
malefactor John 18 30 if he were not a m., we would
malefactors Luke 23 32 there were two other m. led
males Gen 31 10 the males . . . of divers colors. 12
Gen 34 24 all agreed and circumcised all the m.
Exod 12 48 his males shall first be circumcised
23 17 all thy males appear before the Lord
34 23 all thy males shall appear in the sight
Lev 6 18 the males only of the race of Aaron
Num 3 43 the males by their names from one
18 10 the males only shall eat thereof
26 62 m. from one month old and upward
Deut 16 16 all thy males appear before Lord
Josu 5 4 that came out of Egypt that were males
2 Pa 31 16 besides the males from three years
19 to distribute portions to all the m.
malice Gen 50 17 m. they practised against thee
1 K 20 7 that his malice is come to its height
13 if my father shall continue in malice
Esth 8 3 that the malice of Aman the Agagite
Ps 34 17 rescue thou my soul from their malice
51 3 why dost thou glory in malice, thou
5 thou hast loved m. more than goodness
93 23 in their malice he will destroy them
Prov 26 26 his malice shall be laid open in the
Wisd 2 21 for their own malice blinded them
12 10 wicked generation and their m. natural
16 14 a man indeed killeth through malice
Eccu 9 1 she show . . . malice of a wicked lesson
25 26 all m. is short to the m. of a woman
37 3 to cover the earth with thy malice
Eze 16 57 pride, before thy malice was laid open
1 Ma 5 4 remembered the m. of the children of
13 6 together to destroy us out of mere m.
2 Ma 4 4 which increased the malice of Simon
50 Menelaus . . . increasing in malice
9 6 he by no means ceased from his malice
Rom 1 29 being filled with all iniquity, malice
1 C 5 8 nor with leaven of malice and wickedness

14 20 in malice be children, and in sense be
Eph 4 31 be put away from you, with all malice
Col 3 8 put you also all away: anger . . . malice
Titus 3 3 living in malice and envy, hateful and
1 P 2 1 laying away all malice and all guile
16 as making liberty a cloak for malice
malices Jer 2 33 taught thy m. to be thy ways
malicious Ps 82 4 they have taken a m. counsel
Ps 143 10 thy servant David from the m. sword
Wisd 1 4 wisdom will not enter into a m. soul
Eccu 33 28 and fetters are for a malicious slave
3 J 10 with m. words prating against us. And
maliciously Dan 13 43 these men have m. forged
Dan 13 61 as they had m. dealt against their
malignant Job 5 12 nought the designs of the m.
Ps 9 15 arm of the sinner and of the malignant
14 4 the malignant is brought to nothing
21 17 the council of the m. hath besieged me
25 5 I have hated the assembly of the m.
63 3 protected me from assembly of the m.
91 12 shall hear of the downfall of the m.
100 4 the malignant . . . I would not know
118 115 depart from me, ye malignant: and I
malignity Rom 1 29 of envy, murder, contention, m.
Mallos 2 Ma 4 30 they of Tharsus and M. raised
Maloch 1 Es 10 32 of the sons of Herem . . . Maloch
Mambre Gen 13 18 dwelt by the vale of Mambre
Gen 14 13 who dwelt in the vale of Mambre
24 came with me, Aner, Escol, and Mambre
18 1 appeared to him in the vale of Mambre
23 17 double cave, looking towards Mambre
19 the field that looked towards Mambre
25 9 in the field . . . over against Mambre
35 27 he came to Isaac his father in Mambre
49 30 double cave . . . over against M. 50:13
Jdth 2 14 from the torrent of Mambre, till one
Mambres 2 Tim 3 8 as Jannes and M. resisted Moses
mammon Mat 6 24 cannot serve God and m. Luke 16:13
Luke 16 9 friends of the mammon of iniquity
11 not been faithful in the unjust mammon
Mamuchan Esth 1 14 and Marsana and Mamuchan
Esth 1 16 Mamuchan answered, in the hearing of
21 king did according to the counsel of M.
mamzer Deut 23 2 a mamzer . . . shall not enter into
man of God Deut 33 1 the man of God Moses blessed
Josu 14 6 Lord spoke to Moses the man of God
Judg 13 6 said to him: A man of God came to me
8 the man of God, whom thou didst send
1 K 2 27 there came a man of God to Heli, and
9 6 there is a man of God in this city
7 what shall we carry to the man of God
7 no present to make to the man of God
8 let us give it to the man of God
10 into city where the man of God was
3 K 12 22 came to Semeias the man of God, saying
13 1 there came a man of God out of Juda
4 had heard the word of the man of God
5 sign which the man of God had given
6 the king said to the man of God. 7
6 m. . . . besought the face of the Lord
8 the man of God answered the king: If
11 the works that the man of God had done
12 the way by which the man of God went
14 went after the man of God and found
14 art thou the man of God that camest
21 he cried out to the man of God who
26 the man of God that was disobedient
29 took up the body of the man of God
31 wherein the man of God is buried: lay
17 18 I to do with thee, thou man of God
24 I know that thou art a man of God
20 28 a man of God coming, said to the king
4 K 1 9 man of God, the king hath commanded
10 if I be a man of God, let fire. 12
11 man of God, thus saith the king: Make
13 man of God, despise not my life and
4 7 and she came and told the man of God
9 I perceive that this is a holy m. . . .
16 man of God, do not lie to thy handmaid
21 laid him upon the bed of the man of God
22 that I may run to the man of God and
25 came to the man of God to mount Carmel
25 when the man of God saw her coming
27 when she came to the man of God to the
27 and the man of God said: Let her alone
40 death is in the pot, O man of God
42 bringing to the man of God bread of
5 8 Eliseus the man of God had hear this
14 to the word of the man of God. 7:18; 8:2
15 and returning to the man of God with
20 servant of the man of God. 6:15; 8:4
6 6 the man of God said: Where did it fall
9 man of God sent to the king of Israel
10 place which the man of God had told him
7 2 answering the man of God, said: If the
17 as the man of God had said, when the
19 when that lord answered the man of God
8 7 saying: The man of God is come hither
8 presents, and go to meet the m. . . .
11 the man of God wept. And Hazael said
13 19 and the man of God was angry with him
23 16 word of Lord, which man of God spoke
17 it is the sepulcher of the man of God
1 Pa 23 14 sons also of Moses, the man of God
2 Pa 8 14 so David the man of God had commanded
11 2 came to Semeias the man of God, saying
25 7 a man of God came to him and said
9 and Amasias said to the man of God
9 the man of God answered him: The Lord
30 16 law of Moses the m. . . . 1 Es 3:2
2 Es 12 24 commandment of David the man of God
35 instruments of David the man of God
Ps 89 1 a prayer of Moses the man of God
Jer 35 4 the son of Jegedelias the man of God
manacles Ps 149 8 their nobles with m. of iron
Eccu 21 22 and like manacles on the right hand
Isa 45 14 they shall go bound with manacles: and
manage 1 Ma 2 66 shall m. the war of the people
managed Prov 20 18 are to be m. by governments
Prov 24 6 because war is managed by due ordering
Jer 5 28 have not m. the cause of the fatherless
management 1 Ma 13 15 which he had the management of
Manahat Gen 36 23 the sons of Sobal: Alvan and M.
Manahath 1 Pa 1 40 sons of Sobal . . . Manahath
1 Pa 8 6 Gabaa, who were removed into Manahath
Manahem 4 K 15 14 Manahem . . . went up from Thersa
4 K 15 16 then Manahem destroyed Thapsa and
17 reigned M. son of Godi over Israel
19 Manahem gave Phul a thousand talents
20 and Manahem laid a tax upon Israel, on
21 and the rest of the acts of Manahem
22 and Manahem slept with his fathers
23 reigned Phacia the son of Manahem
Manahen Acts 13 1 and Lusius of Cyrene, and Manahen
Manaim Josu 13 26 from M. unto borders of Dabir
Josu 13 30 from M. all Basan and all the kingdoms
21 37 and Manaim and Hesebon and Jaser
3 K 4 14 Abinadab . . . was chief in Manaim
1 Pa 6 80 out of the tribe of Gad . . . Manaim
Manasse 1 Es 10 30 the sons of Phahath . . . Manasse
1 Es 10 33 of the sons of Hasom . . . Manasse
Manasses Gen 41 51 the name of the firstborn M.
Gen 46 20 bore him: Manasses and Ephraim
48 1 taking his two sons Manasses and Ephraim
5 Ephraim and M. shall be reputed to me

13 Israel; but Manasses on his left hand
14 the left upon the head of Manasses
17 to remove it to the head of Manasses
20 to thee as to Ephraim and as to M.
20 and he set Ephraim before Manasses
50 22 Machir the son of Manasses. Num 32:39; 36:1; Josu 13:31; 17:3; 1 Pa 7:17
Num 1 10 of M. Gamaliel the son of Phadassur
34 of the sons of Manasses . . . 32,200
2 20 the tribe of the sons of Manasses. 10:23
7 54 the prince of the sons of M., Gamaliel
13 12 of the scepter of Manasses, Gaddi the
26 28 sons of Joseph . . . Manasses and Ephraim
29 of Manasses was born Machir, of
34 these are the families of Manasses
27 1 of Manasses who was the son of Joseph
32 40 of Galaad to Machir the son of M.
41 Jair the son of Manasses. Deut 3:14; 3 K 4:13
36 12 Manasses, who was the son of Joseph
Deut 33 17 and these the thousands of Manasses
34 2 and the land of Ephraim and Manasses
Josu 14 4 two tribes, of Manasses and Ephraim
16 4 Manasses and Ephraim . . . possessed it
9 midst of possession of children of M.
17 1 to Machir the firstborn of Manasses
2 to the rest of the children of Manasses
2 these are the male children of Manasses
5 there fell ten portions to Manasses
6 the daughters of Manasses possessed
6 the lot of the rest of the children of M.
7 the border of Manasses was from Aser
8 lot of M. took in the land of Taphua
8 which is on the borders of Manasses
9 in the midst of the cities of Manasses
9 the border of Manasses is on the north
10 and on the north that of Manasses
11 the inheritance of Manasses in Issachar
12 neither could children of M. overthrow
17 Josue said . . . to Ephraim and Manasses
Judg 1 27 Manasses also did not destroy Bethsan
6 15 my family is the meanest in Manasses
35 he sent messengers into all Manasses
7 23 from all Manasses pursued after Madian
11 29 going round Galaad and Manasses
12 4 dwelleth in midst of Ephraim and M.
4 K 10 33 the land of . . . Ruben and Manasses
20 21 Manasses his son reigned in his stead
21 1 Manasses was twelve years old when he
9 were seduced by Manasses to do evil
11 because Manasses king of Juda hath done
16 M. shed also very much innocent blood
17 the rest of the acts of Manasses and
18 and Manasses slept with his fathers
20 as Manasses his father had done. And
23 12 the altars which Manasses had made
26 wherewith Manasses had provoked him
24 3 all the sins of Manasses which he did
1 Pa 3 13 Ezechias, of whom was born Manasses
14 M. begot Amon the father of Josias. And
7 14 the son of Manasses, Ezriel: and his
29 by the borders of the sons of Manasses
9 3 of the children of Ephraim and of M.
12 19 some of Manasses that went over to
20 there fled to him of Manasses, Ednas
20 captains of thousands in Manasses
2 Pa 15 9 strangers with them of . . . Manasses
30 1 he wrote letters to Ephraim and M.
10 through the land of Ephraim and of M.
11 some men of Aser and of Manasses and
31 1 out of Ephraim also and Manasses, till
32 33 Manasses his son reigned in his stead
33 1 Manasses was twelve years old when he
9 so Manasses seduced Juda and the
11 took Manasses and carried him bound
13 Manasses knew that the Lord was God
18 the rest of the acts of Manasses and
20 and Manasses slept with his fathers
22 as Manasses his father had done: and
22 idols which M. his father had made
23 as M. his father had humbled himself
34 6 in the cities of M. and of Ephraim and
9 had gathered together from Manasses
Jdth 8 2 her husband was Manasses, who died
16 26 after death of Manasses her husband
Ps 59 9 Galaad is mine, and Manasses is mine
79 3 before Ephraim, Benjamin, and M.
107 9 Galaad is mine: and Manasses is mine
Isa 9 20 shall eat the flesh of his own arm: M. Ephraim, and Ephraim M.
Jer 15 4 because of Manasses . . . for all that
Eze 48 4 of the sea, one portion for Manasses
5 by the border of Manasses, from the east
Mat 1 10 Ezechias begot M. and M. begot Amon

half tribe of Manasses Num 32 33 to the h. . . . the son of Joseph, the kingdom of Sehon
Deut 3 13 the kingdom of Og to the h. . . . , all
29 8 Ruben and Gad and the h. . . . 1 Pa 5:26
Josu 1 12 Rubenites and the Gadites and the h. . . . 12:6; 22:1; 1 Pa 26:32
13 7 to the nine tribes and to the h. . . .
29 to the h. . . . and his children possession
18 7 Gad and Ruben and the h. . . . have
21 5 Ephraim and of Dan and the h. . . .
6 Nephtali and of the h. . . . in Basan
25 and of the h. . . . , Thanac and
28 out of the h. . . . , Gaulon in Basan
22 9 the children of Gad and the h. . . .
11 Ruben and of Gad and the h. . . . 15, 21, 30; 1 Pa 5:18
1 Pa 5 23 children of the h. . . . possessed the
6 61 they gave out of the h. . . . ten cities
70 out of the h. . . . , Aner and its suburbs
71 out of kindred of the h. . . . , Gaulon
12 31 of the h. . . . , 18,000 every one by
27 20 over the h. . . . , Joel the son of
21 over the h. . . . in Galaad, Jaddo the

tribe of Manasses Num 34 14 half of the t. . . .
Num 34 23 the children of Joseph of the t. . . .
Deut 4 43 Golan in Basan, which is in the t. . . .
Josu 4 12 half the t. . . . went armed before
17 1 this lot fell to the t. . . . , for he is
20 8 Gaulon in Basan of the tribe of M.
22 7 to half the t. . . . , Moses had given
1 Pa 6 62 out of the t. . . . in Basan, 13 cities
12 37 of Gad and of the half of the t. . . .
Apoc 7 6 of the tribe of Manasses, 12,000 signed

mandate 2 Ma 4 25 having received the king's m.

mandrakes Gen 30 14 found m.: which he brought
Gen 30 14 give me part of thy son's mandrakes
15 unless thou take also my son's m.
16 I have hired thee for my son's m.
Cant 7 13 the mandrakes give smell. In our

Mane Dan 5 25 is written: Mane, Thecel, Phares
Dan 5 26 Mane: God hath numbered thy kingdom

manes Jer 51 38 shake their m. like young lions

manfully Num 24 18 enemies, but Israel shall do m.
Deut 31 6 do m. and be of good heart: fear not
Josu 1 18 only take courage and do manfully
1 Pa 19 13 and let us behave ourselves manfully
22 13 take courage and act m., fear not nor
Jdth 15 11 for thou hast done manfully and thy
Ps 26 14 do manfully, and let thy heart take
30 25 do ye manfully, and let your heart be
1 Ma 2 64 and behave manfully in the law: for
4 35 ready either to live or to die manfully

5 61 thinking that they should do manfully
67 desiring to do manfully they went out
6 31 burnt them with fire and fought m.
9 10 let us die manfully for our brethren
2 Ma 2 22 that behaved themselves manfully on
6 27 by departing m. out of this life, I
7 5 exhorted one another to die manfully
8 16 against them, but to fight manfully
10 35 approached manfully to the wall, and
13 14 exhorted his people to fight manfully
14 43 and m. threw himself down to the crowd
15 17 fight and to set upon them manfully
1 C 16 13 in the faith, do m., and be strengthened
manger Job 6 5 he standeth before a full manger
Luke 2 7 clothes, and laid him in a manger
12 swaddling clothes, and laid in a m.
16 and the infant lying in the manger
13 15 his ox or his ass from the manger
manhu Exod 16 15 they said one to another: Manhu
manifest Deut 29 29 things that are m., to us and
1 K 3 1 those days there was no m. vision
Prov 10 9 that perverteth his ways, shall be m.
14 4 there the strength of the ox is m.
Wisd 11 8 were diminished for a m. reproof of
Eccu 6 23 and she is not manifest unto many
17 15 Israel was made the m. portion of God
Bar 6 50 it shall be m. that they are no gods
2 Ma 3 17 it was m. to them that beheld him
28 the m. power of God being known. And
9 8 witness to the m. Power of God in
15 35 evident and m. sign of the help of God
John 7 4 things, manifest thyself to the world
14 21 and will manifest myself to him
22 that thou wilt m. thyself to us, and
Acts 2 20 great and manifest day of the Lord
4 16 it is manifest, and we cannot deny it
Rom 1 19 that which is known of God is m. in them
1 C 3 13 every man's work shall be manifest; for
4 5 will make manifest counsels of hearts
2 C 5 11 to men; but to God we are manifest. And
11 in your consciences we are manifest. We
12 to m. our carefulness that we have for
Gal 3 11 it is manifest: because the just man
5 19 now the works of the flesh are manifest
Col 4 4 I may make it manifest as I ought to
1 Tim 4 15 they profiting may be manifest to all
5 24 some men's sins are manifest, going
25 also good deeds are manifest: and they
2 Tim 3 9 their folly shall be manifest to all men
1 J 2 19 that they may be m., that they are not
3 10 in this the children of God are m. and
Apoc 15 4 because thy judgments are manifest
made manifest Ps 24 14 covenant shall be m. m.
Ps 50 8 of thy wisdom thou hast made m. to me
147 20 judgments he hath not made m. to them
Eccu 1 7 of wisdom been revealed and made m.
Dan 2 30 might be made manifest to the king and
1 Ma 11 12 and his enmities were made manifest
15 9 that your glory shall be made manifest
Mark 4 22 which shall not be made m. Luke 8:17
6 14 heard, for his name was made manifest
John 1 31 that he may be made manifest in Israel
3 21 that his works may be made manifest
9 3 works of God should be made manifest
Acts 10 40 gave him to be made manifest, not to
Rom 3 21 the justice of God is made manifest
16 26 now is made manifest by the scriptures
1 C 11 19 may be made manifest among you. When
14 25 secrets of his heart are made manifest
2 C 4 10 life also of Jesus may be made m. 11
11 6 in all things we have been made manifest
Eph 5 13 are m. m. by the light; for all that is m. m. is light
Phil 1 13 my bands are made manifest in Christ, in
2 Tim 1 10 is now made m. by the illumination of
Heb 9 8 the holies was not yet made manifest
manifestation Luke 1 80 the day of his m. to Israel
1 C 1 7 waiting for the m. of our Lord Jesus
12 7 the m. of the Spirit is given to every
2 C 4 2 by m. of the truth commending ourselves
manifestations 2 Ma 2 22 the m. that came from
manifested Luke 19 11 kingdom of God should immediately be m.
John 2 11 m. his glory, and his disciples believed
17 6 I have m. thy name to the men whom
21 14 third time that Jesus was m. to his
Rom 1 19 for God hath manifested it unto them
2 C 3 3 being m., that you are the epistle of
5 10 we must all be m. before the judgment
Col 1 8 who also hath m. to us your love in the
26 but now is manifested to his saints, to
1 Tim 3 16 which was manifested in the flesh, was
Titus 1 3 due times m. his word in preaching
1 P 1 20 but m. in the last times for you, who
1 J 1 2 the life was manifested; and we have
manifesteth 2 C 2 14 m. the odor of his knowledge
manifestly Ps 49 3 God shall come m.: our God
2 Ma 6 30 thou knowest m. that whereas I might
Acts 10 3 in a vision manifestly, about the ninth
1 Tim 4 1 now the Spirit manifestly saith, that
manifold 2 Es 9 35 in thy m. goodness, which thou
Job 11 6 wisdom, and that his law is manifold
22 5 and not for thy manifold wickedness
Wisd 7 22 of understanding: holy, one, manifold
Eze 27 27 thy manifold furniture, thy mariners
Dan 12 4 pass over, and knowledge shall be m.
Osee 8 12 I shall write to him my m. laws, which
Amos 5 12 because I know your manifold crimes
Eph 3 10 that the manifold wisdom of God may be
1 P 4 10 as good stewards of the manifold grace
Manilius 2 Ma 11 34 and Titus M., ambassadors
mankind Gen 9 19 from these was all m. spread
Lev 18 22 shalt not lie with mankind as with
Esth 13 5 one nation in opposition to all mankind
2 Ma 7 28 God made them . . . and mankind also
Acts 17 26 hath made of one, all mankind, to dwell
1 C 6 10 nor effeminate, nor liers with mankind
1 Tim 1 10 who defile themselves with mankind, for
manna Exod 16 31 called the name thereof Manna
Exod 16 33 take a vessel and put manna into it
35 children of Israel ate manna 40 years
Num 11 6 our eyes behold nothing else but manna
7 now the manna was like coriander seed
9 the camp, the manna also fell with it
Deut 8 3 and gave thee manna for thy food
16 feed thee in the wilderness with manna
Josu 5 12 the manna ceased after they ate of it
2 Es 9 20 thy manna thou didst not withhold from
Ps 77 24 had rained down manna upon them to eat
John 6 31 our fathers did eat manna in the desert
49 your fathers did eat manna. 59
Heb 9 4 was a golden pot that had manna, and the
Apoc 2 17 I will give the hidden manna, and will
manners Eccu 20 28 m. of lying men are without
Eze 27 24 were thy merchants in divers manners
2 Ma 4 13 progress of heathenish and foreign m.
5 22 in manners more barbarous than he that
15 12 Onias . . . gentle in his manners
Acts 13 18 endured their manners in the desert
1 C 15 33 evil communications corrupt good manners
Heb 1 1 at sundry times and in divers manners
13 5 let your m. be without covetousness
manners' Eccu 31 20 leave off first for m. sake
man's Mat 10 36 a man's enemies shall be they of
Mark 12 19 if any man's brother die. Luke 20:28
Luke 6 22 as evil, for the Son of man's sake

12 15 a man's life doth not consist in the
16 21 that fell from the rich man's table
John 18 17 thou also one of this man's disciples
Acts 11 12 and we entered into the man's house. And
13 23 this man's seed God according to his
20 33 I have not coveted any man's silver, gold
27 22 there shall be no loss of any man's life
Rom 5 17 if by one man's offence death reigned
14 4 thou that judgest another man's servant
15 20 build upon another man's foundation. But
1 C 3 13 every man's work shall be manifest; for
13 and the fire shall try every man's work
14 if any man's work abide, which he hath
15 if any man's work burn, he shall suffer
4 3 to be judged by you, or by man's day
10 29 judged by another man's conscience? If
2 C 4 2 to every m. conscience, in sight of God
10 16 not to glory in another man's rule, in
Gal 3 15 yet man's testament, if it be confirmed
1 Th 4 11 and that you want nothing of any man's
2 Th 3 8 neither did we eat any man's bread for
James 1 26 this man's religion is vain. Religion
2 P 2 16 speaking with a man's voice, forbade
manservant Exod 20 10 no work . . . nor thy m.
Exod 21 26 any man strike the eye of his m.
27 if he strike out a tooth of his m.
Lev 25 6 you for meat, to thee and to thy m.
Deut 5 14 not do any work . . . nor thy m.
14 thy m. and thy maidservant may rest
21 nor his house nor his field nor his m.
12 18 thou shalt eat . . . and thy manservant
16 11 thou shalt feast . . . and thy manservant
14 shalt make merry . . . thy manservant
Job 31 13 despised to abide judgment with my m.
Jer 34 9 let his manservant . . . go free. 10
16 brought back again every man his m.
mansions Exod 17 1 forward . . . by their mansions
Exod 40 36 of Israel throughout all their mansions
Num 33 1 the mansions of the children of Israel
John 14 2 house there are many mansions. If not
manslaughter Deut 19 3 is forced to flee for m.
manslayer Num 35 28 shall the m. return. Josu 20:6
manslayers 1 Tim 1 9 murderers of mothers, for m.
mantle Judg 8 25 spreading a m. on the ground
Ruth 3 15 spread thy mantle wherewith thou art
1 K 15 27 laid hold upon the skirt of his mantle
28 14 he is covered with a mantle. And Saul
3 K 19 13 he covered his face with his mantle
19 he [Elias] cast his mantle upon him
4 K 2 8 Elias took his mantle and folded it
13 and he took up the mantle of Elias
14 struck the waters with mantle of Elias
4 39 wild gourds . . . and filled his mantle
1 Es 9 3 I [Esdras] rent my mantle and my coat
5 having rent my mantle and my garment
Manue Judg 13 2 name was Manue, and his wife. (And this chapter *passim*)
Judg 16 31 in burying place of his father Manue
Maoch 1 K 27 2 Achis the son of Maoch, king of
Maon Josu 15 55 Maon and Carmel and Ziph and
1 K 23 24 David and his men were in dessert of M.
25 and abode in the wilderness of Maon
25 after David in the wilderness of Maon
25 2 certain man in the wilderness of Maon
1 Pa 2 45 the son of Sammai, Maon: and Maon the father of Bethsur
Maonathi 1 Pa 4 13 sons of Othoniel . . . Maonathi
1 Pa 4 14 Maonathi begot Ophra, and Saraia
Maozim Dan 11 38 he shall worship the god Maozim
Dan 11 39 to fortify Maozim with a strange god
Mapsam 1 Pa 4 25 Mapsam his son, Masma his son
Mara Exod 15 23; Num 33:8, 9; Ruth 1:20
Marai 1 Pa 27 13 for the tenth month, was Marai
Maraia 2 Es 12 12 of Saraia, Maraia: of Jeremias
Maraioth 1 Pa 6 6 begot M. and M. begot Amarias
1 Pa 9 11 the son of Sadoc, the son of Maraioth
1 Es 7 3 son of Azarias, the son of Maraioth
2 Es 12 15 of Maraioth, Helci; of Adaia, Zacharia
maranatha 1 C 16 22 Christ, let him be anathema, m.
marble Exod 31 5 of marble and precious stones
1 Pa 29 2 marble of Paros in great abundance
2 Pa 2 14 in brass and in iron and in marble
3 6 floor . . . with most precious marble
Esth 1 6 and were held up with marble pillars
6 paved with porphyry and white marble
Cant 5 15 his legs as pillars of marble that are
Apoc 18 12 and of brass and of iron and of marble
march Num 2 9 by their troops shall march first
Num 2 16 they shall march in the second place
17 shall march according to their places
24 they shall march in the third place
31 they shall march last. This is the
10 6 the trumpets shall sound for a march
32 27 will march on to the war, as thou
Josu 6 6 and march before the ark of the Lord
14 11 this day, as well to fight as to march
Judg 20 34 to march from the west side of the city
Isa 27 4 shall I march against it, shall I set
Joel 2 7 men shall march every one on his way
Nah 2 5 they shall stumble in their march
1 Ma 5 28 turned their march into the desert, to
6 33 and made his troops march on fiercely
15 39 to march with his army towards Judea
marched Exod 14 29 marched through the midst of the
Exod 15 22 they marched three days through the
Num 2 34 marched by the families and houses
9 17 the children of Israel marched forward
18 at commandment of the Lord they marched
19 kept the watches . . . and marched not
21 they m. forward: and if it departed
22 in the same place, and marched not
23 tents, and by his word they marched
10 12 children of Israel m. by their troops
18 the sons of Ruben also marched by
21 the Caathites also marched carrying
25 the last . . . marched the sons of Dan
33 marched from the mount of the Lord
34 was over them by day when they marched
13 1 the people marched from Haseroth
21 4 they marched from mount Hor by the
18 they marched from the wilderness to
33 8 having m. three days through the desert
Josu 3 17 people marched over against Jericho
4 13 marched through the plains and fields
1 K 29 2 lords of the Philistines marched
2 K 2 32 marched all the night, and they came
15 23 all the people m. towards the way that
1 Pa 19 10 Joab . . . marched against the Syrians
1 Ma 5 36 thence he marched and took Casbon and
6 40 they marched on warily and orderly
13 20 marched to every place whithersoever
2 Ma 12 32 they marched against Gorgias the
13 19 he marched with his army to Bethsura
marches Num 10 28 order of the camps and marches
marching Exod 13 20 m. from Socoth they encamped
Josu 6 7 marching before the ark of the Lord
2 Pa 20 20 and as they were marching Josaphat
Jer 47 3 at the noise of the marching of arms
Haba 1 6 marching upon the breadth of the
1 Ma 6 41 were moved at . . . the m. of the company
2 Ma 12 10 and were marching towards Timotheus
Mardochai 1 Es 2 2 who came with . . . M. 2 Es 7:7
Esth 2 5 there was . . . a Jew, named Mardochai
7 Mardochai adopted her for his daughter
10 M. had charged her to say nothing
15 of Abihail the brother of Mardochai

19 Mardochai stayed at the king's gate
21 when M. abode at the king's gate
22 M. had notice of it, and immediately
3 2 Mardochai did not bend his knee
5 that Mardochai did not bend his knee
6 to lay his hands upon Mardochai alone
4 1 when Mardochai had heard these things
5 she commanded him to go to Mardochai
6 and Athach going out went to Mardochai
7 M. told him all that had happened, how
9 told Esther all that Mardochai had said
10 bade him say to M.: all the king's
12 when Mardochai had heard this, he sent
15 again Esther sent to Mardochai in
17 Mardochai went and did all that Esther
5 9 when he saw Mardochai sitting before
13 so long as I see Mardochai the Jew
14 that Mardochai may be hanged upon it
6 2 Mardochai had discovered the treason
3 what honor and reward hath Mardochai
4 he might order Mardochai to be hanged
10 do as thou hast spoken, to Mardochai
11 arraying M. in the street of the city
12 but M. returned to the palace gate
13 if Mardochai be of the seed of the Jews
7 9 gibbet which he hath prepared for M.
10 which he had prepared for Mardochai
8 1 and Mardochai came in before the king
2 the ring . . . and gave it to Mardochai
2 Esther set Mardochai over her house
7 answered Esther the queen and Mardochai
9 were written, as Mardochai had a mind
15 Mardochai going forth out of the palace
9 3 extolled the Jews for fear of Mardochai
20 Mardochai wrote all these things and
23 which M. by letters had commanded to
29 and Mardochai the Jew wrote also a
31 as Mardochai and Esther had appointed
10 2 and greatness wherewith he exalted M.
3 M. of the race of the Jews was next
4 M. said: God hath done these things
11 2 M. the son of Jair, the son of Semei
12 when M. had seen this and arose out
12 4 M. also committed the memory of the
6 sought to hurt Mardochai and his people
13 8 but Mardochai besought the Lord
15 1 no doubt but he was Mardochai
16 13 he hath sought the destruction of M.
Mardochai's Esth 2 22 to the king in M. name
Mardochias' 2 Ma 15 37 the day before M. day
Mares Esth 1 14 nearest him were . . . Mares
Maresa Josu 15 44 Ceila and Achzib and Maresa
1 Pa 2 42 the sons of Maresa father of Hebron
4 21 Laada the father of Maresa, and the
2 Pa 11 8 Geth and Maresa and Ziph and
14 9 and he [Zara] came as far as Maresa
10 vale of Sephata, which is near Maresa
20 37 Eliezer the son of Dodau of Maresa
Mich 1 15 heir to thee that dwellest in Maresa
2 Ma 12 35 and so Gorgias escaped to Maresa. But
Mareth Josu 15 59 Mareth and Bethanoth and
Mariam 1 Pa 4 17 he begot Mariam and Sammai
Marimuth 1 Es 10 26 of the sons of Bani . . . M.
2 Es 3 3 next to them built Marimuth the son
mariners 2 Pa 8 18 Hiram sent . . . skilful m.
Eze 27 9 the wise men thereof furnished mariners
9 and their mariners were thy factors
27 thy m. and thy pilots who kept thy
29 the m. and all the pilots of the sea
Jon 1 5 the m. were afraid, and the men cried
Apoc 18 17 that sail into the lake, and mariners
mark Gen 4 15 the Lord set a mark upon Cain
Gen 41 21 yet gave no mark of their being full
Num 34 10 thence they shall mark out the bounds
Josu 18 4 mark it out according to the number
6 these mark ye out into seven parts
8 risen up to go to mark out the land
8 go round the land and mark it out
Ruth 3 4 mark the place wherein he sleepeth
1 K 20 20 as if I were exercising myself at a mark
3 K 20 7 mark and see that he layeth snares
4 K 5 7 mark, and see how he seeketh occasions
Job 16 13 and hath set me up to be his mark
Ps 129 3 if thou, O Lord, wilt mark iniquities
Wisd 5 11 passage of which no mark can be found
11 no mark found afterwards of her way
12 as when an arrow is shot at a mark
13 been able to show no mark or virtue
22 shot out, and shall fly to the mark
Eccu 5 17 m. of disgrace upon the double tongued
23 11 is never without a blue mark: so
28 21 stroke of a whip maketh a blue mark
Lam 3 12 and set me as a mark for his arrows
Eze 9 4 mark Thau upon the foreheads of the
44 5 and mark well the ways of the temple
Dan 9 23 do thou mark the word and understand
14 18 mark whose footsteps these are. And the
2 Ma 2 6 came up to mark the place: but they
Rom 16 17 to mark them who make dissensions and
Phil 3 14 I press towards the mark, to the prize
Mark Acts 12 12 John, who was surnamed Mark. 12:25; 15:37
Acts 15 39 Barnabas indeed taking Mark, sailed to
Col 4 10 Mark, the cousin german of Barnabas
2 Tim 4 11 take Mark, and bring him with thee: for
Philem 24 Mark. Aristarchus, Demas, and Luke my
1 P 5 13 and so doth my son Mark. Salute one
marked Deut 1 33 m. out the place wherein you
Josu 18 4 bring back to me what they have marked
Job 19 23 that they may be marked down in a book
market 2 Pa 1 17 m. was made in the kingdoms
Eze 27 14 they brought horses . . . to thy market
16 they set forth . . . in thy market
19 stacte and calamus were in thy market
22 which they set forth in thy market
Mat 11 16 children sitting in the market place. Mark 7:32
20 3 others standing in the market place
23 7 salutations in the market place. Luke 11:43; 20:46
Mark 7 4 and when they come from the market
12 38 and to be saluted in the market place
Luke 7 32 to children sitting in the market place
Acts 16 19 brought them into the market place to
17 17 in m. place every day with them
marking Luke 14 7 marking how they chose the first
marks Gal 6 17 for I bear the marks of the Lord Jesus
Lev 19 28 in yourselves any figures or m.
Marma 1 Pa 8 10 [Saharim] begot . . . Marma
marred Nah 2 2 have marred their vine branches
marriage Gen 29 22 to the feast, made the m.
Gen 29 26 to give the younger in marriage first
30 having at length obtained the marriage
30 4 and she gave him Bala in marriage
Exod 21 10 he shall provide her a marriage and
1 Es 9 14 nor join in marriage with the people
Tob 7 16 they made a writing of the marriage
9 12 but the marriage feast they celebrated
10 1 stay upon occasion of the marriage
Esth 2 18 for the marriage and wedding of Esther
Wisd 13 17 inquiring concerning . . . his marriage
24 neither keep life, nor m. undefiled
26 disorder in m. and the irregularity
1 Ma 1 28 bride that sat in the m. bed, mourned
9 37 children of Jambri made a great m.
41 the marriage was turned into mourning

10 58 he eclebrated her m. at Ptolemais
Mat 22 2 king who made a marriage for his son
3 that were invited to the marriage; and
4 things are ready: come ye to the m.
8 the marriage indeed is ready; but they
9 as you shall find, call to the marriage
10 the marriage was filled with guests
24 38 marrying and giving in marriage, even
25 10 went in with him to the marriage, and
Mark 2 19 can the children of the marriage fast
Luke 17 27 they married and were given in m.
20 34 marry and are given in marriage: but
John 2 1 was a marriage in Cana of Galilee
2 and his disciples, to the marriage
1 C 7 38 he that giveth his virgin in marriage
Heb 13 4 marriage honorable in all, and the
Apoc 19 7 for the marriage of the Lamb is come
9 that are called to the marriage supper
marriageable Lev 19 20 is a bondservant and m.
marriages Gen 34 9 let us contract marriages
Deut 8 3 neither . . . make marriages with them
Josu 23 12 if you . . . make marriages with them
married Gen 11 29 Abram and Nachor married wives
Gen 25 1 Abraham married another wife named
26 34 Esau being forty years old, m. wives
29 28 the week was past, he married Rachel
38 14 and she had not been married to him
Lev 22 12 if the daughter of a priest be married
Num 36 11 were married to the sons of their uncle
Ruth 4 13 Booz . . . took Ruth and married her
1 Pa 2 26 and Jerameel married another wife
2 Pa 11 20 and after her he married Maacha the
21 he [Roboam] had married eighteen wives
2 Es 13 23 that married wives, women of Azotus
Tob 7 14 that this maid might be married to one
Prov 30 23 by an odious woman when she is married
Eccu 15 2 receive him as a wife m. of a virgin
42 9 when she is married, lest she should
Mala 2 11 married the daughter of a strange God
2 Ma 14 25 so he married: he lived quietly
Mat 22 25 the first having married a wife, died
30 shall neither marry nor be m. Mark 12:25
Mark 6 17 because he had married her [Herodias]
10 12 husband, and be married to another
Luke 14 30 I have married a wife, and therefore
17 27 they m. and were given in marriage
20 35 shall neither be m. nor take wives
1 C 7 10 to them that are m., not I but the Lord
34 she that is m. thinketh on the things
marrieth Lev 20 21 he that m. his brother's wife
Deut 24 2 is departed and m. another husband
Luke 16 18 away his wife and marrieth another
18 that marrieth her that is put away
marrow Gen 45 18 you may eat the m. of the land
Deut 32 14 and goats with the marrow of wheat
Job 21 24 his bones are moistened with marrow
Ps 62 6 let my soul be filled as with marrow
65 15 to thee holocausts full of marrow
Isa 25 6 feast . . . of fat things full of marrow
34 6 with the blood of rams full of marrow
Eze 17 3 and took away the marrow of the cedar
22 will take of the m. of the high cedar
Heb 4 12 of the joints also and the marrow, and
marry Gen 28 6 Syria, to marry a wife thence
Gen 38 8 to thy brother's wife, and marry her
Lev 20 14 marrying the daughter marry her mother
Num 36 6 let them marry to whom they will
7 shall marry wives of their own tribe
Deut 22 13 if a man marry a wife and afterwards
25 5 wife of the deceased shall not marry to
Ruth 1 13 you would be old women before you m.
2 Es 13 37 great evil . . . and m. strange women
Eccu 7 27 marry thy daughter well, and thou
Jer 3 1 she go from him and marry another
2 Ma 1 14 as though he would marry her, and
14 25 and he desired him to marry a wife
Mat 5 32 shall marry her that is put away, committed. 19:9
19 9 m. another, committeth adultery. Mark 10:11
10 be so, it is not expedient to marry
22 24 his brother shall marry his wife and
30 neither marry nor be married. Mark 12:25
Luke 20 34 the children of this world marry and
1 C 7 9 do not contain themselves, let them m.
9 it is better to marry than to be burnt
28 if a virgin marry, she hath not sinned
36 will; he sinneth not, if she marry. For
39 let her marry to whom she will; only in
1 Tim 4 3 forbidding to m., to abstain from meats
5 11 grown wanton in Christ, they will marry
14 the younger should marry, bear children
marrying Mat 24 38 m. and giving in marriage
Marsana Esth 1 14 Tharsis and Mares and M.
mart Isa 23 3 is become the mart of the nations
Martha Luke 10 38 woman named M. received him
Luke 10 40 Martha was busy about much serving
41 Martha, Martha, thou art careful and art
John 11 1 the town of Mary and of Martha her
5 Jesus loved M. and her sister Mary and
19 of the Jews were come to M. and Mary
20 M. therefore, as soon as she heard
21 M. therefore said to Jesus: Lord, if
24 Martha saith to him: I know that he
30 that place where Martha had met him
39 Martha, the sister of him that was dead
45 Jews who were come to Mary and Martha
12 2 him a supper there: and Martha served
martyrs Apoc 17 6 with the blood of the m. of Jesus
marvelled Mat 8 10 Jesus hearing this, marvelled; and
Mat 15 31 multitudes marvelled, seeing the dumb
Mark 12 17 that are God's. And they m. at him. And
Luke 7 9 which Jesus hearing, marvelled: and
marvellous 1 P 2 9 darkness into his m. light
Mary Exod 15 20 Mary the prophetess, the sister
Num 12 1 Mary and Aaron spoke against Moses
4 spoke to him and to Aaron and Mary
5 calling to Aaron and Mary. And when
10 Mary appeared white as snow with a
15 Mary therefore was put out of the camp
20 1 Mary died there and was buried in the
26 59 and Moses, and Mary their sister
Deut 24 9 what the Lord your God did to Mary in
1 Pa 6 3 of Amram: Aaron, Moses, and Mary. The
Mich 6 4 thy face Moses and Aaron and Mary
Mat 1 16 Joseph the husband of Mary, of whom
18 his mother Mary was espoused to Joseph
20 fear not to take unto thee Mary thy
2 11 found the child with Mary his mother
13 55 is not his mother called Mary, and his
27 56 Mary the mother of James and Joseph
61 the other Mary sitting over against the
28 1 the other Mary, to see the sepulcher
Mark 6 3 is not this the carpenter the son of M.
15 40 Mary the mother of James the less and
47 and Mary the mother of Joseph beheld
16 1 Mary the mother of James, and Salome
Luke 1 27 David; and the virgin's name was Mary
30 fear not, Mary, for thou hast found
34 Mary said to the angel: How shall this
38 Mary said: Behold the handmaid of the
39 Mary rising up in those days, went into
41 Elizabeth heard the salutation of Mary
46 Mary said: My soul doth magnify the Lord
56 Mary abode with her about three months
2 5 to be enrolled with Mary his espoused

16 they found Mary and Joseph and the
19 Mary kept all these words, pondering them
34 Simeon blessed them and said to Mary
8 2 Mary who is called Magdalen, out of whom
10 39 and she had a sister called Mary, who
42 Mary hath chosen the best part, which
24 10 Mary of James and the other women that
John 11 1 of the town of Mary and of Martha her
2 Mary was she that anointed the Lord with
5 Jesus loved Martha and her sister Mary
19 Jews were come to Martha and Mary to
20 went to meet him: but Mary sat at home
28 she went and called her sister Mary
31 when they saw Mary that she rose up
32 Mary therefore was come where Jesus was
45 who were come to Mary and Martha and
12 3 Mary therefore took a pound of ointment
19 25 his mother's sister, Mary of Cleophas
20 11 but Mary stood at the sepulcher without
16 Jesus saith to her: Mary. She turning
Acts 1 14 the women and Mary the mother of Jesus
12 12 house of Mary the mother of John, who
Rom 16 6 salute Mary, who hath labored much among
Mary Magdalen Mat 27 56 among whom was M. M. and
Mat 27 61 was there M. M. and the other Mary
28 1 first day of the week, came M. M. and
Mark 15 40 among whom was M. M. and Mary the
47 M. M. and Mary the mother of Joseph
16 1 sabbath was past, M. M. and Mary the
9 appeared first to M. M., out of whom he
Luke 8 2 Mary who is called Magdalen, out of
24 10 it was M. M. and Joanna and Mary of
John 19 25 Mary of Cleophas and Mary Magdalen
20 1 M. M. cometh early, when it was yet dark
18 M. M. cometh and telleth the disciples
Masal Josu 21 30 of tribe of Aser, Masal. 1 Pa 6:74
Masaloth 1 Ma 9 2 they camped in Masaloth, which
Masepha Josu 15 38 Delean and Masepha and Jecthel
Maserephoth Josu 13 6 to the waters of M., and
Maserites 1 Pa 2 53 and Semathites and Maserites
Maserophot Josu 11 8 the waters of Maserophot
Masia 2 Es 11 7 Colaia the son of Masia, the son
Masma Gen 25 14 Masma and Duma. 1 Pa 1:30
1 Pa 4 25 Masma his son. The sons of Masma
Masmana 1 Pa 12 10 Masmana the fourth, Jeremias
Masobia 1 Pa 11 46 Obed and Jasiel of Masobia
mason's Amos 7 7 in his hand a mason's trowel
Amos 7 8 I said: A mason's trowel. And the Lord
masons 2 K 5 11 king of Tyre sent . . . masons
3 K 5 18 masons of Solomon and masons of Hiram
4 K 12 11 masons that wrought in the house of the
22 6 that is, to carpenters and masons
1 Pa 14 1 masons and carpenters to build him a
22 15 m. and carpenters and of all trades
2 Pa 34 11 gave it to the artificers and to the m.
1 Es 3 7 money to hewers of stones and to masons
10 when the masons laid the foundations
Maspha Josu 11 3 at foot of Hermon in land of M.
Judg 10 17 themselves together and camped in M.
11 11 all his words before the Lord in Maspha
29 and Manasses and Maspha of Galaad
34 when Jephte returned into Maspha to
20 1 land of Galaad, to the Lord in Maspha
3 children of Israel were come up to M.
21 1 had also sworn in Maspha, saying: None
5 with a great oath, when they were in M.
8 that came not up to the Lord to Maspha
1 K 10 17 together the people to the Lord in M.
22 3 David departed from thence into Maspha
3 K 15 22 Asa built Gabaa of Benjamin and Maspha
4 K 25 23 they came to Godolias to Maspha
25 Chaldees that were with him in Maspha
2 Pa 16 6 he built with them Gabaa and Maspha
2 Es 3 7 the men of Gabaon and Maspha, for the
15 built, lord of the street of Maspha
19 Aser the son of Josue, lord of Maspha
1 Ma 3 46 assembled together and came to Maspha
46 for in Maspha was a place of prayer
5 35 Judas turned aside to M. and assaulted
Masphath 1 K 7 5 gather all Israel to Masphath
1 K 7 6 and they gathered together to Masphath
6 judged the children of Israel in M.
7 were gathered together to M. and the
11 the men of Israel going out of Masphath
12 and laid it between Masphath and Sen
16 to Bethel and to Galgal and to M.
Jer 40 6 to Godolias the son of Ahicam to M.
8 came to Godolias to M. 12, 13; 41:1
10 I dwell in M. that I may answer the
15 spoke to Godolias privately in Masphath
41 3 Jews that were with Godolias in M.
6 forth from Masphath to meet them
10 remnant of the people that were in M.
10 all the people that remained in M.
14 Ismahel had taken, went back to M.
16 took all the remnant . . . from Masphath
Masphe Josu 11 8 field of M. which is on the east
Josu 13 26 from Hesebon unto Ramoth, Masphe
Masreca Gen 36 36 in his stead, Semla of Masreca
1 Pa 1 47 Semla of Masreca reigned in his stead
mass Eccu 22 18 mass of iron is easier to bear
Massa Gen 25 14 [Ismael's] children . . . Massa
1 Pa 1 30 Massa, Hadad, and Thema, Jetur, Naphis
massy Eccu 50 10 as a massy vessel of gold adorned
mast Isa 30 17 be left as the mast of a ship
Isa 33 23 thy mast shall be in such condition
Eze 27 7 for thy sail, to be spread on thy mast
master Exod 21 8 she displease the eyes of her m.
Exod 21 32 thirty sicles of silver to their master
22 8 the master of the house shall be brought
Judg 19 22 calling to the master of the house
1 K 25 14 to salute our master: and he rejected
3 K 22 17 the Lord said: These have no master
4 K 5 18 master goeth into the temple of Remmon
6 22 may eat and drink and go to their m.
23 and they went away to their master
Jdth 3 7 made himself master of every city
6 9 with ropes, and returned to their m.
10 20 her up by the command of their m.
Ps 104 21 he made him master of his house and
Prov 6 7 although she hath no guide nor master
27 18 he that is the keeper of his master
30 10 accuse not a servant to his master
Wisd 12 18 thou being master of power, judgest
18 11 suffered the same punishment as the m.
Isa 50 4 ear, that I may hear him as a master
55 4 a leader and a master to the Gentiles
Dan 1 3 to Asphenez the master of the eunuchs
7 master of the eunuchs gave them names
8 he requested the master of the eunuchs
Mala 1 6 if I be a master, where is my fear
2 12 done this, both the m. and the scholar
1 Ma 6 63 where he found Philip m. of the city
11 56 and made himself master of Antioch
14 6 made himself master of the country
16 13 to make himself master of the country
2 Ma 2 30 as the master builder of a new house
13 13 and make himself master of the city
14 2 made himself master of the countries
Mat 8 19 master, I will follow thee whithersoever
10 24 disciple is not above the m. Luke 6:40
12 38 master, we would see a sign from thee
19 16 good master, what good shall I do that
20 11 murmured against the master of the house
22 16 master, we know that thou. Mark 12:14
24 master, Moses said: If a man die having

36 master, which is the great commandment
26 18 the master saith: My time is near at
Mark 4 38 say to him: Master, doth it not concern
5 35 why dost thou trouble the master any
9 16 Master, I have brought my son to thee
37 Master, we saw one casting out devils
10 17 good M., what shall I do. Luke 18:18
20 Master, all these things I have
35 master, we desire that whatsoever we
12 19 M., Moses wrote unto us. Luke 20:28
32 well, Master, thou hast said in truth
13 1 Master, behold what manner of stones
14 14 say to the master of the house. The master saith, Where is my
Luke 3 12 said to him: Master, what shall we do
5 5 Master, we have labored all the night
7 40 to thee. But he said: Master, say it
8 24 saying: Master, we perish. But he
45 Master, the multitudes throng and
9 33 Master, it is good for us to be here
38 Master, I beseech thee, look upon my
49 Master, we saw a certain man casting
10 25 Master, what must I do to possess
11 45 Master, in saying these things, thou
12 13 Master, speak to my brother that he
13 25 when the master of the house shall be
14 21 the master of the house, being angry
17 13 Jesus, master, have mercy on us
19 39 to him: Master, rebuke thy disciples
20 21 saying: Master, we know that thou
28 saying: Master, Moses wrote unto us
39 to him: Master, thou hast said well
21 7 master, when shall these things be
22 11 the master saith to thee, Where is the
John 1 38 is to say, being interpreted, Master
3 10 art thou a master in Israel and
8 4 master, this woman was even now taken
11 28 the master is come and calleth for
13 13 you call me Master and Lord; and you
14 if then I being your Lord and Master
20 16 Rabboni, which is to say, Master
Acts 27 11 centurion believed . . . the m. of ship
Col 4 1 that you also have a master in heaven
his master Gen 24 61 with speed returned to his m.
Gen 39 4 Joseph found favor in sight of his m.
39 19 his m. hearing these things and giving
Exod 21 4 if his master gave him a wife and she
6 his master shall bring him to the gods
29 they warned his master and he did not
36 and his master did not keep him in: he
Deut 23 15 not deliver to his master the servant
Judg 19 11 the servant said to his master: Come
12 his master answered him: I will not
1 K 20 38 arrows, and brought them to his master
29 4 how can he otherwise appease his master
3 K 11 23 who had fled from his master Adarezer
4 K 5 1 Naaman . . . a great man with his master
25 he went in and stood before his master
8 14 from Eliseus he came to his master
9 31 for Zambri, that hath killed his master
19 4 king of Assyrians his master hath sent
1 Pa 12 19 he will return to his master Saul. So
Job 3 19 and the servant is free from his master
Isa 24 2 as with the servant, so with his master
37 4 king of the Assyrians his m. hath sent
Mala 1 6 the servant [honoreth] his master
Mat 10 25 disciple that he be as his master
Luke 6 40 the disciple is not above his master
40 shall be perfect if he be as his m.
John 15 20 servant is not greater that his master
my master Gen 24 12 the God of my master Abraham
Gen 24 12 show kindness to my master Abraham
14 that thou hast shown kindness to my m.
27 blessed be the Lord God of my m. Abraham
27 away his mercy and truth from my m.
35 and the Lord hath blessed my master
36 borne my master a son in her old age
37 my master made me swear, saying: Thou
39 I answered my master: What if the
42 Lord God of my master Abraham, if thou
48 blessing the Lord God of my m. Abraham
49 according to mercy and truth with my m.
54 let me depart, that I may go to my m.
56 send me away, that I may go to my m.
65 he said to her: That man is my master
39 8 my master hath delivered all things
Exod 21 5 I love my m. and my wife and children
1 K 24 7 I may do no such thing to my master
30 13 my master left me because I began to
15 nor deliver me into hands of my master
4 K 5 3 I wish my m. had been with the prophet
20 my master hath spared Naaman this
22 my master hath sent me to thee [Naaman]
10 9 if I conspired against my master and
18 23 come over to my master the king of
27 hath my m. sent me to thy m. Isa 36:12
thy master 2 K 9 10 Miphiboseth the son of thy m.
3 K 18 8 tell thy master: Elias is here. 11, 14
4 K 2 3 will take away thy master from thee. 5
16 that can go and seek thy master [Elias]
9 7 cut off the house of Achab thy master
18 27 hath my m. sent to thy m. Isa 36:12
your master 1 K 26 16 who have not kept your master
2 K 2 5 shown this mercy to your master Saul
7 although your master Saul be dead
4 K 10 3 and fight for the house of your master
6 take the heads of sons of your master
19 6 thus shall you say to your m. Isa 37:6
Mat 9 11 why doth your master eat with. Mark 2:16
17 23 doth not your m. pay the didrachmas
23 8 for one is your master. 10
mastering Acts 19 16 leaping upon them and m. them
master's Gen 24 10 took ten camels of his m. herd
Gen 24 27 into the house of my master's brother
36 and Sara my master's wife hath borne
44 the Lord hath prepared for my m. son
48 to take the daughter of my m. brother
51 let her be the wife of thy master's son
39 2 [Joseph] dwelt in his master's house
Exod 21 4 woman and her children shall be her m.
2 K 9 9 I have given to thy master's son
10 shalt bring in food for thy m. son
12 8 gave thee thy m. house and thy m. wives
16 3 king said: Where is thy master's son
4 K 6 32 sound of his master's feet is behind
10 2 ye that have your master's sons and
3 please you most of your master's sons
18 24 of the least of my master's servants
Isa 1 3 and the ass [knoweth] his master's crib
36 9 of the least of my master's servants
masters Exod 1 11 he set over them m. of the works
Num 11 16 knowest to be ancients and masters
Josu 23 2 for the judges and for the m. 24:1
1 K 25 10 now a days who flee from their masters
2 Pa 18 16 the Lord said: These have no masters
19 11 you have before you the Levites for m.
30 9 shall find mercy before their masters
34 13 masters of the number of the Levites
Esth 1 22 husbands should be rulers and masters
Ps 122 2 are on the hands of their masters
Prov 5 13 have not inclined my ear to masters
Ecce 12 11 by the counsel of masters are given
Eccu 3 8 and will serve them as his masters
Isa 19 4 Egypt into the hand of cruel masters
Jer 27 4 thus shall you say to your masters
4 command them to speak to their masters

Bar 2 34 and they shall be masters thereof
Amos 4 1 that say to your masters: Bring, and we
1 Ma 9 2 they made themselves masters of it
2 Ma 2 22 made themselves masters of the. 8:30
Mat 6 24 no man can serve two masters. For
15 27 fall from the table of their masters
23 10 neither be ye called masters; for one
Luke 16 13 no servant can serve two masters: for
Acts 16 16 to her masters much gain by divining
19 her masters, seeing that the hope of
30 m., what must I do, that I may be saved
Eph 6 9 and you, masters, do the same things to
Col 3 22 servants, obey in all things your m.
4 1 masters, do to your servants that which
1 Tim 6 1 count their masters worthy of all honor
2 but they that have believing masters
Titus 2 9 servants to be obedient to their masters
Heb 5 12 for the time you ought to be masters
James 3 1 be ye not many masters, my brethren
1 P 2 18 servants, be subject to your masters
mastery 1 C 9 25 and every one that striveth for m.
2 Tim 2 5 he also that striveth for the mastery
mastic Dan 13 54 he said: Under a mastic tree
masts Eze 27 5 from Libanus to make thee masts
match Gen 29 27 up the week of days of this m.
2 C 10 12 we dare not match, or compare ourselves
Mathan 4 K 11 18 they slew also Mathan. 2 Pa 23:17
Jer 38 1 Saphatias the son of Mathan, and
Mat 1 15 Eleazar begot M. and M. begot Jacob
Mathana Num 21 18 marched from the wilderness to M.
Num 21 19 marched . . . from Mathana unto Nahaliel
Mathanai 1 Es 10 33 of the sons of Hasom, Mathanai
2 Es 12 19 of Joiarib, Mathanai; of Jodaia
Mathanaias 1 Pa 25 16 ninth [lot] to Mathanaias
Mathania 1 Pa 9 15 M. son of Micha. 2 Es 11:17, 22
1 Es 10 27 of the sons of Zethua . . . Mathania
37 of the sons of Bani . . . Mathania
2 Es 12 25 Mathania . . . were keepers of the gates
34 Semeia the son of Mathania, the son
13 13 son of Zachur the son of Mathania
Mathanias 2 Pa 20 14 Hehiel the son of Mathanias
2 Pa 29 13 of the sons of Asaph, Zacharias and M.
1 Es 10 30 Banaias and Maasias, Mathanias, Beseleel
37 Mathanias, Mathania, and Jasi and
2 Es 12 8 Cedmihel, Sarebia, Juda, Mathanias
Mathaniau 1 Pa 25 4 sons of Heman, Bocciau, M.
Mathanite 1 Pa 11 43 and Josaphat a Mathanite
Mathat Luke 3 23 who was of Heli, who was of Mathat
Luke 3 29 Jorim, who was of Mathat, who was of
Mathatha 1 Es 10 33 of the sons of Hasom . . . M.
Luke 3 31 Menna, who was of Mathatha, who was
Mathathias 1 Pa 9 31 Mathathias . . . was overseer
1 Pa 15 18 M. and Eliphalu and Macenias. 21
16 5 Mathathias and Eliab and Banaias
25 3 Jeseias and Hasabias and Mathathias
21 the fourteenth lot to Mathathias
1 Es 10 43 Mathathias; Zabad, Zabina, Jeddu
2 Es 8 4 there stood by him M. and Semeia and
1 Ma 2 1 in those days arose Mathathias the
7 M. said: Woe is me, wherefore was I
14 M. and his sons rent their garments
16 Mathathias and his sons stood firm
17 from Antiochus, answering, said to M.
19 M. answered and said with a loud voice
24 and Mathathias saw and was grieved
27 M. cried out in the city with a loud
39 Mathathais and his friends heard of it
45 M. and his friends went round about
49 the days drew near that M. should die
11 70 none was left of them but Mathathias
14 29 Simon the son of Mathathias of the
16 14 to Jericho, he and M. and Judas his
Luke 3 25 Joseph, who was of Mathathias, who
26 Mahath, who was of Mathathias, who
Mathusael Gen 4 18 Maviael begot M., and M. begot
Lamech
Mathusala Gen 4 21 Henoch . . . begot Mathusala
Gen 5 22 Henoch lived after he begot Mathusala
25 Mathusala lived 187 years and begot
26 Mathusala lived after he begot Lamech
27 the days of Mathusala were 969 years
Mathusale 1 Pa 1 3 Henoc, Mathusale, Lamech
Luke 3 37 Lamech, who was of Mathusale, who was
Matred Gen 36 39 Meetabel, daughter of M. 1 Pa 1:50
matrimony Tob 6 17 who in such manner receive m.
matter Gen 30 15 dost thou think it a small m.
Gen 37 8 this matter of his dreams and words
18 22 any great matter soever shall fall out
16 13 is it a small matter to thee, that thou
Deut 3 26 speak no more to me of this matter
17 8 a hard and doubtful matter in judgment
22 28 and the matter come to judgment: he
1 K 10 16 of the matter of the kingdom of which
18 23 doth it seem to you a small matter
20 39 only Jonathan and David knew the matter
22 15 thy servant knew nothing of this matter
30 24 no man shall hearken to you in this m.
2 K 1 4 what is the m. that is come to pass
3 8 charge me with a m. concerning a woman
14 5 to her: What is the matter with thee
19 42 why art thou angry for this matter
20 21 the matter is not so, but a man of
3 K 15 5 except the matter of Urias the Hethite
21 6 the matter that thy soul is so grieved
4 K 20 10 easy m. for the shadow to go forward
1 Es 5 5 the matter should be referred to Darius
17 his pleasure to us concerning this m.
9 15 no standing before thee in this matter
10 13 have exceedingly sinned in this matter
16 sat down . . . to examine the matter
2 Es 13 11 and I pleaded the matter against the
Tob 2 8 for thee to be slain because of this m.
Jdth 6 10 asked him what was the matter, that
Esth 15 12 what is the matter, Esther? I am thy
Job 2 8 scraped the corrupt matter, sitting on
15 11 it a great m. that God should comfort
32 18 for I am full of matter to speak of
Ecce 5 7 wonder not at this matter; for he that
Wisd 11 18 hand, which made the world of matter
15 13 of earthly m. maketh brittle vessels
Eccu 8 21 before stranger do no matter of counsel
11 9 a matter which doth not concern thee
37 14 no heed to these in any m. of counsel
Jer 7 22 concerning the matter of burnt offerings
Dan 2 15 when Arioch had told the m. to Daniel
17 and told the matter to Ananias and
3 16 to answer thee concerning this matter
13 26 back door to see what was the matter
1 Ma 3 18 easy matter for many to be shut up in
10 43 being indebted to the king for any m.
63 no man complain against him of any m.
2 Ma 1 33 when this matter became public, it was
34 and diligently examining the matter
2 25 because of the multitude of the matter
3 14 Heliodorus entered in to order this m.
9 7 commanding the matter to be hastened
11 18 granted as much as the matter permitted
14 18 afraid to try the matter by the sword
15 17 that valor might decide the matter
Acts 8 21 hast no part nor lot in this matter
11 4 began and declared to them the matter
15 6 assembled to consider of this matter
17 32 will hear thee again concerning this m.
18 14 if it were some matter of injustice, or
19 38 are with him have a m. against any man
39 if you inquire after any other matter

1 C 6 1 having a m. against another, go to be
9 11 things, is it a great matter if we reap
2 C 7 11 yourselves to be undefiled in the matter
9 4 ye, should be ashamed in this matter
11 17 foolishness, in this matter of glorying
matters Exod 18 22 let them judge the lesser m. only
1 K 2 3 old matters depart from your mouth
2 Pa 19 11 m. which belong to the king's office
2 Es 11 24 in all matters concerning the people
Ps 130 1 neither have I walked in great matters
Eccu 3 24 in unnecessary m. be not over curious
11 10 son, meddle not with many matters
Dan 1 20 and in all matters of wisdom and
13 6 had any m. of judgment came to them
2 Ma 4 6 that matters should be settled in peace
43 concerning these m., an accusation was
8 9 of great experience in matters of war
9 20 if all matters go with you to your mind
13 26 thus matters went with regard to the
1 C 6 2 you unworthy to judge the smallest m.
Matthanias 4 K 24 17 he appointed M. his uncle
Matthew Mat 9 9 in the custom house, named Matthew
Mat 10 3 Thomas and Matthew the publican, and
Mark 3 18 and Matthew and Thomas and James of
Luke 6 15 Matthew and Thomas, James the son of
Acts 1 13 where abode . . . Matthew, James of
Matthias 2 Ma 14 19 he sent . . . Theodotius and M.
Acts 1 23 appointed two, Joseph . . . and Matthias
26 the lot fell upon Matthias, and he was
maturity 4 K 19 26 withered before it came to m.
Mauman Esth 1 10 he commanded Mauman and Bazatha
Maviael Gen 4 18 Irad begot M., and M. begot
mazers 4 K 25 14 m. and the forks and the cups
meadow Wisd 2 8 let no meadow escape our riot
Eccu 24 42 I will water . . . fruits of my meadow
meadows Prov 27 25 the m. are open, and the green
meal Gen 40 16 I had three baskets of meal
Exod 12 39 they baked the meal, which a little
Lev 2 14 the fire and break it small like meal
Num 5 15 tenth part of a measure of barley meal
1 K 28 24 taking meal kneaded it and baked some
2 K 13 8 and she took meal and tempered it
17 28 barley and meal and parched corn
3 K 4 22 flour and threescore measures of meal
17 12 but only a handful of meal in a pot
13 make for me of the same meal a little
14 the pot of meal shall not waste
16 from that day the pot of m. wasted not
4 K 4 41 he [Eliseus] said: Bring some meal
1 Pa 12 40 to eat: meal, figs, raisins, wine
Isa 47 2 take a millstone and grind meal
Osee 8 7 in it, the bud shall yield no meal
Mat 13 33 hid in three measures of m. Luke 13:21
meal-time Ruth 2 14 at m. come thou hither and
mean Gen 21 29 what mean these seven ewe lambs
Gen 29 25 what is it that thou didst mean to do
33 5 what mean these? And do they belong
42 31 peaceable men, and we mean no plot
Num 22 9 what mean these men that are with thee
Deut 6 20 what mean these testimonies and
Josu 4 6 what mean these stones. 21
Judg 9 15 if indeed you mean to make me king
15 if you mean it not, let fire come out
1 K 29 3 to Achis: What mean these Hebrews
2 K 16 2 said to Siba: What mean these things
4 K 7 3 what mean we to stay here till we die
Prov 11 12 despiseth his friend, is mean of heart
Eze 17 12 know you not what these things mean
24 19 what these things mean that thou doest
2 Ma 14 7 I mean of the high priesthood
Mark 9 9 what that should mean, when he shall
Acts 10 17 the vision that he had seen should mean
17 20 would know . . . what these things mean
21 13 what do you mean weeping and afflicting
39 in Cilicia, a citizen of no mean city
1 C 5 10 I mean not with the fornicators of this
2 C 8 13 I mean that others should be eased
James 2 2 come in also a poor man in mean apparel
in the mean time Gen 35 1 i. . . . God said to Jacob
Gen 43 1 i. . . . the famine was heavy upon all
Exod 1 8 i. . . . there arose a new king over
Num 11 1 i. . . . there arose a murmuring of the
13 31 in the mean time Caleb, to still the
20 14 i. . . . Moses sent messengers from Cades
Josu 22 13 i. . . . they sent to them into the land
2 K 11 2 i. . . . it happened that David arose from
20 11 i. . . . some men of Joab's company
Job 34 37 let him be tied fast i. . . . amongst us
1 Ma 9 1 i. . . . when Demetrius heard that Nicanor
John 4 31 in the mean time the disciples prayed him
meaner 2 K 6 22 make myself m. than I have done
meanest Deut 1 14 is good which thou m. to do
Judg 6 15 my family is the meanest in Manasses
8 1 what is this that thou meanest to do
3 K 13 33 made of the m. of the people priest
4 K 9 8 that is shut up, and the m. in Israel
Eze 33 2 take a man, one of the meanest, and
37 18 not tell us what thou meanest by this
meaneth Gen 37 10 what m. this dream that thou
Deut 21 16 he meaneth to divide his substance
29 24 what meaneth this exceeding great heat
Josu 22 16 what meaneth this transgression? Why
Judg 14 15 to tell thee what the riddle meaneth
1 K 4 14 what meaneth the noise of this uproar
15 14 what m. then this bleating of the
2 K 24 3 what m. my lord . . . by this kind of
3 K 1 41 what meaneth this noise of the city
Eze 20 29 what meaneth the high place to which
Dan 13 47 what m. this word that thou hast
Mat 9 13 this meaneth, I will have mercy. 12:7
Acts 2 12 one to another: What meaneth this
meaning Gen 41 26 the same meaning of the dream
Exod 12 26 what is the meaning of this service
Judg 15 1 Samson came, meaning to visit his wife
1 K 14 41 we may know what the meaning is that
2 K 14 14 m. that he that is cast off should
Jer 11 15 what is the meaning that my beloved
Eze 18 1 to me, saying: What is the meaning
Dan 2 5 you tell me the dream and the meaning
6 if you tell the dream and the m. of it
4 15 are not able to declare the m. of it
5 15 they could not declare to me the m.
8 15 saw the vision and sought the meaning
Acts 22 30 m. to know more diligently for what
23 28 m. to know cause which they objected
27 2 meaning to sail by the coasts of Asia
Heb 6 17 God, meaning more abundantly to show to
meanings Eccu 39 3 will search out the hidden m.
means Gen 30 37 by this m. the color was divers
Num 23 8 by what means should I detect him whom
Lev 25 28 find not the means to repay the price
54 if by these means he cannot be redeemed
3 K 22 21 the Lord said to him: By what means
2 Pa 18 20 by what means wilt thou deceive him
Tob 10 7 but she could by no means be comforted
10 he by no means would hearken to him
Wisd 8 13 by the means of her I shall have
16 3 by m. of those things that were shown
17 9 which could by no means be avoided
1 Ma 5 46 there was no means to turn from it
14 35 sought by all m. to advance his people
2 Ma 3 13 by all means the money must be carried
4 11 by the means of John the father of
8 36 by the m. of the captives of Jerusalem
9 6 he by no means ceased from his malice
11 by this means, being brought from his

11 19 will endeavor to be a m. of your good
15 36 by no means to let this day pass
Luke 5 18 they sought means to bring him in
Acts 4 9 by what means he hath been made whole
2 C 1 11 by the means of many persons, thanks
Phil 1 18 so that by all means, whether by occasion
Heb 9 15 testament: that by means of his death
by any means Exod 32 30 if b. . . . I may be able to
Num 22 6 if b. . . . I may beat them and drive
11 if b. . . . I may fight with them and
Jer 20 10 if b. . . . he may be deceived, and we
Soph 2 3 if b. . . . you may be hid in the day of
Mala 1 9 if b. . . . he will receive your faces
2 Ma 3 12 thing which could not b. . . . be done
Acts 27 12 if by any means they might reach Phenice
Rom 1 10 if by any means now at length I may have
11 14 if, by any means, I may provoke to
Phil 3 11 if by any means I may attain to the
12 after, if I may by any means apprehend
2 Th 2 3 let no man deceive you by any means
meant Exod 1 18 what is that you meant to do
Exod 14 5 what m. we to do, that we let Israel
Deut 19 19 to him as he m. to do to his brother
Judg 2 15 whithersoever they meant to go, the
2 Pa 11 22 for he meant to make him [Abia] king
1 Ma 13 14 that he meant to join battle with him
14 35 to what glory he meant to bring his
2 Ma 14 26 that he meant to make Judas, who was
Luke 15 26 and asked what these things meant
18 36 passing by, he asked what this meant
John 6 72 he meant Judas Iscariot, the son of
Acts 23 15 as if you meant to know something more
20 as if they meant to inquire something
measurable Ps 38 6 thou hast made my days m.
measure Gen 7 19 the waters prevailed beyond m.
Gen 13 13 wicked and sinners . . . beyond measure
41 49 of the sea, and the plenty exceeded m.
Exod 16 18 measured by the measure of a gomor
26 2 all the curtain shall be of one measure
8 m. of all the curtains shall be equal
28 16 it shall be the measure of a span
29 40 wine for libation of the same measure
36 15 all the curtains were of one measure
38 18 according to the m. of all the hangings
39 9 rational . . . of the measure of a span
Lev 5 18 to measure and estimation of the sin
6 6 estimation and measure of the offence
19 35 judgment, in rule, in weight, or in m.
27 16 according to the measure of the seed
Num 5 15 tenth part of a measure of barley meal
15 5 the same measure of wine to pour out
7 same measure of wine for the libation
10 wine for libations of the same measure
28 5 the measure of fourth part of a hin
Deut 3 11 after the m. of the cubit of a man's
21 2 shall measure from the place where the
25 2 according to the m. of the sin shall the m. also of the stripes be
Judg 6 19 unleavened loaves of a measure of flour
Ruth 2 17 she found about the measure of an ephi
3 K 6 3 according to the m. of the breadth of
25 the measure and the work was the same
7 9 sawed by a certain rule and measure
11 were costly stones, of equal measure
20 according to the measure of the pillar
37 ten bases, of one casting and measure
4 K 12 11 they gave it out by number and measure
1 Pa 23 29 of every weight and measure. And the
28 17 according to the m. he gave by weight
2 Pa 3 3 length by the first measure 60 cubits
4 measure of the breadth of the house
1 Es 7 22 bates of oil and salt without measure
2 Es 3 19 built another m. 20, 21, 24, 27, 30
Jdth 7 11 daily given out to the people by m.
Job 11 9 measure of him is longer than the earth
28 25 winds, and weighed the waters by m.
42 3 that above m. exceeded my knowledge
Ps 79 6 give us for our drink tears in measure
Wisd 11 21 thou hast ordered all things in m.
15 14 and unhappy and proud beyond measure
Eccu 50 3 they were filled as the sea above m.
Isa 5 10 vineyard shall yield one little measure
27 8 in m. against m., when it shall be cast
28 17 judgment in weight, and justice in m.
65 7 I will measure back their first work
Jer 13 25 thy lot and the portion of thy measure
Eze 4 11 and thou shalt drink water by measure
16 and they shall drink water by measure
40 10 all three were of one measure, and the fronts of one measure
21 according to the m. of the former gate
22 according to the measure of the gate
41 8 chambers which were the m. of a reed
17 even to the inner house . . . by measure
43 10 and let them measure the building: and
45 3 with this m. thou shalt m. the length
11 shall be equal, and of one measure
11 equal according to the m. of a core
13 the m. of oil also, a bate of oil is
46 22 broad, all the four were of one m.
47 18 thus you shall measure the east side
48 30 side, thou shalt measure 4,500. 33
Osee 1 10 sand of the sea, that is without m.
Amos 8 5 that we may lessen the measure and
Mich 6 10 iniquity, and a scant m. full of wrath
Zach 2 2 he said to me: To measure Jerusalem
2 Ma 7 20 the mother was to be admired above m.
Mat 7 2 what measure you mete. Mark 4:24
23 32 fill ye up then the m. of your fathers
Luke 6 38 good m. and pressed down and shaken
38 with the same measure that you shall
12 42 to give them their measure of wheat
John 3 34 for God doth not give the Spirit by m.
Rom 7 13 might become sinful above measure. For
12 3 divided to every one measure of faith
2 C 1 8 that we were pressed out of m. above our
4 17 worketh for us above m. exceedingly an
10 12 but we measure ourselves by ourselves
13 he will not glory beyond our measure
13 according to the measure of the rule
13 to us, a measure to reach even unto you
14 we stretch not ourselves beyond our m.
15 not glorying beyond m. in other men's
11 23 in stripes above m., in deaths often
12 11 them that are above measure apostles
Gal 1 13 beyond measure, I persecuted the church
Eph 4 7 to the measure of the giving of Christ
13 unto the m. of the age of the fulness
16 operation in the measure of every part
Apoc 11 1 arise, and measure the temple of God
2 measure it not: because it is given
21 15 had a m. of a reed of gold to m. the
17 the m. of a man, which is of an angel
measured Exod 16 18 m. by the measure of a gomor
Ruth 3 15 he measured six measures of barley
2 K 8 2 David . . . measured them with a line
2 m. with two lines, one to put to death
3 K 17 21 [Elias] stretched and measured himself
Eccu 1 2 who hath measured the height of heaven
9 saw her and numbered her and m. her
Isa 40 12 hath m. the waters in the hollow of
48 13 my right hand hath m. the heavens
Jer 31 37 if the heavens above can be measured
33 22 nor the sand of the sea be measured
Eze 40 5 and he m. the breadth of the building
6 he m. the breadth of the threshold. 11

9 and he measured the porch of the gate
13 he m. the gate from the roof of one
19 he m. the breadth from the face of the
20 he m. also both the length and the
23 he m. from gate to gate 100 cubits
24 he measured the front thereof and the
27 he m. from gate to gate towards
28 he m. the gate according to the. 32
35 he m. according to the former measures
47 and he measured the court 100 cubits
48 he m. the porch 5 cubits on this side
41 1 he measured the fronts six cubits broad
2 he m. the length thereof forty cubits
3 he m. the front of the gate two cubits
4 he m. the length thereof twenty cubits
5 he m. the walls of the house six cubits
13 m. the length of the house. 100 cubits
15 he m. the length of the building over
42 15 measured it on every side round about
16 he measured toward the east with the
17 he measured toward the north 500 reeds
18 towards the south he measured 500 reeds
19 toward the west he measured 500 reeds
20 he measured the wall thereof on every
47 3 east he measured a thousand cubits
5 he m. a thousand, and he brought me
Amos 7 17 thy land shall be measured by a line
Haba 3 6 he stood and measured the earth. He
Mat 7 2 it shall be measured to you again. Mark 4:24; Luke 6:38
2 C 10 13 rule, which God hath measured to us, a
Apoc 21 16 he m. the city with the golden reed
17 he m. the wall thereof 144 cubits, the
measures Gen 18 6 together three m. of flour
Ruth 3 15 he measured six measures of barley
17 hath given me six measures of barley
1 K 25 18 five measures of parched corn, and a
3 K 4 22 m. of fine flour and threescore m. of meal
5 11 allowed Hiram 20,000 measures of wheat
11 and twenty measures of the purest oil
2 Pa 2 10 I will give . . . 20,000 measures of oil
4 5 and it held three thousand measures
27 5 gave him . . . 10,000 measures of wheat and as many measures of barley
Job 38 5 who hath laid the measure thereof, if
Prov 20 10 diverse m. both are abominable before
Eze 40 24 according to the former m. 28, 32, 35
29 porch thereof with the same measures
43 13 these are the measures of the altar
48 16 these are the m. thereof, on the north
Dan 14 2 twelve great measures of fine flour
Mat 13 33 hid in three m. of meal. Luke 13:21
John 2 6 containing two or three m. apiece
measuring Jer 31 39 and the m. line shall go out
Eze 40 3 a m. reed in his hand. Zach 2:1
5 in the man's hand a measuring reed
42 15 when he had made an end of m. the
16 measured . . . with the m. reed. 18, 19
meat Gen 1 29 of their own kind, to be your meat
Gen 9 3 moveth and liveth shall be m. for you
27 4 make me savory meat thereof as thou
9 I may make of them meat for thy father
17 and she gave him the savory meat
Exod 12 39 did they think of preparing any meat
16 35 with this meat were they fed until
Lev 7 18 soul shall defile itself with such meat
11 34 any meat which you eat, if water
41 neither shall it be taken for meat
22 7 sanctified things because it is his meat
25 6 but they shall be unto you for meat
Num 11 33 neither had that kind of meat failed
Deut 2 28 sell us meat for money, that we may
28 26 be thy carcass meat for all the fowls
Judg 1 7 gathered up the leavings of the meat
14 14 out of the eater came forth meat, and
19 8 I beseech thee to take a little meat
22 refreshing their bodies with meat and
Ruth 2 18 gave her of the remains of her meat
1 K 20 27 why cometh not the son of Isai to meat
2 K 3 35 when all the people came to take meat
11 8 after him a mess of meat from the king
12 17 neither did he eat meat with them
13 11 when she had presented him the meat
19 35 can meat or drink delight thy servant
3 K 10 5 meat of his table and the apartments
2 Pa 28 15 and refreshed them with meat and drink
1 Es 3 7 meat and drink and oil to the Sidonians
Tob 12 19 but I use an invisible meat and drink
Ruth 12 9 she took her own meat in the evening
Job 20 21 there was nothing left of his meat and
33 20 the meat which before he desired. He
38 41 about, because they have no meat
Ps 73 14 thou hast given him to be meat for
77 18 by asking meat for their desires. And
30 as yet their meat was in their mouth
78 2 to be meat for the fowls of the air
103 21 lions . . . seeking their meat from God
106 18 their soul abhorred all manner of meat
144 15 thou givest them meat in due season
Prov 6 8 provideth her meat for herself in the
30 22 by a fool when he is filled with meat
Wisd 13 12 the chips of his work to dress his meat
16 2 preparing for them quails for their m.
3 want for a short time, tasted a new m.
Eccu 30 18 as messes of meat set about a grave
36 20 the belly will devour all meat, yet
37 32 and pour not out thyself upon any meat
40 30 feedeth his soul with another man's m.
41 2 and that is yet able to take meat
24 of leaning with thy elbow over meat
Isa 44 16 with part of it he dressed his meat
62 8 thy corn to be meat for thy enemies
Jer 7 33 meat for the fowls of the air. 16:4; 19:7
34 20 bodies shall be for meat to the fowls
Lam 4 10 own children: they were their meat
Bar 1 10 make meat offerings, and offerings for
Eze 4 10 thy meat that thou shalt eat, shall be
24 17 thy face, nor eat the meat of mourners
22 nor shall you eat the meat of mourners
29 5 have given thee for meat to the beasts
34 10 and it shall no more be meat for them
Dan 1 5 a daily provision, of his own meat and
10 who hath appointed you meat and drink
13 children that eat of the king's meat
15 children that ate of the king's meat
6 18 meat was not set before him, and even
Osee 11 4 I put his meat to him that he might eat
Haba 1 16 portion is made fat, and his m. dainty
Agge 2 13 and touch with his skirts . . . any meat
Mala 3 10 that there may be meat in my house
Mat 3 4 his meat was locusts and wild honey
6 25 is not the life more than the meat
9 10 as he was sitting at meat in the house
10 10 for the workman is worthy of his meat
24 45 family, to give them meat in season
Mark 2 15 as he sat at meat in his house, many
6 36 they may buy themselves meat to eat
14 3 of Simon the leper, and was at meat
Luke 3 11 he that hath meat, let him do in like
7 36 of the Pharisee, and sat down to meat
37 when she knew that he sat at meat in
49 that sat at meat with him began to
12 23 the life is more than the meat, and
37 and make them sit down to meat, and
17 7 immediately go, sit down to meat: and
John 4 32 I have meat to eat, which you know not

34 34 my meat is to do the will of him that
6 27 labor not for the m. which perisheth
5 6 for my flesh is meat indeed: and my
21 5 children, have you any meat? They
12 none of them who were at meat durst
Acts 2 46 they took their meat with gladness
9 19 and when he had taken meat, he was
27 33 Paul besought them all to take meat
34 I pray you to take some meat for your
36 better cheer, and they also took some m.
Rom 14 15 for if, because of thy meat, thy brother
15 destroy not him with thy meat, for whom
17 for the kingdom of God is not meat and
20 destroy not the work of God for meat
1 C 3 2 I gave you milk to drink, not meat; for
6 13 meat for the belly, and the belly for
8 8 but meat doth not commend us to God. For
10 sit at meat in the idol's temple
13 if meat scandalize my brother, I will
Col 2 16 let no man therefore judge you in meat
Heb 5 12 need of milk, and not of strong meat
14 but strong meat is for the perfect; for
meats Gen 27 7 make me meats that I may eat and
Gen 27 14 she dressed meats, such as she knew
25 bring me the meats of thy hunting, my
31 brought in to his father meats made
40 17 I carried all meats that are made by
Exod 8 3 and into the remains of thy meats; and
16 23 m. that are to be dressed, dress them
Lev 22 13 she shall eat of her father's meats
Deut 2 6 you shall buy meats of them for money
4 K 6 23 provision of meats was set before them
2 Pa 9 4 meats of his table, and the dwelling
35 15 the Levites prepared meats for them
2 Es 8 10 eat fat meats, and drink sweet wine
10 37 would bring the firstfruits of our m.
Tob 1 12 all ate of the meats of the Gentiles
12 and never was defiled with their meats
Esth 1 7 the m. were brought in divers vessels
9 19 portions of their banquets and meats
22 send to one another portions of meats
Job 6 7 now, through anguish, are my meats
34 3 the mouth discerneth meats by the taste
Prov 23 3 be not desirous of his meats, in which
6 envious man, and desire not his meats
8 the meats which thou hadst eaten, thou
Wisd 19 11 appetite they asked for delicate meats
Eccu 13 8 he will shame thee by his meats till
37 33 in many meats there will be sickness
Jer 51 34 filled his belly with my delicate m.
Eze 44 30 firstfruits of your meats to the priest
Dan 14 10 do thou, O king, set on the meats and
13 the king set the meats before Bel: and
1 Ma 1 65 than to be defiled with unclean meats
2 Ma 11 31 the Jews may use their own kind of m.
Mark 7 19 into the privy, purging all meats? But
John 4 8 were gone into the city to buy meats
1 C 6 13 meats for the belly, and the belly for m.
8 4 but as for meats that are sacrificed to
1 Tim 4 3 to abstain from meats, which God hath
Heb 9 9 serveth, only in meats and in drinks
13 9 established with grace, not with meats
Mecherathite 1 Pa 11 36 Hepher a Mecherathite
Mechmas 2 Es 11 31 children of Benjamin . . . at M.
Mechnedebai 1 Es 10 40 of the sons of Bani . . . M.
Medaba Num 21 30 came weary to Nophe and unto M.
Josu 13 9 and all the plains of Medaba, as far
16 all the plain, that leadeth to Medaba
1 Pa 19 7 came and camped over against Medaba
Isa 15 2 to mourn over Nabo and over Medaba
Medad Num 11 26 was called Eldad, and the other M.
Num 11 27 Eldad and Medad prophesy in the camp
Meddin Josu 15 61 Meddin and Sachacha and Nebsan

meddle Prov 20 19 m. not with him that revealeth
Eccu 11 10 meddle not with many matters: and
23 10 meddle not with the names of saints
meddleth Prov 26 17 m. with another man's quarrel
meddling Prov 20 3 fools are m. with reproaches
2 Th 3 11 working not at all, but curiously m.
Mede Isa 21 2 go up, O Elam, besiege, O Mede
Dan 5 31 Darius the M. succeeded to the kingdom
11 1 the first year of Darius the Mede
Medemena Josu 15 31 Siceleg and Medemena and
Isa 10 31 M. is removed: ye inhabitants of
Medes 4 K 17 6 in the cities of the M. 18:11
Tob 1 16 Rages a city of the Medes. 3:7; 4:21; 5:8, 14
5 7 leadeth to the country of the Medes
6 6 Rages the city of the Medes. 9:3, 6
Jdth 1 1 Arphaxad king of the Medes had brought
16 12 constancy, and the M. at her boldness
14 princes of the Persians and the M. 18
19 law of the Persians and of the Medes
10 2 are written in the books of the Medes
Isa 13 17 I will stir up the Medes against them
Jer 25 25 of Elam and all the kings of the Medes
51 11 raise up spirit of the kings of the M.
Dan 5 28 and is given to the Medes and Persians
6 8 what is decreed by the M. and Persians
12 the decree of the Medes and Persians
15 the law of the Medes and Persians is
8 20 is the king of the Medes and Persians
9 1 of Assuerus of the seed of the Medes
1 Ma 1 1 Darius king of the Persians and Medes
8 8 country of the Indians and of the Medes
Acts 2 9 Parthians and Medes and Elamites and
Media 1 Es 6 2 castle in the province of Media
Jer 51 28 nations against her, the kings of M.
1 Ma 6 56 was returned from Persia and M. with
14 1 went into Media to get him succors
2 Arsaces the king of Persia and Media
mediator Deut 5 5 I was the m. and stood between
Judg 11 10 he himself is mediator and witness
Gal 3 19 ordained by angels in the hand of a m.
20 a mediator is not of one: but God is one
1 Tim 2 5 there is one God, and one mediator of
Heb 8 6 he is mediator of a better testament
9 15 mediator of the new testament. 12:24
medicine Eccu 6 16 faithful friend is m. of life
Eccu 18 20 before sickness take a medicine, and
Eze 47 12 and the loaves thereof for medicine
medicines Tob 6 5 are necessary for useful m.
Eccu 38 4 the most High hath created medicines
Jer 30 13 it up: thou hast no healing medicines
46 11 in vain dost thou multiply medicines
meditate Gen 24 63 forth to meditate in the field
Deut 6 7 thou shalt meditate upon them, sitting
11 19 your children that they m. on them
Josu 1 8 thou shalt meditate on it day and
Ps 1 2 on his law he shall meditate day and
34 28 my tongue shall meditate thy justice
36 30 the mouth of the just shall m. wisdom
62 7 I will meditate on thee in the morning
70 24 my tongue shall m. on thy justice all
76 13 and I will meditate on all thy works
118 15 I will meditate on thy commandments
117 I will m. always on thy justifications
148 that I might meditate on thy words
Prov 8 7 my mouth shall meditate truth, and my
Eccu 6 37 m. continually on his commandments
14 22 that shall meditate in his justice
39 10 and in his secrets shall he meditate
16 I will yet meditate that I may declare
Isa 33 18 thy heart shall meditate fear: where is
38 14 I will m. like a dove: my eyes are
Luke 21 14 not to m. before how you shall answer
Acts 4 25 and the people meditate vain things

1 Tim 4 15 meditate upon these things, be wholly
meditated Ps 76 7 I m. in the night with my
Ps 118 47 I m. also on thy commandments, which I
70 but I have meditated on thy law. It is
142 5 I m. on all thy works: I m. upon the works of thy hands
Eccu 39 38 I have m. and thought on these things
Isa 27 8 he hath m. with his severe spirit in
meditation Ps 18 15 the m. of my heart always
Ps 38 4 in my meditation a fire shall flame out
48 4 meditation of my heart understanding
118 24 thy testimonies are my meditation. 99
77 and I shall live: for thy law is my m.
92 unless thy law had been my meditation
97 it is my meditation all the day
143 thy commandments are my meditation
174 thy law is my meditation. My soul
medley Num 35 22 if by chance m., and without
meek Num 12 3 Moses was a man exceeding meek
Jdth 9 16 the prayer of the humble and the meek
Job 24 4 oppressed together the meek of the earth
Ps 24 9 he will teach the meek his ways. All
33 3 praised: let the meek hear and rejoice
36 11 but the meek shall inherit the land
75 10 to save all the meek of the earth. For
146 6 Lord lifteth up the meek and bringeth
149 4 he will exalt the meek unto salvation
Prov 3 34 to the meek he will give grace. The
16 19 better to be humbled with the meek
Eccu 5 13 be meek to hear the word, that thou
10 17 hath set up the meek in their stead
Isa 11 4 with equity for the meek of the earth
29 19 the meek shall increase their joy in
32 7 hath framed devices to destroy the meek
61 1 he hath sent me to preach to the meek
Jer 11 19 I was as a meek lamb, that is carried
Soph 2 3 seek the Lord, all ye meek of the earth
3 seek the just, seek the meek: if by
Mat 5 4 blessed are the meek: for they shall
11 29 because I am meek and humble of heart
21 5 thy king cometh to thee, meek and
1 P 3 4 a quiet and a meek spirit, which is
meekness Ps 44 5 because of truth and meekness
Ps 131 1 remember David and all his meekness
Wisd 2 19 that we may know his meekness and try
Eccu 1 35 agreeable to him, is faith and meekness
3 19 my son, do thy works in meekness, and
10 31 keep my soul in meekness, and give it
45 4 he sanctified him in his faith and m.
Dan 3 42 but deal with us according to thy m.
1 C 4 21 charity, and in the spirit of meekness
Gal 6 1 instruct such a one in the spirit of m.
James 1 21 with m. receive the ingrafted word
3 13 his work in the meekness of wisdom
meet Gen 14 17 king of Sodom went out to m. him
Gen 18 2 as he saw them he ran to meet them
19 1 he rose up and went to meet them: and
24 12 meet me today, I beseech thee, and
17 the servant ran to meet her and said
29 13 son was come, ran forth to meet him
30 16 the field, Lia went out to meet him
32 6 he cometh with speed to meet thee with
17 if thou meet my brother Esau, and he
33 4 then Esau ran to meet his brother and
46 28 and that he should meet him in Gessen
29 Joseph . . . went up to meet his father
Exod 4 14 he [Aaron] cometh forth to meet thee
27 go into the desert to meet Moses. And he went forth to meet him
7 15 shalt stand to meet him on the bank
18 7 and he went out to meet his kinsman
19 17 Moses had brought them forth to m. God
23 4 if thou meet thy enemy's ox or ass
36 12 that the loops might meet one against
Num 20 20 he came forth to meet them with an
21 23 went forth to meet them in the desert
22 26 hand or to the left, stood to meet him
36 he came forth to meet him [Balaam]
23 3 to see if perhaps the Lord will meet me
15 burnt offering while I go to meet him
31 13 forth to meet them without the camp
Deut 2 32 Sehon came out to meet us with all his
3 1 the king of Basan came out to meet us
23 4 they would not meet you with bread
Josu 2 16 lest perhaps they meet you as they
8 22 out of the city to meet their own men
9 11 go meet them, and say: We are your
Judg 4 18 and Jahel went forth to meet Sisara
22 Jahel went out to meet him [Barac]
6 35 and they came to meet him [Gedeon]
7 34 come down to meet Madian, and take
11 31 shall meet me when I return in peace
15 14 Philistines shouting went to meet him
20 42 fired the city came also out to m. them
1 K 10 3 there shall meet thee three men going
5 thou shalt meet a company of prophets
13 10 Saul went forth to meet him and salute
15 to meet the people who fought against
17 48 coming and drew nigh to meet David
48 ran to the fight to meet the Philistine
18 6 singing and dancing to meet king Saul
23 28 Saul . . . went to meet the Philistines
25 32 who sent thee this day to meet me and
34 thou hast not quickly come to meet me
30 21 they came out to meet David: and the
2 K 6 20 Michol . . . coming out to meet David
10 5 he [David] sent to meet them: for the
15 32 Chusai . . . came to meet him [David]
16 1 Siba . . . came to meet him with two
19 15 as far as Galgal to meet the king
16 the men of Juda to meet king David
20 am come down to meet my lord the king
24 came down to meet the King, and he
3 K 2 8 he came down to meet me when I passed
19 the king arose to meet her [Bethsabee]
18 16 Abdias therefore went to meet Achab
16 Achab came to meet Elias. And when
21 18 go down to meet Achab king of Israel
4 K 1 3 go up to meet the messengers of the
2 15 coming to meet him [Eliseus], they
4 26 go therefore to meet her, and say to
29 if any man meet thee, salute him not
31 he [Gieze] returned to meet him, and
5 21 down from his chariot to meet him
26 back from his chariot to meet thee
8 8 go to meet the man of God, and consult
9 Hazael went to meet him, taking with
9 18 went one in a chariot to meet him
21 they went out to meet Jehu, and met
16 10 king Achaz went to Damascus to meet
23 29 king Josias went to meet him: and was
1 Pa 12 17 David went out to meet them and said
19 5 word to David, who sent to meet them
21 21 of the thrashingfloor to meet him
2 Pa 14 10 Asa went out to meet him and set his
15 2 went out to meet Asa and said to him
28 9 [Obed] went out to meet the army
35 20 Josias went out to meet him. But he
Tob 11 10 servant his hand, went to meet his son
Jdth 3 9 went out to meet him at his coming
5 4 and have not come out to meet us that
13 15 all ran to meet her from the least to
Job 5 14 shall meet with darkness in the day
14 3 dost thou think it meet to open thy
39 21 he goeth forward to meet armed men
Ps 58 6 rise up thou to meet me, and behold

Prov 4 12 thou shalt not meet a stumblingblock
7 15 I am come out to meet thee, desirous
13 3 on his speech shall meet with evils
17 12 better to meet a bear robbed of her
Eccu 15 2 she will meet him as an honorable mother
7 and wise men shall meet her, foolish
32 19 shall meet with a stumblingblock
Isa 7 3 go forth to meet Achaz, thou and Jasub
14 9 uproar to meet thee at thy coming
21 14 meet with bread him that fleeth. For
34 14 demons and monsters shall meet and
Jer 41 6 went forth from Masphath to meet them
51 31 one running post shall meet another
31 and messenger shall meet messenger
Osee 13 8 I will meet them as a bear that is
Amos 4 12 be prepared to meet thy God, O Israel
5 19 of a lion, and a bear should meet him
Soph 1 3 the ungodly shall meet with ruin
14 man shall there meet with tribulation
1 Ma 3 11 Judas . . . went forth to meet him
16 Judas went forth to meet him with
17 they saw the army coming to meet them
5 39 Judas went to meet them. And Timotheus
9 39 brethren to meet them with timbrels and
10 56 meet me at Ptolemais, that we may
59 that he should come and meet him. And
86 out of the city to meet him with great
11 2 ordered them to go forth to meet him
6 Jonathan came to meet the king at Joppe
12 11 as it is meet . . . to remember brethren
41 Jonathan went out to meet him with
2 Ma 6 19 to meet most glorious death than a
14 16 to the town of Dessau to meet them
Mat 8 34 the whole city went out to meet Jesus
25 1 went out to meet the bridegroom and the
6 go ye forth to meet him. Then all those
Mark 14 13 there shall meet you a man. Luke 22:10
Luke 14 31 to meet him that, with 20,000, cometh
John 11 20 went to meet him: but Mary sat at home
12 13 went forth to meet him and cried
18 the people came to meet him, because
Acts 10 25 Cornelius came to m. him, and falling
28 15 they came to meet us as far as Appii
1 C 16 4 if it be meet that I also go, they shall
Eph 4 13 until we all m. into the unity of faith
Phil 1 7 as it is meet for me to think this for
1 Th 4 16 with them in the clouds to meet Christ
Heb 6 7 herbs meet for them by whom it is tilled
2 P 1 13 I think it meet as long as I am in
Meetabel Gen 36 39 his wife was called M. 1 Pa 1:50
meetest Eccu 19 26 a wise man, when thou m. him
meeteth Prov 7 10 a woman m. him in harlot's
Prov 30 30 hath no fear of anything he meeteth
Wisd 6 17 and meeteth them with all providence
Eccu 43 24 of a cloud, and a dew that meeteth it
meeting Deut 1 44 m. you, chased you, as bees do
Judg 20 25 m. them made so great a slaughter
1 K 16 4 ancients . . . meeting him, they said
Eccu 40 23 companion m. together in season, but
Isa 21 14 meeting the thirsty bring him water
Mark 11 4 without, in the meeting of the two ways
meetings Ps 15 4 their m. for blood offerings
Megbis 1 Es 2 30 the children of Megbis, 156
Megphias 2 Es 10 20 Megphias, Mosollam, Hazir
Mehusim 1 Pa 8 11 M. begot Agitob and Elphaal
Mejarcon Josu 19 46 and Mejarcon and Arecon
Melcha Gen 11 29 name of Nachor's wife, Melcha
Gen 22 20 that Melcha also had borne children
23 these eight did M. bear to Nachor
24 15 daughter of Bathuel, son of Melcha. 24
47 Bathuel, son of Nachor, whom Melcha bore
Num 26 33 daughters . . . Melcha and Thersa. Josu 17:3
27 1 daughters of Salphaad . . . Hegla and M.
36 11 and Thersa and Hegla and Melcha
Melchi Luke 3 24 Levi, who was of Melchi, who was
Luke 3 28 Neri, who was of Melchi, who was of
Melchia 1 Pa 6 40 Basaia the son of Melchia the
1 Pa 24 9 the fifth to Melchia, the sixth to
1 Es 10 25 of the sons of Pharos . . . Melchia and
2 Es 8 4 Misael and Melchia and Hasum and
12 41 and Melchia and Elam and Ezer. And
Melchias 1 Pa 9 12 Phassur the son of Melchias. Jer 21:1; 38:1
1 Es 10 31 Josue, M., Semeias, Simeon, Benjamin
2 Es 3 11 Melchias the son of Herem, and Hasub
14 Melchias the son of Rechab built, lord
30 Melchias the goldsmith's son built
10 3 Pheshur, Amarias, Melchias, Hattus
11 12 the son of Pheshur, the son of Melchias
Jdth 8 1 the son of Achitob, the son of Melchias
Jer 38 6 cast him into the dungeon of Melchias
Melchiel Gen 46 17 the sons of Beria: Heber and M.
Num 26 45 the sons of Brie: Heber . . . and Melchiel
1 Pa 7 31 the sons of Baria: Haber and Melchiel
Melchielites Num 26 45 is the family of the M.
Melchiram 1 Pa 3 18 sons of Jechonias . . . Melchiram
Melchisedech Gen 14 18 but M. the king of Salem
Ps 109 4 according to the order of Melchisedech
Heb 5 6 according to the order of Melchisedech. 10; 6:20; 7:11, 17
7 1 this Melchisedech was king of Salem
10 his father, when Melchisedech met him
15 if according to the similitude of M.
Melchisua 1 K 14 49 Jonathan and Jessui and M.
1 K 31 2 and M. the sons of Saul. 1 Pa 10:2
1 Pa 8 33 Saul begot Jonathan and M. 9:39
Melchom 4 K 23 13 to M. the abomination of
1 Pa 20 2 and David took the crown of Melchom
Jer 49 1 why then hath Melchom inherited Gad
3 Melchom shall be carried into captivity
Amos 1 15 and Melchom shall go into captivity
Soph 1 5 by the Lord, and swear by Melchom
Melea Luke 3 31 Eliakim, who was of Melea, who was
Melech 1 Pa 8 35 sons of Micha . . . Melech. 9:41
Melita Acts 28 1 knew that the island was called M.
Mello Judg 9 6 the families of the city of Mello
Judg 9 20 and consume . . . the town of Mello
20 of Sichem and from the town of Mello
2 K 5 9 and built round about from Mello and
3 K 9 15 to build . . . his own house and Mello
24 then did he Solomon build Mello
11 27 for Solomon built Mello and filled up
4 K 12 20 and slew Joas in the house of Mello
2 Pa 32 5 he repaired Mello in the city of David
Mellothi 1 Pa 25 4 Mellothi, Othir, Mahazioth
1 Pa 25 26 the nineteenth to Mellothi, to his sons
Melluch 1 Es 10 29 Mosollam and Melluch and Adaia
2 Es 10 27 Hanan, Anan, Melluch, Haran, Baana
12 2 Melluch, Hattus, Sebenias, Rheum
Meloch 1 Pa 6 44 Abdi the son of Meloch the son
melodious Wisd 17 17 or the m. voice of birds
melody 1 Pa 2 55 singing and making melody and
Job 38 7 the sons of God made a joyful melody
Ps 97 4 earth: make melody, rejoice and sing
Eccu 32 8 is the melody of music with pleasant
40 21 and the psaltery make a sweet melody
47 11 by their voices he made sweet melody
50 20 sound of sweet melody was increased
Isa 24 8 ended, the melody of the harp is silent
Mich 2 4 a song shall be sung with melody by
Eph 5 19 making m. in your hearts to the Lord
melons Num 11 5 melons and the leeks and the
Melothus Jdth 2 13 assault the renowned city of M.
melt 2 K 17 10 valiant man . . . shall melt for fear
Jdth 16 18 rocks shall melt as wax before thy

Ps 147 18 send out his word and shall melt them
Wisd 16 29 hope of the unthankful shall melt away
19 20 neither did they melt that good food
20 good food, which was apt to melt as ice
Eccu 3 17 thy sins shall melt away as the ice
28 29 melt down thy gold and silver and make
Isa 13 7 and every heart of man shall melt and
19 1 the heart of Egypt shall melt in the
64 1 the mountains would melt away at thy
2 they would melt as at the burning of
Jer 9 7 behold I will melt, and try them: for
Eze 21 7 it cometh, and every heart shall melt
22 20 I may kindle a fire in it to melt it
20 take my rest, and I will melt you down
Amos 9 5 toucheth the earth, and it shall melt
2 P 3 12 elements shall melt with the burning
melted Exod 16 21 after the sun grew hot, it m.
Josu 7 5 struck with fear and m. like water
Judg 5 5 the mountains melted before the face of
2 K 22 46 the strangers are m. away and shall
Job 6 17 they shall be m. out of their place
28 1 gold hath a place wherein it is melted
2 stone melted with heat is turned into
Ps 74 4 earth is melted, and all that dwell
96 5 the mountains melted like wax, at the
Cant 5 6 my soul melted when he spoke: I sought
Wisd 16 22 endured the force of fire and m. not
27 little sunbeam, presently melted away
Isa 34 3 mountains shall be m. with their blood
64 3 at thy presence the mountains m. away
Jer 6 29 fire, the founder hath melted in vain
Eze 22 21 you shall be m. in the midst thereof
22 as silver is melted in the midst of
24 11 and the brass thereof may be melted
11 let the filth of it be melted in the
Mich 1 4 the mountains shall be melted under
Nah 1 6 fire; and the rock are melted by him
Haba 3 6 he beheld, and melted the nations: and
2 P 3 10 the elements shall be melted with heat
melteth Ps 57 9 like wax that m. they shall be
Ps 67 3 as wax melteth before the fire, so let
Nah 2 10 heart melteth, and the knees fail
Meltias 2 Es 3 7 next to them built Meltias the
melting Ps 21 15 like wax m. in the midst of my
mem Ps 118 97 mem. Lam 1:13; 2:13; 3:37, 38, 39; 4:13
member 1 C 12 14 the body is not one m., but many
1 C 12 19 if they all were one member, where would
26 and if one member suffer anything, all
26 if one member glory, all the members
27 body of Christ, and members of member
James 3 5 the tongue is indeed a little member
members Lev 9 13 to him the head and all the m.
Job 41 14 m. of his flesh cleave one to another
Mat 5 29 that one of thy m. should perish. 30
Rom 6 13 your m. as instruments of iniquity
13 your members as instruments of justice
19 yielded your m. to serve uncleanness
19 now yield your members to serve justice
7 5 did work in our m., to bring forth fruit
23 but I see another law in my members
23 the law of sin, that is in my members
12 4 as in one body we have many members, but
4 but all members have not the same office
5 and every one members one of another
1 C 6 15 your bodies are members of Christ? shall
15 shall I then take members of Christ, and
15 make them the members of an harlot? God
19 your m. are the temple of the Holy Ghost
12 12 as body is one, and hath many members
12 all the members of the body, whereas
18 God hath set the members every one of
20 now there are many members indeed, yet
22 to be the more feeble members of body
23 less honorable m. of the body, about
25 the members might be mutually careful
26 all the members suffer with it; or if
26 glory, all the members rejoice with it
27 body of Christ, and members of member
Eph 4 25 for we are members one of another. Be
5 30 we are members of his body, of his flesh
Col 3 5 your members which are upon the earth
James 3 6 the tongue is placed among our members
4 1 which war in your members? You covet
Memmius 2 Ma 11 34 Quintus M. and Titus Manilius,
memoirs 2 Ma 2 13 m. and commentaries of Nehemias
memorial Exod 3 15 is my m. unto all generations
Exod 12 14 this day shall be for a memorial to
13 9 and as a memorial before thy eyes
17 14 write this for a memorial in a book
28 12 a memorial for the children of Israel
29 a memorial before the Lord forever
30 16 that it may be a memorial of them
39 7 a m. of children of Israel. Num 31:54
Lev 2 2 shall put it a memorial upon the altar
9 he shall take a memorial out of the
16 shall burn for a memorial of the gift
5 12 shall burn it . . . for a memorial. 6:15
23 24 you shall keep a sabbath, a memorial
24 7 for a memorial of the oblation of the
Num 16 38 may see them for a sign and a memorial
Ps 101 13 and thy memorial to all generations
134 13 thy memorial . . . unto all generations
Wisd 10 8 left also unto men a m. of their folly
Eccu 35 9 will not forget the memorial thereof
38 11 give . . . a memorial of fine flour
44 9 some, of whom there is no memorial
45 11 for a m. to the children of his people
13 with precious stones . . . for a memorial
20 for a memorial to make reconciliation
Bar 4 5 people of God, the memorial of Israel
Osee 12 5 God of hosts, the Lord is his memorial
14 8 his memorial shall be as the wine
Zach 6 14 a memorial in the temple of the Lord
1 Ma 8 22 for a m. of the peace and alliance
14 23 be a m. to the people of the Spartans
Mark 14 9 shall be told for a memorial of her
Acts 10 4 for a memorial in the sight of God
memory Exod 17 14 I will destroy the m. of Amalec
Exod 20 24 where the memory of my name shall be
Deut 32 26 I will make the m. of them to cease
Esth 12 4 committed m. of the thing to writing
Job 8 8 search diligently into m. of the fathers
18 17 let the memory of him perish from the
Ps 9 7 their memory hath perished with a noise
29 5 give praise to the m. of his holiness
108 15 let the memory of them perish from
144 7 they shall publish the memory of the
Prov 10 7 the memory of the just is with praise
Ecce 9 5 for the memory of them is forgotten
Wisd 4 1 for the memory thereof is immortal
19 sorrow, and their memory shall perish
8 13 shall leave behind me an everlasting m.
Eccu 10 20 hath made the memory of them to cease
21 hath abolished the memory of the proud
21 preserved the memory of . . . them that
23 36 she shall leave her memory to be cursed
24 28 my m. is unto everlasting generations
29 13 the memory of him shall not depart
45 1 whose memory is in benediction. He
46 14 that their memory might be blessed
49 1 the memory of Josias is like the
Isa 26 14 and hast destroyed all their memory
1 Ma 3 7 works, and his m. is blessed forever
35 take away the m. of them from. 12:54
13 29 upon the pillars arms for a perpetual m.
2 Ma 2 26 they may more easily commit to memory

6 31 the memory of his death for an example
Mat 26 13 shall be told for a memory of her
Acts 20 31 watch, keeping in memory, that for three
2 P 1 15 you may keep a memory of these things
Memphis Isa 19 13 princes of M. are gone astray
Jer 2 16 children also of Memphis and of Taphnes
44 1 in Magdal and in Taphnis and in M.
46 14 and let it be known in Memphis and in
19 Memphis shall be made desolate and
Eze 30 13 will make an end of the idols of M.
16 in M. there shall be daily distresses
Osee 9 6 Memphis shall bury them: nettles shall
mend 4 K 22 6 and to such as mend breaches
2 Pa 34 10 the temple and mend all that was weak
mended 1 K 13 21 the goad, which was to be mended
mending Mat 4 21 mending their nets, and he called them
Mark 1 19 were mending their nets in the ship
Menelaus 2 Ma 4 23 Jason sent M., brother of the
2 Ma 4 27 so Menelaus got the principality: but
29 and M. was removed from the priesthood
32 then M. supposing that he had found a
34 M. coming to Andronicus, desired him
39 sacrileges . . . by the counsel of M.
43 an accusation was laid against M.
45 M. being convicted, promised Ptolemee
47 M. who was guilty of all the evil
50 M. continued in authority, increasing
5 5 M. fled into the castle. But Jason
15 Menelaus, that traitor to the laws and
23 in Gazarim, Andronicus and Menelaus
11 29 Menelaus came to us, saying that you
32 we have sent also M. to speak to you
13 3 M. also joined himself with them: and
7 Menelaus the transgressor of the law
Menna Luke 3 31 Melea, who was of Menna, who was of
Menni Jer 51 27 against her the kings of . . . M.
Mennith Judg 11 33 from Aroer till you come to M.
men's Gen 16 12 all men's hands against him
Exod 22 5 to feed upon that which is other men's
Deut 4 28 gods that were framed with men's hands
3 K 13 2 he shall burn men's bones upon thee
4 K 19 18 the works of m. hands. Ps 134:15; Isa 37:19; Bar 6:50, 51
23 20 altars: and he burnt m. bones upon them
Jdth 10 4 so that she appeared to all men's eyes
Esth 9 4 spread abroad through all men's mouths
16 5 as to be worthy of all men's praise
Wisd 2 15 his life is not like other men's, and
12 5 own children, and eaters of m. bowels
Eccu 21 9 buildeth his house at other m. charges
Eze 12 6 be carried out upon men's shoulders
7 and was carried on men's shoulders
Haba 2 8 shall spoil thee: because of m. blood
1 Ma 15 33 we have neither taken other men's land
33 do we hold that which is other men's
Mat 23 4 and lay them on men's shoulders; but
27 within are full of dead men's bones
Acts 17 25 he served with m. hands, as though he
2 C 10 15 beyond measure in other men's labors
Phil 2 4 his own, but those that are other men's
1 Tim 5 22 neither be partaker of other men's sins
24 some men's sins are manifest, going
1 P 4 15 or a coveter of other men's things
menservants Gen 12 16 he [Abram] had . . . m. and
Gen 24 35 he hath given him . . . menservants and
30 43 he [Jacob] had many . . . menservants
32 5 I have oxen and asses and sheep and m.
Deut 12 12 there shall you feast . . . your m. and
4 K 5 26 vineyards and sheep and oxen and m.
1 Es 2 65 besides their menservants. 2 Es 7:67
Tob 10 10 half of all his substance in m. and
Ecce 2 7 I got me m. and maidservants, and had
Jer 34 11 them into subjection as menservants
Luke 12 45 shall begin to strike the menservants
menstealers 1 Tim 1 10 for m., for liars, for
menstruous Isa 30 22 the uncleanness of a m. woman. Eze 36:17
Isa 64 6 justices as the rag of a m. woman
Lam 1 17 Jerusalem is as a m. woman among them
Bar 6 28 and m. women touch their sacrifices
Eze 18 6 nor come near to a menstruous woman
22 10 the uncleanness of the m. woman in
mention Eccu 49 11 he made mention of the enemies
Isa 48 1 and make mention of the God of Israel
Jer 20 9 I will not make m. of him nor speak
Amos 6 11 and mention not the name of the Lord
1 Ma 12 8 was m. made of the alliance and amity
Heb 11 22 dying, made mention of the going out of
mentioned 1 K 17 12 that Ephrathite . . . before m.
2 Pa 28 15 the men, whom we mentioned above, rose
34 22 they spoke to her the words above m.
Job 28 18 shall not be m. in comparison of it
Jer 2 34 but in all places which I m. before
23 36 burden of Lord shall be m. no more
Mephaath Josu 13 18 and Cedimoth and Mephaath and
Josu 21 36 Jethson and Mephaath, four cities
1 Pa 6 79 out of the tribe of Ruben . . . Mephaath
Jer 48 21 and judgment is come . . . upon Mephaath
Meraioth 1 Pa 6 52 Zarahia his son, M. his son
2 Es 11 11 son of Sadoc, the son of Meraioth
Merala Josu 19 11 it went up from sea and from M.
Merari Gen 46 11 sons of Levi . . . Merari. Exod 6:16; Num 3:17; 26:57; 1 Pa 6:1, 16; 23:6
Num 3 33 of Merari are the families of the
Josu 21 34 to the children of Merari, Levites of
38 all the cities of the children of M.
1 Pa 6 47 the son of Merari, the son of Levi
24 27 the son also of Merari: Oziau, and
Jdth 8 1 who was the daughter of Merari, the
16 8 to him, but Judith the daughter of M.
sons of Merari Exod 6 19 sons of Merari: Moholi and Musi. Num 3:20; 1 Pa 6:19; 23:21; 24:26
Num 4 29 shalt reckon up the sons of Merari
42 the sons of Merari also were numbered
45 this is the number of the sons of M.
7 8 and eight oxen he gave to sons of M.
10 17 the sons of Gerson and M. set forward
Josu 21 7 to the sons of Merari by their kindreds
1 Pa 6 29 the sons of Merari, Moholi: Lobni
44 and the sons of Merari their brethren
63 the sons of Merari . . . twelve cities
77 to the sons of Merari that remained
9 14 son of Hasebia of the sons of Merari
15 6 of the sons of Merari, Asaia the
17 of the sons of Merari, their brethren
26 10 of Hosa, that is, of the sons of Merari
19 of the sons of Core and of Merari
2 Pa 29 12 of the sons of Merari, Cis the son of
34 12 Jahath and Abdias of sons of Merari
1 Es 8 19 with him Isaias of the sons of Merari
Merarites Num 4 33 the family of the M. 26:57
merchandise Prov 3 14 better than the m. of silver
Isa 23 18 her m. and her hire shall be sanctified
18 her m. shall be for them that shall
45 14 labor of Egypt and the m. of Ethiopia
Eze 26 12 they shall make a spoil of thy m.: and
27 24 they had cedars also in thy merchandise
25 of the sea were thy chief in thy m.
33 by thy m. that went from thee by sea
28 16 by the multitude of thy m., thy inner
Mat 22 5 to his farm, and another to his m.
2 P 2 3 with feigned words make m. of you
Apoc 18 11 for no man shall buy their m. any more
12 m. of gold and silver and precious
merchandises Nah 3 16 hast multiplied thy m.
merchant Eccu 26 28 a m. is hardly free from

Eccu 37 12 nor with a merchant about traffic, nor
Eze 27 16 the Syrian was thy merchant: by reason
Zach 14 21 the m. shall be no more in the house
Mat 13 45 is like to a m. seeking good pearls
merchant's Prov 31 14 she is like the m. ship, she
merchants Gen 37 28 when the Madianite m. passed
3 K 10 15 that were over the tributes, and the m.
28 the king's merchants brought them out
2 Pa 1 16 Egypt and from Coa by the king's m.
9 14 the merchants were accustomed to bring
2 Es 3 31 the goldsmiths and the merchants built
13 20 the m. and they that sold all kinds
Job 28 8 children of the m. have not trodden it
40 25 in pieces, shall merchants divide him
Eccu 42 5 of the corruption of buying, and of m.
Isa 23 2 the m. of Sidon passing over the sea
8 Tyre . . . whose merchants were princes
47 15 thy merchants from thy youth, every
Bar 3 23 the m. of Merrha and of Theman and the
17 4 and he set it in a city of merchants
27 12 the Carthaginians thy m. supplied thy
13 and Mosoch, they were thy merchants
15 the men of Dedan were thy m. 20
17 were thy merchants with the best corn
18 the men of Damascus were thy merchants
21 they were the merchants of thy hand
21 thy merchants came to thee with lambs
22 Saba and Reema, they were thy m.
23 Chene and Eden were thy merchants
24 they were thy m. in divers manners
36 the m. of people have hissed at thee
Eze 38 13 Saba and Dedan and the m. of Tharsis
1 Ma 3 41 the m. of the countries heard the fame
2 Ma 8 34 brought 1,000 m. to sale of the Jews
Apoc 18 3 m. of the earth have been made rich by
11 the merchants of the earth shall weep
15 the m. of these things, who were made
23 thy m. were the great men of the earth
mercies Gen 32 10 of the least of all thy m.
2 K 24 14 for his mercies are many. 1 Pa 21:13
2 Pa 6 42 remember the m. of David thy servant
32 32 the acts of Ezechias and of his mercies
35 26 the acts of Josias and of his mercies
2 Es 9 19 in thy mercies, didst not leave them
27 multitude of thy tender mercies. 13:22; Ps 50:3; 68:17; Dan 9:18
28 deliveredst them many times in thy m.
Ps 16 7 show forth thy wonderful mercies: thou
24 6 thy mercies that are from the beginning
39 12 withhold not . . . thy tender mercies
76 10 will he in his anger shut up his m.
78 8 let thy mercies speedily prevent us
88 2 the mercies of the Lord I will sing
50 Lord, where are thy ancient mercies
102 6 the Lord doth mercies and judgment for
105 7 remembered not the multitude of thy m.
45 multitude of his m. Isa 63:7; Lam 3:32
46 and he gave them unto mercies in the
106 8 let m. of Lord give glory. 15, 21, 31
43 will understand the m. of the Lord
118 77 let thy tender mercies come unto me
156 many, O Lord, are thy mercies: quicken
144 9 his tender m. are over all his works
Eccu 17 27 praise God and shalt glory in his m.
36 1 and show us the light of thy mercies
Isa 54 7 with great mercies will I gather thee
55 3 with you, the faithful mercies of David
63 7 I will remember the tender mercies of
15 multitude of thy bowels, and of thy m.
Jer 42 12 I will show m. to you and will take
Lam 3 22 m. of the Lord that we are not consumed
Dan 3 42 according to the multitude of thy m.
Zach 1 16 I will return to Jerusalem in mercies

2 C 1 3 Father of m., and God of all comfort
merciful Exod 30 16 he may be m. to their souls
Exod 33 19 I will be m. to whom it shall please
34 6 Lord God, m. and gracious patient and
Lev 4 20 the Lord will be merciful unto them
23 28 the Lord your God may be m. unto you
Num 14 19 as thou hast been merciful to them from
30 13 and the Lord will be merciful to hear
Deut 4 31 Lord thy God is a merciful God: he
6 25 he will be merciful to us if we keep
21 8 be merciful to thy people Israel, whom
32 43 he will be m. to the land of his people
1 K 24 7 the Lord be merciful unto me. 26:11; 2 K 23:17; 3 K 21:3
2 K 24 25 the Lord became merciful to the land
3 K 20 31 kings of the house of Israel are m.
2 Pa 30 9 the Lord your God is merciful, and will
20 the Lord heard him and was merciful
2 Es 9 17 a forgiving God, gracious and merciful
31 thou art a merciful and gracious God
Job 33 24 found wherein I may be merciful to him
Ps 40 5 O Lord, be thou merciful to me: heal
77 38 he is m. and will forgive their sins
85 15 God of compassion, and m., patient
98 8 thou wast a merciful God to them, and
102 8 is compassionate and merciful. Eccu 2:13
110 4 being a merciful and gracious Lord
111 4 he is m. and compassionate and just
114 5 the Lord is merciful and just, and our
129 4 with thee there is m. forgiveness: and
144 8 is gracious and merciful. Joel 2:13
Prov 11 17 a m. man doth good to his own soul
13 13 the just are merciful and show mercy
19 22 a needy man is merciful: and better is
20 6 many men are called merciful: but who
Eccu 4 10 in judging be m. to the fatherless as
12 4 give to the merciful and uphold not
23 16 from the m. all these things shall be
48 22 called upon the Lord who is merciful
Isa 49 10 he that is m. to them shall be their
Jer 5 1 faith: and I will be merciful unto it
7 how can I be merciful to thee? Thy
50 20 I will be merciful to them whom I
Bar 3 2 mercy, for thou art a merciful God
Amos 7 2 O Lord God, be merciful, I beseech
Jon 4 2 that thou art a gracious and m. God
1 Ma 2 21 God be m. to us: it is not profitable
2 Ma 1 24 dreadful and strong, just and merciful
7 37 calling upon God to be speedily m. to
8 29 besought the m. Lord to be reconciled
10 26 besought him to be merciful to them
11 9 they all together blessed the m. Lord
Mat 5 7 blessed are the merciful: for they shall
Luke 6 36 be ye therefore merciful, as your Father also is merciful
18 13 O God, be merciful to me a sinner
Eph 4 32 merciful, forgiving one another, even
Heb 2 17 he might become a m. and faithful high
8 12 I will be merciful to their iniquities
James 5 11 that the Lord is m. and compassionate
1 P 3 8 m., modest, humble: not rendering evil
mercifully Ruth 1 8 the Lord deal m. with you
1 K 20 8 deal mercifully then with thy servant
merciless Wisd 12 5 m. murderers of their own
Mercury Prov 26 8 stone into the heap of Mercury
Acts 14 11 Barnabas, Jupiter: but Paul, Mercury
mercy Gen 24 49 if you do according to mercy and
Gen 39 21 Lord . . . having mercy upon him [Joseph]
Exod 20 6 showing mercy unto thousands to them
33 19 I will have mercy on whom I will, and
34 7 who keepest mercy unto thousands: who
Lev 19 22 he shall have mercy on him, and the
Num 6 25 show his face to thee, and have mercy

	14	18	the Lord is patient and full of mercy
Deut	5	10	showing mercy unto many thousands, to
	7	9	mercy to them that love him and to
		12	the mercy which he swore to thy fathers
	8	16	at the last he had mercy on thee lest
	13	17	may have mercy on thee and multiply
	30	3	will have mercy on thee and gather thee
	32	36	will have mercy on his servants: he shall
Josu	2	12	as I have shown mercy to you, so you also
Judg	2	18	in their days he was moved to mercy
2 K	2	5	have shown this mercy to your master
		6	the Lord surely will render you mercy
	3	8	who have shown mercy to house of Saul
	7	15	my mercy I will not take away from him
	21	14	God showed mercy again to the land
	22	51	showing mercy to David his anointed
3 K	3	6	hast shown great mercy to thy servant
	8	23	who keepest covenant and mercy. 2 Pa 6:14; 2 Es 1:5; 9:32
		50	give them mercy before them that have
4 K	13	23	and the Lord had mercy on them, and
1 Pa	17	13	I will not take my mercy away from him
	28	11	and of the house for the mercy seat
2 Pa	30	9	brethren and children shall find mercy
1 Es	9	9	but hath extended mercy upon us before
2 Es	1	11	and give him mercy before this man
Tob	3	2	and all thy ways mercy and truth and
	8	10	Sara also said: Have mercy on us, O
	12	9	to find mercy and life everlasting
Jdth	7	20	have thou mercy on us because thou art
		23	let us wait these five days for mercy
	8	12	not a word that may draw down mercy
		13	set a time for mercy of the Lord
	10	12	that they might find mercy in your sight
Esth	10	12	and had mercy on his inheritance
	13	15	have mercy on thy people. Eccu 36:14
Job	6	14	that taketh away mercy from his friend
	10	12	thou hast granted me life and mercy
	24	20	let mercy forget him: may worms be
	31	18	from my infancy mercy grew up with me
	33	24	he shall have mercy on him and shall
Ps	4	2	have mercy on me. 6:3; 9:14; 24:16; 25:11; 26:7; 30:10; 40:11; 50:3; 55:2; 56:2; 85:3, 16; 118:29, 58, 132
	17	51	showing mercy to David his anointed
	20	8	through the mercy of the most High
	23	5	Lord, and mercy from God his Savior
	24	10	ways of the Lord are mercy and truth
	29	11	hath heard and hath had mercy on me
	31	10	mercy shall encompass him that hopeth
	32	5	he loveth mercy and judgment; the earth
		5	earth is full of mercy of the Lord
	36	21	the just showeth mercy and shall give
		26	he showeth mercy, and lendeth all the
	58	6	no mercy on all them that work iniquity
		18	art God my defence: my God my mercy
	59	3	been angry and hast had mercy on us
	61	13	and mercy [belongeth] to thee, O Lord
	66	2	may God have mercy on us and bless
		2	upon us, may he have mercy on us
	83	12	God loveth mercy and truth: the Lord
	84	11	mercy and truth have met each other
	85	5	plenteous in mercy to all that call
		15	a God . . . of much mercy, and true
	88	3	mercy shall be built up forever in the
		15	mercy and truth shall go before thy
		25	truth and my mercy shall be with him
		29	I will keep my mercy for him forever
		34	my mercy I will not take away from him
	91	11	and my old age in plentiful mercy
	100	1	mercy and judgment I will sing to thee
	101	14	shalt arise and have mercy on Sion
		14	for it is time to have mercy on it
	102	4	who crowneth thee with mercy and
		8	longsuffering and plenteous in mercy
	111	5	acceptable is man that showeth mercy
	114	5	and just, and our God showeth mercy
	122	2	our God, until he have mercy on us
		3	have mercy on us, O Lord, have mercy
	129	7	because with the Lord there is mercy
	140	5	the just man shall correct me in mercy
	143	2	my mercy and my refuge: my support
	144	8	patient and plenteous in mercy. The
Prov	3	3	let not mercy and truth leave thee
	14	21	he that showeth mercy to the poor
		21	believeth in the Lord, loveth mercy
		22	mercy and truth prepare good things
	15	27	by mercy and faith sins are purged away
	16	6	by mercy and truth iniquity is redeemed
	19	17	he that hath mercy on the poor, lendeth
	20	28	mercy and truth preserve the king and
	21	3	to do mercy and judgment, pleaseth
		21	followeth justice and mercy, shall find
	22	9	that is inclined to mercy shall be
	27	4	anger hath no mercy, nor fury when
	28	13	and forsake them, shall obtain mercy
Wisd	6	7	to him that is little, mercy is granted
	9	1	God of my fathers, and Lord of mercy
	11	10	were tried and chastised with mercy
		24	thou hast mercy upon all, because
	15	1	patient and ordering all things in mercy
	19	1	came upon them wrath without mercy
Eccu	2	9	and mercy shall come to you for your
	4	11	he will have mercy on thee more than
	5	6	say not: The mercy of the Lord is great
		6	will have mercy on multitude of my sins
		7	mercy and wrath quickly come from him
	12	3	sinners, and hath mercy on the penitent
	16	12	for mercy and wrath are with him. He
		14	patience of him that showeth mercy
		15	all mercy shall make a place for every
	17	28	how great is the mercy of the Lord
	18	13	he hath mercy and teacheth and
		14	he hath mercy on him that receiveth the discipline of mercy
		20	shalt find mercy in the sight of God
	28	4	he hath no mercy on a man like himself
	29	1	he that showeth mercy, lendeth to his
	35	4	he that doth mercy, offereth sacrifice
	36	1	have mercy upon us, O God of all, and
		15	have mercy on Jerusalem, the city which
	40	17	and mercy remaineth forever. The life
		24	mercy shall deliver more than they
	44	10	these were men of mercy, whose godly
		27	he preserved for him men of mercy
	46	9	days of Moses he did a work of mercy
	51	4	the multitude of the mercy of thy name
Isa	9	17	neither shall he have mercy on their
	14	1	the Lord will have mercy on Jacob
	16	5	a throne shall be prepared in mercy
	27	11	made it, shall not have mercy on it
	30	18	waiteth that he may have mercy on you
	33	2	have mercy on us: for we have waited
	44	23	for the Lord hath shown mercy: shout
	47	6	thou hast shown no mercy to them: upon
	49	13	and will have mercy on his poor ones
	54	8	kindness have I had mercy on thee, said
		10	my mercy shall not depart from thee
		10	said the Lord that hath mercy on thee
	55	7	Lord, and he will have mercy on him
	57	1	men of mercy are taken away, because
	60	10	in my reconciliation have I had mercy
Jer	6	23	they are cruel and will have no mercy
	9	24	I am the Lord that exercise mercy
	12	15	I will return and have mercy on them
	13	14	will not pardon; nor will I have mercy

16 5 Lord, my mercy and commiserations
31 9 I will bring them back in mercy: and I
32 18 thou showest mercy unto thousands
33 26 captivity and will have mercy on them
Lam 3 32 hath cast off, he will also have mercy
Bar 2 19 and beg mercy in thy sight, O Lord
27 to all that great mercy of thine
3 2 hear, O Lord, and have mercy, for thou
4 22 because of the mercy which shall come
5 9 will bring Israel . . . with mercy and
Eze 39 25 will have mercy on all the house of
Dan 1 9 God gave to Daniel grace and mercy
2 18 should ask mercy at the face of the God
9 4 and mercy to them that love thee and
9 to thee . . . mercy and forgiveness
Osee 1 6 call her name, Without mercy: for I will
6 I will not add any more to have mercy
7 I will have mercy on the house of Juda
8 weaned her that was called Without mercy
2 1 to your sister: Thou hast obtained mercy
4 I will not have mercy on her children
19 I will espouse thee to me . . . in mercy
23 I will have m. on her that was without m.
4 1 and there is no mercy . . . in the land
6 4 your mercy is as a morning cloud and
6 I desired mercy, and not sacrifice
10 12 reap in the mouth of mercy, break up
12 6 keep mercy and judgment, and hope
14 4 thou wilt have mercy on the fatherless
Joel 2 13 he is . . . patient and rich in mercy
Amos 5 15 may have mercy on the remnant of Joseph
Jon 2 9 vanities, forsake their own mercy
3 10 God had mercy with regard to the evil
Mich 6 8 to do judgment and to love mercy and
7 18 more, because he delighteth in mercy
19 will turn again and have mercy on us
20 wilt perform . . . the mercy to Abraham
Haba 3 2 art angry, thou wilt remember mercy
Zach 1 12 how long wilt thou not have mercy
8 15 I had no mercy: so turning again I
10 6 because I will have mercy on them
Mala 1 9 of God, that he may have mercy on you
1 Ma 3 44 that they might pray and ask mercy and
4 10 the Lord will have mercy on us and
2 Ma 2 7 till God . . . receive them to mercy
18 will shortly have mercy upon us and
23 with all clemency showing mercy to them
5 6 Jason slew his countrymen without mercy
7 29 that in that mercy I may receive thee
8 5 wrath of the Lord was turned into mercy
27 distilling the beginning of mercy upon
9 13 of whom he was not like to obtain mercy
11 10 the Lord who showed mercy to them
Mat 5 7 merciful: for they shall obtain mercy
9 13 I will have mercy and not sacrifice. 12:7
27 have mercy on us, O Son of David
15 22 have mercy on me, O Lord, thou son of
20 30 thou son of David, have mercy on us. 31
23 23 judgment and mercy and faith. These
Mark 5 19 for thee and hath had mercy on thee
10 47 son of David, have mercy on me. 48; Luke 18:38, 39
Luke 1 72 to perform mercy to our fathers and
7 13 being moved with mercy towards her
10 37 he said: He that showed mercy to him
16 24 said: Father Abraham, have mercy on me
17 13 Jesus, master, have mercy on us. Whom
Rom 1 31 without fidelity, without mercy. Who
9 15 I will have mercy on whom I will have m.
16 that runneth, but of God that showeth m.
18 he hath mercy on whom he will; and whom
23 his glory on the vessels of mercy, which
25 that had not obtained mercy, one that hath obtained mercy
11 30 have obtained m., through their unbelief
31 now have not believed, for your mercy
31 that they also may obtain mercy. For God
32 that he may have mercy on all. O the
12 8 he that showeth mercy, with cheerfulness
1 C 7 25 obtained mercy of Lord, to be faithful
2 C 4 1 according as we have obtained mercy, we
Gal 6 16 peace on them, and mercy, and upon the
Eph 2 4 but God, who is rich in mercy, for his
Phil 2 27 but God had mercy on him; and not only
Col 3 12 the bowels of mercy, benignity, humility
1 Tim 1 2 mercy and peace from God the Father. 2 Tim 1:2
16 for this cause have I obtained mercy
2 Tim 1 16 give mercy to the house of Onesiphorus
18 Lord grant unto him to find mercy of
Heb 4 16 we may obtain mercy, and find grace in
10 28 dieth without any mercy under two or
James 2 13 judgment without mercy to him that hath not done mercy
13 mercy exalteth itself above judgment
3 17 full of mercy and good fruits, without
1 P 1 3 who according to his great mercy hath
2 10 who had not obtained mercy; but now have obtained mercy
2 J 3 grace be with you, mercy and peace
Jude 2 mercy unto you, and peace and charity
21 waiting for the mercy of our Lord
23 on others have mercy, in fear, hating

his mercy Gen 24 27 hath not taken away his m.
1 Pa 16 34 his mercy endureth forever. 41; 2 Pa 5:13; 7:3, 6; 20:21; 1 Es 3:11, 41; Jdth 13:21; Ps 99:5; 105:1; 106:1; 117:1, 2, 3, 4, 29; 135 passim; Jer 33:11; Dan 3:89, 90; 1 Ma 4:24
Tob 12 6 because he hath shown his mercy to you
13 5 and he will save us for his own mercy
8 that he will show his mercy to you
Jdth 7 4 would show his mercy upon his people
8 17 so he would show his mercy to us
13 18 he hath fulfilled his mercy, which he
Job 37 13 or in what place soever of his mercy
Ps 30 22 he hath shown his wonderful mercy to me
32 18 and on them that hope in his mercy
41 9 the Lord hath commanded his mercy; and
56 4 God hath sent his mercy and his truth
58 11 my God, his mercy shall prevent me
60 8 his mercy and truth who shall search
65 20 not turned away . . . his mercy from me
76 9 or will he cut off his mercy forever
97 3 he hath remembered his mercy and his
102 11 strengthened his m. towards them that
116 2 his mercy is confirmed upon us: and
146 11 and in them that hope in his mercy
Wisd 4 15 of God, and his m. is with his saints
Eccu 2 7 that fear the Lord, wait for his mercy
23 greatness, so also is his m. with him
16 13 according as his mercy is, so his
18 4 who shall be able to declare his mercy
9 and poureth forth his mercy upon them
11 therefore hath he filled up his mercy
35 25 he shall delight the just with his m.
47 24 but God will not leave off his mercy
50 24 done with us according to his mercy
51 37 let your soul rejoice in his mercy and
Isa 63 9 in his mercy he redeemed them and he
1 Ma 2 57 David by his mercy obtained the throne
2 Ma 6 16 he never withdraweth his mercy from us
7 23 will restore to you again in his mercy
Luke 1 50 his mercy is from generation unto
54 servant, being mindful of his mercy

58 the Lord had showed his great mercy
Rom 15 9 Gentiles are to glorify God for his m.
Titus 3 5 have done, but according to his mercy
mercy of God 2 K 9 3 that I may show the m. . . .
Ps 51 10 have hoped in the mercy of God forever
102 17 but the mercy of God is from eternity
Eccu 18 12 but the mercy of God is upon all flesh
35 26 the mercy of God is beautiful in the
50 26 believe that the mercy of God is with
2 Ma 13 12 craved mercy of God with weeping and
Luke 1 78 through the bowels of the m. of our God
Rom 12 1 brethren, by the mercy of God, that you
1 Tim 1 13 I obtained the mercy of God, because
show mercy Deut 7 2 nor show mercy to them
Josu 2 12 so you also will show mercy to my
14 we will show thee mercy and truth
Judg 1 24 the city, and we will show thee mercy
8 35 neither did they show m. to the house
2 K 9 7 I will surely show thee mercy for
15 20 Lord will show thee mercy and truth
3 K 8 30 and when thou hearest, show them mercy
2 Pa 6 21 that is, from heaven, and show mercy
30 18 the Lord who is good will show mercy
Tob 3 13 thou hast been angry, wilt show mercy
Ps 76 10 will God forget to show mercy or will
108 15 because he remembered not to show m.
Prov 13 13 the just are merciful and show mercy
Eccu 29 11 delay not to show him mercy. Help the
36 25 likewise mitigate and show mercy: her
Jer 21 7 he shall . . . nor show mercy to them
Eze 7 9 neither will I show mercy. 8:18
Zach 7 9 judge true judgment and show ye m.
Rom 9 15 I will show mercy to whom I will show m.
thy mercy Gen 19 19 thou hast magnified thy m.
Exod 15 13 in thy mercy thou hast been a leader
Num 14 19 according to the greatness of thy mercy
3 K 3 6 thou hast kept thy great mercy for him
Tob 3 21 it shall be allowed to come to thy m.
8 18 thou hast shown thy mercy to us and
Jdth 9 17 to thee and presuming of thy mercy
Ps 5 8 in multitude of thy mercy, I will come
12 6 but I have trusted in thy mercy. My
22 6 thy mercy will follow me all the days
24 7 according to thy m. remember thou me
25 3 thy mercy is before my eyes: and I am
30 8 I will be glad and rejoice in thy mercy
17 thy servant: save me in thy mercy
32 22 let thy mercy, O Lord, be upon us
35 6 thy mercy is in heaven, and thy truth
8 how hast thou multiplied thy mercy
11 extend thy mercy to them that know thee
39 11 I have not concealed thy mercy within
12 thy m. and thy truth have always upheld
47 10 we have received thy mercy, O God, in
50 3 O God, according to thy great mercy
56 11 thy mercy is magnified even to the
58 17 and will extol thy mercy in the morning
62 4 thy mercy is better than lives: thee
68 14 in the multitude of thy mercy hear me
17 hear me, O Lord, for thy mercy is king
84 8 show us, O Lord, thy mercy; and grant
85 13 thy mercy is great towards me: and
87 12 any one in sepulcher declare thy m.
89 14 filled in the morning with thy mercy
91 3 to show forth thy mercy in the morning
93 18 moved: thy mercy, O Lord, assisted me
107 5 thy mercy is great above the heavens
108 21 sake: because thy mercy is sweet
26 save me according to thy mercy. And let
113 2 for thy mercy and for thy truth's sake
118 41 let thy mercy also come upon me
64 the earth, O Lord, is full of thy mercy
76 let thy mercy be for my comfort
124 with thy servant according to thy mercy
149 my voice, O Lord, according to thy m.
159 quicken me thou in thy mercy. The
137 2 for thy mercy and for thy truth: for
8 thy mercy, O Lord, endureth forever
142 8 cause me to hear thy mercy in the
12 in thy m. thou wilt destroy my enemies
Wisd 12 22 judged, we may hope for thy mercy
16 10 for thy mercy came and healed them
Eccu 51 11 I remembered thy mercy, O Lord, and
Dan 3 35 take not away thy mercy from us for
39 before thee, that we may find thy mercy
1 Ma 13 46 our evil deeds, but according to thy m.
mercy's Ps 6 5 save me for thy mercy's sake
mere Isa 59 4 but they trust in a mere nothing
1 Ma 13 6 to destroy us out of mere malice. And
Mered 1 Pa 4 17 sons of Esra, Jether and Mered
1 Pa 4 18 Bethia . . . whom Mered took to wife
Meremoth 1 Es 8 33 of our God by the hand of M.
Merezebel 2 Es 3 4 of Barachias the son of M.
Meribbaal 1 Pa 8 34 the son of Jonathan was M.: and
M. begot Micha. 9:40
Merimuth 2 Es 12 3 Sebenias, Rhaum, Merimuth, Addo
2 Es 10 5 Harem, Merimuth, Obdias, Daniel
3 21 after him Merimuth . . . built
merit Eccu 16 15 according to the m. of his works
Eccu 38 18 mourning for him according to his merit
Merob 1 K 18 17 behold my elder daughter Merob
1 K 18 19 when Merob the daughter of Saul should
Merodach Isa 39 1 Merodach Baladan . . . sent letters
Jer 50 2 is confounded, M. is overthrown
Merom Josu 11 5 the waters of Merom. 7
Merome Judg 5 18 to death in the region of M.
Meronathite 1 Pa 27 30 over the asses, Jadias a M.
2 Es 3 7 built . . . and Jadon the Meronathite
Meroz Judg 5 23 curse ye the land of Meroz
Merrha Bar 3 23 merchants of M. and of Theman
merry Gen 43 34 they drank and were m. with him
Deut 16 14 shalt make merry in thy festival time
Judg 16 23 great sacrifices . . . and to make merry
19 6 today, and let us make merry together
22 while they were making merry and
Ruth 3 7 had eaten and drunk and was merry
1 K 25 36 Nabal's heart was merry; for he was
Tob 7 17 afterwards they made merry, blessing
Jdth 12 12 with him and drink wine and be merry
17 drink now and sit down and be merry
20 and Holofernes was made merry on her
Ecce 8 15 but to eat and drink and be merry
Wisd 14 28 they are mad when they are merry
Jer 31 4 in the dances of them that make merry
Luke 15 23 and let us eat and make merry
24 is found. And they began to be merry
29 a kid to make merry with my friends
32 it was fit that we should make merry
Apoc 11 10 shall rejoice over them and make merry
merry-hearted Isa 24 7 all the m. have sighed
Mesa 4 K 3 4 Mesa, king of Moab, nourished
1 Pa 2 42 Mesa his firstborn, who was the father
Meselemia 1 Pa 26 1 of the Corites Meselemia
1 Pa 26 2 the sons of Meselemia. 9
Mesezebel 2 Es 11 24 Phathahia the son of M.
meshes Job 18 8 net, and walketh in its meshes
Mesizabel 2 Es 10 21 Mesizabel, Sadoc, Jeddua
Mesollam 1 Es 10 15 Mesollam and Sebethai, Levites
Mesopotamia Gen 24 10 went on to Mesopotamia
Gen 25 20 of Bathuel the Syrian of Mesopotamia
28 2 take a journey to Mesopotamia of Syria
5 he took his journey and went to M.
6 had sent him Jacob into M. of Syria
31 18 whatsoever he had gotten in Mesopotamia
33 18 after he returned from Mesopotamia. 35:9
35 26 that were born to him in Mesopotamia

46 15 whom she [Lia] bore in Mesopotamia
48 7 when I came out of M., Rachel died
Deut 23 4 hired against thee Balaam . . . from M.
Josu 24 3 Abraham from the borders of Mesopotamia
14 gods which your fathers served in M. 15
Judg 3 8 Chusan Rasathaim king of Mesopotamia
1 Pa 19 6 chariots and horsemen out of M.
Jdth 2 14 over the Euphrates and came into M.
3 1 the cities and provinces of Syria, M.
14 Sobal and all Apamea and all M.
5 7 they dwelt first in M. because they
Ps 59 2 when he set fire to M. of Syria and
Acts 2 9 inhabitants of Mesopotamia, Judea, and
7 2 father Abraham, when he was in M.
Mesphar 1 Es 2 2 who came with . . . Mesphar
2 Es 7 7 who came with . . . Mespharath
Mesphe Josu 18 26 Mesphe and Caphara and Amosa
Mesraim Gen 10 6 sons of Cham: Chus and Mesraim
Gen 10 13 Mesraim begot Ludim. 1 Pa 1:11
1 Pa 1 8 sons of Cham: Chus and Mesraim
mess Gen 43 34 the greater mess came to Benjamin
2 K 11 8 after him a mess of meat from the king
13 5 to make me a mess, that I may eat
7 brother Ammon, and make him a mess
10 bring the mess into the chamber, that
Heb 12 16 for one mess sold his first birthright
Mess Gen 10 23 the sons of Aram: . . . Mess
Messa Gen 10 30 their dwelling was from Messa
4 K 11 6 keep the watch of the house of Messa
message Gen 24 33 will not eat till I tell my m.
Gen 32 5 now I send a message to my lord, that I
50 16 they sent a message to him, saying
Judg 3 19 I have a secret message to thee
2 K 17 17 to carry the message to king David
4 K 19 7 shall hear a message and shall return. Isa 37:7
messages Esth 8 10 former letters with new m. And
Esth 8 14 posts went out carrying the messages
Messal Josu 19 26 and Amaad and Messal: and it
Messalemeth 4 K 21 19 name of his mother was M.
messenger 1 K 23 27 m. came to Saul, saying: Make
2 K 11 19 and he [Joab] charged the messenger
22 m. departed and came and told David
23 m. said to David: The men prevailed
25 David said to the messenger: Thus
15 13 there came a messenger to David, saying
18 20 shalt not be the messenger this day
26 king said: he also is a good messenger
3 K 19 2 Jezabel sent a messenger to Elias
22 13 m. that went to call Micheas. 2 Pa 18:12
4 K 5 10 and Eliseus sent a messenger to him
6 32 before that messenger came, he said
33 the m. appeared who was coming to him
9 18 m. came to them, but he returneth not
10 8 a messenger came and told him, saying
Tob 10 8 I will send a messenger to Tobias, thy
Job 1 14 there came a messenger to Job, and
Prov 13 17 messenger of the wicked shall fall
25 13 so is a faithful m. to him that sent
26 6 he that sendeth words by a foolish m.
Ecce 8 7 to come he cannot know by any messenger
Jer 51 31 m. shall meet m.: to tell the king
Eze 23 40 to whom they had sent a messenger
Agge 1 13 Aggeus the m. of the Lord . . . spoke
messengers Gen 32 6 the m. returned to Jacob
Num 24 12 did I not say to thy messengers, whom
Deut 1 28 the m. have terrified our hearts, saying
Josu 6 17 she hid the messengers whom we sent
25 because she hid the m. whom he had sent
22 11 certain m. had brought them an account
Judg 6 35 he sent m. into all Manasses, and
35 and other m. into Aser and Zabulon and
11 28 which he [Jephte] sent by the m.
1 K 11 3 that we may send m. to all the coasts
4 the m. therefore came to Gabaa of Saul
7 into all the coasts of Israel by m.
9 they said to the messengers that came
9 the messengers therefore came and told
19 16 when the m. were come in, they found
22 17 the king said to the m. that stood about
25 42 she followed the messengers of David
3 K 20 2 sending messengers to Achab king of
5 the m. came again and said: Thus
9 he answered the m. of Benadad: Tell my
10 messengers returning brought him word
4 K 1 3 go up to meet the m. of the king of
5 the messengers turned back to Ochozias
6 32 when the m. shall come, shut the door
7 15 messengers returned and told the king
19 14 letter of the hand of the messengers
2 Pa 20 2 there came m. and told Josaphat, saying
30 5 thus decreed to send m. to all Israel
36 15 sent to them by the hand of his m.
16 but they mocked the m. of God and
Esth 3 13 were sent by the king's m. to all
Prov 16 14 the wrath of a king is as m. of death
Isa 14 32 what shall be answered to the m. of the
30 4 and thy messengers came even to Hanes
37 14 letter from the hand of the messengers
44 26 perform the counsel of my messengers
Jer 27 3 by the hand of the m. that are come to
Eze 30 9 shall m. go forth from my face in ships
Mich 1 14 shall she send m. to the inheritance of
Nah 2 13 voice of thy m. shall be heard no more
Agge 1 13 as one of the m. of the Lord, spoke
1 Ma 1 46 sent letters by the hands of messengers
5 14 there came other m. out of Galilee with
Luke 7 24 when the m. of John were departed, he
James 2 25 receiving the m. and sending them out
sent messengers Gen 32 3 s. m. before him to
Num 20 14 Moses sent m. from Cades to the king
21 21 Israel sent messengers to Sehon king of
22 5 he sent therefore m. to Balaam the son
37 I sent m. to call thee, why didst thou
Deut 2 26 I sent m. from the wilderness of
Judg 6 35 he sent m. into all Manasses, and they
7 24 Gedeon sent m. into all mount Ephraim
9 31 sent m. privately to Abimelech, saying
11 12 he sent m. to the king of the children
17 he sent m. to the king of Edom, saying
19 so Israel sent m. to Sehon king of the
20 12 sent m. to all the tribe of Benjamin
21 13 sent m. to the children of Benjamin
1 K 6 21 and they sent m. to the inhabitants of
16 19 then Saul sent messengers to Isai
19 21 was told Saul, he sent other messengers
21 Saul sent messengers the third time
25 14 David sent m. out of the wilderness
2 K 2 5 David therefore sent m. to the men of
3 12 Abner therefore sent m. to David for
14 David sent m. to Isboseth the son of
26 sent m. after Abner and brought him
5 11 the king of Tyre sent m. to David
11 4 David sent messengers and took her
12 27 Joab sent messengers to David, saying
4 K 1 2 he [Ochozias] sent messengers, saying
16 thou hast sent m. to consult Beelzebub
14 8 then Amasias sent messengers to Joas
16 7 Achaz sent m. to Theglathphalasar king
17 4 had sent m. to Sua the king of Egypt
18 14 Ezechias king of Juda sent messengers
19 9 he sent m. to Ezechias, saying: Thus
1 Pa 14 1 Hiram king of Tyre sent m. to David
19 2 David sent messengers to comfort him
16 the Syrians . . . sent m. and brought to
2 Pa 25 18 he [Joas] sent back the messengers

35 21 he [Nechao] sent messengers to him
2 Es 6 3 I sent messengers to them, saying
Jdth 1 10 Nabuchodonosor . . . sent m. But they all
15 5 Ozias sent m. through all the cities
Isa 37 9 he sent messengers to Ezechias, saying
42 19 deaf, but he to whom I have sent my m.
57 9 thou hast sent thy messengers far off
Eze 23 16 and she sent m. to them into Chaldea
1 Ma 7 10 they sent messengers and spoke to Judas
13 14 he [Tryphon] sent messengers to him
21 were in the castle, sent m. to Tryphon
Luke 9 52 and he sent messengers before his face
messes Gen 43 34 taking the m. which they received
2 K 13 6 and make in my sight two little messes
8 it in his sight, she made little messes
10 and Thamar took the little messes which
Eccu 30 18 are as messes of meat set about a grave
Messias John 1 41 we have found the Messias, which
John 4 25 I know that the Messias cometh, who
Messulam 4 K 22 3 Assia the son of Messulam
met Gen 32 1 the angels of God met him [Jacob]
Gen 33 8 said: What are the droves that I met
Exod 4 24 Lord met him and would have killed him
5 20 they met Moses and Aaron, who stood
Num 23 4 when he was gone with speed, God met him
16 when the Lord had met him and had put
Deut 25 18 how he [Amalec] met thee: and slew the
Judg 11 34 his only daughter met him with timbrels
14 5 young lion met him raging and roaring
19 3 and had seen him, he met him with joy
20 2 all the tribes of Israel met together
1 K 10 10 behold a company of prophets met him
25 20 she met them. And David said: Truly in
2 K 2 13 and met them by the pool of Gabaon. And
18 9 that Absalom met the servants of David
19 25 when he met the king at Jerusalem, the
20 8 Amasa coming met them. And Joab had on
3 K 2 7 they met me when I fled from the face
18 7 as Abdias was in the way, Elias met
20 38 the prophet . . . met the king in the way
4 K 1 6 a man met us and said to us: Go and
7 what manner of man was he who met you
9 21 met him [Jehu] in the field of Naboth
10 13 he met with the brethren of Ochozias
2 Pa 19 2 Jehu . . . the seer met him and said to him
2 Es 13 2 because they met not the children of
Jdth 10 11 the watchmen of the Assyrians met her
Ps 2 2 princes met together against the Lord
84 11 mercy and truth have met each other
114 3 I met with trouble and sorrow: and
Prov 22 2 the rich and poor have met one another
29 13 and the creditor have met one another
Isa 64 5 thou hast met him that rejoiceth and
Jer 41 6 when he had met them, he said to them
1 Ma 4 29 and Judas met them with 10,000 men
5 16 great assembly met together to consider
25 the Nabutheans met them and received
10 58 Alexander met him, and he gave him
60 and he met there the two kings and he
74 Simon his brother met him to help
11 2 opened to him the cities and met him
15 met him with a strong power, and put
60 met him honorably out of the city
68 army of the strangers met him in the
12 25 met them in the land of Amath: for he
2 Ma 6 11 others that had met together in caves
14 30 when they met together as usual he
Mat 8 28 there met him two that were possessed
28 9 Jesus met them, saying: All hail. But
Mark 5 2 met him out of the monuments a man with
Luke 8 27 there met him a certain man who had a
9 37 there met him a great multitude. And
17 12 there met him ten men that were lepers
20 1 scribes with the ancients met together
John 4 51 going down, his servants met him; and
11 30 that place where Martha had met him
Acts 16 16 met us, who brought to her masters
20 14 when he had met with us at Assos, we
27 41 fallen into a place where two seas met
Heb 7 1 who met Abraham returning from the
10 his father, when Melchisedech met him
Metabeel 2 Es 6 10 Delaia the son of Metabeel
metal Exod 35 24 if any man had . . . m. of silver
Exod 38 11 were of same measure and work and metal
mete Ps 59 8 m. out the vale of tabernacles. 107:8
Mat 7 2 with what measure you mete, it shall
Mark 4 24 in what measure you shall mete, it
Luke 6 38 measure that you shall mete withal
Methca Num 33 28 pitched their tents in Methca
Num 33 29 removing from Methca, they camped
methought Gen 41 17 m. I stood upon the bank
Metri 1 K 10 21 lot fell upon the kindred of Metri
Meza Gen 36 13 sons of Rahuel . . . Meza. 17; 1 Pa 1:37
Mezaab Gen 36 39 Matred, daughter of Mezaab. 1 Pa 1:50
Miamin 1 Es 10 25 the sons of Pharos . . . Miamin
2 Es 10 7 Mosollam, Abia, Miamin, Maazia
12 5 Miamin, Madia, Belga, Semeia, and
17 of Miamin and Moadia, Phelti: of Belga
40 Miamin, Michea, Elioenai, Zacharia
Mibahar 1 Pa 11 38 Mibahar the son of Agarai
mice 1 K 5 6 came forth a multitude of mice
1 K 6 5 emerods and five golden mice: for the
5 and the likeness of the mice that
11 box that had in it the golden mice and
18 golden mice according to the number
Jdth 14 12 the mice, coming out of their holes
Micha 2 K 9 12 young son whose name was Micha
4 K 22 12 Achobor the son of Micha, and Saphan
1 Pa 5 5 Micha his son, Reia his son, Baal
8 34 Meribbaal begot Micha. 9:40
35 the sons of Micha were. 9:41
9 15 Micha the son of Zechri, the son of
23 20 sons of Oziel: Micha the first, Jesia
24 24 son of Oziel, M.: the son of M., Samir
25 the brother of Micha, Jesia: and the
2 Pa 34 20 Abdon the son of Micha, and Saphan
2 Es 10 11 Micha, Rohob, Hasebia, Zachur, Serebia
11 17 Mathania the son of Micha. 22
Jdth 6 11 Ozias the son of Micha, of the tribe of
Michael Num 13 14 Sthur the son of Michael. Of the
1 Pa 5 13 their brethren . . . were Michael and
14 Galaad the son of Michael, the son of
6 40 Samaa, the son of Michael, the son of
7 3 Izrahia, of whom were born Michael
8 16 and Michael and Jespha and Joha, the
12 20 there fled to him . . . Michael and
27 18 over Issachar, Amri the son of Michael
2 Pa 21 2 sons of Josaphat . . . Michael and
1 Es 8 8 Zebedia the son of Michael, and with
Dan 10 13 Michael, one of the chief princes
21 none is my helper . . . but M. your
12 1 at that time shall Michael rise up
Jude 9 when Michael the archangel, disputing
Apoc 12 7 Michael and his angels fought with the
Michaia 2 Pa 13 2 his mother's name was Michaia
2 Es 12 34 Mathania the son of Michaia, the son
Michas Judg 17 1 Michas, who said to his mother
Judg 17 4 good which was in the house of Michas
8 aside a little into the house of M.
10 M. said: Stay with me and be unto me
12 Michas filled his hand and had the
18 2 they went into the house of Michas and
4 Michas hath done such and such things
13 they were come to the house of Michas

15 Levite who was in the house of Michas
22 at a distance from the house of Michas
22 men that dwelt in the houses of Michas
23 and said to Michas: What aileth thee
26 Michas seeing that they were stronger
31 the idol of Michas remained with them
Michea 2 Es 12 40 Miamin, Michea . . . with trumpets
Micheas 3 K 22 8 M. the son of Jemla. 2 Pa 18:7, 8
3 K 22 9 make haste and bring hither Micheas
13 that went to call Micheas. 2 Pa 18:12
14 Micheas said to him: As the Lord liveth
15 M., shall we go to Ramoth. 2 Pa 18:14
24 Sedecias . . . struck Micheas. 2 Pa 18:23
25 Micheas said: Thou shalt see in the day
26 take Micheas and let him abide with
28 M. said: If thou return. 2 Pa 18:27
2 Pa 17 7 he sent of his princes . . . Micheas
18 13 M. answered him: As the Lord liveth
24 Micheas said: Thou thyself shalt see
25 take Micheas and carry him to Amon
Jer 26 18 Micheas of Morasthi was a prophet
36 11 Micheas . . . had heard out of the book
13 Micheas told them all the words that
Mich 1 1 word of the Lord that came to Micheas
Michol 1 K 14 49 and the name of the younger Michol
1 K 18 20 Michol the other daughter of Saul
27 Saul therefore gave him Michol his
28 Michol the daughter of Saul loved him
19 11 when Michol David's wife had told him
13 Michol took an image and laid it
17 Saul said to Michol: Why hast thou
17 Michol answered Saul: Because he said
25 44 but Saul gave Michol . . . to Phalti
2 K 3 13 not see my face before thou bring M.
14 David . . . saying: Restore my wife M.
6 16 Michol . . . looking out. 1 Pa 15:29
20 Michol . . . coming out to meet David
21 David said to Michol: Before the Lord
23 M. the daughter of Saul had no child
21 8 and the five sons of M. the daughter of
midday Deut 28 29 mayst thou grope at midday as
3 K 18 29 after midday was past, and while they
2 Es 8 3 gate, from the morning until midday
Cant 1 6 feedest, where thou liest in the midday
Isa 16 3 thy shadow as the night in the midday
Jer 6 4 arise, and let us go up at midday: woe
Amos 8 9 that the sun shall go down at midday
Acts 22 6 drawing nigh to Damascus at midday, that
26 13 at m., O king, I saw in the way a light
middle Gen 6 16 with lower, middle chambers
Exod 14 27 them up in the middle of the waves
39 21 in the upper part at the middle, and a
Num 8 4 gold, both the shaft in the middle and
Josu 12 2 of the middle part in the valley
Judg 9 37 people down from the m. of the land
2 K 3 27 took him aside to the m. of the gate
3 K 6 6 the middle floor was six cubits in
8 door for the m. side was on the right
8 they went up to the middle room and from the middle to the third
8 64 sanctified the m. of the court. 2 Pa 7:7
4 K 20 4 was gone out of the middle of the court
Jer 39 3 came in and sat in the middle gate
Eze 42 6 places, and out of the middle places
Eph 2 14 breaking down the m. wall of partition
midland 2 Ma 8 35 fleeing through the m. country
midnight Exod 11 4 at m. I will enter into Egypt
Exod 12 29 it came to pass at m. the Lord slew
Judg 7 19 at the beginning of the midnight watch
16 3 Samson slept till midnight, and then
Ruth 3 8 was now midnight, the man was afraid
Tob 2 9 in his house, and at m. buried them
Job 34 20 people shall be troubled at midnight
Ps 118 62 I rose at midnight to give praise to
Mat 25 6 and at midnight there was a cry made
Mark 13 35 at even or at m. or at the cockcrowing
Luke 11 5 a friend, and shall go to him at m.
Acts 16 25 at midnight, Paul and Silas praying
20 7 he continued his speech until midnight
27 27 we were sailing in Adria, about midnight
midway Tob 11 1 which is in the midway to Ninive
midwife Gen 35 17 midwife said to her [Rachel]
Gen 38 27 whereon the m. tied a scarlet thread
Exod 1 19 are skilful in the office of a midwife
midwives Exod 1 15 king of Egypt spoke to the m.
Exod 1 16 when you shall do the office of m.
17 but the midwives feared God and did not
20 therefore God dealt well with the m.
21 and because the midwives feared God
might Lev 25 43 afflict him not by might, but
Lev 25 46 oppress not your brethren . . . by might
Deut 8 17 my own might and the strength of my
21 14 her for money nor oppress her by might
2 K 6 14 and David danced with all his might
4 K 20 20 the acts of Ezechias and all his might
1 Pa 13 8 played before God with all their might
29 12 over all, in thy hand is power and m.
Job 24 22 pulled down the strong by his might
Ps 79 3 stir up thy might, and come to save us
88 14 thy arm is with might. Let thy hand
144 6 speak of the might of thy terrible acts
12 to make thy might known to the sons of
Isa 40 26 by the greatness of his m. and strength
29 force and might to them that are not
Jer 10 6 great is thy name in might. Who shall
16 19 O Lord, my might and my strength and
Dan 3 44 let them be confounded in all thy m.
Zach 4 6 not with an army nor by might, but by
Luke 1 51 he hath showed might in his arm: he
Rom 8 38 present, nor things to come, nor might
Eph 1 19 the operation of the might of his power
3 16 Spirit with might unto the inward man
6 10 in the Lord, and in the m. of his power
Col 1 11 strengthened with all might, according
James 2 6 do not the rich oppress you by might
mightier Gen 26 16 art become much m. than we
Num 14 12 nation, and mightier than this is
22 6 people, because it is mightier than I
2 Pa 11 23 he was wiser and mightier than all his
Wisd 10 12 and know that wisdom is m. than all
13 4 that made them is mightier than they
Eccu 8 15 lend not to a man that is mightier
13 12 if thou be invited by one that is m.
Jer 31 11 hand of one that was mightier than he
Dan 7 24 he shall be mightier than the former
Mat 3 11 shall come after me is mightier than I
Mark 1 7 cometh after me one mightier than I
Luke 3 16 there shall come one mightier than I
mighties 1 Pa 11 12 who was one of the three m.
mightily Job 30 22 and thou hast m. dashed me
Ps 59 14 through God we shall do m. 107:14
Wisd 6 7 the mighty shall be mightily tormented
8 1 she reacheth . . . from end to end m.
Acts 19 20 so m. grew the word of God, and was
27 18 we being m. tossed with the tempest
mighty Gen 10 8 he began to be mighty on the earth
Gen 18 18 shall become a great and mighty nation
Exod 15 10 they sunk as lead in the mighty waters
20 5 I am the Lord thy God, mighty, jealous
Lev 19 15 nor honor the countenance of the mighty
Deut 7 21 thy God . . . a God mighty and terrible
10 17 a great God and mighty and terrible
29 3 seen, those mighty signs and wonders
Josu 24 19 he is a holy God, and m. and jealous
1 K 2 4 the bow of the mighty is overcome and
3 K 11 28 Jeroboam was a valiant and mighty man

4 K 15 20 tax . . . on all that were mighty and rich
1 Pa 1 10 Nemrod: he began to be mighty upon earth
1 Es 7 28 and all the mighty princes of the king
2 Es 3 16 labor, and to the house of the mighty
9 11 the depth, as a stone into mighty waters
11 14 their brethren who were very mighty 128
14 their ruler Zabdiel son of the mighty
Jdth 5 20 and all the mighty ones in Hesebon and
11 6 that thou only art excellent and mighty
16 8 their m. ones did not fall by young men
Job 6 23 rescue me out of the hand of the mighty
9 4 he is wise in heart and m. in strength
36 5 God doth not cast away the mighty, whereas he himself also is mighty
19 and all the mighty of strength. Prolong
41 3 I will not spare him nor his m. words
Ps 23 8 the Lord who is strong and mighty: the Lord mighty in battle
49 3 a m. tempest shall be round about him
51 3 malice: thou that art mighty in iniquity
53 5 the mighty have sought after my soul
58 4 the mighty have rushed in upon me
71 12 shall deliver the poor from the mighty
77 65 like a m. man that hath been surfeited
85 14 assembly of the m. have sought my soul
88 9 thou art mighty, O Lord, and thy truth
20 I have laid help upon one that is mighty
102 20 angels: you that are mighty in strength
111 2 his seed shall be mighty upon earth
119 4 the sharp arrows of the mighty, with
126 4 as arrows in the hand of the mighty
134 10 many nations, and slew mighty kings
Prov 8 16 by me . . . the mighty decree justice
18 18 determineth even between the mighty
19 6 many honor the person of him that is m.
Wisd 5 24 a m. wind shall stand up against them
24 shall overthrow the thrones of the m.
6 7 the mighty shall be mightily tormented
9 punishment is ready for the more mighty
8 11 be admired in the sight of the mighty
17 18 the mighty noise of stones tumbling
18 5 them all together in a mighty water
Eccu 4 32 resist not against the face of the m.
5 3 say not: How mighty am I? And who
6 22 to them as a mighty stone of trial
10 27 the judge and the mighty is in honor
16 12 he is mighty to forgive and to pour
21 8 he that is mighty by a bold tongue
25 abashed at the person of the mighty
24 41 brook out of a river of a m. water
29 16 better than the shield of the mighty
47 6 to take away the mighty warrior and
Isa 5 22 woe to you that are mighty to drink
9 6 shall be called . . . God the Mighty
10 13 as a mighty man hath pulled down
21 shall be converted . . . to the mighty God
13 11 will bring down the arrogancy of the m.
25 3 city of mighty nations shall fear thee
4 blast of the m. is like a whirlwind
5 shalt make branch of the m. to wither
26 4 in the Lord God mighty forever. For
28 2 behold the Lord is mighty and strong
30 14 all to pieces with mighty breaking
34 7 bulls [shall go down] with the mighty
42 13 Lord shall go forth as a mighty man
43 16 and a path in the mighty waters
49 24 that which was taken by the mighty. 25
51 10 the water of the mighty deep, who
61 3 called . . . the mighty ones of justice
Jer 14 9 as a mighty man that cannot save
15 21 thee out of the hand of the mighty
50 9 arrows, like those of a mighty man
Bar 2 11 great power and with a mighty arm
6 35 nor save the weak from the mighty
Eze 7 24 will make the pride of the m. to cease
32 12 by swords of the m. I will overthrow
18 the daughters of the mighty nations
27 they were the terror of the mighty
38 15 a great company and a mighty army
39 18 you shall eat the flesh of the mighty
20 with horses and mighty horsemen and
Dan 2 10 any king, though great and mighty
3 100 his wonders, because they are mighty
4 19 art grown great and become mighty
8 24 he shall destroy the mighty and the
11 2 when he shall be grown mighty by his
Joel 1 15 come like destruction from the mighty
Amos 5 9 that bringeth . . . waste upon the mighty
24 water, and justice as a mighty torrent
Mich 4 7 hath been afflicted, a mighty nation
Soph 1 14 the mighty man shall there meet with
3 17 thy God in the midst of thee is mighty
Zach 9 13 will make thee as the sword of the mighty
11 2 fallen, for the mighty are laid waste
1 Ma 4 30 didst break the violence of the mighty
5 6 where he found a mighty power and
8 1 and that they are mighty in power
9 21 how is the mighty man fallen, that
2 Ma 15 5 I am mighty upon the earth, and I
Mat 14 2 mighty works show forth. Mark 6:14
Mark 6 2 m. works as are wrought by his hands
Luke 1 49 he that is m. hath done great things
52 he hath put down the mighty from their
9 44 astonished at the mighty power of God
10 13 m. works that have been wrought in
15 14 came a mighty famine in that country
19 37 for all the mighty works they had seen
24 19 mighty in work and word before God and
Acts 2 2 as of a mighty wind coming, and it
7 22 he was mighty in his words and in his
18 24 Apollo . . . one mighty in the scriptures
1 C 1 26 flesh, not many mighty, not many noble
2 C 10 4 not carnal, but mighty to God unto the
12 12 in signs, and wonders, and mighty deeds
13 3 you is not weak, but is mighty in you
1 Tim 6 15 who is the Blessed and only Mighty, the
Apoc 10 1 I saw another mighty angel come down
18 10 great city Babylon, that mighty city
21 and a mighty angel took up a stone

mighty hand Exod 3 19 let you go, but by a m. h.
Exod 6 1 by a mighty hand shall he let them go
Deut 3 24 hast begun to show . . . most mighty hand
32 27 our m. h. and not the Lord hath done
34 12 all the mighty hand and great miracles
Josu 4 25 learn the most mighty hand of the Lord
Judg 4 24 with a mighty hand overpowered Jabin
3 K 8 41 of thy great name and thy mighty hand
2 Es 1 10 thy great strength and by thy m. hand
Ps 135 12 with a mighty hand and with a stretched
1 P 5 6 under the mighty hand of God, that he

mighty men Gen 6 4 are the mighty men of old
2 K 23 17 these things did these three mighty men
Eccu 11 6 mighty men have been greatly brought
Lam 1 15 hath taken away all my mighty men
Eze 17 13 he shall take away the mighty men
Nah 2 3 shield of his mighty men is like fire
Zach 10 5 they shall be as mighty men, treading
1 Ma 3 38 mighty men of the king's friends. And
Apoc 19 18 tribunes and the flesh of mighty men

mighty one Gen 49 24 hands of the m. one of Jacob
Jdth 1 4 as a m. one in the force of his army
Eccu 46 8 he followed the mighty one. And in the
Isa 1 24 God of hosts, the mighty one of Israel
30 29 Lord, to the M. O. of Israel. And
49 26 Redeemer the M. One of Jacob. 60:16
Eze 31 11 hands of the m. one of the nations

2 Ma 15 3 if there were a mighty one in heaven
4 in heaven the m. one that commanded
most mighty Gen 33 20 invoked upon it m. m. God
Gen 46 3 I am the most mighty God of thy father
Num 16 22 O most mighty, the God of the spirits
Josu 22 22 Lord the most mighty God, he knoweth
2 K 22 18 delivered me from my most mighty enemy
Job 22 8 being the most mighty thou holdest it
Ps 44 4 upon thy thigh, O thou most mighty
Ecce 8 1 the most mighty will change his face
Eccu 24 34 raise up of him a most mighty king
Jer 32 18 O most mighty, great, and powerful
Eze 32 21 the most mighty among the strong
milch Gen 32 15 presents . . . thirty milch camels
mild Ps 24 9 will guide the mild in judgment
Ps 85 5 thou, O Lord, art sweet and mild
Prov 15 1 a mild answer breaketh wrath: but
2 Ma 6 29 had been a little before more mild
2 Tim 2 24 be mild towards all men, apt to teach
mildew 3 K 8 37 a famine arise . . . or m. 2 Pa 6:28
Joel 1 4 hath left, the mildew hath destroyed
2 25 mildew and the palmerworm have eaten
Amos 4 9 with a burning wind and with mildew
Agge 2 18 the works of your hand with the mildew
mildly Gen 45 4 he said m. to them: Come nearer
Gen 50 21 and spoke gently and mildly. And he
mildness 2 K 22 36 and thy m. hath multiplied me
Esth 15 11 changed the king's spirit into mildness
Ps 89 10 for mildness is come upon us: and we
Eccu 4 8 answer him peaceable words with m.
2 C 10 1 by the m. and modesty of Christ, who
Gal 5 23 the fruit of the Spirit is . . . mildness
Eph 4 2 with all humility and m., with patience
1 Tim 6 11 and pursue . . . patience, mildness. Fight
Titus 3 2 showing all mildness towards all men
mile Mat 5 41 will force thee one mile, go with him
Miletus Acts 20 15 and day following we came to M.
Acts 20 17 sending from M. to Ephesus, he called
2 Tim 4 20 and Trophimus I left sick at Miletus
Milicho 2 Es 12 14 of Milicho, Jonathan: of Sabenia
milk Gen 18 8 he took also butter and milk
Gen 49 12 wine, and his teeth whiter than milk
Exod 3 8 floweth with milk and honey. 17; 13:5; 33:3; Num 16:14; Deut 11:9; 31:20; Eccu 46:10
23 19 not boil a kid in the milk of his dam. 34:26; Deut 14:21
Lev 20 24 flowing with milk and honey. Num 13:28; 14:8; Deut 6:3; 26:9, 15; 27:3; Josu 5:6; Jer 11:5; 32:22; Bar 1:20; Eze 20:6, 15
Num 16 13 a land that flowed with milk and honey
Deut 32 14 milk of the sheep with fat of lambs
33 19 suck as milk the abundance of the sea
Judg 4 19 she opened a bottle of milk and gave
5 25 he asked her water and she gave him m.
Job 10 10 hast thou not milked me as milk and
Ps 118 70 their heart is curdled like milk: but
Prov 27 27 let the milk of the goats be enough
30 33 squeezeth the paps to bring out milk
Cant 4 11 honey and milk are under thy tongue
5 1 I have drunk my wine with my milk: eat
12 which are washed with milk, and sit
Eccu 39 31 things necessary . . . salt, milk, and
Isa 7 22 for abundance of m. he shall eat butter
28 9 them that are weaned from the milk
55 1 buy wine and milk without money and
60 16 shalt suck the milk of the Gentiles
66 11 that you may milk out and flow with
Lam 4 7 were whiter than snow, purer than milk
Eze 25 4 fruits: and they shall drink thy milk
34 3 you ate the milk, and you clothed
Joel 3 18 and the hills shall flow with milk
1 C 3 2 I gave you milk to drink, not meat; for
9 7 and eateth not of the milk of the flock
Heb 5 12 you are become such as have need of m.
13 every one that is a partaker of milk, is
1 P 2 2 desire the rational milk without guile
milked Job 10 10 hast thou not milked me as milk
mill Exod 11 5 of the handmaid that is at the m.
Num 11 8 gathering it, ground it in a mill
Jer 25 10 the sound of the mill, and the light
Mat 24 41 women shall be grinding at the mill
Apoc 18 22 the sound of the mill shall be heard no
millet Isa 28 25 in order, and barley and millet
Eze 4 9 and beans and lentils and millet
millstone Deut 24 6 nor the upper m. to pledge
Judg 9 53 woman casting a piece of a millstone
2 K 11 21 woman cast piece of millstone upon him
Isa 47 2 take a m. and grind meal: uncover thy
Mat 18 6 better for him that a m. should be
Mark 9 41 m. were hanged about his neck. Luke 17:2
Apoc 18 21 a great m., and cast it into the sea
mind Gen 26 35 offended the mind of Isaac and
Gen 40 14 to put Pharao in mind to take me out
Exod 19 21 lest they should have a mind to pass
35 21 with a most ready and devout mind
29 with devout mind offered gifts, that
Lev 26 41 until their uncircumcised mind be ashamed
Num 6 21 that which he had vowed in his mind
11 5 the cucumbers come into our mind, and
22 23 had a mind to bring her again to the way
30 15 defer the declaring his mind till another
Deut 5 29 shall give them to have such a mind
17 17 many wives, that may allure his mind
18 6 a longing mind to come to the place
9 lest thou have a mind to imitate the
22 hath forged it by the pride of his mind
28 28 madness and blindness and fury of mind
Josu 22 23 and if we did it with that mind, that
23 14 you shall know with all your mind that
Judg 13 23 if the Lord had a mind to kill us, he
16 15 when thy mind is not with me? Thou
18 he had discovered to her all his mind
20 he said in his mind: I will go out as I
1 K 14 7 do all that pleaseth thy mind: go
7 with thee wheresoever thou hast a mind
20 12 if I shall discover my father's mind
22 2 with debt and under affliction of mind
30 6 the people had a mind to stone him
2 K 17 8 very valiant, and bitter in their mind
18 3 we flee away, they will not much mind
3 K 8 18 in having this same thing in thy mind
9 19 whatsoever he had a mind to build
11 9 his mind was turned away from the Lord
19 3 he went whithersoever he had a mind
1 Pa 28 9 with a perfect heart and a willing mind
29 18 let this mind remain always for the
2 Pa 6 7 had a mind to build a house to the
8 6 that Solomon had a mind and designed
24 4 Joas had a mind to repair the house
26 16 he had a mind to burn incense upon
28 10 you have a mind to keep under the
29 10 I have a mind that we make a covenant
31 and holocausts with a devout mind
32 3 and as they were all of this mind, he
2 Es 6 6 hast a mind to set thyself king over
Tob 1 14 liberty to do whatever he had a mind
4 6 days of thy life have God in thy mind
14 never suffer pride to reign in thy mind
6 17 as to shut out God . . . from their mind
Jdth 5 11 they had a mind to take them again
26 they had a mind to kill him [Achior]
9 14 give me constancy in my mind, that I
11 6 the industry of thy mind is spoken of
Esth 2 15 the keeper of the virgins had a mind
4 1 showing the anguish of his mind. And
5 8 tomorrow I will open my mind to the

6 9 whom the king hath a mind to honor. 11
8 9 were written, as Mardochai had a mind
9 27 a mind to be joined to their religion
11 12 he kept it fixed in his mind, desirous
13 18 all Israel with like mind . . . cried to
15 8 bright eyes, hid a mind full of anguish
16 9 that it cometh of the levity of our mind
10 a Macedonian both in mind and country
Job 5 27 consider it thoroughly in thy mind
13 13 whatsoever my mind shall suggest to me
20 2 my mind is hurried away to different
29 25 if I had a mind to go to them, I sat
Ps 30 23 I said in the excess of my mind: I am
34 25 it is well, it is well, to our mind
67 28 Benjamin a youth, in ecstasy of mind
76 6 I had in my mind the eternal years
Prov 5 2 mind not the deceit of a woman. For the
7 25 let not thy mind be drawn away in
15 13 by grief of mind the spirit is cast
15 secure mind is like a continual feast
28 mind of the just studieth obedience
17 22 a joyful mind maketh age flourishing
18 1 hath a mind to depart from a friend
19 3 he fretteth in his mind against God
8 he that possesseth a mind, loveth his
23 7 to thee: and his mind is not with thee
15 if thy mind be wise, my heart shall
19 be wise: and guide thy mind in the way
24 2 because their mind studieth robberies
28 14 that is hardened in mind, shall fall
29 11 a fool uttereth all his mind: a wise
31 6 wine to them that are grieved in mind
Ecce 1 13 I proposed in my mind to seek and
16 my mind hath contemplated many things
2 3 that I might turn my mind to wisdom
11 all things vanity and vexation of mind
15 speaking with my own mind, I perceived
23 in the night he doth not rest in mind
26 and a fruitless solicitude of the mind
4 6 full with labor and vexation of mind
7 3 we are put in mind of the end of all
4 the mind of the offender is corrected
26 have surveyed all things with my mind
Wisd 4 12 overturneth the innocent mind. Being
9 15 earthly habitation presseth down the m.
14 17 the king whom they had a mind to honor
Eccu 6 27 come to her with all thy mind and
33 wilt apply thy mind, thou shalt be wise
7 9 be not fainthearted in thy mind
9 3 upon a woman that hath a mind for many
23 let the thought of God be in thy mind
10 21 memory of them that are humble in mind
13 15 his cruel mind will lay up thy words
14 2 that hath had no sadness of his mind
22 in his mind shall think of the all seeing
19 8 tell not thy mind to friend or foe
23 6 give me not over to a . . . foolish mind
27 17 shall never find a friend to his mind
29 21 he that is of an unthankful mind will
32 16 do what thou hast a mind, but not in
37 6 forget not thy friend in thy mind and
9 for he will devise to his own mind
38 27 shall give his mind to turn up furrows
28 shall give his mind to the resemblance
31 he setteth his mind to finish his work
34 he shall give his mind to finish the
Isa 44 19 they do not consider in their mind nor
Jer 19 5 neither did it once come into my mind
22 27 they lift up their mind to return
39 12 but as he hath a mind, so do with him
51 11 his mind is against Babylon to destroy
50 and let Jerusalem come into your mind
Bar 4 28 as it was your mind to go astray from
Eze 20 32 neither shall the thought of your mind
21 16 which way soever thou hast a mind to
25 15 revenged themselves with all their mind
36 5 with all the heart, and with the mind
Dan 2 1 and his dream went out of his mind
3 troubled in mind I know not what I saw
5 the thing is gone out of my mind
30 mightest know the thoughts of thy mind
13 9 they perverted their own mind and
Nah 1 11 contriving treachery in his mind. Thus
1 Ma 1 17 a mind to reign over the land of Egypt
3 27 these words, he was angry in his mind
31 and he was greatly perplexed in mind
4 27 not succeeded . . . according to his mind
8 9 had a mind to go and to destroy them
13 they had a mind to help to a kingdom
30 have a mind to add to these articles
10 74 was moved in his mind: and he chose
2 Ma 1 3 with a great heart and a willing mind
2 26 that it might be a pleasure of mind
3 16 declared the inward sorrow of his mind
4 25 but having the mind of a cruel tyrant
37 Antiochus . . . was grieved in his mind
46 and brought him to be of another mind
5 11 out of Egypt with a furious mind, he
17 Antiochus, going astray in mind, did not
21 such was the haughtiness of his mind
6 28 if with a ready mind . . . I suffer
8 19 he put them in mind also of the helps
9 20 if all matters go with you to your mind
11 4 puffed up in mind, and trusting in the
8 going forth together with a willing m.
37 that we may know of what mind you are
13 4 stirred up the mind of Antiochus
9 the king, with his mind full of rage
23 he was in a consternation of mind
14 45 being inflamed in mind he arose: and
15 9 putting them in mind of the battles
30 ready, in body and mind, to die for his
Mat 14 5 having a mind to put him to death
17 12 unto him whatsoever they had a mind
22 37 soul and with thy whole m. Mark 12:30
Luke 5 39 old, hath presently a mind to new
8 35 feet, clothed, and in his right mind
10 27 all thy strength and with all thy mind
13 31 for Herod hath a mind to kill thee
14 28 having a mind to build a tower, doth
24 4 as they were astonished in their mind
John 14 26 and bring all things to your mind
16 19 Jesus knew that they had a mind to ask
Acts 2 6 were confounded in mind because that
5 28 you have a mind to bring the blood of
10 10 came upon him an ecstasy of mind
11 5 I saw in an ecstasy of mind a vision
Rom 7 23 fighting against the law of my mind, and
25 I myself, with mind serve the law of God
8 5 mind the things that are of the flesh
5 mind the things that are of the spirit
11 34 known the mind of the Lord. 1 C 2:16
12 2 be reformed in the newness of your mind
15 15 as it were putting you in mind: because
1 C 1 10 that you be perfect in the same mind
2 16 him? But we have the mind of Christ. And
4 17 who will put you in mind of my ways
2 C 1 15 I had a mind to come to you before, that
5 13 whether we be transported in mind, it is
8 11 as your mind is forward to be willing
9 2 for I know your forward mind: for which
12 6 though I should have a mind to glory
Gal 5 10 that you will not be of another mind
Eph 4 17 walk in the vanity of their mind, having
23 be renewed in the spirit of your mind
Phil 2 5 let this mind be in you, which was also

20 I have no man so of the same mind, who
3 16 come, that we be of the same mind, let
19 in their shame; who mind earthly things
Col 1 21 and enemies in mind in evil works: yet
3 2 mind the things that are above, not
1 Tim 6 5 conflicts of men corrupted in mind, and
2 Tim 1 5 calling to mind that faith which is in
2 14 these things put them in m., charging
3 8 truth, men corrupted in mind, reprobate
Titus 1 15 mind and their conscience are defiled
Heb 8 10 I will give my laws into their mind, and
10 32 God. But call to mind the former days
James 5 13 is he cheerful in mind? Let him sing
1 P 1 13 having the loins of your mind girt up
2 P 3 1 by way of admonition your sincere mind
Apoc 3 3 have in mind therefore in what manner
one mind Josu 9 2 against Josue . . . with one m.
Judg 20 11 against the city, as one man, with one m.
Jdth 1 11 but they all with one mind refused
Ps 54 14 but thou a man of one mind, my guide
1 Ma 10 20 that thou be of one mind with us
2 Ma 14 20 all of one mind to consent to covenants
Acts 1 14 these were persevering with one mind
Rom 12 16 of one mind one towards another. 15:5
15 6 that with one mind, and with one mouth
Phil 1 27 in one spirit, with one mind laboring
15 5 be of one mind. 2 C 13:11; Phil 2:2; 4:2
1 P 3 8 and in fine, be ye all of one mind
minded 2 Pa 25 16 that God is minded to kill thee
1 Es 7 13 that are minded to go into Jerusalem
2 Es 9 34 have not minded thy commandments
Ps 130 2 if I was not humbly m., but exalted
Mat 1 19 was minded to put her away privately
Acts 27 39 m., if they could, to thrust in the ship
2 C 1 17 then I was thus m., did I use lightness
Phil 3 15 as many as are perfect, be thus minded
15 if in anything you be otherwise minded
1 Th 5 14 comfort the feeble minded, support the
James 1 8 a double minded man is inconstant in
4 8 purify your hearts, ye double minded
mindful Lev 19 18 nor be m. of the injury of thy
Num 15 40 mindful of the precepts of the Lord
1 K 1 11 wilt be m. of me and not forget thy
2 K 14 32 if he be m. of my iniquity, let him
Tob 1 13 and because he was mindful of the Lord
4 4 for thou must be m. what and how great
14 11 that they be m. of God and bless him
Jdth 8 21 that they may be m. how our fathers
13 25 men who shall be mindful of the power
Ps 6 6 one in death, that is mindful of thee
8 5 what is man that thou art m. of him
15 4 nor will I be m. of their names by my
19 4 may he be m. of all thy sacrifices
70 16 I will be mindful of thy justice alone
76 12 I will be mindful of thy wonders from
86 4 I will be m. of Rahab and of Babylon
88 51 be mindful, O Lord, of the reproach
102 18 and are mindful of his commandments
105 45 was m. of his covenant: and repented
110 5 he will be m. forever of his covenant
113 12 the Lord hath been mindful of us
118 49 be thou m. of thy word to thy servant
135 23 he was mindful of us in our affliction
Wisd 19 10 they were yet mindful of those things
Eccu 15 8 lying men shall not be mindful of her
48 23 he was not mindful of their sins
Isa 49 1 he hath been mindful of my name. And
57 11 and hast not been mindful of me nor
62 6 you that are mindful of the Lord, hold
Lam 3 20 I will be mindful and remember, and my
Bar 2 32 captivity and shall be m. of my name
Luke 1 54 servant, being mindful of his mercy
1 C 11 2 that in all things you are mindful of me
Gal 2 10 that we should be mindful of the poor
Eph 2 11 for which cause be m. that you, being
Col 4 18 be mindful of my bands. Grace be with
1 Th 1 3 being mindful of the work of your faith
2 Tim 1 4 being mindful of thy tears, that I may
2 8 be mindful that the Lord Jesus Christ
Heb 2 6 what is man, that thou art m. of him
11 15 truly if they had been mindful of that
2 P 3 2 you may be mindful of those words
Jude 17 be mindful of the words which have
Apoc 2 5 be m. therefore from whence thou art
minding Rom 12 16 not m. high things, but consenting to
minds Num 32 7 why do ye overturn the minds of
Deut 11 18 my words in your hearts and minds, and
1 Pa 28 9 understandeth all the thoughts of minds
Jdth 4 2 dread and horror seized upon their m.
14 17 their minds were troubled exceedingly
Eccu 3 26 hath detained their minds in vanity
1 Ma 4 45 a good counsel came into their minds
11 49 they were discouraged in their minds
2 Ma 2 2 that they should not err in their minds
4 40 their minds being filled with anger
10 35 inflamed in their minds because of the
Acts 14 2 and incensed the minds of the Gentiles
28 6 changing their minds, they said, that he
2 C 4 4 hath blinded the minds of unbelievers
11 3 so your minds should be corrupted, and
Phil 4 7 keep your hearts and minds in Christ
Heb 10 16 and on their minds will I write them
12 3 be not wearied, fainting in your minds
mines Deut 8 9 of its hills are dug m. of brass
1 Ma 8 3 under their power the mines of silver
mingle Lev 21 15 not m. the stock of his kindred
Apoc 18 6 mingled, mingle ye double unto her
mingled Lev 7 12 cakes tempered and m. with oil
Num 36 7 of Israel be m. from tribe to tribe
9 tribes be not mingled one with another
1 Es 9 2 they have mingled the holy seed with
Ps 101 10 and mingled my drink with weeping
105 35 they were mingled among the heathens
Prov 9 2 m. her wine and set forth her table
5 the wine which I have mingled for you
14 13 laughter shall be mingled with sorrow
Wisd 14 25 and all things are mingled together
Isa 1 22 dross: thy wine is mingled with water
9 5 and garment mingled with blood, shall
19 14 the Lord hath mingled in the midst
29 10 the Lord hath m. for you the spirit of
30 24 shall eat mingled provender as it was
Eze 46 14 to be mingled with the fine flour
Dan 2 43 they shall be mingled indeed together
Mat 27 34 him wine to drink mingled with gall
Mark 15 23 him to drink wine mingled with myrrh
Luke 13 1 whose blood Pilate had mingled with
Apoc 8 7 hail and fire, mingled with blood, and
14 10 which is mingled with pure wine in the
15 2 a sea of glass mingled with fire, and
18 6 in the cup wherein she hath mingled
mingling Lev 18 20 nor be defiled with m. of seed
Osee 7 4 rested a little from the m. of the leaven
2 Ma 14 3 time of mingling with the heathens
minister Exod 24 13 Moses rose up, and his m. Josue
Exod 28 1 that they may minister to me. 40:13
3 being consecrated may minister to me
43 to minister in the sanctuary. 29:30
Lev 21 18 neither shall he approach to minister
Num 1 50 they shall minister and shall encamp
3 6 to minister to him, and let them watch
10 stranger that approacheth to minister
31 vessels . . . wherewith they m. 4:12
4 3 that go in to stand and to minister
23 that go in and m. in the tabernacle
39 to minister in the tabernacle. 8:24

11 28 Josue . . . the minister of Moses. Josu 1:1
16 9 of the people, and should m. to him
18 2 be ready in hand and minister to thee
2 and thy sons shall m. in the tabernacle
Deut 18 5 to minister to the name of the Lord
7 he shall minister in the name of the
21 5 thy God hath chosen to minister to him
Josu 1 1 Josue the son of Nun, the m. of Moses
1 K 2 30 should minister in my sight forever
3 K 8 11 priests could not stand to minister
1 Pa 15 2 and to minister unto himself forever
16 4 appointed Levites to m. before the ark
37 Asaph and his brethren to minister in
23 13 Aaron was separated to m. in the holy
32 that they may m. in the house of the
2 Pa 5 14 nor could the priests stand and m.
8 14 the Levites . . . to give praise and m.
13 10 the priests who minister to the Lord
23 6 and they that minister of the Levites
29 11 to minister to him and to worship him
31 2 to minister and to praise and to sing
35 2 to minister in the house of the Lord
3 but minister now to the Lord your God
2 Es 10 36 to the priests who m. in the house of
Isa 60 7 the rams of Nabaioth shall m. to thee
10 and their kings shall minister to thee
Eze 40 46 near to the Lord to minister to him
42 14 their vestments, wherein they minister
44 11 in their sight, to minister to them
15 shall come near to me, to m. to me
16 to minister unto me and to keep my
17 when they minister in the gates of the
27 to m. unto me in the sanctuary, he
45 5 Levites, that minister in the house
Mat 20 26 among you, let him be your minister
28 ministered unto, but to m. Mark 10:45
25 44 prison, and did not minister to thee
Mark 9 34 last of all and the minister of all
10 43 will be greater, shall be your m.
Luke 4 20 book, he restored it to the minister
12 37 and passing will minister unto them
John 12 26 if any man minister to me, let him
26 I am, there also shall my minister be
Acts 24 23 prohibit any of his friends to m. unto
26 16 that I may make thee a minister, and a
Rom 13 4 he is God's m. to thee, for good. But
15 8 I say that Christ Jesus was minister of
16 I should be minister of Christ Jesus
25 Jerusalem, to minister unto the saints
27 ought also in carnal things to m. to
Gal 2 17 is Christ then the minister of sin? God
Eph 3 7 of which I am made a minister, according
6 21 Tychicus, my . . . faithful minister in
Col 1 7 who is for you a faithful m. of Christ
23 whereof I Paul am made a minister. 25
4 7 our dearest brother, and faithful m.
1 Th 3 2 minister of God in the gospel of Christ
1 Tim 3 10 so let them minister, having no crime
4 6 thou shalt be a good minister of Christ
5 16 let him minister to them, and let not
Heb 1 14 spirits, sent to minister for them, who
6 10 who have ministered, and do m. to the
8 2 a minister of the holies, and of the
1 P 4 11 if any man minister, let him do it as
2 P 1 5 minister in your faith, virtue; and
ministered Gen 37 8 m. nourishment to their envy
Gen 39 4 in the sight of his master and m. to him
Exod 39 1 when he ministered in the holy places
1 K 2 11 the child ministered in the sight of
18 Samuel m. before the face of the Lord
3 1 the child Samuel ministered to the Lord
2 K 13 17 calling the servants that m. to him
3 K 1 15 and Abisag the Sunamitess m. to him
19 21 followed Elias and ministered to him
4 K 25 14 vessels of brass with which they m.
1 Pa 6 32 they ministered before the tabernacle
26 12 always m. in the house of the Lord
2 Es 13 10 they that m. were fled away every man
Eccu 24 14 in the holy dwelling place I have m.
Eze 44 12 they m. to them before their idols and
19 their garments wherein they ministered
Dan 7 10 thousands of thousands m. to him, and
Mat 4 11 angels came and ministered to him
8 15 she arose and ministered to them
20 28 is not come to be m. unto. Mark 10:45
Mark 1 13 and the angels ministered to him. And
31 she ministered unto them. Luke 4:39
15 41 followed him and ministered to him
Luke 8 3 many others who ministered unto him
Acts 19 22 Macedonia two of them that m. to him
2 C 3 3 you are the epistle of Christ, m. by us
Phil 2 25 and he that hath ministered to my wants
1 Tim 3 13 for they that have ministered well
5 10 have m. to them that suffer tribulation
2 Tim 1 18 in how many things he ministered unto me
Philem 13 in thy stead he might have ministered to
Heb 6 10 you who have m., and do minister to the
1 P 1 12 to you they m. those things which are
2 P 1 11 an entrance shall be ministered to you
ministereth Deut 17 12 priest who m. at that time
2 C 9 10 he that m. seed to the sower, will both
ministering Mat 27 55 from Galilee, ministering unto him
Acts 13 2 as they were m. to the Lord and fasting
Rom 12 7 or ministry, in ministering; or he that
Heb 1 14 they not all ministering spirits, sent
10 11 priest indeed standeth daily ministering
1 P 4 10 ministering the same one to another
ministers Num 8 26 be the m. of their brethren
Josu 7 22 sent ministers: who running to his tent
10 23 the m. did as they were commanded
3 K 10 5 the order of his m. and their apparel
1 Es 7 24 and ministers of the house of this God
8 17 that they should bring us ministers
2 Es 10 39 singing men and the porters and m.
Esth 6 3 his servants and ministers said to him
Ps 102 21 you ministers of his that do his will
103 4 spirits: and thy m. a burning fire
Wisd 6 5 being m. of his kingdom, you have not
Eccu 7 32 that made thee: and forsake not his m.
10 2 is himself, so also are his ministers
Isa 61 6 ye ministers of our God; you shall eat
Jer 33 21 with the Levites and priests my m.
22 my servant, and the Levites my m.
Eze 44 11 gates of the house and m. to the house
45 4 for the priests the m. of the sanctuary
46 24 kitchens wherein the m. of the house
Joel 1 9 priests, the Lord's m., have mourned
13 howl, ye ministers of the altars
13 lie in sackcloth, ye m. of my God
2 17 priests the Lord's m. shall weep
Luke 1 2 eyewitnesses and ministers of the word
John 7 32 rulers and Pharisees sent ministers
45 the m. therefore came to the chief
46 the m. answered: Never did man speak
18 18 the servants and m. stood at a fire
Acts 5 22 when the m. came and opening the
26 went the officer with the ministers
Rom 13 6 they are the ministers of God, serving
1 C 3 5 the m. of him whom you have believed
4 1 account of us as of m. of Christ, and
2 C 3 6 who also hath made us fit ministers of
6 4 exhibit ourselves as the m. of God, in
11 15 it is no great thing if his ministers
15 be transformed as ministers of justice
23 they are the ministers of Christ, I
Heb 1 7 spirits, and his ministers a flame of

ministration Acts 6 1 were neglected in the daily m.
2 C 3 7 if m. of death, engraven with letters
8 shall not m. of the spirit be rather in
9 if the m. of condemnation be glory, much
9 much more m. of justice aboundeth in
4 1 seeing we have this m., according as we
ministries Num 18 6 in the m. of the tabernacle
1 Pa 24 19 courses according to their ministries
2 Pa 5 11 courses and orders of the ministries
8 14 offices of the priests in their m.
1 C 12 5 are diversities of m., but the same Lord
ministry Exod 28 35 with it in the office of his m.
Exod 31 10 vestments in the ministry for Aaron
35 19 to be used in the m. of the sanctuary
39 24 adorned when he discharged his m.
40 to be made for the m. of the tabernacle
Num 3 8 tabernacle, serving in the m. thereof
4 14 vessels that they use in the ministry
26 the cords and the vessels of the m.
30 that go in to the office of their m.
33 their ministry in the tabernacle of the
35 go in to the m. of the tabernacle. 47
7 5 to serve in the m. of the tabernacle
5 according to the order of their m.
8 11 that they may serve in his ministry
18 5 the sanctuary and in the m. of the altar
21 for the m. wherewith they serve me
31 it is your reward for the ministry
Deut 10 8 to stand before him in the ministry
1 Pa 6 32 according to their order in the m.
48 for all the ministry of the tabernacle
9 13 work of the ministry in house of God
28 charge of the vessels for the ministry
33 continually day and night in their m.
23 4 unto the m. of the house of the Lord
24 that did the works of the ministry
28 and in all the works of the ministry
24 3 according to their courses and ministry
25 1 separated for the ministry the sons of
28 14 by weight for every vessel for the m.
21 for every m. of the house of the Lord
2 Pa 7 6 singing the hymns of David by their m.
24 14 vessels for the temple for the ministry
26 18 who are consecrated for this ministry
29 36 ministry of the Lord was accomplished
31 16 there was need of in the ministry, and
21 in all the service of the ministry of
35 10 the m. was prepared, and the priests
2 Es 11 22 in the ministry of the house of God
13 30 and the Levites, and every man in his m.
Wisd 18 21 bringing forth the shield of his m.
Isa 22 19 and depose thee from thy ministry
Jer 52 18 vessels that had been used in the m.
Eze 40 46 that watch over the m. of the altar
45 4 who come near to the m. of the Lord
Osee 12 10 similitudes by the m. of the prophets
1 Ma 10 42 the priests that execute the ministry
2 Ma 3 3 all the charges belonging to the m.
Acts 1 17 and had obtained part of this ministry
25 to take the place of this ministry
6 4 and to the ministry of the word. And
12 25 having fulfilled their ministry, taking
13 5 and they had John also in the ministry
20 24 m. of word which I received from Lord
21 19 God had wrought among Gentiles by his m.
Rom 11 13 Gentiles, I will honor my ministry, if
12 7 or ministry, in ministering; or he that
16 1 who is in the ministry of the church
1 C 16 15 dedicated themselves to m. of the saints
2 C 5 18 hath given to us m. of reconciliation
6 3 man, that our ministry be not blamed
8 4 communication of ministry that is done
9 1 concerning the m. that is done towards
13 by the proof of this m., glorifying God
11 8 receiving wages of them for your m. And
Eph 4 12 the saints, for the work of the ministry
Col 4 17 take heed to the ministry which thou
1 Tim 1 12 me faithful, putting me in the ministry
2 Tim 4 5 evangelist, fulfil thy ministry
11 he is profitable to me for the ministry
Heb 8 6 he hath obtained a better ministry, by
9 21 the vessels of the m., in like manner
Apoc 2 19 faith and thy charity and thy ministry
minstrel 4 K 3 15 but now bring me hither a m.
4 K 3 15 when the minstrel played, the hand of
minstrels Mat 9 23 saw the m. and the multitude
mint Mat 23 23 because you tithe mint. Luke 11:42
Miphiboseth 2 K 4 4 lame: and his name was M.
2 K 9 6 when Miphiboseth . . . was come to David
6 David said: Miphiboseth? And he
10 M. the son of the master shall always
11 and Miphiboseth shall eat at my table
12 Miphiboseth had a young son . . . Micha
12 the kindred of house of Siba served M.
13 but Miphiboseth dwelt in Jerusalem
16 1 Siba the servant of M. came to meet him
4 I give thee all that belonged to M.
19 24 M. the son of Saul came down to
25 why camest thou not with me, M.? And
30 M. answered the king: Yea, let him
21 7 the king spared M. the son of
8 whom she bore to Saul, Armoni and M.
miracle Num 26 10 there was a great m. wrought
1 K 14 15 and there was a miracle in the camp
15 and it happened as a miracle from God
Isa 29 14 people, by a great and wonderful m.
Mark 9 38 no man that doth a miracle in my name
John 4 54 this is again the second miracle that
6 14 when they had seen what a miracle
12 18 heard that he had done this miracle
Acts 4 16 a known miracle hath been done by them
miracles Deut 34 12 m. which Moses did before all
Judg 6 13 where are his m., which our fathers have
Wisd 19 8 thy hand, seeing thy m. and wonders
Eccu 36 6 renew thy signs, and work new miracles
48 15 wonders, and in death he wrought m.
Mat 7 22 and done many miracles in thy name
11 20 were done the most of his miracles
21 the m. that have been wrought in you
23 if in Sodom had been wrought the m.
13 54 came this man by this wisdom and m.
58 he wrought not many miracles there
Mark 6 5 he could not do any miracles there
John 2 11 this beginning of miracles did Jesus
6 2 they saw the miracles which he did on
26 not because you have seen miracles
7 31 shall he do more miracles than these
9 16 man that is a sinner do such miracles
11 47 for his man doth many miracles? If
12 37 whereas he had done so many miracles
Acts 2 22 by miracles and wonders and signs
8 6 and seeing the miracles which he did
13 exceeding great m. that were done
19 11 by the hand of Paul more than common m.
1 C 12 10 to another, the working of miracles; to
28 after that miracles; then the graces
30 are all workers of miracles? Have all
Gal 3 5 Spirit, and worketh miracles among you
Heb 2 4 signs and wonders and divers miracles
miraculous Acts 4 22 in whom that m. cure had been
mire 2 K 22 43 abroad like the m. of the streets
Job 41 21 he shall strew gold under him like mire
Ps 39 3 the pit of misery and the mire of dregs
68 3 I stick fast in the mire of the deep
15 draw me out of the mire, that I may
Isa 10 6 to tread them down like the mire of

57 20 waves thereof cast up dirt and mire
Jer 38 6 wherein there was no water, but mire. And Jeremias sunk into the mire
22 they have plunged thy feet in the mire
Mich 7 10 under foot as the mire of the streets
Zach 9 3 and gold as the mire of the streets
10 5 treading under foot the m. of the ways
2 P 2 22 washed, to her wallowing in the mire
mirror Wisd 7 26 unspotted m. of God's majesty
mirrors Exod 38 8 of the mirrors of the women that
mirth 2 Es 8 12 portions, and to make great m.
Esth 9 22 sorrow were turned into mirth and joy
Ecce 2 2 to mirth I said: Why art thou vainly
7 5 heart of fools where there is mirth
8 15 I commended mirth because there was
Eccu 31 41 wine: and despise him not in his mirth
Isa 24 8 the mirth of timbrels hath ceased, the
11 all mirth is forsaken: the joy of the
Jer 16 9 and in your days the voice of mirth
25 10 take away from them the voice of mirth
Bar 2 23 take away from you the voice of mirth
Osee 2 11 I will cause all her mirth to cease
miry Dan 2 41 iron mixed with the m. clay. 43
Misaam 1 Pa 8 12 sons of Elphaal . . . Misaam
Misach Dan 1 7 them names . . . to Misael, M.
Sidrach, Misach, and Abdenago; *see* **Sidrach**
Misael Lev 10 4 Moses called M. and Elisaphan
2 Es 8 4 Misael and Melchia and Hasum and
Dan 1 6 Daniel, Ananias, Misael. 11, 19
7 gave them names . . . to M., Misach
2 17 told the matter to Ananias and Misael
3 88 Ananias, Azarias, and Misael, bless
1 Ma 2 59 and M. by believing, were delivered
misbehave Eccu 42 10 lest she should m. herself
miscarried Rom 9 6 as though word of God hath m.
miscarry Exod 21 22 if . . . she m. indeed, but live
mischief Gen 42 38 if any m. befall him in the
2 Es 6 2 but they thought to do me mischief
Prov 6 18 feet that are swift to run into m.
10 23 fool worketh m. as it were for sport
12 21 wicked shall be filled with mischief
13 17 messenger of wicked shall fall into m.
1 Ma 9 61 the principal authors of the mischief
2 Ma 3 32 some m. had been done to Heliodorus
7 31 author of all m. against the Hebrews
14 22 some m. might be suddenly practised
mischiefs Prov 26 25 there are seven m. in his
mischievous Wisd 15 4 invention of m. men hath
Eccu 11 35 take heed to thyself of a m. man
27 30 a m. counsel shall be rolled back
Isa 35 9 nor shall any m. beast go up by it
Eze 14 15 if I shall bring m. beasts also upon
21 the famine and the mischievous beasts
38 10 thou shalt conceive a m. design
miserable Deut 28 22 afflict thee with m. want
Ps 37 7 I am become miserable and am bowed
136 8 O daughter of Babylon, miserable
Prov 14 34 but sin maketh nations miserable
Eccu 29 30 it is a m. life to go as a guest from
2 Ma 9 28 died a miserable death in a strange
1 C 15 19 we are of all men most miserable. But
Apoc 3 17 that thou art wretched and m. and poor
miseries Judg 10 16 he was touched with their miseries
Jdth 3 2 or suffer the miseries of slavery. All
Job 14 1 man . . . is filled with many miseries
30 14 rolled themselves down to my miseries
Ps 139 11 in m. they shall not be able to stand
Ecce 2 23 his days are full of sorrows and m.
2 Ma 14 14 thinking the m. and calamities of the
James 5 1 weep and howl in your miseries, which
misery Gen 43 6 you have done this for my misery
Job 3 20 why is light given to him that is in m.
10 15 being filled with affliction and misery
22 a land of misery and darkness, where
11 16 thou shalt also forget misery, and
30 3 disfigured with calamity and misery
36 21 thou hast begun to follow after misery
Ps 11 6 by reason of the misery of the needy
39 3 and brought me out of the pit of misery
68 21 my heart hath expected reproach and m.
87 19 my acquaintance, because of misery
Ecce 5 16 many cares, and in misery and sorrow
6 2 this is vanity and a great misery
Wisd 3 2 their departure was taken for misery
Isa 47 11 misery shall come upon thee suddenly
Soph 1 15 a day of calamity and misery, a day
2 Ma 6 9 to death: then was misery to be seen
Rom 3 16 destruction and misery in their ways
Misor Josu 21 36 Misor and Jaser and Jethson
Misphat Gen 14 7 came to the fountain of Misphat
miss Judg 20 16 not miss by the stone's going on
missed 1 K 19 10 spear m. him and was fastened
1 K 20 18 thou [David] wilt be missed; for thy
2 Ma 14 43 he missed of giving himself a sure
missing 1 K 25 7 neither was there aught m. to
1 K 30 19 was nothing missing small or great
Isa 40 26 power, not one of them was missing
mist Gen 15 17 was set, there arose a dark mist
Job 3 5 let a mist overspread it, and let
9 let the stars be darkened with the mist
10 21 and covered with the mist of death
22 13 he judgeth as it were through a mist
23 17 neither hath the mist covered my face
38 9 wrapped it in a mist as in swaddling
Wisd 2 3 and shall be dispersed as a mist which
Isa 5 30 the light is darkened with the mist
8 22 and a mist following them, and they
44 22 blotted out . . . thy sins as a mist
60 2 a mist [shall cover] the people: but
Amos 4 13 he that maketh the morning mist and
Acts 13 11 there fell a m. and darkness upon him
2 P 2 17 to whom the m. of darkness is reserved
mistake Gen 43 12 lest perhaps it was done by m.
Lev 5 15 if any one shall sin through mistake
19 because by m. he trespassed against
Judg 9 36 heads of men, and this is thy mistake
mistress Gen 16 4 [Agar] despised her mistress
Gen 16 8 I flee from the face of Sarai, my m.
9 return to thy m. and humble thyself
39 7 his mistress cast her eyes on Joseph
3 K 17 17 son of the woman, the m. of the house
4 K 5 3 she said to her mistress: I wish my
Ps 122 2 are on the hands of her mistress: so
Prov 30 23 bondwoman when she is heir to her m.
Isa 24 2 as with the handmaid, so with her m.
Lam 1 1 m. of the Gentiles become as a widow
mistresses 1 Tim 5 14 be m. of families, give no
mists Ps 147 16 scattereth mists like ashes. He
misty Deut 33 28 heavens shall be misty with dew
misused 2 Pa 36 16 his words and m. the prophets
mite Luke 12 59 until thou pay the very last mite
miter Exod 28 4 garment, a miter and a girdle
Exod 28 37 fillet, and it shall be upon the miter
39 thou shalt make a fine linen miter
29 6 put the miter upon his head. Lev 8:9
6 and the holy plate upon the miter
39 30 they fastened it to the miter with
Lev 8 9 upon the miter over the forehead
16 4 shall put a linen miter upon his head
Eccu 45 14 and a crown of gold upon his miter
Zach 3 5 put a clean miter upon his head
miters Exod 28 40 and miters for glory and beauty
Exod 29 9 and thou shalt put miters upon them
39 26 and miters with their little crowns
Lev 8 13 with girdles and put miters on them
Eze 44 18 shall have linen miters on their heads

mites Mark 12 42 poor widow, and she cast in two m.
Luke 21 2 poor widow casting in two brass mites
Mithridates 1 Es 1 8 them forth by the hand of M.
1 Es 4 7 Mithridates . . . wrote to Artaxerxes
mitigate Jdth 3 11 could not for all that m. the
Eccu 36 25 likewise mitigate and show mercy
mitigated Ps 84 4 thou hast m. all thy anger
Wisd 16 18 at one time the fire was mitigated
Mitylene Acts 20 14 we took him in, and came to M.
mixed 2 Ma 3 21 expectation of the mixed multitude
Osee 7 8 Ephraim . . . is mixed among the nations
Exod 9 24 the hail and fire mixed with it
12 38 a mixed multitude without number went
Heb 4 2 not being m. with the faith of those
Dan 2 41 iron m. with the miry clay. 43
43 as iron cannot be mixed with clay
mixt Num 11 4 m. multitude of people, that came
mixture Num 19 13 is not sprinkled with this m.
Ps 74 9 a cup of strong wine full of mixture
John 19 39 bringing a mixture of myrrh and aloes
Mizael Exod 6 22 the sons also of Oziel: Mizael
mna Eze 45 12 and 15 sicles make a mna. And these
Mnason Acts 21 16 with them one Mnason a Cyprian
Mnestheus 2 Ma 4 21 Apollonius the son of M.
Moab Gen 19 37 she called his name Moab: he is
Gen 36 35 defeated Madianites in country of Moab
Exod 15 15 trembling seized on stout men of Moab
Num 21 11 that faceth Moab toward the east. And
13 Arnon is the border of Moab, dividing
20 is a valley in the country of Moab, to
29 woe to thee Moab: thou art undone
22 4 now he was at that time king in Moab
7 the ancients of Moab and the elders of
24 17 shall strike the chiefs of Moab: and
25 1 fornication with the daughters of Moab
Deut 2 8 way that leadeth to the desert of Moab
18 shalt pass this day the borders of Moab
Judg 3 28 Jordan, which are in the way of Moab
30 Moab was humbled that day under the
10 6 gods of Syria and of Sidon and of Moab
11 18 he would not enter the bounds of Moab
Ruth 1 2 and entering into the country of Moab
4 they took wives of the women of Moab
4 3 who is returned from the country of Moab
1 K 14 47 his enemies round about, against Moab
22 3 David departed . . . into Maspha of Moab
2 K 8 2 he defeated Moab and measured them
2 Moab was made to serve David under
12 of Syria and of Moab and of the
23 20 he slew the two lions of Moab, and he
3 K 11 1 king Solomon loved . . . women of Moab
7 a temple for Chamos the idol of Moab
33 Chamos the god of Moab, and Moloch
4 K 1 1 Moab rebelled against Israel after the
10 to deliver us into the hands of Moab
13 to deliver them into the hands of Moab
18 will deliver also Moab into your hands
23 go now, Moab, to the spoils. And they
24 but Israel rising up defeated Moab
13 20 rovers from Moab came into the land
23 13 to Chamos the scandal of Moab, and to
24 2 sent against him . . . the rovers of Moab
1 Pa 4 22 who were princes in Moab and who
11 22 he slew the two ariels of Moab: and
18 2 he defeated Moab, and the Moabites
11 as well from Edom and from Moab, and
2 Pa 20 1 children of Moab . . . were gathered
10 behold the children of Ammon and of M.
22 children of Ammon and Moab. 23; Jdth 7:8
1 Es 2 6 the children of Phahath Moab, of the
10 30 of the sons of Phahath, Moab, Edna
2 Es 3 11 Hasub the son of Phahath Moab, built
7 11 the children of Phahath Moab . . . 2,818
10 14 Pharos, Phahath Moab, Elam, Zethu
13 23 wives, women of Azotus . . . and of Moab
Jdth 5 2 and he called all the princes of Moab
Ps 59 10 Moab is the pot of my hope. Into Edom
82 7 Moab and the Agarens, Gebal and
107 10 Juda is my king: Moab the pot of my hope
Isa 11 14 Edom and Moab shall be under the rule
15 1 the burden of Moab. Because in the
1 in the night Ar of Moab is laid waste
1 the wall of Moab is destroyed in the
2 Moab hath howled: on all their heads
4 shall well appointed men of Moab howl
5 my heart shall cry to Moab, the bars
8 cry is gone round about border of Moab
9 lion upon them that shall flee of Moab
16 2 so shall the daughters of Moab be
4 Moab, be thou a covert to them from
6 we have heard of the pride of Moab, he
7 therefore shall Moab howl to Moab
11 shall sound like a harp for Moab and
12 when it is seen that Moab is wearied
13 the word that the Lord spoke to Moab
14 the glory of Moab shall be taken away
25 10 Moab shall be trodden down under him
Jer 9 26 children of Ammon and upon Moab, and
25 21 and Moab and the children of Ammon
40 11 all the Jews that were in Moab and
48 1 against Moab thus saith the Lord of
2 there is no more rejoicing in Moab
4 Moab is destroyed: proclaim a cry for
11 Moab hath been fruitful from his youth
13 and Moab shall be ashamed of Chamos
15 Moab is laid waste, and they have cast
16 destruction of Moab is near to come
18 the spoiler of Moab is come up to thee
20 Moab is confounded, because he is
20 tell ye it in Arnon, that Moab is wasted
25 the horn of Moab is cut off, and his
26 Moab shall dash his hand in his own
28 dwell in the rock, you that dwell in M.
29 we have heard the pride of Moab, he is
31 therefore will I lament for Moab and
31 and I will cry out to all Moab, for the
35 I will take away from Moab, saith the
36 my heart shall sound for Moab like pipes
38 upon all the housetops of Moab and in
38 I have broken Moab as an useless vessel
39 how hath Moab bowed down the neck and
39 and Moab shall be a derision and an
40 shall stretch forth his wings to Moab
41 the heart of the valiant men of Moab
42 and Moab shall cease to be a people
43 come upon thee, O inhabitant of Moab
44 upon Moab the year of their visitation
45 it shall devour part of Moab, and the
46 woe to thee, Moab, thou hast perished
47 I will bring back the captivity of Moab
47 hitherto the judgments of Moab
Eze 25 8 Moab and Seir have said: Behold the
9 I will open the shoulder of Moab from
11 and I will execute judgments in Moab
Dan 11 41 only shall be saved . . . Edom and Moab
Amos 2 1 for three crimes of Moab and for four
2 I will send a fire into Moab, and it
2 Moab shall die with a noise, with the
Soph 2 8 I have heard the reproach of Moab and
9 Moab shall be as Sodom, and the
king of Moab Num 21 26 fought against the k. . . .
Josu 24 9 Balac son of Sephor k. . . . arose and
Judg 3 12 strengthened against them Eglon k. . . .
14 of Israel served Eglon k. . . . 18 years
15 of Israel sent presents to Eglon k. . . .
17 he presented the gifts to Eglon k. . . .

11 17 he sent also to the k. . . . who likewise
25 Balac the son of Sephor k. . . .
1 K 12 9 into the hand of the king of Moab
22 3 he said to the k. . . . : Let my father
4 left them under the eyes of the k. . . .
4 K 3 4 Mesa k. . . . nourished many sheep and
7 the k. . . . is revolted from me, come
26 when the k. . . . saw this, to wit, that
Jer 27 3 to the king of Edom and to the k. . . .
Mich 6 5 what Balach the k. . . . purposed: and
land of Moab Deut 1 5 beyond the Jordan in l. . . .
Deut 29 1 with the children of Israel in l. . . .
32 49 unto mount Nebo, which is in the l. . . .
34 5 of the Lord died there, in the l. . . .
6 buried him in the valley of the l. . . .
Judg 11 15 Israel did not take away the l. . . .
18 of Edom at the side, and the l. . . .
18 over against east coast of the l. . . .
Ruth 1 1 went to sojourn in the l. . . . with
6 she arose to go from the l. . . . to her
2 6 who came with Noemi from the l. . . .
1 Pa 1 46 defeated the Madianites in l. . . .
8 8 Saharim begot in the l. . . . after he
Jer 48 24 upon all the cities of the l. . . . , far
33 away from Carmel and from the l. . . .
plains of Moab Num 22 1 encamped in the p. . . .
Num 26 3 Eleazar the priest being in the p. . . .
63 in the p. . . . upon the Jordan. 36:13
31 12 they carried to the camp on the p. . . .
33 48 they passed to the p. . . . by the
35 1 these things also to Moses in the p. . . .
Deut 34 1 Moses went up from the p. . . . upon
8 mourned for him in the p. . . . 30 days
Josu 13 32 possession Moses divided in p. . . .
Moabite Deut 23 3 the Moabite . . . not enter into
1 Pa 11 46 Jethma a Moabite, Eliel and Obed
Moabites Gen 19 37 he is the father of the M.
Num 21 13 dividing the M. and the Amorrhites
15 lie down in the borders of the M.
28 and hath consumed Ar of the Moabites
22 3 that the M. were in great fear of him
10 the son of Sephor king of the Moabites
36 to meet him in a town of the Moabites
23 6 offering, with all the princes of the M.
7 Balac king of the M. hath brought me
17 the princes of the Moabites with him
33 44 which is in the borders of the Moabites
49 to Ablesatim in the plains of the M.
Deut 2 9 said to me: Fight not against the M.
11 Enacims. But the M. call them Emims
29 and the Moabites, that abide in Ar
Judg 3 28 Lord hath delivered our enemies the M.
29 they slew of the Moabites at that time
4 K 3 21 all the M. hearing that the kings
22 M. saw the waters over against them
1 Pa 18 2 Moabites were made David's servants
1 Es 9 1 Ammonites and the Moabites and the
2 Es 13 1 M. should not come in to the church
Moabitess Ruth 1 22 Noemi came with Ruth the M.
Ruth 2 2 Ruth the M. said to her mother-in-law
6 this is the M. who came with Noemi
4 5 thou must take also Ruth the Moabitess
10 have taken to wife Ruth the Moabitess
2 Pa 24 26 and Jozabab the son of Semarith a M.
Moadia 2 Es 12 17 of Miamim and Moadia, Phelti
Mobonnai 2 K 23 27 of Anathoth, M. of Husati
Mochona 2 Es 11 28 some dwelt . . . at Mochona
Mochori 1 Pa 9 8 Ozi the son of Mochori: and
mock 1 K 31 4 come and slay me and mock at me
1 Pa 10 4 these uncircumcised come and mock me
Jdth 12 11 if a woman mock a man, by doing so as
Prov 1 26 will mock when that shall come to you
Wisd 12 25 as senseless children to mock them
Isa 28 22 do not mock, lest your bonds be tied
Jer 9 5 and a man shall mock his brother
Mark 10 34 they shall mock him and spit on him
Luke 14 29 all that see it begin to mock him
mocked Gen 27 12 will think I would have m. him
Exod 1 13 and afflicted them and mocked them
Judg 16 10 thou hast mocked me and hast told me
4 K 2 23 mocked him, saying: Go up, thou bald
2 Pa 30 10 they laughed at them and mocked them
36 16 but they mocked the messengers of God
2 Es 4 5 because they have mocked thy builders
Tob 2 15 so his relations and kinsmen mocked at
Job 11 3 when thou hast mocked others, shall no
12 4 he that is mocked by his friends as I
Lam 1 7 her, and have mocked at her sabbaths
1 Ma 7 34 but he mocked and despised them
2 Ma 7 39 taking it grievously that he was m.
Mat 20 19 deliver him to the Gentiles to be m.
Mat 27 29 they mocked him, saying: Hail, king of
31 after they had mocked him. Mark 15:20
Luke 18 32 and shall be mocked and scourged and
22 63 the men that held him, mocked him and
23 11 mocked him, putting on him a white
36 the soldiers also mocked him, coming
Acts 17 32 some indeed mocked, but others said
Gal 6 7 be not deceived, God is not mocked. For
mocker Prov 3 32 every mocker is an abomination
Eccu 33 6 a friend that is a mocker is like a
mockeries Wisd 12 26 that were not amended by m.
Eccu 34 21 m. of the unjust are not acceptable
Isa 66 4 I also will choose their mockeries
Heb 11 36 had trial of mockeries and stripes
mockers Jude 18 there should come mockers, walking
mockery Eccu 27 31 m. and reproach are of the proud
Eze 22 4 Gentiles, and a m. to all countries
Heb 6 6 Son of God, and making him a mockery
mocketh Prov 30 17 the eye that m. at his father
mocking 2 Ma 7 7 next to make him a m. stock
2 Ma 7 27 mocking the cruel tyrant, she said
Mat 27 41 with the scribes and ancients, m., said
Mark 15 31 the chief priests mocking, said with
Acts 2 13 mocking, said: These men are full of
model Phil 2 17 who walk so as you have our model. For
moderate Ecce 31 24 wholesome sleep with a m. man
Eccu 32 8 of music with pleasant and m. wine
moderated Gen 24 67 it m. the sorrow which was
moderately Eccu 31 32 if thou drink it m., thou
moderation Eccu 31 36 drunken with m. is the joy
2 Ma 9 27 that he will behave with moderation
modest 2 Ma 15 12 virtuous man, m. in his looks
1 Tim 3 3 not given to wine, no striker, but m.
Phil 4 8 whatsoever modest, whatsoever just
James 3 17 modest, easy to be persuaded
1 P 3 8 modest, humble: not rendering evil for
modesty Eccu 7 21 grace of her m. is above gold
2 Ma 4 37 sobriety and m. of the deceased
2 C 10 1 by the mildness and m. of Christ, who
Gal 5 23 the fruit of the Spirit is . . . modesty
Phil 4 5 let your modesty be known to all men
Col 3 12 bowels of mercy . . . modesty, patience
1 Tim 2 9 adorning themselves with modesty and
2 Tim 2 25 with m. admonishing them that resist the
1 P 3 16 with modesty and fear, having a good
Modin 1 Ma 2 1 abode in the mountain of Modin
1 Ma 2 15 that were fled into the city of Modin
23 upon the altar in the city of Modin
70 in sepulchers of his fathers in Modin
9 19 buried him . . . in the city of Modin
13 25 his brother, and buried them in Modin
30 the sepulcher that he made in Modin
16 4 against Cendebeus: and they rested in M.
2 Ma 13 14 he placed his army about Modin. And
Mohola 1 Pa 7 18 Goodlyman and Abiezer and M.

Moholi Exod 6 19 the sons of Merari: Moholi. Num 3:20; 1 Pa 6:19, 29; 23:21; 24:26
Num 26 58 family of Moholi, the family of Musi
1 Pa 6 47 Somer the son of Moholi the son of
23 21 the sons of Moholi: Eleazar and Cis
23 the sons of Musi: Moholi and. 24:30
24 28 the son of Moholi: Eleazar, who had
1 Es 8 18 most learned man of the sons of Moholi
Moholites Num 3 33 are the families of the M.
moiety Num 31 30 the m. of the children of Israel
moist Judg 16 7 sinews not yet dry, but still m.
Job 40 16 he sleepeth . . . and in moist places
moistened Job 21 24 his bones are m. with marrow
Eze 31 16 all that were moistened with waters
moistening Prov 3 8 shall be . . . m. to thy bones
moisture Job 6 11 the rush be green without m.
Job 8 16 he seemeth to have moisture before
Jer 17 8 spreadeth out its roots towards m.
Luke 8 6 it withered away because it had no m.
Molada Josu 15 26 Amam, Sama and Molada, and
Josu 19 2 Bersabee and Sabee and Molada and
1 Pa 4 28 they dwelt in Bersabee and Molada and
2 Es 11 26 at Jesue and at Molada and at
Molathi 2 K 21 8 Berzellai, that was of Molathi
Molathite 1 K 18 19 was given to Hadriel the M.
Molchom 1 Pa 8 9 [Saharim] begot . . . Molchom
mole Lev 11 30 stello and the lizard and the mole
moles Isa 2 20 for himself to adore, m. and bats
molest Exod 22 21 shalt not m. a stranger nor. 23:9
Ruth 2 9 charged my young men not to molest thee
1 Ma 10 35 or to molest any of them in any cause
Mark 14 6 let her alone, why do you molest her
molested 1 K 25 7 were shearing; we never m. them
Wisd 17 14 were sometimes m. with the fear of
Mich 6 3 thee, or in what have I molested thee
2 Ma 11 31 that none of them . . . be molested
Molid 1 Pa 2 29 who bore him Ahobban and Molid
mollifying Wisd 16 12 nor m. plaster that healed
Moloch Lev 18 21 to be consecrated to the idol M.
Lev 20 2 give of his seed to the idol Moloch
3 hath given of his seed to Moloch. 4
5 to commit fornication with Moloch
3 K 11 5 and Moloch the idol of the Ammonites
7 Solomon built a temple . . . for Moloch
33 M. the god of the children of Ammon
4 K 23 10 or his daughter through fire to Moloch
Jer 32 35 their sons and their daughters to M.
Amos 5 26 you carried a tabernacle for your M.
Acts 7 43 took unto you the tabernacle of Moloch
molten Exod 32 4 and made of them a molten calf
Exod 32 8 made to themselves a m. calf. 2 Es 9:18
34 17 not make to thyself any molten gods
Lev 19 4 nor make to yourselves molten gods
Deut 9 12 have made to themselves a molten idol
16 had made to yourselves a molten calf
27 15 that maketh a graven and molten thing
Judg 17 3 and made a graven and a molten god
4 to make of them a graven and a m. god
18 14 graven and a molten god: see what
17 and the theraphim and the molten god
18 ephod and the idols and the m. god
3 K 7 16 also two chapiters of molten brass
23 also a molten sea of 10 cubits. 2 Pa 4:2
39 were undersetters under the laver m.
14 9 made thee strange gods and molten gods
4 K 17 16 made to themselves two molten calves
2 Pa 33 7 set also a graven and a molten statue
Job 37 18 as if they were of molten brass
41 6 his body is like molten shields, shut
Isa 30 22 garment of thy molten things of gold
42 17 that say to a molten thing: You are
48 5 my graven and m. things have commanded
Bar 6 23 neither when they were molten did they
Osee 13 2 have made to themselves a molten thing
Nah 1 14 I will destroy the graven and molten
Haba 2 18 graven it, a molten and a false image
moment Lev 15 3 filthy humor at every m. cleaveth
Num 16 45 this moment will I destroy them. And
Ruth 2 7 and hath not gone home for one moment
2 Pa 25 15 so as not to depart one moment from
1 Es 9 8 for a moment has our prayer been made
Job 20 5 joy of the hypocrite but for a moment
21 13 and in a moment they go down to hell
Wisd 18 12 in one moment the noblest offspring
Isa 26 20 hide thyself a little for a moment
54 7 for a small m. have I forsaken thee
8 in m. of indignation have I hid my face
Jer 4 20 my pavilions [are destroyed] in a m.
Lam 4 6 Sodom which was overthrown in a moment
Dan 14 41 they were devoured in a moment before
2 Ma 9 11 his pains increasing every moment
Luke 4 5 of the world in a moment of time
1 C 15 52 in a moment, in the twinkling of an eye
momentary 2 C 4 17 that which is at present m. and
moments Acts 1 7 for you to know the times or m.
1 Th 5 1 of the times and moments, brethren, you
money Gen 23 9 for as much money as it is worth
Gen 23 13 I will give money for the field
16 he [Abraham] weighed out the money
16 sicles of silver of common current money
42 25 every man's money again in their sacks
27 saw the money in the sack's mouth
28 my money is given me again, behold
35 found his money tied in the mouth of
43 12 and take with you double money, and
15 took the presents and double money
18 because of the money which we carried
21 found our money in the mouths of the
22 we have brought other money besides
23 money which you gave me, I have for
44 1 put the money of every one in the top
8 the money that we found in the top of
45 23 sending to his father as much money
47 14 gathered up all the money for the corn
15 and when the buyers wanted money
15 die in thy presence, having now no m.
16 I will give you food, if you have no m.
18 how that our money is spent, and our
Exod 21 11 she shall go out free without money
21 punishment, because it is his money
22 17 shall give m. according to the dowry
25 if thou lend money to any of my
30 16 money received which was contributed
Lev 25 37 shalt not give him thy m. upon usury
50 counting the money that he was sold for
27 18 priest shall reckon the m. according
19 he shall add the fifth part of the money
Num 3 48 thou shalt give the money to Aaron
49 Moses therefore took the money of
35 31 shall not take money of him that is
Deut 2 6 you shall buy meats of them for money
6 you shall draw waters for money and
28 sell us meat for money, that we may
14 25 sell them all and turn them into money
26 thou shalt buy with the same money
21 14 thou mayst not sell her for money nor
23 19 not lend to thy brother money to usury
Judg 16 18 went up taking with them the money
3 K 21 2 I will give thee the worth of it in m.
6 give me thy vineyard and take money
15 would not . . . give it thee for money
4 K 5 26 so now thou hast received money and
12 4 all the money of the sanctified things
7 take you therefore money no more
8 were forbidden to take any more money
9 put therein all the money that was

10 there was very much money in the chest
10 poured it out and counted the money
13 there were not made of the same money
13 of the money that was brought into the
15 with the men that received the money
16 m. for trespass and the money for sins
22 4 that the money may be put together
7 of the money which they receive, but
9 money that was found in the house of
1 Pa 21 22 thou shalt take of me as much money as
24 I will give thee money as much as it
2 Pa 24 5 gather of all Israel money to repair
6 the money that was appointed by Moses
9 money which Moses . . . appointed for
11 for they saw there was much money
11 they poured out the money that was in
11 was gathered an immense sum of money
14 they brought the rest of the m. before
27 concerning his sons and the sum of m.
34 9 received of him [Helcias] the money
14 when they carried out the money that
1 Es 3 7 they gave money to hewers of stones
7 17 buy diligently with this money, calves
2 Es 5 4 let us borrow money for the king's
10 and my servants have lent money and
11 restore . . . hundredth part of the money
15 took . . . in money every day forty sicles
6 13 for he had taken money, that I being
Tob 1 17 he gave him the aforesaid sum of money
4 22 of him the foresaid sum of money and
5 2 how I shall get this money, I cannot
24 I wish the money for which thou hast
9 3 receive of him the money, and desire
6 and received of him all the money. And
10 2 and no man will pay him the money
10 of all his substance . . . in much money
11 18 an abundance of money of his wife's
18 money also which he had received of
12 3 he received the money of Gabelus
Esth 3 11 as to the money which thou promisest
Job 31 39 eaten the fruits thereof without money
4 7 how Aman had promised to pay money
Ps 14 5 hath not put out his money to usury
Prov 2 4 if thou shalt seek her as money and
7 20 he took with him a bag of money: he
8 10 receive my instruction, and not money
Ecce 5 9 shall not be satisfied with money: and
7 13 wisdom is a defence, so m. is a defence
10 19 may feast: all things obey money
Eccu 7 20 against thy friend deferring money
10 10 more wicked thing than to love money
29 8 he will defraud him of his money and
13 lose thy money for thy brother and thy
31 8 nor put his trust in money nor in
46 22 money or anything else, even to a shoe
51 36 discipline as a great sum of money and
Isa 24 2 as with him that calleth for his money
43 24 brought me no sweet cane with money
52 3 you shall be redeemed without money
55 1 you that have no money make haste, buy
1 buy wine and milk without money and
2 why do you spend money for that which
Jer 32 9 I weighed him the money, seven staters
10 weighed him the money in the balances
25 buy a field for m. and take witnesses
44 fields shall be bought for money and
Lam 5 4 we have drunk our water for money: we
Bar 1 6 and they made a collection of money
10 behold we have sent you money, buy
Eze 16 36 because thy money hath been poured out
Amos 8 6 we may possess the needy for money
Mich 3 11 and her prophets divined for money
1 Ma 3 29 perceived that the m. of his treasures
31 countries, and to gather much money
8 26 or furnish them with . . . arms or money
28 not be given . . . arms or money or ships
13 15 m. that he owed in the king's account
17 ordered the m. and the children to be
18 because he sent not the money and the
14 32 laid out much of his money, and armed
15 6 I give thee leave to coin thy own m.
2 Ma 1 14 he might receive great sums of money
3 6 was full of immense sums of money and
7 concerning the m. that he was told of
7 to bring him the foresaid money. So
9 had been given concerning the money
13 the money must be carried to the king
4 1 who was the betrayer of the money and
20 the m. was appointed by him that sent
23 to carry m. to the king and to bring
27 the money he had promised to the king
45 promised Ptolemee to give him much m.
8 10 making so much m. of the captive Jews
25 took the m. of them that came to buy
10 20 were persuaded for the sake of money
21 they had sold their brethren for money
Mat 10 9 nor silver nor money in your purses
21 12 tables of the m. changers. Mark 11:15
25 18 the earth, and hid his lord's money
27 committed my money to the bankers
28 12 a great sum of money to the soldiers
15 they taking the money, did as they
Mark 6 8 no bread, nor money in their purse
12 41 beheld how the people cast money into
14 11 promised him they would give him m.
Luke 9 3 staff nor scrip nor bread nor money
19 15 to whom he had given the money, that
23 why then didst thou not give my money
22 5 and covenanted to give him money. And
John 2 14 and the changers of money sitting
15 money of the changers he poured out
Acts 7 16 Abraham bought for a sum of money of
8 18 he offered them money, saying: Give me
20 keep thy money to thyself to perish
20 gift of God may be purchased with m.
19 19 they found the m. to be 50,000 pieces
23 25 slandered, as if he was to take money
24 26 hoping also withal, that m. should be
1 Tim 6 10 desire of money is the root of all evils

monsters Num 13 34 there we saw certain monsters
Wisd 17 14 molested with the fear of monsters
Isa 34 14 and demons and monsters shall meet
Lam 4 3 even the sea monsters have drawn out

monstrous Tob 6 2 m. fish came up to devour
Eccu 43 27 and the monstrous creatures of whales
Jer 50 38 and they glory in monstrous things

month Gen 7 11 seventeenth day of the month, all
Gen 8 4 seven and twentieth day of the month. 14; 4 K 25:27
5 until the tenth month. 4 K 25:1; 1 Pa 27:13; 1 Es 10:16; Esth 2:16; Jer 39:1; 52:4; Eze 24:1; 29:1; 33:21
5 first day of the month. 13; Exod 40:2; Lev 23:24; Num 28:11; 29:6; 33:38; Deut 1:3; Eze 26:1; 31:1; 32:1; Agge 1:1
29 14 after days of one month were expired
Exod 12 2 this m. shall be to you the beginning
3 on the tenth day of this month let every
6 until fourteenth day of this month
18 fourteenth day of the month. Lev 23:5; Num 9:5, 11; 28:16; Josu 5:10; Eze 45:21
18 one and twentieth day of same month
13 4 m. of new corn. 23:15; 34:18; Deut 16:1
5 manner of sacred rites in this month
19 1 third month. 1 Pa 27:5; 2 Pa 15:10; 31:7; Esth 8:9; Eze 31:1

34 18 in the month of the springtime thou
Lev 15 19 woman, who at the return of the month
16 29 tenth day of the month. 25:9; 4 K 25:1; Jer 52:4, 12; Eze 20:1; 24:1; 40:1
23 6 fifteenth day of the same m. Esth 10:13
32 ninth day of the m. 4 K 25:3; Jer 52:6
27 6 from one month until the fifth year
Num 3 22 from one m. and upward. 28, 34, 39, 40, 43
9 3 fourteenth day of this month in the
22 remained . . . for two days or a month
10 11 twentieth day of the month. 1 Es 10:9
11 20 give you flesh . . . for a month of days
21 give them flesh to eat a whole month
18 16 redemption of it shall be after one m.
26 62 from one month old and upward: for
28 14 shall be the holocaust for every month
33 38 the fifth month. 1 Pa 27:8; 1 Es 7:8, 9; Jer 1:3; 28:1; 52:12; Eze 20:1; Zach 7:3
Deut 1 3 the eleventh month. 1 Pa 27:14; Zach 1:7; 1 Ma 16:14
16 1 in this month the Lord . . . brought thee
21 13 for her father and mother one month
1 K 11 1 it came to pass about a month after
3 K 4 7 each man his month in the year. And
5 14 ten thousand every month by turns, so
6 37 house of Lord founded in the month Zio
38 the eleventh year in the month Bul
38 the eighth month. 12:32, 33; 1 Pa 27:11; Zach 1:1
8 2 festival day in the month of Ethanim
12 32 fifteenth day of the month. Eze 32:17; 45:25
4 K 15 13 Sellum . . . reigned one m. in Samaria
25 8 seventh day of the month. Bar 1:2; Eze 30:20; 45:20
27 the twelfth month. 1 Pa 27:15; Esth 2:12; 3:7, 13; 8:12; 13:6; 16:20; 19:1; Jer 52:31; Eze 32:1
1 Pa 27 1 who came in and went out every month
7 the fourth month. Jer 39:2; 52:6; Eze 1:1; Zach 8:19
9 the sixth month. Eze 8:1; Agge 1:1; 2:1
12 the ninth month. 1 Es 10:9; Jer 36:9, 22; Agge 2:11, 19; Zach 7:1; 1 Ma 4:52
2 Pa 29 3 first year and month of his reign
17 eighth day of the same month they came
17 sixteenth day of the same month they
1 Es 6 15 day of the month of Adar. Esth 9:15, 17, 19, 21; 1 Ma 7:43; 2 Ma 15:37
2 Es 1 1 the month of Casleu. 1 Ma 1:57; 4:52, 59; 2 Ma 1:18; 10:5
2 1 the month of Nisan. Esth 11:2
6 15 five and twentieth day of month of Elul
9 1 four and twentieth day of the month. Agge 2:1; 2:21
Esth 3 7 and what month the nation of the Jews
12 the thirteenth day of the same month
8 9 three and twentieth day of the month
9 18 and fourteenth day of the same month
10 13 the month of Adar. 1 Ma 7:49
Eccu 43 8 the month is called after her name
Isa 66 23 there shall be month after month, and
Jer 39 2 the fifth day of the month. Eze 1:1, 2; 8:1; 33:21
52 31 the five and twentieth day of the month. 1 Ma 1:62
Bar 1 8 the tenth day of the month Sivan, the
Eze 29 1 the eleventh day of the month, the word
17 in the first of the month. 45:18
47 12 every month they shall bring forth
Osee 5 7 now shall a month devour them with
10 12 in justice, reap in the month of mercy
Amos 8 5 when will the month be over, and we
Zach 11 8 I cut off three shepherds in one month
1 Ma 1 61 were found in the cities m. after m.
14 27 the eighteenth day of the month Elul
16 14 the same is the month Sabath. And the
2 Ma 1 9 Scenopegia in the month of Casleu
11 21 day of the month of Dioscorus. But
30 of the month of Xanthicus. 33, 38
Luke 1 26 in the sixth month the angel Gabriel
36 this is the sixth month with her that
Apoc 9 15 prepared for . . . a month and a year
22 2 yielding its fruits every month, and

first month Gen 8 13 in the 601st year, the f. m.
Exod 12 18 first month, the fourteenth day. Lev 23:5; Num 28:16; Eze 45:21
40 2 the first month, the first day
15 in the first month of the second year
Num 9 1 of the land of Egypt, in the first m.
20 1 the desert of Sin in the first month
33 3 from Ramesses the first month, on the fifteenth day of the f. m.
Josu 4 19 Jordan, the tenth day of the first m.
1 Pa 12 15 over the Jordan in the first month
27 2 over the first company the first month
3 captains in the host in the first m.
2 Pa 29 17 first day of f. m. 1 Es 7:9; 10:17
35 1 fourteenth day of the f. m. 1 Es 6:19
1 Es 8 31 on the twelfth day of the first month
Jdth 2 1 two and twentieth day of the first m.
Esth 3 7 the first month, which is called Nisan
12 were called in the first month Nisan
Eze 29 17 first m., the first of the m. 45:18
30 20 in the first month, in the seventh day
Dan 10 4 four and twentieth day of first month
1 Ma 9 3 in the first month of the 152nd year

second month Gen 7 11 life of Noe, in s. m.
Gen 8 14 the second month . . . the earth was dried
Exod 16 1 the fifteenth day of the second month
Num 1 1 the first day of second month. 18
9 11 second m., on the fourteenth day
10 11 the second month, the twentieth day
3 K 6 1 month Zio, same is the second month
1 Pa 27 4 the company of the second month was
2 Pa 3 2 he began to build in the second month
30 2 to keep the phase the second month
13 unleavened bread in the second m.
15 on fourteenth day of the second month
1 Es 3 8 the second year . . . the second month
1 Ma 9 54 in the year 153, the second month
13 51 three and twentieth day of second m.

seventh month Gen 8 4 the ark rested in the s. m.
Lev 16 29 seventh month, the tenth day. 25:9
23 24 the seventh month on the first day
27 the tenth day of this seventh month
34 fifteenth day of this same seventh m.
39 the fifteenth day of the seventh month
41 in the s. m. shall you celebrate this
Num 29 1 first day of the seventh month. 1 Es 3:6; 2 Es 8:2
7 the tenth day of this seventh month
12 on the fifteenth day of the seventh m.
3 K 8 2 Ethanim, the same is the seventh month
4 K 25 25 it came to pass in the seventh month
1 Pa 27 10 for the seventh month, was Helles
2 Pa 5 3 in the solemn day of the seventh month
7 10 three and twentieth day of seventh m.
31 7 in seventh month they finished them
1 Es 3 1 and now the seventh month was come
2 Es 8 1 and the seventh month came: and the
14 on the feast, in the seventh month
Jer 28 17 died in that year, in the seventh month
41 1 it came to pass in the seventh month
Eze 45 25 the seventh month, in the fifteenth day
Agge 2 2 in the seventh month, the word of the
Zach 7 5 mourned in the fifth and the seventh m.

1 Ma 10 21 holy vestment in the seventh month
monthly Lev 12 5 custom of her monthly courses
Lev 15 25 ceaseth not to flow after the m. courses
33 that is separated in her monthly times
Jer 2 24 in her monthly filth they shall find
months Gen 38 24 after three m. they told Juda
Exod 2 2 a goodly child, hid him three months
12 2 shall be to you the beginning of m.
2 be the first in the months of the year
Num 10 10 first days of your months, you shall
Judg 11 37 about the mountains for two months
38 and he sent her away for two months
39 the two m. being expired, she returned
19 2 abode with him four months. And her
20 47 abode in the rock Remmon four months
1 K 6 1 in the land of the Philistines seven m.
27 7 in country of Philistines, was four m.
2 K 2 11 reigning . . . 7 years and 6 months
5 5 he reigned over Juda 7 years and 6 m.
6 11 ark of the Lord abode . . . three months
24 8 after nine months and twenty days they
13 or thou shalt flee three months before
3 K 5 14 so that two months they were at home
11 16 for Joab remained there six months
4 K 15 8 reigned Zacharias . . . in Samaria six m.
23 31 he reigned three m. in Jerusalem. 24:8
1 Pa 3 4 where he reigned 7 years and 6 months
13 14 in the house of Obededom three months
21 12 three months to flee from thy enemies
2 Pa 36 2 he [Joachaz] reigned three months in
9 he reigned three months and ten days
Jdth 8 4 widow now three years and six months
16 24 for three m. the joy of this victory
Esth 2 12 for six months they were anointed with
12 six months they used certain perfumes
Job 3 6 the year, nor numbered in the months
7 3 so I also have had empty months and
14 5 the number of his months is with thee
21 21 if the number of his m. be diminished
29 2 I might be according to the m. past
39 2 hast thou numbered the months of their
Wisd 7 2 in time of ten months I was compacted
Isa 47 13 gazed at the stars and counted the m.
Eze 39 12 shall bury them for seven months to
14 after seven m. they shall begin to seek
Dan 4 26 at the end of twelve m. he was walking
Amos 4 7 were yet three months to the harvest
2 Ma 7 27 upon me that bore thee nine months
Luke 1 24 and hid herself five months, saying
56 Mary abode with her about three months
4 25 was shut up 3 years and 6 months
John 4 35 you say, There are yet four months
Acts 7 20 who was nourished three months in his
18 11 he stayed there a year and 6 months
19 8 spoke boldly for the space of 3 months
20 3 when he had spent 3 months, the Jews laid
28 11 after three months, we sailed in a ship
Gal 4 10 you observe days, and months, and times
Heb 11 23 was hid three months by his parents
James 5 17 rained not for 3 years and 6 months
Apoc 9 5 they should torment them five months
10 their power was to hurt men five months
11 2 tread under foot two and forty months
13 5 given to him to do two and forty months
monument Gen 35 14 he set up a monument of stone
Gen 35 20 this is the pillar of Rachel's monument
Josu 4 7 were these stones set for a monument
2 K 18 18 this shall be the monument of my name
4 K 23 17 what is that monument which I see
2 Pa 35 24 was buried in the m. of his fathers
Jdth 9 15 be a glorious monument for thy name
Wisd 10 7 of salt is a m. of an incredulous soul
Isa 19 19 a monument of the Lord at the borders
22 16 hast hewed out a monument carefully
2 Ma 15 6 thought to set up a public monument
Mat 27 60 and laid it in his own new monument
60 stone to the door of the monument and
monuments Mat 23 29 adorn the monuments of the just
Mark 5 2 there met him out of the m. a man with
5 was always day and night in the m.
Luke 11 47 you who build the m. of the prophets
moon Gen 37 9 as it were the sun and the moon
Deut 4 19 thou see the sun and the moon and all
17 3 and adore them, the sun and the moon
33 14 brought forth by the sun and by the
Josu 10 12 thou, O moon, toward valley of Aialon
13 sun and moon stood still. Haba 3:11
4 K 23 5 to Baal and to the sun and to the moon
Job 25 5 behold even the moon not shine
31 26 the moon going in brightness: and my
Ps 8 4 the moon and the stars which thou hast
71 5 with the sun and before the moon
7 peace, till the moon be taken away
88 38 and as the moon perfect forever
103 19 he hath made the moon for seasons: the
120 6 burn thee by day: nor the moon by night
135 9 moon and the stars to rule the night
148 3 praise ye him. O sun and moon: praise
Prov 7 20 will return home day of the full moon
Ecce 12 2 the moon and the stars be darkened
Cant 6 9 fair as the moon, bright as the sun
Wisd 13 2 or the sun and moon to be the gods
Eccu 27 12 a fool is changed as the moon. In the
43 6 the moon in all in her season is for a
7 moon is the sign of the festival day
50 6 of a cloud, and as the moon at the full
Isa 13 10 moon shall not shine with her light
24 23 the moon shall blush, and the sun
30 26 the light of the moon shall be as the
60 19 neither shall the brightness of the m.
20 thy moon shall not decrease: for the
Jer 8 2 them abroad to the sun and the moon
31 35 the order of the moon and of the stars
Bar 6 59 the sun and the moon and the stars
66 as the sun, nor give light as the moon
Eze 32 7 and the moon shall not give her light
Dan 3 62 sun and moon, bless the Lord: praise
Joel 2 10 the sun and moon are darkened. 3:15
31 moon [shall be turned] into blood
Mat 24 29 m. shall not give her light. Mark 13:24
Luke 21 25 be signs in the sun and in the moon
Acts 2 20 into darkness, and the moon into blood
1 C 15 41 glory of the moon, and another the glory
Apoc 6 12 and the whole moon became as blood
8 12 smitten, and third part of the moon
12 1 and the moon under her feet, and on
21 23 hath no need of the sun nor of the moon
new moon 1 K 20 5 tomorrow is the new m. 18
1 K 20 24 the new moon came, and the king sat
27 second day after the new moon. 34
4 K 4 23 today is neither new moon nor sabbath
Ps 80 4 blow up the trumpet on the new moon
Eze 46 1 day of the new moon it shall be opened
6 on the day of the new moon a calf
Col 2 16 or of the new moon, or of the sabbaths
moons Isa 3 18 of shoes and little moons. And
new moons 1 Pa 23 31 sabbaths and in the new m.
2 Pa 2 4 sabbaths and on the new moons. 8:13; 31:3; 2 Es 10:33; Eze 46:3
1 Es 3 5 holocaust, both of the new moons and
Jdth 8 6 the sabbaths and new moons. 1 Ma 10:34
Isa 1 13 the new moons and the sabbaths and
14 my soul hateth your new moons and
Eze 45 17 on the feasts and on the new moons
Osee 2 11 to cease, her solemnities, her new moons
Moos 1 Pa 2 27 sons of Ram . . . Moos, Jamin

Mophim Gen 46 21 sons of Benjamin: . . . Ros and M.
Morasthi Jer 26 18 Micheas of M. was a prophet
Morasthite Mich 1 1 came to Micheas the M.
Moria 2 Pa 3 1 the Lord in Jerusalem in mount M.
morning Gen 1 5 evening and morning . . . day. 8, 13, 19, 23
Gen 19 15 when it was morning, the angels pressed
29 24 when m. was come he saw it was Lia
32 24 a man wrestled with him till morning
41 8 when m. was come, being struck with
44 3 when the morning arose, they were sent
Exod 10 13 when it was morning, the burning wind
12 10 remain anything of it until morning
22 none of you go out . . . till morning
14 24 now the morning watch was come, and
16 19 let no man leave thereof till the m.
20 some of them left until the morning
23 shall remain, lay it up until the m.
18 13 stood by Moses from morning until night
14 all the people wait from morning till
19 16 third day was come, and the m. appeared
23 18 fat of my solemnity remain until the m.
27 21 light before the Lord until the morning
29 34 if there remain . . . till the morning
41 according to rite of the m. oblation
Lev 6 9 burnt upon the altar, all night until m.
7 15 any of it remain until the morning
9 17 the ceremonies of the m. holocaust
19 13 wages . . . not abide with thee until m.
22 30 not any of it remain until the morning
24 3 shall set them from evening until m.
Num 9 12 not leave anything thereof until morning
15 the appearance of fire until the morning
21 cloud tarried from evening until m.
22 41 when morning was come, he brought
28 8 the rites of the morning sacrifice
23 m. holocaust which you shall always offer
Deut 16 4 first day in the evening until m.
28 67 at evening: Who will grant me morning
Judg 19 8 when morning was come, the Levite
Ruth 2 7 she hath been in the field from m.
3 13 when morning is come, if he will take
13 sleep till the morning. So she slept
1 K 3 15 Samuel slept till morning, and opened
14 36 destroy them till the morning light
17 16 Philistine came out m. and evening
20 35 when the morning came. Jonathan went
25 22 of all that belong to him till the m.
34 not been left to Nabal by the m. light
36 she told him nothing . . . until morning
2 K 11 14 morning was come, David wrote a letter
23 4 as the light of the morning, when the
24 15 from morning unto the time appointed
3 K 18 26 name of Baal from m. even till noon
4 K 7 9 and do not tell it till the morning
10 8 in two heaps . . . until the morning
16 15 offer the morning holocaust and the
1 Pa 16 40 continually, morning and evening
2 Pa 2 4 for the holocausts, m. and evening
13 11 holocausts to Lord . . . m. and evening
31 3 be offered always morning and evening
1 Es 3 3 holocaust to the Lord m. and evening
2 Es 4 21 spears from the rising of the morning
8 3 read it . . . from the m. until midday
Job 4 20 m. till evening they shall be cut
24 17 if the morning suddenly appear, it is
38 7 when the morning stars praised me
12 didst thou . . . command the morning
41 9 his eyes like the eyelids of the morning
Ps 54 18 evening and morning . . . I will speak
64 9 outgoings of the m. and of the evening
73 16 thou hast made the morning light and
118 148 my eyes to thee have prevented the m.
129 6 from the morning watch even until night
Cant 6 9 cometh forth as the morning rising
Wisd 11 23 as a drop of the morning dew, that
Eccu 18 26 from the m. until the evening the time
24 44 to shine forth to all as morning light
31 24 he shall sleep till morning, and his
50 6 shone in his days as the morning star
Isa 8 20 they shall not have the morning light
17 14 morning shall come, and he shall not be
21 12 the morning cometh, also the night
38 12 m. even to night thou wilt make. 13
13 I hoped till morning, as a lion so hath
58 8 shall thy light break forth as the m.
Lam 3 23 they are new every morning, great is
Eze 46 14 offer the sacrifice for it m. by m.
15 the sacrifice and the oil m. by m.
Dan 8 14 unto evening and morning 2,300 days
26 the vision of the evening and the m.
Osee 6 3 going forth is prepared as the m. light
4 your mercy is as a morning cloud
11 1 as the m. passeth, so hath the king
13 3 they shall be as a morning cloud
Joel 2 2 as the m. spread upon the mountains
Amos 4 13 he that maketh the morning mist
5 8 that turneth darkness into morning
Jon 4 7 when the m. arose on the following day
Soph 3 3 they left nothing for the morning
1 Ma 3 58 and be ready against the morning, that
4 52 they arose before the morning on the
9 13 battle was fought from m. even unto
10 80 cast darts at the people from m. till
12 29 Jonathan . . . knew it not till the m.
Mat 27 1 when morning was come, all the chief
John 18 28 and it was morning; and they went not
21 4 when the morning was come, Jesus
Acts 28 23 persuading . . . from m. until evening
Apoc 2 28 and I will give him the morning star
22 16 the bright and morning star, And the
in the morning Gen 19 2 in the morning you shall go on your way
Gen 19 27 Abraham got up early in the morning
21 14 Abraham rose up in the morning, and
24 54 in the morning, the servant arose and
26 31 arising in the morning, they swore
28 18 Jacob, arising in the morning, took
40 6 Joseph was come in to them in the m.
49 27 in the morning shall eat the prey
Exod 7 15 go to him [Pharao] in the morning
9 13 arise in the m. and stand before Pharao
16 7 in the morning you shall see the glory
8 and in the morning bread to the full
13 in the morning you shall have your fill
13 in the morning a dew lay round
21 every one of them gathered in the m.
24 4 rising in the m. he [Moses] built an
29 39 sacrifice . . . one lamb in the morning
30 7 burn . . . incense upon it in the m.
32 6 in the morning, they offered holocausts
34 2 be ready in the morning, that thou
25 remain in the m. anything of the victim
36 3 daily in the morning offered their vows
Lev 6 12 putting wood on it every day in the m.
20 offer . . . half of it in the morning
Num 14 40 rising up very early in the morning
16 5 in the morning the Lord will make known
22 13 he [Balaam] rose in the morning and
28 4 one you shall offer in the morning
Deut 16 7 in the m. rising up thou shalt go into
28 67 in the morning thou shalt say: Who will
Josu 7 14 you shall come in the morning, every one
16 when he rose in the m., made Israel
8 10 rising early in the m., he mustered
14 he made haste in the morning, and went

Judg 6 28 when the men . . . risen in the morning
9 33 in m. at sun rising set upon the city
16 2 that in morning they might kill him
19 5 early in morning he desired to depart
25 they let her go in the morning. But the
27 in morning the man arose and opened
20 19 rising in the morning, camped by Gabaa
1 K 1 19 they rose in morning and worshipped
5 4 in the morning, they found Dagon lying
9 19 I will let thee go in the morning: and
26 when they were risen in the morning
11 10 in the morning we will come out to you
11 into midst of camp in the m. watch
15 12 rose early, to go to Saul in the morning
17 20 David therefore arose in the morning
19 2 look to thyself . . . in the morning
11 that he might be killed in the morning
25 37 in m. when Nabal had digested his wine
29 10 therefore arise in the morning, thou
11 that they might set forward in the m.
2 K 2 27 if thou hadst spoke sooner, even in m.
23 4 shineth in the morning without clouds
24 11 David arose in the morning, and the
3 K 3 21 when I rose in the morning to give my
17 6 brought him bread . . . in the morning
4 K 3 20 and it came to pass in the morning
22 they rose early in the m. 2 Pa 20:20
19 35 when he arose early in the morning
1 Pa 9 27 might open the gates in the morning
23 30 the Levites are to stand in the morning
Esth 2 14 came out in the morning, and from
5 14 in the morning speak to the king
Job 7 18 thou visitest him early in the morning
21 if thou seek me in the m., I shall not
Ps 5 4 in the morning thou shalt hear my voice
5 in the morning I will stand before thee
29 6 have place, and in the morning gladness
45 6 God will help it in the morning early
48 15 dominion over them in the morning
58 17 will extol thy mercy in the morning
62 7 I will meditate on thee in the morning
77 34 came to him early in the morning. And
87 14 in the m., my prayer shall prevent
89 6 in the m., man shall grow up like grass
6 in m. he shall flourish and pass away
14 we are filled in the morning with thy
91 3 to show forth thy mercy in the morning
100 8 in the m. I put to death all the wicked
107 3 I will arise in the morning early. I
138 9 if I take wings early in the morning
142 8 cause me to hear thy mercy in the m.
Prov 1 28 they shall rise in the m. and shall not
8 17 that in the morning early watch for me
Ecce 10 16 when the princes eat in the morning
11 6 in the morning sow thy seed, and in
Eccu 6 36 go to him early in the morning and let
47 12 magnify the holiness of God in the m.
Isa 5 11 woe to you that rise up early in the m.
14 12 Lucifer, who didst rise in the morning
17 11 in the morning thy seed shall flourish
26 9 in the morning early I will watch to thee
28 19 in the m. early it shall pass through
33 2 be thou our arm in the morning, and
37 36 they arose in the morning, and behold
50 4 he wakeneth in the morning, in the morning he wakeneth my ear
Jer 20 16 let him hear a cry in the morning, and
21 12 judge ye judgment in the morning and
32 33 when I taught them early in the morning
Eze 12 8 word of the Lord came to me in the m.
24 18 so I spoke to the people in the morning
18 I did in the m. as he had commanded me
33 22 till he came to me in the morning
46 13 he shall offer it always in the morning
Dan 6 19 the king rising very early in the m.
14 11 when thou comest in the morning, if
15 the king arose early in the morning
Osee 6 4 as the dew that goeth away in the m.
7 6 in the morning he himself was heated
Amos 4 4 bring in the morning your victims
Mich 2 1 in the morning light they execute it
Soph 3 5 in the m. he will bring his judgment
1 Ma 5 30 early in the m., when they lifted up
16 5 they arose in the m. and went into
Mat 16 3 in the morning: Today there will be a
20 1 went out early in the morning to hire
21 18 in the m., returning into the city
Mark 11 20 when they passed by in the morning
13 35 the cockcrowing or in the morning
15 1 in the m. the chief priests holding a
16 2 very early in the m., the first day of
Luke 21 38 came early in the morning to him in
24 1 very early in the morning, they came
John 8 2 early in the m. he came again into
Acts 5 21 in the morning entered into the temple
mornings Ps 72 14 chastisement hath been in the m.
morrow Lev 7 16 if any of it remain until the m.
Lev 23 15 count from the morrow after the sabbath
16 unto the morrow after the seventh week
1 K 31 8 on the morrow the Philistines came
11 11 when the morrow was come that Saul
1 Ma 5 27 to bring their army on the morrow near
Mat 6 34 the morrow will be solicitous for
Acts 4 5 it came to pass on the morrow, that
10 24 the m. after, he entered into Caesarea
20 7 depart on the morrow: and he continued
James 4 14 know not what shall be on the morrow
morsel Gen 18 5 I will set a morsel of bread
Ruth 2 14 bread, and dip thy m. in the vinegar
1 K 2 36 that I may eat a morsel of bread
28 22 let me set before thee a morsel of bread
3 K 17 11 bring . . . a morsel of bread in thy hand
Job 31 17 if I have eaten my morsel alone, and
Prov 17 1 better is a dry morsel with joy than
28 21 for morsel of bread forsaketh the truth
John 13 27 after the morsel, Satan entered into
30 having received the morsel, went out
morsels Ps 147 17 he sendeth his crystal like m.
mortal Job 38 26 wilderness, where no m. dwelleth
Wisd 7 1 I myself also am a mortal man like
9 14 the thoughts of mortal men are fearful
15 17 being mortal himself, he formeth a
17 hath lived, though he were mortal, but
Isa 51 12 that thou . . . afraid of a mortal man
2 Ma 9 12 a mortal man should not equal himself
Rom 6 12 reign in your mortal body, so as to obey
8 11 shall quicken also your mortal bodies
1 C 15 53 and this mortal must put on immortality
54 when this m. hath put on immortality
2 C 4 11 may be made manifest in our mortal flesh
5 4 that that which is m. may be swallowed
mortality 1 K 5 6 was the confusion of a great m.
mortals Job 36 31 and giveth food to many mortals
Acts 14 14 we also are m., men like unto you
mortar Gen 11 3 and slime instead of mortar. And
Lev 14 42 house be plastered with other mortar
Num 7 14 a little mortar of ten sicles of gold
20 a little mortar of gold. 26, 32, 38, 44, 50, 56, 62, 68, 74, 80
11 8 it in a mill or beat it in a mortar
Prov 27 22 shouldst bray a fool in the mortar
Eze 13 14 you have daubed with untempered mortar
15 that daub it without tempering the m.
22 28 daubed them without tempering the mortar
mortars Num 4 7 with it the censers and little m.
Num 7 84 twelve little mortars of gold. 86

3 K 7 50 mortars and censers of most pure gold
4 K 25 14 they took away also . . . the mortars
2 Pa 4 22 bowls and the mortars, of pure gold
Jer 52 18 the bowls and the little mortars and
19 candlesticks and the mortars and the
1 Ma 1 23 vials and the little mortars of gold
Morter Soph 1 11 howl, ye inhabitants of the M.
mortgage 2 Es 5 3 let us m. our lands and our
mortification 2 C 4 10 in our body the m. of Jesus
mortify Rom 8 13 if by the Spirit you m. the deeds
Col 3 5 mortify therefore your members which
mortises Exod 26 17 shall be made two mortises
Exod 36 22 two mortises throughout every board
24 where the mortises of the sides end
Mosa 1 Pa 2 46 concubine of Caleb bore . . . Mosa
1 Pa 8 9 Sebia and Mosa and Molchom and Jehus
37 Zamri begot M., and M. begot Banaa. 9:42
Mosabab 1 Pa 4 34 Mosabab and Jemlech and Josa
Mosallam 1 Pa 9 8 Mosallam the son of Saphatias
Mosel Eze 27 19 and Mosel have set forth in thy
Mosera Deut 10 6 into Mosera where Aaron died
Moseroth Num 33 30 they came to Moseroth. And
Num 33 31 removing from Moseroth, they camped in
Moses Mat 8 4 offer the gift which M. commanded
17 3 appeared to them M. and Elias. Mark 9:3
4 one for Moses. Mark 9:4; Luke 9:33
19 7 M. commanded to give a bill of divorce
8 Moses by reason of the hardness of
22 24 Moses said: If a man die having no son
23 2 have sitten on the chair of Moses. All
Mark 7 10 Moses said: Honor thy father and thy
10 3 what did Moses command you? Who said
4 Moses permitted to write a bill of
12 19 Moses wrote unto us. Luke 20:28
26 in the book of Moses, how in the bush
Luke 5 14 according as Moses commanded, for a
9 30 M. and Elias, appearing in majesty
16 29 they have Moses and the prophets; let
31 if they hear not M. and the prophets
20 37 Moses also showed, at the bush, when
24 27 Beginning at Moses and all the prophets
John 1 17 the law was given by Moses; grace and
45 of whom Moses in the law, and the
3 14 as Moses lifted up the serpent in the
5 45 there is one that accuseth you, Moses
46 if you did believe Moses, you would
6 32 Moses gave you not bread from heaven
7 19 did not Moses give you the law, and
22 Moses gave you circumcision, not
22 not because it is of Moses, but of
8 5 Moses in the law commanded us to stone
9 28 but we are the disciples of Moses. We
29 we know that God spoke to Moses: but
Acts 3 22 Moses said: A prophet shall the Lord
6 11 words of blasphemy against Moses and
14 traditions which M. delivered unto us
7 20 at the same time was Moses born, and
22 Moses was instructed in all the wisdom
29 Moses fled upon this word and was a
31 Moses seeing it, wondered at the sight
32 M. being terrified, durst not behold
35 this Moses, whom they refused, saying
37 that Moses who said to the children
7 40 as for this Moses, who brought us out
44 speaking to Moses, that he should
15 1 circumcised after the manner of M.
21 Moses of old time hath in every city
21 21 among Gentiles, to depart from Moses
26 22 and Moses did say should come to pass
Rom 5 14 death reigned from Adam unto Moses, even
9 15 for he saith to Moses: I will have mercy
10 5 Moses wrote, that the justice which is
19 first, Moses saith: I will provoke you

1 C 10 2 all in Moses were baptized, in the cloud
2 C 3 7 behold the face of Moses, for the glory
13 not as Moses put a veil upon his face
15 when Moses is read, the veil is upon
2 Tim 3 8 as Jannes and Mambres resisted Moses, so
Heb 3 2 him, as was also Moses in all his house
3 counted worthy of greater glory that M.
5 M. indeed was faithful in all his house
16 all that came out of Egypt by Moses. And
8 5 it was answered to Moses, when he was
9 19 the law had been read by Moses to all
11 23 by faith Moses, when he was born, was
24 by faith Moses, when he was grown up
12 21 Moses said: I am frighted, and tremble
Jude 9 contended about the body of Moses, he
law of Moses Josu 8 31 book of the law of Moses. 23:6; 4 K 14:6; 2 Pa 25:4; 2 Es 8:1
Josu 8 32 Deuteronomy of the l. . . . , which he had
3 K 2 3 as it is written in the l. . . . 2 Pa 23:18; 31:3; 1 Es 3:2; 2 Es 10:34
4 K 23 25 strength, according to all the l. . . .
2 Pa 30 16 the disposition and law of Moses the
1 Es 7 6 a ready scribe in the law of Moses
Tob 7 14 according to the law of Moses. Dan 13:3
Bar 2 2 that are written in the law of Moses
Dan 13 62 to fulfil the law of Moses: and they
Mala 4 4 remember the law of Moses my servant
Luke 2 22 purification, according to the l. . . .
24 44 which are written in the law of Moses
John 7 23 that the l. . . . may not be broken
Acts 13 38 not be justified by the law of Moses
15 5 commanded to observe the law of Moses
28 23 out of law of Moses and the prophets
1 C 9 9 for it is written in the law of Moses
Heb 10 28 a man making void the law of Moses
Moses' Exod 17 12 Moses' hands were heavy
Mosoch Gen 10 2 sons of Japheth: . . . M. 1 Pa 1:5
1 Pa 1 17 sons of Sem . . . Gether and Mosoch
Eze 27 13 and Mosoch, they were thy merchants
32 26 there is Mosoch and Thubal and all
38 2 chief of M. and Thubal. 3; 39:1
Mosollam 1 Pa 3 19 Zorobabel begot Mosollam
1 Pa 5 13 Michael and Mosollam and Sebe and
8 17 and Mosollam and Hezeci and Heber
9 7 Salo the son of Mosollam, the son of
11 Helcias the son of Mosollam the son of
12 Mosollam the son of Mosollamith, the
2 Pa 34 12 and Mosollam of the sons of Caath, who
1 Es 8 16 Zacharias and Mosollam, chief men: and
10 29 sons of Bani, Mosollam and Melluch and
2 Es 3 4 next to him built Mosollam the son of
6 Mosollam the son of Besodia built the
30 built Mosollam the son of Barachias
6 18 daughter of M. the son of Barachias
8 4 and Hasbadana, Zacharia and Mosollam
10 7 Mosollam, Abia, Miamin, Maazia, Belgia
20 Megphias, Mosollam, Hazir, Mesizabel
11 7 Sellum the son of Mosollam, the son of
11 Helcias the son of Mosollam the son of
12 13 of Esdras, Mosollam: and of Amaria
16 Zacharia: of Genthon, Mosollam: of
25 Mosollam, Telmon, Accub, were keepers
33 Azarias, Esdras, and Mosollam, Judas
Mosollamia 1 Pa 9 21 Zacharias the son of M.
Mosollamith 1 Pa 9 12 son of M. the son of Emmer
Mosollamoth 2 Pa 28 12 Barachias the son of M.
2 Es 11 13 Ahazi the son of Mosollamoth the son
mote Mat 7 3 why seest thou the mote. Luke 6:41
Mat 7 4 let me cast the mote out of thy eye
5 shalt thou see to cast out the mote
Luke 6 42 let me pull the mote out of thy eye
42 shall not clearly to take out the mote
moth Job 4 19 be consumed as with the moth

Job 27 18 he hath built his house as a moth and
Prov 25 20 as a moth doth by a garment, and a
Eccu 42 13 from garments cometh a moth, and from
Isa 14 11 under thee shall the moth be strewed
50 9 a garment, the moth shall eat them up
51 8 the moth shall consume them as wool
Bar 6 11 themselves from the rust and from the m.
Osee 5 12 and I will be like a moth to Ephraim
Mat 6 19 where the rust and moth consume and
20 neither the rust nor moth doth consume
Luke 12 33 approacheth nor moth corrupteth. For
motheaten Job 13 28 as a garment that is m.
Bar 6 71 the scarlet which are m. upon them
James 5 2 and your garments are motheaten. Your
mother Gen 2 24 a man shall leave father and m.
Gen 3 20 she was the mother of all the living
24 53 also to her brothers and to her mother
55 her brother and mother answered: Let
32 11 and kill the mother with the children
43 29 Benjamin his brother by the same mother
44 20 whose brother by the mother is dead
Exod 2 8 the maid went and called her mother
Lev 18 9 of thy sister by father or by mother
20 14 after marrying daughter, marry the m.
20 father or of his uncle by the mother
Deut 21 13 mourn for her father and mother one
22 15 her father and mother shall take her
Judg 11 2 because thou art born of another m.
2 K 1 26 as the mother loveth her only son, so
17 25 sister of Sarvia, who was m. of Joab
20 19 and to overthrow a mother in Israel
3 K 1 11 Bethsabee the m. of Solomon. 2:13
2 19 a throne was set for the king's mother
3 27 not be killed, for who is the mother
11 26 whose mother was named Sarua, a widow
4 K 4 30 mother of the child said: As the Lord
11 1 Athalia the mother of Ochozias, seeing
24 15 king's mother and the king's wives
1 Pa 2 26 Atara, who was the mother of Onam
2 Pa 15 16 Maacha the mother of king Asa he
Tob 14 12 as soon as you shall bury your mother
Esth 2 7 her father and mother being dead
Ps 112 9 a house, the joyful mother of children
Prov 17 25 sorrow of the mother that bore him
30 11 father and doth not bless their mother
Cant 6 8 she is the only one of her mother, the
Wisd 7 12 that she was the mother of them all
Eccu 4 10 father, and as a husband to their m.
11 will have mercy on thee more than a m.
15 2 will meet him as an honorable mother
24 24 I am the mother of fair love and of
40 1 their burial into the mother of all
41 21 of fornication before father and m.
Isa 8 4 know to call his father and his mother
49 1 from the bowels of my mother he hath
50 1 this bill of the divorce of your mother
1 deeds have I put your mother away
66 13 as one whom the mother caresseth, so
Jer 15 8 against the mother of the young man
16 7 to comfort them for their father and m.
50 12 your m. is confounded exceedingly
Eze 16 44 as the mother was, so also is her
45 your mother was a Cethite, and your
22 7 they have abused father and mother
23 2 two women, daughters of one mother
44 25 no dead . . . only their father and m.
Osee 2 2 judge your mother, judge her; because
5 their mother hath committed fornication
10 14 the mother being dashed in pieces upon
Mich 7 6 daughter riseth up against her mother
2 Ma 7 1 with their mother, were apprehended
5 together with the mother, exhorted
20 the m. was to be admired above measure
25 king called the mother and counselled
41 after the sons the m. also was consumed
Mat 8 14 saw his wife's mother lying and sick
10 35 and the daughter against her mother
37 he that loveth father or mother more
14 8 being instructed before by her mother
11 and she brought it to her mother
15 4 he that shall curse father or mother
5 whosoever shall say to father or mother
19 5 shall a man leave father and mother
29 left . . . father or mother. Mark 10:29
20 20 mother of the sons of Zebedee. 27:56
27 56 Mary the mother of James and Joseph
Mark 1 30 Simon's wife's mother lay in a fit of a
3 35 is my brother and my sister and mother
5 40 father and the mother of the damsel
6 24 said to her mother, What shall I ask
28 and the damsel gave it to her mother
7 10 he that shall curse father or mother
15 40 and Mary the mother of James the less
47 Mary the mother of Joseph, beheld where
16 1 and Mary the mother of James, and
Luke 1 43 mother of my Lord should come to me
4 38 Simon's wife's mother was taken with
8 51 and the father and m. of the maiden
12 53 the m. against the daughter, and the daughter against the m.
John 2 1 and the mother of Jesus was there. And
3 mother of Jesus saith to him: They have
6 42 whose father and mother we know? How
Acts 1 14 the women and Mary the mother of Jesus
12 12 he came to the house of Mary the mother
Gal 4 26 is above, is free: which is our mother
Heb 7 3 without father, without m., without
Apoc 17 5 the mother of the fornications and the
his mother Gen 21 21 his m. took a wife for him
Gen 24 67 her into the tent of Sara his mother
27 13 his mother said to him: Upon me be
14 brought, and gave them to his mother
28 5 Syrian, brother to Rebecca his mother
30 14 which he brought to his mother Lia
44 20 he alone is left of his mother, and his
Exod 21 15 he that striketh his father or mother
17 that curseth his father or m. Lev 20:9
Lev 19 3 every one fear his father and his m.
20 9 he hath cursed his father and mother
17 father, or the daughter of his mother
21 2 for his father and for his mother, and
11 even for his father or his m. Num 6:7
24 11 his mother was called Salumith, the
Deut 21 18 the commandments of his father or m.
27 16 that honoreth not his father and mother
22 daughter of his father or of his mother
33 9 said to his father and to his mother
Judg 5 28 his mother looked out at a window and
14 2 [Samson] told his father and his mother
3 his father and mother said to him: Is
5 Samson went down with his . . . mother
6 not tell this to his father and mother
9 coming to his father and mother, he
17 2 said to his mother: The 1,100 pieces of
3 he restored them to his mother. 4
1 K 2 19 and his mother made him a little coat
3 K 2 22 Solomon answered, and said to his m.
15 2 the name of his mother was. 22:42; 4 K 8:26; 12:1; 14:2; 15:2, 33; 18:2; 21:1, 19; 22:1; 23:31, 36; 24:8, 18; 2 Pa 12:13; 20:31; 22:2; 24:1; 25:1; 26:3; 27:1; 29:1; Jer 52:1
13 he also removed his mother Maacha
17 23 and [Elias] delivered him to his mother
22 53 walked in way of his father and his m.
4 K 3 2 but not like his father and his mother

4 19 take him and carry him to his mother
20 brought him to his mother, she set him
24 12 he and his mother and his servants
1 Pa 4 9 and his mother called his name Jabes
2 Pa 22 3 his mother pushed him on to do wickedly
10 Athalia his mother, seeing that her son
Tob 5 22 bade his father and his mother farewell
23 his mother began to weep and to say
28 his mother ceased weeping, and held her
10 4 but his mother wept and was quite
14 14 after the death of his mother, Tobias
Ps 108 14 let not sin of his m. be blotted out
130 2 that is weaned is towards his mother
Prov 10 1 foolish son is the sorrow of his mother
15 20 the foolish man despiseth his mother
19 26 chaseth away his mother, infamous
20 20 he that curseth his father and mother
28 24 from his father or from his mother
29 15 own will bringeth his mother to shame
30 17 labor of his mother in bearing him
31 1 wherewith his mother instructed him
Cant 3 11 diadem wherewith his mother crowned him
Eccu 3 5 he that honoreth his mother is as one
7 shall be a comfort to his mother. He
18 cursed of God that angereth his mother
Zach 13 3 father and his mother that brought him
3 his mother, his parents shall thrust
1 Ma 13 28 pyramids . . . for his father and his m.
2 Ma 7 4 brethren and his mother looking on
Mat 1 18 as his mother Mary was espoused to
2 11 found the child with Mary his mother
13 take the child and his mother. 20
14 took the child and his mother. 21
12 46 his mother and his brethren stood
13 55 is not his mother called Mary, and his
15 6 shall not honor his father or his mother
Mark 3 31 his m. and his brethren came. Luke 8:19
7 11 man shall say to his father or mother
12 to do anything for his father or mother
10 7 shall leave his father and m. Eph 5:31
Luke 1 60 his mother answering, said: Not so
2 33 his father and mother were wondering
34 said to Mary his mother: Behold this
48 his mother said to him: Son, why hast
51 his m. kept all these words in her
7 12 the only son of his mother; and she
15 speak. And he gave him to his mother
14 26 and hate not his father and mother
John 2 5 his mother saith to the waiters
12 to Capharnaum, he and his mother and
19 25 by the cross of Jesus, his mother and
26 Jesus therefore had seen his mother
26 he saith to his mother: Woman, behold
Rom 16 13 Rufus, elect in the Lord, and his mother
my mother Gen 20 12 not the daughter of my mother
Josu 2 13 that you will save my father and mother
Judg 8 19 my brethren, the sons of my mother
14 16 not tell it to my father and mother
1 K 22 3 let my father and my mother tarry
2 K 19 37 sepulcher of my father and of my mother
3 K 2 20 the king said to her: My mother, ask
19 20 let me . . . kiss my father and my m.
Tob 10 9 my father and mother now count the days
Job 17 14 to worms, my mother and my sister
Ps 21 10 my hope from the breasts of my mother
26 10 my father and my mother have left me
50 7 in sins did my mother conceive me
68 9 an alien to the sons of my mother
Prov 4 3 as an only son in the sight of my m.
Cant 1 5 sons of my m. have fought against me
8 1 sucking the breasts of my mother, that
Wisd 7 1 in womb of my mother I was fashioned
Jer 15 10 woe is me, my mother: why hast thou
20 14 the day in which my mother bore me
17 that my mother might have been my grave
Mat 12 48 who is my mother. Mark 3:33
49 my mother and my brethren. Mark 3:34; Luke 8:21
50 he is my brother and sister and mother
thy mother Gen 37 10 shall I and thy m. and thy
Exod 20 12 honor thy father and thy m. Deut 5:16
Lev 18 7 or the nakedness of thy m.: she is thy m.
20 19 nakedness of thy aunt by thy mother
Deut 13 6 if thy brother the son of thy mother
Josu 2 18 gather together thy father and mother
1 K 15 33 so shall thy mother be childless among
20 30 to confusion of thy shameless mother
4 K 3 13 prophets of thy father and thy mother
9 22 the fornications of Jezabel thy mother
Tob 4 3 thou shalt honor thy mother all the
Prov 1 8 forsake not the law of thy mother. 6:20
23 22 despise not thy mother when she is old
25 let thy father and thy mother be joyful
Cant 8 5 there thy mother was corrupted, there
Eccu 3 16 repaid to thee for the sin of thy m.
7 29 forget not the groanings of thy mother
23 18 remember thy father and thy mother
Jer 1 5 I formed thee in the bowels of thy m.
22 26 I will send thee and thy mother that
Eze 16 3 Amarrhite, and thy mother a Cethite
19 2 why did thy mother the lioness lie down
10 thy mother is like a vine in thy blood
Osee 4 5 I have made thy mother to be silent
Mat 12 47 thy mother and thy brethren stand
15 4 honor thy father and mother. 19:19; Mark 7:10; 10:19; Luke 18:20; Eph 6:2
Mark 3 32 thy m. and thy brethren. Luke 8:20
John 19 27 to the disciple: Behold thy mother
2 Tim 1 5 and in thy mother Eunice, and I am
mother-in-law Deut 27 23 he that lieth with his m.
Judg 5 29 returned this answer to her m.
Ruth 1 14 Ruth stuck close to her m. And Noemi
14 Orpha kissed her m. and returned
2 2 Ruth the Moabitess said to her m.
11 that thou hast done to thy m. after
18 the city, and showed it to her m.
19 her m. said to her: Where hast thou
22 her m. said to her: It is better for
3 1 after she was returned to her m., Noemi
6 and did all that her m. had bid her
16 came to her m.; who said to her: What
17 not have thee return empty to thy m.
Tob 10 13 to honor her father and mother-in-law
14 14 and returned to his father and m.
Mich 7 6 the daughter-in-law against her m.
Mat 10 35 the daughter-in-law against her m.
Luke 12 53 the m. against her daughter-in-law
53 daughter-in-law against her m.
mother's Gen 24 28 ran and told in her m. house
Gen 24 67 which was occasioned by his m. death
27 29 let thy mother's children bow down
28 2 to the house of Bathuel thy m. father
Lev 18 13 not uncover nakedness of thy m. sister
13 because she is thy mother's flesh
Num 12 12 that is cast forth from the m. womb
Judg 9 1 went to Sichem to his mother's brethren
1 to all the kindred of his m. father
3 his mother's brethren spoke of him
13 5 Nazarite . . . from his mother's womb
16 17 consecrated to God from my m. womb: if
3 K 14 21 his mother's name was Naama. 31
2 Pa 13 2 his mother's name was Michaia, the
Job 1 21 naked came I out of my mother's womb
31 18 it came out with me from my m. womb
Ps 21 11 from my mother's womb, thou art my God
49 20 didst lay a scandal against thy m. son

70 6 from my m. womb thou art my protector
138 13 protected me from my mother's womb
Ecce 5 14 came forth naked from his mother's womb
Cant 3 4 till I bring him into my mother's house
8 2 and bring thee into my mother's house
Eccu 3 11 but the mother's curse rooteth up the
40 1 their coming out of their mother's womb
49 9 a prophet from his mother's womb, to
50 24 increased our days from our m. womb
Eze 16 45 thou art thy mother's daughter, that
Mat 19 12 were born so from their mother's womb
Luke 1 15 Ghost, even from his mother's womb
John 3 4 second time into his mother's womb
19 25 his mother and his mother's sister
Acts 3 2 who was lame from his mother's womb
14 7 a cripple from his mother's womb
Gal 1 15 who separated me from my m. womb, and
mothers Ruth 1 8 to them: Go ye home to your m.
Eccu 3 3 seeking the judgment of the mothers
Jer 16 3 concerning their m. that bore them
Lam 2 12 said to their mothers: Where is corn
12 their souls in the bosoms of the m.
5 3 a father: our mothers are as widows
Mark 10 30 brethren and sisters and mothers and
1 Tim 1 9 murderers of mothers, for manslayers
5 2 old women, as mothers: young women, as
motion 2 K 20 8 as to come out with the least m.
Jdth 13 6 and the motion of her lips in silence
14 14 he perceived no motion of one lying
Ps 88 10 and appeasest the motion of the waves
Bar 6 41 sensible that have no m. themselves
John 5 4 pond after the motion of the water
mount Gen 31 21 going on towards mount Galaad
Gen 31 23 overtook him in the mount of Galaad
25 his tent in the same mount of Galaad
Exod 19 12 take heed you go not up into the mount
12 every one that toucheth the mount
13 then let them go up into the mount
14 Moses came down from the mount to the
16 very thick cloud to cover the mount
17 they stood at the bottom of the mount
18 and all the mount was terrible. And the
20 Sinai, in the very top of the mount
23 set limits about the mount and sanctify
20 18 the people saw . . . the mount smoking
24 4 built an altar at the foot of the mount
12 come up to me into the mount. Deut 10:1
13 Moses going up into the mount of God
15 gone up, a cloud covered the mount
17 burning fire upon the top of the mount
25 40 shown thee in the mount. 26:30; 27:8
32 1 delayed to come down from the mount
15 and Moses returned from the mount
19 broke them at the foot of the mount
33 6 aside their ornaments by mount Horeb
34 2 stand with me upon the top of the mount
3 any man be seen throughout all the mount
Num 10 33 marched from the mount of the Lord
20 25 and bring them up into mount Hor: and
27 and they went up into mount Hor before
21 4 they marched from mount Hor by the
23 14 upon the top of mount Phasga, Balaam
28 him upon the top of mount Phogor, which
33 32 they came to mount Gadgad. From thence
37 from Cades, they camped in mount Hor
38 Aaron the priest went up into mount Hor
41 and they departed from mount Hor, and
Deut 3 8 Arnon unto the m. Hermon. Josu 12:1
12 Arnon unto the half of mount Galaad
4 11 you came to the foot of the mount
49 and unto the foot of mount Phasga
5 4 spoke to us face to face in the mount
9 9 I went up into the mount. 10:3
9 I continued in the mount forty days
10 spoke to you in the mount. 10:4
15 I came down from the burning mount
10 5 returning from the mount, I came down
10 I stood in the mount, as before, forty
11 29 put the blessing upon mount Garizim, the curse upon mount Hebal
27 4 set up the stones . . . in mount Hebal
12 these shall stand upon mount Garizim
13 shall stand on mount Hebal to curse
32 49 go up . . . unto mount Nebo, which is
50 Aaron thy brother died in mount Hor
33 2 he hath appeared from mount Pharan
34 1 Moses went up . . . upon mount Nebo
Josu 8 30 Josue built an altar . . . in mount Hebal
33 half of them by mount Garizim, and half by mount Hebal
11 17 by plain of Libanus under mount Hermon
12 4 and had dominion in mount Hermon and
7 mount, part of which goeth up into Seir
13 5 from Baalgad under mount Hermon to the
11 all mount Hermon and all Basan as far
15 9 reacheth to the towns of mount Ephron
10 passeth by the side of mount Jarim
11 to Sechrona, and passeth mount Baala
20 7 Cedes in Galilee of mount Nephtali
24 30 north side of mount Gaas. Judg 2:9
Judg 3 3 Hevites that dwelt in mount Libanus
3 from mount Baal Hermon to the entering
4 6 and lead an army to mount Thabor
14 Barac went down from mount Thabor
7 3 away from mount Galaad and returned
9 7 stood on the top of mount Garizim
48 Abimelech . . . went up into mount Selmon
12 15 Pharathon . . . in the mount of Amalech
1 K 13 2 with Saul in Machmas and in mount Bethel
23 19 of the wood, in mount Hachila, which is
31 1 and fell down slain in mount Gelboe
8 found Saul . . . lying in mount Gelboe
2 K 1 6 I came by chance upon mount Gelboe
3 K 18 19 unto me all Israel, unto mount Carmel
20 together the prophets unto mount Carmel
19 8 walked . . . unto the mount of God, Horeb
11 stand upon the mount before the Lord
4 K 2 25 from thence he went to mount Carmel
4 25 came to the man of God to mount Carmel
27 she came to the man of God to the mount
23 13 on right side of the Mount of Offence
16 the sepulchers that were in the mount
1 Pa 5 23 Hermon and Sanir and mount Hermon, for
10 1 fell down wounded in mount Gelboe. And
8 Saul and his sons lying on mount Gelboe
2 Pa 3 1 house of the Lord . . . in mount Moria
13 4 Abia stood upon mount Semeron, which
33 15 in the mount of the house of the Lord
2 Es 3 20 in the mount Baruch . . . built another
8 15 forth to the mount and fetch branches
Tob 5 8 is situate in the mount of Ecbatana
Job 20 6 if his pride mount up even to heaven
39 27 will the eagle mount up at thy command
Ps 106 26 they mount up to the heavens and they
Cant 4 1 which came up from mount Galaad. Thy
Wisd 9 8 to build a temple on thy holy mount
Eccu 50 13 as the cedar planted in mount Libanus
Isa 16 1 to the mount of the daughter of Sion
27 13 shall adore the Lord in the holy mount
30 16 and we will mount upon swift ones
56 7 I will bring them into my holy mount
57 13 and shall possess my holy mount. And I
65 11 that have forgotten my holy mount, that
Jer 6 23 they shall mount upon horses, prepared
51 53 if Babylon should mount up to heaven
Eze 4 2 cast up a mount and set a camp against

10 16 wings, to mount up from the earth, the
11 23 over the mount that is on the east
21 22 to cast up a mount, to build forts
26 8 shall cast up a mount. Dan 11:15
Abdi 8 understanding out of the mount of Esau
9 may be cut off from the mount of Esau
19 shall inherit the mount of Esau, and
21 to judge the mount of Esau: and the
Haba 1 10 shall cast up a mount and shall take it
3 3 the holy one from mount Pharan: his
Zach 14 4 shall stand . . . upon the mount of Olives
4 the mount of Olives shall be divided
1 Ma 9 15 pursued them even to the mount Azotus
12 36 raise a mount between the castle and
Mark 11 1 to Bethania at the mount of Olives, be
13 3 and as he sat on the mount of Olivet
14 26 they went forth to the mount of Olives
Luke 19 29 unto the mount called Olivet, he sent
21 37 m. that is called Olivet. Acts 1:12
22 39 his custom, to the mount of Olives
Heb 8 5 which was shown thee on the mount. But
12 20 so much as a beast shall touch the m.
2 P 1 18 we were with him in the holy mount
mount Ephraim; *see* **Ephraim**
mount Olivet; *see* **Olivet**
mount Seir; *see* **Seir**
mount Sina; *see* **Sina**
mount Sinai; *see* **Sinai**
mount Sion; *see* **Sion**
mountain Gen 10 30 Sephar, a mountain in the east
Gen 12 8 passing on from thence to a mountain
14 10 that remained fled to the mountain
19 17 save thyself in the mountain, lest
19 I cannot escape to the mountain, lest
30 and Lot . . . abode in the mountain, and
22 14 in the mountain the Lord will see. And
31 25 Jacob had pitched his tent in the m.
54 had offered sacrifices in the mountain
Exod 3 1 mountain of God. 4:27; 18:5; Eze 28:16
12 offer sacrifice to God upon this mountain
15 17 plant them in m. of thy inheritance
19 2 pitched their tents over against the m.
3 Lord called unto him from the mountain
24 18 Moses . . . went up into the mountain
Num 14 40 they went up to the top of the m. 44
45 Chanaanite that dwelt in the mountain
20 29 Aaron being dead in the top of the m.
27 12 go up into this m. Abarim. Deut 32:49
33 23 and camped in the mountain Sepher
24 departing from the mountain Sepher
34 7 great sea, reaching to the most high m.
Deut 1 6 you have stayed long enough in this m.
7 come to the m. of the Amorrhites and
19 mountain of the Amorrhite. 20
41 you went ready armed unto the mountain
43 pride, you went up into the mountain
2 3 you have compassed this m. long enough
3 25 I will see . . . this goodly mountain
5 5 and went not up into the mountain
22 Lord spoke to . . . you in the mountain
23 after you . . . saw the mountain burn
9 21 torrent which cometh down from the m.
32 49 and die thou in the mountain. When thou
33 19 they shall call the people to the m.
Josu 2 23 the spies . . . came down from the mountain
3 16 waters . . . swelling up like a mountain
11 16 Josue took . . . the mountain of Israel
17 part of mountain that goeth up to Seir
21 from all the mountain of Juda and Israel
13 19 Sarathasar in the m. of the valley
14 12 give me therefore this mountain, which
15 8 ascending to the top of the mountain
9 it passeth on from top of the mountain
48 in the mountain Samir and Jether and
16 1 from Jericho to mountain of Bethel
17 18 thou shalt pass to the mountain and
18 13 into Ataroth-addar to the mountain
14 the m. that looketh towards Beth-horon
16 down to that part of the mountain that
20 7 Hebron in the mountain of Juda. 21:11
Judg 1 34 straitened children of Dan in the m.
35 he dwelt in the mountain Hares, that
1 K 17 3 the Philistines stood on a mountain
3 Israel stood on mountain on other side
23 14 in a mountain of the desert of Ziph
26 Saul went on this side of the mountain
25 20 coming down to the foot of the mountain
2 K 13 34 by a by-way on side of the mountain
15 32 David was come to top of the mountain
3 K 5 15 and 80,000 to hew stones in the mountain
4 K 2 16 and cast him upon some mountain or
6 17 behold the mountain was full of horses
Jdth 6 9 out of way by the side of the mountain
Job 14 18 a mountain falling cometh to nought
Ps 10 2 get thee away from hence to the mountain
23 3 the m. of the Lord. Isa 2:3; 30:29; Mich 4:2; Zach 8:3
67 16 the mountain of God is a fat mountain, a curdled mountain, a fat mountain
17 m. in which God is well pleased to dwell
77 54 them into the m. of his sanctuary
54 m. which his right hand had purchased
Cant 4 6 I will go to the mountain of myrrh
Isa 2 2 m. of the house of the Lord. Mich 4:1
10 32 against the m. of the daughter of Sion
13 2 upon the dark m. lift ye up a banner
14 13 I will sit in the m. of the covenant
22 5 and magnificent upon the mountain
25 6 unto all people in this mountain, a feast
7 he shall destroy in this mountain
10 hand of the Lord shall rest in this m.
28 21 up as in the mountain of divisions
30 17 the mast of a ship on the top of a m.
25 there shall be upon every high mountain
40 4 every m. and hill shall be made low
9 get thee up upon a high mountain, thou
57 7 upon a high and lofty m. thou hast laid
Jer 3 6 gone of herself upon every high mountain
16 16 they shall hunt them from every mountain
26 18 m. of the house the high places of woods
50 6 they have gone from mountain to hill
51 25 I come against thee, thou destroying m.
25 and will make thee a burnt mountain
Bar 5 7 appointed to bring down every high m.
Eze 17 22 I will plant it on a mountain high
20 40 in my holy m., in the high m. of Israel
34 6 my sheep have wandered in every mountain
40 2 and set me upon a very high mountain
43 12 of the house upon the top of the m.
Dan 2 34 till a stone was cut out of a mountain
35 the stone . . . became a great mountain
45 that the stone was cut out of the m.
Amos 6 1 that have confidence in m. of Samaria
Mich 3 12 m. of the temple as the high places
7 12 they shall come . . . from mountain to m.
Agge 1 8 go up to the mountain, bring timber
Zach 4 7 who art thou, O great mountain, before
8 3 be called . . . The sanctified mountain
14 4 half of the mountain shall be separated
1 Ma 2 1 he abode in the mountain of Modin
4 18 and his army are near us in the mountain
19 appeared looking forth from the mountain
46 laid up the stones in m. of the temple
9 38 hid themselves under covert of the m.
13 53 he fortified the mountain of the temple
16 20 others to take . . . the m. of the temple

2 Ma 2 4 to the mountain where Moses went up
Mat 4 8 him up into a very high mountain, and
5 1 went up into a m. Luke 9:28; John 6:3
14 a city seated on a mountain cannot be
8 1 when he was come down from the m.
14 23 he went into a mountain alone to pray
15 29 going up into a mountain, he sat there
17 1 them up into a high m. Mark 9:1
9 they came down from the m. Mark 9:8; Luke 9:37
19 shall say to this m. 21:21; Mark 11:23
28 16 the m. where Jesus had appointed them
Mark 3 13 going up into a m., he called unto
5 11 near the m. a great herd of swine
6 46 he went up to the mountain to pray
Luke 3 5 every m. and hill shall be brought
4 5 devil led him into a high mountain
6 12 he went out into a mountain to pray
8 32 many swine feeding on the mountain
John 4 20 our fathers adored on this mountain
21 neither on this m. nor in Jerusalem
6 15 fled again into the m. himself alone
Gal 4 25 Sina is a mountain in Arabia, which hath
Heb 12 18 you are not come to a m. that might be
Apoc 6 14 every m. and the islands were moved
8 8 a great m., burning with fire, was cast
21 10 in spirit to a great and high mountain

holy mountain Ps 2 6 by him over Sion his h. m.
Ps 47 2 in the city of our God, in his holy m.
98 9 Lord our God and adore at his holy m.
Isa 11 9 nor shall they kill in all my holy m.
65 25 not hurt nor kill in all my holy m.
66 20 in coaches to my holy m. Jerusalem
Jer 31 23 the beauty of justice, the holy m.
Eze 28 14 I set thee in the holy m. of God
Dan 9 16 city Jerusalem and from thy holy m.
20 of my God, for the holy m. of my God
11 45 upon a glorious and holy mountain
Joel 2 1 sound an alarm in my holy mountain
3 17 your God, dwelling in Sion my holy m.
Abdi 16 you have drunk upon my holy mountain
Soph 3 11 be lifted up because of my holy m.
1 Ma 11 37 upon the holy m. in a conspicuous

mountains Gen 7 19 mountains under the whole heaven
Gen 8 4 upon the mountains of Armenia. And the
5 the tops of the mountains appeared
14 6 smote . . . the Chorreans in the mountains
22 2 shalt offer him . . . upon one of the m.
Exod 32 12 might kill them in the mountains, and
Num 13 18 when you shall come to the mountains
30 and the Amorrhite in the mountains
23 7 brought me . . . from the m. of the east
33 47 the mountains of Abarim. 48
Deut 1 24 and had gone up to the mountains, came
44 Amorrhite that dwelt in the mountains
2 37 except . . . the cities in the mountains
12 2 worshipped their gods upon high mountains
32 22 shall burn the foundations of the m.
33 15 of the tops of the ancient mountains
Josu 2 16 get ye up to the mountains, lest
22 they went and came to the mountains
9 1 that dwelt in the mountains and in
10 6 who dwell in the m., are gathered
11 2 kings of the north, that dwelt in the m.
3 he sent to . . . Jebusite in the mountains
21 cut off the Enacims from the mountains
12 8 as well in the m. as in the plains
13 6 all that dwell in the m. from Libanus
17 16 we cannot go up to the mountains, for
18 12 thence going up westward to the m.
Judg 1 9 the Chanaanite, who dwelt in the m.
5 5 the mountains melted before the face
6 2 dens and caves in the mountains, and
9 25 ambush . . . on the top of the mountains
36 seest the shadows of the mountains as
36 multitude cometh down from the mountains
11 37 that I may go about the mountains for
38 she mourned her virginity in the m.
1 K 26 20 as the partridge is hunted in the m.
2 K 1 19 of Israel are slain upon thy mountains
21 ye mountains of Gelboe, let neither
22 8 foundations of the mountains were moved
3 K 19 11 wind . . . overthrowing the mountains
4 K 19 23 gone up to the height of the mountains
1 Pa 12 8 like the roebucks on the mountains
2 Pa 2 2 to hew stones in the mountains. 18
18 16 all Israel scattered in the mountains
26 10 dressers of vines in the mountains
27 4 built cities in the mountains of Juda
Jdth 2 12 came to the great mountains of Ange
3 3 all mountains and hills and fields
7 he came down from the mountains with
4 3 seized upon all the tops of the m.
5 possession of the ascents of the m.
5 where the way was narrow between the m.
5 1 had shut up the ways of the mountains
3 is this people that besetteth the m.
5 this people, that dwelleth in the m.
23 are gone up into all these mountains
28 let us go up into the mountains: and
6 8 when they came near the mountains
7 5 lead directly between the mountains
8 but the mountains are their defence
9 because it is situate in the mountains
16 5 the Assyrian came out of the mountains
18 the mountains shall be moved from
Job 9 5 who hath removed mountains, and they
24 8 wet with the showers of the mountains
28 9 overturned mountains from the roots
39 8 he looketh round about the mountains
40 15 to him the mountains bring forth grass
Ps 17 8 the foundations of the m. were troubled
35 7 thy justice is as the mountains of God
45 3 and the mountains shall be removed
4 the m. were troubled with his strength
64 7 thou who preparest the mountains by
67 17 why suspect, ye curdled mountains? A
71 3 let the mountains receive peace for
16 firmament . . . on the tops of mountains
82 15 as a flame burning mountains: so shalt
86 1 foundations thereof are in the holy m.
89 2 before the mountains were made or the
94 4 the heights of the mountains are his
96 5 the mountains melted like wax at the
97 8 the mountains shall rejoice together
103 6 above the m. shall the waters stand
8 the m. ascend and the plains descend
32 toucheth the mountains, and they smoke
113 4 the mountains skipped like rams, and
6 ye mountains, that ye skipped like rams
120 1 have lifted up my eyes to the mountains
124 2 in Jerusalem. M. are round about it
143 5 touch the mountains, and they shall smoke
146 8 maketh grass to grow on the mountains
148 9 mountains and all hills, fruitful trees
Prov 8 25 the mountains . . . had not as yet been
27 25 the hay is gathered out of the mountains
Cant 2 8 he cometh leaping upon the mountains
17 a young hart upon the m. of Bether
4 8 from the mountains of the leopards
8 14 hart upon the m. of aromatical spices
Wisd 17 18 rebounding echo from the highest mountains
Eccu 16 19 the mountains also and the hills
43 4 the sun . . . burneth the mountains
17 at his sight shall the m. be shaken
23 it shall devour the m. and burn the

Isa 2 2 shall be prepared on the top of m.
14 and upon all the high mountains and
5 25 m. were troubled, and their carcasses
13 4 noise of a multitude in the mountains
14 25 upon my mountains tread him under foot
17 2 their green trees upon the high m.
13 as the dust of the m. before the wind
18 3 the sign shall be lifted up on the m.
6 left together to the birds of the m.
34 3 the m. shall be melted with their blood
37 24 I have gone up to the height of the m.
40 12 and weighed the mountains in scales
41 15 thou shalt thrash the mountains and
42 11 they shall cry from the top of the m.
15 I will lay waste the m. and hills
44 23 ye mountains, resound with praise
49 11 I will make all my mountains a way
13 ye m., give praise with jubilation
52 7 how beautiful upon the m. are the feet
54 10 the m. shall be moved, and the hills
55 12 the m. and the hills shall sing praise
64 1 the m. would melt away at thy presence
3 at thy presence the m. melted away
65 7 who have sacrificed upon the mountains
9 out of Juda a possessor of my mountains
Jer 3 23 liars, and the multitude of the m.
4 24 I looked upon the mountains, and behold
9 10 for the m. I will take up weeping
13 16 your feet stumble upon the dark m.
17 26 they shall come . . . from the mountains
31 5 vineyards in the mountains of Samaria
32 44 in the cities on the mountains. 33:13
46 18 as Thabor is among the mountains
50 6 have made them wander in the mountains
Lam 4 19 they pursued us upon the mountains
Bar 6 38 stones that are hewn out of the m.
62 to consume mountains and woods, doth
Eze 6 3 thus saith the Lord God to the m.
13 and on all the tops of mountains, and
7 7 and not of the joy of mountains. Now
16 they shall be in the m. like doves
18 6 hath not eaten upon the mountains. 15
11 but that eateth upon the mountains
22 9 they have eaten upon the m. in thee
31 12 and cast him away upon the mountains
32 5 I will lay thy flesh upon the mountains
6 with thy stinking blood upon the m.
35 8 I will fill his m. with his men that are
36 4 thus saith the Lord God to the mountains
6 say to the mountains and to the hills
38 20 the mountains shall be thrown down
21 sword against him in all my mountains
Dan 3 75 ye mountains and hills, bless the Lord
Osee 4 13 offered sacrifice upon tops of the m.
10 8 they shall say to the m.: Cover us
Joel 2 2 as the morning spread upon the mountains
5 noise of chariots upon the tops of m.
3 18 the mountains shall drop down sweetness
Amos 3 9 assemble yourselves upon m. of Samaria
4 1 that are in the mountains of Samaria
13 he that formeth the m. and createth
9 13 the mountains shall drop sweetness
Jon 2 7 went down to the lowest parts of the m.
Mich 1 4 the m. shall be melted under him: and
4 1 shall be prepared in the top of m. and
6 1 contend thou in judgment against the m.
2 let the m. hear the judgment of the Lord
Nah 1 5 the m. tremble at him, and the hills
15 upon the m. the feet of him that
3 18 thy people are hid in the mountains
Haba 3 6 the ancient m. were crushed to pieces
10 the m. saw thee, and were grieved
Agge 1 11 I called for a drought upon . . . the m.
Zach 6 1 came out from the midst of two mountains
1 the mountains were mountains of brass
14 5 shall flee to the valley of those m.
5 the valley of the m. shall be joined
Mala 1 3 I have made his mountains a wilderness
1 Ma 2 28 he and his sons fled into the mountains
4 5 he [Gorgias] sought them in the m.
38 courts as in a forest or on the m.
6 39 the mountains glittered therewith
40 was distinguished by the high mountains
9 40 the rest fled into the mountains, and
10 70 showest thy power against us in the m.
11 68 they laid an ambush for him in the m.
2 Ma 5 27 lived amongst wild beasts in the m.
9 8 to weigh the heights of the mountains
28 in a strange country among the m.
10 6 when they were in the m. and in dens
Mat 18 12 doth he not leave the 99 in the m.
24 16 Judea, let them flee to the mountains
Mark 5 5 in the monuments and in the m., crying
13 14 that are in Judea, flee into the m.
Luke 21 21 who are in Judea flee to the mountains
23 30 then shall they begin to say to the m.
1 C 13 2 so that I could remove mountains, and
Heb 11 38 wandering in deserts, in m., in dens
Apoc 6 15 the dens and in the rocks of mountains
16 they say to the m. and the rocks: Fall
16 20 away, and the mountains were not found
17 9 the seven heads are seven mountains
mountains of Israel Eze 6 2 set thy face towards the mountains of Israel
Eze 6 3 ye m. of Israel, hear the. 36:1, 4
17 23 on the high m. of Israel will I plant
19 9 no more be heard upon the m. of Israel
33 28 mountains of Israel shall be desolate
34 13 I will feed them in the m. of Israel
14 pastures shall be in the high m. of Israel
14 in fat pastures upon the m. of Israel
35 12 hast spoken against the m. of Israel
36 1 prophesy to the mountains of Israel
8 m. of Israel, shoot ye forth your
37 22 nation in the land on the m. of Israel
38 8 to the mountains of Israel which have
39 2 will bring thee upon the m. of Israel
4 shalt fall upon the mountains of Israel
17 a great victim upon the m. of Israel
mounted Deut 33 26 he that is m. upon the heaven
Judg 12 14 mounted upon seventy ass colts, and he
Ps 75 7 slumbered that mounted on horseback
Eze 23 6 all horsemen, mounted upon horses
Dan 3 47 flame mounted up above the furnace
mounteth Ps 67 34 who m. above the heaven of
mounts Eze 17 17 when he shall cast up mounts
mourn Gen 23 2 Abraham came to m. and weep for
Deut 21 13 mourn for her father and mother one
1 K 16 1 how long wilt thou mourn for Saul
2 K 3 31 and mourn before the funeral of Abner
3 K 13 29 city of the old prophet, to m. for him
14 13 all Israel shall mourn for him and
2 Es 8 9 do not mourn nor weep: for all the
Job 5 11 comforteth with health those that m.
14 22 and his soul shall mourn over him
31 38 and with it the furrows thereof mourn
Ps 77 64 sword: and their widows did not mourn
Prov 5 11 and thou mourn at the last, when thou
29 2 shall bear rule, the people shall m.
Ecce 3 4 a time to mourn and a time to dance
Eccu 7 38 weep, and walk with them that mourn
Isa 3 26 her gates shall lament and mourn and
15 2 to the high places to mourn over Nabo
19 8 the fishers also shall mourn and all
10 all they shall mourn that made pools
32 12 mourn for your breasts, for the

57 18 him, and to them that mourn for him
61 2 to comfort all that mourn: to appoint
66 10 with her, all you that mourn for her
Jer 4 28 the earth shall mourn, and the heavens
12 4 how long shall the land mourn, and
16 5 neither go thou to m. nor to comfort
22 18 they shall not mourn for him, Alas
34 5 and they shall mourn for thee, saying
48 31 the men of the brick wall that mourn
49 3 mourn and go about by the hedges: for
Lam 1 4 the ways of Sion mourn because there
Eze 7 12 buyer rejoice: nor the seller mourn
27 the king shall mourn, and the prince
9 4 and mourn for all the abominations that
13 22 made the heart of the just to mourn
21 6 mourn with the breaking of thy loins
27 30 they shall mourn over thee with a land
32 8 lights of heaven to mourn over thee
Osee 4 3 therefore shall the land mourn and
Joel 1 5 and mourn all ye that take delight in
Amos 8 8 every one m. that dwelleth therein
9 5 and all that dwell therein shall mourn
Zach 12 10 shall mourn for him as one mourneth
12 the land shall mourn: families and
Mat 5 5 blessed are they that mourn: for they
9 15 can children of the bridegroom mourn
24 30 then shall all tribes of the earth m.
Luke 6 25 laugh: for you shall mourn and weep
2 C 12 21 I mourn many of them that sinned before
James 4 9 be afflicted and mourn and weep: let
Apoc 18 11 shall weep and mourn over her: for no
mourned Gen 50 3 Egypt m. for him seventy days
Exod 33 4 hearing these very bad tidings, mourned
Num 14 39 and the people mourned exceedingly
20 30 mourned for him [Aaron] thirty days
Deut 34 8 mourned for him in the plains of Moab
8 they mourned for Moses were ended
Judg 11 38 she m. her virginity in the mountains
1 K 15 35 Samuel mourned for Saul, because the
25 1 they mourned for him and buried him
28 3 all Israel mourned for him [Samuel]
2 K 1 12 they mourned and wept and fasted until
11 26 wife of Urias . . . she mourned for him
13 37 David mourned for his son every day
19 1 the king wept and mourned for his son
3 K 13 30 they m. over him, saying: Alas, alas
31 when they had m. over him, he said to
14 18 Israel mourned for him according to
1 Pa 7 22 Ephraim their father mourned many days
2 Pa 35 24 all Juda and Jerusalem mourned for him
1 Es 10 6 he m. for the transgression of them
2 Es 1 4 I sat down and wept and m. for many
Jdth 16 29 all the people mourned for seven days
Job 29 25 I was a comforter of them that mourned
Isa 24 4 the earth mourned and faded away, and
7 the vintage hath mourned, the vine hath
33 9 the land hath mourned and languished
Jer 12 11 it waste, and it hath mourned for me
14 2 Judea hath mourned, and the gates
22 23 how hast thou mourned when sorrows
23 10 the land hath m. by reason of cursing
Lam 2 8 and the bulwark hath mourned, and
Dan 10 2 I Daniel m. the days of three weeks
Osee 10 5 people thereof have mourned over it
Joel 1 9 the Lord's ministers have mourned: the
10 is destroyed, the ground hath m.: for
Amos 1 2 places of the shepherds have m. and
Zach 7 5 when you fasted and mourned in the
1 Ma 1 27 the princes and the ancients mourned
28 bride that sat in the marriage bed, m.
2 39 they mourned for them exceedingly
70 all Israel mourned for him with great
9 20 they m. for him many days. 13:26

12 52 and Israel m. with great lamentation
Mat 11 17 we have lamented, and you have not m.
Luke 7 32 we have m., and you have not wept
8 52 all wept and mourned for her. But he
1 C 5 2 have not rather mourned, that he might
mourner 2 K 14 2 feign thyself to be a mourner
Jer 48 5 shall the mourner go up with weeping
mourners Ecce 12 5 the m. shall go round about in
Eccu 48 27 and comforted the mourners in Sion
Isa 61 3 to appoint to the mourners of Sion
Eze 24 17 not thy face nor eat the meat of m.
22 nor shall you eat the meat of mourners
Osee 9 4 shall be like the bread of mourners
mournest Eze 21 7 say to thee: Why mournest thou
mourneth Eccu 36 27 mourneth that is in want. Who
Jer 8 18 sorrow, my heart mourneth within me
16 7 that m., to comfort him for the dead
Zach 12 10 mourn for him as one m. for an only
mournful Isa 59 11 and shall lament as m. doves
Eze 27 32 shall take up a m. song for thee and
32 18 sing a m. song for the multitude of
mourning Gen 27 41 days will come of the m. of my
Gen 37 34 sackcloth, m. for his son a long time
35 down to my son into hell, mourning
38 12 had taken comfort after his mourning
50 4 the time of the mourning being expired
11 this is a great m. to the Egyptians
11 that place was called, The m. of Egypt
Deut 26 14 I have not eaten of them in my m.
34 8 days of their mourning in which they
2 K 3 33 the king m. and lamenting over Abner
11 27 the mourning being over, David sent
14 2 and put on mourning apparel and be not
2 had a long time been m. for one dead
1 Es 9 3 my beard, and I sat down mourning
19 2 the victory . . . was turned into m.
Tob 2 5 he ate bread with mourning and fear
6 shall be turned into lamentation and m.
Jdth 6 14 all of them together m. and weeping
Esth 4 3 there was great mourning among the Jews
9 22 their mourning and sorrow were turned
13 17 turn our mourning into joy, that we may
14 2 garments suitable for weeping and m.
16 21 hath turned this day of sadness and m.
Job 23 2 is more grievous than my mourning
30 28 I went mourning without indignation
31 my harp is turned to mourning and my
Ps 29 12 hast turned for me my mourning into joy
34 14 as one mourning and sorrowful so was I
41 10 why go I mourning, whilst my enemy
Prov 14 13 mourning taketh hold of the end of joy
Ecce 7 3 better to go to the house of mourning
5 heart of the wise is where there is m.
Wisd 18 10 a lamentable m. was heard for the
19 3 whilst they were yet mourning and
Eccu 22 6 tale out of time is like music in m.
13 mourning for the dead is seven days
26 8 is the grief and mourning of the heart
38 18 make mourning for him according to his
41 14 mourning of men is about their body
Isa 21 2 have made all the m. thereof to cease
22 12 shall call to weeping and to mourning
29 2 it shall be in sorrow and mourning and
35 10 sorrow and m. shall flee away. 51:11
54 6 as a woman forsaken and m. is spirit
60 20 the days of thy mourning shall be ended
61 3 the oil of joy for mourning, a garment
Jer 6 26 make thee mourning as for an only son
9 10 the beautiful places of the desert, m.
20 every one teach her neighbor mourning
31 13 I will turn their mourning into joy
15 of mourning and weeping, of Rachel
41 5 and their clothes rent, and mourning

48 32 will weep for thee with the m. of Jazer
38 in the streets thereof general mourning
Lam 5 15 our dancing is turning into mourning
Bar 4 9 God hath brought upon me great m.
11 I sent them away with weeping and m.
23 I sent you forth with mourning and
34 and her gladness shall be turned to m.
Bar 5 1 put off, O Jerusalem, garment of thy m.
Eze 3 15 seven days mourning in the midst of
8 14 women sat there mourning for Adonis
24 17 in silence, make no m. for the dead
31 15 I brought in mourning, I covered him
Joel 2 12 be converted . . . in weeping and in m.
Amos 5 16 they shall call the husbandman to m.
8 10 I will turn your feasts into mourning
10 will make it as the m. of an only son
Mich 1 8 and a mourning like the ostriches
11 the house adjoining shall receive m.
Nah 2 7 were led away mourning as doves
1 Ma 1 26 there was great mourning in Israel
41 her festival days were turned into m.
42 her excellency was turned into mourning
2 70 mourned for him with great mourning
3 51 thy priests are in m. and are brought
9 41 the marriage was turned into mourning
Mat 2 18 great mourning; Rachel bewailing her
Mark 16 10 who were mourning and weeping. And
Acts 8 2 and made great mourning over him. But
2 C 7 7 relating to us your desire, your m.
James 4 9 your laughter be turned into mourning
Apoc 18 8 death and mourning and famine, and she
15 weeping and m. and saying: Alas. 19
21 4 death shall be no more, nor mourning
mouse Lev 11 29 the weasel and the mouse and the
Isa 66 17 did eat swine's flesh . . . and the m.
mouth Gen 29 2 mouth thereof was closed with a great
Gen 29 3 to put it on the mouth of the well
8 the stone from the well's mouth, that
42 27 saw the money in the sack's mouth; and
35 money tied in the mouth of his sack
44 2 in the mouth of the younger's sack, put
Exod 4 11 who made man's mouth? Or who made the
23 13 neither shall it be heard out of your m.
Num 12 8 for I speak to him mouth to mouth: and
22 28 the Lord opened the mouth of the ass
Deut 8 3 that proceedeth from the mouth of God
17 6 mouth of two or three witnesses. 19:15
31 19 know it by heart and sing it by mouth
21 take away out of the m. of their seed
Josu 6 10 nor any word go out of your mouth
9 14 consulted not the mouth of the Lord
10 18 roll great stones to mouth of the cave
22 open the mouth of the cave, and bring
27 and put great stones at the mouth
Judg 14 8 swarm of bees in the mouth of the lion
1 K 2 3 old matters depart from your mouth
12 14 and not provoke the mouth of the Lord
2 K 13 32 was appointed by the mouth of Absalom
14 19 these words into mouth of thy handmaid
17 19 a covering over the mouth of the well
3 K 7 31 the mouth also of the laver within
13 26 was disobedient to mouth of the Lord
19 18 mouth that hath not worshipped him
22 13 words of the prophets with one mouth
22 in m. of all his prophets. 2 Pa 18:21
23 in m. of all thy prophets. 2 Pa 18:22
4 K 21 16 till he filled Jerusalem up to the mouth
2 Pa 18 12 with one m. declare good to the king
35 22 words of Nechao from the mouth of God
36 12 speaking to him from mouth of the Lord
21 by the mouth of Jeremias. 22; 1 Es 1:1
1 Es 9 11 filled it from mouth to m. with their
Jdth 13 25 praise shall not depart out of the mouth
Esth 7 8 not yet gone out of the king's mouth
Job 21 5 and lay your finger on your mouth
34 3 mouth discerneth meats by the taste
36 16 thee at large out of the narrow mouth
Ps 8 3 out of the mouth of infants and of
21 22 save me from the lion's mouth; and
36 30 mouth of the just shall meditate wisdom
62 12 mouth is stopped of them that speak
108 2 mouth of the wicked and the mouth of the
125 2 then was our mouth filled with gladness
134 16 they have a mouth, but they speak not
143 8 whose mouth hath spoken vanity. 11
Prov 4 24 remove from thee a forward mouth: and
6 12 walketh with a perverse mouth, he
8 13 I hate . . . mouth with a double tongue
10 6 iniquity covereth the m. of the wicked
11 the m. of the just is a vein of life
11 mouth of the wicked covereth iniquity
14 mouth of the fool is next to confusion
31 mouth of the just shall bring forth
32 mouth of the wicked uttereth perverse
11 11 by m. of wicked it shall be overthrown
12 6 mouth of the just shall deliver them
14 3 in mouth of a fool is the rod of pride
15 2 the mouth of fools bubbleth out folly
14 mouth of fools feedeth on foolishness
28 m. of wicked overfloweth with evils
18 4 words from mouth of a man are as deep
7 the mouth of a fool is his destruction
20 of the fruit of a man's mouth shall
19 28 m. of the wicked devoureth iniquity
22 14 m. of a strange woman is a deep pit
26 7 parable is unseemly in mouth of fools
9 so is a parable in the mouth of fools
28 and a slippery mouth worketh ruin
27 21 is tried by mouth of him that praiseth
30 16 hell, and the mouth of the womb and
Ecce 8 2 I observe the mouth of the king and
10 12 words of the mouth of a wise man are
Wisd 1 11 mouth that belieth, killeth the soul
10 21 wisdom opened the mouth of the dumb
Eccu 13 30 poverty is very wicked in the mouth of
15 9 praise is not seemly in m. of a sinner
10 and shall abound in a faithful mouth
20 21 continually in the mouth of the unwise
22 a parable coming out of a fool's mouth
26 it will be continually in the mouth of
31 presents . . . make them dumb in the m.
21 6 prayer out of the mouth of the poor
20 mouth of the prudent is ought after
29 mouth of wise men is in their heart
22 27 if thou hast opened a sad mouth, fear
23 7 hear . . . the discipline of the mouth
23 is wicked in the mouth of his flesh
24 5 I came out of the mouth of the most High
28 14 quenched: both come out of the mouth
30 18 that are hidden in a mouth that is shut
34 8 plain in the mouth of the faithful
39 41 with the whole heart and mouth praise
40 32 will be sweet in mouth of the unwise
49 2 shall be sweet as honey in every mouth
Isa 1 20 the mouth of the Lord hath spoken it
9 12 shall devour Israel with open mouth
17 every mouth hath spoken folly. For all
10 14 was none that . . . opened the mouth
40 5 mouth of the Lord hath spoken. 58:14
57 4 upon whom have you opened your mouth
59 21 nor out of the mouth of thy seed, nor out of
the mouth of thy seed's seed
62 2 which the mouth of the Lord shall name
Jer 9 12 word of the m. of the Lord may come
23 16 they speak . . . not out of mouth of the
32 4 he shall speak to him mouth to mouth

36 4 Baruch wrote from the m. of Jeremias
27 had written from the mouth of Jeremias
32 wrote in it from the mouth of Jeremias
44 17 that shall proceed out of our own mouth
25 spoken with your mouth and fulfilled
26 in the mouth of any man of Juda, in
45 1 in a book, out of the m. of Jeremias
48 28 maketh her nest in mouth of the hole
Lam 3 38 proceed out of the m. of the Highest
4 20 breath of our mouth, Christ the Lord
Eze 21 22 to open the mouth in slaughter, to lift
29 21 I will give thee an open mouth in the
35 13 you rose up against me with your mouth
Dan 3 51 these three as with one mouth praised
4 28 the word was yet in the king's mouth
6 17 and laid upon the mouth of the den
7 5 there were three rows in the mouth
8 and a mouth speaking great things
20 that horn that had eyes and a mouth
14 26 and put them into the dragon's mouth
Joel 1 5 wine: for it is cut off from your mouth
Amos 3 12 should get out of the lion's mouth
Jon 3 7 in Ninive from the mouth of the king
Mich 4 4 mouth of the Lord of hosts hath spoken
7 16 they shall put the hand upon the mouth
Nah 3 12 shall fall into the mouth of the eater
Zach 5 8 cast the weight of lead upon the mouth
8 9 these words by the m. of the prophets
1 Ma 2 60 was delivered out of m. of the lions
Mat 4 4 that proceedeth from the mouth of God
12 34 of the heart the m. speaketh. Luke 6:45
15 11 not that which goeth into the mouth
11 what cometh out of the mouth, this
17 whatsoever entereth into the mouth
18 things which proceed out of the mouth
17 26 when thou hast opened its mouth, thou
18 16 in m. of two or 3 witnesses. 2 C 13:1
21 16 out of the mouth of infants and of
Luke 1 70 by the mouth of his holy prophets, who
21 15 I will give you a mouth and wisdom
Acts 1 16 spoke before by the mouth of David
3 18 had showed by the mouth of all the
21 spoken by the m. of his holy prophets
4 25 by the mouth of our father David, thy
15 27 who themselves also will, by word of m.
23 2 stood by him to strike him on the mouth
Rom 3 14 mouth is full of cursing and bitterness
19 that every mouth may be stopped, and all
10 10 with the mouth, confession is made unto
15 6 that with one mind, and with one mouth
1 C 9 9 thou shalt not muzzle the m. of the ox
2 C 6 11 our m. is open to you, O ye Corinthians
Eph 4 29 let no evil speech proceed from your m.
Col 3 8 filthy speech out of your mouth. Lie
2 Tim 4 17 delivered out of the mouth of the lion
James 3 10 out of the same mouth proceedeth
3 J 14 and we will speak mouth to mouth. Peace
Apoc 13 2 and his mouth as the mouth of a lion
5 to him a mouth speaking great things
16 13 I saw from the mouth of the dragon
13 and from the mouth of the beast and from
the mouth of the false prophet

her mouth Gen 4 11 earth, which hath opened her m.
Gen 8 11 with green leaves, in her mouth. Noe
Num 16 30 the earth opening her mouth swallow
32 opening her mouth, devoured them with
26 10 opening her mouth, swallowed up Core
30 7 the word once going out of her mouth
Deut 11 6 earth, opening her mouth, swallowed up
1 K 1 12 Heli observed her mouth. Now Anna
2 K 14 3 and Joab put the words in her mouth
Job 5 16 but iniquity shall draw in her mouth
Ps 68 16 let not the pit shut her mouth upon me
106 42 all iniquity shall stop her mouth
Prov 30 20 who eateth, and wiped her mouth and
31 26 she hath opened her mouth to wisdom
Eccu 24 2 shall open her mouth in the churches
26 15 she will open her mouth as a thirsty
Isa 5 14 opened her mouth without any bounds
Osee 2 17 the names of Baalim out of her mouth
Apoc 12 16 earth opened her mouth and swallowed

his mouth Lev 13 45 his m. covered with a cloth
Num 23 5 and the Lord put the word in his mouth
16 and had put the word in his mouth
Deut 18 18 and I will put my words in his mouth
1 K 14 26 but no man put his hand to his mouth
27 and he carried his hand to his mouth
2 K 18 25 there are good tidings in his mouth
22 9 and a devouring fire out of his mouth
3 K 8 15 who spoke with his mouth to David
20 33 in haste caught the word out of his m.
4 K 4 34 and he put his mouth upon his mouth
1 Pa 16 12 his signs and the judgments of his m.
Tob 13 1 and Tobias the elder opening his mouth
Job 3 1 Job opened his mouth and cursed his day
15 30 taken away by breath of his own mouth
20 12 when evil shall be sweet in his mouth
22 22 receive the law of his mouth and lay
23 12 the words of his mouth I have hid in
35 16 therefore Job openeth his mouth in vain
37 2 the sound that cometh out of his mouth
40 18 that the Jordan may run into his mouth
41 4 who can go into the midst of his mouth
10 out of his mouth go forth lamps like
12 a flame cometh forth out of his mouth
Ps 9 7 his mouth is full of cursing and of
32 6 power of them by the spirit of his m.
35 4 the words of his mouth are iniquity
37 14 as a dumb man not opening his mouth
15 and that hath no reproofs in his mouth
104 5 wonders and the judgments of his m.
Prov 2 6 out of his mouth cometh prudence and
11 9 with his mouth deceiveth his friend
12 14 by the fruit of his own mouth shall a
13 2 of the fruit of his own mouth shall
3 that keepeth his m., keepeth his soul
15 23 a man rejoiceth in sentence of his m.
16 10 his mouth shall not err in judgment
23 heart of the wise shall instruct his m.
26 because his m. hath obliged him to it
18 6 and his mouth provoketh quarrels
19 24 not so much as bring it to his mouth
20 17 his mouth shall be filled with gravel
21 23 that keepeth his mouth and his tongue
24 7 in the gate he shall not open his mouth
26 15 grieveth him to turn it to his mouth
30 32 would have laid his hand upon his mouth
Ecce 6 7 all the labor of man is for his mouth
Cant 1 1 him kiss me with the kiss of his mouth
Eccu 14 1 not slipped by a word out of his mouth
15 5 she shall open his mouth and shall fill
20 15 opening of his m. is kindling of a fire
27 26 he will sweeten his m. and will admire
26 at the last he will writhe his mouth
29 30 not deal confidently nor open his mouth
39 7 he will open his mouth in prayer and
22 at words of his mouth the receptacles
Isa 11 4 strike the earth with the rod of his m.
53 7 own will, and he opened not his m.
7 shearer, and he shall not open his m.
9 neither was there deceit in his mouth
Jer 9 8 with his mouth one speaketh peace
20 ears receive the word of his mouth
36 17 write all these words from his mouth
18 with his mouth he pronounced all these
51 44 I will bring forth out of his mouth

Lam 1 18 I have provoked his mouth to wrath
3 29 he shall put his mouth in the dust
4 4 hath stuck to the roof of his mouth
Dan 3 25 opening his mouth in the midst of the
Zach 9 7 will take away his blood out of his m.
Mala 2 6 the law of truth was in his mouth
7 they shall seek the law at his mouth
1 Ma 9 55 and his mouth was stopped, and he was
2 Ma 6 18 to open his mouth to eat swine's flesh
Mat 5 2 opening his mouth, he taught them
Luke 1 64 his mouth was opened, and his tongue
4 22 that proceeded from his mouth, and
11 53 to oppress his mouth about many things
54 to catch something from his mouth
22 71 have heard it from his own mouth
John 19 29 hyssop, put it to his mouth, Jesus
Acts 8 32 shearer, so openeth he not his mouth
35 then Philip, opening his mouth and
10 34 Peter opening his mouth, said: In very
18 14 Paul was beginning to open his mouth
22 14 shouldst hear the voice from his mouth
2 Th 2 8 shall kill with the spirit of his mouth
1 P 2 22 neither was guile found in his mouth
Apoc 1 16 from his mouth came out a sharp two
12 15 the serpent cast out of his mouth after
16 which the dragon cast out of his mouth
13 2 and his mouth as the mouth of a lion
6 he opened his mouth unto blasphemies
19 15 out of his mouth proceedeth a sharp
21 which proceedeth out of his mouth

my mouth Gen 45 12 it is my mouth that speaketh
Num 22 38 that which God shall put in my mouth
Deut 32 1 earth give ear to words of my mouth
Judg 11 35 for I have opened my mouth to the Lord
1 K 2 1 my mouth is enlarged over my enemies
3 K 17 1 but according to the words of my mouth
Tob 4 2 hear, my son, the words of my mouth
Jdth 5 5 not a false word come out of my mouth
9 18 and put thou words in my mouth and
Esth 14 13 give me a well ordered speech in my m.
Job 6 30 neither shall folly sound in my mouth
7 11 wherefore I will not spare my mouth
9 20 my own mouth shall condemn me: if I
19 16 I entreated him with my own mouth. My
23 4 would fill my mouth with complaints
30 11 and hath put a bridle into my mouth
31 27 and I have kissed my hand with my mouth
30 I have not given my mouth to sin by
33 2 now I have opened my mouth, let my
39 34 I will lay my hand upon my mouth. One
Ps 16 4 my m. may not speak the words of men
18 15 words of my mouth shall be such as may
33 2 his praise shall be always in my mouth
38 2 I have set a guard to my mouth when
10 I was dumb, and I opened not my mouth
39 4 he put a new canticle into my mouth
48 4 my mouth shall speak wisdom: and the
50 17 and my mouth shall declare thy praise
53 4 give ear to the words of my mouth. For
62 6 my mouth shall praise thee with joyful
65 14 my mouth hath spoken when I was in
17 I cried to him with my mouth: and I
70 8 let my mouth be filled with praise
15 my mouth shall show forth thy justice
77 1 incline your ears to words of my mouth
2 I will open my mouth in parables: I
88 2 will show forth thy truth with my m.
35 the words that proceed from my mouth
108 30 great thanks to the Lord with my mouth
118 43 word of truth utterly out of my mouth
103 more than honey to my mouth. By thy
108 free offerings of my m. make acceptable
131 I opened my mouth and panted: because
137 1 thou hast heard the words of my mouth
140 3 set a watch, O Lord, before my mouth
144 21 my mouth shall speak the praise of the
Prov 4 5 neither decline from words of my mouth
5 7 depart not from the words of my mouth
7 24 and attend to the words of my mouth
8 7 my mouth shall meditate truth, and my
Eccu 22 33 who will set a guard before my mouth
51 33 I have opened my mouth and have spoken
Isa 6 7 he touched my mouth, and said: Behold
30 2 and have not asked at my mouth, hoping
34 16 that which proceedeth out of my mouth
45 23 word of justice shall go out of my m.
48 3 and they went forth out of my mouth
49 2 hath made my mouth like a sharp sword
55 11 which shall go forth from my mouth: it
Jer 1 9 put forth his hand and touched my mouth
15 19 from the vile, thou shalt be as my m.
36 6 which thou hast written from my mouth
Eze 3 2 I opened my mouth, and he caused me to
4 and it was sweet as honey in my mouth
17 thou shalt hear the word out of my m.
4 14 no unclean flesh hath entered into my m.
33 7 thou shalt hear the word from my mouth
22 he opened my mouth till he came to me
22 my m. being opened, I was silent no
Dan 10 3 flesh nor wine entered into my mouth
16 then I opened my mouth and spoke and
Osee 6 5 slain them by the words of my mouth
Mat 13 35 I will open my mouth in parables
Acts 1 4 you have heard, saith he, by my m.
11 8 unclean hath ever entered into my mouth
15 7 by my mouth the Gentiles should hear
Eph 6 19 may open my mouth with confidence
Apoc 2 16 against them with the sword of my m.
3 16 will begin to vomit thee out of my m.
10 10 it was in my mouth sweet as honey: and

their mouth Judg 7 6 it with the hand to t. m.
1 K 17 35 and delivered it out of their mouth
1 Es 8 17 I put in their m. the words that they
2 Es 9 20 didst not withhold from their mouth
Job 5 15 the needy from the sword of their mouth
29 9 and laid the finger on their mouth
23 opened their m. as for a latter shower
Ps 5 10 for there is no truth in their mouth
13 3 their mouth is full of cursing and
16 10 their mouth hath spoken proudly. They
34 21 they opened their mouth wide against me
48 14 they shall delight in their mouth. They
57 7 in pieces their teeth in their mouth
58 8 they shall speak with their mouth, and
13 for the sin of their mouth, and the
61 5 they blessed with their mouth, but
72 9 have set their mouth against heaven
77 30 as yet their meat was in their mouth
36 and they loved him with their mouth
149 6 praises of God shall be in their mouth
Eccu 21 29 the heart of fools is in their mouth
Isa 52 15 kings shall shut their mouth at him
Jer 7 28 and is taken away out of their mouth
12 2 thou art near in their mouth, and for
Lam 2 16 have opened their mouth against thee
Eze 33 31 they turn them into a song of their m.
34 10 I will deliver my flock from their m.
Dan 13 61 of false witness by their own mouth
Mich 3 5 give not something into their mouth
6 12 their tongue was deceitful in their m.
Soph 3 13 deceitful tongue be found in their m.
Zach 14 12 tongue shall consume away in their m.
Jdth 1 16 and their mouth speaketh proud things
Apoc 14 5 in their mouth there was found no lie

thy mouth Gen 41 40 at the commandment of thy m.
Exod 4 12 I will be in thy mouth: and I will

15 I will be in thy mouth and in his mouth
16 to the people and shall be thy mouth
13 9 law of the Lord be always in thy mouth
Deut 23 23 thy own will and with thy own mouth
30 14 in thy mouth and in thy heart
Josu 1 8 book of this law depart from thy mouth
18 he that shall gainsay thy mouth and
Judg 9 38 where is now thy mouth wherewith thou
11 36 my father, if thou hast opened thy m.
18 19 peace and put thy finger on thy mouth
2 K 1 16 thy own mouth hath spoken against thee
3 K 8 24 with thy mouth thou didst speak, and
17 24 word of the Lord in thy mouth is true
2 Pa 6 15 what thou hast spoken with thy mouth
Job 8 2 words of thy mouth be like a strong wind
15 5 thy iniquity hath taught thy mouth
6 thy own mouth shall condemn thee, and
13 to utter such words out of thy mouth
Ps 49 16 and take my covenant in thy mouth
19 thy mouth hath abounded with evil and
80 11 open thy mouth wide, and I will fill
118 13 pronounced all the judgments of thy m.
72 the law of thy mouth is good to me
88 I shall keep the testimonies of thy m.
137 4 have heard all the words of thy mouth
Prov 3 22 life to thy soul, and grace to thy m.
6 2 art ensnared with the words of thy m.
27 2 another praise thee, and not thy own m.
31 8 open thy mouth for the dumb and for
9 open thy m., decree that which is just
Ecce 5 5 not thy mouth to cause thy flesh to sin
Cant 7 8 the odor of thy mouth like apples
Eccu 5 14 if not, let thy hand be upon thy mouth
23 9 not thy mouth be accustomed to swearing
10 not the naming of God be usual in thy m.
17 not thy m. be accustomed to indiscreet
28 28 and make doors and bars to thy mouth
29 words and a just bridle for thy mouth
31 12 not the first to open thy mouth upon it
Isa 51 16 I have put my words in thy mouth and
59 21 my words that I have put in thy mouth
21 shall not depart out of thy mouth nor
Jer 1 9 I have given my words in thy mouth: lo
5 14 will make my words in thy mouth as fire
34 3 his mouth shall speak with thy mouth
Eze 2 8 open thy m., and eat what I give thee
3 26 tongue stick fast to roof of thy mouth
27 speak to thee, I will open thy mouth
16 56 sister was not heard of in thy mouth
63 mayest no more open thy mouth because
24 27 shall thy mouth be opened to him that
Abdi 12 shalt not magnify thy mouth in the day
Mich 7 5 keep the doors of thy mouth from her
Luke 19 22 out of thy own mouth I judge thee
Rom 10 8 the word is nigh thee, even in thy mouth
9 if thou confess with thy mouth the Lord
Apoc 10 9 in thy m. it shall be sweet as honey
mouths Gen 43 21 our money in the m. of the sacks
Esth 9 4 spread abroad through all men's mouths
13 17 shut not the mouths of them that sing
14 9 shut the mouths of them that praise
10 they may open the mouths of Gentiles
Job 16 11 they have opened their mouths upon me
Ps 21 14 have opened their mouths against me
113 5 they have mouths and speak not: they
134 17 neither . . . any breath in their mouths
Wisd 8 12 shall lay their hands on their mouths
Eccu 39 20 and with canticles of your mouths
Lam 3 46 have opened their mouths against us
Dan 3 33 now we cannot open our mouths: we are
6 22 hath shut up the mouths of the lions
Heb 11 33 promises, stopped the mouths of lions
James 3 3 we put bits into the mouths of horses
Apoc 9 17 from their mouths proceeded fire and
18 which issued out of their mouths. For
19 power of the horses is in their mouths
11 5 fire shall come out of their mouths and
move Gen 1 28 that move upon the earth. 30; 9:2; Lev 11:29; 20:25
Gen 41 44 no man shall move hand or foot in all
Lev 11 10 that move and live in the waters, shall
Deut 2 19 against them nor once move to battle
4 18 creeping things, that move on the earth
6 8 be and shall move between thy eyes
Josu 10 12 move not, O sun, toward Gabaon, nor
21 no man durst move his tongue against
4 K 23 18 him alone, let no man move his bones
Job 13 11 as soon as he shall move himself, he
16 6 would move my lips, as sparing you
Ps 35 12 let not the hand of the sinner move me
77 40 and move him to wrath in the place
Wisd 2 2 and speech a spark to move our heart
Isa 19 16 of hosts, which he shall move over it
Jer 14 10 that have loved to move their feet and
Dan 3 79 all that move in the waters, bless the
Amos 8 12 and they shall move from sea to sea
Agge 2 7 I will move the heaven and the earth
8 I will m. all nations: and the desired
22 I will move both heaven and earth
Mat 23 4 of their own they will not move them
Acts 17 28 for in him we live, and move, and are
Heb 12 26 I will move not only the earth, but
Apoc 2 5 and will move thy candlestick out of
moveable Heb 12 27 the translation of the m. things
moveables Jdth 15 8 and beasts and all their m.
moved Gen 1 2 spirit of God m. over the waters
Gen 7 21 destroyed that moved upon the earth
27 39 Isaac being moved, said to him [Esau]
43 30 his heart was moved upon his brother
Exod 10 23 nor m. himself out of the place where
39 19 and be moved one from the other as
Num 10 22 sons of Ephraim also moved their camp
12 15 the people moved not from that place
25 11 because he was moved with my zeal
Deut 9 19 being moved against you, he would have
25 12 neither shalt thou be m. with any pity
32 19 the Lord saw and was moved to wrath
34 7 not dim, neither were his teeth moved
Josu 15 18 she was moved by her husband to ask
Judg 2 18 in their days he was moved to mercy
21 6 of Israel being moved with repentance
1 K 1 13 only her lips moved, but her voice
15 29 and will not be moved to repentance
2 K 14 17 he is neither moved with blessing nor
18 33 the king therefore being much moved
22 8 foundations of the mountains were m.
3 K 3 26 her bowels were moved upon her child
4 K 21 8 feet of Israel to be m. out of the land
22 19 and thy heart hath been moved to fear
1 Pa 16 30 all the earth be moved at his presence
17 9 and shall be moved no more, neither
21 1 Satan . . . moved David to number Israel
2 Es 4 1 being moved exceedingly, he scoffed at
Tob 6 22 moved rather for love of children than
Jdth 4 14 they being moved by this exhortation
16 18 the mountains shall be moved from the
Job 2 3 thou hast moved me against him, that I
32 2 angry and was moved to indignation
37 1 is moved out of its place. Hear
Ps 9 6 I shall not be moved from generation
12 5 trouble me will rejoice when I am m.
14 5 doth these things shall not be moved
15 8 at my right hand, that I be not moved
16 5 paths: that my footsteps be not moved
17 8 mountains were troubled and were m.
20 8 of the most High he shall not be moved

29 7 abundance I said: I shall never be m.
37 17 whilst my feet are moved, they speak
45 6 midst thereof, it shall not be moved
47 6 they were troubled, they were moved
59 4 thou hast moved the earth and hast
4 breaches thereof, for it has been m.
61 3 protector, I shall be moved no more
7 is my helper, I shall not be moved
65 9 hath not suffered my feet to be moved
67 9 the earth was moved, and the heavens
72 2 my feet were almost moved: my steps
77 58 moved him to jealousy with their graven
81 5 foundations of the earth shall be moved
92 1 the world which shall not be moved
93 18 if I said: My foot is moved: thy
95 9 all the earth be moved at his presence
10 the world, which shall not be moved
11 sea be moved, and the fulness. 97:7
98 1 cherubims: let the earth be moved
103 5 it shall not be moved forever and ever
111 6 because he shall not be moved forever
8 shall not be moved until he look over
113 7 presence of the Lord the earth was m.
120 3 may he not suffer thy foot to be moved
124 he shall not be moved forever that
Prov 10 30 the just shall never be moved: but
12 3 root of the just shall not be moved
Cant 5 4 and my bowels are moved at his touch
Wisd 5 11 she moved her wings, and hath flown
Eccu 15 3 strong in him, and he shall not be m.
16 18 in them, shall be moved in his sight
26 10 yoke of oxen that is moved to and fro
Isa 3 16 their feet and moved in a set pace
6 4 the lintels of the doors were moved at
7 2 upon Ephraim, and his heart was moved
2 as the trees of the woods are moved
10 14 there was none that moved the wing or
13 13 earth shall be moved out of her place
19 1 the idols of Egypt shall be moved at
24 19 with trembling shall the earth be moved
40 20 set up an idol that may not be moved
41 7 with nails, that it should not be moved
54 10 the mountains shall be moved and the
10 covenant of my peace shall not be m.
Jer 4 1 of my sight, thou shalt not be moved
8 16 the land was moved at the sound of the
21 7 and he shall not be moved to pity nor
46 8 waves thereof shall be moved as rivers
49 21 the earth is moved at the noise of
50 46 earth is moved and the cry is heard
Eze 9 5 eyes spare nor be ye moved with pity
38 20 shall be moved at my presence: and the
Joel 2 10 hath trembled, the heavens are moved
3 16 heavens and the earth shall be moved
1 Ma 1 29 the land was moved for the inhabitants
6 8 struck with fear and exceedingly moved
41 inhabitants of the land were moved
10 48 and moved his camp near to Demetrius
74 was moved in his mind: and he chose
13 47 Simon being moved, did not destroy
15 25 king Antiochus moved his camp to Dora
2 Ma 3 21 agony, would have m. any one to pity
4 37 and being moved to pity, shed tears
49 Tyrians being moved with indignation
6 21 being moved with wicked pity, for the
7 25 the young man was not moved with these
Mat 18 27 being moved with pity, let him go and
21 10 the whole city was moved, saying: Who
15 of David; were moved with indignation
29 being moved with repentance, he went
24 29 powers of heaven shall be m. Luke 21:26
Mark 13 25 powers that are in heaven shall be m.
15 11 the chief priests moved the people
Luke 7 13 moved with mercy towards her, he
10 33 seeing him, was moved with compassion
15 20 and was moved with compassion, and
John 5 4 the water was moved. And he that went
Acts 2 25 right hand, that I may not be moved
4 31 the place was moved wherein they were
17 5 the Jews, moved with envy, and taking
1 Th 3 3 that no man should be moved in these
2 Th 2 2 you be not easily moved from your sense
Heb 11 7 moved with fear, framed the ark for the
12 26 whose voice then moved the earth; but
James 1 6 which is moved and carried about by
Apoc 6 14 the islands were m. out of their places
moveth Gen 1 26 that moveth upon the earth. 7:8, 14; Lev 11:44
Gen 9 3 and everything that moveth and liveth
Lev 11 46 creature that moveth in the waters and
Job 15 23 when he moveth himself to seek bread
moving Gen 1 21 every living and m. creature
Isa 19 16 because of the moving of the hand of
John 5 3 waiting for the moving of the water
mower Ps 128 7 wherewith the m. filleth not his
Jer 9 22 as grass behind the back of the mower
mowing Amos 7 1 latter rain after the king's m.
mud Haba 3 15 horses, in the mud of many waters
mulberries 1 Ma 6 34 the blood of grapes and m.
mulberry Ps 77 47 their m. trees with hoarfrost
Luke 17 6 you might say to this mulberry tree
mule 2 K 13 29 up every man upon his mule, and
2 K 18 9 that Absalom . . . riding on a mule
9 the mule went under a thick and large
9 the mule on which he rode passed on
3 K 1 33 and set my son Solomon upon my mule
38 set Solomon upon mule of king David
44 they have set him upon the king's mule
Tob 6 17 to their lust, as the horse and mule
Ps 31 9 not become like the horse and the mule
Zach 14 15 destruction of the horse and the mule
mules 3 K 10 25 and horses and mules every year
3 K 18 5 and save the horses and mules, that
1 Pa 12 40 on camels, and on mules and on oxen
2 Pa 9 24 and spices and horses and mules
1 Es 2 66 horses 736, their mules 245. 2 Es 7:68
Isa 66 20 in chariots and in litters and on mules
Eze 27 14 brought horses and horsemen and mules
mules 4 K 5 17 hence two mules burden of earth
multiplicity Eccu 1 7 the m. of her steps? There
multiplied Gen 1 22 let the birds be m. upon the
Gen 6 1 men began to be multiplied upon the
18 20 the cry of Sodom and Gomorrha is m.
35 11 increase thou and be m. Nations and
39 5 m. all his substance both at home
47 27 and grew and was m. exceedingly. And
48 19 shall become peoples and shall be m.
Exod 1 12 more they were m. and increased: and
20 the midwives: and the people m. and
Lev 26 9 you shall be m., and I will establish
Deut 1 10 your God hath m. you, and you are
6 3 thou mayst be greatly multiplied, as
8 1 that you may live and be m. and going
10 22 hath m. thee as the stars of heaven
11 21 that thy days may be multiplied and
Josu 24 3 the land of Chanaan: and I m. his seed
1 K 1 12 as she m. prayers before the Lord
7 2 abode in Cariathiarim, days were m.
25 10 servants are m. nowadays who flee
2 K 14 11 that the next of kin be not multiplied
22 36 and thy mildness hath multiplied me
4 K 21 6 m. soothsayers to do evil before the
1 Pa 4 38 of their families were m. exceedingly
23 17 sons of Rohobia were m. exceedingly
1 Es 9 6 for our iniquities are m. over our
Jdth 5 9 for 400 years were so m. that the army

Job 5 25 know also that thy seed shall be m.
8 7 thy latter things would be multiplied
27 14 if his sons be m., they shall be for
35 6 if thy iniquities be m., what shalt
Ps 3 2 why, O Lord, are they m. that afflict
4 8 corn, their wine, and oil, they are m.
11 9 thou hast m. the children of men
15 4 their infirmities were m.: afterwards
17 15 he m. lightnings, and troubled them
24 17 troubles of my heart are multiplied
19 consider my enemies for they are m.
35 8 how hast thou multiplied thy mercy
37 20 that hate me wrongfully are multiplied
39 6 hast multiplied thy wonderful works
6 spoken: they are m. above number
13 are m. above the hairs of my. 68:5
70 21 thou hast multiplied thy magnificence
105 29 and destruction was m. among them
106 38 and they were multiplied exceedingly
118 69 the iniquity of the proud hath been m.
138 18 and they shall be m. above the sand
Prov 4 10 that years of life may be m. to thee
9 11 by me shall thy days be multiplied
28 28 when they perish, the just shall be m.
29 16 the wicked are m., crimes shall be m.
Wisd 4 3 the m. brood of the wicked shall not
Eccu 16 1 not in ungodly children, if they be m.
23 3 and my offences be multiplied and my sins
47 29 and their sins were m. exceedingly
Isa 6 12 she shall be m. that was left in the
9 3 thou hast m. the nation and hast not
7 his empire shall be m. and there shall
51 2 alone and blessed him and m. him
57 9 with ointment and hast m. thy perfumes
59 12 our iniquities are m. before thee and
Jer 3 16 when you shall be m. and increase in
5 6 because their transgressions are m.
15 8 their widows are m. unto me above the
23 3 they shall increase and be multiplied
29 6 be ye m. there, and be not few in
46 16 he hath multiplied them that fall, and
23 they are multiplied above locusts and
51 16 the waters are multiplied in heaven
Lam 2 5 hath m. in the daughter of Juda the
Eze 16 25 hast multiplied thy fornications. 26
29 hast also m. thy fornications in the
23 19 for she multiplied her fornications
31 5 his branches were m., and his boughs
36 11 they shall be multiplied and increased
Dan 3 98 peace be multiplied unto you. 6:25
Osee 2 8 and multiplied her silver and gold
10 1 of his fruit he hath multiplied altars
12 1 he multiplied lies and desolation
10 I have m. visions and I have used
Joel 3 13 for their wickedness is multiplied
Nah 3 16 thou hast m. thy merchandise above
Zach 10 8 as they were multiplied before. And I
1 Ma 1 10 and evils were multiplied in the earth
3 42 saw that evils were multiplied and
14 15 m. the vessels of the holy places
Acts 6 7 number of the disciples was multiplied
7 17 the people increased and were m. in
12 24 the word of the Lord increased and m.
1 P 1 2 grace unto you and peace be multiplied

multipliest Job 10 17 and m. thy wrath upon me

multiplieth Job 12 23 m. nations, and destroyeth
Job 35 16 in vain and m. words without knowledge
Ecce 10 14 a fool m. words. A man cannot tell
Eccu 6 5 a sweet word multiplieth friends and
24 36 who m. it as the Jordan in the time of
34 10 experienced in many things, m. prudence
35 1 he that keepeth the law, m. offerings
Eze 21 15 languish in heart, and that m. ruins

multiply Gen 1 22 increase and m. 28; 8:17; 9:1
Gen 3 16 I will multiply thy sorrows and thy
9 7 increase you and multiply, and go upon
16 10 I will multiply thy seed. 22:17; 26:4
17 2 and I will multiply thee exceedingly
20 I will . . . increase and multiply him
26 24 I will bless thee, and m. seed for
28 3 make thee to increase and multiply thee
32 12 m. my seed like the sand of the sea
48 4 I will cause thee to increase and m.
Exod 1 10 wisely oppress them, lest they multiply
7 3 shall multiply my signs and wonders
23 29 and the beasts multiply against thee
32 13 I will m. your seed as the stars of
Deut 7 13 he will love thee and multiply thee
13 17 have mercy on thee, and multiply thee
17 16 he shall not multiply horses to himself
30 16 he may multiply thee and bless thee
1 K 2 3 do not multiply to speak lofty things
2 K 24 3 and again multiply them a hundredfold
1 Pa 27 23 Lord had said that he would m. Israel
2 Es 9 23 thou didst m. their children as the
Job 9 17 and m. my wounds even without cause
29 18 and as a palm tree shall m. my days
Ps 64 11 streams thereof, multiply its fruits
137 3 thou shalt multiply strength in my soul
Eccu 23 21 two sorts of men multiply sins and
47 17 and thou didst m. riddles in parables
20 as copper, and didst m. silver as lead
Isa 1 15 when you m. prayer, I will not hear
Jer 2 22 and multiply to thyself the herb borith
30 19 I will m. them, and they shall. Bar 2:34
33 22 so will I multiply the seed of David
46 11 in vain dost thou multiply medicines
Eze 16 7 I caused thee to m. as the bud of the
36 10 I will multiply men upon you, and all
29 will call for corn and will m. it
30 I will multiply the fruit of the tree
37 I will m. them as a flock of men, as
37 26 I will establish them and will m. them
Dan 3 36 that thou wouldst multiply their seed
Amos 4 4 to Galgal, and multiply transgressions
Zach 10 8 I will m. them as they were multiplied
2 Ma 9 16 to multiply the holy vessels and to
2 C 9 10 will multiply your seed, and increase
1 Th 3 12 may the Lord multiply you, and make you
Heb 6 14 thee, and multiplying I shall m. thee

multiplying Deut 28 63 good to you and m. you
Heb 6 14 bless thee, and m. I shall multiply thee

multitude Gen 16 10 shall not be numbered for m.
Gen 28 3 that thou mayst be a m. of people
32 12 sea, which cannot be numbered for m.
36 7 to bear them, for the m. of their flocks
48 4 I will make of thee a m. of people
16 may they grow into a multitude
Exod 5 5 you see that the m. is increased
12 6 m. of the children of Israel. 16:1; 17:1; 35:1, 20; Lev 16:5; Num 1:53; 8:9, 20; 14:5, 7; 15:25; 16:41; 19:9; 31:12
38 a mixed m. without number went up
15 7 in the m. of thy glory thou hast put
16 22 rulers of the m. came and told Moses
23 2 shalt not follow the multitude to do
Lev 4 21 because it is for the sin of the m.
9 24 when the multitude saw, they praised
Num 1 16 the most noble princes of the multitude
3 7 appertaineth to the service of the m.
10 2 mayest call together the multitude
36 return, O Lord, to the m. of the host
11 4 a mixt m. of people that came up with
12 have I conceived all this multitude
13 flesh to give to so great a multitude
22 shall a m. of sheep and oxen be killed

14 1 whole m. crying wept that night
15 that thou hast killed so great a m.
27 how long doth this wicked m. murmur
35 will I do to all this wicked multitude
36 had made the whole m. to murmur
15 24 and the multitude have forgotten to do
33 him to Moses and Aaron and the whole m.
16 26 he [Moses] said to the multitude
45 get you out from the midst of this m.
47 had run to the midst of the multitude
20 1 the multitude came into the desert of
6 Moses and Aaron leaving the multitude
10 together the multitude before the rock
20 forth to meet them with an infinite m.
25 7 rose up from the midst of the multitude
27 14 in the contradiction of the multitude
16 a man that may be over this multitude
21 m. shall go out and go in at his word
31 26 priest and the princes of the m. 32:2
27 and between the rest of the multitude
43 half that fell to rest of the multitude
35 12 until he stand before the multitude
Deut 1 10 as the stars of heaven for m. 28:62
28 the m. is very great and taller than we
26 5 great and strong and of an infinite m.
33 4 a law, the inheritance of the m. of
Josu 6 20 thundered in the ears of the multitude
8 5 rest of the multitude which is with me
13 last of that m. reached to the west side
22 not one of so great a m. was saved
9 15 princes also of the m. swore to them
18 because the princes of the m. had sworn
21 to serve the whole m. in hewing wood
17 14 whereas I am of so great a multitude
18 4 according to number of each multitude
Judg 4 7 his chariots and all his multitude
15 all his chariots and all his multitude
6 5 m. of men and of camels, wasting
7 6 the rest of the m. had drunk kneeling
8 ordered all rest of the m. to depart
12 in the valley, as a m. of locusts
9 29 gather together the m. of an army
36 behold a multitude cometh down from
11 20 gathering an infinite m., went out
16 30 house fell upon . . . the rest of the m.
1 K 5 6 there came forth a multitude of mice
13 5 and a multitude of people besides
14 16 a m. overthrown and fleeing this way
26 5 rest of the multitude round about him
2 K 18 16 being willing to spare the multitude
3 K 3 8 numbered nor counted for multitude
4 20 as the sand of the sea in multitude
8 65 multitude from the entrance of Emath
4 K 19 23 with the m. of my chariots I have gone
2 Pa 4 18 multitude of vessels was innumerable
5 6 so great was multitude of the victims
14 11 we are come against this multitude
20 12 to be able to resist this multitude
14 spirit . . . came in the midst of the m.
15 be not dismayed at this multitude
24 24 into their hands an infinite multitude
29 23 before the king and the whole multitude
32 holocausts which the multitude offered
30 23 pleased the whole m. to keep other seven
24 Ezechias . . . had given to the m. 1,000
25 the multitude of Juda . . . full of joy
33 25 the rest of the multitude of the people
2 Es 4 2 said before . . . m. of the Samaritans
7 66 all the multitude as it were one man
8 2 brought the law before the multitude
9 27 according to m. of thy tender mercies
13 22 to the multitude of thy tender mercies
Jdth 2 8 before with a m. of innumerable camels
5 3 what is their power or what is their m.
7 4 when they saw the m. of them, prostrated
9 6 trusting . . . in a multitude of warriors
9 trust in their m. and in their chariots
16 thy power, O Lord, is not in a multitude
16 5 Assyrian . . . in the m. of his strength
5 his multitude stopped up the torrents
Esth 5 11 his riches and the m. of his children
Job 20 18 according to multitude of his devices
21 8 their seed . . . a multitude of kinsmen
30 18 with the m. of them my garment is
32 7 that a m. of years would teach wisdom
35 9 by reason of the multitude of oppressors
36 18 neither let m. of gifts turn thee aside
39 7 he scorneth the multitude of the city
Ps 5 8 in the m. of thy mercy, I will come
11 according to m. of their wickedness
9 4 according to the multitude of his wrath
30 20 how great is the m. of thy sweetness
48 7 and glory in the m. of their riches
50 3 the m. of thy tender mercies. 68:17
63 3 from the m. of the workers of iniquity
65 3 in m. of thy strength thy enemies shall
68 14 in the multitude of thy mercy hear me
93 19 according to the m. of my sorrows
105 7 the m. of thy mercies. Dan 3:42
45 m. of his mercies. Isa 63:7; Lam 3:32
150 2 according to the m. of his greatness
Prov 5 23 in m. of his folly he shall be deceived
10 19 in m. of words there shall not want sin
14 28 in the m. of people is the dignity of
20 15 there is gold and a multitude of jewels
Cant 7 4 gate of the daughter of the multitude
Wisd 6 26 multitude of the wise is the welfare
8 10 I shall have glory among the multitude
15 among the m. I shall be found good
11 16 upon them a multitude of dumb beasts
18 to send upon them a multitude of bears
14 20 m. of men, carried away by the beauty
16 1 were destroyed by a multitude of beasts
18 5 tookest away a m. of their children
20 disturbance of the m. in the wilderness
19 10 how the river cast up a m. of frogs
Eccu 5 6 he will have mercy on the m. of my sins
6 35 stand in the multitude of ancients
7 7 offend not against the m. of a city
11 will have respect to m. of my gifts
15 not full of words in a m. of ancients
17 thyself among the m. of the disorderly
15 22 desireth not a multitude of faithless
16 17 in such a multitude I shall not be known
24 4 in the m. of the elect she shall have
34 23 for sins by the m. of their sacrifices
35 23 have taken away the m. of the proud
44 20 was the great father of a m. of nations
51 4 the multitude of the mercy of thy name
Isa 1 11 do you offer me the m. of your victims
5 13 their m. were dried up with thirst
13 4 noise of a multitude in the mountains
17 12 woe to the m. of many people, like the multitude of the roaring sea
29 5 the multitude of them that fan thee
5 the m. of them that have prevailed
7 m. of all nations that have fought
8 so shall be the m. of all the Gentiles
31 4 when a m. of shepherds shall come
4 he will not . . . be afraid of their m.
32 14 the multitude of the city is left
37 24 with the m. of my chariots I have gone
47 9 the multitude of thy sorceries. 12
13 hast failed in the m. of thy counsels
57 10 been wearied in the m. of thy ways
60 5 the m. of the sea shall be concerted

6 the m. of camels shall cover thee
63 7 for the multitude of his good things
15 where is . . . the m. of thy bowels
Jer 3 23 were liars, and the m. of the mountains
10 13 he giveth a m. of waters in the heaven
30 14 by reason of the m. of thy iniquities
15 for the m. of the iniquity and for
47 3 his chariots, and the m. of his wheels
49 32 multitude of their cattle for a booty
51 42 she is covered with the m. of the waves
52 15 Babylon, and the rest of the multitude
Lam 1 5 her for the m. of her iniquities
Bar 4 34 the joy of her m. shall be cut off
6 5 when you see the m. behind and before
Eze 1 24 walked, it was like the voice of a m.
12 19 desolate from the m. that is therein
14 4 according to m. of his uncleannesses
16 40 they shall bring upon thee a multitude
19 11 her height in the m. of her branches
23 24 shall come upon thee . . . a m. of people
42 was in her the voice of a m. rejoicing
42 that were brought of the m. of men
46 bring a m. upon them and deliver them
26 10 by reason of the m. of his horses
13 will make the m. of thy songs to cease
27 12 supplied thy fairs with a m. of all
16 by reason of the multitude of thy works
18 thy merchants in the m. of thy works
18 in the multitude of divers riches
27 thy m. that is in the midst of thee
33 which by the multitude of thy riches
34 m. that was in the midst of thee is fallen
28 16 by the m. of thy merchandise, thy inner
18 defiled . . . by m. of thy iniquities
29 19 and he shall take her multitude, and
30 4 the m. thereof shall be taken away
10 I will make the m. of Egypt to cease
15 and will cut off the m. of Alexandria
31 18 this is Pharao and all his multitude
32 3 with the multitude of many people
12 I will overthrow thy multitude: all
12 and m. thereof shall be destroyed
16 for the m. thereof they shall lament
18 a mournful song for the m. of Egypt
22 Assur is there, and all his multitude
23 his multitude lay round about his grave
24 there is Elam and all his multitude
26 Mosoch and Thubal and all their m.
31 he was comforted concerning all his m.
32 Pharao and all his m., saith the Lord
38 7 make thyself ready and all thy multitude
13 hast gathered thy m. to take a prey
39 11 shall they bury Gog and all his m.
11 be called the valley of the m. of Gog
15 bury it in the valley of the m. of Gog
Dan 9 18 for the m. of thy tender mercies
10 6 voice of his word like voice of a m.
11 10 shall assemble a m. of great forces
11 and a m. shall be given into his hand
12 and he shall take a multitude, and his
13 shall prepare a m. much greater than
13 41 m. believed them as being the elders
Osee 4 7 according to the multitude of them
9 7 for the multitude of thy iniquity and the multitude of thy madness
10 1 according to the m. of his fruit he
13 trusted . . . in the m. of thy strong
Mich 2 12 a tumult by reason of the m. of men
Nah 3 3 the noise . . . of a multitude slain
4 because of the m. of the fornications
Zach 2 4 by reason of the multitude of men
8 4 staff in his hand through m. of days
1 Ma 3 17 able to fight against so great a m.
19 success . . . not in the m. of the army
20 come against us with an insolent m.
4 8 fear ye not their multitude, neither
6 41 were moved at the noise of their m.
9 6 they saw the multitude of the army
63 he gathered together all his multitude
2 Ma 2 22 put to flight the barbarous multitude
25 considering the multitude of books
25 because of the multitude of the matter
3 21 the expectation of the mixed multitude
4 39 the m. gathered themselves together
40 the multitude making an insurrection
5 3 m. of men in helmets with drawn swords
8 5 when Machabeus had gathered a multitude
16 nor to fear the m. of the enemies
9 2 m. running together to arms, put them
10 24 called together a m. of foreign troops
11 4 trusting in the m. of his foot soldiers
12 27 there dwelt a m. of divers nations
13 1 was coming with a m. against Judea
14 20 captain had acquainted the m. with it
41 as the m. sought to rush into his house
15 21 considering the coming of the multitude
Mat 9 8 the m. seeing it, feared, and glorified
23 minstrels and the m. making a rout
25 when the m. was put forth, he went
14 23 having dismissed the m. 15:39
15 33 in the desert, as to fill so great a m.
35 he commanded the m. to sit down upon
17 14 when he was come to the m., there came
20 31 the m. rebuked them that they should
21 26 we are afraid of the m.; for all held
Mark 2 4 not offer him unto him for the m.
3 9 wait on him because of the multitude
20 the m. cometh together again, so that
32 the m. sat about him; and they say to
4 36 sending away the m., they take him
5 30 turning to the m., said: Who hath
31 thou seest the m. thronging thee, and
7 14 calling again the m. unto him, he said
17 into the house from the m., his
33 taking him from the m. apart, he put
8 2 I have compassion on the multitude
34 calling the m. together with his
9 16 one of the m., answering, said: Master
24 when Jesus saw the m. running together
11 18 whole m. was in admiration at his
15 8 when the m. was come up, they began
Luke 2 13 a m. of the heavenly army, praising
5 19 bring him in, because of the m., they
7 9 turning about to the m. that followed
8 40 was returned, the m. received him
9 12 send away the m., that going into the
13 and buy food for all this multitude
16 his disciples to set before the m.
12 13 one of the m. said to him: Master
13 14 said to the m.: Six days there are
18 36 he heard the multitude passing by
19 37 the whole m. of his disciples began
39 Pharisees, from amongst the m., said
22 6 to betray him in the absence of the m.
47 as he was yet speaking, behold a m.
23 1 whole m. of them rising up, led him to
18 whole multitude together cried out
John 5 13 Jesus went aside from the m. standing
6 22 the m. that stood on the other side
24 when therefore the m. saw that Jesus
7 12 there was much murmuring among the m.
20 the m. answered and said: Thou hast a
40 of that m. therefore, when they had
49 this m., that knoweth not the law, are
12 17 the m. therefore gave testimony, which
29 m. therefore that stood and heard, said

34 the m. answered him: We have heard out
21 6 able to draw it for the m. of fishes
Acts 2 6 m. came together and were confounded
4 32 the m. of believers had but one heart
5 14 the m. of men and women who believed
16 a m. out of the neighboring cities
6 2 together the m. of the disciples, said
14 4 and the m. of the city was divided
18 persuading the m., and stoning Paul
15 30 together the m., delivered the epistle
17 13 stirring up and troubling the multitude
19 9 evil of way of the Lord, before the m.
33 they drew forth Alexander out of the m.
21 22 the m. must needs come together: for
34 cried one thing, some another, among m.
36 the multitude of the people followed
23 7 and the multitude was divided. For the
24 18 neither with multitude, nor with tumult
Heb 11 12 as the stars of heaven in multitude, and
James 5 20 and shall cover a multitude of sins
1 P 4 8 charity covereth a multitude of sins

all the multitude Exod 16 3 that you might destroy all the m. with famine
Lev 8 4 a. . . . being gathered together before
9 5 when all the m. stood, Moses said
23 glory of the Lord appeared to a. . . .
24 16 all the m. shall stone him, whether
Num 1 17 with all the m. of the common people
10 3 a. . . . shall gather together unto thee
13 27 speaking to them and to all the m.
14 10 when all the multitude cried out and
15 35 let all the m. stone him without the
16 3 that all the m. consisteth of holy ones
5 speaking to Core and all the multitude
19 and had drawn up all the multitude
20 8 a. . . . and their cattle shall drink
27 went up into mount Hor before a. . . .
30 all the m. seeing that Aaron was dead
27 19 before Eleazar the priest and all the m.
Deut 5 22 these words the Lord spoke to a. . . .
Josu 8 1 take with thee a. . . . of fighting men
Judg 4 16 all the m. of the enemies was utterly
3 K 1 40 all the multitude went up after him
1 Pa 13 4 all the m. answered that it should be
29 10 he blessed the Lord before all the m.
2 Pa 1 3 he went with a. . . . to the high place
6 3 for all the multitude stood attentive
23 3 all the multitude made a covenant with
28 14 before the princes and all the m. And
29 28 and all the multitude adored, and the
31 and all the multitude offered victims
31 18 to all the m., both to their wives
32 7 nor dismayed . . . for all the multitude
1 Es 10 12 all the multitude answered and said
14 let rulers be appointed in all the m.
2 Es 5 13 and all the multitude said: Amen
Eccu 42 11 make thee ashamed before all the m.
Isa 16 14 taken away for all the m. of the people
Eze 7 13 the vision which regardeth all the m.
Mat 13 2 all the multitude stood on the shore
Mark 2 13 all the m. came to him, and he taught
4 1 all the m. was upon the land by the
Luke 1 10 all the m. of the people was praying
6 19 all the m. sought to touch him, for
8 37 all the m. of the country of the
23 48 a. . . . of them that were come together
Acts 6 5 the saying was liked by all the m.
15 12 all the multitude held their peace; and
25 24 you see this man, about whom all the m.

great multitude Exod 19 21 and a very g. m. of them should perish
Josu 11 4 horses also and chariots a very g. m.
3 K 7 47 for exceeding g. m. the brass could
20 13 hast thou seen all this exceeding g. m.
28 I will deliver all this g. m. into thy
2 Pa 1 15 which grow in the plains in great m.
13 8 you have a great multitude of people
16 8 and horsemen and an exceeding g. m.
20 2 cometh a great multitude against thee
32 4 he gathered together a very great m.
Tob 1 17 amongst a great m. of his kindred
Job 31 34 if I have been afraid at a very great m.
Jer 44 15 of whom there stood by a great m.
Bar 2 29 this great m. shall be turned into a
Eze 38 4 a great m., armed with spears and
47 10 fishes of the great sea, a very great m.
Dan 11 11 shall prepare an exceeding great m.
44 he shall come with a great multitude
1 Ma 1 18 he entered into Egypt with a great m.
22 he went up to Jerusalem with a great m.
30 he came to Jerusalem with a great m.
3 18 to deliver with a great m. or with a
2 Ma 5 26 he destroyed a very great multitude
Mat 14 14 saw a great m. and had compassion on
20 29 a g. m. followed him. Mark 3:7; 5:24; John 6:2
21 8 very great m. spread their garments
26 47 with him a g. m. with swords. Mark 14:43
Mark 3 8 they about Tyre and Sidon, a great m.
4 1 g. m. was gathered together unto. Luke 8:4
5 21 a great m. assembled together unto him
6 34 Jesus going out saw a great multitude
8 1 was a great m., and had nothing to eat
9 13 he saw a great m. about them, and the
10 46 with his disciples and a very great m.
12 37 and a great multitude heard him gladly
Luke 5 6 enclosed a very great m. of fishes
6 17 great m. of people from all Judea and
7 11 with him his disciples and a great m.
12 a great m. of the city was with her
9 37 met him a great m. And behold a man
23 27 followed him a great m. of people and
John 5 3 in these lay a great multitude of sick
6 5 a very great m. cometh to him he said
12 9 a great m. therefore of the Jews knew
12 g. m. that was come to the festival
Acts 6 7 a great m. also of the priests obeyed
11 24 a great multitude was added to the Lord
26 they taught a great multitude, so
14 1 so spoke that a very great multitude
17 4 of the Gentiles a great multitude, and
19 26 hath drawn away a great multitude, not
Apoc 7 9 I saw a great m. which no man could
19 6 as it were the voice of the great m. and

multitude of Israel Lev 4 13 if all the multitude of Israel shall be ignorant
Num 10 4 the princes and heads of the m. . . .
2 K 6 19 he distributed to all the m. of Israel
3 K 8 5 the m. . . . that were assembled before
12 3 Jeroboam came and all m. of Israel
4 K 7 13 are no more in the whole m. of Israel
2 Pa 6 3 and blessed all the multitude of Israel
12 in presence of all the m. . . . 13
24 6 for all the m. of Israel to bring

multitudes Exod 1 7 and sprung up into m., and
Deut 33 17 these are the multitudes of Ephraim
1 Es 2 64 all the m. as one man, were 42,360
Prov 1 21 at the head of multitudes she crieth
Wisd 6 3 that please yourselves in m. of nations
2 Ma 12 13 inhabited by m. of different nations
14 23 sent away the flocks of the multitudes
Mat 5 1 seeing the m., he went up into a
8 1 the mountain, great m. followed him
18 Jesus seeing great m. about him, gave
9 33 the m. wondered, saying: Never was the
36 seeing the m., he had compassion on

11 7 Jesus began to say to the m. concerning
12 23 all the m. were amazed and said: Is
46 as he was yet speaking to the m.
13 2 great m. were gathered together unto
34 Jesus spoke in parables to the m.
36 having sent away the m., he came into
14 13 the m. having heard of it, followed
15 send away the m., that going into the
19 when he had commanded the m. to sit
19 and the disciples to the multitudes
15 10 having called together the m. unto him
30 there came to him great m., having
31 the m. marvelled seeing the dumb speak
32 I have compassion on the m., because
19 2 great m. followed him: and he healed
21 9 m. that went before and that followed
46 they feared the m.: because they held
22 33 the m. hearing it, were in admiration
23 1 Jesus spoke to the m. and to his
26 55 Jesus said to the m.: You are come out
Mark 10 1 Jordan: and the m. flock to him again
Luke 3 7 said therefore to the m. that went
4 42 the m. sought him and came unto him
5 1 when the m. pressed upon him to hear
3 he taught the m. out of the ship. Now
15 great m. came together to hear and
7 24 to speak to the m. concerning John
8 42 went, that he was thronged by the m.
45 Master, the m. throng and press thee
11 14 and the m. were in admiration at it
29 the m. running together, he began to
12 1 when great m. stood about him, so
54 he said also to the m.: When you see
14 25 there went great multitudes with him
23 4 said to the chief priests and to the m.
Acts 13 45 Jews seeing m., were filled with envy
14 10 when the m. had seen what Paul had
19 35 when town clerk had appeased the m.
Munim 1 Es 2 50 children of Munim. 2 Es 7:52
murder Exod 22 3 he hath committed murder, and
Num 35 16 he shall be guilty of murder, and he
21 the striker shall be guilty of murder
Deut 21 1 not known who is guilty of the murder
Judg 9 24 the murder of the 70 sons of Jerobaal
Wisd 14 25 are mingled together, blood, murder
Jer 7 9 to steal, to murder, to commit adultery
Osee 6 9 priests who murder in the way those
2 Ma 4 35 for the unjust murder of so great a man
36 complaining of the unjust m. of Onias
Mat 19 18 thou shalt do no murder, Thou shalt
Mark 15 7 in the sedition had committed murder
Luke 23 19 and for a murder, was cast into prison
25 who for murder and sedition had been
Rom 1 29 full of envy, murder, contention, deceit
murdered 3 K 2 32 because he m. two men, just
Ps 93 6 and they have murdered the fatherless
Wisd 10 3 the fury wherewith he m. his brother
1 Ma 2 9 her old men are m. in the streets, and
murderer Num 35 19 kinsman . . . shall kill the m.
Num 35 26 if the m. be found without the limits
30 the m. shall be punished by witnesses
4 K 6 32 this son of a murderer hath sent to cut
Tob 3 9 thou murderer of thy husbands. Wilt
Job 24 14 the m. riseth at the very break of day
Prov 28 24 no sin, is the partner of a murderer
Osee 9 13 shall bring out his children to the m.
2 Ma 9 28 m. and blasphemer, being grievously
John 8 44 he was a murderer from the beginning
Acts 3 14 and desired a m. to be granted to you
28 4 undoubtedly this man is a murderer, who
1 P 4 15 let none of you suffer as a murderer
1 J 3 15 whosoever hateth his brother is a m.
15 no murderer hath eternal life abiding
murderers 4 K 14 6 children of the m. he did not
Wisd 12 5 merciless m. of their own children and
Isa 1 21 justice dwelt in it, but now murderers
2 Ma 4 16 who were their enemies and murderers
12 6 came against those m. of his brethren
Mat 22 7 he destroyed those m., and burnt their
Acts 7 52 been now the betrayers and murderers
21 38 into the desert 4,000 men that were m.
1 Tim 1 9 for murderers of fathers and murderers of mothers, for manslayers
Apoc 21 8 m. and whoremongers and sorcerers and
22 15 sorcerers and unchaste and murderers
murdering Esth 8 6 how can I endure the m. and
Wisd 11 8 reproof of their murdering the infants
murders 2 Ma 4 3 that m. also were committed by
Mat 15 19 come forth evil thoughts, murders
Mark 7 21 murders, thefts, covetousness
Gal 5 21 m., drunkenness, revellings and such like
Apoc 9 21 neither did they penance from their m.
murmur Num 14 27 doth this wicked multitude m.
Num 14 36 had made the whole multitude to murmur
16 11 what is Aaron that you m. against him
17 5 wherewith they murmur against you
20 6 satisfied, they may cease to murmur
Ps 58 16 and shall murmur if they be not filled
Eccu 10 28 will not murmur when he is reproved
31 29 against him . . . the city will murmur
John 6 43 murmur not among yourselves. No man
1 C 10 10 neither do you murmur: as some of them
murmured Exod 15 24 murmured against Moses. 17:3; Num 14:2; 16:41
Num 14 29 you that . . . have murmured against me
Deut 1 27 you murmured in your tents and said
Josu 9 18 common people m. against the princes
Ps 105 25 and they murmured in their tents: they
Isa 29 24 they that murmured shall learn the law
Lam 3 39 why hath a living man murmured, man
1 Ma 11 39 who seeing that all the army murmured
Mat 20 11 they m. against the master of the house
Mark 14 5 they murmured against her. But Jesus
Luke 5 30 Pharisees and the scribes m. 15:2
19 7 all saw it, they murmured, saying
John 6 41 the Jews therefore murmured at him
62 that his disciples murmured at this
1 C 10 10 some of them m., and were destroyed by
murmurers Jdth 1 16 these are m., full of complaints
murmuring Exod 16 7 he hath heard your m. 9
Exod 16 8 your murmuring is not against us, but
12 I have heard the murmuring of the
Num 11 1 arose a murmuring of the people against
13 31 to still the murmuring of the people
Jdth 8 24 reproach of their m. against the Lord
Wisd 1 10 tumult of murmuring shall not be hid
11 keep yourselves therefore from m.
Eccu 29 6 and will return tedious and m. words
46 9 and appeasing the wicked murmuring
Isa 26 16 in tribulation of m. thy instruction
Nah 2 7 as doves, murmuring in their hearts
John 7 12 there was much m. among the multitude
32 Pharisees heard the people murmuring
Acts 6 1 a m. of the Greeks against the Hebrews
1 P 4 9 one towards another, without murmuring
murmurings Exod 16 8 for he hath heard your m.
Num 14 27 I have heard the murmurings of the
17 5 I will make to cease from me the m.
Phil 2 14 do ye all things without murmurings
murrain Exod 9 3 grievous m. upon thy horses
Musach 4 K 16 18 the Musach also for the sabbath
museth Wisd 9 15 that museth upon many things
Musi Exod 6 19 the sons of Merari: Moholi and Musi. Num 3:20; 1 Pa 6:19; 23:21; 24:26
Num 26 58 of Levi: . . . the family of Musi
1 Pa 6 47 the son of Moholi, the son of Musi

23 23 the sons of Musi: Moholi. 24:30
music 2 Pa 7 6 Levites with the instruments of m.
Ecce 12 4 the daughters of music shall grow deaf
Eccu 22 6 tale out of time is like m. in mourning
32 5 knowledge, and hinder not music. Where
7 a concert of music in a banquet of wine
8 so is the melody of music with pleasant
40 20 wine and music rejoice the heart, but
49 2 and as music at a banquet of wine
Isa 22 24 cups even to every instrument of music
Dan 3 5 and of all kind of music. 7, 10, 15
Amos 6 5 to have instruments of music like David
Luke 15 25 house, he heard music and dancing
musical 1 Pa 15 16 be singers with m. instruments
1 Pa 16 42 cymbals and all kinds of m. instruments
2 Pa 5 13 with divers kind of musical instruments
2 Es 12 35 with the musical instruments of David
Eccu 44 5 sought out musical tunes and published
Eze 33 32 thou art to them as a musical song
1 Ma 9 39 with timbrels and musical instruments
41 noise of the musical instruments into
musicians Apoc 18 22 the voice of harpers and of m.
musing Gen 24 21 he m. beheld her with silence
Musites Num 3 33 families of the Moholites and M.
mustard Mat 13 31 like to a grain of mustard seed. 17:19; Mark 4:31; Luke 13:19; 17:6
muster Nah 2 5 he will muster up his valiant men
mustered Josu 8 10 he [Josue] m. his soldiers
3 K 20 15 mustered the servants of the princes
15 he m. after them the people . . . 7,000
26 Benadad mustered the Syrians and went
27 the children of Israel were mustered
4 K 3 6 king Joram . . . mustered all Israel
mutter Exod 16 7 what are we that you m. against
Isa 8 19 who mutter in their enchantments: should
29 4 out of the ground thy speech shall m.
mutual 1 P 4 8 have a constant mutual charity among
mutually Gen 34 16 then will we m. give and take
1 C 12 25 the members might be mutually careful
muzzle Deut 25 4 thou shalt not muzzle the ox
1 C 9 9 thou shalt not m. the mouth of the ox
1 Tim 5 18 shalt not muzzle the ox that treadeth
Myndus 1 Ma 15 23 to Delus and Myndus and Sicyon
myrrh Gen 37 25 spices and balm and myrrh to Egypt
Gen 43 11 myrrh, turpentine, and almonds. And
Exod 30 23 spices, of principal and chosen myrrh
Esth 2 12 they were anointed with oil of myrrh
Ps 44 9 myrrh and stacte and cassia perfume
Prov 7 17 I have perfumed my bed with myrrh
Cant 1 12 a bundle of myrrh is my beloved to me
3 6 smoke . . . of myrrh and frankincense
4 6 I will go to the mountain of myrrh
14 myrrh and aloes with all the chief
5 1 I have gathered my myrrh, with my
5 my hands dropped with myrrh, and my
5 my fingers were full of choicest myrrh
13 lips are as lilies dropping choice m.
Eccu 24 20 yielded sweet odor like the best myrrh
Mat 2 11 gifts; gold, frankincense, and myrrh
Mark 15 23 him to drink wine mingled with myrrh
John 19 39 bringing a mixture of myrrh and aloes
myrtle 2 Es 8 15 branches of m. and branches
Isa 41 19 thorn and the myrtle and the olive
55 13 nettle, shall come up the myrtle tree
Zach 1 8 stood among the myrtle trees. 10, 11
Mysia Acts 16 7 when they were come into Mysia
Acts 16 8 when they had passed through Mysia
mysteries 1 Pa 15 20 sung m. upon psalteries. And
Wisd 6 24 not hide from you the mysteries of God
Dan 2 28 God in heaven that revealeth mysteries
29 he that revealeth mysteries showed
Mat 13 11 it is given to know the mysteries of
1 C 4 1 the dispensers of the mysteries of God
13 2 should know all m., and all knowledge
14 2 yet by the Spirit he speaketh mysteries
mysterious Prov 1 6 wise and their m. sayings
mystery Dan 2 19 was the m. revealed to Daniel
Mark 4 11 to know the m. of the kingdom. Luke 8:10
Rom 11 25 ignorant, brethren, of this mystery
16 25 according to the revelation of the m.
1 C 2 7 we speak wisdom of God in a mystery
15 51 behold, I tell you a mystery. We shall
Eph 1 9 known unto us the mystery of his will
3 3 the mystery has been made known to me
4 my knowledge in the mystery of Christ
9 what is the dispensation of the mystery
6 19 to make known the mystery of the gospel
Col 1 26 the m. which hath been hidden from ages
27 the riches of the glory of this mystery
2 2 unto the knowledge of the mystery of God
4 3 speech to speak the mystery of Christ
2 Th 2 7 the mystery of iniquity already worketh
1 Tim 3 9 holding the mystery of faith in a pure
16 evidently great is the m. of godliness
Apoc 1 20 the m. of the seven stars, which thou
10 7 the mystery of God shall be finished
17 5 was written: A mystery; Babylon the
7 the m. of the woman and of the beast

N

Naalol Josu 19 15 Cateth and Naalol and Semeron
Josu 21 35 and Damna and Naalol, four cities
Judg 1 30 the inhabitants of Cetron and Naalol
Naama Josu 15 41 N. and Maceda, sixteen cities
3 K 14 21 his mother's name was Naama. 31
2 Pa 12 13 the name of his mother was Naama
Naaman Gen 46 21 N. and Echi and Ros and Mophim
4 K 5 1 Naaman, general of the army of the
4 Naaman went in to his lord and told him
6 I have sent to thee Naaman my servant
9 so Naaman came with his horses and
11 N. was angry and went away, saying
17 N. said: As thou wilt; but I beseech
20 my master hath spared Naaman this
21 and Giezi followed after Naaman: and
23 Naaman said: It is better that thou
27 leprosy of N. shall also stick to thee
1 Pa 8 4 Naaman and Ahoe and Gera and Sephuphan
7 N. and Achia and Gera he removed them
Luke 4 27 was cleansed but Naaman the Syrian
Naaman's 4 K 5 2 and she waited upon N. wife. And
Naamathite Job 2 11 Sophar the N. 11:1; 20:1; 42:9
Naara 1 Pa 4 5 had two wives, Halaa and Naara
1 Pa 4 6 Naara bore him Ozam and Hepher and
6 these are the sons of Naara. And the
Naarai 1 Pa 11 37 Naarai the son of Azbai, Joel the
Naaratha Josu 16 7 from Janor into Ataroth and N.
Naaria 1 Pa 3 22 N. and Saphat, six in number
1 Pa 3 23 the sons of Naaria, Elioenai and
4 42 their captains Phaltias and Naaria
Naas 1 K 11 1 Naas the Ammonite came up and began
1 K 11 1 and all the men of Jabes said to Naas
2 Naas the Ammonite answered them: On
12 12 but seeing that Naas king of the
2 K 17 25 in to Abigail the daughter of Naas
27 Sobi the son of Naas of Rabbath of
1 Pa 4 12 Tehinna father of the city of Naas
19 1 it came to pass that Naas . . . died
2 kindness to Hanon the son of Naas
Naasson Tob 1 1 upper parts of Galilee above N.
Mat 1 4 Aminadab begot N. and N. begot Salmon
Luke 3 32 Salmon, who was of Naasson, who was of
Nabaioth Isa 60 7 the rams of N. shall minister
Nabajoth Gen 25 13 the firstborn of Ismael was N.
Gen 28 9 Maheleth . . . the sister of Nabajoth

36 3 and Basemath . . . sister of Nabajoth
1 Pa 1 29 firstborn of Ismahel, Nabajoth, then
Nabal 1 K 25 3 the name of the man was Nabal
1 K 25 4 that Nabal was shearing his sheep, he
5 go up to Carmel, and go to Nabal and
9 they spoke to Nabal all these words
10 Nabal answering the servants of David
14 Abigail the wife of Nabal. 27:3; 30:5; 2 K 2:2; 3:3
19 but she told not her husband Nabal
25 not . . . regard this naughty man Nabal
26 and now let thy enemies be as Nabal
34 there had not been left to Nabal by
36 Abigail came to Nabal: and behold
37 when Nabal had digested his wine, his
38 the Lord struck Nabal, and he died
39 when David had heard that N. was dead
39 cause of my reproach at the hand of N.
39 the wickedness of Nabal upon his head
Nabal's 1 K 25 36 and Nabal's heart was merry
Nabat 3 K 11 26 Jeroboam also the son of Nabat. 12:2, 15; 15:1; 16:3, 26, 31; 21:22; 22:53; 4 K 3:3; 9:9; 10:29; 13:2, 11; 14:24; 15:9, 18, 24, 28; 17:21; 23:15; 2 Pa 9:29; 10:2, 15; 13:6; Eccu 47:29
Nabath Tob 11 20 and N. the kinsmen of Tobias
Nabo Num 32 38 children of Ruben built . . . Nabo
Num 33 47 mountains of Abarim over against Nabo
Isa 15 2 to the high places to mourn over Nabo
Jer 48 1 woe to Nabo, for it is laid waste
22 judgment is come . . . upon Nabo and
Naboth 3 K 21 1 N. . . . had at that time a vineyard
3 K 21 2 Achab spoke to Naboth, saying: Give
3 N. answered him: The Lord be merciful
4 word that Naboth . . . had spoken to him
6 I spoke to Naboth the Jezrahelite
7 I will give thee the vineyard of Naboth
8 his city and that dwelt with Naboth
9 Naboth sit among the chief of. 12
13 saying: Naboth hath blasphemed God
14 saying: Naboth is stoned and is dead
15 Jezabel heard that Naboth was stoned
15 take possession of vineyard of Naboth
15 for Naboth is not alive, but dead. And
16 when Achab heard . . . that N. was dead
16 went down to the vineyard of Naboth
18 he is going down to the vineyard of N.
19 dogs have licked the blood of Naboth
4 K 9 21 and met him in the field of Naboth
25 and cast him into the field of Naboth
26 for the blood of Naboth and for the
Nabuchodonosor 1 Pa 6 15 by the hands of N. So the
2 Pa 36 6 against him came up Nabuchodonosor
10 N. sent and brought him to Babylon
1 Es 1 7 which N. had taken from Jerusalem
5 14 which N. had taken out of the temple
6 5 which N. took out of the temple of
Jdth 1 5 N. king of the Assyrians . . . fought
7 then was the kingdom of N. exalted
10 N. king of Assyrians sent messengers
2 1 the thirteenth year of the reign of N.
1 the house of N. king of the Assyrians
3 2 is better for us to live and serve N.
5 29 may know that N. is god of the earth
6 2 show thee that there is no God, but N.
4 that N. is lord of the whole earth
11 21 thou shalt be great in the house of N.
Jer 29 1 whom N. had carried away from Jerusalem
32 1 the eighteenth year of N. 52:29
52 28 people whom N. carried away captive
30 in the three and twentieth year of N.
Dan 1 18 eunuchs brought them in before N.
2 1 second year of reign of N., N. had dream
3 13 N. in fury and wrath, commanded that
19 then was N. filled with fury: and the
93 N. came to the door of the burning
95 N. breaking forth, said: Blessed be
4 1 I N. was at rest in my house, and
30 same hour the word was fulfilled upon N.
31 I N. lifted up my eyes to heaven, and
34 I N. do now praise and magnify and
5 2 which N. his father had brought away
18 God gave to N. thy father a kingdom
king Nabuchodonosor 2 Pa 36 13 revolted from k. N.
Jdth 1 12 king Nabuchodonosor being angry against
5 27 children of Israel can resist king N.
14 16 confusion in the house of king N.: for
Dan 2 28 who hath shown to thee, O king N., what
46 king N. fell on his face and worshipped
3 1 king N. made a statue of gold of 60
2 statue which king N. had set up. 3, 7
5 the statue which king N. hath set up
9 said to king N.: O king, live forever
16 said to king N.: We have no occasion
4 15 I k. N. saw this dream: thou, therefore
25 all these things came upon king N.
28 to thee, O king N., it is said: Thy
5 11 king N. thy father appointed him prince
Nabuchodonosor king of Babylon; *see* **Babylon**
Nabuchodonosor the king Jdth 2 4 N. the king called Holofernes the
Jdth 3 2 and serve Nabuchodonosor the great king
13 N. the king had commanded him to destroy
11 1 that was willing to serve N. the king
5 as N. the king of the earth liveth
Dan 3 2 N. the king sent to call together the
14 N. the king spoke to them and said
91 N. the king was astonished, and rose up
98 N. the king, to all peoples, nations
Nabusezban Jer 39 13 and N. and Rabsares and
Nabutheans 1 Ma 5 25 the Nabutheans met them
1 Ma 9 35 to desire the N. his friends that they
Nabuzardan 4 K 25 8 came N. commander of the
4 K 25 11 Nabuzardan . . . carried away the rest
20 these Nabuzardan . . . took away and
Jer 39 9 Nabuzardan . . . carried away captive
10 N. the general left some of the poor
11 had given charge to N. the general
13 N. the general sent and took
40 1 N. the general had let him go from Rama
41 10 Nabuzardan . . . committed to Godolias
43 6 which N. the general had left with
52 12 came N. the general of the army, who
15 N. the general carried away captive
16 N. the general left some for
26 N. the general took them and brought
30 N. the general carried away of the Jews
Nachon 2 K 6 6 they came to the floor of Nachon
Nachor Gen 11 22 and Sarug . . . begot Nachor
Gen 11 23 Sarug lived after he begot Nachor
24 Nachor lived nine and twenty years and
25 Nachor lived after he begot Thare
26 Thare . . . begot Abram and Nachor. 27
29 and Abram and Nachor married wives
22 20 borne children to Nachor his brother
23 these eight did Melcha bear to Nachor
24 10 to Mesopotamia to the city of Nachor
15 Bathuel, son of Melcha, wife to Nachor
24 son of Melcha, whom she bore to Nachor
47 daughter of Bathuel, the son of Nachor
29 5 know you Laban the son of Nachor? They
31 53 the God of Nachor . . . judge between us
Josu 24 2 Thare the father of Abraham and Nachor
1 Pa 1 26 Serug, Nachor, Thare, Abram, this is
Luke 3 34 Thare, who was of Nachor, who was of
Nachor's Gen 11 29 name of Nachor's wife, Melcha

Nadab Exod 6 23 Elizabeth . . . bore him Nadab and
Exod 24 1 up to the Lord, thou and Aaron, Nadab
9 Moses and Aaron, Nadab and Abiu, and
28 1 Aaron, Nadab, and Abiu, Eleazar, and
Lev 10 1 Nadab and Abiu, the sons of Aaron
Num 3 2 sons of Aaron: his firstborn Nadab
4 Nadab and Abiu died. 26:61; 1 Pa 24:2
26 60 of Aaron were born Nadab and Abiu and
3 K 14 20 Nadab his son reigned in his stead
15 25 Nadab the son of Jeroboam reigned
27 Nadab and all Israel besieged Gebbethon
31 but the rest of the acts of Nadab
1 Pa 2 28 sons of Semei: Nadab and Abisur. And
30 the sons of Nadab were Saled and Apphaim
6 3 sons of Aaron: Nadab and Abiu. 24:1
8 30 Sur and Cis and Baal and Nadab and
9 36 Cis and Baal and Ner and Nadab, Gedor
Nadabia 1 Pa 3 18 sons of Jechonias . . . Nadabia
Nagge Luke 3 25 Nahum, who was of Nagge, who was of
Nahabi Num 13 15 of Nephtali, N. the son of Vapsi
Nahaliel Num 21 19 from Mathana unto N.: from N. unto Bamoth
Naham 1 Pa 4 15 sons of Caleb . . . Ela and Naham
1 Pa 4 19 sister of Naham the father of Celia
Nahamani 2 Es 7 7 who came with . . . Nahamani
Naharai 2 K 23 37 Naharai the Berothite
1 Pa 11 39 N. a Berothite, the armorbearer of
Nahason Exod 6 23 Elizabeth . . . sister of Nahason
Nahasson Num 2 3 prince of his sons shall be N.
Num 7 12 the first day Nahasson the son of
17 this was the offering of Nahasson
10 14 whose prince was Nahasson the son of
Ruth 4 20 Aminadab begot Nahasson. 1 Pa 2:10
20 Nahasson begot Salmon, Salmon begot
1 Pa 2 11 N. begot Salma, the father of Booz
Nahath Gen 36 13 sons of Rahuel were N. 17; 1 Pa 1:37
1 Pa 6 26 Sophai his son, Nahath his son, Eliab
2 Pa 31 13 Azarias and Nahath . . . overseers
Nahum 2 Es 7 7 Mespharath, Begoia, N., Baana
Nah 1 1 the book of the vision of Nahum the
Luke 3 25 Amos, who was of Nahum, who was of
nail Judg 4 21 Jahel Haber's wife took a nail
Judg 4 21 she put the nail upon the temples of
22 and the nail fastened in his temples
5 26 she put her left hand to the nail
16 13 tying them around about a nail fastenest
14 he drew out the nail with the hairs
1 K 18 11 thinking to nail David to the wall
19 10 Saul endeavored to nail David to the
2 Pa 3 9 weight of every nail was fifty sicles
nailed 1 Es 6 11 set up, and he be nailed upon it
Gal 2 19 God: with Christ I am n. to the cross
nails Num 33 55 be unto you as n. in your eyes
Deut 21 12 shall shave her hair and pare her nails
3 K 6 21 fastened on the plates with n. of gold
1 Pa 22 3 iron for the nails of the gates and
2 Pa 3 9 he made also nails of gold, and the
Ecce 12 11 and as nails deeply fastened in, which
Isa 33 20 neither shall the n. thereof be taken
41 7 he strengthened it with nails that it
Jer 10 4 put it together with nails and hammers
Dan 4 30 eagles, and his nails like birds' claws
John 20 25 in his hands the print of the nails
25 put my finger into the place of the n.
Naim Luke 7 11 went into a city that is called Naim
Najoth 1 K 19 18 and Samuel went and dwelt in N.
1 K 19 19 behold David is in Najoth in Ramatha
22 behold they are in Najoth in Ramatha
23 he [Saul] went to Najoth in Ramatha
23 till he came to Najoth in Ramatha
20 1 David fled from Najoth, which is in
naked Gen 2 25 they were both naked: to wit, Adam
Gen 3 7 they perceived themselves to be naked
10 I was afraid, because I was naked, and
11 who hath told thee that thou wast naked
31 42 now thou hadst sent me away naked: God
Exod 32 25 Moses saw that the people were naked
25 set them naked among their enemies
1 K 19 24 lay down naked all that day and night
2 K 6 20 king of Israel . . . was naked, as if one of the buffoons should be naked
2 Pa 28 15 clothed all them that were naked: and
Tob 1 20 hungry, and gave clothes to the naked
23 Tobias fleeing naked away with his son
4 17 and with thy garments cover the naked
Job 1 21 naked came I out of my mother's womb
21 and naked shall I return thither: the
22 6 stripped the naked of their clothing
24 7 they send men away naked, taking away
10 from the naked . . . they have taken away
26 6 hell is naked before him, and there is
Ecce 5 14 he came forth naked from his mother's
Isa 20 2 did so and went naked and barefoot
3 Isaias hath walked naked and barefoot
4 young and old, naked and barefoot
58 7 when thou shalt see one naked, cover
Lam 4 21 thou shalt be made drunk and naked
Eze 16 7 thou wast naked and full of confusion
22 days of thy youth, when thou wast n.
39 leave thee naked and full of disgrace
18 7 covered the naked with a garment. 16
23 29 shall let thee go naked and full of
26 14 I will make thee like a naked rock
Osee 2 3 lest I strip her naked and set her
Amos 2 16 shall flee away naked in that day
Mich 1 8 and howl: I will go stripped and naked
2 Ma 11 12 and many . . . wounded, escaped naked
Mat 25 36 naked, and you covered me: sick, and
38 thee in? or naked, and covered thee
43 naked, and you covered me not: sick
44 stranger or naked or sick or in prison
Mark 14 51 linen cloth cast about his naked body
52 the linen cloth, fled from them naked
John 21 7 his coat about him, for he was naked
Acts 19 16 fled out of that house n. and wounded
1 C 4 11 thirst, and are naked, and are buffeted
2 C 5 3 so that we be found clothed, not naked
Heb 4 13 all things are n. and open to his eyes
James 2 15 and if a brother or sister be naked
Apoc 3 17 miserable and poor and blind and naked
16 15 lest he walk naked and they see his
17 16 and shall make her desolate and naked
nakedness Gen 9 22 his father's n. was uncovered
Gen 9 23 they saw not their father's nakedness
23 covered the nakedness of their father
Exod 20 26 altar, lest thy nakedness be discovered
28 42 to cover the flesh of their nakedness
Lev 16 4 shall cover his n. with linen breeches
18 6 near of kin to him, to uncover her n.
7 not uncover the n. of thy father or the n. of thy mother
7 thou shalt not uncover her nakedness
8 not uncover n. of thy father's wife
8 for it is the nakedness of thy father
9 not uncover the nakedness of thy sister
10 not uncover n. of thy son's daughter
10 because it is thy own nakedness. Thou
11 the n. of thy father's wife's daughter
12 the nakedness of thy father's sister
13 the nakedness of thy mother's sister
14 nakedness of thy father's brother
15 nakedness of thy daughter-in-law
16 the nakedness of thy brother's wife
16 it is the nakedness of thy brother
17 not uncover the nakedness of thy wife
18 neither shalt thou discover her n.

19 neither shalt thou uncover her n.
20 11 discover the nakedness of his father
17 take his sister . . . and see her n.
17 have discovered one another's nakedness
18 in her flowers and uncover her n., and
19 not uncover the nakedness of thy aunt
21 he hath uncovered his brother's n.
Deut 28 48 in hunger and thirst and nakedness and
Isa 47 3 thy nakedness shall be discovered
Jer 13 22 thy nakedness is discovered, the soles
Eze 16 37 and they shall see all thy nakedness
22 10 have discovered the n. of their father
Nah 3 5 will show thy nakedness to the nations
Haba 2 15 that he may behold his nakedness. Thou
Rom 8 35 or distress? or famine? or nakedness? or
2 C 11 27 in fastings often, in cold and nakedness
Apoc 3 18 shame of thy nakedness may not appear
name Gen 2 11 name of the one is Phison
Gen 2 13 the name of the second river is Gehon
14 the name of the third river is Tigris
19 living creature, the same is its name
3 20 Adam called the name of his wife Eve
4 17 called the name thereof by the name of
19 the name of the one was Ada, and the name of the other Sella
21 his brother's name was Jubal; he was
5 2 called their name Adam, in the day when
10 25 the name of the one was Phaleg . . . and his brother's name Jectan
11 4 let us make our name famous before we
9 the name thereof was called Babel
29 the name of Abram's wife was Sarai: and the name of Nachor's wife, Melcha
19 22 the name of that city was called Segor
21 3 called the name of his son . . . Isaac
26 20 called the name of the well . . . Calumny
21 he called the name of it, Enmity. Going
22 he called the name thereof, Latitude
33 name of the city was called Bersabee
28 19 he called the name of the city Bethel
29 16 the name of the elder was Lia: and the
31 48 the name thereof was called Galaad
32 29 tell me by what name art thou called
30 called the name of the place Phanuel
33 17 he called the name of the place Socoth
35 18 she called the name of her son Benoni
36 39 name of his city was Phau. 1 Pa 1:50
32 name of his city Denaba. 1 Pa 1:43
35 name of his city was Avith. 1 Pa 1:46
38 6 his firstborn, whose name was Thamar
9 should be born in his brother's name
41 51 called name of the firstborn Manasses
48 6 called by the name of their brethren
7 by another name is called Bethlehem
Exod 6 3 to Jacob, by the name of God Almighty
15 23 gave a name also agreeable to the place
17 15 name thereof, The Lord my exaltation
23 13 n. of strange gods you shall not swear
28 21 each stone with the name of one
31 2 I have called by name Beseleel the son
33 7 the name thereof, The tabernacle of the
12 I know thee by name, and thou hast
17 and thee I have known by name. And he
35 30 the Lord hath called by name Beseleel
39 14 Israel, each one with its several name
Lev 18 21 nor defile the name of thy God: I am
19 12 nor profane the name of thy God. I am
21 9 dishonor the name of her father, she
22 2 defile not name of the things sanctified
24 11 when he had blasphemed the name and
Num 4 46 the princes of Israel took by name
16 2 time of assembly were called by name
17 2 write the name of every man upon his rod
3 name of Aaron shall be for tribe of Levi
25 14 the name of the Israelite that was slain
26 46 name of the daughter of Aser was Sara
Deut 9 14 abolish their name from under heaven
18 20 shall speak . . . in name of strange gods
22 14 laying to her charge a very ill name
17 layeth to her charge a very ill name
19 defamed by a very ill name a virgin
25 7 refuseth to raise up his brother's name
Josu 7 9 and cut off our name from the earth
14 15 the name of Hebron before was called
19 47 calling the name of it Lesem Dan by
47 by the name of Dan their father
23 7 should swear by the name of their gods
Judg 1 10 the name . . . in former times Cariath-Arbe
11 Dabir, the ancient name . . . Cariath-Sepher
17 the name of the city was called Horma
4 5 palm tree, which was called by her name
8 31 bore him son, whose name was Abimelech
9 46 thence the place had taken its name
13 2 name was Manue, and his wife was barren
6 and by what name he was called, he would
17 1 whose name was Michas, who said to his
18 29 calling the name of the city Dan after the name of their father
19 10 by another name is called Jerusalem
Ruth 2 1 and very rich, whose name was Booz
19 the man's name, that he was called Booz
4 5 to raise up the name of thy kinsman
10 to raise up the name of the deceased
11 may become a famous name in Bethlehem
1 K 1 2 wives, the name of one was Anna, and the name of the other Phenenna
8 2 name of his firstborn son was Joel: and the name of the second was Abia
9 1 a man of Benjamin whose name was Cis
2 he had a son whose name was Saul
14 4 the name of the one was Boses, and the name of the other was Sene
49 name of the firstborn was Merob, and the name of the younger Michol
50 the name of Saul's wife was Achinoam
50 name of captain of his army was Abner
17 12 name was Isai, who had eight sons
23 base-born man whose name was Goliath
22 20 whose name was Abiathar, escaped and
25 3 the name of the man was Nabal: and the name of his wife was Abigail
9 to Nabal all these words in David's n.
2 K 2 16 name of the place was called. 5:20; 6:8
4 2 the name of the one was Baana, and the name of the other Rechab
7 9 like unto the name of the great ones
23 to make him a name and to do for them
8 13 David also made himself a name, when
9 12 a young son whose name was Micha
13 1 beautiful, and her name was Thamar
14 7 and will leave my husband no name
27 one daughter, whose name was Thamar
20 1 a man of Belial whose name was Seba
3 K 1 47 may God make the name of Solomon
7 21 he called the name thereof Jachin
21 and called the name thereof Booz
13 2 to the house of David, Josias by name
14 21 his mother's name was. 31; 15:10; 2 Pa 13:2
15 2 the name of his mother was. 22:42; 4 K 8:26; 12:1; 14:2; 15:2, 33; 18:2; 21:1, 19; 22:1; 23:31, 36; 24:8, 18; 2 Pa 12:13; 20:31; 22:2; 24:1; 25:1; 26:3; 27:1; 29:1; Jer 52:1
16 24 Samaria, after the name of Semer
18 24 I will call on the name of my Lord
26 and they called on the name of Baal
21 8 so she wrote letters in Achab's name

4 K 14 7 and called the name thereof Jectehel
27 would blot out the name of Israel
18 4 and he called its name Nohestan
1 Pa 1 19 name of the one was Phaleg . . . the name of his brother was Jectan
2 29 name of Abisur's wife was Abihail
4 3 name of their sister was Asalelphuni
7 15 the name of the second was Salphaad
16 the name of his brother was Sares
8 29 the name of his wife was Maacha. 9:35
14 17 the name of David became famous in all
17 8 name like that of one of the great ones
2 Pa 28 9 a prophet . . . whose name was Oded
1 Es 2 61 Galaadite, and was called by their name
5 1 in the name of the God of Israel
2 Es 7 63 and he was called by their name. These
9 5 blessed be the high name of thy glory
7 and gavest him the name of Abraham
10 thou madest thyself a name, as it is at
Tob 6 11 here is one whose name is Raguel, a
13 15 shall call upon the great name in thee
Esth 2 7 who by another name was called Esther
14 and had ordered her by name to come
22 she to the king in Mardochai's name
3 12 wrote . . . in the name of king Assuerus
8 8 write ye . . . in the king's name and
8 which were sent in the king's name. 10
17 a great dread of the name of the Jews
10 8 to destroy the name of the Jews. And
16 17 those letters which he sent in our name
Job 1 1 the land of Hus, whose name was Job
42 14 he called the name of one Dies, and the name of the second Cassia, and the name of the third Cornustibii
Ps 9 6 thou hast blotted out their name
19 2 name of the God of Jacob protect thee
6 in name of our God we shall be exalted
43 21 if we have forgotten name of our God
68 31 I will praise the name of God with a
71 19 blessed be the name of his majesty
82 5 name of Israel be remembered no more
Prov 10 7 the name of the wicked shall rot. The
15 30 a good name maketh the bones fat. The
22 1 good name is better than great riches
30 9 and forswear the name of my God. Accuse
Ecce 7 2 good name is better than precious
Wisd 2 4 our name in time shall be forgotten
14 21 gave the incommunicable name to stones
Eccu 6 23 of doctrine is according to her name
15 6 cause him to inherit an everlasting n.
22 17 what other name hath he but fool
37 1 friend that is only a friend in name
39 15 he shall leave a name above a thousand
40 19 building of a city shall establish a n.
41 14 name of the ungodly shall be blotted out
15 take care of a good name: for this
16 a good name shall continue forever
43 8 the month is called after her name
44 8 have left a name behind them, that
14 their name liveth unto generation and
46 13 all the judges, every one by name
15 and their name continue forever, the
48 12 after death our name shall not be such
Isa 14 22 I will destroy the name of Babylon
44 5 shall call himself by the name of Jacob
5 surname himself by the name of Israel
48 1 that are called by the name of Israel
56 5 a name better than sons and daughters
5 I will give them an everlasting name
62 2 thou shalt be called by a new name
2 the mouth of the Lord shall name
63 12 to make himself an everlasting name
14 to make thyself a glorious name. Look
65 15 shall leave your name for an execration
15 and call his servants by another name
66 22 so shall your seed stand, and your name
Jer 13 11 might be my people, and for a name
23 6 this is the name that they shall call
32 20 hast made thee a name as at this day
33 9 it shall be to me a name and a joy
16 this is the name that they shall call
46 17 call ye the name of Pharao king of
48 15 whose name is the Lord of hosts. 51:57
Bar 2 11 hast made thee a name as at this day
Eze 20 29 the name thereof was called High-place
24 2 write thee the name of this day on which
39 16 the name of the city shall be Amona
48 35 the name of the city from that day
Dan 2 26 Daniel, whose name was Baltassar. 4:16
4 5 Daniel . . . whose name is Baltassar
5 according to the name of my god, who
9 15 hast made thee a name as at this day
13 2 took a wife whose name was Susanna
45 young boy, whose name was Daniel. And
Osee 1 6 call her name, Without mercy: for I
2 17 she shall no more remember their name
Mich 4 5 walk every one in the name of his god
Soph 3 19 I will get them praise and a name
20 I will give you a name and praise
1 Ma 2 51 shall receive . . . an everlasting name
3 14 he said: I will get me a name and will
5 57 he said: Let us also get us a name
63 the nations where their name was heard
6 44 to get himself an everlasting name
8 12 that heard their name, were afraid of
2 Ma 12 13 city . . . name of which is Casphin
Mat 10 41 a prophet in the name of a prophet
41 just man in the name of a just man
42 water only in the name of a disciple
28 19 baptizing them in the name of the
Mark 3 16 to Simon he gave the name Peter: and
Luke 1 5 and her name Elizabeth. And they were
27 and the virgin's name was Mary. And
59 they called him by his father's name
61 kindred that is called by this name
6 22 and cast out your name as evil, for
John 3 18 believeth not in the name of the only
5 43 I am come in the name of my Father
10 3 and he calleth his own sheep by name
25 that I do in the name of my Father
18 10 the name of the servant was Malchus
Acts 4 7 by what power or by what name have you
12 there is no other name under heaven
17 that they speak no more in this name
30 by the name of thy holy Son Jesus
5 28 that you should not teach in this name
9 21 those that called upon this name: and
26 9 contrary to name of Jesus of Nazareth
Rom 2 24 the n. of God through you is blasphemed
1 C 1 13 were you baptized in the name of Paul
Eph 1 21 every name that is named, not only in
Phil 2 9 hath given him a name which is above all
Heb 1 4 inherited a more excellent name than
James 2 7 do not they blaspheme the good name
1 P 4 14 if you be reproached for the name of
16 but let him glorify God in that name
1 J 3 23 should believe in the name of his Son
5 13 believe in the name of the Son of God
3 J 14 salute the friends by name
Apoc 2 17 in the counter, a new name written
3 1 thou hast the name of being alive: and
12 will write upon him the name of my God
12 and the name of the city of my God
8 11 name of the star is called Wormwood
9 11 whose name in Hebrew is Abaddon, and
13 17 or the name of the beast or the number

14 1 his name and the name of his Father
16 9 they blasphemed the name of God, who
17 5 on her forehead a name was written
19 12 he had a name written, which no man

his name Gen 4 25 called his name *N.* 5:3, 29; 16:15; 19:37, 38; 29:32, 33, 34; 30:6, 11, 18, 20, 24; 38:3, 29; 1 K 1:20; 2 K 12:24; 4 K 24:17; 1 Pa 4:9; 7:16, 23

Gen 12 8 to the Lord and called upon his name
16 11 and thou shalt call his name Ismael
17 19 thou shalt call his name Isaac, and I
25 25 a skin: and his name was called Esau
30 which reason his name was called Edom
27 36 rightly is his name called Jacob; for
41 45 he turned his name and called him
Exod 3 13 if they should say to me: What is his name
34 14 the Lord his name is Jealous, he is a
Lev 21 6 and shall not profane his name: for
Num 27 3 why is his name taken away out of his
32 42 he called it by his own name, Nobe
Deut 3 14 he called Basan by his own name, Havoth
5 11 that taketh his name upon a vain thing
6 13 and thou shalt swear by his name. You
10 8 to bless in his name until this present
20 adhere and shalt swear by his name
12 11 choose, that his name may be therein
21 choose, that his name should be there
14 23 his name may be called upon therein
16 2 that his name may dwell there. 6, 11
21 5 to bless in his name, and that by
25 6 have of her he shall call by his name
6 that his name be not abolished out of
10 his name shall be called in Israel
19 thou shalt blot out his name from
26 2 that his name may be invocated there
19 to his own praise and name and glory
28 58 fear his glorious and terrible name
29 20 and the Lord should blot out his name
Josu 6 27 his name was noised throughout all the
Judg 10 4 from his name were called Havoth Jair
11 12 sent messengers . . . to say in his name
Ruth 4 1 said to him, calling him by his name
10 lest his name be cut off from among
14 that his name should be preserved in
17 called his name Obed: he is the father
1 K 1 1 his name was Elcana, the son of Jeroham
18 30 and his name became very famous
21 7 his name was Doeg, an Edomite, the
25 25 according to his name, he is a fool
2 K 4 4 lame, and his name was Miphiboseth
12 25 called his name, Amiable to the Lord
18 18 he called the pillar by his own name
3 K 14 21 to put his name there. Deut 12:5
4 K 23 34 turned his name to Joakim. And he
1 Pa 13 6 where his name is called upon. And
16 8 ye the Lord, and call upon his name
10 praise ye his holy name: let the heart
29 give to the Lord glory to his name
41 every one by his name to give praise
23 13 and to bless his name forever. The
2 Pa 6 2 but I have built a house to his name
12 13 of Israel, to establish his name there
26 8 and his name was spread abroad even
15 and his name went forth far abroad
36 4 turned his name [Eliakim] to Joakim
1 Es 6 12 hath caused his name to dwell there
Tob 1 9 whom he called after his own name, and
Jdth 7 24 and will give glory to his own name
16 2 psalm, extol and call upon his name
3 the Lord is his name. Ps 67:5; Jer 33:2; Amos 5:8; 9:6
Esth 9 4 the fame of his name increased daily
Job 18 17 let not his name be renowned in the

Ps 28 2 to the Lord glory to his name. 95:8
32 21 in his holy name we have trusted
33 4 and let us extol his name together
40 6 when shall he die and his name perish
65 2 sing ye a psalm to his name. 67:5
68 37 that love his name shall dwell therein
71 17 let his name be blessed for evermore
17 his name continueth before the sun
75 2 known: his name is great in Israel
95 2 sing ye to the Lord and bless his name
98 6 Samuel among them that call upon his n.
99 4 glory to him: praise ye his name
102 1 that is within me bless his holy name
104 1 and call upon his name: declare his
3 glory ye in his holy name: let the
108 13 may his name be blotted out. May the
110 9 holy and terrible is his name: the
134 3 sing ye to his name, for it is sweet
144 21 let all flesh bless his holy name
148 13 his name alone is exalted. The praise
149 3 let them praise his name in choir
Prov 30 4 what is his name and what is the name
Ecce 6 4 his name shall be wholly forgotten
10 shall be, his name is already called
Eccu 37 29 and his name shall live forever. My
39 13 and his name shall be in request from
20 magnify his name, and give glory to
45 19 and to glorify his people in his name
46 1 who was great according to his name
47 15 he might build a house in his name
50 22 with his lips and to glory in his name
Isa 7 14 his name shall be called Emmanuel
8 3 call his name, Hasten to take away the
9 6 his name shall be called Wonderful
12 4 ye the Lord and call upon his name
4 remember that his name is high. Sing
48 2 the Lord of hosts is his name. 54:5; Jer 10:16; 31:35; 50:34; 51:19
19 his name should not have perished nor
56 6 to worship him and to love his name
57 15 his name is Holy, who dwelleth in the
Jer 11 19 let his name be remembered no more
20 9 nor speak any more in his name: and
48 17 all you that know his name, say: How
Dan 13 1 in Babylon and his name was Joakim
Osee 1 4 call his name Jezrahel: for yet a
9 call his name, Not my people: for you
Amos 4 13 the God of hosts is his name. 5:27
Zach 6 12 behold a man, the Orient is his name
10 12 they shall walk in his name, saith the
14 9 one Lord, and his name shall be one
Mala 3 16 that fear the Lord and think on his n.
1 Ma 6 17 young: and he called his name Eupator
14 43 writings . . . should be made in his name
2 Ma 8 4 the blasphemies offered to his name
15 for sake of his holy and glorious name
Mat 1 21 shalt call his n. Jesus. Luke 1:31
23 and they shall call his name Emmanuel
25 son: and he called his name Jesus
12 21 in his name the Gentiles shall hope
Mark 6 14 heard, for his name was made manifest
Luke 1 13 and thou shalt call his name John: and
49 things to me; and holy is his name
63 he wrote, saying: John is his name
2 21 his name was called Jesus, which was
24 47 should be preached in his name unto
John 1 12 to them that believe in his name. Who
2 23 many believed in his name, seeing his
5 43 if another shall come in his own name
20 31 you may have life in his name. After
Acts 3 16 in the faith of his name, this man
16 hath his name strengthened; and the
10 43 his name all receive remission of sins

13 8 for so his name is interpreted
15 14 to take of Gentiles a people to his n.
22 16 wash away thy sins, invoking his name
Rom 1 5 to faith, in all nations, for his name
Heb 6 10 love which you have shown in his name
13 15 fruit of lips confessing to his name
3 J 7 for his name they went out, taking
Apoc 3 5 I will not blot out his name out of
5 I will confess his n. before my Father
6 8 sat upon him, his name was Death, and
13 6 blaspheme his name and his tabernacle
17 the beast, or the number of his name
14 1 his name and the name of his Father
11 receiveth the character of his name
15 2 his image, and the number of his name
19 13 his name is called, The Word of God
22 4 his name shall be on their foreheads
holy name Lev 20 3 profaned my holy name. And
Lev 22 32 profane not my holy name, that I may
1 Pa 16 10 praise ye his holy name: let the heart
35 we may give glory to thy holy name
29 16 to build thee a house for thy holy name
Ps 32 21 in his holy name we have trusted
102 1 that is within me bless his holy name
104 3 glory ye in his holy name: let the
105 47 we may give thanks to thy holy name
137 2 hast magnified thy holy name above all
144 21 let all flesh bless his holy name
Wisd 10 20 they sung to thy holy name, O Lord
Eccu 47 12 they should praise the holy name of
Eze 20 39 defile my holy name any more with your
36 20 they profaned my holy name. 43:8
21 and I have regarded my own holy name
39 7 I will make my holy name known in the
7 my holy name shall be profaned no more
25 and I will be jealous for my holy name
43 7 shall no more profane my holy name
Dan 3 52 blessed is the holy name of thy glory
Amos 2 7 young woman, to profane my holy name
2 Ma 8 15 for sake of his holy and glorious name
my name Gen 32 29 why dost thou ask my name
Gen 48 16 and let my name be called upon them
Exod 3 15 this is my name forever, and this
6 3 my name Adonai I did not show them
9 16 my name may be spoken of throughout
20 24 where the memory of my name shall be
23 21 hast sinned, and my name is in him
Lev 19 12 shalt not swear falsely by my name
20 3 hath . . . profaned my holy name. And if
22 32 profane not my holy name, that I may
Num 6 27 shall invoke my name upon the children
Deut 18 19 which he shall speak in my name, I
20 shall speak in my name things that I
Judg 13 18 why askest thou my name, which is
1 K 24 22 nor take away my name from the house
25 5 and salute him in my name with peace
2 K 7 13 he shall build a house to my name. 3 K 5:5; 8:19; 1 Pa 22:10; 2 Pa 6:9
12 28 the victory be ascribed to my name
18 18 this shall be the monument of my name
3 K 8 16 that my name might be there. 11:36; 2 Pa 6:6
18 to build a house to my name. 2 Pa 6:8
29 my name shall be there. 4 K 23:27
9 3 built, to put my name there forever
7 which I have sanctified to my name
4 K 21 4 in Jerusalem I will put my name. And
7 in this temple . . . I will put my name
1 Pa 22 8 canst not build a house to my name
28 3 shalt not build a house to my name
2 Pa 6 5 a house to be built in it to my name
7 16 that my name may be there forever
20 which I have sanctified to my name
33 4 in Jerusalem shall my name be forever
7 in this house . . . will I put my name
2 Es 1 9 have chosen for my name to dwell there
Ps 88 25 in my name shall his horn be exalted
90 14 him because he hath known my name
Isa 29 23 his children . . . sanctifying my name
41 25 he shall call upon my name, and he
42 8 I the Lord, this is my name: I will
43 7 every one that calleth upon my name
49 1 he hath been mindful of my name. And
51 15 swell: the Lord of hosts is my name
52 5 my name is continually blasphemed
6 my people shall know my name in that
65 1 nation that did not call upon my name
Jer 7 10 in which my name is called upon. 14, 30; 32:34
11 in which my name hath been called upon
12 my place in Silo, where my name dwelt
12 16 to swear by my name: The Lord liveth
14 14 prophets prophesy falsely in my name
15 the prophets that prophesy in my name
16 21 shall know that my name is the Lord
23 25 that prophesy lies in my name and
27 seek to make my people forget my name
27 their fathers forgot my name for Baal
25 29 the city wherein my name is called upon
27 15 and they prophesy in my name falsely
29 9 they prophesy falsely to you in my name
21 prophesy unto you in my name falsely
23 have spoken lying words in my name
34 15 house upon which my name is invocated
16 fallen back and have defiled my name
44 26 I have sworn by my great name, saith
26 that my name shall no more be named
Bar 2 32 shall be mindful of my name. And they
Eze 20 14 I spared them for the sake of my name
39 defile my holy name any more with your
36 20 they profaned my holy name. 43:8
21 and I have regarded my own holy name
23 I will sanctify my great name which
39 7 I will make my holy name known in the
7 my holy name shall be profaned no more
25 and I will be jealous for my holy name
43 7 shall no more profane my holy name
Amos 2 7 young woman, to profane my holy name
9 12 because my name is invoked upon them
Zach 5 4 that sweareth falsely by my name
13 9 they shall call on my name, and I will
Mala 1 7 to you, O priests, that despise my name
11 my name is great among the Gentiles
14 my name is dreadful among the Gentiles
2 2 to heart, to give glory to my name
5 and he was afraid before my name
4 2 unto you that fear my name, the Sun of
Mat 18 5 such little child in m. n. Mark 9:36
20 gathered together in my name, there
24 5 many will come in my name. Mark 13:6; Luke 21:8
Mark 5 9 my name is Legion, for we are many
9 38 no man that doth a miracle in my name
40 to drink a cup of water in my name
16 17 in my name they shall cast out devils
Luke 9 48 shall receive this child in my name
John 14 13 shall ask the Father in my name. 15:16
14 if you shall ask me anything in my n.
26 whom the Father will send in my name
16 23 ask the Father anything in my name
24 have not asked anything in my name
26 in that day you shall ask in my name
Acts 9 15 vessel of election to carry my name
15 17 nations upon whom my name is invoked
Rom 9 17 my name may be declared throughout all
1 C 1 15 say that you were baptized in my name
Apoc 2 3 hast endured for my name and hast not

31 thou holdest fast my name and hast not
3 8 my word and hast not denied my name
12 and my new name. He that hath an ear
name of Jesus Acts 2 38 every one of you in the n. . . . Christ, for
Acts 3 6 in the n. . . . Christ of Nazareth, arise
4 18 nor teach in the n. . . . But Peter and
5 40 not speak at all in the name of Jesus
41 suffer reproach for the name of Jesus
8 12 in n. . . . Christ, they were baptized
9 27 he had dealt confidently in the n. . . .
16 18 I command thee, in the n. . . . Christ
26 9 to do many things contrary to the n. . . .
Phil 2 10 that in the n. . . . every knee should
name of our Lord Jesus Christ Acts 4 10 by the n. . . . of Nazareth, whom you
Acts 15 26 have given their lives for the n. . . .
1 C 1 2 with all that invoke the n. . . . in every
10 I beseech you, brethren, by the n. . . .
5 4 done, in the n. . . . , you being gathered
6 11 you are justified in the n. . . . , and
Eph 5 20 in the n. . . . , to God and the Father
2 Th 1 12 that the n. . . . may be glorified in
3 6 we charge you, brethren, in the n. . . .
name of that place Gen 22 14 n. . . . The Lord seeth
Gen 32 2 called n. . . . Mahanaim, that is, Camps
35 7 called the n. . . . The house of God
8 n. . . . was called The oak of weeping
15 calling the n. . . . Bethel. And going
50 11 n. . . . was called The mourning of Egypt
Num 11 3 he called the n. . . . The burning: for
21 3 they called the n. . . . Horma, that is
Josu 5 9 n. . . . was called Galgal, until this
7 26 n. . . . was called the Valley of Achor
Judg 2 5 n. . . . was called The place of weepers
15 17 called the n. . . . Ramathlechi, which is
19 n. . . . was called The Spring of him that
1 Pa 14 11 the n. . . . was called Baalpharasim
name of the Lord Gen 4 26 this man began to call upon the n. . . .
Gen 13 4 and there he called upon the n. . . .
16 3 she called the n. . . . that spoke unto
21 33 there called upon the n. . . . God eternal
26 25 called upon the n. . . . and pitched his
Exod 20 7 not take the n. . . . thy God in vain
7 shall take the n. . . . his God in vain
33 19 I will proclaim in the n. . . . before
34 5 stood with him, calling upon n. . . .
Lev 24 16 that blasphemeth the n. . . . , dying let
Deut 5 11 not take the n. . . . thy God in vain
18 5 stand and to minister to the n. . . .
7 he shall minister in the n. . . . his God
22 prophet foretelleth in the n. . . . and
28 10 shall see that the n. . . . is invocated
32 3 because I will invoke the n. . . .
Josu 9 9 thy servants are come in the n. . . .
18 of the multitude had sworn in n. . . .
19 we have sworn to them in the n. . . .
1 K 17 45 I come to thee in the n. . . . of hosts
20 42 have sworn both of us in the n. . . .
2 K 6 2 upon which the n. . . . of hosts is
18 he blessed the people in the n. . . . of
3 K 3 2 was no temple built to the n. . . .
5 3 could not build a house to the n. . . .
5 purpose to build a temple to the n. . . .
8 17 would have built a house to n. . . .
20 and have built a house to the n. . . .
10 1 the fame of Solomon in the n. . . .
18 32 with the stones an altar to the n. . . .
22 16 but that which is true in the n. . . .
4 K 2 24 saw them and cursed them in n. . . .
5 11 would have invoked the n. . . . his God
1 Pa 16 2 he blessed the people in the n. . . .
21 19 which he spoke to him in the n. . . .
22 7 desire to have built a house to n. . . .
19 the house which is built to the n. . . .
2 Pa 2 1 determined to build house to n. . . .
4 that I may build a house to the n. . . .
6 7 had a mind to build a house to n. . . .
10 and have built a house to the n. . . .
18 15 but the truth to me, in the n. . . .
33 18 seers that spoke to him in the n. . . .
Job 1 21 so is it done: blessed be the n. . . .
Ps 7 18 and will sing to the n. . . . the most
12 6 I will sing to the n. . . . the most
19 8 but we will call upon the n. . . . our
39 5 the man whose trust is in the n. . . .
101 22 that they may declare the n. . . . in
112 1 praise ye the n. . . . 134:1
2 blessed be the n. . . . from henceforth
3 same, the n. . . . is worthy of praise
114 4 sorrow: and I called upon the n. . . .
115 13 I will call upon the n. . . . , I will
17 praise, and I will call upon the n. . . .
117 10 in the n. . . . I have been revenged. 11
12 in the n. . . . I was revenged on them
26 blessed is he that cometh in n. . . .
121 4 of Israel, to praise the n. . . .
123 8 our help is in the n. . . . who made
128 8 we have blessed you in the n. . . .
148 5 above the heavens; praise the n. . . .
12 old with the younger, praise the n. . . .
Prov 18 10 name of the Lord is a strong tower
Eccu 39 41 praise ye him and bless the n. . . .
46 19 called upon the n. . . . Almighty, in
47 12 that they should praise the holy n. . . .
19 at the n. . . . God, whose surname is
51 17 and praise thee and bless the n. . . .
Isa 18 7 to the place of the n. . . . of hosts
24 15 the n. . . . God of Israel in the islands
30 27 the n. . . . cometh from afar, his wrath
48 1 you who swear by the n. . . . and make
50 10 let him hope in the n. . . . and lean
59 19 from the west shall fear the n. . . .
60 9 to the n. . . . thy God and to the Holy
Jer 3 17 be gathered together to it, in n. . . .
11 21 thou shalt not prophesy in the n. . . .
26 9 why hath he prophesied in the n. . . .
16 he hath spoken to us in the n. . . .
20 a man that prophesied in the n. . . .
44 16 which thou hast spoken to us in n. . . .
Dan 2 20 blessed be the name of the Lord
Joel 2 26 you shall praise the name of the Lord
32 that shall call upon the n. . . .
Amos 6 11 and mention not the name of the Lord
Mich 4 5 we will walk in the n. . . . our God
5 4 in the height of the n. . . . his God
Soph 3 9 that all may call upon the n. . . .
12 they shall hope in the name of the Lord
Zach 13 3 because thou hast spoken a lie in n. . . .
Mat 21 9 that cometh in n. . . . 23:39; Mark 11:9; Luke 13:35; 19:38; John 12:13
Acts 2 21 shall call upon the n. . . . Rom 10:13
8 16 were only baptized in the n. . . . Jesus
9 28 and dealing confidently in the n. . . .
10 48 baptized in the n. . . . Jesus Christ
18 34 bringing in the n. . . . Jesus; and he
19 5 they were baptized in the n. . . . Jesus
13 n. . . . Jesus, saying: I conjure you by
17 n. . . . Jesus was magnified. And many of
21 13 die also in Jerusalem, for the n. . . .
Col 3 17 do all in the name of the Lord Jesus
1 Tim 6 1 lest the n. of the Lord and his doctrine
2 Tim 2 19 who nameth the name of the Lord. But in
James 5 10 the prophets, who spoke in the n. . . .
14 anointing him with oil in the n. . . .

thy name Gen 12 2 bless thee and magnify thy n.
Gen 17 5 shall thy name be called any more Abram
32 27 what is thy name? He answered: Jacob
28 thy name shall not be called Jacob
35 10 Israel shall be thy name. 3 K 18:31
Exod 5 23 in to Pharao to speak in thy name
Deut 2 25 that when they hear thy name they
Josu 7 9 what wilt thou do to thy great name
Judg 13 17 he said to him: What is thy name
2 K 7 26 that thy name may be magnified forever
22 50 Gentiles, and will sing to thy name
3 K 1 47 name of Solomon greater than thy name
8 33 thy people . . . confessing to thy name
35 place, shall do penance to thy name
41 hear everywhere of thy great name
43 may learn to fear thy name, as do thy
43 may prove that thy name is called upon
44 which I have built to thy name. 48; 2 Pa 6:34, 38
1 Pa 16 35 we may give glory to thy holy name
17 24 let thy name remain and be magnified
29 13 thee, and we praise thy glorious name
16 to build thee a house for thy holy name
2 Pa 6 20 that thy name should be called upon
24 do penance and call upon thy name and
26 and they shall . . . confess to thy name
32 for the sake of thy great name and
33 people of the earth may know thy name
33 thy name is invoked upon this house
14 11 with confidence in thee and in thy n.
20 8 built in it a sanctuary to thy name
9 house in which thy name is called upon
2 Es 1 11 servants who desire to fear thy name
Tob 3 13 blessed is thy n., O God of our fathers
23 be thy name, O God of Israel, blessed
8 9 in which thy name may be blessed
Jdth 9 10 beginning, and the Lord is thy name
11 defile the dwelling place of thy name
15 be a glorious monument for thy name
10 8 and thy name may be in the number of
11 21 thy name shall be renowned through all
13 25 he hath so magnified thy name this day
31 every nation which shall hear thy name
Esth 13 17 that we may live and praise thy name
Ps 5 12 that love thy name shall glory in thee
8 2 how admirable is thy name in the. 10
9 11 let them trust in thee who know thy n.
17 50 and I will sing a psalm to thy name
21 23 I will declare thy name to my brethren
43 6 through thy name we will despise them
9 and in thy name we will give praise
44 18 they shall remember thy n. throughout
47 11 according to thy name, O God, so also
51 11 I will wait on thy name, for it is
53 3 save me, O God, by thy name, and judge
8 will give praise, O God, to thy name
60 6 inheritance to them that fear thy name
9 so will I sing a psalm to thy name
62 5 in thy name I will lift up my hands
65 4 let it sing a psalm to thy name. Come
73 7 defiled the dwelling place of thy name
10 is the adversary to provoke thy name
18 foolish people hath provoked thy name
21 poor and needy shall praise thy name
74 2 praise, and we will call upon thy name
78 6 that have not called upon thy name
9 for the glory of thy name, O Lord
79 19 and we will call upon thy name. O Lord
82 17 and they shall seek thy name, O Lord
19 them know that the Lord is thy name
85 9 Lord: and they shall glorify thy name
11 heart rejoice that it may fear thy n.
12 I will glorify thy name forever: for
88 13 and Hermon shall rejoice in thy name
17 in thy name they shall rejoice all the
91 2 to sing to thy name, O most high
98 3 let them give praise to thy great name
101 16 and the Gentiles shall fear thy name
105 47 we may give thanks to thy holy name
113 1 not to us; but to thy name give glory
118 55 in the night I have remembered thy name
132 judgment of them that love thy name
134 13 thy name, O Lord, is forever: thy
137 2 and I will give glory to thy name
2 hast magnified thy holy name above all
139 14 they shall give glory to thy name
141 8 of prison, that I may praise thy name
144 1 I will bless thy name forever: yea
2 and I will praise thy name forever
Cant 1 2 thy name is as oil poured out
Wisd 10 20 they sung to thy holy name, O Lord
Eccu 36 14 people, upon whom thy name is invoked
17 the former prophets spoke in thy name
47 17 thy name went abroad to the islands
51 2 I will give glory to thy name: for
4 the multitude of the mercy of thy name
15 I will praise thy name continually
Isa 4 1 only let us be called by thy name
25 1 thee, and give glory to thy name
26 8 thy name and thy remembrance are the
13 only in thee let us remember thy name
43 1 called thee by thy name: thou art mine
45 3 the Lord who call thee by thy name
4 I have even called thee by thy name
63 16 from everlasting is thy name. Why
19 when we were not called by thy name
64 2 that thy name might be made known
7 is none that calleth upon thy name
Jer 10 6 great, and great is thy name in might
25 that have not called upon thy name
11 16 the Lord called thy name, a plentiful
14 9 and thy name is called upon by us
15 16 thy name is called upon me, O Lord
20 3 Lord hath not called thy name Phassur
29 25 thou hast sent letters in thy name
32 18 the Lord of hosts is thy name. Great
Lam 3 55 I have called upon thy name, O Lord
Bar 2 15 that thy name is called upon Israel
26 in which thy name was called upon
3 5 think upon thy hand and upon thy name
7 that we should call upon thy name
5 4 thy name shall be named to thee by God
Dan 3 26 and thy name is worthy of praise
43 give glory to thy name, O Lord: and let
9 6 prophets, that have spoken in thy name
18 the city upon which thy name is called
19 thy name is invocated upon thy city
Mich 6 9 shall be to them that fear thy name
Nah 1 14 that no more of thy name shall be sown
Mala 1 7 wherein have we despised thy name
1 Ma 4 33 let all that know thy name praise thee
7 37 for thy name to be called upon therein
Mat 6 9 hallowed by thy name. Luke 11:2
7 22 have not we prophesied in thy name
22 and cast out devils in thy name, and
22 and done many miracles in thy name
Mark 5 9 what is thy name? Luke 8:30
9 37 saw one casting out devils in thy name
Luke 9 49 casting out devils in thy name, and
10 17 also are subject to us in thy name
John 12 28 Father, glorify thy name. A voice
17 6 I have manifested thy name to the men
11 keep them in thy name whom thou hast
12 with them, I kept them in thy name
26 I have made known thy name to them
Acts 9 14 priests to bind all that invoke thy name

Rom 15 9 Gentiles, and will sing to thy name
Heb 2 12 I will declare thy n. to my brethren; in
Apoc 11 18 to them that fear thy name, little and
15 4 and magnify thy name? For thou only
whose name was Luke 1 27 virgin espoused to a man w. . . . Joseph
Luke 8 41 a man w. . . . Jairus, and he was a ruler
24 18 one of them, w. . . . Cleophas, answering
John 1 6 a man sent from God, w. . . . John
Acts 7 57 the feet of a young man w. . . . Saul
12 13 came to hearken whose name was Rhode
13 6 prophet, a Jew, whose name was Bar-jesu
named Gen 16 1 having a handmaid . . . named Agar
Gen 22 24 concubine, named Roma, bore Tabee
24 29 Rebecca had a brother named Laban
25 1 married another wife named Cetura
11 well named of the living and seeing
29 24 his daughter a handmaid named Zelpha
30 21 she bore a daughter named Dina. The
38 1 in to a certain Odollamite, named Hiras
41 52 he named the second Ephraim, saying
Deut 2 18 borders of Moab, the city named Ar
Josu 2 1 woman that was a harlot named Rahab
Judg 4 2 had a general of his army named Sisara
Ruth 1 2 he was named Elimelech, and his wife
1 K 4 18 and when he had named the ark of God
17 4 named Goliath, of Geth, whose height
2 K 3 7 Saul had a concubine named Respha
9 2 the house of Saul, a servant n. Siba
13 3 Amnon had a friend, named Jonadab
16 5 of the house of Saul named Semei
3 K 11 26 whose mother was named Sarua, a
1 Pa 2 18 and Caleb . . . took a wife named Azuba
26 Jerameel married another wife n. Atara
34 and a servant an Egyptian named Jeraa
4 38 were named princes in their kindreds
7 15 and he had a sister named Maacha
18 his sister named Queen bore Goodlyman
27 4 after him was another named Macelloth
2 Pa 20 16 will come up by the ascent named Sis
Tob 3 8 devil named Asmodeus had killed them
6 11 and he hath a daughter named Sara
Isa 14 20 of the wicked shall not be n. forever
55 13 Lord shall be n. for an everlasting
Jer 37 12 the captain . . . was one named Jerias
44 26 no more be named in the mouth of any
Bar 4 30 he exhorteth thee, that named thee
5 4 thy name shall be named to thee by
Dan 5 12 Daniel: whom the king named Baltassar
Mat 9 9 in the custom house, named Matthew
27 32 found a man of Cyrene, named Simon
57 rich man of Arimathea, named Joseph
Mark 3 17 and he named them Boanerges, which is
5 22 rulers of the synagogue named Jairus
Luke 1 5 a certain priest named Zachary of the
2 25 was a man in Jerusalem named Simeon
5 27 saw a publican named Levi, sitting
6 13 them, whom also he named apostles
10 38 certain woman named Martha, received
16 20 a certain beggar named Lazarus who
19 2 a man named Zacheus, who was the chief
23 50 man named Joseph, who was a counsellor
24 13 same day to a town . . . named Emmaus
John 3 1 there was a man . . . named Nicodemus
5 2 which in Hebrew is named Bethsaida
11 1 was a certain man sick, named Lazarus
49 one of them, named Caiphas, being
Acts 5 1 a certain man named Ananias, with
34 rising up, a Pharisee, named Gamaliel
8 9 a certain man named Simon, who before
9 10 disciple at Damascus, named Ananias
11 one named Saul of Tarsus. For behold he
12 he saw a man named Ananias coming in
33 man named Eneas, who had kept his bed
36 certain disciple named Tabitha, which
10 1 man in Caesarea, named Cornelius, a
11 26 the disciples were first n. Christians
28 one of them named Agabus, rising up
16 1 certain disciple there named Timothy
14 certain woman named Lydia, a seller
17 34 woman n. Damaris, and others with them
18 2 finding a certain Jew, named Aquila
7 house of a certain man, n. Titus Justus
24 a certain Jew, named Apollo, born at
19 24 for a certain man named Demetrius, a
20 9 and a certain young man named Eutychus
21 10 from Judea a certain prophet, n. Agabus
27 1 centurion, n. Julius, of band Augusta
28 7 chief man of island, named Publius, who
Rom 15 20 not where Christ was n., lest I should
1 C 5 11 if any man that is named a brother, be
Eph 1 21 every name that is named, not only in
3 15 paternity in heaven and earth is named
5 3 let it not so much as be named among you
namely 1 Es 9 1 abominations, namely, of the
2 Ma 12 2 that were behind, namely, Timotheus
Acts 15 22 n., Judas, who was surnamed Barsabas
name's 1 K 12 22 for his great name's sake
3 K 8 41 out of a far country for thy n. sake
Ps 22 3 for his own name's sake. 105:8
24 11 for thy name's sake, O Lord. 142:11
30 4 for thy name's sake thou wilt lead me
43 26 and redeem us for thy name's sake
78 9 forgive us our sins for thy name's sake
108 21 do with me for thy name's sake: because
Isa 48 9 for my name's sake I will remove my
66 5 and cast you out for my name's sake
Jer 14 7 do thou it for thy name's sake, for
21 not to be a reproach, for thy n. sake
Eze 20 9 I did otherwise for my name's sake
22 and wrought for my name's sake, that it
44 well by you for my own name's sake
36 22 but for my holy name's sake, which you
Dan 3 34 deliver us not . . . for thy name's sake
Mat 10 22 hated by all men for my name's sake. Mark 13:13; Luke 21:17
19 29 children or lands for my name's sake
24 9 by all nations for my name's sake
Luke 21 12 and governors, for my name's sake
John 15 21 will do to you for my name's sake
Acts 9 16 things he must suffer for my name's sake
1 J 2 12 are forgiven you for his name's sake
names Gen 2 20 called all the beasts by their n.
Gen 25 13 names of his [Ismael's] children
16 these are their names by their castles
26 18 he called them by the same names by
36 10 and these the names of his sons
40 are the names of the dukes of Esau
46 8 the names of the children of Israel. Exod 1:1; 28:9, 11, 21, 29; 39:6
48 16 upon them, and the names of my fathers
Exod 6 16 are the names of the sons of Levi
28 10 six names on one stone, and the other
12 Aaron shall bear their names before the
21 with 12 names shall they be engraved
39 14 engraved with n. of the twelve tribes
Num 1 2 names of every one . . . from twenty years old. 18, 24, 26, 28, 30, 32, 34, 36, 38, 40, 42
5 the princes . . . whose names are these
20 and houses and names of every head
22 were reckoned up by the names and heads
3 2 these the names of the sons of Aaron. 3
17 were found sons of Levi by their names
27 reckoned up by their names. 33
43 the males by their names, from one
13 4 principal men, whose names are these

17 names of the men whom Moses sent to
26 33 daughters, whose n. are these. Josu 17:3
53 according to the number of names. To
27 1 their names and Maala and Noa and
32 38 Baalmeon, their names being changed
38 giving names to the cities which they
34 17 names of the men that shall divide
19 one prince of every tribe, whose names
Deut 7 24 thou shalt destroy their names from under
Josu 9 17 names of which are Gabaon and Caphira
21 9 Josue gave cities: whose n. are these
1 K 14 49 and the names of his two daughters
17 13 names of his three sons that went to
2 K 5 14 names of them that were born to him
23 8 the names of the valiant men of David
3 K 4 8 their names: Benhur, in mount Ephraim
18 24 call ye on the names of your gods. 25
1 Pa 4 41 these whose names are written above
6 17 are the names of the sons of Gerson
65 cities which they called by their names
8 38 Asel had six sons whose names. 9:44
12 31 every one by their names, came to
14 4 names of them that were born to him
1 Es 5 4 we gave them the names of the men
10 we asked also of them their names
10 we have written the names of the men
8 13 sons of Adonicam . . . their names
20 all these were called by their names
10 16 all by their names, went and sat down
Esth 9 6 sons of Aman . . . whose names are these
Ps 15 4 nor will I be mindful of their names
48 12 have called their lands by their names
71 14 their names shall be honorable in his
146 4 calleth them all by their n. Isa 40:26
Eccu 23 10 meddle not with the names of saints
Eze 23 4 their names were Oolla . . . and Ooliba
4 for their names, Samaria is Oolla
48 1 these are the names of the tribes
31 according to the names of the tribes
Dan 1 7 master of the eunuchs gave them names
Osee 2 17 I will take away the names of Baalim
Soph 1 4 names of the wardens of the temples
Zach 13 2 I will destroy the names of idols
Mat 10 2 the names of the twelve apostles are
Luke 10 20 that your names are written in heaven
Acts 18 15 if they be questions of word and names
Phil 2 9 him a name which is above all names
4 3 whose names are in the book of life
Apoc 3 4 but thou hast a few names in Sardis
11 13 in the earthquake names of men 7,000
13 1 and upon his heads names of blasphemy
8 whose n. are not written in book. 17:8
17 3 beast, full of names of blasphemy
21 12 n. written thereon, which are the n. of the twelve tribes
14 in them the 12 names of the 12 apostles
nameth Eccu 23 11 every one that sweareth and n.
2 Tim 2 19 who nameth the name of the Lord. But in
naming Exod 30 13 that passeth at the naming
Eccu 23 10 let not the naming of God be usual
Namsi 3 K 19 16 Jehu the son of Namsi. 4 K 9:20; 2 Pa 22:7
4 K 9 2 Josaphat the son of Namsi. 14
Namuel Num 26 9 his sons were Namuel and Dathan and
Num 26 12 sons of Simeon . . . Namuel. 1 Pa 4:24
Namuelites Num 26 12 is the family of the N.
Nanea 2 Ma 1 13 he fell in the temple of Nanea
2 Ma 1 13 by counsel of the priests of Nanea
15 when the priests of N. had set it forth
Napheg 1 Pa 14 6 and Noga and N. and Japhia
Naphis Gen 25 15 Jethur and Naphis and Cedma
1 Pa 1 31 of Ismahel . . . Jetur, Naphis
5 19 Naphis and Nadab gave them help
napkin Luke 19 20 which I have kept laid up in a n.
John 11 44 was bound about with a napkin. Jesus
20 7 napkin that had been about his head
Narcissus' Rom 16 11 them that are of N. household
narration 2 Ma 2 33 then we will begin the n.
2 Ma 6 17 now we must come to the narration
15 38 will here make an end of my narration
Luke 1 1 to set forth in order a narration of
narrations 2 Ma 2 25 undertake the n. of histories
narrow Num 22 24 angel stood in a narrow place
Num 22 26 the angel going on to a narrow place
Josu 17 15 possession of mount Ephraim is too n.
Jdth 4 5 where the way was narrow between the
7 5 a narrow pathway lead directly between
Job 36 16 at large out of the narrow mouth
Prov 23 27 and a strange woman is a narrow pit
Isa 49 19 the land . . . shall now be too narrow
2 Ma 11 5 Bethsura, which is in a narrow place
Mat 7 13 enter ye in at the narrow gate; for
14 how narrow is the gate, and strait the
Luke 13 24 strive to enter by the narrow gate
Nasia 1 Es 2 54 the children of Nasia. 2 Es 7:56
Nathan Luke 3 31 Mathatha, who was of Nathan, who
2 K 5 14 Sobab and Nathan and Solomon. 1 Pa 3:5
7 3 Nathan said to the king: Go, do all
4 the word of the Lord came to Nathan
17 so did N. speak to David. 1 Pa 17:15
12 1 and the Lord sent Nathan to David
5 he said to Nathan: As the Lord liveth
7 Nathan said to David: Thou art the man
13 David said to Nathan: I have sinned
13 Nathan said to David: The Lord also
15 and Nathan returned to his house
25 and he sent by the hand of Nathan
23 36 Igaal the son of Nathan of Soba
3 K 1 11 Nathan said to Bethsabee the mother
23 Nathan said: My lord, O king, hast thou
4 5 Azarias the son of Nathan over them
5 Zabud the son of Nathan the priest
1 Pa 2 36 Ethei begot N., and N. begot Zabad
11 38 Joel the brother of Nathan, Mibahar
14 4 and Sobad, Nathan, and Solomon
17 2 Nathan said to David: Do all that
3 the word of God came to Nathan, saying
1 Es 8 16 N. and Zacharias and Mosollam, chief
10 39 Salmias and Nathan and Adaias, and
Zach 12 13 families of the house of Nathan apart
Nathan the prophet 2 K 7 2 he [David] said to N. . . . 1 Pa 17:1
2 K 12 25 he sent by the hand of N. . . . and called
3 K 1 8 N. . . . and Semei and Rei and the
10 N. . . . and Banaias and all the valiant
22 speaking with the king, N. . . . came
23 the king, saying: N. . . . is here. And
32 Sadoc the priest and N. . . . and Banaias
34 the priest and N. . . . anoint him there
38 N. . . . went down, and Banaias the son
44 with him Sadoc the priest and N. . . .
45 the priest and N. . . . have anointed him
1 Pa 29 29 the seer, and in the book of N. . . .
2 Pa 9 29 are written in the words of N. . . .
29 25 and of Gad the seer and of N. . . . : for
Ps 50 2 when N. . . . came to him after he had
Eccu 47 1 then N. . . . arose in the days of
Nathanael Num 1 8 Nathanael the son of Suar. 2:5; 7:18, 23; 10:15
1 Pa 2 14 fourth Nathanael, the fifth Raddai
15 24 Nathanael and Amasai and Zacharias
24 6 son of Nathanael the scribe a Levite
26 4 Sachar the fourth, Nathanael the fifth
2 Pa 17 7 N. and Micheas to teach in the cities
35 9 Chonenias and Semeias and Nathanael
1 Es 10 22 Ismael, Nathanael, Jozabed, and Elasa

2 Es 12 21 Hasebia: of Idaia, Nathanael. The
35 Nathanael and Judas and Hanani, with
John 1 45 Philip findeth Nathanael, and saith to
46 N. said to him: Can anything of good
47 Jesus saw Nathanael coming to him and
48 N. saith to him: Whence knowest thou
49 N. answered him and said: Rabbi, thou
21 2 and Nathanael, who was of Cana of
Nathania 1 Pa 25 2 of the sons of Asaph . . . N.
1 Pa 25 12 the fifth [lot] to Nathania, to his
Nathanias 4 K 25 23 Ismael the son of N. 25
2 Pa 17 8 with them the Levites . . . Nathanias
Jdth 8 1 son of Enan the son of Nathanias
Jer 36 14 princes sent Judi the son of Nathanias
40 8 Ismahel the son of Nathanias. 14, 15; 41:1, 2, 6, 7, 9, 10, 11, 12, 15, 16, 18
Nathanmelech 4 K 23 11 near the chamber of N.
Nathineans 1 Pa 9 2 in their cities . . . the N.
Nathinites 1 Es 2 43 N. the children of Siha
1 Es 2 58 N. and the children of servants of Solomon. 2 Es 7:60; 11:3
70 the Nathinites dwelt in their cities
7 7 porters and of the N. to Jerusalem
24 singers and the porters and the N.
8 17 to Eddo and his brethren the Nathinites
20 N. whom David and the princes . . . N. 220
2 Es 3 26 and the Nathinites dwelt in Ophel
30 built unto the house of the Nathinites
7 47 the Nathinites: the children of Soha
73 N. and all Israel dwelt in their cities
10 28 porters and singing men, Nathinites
11 21 the Nathinites, that dwelt in Ophel
21 Siaha and Gaspha of the Nathinites
native Gen 24 7 and out of my native country
Gen 31 13 return into thy native country. And
Lev 24 16 whether he be a native or a stranger
22 whether he be a stranger or a native
Jer 22 10 no more, nor see his native country
natives Num 15 29 whether they be n. or strangers
nativity Gen 11 28 land of his nativity in Ur
Eccu 23 19 lest . . . curse the day of thy nativity
Jer 46 16 to the land of our nativity, from the
Eze 16 3 thy nativity is of the land of Chanaan
4 day of thy n. thy navel was not cut
21 30 created, in the land of thy nativity
29 14 Phatures, in the land of their nativity
2 Ma 7 23 that formed the nativity of man
Luke 1 14 and many shall rejoice in his nativity
James 3 6 inflameth the wheel of our nativity
natural Wisd 12 10 generation, and their malice n.
Rom 1 26 their women have changed the natural use
27 leaving the natural use of the women
11 21 if God hath not spared the n. branches
24 which is natural to thee; and, contrary
24 they that are the natural branches, be
1 C 15 44 it is sown a natural body, it shall rise
44 if there be a natural body, there is
46 but that which is natural; afterwards
naturally 2 P 2 12 n. tending to the snare and to
Jude 10 what things soever they naturally know
nature Deut 23 12 mayst go for the necessities of n.
Judg 3 22 by the secret parts of nature the
24 perhaps he is easing nature in his
19 24 commit not this crime against nature
1 K 24 4 into which Saul went to ease nature
Esth 16 6 judge of others by their own nature
Wisd 14 26 defiling of souls, changing of nature
19 19 the water forgot its quenching nature
Rom 1 26 into that use which is against nature
2 14 do by n. those things that are of law
27 that which by nature is uncircumcision
11 24 natural to thee; and, contrary to nature
1 C 11 14 doth not even nature itself teach you
Gal 2 15 we by nature are Jews, and not of the
4 8 served them, who, by n., are not gods
Eph 2 3 and were by nature children of wrath
James 3 7 every nature of beasts and of birds
7 hath been tamed by the nature of man
2 P 1 4 be made partakers of the divine nature
natures Wisd 7 20 the natures of living creatures
naught Num 14 36 ill of the land that it was n.
naughtiness Deut 29 19 walk on in n. of my heart
James 1 21 and abundance of naughtiness, with
naughty 1 K 25 25 regard this naughty man Nabal
Nave Eccu 46 1 valiant in war was Jesus son of N.
navel Job 40 11 his force in the n. of his belly
Prov 3 8 it shall be health to thy navel
Cant 7 2 thy navel is like a round bowl never
Eze 16 4 thy nativity thy navel was not cut
naves 3 K 7 33 strakes and naves were all cast
navies 3 K 22 49 king Josaphat made n. on the sea
navigable 2 Ma 5 21 might now make the land n.
navy 3 K 10 11 navy also of Hiram which brought
3 K 10 22 king's navy, once in three years went with the navy of Hiram
Dan 11 40 king of the north . . . with great navy
2 Ma 14 1 up with a great power and a navy
nay Gen 18 15 nay; but thou didst laugh
1 K 8 19 nay, but there shall be a king over us
10 19 nay, but set a king over us. Now
12 12 nay, but a king shall reign over us
2 K 13 25 king said to Absalom: Nay, my son, do
16 18 Chusai answered Absalom: Nay, for I
24 24 nay, but I will buy it of thee at a
3 K 3 23 nay, but thy child is dead, and mine
20 7 he sent to me . . . and I said not nay
Nazarene Mat 2 23 that he shall be called a Nazarene
Nazarenes Acts 24 5 of sedition of sect of N.
Nazareth Mat 2 23 he dwelt in city called Nazareth
Mat 4 13 leaving the city Nazareth, he came and
21 11 this is Jesus the prophet from N.
Mark 1 9 Jesus came from Nazareth of Galilee
Luke 1 26 into a city of Galilee called Nazareth
2 4 out of the city of Nazareth into Judea
39 into Galilee to their city Nazareth
51 down with them and came to Nazareth
4 16 he came to N., where he was brought
John 1 46 can anything of good come from N.
Acts 3 6 in the name of Jesus Christ of N.
4 10 name of our Lord Jesus Christ of N.
Nazarite Gen 49 26 upon crown of the N. Deut 33:16
Num 6 18 the hair of the consecration of N.
19 deliver them into the hands of the N.
20 after this the Nazarite may drink wine
Judg 13 5 for he shall be a Nazarite of God
7 the child shall be a Nazarite of God
16 17 upon my head, for I am a Nazarite
Nazarites Lam 4 7 her N. were whiter than snow
Amos 2 11 and of your young men for Nazarites
12 you will present wine to the Nazarites
1 Ma 3 49 stirred up the N. that had fulfilled
Neapolis Acts 16 11 the day following to Neapolis
near Gen 12 11 he was near to enter into Egypt
Gen 24 11 without the town near a well of water
30 camels and near to the spring of water
27 22 he [Jacob] came near to his father
26 come near me, and give me a kiss
27 he came near, and kissed him. And
33 3 seven times until his brother came near
6 handmaids and their children came near
7 Lia . . . came near and bowed down
45 4 when they were come near him, he said
10 thou shalt be near me, thou and thy
48 7 I buried her near the way of Ephrata
Exod 13 17 land of the Philistines which is near
14 10 when Pharao drew near, the children of

	19	15	third day, and come not near your wives
	34	30	Moses horned, were afraid to come near
Lev	13	21	not lower than the flesh that is n. it
		31	equal with the flesh that is near it
	18	6	no man . . . that is near of kin to him
	20	20	uncover the shame of his near akin
	21	2	his kin, such as are near in blood
Num	13	30	and near the streams of the Jordan
	16	40	should come near to offer incense to
	24	6	as watered gardens near the rivers, as
		17	I shall behold him, but not near. A
Deut	11	30	is near the valley that reacheth and
	13	7	that are near or afar off, from one end
	16	21	any tree near the altar of the Lord
	19	3	may have near at hand whither to escape
Josu	3	4	take care you come not near the ark
	5	1	possessed the places near the great sea
	9	1	in the places near the sea and on the
	22	10	an altar immensely great near the Jordan
Judg	4	11	is called Sennim and was near Cedes
	9	34	laid ambushes near Sichem in four places
		52	Abimelech coming near the tower, fought
	11	26	cities near the Jordan for 300 years
	19	11	and now they were come near Jebus
	20	36	which they had set near the city. And
Ruth	3	2	this Booz . . . is our near kinsman, and
		9	for thou art a near kinsman. And he said
		12	do I deny myself to be near of kin
	4	4	there is no near kinsman besides thee
1 K	4	19	was big with child and near her time
	14	36	said: Let us draw near hither unto God
	20	20	and I will shoot three arrows near it
2 K	1	15	go near and fall upon him. And he struck
	11	20	why did you approach so near to the wall
		21	why did you go near the wall? Thou
	13	23	in Baalhasor, which is near Ephraim
	14	30	know the field of Joab near my field
	20	16	say to Joab: Come near hither, and I
		17	when he [Joab] was come near to her
	24	7	they passed near the walls of Tyre and
3 K	1	9	which was near the fountain Rogel
	8	46	the land of their enemies far or near
	18	30	the people coming near unto him, he
		36	Elias the prophet came near and said
	21	1	vineyard near the palace of Achab king
4 K	11	14	the singers and the trumpets near him
	15	25	smote him . . . near Argob and near Arie
	23	11	near the chamber of Nathanmelech the
1 Pa	1	48	of Rohoboth, which is near the river
	12	40	moreover they that were near them even
2 Pa	6	36	land either afar off or near at hand
2 Es	13	4	Eliasib . . . was near akin to Tobias
Tob	6	11	is Raguel, a near kinsman of thy tribe
Jdth	6	8	but when they came near the mountains
Job	33	22	his soul hath drawn near to corruption
Ps	1	3	which is planted near the running waters
	5	6	neither shall the wicked dwell near thee
	21	12	tribulation is very near: for there is
	26	2	whilst the wicked draw near against me
	31	9	their jaws, who come not near unto thee
	37	12	have drawn near and stood against me
		12	they that were near me stood afar off
	54	19	in peace from them that draw near to me
		22	and his heart hath drawn near. His
	84	10	his salvation is near to them that fear
	90	10	nor . . . scourge come near thy dwelling
	93	15	that are near it are all the upright of
	118	151	thou art near, O Lord: and all thy ways
		169	my supplication . . . come near in thy
Prov	7	12	now lying in wait near the corners
	23	11	their near kinsman is strong: and he
	27	10	better is a neighbor that is near than
Wisd	6	20	and incorruption bringeth near to God
Eccu	14	25	he that lodgeth near her house and
	21	2	for if thou comest near them, they will
	24	43	and my river came near to a sea: for
	26	15	and will drink of every water near her
	33	12	hath he sanctified and set near himself
	41	8	that converse near the houses of the
	51	9	and my life was drawing near to hell
		31	draw near to me, ye unlearned and
		34	for she is near at hand to be found
Isa	13	6	ye, for the day of the Lord is near
	14	1	her time is near at hand, and her days
	26	17	draweth near the time of her delivery
	29	13	draw near me with their mouth and with
	33	13	and you that are near know my strength
		24	neither shall he that is near, say: I
	34	1	come near, ye Gentiles, and hear and
	41	1	let them come near and then speak
		1	let us come near to judgment together
		5	the ends of the earth . . . drew near and
		21	bring your cause near, saith the Lord
	45	20	draw near together, ye that are saved
	46	12	I have brought my justice near, it
	48	16	come ye near unto me and hear this: I
	50	8	he is near that justifieth me, who will
		8	my adversary? Let him come near to me
	51	5	my just one is near at hand, my savior
	54	14	terror, for it shall not come near thee
	55	6	found: call upon him while he is near
	56	1	for my salvation is near to come and
	57	3	but draw near hither, you sons of the
		8	thou hast discovered thyself near me
		19	that is far off and to him that is near
	65	5	say: Depart from me, come not near me
Jer	12	2	thou art near in their mouth, and far
	25	26	all the kings of the north far and near
	30	21	and I will bring him near, and he shall
	41	17	in Chamaam, which is near Bethlehem
	42	1	from the least to the greatest came near
	48	16	destruction of Moab is near to come
		24	cities of land of Moab, far or near
	52	8	in the desert which is near Jericho
		25	them that were near the king's person
Lam	3	57	thou drewest near in the day when I
	4	18	our end draweth near: our days are
Bar	4	9	give ear, all you that dwell near Sion
Eze	6	12	he that is near, shall fall by the
	7	7	the day of slaughter is near, and not
	8	3	into Jerusalem, near the inner gate
	18	6	nor come near to a menstruous woman
	22	4	and thou hast made thy days to draw near
		5	those that are near, and those that are
	30	3	day is near, yea the day of the Lord is near
	31	7	for his root was near great waters
	40	46	come near to the Lord to minister to
	44	13	and they shall not come near to me
		13	they come near to any of my holy things
		15	shall come near to me, to minister to
		16	and they shall come near to my table
		25	they shall come near no dead person
	45	4	who come near to the ministry of the
Dan	3	48	Chaldeans as it found near the furnace
	6	20	coming near to the den, cried with a
	7	16	I went near to one of them that stood
	8	7	when he was come near the ram, he was
		17	he came and stood near where I stood
	9	7	to them that are near and to them that
	13	4	rich and had an orchard near his house
Joel	3	14	the day of the Lord is near. Soph 1:7
Soph	3	2	the Lord, she drew not near to her God
1 Ma	2	49	now the days drew near that Mathathias
	3	40	pitched near Emmaus in the plain country
	4	18	Gorgias and his army are near us in the
	5	27	their army . . . near to these cities

40 when Judas . . . come near the torrent
42 when Judas came near the torrent of
50 the men of the army drew near, and he
6 42 Judas and his army drew near for battle
7 39 encamped near to Bethoron, and an army
8 12 had conquered kingdoms that were near
9 12 and the legion drew near on two sides
10 48 moved his camp near to Demetrius. And
75 and they pitched their tents near Joppe
11 4 battle which they had made near the way
4 and when he came near to Azotus, they
13 53 that was near the castle, and he dwelt
15 14 city, and the ships drew near by sea
2 Ma 6 11 together in caves that were near, and
10 25 when he [Timotheus] drew near, prayed
27 they were come very near the enemies
Mat 26 18 my time is near at hand, with thee
Mark 5 11 there was there near the mountain a
11 1 they were drawing near to Jerusalem
13 28 you know that summer is very near
Luke 7 14 he came near and touched the bier
10 32 a Levite, when he was near the place
33 came near him; and seeing him, was
15 1 and sinners drew near unto him to
18 40 when he was come near, he asked him
19 37 coming near the descent of mount
41 when he drew near, seeing the city
22 47 drew near to Jesus, for to kiss him
24 15 Jesus himself also drawing near, went
John 3 23 John also was baptizing near Salim
4 5 near the land which Jacob gave to his
6 4 the pasch . . . was near at hand. When
11 18 Bethania was near Jerusalem, about
54 went into a country near the desert
Acts 7 17 when the time of the promise drew near
31 as he drew near to view it, the voice
8 29 go near and join thyself to this
21 33 then tribune coming near, took him, and
23 15 before he come n., are ready to kill him
Heb 6 8 is reprobate, and very near unto a curse
8 13 decayeth and groweth old, is n. its end
10 22 let us draw near with a true heart in
nearer Gen 44 8 then Juda coming n., said boldly
Gen 45 4 mildly to them: Come nearer to me
Deut 21 3 which they shall perceive to be nearer
Ruth 3 12 but there is another nearer than I
2 K 18 23 Achimaas running by a n. way passed
19 42 because the king is nearer to me: why
Rom 13 11 now our salvation is nearer than when we
Heb 6 9 nearer to salvation; though we speak
nearest Eccu 13 19 him that is n. to himself
neat's Eze 4 15 thee n. dung for man's dung
Nebahaz 4 K 17 31 Hevites made N. and Tharthac
Nebai 2 Es 10 19 Hareph, Anathoth, Nebai, Megphias
Neballat 2 Es 11 34 Hadid, Seboim, and N., Lod
Nebo Num 32 3 Saban and Nebo and Beon, the land
Deut 32 49 mount Nebo, which is in the land of
34 1 then Moses went . . . upon mount Nebo
1 Es 2 29 the children of Nebo, fifty-two. The
10 43 of the sons of Nebo, Jehiel, Mathathias
2 Es 7 33 the men of the other Nebo. 52
Isa 46 1 Bel is broken, Nebo is destroyed: their
Nebsan Josu 15 62 Nebsan and the city of salt
Neceb Josu 19 33 Adami, which is Neceb, and
necessaries Gen 42 2 go ye down and buy us n.
Gen 42 7 from the land of Chanaan to buy n.
43 4 and will buy necessaries for thee
3 K 4 7 every one provided necessaries, each
27 they furnished the n. also for king
5 9 thou shalt allow me n. to furnish food
1 Pa 22 5 I will prepare him n. And therefore
Prov 30 8 give me only the necessaries of life
Eze 12 3 prepare thee all n. for removing, and

2 Ma 13 20 Judas sent n. to them that were within
necessary Gen 42 33 take ye n. provision for
Exod 10 26 they are n. for the service of the Lord
35 21 whatsoever was n. to the service and
36 1 that are n. for the uses of sanctuary
5 the people offereth more than is n.
Lev 11 25 if it be n. that he carry any of these
Num 4 9 necessary for the dressing of the lamps
Judg 19 20 I will furnish all things that are n.
2 K 13 26 is not n. that he should go with thee
1 Es 6 9 if it shall be necessary, let calves
Tob 6 5 are necessary for useful medicines
8 21 provisions that are necessary for such
11 4 gall of the fish, for it will be n.
12 13 it was necessary that temptation should
Ecce 7 17 and be not more wise than is necessary
Wisd 16 3 was necessary to satisfy their desire
Eccu 3 23 it is not necessary for thee to see
29 3 always find that which is n. for thee
38 12 depart from thee, for his works are n.
39 31 things n. for the life of men are
1 Ma 10 39 for the n. charges of the holy things
2 Ma 1 18 thought it n. to signify it to you
4 19 the sacrifices, because it was not n.
23 from him concerning certain n. affairs
7 24 friend, and furnish him with things n.
9 21 n. to take care for the common good
Luke 10 42 but one thing is necessary. Mary
14 28 reckon the charges that are necessary
22 7 n. that the pasch should be killed
Acts 15 28 burden upon you than these n. things
28 10 laded us with such things as were n.
1 C 12 22 members of the body, are more necessary
2 C 9 5 I thought it n. to desire the brethren
Phil 2 25 necessary to send to you Epaphroditus
3 1 not wearisome, but to you is necessary
Titus 3 14 excel in good works for necessary uses
Heb 7 12 it is n. that a translation also be made
8 3 it is necessary that he also should have
9 23 it is n. therefore that the patterns of
10 36 for patience is necessary for you; that
James 2 16 things that are n. for the body, what
necessities Num 18 24 rated for their uses and n.
Deut 15 10 anything craftily in relieving his n.
23 12 thou mayst go for the n. of nature
Ps 24 17 deliver me from my necessities. See
Prov 27 27 and for the necessities of thy house
Eccu 18 25 the n. of poverty in the day of riches
Rom 12 13 communicating to the n. of the saints
2 C 6 4 patience, in tribulation, in necessities
12 10 in my infirmities, in reproaches, in n.
necessity Gen 33 15 [Jacob] said: There is no n.
Num 7 7 sons of Gerson according to their n.
Judg 11 7 you are come to me constrained by n.
1 K 13 12 forced by n., I offered the holocaust
Tob 4 10 a good reward for the day of necessity
Esth 14 16 thou knowest my n., that I abominate
16 9 the quality and necessity of times
Wisd 17 16 necessity from which he could not fly
19 4 necessity . . . brought them to this end
Dan 14 29 constrained by n. he delivered Daniel
Luke 23 17 of n. he was to release unto them one
John 4 4 he was of n. to pass through Samaria
Rom 13 5 be subject of n., not only for wrath
1 C 7 26 that this is good for present necessity
37 having no necessity, but having power
9 16 for a necessity lieth upon me: for woe
2 C 9 7 not with sadness, or of necessity: for
1 Th 3 7 in all our necessity and tribulation
Philem 14 not be as it were of n., but voluntary
Heb 9 16 the testator must of necessity come in
Jdth 1 3 I was under a n. to write unto you
Nechao 4 K 23 29 Pharao N. king of Egypt went

4 K 23 33 Pharao Nechao bound him at Rebla
34 Pharao Nechao made Eliacim . . . king
35 to his ability: to give to Pharao N.
2 Pa 35 20 Nechao king of Egypt came up to fight
22 hearkened not to the words of Nechao
Jer 46 2 against the army of Pharao Nechao
neck Gen 27 16 covered the bare of his neck
Gen 27 40 off and loose his yoke from thy neck
33 4 clasping him fast about the neck and
41 42 put a chain of gold about his neck
45 14 falling upon neck of his brother
14 and Benjamin . . . wept also on his neck
46 29 he fell upon his neck, and embracing
Lev 1 15 twisting back the neck and breaking
5 8 so that it stick to the neck, and be
Deut 10 16 heart, and stiffen your neck no more
28 48 shall put an iron yoke upon thy neck
31 27 thy obstinacy and thy most stiff neck
1 K 4 18 by the door, and broke his neck, and
4 K 17 14 like to the neck of their fathers, who
2 Pa 18 33 between the neck and the shoulders
23 15 they laid hold on her by the neck
36 13 he hardened his neck and his heart
2 Es 9 29 hardened their neck and would not hear
Tob 7 7 Raguel . . . weeping upon his neck, said
Jdth 13 10 she struck twice upon his neck and cut
Esth 15 15 scepter, and laid it upon her neck
Job 15 26 run against him with his neck raised up and is armed with a fat neck
16 13 he hath taken me by my neck, he hath
39 19 or clothe his neck with neighing
41 13 in his neck strength shall dwell and
Prov 1 9 head, and a chain of gold to thy neck
3 3 put them about thy neck, and write
6 21 and put them about thy neck. When
29 1 man that with a stiff neck despiseth
Cant 1 9 the turtle-dove's, thy neck as jewels
4 4 thy neck is as the tower of David
9 eyes, and with one hair of thy neck
7 4 thy neck as a tower of ivory. Thy eyes
Eccu 6 25 fetters, and thy neck into her chains
7 25 down their neck from their childhood
30 12 bow down his neck while he is young
33 27 yoke and the thong bend a stiff neck
38 19 sorrow of the heart boweth down the n.
51 34 and submit your neck to the yoke
Isa 8 8 going over shall reach even to the neck
10 27 his yoke from off thy neck, and the
30 28 even to the midst of the neck, to
48 4 thy neck is as an iron sinew, and thy
52 2 loose the bonds from off thy neck
Jer 7 26 their ear: but have hardened their neck
17 23 hardened their neck, that they might
27 2 and thou shalt put them on thy neck
8 whosoever will not bend his neck
11 nation that shall bend down their neck
28 10 took the chain from neck of Jeremias
11 from off the neck of all the nations
12 chain from off the neck of Jeremias
14 upon the neck of all these nations
30 8 I will break his yoke from off thy neck
48 39 how hath Moab bowed down the neck
Lam 1 14 in his hand, and put upon my neck
Bar 2 21 bow down your shoulder and your neck
30 they are a people of a stiff neck
33 away themselves from their stiff neck
4 25 and thou shalt get up upon his neck
Eze 16 11 hands, and a chain about thy neck
Dan 5 7 shall have a golden chain on his neck
16 have a chain of gold about thy neck
29 a chain of gold was put about his neck
Osee 10 11 I passed over upon the beauty of her n.
Haba 3 13 laid bare his foundation even to the n.
2 Ma 14 44 he came upon the midst of the neck
Luke 15 20 running to him fell upon his neck
Mat 18 6 millstone should be hanged about his neck. Mark 9:41; Luke 17:2
Acts 20 37 falling on neck of Paul, they kissed him
necklaces Isa 3 19 chains and n. and bracelets
necks Gen 49 8 shall be on n. of thy enemies
Lev 26 13 have broken the chains of your necks
Deut 33 29 and thou shalt tread upon their necks
Josu 10 24 set your feet on necks of these kings
24 put their feet upon the necks of them
Judg 5 30 heaped together to adorn the necks
8 26 chains that were about the camels' n.
21 with which the necks of camels of kings
4 K 17 14 hearkened not, but hardened their n.
2 Pa 30 8 harden not your necks, as your fathers
2 Es 3 5 did not put their necks to the work
9 16 hardened their necks and hearkened not
17 they hardened their necks and gave
Job 13 12 your necks shall be brought to clay
Ps 128 4 Lord . . . will cut the necks of sinners
Isa 3 16 have walked with stretched out necks
Jer 19 15 because they have hardened their necks
27 12 bend down your necks under the yoke
Lam 5 5 we were dragged by the necks, we were
Eze 10 12 and their necks . . . were full of eyes
21 29 bring thee upon the n. of the wicked
Mich 2 3 you shall not withdraw your necks
1 Ma 1 64 they hanged the children about their n.
Acts 15 10 to put a yoke upon n. of the disciples
Rom 16 4 for my life laid down their own necks
Necoda 1 Es 2 48 children of N. 50; 2 Es 7:50, 62
need Gen 25 22 what need was there to conceive
Deut 15 8 which thou perceivest he hath need of
1 K 21 15 have we need of madmen, that you have
2 K 19 26 I [Berzellai] need not this recompense
3 K 9 11 gold according to all he had need of
4 K 12 12 wheresoever there was need of expenses
1 Pa 29 5 wheresoever there is need of gold
5 wheresoever there is need of silver
2 Pa 2 14 that there may be need of in the work
31 16 there was need of in the ministry
1 Es 7 20 be need of for the house of thy God
Job 13 7 hath God any need of your lie, that
Prov 22 16 that is richer, and shall be in need
Wisd 11 6 they in their need were benefited. For
13 16 it is an image and hath need of help
Eccu 8 12 to give an answer in time of need
11 25 what need I, and what good shall I
13 7 if he have need of thee he will deceive
29 2 lend . . . in the time of his need
37 9 and know before what need he hath
38 1 physician for the need thou hast of
39 37 shall be ready upon earth when need is
41 3 is welcome to the man that is in need
Dan 10 1 is need of understanding in a vision
Mat 6 32 knoweth that you have need. Luke 12:30
9 12 they that are in health need not a
21 3 that the Lord hath need of them: and
26 65 what further need have we of witnesses
Mark 2 25 what David did when he had need and
11 3 say ye that the Lord hath need of him
14 63 what need we any further witnesses
Luke 5 31 that are whole need not the physician
15 7 upon 99 just who need not penance
19 31 the Lord hath need of his service
34 said: Because the Lord hath need of
22 71 what need we any further testimony
John 13 39 buy those things which we have need of
Acts 2 45 to all according as every one had need
4 35 to every one according as he had need
Rom 3 23 all have sinned, and so n. glory of God
16 2 business she shall have need of you. For

1 C 12 21 I need not thy help; nor again the head
2 C 3 1 or do we need, as some do, epistles of
Eph 4 28 to give to him that suffereth need. Let
Phil 4 12 both to abound, and to suffer need. I
1 Th 1 8 so that we need not to speak anything
5 1 you need not, that we should write to
Heb 5 12 you have need to be taught again what
12 you are become such as have n. of milk
7 11 what further need was there that another
1 J 3 17 and shall see his brother in need and
Apoc 3 17 made wealthy, and have need of nothing
22 5 they shall not need the light of the
no need 1 K 26 8 be no need of a second time
Ps 15 2 for thou hast no need of my goods
Prov 31 11 and he shall have no need of spoils
Eccu 15 12 for he hath no need of wicked men
42 22 he hath no need of any counsellor
Mat 14 16 they have no need to go: give you them
Mark 2 17 they that are well have no need of a
1 C 12 21 head to the feet: I have no need of you
24 but our comely parts have no need: but
1 Th 4 9 we have no need to write to you: for
1 J 2 27 you have no need that any man teach
Apoc 21 23 the city hath no need of the sun nor
needed 1 Ma 12 9 though we needed none of these
John 2 25 he needed not that any should give
Acts 17 25 hands, as though he needed anything
neededst John 16 30 neededst not that any man should
needeth Ecce 7 1 what n. a man to seek things
Eccu 40 27 and it needeth not to seek for help
Luke 11 8 and give him as many as he needeth
John 13 10 needeth not but to wash his feet, but
2 Tim 2 15 a workman that needeth not be ashamed
Heb 7 27 who n. not daily . . . to offer sacrifices
needful Mat 6 8 knoweth what is n. for you, before
Acts 20 34 for such things as were needful for me
Phil 1 24 abide still in the flesh, is n. for you
Heb 9 5 it is not n. to speak now particularly
needle Mat 19 24 pass through eye of a needle. Mark 10:25; Luke 18:25
needs Gen 43 11 if it needs be so, do what you
Jdth 14 3 the watchman must needs run to awake
Mat 18 7 it must needs be that scandals come
Mark 13 7 such things must needs be, but the end
Luke 14 18 and I must needs go out and see it
24 44 that all things must n. be fulfilled
Acts 1 16 the scripture must needs be fulfilled
21 22 the multitude must needs come together
1 C 5 10 otherwise you must n. go out of this
2 C 11 30 if I must needs glory, I will glory of
needy Deut 15 11 open thy hand to thy n. and poor
Deut 24 14 shalt not refuse the hire of the needy
Judg 9 4 he hired to himself men that were needy
11 3 there were gathered to him needy men
1 K 2 8 he raiseth up the needy from the dust
Tob 4 17 thy bread with the hungry and the needy
Job 5 15 he shall save the needy from the sword
16 and to the needy there shall be hope
24 14 he killeth the needy and the poor man
28 4 whom the food of the needy man hath
34 28 the cry of the needy to come to him
Ps 11 6 by reason of the misery of the needy
34 10 needy and the poor from them that strip
36 14 to cast down the poor and needy, to
40 2 understandeth concerning the needy and
69 6 I am needy and poor: O God, help me
71 12 and the needy that had no helper. He
13 he shall spare the poor and needy
73 21 poor and needy shall praise thy name
81 3 judge for the needy and fatherless
4 deliver the needy out of the hand of
85 1 hear me: for I am needy and poor
108 22 deliver me, for I am poor and needy
112 7 raising up the needy from the earth
139 13 the Lord will do justice to the needy
Prov 19 22 a needy man is merciful: and better is
22 22 do not oppress the needy in the gate
30 14 to devour the needy from off the earth
31 9 and do justice to the needy and poor
20 she hath opened her hand to the needy
Eccu 4 3 afflict not the heart of the needy
4 turn not away thy face from the needy
7 23 not of liberty, nor leave him needy
14 10 shall be needy and pensive at his
34 25 bread of the n. is the life of the poor
Isa 25 4 a strength to the needy in his distress
26 6 of the poor, the steps of the needy
41 17 the needy and the poor seek for waters
58 7 bring the needy and the harborless into
Jer 22 16 judged the cause of the poor and needy
Eze 16 49 not put forth their hand to the needy
18 12 that grieveth the needy and the poor
22 29 they afflicted the needy and poor
Amos 4 1 that oppress the needy and crush the
8 4 and make the n. of the land to fall
6 we may possess the needy for money
Soph 3 12 midst of thee a poor and needy people
Acts 4 34 neither was there any one needy among
2 C 6 10 as needy, yet enriching many; as having
Gal 4 9 how turn you again to the weak and needy
neglect Deut 8 11 and n. his commandments and
Deut 22 3 neglect it not as pertaining to another
Judg 18 9 neglect not, lose no time: let us go
3 K 22 3 is ours, and we neglect to take it
Eccu 7 10 neglect not to pray, and to give alms
32 22 counsel will not neglect understanding
38 9 in thy sickness neglect not thyself
16 his body and neglect not his burial
1 Tim 4 14 neglect not the grace that is in thee
Heb 2 3 shall we escape if we neglect so great
12 5 neglect not the discipline of the Lord
neglected 2 Pa 26 16 and he n. the Lord his God
2 Es 6 3 lest it be neglected whilst I come
Prov 1 25 and have neglected my reprehensions
3 10 have n. the just, and have revolted
Mat 22 5 but they neglected, and went their ways
Acts 6 1 that their widows were neglected in
neglecteth Prov 12 26 n. a loss for the sake of
Prov 19 16 he that n. his own way, shall die
Ecce 7 19 that feareth God, neglecteth nothing
neglecting Lev 20 4 if the people of the land n.
2 Ma 4 14 n. the sacrifices, hastened to be
negligence Num 5 6 by n. shall have transgressed
Eccu 26 28 a merchant is hardly free from n.
negligences Eccu 7 34 for thy n. purify thyself
negligent 2 Pa 24 5 the Levites were negligent
2 Pa 29 11 my sons, be not negligent: the Lord
1 Es 4 22 that you be not n. in executing this
2 Ma 12 14 behaved in a more negligent manner
Nehelamite Jer 29 24 to Semeias the N. thou shalt
Jer 29 31 saith the Lord to Semeias the N.
32 I will visit upon Semeias the N.
Nehelescol Num 13 25 place, which was called N.
Nehemia 1 Es 2 2 Nehemia, Saraia, Rahelaia
Nehemias 2 Es 1 1 the words of Nehemias the son
2 Es 3 16 after him built Nehemias the son of
7 7 who came with Zorobabel, Josue, N.
8 9 Nehemias (he is Athersatha) and Esdras
10 1 and the subscribers were Nehemias
12 26 in the days of Nehemias the governor
46 in the days of Nehemias gave portions
Eccu 49 15 let Nehemias be a long time remembered
2 Ma 1 18 when N. offered sacrifices, after the
20 pleased God that N. should be sent by
21 priest N. commanded the sacrifices
24 the prayer of N. was after this manner

31 N. commanded the water that was left
33 with which Nehemias . . . had purified
36 Nehemias called this place Nephthar
2 13 in the memoirs and commentaries of N.
Nehiel Josu 19 27 to Bethemec and Nehiel. And it
neigh Jer 31 7 n. before the head of the Gentiles
neighbor Lev 3 22 every woman shall ask of her neighbor
Exod 11 2 every woman of her neighbor, vessels
Ps 27 3 who speak peace with their neighbor
34 14 as a neighbor and as an own brother
87 19 friend and neighbor thou hast put far
Prov 27 10 better is a neighbor that is near
Ecce 4 4 exposed to the envy of their neighbor
Jer 6 21 neighbor and kinsman shall perish
9 20 every one her neighbor mourning
50 40 Gomorrha and their n. cities, saith the
Bar 6 43 she upbraideth her neighbor, that she
Dan 13 61 had maliciously dealt against their n.
Mark 12 33 to love one's neighbor as one's self
Luke 10 29 said to Jesus: And who is my neighbor
36 was n. to him that fell among the
Rom 13 10 love of our neighbor worketh no evil
his neighbor Gen 11 3 each one said to his n.
Exod 12 4 he shall take unto him his neighbor
21 14 if a man kill his n. on set purpose
18 the one strike his n. with a stone
22 9 he shall restore double to his neighbor
14 if a man borrow of his neighbor any
32 27 let every man kill his . . . friend and n.
Lev 6 2 deny to his n. the things delivered
19 11 neither shall any man deceive his n.
Deut 4 42 who should kill his n. unwillingly
15 2 thing is owing from his friend or n.
19 4 he that killeth his n. ignorantly
11 man hating his neighbor, lie in wait
27 24 he that secretly killeth his neighbor
Josu 20 5 because he slew his neighbor unawares
Judg 7 13 one told his neighbor a dream: and
Ruth 4 7 put off his shoe and gave it to his n.
1 K 14 20 man's sword was turned upon his n.
3 K 8 31 if any man trespass against his n.
2 Pa 6 22 if any man sin against his neighbor
Jdth 15 2 so that no one spoke to his neighbor
Ps 11 3 vain things every one to his neighbor
14 3 nor hath done evil to his neighbor
3 nor taken up a reproach against his n.
4 he that sweareth to his neighbor
23 4 nor sworn deceitfully to his neighbor
100 5 that in private detracted his neighbor
Prov 14 20 shall be hateful even to his own n.
21 that despiseth his neighbor, sinneth
21 10 he will not have pity on his neighbor
25 18 beareth false witness against his n.
27 14 that blesseth his n. with a loud voice
Eccu 11 32 spy that looketh on the fall of his n.
16 28 nor shall any of them straiten his n.
17 12 them commandment concerning his n.
18 12 the compassion of man is toward his n.
27 20 that destroyeth the friendship of his n.
29 that setteth a stone for his neighbor
29 1 that showeth mercy, lendeth to his n.
18 man is surety for his neighbor. 22
34 26 is like him that killeth his neighbor
Isa 3 5 and every man against his neighbor
13 8 every one shall be amazed at his n.
41 6 every one shall help his neighbor
Jer 7 5 judgment between a man and his neighbor
9 4 let every man take heed of his neighbor
22 8 shall say every man to his neighbor
23 27 which they tell every man to his n.
30 steal my words every one from his n.
35 thus shall you say every one to his n.
31 34 teach no more every man his neighbor
Eze 33 30 each man to his neighbor, saying: Come
Zach 8 10 all men go every one against his n.
16 speak ye truth every one to his n.
11 9 devour every one the flesh of his n.
14 13 a man shall take the hand of his n.
Mala 3 16 spoke every one with his neighbor
1 Ma 2 40 every man said to his neighbor: If we
3 43 every man to his n.: Let us raise up
Acts 7 27 he that did the injury to his neighbor
Rom 13 8 he that loveth his n., hath fulfilled
15 2 let every one of you please his n. unto
Eph 4 25 the truth every man with his neighbor
Heb 8 11 they shall not teach every man his n.
thy neighbor Exod 2 13 why strikest thou thy n.
Exod 20 16 false witness against thy neighbor
22 26 if thou take of thy neighbor a garment
Lev 19 13 shalt not calumniate thy neighbor
15 judge thy n. according to justice
16 not stand against the blood of thy n.
25 14 shalt sell anything to thy neighbor
Deut 5 20 thou bear false witness against thy n.
15 3 exact it: of thy countryman and n.
24 10 when thou shalt demand of thy n.
1 K 15 28 hath given it to thy n. who is better
28 17 and will give it to thy neighbor David
2 K 12 11 and give them to thy neighbor, and he
Prov 6 3 art fallen into hands of thy neighbor
24 28 witness without cause against thy n.
25 17 withdraw thy foot from house of thy n.
Eccu 4 27 reverence not thy neighbor in his fall
5 14 thou have understanding, answer thy n.
6 1 become not an enemy to thy neighbor
9 21 beware of thy n. and treat with the
10 6 any injury done thee by thy neighbor
19 10 hast thou heard a word against thy n.
14 reprove thy neighbor, for it may be
17 admonish thy n. before thou threaten
27 18 love thy neighbor and be joined to him
21 so hast thou let thy neighbor go
28 2 forgive thy n. if he hath hurt thee
8 and be not angry with thy neighbor
9 overlook the ignorance of thy neighbor
29 2 lend to thy n. in the time of his need
2 pay thou thy n. again in due time
26 recover thy n. according to thy power
31 18 judge of the disposition of thy n. by
41 rebuke not thy n. in a banquet of wine
41 26 turn not away thy face from thy n.
Mat 5 43 thou shalt love thy n., and hate thy
19 19 love thy n. as thyself. 22:39; Mark 12:31;
Luke 10:27; Rom 13:9; Gal 5:14; James 2:8
James 4 13 who art thou that judgest thy neighbor
neighboring 1 Ma 12 33 Ascalon and n. fortresses
2 Ma 4 32 Tyre and in the neighboring cities
6 8 went out a decree into the n. cities
9 25 n. princes and borderers wait for
Mark 1 38 let us go into the neighboring towns
Acts 5 16 a multitude out of the n. cities
Jdth 1 7 Sodom and Gomorrha and the n. cities
neighbor's Exod 20 17 not covet thy n. house
Exod 22 8 not lay his hand upon his n. goods
10 sheep or any beast to his n. custody
11 not put forth his hand to his n. goods
Lev 18 20 shalt not lie with thy n. wife, nor
20 10 defile his n. wife, let them be
Deut 5 21 shalt not covet thy neighbor's wife
19 14 nor remove thy neighbor's landmark
22 24 because he hath humbled his n. wife
23 24 into thy n. vineyard, thou mayst eat
27 17 that removeth his neighbor's landmarks
Prov 6 29 that goeth in to his neighbor's wife
Eccu 21 25 is soon in his neighbor's house: but
Jer 5 8 every one neighed after his n. wife

Eze 18 6 and hath not defiled his n. wife. 15
11 and that defileth his neighbor's wife
22 11 committed abomination with his n. wife
33 26 every one hath defiled his n. wife
Zach 11 6 every one into his neighbor's hand
14 13 shall be clasped upon his n. hand
neighbors Lev 24 19 a blemish to any of his n.
Num 25 5 let every man kill his n., that have
Ruth 4 17 the women her n., congratulating
1 K 30 26 to the ancients of Juda his neighbors
4 K 4 3 borrow of all thy n. empty vessels
Tob 2 8 all his neighbors blamed him, saying
8 22 banquet to be prepared for all his n.
Ps 30 12 very much [a reproach] to my neighbors
37 12 my friends and my n. have drawn near
43 14 hast made us a reproach to our n.
44 15 her neighbors shall be brought to thee
78 4 we are become a reproach to our n.
12 render to our neighbors sevenfold
79 7 made us to be a contradiction to our n.
88 42 he is become a reproach to his n.
121 8 the sake of my brethren and of my n.
Eccu 15 4 and she shall exalt him among his n.
25 2 concord of brethren and the love of n.
24 in midst of her n., her husband groaned
30 1 not grope after the doors of his n.
Jer 12 14 saith Lord against all my wicked n.
49 10 laid waste, and his brethren and his n.
18 Sodom was overthrown . . . and the n.
Bar 4 24 as the n. of Sion have now seen your
Eze 16 26 fornication with the Egyptians thy n.
22 12 and hast covetously oppressed thy n.
27 4 thy neighbors that built thee, have
Luke 1 58 her n. and kinsfolks heard that the
65 fear came upon all their neighbors
14 12 nor thy neighbors who are rich; lest
15 6 call together his friends and n.
9 and call together her friends and n.
John 9 8 the n., therefore, and they who had
neighed Jer 5 8 n. after his neighbor's wife
neigheth Eccu 33 6 he n. under every one that
neighing Job 39 19 or clothe his neck with n.
Jer 8 16 sound of the neighing of his warriors
13 27 I have seen thy adulteries and thy n.
Nah 3 2 wheels, and of the neighing horse
Nemra Num 32 3 Dibon and Jazer and Nemra
Nemrim Isa 15 6 waters of N. shall be desolate
Jer 48 34 waters also of Nemrim shall be very bad
Nemrod Gen 10 8 Chus begot Nemrod. 1 Pa 1:10
Gen 10 9 even as Nemrod the stout hunter
Mich 5 6 shall feed . . . the land of Nemrod
neophyte 1 Tim 3 6 not a n.: lest being puffed up
Nephath-Dor 3 K 4 11 to whom belonged all N.
Nepheg Exod 6 21 sons also of Isaar: Core and N.
2 K 5 15 Jebahar and Elisua and Nepheg and
1 Pa 3 7 and Noge and Nepheg and Japhia
Nephi 2 Ma 1 36 Nephthat . . . But many call it N.
Nephtali Gen 30 8 and she called him Nephtali
Gen 35 25 the sons of Bala . . . Dan and Nephtali
49 21 Nephtali, a hart let loose, and giving
Exod 1 4 Dan and Nephtali, Gad and Aser. And
Num 1 15 of Nephtali, Ahira the son of Enan
13 15 of the tribe of Nephtali. 34:28
Deut 27 13 on mount Hebal . . . Dan and Nephtali
33 23 to N. he said: N. shall enjoy abundance
34 2 the Lord showed him . . . all Nephtali
Josu 19 39 of the tribe of the children of N.
20 7 and Cedes in Galilee of mount Nephtali
21 6 of Issachar and of Aser and of Nephtali
32 of the tribe also of Nephtali, Cedes
Judg 1 33 N. also destroyed not the inhabitants
4 6 the son of Abinoem out of Cedes in N.
6 fighting men of the children of N. and
10 he called unto him Zabulon and Nephtali
5 18 Zabulon and N. offered their lives
6 35 into Aser and Zabulon and Nephtali
7 23 shouting from Nephtali and Aser and
3 K 4 15 Achimaas in Nephtali: he also had
7 14 widow woman of the tribe of Nephtali
15 20 they smote . . . the land of Nephtali
4 K 15 29 and Galilee and all the land of N.
1 Pa 2 2 Benjamin, Nephtali, Gad and Aser
6 62 out of the tribe of Nephtali. 76
12 34 and of Nephtali, a thousand leaders
40 as far as Issachar and Zabulon and N.
2 Pa 16 4 all the walled cities of Nephtali
34 6 even to Nephtali he demolished all
Tob 1 1 Tobias of the tribe and city of N.
4 younger than any of the tribe of N.
7 4 we are of the tribe of Nephtali, of
Isa 9 1 land of Nephtali was lightly touched
sons of Nephtali Gen 46 24 the sons of N.: Jaziel
Num 1 42 of the sons of Nephtali . . . 53,400
2 29 tribe of sons of N., the prince. 10:27
7 78 the prince of the sons of Nephtali
26 48 the sons of Nephtali by their kindreds
50 are the kindreds of the sons of N.
Josu 19 32 sixth lot came out to the sons of N.
1 Pa 7 13 sons of Nephtali were Jasiel and
Nephtalites 1 Pa 27 19 over the N., Jerimoth
Nephthali Ps 67 28 leaders . . . the princes of N.
Eze 48 3 of the sea, one portion for Nephthali
4 by the border of N., from the east
34 Aser one, the gate of Nephthali one
Apoc 7 6 of the tribe of Nephthali, 12,000 signed
Nephthalim Mat 4 13 borders of Zabulon and of N.
Mat 4 15 land of Zabulon and land of Nephthalim
Nephthar 2 Ma 1 36 Nehemias called this place N.
Nephtoa Josu 15 9 the fountain of the water of N.
Josu 18 15 to fountain of the waters of Nephtoa
Nephtuim 1 Pa 1 11 Mesraim begot . . . Nephtuim
Nephusim 1 Es 2 50 the children of Nephusim
Nephussim 2 Es 7 52 Nathinites . . . children of N.
Nepthuim Gen 10 13 Mesraim begot . . . Nepthuim
Ner 1 K 14 50 Abner the son of Ner. 26:5, 14; 2 K 2:8, 12; 3:6, 25, 28, 37; 3 K 2:5, 32; 1 Pa 26:28
1 K 14 51 Ner the father of Abner, was son of
1 Pa 8 33 Ner begot Cis. 9:39
9 36 Cis and Baal and Ner and Nadab
Neregel Jer 39 3 N., Sereser . . . N., Serezer
Jer 39 13 Neregel and Sereser and Rebmag
Nereus Rom 16 15 salute Philologus and Julia, N.
Nergel 4 K 17 30 and the Culthites made Nergel
Neri Jer 32 12 Baruch the son of Neri. 16
Luke 3 27 Salathiel, who was of Neri, who was
Nerias Jer 36 4 Baruch the son of Nerias. 8, 14, 32; 43:3, 6; 45:1; Bar 1:1
Jer 51 59 Saraias the son of Nerias the son of
Nesib Josu 15 43 Jephtha and Esna and Nesib
Nesroch 4 K 19 37 worshipping in the temple of Nesroch. Isa 37:38
nest Num 24 21 though thou build thy n. in a rock
Deut 22 6 bird's nest in a tree or on the ground
Tob 2 11 hot dung out of a swallow's nest fell
Job 29 18 and I said: I shall die in my nest
39 27 and make her nest in high places
Ps 83 4 the turtle a nest for herself where
Prov 27 8 as bird that wandereth from her nest
Isa 10 14 the strength of the people as a nest
16 2 as young ones flying out of the nest
Jer 22 23 and makest thy nest in the cedars
48 28 maketh her nest in mouth of the hole
49 16 make thy nest as high as an eagle
Eze 17 23 every fowl shall make its nest under
Abdi 1 4 thou set thy nest among the stars
Haba 2 9 house, that his nest may be on high

nests Ps 103 17 the sparrows shall make their n.
Eze 31 6 made their nests in his boughs, and
Mat 8 20 birds of the air nests. Luke 9:58
net Exod 27 4 grate of brass in manner of a net. 38:4
Exod 38 5 at four ends of the net at the top
Jdth 9 13 be caught in the net of his own eyes
Job 18 8 he hath thrust his feet into a net
Ps 9 10 in his net he will bring him down
34 7 they have hidden their net for me
8 let the net which he hath hidden catch
65 11 thou hast brought us into a net, thou
139 6 the proud have hidden a net for me
140 10 the wicked shall fall in his net: I am
Prov 1 17 a net is spread in vain before the eyes
29 5 spreadeth a net for his feet. A snare
Ecce 7 27 her heart is a net, and her hands are
Jer 5 27 as a net is full of birds, so their
Lam 1 13 he hath spread a net for my feet, he
Eze 12 13 I will spread my net over him, and he shall be taken in my net. 17:20
19 8 and they spread their net over him
32 3 I will spread out my net over thee
3 and I will draw thee up in my net
Osee 5 1 over, and a net spread upon Thabor
7 12 I will spread my net upon them, I will
Haba 1 15 drag, and gathered them into his net
16 and he will sacrifice to his net
17 spreadeth his net and will not spare
Mat 4 18 his brother, casting a net into the sea
13 47 is like to a net cast into the sea
Luke 5 5 at thy word I will let down the net
6 of fishes, and their net broke. And
John 21 6 cast the net on the right side of the
8 dragging the net with fishes. As soon
11 went up and drew the net to land, full
11 were so many, the net was not broken
nether Exod 28 27 looketh towards the n. joining
Deut 24 6 not take the nether . . . millstone
Josu 15 19 and the nether watery ground. Judg 1:15
16 3 unto borders of Beth-horon the nether
18 13 on the south of the nether Beth-horon
3 K 9 17 Solomon built . . . Beth-horon the n.
1 Pa 7 24 built Bethoron, the n. and the upper
2 Pa 8 5 he built . . . Beth-horon the nether
Nethuphati 2 Es 12 28 out of the villages of N.
Netophathi 1 Pa 2 54 sons of Salma . . . N.
Jer 40 8 children of Ophi, that were of N.
Netophathite 2 K 23 28 Ahohite, Maharai the N.
2 K 23 29 Heled the son of Baana, also a N.
4 K 25 23 son of Thanehumeth the Netophathite
1 Pa 11 30 Maharai a Netophathite, Heled the son of Baana a Netophathite
27 13 Marai, who was a Netophathite of the
15 twelfth . . . was Holdai a Netophathite
Netophati 1 Pa 9 16 dwelt in the suburbs of N.
nets 3 K 7 17 seven rows of nets were on one
3 K 7 17 and seven nets on the other chapiter
Job 40 26 wilt thou fill nets with his skin
Isa 19 8 they that spread nets upon the waters
Eze 26 5 she shall be a drying place for nets
14 thou shalt be a drying place for nets
47 10 there shall be drying of nets: there
Mat 4 20 leaving their nets, followed. Mark 1:18
21 mending their nets, and he called them
22 forthwith left their nets and father
Mark 1 16 casting nets into the sea, for they
19 were mending their nets in the ship
Luke 5 2 were washing their nets. And going
4 and let down your nets for a draught
nettle Isa 55 13 instead of the n., shall come up
nettles Prov 24 31 it was all filled with nettles
Isa 34 13 nettles shall grow up in its houses
Osee 9 6 n. shall inherit their beloved silver

Netupha 1 Es 2 22 the men of Netupha, 56
2 Es 7 26 children of Bethlehem and N., 188
network 3 K 7 17 a kind of n. and chain work
3 K 7 18 two rows round about each network
20 of the pillar over against the network
42 two rows of pomegranates for each n.
4 K 25 17 and the network . . . all of brass
2 Pa 4 12 the network to cover the chapiters
13 and two wreaths of network, so that
Jer 52 22 network and pomegranates were upon the
23 in all, were compassed with network
networks 3 K 7 41 two n. to cover the two cords
3 K 7 42 and 400 pomegranates for the two n.
never Gen 24 6 thou never bring my son back
Gen 38 22 that there never sat a harlot there
41 19 I never saw the like in land of Egypt
Exod 9 24 bigness, as never before was seen
13 22 never failed the pillar of the cloud
34 10 I will do signs such as were never seen
12 beware thou never join in friendship
Lev 6 13 perpetual fire which shall never go out
Num 22 30 to thee. But he [Balaam] said: Never
Deut 21 4 valley, that never was plowed nor sown
Judg 16 11 with new ropes that were never in work
17 the razor hath never come upon my head
19 30 was never such a thing done in Israel
20 6 there never was so heinous a crime
1 K 25 7 were shearing we never molested them
12 21 vain things which shall n. profit you
2 K 1 22 arrow of Jonathan never turned back
12 10 sword shall n. depart from thy house
2 Pa 9 11 never were there seen such trees in
18 7 for he never prophesieth good to me
Tob 1 12 and never was defiled with their meats
2 18 to those that never change their faith
3 9 may we n. see son or daughter of thee
16 that I never coveted a husband, and
17 never have I joined myself with them
4 6 take heed thou never consent to sin
13 never endure to know a crime. Never
14 n. suffer pride to reign in thy mind
16 see thou never do to another what thou
5 24 I wish the money . . . had never been
Jdth 5 14 Sina, in which never man could dwell
11 1 for I have never hurt a man that was
2 I would never have lifted up my spear
12 20 so much as he had n. drunk in his life
Job 14 2 and never continueth in the same state
Ps 12 4 my eyes that I never sleep in death
29 7 I said: I shall never be moved. O Lord
30 1 I hoped, let me never be confounded
48 20 fathers: and he shall never see light
70 1 let me never be put to confusion
76 8 will he never be more favorable again
102 2 never forget all he hath done for thee
118 93 thy justifications I will never forget
Prov 10 30 the just shall never be moved: but
13 25 belly of the wicked is n. to be filled
27 20 hell and destruction are never filled
20 so the eyes of men are never satisfied
30 15 three things that never are satisfied
15 the fourth never saith: It is enough
16 and the fire never saith: It is enough
Ecce 11 4 considereth the clouds, shall n. reap
Cant 7 2 like a round bowl never wanting cups
Wisd 3 15 and the root of wisdom never faileth
6 13 wisdom is glorious and never fadeth
12 10 their thought could never be changed
15 17 though he were mortal, but they never
Ecce 7 40 last end, and thou shalt never sin
12 10 never trust thy enemy; for as a brass
22 6 of wisdom are never out of time. He
23 11 is never without a blue mark, so

20 will never be corrected all the days
22 it will never be quenched till it
24 6 should rise light that never faileth
27 17 shall never find a friend to his mind
28 20 shall never have rest, neither shall
30 23 a never failing treasure of holiness
32 28 in him, shall fare never the worse
39 12 wisdom, and it shall never be forgotten
43 11 and shall never fall in their watches
34 weary: for you can never go far enough
44 9 perished as if they had never been
9 become as if they had never been born
Isa 56 5 everlasting name which shall n. perish
11 impudent dogs, they never had enough
62 6 they shall never hold their peace
Jer 20 11 reproach, which never shall be effaced
23 40 shame which shall never be forgotten
50 5 covenant which shall n. be forgotten
Bar 2 2 such as never happened under heaven
Eze 27 36 and thou shalt never be any more. 28:19
Dan 2 44 kingdom that shall never be destroyed
9 12 such as never was under all the heaven
11 24 that which his fathers never did
12 1 a time shall come such as never was
13 27 never had there been any such word
14 34 Lord, I never saw Babylon, nor do I
Amos 8 7 I will never forget all their works
Haba 2 5 like death, and he is never satisfied
2 Ma 1 5 and never forsake you in the evil time
6 16 he never withdraweth his mercy from
11 4 never considering the power of God
Mat 7 23 I never knew you: depart from me, you
9 33 never was the like seen in Israel
12 7 you would never have condemned the
21 16 have you never read. 42; Mark 2:25
26 33 in thee, I will never be scandalized
27 14 and he answered him to never a word
Mark 2 12 saying: We never saw the like. And he
3 29 shall never have forgiveness, but
Luke 15 29 I have never transgressed thy
29 thou hast never given me a kid to
23 53 never yet any man had been laid. And
John 6 35 that believeth in me shall never thirst
7 15 know letters, having never learned
46 never did man speak like this man
8 33 we have never been slaves to any man
13 8 thou shalt never wash my feet. Jesus
Acts 10 14 I n. did eat anything that is common
14 7 his mother's womb, who n. had walked
1 C 2 8 they would n. have crucified the Lord of
8 13 I will never eat flesh, lest I should
13 8 charity never falleth away: whether
2 Tim 3 7 ever learning, and never attaining to
Heb 4 8 he would never have afterwards spoken
10 11 which can never take away sins. But this
1 P 5 4 you shall receive a never fading crown
Apoc 16 18 as never had been since men were upon
nevertheless Mat 18 7 n. woe to that man by whom the
Mat 26 39 n. not as I will, but as thou wilt
64 n. I say to you, hereafter you shall
Acts 14 16 ways. N. he left not himself without
1 C 7 28 n., such shall have tribulation of flesh
9 12 n., we have not used this power: but we
Eph 5 33 n. let every one of you in particular
Phil 3 16 n. whereunto we are come, that we be
4 14 n. you have done well in communicating
new Exod 1 8 there arose a new king over Egypt
Exod 13 4 month of new corn. 23:15; 34:18; Deut 16:1
35 35 things, and to invent all new things
Lev 23 16 you shall offer a new sacrifice to the
25 22 till new grow up, you shall eat the old
26 10 new coming on, you shall cast away the
Num 16 30 but if the Lord do a new thing, and
28 26 you shall offer new fruits to the Lord
Deut 20 5 is there, that hath built a new house
22 8 when thou buildest a new house, thou
Josu 9 13 of wine when we filled them were new
Judg 5 8 the Lord chose new wars, and he
10 6 adding new sins to their old ones
15 13 they bound him with two new cords
16 11 if I shall be bound with new ropes
1 K 6 7 therefore take and make a new cart
2 K 6 3 laid the ark of God upon a new cart
3 Oza and Ahio . . . drove the new cart
21 16 girded with a new sword, attempted
3 K 11 29 clad with a new garment, found him
4 K 2 20 bring me a new vessel, and put salt
4 42 of barley, and new corn in his scrip
1 Pa 9 32 prepare always new [loaves] for every
13 7 the ark of God upon a new cart
2 Pa 20 5 of the Lord before the new court
1 Es 6 4 stones, and so rows of new timber
Jdth 16 2 tune unto him a new psalm, extol
10 she took a new robe to deceive him
15 let us sing a new hymn to our God
Job 32 19 is as new wine which wanteth vent, which bursteth the new vessels
Ps 32 3 sing to him a new canticle, sing well
39 4 he put a new canticle into my mouth
80 10 there shall be no new god in thee
95 1 ye to the Lord a new canticle. 97:1; 149:1
143 9 I will sing a new canticle: on the
12 whose sons are as new plants in their
Ecce 1 10 nothing under the sun is new, neither
10 man able to say: Behold, this is new
Cant 7 13 are all fruits: the new and the old
8 2 and new wine of my pomegranates. His
Wisd 11 19 beasts of a new kind, full of rage
16 2 of delicious food, of a new taste
3 for a short time, tasted a new meat
19 5 but they might find a new death. For
11 they saw a new generation of birds
Eccu 9 14 for the new will not be like to him
15 a new friend is as new wine: it shall
24 35 Tigris in the days of the new fruits
36 6 thy signs, and work new miracles
46 16 established a new government and
Isa 41 1 and the nations take new strength
15 made thee as a new thrashing wain
42 9 and new things do I declare: before
10 sing ye to the Lord a new song, his
43 19 I do new things, and now they shall
48 6 I have shown thee new things from
49 26 with their own blood, as with new wine
62 2 thou shalt be called by a new name
65 17 I create new heavens and a new earth
66 22 as the new heavens and the new earth
Jer 26 10 sat in the entry of the new gate
31 22 hath created a new thing upon the
31 I will make a new covenant with the
36 10 in the entry of the new gate of the
Lam 3 23 they are new every morning, great
Eze 3 15 to the heap of new corn, to them
11 19 will put a new spirit in their bowels
18 31 a new heart and a new spirit: and
36 26 I will give you a new heart and put a new spirit within you
Mich 6 15 and the new wine, but shalt not drink
1 Ma 4 47 built a new altar according to the
49 they made new holy vessels and brought
53 upon the new altar of holocausts
13 11 and with him a new army into Joppe
2 Ma 2 30 the master builder of a new house
9 6 others with many and new torments
Mat 9 17 neither do they put new wine into old
17 new wine they put into new bottles

13 52 out of his treasure new things and old
26 28 my blood of new testament. Mark 14:24
29 when I shall drink it with you new in
27 60 and laid it in his own new monument
Mark 1 27 what is this new doctrine? For with
2 22 putteth new wine into old. Luke 5:37
22 new wine must be put into new bottles. Luke 5:38
14 25 when I shall drink it new in the
16 17 they shall speak with new tongues
Luke 5 36 putteth a piece from a new garment
36 otherwise he both rendeth the new
36 piece taken from the new agreeth not
37 otherwise the new wine will break the
22 20 new testament in my blood. 1 C 11:25
John 13 34 a new commandment I give unto you
19 41 and in the garden a new sepulcher
Acts 17 18 a setter forth of new gods because
19 may we know what this new doctrine is
20 thou bringest in certain new things
21 in telling or in hearing some new thing
1 C 5 7 that you may be a new paste, as you
2 C 3 6 made us fit ministers of new testament
5 17 any be in Christ a new creature, the old
17 away, behold all things are made new
Gal 6 15 nor uncircumcision, but a new creature
Eph 2 15 himself into one new man, making peace
4 24 put on the new man, who according to God
Col 3 10 putting on the new, him who is renewed
Heb 8 8 unto the house of Juda, a new testament
13 now in saying a new, he hath made the
9 15 mediator of the new testament. 12:24
10 20 Christ; a new and living way which he
1 P 4 12 as if some new thing happened to you
2 P 3 13 we look for new heavens and a new earth
1 J 2 7 I write not a new commandment to you
8 a new commandment I write unto you
2 J 5 not as writing a new commandent to
Apoc 2 17 in the counter, a new name written
3 12 the new Jerusalem, which cometh down
12 and my new name. He that hath an ear
5 9 they sung a new canticle. 14:3
21 1 I saw a new heaven and a new earth
2 saw the holy city, the new Jerusalem
New Asor Josu 15 25 cities . . . New Asor and
new moon; *see* **moon**
new moons; *see* **moons**
newborn 1 P 2 2 as n. babes, desire the rational
newly Deut 32 17 knew not: that were n. come up
newness Rom 6 4 so we also may walk in n. of life
Rom 7 6 we should serve in newness of spirit
12 2 but be reformed in the n. of your mind
news 1 K 4 17 he that brought the news answered
1 K 4 19 hearing the news that the ark of God
2 K 4 10 should have been rewarded for his news
18 27 good man; and cometh with good news
3 K 1 42 a valiant man and bringest good news
2 28 the news came to Joab, because Joab
Tob 8 16 returning she brought the good news
11 9 as if he had brought the news, showed
2 Ma 9 3 news of what had happened to Nicanor
Nicanor 1 Ma 3 38 N. and Gorgias, mighty men of
1 Ma 7 26 the king sent Nicanor one of his
27 N. came to Jerusalem with a great army
31 N. knew that his counsel was discovered
33 Nicanor went up into mount Sion: and
39 then Nicanor went out from Jerusalem
43 and the army of Nicanor was defeated
44 when his army saw that N. was slain
9 1 heard that N. and his army were fallen
2 Ma 8 9 and he with all speed sent Nicanor
10 Nicanor purposed to raise for the king
12 when Judas found that N. was coming
14 would deliver them from the wicked N.
23 first band, he joined battle with N.
34 as for that most wicked man Nicanor
9 3 news of what had happened to Nicanor
12 2 N. the governor of Cyprus would not
14 12 N. the commander over the elephants
14 Gentiles . . . came to Nicanor by flocks
17 had joined battle with Nicanor, but
18 Nicanor hearing of the valor of Judas'
23 N. abode in Jerusalem and did no wrong
26 N. assented to the foreign interest
27 wrote Nicanor, signifying that he was
28 N. was in a consternation and took it
30 perceived that N. was more stern to
30 his men, and hid himself from Nicanor
37 Razias . . . was accused to Nicanor
39 N. being willing to declare the hatred
15 1 when N. understood that Judas was in
6 N. being puffed up with exceeding great
25 Nicanor . . . came forward with trumpets
28 that Nicanor was slain in his armor
32 and showing them the head of Nicanor
33 that the tongue of the wicked Nicanor
38 being done with relation to Nicanor
Acts 6 5 Philip and Prochorus and Nicanor and
Nicanor's 1 Ma 7 32 there fell of N. army almost
1 Ma 7 47 they cut off Nicanor's head and his
2 Ma 8 24 disabled the greater part of N. army
14 15 when the Jews heard of Nicanor's coming
15 30 commanded that N. head and his hand
35 he hung up N. head in the top of the
nice Deut 28 54 the man that is nice among you
2 Ma 2 32 avoid nice declarations of things
nicely 2 Ma 15 40 the speech be always n. framed
niceness Deut 28 56 down her foot for overmuch n.
Nicodemus John 3 1 there was a man . . . named N.
John 3 4 N. said to him: How can a man be born
9 N. answered and said to him: How can
7 50 N. said to them, he that came to him
19 39 N. also came, he who at the first came
Nicolaites Apoc 2 6 hatest the deeds of the N.
Apoc 2 15 them that hold the doctrine of the N.
Nicolas Acts 6 5 and Nicolas, a proselyte of Antioch
Nicopolis Titus 3 12 make haste to come unto me at N.
Niger Acts 13 1 Simon who was called N., and Lucius
niggard Eccu 14 3 for a covetous man and a niggard
niggardliness Eccu 31 29 testimony of his n. is
niggardly Eccu 31 29 him that is n. of his bread
nigh Gen 18 23 drawing nigh he said: Wilt thou
Gen 24 13 I stand nigh the spring of water
37 18 before he [Joseph] came nigh them
47 29 saw that the day of his death drew n.
Exod 3 5 come not nigh hither, put off the shoes
24 2 but they shall not come nigh: neither
32 19 when he came nigh to the camp, he saw
Num 18 3 they shall not come nigh the vessels
Deut 2 19 when thou comest nigh the frontiers
4 7 that hath gods so nigh them, as our
15 9 seventh year of remission draweth nigh
22 2 if thy brother be not nigh, or thou
30 14 the word is very nigh unto thee, in
31 14 behold the days of thy death are nigh
Josu 9 16 they heard that they dwelt nigh and
1 K 17 41 came on and drew nigh against David
48 coming and drew nigh to meet David
2 K 1 6 and horsemen drew nigh unto him [Saul]
3 K 2 1 days of David drew nigh that he should
8 59 be nigh unto the Lord our God day
21 2 it is nigh and adjoining to my house
Ps 31 6 they shall not come nigh unto him
33 19 the Lord is nigh unto them that are of
72 2 moved: my steps had well nigh slipped
87 4 and my life hath drawn nigh to hell

90 7 hand: but it shall not come nigh thee
106 18 drew nigh even to the gates of death
118 150 persecute me have drawn n. to iniquity
144 18 Lord is nigh unto all them that call
Prov 5 8 come not nigh the doors of her house
7 8 and goeth nigh the way of her house
12 13 ruin draweth nigh to the evil man
Ecce 4 17 house of God, and draw nigh to hear
12 1 and the years draw nigh of which thou
Eccu 14 25 shall set up his tent nigh unto her
35 21 till it come nigh he will not be
Joel 2 1 cometh, because it is nigh at hand
Mat 15 29 he came nigh the sea of Galilee. And
21 1 when they drew nigh to Jerusalem and
34 when the time of the fruits drew nigh
24 32 you know that summer is nigh. So you
33 know ye that it is nigh, even at the
Mark 5 21 he was nigh unto the sea. And there
13 29 know ye that it is very nigh, even at
Luke 7 12 when he came nigh to the gate of the
10 9 kingdom of God is come nigh unto you
15 25 when he came and drew nigh to the
18 35 when he drew nigh to Jericho, that a
19 11 because he was nigh to Jerusalem and
29 when he was come nigh to Bethphage
21 30 fruit, you know that summer is nigh
24 28 they drew nigh to the town whither
John 6 19 and drawing nigh to the ship, and they
23 nigh unto the place where they had
19 20 was crucified was nigh to the city
42 because the sepulcher was n. at hand
Acts 1 12 called Olivet, which is nigh Jerusalem
9 3 he drew nigh to Damascus; and suddenly
38 Lydda was nigh to Joppe, the disciples
10 9 drawing nigh to the city, Peter went
22 6 pass, as I was going, and drawing nigh
27 8 nigh to which was the city of Thalassa
Rom 10 8 the word is nigh thee, even in thy mouth
Eph 2 13 are made nigh by the blood of Christ
17 afar off, and peace to them that were n.
Phil 2 27 indeed he was sick, nigh unto death; but
4 5 known to all men. The Lord is nigh
Heb 7 19 hope, by which we draw nigh to God
James 4 8 draw n. to God, and he will draw n. to you

night Gen 1 5 and the darkness Night; and there
Gen 1 16 a lesser light to rule the night: and
19 5 men that came in to thee at night
34 I lay last night with my father, let us
29 23 at night he brought in Lia his daughter
40 5 both dreamed a dream the same night
41 11 in one n. both of us dreamed a dream
Exod 12 42 this is the observable n. of the Lord
14 20 a dark cloud, and enlightening the n.
18 13 stood by Moses from morning until n.
14 all the people wait from morning till n.
Deut 14 17 the night crow, the bittern and the
Judg 7 9 the same night the Lord said to him
20 23 and wept before the Lord until night
Ruth 3 14 at his feet till the night was going
1 K 14 34 every man his ox with him till the n.
3 K 3 20 rising in the dead time of the night
2 Pa 35 14 were busied in offering . . . until night
Tob 6 1 he lodged the first night by the river
20 second night thou shalt be admitted
21 third n. thou shalt obtain a blessing
22 when the third night is past, thou
8 4 when the third night is over, we will
Jdth 12 5 liberty to go out at night and before
Job 3 3 the night in which it was said: A man
17 12 they have turned night into day, and
20 8 he shall pass as a vision of the night
34 25 therefore he shall bring night on them
36 20 prolong not the night that people
Ps 6 7 every night I will wash my bed: I will
15 7 have corrected me even till night
18 3 night to night showeth knowledge
73 16 thine is the day, and thine is the n.
90 5 not be afraid of the terror of the n.
101 7 I am like a night raven in the house
103 20 hast appointed darkness, and it is n.
129 6 from the morning watch even until night
135 9 moon and the stars to rule the night
138 11 night shall be my light in my pleasures
12 and night shall be light as the day
Prov 7 9 in darkness and obscurity of the night
Wisd 7 30 after this cometh night, but no evil
17 2 bonds of darkness and a long night
5 the stars enlighten that horrible night
20 over them only was spread a heavy night
18 14 night was in the midst of her course
Eccu 36 28 lodgeth wheresoever the n. taketh him
40 5 sleep of the n. changeth his knowledge
Isa 16 3 thy shadow as the night in the midday
21 11 watchman, what of the night? Watchman
12 the morning cometh, also the night
24 20 be removed as the tent of one night
38 12 even to night thou wilt make an end. 13
60 11 they shall not be shut day nor night
Jer 31 35 of the stars, for the light of the n.
33 20 void, and my covenant with the night
Bar 2 25 the sun, and to the frost of the night
Dan 5 30 the same night Baltasar . . . was slain
7 7 I beheld in the vision of the night
13 beheld therefore in vision of the n.
Amos 5 8 and that changeth day into night
Jon 4 10 which in one night came up, and in one night perished
Mich 3 6 n. shall be to you instead of vision
Zach 14 7 shall be one day . . . not day nor night
1 Ma 9 58 he shall take them all in one night
Mat 14 25 in the fourth watch of the night, he
Mark 6 48 about the fourth watch of the night
Luke 2 8 keeping the night watches over their
21 37 at night, going out, he abode in the
John 9 4 night cometh, when no man can work
13 30 went out immediately. And it was night
Acts 12 6 same night Peter was sleeping between
16 33 taking them the same hour of the night
23 11 n. following the Lord standing by him
23 spearmen for third hour of the night
27 27 after the 14th night was come, as we
Rom 13 12 night is passed, and the day is at hand
1 C 11 23 the same night in which he was betrayed
2 C 11 25 a n. and a day I was in depth of the sea
1 Th 5 5 we are not of the night, nor of darkness
Apoc 8 12 of it, and the night in like manner
14 11 neither have they rest day nor night
21 25 for there shall be no night there. And
22 5 night shall be no more: and they shall

all (the) night Exod 14 20 not come at one another all the night
Exod 14 21 and burning wind blowing all the night
Lev 6 9 be burnt upon the altar, all night
Josu 10 9 Josue going up from Galgal all the n.
Judg 16 2 watching there all the night in silence
19 25 when they had abused her all the night
1 K 15 11 [Samuel] cried unto the Lord all night
31 12 valiant men arose and walked all the n.
2 K 2 32 were with him, marched all the night
4 7 way of the wilderness, walking all n.
Jdth 6 21 and they prayed all the night long
Ps 77 14 all the night with a light of fire
Isa 62 6 watchmen all the day and all the night
Osee 7 6 he slept all the night baking them
1 Ma 5 50 that city all the day and all the night
12 27 to be in arms all night long ready to

Luke 5 5 we have labored all the night, and
by night Gen 20 3 to Abimelech in a dream by n.
Exod 13 21 and by night in a pillar of fire
22 by day nor the pillar of fire by night
40 36 tabernacle by day, and a fire by night
Num 9 16 by night as it were the appearance of
14 14 in a pillar of fire by night. 2 Es 9:12
Deut 16 1 brought thee out of Egypt by night
23 10 that is defiled in a dream by night
Josu 2 2 there are men come in hither by night
Judg 6 27 not do it by day, but did all by night
9 34 arose with all his army by night and
1 K 14 36 let us fall upon Philistines by night
25 16 a wall unto us both by night and day
26 7 David . . . came to the people by night
28 8 and they came to the woman by night
2 K 21 10 tear them . . . nor the beasts by night
3 K 3 5 appeared to Solomon in a dream by night
4 K 6 14 they came by night and beset the city
2 Pa 7 12 the Lord appeared to him by night
2 Es 2 13 I went out by night by the gate of the
Tob 12 12 when thou didst . . . bury them by night
Job 4 13 in the horror of a vision by night
33 15 by a dream in a vision by night when
Ps 16 3 proved my heart and visited it by night
21 3 by night, and it shall not be reputed
120 6 burn thee by day: nor the moon by night
Cant 3 1 in my bed by night I sought him whom
Wisd 10 17 and for the light of stars by night
Isa 29 7 be as the dream of a vision by night
Jer 29 19 rising by night, and sending: and you
36 30 heat by day, and to the frost by night
Dan 7 2 I saw in my vision by night, and behold
14 14 but the priests went in by night
Abdi 5 gone in to thee, if robbers by night
Zach 1 8 saw by night, and behold a man riding
1 Ma 4 1 they removed out of the camp by night
5 Gorgias came by night into the camp of
5 29 they removed from thence by night
2 Ma 12 9 he came upon the Jamnites also by night
13 15 he set upon the king's quarter by night
Mat 2 14 took the child and his mother by night
28 13 say you, His disciples came by night
John 3 2 this man came to Jesus by night and
7 50 he that came to him by night, who was
19 39 at the first came to Jesus by night
Acts 5 19 angel of the Lord by night opening
17 10 sent away Paul and Silas by night unto
23 31 Paul, brought him by night to Antipatris
day and night (night and day) Gen 1 14 to divide the day and the night
Gen 1 18 to rule the day and the night and to
8 22 night and day, shall not cease. And
31 40 day and night was I parched with heat
Exod 10 13 a burning wind all that day and night
Lev 8 35 day and night shall you remain in the
Num 9 21 if it departed after a day and a night
11 32 rising up all that day and night and
Deut 28 66 thou shalt fear night and day, neither
Josu 1 8 shalt meditate on it day and night that
1 K 19 24 lay down naked all that day and night
25 16 a wall unto us both by night and day
3 K 8 29 be open upon this house night and day
59 nigh unto Lord our God day and night
1 Pa 9 33 might serve continually day and night
2 Pa 6 20 eyes upon this house day and night
2 Es 1 6 I pray before thee now, night and day
4 9 watchmen upon the wall day and night
Jdth 7 5 they guarded them all day and night
Ps 1 2 on his law he shall meditate d. . . .
31 4 day and night thy hand was heavy upon
41 4 my tears have been my bread d. . . .
54 11 day and night shall iniquity surround
Ecce 8 16 that day and night take no sleep with
Eccu 38 28 that laboreth night and day, he who
Isa 27 3 I keep it night and day. There is no
34 10 night and day it shall not be quenched
Jer 9 1 I will weep day and night for the slain
14 17 shed down tears night and day and let
16 13 shall serve strange gods day and night
33 20 that there should not be day and night
25 set my covenant between day and night
Lam 2 18 tears run down like a torrent d. . . .
2 Ma 13 10 to call upon the Lord day and night
Mark 4 27 should sleep and rise night and day
5 5 day and night in the monuments, crying
Luke 2 37 [Anna] serving night and day. Now she
18 7 his elect who cry to him day and night
Acts 9 24 they watched the gates day and night
20 31 to admonish every one of you n. . . .
26 7 our twelve tribes, serving n. . . . , hope
1 Th 2 9 working n. . . . lest we should. 2 Th 3:8
3 10 n. . . . more abundantly praying that
1 Tim 5 5 continue in . . . prayers night and day
2 Tim 1 3 remembrance of thee in my prayers n. . . .
Apoc 4 8 they rested not day and night, saying
7 15 they serve him d. . . . in his temple: and
12 10 who accused them . . . day and night. And
20 10 false prophet shall be tormented d. . . .
in the night Gen 14 15 rushed upon them i. . . .
Gen 20 8 Abimelech forthwith rising up in the n.
22 3 so Abraham rising up in the night
31 55 Laban arose in the night and kissed
46 2 he heard him by a vision in the night
Exod 12 30 Pharao arose in the night, and all
31 calling Moses and Aaron in the night
Num 11 9 when the dew fell in the night upon
22 20 came to Balaam in the night and said
Deut 1 33 in the night showing you the way by
Josu 8 3 30,000 chosen valiant men in the night
Judg 9 32 arise therefore in the night with the
20 5 in the night beset the house wherein
1 K 29 11 David and his men arose in the night
3 K 3 19 this woman's child died in the night
4 K 7 12 arose i. . . . and said to his servants
8 21 he arose in the night and defeated
25 4 all the men of war fled in the night
2 Pa 21 9 Joram . . . rose in the n. and defeated
2 Es 2 12 and I arose in the night, I and some
15 I went up in the night by the torrent
4 22 let us take our turns in the night
6 10 in the n. they will come to slay thee
Job 5 14 grope at noonday as in the night
24 14 but in the night he will be as a thief
27 20 tempest shall oppress him in the night
30 17 in the night my bone is pierced with
35 10 who hath given songs in the night
Ps 41 9 and a canticle to him in the night
76 3 my hands lifted up to him in the night
7 I meditated in the night with my own
87 2 I have cried in the day and in the night
89 4 as a watch in the night, things that
91 3 morning, and thy truth in the night
104 39 fire to give them light in the night
118 55 in the night I have remembered thy name
Prov 27 14 with a loud voice, rising in the night
31 15 she hath risen in the night and given
18 her lamp shall not be put out in night
Ecce 2 23 even in the night he doth not rest
Cant 3 8 his thigh, because of fears in the night
Isa 4 5 brightness of a flaming fire in the n.
15 1 in the night Ar of Moab is laid waste
1 wall of Moab is destroyed in the night
26 9 my soul hath desired thee in the night
28 19 pass through, in the day and in the n.
30 29 in the n. of the sanctified solemnity

Jer 6 5 let us go up in the night and destroy
39 4 and they went forth in the night
49 9 if thieves in the night, they would
52 7 went out of the city in the night
Lam 1 2 weeping she hath wept in the night
2 19 arise, give praise in the night
Dan 2 19 to Daniel by a vision in the night
Osee 4 5 in the n. I have made thy mother to be
1 Ma 12 26 they designed to come upon them i. . . .
2 Ma 12 6 and set the haven on fire in the night
John 11 10 if he walk in the night, he stumbleth
Acts 9 25 disciples taking him i. . . . , conveyed
16 9 vision was showed to Paul in the night
18 9 the Lord said to Paul in the night, by
1 Th 5 2 shall so come, as a thief in the night
7 they that sleep, sleep in the night, and
7 that are drunk, are drunk in the night
that night Gen 19 33 made their father drink wine that night. 35
Gen 26 24 Lord appeared to him that same night
30 16 he [Jacob] slept with her that night
32 13 when he had slept there that night
21 himself lodged that night in the camp
Exod 12 8 they shall eat the flesh that night
12 through the land of Egypt that night
Num 14 1 whole multitude crying wept that night
Deut 24 12 pledge shall not lodge with thee that n.
Josu 8 9 Josue stayed that night in the midst of
13 Josue went that night and stood in the
Judg 6 25 that night the Lord said to him: Take
40 God did that night as he had requested
1 K 19 10 and David fled and escaped that night
28 25 they rose up and walked all that night
2 K 2 29 Abner and his men walked all that night
7 4 that night, that the word of the Lord
4 K 19 35 came to pass that night, that an angel
1 Pa 17 3 that night the word of God came to
2 Pa 1 7 that n. God appeared to him [Solomon]
Tob 6 19 on that night lay the liver of the fish
Esth 6 1 that n. the king passed without sleep
Job 3 6 whirlwind seize upon that night, let
7 let that night be solitary, and not
Wisd 17 13 that night, in which nothing could be
18 6 that n. was known before by our fathers
1 Ma 13 22 all his horsemen to come that night
Luke 17 34 in that night there shall be two men
John 21 3 and that night they caught nothing
this night Exod 12 42 this night all the children of Israel must observe
Num 22 8 tarry here this night and I will answer
19 I pray you to stay here this night
Josu 4 3 you shall pitch your tents this night
Ruth 1 12 although I might conceive this night
3 2 this night he winnoweth barley in the
13 rest thou this night; and when morning
1 K 15 16 what the Lord hath said to me this n.
19 11 unless thou save thyself this night
2 K 17 1 and pursue after David this night
16 tarry not this night in the plains
19 7 tarry with thee so much as one this n.
Jdth 8 32 you shall stand at the gate this night
13 18 of his people by my hand this night
27 the unbelievers this night by my hand
Mat 26 31 shall be scandalized in me this night
34 in this night before the cock crow
Mark 14 27 be scandalized in my regard this night
30 even in this night, before the cock
Luke 12 20 this night do they require thy soul
Acts 27 23 whom I serve, stood by me this night
nights Gen 7 4 earth 40 days and 40 nights. 12
Exod 24 18 he was there 40 days and 40 nights
34 28 with the Lord 40 days and 40 nights
Deut 9 9 continued in the mount 40 days and n.
11 forty days were passed, and as many n.
18 forty days and nights neither eating
25 before the Lord forty days and nights
10 10 mount as before, 40 days and nights
1 K 30 12 nor drunk water 3 days and 3 nights
3 K 19 8 of that food forty days and forty nights
Tob 3 10 and three nights did neither eat nor
8 4 these three nights we are joined to God
Jdth 12 7 she went out in the nights into the
Esth 4 16 nor drink for three days and three n.
Job 2 13 on the ground 7 days and 7 nights
7 3 numbered to myself wearisome nights
Ps 133 2 in the nights lift up your hands
Cant 5 2 my locks [full] of drops of the nights
Isa 21 8 upon my ward, standing whole nights
Dan 3 71 ye nights and days, bless the Lord
Jon 2 1 of the fish three days and three nights
2 Ma 8 7 nights he went upon these expeditions
Mat 4 2 had fasted 40 days and 40 nights
12 40 the whale's belly 3 days and 3 nights
40 heart of the earth 3 days and 3 nights
Mark 1 13 desert forty days and forty nights
Nile Isa 23 3 seed of the Nile in many waters
Ninive Gen 10 11 came forth Assur, and built N.
Gen 10 12 Resen also between Ninive and Chale
4 K 19 36 and he returned and abode in Ninive
Tob 1 11 tribe was come to the city of Ninive
7 4 tribe of Nephtali, of the captivity of N.
11 1 Charan, which is in the midway to N.
14 2 he was buried honorably in Ninive
6 the destruction of Ninive is at hand
14 Tobias departed out of Ninive with his
Isa 37 37 and returned and dwelt in Ninive
Jon 1 2 and go to N. the great city. 3:2
3 3 and Jonas arose and went to Ninive
3 Ninive was a great city of three days'
4 and Ninive shall be destroyed. And the
5 the men of Ninive believed in God
6 the word came to the king of Ninive
7 caused it to be . . . published in N.
4 11 shall not I spare Ninive, that great
Nah 1 1 the burden of Ninive. The book of
2 8 as for Ninive, her waters are like
3 7 shall say: Ninive is laid waste: who
Mat 12 41 men of Ninive shall rise. Luke 11:32
Ninivites Luke 11 30 as Jonas was a sign to the N.
Nisan 2 Es 2 1 came to pass in the month of Nisan
Esth 3 7 the first month, which is called Nisan
12 were called in the first month Nisan
11 2 in the first day of the month Nisan
niter Prov 25 20 as vinegar upon niter, so is he
Jer 2 22 though thou wash thyself with niter
Noa Num 26 33 Maala and Noa and Hegla. 27:1; Josu 17:3
Num 36 11 Melcha and Noa were married to the
Josu 19 13 goeth out to Remmon, Amthar and Noa
Noadaia 1 Es 8 33 Noadaia the son of Benoi
Noadias 2 Es 6 14 N. the prophet and the rest of
Nob 2 Es 11 32 at Anathoth, Nob, Anania, Asor
Nobe Num 32 42 Nobe also went and took Canath
Num 32 42 he called it by his own name, Nobe
Judg 8 11 on the east of Nobe and Jegbaa, and
1 K 21 1 David came to Nobe to Achimelech the
22 9 I saw the son of Isai in Nobe with
11 priests that were in Nobe, and they
19 Nobe the city of the priests he smote
Isa 10 32 it is yet day enough, to remain in Nobe
nobility Wisd 8 3 she glorifieth her nobility
noble Gen 12 6 Sichem, as far as the noble vale
Num 1 16 these are the most noble princes of
25 15 most noble prince among the Madianites
Prov 4 9 and protect thee with a noble crown
Ecce 10 17 blessed is the land whose king is n.

Jer 22 18 my Lord, or, Alas, the noble one. He
Lam 4 2 the noble sons of Sion, and they that
Eze 25 9 the noble cities of the land of
1 Ma 8 2 of their battles and their noble acts
9 22 and of the noble acts that he did
2 Ma 14 42 abuses unbecoming his noble birth
Mark 15 43 Joseph of Arimathea, a noble counsellor
Acts 17 4 of noble women not a few. But the Jews
11 these were more noble than those in
1 C 1 26 flesh, not many mighty, not many noble
nobleman 1 Ma 3 32 Lysias, a n. of the blood royal
Luke 19 12 nobleman went into a far country to
nobles 2 K 19 6 that thou carest not for thy n.
3 K 21 11 men of his city, the ancients and n.
4 K 24 12 servants and his n. and his eunuchs
2 Es 2 16 or to the nobles or to the magistrates
4 19 I said to the nobles and to the
5 7 I rebuked the nobles and magistrates
Jdth 3 9 princes and n. as well as the people
Esth 1 3 Persians and the nobles of the Medes
8 set over every table one of his nobles
6 9 first of the king's princes and nobles
Job 12 19 without glory, and overthroweth nobles
Ps 149 8 their nobles with manacles of iron
Isa 5 13 their nobles have perished with famine
23 8 her traders the nobles of the earth
34 12 the nobles thereof shall not be there
Jer 39 6 king of Babylon slew all the n. of Juda
13 and all the n. of the king of Babylon
41 1 nobles of the king and ten men with
Bar 1 4 and in the hearing of the nobles
Eze 23 23 the nobles and the kings and princes
Dan 3 2 king sent to call together the nobles
3 n., the magistrates, and the judges. 94
91 said to his nobles: Did we not cast
4 33 my nobles and my magistrates sought
5 1 feast for a thousand of his nobles
2 king and his nobles, his wives and. 3
9 and his nobles also were troubled
23 thou and thy nobles and thy wives
6 17 ring, and with the ring of his nobles
Nah 3 10 they cast lots upon her nobles, and all
1 Ma 1 7 he called his servants the nobles
2 Ma 4 21 to treat with the n. of king Philometor
31 leaving Andronicus, one of his nobles
noblest 2 K 23 19 n. of three and was their chief
Wisd 18 12 the n. offspring of them was destroyed
nobly 2 Ma 14 42 choosing to die n. rather than
nobody Gen 40 8 there is n. to interpret it to
Dan 13 16 there was n. there but the two old men
20 nobody seeth us, and we are in love
Mat 9 16 nobody putteth a piece of raw cloth
Mark 8 26 thou enter into the town, tell nobody
Nodab 1 Pa 5 19 Naphis and Nodab gave them help
Noe Gen 5 29 and he [Lamech] called his name Noe
Gen 5 30 Lamech lived after he begot Noe
31 Noe . . . begot Sem, Cham, and Japheth
6 8 but Noe found grace before the Lord
9 these are the generations of Noe: Noe
9 Noe was a just and perfect man in his
13 he said to Noe: The end of all flesh
22 Noe did all things which God commanded
7 5 Noe did all things which the Lord
7 Noe went in and his sons, his wife and
9 went in to Noe into the ark. 15
9 as the Lord had commanded Noe. And
11 in the 600th year of the life of Noe
13 in the selfsame day Noe and Sem and
23 Noe only remained, and they that were
8 1 and God remembered Noe and all the
6 Noe, opening the window of the ark
11 Noe understood that the waters were
13 Noe opening the covering of the ark
15 God spoke to Noe, saying: Go out of
18 Noe went out, he and his sons: his wife
20 Noe built an altar unto the Lord: and
9 1 God blessed Noe and his sons. And he
8 said God to Noe and to his sons with
17 God said to Noe: This shall be the sign
18 sons of Noe who came out of the ark
19 these three are the sons of Noe: and
20 Noe, a husbandman, began to till the
24 Noe awaking from the wine, when he had
28 Noe lived after the flood 350 years
10 1 the generations of the sons of Noe
32 these are the families of Noe according
1 Pa 1 4 Lamech, Noe, Sem, Cham, and Japheth
Eccu 44 17 Noe was found perfect, just, and in
Isa 54 9 this thing is to me as in days of Noe
9 no more bring in the waters of Noe
Eze 14 14 these three men, Noe, Daniel, and Job
20 Noe and Daniel and Job be in the midst
Mat 24 37 as in the days of Noe, so shall also
38 day in which Noe entered. Luke 17:27
Luke 3 36 Sem, who was of Noe, who was of
17 26 as it came to pass in the days of Noe
Heb 11 7 by faith Noe, having received an answer
1 P 3 20 patience of God in the days of Noe
2 P 2 5 but preserved Noe, the eighth person
Noema Gen 4 22 sister of Tubalcain was Noema
Noeman Num 26 40 sons of Bela: Hered and Noeman
Num 26 40 of N., the family of the Noemanites
Noemanites Num 26 40 of Noeman, the family of the N.
Noemi Ruth 1 2 named Elimelech, and his wife N.
Ruth 1 3 Elimelech the husband of Noemi died
15 Noemi said to her: Behold thy kinswoman
18 Noemi, seeing that Ruth was steadfastly
19 the women said: This is that Noemi
20 call me not Noemi, that is, beautiful
21 why then do you call me Noemi, whom
22 Noemi came with Ruth the Moabitess
2 6 this is the Moabitess who came with N.
20 Noemi answered her: Blessed be he
3 1 Noemi said to her: My daughter, I will
18 Noemi said: Wait my daughter, till we
4 3 Noemi, who is returned from the country
9 I have bought . . . of the hand of Noemi
14 the women said to Noemi: Blessed be
16 Noemi taking the child laid it in her
17 there is a son born to Noemi: called
Noga 1 Pa 14 6 born to him [David] . . . Noga and
Noge 1 Pa 3 7 Noge and Nepheg and Japhia and
Nohaa 1 Pa 8 2 Benjamin begot . . . Nohaa the fourth
Nohesta 4 K 24 8 the name of his mother was N.
Nohestan 4 K 18 4 he called its name Nohestan
noise Exod 11 7 shall not a dog make the least n.
Exod 19 16 and the noise of the trumpet sounded
32 17 Josue hearing the noise of the people
17 noise of battle is heard in the camp
Num 10 6 like noise of the trumpet, they who lie
1 K 4 6 Philistines heard the n. of the shout
6 what is this noise of a great shout
14 Heli heard the noise of the cry and he
14 what meaneth the noise of this uproar
3 K 1 40 earth rang with the noise of their cry
41 what meaneth this noise of the city
45 this is the noise that you have heard
4 K 7 6 in camp of Syria the noise of chariots
11 13 heard the n. of the people. 2 Pa 23:12
1 Pa 15 16 that the joyful noise might resound
1 Es 3 13 the noise of the weeping of the people
Jdth 14 7 they went out with a great noise and
9 made a noise before the door of the
9 not by their calling him, but by their n.
Job 37 4 after it a noise shall roar, he shall
39 24 when the noise of the trumpet soundeth

Ps 9 7 their memory hath perished with a noise
32 3 sing well unto him with a loud noise
41 5 and praise: the noise of one feasting
8 deep, at the noise of thy flood-gates
64 8 depth of the sea, the n. of its waves
76 18 great was the noise of the waters: the
82 3 thy enemies have made a noise: and
92 4 the noise of many waters. Isa 17:12; Eze 43:2
94 2 a joyful noise to him with psalms
97 6 make a joyful noise before the Lord
Wisd 17 18 mighty noise of stones tumbling down
Eccu 38 30 noise of the hammer is always in his
40 13 with a noise like a great thunder
15 a noise as unclean roots upon top of
43 18 the noise of his thunder shall strike
45 11 might be a sound, and a noise made
46 20 with a great noise made his voice
50 18 and made a great noise to be heard
Isa 3 16 and made a noise as they walked with
5 30 they shall make a noise against them
10 14 the mouth, or made the least noise
13 4 noise of a multitude in the mountains . . . noise of the sound of kings
17 13 n. like the n. of waters overflowing
24 8 noise of them that rejoice is ended
14 they shall make a joyful noise from
18 that shall flee from noise of the fear
27 13 n. shall be made with a great trumpet
29 6 and with a great noise of whirlwind
54 1 forth praise, and make a joyful noise
Jer 2 15 roared upon him and have made a noise
10 22 the sound of a noise cometh, a great
11 16 at the noise of a word, a great fire
25 31 the noise is come even to the ends of
47 3 at the noise of the marching of arms
49 2 I will cause the noise of the war to
21 earth is moved at the n. of their fall
50 22 a noise of war in the land, and a
46 at the noise of the taking of Babylon
51 54 the noise of a cry from Babylon and
55 waters: their voice hath made a noise
Lam 2 7 made a noise in the house of the Lord
Eze 1 24 I heard the noise of their wings, like the noise of many waters
24 like the noise of an army, and when
3 13 noise of the wings of the living
13 and the noise of the wheels following
13 and the noise of a great commotion
7 11 people, nor of the noise of them: and
26 10 shall shake at noise of the horsemen
37 7 as I prophesied there was a noise
Joel 2 5 shall leap like the noise of chariots
5 like the noise of a flame of fire
Amos 2 2 Moab shall die with a noise, with the
Nah 3 2 n. of the whip and the n. of the rattling of the wheels
Soph 1 10 the noise of a cry from the fish gate
1 Ma 6 41 were moved at noise of their multitude
9 13 earth shook at the noise of the armies
41 noise of the musical instruments into
2 Ma 15 29 making a shout and a great noise
Apoc 9 9 the noise of their wings was as the noise of chariots
14 2 as the noise of many waters and as
noised Josu 6 27 his name was n. throughout all
Judg 16 2 and it was noised about among them
2 Pa 31 5 which when it was noised abroad in the
Luke 1 65 all these things were noised abroad
Acts 2 6 and when this was noised abroad, the
noises Wisd 17 4 n. coming down troubled them
noisome 2 Ma 9 9 his smell was n. to the army
noisy Job 38 25 who gave . . . a way for n. thunder
none Gen 31 50 none is witness of our speech but
Exod 8 10 there is none like to the Lord our God
9 14 there is none like me in all the earth
12 22 let none of you go out of the door
15 26 none of the evils that I laid upon
16 27 going forth to gather, found none
29 let none go forth out of his place
30 32 none other of the same composition
Lev 10 18 none of the blood . . . been carried within
26 6 shall be none to make you afraid
37 none of you shall dare to resist
Num 24 9 lioness whom none shall dare to rouse
26 65 none remained of them but Caleb the
35 30 none shall be condemned upon the
Deut 11 25 none shall stand against you: the
20 16 thou shalt suffer none at all to live
23 24 but must carry none out with thee
28 26 and be there none to drive them away
31 and may there be none to help thee
32 5 are none of his children in their filth
39 there is none that can deliver out of
Josu 10 8 none of them shall be able to stand
33 his people, so as to leave none alive
21 42 none of their enemies durst stand
Judg 3 29 valiant men: none of them could escape
4 20 here? thou shalt say: There is none
19 18 none will receive us under his roof
21 1 none of us shall give of his daughters
1 K 2 2 there is none holy as the Lord is: for
2 there is none strong like our God
10 24 is none like him among all the people
14 24 so none of the people tasted any food
39 in this none of the people gainsaid
21 9 David said: There is none like that
2 K 7 22 because there is none like to thee
14 6 there was none to part them; and the
22 42 cry, and there shall be none to save
3 K 12 20 none that followed the house of David
4 K 5 16 I [Eliseus] will receive none. And
10 19 let none be wanting, for I have a great
18 5 was none like him among all the kings
24 14 none were left, but the poor sort of
1 Pa 17 20 O Lord, there is none like thee: and
2 Pa 1 12 so that none of the kings before thee
8 9 but of . . . Israel he set none to serve
23 19 none who was unclean . . . should enter
1 Es 8 15 sons of Levi, and found none there
2 Es 13 19 that none should bring in burthens on
Tob 13 2 there is none that can escape thy hand
Jdth 16 30 there was none that troubled Israel
Job 1 8 is none like him in the earth. 2:3
5 4 there shall be none to deliver them
6 25 is none of you that can reprove me
9 33 none that may be able to reprove both
11 19 there shall be none to make thee afraid
12 14 there is none that can open. If he
15 15 among his saints none is unchangeable
19 7 cry aloud, and there is none to judge
30 13 prevailed, and there was none to help
32 12 none of you that can convince Job
36 22 none is like him among the lawgivers
Ps 13 1 none that doth good. 3; 52:2, 4
17 42 cried, but there was none to save them
21 12 very near: for there is none to help me
24 3 none of them that wait on thee shall be
33 23 none of them that trust in him shall
49 22 and there be none to deliver you
68 21 together with me, but there was none
21 would comfort me, and I found none
26 be none to dwell in their tabernacles
70 11 for there is none to deliver him
78 3 and there was none to bury them
85 8 none among the gods like unto thee
8 there is none according to thy works

106 12 and there was none to help them
108 12 be none to help him: nor none to pity
Prov 1 24 hand, and there was none that regarded
2 19 none that go in unto her shall return
30 31 and a king, whom none can resist
Ecce 4 10 falleth, he hath none to lift him up
Cant 4 2 there is none barren among them. 6:5
Wisd 2 9 let none of us go without his part in
7 5 none of the kings had any other
28 God loveth none but him that dwelleth
11 25 hatest none of the things which thou
17 19 none were hindered in their labors
Eccu 10 27 none greater than he that feareth God
14 6 none worse than he that envieth himself
25 13 none above him that feareth the Lord
45 15 there were none so beautiful even from
51 10 succor of men, and there was none that
Isa 1 31 and there shall be none to quench it
5 27 there is none that shall faint nor
29 and there shall be none to deliver it
10 14 there was none that moved the wing
13 14 there shall be none to gather them
14 8 hath none come up to cut us down. Hell
31 is none that shall escape his troop
17 2 shall be none to make them afraid
22 22 he shall open, and none shall shut
34 10 none shall pass through it forever
41 17 seek for waters, and there are none
26 there is none that showeth nor that
42 22 and there is none to deliver them
22 there is none that saith: Restore
43 10 and after me there shall be none
13 there is none that can deliver out of
44 24 the earth, and there is none with me
45 5 the Lord, and there is none else. 6
6 there is none besides me. I am the Lord
21 a savior, there is none besides me
47 8 and there is none else besides me
10 said: There is none that seeth me
15 there is none that can save thee
50 2 and there was none that would hear
51 18 there is none that can uphold her
18 there is none that taketh her by the
57 1 there is none that understandeth; for
59 4 is none that calleth upon justice
11 looked for judgment, and there is none
16 there is none to oppose himself: and
60 15 was none that passed through thee
63 5 about, and there was none to help
5 sought, and there was none to give aid
64 7 is none that calleth upon thy name
66 4 and there was none that would answer
Jer 2 15 and there is none to dwell in them
24 none shall turn her away: all that
4 4 there be none that can quench it
7 33 shall be none to drive them away. And
8 6 there is none that doth penance for
9 12 wilderness, which none passeth through
22 and there is none to gather it. Thus
10 6 there is none like to thee. 7
20 none to stretch forth my tent any more
12 11 none that considereth in the heart
13 19 and there is none to open them: all
14 16 there shall be none to bury them: they
21 12 and there be none to quench it because
23 4 none shall be wanting of their number
30 10 there shall be none whom he may fear
13 there is none to judge thy judgment
17 that hath none to seek after her
35 14 they have drunk none to this day
36 30 none to sit upon the throne of David
42 17 none of them shall remain nor escape
44 14 there shall be none that shall escape
14 there shall none return but they that
46 27 there shall be none to terrify him
50 3 there shall be none to dwell therein
20 sought for, and there shall be none
20 sin of Juda, and there shall none be
29 round about, and let none escape
32 there shall be none to lift him up
51 43 a land wherein none can dwell nor son
Lam 1 2 there is none to comfort her. 17
4 none that come to the solemn feast
21 and there is none to comfort me: all
2 22 there was none in the day of the wrath
4 4 there was none to break it unto them
5 8 there was none to redeem us out of
Bar 3 31 none that is able to know her ways
Eze 7 14 there is none to go to the battle
25 for peace, and there shall be none
14 15 so that there is none that can pass
22 30 for a man . . . and I found none. And I
31 14 none of the trees by the waters shall
33 16 none of his sins, which he hath
28 because there is none to pass by them
34 6 and there was none that sought them
6 there was none, I say, that sought
Dan 2 27 none of the wise men . . . can declare
4 32 is none that can resist his hand
8 7 none could deliver the ram out of
27 was none that could interpret it
10 21 none is my helper in all these things
11 16 be none to stand against his face
45 top thereof, and none shall help him
12 10 none of the wicked shall understand
13 43 whereas I have done none of these
Osee 2 3 a land that none can pass through
5 14 there is none that can rescue. I will
7 7 none amongst them that calleth unto
Joel 2 27 your God, and there is none besides
Amos 5 2 there is none to raise her up. For
6 there shall be none to quench Bethel
Mich 2 5 shalt have none that shall cast a
4 4 shall be none to make them afraid
5 8 and take, there is none to deliver
7 2 there is none upright among men: they
Nah 2 8 there is none that will return back
11 was none to make them afraid. 1 Ma 14:12
3 18 there is none to gather them together
Soph 2 15 I am, and there is none beside me
3 6 so that there is none that passeth by
13 shall be none to make them afraid
Agge 2 18 none among you that returned to me
Zach 1 21 and none of them lifted up his head
8 17 let none of you imagine evil in your
1 Ma 2 61 none that trust in him fail in strength
3 45 none of her children that went in
7 17 and there was none to bury them. Then
8 14 none of all these wore a crown or was
11 70 none was left of them but Mathathias
12 9 we needed none of these things, having
14 7 there was none that resisted him. And
13 none left in the land to fight against
15 14 suffered none to come in or to go out
2 Ma 11 31 that none of them . . . be molested
Mat 8 28 so that none could pass by that way
12 43 places seeking rest, and findeth none
23 9 call none your father upon earth; for
Mark 10 18 none is good but one, that is God
14 55 put him to death, and found none. For
Luke 1 61 there is none of thy kindred that is
3 11 let him give to him that hath none
4 26 to none of them was Elias sent, but
27 none of them was cleansed but Naaman
13 6 seeking fruit on it, and found none
7 on this fig tree, and I find none

14 24 none of those men that were invited
18 19 me good? None is good but God alone
34 they understood none of these things
John 7 19 yet none of you keepeth the law
16 5 none of you asketh me: Whither goest
17 12 none of them is lost but the son of
21 12 none of them who were at meat durst
Acts 1 20 and let there be none to dwell therein
3 6 silver and gold I have none; but what
8 24 that none of these things which you
11 19 speaking the word to n., but to Jews
18 17 Gallio cared for none of those things
20 24 I fear none of these things, neither do
25 11 if there be none of these things whereof
26 26 for I am persuaded that none of these
Rom 3 11 there is none that understandeth, there
11 there is none that seeketh after God
12 there is none that doth good, there is
8 9 not the Spirit of Christ, he is none of
14 7 for none of us liveth to himself; and
1 C 1 14 I baptized none of you but Crispus and
2 8 which n. of princes of this world knew
7 29 who have wives, be as if they had none
9 15 but I have used none of these things
14 10 this world; and none is without voice
Gal 1 19 but other of the apostles I saw none
1 Th 5 15 see that none render evil for evil to
Heb 3 13 that none of you be hardened through
1 P 4 15 let none of you suffer as a murderer
Apoc 2 10 fear none of those things which thou
noon Gen 43 16 they shall eat with me at noon
Gen 43 25 presents against Joseph came at noon
2 K 4 5 he was sleeping upon his bed at noon
11 2 David arose from his bed after noon
3 K 18 26 name of Baal from morning even till **n.**
27 when it was now noon, Elias jested
20 16 they went out at noon. But Benadad
4 K 4 20 she set him on her knees until noon
Job 24 11 they have taken their rest at noon
Ps 54 18 and at noon I will speak and declare
Eccu 34 19 and a cover from the sun at noon
43 3 at noon he burneth the earth, and who
Isa 18 4 as the noon light is clear, and as a
Dan 13 7 when the people departed away at noon
noonday Job 5 14 grope at n. as in the night
Job 11 17 brightness like that of the noonday
Ps 36 6 light, and thy judgment as the noonday
90 6 not be afraid . . . of the noonday devil
Isa 58 10 thy darkness shall be as the noonday
59 10 we have stumbled at noonday as in
Jer 15 8 upon them . . . a spoiler at noonday
Soph 2 4 they shall cast out Azotus at noonday
noontide Jer 20 16 morning, and howling at n.
Nophe Num 21 30 they came weary to Nophe and
Nopheth Josu 17 11 third part of the city of N.
Noran 1 Pa 7 28 their possessions . . . eastward N.
north Gen 13 14 look . . . to the north and to the
Gen 28 14 shalt spread abroad . . . to the north
Exod 26 20 looketh to the north. Lev 1:11; Josu 16:6; Eze 9:2; 40:44
36 25 looketh toward the n. Eze 40:40, 44, 46
Num 8 2 the lamps look over against the north
Deut 2 3 long enough: go toward the north
3 27 cast thy eyes round about . . . to the n.
Josu 11 2 he sent . . . to the kings of the north
15 5 towards the north, from the bay of the
6 passeth by the north into Betharaba
10 by side of mount Jarim to the north
17 10 on the north that of Manasses and the
10 in the tribe of Aser on the north, and
18 5 and the house of Joseph on the north
16 and is over against the north quarter
17 passing thence to the north, and going
19 towards the north of the most salt sea
19 14 turneth about to the north of Hanathon
27 towards the north to Bethemec and
Judg 12 1 passing towards the north, they said
21 19 on the north of the city of Bethel, and
1 K 14 5 one rock stood out towards the north
3 K 7 25 looked towards n. 2 Pa 4:4; Eze 8:3; 46:19
4 K 16 14 at side of the altar toward the north
1 Pa 26 14 learned man the north gate fell by lot
17 and towards the north four a day: and
Jdth 16 5 out of the mountains from the north
Job 26 7 he stretched out the north over the
37 22 cold cometh out of the north, and to
Ps 47 3 Sion founded, on the sides of the north
88 13 the north and the sea thou hast created
106 3 the sun, from the north and from the sea
Prov 25 23 the north wind driveth away rain, as
Ecce 1 6 south, and turneth again to the north
11 3 tree fall to the south or to the north
Cant 4 16 arise, O north wind, and come, O south
Isa 14 13 I will sit . . . in the sides of the n.
31 for a smoke shall come from the north
41 25 I have raised up one from the north and
43 6 I will say to the north: Give up: and
49 12 behold these from the north and from
Jer 1 13 face thereof from the face of the north
14 from the n. shall an evil break forth
15 families of the kingdoms of the north
3 12 proclaim these words towards the north
4 6 I bring evil from the north, and great
6 1 evil is seen out of the north, and a
13 20 and see, you that come from the north
15 12 allied with the iron from the north
25 9 and take all the kindreds of the north
26 all the kings of the north far and near
31 8 will bring them from the north country
46 6 towards the n. by the river Euphrates
10 a sacrifice . . . in the north country
20 from the north one that shall goad her
24 into hand of the people of the north
47 2 there come up waters out of the north
50 3 is come up against her out of the north
41 behold a people cometh from the north
51 48 spoilers shall come to her from the n.
Eze 1 4 behold a whirlwind came out of the north
8 5 my eyes towards the way of the north
14 looked to the north. 40:35
20 47 from the south even to the north. 21:4
26 7 the king of kings, from the north, with
32 30 there are all the princes of the north
40 19 hundred cubits to east and to the north
23 over against the gate of the north
41 11 one door was toward the north, and
42 1 by the way that leadeth to the north
1 over against the house toward the north
2 in the face of the north door was the
4 and their doors were toward the north
11 chambers which were toward the north
13 chambers of the north . . . holy chambers
17 he measured toward the north 500 reeds
44 4 by the way of the north gate. 46:9; 47:2
46 9 he that goeth in by the north gate
48 1 from the borders of the north by the way
10 toward the n. five and twenty thousand
17 suburbs . . . to the north 250
Dan 8 4 with his horns . . . against the north
11 6 the king of the north. 7, 8, 11, 13, 15, 40
44 tidings out of the . . . north shall
Amos 8 12 they shall move . . . from the north to
Soph 2 13 will stretch out his hand upon the north
Zach 14 4 shall be separated to the north, and
Luke 13 29 west and the north and the south
Apoc 21 13 on the north, three gates: and on the

land of the north Jer 3 18 they shall come together out of l. . . .
Jer 6 22 cometh from the land of the north
10 22 a great commotion out of the l. . . .
16 15 children of Israel out of the l. . . .
23 8 seed of house of Israel from l. . . .
50 9 assembly of great nations from l. . . .
Zach 2 6 flee ye out of the land of the north
6 6 black horses went forth into l. . . .
8 they that go forth into the l. . . . have quieted my spirit in the l. . . .
north side Exod 26 35 table shall stand in the n. s.
Exod 27 11 on n. s. there shall be hangings of
38 11 in like manner at the n. s. the hangings
40 20 testimony at the n. s. without the veil
Num 2 25 on the n. s. camped the sons of Dan
3 35 they shall camp on the north side
34 7 toward n. s. the borders shall begin
9 these shall be the borders on n. s.
35 5 n. s. shall be bounded with the like
Josu 8 11 they stood on the n. s. of the city
13 army went in battle array on the n. s.
17 9 is on the north side of the torrent
18 12 by the side of Jericho on the n. s.
18 passeth on the n. s. to the champaign
24 30 on the north side of mount Gaas. Judg 2:9
Judg 7 1 valley on the n. s. of the high hill
Eze 8 5 on the n. s. of the gate of the altar
47 15 toward the n. s., from the great sea
17 the border of Emath, this is the n. s.
48 16 on the north side 4,500; and on the
30 on the n. s. thou shalt measure 4,500
31 three gates on the north side, the gate
northern Eccu 43 18 so doth the n. storm and the
Eze 38 6 northern parts and all his strength
15 out of thy place from the n. parts
39 2 will make thee go up from the n. parts
Joel 2 20 far off from you the n. enemy
northwest Acts 27 12 looking towards southwest and n.
nose Lev 21 18 if he have . . . a crooked nose
4 K 19 28 will put a ring in thy nose. Isa 37:29
Job 40 21 canst thou put a ring in his nose
Prov 30 33 he that violently bloweth his nose
Cant 7 4 thy nose is as the tower of Libanus
Eze 8 17 behold they put a branch to their nose
23 25 they shall cut off thy nose and thy ears
noses Ps 113 6 they have noses and smell not
Wisd 15 15 eyes to see, nor noses to draw breath
nostrils Num 11 20 till it come out at your n.
2 K 22 9 a smoke went up from his nostrils
Job 27 3 and the spirit of God in my nostrils
39 20 the glory of his nostrils is terror
40 19 bore through his nostrils with stakes
41 11 out of his nostrils goeth smoke, like
Wisd 2 2 the breath in our nostrils is smoke
Isa 2 22 man, whose breath is in his nostrils
Amos 4 10 of your camp to come up into your n.
notable Dan 8 5 had a n. horn between his eyes
notably 2 Ma 14 31 finding himself n. prevented
note Tob 1 17 taking a note of his hand, he gave
Tob 4 21 I have a note of his hand with me. 5:3
22 restore to him the note of his hand
9 3 to restore to him his note of hand
6 Gabelus, gave him his note of hand
Isa 30 8 and note it diligently in a book
Rom 16 7 who are of note among the apostles, who
2 Th 3 14 note that man, and do not keep company
noted Ps 80 4 the noted day of your solemnity
Eze 39 11 I will give Gog a noted place for
13 it shall be unto them a noted day
nothing Gen 45 20 leave nothing of your household
Exod 21 2 he shall go out free for nothing
Num 6 4 eat nothing that cometh of the vineyard
11 6 our eyes behold n. else but manna
16 26 touch nothing of theirs lest you be
18 20 you shall possess nothing in their land
Deut 2 7 years, and thou hast wanted nothing
34 we left nothing of them except the
5 22 adding nothing more: and he wrote them
9 3 bring them to nothing before thy face
13 17 nothing of that anathema stick to thy
18 2 they shall receive nothing else of the
22 26 the damsel shall suffer nothing, neither
28 55 because he hath nothing else in the
Josu 8 35 he left out nothing of those things
Judg 6 4 they left nothing at all in Israel
7 14 this is nothing else but the sword of
11 26 attempted nothing about this claim
13 14 let her eat n. that cometh of the vine
14 6 having nothing at all in his hand
19 19 with me: we want nothing but lodging
1 K 15 9 good for nothing, that they destroyed
20 26 and Saul said nothing that day, for he
22 15 thy servant knew nothing of this matter
25 21 nothing was lost of all that pertained
36 she told him nothing less or more until
30 19 there was nothing missing small or great
2 K 3 26 of Sira, David knowing nothing of it
12 3 the poor man had nothing at all but
15 11 and knowing nothing of the design
18 29 me thy servant: I know nothing else
23 7 be set on fire and burnt to nothing
3 K 6 22 n. in temple that was not covered with
11 22 but he answered: Nothing: yet I beseech
18 43 looked and said: There is nothing
22 16 tell me nothing but that which is true
4 K 4 2 nothing in my house but a little oil
9 35 they found nothing but the skull and
20 13 nothing in his house . . . that Ezechias
15 there is nothing among my treasures
17 into Babylon; nothing shall be left
2 Pa 5 10 there was nothing else in the ark
18 15 to say nothing but the truth to me
28 21 yet it availed him [Achaz] nothing
1 Es 4 3 you have nothing to do with us to build
2 Es 5 12 and we will require nothing of them
9 21 and nothing was wanting to them: their
Tob 2 22 is evident thy hope is come to nothing
Jdth 8 28 is n. to be reprehended in thy words
Esth 2 10 Mardochai had charged her to say nothing
3 6 he counted it nothing to lay his hands
5 13 I think I have nothing, so long as
10 5 things: and nothing thereof hath failed
16 10 having nothing of the Persian blood
Job 5 6 n. upon earth is done without a cause
7 16 spare me, for my days are nothing
13 9 from whom nothing can be concealed
19 20 n. but lips are left about my teeth
20 21 there was nothing left of his meat
21 nothing shall continue of his goods
22 17 the Almighty as if he could do nothing
26 7 and hangeth the earth upon nothing
27 19 he shall open his eyes and find nothing
19 shall take away nothing with him
29 22 to my words they durst add nothing
30 2 strength of whose hands was to me as n.
32 14 he hath spoken nothing to me, and I
Ps 14 4 the malignant is brought to nothing
22 1 Lord ruleth me; and I shall want nothing
36 20 shall come to n. and vanish like smoke
38 6 my substance is as nothing before thee
48 18 he shall die he shall take nothing away
55 8 for nothing shalt thou save them
57 8 they shall come to nothing, like water
58 9 shalt bring all the nations to nothing

59 14 shall bring to n. them that afflict us
70 13 come to nothing that detract my soul
72 20 shalt bring their image to nothing
75 6 have found nothing in their hands
77 59 reduced Israel . . . as it were to nothing
89 5 things that are counted nothing, shall
107 14 he will bring our enemies to nothing
Prov 8 8 is nothing wicked nor perverse in them
9 13 full of allurements and knowing nothing
10 2 treasures of wickedness shall profit n.
20 heart of the wicked is nothing worth
13 7 as it were rich, when he hath nothing
14 35 good for nothing shall feel his anger
19 7 after words only, shall have nothing
24 12 n. deceiveth the keeper of thy soul
21 have nothing to do with detracters
Ecce 1 10 nothing under the sun is new, neither
2 11 nothing was lasting under the sun
3 19 and man hath nothing more than beast
22 n. is better than for a man to rejoice
5 14 shall take nothing away with him of
6 2 wanteth nothing of all that he desireth
7 19 that feareth God, neglecteth nothing
8 15 take nothing else with him of his labor
9 5 but the dead know nothing more
10 11 he is nothing better that backbiteth
Cant 8 7 for love, he shall despise it as nothing
Wisd 1 11 murmuring, which profiteth nothing
2 2 we are born of nothing, and after this
11 feeble, is found to be nothing worth
3 17 they shall be nothing regarded, and
4 5 their fruits . . . fit for nothing
7 8 esteemed riches nothing in comparison
22 which nothing hindereth, beneficent
8 7 men can have nothing more profitable
9 6 with him, he shall be nothing regarded
13 13 left thereof, which is good for nothing
13 when he hath nothing else to do and
17 11 fear is nothing else but a yielding
13 night, in which nothing could be done
Eccu 6 15 n. can be compared to a faithful friend
8 19 blood is as nothing in his sight
10 6 do thou nothing by deeds of injury
9 n. is more wicked than the covetous man
13 5 if thou have nothing, he will forsake
17 26 praise perisheth from the dead as n.
18 5 nothing may be taken away nor added
22 let nothing hinder thee from praying
33 when thou hast nothing in thy purse
20 25 maketh him his enemy for nothing
23 37 is nothing better than the fear of God
37 nothing sweeter than to have regard
26 18 there is nothing so much worth as a
32 24 son, do thou nothing without counsel
34 16 feareth the Lord shall tremble at nothing
36 24 and a man desireth nothing more. If she
39 24 there is nothing hid from his eyes
25 there is nothing wonderful before him
40 6 a little and as nothing is his rest
42 21 eternity, and to him n. may be added
25 and he hath made nothing defective
Isa 14 4 how is the oppressor come to nothing
30 28 to destroy the nations unto nothing
34 11 out upon it, to bring it to nothing
12 all the princes thereof shall be nothing
39 2 there was nothing in his house, nor
40 17 counted to him as nothing, and vanity
22 that stretcheth out the heavens as n.
23 bringeth searchers of secrets to nothing
41 11 fight against thee . . . shall be as n.
12 resist thee: they shall be as nothing
24 you are of nothing, and your work of
44 9 makers of idols are all of them nothing
10 thing that is profitable for nothing
59 4 trust in a mere n. and speak vanities
63 18 have possessed thy holy people as n.
Jer 2 21 into that which is good for nothing
37 shalt have nothing prosperous therein
4 23 earth, and lo it was void and nothing
10 24 thy fury, lest thou bring me to nothing
15 13 I will give unto spoil for nothing
38 14 ask thee a thing, hide n. from me
27 they left him: for n. had been heard
39 10 of the poor people that had n. at all
42 4 and I will hide nothing from you
46 15 why are thy valiant men come to nothing
50 26 destroy her, and let n. of her be left
51 58 labors of the people shall come to n.
Lam 4 6 moment, and hands took nothing in her
Bar 6 27 give nothing of it either to the sick
30 shaven, and nothing upon their heads
45 shall be n. else but what the priests
53 because they can do nothing and are
69 as a scarecrow . . . keepeth nothing
Eze 7 11 nothing of them shall remain, nor of
13 3 follow their own spirit and see nothing
18 7 hath taken nothing away by violence
26 21 I will bring thee to nothing, and
Dan 4 32 are reputed as nothing before him
6 17 that n. should be done against Daniel
Amos 3 4 out of his den, if he have taken nothing
7 God doth nothing without revealing his
Soph 3 3 they left nothing for the morning
Agge 2 4 is it not in comparison to that as n.
1 Ma 2 63 and his thought is come to nothing
11 36 n. hereof shall be revoked from this
38 seeing that . . . nothing resisted him
2 Ma 4 25 nothing worthy of the high priesthood
7 12 he esteemed the torments as nothing
28 consider that God made them out of n.
12 4 suspecting nothing, because of the peace
14 35 Lord of all things, who wantest nothing
Mat 5 13 it is good for nothing any more but to
10 26 nothing is covered that shall not be
17 19 and nothing shall be impossible to you
21 19 found n. on it but leaves. Mark 11:13
23 16 swear by the temple, it is nothing; but
18 shall swear by the altar, it is nothing
26 62 answerest thou nothing. Mark 14:60; 15:4
27 12 he answered nothing. Then Pilate saith
19 have thou n. to do with that just man
24 Pilate seeing that he prevailed n.
Mark 4 22 there is n. hid which shall not be
5 26 was n. the better, but rather worse
6 8 they should take nothing for the way
7 15 n. from without a man that entering
8 1 multitude, and had nothing to eat
2 three days and have nothing to eat
9 28 this kind can go out by nothing but
14 61 he held his peace and answered nothing
15 5 but Jesus still answered nothing; so
16 8 they said nothing to any man; for they
Luke 3 13 do nothing more than that which is
4 2 and he ate nothing in those days
5 5 the night, and have taken nothing
6 35 do good, and lend, hoping for nothing
9 3 take nothing for your journey; neither
10 19 enemy: and nothing shall hurt you
12 2 there is n. covered, that shall not
22 36 anything? But they said: Nothing. Then
23 9 words. But he answered him nothing
15 nothing worthy of death is done to him
John 1 3 without him was made nothing that was
4 11 sir, thou hast nothing wherein to draw
6 39 hath given me, I should lose nothing
64 the flesh profiteth nothing. The words

7 26 openly, and they say nothing to him
8 28 I do nothing of myself, but as the
54 if I glorify myself, my glory is n.
11 49 said to them: You know nothing
12 19 do you see that we prevail nothing
15 5 for without me you can do nothing
18 20 and in secret I have spoken nothing
21 3 and that night they caught nothing
Acts 4 14 they could say nothing against it. But
9 8 he saw nothing. But they leading him by
10 20 and go with them, doubting nothing: for
11 8 not so, Lord; for nothing common or
12 should go with them, nothing doubting
17 21 employed themselves in nothing else
19 27 great Diana shall be reputed for nothing
36 ought to be quiet and to do n. rashly
20 20 now I have kept back nothing that was
23 14 we will eat n. till we have slain Paul
29 but having nothing laid to his charge
25 25 yet have I found nothing that he hath
26 I have n. certain to write to my lord
26 31 this man hath done n. worthy of death
27 33 and continued fasting, taking nothing
28 17 I, having done n. against the people, or
Rom 14 14 that nothing is unclean of itself; but
1 C 1 7 that n. is wanting to you in any grace
7 19 circumcision is n., and uncircumcision
19 nothing, and uncircumcision is nothing
8 4 we know that an idol is n. in the world
13 2 and have not charity, I am nothing. And
3 and have not charity, it profiteth me n.
2 C 6 10 as having n., and possessing all things
7 9 you might suffer damage by us in nothing
8 15 he that had much, had nothing over; and
11 5 done n. less than the great apostles
12 5 for myself I will glory nothing, but in
11 measure apostles, although I be nothing
13 8 we can do nothing against the truth; but
Gal 2 6 what they were some time, it is n. to me
6 that seemed to be something added n.
4 1 he differeth nothing from a servant
5 2 Christ shall profit you nothing. And I
6 3 something, whereas he is nothing, he
Phil 1 20 that in nothing I shall be confounded
27 in n. be ye terrified by the adversaries
2 3 let nothing be done through contention
4 6 be n. solicitous; but in everything
1 Th 4 11 and that you want nothing of any man's
2 Th 3 8 did we eat any man's bread for nothing
1 Tim 4 4 nothing to be rejected that is received
5 21 doing n. by declining to either side
6 4 he is proud, knowing nothing, but sick
7 we brought nothing into this world: and
7 and certainly we can carry nothing out
Titus 1 15 and to unbelievers, nothing is clean
3 13 care, that nothing be wanting to them
Philem 14 without thy counsel I would do nothing
Heb 2 8 he left nothing not subject to him. But
7 14 in which tribe Moses spoke nothing
19 the law brought nothing to perfection
James 1 4 perfect and entire, failing in nothing
6 let him ask in faith, nothing wavering
3 J 7 out, taking nothing of the Gentiles
Apoc 3 17 made wealthy, and have need of nothing
brought to nothing Job 16 8 my limbs are b. . . .
Job 17 7 my limbs are b. as it were to nothing
30 15 I am brought to nothing: as a wind
Ps 72 22 I am brought to nothing, and I knew not
Prov 15 22 designs are brought to nothing when
Eccu 21 5 shall be brought to nothing by pride
Eze 27 36 thou art brought to nothing and. 28:19
1 Ma 1 41 her honors were brought to nothing
Acts 5 36 believed him were . . . b. to nothing

notice Exod 2 4 taking n. what would be done
Exod 23 21 take notice of him and hear his voice
Ruth 2 10 to take notice of me a woman of another
2 K 13 28 take notice when Amnon shall be drunk
20 10 Amasa did not take notice of the sword
1 Pa 19 3 dost not take notice that his servants
1 Es 5 10 names, that we might give thee notice
Prov 8 5 subtilty: and ye unwise, take notice
28 5 seek after the Lord, take n. of all
29 7 taketh notice of the cause of the poor
Isa 58 3 souls, and thou hast not taken notice
Jer 4 15 giving notice of the idol from mount
Dan 9 25 know thou therefore and take notice
2 Ma 3 7 when Apollonius had given the king n.
Acts 21 26 entered into the temple, giving notice
notified 1 Ma 14 28 these things were notified
notorious Mat 27 16 he had then a notorious prisoner
nought Deut 28 63 destroying and bringing you to n.
Deut 33 27 shall say: Be thou brought to nought
Jdth 13 22 he hath brought our enemies to nought
Job 5 12 who bringeth to nought the designs of
14 18 a mountain falling cometh to nought
Ps 7 10 of sinners shall be brought to nought
17 43 I shall bring them to nought, like the
32 9 bringeth to n. the counsels of nations
105 24 they set at nought the desirable land
Prov 20 14 it is n., it is n., saith every buyer
Wisd 1 11 obscure speech shall not go for nought
Amos 6 14 you that rejoice in a thing of nought
2 Ma 4 15 setting nought by the honors of their
Luke 23 11 Herod with his army set him at nought
Acts 5 38 be of men, it will come to nought
19 27 craft is in danger to be set at nought
1 C 1 28 he might bring to nought things that are
2 6 princes of this world that come to n.
15 24 when he shall have brought to nought
Apoc 18 17 are so great riches come to nought
nourish Ps 30 4 thou wilt lead me and n. me
Isa 7 21 that a man shall nourish a young cow
Zach 11 16 nor nourish that which standeth, and
2 Ma 14 6 nourish wars and raise seditions and
1 C 11 14 that a man indeed, if he n. his hair
15 if a woman nourish her hair, it is glory
nourished Gen 47 12 he [Joseph] nourished them
2 K 12 3 lamb, which he had bought and n. up
4 K 3 4 Mesa, king of Moab, n. many sheep
Wisd 16 23 that the just might be n., did even
Isa 23 4 nor have I nourished up young men
44 14 pine tree, which the rain hath n.
Lam 2 22 those that I brought up and nourished
Bar 4 11 I nourished them with joy: but I
Eze 31 4 the waters nourished him, the deep
Dan 1 5 being n. three years, afterwards
2 Ma 7 27 and n. thee and brought thee up
Acts 7 20 who was nourished three months in his
21 and nourished him for her own son. And
12 20 their countries were nourished by him
1 Tim 4 6 nourished up in the words of faith, and
James 5 5 in riotousness you have n. your hearts
Apoc 12 14 she is n. for a time and times, and
nourisheth Prov 29 21 n. his servant delicately
Wisd 16 25 was obedient to thy grace that n. all
26 not the growing of fruits that n. men
Eccu 28 5 he that is but flesh, n. anger, and
Eph 5 29 but nourisheth and cherisheth it, as
nourishing Exod 35 14 the oil for the n. of fires
nourishment Gen 37 8 ministered n. to their envy
Isa 30 33 the nourishment thereof is fire and
Col 2 19 being supplied with nourishment and
novelties 1 Tim 6 20 avoiding the profane n. of
nowadays 1 K 25 10 servants are multiplied n. who
nowhere Heb 2 16 n. doth he take hold of the angels
nowise Eccu 4 30 in n. speak against the truth

number Gen 13 16 any man be able to number the dust
Gen 13 16 he shall be able to number thy seed
15 5 and number the stars, if thou canst
29 22 invited a great number of his friends
Exod 5 18 deliver the accustomed number of bricks
10 6 number as thy fathers have not seen
12 4 but if the number be less than may
38 multitude without number went up also
23 26 I will fill the number of thy days
30 12 children of Israel according to their n.
14 he that is counted in the number from
Lev 15 13 he shall number seven days after his
25 8 number to thee seven weeks of years
26 22 cattle, and make you few in number
Num 1 3 you shall number them by their troops
45 whole number of the children of Israel
49 number not the tribe of Levi, neither
2 6 the whole number of his fighting men
32 the number of the children of Israel. 26:63; Josu 4:5
3 15 number the sons of Levi by the
40 number the firstborn of the male sex
46 that exceed the number of the Levites
4 23 n. them all that go in and minister
37 the number of the people of Caath
37 these did Moses and Aaron number
45 this is the n. of the sons of Merari
13 19 strong or weak: few in number or many
16 49 the number of them that were slain was
23 1 prepare . . . same number of rams. 29
10 know the number of the stock of Israel
26 2 number the whole sum of the children of
4 this is the number of them: Ruben the
7 whose number was found to be 43,730
14 number was. 18, 22, 25, 27, 37, 41, 43, 50; 1 Pa 7:7, 40
34 the number of them 52,700
47 of Aser, and their number 53,400
54 to the greater number thou shalt give
57 the number of the sons of Levi by their
31 41 delivered the number of the firstfruits
49 the number of the fighting men whom
Deut 1 11 God of your fathers add to this number
7 7 not because you surpass all nations in n.
16 9 thou shalt number unto thee seven weeks
17 15 shall choose out of the number of thy
16 lifted up with the number of his horsemen
19 9 double the number of the three cities
20 19 number of them that fight against thee
21 11 seest in the number of the captives a
25 3 they exceed not the number of forty
26 5 sojourned there in a very small number
28 62 and you shall remain few in number
33 6 and be he [Ruben] small in number
Josu 8 25 the number of them that fell that day
Judg 7 6 number of them that had lapped water
8 and trumpets according to their number
12 5 any one of the number of Ephraim came
9 wives for his sons of the same number
20 22 trusting in their strength and their n.
47 remained of all the number of Benjamin
21 23 according to their n. they carried off
1 K 13 5 like sand on the seashore for number
2 K 2 11 the number of the days that David abode
15 went over twelve in n. of Benjamin
24 1 saying: God, number Israel and Juda
2 number ye the people, that I may know the number of them
4 out . . . to number the people of Israel
9 the sum of the number of the people
3 K 5 16 overseers . . . in number three thousand
20 15 he found the number of 232: and he
25 and make up the number of soldiers
4 K 12 11 they gave it out by number and measure
24 14 to the number of 10,000 into captivity
1 Pa 3 22 Semeia, whose sons . . . six in number
5 9 they possessed a great n. of cattle
23 for their number was great. And these
9 26 were committed the whole number of porters
28 brought in and carried out by number
11 11 is the number of the heroes of David
12 22 till they became a great number, like
23 the number of the chiefs of the army
21 1 Satan . . . moved David to number Israel
2 said to Joab . . . go and number Israel
2 bring me the number of them that I may
5 and he gave David the number of them
5 the number of Israel was found to be
6 Levi and Benjamin he did not number
22 4 and the cedar trees were without number
16 and in iron, whereof there is no number
23 24 the number of every head that did the
25 1 according to their number serving in
7 the number of them with their brethren
27 1 children of Israel according to their n.
23 would not number them from 20 years
24 began to number but he finished not
24 number of them . . . was not registered
2 Pa 5 6 sacrificed rams and oxen without number
12 3 and the people were without number
14 15 and took an infinite number of cattle
17 14 this is the number of the houses and
26 12 the whole number of the chiefs by the
29 32 the number of the holocausts which the
30 17 because a great n. was not sanctified
24 great number of priests was sanctified
32 29 [Ezechias] had . . . herds without number
34 13 masters of the number of the Levites
1 Es 1 9 number of them: thirty bowls of gold
2 2 the number of the men of the people of
2 Es 5 17 to the n. of 150 men were at my table
7 5 I assembled . . . to number them: and I found a book of the number of them
7 number of the men of people of Israel
Jdth 2 8 and flocks of sheep, without number
10 8 may be in the number of the holy and
16 31 in the number of holy days and is
Esth 2 8 to be kept in the number of the women
9 11 the number of them that were killed. 16
11 4 he was of the number of the captives
Job 5 9 doth . . . wonderful things without number
9 10 wonderful, of which there is no number
14 5 the number of his months is with thee
15 20 the number of the years of his tyranny
21 21 if number of his months be diminished
31 4 consider my ways and n. all my steps
36 26 the number of his years is inestimable
38 21 didst thou know the number of thy days
Ps 38 5 what is the number of my days: that I
39 6 they are multiplied above number
13 evils without n. have surrounded me
89 12 who . . . can number thy wrath? So make
103 25 are creeping things without number
104 34 bruchus, of which there was no number
138 18 I will number them, and they shall be
146 4 who telleth the number of the stars
5 and of his wisdom there is no number
Ecce 1 15 and the number of fools is infinite
4 16 number of the people . . . is infinite
5 6 many vanities and words without number
12 3 grinders shall be idle in a small number
Cant 6 7 and young maidens without number. One
Wisd 4 8 nor counted by the number of years
11 21 all things in measure and number and
Eccu 7 17 number not thyself among the multitude
17 3 he gave him the number of his days

18 8 the number of the days of men at the
19 3 soul shall be taken away out of the n.
26 1 for the number of his years is double
33 10 he put in the number of ordinary days
37 28 life of a man is in the n. of his days
38 32 and maketh all his work by number
41 16 a good life hath its number of days
42 7 deliver all things in number and weight
45 13 according to n. of the tribes of Israel
46 10 from among the number of 600,000 men
Isa 21 17 residue of the number of strong archers
40 26 who bringeth out their host by number
65 12 I will number you in the sword, and you
Jer 2 32 hath forgotten me days without number
23 4 none shall be wanting of their number
29 6 multiplied there, and be not few in n.
46 23 above locusts, and are without number
51 27 number Taphsar against her, bring the
6 18 candles to them, and in great number
Bar 6 18 candles to them, and in great number
Dan 9 2 understood by books the n. of the years
Osee 1 10 the number of the children of Israel
Joel 1 6 a nation is come . . . without number
1 Ma 1 18 into Egypt with . . . great n. of ships
2 18 be in the number of the king's friends
38 to the number of a thousand persons
4 15 fell of them to the number of 3,000 men
5 30 people without number, carrying ladders
6 30 number of his army was 100,000 footmen
9 65 Jonathan . . . came with a number of men
10 21 army, and made a great number of arms
36 to the number of 30,000 of the Jews
78 because he had a great n. of horsemen
11 45 together to the number of 120,000 men
14 7 gathered together great n. of captives
2 Ma 10 19 in sufficient number to besiege them
12 19 slew . . . to the number of 10,000 men
Mat 14 21 the number of them that did eat, was
John 6 10 sat down, in number about 5,000. And
Acts 1 15 n. of persons together was about 120
4 4 the number of the men was made 5,000
5 36 to whom a number of men, about 400
6 1 the number of the disciples increasing
7 n. of the disciples was multiplied
11 21 great n. believing, were converted to
16 5 faith, and increased in number daily
20 8 there were a great number of lamps in
Rom 9 27 if the number of the children of Israel
Apoc 5 11 the number of them was thousands of
7 4 I heard the number of them that were
9 multitude which no man could number
9 16 the number of the army of horsemen was
16 I heard the number of them. And thus
13 17 the beast, or the number of his name
18 let him count the number of the beast
18 it is the number of a man: and the number is 666
15 2 his image, and the number of his name
20 7 n. of whom is as the sand of the sea

according to the number Exod 12 4 a. . . . of souls which may be enough
Exod 16 16 a. . . . of your souls that dwell in a
Lev 25 14 a. . . . of years from the jubilee. And
50 that he was sold for, a. . . . of the years
52 reckoning with him a. . . . of the years
27 18 a. . . . of years that remain until the
23 a. . . . of years unto the jubilee: and
Num 14 34 a. . . . of the forty days wherein you
26 53 for their possessions a. . . . of names
34 14 children of Gad, a. . . . of their kindreds
Deut 32 8 a. . . . of children of Israel. Josu 4:8
Josu 18 4 mark it out a. . . . of each multitude
1 K 6 5 a. . . . of provinces of the Philistines
18 a. . . . of the cities of the Philistines
3 K 18 31 a. . . . of the tribes of the sons of Jacob
1 Pa 23 31 a. . . . and ceremonies prescribed for
1 Es 6 17 a. . . . of the tribes of Israel. And they
8 34 a. . . . and weight of every thing: and
Jer 2 28 a. . . . of thy cities were thy gods. 11:13
11 13 a. . . . of the streets of Jerusalem thou
Eze 4 4 according to the n. of the days. 5, 9

small number Deut 26 5 sojourned there in a very small number
1 Pa 16 19 they were but a s. n. Ps 104:12
2 Pa 24 24 a very small number of the Syrians
Prov 14 28 in the small n. of people the dishonor
Ecce 12 3 grinders shall be idle in a s. number
Eccu 48 2 were reduced to a small number, for
Bar 2 29 shall be turned into a very small n.
Eze 5 3 thou shalt take thereof a small number

numbered Gen 14 14 he n. of the servants born in
Gen 16 10 it shall not be numbered for multitude
32 12 which cannot be numbered for multitude
Exod 38 25 offered by them that went to be n.
Num 1 19 they were n. in the desert of Sinai
44 these are they who were numbered by
47 families were not numbered with them
2 9 that were n. in the camp of. 24, 31
11 of his fighting men, that were numbered. 13, 15, 19, 21, 26, 28
33 the Levites were not numbered among
3 16 Moses numbered them as the Lord had
22 were n., people of the male sex from
39 Levites, that Moses and Aaron numbered
4 38 sons of Gerson also were numbered
41 Gersonites, whom Moses and Aaron n.
42 sons of Merari also were numbered
7 2 rulers of them who had been numbered
14 29 that were n. from twenty years old
26 62 that were numbered were 23,000 males
64 that were numbered before by Moses
1 K 11 8 and he [Saul] numbered them in Bezec
13 15 Saul n. the people that were found with
15 4 people, and numbered them as lambs
18 27 brought their foreskins and n. them
2 K 17 11 the sand of the sea which cannot be n.
24 10 struck him after the people were n.
3 K 3 8 an immense people which cannot be n.
8 5 oxen that could not counted or n.
1 Pa 5 7 when they were n. by their families
17 all these were numbered in the days of
7 2 the posterity of Thola were n. in the
5 of Issachar, were numbered 87,000 most
9 and they were numbered by the families
9 1 all Israel was numbered: and the sum
21 17 that commanded the people to be n.
23 3 the Levites were n. from the age of 30
14 were numbered in the tribe of Levi
27 the sons of Levi are to be numbered
26 31 they were n., and there were found
27 24 the number of them that were numbered
2 Pa 2 2 he n. out 70,000 men to bear burdens
17 Solomon numbered all the proselytes
25 5 he numbered them from twenty years old
1 Es 1 8 and numbered them to Sassabasar the
8 3 and with him were numbered 150 men
2 Es 7 1 and n. the porters and singing men
Jdth 5 9 that the army of them could not be n.
Job 3 6 of the year nor n. in the months. Let
7 3 and have n. to myself wearisome nights
14 16 thou indeed hast numbered my steps
39 2 hast thou n. the months of their
Ps 21 18 they have numbered all my bones. And
Wisd 5 5 they are n. among the children of God
Eccu 1 2 who hath numbered the sand of the sea
9 saw her and n. her and measured her
23 it hath seen and numbered her: but
Isa 10 19 that they shall easily be numbered

22 10 have numbered the houses of Jerusalem
Jer 33 22 stars of heaven cannot be numbered
Dan 5 26 God hath numbered thy kingdom and
Osee 1 10 without measure and shall not be n.
Mat 10 30 hairs of your head are all n. Luke 12:7
Acts 1 17 who was n. with us and had obtained
26 and he was numbered with the eleven
Heb 7 6 he, whose pedigree is not n. among them
numbereth Tob 9 4 that my father n. the days
Jer 33 13 under the hand of him that n. them
numbering 2 Pa 2 17 n. which David his father had
Jdth 15 8 there was no numbering of their cattle
Job 25 3 is there any numbering of his soldiers
numbers Deut 20 1 n. of enemy's army greater than
2 Pa 17 2 he placed numbers of soldiers in all
1 Ma 4 35 again into Judea with greater numbers
2 Ma 1 12 made numbers of men swarm out of Persia
Numenius 1 Ma 12 16 we have chosen therefore N.
1 Ma 14 22 N. the son of Antiochus, and Antipater
24 Simon sent Numenius to Rome with a
15 15 N. and they that had been with him
numerous Exod 1 9 are n. and stronger than we
Exod 5 5 the people of the land is numerous
Deut 7 1 nations much more n. than thou art
30 5 thee more n. than were thy fathers
Josu 11 4 a people exceeding n. as the sand
3 K 3 9 this people, thy people which is so n.
5 7 a very wise son over this n. people
2 Pa 16 8 the Libyans much more n. in chariots
Joel 2 2 a n. and strong people as the morning
1 Ma 3 10 a n. and great army from Samaria
16 7 horsemen of the enemies were very n.
nun Ps 118 105 nun. Lam 1:14; 2:14; 3:40, 41, 42; 4:14
Nun Exod 33 11 Josue the son of Nun. Num 11:28; 14:6, 30, 38; 26:65; 27:18; 32:12, 28; 34:17; Deut 1:38; 31:23; 34:9; Josu 1:1; 2:1, 23; 6:6; 14:1; 17:4; 19:49, 51; 21:1; 24:29; 3 K 16:34; 2 Es 8:17
Num 13 9 Osee the son of Nun, 17
1 Pa 7 27 Elisama, of whom was born Nun, who
nurse Gen 24 59 they sent her away, and her nurse
Gen 35 8 Debora the nurse of Rebecca died and
Exod 2 7 a Hebrew woman, to nurse the babe
9 take this child and nurse him for me
Num 11 12 as the nurse is wont to carry the
Ruth 4 16 she carried it and was a nurse unto it
2 K 4 4 and his nurse took him up and fled
4 K 11 2 out of the bedchamber with his nurse
2 Pa 22 11 hid him with his nurse in a bedchamber
1 Th 2 7 as if a n. should cherish her children
nursed Exod 2 9 the woman took and n. the child
Wisd 7 4 I was nursed in swaddling clothes and
Isa 60 16 shalt be n. with the breasts of kings
Bar 4 8 have grieved Jerusalem that nursed you
nurses Isa 49 23 queens [shall be] thy nurses
nursing Isa 49 23 kings shall be thy n. fathers
nut Exod 25 34 four cups in the manner of a nut
Exod 37 19 three cups in manner of a nut on each
19 three cups of the fashion of a nut in
20 four cups after the manner of a nut
nuts Exod 25 33 three cups as it were nuts to
Exod 25 33 three cups, likewise of fashion of nuts
Cant 6 10 I went down into the garden of nuts
Nymphas Col 4 15 brethren who are at Laodicea, and N.

O

oak Gen 35 8 at the foot of Bethel under an oak
Gen 35 8 was called, The oak of weeping
Josu 24 26 set it under the oak that was in the
Judg 6 11 sat under an oak that was in Ephra
19 into a pot, he carried all under the oak
9 6 king, by the oak that stood in Sichem
37 the way that looketh towards the oak
1 K 10 3 and shalt come to the oak of Thabor
2 K 18 9 mule went under a thick and large oak
9 his head stuck in the oak: and while
10 I saw Absalom hanging upon an oak. And
14 panted for life, sticking on the oak
1 Pa 10 12 buried their bones under the oak that
Isa 1 30 when you shall be as an oak with the
6 13 as an oak that spreadeth its branches
44 14 the oak that stood among the trees of
Eze 6 13 and under every thick oak, the place
Osee 4 13 hills: under the oak and the poplar
Amos 2 9 and who was strong as an oak: and I
oaks Isa 2 13 upon all the oaks of Basan
Eze 27 6 cut thy oars out of the oaks of Basan
Zach 11 2 howl, ye oaks of Basan, because the
oar Eze 27 29 that handled the oar shall come
oars Exod 35 11 the board work with the oars
Isa 33 21 no ship with oars shall pass by it
Eze 27 6 they have cut thy oars out of the oaks
oath Gen 21 32 made a league for the well of oath
Gen 24 8 thou shalt not be bound by the oath
26 3 the oath which I swore to Abraham
28 let there be an oath between us and
43 3 unto us with the attestation of an oath
46 1 he had, came to the well of the oath
5 Jacob rose up from the well of the o.
Exod 22 11 there shall be an oath between them
11 the owner shall accept of the oath
Lev 5 4 and bindeth the same with an oath, and
Num 30 3 to the Lord or bind himself by an oath
4 anything, and bind herself by an oath
4 the oath wherewith she hath bound her
7 mouth shall bind her soul by an oath
11 hath bound herself by vow and by oath
14 if she vow and bind herself by oath
32 11 which I promised with an oath. Deut 1:35
Deut 7 8 loved you and hath kept his oath
9 5 he promised by oath to thy fathers
11 9 Lord promised by oath to your fathers
29 12 in the oath which this day the Lord
19 when he shall hear words of this oath
Josu 2 17 we shall be blameless of this oath
20 shall be quit of this oath which thou
6 22 are hers, as you assured her by oath
Judg 21 5 had bound themselves with a great oath
18 being bound with an oath and a curse
1 K 14 26 for the people feared the oath. But
28 hath bound the people with an oath
2 K 21 7 because of the oath of the Lord, that
3 K 2 43 hast thou not kept the oath of the Lord
8 31 have an oath upon him wherewith he
31 come because of the oath before thy
18 10 he took an oath of every kingdom and
4 K 11 4 taking an oath of them in the house of
1 Pa 4 21 wrought fine linen in the House of oath
16 16 with Abraham: and his oath to Isaac
2 Es 5 12 the priests, and took an oath of them
Ps 104 9 made to Abraham: and his oath to Isaac
Prov 29 24 he heareth one putting him to his oath
Eccu 44 22 by an oath he gave him glory in his
Jer 11 5 the oath which I swore to your fathers
Bar 2 34 the land which I promised with an oath
Eze 16 59 as thou hast despised the oath, in
17 13 and take an oath of him. Yea, and he
16 king, whose oath he hath made void
18 he had despised the oath, breaking his
19 upon his head the oath he hath despised
Zach 8 17 love not a false oath: for all these
1 Ma 6 62 quickly broke the oath that he had
7 18 and the oath which they made
2 Ma 4 34 gave him his right hand with an oath
7 24 but also assured him with an oath that
Mat 14 7 he promised with an oath, to give her
9 because of his oath, and for them that

20 72 again he [Peter] denied with an oath
Mark 6 26 yet because of his oath and because of
Luke 1 73 the oath which he swore to Abraham our
Acts 2 30 God hath sworn to him with an oath
23 21 who have bound themselves by oath
Heb 6 16 an oath for confirmation is the end of
17 of his counsel, interposed an oath: that
7 20 inasmuch as it is not without an oath
20 were made priests without an oath
21 but this with an oath, by him that said
28 the word of the oath, which was since
James 5 12 by the earth, nor by any other oath
oaths Num 30 6 her vows and her o. shall be void
Deut 29 14 make this covenant and confirm these **o.**
Wisd 18 6 knowing what oaths they had trusted to
22 alleging the oaths and covenant made
Haba 3 9 according to the oaths which thou hast
2 Ma 15 10 of the Gentiles, and their breach of o.
Mat 5 33 shalt perform thy oaths to the Lord
Obadia 1 Pa 7 3 were born Michael and O. and
Obdia 1 Pa 3 21 Arnan, of whom was born Obdia
1 Pa 8 38 Asel had six sons . . . Obdia. 9:44
9 16 Obdia the son of Semeia, the son of
Obdias 1 Pa 12 9 O. the second, Eliab the third
2 Es 10 5 Harem, Merimuth, Obdias, Daniel
Obed Judg 9 26 Gaal the son of Obed. 28, 30, 31, 35
Ruth 4 17 name Obed: he is the father of Isai
21 Booz begot O., O. begot Isai. 1 Pa 2:12
1 Pa 2 37 Ophlal begot Obed. Obed begot Jehu
11 46 Eliel and Obed and Jasiel of Masobia
26 7 were Othni and Raphael and Obed
2 Pa 23 1 Azarias the son of Obed, and Maasias
Mat 1 5 Booz begot Obed of Ruth. And Obed begot
Luke 3 32 Jesse, who was of Obed, who was of
Obededom 2 K 6 10 carried into the house of O.
2 K 6 11 ark of the Lord abode in house of O.
11 the Lord blessed Obededom and all that
12 that the Lord had blessed Obededom
12 the ark of God out of the house of O.
1 Pa 13 13 carried it aside into the house of O.
14 ark of God remained in house of O.
15 18 Obededom and Jehiel, the porters. Now
21 Macenias and Obededom and Jehiel and
24 Obededom and Jehias were porters of
25 out of the house of Obededom with joy
16 5 Eliab and Banaias and Obededom: and
38 Obededom with his brethren sixty-eight
38 O. the son of Idithun, and Hosa he
26 4 the sons of Obededom. 8
8 for service, sixty-two of Obededom
15 to O. and his sons that towards the
2 Pa 25 24 in the house of God and with Obededom
Obedia 1 Es 8 9 of the sons of Joab, Obedia the
2 Es 12 25 Obedia and Mosollam, Telmun, Accub
obedience Deut 21 18 being corrected, slighteth o.
1 K 15 22 obedience is better than sacrifices
Prov 15 28 mind of the just studieth obedience
Ecce 4 17 better is obedience than the victims
Eccu 3 1 their generation, obedience and love
Rom 1 5 apostleship for obedience to the faith
5 19 also by o. of one, many shall be made
6 16 sin unto death, or of o. unto justice
15 18 for the o. of the Gentiles, by word and
16 19 your o. is published in every place. I
26 eternal God, for the obedience of faith
2 C 7 15 remembering the o. of you all, how with
9 13 glorifying God for obedience of your
10 5 every understanding unto o. of Christ
6 when your obedience shall be fulfilled
Philem 21 trusting in thy o., I have written to
Heb 5 8 he learned o. by the things which be
1 P 1 2 unto o. and sprinkling of the blood of
14 as children of o., not fashioned
22 your souls in the obedience of charity
obedient Exod 24 7 we will do, we will be o.
Josu 24 24 we will be o. to his commandments
3 K 13 21 hast not been obedient to the Lord
Prov 21 28 an obedient man shall speak of victory
25 12 reproveth the wise, and the o. ear
Wisd 16 25 was o. to thy grace that nourisheth
Eccu 4 11 shalt be as o. son of the most High
33 30 if he be not obedient, bring him
Isa 11 14 children of Ammon shall be obedient
Jer 35 10 have been obedient according to all
Bar 1 18 we were not obedient to him and we
6 59 forth for profitable uses, are obedient
2 C 2 9 whether you be obedient in all things
Eph 6 5 be obedient to them that are your lords
Phil 2 8 himself, becoming obedient unto death
Titus 2 5 gentle, obedient to their husbands
9 exhort servants to be obedient to their
obeisance Gen 43 28 they made o. to him [Joseph]
obey Gen 41 40 thy mouth all the people shall obey
Exod 15 26 obey his commandments and keep all his
Lev 26 18 if you will not yet for all this obey
Deut 11 13 if then you obey my commandments which
27 blessing, if you obey the commandments
28 curse, if you obey not the commandments
17 12 refuse to obey the commandment of the
26 17 and judgments and obey his command. And
30 2 to him and obey his commandments
20 and obey his voice and adhere to him
Josu 1 17 all things, so will we obey thee [Josue]
18 not obey all thy words that thou
1 K 15 23 like sin of idolatry, to refuse to obey
28 18 didst not obey the voice of the Lord
2 K 22 45 hearing of the ear they will obey me
4 K 10 6 if you be mine and will obey me, take
17 14 who would not obey the Lord their God
Jdth 11 5 also the beasts of the field obey him
Ecce 10 19 may feast: and all things obey money
Eccu 42 24 for every use all things obey him
46 12 that it is good to obey the holy God
Jer 18 10 in my sight, that it obey not my voice
35 13 instruction, to obey my words, saith
37 2 did obey the words of the Lord that he
42 6 we will obey the voice of the Lord
Dan 7 27 shall serve him and shall obey him
1 Ma 2 18 and obey the king's commandment, as
19 although all nations o. king Antiochus
20 will obey the law of our fathers
34 neither will we obey the king's edict
6 23 to his orders and obey his edicts
8 26 they shall obey their orders without
10 38 obey no other authority but that of
12 43 his troops to obey him as himself. And
2 Ma 3 24 that all that had presumed to obey him
7 30 I will not obey the commandment of the
Mat 8 27 winds and the sea obey him. Luke 8:25
Mark 1 27 unclean spirits, and they obey him
4 40 that both wind and sea obey him
Luke 17 6 into the sea: and it would obey you
Acts 5 29 ought to obey God, rather than men
32 God hath given to all that obey him
7 39 whom our fathers would not obey; but
Rom 2 8 who obey not the truth, but give credit
6 12 body, so as to obey the lusts thereof
16 you yield yourselves servants to obey
16 obey, his servants you are whom you obey
10 16 but all do not obey the gospel. For
Gal 3 1 that you should not obey the truth. 5:7
Eph 6 1 children, obey your parents. Col 3:20
Col 3 22 servants, o. in all things your masters
2 Th 1 8 who obey not the gospel of our Lord
3 14 if any man obey not our word by this
Titus 3 1 to obey at a word, to be ready to every

Heb 5 9 he became, to all that obey him, the
12 9 obey the Father of spirits and live
13 17 obey your prelates, and be subject to
James 3 3 horses, that they may obey us, and we
obeyed Gen 22 18 because thou hast o. my voice
Gen 26 5 because Abraham obeyed my voice and
Num 14 22 have not obeyed my voice, shall not
Deut 26 14 I have obeyed the voice of the Lord
34 9 children of Israel obeyed him [Josue]
Josu 1 17 as we obeyed Moses in all things
3 6 they obeyed his commands and took it up
22 2 you have also obeyed me in all things
1 K 15 22 that the voice of the Lord should be o.
28 21 thy handmaid hath obeyed thy voice
1 Pa 29 23 and all Israel obeyed him [Solomon]
Tob 3 4 we have not obeyed thy commandments
Ps 17 45 at hearing of the ear they have o. me
Jer 11 8 they obeyed not nor inclined their ear
32 23 but they obeyed not thy voice and they
34 10 and they obeyed and let them go free
35 8 have obeyed the voice of Jonadab. 18
14 they have obeyed the commandment of
14 speaking, and you have not obeyed me
16 but this people hath not obeyed me
42 21 you have not obeyed the voice of the
43 4 obeyed not the voice of the Lord. 7
44 23 have not obeyed the voice of the Lord
1 Ma 14 43 that he should be obeyed by all, and
Acts 6 7 also of the priests obeyed the faith
Rom 6 17 but have o. from the heart, unto that
Phil 2 12 as you have always obeyed, not as in my
Heb 11 8 obeyed to go out into a place which he
1 P 3 6 as Sara obeyed Abraham, calling him
obeyeth Prov 17 4 evil man o. an unjust tongue
Eccu 3 7 he that obeyeth the father, shall be
Bar 3 33 hath called it, and it obeyeth him
obeying Gen 28 7 Jacob o. his parents was gone
Josu 10 14 the Lord obeying the voice of a man
1 K 15 24 fearing the people and o. their voice
Wisd 19 6 o. thy commandments, that thy children
Bar 2 5 our God, by not obeying his voice
objected Acts 23 28 to know the cause which they o.
objecting Acts 25 7 o. many and grievous causes
oblation Exod 29 18 it is an oblation to the Lord
Exod 29 25 of the Lord, because it is his oblation
41 according to rite of the morning o.
42 perpetual o. unto your generations
30 9 of another composition nor oblation
Lev 1 14 if the oblation of a holocaust to the
17 and o. of most sweet savor to the Lord
2 1 shall offer an oblation of sacrifice
5 if thy oblation be from the fryingpan
11 every o. that is offered to the Lord
15 because it is the oblation of the Lord
3 1 if his oblation be a sacrifice of peace
3 peace offerings, for an o. to the Lord
5 for an oblation of most sweet savor
6 his oblation and the sacrifice of peace
11 for the food of the fire and of the o.
6 20 this is the oblation of Aaron and of
7 12 if the oblation be for thanksgiving
18 the oblation shall be of no effect
8 28 it was the oblation of consecration
10 12 sacrifice that is remaining of the o.
17 4 of the tabernacle an o. to the Lord
22 18 that offereth his o., either paying his
24 7 for a memorial of the o. of the Lord
Num 5 15 shall offer an oblation for her, the tenth
15 an oblation searching out adultery
18 on her hands . . . the o. of jealousy
6 14 shall offer his oblation to the Lord
21 when he hath vowed his oblation to the
7 10 their oblation before the altar. And
29 this is the oblation of Eliab the son
8 15 consecrate them for an oblation of the
18 24 be content with the oblation or tithes
27 reckoned to you as an o. of firstfruits
28 2 offer ye my oblation and my bread and
8 an o. of most sweet odor to the Lord
Deut 16 10 a voluntary oblation of thy hand which
1 K 10 8 that thou mayest offer an oblation
1 Pa 23 31 as well in the o. of the holocausts
2 Pa 29 29 and when the o. was ended, the king
Ps 39 7 sacrifice and o. thou didst not desire
Eccu 35 8 the oblation of the just maketh the
50 15 oblation of the Lord was in their hands
Isa 66 3 he that offereth an oblation, as if he
Dan 3 38 or sacrifice or oblation or incense
Acts 21 26 until an o. should be offered for every
Rom 15 16 that the o. of the Gentiles may be made
31 that the oblation of my service may be
Eph 5 2 an oblation and a sacrifice to God for
Heb 10 5 sacrifice and oblation thou wouldest not
10 by the oblation of the body of Jesus
14 by one o. he hath perfected forever them
18 there is no more an oblation for sin
oblations Lev 2 13 all thy o. thou shalt offer
Lev 7 38 that they should offer their oblations
10 13 and thy sons of the o. of the Lord
23 37 shall offer on them o. to the Lord
Num 18 32 lest you profane the oblations of the
29 39 and voluntary oblations for holocaust
Deut 12 27 shalt offer thy oblations the flesh and
18 1 the sacrifices of the Lord and his o.
1 Es 6 10 let them offer oblations to the God
Ps 50 21 oblations and whole burnt offerings
Eccu 34 23 respect to the oblations of the unjust
Isa 43 23 not caused thee to serve with oblations
1 Ma 15 5 I confirm unto thee all the oblations
Heb 10 8 sacrifices and o. and holocausts for sin
oblige 2 Pa 24 6 to o. the Levites to bring in
2 Ma 6 8 Jews, to oblige them to sacrifice
obliged Exod 22 14 shall be o. to make restitution
2 K 2 22 lest I be obliged to stab thee to the
Prov 16 26 because his mouth hath o. him to it
2 Ma 8 24 Nicanor's army, they o. them to fly
Mat 14 22 Jesus obliged his diciples to go up
Mark 6 45 he o. his disciples to go up into ship
oblique 3 K 6 4 made in the temple o. windows
Eze 41 16 thresholds and the oblique windows
26 upon which were the oblique windows
oblivion Deut 31 21 which no o. shall take away
Jdth 16 23 offered for an anathema of oblivion
Ecce 2 16 shall cover all things together with o.
obols Exod 30 13 sicle hath twenty obols. Lev 27:25; Num 3:47; 18:16; Eze 45:12
Oboth Num 21 10 camped in Oboth. 33:43
Num 33 44 from Oboth they came to Ijeabarim
obscenity Eph 5 4 or o. or foolish talking or
obscure Lev 13 7 if the leprosy be somewhat o.
Lev 13 21 color, and the scar somewhat obscure
26 appearance of the leprosy be somewhat o.
Ps 73 20 they that are the obscure of the earth
104 28 he sent darkness and made it obscure
Prov 22 29 shall not be before those that are o.
Wisd 1 11 obscure speech shall not go for nought
17 3 thought to lie hid in their o. sins
Jer 14 2 and are become obscure on the ground
Dan 5 17 that thou canst interpret o. things
obscureth Wisd 4 12 of vanity o. good things
obscurity Deut 4 11 a cloud and obscurity in it
Prov 7 9 in the darkness and o. of the night
Isa 29 18 out of darkness and obscurity the eyes
32 14 darkness and o. are come upon its dens
Lam 2 1 covered with o. the daughter of Sion
Amos 5 20 and obscurity and no light in it

Soph 1 15 a day of darkness and obscurity, a day
obsequies Gen 23 3 rose up from the funeral o.
observable Exod 12 42 is the o. night of the Lord
observance Exod 12 14 with an everlasting o. Seven
Exod 12 17 by a perpetual o. The first month
13 10 thou shalt keep this observance at
27 21 it shall be a perpetual observance
Lev 7 36 by a perpetual o. in their generations
Num 19 2 this is the observance of the victim
2 Es 12 44 kept . . . the observance of expiation
2 Ma 6 11 reason of the religious o. of the day
1 C 7 19 but the observance of the commandments
observances 1 Pa 23 32 and let them keep the o.
1 Ma 12 11 remember you . . . in our observances
observation Luke 17 20 of God cometh not with o.
observe Gen 17 10 my covenant which you shall o.
Exod 12 17 observe the feast of the unleavened
25 you shall observe these ceremonies
42 this night all . . . must observe in
34 11 observe all things which this day I
Lev 18 4 and shall observe my precepts, and
19 26 you shall not divine nor observe dreams
25 2 observe the rest of the sabbath to
Num 3 7 observe whatsoever appertaineth to the
9 12 they shall observe all the ceremonies
19 10 shall observe this for a holy thing
Deut 4 6 and you shall observe and fulfil them
5 12 observe the day of the sabbath, to
15 thou shouldst observe the sabbath day
6 3 observe to do the things which the
8 1 take great care to observe: that you
11 1 observe his precepts and ceremonies
12 28 observe and hear all the things that
16 1 observe the month of new corn, which is
23 23 out of thy lips, thou shalt observe
24 8 observe diligently that thou incur not
32 46 you shall command your children to o.
Josu 1 7 thou mayst observe and do all the law
8 mayst observe and do all things that
22 5 yet so that you observe attentively
23 6 to observe all things that are written
Judg 13 14 commanded her, let her fulfil and o.
21 11 this is what you shall observe: Every
3 K 2 3 and o. his ceremonies and his precepts
4 K 17 37 you shall observe to do them always
21 8 if they will o. to do all that I have
Tob 1 8 and such like things did he observe
Job 36 11 if they shall hear and observe, they
104 45 that they might o. his justifications
Ecce 8 2 I observe the mouth of the king and
Eccu 4 23 observe the time and fly from evil
37 15 shalt know to observe the fear of God
Isa 42 20 things, wilt thou not observe them
Eze 17 14 but keep his covenant and observe it
20 18 and observe not their judgments nor
19 and observe my judgments and do them
45 21 shall o. the solemnity of the pasch
Jon 2 9 they that are vain observe vanities
1 Ma 2 67 take to you all that observe the law
8 28 shall o. their orders without deceit
13 48 in it men that should observe the law
Mat 23 3 they shall say to you, observe and do
28 20 teaching them to observe all things
Mark 7 4 been delivered to them to observe
Acts 15 5 be commanded to o. the law of Moses
16 21 not lawful for us to receive nor o.
Gal 4 10 you observe days, and months, and times
Phil 3 17 and observe them who walk so as you
1 Tim 5 21 that you observe these things without
Heb 2 1 ought we more diligently to observe the
Apoc 3 3 observe and do penance. If then thou
observed Gen 26 5 and o. my ceremonies and laws
Exod 26 24 the like joining shall be observed for
Deut 33 9 kept thy word and o. thy covenant
1 K 1 12 that Heli observed her mouth. Now
13 14 because thou hast not observed that
4 K 21 6 he used divination and observed omens
2 Pa 33 6 observed dreams, followed divinations
Jdth 16 31 is religiously observed by the Jews
Job 13 27 and hast observed all my paths, and
33 11 stocks: he hath observed all my paths
39 1 hast thou o. the hinds when they fawn
Jer 8 7 have observed the time of their coming
Eze 20 21 nor observed my judgments to do them
Dan 3 30 nor have we observed nor done as thou
1 Ma 1 60 whosoever observed the law of the Lord
2 Ma 6 6 the solemn days of the fathers o.
Mark 10 20 these things I have o. from my youth
observeth Deut 18 10 or observeth dreams and omens
Job 24 15 the eye of the adulterer o. darkness
Prov 10 17 way of life, to him that o. correction
Ecce 11 4 that observeth the wind, shall not sow
observing Lev 8 35 o. the watches of the Lord
Ps 118 9 his way? by observing thy words
Osee 4 10 forsaken the Lord in not o. his law
obstetric Job 26 13 his o. hand brought forth
obstinacy Deut 31 27 I know thy o. and thy most
obstinate Eze 2 4 hard face and of an o. heart
Eze 3 7 of a hard forehead and an o. heart
obtain Num 15 28 and he shall obtain his pardon
Num 32 22 you shall o. the countries that you
2 K 19 38 thou shalt ask of me, thou shalt o.
Tob 6 21 third night thou shalt o. a blessing
22 mayst obtain a blessing in children
Prov 28 13 and forsake them, shall obtain mercy
Eccu 3 4 that loveth God, shall obtain pardon
15 7 but foolish men shall not obtain her
16 8 the ancient giants did not o. pardon
27 9 followest justice, thou shalt o. her
28 5 who shall obtain pardon for his sins
29 15 it shall obtain help for thee against
Isa 35 10 they shall o. joy and gladness. 51:11
Dan 11 6 but she shall not obtain the strength
21 and shall obtain the kingdom by fraud
2 Ma 9 13 of whom he was not like to o. mercy
Mat 5 7 merciful: for they shall obtain mercy
Rom 11 31 that they also may obtain mercy. For God
1 C 9 24 the prize? So run that you may obtain
Gal 5 21 shall not obtain the kingdom of God. But
2 Tim 2 10 that they also may obtain the salvation
Heb 4 16 we may obtain mercy, and find grace in
James 4 2 you kill and envy, and cannot obtain
obtained Gen 29 30 o. the marriage he wished for
Josu 22 9 had o. according to the commandment
Judg 5 11 to the gates and o. the sovereignty
11 24 what the Lord our God hath obtained
Ps 72 12 in the world they have obtained riches
Eccu 49 19 Seth and Sem obtained glory among
50 5 o. glory in his conversation with the
Dan 7 22 and the saints obtained the kingdom
Osee 2 1 your sister: Thou hast obtained mercy
1 Ma 2 57 obtained the throne of an everlasting
Acts 1 17 and had obtained part of this ministry
22 28 I o. the being free of this city with
27 13 thinking that they had o. their purpose
Rom 9 25 that had not obtained mercy, one that
25 one that hath obtained mercy. And it
11 7 Israel sought, he hath not obtained: but
7 but the election hath obtained it; and
30 have o. mercy, through their unbelief
1 C 7 25 obtained mercy of Lord, to be faithful
2 C 1 11 that for this gift obtained for us, by
4 1 according as we have obtained mercy, we
Heb 6 15 so patiently enduring he o. the promise
8 6 he hath obtained a better ministry, by
9 12 having obtained eternal redemption. For

15 we are the good odor of Christ unto God
16 to the one indeed the odor of death unto
16 to the others the odor of life unto life
Eph 5 2 sacrifice to God for an o. of sweetness
Phil 4 18 things you sent, and odor of sweetness
odoriferous 2 Pa 16 14 of spices and o. ointments
odors Lev 26 31 will receive no more your sweet o.
4 K 20 13 the silver and divers precious odors
Isa 39 2 sweet odors and of the precious
Eze 20 28 and there they set their sweet odors
Apoc 5 8 golden vials full of odors, which are
18 13 odors and ointment and frankincense
Odovia 1 Es 2 40 the children of Odovia, 74
Oduia 1 Pa 3 24 the sons of Elioenai, Oduia
1 Pa 9 7 son of Mosollam, the son of Oduia
2 Es 7 44 Josue and Cedmihel, the sons of Oduia
9 5 Oduia, Sebnia, and Phathahia said
10 10 Sebenia, Oduia, Celita, Phalaia
Odullam Josu 12 15 the king of Odullam one
offence Lev 5 3 he shall be guilty of an offence
Lev 5 4 afterwards understandeth his offence
15 he shall offer for his offence a ram
6 4 convicted of the o., he shall restore
6 the estimation and measure of the o.
3 K 15 30 for the offence wherewith he provoked
4 K 23 13 on right side of the Mount of Offence
1 Es 10 19 to offer for their offence a ram
Jdth 5 25 if there be no offence of this people
Prov 15 19 the way of the just is without offence
Eccu 30 13 lest his lewd behavior be an o. to thee
38 10 cleanse thy heart from all offence
41 22 of an offence before a prince and a
Isa 8 14 a rock of offence to the two houses
Bar 3 8 reproach and a curse and an offence
Dan 6 22 before thee, O king, I have done no o.
Acts 24 16 a conscience without o. towards God
Rom 5 15 but not as the offence, so also the gift
15 for if by the offence of one, many died
17 if by one man's offence death reigned
18 as by the offence of one, unto all men
11 11 by their offence, salvation is come to
12 now if offence of them by the riches of
14 20 for that man who eateth with offence. It
1 C 10 32 be without offence to the Jews, and to
2 C 6 3 giving no offence to any man, that our
Phil 1 10 you may be sincere and without offence
Col 2 13 together with him, forgiving you all o.
offences Lev 16 21 all their offences and sins
2 Pa 28 13 and heap up upon our former offences
Tob 3 3 neither remember my offences nor those
Job 13 23 make me know my crimes and offences
14 17 thou hast sealed up my offences as it
Ps 68 6 my offences are not hidden from thee
Eccu 23 3 and my offences be multiplied and my
Eze 5 11 violated my sanctuary with all thy o.
20 26 they offered . . . for their offences
Dan 4 24 perhaps he will forgive thy offences
Mat 6 14 you will forgive men their offences
14 will forgive you also your offences
15 your Father forgive you your offences
Rom 5 16 many offences, unto justification. For
16 17 offences contrary to the doctrine which
Eph 2 1 you were dead in your offences and sins
Col 2 13 with him, forgiving you all offences
offend Lev 4 3 making the people to offend, he
Deut 7 25 anything thereof lest thou offend
1 K 29 7 offend not the eyes of the princes
Ps 33 23 none of them that trust in him shall o.
Ecce 9 18 he that shall offend in one, shall lose
Wisd 12 2 concerning the things wherein they o.
Eccu 7 7 offend not against the multitude of
17 22 the face of the Lord, and offend less
31 20 and exceed not, lest thou offend
Jer 2 3 all they that devour him offend: evils
Osee 4 15 O Israel, at least let not Juda offend
Mat 18 15 if thy brother shall offend against
21 how often shall my brother offend
James 2 10 whole law, but offend in one point
3 2 in many things we all offend. If any
2 if any man offend not in word, the
offended Gen 20 9 what have we offended thee in
Gen 26 35 offended the mind of Isaac and Rebecca
40 1 two eunuchs . . . offended their lord
Exod 32 22 let not my lord be offended: for thou
Lev 5 2 uncleanness, he is guilty and hath o.
Num 5 6 the commandment of the Lord and o.
27 14 because you o. me in the desert of Sin
4 K 17 9 children of Israel offended the Lord
18 14 I have offended, depart from me: and
Jdth 11 8 that our God is so offended with sins
9 of Israel know they have o. their God
Job 33 27 I have sinned, and indeed I have o.
Ps 94 10 was I offended with that generation
118 67 before I was humbled I offended
Eccu 19 17 that hath not offended with his tongue
23 33 she hath offended against her husband
Jer 37 17 in what have I offended against thee
Bar 6 17 upon one that hath offended the king
Eze 25 12 hath greatly offended and hath sought
Zach 12 8 he that hath o. among them in that
Acts 25 8 nor against Caesar, have I o. in any
Rom 14 21 whereby thy brother is o. or scandalized
Heb 3 10 for which cause I was offended with this
17 with whom was he o. forty years? Was
offender Deut 25 2 the o. be worthy of stripes
Job 9 28 knowing that thou didst not spare the o.
Ecce 7 4 the mind of the offender is corrected
offenders 3 K 1 21 shall be counted offenders
offendeth Wisd 15 13 that he o. above all others
Eccu 23 13 if he dissemble it, he o. double
Bar 6 13 cannot put to death one that o. him
offending Lev 4 27 o., and shall come to know
offends Lev 24 22 a stranger, or a native that o.
offerer Lev 7 18 neither shall it profit the o.
offerers Exod 29 33 hands of the offerers may be
offering Exod 36 6 so they ceased from o. gifts
Exod 40 27 o. the holocaust and the sacrifices
Lev 1 2 offering victims of oxen and sheep, if
3 if his offering be a holocaust and of
10 and if the offering be of the flocks
2 1 his offering shall be of fine flour
3 6 the sacrifice of peace o. be of the flock
12 if his offering be a goat, and he offer
5 16 shall pray for him, offering the ram
9 4 o. for the sacrifice of every one of
15 then offering for the sin of the people
10 1 offering before the Lord strange fire
13 victim for a trespass o. pertaineth
21 a lamb for an offering for trespass
16 1 slain upon their offering strange fire
19 5 if ye offer in sacrifice a peace o.
22 18 or offering of his own accord. 21
Num 6 12 offering a lamb of one year for sin
14 for a victim of peace offering, a
17 for a sacrifice of peace offering to the
17 offering at the same time the basket of
7 12 first day Nahasson . . . offered his o.
13 and his offering was a silver dish
17 this was the offering of *N.* 23, 35, 41, 47, 53, 59, 65, 71, 77, 83
18 second day Nathanael . . . made his o.
8 8 for the offering thereof fine flour
9 7 not offer in its season the o. to the
15 3 shall make an offering to the Lord
3 vows, or voluntarily offering gifts
10 for an offering of most sweet savor

25 o. notwithstanding a burnt offering
16 17 offering to the Lord 250 censers: let
18 9 every o. and sacrifice and whatsoever
28 13 and an offering by fire to the Lord
Deut 12 31 offering their sons and daughters
Judg 13 19 upon a rock, offering to the Lord
1 K 7 10 when Samuel was offering the holocaust
13 10 had made an end of o. the holocaust
15 12 Saul was offering a holocaust to the
2 K 6 18 had made an end of offering holocausts
15 12 while he was o. sacrifice, there was
3 K 18 29 the time was come of offering sacrifice
1 Pa 16 2 David had made an end of o. holocausts
2 Pa 8 13 every day an offering might be made
35 14 for the priests were busied in offering
16 in keeping the phase and o. holocausts
1 Es 3 5 in which a free-will offering was made
2 Es 10 34 for the offering of wood, that it
13 31 the offering of wood at times appointed
Tob 1 6 offering faithfully all his firstfruits
Wisd 18 9 were offering sacrifice secretly and
Eccu 30 19 what good shall an o. do to an idol
34 21 the offering of him that sacrificeth
38 11 of fine flour and make a fat offering
47 7 in offering to him a crown of glory
50 15 to honor the o. of the most high King
Isa 66 20 should bring an o. in a clean vessel
Jer 11 17 provoke me, o. sacrifice to Baalim
17 26 they shall bring in an offering
Bar 4 7 o. sacrifice to devils, and not to
Eze 20 31 in the offering of your gifts, when you
40 39 trespass o. might be slain thereon
43 upon the tables was the flesh of the o.
42 13 the offering for sin and for trespass
46 20 priests shall boil . . . the trespass o.
Osee 12 11 in Galgal o. sacrifices with bullocks
Soph 3 10 of my dispersed people bring me an o.
Mala 1 13 and the sick, and brought in an o.
2 12 him that offereth an o. to the Lord
2 Ma 4 24 by offering more than Jason by 300
14 31 that were o. the accustomed sacrifices
Mat 5 24 leave there thy offering before the
Luke 23 36 coming to him, and o. him vinegar, and
Heb 5 7 offering up prayers and supplications
7 27 this he did once, in offering himself
10 11 and often offering the same sacrifices
12 this man offering one sacrifice for sins
James 2 21 o. up Isaac his son upon the altar
burnt offering Exod 29 13 shalt offer a b. o.
Exod 29 18 offer the whole ram for a burnt o.
Lev 21 6 they offer the burnt o. of the Lord
23 13 flour tempered with oil for a burnt o.
Num 15 25 a burnt o. to the Lord for themselves
23 3 stand a while by thy burnt offering
6 found Balac standing by his burnt o.
15 stand here by thy burnt offering while
3 K 18 34 and pour it upon the burnt offering
4 K 3 27 and offered him for a burnt offering
10 25 when the burnt offering was ended
Ps 19 4 thy whole burnt offering be made fat
39 7 burnt o. and sin o. thou didst not
Isa 40 16 beasts thereof sufficient for a b. o.
sin offering Lev 4 8 fat of the calf for the s. o.
Num 6 14 without blemish for a sin offering
16 shall offer both the sin offering and
8 8 another ox of the herd for a sin o.
19 17 of the burning and of the sin o.
28 15 buck goat . . . for a sin o. 29:19
2 Pa 29 24 sin o. should be made for all Israel
1 Es 6 17 for a sin offering for all Israel
2 Es 10 33 for the holy things and for the sin o.
Ps 39 8 sin offering thou didst not require
Eze 40 39 the sin o. and the trespass o. might
45 19 shall take of the blood of the sin o.
25 as well in regard to the sin offering
46 20 where the priests shall boil the sin o.
2 Ma 2 11 because the sin offering was not eaten
offerings Gen 4 4 respect to Abel and to his o.
Gen 4 5 to Cain and his o. he had no respect
35 14 pouring drink offerings upon it, and
Exod 28 38 and sanctified in all their gifts and o.
35 29 dedicated voluntary o. to the Lord
36 3 he delivered all the offerings of the
Lev 2 3 holy of holies of the o. of the Lord. 10
Num 7 84 these were the o. made by the princes
Deut 32 38 drank the wine of their drink offerings
1 K 3 14 not be expiated with victims nor o.
1 Pa 29 9 when they promised their offerings
17 here present offer thee their offerings
Esth 14 17 have not drunk the wine of the drink o.
Ps 15 4 their meetings for blood offerings: nor
118 108 free o. of my mouth make acceptable
Eccu 7 11 high God, he will accept my offerings
14 11 and offer to God worth offerings
35 1 keepeth the law, multiplieth offerings
Isa 19 21 shall worship him with sacrifices and o.
Jer 19 13 poured out drink o. to strange. 32:29
41 5 they had o. and incense in their hand
44 17 pour out drink o. to her. 18, 19, 25
Bar 1 10 make meat o. and o. for sin
6 29 women set offerings before the gods
Eze 20 28 presented the provocation of their o.
Amos 4 5 call free offerings, and proclaim it
Luke 21 4 cast into the o. of God: but she of
Acts 24 17 I came to bring alms . . . and offerings
burnt offerings Exod 10 25 also sacrifices and b. o.
4 K 10 24 to offer sacrifices and burnt offerings
1 Pa 6 49 Aaron and his sons offered burnt o.
Ps 49 8 thy burnt o. are always in my sight
50 18 with b. o. thou wilt not be delighted
21 oblations and whole burnt offerings
65 13 I will go into thy house with burnt o.
15 full of marrow with burnt o. of rams
Jer 7 21 add your burnt o. to your sacrifices
22 concerning the matter of burnt o.
peace offerings Exod 20 24 your holocausts and p. o.
Lev 3 1 if his oblation be a sacrifice of p. o.
3 the sacrifice of p. o. 4:10; 7:11, 20; Num 7:17, 23, 29
9 victim of peace o. 7:18, 29, 32; 22:21
4 26 victims of p. o. 31; 7:34, 37; 10:14; Num 7:35; 15:8; Josu 8:31; 3 K 3:15; 8:63; 9:25; 2 Pa 30:22; 35:13
35 ram that is offered for peace offerings
6 12 the fat of the peace offerings. 3 K 8:64; 2 Pa 7:7
7 13 which is offered for peace offerings
9 4 bullock and a ram for peace offerings
18 the peace offerings of the people
22 the peace offerings being finished, he
17 5 may sacrifice them for peace offerings
23 19 sacrifices of peace o. Num 7:41, 47, 53, 59, 65, 71, 77, 83, 88; 10:10; Josu 22:27
Num 6 18 is under the sacrifice of the peace o.
1 K 13 9 bring me the holocaust and the p. o.
2 K 6 17 holocausts and p. o. 18; 24:25; 1 Pa 16:1, 2; 21:26
4 K 16 13 poured the blood of the peace offerings
2 Pa 29 35 the fat of peace o. and the libations
31 2 for holocausts and for peace offerings
33 16 sacrificed upon it victims and peace o.
Eze 43 27 upon the altar and the peace offerings
45 15 for holocausts and for p. o.
17 the holocaust and the peace offerings
46 2 offer his holocaust and his p. o. 12
12 holocaust or voluntary peace o.

office Gen 40 13 him the cup according to thy o.
Gen 41 13 for I was restored to my office: and he
Exod 1 16 when you shall do the o. of midwives
19 are skilful in the office of a midwife
28 1 may minister to me in the priest's o.
4 they may do the office of priesthood. 41; 30:30
35 vested with it in the o. of his ministry
29 44 to do the o. of priesthood unto me
31 10 that they may execute their office
35 19 to do the office of priesthood to me
Lev 7 35 they might do the office of priesthood
16 32 to do the office of the priesthood
Num 3 4 and Ithamar performed the priestly o.
4 24 the o. of the family of the Gersonites
30 that go in to the o. of their ministry
33 the o. of the family of the Merarites
49 every one according to their office
18 8 and to thy sons for the priestly office
Deut 10 6 succeeded him in the priestly office
20 6 and another man execute his office
1 K 2 13 nor the o. of the priests to the people
36 to somewhat of the priestly office
3 K 14 28 whose office it was to go before him
1 Pa 6 19 he that executed the priestly office
23 26 it shall not be the o. of the Levites
24 2 Ithamar did the o. of the priesthood
25 1 serving in their appointed office
2 Pa 11 14 from executing the priestly office
19 11 matters which belong to the king's o.
29 28 and the trumpeters were in their office
30 21 instruments that agreed to their o.
31 2 every man in his own office, to wit
35 10 and the priests stood in their office
2 Es 12 9 their brethren every one in his office
Eccu 45 19 to execute the office of the priesthood
50 21 and they had finished their office
Eze 44 13 to do the office of priest to me
Osee 4 6 shalt not do the office of priesthood
1 Ma 14 47 to execute o. of the high priesthood
Luke 1 9 the custom of the priestly office
23 days of his office were accomplished
Rom 12 4 but all members have not the same office
2 C 9 12 this o. doth not only supply the want
1 Tim 3 1 if a man desire the office of a bishop
officer Jer 52 25 a scribe, an o. of the army
Mat 5 25 the judge deliver thee to the officer
Acts 4 1 the priests and the o. of the temple
5 24 when the officer of the temple and the
26 went the officer with the ministers
officers Exod 5 15 o. of the children of Israel. 19
Num 2 17 shall be carried by o. of the Levites
31 14 Moses being angry with the chief o.
Deut 1 15 officers over fifties and over tens, who
1 K 19 14 Saul sent officers to seize David
20 so Saul sent officers to take David
3 K 9 23 there were 550 chief officers set over
1 Pa 27 1 and officers, that served the king
28 1 his sons with the officers of the court
2 Pa 9 4 and the attendance of his officers
2 Es 5 15 and their o. also oppressed the people
Jdth 2 2 the governors and his officers of war
7 Holofernes called the captains and o.
7 10 words pleased Holofernes and his o.
10 18 his officers said to him: Who can
Esth 2 2 king's servants and his officers said
Eze 44 11 they shall be officers in my sanctuary
1 Ma 13 37 to write to the king's chief officers
offices Num 7 8 of Merari according to their o.
2 Pa 7 6 and the priests stood in their offices
8 14 the o. of the priests in their ministries
31 16 their o. according to their courses
35 2 and he set the priests in their offices
Esth 16 5 such as observe diligently the offices
2 Ma 4 14 now occupied about the o. of the altar
Heb 9 6 accomplishing the offices of sacrifices
offscouring 1 C 4 13 the o. of all even until now
offspring Gen 46 7 daughters, and all his o.
Num 32 14 increase and offspring of sinful men
Jdth 5 6 people is of the o. of the
Job 5 25 thy offspring like the grass of the
18 19 nor his offspring among his people
20 28 offspring of his house shall be exposed
31 8 and let my offspring be rooted out
Ps 28 1 bring to the Lord the offspring of rams
108 12 none to pity his fatherless offspring
Prov 18 20 offspring of his lips shall fill him
Wisd 3 13 their offspring is cursed: for happy
18 12 noblest offspring of them was destroyed
Eccu 24 46 will not cease to instruct their o.
38 26 whole talk is about the o. of bulls
39 17 hear me, ye divine offspring, and bud
40 15 o. of the ungodly shall not bring forth
47 24 by the roots the offspring of his elect
Isa 14 22 the remains and the bud and the o.
48 19 offspring of thy bowels like the gravel
61 9 their o. in the midst of peoples
Luke 3 7 ye o. of vipers, who hath showed you
Acts 17 28 said: For we are also his offspring
29 being . . . the o. of God, we must not
19 35 great Diana, and of Jupiter's offspring
often Gen 43 5 the man, as we have often said
Exod 10 2 how often I have plagued the Egyptians
4 K 4 8 as he [Eliseus] passed often that way
9 man of God who often passeth by us
21 13 draw the pencil often over the face
Tob 5 8 have often walked through all the ways
Job 16 2 have often heard such things as these
21 17 how often shall the lamp of the wicked
Ps 77 40 how often did they provoke him in the
128 1 often have they fought against me. 2
Ecce 7 23 also hast often spoken evil of others
Eccu 19 15 for there is often a fault committed
20 18 how often and how many will laugh him
Jer 20 8 and I often proclaim devastation: and
1 Ma 14 28 as there have often been wars in our
2 Ma 9 25 whom I often recommended to many of
10 14 often fought against the Jews. And the
12 22 they were often thrown down by their
Mat 9 14 why do we and the Pharisees fast often
17 14 o. into the fire and o. into the water
18 21 how often shall my brother offend
23 37 how o. would I have gathered. Luke 13:34
Mark 5 4 having often been bound with fetters
7 3 eat not without often washing their
Luke 5 33 the disciples of John fast often and
John 18 2 Jesus had often resorted thither
Rom 1 13 I have o. purposed to come unto you, and
1 C 11 25 this do ye, as often as you shall drink
26 for as often as you shall eat this bread
2 C 8 22 brother also, whom we have often proved
11 23 in stripes above measure, in deaths o.
26 in journeying often, in perils of waters
27 in fastings often, in cold and nakedness
Phil 3 18 many walk, of whom I have told you often
2 Tim 1 16 he hath often refreshed me, and hath not
Heb 6 7 rain which cometh often upon it, and
9 25 yet that he should offer himself often
26 he ought to have suffered often from
10 11 and often offering the same sacrifices
Apoc 11 6 with all plagues as often as they will
oftentimes Prov 14 23 many words, there is o. want
1 Ma 16 2 that we have delivered Israel o.
2 Ma 10 13 being oftentimes called traitor
Mark 9 21 o. hath he cast him into the fire
Acts 24 26 for which cause also o. sending for him

26 11 o. punishing them, in every synagogue
Og Deut 3 4 the kingdom of Og in Basan. 10; Josu 13:12, 31
Deut 3 13 and all Basan the kingdom of Og
31 4 to them as he did to Sehon and Og
Josu 2 10 Sehon and Og whom you slew. And
Og king of Basan Num 21 33 O. . . . came against them with all his
Num 32 33 the kingdom of O. . . . and their land
Deut 1 4 O. . . . who abode in Astaroth and in
3 1 and O. . . . came out to meet us with
11 only O. . . . remained of the race of
4 47 possessed his land and land of O. . . .
29 7 and O. . . . came out against us to
Josu 9 10 and O. . . . that was in Astaroth
12 4 the border of O. . . . of the remnant
13 30 all the kingdoms of O. . . . and all the
3 K 4 19 of O. . . . over all that were in that
2 Es 9 22 of Hesebon and the land of O. . . .
Ps 134 11 and O. . . . and all the kingdoms of
135 20 and O. . . . : for his mercy endureth
Oham Josu 10 3 sent to Oham king of Hebron and
Ohol 1 Pa 3 20 Ohol and Barachias and Hasadias
Oholai 1 Pa 2 31 begot Sesan. And Sesan begot O.
Oholi 1 Pa 11 41 Zabad the son of Oholi, Adina
oil Gen 28 18 pouring oil upon the top of it
Gen 35 14 upon it, and pouring oil thereon
Exod 25 6 oil to make lights: spices for ointment
27 20 that they bring thee the purest oil of
29 2 wafers also unleavened anointed with oil
40 part of flour tempered with beaten oil
30 24 of oil of olives the measure hin: and
35 8 oil to maintain lights and to make
14 and the oil for the nourishing of fires
28 and spices and oil for the lights
37 29 he compounded also the oil for the
39 36 and the furniture of them with the oil
Lev 2 1 fine flour, and he shall pour oil upon
2 shall take a handful of the flour and oil
4 unleavened wafers anointed with oil. 7:12
6 little pieces, and pour oil upon it
15 pouring oil upon it and putting on
16 the corn broken small and of the oil
5 11 he shall not put oil upon it nor put
7 12 cakes tempered and mingled with oil
8 11 the laver . . . he sanctified with the oil
10 7 the oil of the holy unction is on you
14 10 for a sacrifice, and sextary of oil. 21
12 trespass offering with the sextary of oil
15 he shall pour of the sextary of oil into
17 and the rest of the oil in his left hand
24 for trespass, and the sextary of oil
26 part of the oil into his own left hand
29 part of the oil that is in his left hand
21 12 the oil of the holy unction of his God
24 2 the finest and clearest oil of olives
Num 4 9 and the snuffers and all the oil vessels
16 the oil to dress the lamps and the sweet
5 15 he shall not pour oil thereon nor put
6 15 wafers without leaven anointed with oil
15 4 with the fourth part of a hin of oil
6 with the third part of a hin of oil
9 flour tempered with half a hin of oil
18 12 all the best of the oil and of the wine
28 5 shall be tempered with the purest oil
35 25 that is anointed with the holy oil
Deut 7 13 thy vintage, thy oil, and thy herds
8 8 land of oil and honey. Where without
11 14 your corn and your wine and your oil
12 17 corn and thy wine and thy oil. 14:23
18 4 firstfruits of corn, of wine, and of oil. 2 Pa 31:5; 2 Es 10:39
28 40 and shalt not be anointed with the oil
51 leave thee no wheat nor wine nor oil
32 13 rock, and oil out of the hardest stone
33 24 and let him dip his foot in oil. His
1 K 10 1 Samuel took a little vial of oil and
16 1 fill thy horn with oil, and come, that
13 then Samuel took the horn of oil and
2 K 1 21 as though . . . not been anointed with oil
6 19 beef, and fine flour fried with oil: and
14 2 and be not anointed with oil, that thou
3 K 1 39 Sadoc the priest took a horn of oil
5 11 and twenty measures of the purest oil
17 12 in a pot, and a little oil in a cruse
14 nor the cruse of oil be diminished
16 and the cruse of oil was not diminished
4 K 4 2 nothing in my house but a little oil
6 I have no more. And the oil stood. And
7 go, sell the oil and pay thy creditor
9 1 this little bottle of oil in thy hand
3 taking the little bottle of oil, thou
6 and he poured the oil upon his head
18 32 a land of olives and oil and honey, and
1 Pa 9 29 of the fine flour and wine and oil
12 40 meal, figs, raisins, wine, oil, and oxen
16 3 roasted beef, and flour fried with oil
27 28 over the oil cellars, Joas. And over
2 Pa 2 10 I will give . . . 20,000 measures of oil
15 and the oil . . . send to thy servants
11 11 provisions, that is, of oil and of wine
32 28 storehouses . . . of wine and of oil, and
1 Es 3 7 meat and drink and oil to the Sidonians
6 9 wheat, salt, wine, and oil, according
7 22 unto a hundred bates of oil and unto
2 Es 5 11 and of the corn, the wine, and the oil
10 37 would bring the firstfruits . . . of oil
13 5 tithes . . . of the wine and of the oil
12 tithe of the corn . . . and the oil
Jdth 10 5 wine to carry, and a vessel of oil and
11 12 consecrated things . . . wine and oil
Esth 2 12 they were anointed with oil of myrrh
Job 29 6 the rock poured me out rivers of oil
Ps 4 8 by the fruit of . . . their wine and oil
22 5 thou hast anointed my head with oil
44 8 anointed thee with the oil of gladness
54 22 his words are smoother than oil, and
88 21 with my holy oil I have anointed him
103 15 he may make the face cheerful with oil
108 18 it went in . . . like oil in his bones
140 5 not oil of the sinner fatten my head
Prov 5 3 throat is smoother than oil. But her
21 20 and oil in the dwelling of the just
27 16 shall call in the oil of his right hand
Ecce 9 8 and let not oil depart from thy head
Cant 1 2 thy name is as oil poured out: therefore
Eccu 39 31 things necessary . . . oil and clothing
45 18 Moses . . . anointed him with holy oil
Isa 1 6 nor dressed nor fomented with oil
10 27 shall putrify at presence of the oil
61 3 the oil of joy for mourning, a garment
Jer 31 12 the corn and wine and oil, and the
40 10 gather ye . . . the oil, and lay it up
41 8 of wheat and barley and oil and honey
Eze 16 9 from thee: and I anointed thee with oil
13 didst eat fine flour and honey and oil
18 settest my oil and my sweet incense
19 and oil and honey wherewith I fed thee
27 17 they set forth balm and honey and oil
32 14 and cause their rivers to run like oil
45 14 the measure of oil also, a bate of oil
24 a hin of oil for every ephi. 46:7
25 holocaust and the sacrifice and the oil
46 11 find: and a hin of oil to every ephi
14 third part of a hin of oil to be mingled
15 and the oil morning by morning

Dan 13 17 bring me oil and washing balls, and
Osee 2 5 that give me my bread . . . my oil and
8 I gave her corn and wine and oil
22 hear the corn and the wine and the oil
12 1 Assyrians, and carried oil into Egypt
Joel 1 10 confounded, the oil hath languished
2 19 I will send you corn and wine and oil
24 presses shall overflow with wine and oil
Mich 6 15 but shalt not be anointed with the oil
Agge 1 11 called for a drought . . . upon the oil
2 13 touch with his skirt . . . wine or oil
Mat 25 3 lamps, did not take oil with them
4 but the wise took oil in their vessels
8 give us of your oil, for our lamps are
Mark 6 13 anointed with oil many that were sick
Luke 7 46 my head with oil thou didst not
10 34 his wounds, pouring in oil and wine
16 6 he said: An hundred barrels of oil
Heb 1 9 anointed thee with the oil of gladness
James 5 14 anointing him with oil in the name of
Apoc 6 6 see thou hurt not the wine and the oil
18 13 wine and oil and fine flour and wheat
oil of unction Exod 29 7 the o. . . . upon his head
Exod 29 21 oil of unction, thou shalt sprinkle
30 25 shalt make the holy oil of unction
31 this oil of unction shall be holy unto
31 11 oil of unction and the incense. 35:15
40 9 thou shalt take the oil of unction and
11 consecrate all with the oil of unction
Lev 8 2 their vestments and the oil of unction
10 he took also the oil of unction with
21 10 the oil of unction hath been poured
Num 4 16 oil of unction and whatever pertaineth
tempered with oil Exod 29 2 and a cake without leaven, tempered with oil
Exod 29 23 and one roll of bread, a cake t. . . .
Lev 2 4 to wit, loaves without leaven t. . . .
5 of flour t. . . . and without leaven. Thou
7 like manner the flour shall be t. . . .
6 21 it shall be t. . . . and shall be fried
7 10 whether they be t. . . . or dry, all the
12 offer loaves without leaven t. . . . and
13 full of flour t. . . . 19, 25, 31, 37, 43, 49, 55, 61, 67, 73, 79
8 26 a loaf without leaven and a cake t. . . .
9 4 of every one of them flour t. . . . ; for
14 10 tenths of flour t. . . . 23:13; Num 28:9, 12, 28; 29:3, 9, 14
21 and a tenth part of flour t. . . . for a
Num 6 15 of unleavened bread tempered with oil
8 8 the offering thereof fine flour t. . . .
11 8 thereof of the taste of bread t. . . .
13 the tenth of a tenth of flour t. . . .
20 tenths of flour which shall be t. . . . to
ointment Exod 25 6 to make lights: spices for o.
Exod 30 25 an o. compounded after the art of the
35 8 to make ointment and most sweet incense
28 for the preparing of ointment and to
37 29 oil for the ointment of sanctification
39 37 the ointment and the incense of spices
Lev 8 30 taking the ointment and the blood that
Jdth 10 3 anointed herself with the best ointment
16 10 she anointed her face with ointment and
Ps 132 2 like the precious ointment on the head
Prov 27 9 ointment and perfumes rejoice the heart
Ecce 10 1 dying flies spoil sweetness of the o.
Isa 39 2 odors and of the precious ointment and
57 9 adorned thyself for the king with o.
Eze 23 41 didst set my incense and my ointment
Dan 10 3 neither was I anointed with ointment
Mat 26 7 an alabaster box of precious ointment
12 she in pouring this o. upon my body
Mark 14 3 alabaster box of ointment. Luke 7:37
4 why was this waste of the ointment
5 this o. might have been sold for more
Luke 7 38 and anointed them with the ointment
46 she with ointment hath anointed my feet
John 11 2 that anointed the Lord with ointment
12 3 took a pound of o. of right spikenard
3 filled with the odor of the ointment
5 why was not this o. sold for 300 pence
Apoc 18 13 odors and ointment and frankincense
ointments 1 K 8 13 to make him ointments and to be
4 K 20 13 and divers precious odors and ointments
1 Pa 9 30 sons of the priests made the ointments
2 Pa 16 14 bed full of spices and odoriferous o.
Esth 14 2 instead of divers precious ointments
Ecce 7 2 good name is better than precious o.
Cant 1 2 smelling sweet of the best ointments
3 after thee to the odor of thy ointments
4 10 sweet smell of thy ointments above all
Wisd 2 7 fill ourselves with costly wine and o.
Eccu 38 7 and shall make up ointments of health
Amos 6 6 and anoint themselves with the best o.
Luke 23 56 they prepared spices and ointments
old Gen 6 4 these are the mighty men of old
Gen 17 12 an infant of eight days old shall be
18 12 after I am grown old, and my lord is an
13 saying: Shall I who am an old woman
19 4 beset the house, both young and old
31 our father is old, and there is no man
24 1 Abraham was old, and advanced in
26 18 the Palestines had of old stopped up
27 1 Isaac was old, and his eyes were dim
2 thou seest that I am old and know not
37 20 let us . . . cast him into some old pit
24 and cast him into an old pit, where
Exod 10 9 we will go with our young and old, with
Lev 25 22 and shall eat of the old fruits until
22 grow up, you shall eat the old store
26 10 shall eat the oldest of the old store
10 coming on, you shall cast away the old
Num 26 62 males from one month old and upward
Josu 6 21 all that were in it . . . young and old
9 4 laying old sacks upon their asses, and
5 very old shoes, which for a show of age
5 patches, and old garments upon them
12 in pieces by being exceeding old
11 10 Asor of old was the head of all these
13 1 Josue was old and far advanced in years
1 thou art grown old and advanced in age
23 1 Josue being now old and far advanced
2 [Josue] said to them: I am old and far
24 2 your fathers dwelt of old on the other
Judg 10 6 adding new sins to their old ones, did
19 22 came and beset the old man's house and
Ruth 1 13 you would be old women before you marry
1 K 2 3 let old matters depart from your mouth
22 Heli was very old, and he heard all
8 1 when Samuel was old, that he appointed
5 thou art old, and thy sons walk not in
12 2 but I [Samuel] am old and grayheaded
24 14 as also it is said in the old proverb
27 8 these were of old the inhabitants of
2 K 20 18 a saying was used in the old proverb
3 K 1 1 now king David was old and advanced in
15 now the king was very old, and Abisag
11 4 when he was now old, his heart was
13 11 a certain old prophet dwelt in Bethel
25 city, wherein that old prophet dwelt
29 it into the city of the old prophet
4 K 4 14 hath no son, and her husband is old
17 34 this day they followed the old manner
41 but did according to their old custom
1 Pa 4 22 now these are things of old. These are
23 1 and David being old and full of days

2 Pa 24 15 Joiada grew old and was full of days
1 Es 4 15 wars were raised therein of old time
19 this city of old time hath rebelled
2 Es 3 6 built the old gate: they covered it and
9 21 their garments did not grow old and
12 38 above the old gate and above the fish
Tob 8 10 us grow old both together in health
Jdth 9 4 for thou hast done the things of old
Job 14 8 if its root be old in the earth, and its
41 23 shall esteem the deep as growing old
Ps 6 8 have grown old amongst all my enemies
31 3 because I was silent, my bones grew old
36 25 I have been young, and now am old: and
92 2 thy throne is prepared from of old
101 27 of them shall grow old like a garment
118 52 I remembered . . . thy judgments of old
138 5 all things, the last and those of old
142 3 as those that have been dead of old
148 12 let the old with the younger, praise
Prov 8 23 and of old before the earth was made
22 6 when he is old he will not depart from
23 22 despise not thy mother when she is old
Ecce 4 13 than a king that is old and foolish
Cant 7 13 and the old . . . I have kept for thee
Eccu 2 6 keep his fear, and grow old therein
8 7 for we also shall become old. Rejoice
9 14 forsake not an old friend, for the new
15 as new wine: it shall grow old, and thou
11 16 glory in evil things, grow old in evil
21 and grow old in the work of thy
Isa 1 26 before, and thy counsellors as of old
20 4 the captivity of Egypt, young and old
22 11 ditch . . . for the water of the old pool
23 7 gloried from of old in her antiquity
25 1 things, thy designs of old faithful
26 3 the old error is passed away: thou
37 26 heard what I have done to him of old
41 26 and from time of old, that we may say
43 18 things, and look not on things of old
48 3 former things of old I have declared
5 I foretold thee of old, before they
7 they are created now, and not of old
8 neither was thy ear opened of old. For
61 4 places that have been waste from of old
Jer 2 20 of old time, thou hast broken my yoke
6 16 see, and ask for the old paths, which
38 11 thence old rags and old rotten things
12 put these old rags and these rent
Lam 3 4 skin and my flesh he hath made old
4 7 more ruddy than the old ivory, fairer
Bar 3 11 art grown old in a strange country
Eze 9 6 utterly destroy old and young, maidens
25 15 destroying and satisfying old enmities
26 20 as places desolate of old, with them
Dan 13 52 thou that art grown old in evil days
1 Ma 3 29 might take away the laws of old times
16 3 now I am old, but be you instead of me
2 Ma 5 13 there was a slaughter of young and old
6 21 for the old friendship they had with
22 for the sake of their old friendship
Mat 5 21 was said to them of old. 27, 33
9 16 cloth unto an old garment. Mark 2:21
17 new wine into old bottles. Mark 2:22; Luke 5:37
13 52 out of his treasure new things and old
Mark 2 21 new piecing taketh away from the old
Luke 5 36 a new garment upon an old garment
36 the new agreeth not with the old
39 no man drinking old, hath presently
39 for he saith: The old is better
12 33 to yourselves bags which grow not old
John 3 4 a man be born again when he is old
21 18 when thou shalt be old, thou shalt
Acts 15 21 Moses of old time hath in every city
21 16 one Mnason a Cyprian, an old disciple
1 C 5 7 purge out the old leaven, that you may
8 let us feast, not with the old leaven
2 C 3 14 veil, in reading of the old testament
5 17 the old things are passed away, behold
12 19 steps? Of old, think you that we excuse
1 Tim 4 7 but avoid foolish and old wives' fables
5 2 old women, as mothers: young women, as
Heb 8 13 a new, he hath made the former old. And
13 decayeth and groweth old, is near its
2 P 1 9 that he was purged from his old sins
1 J 2 7 but an old commandment which you had
7 the old commandment is the word which
Apoc 12 9 dragon was cast out, that old serpent
20 2 laid hold of the dragon the old serpent
days of old Deut 4 32 ask of the days of old
Deut 32 7 remember the days of old, think upon
4 K 19 25 from the days of old I have formed it
Ps 43 2 in their days and in the days of old
76 6 I thought upon the days of old
142 5 I remembered the days of old
Isa 37 26 from the days of old I have formed it
51 9 arise as in the days of old
63 9 lifted them up all the days of old
11 he remembered the days of old of Moses
Jer 46 26 be inhabited as in the days of old
Lam 1 7 which she had from the days of old
2 17 which he commanded in the days of old
Eze 38 17 of whom I have spoken in the d. . . .
Amos 9 11 I will rebuild it as in the d. . . .
Mich 7 14 Basan and Galaad according to d. . . .
20 sworn to our fathers from the d. . . .
Mala 3 4 shall please the Lord, as in the d. . . .
old age; *see* **age**
old man Gen 18 12 and my lord is an old man
Gen 43 27 is the old man your father in health
44 20 we have a father an old man, and a
46 5 Pharao had sent to carry the old man
48 2 and it was told the old man [Jacob]
Judg 19 16 they saw an old man returning out of
17 the old man lifting up his eyes, saw
20 the old man answered him: Peace be
23 the old man went out to them and said
1 K 2 31 not be an old man in thy house. 32
4 18 for he [Heli] was an old man
17 12 was an old man in the days of Saul
28 14 she said: An old man cometh up, and he
2 Pa 36 17 old man or even him that stooped for
Eccu 25 4 an old man that is a fool and doting
Isa 65 20 nor an old man that shall not fill up
Jer 51 22 I will break in pieces the old man
Lam 2 21 the child and the old man lie without
2 Ma 6 1 king sent a certain old man of Antioch
Luke 1 18 for I am an old man, and my wife is
Rom 6 6 knowing this, that our old man is
Eph 4 22 the old man, who is corrupted according
Col 3 9 stripping yourselves of the old man
Philem 9 as Paul an old man, and now a prisoner
old men 3 K 12 6 took counsel with the old men
3 K 12 8 but he left the counsel of the old men
13 leaving the counsel of the old men
Job 29 8 and the old men rose up and stood
Prov 17 6 children's children are crown of old men
20 29 dignity of old men, their gray hairs
Eccu 25 8 experience is the crown of old men
Jer 31 13 the young men and old men together
Dan 13 8 the old men saw her going in every day
16 was nobody there but the two old men
27 after the old men had spoken, the
50 the old men said to him: Come and sit
Joel 1 2 hear this, ye old men, and give ear
2 28 your old men shall dream dreams, and

Zach 8 4 shall yet old men and old women dwell
1 Ma 2 9 her old men are murdered in the streets
Acts 2 17 and your old men shall dream dreams
year old Exod 29 38 two lambs of a year old every
Lev 9 3 calf and a lamb, both of a year old
12 6 a lamb of a year old for a holocaust
14 10 ewe of a year old without blemish
Num 6 14 one he lamb of a year old without
14 one ewe lamb of a year old without
7 15 a lamb of a year old for a holocaust. 21, 27, 33, 39, 45, 51, 57, 63, 69, 75, 81
17 five lambs of a year old. 23, 29, 35, 41, 47, 53, 59, 65, 71, 77, 83
87 twelve lambs of a year old and their
88 goats sixty, lambs of a year old sixty
15 27 he shall offer a she goat of a year old
28 3 two lambs of a year old without. 9
11 seven lambs of a year old. 19, 27; 29:2, 8, 36
29 13 and fourteen lambs of a year old. 17, 20, 23, 26, 29, 32
Mich 6 6 unto him and calves of a year old
years old Gen 5 31 Noe, when he was 500 y. o.
Gen 7 6 he [Noe] was 600 years old when the
11 10 Sem was 100 years old when he begot
12 4 Abram was 75 years old when he went
15 9 take me a cow of three years old and
16 16 Abram was fourscore and six years old
17 1 began to be ninety and nine years old
17 be born to him that is 100 years old
17 shall Sara that is 90 years old bring
24 Abraham was ninety and nine years old
25 Ismael his son was full 13 years old
21 5 when he was a hundred years old: for
25 20 when he [Isaac] was forty years old
26 Isaac was threescore years old when
26 34 Esau being forty years old, married
37 2 Joseph, when he was sixteen years old
41 46 was 30 years old when he stood before
50 25 he [Joseph] died being 110 years old
Exod 7 7 Moses was eighty years old, and Aaron
38 25 from 20 years old and upward. Num 1:3, 18, 20, 22, 24, 26, 28, 30, 32, 34, 36, 38, 40, 42, 45; 14:29; 25:4; 26:2; 32:11; 1 Pa 23:27; 2 Pa 25:5
Lev 27 2 if it be a man from 20 years old unto 60 years old
7 a man that is 60 years old or upward
Num 4 3 from 30 years old and upward. 23, 30, 35, 39, 43, 47
3 from thirty . . . to fifty years old
8 24 from 25 years old and upwards
33 39 when he [Aaron] was 123 years old
Deut 31 2 I am this day 120 years old, I can
34 7 Moses was 120 years old when he died
Josu 14 7 I was forty years old when Moses the
10 this day I am eighty-five years old
24 29 died, being 110 years old. Judg 2:8
1 K 4 15 Heli was 98 years old and his eyes
2 K 2 10 was 40 years old when he began to
4 4 he was 5 years old when the tidings
5 4 David was 30 years old when he began
19 32 fourscore years old, and he provided
35 I am this day fourscore years old, are
3 K 14 21 Roboam was one and forty years old
22 42 he [Josaphat] was 5 and 30 years old
4 K 8 17 he [Joram] was 2 and 30 years old when
26 Ochozias was 2 and 20 years old when
11 21 Joas was seven years old when he began
14 2 he [Amasias] was 5 and 20 years old
21 took Azarias, who was 16 years old
15 2 he [Azarias] was 16 years old when he
33 he [Joatham] was 5 and 20 years old
16 2 Achaz was 20 years old when he began
18 2 [Ezechias] was 5 and 20 years old when
21 1 Manasses was 12 years old when he
1 Pa 2 21 wife when he was threescore years old
23 24 house of the Lord from 20 years old
27 23 not number them from 20 years old and
2 Pa 12 13 [Roboam] was one and forty years old
20 31 he was five and thirty years old when
21 5 Joram was two and thirty years old
20 he was two and thirty years old when
22 2 Ochozias was forty-two years old when
24 1 Joas was seven years old when he began
15 died when he was 130 years old
25 1 Amasias was five and twenty years old
26 1 son Ozias who was sixteen years old
3 Ozias was sixteen years old when he
27 1 Joatham was 5 and 20 years old when he
8 [Joatham] was five and twenty years old
28 1 Achaz was twenty years old when he
29 1 he [Ezechias] was five and 20 years old
31 16 males from three years old and upward
Isa 15 5 unto Segor a heifer of three years old
65 20 child shall die a hundred years old
Mat 2 16 from two years old and under, according
Mark 5 42 walked: and she was twelve years old
Luke 2 42 when he was 12 years old, they going
8 42 daughter almost twelve years old
John 8 57 thou art not yet fifty years old, and
Acts 4 22 the man was above forty years old
7 23 when he was full forty years old, it
Rom 4 19 whereas he was almost an 100 years old
Olda 2 Pa 34 22 went to Olda the prophetess
oldest Lev 26 10 eat the o. of the old store
oldness Rom 7 6 not in the oldness of the letter. What
olive Deut 24 20 gathered the fruit of thy o. trees
Deut 28 40 thou shalt have olive trees in all thy
2 Es 8 15 mount, and fetch branches of olive
Ps 127 3 thy children as olive plants round
Bar 6 42 sit in the ways, burning o. stones
Amos 4 9 your olive groves and fig groves
Zach 4 3 and two olive trees over it: one upon
11 what are these two olive trees upon the
12 what are the two olive branches that
Rom 11 17 being wild olive, art ingrafted in them
Apoc 11 4 these are the two olive trees and the
olive tree Gen 8 11 carrying a bough of an o. t.
Judg 9 8 they said to the olive tree: Reign thou
3 K 6 23 in the oracle two cherubims of o. t.
31 he made little doors of olive tree
32 and two doors of olive tree: and he
33 temple posts of olive tree foursquare
Job 15 33 an olive tree that casteth its flower
Ps 51 10 a fruitful olive tree in house of God
Eccu 24 19 as a fair olive tree in the plains
50 11 as an olive tree budding forth and
Isa 17 6 and as the shaking of the olive tree
24 13 should be shaken out of the olive tree
41 19 and the myrtle and the olive tree
Jer 11 16 thy name, a plentiful olive tree
Osee 14 7 his glory shall be as the olive tree
Haba 3 17 the labor of the olive tree shall fail
Agge 2 20 and the olive tree as yet flourished
Rom 11 17 and of the fatness of the olive tree
24 if thou wert cut out of wild olive tree
24 were grafted into the good olive tree
24 be grafted into their own olive tree
olives Exod 27 20 thee the purest oil of the o.
Exod 30 24 of oil of olives the measure hin: and
Lev 24 2 the finest and clearest oil of olives
Deut 28 40 the olives shall fall off and perish
4 K 18 32 a land of olives and oil and honey
Isa 24 13 as if a few olives, that remain
Mich 6 15 thou shalt tread the olives, but shalt
Zach 14 4 shall stand . . . upon the mount of O.

34 17 malice: my only one from the lions
Prov 4 3 as an only son in the sight of my mother
Jer 6 26 make thee mourning as for an only son
Dan 3 45 thou art the Lord the only God
Amos 8 10 make it as the mourning of an only son
Zach 12 10 as one mourneth for an only son, and
Mat 4 10 adore, and him only shalt thou serve
21 19 found nothing on it but leaves only
Mark 2 7 who can forgive sins but God only
4 17 but are only for a time; and then when
6 5 only that he cured a few that were
8 nothing for the way, but a staff only
9 7 any more, but Jesus only with them
Luke 4 8 God, and him only shalt thou serve
7 12 the only son of his mother; and she
8 42 he had an only daughter, almost
9 38 upon my son, because he is my only one
John 1 14 of the only begotten of the Father
18 the only begotten Son who is in the
3 16 as to give his only begotten Son
18 name of the only begotten Son of God
12 9 they came not for Jesus' sake only
17 3 they may know thee, the only true God
Acts 11 19 the word to none, but to the Jews only
18 25 Jesus, knowing only baptism of John
21 25 they should only refrain themselves from
24 21 except it be for this one voice only
27 22 life among you, but only of the ship
Rom 3 29 is he the God of the Jews only? Is he
4 9 doth it remain in the circumcision only
12 not to them o., that are of circumcision
16 27 to God the only wise, through Jesus
Phil 4 16 giving and receiving, but you only: for
1 Tim 1 17 the only God, be honor and glory for
6 15 who is the Blessed and only Mighty, the
16 lords; who only hath immortality, and
Heb 11 17 offered up his only begotten son; to
1 J 4 9 God hath sent his only begotten Son
Jude 4 denying the only sovereign Ruler, and
25 to the only God our Savior through
Ono 1 Pa 8 12 who built Ono and Lod and its
1 Es 2 33 the children of Lod, Hadid, and Ono
2 Es 6 2 in the villages, in the plain of Ono
7 37 children of . . . Hadid and Ono, 721
11 35 and Ono the valley of craftsmen
onset Josu 10 42 he took and wasted at one onset
2 K 23 8 who killed 800 men at one onset
onycha Exod 30 34 spices, stacte and onycha
onyx Gen 2 12 found bdellium and the o. stone
Exod 27 7 onyx stones and precious stones. 35:9
28 9 and thou shalt take two onyx stones
35 27 the princes offered onyx stones and
39 6 he prepared also two onyx stones, fast
1 Pa 29 2 onyx stones and stones like alabaster
Eccu 24 21 galbanum and onyx and aloes and as
Eze 28 13 thy covering . . . onyx and the beryl
Ooliab Exod 31 6 given him for his companion O.
Exod 36 1 Beseleel and Ooliab . . . made the
38 23 having for his companion Ooliab
Ooliba Eze 23 4 Ooliba her younger sister
Eze 23 4 Samaria is Oolla, and Jerusalem is O.
11 when her sister Ooliba saw this, she
22 Ooliba, thus saith the Lord God: Behold
36 dost thou judge Oolla and Ooliba, and
44 so went they in unto Oolla and Ooliba
Oolibama Gen 36 2 Esau took wives . . . Oolibama
Gen 36 5 Oolibama bore Jehus and Ihelon and
14 and these were the sons of Oolibama
18 the sons of Oolibama the wife of Esau
18 these are the dukes of Oolibama, the
25 a son Dison and a daughter Oolibama
41 dukes of Esau . . . duke Oolibama
1 Pa 1 52 dukes in Edom . . . duke Oolibama

Oolla Eze 23 4 Oolla the elder, and Ooliba
Eze 23 4 Samaria is O., and Jerusalem is Ooliba
5 Oolla committed fornication against me
36 dost thou judge Oolla and Ooliba
44 so went they in unto Oolla and Ooliba
open Gen 19 9 point of breaking open the doors
Exod 21 33 if a man open a pit and dig one and
22 2 a thief be found breaking open a house
Lev 20 18 and she open the fountain of her blood
Num 8 16 of the firstborn that open every womb
20 6 open to them thy treasure, a fountain
Deut 15 8 but shalt open it to the poor man
11 to open thy hand to thy needy and poor
20 11 if they receive it and open the gates
28 12 Lord will open his excellent treasure
Josu 8 17 leaving the towns open as they had
10 22 open the mouth of the cave and bring
2 K 22 16 foundations of the world were laid o.
3 K 8 29 thy eyes may be open upon this house
52 that thy eyes may be open to the
4 K 6 17 Lord, open his eyes, that he may see
20 open the eyes of these men, that they
9 3 thou shalt open the door and flee
13 17 and said: Open the window to the east
15 16 because they would not open to him
19 16 hear: open, O Lord, thy eyes and see
1 Pa 9 27 when it was time, they might open the
2 Pa 6 20 thou mayest open thy eyes upon this
40 let thy eyes, I beseech thee, be open
7 15 my eyes also shall be open and my ears
18 9 they sat in the open court by the gate
2 Es 1 6 ears be attentive, and thy eyes open
13 19 not open them till after the sabbath
Jdth 13 13 open the gates for God is with us, who
14 10 no man durst knock or open and go into
Job 11 5 and would open his lips to thee, that
12 14 up a man, there is none that can open
14 3 meet to open thy eyes upon such an one
27 19 shall open his eyes and find nothing
31 32 my door was open to the traveller. If
32 20 I will open my lips and will answer
34 26 them, as being wicked, in open sight
36 10 also shall open their ear, to correct
15 and shall open his ear in affliction
41 5 who can open the doors of his face
Ps 5 11 their throat is an o. sepulcher. 13:3
48 5 I will open my proposition on the
50 17 O Lord, thou wilt open my lips: and
77 2 I will open my mouth in parables: I
80 11 open thy mouth wide, and I will fill it
117 19 open ye to me the gates of justice
118 18 open thou my eyes: and I will consider
Prov 13 16 that is a fool, layeth open his folly
16 2 the ways of a man are open to his eyes
3 lay open thy works to the Lord: and
20 13 open thy eyes and be filled with bread
24 7 in the gate he shall not open his mouth
25 28 as a city that lieth open and is not
26 26 his malice shall be laid open in the
27 5 open rebuke is better than hidden love
19 hearts of men are laid open to the wise
25 the meadows are open, and the green
31 8 open thy mouth for the dumb, and for
9 open thy mouth, decree that which is
Cant 5 2 open to me, my sister, my love, my
5 I arose up to open to my beloved: my
Eccu 8 22 open not thy heart to every man: lest
15 15 she shall open his mouth and shall
24 2 shall open her mouth in the churches
26 15 she will open her mouth as a thirsty
15 open her quiver against every arrow
29 30 deal confidently, nor open his mouth
31 12 be not the first to open thy mouth

39 7 he will open his mouth in prayer and
Isa 9 12 shall devour Israel with open mouth
22 22 shall open, and none shall shut: and he shall shut, and none shall open
26 2 open ye the gates and let the just
28 24 shall be open and harrow his ground
37 17 open, O Lord, thy eyes, and see, and
41 18 I will open rivers in the high hills
42 20 thou that hast ears open, wilt thou
45 1 and to open the doors before him and
51 14 come that is going to open unto you
53 7 will, and he shall not open his mouth
57 8 hast loved their bed with open hand
59 15 from evil, lay open to be a prey: and
60 11 thy gates shall be open continually
Jer 5 16 their quiver is as an open sepulcher
13 19 and there is none to open them: all
20 12 for to thee I have laid open my cause
32 14 sealed up, and this deed that is open
19 whose eyes are open upon all the ways
50 26 open that they may go forth that shall
Bar 2 17 open thy eyes, and behold: for the
Lam 2 14 they have not laid open thy iniquity
Eze 2 8 open thy mouth, and eat what I give
3 27 I will open thy mouth, and thou shalt
16 57 before thy malice was laid open: as it
63 and mayest no more open thy mouth
21 22 to open the mouth in slaughter, to lift
25 9 I will open the shoulder of Moab from
29 21 I will give thee an open mouth in the
32 4 will cast thee away into the open field
37 12 I will open your graves and will bring
Dan 3 33 and now we cannot open our mouths
9 18 open thy eyes and see our desolation
Osee 2 10 I will lay open her folly in the eyes
Amos 8 5 sabbath, and we shall open the corn
Mich 2 13 that shall open the way before them
Nah 3 13 shall be set wide open to thy enemies
Zach 11 1 open thy gates, O Libanus, and let
12 4 I will open my eyes upon the house of
13 1 there shall be a fountain open to the
Mala 3 10 if I open not unto the flood-gates
1 Ma 3 48 they laid open the books of the law
5 48 foot. But they would not open to them
2 Ma 1 4 may he open your heart in his law
6 18 was pressed to open his mouth to eat
14 41 to break open the door and to set fire
Mat 13 35 I will open my mouth in parables
24 43 his house to be broken open. Luke 12:39
25 11 Lord, open to us. Luke 13:25
Luke 12 36 they may open to him immediately
John 9 26 how did he open thy eyes? He answered
10 21 can a devil open the eyes of the blind
Acts 16 27 seeing the doors of the prison open
18 14 Paul was beginning to open his mouth
19 38 courts of justice are open, and there
26 18 to open their eyes, that they may be
Rom 3 13 their throat is an open sepulcher; with
2 C 3 18 the glory of the Lord with open face
6 11 our mouth is o. to you, O ye Corinthians
Eph 6 19 that I may open my mouth with confidence
Col 2 15 exposed them confidently in open show
4 3 God may open unto us a door of speech
Heb 4 13 all things are naked and o. to his eyes
Apoc 3 20 my voice, and open to me the door, I
5 2 who is worthy to open the book and to
3 to open the book nor to look on it
4 worthy to open the book nor to see it
5 hath prevailed to open the book and to
9 to take the book and to open the seals
10 2 he had in his hand a little book open
8 take the book that is open, from the

opened Gen 3 5 your eyes shall be opened: and
Gen 3 7 and the eyes of them both were opened
4 11 earth, which hath opened her mouth
7 11 the flood gates of heaven were opened
21 19 God opened her eyes: and she saw a well
29 31 opened her womb, but her sister
30 22 heard her [Rachel] and opened her womb
41 56 Joseph opened all the barns and sold
43 21 opened our sacks and found our money
44 11 every man opened his sack. Which when
Exod 2 6 she opened it and seeing within it an
Num 22 28 the Lord opened the mouth of the ass
31 the Lord opened the eyes of Balaam
24 4 that falleth, and so his eyes are o.
16 who falling hath his eyes opened: I
Judg 3 26 and seeing that no man opened the door
4 19 opened a bottle of milk and gave him
11 35 for I have opened my mouth to the Lord
36 if thou hast o. thy mouth to the Lord
15 19 then the Lord opened a great tooth
16 18 now he hath opened his heart to me
19 27 the men arose and opened the door that
1 K 3 15 o. the doors of the house of the Lord
3 K 6 34 double, and so o. with folding leaves
4 K 4 35 child gaped . . . and opened his eyes
6 17 Lord opened the eyes of the servant
20 Lord opened their eyes, and they saw
9 10 he opened the door and fled. Then Jehu
13 17 when he had opened it, Eliseus said
2 Pa 29 3 he o. the doors of the house of the
2 Es 7 3 let not the gates of Jerusalem be o.
8 5 Esdras opened the book before all the
5 when he had o. it, all the people stood
Tob 11 8 that his eyes shall be presently opened
Jdth 5 12 God of heaven opened the sea to them
Job 3 1 Job o. his mouth and cursed his day
16 11 they have opened their mouths upon me
29 19 my root is opened beside the waters
23 o. their mouth as for a latter shower
30 11 he hath opened his quiver and hath
14 as when a wall is broken and a gate o.
33 2 behold now I have opened my mouth
38 17 have the gates of death been opened
Ps 7 16 he hath opened a pit and dug it: and
21 14 they have opened their mouths against
34 21 they opened their mouth wide against
38 10 I was dumb, and I opened not my mouth
77 23 and had opened the doors of heaven
104 41 he opened the rock, and the waters flowed
105 17 earth opened and swallowed up Dathan
108 2 of the deceitful man is opened against
118 131 I opened my mouth and panted: because
Prov 8 6 my lips shall be o. to preach right
31 20 she hath opened her hand to the needy
26 she hath opened her mouth to wisdom
Cant 5 6 I opened the bolt of my door to my
Wisd 10 21 wisdom opened the mouth of the dumb
Eccu 22 27 if thou hast opened a sad mouth, fear
43 15 through this are the treasures opened
51 33 I have opened my mouth and have spoken
Isa 5 14 hath hell . . . opened her mouth without
10 14 moved the wing or opened the mouth or
14 17 opened not the prison to his prisoners
24 18 flood-gates from on high are opened
35 5 shall the eyes of the blind be opened
45 8 let the earth be opened and bud forth
48 8 neither was thy ear opened of old. For
50 5 the Lord God hath opened my ear, and
53 7 he opened not his mouth: he shall be
57 4 upon whom have you opened your mouth
Jer 39 2 the city was opened. And all the
50 25 the Lord hath opened his armory, and
Lam 2 16 have opened their mouth against thee
3 46 our enemies have opened their mouths

Eze 1 1 the heavens were opened and I saw the
3 2 I opened my mouth, and he caused me to
20 26 they offered all that opened the womb
24 27 thy mouth be opened to him that hath
33 22 he opened my mouth till he came to me
22 my mouth being opened, I was silent
37 13 when I shall have o. your sepulchers
44 2 it shall not be opened, and no man
46 1 on the sabbath day it shall be opened
1 the day of the new moon it shall be o.
12 shall be opened to him, and he shall
Dan 7 10 and the books were opened. I beheld
10 17 then I opened my mouth and spoke and
13 25 to the door of the orchard and o. it
14 17 as soon as he had opened the door, the
Nah 2 6 the gates of the rivers are opened
1 Ma 3 28 he opened his treasury and gave out
10 76 opened the gates to him [Jonathan]: so
11 2 they opened to him the cities and met
Mat 3 16 lo, the heavens were opened to him
7 7 knock and it shall be o. Luke 11:9
8 knocketh, it shall be o. Luke 11:10
9 30 their eyes were opened. Luke 24:31
17 26 when thou hast opened its mouth, thou
20 33 Lord, that our eyes be opened. And
27 52 the graves were opened: and many bodies
Mark 1 10 he saw the heavens opened and the
7 34 ephpheta, which is, Be thou opened
35 his ears were opened, and the string
Luke 1 64 immediately his mouth was opened, and
3 21 heaven was opened; and the Holy Ghost
24 32 way, and opened to us the scriptures
45 then he opened their understanding
John 1 51 you shall see the heaven opened and
9 10 how were thy eyes opened? He answered
14 made the clay and opened his eyes
17 of him that hath opened thy eyes? and
21 who hath opened his eyes, we know not
30 he is, and he hath opened my eyes
32 hath opened the eyes of one born blind
11 37 could not he that opened the eyes of
19 34 with a spear opened his side, and
Acts 7 55 I see the heavens opened, and the Son
9 8 when his eyes were o., he saw nothing
40 she opened her eyes; and seeing Peter
10 11 the heaven opened, and a certain vessel
12 10 city, which of itself opened to them
14 voice, she opened not the gate for joy
16 when they had opened they saw him
14 26 had o. door of faith to the Gentiles
16 14 whose heart the Lord opened to attend
26 immediately all the doors were o., and
1 C 16 9 a great door and evident is o. unto me
2 C 2 12 door was opened unto me in the Lord, I
Apoc 3 8 I have given before thee a door opened
4 1 a door was opened in heaven, and the
5 8 when he had opened the book, the four
6 1 had opened one of the seven seals and
3 when he had opened the . . . seal. 5, 7, 9, 12; 8:1
9 2 and he opened the bottomless pit: and
11 19 the temple of God was opened in heaven
12 16 earth opened her mouth and swallowed
13 6 he opened his mouth unto blasphemies
15 5 the temple . . . in heaven was opened
19 11 I saw heaven opened, and behold a white
20 12 throne, and the books were opened; and
12 another book was opened, which is the

openest Ps 103 28 when thou o. thy hand, they
Ps 144 16 thou openest thy hand, and fillest

openeth Exod 13 2 that o. the womb. 12, 15; 34:19; Num 3:12
Job 33 16 then he openeth the ears of men and
35 16 therefore Job openeth his mouth in vain
Prov 20 19 deceitfully, and openeth wide his lips
Eccu 40 14 while he o. his hands he shall rejoice
Jer 22 14 who openeth to himself windows, and
John 10 3 to him the porter openeth; and the
Acts 8 32 shearer, so openeth he not his mouth
Apoc 3 7 he that openeth, and no man shutteth
7 shutteth, and no man openeth: I know

opening Gen 8 6 opening the window of the ark
Gen 8 13 Noe opening the covering of the ark
42 27 one of them opening his sack, to give
Num 16 30 if . . . the earth o. her mouth swallow
32 earth . . . opening her mouth, devoured
26 10 earth o. her mouth swallowed. Deut 11:6
Judg 3 25 opening, they found their lord lying
16 17 opening the truth of the thing, he said
Tob 13 1 Tobias the elder opening his mouth
Ps 37 14 as a dumb man not opening his mouth
Eccu 20 15 o. of his mouth is kindling of a fire
Dan 3 25 o. his mouth in the midst of the fire
6 10 o. the windows in his upper chamber
13 39 and opening the doors he leaped out
Osee 2 15 valley of Achor for an opening of hope
Zach 14 4 to the west with a very great opening
2 Ma 1 16 o. a secret entrance of the temple
Mat 2 11 opening their treasures, they offered
5 2 opening his mouth, he taught them
Mark 2 4 opening it, they let down the bed
Luke 2 23 every male opening the womb shall be
Acts 5 19 opening the doors of the prison, and
22 opening the prison, found them not
23 but opening it, we found no man within
8 35 then Philip, opening his mouth and
10 34 Peter opening his mouth, said: In every

openly Lev 19 17 reprove him o. lest thou incur
Eccu 51 18 I sought for wisdom o. in my prayer
2 Ma 6 10 when they had openly led about through
Mark 1 45 he could not openly go into the city
8 32 he spoke the word openly. And Peter
John 7 4 himself seeketh to be known openly
10 not openly, but as it were in secret
13 no man spoke openly of him for fear
26 he speaketh o., and they say nothing
11 54 Jesus walked no more openly among the
18 20 I have spoken openly to the world: I
Acts 18 28 he convinced the Jews openly, showing
Rom 10 20 I appeared openly to them that asked not

operation Eph 1 19 the operation of the might of his power
Eph 3 7 according to the operation of his power
4 16 operation in the measure of every part
Phil 3 21 operation whereby also he is able to
Col 2 12 again by the faith of the o. of God
2 Th 2 10 shall send them the operation of error

operations Ps 27 5 Lord and the o. of his hands
1 C 12 6 there are diversities of operations, but

Ophaz Jer 10 9 from Tharsis, and gold from O.

Ophel 2 Pa 27 3 on the wall of Ophel he built
2 Pa 33 14 of the fish gate round about to Ophel
2 Es 3 26 and the Nathinites dwelt in Ophel
11 21 the Nathinites, that dwelt in Ophel

Opher Gen 25 4 of Madian was born Epha and O.
Josu 12 17 of Taphau one, the king of Opher one
4 K 14 25 who was of Geth, which is in Opher

Ophera Josu 18 23 Avim and Aphara and Ophera

Ophi Jer 40 8 to Masphath . . . the children of O.

Ophim Gen 46 21 sons of Benjamin: . . . Ophim and

ophiomachus Lev 11 22 you shall eat . . . the o.

Ophir Gen 10 29 Jectan begot . . . O. 1 Pa 1:23
3 K 9 28 they came to Ophir and they brought
10 11 which brought gold from O., brought from O. great plenty of thyine
22 49 to sail into Ophir for gold: but they
1 Pa 29 4 talents of gold of the gold of Ophir

2 Pa 8 18 went with Solomon's servants to Ophir
9 10 brought gold from Ophir, and thyine
Ophlal 1 Pa 2 37 Zabad begot O., and O. begot Obed
Ophni Josu 18 24 the town Emona and Ophni and
1 K 1 3 sons of Heli, Ophni and Phinees
2 34 upon thy two sons, Ophni and Phinees
4 4 Ophni and Phinees, were with the ark
11 two sons of Heli, Ophni and Phinees
17 sons, Ophni and Phinees, are dead
Ophra 1 Pa 4 14 Maonathi begot Ophra, and
opinion Exod 23 2 to opinion of the most part
Job 32 6 I was afraid to show you my opinion
Eccu 41 20 do not please all men in opinion
Mat 17 24 what is thy opinion, Simon? The kings
Luke 3 15 as the people were of opinion, and
10 36 which of these three, in thy opinion
opinions Job 13 4 and maintainers of perverse o.
opportunities 2 Ma 9 25 and borderers wait for o.
opportunity Eccu 8 6 and o. for every business
Eccu 12 16 if he find an opportunity he will not
19 25 if he shall find opportunity to do evil
20 7 hold his peace till he see opportunity
26 13 lest finding an o. she abuse herself
1 Ma 11 42 and thy nation when o. shall serve
15 34 we having o. claim the inheritance of
2 Ma 14 29 watched an o. to comply with the orders
Mat 26 16 he sought o. to betray him. Luke 22:6
oppose Judg 18 7 having no man at all to o. them
Jdth 16 8 nor tall giants o. themselves to him
Isa 59 16 because there is none to oppose himself
2 Ma 14 29 but because he could not o. the king
opposed 1 K 15 2 he [Amalec] o. them in the way
opposeth 2 Th 2 4 who o., and lifted up above
opposite Lev 26 28 against you with opposite fury
Josu 15 7 which is o. to the ascent of Adommin
2 Es 12 37 choir . . . went on the opposite side
Job 7 20 why hast thou set me opposite to thee
Eccu 23 15 is also another speech o. to death
opposition Judg 11 20 and made strong opposition
Esth 13 4 violated by their o. the concord of all
Haba 1 3 is a judgment, but o. is more powerful
2 Ma 3 4 strove in opposition to the high priest
Heb 12 3 endured such opposition from sinners
oppositions 1 Tim 6 20 oppositions of knowledge falsely
oppress Gen 41 36 which shall oppress Egypt
Gen 44 34 calamity that will oppress my father
Exod 1 10 let us wisely oppress them lest they
22 25 nor oppress them with usuries. If thou
Lev 19 13 neighbor nor oppress him by violence
25 39 shalt not oppress him with the service
46 oppress not your brethren the children
Deut 21 14 for money nor oppress her by might
28 53 wherewith thy enemy shall o. thee. 57
Judg 10 12 and Amalec and Chanaan oppress you
Job 10 3 thou shouldst calumniate me and o. me
19 3 and are not ashamed to oppress me. For
27 20 a tempest shall o. him in the night
Ps 88 43 up the right hand of them that o. him
Prov 20 13 love not sleep, lest poverty o. thee
22 22 do not oppress the needy in the gate
28 16 prince void of prudence shall o. many
Wisd 2 10 let us oppress the poor just man, and
Eccu 36 11 let them perish that o. thy people
Isa 10 2 to oppress the poor in judgment and
24 12 and a calamity shall oppress the gates
58 6 undo the bundles that oppress, let
Jer 7 6 if you oppress not the stranger, the
22 3 nor oppress them unjustly: and shed
13 that will o. his friend without cause
Amos 4 1 you that oppress the needy and crush
Zach 7 10 o. not the widow and the fatherless
Mala 3 5 that oppress the hireling in his wages
5 o. the stranger and have not feared
2 Ma 1 28 punish them that oppress us and that
9 2 the temple, and to oppress the city
Luke 11 53 to oppress his mouth about many things
James 2 6 do not the rich oppress you by might
oppressed Gen 41 56 the famine had o. them also
Gen 47 13 and a famine had oppressed the land
Exod 1 12 the more they oppressed them, the more
3 9 affliction wherewith they are oppressed
5 9 let them be oppressed with works, and
6 5 wherewith the Egyptians have o. them
Deut 28 29 be oppressed with violence and mayst
Judg 2 16 from the hands of those that o. them
4 3 for 20 years had grievously o. them
6 2 and they were grievously o. by them
10 8 grievously oppressed for 18 years
1 K 12 3 if I [Samuel] have oppressed any man
4 hast not wronged us nor oppressed us
22 2 that were in distress and o. with debt
2 K 21 5 man that crushed us and o. us unjustly
4 K 13 4 because the king of Syria had o. them
1 Pa 4 10 save me from being oppressed by evil
2 Pa 10 4 thy father oppressed us with a most
2 Es 1 15 and their officers also o. the people
Jdth 5 10 when the king of Egypt oppressed them
Job 12 21 relieveth them that were oppressed
16 8 but now my sorrow hath oppressed me
20 10 his children shall be oppressed with
23 4 have o. together the meek of the earth
6 whom by violence they have oppressed
Prov 11 27 after evil things shall be o. by them
Wisd 10 14 and power against those that o. him
15 from the nations that o. them. She
Isa 1 17 seek judgment, relieve the oppressed
23 12 daughter of Sidon, who art oppressed
51 23 the hand of them that have o. thee
52 4 the Assyrian hath o. them without any
Jer 21 12 him that is oppressed by violence out
50 33 the children of Juda are o. together
Lam 1 4 and she is oppressed with bitterness
5 11 they oppressed the women in Sion, and
Eze 18 18 because he o. and offered violence
22 7 they have o. the stranger in the midst
11 the brother hath oppressed his sister
12 and hast covetously o. thy neighbors
29 they o. the stranger by calumny without
Mich 2 2 and oppressed a man and his house
1 Ma 8 18 saw that they o. the kingdom of Israel
Acts 10 38 healing all that were o. by the devil
20 9 being oppressed with a deep sleep, as
2 P 2 7 Lot, o. by the injustice and lewd
oppresseth Prov 14 31 o. the poor, upbraideth his
Prov 22 16 he that o. the poor to increase his
28 3 a poor man that o. the poor is like a
oppressing Eccu 4 35 o. them that are under thee
Dan 13 53 o. the innocent, and letting the guilty
Amos 5 12 and oppressing the poor in the gate
oppression Lev 6 2 extort anything or commit o.
Deut 28 33 and mayst thou always suffer oppression
Eccu 7 8 oppression troubleth the wise, and
51 6 from the oppression of the flame which
Isa 30 12 have trusted in oppression and tumult
33 15 that casteth away avarice by oppression
54 14 depart far from oppression, for thou
Jer 6 6 all oppression is in the midst of her
22 17 upon o. and running after evil works
Bar 6 53 nor deliver countries from oppression
Eze 22 29 the people of the land have used o.
Osee 5 11 Ephraim is under oppression, and
12 7 he hath loved oppression. And Ephraim
Amos 3 9 them that suffer o. in the inner rooms
oppressions Ecce 4 1 I saw the o. that are done
Ecce 5 7 shalt see the oppressions of the poor
Eccu 30 9 oppressions . . . created for the wicked

oppressor Job 3 18 not heard the voice of the o.
Ps 71 4 and he shall humble the oppressor
Isa 9 4 the scepter of their oppressor thou
14 4 how is the oppressor come to nothing
19 20 shall cry to the Lord because of the
51 13 where is now the fury of the oppressor
Jer 21 12 out of the hand of the oppressor. 22:3
Lam 1 5 captivity: before the face of the o.
Zach 9 8 the o. shall no more pass through them
oppressors Judg 2 18 from the slaughter of the o.
Job 35 9 by reason of the multitude of o. they
Isa 3 12 their oppressors have stripped them
14 2 and shall subdue their oppressors
opprobrious Eccu 23 20 is accustomed to o. words
oracle Exod 25 18 on the two sides of the oracle
Exod 25 20 their wings and covering the oracle
37 6 the propitiatory, that is, the oracle
40 18 bars underneath and the oracle above
Lev 16 2 I will appear in a cloud over the o.
13 vapor thereof may cover the oracle
15 may sprinkle it over against the oracle
Num 7 89 of the covenant to consult the oracle
2 K 21 1 David consulted the oracle of the Lord
3 K 6 5 round about the temple and the oracle
16 made the inner house of the oracle
17 temple itself before doors of the o.
19 made the o. in the midst of the house
20 the oracle was twenty cubits in length
21 the house before the oracle he overlaid
22 altar of the oracle he covered also
23 he made in the oracle two cherubims
31 in the entrance of the oracle he made
7 49 candlesticks . . . over against the o.
8 6 into the oracle of the temple, into
8 in the sanctuary before the oracle
2 Pa 3 16 as it were little chains in the oracle
4 20 lamps to give light before the oracle
5 7 that is, to the oracle of the temple
9 longer, were seen before the oracle
Eze 21 33 as one consulting the oracle in vain
oration Acts 12 21 [Herod] made an oration to them
orator Acts 24 1 ancients, and one Tertullus an o.
oratory Jdth 9 1 Judith went into her oratory
orchard Cant 4 13 with the fruits of the orchard
Dan 13 4 had an orchard near his house: and the
7 and walked in her husband's orchard
15 was desirous to wash herself in the o.
17 and shut the doors of the orchard, that
18 and they shut the doors of the orchard
20 the doors of the orchard are shut and
25 ran to the door of the orchard and
26 heard the cry in the orchard, they
36 as we walked in the orchard alone, this
36 shut the doors of the orchard and sent
38 we that were in a corner of the o.
orchards Ecce 2 5 I made gardens and orchards
Jer 29 5 plant orchards and eat the fruit of
ordain Num 9 8 what he will o. concerning you
1 C 11 17 now this I ordain: not praising you
Titus 1 5 shouldst ordain priests in every city
ordained Num 19 2 which the Lord hath ordained
Deut 15 5 keep all things that he hath ordained
3 K 12 33 o. a feast to the children of Israel
Ps 80 6 he o. it for a testimony in Joseph
Eccu 7 16 husbandry ordained by the most High
1 Ma 7 49 he ordained that this day should be
13 52 he o. that these days should be kept
2 Ma 10 8 they ordained by a common statute and
11 25 we have ordained and decreed that the
15 36 all ordained by a common decree, by no
Acts 13 48 as many as were o. to life everlasting
14 22 when they had o. to them priests in
Rom 7 10 commandment that was ordained to life
13 1 those that are, are ordained of God
1 C 2 7 which God ordained before the world
9 14 the Lord o. that they who preach the
2 C 8 19 he was also ordained by the churches
Gal 3 19 o. by angels in the hand of a mediator
Heb 5 1 is ordained for men in the things that
order Gen 22 9 laid the wood in order upon it
Gen 41 28 which shall be fulfilled in this order
45 27 told the whole order of the thing
Exod 27 21 Aaron and his sons shall order it
28 10 according to the order of their birth
40 21 setting there in order the loaves of
23 placing the lamps in order according
Lev 1 7 having before laid in order a pile of
8 lay the parts that are cut out in order
Num 7 5 according to the o. of their ministry
8 26 thus shalt thou order the Levites
10 28 this was the order of the camps and
Deut 15 2 which shall be celebrated in this o.
Judg 5 20 the stars remaining in their order and
2 K 17 23 putting his house in order, hanged
3 K 10 5 the order of his ministers and their
18 33 he laid the wood in order, and cut the
4 K 12 5 priests take it according to their o.
7 money no more according to your order
23 4 and the priests of the second order
1 Pa 6 32 according to their o. in the ministry
2 Pa 8 14 appointed according to order of David
14 Levites in their order to give praise
13 10 and the Levites are in their order
30 16 they stood in their order according
35 15 sons of Asaph stood in their order
2 Es 4 13 behind the wall round about in order
11 23 order among the singing men day by day
12 24 of God, and to wait equally in order
Tob 5 27 doth order all things well that are
Jdth 15 4 they went without order in their flight
Esth 1 6 placed in order upon a floor paved
15 9 she passed through all the doors in o.
Job 10 22 the shadow of death and no order
38 33 dost thou know the order of heaven
37 can declare the o. of the heavens
Ps 109 4 according to the order of Melchisedech
111 5 he shall order his words with judgment
Cant 2 4 he set in order charity in me. Stay
Wisd 7 29 and above all the order of the stars
8 14 I shall set the people in order: and
9 3 that he should o. the world according
Eccu 33 13 in his hand, to fashion and order it
38 10 from sin and order thy hands aright
47 12 set in order the solemn times even to
Isa 5 17 lambs shall feed according to their o.
38 1 take order with thy house, for thou
44 7 and let him set before me the order
54 11 behold I will lay thy stones in order
Jer 7 5 if you will order well your ways and
30 18 shall be founded according to the order
31 35 the order of the moon and of the stars
41 17 in order to go forward and enter into
48 12 shall order and overturn his bottles
Eze 43 11 all its order and all its laws, and
1 Ma 5 15 with strangers in order to consume us
6 45 horsemen set in order were chosen for
57 to take order for the affairs of the
9 55 nor give order concerning his house
2 Ma 3 14 Heliodorus entered in to o. this matter
5 3 horses set in order by ranks, running
8 in order for his destruction, flying
Luke 1 1 to set forth in order a narration of
3 to write to thee in order, most
8 in the order of his course before God
Acts 8 2 took order for Stephen's funeral and
11 4 declared to them the matter in order

18 23 in order, confirming all the disciples
1 C 11 34 rest I will set in order, when I come
14 40 be done decently, and according to order
15 23 but every one in his own order: the
16 1 have given o. to the churches of Galatia
Col 2 5 rejoicing, and beholding your order
Titus 1 5 thou shouldest set in order the things
Heb 5 6 according to the order of Melchisedech. 10; 6:20; 7:11, 17
7 11 called according to the order of Aaron
ordered Gen 45 22 he o. also to be brought out
Josu 6 15 went about the city, as it was ordered
8 32 which he had ordered before the
Judg 7 8 he o. all the rest of the multitude
1 K 30 21 ordered them to abide at the torrent
1 Pa 19 5 ordered them to stay at Jericho till
1 Es 7 21 I Artaxerxes the king have ordered
Tob 8 11 Raguel o. his servants to be called
Jdth 12 1 then he ordered that she should go in
Prov 16 24 well ordered words are as a honeycomb
Wisd 11 21 hast ordered all things in measure and
18 9 unanimously ordered a law of justice
Eccu 33 9 he ordered the seasons and holidays
Isa 38 21 Isaias had o. that they should take
Dan 1 18 had ordered they should be brought in
1 Ma 10 11 he ordered workmen to build the walls
11 2 Alexander had ordered them to go forth
13 17 he ordered the money and the children
2 Ma 14 22 Judas ordered men to be ready in
Heb 9 6 now these things being thus ordered
orderest Wisd 12 15 thou o. all things justly
ordereth Wisd 8 1 and o. all things sweetly
ordering Prov 24 6 war is managed by due o.
Wisd 15 1 and ordering all things in mercy
Eccu 33 14 all his ways are according to his o.
1 Ma 16 14 care for the good ordering of them
orderly 1 Es 3 4 the holocaust every day o.
1 Ma 6 40 they marched on warily and orderly
orders Gen 12 20 and Pharao gave his men orders
Gen 45 17 he should give orders to his brethren
19 give orders also that they take wagons
47 4 we pray thee to give orders that we
Exod 25 22 thence will I give orders and will
Lev 13 54 he shall give orders, and they shall
Num 8 2 give orders therefore that the lamps
Josu 9 27 he gave orders in that day that they
10 22 Josue gave o. saying: Open the mouth
1 K 16 16 let our lord give o., and thy servants
3 K 5 6 give orders therefore that thy servants
1 Pa 21 6 Joab unwillingly executed king's orders
2 Pa 5 11 courses and orders of the ministries
7 13 if I give orders and command the locust
30 6 according to the king's orders: Ye
1 Es 3 7 according to the orders which Cyrus
4 21 till further orders be given by me
10 4 it is thy part to give orders, and we
Jdth 7 1 gave orders to his army, to go up
Esth 8 3 would give orders that the malice of
Ps 102 20 hearkening to the voice of his orders
Dan 2 15 that had received the o. of the king
24 given orders to destroy the wise men
1 Ma 3 39 destroy it according to the king's o.
42 knew the orders the king had given
6 23 to do according to his orders and obey
8 26 they shall obey their orders without
28 shall observe their o. without deceit
2 Ma 3 13 by reason of the o. he had received
11 20 I have given orders by word both to
14 29 opportunity to comply with the orders
Mat 8 18 gave orders to pass over the water
ordinance Exod 29 9 by a perpetual o. Num 18:19; 19:10
Lev 6 18 it shall be an ordinance everlasting
16 29 shall be to you an everlasting ordinance
34 shall be an o. forever. 17:7; Num 10:8
23 21 it shall be an everlasting ordinance. 31, 41; Num 18:23
Num 9 14 same o. shall be with you both for
10 21 this precept shall be an ordinance
31 21 this is the ordinance of the law
35 29 for an ordinance in all your dwellings
1 K 30 25 was made a statute and an ordinance
2 Pa 8 13 according to the ordinance of Moses
13 11 made according to the o. of the law
Esth 2 8 when the king's ordinance was noised
Ps 118 91 by thy ordinance the day goeth on
Eccu 38 38 and the o. of judgment they shall not
Isa 24 5 the laws, they have changed the o.
Jer 5 22 for the sea, an everlasting ordinance
Eze 46 14 a sacrifice to the Lord by ordinance
Rom 13 2 power, resisteth the ordinance of God
ordinances Exod 15 25 there he appointed him o.
Lev 10 11 teach the children of Israel all my o.
18 3 nor shall you walk in their ordinances
26 keep ye my ordinances and my
Num 18 8 the priestly office, by everlasting o.
Deut 6 24 that we should do all these ordinances
3 K 9 4 wilt keep my o. and my judgments
4 K 17 15 they rejected his ordinances and the
26 know not the ordinances of the God of
27 let him teach them the ordinances of
2 Es 10 32 we made o. for ourselves, to give the
Esth 3 8 moreover despise the king's ordinances
Jer 31 36 if these ordinances shall fail before
Eze 43 11 plan thereof and all its ordinances
11 form thereof and its o. and do them
44 8 have not kept the o. of my sanctuary
24 they shall keep my laws and my o. in
Zach 1 6 my o., which I gave in charge to my
Mala 3 7 you have departed from my ordinances
14 profit is it that we have kept his o.
1 Ma 1 14 to do after the o. of the heathens
2 Ma 4 11 disannulled the lawful o. of the
16 followed earnestly their ordinances
6 23 according to the o. of the holy law
8 17 their destroying the o. of the fathers
1 C 11 2 keep my ordinances as I have delivered
ordinary Lev 15 25 many days out of her o. time
Eccu 33 10 he put in the number of ordinary days
Oreb Judg 7 25 two men of Madian, Oreb and Zeb
Judg 7 25 Oreb they slew in the rock of Oreb
25 carrying the heads of Oreb and Zeb
8 3 the princes of Madian, Oreb and Zeb
Ps 82 12 make their princes like Oreb and Zeb
Isa 10 26 slaughter of Madian in the rock of Oreb
organ Job 21 12 rejoice at the sound of the o.
Job 30 31 my o. into the voice of those that weep
organs Gen 4 21 play upon the harp and the organs
2 Pa 5 13 and voice and cymbals and organs
Ps 150 4 praise him with strings and organs
Orient Zach 3 8 I will bring my servant the Orient
Zach 6 12 behold a man, the Orient is his name
Luke 1 78 the Orient from on high hath visited us
Orientals 3 K 4 30 surpassed wisdom of all the O.
origin Wisd 6 24 wisdom is and what was her o.
Dan 2 41 it shall take its origin from the iron
2 Ma 7 23 and that found out the origin of all
original 2 P 2 5 and spared not the original world
Orion Job 9 9 maketh Arcturus and O. Amos 5:8
ornament Eccu 21 24 is as an ornament of gold
Eccu 26 21 good wife for the ornament of her house
32 3 receive a crown as an o. of grace
45 14 Holiness, an ornament of honor
Isa 49 18 clothed with all these as with an o.
Jer 2 32 will a virgin forget her ornament
Eze 8 20 have turned the o. of their jewels
16 7 and camest to woman's ornament: they

20 3 he saw others standing in the market
6 went out and found others standing
21 8 others cut boughs from. Mark 11:8
26 67 others struck his face with the palms
27 42 he saved others. Mark 15:31; Luke 23:35
49 the others said: Let be, let us see
Mark 4 18 others there are who are sown among
6 15 others said: It is Elias. But others
8 28 but some Elias, and others as one of
12 5 many others, of whom some they beat
5 some they beat, and others they killed
9 and will give the vineyard to others
Luke 5 29 company of publicans and of others
8 3 many others who ministered unto him
9 8 by others, that one of the old
19 others say that one of the former
11 16 others tempting, asked of him a sign
18 9 as just, and despised others, he
20 16 and will give the vineyard to others
John 4 38 others have labored, and you have
7 12 others said: No, but he seduceth the
41 others said: This is the Christ. But
9 9 others said: No, but he is like him
16 others said: How can a man that is a
10 8 all others, as many as have come, are
21 others said: These are not the words
12 29 others said: An angel spoke to him
18 34 or have others told it thee of me
19 18 crucified him, and with him two others
21 2 and two others of his disciples. Simon
Acts 2 13 others mocking, said: These men are
15 2 certain o. of the other side, should
35 and preaching, with many others, the
17 18 would say? But others: He seemeth to
32 others said: We will hear thee again
1 C 9 2 and if unto others I be not an apostle
12 if others be partakers of this power
27 when I have preached to others, I myself
14 19 that I may instruct others also; than
2 C 2 16 to the others the odor of life unto life
8 8 by the carefulness of others, approving
13 I mean not that others should be eased
Phil 2 3 but in humility, let each esteem others
1 Th 2 6 glory of men, neither of you, nor of o.
4 12 even as others who have no hope. For
5 6 let us not sleep, as others do; but let
1 Tim 6 18 to give easily, to communicate to others
2 Tim 2 2 who shall be fit to teach others also
Heb 7 20 the others indeed were made priests
23 others indeed were made many priests
8 4 there would be others to offer gifts
9 25 every year with the blood of others: for
11 35 others were racked, not accepting
36 others had trial of mockeries and
Jude 23 others save, pulling them out of the
23 on others have mercy, in fear, hating
otherwise Deut 18 14 thou art o. instructed by
1 K 20 9 I could do no otherwise than tell thee
25 34 otherwise as the Lord liveth the God of
29 4 how can he otherwise appease his master
3 K 1 21 o. it shall come to pass . . . that I
22 20 words of this manner, and another o.
2 Pa 18 19 spoke in this manner, and another o.
30 18 ate the phase o. than it is written
Wisd 8 21 that I could not otherwise be continent
Eze 20 9 I did otherwise for my name's sake
1 Ma 14 45 whosoever shall do otherwise or shall
2 Ma 5 18 o. had they not been involved in
Mat 6 1 o. you shall not have a reward of your
9 17 o. the bottles break, and the wine
Mark 2 21 o. the new piecing taketh away from
22 o. the wine will burst the bottles, and
Luke 5 36 otherwise he doth rendeth the new
37 otherwise the new wine will break the
John 14 12 o. believe for the very works' sake
Acts 13 9 Saul, otherwise Paul, filled with Holy
Rom 3 6 otherwise how shall God judge this world
11 6 works: otherwise grace is no more grace
22 otherwise thou also shalt be cut off
1 C 5 10 o. you must needs go out of this world
7 14 o. your children should be unclean; but
15 29 o. what shall they do that are baptized
2 C 11 16 otherwise take me as one foolish, that
Phil 3 15 if in anything you be otherwise minded
1 Tim 1 3 charge some not to teach otherwise, not
5 25 they that are otherwise cannot be hid
6 3 if any man teach otherwise, and consent
Heb 9 17 otherwise it is as yet of no strength
Othir 1 Pa 25 4 sons of Heman . . . Othir
1 Pa 25 28 one and twentieth [lot] to Othir
Othni 1 Pa 26 7 sons of Semeias were Othni
Otholia 1 Pa 8 26 and Otholia . . . sons of Jeroham
Othoniel Josu 15 17 O. the son of Cenez. Judg 1:13; 3:9, 11
1 Pa 4 13 the sons of Cenez were Othoniel and
13 the sons of Othoniel, Hethath and
ought Josu 6 18 lest you touch ought of those
1 K 12 4 nor taken ought at any man's hand
25 7 neither was there ought missing to
2 K 14 10 if any one shall say ought against
23 5 ought thereof that springeth not up
ounces 2 K 21 16 iron of whose spear weighed 300 o.
outcast Ps 21 7 and the outcast of the people
Jer 30 17 have called thee, O Sion, an outcast
Lam 3 45 thou hast made me as an outcast
outcasts Isa 27 13 were o. in the land of Egypt
outgoings Josu 17 9 the o. of it are at the sea
Josu 18 14 outgoings thereof are into Cariathbaal
19 outgoings thereof are towards the north
19 14 the o. thereof are valley of Jephtahel
22 the o. thereof shall be at the Jordan
29 outgoings thereof shall be at the sea
33 their outgoings unto the Jordan
Ps 64 9 the outgoings of the morning and of
outmost Exod 28 32 made in the o. parts of garments
outrageous 2 Ma 4 4 that Apollonius . . . was o.
outrages Wisd 2 19 let us examine him by outrages
outrun John 20 4 that other disciple did outrun Peter
outside Gen 7 16 the Lord shut him in on the o.
Gen 37 23 stript him of his outside coat that
Lev 13 55 leprosy has taken hold of the outside
3 K 6 6 and he put beams . . . on the outside
2 Pa 4 3 and certain engravings on the outside
24 8 set it by the gate . . . on the outside
Jer 32 11 the seals that were on the outside
Eze 40 5 was a wall on the outside of the house
Mat 23 25 make clean the outside. Luke 11:39
26 that the outside may become clean
outstretched Jer 21 5 with an o. hand and with
outward Num 35 4 from the walls of the cities o.
2 Pa 5 9 but if a man were a little outward
2 Es 11 16 over all the o. business of the house
Eze 40 40 on the outward side, which goeth up
42 7 the outward wall that went about by
10 in the breadth of the outward wall of
44 1 of the gate of the outward sanctuary
47 2 to the way without the outward gate
2 C 4 16 though our outward man is corrupted, yet
10 7 the things that are according to outward
1 P 3 3 not be the o. plaiting of the hair or
outward court; *see* **court**
outwardly Mat 23 27 o. appear to men beautiful
Mat 23 28 you also o. indeed appear to men just
Rom 2 28 not he is a Jew, who is so outwardly
28 circumcision which is outwardly in flesh
outwards Eze 41 6 they bore o. that they might

oven Lev 2 4 sacrifice baked in the oven
Lev 7 9 of flour that is baked in the oven
26 26 shall bake your bread in one oven
Ps 20 10 thou shalt make them as an oven of fire
Lam 5 10 our skin was burnt as an oven, by
Osee 7 4 like an oven heated by the baker: the
6 have applied their heart like an oven
7 they were all heated like an oven and
Mat 6 30 tomorrow is cast into the oven
ovens Exod 8 3 into thy ovens and into the
over 2 K 11 27 mourning being over, David sent
Eccu 3 24 be not over curious, and in many
Mat 5 37 that which is over and above these
25 20 have gained other five over and above
Luke 10 35 thou shalt spend over and above, I
John 6 13 remained over and above to them that
2 C 8 15 he that had much, had nothing over; and
overcame Exod 17 11 lifted up his hands, Israel o.
Exod 17 11 if he let them down a little, Amalec o.
1 K 14 47 withersoever he turned himself he o.
2 Pa 27 5 children of Ammon and overcame them
Jdth 1 5 fought against Arphaxad and o. him
4 12 remember Moses . . . who overcame Amalec
5 16 their God fought for them and overcame
Wisd 16 10 of venemous serpents o. thy children
18 22 he o. the disturbance, not by strength
Apoc 12 11 they overcame him by the blood of the
overcharged Exod 1 14 wherewith they were o.
Jdth 13 2 they were all overcharged with wine
Luke 21 34 your hearts be o. with surfeiting
overcome Gen 25 23 one people shall o. the other
Gen 32 25 saw that he could not overcome him
Exod 1 10 having overcome us, depart out of
24 24 they shall overcome the Assyrians
31 7 the Madianites, and had overcome them
Judg 16 5 how we may be able to o. him [Samson]
1 K 2 4 the bow of the mighty is overcome and
2 K 10 19 kings . . . seeing themselves o. by Israel
3 K 20 23 therefore they have overcome us: but
23 in the plains, and we shall o. them
25 thou shalt see that we shall o. them
4 K 16 5 but were not able to o. him [Achaz]
1 Pa 19 19 of Adarezer saw themselves o. by Israel
2 Pa 6 24 if thy people Israel be o. by their
25 8 God will make thee to be overcome by
Jdth 6 13 when he should o. the children
7 9 that thou mayst overcome them without
16 16 and no one can overcome thee
Job 36 18 let not anger o. thee to oppress
50 6 and mayst o. when thou art judged
Wisd 7 30 but no evil can overcome wisdom
10 12 a strong conflict, that he might o.
Eccu 48 14 no word could overcome him [Elias]
Isa 8 9 be o. and give ear, all ye lands afar
9 be o., gird yourselves, and be o.
9 4 scepter of their oppressor thou hast o.
Dan 11 22 arms of the fighter shall be overcome
23 and shall overcome with a small people
2 Ma 3 5 when he could not overcome Onias, he
10 24 who before had been o. by the Jews
11 13 that the Hebrews could not be o.
12 11 rest of the Arabians being overcome
13 23 he fought with Judas, and was o.
Luke 11 22 come upon him and overcome him; he
John 16 33 confidence, I have overcome the world
Rom 3 4 and mayest o. when thou art judged. But
8 37 but in all these things we overcome
12 21 be not o. by evil, but o. evil by good
2 P 2 19 by whom a man is o., of the same also
20 they be again entangled in them and o.
1 J 2 13 you have overcome the wicked one. 14
4 4 you are of God . . . and have o. him
Apoc 2 11 he that shall o. 26; 3:5, 12; 21:7
3 21 to him that shall o., I will give to
21 as I also have o. and am set down with
11 7 shall o. them and kill them. And their
13 7 war with the saints and to overcome
15 2 that had o. the beast and his image
17 14 the Lamb shall o. them because he is
overcometh 1 J 5 4 is born of God, o. the world
1 J 5 4 victory which o. the world, our faith
5 who is he that o. the world, but he
Apoc 2 7 to him that o., I will give. 17
overcoming Num 21 1 o. them carried off their
overdriven Gen 33 13 if I should cause to be o.
overflow Ecce 1 7 yet the sea doth not overflow
Isa 8 7 and shall overflow all his banks and
10 22 the consumption abridged shall o. with
28 17 waters shall overflow its protection
Joel 2 24 presses shall o. with wine and oil
overflowed Gen 7 6 waters of the flood o. 10
Gen 7 18 they overflowed exceedingly: and filled
Ps 77 20 waters gushed out and the streams o.
Eccu 39 27 his blessing hath o. like a river
Osee 4 2 killing and theft and adultery have o.
2 P 3 6 being overflowed with water, perished
overfloweth Prov 15 28 the wicked o. with evils
overflowing Job 3 24 as o. waters, so is my
Job 22 11 covered with the violence of o. waters
Prov 18 4 fountain of wisdom as an o. stream
Isa 8 8 shall pass through Juda, overflowing
17 13 like the noise of waters overflowing
28 2 as the violence of many waters o.
15 when the o. scourge shall pass. 18
30 28 his breath as a torrent overflowing
66 12 as an o. torrent the glory of the
Jer 47 2 shall be as an overflowing torrent
Eze 13 11 there shall be an overflowing shower
13 shall be an o. shower in my anger
overflowings 2 K 22 16 the o. of the sea appeared
overlaid Exod 26 32 also shall be o. with gold
Exod 36 34 he overlaid with gold, casting for. 36
37 1 overlaid it with the purest gold. 26
4 setim wood, which he o. with gold
11 o. it with the finest gold. 3 K 10:15
15 overlaid them with gold. 3 K 6:32
28 and overlaid them with plates of gold
38 2 he overlaid it with plates of brass
6 overlaid them with plates of brass
17 he overlaid the pillars of the court
28 which also he overlaid with silver
3 K 3 19 for in her sleep she overlaid him
6 20 covered and o. it with most pure gold
21 he o. with most pure gold and
28 he overlaid the cherubims with gold
30 the floor . . . he o. with gold within
35 he overlaid all with golden plates
2 Pa 3 4 he overlaid it within with pure gold
5 o. them with plates of fine gold
7 plates with which he o. the house
8 he overlaid it with plates of gold
9 upper chambers also he o. with gold
10 work, and he overlaid them with gold
9 17 of ivory, and o. it with pure gold
overlay Exod 25 11 shalt overlay it with the purest gold. 24; 30:3
Exod 25 13 shalt o. them with gold. 28; 30:5
26 29 thou shalt overlay with gold and
37 shalt overlay with gold five pillars
1 Pa 29 4 silver, to o. the walls of the temple
overlook Eccu 28 9 o. the ignorance of thy neighbor
overlookest Wisd 11 24 o. the sins of men for the
overmaster Eccu 12 6 lest thereby he o. thee
overmuch Deut 28 56 down her foot for o. niceness
Ecce 7 18 be not overmuch wicked: and be not
2 C 2 7 be swallowed up with overmuch sorrow

overpass Eccu 14 14 part of a good gift o. thee
overplus Lev 25 27 the o. he shall restore to
overpower Eccu 43 24 heat that cometh, shall o. it
overpowered Judg 4 24 o. Jabin king of Chanaan
2 K 13 14 o. her [Thamar] and lay with her
Wisd 2 3 the sun and o. with the heat thereof
Jer 52 6 a famine overpowered the city: and
overreach 2 C 12 17 did I overreach you by any of them
2 C 12 18 did Titus overreach you? Did we not walk
1 Th 4 6 that no man overreach, nor circumvent
overreached Wisd 10 11 deceit of them that o. him
2 C 2 11 that we be not o. by Satan. For we are
7 2 no man, we have overreached no man. I
oversee 2 Pa 2 2 and 3,600 to oversee them
1 Ma 3 32 to oversee the affairs of the kingdom
overseer 1 Pa 9 31 o. of such things as were fried
2 Pa 31 12 the overseer of them was Chonenias
14 o. of the things which were freely
2 Es 11 22 overseer of the Levites in Jerusalem
12 41 loud, and Jezraia was their overseer
Esth 2 3 the o. and keeper of the king's women
2 Ma 3 4 who was appointed o. of the temple
overseers Gen 41 34 that he may appoint o.
Exod 5 6 he commanded the same day the o.
10 o. of the works and the taskmasters
13 overseers of the works pressed them
3 K 5 16 besides the overseers who were over
9 22 overseers of the chariots and horses
4 K 10 5 o. of the house and the rulers of the
22 5 given to the workmen by the o. 9
1 Pa 23 4 and 6,000 were overseers and judges
29 6 overseers of the king's possessions
2 Pa 2 18 and 3,600 to be overseers of the work
23 18 Joiada appointed overseers in the house
31 13 overseers under the hand of Chonenias
34 12 the overseers of the workmen were
17 it is given to the o. of the artificers
Isa 60 17 visitation peace, and thy o. justice
overshadow Ps 90 4 he will o. thee with his
Luke 1 35 power of the most High shall o. thee
Acts 5 15 might overshadow them and they might
overshadowed Ps 139 8 hast o. my head in the
Wisd 19 7 a cloud overshadowed their camp
Bar 5 8 sweet-smelling tree have o. Israel
Mat 17 5 a bright cloud overshadowed them. And
Luke 9 34 a cloud, and overshadowed them
overshadowing Mark 9 6 there was a cloud o. them
Heb 9 5 cherubims of glory o. the propitiatory
oversight 1 Ma 13 39 for any o. or fault committed
oversowed Mat 13 25 his enemy came and o. cockle
overspread Job 3 5 let a mist overspread it
overtake Exod 15 9 said: I will pursue and overtake
Num 32 23 know ye that your sin shall o. you
Deut 28 2 blessings shall come upon thee and o.
15 curses shall come upon thee and o.
45 upon thee and shall pursue and o. thee
Josu 2 5 quickly, and you will overtake them
1 K 30 8 and shall I overtake them or not
8 thou shalt surely overtake them and
2 K 15 14 lest he [Absalom] come and overtake us
Ps 17 38 after my enemies, and overtake them
Eccu 11 10 thou pursue after, thou shalt not o.
Isa 59 9 and justice shall not overtake us. We
Jer 42 16 shall o. you there in land of Egypt
Osee 2 7 lovers, and shall not overtake them
10 9 of iniquity shall not overtake them
Amos 9 13 when the plowman shall o. the reaper
John 12 35 that the darkness overtake you not
1 Th 5 4 that day should overtake you as a thief
overtaken Gen 31 25 had o. him, he pitched
Gen 44 4 when thou hast overtaken them, say
6 having o. them, he spoke to them
Ps 39 13 my iniquities have overtaken me, and
Wisd 17 16 in the field and was suddenly o., he
Gal 6 1 if a man be overtaken in any fault, you
overthrew Exod 14 25 o. the wheels of the chariots
Josu 13 12 Moses overthrew and destroyed them
Judg 3 10 and he [Othoniel] overthrew him
13 he went and o. Israel and possessed
5 8 himself o. the gates of the enemies
3 K 20 21 going out, o. the horses and chariots
2 Pa 28 5 king of Israel, who o. him with a
Jdth 5 20 overthrew the king of the Chanaanites
Job 9 5 whom he o. in his wrath, knew it not
Ps 135 15 o. Pharao and his host in the Red Sea
Eccu 48 24 he o. the army of the Assyrians and
Jer 50 40 as the Lord o. Sodom and Gomorrha
1 Ma 3 11 he overthrew him and killed him
Mat 21 12 o. the tables of the. Mark 11:15
John 2 15 poured out, and the tables he o.
overthrow Num 32 21 until the Lord o. his enemies
Deut 12 3 overthrow their altars and break down
Josu 17 12 children of Manasses o. these cities
2 K 10 3 spy into the city and overthrow it
11 25 exhort them that thou mayest o. it
20 19 city and to o. a mother in Israel
Jdth 9 14 and fortitude that I may overthrow him
Job 6 27 you endeavor to overthrow your friend
8 3 doth the Almighty o. that which is just
Ps 34 1 overthrow them that fight against me
105 26 over them: to o. them in the desert
Wisd 5 24 wickedness shall o. the thrones of the
Eccu 4 33 and God will o. thy enemies for thee
8 19 there is no help, he will o. thee
11 36 he shall o. thee with a whirlwind
13 29 and if he stumble, they will o. him
46 2 to o. the enemies that rose up against
49 9 to overthrow, and pluck up and destroy
Isa 30 32 in great battles he shall o. them
Eze 21 13 when it shall overthrow the scepter
32 12 I will overthrow thy multitude: all
Dan 11 17 a daughter of women to overthrow it
Agge 2 23 I will o. the throne of kingdoms and
23 I will o. the chariot and him that
1 Ma 3 14 and will o. Judas and those that are
22 the Lord himself will overthrow them
4 18 against our enemies and o. them and
5 60 and there was a great o. of the people
2 Ma 15 16 shalt o. the adversaries of my people
Acts 5 39 be of God, you cannot overthrow it
overthroweth Job 12 19 without glory, and o. nobles
Prov 13 6 but wickedness o. the sinner. One is
overthrowing 3 K 19 11 o. the mountains and
overthrown Gen 14 10 turned their backs and were o.
Josu 2 24 inhabitants thereof are o. with fear
1 K 4 10 Philistines fought, and Israel was o.
7 10 they were o. before the face of Israel
14 16 a multitude o. and fleeing this way
1 Pa 18 10 that he had defeated and o. Adarezer
2 Pa 25 19 thou hast said: I have overthrown Edom
Job 12 23 restoreth them again after they were o.
22 16 flood hath overthrown their foundation
30 12 have overthrown my feet and have
34 5 and God hath overthrown my judgment
Ps 88 40 hast o. the covenant of thy servant
Prov 11 11 by mouth of the wicked it shall be o.
22 12 the words of the unjust are overthrown
Eccu 10 19 Lord hath o. the lands of the Gentiles
27 4 thy house shall quickly be o. As
28 17 and hath o. the houses of great men
Jer 18 23 let them be o. before thy eyes in the
20 16 as the cities which the Lord hath o.
46 6 they are overthrown and fallen down
15 because the Lord hath o. them. He hath
48 20 Moab is confounded, because he is o.
39 how it is o., and they have howled

49 18 as Sodom was o. and Gomorrha and the
50 2 Bel is confounded, Merodach is o.
2 are confounded, their idols are o.
Lam 2 5 he hath o. all the walls thereof: he
4 6 of Sodom, which was o. in a moment
Dan 11 26 his army shall be overthrown: and many
1 Ma 1 1 had o. Darius king of the Persians and
3 23 Seron and his host were overthrown
8 4 and had o. them with great slaughter
10 52 have o. Demetrius and possessed
1 C 10 5 for they were overthrown in the desert
Heb 3 17 whose carcasses were o. in the desert
2 P 2 6 condemned them to be o., making them
overtook Gen 31 23 o. him in the mount of Galaad
1 K 31 3 the archers overtook him [Saul], and
4 K 35 5 overtook him in the plains of Jericho
Jer 52 8 they overtook Sedecias in the desert
1 Ma 12 30 after them, but overtook them not
overturn Num 32 7 why do ye o. the minds of the
Job 11 10 if he shall o. all things or shall
12 15 send them out, they shall o. the earth
Isa 28 17 hail shall o. the hope of falsehood
Jer 48 12 shall order and overturn his bottles
overturned Num 32 9 they o. the hearts of the
Job 24 4 they have o. the way of the poor and
28 5 in its place, hath been o. with fire
9 he hath o. mountains from the roots
Ps 117 13 being pushed I was o. that I might
Eccu 10 17 God hath o. the thrones of proud
overturneth Wisd 4 12 o. the innocent mind
overwhelm Job 23 6 nor o. me with the weight
Ps 139 10 the labor of their lips shall o. them
overwhelmed Jdth 5 13 they were so o. with the
Jdth 9 8 feet, and the waters overwhelmed them
Job 30 12 have o. me with their paths as with
Ps 68 3 of the sea: and a tempest hath o. me
77 53 and the sea overwhelmed their enemies
Prov 25 27 searcher of majesty, shall be o. by
overwhelmeth Eccu 38 19 it o. the strength and
owe 1 K 6 3 render unto him what you owe for
Luke 16 5 how much dost thou owe. 7
Rom 13 8 owe no man anything but to love
owed 1 Ma 13 15 money that he owed in the king's
1 Ma 13 39 and the crown which you owed: and if
Mat 18 24 that owed him ten thousand talents
28 that owed him an hundred pence: and
Luke 7 41 the one owed 500 pence, and the other
owest Eccu 4 8 the poor, and pay what thou owest
Mat 18 28 him, saying: Pay what thou owest. And
Philem 19 that thou owest me thy own self also
oweth Deut 24 10 any thing that he oweth thee
Isa 24 2 for his money, so with him that oweth
owing Deut 15 2 he to whom anything is owing
2 Es 5 10 us forgive the debt that is o. to us
owl Lev 11 16 ostrich and the owl and. Deut 14:15
Lev 11 17 the screech owl and the cormorant
owls Isa 13 22 owls shall answer one another
Bar 6 21 owls and swallows and other birds
owner Exod 21 28 owner of the ox shall be quit
Exod 21 29 the owner also shall be put to death
34 the owner of the pit shall pay the
22 11 and the owner shall accept of the oath
12 shall make the loss good to the owner
14 or die, the owner not being present
15 but if the owner be present, he shall
Lev 6 5 the fifth part besides to the owner
25 28 that is sold shall return to the owner
31 in the jubilee it shall return to o.
27 24 it shall return to the former owner
Ruth 2 3 that the owner of that field was Booz
3 K 16 24 name of Semer the owner of the hill
Ecce 5 10 what doth it profit the owner but that
12 riches kept to the hurt of the owner
Isa 1 3 the ox knoweth his owner, and the
Jer 9 10 have not heard the voice of the owner
Bar 6 58 owner thereof will be well satisfied
owners Lev 25 33 they shall all return to the o.
Tob 2 21 be stolen, restore ye it to its owners
Luke 19 33 the owners thereof said to them: Why
Acts 4 34 as many as were owners of lands or
ox Exod 20 17 nor his ox nor his ass nor
Exod 21 28 if an ox gore a man or a woman
28 the owner of the ox shall be quit. But
29 if the ox was wont to push with his
29 the ox shall be stoned, and his owner
32 master, and the ox shall be stoned
33 an ox or an ass fall into it, the owner
35 if one man's ox gore another man's ox
35 they shall sell the live ox and shall
36 if he knew that his ox was wont to push
36 he shall pay ox for ox, and shall
22 1 if any man steal an ox or a sheep
1 he shall restore five oxen for one ox
4 be found with him, alive, either ox or
9 to do any fraud, either in ox or in ass
10 if a man deliver ass, ox, sheep, or
23 4 if thou meet thy enemy's ox or ass
12 that thy ox and thy ass may rest: and
Lev 7 23 fat of a sheep and of an ox and
17 3 if he kill an ox or a sheep or a goat
22 23 ox or a sheep, that hath the ear and
Num 7 3 offered one wagon, and each one an ox
15 an ox of the herd, and a ram. 21, 27, 33, 39, 45, 51, 57, 63, 69, 75, 81
8 8 they shall take an ox of the herd, and
8 another ox of the herd for a sin
15 9 for every ox three tenths of flour
12 for every ox and ram and lamb and kid
22 4 as the ox is wont to eat the grass
Deut 5 14 nor thy ox nor thy ass nor any of thy
21 nor his ox nor his ass nor anything
14 4 beasts that you shall eat, the ox and
17 1 ox wherein there is blemish or any
18 3 whether they sacrifice an ox or a sheep
22 1 seest thy brother's ox or his sheep
4 his ox to be fallen down in the way
10 shalt not plow with an ox and an ass
25 4 thou shalt not muzzle the ox that
28 31 may thy ox be slain before thee and
1 K 12 3 whether I have taken any man's ox or
14 34 tell them to bring me every man his ox
34 the people brought every man his ox
15 3 ox and sheep, camel and ass. So Saul
22 19 ox and ass and sheep with the edge
2 K 6 13 he [David] sacrificed an ox and a ram
1 Pa 13 9 the ox being wanton had made it lean
2 Es 5 18 was prepared for me day by day one ox
Job 6 5 will the ox low when he standeth before
24 3 taken away the widow's ox for a pledge
40 10 with thee, he eateth grass like an ox
Prov 7 22 followeth her as an ox led to be victim
14 4 the strength of the ox is manifest
Isa 1 3 the ox knoweth his owner, and the
7 25 they shall be for the ox to feed on
11 7 the lion shall eat straw like the ox
32 20 thither the foot of the ox and the ass
51 20 as the wild ox that is snared: full of
65 25 the lion and the ox shall eat straw
66 3 he that sacrificeth an ox, is as if
Eze 1 10 the face of an ox on the left side
Dan 4 22 thou shalt eat grass as an ox. 29
30 did eat grass like an ox. 5:21
Luke 13 15 loose his ox or his ass from the
14 5 have an ass or an ox fall into a pit
1 C 9 9 shalt not muzzle the mouth of the ox
1 Tim 5 18 shalt not muzzle the ox that treadeth

oxen Gen 12 16 he [Abram] had sheep and oxen
Gen 20 14 and Abimelech took sheep and oxen
21 27 Abraham took sheep and oxen and gave
24 35 and he hath given him sheep and oxen
32 5 I have oxen and asses and sheep and
7 flocks and the sheep and the oxen
47 17 for their horses and sheep and oxen
Exod 9 3 grievous murrain upon thy . . . oxen
20 24 peace offerings, your sheep and oxen
22 1 he shall restore five oxen for one ox
30 same with the firstborn of thy oxen
34 3 nor the sheep nor oxen fed over against
19 of oxen and of sheep, it shall be mine
Lev 1 2 offering victims of oxen and sheep
27 32 of all the tithes of oxen and sheep
Num 7 3 six wagons covered, and twelve oxen
6 receiving the wagons and the oxen
7 two wagons and four oxen he gave
8 four wagons and eight oxen he gave
9 sons of Caath he gave no wagons or o.
17 peace offerings, two oxen. 23, 29, 35, 41, 47, 53, 59, 65, 71, 77, 83
87 twelve oxen out of the herd for a
88 peace offerings, oxen twenty-four
8 12 their hands upon the heads of the oxen
11 22 shall multitude of sheep and oxen be
15 3 unto the Lord, of oxen or of sheep
8 a holocaust or sacrifice of oxen
22 40 when Balac had killed oxen and sheep
31 28 well of persons as of oxen and asses
30 fiftieth head of persons and of oxen
33 taken, was 675,000 sheep, 72,000 oxen
38 and out of the 36,000 oxen, 72 oxen
44 out of the 36,000 oxen . . . Moses took
Deut 8 13 shalt have herds of oxen and flocks
16 2 the phase . . . of sheep and of oxen
28 18 of thy ground, the herds of thy oxen
51 nor wine nor oil nor herds of oxen
Josu 6 21 the oxen also and the sheep and the
7 24 his oxen and asses and sheep, the
Judg 6 4 of life, nor sheep nor oxen nor asses
1 K 11 5 came, following oxen out of the field
7 taking both the oxen, he cut them in
7 so shall it be done to his oxen. And
14 14 which a yoke of oxen is wont to plow
32 they took sheep and oxen and calves
15 21 took of the spoils sheep and oxen
27 9 took away the sheep and the oxen and
2 K 6 6 the oxen kicked and made it lean aside
12 2 man had exceeding many sheep and oxen
4 spared to take of his own sheep and o.
24 22 thou hast here oxen for a holocaust
22 and the yokes of the oxen for wood
24 David bought the floor and the oxen
3 K 1 19 he hath killed oxen and all fat cattle
25 and hath killed oxen and fatlings
4 23 ten fat oxen and twenty out of the
7 25 it stood upon twelve oxen, of which
29 were lions and oxen and cherubims
29 under the lions and oxen, as it were
44 one sea, and twelve oxen under the sea
8 5 and they sacrificed sheep and oxen
63 to the Lord, 2 and 20 thousand oxen
19 19 plowing with twelve yoke of oxen
20 left the oxen and ran after Elias
21 took a yoke of oxen and killed them
21 boiled the flesh with plow of the oxen
4 K 5 26 and sheep and oxen and menservants
16 17 took down the sea from the brazen oxen
1 Pa 12 40 on camels and on mules and on oxen
40 figs, raisins, wine, oil, and oxen
15 26 in sacrifice 7 oxen and 7 rams
21 23 the oxen also I give for a holocaust
27 29 over the oxen in the valleys, Saphat
2 Pa 4 3 under it there was the likeness of oxen
4 the oxen were cast: and the sea itself
4 sea itself was set upon the 12 oxen
4 the hinder parts of the oxen were
15 one sea and twelve oxen under the sea
5 6 sacrificed rams and oxen without number
7 5 offered a sacrifice of 22,000 oxen
15 11 brought, 700 oxen and 7,000 rams
18 2 at his coming killed sheep and oxen
29 33 they consecrated to the Lord 600 oxen
31 6 brought in the tithes of o. and sheep
35 7 of oxen 3,000, all these were of
8 phase, 2,600 small cattle and 300 oxen
9 phase, 5,000 small cattle and 500 oxen
12 with the oxen they did in like manner
2 Es 10 36 the firstlings of our oxen and of
Jdth 2 8 herds of oxen and flocks of. 3:3; 8:7
Job 1 3 camels and five hundred yoke of oxen
14 the oxen were plowing, and the asses
42 8 take unto you therefore seven oxen
12 camels and a thousand yoke of oxen
Ps 8 8 under his feet, all sheep and oxen
49 10 the cattle on the hills, and the oxen
143 14 their goings forth: their oxen fat
Prov 14 4 where there are no oxen, the crib is
Ecce 2 7 had a great family: and herds of oxen
Eccu 22 2 sluggard is pelted with dung of oxen
26 10 as a yoke of oxen that is moved to
38 26 goad, that driveth the oxen therewith
Isa 30 24 thy oxen and the ass colts that till
Jer 51 23 the husbandman and his yoke of oxen
52 20 twelve oxen of brass that were under
Jon 3 7 oxen nor sheep, taste anything: let
Luke 14 19 I have bought five yoke of oxen and
John 2 14 them that sold oxen and sheep and
15 the sheep also and the oxen and the
Acts 14 12 bringing oxen and garlands before gate
1 C 9 9 doth God take care for oxen? Or doth he
Heb 9 13 if the blood of goats and of oxen, and
10 4 with the blood of oxen and goats sin

Oza 2 K 6 3 Oza and Ahio sons of Abinadab
2 K 6 6 Oza put forth his hand to the ark
7 Lord was enkindled against Oza
8 because the Lord had struck Oza, and
8 place was called: The striking of Oza
4 K 21 18 in the garden of Oza. 26
1 Pa 6 29 Semei his son, Oza his son
8 7 begot Oza and Ahiud. And Saharim
13 7 Oza and his brother drove the cart
9 Oza put forth his hand to hold up
10 and the Lord was angry with Oza
11 because the Lord had divided Oza
11 he called that place the Breach of Oza

Ozam 1 Pa 4 6 Naara bore him Ozam, and Hepher

Ozan Num 34 26 Phaltiel the prince, the son of O.

Ozaziu 1 Pa 15 21 Ozaziu sung a song of victory
1 Pa 27 20 of Ephraim, Osee the son of Ozaziu

Ozensara 1 Pa 7 24 who built Bethoron . . . and O.

Ozi 1 Pa 6 5 Bocci begot Ozi. Ozi begot Zaraias
1 Pa 6 51 Bocci his son, Ozi his son, Zarahia
7 2 the sons of Thola: Ozi and Raphaia
3 the sons of Ozi: Izrahia, of whom
7 the sons of Bela: Esbon and Ozi and
9 8 Ela the son of Ozi, the son of
1 Es 7 4 Zarahias, the son of Ozi, the son of
2 Es 3 25 Phalel the son of Ozi, over against

Ozia 1 Pa 11 44 Ozia an Astarothite, Samaa

Ozial 1 Pa 7 7 Ozi and Ozial and Jerimoth

Ozias 4 K 15 30 Joatham the son of Ozias. 32
4 K 15 34 all that his father Ozias had done
1 Pa 6 24 Uriel his son, Ozias his son, Saul
27 25 castles, was Jonathan the son of Ozias

2 Pa 26 1 people of Juda took his son Ozias
3 Ozias was sixteen years old when he
8 the Ammonites gave gifts to Ozias
9 and Ozias built towers in Jerusalem
14 Ozias prepared for them, that is, for
18 not belong to thee, Ozias, to burn
19 Ozias was angry and holding in his hand
21 and Ozias the king was a leper unto
22 but the rest of the acts of Ozias
23 Ozias slept with his fathers, and they
27 2 according to all that Ozias his father
1 Es 10 21 and Semeia and Jehiel and Ozias
Jdth 6 11 the rulers there were Ozias the son of
19 O., after the assembly was broken up
7 12 gathering themselves together to Ozias
23 Ozias rising up all in tears, said
8 1 the son of Joseph, the son of Ozias
9 she had heard that Ozias had promised
10 by which Ozias hath consented to give
28 Ozias and the ancients said to her
34 Ozias the prince of Juda said to her
10 6 they found Ozias and the ancients of
13 23 Ozias the prince of the people of
15 5 Ozias sent messengers through all the
Isa 1 1 and Jerusalem in the days of Ozias
6 1 in the year that king Ozias died
7 1 Joathan the son of Ozias, king of
Osee 1 1 in the days of Ozias, Joathan, Achaz
Amos 1 1 days of Ozias king of Juda. Zach 14:5
Mat 1 8 Joram begot O. And O. begot Joatham
Oziau 1 Pa 24 26 the son of Oziau, Benno
1 Pa 24 27 the son also of Merari: Oziau
Oziel Exod 6 18 the sons of Caath: . . . Oziel. Num 3:19; 1 Pa 6:2, 18; 23:12
Exod 6 22 the sons also of Oziel. Lev 10:4; 1 Pa 15:10; 23:20
Num 3 30 shall be Elisaphan the son of Oziel
1 Pa 4 42 Raphaia and Oziel the sons of Jesi
15 20 Oziel and Semiramoth and Jehiel
24 24 the son of Oziel, Micha: the son of
25 4 Oziel, Subuel, and Jerimoth, Hananias
2 Pa 29 14 sons of Idithun, Semeias and Oziel
Ozielites Num 3 27 and Hebronites and O.
1 Pa 26 23 and Isaarites and Hebronites and O.
Ozni Num 26 16 Ozni, of him is the family of
Oznites Num 26 16 of him is the family of the O.
Ozriel 1 Pa 27 19 Jerimoth the son of Ozriel

P

pace Isa 3 16 their feet and moved in a set pace
Acts 7 5 in it; no, not the pace of a foot: but
paces Num 35 4 a thousand paces on every side
pacific Exod 24 5 sacrificed p. victims of calves
pacified Ps 195 30 Phinees stood up and p. him
Eccu 34 23 nor will he be p. for sins by the
Isa 19 22 he shall be pacified towards them
Jer 24 6 my eyes upon them to be pacified
Eze 16 63 when I shall be p. toward thee for
24 14 pass by nor spare nor be pacified
43 27 and I will be pacified towards you
pacify Prov 16 14 the wise man will pacify it
packs Luke 11 46 yourselves touch not the packs with
paddle Deut 23 13 carrying a paddle at thy girdle
pages Jer 36 23 Judi had read three or four p.
paid Gen 47 26 fifth part is paid to the king
Lev 22 23 but a vow may not be paid with them
1 K 6 8 which you have paid him for sin
2 K 18 12 if thou wouldst have paid down in my
4 K 3 4 paid to king of Israel 100,000 lambs
17 3 his servant and paid him tribute
1 Es 6 8 tribute that is p. out of the country
Ps 64 2 vow shall be paid to thee in Jerusalem
136 8 thy payment which thou hast paid us
Prov 7 14 this day I have paid my vows
Jon 1 3 to Tharsis: and he paid the fare
1 Ma 10 41 affairs the years before, had not paid
Mat 18 30 him into prison, till he paid the debt
34 torturers until he paid all the debt
Heb 7 9 received tithes, paid tithes in Abraham
pain Gen 34 25 when the pain of the wound was
Gen 35 18 when her soul was departing for pain
18 Benoni, that is The son of my pain
Deut 2 25 and be in pain like women in travail
2 Pa 16 12 of a most violent pain in his feet
Job 14 22 while he shall live, shall have pain
16 7 if I speak, my pain will not rest
Prov 23 35 but I was not sensible of pain: they
Eccu 31 22 with it, and thou shalt feel no pain
48 21 they were in pain as women in travail
Isa 13 8 shall be in pain as a woman in labor
21 3 therefore are my loins filled with pain
26 17 is in pain and crieth out in her pangs
Jer 4 19 my bowels are in pain, the senses of
51 8 howl for her, take balm for her pain
Eze 28 24 nor a thorn causing pain on every side
30 16 Pelusium shall be in pain like a woman
Mich 4 10 in pain and labor, O daughter of Sion
2 Ma 7 36 having now undergone a short pain, are
9 5 a dreadful pain in his bowels came
9 whilst he lived in sorrow and pain
Rom 8 22 every creature . . . and travaileth in p.
1 J 4 18 casteth out fear because fear hath p.
Apoc 12 2 and was in pain to be delivered. And
16 10 and they gnawed their tongues for pain
pained 2 Ma 9 7 that his limbs were much pained
painful Exod 6 9 anguish of spirit and most p. work
Ecce 1 13 this painful occupation hath God given
painfulness 2 C 11 27 brethren. In labor and p.
pains 1 K 4 19 her p. came upon her on a sudden
Job 9 23 not laugh at the pains of the innocent
10 17 upon me, and pains war against me
16 11 cheek, they are filled with my pains
Ps 47 7 were pains as of a woman in labor
Eccu 21 11 end is hell and darkness and pains
38 7 shall cure and shall allay their pains
Isa 13 8 gripings and pains shall take hold of
Jer 22 23 thee, as the pains of a woman in labor
Bar 2 25 and they have died in grievous pains
Eze 24 12 great pains have been taken, and the
Joel 2 6 the people shall be in grievous pains
2 Ma 6 30 I suffer grievous pains in body: but
9 11 his pains increasing every moment. And
18 but his pains not ceasing, for the
1 Th 5 3 as the pains upon her that is with child
Apoc 16 11 because of their pains and wounds, and
paint Eze 23 40 thyself, and didst p. thy eyes
2 Ma 2 30 he that taketh care to paint it
painted 4 K 9 30 painted her face with stibic
Prov 7 16 I have covered it with p. tapestry
Eze 8 10 were painted on the wall all round
23 14 she had seen men painted on the wall
paintest Jer 4 30 p. thy eyes with stibic stone
painteth Jer 22 14 and p. them with vermilion
painting Esth 1 6 which was embellished with p.
Wisd 13 14 painting it red and covering every
pair Amos 2 6 the poor man for a pair of shoes
Amos 8 6 and the poor for a pair of shoes
Luke 2 24 a pair of turtledoves or two young
Apoc 6 5 he that sat on him had a pair of scales
palace 3 K 16 18 into the p. and burnt himself
3 K 21 1 a vineyard near the palace of Achab
4 K 7 11 and told it within the king's palace
11 16 by the palace, and she was slain there
19 gate of the shieldbearers into the p.
12 18 in the king's p., and sent it to Hazael

15 5 Joatham the king's son governed the p.
20 18 they shall be eunuchs in the palace
2 Pa 2 1 the Lord, and a palace for himself. 12
12 10 who guarded the entrance of the palace
23 15 within the horse gate of the palace
Esth 1 9 a feast for the women in the palace
2 21 presided in first entry of the palace
3 2 that were at the doors of the palace
3 were chief at the doors of the palace
4 2 even to the gate of the palace: for no
6 street of the city, before the p. gate
14 salt that we have eaten in the palace
5 1 upon his throne in the hall of the p.
9 sitting before the gate of the palace
6 10 sitteth before the gates of the palace
12 Mardochai returned to the palace gate
8 15 Mardochai going forth out of the palace
9 4 they knew him to be prince of the p.
12 1 eunuchs who were porters of the p.
5 to abide in the court of the palace
Isa 39 7 eunuchs in p. of the king of Babylon
Dan 1 4 as might stand in the king's palace
2 49 Daniel himself was in the king's palace
4 1 in my house, and flourishing in my p.
26 was walking in the palace of Babylon
5 5 surface of the wall of the king's p.
1 Ma 11 46 and the king fled into the palace
Mark 15 16 led him away into the court of the p.
palate Job 12 11 p. of him that eateth, the taste
Ps 118 103 how sweet are thy words to my palate
Cant 2 3 his fruit was sweet to my palate
Eccu 36 21 the palate tasteth venison and the
pale Apoc 6 8 a pale horse, and he that sat upon him
paleness Lev 14 37 dints, disfigured with p.
Jdth 6 5 paleness that is in thy face depart
Ps 67 14 her back with the paleness of gold
pales Eccu 22 21 as pales set in high places
Palestine Jer 47 1 against the people of P.
Eze 16 57 Syria and of all the daughters of P.
Palestines Gen 21 33 returned to land of the P.
Gen 21 34 sojourner in the land of the Palestines
26 1 Abimelech king of the Palestines. 8
14 wherefore the Palestines envying him
18 the Palestines had of old stopped up
Exod 23 31 Red Sea to the sea of the Palestines
palm Judg 3 16 the length of the palm of the hand
2 Es 8 15 of myrtle and branches of palm
Isa 40 12 weighed the heavens with his palm
1 Ma 13 37 palm, which you sent, we have received
2 Ma 14 4 unto him a crown of gold and a palm
palm tree Judg 4 5 [Debbora] sat under a p. t.
Job 29 18 as a palm tree shall multiply my days
Ps 91 13 just shall flourish like the palm tree
Cant 7 7 thy stature is like to a palm tree
8 I will go up into the palm tree
Eccu 24 18 I was exalted like a p. tree in Cades
Jer 10 5 framed after the likeness of a p. tree
Eze 41 18 palm tree was between a cherub and a
19 face of a man was toward the palm tree
19 face of a lion was toward the p. tree
Joel 1 12 and the palm tree . . . are withered
palm trees Exod 15 27 water and seventy palm trees. Num 33:9
Lev 23 40 branches of palm trees and boughs
Deut 34 3 plain of Jericho the city of p. trees
Judg 3 13 and possessed the city of palm trees
3 K 6 29 he made in them cherubims and p. trees
32 cherubims and figures of palm trees
32 the cherubims and the palm trees
35 he carved cherubims and palm trees
7 36 cherubims and lions and palm trees
2 Pa 3 5 and he graved in them palm trees
28 15 to Jericho the city of palm trees
Cant 5 11 his locks as branches of palm trees
Eccu 50 14 as branches of palm trees, they stood
Eze 40 16 the representation of palm trees
26 there were graven palm trees, one
31 the palm trees thereof in the front
34 the graven palm trees in the front
37 the graving of palm trees in the front
41 18 cherubims and palm trees wrought. 20
25 temple, and the figures of palm trees
26 and the representation of palm trees
1 Ma 13 51 with branches of palm trees and harps
John 12 13 took branches of palm trees and went
palmerworm Joel 1 4 which the p. hath left
Joel 2 25 mildew and the palmerworm have eaten
Amos 4 9 p. hath eaten up your many gardens
Palmira 3 K 9 18 P. in the land of the wilderness
2 Pa 8 4 and he built Palmira in the desert
palms Judg 1 16 went up from the city of palms
Judg 8 6 p. of the hands of Zebee and Salmana
1 K 5 4 the palms of his hands were cut off
2 Ma 10 7 green branches and palms for him
Mat 26 67 his face with the palms of their hands
Mark 14 65 struck him with the p. of their hands
Apoc 7 9 white robes, and palms in their hands
palsy 1 Ma 9 55 he was taken with a palsy
Mat 4 24 lunatics, and those that had the palsy
8 6 lieth at home sick of the palsy, and
9 2 brought to him one sick of the palsy
2 said to the man sick of the palsy. 6
Mark 2 3 to him, bringing one sick of the palsy
4 wherein the man sick of the palsy lay
5 he saith to the sick of the palsy. 10; Luke 5:24
9 easier, to say to the sick of the palsy
Luke 5 18 in a bed a man who had the palsy
Acts 8 8 many, taken with the palsy, and that
9 33 for eight years, who was ill of palsy
Pamphylia 1 Ma 15 23 Samus and P. and Lycia
Acts 2 10 Pamphylia, Egypt, and the parts of
13 13 Paphos, they came to Perge in Pamphylia
14 23 through Pisidia, they came into P.
15 38 having departed from them out of P.
27 5 sailing over the sea of Cilicia and P.
pan 1 K 2 14 or into the pot or into the pan
Eze 4 3 take unto thee an iron pan and set it
pangs 2 K 22 5 p. of death have surrounded me
Isa 26 17 is in pain and crieth out in her pangs
Jer 50 43 of him, pangs as a woman in labor
pans Exod 27 3 make . . . pans to receive the ashes
pant Tob 6 4 he began to pant before his feet
panted 2 K 18 14 whilst he yet panted for life
Ps 118 131 I opened my mouth and panted because
panteth Ps 41 2 hart p. after the fountains
Ps 41 2 so my soul panteth after thee, O God
paper Tob 7 16 taking paper they made a writing
2 J 12 I would not by paper and ink: for I
Paphos Acts 13 6 through whole island, as far as P.
Acts 13 13 sailed from Paphos, they come to Perge
paps Prov 30 33 that strongly squeezeth the paps
Eze 23 21 and the paps of thy virginity broken
Luke 11 27 and the paps that gave thee suck
23 29 and the paps that have not given suck
Apoc 1 13 girt about the paps with a golden
parable Num 23 7 taking up his p. he said: Balac king
Num 23 18 taking up his p., said: Stand, O Balac
24 3 took up his p. and said. 20, 21
15 taking up his p. again he said. 23
Job 27 1 Job also added, taking up his p. 29:1
Ps 48 5 I will incline my ear to a parable
Prov 1 6 he shall understand a parable and the
26 7 a p. is unseemly in the mouth of fools
9 so is a parable in the mouth of fools
Wisd 5 3 in derision and for a p. of reproach

Eccu 20 22 a parable coming out of a fool's mouth
Isa 14 4 thou shalt take up this p. against
Eze 17 2 speak a parable to the house of Israel
18 2 that you use among you this parable
3 this parable shall be no more to you a
24 3 thou shalt speak by a figure a parable
Mich 2 4 a parable shall be taken up upon you
Haba 2 6 shall not all these take up a parable
Mat 13 18 hear you . . . the p. of the sower
24 another p. he proposed to them. 31
33 another parable he spoke to them
36 expound to us the p. of the cockle
15 15 to him: Expound to us this parable
21 33 hear ye another parable. There was a
24 32 from the fig tree learn a p. Mark 13:28
Mark 4 10 the twelve . . . asked him the parable
13 are you ignorant of this parable? And
30 to what parable shall we compare it
34 without p. he did not speak unto them
7 17 his disciples asked him the parable
12 12 knew that he spoke this p. Luke 20:19
Luke 8 9 asked him what this parable might be
11 the p. is this: The seed is the word
12 41 Lord, dost thou speak this p. to us
13 6 he spoke also this parable: A certain
14 7 he spoke a parable also to them that
15 3 he spoke to them this parable, saying
18 1 he spoke also a parable to them
9 he spoke this parable: Two men went
19 11 and spoke a parable, because he was
20 9 began to speak to the people this p.
Heb 9 9 which is a parable of the time present
11 19 whereupon also he received him for a p.
parables 3 K 4 32 Solomon also spoke 3,000 p.
Ps 77 2 I will open my mouth in parables
Prov 1 1 the parables of Solomon, the son of
25 1 these are also p. of Solomon which
Ecce 12 9 he set forth many parables. He
Eccu 38 38 not be found where p. are spoken
39 2 withal into the subtilties of parables
3 conversant in the secrets of parables
47 17 thou didst multiply riddles in p.
18 canticles and proverbs and parables
Eze 20 49 doth not this man speak by parables
Mat 13 3 spoke to them many things in parables
10 why speakest thou to them in parables
13 therefore do I speak to them in p.
34 Jesus spoke in parables to the
34 without p. he did not speak to them
35 I will open my mouth in parables
53 when Jesus had finished these parables
21 45 and Pharisees had heard his parables
22 1 spoke again in parables to them, saying
Mark 3 23 he said to them in parables: How can
4 2 he taught them many things in parables
11 all things are done in parables; that
13 and how shall you know all parables
33 with many such parables he spoke to
12 1 he began to speak to them in parables
Luke 8 10 but to the rest in parables, that
Paraclete John 14 16 he shall give you another P.
John 14 26 the Paraclete, the Holy Ghost, whom
15 26 when the P. cometh, whom I will send
16 7 if I go not, the P. will not come to
paradise Gen 2 8 had planted a p. of pleasure
Gen 2 9 tree of life also in the midst of p.
10 out of place of pleasure to water p.
15 and put him into the p. of pleasure
16 of every tree of p. thou shalt eat
3 1 you should not eat of every tree of p.
2 the trees that are in p. we do eat
3 the tree which is in the midst of p.
8 the Lord God walking in paradise
8 hid . . . amidst the trees of paradise
10 I heard thy voice in paradise: and I was
23 God sent him out of the p. of pleasure
24 before the p. of pleasure cherubims
13 10 as the paradise of the Lord and like
Cant 4 13 thy plants are a p. of pomegranates
Eccu 24 41 like an aqueduct, came out of paradise
40 17 grace is like a paradise in blessings
28 fear of the Lord is like p. of blessing
44 16 was translated into p. that he may
Eze 28 13 was in the pleasures of the p. of God
31 8 the cedars in the paradise of God
8 no tree in the paradise of God was like
9 that were in the p. of God, envied him
Luke 23 43 this day thou shalt be with me in p.
2 C 12 4 that he was caught up into paradise, and
Apoc 2 7 which is in the paradise of my God
Parasceve Mark 15 42 because it was the P. John 19:31
Luke 23 54 it was the day of the Parasceve, and
John 19 14 it was the Parasceve of the pasch
42 because of the Parasceve of the Jews
parcel Ruth 4 3 will sell a parcel of land that
parched Gen 31 40 and night was I p. with heat
Lev 23 14 not eat either bread or parched corn
1 K 25 18 and five measures of parched corn
2 K 17 28 parched corn and beans and lentils
Jdth 10 5 and a vessel of oil and parched corn
16 13 my lowly ones appeared, p. with thirst
James 1 11 burning heat and parched the grass and
parchments 2 Tim 4 13 the books, especially the p.
pardon Gen 4 13 greater than that I may deserve p.
Num 15 28 and he shall obtain his pardon and it
4 K 5 18 that the Lord pardon me thy servant
Jdth 8 14 with many tears let us beg his pardon
Ps 24 11 thou wilt pardon my sin: for it is
64 4 thou wilt pardon our transgressions
Wisd 12 11 neither didst . . . give pardon to their
Eccu 3 4 that loveth God, shall obtain pardon
16 8 the ancient giants did not obtain p.
28 5 who shall obtain pardon for his sins
35 3 and a begging of pardon for sins
Jer 13 14 I will not spare, and I will not p.
2 C 12 13 burthensome to you? P. me this injury
pardoned Wisd 13 8 again they are not to be p.
2 Ma 15 39 not so perfectly, it must be p. me
2 C 2 10 to whom you have p. anything, I also
10 what I have p., if I have p. anything
pare Deut 21 12 shave her hair and pare her nails
parent 1 Ma 11 31 have written to Lasthenes our p.
1 Ma 11 32 king Demetrius to Lasthenes his parent
parents Gen 28 7 that Jacob obeying his p. was
Josu 6 23 brought out Rahab and her parents
Judg 14 4 his parents knew not that the thing
Ruth 2 11 how thou hast left thy parents and the
Tob 3 3 remember my offences nor those of my p.
6 15 I am the only child of my parents
9 10 a blessing come . . . upon your parents
10 11 find all things well about your parents
12 the p. taking their daughter kissed her
11 19 told his p. all the benefits of God
12 3 he gave joy to her parents, myself
Esth 2 7 she had lost both her parents: and was
Prov 19 14 house and riches are given by parents
Wisd 4 6 witnesses of wickedness against their p.
12 6 those p. sacrificing with their own
6 to destroy by the hands of our parents
21 to whose parents thou hast sworn
Eccu 3 8 that feareth the Lord, honoreth his p.
Dan 13 3 her parents being just, had instructed
30 she came with her p. and children
Zach 13 3 his parents shall thrust him through
1 Ma 10 9 he restored them to their parents
2 Ma 12 24 because he had the p. and brethren

Mat 10 21 rise up against their p. Mark 13:12
Luke 2 27 when his parents brought in the child
41 and his parents went every year to
43 and his parents knew it not. And
8 56 and her parents were astonished
18 29 that hath left house or parents or
21 16 you shall be betrayed by your parents
John 9 2 hath sinned, this man or his parents
3 hath this man sinned, nor his parents
18 called the p. of him that had received
20 his p. answered them and said: We
22 these things his parents said because
23 parents say: he is of age, ask himself
Rom 1 30 evil things, disobedient to parents
2 C 12 14 children to lay up for the parents, but the parents for children
Eph 6 1 children, obey your p. Col 3:20
1 Tim 5 4 to make a return of duty to her parents
2 Tim 3 2 disobedient to parents, ungrateful
Heb 11 23 was hid three months by his parents
parlor Judg 3 20 he was sitting in a summer p.
Judg 3 23 shutting the doors of the parlor and
24 saw the doors of the parlor shut
24 easing nature in his summer parlor
1 K 9 22 brought them into the parlor and gave
2 K 4 7 was sleeping upon his bed in a parlor
Parmenas Acts 6 5 and Timon and Parmenas and Nicolas
Paros 1 Pa 29 2 marble of P. in great abundance
part Gen 26 29 on our part have touched nothing of
Gen 30 14 give me part of thy son's mandrakes
37 rods . . . and pilled them in part
33 19 he bought that part of the field in
Exod 21 35 carcass . . . they shall part between them
23 2 to opinion of the most part, to stray
29 40 the fourth part of a hin. Lev 23:13; Num 15:4; 28:5, 7
39 21 a hole for the head in the upper part
Lev 2 16 shall burn . . . part of the corn
5 13 part that is left, he himself shall have
6 16 and the part of the flour that is left
17 part thereof is offered for the burnt
13 43 leprosy which is risen in the bald part
54 wash that part wherein the leprosy is
14 26 part of the oil into his own left hand
29 the other part of the oil that is in
Num 8 2 against that part shall they give light
11 1 were at the uttermost part of the camp
22 41 beheld the uttermost part of the people
23 13 whence thou mayest see part of Israel
27 20 the sight of all, and part of thy glory
33 54 to the more you shall give a larger part
Deut 3 13 I delivered the other part of Galaad
12 12 he hath no other part and possession
14 27 hath no other part in thy possession
29 the Levite that hath no other part
16 19 and not go aside to either part
18 4 and of oil and a part of the wool
28 27 part of thy body by which the dung
34 3 south part, and the breadth of the plain
Josu 3 8 have entered into part of the water of
15 feet were dipped in part of the water
11 17 part of mountain that goeth up to Seir
12 2 and of the middle part in the valley
7 mount, part of which goeth up into Seir
13 6 as a part of the inheritance of Israel
27 other part of the kingdom of Sehon
27 uttermost part of the sea of Cenereth
15 1 to the uttermost part of the south coast
11 northward to a part of Accaron at
18 15 goeth out from part of Cariathiarim
16 down to that part of the mountain
16 furthermost part of valley of Raphaim
24 32 in Sichem, in that part of the field
Judg 7 11 into part of the camp, where was the
17 I will go into one part of the camp and
19 Gedeon . . . went into part of the camp
16 27 from roof and higher part of the house
21 22 and the fault was committed on your part
Ruth 1 17 if aught but death part me and thee
1 K 2 33 a great part of thy house shall die
9 8 in my hand the fourth part of a sicle
10 26 there went with him a part of the army
14 2 Saul abode in uttermost part of Gabaa
24 4 lay hid in the lower part of the cave
2 K 2 15 of the part of Isboseth the son of
14 6 there was none to part them; and the
30 have set part of the field on fire
3 K 6 16 cedar at the hinder part of the temple
19 made the oracle . . . in the inner part
19 20 that which was my part, I have done
4 K 3 25 and a great part thereof destroyed
6 25 fourth part of a cabe of pigeon's dung
7 5 were come to the first part of the camp
1 Pa 12 29 great part of them followed house of
26 15 in which part of the house was the
27 4 who commanded a part of the army of
2 Pa 2 16 and it will be thy part to bring them
30 18 great part of the people from Ephraim
31 3 the king's part was that, of his proper
34 22 dwelt in Jerusalem in the Second part
1 Es 10 4 arise, it is thy part to give orders
2 Es 2 20 but you have no part . . . in Jerusalem
5 11 and the hundredth part of the money
11 1 one part in ten to dwell in Jerusalem
Tob 8 2 took out of his bag part of the liver
Jdth 8 5 in the upper part of her house
Esth 2 9 to deliver to her her part and seven
Job 26 14 these things are said in part of his
31 2 what part should God from above have
32 17 I also will answer my part and will
Prov 16 1 is the part of man to prepare the soul
Ecce 9 6 neither have they any part in this
Wisd 1 16 are worthy to be of the part thereof
2 9 none of us go without his part in
Eccu 13 22 what part hath the rich with the poor
14 14 not the part of a good gift overpass
Isa 36 8 wilt be able on thy part to find riders
44 16 part of it he burnt with fire, and with part of it he dressed his meat
19 I have burnt part of it in the fire
20 part thereof is ashes: his foolish heart
49 6 even to the farthest part of the earth
61 7 they shall praise their part: therefore
Jer 48 45 it shall devour part of Moab, and the
Eze 4 11 shalt drink . . . sixth part of a hin
32 18 to the lowest part of the earth, with
45 7 the length according to every part
13 sixth part of an ephi of a core of
46 14 shall offer . . . sixth part of an ephi
47 1 temple to the south part of the altar
Dan 1 2 part of the vessels of the house of God
2 33 the feet part of iron and part of clay
41 part of potter's clay, and part of iron
42 were part of iron and part of clay
5 24 he hath sent the part of the hand which
11 31 arms shall stand on his part and they
Joel 2 20 his hinder part towards the utmost sea
Amos 7 4 and ate up a part at the same time
Jon 1 5 down into the inner part of the ship
Mich 3 1 is it not your part to know judgment
1 Ma 3 9 renowned even to the utmost part of the
4 19 part of them appeared looking forth from
6 40 part of king's army was distinguished
40 and the other part by the low places
9 14 stronger part of the army of Bacchides
11 73 and they of his part that fled saw this

12 34 to them that took part with Demetrius
2 Ma 3 11 some part of that which wicked Simon
8 8 that things for the most part succeeded
24 disabled the greater part of Nicanor's
10 28 the one part having . . . the Lord for a
Mark 4 38 he was in the hinder part of the ship
13 27 earth to the uttermost part of heaven
John 19 23 four parts, to every soldier a part
Acts 1 8 even to the uttermost part of the earth
17 and had obtained part of this ministry
5 2 by fraud kept back part of the price
2 bringing a certain part of it, laid it
3 by fraud keep part of the price of the
13 47 salvation unto the utmost part of earth
16 12 is the chief city of part of Macedonia
19 32 the greater part knew not for what cause
23 6 knowing that one part were Sadducees
27 12 greatest p. gave counsel to sail thence
41 hinder part was broken with the violence
Rom 11 25 that blindness in part has happened in
15 24 if first, in part, I shall have enjoyed
1 C 11 18 among you; and in part I believe it. For
13 9 we know in part, and we prophesy in part
10 that which is in part shall be done away
12 I know in part; but then I shall know
16 17 that which was wanting on your p., they
2 C 1 14 you have known us in part, that we are
2 5 but in part, that I may not burden you
3 10 even that which was glorious in this p.
6 15 or what part hath the faithful with the
11 21 we had been weak in this part. Wherein
Eph 4 16 operation in the measure of every part
Phil 2 30 that which on your part was wanting
Titus 2 8 that he, who is on the contrary part
Heb 9 4 covered about on every part with gold
Apoc 20 6 that hath part in the first resurrection
22 19 his part out of the book of life and
fifth part Gen 41 34 fifth part of the fruits
Gen 47 24 fifth part you shall give to the king
26 the fifth part is paid to the king
Lev 5 16 and shall add the fifth part besides
6 5 principal and the fifth part besides
22 14 shall add the fifth part with that
27 13 above the estimation the fifth part
15 give the fifth part of the estimation
19 shall add the fifth part of the money
27 shall add the fifth part of the price
31 he shall add the fifth part of them
Num 5 7 restore . . . fifth part over and above
no part Deut 10 9 Levi hath no p. nor possession
Deut 18 1 shall have no part nor inheritance
Josu 18 7 the Levites have no part among you
22 25 you have no part in the Lord. 27
2 K 20 1 we have no part in David. 2 Pa 10:16
2 Es 2 20 but you have no part nor justice nor
Luke 11 36 having no part of darkness; the whole
John 13 8 thou shalt have no part with me. Simon
Acts 8 21 thou hast no part nor lot in this
tenth part Exod 16 36 the tenth part of an ephi. Lev 5:11; 6:20; Num 15:4; 28:5
Exod 29 40 t. p. of flour tempered with oil. Lev 14:21
Num 5 15 tenth part of a measure of barley meal
18 26 to say, the tenth part of the tenth
Eze 45 11 bate may contain tenth part of a core
11 and the ephi the tenth part of a core
14 bate of oil is tenth part of a core
Apoc 11 13 the tenth part of the city fell: and
third part Num 15 6 third part of a hin of oil
Num 15 7 third part of the same measure of wine
Josu 17 11 third part of the city of Nopheth
2 K 18 2 sent forth a third part of the people
2 a third part under the hand of Abisai
2 third part under the hand of Ethai
4 K 11 6 third part of you go in on the sabbath
6 let a third part be at the gate of
6 third part be at the gate behind the
2 Pa 23 5 a third part of you that come to the
5 and a third part at the king's house
2 Es 10 32 to give the third part of a sicle
Eze 5 2 third part thou shalt burn with fire
2 thou shalt take a third part and cut it
2 other third part thou shalt scatter
12 a third part of thee shall die with
12 a third part of thee shall fall by the
12 a third part of thee will I scatter
46 14 third part of a hin of oil to be
Zach 13 8 the third part shall be left therein
9 will bring the third part through the
Apoc 8 7 third part of the earth was burnt up
7 third part of the trees was burnt up
8 the third part of the sea became blood
9 the third part of those creatures died
9 third part of the ship was destroyed
10 it fell on the third part of the rivers
11 t. p. of the waters became wormwood
12 the third part of the sun was smitten
12 third part of the moon and the third part of the stars, so that the third part of them was darkened
12 the day did not shine for a third part
9 15 for to kill the third part of men. And
18 was slain the third part of men, by
12 4 his tail drew the third part of the
partake 1 C 9 13 serve the altar, p. with the altar
1 C 10 17 one body, all that partake of one bread
30 if I partake with thanksgiving, why am
2 Tim 2 6 laboreth, must first p. of the fruits
1 P 4 13 if you p. of the sufferings of Christ
partaker Tob 3 17 p. with them that walk in
Esth 16 24 that will not be p. of this solemnity
Ps 49 18 with adulterers thou hast been a p.
118 63 I am a partaker with all them that fear
Prov 29 24 he that is a partaker with a thief
Wisd 6 25 such a man shall not be p. of wisdom
Osee 4 17 Ephraim is a partaker with idols
1 Ma 10 65 him governor and p. of his dominion
2 Ma 5 10 nor being p. of the sepulcher of his
20 was made p. of the evils of the people
Rom 11 17 and art made partaker of the root, and
1 C 9 23 that I may be made partaker thereof
1 Tim 5 22 neither be partaker of other men's sins
Heb 2 14 hath been partaker of the same: that
5 13 every one that is a partaker of milk, is
1 P 5 1 as also a partaker of that glory which
partakers Prov 5 17 neither let strangers be p.
Isa 44 11 partakers thereof shall be confounded
2 Ma 4 14 hastened to be partakers of the games
5 27 they might not be p. of the pollution
Mat 23 30 we would not have been p. with them
Rom 15 27 if Gentiles have been made partakers of
1 C 9 12 if others be partakers of this power
10 18 eat of the sacrifices, p. of the altar
20 that you should be made p. with devils
21 you cannot be p. of table of the Lord
2 C 1 7 knowing that as you are partakers of
Eph 5 7 be ye not therefore partakers with them
Phil 1 7 gospel, you all are partakers of my joy
Col 1 12 who hath made us worthy to be partakers
1 Tim 6 2 who are partakers of the benefit. These
Heb 2 14 children are p. of flesh and blood, he
3 1 partakers of the heavenly vocation
14 for we are made partakers of Christ
6 4 were made partakers of the Holy Ghost
12 8 whereof you are made partakers, then
2 P 1 4 be made partakers of the divine nature
Apoc 18 4 that you be not partakers of her sins

partaking 1 C 10 16 is it not the p. of the body
parted Josu 22 9 p. from the children of Israel
4 K 2 11 and fiery horses parted them both
Ps 21 19 they parted my garments amongst them
Joel 3 2 nations, and have parted my land
John 19 24 they have parted my garments among
Acts 2 3 parted tongues as it were of fire, and
21 1 being parted from them, we set sail
Parthians Acts 2 9 Parthians and Medes and Elamites
participation 2 C 6 14 what p. hath justice with
particular 2 Ma 2 29 exact handling of every p.
2 Ma 2 31 to discuss every particular point
Eph 5 33 you in p. love his wife as himself: and
particularly Acts 21 19 related p. what things God
Heb 9 5 it is not needful to speak now p. Now
2 Pa 35 25 mourned for him, p. Jeremias
particulars 2 Ma 11 20 as concerning other p., I
parties Exod 22 9 cause of both p. shall come to
parting Wisd 5 11 p. it by the force of her flight
partition Gen 38 29 why is the p. divided for thee
Eph 2 14 breaking down the middle wall of p., the
partly Dan 2 42 be p. strong, and p. broken
partner 2 Pa 20 36 p. with him in making ships
Esth 16 13 of Esther the partner of our kingdom
Prov 28 24 no sin, is the partner of a murderer
Mala 2 14 yet she was thy partner, and the wife
2 Ma 7 29 made a worthy partner with thy brethren
Philem 17 if therefore thou count me a partner
Apoc 1 9 I John, your brother and your partner
partners Luke 5 7 they beckoned to their partners
Luke 5 10 who were Simon's partners. And Jesus
partridge 1 K 26 20 as the partridge is hunted
Eccu 11 32 as the p. is brought into the cage
Jer 17 11 as the partridge hath hatched eggs
parts Gen 16 13 here have I seen the hinder parts
Gen 30 37 in the parts that were pilled there
37 parts that were whole remained green
42 9 you are come to view the weaker parts
12 to consider the unfenced parts of
43 34 so that it exceeded by five parts
Exod 3 1 drove the flock to inner parts of the
26 12 cover the back parts of the tabernacle
28 26 put in the top parts of the rational
26 look towards the back parts thereof
32 made in the outmost parts of garments
33 23 thou shalt see my back parts: but my
Lev 1 8 shall lay the parts that are cut out
3 14 and that covereth all the vital parts
13 58 wash with water the parts that are pure
Num 25 8 man and the woman in the genital parts
Deut 14 6 that divideth the hoof in two parts
19 3 of thy land equally into three parts
28 64 from the farthest parts of the earth
Josu 15 21 the cities from the uttermost parts
18 5 to yourselves the land into seven parts
6 these mark ye out into seven parts
9 surveying it divided it into 7 parts
10 to the children of Israel into seven p.
Judg 3 22 by the secret parts of nature the
7 16 he divided the 300 men into three parts
19 29 wife with her bones into 12 parts
20 6 and sent the parts into all the borders
1 K 5 9 they had emerods in their secret parts
2 K 19 43 I have ten parts in the king more than
3 K 7 25 their hinder parts were all hid within
11 30 was clad, divided it into twelve parts
16 21 people of Israel divided into two p.
4 K 11 7 let two parts of you, all that go forth
19 23 I have entered into the furthest parts
2 Pa 4 4 hinder parts of the oxen were inward
21 15 till thy vital parts come out by little
2 Es 1 9 away to the uttermost p. of the world
11 1 and nine parts in the other cities
Tob 1 1 which is in the upper parts of Galilee
Job 9 9 and the inner parts of the south
30 27 my inner parts have boiled without any
37 9 out of the inner parts shall a tempest
38 16 walked in the lowest parts of the deep
Ps 2 8 utmost p. of earth for thy possession
62 10 they shall go into the lower parts of
67 14 hinder parts of her back with the
77 66 smote his enemies on the hinder parts
135 13 who divided the Red Sea into parts
138 9 dwell in the uttermost parts of the sea
15 my substance in lower p. of the earth
Prov 18 8 even to the inner parts of the bowels
20 30 in the more inward parts of the belly
26 22 reach to innermost parts of the belly
Eccu 16 26 he distinguished their parts and their
23 28 hearts of men, into most hidden parts
24 45 I will penetrate to all the lower parts
Isa 7 18 fly, that is in the uttermost parts
16 11 my inward parts for the brick wall
41 9 from the remote p. thereof have called
57 6 in the parts of the torrent is thy
Jer 34 18 and passed between the parts thereof
19 passed between the parts of the calf
Eze 1 17 they went by their four parts: and
26 20 set thee in lowest parts of the earth
28 16 thy inner p. were filled with iniquity
31 14 unto death to the lowest parts of the
16 comforted in the lowest p. of the earth
18 to the lowest parts of the earth: thou
32 23 are set in the lowest parts of the pit
34 down uncircumcised to the lowest parts
38 6 the northern parts and all his strength
15 out of thy place from the northern p.
39 2 make thee go up from the northern p.
40 10 fronts of one measure, on both parts
41 7 temple broader in the higher parts
7 from lower p. they went to the higher
20 even to the upper parts of the gate
42 4 looking to the inner parts of a way
5 out of them from the lower parts
Osee 13 8 I will rend inner parts of their liver
Jon 2 7 I went down to the lowest parts
Zach 13 8 two parts in it shall be scattered
2 Ma 7 5 when he was now maimed in all parts
9 5 and bitter torments of the inner parts
Mat 24 31 from the farthest parts of the heavens
Mark 8 10 he came into the parts of Dalmanutha
Luke 17 24 shineth unto the parts that are under
John 19 23 they made four parts, to every soldier
Acts 2 10 and the parts of Libya about Cyrene
10 9 the higher parts of the house to pray
20 2 when he had gone over those parts, and
1 C 12 23 and those that are our uncomely parts
24 but our comely parts have no need: but
Eph 4 9 first into the lower parts of the earth
Apoc 6 8 over the four parts of the earth, to
16 19 great city was divided into three p.
party Exod 21 21 if the p. remain alive a day or
1 Ma 8 30 if after this one party or the other
11 39 Tryphon who had been of Alexander's p.
pasch Eze 45 21 observe the solemnity of the p.
Mat 26 2 after two days shall be the pasch, and
17 prepare for thee to eat the pasch. Mark 14:12
18 with thee I make the pasch with my
19 they prepared the pasch. Mark 14:16
Mark 14 1 the feast of the pasch and of the
12 when they sacrificed the pasch, the
14 where I may eat the pasch. Luke 22:11
Luke 2 41 at the solemn day of the pasch, and
22 1 which is called the pasch, was at
7 necessary that the p. should be killed

8 prepare for us the pasch, that we may
13 and made ready the pasch. And when the
15 desired to eat this pasch with you
John 2 13 pasch of the Jews was at hand. 11:55
23 when he was at Jerusalem at the pasch
6 4 the pasch, the festival day of the
11 55 before the pasch to purify themselves
12 1 six days before the pasch, came to
13 1 before the festival day of the pasch
18 28 but that they might eat the pasch
39 release one unto you at the pasch
19 14 it was the parasceve of the pasch
Acts 12 4 after the pasch, to bring him forth to
1 C 5 7 for Christ our pasch is sacrificed
Heb 11 28 by faith he celebrated the pasch, and
pass Gen 13 9 right hand, I will pass to the left
Gen 18 5 heart, afterwards you shall pass on
31 52 if either I shall pass beyond it going
52 or thou shalt pass beyond it, thinking
41 32 that the word of God cometh to pass
Exod 19 21 a mind to pass the limits to see
24 let not . . . the people pass the limits
33 22 when my glory shall pass, I will set
22 thee with my right hand till I pass
Lev 27 32 that pass under the shepherd's rod
Num 20 19 the price, only let us pass speedily
20 he answered: Thou shalt not pass
27 8 inheritance shall pass to his daughter
32 7 that they may not dare to pass into
29 pass with you over the Jordan, all
30 if they will not pass armed with you
36 4 of the one shall pass to the others
Deut 2 13 rising up to pass the torrent Zared
18 thou shalt pass this day the borders
24 arise ye and pass the torrent Arnon
29 and pass to the land which the Lord
30 king of Hesebon would not let us pass
3 21 the kingdoms to which thou shalt pass
27 for thou shalt not pass this Jordan
4 22 you shall pass, and possess the goodly
13 2 and that come to pass which he spoke
18 22 and it cometh not to pass: that thing
29 12 that thou mayst pass in the covenant
Josu 17 18 thou shalt pass to the mountain
21 43 was made void, but all came to pass
Judg 12 5 and said: I beseech you let me pass
1 K 3 21 word of Samuel came to pass to all
9 6 that he saith, cometh certainly to pass
27 servant to go before us and pass on
2 K 18 30 king said to him: Pass and stand here
4 K 6 9 that thou pass not to such a place
9 19 to do with peace? Pass, and follow me
12 4 by those that pass, which is offered
2 Pa 15 3 and many days shall pass in Israel
20 10 lands thou didst not allow Israel to p.
2 Es 2 14 for the beast on which I rode to pass
Jdth 9 12 bring to pass, O Lord, that his pride
10 8 they let her pass, saying: The God of
12 11 by doing so as to pass free from him
13 7 that I may bring to pass that which I
Job 14 13 hell, and hide me till thy wrath pass
19 8 path round about, and I cannot pass
20 8 he shall pass as a vision of the night
24 12 doth not suffer it to pass unrevenged
19 let him pass from the snow waters to
34 20 they shall pass and take away the
37 21 wind shall pass and drive them away
Ps 65 6 in the river they shall pass on foot
76 18 thy arrows pass: the voice of thy
102 16 the spirit shall pass in him, and he
103 10 midst of the hills the water shall p.
140 10 in his net: I am alone until I pass
Prov 8 29 that they should not pass their limits
22 28 pass not beyond the ancient bounds
23 30 they that pass their time in wine and
31 8 causes of all the children that pass
Ecce 3 1 their times all things p. under heaven
Eccu 11 20 he knoweth not what time shall pass
39 5 he shall pass into strange countries
Isa 10 28 into Aiath, he shall pass into Magron
23 10 pass thy land as a river, O daughter
28 18 the overflowing scourge shall pass
41 3 he shall pass in peace, no path
46 11 have spoken and will bring it to pass
54 3 thou shalt pass on to the right hand
Jer 33 13 shall the flocks pass again under the
Eze 14 15 so that there is none that can pass
Dan 4 28 thy kingdom shall pass from thee
Osee 6 9 way those that pass out of Sichem
10 7 hath made her king to pass as froth
Mich 2 13 and their king shall pass before them
Nah 1 12 they be cut off, and he shall pass
Haba 1 11 be changed, and he shall pass and
2 Ma 4 17 wickedly . . . doth not pass unpunished
15 36 by no means to let this day pass
Mat 5 18 till heaven and earth pass, one jot or
18 or one tittle shall not pass of the law
24 34 this generation shall not p. Mark 13:30
35 shall pass, but my words shall not pass
26 39 possible, let this chalice pass from me
Mark 14 35 the hour might pass from him. And he
Luke 12 55 will be heat: and it cometh to pass
16 17 is easier for heaven and earth to pass
26 they who would pass from hence to you
19 4 see him; for he was to pass that way
John 7 3 pass from hence and go into Judea
13 1 that he should pass out of this world
Rom 15 24 I hope that as I pass, I shall see you
pass away Gen 18 3 p. not away from thy servant
Job 14 20 that he may pass away forever: thou
16 23 short years pass away, and I am
Ps 56 2 will I hope, until iniquity pass away
89 6 he shall flourish and pass away: in
143 4 his days pass away like a shadow
148 6 a decree, and it shall not pass away
Ecce 8 13 as a shadow let them pass away that
Wisd 2 3 our life shall pass away as the trace
Eccu 40 13 shall pass away with a noise like a
42 9 lest she pass away the flower of her
51 13 I have prayed for death to pass away
Isa 26 20 until the indignation pass away. For
31 9 and his strength shall pass away with
Dan 2 9 before me till the time pass away
Mich 1 11 pass away, O thou that dwellest in
Mat 26 42 if this chalice may *not* pass away, but
Mark 13 31 heaven and earth shall p. away, but my words shall not p. away. Luke 21:33
Luke 21 32 this generation shall not pass away
James 1 10 flower of the grass shall he pass away
2 P 3 10 the heavens shall pass away with great
pass by Exod 15 16 until thy people, O Lord, pass by: until this thy people pass by
Exod 23 5 thou shalt not pass by, but shalt lift
Num 20 18 thou shalt not pass by me: if thou
21 23 that Israel should pass by his borders
Deut 2 4 you shall pass by the borders of
22 1 thou shalt not pass by if thou seest
3 K 9 8 every one that shall pass by it shall
4 K 9 37 they who pass by shall say: Is this
2 Pa 7 21 be for a proverb to all that pass by
Job 36 12 hear not, they shall pass by the sword
Ps 79 13 they who pass by the way do pluck it
Prov 4 15 flee from it, pass not by it: go aside
9 15 to call them that pass by the way
Wisd 1 8 the chastising judgment pass him by
2 7 let not the flower of the time p. by

Isa 8 21 they shall pass by it, they shall fall
33 21 no ship with oars shall pass by it
Jer 18 16 every one that shall pass by, shall
19 8 that shall pass by it shall. 49:17
22 8 many nations shall pass by this city
20 and cry to them that pass by, for
50 13 every one that shall pass by Babylon
Lam 1 12 all ye that pass by the way, attend
Eze 24 14 I will not pass by nor spare nor be
33 28 because there is none to pass by them
39 11 astonishment in them that pass by
Amos 8 2 I will not again pass by them any
Mat 8 28 so that none could pass by that way
2 C 1 16 and to pass by you into Macedonia, and
pass over Exod 12 13 blood and shall p. over you
Exod 12 23 will pass over the door of the house
Num 6 5 no razor shall pass over his head
32 5 make us not pass over the Jordan
21 every fighting man pass over the Jordan
Deut 3 25 I will pass over therefore and will see
27 for thou shalt not pass this Jordan
4 21 that I should not pass over the Jordan
22 I shall not pass over the Jordan
6 1 the land into which you pass over
9 3 himself will pass over before thee
11 31 you shall pass over the Jordan. 12:10
30 18 to which thou shalt p. over the Jordan
31 2 thou shalt not pass over this Jordan
3 God then will pass over before thee
34 4 eyes, and shalt not pass over to it
Josu 1 2 arise and pass over this Jordan, thou
11 you shall pass over the Jordan
14 pass you over armed before your
3 14 out of their tents, to pass over the
22 19 pass over to the land wherein is the
Judg 3 28 they suffered no man to pass over
19 12 I will pass over to Gabaa: and when I
2 K 15 22 David said to Ethai: Come and pass over
17 16 without delay pass over: lest the king
21 arise and pass quickly over the river
3 K 2 37 and shalt pass over the brook Cedron
Ps 103 9 a bound which they shall not pass over
Prov 19 11 and his glory is to pass over wrongs
Wisd 6 24 light, and will not p. over the truth
Isa 23 6 of Tyre: pass over the seas, howl
35 8 the unclean shall not pass over it
47 2 bare thy legs, pass over the rivers
51 10 that the delivered might pass over
Jer 2 10 pass over to the isles of Cethim and
5 22 which it shall not pass over: and the
22 shall swell and shall not pass over
Eze 5 1 and cause it to pass over thy head
47 5 torrent, which I could not pass over
Dan 4 13 and let seven times pass over him
20 beasts, till seven times pass over him
22 seven times shall pass over thee. 29
12 4 many shall pass over, and knowledge
Amos 5 5 shall you pass over to Bersabee: for
6 2 pass ye over to Chalane and see and
Zach 10 11 he shall pass over the strait of the
1 Ma 5 40 if he pass over unto us first, we
41 but if he be afraid to pass over
41 we will pass over to them and shall
Mat 8 18 gave orders to pass over the water
Mark 4 35 let us pass over to the other side
Luke 11 42 and pass over judgment and the charity
Acts 16 9 beseeching him, and saying: Pass over
pass through Exod 12 12 I will p. t. the land of
Exod 12 23 the Lord will pass through striking
Lev 26 6 the sword shall not pass through your
Num 20 17 we may have leave to pass through thy
31 23 all that may pass through the fire
Deut 2 27 we will pass through thy land, we will
28 that thou wilt let us pass through
18 10 making them to pass through the fire
Josu 1 10 pass through the midst of the camp
Judg 11 17 suffer me to pass through thy land. 19
20 suffered him not to pass through his
3 K 12 31 and made them pass through brickkilns
4 K 16 3 son, making him pass through the fire
21 6 he made his son pass through fire
2 Pa 33 6 made his sons to pass through the fire
Jdth 6 4 sword of my soldiers shall p. through
Ps 8 9 that pass through the paths of the sea
67 8 thou didst pass through the desert
Wisd 19 5 people might wonderfully pass through
Isa 8 8 shall pass through Juda, overflowing
11 15 so that men may pass through it in
28 15 overflowing scourge shall pass through
19 whensoever it shall pass through, it
19 morning early it shall pass through
33 21 shall the great galley pass through it
34 10 none shall pass through it forever
43 2 when thou shalt pass through the
52 1 shall no more pass through thee
Jer 51 43 dwell, nor son of man pass through it
Lam 3 44 that our prayer may not pass through
Eze 5 17 and blood shall pass through thee
14 17 to the sword: Pass through the land
20 31 your children pass through the fire
29 11 foot of man shall not pass through
44 2 and no man shall pass through it
Dan 11 40 and shall destroy and pass through
43 he shall pass through Libya and
Osee 2 3 a land that none can pass through
Joel 3 17 strangers shall pass through it no
Amos 5 17 I will pass through in the midst of
Mich 2 13 they shall . . . pass through the gate
Nah 1 15 Belial shall no more pass through
Zach 9 8 oppressor shall no more pass through
1 Ma 5 48 let us pass through your land to go
48 we will only pass through on foot. But
Mat 19 24 to p. t. eye of a needle. Mark 10:25; Luke 18:25
1 C 16 5 for I shall pass through Macedonia. And
passable Eze 19 13 desert, in a land not p. and
Soph 2 13 as a place not passable and as a
2 Ma 5 21 and the sea passable on foot: such
passage Exod 12 27 the victim of the p. of the Lord
Exod 12 11 it is the Phase, that is the Passage,
Num 20 21 to grant them p. through his borders
Judg 11 17 likewise refused to give him passage
12 6 killed him in the very p. of the Jordan
Jdth 2 9 out of all Syria in his passage
4 5 by whom there might be a passage of way
Ps 143 14 there is no breach of wall nor passage
Wisd 5 11 passage of which no mark can be found
12 the passage thereof is not known
19 16 sought the passage of his own door
Isa 16 2 daughters of Moab be in the p. of Arnon
30 32 p. of the rod shall be strongly grounded
57 14 make a way; give free passage, turn
Eze 41 7 there was a broad passage round about
passages Deut 32 49 Abarim, that is to say, of p.
1 Ma 11 46 they of the city kept the passages
passed Gen 7 10 after the seven days were passed
Gen 8 6 after that forty days were passed
26 8 when very many days were passed, Noe
31 21 [Jacob] having passed the river, was
34 7 hearing what had passed, they were
40 4 some little time passed, and they were
50 3 there passed forty days: for this was
Exod 34 6 when he passed before him, he said
Num 33 48 they passed to the plains of Moab by
Deut 9 11 when forty days were passed and as
27 12 people, when you are passed the Jordan

Josu 10 29 he passed from Maceda with all Israel
31 from Lebna he passed unto Lachis
34 and he passed from Lachis to Eglon
23 1 when a long time was passed, after
Judg 18 13 thence they passed into mount Ephraim
1 K 15 12 had passed on and gone down to Galgal
25 38 after ten days had passed, the Lord
2 K 2 29 they passed the Jordan, and having
15 22 and Ethai the Gethite passed, and all
17 20 answered them: They p. on in haste
18 9 the mule on which he rode passed on
23 running by a nearer way p. Chusai
31 when he had passed and stood still
19 18 they passed the fords before the king
20 12 that they who p. might not stop on
24 5 when they had passed the Jordan, they
6 by Jazer they passed into Galaad
7 they passed near the walls of Tyre
3 K 22 1 there passed three years without war
4 K 4 8 as he [Eliseus] passed often that way
14 9 passed and trod down the thistle
1 Pa 16 20 passed from nation to nation. Ps 104:13
19 17 passed the Jordan and came upon them
29 30 and of the times that passed under him
2 Pa 21 19 time rolled on, two whole years passed
2 Es 2 14 I passed to the gate of the fountain
Jdth 5 12 of the sea, and passed it dry foot
13 12 and they passed the camp, and having
Job 4 15 when a spirit p. before me, the hair
7 6 my days have passed more swiftly than
11 16 only as waters that are passed away
14 5 his bounds which cannot be passed
15 19 no stranger hath passed among them
17 11 my days have passed away, my thoughts
30 15 my prosperity hath passed away like a
Ps 17 13 clouds passed, hail and coals of fire
72 7 passed into the affection of the heart
Prov 22 3 the simple p. on, and suffered loss
Ecce 2 12 I passed further to behold wisdom and
Wisd 5 9 all those things are passed away like
19 8 through which all the nation passed
18 swam in the water passed upon the land
Eccu 28 23 that hath not passed into the wrath
Isa 10 29 they have passed in haste, Gaba is
26 3 the old error is passed away: thou
Jer 8 13 them the things that passed away
34 18 and passed between the parts thereof
19 that p. between the parts of the calf
Dan 3 94 nor smell of the fire had p. on them
Osee 11 1 so hath the king of Israel passed away
Mich 2 8 that passed harmless you have turned
Nah 3 19 upon whom hath not thy wickedness p.
Haba 3 10 great body of waters passed away
1 Ma 12 10 long time passed since you sent to
30 they had passed the river Eleutherus
2 Ma 1 20 but when many years had passed, and it
Mat 9 9 when Jesus passed on from thence, he
27 as Jesus passed from thence, there
11 1 he passed from thence. 13:53
12 9 when he had passed from thence
14 34 having passed the water, they came
15 29 when Jesus had passed away from thence
Mark 5 21 when Jesus had p. again in the ship
8 13 passed to the other side of the water
Luke 6 12 he p. the whole night in the prayer
John 5 24 but is passed from death to life
Acts 9 23 when many days were passed, the Jews
Rom 5 12 and so death passed upon all men, in
13 12 night is passed, and the day is at hand
2 C 5 17 the old things are passed away, behold
Heb 4 14 priest that hath passed into the heavens
1 J 2 8 the darkness is passed, and the true
3 14 that we have passed from death to life

Apoc 21 4 for the former things are passed away
passed by Gen 37 28 the Madianite merchants p. by
Deut 2 8 when we had passed by our brethren
Judg 3 26 and passed by the place of the idols
9 25 taking spoils of all that passed by
19 14 so they passed by Jebus and went on
3 K 20 39 as the king passed by, he cried to the
4 K 4 8 a day when Eliseus passed by Sunam
6 30 passed by upon the wall. And all the
2 Pa 25 18 passed by and trod down the thistle
Job 6 15 my brethren have passed by me as the
9 26 they have passed by as ships carrying
28 8 neither hath the lioness passed by it
Ps 36 36 I passed by, and lo, he was not: and
128 8 and they that passed by have not said
Prov 24 30 I passed by the field of the slothful
Cant 3 4 when I had a little passed by them
Lam 2 15 that pass by the way have clapped
Eze 16 8 and I passed by thee and saw thee
25 thyself to every one that passed by
36 24 in the sight of all that passed by
Mat 20 30 heard that Jesus passed by, and they
27 39 they that passed by blasphemed. Mark 15:29
Mark 6 48 and he would have passed by them
11 20 when they passed by in the morning
15 21 one Simon a Cyrenian who passed by
Luke 10 31 same way: and seeing him, passed by
32 near the place and saw him, passed by
passed over Gen 32 10 with my staff I p. over
Gen 32 22 and passed over the ford of Jaboc
33 18 he passed over to Salem, a city of
Exod 12 27 when he passed over the houses of
Num 33 51 when you shall have passed over the Jordan. 35:10
Deut 2 14 till we passed over the torrent Zared
4 26 when you have passed over the Jordan. 27:2, 4, 12
27 3 when thou art passed over the Jordan
Josu 3 17 people passed over through the channel
4 1 when they were passed over, the Lord
7 when it [ark] passed over the same
10 the people made haste and passed over
11 when they had all passed over, the ark also of the Lord passed over
22 Israel passed over this Jordan through
23 in your sight, until you passed over
5 1 children of Israel, till they passed over
24 11 you passed over the Jordan, and you
Judg 8 4 he passed over it with the 300 men
11 32 Jephte passed over to the children
12 3 p. over against the children of Ammon
1 K 13 7 passed over the Jordan into the land
2 K 10 17 passed over the Jordan and came to
15 23 and all the people passed over: the
17 22 they passed over the Jordan until it
24 and Absalom passed over the Jordan
19 39 the king had passed over the Jordan
3 K 2 8 to meet me when I p. over the Jordan
4 K 2 8 they both passed over on dry ground
14 and thither, and Eliseus passed over
1 Pa 12 15 are they who passed over the Jordan
Jdth 2 14 he passed over the Euphrates and came
Ps 41 8 and thy billows have passed over me
Isa 40 27 my judgment is passed over from my
Bar 3 30 who hath passed over the sea and found
Eze 47 5 torrent which could not be passed over
Osee 10 11 I passed over upon the beauty of her
Jon 2 4 thy waves have passed over me. And I
1 Ma 3 37 and he passed over the river Euphrates
5 6 he passed over to the children of
24 his brother passed over the Jordan and
43 he passed over to them first, and all

52 they passed over the Jordan to the
16 6 men seeing him, passed over after him
Mat 9 1 he passed over the water and came into
Mark 6 53 when they had passed over, they came
passed through Gen 12 6 Abram p. t. the country
Num 33 8 they p. through the midst of the sea
Deut 1 19 we passed through the terrible and
2 7 how thou hast passed through this
29 16 how we have passed through the midst
Josu 4 24 which he dried up till we p. through
24 17 all the people through whom we passed
1 K 9 3 they had p. through mount Ephraim
4 they p. also through the land of Salim
2 K 20 14 had passed through all the tribes of
2 Es 9 11 passed through the midst of the sea
Jdth 2 12 when he had p. through the borders of
3 14 when he had passed through all Syria
8 23 passed through many tribulations
10 10 passed through the gates, she and her
Ps 65 12 we have passed through fire and water
72 9 their tongue hath p. through the earth
123 5 our soul hath passed through a torrent
5 our soul had passed through a water
Isa 60 15 there was none that passed through thee
Zach 7 14 no man passed through or returned
1 Ma 5 51 passed through all the city over
11 60 passed through the cities beyond
12 32 and passed through all that country
Mark 9 29 they passed through Galilee, and he
Luke 17 11 he p. through the midst of Samaria
Acts 9 32 Peter, as he passed through, visiting
12 10 they passed on through one street
15 3 they . . . passed through Phenice, and
16 4 as they passed through the cities, they
6 they had passed through Phrygia, and
8 when they had passed through Mysia
17 1 when they had p. t. Amphipolis and
19 1 having passed through the upper coasts
21 when he had passed through Macedonia and
1 C 10 1 the cloud, and all passed through sea
16 5 I shall have passed through Macedonia
Heb 11 29 by faith they p. through the Red Sea
passedst Judg 5 4 and p. by the regions of Edom
passenger Bar 6 43 drawn away by some p., lieth
Eze 16 15 prostituted thyself to every passenger
passengers Eze 39 11 valley of the p. on the east
passest Mich 7 18 p. by the sin of the remnant
passeth Gen 2 14 same p. along by the Assyrians
Exod 30 13 that p. at the naming, half a sicle
Josu 15 3 of the Scorpion and passeth on to Sina
6 passeth by the north into Beth Araba
7 border passeth the waters that are
9 it p. on from the top of the mountain
10 passeth by the side of Mount Jarim
10 Bethsames, and passeth into Thamna
11 to Sechrona, and passeth mount Baala
16 2 and p. the border of Archi to Ataroth
6 and p. along on the east side to Janoe
8 Taphua it passeth on towards the sea
18 18 it passeth along to the hills that
18 p. on north side to the champaign
19 it passeth by Bethhagla northward
19 13 it passeth along from thence to the
27 and passeth along to Zabulon and to
34 passeth along to Zabulon southward
3 K 19 11 behold the Lord passeth and a great
4 K 4 9 man of God who often passeth by us
Job 6 15 as the torrent that passeth swiftly
7 9 as a cloud is consumed and p. away
23 10 as gold that passeth through the fire
Ps 38 7 man passeth as an image: yea and he is
Prov 7 8 p. through the street by the corner
10 25 a tempest that passeth, so the wicked
26 17 so is he that passeth by in anger and
Ecce 1 4 generation passeth away and another
7 1 and the time that p. like a shadow
Wisd 5 10 as a ship that p. through the waves
15 a guest of one day that passeth by
Eccu 23 25 man that passeth beyond his own bed
26 27 he that p. over from justice to sin
Isa 33 8 desolate, no one passeth by the road
Jer 9 10 not a man that passeth through them
12 a wilderness, which none p. through
Eze 5 14 sight of every one that passeth by
Osee 11 1 as the morning passeth, so hath the
13 3 as the early dew that passeth away
Nah 1 8 with a flood that passeth by, he
Soph 2 15 that passeth by her shall hiss and
3 6 so that there is none that passeth by
1 C 7 31 the fashion of this world passeth away
1 J 2 17 and the world passeth away, and the
passible James 5 17 Elias was a man passible like unto us
passing Gen 12 8 p. on from thence to a mountain
Gen 15 17 fire passing between those divisions
Deut 29 16 passing through them, you have seen
Josu 2 23 passing over the Jordan, they came
15 4 from thence passing along into Asemona
18 13 and passing along southward by Luza
17 passing thence to the north and going
Judg 4 21 passing from deep sleep to death, he
6 33 passing over the Jordan, camped in
10 9 children of Ammon p. over the Jordan
11 29 [Jephte] passing over from thence to
12 1 passing towards the north, they said
2 K 15 24 come out of the city had done passing
3 K 13 25 men passing by saw the dead body cast
4 K 6 26 the king of Israel was p. by the wall
2 Pa 11 14 passing over to Juda and Jerusalem
Ps 106 40 to wander where there was no passing
Job 33 18 and his life from passing to the sword
Prov 12 11 delighted in p. his time over wine
27 12 little ones p. on have suffered losses
Wisd 2 5 our time is as the passing of a shadow
14 5 p. over the sea by ship are saved
17 9 sacred with the passing by of beasts
Isa 23 2 merchants of Sidon p. over the sea
29 5 as ashes passing away, the multitude
31 5 delivering, passing over and saving
Eze 16 6 passing by thee, I saw that thou wast
39 15 shall go about passing through the land
Soph 2 2 forth the day as dust passing away
Mark 1 16 passing by the sea of Galilee, he saw
2 14 when he was passing by, he saw Levi
Luke 4 30 he p. through the midst of them, went
12 37 passing will minister unto them. And
18 36 when he heard the multitude passing by
37 that Jesus of Nazareth was passing by
John 9 1 Jesus passing by, saw a man who was
Acts 8 40 p. through, he preached the gospel to
12 10 p. through first and second ward
13 14 they passing through Perge, came to
14 23 p. through Pisidia, they came into
17 23 passing by, and seeing your idols, I
passion Jdth 6 1 Holofernes being in a violent p.
Acts 1 3 showed himself alive after his passion
1 Th 4 5 not in the p. of lust, like the Gentiles
Heb 2 10 author of their salvation, by his p.
passionate Prov 15 18 a p. man stirreth up strifes
Prov 21 19 than with a quarrelsome and p. woman
29 22 a passionate man provoketh quarrels
Eccu 8 19 quarrel not with a passionate man, and
28 11 for a passionate man kindleth strife
passions Rom 7 5 p. of sins, which were by the law
past Gen 29 28 the week was past, he married
Gen 38 12 after many days were past, the daughter
41 53 years of the plenty . . . were past

Num 20 17 the left, till we are past thy borders
21 22 highway till we be past thy borders
1 K 9 9 in time past in Israel, when a man went
9 prophet, in time past was called seer
2 K 16 1 was a little past the top of the hill
3 K 18 29 after midday was past, and while they
Tob 6 22 and when the third night is past, thou
Jdth 7 25 if after five days be past there come
Job 29 2 I might be according to the months p.
Ps 89 4 thy sight are as yesterday, which is p.
Ecce 3 15 and God restoreth that which is past
8 7 because he is ignorant of things past
11 8 things past shall be accused of vanity
Cant 2 11 winter is now past, the rain is over
Wisd 8 8 she knoweth things past and judgeth of
11 13 for the remembrance of things past
12 27 in time past they denied that they
Eccu 42 19 he declareth the things that are past
Isa 2 6 they are filled as in times past and
Jer 8 20 the harvest is past, the summer is
Mat 14 15 this is a desert place, and the hour is now past. Mark 6:35
Mark 16 1 when the sabbath was past, Mary
Acts 14 15 times past suffered all nations to walk
27 9 because the fast was now past, Paul
Rom 11 30 as you also in times p. did not believe
15 23 desire these many years past to come
2 C 9 2 Achaia also is ready from the year past
Gal 1 13 my conversation in time past in Jews'
23 he, who persecuted us in times past
Eph 2 2 in time past you walked according to the
3 also we all conversed in time past, in
2 Tim 2 18 saying, that the resurrection is past
Heb 1 1 spoke in times past to the fathers by
11 11 even past the time of age; because she
1 P 2 10 who in time past were not a people
4 3 the time past is sufficient to have
Apoc 9 12 one woe is past, and behold there come
11 14 the second woe is past: and behold the
paste 1 C 5 7 that you may be a new paste, as you
pastime Wisd 15 12 they have counted our life a p.
Eccu 32 15 thyself, and there take thy pastime
pastor Gen 49 24 thence he came forth a pastor
Jer 17 15 not troubled, following thee for my p.
Heb 13 20 the great pastor of the sheep, our
pastors Jer 2 8 the p. transgressed against me
Jer 3 15 I will give you pastors according to
10 21 the pastors have done foolishly
12 10 many p. have destroyed my vineyard
22 22 the wind shall feed all thy pastors
23 1 woe to the pastors, that destroy
2 to the pastors that feed my people
4 and I will set up pastors over them
Eph 4 11 and other some pastors and doctors, for
1 P 5 4 when the prince of p. shall appear
pasture Gen 41 18 on green places in a marshy p.
Job 39 8 round about the mountains of his p.
Ps 22 2 he hath set me in a place of pasture
73 1 enkindled against the sheep of thy p.
78 13 we thy people and the sheep of thy p.
94 7 we are the people of his pasture and
99 3 are his people and the sheep of his p.
Isa 34 13 dragons and the pasture of ostriches
37 27 the field and the herb of the pasture
Jer 23 1 destroy and tear the sheep of my p.
Eze 34 31 the flocks of my pasture are men: and
Joel 1 18 because there is no pasture for them
pastures 1 K 16 19 David thy son, who is in the p.
2 K 7 8 I took thee out of the pastures from
3 K 4 23 oxen and twenty out of the pastures
1 Pa 4 39 valley, to seek p. for their flocks
40 they found fat pastures and very good
41 because they found there fat pastures
17 7 I took thee [David] from the pastures
Isa 32 14 joy of wild asses, the p. of flocks
49 9 their pastures shall be in every plain
Jer 25 36 the Lord hath wasted their pastures
Lam 1 6 become like rams that find no p.
Eze 34 14 will feed them in the most fruitful p.
14 their p. shall be in the high mountains
14 and be fed in fat pastures upon the
34 18 not enough for you to feed upon good p.
18 with your feet the residue of your p.
Osee 13 6 according to their p. they were filled
2 Ma 12 11 promising to give him pastures and
John 10 9 and go out and shall find pastures
Patara Acts 21 1 to Rhodes, and from thence to P.
patches Josu 9 5 were clouted with patches, and old
paternity Eph 3 15 of whom all p. in heaven and
path Gen 49 17 a serpent in the path, that biteth
Job 16 23 in a path by which I shall not return
18 10 the earth, and his trap upon the path
19 8 he hath hedged in my path round about
22 15 dost thou desire to keep path of ages
28 7 the bird hath not known the path
41 23 a path shall shine after him, he shall
Ps 26 11 guide me in the right path, because of
77 50 he made a way for a path to his anger
118 35 me into the path of thy commandments
138 3 my path and my line thou hast searched
Prov 2 9 and equity and every good path
4 18 path of the just, as a shining light
26 make straight the path for thy feet
5 6 they walk not by the path of life, her
12 28 in the path of justice is life: but
15 24 the path of life is above for the wise
16 17 path of the just departeth from evils
Wisd 5 10 nor the path of its keel in the waters
14 3 and a most sure path among the waves
Isa 26 7 path of the just is right to walk in
30 11 turn away the path from me, let the
35 8 a path and a way shall be there, and
40 14 and taught him the path of justice
41 3 no path shall appear after his feet
43 16 sea, and a path in the mighty waters
57 14 give free passage, turn out of the path
Joel 2 8 they shall walk every one in his path
paths Judg 5 6 in the days of Jahel the p. rested
Jdth 15 2 the fields and the paths of the hills
Job 6 18 the paths of their steps are entangled
19 consider the paths of Thema, the ways
13 27 stocks, and hast observed all my paths
24 13 neither have they returned by his p.
30 12 have overwhelmed me with their paths
33 11 stocks, he hath observed all my paths
37 16 knowest thou the great p. of the clouds
38 20 and understand the paths of the house
Ps 8 9 that pass through the paths of the sea
16 5 perfect thou my goings in thy paths
17 46 away and have halted from their paths
22 3 he hath led me on the paths of justice
24 4 ways to me and teach me thy paths
76 20 the sea, and thy paths in many waters
118 105 thy word . . . a light to my paths
138 23 heart: examine me and know my paths
141 4 failed me, then thou knewest my paths
Prov 1 15 restrain thy foot from their paths
2 8 keeping the paths of justice, and
18 unto death, and her paths to hell
20 and mayst keep the paths of the just
3 17 ways, and all her paths are peaceable
4 11 I will lead thee by the paths of equity
14 not delighted in the p. of the wicked
7 25 neither be thou deceived with her p.
8 2 by the way, in the midst of the paths
20 in the midst of the paths of judgment

17 23 he may pervert the paths of judgment
31 27 looked well to the paths of her house
Isa 2 3 ways, and we will walk in his paths
21 13 you shall sleep, in the p. of Dedanim
40 3 in the wilderness the paths of our God
42 16 in the p. which they were ignorant of
49 11 a way, and my paths shall be exalted
58 12 fences, turning the paths into rest
59 8 their paths are become crooked to them
Jer 6 16 ask for the old paths, which is the good
18 15 stumbling in their ways, in ancient p.
Lam 3 9 he hath turned my paths upside down
11 he hath turned aside my paths, and
Bar 3 21 nor have they understood the paths
23 neither have they remembered her paths
31 nor that can search out her paths
4 13 entered by the paths of his truth
Osee 2 6 wall, and she shall not find her paths
Mich 4 2 ways: and we will walk in his paths
Mat 3 3 make straight his paths. Mark 1:3; Luke 3:4
pathway Jdth 7 5 by a narrow p. lead directly
patience Tob 2 12 be given to posterity of his p.
Job 4 6 where is thy fear, thy fortitude, thy p.
6 11 what is my end that I should keep p.
17 15 and who considereth my patience? All
Ps 9 19 patience of the poor shall not perish
61 6 to God: for from him is my patience
70 5 thou art my patience, O Lord: my hope
Prov 19 11 learning of a man is known by patience
25 15 by patience a prince shall be appeased
Ecce 8 12 by patience be borne withal, I know
Wisd 2 19 know his meekness and try his p.
Eccu 2 3 wait on God with patience: join
4 in thy humiliation keep patience
16 woe to them that have lost patience
21 will have p. even until his visitation
3 9 father, in work and word and all p.
15 if his understanding fail, have p.
16 14 patience of him that showeth mercy
17 20 them that were fainting in patience
35 22 the Almighty will not have patience
41 4 to the distrustful that loseth patience
Jer 15 15 do not defend me in thy patience: know
29 11 affliction, to give you an end and p.
1 Ma 8 3 of all the place by their counsel and p.
Mat 18 26 have p. with me, and I will pay. 29
Luke 8 15 keep it and bring forth fruit in p.
18 7 will he have patience in their regard
21 19 in your p. you shall possess your souls
Rom 2 4 despisest thou the riches of his . . . p.
7 who according to p. in good work, seek
5 3 knowing that tribulation worketh p.; and
4 and patience trial; and trial hope; and
8 25 we see not, we wait for it with patience
9 22 endured with much p. vessels of wrath
15 4 through p. and comfort of the scriptures
5 God of p. and of comfort grant you to be
2 C 6 4 of God, in much patience, in tribulation
12 12 been wrought on you, in all patience
Gal 5 22 the fruit of the Spirit is . . . patience
Eph 4 2 with all humility and mildness, with p.
Col 1 11 in all patience and longsuffering with
3 12 bowels of mercy . . . modesty, patience
2 Th 1 4 of God, for your patience and faith, and
3 5 charity of God, and the p. of Christ
1 Tim 1 16 Jesus might show forth all patience, for
6 11 and pursue . . . patience, mildness. Fight
2 Tim 3 10 faith, longsuffering, love, patience
4 2 reprove, entreat, rebuke in all patience
Titus 2 2 sound in faith, in love, in patience
Heb 6 12 faith and p. shall inherit the promises
10 36 for patience is necessary for you; that
12 1 let us run by patience to the fight
James 1 3 the trying of your faith worketh p.
4 and patience hath a perfect work; that
5 10 of suffering evil, of labor and p.
11 you have heard of the patience of Job
1 P 3 20 when they waited for the p. of God
2 P 1 6 in abstinence, p.; and in p., godliness
Apoc 1 9 kingdom, and patience in Christ Jesus
2 2 thy works and thy labor and thy patience
3 thou hast p. and hast endured for my
19 charity and thy ministry and thy p.
3 10 thou hast kept the word of my patience
13 10 here is the p. and the faith of the
14 12 here is the patience of the saints
patient Exod 34 6 patient and of much compassion
Num 14 18 the Lord is patient and full of mercy
Jdth 8 14 but forasmuch as the Lord is patient
Ps 7 12 is a just judge, strong and patient
85 15 God of compassion, merciful, patient
144 8 merciful: p. and plenteous in mercy
Prov 14 29 he that is patient is governed with
15 18 that is patient appeaseth those that
16 32 the p. man is better than the valiant
Ecce 7 9 better is the patient man than the
Wisd 15 1 p. and ordering all things in mercy
Eccu 1 29 a patient man shall bear for a time
5 4 the most High is a patient rewarder
Isa 42 14 have kept silence, I have been patient
Joel 2 13 patient and rich in mercy and ready
Jon 4 2 gracious and merciful God, patient and
Nah 1 3 the Lord is patient and great in power
Rom 12 12 rejoicing in hope. P. in tribulation
1 C 13 4 charity is patient, is kind: charity
1 Th 5 14 weak, be patient towards all men. See
2 Tim 2 24 mild towards all men, apt to teach, p.
James 5 7 be patient therefore, brethren, until
8 be you therefore also patient and
patiently Eccu 36 18 reward them that p. wait
Isa 25 9 we have patiently waited for him, we
26 8 we have patiently waited for thee: thy
51 5 and shall patiently wait for my arm
Bar 4 25 suffer patiently the wrath that is
2 Ma 6 14 whom the Lord patiently expecteth
20 he was come to it, patiently bearing
7 17 but stay patiently a while, and thou
Acts 26 3 I beseech thee to hear me patiently. And
Heb 6 15 so p. enduring he obtained the promise
James 5 7 p. bearing till he receive the early
1 P 2 20 but if doing well you suffer patiently
2 P 3 9 but dealeth patiently for your sake
Patmos Apoc 1 9 in the island which is called Patmos
patriarch Acts 2 29 speak to you of the p. David
Heb 7 4 to whom also Abraham the p. gave tithes
patriarchs Tob 6 20 the society of the holy p.
Acts 7 8 and Jacob begot the 12 patriarchs
9 the p. through envy sold Joseph into
Patrobas Rom 16 14 salute . . . Hermas, Patrobas
Patroclus 2 Ma 8 9 Nicanor the son of Patroclus
pattern Exod 25 40 p. that was shown thee. 26:30
Num 8 4 p. which the Lord had shown to Moses
4 K 16 10 sent to Urias the priest a pattern of
1 Pa 28 19 understand all the works of the pattern
Eccu 38 30 the pattern of the vessel he maketh
1 Th 1 7 you were made a pattern to all that
2 Th 3 9 might give ourselves a pattern unto you
Heb 8 5 according to the p. which was shown thee
1 P 5 3 a pattern of the flock from the heart
patterns Heb 9 23 p. of heavenly things should be
Heb 9 24 with hands, the patterns of the true
Paul Acts 13 9 Saul, otherwise Paul, filled with
Acts 13 13 when P. and they that were with him
16 Paul rising up, and with his hand
43 the strangers . . . followed Paul and
45 those things which were said by Paul

46 Paul and Barnabas said boldly: To you
50 persecution against Paul and Barnabas
14 8 this same heard Paul speaking. Who
10 multitudes had seen what P. had done
11 Barnabas, Jupiter: but Paul, Mercury
13 when . . . Barnabas and Paul had heard
18 stoning Paul, drew him out of the city
15 2 when Paul and Barnabas had no small
2 they determined that P. and Barnabas
12 they heard Barnabas and Paul telling
22 send to Antioch, with P. and Barnabas
25 with our well beloved Barnabas and P.
35 Paul and Barnabas continued at Antioch
36 after some days, Paul said to Barnabas
38 but Paul desired that he, as having
40 Paul choosing Silas, departed, being
16 3 P. would have to go along with him: and
9 a vision was showed to P. in the night
14 to those things which were said by Paul
17 this same following Paul and us, cried
18 Paul being grieved, turned, and said to
19 apprehending Paul and Silas, brought
25 at midnight, Paul and Silas praying
28 Paul cried with a loud voice, saying
29 fell down at the feet of Paul and Silas
36 of the prison told these words to Paul
37 Paul said to them: They have beaten
17 2 Paul, according to his custom, went
4 were associated to Paul and Silas; and
10 sent away Paul and Silas by night unto
13 word of God was also preached by Paul
14 immediately brethren sent away Paul
15 they that conducted Paul, brought him
16 whilst Paul waited for them at Athens
22 but Paul standing in the midst of the
33 so Paul went out from among them. But
18 5 P. was earnest in preaching, testifying
9 the Lord said to Paul in the night, by
12 with one accord rose up against Paul
14 Paul was beginning to open his mouth
18 P., when he had stayed yet many days
19 1 Paul having passed through the upper
4 Paul said: John baptized the people
6 when Paul had imposed his hands on
11 God wrought by the hand of Paul more
13 conjure you by Jesus, whom P. preacheth
15 Jesus I know, and Paul I know; but who
21 Paul purposed in the spirit, when he had
26 this P. by persuasion hath drawn away
30 when Paul would have entered in unto
20 1 Paul calling to him the disciples, and
7 Paul discoursed with them, being to
9 deep sleep, as Paul was long preaching
10 when Paul had gone down, he laid himself
13 to Assos, being there to take in Paul
16 Paul had determined to sail by Ephesus
37 falling on neck of Paul, they kissed him
21 4 who said to Paul through the Spirit
13 Paul answered, and said: What do you
18 Paul went in with us unto James; and all
26 Paul took the men, and the next day
29 they supposed that Paul had brought into
30 taking Paul, they drew him out of temple
32 they left off beating Paul. Then the
37 as Paul was about to be brought into the
39 Paul said to him: I am a Jew of Tarsus
40 Paul standing on the stairs, beckoned
22 25 Paul saith to the centurion that stood
28 and Paul said: But I was born so
30 bringing forth Paul, he set him before
23 1 Paul looking upon the council, said: Men
3 Paul said to him: God shall strike thee
5 Paul said: I knew not, brethren, that
6 and Paul knowing that the one part were
10 lest Paul should be pulled in pieces by
12 eat, nor drink, till they killed Paul
14 will eat nothing till we have slain Paul
16 entered into the castle and told Paul
17 P., calling to him one of the centurions
18 said: Paul, the prisoner, desired me to
20 that thou wouldst bring forth Paul
24 provide beasts, that they may set Paul
31 soldiers . . . taking Paul, brought him
33 did also present Paul before him. And
24 1 who went to the governor against Paul
2 Paul being called for, Tertullus began
10 Paul answered, the governor making sign
24 sent for P., and heard of him the faith
26 that money should be given him by Paul
27 to show Jews a pleasure, left Paul bound
25 2 the Jews, went unto him against Paul
4 that Paul was kept in Caesarea, and that
6 seat; and commanded Paul to be brought
8 Paul making answer for himself: Neither
9 Festus . . . answering Paul, said: Wilt
10 Paul said: I stand at Caesar's judgment
14 Festus told the king of Paul, saying: A
19 deceased, whom Paul affirmed to be alive
21 Paul appealing to be reserved unto the
23 commandment, Paul was brought forth
26 1 Agrippa said to Paul: Thou art permitted
1 Paul stretching forth his hand, began
24 voice: Paul, thou art beside thyself
25 Paul said: I am not mad, most excellent
28 Agrippa said to Paul: In a little thou
29 Paul said: I would to God, that both in
27 1 Paul, with the other prisoners, should
3 and Julius treating Paul courteously
9 Paul comforted them, saying to them
11 those things which were said by Paul
21 Paul standing forth in the midst of them
23 fear not, Paul, thou must be brought
31 Paul said to centurion, and to soldiers
33 Paul besought them all to take meat
43 the centurion, willing to save Paul
28 3 Paul had gathered together a bundle of
8 to whom Paul entered in; and when he had
15 whom when Paul saw, he gave thanks to
16 Paul was suffered to dwell by himself
25 Paul speaking this one word: Well did
Rom 1 1 Paul, a servant of Jesus Christ, called
1 C 1 1 Paul, called to be an apostle of Jesus
12 I indeed am of Paul. 3:4
13 was Paul then crucified for you? or were
3 4 what then is Apollo, and what is Paul
22 yours, whether it be Paul or Apollo
16 21 salutation of me Paul, with my own hand
2 C 1 1 Paul, an apostle of Jesus Christ. Eph 1:1; Col 1:1; 1 Tim 1:1; 2 Tim 1:1
10 1 now I Paul myself beseech you, by the
Gal 1 1 Paul, an apostle, not of men, neither
5 2 behold, I Paul tell you, that if you be
Eph 3 1 I Paul, the prisoner of Jesus Christ
Phil 1 1 Paul and Timothy, the servants of Jesus
Col 1 23 whereof I Paul am made a minister. Who
4 18 salutation of P. with my own. 2 Th 3:17
1 Th 1 1 P. and Sylvanus and Timothy. 2 Th 1:1
2 18 I Paul indeed, once and again: but Satan
2 Th 3 17 the salutation of Paul with my own hand
Titus 1 1 Paul, a servant of God, and an apostle
Philem 1 Paul, a prisoner of Christ Jesus, and
9 as Paul an old man, and now a prisoner
19 I Paul have written it with my own hand
2 P 3 15 our most dear brother Paul, according

Paul's Acts 19 29 men of Macedonia, P. companions
Acts 21 11 when he was come to us, took P. girdle

23 16 when Paul's sister's son had heard, of
Paulus Acts 13 7 was with the proconsul Sergius P.
paved 2 Pa 3 6 p. also the floor of the temple
Tob 13 22 be paved with white and clean stones
Eze 42 3 outward court that was p. with stone
pavement Num 5 17 cast a little earth of the p.
4 K 16 17 and put it upon a pavement of stone
2 Pa 7 3 upon the stone pavement, they adored
Ps 118 25 my soul hath cleaved to the pavement
Eccu 20 20 as one that falleth on the pavement
Eze 40 17 a pavement of stone in the court
17 thirty chambers encompassed the p.
18 the pavement in the front of the gates
42 3 the pavement of the outward court that
Dan 14 18 behold the p., mark whose footsteps
pavilion Exod 33 8 stood in the door of his p.
3 K 20 16 drinking himself drunk in his pavilion
Ps 17 12 covert, his pavilion round about him
103 2 stretchest out the heaven like a p.
pavilions Num 16 27 stood in entry of their p.
3 K 20 12 the kings were drinking in pavilions
4 K 13 5 children of Israel dwelt in their p.
23 7 destroyed also the p. of the effeminate
Ps 77 28 fell . . . round about their pavilions
Jer 4 20 on a sudden, and my p. in a moment
30 18 back the captivity of the p. of Jacob
paving Deut 19 3 paving diligently the way
paw 1 K 17 37 me out of the paw of the lion and out of the paw of the bear
pay Exod 21 34 owner of the pit shall pay the
Exod 21 36 he shall pay ox for ox and shall take
22 29 thou shalt not delay to pay thy tithes
Lev 27 8 and not able to pay the estimation
8 see him able to pay, so much shall
Deut 23 21 shalt not delay to pay it: because
24 15 shalt pay him the price of his labor
Judg 15 10 to pay him for what he hath done
2 K 15 7 let me go and pay my vows which I have
3 K 20 39 or thou shalt pay a talent of silver
4 K 4 7 go, sell the oil and pay thy creditor
17 4 that he [Osee] might not pay tribute
1 Es 4 13 they will not pay tribute nor toll nor
Tob 4 15 immediately pay him his hire and let
5 3 shalt show him, he will presently pay
14 thou shalt return, I will pay thee
10 2 and no man will pay him the money
Job 22 27 hear thee, and thou shalt pay vows
Ps 21 26 will pay my vows in the sight of them
36 21 sinner shall borrow, and not pay again
49 14 and pay thy vows to the most High
55 12 are vows to thee, which I will pay
60 9 that I may pay my vows from day to day
65 13 I will pay thee my vows, which my lips
68 5 then did I pay that which I took not
75 12 vow ye, and pay to the Lord your God
115 14 I will pay my vows to the Lord. 18
Ecce 5 3 anything to God, defer not to pay it
3 but whatsoever thou hast vowed, pay it
Eccu 4 8 the poor, and pay what thou owest
8 16 surety, think as if thou wert to pay it
29 2 pay thou thy neighbor again in due
7 if he be able to pay he will stand
9 he will pay him with reproaches and
Jer 22 13 and will not pay him his wages. Who
50 29 escape: pay her according to her work
Jon 2 10 I will pay whatsoever I have vowed
Nah 1 15 keep thy festivals and pay thy vows
1 Ma 3 28 gave out pay to the army for a year
8 4 the rest pay them tribute every year
7 after him, should pay a great tribute
Mat 17 23 doth not your master pay the didrachmas
18 25 as he had not wherewith to pay it
26 with me, and I will pay thee. 29
28 him, saying: Pay what thou owest
20 8 pay them their hire, beginning from
Luke 3 14 and be content with your pay. And as
7 42 whereas they had not wherewith to pay
12 59 until thou pay the very last mite
paying Lev 22 18 p. his vows or offering. 21
Num 15 3 paying your vows, or voluntarily
Deut 20 11 shall serve thee paying tribute
Josu 16 10 Chanaanite dwelt . . . paying tribute
Rom 13 6 for therefore also you pay tribute. For
payment Ps 136 8 who shall repay thee thy p.
Mat 18 25 all that he had, and p. to be made
payments 1 Ma 11 34 instead of the p. which the
peace Gen 15 15 shalt go to thy fathers in peace
Gen 26 29 with peace have sent thee away
34 5 he held his peace. Lev 10:3; 2 Ma 14:4
43 23 he answered: Peace be with you
Exod 4 18 go in peace. Judg 18:6; 1 K 1:17; 20:13, 22, 42; 25:35; 29:7; 2 K 15:9; 4 K 5:19
14 14 hold your peace. 4 K 2:3, 5; 2 Es 8:11; Job 13:13
18 7 saluted one another with words of peace
23 shall return to their places with peace
29 28 peace victims. 32:6; Deut 27:7
Lev 3 6 peace offering. 19:5; Num 6:14, 17
26 6 I will give peace in your coasts: you
Num 6 26 to thee, and give thee peace. And they
25 12 I give him the peace of my covenant
30 4 if the father knew . . . and held his peace
12 if her husband hear, and hold his peace
15 if the husband hearing it hold his peace
15 as he heard it, he held his peace
Deut 20 9 when the captains . . . shall hold their p.
10 thou shalt first offer it peace. If
12 if they will not make peace and shall
23 6 thou shalt not make peace with them
29 19 I shall have peace and will walk on
Josu 9 6 desiring to make peace with you. And
21 42 he gave them peace from all nations
22 4 hath given your brethren rest and peace
23 1 the Lord had given peace to Israel
Judg 4 17 peace between Jabin the king of Asor
6 23 peace be with thee. 19:20; Jdth 8:34
24 and called it the Lord's peace, until
8 9 when I shall return a conqueror in peace
11 31 shall meet me when I return in peace
18 15 they saluted him with words of peace
19 hold thy peace. Tob 10:6; Job 33:31, 33; Amos 6:11
21 4 victims of peace. 1 K 10:8; 11:15
13 commanded them to receive them in peace
1 K 7 14 p. between Israel and the Amorrhites
20 7 it is well; thy servant shall have peace
22 because there is peace to thee and
25 5 and salute him in my name with peace
6 peace be to my brethren and to thee
6 peace to thy house and peace to all that
9 David's servants . . . then held their peace
2 K 3 21 and he [Abner] was gone in peace. 22
10 19 and they made peace with Israel: and
13 20 sister, hold thy peace, he is thy brother
15 27 O seer, return into the city in peace
19 24 until the day of his return in peace
3 K 2 5 and shed the blood of war in peace
6 his hoary head go down to hell in peace
33 and to his throne be peace forever
4 24 he had peace on every side round about
5 12 was peace between Hiram and Solomon
20 18 they come for peace, take them alive
22 17 of them return to his house in peace
27 till I return in peace. 2 Pa 18:26
28 Micheas said: if thou return in peace
45 Josaphat had peace with king of Israel

4 K	7	9	if we hold our peace and do not tell
	9	18	what hast thou to do with peace. 19
		19	is there peace? And Jehu said
		22	is there peace, Jehu? And he answered: What peace
		31	said: Can there be peace for Zambri
	18	36	but the people held their peace
	20	19	let peace and truth be in my days
	22	20	gathered to thy sepulcher in peace
1 Pa	12	18	peace, peace be to thee, and peace to
	18	10	to desire peace of him [David]
	22	9	I will give peace and quietness to
2 Pa	14	5	and [Asa] reigned in peace
		6	no wars . . . the Lord giving peace
		7	he hath given us peace round about
	18	16	man return to his own house in peace
		27	Micheas said: If thou return in peace
	19	1	returned to his house in peace
	20	30	and God have him peace round about
	34	28	shalt be brought to thy tomb in peace
1 Es	4	10	and made to dwell . . . in peace
		17	king . . . sending greeting and peace
	5	7	to Darius the king all peace
	9	12	seek not their peace nor their
2 Es	5	8	they held their peace and found not
Tob	3	6	command my spirit to be received in peace
	5	28	mother ceased weeping, and held her peace
	12	17	the angel said to them: Peace be to you
	13	18	and that rejoice in thy peace
	14	4	the fear of God he departed in peace
Jdth	5	4	that they might receive us with peace
	7	22	they held their peace. Job 29:10, 21; Isa 36:21
	13	16	when all had held their peace, Judith
Esth	4	14	if thou wilt now hold thy peace
	9	30	that they should have peace and
	13	2	any terror, and might enjoy peace
		5	disturbing the peace and concord of
		7	may restore to our empire the peace
	15	15	as she held her peace, he took the
	16	8	we must provide for the peace of all
Job	5	23	of the earth shall be at peace with thee
		24	know that thy tabernacle is in peace
	6	24	teach me, and I will hold my peace
	9	4	who hath resisted him and hath had peace
	13	5	I wish you would hold your peace
		19	why am I consumed holding my peace
	15	21	when there is peace, he always suspecteth
	16	7	if I hold my peace, it will not depart
	22	21	submit thyself then to him and be at p.
	25	2	who maketh peace in his high places
	31	34	and I have not rather held my peace
	34	29	when he granteth peace, who is there
Ps	4	9	in peace in the selfsame I will sleep
	13	3	the way of peace they have not known
	27	3	who speak peace with their neighbor
	28	10	Lord will bless his people with peace
	33	15	seek after peace and pursue it
	34	27	who delights in the peace of his servant
	36	11	shall delight in abundance of peace
	40	10	the man of my peace, in whom I trusted
	54	19	he shall redeem my soul in peace
	71	3	let the mountains receive peace
		7	in his days . . . abundance of peace
	75	3	his place is in peace: and his abode
	82	2	hold not thy peace, neither be thou
	84	9	he will speak peace unto his people
		11	justice and peace have kissed. Truth
	118	165	much peace have they that love thy law
	119	7	with them that hated peace I was
	121	6	that are for the peace of Jerusalem
		7	peace be in thy strength: and abundance
		8	my neighbors, I spoke peace of thee
	124	5	peace upon Israel. 127:6
	147	14	who hath placed peace in thy borders
Prov	3	2	shall add . . . years of life and peace
	4	27	he will bring forward thy ways in peace
	11	12	the wise man will hold his peace
	12	20	them that take counsels of peace
	13	13	the commandment, shall dwell in peace
	16	7	will convert even his enemies to peace
	17	28	even a fool, if he will hold his peace
Ecce	3	8	a time of war and a time of peace
Cant	8	10	in his presence as one finding peace
Wisd	3	3	utter destruction: but they are in peace
		9	grace and peace is to his elect
	8	12	shall wait for me when I hold my peace
	14	22	call so many and so great evils peace
Eccu	1	22	filling up peace and the fruit of
	5	12	word of peace and justice keep with
	6	6	be in peace with many, but let one
	13	4	poor is wronged and must hold his peace
		28	rich man spoke, and all held their peace
	19	28	is one that holdeth his peace. 20:5, 6
	20	6	is another that holdeth his peace
		7	a wise man will hold his peace till he
	26	2	fulfil the years of his life in peace
	28	11	in the midst of them that are at peace
		15	hath troubled many that were at peace
	38	8	the peace of God is over all the face
	41	1	man that hath peace in his possessions
		17	my children, keep discipline in peace
	44	6	living at peace in their houses
		14	their bodies are buried in peace
	45	30	he made to him a covenant of peace
	47	15	Solomon reigned in days of peace
		17	and thou wast beloved in thy peace
	50	25	that there be peace in our days
Isa	6	5	woe is me because I have held my peace
	9	6	shall be called . . . the Prince of Peace
		7	and there shall be no end of peace
	26	3	thou wilt keep peace: peace because we
		12	Lord, thou wilt give us peace: for thou
	27	5	strength, shall it make peace with me
	32	17	the work of justice shall be peace
		18	my people shall sit in the beauty of p.
	33	7	angels of peace shall weep bitterly
	38	17	in peace is my bitterness most bitter
	39	8	let peace and truth be in my days
	41	3	pursue them, he shall pass in peace
	42	14	I have always held my peace, I have
	45	7	I make peace and create evil: I the
	48	18	thy peace had been as a river, and
	52	7	feet of him . . . that preacheth peace
	53	5	chastisement of our peace was upon him
	54	10	covenant of my p. shall not be moved
		13	great shall be the peace of thy children
	55	12	you shall . . . be led forth with peace
	57	2	let peace come, let him rest in his bed
		19	peace, peace to him that is far off
	59	8	they have not known the way of peace
	60	17	and I will make thy visitation peace
	62	6	they shall never hold their peace
		6	mindful of the Lord, hold not your peace
	64	12	wilt thou hold thy peace and afflict
	66	12	upon her as it were a river of peace
Jer	4	10	saying: You shall have peace: and
		19	I will not hold my peace, for my soul
	8	15	we looked for peace and no good came
	9	8	one speaketh peace with his friend
	12	5	hast been secure in a land of peace
	14	13	he will give you true peace in this
		19	we have looked for peace, and there is
	15	5	who shall go to pray for thy peace
	16	5	I have taken away my peace from this
	23	17	Lord hath said: You shall have peace

	25	37	the fields of peace have been silent
	28	9	the prophet that prophesied peace
	29	7	in the peace thereof shall be your peace
		7	seek the peace of the city, to which
		11	saith the Lord, thoughts of peace
	33	6	will reveal to them the prayer of peace
		9	be troubled . . . for all the peace that
	34	5	but thou shalt die in peace, and
	38	4	seeketh not peace to this people, but
		22	thy men of peace have deceived thee
	43	12	he shall go forth from thence in peace
	47	5	Ascalon hath held her peace with the
	48	2	shalt thou in silence hold thy peace
	50	30	her men of war shall hold their peace
Lam	2	10	they have held their peace: they have
	3	17	my soul is removed far off from peace
		28	he shall sit solitary and hold his peace
Bar	3	13	hadst surely dwelt in peace forever
		14	where is the light of the eyes, and p.
	4	20	I have put off the robe of peace
	5	4	the peace of justice and honor of piety
	6	2	will bring you away from thence with p.
Eze	7	25	they will seek for peace, and there
	13	16	that see visions of peace for her: and there
	34	25	I will make a covenant of peace. 37:26
Dan	3	98	peace be multiplied unto you. 6:25
	10	15	to the ground, and held my peace
		19	peace be to thee: take courage and be
Abdi		5	how wouldst thou have held thy peace
		7	the men of thy peace have prevailed
Mich	3	5	bite with their teeth and preach peace
Nah	1	15	feet of him . . . that preacheth peace
Haba	1	13	holdest thy peace when the wicked
Agge	2	10	in this place I will give peace
Zach	6	13	counsel of p. shall be between them
	8	10	neither . . . peace to him that came in
		12	there shall be the seed of peace
		16	judge ye truth and judgment of peace
		19	only love ye truth and peace. Thus
	9	10	he shall speak peace to the Gentiles
Mala	2	5	covenant was with him of life and peace
		6	he walked with me in peace and in
1 Ma	5	54	slain, till they had returned in peace
	6	49	he made peace with them that were in
		58	let us . . . make peace with them
		60	he sent to them to make peace: and
	7	13	Israel, and they sought peace of them
		28	few men to see your faces with peace
		35	as soon as ever I return in peace
	8	20	to make alliance and peace with you
		22	a memorial of the peace and alliance
	9	70	sent ambassadors to him to make peace
	10	4	let us first make a peace with him
		47	promoter of peace in their regard
		66	into Jerusalem with peace and joy
	11	5	him odious: but the king held his peace
		50	grant us peace, and let the Jews cease
		51	threw down their arms and made peace
		66	and they desired him to make peace
	12	4	them into the land of Juda with peace
	13	37	ready to make a firm peace with you
		40	and let there be peace between us
		45	beseeching Simon to grant them peace
		50	and they cried to Simon for peace
	14	8	every man tilled his land with peace
		11	he made peace in the land, and Israel
	16	10	and he returned into Judea in peace
2 Ma	1	1	of Judea, send health and good peace
		4	commandments, and send you peace
	3	1	holy city was inhabited with all peace
	4	6	that matters should be settled in peace
	5	25	was come to Jerusalem, pretending peace
	11	26	to send to them and grant them peace
	12	2	would not suffer them to live in peace
		4	suspecting nothing, because of the peace
		11	besought Judas for peace, promising
		12	Judas . . . promised them peace, and
	13	25	displeased with the conditions of the p.
	14	6	will not suffer the realm to be in peace
Mat	10	12	p. be to this house. Luke 10:5
		13	your peace shall come upon it; but if
		13	your peace shall return to you
		34	that I came to send peace upon earth
		34	not to send peace, but the sword
	20	31	them that they should hold their peace
	26	63	but Jesus held his peace. And the high
Mark	3	4	they held their peace. 9:33; Luke 9:36; 14:4; 20:26; Acts 11:18; 12:17
	4	39	said to the sea: Peace, be still. And
	5	34	go in peace, and be thou whole of thy
	9	49	salt in you, and have peace among you
	10	48	him, that he might hold his peace
	14	61	but he held his peace and answered
Luke	1	79	to direct our feet into the way of p.
	2	14	on earth peace to men of good will
		29	Lord, according to thy word in peace
	4	35	rebuked him, saying: Hold thy peace
	7	50	faith hath made thee safe, go in peace
	8	48	made thee whole; go thy way in peace
	10	6	if the son of peace be there, your
		6	your peace shall rest upon him; but
	11	21	those things are in peace which he
	12	51	think ye that I am come to give peace
	14	32	he desireth conditions of peace. So
	18	39	that he should hold his peace: but
	19	38	peace in heaven, and glory on high
		40	if these shall hold their peace, the
		42	the things that are to thy peace; but
	24	36	peace be to you; it is I, fear not
John	14	27	peace I leave with you, my peace I
	16	33	that in me you may have peace. In the
	20	19	peace be to you. 21, 26
Acts	7	26	would have reconciled them in peace
	9	31	church had peace throughout all Judea
	10	36	preaching peace by Jesus Christ: he
	12	20	they desired p., because their countries
	15	12	multitude held their peace; and they
		13	after they had held their peace, James
		33	let go with peace by the brethren, unto
	16	36	depart, and go in peace. But Paul said
	18	9	fear, but speak; and hold not thy peace
	24	2	through thee we live in much peace, and
Rom	1	7	peace from God our Father. 1 C 1:3; 2 C 1:2; Phil 1:2; Col 1:3; 2 Th 1:2; Philem 3
	2	10	peace to every one that worketh good
	3	17	the way of peace they have not known
	5	1	let us have peace with God, through our
	8	6	wisdom of the spirit is life and peace
	10	15	them that preach the gospel of peace
	12	18	as is in you, have peace with all men
	14	17	not meat and drink; but justice and p.
		19	after the things that are of peace; and
	15	13	fill you with all joy and peace in
		33	now the God of peace be with you all
	16	20	the God of peace crush Satan under your
1 C	7	15	cases. But God hath called us in peace
	14	28	let him hold his peace in the church
		30	sitting, let the first hold his peace
		33	not the God of dissension, but of peace
	16	11	but conduct ye him on his way in peace
2 C	13	11	have peace; and the God of peace and of
Gal	1	3	peace from God the Father. Eph 1:2; 1 Tim 1:2; 2 Tim 1:2; Titus 1:4; 2 J 3
	5	22	the fruit of the Spirit is . . . peace
	6	16	peace on them, and mercy, and upon the
Eph	2	14	he is our peace, who hath made both one

15 himself into one new man, making peace
17 coming, he preached peace to you that
17 afar off, and p. to them that were nigh
4 3 unity of Spirit in the bond of peace
6 15 the preparation of the gospel of peace
23 peace be to the brethren and charity
Phil 4 7 the peace of God, which surpasseth all
9 and the God of peace shall be with you
Col 1 20 making p. through the blood of his cross
3 15 let the peace of Christ rejoice in your
1 Th 1 2 grace be to you and peace. We give
5 3 when they shall say, peace and security
13 their work's sake. Have peace with them
23 may the God of peace himself sanctify
2 Th 3 16 now the Lord of peace himself give you everlasting peace
2 Tim 2 22 pursue justice, faith, charity and peace
3 3 wicked, without affection, without p.
Heb 7 2 king of Salem, that is, king of peace
11 31 receiving the spies with peace. And what
12 14 follow peace with all men, and holiness
13 20 may the God of peace, who brought
James 2 16 go in peace, be ye warmed and filled
3 18 fruit of justice is sown in peace, to them that make peace
1 P 1 2 grace unto you and peace be multiplied
3 11 let him seek after peace and pursue it
2 P 1 2 peace be accomplished in the knowledge
3 14 unspotted and blameless in peace, and
3 J 14 peace be to thee. Our friends salute
Jude 2 mercy to you, and peace, and charity
Apoc 1 4 grace be unto you and peace from him
6 4 that he should take p. from the earth
no peace 2 Pa 15 5 that time there shall be no p.
Ps 37 4 there is no peace for my bones because
Isa 48 22 there is no p. to the wicked. 57:21
59 8 treadeth in them, knoweth no peace
Jer 6 14 peace, peace: and there was no peace
8 11 peace, peace: when there was no peace
12 12 there is no peace for all flesh. They
30 5 of terror: there is fear and no peace
Eze 13 10 and there is no peace. 16
peacemakers Mat 5 9 blessed are the peacemakers: for
peace offerings; *see* **offerings**
peaceable Gen 34 21 these men are p. and willing
Gen 42 11 we are come as peaceable men, neither
19 if you be peaceable men, let one
31 we are peaceable men, and we mean
33 shall I know that you are peaceable men
Deut 2 26 the king of Hesebon with p. words
1 K 16 4 is thy coming hither peaceable? And
5 he said: It is peaceable: I am come
3 K 2 13 is thy coming peaceable? He answered: P.
4 K 9 18 thus saith the king: Are all things p.
1 Pa 22 9 therefore he shall be called Peaceable
Jdth 3 6 come to us a peaceable lord and use
Job 8 6 make the dwelling of thy justice p.
21 9 their houses are secure and peaceable
Ps 36 37 there are remnants for the p. man
119 7 with them that hated peace I was p.
Prov 3 17 and all her paths are p. She is a
15 4 a peaceable tongue is a tree of life
Cant 8 11 the p. had a vineyard in that which
12 a thousand are for thee, the peaceable
Eccu 4 8 and answer him p. words with mildness
1 Ma 1 31 he spoke to them p. words in deceit
5 25 received them in a p. manner and told
47 and Judas sent to them with p. words
7 10 to Judas . . . with p. words deceitfully
10 3 a letter to Jonathan with p. words
11 2 he went out into Syria with p. words
1 Tim 2 2 we may lead a quiet and a peaceable life
Heb 12 11 the most peaceable fruit of justice
James 3 17 first indeed is chaste, then peaceable
peaceably Gen 26 31 Isaac sent them away p. to
Gen 37 4 and could not speak peaceably to him
Judg 11 13 therefore restore the same p. to me
1 K 30 21 coming to the people, saluted them p.
2 K 19 30 my lord the king is returned p. into
1 Pa 12 17 if you are come p. to me to help me
Jdth 7 13 in that thou wouldst not speak p. with
Ps 34 20 for they spoke indeed peaceably to me
1 Ma 7 15 he spoke to them p.: and he swore
29 and they saluted one another peaceably
33 the people came out to salute him p.
12 52 they all came p. into the land of Juda
2 Ma 10 12 done them and to deal p. with them
peacocks 3 K 10 22 brought . . . apes and p. 2 Pa 9:21
pear 2 K 5 23 over against the p. trees. 1 Pa 14:14
2 K 5 24 in the tops of the pear trees. 1 Pa 14:15
pearl Lev 21 20 if he . . . have a p. in his eye
Prov 25 12 an earring of gold and a bright pearl
Mat 13 46 when he had found one p. of great price
Apoc 21 21 several gate was of one several pearl
pearls Mat 7 6 neither cast ye your pearls before
Mat 13 45 like to a merchant seeking good pearls
1 Tim 2 9 not with plaited hair, or gold, or p.
Apoc 17 4 gold and precious stones and p. 18:6
18 12 silver and precious stones and of p.
21 21 the twelve gates are twelve pearls
pebble Eccu 18 8 as a pebble of the sand
peculiar Exod 19 5 you shall be my p. possession
Deut 7 6 to be his peculiar people. 14:2; 26:18
Jdth 15 14 to be the peculiar goods of Holofernes
pedagogue Gal 3 24 law was our pedagogue in Christ
Gal 3 25 we are no longer under a pedagogue. For
pedigree Heb 7 6 he, whose p. is not numbered among
peeled Eze 29 18 bald, and every shoulder was p.
peep Eccu 21 26 fool will peep through window
peg Isa 22 23 I will fasten him as a peg in a
Isa 22 25 shall the peg be removed, that was
pelican Ps 101 7 I am become like to a pelican
pelted Eccu 22 1 the sluggard is p. with a dirty
Eccu 22 2 sluggard is pelted with the dung of
Pelusium Eze 30 15 out my indignation upon P.
Eze 30 16 Pelusium shall be in pain like a woman
pen Job 19 24 with an iron pen and in a plate of
Ps 44 2 my tongue is the pen of a scrivener
Isa 8 1 and write in it with a man's pen
Jer 8 8 lying pen of the scribes hath wrought
3 J 13 I would not by ink and pen write to
penance Lev 5 5 let him do penance for his sin
3 K 8 33 doing penance and confessing to thy
35 this place, shall do p. to thy name
47 if they do penance in their heart in
2 Pa 6 24 and being converted shall do penance
37 do penance and pray to thee in the
7 14 and seek out my face and do penance
33 12 and did penance exceedingly before
19 and statues before he did penance
Job 21 2 I beseech you, my words, and do p.
24 23 God hath given him place for penance
42 6 do penance in dust and ashes. And after
10 Lord also was turned at the p. of Job
Eccu 2 22 if we do not penance, we shall fall
48 8 who anointedst kings to penance and
Jer 8 6 none that doth penance for his sin
31 19 thou didst convert me, I did penance
Lam 2 14 thy iniquity, to excite thee to penance
Eze 18 21 if the wicked do penance for all his
30 and do penance for all your iniquities
33 14 do p. for his sin and do judgment
Mat 3 2 do p.: for the kingdom of heaven. 4:17
8 forth therefore fruit worthy of penance
11 baptize you in water unto penance, but
11 20 for that they had not done penance

21 they had long ago done penance in
12 41 p. at the preaching of Jonas. Luke 11:32
Mark 1 4 preaching the baptism of p. Luke 3:3
6 12 preached that men should do penance
Luke 3 8 forth therefore fruits worthy of p.
5 32 not to call the just, but sinners to p.
10 13 they would have done penance long ago
13 3 unless you do penance, you shall all
5 except you do penance, you shall all
15 7 one sinner that doth penance, more
7 upon 99 just who need not penance
10 of God upon one sinner doing penance
16 30 from the dead, they will do penance
17 3 and if he do penance, forgive him
24 47 that p. and remission of sins should
Acts 2 38 do penance and be baptized every one
8 22 do penance therefore for this thy
13 24 baptism of p. to all the people of
17 30 men, that all should everywhere do p.
19 4 baptized people with the baptism of p.
20 21 testifying both to Jews and Gentiles p.
26 20 I preach, that they should do penance
20 turn to God, doing works worthy of p.
Rom 2 4 benignity of God leadeth thee to p.
2 C 7 9 you were made sorrowful unto penance
10 worketh p., steadfast unto salvation
12 21 have not done p. for the uncleanness
Heb 6 1 not laying again the foundation of p.
6 away: to be renewed again to penance
2 P 3 9 but that all should return to penance
Apoc 2 5 and do penance, and do the first works
5 out of its place, except thou do p.
16 do penance: if not, I will come to thee
21 I gave her a time that she might do p.
22 except they do p. from their deeds
3 3 observe and do penance. If then thou
19 be zealous therefore and do penance
9 20 did not do penance from the works of
21 neither did they p. from their murders
16 9 neither did they p. to give him glory
11 and did not penance for their works
pence Mat 18 28 that owed him an hundred pence: and
Mark 6 37 let us go and buy bread for 200 pence
14 5 been sold for more than 300 pence and
Luke 7 41 the one owed 500 pence, and the other
10 35 he took out two pence and gave to
John 12 5 this ointment sold for 300 pence, and
pencil 4 K 21 13 the pencil often over the face
penetrate Eccu 24 45 I will p. to all the lower
penetrated Eccu 24 8 have p. into the bottom of
penitent Jdth 5 19 and as often as they were p.
Jdth 8 14 let us be penitent for this same thing
Eccu 12 3 sinners, and hath mercy on the p.
17 20 to the p. he hath given way of justice
Acts 3 19 be penitent, therefore, and be
penknife Jer 36 23 he cut it with the penkife
penny Mat 20 2 with the laborers for a penny a day
Mat 20 9 they received every man a penny
10 they also received every man a penny
13 didst thou not agree with me for a p.
22 19 tribute. And they offered him a penny
Mark 12 15 bring me a penny that I may see it
Luke 20 24 show me a penny. Whose image and
Apoc 6 6 two pounds of wheat for a penny, and
6 thrice two pounds of barley for a penny
pennyworth John 6 7 two hundred p. of bread is not
pensions 2 Pa 21 3 of silver and of gold and p.
pensive Job 23 15 I am made pensive with fear
Eccu 14 10 needy and pensive at his own table
pensiveness Deut 28 65 a soul consumed with p.
Eccu 30 26 p. will bring old age before the time
Pentapolis Wisd 10 6 the fire came down upon P.
Pentecost 2 Ma 12 32 after P. they marched against
Acts 2 1 when the days of P. were accomplished
20 16 possible for him, to keep the day of P.
1 C 16 8 I will tarry at Ephesus until Pentecost
peopled Eze 36 35 destroyed, are p. and fenced
people's Exod 19 8 Moses had related the p. words
Lev 9 7 when thou hast slain the people's victim
2 Pa 10 15 not to the people's requests: for it
Jdth 6 16 was ended, and the people's prayer
Eze 46 18 shall not take of the p. inheritance
2 Ma 5 19 but the place for the people's sake
Heb 7 27 his own sins, and then for the people's
Heb 9 7 for his own, and the people's ignorance
peoples Gen 10 32 of Noe, according to their p.
Gen 25 23 two p. shall be divided out of
27 29 let peoples serve thee, and tribes
35 11 peoples of nations shall be from thee
48 19 this also shall become peoples and
Deut 7 6 to be his peculiar people of all peoples
1 Pa 7 4 with them by their families and peoples
Esth 8 13 be notified in all lands and peoples
17 in all peoples, cities, and provinces
Ps 86 6 shall tell in his writings of peoples
Wisd 6 23 all ye that bear rule over peoples
Isa 61 9 their offspring in the midst of p.
Eze 11 17 will gather you from among the peoples
34 13 I will bring them out from the peoples
38 6 strength, and many peoples with thee
Dan 3 98 to all peoples, nations, and tongues
7 14 all p., tribes and tongues shall serve
Mich 4 13 thou shalt beat in pieces many peoples
5 7 shall be in the midst of many peoples
8 in midst of many p. as a lion among
Zach 8 22 many p. and strong nations shall come
10 9 and I will sow them among peoples
Luke 2 31 prepared before the face of all p.
Apoc 7 9 of all nations and tribes and peoples
10 11 and peoples and tongues and kings
11 9 they of the tribes and peoples and
17 15 are peoples and nations and tongues
peradventure Gen 31 42 p. now thou hadst sent me
Num 23 27 if peradventure it please God that thou
Judg 8 6 p. the palms of the hands of Zebee
15 p. the hands of Zebee and Salmana are
Job 11 7 p. thou wilt comprehend the steps of
2 Tim 2 25 if p. God may give them repentance to
perceive Gen 19 25 neither then did he perceive
Gen 27 12 father shall feel me, and perceive it
Lev 13 31 if he perceive the place of the spot
43 priest p. this, he shall condemn him
14 44 perceive that the leprosy is returned
48 perceive that the leprosy is not spread
Deut 17 8 if thou perceive that there be among
21 3 city which they shall p. to be nearer
25 1 to him whom they perceive to be just
2 K 19 6 I now plainly p. that if Absalom had
4 K 4 9 I p. that this is a holy man of God
Job 21 29 you shall p. that he knoweth these
Wisd 16 18 that they might see and perceive that
Bar 6 41 when they shall p. this, will leave
Mat 13 14 shall see, and shall not p. Acts 28:26
Mark 4 12 seeing they may see and not perceive
John 4 19 I perceive that thou art a prophet
Acts 10 34 in very deed I perceive, that God
17 22 men of Athens, I p. that in all things
perceived Gen 3 7 p. themselves to be naked
Gen 19 33 perceived not neither when his daughter
Judg 20 40 perceived as it were a pillar of smoke
3 K 3 15 Solomon . . . p. that it was a dream
22 33 p. that he was not the king of Israel
1 Pa 14 2 David p. that the Lord had confirmed
2 Pa 13 13 he encompassed Juda, who p. it not
2 Es 6 16 they p. that this work was the work of
13 10 I p. that the portions of the Levites

Tob 11 6 off and presently p. it was her son
Jdth 14 14 he perceived no motion of one lying
Ecce 1 17 I have perceived that in these also
2 15 I perceived that this also was vanity
Wisd 19 17 may clearly be p. by the very sight
Eccu 3 30 root in them, and it shall not be p.
Isa 64 4 they have not heard nor perceived
1 Ma 3 29 he p. that the money of his treasurer
9 14 Judas p. that the stronger part of
15 12 for he p. that evils were gathered
2 Ma 2 7 when Jeremias p. it, he blamed them
4 41 when they perceived the attempt of
14 30 when Machabeus p. that Nicanor was
Luke 9 45 so that they perceived it not. And
Acts 19 34 soon as they perceived him to be a Jew
perceivest Deut 15 8 which thou p. he hath need
perceiveth 1 C 2 14 the sensual man p. not these
perceiving Gen 16 4 p. that she was with child
Gen 16 5 perceiving herself to be with child
30 9 Lia, perceiving that she had left off
31 2 p. also that Laban's countenance
Judg 19 28 perceiving she was dead, he took her
Dan 6 15 those men p. the king's design, said
2 Ma 11 13 and p. that the Hebrews could not be
Mat 2 16 Herod p. that he was deluded by the
perdition Tob 4 14 from it all p. took its
John 17 12 is lost but the son of perdition
Phil 1 28 which to them is a cause of perdition
2 Th 2 3 of sin be revealed, the son of perdition
1 Tim 6 9 drown men into destruction and perdition
Heb 10 29 children of withdrawing unto p., but of
2 P 2 1 who shall bring in sects of perdition
3 and their perdition slumbereth not
3 7 and perdition of the ungodly men. But
perfect Gen 6 9 Noe was a just and p. man in his
Gen 17 1 walk before me, and be perfect. And I
Deut 18 13 shalt be p. and without spot before the
32 4 the works of God are perfect, and all
Josu 24 14 serve him with a p. and most sincere
2 K 22 24 I shall be perfect with him: and shall
26 wilt be holy: and with the valiant p.
33 with strength, and made my way perfect
3 K 8 61 let our hearts also be perfect with
11 4 his heart was not p. with the. 15:3
15 14 the heart of Asa was perfect with the
4 K 20 3 thee in truth and with a perfect heart
1 Pa 12 38 came with a perfect heart to Hebron
28 9 and serve him with a perfect heart
29 19 give to Solomon my son a perfect heart
2 Pa 15 17 heart of Asa was perfect all his days
16 9 who with a perfect trust in him
19 9 faithfully and with a perfect heart
25 2 but yet not with a perfect heart
1 Es 2 63 there arose a priest learned and p.
Jdth 11 4 the Lord will do with thee a p. thing
Job 22 2 though he were of perfect knowledge
36 4 p. knowledge shall be proved to thee
37 16 clouds, and the perfect knowledge
Ps 16 5 perfect thou my goings in thy paths
50 14 strengthen me with a perfect spirit
67 10 was weakened, but thou hast made it p.
79 16 and perfect the same, which thy right
88 38 and as the moon perfect forever, and
100 6 the man that walked in the perfect way
138 22 have hated them with a perfect hatred
Prov 4 18 and increaseth even to perfect day
Ecce 9 14 about it, and the siege was perfect
Cant 6 8 my perfect one is but one, she is the
Wisd 4 5 the branches not being perfect, shall
13 being made perfect in a short space
6 16 upon her, is perfect understanding
9 6 if one be p. among the children of
15 3 to know thee is perfect justice: and
Eccu 24 38 who first hath perfect knowledge of
31 10 been tried thereby and made perfect
44 17 Noe was found perfect, just, and in
Isa 18 5 it shall bud without perfect ripeness
38 3 in truth and with a perfect heart and
Lam 2 15 is this the city of perfect beauty
Eze 16 14 thou wast perfect through my beauty
27 3 thou hast said; I am of perfect beauty
28 12 full of wisdom and perfect in beauty
15 thou wast perfect in thy ways from
Amos 1 6 have carried away a perfect captivity
Nah 1 12 though they were perfect: and many
2 Ma 5 24 to kill all that were of p. age
Mat 5 48 be you therefore perfect, as also your heavenly Father is perfect
19 21 if thou wilt be perfect, go sell what
Luke 1 17 to prepare unto the Lord a p. people
6 40 every one shall be perfect if he be
8 15 they who in a good and perfect heart
John 4 34 sent me, that I may perfect his work
5 36 the Father hath given me to perfect
17 23 that they may be made perfect in one
Acts 3 16 hath given him perfect soundness in
Rom 12 2 acceptable, and the perfect will of God
1 C 1 10 that you be perfect in the same mind
2 6 we speak wisdom among the perfect: yet
13 10 when that which is perfect is come, that
14 20 malice be children, and in sense be p.
2 C 12 9 for power is made perfect in infirmity
13 11 the rest, brethren, rejoice, be perfect
Gal 3 3 you would now be made perfect by flesh
Eph 4 13 unto a perfect man, unto the measure of
6 13 day, and to stand in all things perfect
Phil 1 6 will perfect it unto the day of Christ
3 12 had already attained, or were already p.
15 as many as are perfect, be thus minded
Col 1 28 that we may present every man perfect
4 12 that you may stand perfect, and full in
2 Tim 3 17 that the man of God may be perfect
Heb 2 10 to perfect the author of their salvation
5 14 but strong meat is for the perfect; for
6 1 let us go on to things more perfect, not
8 8 I will perfect unto the house of Israel
9 9 make him perfect that serveth, only in
11 by a greater and more perfect tabernacle
10 1 never make the comers thereunto perfect
12 23 to the spirits of the just made perfect
James 1 4 patience hath a perfect work; that you
4 that you may be perfect and entire
17 and every perfect gift is from above
25 looked into the perfect law of liberty
2 22 and by works faith was made a perfect
3 2 not in word, the same is a perfect man
1 P 5 10 will himself perfect you and confirm
1 J 4 18 perfect charity casteth out fear
perfected Exod 40 31 after all things were p.
Ps 8 3 and of sucklings thou hast p. praise
Eccu 7 36 and thy blessing may be perfected
23 29 so also after they were perfected he
50 21 until the worship of the Lord was p.
Eze 27 4 that built thee, have p. thy beauty
11 round about: they perfected thy beauty
Mat 21 16 of sucklings thou hast perfected praise
Heb 7 28 the Son who is perfected for evermore
10 14 by one oblation he hath p. forever them
11 40 they should not be perfected without
1 J 2 5 the charity of God is perfected; and
4 12 in us, and his charity is p. in us
17 is the charity of God p. with us
18 he that feareth is not p. in charity
perfecting 2 C 7 1 p. sanctification in fear of
Eph 4 12 for the perfecting of the saints, for
perfection 3 K 7 1 years and brought it to p.

Job 4 6 thy patience and the p. of thy ways
Ps 118 96 I have seen an end of all perfection
Wisd 3 16 of adulterers shall not come to p.
Eccu 21 13 perfection of the fear of God is wisdom
38 31 watching to polish them to perfection
43 7 light that decreaseth in her perfection
8 name, increasing wonderfully in her p.
50 11 clothed with perfection of power. When
2 C 13 9 this also we pray for, your perfection
Col 3 14 charity, which is the bond of perfection
Heb 7 11 if then perfection was by the Levitical
19 the law brought nothing to perfection
perfectly Job 11 7 wilt find out the Almighty p.
Amos 5 10 abhorred him that speaketh perfectly
2 Ma 15 39 if not so p., it must be pardoned
1 Th 5 2 yourselves know perfectly, that the day
1 P 1 13 trust perfectly in the grace which is
perform Josu 21 43 which he had promised to p. unto
Josu 23 14 which the Lord promised to perform
2 K 14 15 it may be the king will p. the request
4 K 23 3 to perform the words of this covenant
24 that he might p. the words of the law
Ecce 5 4 than after a vow not to perform the
Eccu 15 16 perform acceptable fidelity forever
Isa 9 7 zeal of the Lord of hosts will p. this
19 21 vows to the Lord and perform them
28 21 work, that he may perform his work
44 26 and p. the counsel of my messengers
28 thou shalt perform all my pleasures
Jer 1 12 I will watch over my word to p. it
28 6 the Lord perform thy words, which
29 10 I will p. my good word in your favor
33 14 I will perform the good word that I
44 25 let us perform our vows which we have
Bar 6 34 make a vow to them and perform it not
Mich 7 20 thou wilt perform the truth of Jacob
Agge 2 5 and perform, for I am with you, saith
Mat 5 33 thou shalt p. thy oaths to the Lord
Luke 1 72 to perform mercy to our fathers and
Rom 4 21 he has promised, he is able also to p.
2 C 8 11 perform ye it also in deed; that as your
11 so it may be also to perform, out of
performed Num 3 4 and Ithamar p. the priestly
3 K 8 20 Lord hath p. his word which he spoke
24 with thy hands thou hast performed
2 Pa 6 15 hast performed to thy servant David
Isa 10 12 Lord shall have p. all his works in
Jer 30 24 and p. the thought of his heart: in
34 18 have not p. the words of the covenant
44 25 vows, and have performed them indeed
Luke 2 39 after they had p. all things according
perfume Lev 16 12 the compounded p. for incense
2 Pa 2 4 and to perfume with aromatical spices
Ps 44 9 stacte and cassia perfume thy garments
perfumed Prov 7 17 I have p. my bed with myrrh
Eccu 24 21 I perfumed my dwelling as storax
perfumer Exod 30 25 after the art of the perfumer
Exod 30 35 compounded by the work of the perfumer
37 29 according to the work of a perfumer
2 Es 3 8 built Ananias the son of the perfumer
Cant 3 6 of all the powders of the perfumer
Eccu 49 1 smell made by the art of a perfumer
perfumers 2 Pa 16 14 made by the art of the p.
Cant 5 13 beds of aromatical spices set by the p.
perfumes Lev 16 13 the p. are put upon the fire
2 Pa 4 22 the vessels also for the perfumes
Esth 2 12 used certain perfumes and sweet spices
Prov 27 9 ointment and perfumes rejoice the heart
Cant 4 14 and aloes with all the chief perfumes
Isa 57 9 and hast multiplied thy perfumes
Pergamus Apoc 1 11 to Smyrna and to Pergamus and to
Apoc 2 12 to the angel of the church of Pergamus
Perge Acts 13 13 they came to Perge in Pamphylia
Acts 13 14 passing through Perge, came to Antioch
14 24 spoken the word of the Lord in Perge
perhaps Mat 4 6 lest p. thou dash thy foot. Luke 4:11
Mat 5 25 lest p. the adversary deliver thee to
7 6 lest perhaps they trample them under
11 23 perhaps it had remained unto this day
13 29 lest perhaps gathering up the cockle
25 9 lest perhaps there be not enough for
26 5 lest perhaps there should be a tumult
27 64 lest perhaps his disciples come and
Mark 11 13 if perhaps he might find anything on
Luke 3 15 that perhaps he might be the Christ
9 13 unless perhaps we should go and buy
12 58 lest perhaps he draw thee to the judge
14 8 lest perhaps one more honorable than
12 lest perhaps they also invite thee
21 34 lest p. your hearts be overcharged
John 4 10 thou p. wouldst have asked of him and
5 46 you would perhaps believe me also
8 19 perhaps you would know my Father also
Acts 5 39 lest p. you be found even to fight
8 22 that p. this thought of thy heart
23 25 he feared lest p. the Jews might take
28 27 lest p. they should see with their eyes
Rom 5 7 yet perhaps for a good man some one
11 21 fear lest perhaps he also spare not thee
1 C 7 5 except, perhaps, by consent, for a time
8 9 take heed lest perhaps this your liberty
9 27 lest p., when I have preached to others
16 6 with you perhaps I shall abide, or even
2 C 2 7 lest perhaps such a one be swallowed up
12 20 I fear lest perhaps when I come I shall
20 lest perhaps contentions, envyings
13 5 in you, unless perhaps you be reprobates
Gal 2 2 lest p. I should run, or had run in vain
4 11 lest perhaps I have labored in vain
1 Th 3 5 lest perhaps he that tempteth should
Philem 15 for perhaps he therefore departed for
Heb 2 1 lest perhaps we should let them slip
3 12 lest perhaps there be in any of you an
3 J 9 I had written perhaps to the church
peril 2 K 23 17 went, and the p. of their lives
Lam 5 9 fetched our bread at peril of our lives
perils Tob 4 4 how great p. she suffered for
Ps 114 3 the perils of hell have found me
2 Ma 2 19 hath delivered us out of great perils
2 C 11 26 in journeying often, in p. of waters, in p.
of robbers, in p. from my own nation, in p.
from the Gentiles, in p. in the city, in p.
in the wilderness, in p. in the sea, in p.
from false brethren
perish Gen 18 24 shall they perish withal
Gen 19 15 lest thou also p. in the wickedness
43 8 lest both we and our children perish
45 11 lest both thou perish and thy house
Exod 9 15 and thou shalt perish from the earth
12 15 that soul shall perish out of Israel
19 his soul shall p. out of the. 31:14; Num 19:20
19 21 great multitude of them should perish
30 38 he shall p. out of his people. Lev 7:25
Lev 7 27 shall perish from among the people
10 7 not go out . . . otherwise you shall perish
17 4 so shall he perish from the midst of
9 shall p. from among his people. 19:8; 23:29
18 29 shall p. from the midst of his people
22 3 shall perish before the Lord. I am
26 38 you shall perish among the Gentiles
Num 17 12 behold we are consumed, we all perish
18 3 lest both they die and you also perish
19 13 the Lord, and shall perish out of Israel
24 24 last they themselves also shall perish

26 11 Core perished, his sons did not perish
Deut 2 15 that they should p. from the midst of
4 26 you shall quickly p. out of the land
8 19 foretell thee that thou shalt utterly p.
20 so shall you also perish if you be
11 17 beware lest . . . you perish quickly
28 22 and pursue thee till thou perish. Be
40 for the olives shall fall off and perish
45 curses shall come . . . till thou perish
30 18 thou shalt perish and shalt remain
Judg 5 31 so let all thy enemies perish, O Lord
18 25 and thou perish with all thy house
1 K 12 25 you and your king shall p. together
26 10 he shall go down to battle and perish
2 K 14 14 neither will God have a soul to perish
14 is cast off should not altogether perish
3 K 18 5 that the beasts may not utterly perish
Jdth 3 2 subject to thee, than to die and to p.
6 3 and all Israel shall perish with thee
Job 3 3 let the day perish wherein I was born
11 why did I not p. when I came out of
4 20 they shall perish forever. And they
6 17 shall be scattered they shall perish
18 they shall walk in vain and shall perish
8 13 the hope of the hypocrite shall perish
15 32 before his days be full he shall perish
18 17 let the memory of him perish from the
29 13 blessing of him that was ready to perish
34 15 all flesh shall perish together and
Ps 1 6 and the way of the wicked shall perish
2 12 angry, and you perish from the just way
9 4 shall be weakened and p. before thy
16 ye Gentiles shall perish from his land
19 patience of the poor shall not perish
36 20 filled: because the wicked shall perish
22 but such as curse him shall perish
28 the seed of the wicked shall perish
34 when the sinners shall p., thou shalt
38 the remnants of the wicked shall perish
40 6 when shall he die and his name perish
48 11 senseless and the fool shall perish
72 27 they that go far from thee shall perish
79 17 things set on fire . . . shall perish at
82 18 let them be confounded and perish
91 8 that they may perish forever and ever
10 for behold thy enemies shall perish
101 27 they shall perish but thou remainest
108 15 memory of them perish from the earth
111 10 the desire of the wicked shall perish
145 4 that day all their thoughts shall perish
Prov 10 28 the hope of the wicked shall perish
31 tongue of the perverse shall perish
11 7 expectation of the solicitous shall p.
10 the wicked p. there shall be praise
19 9 he that speaketh lies, shall perish
21 28 lying witness shall perish: an obedient
24 14 the end, and thy hope shall not perish
28 28 when they perish, the just shall be
Wisd 4 19 sorrow, and their memory shall perish
11 15 his being wickedly exposed to perish
12 12 accuse thee, if the nations perish
18 19 lest they should perish and not know
Eccu 3 27 that loveth danger shall perish in it
8 18 thou shalt p. together with his folly
9 4 lest thou perish by the force of her
23 7 keep it shall not perish by his lips
27 29 snare for another, shall perish in it
32 they shall perish in a snare that are
31 7 and every fool shall perish by it
36 11 let them p. that oppress thy people
41 9 of the children of sinners shall perish
Isa 11 13 the enemies of Juda shall perish
14 30 I will make thy root p. with famine
22 25 that which hung thereon shall perish
29 14 wisdom shall p. from their wise men
38 17 delivered my soul that it should not p.
41 11 men shall p. that strive against thee
48 9 bridle thee, lest thou shouldst perish
51 6 inhabitants thereof shall p. in like
60 12 that will not serve thee, shall perish
Jer 4 9 the heart of the king shall perish
6 21 neighbor and kinsman shall perish
10 11 let them perish from the earth and
15 time of their visitation they shall p.
18 18 the law shall not p. from the priest
27 10 cast you out and to make you perish
15 you out and that you may perish
40 15 lest . . . the remnant of Juda perish
44 8 and that you should perish and be a
48 8 the valleys shall perish, and the
51 18 time of their visitation they shall p.
58 shall go to the fire and shall perish
Bar 3 3 and shall we perish everlastingly
27 knowledge, therefore did they perish
4 31 have afflicted thee, shall perish
Eze 7 26 the law shall perish from the priest
Dan 2 18 and his companions might not perish
7 26 be broken in pieces and perish
Osee 8 4 made idols . . . that they might perish
10 2 now they shall perish: he shall break
14 1 let Samaria perish, because she hath
1 let them perish by the sword, let
Amos 1 8 rest of the Philistines shall perish
2 14 flight shall perish from the swift
3 15 and the houses of ivory shall perish
Abdi 10 thee, and thou shalt perish forever
Jon 1 6 think of us that we may not perish
14 let us not perish for this man's
3 9 fierce anger, and we shall not perish
Nah 3 15 thou shalt perish by the sword
Soph 3 7 and her dwelling shall not perish
Zach 9 5 the king shall perish from Gaza
13 8 shall be scattered and shall perish
1 Ma 6 13 I perish with great grief in a
Mat 5 29 that one of thy members should p. 30
8 25 saying: Lord, save us, we perish. And
9 17 runneth out, and the bottles perish
18 14 one of these little ones should perish
26 52 the sword shall perish with the sword
Mark 4 38 it not concern thee that we perish
Luke 9 24 saying: Master, we perish. But he
13 3 penance, you shall all likewise p. 5
33 that a prophet p. out of Jerusalem
15 17 bread, and I here perish with hunger
21 18 a hair of your head shall not perish
John 3 15 believeth in him, may not perish. 16
10 28 they shall not perish forever, and no
11 50 and that the whole nation perish not
Acts 8 20 thy money to thyself to p. with thee
13 41 ye despisers, and wonder, and perish
27 34 not an hair of the head of any of you p.
Rom 2 12 the law, shall perish without the law
1 C 1 18 to them indeed that p., is foolishness
8 11 the weak brother perish for whom Christ
2 C 2 15 that are saved, and in them that perish
4 9 we are cast down, but we perish not
2 Th 2 10 seduction of iniquity to them that p.
Heb 1 11 they shall p., but thou shalt continue
2 P 2 12 shall p. in their corruption, receiving
3 9 not willing that any should perish

perished Num 16 33 they p. from among the people
Num 16 49 had perished in the sedition of Core
20 3 would God we had perished among our
21 30 their yoke is perished from Hesebon
26 11 when Core p., his sons did not perish
Josu 22 17 and many of the people perished

26 11 them, I p. them even unto foreign cities
1 C 4 12 we are persecuted, and we suffer it
15 9 because I persecuted the church of God
Gal 1 13 I p. the church of God, and wasted it
23 he, who p. us in times past, doth now
4 29 p. him that was after the spirit; so
1 Th 2 15 the prophets, and have persecuted us
Apoc 12 13 he p. the woman who brought forth the
persecutest Acts 9 4 why persecutest thou me. 22:7; 26:14
Acts 9 5 I am Jesus whom thou persecutest. 26:15
22 7 Saul, Saul, why persecutest thou me? And
8 I am Jesus of Nazareth, whom thou p.
persecuting Phil 3 6 persecuting the church of God
persecution Mat 5 10 that suffer p. for justice' sake
Mat 13 21 when there ariseth tribulation and p.
Mark 4 17 when tribulation and p. ariseth for
Acts 8 1 was raised a great persecution against
11 19 p. that arose on occasion of Stephen
13 50 raised p. against Paul and Barnabas
Rom 8 35 or danger? or p.? or the sword? As it is
2 C 4 9 we suffer p., but are not forsaken; we
Gal 5 11 why do I yet suffer persecution? Then
6 12 they may not suffer the persecution of
2 Tim 3 12 godly in Christ Jesus, shall suffer p.
persecutions Mark 10 30 children and lands with p.
2 C 12 10 in reproaches, in necessities, in p.
2 Th 1 4 in all your p. and tribulations, which
2 Tim 3 11 p., afflictions: such as came upon me
11 what p. I endured, and out of them all
persecutor Ps 43 17 the face of the enemy and p.
1 Tim 1 13 who before was a blasphemer, and a p.
persecutors 2 Es 9 11 their p. thou threwest
Esth 9 2 hands on their enemies and their p.
16 and slew their enemies and persecutors
Ps 108 31 of the poor, to save my soul from p.
141 7 deliver me from my persecutors; for
Lam 1 3 all her persecutors have taken her
4 19 our p. were swifter than the eagles
Persepolis 2 Ma 9 2 into the city called P.
Perses 1 Ma 8 5 defeated in battle Philip and P.
perseverance Jdth 4 11 if you continue with p. in
persevere Jdth 4 13 if you p. in this work which
2 Ma 14 38 life, that he might persevere therein
Mat 10 22 he that shall p. unto the end. 24:13
Heb 12 7 p. under discipline. God dealeth with
persevering Acts 1 14 were persevering with one mind
Acts 2 42 they were p. in the doctrine of the
Persia 2 Pa 36 20 till the reign of the king of P.
1 Es 1 8 Cyrus king of Persia brought them forth
4 5 all the days of Cyrus king of Persia
Dan 11 2 shall stand yet three kings in Persia
1 Ma 3 31 purposed to go into Persia and to take
6 1 heard that the city of Elymais in P.
5 whilst he was in Persia, there came
56 was returned from Persia and Media
14 2 Arsaces the king of Persia and Media
2 Ma 1 12 made numbers of men swarm out of Persia
13 when the leader himself was in Persia
19 when our fathers were led into Persia
20 should be sent by the king of Persia
33 it was told to the king of Persia
9 1 returned with dishonor out of Persia
21 returning out of the places of Persia
Persian 2 Es 12 22 in the reign of Darius the P.
Dan 6 28 unto . . . reign of Cyrus the Persian
13 65 Cyrus the P. received his kingdom
Persians 2 Pa 36 22 Cyrus king of the Persians. 23; 1 Es 1:1, 2; 3:7; 4:3; Dan 10:1
1 Es 4 5 Darius king of the P. 24; 1 Ma 1:1
7 Artaxerxes king of the P. 6:14; 7:1
9 9 mercy upon us before the king of the P.
Jdth 16 12 the Persians quaked at her constancy
Esth 1 3 for the most mighty of the Persians
14 seven princes of the Persians and of
18 wives of the princes of the Persians
19 the law of the P. and of the Medes
10 2 books of the Medes and of the P.
16 14 might transfer the kingdom of the P.
23 all they who faithfully obey the P.
Eze 27 10 the P. and Lydians and Libyans
38 5 P., Ethiopians, and Libyans with them
Dan 5 28 and is given to the Medes and Persians
6 8 what is decreed by the Medes and P.
12 the decree of the Medes and Persians
15 the law of the Medes and Persians is
8 20 is the king of the Medes and Persians
10 13 prince of the kingdom of the Persians
13 remained there by the king of the P.
20 to fight against the prince of the P.
Persis Rom 16 12 salute Persis, the dearly beloved
persisted Judg 7 22 p. sounding the trumpets, And
Eze 13 6 they have p. to confirm what they
person Exod 23 1 bear false witness for a wicked p.
Exod 23 7 and just p. thou shalt not put to death
Lev 5 4 the person that sweareth and uttereth
14 29 pour upon the head of the purified p.
15 11 every p. whom such a one shall touch
19 15 respect not the person of the poor
32 and honor the person of the aged man
21 11 nor shall he go in at all to any dead p.
Num 19 22 whatsoever a p. toucheth who is unclean
22 p. that toucheth any of these things
Deut 1 17 neither shall you respect any man's p.
10 17 accepteth no person nor taketh bribes
16 19 thou shalt not accept person nor gifts
21 6 shall come to the person slain and
27 25 taketh gifts, to slay an innocent p.
Josu 20 3 whosoever shall kill a p. unawares
1 K 9 2 children of Israel a goodlier p. than he
16 18 prudent in his words, and a comely p.
30 2 and they had not killed any person
3 K 3 18 no other person with us in the house
Tob 4 7 away thy face from any poor person
Esth 1 13 were always near his person, and all
Job 1 12 put not forth thy hand upon his person
13 8 do you accept this person and do you
10 because in secret you accept his person
32 21 I will not accept the person of man
Prov 18 5 not good to accept p. of the wicked
19 6 many honor p. of him that is mighty
28 17 doth violence to the blood of a person
21 he that hath respect to a person
Wisd 6 8 God will not except any man's person
Eccu 4 26 accept no p. against thy own p.
7 6 lest thou fear person of the powerful
8 14 against the face of an injurious person
10 5 upon the person of the scribe he shall
20 24 by occasion of an unwise person he
24 by respect of person he will destroy
21 25 abashed at the person of the mighty
28 16 tongue of a third p. hath disquieted
19 tongue of a third person hath cast out
35 15 there is not with him respect of person
16 the Lord will not accept any person
42 1 and accept no person to sin thereby
Isa 42 2 not cry nor have respect to person
Jer 52 25 of them that were near the king's p.
Eze 44 25 they shall come near no dead person
Mat 22 16 thou dost not regard the person of men
Mark 12 14 thou regardest not the person of men
Luke 20 21 thou dost not respect any person, but
1 C 14 24 an unlearned person, he is convinced of
2 C 2 10 have I done it in the person of Christ
Gal 2 6 God accepteth not the person of man
Eph 5 5 unclean, or covetous person, which is a
Heb 12 16 there be any fornicator or profane p.

2 P 2 5 but preserved Noe, the eighth person
persons Gen 14 21 give me the p., and the rest take
Gen 18 28 there be five less than fifty just p.
Num 31 28 as well of persons as of oxen and
30 shalt take the fiftieth head of persons
35 and 32,000 persons of the female sex
40 out of the 16,000 persons, there fell to
46 out of the 16,000 persons, Moses took
Deut 1 17 there shall be no difference of persons
Josu 8 25 12,000 persons all of the city of Hai
Judg 9 49 thousand persons were killed, men and
16 27 about 3,000 persons of both sexes from
2 K 13 9 said: Put out all persons from me
9 and when they had put all persons out
4 K 10 7 slew 70 persons and put their heads
14 26 up in prison, and the lowest persons
2 Pa 19 7 nor respect of persons nor desire of
Esth 2 3 let some persons be sent through all
Job 34 19 accepteth not the persons of princes
Ps 81 2 and accept persons of the wicked
Prov 24 23 not good to have respect to persons
Lam 4 16 respected not the p. of the priests
5 12 did not respect the p. of the ancient
Eze 13 18 for the heads of persons of every age
Jon 4 11 more than 120,000 persons that know not
Mala 2 9 and have accepted persons in the law
1 Ma 2 38 to the number of a thousand persons
2 Ma 6 24 many young p. might think that Eleazar
12 26 he slew five and twenty thousand p.
Acts 1 15 number of p. together was about 120
5 16 bring sick persons and such as were
10 34 that God is not a respecter of persons
Rom 2 11 is no respect of p. with God. Col 3:25
1 C 14 23 there come in unlearned p. or infidels
2 C 1 11 by the means of many persons, thanks
Eph 6 9 there is no respect of persons with him
1 Tim 1 10 for perjured persons, and whatever other
James 2 1 of glory with respect of persons. For
9 but if you have respect to persons
1 P 1 17 without respect of persons, judgeth
Jude 16 admiring persons for gain's sake. But
persuade Deut 13 6 would p. thee secretly, saying
Judg 14 15 persuade him to tell thee what the
Ruth 1 18 nor p. her any more to return to her
Jdth 12 10 go and persuade that Hebrew woman, to
2 Ma 4 45 to persuade the king to favor him
11 14 persuade the king to be their friend
Mat 28 14 we will persuade him and secure you
Acts 21 14 but when we could not persuade him, we
Gal 1 10 for do I now persuade men, or God? Or
1 J 3 19 and in his sight shall p. our hearts
persuaded 2 Pa 18 2 he p. him to go up to Ramoth
Wisd 13 7 they are p. that the things are good
1 Ma 1 12 they p. many, saying: Let us go
2 Ma 4 34 p. him to come forth out of the
10 20 were p. for the sake of money by
Mat 27 20 p. the people that they should ask
Luke 20 6 they are p. that John was a prophet
Acts 13 43 speaking to them, p. them to continue
18 4 he persuaded the Jews and the Greeks
26 26 for I am persuaded that none of these
James 3 17 then peaceable, modest, easy to be p.
persuadest Acts 26 28 p. me to become a Christian
persuadeth Acts 18 13 p. men to worship God contrary
persuading Acts 14 18 p. multitude, and stoning Paul
Acts 28 23 p. them concerning Jesus, out of the law
persuasion 2 Pa 32 15 nor delude you with a vain p.
Acts 19 26 this Paul by p. hath drawn away a great
2 C 5 11 we use persuasion to men; but to God we
Gal 5 8 this p. is not from him that calleth you
persuasive 1 C 2 4 was not in the p. words of
pertain Exod 4 16 things that p. to God. 18:19
Num 3 36 that pertain to this kind of service
4 26 all things that pertain to the altar
18 7 that p. to the service of the altar
pertained 1 K 25 21 lost of all that p. unto him
pertaineth Lev 14 13 offering p. to the priest
Lev 27 21 pertaineth to the right of the priests
Num 1 50 and whatsoever p. to the ceremonies
4 16 to whose charge pertaineth the oil to
16 p. to the service of the tabernacle
pertaining Gen 41 32 a dream p. to the same thing
Deut 22 3 neglect it not as pertaining to another
2 Ma 9 16 charges pertaining to the sacrifices
1 C 6 4 you have judgments of things p. to this
perverse Num 22 32 thy way is p. and contrary to
Deut 32 5 they are a wicked and p. generation
20 for it is a perverse generation and
2 K 22 27 with the p. thou wilt be perverted. Ps 17:27
Job 13 4 of lies, and maintainers of p. opinions
Ps 77 8 a perverse and exasperating generation
100 4 the perverse heart did not cleave to me
Prov 2 12 from the man that speaketh p. things
15 whose ways are p., and their steps
4 27 those are p. which are on the left hand
6 12 unprofitable man, walketh with p. mouth
8 8 nothing wicked nor perverse in them
10 31 the tongue of the perverse shall perish
32 mouth of the wicked uttereth p. things
11 20 a p. heart is abominable to the Lord
16 28 a perverse man stirreth up quarrels
17 20 he that is of a p. heart, shall not
19 1 rich man that is perverse in his lips
21 8 the perverse way of a man is strange
22 5 arms and swords are in way of the p.
23 33 thy heart shall utter perverse things
28 18 he that is p. in his ways shall fall
Ecce 1 15 the perverse are hard to be corrected
Wisd 1 3 perverse thoughts separate from God
Eccu 3 28 the p. of heart shall be scandalized
36 22 a perverse heart will cause grief
Isa 29 16 this thought of yours is perverse
Jer 17 9 the heart is p. above all things, and
Eze 18 25 are not rather your ways perverse. 29
2 Ma 4 11 brought in fashions that were perverse
Mat 17 16 unbelieving and p. generation, how long
Luke 9 41 faithless and p. generation, how long
Acts 2 40 save yourselves from this p. generation
20 30 shall arise men speaking p. things, to
Phil 2 15 of a crooked and perverse generation
perversely Isa 1 16 cease to do p., learn to do
1 C 13 4 charity envieth not, dealeth not p.; is
perverseness Jer 9 14 after the p. of their own
Jer 11 8 every one in p. of his own wicked heart
13 10 that walk in the p. of their heart
16 12 walketh after the p. of his evil heart
18 12 according to the p. of his evil heart
23 17 that walketh in the p. of his own heart
Eze 9 9 the city is filled with perverseness
perversity Jer 3 17 after the p. of their most
Jer 7 24 in the perversity of their wicked heart
pervert Exod 23 8 and p. the words of the just
Deut 24 17 not p. the judgment of the stranger
Job 8 3 doth God pervert judgment, or doth the
34 12 neither will the Almighty p. judgment
Prov 17 23 that he may p. the paths of judgment
31 5 and pervert the cause of the children
Mich 3 9 judgment and pervert all that is right
Acts 13 10 not to p. the right ways of the Lord
Gal 1 7 and would pervert the gospel of Christ
perverted 1 K 8 3 took bribes and p. judgment
2 K 22 27 with the perverse thou wilt be p. Ps 17:27
Ecce 5 7 and justice perverted in the province
Eccu 8 3 to the heart of kings and p. them
Jer 23 36 you have p. the words of the living
Dan 13 9 they perverted their own mind and

56 and lust hath perverted thy heart
perverteth Deut 27 19 that p. the judgment of the
Prov 10 9 he that p. his ways, shall be manifest
17 20 p. his tongue, shall fall into evil
Luke 23 14 as one that perverteth the people
perverting Luke 23 2 found this man p. our nation
pestilence Exod 5 3 p. or the sword fall upon us
Exod 9 15 to strike thee and thy people with p.
Lev 26 25 I will send the p. in the midst of you
Num 14 12 I will strike them with pestilence
Deut 28 21 may the Lord set the p. upon thee
2 K 24 13 three days there shall be a pestilence
15 the Lord sent a pestilence upon Israel
3 K 8 37 arise in the land, or a p. 2 Pa 6:28
1 Pa 21 12 sword of Lord and p. in the land
14 the Lord sent a pestilence upon Israel
2 Pa 7 13 if I send pestilence among my people
20 9 upon us the sword of judgment or p.
Ps 1 1 nor sat in the chair of pestilence
Jer 14 12 by famine and by the p. 21:9; 27:13; 32:24, 36; 38:2; 42:22; 44:13; Eze 6:11
21 6 men and beasts shall die of a great p.
7 as are left in this city from the p.
24 10 sword and the famine and the p. 29:17
27 8 sword and with famine and with p. 29:18
34 17 sword, to the p., and to the famine
42 17 into Egypt . . . shall die . . . by pestilence
Eze 5 12 third part of thee shall die with the p.
17 p. and blood shall pass through thee
6 12 he that is far off shall die of the p.
7 15 the pestilence and the famine within
15 in the city, shall be devoured by the p.
12 16 from the famine and from the p.
14 19 if I also send the p. upon that land
21 and the p. to destroy out of it
28 23 I will send into her p., and blood
33 27 and caves, shall die of the pestilence
38 22 and I will judge him with pestilence
pestilences Mat 24 7 shall be p. and. Luke 21:11
pestilent Prov 21 11 when a p. man is punished
1 Ma 10 61 and some pestilent men of Israel, men
15 3 certain pestilent men have usurped
21 if therefore any p. men are fled out
Acts 24 5 we have found this to be a p. man, and
pestilential Jer 51 1 a p. wind against Babylon
pestle Exod 16 14 as it were beaten with a pestle
Exod 27 20 oil of the olives, and beaten with a p.
Prov 27 22 when pestle striketh upon sodden barley
Peter Mat 4 18 Simon who is called Peter. 10:2
Mat 14 28 Peter making answer, said: Lord, if it
29 Peter going down out of the boat
16 18 thou art Peter; and upon this rock I
22 P. taking him, began to rebuke. Mark 8:32
23 said to Peter: Go behind me, Satan
17 23 came to Peter and said to him: Doth not
18 21 came Peter unto him and said: Lord
26 40 he saith to Peter: What? Could you not
58 P. followed him afar off. Mark 14:54
69 Peter sat without in the court: and
73 said to Peter: Surely thou also art
75 P. remembered the word. Mark 14:72; Luke 22:61
Mark 3 16 to Simon he gave the name Peter: and
8 33 threatened Peter, saying: Go behind me
10 28 Peter began to say unto him: Behold
11 21 P. remembering, said to him: Rabbi
14 37 he saith to Peter: Simon, sleepest
66 when Peter was in the court below
67 she had seen Peter warming himself
70 they that stood by said again to Peter
16 7 tell his disciples and Peter that he
Luke 6 14 Simon, whom he surnamed Peter, and
8 45 P. and they that were with him. 9:32
22 8 he sent Peter and John, saying: Go
34 Peter, the cock shall not crow this
54 but Peter followed afar off. And when
61 the Lord turning, looked on Peter
62 and Peter going out, wept bitterly
24 12 Peter rising up, ran to the sepulcher
John 1 42 Cephas, which is interpreted Peter
44 Bethsaida, the city of Andrew and P.
18 11 said to Peter: Put up thy sword into
16 but Peter stood at the door without
16 to the portress, and brought in Peter
18 Peter also, standing and warming. 25
26 a kinsman to him whose ear P. cut off
27 again therefore Peter denied; and
20 3 Peter therefore went out, and that
4 that other disciple did outrun Peter
21 7 said to Peter: It is the Lord. Simon
17 Peter was grieved because he had said
20 P. turning about, saw that disciples
21 him therefore when Peter had seen
Acts 1 13 where abode Peter and John, James and
15 Peter rising up in the midst of the
2 14 Peter standing up with the eleven
37 said to Peter and to the rest of the
3 1 Peter and John went up into the temple
3 when he had seen Peter and John about
4 Peter with John fastening his eyes
11 as he held Peter and John, all the
12 Peter seeing, make answer to the
4 13 seeing the constance of Peter and of
19 Peter and John answering, said to them
5 15 that when Peter came, his shadow at
29 Peter and the apostles answering
8 14 they sent unto them Peter and John
9 32 it came to pass that Peter, as he
38 disciples hearing that Peter was there
39 Peter rising up, went with them. And
40 put forth, Peter kneeling down prayed
40 she opened her eyes; and seeing Peter
10 5 Simon, who is surnamed P. 18, 32; 11:13
9 city, Peter went up to the higher parts
13 voice to him: Arise, Peter; kill and
17 whilst Peter was doubting within himself
19 as Peter was thinking of the vision
21 Peter, going down to the men, said
25 when Peter was come in, Cornelius came
26 Peter lifted him up, saying: Arise, I
34 Peter opening his mouth, said: In every
44 while Peter was yet speaking these
45 faithful . . . who came with Peter, were
47 P. answered: Can any man forbid water
11 2 when Peter was come up to Jerusalem
4 P. began and declared to them the matter
7 to me: Arise, Peter; kill and eat
12 3 he proceeded to take up Peter also
5 Peter therefore was kept in prison
6 P. was sleeping between two soldiers
7 striking P. on the side, raised him
11 Peter coming to himself, said: Now I
14 running in she told that Peter stood
16 Peter continued knocking. And when
18 stir . . . what was become of Peter
15 7 Peter, rising up, said to them: Men
Gal 1 18 I went to Jerusalem, to see Peter, and I
2 7 as to Peter was that of the circumcision
8 wrought in Peter to the apostleship of
1 P 1 1 Peter, an apostle of Jesus Christ, to
Peter and James and John Mat 17 1 Jesus taketh unto him P. . . .
Mark 5 37 any man to follow him but P. . . .
9 1 Jesus taketh with him P. . . . and
13 3 P. . . . and Andrew asked him apart
14 33 he taketh P. . . . with him; and he began

Luke 8 51 man to go in with him, but P. . . .
9 28 he took P. . . . and went up into a
Peter answering said Mat 15 15 P. . . . to him: Expound to us this
Mat 17 4 P. . . . to Jesus: Lord, it is good
19 27 P. . . . to him: Behold we have left
26 33 P. . . . to him: Although all shall be
Mark 8 29 P. . . . to him: Thou art the Christ
9 4 P. . . . to Jesus: Rabbi, it is good for
Luke 9 20 P. . . . : The Christ of God. But he
Peter said Luke 12 41 Peter said to him: Lord, dost thou
Luke 18 28 Peter said: Behold, we have left all
22 58 but Peter said: O man, I am not. And
60 Peter said: Man, I know not what thou
Acts 2 38 Peter said to them: Do penance and
3 6 Peter said: Silver and gold I have
4 8 P., filled with the Holy Ghost, said
5 3 Peter said: Ananias, why hath Satan
8 Peter said to her: Tell me, woman
9 Peter said unto her: Why have you
8 19 Peter said to him: Keep thy money to
9 34 Peter said to him: Eneas, the Lord
10 14 Peter said: Far be it from me; for I
Peter saith Mat 26 35 P. saith to him: Yea, though
Mark 14 29 Peter saith to him: Although all shall
Luke 9 33 Peter saith to Jesus: Master, it is
John 13 6 Peter saith to him: Lord, dost thou
8 Peter saith to him: Thou shalt never
9 P. saith to him: Lord not only my feet
36 P. saith to him: Lord, whither goest thou
37 Peter saith to him: Why cannot I
21 3 Peter saith to them: I go a fishing
Peter's Mat 8 14 Jesus was come into Peter's house
Acts 12 14 as soon as she knew Peter's voice
petition 1 K 1 17 God of Israel grant thee thy p.
1 K 1 27 the Lord hath granted me my petition
3 K 2 16 I ask one petition of thee: Turn not
20 I desire one small petition of thee
12 7 grant their petition and wilt speak
Tob 7 10 unless thou first grant me my petition
11 and gave no answer to his petition
Esth 5 7 my petition and request is this: If I
8 to fulfil my petition: let the king
7 2 what is thy petition, Esther, that it
Ps 85 6 attend to the voice of my petition
87 3 thee: incline thy ear to my petition
101 18 he hath not despised their petition
Eccu 4 4 reject not the p. of the afflicted
Jer 37 19 let my p. be accepted in thy sight
Dan 6 7 whosoever shall ask any p. of any god
petitioneth Wisd 13 19 p. him that cannot walk
petitions Deut 4 7 God is present to all our p.
Ps 19 7 the Lord fulfil all thy petitions
Bar 2 14 hear, O Lord, our prayers and our p.
Phil 4 6 let your petitions be made known to God
1 J 5 15 we have the p. which we request of him
Petra Isa 16 1 from P. of the desert, to the
Isa 42 11 ye inhabitants of Petra, give praise
Phacee 4 K 15 25 Phacee . . . conspired against him
4 K 14 27 reigned P. the son of Romelia over
29 in the days of Phacee king of Israel
30 and formed a plot against Phacee
31 but the rest of the acts of Phacee
32 in the second year of Phacee the son
37 into Juda Rasin king of Syria and P.
16 1 in the seventeenth year of Phacee
5 Phacee . . . came up to Jerusalem. Isa 7:1
2 Pa 28 6 Phacee . . . slew of Juda 120,000
Phaceia 4 K 15 22 P. his son reigned in his stead
4 K 15 23 reigned Phaceia the son of Manahem
26 and the rest of the acts of Phaceia
Phadaia 4 K 23 36 Zebida the daughter of Phadaia
1 Pa 3 18 P., Senneser, and Jacemia, Sama
19 of Phadaia were born Zorobabel and
27 20 of Manasses, Joel the son of Phadaia
2 Es 3 25 after him Phadaia the son of Pharos
8 4 P., Misael, and Melchia, and Hasum
11 7 the son of Joed, the son of Phadaia
13 13 of the Levites Phadaia, and next to
Phadassur Num 1 10 Gamaliel the son of Phadassur. 2:20; 7:54, 59; 10:23
Phadon 1 Es 2 44 children of Phadon. 2 Es 7:48
Phahath 1 Es 2 6 children of Phahath Moab. 2 Es 7:11
1 Es 8 4 of the sons of Phahath Moab. 10:30
2 Es 3 11 Hasub the son of Phahath Moab, built
10 14 Pharos, Phahath Moab, Elam, Zethu
Phalaia 2 Es 8 7 Hanan, Phalaia, the Levites
2 Es 10 10 Celita, Phalaia, Hanan, Micha, Rohob
Phalea 2 Es 10 24 Alohes, Phalea, Sobec, Rehum
Phaleg Gen 10 25 name of the one was P. 1 Pa 1:19
Gen 11 16 lived 34 years, and begot Phaleg
17 Heber lived after he begot Phaleg
18 P. also lived thirty years and begot
19 Phaleg lived after he begot Reu
1 Pa 1 25 Heber, Phaleg, Ragau, Serug, Nachor
Luke 3 35 Ragan, who was of Phaleg, who was of
Phalel 2 Es 3 25 P. the son of Ozi over against
Phalet 1 Pa 2 47 Phalet and Epha and Saaph. And
Phaleth 1 Pa 2 33 Jonathan begot Phaleth and
Phallet 1 Pa 12 3 and P. the sons of Azmoth, and
Phallonite 1 Pa 27 10 was Helles a Phallonite
Phallu Gen 46 9 the sons of Ruben . . . Phallu. Exod 6:14; 1 Pa 5:3
Num 26 5 his sons were Henoch . . . and Phallu
8 the son of Phallu was Eliab. His sons
Phalluites Num 26 5 of whom is family of the P.
Phalonite 1 Pa 11 27 valiant men . . . Helles a P.
Phalti Num 13 10 Phalti the son of Raphu
1 K 25 44 gave Michol . . . David's wife, to Phalti
2 K 23 26 Heles of Phalti, Hira the son of
Phaltias 1 Pa 4 42 their captains P. and Naaria
Phaltiel Num 34 26 of the tribe of Issachar, P.
2 K 3 15 took her from her husband Phaltiel
Phanuel Gen 32 30 called the name of the place P.
Gen 32 31 rose upon him after he was past P.
Judg 8 8 from thence, he came to Phanuel
17 he demolished the tower of Phanuel
3 K 12 25 going out from thence he built Phanuel
1 Pa 4 4 Phanuel the father of Gedor, and Ezar
8 25 Jephdaia and P. the sons of Sesac
Luke 2 36 the daughter of Phanuel, of the tribe
Phara Judg 7 10 let Phara thy servant go down
Judg 7 11 he went down with Phara his servant
1 Ma 9 50 Phara and Thopo, with high walls
Pharai 2 K 23 35 Hesrai of Carmel, P. of Arbi
Pharam Josu 10 3 and to Pharam king of Jerimoth
Pharan Gen 14 6 even to the plains of Pharan
Gen 21 21 he dwelt in the wilderness of Pharan
Num 10 12 cloud rested in the wilderness of P.
13 1 pitched their tents in the desert of P.
4 sending from the desert of Pharan
27 to the desert of Pharan, which is in
Deut 1 1 between Pharan and Thophel and
33 2 he hath appeared from mount Pharan
1 K 25 1 went down into the wilderness of P.
3 K 11 18 arose out of Madian and came into P.
18 they took men with them from Pharan
Haba 3 3 and the holy one from mount Pharan
Pharao Gen 12 15 told Pharao and praised her
Gen 12 15 was taken into the house of Pharao
17 Lord scourged Pharao . . . for Sarai
18 Pharao called Abram and said to him
20 and Pharao gave his men orders
37 36 Putiphar, an eunuch of Pharao. 39:1
40 2 and Pharao being angry with them
11 the cup of Pharao was in my hand

11 and I gave the cup to Pharao
13 Pharao will remember thy service
14 to put Pharao in mind to take me out
19 Pharao will take thy head from thee
20 third day . . . was the birthday of Pharao
41 1 after two years Pharao had a dream
4 so Pharao awoke. He slept again and
7 Pharao awaked after his rest: and when
16 God shall give P. a prosperous answer
17 Pharao told what he had dreamed
25 God hath shown to P. what he is about
41 again Pharao said to Joseph: Behold
44 king said to Joseph: I am Pharao
46 when he stood before king Pharao
55 the people cried to Pharao for food
42 15 by the health of Pharao you shall not
44 18 for after Pharao thou art, my lord
45 2 and all the house of Pharao heard
8 made me as it were a father to Pharao
16 Pharao with all his family was glad
46 5 in the wagons which Pharao had sent
31 I will go up and will tell Pharao
47 1 Joseph went in and told Pharao, saying
11 in Ramesses as Pharao had commanded
23 you and your lands belong to Pharao
50 4 Joseph spoke to the family of Pharao
4 speak in the ears of Pharao: for my
6 Pharao said to him: Go up and bury thy
Exod 1 11 built for Pharao cities of tabernacles
22 Pharao therefore charged all his people
2 5 daughter of Pharao came down to wash
15 Pharao heard of this word and sought
22 delivered me out of the hand of Pharao
3 10 I will send thee to Pharao, that thou
11 who am I that I should go to Pharao
4 21 thou do all the wonders before Pharao
5 1 said to Pharao: Thus saith the Lord
5 Pharao said: The people . . . is numerous
10 thus saith Pharao, I allow you no straw
15 the officers . . . cried out to Pharao
20 then as they came out from Pharao
21 made our savor to stink before Pharao
23 since the time that I went in to Pharao
6 1 shalt see what I will do to Pharao
11 go in and speak to Pharao king of
12 how will Pharao hear me, especially
13 he gave them a charge . . . unto Pharao
27 these are they that speak to Pharao
29 speak thou to Pharao king of Egypt
30 how will Pharao hear me? And the Lord
7 1 I have appointed thee the God of Pharao
2 he [Aaron] shall speak to Pharao
7 Aaron 83, when they spoke to Pharao
9 when P. shall say to you, Show signs
9 take thy rod and cast it down before P.
10 so Moses and Aaron went in unto Pharao
10 Aaron took the rod before Pharao and
11 Pharao called the wise men and the
20 he struck the water . . . before Pharao
8 1 go in to Pharao. 9:1; 10:1
8 Pharao called Moses and Aaron. 25; 9:27; 10:24
9 Moses said to Pharao: Set me a time
12 Moses and Aaron went forth from Pharao
12 promise which he had made to Pharao
15 Pharao seeing that rest was given
19 the magicians said to Pharao: This is
20 arise early and stand before Pharao
24 swarm of flies into the houses of Pharao
28 Pharao said: I will let you go to
29 the flies shall depart from Pharao
31 he took away the flies from Pharao
9 7 Pharao sent to see: and there was not
8 it in the air in the presence of Pharao
10 the chimney and stood before Pharao
13 the morning and stand before Pharao
33 when Moses was gone from Pharao out of
34 Pharao seeing that the rain . . . ceased
10 3 Moses and Aaron went in to Pharao
6 himself away and went forth from Pharao
8 called back Moses and Aaron to Pharao
10 P. answered: So be the Lord with you
16 Pharao in haste called Moses and Aaron
18 going forth from the presence of Pharao
28 Pharao said to Moses: Get thee from me
11 1 one plague more will I bring upon P.
5 shall die from the firstborn of Pharao
9 he went out from P. exceeding angry
9 Pharao will not hear you, that many
10 did all the wonders . . . before Pharao
12 29 from the firstborn of Pharao, who sat
30 Pharao arose in the night, and all his
31 Pharao calling Moses and Aaron in the
13 15 when Pharao was hardened . . . Lord slew
17 when Pharao had sent out the people
14 3 Pharao will say of the children of Israel
4 I shall be glorified in Pharao. 17, 18
5 the heart of Pharao . . . was changed
8 the Lord hardened the heart of Pharao
10 when Pharao drew near, the children
28 horsemen of all the army of Pharao
15 19 Pharao went in on horseback with his
18 4 delivered me from the sword of Pharao
8 all that the Lord had done to Pharao
10 delivered you out of the hand of Pharao
Deut 6 21 we were bondmen of Pharao in Egypt
22 signs and wonders . . . against Pharao
7 18 remember what the Lord . . . did to Pharao
11 3 which he did . . . to king Pharao and to
29 2 things that the Lord did . . . to Pharao
34 11 to do in the land of Egypt to Pharao
1 K 2 27 were in Egypt in the house of Pharao
6 6 as Egypt and Pharao hardened their
3 K 3 1 and he made affinity with Pharao
7 8 a house for the daughter of Pharao
9 16 Pharao the king of Egypt came up
24 the daughter of Pharao came up
11 1 women besides the daughter of Pharao
18 and went into Egypt to Pharao
19 Adad found great favor before Pharao
20 Taphnes brought him up in house of P.
20 and Genubath dwelt with Pharao
21 he said to Pharao: Let me depart
22 Pharao said to him: Why, what is wanting
4 K 17 7 from under the hand of Pharao
18 21 so is Pharao king of Egypt, to all
23 29 Pharao Nechao . . . went up against
33 Pharao Nechao bound him at Rebla
34 Pharao Nechao made Eliacim . . . king
35 gave the silver and the gold to Pharao
35 according to the commandment of Pharao
35 his ability: to give to Pharao Nechao
1 Pa 4 18 Bethia the daughter of Pharao
2 Pa 8 11 he removed the daughter of Pharao
2 Es 9 10 showedst signs and wonders upon Pharao
Ps 134 9 upon Pharao, and upon all his servants
135 15 overthrew Pharao and his host
Isa 19 11 counsellors of P. have given foolish
11 how will you say to Pharao: I am the
30 2 hoping for help in strength of Pharao
3 strength of P. shall be to your confusion
36 6 so is Pharao . . . to all that trust in
Jer 25 19 Pharao the king of Egypt and his
37 4 army of Pharao was come out of Egypt
6 the army of Pharao . . . shall return
44 30 I will deliver Pharao Ephree king of

46 2 against the army of Pharao Nechao
17 call ye the name of P. king of Egypt
25 I will visit . . . upon Pharao and
47 1 Palestine, before Pharao took Gaza
Eze 17 17 nor with much people shall P. fight
29 2 set thy face against P. king of Egypt
3 I come against thee, P. king of Egypt
30 21 I have broken the arm of Pharao king
22 I come against Pharao king of Egypt
24 I will break the arms of Pharao
25 and the arms of Pharao shall fall
31 2 speak to Pharao king of Egypt and to
18 this is Pharao and all his multitude
32 2 take up a lamentation for Pharao
31 P. saw them, and he was comforted
31 Pharao and all his army, saith the Lord
32 P. and all his multitude, saith the
1 Ma 4 9 when P. pursued them with a great army
Acts 7 10 and wisdom in the sight of Pharao
13 his kindred was made known to Pharao
Rom 9 17 for the scripture saith to Pharao: To
Pharao's Gen 41 35 corn be laid up under P. hands
Gen 45 21 them wagons according to P. commandment
47 20 he brought it into Pharao's hands
50 7 with him all the ancients of P. house
Exod 2 9 Pharao's daughter said to her: Take
9 she delivered him to Pharao's daughter
5 14 were scourged by Pharao's taskmasters
7 13 Pharao's heart was hardened. 22; 8:19, 32; 9:7
14 P. heart is hardened, he will not
9 12 the Lord hardened Pharao's heart. 10:20, 27; 11:10
20 word of the Lord among P. servants
10 7 P. servants said to him: how long
11 they were cast out from P. presence
11 3 in the sight of Pharao's servants and
14 9 all Pharao's horse and chariots and
23 went in after them, and all P. horses
15 4 P. chariots and his army he hath
Cant 1 8 company of horsemen, in P. chariots
Jer 37 10 from Jerusalem, because of P. army
43 9 the brick wall at the gate of P. house
Acts 7 21 Pharao's daughter took him up and
Heb 11 24 to be the son of Pharao's daughter
Pharathon Judg 12 15 he died and was buried in P.
Pharathonite Judg 12 13 the son of Illel, a P.
2 K 23 30 Banaia the Pharathonite, Heddai of
1 Pa 11 31 of Benjamin, Banai a Pharathonite
27 14 Banaias, a Pharathonite of the sons
Phares Gen 38 29 therefore called his name P.
Gen 46 12 Onan and Sela and Phares and Zara
12 sons were born to Phares: Hesron
Num 26 20 Phares, of whom is the family of
21 sons of Phares were: Hesron, of whom
Ruth 4 12 house may be as the house of Phares
18 generations of P.: P. begot Esron
1 Pa 2 4 Thamar . . . bore him Phares and Zara
5 the sons of P. were Hesron and Hamul
4 1 sons of Juda: Phares, Hesron, and
7 16 she [Maacha] called his name Phares
9 4 of the sons of Phares the son of Juda
27 3 of the sons of Phares, the chief
2 Es 11 4 of the sons of Phares, Maasia
6 all these the sons of Phares, who
Dan 5 25 that is written: Mane, Thecel, Phares
28 Phares: thy kingdom is divided, and
Mat 1 3 Judas begot Phares and Zara of Thamar
3 Phares begot Esron. And Esron begot
Luke 3 33 Esron, who was of Phares, who was of
Pharesites Num 26 20 is the family of the P.
Pharida 2 Es 7 57 Nathinites . . . children of P.
Pharisee Mat 23 26 blind P., first made clean the
Luke 7 36 went into the house of the Pharisee
39 the Pharisee, who had invited him
11 37 P. prayed him that he would dine with
38 the P. began to say, thinking within
18 10 one a P., and the other a publican
11 the P. standing, prayed thus with
Acts 5 34 one in the council rising up, a P.
23 6 I am a Pharisee, the son of Pharisees
26 5 sect of our religion I lived a Pharisee
Phil 3 5 according to the law, a Pharisee
Pharisee's Luke 7 37 he sat at meat in the P. house
Pharisees Mat 3 7 seeing many of P. and Sadducees
Mat 9 11 seeing it, said to his disciples
14 why do we and the P. fast often, but
34 the P. said, By the prince of devils
12 2 P. seeing them, said to him: Behold
14 the P. going out made a consultation
24 the P. hearing it, said: This man
15 12 the P., when they heard this word
16 1 came to him the P. and Sadducees
6 beware of the leaven of the Pharisees. Mark 8:15; Luke 12:1
12 the doctrine of the P. and Sadducees
19 3 came to him the P. tempting him and
22 15 the P. going, consulted among themselves
34 the P. hearing that he had silenced
41 the P. being gathered together, Jesus
Mark 2 18 disciples of John and the P. used to
24 the P. said to him: Behold, why do they
3 6 the P. going out, immediately made a
7 1 unto him the P. and some of the scribes
3 P. and all the Jews eat not without
5 P. and scribes asked him: Why do not
8 11 the P. came forth and began to question
9 10 why then do the P. and scribes say
10 2 the P. coming to him asked him: Is it
12 13 they sent to him some of the Pharisees
Luke 5 17 there were also P. and doctors of
30 the P. and scribes murmured, saying
33 the disciples of the P. in like manner
6 2 some of the P. said to them: Why do
7 30 the Pharisees and the lawyers despised
35 one of the P. desired him to eat with
11 39 you P. make clean the outside of the
42 woe to you Pharisees. 43
53 the Pharisees and the lawyers began
13 31 some of the P., saying to him: Depart
14 1 house of one of the chief of the P.
3 spoke to the lawyers and Pharisees
15 2 and the P. and the scribes murmured
16 14 the P., who were covetous, heard all
17 20 being asked by the P., when the
19 39 P., from amongst the multitude, said
John 1 24 they that were sent were of the P.
3 1 there was a man of the Pharisees, named
4 1 P. had heard that Jesus maketh more
7 32 the P. heard the people murmuring
32 rulers and Pharisees sent ministers
47 P. therefore answered them: Are you
48 believed in him, or of the Pharisees
8 13 the Pharisees therefore said to him
9 13 bring him that had been blind to the P.
15 the P. asked him how he had received
16 some therefore of the P. said: This
40 some of the P., who were with him
11 46 some of them went to the P. and told
12 19 the P. therefore said among themselves
42 because of the P. they did not confess
Acts 15 5 arose some of the sect of Pharisees
23 6 one part were Sadducees, and other P.
6 I am a Pharisee, the son of Pharisees
7 dissension between P. and Sadducees; and
8 nor spirit: but the P. confess both

9 some of P. rising up, strove, saying
scribes and Pharisees Mat 5 20 abound more than that of the s. . . .
Mat 7 29 power, and not as the s. . . . And when
12 38 some of the s. and P. answered him
15 1 came to him from Jerusalem s. . . .
23 2 s. . . . have sitten on the chair of
13 woe to you scribes and Pharisees. 14, 15, 23, 25, 27, 29
Mark 2 16 the s. . . . seeing that he ate with
Luke 5 21 the s. . . . began to think, saying
6 7 the s. . . . watched if he would heal
John 8 3 the s. . . . bring unto him a woman
Pharisim 2 K 5 20 and David came to Baal Pharisim
2 K 5 20 name of place was called Baal Pharisim
Pharnach Num 34 25 Elisaphan the son of Pharnach
Pharos 1 Es 2 3 children of P. 2,172. 2 Es 7:8
1 Es 8 3 the son of Pharos, Zacharias, and with
10 25 of the sons of Pharos, Remeia and
2 Es 3 25 after him Phadaia the son of Pharos
10 14 Pharos, Phahath, Moab, Elam, Zethu
Pharphar 4 K 5 12 are not the Abana and the P.
Pharsandatha Esth 9 7 P. and Delphon and
Pharuda 1 Es 2 55 the children of Pharuda
Pharue 3 K 4 17 Josaphat the son of Pharue
Pharurim 4 K 23 11 Nathanmelech . . . who was in P.
phase Exod 12 11 Phase, that is the Passage
Exod 12 21 sacrifice the phase. Deut 16:2
43 this is the service of the phase: no
48 among you and to keep the phase
34 25 victim of the solemnity of the phase
Lev 23 5 at evening, is the phase of the Lord
Num 9 2 let the children of Israel make the p.
4 that they should make the phase. And
6 could not make the phase on that day
10 let him make the phase of the Lord
12 observe all the ceremonies of the p.
13 if any man . . . did not make the phase
14 be among you, shall make the phase
28 16 day of the month shall be the phase
33 3 the first month, the day after the phase
Deut 16 1 that thou mayst celebrate the phase
5 not immolate the phase in any one of
6 shalt immolate the p. in the evening
Josu 5 10 kept the p. on the 14th. 1 Es 6:19
4 K 23 21 keep the phase to the Lord. 2 Pa 30:1
22 there was no such a phase kept from
23 as was this phase that was kept to
2 Pa 30 2 to keep the phase the second month
5 they should come and keep the phase
15 immolated the p. on the fourteenth
17 Levites immolated the phase for them
18 ate the phase otherwise than it is
35 1 and Josias kept a phase to the Lord
6 being sanctified kill the phase and
7 found there in the solemnity of the p.
8 gave to the priests to keep the phase
9 to rest of Levites to celebrate the p.
11 and the phase was immolated: and the
13 and they roasted the phase with fire
16 in keeping the phase and offering
17 kept the phase at that time, and the
18 was no phase like to this in Israel
18 keep such a phase as Josias kept
19 reign of Josias was this p. celebrated
1 Es 6 20 all were clean to kill the phase
Phasea 1 Es 2 49 the children of P. 2 Es 7:51
2 Es 3 6 Joiada the son of Phasea, and Mosollam
Phaselis 1 Ma 15 23 Aradus and Rhodes and P.
Phaseron 1 Ma 9 66 children of P. in their tents
Phasga Num 21 20 country of Moab to top of P.
Num 23 14 top of mount Phasga, Balaam built
Deut 3 17 salt sea, to the foot of mount Phasga
27 go up to the top of Phasga and cast
4 49 and unto the foot of mount Phasga
34 1 mount Nebo to the top of Phasga
Josu 12 3 that lieth under Asedoth, Phasga
Phashur 2 Es 7 41 children of Phashur, 1,247
Phaspha 1 Pa 7 38 sons of Jether: Jephone and P.
Phassur 1 Pa 9 12 Jeroham the son of Phassur
Jer 20 1 Phassur the son of Emmer the priest
2 Phassur struck Jeremias the prophet
3 P. brought Jeremias out of the stocks
3 Lord hath not called thy name Phassur
6 thou Phassur, and all that dwell in
21 1 when king Sedecias sent unto him P.
38 1 Gedelias the son of Phassur, and Juchal
1 Phassur the son Melchias heard the
Phataia 1 Es 10 23 Calita, P., Juda, and Eliezer
Phathahia 2 Es 9 5 Sebnia and Phathahia said
2 Es 11 24 Phathahia the son of Mesezebel of
Phatuel Joel 1 1 Joel the son of Phatuel
Phatures Jer 44 1 in the land of P. Eze 29:14
Jer 44 15 that dwelt in the land of Egypt in P.
Eze 30 14 I will destroy the land of Phatures
Phau Gen 36 39 name of his city was Phau. 1 Pa 1:50
phe Ps 118 129 phe. Lam 1:17; 2:16; 3:46, 47, 48; 4:16
Phebe Rom 16 1 I commend to you Phebe, our sister
Phedael Num 34 28 of the tribe of Nephtali, P.
Phegiel Num 1 13 P. the son of Ochran. 2:27; 7:72, 77; 10:26
Pheldas Gen 22 22 Pheldas and Jedlaph and
Pheleia 1 Pa 3 24 sons of Elioenai . . . Pheleia
Phelelia 2 Es 11 12 Jeroham the son of Phelelia
Pheleth Num 16 1 Hon the son of Pheleth
Phelethi 2 K 8 18 the Cerethi and P. 15:18; 20:7; 3 K 1:38, 44; 4 K 11:19; 1 Pa 18:17
Phelethites 2 K 20 23 over the Cerethites and P.
Phelonite 1 Pa 11 36 Ahia a Phelonite, Hesro a
Phelti 2 Es 12 17 of Miamin and Moadia, Phelti
Pheltia 2 Es 10 22 Pheltia, Hanan, Anaia
Pheltias Eze 11 1 Pheltias the son of Banaias. 13
Phenenna 1 K 1 2 the name of the other P. P. had children; but Anna
1 K 1 4 sacrifice, and gave to P. his wife
Phenice Acts 11 19 they . . . went about as far as Phenice
Acts 15 3 they . . . passed through Phenice, and
21 2 we had found ship sailing over to P., we
27 12 if by any means they might reach Phenice
Phenicia 2 Ma 3 5 governor of Celesyria and P. 4:4; 2 Ma 8:8
2 Ma 3 8 visiting the cities of Celesyria and P.
4 22 returned with his army into Phenicia
10 11 general of the army of P. and Syria
Pherezite Gen 13 7 the P. dwelled in that country
Exod 3 8 the P. and the Hevite and the Jebusite. 17; 33:3; 34:11; Deut 7:1; 20:17; Josu 9:1; 12:8; 17:15; Judg 3:5
23 23 Amorrhite and the Hethite and the P.
Josu 3 10 he shall destroy . . . the Pherezite
11 3 Hethite and the P. and the Jebusite
24 11 the P. and the Chanaanite and the
Judg 1 4 and the Pherezite into their hands
5 defeated the Chanaanite and the P.
2 Es 9 8 to give him the land of . . . the P.
Pherezites Gen 15 20 and the Hethites and the P.
Gen 34 30 me hateful to the Chanaanites and P.
3 K 9 20 that were left of the . . . P. 2 Pa 8:7
1 Es 9 1 P. and the Jebusites and the Ammonites
Jdth 5 20 the P. and of the Hethites and of the
Phermesta Esth 9 9 sons of Aman . . . Phermesta
Phesdomim 1 Pa 11 13 he was with David in P.
Pheshur 1 Es 2 38 children of Pheshur, 1,247
1 Es 10 22 of the sons of Pheshur, Elioenai
2 Es 10 3 Pheshur, Amarias, Melchias, Hattus

11 12 Zacharias the son of Pheshur, the son
Phesse 1 Pa 4 12 Esthon begot Bethrapha and P.
Pheteia 1 Pa 24 16 the nineteenth [lot] to P.
Phetros Isa 11 11 and from P. and from Ethiopia
Phetrusim Gen 10 14 Mesraim begot . . . P. 1 Pa 1:12
phials Zach 14 20 as the phials before the altar
Phicol Gen 21 22 P. the general of his army. 33
Gen 26 26 Phicol chief captain of his soldiers
Phigellus 2 Tim 1 15 of whom are P. and Hermogenes
Phihahiroth Exod 14 2 encamp over against P.
Exod 14 9 the whole army were in Phihahiroth
Num 33 7 they came over against Phihahiroth
8 departing from P., they passed through
Philadelphia Apoc 1 11 to Sardis and to P. and to
Apoc 3 7 to the angel of the church of P., write
Philarches 2 Ma 8 32 they slew also Philarches
Philemon Philem 1 to P., our beloved and fellow
Philetus 2 Tim 2 17 of whom are Hymeneus and P.
Philip 1 Ma 1 1 Alexander the son of P. 6:2
1 Ma 6 14 he called Philip, one of his friends
55 heard that Philip . . . was returned
63 he found Philip master of the city
8 5 that they had defeated in battle Philip
2 Ma 5 22 governors . . . at Jerusalem, Philip
6 11 being discovered by Philip, were burnt
8 8 Philip, seeing that the man gained
9 29 Philip that was brought up with him
13 23 that Philip . . . had rebelled at Antioch
Mat 10 3 Philip and Bartholomew, Thomas and
Mark 3 18 Andrew and Philip and Bartholomew and
6 17 Herodias the wife of P. his brother
Luke 3 1 Philip his brother tetrarch of Iturea
6 14 Philip and Bartholomew, Matthew and
John 1 43 he findeth Philip. And Jesus saith to
44 Philip was of Bethsaida, the city of
45 Philip findeth Nathanael, and saith to
46 Philip saith to him: Come and see
48 before that P. called thee, when thou
6 5 he said to Philip: Whence shall we buy
7 Philip answered him: Two hundred
12 21 these therefore came to Philip, who
22 Philip cometh and telleth Andrew
22 again Andrew and Philip told Jesus
14 8 Philip saith to him: Lord, show us the
9 Philip, he that seeth me seeth the
Acts 1 13 where abode . . . Philip and Thomas
6 5 Philip and Prochorus and Nicanor and
8 5 P. going down to the city of Samaria
6 those things which were said by Philip
12 when they had believed P. preaching
13 being baptized, he adhered to Philip
26 an angel of the Lord spoke to Philip
29 the Spirit said to Philip: Go near
30 Philip running thither, heard him
31 he desired Philip that he would come
34 the eunuch, answering Philip, said: I
35 then Philip, opening his mouth and
37 Philip said: If thou believest with
38 the water, both Philip and the eunuch
39 Spirit of the Lord took away Philip
40 but Philip was found in Azotus; and
21 8 entering into house of Philip evangelist
Philippi Mat 16 13 into the quarters of Caesarea P.
Mark 8 27 into the towns of Caesarea Philippi
Acts 16 12 thence to Philippi, which is chief city
20 6 we sailed from Philippi after the days
Phil 1 1 saints in Christ Jesus, who are at P.
1 Th 2 2 been shamefully treated . . . at Philippi
Philippians Phil 4 15 you also know, O P., that in
Philisthiim Exod 15 14 hold on inhabitants of P.
Philistia Josu 13 2 Galilee, P. and all Gessuri
Isa 14 29 rejoice not thou, whole Philistia
31 O city: all Philistia is thrown down
Philistine 1 K 17 8 am not I a P., and you the
1 K 17 10 P. said: I have defied the bands of
11 hearing these words of the P.
23 whose name was Goliath, the P., of Geth
26 to the man that shall kill this P.
26 who is this uncircumcised Philistine. 36
32 will go and will fight against the P.
33 thou art not able to withstand this P.
36 this uncircumcised P. shall be also as
37 will deliver me out of hand of this P.
40 and went forth against the Philistine
41 the Philistine came on and drew nigh
42 when the P. looked, and beheld David
43 the P. said to David: Am I a dog
43 the Philistine cursed David by his gods
45 David said to the P.: Thou comest
48 when the P. arose and was coming
48 ran to the fight to meet the P.
49 struck the Philistine in the forehead
50 David prevailed over the Philistine
50 and he struck and slew the Philistine
51 stood over the P. and took his sword
54 David taking the head of the Philistine
57 returned, after the P. was slain
57 head of the Philistine in his hand
18 6 returned after he slew the P., the
19 5 his life in his hand, and slew the P.
21 9 the sword of Goliath the P. 22:10
2 K 21 17 Abisai . . . striking the P. killed him
Philistines Gen 10 14 of whom came forth the P.
Josu 13 3 divided among the lords of the P.
Judg 3 31 who slew of the Philistines 600 men
10 6 the gods . . . of the Philistines
7 into the hands of the P. 13:1; 15:12; 1 K 12:9
11 the children of Ammon and the Philistines
13 5 from the hands of the P. 1 Pa 18:1
14 1 a woman of the daughters of the P.
2 woman . . . of the daughters of the P.
3 that thou wilt take a wife of the P.
4 sought an occasion against the P.
4 the Philistines had dominion over Israel
15 3 blameless in what I do against the P.
5 into the standing corn of the Philistines
6 the P. said: Who hath done this thing
6 the P. went up and burnt both the woman
9 the P. going up into the land of Juda
11 that the Philistines rule over us
14 the P. shouting went to meet him
20 he judged Israel in days of the P.
16 2 when the Philistines had heard this
9 the P. are upon thee, Samson. 12, 14, 20
21 the P. seized upon him and forthwith
30 he said: Let me die with the Philistines
1 K 4 1 the P. gathered themselves together
1 Israel went out to war against the P.
1 and the Philistines came to Aphec
2 Israel turned their backs to the P.
3 Lord defeated us today before the P.
6 the P. heard the noise of the shout
7 and the Philistines were afraid, saying
9 and behave like men, ye Philistines
10 P. fought, and Israel was overthrown
17 Israel has fled before the Philistines
5 1 the Philistines took the ark of God. 2
8 together all the lords of the P. 11
6 2 the Philistines called for the priests
5 the number of the provinces of the P.
12 lords of the Philistines followed them
17 which the Philistines returned for sin
18 the number of the cities of the P.
21 the P. have brought back the ark of
7 3 out of the hand of the P. 8; 9:16

7 the P. heard that the children of Israel
7 lords of the P. went up against Israel
7 they were afraid of the Philistines
10 the P. began the battle against Israel
10 with a great thunder . . . upon the P.
11 men of Israel . . . pursued after the P.
13 and the Philistines were humbled
13 hand of the Lord was against the P.
14 cities which the Philistines had taken
14 from the hand of the Philistines
10 5 where garrison of the Philistines is
13 3 Jonathan smote the garrison of the P.
3 when the P. had heard of it, Saul
4 had smitten the garrison of the P.
4 and Israel took courage against the P.
5 P. also were assembled to fight against
11 P. were gathered together in Machmas
12 now will the P. come down upon me to
16 the Philistines encamped in Machmas
17 there went out of the camp of the P.
19 the P. had taken this precaution
20 Israel went down to the P., to sharpen
23 the army of the Philistines went out
14 1 go over to the garrison of the P. 4
11 discovered themselves to garrison of P.
11 the P. said: Behold the Hebrews come
19 a great uproar in the camp of the P.
21 the Hebrews that had been with the P.
22 hearing that the P. fled, joined
30 greater slaughter among the Philistines
31 they smote that day the Philistines
36 let us fall upon the P. by night
37 shall I pursue after the Philistines
46 did not pursue after the Philistines
46 the Philistines went to their own places
47 against . . . kings of Soba and the P.
52 war against the P. all the days of Saul
17 1 the P. gathering together their troops
2 army in array to fight against the P.
3 the Philistines stood on a mountain
4 a man baseborn from the camp of the P.
19 fighting against the Philistines
21 P. who stood against them were prepared
23 coming up from camp of the Philistines
46 the carcasses of the army of the P.
51 P. seeing that their champion was dead
52 after the P. till they came to the valley
52 there fell many wounded of the P.
53 after they had pursued the Philistines
55 Saul saw David going out against the P.
18 17 let the hands of the P. be upon him
21 hand of the P. may be upon him
25 only 100 foreskins of the Philistines
25 to deliver David into hands of the P.
27 he slew of the Philistines 200 men
19 8 went out and fought against the P.
23 1 the Philistines fight against Ceila
2 shall I go and smite these Philistines
2 shalt smite the P. and shalt save Ceila
3 to Ceila against the bands of the P.
4 I will deliver the P. into thy hand
5 went to Ceila and fought against the P.
27 the P. have poured in themselves upon
28 and [Saul] went to meet the Philistines
24 2 Saul was returned from following the P.
27 7 David dwelt in the country of the P.
11 days that he dwelt in country of the P.
28 1 the P. gathered together their armies
4 the Philistines were gathered together
5 Saul saw the army of the Philistines
15 for the Philistines fight against me
19 Israel with thee into hands of the P.
19 army of Israel into the hands of the P.
29 1 the troops of the P. were gathered
2 the lords of the Philistines marched
11 and the Philistines went up to Jezrahel
31 1 the Philistines fought against Israel
1 men of Israel fled from before the P.
2 and the Philistines fell upon Saul
7 the Philistines came and dwelt there
8 the Philistines came to strip the slain
11 heard all that the P. had done to Saul
2 K 1 20 lest the daughters of the P. rejoice
3 14 for a hundred foreskins of the P.
18 I will save . . . from hands of the P.
5 17 the P. heard that they had anointed
18 the P. coming spread themselves
19 shall I go up to the Philistines
19 I will surely deliver the P. into thy
22 and the Philistines came up again
23 shall I go up against the Philistines
24 to strike the army of the P. 1 Pa 14:15
25 he smote the Philistines from Gabaa
8 1 David defeated the Philistines and
1 bridle of tribute out of hand of P.
12 silver and gold . . . of the Philistines
19 9 saved us out of the hand of the P.
21 12 where the Philistines had hanged them
15 the P. made war again against Israel
15 [David] fought against the Philistines
18 battle in Gob against the P. 19
23 9 with David when they defied the P.
10 smote the P. till his hand was weary
11 P. were gathered together in a troop
11 were fled from the face of the P.
12 [Semma] defeated the Philistines
13 the camp of the P. was in the valley
14 a garrison of the P. then in Bethlehem
16 broke through the camp of the Philistines
3 K 15 27 Gebbethon a city of the P. 16:15
4 K 18 8 he smote the Philistines as far as Gaza
1 Pa 1 12 from whom came the Philistines, and
10 1 the Philistines fought against Israel
1 Israel fled from before the Philistines
2 the P. drew near pursuing after Saul
7 Philistines came, and dwelt in them
8 the Philistines taking away the spoils
11 that the Philistines had done to Saul
11 13 when the P. were gathered to that place
13 people fled from before the Philistines
14 and defended it: and they slew the P.
15 P. encamped in the valley of Raphaim
16 and the garrison of the P. in Bethlehem
18 through midst of the camp of the P.
12 19 when he came with the P. against Saul
19 lords of the P. taking counsel, sent him
14 8 P. hearing that David was anointed
9 the P. came and spread themselves in
10 shall I go up against the Philistines
13 the P. made an irruption and spread
16 defeated the army of the P., slaying
18 1 David defeated the P. and humbled
11 from the Philistines and from Amalec
20 4 a war at Gazer against the Philistines
5 battle also was fought against the P.
2 Pa 17 11 the Philistines also brought presents
21 16 against Joram the spirit of the P.
26 6 and fought against the Philistines
6 he [Ozias] built towns . . . among the P.
7 God helped him against the Philistines
28 18 the Philistines also spread themselves
Ps 55 1 when the Philistines held him in Geth
82 8 the P. with the inhabitants of Tyre
Eccu 46 21 Tyrians and all the lords of the P.
47 8 extirpated the P. the adversaries
50 28 that sit on mount Seir, and the P.

Isa 2 6 and have had soothsayers as the P.
9 12 and the Philistines from the west
11 14 shall fly upon the shoulders of the P.
Jer 47 4 in which all the P. shall be laid waste
4 for the Lord hath wasted the Philistines
Eze 16 27 to the will of the daughters of the P.
25 15 because the P. have taken vengeance
16 will stretch forth my hand upon the P.
Joel 3 4 and all the coast of the Philistines
Amos 1 8 rest of the Philistines shall perish
6 2 go down into Geth of the Philistines
9 7 and the Philistines out of Cappadocia
Abdi 19 and they that are in the plains, the P.
Zach 9 6 I will destroy the pride of the P.
land of the Philistines Gen 21 33 of his army arose and returned to the l. . . .
Gen 21 34 was a sojourner in the l. . . . many days
Exod 13 17 led them not by the way of the l. . . .
1 K 6 1 ark of God was in l. . . . seven months
27 1 me to flee and to be saved in the l. . . .
29 11 morning, and returned to the l. . . . : and
30 16 which they had taken out of the l. . . .
31 9 sent into the l. . . . round about to
3 K 4 21 kingdoms from the river to the l. . . .
4 K 8 2 she sojourned in the l. . . . many days
2 Pa 9 26 from the river Euphrates to the l. . . .
Jer 25 20 all the kings of the l. . . . and Ascalon
Soph 2 5 Lord upon you, O Chanaan, the l. . . .
1 Ma 3 24 men, and the rest fled into the l. . . .
princes of the Philistines Judg 3 3 the five p. . . .
Judg 16 3 p. . . . came to her and said: Deceive
8 p. . . . brought unto her seven cords
18 she sent to the p. . . . , saying: Come
23 p. . . . assembled together to offer
27 men and women, and all the p. . . . were
1 K 6 16 the p. . . . saw, and they returned to
18 30 the p. . . . went forth: and from the
29 3 p. . . . said to Achis: What mean these
3 Achis said to the p. . . . : Do you not
4 p. . . . were angry with him, and they
7 offend not the eyes of the p. . . .
9 p. . . . have said: He shall not go up
Philologus Rom 16 15 salute P. and Julia, Nereus
Philometor 2 Ma 4 21 with the nobles of king P.
2 Ma 9 29 went into Egypt to Ptolemee Philometor
10 13 Cyprus which P. had committed to him
philosophers Dan 2 27 or the p. or the diviners
Acts 17 18 certain p. of the Epicureans and of
philosophy Col 2 8 beware lest any man cheat you by p.
Phinees Exod 6 25 of Phutiel: and she bore him P.
Num 25 7 Phinees the son of Eleazar. 11; 31:6; Josu 22:13; Judg 20:28; 1 Pa 9:20; 1 Es 7:5; Eccu 45:28
Josu 22 30 when Phinees the priest, and the princes
31 Phinees the priest the son of Eleazar
24 33 in Gabaath that belongeth to Phinees
1 K 1 3 sons of Heli, Ophni and Phinees. 4:11
2 34 upon thy two sons, Ophni and Phinees
4 4 Ophni and Phinees, were with the ark
17 sons, Ophni and Phinees, are dead
19 the wife of Phinees was big with child
14 3 brother to Ichabod the son of P.
1 Pa 6 4 Eleazar begot P., and P. begot Abisue
50 Eleazar his son, Phinees his son
1 Es 8 2 of the sons of Phinees, Gersom
33 with him was Eleazar the son of P.
Ps 105 30 Phinees stood up and pacified him
1 Ma 2 26 as Phinees did by Zamri the son of
54 Phinees our father, by being fervent
Phinon Gen 36 41 duke Phinon, duke Cenez. 1 Pa 1:52
Phison Gen 2 11 the name of the one is Phison
Eccu 24 35 filleth up wisdom as the Phison
Phithom Exod 1 11 built for Pharao cities . . . P.
Phithon 1 Pa 8 35 sons of Micha were Phithon. 9:41
Phlegon Rom 16 14 salute Asyncritus, Phlegon, Hermas
Phochereth 1 Es 2 57 children of P. 2 Es 7:59
Phogor Num 23 28 him upon the top of mount P.
Num 25 18 deceived you by the idol Phogor and
18 the plague for the sacrilege of Phogor
31 16 against the Lord by the sin of Phogor
Deut 3 29 valley over against the temple of P. 4:46
34 6 the land of Moab over against Phogor
Phollathi 1 Pa 26 5 sons of Obededom . . . Phollathi
Phoratha Esth 9 8 sons of Aman . . . Phoratha
Phosech 1 Pa 7 33 sons of Jephlat: Phosech
Phrygia Acts 2 10 Phrygia and Pamphylia, Egypt and
Acts 16 6 when they had passed through Phrygia
18 23 through the country of Galatia and P.
Phrygian 2 Ma 5 22 Philip, a Phrygian by birth
Phua Gen 46 13 Thola and Phua and Job
Exod 1 15 midwives of the Hebrews . . . the other P.
Num 26 23 Phua, of whom is the family of the
Judg 10 1 ruler in Israel, Thola son of Phua
1 Pa 7 1 and Phua, Josub and Simeron four
Phuaites Num 26 23 whom is the family of the P.
Phul 4 K 15 19 Phul king of the Assyrians. 1 Pa 5:26
4 K 15 19 Manahem gave Phul a thousand talents
Phunon Num 33 42 they removed and came to Phunon
Num 33 43 departing from Phunon, they camped
Phur Esth 3 7 which in Hebrew is called Phur
Esth 9 24 and had cast Phur, that is, the lot
26 because Phur, that is, the lot was cast
Phurim Esth 9 26 these days are called Phurim
Esth 9 28 any city wherein the days of Phurim
11 1 his son brought this epistle of Phurim
Phut 1 Pa 1 8 sons of Cham . . . Phut and Chanaan
Phuth Gen 10 6 sons of Cham: . . . Phuth and
Phutiel Exod 6 25 a wife of the daughters of P.
phylacteries Mat 23 5 they make their p. broad
physician Eccu 10 11 is troublesome to the p.
Eccu 10 12 physician cutteth off a short sickness
38 1 honor the p. for the need thou hast
3 skill of the p. shall lift up his head
11 and then give place to the physician
15 shall fall into the hands of the p.
Jer 8 22 is in Galaad? Or is there no p. there
Mat 9 12 that are in health need not a physician
Mark 2 17 well have no need of a physician, but
Luke 4 23 physician, heal thyself: as great
5 31 that are whole need not the physician
Col 4 14 Luke, the most dear physician, saluteth
physicians Gen 50 2 physicians to embalm his father
Exod 21 19 for his expenses upon the physicians
2 Pa 16 12 rather trusted in the skill of p.
Ps 87 11 shall physicians raise to life and
Mark 5 26 suffered many things from many p.
Luke 8 43 bestowed all her substance on p.
pick Prov 30 17 ravens of the brooks pick it out
Isa 62 10 the road plain, pick out the stones
Eze 20 38 I will pick out from among you the
picked Isa 5 2 picked the stones out of it and
picture Wisd 15 4 us, nor the shadow of a p.
Eccu 38 28 his mind to the resemblance of the p.
pictures Eze 8 11 them that stood before the p.
piece Judg 9 53 woman casting a piece of a millstone
1 K 2 36 and shall offer a piece of silver
30 12 as also a piece of a cake of figs
2 K 6 19 a piece of roasted beef. 1 Pa 16:3
11 21 woman cast piece of millstone upon him
4 K 6 2 every man a piece of timber, that we
6 he cut off a piece of wood and cast it
Tob 6 8 if thou put a little piece of its heart
Cant 4 3 cheeks are as a piece of a pomegranate
Wisd 13 13 being a crooked piece of wood and
14 1 calleth upon a piece of wood more frail
Jer 37 20 should give him daily a piece of bread

Eze 13 19 handful of barley and a piece of bread
24 4 every good piece, the thigh and the
6 cast it out piece by piece, there hath
Amos 3 12 that dwell in Samaria in p. of a bed
4 7 one p. was rained upon; and the p. whereupon I rained not, withered
Mat 9 16 nobody putteth a piece of raw cloth
Mark 2 21 no man seweth a piece of raw cloth to
Luke 5 36 no man putteth a piece from a new
36 the piece taken from the new agreeth
24 42 offered him a piece of a broiled fish
Acts 5 1 Ananias . . . sold a piece of land, and
pieces Gen 15 10 laid the two pieces of each one
Exod 29 17 and thou shalt cut the ram in pieces
17 upon the flesh that is cut in pieces
Lev 1 6 they shall cut the joints into pieces
2 6 thou shalt divide it into little pieces
8 20 cutting the ram into pieces, the head
9 13 the victim being cut into pieces, they
Num 33 52 break in pieces their statues, and waste
Deut 9 21 breaking it into pieces until it was
12 3 break their idols in pieces, destroy
Josu 9 5 loaves . . . hard and broken into pieces
12 are become dry, and broken in pieces
Judg 8 16 cut in pieces the men of Soccoth
14 6 as he would have torn a kid in pieces
19 29 sent the pieces into all the borders
20 6 I took her and cut her in pieces
1 K 6 14 they cut in pieces the wood of the cart
11 7 both the oxen, he cut them in pieces
15 33 Samuel hewed him in pieces before the
2 K 22 39 I will . . . break them in pieces
3 K 11 31 said to Jeroboam: Take to thee ten pieces
15 13 and broke in pieces the filthy idol
18 23 cut it in pieces and lay it upon wood
33 cut the bullock in pieces and laid it
19 11 and breaking the rocks in pieces
4 K 2 12 garments, and rent them in two pieces
5 5 took . . . six thousand pieces of gold
10 27 burnt it and broke it in pieces
11 18 his images they broke in pieces
18 4 and broke the statues in pieces
23 14 and he broke in pieces the statues
24 13 cut in pieces all the vessels of
25 13 the Chaldees broke in pieces and carried
1 Pa 20 3 they were cut and bruised to pieces
2 Pa 9 15 sum of six hundred pieces of gold
16 shields of three hundred pieces of gold
15 16 breaking it into pieces, burnt it
25 12 and they all were broken to pieces
34 4 graven things, and broke them in pieces
7 and had broken the idols in pieces
Job 16 13 am all on a sudden broken to pieces
19 2 and break me in pieces with words
22 9 arms . . . thou hast broken in pieces
24 20 broken in p. as an unfruitful tree
34 24 he shall break in pieces many and
40 25 shall friends cut him in pieces, shall
Ps 2 9 shalt break them in pieces like a
28 6 and shall reduce them to pieces
36 17 of the wicked shall be broken in pieces
47 8 shalt break in p. the ships of Tharsis
55 8 thou shalt break the people in pieces
57 7 God shall break in pieces their teeth
104 16 broke in p. all the support of bread
33 and he broke in pieces the trees
Eccu 28 18 hath cut in pieces the forces of people
33 2 he shall not be dashed in pieces
48 6 brokest easily their power in pieces
Isa 8 15 very many . . . shall be broken in pieces
13 16 their infants shall be dashed in pieces
14 29 that the rod . . . is broken in pieces
18 2 to a nation rent and torn in pieces
7 from a people rent and torn in pieces
25 10 as straw is broken in p. with the wain
27 9 as burnt stones broken in pieces, the
30 14 as potter's vessel is broken all to p.
14 not a sherd be found of the pieces
30 he shall crush to p. with whirlwind
37 19 and they broke them in pieces. And now
41 15 mountains, and break them in pieces
45 2 in pieces the gates of brass, and will
Jer 23 29 hammer that breaketh the rock in pieces
51 21 I will break in pieces the horse and
21 I will break in pieces the chariot
22 I will break in pieces man and woman
22 I will break in pieces the old man
22 I will break in pieces the young man
23 I will break in pieces the shepherd
23 I will break in pieces the husbandman
23 I will break in pieces captains and
52 17 also broke in pieces the brazen pillars
Lam 3 11 and hath broken me in pieces, he hath
Eze 4 16 will break in p. the staff of bread
5 2 and cut it in pieces with the knife
11 I will also break thee in pieces, and
6 4 your idols shall be broken in pieces
6 your altars . . . shall be broken in p.
24 4 heap together into it the pieces thereof
4 choice pieces and full of bones. Take
25 7 I will . . . break thee in pieces: and
30 22 I will break in pieces his strong arm
Dan 2 34 upon the feet . . . and broke them in p.
35 silver and the gold broken to pieces
40 as iron breaketh into pieces and
44 it shall break in p. and shall consume
45 broke in pieces the clay and the iron
6 24 and broke all their bones in pieces
7 7 iron teeth, eating and breaking in p.
19 he devoured and broke in pieces
23 shall tread it down and break it in p.
26 his power may . . . be broken in pieces
11 4 his kingdom shall be rent in pieces
Osee 1 5 I will break in p. the bow of Israel
10 14 the mother being dashed in pieces upon
Mich 1 7 her graven things shall be cut in pieces
4 13 shalt beat in pieces many peoples
Nah 1 13 I will break in pieces his rod with
3 10 her young children were dashed in pieces
Haba 1 4 therefore the law is torn in pieces
3 6 ancient mountains were crushed to pieces
1 Ma 1 23 he broke them all in pieces. And he
59 in pieces . . . the books of the law
6 51 and pieces to shoot arrows, and slings
2 Ma 1 16 hewed them in pieces, and cutting off
15 33 be cut out and given by pieces to birds
Mark 5 4 and broken the fetters in pieces and
Acts 23 10 fearing lest Paul should be pulled in p.
pieces of silver; *see* **silver**
piecing Mark 2 21 new p. taketh away from the old
pierce Num 24 8 bones, and p. them with arrows
4 K 18 21 and go into his hand and pierce it
Ps 118 120 pierce thou my flesh with thy fear
Prov 7 23 till the arrow pierce his liver: as if
Eccu 35 21 humbleth himself, shall p. the clouds
Isa 36 6 it will go into his hand and pierce it
Luke 2 35 and thy own soul a sword shall pierce
pierced Jdth 13 28 will command thy sides to be p.
Jdth 16 14 of the damsels have p. them through
Job 30 17 in the night my bone is p. with sorrows
39 7 but thou hast pierced ears for me
Ps 104 18 in fetters: the iron pierced his soul
Zach 12 10 look upon me whom they have pierced
John 19 37 shall look on him whom they pierced
Apoc 1 7 see him, and they also that p. him
piercing Judg 5 26 strongly p. through his temples

Jer 9 8 their tongue is a piercing arrow, it
Heb 4 12 more piercing than any two-edged sword
piety Eccu 37 13 nor with the ungodly of piety
Bar 5 4 the peace of justice and honor of piety
1 Tim 2 2 a peaceable life in all p. and chastity
pigeon Gen 15 9 a turtle also and a pigeon
Lev 12 6 a young pigeon or a turtle for sin
14 30 shall offer a turtle or young pigeon
pigeon's 4 K 6 25 part of a cabe of p. dung
pigeons Lev 1 14 of turtles or of young pigeons
Lev 5 7 two turtles or two young p. 11; 12:8; 14:22; 15:14, 29; Num 6:10
Luke 2 24 or turtledoves or two young pigeons
pikes Jdth 9 9 in their chariots and in their p.
Eze 39 9 and the handstaves and the pikes
Amos 4 2 when they shall lift you up on pikes
Pilate Mat 27 2 and delivered him to Pontius Pilate
Mat 27 13 Pilate saith to him: Dost thou hear
17 Pilate said: Whom will you that I
22 Pilate saith to them: What shall I
24 Pilate seeing that he prevailed nothing
58 he went to Pilate and asked the body
58 Pilate commanded that the body should
62 came together to Pilate, saying: Sir
65 Pilate saith to them: You have a guard
Mark 15 1 led him away and delivered him to P.
2 Pilate asked him: Art thou the king
4 and Pilate again asked him, saying
5 nothing; so that Pilate wondered. Now
9 P. answered them and said: Will you
12 P. again answering, saith to them
14 P. saith to them: Why, what evil hath
15 P. being willing to satisfy the people
43 went in boldly to Pilate and begged
44 P. wondered that he should be already
Luke 3 1 Pontius Pilate being governor of Judea
13 1 whose blood Pilate had mingled with
23 3 Pilate asked him, saying: Art thou
4 Pilate said to the chief priests and
6 Pilate hearing Galilee, asked it the
11 garment, and sent him back to Pilate
12 Herod and Pilate were made friends
13 Pilate, calling together the chief
20 Pilate again spoke to them, desiring
24 Pilate gave sentence that it should be
52 this man went to Pilate, and begged
John 18 29 Pilate therefore went out to them
31 Pilate therefore said to them: Take
33 Pilate therefore went into the hall
35 Pilate answered: Am I a Jew? Thy own
37 Pilate therefore said to him: Art thou
38 Pilate saith to him: What is truth
19 1 Pilate took Jesus and scourged him
4 Pilate therefore went forth again and
6 Pilate saith to them: Take him you
8 when Pilate therefore had heard this
10 Pilate therefore saith to him
12 Pilate sought to release him. But the
13 when Pilate had heard these words, he
15 Pilate saith to them: Shall I crucify
19 Pilate wrote a title also, and he put
21 said to Pilate: Write not, the King
22 Pilate answered: What I have written
31 besought Pilate that their legs might
38 besought Pilate that he might take
38 Pilate gave leave. He came therefore
Acts 3 13 and denied before the face of Pilate
4 27 Herod and Pontius Pilate with the
13 28 desired of P., that they might kill him
1 Tim 6 13 who gave testimony under Pontius Pilate
pile Gen 22 9 him on the altar upon the p. of wood
Lev 1 7 having before laid in order a pile of
4 12 he shall burn them upon a pile of wood
Judg 6 26 a holocaust upon a pile of the wood
piles Eze 24 5 lay together p. of bones under it
pilgrimage Gen 47 9 days of my p. are 130 years
Gen 47 9 up to the days of the p. of my fathers
Exod 6 4 Chanaan, the land of their pilgrimage
Ps 118 54 song, in the place of my pilgrimage
Ecce 7 1 in all the days of his pilgrimage
pilgrims Heb 11 13 confessing that they are pilgrims
1 P 2 11 you as strangers and p., to refrain
pillage Jdth 8 19 to the sword and to pillage
Jer 20 5 they shall pillage them and take them
1 Ma 6 3 to take the city and to pillage it
pillaged 1 K 27 8 pillaged Gessuri and Gerzi
4 K 7 16 pillaged the camp of the Syrians
2 Pa 14 14 they pillaged the cities and carried off
Jdth 2 13 pillaged all the children of Tharsis
Isa 13 16 their houses shall be pillaged, and
2 Ma 10 37 pillaged and sacked the fortress
pillaging Jer 50 11 great things, p. my inheritance
pillar Gen 35 20 erected a p. over the sepulcher
Gen 35 20 this is the pillar of Rachel's monument
Exod 13 21 the way by day in a pillar of a cloud
21 and by night in a pillar of fire
22 never failed the p. of the cloud by day nor the p. of fire by night
14 19 p. of the cloud, leaving the forepart
24 through the p. of fire and of the cloud
33 9 the pillar of the cloud came down and
10 pillar of the cloud stood at the door
Num 12 5 Lord came down in a pillar of the cloud
14 14 goest before them in a p. of a cloud
14 in a pillar of fire by night and
Deut 1 33 in the day by the pillar of a cloud
31 15 appeared there in the pillar of a cloud
20 40 perceived as it were a pillar of smoke
2 K 18 18 he called the pillar by his own name
18 Absalom had reared . . . a pillar which
3 K 7 15 each pillar was eighteen cubits high
20 according to the measure of the pillar
21 when he had set up pillar on the right
21 in like manner he set up the second p.
4 K 25 17 one pillar was eighteen cubits high
17 that were upon the chapiter of the p.
17 second pillar had the like adorning
2 Es 9 12 in a pillar of fire by night that they
12 and in a pillar of a cloud thou wast
19 the pillar of the cloud departed not
19 the pillar of fire by night to show
Jdth 13 8 she went to the pillar that was at his
Ps 55 1 an inscription of a title (or pillar)
98 7 spoke to them in the p. of the cloud
Cant 3 6 as a pillar of smoke of aromatical
Wisd 10 7 standing pillar of salt is a monument
18 3 they received a burning pillar of fire
Eccu 24 7 my throne is in a pillar of a cloud
36 26 a help like to himself and a p. of rest
Jer 1 18 a fortified city and a pillar of iron
21 one pillar was eighteen cubits high
52 22 the same of the second pillar, and
1 Tim 3 15 God, the pillar and ground of the truth
Apoc 3 12 I will make him a pillar in the temple
pillars Exod 26 32 hang it up before four pillars
Exod 26 37 overlay with gold five p. of setim
27 10 twenty p. with as many sockets. 11
12 and ten pillars and as many sockets
14 three p. and as many sockets. 15; 38:15
16 four pillars with as many sockets
17 the pillars of the court round about
35 11 the oars, the pillars and the sockets
17 curtains of the court with the pillars
36 36 four pillars of setim wood, which with
38 five pillars with their heads, which
38 10 twenty pillars of brass with their

10 heads of the pillars . . . of silver. 12
11 p. and the sockets and heads of the p.
12 ten pillars of brass with their sockets
14 with three pillars and their sockets
17 sockets of the pillars were of brass
17 he overlaid the pillars of the court
19 the pillars in the entry were four
28 he made the heads of the pillars
39 32 the bars, the pillars, and their sockets
39 and the pillars with their sockets
40 16 and the bars, and set up the pillars
Lev 26 1 neither shall you erect pillars nor
Num 3 36 bars and the pillars and their sockets
37 the pillars of the court round about
4 31 bars thereof, the p. and their sockets
32 pillars also of the court round about
33 52 beat down their pillars and break
Judg 16 25 them made him stand between two pillars
26 suffer me to touch the pillars which
29 and laying hold on both the pillars
30 when he had strongly shook the pillars
3 K 7 2 four galleries between pillars of cedar
2 for he had cut cedar trees into pillars
3 was held up with five and forty pillars
3 and one row had fifteen pillars, set
5 with equal space between the pillars
5 over the pillars were square beams
6 he made a porch of pillars of 50 cubits
6 pillars, and chapiters upon the pillars
15 and he cast two pillars in brass
15 a line of 12 cubits compassed both p.
16 to be set upon the tops of the pillars
17 the chapiters of the pillars were cast
18 he made the pillars, and two rows
19 were upon the top of the pillars. 41
20 other chapiters in top of the pillars
21 he set up the two pillars in the porch
22 upon tops of pillars he made lily work
22 the work of the pillars was finished
31 in the corners of the pillars were
31 spaces between the pillars were square
41 the two pillars and the two cords of
41 upon the chapiters of the pillars
42 which were upon the tops of the pillars
4 K 25 13 p. of brass that were in the temple
16 two pillars, one sea, and the bases
1 Pa 18 8 the pillars and the vessels of brass
2 Pa 3 15 before doors of the temple two pillars
16 put them on the heads of the pillars
17 these pillars he put at the entrance
4 12 the two pillars and the pommels
13 pommels and the chapiters of the p.
Jdth 13 10 took off his canopy from the pillars
Esth 1 6 and were held up with marble pillars
Job 9 6 place, and the pillars thereof tremble
26 11 the pillars of heaven tremble, and
Ps 74 4 I have established the pillars thereof
Prov 9 1 she hath hewn her out seven pillars
Cant 3 10 the pillars thereof he made of silver
5 15 his legs as pillars of marble that are
Eccu 26 23 as golden pillars upon bases of silver
Jer 27 19 saith the Lord of hosts to the pillars
52 17 also broke in pieces the brazen pillars
20 the two pillars and one sea and twelve
21 concerning the pillars, one pillar was
Eze 40 49 and there were pillars in the fronts
42 6 had not p., as the p. of the courts
1 Ma 13 29 round about these he set great pillars
29 upon the p. arms for a perpetual memory
14 26 and set it upon pillars in mount Sion
Gal 2 9 John, who seemed to be pillars, gave to
Apoc 10 1 his feet as pillars of fire. And he
pilled Gen 30 37 and pilled them in part: so
Gen 30 37 in the parts that were pilled, there
Joel 1 7 hath pilled off the bark of my fig
pillow Mark 4 38 part of the ship, sleeping upon a p.
pillows Eze 13 18 make pillows for the heads of
Eze 13 21 I will tear your pillows and will
pilot Prov 23 34 as a pilot fast asleep, when the
Acts 27 11 but the centurion believed the pilot
pilots Eze 27 8 thy wise men, O Tyre, were thy p.
Eze 27 27 thy mariners and thy pilots who kept
29 all the pilots of the sea shall stand
pin 1 Es 9 8 give us a pin in his holy place
Eccu 14 25 fastening a pin in her walls shall set
Eze 15 3 shall a pin be made of it for any
Zach 10 4 out of him the pin, out of him the bow
pine Lev 26 39 shall pine away in their iniquities
2 Pa 2 8 cedars and fir trees and pine trees
Ps 111 10 gnash with his teeth and pine away
118 139 my zeal hath made me pine away
Eccu 40 14 transgressors shall pine away in the
Isa 34 4 host of the heavens shall pine away
44 14 he hath planted the pine tree, which
60 13 and the box tree and the pine tree
Eze 4 17 they may pine away in their iniquities
24 23 shall pine away for your iniquities
33 10 are upon us, and we pine away in them
pined Ps 106 26 their soul pined away with evils
Ps 118 158 beheld the transgressors and I p. away
138 21 and pined away because of thy enemies
Lam 1 19 and my ancients pined away in the city
4 9 these pined away being consumed for
pineth Mark 9 17 with the teeth, and pineth away
pining 2 K 13 20 Thamar remained p. away in the
pinions Lev 1 17 he shall break the p. thereof
Lev 5 8 back the head of it to the little p.
pinnacle Mat 4 5 set him upon the p. Luke 4:9
pins Exod 27 19 pins both of it and of the court
Exod 35 18 the pins of the tabernacle and of the
38 20 the pins also of the tabernacle and of
39 40 the little cords and the pins thereof
Num 3 37 sockets and the pins with their cords
4 32 with their sockets and pins and cords
Isa 3 22 and fine linen and crisping pins and
pipe 1 K 10 5 and a pipe and harp before them
Isa 5 12 the pipe and wine are in your feasts
30 29 heart, as when one goeth with a pipe
1 Ma 3 45 and the pipe and harp ceased there
1 C 14 7 that give sound, whether pipe or harp
Apoc 18 22 that play on the pipe and on the trumpet
piped Mat 11 17 we have piped to you. Luke 7:32
1 C 14 7 how shall it be known what is piped or
pipes 3 K 1 40 and the people played with pipes
Job 40 13 his bones are like pipes of brass, his
Jer 48 36 my heart shall sound for Moab like p.
36 my heart shall sound like pipes for
Eze 28 13 thy pipes were prepared in the day that
Pisidia Acts 13 14 Perge, came to Antioch in P.
Acts 14 23 passing through P., they came into
piss 3 K 16 11 not one thereof to piss against
pisseth 1 K 25 22 that pisseth against the wall. 34; 3 K 14:10; 21:21; 4 K 9:8
pit Gen 37 20 cast him into some old pit: and we
Gen 37 22 but cast him into this pit that is
24 and cast him into an old pit, where
28 they drew him out of the pit and sold
29 Ruben, returning to the pit, found not
Exod 21 34 owner of the pit shall pay the price
23 13 they shall be a pit and a snare in your
Judg 5 15 as one going headlong and into a pit
2 K 18 17 cast him [Absalom] into a great pit
23 20 and slew a lion in the midst of a pit
4 K 10 14 and killed them at the pit by the cabin
1 Pa 11 22 killed a lion in the midst of a pit
Tob 8 13 when they had prepared the pit, Raguel

20 20 to fill up the pit they had made
Job 17 16 shall go down into the deepest pit
40 8 and plunge their faces into the pit
Ps 7 15 he hath opened a pit and dug it: and
27 1 that go down into the pit. 29:4; 87:5; 142:7; Eze 31:14; 32:18, 24, 29, 30
39 3 and brought me out of the pit of misery
54 24 down into the pit of destruction
56 7 they dug a pit before my face, and they
68 16 let not the pit shut her mouth upon me
87 7 they have laid me in the lower pit
93 13 till a pit be dug for the wicked
Prov 1 12 as one that goeth down into the pit
13 15 in the way of scorners is a deep pit
22 14 mouth of a strange woman is a deep pit
23 27 a strange woman is a narrow pit
26 27 he that diggeth a pit, shall fall into it. Ecce 10:8; Eccu 27:29
28 17 if he flee even to the pit, no man
Wisd 10 13 she went down with him into the pit
Eccu 12 15 lieth in wait, to throw thee into a pit
Isa 2 19 hide thee in the pit from the face of
14 15 down to hell, into the depth of the pit
19 art gone down to the bottom of the pit
24 17 the pit and the snare are upon thee
18 noise of the fear, shall fall into the pit
18 that shall rid himself out of the pit
22 gathering of one bundle into the pit
30 14 a little water be drawn out of the pit
51 1 hole of the pit from which you are dug
Jer 18 20 they have digged a pit for my soul
22 they have digged a pit to take me
41 7 cast them into the midst of the pit
9 the pit into which Ismahel cast all
48 43 fear and the pit and the snare come
44 from the fear, shall fall into the pit
44 he that shall get up out of the pit
Lam 3 53 my life is fallen into the pit, and
55 thy name O Lord, from the lowest pit
Eze 26 20 with those that descend into the pit. 31:16; 32:25
20 that are brought down into the pit
32 23 are set in the lowest parts of the pit
Zach 9 11 sent forth thy prisoners out of the pit
1 Ma 7 19 killed, and threw them into a great pit
2 Ma 1 19 there was a deep pit without water
Mat 12 11 if the same fall into a pit on the
15 14 lead the blind, both fall into the pit
Luke 14 5 have an ass or an ox fall into a pit
Apoc 9 1 to him the key of the bottomless pit
2 and he opened the bottomless pit: and
2 the smoke of the pit arose, as the
2 darkened with the smoke of the pit
3 from the smoke of the pit there came
11 king, the angel of the bottomless pit
17 8 come up out of the bottomless pit
20 1 having the key of the bottomless pit
3 he cast him into the bottomless pit

pitch Gen 6 14 thou shalt pitch it within and
Gen 16 12 he shall pitch his tents over against
Exod 2 3 and daubed it with slime and pitch
Num 1 53 the Levites shall pitch their tents
2 3 on the east Juda shall pitch his tents
3 24 these shall pitch behind the tabernacle
Deut 1 33 wherein you should pitch your tents
Josu 4 3 where you shall pitch your tents this
Eccu 13 1 that toucheth pitch, shall be defiled
Isa 13 20 neither shall the Arabian pitch his
34 9 streams thereof shall be turned into p.
9 land thereof shall become burning pitch
Dan 3 46 brimstone and tow and pitch and dry
14 26 Daniel took pitch and fat and hair

pitched Gen 12 8 of Bethel, he there p. his tent
Gen 13 3 where before he had pitched his tent
26 25 name of the Lord, and p. his tent
25 he pitched his tent in the same mount
31 25 Jacob had pitched his tent in the
33 17 having built a house and pitched tents
19 field in which he pitched his tents
35 21 pitched his tent beyond the Flock tower
Exod 19 2 there Israel pitched their tents
33 7 tabernacle, pitched it without the camp
Num 2 27 of the tribe of Aser p. their tents
9 18 they pitched the tabernacle. All the
20 at commandment of Lord they p. their
23 by word of Lord they p. their tents
13 1 p. their tents in the desert of Pharan
21 11 they pitched their tents in Jeabarim
24 6 as tabernacles which the Lord hath p.
33 10 they pitched their tents by the Red Sea
14 they pitched their tents in Raphidim
28 and pitched their tents in Methca
45 they pitched their tents in Dibongab
Josu 4 20 the Jordan, Josue pitched in Galgal
Judg 4 11 had pitched his tents unto the valley
10 17 together, pitched their tents in Galaad
2 K 6 17 tabernacle which David had p. for it
1 Pa 15 1 of God, and p. a tabernacle for it
16 1 tent, which David had pitched for it
2 Pa 1 4 and where he p. a tabernacle for it
Wisd 11 2 in desert places they p. their tents
Jer 6 3 they have pitched their tents against
1 Ma 3 40 p. near Emmaus in the plain country
57 pitched on the south side of Emmaus
4 29 and pitched their tents in Bethoron
5 39 p. their tents beyond the torrent
6 48 the king's army pitched their tents
7 19 pitched in Bethzecha; and he sent
40 Judas pitched in Adarsa with 3,000
9 5 Judas had pitched his tents in Laisa
33 p. by the water of the lake Asphar
10 75 they pitched their tents near Joppe
13 13 Simon pitched in Addus, over against
16 6 pitched their camp over against them
Heb 8 2 which the Lord hath pitched, and not men

pitcher Gen 24 14 let down thy p. that I may drink
Gen 24 15 having a pitcher on her shoulder: an
16 to the spring and filled her pitcher
17 little water to drink of thy p. 43
18 and quickly she let down the pitcher
20 pouring out the p. into the troughs
45 Rebecca appeared coming with a pitcher
46 she speedily let down the pitcher
Ecce 12 6 the pitcher be crushed at the fountain
Mark 14 13 a man carrying a pitcher. Luke 22:10

pitchers Judg 7 16 empty p., and lamps within the p.
Judg 7 19 to clap the p. one against another
20 and had broken their pitchers, they
Jer 52 19 the general took away the pitchers

pitching Judg 6 4 and p. their tents among them

pitied 1 K 23 21 for you have pitied my case
Bar 4 16 the ancient, nor pitied children, and

pitieth 1 K 22 8 not one of you that p. my case

pitiful Lam 4 10 the hands of the p. women have

pits Gen 14 10 vale had many pits of slime
1 K 13 6 and in rocks and in dens and in pits
2 K 17 9 perhaps he now lieth hid in pits
Prov 23 29 who falls into pits? Who hath wounds

pity Deut 13 8 spare him to pity and conceal him
Deut 19 13 thou shalt not pity him. 21
25 12 neither shalt thou be moved with any p.
28 50 ancients, nor have pity on the infant
Judg 21 22 have pity on them; for they took them
Ruth 2 19 be he that hath had pity on thee
2 K 12 6 because he did this thing and had no p.
24 16 the Lord had pity on the affliction

1 Pa 21 15 took pity for the greatness of the evil
Tob 8 19 hast taken pity upon two only children
Esth 13 6 and that none shall have pity on them
Job 19 21 pity on me, at least you my friends
Ps 101 16 shall have pity on the earth thereof
108 12 none to pity his fatherless offspring
Prov 14 31 but he that hath pity on the poor
21 10 he will not have pity on his neighbor
Eccu 12 13 who will pity an enchanter struck
16 10 he had not pity on them, destroying
30 24 have pity on thy own soul, pleasing
Isa 13 18 shall have no pity upon the sucklings
26 10 let us have pity on the wicked, but
30 19 he will surely have pity on thee: at
49 15 not to have pity on the son of her womb
Jer 15 5 for who shall have pity on thee, O
21 7 and he shall not be moved to pity
30 18 Jacob, and will have pity on his houses
31 3 have I drawn thee, taking pity on thee
20 pitying I will p. him, saith the Lord
42 12 will take pity on you and will cause
Lam 2 21 thou hast killed, and shown them no p.
4 16 neither had they pity on the ancient
Bar 3 2 have pity on us: for we have sinned
6 37 they shall not pity the widow nor do
5 11 not spare, and I will not have any pity
7 4 I will show thee no pity: but I will
Eze 9 5 spare, nor be ye moved with pity
10 my eye spare, nor will I have pity
Amos 1 11 the sword, and hath cast off all pity
7 3 the Lord had pity upon this. 6
2 Ma 3 21 would have moved any one to pity. And
4 37 Antiochus . . . moved to pity, shed tears
6 21 stood by, being moved with wicked pity
7 27 son, have pity upon me that bore thee
8 2 and would have pity on the temple
3 would have pity also upon the city
Mat 17 14 have pity on my son, for he is a
18 27 being moved with pity, let him go and
pitying Jer 2 2 remembered thee, p. thy youth
Jer 31 20 pitying I will pity him, saith the Lord
place (verb) Exod 30 8 when he shall place them
Num 8 2 when thou shalt place the seven lamps
Deut 11 18 and place them between your eyes
Ps 112 8 that he may place him with princes
Eccu 29 14 place thy treasure in the commandments
Isa 22 7 the horsemen shall place themselves in
Eze 4 2 place battering rams round about it
14 4 that shall place his uncleannesses
7 place his idols in his heart and set
25 4 shall place their sheepcotes in thee
29 14 place them in the land of Phatures
Dan 11 31 they shall place there the abomination
Osee 11 11 I will place them in their own houses
1 Ma 10 32 to place therein such men as he shall
Mat 24 47 he shall place him over all his goods
25 21 I will place thee over many things. 23
2 C 4 14 also with Jesus, and place us with you
placed Gen 2 8 he p. man whom he had formed
Gen 3 24 placed before the paradise of pleasure
Exod 40 16 placed the boards and the sockets
1 K 17 18 and learn with whom they are placed
2 K 8 14 in Edom, and placed there a garrison
3 K 2 24 and placed me upon the throne of David
7 47 and Solomon placed all the vessels
12 32 placed in Bethel priests of the high
4 K 17 6 he placed them in Hala and Habor
24 placed them in the cities of Samaria
32 p. them in the temples of the high
18 11 and placed them in Hala and in Habor
1 Pa 6 31 after that the ark was placed. And
2 Pa 1 14 he placed them in the cities of the chariots. 9:25
17 2 placed numbers of soldiers in all the
26 15 kinds, which he placed in the towers
1 Es 6 5 also were placed in the temple of God
Jdth 7 10 placed all round about a hundred men
9 5 in thy providence thou hast placed thy
Job 20 4 since man was placed upon the earth
Ps 106 36 and hath placed there the hungry; and
147 14 who hath placed peace in thy borders
Isa 28 15 for we have placed our hope in lies
Bar 6 16 when they are placed in the house
Eze 14 3 men have placed their uncleannesses in
Dan 3 3 great men that were placed in authority
7 9 I beheld till thrones were placed, and
1 Ma 1 36 and they placed there a sinful nation
4 61 he placed a garrison there to keep
6 38 the rest of the horsemen he placed on
50 he placed there a garrison to keep
9 51 he placed garrisons in them that they
10 53 we are placed in the throne of his
11 66 the city and placed a garrison in it
13 48 placed in it men that should observe
14 33 he placed there a garrison of Jews
34 he placed Jews here: and furnished
37 he placed therein Jews for the defence
15 41 he placed there horsemen and an army
2 Ma 13 14 he placed his army about Modin
Acts 20 28 the Holy Ghost hath placed you bishops
2 C 5 19 he hath p. in us word of reconciliation
James 3 6 tongue is placed among our members
place's 2 Ma 5 19 the people for the place's sake
placeth Job 36 7 p. kings on the throne forever
placing Exod 40 23 placing the lamps in order
plague Exod 11 1 one plague more will I bring
Exod 12 13 and the plague shall not be upon you
Lev 13 20 the plague of leprosy is broken out
14 34 there be the p. of leprosy in a house
35 is the plague of leprosy in my house
Num 8 19 lest there should be a plague among
11 33 struck them with an exceeding great p.
16 29 and if they be visited with a plague
46 from the Lord, and the plague rageth
48 for the people, and the plague ceased
25 18 who was slain in the day of the plague
1 K 5 7 men of Azotus seeing this kind of p.
6 5 same plague hath been upon you all
2 K 24 21 that the plague, which rageth among
25 and the plague was stayed from Israel
3 K 8 37 whatsoever p., whatsoever infirmity
1 Pa 21 22 that the plague may cease from the
2 Pa 21 14 will strike thee with a great plague
Jdth 5 11 and the plague had ceased from them
Eccu 25 17 the sadness of the heart is every p.
18 a man will choose any plague but the plague of the heart
Zach 14 12 this shall be the plague wherewith
2 Ma 9 5 with an incurable and an invisible p.
Apoc 16 21 and men blasphemed God for the plague
plagued Exod 10 2 often I have p. the Egyptians
plagues Exod 9 14 at this time send all my p.
Lev 26 21 I will bring seven times more plagues
28 I will chastise you with seven plagues
Deut 8 19 great plagues which thy eyes saw and
28 59 the Lord shall increase thy plagues
59 plagues of thy seed, plagues great and
61 upon thee all the diseases and plagues
29 22 seeing the plagues of that land and
1 K 4 8 struck Egypt with all the plagues in
Jdth 5 10 the whole land of Egypt with divers p.
Jer 19 8 shall hiss because of all the plagues
49 17 and shall hiss at all its plagues
50 13 and shall hiss at all her plagues
Apoc 9 18 by these three plagues was slain the
20 who were not slain by these plagues

11 6 and to strike the earth with all p.
15 1 seven angels having the 7 last plagues
6 having the seven plagues, clothed with
8 till the seven plagues of the seven
16 9 God, who hath power over these plagues
18 4 that you receive not of her plagues
8 shall her plagues come in one day
21 9 vials full of the seven last plagues
22 18 God shall add unto him the plagues
plain Gen 11 2 they found a plain in the land
Gen 25 27 Jacob a plain man dwelt in tents
Num 10 7 sound of the trumpets shall be plain
Deut 1 1 Moses spoke . . . in the p. wilderness
2 8 by the way of the plain from Elath
3 10 the cities that are situated in the p.
17 plain of the wilderness and the Jordan
4 49 all the plain beyond the Jordan at
11 30 who dwelleth in the plain country
34 3 and the breadth of the plain of Jericho
Josu 10 40 of the plain and of Asedoth, with
11 17 as far as Baalgad, by plain of Libanus
13 16 all the plain, that leadeth to Medaba
21 and all the cities of the plain
18 18 and goeth down into the plain, and
20 8 is upon the plain of the wilderness
Judg 1 34 them not place to go down to the plain
1 K 23 24 the plain at the right hand of Jesimon
2 Es 6 2 in the villages, in the plain of Ona
12 28 out of the p. country about Jerusalem
Jdth 1 6 the great plain which is called Ragua
6 in the plain of Erioch, the king of the
8 Galilee in the great plain of Esdrelon
4 5 Esdrelon, which faceth the great plain
Eccu 21 11 way of sinners is made plain with
34 8 wisdom shall be made plain in the
39 29 his ways were made plain for their
Isa 28 25 when he hath made plain the surface
32 4 stammerers shall speak readily and p.
40 4 straight, and the rough ways plain
49 9 their pastures shall be in every plain
62 10 make the road plain, pick out the
Jer 21 14 in a valley upon a rock above a plain
39 5 took Sedecias in plain of the desert
48 21 judgment is come upon the plain country
Eze 3 22 rise and go forth into the plain
23 I rose up and went forth into the plain
8 4 the vision which I had seen in the p.
37 1 midst of a plain that was full of bones
2 very many upon the face of the plain
Dan 3 1 and he set it up in the plain of Dura
Amos 1 5 inhabitants from the plain of the idol
Haba 2 2 write the vision and make it plain
Zach 4 7 thou shalt become a plain: and he
7 7 towards the south and in the plain
12 11 of Adadremmon in the plain of Mageddon
1 Ma 3 24 he pursued him . . . even to the plain
40 near Emmaus in the plain country
4 6 Judas showed himself in the plain
14 were routed, and fled into the plain
21 Judas and his army in the plain
5 52 great p. that is over against Bethsan
10 71 come down to us into the plain and
73 and so great an army in the plain
78 immediately he went forth into the p.
83 that were scattered about the plain
11 67 they were ready in the plain of Asor
68 army of the strangers met him in the p.
12 49 into Galilee, into the great plain
13 13 pitched in Addus, over against the p.
16 5 in the morning and went into the plain
11 appointed captain in the p. of Jericho
Luke 3 5 straight; and the rough ways plain
6 17 he stood in a plain place and the

1 C 14 9 except you utter by the tongue p. speech
plainly Num 12 8 plainly and not by riddles
Deut 27 8 words of this law plainly and clearly
1 K 2 27 did I not p. appear to thy father's
2 K 19 6 I now p. perceive that if Absalom had
1 Es 4 18 sent to us, hath been p. read before me
2 Es 8 3 he read it plainly in the street that
8 distinctly and plainly to be understood
2 Ma 6 6 neither did any man plainly profess
12 40 all plainly saw that for this cause
John 10 24 if thou be the Christ, tell us plainly
11 14 Jesus said to them plainly: Lazarus
16 25 will show you plainly of the Father
29 thou speakest plainly, and speakest no
1 C 6 7 there is plainly a fault among you, that
plains Gen 14 6 even to the plains of Pharan
Num 33 49 Ablesatim in the p. of the Moabites
Deut 1 7 the plains and the hills and the vales
4 43 in the plains of the tribe of Ruben
8 7 in the plains of which and the hills
11 11 but it is a land of hills and plains
Josu 4 13 marched through the plains and fields
5 10 at evening the plains of Jericho
9 1 dwelt in the mountains and in the p. **11:2**
11 16 and the plains and the west country
16 mountain of Israel and plains thereof
12 8 as well in the mountains as in the p.
13 9 and all the plains of Medaba, as far
17 their villages, which are in the plains
15 33 but in the plains: Estaol and Sarea
Judg 1 9 and in the south and in the plains
2 K 2 29 walked all that night through the p.
15 28 will lie hid in p. of the wilderness
17 16 tarry not this night in the plains
3 K 7 46 in plains of the Jordan did the king
10 27 as sycamores which grow in the plains
20 24 fight against them in the plains. 25
4 K 25 4 leadeth to the plains of the wilderness
5 overtook him in the plains of Jericho
1 Pa 10 7 men of Israel, that dwelt in the plains
27 28 fig groves, which were in the plains
2 Pa 1 15 sycamores, which grow in the p. 9:27
26 10 he had much cattle both in the plains
28 18 themselves among the cities of the p.
2 Es 3 22 the men of the plains of the Jordan
Jdth 2 17 went down into the plains of Damascus
6 8 taking, him, went through the plains
Ps 103 8 and the plains descend into the place
Eccu 24 19 as a fair olive tree in the plains
Isa 41 18 fountains in the midst of the plains
65 10 the plains shall be turned to folds
Jer 17 26 land of Benjamin and from the p.
32 44 in the cities of the plains. 33:13
48 8 and the plains shall be destroyed
Eze 47 8 go down to the plains of the desert
Abdi 19 that are in the plains, the Philistines
1 Ma 4 15 even to the plains of Idumea and of
plains of Moab; *see* **Moab**
plaited Jdth 10 3 plaited the hair of her head
1 Tim 2 9 not with p. hair, or gold, or pearls, or
plaiting 1 P 3 3 the outward plaiting of the hair
plan Eze 4 1 draw upon it the plan of the city
Eze 43 11 plan thereof and all its ordinances
2 Ma 2 29 according to the p. proposed, studying
plane Gen 30 37 of almond and of plane trees
Eccu 24 19 as a plane tree by the water in the
Isa 44 13 rule, he hath formed it with a plane
Eze 31 8 neither were the p. trees to be compared
planks Gen 6 14 make thee an ark of timber p.
3 K 6 15 covered floor of house with p. of fir
7 11 and, in like manner, planks of cedar
12 stones and one row of planks of cedar
Eze 27 5 have built thee with all sea planks

41 25 the planks were thicker in the front
plant Gen 2 5 every plant of the field before
Exod 15 17 p. them in mountain of thy inheritance
Deut 6 11 oliveyards which thou didst not plant
16 21 thou shalt plant no grove nor any
28 30 mayest thou plant a vineyard and not
39 thou shalt plant a vineyard and dig it
2 K 7 10 I will plant them, and they shall dwell
4 K 19 29 plant vineyards and eat the fruit of
Ecce 3 2 a time to plant and a time to pluck up
Eccu 3 30 plant of wickedness shall take root
24 18 Cades, and as a rose plant in Jericho
Isa 5 7 the man of Juda, his pleasant plant
17 10 shalt thou plant good plants, and
37 30 plant vineyards and eat the fruit of
41 19 I will plant in the wilderness the
51 16 that thou mightest plant the heavens
53 2 he shall grow up as a tender plant
65 21 they shall plant vineyards and eat the
22 they shall not plant, and another eat
Jer 1 10 to destroy and to build and to plant
18 9 of a kingdom, to build up and plant it
24 6 I will plant them, and not pluck them
29 5 plant orchards, and eat the fruit of
28 plant gardens and eat the fruit of
31 5 thou shalt yet plant vineyards in the
5 the planters shall plant, and they
28 to build up and to plant them, saith
32 41 I will plant them in this land in
35 7 nor sow seed nor plant vineyards nor
42 10 I will plant you, and not pluck you up
Eze 17 22 I will plant it on a mountain high
23 mountains of Israel will I plant it
28 26 houses, and shall plant vineyards
Dan 11 7 a plant of the bud of her roots shall
Amos 5 11 you shall p. most delightful vineyards
9 14 they shall plant vineyards and drink
14 I will plant them upon their own land
Soph 1 13 they shall plant vineyards and shall not
Mat 15 13 every plant which my heavenly Father
plantation Eze 17 7 it by the furrows of her p.
plantations 1 Pa 4 23 they dwelt in Plantations
planted Gen 2 8 had p. a paradise of pleasure
Gen 9 20 planted a vineyard, and drinking of
21 33 Abraham planted a grove in Bersabee
Lev 19 23 shall have planted in it fruit trees
Deut 20 6 is there, that hath planted a vineyard
Josu 24 13 oliveyards which you planted not
3 K 16 33 he planted a grove: and Achab did more
1 Pa 17 9 they shall be planted and shall dwell
Job 14 9 leaves, as when it was first planted
Ps 1 3 which is p. near the running waters
79 9 hast cast out the Gentiles and p. it
16 which thy right hand hath planted
91 14 that are p. in the houses of the Lord
93 9 he that planted the ear, shall he not
103 16 cedars of Libanus which he hath p.
106 37 they sowed fields and planted vineyards
Prov 31 16 of her hands she hath p. a vineyard
Ecce 2 4 I built me houses and planted vineyards
3 2 time to pluck up that which is planted
Eccu 10 18 hath p. the humble of these nations
39 17 as the rose p. by the brooks of waters
43 25 the Lord hath planted islands therein
50 13 as the cedars planted in mount Libanus
Isa 5 2 planted it with the choicest vines
40 24 their stock was neither p. nor sown
44 14 he hath planted the pine tree which
Jer 2 21 yet I planted thee a chosen vineyard
11 17 the Lord of hosts that planted thee
12 2 thou hast planted them, and they have
17 8 tree that is planted by the waters
45 4 whom I have planted, I do pluck up
Eze 17 5 he p. it on the surface of the earth
8 it was planted in a good ground upon
10 it is planted: shall it prosper them
19 10 vine in thy blood planted by the water
36 36 and planted what was desolate, that
Mich 1 6 in the field when a vineyard is p.
Mat 15 13 my heavenly Father hath not planted
21 33 planted a vineyard and made a hedge
Mark 12 1 a certain man p. a vineyard. Luke 20:9
Luke 13 6 a fig tree planted in his vineyard
17 28 and sold, they planted and built
Rom 6 5 for if we have been planted together in
1 C 3 6 I have planted, Apollo watered, but God
plantedst Ps 43 3 thou p. them: thou didst
Ps 79 10 thou plantedst the roots thereof and it
planters Jer 31 5 the p. shall plant, and they
planteth 1 C 3 7 neither he that planteth is anything
1 C 3 8 he that p., and he that watereth, are
9 7 who planteth vineyard, and eateth not
planting Isa 60 21 the branch of my planting
Isa 61 3 planting of the Lord to glorify him
1 Ma 3 56 wives or were planting vineyards or
plants Ps 127 3 thy children as olive plants
Ps 143 12 whose sons are as new plants in their
Cant 4 13 thy p. are a paradise of pomegranates
Wisd 7 20 diversities of plants and the virtues
Eccu 24 42 I will water my garden of plants and
Isa 17 10 therefore shalt thou plant good plants
plaster Deut 27 2 shalt p. them over with p.
Deut 27 4 thou shalt plaster them with plaster
Wisd 16 12 nor mollifying plaster that healed them
Isa 38 21 lay it as a plaster upon the wound
Amos 7 8 I will plaster them over no more
plastered Lev 14 42 house be p. with other mortar
Lev 14 43 and it be plastered with other earth
48 after it was plastered again, he shall
Amos 7 7 the Lord was standing upon a p. wall
plasterings Eccu 22 21 and p. made without cost
plate Exod 28 36 make also a p. of the purest gold
Exod 28 38 plate shall be always on his forehead
29 6 and the holy plate upon the miter
39 29 also the plate of sacred veneration
Lev 8 9 forehead, he put the plate of gold
Job 19 24 with an iron pen and in a p. of lead
plates Exod 27 6 thou shalt cover with p. of brass
Exod 27 17 shall be garnished with p. of silver
38 2 he overlaid it with plates of brass
6 overlaid them with plates of brass
Num 16 38 let him beat them into plates and
39 beat them into plates, fastening them
3 K 6 21 fastened on the p. with nails of gold
35 and he overlaid all with golden plates
7 36 he engraved also in those plates which
10 16 sicles of gold for the plates of one
2 Pa 3 5 overlaid them with plates of fine gold
7 gold of the plates with which he overlaid
Job 40 13 brass, his gristle like plates of iron
Isa 30 22 shalt defile the plates of thy graven
40 19 the silversmith with plates of silver
Jer 10 9 silver spread into plates is brought
plates of gold Exod 26 29 cover with p. . . .
Exod 36 34 bars themselves with plates of gold
37 28 and overlaid them with plates of gold
39 3 he cut thin plates of gold and drew
4 K 18 16 plates of gold which he had fastened
2 Pa 3 8 and he overlaid it with plates of gold
platter Luke 11 39 outside of the cup and of the p.
plattest Judg 16 13 if thou p. the seven locks of
platting Mat 27 29 p. crown of. Mark 15:17; John 19:2
play Gen 4 21 of them that play upon the harp
Exod 32 6 and drink, and they rose up to play
Deut 22 21 to play the whore in her father's house
Judg 16 25 that Samson . . . should play before them

1 K 16 16 he may play with his hand, and thou
17 some man that can play well, and
21 15 to play the madman in my presence
2 K 2 14 young men rise and play before us
6 22 will both play and make myself meaner
2 Pa 34 12 Levites skilful to play on instruments
Tob 3 17 have I joined myself with them that play
Job 21 11 and their children dance and play
40 15 all the beasts of the field shall play
24 thou play with him, as with a bird
Ps 103 26 which thou hast formed to play therein
Eccu 30 9 play with him, and he shall make thee
Isa 11 8 the sucking child shall play on the
Jer 30 19 praise and the voice of them that play
Osee 3 3 thou shalt not play the harlot and
4 15 if thou play the harlot, O Israel
Amos 7 17 thy wife shall play the harlot in
1 C 10 7 to eat and drink, and rose up to play
Apoc 18 22 that play on the pipe and on the trumpet
played Gen 38 24 Thamar . . . hath p. the harlot
Judg 16 25 out of prison he played before them
1 K 16 23 took his harp and played with his hand
18 7 the women sung as they played and they
10 David played with his hand. 19:9
2 K 6 5 and all Israel played before the Lord
3 K 1 40 the people p. with pipes and rejoiced
4 K 3 15 when the minstrel played, the hand of
1 Pa 13 8 David and all Israel played before God
16 42 trumpet and played on the cymbals
Eccu 47 3 he played with lions as with lambs
Jer 3 6 and hath played the harlot there
8 rebellious Israel p. the harlot
8 went and played the harlot also herself
9 played the harlot with stones and with
Eze 16 16 hast played the harlot upon them, as
28 hadst played the harlot with them, even
23 19 she played the harlot in the land of
30 because thou hast played the harlot
playedst Eze 16 15 thou playedst the harlot
player 1 K 16 18 skilful player and one of great
playing Gen 21 9 p. with Isaac her son, she said
Gen 26 8 saw him playing with Rebecca his wife
1 K 16 16 a man skilful in playing on the harp
1 Pa 15 29 saw king David dancing and playing
2 Pa 23 13 playing on instruments of divers kinds
Jdth 15 15 men, playing on instruments and harps
Ps 67 26 midst of young damsels p. on timbrels
Prov 7 22 as a lamb playing the wanton, and not
8 30 playing before him at all times. Playing in the world: and my
Wisd 17 18 be seen of beasts playing together
Zach 8 5 boys and girls playing in the streets
plead 1 K 12 7 that I may p. in judgment
Job 13 19 who is he that will plead against me
Isa 43 26 let us plead together: tell if thou
Jer 2 9 and I will plead with your children
12 1 art just, if I plead with thee, but
Eze 20 35 there will I plead with you face to
Joel 3 2 I will plead with them there for my
Mich 6 2 and he will plead against Israel
2 Ma 4 44 ancients to plead the cause before him
Acts 23 30 also to his accusers to plead before
pleaded 2 Es 13 11 I p. the matter against the
Eze 20 36 as I pleaded against your fathers in
2 Ma 4 47 if they had pleaded their cause even
pleasant Gen 2 9 to behold, and p. to eat of
Ps 80 3 the pleasant psaltery with the harp
132 1 how good and how pleasant it is for
Prov 9 17 and hidden bread is more pleasant. And
Eccu 24 23 I have brought forth a pleasant odor
32 8 of music with p. and moderate wine
40 21 a pleasant tongue is above them both
Isa 5 7 the man of Juda, his pleasant plant
30 10 speak unto us pleasant things, see
1 Ma 6 11 I that was pleasant and beloved in
2 Ma 15 40 p. to use sometimes the one and
pleasantly Prov 23 31 it goeth in p., but in the
please Gen 19 8 abuse you them as it shall p.
Gen 20 15 dwell wheresoever it shall please thee
23 8 if it p. your soul that I should bury
24 49 if it please you otherwise, tell me
33 14 may it please my lord to go before
Exod 33 19 merciful to whom it shall please me
Lev 10 19 or p. the Lord in the ceremonies
Num 23 27 it please God that thou mayest curse
Deut 21 14 if afterwards she please thee not
23 16 with thee in place that shall p. him
Ruth 4 4 if it please thee not, tell me so
1 K 11 10 you shall do what you please with us
2 K 19 38 do for him whatsoever shall p. thee
3 K 21 6 it p. thee, I will give thee a better
4 K 9 15 said: If it please you, let no man
10 3 him that shall please you most of your
1 Pa 13 2 if it please you: and if the words
2 Pa 10 7 if thou please this people and soothe
Tob 11 3 if it p. thee, therefore, let us go
14 10 seek to do the things that please him
Jdth 3 6 our service as it shall please thee
6 18 that as it shall please thee, so thou
12 14 and whatsoever shall please him, that
Job 8 14 his folly shall not please him and his
13 9 shall it please him, from whom nothing
21 3 after, if you please, laugh at my words
34 9 man shall not please God, although he
35 3 which is right doth not please thee
Ps 18 15 of my mouth shall be such as may please
34 14 and as an own brother, so did I please
52 6 scattered the bones of them that p. men
55 13 that I may please in the sight of God
68 32 shall p. God better than a young calf
114 9 I will please the Lord in the land of
Prov 2 10 heart, and knowledge please thy soul
4 14 neither let the way of evil men p. thee
12 22 they that deal faithfully please him
16 7 when the ways of man shall p. the Lord
Ecce 9 7 gladness: because thy works please God
12 1 thou shalt say: They please me not
Cant 2 7 make the beloved to awake till she p.
3 5 nor awake my beloved till she please
8 4 nor awake my love till she please
Wisd 6 3 that please yourselves in multitudes of
9 18 men may learn the things that p. thee
14 19 willing to p. him that employed him
Eccu 8 20 love but such things as please them
9 17 even to hell the wicked shall not p.
20 29 prudent man shall p. the great ones
39 8 if it shall please the great Lord
41 20 all things do not please all men
Isa 55 11 but it shall do whatsoever I please
56 4 shall choose the things that please me
7 their victims shall please me upon my
Jer 9 24 these things please me, saith the Lord
40 4 if it please thee to come with me to
4 if it do not please thee to come with
4 whither it shall please thee to go. 5
Eze 20 40 the land in which they shall please me
Dan 3 40 this day, that it may please thee: for
4 14 it to whomsoever it shall please him
5 21 over it whomsoever it shall please him
Osee 9 4 neither shall they please him: their
Mala 2 17 sight of the Lord, and such please him
3 4 shall p. the Lord as in the days of
Mat 11 27 it shall please the Son to reveal him
John 8 29 I do always the things that p. him
Rom 8 8 they who are in the flesh cannot p. God
15 1 of the weak, and not to please ourselves

2 let every one of you p. his neighbor
3 for Christ did not please himself, but
1 C 7 32 how he may please God. But he that is
33 the world, how he may please his wife
34 world, how she may please her husband
10 33 as I also in all things please all men
16 2 laying up what it shall well please him
2 C 5 9 whether absent or present, to please him
12 10 cause I p. myself in my infirmities, in
Gal 1 10 or do I seek to please men? If I yet
6 12 as many as desire to please in the flesh
1 Th 2 15 persecuted us, and please not God, and
4 1 how you ought to walk, and to please
2 Tim 2 4 that he may please him to whom he hath
Heb 10 6 holocausts for sin did not please thee
38 himself, he shall not please my soul
11 6 faith it is impossible to please God
pleased Gen 28 8 not well p. with the daughters
Gen 34 18 their offer pleased Hemor and Sichem
41 37 the counsel pleased Pharao and all
Exod 28 38 Lord may be well pleased with them
Num 24 1 pleased the Lord that he should bless
Deut 1 23 because the saying pleased me, I sent
Josu 22 33 the saying pleased all that heard it
Judg 14 3 for me, for she hath pleased my eyes
7 to the woman that had pleased his eyes
18 14 molten god: see what you are p. to do
1 K 2 26 and pleased both the Lord and men
18 20 it was told Saul, and it pleased him
2 K 3 36 people heard, and they were pleased
17 4 and his saying pleased Absalom and all
19 6 slain, then it would have pleased thee
22 20 he delivered me, because I pleased him
3 K 9 1 all that he desired and was p. to do
12 given him, and they pleased him not
10 9 Lord thy God, whom thou hast pleased
13 4 for the word pleased all the people
28 4 it pleased him to choose me king over
29 23 and he p. all: and all Israel obeyed him
2 Pa 1 11 because this choice hath p. thy heart
9 8 God, who hath been pleased to set thee
30 4 the things pleased the king and all the
23 it pleased the whole multitude to keep
2 Es 2 6 it pleased the king, and he sent me
9 24 might do with them as it pleased them
Tob 11 4 and as this their going pleased him
Jdth 2 4 and when this saying pleased them all
7 10 these words pleased Holofernes. 11:18
8 23 Moses and all that have pleased God
9 6 as thou wast pleased to look upon the
16 and the meek hath always pleased thee
11 3 why it hath pleased thee to come to us
12 6 to adore her God as she p. for three
Job 1 21 as it hath pleased the Lord so is it
30 7 they pleased themselves among these
Ps 17 20 saved me because he was well p. with
39 14 be pleased, O Lord, to deliver me
43 4 because thou wast pleased with them
101 15 stones thereof have p. thy servants
134 6 whatsoever the Lord pleased he hath
Ecce 2 26 to give it to him that hath pleased God
Wisd 4 10 he pleased God and was beloved, and
14 his soul p. God: therefore he hastened
9 19 whosoever have pleased thee, O Lord
Eccu 9 17 be not p. with the wrong done by the
25 1 with three things my spirit is pleased
44 16 Henoch pleased God and was translated
45 23 the Lord God saw and it pleased him
48 18 some of these did that which p. God
25 Ezechias did that which pleased God
Isa 53 10 Lord was pleased to bruise him in
62 4 Lord hath been well pleased with thee
Jer 14 10 have not pleased the Lord: he will
Jon 1 14 Lord, hast done as it pleased thee
Mala 1 8 prince, if he will be pleased with
1 Ma 14 4 power and his glory pleased them
23 it pleased the people to receive the
46 it pleased all the people to establish
47 well pleased to execute the office
2 Ma 1 20 it pleased God that Nehemias should
14 35 wast pleased that the temple of thy
Mat 3 17 in whom I am well p. 17:5; 2 P 1:17
12 18 in whom my soul hath been well pleased
14 6 danced before them: and pleased Herod
Mark 1 11 Son; in thee I am well p. Luke 3:22
6 22 danced and pleased Herod and them that
Luke 12 32 it hath p. your Father to give you a
Acts 12 3 seeing that it pleased the Jews, he
15 22 it p. the apostles and ancients, with
Rom 15 26 it hath pleased them of Macedonia and
27 for it hath pleased them: and they are
1 C 1 21 it pleased God, by the foolishness
10 5 with most of them God was not well p.
12 18 them in the body as it hath pleased him
Gal 1 10 if I yet pleased men, I should not be
15 when it p. him, who separated me from
Col 1 19 in him, it hath well pleased the Father
Heb 11 5 had testimony that he pleased God. But
pleasest Deut 23 24 eat as many grapes as thou p.
1 K 18 22 behold thou [David] pleasest the king
29 6 but thou p. not the lords. Return
2 K 15 26 if he shall say to me: Thou p. me not
Eccu 37 31 every kind pleaseth not every soul
pleaseth Deut 12 21 eat in thy towns, as it p. thee
Deut 14 26 the same money whatsoever p. thee
Josu 24 15 choose this day that which pleaseth you
Judg 10 15 do thou unto us whatsoever p. thee
1 K 14 7 do all that pleaseth thy mind: go
2 K 19 27 angel of God, do what pleaseth thee
3 K 20 6 all that p. them, they shall put in
4 K 10 5 a king: do thou all that pleaseth thee
1 Pa 21 23 my lord the king do all that p. him
29 5 and offer what he pleaseth to the Lord
Prov 3 12 as a father in the son he p. himself
21 3 pleaseth the Lord more than victims
Ecce 7 27 he that pleaseth God shall escape from
8 3 for he will do all that pleaseth him
Eccu 20 30 that p. great men shall escape iniquity
35 5 is that which pleaseth the Lord, and
Dan 11 3 and he shall do what he pleaseth
Rom 14 18 pleaseth God and is approved of men
Apoc 17 17 to do that which pleaseth him: that
pleasing Deut 6 18 p. and good in the sight of
Deut 12 25 p. in the sight of the Lord. 28; 13:18; 4 K 16:2; 2 Pa 14:2; 29:2
1 K 18 26 the word was p. in the eyes of David
3 K 3 10 the word was pleasing to the Lord
11 6 did that which was not p. before
14 8 that which was well p. in my sight
4 K 10 30 which was right and p. in my eyes
15 3 pleasing before the Lord. 2 Pa 20:32
20 3 have done that which is p. before thee
Eccu 2 19 things that are well pleasing to him
30 24 pity on thy own soul, pleasing God
Jer 6 20 nor are your sacrifices pleasing to
Bar 4 4 the things that are pleasing to God
1 Ma 8 21 the proposal was p. in their sight
Rom 12 1 your bodies living sacrifice, holy, p.
16 18 by p. speeches and good words, seduce
Eph 5 10 proving what is well pleasing to God
6 6 to the eye, as it were pleasing men, but
Phil 4 18 acceptable sacrifice, pleasing to God
Col 1 10 walk worthy of God, in all things p.
3 20 for this is well pleasing to the Lord
22 not serving to the eye, as pleasing men
1 Th 2 4 even so we speak, not as pleasing men

Titus 2 9 in all things pleasing, not gainsaying
Heb 10 8 not, neither are they pleasing to thee
12 28 let us serve, pleasing God, with fear
13 21 which is well pleasing in his sight
1 J 3 22 those things which are p. in his sight
pleasure Gen 2 8 had planted a paradise of p.
Gen 2 10 a river went out of the place of p.
15 put him into the paradise of pleasure
3 23 sent him out of the paradise of p.
24 before the paradise of p. cherubims
18 12 shall I [Sara] give myself to pleasure
24 50 speak any other thing to thee but his p.
29 28 [Jacob] yielded to his pleasure
4 K 16 15 altar of brass shall be ready at my p.
1 Es 5 17 let the king send his pleasure to us
10 11 do his pleasure and separate yourselves
Jdth 8 13 him a day according to your pleasure
Ps 35 9 them drink of the torrent of thy p.
68 14 for the time of thy good pleasure
88 18 thy good p. shall our horn be exalted
146 10 nor take pleasure in the legs of a man
11 taketh pleasure in them that fear him
Prov 18 22 shall receive a pleasure from the Lord
Ecce 2 10 my heart from enjoying every pleasure
11 10 flesh. For youth and pleasure are vain
Wisd 1 13 neither hath he p. in the destruction
7 2 the pleasure of sleep concurring
Eccu 9 15 thou shalt drink it with pleasure
14 5 he shall not take pleasure in his goods
18 32 take no pleasure in riotous assemblies
30 16 no pleasure above the joy of the heart
41 6 by the good pleasure of the most high
Isa 13 22 and sirens in the temples of pleasure
44 28 thou shalt perform all my pleasure
48 14 he will do his pleasure in Babylon
51 3 will make her desert as a place of p.
62 4 shalt be called My pleasure in her
Jer 22 28 is he a vessel wherein is no pleasure
Eze 16 37 with whom thou hast taken pleasure
31 9 all the trees of pleasure that were in
16 trees of pleasure, the choice and best
18 and lofty among the trees of pleasure
18 art brought down with the trees of p.
36 35 is become as a garden of pleasure
Dan 11 16 upon him and do according to his p.
Joel 2 3 the land is like a garden of pleasure
Amos 1 5 scepter from the house of pleasure
Mala 1 10 I have no pleasure in you, saith the
1 Ma 8 30 they may do it at their pleasure: and
2 Ma 2 26 that it might be a pleasure of mind
7 6 truth, and will take pleasure in us
6 in his servants he will take pleasure
11 26 our p. being known, they may be of good
Acts 24 27 willing to show Jews a p. 25:9
Eph 1 9 according to his good pleasure, which he
2 Th 1 11 fulfil all the good p. of his goodness
Heb 11 25 to have the pleasure of sin for a time
12 10 days, according to their own pleasure
2 P 2 13 counting for a p. the delights of a
pleasures 2 Pa 10 10 and brought up with him in p.
Ps 138 11 night shall be my light in my pleasures
Eccu 27 14 their laughter is at pleasures of sin
Eze 28 13 wast in the p. of the paradise of God
Luke 8 14 riches and p. of this life, and yield
1 Tim 5 6 for she that liveth in pleasures, is
2 Tim 3 4 lovers of pleasures more than of God
Titus 3 3 slaves to divers desires and pleasures
pledge Gen 38 17 if thou give a pledge, till
Gen 38 18 what wilt thou have for a pledge? She
20 that he might receive the pledge again
Exod 22 26 garment in pledge, thou shalt give it
Deut 24 6 nor the upper millstone to pledge
10 into his house to take away a pledge
12 the pledge shall not lodge with thee
17 the widow's raiment for a pledge
Job 22 6 taken away the pledge of thy brethren
24 3 taken away the widow's ox for a pledge
Prov 20 16 take a pledge from him for strangers
27 13 take from him a pledge for strangers
Eze 18 7 hath restored the pledge to the debtor
12 that restoreth not the pledge, and
16 nor withholden the pledge not taken
33 15 if that wicked man restore the pledge
Amos 2 8 sat down upon garments laid to pledge
2 C 1 22 given pledge of the Spirit in our hearts
5 5 who hath given us the p. of the Spirit
Eph 1 14 who is the pledge of our inheritance
pledged Deut 24 6 for he hath p. his life to thee
Pleiades Job 38 31 together the shining stars the P.
plenteous Ps 85 5 p. in mercy to all that call
Ps 102 8 longsuffering and plenteous in mercy
144 8 merciful: patient and p. in mercy
plentiful Gen 27 27 as the smell of a p. field
3 K 10 27 as plentiful in Jerusalem as stones
4 K 18 32 fruitful land and plentiful in wine
2 Pa 9 27 silver as p. in Jerusalem as stones
Ps 91 11 and my old age in plentiful mercy
129 7 and with him plentiful redemption
Isa 30 23 the corn of the land shall be most p.
Jer 11 16 called thy name, a plentiful olive tree
Dan 11 24 shall enter into rich and p. cities
plentifully Deut 33 22 he shall flow p. from Basan
Ps 64 10 the earth, and hast plentifully watered
11 fill up plentifully the streams thereof
1 Ma 16 16 when Simon and his sons had drunk p.
plenty Gen 33 9 I have plenty, my brother
Gen 41 26 seven full ears are seven years of p.
29 shall come seven years of great plenty
31 shall destroy the greatness of the p.
49 sea, and the plenty exceeded measure
53 when the seven years of the plenty
Deut 8 13 plenty of gold and of silver and of
30 9 land and in the plenty of all things
3 K 10 11 from Ophir great p. of thyine trees
Ps 35 9 inebriated with the plenty of thy house
64 12 thy fields shall be filled with plenty
Osee 10 1 according to the plenty of his land
Joel 2 26 shall eat in plenty and shall be filled
Luke 12 16 brought forth plenty of fruits. And
plot Gen 42 31 peaceable men, and we mean no p.
4 K 15 30 and formed a plot against Phacee
1 Pa 12 17 if you plot against me for my enemies
plots Prov 6 18 a heart that deviseth wicked p.
plotted 4 K 21 23 his servants p. against him
Ps 139 9 wicked: they have plotted against me
plotting 1 K 22 8 p. against me to this day
plow Exod 34 21 seventh day thou shalt cease to p.
Deut 22 10 not plow with an ox and an ass together
1 K 8 12 to plow his fields and to reap his
14 14 which a yoke of oxen is wont to plow
Job 39 10 rhinoceros with thy thong to plow
Prov 20 4 the sluggard would not plow: he shall
Eccu 38 26 he be furnished that holdeth the plow
Isa 28 24 shall the plowman plow all the day
Osee 10 11 Juda shall plow, Jacob shall break
Luke 9 62 no man putting his hand to the plow
1 C 9 10 he that ploweth should plow in hope
plowed Deut 21 3 in the yoke nor p. the ground
Deut 21 4 valley, that never was plowed nor sown
Judg 14 18 if you had not plowed with my heifer
Jer 26 18 Sion shall be plowed like a field
Eze 36 9 you shall be plowed and sown. And I
Osee 10 13 you have plowed wickedness, you have
Mich 3 12 Sion shall be plowed as a field, and
ploweth Eccu 6 19 come to her as one that p. and
1 C 9 10 that he that p., should plow in hope

plowing Gen 45 6 there can be neither p. nor
3 K 19 19 plowing with twelve yoke of oxen.
Job 1 14 the oxen were plowing and the asses
Luke 17 7 a servant plowing or feeding cattle
plowman Isa 28 24 shall the p. plow all the day
Amos 9 13 then the p. shall overtake the reaper
plows Isa 17 9 shall be forsaken, as the plows
plowshare Judg 3 31 600 men with plowshare
1 K 13 20 to sharpen every man his plowshare
plowshares Isa 2 4 turn their swords into p.
Joel 3 10 cut your plowshares into swords
Mich 4 3 they shall beat their swords into p.
pluck 1 K 11 2 that I may p. out all your right
2 Pa 7 20 I will pluck you up by the root out
Ps 24 15 shall pluck my feet out of the snare
51 7 he will pluck thee out and remove thee
79 13 they who pass by the way do pluck it
Ecce 3 2 a time to plant and a time to pluck up
Eccu 49 9 to overthrow and pluck up and destroy
Jer 12 14 I will pluck them out of their land
14 I will pluck the house of Juda out
17 I will utterly pluck out and destroy
22 24 right hand, I would pluck him thence
24 6 will plant them, and not pluck them
31 28 to pluck up and to throw down and
42 10 I will plant you, and not pluck you up
45 4 whom I have planted, I do pluck up
Eze 17 9 people, to pluck it up by the root
Amos 9 14 no more pluck them out of their
Mich 3 2 that violently pluck off their skins
5 13 I will pluck up thy groves out of
Mat 5 29 pluck it out. 18:9; Mark 9:46
12 1 began to pluck the ears and to eat
Mark 2 23 forward and to pluck the ears of corn
John 10 28 no man shall pluck them out of my hand
plucked 2 K 23 6 shall all of them be p. up
1 Pa 11 23 plucked away the spear that he held
1 Es 9 3 plucked off the hairs of my head and
Job 8 12 and is not plucked up with the hand
19 10 as from a tree that is plucked up
Ps 128 6 which withereth before it be plucked up
Isa 50 6 my cheeks to them that plucked them
Jer 12 15 when I shall have plucked them out
31 40 it shall not be plucked up and it
Eze 19 12 she was plucked up in wrath and cast
Dan 7 4 till her wings were plucked off and
8 horns were plucked up at the presence
Amos 4 11 firebrand plucked out of the burning
Zach 3 2 is not this a brand p. out of the fire
Luke 6 1 his disciples plucked the ears and
Gal 4 15 you would have p. out your own eyes, and
Jude 12 twice dead, plucked up by the roots
plucking Amos 7 14 am a herdsman p. wild figs
plummet Isa 34 11 and a plummet, unto desolation
Zach 4 10 shall see the tin plummet in the hand
plunder 1 K 13 17 three companies to plunder
1 K 14 15 garrison, who had gone out to plunder
Ps 108 11 and let strangers plunder his labors
Mark 3 27 and then shall he plunder his house
plundered Gen 34 27 p. the city in revenge of the
Num 31 9 all their possessions they plundered
2 Pa 28 20 plundered him without any resistance
Ps 43 11 they that hated us p. for themselves
plunderers Judg 2 14 them into the hands of p.
plunge Job 9 31 yet thou shalt p. me in filth
Jon 40 8 and plunge their faces into the pit
plunged Jer 38 22 have p. thy feet in the mire
poems 3 K 4 32 his p. were a thousand and five
poets Acts 17 28 some also of your own poets said
point Gen 19 9 point of breaking open the doors
Num 18 32 you shall not sin in this point
1 K 4 20 when she was upon the p. of death
Wisd 8 21 and this also was a point of wisdom
Eccu 9 6 give not thy soul to harlots in any p.
Jer 17 1 with the p. of a diamond it is graven
2 Ma 2 31 to discuss every particular point
8 20 when it came to the point, and the
Mark 5 23 my daughter is at the point of death
John 4 47 son; for he was at the point of death
Phil 2 30 Christ he came to the point of death
James 2 10 whole law, but offend in one point
pointed Eze 38 21 man's sword shall be p. against
poised Prov 8 28 poised the fountains of waters
Isa 40 12 hath poised with three fingers the
poison Ps 13 3 poison of asps is under their
Prov 23 32 spread abroad poison like a basilisk
Wisd 1 14 is no poison of destruction in them
2 Ma 10 13 he put an end to his life by poison
James 3 8 an unquiet evil, full of deadly poison
poles Deut 30 4 be driven as far as the p. of
1 K 2 8 the poles of the earth are the Lord's
Job 22 14 he walketh about the poles of heaven
Prov 8 26 the rivers nor the poles of the world
policy 2 Ma 13 18 to take the strong places by p.
polish 1 Pa 22 2 to hew stones and polish them
Eccu 38 31 watching to polish them to perfection
polished Exod 25 25 to the ledge itself a p. crown
Exod 37 12 he made a polished crown of gold of
Deut 27 6 of stones not fashioned nor polished
3 K 6 36 court with three rows of p. stones and
Bar 6 7 their tongue what is polished by the
1 Ma 13 27 of polished stone behind and before
poll Eze 44 20 but they shall only poll their heads
polled 2 K 14 26 when he polled his hair, now he was polled once a year
Jer 9 26 all that have their hair polled round
Mich 1 16 make thee bald, and be polled for
pollute Jer 7 30 in the house . . . to pollute it
polluted Ps 105 38 and the land was p. with blood
Isa 47 6 have polluted my inheritance and have
Jer 2 23 how canst thou say: I am not p., I
3 1 shall not that woman be polluted and
2 and thou hast p. the land with thy
Eze 14 11 nor be p. with all their transgressions
20 26 I polluted them in their own gifts
22 26 nor have distinguished between the p.
23 17 she was polluted by them, and her
38 they p. my sanctuary on the same day
Amos 7 17 and thou shalt die in a polluted land
Soph 3 4 her priests have p. the sanctuary
Mala 1 7 you offer polluted bread upon my altar
7 wherein have we polluted thee? In
2 Ma 10 5 same day that the temple had been p. by
pollution Jdth 13 20 back to you without p. of sin
2 Ma 5 27 they might not be partakers of the p.
pollutions Acts 15 20 refrain themselves from p. of
2 P 2 20 flying from the p. of the world through
pomegranate Exod 28 34 shall be a golden bell and a p.
Exod 28 34 another golden bell and a pomegranate
1 K 14 2 under the p. tree, which was in Magron
Cant 4 3 are as a piece of a p. besides that
6 6 thy cheeks are as the bark of a p.
Joel 1 12 the p. tree and the palm tree and the
Agge 2 20 p. and the olive tree as yet flourished
pomegranates Exod 28 33 shalt make as it were p.
Exod 39 22 at the feet pomegranates of violet
23 which they put between the p. at the
Num 13 24 they took also of the p. and of the figs
20 5 bringeth forth figs nor vines nor p.
Deut 8 8 fig trees and p. and oliveyards grow
3 K 7 18 that were upon the top, with p.
20 of pomegranates there were 200 in rows
42 and 400 p. for the two networks: two rows of p. for each network
4 K 25 17 p. that were upon the chapiter of the
2 Pa 3 16 p. which he put between the little

4 13 and 400 p. and two wreaths of network
13 two rows of p. were joined to each
Cant 4 13 thy plants are a paradise of p. with
6 10 had flourished and the p. budded
7 12 bring forth fruits, if the p. flourish
8 2 spiced wine and new wine of my p.
Jer 52 22 and p. were upon the chapiters round
22 same of the second pillar and the p.
23 there were ninety-six p. hanging down
23 the p. being a hundred in all, were
pommels 2 Pa 4 12 the two pillars and the p. and
2 Pa 4 13 to cover the pommels and the chapiters
pomp 2 Pa 16 14 them over him with very great pomp
1 Ma 9 37 princes of Chanaan with great pomp
Acts 25 23 were come with great pomp, and had
pond John 5 2 at Jerusalem a pond called Probatica
John 5 4 at certain times into the pond; and
4 he that went down first into the pond
7 to put me into the pond. For whilst I
pondered Gen 24 45 whilst I pondered these things
pondereth Isa 33 18 where is he that p. the words
pondering Wisd 8 17 and p. them in my heart
Luke 2 19 words, pondering them in her heart
ponds Exod 7 19 and all the ponds of waters
Ecce 2 6 I made me ponds of water to water
Pontius Mat 27 2 and delivered him to Pontius Pilate
Luke 3 1 Pontius Pilate being governor of Judea
Acts 4 27 Herod and Pontius Pilate with the
1 Tim 6 13 who gave testimony under Pontius Pilate
Pontus Gen 14 1 Arioch king of Pontus. 9
Acts 2 9 inhabitants of . . . Pontus and Asia
18 2 Aquila, born in Pontus, lately come
1 P 1 1 to the strangers dispersed through P.
pool 2 K 2 13 met them by the pool of Gabaon
2 K 2 13 the one on the one side of the pool
4 12 hanged them up over the pool in Hebron
3 K 22 38 washed his chariot in pool of Samaria
4 K 18 17 stood by the conduit of the upper pool
20 20 how he made a pool and a conduit and
2 Es 3 15 and the walls of the pool of Siloe
16 pool, that was built with great labor
Isa 7 3 to the conduit of the upper pool, in
22 9 together the waters of the lower pool
11 walls for the water of the old pool
35 7 which was dry land, shall become a p.
36 2 stood by the conduit of the upper pool
Nah 2 8 her waters are like a great pool, but
2 Ma 12 16 a pool adjoining of two furlongs broad
John 9 7 go, wash in the pool of Siloe, which
11 go to the pool of Siloe and wash
Apoc 19 20 were cast alive into the pool of fire
20 9 was cast into the pool of fire. 15
14 and death were cast into the p. of fire
21 8 portion in the pool burning with fire
pools Exod 7 19 their rivers and streams and p.
Exod 8 5 and upon the rivers and the pools
Lev 11 9 sea, as in the rivers and the pools
Ps 106 35 turned wilderness into pools of waters
113 8 who turned the rock into pools of water
Isa 14 23 for the ericius and pools of waters
19 10 mourn that made pools to take fishes
41 18 will turn the desert into p. of waters
42 15 and will dry up the standing pools
poor Exod 22 25 any of my people that is poor
Exod 23 11 that the poor of thy people may eat
Lev 14 21 if he be poor and his hand cannot find
19 10 shalt leave them to the poor and the
15 respect not the person of the poor nor
23 22 but you shall leave them for the poor
27 8 if he be poor and not able to pay the
Deut 15 4 be no poor nor beggar among you
9 away thy eyes from thy poor brother
11 there will not be wanting poor in the
11 hand to thy needy and poor brother
24 12 if he be poor, the pledge shall not
14 the hire of the needy and the poor
15 shalt pay him . . . because he is poor
Ruth 3 10 not followed young men either poor or
1 K 2 7 the Lord maketh poor and maketh rich
8 lifteth up the poor from the dunghill
2 K 12 1 two men . . . one rich and the other poor
4 took the poor man's ewe and dressed it
22 28 and the poor people thou wilt save
4 K 24 14 none were left, but the poor sort of
25 12 of the poor of the land he left some
Tob 4 7 not away thy face from any poor person
23 we lead indeed a p. life, but we shall
Jdth 9 17 me a poor wretch making supplication
Esth 9 22 and should give gifts to the poor
Job 5 15 the poor from the hand of the violent
20 19 he broke in and stripped the poor
24 4 have overturned the way of the poor
9 and stripped the poor common people
29 16 I was the father of the poor: and the
30 25 my soul had compassion on the poor
31 16 if I have denied to the poor what
34 28 and he heard the voice of the poor
36 6 and he giveth judgment to the poor
15 he shall deliver the poor out of his
Ps 9 2 man is proud, the poor is set on fire
10 Lord is become a refuge for the poor
10 when he shall have power over the poor
12 hand be exalted: forget not the poor
13 hath not forgotten the cry of the poor
17 Lord hath heard the desire of the poor
19 patience of the poor shall not perish
11 6 the needy, and the groans of the poor
21 27 the poor shall eat and shall be filled
24 16 mercy on me: for I am alone and poor
34 10 who deliverest the poor from the hand
10 and the poor from them that strip him
36 14 to cast down the poor and needy, to
39 18 but I am a beggar and poor: the Lord
40 2 concerning the needy and the poor
48 3 sons of men: both rich and poor together
67 11 O God, thou hast provided for the poor
68 30 but I am poor and sorrowful: thy salvation
33 let the poor see and rejoice: seek ye
34 the Lord hath heard the poor: and hath
69 6 I am needy and poor. 85:1
71 2 to judge . . . thy poor with judgment
4 he shall judge the poor of the people
4 he shall save the children of the poor
12 shall deliver the poor from the mighty
13 he shall spare the poor and needy
13 he shall save the souls of the poor
73 19 forget not . . . the souls of thy poor
21 poor and needy shall praise thy name
78 8 we are become exceeding poor. Help us
81 3 do justice to the humble and the poor
4 rescue the poor: and deliver the needy
87 16 I am poor, and in labors from my youth
106 41 he helped the poor out of poverty
108 22 deliver me, for I am poor and needy
31 stood at the right hand of the poor
111 9 distributed, he hath given to the poor
112 7 lifting up the poor out of the dunghill
131 15 I will satisfy her poor with bread
139 13 to the needy and will revenge the poor
Prov 10 15 the fear of the poor is their poverty
13 7 as it were poor, when he hath great
8 he that is poor beareth not reprehension
14 21 but he that showeth mercy to the poor
31 that oppresseth the poor, upbraideth
31 but he that hath pity on the poor
15 15 all the days of the poor are evil

17 5 that despiseth the poor, reproacheth
18 23 the poor will speak with supplications
19 17 that hath mercy on the poor, lendeth
22 better is the poor than the lying man
21 13 stoppeth his ear against cry of the poor
22 2 the rich and poor have met one another
7 the rich ruleth over the poor: and
9 of his bread he hath given to the poor
16 that oppresseth the poor, to increase
22 do no violence to the poor, because he is poor
28 3 a poor man that oppresseth the poor
8 for him that will be bountiful to poor
15 a wicked prince over the poor people
27 that giveth to the poor, shall not want
29 7 taketh notice of the cause of the poor
14 the king that judgeth the poor in truth
30 14 to devour . . . the poor from among men
31 5 pervert cause of children of the poor
9 do justice to the needy and poor
20 stretched out her hands to the poor
Ecce 4 13 better is a child that is poor and wise
5 7 shalt see the oppressions of the poor
9 15 was found in it a man poor and wise
Eccu 4 1 son, defraud not the poor of alms
1 turn not away thy eyes from the poor
2 provoke not the poor in his want
5 turn not away thy eyes from the poor
7 affable to the congregation of the poor
8 down thy ear cheerfully to the poor
7 36 stretch out thy hand to the poor
10 25 fear of God is glory . . . of the poor
26 despise not a just man that is poor
13 4 poor is wronged and must hold his peace
22 what part hath the rich with the poor
23 also the poor are devoured by the rich
24 also the rich man abhorreth the poor
14 13 stretching out thy hand give to the poor
18 33 make not thyself poor by borrowing
21 6 prayer out of the mouth of the poor
26 4 rich or poor, if his heart is good
29 11 towards the poor be thou more hearty
12 help the poor because of the commandment
15 shut up alms in the heart of the poor
31 4 of life, and in the end he is still poor
34 24 sacrifice of the goods of the poor
25 bread of the needy is life of the poor
38 20 substance of the poor is according to
Isa 3 14 the spoil of the poor is in your house
15 why . . . grind the faces of the poor
10 2 to oppress the poor in judgment
11 4 he shall judge the poor with justice
14 30 firstborn of the poor shall be fed, and the poor shall rest with confidence
32 the poor of his people shall hope in
25 4 thou hast been a strength to the poor
26 6 tread it down, the feet of the poor
29 19 poor men shall rejoice in the Holy
41 17 the needy and the poor seek for waters
49 13 will have mercy on his poor ones
51 21 hear this, thou poor little one and
54 11 poor little one, tossed with tempest
66 2 but to him that is poor and little and
Jer 2 34 the blood of the souls of the poor
5 4 perhaps these are poor and foolish
28 not judged the judgment of the poor
20 13 he hath delivered the soul of the poor
22 16 he judged the cause of the poor and
39 10 general left some of the poor people
40 7 of the poor of the land, them that had
52 15 captives some of the poor people
16 of the poor of the land, Nabuzardan
Bar 6 27 of it either to the sick or to the poor
Eze 16 49 not put forth their hand . . . to the poor

18 12 that grieveth the needy and the poor
17 away his hand from injuring the poor
22 29 they afflicted the needy and poor
Dan 4 24 with works of mercy to the poor
Amos 2 7 they bruise the heads of the poor
4 1 oppress the needy and crush the poor
5 11 because you robbed the poor and took
12 and oppressing the poor in the gate
8 4 hear this, you that crush the poor
6 and the poor for a pair of shoes
Soph 3 12 midst of thee a poor and needy people
Zach 7 10 oppress not the widow . . . and the poor
9 9 he is poor, and riding upon an ass
11 7 ye poor of the flock. And I took
11 the poor of the flock that keep for me
2 Ma 4 47 those poor men, who, if they had
Mat 5 3 blessed are the poor in spirit: for
11 5 the poor have the gospel preached to
19 21 what thou hast, and give to the poor. Mark 10:21; Luke 18:22
26 9 sold for much, and given to the poor
11 the poor you have always with you. Mark 14:7; John 12:8
Mark 12 42 there came a certain poor widow and
43 p. widow hath cast in more. Luke 21:3
14 5 than 300 pence and given to the poor
Luke 4 18 to preach the gospel to the poor, he
6 20 blessed are ye poor, for yours is the
7 22 to the poor the gospel is preached
14 13 call the poor, the maimed, the lame
21 in hither the poor and the feeble
19 8 half of my goods I give to the poor
21 2 and he saw also a certain poor widow
John 12 5 for 300 pence, and given to the poor
6 not because he cared for the poor; but
13 29 he should give something to the poor
Rom 15 26 contribution for the poor of the saints
1 C 13 3 distribute all my goods to feed the poor
2 C 8 9 being rich he became p., for your sakes
9 9 abroad, he hath given to the poor: his
Gal 2 10 that we should be mindful of the poor
James 2 5 hath not God chosen the poor in this
Apoc 3 17 art wretched and miserable and poor
13 16 both little and great, rich and poor

poor man Deut 15 8 open it to the poor man
1 K 18 23 I am a poor man and of small ability
2 K 12 3 but the poor man had nothing at all
Job 29 12 because I had delivered the poor man
Ps 101 1 the prayer of the poor man when he was
108 17 persecuted the poor man and the beggar
Prov 12 9 better is the poor man that provideth
14 20 the poor man shall be hateful even to
19 1 better is the poor man that walketh
4 from poor man, even they whom he had
7 the brethren of the poor man hate him
28 3 a poor man that oppresseth the poor
6 better is the poor man walking in his
11 poor man that is prudent shall search
29 13 the poor man and the creditor have met
Ecce 6 8 what the poor man, but to go thither
9 16 the wisdom of the poor man slighted
Wisd 2 10 let us oppress the poor just man, and
Eccu 10 33 p. man is glorified by his discipline
11 23 a sudden to make the poor man rich
25 4 a poor man that is proud: a rich man
30 14 better is a poor man who is sound and
31 4 poor man hath labored in his low way
35 16 accept any person against a poor man
Isa 32 7 when the poor man speaketh judgment
Amos 2 6 and the poor man for a pair of shoes
Haba 3 14 that devoureth the poor man in secret
James 2 2 come in also a poor man in mean attire
3 but say to the poor man: Stand thou

6 but you have dishonored the poor man
poplar Gen 30 37 Jacob took green rods of poplar
Osee 4 13 under the oak and the poplar and the
populous Isa 22 2 a p. city, a joyous city: thy
Nah 3 8 art thou better than the p. Alexandria
porch 3 K 6 3 was a porch before the temple
3 K 7 6 he made a porch of pillars of 50 cubits
6 another porch before the greater porch
7 he made also the porch of the throne
8 midst of the porch was a small house
8 of the same work as this porch, all of
12 in the porch of the house. And king
19 pillars, were of lily work in the porch
21 two pillars in the porch of the temple
1 Pa 28 11 a description of the porch and of the
2 Pa 3 4 porch in the front which was extended
15 8 which was before the porch of the Lord
29 7 up the doors that were in the porch
17 they came into the porch of the temple
Eze 8 16 between the porch and the altar, were
40 8 threshold of the gate by the porch
9 and he measured the porch of the gate
9 and the porch of the gate was inward
15 to the face of the porch of inner gate
21 p. thereof according to the measure
22 the windows thereof and the porch
22 seven steps, and a porch was before it
24 p. thereof according to the former
26 and a porch before the doors thereof
29 porch thereof with the same measures
29 porch thereof round about it was
30 p. round about was 5 and 20 cubits
31 porch thereof to the outward court
33 p. thereof as before: and the windows
34 p. thereof, that is, of the outward
36 porch thereof and the windows thereof
37 p. thereof looked to the outward court
39 in porch of the gate were two tables
40 before p. of the gate were two tables
48 brought me into the porch of the temple
48 he measured the porch five cubits on
49 length of the porch was twenty cubits
41 25 were thicker in the front of the porch
26 in the sides of the porch according
42 12 way was before the porch, separated
44 3 way of the p. of the gate. 46:2, 8
Joel 2 17 between the porch and the altar the
John 10 23 in the temple, in Solomon's porch. The
Acts 3 11 the porch which is called Solomon's
5 12 all with one accord in Solomon's p.
porches 1 Pa 23 28 in the p. and in the chambers
Eze 40 16 there were also in the porches windows
25 the windows thereof and the porches
33 and the porches thereof round about it
41 15 inner temple and the p. of the court
John 5 2 named Bethsaida, having five porches
porphirion Deut 14 17 eat not . . . the porphirion
porphyrion Lev 11 18 you must not eat . . . the p.
porphyry Esth 1 6 upon a floor paved with p. and
portending Zach 3 8 for they are portending men
porter 1 Pa 9 21 Zacharias . . . was p. of the gate
2 Pa 31 14 Levite, the porter of the east gate
Mark 13 34 and commanded the porter to watch
John 10 3 to him the porter openeth; and the
porters 1 Pa 9 17 the porters were Sellum and
1 Pa 9 22 were chosen to be porters at the gates
24 in four quarters were the porters
26 were committed the whole number of p.
15 18 Obededom and Jehiel, the porters
24 Obededom and Jehias were porters of
16 42 the sons of Idithun he made porters
23 5 moreover four thousand were porters
26 1 the divisions of the p. 12, 19
18 in the cells also of the porters toward
2 Pa 8 14 and the porters in their divisions
23 5 of the porters shall be at the gates
19 he appointed also porters in the gates
34 9 which the Levites and p. had gathered
13 the number of the Levites, and porters
35 15 the porters kept guard at every gate
1 Es 2 42 the children of the porters: the
70 p. and the Nathinites dwelt in their
7 7 and of the singing men and of the p.
24 Levites and the singers and the p.
10 24 of the porters, Sellum and Telem and
2 Es 7 1 numbered the porters and singing men
46 the porters: the children of Sellum
73 Levites and the p. and the singing men
10 28 priests, Levites, porters, and singing
39 the singing men and the porters. 12:44
11 19 the porters, Accub, Telmon, and their
12 46 to the singing men and to the porters
13 5 of the singing men and of the porters
Esth 12 1 eunuchs, who were p. of the palace
portion Gen 48 22 thee a p. above thy brethren
Lev 7 33 right shoulder also for his portion
8 29 the breast for his portion, elevating it
Num 18 20 neither shall you have a p. among them
20 I am thy p. and inheritance in the
26 54 thou shalt give a greater portion, and
31 28 thou shalt separate a p. to the Lord
37 for the p. of the Lord were reckoned
40 to the portion of the Lord, 32 souls
34 15 received their p. beyond the Jordan
Deut 18 8 shall receive the same portion of food
21 17 shall give him a double portion of all
32 9 but the Lord's portion is his people
33 21 in his portion the teacher was laid up
Josu 14 4 neither did Levites receive other p.
15 13 a p. in midst of the children of Juda
17 14 given me but one lot and one portion
1 K 1 5 to Anna he gave one p. with sorrow
9 23 bring the portion which I gave thee
30 24 but equal shall be the portion of him
3 K 12 16 what portion have we in David? Or
31 4 priests and the Levites their portion
Esth 13 16 despise not thy portion, which thou
Job 20 29 this is the p. of a wicked man. 27:13
24 18 cursed be his portion on the earth
Ps 10 7 winds shall be the portion of their cup
15 5 Lord is the portion of my inheritance
72 26 the God that is my portion forever
118 57 O Lord, my portion, I have said, I
141 6 my portion in the land of the living
Ecce 2 10 my portion, to make use of my own labor
3 22 in his work and that this is his portion
5 17 hath given him: and this is his portion
18 to eat thereof and to enjoy his portion
9 9 this is thy portion in life, and in thy
11 2 give a portion to seven and also to
Wisd 2 9 this is our portion and this our lot
Eccu 7 34 give them their portion, as it is
11 18 and this is the portion of his reward
14 9 insatiable in his portion of iniquity
17 15 Israel was made the manifest p. of God
24 16 the portion of my God his inheritance
26 3 a good wife is a good portion, she
3 in the portion of them that fear God
41 12 in malediction shall be your portion
26 of taking away a p. and not restoring
44 26 divided him his p. in twelve tribes
45 27 he hath no portion among the people
27 himself is his portion and inheritance
Isa 17 14 portion of them that have wasted us
57 6 in the parts of the torrent is thy p.
Jer 10 16 the portion of Jacob is not like these

12 10 have trodden my portion under foot
10 have changed my delightful portion
13 25 thy lot and the portion of thy measure
51 19 the portion of Jacob is not like them
52 34 every day a portion, until the day of
Lam 3 24 the Lord is my portion, said my soul
Eze 45 1 a portion of the land to be holy, in
4 the holy portion of the land shall be
8 shall have a p. of the land in Israel
47 13 for Joseph hath a double portion. And
48 1 to the sea, shall be one p. for Dan
2 the side of the sea, one portion for. 3, 4, 5, 6, 7, 27
21 shall likewise be the p. of the prince
48 23 to the west side, one portion for. 24, 25, 26
Dan 4 12 let its portion be with the wild beasts
Mich 2 4 the portion of my people is changed
Haba 1 16 through them his portion is made fat
Soph 2 7 the portion of him that shall remain
Zach 2 12 the Lord shall possess Juda his portion
2 Ma 1 26 preserve thy own p. and sanctify it
14 15 protected his portion by evident signs
Mat 24 51 appoint his portion with the hypocrites
Luke 12 46 appoint him his p. with unbelievers
15 12 give me the portion of substance that
Apoc 21 8 shall have their portion in the pool
portions Josu 17 5 there fell ten p. to Manasses
1 K 1 4 to all her sons and daughters, portions
2 Pa 31 15 to distribute faithfully portions to
19 to distribute portions to all the males
2 Es 8 10 send portions to them that have not
12 to eat and drink and to send portions
11 36 of the Levites were portions of Juda
12 46 Nehemias gave p. to the singing men
13 5 the portions of the Levites and of the
10 portions of the Levites had not been
13 committed the portions of their brethren
Esth 9 19 send one another p. of their banquets
22 send one to another portions of meats
Ps 62 11 they shall be the portions of foxes
Eccu 50 13 when he took the portions out of the
Eze 48 8 as every one of the portions from the
22 are in the midst of the prince's p.
29 and these are the portions of them
Dan 1 16 Malasar took their portions and the
Osee 5 7 a month devour them with their portions
2 Ma 8 30 giving equal portions to the feeble
Portius Acts 24 27 for successor P. Festus
portress John 18 16 went out and spoke to the p.
John 18 17 the maid therefore that was portress
Posidonius 2 Ma 14 19 he sent P. and Theodotius
possess Gen 15 7 that thou mightest possess it
Gen 15 8 may I know that I shall possess it
24 60 may thy seed possess the gates of
28 4 mayst possess the land. Deut 4:1
34 10 till, trade, and possess it. Sichem
23 all that they possess, shall be ours
Exod 6 8 and I will give it you to possess
23 30 till thou . . . dost possess the land
32 13 seed, and you shall possess it forever
34 9 take away our . . . sin, and possess us
Lev 20 24 p. their land which I will give you
25 30 the buyer shall possess it, and his
46 posterity, and shall p. them forever
27 19 add the fifth part . . . and shall p. it
Num 13 31 let us go up and possess the land
14 24 Caleb . . . his seed shall possess it
18 20 you shall possess nothing in their land
23 they shall not possess any other thing
24 18 he shall p. Idumea: the inheritance
32 18 until the children of Israel p. their
34 13 land which you shall p. Deut 4:5, 14, 26
Deut 1 8 go in and possess it. 2 Es 9:23
21 go up and possess it, as the Lord
39 the land, and they shall possess it
2 22 to them, which they possess to this day
24 and begin thou to possess his land
31 Sehon and his land, begin to possess it
3 20 until . . . they also p. the land. Josu 1:15
4 22 possess the goodly land. 6:18
6 1 into which you pass over to possess it
7 1 which thou art going in to possess
8 1 and going in may possess the land
9 1 this day; to possess nations very great
4 brought me in to possess this land
5 thou shalt go in to possess their lands
23 possess the land that I have given you
10 11 that they may . . . possess the land
11 8 and may go in and possess the land
10 the land, which thou goest to possess
23 these nations . . . and you shall p. them
31 to p. the land which the Lord. Josu 18:3
31 that you may have it and possess it
12 1 will give thee, to possess it all the
2 the nations, that you shall possess
29 which thou shalt go in to possess. 23:20; 28:21, 63
29 when thou shalt possess them and dwell
16 20 mayst live and possess the land
18 14 nations whose land thou shalt possess
19 1 to thee, and thou shalt possess it
10 thy God will give thee to p. 24:4; 26:1
14 which thou shalt receive to possess
30 5 bring thee . . . and thou shalt possess it
16 shalt go in to possess. 18
31 3 nations . . . and thou shalt possess them
13 are going over the Jordan to p. it. 32:47
32 49 to the children of Israel to possess
33 23 he shall possess the sea and the south
Josu 1 11 shall go in to possess the land
17 14 but one lot and one portion to possess
18 11 to p. the land between the children
23 5 you shall possess the land. Eze 47:13
Judg 11 23 and wilt thou now possess this land
18 9 lose no time; let us go and possess it
Ruth 4 4 buy it and possess it; but if it
1 Pa 28 8 that you may possess the good land
2 Pa 6 27 hast given to thy people to possess
1 Es 9 11 land which you go to p., is an unclean
2 Es 5 5 and our vineyards other men possess
9 15 they should go in and possess the land
Jdth 5 23 possess Jerusalem again, where their
Job 3 15 or with princes, that possess gold
20 20 he shall not be able to possess them
22 8 of thy arm thou didst possess the land
30 16 and the days of affliction possess me
Ps 68 37 the seed of his servants shall possess it
82 13 said: Let us p. the sanctuary of God
Prov 3 35 the wise shall possess glory: the
14 18 the childish shall possess folly, and
28 10 and the upright shall possess his goods
Eccu 28 26 it shall p. the ways of the unjust
51 29 therefore shall I p. a good possession
36 and possess abundance of gold by her
Isa 11 11 to possess the remnant of his people
14 2 house of Israel shall possess them
34 11 bittern and ericius shall possess it
17 they shall possess it forever, from
49 8 p. inheritances that were destroyed
57 13 and shall possess my holy mount
60 18 salvation shall possess thy walls
Jer 30 3 their fathers, and they shall p. it
32 8 thou art next of kin to possess it
49 2 Israel shall possess them that have
Eze 7 24 they shall possess their houses
24 they shall possess their sanctuary

22 16 I will possess thee in the sight of
33 25 shall you p. the land by inheritance. 26
35 10 I will possess them by inheritance
36 12 shall p. thee for their inheritance
38 12 which hath begun to possess and to
45 5 they shall possess store chambers
46 16 they shall possess it by inheritance
47 14 you shall p. it, every man in like
Dan 7 18 they shall p. the kingdom forever
11 17 to come to possess all his kingdom
Amos 2 10 that you might p. the land of the
14 valiant shall not p. his strength
8 6 that we may possess the needy for
9 12 they may possess the remnant of Edom
Abdi 17 house of Jacob shall p. those that
19 they shall p. the country of Ephraim
19 and Benjamin shall possess Galaad
20 shall possess the cities of the south
Haba 1 6 to p. the dwelling places that are
Soph 2 9 residue of my nation shall p. them
Zach 2 12 and the Lord shall possess Juda
8 12 this people to p. all these things
9 4 Lord shall p. her and shall strike
Mat 5 4 meek: for they shall possess the land
10 9 do not possess gold nor silver nor
19 29 and shall possess life everlasting
25 34 possess you the kingdom prepared for
Luke 10 25 what must I do to possess eternal life
12 33 sell what you possess and give alms
18 12 I give tithes of all that I possess
18 shall I do to possess everlasting life
21 19 your patience you shall p. your souls
1 C 6 9 unjust shall not p. the kingdom of God
10 shall possess the kingdom of God. And
15 50 flesh and blood cannot p. kingdom of God
50 neither shall corruption p. incorruption
1 Th 4 4 you should know how to p. his vessel
Apoc 21 7 shall overcome shall p. these things
possessed Gen 47 27 the land of Gessen, and p. it
Exod 9 7 dead of that which Israel possessed
15 16 people pass by, which thou hast p.
Num 21 24 and they possessed his land. 35
Deut 3 12 we p. the land at that time from Aroer
14 p. all the country of Argob unto the
4 47 coming out of Egypt, possessed his land
20 8 as he himself is possessed with fear
30 5 thee into the land which thy fathers p.
32 6 is not he thy father, that hath p. thee
Josu 5 1 who p. the places near the great sea
12 1 and p. their land beyond the Jordan
13 8 Ruben and Gad have possessed the land
14 1 what the children of Israel possessed
16 4 Ephraim the children of Joseph p. it
17 6 daughters of Manasses p. inheritance
19 47 possessed it and dwelt in it. 21:41
24 8 you possessed their land and slew them
Judg 1 19 he Juda possessed the hill country
3 13 and possessed the city of palm trees
11 21 and p. all the land of the Amorrhite
1 Pa 5 9 possessed a great number of cattle
23 the half tribe of Manasses p. the land
2 Pa 8 3 he went also into Emath Suba and p. it
2 Es 9 22 and they possessed the land of Sehon
24 children came and possessed the land
25 and possessed houses full of all goods
Tob 8 24 of all things which Raguel possessed
Jdth 5 20 they possessed their hands and their
Ps 73 2 thy congregation which thou hast p.
104 44 they possessed the labors of the people
138 13 for thou hast possessed my reins: thou
Prov 8 22 Lord p. me in the beginning of his ways
Eccu 51 28 I p. my heart with her from the
Isa 63 18 have p. thy holy people as nothing
Jer 16 19 surely our fathers have possessed lies
32 15 vineyards shall be p. again in this
23 and they came in and possessed it
49 2 shall possess them that have p. him
Abdi 17 Jacob shall possess those that p. them
Zach 11 5 which they that possessed, slew and
1 Ma 1 34 the children, and the cattle they p.
10 52 p. our country and have joined
14 17 and was possessed of all the country
15 33 which was for some time unjustly p.
2 Ma 15 38 the city being p. by the Hebrews, I
Mat 4 24 such as were possessed by devils and
8 16 brought to him many that were possessed
28 met him two that were p. with devils
33 that had been possessed by the devils
9 32 a dumb man, possessed with a devil
12 22 one p. with a devil, blind and dumb
Mark 1 32 ill and that were p. with devils. And
Acts 1 18 hath p. a field of the reward of
4 32 aught of the things which he p. was
1 C 7 30 they that buy as though they p. not
possessest Deut 17 14 will give thee . . . and p. it
possesseth Judg 11 24 which thy god Chamos p.
2 Pa 13 8 he possesseth by the sons of David
Prov 15 32 yieldeth to reproof p. understanding
16 22 a fountain of life to him that p. it
19 8 he that p. a mind, loveth his own soul
Ecce 7 13 that they give life to him that p. them
Eccu 15 1 he that p. justice, shall lay hold
36 26 he that p. a good wife, beginneth
Luke 11 21 things are in peace which he p.
12 15 the abundance of things which he p.
44 he will set him over all that he p.
14 33 that doth not renounce all that he p.
possessing 2 C 6 10 as having nothing, and p. all
possession Gen 13 2 [Abram] rich in p. of gold
Gen 17 8 land of Chanaan for a perpetual p.
23 9 before you for a p. of a buryingplace
18 made sure to Abraham for a possession
20 that was in it, for a p. to bury in
30 29 how great thy possession hath been in
47 11 Joseph gave a possession to his father
48 4 seed after thee for an everlasting p.
49 30 Ephron the Hethite for a p. to bury in
50 13 for a possession of a buryingplace
Exod 19 5 you shall be my peculiar possession
Lev 14 34 which I will give you for a possession
25 34 because it is a perpetual possession
41 kindred and to the p. of his fathers
27 21 and as a possession consecrated
22 not of a man's ancestors' possession
Num 18 21 all the tithes of Israel for a p.
26 54 reckoned up shall a p. be delivered
62 neither was a possession given to
27 3 give us a possession among the kinsmen
6 give them a p. among their father's
32 5 thou give it to us thy servants in p.
19 our possession on the east side thereof
29 give them Galaad in possession. But
32 we have already received our possession
33 53 I have given it you for a possession
54 the possession shall be divided by the
36 2 the possession due to their father
4 p. of the one shall pass to the others
7 lest the p. of the children of Israel be
12 the p. that had been allotted to them
Deut 2 5 mount Seir to Esau, for a possession
9 Ar to the children of Lot in possession
19 it to the children of Lot for a p.
4 38 give thee their land for a possession
5 31 which I will give them for a possession
9 6 thee not this excellent land in p.
10 9 Levi hath no part nor possession with

12 9 to the p. which the Lord your God
12 he hath no other part and possession
14 27 hath no other part in thy possession
29 Levite that hath no other part nor p.
15 4 which he will give thee in possession
18 2 shall receive nothing else of the p.
19 2 which the Lord will give thee in p.
14 thy predecessors have set in thy p.
20 15 cities which thou shalt receive in p.
21 23 Lord thy God shall give thee in p.
29 8 delivered it for a possession to Ruben
Josu 11 23 delivered it in p. to the children of
12 6 Moses delivered their land in p. to the
7 Josue delivered it in p. to the tribes
13 7 now divide the land in possession
14 to the tribe of Levi he gave no p.
15 gave a p. to the children of Ruben
23 this is the possession of the Rubenites
24 his children by their kindreds a p.
28 the possession of the children of. 16:9; 18:20, 28; 19:2, 31; 21:39
29 possession according to their kindreds
32 this possession Moses divided in the
33 to tribe of Levi he gave no possession
14 3 had given possession beyond the Jordan
9 trodden upon shall be thy possession
13 and gave him Hebron in possession
15 20 this is the possession of the tribe. 16:8; 19:39, 48
17 1 had for possession Galaad and Basan
4 that a possession should be given us
4 a p. amongst brethren of their father
10 possession of Ephraim is on the south
15 the p. of mount Ephraim is too narrow
19 9 in the p. and lot of children of Juda
23 the possession of the sons of Issachar
49 children of Israel gave a p. to Josue
21 20 race of Levi was given this possession
22 7 Moses had given a possession in Basan
24 32 it was in the p. of the sons of Joseph
Judg 11 24 obtained by conquest, shall be our p.
Ruth 4 4 if thou wilt take possession of it by
3 K 8 36 hast given to thy people in possession
21 15 take possession of vineyard of Naboth
18 to the vineyard of Naboth, to take p.
19 slain, moreover also thou hast taken p.
4 K 14 5 when he had possession of the kingdom
1 Pa 6 61 they gave . . . ten cities in possession
2 Pa 20 11 out of the p. which thou hast delivered
1 Es 4 16 shalt have no p. on this side of the
Jdth 3 15 he took possession of their cities
4 5 should take possession of the ascents
Ps 2 8 utmost parts of the earth for thy p.
43 4 they got not the possession of the land
78 11 take possession of the children of them
104 21 of his house, and ruler of all his p.
134 4 unto himself; Israel for his own p. For
Prov 4 7 with all thy p. purchase prudence
Eccu 36 26 possesseth a good wife, beginneth a p.
27 no hedge, the p. shall be spoiled
51 29 therefore shall I possess a good p.
Isa 14 23 I will make it a p. for the ericius
30 23 shall feed at large in thy possession
Jer 37 11 to divide a p. there in the presence
Bar 3 24 how vast is the place of his possession
Eze 11 15 the land is given in possession to us
44 28 neither shall you give them any p. in Israel, for I am their p.
45 6 you shall appoint the p. of the city
7 and according to the p. of the city
7 over against the possession of the city
46 18 by violence nor of their possession
18 out of his own p. he shall give an
18 not dispersed every man from his p.
47 14 this land shall fall unto you for a p.
22 they shall divide the p. with you in
23 there shall you give him possession
48 20 and for the possession of the city
21 sanctuary, and of the p. of the city
22 from the p. of the Levites and from the p. of the city
Mala 3 17 they shall be my special possession
1 Ma 8 3 had gotten p. of all the place by their
10 and took possession of their land
10 89 Accaron and all borders thereof in p.
12 33 to Joppe, and took possession of it
2 Ma 2 14 we had, and they are in our possession
4 7 had taken possession of the kingdom
8 6 taking p. of the most commodious places
Acts 7 5 he promised to give it him in p.
45 into the possession of the Gentiles

his possession Lev 25 10 every man shall return to his possession
Lev 25 25 being impoverished, sell his little p.
27 so shall receive his possession again
27 16 if he vow the field of his possession
24 had it in the lot of his possession
Deut 2 12 as Israel did in the land of his p.
3 20 then shall every man return to his p.
10 9 the Lord himself is his possession
Josu 21 12 to Caleb the son of Jephone for his p.
24 4 to Esau mount Seir for his possession
30 they buried him in the border of his p.
Judg 2 6 went every one to his own p. to hold it
9 they buried him in the borders of his p.
2 Es 11 3 and every one dwelt in his possession
20 the cities of Juda, every man in his p.
Job 1 3 his possession was 7,000 sheep and
10 his p. hath increased on the earth
36 33 that it is his possession and that he

their possession Num 36 3 their p. will follow
Josu 13 33 the God of Israel himself is their p.
16 5 their possession towards the east was
7 have already received their p. beyond
9 the children of Simeon had their p.
19 10 the border of their p. was unto Sarid
41 the border of their p. was Saraa and
22 9 go into Galaad the land of their p.
33 destroy the land of their possession
24 28 away every one to their own possession
Judg 21 23 and they went into their possession

your possession Lev 25 24 the country of your p.
Num 34 2 it shall be fallen into your p. by lot
35 34 thus shall your possession be cleansed
Deut 5 33 days may be long in land of your p.
Josu 1 15 shall return into the land of your p.
22 4 and to the land of your possession
19 if you think the land of your p. to be
Judg 20 6 parts into all the borders of your p.

possessions Gen 25 5 gave all his p. to Isaac
Gen 26 14 he had possessions of sheep and of
47 20 every man selling his p., because of
22 they were not forced to sell their p.
48 6 the name of their brethren in their p.
Exod 9 4 difference between the p. of Israel and the possessions of the Egyptians
Lev 25 13 all shall return to their possessions
23 cities of the Levites are for their p.
Num 16 14 hast given us possessions of fields
26 53 land be divided for their possessions
31 9 all their possessions they plundered
35 2 give to the Levites out of their p.
8 shall be given out of the possessions
Josu 18 2 which as yet had not received their p.
19 55 these are the possessions which Eleazar
21 3 gave out of their possessions according

1 K 25 2 his possessions were in Carmel, and the
2 K 19 29 thou and Siba divide the possessions
1 Pa 7 21 came down to invade their possessions
28 their p. and habitations were Bethel
9 2 first that dwelt in their possessions
28 1 charge over the substance and p. of the
29 6 overseers of the king's possessions
2 Pa 11 14 leaving their suburbs and their p.
31 1 returned to their p. and cities. And
Jdth 3 3 all our cities and our possessions
8 7 large possessions of herds of oxen and
Eccu 5 1 set not thy heart upon unjust p.
41 1 man that hath peace in his possessions
1 Ma 12 23 cattle and our possessions are yours
Mat 19 22 for he had great p. Mark 10:22
Acts 2 45 their goods and p. they sold and
28 7 in those places were p. of chief man of
possessor Gen 14 22 the p. of heaven and earth
Lev 25 28 to the owner and to the ancient p.
Isa 65 9 out of Juda a possessor of my mountains
possessors Prov 1 19 destroy the souls of the p.
possible Tob 10 7 that she might if p. see him
Eccu 18 5 neither is it p. to find out the
2 Ma 3 6 p. to bring all into the king's
14 10 not p. that the state should be
Mat 19 26 but with God all things are possible
24 24 to deceive, if possible, even the elect
26 39 if it be possible, let this chalice
Mark 9 22 all things are possible to him that
10 27 for all things are possible with God
13 22 to seduce, if it were possible, even
14 36 all things are possible to thee: remove
Luke 18 27 impossible with men, are p. with God
Acts 20 16 he hasted, if it were possible for him
Rom 12 18 if it be possible, as much as is in you
possibly 4 K 7 2 can that p. be which thou
post Job 9 25 have been swifter than a post
Wisd 5 9 shadow and like a post that runneth on
Isa 57 8 behind the post thou hast set up thy
Jer 51 31 one running post shall meet another
Soph 2 14 window, the raven on the upper post
posted Jdth 7 5 they posted themselves at the places
posterity Gen 21 23 wilt not hurt me nor my p.
Gen 26 4 I will give to thy posterity all these
Lev 17 7 ordinance forever to them and to their p.
22 3 say to them and to their posterity
23 43 that your posterity may know that I
25 30 possess it, and his posterity forever
46 shall leave them to your posterity
Josu 22 27 us and you, and our posterity and yours
Ruth 4 6 not cut off the p. of my own family
3 K 16 3 I will cut down the posterity of Baasa
3 Baasa and the posterity of his house
21 21 and I will cut down thy posterity
1 Pa 4 3 and this is the posterity of Etam
7 2 of the posterity of Thola were numbered
2 Pa 8 8 of the posterity whom the children of
Tob 2 12 example might be given to posterity
8 9 but only for the love of posterity
10 4 of our life, the hope of our posterity
Jdth 5 13 to tell what had happened to posterity
Esth 9 28 observed by the Jews, and by their p.
Ps 108 13 may his posterity be cut off; in one
Eccu 41 9 with their p. shall be a perpetual
44 12 their posterity are a holy inheritance
22 he gave him glory in his posterity
Isa 65 23 blessed of the Lord, and their p. with
Bar 2 15 is called upon Israel and upon his p.
Dan 11 4 but not to his p. nor according to his
2 Ma 1 20 sent some of the p. of those priests
postern Judg 3 24 went out by a postern door
posts Exod 12 7 put it upon both the side posts and on
the upper door posts
Exod 12 23 on the transom and on both the posts
21 6 shall be set to the door and the posts
Deut 11 20 thou shalt write them upon the posts
Judg 16 3 the doors of the gate with the posts
3 K 6 31 of olive tree and posts of five corners
33 posts of olive tree foursquare: and two
2 Pa 3 7 posts and the walls and the doors
30 6 and the posts went with letters by
10 the posts went speedily from city to
Esth 8 10 sealed with his ring and sent by posts
14 the swift posts went out carrying
Prov 8 34 and waiteth at the posts of my doors
Eze 43 8 their p. by my p., and there was but a
45 19 shall put it on the posts of the house
19 on the posts of the gate of inner court
pot Num 11 8 boiled it in a pot and made cakes
Judg 6 19 the broth of the flesh into a pot
1 K 2 14 caldron or into the pot or into the pan
3 K 14 3 and a pot of honey and go to him
17 12 but only a handful of meal in a pot
14 the pot of meal shall not waste nor
16 from that day the pot of meal wasted not
4 K 4 38 set on the great pot and boil pottage
39 he shred them into the pot of pottage
40 cried out, saying: Death is in the pot
41 he cast it into the pot and said
41 there was now no bitterness in the pot
Job 41 11 like that of a pot heated and boiling
22 make the deep sea to boil like a pot
Ps 59 10 Moab is the pot of my hope. 107:10
Ecce 7 7 crackling of thorns burning under a pot
Eccu 12 10 as a brass pot his wickedness rusteth
13 3 what agreement shall the earthen pot
Eze 24 3 set on a pot, set it on, I say
6 to the pot whose rust is in it, and
Heb 9 4 was a golden pot that had manna, and the
pothooks Exod 38 3 he prepared . . . fleshhooks, p.
Num 4 14 all the vessels . . . forks, pothooks
pots Exod 16 3 when we sat over the flesh pots
Lev 11 35 whether it be oven or pots with feet
3 K 7 50 and pots and fleshhooks and bowls
4 K 25 14 they took away also the pots of brass
2 Pa 35 13 boiled in caldrons and kettles and pots
Isa 45 9 a sherd of the earthen pots: shall the
Jer 35 5 pots full of wine, and cups: and I said
52 19 censers and the pots and the basins
Amos 4 2 what shall remain of you in boiling p.
Mark 7 4 the washing of cups and of pots and
8 the washings of pots and of cups: and
potsherd Job 2 8 took a potsherd and scraped
Ps 21 16 my strength is dried up like a potsherd
Eccu 22 7 like one that glueth a p. together
potsherds Judg 1 35 mountain Hares, that is, of p.
pottage Gen 25 29 Jacob boiled pottage: to whom
Gen 25 30 give me of this red pottage, for I am
34 taking bread and the pottage of lentils
4 K 4 38 boil p. for the sons of the prophets
39 he shred them into the pot of pottage
40 when they had tasted of the pottage
Isa 44 16 he boiled pottage, and was filled
Dan 14 32 Habacuc, and he had boiled pottage
Agge 2 13 and touch with his skirt, bread or p.
potter Wisd 15 7 the p. also tempering soft earth
Wisd 15 7 these vessels, the potter is the judge
Eccu 38 32 the potter sitting at his work, turning
Isa 29 16 clay should think against the potter
41 25 as dirt, and as the potter treading clay
Jer 18 6 cannot I do with you, as this potter
Rom 9 21 hath not the potter power over the clay
Apoc 2 27 as the vessel of a potter they shall be
potter's Ps 2 9 them in pieces like a p. vessel
Eccu 27 6 the furnace trieth the potter's vessels
33 13 as the potter's clay is in his hand

Isa 30 14 as the potter's vessel is broken
Jer 18 2 go down into the potter's house and
3 I went down into the potter's house
19 1 go, and take a potter's earthen bottle
11 as the potter's vessel is broken
Lam 4 2 vessels, the work of the potter's hands
Dan 2 41 feet and the toes, part of p. clay
Mat 27 7 bought with them the potter's field
10 they gave them unto the potter's field
potters 1 Pa 4 23 these are the potters, and they
pound Luke 19 16 Lord, thy pound hath gained ten
Luke 19 18 thy pound hath gained five pounds
20 here is thy pound, which I have kept
24 take the pound away from him and give
John 12 3 Mary therefore took a p. of ointment
19 39 aloes, about an hundred pound weight
pounds 3 K 10 17 300 p. of gold covered one target
1 Es 2 69 gold, 5,000 pounds of silver and a
2 Es 7 71 of gold, and 2,200 pounds of silver
72 of gold, and 2,000 pounds of silver
1 Ma 14 24 of gold of the weight of 1,000 pounds
15 18 a shield of gold of a thousand pounds
Luke 19 13 servants, he gave them ten pounds, and
16 Lord, thy pound hath gained ten pounds
18 thy pound hath gained five pounds
24 give it to him that hath ten pounds
25 said to him: Lord, he hath ten pounds
Apoc 6 6 two pounds of wheat for a penny, and
6 thrice two pounds of barley for a penny
pour Exod 29 7 shalt pour the oil of unction
Exod 29 12 rest of the blood thou shalt pour at
16 pour round about the altar: and thou
20 shalt pour the blood upon the altar
Lev 1 11 shall pour the blood thereof. 3:8, 13
2 1 and he shall pour oil upon it and put
6 little pieces, and shalt pour oil upon
3 2 shall pour the blood round about
4 7 he shall pour all the rest of the blood
18 the rest of the blood he shall pour
11 38 if any man pour water upon the seed
14 15 he shall pour of the sextary of oil
17 shall pour upon the tip of the right
26 he shall pour part of the oil into
29 he shall pour upon the head of the
16 18 let him pour it upon the horns thereof
17 6 the priest shall pour the blood upon
Num 5 15 he shall not pour oil thereon nor put
18 17 thou shalt pour upon the altar, and
19 9 shall pour them forth without the camp
17 shall pour living waters upon them
Deut 12 16 shalt pour it upon the earth. 24
27 thou shalt pour on the altar: and the
3 K 18 34 and pour it upon the burnt offering
4 K 9 3 of oil, thou shalt pour it on his head
Eccu 39 9 he will pour forth the words of his
43 21 he shall pour frost as salt upon the
Eze 36 25 and I will pour upon you clean water
Joel 2 29 those days I will pour forth my spirit
Soph 3 8 and to pour upon them my indignation
pour out Exod 4 9 pour it out upon the dry
Lev 4 30 shall pour out the rest at the foot
34 the rest he shall pour out at the foot
7 14 shall pour out the blood of the victim
16 10 that he may pour out prayers upon him
17 13 let him pour out its blood and cover it
Num 4 7 and bowls to pour out the libations
15 5 of wine to pour out in libations for
Deut 12 16 thou shalt pour it out upon the earth
15 23 but pour it out on the earth as water
Judg 6 20 rock, and pour out the broth thereon
4 K 4 4 pour out thereof into all those vessels
41 pour out for the people, that they may
16 15 of the victim thou shalt pour out

Ps 61 9 pour out your hearts before him. God
68 25 pour out thy indignation upon them
78 6 pour out thy wrath upon the nations
141 3 in his sight I pour out my prayer: and
Ecce 2 8 and vessels to serve to pour out wine
11 3 clouds be full, they will pour out rain
Eccu 16 12 forgive, and to pour out indignation
24 46 I will yet pour out doctrine as
32 6 there is no hearing, pour not out words
36 8 raise up indignation and pour out wrath
37 32 pour not out thyself upon any meat
39 34 they shall pour out their force; and
Isa 44 3 I will pour out waters upon the thirsty
3 I will pour out my spirit upon thy seed
58 10 when thou shalt pour out thy soul to
Jer 6 11 pour it out upon the child abroad and
10 25 pour out thy indignation upon the
14 16 I will pour out their own wickedness
44 17 p. out drink offerings to her. 18, 19, 25
Lam 2 19 pour out thy heart like water before
Bar 2 19 that we pour out our prayers and beg
Eze 7 8 I will pour out my wrath upon thee
10 2 and pour them out upon the city. And
14 19 and pour out my indignation upon it in
20 8 I would pour out my indignation. 13
21 threatened to pour out my indignation
21 31 and I will pour out upon thee my
30 15 I will pour out my indignation upon
Osee 5 10 I will pour out my wrath upon them
Joel 2 28 I will pour out my spirit upon all
Zach 12 10 I will pour out upon the house of
Mala 3 10 and pour you out a blessing even
Acts 2 17 I will pour out of my Spirit upon
18 will I pour out in those days of my
Apoc 16 1 pour out the seven vials of the wrath
poured Exod 24 6 rest he poured upon the altar
Lev 7 2 the blood thereof shall be poured round
8 12 he poured it upon Aaron's head and he
15 he poured the rest of the blood at the
19 poured the blood thereof round about
24 the rest he poured on the altar round
9 9 poured the rest at the foot thereof
12 he poured round about on the altar
18 which he poured upon the altar round
11 34 if water from such a vessel be poured
21 10 the oil of unction hath been poured
1 K 10 1 oil, and poured it upon his head
23 27 for the Philistines have poured in
4 K 3 11 who poured water on the hands of Elias
4 5 brought her the vessels, and she p. it
8 15 took a blanket and poured water on it
9 6 he poured the oil upon his head and
16 13 poured the blood of the peace offerings
2 Pa 29 22 priests took the blood and poured it
22 their blood they p. also upon the altar
22 the lambs and poured the blood upon
Job 38 38 when was the dust poured on the earth
Ps 44 3 grace is poured abroad in thy lips
106 40 contempt was poured forth upon their
Wisd 2 3 our spirit shall be poured abroad as
Eccu 18 29 and have poured forth proverbs and
Isa 32 15 until the spirit be poured upon us
Jer 44 6 and my fury was poured forth and was
Eze 20 28 odors and poured forth their libations
Mat 26 7 poured it on his head as he was at
Mark 14 3 box, she poured it out upon his head
Acts 2 33 he hath poured forth that which you
Rom 5 5 charity of God is p. forth in our hearts
Titus 3 6 he hath p. forth upon us abundantly
poured out Gen 30 38 where the water was p. out
Gen 42 35 they poured out their corn, and every
49 4 thou art poured out as water, grow
Lev 1 16 the ashes are wont to be poured out

	11	5	and his power liveth which is in thee
	13	13	who hath shown his power in Israel
		22	Lord hath blessed thee by his power
		25	mindful of the power of the Lord
	14	6	seeing the power that the God of Israel
	16	16	glorious in thy power, and no one can
Esth	1	4	and boasting of his power, for a long
	7	5	who is this, and of what power, that he
	9	2	fear of their power had gone through
		4	knew him . . . to have great power
	13	2	to abuse the greatness of my power
		9	for all things are in thy power
	14	8	their hands to the power of their idols
		12	O Lord, king of gods, and of all power
Job	13	25	against a leaf . . . thou showest thy p.
	25	2	power and terror are with him, who
	26	12	by his power the seas are suddenly
	34	23	it is no longer in the power of man
	41	24	no p. on earth that can be compared
Ps	20	14	we will sing and praise thy power
	28	4	the voice of the Lord is in power
	32	6	the p. of them by spirit of his mouth
	58	12	scatter them by thy power; and bring
	61	12	have I heard, that p. belongeth to God
	62	3	to see thy power and thy glory. For
	64	7	thy strength, being girded with power
	65	7	who by his power ruleth forever: his
	67	12	that preach good tidings with great p.
		34	will give to his voice the voice of p.
		35	his magnificence and his p. is in the
		36	will give p. and strength to his people
	70	18	thy power and thy justice, O God
	76	15	thou hast made thy power known among
	77	26	by his power brought in the southwest
	88	10	thou rulest the power of the sea: and
		23	son of iniquity have power to hurt him
	89	11	who knoweth the power of thy anger
	104	27	he gave them power to show his signs
	105	8	that he might make his power known
	109	2	will send forth the scepter of thy p.
	110	6	to his people the power of his works
	144	4	and they shall declare thy power
		11	kingdom: and shall tell of thy power
	146	5	great is our Lord and great is his power
	150	1	praise ye him in firmament of his power
Prov	3	25	power of the wicked falling upon thee
	18	21	and life are in the p. of the tongue
	23	2	thou have thy soul in thy own power
	27	24	for thou shalt not always have power
Ecce	5	18	hath given him power to eat thereof
	6	2	doth not give him power to eat thereof
	8	4	his word is full of power: neither
		8	not in man's power to stop the spirit
		8	neither hath he p. in the day of death
	10	4	if the spirit of him that hath power
Wisd	1	3	his power . . . reproveth the unwise
	6	4	for power is given you by the Lord
	7	23	having all p., overseeing all things
		25	she is a vapor of the power of God
	9	11	and shall preserve me by her power
	10	2	gave him power to govern all things
		14	power against those that oppressed him
	11	21	scattered by the breath of thy power
		22	great power always belonged to thee
	12	15	thinking it not agreeable to thy power
		16	thy power is the beginning of justice
		17	thou showest thy power, when men will
		17	not believe thee to be absolute in p.
		18	thou being master of power, judgest
		18	thy power is at hand when thou wilt
	13	4	if they admired their power and their
	14	31	not the p. of them by whom they swear
	15	3	to know thy justice and thy power
	16	13	that hast power of life and death
		19	the fire, above its own power, burned
	17	5	no power of fire could give them light
	19	19	the fire had power in water above its
Eccu	6	27	keep her ways with all thy power
	8	16	be not surety above thy power; and if
	9	2	give not power of thy soul to a woman
		18	from the man that hath power to kill
		21	according to thy power beware of thy
	10	4	power of the earth is in the hand of
		11	all power is of short life. A long
	15	19	he is strong in power, seeing all men
	17	3	gave him power over all things that
		31	beholdeth the power of the height
	18	4	shall show forth the p. of his majesty
	19	25	hindered from sinning for want of power
	24	2	glorify herself in the sight of his p.
		11	by my p. I have trodden under my feet
		15	I rested, and my p. was in Jerusalem
	29	26	recover thy neighbor according to thy p.
	33	20	give not . . . power over thee while thou
	36	3	nations, that they may see thy power
	37	30	and if it be wicked, give it no power
	41	21	lie before a governor and a man in p.
	43	31	great, and his power is admirable
	45	14	a work of power, and delightful to the
		21	gave him power in his commandments
	46	8	that the nations might know his power
	47	10	he gave him power against his enemies
		14	cast down all the power of the enemies
	48	6	brokest easily their power in pieces
		20	and became proud through his power
	50	11	clothed with the perfection of power
Isa	22	21	and will give thy power into his hand
	40	26	of his might and strength and power
	47	14	from the power of the flames: there
Jer	10	12	he that maketh the earth by his power
	16	21	I will show them my hand and my power
	22	30	and have power any more in Juda
	26	21	Joakim and all his men in power and
	27	5	of the earth, by my great power
	32	17	heaven and earth by thy great power
	34	1	that were under the power of his hand
	51	15	he that made the earth by his power
Bar	1	6	money according to every man's power
	2	11	hast brought . . . with thy great power
	6	58	to be a king that showeth his power
		62	nor in power are like to any one of
Eze	30	18	pride of her power shall cease in her
Dan	2	37	hath given thee . . . power and glory
		38	hath put all things under thy power
	3	94	that the fire had no power on their
		100	and his power to all generations
	4	19	thy power unto the ends of the earth
		23	have known that power is from heaven
		27	kingdom, by the strength of my power
		31	his power is an everlasting power
	5	29	that he had power as the third man
	6	26	his power shall be forever. He is
	7	6	four heads, and power was given to it
		12	p. of the other beasts was taken away
		14	he gave him power and glory and a
		14	his power is an everlasting power
		26	that his power may be taken away
		27	kingdom and power . . . may be given to
	8	24	his power shall be strengthened, but not
	11	3	king, and shall rule with great power
		4	posterity, nor according to his power
		5	and he shall rule with great power
		39	and shall give them power over many
		43	he shall have power over the treasures
	14	4	earth, and hath power over all flesh
		21	delivered Bel into the power of Daniel

Mich 3 8 I am filled . . . with judgment and power
4 8 yea the first power shall come
Nah 1 3 the Lord is patient and great in power
2 1 loins, strengthen thy power exceedingly
Zach 9 10 his power shall be from sea to sea
1 Ma 1 4 he [Alexander] gathered a power
61 by their power did they deal with the
3 40 they went forth with all their power
5 6 where he found a mighty power and much
6 6 Lysias went with a very great power
6 grown strong by the armor and power
11 was pleasant and beloved in my power
7 22 they got the land of Juda into their p.
8 1 and that they are mighty in power
3 brought under their power the mines
11 destroyed and brought under their power
9 43 the bank of the Jordan with a great p.
10 19 that thou art a man of great power
32 I yield up also the p. of the castle
35 no man shall have power to do anything
70 thou showest thy power against us
11 15 met him with a strong power and put
14 4 his power and his glory pleased them
2 Ma 4 24 magnified the appearance of his power
50 covetousness of them that were in power
7 16 whereas thou hast power among men
17 thou shalt see his great power, and in
12 28 who with his p. breaketh the strength
14 1 was come up with a great power and a
15 21 not according to the p. of their arms
Mat 7 29 teaching them as one having p. Mark 1:22
9 6 hath power on earth to forgive sins. Mark 2:10; Luke 5:24
8 God that gave such power to men. And
10 1 p. over unclean spirits. Mark 6:7
20 25 the greater, exercise power upon them
24 30 heaven with much power and majesty
28 18 all power is given to me in heaven and
Mark 1 27 with power he commandeth even the
3 15 he gave them power to heal sicknesses
8 39 the kingdom of God coming in power
10 42 their princes have power over them
13 26 clouds, with great power and glory
Luke 1 17 in the spirit and power of Elias; that
35 p. of the most High shall overshadow
4 6 to thee will I give all this power
32 for his speech was with power. And
36 with authority and p. he commandeth
5 17 power of the Lord was to heal them
9 1 he gave them power and authority over
10 19 I have given you power to tread upon
19 and upon all the power of the enemy
12 5 killed, hath power to cast into hell
19 17 thou shalt have power over ten cities
20 20 authority and power of the governor
21 27 a cloud, with great power and majesty
22 25 they that have power over them are
53 your hour and the power of darkness
24 49 till you be endued with power from on
John 5 27 he hath given him power to do judgment
10 18 I have power to lay it down: and I have power to take it up again
17 2 as thou hast given him power over all
19 10 that I have power to crucify thee and I have power to release thee
11 shouldst not have any p. against me
Acts 1 7 the Father hath put in his own power
8 shall receive the power of the Holy
3 12 as if by our strength or power we had
4 7 by what power or by what name have you
33 with great power did the apostles give
5 4 it was sold, was it not in thy power
8 19 give me also this power, that on
10 38 with the Holy Ghost, and with power
26 18 converted from . . . power of Satan to God
Rom 1 20 his eternal power also, and divinity: so
9 17 that I may show my power in thee, and
21 hath not the potter power over the clay
22 his wrath, and to make his power known
13 1 for there is no power but from God: and
2 he that resisteth the power, resisteth
3 wilt thou then not be afraid of the p.
15 13 and in the power of the Holy Ghost. 19
1 C 2 4 but in showing of the Spirit and power
4 19 of them that are puffed up, but the p.
20 of God is not in speech, but in power
5 4 spirit, with the power of our Lord Jesus
6 12 will not be brought under the p. of any
14 and will raise us up also by his power
7 4 wife hath not power of her own body, but
4 also hath not power of his own body, but
35 which may give you power to attend upon
37 but having power of his own will; and
9 4 have not we power to eat and to drink
5 have we not power to carry about woman
6 Barnabas, have not we power to do this
12 if others be partakers of this power
12 we have not used this power: but we bear
18 that I abuse not my power in the gospel
11 10 ought the woman to have a power over her
14 11 if then I know not the p. of the voice
15 24 brought to nought all . . . power, and
43 sown in weakness, it shall rise in power
56 is sin: and the power of sin is the law
2 C 8 3 for according to their power, I bear
3 beyond their power, they were willing
10 8 should boast somewhat more of our p.
12 9 for power is made perfect in infirmity
9 that power of Christ may dwell in me
13 10 power which the Lord hath given me unto
Eph 1 19 is the exceeding greatness of his power
19 the operation of the might of his power
21 above all principality, and power and
2 2 according to the prince of the power of
3 7 according to the operation of his power
20 according to the p. that worketh in us
6 10 in the Lord, and in the might of his p.
Phil 3 10 him, and the power of his resurrection
Col 1 11 according to the power of his glory
13 who hath delivered us from the power
29 working which he worketh in me in powei
2 10 is the head of all principality and p.
1 Th 1 5 unto you in word only, but in power also
2 Th 1 7 from heaven, with the angels of his p.
9 Lord, and from the glory of his power
11 goodness and the work of faith in power
2 9 the working of Satan, in all power, and
3 9 not as if we had not power: but that we
2 Tim 1 7 but of power and of love and of sobriety
3 5 godliness, but denying the p. thereof
Heb 1 3 all things by the word of his p., making
7 16 according to the p. of an indissoluble
13 10 they have no power to eat who serve
1 P 4 11 let him do it as of the power, which
2 P 1 3 as all things of his divine power
16 the power and presence of our Lord
2 11 who are greater in strength and power
Jude 25 magnificence, empire and power, before
Apoc 1 16 face was as the sun shineth in his p.
2 26 I will give him power over the nations
4 11 to receive glory and honor and power
5 12 to receive power and divinity and
13 honor and glory and power forever and
6 8 power was given to him over the four
7 12 power and strength to our God forever
9 3 p. was given to them, as the scorpions

3 as the scorpions of the earth have p.
10 their power was to hurt men five months
19 power of the horses is in their mouths
11 6 these have power to shut heaven, that
6 they have power over waters to turn
17 hast taken to thee thy great power
12 10 of our God and the power of his Christ
13 2 him his own strength and great power
4 dragon which gave power to the beast
5 power was given to him to do two and
7 power was given him over every tribe
12 executed all the power of the former
14 18 who had power over fire; and he cried
15 8 majesty of God and from his power
16 9 God, who hath power over these plagues
17 12 shall receive power as kings one hour
13 their strength and power they shall
18 1 from heaven, having great power: and
3 rich by the power of her delicacies
19 1 and glory and power is to our God. For
20 6 in these the second death hath no power
power of God Eccu 3 21 great is the p. . . . alone
Eccu 50 23 his prayer, willing to show the p. . . .
2 Ma 3 24 falling down by the p. . . . , were struck
28 the manifest power of God being known
29 he indeed by the p. . . . lay speechless
34 all men the great works and the p. . . .
38 in that place a certain power of God
9 8 bearing witness to the manifest p. . . .
17 place of the earth and declare the p. . . .
11 4 never considering the power of God
Mat 22 29 Scriptures nor the p. . . . Mark 12:24
26 64 right hand of the p. . . . Mark 14:62; Luke 22:69
Luke 9 44 all were astonished at the mighty p. . . .
Acts 8 10 this man is the power of God, which
Rom 1 16 for it is the power of God. 1 C 1:18
1 C 1 24 power of God, and the wisdom of God
2 5 wisdom of men, but on the power of God
2 C 4 7 excellency may be of the power of God
6 7 in word of truth, in the power of God
13 4 yet he liveth by the power of God. For
4 we shall live with him by power of God
2 Tim 1 8 gospel, according to the power of God
1 P 1 5 by the p. . . . are kept by faith unto
4 14 is of the honor, glory, and p. . . .
powerful Ruth 2 1 a p. man and very rich, whose
1 Pa 5 24 valiant and powerful men and famous
2 Pa 28 7 Zechri a powerful man of Ephraim slew
1 Es 4 20 there have been p. kings in Jerusalem
Eccu 1 8 and a p. king and greatly to be feared
7 6 lest thou fear the person of the p.
8 1 strive not with a powerful man, lest
29 24 hath made p. men to go from place to
34 19 he is their powerful protector and
48 13 and no man was more powerful than he
Jer 32 18 O most mighty, great, and powerful
Bar 1 9 the princes and all the powerful men
Haba 1 3 judgment, but opposition is more p.
1 Ma 8 1 the Romans, that they are p. and strong
2 C 12 10 for when I am weak, then am I powerful
powers Ps 19 7 of his right hand is in powers
Ps 67 13 the king of powers is of the beloved
70 16 I will enter into the powers of the Lord
75 4 hath he broken the powers of bows
77 4 declaring praises of Lord and his p.
105 2 who shall declare the p. of the Lord
Dan 3 61 all ye powers of the Lord, bless the
4 32 as well with the powers of heaven
Mat 24 29 p. of heaven shall be moved. Luke 21:26
Mark 13 25 p. that are in heaven shall be moved
Luke 12 11 and to magistrates and powers, be not
Rom 8 38 powers, nor things present, nor things
13 1 let every soul be subject to higher p.
Eph 3 10 made known to the principalities and p.
6 12 but against principalities and powers
Col 1 16 dominations, or principalities, or p.
2 15 despoiling the principalities and p.
Titus 3 1 to be subject to princes and powers
Heb 6 5 and the powers of the world to come
1 P 3 22 the angels and powers and virtues being
practice Deut 4 6 observe and fulfil them in p.
Prov 1 18 and p. deceits against their own souls
3 29 practice not evil against thy friend
Eccu 27 10 truth will return to them that p. her
Isa 32 6 to practice hypocrisy and speak to
practiced Gen 50 17 malice they p. against thee
Exod 8 18 magicians . . . practiced in like manner
2 Ma 14 22 mischief might be suddenly p. by
practices Prov 10 3 disappoint the deceitful p.
Acts 8 11 bewitched them with his magical p.
praise (noun) Exod 15 2 is my strength and my p.
Lev 19 24 be sanctified, to the praise of the Lord
Deut 10 21 he is thy praise and thy God
26 19 to his own praise and name and glory
1 Pa 16 7 to give praise to the Lord. 41
27 praise and magnificence are before him
33 the trees of the wood give praise
29 11 to thee is praise: for all that is in
2 Pa 8 14 Levites in their order to give praise
33 16 victims and peace offerings and praise
1 Es 3 11 they sung together hymns and praise
2 Es 9 5 thy glory with all blessing and praise
12 31 two great choirs to give praise. And
39 two choirs of them that gave praise
Tob 8 19 up to thee a sacrifice of thy praise
Jdth 13 25 thy praise shall not depart out of
Esth 16 5 as to be worthy of all men's praise
Job 3 7 be solitary and not worthy of praise
20 5 that the praise of the wicked is short
37 22 the north, and to God praise with fear
Ps 8 3 of sucklings thou hast perfected praise
9 2 I will give praise to thee. 29:13; 56:10
21 4 in the holy place, the praise of Israel
26 with thee is my praise in a great church
25 7 that I may hear the voice of thy praise
27 7 with my will I will give praise to him
29 5 give praise to the memory of his holiness
32 1 ye just: praise becometh the upright
2 give praise to the Lord on the harp
33 2 his praise shall be always in my mouth
34 28 thy justice, thy praise all the day long
41 5 with the voice of joy and praise
6 in God, for I will give praise to him
12 I will still give praise to him. 42:6
42 5 I will give praise upon the harp: why
43 9 and in thy name we will give praise
47 11 thy praise unto the end of the earth
49 14 offer to God the sacrifice of praise
23 sacrifice of praise shall glorify me
50 17 my mouth shall declare thy praise
53 8 will give praise, O God, to thy name
65 2 to his name: give glory to his praise
8 make voice of his praise to be heard
66 4 let all people give praise to thee. 6
68 31 and I will magnify him with praise
70 8 let my mouth be filled with praise
14 I will . . . add to all thy praise
78 13 we will show forth thy praise unto
87 11 raise to life and give praise to thee
90 1 the praise of a canticle for David
91 2 it is good to give praise to the Lord
92 1 praise in the way of a canticle, for
94 1 praise of a canticle for David himself
95 6 praise and beauty are before him
96 12 give praise to the remembrance of his

97 5 sing praise to the Lord on the harp
98 3 let them give praise to thy great name
99 1 a psalm of praise for David himself
4 go ye into his gates with praise, into
101 22 may declare . . . his praise in Jerusalem
103 1 thou hast put on praise and beauty
33 I will sing praise to my God while I
105 47 name and may glory in thy praise
106 22 them sacrifice the sacrifice of praise
107 2 I will sing and will give praise with
108 2 be not thou silent in my praise: for
110 3 his work in praise and magnificence
10 his praise continueth forever and ever
112 3 name of the Lord is worthy of praise
115 17 sacrifice to thee the sacrifice of p.
117 1 give praise to the Lord for he is good
14 the Lord is my strength and my praise
19 I will . . . give praise to the Lord
118 62 I rose at midnight to give praise to
164 seven times a day I have given praise
137 1 I will sing praise to thee in the sight
144 1 praise, for David himself. I will
21 shall speak the praise of the Lord
146 1 to our God be joyful and comely praise
7 sing ye to the Lord with praise: sing
148 14 the praise of him is above heaven
149 1 let his praise be in the church of the
Prov 11 10 wicked perish there shall be praise
Wisd 15 19 they have fled from the praise of God
Eccu 6 35 sayings of praise may not escape thee
15 9 praise is not seemly in mouth of a sinner
10 praise shall be with the wisdom of God
10 sovereign Lord will give praise unto it
17 25 with them that . . . give praise to God
26 p. perisheth from the dead as nothing
18 28 will give praise to him that findeth her
24 4 she shall have praise, and among the
39 14 the church shall show forth his praise
43 33 as you can: for he is above all praise
44 15 let . . . the church declare their praise
45 19 to have praise and to glorify his people
51 37 you shall not be confounded in his p.
Isa 12 2 the Lord is my strength and my praise
24 14 up their voice, and shall give praise
26 19 give praise, ye that dwell in the dust
35 2 and shall rejoice with joy and praise
10 and shall come into Sion with praise
38 19 the living, he shall give praise to thee
42 8 nor my praise to graven things
10 his praise is from the ends of the earth
11 ye inhabitants of Petra, give praise
12 shall declare his praise in the islands
43 21 they shall show forth my praise. But
44 23 give praise, O ye heavens. 49:13
23 ye mountains, resound with praise
48 9 for my praise I will bridle thee
49 13 ye mountains, give praise with
51 3 thanksgiving and the voice of praise
54 1 give praise, O thou barren, that
1 sing forth praise, and make a joyful
55 12 and the hills shall sing praise before
60 6 and showing forth praise to the Lord
18 and praise [shall possess] thy gates
61 3 garment of p. for the spirit of grief
11 and praise before all the nations
62 7 till he make Jerusalem a p. in the earth
63 7 the praise of the Lord for all the
Jer 7 16 nor take to thee praise and supplication
11 14 do not take up praise . . . for them
13 11 be my people . . . and for a praise
17 14 shall be saved: for thou art my praise
30 19 out of them shall come forth praise
31 12 and shall give praise in mount Sion
33 9 it shall be to me . . . a praise and a
51 48 in them shall give praise for Babylon
Lam 2 19 arise, give praise in the night
Dan 3 26 thy name is worthy of praise and. 56
Amos 4 5 offer a sacrifice of praise with leaven
Jon 2 10 I with the voice of p. will sacrifice
Mich 2 9 you have taken my praise forever from
Haba 3 3 the earth is full of his praise
Soph 3 14 give praise, O daughter of Sion: shout
17 he will be joyful over thee in praise
19 I will get them praise and a name
20 I will give you a name and praise
Zach 2 10 sing praise and rejoice, O daughter of
1 Ma 4 56 sacrifices of salvation and of praise
Mat 21 16 of sucklings thou hast perfected praise
Luke 18 43 when they saw it, gave praise to God
Rom 2 29 whose praise is not of men, but of God
13 3 thou shalt have praise from the same
1 C 4 5 shall every man have praise from God
2 C 8 18 brother, whose praise is in the gospel
Eph 1 6 unto the p. of the glory of his grace
12 unto the praise of his glory. 14
Phil 1 11 Christ, unto the glory and praise of God
4 8 if any praise of discipline, think on
Heb 13 15 let us offer the sacrifice of praise
1 P 1 7 may be found unto praise and glory and
2 14 and for the praise of the good: for so
Apoc 19 5 give praise to our God, all ye his
praise (verb) Gen 29 35 now will I praise the Lord
Gen 49 8 thee shall thy brethren praise
Deut 32 43 praise his people, ye nations, for he
1 Pa 16 4 to glorify and praise the Lord God of
8 praise ye the Lord and call upon his
10 praise ye his holy name: let the heart
29 13 thee: and we praise thy glorious name
2 Pa 5 13 when they began to praise the Lord
7 6 which king David made to p. the Lord
20 21 to praise him by their companies, and
29 30 commanded the Levites to p. the Lord
31 2 to minister and to praise and to sing
1 Es 3 10 to praise God by the hands of David
2 Es 11 17 was the principal man to praise and to
12 24 to praise and to give thanks according
45 appointed to praise with canticles
Tob 13 3 praise him in the sight of the Gentiles
7 I will praise him in the land of my
Jdth 13 17 Judith said: praise ye the Lord our God
Job 37 22 the north and to God praise with fear
Ps 17 28 I will praise thee, because thou hast
20 14 we will sing and praise thy power
21 23 midst of the church I will praise thee
24 ye that fear the Lord, praise him: all
27 shall praise the Lord that seek him
34 18 I will praise thee in a strong people
44 18 therefore shall people praise thee
48 19 he will praise thee when thou shalt do
51 11 I will praise thee forever, because
55 5 in God I will praise my words, in God
11 in God will I praise the word, in the Lord will I praise his speech
62 4 than lives: thee my lips shall praise
6 my mouth shall praise thee with joyful
68 31 I will praise the name of God with a
35 let the heavens and the earth p. him
73 21 the poor and needy shall p. thy name
74 2 we will p. thee, O God: we will p.
83 5 they shall praise thee forever and ever
85 12 I will praise thee, O Lord my God
94 1 come, let us praise the Lord with joy
99 4 praise ye his name: for the Lord is
101 19 that shall be created shall p. the Lord
106 32 praise him in the chair of the ancients
107 4 I will praise thee, O Lord, among the

108 30 in the midst of many I will praise him
110 1 I will praise thee, O Lord, with my
112 1 praise the Lord, ye children: praise ye the name of the Lord
113 17 the dead shall not praise thee, O Lord
116 1 praise the Lord, all ye nations: praise him, all ye people
117 28 thou art my God, and I will praise thee
29 praise ye the Lord, for he is good
118 7 I will praise thee with uprightness of
175 my soul shall live and shall p. thee
121 4 Israel, to praise the name of the Lord
134 1 praise ye the name of the Lord: O you
1 O you his servants, praise the Lord
3 p. ye the Lord, for the Lord is good
135 1 praise the Lord, for he is good: for his
2 praise ye the God of gods: for his
3 praise ye the Lord of lords: for his
137 1 I will praise thee, O Lord, with my
138 14 I will praise thee, for thou art
141 8 of prison, that I may praise thy name
144 2 and I will praise thy name forever
4 and generation shall praise thy works
10 let all thy works, O Lord, praise thee
145 2 praise the Lord, O my soul, in my life I will praise the Lord
146 1 praise ye the Lord, because psalm is
147 12 praise the Lord, O Jerusalem: praise thy God, O Sion
148 1 praise ye the Lord from the heavens
1 praise ye him in the high places
2 praise ye him, all his angels: praise ye him, all his hosts
3 praise ye him, O sun and moon: praise him, all ye stars and light
4 praise him, ye heavens of heavens
5 praise the name of the Lord. For he
7 praise the Lord from the earth, ye
12 younger, praise the name of the Lord
149 3 let them praise his name in choir: let
150 1 praise ye the Lord in his holy places
1 p. ye him in the firmament of his power
2 praise ye him for his mighty acts: praise ye him according to the multitude
3 praise him with sound of trumpet: praise him with psaltery and harp
4 praise him with timbrel and choir: praise him with strings and organs
5 praise him on high sounding cymbals: praise him on cymbals of joy
5 joy: let every spirit praise the Lord
Prov 27 2 let another praise thee, and not thy
28 4 forsake the law, praise the wicked man
29 6 and the just shall praise and rejoice
31 31 let her works praise her in the gates
Eccu 11 2 praise not a man for his beauty
30 praise not any man before death, for
17 8 that they might praise the name which
27 shalt praise God and shalt glory in
21 18 man of sense will p. every wise word
24 1 wisdom shall praise her own self and
27 8 praise not a man before he speaketh
31 9 who is he, and we will praise him
37 27 and they that see shall praise him
39 12 many shall praise his wisdom and it
19 and praise with canticles and bless
41 praise ye him and bless the name of
44 1 let us now praise men of renown, and
47 12 that they should praise the holy name
51 1 I will praise thee, O God my Savior
8 my soul shall praise the Lord even
15 I will praise thy name continually
15 and will praise it with thanksgiving
17 I will give thanks and praise thee
30 reward: and with it I will praise him
Isa 12 4 praise ye the Lord and call upon his
6 rejoice and praise, O thou habitation
25 3 shall a strong people praise thee
38 18 neither shall death praise thee: nor
52 8 lifted up their voice, they shall praise
61 7 shame, they shall praise their part
62 9 shall eat it and shall praise the Lord
65 14 my servants shall p. for joyfulness
Jer 4 2 shall bless him and shall praise him
20 13 sing ye to the Lord, praise the Lord
Bar 2 32 they shall praise me in the land of
3 6 God, and we will praise thee, O Lord
7 name and praise thee in our captivity
Dan 2 23 I give thanks, and I praise thee
3 57 praise and exalt him. (and so to verse 88)
90 praise him and give him thanks because
4 34 I Nabuchodonosor do now praise and
Joel 2 26 you shall praise the name of the Lord
1 Ma 4 33 know thy name, praise thee with hymns
Luke 19 37 began with joy to praise God with a
Rom 15 11 and again: Praise the Lord, all ye
1 C 11 2 I praise you, brethren, that in all
22 do I praise you? In this I praise you
Heb 2 12 in the midst of the church will I praise
praised Gen 12 15 Pharao, and p. her before him
Lev 9 24 multitude saw, they praised the Lord
Josu 22 33 the children of Israel praised God
Judg 16 24 also seeing this, praised their god
2 K 22 4 the Lord who is worthy to be praised
1 Pa 16 25 Lord is great and exceedingly to be p.
2 Pa 7 3 they adored and praised the Lord
23 13 and the voice of those that praised
29 30 and they praised him with great joy
2 Es 5 13 they praised God. And the people did
6 19 and they praised him also before me
Job 38 7 when the morning stars praised me
Ps 9 3 the sinner is praised in the desires of
33 3 in the Lord shall my soul be praised
47 2 the Lord, and exceedingly to be praised
62 12 they shall be praised that swear by him
63 11 the upright in heart shall be praised
95 4 Lord is great and exceedingly to be p.
101 9 they that p. me did swear against me
105 5 that thou mayst be praised with thy
144 3 great is the Lord, and greatly to be p.
Prov 24 25 they that rebuke him, shall be praised
28 20 a faithful man shall be much praised
31 28 her husband, and he praised her. Many
30 that feareth the Lord, she shall be p.
Ecce 4 2 I p. the dead rather than the living
8 10 were praised . . . as men of just works
Cant 6 8 and concubines, and they praised her
Wisd 10 20 and they praised with one accord thy
Eccu 9 24 works shall be p. for the hand of
30 2 instructeth his son shall be p. in him
38 3 in sight of great men he shall be p.
44 7 generation, and were p. in their days
47 10 with his whole heart he p. the Lord
Isa 45 26 seed of Israel be justified and p.
64 11 where our fathers praised thee, is
Dan 3 51 praised and glorified and blessed God
52 and worthy to be praised and glorified
52 and worthy to be praised and exalted
53 and exceedingly to be praised. 54
4 31 I praised and glorified him that liveth
5 4 and praised their gods of gold and
23 thou hast praised the gods of silver
13 63 but Helcias and his wife praised God
2 Ma 3 30 they praised the Lord because he had
Acts 16 25 Paul and Silas praying, praised God
praises 1 Pa 16 9 sing praises to him: and relate

1 Pa 16 35 and may rejoice in singing thy praises
42 instruments to sing praises to God: and
23 30 thanks and to sing praises to the Lord
2 Pa 20 22 they began to sing praises. 29:27
29 31 come and offer victims and praises
31 multitude offered victims and praises
Tob 12 18 bless ye him and sing praises to him
Ps 9 15 that I may declare all thy praises
46 7 sing praises to our God, sing ye
7 sing praises to our king, sing ye
55 12 thee, which I will pay, praises to thee
71 20 p. of David, the son of Jesse, are ended
72 28 that I may declare all thy praises
75 1 the end, in praises, a psalm for Asaph
77 4 declaring the praises of the Lord and
104 2 yea sing praises to him: relate all his
105 2 who shall set forth all his praises
12 his words: and they sang his praises
143 9 ten strings I will sing praises to thee
149 6 praises of God shall be in their mouth
Prov 10 7 the memory of the just is with praises
Wisd 18 9 singing now the praises of the fathers
Eccu 44 8 that their praises might be related
Isa 24 16 we have heard praises, the glory of
51 11 shall come into Sion singing praises
2 Ma 4 22 came in with torch lights and with p.
praiseth Prov 27 21 by the mouth of him that p.
praiseworthy Exod 15 11 terrible and p., doing
praising 2 Pa 23 12 people running and p. the king
2 Pa 30 21 joy, praising the Lord every day
22 praising the Lord the God of their
1 Es 3 11 with a great shout, praising the Lord
Ps 17 4 praising I will call upon the Lord
Wisd 19 9 they skipped like lambs, praising thee
Eccu 39 20 in praising him, you shall say in this
Dan 3 24 praising God and blessing the Lord
Luke 2 13 heavenly army, p. God, and saying
20 shepherds returned, glorifying and p.
24 53 in the temple, p. and blessing God
Acts 2 47 p. God and having favor with all the
3 8 walking and leaping and praising God
9 the people saw him walking and p. God
1 C 11 17 now this I ordain: not praising you
pranceth Job 39 21 he p. boldly, he goeth forward
prating 3 J 10 with malicious words p. against
pray Gen 12 13 I pray thee. 13:9; 1 K 9:18; 26:19; 2 K 13:5, 6; 24:10; 3 K 2:17; 19:20; Tob 5:16, 19; 9:1; Job 4:7; Mich 6:5
Gen 20 7 he shall pray for thee, and thou shalt
47 4 we pray thee to give orders that we
50 17 we also pray thee, to forgive the
Exod 8 8 pray ye to the Lord to take away the
9 me a time when I shall pray for thee
28 but go no farther: pray for me. And
29 from thee, and will pray to the Lord
9 28 pray ye to the Lord, that the
10 17 pray to the Lord . . . that he take away
30 10 Aaron shall pray upon the horns thereof
Lev 4 26 the priest shall pray for him. 5:6, 10, 18; 19:22
31 he shall pray for him. 35; 6:7; 14:19; 15:15
5 16 to the priest, who shall pray for him
9 7 pray for thyself and for the people
7 slain the people's victim, pray for
10 17 and may pray for them in the sight of
12 7 shall pray for her, and so she. 8
14 21 that the priest may pray for him, and
53 he shall pray for the house, and it
15 30 he shall pray for her before the Lord
16 17 to pray for himself and his house
18 let him pray for himself, and taking
24 he shall pray both for himself and for
34 that you p. for the children of Israel
26 41 then shall they pray for their sins
43 they shall pray for their sins because
Num 6 11 the priest . . . shall pray for him. 15:28
8 12 holocaust to the Lord, to pray for them
19 to pray for them, lest there should be
15 25 priest shall pray for all the multitude
16 46 quickly to the people to pray for them
21 7 pray that he may take away these
22 19 I pray you to stay here this night also
31 50 that thou mayst pray to the Lord for
32 5 we pray thee . . . thou give it to us
Judg 6 39 I pray that the fleece only may be dry
19 23 I pray you. 1 K 23:22; Job 14:10; Lam 1:18; 2 Ma 9:26
1 K 1 23 I pray that the Lord may fulfil his word
27 for this child did I pray, and the
2 25 against the Lord, who shall p. for him
7 5 that I may pray to the Lord for you
12 19 pray for thy servants to the Lord
23 that I should cease to pray for you
25 25 let not my lord the king, I pray, regard
2 K 7 27 in his heart to pray this prayer to
13 24 let the king, I pray, with his servants
3 K 8 30 whatsoever they shall pray for in this
33 if thy people . . . shall come and pray
42 when he . . . shall pray in this place
44 pray to thee towards the way. 48
13 6 pray for me, that my hand may be
4 K 18 26 we pray thee speak to us thy servants
1 Pa 17 25 found confidence to pray before thee
21 30 David could not go . . . there to pray
2 Pa 6 21 whosoever shall pray in this place
24 and call upon thy name and pray to thee
26 they shall pray to thee in this place
29 shall pray and shall spread forth his
37 and do penance and pray to thee
7 15 prayer of him that shall p. in this
20 3 betook himself wholly to pray to the
4 Juda gathered . . . to pray to the Lord
34 21 go and pray to the Lord for me
1 Es 6 10 and pray for the life of the king
2 Es 1 6 which I pray before thee now, night and
Tob 3 1 then Tobias sighed and began to pray
8 4 Sara, arise and let us pray to God
12 12 when thou didst pray with tears and
Jdth 8 31 pray that God may strengthen my design
32 and pray ye, that as you have said
33 but to pray for me to the Lord our God
11 14 will go out and I will pray to God
Job 5 8 I will pray to the Lord and address my
21 15 it profit us if we pray to him
22 27 thou shalt pray to him, and he will
33 26 he shall pray to God, and he will be
42 8 my servant Job shall pray for you
Ps 5 4 to thee will I pray: O Lord, in the
27 2 my supplication, when I pray to thee
31 6 holy pray to thee in a seasonable time
36 7 be subject to the Lord and pray to him
121 6 pray ye for the things that are for
Wisd 18 21 man made haste to pray for the people
Eccu 7 10 neglect not to pray, and to give alms
21 1 pray that they may be forgiven thee
37 19 pray to the most High, that he may
38 9 pray to the Lord and he shall heal
39 6 he will pray in the sight of the most
50 19 to pray to the Almighty God the most
24 now pray ye to the God of all, who
Isa 16 12 go in to his sanctuaries to pray
45 20 and pray to a god that cannot save
Jer 7 16 do not thou pray for this people. 11:14
14 11 pray not for this people for their
15 5 who shall go to pray for thy peace
29 7 and pray to the Lord for it: for in

12 you shall pray to me, and I will hear
37 3 saying: Pray to the Lord our God for us
42 2 pray thou for us to the Lord thy God
4 behold I will pray to the Lord your God
20 pray for us to the Lord our God, and
Bar 1 11 pray ye for the life of Nabuchodonosor
13 pray ye for us to the Lord our God
Dan 9 3 to pray and make supplication with
1 Ma 3 44 that they might pray and ask mercy
2 Ma 12 44 and vain to pray for the dead
46 to pray for the dead, that they may
Mat 5 44 pray for them that persecute and
6 5 when ye pray, you shall not be as the
5 that love to stand and pray in the
6 when thou shalt pray, enter into thy
6 the door, pray to thy Father in secret
9 thus therefore shall you pray: Our
9 38 p. ye therefore the Lord. Luke 10:2
14 23 he went into a mountain alone to pray
19 13 impose hands upon them and pray. And
24 20 pray that your flight be not in the
26 36 you here, till I go yonder and pray
41 pray that ye enter not. Mark 14:38
Mark 5 17 to pray him that he would depart from
6 46 he went up to the mountain to pray
11 24 whatsoever you ask when ye pray
25 when you shall stand to pray, forgive
13 18 but pray ye, that these things happen
33 take ye heed, watch and pray. For ye
14 32 sit you here, while I pray. And he
Luke 6 12 he went out into a mountain to pray
28 pray for them that calumniate you
9 28 and went up into a mountain to pray
11 1 Lord, teach us to pray, as John also
2 when you pray, say: Father, hallowed
14 18 I pray thee, hold me excused. 19
18 1 that we ought always to pray, and not
22 40 p., lest ye enter into temptation. 46
John 17 9 I pray for them: I pray not for the
15 I pray not that thou shouldst take
20 not for them only do I pray, but for
Acts 8 22 pray to God that perhaps this thought
10 9 the higher parts of the house to pray
27 34 I pray you to take some meat for your
Rom 8 26 we know not what we should pray for as
1 C 11 13 a woman, to pray unto God uncovered
14 13 let him pray that he may interpret. For
14 if I pray in a tongue, my spirit prayeth
15 I will pray with the spirit, I will pray
2 C 13 7 now we pray God, that you may do no evil
9 this also we pray for, your perfection
Eph 3 13 I p. you not to faint at my tribulations
Phil 1 9 this I pray, that your charity may more
Col 1 9 cease not to pray for you, and to beg
1 Th 4 1 we pray and beseech you in the Lord
5 17 always rejoice. Pray without ceasing
25 pray for us. 2 Th 3:1; Heb 13:18
2 Th 1 11 we pray always for you; that our God
1 Tim 2 8 that men pray in every place, lifting up
James 5 13 is any of you sad? Let him pray. Is
14 let them pray over him, anointing him
16 pray one for another, that you may be

prayed Gen 20 17 when Abraham prayed, God healed
Exod 8 30 Moses . . . prayed to the Lord. 10:18
Lev 16 6 p. for himself and for his own house
Num 8 21 sight of the Lord and prayed for them
11 2 Moses prayed to the Lord, and the fire
16 48 prayed for the people, and the plague
21 7 Moses prayed for the people. And the
Deut 9 20 and I prayed in like manner for him
Judg 13 8 then Manue prayed to the Lord and said
1 K 1 10 she [Anna] prayed to the Lord, shedding
28 and Anna prayed and said: My heart
2 36 shall come that he may be prayed for
8 6 Samuel prayed to the Lord. And the
3 K 8 59 wherewith I have p. before the Lord
18 29 answer nor regard them as they prayed
4 K 4 33 upon the child, and prayed to the Lord
6 17 Eliseus prayed and said: Lord, open
18 Eliseus prayed to the Lord, saying
19 15 he [Ezechias] prayed in his sight
20 2 [Ezechias] prayed to the Lord, saying
1 Pa 4 10 God granted him the things he prayed
2 Pa 23 11 and they prayed for him and said
30 18 and Ezechias prayed for them, saying
32 20 prayed against this blasphemy and
24 to death, and prayed to the Lord
33 12 after that he was in distress he p. to
2 Es 1 4 I fasted and prayed before the face of
2 4 and I prayed to the God of heaven
4 9 we prayed to our God and set watchmen
Tob 8 6 so they both arose and prayed earnestly
Jdth 4 14 prayed to the Lord and continued in
6 21 and they prayed all the night long
12 8 as she came up, she prayed to the Lord
Job 42 10 Job, when he prayed for his friends
Eccu 33 4 and so having prayed he shall be heard
51 13 I have prayed for death to pass away
19 I prayed for her before the temple
Isa 37 15 and Ezechias prayed to the Lord, saying
38 2 toward the wall, and p. to the Lord
53 12 and hath prayed for the transgressors
Jer 32 16 I prayed to the Lord, saying: Alas
Bar 1 5 fasted, and prayed before the Lord
Dan 3 25 Azarias standing up prayed in this
9 4 I prayed to the Lord my God and I made
Jon 2 2 Jonas prayed to the Lord his God out
4 2 and he prayed to the Lord and said
1 Ma 4 30 he prayed and said: Blessed art thou
7 40 Judas prayed and said: O Lord, when
11 71 cast earth upon his head and prayed
2 Ma 1 8 we prayed to the Lord and were heard
2 8 when Solomon prayed that the place
10 as Moses prayed to the Lord, and fire
10 so Solomon also prayed, and fire came
5 4 prayed that these prodigies might turn
9 13 this wicked man prayed to the Lord
10 25 prayed to the Lord, sprinkling earth
15 12 prayed for all the people of the Jews
Mat 26 42 the second time, he went and prayed
44 he prayed the third time, saying the
Mark 1 35 a desert place: and there he prayed
14 35 he prayed, that if it might be, the
39 he prayed, saying the same words. And
Luke 5 16 he retired into the desert and prayed
9 29 whilst he prayed, the shape of his
11 37 Pharisee p. him that he would dine
18 11 Pharisee standing, prayed thus with
22 32 but I have prayed for thee, that thy
41 he prayed, saying: Father, if thou
43 in an agony, he prayed the longer
John 4 31 disciples prayed him, saying: Rabbi
47 prayed him to come down and heal his
Acts 4 31 when they had prayed, the place was
8 15 prayed for them, that they might
9 40 Peter kneeling down prayed, and
14 22 when they . . . had prayed with fasting
20 36 kneeling down, he prayed with them all
21 5 kneeled down on the shore, and we prayed
28 8 when he had p., and laid his hands on
James 5 17 he prayed that it might not rain upon
18 prayed again: and the heaven gave rain

prayer Judg 13 9 Lord heard the prayer of Manue
2 K 7 27 his heart to pray this prayer to thee
3 K 8 28 have regard to prayer of thy servant
28 hear the hymn and the prayer which thy

29 that thou mayest hearken to the prayer
54 made an end of praying all this prayer
9 3 I have heard thy prayer. 4 K 20:5; 2 Pa 7:12; Isa 38:5
4 K 19 4 do thou offer prayer for the remnants
20 I have heard the prayer thou hast made
2 Pa 6 19 mayest regard the p. of thy servant
21 that thou wouldst hear the prayer which
40 let thy ears be attentive to the prayer
7 1 Solomon had made an end of his prayer
15 prayer of him that shall pray in this
30 27 their prayer came to the holy dwelling
33 13 he heard his prayer, and brought him
18 Manasses, and his prayer to his God
19 his prayer also and his being heard
1 Es 9 8 our prayer been made before the Lord
2 Es 1 6 open to hear the prayer of thy servant
11 attentive to the prayer of thy servant and to the prayer of thy servants
11 17 to praise, and to give glory in prayer
Tob 3 11 but continuing in prayer with tears
12 when she was making an end of her p.
4 1 Tobias thought that his p. was heard
12 8 prayer is good with fasting and alms
12 I offered thy prayer to the Lord. And
Jdth 6 16 the people's prayer . . . was concluded
9 16 the prayer of the humble and the meek
12 5 out at night and before day to prayer
13 12 to their custom, as it were to prayer
Ps 4 2 hear my prayer. 38:13; 53:4; 54:2; 63:2; 64:3; 83:9; 101:2; 142:1
5 3 hearken to the voice of my prayer, O my
6 10 the Lord hath received my prayer. Let
16 1 the prayer of David. Hear, O Lord, my
1 give ear unto my p., which proceedeth
30 23 thou hast heard the voice of my prayer
34 13 my prayer shall be turned into my bosom
41 9 with me is prayer to the God of my life
60 2 be attentive to my prayer. To thee
6 thou, my God, hast heard my prayer
65 20 who hath not turned away my prayer
68 14 as for me, my prayer is to thee
79 5 angry against the prayer of thy servant
85 1 a prayer for David himself. Incline
6 give ear, O Lord, to my prayer: and
87 3 let my prayer come in before thee
14 in morning my prayer shall prevent thee
15 Lord, why castest thou off my prayer
89 1 a prayer of Moses the man of God
101 1 the prayer of the poor man, when he was
18 had regard to the prayer of the humble
105 44 tribulation: and he heard their prayer
108 4 but I gave myself to prayer. And they
7 and may his prayer be turned to sin
114 1 Lord will hear the voice of my prayer
140 2 let my prayer be directed as incense
5 my prayer also shall still be against
141 1 a prayer when he was in the cave
3 in his sight I pour out my prayer
144 19 he will hear their prayer and save
Prov 28 9 his prayer shall be an abomination
Wisd 13 17 then maketh prayer to it, inquiring
18 21 the shield of his ministry, prayer
Eccu 3 4 obtain pardon for his sins by prayer
4 shall be heard in the prayer of days
6 in day of his prayer he shall be heard
4 6 the prayer of him that curseth thee
7 15 and repeat not the word in thy prayer
17 22 make thy prayer before the face of the
24 and in prayer to the most high God
18 23 before prayer prepare thy soul: and
20 1 not to hinder him that confesseth in p.
21 6 the prayer out of the mouth of the poor
34 31 profit him? Who will hear his prayer
35 16 will hear p. of him that is wronged
20 his prayer shall approach even to the
21 the prayer of him that humbleth himself
38 39 their prayer shall be in the work of
39 7 he will open his mouth in prayer and
9 in his p. he will confess to the Lord
50 21 the people in prayer besought the Lord
23 he repeated his prayer, willing to
51 1 a prayer of Jesus the son of Sirach
15 thanksgiving, and my prayer was heard
Isa 1 15 when you multiply prayer, I will not
37 4 lift up thy prayer for the remnant that
21 for the prayer thou hast made to me
51 18 I sought for wisdom openly in my prayer
56 7 make them joyful in my house of prayer
7 shall be called the house of prayer
Jer 11 14 not take up praise and prayer for them
33 6 will reveal to them the prayer of peace
Lam 3 8 entreat, he hath shut out my prayer
44 that our prayer may not pass through
Bar 3 4 hear now the p. of the dead of Israel
Eze 41 11 was turned towards the place of prayer
11 the breadth of the place for prayer
Dan 6 13 three times a day he maketh his prayer
9 21 as I was yet speaking in prayer
Jon 2 8 that my prayer may come to thee, unto
Haba 3 1 a prayer of Habacuc the prophet for
1 Ma 3 46 for in Maspha was a place of prayer
5 33 their trumpets, and cried out in prayer
7 37 that it might be a house of prayer
2 Ma 1 23 all the priests made prayer while the
24 p. of Nehemias was after this manner
10 27 after prayer taking their arms, they
15 22 in his prayer he said after this manner
24 and thus he concluded his prayer
Mat 17 20 not cast out but by prayer and fasting
21 13 be called the house of p. Mark 11:17
22 whatsoever you shall ask in prayer
Mark 9 28 by nothing but by prayer and fasting
12 40 under the pretence of long prayer
Luke 1 13 Zachary, for thy prayer is heard; and
6 12 the whole night in the prayer of God
19 46 my house is the house of prayer. But
20 47 houses of widows, feigning long prayer
22 45 when he rose up from prayer and was
Acts 1 14 one mind in prayer with the women and
3 1 temple at the ninth hour of prayer
6 4 give ourselves continually to prayer
10 31 thy p. is heard, and thy alms are had
12 5 prayer was made without ceasing by
16 13 where it seemed that there was p.; and
16 as we went to prayer, a certain girl
Rom 10 1 and my prayer to God, is for them unto
12 12 patient in tribulation. Instant in p.
1 C 7 5 that you may give yourselves to prayer
2 C 1 11 you helping withal in prayer for us
Eph 6 18 by all p. and supplication praying at
Phil 1 19 me unto salvation, through your prayer
4 6 in everything, by p. and supplication
Col 4 2 be instant in prayer; watching in it
1 Tim 4 5 is sanctified by the word of God and p.
James 5 15 the prayer of faith shall save the
16 continual p. of a just man availeth
17 with prayer he prayed that it might
3 J 2 I make it my prayer that thou mayest

prayers Gen 19 21 in this I have heard thy p.
Gen 30 17 and God heard her prayers: and she
Lev 16 10 that he may pour out prayers upon him
Num 21 3 the Lord heard the prayers of Israel
1 K 1 12 as she multiplied prayers before the
2 K 13 14 he would not hearken to her prayers
3 K 8 45 hear thou in heaven their prayers

49 hear thou in heaven . . . their p. 2 Pa 6:39
2 Pa 6 19 mayest hear the p. which thy servant
21 hearken then to the prayers of thy
35 hear thou from heaven their prayers
Tob 3 24 the prayers of them both were heard
25 whose p. at one time were rehearsed
6 18 to nothing else but to prayers with her
7 13 God hath regarded my prayers and tears
Jdth 4 7 humbled their souls in fastings and p.
11 the Lord will hear your prayers if you
11 continue . . . in fastings and prayers
12 Moses . . . overcame . . . by holy prayers
6 14 and weeping poured out their prayers
Job 15 4 hast taken away p. from before God
16 18 when I offered pure prayers to God
Ps 33 16 just: and his ears unto their prayers
39 3 he heard my prayers, and brought me
Prov 6 35 nor will he yield to any man's prayers
15 29 he will hear the prayers of the just
Eccu 35 17 will not despise p. of the fatherless
36 18 and hear the prayers of thy servants
Jer 14 12 when they fast I will not hear their p.
Bar 2 14 hear, O Lord, our prayers and our
19 we pour out our prayers and beg mercy
Dan 9 17 supplication of thy servant, and his p.
18 that we present our p. before thy face
23 from the beginning of thy prayers
Zach 12 10 the spirit of grace and of prayers
2 Ma 1 5 may he hear your prayers and be
10 16 beseeching the Lord by p. to be their
12 24 with many prayers he besought them
42 betaking themselves to prayers they
15 26 encountered them, calling upon God by p.
Mat 23 14 houses of widows, praying long prayers
Luke 2 37 by fastings and p. serving night and
5 33 of John fast often and make prayers
Acts 2 42 the breaking of bread, and in prayers
10 4 thy prayers and thy alms are ascended
Rom 1 10 always in my p. making request, if by
15 30 help me in your prayers for me to God
Eph 1 16 making commemoration of you in my p.
Phil 1 4 always in all my p. making supplication
4 12 who is always solicitous for you in p.
1 Th 1 2 making a remembrance of you in our p.
1 Tim 2 1 p., intercessions, and thanksgivings be
5 5 continue in supplications and prayers
2 Tim 1 3 remembrance of thee in my p., night and
Philem 4 remembrance of thee in my prayers
22 I hope that through your prayers I shall
Heb 5 7 offering up prayers and supplications
1 P 3 7 that your prayers be not hindered
12 and his ears unto their prayers: but
4 7 prudent therefore, and watch in p.
Apoc 5 8 odors, which are the prayers of saints
8 3 should offer of the p. of all saints
4 incense of the prayers of the saints
prayest Eccu 28 2 forgiven to thee when thou p.
prayeth 3 K 8 28 which thy servant p. before thee
3 K 8 29 which thy servant prayeth in this place
2 Pa 6 21 prayer which thy servant prayeth in it
Wisd 13 18 for life prayeth to that which is dead
Eccu 34 29 when one prayeth and another curseth
Isa 44 17 prayeth unto it, saying: Deliver me
2 Ma 15 14 he that prayeth much for the people
Acts 9 11 Saul of Tarsus. For behold he prayeth
1 C 14 14 if I pray in a tongue, my spirit prayeth
praying Lev 4 20 priest p. for them, the Lord
Lev 5 13 praying for him and making atonement
16 11 praying for himself and for his own
21 praying that they may light on his head
Deut 9 26 p., I said: O Lord God, destroy not
1 K 1 26 stood before thee here p. to the Lord
3 K 8 35 they p. in this place, shall do penance
54 had made an end of p. all this prayer
1 Es 10 1 when Esdras was thus praying and
Jdth 7 4 praying with one accord, that the God
10 10 but Judith praying to the Lord, passed
13 6 Judith stood before the bed praying
Eccu 18 22 let nothing hinder thee from praying
Dan 6 11 found Daniel praying and making
9 20 while I was yet speaking and praying
2 Ma 1 6 and now here we are praying for you
3 18 p. and making public supplication
33 and when the high priest was praying
15 27 praying to the Lord with their hearts
Mat 6 7 when you are praying, speak not much
23 14 the houses of widows, p. long prayers
26 39 he fell upon his face, praying and
Luke 1 10 of the people was praying without at
3 21 Jesus also being baptized and praying
9 18 as he was alone praying, his disciples
11 1 as he was in a certain place praying
21 36 watch ye, therefore, p. at all times
Acts 1 24 praying, they said: Thou, Lord, who
6 6 they praying, imposed hands upon them
10 2 the people, and always praying to God
30 I was p. in my house, at ninth hour
11 5 I was in the city of Joppe praying
12 12 many were gathered together and p.
13 3 they fasting and p., and imposing their
16 25 at midnight, Paul and Silas praying
22 17 was p. in temple, that I was in a trance
1 C 11 4 every man praying or prophesying with
5 every woman p. or prophesying with her
2 C 9 14 in their p. for you, being desirous of
Eph 6 18 by all prayer and supplication praying
Col 1 3 Lord Jesus Christ, praying always for
4 3 praying withal for us also, that God
1 Th 3 10 night and day more abundantly praying
Jude 20 holy faith, praying in the Holy Ghost
preach 2 Es 6 7 to preach of thee at Jerusalem
Ps 67 12 word to them that preach good tidings
Prov 8 6 my lips shall be opened to p. right
Isa 61 1 he hath sent me to preach to the meek
1 to preach a release to the captives
Jon 1 2 Ninive the great city, and p. in it. 3:2
3 5 with their teeth, and preach peace
Mat 4 17 from that time Jesus began to preach
10 7 going, preach, saying: The kingdom of
27 the ear, preach ye upon the housetops
11 1 to teach and preach in their cities
Mark 1 38 cities, that I may preach there also
3 14 that he might send them to preach
16 15 preach the gospel to every creature
Luke 3 18 exhorting, did he preach to the people
4 18 to preach the gospel to the poor, he
19 to preach deliverance to the captives
19 to p. the acceptable year of the Lord
43 to other cities also I must preach
9 2 he sent them to preach the kingdom of
60 but go thou and p. the kingdom of God
Acts 5 42 to teach and preach Christ Jesus. And
10 42 he commanded us to p. to the people
15 21 them that p. him in the synagogues
16 6 forbidden by Holy Ghost to preach the
10 God had called us to preach the gospel
17 who p. unto you the way of salvation
21 preach a fashion which it is not lawful
17 3 Jesus Christ, whom I preach to you. And
23 without knowing it, that I preach to you
26 20 Judea, and to the Gentiles did I preach
Rom 1 15 I am ready to preach the gospel to you
10 8 this is the word of faith, which we p.
15 how shall they p. unless they be sent
15 beautiful are feet of them that preach
1 C 1 17 not to baptize, but to preach the gospel

23 but we preach Christ crucified, unto
9 14 that they who preach the gospel, should
16 if I preach the gospel, it is no glory
16 woe is unto me if I preach not gospel
15 11 so we preach, and so you have believed
2 C 4 5 we p. not ourselves, but Jesus Christ
10 16 beyond you, to preach the gospel, not
Gal 1 8 preach gospel to you besides that. 9
16 I might preach him among the Gentiles
23 now p. the faith which once he impugned
2 2 which I preach among the Gentiles, but
5 11 if I yet preach circumcision, why do I
Eph 3 8 this grace, to preach among the Gentiles
Phil 1 15 some also for good will preach Christ
17 some . . . preach Christ not sincerely
Col 1 28 whom we preach, admonishing every man
2 Tim 4 2 preach the word: be instant in season
Apoc 14 6 to preach unto them that sit upon the
preached Mat 11 5 poor have the gospel p. to them
Mat 24 14 shall be preached in the whole world
26 13 wheresoever this gospel shall be preached. Mark 14:9
Mark 1 7 he p., saying: There cometh after me
6 12 they p. that men should do penance
13 10 the gospel must first be preached. And
16 20 they going forth preached everywhere
Luke 7 22 to the poor the gospel is preached
12 3 shall be preached on the housetops
16 16 the kingdom of God is preached and
24 47 should be p. in his name unto all
Acts 3 20 he shall send him who hath been p.
4 2 p. in Jesus the resurrection from the
8 5 of Samaria, preached Christ unto them
25 having testified and p. the word of
25 p. the gospel to many countries of the
35 Philip . . . preached unto him Jesus
40 he preached the gospel to all the
9 20 he p. Jesus in the synagogues, that he
10 37 after the baptism which John preached
13 5 they p. word of God in the synagogues
38 forgiveness of sins is p. to you: and
14 20 when they had p. the gospel to that
15 36 we have p. the word of the Lord, to
16 32 they p. the word of the Lord to him
17 13 word of God was also p. by Paul at
18 because he p. to them Jesus and the
20 20 but have preached it to you, and taught
Rom 15 20 and I have so preached this gospel, not
1 C 9 27 lest perhaps, when I have p. to others
15 1 gospel which I preached to you, which
2 hold fast after what manner I preached
12 if Christ be preached, that he arose
2 C 1 19 Jesus Christ who was preached among you
11 4 other Christ, whom we have not preached
7 I p. unto you the gospel of God freely
Gal 1 8 besides that which we have p. to you
11 gospel which was preached by me is not
4 13 I preached the gospel to you heretofore
Eph 2 17 coming, he preached peace to you that
Phil 1 18 or by truth, Christ be preached; in this
Col 1 23 which is preached in all the creation
1 Th 2 9 we preached among you the gospel of God
1 Tim 3 16 hath been preached unto the Gentiles
Heb 4 6 they, to whom it was first preached, did
1 P 1 12 by them that have p. the gospel to you
25 by the gospel hath been p. unto you
3 19 he p. to those spirits that were in
4 6 was the gospel p. also to the dead
preacher Rom 10 14 how shall they hear, without a p.
1 Tim 2 7 I am appointed a preacher. 2 Tim 1:11
2 P 2 5 eighth person, the preacher of justice
preachest Rom 2 21 p. that men should not steal
preacheth Prov 1 20 wisdom p. abroad, she uttereth
Isa 52 7 tidings, and that p. peace. Nah 1:15
7 forth good, that preacheth salvation
Acts 19 13 I conjure you by Jesus, whom Paul p.
2 C 11 4 if he that cometh p. another Christ
preaching Ps 2 6 mountain, preaching his commandment
Jon 3 2 preach in it the preaching that I bid
Mat 3 1 Baptist preaching in the desert of Judea
4 23 p. gospel of the kingdom. 9:35; Mark 1:14
12 41 penance at the p. of Jonas. Luke 11:32
Mark 1 4 p. the baptism of penance. Luke 3:3
39 he was preaching in their synagogues
Luke 4 44 he was p. in the synagogues of Galilee
8 1 p. and evangelizing the kingdom of
9 6 p. the gospel and healing everywhere
20 1 in the temple, and p. the gospel, the
Acts 8 4 went about preaching the word of God
12 Philip p. of the kingdom of God, in
10 36 sent the word . . . p. peace by Jesus
11 20 spoke also to the Greeks, p. the Lord
13 24 John first p., before his coming, the
35 teaching and p., with many others, the
14 6 and were there preaching the gospel
14 men like unto you, p. to you to be
18 5 Paul was earnest in p., testifying to
20 9 deep sleep, as Paul was long preaching
25 preaching the kingdom of God. 28:31
Rom 16 25 p. of Jesus Christ, according to the
1 C 1 21 by the foolishness of our p., to save
2 4 and my speech and my p. was not in the
9 18 that p. the gospel, I may deliver gospel
15 14 then is our p. vain, and your faith is
2 C 1 18 our p. which was to you, was not, It is
2 Tim 4 17 by me the p. may be accomplished, and
Titus 1 3 manifested his word in preaching, which
precaution 1 K 13 19 Philistines had taken this precaution
precept Exod 40 23 according to p. of the Lord. Num 3:39
Lev 10 7 according to the precept of Moses
9 because it is an everlasting precept
23 14 it is a precept forever throughout
Num 15 31 the Lord made void his precept
19 21 this precept shall be an ordinance
1 Pa 16 17 appointed same to Jacob for a precept
2 Pa 29 15 according to . . . precept of the Lord
Ps 7 7 in the p. which thou hast commanded
Mark 10 5 he wrote you that precept. But from
Rom 16 26 according to p. of the eternal God, for
1 Tim 1 18 this precept I commend to thee, O son
preceptor 2 Ma 1 10 Aristobolus the p. of king
precepts Gen 26 5 and kept my precepts
Exod 15 26 commandments and keep all his p.
18 16 to show the precepts of God and his
23 shalt be able to bear his precepts
Lev 18 4 shall observe my precepts and shall
19 37 keep all my precepts and all my
20 8 keep my precepts and do them. I am
22 9 let them keep my precepts, that they
25 18 do my p. and keep my judgments
26 3 if you walk in my precepts and keep
45 precepts and laws which the Lord gave
27 34 the precepts which the Lord commanded
Num 15 40 mindful of the precepts of the Lord
27 20 thou shalt give him precepts in the
Deut 4 6 hearing all these precepts, they may
40 keep his precepts and commandments
6 1 these are the precepts and ceremonies
2 keep all his commandments and precepts
17 keep the precepts of the Lord thy
25 if we keep and do all his precepts
7 11 keep therefore the p. and ceremonies
11 1 observe his precepts and ceremonies
12 1 these are the precepts and judgments
13 18 keeping all his precepts, which I

26 13 commandments nor forgotten thy p.
17 and keep his ceremonies and precepts
28 2 thee: yet so if thou hear his precepts
30 10 and keep his precepts and ceremonies
2 K 22 23 his precepts I have not removed from me
3 K 2 3 observe his ceremonies and his p.
3 3 walking in the precepts of David his
14 walk in my ways and keep my precepts
11 11 not kept my covenant and my precepts
33 before me and to keep my precepts
34 kept my commandments and my precepts
38 keeping my commandments and my precepts
4 K 17 13 and keep my precepts and ceremonies
16 they forsook all the precepts of Lord
1 Pa 23 27 according to last precepts of David
2 Pa 13 11 for we keep the precepts of the Lord
2 Es 9 13 truth, ceremonies and good precepts
Tob 3 5 we have not done according to thy p.
Ps 118 40 I have longed after thy precepts
110 I have not erred from thy precepts
173 to save me; for I have chosen thy p.
Prov 7 1 and lay up my precepts with thee. Son
10 8 the wise of heart receiveth precepts
Eccu 6 37 thy thoughts be upon the p. of God
15 15 he added his commandments and precepts
24 33 commanded a law in the p. of justices
Jer 35 18 kept all his precepts and have done
Mala 4 4 Israel, the precepts and judgments
1 Ma 2 68 take heed to the precepts of the law
Mark 7 7 teaching doctrines and precepts of men
Acts 15 41 commanding them to keep the precepts
Col 2 22 according to the p. and doctrines of men
1 Th 4 2 you know what precepts I have given
2 P 3 2 the precepts of the Lord and Savior
precinct 4 K 11 8 enter the p. of the temple
4 K 11 15 without the p. of the temple. 2 Pa 23:14
precious 1 K 3 1 of the Lord was p. in those
1 K 26 21 my life hath been precious in thy eyes
4 K 20 13 divers precious odors and ointments
2 Pa 36 19 whatsoever was precious they destroyed
Job 28 10 his eye hath seen every precious thing
Ps 115 15 p. in the sight of the Lord is the
132 2 like the precious ointment on the head
Prov 1 13 we shall find all precious substance
3 15 she is more precious than all riches
6 26 the woman catcheth the p. soul of a man
8 19 is better than gold and the p. stone
12 27 substance of just man shall be p. gold
16 16 for it is more precious than silver
17 27 man of understanding is of a p. spirit
20 15 the lips of knowledge are a p. vessel
24 4 filled with all p. and most beautiful
Ecce 7 2 good name is better than p. ointments
10 1 wisdom and glory is more precious than
Wisd 3 14 the p. gift of faith shall be given to
7 9 did I compare unto her any p. stone
Eccu 41 15 thousand treasures precious and great
50 10 adorned with every precious stone
Isa 13 12 man shall be more precious than gold
28 16 a corner stone, a precious stone
39 2 odors and of the precious ointment
Jer 15 19 separate the precious from the vile
25 34 you shall fall like precious vessels
Lam 1 11 have given all their precious things
Eze 27 24 of embroidered work and of p. riches
28 13 every precious stone was thy covering
Dan 11 8 their p. vessels of gold and silver
43 and all the precious things of Egypt
Nah 2 9 riches of all the precious furniture
1 Ma 1 24 and the precious vessels: and he took
Mat 26 7 an alabaster box of precious ointment
Mark 14 3 box of ointment of precious spikenard
Acts 20 24 neither do I count my life more precious
James 5 7 husbandman waiteth for the p. fruit
1 P 1 7 faith, much more precious than gold
19 but with the precious blood of Christ
2 6 a chief corner stone, elect, precious
2 P 1 4 us most great and precious promises
Apoc 18 12 all manner of vessels of precious stone
21 11 light thereof was like to a p. stone
most precious 2 K 12 30 set with m. p. stones
1 Pa 20 2 weight of gold and most precious stones
2 Pa 3 6 most precious marble of great beauty
20 25 garments and most precious vessels
36 10 most precious vessels of the house of
Job 28 16 with the most precious stone sardonyx
Prov 8 11 better than all the most p. things
precious stones Exod 25 7 p. s. to adorn the ephod
Exod 31 5 of marble and precious stones and
35 9 p. s. for the adorning of the ephod
27 p. s. for the ephod and the rational
39 10 he set four rows of precious stones in
2 K 12 30 of gold set with most precious stones
3 K 10 2 quantity of gold and precious stones
10 spices a very great store, and p. s.
11 great plenty of thyine trees and p. s.
1 Pa 20 2 weight of gold and most precious stones
29 2 and all manner of precious stones
2 Pa 9 1 abundance of gold and precious stones
9 in great abundance, and most p. s.
10 thyine trees and most precious stones
32 27 of precious s., of spices, and of arms
Tob 13 21 walls thereof round about of p. s.
Jdth 10 19 with emeralds and precious stones
15 14 and silver and garments and p. s.
Esth 15 9 glittering with gold and precious s.
Ps 18 11 desired than gold and many precious s.
20 4 on his head a crown of precious stones
Eccu 45 13 with precious s. cut and set in gold
Eze 27 16 they set forth precious stones and
22 all the best spices and precious stones
Dan 11 38 worship with gold and silver and p. s.
1 C 3 12 build upon this foundation . . . p. s.
Apoc 17 4 gilt with gold and precious s. 18:16
18 12 merchandise of gold and silver and p. s.
21 19 adorned with all manner of p. stones
precipices Jdth 7 8 steep hills and p. guard
predecessors Deut 19 14 landmark which thy p. have
Esth 14 5 our fathers from all their predecessors
1 Ma 11 26 treated him as his p. had done before
predestinated Rom 1 4 was p. the Son of God
Rom 8 29 whom he foreknew, he also p. to be made
30 and whom he p., them he also called. And
Eph 1 5 who hath p. us unto the adoption of
11 being p. according to the purpose of him
prediction Eccu 49 8 according to p. of Jeremias
pre-eminence Deut 33 21 and he saw his p.
Eccu 7 4 seek not of the Lord a pre-eminence
33 23 in all thy works keep the pre-eminence
3 J 9 who loveth to have the pre-eminence
preface 2 Ma 2 33 this be enough by way of a p.
prefer Deut 21 16 p. him before the son of the
preferable Eccu 28 25 death: and hell is p. to it
preferably Bar 3 30 brought her p. to chosen gold
preferred Gen 29 30 he p. the love of the latter
3 K 2 15 all Israel had p. me to be their king
Wisd 7 8 I p. her before kingdoms and thrones
John 1 15 is preferred before me. 27, 30
preferreth Wisd 2 16 he p. the latter end of the
prefixed Dan 11 40 at the time p. the king of
pregnant 4 K 8 12 rip up their pregnant women
prejudice 1 Tim 5 21 observe these things without p.
prelates Heb 13 7 remember your p. who have
Heb 13 17 obey your prelates, and be subject to
24 salute all your p. and all the saints
preordained Acts 10 41 witnesses p. by God, even

Acts 22 14 God of our fathers hath p. thee that
preparation Ps 9 17 heard the p. of their heart
Ps 64 10 their food: for so is its preparation
88 15 are the preparation of thy throne
Nah 2 3 are flaming in the day of his p.
1 Ma 9 39 behold a tumult and great preparation
Mat 27 62 which followed the day of preparation
Eph 6 15 shod with the p. of the gospel of peace
preparations Jdth 2 8 he made all his warlike p.
Jdth 7 2 besides the preparations of those men
2 Ma 15 21 and the divers preparations of armor
prepare Gen 43 16 kill victims and p. a feast
Exod 25 26 shalt prepare also four golden rings
29 thou shalt prepare also dishes and
28 40 thou shalt prepare linen tunicks and
Num 23 1 seven altars, and p. as many calves. 29
Deut 20 9 every man shall prepare their bands
Josu 1 11 prepare you victuals: for after the third
3 12 prepare ye twelve men of the tribes
1 K 7 3 prepare your hearts unto the Lord
3 K 18 44 prepare thy chariot and go down, lest
4 K 18 20 taken counsel, to p. thyself for battle
1 Pa 9 32 prepare always new for every sabbath
22 5 therefore I will p. him necessaries
2 Pa 12 14 did not p. his heart to seek the Lord
31 11 Ezechias commanded to p. storehouses
35 4 and prepare yourselves by your houses
6 prepare your brethren that they may do
2 Es 4 8 against Jerusalem and to p. ambushes
Tob 7 18 and bade her prepare another chamber
8 21 prepare all kind of provisions that
Job 27 16 as earth, and prepare raiment as clay
17 he shall prepare indeed, but the just
Ps 20 13 in thy remnants thou shalt p. their
Prov 14 22 mercy and truth prepare good things
16 1 it is the part of man to p. the soul
24 27 p. thy work without, and diligently
Eccu 2 1 and prepare thy soul for temptation
20 fear the Lord, will p. their hearts
18 19 before judgment p. thee justice and
23 before prayer prepare thy soul: and be
33 4 shall prepare what to say, and so
47 15 name, and prepare a sanctuary forever
Isa 14 21 prepare his children for slaughter
21 5 prepare the table, behold in the
36 5 strength dost thou prepare for war
40 3 prepare ye the way of the Lord, make
62 10 prepare the way for the people, make
Jer 6 4 prepare ye war against her: arise and
12 3 prepare them for the day of slaughter
22 7 I will p. against thee the destroyer
33 2 will do and will form it and p. it
46 3 prepare ye the shield and buckler and
14 stand up and prepare thyself: for the
50 14 prepare yourselves against Babylon
51 12 the watchmen, prepare the ambushes
27 prepare the nations against her. 28
Eze 12 3 p. thee all necessaries for removing
38 7 prepare and make thyself ready, and
Dan 11 11 shall p. an exceeding great multitude
13 shall p. a multitude much greater
Joel 3 9 prepare war, rouse up the strong: let
Mich 3 5 mouth, they prepare war against him
Mala 3 1 he shall p. the way before my face
2 Ma 2 28 as they that prepare a feast and seek
Mat 3 3 prepare ye the way of the Lord. Mark 1:3; Luke 3:4
11 10 who shall prepare thy way before thee. Mark 1:2; Luke 7:27
26 17 where wilt thou that we p. Luke 22:9
Mark 14 12 and prepare for thee to eat the pasch
15 furnished; and there prepare ye for us
Luke 1 17 to p. unto the Lord a perfect people
76 face of the Lord to prepare his ways
9 52 city of the Samaritans to p. for him
22 8 go, and prepare for us the pasch. that
12 dining room furnished; and there p.
John 14 2 because I go to p. a place for you
3 if I shall go and prepare a place for
1 C 14 8 who shall prepare himself to the battle
2 C 9 5 prepare this blessing before promised
Philem 22 but withal prepare me also a lodging
prepared Gen 24 31 I have prepared the house and
Gen 24 44 whom the Lord hath prepared for my
Exod 23 20 into the place that I have prepared
26 12 the curtains, that are p. for the roof
17 this manner shall all the boards be p.
38 3 he prepared divers vessels of brass
13 he prepared hangings of fifty cubits
39 6 he prepared also two onyx stones, fast
Num 21 18 and the chiefs of the people prepared
Judg 16 12 there being an ambush p. for him
19 8 Levite prepared to go on his journey
20 17 that drew swords and were p. to fight
36 to the ambushes that were prepared
1 K 2 3 and to him are thoughts prepared
9 25 he [Samuel] prepared a bed for Saul
17 8 why are you come out prepared to fight
21 who stood against them were prepared
23 9 that Saul secretly p. evil against him
28 1 to be prepared for war against Israel
2 K 10 9 seeing that the battle was p. against
3 K 5 18 the Giblians p. timber and stones to
4 K 10 24 Jehu had p. him fourscore men without
1 Pa 12 35 of Dan also 28,600 prepared for battle
39 for their brethren had prepared for
15 3 place, which he had prepared for it
12 to the place which is prepared for it
22 3 p. in abundance iron for the nails
5 before his death he p. all the charges
14 I in my poverty have p. the charges
14 and stones I have prepared for all
28 2 I prepared all things for the building
29 1 a house is p. not for man but for God
2 I have p. the expenses for the house
3 what things I have p. for the holy
16 that we have p. to build thee a house
2 Pa 1 4 place, which he had prepared for it
3 1 the place which David had prepared in
8 16 Solomon had all charges prepared, from
16 6 timber that Baasa had prepared for the
17 13 he p. many works in the cities of Juda
19 3 hast prepared thy heart to seek the
26 14 Ozias prepared for them . . . shields
29 27 which David the king of Israel had p.
35 10 and the ministry was prepared and the
14 wherefore the Levites p. for themselves
15 the Levites prepared meats for them
22 Josias would not return but p. to fight
1 Es 7 10 Esdras had p. his heart to seek the law
8 10 send portions to them that have not p.
2 Es 5 18 was p. for me day by day one ox and
Tob 2 1 a good dinner was p. in Tobias' house
7 9 be killed, and a feast to be prepared
8 13 and when they had prepared the pit
22 a banquet to be prepared for all his
Jdth 2 9 he appointed corn to be prepared out of
5 1 children of Israel prepared themselves
7 3 all these prepared themselves together
9 5 for all thy ways are prepared, and in
12 19 what her maid had prepared for her
Job 15 24 as a king that is p. for the battle
28 27 he saw it and declared and prepared
29 7 in the street they prepared me a chair
38 23 which I have p. for the time of the
Ps 7 14 he hath p. the instruments of death

9 8 he hath prepared his throne in judgment
16 fast in the destruction which they p.
10 3 they have p. their arrows in the quiver
16 12 taken me, as a lion p. for the prey
22 5 thou hast prepared a table before me
23 2 and hath prepared it upon the rivers
32 14 from his habitation which he hath p.
56 7 they prepared a snare for my feet
64 10 thou hast prepared their food; for so
88 3 thy truth shall be prepared in them
92 2 thy throne is prepared from of old
98 4 thou hast p. directions; thou hast done
102 19 the Lord hath p. his throne in heaven
131 17 I have prepared a lamp for my anointed
Prov 7 10 in harlot's attire p. to deceive souls
8 27 when he p. the heavens, I was present
19 29 judgments are prepared for scorners
21 31 the horse is p. for the day of battle
Ecce 2 10 in the things which I had prepared
Wisd 9 8 which thou hast p. from the beginning
16 20 bread from heaven p. without labor
Eccu 26 27 God hath p. such a one for the sword
30 27 his banquets are p. with diligence
45 26 he p. them bread in the first place
49 14 to the Lord, p. for everlasting glory
51 4 them that did roar, prepared to devour
Isa 2 2 shall be p. on the top of the mountains
16 5 a throne shall be prepared in mercy
30 33 is p. from yesterday, p. by the king
51 13 had prepared himself to destroy thee
52 10 the Lord hath prepared his holy arm
64 4 what things thou hast prepared for them
Jer 6 23 prepared as men for war, against thee
50 9 they shall be prepared against her
42 like a man prepared for battle against
51 15 that hath p. the world by his wisdom
Bar 3 32 he that p. the earth for evermore
Eze 28 13 thy pipes were prepared in the day
Osee 6 3 his going forth is prepared as the
Joel 2 5 a strong people prepared to battle
Amos 4 12 be prepared to meet thy God, O Israel
Jon 2 1 the Lord p. a great fish to swallow up
4 6 the Lord God prepared an ivy, and it
7 God prepared a worm, when the morning
Mich 4 1 shall be p. in the top of mountains
Nah 2 5 and a covering shall be prepared. The
Soph 1 7 for the Lord hath prepared a victim
1 Ma 7 29 were p. to take away Judas by force
2 Ma 5 1 p. for a second journey into Egypt
12 3 into the boats which they had prepared
Mat 20 23 to them for whom it is p. Mark 10:40
22 4 behold, I have prepared my dinner; my
25 34 possess you the kingdom p. for you
41 which was p. for the devil and his
26 19 and they p. the pasch. Mark 14:16
Luke 2 31 which thou hast p. before the face of
12 47 will of his Lord and p. not himself
23 56 they prepared spices and ointments
24 1 bringing the spices which they had p.
Acts 21 15 being prepared we went up to Jerusalem
23 30 ambushes that they had p. for him, I
Rom 9 23 of mercy, which he hath p. unto glory
1 C 2 9 what things God hath prepared for them
Eph 2 10 God hath prepared that we should walk in
2 Tim 2 21 prepared unto every good work. But flee
Heb 11 16 their God; for he hath p. for them city
Apoc 8 6 p. themselves to sound the trumpet. And
9 7 like unto horses prepared unto battle
15 who were p. for an hour and a day and
12 6 where she had a place prepared by God
16 12 that a way might be prepared for the
12 a way might be p. for the kings from
19 7 is come, and his wife hath p. herself

21 2 p. as a bride adorned for her husband
preparest Ps 64 7 who p. the mountains by thy
prepareth Job 15 35 and his womb p. deceits
Ps 28 9 voice of the Lord prepareth the stags
146 8 with clouds, and p. rain for the earth
Prov 11 19 clemency p. life: and the pursuing of
Jer 10 12 that p. the world by his wisdom and
Haba 2 12 and prepareth a city by iniquity. Are
preparing Exod 12 39 think of preparing any meat
Exod 35 28 for the preparing of ointment and to
Wisd 16 2 p. for them quails for their meat
1 Ma 5 11 they are p. to come and to take the
Acts 10 10 as they were p., there came upon him
prepuces 1 Ma 1 16 they made themselves prepuces
prescribe 2 Es 9 14 didst p. to them commandments
prescribed 1 Pa 23 31 ceremonies p. for every thing
1 Pa 29 21 every thing prescribed most abundantly
2 Pa 30 5 had not kept it as it is prescribed
presence Gen 23 11 p. of the children of my people
Gen 23 13 spoke to Ephron in p. of the people
25 18 died in presence of all his brethren
42 25 binding him [Simeon] in their presence
47 15 why should we die in thy presence
Exod 8 26 in their presence, they will stone us
9 8 sprinkle it in the air in p. of Pharao
10 11 they were cast out from Pharao's p.
18 going forth from the presence of Pharao
35 20 going out from the presence of Moses
Num 3 4 priestly office in presence of Aaron
Josu 17 4 they came in the presence of Eleazar
1 K 18 11 David stept aside out of his presence
19 10 slipt away out of the presence of Saul
21 15 to play the madman in my presence
2 K 24 4 went out from the presence of the king
1 Pa 16 30 all the earth be moved at his presence
37 to minister in the presence of the ark
2 Pa 6 12 in p. of all multitude of Israel. 13
20 9 we will stand in thy presence before
Jdth 6 12 and in the presence of all the people
10 13 I will go to the presence of the prince
17 when she was come into his presence
13 25 prevented our ruin in the p. of our God
Esth 1 10 eunuchs that served in his presence
19 let an edict go out from thy presence
7 8 will force the queen also in my p.
8 15 palace and from the king's presence
14 13 in my mouth in the p. of the lion
Job 1 12 Satan went forth from the p. 2:7
13 16 no hypocrite shall come before his p.
23 15 I am troubled at his presence, and when
Ps 67 3 let the wicked perish at the presence
5 the wicked shall be troubled at his p.
9 at the presence of the God of Sina
9 at the presence of the God of Israel
94 2 let us come before his presence with
96 5 like wax, at the presence of the Lord
97 9 shall rejoice together at p. of the
99 2 come in before his presence with
113 7 at p. of the Lord the earth was moved
7 at the presence of the God of Jacob
Cant 8 10 in his presence as one finding peace
Wisd 14 17 whom men could not honor in presence
Eccu 29 33 the honorable presence of my friends
34 24 sacrificeth son in the p. of his father
36 4 be magnified among them in our presence
Isa 10 27 putrify at the presence of the oil
19 1 idols of Egypt shall be moved at his p.
26 17 pangs: so are we become in thy presence
51 13 at the presence of his fury who
63 9 the angel of his presence saved them
64 1 the mountains would melt away at thy p.
2 the nations might tremble at thy p.
3 at thy p. the mountains melted away

Jer 1 8 be not afraid at their presence. 17
4 26 were destroyed at the p. of the Lord
26 at p. of the wrath of his indignation
5 22 will you not repent at my presence
15 17 a boast of the presence of thy hand
23 9 man full of wine, at the p. of the Lord
9 at the presence of his holy words
39 to your fathers, out of my presence
28 5 in the presence of all the people. 11
32 12 in p. of the witnesses that subscribed
34 18 which they agreed to in my presence
37 11 there in the presence of the citizen
52 3 till he cast them out from his presence
Bar 4 2 in the presence of the light thereof
Eze 3 9 neither be thou dismayed at their p.
12 4 forth in the evening in their presence
38 20 earth, shall be moved at my presence
Dan 1 19 and they stood in the king's presence
7 8 horns were plucked up at the p. thereof
Joel 2 6 at their presence the people shall be
10 at their p. the earth hath trembled
Nah 1 5 the earth hath quaked at his presence
Zach 2 13 flesh be silent at the p. of the Lord
1 Ma 1 19 Ptolemee was afraid at his presence
2 Ma 3 24 gave a great evidence of his presence
12 22 struck with fear by the presence of God
15 27 greatly cheered with the p. of God
Luke 13 26 have eaten and drunk in thy presence
Acts 3 20 shall come from the p. of the Lord
5 41 went from the presence of the council
1 C 16 17 I rejoice in the presence of Stephanas
2 C 10 1 who in p. indeed am lowly among you, but
10 but his bodily presence is weak, and his
Phil 2 12 not as in my presence only, but much
1 Th 2 19 are not you, in the presence of our Lord
Heb 9 24 may appear now in the p. of God for us
2 P 1 16 the power and presence of our Lord
Jude 24 spotless before the p. of his glory
Apoc 8 2 seven angels standing in the p. of God
20 12 standing in the presence of the throne
present Gen 4 7 shall not sin forthwith be p.
Gen 15 16 not at the full until this present time
24 53 he gave them to Rebecca for a present
31 50 but God, who is present and beholdeth
32 18 sent them as a present to my lord Esau
33 10 receive a little present at my hands
40 13 and thou shalt present him the cup
21 to his place to present him the cup
45 1 no stranger be present at their knowing
50 20 exalt me, as at present you see
Exod 9 18 was founded, until this present time
22 14 or die, the owner not being present
15 if the owner be present, he shall not
29 10 thou shalt present also the calf before
Lev 8 34 as at this present it hath been done
16 10 he shall present alive before the Lord
Num 6 16 the priest shall present them before
Deut 4 7 as our God is p. to all our petitions
20 inheritance, as it is this present day
38 as thou seest at this present day
5 3 us, who are now present and living
8 18 fathers, as this present day showeth
10 5 they are there till this present, as
12 9 until this present time you are not
29 4 ears that may hear, unto this p. day
15 with all that are present and that are
Josu 5 12 ate of the corn of the present year
9 27 carrying water, until this present time
Judg 20 34 understood not that p. death threatened
1 K 9 7 we have no present to make to the man
13 16 the people that were present with them
2 K 20 4 third day, and be thou here present
4 K 5 26 was not my heart present when the man
8 6 day that she left the land to this p.
16 8 for a present to king of the Assyrians
1 Pa 15 13 struck us, because you were not present
29 17 thy people, which are here present
2 Pa 6 15 as also the present time proveth. Now
18 4 inquire . . . at present the word of the
Job 1 6 Satan also was present among them. And
Ps 138 8 I descend into hell, thou art present
Prov 3 28 thee: when thou canst give at present
8 12 and am present in learned thoughts
27 when he prepared the heavens, I was p.
21 14 a secret present quencheth anger: and
Wisd 2 6 us enjoy the good things that are p.
4 2 when it is present, they imitate it
9 9 which then also was present when thou
11 12 whether absent or present, they were
14 17 they might honor as present, him that
Eccu 32 13 when the ancients are present, speak
43 24 a present remedy of all is the speedy
44 4 and ruling over the present people
Isa 18 7 at that time shall a present be brought
Jer 36 7 may present their supplication before
42 9 to p. your supplications before him
Lam 1 22 let all their evil be p. before thee
Bar 6 40 they present him to Bel, entreating
Dan 9 18 we present our prayers before thy face
Osee 10 6 Assyria, a present to the avenging king
Amos 2 12 you will present wine to the Nazarites
Zach 3 7 that are now present here to walk
1 Ma 15 8 the king's hereafter, from this present
2 Ma 3 23 himself being present in the same
4 18 kept at Tyre, the king being present
6 26 though for the present time I should
7 9 destroyest us out of this present life
14 19 to present and receive the right hands
Luke 2 22 to Jerusalem to p. him to the Lord
13 1 there were present at that very time
18 30 receive much more in this p. time
John 13 19 at present I tell you, before it come
Acts 2 29 sepulcher is with us to this p. day
10 33 all we are present in thy sight, to hear
13 31 who to this p. are his witnesses to
23 33 did also present Paul before him. And
24 19 certain Jews of Asia, who ought to be p.
25 16 he who is accused have his accusers p.
24 Agrippa, and all ye men who are here p.
28 2 because of the p. rain, and of the cold
Rom 6 13 present yourselves to God, as those that
7 18 for to will, is present with me; but to
21 have a will to do good, evil is p. with
8 38 powers, nor things present, nor things
11 5 even so then at this present time also
12 1 you p. your bodies a living sacrifice
1 C 3 22 world, or life, or death, or things p.
5 3 I indeed, absent in body, but p. in
3 already judged, as though I were present
7 26 that this is good for present necessity
8 7 some until this p., with conscience of
15 6 of whom many remain until this present
2 C 4 17 that which is at p. momentary and light
5 8 rather from the body, and to be present
9 we labor, whether absent or present, to
8 14 in this present time let your abundance
10 2 that I may not be bold when I am present
11 such also we will be indeed when present
11 2 present you as a chaste virgin to Christ
9 when I was p. with you, and wanted, I
13 2 I have told before, and foretell, as p.
10 being p., I may not deal more severely
Gal 1 4 deliver us from this p. wicked world
4 18 and not only when I am present with you
20 I would willingly be present with you
Eph 5 27 might p. it to himself a glorious church

Col 1 22 to present you holy and unspotted, and
28 that we may present every man perfect
2 Tim 2 15 study to p. thyself approved unto God
Heb 9 9 which is a parable of the time present
12 11 now all chastisement for the present
2 P 1 12 and are confirmed in the present truth
Jude 24 to present you spotless before the
until this present day Exod 10 6 time they were first upon the earth u. . . .
Deut 3 14 is to say, to towns of Jair, u. . . .
4 4 the Lord your God, are all alive u. . . .
10 8 and to bless in his name u. . . .
11 4 and how the Lord destroyed them u. . . .
34 6 man hath known of his sepulcher u. . . .
Josu 5 9 of that place was called Galgal u. . . .
6 25 in the midst of Israel u. . . . 13:13
7 26 of stones which remaineth u. . . . 8:29
14 10 granted me life as he promised u. . . .
14 the son of Jephone the Cenezite u. . . .
15 63 children of Juda in Jerusalem u. . . .
22 3 your brethren this long time u. . . .
Judg 1 21 sons of Benjamin in Jerusalem u. . . .
6 24 and called it the Lord's peace, u. . . .
Jdth 14 6 the succession of his kindred u. . . .
Acts 23 1 conscience before God until this p. day
Rom 11 8 should not hear, until this present day
2 C 3 14 until this present day, the selfsame
presented Gen 47 2 he presented before the king
Gen 47 7 father to the king, and presented him
Lev 14 11 purifieth the man, hath presented him
Judg 3 17 and he presented the gifts to Eglon
18 when he had presented the gifts unto
6 19 under the oak, and presented to him
1 K 15 32 Agag was presented to him very fat
17 16 and evening, and p. himself forty days
2 K 13 11 when she had p. him the meat, he took
2 Pa 25 21 p. themselves to be seen by one another
Jer 25 17 I p. it to all the nations to drink
38 26 I p. my supplication before the king
Eze 20 28 there they p. the provocation of their
Dan 7 13 and they presented him before him
1 Ma 11 35 the crowns that were presented to us
Mat 4 24 they presented to him all sick people
19 13 then were little children presented
Luke 23 14 you have presented unto me this man
Acts 9 41 and the widows, he presented her alive
presenteth Lev 22 18 whatsoever it be which he p.
Haba 2 15 p. his gall, and maketh him drunk
presenting Dan 9 20 p. my supplications in the
2 Ma 14 4 presenting unto him a crown of gold
Acts 16 20 p. them to the magistrates, they said
presently Gen 41 35 years, that shall now p. ensue
Gen 42 15 I shall now presently try what you are
Exod 9 19 send therefore now presently and gather
33 5 now presently lay aside thy ornaments
Lev 25 12 as they grow you shall presently eat
Num 11 23 shalt presently see whether my word
16 21 that I may presently destroy them
Deut 13 9 thou shalt presently put him to death
24 13 thou shalt restore it to him presently
Josu 2 7 gone out, the gate was presently shut
11 10 presently turning back he took Asor
Judg 12 6 presently they took him and killed him
15 5 they p. went into the standing corn
1 K 20 31 presently send and fetch him to me
2 K 10 18 the captain of the army, who p. died
11 4 presently she was purified from her
4 K 3 27 p. they departed from him and returned
2 Pa 26 19 presently there rose a leprosy in his
Tob 5 3 shalt show him, he will presently pay
11 6 afar off and p. perceived it was her
8 that his eyes shall be presently opened
Job 8 6 he will presently awake unto thee
Ps 36 20 presently after they shall be honored
69 4 let them be presently turned away
Prov 6 15 his destruction shall presently come
Wisd 5 12 the divided air p. cometh together
16 27 with a little sunbeam, p. melted away
Dan 3 8 p. at that very time some Chaldeans
13 29 and presently they sent. And she came
14 38 angel of the Lord presently set Habacuc
Mala 3 1 p. the Lord, whom you seek, and the
2 Ma 6 13 long time, but are presently punished
Mat 13 21 of the word, he is p. scandalized
21 20 how is it presently withered away
26 53 he will give me presently more than
Mark 2 8 Jesus presently knowing in his spirit
4 17 for the word, they are p. scandalized
9 14 presently all the people seeing Jesus
Luke 5 39 old, hath presently a mind to new
12 54 presently you say: A shower is coming
21 9 but the end is not yet presently
John 6 21 and presently the ship was at the land
11 44 presently he that had been dead came
Acts 10 16 and presently the vessel was taken up
James 1 24 p. forgot what manner of man he was
presents Gen 32 13 presents for his brother Esau
Gen 32 20 I will appease him with the presents
21 so the presents went before him, but
43 11 and carry down presents to the man
15 so the men took the presents and
25 but they made ready the presents
26 and they offered him the presents
Num 22 40 he sent presents to Balaam and to the
Judg 3 15 sent presents to Eglon king of Moab
1 K 10 27 despised him and brought him no p.
30 26 sent presents of prey to the ancients
3 K 4 21 they brought him [Solomon] presents
10 25 and every one brought him presents
13 7 to dine, and I will make thee presents
15 19 I have sent thee presents of silver
4 K 8 8 said to Hazael: Take with thee presents
9 Hazael . . . taking with him presents
20 12 sent letters and presents to Ezechias
2 Pa 9 24 every year they brought him presents
17 5 all Juda brought presents to Josaphat
11 the Philistines also brought presents
32 23 presents to Ezechias king of Juda
Esth 12 5 gave him presents for the information
Ps 67 30 kings shall offer presents to thee
71 10 kings of Tharsis . . . shall offer p.
75 12 you that are round about him bring p.
Prov 22 9 maketh presents shall purchase victory
Eccu 20 31 p. and gifts blind the eyes of judges
Isa 39 1 sent letters and presents to Ezechias
45 13 not for ransom nor for presents, saith
Jer 40 5 gave him victuals and presents and let
1 Ma 2 18 gold and silver and many presents
10 60 much silver and gold and presents
11 24 and raiment and many other presents
12 43 and gave him [Jonathan] presents
2 Ma 1 35 the priests many good and divers p.
preservation Gen 45 5 into Egypt for your p.
Eccu 34 20 a p. from stumbling and a help from
preserve Gen 19 32 we may p. seed of our father
2 Pa 9 8 loveth Israel and will preserve them
Ps 11 8 O Lord, wilt preserve us: and keep
15 1 p. me, O Lord, for I have put my trust
35 7 men and beasts thou wilt p., O Lord
40 3 Lord preserve him and give him life
85 2 preserve my soul, for I am holy: save
Prov 2 11 thee, and prudence shall preserve thee
4 6 love her, and she shall preserve thee
5 2 and thy lips may preserve instruction
14 3 but the lips of the wise preserve them
20 28 mercy and truth preserve the king

22 12 eyes of the Lord preserve knowledge
Wisd 9 11 and shall preserve me by her power
Eccu 15 16 fidelity forever, they shall p. thee
17 18 shall p. the grace of a man as the
Eze 34 16 was fat and strong I will preserve
2 Ma 1 26 p. thy own portion and sanctify it
3 15 kept, that he would preserve them safe
22 to p. the things that had been
Luke 17 33 whosoever shall lose it, shall p. it
2 Tim 4 18 will p. me unto his heavenly kingdom
Jude 24 is able to preserve you without sin
preserved Gen 45 7 that you may be p. upon the
Josu 24 17 preserved us in all the way by which
Ruth 4 14 that his name should be p. in Israel
2 K 8 6 Lord p. David in all his enterprises
14 Lord p. David in all enterprises he
1 Pa 18 13 the Lord preserved David in all things
Job 10 12 thy visitation hath preserved my spirit
Ps 36 28 his saints: they shall be p. forever
Wisd 10 1 she p. him, that was first formed by
5 and preserved him without blame to God
11 26 or be preserved if not called by thee
Eccu 10 21 hath p. the memory of them that are
44 27 he preserved for him men of mercy
51 3 and hast p. my body from destruction
Isa 42 6 taken thee by the hand and p. thee
49 8 I have p. thee and given thee to be a
Osee 12 13 and he was preserved by a prophet
Mala 3 15 and they have tempted God and are p.
Mat 9 17 bottles: and both are p. Luke 5:38
1 Th 5 23 may be p. blameless in the coming of our
2 P 2 5 but preserved Noe, the eighth person
Jude 1 preserved in Jesus Christ, and called
preserveth Ps 96 10 the Lord p. the souls of
Wisd 16 26 thy word p. them that believe in thee
Jer 5 24 who p. for us the fulness of the yearly
1 J 5 18 the generation of God preserveth him
preside Deut 17 10 shall say, that p. in the place
presided Judg 8 28 for forty years, while Gedeon p.
1 Pa 15 22 presided over the prophecy, to give
presiding 1 K 19 20 Samuel presiding over them
press Judg 13 16 if thou press me, I will not eat
2 K 16 8 thy evils press upon thee, because thou
Job 11 10 things or shall press them together
Eccu 31 42 and press him not in demanding again
Isa 16 10 shall not tread out wine in the press
Joel 2 8 no one shall press upon his brother
3 13 and go down, for the press is full
Agge 2 17 you went into the press, to press out
Mat 21 33 dug in it a press and built a tower and
Luke 8 45 the multitudes throng and press thee
Phil 3 14 I press towards the mark, to the prize
Apoc 14 19 the great press of the wrath of God
20 the press was trodden without the city
20 blood came out of the press up to the
pressed Gen 19 3 he p. them very much to turn in
Gen 19 9 they pressed very violently upon Lot
15 the angels pressed him, saying: Arise
40 11 grapes, and pressed them into the cup
Exod 5 13 overseers of the works pressed them
12 33 pressed the people to go forth out of
Num 6 3 thing that is pressed out of the grape
Judg 11 5 and as they pressed hard upon them
16 16 and when she pressed him much and
19 7 father-in-law earnestly pressed him
2 K 13 25 when he pressed him, and he would not
27 Absalom pressed him, so that he let
4 K 2 17 they pressed him till he consented
5 16 when he pressed him, he still refused
Tob 10 10 when Raguel had pressed Tobias with
Wisd 19 3 whom they had pressed to be gone: for
Eze 23 3 there were their breasts pressed down
21 then thy breasts were pressed in Egypt
Dan 14 29 that they pressed upon him violently
1 Ma 9 7 the battle pressed upon him, and his
10 49 after him and pressed them close. And
11 40 he pressed him much to deliver him
2 Ma 6 18 was pressed to open his mouth to eat
Mark 3 10 they pressed upon him for to touch him
Luke 5 1 pressed upon him to hear the word
6 38 good measure and p. down and shaken
2 C 1 8 that we were p. out of measure above our
presses 2 Es 13 15 treading the p. on the sabbath
Ps 8 1 unto the end, for the presses: a psalm
Prov 3 10 thy presses shall run over with wine
Jer 48 33 taken away the wine out of the presses
Joel 2 24 presses shall overflow with wine and oil
presseth Prov 6 13 p. with the foot, speaketh with
Wisd 9 15 presseth down the mind that museth
2 C 5 14 for the charity of Christ presseth us
pressing Gen 33 11 at his brother's earnest p.
Exod 12 39 the Egyptians pressing them to depart
Job 41 6 with scales pressing upon one another
presume Num 8 19 if they should p. to approach
Jdth 6 15 humblest them that p. of themselves
Ps 9 18 may no more presume to magnify himself
presumed Jdth 14 12 have presumed to challenge us
2 Ma 3 24 that all that had presumed to obey him
4 2 he presumed to call him a traitor
5 15 he p. also to enter into the temple
presuming Jdth 9 17 to thee, and p. of thy mercy
presumption Ecce 6 9 is vanity and p. of spirit
Eccu 18 10 seen the presumption of their heart
35 24 of Adam, and according to his p.
37 3 wicked presumption, whence camest thou
2 Ma 5 18 and put back from his presumption
presumptuous Ecce 7 9 the patient man than the p.
pretence Mark 12 40 under pretence of long prayer
pretendeth Eccu 12 18 while he p. to help thee
pretending 2 Ma 5 25 come to Jerusalem, p. peace
prevail Gen 32 28 more shalt thou p. against men
1 K 2 9 no man shall p. by his own strength
17 9 if I prevail against him and kill him
26 25 do, and prevailing thou shalt prevail
3 K 22 22 thou shalt deceive him and shalt p.
2 Pa 14 11 God, let not man prevail against thee
18 21 thou shalt go out and shalt prevail
Tob 6 16 they are, over whom the devil can p.
Ps 128 2 but they could not prevail over me
Ecce 4 12 and if a man prevail against one, two
Isa 7 1 but they could not prevail over it
16 12 sanctuaries to pray, and shall not p.
29 20 for he that did prevail hath failed
42 13 he shall prevail against his enemies
Jer 1 19 against thee and shall not prevail
5 22 toss themselves and shall not prevail
15 20 against thee, and shall not prevail
20 10 and we may prevail against him and be
Eze 22 14 shall thy hands prevail in the days
Dan 11 5 one of his princes shall prevail over
7 he shall abuse them and shall prevail
8 shall p. against the king of the north
12 thousands: but he shall not prevail
32 that know their God shall prevail and
1 Ma 5 40 for he will certainly prevail over us
41 to them and shall prevail against him
Mat 16 18 the gates of hell shall not prevail
John 12 19 do you see that we prevail nothing
prevailed Gen 7 19 the waters p. beyond measure
Gen 7 24 the waters prevailed upon the earth
30 8 with my sister, and I have prevailed
41 54 famine prevailed in the whole world
1 K 17 50 David prevailed over the Philistine
2 K 11 23 said to David: the men p. against us
24 4 but the king's words p. over the words
3 K 16 22 that were with Amri p. over the people

4 K 3 26 that the enemies had prevailed, he
14 10 hast beaten and prevailed over Edom
25 3 and a famine prevailed in the city
1 Pa 21 4 but the king's word rather prevailed
2 Pa 13 7 and they prevailed against Roboam
Job 30 13 have p. and there was none to help
Ps 12 5 my enemy say: I have p. against him
51 9 of his riches: and p. in his vanity
64 4 words of the wicked have p. over us
140 6 shall hear my words, for they have p.
Eccu 50 5 he prevailed to enlarge the city and
Isa 29 5 them that have prevailed against thee
7 and besieged and prevailed against it
Jer 20 7 been stronger than I, and thou hast p.
35 14 not to drink wine, have prevailed
38 22 have prevailed against thee: they have
Lam 1 16 desolate because the enemy hath p.
Dan 7 21 against the saints, and p. over them
Osee 12 4 he prevailed over the angel and was
Abdi 7 men of thy peace have p. against thee
1 Ma 6 54 few, for the famine had p. over them
7 25 Alcimus saw that Judas . . . prevailed
2 Ma 15 5 he p. not to accomplish his design
Mat 27 24 Pilate seeing that he p. nothing, but
Luke 23 23 crucified; and their voices prevailed
Acts 19 16 mastering them both, p. against them
Apoc 5 5 hath prevailed to open the book and to
12 8 they p. not, neither was their place
prevaileth Haba 1 4 wicked p. against the just
prevailing 1 K 26 25 and p. thou shalt prevail
Wisd 14 16 wicked custom p., this error was kept
prevaricated Isa 24 16 have p., and with the prevarication of transgressors they have p.
Eze 18 24 by which he hath prevaricated and
prevarication Isa 24 16 the p. of transgressors
Lam 1 7 and p. of all her desirable things
Eze 18 24 in the prevarication by which he hath
prevarications Eze 21 24 have discovered your p.
prevaricator Gal 2 18 destroyed, I make myself a p.
prevaricators Ps 118 119 sinners of the earth p.
Isa 24 16 the prevaricators have prevaricated
Dan 3 32 enemies that are unjust . . . and p.
11 14 the children of p. of thy people
prevent 3 K 18 44 go down, lest the rain p. thee
Ps 58 11 my God, his mercy shall prevent me
78 8 let thy mercies speedily prevent us
87 14 in the morning my prayer shall p. thee
Wisd 16 28 that we ought to prevent the sun to
1 Ma 6 27 unless thou speedily prevent them
1 Th 4 14 shall not prevent them who have slept
prevented 2 K 22 6 snares of death p. me. Ps 17:6
2 K 22 19 he p. me in the day of my affliction
4 K 6 10 man of God had told him, and p. him
Jdth 13 25 but hast prevented our ruin in the
Job 30 27 days of affliction have prevented me
Ps 17 19 they p. me in the day of my affliction
20 4 thou hast prevented him with blessings
76 5 my eyes prevented the watches: I was
118 147 I prevented the dawning of the day
148 my eyes to thee have p. the morning
Wisd 4 7 the just man, if he be p. with death
1 Ma 10 23 that Alexander hath p. us to gain the
2 Ma 14 31 finding himself notably prevented by
Mat 17 24 Jesus p. him [Peter], saying: What is
preventeth Wisd 6 14 she p. them that covet her
preventing Rom 12 10 with honor p. one another
prey Gen 49 9 to the prey, my son, thou art gone
Gen 49 27 in the morning shall eat the prey, and
Num 14 31 they should be a prey to the enemies
23 24 not lie down till it devour the prey
Deut 3 7 spoils of the cities we took for our p.
20 14 shalt divide all the prey to the army
Josu 8 2 the cattle you shall take for a prey
27 divided among them the cattle and the p.
22 8 divide the prey of your enemies
Judg 5 30 are given to Sisara for his prey, and
1 K 14 30 if the people had eaten of the prey
15 19 but hast turned to the prey and hast
30 8 overtake them and recover the prey
16 keeping festival day, for all the prey
20 they said: This is the prey of David
22 not give them anything of the prey
26 sent presents of prey to the ancients
26 receive a blessing of the prey of the
4 K 21 14 they shall become a prey and a spoil
2 Pa 15 11 that day of the spoils and of the prey
Jdth 4 9 their children might not be made a prey
9 3 gavest their wives to be made a prey
10 12 I knew they would be made a prey to you
16 6 to make my infants a prey, and my
Job 4 11 the tiger hath perished for want of prey
9 26 fruits, as an eagle flying to the prey
17 5 he promiseth a prey to his companions
24 5 by watching for a prey they get bread
29 17 out of his teeth I took away the prey
38 39 wilt thou take the prey for the lioness
Ps 16 12 me, as a lion prepared for the prey
Job 39 29 from thence she looketh for the prey
Ps 103 21 young lions roaring after their prey
123 6 not given us to be a prey to their
Prov 31 15 and given a prey to her household
Eccu 13 23 the wild ass is the lion's prey
27 11 the lion always lieth in wait for prey
Isa 5 29 shall roar and take hold of the prey
8 1 with speed, quickly take the prey
3 make haste to take away the prey. For
9 3 conquerors rejoice after taking a prey
10 2 that widows might be their prey, and
6 spoils, and to lay hold on the prey
31 4 and the lion's whelp upon his prey
33 23 the spoils of much prey be divided
42 22 they are made a prey, and there is none
49 24 shall the prey be taken from the strong
59 15 departed from evil, lay open to be a p.
Jer 2 14 slave? Why then is he become a prey
30 16 prey upon thee will I give for a prey
50 10 and Chaldea shall be made a prey
Bar 4 26 as a flock made a prey by the enemies
Eze 7 21 to the wicked of the earth for a prey
13 21 any more in your hands to be a prey
19 3 and he learned to catch the prey. 6
22 25 lion that roareth and catcheth the prey
27 are like wolves ravening the prey
29 19 and take the booty thereof for a prey
34 5 they became the prey of all the beasts
8 my sheep are become a prey to all the
38 12 to take spoils and lay hold on the prey
13 gathered thy multitude to take a prey
39 10 and shall make a prey of them to whom they had been a prey
Dan 11 24 shall scatter their spoils and their p.
Amos 3 4 roar in the forest if he leave no prey
5 11 and took the choice prey from him
Nah 2 12 filled his holes with prey, and his den
13 I will cut off thy prey out of the land
Haba 1 9 they shall all come to the prey, their
Zach 2 9 they shall be a prey to those that
1 Ma 3 4 like a lion's whelp roaring for his p.
Priapus 3 K 15 13 princess in the sacrifices of P.
2 Pa 15 16 had made in a grove an idol of Priapus
price Gen 23 15 is the price between me and thee
Gen 31 15 sold us and eaten up the price of us
44 2 the price which he gave for the wheat
Exod 13 13 of men thou shalt redeem with a price

21 10 he refuse the price of her chastity
30 if they set a price upon him, he shall
34 shall pay the price of the beasts: and
35 the live ox and shall divide the price
30 12 shall give a price for their souls
14 and upwards, shall give the price
34 20 if thou wilt not give a price for it
Lev 19 20 and yet not redeemed with a price
25 16 the more shall the price increase
26 himself can find the price to redeem it
28 find not the means to repay the price
51 shall he repay the price. If few
27 2 his soul to God, shall give the price
12 it be good or bad, shall set the price
14 it shall be sold according to the price
16 the price shall be rated according to
18 jubilee, and the price shall be abated
23 the priest shall reckon the price
27 shall add the fifth part of the price
Num 3 46 but for the price of the 273 of the
48 the price of them that are above
18 15 firstborn of man thou shalt take a p.
20 19 shall be no difficulty in the price
22 7 went with the price of divination
Deut 23 18 of a strumpet nor the price of a dog
24 7 and selling him shall take a price
15 shalt pay him the price of his labor
2 K 24 24 but I will buy it of thee at a price
3 K 10 28 of Coa and bought them at a set price
4 K 12 4 is offered for the price of a soul
2 Pa 1 16 who went and bought at a price, a
32 27 kinds, and of vessels of great price
2 Es 5 2 let us take up corn for price of them
Job 15 31 that he may be redeemed with any price
28 13 man knoweth not the price thereof
Ps 43 13 thou hast sold thy people for no price
48 9 nor price of the redemption of his soul
61 5 have thought to cast away my price
Prov 6 26 price of a harlot is scarce one loaf
27 26 and kids for the price of the field
31 10 from uttermost coasts is the p. of her
Eccu 20 12 that buyeth much for a small price
26 20 no price is worthy of a continent soul
Isa 55 1 without money and without any price
Bar 6 24 men buy them at a high price whereas
Eze 16 31 that by disdain enhanceth her price
27 15 exchanged for thy price teeth of ivory
Dan 11 38 stones and things of great price
Zach 11 13 cast it to the statuary, a handsome p.
Mat 13 46 he had found one pearl of great price
27 6 because it is the price of blood. And
9 the price of him that was prized
John 12 3 of right spikenard of great price
Acts 4 34 brought the p. of the things they sold
37 brought the price and laid it at the
5 2 by fraud kept back part of the price
3 by fraud keep part of the price of the
19 19 the price of them, they found the money
1 C 6 20 for you are bought with a great price
7 23 you are bought with a price; be not made
prices Apoc 18 19 at sea, by reason of her p.
pricked Prov 12 18 p. as it were with a sword of
Eccu 12 12 and be pricked with my sayings
14 1 is not p. with the remorse of sin
20 23 and in his rest he shall be pricked
pricketh Eccu 22 24 that p. the eye, bringeth out
Eccu 22 24 he that p. the heart, bringeth forth
pride Lev 26 19 I will break the pride of your
Num 15 30 that committeth anything through pride
Deut 1 43 swelling with pride, you went up into
17 13 that no one afterwards swell with pride
20 his heart be not lifted up with pride
18 20 prophet who being corrupted with pride
22 hath forged it by the pride of his mind
1 K 17 28 I know thy pride and the wickedness
4 K 19 28 thy pride hath come up to my ears
2 Pa 25 19 thy heart is lifted up with pride
Tob 4 14 never suffer pride to reign in thy mind
Jdth 6 15 behold their pride and look on our
8 17 as our heart is troubled by their pride
9 12 that his pride may be cut off with his
13 28 in the contempt of his pride despised
Esth 13 12 it was not out of pride and contempt
14 16 that I abominate the sign of my pride
16 2 many have abused unto p. the goodness
Job 10 16 for pride thou wilt take me as a lioness
11 12 a vain man is lifted up into pride
20 6 if his pride mount up even to heaven
24 23 he abuseth it unto pride: but his eyes
33 17 doing, and may deliver him from pride
35 12 hear, because of the pride of evil men
41 25 is king over all the children of pride
Ps 30 19 against the just, with pride and abuse
35 12 let not the foot of pride come to me
58 13 let them be taken in their pride
72 6 therefore pride hath held them fast
73 3 lift up thy hands against their pride
23 the pride of them that hate thee
100 7 he that worketh pride shall not dwell
Prov 8 13 I hate arrogance and pride and every
11 2 pride is, there also shall be reproach
14 3 in mouth of a fool is the rod of pride
16 18 pride goeth before destruction: and
21 24 who in anger worketh pride. Desires
Wisd 5 8 what hath pride profited us? Or what
Eccu 10 7 pride is hateful before God and men
14 the beginning of the pride of man
15 pride is the beginning of all sin
22 pride was not made for men: nor wrath
13 1 with the proud, shall put on pride
15 7 she is far from pride and deceit
16 9 abhorred them for pride of their word
21 5 rich shall be brought to nothing by p.
22 27 except upbraiding and reproach and pride
Isa 9 9 that say in the pride . . . of their heart
13 11 I will make pride of infidels to cease
19 the famous pride of the Chaldeans
14 11 thy pride is brought down to hell
16 6 we have heard of the pride of Moab
6 his pride and his arrogancy and his
23 9 to pull down the pride of all glory
28 1 woe to the crown of pride, to the
3 the crown of pride of the drunkards
30 7 it is pride only, sit still. Now
37 29 thy pride came up to my ears: therefore
61 6 shall pride yourselves in their glory
Jer 13 9 will I make the pride of Juda and the great
pride of Jerusalem to rot
17 shall weep in secret for your pride
48 29 we have heard the pride of Moab, he is
29 his pride and the loftiness of his heart
49 16 deceived thee, and the pride of thy heart
Eze 7 10 rod hath blossomed, pride hath budded
20 the ornament of their jewels into pride
24 will make the p. of the mighty to cease
16 49 iniquity of Sodom . . . pride, fulness of
56 in day of thy pride, before thy malice
30 6 pride of her empire shall be brought
18 pride of her power shall cease in her
32 12 they shall waste the pride of Egypt
Dan 4 34 that walk in pride he is able to abase
5 20 when . . . his spirit hardened unto pride
Osee 5 5 pride of Israel shall answer in his face
7 10 the pride of Israel shall be humbled

Amos 6 8 I detest the pride of Jacob, and I hate
8 7 hath sworn against the pride of Jacob
Abdi 3 pride of thy heart hath lifted thee up
Nah 2 2 Lord hath rendered the pride of Jacob as the pride of Israel
Soph 2 10 this shall befall them for their pride
Zach 9 6 I will destroy the p. of the Philistines
10 11 the pride of Assyria shall be humbled
11 3 the pride of the Jordan is spoiled
1 Ma 2 47 they pursued after the children of pride
49 now hath pride . . . gotten strength
3 20 they come against us . . . with pride
2 Ma 1 28 that treat us injuriously with pride
5 21 thinking through pride that he might now
7 36 shalt receive just punishment for thy p.
9 7 filled with pride, breathing out fire
11 being brought from his great pride
15 6 puffed up with exceeding great pride
Mark 7 22 blasphemy, pride, foolishness. All
1 Tim 3 6 lest being puffed up with pride, he fall
1 J 2 16 of the eyes, and the pride of life
priest Gen 14 18 the priest of the most high God
Gen 41 45 daughter of Putiphare priest of Heliopolis. 50; 46:20
Exod 2 16 priest of Madian had seven daughters
3 1 Jethro . . . the priest of Madian. 18:1
Lev 1 9 priest shall burn them upon the altar. 3:11, 16; 7:5
13 the priest shall offer it all and burn
15 the priest shall offer it at the altar
2 8 shalt deliver it to the hands of the p.
16 the priest shall burn for a memorial of
4 3 if the priest that is anointed shall sin
16 the priest . . . shall carry of the blood
20 the priest praying for them, the Lord
25 the p. shall dip his finger in the blood
26 the priest shall pray for him. 5:6, 10, 18; 19:22; Num 15:28
30 the priest shall take of the blood. 34
5 8 shall give them to the priest. 15:14
12 and he shall deliver it to the priest
16 delivering it to the p., who shall pray
18 a ram without blemish to the priest
6 6 shall give it to the priest according
10 the priest shall be vested with the
12 the priest shall feed it, putting wood
15 priest shall take a handful of the flour
22 priest that rightfully succeedeth his father
23 sacrifice of the p. shall be consumed
26 the priest that offereth it, shall eat
7 7 shall belong to the priest that offereth
8 the priest that offereth the victim of
30 shall deliver them to the priest. 12:6
32 shall fall to the priest for firstfruits
12 8 the priest shall pray for her, and so
13 4 priest shall shut him up seven days
7 after he was seen by the priest and
9 he shall be brought to the priest, and
11 therefore shall declare him unclean
13 the priest shall view him and. 17
15 by the judgment of the p. he shall be
19 the man shall be brought to the priest
25 the priest shall view it, and if he see
29 the priest shall see them. And if the
39 the priest shall view them. If he find
43 and the priest perceive this, he shall
44 separated by the judgment of the priest
49 shall be shown to the priest. And he
14 2 cleansed: he shall be brought to the p.
11 when the priest that purifieth the man
13 trespass offering pertaineth to the p.
14 priest taking of the blood of the victim
21 that the priest may pray for him, and
23 shall offer them . . . to the priest
24 priest receiving the lamb for trespass
35 shall go and tell the priest, saying: It
44 p. going in perceive that the leprosy. 48
15 29 offer for herself to the p., two turtles
16 32 the priest . . . shall make atonement
33 the priest also and all the people
17 5 shall bring to the priest their victims
6 the priest shall pour the blood upon
21 1 let not a priest incur an uncleanness
9 if the daughter of a priest be taken
10 high priest, that is to say, the priest
22 11 he whom the priest hath bought, and he
12 if the daughter of a priest be married
14 and shall give it to the priest into
23 10 firstfruits of your harvest to the p.
20 and when the priest hath lifted them
27 8 he shall stand before the priest: and
11 shall be brought before the priest
14 the priest shall consider it, whether
18 the priest shall reckon the money
23 the priest shall reckon the price
Num 5 9 the firstfruits . . . belong to the priest
10 is delivered into the hands of the priest
15 he shall bring her to the priest and
16 the priest therefore shall offer it and
23 the priest shall write these curses in
25 the priest shall take from her hand the
30 priest do to her according to all things
6 10 or two young pigeons to the priest in
11 and the priest shall offer one for sin
16 the priest shall present them before
20 being sanctified shall belong to the p.
15 25 priest shall pray for all the multitude
19 6 the priest shall also take cedar wood
Deut 17 12 to obey the commandment of the priest
18 3 shall give to the priest the shoulder
20 2 the priest shall stand before the army
26 3 thou shalt go to the priest that shall
4 the priest taking the basket at thy
Josu 22 30 Phinees the priest . . . had heard this
31 Phinees the priest . . . said to them
Judg 17 5 one of his sons, and he became his p.
10 be unto me a father and a priest, and I
12 the young man with him, for his priest
13 I have a p. of the race of the Levites
18 4 and hath hired me to be his priest
17 and the priest stood before the door
18 priest said to them: What are you doing
19 we may have thee for a father and a p.
19 to be a priest in the house of one man
24 taken away my gods . . . and the priest
27 the six hundred men took the priest
1 K 1 9 Heli the priest sitting upon a stool
2 11 before the face of Heli the priest. Now
13 the servant of the priest came while
14 brought up, the priest took to himself
15 the servant of the priest came and said
15 give me flesh to boil for the priest
28 to be my priest, to go up to my altar
35 I will raise me up a faithful priest
14 3 Phinees the son of Heli the priest
19 while Saul spoke to the priest, there
19 Saul said to the priest: Draw in thy
36 the priest said: Let us draw near hither
21 1 David came . . . to Achimelech the priest
2 David said to Achimelech the priest
4 the priest answered David, saying
5 David answered the priest and said
6 p. therefore gave him hallowed bread
9 the priest said: Lo, here is the sword
22 9 Achimelech the son of Achitob the priest
11 sent to call for Achimelech the priest

23 9 he said to Abiathar the priest: Bring
2 K 20 26 Ira the Jairite was the priest of David
3 K 1 7 he conferred . . . with Abiathar the priest
19 and invited . . . Abiathar the priest. 25
42 Jonathan the son of Abiathar the priest
2 22 and hath Abiathar the priest, and Joab
26 king said also to Abiathar the priest
27 from being the priest of the Lord
4 5 Zabud the son of Nathan the priest
13 33 was made a priest of the high places
4 K 11 9 that Joiada the priest had commanded
9 centurions . . . came to Joiada the priest
15 p. had said: Let her not be slain in
18 Mathan the priest of Baal. 2 Pa 23:17
18 priest set guards in house of the Lord
12 2 days that Joiada the priest taught him
22 10 Helcias the priest hath delivered to me
12 he commanded Helcias the priest and
14 Helcias the priest . . . went to Holda
23 24 which Helcias the priest had found
25 18 took . . . Sophonias the second priest
1 Pa 27 5 Banaias the son of Joiada the priest
2 Pa 13 9 made a priest of those who are no gods
15 3 without a priest a teacher and without
19 11 Amarias the priest . . . shall be chief
23 9 Joiada the priest gave to the captains
14 priest commanded that she should not
24 2 all the days of Joiada the priest
20 Zacharias the son of Joiada the priest
25 the blood of the son of Joiada the p.
26 17 Azarias the priest going in after him
31 10 Azarias the chief p. of the race of
34 14 Helcias the priest found the book of
18 Helcias the priest gave me this book
1 Es 2 63 till there arose a priest learned and
7 11 Artaxerxes gave to Esdras the priest
12 Artaxerxes . . . to Esdras the priest
21 Esdras the priest . . . shall require
10 10 Esdras the priest stood up and said
16 Esdras the priest . . . went and sat
2 Es 7 65 until there stood up a priest learned
8 2 Esdras the p. brought the law before
9 Esdras the priest and scribe. 12:26
10 38 the priest the son of Aaron shall be
13 4 over this thing was Eliasib the priest
13 over the storehouses Selemias the priest
Jdth 4 5 Eliachim the priest wrote to all that
6 as the priest of the Lord Eliachim had
Esth 11 1 Dositheus, who said he was a priest
Ps 109 4 thou art a priest forever
Isa 24 2 as with the people, so with the priest
28 7 p. and the prophet have been ignorant
Jer 6 13 from the prophet even to the priest
8 10 even to the priest all deal deceitfully
14 18 and the priest are gone into a land
18 18 the law shall not perish from the priest
20 1 Phassur . . . the p., who was appointed
21 1 Sophonias the son of Maasias the priest. 29:25; 37:3
23 11 the prophet and the priest are defiled
33 or the priest shall ask thee, saying
34 as for the prophet and the priest and
29 26 the Lord hath made thee priest instead of Joiada the priest
29 Sophonias the priest read this letter
52 24 took . . . Sophonias the second priest
Lam 2 6 delivered up king and p. to reproach
20 shall the p. and the prophet be slain
Bar 1 7 sent it to Jerusalem to Joakim the p.
Eze 1 3 word of Lord came to Ezechiel the priest
7 26 the law shall perish from the priest
44 21 no priest shall drink wine when he is
22 widow also, that is, the widow of a p.
30 firstfruits of your meats to the priest
45 19 the priest shall take of the blood
Osee 4 4 are as they that contradict the priest
9 there shall be like people like priest
Amos 7 10 Amasias the priest of Bethel sent
Zach 6 13 he shall be a priest upon his throne
Mala 2 7 the lips of the p. shall keep knowledge
1 Ma 2 1 Mathathias . . . a priest of the sons of
7 14 that is a priest of the seed of Aaron
15 1 sent letters . . . to Simon the priest
2 Ma 1 21 p. Nehemias commanded the sacrifices
3 33 give thanks to Onias the priest
4 13 Jason, that impious wretch and no p.
Mat 8 4 go, show thyself to the p. Luke 5:14
Luke 1 5 a certain priest named Zachary of the
10 31 certain priest went down the same way
Acts 14 12 p. also of Jupiter that was before city
1 Tim 5 19 against a p. receive not an accusation
Heb 5 6 thou art a priest forever. 7:17, 21
7 1 priest of the most high God, who met
3 Son of God, continueth a priest forever
11 another priest should rise according to
15 Melchisedech there ariseth another p.
8 4 were on earth, he would not be a priest
10 11 priest indeed standeth daily ministering

Aaron the priest Exod 31 10 holy vestments in the ministry of Aaron the priest
Exod 38 21 Ithamar son of A. . . . Num 4:28, 33; 7:8
Lev 7 34 have given them to Aaron the priest
13 2 shall be brought to A. . . . or any one
21 21 whosoever of the seed of A. . . . hath a
Num 3 6 make them stand in the sight of A. . . .
32 Eleazar the son of A. . . . 4:16; 16:37; 25:7, 11; 26:1; 1 Es 7:5
10 8 sons of A. . . . shall sound trumpets
18 28 to the Lord and give them to A. . . .
33 38 A. . . . went up into mount Hor at the
Josu 21 4 family of Caath of children of A. . . .
13 to the children of A. . . . , Hebron a

Eleazar the priest; *see* **Eleazar**

high priest Exod 28 38 over forehead of the h. p.
Exod 29 30 he appointed high priest in his stead
35 19 the vesture of Aaron the high priest
39 24 wherewith the high priest went adorned
Lev 8 7 he vested the high priest with the
16 17 when the h. p. goeth into the sanctuary
21 10 high priest . . . is the greatest among
Num 35 25 shall abide there until death of h. p.
28 in the city until the death of the h. p.
32 before death of the h. p. may by no
Josu 20 6 till the death of the high priest, who
4 K 12 7 king Joas called Joiada the high priest
9 and Joiada the high priest took a chest
10 king's scribe and the high priest came
22 4 go to Helcias the high priest, that the
8 Helcias the high priest said to Saphan
23 4 king commanded Helcias the high priest
1 Pa 9 11 Achitob, high priest of house of God
29 22 be prince, and Sadoc to be high priest
2 Pa 19 11 Amarias the priest your high priest
22 11 Josabeth . . . wife of Joiada the h. p.
23 8 Joiada the high priest had commanded
8 Joiada the high priest permitted not
11 Joiada the high priest . . . anointed
14 Joiada the high priest going out to
24 11 he whom the high priest had appointed
26 20 Azarias the high priest and all the
31 13 Azarias the high priest of the house
34 9 they came to Helcias the high priest
2 Es 3 1 then Eliasib the high priest arose
20 of the house of Eliasib the high priest
13 28 the son of Eliasib the high priest
Jdth 4 10 Eliachim the h. p. of the Lord went

15 9 Joachim the high priest came from
Eccu 50 1 Simon the high priest the son of Onias
Agge 1 1 Jesus the son of Josedec the h. p. 12, 14; 2:3, 5; Zach 6:11
Zach 3 1 Lord showed me Jesus the high priest
8 hear, O Jesus thou high priest, thou
1 Ma 7 5 who desired to be made high priest
9 the wicked Alcimus he made high priest
10 20 we make thee this day high priest of
32 I give it to the high priest, to place
38 other authority but that of the h. p.
69 he sent to Jonathan the high priest
12 3 Jonathan the h. p. and the nation of
6 Jonathan the h. p. and the ancients
7 sent long ago to Onias the high priest
20 Spartans to Onias the h. p., greeting
13 36 king Demetrius to Simon the high priest
42 first year of Simon the high priest
14 17 that Simon his brother was made h. p.
20 the Spartans to Simon the high priest
23 a copy of them to Simon the high priest
27 third year under Simon the high priest
30 Jonathan . . . was made their high priest
35 made him their prince and high priest
41 he should be their prince and high p.
15 2 king Antiochus to Simon the high priest
17 being sent from Simon the high priest
21 deliver them to Simon the high priest
24 a copy thereof to Simon the high priest
16 12 he was son-in-law of the high priest
24 from time that he was made high priest
2 Ma 3 1 because of godliness of Onias the h. p.
4 strove in opposition to the high priest
9 received in the city by the high priest
10 h. p. told him that these were sums
16 saw the countenance of the high priest
21 of the high priest who was in an agony
32 h. p. considering that the king might
33 when the high priest was praying, the
14 13 and to make Alcimus the high priest
15 12 Onias who had been h. p., a good and
Sadoc the priest; *see* **Sadoc**
Urias the priest; *see* **Urias**
priesthood Exod 28 4 do the office of p. 41; 29:44; 30:30; 35:19; Lev 7:35; 16:32
Exod 29 1 may be consecrated to me in priesthood
40 13 them may prosper to an everlasting p.
Lev 21 10 hands have been consecrated for the p.
Num 3 3 consecrated to do the functions of p.
10 and his sons over the service of p.
16 10 challenge to yourselves the p. also
18 1 shall bear the sins of your priesthood
7 thou and thy sons look ye to the p.
25 13 covenant of the p. forever shall be
Josu 18 7 p. of the Lord is their inheritance
1 Pa 24 2 did the office of the priesthood. And
1 Es 2 62 they were cast out of the p. 2 Es 7:64
2 Es 13 29 that defile the priesthood and the law
Eccu 45 8 gave him the priesthood of the nation
19 to execute office of the priesthood
30 dignity of priesthood should be to him
Osee 4 6 shalt not do the office of p. to me
1 Ma 2 54 received covenant of an everlasting p.
7 21 what he could to maintain his chief p.
11 27 confirmed him in the high priesthood. 14:38
57 I confirm thee in the high priesthood
14 47 to execute the office of the high p.
16 24 the book of the days of his priesthood
2 Ma 2 17 kingdom and the p. and the sanctuary
4 7 Jason . . . sought the high priesthood
24 got the high priesthood for himself
25 bringing nothing worthy of the high p.
29 and Menelaus was removed from the p.
11 3 to set the high p. to sale every year
14 7 ancestor's glory, I mean of the high p.
1 Tim 4 14 with imposition of the hands of the p.
Heb 7 5 Levi, who receive the priesthood, have a
11 perfection was by the Levitical p., for
12 the priesthood being translated, it is
24 forever, hath an everlasting priesthood
1 P 2 5 a spiritual house, a holy priesthood
9 are a chosen generation, a kingly p.
priestly Exod 19 6 shall be to me a p. kingdom
Lev 6 29 every male of the p. race shall. 7:6
Num 3 4 and Ithamar performed the p. office
18 8 and to thy sons for the priestly office
Deut 10 6 succeeded him in the priestly office
Judg 17 5 theraphim, that is to say, a p. garment
1 K 2 36 to somewhat of the p. office, that I
1 Pa 24 6 of the p. and Levitical families. 31
2 Pa 11 14 from executing the p. office of the
Wisd 18 24 in the priestly robe which he wore
1 Ma 3 49 they brought the priestly ornaments
Luke 1 8 when he executed the p. function in
9 the custom of the priestly office
priest's Exod 28 1 minister to me in the p. office
Lev 7 9 shall be the priest's that offereth it
14 the priest's that shall pour out the
Num 5 8 to the Lord, and it shall be the priest's
Deut 18 3 this shall be the priest's due from the
Eze 44 30 firstfruits . . . shall be the priest's
Luke 22 54 led him to the high priest's house
priests Gen 47 22 except the land of the priests. 26
Exod 19 22 the priests also that come to the Lord
24 let not the p. and the people pass the
29 9 they shall be priests to me by a
39 41 the priests . . . used in the sanctuary
Lev 1 5 the priests . . . shall offer the blood
2 2 bring it to the sons of Aaron the p.
3 2 the priests shall pour the blood round
8 22 second ram, in the consecration of p.
21 1 speak to the priests the sons of Aaron
22 10 sojourner of the p. or a hired servant
27 21 pertaineth to the right of the priests
Num 3 3 names of the sons of Aaron the priests
18 7 shall be executed by the priests. If
Deut 17 9 thou shalt come to the priests of the
18 taking the copy of the priests of the
18 1 the priests . . . shall have no part nor
19 17 before the Lord in the sight of the p.
21 5 the priests the sons of Levi shall come
24 8 whatsoever the priests . . . shall teach
27 9 and the priests of the race of Levi
31 9 this law, and delivered it to the priests
Josu 3 3 priests of the race of Levi carrying
6 he said to the priests: Take up the ark
8 the priests that carry the ark. 13; 4:16
14 the priests that carried the ark. 17; 4:10; 8:33
4 3 where the feet of the priests stood
9 the Jordan, where the priests stood
11 and the priests went before the people
6 4 the p. shall take the seven trumpets
4 the priests shall sound the trumpets
6 Josue the son of Nun called the priests
6 let 7 other priests take the 7 trumpets
8 and the seven priests blew the seven
12 the priests took the ark of the Lord
16 the priests sounded with the trumpets
Judg 18 30 Jonathan . . . and his sons were priests
1 K 1 3 sons of Heli . . . were there priests
2 13 not knowing . . . office of the priests
5 5 neither the priests of Dagon . . . tread
6 2 the Philistines called for the priests
22 11 to call for . . . priests that were in
17 turn, and kill the priests of the Lord

17 their hands against the p. of the Lord
18 turn thou and fall upon the priests
18 and fell upon the priests and slew in
19 Nobe the city of the priests he smote
21 told him that Saul had slain the priests
28 6 answered him not . . . nor by priests
2 K 8 17 Sadoc . . . and Achimelech . . . p. 1 Pa 18:16
15 35 Sadoc and Abiathar the p. 17:15; 19:11; 20:25; 3 K 4:4; 1 Pa 15:11
3 K 8 3 and the priests took up the ark
4 priests and the Levites carried them
6 the priests brought in the ark of the
10 when the priests were come out of the
11 the p. could not stand to minister
12 31 priests of the lowest of the people
32 in Bethel priests of the high places
13 2 immolate . . . priests of the high places
33 made of the meanest of the people priests
4 K 10 11 Jehu slew . . . and his priests, till there
19 call to me . . . all his priests: let
12 4 Joas said to the priests: All the money
5 let the priests take it according to
6 the priests did not make the repairs
7 Joas called Joiada . . . and the priests
8 priests were forbidden to take any more
9 the priests that kept the doors put
16 Lord, because it was for the priests
17 27 carry thither one of the priests whom
32 made . . . priests of the high places
19 2 sent . . . the ancients of the priests
23 2 with him, the priests and the prophets
4 and the priests of the second order
8 he gathered together all the priests
8 high places, where the priests offered
9 priests of the high places came not
20 slew all the priests of the high places
1 Pa 9 2 in their cities were . . . the priests
10 of the priests: Jedaia, Joiarib
30 sons of the priests made the ointments
13 2 let us send . . . to the priests and
15 14 priests and the Levites were sanctified
24 the priests, sounded with trumpets
16 6 the priests, to sound the trumpet
39 Sadoc . . . and his brethren priests
23 2 he gathered . . . the priests and Levites
29 priests have the charge of the loaves
28 13 of the divisions of the priests and
21 behold the courses of the priests
2 Pa 4 6 the sea was for the priests to wash in
9 he made also the court of the priests
5 5 the priests with the Levites carried
7 and the priests brought in the ark
11 priests were come out of the sanctuary
11 all the priests that could be found
12 with them 120 priests, sounding with
14 nor could the p. stand and minister
6 41 let thy priests . . . put on salvation
7 2 neither could the priests enter into
6 and the priests stood in their offices
6 and the priests sounded with trumpets
8 14 appointed . . . the offices of the priests
14 and minister before the priests
15 the priests and Levites departed not
11 13 priests and Levites . . . came to him
15 he made to himself priests for the
13 9 have cast out the priests of the Lord
9 you have made you priests, like all
10 the priests who minister to the Lord
12 his priests who sound with trumpets
14 the priests began to sound with the
17 8 with them Elisama and Joram priests
19 8 Josaphat appointed Levites and priests
23 5 third part . . . of the priests and of
6 into the house of the Lord, but the p.
18 under the hands of the priests and
24 5 he [Joas] assembled the priests and
26 17 and with him fourscore priests of the
18 to burn incense . . . but to the priests
19 burn incense, threatened the priests
19 leprosy in his forehead before the p.
20 the rest of the priests looked upon him
29 4 he brought the priests and the Levites
16 and the priests went into the temple
21 spoke to the priests the sons of Aaron
22 the priests took the blood and poured
24 the p. immolated them and sprinkled
26 Levites . . . and the priests with trumpets
34 priests were few and were not enough
34 was ended and priests were sanctified
34 with an easier rite than the priests
30 3 were not priests enough sanctified
15 priests and Levites being at length
16 the priests received the blood which
21 and the priests with instruments that
24 great number of priests was sanctified
25 with the priests . . . were full of joy
27 the priests and the Levites rose up
31 2 both of the priests and of the Levites
4 to give to the priests and the Levites
9 Ezechias asked the priests and the
15 Sechenias, in the cities of the priests
17 to the priests by their families
19 males, among the priests and the Levites
34 5 he burnt the bones of the priests
30 went up . . . the priests and the Levites
35 2 and he set the priests in their offices
8 both to the people and to the priests
8 gave to the priests to keep the phase
10 and the priests stood in their office
11 and the priests sprinkled the blood
14 ready for themselves and for the priests
14 the priests were busied in offering
14 prepared for themselves and for the p.
18 as Josias kept, with the priests
36 14 chief of the priests . . . transgressed
1 Es 1 5 rose up . . . the priests and Levites
2 36 the priests: the children of Jedaia
61 and of the children of the priests
69 a hundred garments for the priests
70 priests . . . dwelt in their cities. 2 Es 7:73
3 2 Josue . . . and his brethren the priests
8 the rest of their brethren the priests
10 the priests stood in their ornaments
12 but many of the priests . . . wept
6 9 according to the custom of the priests
16 priests and the Levites . . . kept the
18 set aside the p. in their divisions
20 and for their brethren the priests
20 priests and the Levites were purified
7 7 went up . . . of the children of the p.
13 priests and of the Levites in my realm
16 and that the priests shall offer
24 understand concerning all the priests
8 15 among the people and among the priests
24 I separated 12 of the chief of priests
29 before the chief of the priests and
30 the priests and the Levites received
9 1 priests and Levites have not separated
7 our priests have been delivered into
10 5 made the chiefs of the priests . . . swear
18 were found among the sons of the priests
2 Es 2 16 told anything to the Jews or to the p.
3 1 Eliasib . . . and his brethren the priests
22 after him built the priests, the men
28 from the horse gate the priests built

5 12 I called the priests and took an oath
7 39 the priests: the children of Idaia in the
63 of the priests, the children of Habia
70 and 530 garments for priests. And
72 gave . . . and 67 garments for priests
8 13 priests and the Levites were gathered
9 32 labor which hath come upon . . . our p.
34 our priests . . . have not kept thy law
38 our Levites and our priests sign it
10 8 subscribers . . . these were priests
28 priests, Levites, porters, and singing
34 and we cast lots among the priests
36 to the priests who minister in the
37 that we would bring . . . to the priests
39 the priests and the singing men and
11 3 in their cities: Israel, the priests
10 of the priests, Idaia the son of Joarib
20 priests and the Levites were in all
12 1 these are the priests and the Levites
7 these were the chief of the priests
12 priests and heads of the families were
22 the priests in the reign of Darius
30 priests and the Levites were purified
34 of the sons of the priests with trumpets
40 and the priests . . . with trumpets
43 the priests and Levites that assisted
43 thanksgiving, for the priests and Levites
13 5 laid up . . . the firstfruits of the priests
29 and the law of priests and Levites
30 I appointed the courses of the priests
Jdth 4 8 and the priests put on haircloths
Job 12 19 he leadeth away priests without glory
Ps 77 64 their priests fell by the sword
98 6 Moses and Aaron among his priests
131 9 let thy priests be clothed with justice
16 I will clothe her p. with salvation
Eccu 7 31 fear the Lord and reverence his priests
33 give honor to the priests and purify
50 13 portions out of the hands of the priests
Isa 37 2 he sent . . . the ancients of the priests
61 6 you shall be called the p. of the Lord
66 21 I will take of them to be priests
Jer 1 1 of the priests that were in Anathoth
18 to the princes thereof and to the p.
2 8 the priests did not say: Where is
26 and their priests and their prophets
4 9 and the priests shall be astonished
5 31 and the priests clapped their hands
8 1 shall cast out . . . bones of the priests
13 13 I will fill . . . the priests and the
19 1 take of . . . the ancients of the priests
26 7 the priests . . . heard Jeremias speaking
8 the priests . . . laid hold on him
11 priests and the prophets spoke to the
16 and all the people said to the priests
27 16 I spoke also to the priests and to
28 1 spoke to me . . . before the priests
29 1 to the priests and to the prophets
25 letters . . . to all the priests, saying
31 14 I will fill the soul of the priests
32 32 to wrath . . . princes and their priests
33 18 neither . . . cut off from the priests
21 my covenant . . . with the Levites and p.
34 19 the eunuchs and the priests and all
48 7 into captivity, his priests and. 49:3
Lam 1 4 gates are broken down: her priests sigh
19 my priests and my ancients pined away
4 13 and the iniquities of her priests
16 respected not the persons of the priests
Bar 1 7 they sent it . . . to the priests
16 to our princes and to our priests
6 9 whereof the priests secretly convey away
17 so do the priests secure the doors
27 sacrificed to them, their priests sell
30 and priests sit in their temples
32 the priests take away their garments
45 but what the p. will have them to be
48 the priests consult with themselves
54 their priests indeed will flee away
Eze 22 26 her priests have despised my law
40 45 chamber . . . shall be for the priests. 46
42 13 chambers in which the priests shall eat
14 when the priests shall have entered in
43 19 shalt give to the priests and Levites
24 the priests shall put salt upon them
27 the priests shall offer your holocausts
44 15 the priests . . . who kept the ceremonies
31 p. shall not eat of anything . . . dead
45 4 portion of the land shall be for the p.
46 2 the priests shall offer his holocaust
19 chambers . . . that were for the priests
20 where the p. shall boil the sin offering
48 10 firstfruits of the sanctuary for the p.
11 the sanctuary shall be for the priests
13 Levites . . . by the borders of the priests
Dan 3 84 ye priests of the Lord, bless the Lord
14 7 king being angry called for his priests
9 the priests of Bel were seventy
10 the priests of Bel said: Behold we go
14 but the priests went in by night
20 he took the priests and their wives
27 he hath put the priests to death
Osee 5 1 hear ye this, O priests, and hearken
6 9 they conspire with the p. who murder
Joel 1 9 p. the Lord's ministers, have mourned
13 gird yourselves, and lament, O ye p.
2 17 the p. the Lord's ministers shall weep
Mich 3 11 her priests have taught for hire
Soph 1 4 names of the wardens . . . with the p.
3 4 her p. have polluted the sanctuary
Agge 2 12 ask the priests the law, saying: If a
13 the priests answered and said: No
14 the p. answered . . . It shall be defiled
Zach 7 3 to speak to the priests of the house of
5 speak . . . to the priests, saying: When
Mala 1 7 to you, O priests, that despise my name
2 1 O ye p., this commandment is to you
1 Ma 3 51 and thy priests are in mourning
4 42 he chose priests without blemish
5 67 in that day some priests fell in battle
7 33 some of the priests and the people came
36 the priests went in and stood before
10 42 to the p. that execute the ministry
11 23 and he chose some . . . of the priests
12 6 and the priests . . . to the Spartans
14 20 and to the ancients and the priests
28 in a great assembly of the priests
41 Jews and their p. had consented that he
44 not be lawful for any . . . of the priests
47 Simon . . . prince . . . of the priests
2 Ma 1 10 of the stock of the anointed priests
13 deceived by counsel of the p. of Nanea
15 when the p. of Nanea had set it forth
19 the priests that then were worshippers
20 posterity of those p. that had hid it
23 and all the priests made prayer
30 the p. sung hymns till the sacrifice
33 where the priests . . . had hid the fire
35 he gave the priests many goods
3 15 the priests prostrated themselves before
4 14 the p. were not now occupied about the
14 31 commanded the p. that were offering
34 the p. stretching forth their hands
15 31 called . . . the priests to the altar
Mat 12 4 with him, but for the priests only
5 the priests in the temple break the

Mark 2 26 not lawful to eat but for the priests
8 31 by the ancients and by the high priests
14 53 all the priests . . . assembled together
Luke 3 2 under the high priests Annas and
6 4 lawful to eat but only for the p.
17 14 go, show yourselves to the priests
John 1 19 from Jerusalem priests and Levites to
Acts 4 1 the p. and the officer of the temple
6 7 also of the priests obeyed the faith
14 22 when they had ordained to them p. in
15 2 should go up to apostles and priests
22 30 he loosed him, and commanded the p. to
1 Tim 5 17 let the p. that rule well, be esteemed
Titus 1 5 shouldest ordain priests in every city
Heb 7 14 Moses spoke nothing concerning priests
20 the others indeed were made priests
23 others indeed were made many priests
27 needeth not daily, as the other priests
28 the law maketh men priests, who have
9 6 the priests indeed always entered
James 5 14 let him bring in the priests of the
Apoc 1 6 made us a kingdom and priests to God
5 10 made us to our God a kingdom and p.
20 6 shall be priests of God and of Christ

chief priests; *see* **chief**

priests' 2 Ma 3 15 altar in their p. vestments

primacy Col 1 18 in all things he may hold the primacy

prince Gen 23 6 thou art a prince of God
Gen 34 2 Hemor . . . the prince of that land
Exod 2 14 who hath appointed thee prince and
22 28 p. of thy people thou shalt not curse
Lev 4 22 if a prince shall sin, and through
21 4 not even for the prince of his people
Num 2 3 the prince of his sons shall be Nahasson
5 whose prince was *N.* 12, 18, 20, 25, 27; 10:14, 18
7 the prince was *N.* 14, 22, 29; 10:15, 16, 19–27
10 the prince shall be Elisur the son of
3 24 under their prince Eliasaph, the son
30 and their prince shall be Elisaphan
32 the prince of the princes of the Levites
35 their prince Suriel the son of Abihaiel
7 18 prince of the tribe of Issachar, made
24 the prince of the sons of *N.* 30, 36, 42, 48, 54, 60, 66, 72, 78
25 14 p. of the kindred and tribe of Simeon
15 most noble prince among the Madianites
18 a daughter of a prince of Madian
34 18 one prince of every tribe, whose names
26 tribe of Issachar, Phaltiel the son
Josu 5 15 I am prince of the host of the Lord
Judg 11 3 and they followed him as their prince
6 come thou and be our prince and fight
9 into my hand, shall I be your prince
11 all the people made him their prince
1 K 10 1 that God hath anointed thee to be prince
13 14 commanded to be prince over his people
22 2 and he [David] became their prince, and
25 30 shall have made thee prince over Israel
2 K 3 38 a prince and a great man is slain
5 2 and thou shalt be prince over Israel
3 K 11 34 I will make him prince all the days
14 7 made thee prince over my people. 16:2
4 K 9 5 I have a word to thee, O prince. And
5 and he said: To thee, Jehu O prince
1 Pa 2 10 Nahasson, prince of children of Juda
5 6 he was prince in the tribe of Ruben
9 17 their brother Sellum was the prince
20 Phinees . . . was their prince before the
11 42 Adina . . . the prince of the Rubenites
12 27 Joiada prince of the race of Aaron
29 22 anointed him to the Lord to be prince
1 Es 1 8 to Sassabasar the prince of Juda
2 Es 11 11 Achitob the prince of the house of God
Jdth 8 34 Ozias the prince of Juda said to her
10 13 the presence of the prince Holofernes
13 23 Ozias the prince of the people of Israel
24 the head of the prince of our enemies
14 3 to awake their prince for the battle
Esth 9 4 they knew him to be prince of the palace
Job 21 28 where is the house of the prince
31 37 I would . . . offer it as to a prince
Prov 14 28 of people the dishonor of the prince
17 7 nor lying lips [become] a prince. The
26 no good thing . . . to strike the prince
23 1 when thou shalt sit to eat with a p.
25 7 shouldst be humbled before the prince
15 by patience a p. shall be appeased
28 2 life of the prince shall be prolonged
15 a wicked prince over the poor people
16 prince void of prudence shall oppress
29 12 prince that gladly heareth lying words
26 many seek the face of the prince
Ecce 9 17 than the cry of a prince among fools
10 5 error proceeding from face of the prince
Eccu 9 24 prince of the people for the wisdom
41 22 of an offence before a prince and a
45 30 to be the prince of the sanctuary
48 13 in his days he feared not the prince
17 and a prince in the house of David
49 17 was a man born prince of his brethren
50 17 a divine odor to the most high Prince
Isa 9 6 the world to come, the Prince of Peace
32 5 the fool shall no more be called prince
8 the prince will devise such things as are worthy of a prince
Jer 30 21 their prince shall come forth from the
Eze 7 27 the prince shall be clothed with sorrow
12 10 this burden concerneth my prince that
12 the prince that is in the midst of them
21 25 thou profane wicked prince of Israel
28 2 say to the prince of Tyre: Thus saith
30 13 no more a prince of the land of Egypt
34 24 David the prince in the midst of them
37 25 David my servant shall fear their prince
38 2 prince of Mosoch and Thubal. 3; 39:1
44 3 it shall be shut for the prince. The prince himself shall sit in it
45 7 for the prince also on the one side
16 these firstfruits for the prince
17 the prince shall give the holocaust
22 the prince on that day shall offer for
46 2 the prince shall enter by the way of
4 holocaust that the prince shall offer
8 when the prince is to go in, let him
10 the prince in the midst of them shall
12 when the prince shall offer a voluntary
16 if the prince give a gift to any of
17 and it shall return to the prince
18 prince shall not take of the people's
48 21 the residue shall be for the prince
21 shall likewise be the portion of the p.
22 shall also belong to the prince. And
Dan 1 9 prince of the eunuchs. 10, 11, 18
3 38 neither is there at this time prince
4 6 Baltassar, prince of the diviners
5 11 appointed him prince of the wise men
16 shalt be the third prince in my kingdom
8 11 it was magnified even to the prince
25 rise up against the p. of princes
9 25 from . . . unto Christ the prince, there
10 13 prince of the kingdom of the Persians
20 to fight against the p. of the Persians
20 there appeared the prince of the Greeks
21 is my helper . . . but Michael your p.

11 18 shall cause the p. of his reproach to
22 yea also the prince of the covenant
12 1 shall Michael rise up, the great prince
Osee 3 4 many days without king and without p.
Mich 7 3 p. requireth, and the judge is for giving
5 not a friend, and trust not in a prince
Haba 1 10 their prince shall triumph over kings
Mala 1 8 offer it to thy prince, if he will be
1 Ma 9 30 chosen this day to be our prince
12 45 they have no prince nor anyone to help
13 42 great captain and prince of the Jews
14 35 made him their prince and high priest
41 consented that he should be their prince
47 prince of the nation of the Jews. 15:1
2 Ma 5 24 he sent that hateful prince Apollonius
13 24 p. from Ptolemais unto the Gerrenians
Mat 9 34 by the prince of devils he casteth out. Mark 3:22
12 24 Beelzebub the p. of devils. Luke 11:15
Luke 12 58 with thy adversary to the prince
John 12 31 the prince of this world be cast out
14 30 the prince of this world cometh, and
16 11 prince of this world is already judged
Acts 5 31 to be Prince and Savior, to give
7 27 who hath appointed thee prince. 35
35 him God sent to be prince and redeemer
23 5 thou shalt not speak evil of the prince
Eph 2 2 according to the prince of the power of
1 P 5 4 when the p. of pastors shall appear
Apoc 1 5 the prince of the kings of the earth
prince's Cant 7 1 in shoes, O prince's daughter
Eze 48 22 are in the midst of the p. portions
princes Gen 12 15 the princes told Pharao and
Gen 25 16 twelve princes of their tribes. And the
Exod 15 15 were the p. of Edom troubled, trembling
35 27 but the princes offered onyx stones
Num 1 4 princes of the tribes. 17:2; 30:2; Deut 5:23; 3 K 8:1; 1 Pa 28:1; 29:6; 2 Pa 5:2
16 p. of the multitude. 31:26; 32:2; Josu 9:15, 18
3 32 the prince of the princes of the Levites
4 34 and the princes of the synagogue reckoned
7 3 two princes offered one wagon, and
10 the princes offered for the dedication
11 let each of the princes . . . offer their
10 4 if thou sound but once, the princes
17 6 all the princes gave him rods one for
21 18 the well which the princes dug and the
22 13 said to the princes: Go into your
14 the princes returning, said to Balac
35 he went therefore with the princes. And
40 presents to Balaam and to the princes
23 6 Balac . . . with all the p. of the Moabites
17 the princes of the Moabites with him
31 8 five p. of the nation . . . they killed
13 all the princes of the synagogue went
32 28 p. of the families. 36:1; Josu 14:1; 19:51; 21:1
Deut 29 10 your princes and tribes and ancients
Josu 8 33 ancients and the princes and judges
9 18 people murmured against the princes
13 21 Moses slew with the princes of Madian
17 4 came in the presence of . . . the princes
21 1 came to the princes of the kindreds
22 14 and ten princes with him [Phinees]
21 answered the princes of the embassage
30 princes of the embassage who were with
32 and he returned with the princes
23 2 Josue called . . . and for the princes
24 1 called for the ancients and the princes
Judg 5 3 hear, O ye kings, give ear, ye princes
14 out of Machir there came down princes
25 butter in a dish fit for princes
8 3 into your hands the princes of Madian
6 the princes of Soccoth answered
9 24 upon rest of princes of the Sichemites
51 all the princes of the city, and having
10 4 and were princes of thirty cities, which
18 princes of Galaad said one to another
11 8 the princes of Galaad said to Jephte
11 went with the princes of Galaad, and
16 30 the house fell upon all the princes
1 K 2 8 that he may sit with princes and hold
29 7 and offend not the eyes of the princes
2 K 8 18 and the sons of David were the princes
10 3 p. of the children of Ammon. 1 Pa 19:3
18 5 king giving charge to all the princes
23 13 three who were p. among the thirty
3 K 4 2 these were the princes which he had
9 22 servants and his princes and captains
20 14 the princes of the provinces. 15, 17, 19; Lam 1:1; Dan 3:3
4 K 24 14 he carried away . . . all the princes
1 Pa 4 22 who were princes in Moab and who
38 were named princes in their kindreds
5 2 of the race of Juda . . . came the p.
7 had for princes Jehiel and Zacharias
9 34 the Levites, princes in their families
23 24 and families, princes by their courses
24 5 p. of the sanctuary and p. of God
6 down before the king and the princes
6 p. also of the priestly . . . families
31 p. of the priestly and Levitical families
27 22 the princes of the children of Israel
28 4 of Juda he chose the princes: and of
21 princes and the people know how to
29 11 Lord, and thou art above all princes
24 all the princes . . . gave their hand
2 Pa 17 7 he sent of his p. Benhail and Abdias
21 9 Joram went over with his princes and
23 13 she saw the king . . . and the princes
24 10 princes and all the people rejoiced
28 14 lift the spoils . . . before the princes
21 house of the kings and of the princes
29 30 Ezechias and the princes commanded
30 2 king, taking counsel, and the princes
6 by commandment of the king and his p.
12 commandment of the king and of the p.
24 the princes had given the people
31 8 when Ezechias and his princes came in
32 3 he took counsel with the princes and
31 in embassy of the princes of Babylon
35 8 his princes willingly offered what they
9 princes of the Levites, gave to the rest
36 18 treasures . . . of the king and of the p.
1 Es 7 28 all the mighty princes of the king
8 20 whom David and the princes gave for
25 and his princes . . . had offered. And I
9 15 the princes came to me, saying: The
10 8 according to the counsel of the princes
2 Es 7 5 I assembled the princes and magistrates
9 32 labor which hath come upon . . . our p.
34 our princes . . . have not kept thy law
38 and our princes . . . and our priests sign
11 16 of God, of the princes of the Levites
Jdth 3 1 kings and the princes of all the cities
9 both princes and nobles . . . went out to
5 2 and he called all the princes of Moab
Esth 1 3 made a great feast for all the princes
11 her beauty to all the people and the p.
14 seven princes of the Persians and of
16 in the hearing of the king and the p.
16 but also all the people and princes
18 wives of the princes of the Persians
21 counsel pleased the king and the princes
2 18 feast to be prepared for all the princes

3 1 set his throne above all the princes
5 11 advanced him above all his princes
6 9 let the first of the king's princes
13 1 to the princes and governors of the
16 1 to the governors and princes of
2 abused unto pride the goodness of p.
6 fraud they deceive the ears of princes
Job 3 15 with princes, that possess gold and
12 21 he poureth contempt upon princes and
24 he changeth the heart of the princes
29 9 the princes ceased to speak, and laid
34 19 accepteth not the persons of princes
Ps 2 2 and the princes met together against the
23 7 lift up your gates, O ye princes. 9
32 10 casteth away the counsels of princes
44 17 shalt make them princes over all the
67 26 princes went before joined with singers
28 the p. of Zabulon, the p. of Nephthali
75 13 who taketh away the spirit of princes
81 7 and shall fall like one of the princes
82 12 make their princes like Oreb and Zeb
12 all their princes who have said: Let
86 6 tell in his writings of peoples and of p.
104 22 that he might instruct his princes
106 40 contempt was poured forth upon their p.
112 8 may place him with p., with the p. of
117 9 Lord, rather than to trust in princes
118 23 for princes sat and spoke against me
161 p. have persecuted me without cause
145 2 put not your trust in princes: in the
148 11 princes and all judges of the earth
Prov 8 16 by me princes rule, and the mighty
16 28 one full of words separateth princes
18 16 and maketh him room before princes
19 10 nor for servant to have rule over p.
28 2 the land many are the princes thereof
Ecce 7 20 more than ten princes of the city
10 7 p. walking on the ground as servants
16 when the princes eat in the morning
17 and whose princes eat in due season
Wisd 8 11 faces of princes shall wonder at me
Eccu 10 17 overturned the thrones of proud princes
36 12 crush the head of the princes of the
46 16 and anointed princes over his people
21 he crushed the princes of the Tyrians
Isa 1 23 thy p. are faithless, companions of
3 4 I will give children to be their princes
14 the ancients of his people and its p.
10 9 are not my princes as so many kings
13 and have taken the spoils of the princes
14 9 all the princes of the earth are risen . . . all the princes of nations
19 11 princes of Tanis are become fools. 13
13 the princes of Memphis are gone astray
21 5 arise, ye princes, take up the shield
22 3 all the princes are fled together
23 8 Tyre . . . whose merchants were princes
29 10 he will cover your prophets and princes
30 4 for thy princes were in Tanis, and thy
31 9 his princes fleeing shall be afraid
32 1 and princes shall rule in judgment
34 12 the princes thereof shall be nothing
41 25 he shall make princes to be as dirt
43 28 and I have profaned the holy princes
49 7 kings shall see, and princes shall rise
Jer 1 18 to the kings of Juda, to the princes
2 26 their princes and their priests. 32:32
4 9 shall perish, and the heart of the p.
6 28 all these princes go out of the way
8 1 shall cast out . . . bones of the princes
17 25 by the gates of this city kings and p.
25 they and their princes, the men of Juda
24 8 Sedecias the king of Juda and his p.
25 18 cities of Juda . . . and the p. thereof
19 Pharao . . . and his servants and his p.
26 11 priests and the prophets spoke to the p.
12 Jeremias spoke to all the princes
16 p. and all the people said to the priests
21 and his princes heard these words
34 10 all the princes . . . heard that every
19 of Juda and the p. of Jerusalem
21 Sedecias the king of Juda and his p.
35 4 was by the treasure house of the princes
36 12 all the p. sat there . . . and all the p.
14 the princes sent Judi . . . to Baruch
19 princes said to Baruch: Go and hide
21 all the p. that stood about the king
37 13 took Jeremias and brought him to the p.
14 the princes were angry with Jeremias
38 4 princes said to the king: We beseech
17 princes of king of Babylon. 18, 22; 39:3
25 if the princes shall hear that I have
27 all the princes came to Jeremias
44 17 have done, our kings and our princes
21 that you offered . . . and your princes
48 7 captivity, his priests and his p. 49:3
49 38 Elam, and destroy kings and princes
50 35 a sword is . . . upon her princes and
51 57 I will make her princes drunk and
Lam 1 6 her princes are become like rams
2 2 kingdom unclean, and the p. thereof
9 and her princes are among the Gentiles
5 12 the p. were hanged up by their hand
Bar 1 9 carried away Jechonias and the princes
16 to our kings and to our princes. 2:1
3 16 where are the princes of the nations
4 21 you out of the hand of the princes
Eze 17 12 shall take away the king and the p.
22 27 her princes in the midst of her are like
23 6 princes and rulers, beautiful youths
12 the princes and rulers that came to her
23 the nobles and the kings and princes
23 and rulers, the princes of princes
26 16 all the princes of the sea shall come
27 21 p. of Cedar, they were the merchants
32 29 there is Edom and . . . all her princes
30 there are all the princes of the north
39 18 you shall drink the blood of the p.
45 8 the princes shall no more rob my people
Dan 1 3 of the king's seed and of the princes
6 2 three princes over them, of whom Daniel
3 Daniel excelled all the princes and
4 the princes and the governors. 6
7 all the princes . . . have consulted
8 25 shall rise up against the prince of p.
9 6 spoken in thy name . . . to our princes
8 confusion of face, to our princes
12 spoke against us and against our p.
10 13 Michael, one of the chief princes
11 5 one of his princes shall prevail over
Osee 7 3 the princes [glad] with their lies
5 the princes began to be mad with wine
16 their princes shall fall by the sword
8 4 they have been princes, and I knew not
10 from the burden of the king and the p.
9 15 no more, all their princes are revolters
13 10 thou saidst: Give me kings and princes
Amos 1 15 into captivity, both he and his princes
2 3 will slay all his princes with him
Jon 3 7 from mouth of the king and of his p.
Mich 3 1 hear, O ye princes of Jacob, and ye
9 hear this, ye p. of the house of Jacob
11 her princes have judged for bribes
Nah 3 18 Assyria, thy princes shall be buried
Haba 1 10 princes shall be his laughingstock
Soph 1 8 I will visit upon the princes and upon

3 3 her princes are . . . as roaring lions
1 Ma 1 5 subdued countries of nations, and p.
27 the princes and the ancients mourned
6 60 in the sight of the king and of the p.
61 the king and the princes swore to them
9 37 daughter of one of the great princes
10 63 said to his princes: Go out with him
14 2 sent one of his princes to take him
20 princes and the cities of the Spartans
28 assembly of . . . the p. of the nation
2 Ma 3 2 and the p. esteemed the place worthy
9 25 considering that neighboring princes
Mat 2 6 not the least among the princes of Juda
20 25 princes of the Gentiles lord it over
Mark 6 21 for the princes and tribunes and chief
10 42 and their p. have power over them
Luke 24 20 our chief priests and p. delivered him
Acts 4 5 their p. and ancients and scribes were
26 the princes assembled together against
Rom 13 3 princes are not a terror to good work
1 C 2 6 neither of the princes of this world
8 which none of the p. of this world knew
Titus 3 1 admonish them to be subject to princes
Apoc 6 15 princes and the tribunes and the rich
princes of Israel Eze 19 1 lamentation for p. . . .
Eze 21 12 it is upon all the princes of Israel
22 6 p. . . . , every one hath employed his
45 9 let it suffice you, O p. . . . : cease
princes of Juda 2 Pa 12 5 Roboam and to p. . . .
2 Pa 22 8 he found the princes of Juda and the
24 17 the p. of Juda went in and worshipped
2 Es 12 31 I made the princes of Juda go up upon
32 went . . . half of the princes of Juda
Ps 67 28 the princes of Juda are their leaders
Jer 26 10 the princes of Juda heard these words
29 2 the princes of Juda . . . were departed
34 19 princes of Juda . . . that passed between
52 10 slew all the p. of Juda in Reblatha
Osee 5 10 the princes of Juda are become as
princes of the people Num 25 4 take all the p. . . .
Num 26 9 these are Dathan and Abiron the p. . . .
27 2 p. . . . at the door of the tabernacle
Deut 33 5 p. . . . being assembled with the tribes
21 who was with the p. . . . and did the
Josu 1 10 Josue commanded the p. . . . , saying: Pass,
2 Pa 24 23 killed all the princes of the people
2 Es 11 1 p. of the people dwelt at Jerusalem
Ps 46 10 the princes of the people are gathered
Eze 11 1 Pheltias the son of Banaias, p. . . .
Acts 4 8 ye p. . . . and ancients, hear: If we
princes of the Philistines; *see* **Philistines**
princess 3 K 15 13 p. in the sacrifices of Priapus
principal Gen 23 6 thy dead in our p. sepulchers
Exod 30 23 spices, of principal and chosen myrrh
Lev 6 5 he shall restore . . . in the p., and the
Num 5 7 restore the principal itself and the
13 4 principal men, whose names are these
1 Pa 12 28 the house of his father 22 p. men
32 of the sons of Issachar . . . 200 p. men
24 4 the sons of Eleazar among the p. men
2 Es 6 17 many letters were sent by the p. men
11 17 was the p. man to praise and to give
Eccu 39 31 the p. things necessary for the life
Jer 25 36 a howling of the principal of the flock
Mich 5 5 seven shepherds and eight p. men
1 Ma 7 26 Nicanor one of his principal lords
9 61 the principal authors of the mischief
2 Ma 15 18 p. fear was for the holiness of the
Acts 25 2 chief priests, and p. men of the Jews
23 with tribunes, and p. men of the city
Heb 7 4 gave tithes out of the principal things
principalities Rom 8 38 life, nor angels, nor p.
Eph 3 10 may be made known to the p. and powers
6 12 but against p. and powers, against the
Col 1 16 dominations, or p., or powers: all
2 15 despoiling the p. and powers, he hath
principality Ps 109 3 with thee is the p. in the
Ps 138 17 their p. is exceedingly strengthened
Dan 11 41 and the p. of the children of Ammon
2 Ma 4 27 so Menelaus got the principality: but
5 7 yet he [Jason] did not get the p., but
1 C 15 24 shall have brought to nought all p., and
Eph 1 21 above all principality, and power and
Col 2 10 who is the head of all p. and power: in
Jude 6 angels who kept not their principality
principally 2 Ma 14 8 p. indeed out of fidelity
print John 20 25 in his hands the print of the nails
Prisca Rom 16 3 salute P. and Aquila. 2 Tim 4:19
Priscilla Acts 18 2 lately come from Italy with P.
Acts 18 18 Syria, and with him P. and Aquila
26 when Priscilla and Aquila had heard
1 C 16 19 Aquila and P. salute you much in Lord
prison Gen 39 21 sight of chief keeper of the p.
Gen 40 3 he [Pharao] sent them to the prison
4 keeper of the prison delivered them to
14 Pharao in mind to take me out of this p.
41 14 Joseph was brought out of the prison
42 16 you shall be in prison, till what you
17 so he put them in prison three days
18 third day he brought them out of prison
19 one of your brethren be bound in p.
34 this man again, that is kept in prison
Exod 6 6 out from the work prison. 7
12 29 captive woman that was in the prison
Lev 24 12 they put him into prison till they
Num 15 34 they put him into prison, not knowing
Judg 16 21 shutting him [Samson] up in prison
25 brought out of prison he played before
3 K 22 27 saith the king: Put this man in prison
4 K 14 26 to them that were shut up in prison
25 27 Joachin king of Juda out of prison
29 his garments which he had in prison
2 Pa 16 10 and commanded him to be put in prison
18 26 put this fellow in prison and give him
1 Es 7 26 confiscation of goods or at least to p.
2 Es 3 25 house, that is, in the court of the p.
Job 7 12 that thou hast enclosed me in a prison
Ecce 4 14 out of prison and chains sometimes a
Wisd 17 15 kept shut up in prison without irons
Isa 14 17 opened not the prison to his prisoners
24 22 they shall be shut up there in prison
42 7 bring forth the prisoner out of prison
7 sit in darkness out of the prison house
Jer 29 26 to put him in the stocks and into p.
32 2 shut up in court of the p. 33:1; 39:15
8 to the entry of the prison, and said
12 Jews that sat in the court of the p.
37 14 he [Jonathan] was chief over the prison
15 Jeremias went into house of the prison
20 be committed into the entry of the p.
20 Jeremias remained in the entry of the prison. 38:13, 28
38 6 which was in the entry of the prison
39 14 Jeremias out of the court of the prison
52 11 put him in p. till the day of his death
31 and brought him forth out of prison
33 he changed his prison garments and he
2 Ma 13 21 out, and taken up and put in prison
Mat 11 2 when John had heard in prison the
14 3 bound him and put him in prison
10 he sent and beheaded John in the prison
25 36 I was in prison, and you came to me
39 when did we see thee sick or in prison
43 sick and in prison, and you did not
44 stranger or naked or sick or in prison
Mark 6 17 bound him in prison for the sake of

28 he beheaded him in the prison and
15 7 was put in p. with some seditious men
Luke 3 20 above all, and shut up John in prison
22 33 with thee, both into prison and to
Acts 5 18 and put them in the common prison
19 opening the doors of the prison, and
22 opening the prison, found them not
23 the prison indeed we found shut with
25 the men whom you put in prison are in
8 3 and women, committed them to prison
12 5 Peter therefore was kept in prison
6 keepers before the door kept the p.
17 the Lord had brought him out of prison
16 24 thrust them into the inner prison, and
25 they that were in prison, heard them
26 foundations of prison were shaken
27 the keeper of the prison, awaking out
27 seeing the doors of the prison open
36 keeper of the p. told these words to
40 they went out of the prison, and entered
26 10 many of saints did I shut up in prison
1 P 3 19 to those spirits that were in prison
Apoc 2 10 devil will cast some of you into prison
20 7 Satan shall be loosed out of his prison
cast into prison; *see* **cast**
prisoner Gen 40 3 in which Joseph also was p., but
Isa 42 7 bring forth the prisoner out of prison
2 Ma 14 27 to send Machabeus prisoner in all haste
33 unless you deliver Judas prisoner to me
Mat 27 15 one prisoner, whom they would. And he
16 he had then a notorious prisoner
Acts 23 18 said: Paul, the prisoner, desired me to
25 14 a certain man was left prisoner by Felix
27 unreasonable to send a prisoner, and not
28 17 was delivered p. from Jerusalem into
Eph 3 1 I Paul, the prisoner of Jesus Christ
4 1 I therefore, a prisoner in the Lord
Col 4 10 you. Aristarchus, my fellow prisoner
2 Tim 1 8 of our Lord, nor of me his prisoner: but
Philem 1 Paul, a prisoner of Christ Jesus, and
9 now a prisoner also of Jesus Christ
23 Epaphras, my fellow prisoner in Christ
prisoners Gen 39 20 where the king's p. were kept
Gen 39 22 delivered into his hand all the p.
Ps 68 34 and hath not despised his prisoners
78 11 let the sighing of the prisoners come
Isa 14 17 opened not the prison to his prisoners
20 4 lead away the prisoners of Egypt and
Lam 3 34 under his feet all the p. of the land
Zach 9 11 hast sent forth thy p. out of the pit
12 to the stronghold, ye prisoners of hope
1 Ma 9 70 and to restore to him the prisoners
72 he restored to him the prisoners which
15 40 take the people prisoners and to kill
2 Ma 5 14 forty thousand were made prisoners
Mark 15 6 release unto them one of the prisoners
Rom 16 7 my kinsmen and fellow prisoners: who
Acts 16 27 supposing that the p. had been fled
27 1 Paul, with the other prisoners, should
42 they should kill the prisoners, lest any
prisons Isa 42 22 are hid in the houses of p.
Luke 21 12 to the synagogues and into prisons
Acts 22 4 delivering into p. both men and women
2 C 6 5 in stripes, in prisons, in seditions, in
11 23 many more labors, in p. more frequently
Heb 11 36 moreover also of bands and prisons
private Jdth 8 5 she made herself a p. chamber
Job 4 12 was a word spoken to me in private
Ps 9 8 in ambush with the rich in p. places
100 5 the man that in private detracted his
Ecce 10 20 of the rich man in thy private chamber
Jer 38 16 Sedecias swore to Jeremias, in private
Eze 8 12 every one in private in his chamber
Dan 14 20 they showed him the private doors by
2 Ma 9 26 favors both public and private, you
2 P 1 20 scripture is made by p. interpretation
privately Gen 31 27 why wouldst thou run away p.
Judg 9 31 sent messengers privately to Abimelech
16 9 men lying privately in wait with her
1 K 18 22 his servants to speak to David p.
2 Es 6 10 I went into the house of Samai . . . p.
Tob 2 4 it up, carried it privately to his house
Jer 40 15 spoke to Godolias privately in Masphath
Dan 11 21 he shall come privately and shall
1 Ma 10 79 and Apollonius left p. in the camp
2 Ma 1 19 took p. the fire from the altar and
6 11 and were keeping the sabbath day p.
8 1 with him went privately into the towns
Mat 1 19 was minded to put her away privately
2 7 Herod, privately calling the wise men
24 3 disciples came to him privately, saying
Acts 16 37 they thrust us out p.? Not so; but let
23 19 went aside with him privately, and asked
Gal 2 4 who came in privately to spy our liberty
privilege Ruth 4 6 do thou make use of my p.
privy Lev 5 1 himself hath seen or is p. to it
2 K 23 23 David made him of his privy council
4 K 6 12 that thou speakest in thy p. chamber
Mat 15 17 belly, and is cast out into the privy
Mark 7 19 and goeth out into the privy, purging
Acts 5 2 land, his wife being privy thereunto
prize Deut 25 1 shall give the prize of justice
1 C 9 24 all run indeed, but one receiveth prize
Phil 3 14 to the prize of the supernal vocation
prized Zach 11 13 price that I was p. at by them
Mat 27 9 the price of him that was prized, whom
9 whom they prized of the children of
Probatica John 5 2 at Jerusalem a pond called P.
proceed Josu 17 18 mayst p. farther, when thou
2 K 7 12 which shall proceed out of thy bowels
Jdth 10 4 dressing up did not p. from sensuality
Ps 44 5 out, proceed prosperously, and reign
88 35 the words that proceed from my mouth
Isa 29 14 I will proceed to cause an admiration
Jer 44 17 that shall p. out of our own mouth
Lam 3 38 both evil and good p. out of the mouth
Haba 1 7 their judgment and their burden p.
Mat 15 18 the things which p. out of the mouth
Mark 7 21 out of the heart of men proceed evil
Eph 4 29 let no evil speech p. from your mouth
2 Tim 3 9 they shall proceed no farther: for their
3 J 2 that thou mayest p. prosperously and
proceeded Gen 24 50 word hath p. from the Lord
Job 36 1 Eliu also proceeded and said: Suffer
Jer 9 3 they have proceeded from evil to evil
2 Ma 4 3 when the enmities proceeded so far
Mark 5 30 the virtue that had p. from him
Luke 4 22 that p. from his mouth, and they said
John 8 42 for from God I proceeded and came
Acts 12 3 he p. to take up Peter also. Now it
Apoc 4 5 from the throne proceeded lightnings
9 17 from their mouths proceeded fire and
proceedeth Deut 8 3 word that p. from the mouth
Ps 16 1 prayer, which p. not from deceitful
Isa 34 16 that which p. out of my mouth, he hath
Mat 4 4 that proceedeth from the mouth of God
15 5 whatsoever p. from me, shall profit
John 15 26 who proceedeth from the Father, he
James 3 10 out of the same mouth p. blessing and
Apoc 19 15 out of his mouth proceedeth a sharp
21 which proceedeth out of his mouth
proceeding Gen 12 9 going and p. on to the south
1 K 27 11 such was the proceeding all the days
Ecce 10 5 as it were by an error proceeding from
Apoc 22 1 proceeding from the throne of God and
proceedings 2 Ma 14 8 the evil p. of those men

process Wisd 14 16 in p. of time, wicked custom
Prochorus Acts 6 5 Philip and P. and Nicanor and
proclaim Exod 33 19 I will p. in the name of the
Lev 25 10 shalt proclaim remission to all the
Deut 20 5 the captains shall proclaim through
Josu 3 3 began to proclaim: When you shall see
Judg 7 3 and proclaim in the hearing of all
3 K 21 9 proclaim a fast and make Naboth sit
4 K 10 20 proclaim a festival for Baal. And he
2 Es 8 15 they should p. and publish the word in
Isa 61 2 to p. the acceptable year of the Lord
Jer 3 12 proclaim these words towards the north
7 2 and proclaim there this word and say
11 6 proclaim aloud all these words in the
19 2 shalt p. the words that I shall tell
20 8 and I often proclaim devastation: and
34 17 I proclaim a liberty for you, saith
48 4 proclaim a cry for her little ones
50 2 proclaim, and conceal it not: say
Joel 3 9 p. ye this among the nations: prepare
Amos 4 5 call free offerings and proclaim it
proclaimed 3 K 21 12 they p. a fast and made
3 K 22 36 herald p. through all the army before
2 Pa 20 3 and he proclaimed a fast for all Juda
36 22 who commanded it to be proclaimed
1 Es 8 21 I p. there a fast by the river Ahava
Isa 3 9 they have proclaimed abroad their sin
Jer 36 9 they p. a fast before the Lord to all
Dan 5 29 it was p. of him that he had power as
Jon 3 5 they p. a fast and put on sackcloth
7 he caused it to be p. and published
1 Ma 10 64 his accusers saw his glory proclaimed
proclaiming Gen 41 43 crier p. that all should
2 Pa 30 6 proclaiming according to the king's
Jer 34 15 in proclaiming liberty every one to
17 in p. every man to his brother and
Apoc 5 2 a strong angel, p. with a loud voice
proclamation Exod 32 5 made p. by crier's voice
Exod 36 6 Moses commanded proclamation to be made
2 Pa 24 9 and they made a proclamation in Juda
1 Es 1 1 made a p. throughout all his kingdom
10 7 proclamation was made in Juda and
Jer 34 8 Sedecias . . . making a proclamation
1 Ma 5 49 Judas commanded proclamation to be made
10 63 make p. that no man complain against
proconsul Acts 13 7 was with the p. Sergius Paulus
Acts 13 8 seeking to turn away the p. from faith
12 p., when he had seen what was done
18 12 when Gallio was proconsul of Achaia
proconsuls Acts 19 38 there are p.: let them
procure Wisd 1 12 neither p. ye destruction by
1 C 7 18 let him not procure uncircumcision. Is
prodigies Eccu 45 2 words he made p. to cease
2 Ma 5 4 that these prodigies might turn to good
profane Gen 43 32 they think such a feast profane
Exod 31 14 that shall profane it, shall be put to
Lev 19 7 eat thereof, he shall be profane
12 nor profane the name of thy God. I am
21 6 and shall not profane his name: for
22 15 they shall not profane the sanctified
32 profane not my holy name, that I
Num 18 32 lest you profane the oblations of the
19 13 shall profane the tabernacle of the
2 Pa 34 7 and had demolished all profane temples
Ps 88 32 if they p. my justice: and keep not
35 neither will I profane my covenant
Isa 65 4 and profane broth is in their vessels
Eze 21 25 thou profane wicked prince of Israel
22 26 no difference between holy and profane
23 39 into my sanctuary . . . to profane it
24 21 I will profane my sanctuary, the glory
43 7 shall no more profane my holy name
44 23 the difference between holy and profane
48 15 shall be a profane place for the city
Amos 2 7 young woman, to profane my holy name
1 Ma 2 34 edict, to profane the sabbath day
2 Ma 12 23 earnest in punishing the profane, of
Acts 24 6 hath gone about to profane the temple
1 Tim 6 20 avoiding the profane novelties of words
2 Tim 2 16 but shun profane and vain babblings: for
Heb 12 16 there be any fornicator or p. person
profaned Lev 20 3 profaned my holy name. And if
Num 6 12 because his sanctification was profaned
19 20 because he hath profaned the sanctuary
Jdth 4 9 destroyed and their holy things p.
Ps 88 40 thou hast profaned his sanctuary on
Isa 43 28 and I have profaned the holy princes
Jer 19 4 and have profaned this place: and have
Eze 20 14 lest it should be profaned before the
22 8 and profaned my sabbaths. 23:38
26 I was profaned in the midst of them
25 3 my sanctuary, because it was profaned
36 20 they profaned my holy name when it
21 name which the house of Israel hath p.
22 which you have profaned among the
23 name, which was p. among the Gentiles
23 which you have p. in the midst of them
39 7 and my holy name shall be p. no more
43 8 and they profaned my holy name by the
Mala 1 12 and you have p. it in that you say
2 11 Juda hath p. the holiness of the Lord
1 Ma 1 45 sacrificed to idols and p. the sabbath
49 commanded the holy places to be p.
3 51 are trodden down and are profaned
4 38 the altar profaned and the gates burnt
44 altar of holocausts that had been p.
14 36 p. all places round about the sanctuary
2 Ma 5 16 he unworthily handled and p. them
profaning 2 Es 13 17 are doing, p. the sabbath day
Isa 56 2 keepeth the sabbath from p. it. 6
profess Deut 26 3 I profess this day before the Lord
Ruth 4 6 which I profess I do willingly forego
2 Ma 6 6 plainly profess himself to be a Jew
Mat 7 23 then will I profess unto them, I never
Titus 1 16 they profess that they know God: but
professed 2 Ma 8 36 p. that the Jews had God for
professing Rom 1 22 p. themselves to be wise
1 Tim 2 10 but as it becometh women p. godliness
profession 2 Ma 7 6 declared in the p. of the
profit Gen 37 26 what will it p. us to kill our
Lev 7 18 neither shall it profit the offerer
1 K 12 21 vain things which shall never p. you
Esth 16 9 as p. of the commonwealth requireth
Job 21 15 what doth it profit us if we pray to
22 3 what doth it profit God if thou be just
35 3 or what will it profit thee if I sin
Ps 29 10 what p. is there in my blood whilst
Prov 10 2 of wickedness shall profit nothing
11 4 riches shall not p. in day of revenge
Ecce 2 22 what profit shall a man have of all his
5 10 and what doth it profit the owner, but
15 what then doth it profit him that he
Eccu 5 10 they shall not profit thee in the day
7 24 if they be for thy profit, keep them
20 32 what profit is there in them both
29 14 shall bring thee more profit than gold
30 25 killed many, there is no profit in it
34 28 what profit have they but the labor
31 doth his humbling himself profit him
41 17 what profit is there in them both
Isa 30 5 a people that could not profit them
5 they were no help nor to any profit
44 9 beloved things shall not profit them
47 12 if so be it may profit thee anything
57 12 and thy works shall not profit thee
Jer 7 8 lying words, which shall not p. you

12 13 inheritance, and it shall not p. them
Mala 3 14 what profit is it that we have kept his
2 Ma 2 26 that all that read might receive profit
Mat 15 5 proceedeth from me, shall profit thee
16 26 what doth it profit a man if he gain
Mark 7 11 whatsoever is from me shall p. thee
8 36 what shall it profit a man if he gain
Rom 3 1 or what is the profit of circumcision
1 C 7 35 and this I speak for your profit: not
12 7 Spirit is given to every man unto profit
14 6 what shall I profit you, unless I speak
15 32 what doth it profit me, if the dead rise
Gal 5 2 Christ shall profit you nothing. And I
2 Tim 2 14 contend not in words, for it is to no p.
Heb 4 2 the word of hearing did not profit them
12 10 he, for our profit, that we might
James 2 14 what shall it profit, my brethren, if
16 give them not . . . what shall it profit
profitable 2 K 17 14 p. counsel of Achitophel was
Ecce 2 3 till I might see what was profitable
7 1 whereas he knoweth not what is p. for
12 10 he sought profitable words, and wrote
Wisd 6 27 by my words, and it shall be p. to you
8 7 men can have nothing more p. in life
13 11 vessel p. for the common uses of life
Eccu 10 4 he will raise up a p. ruler over it
20 10 there is a gift that is not profitable
Isa 44 10 graven thing that is p. for nothing
48 17 thy God that teach thee p. things
Bar 6 58 else a profitable vessel in the house
59 and sent forth for profitable uses
1 Ma 2 21 it is not p. for us to forsake the law
2 Ma 12 12 Judas thinking that they might be p.
Luke 14 35 it is neither p. for the land nor for
Acts 20 20 I have kept back nothing that was p.
Rom 2 18 approvest the more profitable things
1 C 10 33 not seeking that which is p. to myself
2 C 8 10 for this is profiable for you, who have
1 Tim 4 8 bodily exercise is profitable to little
8 godliness is profitable to all things
2 Tim 2 21 sanctified and profitable to the Lord
3 16 is profitable to teach, to reprove, to
4 11 he is profitable to me for the ministry
Titus 3 8 these things are good and profitable
Philem 11 now is profitable both to me and thee
profited Wisd 5 8 what hath pride p. us? or
Eccu 51 22 in myself, and I profited therein
Jer 16 19 a vanity which hath not profited them
23 32 who have not profited this people
Heb 13 9 have not p. those that walk in them
profiteth Wisd 1 11 murmuring, which p. nothing
Isa 58 9 and to speak that which profiteth not
John 6 64 the flesh profiteth nothing. The words
Rom 2 25 circumcision p. indeed, if thou keep
1 C 13 3 and have not charity, it p. me nothing
profiting 1 Tim 4 15 that thy p. may be manifest
profound Isa 33 19 the people of p. speech: so
Eze 3 5 to a people of a profound speech
progress 2 Ma 4 13 p. of heathenish and foreign
Gal 1 14 I made progress in the Jews' religion
prohibit 1 Ma 1 48 and should p. the sabbath and
Acts 24 23 he should not p. any of his friends to
prohibiting 1 Th 2 16 p. us to speak to the Gentiles
prohibition Acts 28 31 all confidence, without p.
projecting 3 K 6 18 wrought, and carvings p. out
3 K 6 32 and carvings very much projecting
projects Esth 12 2 searched into their projects
Eze 38 10 projects shall enter into thy heart
prologue 2 Ma 2 33 foolish thing to make a long p.
prolong Job 36 20 p. not the night that people
Prov 10 27 fear of the Lord shall prolong days
28 16 hateth covetousness, shall p. his days
Eccu 37 34 he that is temperate shall p. life
prolonged Deut 6 2 life, that thy days may be p.
Ps 119 5 woe is me, that my sojourning is p.
Prov 28 2 life of the prince shall be prolonged
Ecce 8 13 neither let his days be prolonged, but
Isa 14 1 and her days shall not be prolonged
Eze 12 22 the days shall be prolonged and every
25 and shall not be prolonged any more
28 not one word of mine shall be p. any
promise Exod 8 12 p. which he had made to Pharao
Num 30 12 and doth not disallow the promise
13 she shall not be bound by the promise
32 20 if you do what you promise, go on
Deut 23 22 if thou wilt not promise, thou shalt
Judg 15 12 promise me that you will not kill me
1 Pa 29 14 that we should be able to promise thee
2 Es 10 29 they came to promise and swear that
Tob 7 10 promise to give me Sara thy daughter
Jdth 9 11 who promise themselves to violate thy
11 21 because thy promise is good, if thy
Ps 55 9 in thy sight, as also in thy promise
Ecce 5 3 and foolish promise displeaseth him
Luke 24 49 I send the promise of my Father upon
Acts 1 4 should wait for the p. of the Father
2 33 Father the promise of the Holy Ghost
39 the p. is to you and to your children
7 17 when the time of the promise drew near
13 23 man's seed God according to his p.
32 the p. which was made to our fathers
23 21 now ready, looking for a p. from thee
26 6 hope of promise that was made by God to
Rom 4 13 not through law was the p. to Abraham
14 void, the promise is made of no effect
16 according to grace the p. might be firm
20 in the p. also of God he staggered not
9 8 that are the children of the promise
9 this is the word of promise: According
Gal 3 14 that we may receive the p. of the Spirit
17 to make the promise of no effect. For
18 be of the law, it is no more of promise
18 but God gave it to Abraham by promise
19 come, to whom he made the promise, being
22 the promise, by faith of Jesus Christ
29 heirs according to the promise. Now I
4 23 but he of the free woman, was by promise
28 as Isaac was, are children of promise
Eph 1 13 signed with the holy Spirit of promise
2 12 having no hope of the promise, and
3 6 copartners of his promise in Christ
6 2 is the first commandment with a promise
1 Tim 4 8 having promise of the life that now is
2 Tim 1 1 according to the promise of life, which
Heb 4 1 lest the p. being left of entering into
6 13 God making p. to Abraham, because he
15 so patiently enduring he obtained the p.
17 to show to the heirs of the promise the
9 15 they that are called may receive the p.
10 36 will of God, you may receive the promise
11 9 Jacob, the coheirs of the same promise
39 received not the promise; God providing
2 P 3 4 where is his promise or his coming
9 the Lord delayeth not his promise
1 J 2 25 the promise which he hath promised us
promised Gen 21 1 Lord visited Sara as he had p.
Gen 28 4 which he promised to thy grandfather
38 23 I sent the kid which I promised: and
44 32 promised, saying: If I bring him not
Exod 12 25 will give you as he hath promised
Lev 27 2 vow, and promised his soul to God
Num 10 29 hath promised good things to Israel
30 3 but shall fulfil all that he promised
4 knew the vow that she hath promised
5 whatsoever she promised and swore
6 shall she be bound to what she p.

8 shall give whatsoever she promised
12 shall accomplish whatsoever she had p.
15 whatsoever she had vowed and promised
32 24 accomplish what you have promised
Deut 1 35 land, which I promised. 32:11; Bar 2:34
6 3 hath p. thee a land flowing with milk
9 5 which he p. by oath to thy fathers
28 into the land that he promised them
10 9 as the Lord thy God promised him
11 9 which the Lord promised by oath
15 5 he will bless thee as he hath promised
19 8 all the land that he promised them
23 23 shalt do as thou hast promised to the
25 19 the land which he hath promised thee
31 21 the land which I have promised. 23
Josu 9 15 promised that they should not be slain
24 had promised his servant Moses to give
14 10 granted me life, as he promised until
12 this mountain, which the Lord promised
12 to destroy them, as he promised me
21 43 word which he had promised to perform
22 4 brethren rest and peace, as he promised
23 5 the land as he hath promised you
10 will fight for you, as he hath promised
14 which the Lord promised to perform
15 fulfilled in deed, what he promised
Judg 2 1 I promised that I would not make void
11 10 that we will do as we have promised
36 do unto me whatsoever thou hast p.
16 18 the money which they had promised
3 K 2 24 who hath made me a house, as he p.
5 12 gave wisdom to Solomon, as he p. him
8 20 upon throne of Israel, as the Lord p.
24 what thou hast promised him [David]
56 according to all that he promised
56 all the good things that he promised
9 5 as I promised David thy father, saying
4 K 8 19 as he had p. him [David], to give him
1 Pa 17 26 thou hast promised to thy servant such
29 6 overseers of the king's possessions p.
9 when they p. their offerings willingly
2 Pa 1 9 which thou hast promised to David my
2 15 hast promised, send to thy servants
6 1 Lord p. that he would dwell in a cloud
10 upon throne of Israel, as the Lord p.
15 father all that thou hast promised him
16 whatsoever thou hast promised him
20 place wherein thou hast p. that thy
7 18 as I p. to David thy father, saying
21 7 he had promised to give a lamp to him
Jdth 8 9 Ozias had p. that he would deliver
13 7 as thou hast promised, thou mayst
18 which he p. to the house of Israel
Ecce 5 4 not to perform the things promised
Wisd 17 8 they who p. to drive away fears and
1 Ma 11 28 he promised him 300 talents. And the
2 Ma 2 18 as he promised in the law, will shortly
4 9 he promised also 150 more, if he might
27 money he had promised to the king
45 promised Ptolemee to give him much
7 26 she p. that she would counsel her
8 36 that had p. to levy the tribute
11 14 and p. that he would agree to all
12 12 promised them peace, and after having
Mat 14 7 he promised with an oath, to give her
Mark 14 11 they promised him they would give him
Luke 22 6 to give him money. And he promised
Acts 7 5 he p. to give it him in possession
17 which God had promised to Abraham
Rom 1 2 he had p. before, by his prophets, in
4 21 whatsoever he has p., he is able also to
2 C 9 5 prepare this blessing before promised
Titus 1 2 which God, who lieth not, hath promised
Heb 10 23 for he is faithful that hath promised
11 11 that he was faithful who had promised
James 1 12 God hath p. to them that love him. 2:5
1 J 2 25 the promise which he hath promised us
promises Num 30 9 make her p. and the words
Esth 14 9 they design to change thy promises
Prov 25 14 and doth not fulfil his promises
Wisd 12 21 and made covenants of good promises
Eccu 24 33 of Jacob, and the promises to Israel
29 5 in promises they humble their voice
1 Ma 10 15 the p. that Demetrius had made Jonathan
Rom 9 4 the service of God, and the promises
15 8 to confirm the p. made unto the fathers
2 C 1 20 all the promises of God are in him, It
7 1 having therefore these promises, dearly
Gal 3 16 to Abraham were the promises made
21 was the law then against the p. of God
Heb 6 12 and patience shall inherit the promises
7 6 and blessed him that had the promises
8 6 which is established on better promises
11 13 not having received the promises, but
17 and he that had received the promises
33 wrought justice, obtained promises
2 P 1 4 us most great and precious promises
3 13 new earth according to his promises
promisest Gen 38 17 till thou send what thou promisest
promiseth Job 17 5 p. a prey to his companions
Prov 12 18 there is that p. and is pricked as it
Eccu 20 25 p. to his friend and maketh him his
2 Ma 9 15 he now p. to make equal with the
16 he p. to adorn with goodly gifts
Heb 12 26 now he p., saying: Yet once more, and
promising 2 Es 10 29 p. for their brethren, with
Dan 3 36 p. that thou wouldst multiply their
2 Ma 4 8 promising him 360 talents of silver
8 11 p. that they should have 90 slaves
12 11 promising to give him pastures and to
1 Tim 6 21 some promising, have erred concerning
2 P 2 19 promising them liberty, whereas they
promoted Judg 9 9 come to be p. among the trees
Judg 9 11 be promoted among the other trees. 13
Dan 3 97 the king promoted Sidrach, Misach
promoter 1 Ma 10 47 been the chief p. of peace
2 Ma 4 1 and had been the promoter of evils
promoters 1 Es 5 4 were the p. of that building
promotion Prov 3 35 the p. of fools is disgrace
promulgated Num 36 6 is the law p. by the Lord
prone Gen 8 21 are p. to evil from his youth
Exod 32 22 this people, that they are p. to evil
Prov 29 22 to wrath, shall be more prone to sin
pronounce Lev 13 37 him confidently p. him clean
Deut 27 14 the Levites shall pronounce and say
Job 31 37 every step of mine I would p. it
Ps 118 173 my tongue shall pronounce thy word
Ecce 6 3 of this man I p. that the untimely
Jer 1 16 I will p. my judgments against them
pronounced Lev 13 59 to be cleansed or p. unclean
Ps 118 13 I have p. all the judgments of thy
Ecce 8 11 because sentence is not speedily p.
Jer 11 17 hath pronounced evil against thee
16 10 wherefore hath the Lord pronounced
35 17 the evil that I have p. against them
36 7 the Lord hath p. against this people
18 he p. all these words as if he were
31 the evil that I have p. against them
40 2 thy God hath p. this evil upon this
Bar 2 7 Lord hath p. against us all these
proof Gen 39 16 a p. therefore of her fidelity
1 K 14 41 or in my son Jonathan, give a proof
Wisd 18 25 the proof only of wrath was enough
2 C 9 13 by the p. of this ministry, glorifying
13 3 do you seek a proof of Christ that
Phil 2 22 know ye the proof of him, that as a son

proofs Acts 1 3 alive after his passion, by many p.
prop Job 8 15 shall prop it up, and it shall not
proper Gen 44 32 let me be thy proper servant
Gen 49 28 every one with their proper blessings
Num 9 5 and they made it in its proper time
1 Pa 9 22 they were registered in their p. towns
29 3 I give my own proper goods, gold
2 Pa 31 3 part was, that of his p. substance
Wisd 13 11 cut down a tree proper for his use
Eccu 20 6 his peace, knowing the proper time
Bar 1 14 on feasts and proper days. And you
2 Ma 14 1 to places proper for his purpose
15 17 and proper to stir up the courage
Mat 25 15 every one according to his p. ability
1 C 7 7 every one hath his proper gift from God
15 38 will: and to every seed its proper body
2 C 5 10 every one may receive the proper things
2 P 1 3 by his own proper glory and virtue
properly Prov 19 14 a prudent wife is p. from the
prophecies Eccu 36 17 raise up the p. which the
1 C 13 8 whether prophecies shall be made void
14 22 p. not to unbelievers, but to believers
1 Th 5 20 despise not prophecies. But prove all
1 Tim 1 18 according to the p. going before on thee
prophecy 1 Pa 15 22 presided over the prophecy to
1 Pa 15 27 Chonenias the ruler of the prophecy
2 Pa 15 8 words, and the prophecy of Azarias
1 Es 6 14 according to the prophecy of Aggeus
Jdth 6 5 if thou think thy prophecy true, let
Prov 29 18 when prophecy shall fail, the people
Eccu 24 46 I will yet pour out doctrine as p.
46 23 in prophecy to blot out the wickedness
51 59 Saraias was chief over the prophecy
Lam 3 47 prophecy is become to us a fear and
Dan 9 24 vision and prophecy may be fulfilled
Mat 13 14 the p. of Isaias is fulfilled in them
Rom 12 6 either prophecy, to be used according to
1 C 12 10 to another, prophecy; to another, the
13 2 if I should have p. and should know all
14 6 in revelation, or in knowledge, or in p.
1 Tim 4 14 which was given thee by prophecy, with
2 P 1 20 no p. of scripture is made by private
21 p. came not by the will of man at any
Apoc 1 3 and heareth the words of this prophecy
11 6 it rain not in the days of their p.
19 10 testimony of Jesus is the spirit of p.
22 7 words of the p. of this book. 9, 10, 18
19 the words of the book of this prophecy
prophesied Num 11 25 had rested on them, they p.
Num 11 27 when they p. in the camp, there ran a
1 K 10 10 and he [Saul] p. in the midst of them
11 that he was with the prophets and p.
18 10 [Saul] p. in the midst of his house
19 21 messengers; but they also prophesied
21 messengers third time and they p. also
23 p. till he came to Najoth in Ramatha
24 [Saul] p. with the rest before Samuel
3 K 22 10 the prophets p. before them. 2 Pa 18:9
12 and all the prophets p. in like manner
1 Pa 25 3 Idithun, who prophesied with a harp
2 Pa 18 11 the prophets prophesied in like manner
20 37 p. to Josaphat, saying: Because thou
1 Es 5 1 p. to the Jews that were in Judea
Jdth 6 2 because thou hast prophesied unto us
Eccu 48 14 and after death his body prophesied
49 18 and after death they prophesied
Jer 2 8 the prophets p. in Baal and followed
5 31 the prophets prophesied falsehood
20 6 to whom thou hast prophesied a lie
23 13 they p. in Baal and deceived my people
21 have not spoken to them, yet they p.
25 13 Jeremias hath p. against all nations
26 9 why hath he p. in the name of the Lord
11 because he hath p. against this city
20 there was a man who p. in the name
20 he [Urias] prophesied against this
28 6 thy words which thou hast prophesied
8 have p. concerning many countries
9 prophet that p. peace: when his word
29 31 because Semeias hath p. to you, and
37 18 your prophets that p. to you and said
Eze 11 13 it came to pass when I prophesied that
37 7 I p. as he had commanded me. 10
7 and as I prophesied there was a noise
38 17 who p. in the days of those times
Mat 7 22 have not we prophesied in thy name
11 13 prophets and the law p. until John
15 7 well hath Isaias prophesied of you
Luke 1 67 he p., saying: Blessed be the Lord God
John 11 51 he p. that Jesus should die for the
Acts 19 6 they spoke with tongues and prophesied
1 P 1 10 who p. of the grace to come in you
Jude 14 Enoch also, the seventh from Adam, p.
prophesieth 3 K 22 18 thee that he p. no good
2 Pa 18 7 for he never prophesieth good to me
Jer 29 26 over every man that raveth and p., to
27 the Anathothite who p. to you
Eze 12 27 and this man p. of times afar off
1 C 14 3 he that prophesieth, speaketh to men
4 he that propesieth, edifieth the church
5 greater is he that p., than he that
prophesy Num 11 27 Eldad and Medad p. in the camp
Num 11 29 O that all the people might prophesy
1 K 10 6 and thou shalt prophesy with them
19 20 and they likewise began to prophesy
3 K 22 8 he [Micheas] doth not p. good to me
1 Pa 25 1 to p. with harps and with psalteries
2 Pa 18 17 that this man would not p. me any good
Wisd 14 28 they p. lies or they live unjustly
Jer 11 21 shalt not p. in the name of the Lord
14 14 the prophets p. falsely in my name
14 they p. unto you a lying vision and
15 the prophets that prophesy in my name
16 the people to whom they prophesy shall
19 14 whither Lord had sent him to p., and
23 16 words of the prophets that p. to you
25 that prophesy lies in my name and say
26 that p. lies and that p. the delusions
25 30 thou shalt p. unto them all these words
26 12 Lord sent me to p. concerning this
27 10 they prophesy lies to you: to remove
15 and they prophesy in my name falsely
15 you and the prophets that p. to you
16 words of your prophets, that p. to you
16 for they prophesy a lie unto you
29 9 they p. falsely to you in my name
21 who p. unto you in my name falsely
32 3 why dost thou prophesy, saying: Thus
Eze 4 7 and thou shalt prophesy against it
6 2 mountains of Israel and p. against
11 4 p. against them, p., thou son of man
13 2 prophesy thou against the prophets of Israel that prophesy
2 that p. out of their own heart. 17
16 of Israel that p. to Jerusalem and
17 and do thou prophesy against them
20 46 p. against the forest of the south
21 2 prophesy against the land of Israel
9 prophesy and say: Thus saith the Lord
14 prophesy; and strike thy hands together
28 son of man, prophesy and say. 30:2
25 2 and thou shalt prophesy of them
28 21 Sidon: and thou shalt prophesy of it
29 2 thou shalt p. of him and of all Egypt
34 2 p. concerning the shepherds of Israel
2 prophesy and say to the shepherds

35 2 mount Seir, and p. concerning it
36 1 prophesy to the mountains of Israel
3 p. and say: Thus saith the Lord God
6 p. therefore concerning the land of
37 4 prophesy concerning these bones; and
9 p. to the spirit, p., O son of man
12 p. and say to them: Thus saith the
38 2 prophesy of him and say to him
14 prophesy and say to Gog: Thus saith
39 1 prophesy against Gog and say: Thus
Joel 2 28 sons and your daughters shall prophesy
Amos 2 12 command the prophets, saying: P. not
3 8 Lord God hath spoken, who shall not p.
7 12 eat bread there and prophesy there
13 but p. not again any more in Bethel
15 go, prophesy to my people Israel. And
16 thou shalt not prophesy against Israel
Zach 13 3 that when any man shall p. any more
3 him through, when he shall prophesy
4 by his own vision, when he shall p.
Mat 26 68 prophesy unto us, O Christ, who is he
Mark 7 6 well did Isaias prophesy of you
14 65 and to say unto him: Prophesy: and
Luke 22 64 saying: Prophesy, who is it that
Acts 2 17 your sons and your daughters shall p.
18 of my spirit, and they shall prophesy
21 9 four daughters, virgins, who did p.
1 C 13 9 we know in part, and we prophesy in part
14 1 gifts; but rather that you may prophesy
5 with tongues, but rather to prophesy
24 but if all prophesy, and there come in
31 you may all p. one by one; that all may
39 brethren, be zealous to prophesy; and
Apoc 10 11 thou must p. again to many nations and
11 3 they shall prophesy 1,260 days, clothed
prophesying 1 K 10 5 them and they shall be p.
1 K 10 13 when he had made an end of p., he came
19 20 they saw a company of prophets p.
3 K 18 29 while they were p., the time was come
1 Pa 25 2 under the hand of Asaph p. near the
2 Es 6 12 had spoken to me as if he had been p.
Jer 20 1 heard Jeremias p. these words. And
1 C 11 4 every man praying or p. with his head
5 every woman praying or p. with her head
prophet Gen 20 7 he [Abraham] is a prophet: and
Exod 7 1 Aaron thy brother shall be thy prophet
Num 12 6 if there be among you a prophet of
Deut 13 1 if there rise in the midst of thee a p.
3 shalt not hear the words of that prophet
5 that p. or forger of dreams shall be
18 15 God will raise up to thee a prophet
18 I will raise them up a prophet out of
20 prophet who being corrupted with pride
22 whatsoever that same p. foretelleth
22 but the prophet hath forged it by the
34 10 there arose no more a prophet in Israel
Judg 6 8 he sent unto them a p. and he spoke
1 K 3 20 knew that Samuel was a faithful prophet
22 5 Gad the p. said to David: Abide not
2 K 24 11 Gad the prophet and the seer of David
3 K 11 29 the prophet Ahias the Silonite, clad
13 11 a certain old prophet dwelt in Bethel
18 I also am a prophet like unto thee
20 word of the Lord came to the prophet
23 he saddled his ass for the prophet
25 city wherein that old prophet dwelt
26 that prophet, who has brought him back
29 the p. took up the body of the man
29 brought it unto the city of the old p.
14 2 go to Silo where Ahias the prophet is
18 by hand of his servant Ahias the p.
16 7 Jehu the son of Hanani, the prophet
12 to Baasa in the hand of Jehu the p.
18 22 I only remain a prophet of the Lord
36 Elias the prophet came near and said
19 16 shalt anoint to be prophet in thy room
20 13 a p. coming to Achab king of Israel
22 a prophet coming to the king of Israel
38 the prophet went and met the king
22 7 is there not here some p. of the Lord
4 K 3 11 is there not here a prophet of the Lord
5 3 with the prophet that is in Samaria
8 know that there is a prophet in Israel
13 if the prophet had bid thee do some
6 12 Eliseus the p. that is in Israel telleth
9 1 Eliseus the prophet called one of the
4 young man, the servant of the prophet
14 25 Jonas the son of Amathi, the prophet
19 2 to Isaias the prophet the son of Amos
20 1 Isaias the son of Amos. Isa 37:2; 38:1
11 Isaias the prophet called upon the Lord
14 Isaias the p. came to king Ezechias
23 18 the prophet that came out of Samaria
2 Pa 12 5 Semeias the prophet came to Roboam
15 in the books of Semeias the prophet
13 22 in the book of Addo the prophet
15 8 Azarias the son of Oded the prophet
16 7 at that time Hanani the prophet came
18 6 is there not here a prophet of the Lord
21 12 letter brought him from Elias the p.
25 15 sent a prophet to him [Amasias], to say
16 the prophet departing, said: I know
26 22 were written by Isaias . . . the prophet
28 9 prophet of the Lord there, whose name
32 20 Isaias the prophet . . . prayed against
35 18 from the days of Samuel the prophet
1 Es 5 1 Aggeus the prophet . . . prophesied
6 14 to the prophecy of Aggeus the prophet
2 Es 6 14 Noadias the prophet and the rest of
Tob 2 6 the Lord spoke by Amos the prophet
Ps 73 9 have not seen, there is now no prophet
Wisd 11 1 works in the hands of the holy prophet
Ecce 46 16 Samuel the prophet of the Lord, the
17 by his fidelity he was proved a p.
48 1 Elias the prophet stood up, as a fire
23 by the hand of Isaias, the holy p.
25 Isaias, the great prophet and faithful
49 9 who was consecrated a prophet from his
Isa 3 2 the judge and the prophet and the
9 15 prophet that teacheth lies, he is the tail
28 7 priest and the p. have been ignorant
39 3 Isaias the p. came to king Ezechias
Jer 1 5 made thee a prophet unto the nations
6 13 from the p. even to the priest. 8:10
14 18 the prophet also and the priest are gone
18 18 nor the word [perish] from the prophet
23 11 the prophet and the priest are defiled
28 the p. that hath a dream, let him tell
33 the p. or the priest shall ask thee
34 as for the prophet and the priest
37 thus shalt thou say to the prophet
26 18 Micheas of Morasthi was a prophet in
28 1 Hananias the son of Azur, a prophet
5 said to Hananias the prophet. 15
9 the prophet that prophesied peace
9 the p. shall be known, whom the Lord
10 Hananias the prophet took the chain
12 after that Hananias the p. had broken
17 Hananias the prophet died in that year
Lam 2 20 shall the priest and the p. be slain
Eze 2 5 that there hath been a p. in the midst
7 26 they shall seek a vision of the prophet
14 4 to the prophet inquiring of me by him
7 to the prophet to inquire of me by him
9 when the p. shall err and speak a word
9 I the Lord have deceived that prophet

10 so shall the iniquity of the prophet
33 33 that a prophet hath been among them
Dan 3 38 this time prince or leader or prophet
14 42 was in Judea a prophet called Habacuc
Osee 4 5 the prophet also shall fall with thee
9 7 know ye . . . that the p. was foolish
8 the prophet is become a snare of ruin
12 13 Lord by a prophet brought Israel out
13 and he was preserved by a prophet
Amos 7 14 I am not a p. nor am I the son of a p.
Haba 3 1 a prayer of Habacuc the prophet for
Agge 1 1 by the hand of Aggeus the p. 3; 2:2
12 to the words of Aggeus the prophet
2 11 word of the Lord came to Aggeus the p.
Zach 1 1 of Lord came to Zacharias . . . the p. 7
13 5 I am no prophet, I am a husbandman
Mala 4 5 I will send you Elias the prophet
1 Ma 4 46 till there should come a prophet and
9 27 that there was no p. seen in Israel
14 41 till there should arise a faithful p.
2 Ma 2 4 how the prophet, being warned by God
Mat 1 22 which the Lord spoke by the p. 2:15
2 5 for so it is written by the prophet
3 3 was spoken of by Isaias the prophet
4 14 which was said by Isaias the prophet
8 17 spoken by the prophet Isaias, saying
10 41 receiveth a p. in the name of a p.
41 shall receive the reward of a prophet
11 9 what went you out to see? A p. Luke 7:26
9 you, and more than a p. Luke 7:26
12 17 which was spoken by Isaias the prophet
39 sign of Jonas the p. 16:4; Luke 11:29
13 35 which was spoken by the p. 21:4; 27:35
57 a p. is not without honor. Mark 6:4
14 5 because they esteemed him as a prophet
21 11 this is Jesus the p. from Nazareth
26 for all held John as a prophet. And
46 because they held him as a prophet
24 15 was spoken of by Daniel the prophet
Mark 1 2 as it is written in Isaias the prophet
6 15 it is a p., as one of the prophets
11 32 counted John that he was a prophet
Luke 1 76 shalt be called the p. of the Highest
3 4 of the sayings of Isaias the prophet
4 17 book of Isaias the p. was delivered
24 no p. is accepted in his own country
27 in the time of Eliseus the prophet
7 16 a great prophet is risen up among us
28 is not a greater prophet than John
13 33 that a p. perish out of Jerusalem
20 6 are persuaded that John was a prophet
24 19 who was a prophet, mighty in work and
John 1 21 art thou the p.? And he answered: No
23 as said the prophet Isaias. And they
25 not Christ nor Elias nor the prophet
4 19 I perceive that thou art a prophet
44 a p. hath no honor in his own country
6 14 this is of a truth the prophet that is
7 40 some said: This is the prophet indeed
52 out of Galilee a prophet riseth not
9 17 he said: He is a prophet. The Jews
12 38 that the saying of Isaias the prophet
Acts 2 16 was spoken of by the prophet Joel
30 he was a p. and knew that God hath
3 22 a p. shall the Lord your God raise up
23 soul which will not hear that prophet
7 37 a prophet shall God raise up to you
48 as the prophet saith: Heaven is my
8 28 chariot, and reading Isaias the p.
30 heard him reading the prophet Isaias
34 of whom doth the prophet speak this
13 6 certain man, a magician, a false p.
20 unto them judges, until Samuel the p.
21 10 from Judea a certain p., named Agabus
28 25 speak to our fathers by Isaias the p.
1 C 14 37 if any seem to be prophet, or spiritual
Titus 1 12 one of them a prophet of their own
2 P 2 16 voice, forbade the folly of the prophet
Apoc 16 13 from the mouth of the false prophet
19 20 taken, and with him the false prophet
20 10 the false prophet shall be tormented
Jeremias the prophet; ***see*** **Jeremias**
Nathan the prophet; ***see*** **Nathan**
prophetess Exod 15 20 Mary the p., the sister of
Judg 4 4 was at that time Debbora a prophetess
4 K 22 14 and Asaia went to Holda the prophetess
2 Pa 34 22 went to Olda the prophetess the wife
Isa 8 3 I went to the prophetess and she
Luke 2 36 there was one Anna, a prophetess, the
Apoc 2 20 Jezabel, who calleth herself a p., to
prophetical 2 P 1 19 we have the more firm p. word
prophets 1 K 10 5 thou shalt meet a company of p.
1 K 10 10 behold a company of prophets met him
11 seeing that he was with the prophets
11 is Saul also among the p.? 12; 19:24
19 20 when they saw a company of prophets
28 6 by dreams nor by priests nor by p.
15 hear me, neither by the hand of p.
3 K 18 4 when Jezabel killed the prophets. 13
4 he took a hundred prophets and hid them
13 I hid a hundred men of the prophets
19 and the prophets of Baal 450. 22
19 and the prophets of the groves 400
20 and gathered together the prophets unto
25 then Elias said to the prophets of Baal
40 take the prophets of Baal, and let not
19 1 how he had slain all the prophets with
10 they have slain thy prophets. 14
20 35 certain man of the sons of the prophets
41 knew him, that he was one of the p.
22 6 the king of Israel assembled the p.
10 the p. prophesied before them. 2 Pa 18:9
12 the p. prophesied in like. 2 Pa 18:11
13 words of the prophets with one mouth
22 spirit in mouth of all his p. 2 Pa 18:21
23 lying spirit in mouth of all thy prophets
4 K 2 3 sons of the p. that were at Bethel
5 sons of the p. that were at Jericho
7 fifty men of the sons of the prophets
15 and the sons of the prophets at Jericho
3 13 go to the prophets of thy father and
4 1 certain woman of the wives of the p.
38 the sons of the p. dwelt before him
38 boil pottage for the sons of the p.
5 22 two young men of the sons of the p.
6 1 sons of the prophets said to Eliseus
9 1 called one of the sons of the prophets
7 the blood of my servants the prophets
10 19 call to me all the prophets of Baal
17 13 by the hand of all the p. and seers
13 in the hand of my servants the p.
23 hand of all his servants the prophets
21 10 in the hand of his servants the p.
23 2 with him, the priests and the prophets
24 2 had spoken by his servants the prophets
1 Pa 16 22 and do no evil to my p. Ps 104:15
2 Pa 18 5 gathered together of the p. 400 men
12 the words of all the prophets with one
22 in the mouth of all thy prophets
20 20 believe his prophets, and all things
24 19 he sent prophets to them to bring
29 25 commandment of Lord by hand of his p.
35 15 Heman and Idithun the p. of the king
36 16 despised his words and misused the p.
1 Es 5 2 with them were the prophets of God
9 11 by hand of thy servants the prophets

15 15 to this agree words of the prophets
32 Judas and Silas, being prophets also
24 14 are written in the law and the prophets
26 22 other things than those which the p., and
27 believest thou the prophets, O King
28 23 out of law of Moses and the prophets
Rom 1 2 he had promised before by his p., in
3 21 witnessed by the law and the prophets
11 3 Lord, they have slain thy prophets, they
16 26 made manifest by the scriptures of p.
1 C 12 28 first apostles, secondly p., thirdly
29 are all apostles? Are all prophets? Are
14 29 let the prophets speak, two or three
32 spirits of the p. are subject to the p.
Eph 2 20 foundation of the apostles and prophets
3 5 revealed to his holy apostles and p.
4 11 he gave some apostles, and some prophets
1 Th 2 15 both killed the Lord Jesus, and the p.
Heb 1 1 to the fathers by the prophets, last
11 32 Jephthe, David, Samuel and the prophets
James 5 10 the prophets, who spoke in the name of
1 P 1 10 the p. have inquired and diligently
2 P 2 1 there were also false prophets among
3 2 told you before from the holy prophets
1 J 4 1 many false prophets are gone out into
Apoc 10 7 hath declared by his servants the p.
11 10 these two prophets tormented them that
18 render reward to thy servants the p.
16 6 have shed the blood of saints and p.
18 20 and ye holy apostles and prophets; for
24 in her was found the blood of prophets
22 6 God of the spirits of the prophets
9 and of thy brethren the prophets, and
propitiation Lev 23 28 because it is a day of p.
Rom 3 25 Jesus, whom God hath proposed to be a p.
Heb 2 17 might be a p. for the sins of the people
1 J 2 2 he is the p. for our sins: and not
4 10 sent his Son to be a p. for our sins
propitiatory Exod 25 17 thou shalt make also a p.
Exod 25 20 let them cover both sides of the p.
20 their faces being turned towards the p.
22 and will speak to thee over the p.
26 34 thou shalt set the p. upon the ark
30 6 the ark of the testimony before the p.
31 7 the p. that is over it, and all the
35 12 the p. and the p. veil that is drawn
37 6 made also the p., that is, the oracle
7 he set on the two sides of the p.
8 cherubims at the two ends of the p.
9 covering the p. and looking one
39 34 the veil, the ark, bars, the p.
Lev 16 2 which is within the veil before the p.
14 seven times towards the propitiatory
Num 7 89 of one speaking to him from the p.
Eccu 35 3 is to offer a p. sacrifice for
Heb 9 5 cherubims of glory overshadowing the p.
proposal 3 K 18 24 answering said: A very good p.
1 Ma 6 60 proposal was acceptable in the sight
8 21 proposal was pleasing in their sight
propose Judg 14 12 I will propose to you a riddle
Job 23 7 let him propose equity against me and
proposed Judg 14 16 the riddle which thou hast p.
3 K 10 3 of all the things she proposed to him
2 Pa 9 1 p. to him all that was in her heart
2 Solomon explained to her all that she p.
Ps 139 5 who have proposed to supplant my steps
Ecce 1 13 and I proposed in my mind to seek and
2 Ma 2 29 according to the plan p., studying
Mat 13 24 another parable he proposed to them. 31
Rom 1 13 I have often p. to come unto you, and
3 25 whom God hath p. to be a propitiation
Heb 12 1 run by patience to the fight p. to us
proposing 1 Tim 4 6 these things p. to the brethren

proposition Num 4 7 up also the table of p.
Judg 20 13 would not hearken to the proposition
1 Pa 28 16 also gold for the tables of proposition
2 Pa 29 18 and the table of p. with all its vessels
Ps 48 5 I will open my p. on the psaltery
1 Ma 1 23 table of p. and the pouring vessels
Mat 12 4 and did eat the loaves of p. Mark 2:26
Luke 6 4 and took and ate the bread of p.
loaves of proposition; *see* **loaves**
propositions Ps 77 2 I will utter p. from the
propped Eccu 50 1 who in his life p. up the house
propriety Gen 31 47 to the p. of his language
prosecuted 2 Ma 4 48 that p. the cause for the
proselyte Exod 12 49 to the p. that sojourneth with
Mat 23 15 to make one proselyte; and when he is
Acts 6 5 and Nicolas, a proselyte of Antioch
proselytes 1 Pa 22 2 gather together all the p.
2 Pa 2 17 Solomon numbered all the proselytes
30 25 and the proselytes of the land of Israel
Tob 1 7 gave all his tithes to the proselytes
Eze 14 7 every stranger among the proselytes
Acts 2 11 Jews also, and proselytes, Cretes and
prospect Eze 40 44 their p. was towards the south
2 Ma 13 5 side: this had a prospect steep down
prosper Gen 39 3 made all that he did to p. 23
Exod 40 13 that the unction of them may prosper
3 K 22 12 go up to Ramoth Galaad and prosper, for
15 up and p., and the Lord shall deliver
1 Pa 22 11 do thou prosper and build the house to
13 for then thou shalt be able to prosper
2 Pa 18 11 up to Ramoth Galaad and thou shalt p.
Ps 1 3 whatsoever he shall do shall prosper
100 7 that speaketh unjust things did not p.
Prov 12 12 but the root of the just shall prosper
14 15 wise servant shall p. in his dealings
38 13 that hideth his sins, shall not prosper
Eccu 38 14 that he would p. what they give for
Isa 54 17 that is formed against thee shall p.
55 11 shall p. in the things for which I sent
Jer 12 1 why doth the way of the wicked p.
2 they prosper and bring forth fruit
22 30 a man that shall not p. in his days
46 27 Jacob shall return . . . and prosper
Eze 17 9 shall it prosper then? Shall he not
10 it is planted: shall it prosper then
15 shall he that hath done thus prosper
Dan 8 12 and he shall do and shall prosper
24 lay all things waste and shall prosper
11 27 one table, and they shall not prosper
36 shall p. till the wrath be accomplished
prospered Gen 24 42 if thou hast p. my way
Gen 24 56 because the Lord hath p. my way
40 23 chief butler, when things p. with him
2 Pa 7 11 and in his own house and he prospered
31 21 and he [Ezechias] did it and prospered
1 Es 6 14 the ancients of the Jews built and p.
Wisd 11 1 she p. their works in the hands of
1 Ma 2 47 and the work prospered in their hands
3 6 and salvation prospered in his hand
4 55 to heaven, him that had p. them
14 36 in his days things p. in his hands
16 2 things have p. so well in our hands
prospereth Ps 36 7 envy not the man who p. in
prospering Gen 26 13 he went on p. and increasing
2 K 3 1 David p. and growing always
5 10 [David] went on p. and growing up
prosperity Gen 24 60 wishing p. to their sister
Deut 23 6 neither shalt thou seek their prosperity
1 K 2 32 temple, in all the prosperity of Israel
2 Es 2 10 sought the p. of the children of Israel
Job 30 15 my p. hath passed away like a cloud
Ps 72 3 seeing the prosperity of sinners. For
Prov 1 32 prosperity of fools shall destroy them

7 14 I vowed victims for p., this day I
Eccu 10 5 prosperity of man is in the hand of God
12 8 friend shall not be known in prosperity
9 in the prosperity of a man, his enemies
22 28 in his p. also thou mayst rejoice
Jer 22 21 I spoke to thee in thy prosperity
1 Ma 12 22 you do well to write to us of your p.
2 Ma 5 6 p. against one's own kindred is a
prosperous Gen 24 21 made his journey p. or not
Gen 39 2 he was a prosperous man in all things
41 16 God shall give Pharao a p. answer
Josu 23 15 and all things prosperous have come
Judg 18 5 whether their journey should be p.
Ps 67 20 will make our journey prosperous to us
Prov 11 5 of the upright shall make his way p.
Eccu 41 2 and whose ways are p. in all things
Isa 48 15 brought him, and his way is made p.
53 10 will of the Lord shall be p. in his
Jer 2 37 thou shalt have nothing p. therein
Rom 1 10 I may have a p. journey, by the will of
prosperously Gen 28 21 I shall return p. to my
Num 14 41 which shall not succeed p. with you
2 Pa 18 14 for all shall succeed prosperously
32 30 in all his works he did prosperously
1 Es 8 23 and it fell out prosperously unto us
Ps 44 5 out, proceed prosperously, and reign
2 Ma 8 8 most part succeeded p. with him
3 J 2 that thou mayest proceed p. and fare well as thy soul doth p.
prostitute Lev 21 7 to wife a harlot or a vile p.
Deut 23 2 one born of a p. shall not enter into
Jer 2 20 every green tree thou didst p. thyself
Eze 16 30 the works of a shameless prostitute
prostituted Jer 3 1 hast p. thyself to many
Jer 3 2 see where thou hast not p. thyself
Eze 16 15 hast p. thyself to every passenger
25 hast p. thyself to every one that
prostitutes Bar 6 10 and they give thereof to p.
prostituting Eze 23 12 p. herself to the children
prostitution Eze 16 25 set up a sign of thy p.
prostrate Gen 19 1 worshipped p. to the ground
Gen 50 18 worshipping prostrate on the ground
Exod 34 8 bowed down prostrate unto the earth
Deut 9 25 I lay prostrate before the Lord
Tob 12 22 they lying prostrate for three hours
Jdth 4 8 the little children to lie p. before the
9 1 falling down prostrate before the Lord
10 1 wherein she lay prostrate before the
Dan 3 10 shall prostrate himself and adore
15 prostrate yourselves and adore the
2 Ma 10 4 besought the Lord, lying p. on the
26 lying p. at the foot of the altar
13 12 lying p. on the ground for three days
prostrated 2 K 14 33 p. himself on the ground
Jdth 7 4 prostrated themselves upon the ground
2 Ma 3 15 the priests p. themselves before the
prostrating Jdth 10 20 p. herself to the ground
protect Exod 33 22 and p. thee with my right hand
Deut 32 38 help you and p. you in your distress
4 K 19 34 I will p. this city and will save it
20 6 I will p. this city for my own sake
Job 14 13 that thou mayst protect me in hell
Ps 16 8 p. me under the shadow of thy wings
19 2 name of the God of Jacob protect thee
30 21 shalt protect them in thy tabernacle
47 4 be known, when he shall protect her
90 14 I will p. him because he hath known my
Prov 2 7 and p. them that walk in simplicity
4 9 and protect thee with a noble crown
Eccu 27 9 she shall protect thee forever, and in
Isa 31 5 will the Lord of hosts p. Jerusalem
37 35 I will protect this city and will
38 6 the Assyrians, and I will protect it
Osee 11 8 shall I protect thee, O Israel? How
Zach 9 15 the Lord of hosts will protect them
12 8 the Lord protect the inhabitants of
protected Ps 3 6 because the Lord hath p. me
Ps 26 5 he hath p. me in the secret place of
60 5 I shall be p. under the covert of thy
63 3 thou hast p. me from the assembly of
138 13 thou hast p. me from my mother's womb
Wisd 19 8 which was protected with thy hand
Eccu 2 15 they shall not be protected by him
14 27 he shall be p. under her covering from
Isa 28 15 lies and by falsehood we are protected
49 2 in shadow of his hand he hath p. me
51 16 have p. thee in the shadow of my hand
Osee 4 18 that should have p. them have loved
1 Ma 3 3 and protected the camp with his sword
11 16 into Arabia, there to be protected
2 Ma 14 15 who p. his portion by evident signs
protecteth Num 14 14 thy cloud p. them, and thou
Eccu 4 12 and p. them that seek after her
protecting Isa 31 5 p. and delivering, passing
Eze 28 14 a cherub stretched out and protecting
protection Gen 14 20 by whose p. the enemies are
Ps 17 36 hast given me the p. of thy salvation
21 1 for the morning protection, a psalm
88 19 our protection is of the Lord and of
90 1 under the protection of the God of
104 39 he spread a cloud for their protection
107 9 Ephraim the protection of my head
120 5 the Lord is thy protection upon thy
Isa 4 5 for over all the glory shall be a p.
28 17 waters shall overflow its protection
2 Ma 10 1 by the p. of the Lord, recovered the
13 17 by the protection and help of the Lord
protector Gen 15 1 fear not, Abram, I am thy p.
Ps 3 4 but thou, O Lord, art my protector
17 3 my p. and the horn of my salvation
19 the Lord became my protector. And he
31 the protector of all that trust in him
26 1 the Lord is the protector of my life
27 7 Lord is my helper and my protector
8 the p. of the salvation of his anointed
30 3 be thou unto me a God, a protector
5 thou art my protector. Into thy
32 20 for he is our helper and protector
36 39 he is their p. in the time of trouble
39 18 thou art my helper and my protector
45 8 the God of Jacob is our protector
53 6 the Lord is the protector of my soul
58 10 to thee: for thou art my protector
12 bring them down, O Lord, my protector
61 3 he is my protector, I shall be moved
70 3 be thou unto me a God, a protector
6 from my mother's womb thou art my p.
83 10 behold, O God our protector: and look
90 2 thou art my protector and my refuge
113 9 he is their helper and their p. 10, 11
118 114 thou art my helper and my protector
143 2 my protector, and I have hoped in him
Eccu 2 13 he is a protector to all that seek him
34 19 that fear him, he is their powerful p.
51 2 hast been a helper and protector to me
2 Ma 3 39 is the visitor and p. of that place
8 36 that the Jews had God for their p.
protest 3 K 2 42 did I [Solomon] not p. to thee
1 C 15 31 I die daily, I protest by your glory
protested Eccu 46 22 he p. before the Lord and
Zach 3 6 angel of the Lord protested to Jesus
protesting Jer 11 7 p. I conjured your fathers
proud Deut 17 12 he that will be p. and refuse to
Deut 32 27 lest perhaps their enemies might be p.
Jdth 9 16 have the proud been acceptable to
Job 15 20 the wicked man is proud all his days

26 12 his wisdom has struck the proud one
40 6 scatter the proud in thy indignation
7 look on all that are p. and confound
Ps 9 2 whilst the wicked man is proud, the
11 4 the tongue that speaketh proud things
17 28 wilt bring down the eyes of the proud
88 11 thou hast humbled the proud one, as
93 2 earth: render a reward to the proud
100 5 with him that had a proud eye, and an
118 21 thou hast rebuked the proud: they are
51 the proud did iniquitously altogether
69 iniquity of the p. hath been multiplied
78 let the proud be ashamed, because
122 good: let not the proud calumniate me
122 4 to the rich, and contempt to the proud
139 6 the proud have hidden a net for me
Prov 13 10 among p. there are always contentions
15 25 Lord will destroy the house of the p.
16 5 every proud man is an abomination to
19 than to divide spoils with the proud
21 24 p. and the arrogant is called ignorant
29 23 humiliation followeth the proud: and
Wisd 14 6 when the proud giants perished, the
15 14 are foolish and unhappy and proud
Eccu 3 30 congregation of the proud shall not
4 9 wrong out of the hand of the proud
10 9 why is earth and ashes proud? There
17 overturned thrones of proud princes
18 the roots of proud nations to wither
21 hath abolished the memory of the proud
11 32 so also is the heart of the proud
13 1 he that hath fellowship with the proud
24 humility is an abomination to the proud
26 he hath spoken proud things, and they
21 5 substance of the proud shall be rooted
23 8 proud and the evil speakers shall fall
25 4 a poor man that is proud: rich man
27 16 in the quarrels of the proud is the
31 mockery and reproach are of the proud
31 31 shall rebuke the heart of the proud
32 16 but not in sin or proud speech
22 and proud man will not dread fear
35 23 taken away the multitude of the proud
51 14 in the time of the proud without help
Isa 2 12 shall be upon everyone that is proud
10 12 I will visit the fruit of the p. heart
16 6 pride of Moab, he is exceeding proud
51 9 hast not thou struck the proud one
Jer 13 15 be not proud, for the Lord hath
43 2 and all the proud men, made answer
48 29 pride of Moab, he is exceeding proud
50 31 I come against thee, O proud one
32 the proud one shall fall, he shall
Eze 33 28 proud strength thereof shall fail
Haba 2 5 so shall the proud man be, and he
Soph 3 11 the midst of thee thy proud boasters
Mala 3 15 now we call the proud people happy
4 1 the proud and all that do wickedly
2 Ma 9 8 being proud above the condition of man
15 32 had stretched out with proud boasts
Luke 1 51 he hath scattered the proud in the
Rom 1 30 hateful to God, contumelious proud
1 Tim 6 4 he is proud, knowing nothing, but sick
2 Tim 3 2 covetous, haughty, proud, blasphemers
Titus 1 7 not proud, not subject to anger, not
James 4 6 God resisteth the proud. 1 P 5:5
2 P 2 18 speaking proud words of vanity, they
Jude 16 and their mouth speaketh proud things
proudly Exod 18 11 because they dealt p. against
2 Es 9 10 thou knowest that they dealt proudly
16 they and our fathers dealt proudly
29 they dealt proudly and hearkened not
Ps 16 10 fat: their mouth hath spoken proudly
30 24 will repay them abundantly that act p.
Joel 2 20 go up because he hath done proudly
1 Ma 1 23 he p. entered into the sanctuary
25 slaughters of men and spoke very p.
7 34 and abused them: and he spoke proudly
47 which he had proudly stretched out
2 Ma 9 4 because he had spoken so proudly that
prove Gen 27 21 p. whether thou be my son Esau
Exod 16 4 that I may prove them whether they
20 20 fear not: for God is come to p. you
Deut 8 2 to afflict thee and to prove thee
Josu 20 4 such things as prove him innocent
3 K 8 43 may prove that thy name is called upon
Tob 12 13 that temptation should prove thee
Jdth 8 31 that which I intend to do prove ye if
Job 9 20 innocent, he shall prove me wicked
36 3 and I will prove my maker just. For
13 and crafty men prove the wrath of God
Ps 25 2 prove me, O Lord, and try me: burn my
138 23 prove me, O God, and know my heart
Ecce 3 18 of men, that God would prove them sons
Wisd 2 17 let us prove what shall happen to him
Eccu 37 30 prove thy soul in thy life: and if
Jer 6 27 thou shalt know and prove their way
17 10 who search the heart and p. the reins
2 Ma 1 34 he might prove what had happened
Acts 24 13 neither can they prove unto thee the
25 7 grievous causes, which they could not p.
Rom 12 2 that you may prove what is the good, and
1 C 11 28 let a man prove himself: and so let him
2 C 13 5 you be in faith; prove ye yourselves
Gal 6 4 let every one prove his own work, and
1 Th 5 21 but prove all things; hold fast that
proved Gen 41 13 the event of the thing p. to be
Gen 42 16 till what you have said be proved
Num 5 13 and cannot be proved by witnesses
35 24 and this be proved in the hearing of
Deut 5 24 have proved this day God speaking
8 16 after he had afflicted and proved thee
10 15 of all nations, as this day it is proved
19 4 is proved to have had no hatred. 6
33 8 thou hast proved in the temptation
Josu 20 5 is not proved to have been his enemy
2 Pa 9 6 I had proved that scarce one half of
Jdth 8 21 were tempted that they might be proved
22 and being proved by many tribulations
15 14 all those things that were p. to be
Job 36 4 perfect knowledge shall be p. to thee
Ps 16 3 thou hast proved my heart, and visited
65 10 thou, O God, hast proved us: thou hast
80 8 p. thee at the waters of contradiction
94 9 they proved me, and saw my works
138 1 Lord, thou hast proved me and known me
Prov 17 17 and a brother is proved in distress
Wisd 3 6 as gold in the furnace he hath p. them
Eccu 5 11 every sinner proved by a double tongue
46 17 by his fidelity he was p. a prophet
Jer 10 8 they shall be all proved together
12 3 hast seen me and proved my heart
2 Ma 1 35 when he had proved it, he gave the
2 C 8 22 brother also, whom we have often proved
1 Tim 3 10 let these also first be proved: and so
Heb 3 10 tempted me, proved and saw my works
James 1 12 when he hath been proved, he shall
provender Gen 42 27 to give his beast provender
Gen 43 24 and he gave provender to their asses
Judg 19 19 we have straw and hay for provender
21 and gave provender to his asses
Isa 30 24 as it was shall eat mingled provender
prover Jer 20 12 Lord of hosts, p. of the just
proverb Gen 10 9 came a p.: Even as Nemrod
Num 21 27 it is said in the proverb: Come into
Deut 28 37 and thou shalt be lost, as a proverb

1 K 10 12 became a proverb: Is Saul also among
19 24 this gave occasion to a proverb
24 14 in the old proverb: From the wicked
2 K 5 8 it is said in the proverb: The blind
20 18 a saying was used in the old proverb
3 K 9 7 and Israel shall be a proverb and a
2 Pa 7 21 and this house shall be for a proverb
Prov 22 6 it is a proverb: A young man according
Jer 24 9 a reproach and a byword and a proverb
Eze 12 22 what is this proverb that you have
23 I will make this proverb to cease
14 8 will make him an example and a proverb
16 44 every one that useth a common proverb
18 2 among you this parable as a proverb
3 parable shall be no more to you a p.
John 10 6 this proverb Jesus spoke to them
16 29 plainly, and speakest no proverb. Now
2 P 2 22 that of the true proverb has happened
proverbs Eccu 8 9 acquaint thyself with their p.
Eccu 18 29 have poured forth p. and judgments
39 3 search out the hidden meanings of p.
47 18 for thy canticles and p. and parables
John 16 25 I have spoken to you in proverbs. The
25 will no more speak to you in proverbs
provest 1 Pa 29 17 my God that thou p. hearts
Job 7 18 and thou provest him suddenly. How
proveth 3 K 8 24 hast performed, as this day p.
2 Pa 6 15 as also the present time proveth
1 Th 2 4 men, but God, who proveth our hearts
provide Gen 22 8 God will p. himself a victim
Gen 30 30 I should now provide also for my own
41 33 let the king provide a wise and
Exod 16 5 let them provide for to bring in: and
18 21 provide out of all the people able men
21 10 he shall provide her a marriage and
Num 27 16 provide a man that may be over this
Deut 32 29 and would provide for their last end
Judg 21 17 p. with great diligence that one tribe
Ruth 3 1 will p. that it may be well with thee
1 K 16 17 provide me then some man that can play
2 Pa 2 9 to provide me timber in abundance
Ps 77 20 can he also give bread, or p. a table
Prov 30 25 which p. themselves food in the harvest
2 Ma 14 8 to p. for the good of my countrymen
Acts 23 24 provide beasts, that they may set Paul
provided Gen 24 14 thou hast p. for thy servant
Exod 16 18 did he find less that had provided less
Josu 9 24 and p. for our lives, compelled by
1 K 16 1 I have p. me a king among his sons
2 K 19 32 he p. the king with sustenance
3 K 4 7 who provided victuals for the king and
7 every one p. necessaries, each man his
1 Pa 29 19 house for which I have p. the charges
2 Pa 2 7 whom my father David provided. Send
Ps 67 11 O God, thou hast provided for the poor
Eze 20 6 into a land which I had p. for them
1 Ma 14 10 he provided victuals for the cities
2 Ma 4 2 who p. for the city and defended
Luke 12 20 things be which thou hast provided
providence Jdth 9 5 in thy p. thou hast placed
Jdth 11 16 are told me by the providence of God
Ecce 5 5 say not . . . There is no providence
Wisd 6 17 meeteth them with all providence
14 3 thy providence, O Father, governeth it
17 2 lay there exiled from the eternal p.
Acts 24 2 many things are rectified by thy p.
provideth Job 38 41 who p. food for the raven
Prov 6 8 p. her meat for herself in the summer
12 9 the poor man that p. for himself
Eccu 3 34 God p. for him that showeth favor
providing Num 10 33 p. a place for the camp
Wisd 13 16 providing for it, lest it should fall
2 Ma 11 15 providing for the common good in all

Rom 12 17 p. good things, not only in the sight
Heb 11 40 God p. some better thing for us, that
province Deut 19 3 thou shalt divide the whole p.
Josu 12 23 king of Dor, and of the p. of Dor one
1 Es 2 1 are the children of the p. 2 Es 7:6
5 8 that we went to the province of Judea
6 2 a castle in the province of Media
7 16 find in all the province of Babylon
2 Es 1 3 of the captivity there in the province
11 3 are the chief men of the province
Esth 8 9 to p. and p., to people and people
Ecce 5 7 justice perverted in the province
Dan 2 49 the works of the p. of Babylon. 3:12
3 1 plain of Dura of the p. of Babylon
97 and Abdenago in the p. of Babylon
8 2 Susa, which is in the province of Elam
11 7 into the p. of the king of the north
Acts 23 34 and had asked of what province he was
25 1 when Festus was come into the p., after
provinces Gen 41 57 all provinces came into Egypt
1 K 6 5 according to the number of the p.
18 the cities . . . of the five provinces
3 K 20 14 the servants of the princes of the provinces. 15, 17, 19
1 Es 4 15 hurtful to the kings and provinces
Jdth 3 1 all the cities and provinces of Syria
9 great a fear lay upon all those p.
7 2 brought away out of the provinces
11 6 thy discipline is cried up in all p.
Esth 1 1 to Ethiopia over 127 provinces
3 and the governors of the provinces
16 in all the provinces of king Assuerus
20 be published through all the provinces
22 he sent letters to all the provinces
2 3 be sent through all the provinces
18 and he gave rest to all the provinces
3 8 scattered through all the provinces
12 and to the judges of the provinces
13 sent by the king's messengers to all p.
14 all provinces might know and be ready
4 3 in all provinces, towns, and places
11 provinces that are under his dominion
8 5 destroyed in all the king's provinces
9 who were rulers over the 127 provinces
10 were to run through all the provinces
12 was appointed through all the p.
17 in all peoples, cities, and provinces
9 3 judges of the p. and the governors and
12 think they have slain in all the p.
16 through all the p. which were subject
20 abode in all the king's provinces
28 all provinces in the whole world shall
30 Jews that were in the 127 provinces
13 1 to princes and governors of the 127 p.
5 the peace and concord of the provinces
6 who is chief over all the provinces
16 1 to the . . . princes of 127 provinces
8 must provide for the peace of all p.
Ecce 2 8 the wealth of kings and provinces
Jer 10 25 p. that have not called upon thy name
Lam 1 1 the princes of provinces made tributary
Eze 19 8 against him on every side out of the p.
Dan 2 48 governor over all the p. of Babylon
3 2 to call . . . chief men of the provinces
3 and all the princes of the provinces
1 Ma 8 8 the Lydians, some of their best p.
2 Ma 9 25 when I went into the higher provinces
proving Eph 5 10 p. what is well pleasing to God
provision Gen 42 33 take ye necessary provision
Exod 16 29 sixth day he giveth you a double p.
3 K 4 22 provision of Solomon for each day
5 11 wheat, for provision for his house
4 K 6 23 provision of meats was set before them

Jdth 4 4 together corn for provision for war
Jer 52 34 for his diet a continual provision
Dan 1 5 the king appointed them a daily p.
1 Ma 6 57 our provision of victuals is small
2 Ma 10 18 manner of provision to sustain a siege
12 14 of the walls, and the p. of victuals
27 engines of war and a provision of darts
Rom 13 14 and make not provision for the flesh in
provisions Gen 42 25 to give them besides p.
Gen 45 21 Joseph gave . . . provisions for the way
Josu 9 4 took for themselves provisions, laying
5 which they carried for provisions
2 K 20 3 them in ward, allowing them provisions
2 Pa 11 11 governors and storehouses of p.
23 he gave them provisions in abundance
Jdth 2 8 with all provisions sufficient for
Ps 77 25 he sent them provisions in abundance
1 Ma 9 52 garrisons in them, and p. of victuals
2 Ma 3 10 p. for the subsistence of the widows
provocation Ps 94 9 as in the p. according
Eze 20 28 presented the p. of their offerings
Jer 32 31 this city hath been to me a provocation
Heb 3 8 harden not your hearts, as in the p. 15
provocations 4 K 23 26 p. wherewith Manasses had
provoke Deut 4 25 your God, to p. him to wrath
Deut 9 8 in Horeb also thou didst provoke him
31 29 to provoke him by the works of your
32 21 I will p. them with that which is no
1 K 12 14 and not provoke the mouth of the Lord
3 K 14 9 and molten gods, to p. me to anger
15 made to themselves groves, to p. the
16 2 to provoke me to anger with their sins
7 to provoke him to anger by the works
26 to provoke the Lord the God of Israel
33 Achab did more to provoke the Lord
21 22 hast done, to provoke me to anger
4 K 17 17 evil before the Lord, to provoke him
21 6 evil before the Lord and to provoke him
23 19 kings of Israel had made to p. the
2 Pa 25 19 why dost thou provoke evil against
33 6 before the Lord, to p. him to anger
34 25 to p. me to wrath with all the works
Job 12 6 abound, and they provoke God boldly
34 37 then let him provoke God to judgment
Ps 65 7 not them that provoke him be exalted
67 7 them that p., that dwell in sepulchers
73 10 is the adversary to provoke thy name
77 40 often did they p. him in the desert
Eccu 4 2 and provoke not the poor in his want
Isa 1 20 will not, and will provoke me to wrath
3 8 to provoke the eyes of his majesty
65 3 people that continually p. me to anger
Jer 7 18 strange gods, and to p. me to anger
19 do they provoke me to anger, saith
11 17 to p. me, offering sacrifice to Baalim
25 6 nor provoke me to wrath by the works
7 that you might p. me to anger with
32 29 strange gods, to provoke me to wrath
30 p. me with the work of their hands
44 3 committed to provoke me to wrath
8 in that you provoke me to wrath with
Eze 2 7 forbear: for they provoke me to anger
8 do not thou provoke me, as that house
8 3 idol of jealousy to p. to jealousy
17 have turned to provoke me to anger
16 26 multiplied thy fornications to p. me
32 9 I shall p. to anger the heart of many
1 Ma 6 34 mulberries, to provoke them to fight
15 40 and began to provoke the people and
Rom 10 19 I will p. you to jealousy by that which
11 14 by any means, I may p. to emulation
1 C 10 22 do we provoke the Lord to jealousy? Are
Eph 6 4 provoke not your children to anger; but
Col 3 21 fathers, provoke not your children to
Heb 3 10 for some who heard did provoke: but not
10 24 to p. unto charity and to good works
provoked Gen 49 23 they that held darts p. him
Num 11 33 wrath of the Lord being p. against the
Deut 9 18 Lord, and had provoked him to wrath
22 at the graves of lust you p. the Lord
32 16 they provoked him by strange gods
19 his own sons and daughters provoked him
21 have p. me with that which was no god
Judg 2 12 and they provoked the Lord to anger
1 K 1 7 she provoked her; but Anna wept
3 K 14 22 p. him above all that their fathers
15 30 offence wherewith he p. the Lord the
22 54 served also Baal . . . and p. the Lord
4 K 23 26 wherewith Manasses had provoked him
2 Pa 28 25 and he provoked the wrath of the Lord
1 Es 5 12 our fathers had p. the God of heaven
2 Es 9 26 they p. thee to wrath and departed from
Ps 5 11 for they have provoked thee, O Lord
9 4 the sinner hath provoked the Lord
13 wherefore hath the wicked provoked God
73 18 foolish people hath provoked thy name
77 17 they provoked the most High to wrath
56 they tempted and p. the most high God
58 they p. him to anger on their hills
105 7 they p. to wrath going up to the sea
16 and they provoked Moses in the camp
29 they provoked him with their inventions
32 they p. him also at the waters of
43 they provoked him with their counsel
106 11 provoked the counsel of the most High
Prov 27 4 who can bear the violence of one p.
Eccu 48 2 they that provoked him in their envy
Isa 63 10 they p. to wrath and afflicted the
Jer 4 17 because she hath provoked me to wrath
8 19 have they provoked me to wrath with
50 24 because thou hast provoked the Lord
Lam 1 18 I have provoked his mouth to wrath
3 42 done wickedly, and p. thee to wrath
Bar 4 6 because you provoked God to wrath
7 you have provoked him who made you
Eze 16 43 but hast p. me in all these things
20 8 they p. me and would not hearken to
13 house of Israel p. me in the desert
21 but their children provoked me, they
Dan 11 10 his sons shall be provoked, and they
11 king of the south being provoked shall
Osee 12 14 Ephraim hath provoked me to wrath
Zach 8 14 your fathers had provoked me to wrath
1 Ma 6 59 they have been p. and have done all
2 Ma 12 14 and provoked Judas with railing and
14 27 p. with this man's wicked accusations
1 C 13 5 is not provoked to anger, thinketh no
2 C 9 2 your emulation hath provoked very many
provokedst Deut 9 7 how thou p. the Lord thy
provokest 4 K 14 10 why p. thou evil, that thou
provoketh Prov 18 6 his mouth provoketh quarrels
Prov 20 2 that p. him, sinneth against his own
29 22 a passionate man provoketh quarrels
30 33 that p. wrath bringeth forth strife
Isa 30 9 for it is a people that p. to wrath
Eze 2 8 provoke me, as that house p. me
44 6 the house of Israel that provoketh me
provoking 3 K 16 13 Israel to sin, p. the Lord
4 K 17 11 they did wicked things, p. the Lord
22 17 p. me by all the works of their hands
Jer 5 23 people is become hard of belief and p.
32 32 they have done, provoking me to wrath
Eze 2 5 they are a provoking house. 6; 3:9, 26, 27; 12:2, 3
12 2 dwellest in the midst of a p. house
9 house of Israel, the p. house, said

25 25 but in your days, ye provoking house
17 12 say to the p. house: Know you not
24 3 by a figure a parable to the p. house
Soph 3 1 woe to the p. and redeemed city, the
Gal 5 26 glory, provoking one another, envying
prudence 2 Pa 2 12 with understanding and p.
Job 12 12 wisdom, and in length of days prudence
Prov 1 3 to understand the words of prudence
2 2 incline thy heart to know prudence
3 and incline thy heart to prudence
11 keep thee, and p. shall preserve thee
3 5 and lean not upon thy own prudence
13 that findeth wisdom and is rich in p.
19 hath established the heavens by p.
4 1 attend that you may know prudence
5 get wisdom, get prudence: forget not
7 with all thy possession purchase p.
5 1 and incline thy ear to my prudence
7 4 my sister: and call prudence thy friend
8 1 and prudence put forth her voice
14 prudence is mine, strength is mine
9 6 and live: and walk by the ways of p.
10 the knowledge of the holy is prudence
10 23 for sport: but wisdom is p. to a man
14 7 he knoweth not the lips of prudence
16 16 purchase p., for it is more precious
18 2 a fool receiveth not the words of p.
19 8 he that keepeth prudence shall find
21 30 there is no wisdom, there is no p.
23 4 rich: but set bounds to thy prudence
24 3 by prudence it shall be strengthened
28 16 prince void of prudence shall oppress
Ecce 1 17 I have given my heart to know prudence
Wisd 8 7 who teacheth temperance and prudence
Eccu 1 4 understanding of p. from everlasting
24 knowledge, and understanding of p.
10 3 inhabited through the p. of the rulers
19 19 the device of sinners is not prudence
34 10 in many things, multiplieth prudence
Bar 3 23 of fables, and searchers of prudence
1 C 1 19 prudence of the prudent I will reject
Eph 1 8 superbounded in us in all . . . prudence
prudent 1 K 16 18 fit for war and p. in his words
1 K 18 15 Saul saw that he was exceeding p.
25 3 she was a p. and very comely woman
Prov 18 16 p. man doth all things with counsel
14 18 the prudent shall look for knowledge
33 in heart of the prudent resteth wisdom
15 5 regardeth reproofs shall become prudent
16 21 wise in heart shall be called prudent
19 14 prudent wife is properly from the Lord
22 3 p. man saw the evil and hid himself
27 12 the p. man seeing evil hideth himself
28 11 poor man that is p. shall search him
Eccu 9 21 and treat with the wise and prudent
10 1 government of a p. man shall be steady
28 that is prudent and well instructed
19 2 fall off, and shall rebuke the prudent
20 29 p. man shall please the great ones
21 20 mouth of the prudent is sought after
24 learning to the p. is as an ornament
Isa 5 21 and prudent in your own conceits. Woe
29 14 understanding of their p. men shall be
Amos 5 13 the prudent shall keep silence at that
Mat 11 25 things from the wise and p. Luke 10:21
Acts 13 7 Sergius Paulus, a p. man. He sending
1 C 1 19 prudence of the prudent I will reject
1 Tim 3 2 the husband of one wife, sober, prudent
Titus 2 2 that the aged men be sober, chaste, p.
1 P 4 7 be p. therefore, and watch in prayers
prune Lev 25 3 six years thou shalt prune thy
Lev 25 4 sow thy field nor prune thy vineyard
pruned Isa 5 6 it desolate; it shall not be p.

pruning Cant 2 12 the time of pruning is come
Isa 18 5 shall be cut off with pruning hooks
psalm Jdth 16 2 tune unto him a new psalm, extol
Ps 3 1 psalm of David. 7:1; 14:1; 26:1; 50:1; 61:1; 62:1; 64:1; 136:1; 138:1; 139:1; 140;1; 142:1; 143:1
4 1 a psalm for David. 5:1; 6:1; 8:1; 9:1; 10:1; 11:1; 12:1; 13:1; 18:1; 19:1; 20:1; 21:1; 22:1; 23:1; 24:1; 25:1; 27:1; 28:1; 30:1; 32:1; 36:1; 37:1; 39:1; 40:1; 42:1; 63:1; 69:1; 70:1; 93:1; 97:1; 98:1; 100:1; 107:1; 108:1; 109:1
17 50 and I will sing a psalm to thy name
26 6 I will sing and recite a psalm to the
29 1 psalm of a canticle at the dedication
47 1 psalm of a canticle for sons of Core
48 1 a psalm for the sons of Core. 83:1
49 1 a psalm for Asaph. 72:1; 75:1; 78:1; 80:1; 81:1; 82:1
56 8 I will sing, and rehearse a psalm
10 I will sing a psalm to thee among the
60 9 so will I sing a psalm to thy name
65 1 canticle of a psalm of the resurrection
2 sing ye a psalm to his name: give glory
4 let it sing a psalm to thy name. Come
66 1 a psalm of a canticle for David. 67:1
67 5 sing a psalm to his name, make a way
71 1 a psalm on Solomon. Give to the king
74 1 a psalm of a canticle for Asaph
76 1 a psalm of Asaph. I cried to the Lord
79 1 a testimony for Asaph, a psalm. Give
80 3 take a p. and bring hither the timbrel
84 1 for the sons of Core, a psalm
86 1 for sons of Core a psalm of a canticle
87 1 a canticle of a psalm for the sons
91 1 a psalm of a canticle on the sabbath
97 5 on the harp and with voice of a psalm
99 1 a psalm of praise. Sing joyfully
146 1 praise ye the Lord, because p. is good
Acts 13 33 in the second psalm also is written
1 C 14 26 every one of you hath a psalm, hath a
psalmist 2 K 23 1 excellent p. of Israel said
psalms Ps 94 2 a joyful noise to him with psalms
Isa 38 20 we will sing our psalms all the days
Haba 3 19 lead me upon my high places singing p.
Luke 20 42 himself saith in the book of Psalms
24 44 and in the psalms concerning me. Then
Acts 1 20 it is written in the book of Psalms
Eph 5 19 speaking to yourselves in psalms, and
Col 3 16 admonishing one another in psalms, hymns
psalteries 1 Ps 13 8 with harps and with p. 25:1
1 Pa 15 16 on psalteries and harps and cymbals
20 sung mysteries upon psalteries. And
28 cymbals and p. 25:6; 2 Pa 5:12; 29:25; 2 Es 12:27; 1 Ma 13:51
2 Pa 9 11 harps and p. for the singing men
20 28 they came into Jerusalem with p.
Jer 52 18 the p. and the bowls and the little
psaltery 1 K 10 5 with a psaltery and a timbrel
1 Pa 16 5 Jehiel over the instruments of psaltery
Ps 32 3 the harp: sing to him on the psaltery
48 5 I will open my proposition on the p.
56 9 arise, psaltery and harp. 107:3
70 22 thy truth with the instruments of p.
80 3 the pleasant psaltery with the harp
91 4 upon the psaltery: with a canticle
143 9 on the p. and an instrument of ten
149 3 to him with the timbrel and the p.
150 3 praise him with psaltery and harp
Dan 3 5 hear the sound . . . of the p. 7, 10, 15
Amos 6 5 that sing to the sound of the psaltery
Ptolemais 1 Ma 5 15 they of P. and of Tyre and
1 Ma 5 21 pursued them even to the gate of P.

55 Simon his brother in Galilee before P.
10 1 the Illustrious, came up and took P.
39 P. and the confines thereof I give as
56 meet me at Ptolemais, that we may see
57 he [Ptolemee] came to Ptolemais
58 he celebrated her marriage at P.
60 and he went honorable to Ptolemais
11 22 he came to P. and wrote to Jonathan
24 and went to the king to Ptolemais
12 45 come with me to Ptolemais and I will
48 as soon as Jonathan entered into P.
48 they of Ptolemais shut the gates of
13 12 Tryphon removed from Ptolemais with
2 Ma 13 24 prince from P. unto the Gerrenians
25 when he was come to P., the men of that
Acts 21 7 sea, from Tyre came down to Ptolemais
Ptolemeans 2 Ma 6 8 by the suggestion of the P.
Ptolemee 1 Ma 1 19 he made war against Ptolemee
1 Ma 1 19 but P. was afraid at his presence
3 38 Lysias chose P. the son of Dorymenus
10 51 Alexander sent ambassadors to Ptolemee
57 so P. went out of Egypt with Cleopatra
11 3 when Ptolemee entered into the cities
13 Ptolemee entered into Antioch and set
17 Alexander's head, and sent it to P.
16 11 Ptolemee . . . was appointed captain
16 Ptolemee and his men rose up and took
18 P. wrote these things, and sent to
2 Ma 4 45 promised P. to give him much money
46 P. went to the king in a certain court
8 8 Ptolemee the governor of Celesyria
9 29 went into Egypt to P. Philometor
10 12 Ptolemee that was called Macer was
king Ptolemee 1 Ma 10 55 king P. answered, saying
1 Ma 11 8 king P. got the dominion of the cities
15 king Ptolemee brought forth his army
16 king Ptolemee was exalted. And Zabdiel
18 king Ptolemee died the third day after
15 16 Lucius . . . to king Ptolemee, greeting
2 Ma 1 10 Aristobolus the preceptor of king P.
Ptolemy Esth 11 1 fourth year of the reign of P.
Esth 11 1 Ptolemy his son brought this epistle
1 Lysimachus the son of Ptolemy had
public Gen 47 22 was given out of the p. stores
Deut 24 5 neither shall any public business be
1 Es 7 21 to all the keepers of the public chest
Prov 26 26 laid open in the public assembly
1 Ma 13 42 in the instruments and p. records
14 23 of their words in the public records
2 Ma 1 33 when this matter became public, it was
3 18 praying and making public supplication
9 26 remembering favors both p. and private
15 6 to set up a p. monument of this victory
publican Mat 10 3 Thomas and Matthew the p., and
Mat 18 17 him be to thee as the heathen and p.
Luke 5 27 he saw a publican named Levi sitting
18 10 one a Pharisee, and the other a p.
11 as also is this publican. I fast
13 the p., standing afar off, would not
publicans Mat 5 46 do not even the p. this? And
Mat 9 10 many publicans and sinners came and
11 your master eat with p. and sinners
11 19 friend of p. and sinners. Luke 7:34
21 31 the p. and the harlots shall go into
32 the p. and the harlots believed him
Mark 2 15 many publicans and sinners sat down
16 seeing that he ate with publicans and
16 and drink with publicans and sinners
Luke 3 12 the p. also came to be baptized and
5 29 was a great company of publicans and
30 you eat and drink with p. and sinners
7 29 all the people hearing, and the p.
15 1 the p. and sinners drew near unto him
19 2 who was the chief of the publicans
publicly 4 K 15 10 struck him p. and killed him
Mat 1 19 not willing publicly to expose her
Acts 16 37 they have beaten us p., uncondemned
20 20 preached it to you, and taught you p.
publish 1 K 31 9 to publish it in the temples
2 K 1 20 p. it not in the streets of Ascalon
2 Es 2 15 they should proclaim and p. the word
Tob 12 20 God, and p. all his wonderful works
Ps 144 7 they shall publish the memory of the
Jer 5 20 and publish it in Juda, saying: Hear
46 14 publish it in Magdal, and let it be
50 2 ye among the nations, and publish it
Dan 3 99 to publish his signs, because they
Amos 3 9 publish it in the houses of Azotus
Mark 1 45 began to publish and to blaze abroad
5 20 began to p. in Decapolis how great
7 36 more a great deal did they publish it
published Eccu 44 5 p. canticles of the scriptures
Dan 6 7 imperial decree and an edict be p.
Jon 3 7 caused it to be proclaimed and p.
Luke 4 37 the fame of him was published into
12 3 shall be published in the light: and
Acts 10 37 word which hath been p. through all
13 49 was p. throughout the whole country
Rom 16 19 your obedience is p. in every place. I
publisheth Prov 12 23 the heart of fools p. folly
publishing Luke 8 39 p. how great things Jesus
Publius Acts 28 7 chief man of island named P.
Acts 28 8 it happened that father of P. lay sick
Pudens 2 Tim 4 21 Pudens and Linus and Claudia
puffed Wisd 4 19 shall burst them puffed up and
Dan 8 25 and his heart shall be puffed up
Mala 1 13 our labor, and you puffed it away
2 Ma 11 4 puffed up in mind and trusting in
15 6 so Nicanor being puffed up with
1 C 4 6 one be not puffed up against the other
18 not come to you, so some are puffed up
19 not the speech of them that are p. up
5 2 you are puffed up; and have not rather
13 4 dealeth not perversely; is not p. up
Col 2 18 in vain p. up by the sense of the flesh
1 Tim 3 6 lest being puffed up with pride, he fall
2 Tim 3 4 traitors, stubborn, p. up and lovers of
puffeth Prov 28 25 he that boasteth and p. himself
1 C 8 1 knowledge p. up; but charity edifieth
pull Num 16 14 wilt thou also pull out our eyes
Job 12 14 if he pull down, there is no man that
Prov 14 1 the foolish will pull down with her
Isa 23 9 to pull down the pride of all glory
26 5 he shall pull it down even to the dust
19 land of the giants thou shalt p. down
Jer 1 10 to root up and to pull down and to
18 7 to root out and to pull down and to
24 6 build them up, and not pull them down
42 10 build you up, and not pull you down
50 45 of the flocks shall pull them down
Eze 17 9 shall he not pull up the roots thereof
26 12 and pull down thy fine houses: and
1 Ma 4 45 into their minds, to pull it down
Luke 6 42 let me pull the mote out of thy eye
12 18 I will pull down my barns and will
pulled Judg 16 21 forthwith pulled out his eyes
Job 20 28 he shall be pulled down in the day of
24 22 he hath pulled down the strong by his
Eccu 40 16 shall be pulled up before all grass
Isa 10 13 pulled down them that sat on high
25 12 shall be pulled down to the ground
1 Ma 2 25 Mathathias . . . pulled down the altar
2 Ma 7 7 when they had pulled off the skin
Acts 23 10 fearing lest Paul should be p. in pieces
pulling 2 C 10 4 the p. down of fortifications
Jude 23 save, pulling them out of the fire

pulse 2 K 17 28 beans and lentils and fried pulse
Dan 1 12 let pulse be given us to eat, and water
16 should drink: and he gave them pulse
punish Josu 22 22 him not save us, but punish us
Jdth 7 20 punish our iniquities by chastising us
Wisd 12 20 if thou didst p. the enemies of thy
18 8 as thou didst punish the adversaries
Jer 25 12 I will punish the king of Babylon and
36 31 I will punish him and his seed and his
44 29 that I will punish you in this place
50 21 and punish the inhabitants thereof
1 Ma 7 7 let him p. all his friends and their
15 21 that he may punish them according to
2 Ma 1 28 punish them that oppress us and that
6 14 he may punish them in the fulness of
Acts 4 21 not finding how they might punish them
punished Gen 4 15 shall be punished sevenfold
Lev 24 21 that striketh a man shall be punished
Num 31 16 for which also the people was punished
35 17 shall be punished in the same manner
30 the murderer shall be p. by witnesses
Deut 21 22 for which he is to be p. with death
Job 20 18 shall be punished for all that he did
Ps 36 28 the unjust shall be punished, and the
Prov 21 11 when a pestilent man is punished, the
Wisd 3 10 wicked shall be p. according to their
11 5 by what things their enemies were p.
12 15 him who deserveth not to be punished
14 30 for two things they shall be justly p.
16 1 they were worthily punished and were
18 22 he subdued him that punished them
Eccu 23 30 this man shall be p. in the streets
Bar 4 31 have rejoiced at thy ruin, shall be p.
32 thy children have served, shall be p.
1 Ma 14 45 void any of these things, shall be p.
2 Ma 6 13 time, but are presently punished
7 7 if he would eat, before he were p.
Acts 22 5 from thence to Jerusalem to be punished
punisheth Wisd 14 31 p. the transgression of the
punishing 2 Ma 12 23 earnest in p. the profane
Acts 26 11 oftentimes p. them, in every synagogue
punishment Exod 21 21 not be subject to the p.
Jdth 6 6 when they shall receive the punishment
Wisd 6 9 greater p. is ready for the more mighty
16 2 instead of which punishment, dealing
24 against the unjust for their punishment
18 11 servant suffered the same punishment
19 4 that their punishment might fill up
Eccu 23 14 his house shall be filled with his p.
2 Ma 4 38 the Lord repaying him his deserved p.
48 did soon suffer unjust punishment
7 36 shalt receive just p. for thy pride
Mat 25 46 these shall go into everlasting p.
2 Th 1 9 shall suffer eternal p. in destruction
1 P 2 14 sent by him for the p. of evildoers
Jude 7 suffering the p. of eternal fire. In
punishments Jdth 8 27 p. to be less than our
Job 33 25 his flesh is consumed with punishments
Wisd 11 14 by their p. the others were benefited
19 12 punishments came upon the sinners
2 Ma 6 26 should be delivered from the p. of men
Heb 10 29 think he deserveth worse punishments
purchase Lev 25 16 the less shall the p. cost
Job 28 15 the finest gold shall not purchase it
Prov 4 7 with all thy possession p. prudence
16 16 p. prudence, for it is more precious
22 9 shall purchase victory and honor: but
Jer 32 11 and I took the deed of the purchase
12 and I gave the deed of the purchase to
12 subscribed the book of the purchase
14 deed of the purchase that is sealed up
16 I had delivered the deed of purchase
Rom 13 2 that resist, p. to themselves damnation
1 Tim 3 13 shall p. to themselves a good degree
purchased Ps 77 54 which his right hand had p.
Ps 118 111 I have purchased thy testimonies for
Jer 32 43 fields shall be p. in this land
Acts 8 20 that the gift of God may be purchased
20 28 the church of God, which he hath p. with
1 P 2 9 a holy nation, a purchased people
Apoc 14 3 who were purchased from the earth
4 these were p. from among men, the
purchasing Prov 3 14 p. thereof is better than
1 Th 5 9 wrath, but unto the p. of salvation by
2 Th 2 13 unto the purchasing of the glory of our
pure Exod 30 35 incense pure and most worthy
Exod 31 8 the most pure candlestick with the
37 16 and cups, and censers of pure gold
Lev 13 58 with water the parts that are pure
24 4 be set upon the most pure candlestick
3 K 6 20 and overlaid it with most pure gold
21 oracle he overlaid with most pure gold
7 49 golden candlestick . . . of pure gold
50 mortars and censers of most pure gold
10 21 the furniture . . . of most pure gold
2 Pa 3 4 he overlaid it within with pure gold
4 20 candlestick also of most pure gold
22 bowls and the mortars of pure gold
9 17 ivory and overlaid it with pure gold
Jdth 12 9 going in, she remained p. in the tent
Job 4 17 shall a man be more pure than his maker
11 4 thou hast said: My word is pure and I
15 15 the heavens are not pure in his sight
16 18 when I offered pure prayers to God
25 5 the stars are not pure in his sight
33 3 my lips shall speak a pure sentence
Ps 11 7 the words of the Lord are pure words
Prov 15 26 pure words most beautiful shall be
20 9 my heart is clean, I am pure from sin
21 8 as for him that is pure, his work is
25 4 shall come forth a most pure vessel
30 12 that are pure in their own eyes, and
Wisd 7 23 all spirits, intelligible, pure, subtile
25 a certain pure emanation of the glory
18 4 by whom the pure light of the law was
23 11 shall not be wholly pure from sin
Isa 27 2 singing to the vineyard of pure wine
Haba 1 13 thy eyes are too pure to behold evil
2 Ma 14 38 himself pure in the Jews' religion
1 Tim 1 5 from a p. heart, and a good conscience
2 8 lifting up pure hands, without anger
3 9 mystery of faith in a pure conscience
2 Tim 1 3 with a pure conscience, that without
2 22 that call on the Lord out of a p. heart
Apoc 14 10 which is mingled with pure wine in the
21 18 the city itself pure gold, like to
21 the street of the city was pure gold
purer Lam 4 7 whiter than snow, p. than milk
purest Exod 25 11 shalt overlay it with the purest gold. 24; 30:3
Exod 25 17 also a propitiatory of the purest gold
29 dishes and bowls . . . of the purest gold
36 same beaten work of the purest gold
38 snuffers . . . be made of the purest gold
39 shall be a talent of the purest gold
27 20 that they bring thee the purest oil
28 14 two little chains of the purest gold
22 linked one to another of the purest gold
36 make also a plate of the purest gold
37 1 he overlaid it with the p. gold. 26
6 that is, the oracle, of the purest gold
22 all beaten work of the purest gold
23 the seven lamps . . . of the purest gold
29 and incense of the purest spices
39 15 little chains . . . of the purest gold
23 and little bells of the purest gold

29 of sacred veneration of the p. gold
Num 28 5 shall be tempered with the purest oil
Deut 32 14 might drink the p. blood of the grape
3 K 5 11 twenty measures of the purest oil
10 16 made 200 shields of the purest gold
1 Pa 28 18 altar of incense, he gave the p. gold
Prov 3 14 than the chiefest and purest gold
Eccu 24 21 and my odor is as the purest balm
purgation Heb 1 3 making p. of sins, sitteth
purge Isa 1 25 I will clean p. away thy dross
Luke 3 17 he will purge his floor, and will
John 15 2 he will purge it, that it may bring
1 C 5 7 purge out the old leaven, that you may
purged Ps 11 7 p. from the earth, refined seven
Prov 15 27 by mercy and faith sins are p. away
2 P 1 9 that he was purged from his old sins
purgeth Tob 12 9 same is that which p. away sins
purging Mark 7 19 into the privy, p. all meats
purification Lev 12 4 until the days of her p.
Lev 12 4 and thirty days in the blood of her p.
5 the blood of her p. 66 days
6 the days of her p. are expired
14 23 offer them on the eighth day of his p.
49 for the p. thereof he shall take two
15 28 she shall count seven days of her p.
Num 6 9 forthwith on the same day of his p.
8 7 them be sprinkled with the water of p.
19 20 not sprinkled with the water of p.
1 Pa 23 28 the chambers and in the place of p.
Ps 88 45 hast made his purification to cease
2 Ma 1 18 purpose to keep the p. of the temple
36 Nephthar, which is interpreted p.
2 16 we are then about to celebrate the p.
20 concerning . . . p. of the great temple
Luke 2 22 after the days of her purification
John 3 25 and the Jews concerning purification
Acts 21 26 the accomplishment of the days of p.
purifications Eccu 7 34 their portion . . . of p.
purified Lev 14 4 command him that is to be p.
Lev 14 7 seven times that he may be rightly p.
8 being p., he shall enter into the camp
29 upon the head of the purified person
22 7 being p., he shall eat of the sanctified
Num 8 21 they were purified and washed their
22 that being p. they might go into the
31 19 shall be purified the third day and
20 of goats or of wood, shall be purified
23 shall be p. by fire, but whatsoever
24 being p., you shall afterwards enter
1 K 20 26 that he was not clean nor p.
2 K 11 4 she was purified from her uncleanness
2 Pa 29 17 they purified the temple in eight days
2 Es 12 30 the priests and the Levites were p., and they p. the people
13 22 that they should be p. and should come
Jdth 16 22 as soon as they were purified, they
Eccu 48 23 he p. them by the hand of Isaias the
Isa 25 6 of wine purified from the lees. And he
2 Ma 1 33 were with him had p. the sacrifices
10 3 having p. the temple, they made another
12 38 they p. themselves according to the
Acts 21 26 next day being p. with them, entered
24 18 I was found p. in the temple; neither
purifieth Lev 14 11 the priest that p. the man
purify Lev 14 48 he shall p. it, it being cured
Lev 14 52 shall purify it as well with the blood
Num 8 6 and thou shalt purify them [Levites]
15 shalt thou purify and consecrate them
19 19 that is clean shall purify the unclean
2 Pa 29 5 purify the house of the Lord the God of
15 to purify the house of God. And the
Job 41 16 being affrighted, shall p. themselves
Eccu 7 33 and purify thyself with thy arms
34 thy negligences, p. thyself with a few
Mala 4 3 and he shall purify the sons of Levi
John 11 55 before the pasch to purify themselves
James 4 8 purify your hearts, ye double-minded
purifying John 2 6 manner of the p. of the Jews
Acts 15 9 them, purifying their hearts by faith
1 P 1 22 p. your souls in the obedience of
purity Wisd 7 24 everywhere by reason of her p.
1 Ma 14 36 sanctuary and did much evil to its p.
purple Exod 25 4 violet and purple and scarlet. 26:1, 31, 36; 27:16; 28:5, 6, 8, 15, 33; 35:6, 23, 25; 36:8, 35, 37; 38:18, 23; 39:1, 2, 8, 22, 28; 2 Pa 3:14
Exod 35 35 embroidery in blue and purple
Num 4 13 shall wrap it up in a purple cloth
Judg 8 26 ornaments and jewels and p. raiment
2 Pa 2 7 in purple, in scarlet, and in blue, and
14 in purple also and violet and silk and
Jdth 10 19 which was woven of purple and gold
Esth 1 6 fastened with cords of silk and of p.
8 15 clothed with a cloak of silk and purple
Prov 31 22 fine linen and purple is her covering
Cant 3 10 the seat of gold, the going up of purple
7 5 as the purple of the king bound in the
Eccu 40 4 from him that weareth purple and
45 12 holy robe of gold and blue and purple
Jer 10 9 violet and purple is their clothing
Bar 6 12 covered them with a purple garment
71 by the purple also and the scarlet
Eze 27 7 blue and p. from the islands of Elisa
16 they set forth precious stones and p.
Dan 5 7 shall be clothed with purple and shall
16 thou shalt be clothed with purple and
29 Daniel was clothed with purple and a
1 Ma 4 23 and blue silk and purple of the sea
8 14 wore a crown or was clothed in purple
10 20 he sent him a purple robe and a crown
62 that he should be clothed with purple
64 proclaimed, and him clothed with p.
11 58 to be clothed in purple and to wear
14 43 that he should be clothed with purple
44 to be clothed with purple or to wear a
2 Ma 4 38 Andronicus to be stripped of his purple
Mark 15 17 and they clothe him with purple and
20 they took off the purple from him and
Luke 16 19 rich man who was clothed in purple
John 19 2 and they put on him a purple garment
5 crown of thorns and the p. garment
Acts 16 14 woman named Lydia, a seller of p., of
Apoc 17 4 clothed round about with p. and scarlet
18 12 and fine linen and purple and silk and
16 with fine linen and purple and scarlet
purpose Exod 21 14 man kill his neighbor on set p.
Judg 14 15 to the wedding on purpose to strip us
Ruth 2 16 let fall some of your handfuls of p.
1 K 9 24 it was kept of purpose for thee when
3 K 5 5 I p. to build a temple to the name of
Job 34 27 on purpose have revolted from him and
Ps 30 7 that regard vanities to no purpose
40 7 he went out and spoke to the same p.
Isa 1 11 to what purpose do you offer me the
30 7 Egypt shall help in vain and to no p.
Jer 6 20 to what p. do you bring me frankincense
36 3 evils that I purpose to do unto them
38 4 on purpose he weakeneth the hands of
1 Ma 15 3 my purpose is to challenge the kingdom
2 Ma 1 18 we p. to keep the purifications of
3 8 but indeed to fulfil the king's purpose
14 1 of Tripolis to places proper for his p.
38 had held fast his p. of keeping himself
Mat 26 8 to what purpose is this waste? For
Mark 1 38 also; for to this purpose am I come
John 13 28 knew to what purpose he said this to

Acts 11 23 exhorted them all with purpose of heart
27 13 thinking that they had obtained their p.
Rom 4 5 according to the p. of the grace of God
8 28 to such as, according to his purpose
9 11 the p. of God, according to election
17 to this purpose have I raised thee, that
13 6 ministers of God, serving unto this p.
2 C 1 17 the things that I purpose, do I purpose
Eph 1 5 according to the purpose of his will
11 purpose of him who worketh all things
3 11 according to the eternal purpose, which
5 4 scurrility, which is to no purpose; but
6 22 sent to you for this same p. Col 4:8
2 Tim 1 9 according to his own purpose and grace
3 10 thou hast fully known my . . . purpose
Philem 8 command thee that which is to the p.
1 J 3 8 for this purpose the Son of God

purposed Jdth 11 12 these they have p. to make use
Jdth 12 4 do by my hand that which I have p.
13 7 bring to pass that which I have p.
Wisd 8 9 I p. therefore to take her to me to
Isa 14 24 as I have purposed, so shall it fall
26 this is the counsel that I have p.
19 12 the Lord of hosts hath p. upon Egypt
Jer 4 28 I have purposed and I have not repented
51 12 the Lord hath both purposed and done
Lam 2 8 Lord hath p. to destroy the wall of
17 the Lord hath done that which he p.
Dan 1 8 Daniel purposed in his heart that he
Mich 6 5 thee, what Balach the king of Moab p.
Zach 8 14 as I p. to afflict you, when your
1 Ma 3 31 and p. to go into Persia and to take
6 19 and Judas purposed to destroy them
9 69 he p. to return with the rest into
16 13 he purposed treachery against Simon
2 Ma 8 10 Nicanor p. to raise for the king the
15 1 he purposed to set upon him with all
Acts 11 29 p. to send relief to the brethren who
19 21 Paul p. in spirit, when he had passed
Eph 1 9 pleasure, which he hath purposed in him

purposing 1 Ma 11 63 p. to remove him from the
Acts 29 13 himself purposing to travel by land. And

purse Prov 1 14 lot with us, let us all have one p.
Eccu 18 33 when thou hast nothing in thy purse
Mark 6 8 no bread, nor money in their purse
Luke 10 4 carry neither purse nor scrip nor
22 35 when I sent you without purse and
36 he that hath a purse, let him take it
John 12 6 having the purse, carried the things
13 29 thought, because Judas had the purse

purses Mat 10 9 nor silver nor money in your p.

pursue Gen 35 5 they durst not p. after them
Gen 44 4 arise, and pursue after the men: and
Exod 14 4 and he will pursue you: and I shall be
17 heart of the Egyptians to pursue you
15 9 the enemy said: I will p. and overtake
Lev 26 7 you shall pursue your enemies, and
Deut 19 6 should pursue and apprehend him
28 22 blasting, and p. thee till thou perish
45 and shall pursue and overtake thee
32 30 how should one pursue after a thousand
Josu 2 5 pursue after them quickly, and you
8 17 that did not pursue after Israel
10 19 but pursue after the enemies and kill
20 5 when the avenger of blood shall p. him
Judg 8 4 they could not pursue after them that
5 that we may pursue Zebee and Salmana
1 K 14 37 shall I pursue after the Philistines
46 [Saul] did not p. after the Philistines
24 15 after whom dost thou pursue? After a
30 8 shall I pursue after these robbers
8 Lord said to him: Pursue after them
2 K 2 28 did not pursue after Israel any farther
13 38 David ceased to pursue after Absalom
17 1 and I will arise and pursue after David
20 6 and p. after him [Seba] lest he find
7 went out of Jerusalem to p. after Seba
13 went on following Joab to p. after Seba
22 38 I will p. after my enemies and crush
24 13 adversaries and they shall p. thee
Ps 7 6 let the enemy p. my soul and take it
17 38 I will p. after my enemies and overtake
33 15 do good: seek after peace and pursue it
34 6 let the angel of the Lord pursue them
70 11 pursue and take him, for there is none
82 16 so shalt thou p. them with thy tempest
Eccu 11 10 if thou pursue after thou shalt not
Isa 30 16 swifter that shall pursue after you
41 3 he shall pursue them, he shall pass
Eze 35 6 to blood, and blood shall pursue thee
6 hast hated blood, blood shall p. thee
Osee 8 3 is good, the enemy shall pursue him
Nah 1 8 and darkness shall pursue his enemies
2 Ma 2 32 to pursue brevity of speech and to
1 Tim 6 11 and pursue justice, godliness, faith
2 Tim 2 22 pursue justice, faith, charity and peace
1 P 3 11 let him seek after peace and pursue it

pursued Gen 14 14 appointed: and p. them to Dan
Gen 14 15 and pursued them as far as Hoba
31 23 pursued after him [Jacob] seven days
36 on my part hast thou so hotly p. me
Exod 14 8 and he pursued the children of Israel
Num 14 45 them pursued them as far as Horma
Deut 11 4 covered them when they pursued you
26 5 the Syrian pursued my father, who
Josu 2 7 they that were sent, pursued after them
22 till they that p. them were returned
7 5 enemies p. them from the gate as far
8 16 and encouraging one another, p. them
20 men of the city, that p. after Josue
20 valiantly against them that pursued
24 being slain that had p. after Israel
10 10 p. them by the way of the ascent to
24 6 the Egyptians pursued your fathers
Judg 1 6 they pursued after him [Adonibezec]
4 16 Barac p. after the fleeing chariots
7 23 from all Manasses pursued after Madian
25 and they pursued Madian, carrying the
8 12 Gedeon pursued and took the, all their
20 31 pursued them a long way, so as to wound
39 thought they fled and pursued them
45 they still pursued them and slew also
1 K 7 11 of Masphath p. after the Philistines
17 35 I [David] p. after them and struck them
52 shouted and p. after the Philistines
53 after they had p. the Philistines, fell
23 25 he p. after David in the wilderness of
30 10 David pursued, he and 400 men: for
2 K 2 19 Asael p. after Abner, and turned not
24 while Joab and Abisai p. after Abner
11 23 p. them even to the gate of the city
20 10 and Abisai his brother p. after Seba
3 K 20 20 Syrians fled, and Israel p. after them
4 K 9 27 Jehu p. him [Ochozias] and said: Strike
25 5 army of the Chaldees p. after the king
2 Pa 13 19 Abia pursued after Jeroboam, and took
14 13 with him pursued them to Gerara
Jdth 5 13 when . . . the Egyptians pursued after
9 6 the Egyptians, when they pursued armed
15 6 they pursued them with the edge of the
Ps 142 1 David, when his son Absalom pursued him
Wisd 19 2 they repented and pursued after them
3 p. them as fugitives whom they had
Jer 39 5 army of the Chaldeans p. after. 52:8
Lam 4 19 they pursued us upon the mountains
Amos 1 11 he hath p. his brother with the sword

1 Ma 2 47 they p. after the children of pride
3 5 he p. the wicked and sought them out
24 and he pursued him by the descent of
4 9 when Pharao pursued them with a great
15 they pursued them as far as Gezeron
5 21 and he p. them even to the gate of
60 were p. unto the borders of Judea
7 45 they pursued after them one day's
9 15 he p. them even to the mount Azotus
10 49 Alexander pursued after him and pressed
11 73 they all with him p. the enemies even
12 30 and Jonathan pursued after them, but
15 11 king Antiochus pursued after him and
39 the king himself pursued after Tryphon
16 9 John pursued after them till he came
2 Ma 8 25 and they pursued them on every side
pursuer Lam 1 6 before the face of the pursuer
Titus 2 14 acceptable, a pursuer of good works
pursuest Job 13 25 and thou pursuest a dry straw
pursueth Lev 26 17 you shall flee when no man p.
Lev 26 36 they shall fall when no man pursueth
Prov 12 11 that pursueth idleness is very foolish
13 21 evil pursueth sinners: and to the just
28 1 the wicked man fleeth when no man p.
pursuing Exod 14 23 the Egyptians p. went in after
Josu 8 6 till they p. us be drawn farther from
7 whilst we are fleeing, and they p.
Judg 4 22 Barac came pursuing after Sisara: and
20 42 the enemy pursuing them thither also
2 K 2 26 to bid the people cease from p. after
27 the people should have retired from p.
18 16 back the people from p. after Israel
1 Pa 10 2 the Philistines drew near p. after Saul
Jdth 15 4 children of Israel pursuing in one body
Prov 11 19 and the pursuing of evil things, death
Jer 2 23 as a swift runner pursuing his course
Rom 12 13 the saints. Pursuing hospitality. Bless
pursuit 1 K 23 28 returned, leaving the p. of David
2 Ma 8 26 therefore they did not continue the p.
push Exod 21 29 if the ox was wont to push with
Exod 21 36 if he knew that his ox was wont to push
Num 25 20 if through hatred any one push a man
Deut 33 17 with them shall he push the nations
3 K 22 11 shalt thou push Syria till. 2 Pa 18:10
Job 15 29 neither shall he push his root in the
Ps 43 6 we will push down our enemies with the
Eze 32 2 thou didst push with the horn in thy
pushed Deut 19 6 p. on by his grief should pursue
2 Pa 22 3 his mother pushed him on to do wickedly
Ps 117 13 being pushed I was overturned that
1 Ma 7 46 and they pushed them with the horns
pushing Dan 8 4 saw the ram p. with his horns
2 Ma 10 35 pushing forward with fierce courage
pusillanimity Ps 54 9 saved me from p. of spirit
Puteoli Acts 28 13 we came the second day to P.
Putiphar Gen 37 36 sold Joseph in Egypt to P.
Gen 39 1 P. an eunuch of Pharao, chief captain
Putiphare Gen 41 45 daughter of Putiphar priest. 50; 46:20
putrefied Exod 16 20 be full of worms, and it p.
putrefy Exod 16 24 it did not putrefy, neither
putrified Ps 37 6 my sores are p. and corrupted
putrify Eze 10 27 yoke shall p. at the presence
pygarg Deut 14 5 you shall eat . . . the p.
Pygmeans Eze 27 11 P. also that were in thy
pyramids 1 Ma 13 28 and he set up seven pyramids
Pyrrhus Acts 20 4 Sopater the son of P., of Berea
python Isa 29 4 like that of the python, and
pythonic Deut 18 11 that consulteth p. spirits
pythonical Lev 20 27 a p. or divining spirit
Acts 16 16 girl, having a p. spirit, met us, who
pythons 4 K 21 6 observed omens and appointed p.
Isa 8 19 shall say to you: Seek of pythons

Q

quail Ps 104 40 they asked, and the quail came
Wisd 19 12 the quail came up to them from the sea
quails Exod 16 13 q. coming up, covered the camp
Num 11 31 taking q. up beyond the sea, brought
32 next day gathered together of quails
Wisd 16 2 preparing for them quails for their
quake 1 Ma 4 32 them q. at their own destruction
quaked Jdth 16 12 the Persians q. at her constance
Nah 1 5 the earth hath quaked at his presence
Mat 27 51 and the earth quaked, and the rocks
quality Esth 16 9 the q. and necessity of times
Wisd 19 17 the sound of the quality is changed
quantity 2 K 8 8 an exceeding great q. of brass
3 K 10 2 immense quantity of gold and precious
2 Pa 18 26 bread and water in a small quantity
2 Ma 4 39 q. of gold being already carried away
quarrel Gen 13 8 said to Lot: Let there be no q.
Exod 21 18 if men quarrel, and the one strike his
22 if men quarrel, and one strike a woman
Prov 25 8 utter not hastily in a quarrel: lest
26 17 meddleth with another man's quarrel
Eccu 8 19 quarrel not with a passionate man, and
28 13 and a hasty quarrel sheddeth blood
quarrelled Gen 26 21 for that they q. likewise
Gen 49 23 quarrelled with him and envied him
2 K 14 6 two sons: and they q. with each other
Lam 4 15 they quarrelled, and being removed
quarrelling Exod 2 13 he saw two Hebrews q.: and
quarrels Prov 16 28 a perverse man stirreth up q.
Prov 17 11 an evil man always seeketh quarrels
14 beginning of q. is as when one letteth
19 that studieth discords, loveth quarrels
18 6 and his mouth provoketh quarrels
20 3 for a man to separate himself from q.
22 10 quarrels and reproaches shall cease
28 25 puffeth up himself, stirreth up q.
29 22 a passionate man provoketh quarrels
Eccu 27 16 in the quarrels of the proud is the
31 38 wine drunken with excess raiseth q.
Gal 5 20 wraths, quarrels, dissensions, sects
quarrelsome Prov 21 19 a q. and passionate woman
1 Tim 3 3 not quarrelsome, not covetous, but one
quarries 4 K 22 6 stones out of the q. 2 Pa 34:11
quarter Josu 18 16 is over against the north q.
Josu 19 8 Baalath Beer Ramath to the south q.
2 Ma 13 15 he set upon the king's quarter by night
quarters Lev 26 6 shall not pass through your q.
1 Pa 9 24 in four quarters were the porters
Isa 11 12 from the four quarters of the earth
Jer 49 36 winds from the four quarters of heaven
Eze 7 2 the end is come upon the four quarters
1 Ma 5 9 Israelites that were in their quarters
Mat 2 22 retired into the quarters of Galilee
16 13 into the quarters of Caesarea Philippi
Luke 16 7 said: An hundred quarters of wheat
Apoc 20 7 are over the four quarters of the earth
Quartus Rom 16 23 saluteth you, and Q., a brother
quashed Eccu 6 2 thy strength be quashed by folly
queen 3 K 10 1 the queen of Saba, having heard
3 K 10 4 when the queen of Saba saw all the
10 q. of Saba gave to king Solomon. 2 Pa 9:9
13 Solomon gave the q. of Saba. 2 Pa 9:12
11 19 sister of his wife Taphnes the queen
4 K 10 13 of the king and the sons of the queen
2 Pa 9 1 when the queen of Saba heard of the
2 Es 2 6 the king said to me, and the queen
Esth 1 9 also Vasthi the queen made a feast
11 to bring in q. Vasthi before the king
15 ought to pass upon Vasthi the queen
16 queen Vasthi hath not only injured the
17 this deed of the queen will go abroad

17 that q. Vasthi should come in to him
19 than her, be made queen in her place
2 4 let her be queen instead of Vasthi
17 and made her queen instead of Vasthi
22 immediately he told it to queen Esther
4 8 that he should show it to the queen
5 2 when he saw Esther the queen standing
3 what wilt thou, queen Esther? What is
5 which the queen had prepared for them
12 queen Esther also hath invited no other
7 1 Aman went in to drink with the queen
6 countenance of the king and of the q.
7 to entreat Esther the queen for his
8 he will force the queen also in my
8 1 the house of Aman . . . to queen Esther
7 Assuerus answered Esther the queen
9 12 he said to the queen: The Jews have
29 Esther the queen . . . wrote also a
10 6 whom the king married and made queen
14 1 queen Esther also, fearing the danger
15 10 the q. sunk down and her color turned
Ps 44 10 the queen stood on thy right hand in
Jer 7 18 to make cakes to the queen of heaven
13 18 say to the king and to the queen
29 2 Jechonias the king and the queen
44 17 sacrifice to the q. of heaven. 18, 19, 25
Eze 16 13 and wast advanced to be a queen. And
Mat 12 42 q. of the south shall rise. Luke 11:31
Acts 8 27 Candace the queen of the Ethiopians
Apoc 18 7 saith in her heart: I sit a queen, and
Queen 1 Pa 7 18 sister named Queen bore Goodlyman
queens 3 K 11 3 he had seven hundred wives as q.
Cant 6 7 there are threescore queens and
8 q. and concubines, and they praised her
Isa 49 23 nursing fathers, and q. thy nurses
quench 2 K 14 7 seek to quench my spark which
Cant 8 7 many waters cannot quench charity
Isa 1 31 and there shall be none to quench it
42 3 and smoking flax he shall not quench
Jer 4 4 and there be none that can quench it
21 12 and there be none to quench it because
Amos 5 6 there shall be none to quench Bethel
quenched 4 K 22 17 and shall not be q. 2 Pa 34:25
Eccu 23 22 it will never be quenched till it
28 14 spit upon it, it shall be quenched
27 burn in them and shall not be quenched
Isa 34 10 night and day it shall not be quenched
66 24 and their fire shall not be quenched
Jer 7 20 it shall burn and shall not be quenched
17 27 of Jerusalem, and it shall not be q.
Eze 20 47 the flame of the fire shall not be q.
48 have kindled it, and it shall not be q.
Heb 11 34 quenched the violence of fire, escaped
quencheth Prov 21 14 a secret present q. anger
Eccu 3 33 water q. a flaming fire, and alms
quenching Wisd 19 19 water forgot its q. nature
question Exod 24 14 if any question shall arise
Exod 33 7 all the people that had any question
2 Pa 19 10 there is question concerning the law
Jdth 10 8 but they asked her no question, only
Eccu 23 11 as a slave daily put to the question
33 4 he that cleareth up a question, shall
Dan 2 16 give him time to resolve the question
25 will resolve the question to the king
Mark 8 11 came forth and began to question him
9 15 what do you question about among you
12 34 no man after that durst ask him any q.
John 3 25 a q. between some of John's disciples
Acts 15 2 and priests to Jerusalem about this q.
23 6 resurrection of dead I am called in q.
25 20 being in a doubt of this manner of q.
1 C 10 25 asking no q. for conscience' sake. 27
questioned Mark 1 27 they q. among themselves
Luke 23 9 and he questioned him in many words
questioning Mark 9 9 q. together what that
questions 3 K 10 1 to try him with hard q. 2 Pa 9:1
Ecce 7 30 entangled himself with infinity of q.
Mat 22 46 day forth ask him any more questions
Luke 2 46 hearing them and asking them questions
20 40 they durst not ask him any more q.
Acts 18 15 but if they be q. of word and names
23 29 I found to be accused concerning q. of
25 19 had certain q. of their own superstition
26 3 both customs and q. that are among the
1 Tim 1 4 which furnish questions rather than the
6 4 sick about questions and strifes of
2 Tim 2 23 avoid foolish and unlearned questions
Titus 3 9 avoid foolish questions and genealogies
quick 2 K 19 35 my senses quick to discern sweet
Wisd 7 22 loving that which is good, quick, which
8 11 I shall be found of a quick conceit in
Eccu 31 27 in all thy works be quick, and no
quicken Ps 79 19 not from thee, thou shalt q. us
Ps 118 25 quicken thou me according to thy word
37 not behold vanity: q. me in thy way
40 quicken me in thy justice. 142:11
88 quicken thou me according to thy mercy
107 quicken thou me according to thy word
149 q. me according to thy judgment. 156
154 quicken thou me for thy word's sake
159 O Lord; quicken me thou in thy mercy
137 7 of tribulation, thou wilt quicken me
Rom 8 11 shall quicken also your mortal bodies
quickened 1 C 15 36 which thou sowest is not q.
Eph 2 5 hath quickened us together in Christ, by
Col 2 13 he hath quickened together with him
quickeneth John 6 64 it is the spirit that q.
Rom 4 17 God, whom he believed, who q. the dead
2 C 3 6 the letter killeth, but the spirit q.
1 Tim 6 13 before God, who quickeneth all things
quickening 1 C 15 45 last Adam into a q. spirit
quickly Gen 24 18 q. she let down the pitcher
Gen 24 65 she quickly took her cloak and covered
27 20 how couldst thou find it so quickly
20 what I sought came quickly in my way
Exod 32 8 they have quickly strayed from the way
Lev 26 16 I will quickly visit you with poverty
Num 16 46 go quickly to the people to pray for
Deut 4 26 you shall q. perish out of the land
7 4 be kindled, and will q. destroy thee
9 3 them to nothing before thy face q.
12 arise and go down from hence quickly
12 have quickly forsaken the way that thou
16 and had quickly forsaken his way which
11 17 perish quickly from the excellent land
28 20 until he consume and destroy thee q.
31 29 will quickly turn aside from the way
Josu 2 5 pursue after them quickly and you will
10 6 come up quickly and save us, and
23 16 indignation of the Lord rise up q.
Judg 2 17 they q. forsook the way in which their
23 and would not quickly destroy them
Ruth 1 19 the report was quickly spread among all
1 K 20 19 thou shalt go down quickly and come
29 I will go quickly and see my brethren
25 34 if thou hadst not quickly come to meet
2 K 17 16 send q. and tell David, saying: Tarry
21 arise and pass quickly over the river
2 Pa 18 8 call quickly Micheas the son of Jemla
26 20 because he had quickly felt the stroke
Ps 36 2 as the green herbs shall quickly fall
105 13 they had quickly done, they forgot his
Prov 29 25 he that feareth man, shall quickly fall
Ecce 7 10 be not quickly angry; for anger resteth
Wisd 3 18 if they die q., they shall have no hope
6 16 watcheth for her, shall q. be secure

14 15 his son who was quickly taken away
16 11 and were quickly healed, lest falling
Eccu 5 7 for mercy and wrath q. come from him
6 20 and shalt quickly eat of her fruits
27 4 thy house shall q. be overthrown. As
48 22 the Lord God quickly heard their voice
Isa 5 19 haste, and let his work come quickly
8 1 with speed, quickly take the prey. And
16 5 and q. rendering that which is just
51 14 he shall quickly come that is going to
Bar 4 25 thou shalt quickly see his destruction
Dan 4 15 tell me quickly the interpretation
Nah 2 5 they shall quickly get upon the walls
1 Ma 2 40 they will now quickly root us out of
6 62 he q. broke the oath that he had taken
2 Ma 7 10 he quickly put forth his tongue and
14 44 they quickly making room for his fall
Mat 28 7 going quickly, tell ye his disciples
8 they went out q. from the sepulcher
Luke 14 21 go out quickly into the streets and
15 22 bring forth quickly the first robe
16 6 and sit down quickly and write fifty
18 8 that he will quickly revenge them
John 11 29 riseth quickly and cometh to him. For
13 27 that which thou dost, do quickly. Now
Acts 12 7 raised him up, saying: Arise quickly
22 18 and get thee quickly out of Jerusalem
2 Tim 4 8 make haste to come to me quickly. For
Apoc 2 16 I will come to thee quickly and will
3 11 I come quickly. 22:7, 12, 20
11 14 behold the third woe will come quickly
quicksands Acts 27 17 they should fall into q.
quiet Deut 28 65 neither shalt thou be quiet, even
Judg 15 7 revenged of you and then I will be q.
18 27 to a people that was quiet and secure
4 K 11 20 rejoiced, and the city was q. 2 Pa 23:21
1 Pa 4 40 country spacious and quiet and fruitful
22 9 born to thee, shall be most q. man
2 Pa 14 1 his days the land was quiet ten years
6 he was quiet and there had no wars
7 us build . . . while all is q. from wars
20 30 and the kingdom of Josaphat was quiet
25 16 be quiet, lest I kill thee. And the
Job 3 26 kept silence? Have I not been quiet
Prov 7 11 not bearing to be quiet, not able to
Wisd 18 14 while all things were in quiet silence
Eccu 25 27 a wife full of tongue to a quiet man
Isa 7 4 see thou be quiet: fear not, and let
14 7 the whole earth is quiet and still
30 15 if you return and be quiet, you shall
Jer 42 10 if you will be quiet and remain in
47 6 how long wilt thou not be quiet? Go
7 how shall it be quiet, when the Lord
Lam 3 49 is afflicted and hath not been quiet
Zach 11 12 hither my wages: and if not, be quiet
1 Ma 1 3 and the earth was quiet before him
7 50 land of Juda was quiet for a short
9 57 and the land was quiet for two years
11 38 seeing that the land was quiet before
52 land was quiet before him. And he
2 Ma 12 2 them to live in peace and to be quiet
14 10 possible that the state should be quiet
19 36 ought to be q., and to do nothing rashly
1 Th 4 11 that you use your endeavor to be quiet
1 Tim 2 2 we may lead a quiet and a peaceable life
1 P 3 4 a quiet and a meek spirit, which is
quieted Zach 6 8 have q. my spirit in the land
quietly 2 Ma 11 23 in our realm should live q.
2 Ma 14 25 he lived q. and they lived in common
quietness 1 Pa 22 9 I will give peace and q. to
Isa 32 17 service of justice q. and security
Quintus 2 Ma 11 34 Q. Memmius and Titus Manilius
quit Exod 21 19 he that struck him shall be quit
Exod 21 28 but the owner of the ox shall be quit
Josu 2 19 his own head, and we shall be quit
20 abroad, we shall be quit of this oath
quite Lev 26 44 they should be quite consumed
Judg 4 24 till they quite destroyed him [Jabin]
Ruth 1 20 hath quite filled me with bitterness
Tob 10 4 his mother wept and was q. disconsolate
Zach 11 17 eye: his arm shall quite wither away
quiver Gen 27 3 take thy arms, thy quiver and
Job 30 11 for he hath opened his quiver and hath
39 23 above him shall the quiver rattle, the
Ps 10 3 have prepared their arrows in the q.
Eccu 26 15 open her quiver against every arrow
Isa 22 6 Elam took the quiver, the chariot, of
49 2 in his quiver he hath hidden me. And
Jer 5 16 their quiver is as an open sepulcher
quivers 1 Pa 18 7 David took the golden quivers
Jer 51 11 sharpen the arrows, fill the quivers
Lam 3 13 into my reins the daughters of his q.
Eze 27 11 hung up their quivers on thy walls

R

Raaia 1 Es 2 47 the children of R. 2 Es 2:47; 7:50
Raamias 2 Es 7 7 R., Nahamani, Mardochai, Belsam
Rabba Josu 13 25 Aroer which is over against R.
2 K 11 1 besieged Rabba; but David remained
1 Pa 20 1 Ammon: and went and besieged Rabba
1 when Joab smote Rabba and destroyed it
Amos 1 14 I will kindle a fire in the wall of R.
Rabbath Deut 3 11 of iron is shown, which is in R.
2 K 12 26 and Joab fought against Rabbath
27 I have fought against Rabbath and the
29 together and went out against Rabbath
Jer 49 2 noise of the war to be heard in R.
3 cry, ye daughters of Rabbath, gird
Eze 21 20 that the sword may come to Rabbath
25 5 I will make R. a stable for camels
rabbi Mat 23 7 and to be called by men, Rabbi
Mat 23 8 be not you called Rabbi. For one is
26 25 answering, said: Is it I, Rabbi? He
49 hail, R. and he kissed him. Mark 14:45
Mark 9 4 said to Jesus: Rabbi, it is good for
11 21 Rabbi, behold the fig tree which thou
John 1 38 who said to him, Rabbi, which is to
49 said: Rabbi, thou art the Son of God
3 2 said to him: Rabbi, we know that thou
26 to him: Rabbi, he that was with thee
4 31 prayed him, saying: Rabbi, eat. But he
6 25 Rabbi, when camest thou hither? Jesus
9 2 disciples asked him: Rabbi, who hath
11 8 say to him: Rabbi, the Jews but now
rabbit Prov 30 26 the rabbit, a weak people, which
rabboni Mark 10 51 to him: Rabboni, that I may see
John 20 16 she turning, saith to him: Rabboni
Rabboth Josu 19 20 Rabboth and Cesion, Abes
Rabsaces 4 K 18 17 Tharthan and Rabsaris and R.
4 K 18 19 R. said to them: Speak to Ezechias
27 Rabsaces answered them, saying: Hath
28 Rabsaces stood and cried out. Isa 36:13
37 told him the words of R. Isa 36:22
19 4 will hear all the words of Rabsaces
8 R. returned and found the king. Isa 37:8
Eccu 48 20 Sennacherib came up and sent R.
Isa 36 2 sent R. from Lachis to Jerusalem, to
4 Rabsaces said to them: Tell Ezechias
11 and Sobna and Joahe said to Rabsaces
12 R. said to them: Hath my master sent
37 4 will hear the words of Rabsaces, whom
Rabsares Jer 39 3 Rabsares, Neregel, Sereser. 13
Ransaris 4 K 18 17 sent Tharthan and Rabsaris
raca Mat 5 22 say to his brother, Raca, shall
race Lev 6 18 males only of the race of Aaron

Lev 6 29 every male of the priestly race. 7:6
22 3 posterity: every man of your race
23 42 every one that is of the r. of Israel
Num 13 29 we saw there the race of Enac. Amalec
Rahab Josu 2 1 woman that was a harlot named R.
Josu 2 3 and the king of Jericho sent to Rahab
6 17 let only Rahab the harlot live, with
23 brought out Rahab and her parents
25 Josue saved Rahab the harlot and her
Ps 86 4 I will be mindful of Rahab and of
Mat 1 5 Salmon begot Booz of Rahab. And Booz
Heb 11 31 by faith Rahab the harlot perished not
James 2 25 Rahab the harlot, was not she justified
Raham 1 Pa 2 44 Samma begot Raham, the father of
Rahelaia 1 Es 2 2 Rahelaia, Mardochai, Belsan
Rahuel Gen 36 4 Eliphaz: Basemath bore Rahuel
Gen 36 10 Esau: and Rahuel the son of Basemath
13 the sons of Rahuel were Nahath and Zara
17 the sons of Rahuel, the son of Esau
17 these are the dukes of Rahuel in the
1 Pa 1 35 sons of Esau: Eliphaz, Rahuel, Jehus
37 sons of Rahuel: Nahath, Zara, Samma
9 8 the son of Rahuel, the son of Jebania
Raia 1 Pa 4 2 Raia the son of Sobal begot
railer 1 C 5 11 a server of idols, or a railer, or
1 P 4 15 as a murderer or a thief or a railer
railers 1 C 6 10 nor r., nor extortioners, shall
railing 2 Ma 12 14 and provoked Judas with r. and
1 P 3 9 nor r. for r., but contrariwise
2 P 2 11 not against themselves a r. judgment
Jude 9 against him the judgment of r. speech
rails 3 K 10 12 rails of the house of the Lord
raiment Gen 28 20 bread to eat and r. to put on
Gen 45 23 to his father as much money and raiment
Exod 3 22 vessels of silver and of gold, and r.
12 35 of silver and gold and very much r.
21 3 with what raiment he came in, with
4 himself shall go out with his raiment
10 shall provide her a marriage and r.
22 9 in ox or in ass or sheep or raiment
Deut 8 4 thy r. with which thou wast covered
10 18 stranger, and giveth him food and r.
21 13 put off the r. wherein she was taken
22 3 manner with his ass and with his r.
24 13 that he may sleep in his own raiment
Josu 22 8 brass and iron, and variety of raiment
Judg 8 26 purple r. which the kings of Madian
4 K 5 5 pieces of gold and ten changes of r.
7 8 from thence silver and gold and raiment
Job 27 16 as earth, and prepare raiment as clay
Bar 6 57 raiment wherewith they are clothed
1 Ma 11 24 he took gold and silver and raiment
2 Ma 5 2 in gilded r. and armed with spears
Mat 6 25 and the body more than the raiment
28 for raiment why are you solicitous
28 3 as lightning, and his raiment as snow
Luke 9 29 his r. became white and glittering
12 23 and the body is more than the raiment
rain Gen 7 4 I will rain upon the earth forty
Gen 7 12 the rain fell upon the earth forty days
8 2 the rain from heaven was restrained
Exod 9 18 I will cause it to rain tomorrow at
33 drop any more rain upon the earth
34 Pharao seeing that the rain and the
16 4 I will rain bread from heaven for you
Lev 26 3 I will give you rain in due seasons
Deut 11 11 plains, expecting rain from heaven
14 land the early rain and the latter rain
17 that the rain come not down nor the
28 12 that it may give rain in due season
24 Lord give thee dust for rain upon thy
32 2 let my doctrine gather as the rain
1 K 12 17 and he shall send thunder and rain
18 and the Lord sent thunder and rain
2 K 1 21 let neither dew nor rain come upon you
23 4 springeth out of the earth by rain
3 K 8 35 shut up, and there shall be no rain
36 and give rain upon thy land, which
17 1 shall not be dew nor rain these years
14 the day wherein the Lord will give rain
18 1 that I may give rain upon the face of
41 there is a sound of abundance of rain
44 go down, lest the rain prevent thee
45 and wind and there fell a great rain
4 K 3 17 you shall not see wind nor rain: and
2 Pa 6 26 fall no rain by reason of the sins
27 and give rain to thy land which thou
7 13 shut up heaven and there fall no rain
1 Es 10 9 trembling because of the sin and the r.
13 it is time of rain, and we are not
Job 5 10 giveth rain upon the face of the earth
20 23 him, and rain down his war upon him
28 26 when he gave a law for the rain and
29 23 they waited for me as for rain, and
36 27 he lifteth up the drops of rain, and
37 6 upon the earth, and the winter rain
38 26 that it should rain on the earth
28 who is the father of rain? Or who
Ps 10 7 he shall rain snares upon sinners
67 10 aside for thy inheritance a free rain
71 6 he shall come down like rain upon the
104 32 he gave them hail for rain, a burning
134 7 he hath made lightnings for the rain
146 8 and prepareth rain for the earth. Who
Prov 16 15 his clemency is like the latter rain
25 14 and wind, when no rain followeth, so
23 the north wind driveth away rain, as
26 1 as snow in summer, and rain in harvest
Ecce 11 3 they will pour out rain upon the earth
12 2 and the clouds return after the rain
Cant 2 11 winter is now past, the rain is over
Wisd 16 16 by strange waters and hail and rain
22 in the hail and flashing in the rain
Eccu 1 2 the drops of rain and the days of the
35 26 as cloud of rain in the time of drought
40 13 a noise like a great thunder in rain
49 11 the enemies, under the figure of rain
Isa 4 6 covert from whirlwind and from rain
5 6 will command the clouds to r. no r.
30 23 and rain shall be given to thy seed
44 14 pine tree, which the rain hath nourished
45 8 and let the clouds rain the just
55 10 as the rain and the snow come down
Jer 3 3 and there was no lateward rain: thou
5 24 giveth us the early and the latter r.
10 13 he maketh lightnings for rain, and
14 4 because there came no rain upon the
22 of the Gentiles that can send rain
51 16 he hath turned lightning into rain
Bar 6 52 over the land, nor give rain to men
Eze 34 26 will send down the rain in its season
38 22 and with blood and with violent rain
22 I will rain fire and brimstone upon
Osee 6 3 to us as the early and the latter rain
Joel 1 20 as garden bed that thirsteth after rain
2 23 early and the latter rain to come down
Amos 4 7 I also have withholden the rain from
7 to rain upon one city . . . not to rain upon another city
7 1 of the shooting up of the latter rain
1 the latter rain after the king's mowing
Zach 10 1 ask ye of the Lord rain in the latter
1 and will give them showers of rain
14 17 there shall be no rain upon them. And
Mat 7 25 the rain fell, and the floods came. 27
28 2 because of present r., and of the cold

Heb 6 7 the earth that drinketh in the rain
James 5 7 he receive the early and latter rain
17 he prayed that it might not rain upon
18 prayed again: and the heaven gave rain
Apoc 11 6 that it rain not in the days of their
rainbow Eccu 43 12 look upon the r. and bless him
Eccu 50 8 as the rainbow giving light in the
Eze 1 28 as the appearance of the rainbow when
Apoc 4 3 there was a r. round about the throne
10 1 and a rainbow was on his head, and his
rained Gen 2 5 God had not rained upon the earth
Gen 19 24 Lord rained upon Sodom and Gomorrha
Exod 9 23 the Lord rained hail upon the land
3 K 17 7 for it had not rained upon the earth
Ps 77 24 had rained down manna upon them to eat
27 and he rained upon them flesh as dust
Eze 22 24 land that is unclean and not r. upon
Amos 4 7 one piece was rained upon: and the piece whereon I rained not, withered
Luke 17 29 it rained fire and brimstone from
James 5 17 it rained not for three years and six
raineth Mat 5 45 r. upon the just and the unjust
rains Job 37 15 when God commanded the rains
Acts 14 16 doing good from heaven, giving rains
rainy Eze 1 28 when it is in a cloud on a r. day
raise Gen 34 12 raise the dowry and ask gifts
Gen 38 8 thou mayst raise seed to thy brother
1 Es 4 2 are they able to raise stones out of
Ps 87 11 shall physicians raise to life, and
Mich 5 5 we shall r. against him 7 shepherds
1 Ma 12 36 and raise a mount between the castle
2 Ma 8 10 to raise for the king the tribute
14 6 nourish wars and raise seditions, and
Mat 10 8 heal the sick, raise the dead, cleanse
Acts 21 38 who before these days didst r. a tumult
26 8 that God should raise the dead? And I
Phil 1 17 that they raise affliction to my bands
raise up Deut 18 15 will r. up to thee a prophet
Deut 18 18 I will raise them up a prophet out of
25 5 take her and r. up seed for his brother
7 refuseth to r. up his brother's name
28 9 Lord will raise thee up to be a holy
29 13 he may r. thee up a people to himself
Josu 6 26 that shall raise up and build the city
Ruth 4 5 to raise up the name of thy kinsman
10 to raise up the name of the deceased
1 K 2 35 I will raise me up a faithful priest
3 12 I will raise up against Heli all the
2 K 7 12 I will raise up thy seed after thee
25 r. up forever the word that thou hast
12 11 I will raise up evil against thee out
1 Pa 17 11 I will raise up thy seed after thee
2 Pa 7 18 will raise up the throne of thy kingdom
Jdth 13 7 thou mayst raise up Jerusalem thy city
Job 3 8 who are ready to raise up a leviathan
41 16 when he shall raise him up, the angels
Ps 40 11 have mercy on me, and raise me up again
Eccu 10 4 he will raise up a profitable ruler
24 34 to raise up of him a most mighty king
36 8 r. up indignation and pour out wrath
17 raise up the prophecies which the
Isa 10 26 shall raise up a scourge against him
29 3 and raise up bulwarks to besiege thee
44 26 that raise up the word of my servant
26 I will raise up the wastes thereof
49 6 to raise up the tribes of Jacob and to
8 that thou mightest raise up the earth
58 12 thou shalt raise up the foundations
61 4 and shall raise up ancient ruins and
Jer 23 5 I will raise up to David a just branch
30 9 king, whom I will raise up to them
50 9 I raise up, and will bring against
51 1 behold I will raise up as it were a
Eze 23 22 I will raise up against thee all thy
34 29 I will r. up for them a bud of renown
Osee 6 3 on the third day he will raise us up
Joel 3 7 I will raise them up out of the place
Amos 5 2 her land, there is none to raise her up
6 15 I will raise up a nation against you
7 2 who shall r. up Jacob, for he. 5
9 11 I will raise up the tabernacle of David
Haba 1 6 I will raise up the Chaldeans, a
Zach 9 13 I will raise up thy sons, O Sion
11 16 I will raise up a shepherd in the
1 Ma 3 43 let us raise up the low condition of
2 Ma 7 9 King of the world will raise us up
Mat 3 9 to r. up children to Abraham. Luke 3:8
22 24 wife, and raise up issue to his brother
Mark 12 19 r. up seed to his brother. Luke 20:28
John 2 19 and in three days I will raise it up
20 and wilt thou raise it up in three days
6 39 should raise it up again in the last
40 I will r. him up in the last day. 44, 45
Acts 3 22 shall the Lord your God raise up
7 37 a prophet shall God raise up to you
1 C 6 14 and will raise us up also by his power
2 C 4 14 will raise us up also with Jesus, and
Heb 11 19 God is able to r. up even from the dead
James 5 15 the Lord shall raise him up: and if
raised Exod 9 16 therefore have I r. thee, that I
Exod 10 13 the burning wind raised the locusts
Num 27 3 not in the sedition that was raised
Deut 17 18 after he is raised to the throne of
4 K 8 5 how he had raised one dead to life
5 this is her son whom Eliseus r. to life
25 1 and raised works round about it. And
1 Es 4 15 wars were raised therein of old time
19 and wars have been raised therein
Eze 10 19 were raised from the earth before me
Jon 1 4 a great tempest was raised in the sea
1 Ma 14 29 raised their nation to great glory
2 Ma 4 30 they of Tharsus . . . raised a sedition
John 12 1 been dead, whom Jesus raised to life
9 whom he raised from the dead. But
17 grave, and raised him from the dead
Acts 2 32 this Jesus hath God raised again
3 15 God hath r. from the dead. 4:10; 13:37
8 1 was raised a great persecution against
13 22 he raised them up David to be king
50 r. persecution against Paul and Barnabas
Rom 9 17 to this purpose have I raised thee, that
Gal 1 1 Father, who raised him from the dead
Heb 11 35 women received their dead r. to life
raised up Judg 2 16 Lord r. up judges to deliver
Judg 2 18 when the Lord raised them up judges
3 9 who raised them up a savior. 15
1 K 22 8 my son hath r. up my servant against
3 K 11 14 Lord raised up an adversary to Solomon
23 God also raised up against him an
2 Pa 33 14 and raised it up to a great height
1 Es 1 5 every one whose spirit God had r. up
Job 15 26 run against him with his neck raised up
17 8 the innocent shall be raised up against
Prov 30 4 who hath raised up all the borders of
Cant 8 5 under the apple tree I raised thee up
Eccu 36 14 hast raised up to be thy firstborn
49 15 who raised up for us our walls that
Isa 41 2 who hath raised up the just one from
25 I have raised up one from the north
45 13 I have raised him up to justice and I
Jer 29 15 Lord hath r. us up prophets in Babylon
51 11 Lord hath raised up the spirit of the
Dan 13 45 Lord raised up the holy spirit of
Amos 2 11 I raised up of your sons for prophets
1 Ma 14 37 he raised up the walls of Jerusalem
2 Ma 7 14 from God, to be r. up again by him

Luke 1 69 hath raised up an horn of salvation
Acts 1 9 while they looked on, he was raised up
2 24 whom God hath raised up, having loosed
5 30 God of our fathers hath raised up Jesus
10 40 him God raised up the third day, and
12 7 side, r. him up, saying: Arise quickly
13 23 hath r. up to Israel a Savior, Jesus
30 God raised him up from the dead the
34 show that he r. him up from the dead
Rom 4 24 that raised up Jesus Christ, our Lord
8 11 if the Spirit of him that r. up Jesus
11 he that raised up Jesus Christ from dead
10 9 God hath raised him up from the dead
1 C 6 14 God hath both raised up the Lord, and
15 15 God, that he hath raised up Christ
15 Christ; whom he hath not raised up, if
2 C 4 14 knowing that he who r. up Jesus, will
Eph 2 6 hath r. us up together, and hath made us
Col 2 12 who hath raised him up from the dead
1 Th 1 10 whom he raised up from the dead, Jesus
1 P 1 21 who raised him up from the dead and
raisedst Eccu 48 5 who r. up a dead man from
raiseth 1 K 2 8 r. up the needy from the dust
Eccu 31 38 wine drunken with excess r. quarrels
34 20 he r. up the soul and enlighteneth
John 5 21 as the Father raiseth up the dead and
2 C 1 9 but in God who raiseth the dead. Who
raisin Num 6 4 from the r. even to the kernel
raising Gen 33 20 r. an altar there, he invoked
Ps 112 7 raising up the needy from the earth
Acts 3 26 God, raising up his Son, hath sent
13 33 fulfilled to our children, r. up Jesus
17 31 raising him up from the dead. Eph 1:20
24 5 raising seditions among all the Jews
raisins 1 K 25 18 and a hundred clusters of raisins
1 K 30 12 of figs and two bunches of raisins
1 Pa 12 40 to eat: meal, figs, raisins, wine
rake 1 K 13 20 his spade and his axe and his rake
Isa 7 25 hills that shall be raked with a rake
raked Isa 7 25 hills that shall be raked with a
ram Gen 15 9 a ram of three years, a turtle
Gen 22 13 saw behind his back a ram amongst the
30 41 when the ewes went first to ram, Jacob
Exod 29 15 thou shalt take also one ram upon the
17 and thou shalt cut the ram in pieces
18 offer the whole ram for a burnt offering
19 thou shalt take also the other ram
22 thou shalt take the fat of the ram
22 because it is the ram of consecration
26 ram wherewith Aaron was consecrated. 27
31 shalt take the ram of the consecration
Lev 4 35 ram that is offered for peace offerings
5 15 a ram without blemish. 18; 6:6
16 shall pray for him, offering the ram
8 18 he offered also a ram for a holocaust
20 cutting the ram into pieces, the head
21 whole ram together he burnt upon the
22 he offered also the second ram in the
24 blood of the ram that was immolated
29 he took of the ram of consecration
9 2 for sin and a ram for a holocaust. 16:3
4 bullock and a ram for peace offerings
18 immolated also the bullock and the ram
19 rump of the ram and the two little
16 5 for sin, and one ram for a holocaust
19 21 for his trespass he shall offer a ram
Num 5 8 ram that is offered for expiation
6 14 one ram without blemish for a victim
17 ram he shall immolate for a sacrifice
19 take the boiled shoulder of the ram
7 15 an ox of the herd, and a ram. 21, 27, 33, 39, 45, 51, 57, 63, 69, 75, 81
15 6 for every ram there shall be sacrifice
12 for every ox and ram and lamb and
23 2 a calf and a ram upon every altar
4 laid on every one a calf and a ram
14 laying on every one a calf and a ram
30 he laid on every altar a calf and a ram
28 11 one ram and seven lambs of a year. 19, 27; 29:2, 8, 36
12 flour tempered with oil for every ram
14 calf, a third [of a hin] for a ram
20 two tenths to every ram. 28
29 3 two tenths [of flour] to a ram. 9
1 K 14 34 bring me every man his ox and his ram
17 34 took a ram out of midst of the flock
2 K 6 13 he [David] sacrificed an ox and a ram
1 Es 10 19 to offer for their offence a ram of
Prov 30 31 cock girded about the loins: and a ram
Isa 43 23 not offered me the ram of thy holocaust
Eze 43 23 a ram of the flock without blemish. 25
45 15 one ram out of a flock of two hundred
24 every calf, and an ephi for every ram
46 4 six lambs without blemish and
5 the sacrifice of an ephi for a ram
7 ephi for a calf, an ephi also for a ram
11 ephi to a calf, and an ephi to a ram
Dan 8 3 a ram stood before the water, having
4 I saw the ram pushing with his horns
6 he went up to the ram that had the
7 and when he was come near the ram
7 enraged against him, and struck the ram
7 the ram could not withstand him: and
7 none could deliver the ram out of his
20 ram which thou sawest with horns
Ram 1 Pa 2 9 Jerameel and Ram and Calubi
1 Pa 2 10 Ram begot Aminadab, and Aminadab
25 Ram his firstborn and Buna and
27 sons of Ram the firstborn of Jerameel
Job 32 2 the Buzite, of the kindred of Ram
Rama Josu 18 25 Gabaon and Rama and Beroth
Judg 4 5 between R. and Bethel in mount Ephraim
19 13 there, or at least in the city of Rama
1 K 22 6 was in the wood, which is by Rama
3 K 15 17 up against Juda and built Rama
21 he [Baasa] left off building Rama
22 they took away the stones from Rama
2 Pa 16 1 built a wall about Rama, that no one
5 he left off the building of Rama and
6 they carried away from Rama the stones
1 Es 2 26 the children of Rama and Gabaa, 621
2 Es 7 30 the men of Rama and Geba, 621. The
11 33 Rama, Gethaim, Hadid, Seboim, and
Isa 10 29 Rama was astonished, Gabaath of Saul
Jer 40 1 the general had let him go from Rama
Osee 5 8 cornet in Gabaa, the trumpet in Rama
Mat 2 18 a voice in Rama was heard, lamentation
Ramath Josu 19 8 to Baalath Beer R. to the south
Ramatha 1 K 1 19 and came into their house at R.
1 K 2 11 Elcana went to Ramatha, to his house
7 17 and he returned to Ramatha, for there
8 4 assembled, came to Samuel to Ramatha
15 34 and Samuel departed to Ramatha; but
16 13 Samuel rose up and went to Ramatha
19 18 came to Samuel in Ramatha and told
19 behold David is in Najoth in Ramatha
22 went also himself to Ramatha and
22 behold they are in Najoth in Ramatha
23 he [Saul] whent to Najoth in Ramatha
23 till he came to Najoth in Ramatha
20 1 fled from Najoth, which is in Ramatha
25 1 buried him in his house in Ramatha
28 3 buried him [Samuel] in Ramatha his city
1 Ma 11 34 three cities, Apherema, Lydia, and R.
Ramathaimsophim 1 K 1 1 there was a man of R.
Ramathlechi Judg 15 17 called name of that place R.

Ramesse Exod 12 37 set forward from R. to Socoth
Ramesses Gen 47 11 best place of the land, in R.
Exod 1 11 cities of tabernacles, Phithom and R.
Num 33 3 children of Israel departed from R.
Rameth Josu 19 21 Rameth and Engannim and
Ramoth Deut 4 43 R. in Galaad, which is in the
Josu 13 26 from Hesebon unto Ramoth, Masphe and
20 8 Ramoth in Galaad of the tribe of Gad
21 37 Ramoth in Galaad, one of the cities
1 K 30 27 and that were in Ramoth to the south
4 K 8 29 Syrians had wounded him in Ramoth
1 Pa 6 73 Ramoth also and its suburbs, and Anem
80 out of the tribe of Gad, Ramoth in
1 Es 10 29 Adaia, Jasub, and Saal, and Ramoth
Ramoth Galaad; *see* **Galaad**
rampart Isa 29 3 will cast up a r. against thee
ramparts 1 Es 4 12 setting up the r. thereof and
rams Gen 30 35 the rams of divers colors and
Gen 30 40 before the eyes of the rams. 41
31 38 the rams of thy flocks I did not eat
32 14 20 he goats, 220 ewes, and 20 rams
Exod 29 1 a calf from the herd and two rams
3 and the calf and the two rams. And
Lev 8 2 a calf for sin, two rams, a basket
23 18 one calf from the herd and two rams
Num 7 17 two oxen, five rams. 23, 29, 35, 41, 47, 53, 59, 65, 71, 77, 83
87 twelve rams, twelve lambs of a year
88 rams sixty, buck goats sixty, lambs
23 1 calves and the same number of rams. 29
29 13 thirteen calves of the herd, two rams
14 two tenths to each ram, being two rams
17 twelve calves of the herd, two rams
18 for the calves and for the rams. 21, 24, 27, 30, 33, 37
20 you shall offer . . . calves two rams. 23, 26, 29, 32
Deut 32 14 of the rams of the breed of Basan
1 K 15 9 herds and the garments and the rams
22 rather than to offer the fat of rams
3 K 1 9 Adonias having slain rams and calves
19 and all fat cattle and many rams, and
25 oxen and fatlings and many rams, and
4 23 hundred rams besides venison of harts
4 K 3 4 and 100,000 rams with their fleeces
1 Pa 15 26 in sacrifice seven oxen and seven rams
29 21 thousand bullocks, a thousand rams
2 Pa 5 6 sacrificed r. and oxen without number
7 5 sacrifice of 22,000 oxen and 120,000 r.
13 9 of the herd, and with seven rams, is
15 11 brought 700 oxen and 7,000 rams. And he
17 11 brought him cattle, 7,700 rams and as
29 21 and seven rams and seven lambs and
22 they killed also the rams, and their
32 a hundred rams and 200 lambs. And they
1 Es 6 17 a hundred calves, two hundred rams
7 17 with this money, calves, rams, lambs
8 35 ninety-six rams, seventy-seven lambs
2 Es 5 18 day by day one ox and six choice rams
Job 42 8 seven oxen and seven rams, and go to
Ps 28 1 bring to the Lord the offspring of rams
64 14 the rams of the flock are clothed, and
65 15 marrow, with burnt offerings of rams
113 4 the mountains skipped like rams, and
6 ye mountains, that ye skipped like rams
Isa 1 11 I desire not holocausts of rams and
22 13 killing calves and slaying rams, eating
34 6 with the blood of rams full of marrow
60 7 the rams of Nabaioth shall minister
Jer 51 40 the slaughter, and like rams with kids
Lam 1 6 her princes are become like rams that
Eze 4 2 place battering rams round about it
21 22 set battering rams, to open the mouth
26 9 and battering rams against thy walls
27 21 came to thee with lambs and rams and
34 17 and cattle, of rams and of he goats
39 18 of rams and of lambs and of he goats
45 23 to the Lord, 7 calves and 7 rams
46 6 and the rams shall be without blemish
Dan 3 40 as in holocausts of rams and bullocks
Mich 6 7 be appeased with thousands of rams
2 Ma 12 15 who without any rams or engines of
rams Exod 25 5 rams' skins dyed red. 26:14; 35:7, 23; 36:19; 39:33
ran Gen 16 6 Sarai afflicted her, she ran away
Gen 18 2 he ran to meet them from the door of
7 he himself ran to the herd and took
24 17 the servant ran to meet her and said
20 she ran back to the well to draw water
28 then the maid ran and told in her
29 13 [Laban] ran forth to meet him: and
Num 11 27 there ran a young man and told Moses
Josu 3 16 ran down into the sea of the wilderness
4 7 waters of the Jordan ran off before
18 and ran as they were wont before
Judg 13 10 she made haste and ran to her husband
1 K 3 5 he ran to Heli and said: Here am I
4 12 there ran a man of Benjamin out of
10 23 they ran and fetched him [Saul] thence
17 22 ran to the place of the battle and
48 ran to the fight to meet the Philistine
51 he ran and stood over the Philistine
20 36 when the boy ran, he shot another arrow
21 13 his spittle ran down upon his beard
2 K 18 15 ran up and, striking him slew him
21 Chusai bowed down to Joab, and ran
3 K 2 39 servants of Semei ran away to Achis
18 46 and ran before Achab till he came to
19 20 left the oxen and ran after Elias and
22 35 the blood ran out of the wound into
4 K 23 12 he ran from thence and cast the ashes
2 Pa 32 4 the brook, that ran through the midst
Tob 11 9 been with them in the way, ran before
Jdth 7 6 with water, ran through an aqueduct
13 15 all ran to meet her from the least to
14 8 ran to the tent of Holofernes. And
15 not finding her, he ran out to the
Job 30 5 of them, they ran to them with a cry
Ps 61 5 I ran in thirst: they blessed with
104 41 flowed: rivers ran down in the dry land
132 2 that ran down upon the beard, the beard
2 which ran down to the skirt of his
Jer 23 21 did not send prophets, yet they ran
Eze 1 14 living creatures ran and returned like
31 4 ran round about his roots, and it sent
47 2 there ran out waters on the right side
Dan 8 6 he ran towards him in the force of
13 19 the two elders arose and ran to her
25 ran to the door of the orchard and
38 ran up to them, and we saw them like
1 Ma 6 45 he ran up to it boldly in the midst
2 Ma 3 25 he ran fiercely and struck Heliodorus
5 5 the citizens ran together to the wall
14 43 the doors, he ran boldly to the wall
45 while his blood ran down with a great
45 wounded, he ran through the crowd
Mat 8 32 herd ran violently down. Luke 8:33
Mark 5 6 he ran and adored him. And crying with
6 33 they ran flocking thither on foot from
24 12 Peter rising up, ran to the sepulcher
John 20 2 she ran therefore and cometh to Simon
4 they both ran together, and that other
Acts 3 11 the people ran to them to the porch
7 56 with one accord ran violently upon him
16 22 the people ran together. 21:30
21 32 ran down to them. And when they saw the

rang 1 K 4 5 great shout, and the earth rang
3 K 1 40 the earth rang with the noise of their
45 rejoicing, so that the city rang again
ranged 2 Ma 15 20 horsemen r. in convenient places
rank 1 Pa 15 18 in the second rank, Zacharias
ranks Num 2 17 according to their places and r.
Num 10 18 marched by their troops and ranks
Joel 2 7 shall not turn aside from their ranks
2 Ma 5 3 and horses set in order by ranks
Mark 6 40 they sat down in ranks, by hundreds
Ransaces 4 K 18 26 and Sobna and Joahe said to R.
ransom Ps 48 8 he shall not give to God his r.
Prov 13 8 ransom of a man's life are his riches
Isa 45 13 not for ransom nor for presents, saith
rape Gen 34 27 the city in revenge of the rape
Rapha 1 Pa 7 25 Rapha was his son, and Reseph
1 Pa 8 2 Nohaa the fourth, and Rapha the fifth
37 Mosa begot Banaa, whose son was R.
20 6 also was born of the stock of Rapha
7 these were the sons of Rapha in Geth
Raphael 1 Pa 26 7 of Semeias were Othni and Raphael
Tob 3 25 R. was sent to heal them both, whose
5 7 Raphael the angel answered: Dost thou
6 16 the angel Raphael said to him: Hear me
8 3 then the angel Raphael took the devil
9 6 Raphael took four of Raguel's servants
11 4 Raphael said to Tobias: Take with thee
7 Raphael said to Tobias: As soon as thou
12 15 I am the angel R., one of the seven
Raphaia 1 Pa 4 42 R. and Oziel the sons of Jesi
1 Pa 7 2 the sons of Thola: Ozi and Raphaia
9 43 Banaa: whose son Raphaia begot Elasa
2 Es 3 9 next to him built Raphaia the son of
Raphaim Gen 14 5 and they smote the Raphaim in
Gen 15 20 and the Pherezites, the Raphaim also
Josu 15 8 in the end of the valley of Raphaim
18 16 in furthermost part of valley of R.
2 K 5 18 spread themselves in valley of R. 22
1 Pa 11 15 Philistines encamped in valley of R.
14 9 spread themselves in vale of Raphaim
20 4 slew Saphai of the race of Raphaim
Jdth 8 1 the son of Gedeon the son of Raphaim
Isa 17 5 that seeketh ears in the vale of R.
Raphaims Josu 12 4 the R. who dwelt in Astaroth
Josu 13 12 he was of the remains of the Raphaims
17 15 in land of the Pherezite and the R.
Raphidim Exod 17 1 encamped in R., where there
Exod 17 8 and fought against Israel in Raphidim
19 2 departing out of R. and coming to
Num 33 15 departing from Raphidim, they camped
Raphon 1 Ma 5 37 and camped over against Raphon
Raphu Num 13 10 Phalti the son of Raphu. Of the
rapine Eze 23 46 them over to tumult and rapine
Nah 2 12 with prey, and his den with rapine
3 1 rapine shall not depart from thee
Haba 1 3 to see rapine and injustice before me
Mala 1 13 you brought in of rapine the lame
Mat 23 25 you are full of rapine and uncleanness
Luke 11 39 but your inside is full of rapine and
rapines Eccu 16 14 shall not escape in his r.
Rasathaim Judg 3 8 into the hands of Chusan R.
Judg 3 10 delivered into his hands Chusan R.
rase Ps 136 7 who say: Rase it, rase it, even
rash Eccu 9 25 that is rash in his word shall
rashly Ecce 5 1 speak not anything r., and let
Acts 19 36 ought to be quiet and to do nothing r.
rashness 2 K 6 7 he struck him [Oza] for his r.
Rasin 4 K 15 37 to send into Juda Rasin king of
4 K 16 5 Rasin . . . came up to Jerusalem. Isa 7:1
6 Rasin king of Syria restored Aila to
9 but Rasin he [Theglathphalasar] slew
1 Es 2 48 the children of Rasin. 2 Es 7:50
Isa 7 4 with the wrath of the fury of Rasin
8 and the head of Damascus is Rasin
8 6 hath rather taken Rasin and the son of
9 11 Lord shall set up the enemies of Rasin
rated Lev 27 16 price shall be rated according to
Lev 27 17 be worth, at so much it shall be rated
rather Mat 10 6 go ye rather to the lost sheep of
Mat 10 28 rather fear him that can destroy both
25 9 go ye rather to them that sell and
27 24 but that rather a tumult was made
Mark 5 26 nothing the better, but rather worse
15 11 that he should r. release Barabbas to
Luke 11 28 yea rather, blessed are they who hear
17 8 will not r. say to him: Make ready
John 3 19 men loved darkness rather than the
Acts 5 29 ought to obey God, rather than men
20 35 thing to give, rather than to receive
Rom 1 25 served the creature r. than the Creator
3 8 and not rather, as we are slandered, and
14 13 but judge this rather, that you put not
1 C 5 2 have not rather mourned, that he might
6 7 why do you not rather take wrong? Why
7 do you not rather suffer yourselves to
7 21 thou mayest be made free, use it rather
9 12 this power over you, why not we rather
15 rather than that any man should make my
14 1 gifts; but rather that you may prophesy
5 with tongues, but rather to prophesy
19 I had rather speak five words with my
2 C 2 7 you should r. forgive him and comfort
3 8 ministration of spirit be r. in glory
5 8 rather from the body, and to be present
Gal 4 9 known God, or rather are known by God
Eph 4 28 rather let him labor, working with his
5 4 purpose; but rather giving of thanks
11 of darkness, but rather reprove them
Phil 1 12 rather to the furtherance of the gospel
1 Tim 1 4 which furnish questions rather than the
6 2 but serve them the rather, because they
Philem 9 for charity sake I rather beseech
Heb 11 25 rather choosing to be afflicted with
12 13 out of the way; but rather be healed
ratifications Jer 32 11 the r. with the seals that
ratified 1 Ma 8 30 take away, shall be ratified
1 Ma 11 34 we have r. therefore unto them all
rational Exod 25 7 to adorn the ephod and the r.
Exod 28 4 a rational and an ephod, a tunick
15 shalt make the rational of judgment
22 thou shalt make on the rational chains
23 in the two ends at top of the rational
25 ephod, which is towards the rational
26 put in the top parts of the rational
27 rational may be fitted with the ephod
28 rational and ephod may not be loosed
29 rational of judgment upon his breast
30 and thou shalt put in the rational
29 5 tunick and the ephod and the rational
35 9 for adorning of the ephod and the r.
27 stones, for the ephod and the rational
39 8 made also a r. with embroidered work
15 in the rational little chains linked
18 ephod and rational were bound together
Lev 8 8 girdle, he fitted it to the rational
1 P 2 2 desire the rational milk without guile
rattle Job 39 23 above him shall the quiver r.
rattling Nah 3 2 noise of the r. of the wheels
1 Ma 6 41 r. of the armor, for the army was
ravage 1 Ma 15 40 r. Judea and to take the people
ravaged 4 K 10 32 Hazael r. them in all the coasts
1 Ma 1 21 after Antiochus had r. Egypt in the
ravaging Jer 2 30 generation is like a r. lion
Haba 2 17 the ravaging of beasts shall terrify
raven Gen 8 6 sent forth a raven: which went
Lev 11 15 and all that is of the raven kind

Job 38 41 who provideth food for the raven when
Ps 101 7 I am like a night raven in the house
Cant 5 11 branches of palm trees, black as a r.
Isa 34 11 ibis and the raven shall dwell in it
Soph 2 14 window, the raven on the upper post
ravening Ps 21 14 me, as a lion r. and roaring
Eze 22 27 like wolves ravening the prey to
Mat 7 15 inwardly they are ravening wolves
Acts 20 29 r. wolves will enter in among you, not
ravenous Gen 49 27 Benjamin a ravenous wolf
raven's Deut 14 14 raven's kind: and the ostrich
ravens 3 K 17 4 commanded the r. to feed thee
3 K 17 6 the ravens brought him [Elias] bread
Ps 146 9 to the young ravens that call upon him
Prov 30 17 let the ravens of the brooks pick it
Luke 12 24 consider the ravens, for they sow not
raveth Jer 29 26 over every man that raveth and
ravished 2 K 13 22 because he had r. his sister
2 K 13 32 the day that he r. his sister Thamar
Jdth 16 11 her sandals ravished his eyes, her
Isa 13 16 and their wives shall be ravished
ravisher 1 K 20 30 woman that is the r. of a man
ravishing Gen 34 2 lay with her, r. the virgin
Gen 34 7 unlawful act in r. Jacob's daughter
raw Exod 12 9 shall not eat thereof anything raw
1 K 2 15 not take of thee sodden flesh, but raw
Mat 9 16 nobody putteth a piece of raw cloth
Mark 2 21 no man seweth a piece of raw cloth
razed 1 Ma 5 51 he r. the city and took the spoils
Razias 2 Ma 14 37 R., one of ancients of Jerusalem
Razon 3 K 11 23 Razon the son of Eliada, who had
razor Num 6 5 no r. shall pass over his head
Judg 13 5 no razor shall touch his head: for he
16 17 the razor hath never come upon my head
1 K 1 11 no razor shall come upon his head
Ps 51 4 as a sharp r. thou hast wrought deceit
Isa 7 20 the Lord shall shave with a razor
reach Gen 11 4 top whereof may reach to heaven
Lev 26 5 harvest shall reach unto the vintage
5 vintage shall r. unto the sowing time
Num 34 4 reach toward the south as far as
4 and shall reach as far as Asemona. And
12 and shall reach as far as the Jordan
35 4 which suburbs shall r. from the walls
1 Pa 4 27 whole kindred could not reach to the
Job 8 20 nor r. out his hand to the evildoer
14 15 thou shalt reach out thy right hand
Ps 138 6 it is high, and I cannot reach to it
Prov 18 8 they reach even to the inner parts of
26 22 they reach to the innermost parts of
Eccu 21 6 the poor shall reach the ears of God
31 21 reach not thy hand out first of all
Isa 8 8 going over shall reach even to the neck
Dan 6 24 they did not reach the bottom of the
2 Ma 9 10 he could reach to the stars of heaven
Mat 7 9 ask bread, will he reach him a stone
10 a fish, will he reach him a serpent
Luke 11 12 an egg, will he reach him a scorpion
John 13 26 to whom I shall reach bread dipped
Acts 27 12 if by any means they might reach Phenice
2 C 10 13 to us, a measure to reach even unto you
reached Exod 16 35 until they r. the borders of
Josu 8 13 reached to the west side of the city
1 Pa 10 3 the archers reached him and wounded him
2 Pa 3 11 and reached to the wall of the house
11 and r. to the wing of the other cherub
28 9 your cruelty hath reached up to heaven
Wisd 18 16 standing on the earth r. even to heaven
Eccu 8 3 hath r. even to the heart of kings
Isa 16 8 branches thereof have reached even to
Jer 51 9 her judgment hath reached even to the
Eze 40 15 reached even to the face of the porch
Dan 4 8 height thereof reached unto heaven
17 whose height reached to the skies
19 hath grown and hath reached to heaven
2 C 10 14 measure, as if we reached not unto you
Apoc 18 5 her sins have reached unto heaven, and
reacheth Deut 11 30 valley that r. and entereth far
Josu 15 9 reacheth to the towns of mount Ephron
11 reacheth northward to a part of Accaron
19 26 it reacheth to Carmel by the sea
Ps 35 6 thy truth reacheth even to the clouds
Wisd 7 24 r. everywhere by reason of her purity
8 1 r. therefore from end to end mightily
Jer 4 10 the sword reacheth even to the soul
reaching Gen 49 13 reaching as far as Sidon
Num 34 7 reaching to the most high mountain
Josu 15 4 and reaching the torrent of Egypt: and
7 reaching as far as borders of Debara
18 12 reaching to the wilderness of Bethaven
Prov 7 27 r. even to the inner chambers of death
Heb 4 12 reaching into the division of the soul
read Exod 24 7 r. it in the hearing of the people
Deut 17 19 and shall read it all the days of his
31 11 thou shalt read the words of this law
Josu 8 34 he read all the words of the blessing
4 K 5 7 the king of Israel had read the letter
19 14 had read it, he went up to the house
22 8 gave the book to Saphan, and he read it
10 when Saphan had read it before the king
16 law which the king of Juda hath read
23 2 he read all the words of the book of
2 Pa 34 18 book. And he read it before the king
24 book which they r. before the king of
30 and the king read in their hearing
31 written in that book which he had read
1 Es 4 7 and was read in the Syrian tongue
18 hath been plainly read before me
23 was read before Reum Beelteem and
2 Es 8 3 he read it plainly in the street that
8 read in the book of the law. 18; 9:3
8 and they understand when it was read
13 1 they read in the book of Moses in the
Isa 29 11 is learned, they shall say: Read this
12 it shall be said to him: Read: and
34 16 in the book of the Lord, and read
37 14 the hand of the messengers and read it
Jer 29 29 Sophonias the priest read this letter
36 6 and read out of the volume, which
6 shalt read them in the hearing of all
10 and Baruch read out of the volume the
14 the volume in which thou hast read
15 and read these things in our hearing
15 and Baruch read in their hearing. And
21 read it in the hearing of the king
23 when Judi had read three or four pages
51 61 see, and shalt read all these words
Bar 1 3 Baruch read the words of this book
14 read ye this book, which we have sent
14 to be read in the temple of the Lord
Dan 5 7 whosoever shall read this writing and
8 they could neither read the writing
15 to read this writing and show me the
16 art able to read the writing and to
17 but the writing I will read to thee
1 Ma 10 7 read the letters in the hearing of
14 19 they were read before the assembly
2 Ma 2 26 those indeed that are willing to read
26 all that read might receive profit
6 12 beseech those that shall r. this book
8 23 the holy Book had been read to them
Mat 21 16 have you never read: Out of the mouth
42 have you never read in the Scriptures
Mark 2 25 have you never read what David did
Luke 4 16 sabbath day; and he rose up to read
John 19 20 many of the Jews did read: because

Acts 13 27 prophets, which are r. every sabbath
15 21 where he is read every sabbath. Then
31 when they had read, they rejoiced for
23 34 when he had read it, and had asked of
2 C 1 13 than what you have read and known, and
3 2 which is known and read by all men
15 when Moses is read, the veil is upon
Col 4 16 when this epistle shall have been read
16 cause that it be read in the church
16 you read that which is of the Laodiceans
1 Th 5 27 epistle be read to all the holy brethren
Heb 9 19 the law had been read by Moses to all
have you not read Mat 12 3 h. . . . what David. Luke 6:3
Mat 12 5 h. . . . in the law, that on the sabbath
19 4 h. . . . that he who made man from the
22 31 h. . . . that which was spoken by God
Mark 12 10 h. . . . this scripture, The stone which
26 h. . . . in the book of Moses, how in the
Gal 4 21 under the law, have you not read the law
readers 2 Ma 6 17 few words for a warning to the r.
2 Ma 15 40 it will not be grateful to the readers
readest Luke 10 26 written in the law? How r. thou
Acts 8 30 thou understandest what thou readest
readeth Haba 2 2 he that r. it may run over it
Mat 24 15 that r. let him understand. Mark 13:14
Apoc 1 3 blessed is he that r. and heareth the
readily Isa 32 4 of stammerers shall speak r.
readiness Gen 41 36 it be in r. against the famine
Eccu 45 29 in goodness and readiness of his soul
2 C 10 6 having in r. to revenge all disobedience
reading Jer 36 8 r. out of the volume the words
Jer 36 18 words as if he were reading to me
51 63 have made an end of reading this book
1 Ma 5 14 they were yet reading these letters
Acts 8 28 in his chariot, and reading Isaias the
30 heard him reading the prophet Isaias
32 the scripture which he was reading was
13 15 after the r. of the law and prophets
2 C 3 14 veil, in reading of the old testament
Eph 3 4 you r., may understand my knowledge in
1 Tim 4 13 till I come, attend unto reading, to
ready Gen 37 14 [Joseph] answered: I am ready
Gen 38 27 when she was r. to be brought to bed
Exod 19 11 let them be ready against the third day
15 be r. against the third day and come
34 2 be ready in the morning, that thou
35 5 that is willing and hath a ready heart
21 with a most ready and devout mind, to
Lev 16 21 shall turn him out by a man r. for it
Num 14 40 we are ready to go up to the place
18 2 let them be ready in hand and minister
22 17 I am ready to honor thee [Balaam]
32 17 will go armed and ready for battle
Deut 1 41 when you went ready armed unto the
Josu 8 4 not very far from it: and be ye all r.
1 K 25 18 of wine, and five sheep ready dressed
2 K 15 26 I am ready, let him do that which is
19 31 being r. also to wait on him beyond
4 K 9 12 Joram said: Make ready the chariot
16 15 altar of brass shall be ready at my
1 Pa 7 4 six and 30,000 most valiant men r. for
28 21 stand by thee and are ready, and both
2 Pa 17 18 Jozabad and with him 180,000 ready for
1 Es 7 6 he was a ready scribe in the law of
2 Es 4 16 and half were ready for to fight, with
Tob 5 5 girded, and as it were ready to walk
22 all things being ready, that were to be
8 21 to his wife to make ready a feast
Job 3 8 who are ready to raise up a leviathan
12 5 is ready for the time appointed. The
15 23 day of darkness is ready at his hand
29 13 blessing of him that was r. to perish
Ps 37 18 I am ready for scourges: and my sorrow
56 8 is r. O God, my heart is r. 107:2
111 7 his heart is ready to hope in the Lord
118 60 I am ready and am not troubled: that
Cant 7 12 if the flowers be ready to bring forth
Wisd 6 9 greater punishment is ready for the
Eccu 39 37 they shall be ready upon earth when
Isa 41 7 it is ready for soldering: and he
Dan 3 15 if you be ready at what hour soever
14 10 meats, and make ready the wine and shut
Joel 2 13 mercy, and ready to repent of the evil
1 Ma 3 15 made himself ready: and the host of
17 we are ready to faint with fasting
28 they should be ready for all things
44 that they might be ready for battle
58 be ready against the morning that you
4 21 army in the plain ready to fight. So
35 they were ready either to live or to
5 39 ready to come to fight against thee
6 33 made themselves ready for the battle
11 67 they were ready in the plain of Asor
12 27 in arms all night long ready to fight
28 and his men were ready for battle
50 went out ready for battle. Then they
13 37 we are ready to make a firm peace with
2 Ma 3 31 who was ready to give up the ghost
6 28 if with a ready mind and constancy
30 when he was now ready to die with the
7 2 we are ready to die rather than to
14 when he was now ready to die, he
18 he being ready to die, spoke thus
8 3 that was ready to be made even with
11 9 courage, being ready to break through
13 12 exhorted them to make themselves ready
14 22 but Judas ordered men to be ready in
38 was ready to expose his body and life
41 when he was r. to be taken, he struck
15 30 altogether ready in body and mind to
Mat 22 4 all things are ready: Come ye to the
8 the marriage indeed is ready; but they
24 44 ready, because at what hour. Luke 12:40
25 10 they that were ready went in with him
Luke 7 2 to him, being sick, was ready to die
14 17 come, for now all things are ready
17 8 make ready my supper and gird thyself
22 33 Lord, I am ready to go with thee, both
John 7 6 come; but your time is always ready
Acts 21 13 I am ready not only to be bound, but to
23 15 before he come near, are r. to kill him
21 they are now r., looking for a promise
23 make ready 200 soldiers to go as far as
27 and r. to be killed by them, I rescued
Rom 1 15 I am r. to preach the gospel to you also
2 C 9 2 Achaia also is ready from the year past
3 that, as I have said, you may be ready
5 promised, to be ready, so as a blessing
12 14 the third time I am ready to come to you
2 Tim 4 6 I am even now ready to be sacrificed
Titus 3 1 to be ready to every good work. To
1 P 1 5 ready to be revealed in the last time
3 15 being ready always to satisfy every
4 5 who is ready to judge the living and
Apoc 3 2 things that remain, which are r. to die
12 4 woman who was ready to be delivered
made ready Gen 43 25 they made r. the presents
Exod 14 6 he made ready his chariot, and took
3 K 6 7 built of stones hewed and made ready
4 K 9 21 they made ready his chariot, and Joram
2 Pa 35 14 they made ready for themselves and for
Ps 7 13 he hath bent his bow and made it ready
14 he hath made ready his arrows for them
Eze 7 14 blow the trumpet, let all be made ready
21 15 glitter, that is made r. for slaughter

1 Ma 13 22 Tryphon made ready all his horsemen
Luke 22 13 and made ready the pasch. And when the
2 C 10 16 things that are made ready to our hand
really Deut 13 14 hath been really committed
realm 1 Es 7 13 Levites in my r. that are minded
1 Es 7 23 enkindled against the realm of the king
Eze 24 21 my sanctuary, the glory of your realm
1 Ma 11 51 in the sight of all that were in his r.
15 4 made many cities desolate in my realm
2 Ma 10 11 appointed over the affairs of his realm
11 23 that are in our r. should live quietly
14 6 will not suffer the r. to be in peace
realms 1 Ma 6 29 came also to him from other r.
reap Exod 34 21 shalt cease to plow and to reap
Lev 23 10 and shall reap your corn, you shall
22 when you reap the corn of your land
25 5 forth of itself, thou shalt not reap
11 nor reap the things that grow in the
Deut 23 25 hand: but not reap them with a sickle
Ruth 2 9 my maids, and follow where they reap
15 if she would even reap with you, hinder
22 to go out to reap with his maids, lest
1 K 8 12 his fields, and to reap his corn and
4 K 19 29 in the third year sow and reap: plant
Job 4 8 iniquity, and sow sorrows and r. them
24 6 they reap the field that is not their
Ps 125 5 that sow in tears shall reap in joy
Prov 22 8 that soweth iniquity shall reap evils
Ecce 5 9 loveth riches, shall r. no fruit from
11 4 considereth the clouds, shall never r.
Eccu 7 3 thou shalt not reap them sevenfold
Isa 37 30 but in the third year sow and reap
Osee 8 7 shall sow wind, and reap a whirlwind
10 12 and reap in the mouth of mercy, break
Mich 6 15 thou shalt sow, but shalt not reap
Mat 6 26 they neither sow nor do they reap nor
25 26 knewest that I reap where I sow not
Luke 12 24 for they sow not neither do they reap
John 4 38 I have sent you to reap that in which
1 C 9 11 things, is it a great matter if we reap
2 C 9 6 sparingly, shall also reap sparingly
6 who soweth in blessings, shall also reap
Gal 6 8 shall sow, those also shall he reap. For
8 of the flesh also shall reap corruption
8 of spirit shall reap life everlasting
9 in due time we shall reap, not failing
Apoc 14 15 thrust in thy sickle and reap, because
15 the hour is come to reap: for the
reaped Deut 24 19 when thou hast reaped the corn
Ruth 2 21 till all the corn should be reaped
2 K 21 9 when the barley began to be reaped
Jer 12 13 they have sown wheat and reaped thorns
Osee 10 13 wickedness, you have reaped iniquity
James 5 4 who have reaped down your fields which
Apoc 14 16 into the earth, and the earth was r.
reaper Amos 9 13 plowman shall overtake the r.
reapers Ruth 2 2 that escape the hands of the r.
Ruth 2 3 gleaned the ears of corn after the r.
4 said to the reapers: The Lord be with
5 young man that was set over the r.
7 following the steps of the reapers
14 so she sat at the side of the reapers
21 that I should keep close to his reapers
4 K 4 18 went out to his father to the reapers
Dan 14 32 into the field, to carry it to the r.
Mat 13 30 I will say to the reapers: Gather up
39 and the reapers are the angels. Even
reapest Lev 19 9 when thou r. the corn of thy land
Mat 25 24 thou reapest where thou hast not sown
Luke 19 21 thou r. that which thou didst not sow
reapeth John 4 36 he that r. receiveth wages and
John 4 36 he that soweth and he that reapeth
37 and it is another that reapeth. I have
reaping Gen 45 6 can be neither plowing nor r.
1 K 6 13 the Bethsamites were reaping wheat
Luke 19 22 and reaping that which I did not sow
rear Exod 26 30 thou shalt rear up the tabernacle
1 K 29 2 David and his men were in the rear
reared Exod 40 16 Moses reared it up and placed
Num 9 15 day that the tabernacle was reared up
2 K 18 18 Absalom had reared up for himself in
rearing Eccu 50 11 cypress tree r. itself on high
reason Gen 25 30 for which r. his name was called
Gen 35 17 by reason of her hard labor she began
Exod 16 29 for this reason on the sixth day he
Josu 9 13 by reason of the very long journey
1 K 27 6 for which reason Siceleg belongeth
2 K 13 4 thou not tell me the reason of it? And
3 K 14 4 his eyes were dim by reason of his age
2 Pa 5 14 and minister by reason of the cloud
6 26 fall no rain by reason of the sins
Tob 1 21 from Judea by reason of the slaughter
Jdth 10 13 for this reason I thought with myself
13 25 by r. of the distress and tribulation
Job 13 3 Almighty, and I desire to r. with God
21 4 should not have just r. to be troubled
35 9 by r. of the multitude of oppressors
38 33 and canst thou set down the reason
Ps 11 6 by reason of the misery of the needy
40 13 upheld me by reason of my innocence
72 19 perished by reason of their iniquity
129 4 by reason of thy law, I have waited
Ecce 7 26 seek out wisdom and reason: and to
8 17 can find no reason of all those works
9 10 nor reason nor wisdom nor knowledge
Wisd 7 24 reacheth everywhere by r. of her purity
18 13 before by reason of the enchantments
Isa 49 19 too narrow by reason of the inhabitants
Jer 23 10 land hath mourned by reason of cursing
30 14 r. of the multitude of thy iniquities
Lam 5 10 by reason of the violence of the famine
Eze 26 10 by reason of the multitude of his horses
27 16 by reason of the multitude of thy works
43 8 for which reason I consumed them in my
Dan 9 16 by r. of our sins and the iniquities
Osee 6 5 for this reason have I hewed them
Jon 4 4 think thou hast reason to be angry. 9
9 I am angry with reason even unto death
Mich 2 12 by r. of the multitude of men. Zach 2:4
1 Ma 1 40 fled away by reason of them, and the
13 4 by reason whereof all my brethren have
15 by reason of the affairs which he had
2 Ma 3 13 by r. of the orders he had received
6 11 by reason of the religious observance
10 12 by reason of the wrong that had been
12 21 by r. of the straitness of the places
13 26 judgment seat and set forth the reason
Mat 19 8 by reason of the hardness of your
Mark 8 17 why do you reason, because you have
Luke 21 25 by reason of the confusion of the
John 6 18 sea arose, by r. of a great wind that
12 11 many of the Jews, by reason of him
18 for which reason also the people came
15 3 you are clean by reason of the word
Acts 6 2 it is not reason that we should leave
18 14 I should with reason bear with you. But
Rom 8 20 by reason of him that made it subject
2 C 3 10 by reason of the glory that excelleth
Heb 7 23 by r. of death they were not suffered to
1 P 3 15 a reason of that hope which is in you
Apoc 8 13 by reason of the rest of the voices of
18 19 had ships at sea, by r. of her prices
reasonable Gen 30 30 r. therefore that I should now
Job 32 2 they had not found a reasonable answer
2 Ma 13 23 he swore to all things that seemed r.
Rom 12 1 holy, pleasing unto God, your r. service

reasoned Mark 8 16 they r. among themselves, saying
Luke 24 15 while they talked and reasoned with
Acts 17 2 three sabbath days he reasoned with them
18 4 he r. in the synagogue every sabbath
reasoning Wisd 2 1 said, r. with themselves, but
Mark 12 28 had heard them reasoning together
Acts 28 29 having much reasoning among themselves
reasonings Wisd 7 20 force of winds, the r. of men
Rebe Num 31 8 and Hur and Rebe, five princes
Josu 13 21 and Hur and Rebe, dukes of Sehon
Rebecca Gen 22 23 Bathuel of whom was born R.
Gen 24 15 R. came out, the daughter of Bathuel
29 Rebecca had a brother named Laban
45 Rebecca appeared coming with a pitcher
51 behold Rebecca is before thee, take
53 he gave them to Rebecca for a present
61 Rebecca and her maids, being set upon
64 Rebecca also, when she saw Isaac
25 20 took to wife Rebecca, the daughter of
21 made Rebecca to conceive. But the
28 his hunting: and Rebecca loved Jacob
26 8 saw him playing with Rebecca his wife
35 offended the mind of Isaac and Rebecca
27 5 when Rebecca had heard this, and he
42 these things were told to Rebecca
46 Rebecca said to Isaac: I am weary of
28 5 Syrian, brother to Rebecca his mother
29 12 her father's brother and the son of R.
35 8 Debora the nurse of Rebecca died and
49 31 there was Isaac buried with Rebecca
Rom 9 10 when Rebecca also had conceived at once
rebel 1 K 12 15 will rebel against his words
1 K 15 23 like the sin of witchcraft, to rebel
4 K 17 4 Osee endeavoring to rebel had sent
18 20 thou trust, that thou darest to rebel
2 Es 2 19 you going to rebel against the king
6 6 that thou and the Jews think to rebel
rebelled Num 26 9 when they r. against the Lord
3 K 16 9 servant Zambri . . . rebelled against him
16 when they heard that Zambri had r.
4 K 1 1 Moab r. against Israel after the death
18 7 r. against the king of the Assyrians
24 1 again he [Joakim] rebelled against him
2 Pa 13 6 rose up and r. against his lord. And
1 Es 4 19 this city of old time hath r. against
Amos 7 10 Amos hath rebelled against thee in the
1 Ma 11 14 that were in those places had rebelled
2 Ma 12 23 had rebelled at Antioch, he was in a
rebellion 3 K 11 27 this is the cause of his r.
rebellions Jer 3 22 and I will heal your r. Behold
Jer 5 6 their rebellions are strengthened. How
14 7 our rebellions are many, we have sinned
rebellious Num 14 9 be not r. against the Lord
Num 15 30 hath been rebellious against the Lord
17 10 a token of the r. children of Israel
20 10 hear, ye rebellious and incredulous
Deut 9 24 but were always rebellious from the
21 20 this our son is r. and stubborn, he
31 27 you have always been rebellious against
1 Es 4 12 to Jerusalem, a r. and wicked city
15 shalt know that this city is a r. city
Job 24 13 they have been rebellious to the light
Eccu 47 23 out of Ephraim a r. kingdom to rule
Jer 3 6 thou seen what r. Israel hath done
8 because the r. Israel had played the
11 the r. Israel hath justified her soul
12 return, O rebellious Israel, saith the
22 return, you rebellious children, and I
Eze 2' 3 children of Israel, to a r. people
Rebla Num 34 11 bounds shall go down to Rebla
4 K 23 33 Pharao Nechao bound him at Rebla
Reblatha 4 K 25 6 to the king of Babylon to Reblatha. 20; Jer 52:9, 26
4 K 25 21 smote them and slew them at Reblatha
Jer 39 5 Reblatha which is in land of Emath
6 slew the sons of Sedecias in Reblatha
52 10 slew all the princes of Juda in R.
Rebmag Jer 39 3 Meregel, Serezer, Rebmag. 13
rebounding Wisd 17 18 r. echo from the highest
rebuild Tob 13 12 that he may r. his tabernacle
1 Es 9 9 and to rebuild the desolations thereof
Amos 9 11 I will r. it as in the days of old
Mat 26 61 and after three days to rebuild it
27 40 and in three days dost rebuild it
Acts 15 16 and will rebuild the tabernacle of David
16 and the ruins thereof I will rebuild
rebuilt Judg 18 28 they r. it and dwelt therein
Tob 14 7 is burnt in it, shall again be rebuilt
Eccu 49 15 Nehemias . . . who rebuilt our houses
rebuke Deut 28 20 a rebuke upon all the works
Ruth 2 16 let no man r. her when she gathereth
2 K 22 16 were laid open at the r. of the Lord
3 K 1 6 neither did his father rebuke him
4 K 19 3 is a day of tribulation and of rebuke
Job 6 26 you dress up speeches only to rebuke
Ps 6 2 Lord, rebuke me not in thy indignation
17 16 at thy rebuke, O Lord, at the blast
37 2 rebuke me not O Lord, in thy
67 31 rebuke the wild beasts of the reeds
75 8 at thy rebuke, O God of Jacob, they
79 17 shall perish at r. of thy countenance
93 10 chastiseth nations, shall he not r.
103 7 at thy rebuke they shall flee: at the
Prov 9 8 rebuke not a scorner lest he hate thee
8 r. a wise man, and he will love thee
19 25 if thou rebuke a wise man he will
24 25 they that rebuke him, shall be praised
27 5 open rebuke is better than hidden love
Eccu 19 2 fall off, and shall rebuke the prudent
28 there is a lying rebuke in the anger
31 31 shall rebuke the hearts of the proud
41 rebuke not thy neighbor in a banquet
Isa 2 4 rebuke many people: and they shall turn
17 13 he shall rebuke him, and he shall flee
37 3 is a day of tribulation and of rebuke
50 2 at my r. I will make the sea a desert
51 20 of the Lord, of the rebuke of thy God
54 9 angry with thee and not to rebuke thee
66 15 and his rebuke with flames of fire
Jer 2 19 and thy apostasy shall rebuke thee
Osee 5 9 shall be in desolation in the day of r.
Mich 4 3 and rebuke strong nations afar off
Zach 3 2 the Lord rebuke thee, O Satan: and the
2 Lord that chose Jerusalem rebuke thee
Mala 3 11 I will r. for your sakes the devourer
Mat 16 22 taking him, began to r. him. Mark 8:32
18 15 r. him between thee and him alone
19 39 to him: Master, rebuke thy disciples
2 C 2 6 this rebuke is sufficient, which is
1 Th 5 14 rebuke the unquiet, comfort the feeble
1 Tim 5 1 an ancient man rebuke not, but entreat
2 Tim 4 2 reprove, entreat, rebuke in all patience
Titus 1 13 rebuke them sharply, that they may be
2 15 exhort and rebuke with all authority
Apoc 3 19 such as I love, I rebuke and chastise
rebuked Gen 31 42 and rebuked thee yesterday
Gen 37 10 his father r. him and said: What
2 Es 5 7 I rebuked the nobles and magistrates
13 17 I rebuked the chief men of Juda and
Tob 2 17 Tobias rebuked them saying: speak not
Ps 9 6 thou hast rebuked the Gentiles, and the
105 9 he r. the Red Sea, and it was dried up
118 21 thou hast rebuked the proud: they are
Ecce 7 6 is better to be rebuked by a wise man
Wisd 17 7 boasting of wisdom was reproachfully r.
Eccu 13 27 was deceived and he is rebuked also

Isa 50 6 my face from them that rebuked me
Osee 4 4 judge: and let not a man be rebuked
Mat 17 17 Jesus r. him, and the devil went out
19 13 disciples rebuked them. Mark 10:13
20 31 r. them that they should hold their
Mark 4 39 he r. the wind and said to the sea
10 48 r. him, that he might hold his peace. Luke 18:39
Luke 4 35 Jesus r. him, saying: Hold thy peace
8 24 he arising, rebuked the wind and the
9 43 Jesus rebuked the unclean spirit and
55 he r. them, saying: You know not of
18 15 the disciples saw, they rebuked them
23 40 the other answering, r. him, saying
Heb 12 5 wearied whilst thou art rebuked by him
rebukes Ps 38 11 hath made me faint in rebukes
Eze 5 15 in indignation and in wrathful rebukes
rebuketh Job 33 19 r. also by sorrow in the bed
Prov 9 7 that r. a wicked man, getteth himself
28 23 he that r. a man, shall afterward find
Amos 5 10 have hated him that r. in the gate
Nah 1 4 he rebuketh the sea and drieth it up
rebuking Eccu 8 13 coals of sinners by rebuking them
Eze 25 17 upon them, rebuking them in fury: and
Luke 4 41 rebuking them he suffered them not to
recalleth 2 K 14 14 but r., meaning that he that
Reccath Josu 19 35 Ser and Emath and Reccath
receipt Mark 2 14 at the r. of custom. Luke 5:27
receive Gen 4 7 do well, shalt thou not receive
Gen 33 10 receive a little present at my hands
37 35 he would not r. comfort, but said: I
38 20 that he might receive the pledge again
42 34 and you may receive this man again
Exod 22 17 dowry which virgins are wont to receive
23 1 shalt not receive the voice of a lie
27 3 pans to receive the ashes, and tongs
Lev 16 5 he shall r. from the whole multitude
22 25 and defiled: you shall not receive them
25 27 so shall receive his possession again
35 receive him as a stranger and sojourner
26 31 will receive no more your sweet odors
Num 4 32 shall receive by account all the vessels
5 8 but if there be no one to receive it
7 5 receive them from them to serve in the
14 34 forty years you shall r. your iniquities
18 26 when you shall r. of the children of
28 all the things of which you receive
32 30 let them r. places to dwell in among you
Deut 9 9 the mount to r. the tables of stone
18 2 they shall receive nothing else of the
8 he shall receive the same portion of
19 14 in the land which thou shalt receive
20 11 if they receive it and open the gates
15 these cities which thou shalt receive
22 2 until thy brother seek them and r. them
28 8 in the land that thou shalt receive
33 3 shall receive of his doctrine. Moses
11 r. the works of his hands. Strike the
Josu 14 4 neither did the Levites receive other
20 4 so shall they receive him and give him
Judg 17 3 that my son may receive it at my hand
19 15 for no man would receive them to lodge
18 none will receive us under his roof
21 13 and commanded them to r. them in peace
Ruth 1 17 the land that shall receive thee dying
2 12 mayest thou receive a full reward of
1 K 25 27 r. this blessing which thy handmaid
30 26 receive a blessing of the prey of the
2 K 24 23 the Lord thy God receive thy vow. And
3 K 5 9 land them there, and thou shalt r. them
8 64 was too little to receive the holocaust
4 K 5 6 when thou shalt r. this letter, know
16 I will r. none. And when he pressed him
10 2 as soon as you receive these letters
22 7 of the money which they receive, but
2 Es 10 37 the Levites also shall r. the tithes of
Tob 4 22 and receive of him the foresaid sum of
5 4 that thou mayst r. it, while I yet live
6 17 they who in such manner r. matrimony
9 3 r. of him the money, and desire him
Jdth 5 4 that they might receive us with peace
6 6 when they shall receive the punishment
8 24 did not r. the trials with the fear of
11 4 receive the words of thy handmaid, for
Job 2 10 hand of God, why should we not r. evil
13 17 receive with your ears hidden truths
22 22 r. the law of his mouth, and lay up his
27 13 which they shall r. of the Almighty
35 7 or what shall he receive of thy hand
Ps 2 10 r. instruction, you that judge the earth
23 5 he shall r. a blessing from the Lord
48 16 from hand of hell, when he shall r. me
71 3 let the mountains receive peace for the
138 20 they shall receive thy cities in vain
Prov 1 3 to receive the instruction of doctrine
2 1 my son, if thou wilt receive my words
4 4 let thy heart receive my words, keep
10 hear, O my son, and receive my words
8 10 receive my instruction, and not money
9 9 and he shall make haste to receive it
11 31 if the just man receive in the earth
18 22 shall receive a pleasure from the Lord
19 20 hear counsel and receive instruction
21 11 follow the wise, he will r. knowledge
Wisd 5 17 shall they receive a kingdom of glory
6 27 r. therefore instruction by my words
12 7 dear to thee might r. a worthy colony of
18 9 that the just should r. both good and
Eccu 2 2 and receive the words of understanding
4 36 not thy hand be stretched out to receive
6 18 from thy youth up receive instruction
34 ear, thou shalt receive instruction
11 36 receive a stranger in, and he shall
12 5 give to the good, and r. not a sinner
7 thou shalt r. twice as much evil for
15 2 will r. him as a wife married of a
29 5 till they r., they kiss the hands of
32 3 and r. a crown as an ornament of grace
18 feareth the Lord, will r. his discipline
35 14 gifts, for such he will not receive
36 23 a woman will receive every man: yet
38 2 and he shall receive gifts of the king
25 less in action, shall receive wisdom
51 34 and let your soul receive discipline
Isa 61 7 shall they receive double in their land
Jer 3 1 saith the Lord, and I will receive thee
5 3 they have refused to receive correction
6 10 reproach: and they will not receive it
9 20 your ears receive the word of his mouth
14 12 and victims, I will not receive them
17 23 me, and might not receive instruction
32 33 would not hearken to r. instruction
35 13 will you not r. instruction, to obey my
Bar 6 10 when they receive it of the harlots
Eze 3 10 receive in thy heart, and hear with thy
16 61 when thou shalt receive thy sisters
Dan 2 6 you shall receive of me rewards and
Osee 8 13 eat it, and the Lord will not r. them
14 3 take away all iniquity, and r. the good
Amos 5 21 I will not receive the odor of your
22 your gifts, I will not receive them
Mich 1 11 shall receive mourning from you, which
Soph 3 7 wilt fear me, thou wilt r. correction
Mala 1 9 if by any means he will r. your faces
10 and I will not r. a gift of your hand
1 Ma 2 51 you shall receive great glory and an

14 23 to receive the men honorably and to put
15 20 good to us to receive the shield of them
27 he would not receive them, but broke
2 Ma 1 14 that he might r. great sums of money
26 r. the sacrifice for all thy people
2 7 the people and receive them to mercy
26 that all that read might receive profit
3 38 and thou shalt r. him again scourged
7 11 I hope to receive them again from him
29 partner with thy brethren, receive death
29 I may r. thee again with thy brethren
36 shalt r. just punishment for thy pride
14 19 to present and receive the right hands
Mat 10 14 whosoever shall not receive you. Mark 6:11; Luke 9:5
41 shall r. the reward of a prophet
41 shall r. the reward of a just man
11 14 if you will receive it, he is Elias
17 24 of whom do they receive tribute or
18 5 he that shall r. one such little child
19 29 shall receive an hundredfold and shall
21 22 in prayer, believing, you shall receive
34 that they might r. the fruits thereof
23 14 you shall r. the greater judgment. Woe
Mark 4 16 r. it with joy. And they have no root
20 who hear the word and receive it and
9 36 whosoever shall r. me, receiveth not
10 15 whosoever shall not r. the kingdom of
17 that I may receive life everlasting
30 who shall not r. an hundred times as
11 24 believe that you shall receive; and
12 2 to r. of the husbandmen of the fruit
40 these shall receive greater judgment
Luke 6 34 also lend to sinners for to r. as much
34 to them of whom you hope to receive
8 13 when they hear, r. the word with joy
9 48 r. this child in my name, receiveth
48 shall r. me, receiveth him that sent
10 8 and they r. you, eat such things as
10 and they r. you not, going forth into
16 4 they may receive me into their houses
9 may r. you into everlasting dwellings
25 didst r. good things in thy lifetime
18 17 shall not r. the kingdom of God as a
30 who shall not r. much more in this
42 receive thy sight: thy faith hath made
19 12 to receive for himself a kingdom and
20 47 these shall receive greater damnation
23 41 we r. the due reward of our deeds; but
John 3 11 and you receive not our testimony
27 a man cannot receive anything unless
5 34 I r. not testimony from man: but I say
41 I receive not glory from men. But I
43 my Father, and you receive me not: if
43 in his own name, him you will receive
44 who receive glory one from another
7 23 man r. circumcision on the sabbath
39 the Spirit which they should receive
14 17 whom the world cannot receive because
16 14 he shall receive of mine and shall
24 ask, and you shall receive; that your
20 22 receive ye the Holy Ghost. Whose sins
Acts 1 8 you shall r. the power of the Holy
2 14 and with your ears receive my words
38 you shall r. the gift of the Holy
3 3 the temple, asked to receive an alms
5 hoping that he should receive something
21 whom heaven indeed must receive until
7 58 saying: Lord Jesus, receive my spirit
8 15 that they might r. the Holy Ghost. For
19 he may receive the Holy Ghost. But
9 12 upon him, that he might r. his sight
17 that thou mayest receive thy sight, and
10 43 his name all receive remission of sins
16 21 not lawful for us to r. nor observe
18 27 wrote to the disciples to receive him
20 25 thing to give, rather than to receive
22 18 because they will not r. thy testimony
26 18 that they may r. forgiveness of sins
Rom 5 17 they who receive abundance of grace, and
15 7 receive one another, as Christ also hath
16 2 r. her in the Lord as becometh saints
1 C 3 8 every man shall receive his own reward
14 built thereupon, he shall r. a reward
9 10 that thrasheth, in hope to receive fruit
14 5 that the church may receive edification
2 C 5 10 every one may receive the proper things
6 1 you receive not the grace of God in vain
18 and I will receive you; and I will be
11 4 or if you receive another Spirit, whom
24 five times did I receive forty stripes
Gal 1 12 neither did I receive it of man, nor did
3 2 did you r. the Spirit by the works of
14 that we may r. the promise of the Spirit
4 5 we might receive the adoption of sons
Eph 6 8 the same shall he receive from the Lord
Phil 2 29 receive him therefore with all joy in
Col 3 24 knowing that you shall r. of the Lord
25 shall receive for that which he hath
4 10 if he come unto you, receive him: and
2 Th 2 10 receive not the love of the truth, that
1 Tim 5 19 against a priest r. not an accusation
Philem 12 do thou receive him as my own bowels
15 thou mightest receive him again forever
17 count me partner, receive him as myself
Heb 1 14 them, who shall receive the inheritance
7 5 Levi, who receive the priesthood, have a
8 indeed, men that die, receive tithes
9 15 they that are called may r. the promise
10 36 will of God, you may receive the promise
11 8 which he was to r. for an inheritance
12 10 that we might r. his sanctification
James 1 7 that he shall r. anything of the Lord
12 he shall r. the crown of life, which
21 with meekness r. the ingrafted word
3 1 that you receive the greater judgment
4 3 you ask, and receive not; because you
5 7 till he r. the early and latter rain
1 P 5 4 you shall r. a never fading crown of
1 J 3 22 we shall ask, we shall receive of him
5 9 if we receive the testimony of men
2 J 8 but that you may receive a full reward
10 r. him not into the house nor say to
3 J 8 we therefore ought to receive such
9 Diotrephes . . . doth not receive us
10 neither doth he himself r. the brethren
10 them that do r. them he forbiddeth and
Apoc 4 11 to receive glory and honor and power
5 12 slain is worthy to receive power and
14 9 and r. his character in his forehead
17 12 shall r. power as kings one hour after
18 4 that you receive not of her plagues

received Gen 4 11 received the blood of thy brother
Gen 43 34 messes which they received of him
Exod 22 7 be stolen away from him that received
30 16 money received which was contributed
32 4 when he [Aaron] had received them, he
Lev 12 2 if a woman having received seed shall
24 8 being r. of the children of Israel
Num 17 9 saw, and every one received their rods
31 51 received all the gold in divers kinds
54 that which was r. they brought into
32 32 we have already received our possession
34 15 have r. their portion beyond the Jordan
Josu 14 3 the Levites, who received no land among
18 2 as yet had not r. their possessions

7 have already r. their possessions
Judg 13 23 he would not have received a holocaust
18 1 they had not received their lot among
19 3 she r. him and brought him into her
21 16 the rest that have not received wives
1 K 25 35 David r. at her hand all that she had
4 K 5 26 thou hast r. money and received garments
12 15 that r. the money to distribute it to
18 36 they had r. commandment from the king
19 14 when Ezechias had r. the letter of the
24 12 the king of Babylon r. him [Joachin]
1 Pa 29 14 have given thee what we r. of thy hand
2 Pa 22 6 for he received many wounds in the
30 16 the priests received the blood which
32 25 to the benefits which he had received
34 9 received of him the money which had
1 Es 4 20 have r. tribute and toll and revenues
8 30 Levites r. the weight of the silver and
Tob 2 20 she received a young kid and brought it
3 6 command my spirit to be received in peace
7 received a reproach from one of her
7 1 and Raguel received them with joy
9 6 and received of him all the money. And
11 18 money also which he had r. of Gabelus
12 3 he received the money of Gabelus
Jdth 3 10 received him with garlands and lights
5 15 forty years they r. food from heaven
6 19 Ozias . . . received him into his house
16 31 day . . . of this victory is r. by the
Job 2 10 if we have r. good things at the hand of
3 12 why received upon the knees? Why
4 12 as it were, r. the veins of its whisper
33 27 and I have not r. what I have deserved
Ps 6 10 the Lord hath received my prayer. Let
17 17 took me: and r. me out of many waters
47 10 we have received thy mercy, O God, in
62 9 thy right hand hath received me. But
67 19 captive: thou hast r. gifts in men
72 24 with thy glory thou hast received me
Prov 1 29 and received not the fear of the Lord
5 23 die, because he hath not r. instruction
24 32 by the example I received instruction
Wisd 3 6 as a victim . . . he hath received them
8 19 child, and had received a good soul
16 14 shall he call back the soul that is r.
18 3 they r. a burning pillar of fire for
7 thy people r. the salvation of the just
19 13 others indeed received not strangers
14 against their will r. the strangers
15 whom they had received with joy and
Eccu 23 38 length of days shall be r. from him
51 21 down my ear a little and received her
36 r. ye discipline as a great sum of
Isa 40 2 she hath r. of the hand of the Lord
57 8 and hast received an adulterer: thou
Jer 2 30 they have not received correction
7 28 their God, nor received instruction
12 13 they have received an inheritance
Bar 1 8 when he r. the vessels of the temple
3 21 neither have their children r. it
4 32 be punished: and she that r. thy sons
Dan 2 15 that had r. the orders of the king
13 55 angel of God having r. the sentence
65 and Cyrus the Persian r. his kingdom
Soph 3 2 neither hath she received discipline
1 Ma 2 54 r. the covenant of an everlasting
56 Caleb . . . received an inheritance
5 25 the Nabutheans met them and r. them
10 1 and they r. him, and he reigned there
42 sicles of silver which they r. from
46 gave no credit to them nor r. them
11 34 the payments which the king r. of them
53 the benefits he had received from him
12 8 Onias r. the ambassador with honor
8 and r. the letters wherein there was
43 r. him with honor and commended
13 37 the palm which you sent, we have r.
14 40 they r. Simon's ambassadors with honor
16 15 the son of Abobus r. them deceitfully
2 Ma 3 9 had been courteously r. in the city by
13 the orders he had r. from the king
4 22 he was r. in a magnificent manner by
25 having received the king's mandate
5 7 but received confusion at the end
7 2 the laws of God r. from our fathers
8 received the torments of the first
8 19 helps their fathers had r. from God
20 and for this they received many favors
9 3 he r. the news of what had happened
10 15 received those that were driven out of
14 28 having received no injury from the man
15 8 help they had before r. from heaven
Mat 2 12 having received an answer in sleep
6 2 they have received their reward. 5, 16
10 8 freely have you received, freely give
13 19 is he that r. the seed by the wayside
20 that r. the seed upon stony ground
22 that r. the seed among thorns is he
23 that r. the seed upon good ground is
17 23 they that r. the didrachmas, came to
20 9 they received every man a penny. 10
25 16 he that had r. the five talents. 20
17 he that had received the two. 22
18 but he that had received the one. 24
27 have received my own with usury. Take
Luke 1 54 he hath received Israel his servant
2 26 he had r. an answer from the Holy
8 40 was returned, the multitude r. him
9 11 he received them and spoke to them of
53 they r. him not, because his face was
10 38 named Martha, r. him into her house
15 27 because he hath received him safe
19 6 came down; and received him with joy
15 he returned, having r. the kingdom
John 1 11 and his own r. him not. But as many
12 as many as r. him, he gave them power
16 of his fulness we all have received
3 33 he that hath received his testimony
4 45 the Galileans r. him, having seen all
9 15 asked him how he had r. his sight
18 been blind and had received his sight
18 parents of him that had r. his sight
10 18 commandment have I r. from my Father
13 30 having received the morsel, went out
17 8 they have r. them, and have known in
18 3 Judas therefore having r. a band of
Acts 1 9 cloud received him out of their sight
2 33 having r. of the Father the promise of
41 that received his word, were baptized
3 7 his feet and soles received strength
7 38 who r. the words of life to give unto
53 who have received the law by the
8 14 heard that Samaria had r. the word of
17 and they received the Holy Ghost. And
9 18 he received his sight; and rising up
10 22 received an answer of an holy angel, to
47 baptized, who have r. the Holy Ghost
11 1 heard that the Gentiles also had r.
15 4 they were received by the church, and
38 that he . . . might not be received. And
16 24 having received such a charge, thrust
17 7 hither also: whom Jason hath received
11 who r. the word with all eagerness
19 2 have you r. the Holy Ghost since ye
20 24 ministry of the word which I received
21 17 the brethren received us gladly. And the

26 10 having r. authority of chief priests
28 21 we neither received letters concerning
30 and he received all that came to him
Rom 1 5 by whom we have received grace and
4 11 he received the sign of circumcision
5 11 by whom we have now r. reconciliation
8 15 for you have not received the spirit of
15 you have r. the spirit of adoption of
15 7 as Christ also hath r. you unto honor
1 C 2 12 we have r. not the spirit of this world
4 7 what hast thou that thou hast not r.
7 if thou hast r., why dost thou glory
7 glory, as if thou hadst not received it
9 25 they may receive a corruptible crown
11 23 I have received of the Lord that which
15 1 to you, which also you have received
3 which I also received: how that Christ
2 C 7 15 with fear and trembling you received him
11 4 another Spirit, whom you have not r.: or
4 another gospel which you have not r.
Gal 1 9 besides that which you have received
4 14 received me as an angel of God, even as
Phil 4 9 you have both learned, and received
18 having r. from Epaphroditus the things
Col 2 6 you have received Jesus Christ, the Lord
4 10 Barnabas, touching whom you have r.
17 heed to the ministry which thou hast r.
1 Th 2 13 when you had received of us the word
13 you received it not as the word of men
4 1 as you have received from us, how you
2 Th 3 6 tradition which they have received of us
1 Tim 4 3 created to be r. with thanksgiving by
4 nothing to be rejected that is received
5 10 if she have received to harbor, if she
Heb 2 2 received a just recompense of reward
7 6 received tithes of Abraham, and blessed
9 Levi who received tithes, paid tithes
11 under it the people received the law
11 7 by faith Noe, having received an answer
11 received strength to conceive seed, even
13 not having received the promises, but
17 and he that had received the promises
19 whereupon also he r. him for a parable
35 women received their dead raised to
39 r. not the promise; God providing some
1 P 4 10 as every man hath received grace
2 P 1 17 he r. from God the Father, honor and
1 J 2 27 unction which you have r. from him
2 J 4 as we have r. a commandment from the
Apoc 2 28 as I also have r. of my Father: and I
3 3 in what manner thou hast r. and heard
17 12 who have not yet received a kingdom
19 20 who r. the character of the beast and
20 4 nor r. his character on their foreheads
receivers Prov 22 9 away the souls of the r. Cast
receivest Eccu 42 7 that thou givest out or r. in
receiveth Prov 10 8 the wise of heart r. precepts
Prov 18 2 a fool r. not the words of prudence
Eccu 18 14 him that r. the discipline of mercy
Mat 7 8 every one that asketh, r. Luke 11:10
10 40 he that r. you, r. me: and he that r. me, r. him that sent me
41 he that r. a prophet in the name of
41 he that r. a just man in the name of
13 20 word, and immediately r. it with joy
18 5 little child in my name, receiveth me
Mark 9 36 shall receive me, r. not me, but him
Luke 9 48 receive this child in my name, r. me
48 receive me, r. him that sent me. For
15 2 this man r. sinners and eateth with
John 3 32 and no man receiveth his testimony. He
4 36 he that reapeth receiveth wages and
12 48 despiseth me and r. not my words, hath
13 20 he that r. whomsoever I send, r. me
20 he that r. me, r. him that sent me
1 C 9 24 all run indeed, but one receiveth prize
Heb 6 7 it is tilled, receiveth blessing from
12 6 he scourgeth every son whom he r.
Apoc 2 17 which no man knoweth but he that r. it
14 11 whoever r. the character of his name
receiving Lev 14 24 r. the lamb for trespass
Num 6 20 r. them again from him, he shall elevate
7 6 receiving the wagons and the oxen
4 K 5 20 in not r. of him that which he brought
Tob 11 11 receiving him kissed him, as did also
Eze 19 4 but not without receiving wounds: and
Mat 20 11 receiving it they murmured against the
Acts 7 45 our fathers r., brought in with Jesus
17 15 r. a commandment from him to Silas
22 5 from whom also r. letters to brethren
28 7 Publius, who receiving us, for 3 days
Rom 1 27 and r. in themselves the recompense
11 15 what shall the receiving of them be, but
2 C 11 8 r. wages of them for your ministry. And
Phil 4 16 as concerning giving and receiving, but
1 Th 1 6 receiving the word in much tribulation
Heb 11 31 unbelievers, r. the spies with peace
12 28 r. an immoveable kingdom, we have grace
James 2 25 r. the messengers, and sending them
1 P 1 9 receiving the end of your faith, even
2 P 2 13 r. the reward of their injustice
Recem Num 31 8 their kings Evi and Recem and Sur
Josu 13 21 princes of Madian: Hevi and Recem and
18 27 Recem, Jarephel, and Tharela and Sela
1 Pa 2 43 Thaphua and Recem and Samma. And
44 Jercaam, and Recem begot Sammai. The
Recen 1 Pa 7 16 his sons were Ulam and Recen. And
receptacles Eccu 39 22 his mouth the r. of waters
Recha 1 Pa 4 12 these are the men of Recha. And
Rechab 2 K 4 2 the name of the other Rechab
2 K 4 5 Rechab and Baana coming, went into the
6 Rechab and Baana his brother stabbed
9 but David answered Rechab and Baana
4 K 10 15 Jonadab the son of Rechab. 23; Jer 35:8, 14, 16, 19
1 Pa 2 55 father of the house of Rechab. Now
2 Es 3 14 Melchias the son of Rechab built, lord
reckon Lev 11 4 shall r. it among the unclean
Lev 27 18 the priest shall reckon the money
23 the priest shall reckon the price
Num 4 29 shalt reckon up the sons of Merari
Eze 44 26 they shall reckon unto him seven days
Luke 14 28 doth not first sit down and reckon
Rom 6 11 so do you also reckon, that you are dead
8 18 I r. that the sufferings of this time
2 C 10 2 who reckon us as if we walked according
reckoned Exod 38 27 talent being r. for every socket
Exod 30 12 when they shall be reckoned. And this
Lev 11 29 shall be r. among unclean. 13:15
Num 1 22 were r. up by the names. 24, 30, 32, 34, 36, 38, 40, 42
27 forth to war, were reckoned up. 29
2 16 were reckoned up in the camp of Ruben
23 of his fighting men, that were r. up
3 27 reckoned up by their names. 33
42 Moses reckoned up, as the Lord had
4 34 reckoned up the sons of Caath by their
45 Merari, whom Moses and Aaron reckoned
46 that were reckoned up of the Levites
49 Moses reckoned them up according to
18 27 may be r. to you as an oblation of
30 if shall be r. to you as if you had
23 9 shall not be reckoned among the nations
24 9 that curseth thee shall be r. accursed
26 51 children of Israel, that were reckoned
54 as they have now been reckoned up

62 they were not reckoned up among the
31 37 portion of Lord, were r. 675 sheep
49 r. up the number of the fighting men
1 K 15 2 I have reckoned up all that Amalec
2 K 4 2 Beroth also was reckoned in Benjamin
4 K 12 15 they r. not with the men that received
Mat 25 19 lord . . . came and reckoned with them
Luke 22 37 and with the wicked was he reckoned
Rom 4 4 reward is not r. according to grace, but
reckoning Exod 26 25 r. two sockets for each board
Lev 25 50 and the reckoning of a hired servant
52 he shall make the reckoning with him
Num 1 18 reckoning them up by the kindreds
4 K 22 7 there be no reckoning made with them
Ps 43 13 there was no reckoning in the exchange
recommended 2 Ma 4 24 he being r. to the king
2 Ma 9 25 whom I often r. to many of you
recompense 2 K 19 36 I need not this recompense
2 K 22 25 Lord will r. me according to my justice
Ps 68 23 become as a snare before them and a r.
Eccu 12 2 and thou shalt find great recompense
20 10 gift the recompense of which is double
35 13 the Lord maketh recompense and will
Isa 35 4 will bring the revenge of recompense
66 6 Lord that rendereth r. to his enemies
Lam 3 64 thou shalt render them a recompense
Bar 6 33 they are not able to recompense it
Joel 3 4 I will very soon return you a r. upon
7 I will return your r. upon your own
Luke 14 12 and a recompense be made to thee. But
14 wherewith to make thee recompense: for
14 recompense shall be made thee at the
Rom 1 27 and receiving in themselves the r. which
11 9 stumblingblock and recompense unto them
35 given to him, and r. shall be made him
2 C 6 13 but having the same recompense, I speak
Heb 2 2 received a just recompense of reward
recompenses Isa 34 8 year of r. of the judgment
reconcile Eccu 48 10 to r. the heart of the father
Eph 2 16 might reconcile both to God in one
Col 1 20 through him to reconcile all things
reconciled Judg 19 3 willing to be r. with her
2 Ma 1 5 be r. unto you and never forsake you
5 20 when the great Lord shall be r.
7 33 he will be r. again to his servants
8 16 not to be reconciled to the enemies
29 Lord to be r. to his servants unto
13 23 being reconciled, offered sacrifices
Mat 5 24 go first to be r. to thy brother, and
Acts 7 26 would have reconciled them in peace
Rom 5 10 we were r. to God by death of his Son
10 being r., shall we be saved by his life
1 C 7 11 or be reconciled to her husband. And let
2 C 5 18 God, who hath r. us to himself by Christ
20 we beseech you, be reconciled to God
Col 1 22 now he hath r. in the body of his flesh
reconciliation Eccu 22 27 for there may be a r.
Eccu 27 23 of a curse there is reconciliation
44 17 the time of wrath he was made a r.
45 20 to make reconciliation for his people
Isa 60 10 in my r. have I had mercy upon thee
Rom 5 11 Christ, by whom we have received r.
11 15 if loss of them be r. of the world, what
2 C 5 18 hath given to us the ministry of r. For
19 and he hath placed in us the word of r.
reconciling 2 C 5 19 r. the world to himself
record 1 Es 6 2 in which this r. was written
2 Es 7 64 they sought their writing in the record
Esth 12 4 the king made a record of what was done
recorded 2 Pa 12 15 the seer and diligently r.
2 Es 12 22 the Levites . . . were recorded, and the
recorder 2 K 8 16 Josaphat . . . was recorder. 20:24; 3 K 4:3; 1 Pa 18:15
4 K 18 18 Joahe the son of Asaph the recorder. 37; Isa 36:3, 22
2 Pa 34 8 Joha the son of Joachaz the recorder
records 1 Es 4 15 shalt find written in the r.
1 Ma 13 42 in the instruments and public records
14 23 copy of their words in the public r.
recount Isa 38 15 I will r. to thee all my years
recourse Esth 14 1 Esther . . . had r. to the Lord
recover 1 K 28 22 mayest eat and r. strength
1 K 30 8 overtake them and recover the prey
4 K 1 2 whether I shall r. of this my illness
5 10 and thy flesh shall recover health
8 8 can I recover from this my illness
9 can I recover of this my illness
14 [Eliseus] told me: Thou shalt recover
Job 36 17 cause and judgment thou shalt recover
Eccu 2 6 believe God, and he will recover thee
29 26 r. thy neighbor according to thy
Eze 30 21 that it might recover strength and
Mark 16 18 upon the sick, and thy shall recover
2 Tim 2 26 may r. themselves from the snares of the
recovered Judg 15 19 spirit and r. his strength
1 K 30 18 David r. all that the Amalecites had
19 they had taken; David recovered all
22 of the prey which we have recovered
Tob 11 15 and immediately he recovered his sight
14 3 and sixty when he recovered it again
Jdth 13 30 but after he had recovered his spirits
Isa 38 9 been sick and was r. of his sickness
39 1 he had been sick and was recovered
Jer 41 16 whom they had recovered from Ismahel
1 Ma 2 48 they r. the law out of the hands of
15 9 when we shall have r. our kingdom, we
2 Ma 2 23 r. again the most renowned temple
10 1 r. the temple and the city again
Heb 11 34 r. strength from weakness, became
recovery 2 Ma 3 29 without all hope of recovery
2 Ma 3 32 sacrifice of health for the r. of the
rectified Acts 24 2 are r. by thy providence
red Gen 25 25 he that came forth first was red
Gen 25 30 give me of this red pottage, for I am
Exod 25 5 rams' skins dyed red. 26:14; 35:7, 23; 36:19; 39:33
Lev 13 19 white scar, or somewhat red, the man
24 is healed hath a white or a red scar
49 be infected with a white or red spot
Num 19 2 that they bring unto thee a red cow
4 K 3 22 saw the waters over against them red
Ps 67 24 tongue of thy dogs be red with the
Wisd 13 14 painting it red and covering every
Isa 1 18 if they be red as crimson, they shall
63 2 why then is thy apparel red and thy
Zach 1 8 a man riding upon a red horse, and
8 horses, red, speckled, and white
6 2 in the first chariot were red horses
Mat 16 2 for the sky is red. 3
Apoc 6 4 went out another horse that was red
12 3 a great red dragon having seven heads
Red Sea Exod 10 19 cast them into the Red Sea
Exod 13 18 of the desert, which is by the Red Sea
15 4 captains are drowned in the Red Sea
22 Moses brought Israel from the Red Sea
23 31 I will set thy bounds from the Red Sea
Num 14 25 wilderness by the way of the Red Sea
21 4 by the way that leadeth to the Red Sea
14 as he did in the Red Sea, so will he
33 10 they pitched their tents by the Red Sea
10 departing from the Red Sea, they camped
Deut 1 1 wilderness over against the Red Sea
40 into wilderness by way of the Red Sea
2 1 wilderness that leadeth to the Red Sea
11 4 how the waters of the Red Sea covered
Josu 2 10 dried up the water of the Red Sea

4 24 as he had done before in the Red Sea
24 6 and horsemen, as far as the Red Sea
Judg 11 16 walked through the desert to Red Sea
3 K 9 26 by Ailath on the shore of the Red Sea
2 Pa 8 17 Ailath on the coast of the Red Sea
2 Es 9 9 didst hear their cry by the Red Sea
Jdth 5 14 after they came out of the Red Sea
Ps 105 7 going up to the sea, even the Red Sea
9 he rebuked the Red Sea, and it was
22 terrible things in the Red Sea. And he
135 13 who divided the Red Sea into parts
15 Pharao and his host in the Red Sea
Wisd 10 18 she brought them through the Red Sea
19 7 in the Red Sea a way without hinderance
Jer 49 21 of their voice is heard in the Red Sea
1 Ma 4 9 our fathers were saved in the Red Sea
Acts 7 36 and in the Red Sea and in the desert
Heb 11 29 they passed through the Red Sea, as
reddish Lev 13 42 be risen a white or r. color
redeem Exod 6 6 and redeem you with a high arm
Exod 13 13 if thou do not redeem it, thou shalt
13 of men thou shalt redeem with a price
15 all the firstborn of my sons I redeem
34 20 ass thou shalt redeem with a sheep
20 firstborn of thy sons thou shalt r.
Lev 25 25 he may redeem what he had sold. But
26 he himself can find the price to r. it
29 shall have the liberty to redeem it
30 if he redeem it not, and the whole year
48 that will of his brethren shall r. him
49 be able also, he shall redeem himself
27 15 but if he that vowed will redeem it
19 if he that had vowed will r. his field
20 if he will not redeem it, but it be
20 vowed it, may not redeem it any more
27 he that offereth it shall redeem it
27 if he will not redeem it, it shall be
31 and if any man will redeem his tithes
2 K 7 23 whom God went to r. for a people to
2 Es 5 5 neither have we wherewith to r. them
8 sell your brethren, for us to r. them
Ps 7 3 while there is no one to redeem me nor
25 11 redeem me, and have mercy on me. My
33 23 Lord will r. the souls of his servants
43 26 and redeem us for thy name's sake
48 8 no brother can r., nor shall man r.
16 God will redeem my soul from the hand
54 19 he shall redeem my soul in peace from
71 14 he shall r. their souls from usuries
118 134 redeem me from the calumnies of man
154 judge my judgment and redeem me
129 8 he shall redeem Israel from all his
Isa 50 2 become little, that I cannot redeem
Jer 15 21 I will redeem thee out of the hand of
Lam 5 8 none to redeem us out of their hand
Dan 4 24 and redeem thou thy sins with alms
Mich 4 10 Lord will r. thee out of the hand of
Gal 4 5 he might r. them who were under the law
Titus 2 14 he might redeem us from all iniquity
redeemed Exod 15 13 the people which thou hast r.
Lev 19 20 and yet not redeemed with a price
25 30 it cannot be r., not even in the jubilee
31 if it be not redeemed before, in the
32 which are in cities, may always be r.
33 if they be not r., in the jubilee they
48 after the sale he may be redeemed
54 if by these means he cannot be redeemed
27 28 shall not be sold, neither may it be r.
29 that is offered by man, shall not be r.
33 to the Lord and shall not be redeemed
Num 3 49 whom they had r. from the Levites
18 15 is unclean thou shalt cause to be r.
17 thou shalt not cause to be redeemed
Deut 7 8 r. you from the house of bondage. 13:5
9 26 inheritance, which thou hast redeemed
21 8 thy people Israel, whom thou hast r.
2 Es 1 10 thou hast r. by thy great strength and
5 8 we, as you know, have r. according
Job 15 31 that he may be redeemed with any price
Ps 30 6 I commend my spirit: thou has r. me
70 23 and my soul which thou hast redeemed
73 2 inheritance which thou hast redeemed
76 16 arm thou hast redeemed thy people
77 42 day that he r. them from the hand of
105 10 he r. them from the hand of the enemy
106 2 say so that have been r. by the Lord
2 whom he hath r. from the hand of the
135 24 and he redeemed us from our enemies
143 10 who hast r. thy servant David from the
Prov 16 6 by mercy and truth iniquity is redeemed
Eccu 49 12 and r. themselves by strong faith
Isa 1 27 Sion shall be redeemed in judgment
29 22 he that r. Abraham: Jacob shall not
35 10 the redeemed of the Lord shall return
43 1 fear not, for I have redeemed thee
44 22 return to me, for I have redeemed thee
23 for the Lord hath redeemed Jacob and
48 20 the Lord hath r. his servant Jacob
51 11 that are r. by the Lord, shall return
52 3 you shall be redeemed without money
9 people: he hath redeemed Jerusalem
62 12 the holy people, the r. of the Lord
63 9 in his mercy he redeemed them and he
Jer 31 11 for the Lord hath redeemed Jacob and
Osee 7 13 against me: and I redeemed them: and
Soph 3 1 woe to the provoking and r. city
Zach 10 8 because I have redeemed them: and
Luke 24 21 was he that should have r. Israel: and
Gal 3 13 Christ hath r. us from the curse
1 P 1 18 you were not r. with corruptible things
Apoc 5 9 thou wast slain and hast redeemed us
redeemedst 2 K 7 23 whom thou r. to thyself
redeemer Job 19 25 I know that my redeemer liveth
Ps 18 15 O Lord, my helper and my redeemer
77 35 and the most high God their redeemer
Isa 41 14 thy redeemer the Holy One of Israel
43 14 thus saith the Lord your redeemer
44 6 and his redeemer the Lord of hosts
24 thus saith the Lord thy redeemer and
47 4 our redeemer, the Lord of hosts is
48 17 thus saith the Lord thy redeemer, the
49 7 saith the Lord the redeemer of Israel
26 thy redeemer the Mighty One of Jacob
54 5 thy redeemer, the Holy One of Israel
8 on thee, said the Lord thy redeemer
59 20 there shall come a redeemer to Sion
60 16 I am the Lord thy Savior and thy r.
63 16 O Lord, art our father, our redeemer
Jer 50 34 their r. is strong, the Lord of hosts
Lam 3 58 my soul, thou the redeemer of my life
Acts 7 35 him God sent to be prince and redeemer
redeemeth Ps 102 4 r. thy life from destruction
1 Ma 4 11 one that r. and delivereth Israel
redeeming Eph 5 16 r. the time, because the days
Col 4 5 that are without, redeeming the time
redemption Lev 25 24 be under the condition of r.
Num 18 16 r. of it shall be after one month
Ps 48 9 nor the price of the r. of his soul
110 9 he hath sent redemption to his people
129 7 and with him plentiful redemption
Isa 63 4 the year of my redemption is come
Mat 20 28 to give his life a r. Mark 10:45
Luke 1 68 and wrought the r. of his people: and
2 38 all that looked for the r. of Israel
21 28 because your redemption is at hand
Rom 3 24 through the r., that is in Christ Jesus

8 23 sons of God, the r. of our body. For we
1 C 1 30 is made unto us wisdom and . . . r.: that
Eph 1 7 in whom we have redemption. Col 1:14
14 unto the redemption of acquisition, unto
4 30 are sealed unto the day of redemption
1 Tim 2 6 who gave himself a redemption for all
Heb 9 12 having obtained eternal redemption. For
15 for the r. of those transgressions
redness Lev 14 37 disfigured with paleness or r.
Prov 23 29 who hath redness of eyes? Surely
redound 2 Pa 19 6 you judge, it shall r. to you
reduced 4 K 23 6 it there and r. it to dust
4 K 23 15 and burnt and reduced to powder
Job 15 28 desert houses that are r. into heaps
Ps 77 59 r. Israel exceedingly, as it were to
Eccu 48 2 were reduced to a small number, for
Isa 25 2 for thou hast r. the city to a heap
Jer 51 37 Babylon shall be reduced to heaps
Eze 15 4 the midst thereof is reduced to ashes
reducing 2 P 2 6 r. the cities of the Sodomites
reed 3 K 14 15 as a reed is shaken in the water
4 K 18 21 Egypt a staff of a broken reed, upon
Job 40 16 the shadow, in the covert of the reed
Isa 19 6 the reed and the bulrush shall wither
35 7 shall rise up the verdure of the reed
36 6 trustest upon this broken staff of a r.
42 3 the bruised reed he shall not break
Eze 29 6 thou hast been a staff of a reed
40 3 and a measuring reed in his hand
5 in the man's hand a measuring reed
5 the breadth of the building one reed, and the height one reed
6 of the threshold of the gate one reed
6 one threshold was one reed broad
7 every little chamber was one reed long and one reed broad
8 porch of the gate within was one reed
41 8 which were the measure of a reed
42 16 with the measuring reed. 17, 18, 19
Mat 11 7 reed shaken with the wind. Luke 7:24
12 20 the bruised reed he shall not break
27 29 his head, and a reed in his right hand
30 they took the reed and struck his head
48 put it on a r. and gave him. Mark 15:36
Mark 15 19 and they struck his head with a reed
Apoc 11 1 was given me a reed like unto a rod
21 15 had a measure of a reed of gold to
16 measured the city with the golden reed
reeds Josu 16 8 the sea into the valley of r.
Josu 17 9 goeth down to the valley of the r.
Ps 67 31 rebuke the wild beasts of the reeds
Wisd 3 7 to and fro like sparks among the reeds
Eze 42 16 he measured . . . five hundred reeds. 17
18 he measured five hundred reeds. 19
reeled Ps 106 27 and reeled like a drunken man
Reema Eze 27 22 the sellers of Saba and Reema
re-establish Eph 1 10 to r. all things in Christ
refectory Mark 14 14 where is my r., where I may
refer Exod 18 22 fall out, let them r. it to thee
Exod 24 14 shall arise, you shall refer it to them
Deut 1 17 refer it to me, and I will hear it
referred Exod 18 26 greater difficulty they r. to
Num 27 4 Moses referred their cause to the
1 Es 5 5 that the matter should be r. to Darius
2 Ma 11 36 thought should be referred to the king
refine Zach 13 9 will refine them as silver is
Mala 3 3 shall refine them as gold and as
refined 1 Pa 29 4 and 7,000 talents of r. silver
Ps 11 7 purged from the earth, r. seven times
118 140 thy word is exceedingly refined: and
Isa 48 10 I have refined thee, but not as silver
Zach 13 9 will refine them as silver is refined
refining Mala 3 2 for he is like a r. fire
Mala 3 3 he shall sit refining and cleansing
reflect 1 K 24 12 r. and see that there is no
Ecce 4 8 neither doth he r., saying: For whom
reflecting 2 Ma 8 11 not r. on the vengeance
reform Phil 3 21 will r. the body of our lowness
reformed Rom 12 2 but be r. in the newness of
refrain Gen 45 1 could not longer r. himself
Judg 13 13 thy wife, let her refrain herself
Prov 25 28 cannot r. his own spirit in speaking
Wisd 1 11 refrain your tongue from detraction
Eccu 3 4 shall refrain himself from them and
4 28 and r. not to speak in the time of
28 10 refrain from strife, and thou shalt
Isa 64 12 wilt thou refrain thyself, O Lord, upon
Acts 5 38 refrain from these men, and let them
15 20 they r. themselves from pollutions of
21 25 they should only refrain themselves from
1 Th 5 22 from all appearance of evil refrain
1 P 2 11 to r. yourselves from carnal desires
3 10 let him refrain his tongue from evil
refrained Gen 43 31 refrained himself, and said
1 K 21 5 we have r. ourselves from yesterday
refraineth Prov 10 19 he that r. his lips is most
1 C 9 25 striveth for the mastery, r. himself
refresh Jdth 7 7 r. themselves a little rather
Prov 29 17 instruct thy son, and he shall r. thee
Eccu 31 25 vomit: and it shall refresh thee
Isa 28 12 this is my rest, refresh the weary
Mat 11 28 are burdened, and I will refresh you
Philem 20 Lord. Refresh my bowels in the Lord
refreshed Exod 23 12 and the stranger may be r.
Deut 12 18 thou shalt rejoice and be refreshed
Judg 15 19 drank them, he refreshed his spirit
1 K 16 23 Saul was refreshed and was better
30 12 spirit returned and he was refreshed
2 K 16 14 came weary and r. themselves there
2 Pa 28 15 and refreshed them with meat and drink
Jdth 6 20 and they refreshed themselves together
Ps 38 14 that I may be r., before I go hence
Acts 28 2 kindling a fire, they refreshed us all
Rom 15 32 and may be refreshed with you. Now God
1 C 16 18 they have r. both my spirit and yours
2 C 7 13 because his spirit was refreshed by you
2 Tim 1 16 he hath often refreshed me, and hath not
Philem 7 bowels of the saints have been refreshed
refresheth Prov 25 13 sent him, for he r. his soul
refreshing Judg 19 22 r. their bodies with meat
Isa 28 12 refresh the weary, and this is my r.
refreshment Ps 22 2 me up on the water of r.
Ps 65 12 hast brought us out into a refreshment
Ecce 10 17 whose princes eat in due season for r.
Wisd 11 4 r. of their thirst out of the hard stone
Jer 6 16 and you shall find r. for your souls
Acts 3 20 that when the times of r. shall come
refuge Num 35 6 for r. to fugitives. 11, 13
Deut 19 12 and take him out of the place of refuge
Josu 20 2 appoint cities of refuge, of which I
21 13 Hebron a city of refuge, and the suburbs
21 one of the cities of refuge. 27, 32, 37
2 K 22 3 he lifteth me up and is my refuge
1 Pa 6 57 cities for refuge Hebron and Lobria
67 the cities of refuge Sichem with its
Ps 9 10 Lord is become a refuge for the poor
17 3 the Lord is my firmament, my refuge
30 3 and a house of refuge, to save me
4 thou art my strength and my refuge
31 7 thou art my refuge from the trouble
45 2 our God is our refuge and strength
58 17 art become my support and my refuge
70 3 thou art my firmament and my refuge
89 1 Lord, thou hast been our refuge from
90 2 thou art my protector and my refuge
9 hast made the most High thy refuge

Regma Gen 10 7 Hevila and Sabatha and R. 1 Pa 1:9
Gen 10 7 sons of Regma: Saba and. 1 Pa 1:9
regret Ps 29 13 sing to thee, and I may not r.
regularly Gen 43 7 we answered him regularly
Num 28 10 which r. are poured out every sabbath
regulated Eccu 43 28 by his word all things are r.
regulation 2 Pa 29 25 according to the r. of David
rehearse Ps 56 8 I will sing, and r. a psalm
Eccu 19 7 r. not again wicked and harsh word
rehearsed Judg 5 11 justices of the Lord be r.
1 K 8 21 and r. them in the ears of the Lord
17 31 heard, and were rehearsed before Saul
Tob 3 25 whose prayers at one time were r.
Rehum 1 Es 2 2 Beguai, Rehum, Baana. The number
2 Es 3 17 after him built the Levites, Rehum
10 25 Rehum, Hasebna, Maasia, Echaia, Hanan
Rei 3 K 1 8 the prophet and Semei and Rei and
Reia 1 Pa 5 5 Micha his son, Reia his son, Baal
reign Exod 15 18 the Lord shall reign forever and
Deut 17 20 sons may reign a long time over Israel
Judg 9 8 to the olive tree: Reign thou over us
10 come thou and reign over us. 12, 14
1 K 8 7 me, that I should not reign over them
9 of the king that shall reign over. 11
9 17 this man shall reign over my people
11 12 who is he that said: Shall Saul r. over
12 12 nay, but a king shall reign over us
13 1 when he began to reign. 2 K 2:10; 5:4; 3 K 14:21; 22:42; 4 K 8:17, 26; 11:21; 14:2; 15:2, 33; 16:2; 18:2; 21:1; 2 Pa 12:13; 20:31; 21:5, 20; 22:2; 24:1; 25:1; 26:3; 27:1, 8; 28:1; Jer 52:1
23 17 thou [David] shalt reign over Israel
2 K 3 17 sought for David that he might r. over
21 that thou mayest reign over all as thy
3 K 1 13 Solomon thy son shall reign after me. 17, 30
13 throne? Why then doth Adonias reign
24 let Adonias reign after me, and let
35 he [Solomon] shall reign in my stead
6 1 in the . . . year of the reign of. 14:25; 15:1; 1 Pa 26:31; 2 Pa 12:2; 15:10; 35:19; 1 Es 6:15; Jdth 2:1; Esth 3:7; 11:1; Dan 1:1; 2:1; 8:1
11 37 thou shalt reign over all that thy soul
14 2 told me that I should reign over this
22 41 Josaphat . . . began to reign over Juda
52 Ochozias . . . began to r. over Israel
4 K 12 1 year of Jehu, Joas began to reign: and
15 13 Sellum the son of Jabes began to reign
23 33 that he should not reign in Jerusalem
24 12 in the . . . year of his reign. 25:1; 2 Pa 3:2; 16:12, 13; 17:7; 34:3, 8; Jdth 1:5; Esth 1:3; 2:16; Jer 1:2; 51:59; 52:4, 31; Dan 9:2
1 Pa 4 31 their cities unto the reign of David
29 25 glory of a reign, such as no king of
30 and of all his reign and his valor and
2 Pa 22 9 should reign of the race of Ochozias
23 3 behold the king's son shall reign
29 3 in the first year and month of his r.
19 king Achaz in his reign had defiled
36 20 till the reign of the king of Persia
1 Es 4 5 even until the reign of Darius king
6 in the reign of Assuerus, in beginning of his reign, they wrote
24 till second year of the reign of Darius
7 1 in the reign of Artaxerxes. 8:1
2 Es 12 22 the priests in the reign of Darius
Tob 4 14 never suffer pride to r. in thy mind
13 23 may he reign over it forever and ever
Job 34 30 to reign for the sins of the people
Ps 9 16 the Lord shall reign to eternity, yea
44 5 set out, proceed prosperously, and reign
46 9 God shall reign over the nations: God
145 10 the Lord shall reign forever: thy God
Prov 8 15 by me kings reign, and lawgivers
28 12 when the wicked reign, men are ruined
Wisd 3 8 and their Lord shall reign forever
6 22 love wisdom, that you may reign forever
Isa 24 23 Lord of hosts shall r. in mount Sion
32 1 behold a king shall reign in justice and
52 7 that saith to Sion: Thy God shall reign
Jer 22 15 shalt thou r., because thou comparest
23 5 a king shall reign and shall be wise
26 1 beginning of the reign of Joakim. 27:1
28 1 beginning of the r. of Sedecias. 49:34
33 21 have a son to reign upon his throne
Eze 20 33 I will r. over you with a strong. 34
Dan 6 28 Daniel continued unto reign of Darius and the reign of Cyrus
8 23 and after their reign, when iniquities
Mich 4 7 the Lord will reign over them in mount
1 Ma 1 17 mind to reign over the land of Egypt
17 that he might reign over two kingdoms
6 17 set up Antiochus his son to reign. 55
8 7 and they that should reign after him
11 9 shalt r. in the kingdom of thy father
2 Ma 9 23 appointed who should reign after him
Luke 1 32 he shall reign in the house of Jacob
3 1 year of the reign of Tiberius Caesar
19 14 not have this man to reign over us
27 would not have me reign over them
Rom 5 17 shall reign in life through one, Jesus
21 so also grace might reign by justice
6 12 let not sin therefore reign in your
1 C 4 8 you r. without us; and I would to God you did r., that we also might r.
15 25 he must reign, until he hath put all his
2 Tim 2 12 if we suffer, we shall also r. with him
Apoc 5 10 we shall reign on the earth. And I
11 15 Christ's, and he shall reign forever
20 6 shall reign with him a thousand years
22 5 and they shall reign forever and ever
reigned Gen 36 33 reigned in his stead. 34, 35, 36, 37; 2 K 10:1; 3 K 11:43; 14:20, 31; 15:8; 16:6, 10, 28; 22:40, 51; 4 K 1:17; 3:27; 8:15, 24; 10:35; 12:21; 13:9, 24; 14:16, 29; 15:7, 14, 22, 25, 30, 38; 16:20; 19:37; 20:21; 1 Pa 1:44, 45, 46, 47, 48, 50; 19:1; 29:28; 2 Pa 12:16; 14:1; 17:1; 21:1; 24:27; 26:23; Isa 37:38
Gen 36 39 being dead, Adar reigned in his place
Josu 13 10 who reigned in Hasebon. 21
12 who reigned in Astaroth and Edrai
Judg 4 2 who reigned in Asor: and he had
9 22 so Abimelech reigned over Israel for
1 K 13 1 he [Saul] r. two years over Israel
2 K 2 10 he [Isboseth] reigned two years: and
5 4 reign, and he [David] reigned 40 years
5 in Hebron he reigned over Juda 7 years
5 in Jerusalem he r. 3 and 30 years. 1 Pa 3:4
8 15 and David reigned over all Israel
3 K 2 11 days that David reigned in Israel were
11 in Hebron he reigned seven years
4 1 king Solomon reigned over all Israel
11 25 against Israel, and he reigned in Syria
42 days that Solomon reigned in Jerusalem
12 17 cities of Juda, Roboam r. over them
14 19 how he fought and how he reigned
20 the days that Jeroboam reigned were
21 Roboam the son of Solomon r. in Juda.
21 reigned . . . years in Jerusalem. 15:2, 10; 22:42; 4 K 8:17; 12:1; 15:2, 33; 16:2; 18:2; 21:1, 19; 22:1; 23:36; 24:8, 18; 2 Pa 12:12; 20:31; 21:5, 20; 24:1; 25:1; 26:3; 27:1, 8; 28:1; 33:1, 21; 34:1; 36:5, 11; Jer 52:1
15 1 son of Nabat, Abiam reigned over Juda

9 of Israel, reigned Asa king of Juda
10 he [Asa] reigned one and forty years
24 Josaphat his son reigned in his place
25 reigned over Israel the second year of
25 [Nadab] reigned over Israel two years
28 so Saasa . . . reigned in his place
33 reigned over all Israel in Thersa
16 8 Ela the son of Baasa r. over Israel
15 Zambri reigned seven days in Thersa
22 and Thebni died, and Amri reigned
23 Amri reigned over Israel twelve years
23 in Thersa he [Amri] reigned six years
29 Achab the son of Amri r. over Israel
22 52 and he [Ochozias] r. over Israel two
4 K 3 1 reigned over Israel in Samaria. 10:36; 13:1, 10
1 and [Joram] reigned twelve years
8 16 reigned Joram son of Josaphat king of
25 r. Ochozias son of Joram king of Juda
26 r. one year in Jerusalem. 2 Pa 22:2
9 29 Ochozias reigned over Juda, and Jehu
11 3 and Athalia reigned over the land
14 1 r. Amasias son of Joas king of Juda
23 reigned Jeroboam the son of Joas
15 1 reigned Azarias son of Amasias, king
2 he [Azarias] r. 2 and 50 years in
8 reigned Zacharias son of Jeroboam
10 killed him and reigned in his place
13 and reigned one month in Samaria
17 reigned Manahem son of Gadi over Israel
23 reigned Phaceia the son of Manahem
27 reigned Phacee the son of Romelia
32 reigned Joatham son of Ozias king
16 1 reigned Achaz the son of Joatham king
2 he [Achaz] r. 16 years in Jerusalem
17 1 Osee the son of Ela reigned in Samaria
18 1 reigned Ezechias the son of Achaz
2 he [Ezechias] reigned 9 and 20 years
21 1 [Manasses] reigned 5 and 50 years
22 1 [Josias] r. one and thirty years in
23 31 r. 3 months in Jerusalem. 24:8; 2 Pa 36:2
1 Pa 1 43 these are the kings that reigned in
3 4 in Hebron where he r. seven years and
16 31 among the nations: the Lord hath r.
18 14 so David reigned over all Israel
29 26 so David . . . reigned over all Israel
27 and the days that he reigned over Israel
27 in Hebron he reigned seven years
2 Pa 1 13 then Solomon . . . reigned over Israel
9 30 Solomon reigned in Jerusalem over
10 17 Roboam r. over the children of Israel
11 12 and he reigned over Juda and Benjamin
12 13 strengthened in Jerusalem and r.
13 he [Roboam] reigned seventeen years
13 1 king Jeroboam, Abia reigned over Juda
2 three years he reigned in Jerusalem
14 5 and temples, and [Asa] reigned in peace
20 31 and Josaphat reigned over Juda, and
31 he reigned five and twenty years
22 1 the son of Joram king of Juda reigned
12 during which Athalia r. over the land
29 1 [Ezechias] r. nine and twenty years
34 1 [Josias] r. one and thirty years in
36 9 he reigned three months and ten days
Tob 1 18 Sennacherib . . . who r. in his place
Jdth 1 5 Nabuchodonosor . . . who r. in Ninive
Ps 92 1 the Lord hath reigned, he is clothed
95 10 the Lord hath reigned. For he hath
96 1 the Lord hath reigned, let the earth
98 1 the Lord hath reigned, let the people
Eccu 47 15 Solomon reigned in days of peace, and
Jer 22 11 who reigned instead of his father
37 1 Sedecias . . . r. instead of Jechonias

Dan 9 1 r. over the kingdom of the Chaldeans
Osee 8 4 they have reigned, but not by me
1 Ma 1 1 who first reigned in Greece, coming
8 and Alexander reigned twelve years
11 and he reigned in the 137th year of
6 2 that reigned first in Greece, had left
7 1 a city of the seacoast and r. there
8 13 mind to help to a kingdom, those r.
10 1 received him, and he reigned there
11 19 Demetrius reigned in the 167th year
12 7 Arius who reigned then among you
13 32 and [Tryphon] reigned in his place
2 Ma 1 7 when Demetrius reigned, in the year
Mat 2 22 hearing that Archelaus reigned in Judea
Rom 5 14 death reigned from Adam unto Moses, **even**
17 if by one man's offence death reigned
21 that as sin hath reigned to death; so
Apoc 11 17 thy great power and thou hast reigned
19 6 Lord our God the Almighty hath reigned
20 4 and they lived and reigned with Christ
reigneth 1 K 12 14 and the king who r. over you
2 K 15 10 say ye: Absalom reigneth in Hebron
3 K 1 11 that Adonias the son of Haggith r.
18 and behold now Adonias reigneth, and
Tob 9 11 God of Israel, who reigneth forever and
Prov 30 22 by a slave when he reigneth: by a fool
31 4 there is no secret where drunkenness r.
Ecce 5 8 king that reigneth over all the land
reigning 1 K 16 1 have rejected from r. over Israel
2 K 2 11 that David abode, reigning in Hebron
reins Exod 12 11 you shall gird your reins and you
Exod 28 42 from the reins to the thighs: and
3 K 22 38 and they washed the reins, according
2 Es 4 18 was girded with a sword about his reins
Ps 7 10 the searcher of hearts and reins is God
15 7 moreover my r. also have corrected me
25 2 try me; burn my reins and my heart
72 21 and my reins have been changed: and
138 13 for thou hast possessed my reins: thou
Prov 23 16 my reins shall rejoice, when thy lips
Wisd 1 6 God is witness of his reins, and he is
Isa 11 5 and faith the girdle of his reins
Jer 11 20 and triest the reins and the hearts
12 2 in their mouth and far from their reins
17 10 who search the heart and prove the r.
20 12 who seest the reins and the heart
Lam 3 13 he hath shot into my r. the daughters
Eze 9 2 had a writer's inkhorn at his reins
23 15 girded with girdles about their reins
Nah 2 3 the reins of the chariot are flaming
1 Ma 2 24 his reins trembled and his wrath was
Apoc 2 23 he that searcheth the reins and hearts
reject Prov 3 11 r. not the correction of the Lord
Eccu 4 4 r. not the petition of the afflicted
Osee 4 6 rejected knowledge, I will r. thee
Acts 13 46 but because you reject it, and judge
1 C 1 19 prudence of the prudent I will reject
rejected Lev 26 43 because they r. my judgments
1 K 8 7 they have not rejected thee, but me
10 19 you this day have rejected your God
15 23 as thou hast r. the word of the Lord
23 Lord hath also r. thee from being king
26 thou hast r. the word of the Lord
26 Lord hath r. thee from being king
16 1 Saul, whom I have r. from reigning
7 I have r. him, nor do I judge according
25 14 to salute our master; and he r. them
4 K 17 15 they r. his ordinances and the covenant
Jdth 1 11 empty, and rejected them without honor
Ps 77 67 he rejected the tabernacle of Joseph
88 39 but thou hast rejected and despised
117 22 the stone which the builders rejected
Eccu 20 22 out of a fool's mouth shall be r.

Isa 30 12 because you have rejected this word
33 8 he hath rejected the cities, he hath
Jer 6 30 silver, for the Lord hath rejected them
7 29 for the Lord hath rejected and forsaken
Lam 5 22 but thou hast utterly rejected us
Osee 4 6 because thou hast r. knowledge, I will
Amos 5 21 and have rejected your festivities
Mat 21 42 the stone which the builders rejected. Mark 12:10; Luke 20:17; 1 P 2:7
Mark 8 31 and be r. by the ancients. Luke 9:22
17 25 and be rejected by this generation
Acts 4 11 is the stone which was rejected by you
Gal 4 14 you despised not, nor r.: but received
1 Tim 4 4 nothing to be rejected that is received
Heb 12 17 he [Esau] was rejected; for he found
1 P 2 4 r. indeed by men, but chosen and made
rejecteth Ps 32 10 rejecteth the devices of people
Prov 15 32 that r. instruction, despiseth
Wisd 3 11 he that r. wisdom and discipline is
rejecting 1 Tim 1 19 some r. have made shipwreck
rejoice Lev 23 40 you shall r. before the Lord
Deut 12 7 you shall r. in all things whereunto
18 thou shalt rejoice and be refreshed
24 5 one year he may rejoice with his wife
28 63 so he shall rejoice destroying you
30 9 Lord will return to rejoice over thee
33 18 rejoice, O Zabulon, in thy going out
Judg 9 19 rejoice ye this day in Abimelech and may he rejoice in you
1 K 19 5 thou sawest it and didst rejoice. Why
2 K 1 20 lest daughters of the Philistines r.
1 Pa 16 10 the heart of them r. that seek the Lord
31 let the heavens rejoice and the earth
• 32 let the fields r. and all things that
35 and may rejoice in singing thy praises
2 Pa 6 41 and thy saints rejoice in good things
20 27 because the Lord had made them rejoice
2 Es 12 27 dedication, and to r. with thanksgiving
Tob 11 8 and shall rejoice in the sight of thee
13 9 and I and my soul will rejoice in him
12 and thou mayst rejoice forever and ever
17 but thou shalt rejoice in thy children
18 love thee and that rejoice in thy peace
14 9 the kings of the earth shall r. in it
Job 3 22 r. exceedingly when they have found
21 12 and rejoice at the sound of the organ
22 19 the just shall see and shall rejoice
Ps 2 11 and rejoice unto him with trembling
5 12 they shall r. forever and thou shalt
9 3 I will be glad and rejoice in thee: I
16 I will rejoice in thy salvation: the
12 5 trouble me will rejoice when I am moved
6 my heart shall rejoice in thy salvation
13 7 Jacob shall r. and Israel shall be glad
19 6 we will rejoice in thy salvation; and
20 2 and in thy salvation he shall rejoice
29 2 hast not made my enemies to r. over me
30 8 I will be glad and rejoice in thy mercy
31 11 glad in the Lord, and rejoice, ye just
32 1 rejoice in the Lord, O ye just: praise
21 for in him our heart shall rejoice
33 3 praised: let the meek hear and rejoice
34 9 but my soul shall rejoice in the Lord
19 my enemies wrongfully r. over me
24 justice: and let them not r. over me
26 be ashamed together, who r. at my evils
27 let them rejoice and be glad, who are
37 17 lest at any time my enemies r. over me
39 17 let all that seek thee r. and be glad
40 12 because my enemy shall not r. over me
47 12 let mount Sion r. and the daughters
50 10 bones that have been humbled shall r.
52 7 Jacob shall r. and Israel shall be
57 11 the just shall r. when he shall see the
59 8 will rejoice, and I will divide Sichem
62 8 I will rejoice under the covert of the
12 but the king shall rejoice in God
63 11 the just shall rejoice in the Lord and
64 11 shall spring up and r. in its showers
65 6 on foot: there shall we rejoice in him
66 5 let the nations be glad and rejoice
67 4 let the just feast and r. before God
5 rejoice ye before him: but the wicked
18 thousands of them that rejoice: the
68 33 let the poor see and rejoice: seek ye
69 5 let all that seek thee rejoice and be
70 23 my lips shall greatly rejoice, when I
80 2 rejoice to God, our helper: sing aloud
84 7 and thy people shall rejoice in thee
85 11 let my heart rejoice that it may fear
88 13 Thabor and Hermon shall r. in thy name
17 in thy name they shall r. all the day
43 thou hast made all his enemies to r.
91 5 in the works of thy hands I shall r.
95 11 let the heavens rejoice, and let the
12 shall all the trees of the woods r.
96 1 Lord hath reigned, let the earth r.
12 rejoice, ye just, in the Lord: and give
97 4 earth: make melody, rejoice and sing
8 the mountains shall rejoice together
103 31 the Lord shall rejoice in his works
104 3 let the heart of them rejoice that seek
105 5 we may rejoice in the joy of the nations
106 42 the just shall see and shall rejoice
107 8 I will rejoice and I will divide Sichem
108 28 confounded: but thy servant shall r.
117 24 let us be glad and rejoice therein
118 162 I will rejoice at thy words, as one
131 9 with justice: and let thy saints r.
16 saints shall r. with exceeding great
144 7 and shall rejoice in thy justice
149 2 let Israel rejoice in him that made him
5 the saints shall rejoice in glory: they
Prov 2 14 and rejoice in most wicked things
5 18 and rejoice with the wife of thy youth
11 10 well with the just, the city shall r.
17 21 even his father shall not r. in a fool
23 15 be wise, my heart shall r. with thee
16 my reins shall r. when thy lips shall
25 and let her rejoice that bore thee
24 17 in his ruin let not thy heart rejoice
27 9 ointment and perfumes r. the heart
29 2 just men increase, the people shall r.
6 and the just shall praise and rejoice
Ecce 3 22 than for a man to rejoice in his work
4 16 come afterwards, shall not r. in him
5 18 portion, and to rejoice of his labor
11 9 rejoice therefore, O young man, in thy
Cant 1 3 we will be glad and rejoice in thee
Eccu 8 8 rejoice not at the death of thy enemy
8 not willing that others should r. at
16 1 rejoice not in ungodly children, if
22 28 in his prosperity also thou mayst r.
23 3 and my enemy rejoice over me? O Lord
30 1 that he may rejoice in his latter end
32 3 that thou mayst rejoice for them and
40 14 while he openeth his hands he shall r.
20 wine and music rejoice the heart, but
51 37 let your soul rejoice in his mercy and
Isa 9 3 they shall r. before thee as they that r. in the harvest, as conquerors r.
12 6 rejoice and praise, O thou habitation
13 3 wrath, them that rejoice in my glory
14 29 rejoice not thou, whole Philistia, that
16 7 to them that r. upon the brick walls
24 8 noise of them that rejoice is ended

25 9 we shall rejoice and be joyful in his
29 19 poor men shall r. in the Holy One of
35 1 and the wilderness shall rejoice and
2 and shall rejoice with joy and praise
41 16 and thou shalt rejoice in the Lord
49 13 ye heavens, and rejoice, O earth
52 9 rejoice and give praise together, O ye
62 5 the bridegroom shall r. over the bride
5 and thy God shall rejoice over thee
65 14 servants shall rejoice, and you shall
18 but you shall be glad and r. forever
19 I will rejoice in Jerusalem and joy
66 10 rejoice with Jerusalem, and be glad
10 rejoice with joy with her, all you that
14 you shall see and your heart shall r.
Jer 20 15 to thee: and made him greatly rejoice
31 7 rejoice ye in the joy of Jacob and
13 then shall the virgin rejoice in the
32 41 I will rejoice over them, when I shall
50 11 because you rejoice and speak great
Lam 2 17 caused the enemy to rejoice over thee
4 21 rejoice and be glad, O daughter of
Bar 4 12 let no man rejoice over me, a widow
Eze 7 12 let not the buyer rejoice: nor the
35 14 when the whole earth shall rejoice, I
Osee 9 1 r. not, O Israel: r. not as the nations
Joel 2 21 O land, be glad and rejoice: for the
23 children of Sion, rejoice and be joyful
Amos 6 14 you that rejoice in a thing of nought
Abdi 12 shalt not r. over the children of
Mich 7 8 rejoice not, thou, my enemy, over me
Haba 1 15 for this he will be glad and rejoice
3 18 but I will rejoice in the Lord: and I
Soph 3 14 O Israel: be glad and rejoice with
17 he will r. over thee with gladness
Zach 2 10 rejoice, O daughter of Sion: for behold
4 10 they shall r. and shall see the tin
9 9 rejoice greatly, O daughter of Sion
10 7 their heart shall r. as through wine
7 their children shall see and shall r.
1 Ma 12 12 and we rejoice at your glory. But we
Mat 5 12 be glad and rejoice, for your reward
Luke 1 14 and many shall rejoice in his nativity
6 23 be glad in that day and rejoice; for
10 20 yet rejoice not in this, that spirits
20 rejoice in this, that your names are
15 6 r. with me, because I have found. 9
John 4 36 he that reapeth, may rejoice together
5 35 willing for a time to r. in his light
16 20 and weep, but the world shall rejoice
22 your heart shall rejoice; and your joy
Rom 12 15 rejoice with them that rejoice; weep
15 10 rejoice, ye Gentiles, with his people
16 19 I rejoice therefore in you. But I would
1 C 7 30 that rejoice, as if they rejoiced not
12 26 glory, all the members rejoice with it
16 17 I rejoice in the presence of Stephanas
2 C 2 3 from them of whom I ought to rejoice
7 13 we did the more abundantly rejoice for
16 I rejoice that in all things I have
13 9 we rejoice that we are weak, and you are
11 the rest, brethren, rejoice, be perfect
Gal 4 27 rejoice, thou barren, that bearest not
Phil 1 18 in this also I rejoice, yea, and will r.
2 17 I rejoice, and congratulate with you
18 for the selfsame thing do you also r.
28 that seeing him again, you may rejoice
3 1 rest, my brethren, rejoice in the Lord
4 4 r. in the Lord always; again, I say, r.
10 now I rejoice in the Lord exceedingly
Col 1 24 who now rejoice in my sufferings for
3 15 let the peace of Christ rejoice in your
1 Th 3 9 in all the joy wherewith we rejoice for
5 16 always rejoice. Pray without ceasing
James 4 16 now you rejoice in your arrogancies
1 P 1 6 wherein you shall greatly r. if now
8 believing shall r. with joy unspeakable
4 13 rejoice that when his glory shall be
1 J 1 4 that you may r. and your joy may be
Apoc 11 10 shall rejoice over them and make merry
12 12 rejoice, O heavens, and you that dwell
18 20 rejoice over her, thou heaven, and
19 7 let us be glad and rejoice and give

rejoiced Exod 18 9 Jethro r. for all the good
Deut 28 63 and as the Lord rejoiced upon you
30 9 things, as he rejoiced in thy fathers
1 K 2 1 my heart hath rejoiced in the Lord
6 13 saw the ark, and rejoiced to see it
11 15 Saul and all the men of Israel rejoiced
3 K 1 40 rejoiced with a great joy, and the
5 7 [Hiram] rejoiced exceedingly and said
4 K 11 20 all the people of the land rejoiced
20 13 Ezechias rejoiced at their coming
1 Pa 29 9 the people rejoiced when they promised
9 king rejoiced also with a great joy
2 Pa 23 21 all the people of the land rejoiced
24 10 all the princes and all the people r.
29 36 Ezechias and all the people rejoiced
2 Es 12 42 they r.: for God had made them joyful
42 their wives also and their children r.
Tob 11 21 feasted and rejoiced all with great
Jdth 15 15 all the people rejoiced with the women
Job 31 25 if I have rejoiced over my great riches
27 and my heart in secret hath rejoiced
29 have rejoiced that evil had found him
Ps 15 9 hath been glad, and my tongue hath r.
18 6 hath rejoiced as a giant to run the way
34 15 they r. against me and came together
83 3 and my flesh have r. in the living God
89 14 we have rejoiced and are delighted all
15 we have rejoiced for the days in which
96 8 the daughters of Juda rejoiced, because
106 30 they rejoiced because they were still
121 1 I r. at the things that were said to
Ecce 11 8 years, and have rejoiced in them all
Wisd 7 12 rejoiced in all these: for this wisdom
11 5 Israel abounded therewith and rejoiced
Eccu 30 5 while he lived he saw and r. in him
Isa 14 7 still, it is glad and hath rejoiced
8 fir trees also have rejoiced over thee
32 12 houses of joy of the city that r.
39 2 Ezechias r. at their coming and he
Jer 41 13 men that were with him, they rejoiced
Lam 1 21 they have r. that thou hast done it
Bar 3 34 given light in their watches and r.
4 31 they that have rejoiced at thy ruin
33 for as she rejoiced at thy ruin and
Eze 25 6 hast rejoiced with all thy heart
35 15 hast rejoiced over the inheritance
Osee 10 5 that rejoiced over it in its glory
1 Ma 7 48 and the people rejoiced exceedingly
14 11 and Israel rejoiced with great joy
21 joy: and we rejoiced at their coming
2 Ma 15 11 believed, whereby he rejoiced them all
Mat 2 10 seeing the star they rejoiced with
Luke 1 47 my spirit hath rejoiced in God my
10 21 he r. in the Holy Ghost and said: I
13 17 all the people r. for all the things
John 8 56 Abraham your father r. that he
Acts 2 26 been glad, and my tongue hath rejoiced
7 41 r. in the works of their own hands
11 23 and had seen the grace of God, rejoiced
15 31 when they had read, they rejoiced for
16 34 rejoiced with all his house, believing
1 C 7 30 they that rejoice, as if they r. not
2 C 7 7 zeal for me, so that I rejoiced the more

rejoiceth Prov 15 23 a man r. in the sentence of
Prov 15 30 light of the eyes rejoiceth the soul
17 5 he that r. at another man's ruin
23 24 the father of the just rejoiceth greatly
29 3 a man that loveth wisdom, r. his father
Eccu 19 5 he that rejoiceth in iniquity shall be
26 2 a virtuous woman r. her husband, and
37 4 who r. with his friend in his joys
Isa 64 5 thou hast met him that rejoiceth
Mat 18 13 he r. more for that than for the
John 3 29 r. with joy because of the bridegroom's
1 C 13 6 r. not in iniquity, but r. with truth
rejoicing Judg 16 25 r. in their feasts, when they
3 K 1 45 they are gone up from thence rejoicing
4 20 eating and drinking and rejoicing
8 66 and went to their dwellings rejoicing
4 K 11 14 people of the land r. and sounding the
2 Pa 23 13 all the people of the land rejoicing
Tob 11 20 kinsmen of Tobias came, r. for Tobias
Jdth 13 20 r. for his victory, for my escape and
Esth 8 17 there was wonderful rejoicing, feasts
Job 8 21 with laughter, and thy lips with r.
Ps 18 9 justices of Lord are right, r. hearts
44 16 shall be brought with gladness and r.
86 7 dwelling in thee is as it were of all r.
117 15 the voice of rejoicing and of salvation
Isa 16 10 there shall be no r. nor shouting
65 18 behold I create Jerusalem a rejoicing
Jer 48 2 there is no more rejoicing in Moab
Bar 4 37 Holy One rejoicing for the honor of God
5 5 rejoicing in the remembrance of God
Eze 23 42 the voice of a multitude rejoicing
Luke 15 5 lay it upon his shoulders, rejoicing
Acts 5 41 r. that they were accounted worthy
8 39 and he went on his way rejoicing. But
Rom 12 12 r. in hope. Patient in tribulation
2 C 6 10 as sorrowful, yet always rejoicing; as
Phil 1 26 your r. may abound in Christ Jesus for
Col 2 5 rejoicing, and beholding your order
James 4 16 all such rejoicing is wicked. To him
relate Ps 9 2 will r. all thy wonders. I will
Ps 47 14 that ye may r. it in another generation
74 2 we will relate thy wondrous works
104 2 to him: relate all his wondrous works
2 Ma 10 10 we will relate the acts of Eupator
Mat 11 4 r. to John what you have heard. Luke 7:22
Acts 28 21 hither r. or speak any evil of thee
1 Th 1 9 for they themselves relate of us, what
related Gen 24 30 had heard all that she related
Exod 19 8 when Moses had related the people's
Num 13 28 they related and said: We came into
Judg 7 13 in this manner r. what he had seen
2 Es 6 19 and they related my words to him
Jdth 6 12 and Achior related in the midst of the
Eccu 44 8 that their praises might be related
1 Ma 5 14 rent, who r. according to these words
Mark 6 30 related to him all things that they had
Acts 4 23 related all that the chief priests and
10 8 he had r. all, he sent them to Joppe
14 26 they r. what great things God had done
15 14 Simon hath r. how God first visited
21 19 he r. particularly what things God had
1 Th 3 6 related to us your faith and charity
relating 2 Es 13 14 I have done r. to the house of
Dan 7 1 and relating the sum of it in short
Acts 15 3 r. the conversion of the Gentiles
2 C 7 7 r. to us your desire, your mourning
relations Tob 2 15 so his r. and kinsmen mocked
release 2 Pa 28 11 my counsel and r. the captives
Ps 101 21 might release the children of the slain
Isa 61 1 to preach a release to the captives
Eze 46 17 shall be his until the year of release
1 Ma 10 29 I release you from the customs of salt
13 16 revolt from us, and we will r. him
37 to r. you the things that we have
Mat 27 15 the governor was accustomed to r. to
17 whom will you that I release to you
Mark 15 6 he was wont to release unto them one
9 that I r. to you the king. John 18:39
11 that he should rather r. Barabbas to
Luke 23 16 will chastise him therefore and r. him
17 he was to r. unto them one upon the
18 r. unto us Barabbas: who, for a certain
20 desiring to r. Jesus. But they cried
John 18 39 that I should release one unto you
19 10 and I have power to release thee
12 Pilate sought to release him. But the
12 if thou r. this man, thou art not
released Ps 104 20 king sent and he released him
1 Ma 13 37 you the things that we have released
Mat 27 21 of the two to be released unto you
26 he r. to them Barabbas. Mark 15:15
Luke 23 25 he r. unto them him who for murder
Acts 3 13 when he judged he should be released
28 18 would have r. me, for that there was no
relict Jdth 8 4 Judith his r. was a widow now
relied Ps 129 4 my soul hath relied on his word
1 Ma 8 12 friends and such as r. upon them
2 Ma 11 13 relied upon the help of the Almighty
14 5 and asked what the Jews relied upon
relief Gen 41 57 to seek some r. of their want
1 K 11 9 sun shall be hot, you shall have relief
Lam 1 16 the relief of my soul, is far from me
Acts 11 29 purposed to send r. to the brethren
relieve Isa 1 17 seek judgment, r. the oppressed
Lam 1 11 for food to relieve the soul: see
19 their food, to relieve their souls
relieved Job 7 13 I shall be r. speaking with
Dan 11 34 they shall be r. with a small help
relieveth Job 12 21 r. them that were oppressed
relieving Deut 15 10 craftily in r. his necessities
Eccu 3 15 r. of the father shall not be forgotten
religion Lev 16 31 your souls by a perpetual r.
Jdth 14 6 leaving the religion of the Gentiles
Esth 8 17 many of other nations and religion
9 27 that had a mind to be joined to their r.
Eccu 37 12 treat not with a man without religion
2 Ma 8 1 such as continued in the Jews' religion
14 38 himself pure in the Jews' religion
Acts 26 5 to the most sure sect of our religion I
Gal 1 13 my conversation in time past in Jews' r.
14 I made progress in the Jews' religion
Col 2 18 humility, and r. of angels, walking in
James 1 26 this man's r. is vain. R. clean and
religious Dan 3 90 all ye r., bless the Lord
2 Ma 6 11 reason of the r. observance of the
Acts 10 2 a religious man, and fearing God with
13 50 Jews stirred up religious . . . women
James 1 26 if any man think himself to be r., not
religiously Jdth 16 31 is r. observed by the Jews
2 Ma 12 43 thinking well and r. concerning the
religiousness Eccu 1 17 is the r. of knowledge
Eccu 1 18 r. shall keep and justify the heart
26 understanding and r. of knowledge
remain Gen 6 3 my spirit shall not remain in man
Gen 38 11 remain the widow in thy father's house
45 6 and five years more remain, wherein
Exod 8 9 people: and may r. only in the river
11 and shall remain only in the river
10 24 let your sheep only and herds remain
26 there shall not a hoof remain of them
12 10 neither shall there remain anything
14 28 there so much as one of them remain
16 23 whatsoever shall remain, lay it up
21 21 if the party remain alive a day or two
23 18 neither shall the fat of my solemnity r.

26 12 that which shall r. of the curtains
29 34 if there r. of the consecrated flesh
34 25 neither shall there r. in the morning
Lev 7 15 any of it remain until the morning
16 if any of it remain until the morrow
8 35 shall you remain in the tabernacle
12 4 she shall remain three and thirty days
5 shall r. in blood of her purification
19 9 nor shalt thou gather the ears that r.
20 14 neither shall so great an abomination r.
22 30 not any of it r. until the morning
23 22 shall you gather the ears that remain
25 16 the more years remain after the jubilee
51 years that r. until the jubilee. 27:18
26 36 as to them that shall remain of you
39 and if of them also some remain, they
Num 19 13 his uncleanness shall remain upon him
33 55 they that r. shall be unto you as nails
36 8 the inheritance may r. in the families
9 mingled one with another, but r. so
Deut 3 19 and they must remain in the cities
4 27 you shall r. a few among the nations
40 thou mayst remain a long time upon
16 4 in the evening remain until morning
21 13 shall remain in thy house and mourn
23 his body shall not r. upon the tree
24 21 not gather the clusters that remain
28 62 and you shall remain few in number
30 18 shalt remain but a short time in the
Josu 1 14 children and cattle shall remain
2 11 neither did there remain any spirit
10 27 mouth thereof, which r. until this day
23 4 great sea, and many nations yet remain
7 Gentiles, who will remain among you
Ruth 2 7 to glean the ears of corn that remain
1 K 2 36 whosoever shall remain in thy house
20 19 thou shalt remain beside the stone
3 K 11 32 one tribe shall remain to him for the
36 that there may remain a lamp for my
18 22 I only remain a prophet of the Lord
4 K 7 4 if we will r. here, we must also die
1 Pa 17 24 let thy name remain and be magnified
29 18 and let this mind remain always for the
2 Pa 7 16 my heart may remain there perpetually
1 Es 9 15 for we remain yet to be saved as at
Tob 13 20 if there shall remain of my seed
Job 11 14 let not injustice r. in thy tabernacle
27 15 they that shall remain of him, shall be
Eccu 3 10 his blessing may r. in the latter end
4 16 looketh upon her, shall r. secure
23 37 and they that remain shall know that
27 5 with a sieve, the dust will remain
42 24 these things live and r. forever
44 13 their children for their sakes remain
Isa 4 3 that shall r. in Jerusalem, shall be
10 19 they that remain of the trees of
32 yet day enough to remain in Nobe
24 13 if a few olives, that remain, should
Jer 8 3 all that shall remain of this wicked
27 11 I will let them remain in their own
19 the vessels that remain in this city
38 2 whosoever shall remain in this city
4 men of war that remain in this city
42 10 if you will be quiet and r. in this
17 none of them shall remain, nor escape
43 4 Lord, to remain in the land of Juda
44 14 and remain of the remnant of the Jews
Lam 5 19 thou, O Lord, shalt remain forever
Bar 2 21 you shall remain in the land which
Eze 7 11 nothing of them shall remain, nor of
48 15 the 5,000 that remain in the breadth
Dan 4 23 thy kingdom shall remain to thee after
Amos 4 2 what shall r. of you in boiling pots
6 9 if there remain ten men in one house
Abdi 14 shalt not shut up them that remain
Soph 2 7 portion of him that shall remain of
Zach 5 4 it shall remain in the midst of his
1 Ma 2 18 and they that remain in Jerusalem
15 7 in thy hands, let them remain to thee
Luke 10 7 in the same house remain, eating and
John 6 12 gather up the fragments that remain
12 46 in me, may not remain in darkness
15 16 and your fruit should remain: that
19 31 that the bodies might not r. upon the
21 22 so I will have him to r. till I come. 23
Acts 5 4 whilst it remained, did it not r. to
15 34 it seemed good unto Silas to r. there
Rom 4 9 doth it remain in the circumcision only
1 C 7 11 if she depart, that she r. unmarried
40 more blessed shall she be, if she so r.
13 13 now there r. faith, hope, and charity
15 6 of whom many remain until this present
1 Th 3 1 we thought it good to remain at Athens
4 14 who remain unto the coming of the Lord
1 Tim 1 3 I desired thee to remain at Ephesus
Heb 12 27 things may remain which are immoveable
Apoc 3 2 and strengthen the things that remain
17 10 is come, he must remain a short time
remainder Exod 29 34 shalt burn the r. with fire
2 K 14 7 no name nor remainder upon the earth
remainders Ps 75 11 r. of the thought shall
remained Gen 7 23 Noe only r., and they that
Gen 14 10 they that remained fled to the mountain
29 31 womb, but her sister remained barren
30 37 parts that were whole remained green
32 24 he [Jacob] remained alone: and behold
Exod 10 15 remained not anything that was green
19 remained not so much as one in all
40 35 r. in same place. Num 9:18, 22; Josu 5:8
Num 9 22 if it remained over the tabernacle
11 26 there r. in the camp two of the men
26 65 and none remained of them but Caleb
36 12 remained in the tribe and family
Deut 3 11 for only Og king of Basan remained
32 36 and they that remained are consumed
Josu 5 1 there remained no spirit in them
8 17 not one remained in the city of Hai
18 2 but there remained seven tribes of
21 5 that is, to the Levites, who remained
22 7 to the half that remained Josue gave
Judg 7 3 and returned home, and only 10,000 r.
9 5 there r. only Joatham the youngest son
18 31 the idol of Michas r. with them all
20 45 when they that r. of Benjamin saw this
47 there r. of all the number of Benjamin
Ruth 1 3 she [Noemi] remained with her sons
1 K 5 5 only the stump of Dagon r. in its place
23 14 he [David] remained in a mountain
25 13 and 200 remained with the baggage
2 K 11 1 Rabba: but David remained in Jerusalem
13 20 Thamar r. pining away in the house of
16 3 he r. in Jerusalem, saying: Today
3 K 11 16 Joab r. there six months with all
15 18 took all the silver and gold that r.
20 30 they that remained fled to Aphec
22 47 also of the effeminate who remained
4 K 3 25 so that brick walls only remained
13 6 there still remained a grove in Samaria
17 18 there remained only the tribe of Juda
25 11 rest of the people that r. in the city
22 over the people that r. in the land
1 Pa 6 61 to the sons of Caath that remained
13 14 ark of God r. in the house of Obededom
17 5 for I have not remained in a house
2 Pa 4 4 three that remained toward the east
2 Es 1 2 concerning the Jews that r. and were

Tob 8 24 a writing that the half that remained
Jdth 12 9 going in, she remained pure in the tent
Ecce 2 9 Jerusalem: my wisdom also r. with me
Jer 24 8 that have remained in this city and
34 7 these remained of the cities of Juda
35 11 and we have remained in Jerusalem
37 15 Jeremias remained there many days
20 Jeremias r. in the entry of. 38:13, 28
39 9 the people that remained in the city
9 rest of the people that remained
41 10 all the people that r. in Masphath
48 11 his taste hath remained in him and
52 15 common sort who remained in the city
Eze 3 15 and I r. there seven days mourning
Dan 10 8 there remained no strength in me
13 and I remained there by the king of
16 and no strength hath remained in me
1 Ma 3 37 took the half of the army that r.
6 9 and he remained there many days: for
54 there r. in the holy places but a few
9 6 there r. of them no more than 800 men
8 then he said to them that remained
10 14 in Bethsura there r. some of them
11 40 and he remained there many days
13 11 in it, and himself remained there
Mat 11 23 perhaps it had r. unto this day
14 20 took up what remained, twelve full
15 37 of what remained of the fragments
21 17 of the city into Bethania and r. there
Luke 1 22 made signs to them and remained dumb
2 43 the child Jesus remained in Jerusalem
9 17 of fragments that remained to them
John 1 32 from heaven, and he remained upon him
2 12 they remained there not many days
6 13 which r. over and above to them that
8 9 Jesus alone remained, and the woman
11 6 he still remained in the same place
Acts 5 4 whilst it r., did it not remain to
17 14 but Silas and Timothy remained there
18 3 he remained with them, and wrought
19 22 he himself remained for a time in Asia
27 41 sticking fast, remained unmoveable: but
28 30 he r. two whole years in his own hired
2 Tim 4 20 Erastus r. at Corinth. And Trophimus
1 J 2 19 would no doubt have remained with us
remainest Ps 101 27 they shall perish but thou r.
Bar 3 3 thou remainest forever, and shall
remaineth Lev 25 52 of what r. of the years, his
Deut 24 20 whatsoever remaineth on the trees
Josu 7 26 which r. until this present day. 8:29
22 17 stain of that crime remaineth in us
1 K 16 11 there remaineth yet a young one who
1 Pa 17 24 house of David his servant r. before
Job 17 1 and only the grave remaineth for me
27 3 as long as breath remaineth in me
Ps 9 8 noise: but the Lord remaineth forever
111 3 his justice r. forever and ever. 9
116 2 the truth of the Lord remaineth forever
Eccu 18 1 and he remaineth an invincible king
38 20 in withdrawing aside sorrow remaineth
40 17 in blessings and mercy r. forever
Isa 17 5 in the harvest that which remaineth
Jer 32 43 there remaineth neither man nor beast
Eze 6 12 he that r. and is besieged, shall
Dan 10 17 for no strength r. in me, moreover
Luke 11 41 yet that which remaineth, give alms
John 9 41 you say: We see. Your sin remaineth
12 25 itself remaineth alone. But if it die
1 C 7 29 time is short; it remaineth, that they
2 C 3 11 much more that which r. is in glory
9 9 the poor: his justice remaineth forever
Heb 4 6 seeing then it r. that some are to enter
9 there r. therefore a day of rest for
1 P 1 23 who liveth and remaineth forever
remaining Gen 29 7 there is yet much day r.
Gen 45 11 are yet five years of famine remaining
Lev 10 12 take the sacrifice that is remaining
Judg 5 20 the stars remaining in their order
4 K 7 13 five horses that are r. in the city
Jdth 8 23 through many tribulations, r. faithful
Wisd 7 27 r. in herself the same, she reneweth
Eccu 46 15 glory of the holy men r. unto their
Jer 4 7 waste, remaining without an inhabitant
Eze 39 14 to seek out them that were remaining
Soph 3 6 there is not a man remaining nor any
Mark 1 10 dove descending, and r. John 1:33
remains Exod 8 3 into the remains of thy meats
Num 24 19 shall destroy the remains of the city
Josu 10 28 he left not in it the least remains
30 left not in it any remains. 39; 11:11
37 in it: he left not therein any remains
40 he left not any remains therein but
11 8 so as to leave no remains of them
13 12 he was of the remains of the Raphaims
Judg 20 48 put all the r. of the city to the sword
Ruth 2 18 gave her of the remains of her meat
2 K 21 2 but the remains of the Amorrhites
4 K 10 11 till there were no remains left of him
Isa 14 22 the r. and the bud and the offspring
Jer 6 9 they shall gather the remains of Israel
11 23 there shall be no remains of them
Eze 23 25 what remains shall fall by the sword
Abdi 18 be no remains of the house of Esau
Luke 24 43 taking the remains, he gave to them
remarkable Lev 26 1 nor set up a r. stone in your
1 Pa 17 17 hast made me remarkable above all men
remarked Ecce 4 4 I r. that their industries are
remedies Tob 6 7 what r. are these things good
remedy 2 Pa 36 16 his people, and there was no r.
Prov 6 15 and shall no longer have any remedy
Wisd 2 1 in the end of a man there is no remedy
16 9 there was found no r. for their life
Eccu 21 4 there is no r. for the wound thereof
28 3 anger, and doth he seek remedy of God
38 14 what they give for ease and remedy
43 24 remedy of all is the speedy coming of
Remeia 1 Es 10 25 of the sons of Pharos, Remeia
remember Gen 9 15 I will remember my covenant with
Gen 9 16 and shall r. the everlasting covenant
20 16 thou shalt go: and r. thou wast taken
40 13 Pharao will r. thy service and will
14 r. me when it shall be well with thee
50 15 he should r. the wrong he suffered
Exod 13 3 r. this day in which you came forth
20 8 r. that thou keep holy the sabbath
32 13 remember Abraham, Isaac, and Israel
Lev 26 42 I will r. my covenant that I made
42 and Abraham. I will r. also the land
45 I will r. my former covenant, when I
Num 11 5 we r. the fish that we ate in Egypt
15 39 they may remember all the commandments
Deut 5 15 r. that thou also didst serve in Egypt
7 18 remember what the Lord thy God did to
8 2 shalt r. all the way through which the
14 and thou r. not the Lord thy God
18 r. the Lord thy God, that he hath
9 7 r. and forget not how thou provokedst
27 r. thy servants Abraham, Isaac, and
15 15 r. that thou also wast a bondservant
16 3 mayst r. the day of thy coming out of
12 shalt r. that thou wast a servant in
24 9 r. what the Lord . . . did to Mary
18 r. that thou wast a slave in Egypt and
22 r. what thou also was a bondman in
25 17 r. what Amalec did to thee in the
32 7 remember the days of old, think upon

Josu	1	13	r. the word which Moses the servant
Judg	16	28	r. me, and restore to me now my
1 K	25	31	my lord, thou shalt r. thy handmaid
2 K	14	11	let the king remember the Lord his God
	19	19	nor r. the injuries of thy servant on
4 K	9	25	for I r. when I and thou sitting in a
	20	3	r. how I have walked before thee in
1 Pa	16	4	to remember his works and to glorify
		12	r. his wonderful works which he hath
		15	r. forever his covenant: the word
2 Pa	6	42	r. the mercies of David thy servant
	24	22	king Joas did not r. the kindness that
2 Es	1	8	r. the word that thou commandedst to
	4	14	r. the Lord who is great and terrible
	5	19	r. me O my God, for good according
	6	14	remember me, O Lord, for Tobias and
	13	14	r. me, O my God, for this thing, and
		22	for this also r. me, O my God, and spare
		29	r. them, O Lord my God, that defile the
		31	remember me, O my God, unto good
Tob	3	3	neither remember my offences nor those
Jdth	4	12	remember Moses the servant of the Lord
	8	22	they must r. how our father Abraham was
	9	18	remember, O Lord, thy covenant and put
Job	4	7	r., I pray thee, who ever perished
	7	7	r. that my life is but wind, and my
	10	9	r., I beseech thee, that thou hast made
	11	16	r. it only as waters that are passed
	14	13	appoint me a time when thou wilt r. me
	21	6	when I remember, I am afraid, and
	36	24	r. that thou knowest not his work
	40	27	remember the battle, and speak no more
Ps	21	28	the ends of the earth shall remember
	24	6	r., O Lord, thy bowels of compassion
		7	youth and my ignorance do not remember
		7	according to thy mercy remember thou me
	41	7	therefore will I r. thee from the land
	44	18	they shall remember thy name throughout
	73	2	r. thy congregation which thou hast
		18	r. this, the enemy hath reproached the
		22	remember thy reproaches with which the
	78	8	r. not our former iniquities: let thy
	88	48	r. what my substance is: for hast thou
	104	5	r. his marvellous works which he hath
	105	4	r. us, O Lord, in the favor of thy people
	131	1	remember David and all his meekness
	136	6	cleave to my jaws, if I do not r. thee
		7	r., O Lord, the children of Edom in
Prov	31	7	and remember their sorrow no more
Ecce	5	19	he shall not much r. the days of his
	11	8	he must remember the darksome time and
	12	1	remember thy Creator in the days of thy
Eccu	7	18	r. wrath, for it will not tarry long
		30	r. that thou hadst not been born but
		40	r. thy last end, and thou shalt never
	8	6	r. that we are all worthy of reproach
	10	6	r. not any injury done thee by thy
	14	12	remember that death is not slow and
	16	16	who shall r. me from on high? In such
	18	24	r. the wrath that shall be at the last
		25	r. poverty in the time of abundance
	23	18	r. thy father and thy mother, for thou
		26	the most High will not r. my sins
	28	6	r. thy last things, and let enmity
		8	r. the fear of God, and be not angry
		9	r. the covenant of the most High and
	31	14	remember that a wicked eye is evil
	36	10	hasten the time and remember the end
	38	21	it from thee: and r. the latter end
		23	r. my judgment: for thine also shall
	41	5	r. what things have been before thee
	42	15	I will now r. the works of the Lord
Isa	12	4	the people: r. that his name is high
	19	17	that shall remember it shall tremble
	26	13	only in thee let us remember thy name
	38	3	r. how I have walked before thee in
	43	18	r. not former things, and look not on
		25	own sake, and I will not r. thy sins
	44	21	r. these things, O Jacob and Israel
	46	8	r. this and be ashamed: return, ye
		9	r. the former age, for I am God and
	54	4	shalt r. no more the reproach of thy
	63	7	I will r. the tender mercies of the
	64	5	in thy ways they shall remember thee
		9	and remember no longer our iniquity
Jer	3	16	the heart, neither shall they r. it
	14	10	he will now remember their iniquities
		21	r., break not thy covenant with us
	15	15	r. me and visit me and defend me
	17	2	when their children shall r. their
	18	20	r. that I have stood in thy sight to
	31	20	I spoke of him, I will still r. him
		34	and I will remember their sin no more
	51	50	remember the Lord afar off, and let
Lam	3	19	r. my poverty and transgression, the
		20	I will be mindful and r., and my soul
	5	1	r., O Lord, what is come upon us
Bar	2	33	they shall r. the way of their fathers
	3	5	r. not the iniquities of our fathers
	4	14	remember the captivity of my sons and
Eze	6	9	shall r. me amongst the nations to
	16	60	I will r. my covenant with thee in
		61	shalt r. thy ways and be ashamed
		63	that thou mayest r. and be confounded
	18	22	I will not r. all his iniquities that
	20	43	there you shall remember your ways and
	23	27	eyes to them, nor r. Egypt any more
	36	31	you shall r. your wicked ways and your
Dan	13	9	unto heaven nor r. just judgments
Osee	2	17	she shall no more remember their name
	7	2	that I remember all their wickedness
	8	13	now will he remember their iniquity
	9	9	he will r. their iniquity and will
Mich	6	5	r., I pray thee, what Balach the king
Haba	3	2	thou art angry, thou wilt r. mercy
Zach	10	9	and from afar they shall remember me
Mala	4	4	remember the law of Moses my servant
1 Ma	4	9	r. in what manner our fathers were
		10	will r. the covenant of our fathers
	6	12	now I r. the evils that I have done in
	7	38	r. their blasphemies, and suffer them
	10	5	he will r. all the evils that we have
	12	11	r. you in the sacrifices that we offer
		11	is meet and becoming to r. brethren
2 Ma	1	2	and r. his covenant that he made with
	8	4	that he would r. also the most unjust
	15	8	but to r. the help they had before
Mat	5	23	thou r. that thy brother hath any
	16	9	neither do you r. the five loaves
Mark	8	18	hear you not? Neither do you r.
Luke	1	72	and to remember his holy testament
	16	25	r. that thou didst receive good things
	17	32	not return back. Remember Lot's wife
	23	42	Lord, r. me when thou shalt come into
	24	6	r. how he spoke unto you when he was
John	15	20	r. my word that I said to you: The
	16	4	you may r. that I told you of them
Acts	20	35	remember the word of the Lord Jesus, how
1 Th	2	9	you r., brethren, our labor and toil
2 Th	2	5	remember you not, that when I was yet
Heb	8	12	and their sins I will remember no more
	10	17	sins and iniquities I will r. no more
	13	3	r. them that are in bands, as if you
		7	r. your prelates who have spoken the

remembered Gen 8 1 God r. Noe and all the living

Gen	40	20	at the banquet r. the chief butler

Exod 2 24 r. the covenant which he made with
6 5 them: and I have remembered my covenant
Judg 8 34 they remembered not the Lord their God
1 K 1 19 and the Lord remembered her [Anna]
3 K 17 18 to me that my iniquities should be r.
2 Es 9 17 they r. not thy wonders which thou
Job 24 20 let him be r. no more, but be broken
Ps 9 13 he hath r. them: he hath not forgotten
41 5 these things I r., and poured out my
62 7 if I have remembered thee upon my bed
76 4 I r. God and was delighted and was
12 I remembered the works of the Lord
77 35 they r. that God was their helper
39 and he remembered that they are flesh
42 they r. not his hand in the day that he
82 5 let the name of Israel be r. no more
97 3 he hath r. his mercy and truth toward
104 8 he hath r. his covenant forever: the
42 because he remembered his holy word
105 7 they r. not the multitude of thy mercies
108 14 may the iniquity of his fathers be r.
16 because he r. not to show mercy, but
118 52 I r., O Lord, thy judgments of old
55 in the night I have remembered thy name
136 1 we sat and wept: when we remembered Sion
142 5 I r. the days of old, I meditated on
Ecce 9 15 no man afterward r. the poor man
Wisd 11 14 they r. the Lord, wondering at the
Eccu 3 17 in day of affliction thou shalt be r.
49 15 let Nehemias be a long time remembered
51 11 I remembered thy mercy, O Lord, and thy
Isa 17 10 and hast not r. thy strong helper
23 16 song, that thou mayst be remembered
47 7 neither hast thou r. thy latter end
63 11 he r. the days of old and of Moses
Jer 2 2 I have r. thee, pitying thy youth
11 19 let his name be remembered no more
44 21 which the Lord hath remembered and
Lam 1 7 Jerusalem hath r. the days of her
9 and she hath not remembered her end
2 1 hath not r. his footstool in the day
Bar 3 23 neither have they remembered her paths
4 27 you shall be r. by him that hath
Eze 3 20 which he hath done, shall not be r.
16 22 hast not r. the days of thy youth. 43
18 24 which he hath done, shall not be r.
21 24 because you have r. your iniquity
24 because, I say, you have r., you
Dan 14 37 thou hast remembered me, O God, and
Amos 1 9 have not r. the covenant of brethren
Jon 2 8 in distress within me, I r. the Lord
Zach 13 2 and they shall be remembered no more
1 Ma 5 4 he r. the malice of the children of
9 38 they remembered the blood of John their
10 46 they r. the great evil that he had
2 Ma 7 20 worthy to be remembered by good men
Mat 26 75 Peter r. the word of Jesus. Mark 14:72;
Luke 22:61
27 63 we have r. that that seducer said
Luke 24 8 they r. his words. And going back from
John 2 17 his disciples r. that it was written
22 his disciples r. that he had said this
12 16 they r. that these things were written
Acts 11 16 I r. the word of the Lord, how that
Apoc 18 5 Lord hath remembered her iniquities
rememberest Job 10 13 that thou r. all things
Ps 87 6 whom thou rememberest no more: and they
remembereth Ps 102 14 he r. that we are dust: man's
Eccu 3 34 he r. him afterwards, and in the time
Isa 66 3 he that r. incense, as if he should
John 16 21 she remembereth no more the anguish
remembering Gen 19 29 r. Abraham, he delivered Lot
Gen 30 22 Lord also remembering Rachel, heard
41 9 the chief butler remembering, said
42 9 remembering the dreams, which formerly
1 Es 4 14 we r. the salt that we have eaten in
Tob 2 6 remembering the word which the Lord
8 2 Tobias remembering the angel's word
Cant 1 3 remembering thy breasts more than wine
Eze 23 19 remembering the days of her youth
2 Ma 4 37 remembering the sobriety and modesty
9 21 infirm, but yet kindly remembering you
26 r. favors both public and private
10 6 remembering that not long before they
Mark 11 21 Peter r., said to him: Rabbi, behold
2 C 7 15 r. the obedience of you all, how with
remembrance Exod 13 16 between thy eyes for a r.
Exod 28 12 upon both shoulders for a remembrance
Num 5 18 her hands the sacrifice of r., and
10 9 shall be a r. of you before Lord
10 may be to you for a r. of your God
2 Es 2 20 part nor justice nor r. in Jerusalem
Job 13 12 your r. shall be compared to ashes
Ps 33 17 to cut off the r. of them from the
37 1 for a remembrance of the sabbath
69 1 to bring to r. that the Lord saved him
96 12 give praise to the r. of his holiness
110 4 he hath made a r. of his wonderful
111 7 the just shall be in everlasting r.
Ecce 1 11 is no remembrance of former things
11 are to come, shall there be any r.
2 16 shall be no remembrance of the wise
Wisd 2 4 no man shall have any remembrance
5 15 as remembrance of a guest of one day
11 13 for the remembrance of things past
16 6 to put them in r. of the commandment
11 were examined for the r. of thy words
19 4 they lost the r. of those things which
Eccu 28 1 he will surely keep his sins in r.
38 24 at rest, let his remembrance rest
41 1 death, how bitter is the r. of thee
49 2 his remembrance shall be sweet as honey
50 18 a great noise to be heard for a r.
Isa 26 8 and thy r. are the desire of the soul
43 26 put me in remembrance, and let us
57 8 behind the post thou hast set up thy r.
65 17 former things shall not be in r.
Bar 5 5 rejoicing in the remembrance of God
Eze 21 23 he will call to r. the iniquity that
25 10 no more any r. of the children of Ammon
Mala 3 16 a book of r. was written before him
1 Ma 2 51 call to r. the works of the fathers
Acts 10 31 thy alms are had in r. in the sight
Phil 1 3 I give thanks to my God in every r. of
1 Th 1 2 all; making a r. of you in our prayers
3 6 you have a good remembrance of us always
2 Tim 1 3 r. of thee in my prayers. Philem 4
2 P 1 12 put you always in r. of these things
13 to stir you up by putting you in r.
Apoc 16 19 great Babylon came in r. before God
remiss Eccu 4 34 and slack and r. in thy works
remission Lev 25 10 proclaim remission to all the
Num 36 4 jubilee, that is, the 50th year of r.
Deut 15 1 in seventh year thou shalt make a r.
2 because it is the year of remission
9 seventh year of remission draweth nigh
31 10 after seven years, in the year of r.
Mat 26 28 shall be shed for many unto r. of sins
Mark 1 4 baptism of penance, unto r. of sins
Luke 1 77 his people, unto the r. of their sins
3 3 baptism of penance for the r. of sins
24 47 r. of sins should be preached in his
Acts 2 38 for the r. of your sins: and you shall
5 31 to give repentance to Israel and r.
10 43 his name all receive remission of sins
Rom 3 25 justice, for remission of former sins

Eph 1 7 through his blood, the r. Col 1:14
Heb 9 22 without shedding of blood there is no r.
10 18 where there is a remission of these
remit 1 Ma 10 28 we will r. to you many charges
1 Ma 10 29 and remit the crowns and the thirds
remitted 1 Ma 15 5 kings before me r. to thee
1 Ma 15 5 what other gifts soever they remitted
Remmomphares Num 33 19 they camped in R. And
Remmon Josu 15 32 and Selim and Aen and Remmon
Josu 19 7 Ain and Remmon and Athor and Asan
13 goeth out to Remmon, Amthar and Noa
Judg 20 45 made towards the rock that is called R.
47 and they abode in the rock Remmon
21 13 that were in the rock Remmon, and
2 K 4 2 the sons of Remmon a Berothite of the
5 the sons of Remmon the Berothite. 9
4 K 5 18 master goeth into temple of Remmon
18 if I bow down in the temple of Remmon
1 Pa 4 32 R. and Thocean and Asan, five cities
2 Es 11 29 at Remmon and at Saraa and at
Zach 14 10 to Remmon to the south of Jerusalem
Remmono 1 Pa 6 77 out of the tribe of Zabulon, R.
remnant Lev 2 3 r. of the sacrifice shall be
Josu 12 4 of the remnant of the Raphaims who
3 K 14 10 I will sweep away the r. of the house
22 47 the remnant also of the effeminate
4 K 19 31 out of Jerusalem shall go forth a r.
25 11 and the remnant of the common people
1 Pa 4 43 slew the remnant of the Amalecites
2 Pa 30 6 he will return to the remnant of you
34 9 and all the remnant of Israel and from
21 for the remnant of Israel and Juda
1 Es 9 8 to leave us a remnant and give us a pin
14 not to leave us a remnant to be saved
Eccu 44 18 therefore was there a remnant left
47 25 whereof he gave a remnant to Jacob
Isa 10 20 r. of Israel and they that shall escape
21 the remnant shall be converted, the remnant, I say, of Jacob
22 a remnant of them shall be converted
11 11 to possess the remnant of his people
16 highway for the remnant of my people
14 30 famine, and I will kill thy remnant
15 9 Moab, and upon the remnant of the land
17 3 remnant of Syria shall be as the glory
37 4 lift up thy prayer for the remnant
32 out of Jerusalem shall go forth a r.
46 3 all the remnant of the house of Israel
Jer 15 11 assuredly it shall be well with thy r.
23 3 together the remnant of my flock, out
25 20 Accaron, and the remnant of Azotus
31 7 O Lord, thy people, the r. of Israel
39 9 to Babylon the remnant of the people
40 11 king of Babylon had left a r. in Judea
15 thee, and the remnant of Juda perish
41 10 away captive all the r. of the people
16 took all the remnant of the people
42 2 to the Lord thy God for all this r.
15 the word of the Lord, ye r. of Juda
19 concerning you, O ye remnant of Juda
43 5 the soldiers took all the r. of Juda
44 7 and no remnant should be left you
12 and I will take the remnant of Juda
14 remain of the remnant of the Jews
28 r. of Juda that are gone into the land
47 4 the remnant of the isle of Cappadocia
5 with the remnant of their valley
Eze 5 10 I will scatter thy whole remnant
9 8 wilt thou then destroy all the remnant
11 13 and end of all the remnant of Israel
25 16 will destroy the r. of the seacoast
Amos 5 15 may have mercy on the remnant of Joseph
9 12 that they may possess the r. of Edom
Mich 2 12 I will bring together the r. of Israel
4 7 I will make her that halted, a remnant
5 3 r. of his brethren shall be converted
7 remnant of Jacob shall be in the midst
8 remnant of Jacob shall be among the
7 18 the sin of the r. of thy inheritance
Soph 1 4 out of this place the remnant of Baal
2 9 the r. of my people shall make a spoil
3 13 the r. of Israel shall not do iniquity
Agge 1 12 all the r. of the people hearkened to
Zach 8 6 in the eyes of the r. of this people
11 I will not deal with the r. of this
12 r. of this people to possess all these
1 Ma 3 35 the r. of Jerusalem and to take away
Rom 9 27 of the sea, a remnant shall be saved
11 5 there is a remnant saved according to
remnants Judg 5 13 the r. of the people are saved
4 K 19 4 do thou offer prayer for the remnants
21 14 will leave the r. of my inheritance
Job 18 19 people, nor any remnants in his country
22 20 hath not fire devoured the remnants
Ps 20 13 in thy r. thou shalt prepare their face
36 37 there are r. for the peaceable man
38 the remnants of the wicked shall perish
remorse Eccu 14 1 not pricked with the r. of sin
remote Isa 41 9 the earth, and from the r. parts
remove Gen 29 8 we r. the stone from the well's
Gen 48 17 to remove it to the head of Manasses
Num 14 25 tomorrow remove the camp and return
Deut 19 14 nor remove thy neighbor's landmark
22 30 his father's wife, nor r. his covering
Judg 9 29 that I might remove Abimelech out
3 K 2 31 thou shalt remove the innocent blood
20 24 remove all the kings from the army
4 K 4 27 feet: and Giezi came to remove her
23 27 Lord said: I will remove Juda also from
24 3 to r. them from before him for all the
Job 7 21 why dost thou not remove my sin, and
18 18 and shall remove him out of the world
Ps 21 20 r. not thy help to a distance from me
38 11 r. thy scourges from me. The strength
51 7 and remove thee from thy dwelling place
118 22 r. from me reproach and contempt
29 remove from me the way of iniquity
Prov 4 24 remove from thee a forward mouth
5 8 remove thy way far from her, and come
30 8 remove far from me vanity and lying
Ecce 11 10 remove anger from thy heart, and put
Isa 6 12 the Lord shall remove men far away
48 9 I will remove my wrath far off: and
Jer 27 10 to remove you far from your country
50 8 remove out of the midst of Babylon
Bar 2 35 I will no more remove my people
Eze 12 3 and remove by day in their sight
3 shalt remove out of thy place to
21 26 remove the diadem, take off the crown
Joel 2 20 I will remove far off from you the
3 6 that you might remove them far off
1 Ma 11 63 to r. him from the affairs of the
2 Ma 2 3 not remove the law from their heart
Mat 17 19 to his mountain, Remove from hence hither, and it shall remove
Mark 14 36 r. this chalice from me. Luke 22:42
Luke 10 7 remove not from house to house. And
1 C 13 2 so that I could remove mountains, and
removed Gen 11 2 when they r. from the east
Gen 20 1 Abraham removed from thence to the south
29 10 he removed the stone wherewith the well
Exod 40 34 if at any time the cloud removed from
Num 9 22 as it departed, they removed the camp
10 2 multitude when the camp is to be r.
20 22 when they had r. the camp from Cades
24 7 for Agag his king shall be removed

33 12 they removed from thence. 23, 36
42 from whence they removed and came
Deut 10 6 Israel removed their camp from Beroth
Josu 3 1 before daylight and r. the camp
9 17 children of Israel removed the camp
1 K 18 13 Saul removed him [David] from him
2 K 7 15 Saul, whom I r. from before my face
20 12 so he removed Amasa out of the highway
13 when he [Amasa] was r. out of the way
22 23 his precepts I have not r. from me
3 K 15 12 he removed all the filth of the idols
13 he also removed his mother Maacha
4 K 16 14 he r. from the face of the temple
17 11 nations which the Lord had removed
18 and removed them from his sight
23 till the Lord r. Israel from his face
26 the nations which thou hast removed
23 27 before my face, as I have r. Israel
1 Pa 8 6 in Gabaa, who were r. into Manahath
2 Pa 8 11 and he removed the daughter of Pharao
33 8 Israel to be removed out of the land
35 24 and they removed him from the chariot
Job 9 5 who hath removed mountains, and they
14 18 and a rock is removed out of its place
18 4 shall rocks be r. out of their place
24 2 some have removed landmarks, have taken
Ps 9 5 thy judgments are r. from his sight
45 3 mountains shall be r. into the heart of
55 1 for a people that is removed at a
77 26 he removed the south wind from heaven
80 7 he removed his back from the burdens
102 12 far hath he r. our iniquities from us
Eccu 47 30 they r. them far away from their land
Isa 10 13 I have r. the bounds of the people
31 Medemena is removed: ye inhabitants
22 25 shall the peg be removed, that was
24 20 shall be r. as the tent of one night
26 15 thou hast r. all the ends of the earth
31 2 evil, and hath not removed his words
33 20 a tabernacle that cannot be removed
Jer 10 5 they must be carried to be removed
22 12 place to which I have removed him
34 17 I will cause you to be removed to
50 3 yea they are removed and gone away
Lam 1 3 Juda hath removed her dwelling place
3 17 and my soul is removed far off from
4 15 being removed, they said among the
Bar 2 24 should be removed out of their place
Eze 11 16 I have removed them far off among
12 11 they shall be r. from their dwellings
Mich 7 11 in that day shall the law be far r.
Nah 3 10 she also was removed and carried
1 Ma 3 57 so they r. the camp and pitched on
4 1 they removed out of the camp by night
5 29 they removed from thence by night
66 he r. his camp to go into the land
6 32 and removed the camp to Bethzacharam
7 19 Bacchides r. the camp from Jerusalem
9 11 and the army removed out of the camp
10 86 Jonathan removed his army from thence
13 12 and Tryphon removed from Ptolemais
2 Ma 4 29 Menelaus was r. from the priesthood
12 27 he removed his army to Ephron, a strong
14 16 removed from the place where they
Mark 11 23 be thou r. and be cast into the sea
16 4 I shall be r. from the stewardship
Acts 5 6 the young men rising up, removed him
7 4 he removed him into this land, wherein
13 22 when he had removed him, he raised
27 6 sailing into Italy, removed us into it
Gal 1 6 I wonder that you are so soon removed
removest Eze 21 10 thou r. the scepter of my son
removeth Deut 27 17 he that r. his neighbor's
Ecce 10 9 he that removeth stones, shall be hurt
Eze 12 4 goeth forth that removeth his dwelling
7 as the goods of one that removeth
removing Gen 13 18 Abram removing his tent came
Exod 14 19 camp of Israel, removing, went behind
Num 4 15 at the removing the camp, then shall
21 12 r. from thence they came to the torrent
33 21 r. from Lebna they camped in Ressa
27 r. from Thahath they camped in Thare
29 removing from Methca, they camped in
31 and r. from Moseroth, they camped in
Eze 12 3 prepare thee all necessaries for r.
4 of one that is removing by day in
Rempham Acts 7 43 and the star of your god R.
rend Lev 10 6 and rend not your garments lest
Lev 21 10 head, he shall not rend his garments
1 K 28 17 will rend thy kingdom out of thy hand
2 K 3 31 rend your garments and gird yourselves
3 K 11 11 I will divide and rend thy kingdom
12 but I will rend it out of the hand of
31 I will rend the kingdom out of the
Ecce 3 7 a time to rend and a time to sew
Isa 64 1 that thou wouldst rend the heavens
Jer 36 24 afraid, nor did they rend their garments
Eze 23 34 thou shalt rend thy breasts: because
Osee 13 8 I will rend the inner parts of their
Joel 2 13 r. your hearts, and not your garments
render Gen 29 27 the service that thou shalt r.
Exod 21 23 thereupon he shall r. life for life
Lev 24 21 striketh a beast, shall render another
Deut 19 19 they shall render to him as he meant
32 41 I will render vengeance to my enemies
43 and will r. vengeance to their enemies
Judg 20 10 and render to it for its wickedness
Ruth 2 12 Lord render unto thee for thy work
1 K 6 3 render unto him what you owe for sin
4 what is it we ought to r. unto him for
2 K 2 6 the Lord surely will render you mercy
16 12 Lord may r. me good for the cursing of
22 21 cleanness of my hands he will r. to me
2 Pa 6 30 r. to every one according to his ways
32 25 he did not render again according to
Job 20 10 his hands shall r. to him his sorrow
33 26 and he will render to man his justice
34 11 for he will render to a man his work
39 12 that he will render thee the seed
Ps 27 4 to them: render to them their reward
37 21 they that render evil for good, have
61 13 thou wilt render to every man according
78 12 render to our neighbors sevenfold in
93 2 earth: render a reward to the proud
23 he will render them their iniquity
115 12 what shall I render to the Lord for all
Prov 24 12 he shall render to a man according to
29 I will render to every one according
31 12 she will render him good, and not evil
Eccu 17 19 and shall render them their reward
33 14 he will render to him according to
Isa 65 6 I will render and repay into their
66 15 to render his wrath in indignation and
Jer 32 19 to render unto every one according to
51 6 he will render unto her what she hath
24 I will render to Babylon and to all
Lam 3 64 thou shalt render them a recompense
Eze 23 49 shall render your wickedness upon
33 15 and render what he had robbed, and
Osee 12 2 he will render to him according to
14 his Lord will render his reproach
14 3 we will render the calves of our
Zach 9 12 I will r. thee double as I declare
1 Ma 2 68 render to the Gentiles their reward
Mat 12 36 they shall render an account for it
16 27 then will he render to every man

21 41 shall r. him the fruit in due season
22 21 render therefore to Caesar. Mark 12:17; Luke 20:25
Rom 2 6 who will render to every man according
13 7 render therefore to all men their dues
14 12 every one of us shall render account to
1 C 7 3 let the husband r. the debt to his wife
1 Th 5 15 see that none render evil for evil to
2 Tim 4 8 just judge will r. to me in that day
Heb 13 17 they watch as being to r. an account
1 P 4 5 who shall render account to him who is
Apoc 11 18 shouldest render reward to thy servants
18 6 render to her as she also hath
22 12 to r. to every man according to his
rendered Gen 30 26 service that I have r. thee
Num 18 9 whatsoever is rendered to me for sin
Ps 7 5 if I have r. to them that repaid me
115 12 all the things that he hath r. to me
Wisd 10 17 she rendered to the just the wages of
Eccu 35 24 till he have r. to men according to
Isa 3 9 souls, for evils are rendered to them
Jer 18 20 shall evil be rendered for good, because
Eze 22 31 I have r. their way upon their own
29 18 service that he rendered me against
Nah 2 2 the Lord hath r. the pride of Jacob
1 Ma 16 17 in Israel, and r. evil for good
2 Ma 2 17 and hath r. to all the inheritance
8 35 being rendered very unhappy by the
Apoc 18 6 as she also hath rendered to you
renderest Exod 34 7 r. the iniquity of the fathers
rendereth Prov 17 13 he that r. evil for good
Isa 66 6 that r. recompense to his enemies
rendering Deut 7 10 r. to them what they deserve
Isa 16 5 quickly r. that which is just. We have
2 Ma 8 33 r. to him a worthy reward for his
Rom 12 17 to no man rendering evil for evil
1 P 3 9 not rendering evil for evil, nor
rendeth Luke 5 36 otherwise he both r. the new
rending Gen 37 30 r. his garments, he went to his
Job 2 12 rending their garments they sprinkled
Mark 14 63 the high priest rending his garments
Acts 14 13 rending their clothes, they leaped out
16 22 the magistrates r. off their clothes
renew 1 K 11 14 let us renew the kingdom there
Ps 50 12 renew a right spirit within my bowels
103 30 thou shalt renew the face of the earth
Eccu 36 6 r. thy signs, and work new miracles
49 9 destroy, and to build again and renew
Isa 40 31 in the Lord shall r. their strength
Lam 5 21 renew our days, as from the beginning
1 Ma 12 1 and to renew the amity with them
3 Jews have sent us to renew the amity
10 to r. the brotherhood and friendship
16 to renew with them the former amity
14 18 to renew the friendship and alliance
22 to r. the former friendship. 15:17
renewed Job 29 20 my glory shall always be renewed
Ps 38 3 good things: and my sorrow was renewed
102 5 thy youth shall be r. like the eagle's
Eccu 50 29 who renewed wisdom from his heart
Eze 23 21 hast r. the wickedness of thy youth
1 Ma 4 57 they r. the gates and the chambers
2 C 4 16 the inward man is renewed day by day
Eph 4 23 be renewed in the spirit of your mind
Col 3 10 new, him who is renewed unto knowledge
Heb 6 6 are fallen away: to be renewed again
renewest Job 10 17 r. thy witnesses against me
reneweth Wisd 7 27 the same, she r. all things
renewing 1 Ma 12 17 the renewing of our brotherhood
renounce Luke 14 33 that doth not r. all that he
2 C 4 2 we r. the hidden things of dishonesty
renounced Ecce 2 20 my heart r. laboring any more
renovation Titus 3 5 laver of regeneration and r.
renown Gen 6 4 the mighty men of old, men of r.
Eccu 44 1 let us now praise men of renown and
Jer 49 25 how have they forsaken the city of r.
Eze 16 14 thy renown went forth among the nations
15 playedst the harlot because of thy r.
34 29 I will raise up for them a bud of r.
renowned Deut 4 8 other nation is there so r.
2 K 23 18 r. among the three. 23; 1 Pa 11:20, 24
3 K 4 31 he was r. in all nations round about
1 Pa 12 30 of great valor r. in their kindreds
17 8 great ones that are r. in the earth
22 5 such as to be renowned in all countries
Jdth 2 13 took by assault the r. city of Melothus
8 8 she was greatly renowned among all
11 21 thy name shall be renowned through all
16 25 she was most renowned in all the land
Job 18 17 let not his name be r. in the streets
Eccu 39 2 keep the sayings of renowned men
Jer 51 41 r. one of all the earth surprised
Bar 3 26 the giants, those renowned men that
Eze 23 23 princes, and the renowned horsemen
26 17 r. city that wast strong in the sea
1 Ma 3 9 he was r. even to the utmost part
6 1 city of Elymais in Persia was greatly r.
11 51 and were r. throughout the kingdom
14 10 the fame of his glory was renowned
rent Gen 44 13 then they rent their garments
Num 14 6 viewed the land, rent their garments
Josu 7 6 Josue rent his garments and fell flat
9 4 wine bottles rent and sewed up again
13 were new, now they are r. and burst
Judg 11 35 he rent his garments and said. 4 K 5:7
1 K 4 12 his clothes rent and his head strewed
15 27 the skirt of his mantle, and it rent
28 Lord hath rent the kingdom of Israel
2 K 1 2 with his garments rent and dust strewed
11 hold of his garments and rent them
13 19 ashes on her head and r. her long robe
31 the king rose up and rent his garments
31 stood about him, rent their garments
14 30 with their garments rent. 1 Ma 13:45
15 32 garments rent and his head covered
3 K 13 3 the altar shall be rent, and the ashes
5 the altar also was rent, and the ashes
14 8 and rent the kingdom away from the
21 27 he [Achab] rent his garments and put
4 K 2 12 garments and rent them in two pieces
5 8 that the king of Israel had rent his
8 why hast thou rent thy garments? let
6 30 king heard this, he rent his garments
11 14 [Athalia] rent her garments and cried
17 21 when Israel was rent from the house of
18 37 Ezechias, with their garments r. Isa 36:22
19 1 [Ezechias] r. his garments. Isa 37:1
22 19 r. thy garments and wept. 2 Pa 34:27
2 Pa 23 13 rent her garments and said: Treason
34 19 words of the law, he rent his garments
1 Es 9 3 I rent my mantle and my coat and
5 having rent my mantle and my garment
Jdth 14 14 with weeping, and rent his garments
17 heard this, they all r. their garments
Isa 18 2 to a nation rent and torn in pieces
7 from a people r. and torn in pieces
Jer 38 12 these rent and rotten things under
41 5 beards shaven and their clothes rent
Bar 6 30 having their garments rent, and their
Eze 29 7 didst break and rent all their shoulder
Dan 11 4 his kingdom shall be rent in pieces
Nah 2 10 she is destroyed and rent and torn
Zach 12 3 lift it up shall be rent and torn
1 Ma 2 14 and his sons rent their garments
3 47 they rent their garments and. 4:39
5 14 out of Galilee with their garments r.

1 Pa 18 4 100 chariots, which he r. for himself
Job 21 30 man is r. to the day of destruction
Acts 25 21 Paul appealing to be r. unto the hearing
1 P 1 4 cannot fade, r. in heaven for you
2 P 2 4 unto torments to be r. unto judgment
17 to whom the mist of darkness is r.
3 7 reserved unto fire against the day of
Jude 6 he hath reserved under darkness in
13 storm of darkness is reserved forever
reserveth Eccu 28 3 man to man r. anger and
reserving Num 18 32 r. the choicest and fat things
Resia 1 Pa 7 39 of Olla: Aree and Haniel and Resia
residue Isa 38 10 I sought for the r. of my years
Isa 44 17 the residue thereof he made a god
19 of residue thereof shall I make an idol
Jer 15 9 the residue of them I will give up
21 17 residue of number of strong archers
24 8 princes and the residue of Jerusalem
Isa 28 5 of joy to the residue of his people
Jer 29 1 to the residue of the ancients that
Eze 17 21 the residue shall be scattered
23 25 thy residue shall be devoured by fire
34 18 with your feet the r. of your pastures
48 18 residue in length by the firstfruits
21 the residue shall be for the prince
Joel 2 32 in the residue whom the Lord shall call
Soph 2 9 the r. of my nation shall possess them
Mala 2 15 she is the residue of his spirit
1 Ma 6 53 had eaten the residue of all that which
2 Ma 8 31 residue of their spoils they carried to
Acts 15 17 r. of men may seek after the Lord, and
resist Gen 50 19 can we resist the will of God
Exod 10 4 if thou resist and wilt not let them go
Lev 26 37 none of you shall dare to resist your
Deut 7 24 no man shall be able to resist thee
Josu 1 5 no man shall be able to r. you. 23:9
Judg 6 2 in the mountains and strongholds to r.
Ruth 2 22 another man's field some one r. thee
2 K 22 45 sons of the stranger will resist me
49 liftest me up from them that resist me
4 K 10 4 and how shall we be able to resist
2 Pa 13 7 fearful heart and could not resist them
20 Jeroboam was not able to r. any more
20 6 power, and no one can resist thee
12 to be able to resist this multitude
1 Es 6 12 that shall put out their hand to resist
Jdth 5 1 of Israel prepared themselves to resist
19 the God of heaven gave them power to r.
25 we cannot r. them, because their God
27 of Israel can r. king Nabuchodonosor
16 17 there is no one that can r. thy voice
Job 9 13 God, whose wrath no man can resist
41 1 for who can resist my countenance
Ps 16 8 from them that resist thy right hand
75 8 art terrible, and who shall resist thee
Prov 30 31 and a king, whom none can resist
Ecce 4 1 they were not able to r. their violence
Wisd 11 22 who shall r. the strength of thy arm
Eccu 4 32 r. not against the face of the mighty
22 22 shall not resist against the violence
36 33 a man of experience will resist it
Isa 41 12 shalt not find the men that r. thee
47 3 vengeance, and no man shall resist me
50 5 opened my ear, and I do not resist
Dan 4 32 there is none that can resist his hand
11 15 his chosen ones shall rise up to r.
Nah 1 6 who shall resist in the fierceness
1 Ma 2 33 do you still resist? come forth and
Mat 5 39 but I say to you not to resist evil
Luke 21 15 shall not be able to r. and gainsay
Acts 6 10 were not able to resist the wisdom
7 51 you always resist the Holy Ghost: as
Rom 13 2 they that resist, purchase to themselves
Eph 6 13 you may be able to resist in the evil
2 Tim 2 25 admonishing them that resist the truth
3 8 Moses, so these also resist the truth
James 4 7 r. the devil, and he will fly from you
1 P 5 9 whom r. ye, strong in faith: knowing
resistance 2 Pa 28 20 plundered him without any r.
2 Ma 12 27 upon the walls made a vigorous r.
resisted 2 K 22 40 made them that r. me to bow
Jdth 2 16 and all that resisted him he slew with
Job 9 4 who hath r. him, and hath had peace
Eccu 46 4 who before him hath so resisted for
Dan 10 13 kingdom of the Persians resisted me
1 Ma 8 11 that at any time had resisted them
11 38 and nothing resisted him, sent away
14 7 there was none that resisted him
29 and r. the enemies of their nation
32 Simon resisted and fought for his
2 Tim 3 8 as Jannes and Mambres resisted Moses, so
Heb 12 4 you have not yet resisted unto blood
James 5 6 the Just One, and he resisted you not
resisteth Eccu 3 33 fire, and alms r. sins
Isa 54 17 tongue that resisteth thee in judgment
Rom 9 19 find fault? for who resisteth his will
13 2 he that r. the power, r. the ordinance
James 4 6 God resisteth the proud. 1 P 5:5
resisting Deut 1 43 r. the commandment of the
resolute Ps 63 6 they are r. in wickedness
resolutely Eze 4 3 set thy face r. against it
resolution Josu 9 2 with one mind and one r.
2 Pa 29 36 the r. of doing this thing was taken
Jdth 9 18 strengthen the resolution in my heart
10 15 hast saved thy life by taking this r.
Esth 3 4 whether he would continue in his r.
Ecce 7 30 hath known the resolution of the word
Jer 38 17 if thou wilt take a r. and go out to
1 Ma 12 35 and he took a r. with them to build
Acts 20 3 he took a r. to return through Macedonia
resolve Dan 2 16 him time to resolve the question
Dan 2 25 that will r. the question to the
5 16 obscure things and r. difficult things
resolved Eccu 39 38 from the beginning I was r.
2 Ma 3 23 that which he had resolved on, himself
15 17 they resolved to fight and to set
resolving Dan 5 12 r. of difficult things were
resort Eccu 27 10 birds r. unto their like: so
Eccu 39 6 his heart to resort early to the Lord
John 18 20 temple, whither all the Jews resort
resorted Dan 13 4 the Jews r. to him because
1 Ma 7 22 that disturbed the people r. to him
John 10 41 many resorted to him and they said
18 2 Jesus had often resorted thither
resound 1 Pa 15 16 that the joyful noise might r.
2 Pa 13 12 sound with trumpets and r. against you
Isa 44 23 ye mountains, resound with praise
respect Gen 4 4 Lord had r. to Abel and to his
Gen 4 5 to Cain and his offerings he had no r.
Lev 19 15 respect not the person of the poor
Num 16 15 respect not their sacrifices: thou
Deut 1 17 neither shall you r. any man's person
2 Pa 19 7 nor respect of persons nor desire of
Prov 24 23 not good to have respect to persons
28 21 he that hath respect to a person
Wisd 2 20 shall be r. had unto him by his words
3 6 there shall be respect had to them
4 15 that he hath respect to his chosen
7 9 silver in r. to her shall be counted
14 11 be no respect had even to the idols
19 14 in another r. also they were worse
Eccu 7 11 say not: God will have respect to the
16 2 their life, and r. not their labors
20 24 by r. of person he will destroy himself
34 23 neither hath he r. to the oblations
35 15 there is not with him respect of person

Isa 17 8 he shall not have respect to the things
42 2 not cry nor have respect to person
66 2 but to whom shall I have respect but
Lam 5 12 did not r. the persons of the ancient
Luke 20 21 thou dost not respect any person, but
Rom 2 11 is no r. of persons with God. Col 3:25
Eph 6 9 there is no respect of persons with him
Col 2 16 in drink or in respect of a festival
James 2 1 of glory with respect of persons. For
3 respect to him that is clothed with
9 but if you have respect to persons
1 P 1 17 without respect of persons, judgeth
respected Lam 4 16 they r. not the persons of
Acts 5 34 doctor of the law, r. by all the
respecter Acts 10 34 God is not a r. of persons
Respha 2 K 3 7 Saul had a concubine named Respha
2 K 21 8 the king took the two sons of Respha
10 Respha the daughter of Aia. 11
Ressa Num 33 21 from Lebna they camped in Ressa
Num 33 22 departing from Ressa, they came to
restitution Exod 21 19 he make r. for his work
Exod 22 3 not wherewith to make r. for the theft
11 not be compelled to make restitution
13 and he shall not make restitution. 15
14 shall be obliged to make restitution
Acts 3 21 until the times of the r. of all
restore Gen 20 7 restore the man his wife, for he
Gen 20 7 if thou wilt not restore her, know that
37 22 hands and to restore him to his father
40 13 will restore thee to thy former place
42 37 hand, and I will restore him to thee
43 9 I bring him again and r. him to thee
Exod 22 1 he shall restore five oxen for one ox
4 ass or sheep: he shall restore double
5 he shall restore the best of whatsoever
7 thief be found he shall restore double
9 judgment, he shall restore double
Lev 6 4 he shall restore all that he would have
24 20 tooth for tooth, shall he restore
25 27 overplus he shall restore to the buyer
Num 5 7 r. the principal itself and the fifth
Deut 24 13 thou shalt restore it to him presently
Judg 11 13 restore the same peaceably to me
16 28 restore to me now my former strength
1 K 12 3 it this day and will restore it to you
2 K 3 14 restore my wife Michol, whom I espoused
9 7 I will restore the land of Saul thy
12 6 he shall restore the ewe fourfold
16 3 today will the house of Israel r. me
3 K 20 34 took from thy father I will restore
4 K 8 6 restore her all that is hers, and all
12 7 r. it for the repairing of the temple
2 Es 5 11 r. ye to them this day their fields
12 we will r. and we will require nothing
Tob 2 21 restore ye it to its owners, for it is
4 22 and restore to him the note of his hand
9 3 and to restore to him his note of hand
Ps 15 5 thou wilt restore my inheritance to me
50 14 r. unto me the joy of thy salvation
Prov 6 31 if he be taken he shall r. sevenfold
22 27 if thou have not wherewith to restore
Eccu 48 10 and to restore the tribes of Jacob
Isa 1 26 I will r. thy judges as they were before
42 22 there is none that saith: Restore
Bar 6 36 thy cannot restore the blind man
Eze 16 53 I will bring back and restore them
33 15 and if that wicked man r. the pledge
Joel 2 25 I will restore to you the ears which
Soph 3 9 I will r. to the people a chosen lip
1 Ma 9 70 and to restore to him the prisoners
15 3 to restore it to its former estate
2 Ma 7 23 he will restore to you again in his
12 25 faith that he would r. them according
14 46 and spirit, to restore these to him again
Mat 17 11 Elias indeed shall come and r. all
Mark 9 11 shall come first, shall restore all
Luke 19 8 of anything, I restore him fourfold
Acts 1 6 at this time r. again the kingdom to
restored Gen 20 14 and r. to him Sara, his wife
Gen 40 21 he restored the one to his place
41 13 I was restored to my office: and he
Lev 13 7 by the priest and r. to cleanness
Deut 28 31 taken away in thy sight and not r. to
Judg 17 3 he restored them to his mother. 4
1 K 7 14 taken from Israel, were r. to Israel
3 K 13 6 that my hand may be restored to me
6 the king's hand was restored to him
4 K 5 14 his flesh was restored like the flesh of
8 1 whose son he had restored to life. 5
13 25 [Joas] restored the cities to Israel
14 22 [Azarias] built Elath and r. it to Juda
25 he restored the borders of Israel from
28 how he restored Damascus and Emath
16 6 king of Syria restored Aila to Syria
2 Pa 26 2 Ailath and restored it to the dominion
1 Es 6 5 be r. and carried back to the temple
Tob 1 25 all his substance was restored to him
14 1 after Tobias was restored to his sight
Job 38 14 the seal shall be restored as clay
Ps 96 1 when his land was r. again to him
Eccu 1 29 afterwards joy shall be r. to him
Isa 57 18 him back, and r. comforts to him and
Jer 27 22 be brought and to be r. in this place
Eze 18 7 but hath r. the pledge to the debtor
38 12 had been wasted and afterwards r.
Dan 4 31 and my sense was restored to me: and
33 for me, and I was r. to my kingdom
1 Ma 9 72 he restored to him the prisoners which
10 9 he restored them to their parents
14 26 he hath restored his brethren and
2 Ma 2 23 and r. the laws that were abolished
11 25 that the temple should be r. to them
Mat 12 13 it was r. to health even as the other
Mark 3 5 and his hand was restored unto him
8 25 and he began to see and was restored
Luke 4 20 book, he restored it to the minister
6 10 forth, and his hand was restored
9 43 boy, and restored him to his father
Heb 13 19 that I may be r. to you the sooner
restoreth Job 12 23 r. them again after they were
Ecce 3 15 and God restoreth that which is past
Eccu 20 12 price, and r. the same sevenfold
Eze 18 12 that restoreth not the pledge and
restoring Eccu 41 26 away a portion and not r.
restrain Ps 39 10 I will not r. my lips: O Lord
Prov 1 15 restrain thy foot from their paths
Eccu 7 37 restrain not grace from the dead
restrained Gen 8 2 the rain from heaven was r.
Gen 16 2 Lord hath restrained me from bearing
Ps 118 101 I have r. my feet from every evil way
Eze 31 15 rivers, and restrained the many waters
Acts 14 17 they scarce r. people from sacrificing
resurrection Ps 65 1 canticle of a psalm of the r.
Soph 3 8 in the day of my r. that is to come
2 Ma 7 9 raise us . . . in the r. of eternal life
14 thou shalt have no r. unto life
12 43 and religiously concerning the r.
Mat 22 23 say there is on r. Mark 12:18; Acts 23:8
28 at the r. therefore whose wife of the
30 in the r. they shall neither marry nor
31 concerning the r. of the dead, have
27 53 out of the tombs after his resurrection
Mark 12 23 in the r. therefore, when they shall
Luke 2 34 for the fall and for the r. of many
14 14 be made thee at the r. of the just
20 27 who deny that there is any r., and

33 in the r. therefore, whose wife of them
35 of the resurrection from the dead
36 of God, being the children of the r.
John 5 29 shall come forth unto the r. of life
29 done evil, unto the r. of judgment
11 24 he shall rise again in the r. at the
25 I am the r. and the life: he that
Acts 1 22 be made a witness with us of his r.
2 31 he spoke of the resurrection of Christ
4 2 preached in Jesus the r. from the dead
33 give testimony of the resurrection of
17 18 because he preached to them Jesus and r.
32 they had heard of the r. of the dead
23 6 concerning the hope and r. of the dead I
24 15 there shall be a r. of just and unjust
21 them, concerning the r. of the dead am I
Rom 1 4 by the r. of our Lord Jesus Christ from
6 5 be also in likeness of his resurrection
1 C 15 12 say, that there is no r. of the dead
13 if there be no r. of the dead, then
21 by a man the resurrection of the dead
42 so also is the resurrection of the dead
Phil 3 10 him, and the power of his resurrection
11 attain to the r. which is from the dead
2 Tim 2 18 saying, that the r. is past already, and
Heb 6 2 hands, and of the r. of the dead, and
11 35 they might find a better resurrection
1 P 1 3 by the r. of Jesus Christ. 3:21
Apoc 20 5 were finished. This is the first r.
6 is he that hath part in the first r.
retail 3 K 10 15 and they that sold by retail
retain Prov 3 18 he that shall r. her is blessed
John 20 23 whose sins you shall retain, they are
retained Dan 10 8 I fainted away and r. no
John 20 23 you shall retain, they are retained
Philem 13 whom I would have retained with me, that
retaineth Prov 27 16 he that r. her is as he that
Rethma Num 33 18 from Haseroth they came to R.
Num 33 19 departing from Rethma, they camped in
retire Cant 2 17 day break and the shadows r. 4:6
retired Exod 24 11 that r. afar off, and they saw
2 K 2 27 the people should have r. from pursuing
Ps 9 1 why, O Lord, hast thou r. afar off
1 Ma 9 62 that were with him r. into Bethbessen
Mat 2 14 by night and retired into Egypt: and
22 retired into the quarters of Galilee
4 12 delivered up, he retired into Galilee
12 15 Jesus knowing it, retired from thence
14 13 Jesus had heard, he retired from thence
15 21 r. into the coasts of Tyre and Sidon
Mark 3 7 Jesus r. with his disciples to the sea
Luke 5 16 he r. into the desert and prayed. And
retract Prov 20 25 it is ruin . . . after vows to r.
Reu Gen 11 18 lived 30 years and begot Reu
Gen 11 19 Phaleg lived after he begot Reu
20 Reu lived 32 years and begot Sarug
21 Reu lived after he begot Sarug
Reum 1 Es 4 8 Reum Beelteem and Samsai the
1 Es 4 23 was read before Reum Beelteem and
17 the king sent word to Reum Beelteem
reveal Tob 12 7 to r. and confess the works of
Job 20 27 the heavens shall reveal his iniquity
Jer 33 6 I will r. to them the prayer of peace
Mat 11 27 it shall please the Son to r. him
Luke 10 22 and to whom the Son will reveal him
Gal 1 16 to reveal his Son in me, that I might
Phil 3 15 minded, this also God will reveal to you
revealed 1 K 3 7 the word of the Lord been r.
1 K 3 21 Lord revealed himself to Samuel in Silo
9 15 Lord had revealed to the ear of Samuel
2 K 7 27 hast r. to ear of thy servant. 1 Pa 17:25
Ps 97 2 he hath r. his justice in the sight of
Eccu 1 6 to whom hath the root of wisdom been r.
7 hath the discipline of wisdom been r.
Isa 22 14 of the Lord of hosts was r. in my ears
23 1 from the land of Cethim it is r. to
40 5 the glory of the Lord shall be r.
53 1 to whom is the arm of the Lord r.
56 1 near to come, and my justice to be r.
Jer 11 20 to thee have I revealed my cause
49 10 I have revealed his secrets, and he
Dan 2 19 was the mystery revealed to Daniel
30 to me also this secret is revealed
10 1 a word was revealed to Daniel surnamed
Amos 5 24 but judgment shall be r. as water
Mat 10 26 covered that shall not be r. Luke 12:2
11 25 hast r. them to little ones. Luke 10:21
16 17 flesh and blood hath not r. it to thee
Luke 2 35 many hearts, thoughts may be revealed
17 30 when the Son of man shall be revealed
John 12 38 hath the arm of the Lord been revealed
Rom 1 17 for the justice of God is r. therein
18 for the wrath of God is revealed from
8 18 glory to come, that shall be r. in us
1 C 2 10 but to us God hath revealed them, by his
3 13 because it shall be revealed in fire
14 30 but if anything be revealed to another
Gal 3 23 unto that faith which was to be revealed
Eph 3 5 as it is now r. to his holy apostles and
2 Th 1 7 Jesus shall be revealed from heaven
2 3 first, and the man of sin be revealed
6 that he may be revealed in his time
8 then that wicked one shall be revealed
1 P 1 5 ready to be revealed in the last time
12 to whom it was revealed that not to
4 13 when his glory shall be revealed, you
5 1 which is to be r. in time to come
revealer Dan 2 47 a revealer of hidden things
revealeth Prov 11 13 deceitfully r. secrets
Prov 20 19 meddle not with him that r. secrets
Eccu 42 19 revealeth the traces of hidden things
Dan 2 22 he r. deep and hidden things and
28 a God in heaven that r. mysteries
29 he that r. mysteries showed thee what
revealing Amos 3 7 without r. his secret to his
revelation Luke 2 32 to the r. of the Gentiles
Rom 2 5 against the day of wrath, and revelation
8 19 waiteth for revelation of sons of God
16 25 according to the r. of the mystery
1 C 14 6 to you either in r., or in knowledge
26 psalm, hath doctrine, hath a revelation
Gal 1 12 it; but by revelation of Jesus Christ
2 2 me. And I went up according to r.; and
Eph 1 17 the spirit of wisdom and of revelation
3 3 how that, according to r., the mystery
1 P 1 13 is offered you in the r. of Jesus
Apoc 1 1 the r. of Jesus Christ, which God gave
revelations Lam 2 14 have seen for thee false r.
2 C 12 1 I will come to visions and r. of Lord
7 lest the greatness of the r. should
revelling Deut 21 20 he giveth himself to r. and
revellings Prov 23 20 great drinkers nor in their r.
2 Ma 6 4 riot and r. of the Gentiles: and of
Gal 5 21 drunkenness, revellings and such like
1 P 4 3 excess of wine, revellings, banquetings
revenge Gen 34 27 plundered the city in r. of the
Lev 19 18 seek not revenge nor be mindful of
Num 14 34 your iniquities and shall know my r.
31 2 revenge first the children of Israel
3 who may take the revenge of the Lord
Deut 32 43 he will r. the blood of his servants
Josu 20 9 coveting to r. the blood that was shed
Judg 6 31 if he be a god, let him r. himself
32 let Baal revenge himself on him that
11 36 granted to thee, and r. of thy enemies
16 28 that I may r. myself on my enemies

28 loss of my two eyes, I may take one r.
1 K 24 13 and the Lord revenge me of thee [Saul]
2 K 3 27 in revenge of the blood of Asael
14 11 be not multiplied to take revenge
22 48 God who giveth me r. and bringest
4 K 9 7 I will r. the blood of my servants the
2 Pa 6 23 and to r. the just, rewarding him
35 and their supplications and r. them
24 25 revenge of the blood of son of Joiada
Tob 3 3 of me and take not revenge of my sins
Jdth 2 1 Assyrians, that he would r. himself
8 26 let us not revenge ourselves for these
34 thee to take revenge of our enemies
16 20 Lord almighty will take r. on them
Esth 8 12 and one day of revenge was appointed
Job 35 15 neither doth he revenge wickedness
Ps 57 11 shall rejoice when he shall see the r.
93 1 the God to whom revenge belongeth
1 the God of revenge hath acted freely
139 13 the needy, and will revenge the poor
Prov 6 34 will not spare in the day of revenge
11 4 riches shall not profit in day of r.
Wisd 5 18 he will arm the creature for the r.
Eccu 5 3 for God will surely take revenge. Say
10 in the day of calamity and revenge
25 21 and any r. but the r. of enemies
28 1 he that seeketh to revenge himself
Isa 35 4 will bring the revenge of recompense
59 18 as unto revenge, as it were to repay
Jer 5 9 shall not my soul take revenge. 29
11 20 let me see thy revenge on them: for
46 10 he may revenge himself of his enemies
50 28 the r. of the Lord our God, the r. of his temple
51 6 it is the time of revenge from the Lord
Eze 25 12 to r. herself of the children of Juda
12 and hath sought revenge of them
Joel 3 4 will you r. yourselves on me? And if you r. yourselves on me
1 Ma 2 67 and r. ye the wrong of your people
6 22 the judgment, and to r. our brethren
7 9 to take r. upon the children of Israel
9 42 took r. for the blood of their brother
15 4 that I may take revenge of them that
2 Ma 9 4 he thought to revenge upon the Jews
Luke 18 7 and will not God revenge his elect
8 that he will quickly revenge them
Rom 12 19 r. not yourselves, my dearly beloved
19 revenge is mine, I will repay, saith the
2 C 7 11 fear, yea desire, yea zeal, yea revenge
10 6 readiness to revenge all disobedience
Apoc 6 10 dost thou not judge and r. our blood
revenged Num 35 18 he shall be r. by the blood of
Josu 10 13 till the people revenged themselves
Judg 15 7 yet will I be revenged of you and
1 K 14 24 till I [Saul] be revenged of my enemies
25 31 innocent blood, or hast r. thyself
2 K 4 8 the Lord hath r. my lord the king
Jdth 1 12 that he would revenge himself of all
Ps 117 10 I have been revenged on them. 11
12 name of the Lord I was r. on them
Wisd 11 3 and r. themselves of their adversaries
Isa 1 24 and I will be revenged of my enemies
Jer 9 9 shall not my soul be r. on such a
20 10 against him and be revenged on him
Eze 25 15 have r. themselves with all their
1 Ma 3 15 to be r. of the children of Israel
Apoc 19 2 and hath r. the blood of his servants
revenger Num 35 25 delivered from hand of the r.
Deut 18 19 in my name, I will be the revenger
Job 19 29 the sword is the revenger of iniquities
Wisd 12 12 shall come before thee to be a revenger
Jer 51 56 the Lord, who is a strong revenger
Nah 1 2 the Lord is a jealous God and a r.
2 the Lord is a revenger and hath wrath
revengeth Jdth 13 27 he r. himself of his enemies
revenging 1 K 25 33 r. me with my own hand
Ps 78 10 by the r. the blood of thy servants
revenue Isa 23 3 harvest of the river is her r.
revenues 1 K 8 15 of the r. of your vineyards
4 K 8 6 hers, and all the revenues of the lands
1 Es 4 13 tribute nor toll nor yearly revenues
20 received tribute and toll and revenues
Prov 16 8 than great revenues with iniquity
Eccu 30 15 a sound body, than immense revenues
1 Ma 10 44 shall be given out of the king's r.
2 Ma 3 3 allowed out of his r. all the charges
4 8 out of other revenues fourscore talents
9 16 to allow out of his r. the charges
reverence Lev 19 30 sabbaths and r. my sanctuary. 26:2
4 K 3 14 if I did not r. the face of Josaphat
2 Pa 36 12 did not reverence the face of Jeremias
Eccu 4 27 r. not thy neighbor in his fall: and
7 31 fear the Lord and r. his priests. With
32 9 for thy r. good grace shall come. 14
2 Ma 3 12 for the reverence and holiness of it
15 2 and r. him that beholdeth all things
Mat 21 37 they will reverence my son. Mark 12:6
Luke 20 13 see him, they will reverence him
Heb 5 7 from death, was heard for his reverence
12 28 pleasing God with fear and reverence
reverenced Jdth 13 30 down at her feet and r. her
Bar 4 16 who have neither r. the ancient nor
Heb 12 9 instructors, and we reverenced them
reverencing 2 Pa 34 27 r. my face, hast rent thy
reviewed 2 K 18 1 David having r. his people
revile Mat 5 11 when they shall revile you and
Acts 23 4 dost thou revile the high priest of God
1 P 2 23 when he was reviled, did not revile
reviled 1 Pa 20 7 reviled Israel: but Jonathan
Ps 54 13 if my enemy had reviled me, I would
Mark 15 32 that were crucified with him r. him
John 9 28 they reviled him therefore, and said
1 C 4 12 we are reviled, and we bless; we are
1 Tim 4 10 for therefore we labor and are reviled
1 P 2 23 when he was reviled, did not revile
reviling Ecce 7 22 thou hear thy servant r. thee
revive Isa 57 15 to r. the spirit of the humble
Isa 57 15 to revive the heart of the contrite
Osee 6 3 he will revive us after two days: on
revived Gen 45 27 that he had sent, and his spirit r.
3 K 17 22 returned into him and he revived
Rom 7 9 when the commandment came, sin revived
revoked 1 Ma 11 36 and nothing hereof shall be r.
revolt Deut 11 28 revolt from the way which now I
Josu 22 29 that we should revolt from the Lord
31 because you are not guilty of this r.
Jer 32 40 that they may not revolt from me. And
1 Ma 13 16 he may not revolt from us, and we
2 Th 2 3 unless there come a revolt first, and
revolted Gen 14 4 in the 13th year they r. from
3 K 12 19 Israel r. from the house of David
4 K 3 7 the king of Moab is revolted from me
8 20 Edom r. from being under Juda. 22
24 20 Sedecias r. from the king of Babylon
2 Pa 10 18 Israel revolted from the house of David
21 8 Edom r. from being subject to Juda
10 Edom revolted from being under the
10 at that time Lobna also revolted from
25 27 after he [Amasias] revolted from the Lord
36 13 he also r. from king Nabuchodonosor
Jdth 5 19 for having revolted from the worship of
22 some years ago when they had revolted
Job 34 27 on purpose have revolted from him
Wisd 3 10 just, and have revolted from the Lord
Isa 31 6 return as you had deeply revolted

36 5 trust, that thou art revolted from me
Jer 2 31 we are revolted, we will come to thee
5 23 provoking, they are r. and gone away
52 3 Sedecias revolted from the king of
Eze 2 3 people, that hath revolted from me
6 9 was faithless and revolted from me
17 15 he hath revolted from him and sent
Dan 9 5 we have done wickedly and have r.
1 Ma 7 24 vengeance upon the men that had r.
2 Ma 10 13 had r. also from him, he put an end to
revolters Osee 9 15 all their princes are r.
revolteth 2 J 9 whosoever r. and continueth not
revolting Josu 22 16 r. from the worship of him
3 K 9 6 r. shall turn away from following me
Jer 3 14 return, O ye revolting children, saith
8 5 turned away with a stubborn revolting
revolutions Wisd 7 19 the r. of the year and
reward Gen 15 1 thy reward exceeding great
Gen 30 18 God hath given me a reward because
Num 18 31 it is your reward for the ministry
22 37 was it because I am not able to reward
Ruth 2 12 mayest thou receive a full reward of
1 K 24 20 the Lord reward thee for this good turn
26 23 Lord will reward every one according
2 K 3 39 Lord r. him that doth evil according
5 8 David had offered that day a reward
22 21 Lord will r. me according to my justice. Ps 17:21, 25
2 Pa 15 7 there shall be a reward for your work
Tob 4 10 storest up to thyself a good reward
Esth 6 3 what honor and reward hath Mardochai
3 he hath received no reward at all
16 23 receive a worthy r. for their fidelity
Job 34 11 ways of every one he will reward them
Ps 18 12 in keeping them there is a great reward
27 4 to them: render to them their reward
90 8 shalt see the reward of the wicked
93 2 the earth: render a reward to the proud
118 112 thy justifications forever, for the r.
126 3 the reward, the fruit of the womb. As
130 2 towards his mother, so r. in my soul
141 8 the just wait for me until thou r. me
Prov 11 18 soweth justice, there is a faithful r.
25 22 his head, and the Lord will r. thee
Ecce 9 5 neither have they a reward any more
Wisd 4 2 winning reward of undefiled conflicts
5 16 their reward is with the Lord and the
Eccu 2 8 your reward shall not be made void
11 18 this is the portion of his reward
24 maketh haste to reward the just and
28 to reward every one according to his
14 6 this is the reward of his wickedness
17 19 and shall render them their reward
18 22 the reward of God continueth forever
30 20 bearing the reward of his iniquity
36 18 r. them that patiently wait for thee
51 30 hath given me a tongue for my reward
38 he will give you your reward in his
Isa 3 11 reward of his hands shall be given him
40 10 his r. is with him, and his work. 62:11
59 18 a reward to his enemies: he will repay
Jer 31 16 for there is a reward for thy work
Eze 29 18 there hath been no reward given him
Osee 9 1 hast loved a r. upon every cornfloor
Abdi 15 he will turn thy r. upon thy head
1 Ma 2 68 render to the Gentiles their reward
10 27 and we will r. you with good things
11 53 did not reward him according to the
2 Ma 5 7 for the r. of his treachery, and fled
8 33 to him a worthy r. for his impieties
Mat 5 12 for your reward is very great in heaven
46 what reward shall you have? Do not even
6 1 you shall not have a reward of your
2 they have received their reward. 5, 16
10 41 shall receive the reward of a prophet
41 shall receive the r. of a just man
42 he shall not lose his r. Mark 9:40
Luke 4 19 year of the Lord and the day of r.
6 23 your reward is great in heaven. For
35 your reward shall be great, and you
23 41 we receive the due reward of our deeds
Acts 1 18 a field of the reward of iniquity and
4 4 r. is not reckoned according to grace
1 C 3 8 every man shall receive his own reward
14 built thereupon, he shall receive a r.
9 17 if I do this thing willingly, I have r.
18 what is my reward then? That preaching
Col 3 24 shall receive of the Lord the reward
1 Tim 5 18 the laborer is worthy of his reward
Heb 2 2 received a just recompense of reward
10 35 confidence, which hath a great reward
11 26 for he looked unto the reward. By faith
2 P 2 13 receiving the r. of their injustice
2 J 8 but that you may receive a full reward
Jude 11 they have for reward poured out
Apoc 11 18 shouldest render r. to thy servants
22 12 my r. is with me to render to every
rewarded Judg 9 57 the Sichemites also were r.
1 K 24 18 I [Saul] have rewarded thee with evil
2 K 4 10 who should have been r. for his news
Ps 102 10 nor r. us according to our iniquities
Wisd 3 5 in many they shall be well rewarded
rewarder Eccu 5 4 the most High is a patient r.
Heb 11 6 is a rewarder to them that seek him
rewarding 3 K 8 32 rewarding him according to his justice. 2 Pa 6:23
rewards Isa 1 23 love bribes, they run after r.
Eze 16 34 in that thou gavest rewards, and didst not take rewards
Dan 2 6 you shall receive of me rewards and
5 17 thy rewards be to thyself, and the
Osee 2 12 these are my rewards, which my lovers
Reza Luke 3 27 Joanna, who was of Reza, who was
Rhegium Acts 28 13 we came to Rhegium: and after
Rheum 2 Es 12 3 Rheum, Merimuth, Addo, Genthon
rhinoceros Num 23 22 strength is like to the r. 24:8
Deut 33 17 his horns as the horns of a rhinoceros
Job 39 9 shall the r. be willing to serve thee
10 canst thou bind the r. with thy thong
Rhode Acts 12 13 came to hearken whose name was R.
Rhodes 1 Ma 15 23 Side and Aradus and Rhodes
Acts 21 1 course to Coos, and day following to R.
Rhodocus 2 Ma 13 21 R., one of the Jews' army
rib Gen 2 22 God built the rib which he took
Ribai 2 K 23 29 Ithai the son of R. of Gabaath
1 Pa 11 31 Ethai the son of Ribai of Gabaath
ribands Num 15 38 putting in them r. of blue
ribs Gen 2 21 he took one of his ribs and filled
Job 18 12 famine, and let hunger invade his ribs
rich Gen 13 2 very rich in possession of gold
Gen 30 30 now thou art become rich: and the
36 7 exceeding rich, and could not dwell
Judg 18 7 at all to oppose them, being very rich
9 land which is exceeding rich and fruitful
Ruth 2 1 and very rich, whose name was Booz
3 10 followed young men either poor or rich
1 K 2 7 the Lord maketh poor and maketh rich
2 K 12 1 were two men in one city, the one rich
19 32 [Berzellai] was a man exceeding rich
4 K 5 1 he was a valiant man and rich, but
15 20 on all that were mighty and rich, to
2 Pa 18 1 Josaphat was rich and very glorious
25 9 the Lord is rich enough to be able to
32 27 Ezechias was rich and very glorious
Jdth 15 8 all were made rich by their spoils
Job 12 5 lamp despised in the thoughts of the r.

21 23 dieth strong and hale, rich and happy
Ps 9 8 he sitteth in ambush with the rich
33 11 the rich have wanted and have suffered
44 13 all the rich among the people, shall
48 3 sons of men: both rich and poor together
17 when a man shall be made rich, and when
122 4 filled: we are a reproach to the rich
Prov 3 13 findeth wisdom and is rich in prudence
10 22 blessing of the Lord maketh men rich
13 7 as it were rich, when he hath nothing
14 20 but the friends of the rich are many
18 23 and the rich will speak roughly. A man
21 17 wine and fat things, shall not be rich
22 2 the rich and poor have met one another
7 the rich ruleth over the poor: and
23 4 labor not to be rich: but set bounds
28 6 simplicity than the rich in crooked ways
20 that maketh haste to be rich. 22
Ecce 5 11 fulness of the r. will not suffer him
10 6 dignity, and the rich sitting beneath
Eccu 10 25 fear of God is the glory of the rich
26 not magnify a sinful man that is rich
11 10 if thou be rich, thou shalt not be
23 a sudden to make the poor man rich
13 22 what part hath the rich with the poor
23 also the poor are devoured by the rich
19 1 that is a drunkard shall not be rich
21 5 the house that is very rich shall be
26 4 rich or poor, if his heart is good
28 17 destroyed the strong cities of the rich
44 6 rich men in virtue, studying
Isa 32 9 rise up, ye rich women, and hear my
11 be astonished, ye rich women, be
33 20 shall see Jerusalem, a rich habitation
53 9 his burial, and the rich for his death
Jer 51 13 upon many waters, rich in treasures
Eze 27 18 in rich wine, in wool of the best
38 13 substance, and to take rich spoils
Dan 11 24 shall enter into rich and plentiful
13 4 Joakim was very rich and had an orchard
Joel 2 13 merciful, patient and rich in mercy
Mich 6 12 her rich men were filled with iniquity
Zach 11 5 we are become rich: and their shepherds
1 Ma 6 2 was in it a temple exceeding rich
2 Ma 3 25 adorned with a very rich covering: and
Mark 12 41 and many that were rich cast in much
Luke 1 53 and the rich he hath sent empty away
6 24 woe to you that are rich: for you
12 21 himself, and is not rich towards God
14 12 nor thy neighbors who are rich; lest
16 21 that fell from the rich man's table
18 23 sorrowful; for he was very rich. And
19 2 chief of the publicans and he was rich
21 1 he saw the rich men cast their gifts
Rom 10 12 all, rich unto all that call upon him
1 C 1 5 in all things you are made rich in him
4 8 you are now full; you are now become r.
2 C 8 9 being r. he became poor, for your sakes
9 through his povery you might be rich
Eph 2 4 but God, who is rich in mercy, for his
1 Tim 6 9 for they that will become rich, fall
17 charge the rich of this world not to be
18 to do good, to be rich in good works, to
James 1 10 and the rich, in his being low; because
2 5 the poor in this world, rich in faith
6 do not the rich oppress you by might
5 1 go to, now, ye rich men, weep and howl
1 P 3 4 spirit, which is rich in the sight of
Apoc 2 9 and thy poverty, but thou art rich
3 17 thou sayest: I am rich and made wealthy
18 that thou mayest be made rich; and
6 15 princes and the tribunes and the rich
13 16 both little and great, rich and poor
18 3 have been made rich by the power of her
15 of these things, who were made rich
19 all were made rich that had ships at

rich man 2 K 12 2 rich man had exceeding many
2 K 12 4 certain stranger was come to the r. man
Job 27 19 the rich man when he shall sleep shall
Prov 10 15 substance of a rich man is the city
Ecce 10 20 and speak not evil of the rich man
Eccu 8 2 contend not with a rich man, lest he
25 4 that is proud: a rich man that is a liar
30 14 a rich man who is weak and afflicted
31 3 rich man hath labored in gathering
8 rich man that is found without blemish
Jer 9 23 let not the rich man glory in his
2 Ma 7 24 make him a rich and a happy man, and
Mat 19 23 a rich man shall hardly enter into the
24 than for a rich man to enter. Mark 10:25; Luke 18:25
27 57 came a certain rich man of Arimathea
Luke 12 16 the land of a certain rich man brought
16 1 a certain rich man who had a steward
19 certain rich man who was clothed in
22 the rich man also died: and he was
James 1 11 so also shall the rich man fade away

richer Prov 11 24 their own goods, and grow richer
Wisd 8 5 what is r. than wisdom, which maketh
Eccu 13 2 with one that is richer than thyself

riches Gen 31 16 God hath taken our father's r.
Gen 45 20 all the riches of Egypt shall be yours
23 to carry off all the riches of Egypt
Num 10 32 give thee what is the best of the r.
Deut 6 11 houses full of riches, which thou didst
Josu 22 8 with much substance and riches, you
1 K 17 25 the king will enrich with great riches
3 K 3 11 nor asked for thyself long life or r.
13 I have given to thee: to wit, riches
10 2 with a great train and riches and
23 all the kings of the earth in riches
1 Pa 29 12 thine are riches and thine is glory
28 full of days and riches and glory
2 Pa 1 11 thou hast not asked riches and wealth
12 and I will give thee riches and wealth
9 1 with great riches and camels, which
22 kings of the earth for riches and glory
17 5 [Josaphat] acquired immense riches
Tob 5 25 that we might account it as riches
Jdth 2 16 and stripped them of all their riches
8 7 her husband left her great riches and
Esth 5 11 to them the greatness of his riches
Job 5 5 the thirsty shall drink up his riches
20 15 the riches which he hath swallowed
21 7 advanced, and strengthened with riches
25 in bitterness of soul without any riches
31 25 if I have rejoiced over my great riches
Ps 36 3 and thou shalt be fed with its riches
16 than the great riches of the wicked
48 7 and glory in the multitude of their r.
11 shall leave their riches to strangers
51 9 trusted in the abundance of his riches
61 11 if riches abound, set not your heart
72 12 in the world they have obtained r.
75 6 men of riches have found nothing in
103 24 the earth is filled with thy riches
118 14 way of thy testimonies, as in all r.
Prov 3 15 she is more precious than all riches
16 in her left hand riches and glory
8 18 with me are r. and glory, glorious r.
10 4 hand of the industrious getteth riches
11 4 r. shall not profit in day of revenge
16 glory: and strong shall have riches
28 that trusteth in his riches shall fall
13 7 were poor, when he hath great riches
8 ransom of a man's life are his riches

14 25 the crown of the wise is their riches
17 16 what doth it avail a fool to have r.
19 4 riches make many friends: but from
14 house and riches are given by parents
22 1 a good name is better than great riches
4 the fear of the Lord, riches and glory
16 the poor, to increase his own riches
23 5 lift not up thy eyes to riches which
28 8 that heapeth together riches by usury
30 8 give me neither beggary nor riches
31 3 thy riches to destroy kings. Give not
29 daughters have gathered together riches
Ecce 2 9 I surpassed in riches all that were
4 8 neither are his eyes satisfied with r.
5 9 that loveth riches shall reap no fruit
10 where there are great riches, there are
10 that he seeth the riches with his eyes
12 riches kept to the hurt of the owner
18 man to whom God hath given riches. 6:2
7 12 wisdom with riches is more profitable
9 11 nor riches to the learned, nor favor
Wisd 5 8 what advantage hath boasting of riches
7 8 esteemed riches nothing in comparison
11 innumerable riches through her hands
13 without envy, and her riches I hide not
8 5 if riches be desired in life, what is
18 riches in the works of her hands and
Eccu 9 16 envy not glory and riches of a sinner
11 14 death, poverty and riches are from God
13 30 riches are good to him that hath no sin
14 3 riches are not comely for a covetous
18 25 necessities of poverty in day of riches
21 5 injuries and wrongs will waste riches
24 23 are the fruit of honor and riches
28 12 according to his r. he shall increase
30 16 there is no riches above the riches of the health of the body
31 1 watching for riches consumeth the flesh
3 labored in gathering riches together
37 6 be not unmindful of him in thy riches
40 13 riches of the unjust shall be dried up
26 riches and strength lift up the heart
Isa 30 6 carry their r. upon shoulders of beasts
33 6 riches of salvation, wisdom and
45 3 the concealed riches of secret places
61 6 you shall eat the riches of the Gentiles
Jer 9 23 let not the rich man glory in his r.
15 13 thy r. and thy treasures I will give
17 11 so is he that hath gathered riches
Bar 6 34 can neither give r. nor requite evil
Eze 22 25 they have taken riches and hire, they
26 12 they shall waste thy riches, they shall
27 12 with a multitude of all kinds of riches
18 in the multitude of divers riches
24 embroidered work and of precious r.
27 thy riches and thy treasures and thy
33 which by the multitude of thy riches
34 thy r. are in the bottom of the waters
Dan 11 2 he shall be grown mighty by his riches
13 haste with a great army and much riches
24 spoils and their prey and their riches
28 shall return into his land with much r.
Nah 2 9 there is no end of the riches of all
3 8 the sea is its riches, its waters are its
Zach 14 14 riches of all nations round about shall
1 Ma 4 23 purple of the sea and great riches
Mat 13 22 deceitfulness of riches choketh up
Mark 4 19 the deceitfulness of riches and the
10 23 hardly shall they that have r. Luke 18:24
24 hard is it for them that trust in r.
Luke 8 14 are choked with the cares and riches
Rom 2 4 or despisest thou the riches of his
9 23 that he might show riches of his glory
11 12 offence of them be the r. of the world
12 riches of the Gentiles: how much more
33 O the depth of the r. of the wisdom and
2 C 8 2 abounded unto the r. of their simplicity
Eph 1 7 according to the riches of his grace
18 and what are the riches of the glory of
2 7 come the abundant riches of his grace
3 8 Gentiles, the unsearchable r. of Christ
16 according to the riches of his glory, to
Phil 4 19 according to his riches in glory in
Col 1 27 to whom God would make known the riches
2 2 riches of fulness of understanding, unto
1 Tim 6 17 nor to trust in the uncertainty of r.
Heb 11 26 greater riches than the treasure of the
James 5 2 your riches are corrupted: and your
Apoc 18 17 are so great riches come to nought
rid Isa 24 18 shall rid himself out of the pit
riddle Judg 14 12 I will propose to you a riddle
Judg 14 13 put forth the riddle that we may hear
14 could not in three days expound riddle
15 to tell thee what the riddle meaneth
16 thou wilt not expound to me the riddle
18 you had not found out my riddle. And
19 gave to them that had declared the r.
Eze 17 2 put forth a riddle and speak a parable
riddles Num 12 8 not by r. and figures doth he
Eccu 47 17 didst multiply riddles in parables
ride Num 22 30 hast been always accustomed to r.
Judg 5 10 speak, you that ride upon fair asses
4 K 10 16 so he made him ride in his chariot
Jer 50 42 and they shall ride upon horses: like
Osee 10 11 I will ride upon Ephraim, Juda shall
14 4 we will not ride upon horses neither
Haba 3 8 who will ride upon thy horses: and
rider Gen 49 17 that his rider may fall backward
Exod 15 1 the horse and the rider he hath thrown
21 and his r. he hath thrown into the sea
Num 22 25 bruised the foot of the rider. But he
27 she fell under the feet of the rider
Job 39 18 she scorneth the horse and his rider
Isa 21 7 a r. upon an ass and a r. upon a camel
9 the rider upon the chariot with two
Jer 51 21 in pieces the horse and his rider
Amos 2 15 neither shall the rider of the horse
Zach 12 4 and his rider with madness: and I will
2 Ma 3 25 a horse with a terrible rider upon him
riders 4 K 18 23 whether you be able to have r.
Isa 36 8 wilt be able on thy part to find riders
Agge 2 23 horses and their r. shall come down
Zach 10 5 the riders of horses shall be confounded
rideth Agge 2 23 chariot and him that r. therein
ridges Eze 36 6 the ridges and to the valley
ridiculous Jer 10 15 vain things and a r. work
riding 2 K 18 9 r. on a mule: and as the mule
Jer 17 25 riding in chariots and on horses. 22:4
Eze 38 15 thee, all of them riding upon horses
Zach 1 8 a man riding upon a red horse, and
9 9 he is poor and riding upon an ass and
rifle Eze 29 19 a prey, and r. the spoils thereof
Mat 12 29 house of the strong and rifle his goods
29 and then he will rifle his house. He
rifled Zach 14 2 and the houses shall be rifled
right Gen 13 9 I will take the right: if thou
Gen 23 4 give me the right of a burying-place
Exod 15 26 God, and do what is right before him
29 20 tip of the right ear. Lev 8:24; 14:14, 17, 25, 28
22 thou shall take . . . the right shoulder
28 and his sons' by a perpetual right
Lev 7 32 right shoulder also of the victims
33 he shall have the right shoulder also
8 23 touched the tip of Aaron's right ear
23 toe of his r. foot. 14:14, 17, 25, 28

24 and the great toes of their right feet
25 with the right shoulder, he separated
26 upon the fat and the right shoulder
9 21 Aaron separated . . . the right shoulders
14 16 and shall dip his right finger in it
24 9 of the Lord by a perpetual right
25 46 by right of inheritance shall leave them
27 21 pertaineth to the right of the priests
Num 18 18 the right shoulder shall be thine
29 24 you shall celebrate in right manner
Deut 32 4 any iniquity, he is just and right
33 5 he shall be king with the most right
Josu 9 25 as it seemeth good and right unto thee
22 27 that we may have a right to offer God
Judg 3 15 left hand as well as the right. 20:16
16 under his garment on the right thigh
21 took the dagger from his right thigh
7 20 with their right hands the trumpets
11 24 possesseth, due to thee by right
17 6 did that which seemed right to himself
21 22 took them not away as by right of war
24 did that which seemed right to himself
Ruth 3 13 will take thee by the right of kindred
4 6 I yield up my right of next akin
7 if at any time one yielded his right
7 this was a testimony of cession of right
1 K 8 9 foretell them the right of the king
11 this will be the right of the king
11 2 I may pluck out all your right eyes
12 23 will teach you the good and right way
2 K 14 19 neither on the left hand nor on the r.
16 6 warriors walked on the right and on
19 28 what right to cry any more to the king
3 K 11 38 do what is right before me, keeping
15 5 David had done that which was right
11 did that which was right. 22:43; 4 K 12:2; 14:3; 15:34; 22:2; 2 Pa 26:4; 27:2; 34:2; Jer 34:15
4 K 10 15 is thy heart right as my heart is
30 which was right and pleasing in my
17 9 God with things that were not right
2 Pa 28 1 he [Achaz] did not that which was right
31 20 wrought that which was good and right
1 Es 8 21 might ask of him a right way for us
2 Es 9 13 and thou gavest them right judgments
Job 35 2 doth thy thought seem right to thee
3 that which is right doth not please
42 7 not spoken the thing that is right
8 have not spoken right things before me
Ps 18 9 the justices of the Lord are right
26 11 and guide me in the right path, because
31 11 and glory, all ye right of heart
32 4 for the word of the Lord is right
35 11 justice to them that are right in heart
50 12 renew a right spirit within my bowels
57 2 judge right things, ye sons of men
72 1 to them that are of a right heart
77 37 but their heart was not right with him
96 11 the just, and joy to the right of heart
105 7 and he led them into the right way
118 137 O Lord: and thy judgment is right
138 14 works, and my soul knoweth right well
142 10 spirit shall lead me into the right land
Prov 2 13 who leave the right way, and walk by
8 6 shall be opened to preach right things
9 they are right to them that understand
12 15 way of a fool is right in his own eyes
14 2 he that walketh in the right way and
16 13 speaketh right things shall be loved
25 is a way that seemeth to a man right
17 26 to strike the prince, who judgeth right
20 11 known, if his works be clean and right
21 2 way of a man seemeth right to himself
8 him that is pure, his work is right
23 16 when thy lips shall speak what is right
24 26 kiss the lips, who answereth right words
29 27 loathe them that are in the right way
Ecce 7 30 I have found, that God made man right
12 10 and wrote words most right and full of
Wisd 2 1 reasoning with themselves, but not right
9 9 what was right in thy commandments
10 10 the just . . . through the right ways
Eccu 2 16 and that have forsaken the right ways
20 19 not distribute with right understanding
21 24 like a bracelet upon his right arm
36 7 glorify thy hand and thy right arm
49 11 good to them that showed right ways
51 20 my foot walked in the right way, from
Isa 26 7 the way of the just is right, the path of the just is right
30 10 not for us those things that are right
45 19 justice, that declare right things
Jer 17 11 hath gathered riches, and not by right
16 my lips, hath been right in thy sight
26 14 what is good and right in your eyes
31 9 I will bring them . . . in a right way
21 direct thy heart into the right way
32 7 it is thy right to buy it, being next
8 the right of inheritance is thine
Eze 18 25 way of the Lord is not right. 29; 33:19
29 are not my ways right, O house of
Dan 3 27 works, are true, and thy ways right
Osee 14 10 for the ways of the Lord are right
Amos 3 10 have not known to do the right thing
Haba 2 4 his soul shall not be right in himself
Zach 11 17 the sword . . . and upon his right eye
17 right eye shall be utterly darkened
1 Ma 8 15 might do the things that were right
9 1 the right wing of his army with them
12 and Bacchides was in the right wing
15 right wing was discomfited. 16
2 Ma 14 19 present and receive the right hands
Mat 5 29 if thy right eye scandalize thee, pluck
39 if one strike thee on thy right cheek
Mark 7 35 tongue was loosed and he spoke right
Luke 8 35 feet, clothed, and in his right mind
10 28 thou hast answered right: this do and
22 50 struck . . . and cut off his right ear
John 12 3 pound of ointment of right spikenard
18 10 Simon Peter . . . cut off his right ear
Acts 8 21 thy heart is not right in the sight of
13 10 pervert the right ways of the Lord
Gal 2 9 gave to me and Barnabas the right hands
2 P 2 15 leaving the right way they have gone
Apoc 10 2 and he set his right foot upon the sea
22 14 may have a right to the tree of life

right hand Gen 13 9 if thou choose the r. h.
Gen 24 49 that I may go to the r. h. or to the
35 18 Benjamin, that is, the son of the r. h.
48 13 he set Ephraim on his right hand, that
13 towards his father's right hand, and
14 he stretching forth his r. h., put it
17 his r. h. upon the head of Ephraim
18 put thy r. h. upon his head. But he
Exod 14 22 was as a wall on their right hand
29 were to them as a wall on the r. h.
15 6 thy right hand, O Lord, is magnified
6 thy right hand, O Lord, hath slain the
29 20 and upon the thumbs . . . of their r. h.
33 22 protect thee with my r. h. till I pass
Lev 8 23 he touched . . . thumb of his right hand
14 14 thumb of his r. h. and the. 17, 25, 28
27 dipping the finger of his r. h. in it
Num 20 17 neither turning aside to the r. h. nor
22 26 to turn aside either to the right hand
Deut 2 27 not turn aside neither to the r. h.

	5	32	not go aside neither to the right hand
	17	11	decline to the right hand nor to the
	28	14	away from them neither to the r. h. nor
	33	2	in his right hand is a fiery law. He hath
Josu	1	7	turn not from it to the right hand or
	17	7	it goeth out on the right hand by the
	23	6	aside from them neither to the r. h.
Judg	5	26	her r. h. to the workman's hammer, and
	16	29	holding the one with his right hand and
1 K	6	12	turned not aside neither to the r. h.
	23	19	which is on the r. h. of the desert
		24	in the plain at the r. h. of Jesimon
2 K	2	19	Asael . . . turned not to the r. h. nor
		21	Abner said to him: Go to the r. h. or
	20	9	Amasa by the chin with his right hand
3 K	2	19	she sat on his right hand. And she
	6	8	door . . . was on the r. h. of the house
	7	21	set up the pillar on the right hand, he
		49	candlesticks, five on the right hand
	22	19	standing by him on the r. h. 2 Pa 18:18
4 K	12	9	at the r. h. of them that came into
	22	2	he turned not aside to the right hand
1 Pa	6	39	Asaph, who stood on his right hand
2 Pa	3	17	pillars . . . one on the right hand and
		17	was on the right hand, he called Jachin
	4	6	he set five lavers on the right hand
		7	five candlesticks on the right hand
	34	2	declined not, neither to the right hand
2 Es	8	4	Helcia and Maasia on his right hand: and
	12	31	went on the right hand upon the wall
Tob	1	1	having on the r. h. the city of Sephet
	7	15	taking the right hand of his daughter
		15	gave it into the right hand of Tobias
Job	14	15	thou shalt reach out thy right hand
	23	9	if I turn myself to the right hand, I
	30	12	at the right hand of my rising, my
	40	9	that thy r. h. is able to save thee
Ps	15	8	at my right hand, that I be not moved
		11	at thy right hand are delights even
	16	8	from them that resist thy right hand
	17	36	and thy right hand hath held me up
	19	7	salvation of his r. h. is in powers
	20	9	thy r. h. find out all them that hate
	25	10	their right hand is filled with gifts
	43	4	save them. But thy right hand and thy
	44	5	and thy right hand shall conduct thee
		10	the queen stood on thy right hand in
	47	11	thy right hand is full of justice. Let
	59	7	save me with thy right and and hear
	62	9	thy right hand hath received me. But
	72	24	thou hast held me by my right hand; and
	73	11	thy r. h. out of the midst of thy bosom
	76	11	the change of the r. h. of the most High
	77	54	mountain which his r. h. had purchased
	79	16	same which thy right hand hath planted
		18	hand be upon the man of thy right hand
	88	14	be strengthened, and thy r. h. exalted
		26	in the sea, and his r. h. in the rivers
		43	hast set up the right hand of them that
	89	12	so make thy right hand known; and men
	90	7	and 10,000 [shall fall] at thy r. h.
	97	1	his right hand hath wrought for him
	107	7	save with thy right hand and hear me
	108	6	may the devil stand at his right hand
		31	he hath stood at the r. h. of the poor
	109	1	sit thou at my right hand until I make
		5	the Lord at thy right hand hath broken
	117	16	r. h. of the Lord hath wrought strength
		16	the right hand of Lord hath exalted me
	120	5	is thy protection upon thy right hand
	136	5	Jerusalem, let my r. h. be forgotten
	137	7	thy right hand hath saved me. The Lord
	138	10	lead me: and thy r. h. shall hold me
	141	5	I looked on my r. h. and beheld, and
	143	8	their r. h. is r. h. of iniquity. 11
Prov	3	16	length of days is in her right hand
	4	27	decline not to the right hand nor to
		27	the ways that are on the right hand
	27	16	shall call in the oil of his right hand
Ecce	10	2	heart of a wise man is in his r. h.
Cant	2	6	his right hand shall embrace me. 8:3
Wisd	5	17	with his right hand he will cover them
Eccu	12	12	neither let him sit on the right hand
	21	22	and like manacles on the right hand
	47	6	he gave strength in his right hand to
	49	13	he was as a signet on the right hand
Isa	9	20	he shall turn to the r. h. and shall
	30	21	go not aside neither to the right hand
	41	10	r. h. of my just one hath upheld thee
	44	20	perhaps there is a lie in my right hand
	45	1	whose right hand I have taken hold of
	48	13	my r. h. hath measured the heavens
	54	3	thou shalt pass on to the right hand
	62	8	the Lord hath sworn by his right hand
	63	12	brought out Moses by the right hand
Jer	22	24	were a ring on my r. h., I would pluck
Lam	2	3	he hath drawn back his right hand from
		4	hath fixed his r. h. as an adversary
Eze	16	46	sister that dwelleth at thy right hand
	21	16	go to the right hand or to the left
		22	on his right hand was the divination
	39	3	thy arrows to fall out of thy r. h.
Dan	12	7	when he had lifted up his right hand
Jon	4	11	to distinguish between their right hand
Haba	2	16	the cup of the right hand of the Lord
Zach	3	1	Satan stood on his right hand to be
	12	6	shall devour . . . to the right hand and
1 Ma	5	46	no means to turn from it on the r. h.
	6	45	killing on the r. h. and on the left
	7	27	cut off Nicanor's head and his r. h.
	11	62	Jonathan, and he gave them the r. h.
2 Ma	4	34	he went to Onias and gave him his r. h.
	13	22	gave his right hand: took theirs: and
	15	15	Jeremias stretched forth his right hand
Mat	5	30	if thy right hand scandalize thee, cut
	6	3	know what thy right hand doth. That
	20	21	one on thy r. h. 27:38; Mark 10:37; 15:27
		23	to sit on my right or left hand is not
	22	44	sit on my right hand. Mark 12:36; Luke 20:42; Acts 2:34; Heb 1:13
	25	33	shall set the sheep on his right hand
		34	that shall be on his right hand: Come
	26	64	on the right hand of the power of God. Mark 14:62; Luke 22:69
	27	29	his head, and a reed in his right hand
Mark	10	40	but to sit on my right hand or on my
	15	27	the one on his right hand, and the
	16	19	sitteth on the right hand. Heb 1:3; 10:12; 12:2
Luke	6	6	a man whose right hand was withered
	23	33	and the robbers, one on the right hand
Acts	2	25	because he is at my right hand, that
		33	exalted therefore by the r. h. of God
	3	7	taking him by the right hand, he lifted
	5	31	him hath God exalted with his r. h.
	7	55	standing on the r. h. of God. 55
Rom	8	34	is at the right hand of God. 1 P 3:22
2 C	6	7	by armor of justice on the right hand
Eph	1	20	dead, and setting him on his right hand
Col	3	1	Christ is sitting at the right hand of
Heb	8	1	who is set on the r. h. of the throne
Apoc	1	16	he had in his right hand seven stars
		17	he laid his right hand upon me, saying
		20	which thou sawest in my right hand and
	2	1	holdeth the seven stars in his r. h.
	5	1	I saw in the right hand of him that

22 22 their destruction shall rise suddenly
Cant 3 2 I will rise and will go about the city
Eccu 24 6 should rise light that never faileth
Isa 14 12 Lucifer, who didst rise in the morning
24 20 and it shall fall and not rise again
26 14 live, let not the giants rise again
19 shall live, my slain shall rise again
34 3 of their carcasses shall rise a stink
43 17 and they shall not rise again: they are
Jer 8 4 shall not he that falleth, rise again
25 27 and fall, and rise no more, because
50 41 many kings shall rise from the ends of
Lam 1 14 out of which I am not able to rise
Eze 3 22 rise and go forth into the plain and
6 1 they will rise early to me: Come and
13 15 wind that shall rise from the desert
Amos 5 1 is fallen, and it shall rise no more
8 14 they shall fall and shall rise no more
Nah 1 9 shall not rise a double affliction
2 Ma 12 44 they that were slain should rise again
Mat 5 45 maketh his sun to rise upon the good
11 5 deaf hear, the dead r. again. Luke 7:22
12 41 men of Ninive shall rise. Luke 11:22
42 queen of the south shall r. Luke 11:31
16 21 the third day rise again. Luke 9:22
17 22 the third day he shall rise again. 20:19; Mark 10:34; Luke 18:33
24 7 nation shall rise against nation. Mark 13:8; Luke 21:10
11 many false prophets shall rise and
26 46 rise, let us go: behold he is at hand
27 63 after three days I will rise again
Mark 4 27 and should sleep, and rise, night and
8 31 and after three days rise again. And
9 30 he shall rise again the third day. But
12 23 when they shall rise again. 25
26 concerning the dead that they r. again
Luke 11 7 in bed; I cannot rise and give thee
8 although he will not rise and give
8 he will rise and give him as many as
16 31 if one rise again from the dead
20 37 that the dead rise again, Moses also
24 7 crucified, and the third day rise again
46 and to rise again from the dead the
John 11 23 to her: Thy brother shall rise again
24 he shall rise again in the resurrection
20 9 that he must rise again from the dead
Acts 17 3 Christ was to suffer, and to rise again
26 23 he should be the first that should rise
Rom 13 11 now the hour for us to rise from sleep
1 C 15 15 if the dead r. not again. 16, 29, 32
35 how do the dead rise again? or with what
42 corruption, it shall r. in incorruption
43 sown in dishonor, it shall rise in glory
43 sown in weakness, it shall rise in power
44 body, it shall rise a spiritual body
51 we shall all indeed rise again: but we
52 the dead shall rise again incorruptible
Eph 5 14 rise thou that sleepest, and arise from
1 Th 4 15 the dead who are in Christ, shall rise
Heb 7 11 another priest should rise according to
rise up Gen 19 28 he saw the ashes rise up from
Gen 31 35 that I cannot rise up before thee
Lev 19 32 rise up before the hoary head, and
Num 23 24 the people shall rise up as a lioness
Deut 19 15 one witness shall not rise up against
28 7 thy enemies, that rise up against thee
43 shall rise up over thee and shall be
Josu 3 3 rise you up also and follow them
8 20 seeing the smoke of the city rise up
23 16 shall indignation of the Lord rise up
Judg 12 3 you should rise up to fight against me
20 40 pillar of smoke rise up from the city
1 K 22 13 that he should rise up against me
2 K 12 21 was dead, thou didst rise up and eat
4 K 9 2 thou shalt make him [Jehu] rise up
2 Es 2 18 let us rise up, and build. 20
Jdth 8 20 nations that shall rise up against us
Job 14 12 not awake nor rise up out of his sleep
20 27 the earth shall rise up against him
Ps 3 2 many are they who rise up against me
7 7 rise up, O Lord, in thy anger; and be
17 49 above them that rise up against me
26 3 if a battle should rise up against me
34 2 arms and shield: and rise up to help me
43 6 will despise them that rise up against
58 2 me from them that rise up against me
6 rise up thou to meet me, and behold
77 6 that should be born and should rise up
91 12 of the malignant that r. up against me
93 16 who shall rise up for me against the
108 28 that rise up against me be confounded
Prov 28 28 when the wicked rise up, men shall hide
Ecce 4 15 young man, who shall r. up in his place
12 4 they shall rise up at the voice of the
Eccu 17 19 he shall rise up and shall render
33 33 and if he rise up and depart, thou
Isa 2 19 shall rise up to strike the earth. 21
5 11 woe to you that rise up early in the
11 1 flower shall rise up out of his root
14 21 they shall not rise up nor inherit
22 I will rise up against them, saith thee
31 2 he will rise up against the house of
32 9 rise up, ye rich women, and hear my
33 10 now will I rise up, saith the Lord
35 7 shall rise up the verdure of the reed
49 7 and princes shall rise up and adore
58 10 then shall thy light r. up in darkness
60 4 thy daughters shall rise up at thy side
Jer 6 22 a great nation shall rise up from the
37 9 they shall rise up, every man from his
49 14 against her, and let us r. up to battle
51 64 shall not rise up from the affliction
Lam 3 62 lips of them that rise up against me
Bar 6 26 they rise not up again of themselves
Eze 26 3 to thee, as the waves of the sea rise up
Dan 2 39 after thee shall r. up another kingdom
7 24 and another shall rise up after them
8 22 four kings shall rise up of his nation
25 he shall rise up against the prince
11 3 but there shall rise up a strong king
14 many shall rise up against the king
15 his chosen ones shall rise up to resist
37 he shall rise up against all things
12 1 at that time shall Michael rise up
Amos 7 9 I will rise up against the house of
8 8 rise up altogether as a river and be
9 5 it shall rise up as a river and shall
Abdi 1 let us rise up to battle against him
Jon 1 6 rise up, call upon thy God, if so be
Haba 2 7 shall they not rise up suddenly that
Mat 10 21 the children shall r. up. Mark 13:12
Mark 13 22 there will rise up false Christs and
14 42 rise up, let us go. Behold, he that
Acts 22 16 now why tarriest thou? Rise up, and be
26 16 rise up, and stand upon thy feet: for
Rom 15 12 he that shall rise up to rule Gentiles
risen Gen 19 23 the sun was risen upon the earth
Exod 22 3 if he did this when the sun is risen
Lev 13 42 be risen a white or reddish color
43 leprosy which is risen in the bald part
Judg 6 28 when the men of that town were risen
1 K 9 26 when they were risen in the morning
4 K 4 31 told him, saying: The child is not r.
2 Pa 14 6 there had no wars risen in his time
Ps 19 9 but we are risen and are set upright

96 11 light is risen to the just, and joy to
Prov 31 15 she hath risen in the night and given
Wisd 5 6 of understanding hath not risen upon us
Isa 9 2 of the shadow of death, light is risen
60 1 glory of the Lord is risen upon thee
Eze 47 5 the waters were risen so as to make
Jon 4 8 and when the sun was risen, the Lord
2 Ma 10 28 as soon as the sun was risen both sides
Mat 11 11 hath not risen among them that are born
14 2 the Baptist: he is risen from the dead
17 9 till the Son of man be risen. Mark 9:8
26 32 after I shall be r. again. Mark 14:28
27 64 to the people: he is risen from the
28 6 is not here, for he is risen as he said
7 tell ye his disciples that he is risen
Mark 4 6 when sun was risen, it was scorched
6 14 John the Baptist is risen again from
16 John . . . is risen again from the dead
9 9 when he shall be risen from the dead
16 2 the sepulcher, the sun being now risen
6 he is risen, he is not here, behold
14 seen him after he was risen again
Luke 9 8 by some, that John was risen from the
8 that one of the old prophets was risen
19 one of the former prophets is risen
24 6 he is not here, but is risen. Remember
34 the Lord is risen indeed and hath
John 2 22 when therefore he was risen again
21 14 after he was risen from the dead
Rom 6 4 Christ is r. from the dead. 1 C 15:20
7 4 who is risen again from the dead, that
8 34 Jesus that died, yea that is risen also
1 C 15 13 the dead, then Christ is not risen again
14 if Christ be not risen again. 17
16 not again, neither is Christ risen again
Col 2 12 in whom also you are risen again by
3 1 if you be risen with Christ, seek the
2 Tim 2 8 Jesus Christ is risen again from the
risen up Num 14 35 hath r. up together against
Num 32 14 you are r. up instead of your fathers
Josu 18 8 when the men were risen up to go to
Judg 9 18 you are now r. up against my father's
2 K 18 31 of all that have risen up against thee
4 K 16 7 who are risen up together against me
2 Pa 6 10 I am risen up in the place of David my
Ps 3 6 I have risen up, because the Lord hath
26 12 unjust witnesses have risen up against
53 5 strangers have risen up against me
85 14 the wicked are risen up against me
111 4 to the righteous a light is risen up
Isa 14 9 are risen up from their thrones, all
Bar 3 19 others are risen up in their place
Eze 7 11 iniquity is risen up into a rod of
Dan 8 27 when I was risen up, I did the king's
Mich 2 8 contrary, are risen up as an enemy
Zach 2 13 is risen up out of his holy habitation
1 Ma 13 14 that Simon was risen up in the place
Mark 3 26 if Satan be risen up against himself
Luke 7 16 a great prophet is risen up among us
risest Deut 11 19 when thou liest down and r. up
riseth Deut 22 26 as a robber riseth against his brother
2 K 23 4 light of the morning when the sun r.
Jdth 16 20 woe be to the nation that riseth up
Job 9 7 commandeth the sun and it riseth not
16 9 false speaker riseth up against my face
24 14 murderer r. at the very break of day
Ecce 1 5 the sun riseth and goeth down and
Eccu 24 37 riseth up as Gehon in the time of
26 21 as the sun when it riseth to the world
Isa 64 7 that riseth up and taketh hold of thee
Jer 46 8 Egypt riseth up like a flood, and the
Mich 7 6 the daughter riseth up against her
John 7 52 out of Galilee a prophet riseth not
11 29 riseth quickly and cometh to him. For
13 4 he riseth from supper and layeth aside
rising Gen 32 22 r. early he took his two wives
Exod 24 4 rising in the morning he built an altar
32 6 rising in the morning, they offered
34 4 rising very early he went up into the
Deut 4 47 towards the rising of the sun. Josu 1:15; 12:1; 19:34; Eze 8:16; 11:1
6 7 walking on thy journey, sleeping and r.
Josu 6 12 Josue rising before day, the priests
8 10 r. early in the morning, he mustered
Judg 5 31 shine, as the sun shineth in his rising
6 38 rising before day, wringing the fleece
8 13 from the battle before the sun rising
9 33 morning at sun r. set upon the city
16 3 rising he [Samson] took both the doors
19 5 r. early in the morning he desired to
20 19 children of Israel r. in the morning
38 by the smoke rising on high, they might
21 4 rising early the next day, they built
2 K 14 7 whole kindred r. against thy handmaid
3 K 3 20 r. in the dead time of the night, she
4 K 6 15 servant of the man of God rising early
2 Pa 29 20 Ezechias, rising early assembled all
36 15 rising early and daily admonishing them
2 Es 4 21 spears from the rising of the morning
Job 3 9 nor the r. of the dawning of the day
8 16 at his rising his blossom shall shoot
30 12 at the right hand of my rising, my
Ps 49 1 from the rising of the sun to the. 112:3; Mala 1:11
106 3 from the rising and from the setting
Prov 27 14 with a loud voice, rising in the night
Ecce 1 5 there rising again, maketh his round by
Cant 6 9 cometh forth as the morning rising
Eccu 32 15 at the time of rising be not slack
43 2 appeareth showing forth at his rising
Isa 13 10 the sun shall be darkened in his rising
41 25 he shall come from the r. of the sun
45 6 who are from the rising of the sun
47 11 thou shalt not know the rising thereof
59 19 from the rising of the sun his glory
60 3 kings in the brightness of thy rising
Jer 11 7 rising early I conjured them and said
25 3 have spoken to you, rising before day
4 rising early and sending, and you have
29 19 rising by night and sending: and you
35 14 I have spoken to you, rising early
15 rising early and sending and. 44:4
Bar 5 5 from the rising to the setting sun
Dan 6 19 king rising very early in the morning
Mark 1 35 rising very early, going out, he went
7 24 rising from thence he went into the
16 9 he rising early the first day of the
Luke 4 39 immediately rising, she ministered to
6 8 the midst. And rising he stood forth
12 54 when you see a cloud rising from the
Rom 6 9 Christ r. again from dead, dieth now
Apoc 7 2 ascending from the rising of the sun
16 12 for the kings from the r. of the sun
rising up Gen 20 8 Abimelech forthwith r. up in
Gen 22 3 Abraham rising up in the night saddled
Num 11 32 rising up all that day and night and
14 40 rising up very early in the morning
Deut 2 13 rising up to pass the torrent Zared
16 7 rising up thou shalt go into thy
31 16 this people r. up will go a fornicating
Josu 6 15 seventh day, rising up early, they went
Judg 7 1 the same as Gedeon, rising up early
19 7 he rising up began to be for departing
20 33 rising up out of the places where they
1 K 17 52 the men of Israel and Juda rising up
24 8 Saul rising up out of the cave, went

2 K 15 2 Absalom rising up early stood by the
3 K 14 4 rising up went to Silo, and came to
19 3 Elias was afraid, and rising up, he went
21 r. up he went away and followed Elias
4 K 3 24 but Israel rising up defeated Moab
25 26 rising up, went to Egypt, fearing the
1 Pa 28 2 the king rising up and standing, said
Tob 11 10 his father that was blind, rising up
12 22 rising up, they told all his wonderful
Jdth 7 23 Ozias rising up all in tears, said
Job 1 5 rising up early offered holocausts
Ps 34 11 unjust witnesses rising up have asked
138 2 known my sitting down and my rising up
Jer 7 13 I have spoken to you rising up early
25 day to day, rising up early and sending
26 5 whom I sent to you rising up early
Lam 3 63 their sitting down and their rising up
Dan 13 34 the two elders rising up in the midst
Mat 1 24 Joseph rising up from sleep, did as
8 26 rising up, he commanded the winds and
9 19 Jesus rising up followed him, with his
26 62 the high priest rising up, said to him
Mark 2 14 follow me. And rising up he followed
4 39 rising up, he rebuked the wind, and
10 1 rising up, from thence, he cometh into
14 57 some rising up, bore false witness
60 high priest, rising up in the midst
Luke 1 39 Mary rising up in those days went
4 38 Jesus rising up out of the synagogue
5 25 rising up before them, he took up the
15 20 rising up he came to his father, and
23 1 multitude of them r. up, led him to
24 12 Peter rising up, ran to the sepulcher
33 rising up the same hour, they went
Acts 1 15 Peter rising up in the midst of the
5 6 the young men rising up, removed him
17 then the high priest rising up, and
34 but one in the council rising up, a
8 27 rising up, he went. And behold a man
9 18 sight: and rising up, he was baptized
39 Peter rising up, went with them. And
11 28 Agabus rising up, signified by the
13 16 Paul rising up, and with his hand
15 7 Peter, rising up, said to them: Men
23 9 some of the Pharisees rising up, strove
rite Exod 12 5 according to which rite also you
Exod 29 7 by this rite shall he be consecrated
41 according to rite of morning oblation
40 4 that are commanded according to the r.
Lev 8 34 that the rite of the sacrifice might be
14 2 this is the rite of a leper, when he
16 16 according to this rite shall he do
23 37 according to the rite of every day
24 3 by a perpetual service and rite in your
Num 3 26 whatsoever belongeth to rite of the
8 7 shalt purify them according to this rite
15 14 offer sacrifices after the same rite
19 20 man be not expiated after this rite
29 21 you shall offer according to the rite
27 shall celebrate according to the rite
30 celebrate according to the r. 33, 37
2 Pa 29 34 with an easier rite than the priests
rites Exod 13 5 celebrate this manner of sacred r.
Num 4 43 that go in to fulfil the rites of the
28 8 the rites of the morning sacrifice
1 Es 7 23 all that belongeth to the rites of
Wisd 14 15 appointed him rites and sacrifices
2 Ma 11 24 to turn to the rites of the Greeks
rival Lev 18 18 wife's sister for a harlot to r. her
1 K 1 6 her rival also afflicted her and
2 32 thou shalt see thy rival in the temple
28 16 from thee, and is gone over to thy r.
river Gen 2 10 river went out of the place of
Gen 2 13 the name of the second river is Gehon
14 the name of the third river is Tigris
14 and the fourth river is Euphrates
31 21 having passed the river, was going on
36 37 Saul of the river Rohoboth reigned
41 1 he thought he stood by the river, out
3 other seven also came up out of the r.
3 they fed on the very bank of the river
17 methought I stood upon bank of the r.
18 seven kine came up out of the river
Exod 1 22 male sex, ye shall cast into the river
2 5 came down to wash herself in the river
4 9 take of the river water, and pour it
9 drawest out of river shall be turned
7 15 to meet him on the bank of the river
17 water of the r., and it shall be turned
18 fishes that are in the river shall die
18 when they drink the water of the river
20 he struck the water of the river before
21 the fishes that were in the river died
21 died: and the river corrupted, and the
21 could not drink the water of the river
24 Egyptians dug round about the river
24 could not drink of the water of the r.
25 after that the Lord struck the river
8 3 river shall bring forth abundance of
9 and may remain only in the river
11 and shall remain only in the river
17 5 wherewith thou didst strike the river
23 31 and from the desert to the river: I will
Num 22 5 a soothsayer who dwelt by the river
Josu 13 3 from the troubled river, that watereth
24 2 dwelt of old on other side of the river
Judg 11 19 to pass through thy land to the river
2 K 10 16 Syrians that were beyond the river
17 13 and we will draw it into the river
21 arise and pass quickly over the river
22 left that was not gone over the river
19 31 ready also to wait on him beyond the r.
3 K 4 21 from the river to land of Philistines
24 all country which was beyond the river
8 65 from entrance of Emath to r. of Egypt
14 15 and shall scatter them beyond the river
4 K 17 6 in Hala and Habor by the river of Gozan
1 Pa 1 48 Rohoboth, which is near the river
5 26 and to Ara and to the river of Gozan
19 16 Syrians that were beyond the river
1 Es 4 10 the countries of this side of the river
11 that are on this side of the river
16 no possession on this side of the r.
17 to the rest beyond the river, sending
20 over all country that is beyond the r.
5 3 who was governor beyond the river
6 of country beyond the river. 6:6, 13
6 Arphasachites, who dwelt beyond the r.
6 6 who are beyond the river, depart far
8 out of the country beyond the river
7 21 keepers . . . that are beyond the river
25 all the people that is beyond the river
8 15 I gathered them together to the river
21 there a fast by the river Ahava, that
31 we set forward from the river Ahava
36 and the governors beyond the river
2 Es 2 7 governors of country beyond the r. 9
3 7 was in the country beyond the river
Tob 6 1 lodged first night by the r. of Tigris
Esth 10 6 little fountain which grew into a river
11 10 fountain grew into a very great river
Job 14 11 and an emptied river should be dried up
20 17 let him not see the streams of the r.
40 18 he will drink up a river and not wonder
Ps 45 5 the stream of the river maketh the city
64 10 the river of God is filled with water

65 6 in the river they shall pass on foot
71 8 from the r. unto the ends of the earth
79 12 the sea, and its boughs unto the river
Wisd 11 7 instead of fountain of ever running r.
19 10 river cast up a multitude of frogs
Eccu 4 32 not strive against stream of the river
24 41 like a brook out of a river of a
41 like a channel of a river and like an
43 my brook became a great river, and my river came near to a sea
39 27 his blessing hath overflowed like a r.
40 13 of the unjust shall be dried up like a r.
16 and at the bank of the river, shall be
44 23 from the river to the ends of the earth
47 16 thou wast filled as a river with wisdom
Isa 7 20 hired by them that are beyond the river
8 7 upon them the waters of the river
11 15 shall lift up his hand over the river
19 5 and the river shall be wasted and dry
7 channel of the r. shall be laid bare
8 all that cast a hook into the river
23 3 the harvest of the river is her revenue
10 pass thy land as a river, O daughter
27 12 will strike from the channel of the r.
48 18 thy peace had been as a river, and thy
66 12 upon her as it were a river of peace
Jer 2 18 to drink the water of the river? Thy
Bar 1 4 dwelt in Babylonia, by the river Sodi
Eze 29 3 the river is mine, and I made myself
5 desert, and all the fish of thy river
9 the river is mine, and I made it
Dan 10 4 by the great river which is the Tigris
12 5 on this side upon the bank of the river
5 side, on the other bank of the river
6 that stood upon the waters of the r. 7
Amos 8 8 rise up altogether as a river and be
8 run down as the river of Egypt. 9:5
9 5 it shall rise up as a river and shall
Mich 7 12 the fortified cities even to the r.
Zach 10 11 depths of the r. shall be confounded
1 Ma 5 41 camp on the other side of the river
7 8 that ruled beyond the great river in
11 7 as far as the river, called Eleutherus
60 passed through the cities beyond the r.
12 30 they had passed the river Eleutherus
16 5 there was a running river between them
6 were afraid to go over the river, so he
Mark 1 5 baptized by him in the river of Jordan
Acts 16 13 forth without the gate by a river side
Apoc 12 15 after the woman, water as it were a r.
15 her to be carried away by the river
16 swallowed up the river which the dragon
22 1 he showed me a river of water of life
2 and on both sides of the river was the
river Chobar; *see* **Chobar**
river Euphrates; *see* **Euphrates**
river Jordan Josu 7 7 thou bring this people over the river Jordan
Josu 13 23 river Jordan was the border of the
15 5 bay of the sea unto the same r. J.
22 25 hath put the r. J. for a border
Jdth 1 9 in Samaria and beyond the r. J. even
river's Exod 2 3 in the sedges by the r. brink
Exod 2 5 her maids walked by the river's brink
rivers Exod 7 19 upon their r. and streams and
Exod 8 5 upon the rivers and the pools and
Lev 11 9 as well in the sea as in the rivers
Num 16 14 land that floweth with rivers of milk
24 6 as watered gardens near the rivers
Deut 8 7 in the hills deep rivers break out
4 K 5 12 Abana and the Pharphar, r. of Damascus
18 11 and in Habor by the rivers of Gozan
Tob 8 7 fountains and the rivers and all thy
Job 28 10 in the rocks he hath cut out rivers
11 depths also of rivers he hath searched
29 6 the rock poured me out rivers of oil
Ps 23 2 and hath prepared it upon the rivers
73 15 thou hast dried up the Ethan rivers
77 16 and made streams run down as rivers
44 he turned their rivers into blood
88 26 sea; and his right hand in the rivers
97 8 the rivers shall clap their hands, the
104 41 flowed: rivers ran down in the dry land
106 33 hath turned rivers into a wilderness
136 1 upon the rivers of Babylon, there we
Prov 8 26 not yet made the earth nor the rivers
Ecce 1 7 all the rivers run into the sea, yet
7 the place from whence the rivers come
Wisd 5 23 the rivers shall run together in a
Eccu 24 40 I, wisdom, have poured out rivers
Isa 7 18 uttermost parts of the rivers of Egypt
18 1 which is beyond the rivers of Ethiopia
2 whose land the rivers have spoiled. 7
19 6 and the rivers shall fail: the streams
30 25 elevated hill rivers of running waters
32 2 as rivers of waters in drought, and the
33 21 a place of rivers, very broad and
37 25 foot, all the rivers shut up in banks
41 18 I will open rivers in the high hills
42 15 and I will turn rivers into islands
43 2 and the rivers shall not cover thee
19 the wilderness and r. in the desert. 20
44 27 desolate, and I will dry up thy rivers
47 2 make bare thy legs, pass over the r.
50 2 I will turn the rivers into dry land
Jer 46 7 his streams swell like those of rivers
8 waves thereof shall be moved as rivers
Eze 29 3 that liest in the midst of thy rivers
4 fish of thy r. to stick to thy scales
4 thee out of the midst of thy rivers
10 I come against thee and thy rivers
30 12 will make the channels of the r. dry
31 15 I withheld its rivers, and restrained
32 2 didst push with the horn in thy rivers
14 and cause their rivers to run like oil
34 13 the mountains of Israel, by the rivers
Dan 3 78 ye seas and rivers, bless the Lord
Joel 3 18 waters shall flow through all the r.
Nah 1 4 bringeth all the rivers to be a desert
2 6 the gates of the rivers are opened
3 8 Alexandria, that dwelleth among the r.
Haba 3 8 wast thou angry, O Lord, with the r.
8 or was thy wrath upon the rivers
9 thou wilt divide the r. of the earth
Soph 3 10 from beyond the rivers of Ethiopia
Zach 9 10 the r. even to the end of the earth
John 7 38 out of his belly shall flow rivers of
Apoc 8 10 it fell on the third part of the rivers
16 4 poured out his vial upon the rivers
rivulets Eze 31 4 sent forth its r. to all the
road Gen 49 13 seashore and in the road of ships
Isa 33 8 no one passeth by the r., the covenant
62 10 for the people make the road plain
1 Ma 9 2 took the road that leadeth to Galgal
roads Prov 26 13 in the way, and a lioness in the r.
Roaga 1 Pa 7 34 sons of Somer: Ahi and Roaga
roar 1 Pa 16 32 let the sea roar and the fulness
Job 37 4 after it a noise shall roar, he shall
Eccu 51 4 from them that did roar, prepared
Isa 5 29 they shall roar like young lions yea
29 they shall roar and take hold of the
59 11 we shall roar all of us like bears
Jer 6 23 their voice shall r. like the sea. 50:42
25 30 the Lord shall roar from on high
30 shall roar upon place of his beauty
31 35 and the waves thereof roar, the Lord

51 38 they shall roar together like lions
55 their wave shall r. like many waters
Bar 6 31 they roar and cry before their gods
Joel 3 16 and the Lord shall roar out of Sion
Osee 11 10 shall roar as a lion: because he
Amos 1 2 the Lord will roar from Sion and utter
3 4 will a lion roar in the forest if
8 the lion shall roar, who will not
roared Gen 27 34 Esau . . . roared out with a great
Ps 37 9 I roared with the groaning of my heart
45 4 their waters roared and were troubled
Jer 2 15 the lions have roared upon him and
roareth Isa 31 4 like as the lion roareth and the
Eze 22 25 like a lion that roareth and catcheth
Apoc 10 3 a loud voice as when a lion roareth
roaring Judg 14 5 young lion met him raging and r.
Job 3 24 as overflowing waters, so is my roaring
4 10 the roaring of the lion, and the voice
Ps 21 14 against me, as a lion ravening and r.
103 21 young lions, roaring after their prey
Prov 19 12 as the r. of a lion, so also is. 20:2
28 15 as a roaring lion and a hungry bear
Wisd 17 18 the roaring voice of wild beasts
Isa 5 29 their roaring like that of a lion
30 like the roaring of the sea; we shall
17 12 like the multitude of the roaring sea
Jer 25 30 roaring he shall roar upon the place
Eze 19 7 thereof by the noise of his roaring
7 fulness thereof by the noise of his r.
Soph 3 3 in the midst of her as roaring lions
Zach 11 3 the voice of the roaring of the lions
1 Ma 3 4 lion's whelp roaring for his prey
Luke 21 25 the r. of the sea and of the waves
1 P 5 8 adversary the devil, as a roaring lion
roarings Job 39 3 cast them and send forth r.
roasted Exod 12 8 that night roasted at the fire
Exod 12 9 in water, but only roasted at the fire
2 K 6 19 of bread and a piece of roasted beef
1 Pa 16 3 piece of r. beef and flour fried
2 Pa 35 13 and they roasted the phase with fire
Tob 6 6 when he had done so, he r. the flesh
roasting 1 Pa 23 29 of the fryingpan and of the r.
rob 1 K 23 1 against Ceila, and they rob the
Isa 10 2 that they might rob the fatherless
Eze 39 10 they shall rob those that robbed
45 8 princes shall no more rob my people
2 Ma 5 18 by king Seleucus to rob the treasury
9 2 attempted to rob the temple and to
Mark 3 27 and rob him of his goods, unless he
robbed Job 24 9 have violently r. the fatherless
Ps 88 42 that pass by the way have robbed him
Prov 17 12 to meet a bear robbed of her whelps
Isa 42 22 this is a people that is robbed and
Eze 33 15 and render what he had robbed and
39 10 shall rob those that robbed them
Osee 13 8 bear that is robbed of her whelps
Amos 5 11 because you robbed the poor and
Zach 2 8 to the nations that have robbed you
robber Deut 22 26 as r. riseth against his brother
Prov 23 28 lieth in wait in the way as a robber
Eccu 36 28 as a r. well appointed that skippeth
Jer 3 2 waiting for them as a robber in the
4 7 robber of nations hath roused himself
18 22 shalt bring the r. upon them suddenly
48 32 robber hath rushed in upon the harvest
Eze 18 10 if he beget a son that is a robber
Osee 7 1 in to steal, the robber is without
Mich 5 1 be laid waste, O daughter of the robber
Mat 26 55 come out as it were to a r. Mark 14:48
John 10 1 way, the same is a thief and a robber
18 40 Barabbas. Now Barabbas was a robber
robberies Judg 9 25 they committed r. taking
Ps 61 11 iniquity, and cover not robberies
Prov 21 7 r. of the wicked shall be their downfall
24 2 their mind studieth robberies and
Eze 45 9 cease from iniquity and robberies
Amos 3 10 iniquity and robberies in their houses
robbers Judg 11 3 to him needy men and robbers
1 K 30 8 shall I pursue after these robbers
23 hath delivered the robbers that invaded
2 K 3 22 came, after having slain the robbers
3 K 11 24 and he became a captain of robbers
4 K 5 2 there had gone out robbers from Syria
6 23 and the robbers of Syria came no more
Job 12 6 the tabernacles of robbers abound
Isa 42 24 Jacob for a spoil, and Israel to robbers
Jer 7 11 in your eyes become a den of robbers
Bar 6 14 save himself from war or from robbers
56 deliver themselves from thieves or r.
Eze 7 22 robbers shall enter into it and defile
Abdi 5 gone in to thee, if robbers by night
Luke 10 30 to Jericho, and fell among robbers
36 to him that fell among the robbers
23 33 and the robbers, one on the right hand
39 one of those robbers who were hanged
John 10 8 as have come, are thieves and robbers
2 C 11 26 perils of waters, in perils of robbers
robbery Isa 61 8 and hate r. in a holocaust: and
Eze 22 29 have used oppression and committed r.
Phil 2 6 thought it not r. to be equal with God
robe Gen 41 42 he put upon him a robe of silk
Gen 49 11 he shall wash his robe in wine and his
Lev 61 32 he shall be vested with the linen robe
1 K 24 5 cut off the hem of Saul's robe. 6
12 the hem of thy robe in my hand, that
12 when I cut off the hem of thy robe
2 K 13 18 and she was clothed with a long robe
19 and rent her long robe and laid her
1 Pa 15 27 was clothed with robe of fine linen
Jdth 16 10 she took a new robe to deceive him
Esth 6 10 take the robe and the horse, and do as
11 Aman took the robe and the horse
Job 29 14 judgment, as with a r. and a diadem
Wisd 18 24 in the priestly robe which he wore
Eccu 6 30 her chain a robe of glory: for in her
32 shalt put her on as a robe of glory
27 9 shalt put her on as a long r. of honor
45 9 and clothed him with a robe of glory
12 he gave him a holy robe of gold and
50 11 when he put on the robe of glory
Isa 22 21 and I will clothe him with thy robe
61 10 with robe of justice he hath covered me
63 1 this beautiful one in his r. walking
Bar 4 20 I have put off the robe of peace
Job 3 6 and cast away his robe from him and
1 Ma 6 15 he gave him the crown and his robe
10 20 he sent him a purple robe and a crown
Mark 16 5 right side, clothed with a white robe
Luke 15 22 bring forth quickly the first robe
robes Gen 45 22 out for every one of them two r.
Gen 45 22 of silver with five robes of the best
3 K 22 10 on his throne clothed with royal robes
2 Pa 18 9 on their thrones, clothed in royal r.
Esth 15 5 glittering in royal robes, after she
9 throne, clothed with his royal robes
Eze 26 16 take off their robes and cast away their
1 Ma 14 9 put on them glory and the robes of war
Mark 12 38 who love to walk in long robes and to
Luke 20 46 who desire to walk in long robes and
Apoc 6 11 white robes were given to every one of
7 9 clothed with white robes. 13
14 have washed their robes and have made
22 14 that wash their robes in the blood of
Roboam 3 K 11 43 R. his son reigned in. 2 Pa 9:31
3 K 12 1 Roboam went to Sichem. 2 Pa 10:1
3 and they spoke to Roboam, saying

12 and all the people came to Roboam
17 of Juda, Roboam reigned over them
21 Roboam came to Jerusalem and gathered
21 to bring the kingdom again under Roboam
23 speak to Roboam the son of Solomon
27 will turn to their lord Roboam the
14 21 Roboam the son of Solomon reigned
21 Roboam was one and forty years old
25 in the fifth year of the reign of R.
27 and Roboam made shields of brass
29 now the rest of the acts of Roboam
30 was war between R. and Jeroboam. 15:6
31 R. slept with his fathers. 2 Pa 12:16
1 Pa 3 10 and Solomon's son was Roboam whose
2 Pa 10 3 they spoke to R., saying: Thy father
12 and all the people came to Roboam
17 Roboam reigned over children of Israel
11 1 Roboam came to Jerusalem and called
3 speak to Roboam the son of Solomon
5 Roboam dwelt in Jerusalem and built
17 established R. the son of Solomon
18 and Roboam took to wife Mahalath the
21 Roboam loved Maacha the daughter of
12 1 when the kingdom of R. was strengthened
2 in the fifth year of the reign of R.
5 Semeias the prophet came to Roboam
15 the acts of Roboam first and last
13 7 and they prevailed against Roboam
7 for Roboam was unexperienced and of
Eccu 47 28 even Roboam that had little wisdom
Mat 1 7 Solomon begot R. and R. begot Abia
king Roboam 3 K 12 6 king R. took counsel with
3 K 12 18 king Roboam sent Aduram. 2 Pa 10:18
18 k. R. made haste to get him. 2 Pa 10:18
2 Pa 12 13 king Roboam therefore was strengthened
rock Exod 17 6 before thee upon the rock Horeb
Exod 17 6 and thou shalt strike the rock and
33 21 and thou shalt stand upon the rock
22 I will set thee in a hole of the rock
Num 20 8 and speak to the rock before them and
8 hast brought forth water out of the r.
10 gathered multitude before the rock
10 bring you forth water out of this rock
11 struck the rock twice with the rod
24 21 though thou build thy nest in a rock
Deut 8 15 forth streams out of the hardest rock
32 13 that he might suck honey out of the r.
Judg 1 36 the ascent of the scorpion, the rock
6 20 lay them upon that rock, and pour out
21 and there arose a fire from the rock
26 build an altar . . . in top of this rock
7 25 Oreb they slew in the rock of Oreb
13 19 put them upon a rock, offering to the
15 8 he dwelt in a cavern of the rock Etam
11 went down to the cave of the rock Etam
13 brought him [Samson] from the rock Etam
20 45 towards the rock that is called Remmon
47 and they abode in the rock Remmon
21 13 that were in the rock Remmon and
1 K 14 5 one rock stood out towards the north
23 25 he [David] went down to the rock
28 called that place, the Rock of division
2 K 21 10 spread it under her upon the rock
22 2 the Lord is my rock and my strength
4 K 14 7 and took the rock by war and called
1 Pa 11 15 down to the rock wherein David was
2 Pa 25 12 brought to the steep of a certain rock
2 Es 9 15 water for them out of the rock in their
Job 14 18 and a rock is removed out of its place
29 6 the rock poured me out rivers of oil
Ps 26 6 he hath exalted me upon a rock. 60:3
39 3 and he set my feet upon a rock and
77 15 he struck the rock in the wilderness
16 he brought forth water out of the rock
20 he struck the rock, and the waters gushed
80 17 filled them with honey out of the rock
103 18 the rock [a refuge] for the irchins
104 41 he opened the rock, and waters flowed
113 8 who turned the r. into pools of water
136 9 dash thy little ones against the rock
140 6 their judges falling upon the rock
Prov 30 19 the way of a serpent upon a rock, the
26 which maketh its bed in the rock: the
Cant 2 14 my dove in the clefts of the rock
Wisd 11 4 was given them out of the high rock
Eccu 26 24 foundations upon a solid rock, so
40 15 as unclean roots upon the top of a rock
48 19 and he digged a rock with iron and
Isa 2 10 enter thou into the rock and hide thee
8 14 a rock of offence to the two houses
10 26 slaughter of Madian in the rock of Oreb
22 16 a dwelling for thyself in a rock
32 2 shadow of a rock that standeth out
48 21 he brought forth water out of the rock
21 he clove the rock, and the waters gushed
50 7 have I set my face as a most hard rock
51 1 look unto the rock whence you are hewn
Jer 5 3 made their faces harder than the rock
13 4 hide it there in a hole of the rock
18 14 fail from the rock of the field? Or can
21 13 that dwellest in a valley upon a rock
23 29 as a hammer that breaketh the rock
48 28 leave the cities and dwell in the rock
49 16 that dwellest in the clefts of the rock
Eze 24 7 she hath shed it upon the smooth rock
8 have shed her blood upon the smooth r.
26 4 her, and make her like a smooth rock
14 I will make thee like a naked rock
31 12 branches shall be broken on every rock
1 Ma 10 73 no stone nor rock nor place to flee to
2 Ma 14 46 standing upon a steep rock when he
7 24 man that built his house upon a rock
25 it was founded upon a rock. Luke 6:48
16 18 upon this rock I will build my church
27 60 which he had hewed out in a rock. And
Mark 15 46 which was hewed out of a rock. And he
Luke 6 48 and laid the foundation upon a rock
8 6 other some fell upon a rock: and as
13 they upon the rock, are they who when
Rom 9 33 I lay in Sion a . . . rock of scandal; and
1 C 10 4 they drank of the spiritual rock that
4 followed them, and the rock was Christ
2 8 of stumbling, and a rock of scandal
rocks Num 21 15 rocks of the torrents were bowed
Num 23 9 shall see him from the tops of the r.
1 K 13 6 in thickets and in rocks and in dens
14 4 rocks standing upon both sides and
24 3 even upon the most craggy rocks which
3 K 19 11 and breaking the rocks in pieces: the
Jdth 16 18 the rocks shall melt as wax before thy
Job 18 4 shall r. be removed out of their place
28 10 in the rocks he hath cut out rivers
39 1 wild goats bring forth among the rocks
28 she abideth among the r. and dwelleth
Ps 103 12 from midst of r. they shall give forth
Isa 2 19 they shall go into the holes of rocks
2 21 he shall go into the clefts of rocks
7 19 and in the holes of the rocks and
33 16 fortifications of rocks shall be his
57 5 in the torrents, under the high rocks
Jer 4 29 and have climbed up the rocks: all the
14 6 the wild asses stood upon the rocks
16 16 hill, and out of the holes of the rocks
51 25 and will roll thee down from the rocks
Bar 5 7 high mountain and the everlasting r.
Eze 6 3 hills and to the r. and the valleys

Amos 6 13 can horses run upon the rocks or can
Abdi 3 who dwellest in the clefts of the r.
Nah 1 6 and the rocks are melted by him. The
Mat 27 51 earth quaked, and the rocks were rent
Apoc 6 15 the dens and in the rocks of mountains
16 they say to the mountains and the rocks
rod Exod 4 2 in thy hand? He answered: A rod. And
Exod 4 4 hold of it, and it was turned into a rod
17 and take this rod in the hand wherewith
20 carrying the rod of God in his hand
7 9 take thy rod and cast it down before
10 Aaron took the rod before Pharao and
12 but Aaron's rod devoured their rods
15 thou shalt take in thy hand the rod
17 behold I will strike with the rod
19 take thy rod, and stretch forth thy
20 lifting up the rod he struck the water
8 16 stretch forth thy rod and strike the
17 forth his hand, holding the rod: and
9 23 Moses stretched forth his rod. 10:13
14 16 lift thou up thy rod and stretch forth
17 5 and take in thy hand the rod wherewith
9 having the rod of God in my hand. Josue
21 20 bondman or bondwoman with a rod, and
Lev 27 32 that pass under the shepherd's rod
Num 17 2 and take of every one of them a rod
2 the name of every man upon his rod
3 one rod shall contain all their families
5 his rod shall blossom and I will make
6 were twelve rods besides the rod of
8 the rod of Aaron for the house of Levi
10 carry back the rod of Aaron into the
20 8 take the rod and assemble the people
9 Moses therefore took the rod which
11 struck the rock twice with the rod
Judg 6 21 angel of Lord put forth tip of the rod
Ruth 2 17 beating out with a rod and threshing
1 K 14 27 and he put forth the end of the rod
43 a little honey with the end of the rod
2 K 7 14 I will correct him with the rod of men
23 21 but he went down to him with a rod and
Job 9 34 let him take his rod away from me, and
21 9 and the rod of God is not upon them
Ps 2 9 thou shalt rule them with a rod of iron
22 4 thy rod and thy staff, they have
88 33 will visit their iniquities with a rod
124 3 Lord will not leave the rod of sinners
Prov 10 13 rod on back of him that wanteth sense
13 24 he that spareth the rod hateth his son
14 3 in mouth of a fool is the rod of pride
22 8 with rod of his anger he shall be
15 rod of correction shall drive it away
23 13 for if thou strike him with the rod
14 thou shalt beat him with the rod, and
26 3 an ass, and a rod for the back of fools
29 15 the rod and reproof give wisdom but
Isa 9 4 the rod of their shoulder, and the
10 5 he is the rod and the staff of my anger
15 as if a rod should lift itself up
24 he shall strike thee with his rod
26 and his rod over the sea and he shall
11 1 there shall come forth a rod out of
4 the earth with the rod of his mouth
14 5 of the wicked, the rod of the rulers
29 rod of him that struck thee is broken
28 27 gith shall be beaten out with a rod
30 31 shall fear being struck with the rod
32 passage of the rod shall be strongly
Jer 1 11 and I said: I see a rod watching
10 16 Israel is the rod of his inheritance
48 17 strong staff broken, the beautiful rod
Lam 3 1 poverty by the rod of his indignation
Eze 7 10 rod hath blossomed, pride hath budded
11 is risen up into a rod of impiety
19 14 a fire is gone out from a rod of her
14 so that she now hath no strong rod
Mich 5 1 with a rod shall they strike the cheek
7 14 feed thy people with thy rod, the flock
Nah 1 13 now I will break in pieces his rod
Zach 11 10 I took my rod that was called Beauty
14 and I cut off my second rod that was
1 C 4 21 shall I come to you with a rod: or in
Heb 9 4 had manna, and the rod of Aaron, that
11 21 Joseph, and adorned the top of his rod
Apoc 2 27 rule them with a rod of iron. 19:15
11 1 was given me a reed like unto a rod
12 5 to rule all nations with an iron rod
rode Judg 10 4 having 30 sons who rode on 30 ass
2 K 18 9 the mule on which he rode passed on
22 11 he rode upon the cherubims, and flew
2 Es 2 12 with me but the beast that I rode upon
14 no place for the beast on which I rode
Eze 23 12 the horsemen that rode upon horses
rods Gen 30 37 Jacob took green rods of poplar
Gen 30 38 might have the rods before their eyes
39 the sheep beheld the rods and brought
40 put the rods in the troughs. 41
Exod 7 12 every one cast down their rods and they
12 but Aaron's rod devoured their rods
Num 17 2 the princes of the tribes, twelve rods
6 all the princes gave him rods, one for
6 twelve rods besides the rod of Aaron
9 Moses therefore brought out all the r.
9 that every one received their rods
Eze 19 11 she hath strong rods to make scepters
12 her strong rods are withered and dried
Zach 11 7 I took unto me two rods, one I called
Acts 16 22 commanded them to be beaten with rods
2 C 11 25 thrice was I beaten with rods, once I
roe Deut 12 15 such as may be offered, as the roe
Deut 12 22 even as the roe and the hart is eaten
14 5 the hart and the roe, the buffle, the
15 22 them alike, as the roe and as the hart
Cant 2 9 my beloved is like a roe or a young
17 be like, my beloved, to a roe or to a
8 14 my beloved, and be like to the roe
Eccu 11 32 as the roe [is brought] into the snare
27 22 as a roe escaped out of the snare
roebucks 1 Pa 12 8 they were swift like the r.
roes 2 K 2 18 swift runner, like one of the r.
3 K 4 23 venison of harts, roes, and buffles
Cant 2 7 by the roes and the harts of the. 3:5
4 5 breasts like two young roes. 7:3
Rogel Josu 15 7 the fountain Rogel. 18:16; 2 K 17:17; 3 K 1:9
Rogelim 2 K 17 27 Berzellai the Galaadite of R.
2 K 19 31 coming down from Rogelim, brought
Rogom 1 Pa 2 47 sons of Jahaddai, Rogom and
Rogommelech Zach 7 2 R. and the men that were
Rohob Num 13 22 the land from desert of Sin unto R.
Josu 19 28 and to Abran and Rohob and Hamon
30 and Amma and Aphec and Rohob, twenty
21 31 and Helcath and R. with their suburbs
Judg 1 31 and of Aphec and of Rohob: and he dwelt
18 28 the city was in the land of Rohob
2 K 8 3 Adarezer the son of Rohob. 12
10 6 sent and hired the Syrians of Rohob
8 the Syrians of Soba and of Rohob and
1 Pa 6 75 Rohob with its surburbs. And out of
2 Es 10 11 Micha, Rohob, Hasebia, Zachur
Rohobia 1 Pa 23 17 sons of Eliezer were: Rohobia
1 Pa 23 17 the sons of Rohobia were multiplied
24 21 of the sons of Rohobia the chief Jesias
26 25 Eliezer, whose son Rohobia and his
Rohoboth Gen 36 37 Saul of the river R. reigned
1 Pa 1 48 Rohoboth, which is near the river

roll Gen 29 3 to roll away the stone and after
Exod 29 23 and one roll of bread, a cake
Josu 10 18 roll great stones to the mouth of the
1 K 2 36 a piece of silver and a roll of bread
14 33 roll here to me now a great stone
Jer 36 2 take thee a roll of a book and thou
4 spoke to him, upon the roll of a book
51 25 will roll thee down from the rocks
Mark 16 3 who shall roll us back the stone from
rolled Judg 5 27 he [Sisara] r. before her feet
Judg 7 13 as if hearth cake of barley bread r.
2 Pa 21 19 day came after day and time rolled on
Jdth 13 10 and rolled away his headless body
Job 30 14 rolled themselves down to my miseries
Eccu 27 30 shall be rolled back upon the author
Isa 38 12 an end, and it is rolled away from me
Eze 2 9 wherein was a book rolled up: and he
Mat 27 60 he rolled a great stone to the door of
28 2 rolled back the stone, and sat upon it
Mark 9 19 the ground, he rolled about foaming
15 46 he rolled a stone to the door of the
16 4 they saw the stone rolled back. For
Luke 24 2 and they found the stone rolled back
rolleth Prov 26 27 he that r. a stone, it shall
rolling Eccu 33 5 thoughts are like a r. axletree
Roma Gen 22 24 concubine, named Roma, bore Tabee
Roman Acts 22 25 that is a R., and uncondemned
Acts 22 26 do? For this man is a Roman citizen. And
27 tell me, art thou a Roman? But he said
29 understood that he was a Roman citizen
23 27 an army, understanding that he is a R.
Romans Dan 11 30 and the R. shall come upon him
1 Ma 8 1 Judas heard of the fame of the Romans
23 good success be to the Romans and
24 if there come first any war upon the R.
26 it hath seemed good to the Romans. 28
27 the Romans shall help them with all
29 did the Romans covenant with the people
12 16 have sent them to the Romans to renew
14 40 R. had called the Jews their friends
15 16 Lucius the consul of the Romans, to
2 Ma 8 10 that was to be given to the Romans
36 promised to levy the tribute for the R.
11 34 the Romans also sent them a letter
34 ambassadors of the R., to the people
John 11 48 the Romans will come and take away
Acts 16 21 to receive nor observe, being Romans
37 men that are Romans, and have cast us
38 were afraid hearing that they were R.
25 16 it is not custom of R. to condemn any
28 17 into the hands of the Romans; who, when
Romathite 1 Pa 27 27 was Semeias a Romathite
Rome 1 Ma 1 11 who had been a hostage at Rome
1 Ma 7 1 departed from the city of Rome and
8 17 sent them to Rome to make a league
19 they went to Rome, a very long journey
12 1 chose certain men and sent them to Rome
3 they went to Rome and entered into the
14 16 it was heard at Rome, and as far as
24 Simon sent Numenius to Rome with a
24 when the people of Rome had heard these
15 15 from the city of Rome, having letters
2 Ma 4 11 Eupolemus who went ambassador to Rome
Acts 2 10 about Cyrene, and strangers of Rome
18 2 commanded all Jews to depart from R.
19 21 I have been there, I must see Rome also
23 11 so must thou bear witness also at Rome
28 14 seven days: and so we went to Rome. And
16 when we were come to Rome, Paul was
Rom 1 7 to all that are at Rome, the beloved
15 the gospel to you also that are at Rome
2 Tim 1 17 when he was come to Rome, he carefully
Romelia 4 K 15 25 Phacee the son of Romelia. 27, 30, 32, 37; 16:1, 5; 2 Pa 28:6; Isa 7:1
Isa 7 4 king of Syria, and of the son of R.
5 the evil of Ephraim and the son of R.
9 the head of Samaria the son of Romelia
8 6 taken Rasin, and the son of Romelia
Romenthiezer 1 Pa 25 4 and R. and Jesbacassa
1 Pa 25 30 four and twentieth to R., to his
roof Gen 19 8 in under the shadow of my roof
Exod 26 9 sixth curtain in the front of the roof
12 curtains that are prepared for the roof
14 make also another cover to the roof
35 11 the tabernacle and the roof thereof
36 14 to cover the roof of the tabernacle
18 wherewith the r. might be knit together
39 31 roof of the testimony was finished
32 offered the tabernacle and the roof
40 the roof of the covenant. Num 4:25
40 17 spread the roof over the tabernacle
24 of gold under the roof of the testimony
Deut 22 8 shalt make a battlement to the roof
Judg 16 27 from roof and higher part of the house
19 18 none will receive us under his roof
2 K 11 2 walked upon roof of the king's house
2 he saw from the roof of his house
Prov 19 13 like a r. continually dropping through
Eccu 29 28 poor man's fare under a roof of boards
Lam 4 4 hath stuck to the roof of his mouth
Eze 3 26 tongue stick fast to roof of thy mouth
40 13 from the roof of one little chamber to the roof of another
Mat 8 8 shouldst enter under my r. Luke 7:6
Mark 2 4 they uncovered the roof where he was
Luke 5 19 they went up upon the roof, and let
roofs Prov 27 15 r. dropping through in a cold day
Jer 19 13 upon whose roofs they have sacrificed
22 14 and maketh roofs of cedar and painteth
32 29 houses upon whose roofs they offered
3 K 6 9 covered the house with roofs of cedar
15 the top of the walls and to the roofs
room Gen 26 22 now hath the Lord given us room
Josu 17 15 and cut down room for thyself in the
18 and make thyself room to dwell in
Judg 5 28 and she spoke from the dining room
3 K 2 35 in his room over the army, and Sadoc
5 1 anointed him king in room of his father
6 8 they went up to the middle room and
8 20 I stand in the room of David my father
19 16 shalt anoint to be prophet in thy room
4 K 23 34 king in the room of Josias his father
2 Pa 26 1 made him king in the room of Amasias
Prov 18 16 and maketh him room before princes
Isa 49 20 strait for me, make me room to dwell in
2 Ma 14 44 they quickly making room for his fall
Mat 2 22 in the room of Herod his father, he
Mark 2 2 was no room; no, not even at the door
14 15 show you a large dining r. Luke 22:12
Luke 2 7 there was no room for them in the inn
12 17 I have no room to bestow my fruits
14 22 commanded, and yet there is room
Acts 1 13 they went up into an upper room, where
12 7 a light shined in the room: and he
rooms Gen 6 14 thou shalt make little rooms in
Ps 103 3 coverest higher r. thereof with water
13 waterest the hills from thy upper r.
Amos 3 9 that suffer oppression in the inner r.
6 10 that is in the inner r. of the house
Luke 20 46 and the chief rooms at feasts: who
root Deut 29 18 among you a r. bringing forth gall
3 K 14 14 he shall root up Israel out of this
4 K 19 30 shall take root downward, and bear
2 Pa 7 20 I will pluck you up by the root out
Job 5 3 I have seen a fool with a strong root
15 29 neither shall he push his r. in the

29 19 my root is opened beside the waters
30 4 the root of junipers was their food
Ps 51 7 thy root out of the land of the living
Prov 12 3 root of the just shall not be moved
12 the root of the just shall prosper
Wisd 3 15 the root of wisdom never faileth
4 3 bastard slips shall not take deep root
15 3 thy power is the root of immortality
Eccu 1 6 to whom hath the root of wisdom been
25 the root of wisdom is to fear the Lord
3 30 plant of wickedness shall take root
23 35 her children shall not take root
24 13 in Israel, and take root in my elect
16 I took root in an honorable people
Isa 5 24 so shall their root be as ashes and
11 1 forth a rod out of the root of Jesse
1 flower shall rise up out of his root
10 the root of Jesse, who standeth for
14 29 out of the root of the serpent shall
30 will make thy root perish with famine
37 31 shall take root downward, and shall
53 2 as a root out of a thirsty ground
Jer 1 10 to root up and to pull down and to
12 2 planted them, and they have taken root
18 7 to root out and to pull down and to
Eze 16 3 thy root and thy nativity is of the
17 5 that it might take a firm root over
9 many people to pluck it up by the r.
31 7 for his root was near great waters
Osee 9 16 their root is dried up, they shall yield
14 6 his root shall shoot forth as that of
Mala 4 1 it shall not leave them root nor branch
1 Ma 1 11 there came out of them a wicked root
2 40 they will now quickly root us out
3 35 and root out the strength of Israel
2 Ma 8 9 to root out the whole race of the
12 7 again and root out all the Joppites
Mat 3 10 axe is laid to the root. Luke 3:9
13 6 they had not root, they withered away
21 yet hath he not root in himself, but
29 you root up the wheat also together
Mark 4 6 because it had no root, it withered
17 they have no root in themselves, but
Rom 11 16 if the root be holy, so are the branches
17 and art made partaker of the root, and
18 bearest not the root, but the root thee
15 12 there shall be a root of Jesse; and he
1 Tim 6 10 desire of money is the root of all evils
Heb 12 15 lest any root of bitterness springing
Apoc 5 5 of the tribe of Juda, the root of David
22 16 I am the root and stock of David, the
rooted 1 K 20 15 shall have r. out the enemies
1 K 28 9 how he hath rooted out the magicians
Job 18 14 let his confidence be rooted out of
31 8 and let my offspring be rooted out
Prov 15 5 devices of the wicked shall be r. out
Wisd 3 16 of the unlawful bed shall be r. out
4 4 force of winds they shall be rooted out
Eccu 21 5 of the proud shall be rooted out
Isa 40 24 nor sown nor rooted in the earth
Soph 2 4 noonday, and Accaron shall be r. up
Mat 15 13 hath not planted, shall be rooted up
Luke 17 6 be thou rooted up, and be thou
Eph 3 17 being rooted and founded in charity, you
Col 2 7 him; rooted and built up in him, and
rooteth Job 31 12 r. up all things that spring
Eccu 3 11 mother's curse r. up the foundation
rooting 2 Pa 22 8 when Jehu was r. out the house
roots Num 22 4 wont to eat the grass to the very r.
Job 8 17 his roots shall be thick upon a heap
14 8 if its roots be old in the earth
18 16 let his roots be dried up beneath
28 9 overturned mountains from the roots
Ps 79 10 thou plantedst the roots thereof
Wisd 7 20 and the virtues of roots and all such
Eccu 10 18 made the r. of proud nations to wither
40 15 unclean roots upon the top of a rock
47 24 neither will he cut up by the roots
Jer 17 8 spreadeth out its r. towards moisture
Eze 17 6 the roots thereof were under him
7 bending as it were her r. towards him
9 shall he not pull up the roots thereof
31 4 streams thereof ran round about his r.
Dan 4 12 leave the stump of its roots in the
20 leave the stump of the roots thereof
23 that the stump of the roots thereof
11 7 and a plant of the bud of her roots
Amos 2 9 fruit from above, and his roots beneath
Mark 11 20 the fig tree dried up from the roots
Luke 8 13 these have no roots; for they believe
Jude 12 twice dead, plucked up by the roots
rope Isa 5 18 and sin as the rope of a cart. That
ropes Judg 16 11 if I shall be bound with new r.
2 K 17 13 all Israel shall cast ropes round
3 K 20 31 on our loins, and ropes on our heads
32 and put ropes on their heads and came
Jdth 6 9 left him [Achior] bound with ropes
Prov 5 22 bound with the ropes of his own sins
Jer 38 6 and they let down Jeremias by ropes
Acts 27 32 soldiers cut off the ropes of the boat
2 P 2 4 drawn down by infernal ropes to the
Ros Gen 46 21 Ros and Mophim and Ophim and Ared
rose Gen 2 6 a spring rose out of the earth
Gen 32 31 immediatey the sun rose upon him
Num 13 31 murmuring of the people that rose
22 13 and he [Balaam] rose in the morning
24 25 Balaam rose and returned to his place
26 9 that rose against Moses and Aaron
Josu 3 1 Josue rose before daylight and removed
7 16 when he [Josue] rose in the morning
1 K 1 19 they rose in the morning and worshipped
5 4 when they rose in the morning, they
15 12 when Samuel rose early, to go to Saul
20 34 Jonathan rose from the table in great
41 David rose out of his place which was
25 1 David rose and went down into the
3 K 3 21 when I rose in the morning to give my
8 54 he rose from before the altar of the
4 K 3 22 rose early in the morning. 2 Pa 20:20
2 Pa 21 9 rose in the night and defeated the
26 19 there rose a leprosy in his forehead
Jdth 10 1 that she rose from the place wherein
Ps 118 62 I rose at midnight to give praise to
Eccu 24 18 and as a rose plant in Jericho, as a
39 17 bud forth as the rose planted by the
Soph 3 7 they rose early and corrupted all
1 Ma 6 33 the king rose before it was light
11 69 in ambush rose out of their places
John 10 19 dissension rose again among the Jews
Rom 4 25 and rose again for our justification
14 9 for to this end Christ died and rose
1 C 15 4 and that he rose again the third day
2 C 5 15 him who died for them, and rose again
1 Th 4 13 if we believe that Jesus died and rose
James 1 11 the sun rose with a burning heat
rose up Gen 4 8 Cain r. up against his brother
Gen 18 16 when the men rose up from thence, they
19 1 he rose up and went to meet them: and
33 daughter lay down nor when she r. up. 35
21 14 Abraham rose up in the morning and
23 3 after he rose up from the funeral
7 Abraham rose up and bowed down to the
46 5 Jacob rose up from the well of the oath
Exod 15 14 nations rose up and were angry: sorrows
24 13 Moses rose up, and his minister Josue
32 6 and drink and they rose up to play

33 8 all the people rose up and every one
Num 16 2 rose up against Moses, and with them
25 7 he [Phinees] rose up from the midst
Deut 33 2 and from Seir he rose up to us: he
Josu 8 19 the ambush that lay hid, rose up
21 that the smoke of the city rose up
Judg 3 20 he forthwith rose up from his throne
8 21 Gedeon rose up and slew Zebee and
9 35 Abimelech rose up and all his army
13 11 he rose up and followed his wife
1 K 16 13 Samuel rose up and went to Ramatha
17 35 they rose up against me and I caught
18 27 David rose up and went with the men
24 9 and David also rose up after him
28 25 they rose up and walked all that night
2 K 13 31 the king rose up and rent his garments
1 Pa 21 1 and Satan rose up against Israel
2 Pa 13 6 rose up: and rebelled against his lord
20 23 rose up against the inhabitants of
21 4 Joram rose up over the kingdom of his
22 10 rose up and killed all the royal family
24 25 and his servants rose up against him
28 15 rose up and took the captives and
30 27 Levites rose up and blessed the people
1 Es 3 2 Josue the son of Josedec rose up, and
5 2 rose up Zorobabel the son of Salathiel
9 5 I rose up from my affliction and
10 6 Esdras rose up from before the house
2 Es 4 14 I looked and rose up: and I said to the
9 3 they rose up to stand: and they read
Job 1 20 then Job rose up and rent his garments
29 8 and the old men rose up and stood. The
Ps 17 40 under me them that rose up against me
123 2 when men rose up against us, perhaps
138 18 I rose up and am still with thee. If
Prov 31 28 her children rose up and called her
Eccu 40 7 in the time of his safety he rose up
46 2 overthrow the enemies that rose up
Jer 26 17 of the ancients of the land rose up
Eze 3 23 I rose up and went forth into the
35 13 you rose up against me with your
Dan 3 91 rose up in haste and said to his nobles
13 61 they rose up against the two elders
Jon 1 3 Jonas rose up to flee into Tharsis
3 6 he rose up out of his throne and cast
1 Ma 3 1 called Machabeus, rose up in his stead
4 3 Judas heard of it and rose up, he and
6 4 they rose up against him in battle and
9 23 all the workers of iniquity rose up
31 and rose up in the place of Judas his
40 and they rose up against them from
12 40 so he rose up and came to Bethsan. And
16 16 Ptolemee and his men rose up and took
Mark 5 42 the damsel rose up and walked: and she
Luke 4 16 sabbath day; and he rose up to read
29 they rose up and thrust him out of the
5 28 leaving all things, he rose up and
22 45 when he rose up from prayer and was
John 11 31 when they saw Mary that she rose up
Acts 5 36 for before these days rose up Theodas
37 rose up Judas of Galilee in the days
14 19 he rose up and entered into the city
18 12 with one accord rose up against Paul
26 30 the king rose up, and the governor, and
1 C 10 7 to eat and drink, and rose up to play
roses Wisd 2 8 let us crown ourselves with roses
Eccu 50 8 as the flower of roses in the days
rosin Eze 27 17 and oil and rosin in thy fairs
rot Num 5 21 may he make thy thigh to rot and
Num 5 22 may thy womb swell and thy thigh rot
27 belly swelling, her thigh shall rot
Prov 10 7 and the name of the wicked shall rot
Isa 40 20 strong wood and that will not rot: the
50 2 the fishes shall rot for want of water
rotted Joel 1 17 beasts have rotted in their dung
rotten Job 41 18 as straw, and brass and r. wood
Prov 25 19 is like a rotten tooth and weary foot
Isa 14 19 bottom of the pit, as a rotten carcass
Jer 13 7 and behold the girdle was rotten
22 19 r. and cast forth without the gates
38 11 thence old rags and old rotten things
12 these rent and rotten things under
rottenness Job 7 5 my flesh is clothed with r.
Job 13 28 who am to be consumed as rottenness
17 14 I have said to rottenness: Thou art my
25 6 how much less man that is rottenness
Prov 12 4 confusion is a rottenness in his bones
14 30 envy is the rottenness of the bones
Eccu 19 3 rottenness and worms shall inherit him
Osee 5 12 like rottenness to the house of Juda
Joel 2 20 and his r. shall go up because he
Haba 3 16 let rottenness enter into my bones
rough Deut 21 4 her into a rough and stony valley
Wisd 12 9 with one rough word to destroy them
Eccu 40 4 that is covered with rough linen
Isa 40 4 straight, and the rough ways plain
Bar 4 26 delicate ones have walked rough ways
2 Ma 14 30 behaved himself in a rough manner
30 that this rough behavior came not of
Luke 3 5 straight; and the rough ways plain
Acts 27 29 lest we should fall upon rough places
roughly Gen 42 7 somewhat r., asking them: Whence
Gen 42 30 lord of the land spoke roughly to us
3 K 12 13 the king answered the people roughly
2 Pa 10 13 and the king answered roughly leaving
16 the people upon the king's speaking r.
round 3 K 7 12 greater court was made r. with
3 K 7 31 between the pillars were square, not r.
35 a round compass of half a cubit
10 19 the top of the throne was round behind
2 Pa 4 2 from brim to brim, round in compass
Ecce 1 6 maketh his round by the south and
Cant 7 2 thy navel is like a round bowl never
Isa 44 13 fashioned it round with the compass
Jer 9 26 all that have their hair polled round
25 23 that have their hair cut round. 49:32
Luke 19 43 and compass thee round and straiten
roundwise Lev 19 27 shall you cut your hair r.
rouse Gen 49 9 and as a lioness, who shall r. him
Num 24 9 lioness whom none shall dare to rouse
Isa 7 6 let us go up to Juda and rouse it up
Joel 3 9 prepare war, rouse up the strong
roused Jer 4 7 robber of nations hath r. himself
rout Mat 9 23 and the multitude making a rout
routed 1 Ma 4 14 the Gentiles were r., and fled
1 Ma 8 6 very great army, was routed by them
rovers 4 K 13 20 r. from Moab came into the land
4 K 13 21 saw the rovers, and cast the body
24 2 against him the r. of the Chaldees and the r. of Syria and the r. of Moab and the r. of the children of Ammon
1 Pa 12 21 these helped David against the rovers
2 Pa 22 1 the rovers of the Arabians, who had
row Exod 28 17 in the first row shall be a sardius
Exod 39 10 in the first row was a sardius, a topaz
3 K 6 36 stones, and one row of beams of cedar
7 3 and one row had fifteen pillars set
12 stones, and one row of planks of cedar
rowed Jon 1 13 the men rowed hard to return to
John 6 19 when they had rowed therefore about
rowers Eze 27 8 the Arabians were thy rowers
Eze 27 26 thy rowers have brought thee into great
rowing Mark 6 48 seeing them laboring in rowing
rows Exod 28 17 set in it four rows of stones
Exod 28 20 they shall be set in gold by their rows
39 10 he set four rows of precious stones

13 set and enclosed in gold by their rows
3 K 6 36 with three rows of polished stones
7 12 round with three rows of hewed stones
17 seven rows of nets were on one chapiter
18 two rows round about each network
20 of pomegranates there were 200 in rows
24 two rows cast of chamfered sculptures
42 two rows of pomegranates for each
2 Pa 4 3 of the sea, as it were with two rows
13 two rows of pomegranates were joined
1 Es 6 4 three rows of unpolished stones and so rows of new timber: and the
Wisd 18 24 and in the four rows of the stones
Eze 46 23 there were kitchens built under the **r.**
Dan 7 5 there were three rows in the mouth
royal Josu 10 2 great city and one of the r. cities
1 K 27 5 thy servant dwell in the royal city
2 K 12 26 and laid close siege to the royal city
3 K 10 13 offered her of himself of his r. bounty
22 10 on his throne clothed with royal robes
4 K 11 1 arose and slew all the royal seed
25 25 the son of Elisama of the seed royal
2 Pa 15 16 he deposed from the royal authority
18 9 on their thrones, clothed in r. robes
22 10 arose and killed all the royal family
23 20 and set him [Joas] on the royal throne
26 23 him in the field of the r. sepulchers
Wisd 18 15 from heaven from thy royal throne
Isa 62 3 a royal diadem in the hand of thy God
Jer 41 1 the son of Elisama of the royal blood
1 Ma 3 32 Lysias, a nobleman of the blood royal
10 89 given to such as are of the royal blood
James 2 8 if then you fulfil the royal law
rub Deut 23 25 the ears and rub them in thy hand
rubbing Luke 6 1 rubbing them in their hands
rubbish 2 Es 4 2 out of the heaps of the rubbish
2 Es 4 10 and the rubbish is very much and we
Ruben Gen 29 32 called his name Ruben, saying
Gen 30 14 Ruben, going out in the time of the
35 22 Ruben went and slept with Bala the
23 the sons of Lia: Ruben the firstborn
37 21 R. hearing this, endeavored to deliver
29 Ruben, returning to the pit, found not
42 22 Ruben, one of them, said: Did not I
37 Ruben answered him: Kill my two sons
46 8 and his children. His firstborn Ruben
48 5 shall be reputed to me as R. and Simeon
49 3 R., my firstborn, thou art my strength
Exod 1 2 Ruben, Simeon, Levi, Juda. 1 Pa 2:1
6 15 these are the kindreds of Ruben. The
Num 1 5 of Ruben, Elisur the son of Sedeur
20 of Ruben the eldest son of Israel
2 16 were reckoned in the camp of Ruben
13 5 of the tribe of Ruben, Sammua the son
26 5 them: Ruben the firstborn of Israel
7 the families of the stock of Ruben
32 25 children of Gad and Ruben said to Moses
33 gave to the children of Gad and of R.
Deut 3 12 I gave the cities thereof to Ruben and
16 to the tribes of Ruben and Gad I gave
4 43 in the plains of the tribe of Ruben
11 6 sons of Eliab who was the son of Ruben
27 13 Ruben, Gad, and Aser, and Zabulon
29 8 delivered it for a possession to Ruben
33 6 let Ruben live, and not die and be he
Josu 13 8 with whom Ruben and Gad have possessed
15 6 to the stone of Boen the son of Ruben
18 7 Ruben and the half tribe of Manasses
18 the stone of Boen the son of Ruben
20 8 the wilderness of the tribe of Ruben
21 7 of the tribes of Ruben and of Gad
36 of the tribe of Ruben beyond the Jordan
Judg 5 15 Ruben being divided against himself. 16
4 K 10 33 the land of Galaad and Gad and Ruben
1 Pa 5 6 he was prince in the tribe of Ruben
26 and he carried away Ruben and Gad
6 63 families out of the tribe of Ruben
78 out of the tribe of Ruben, Bosor in
Jdth 8 1 the son of Simeon the son of Ruben
Eze 48 6 side of the sea, one portion for Ruben
7 and by the border of Ruben from the
31 the north side, the gate of Ruben one
Apoc 7 5 of the tribe of Ruben, 12,000 signed
children of Ruben Num 16 1 of Pheleth of c. . . .
Num 32 25 children of Gad and R. said to Moses
29 c. . . . pass with you over the Jordan
31 and the c. . . . answered: As the Lord hath
37 the c. . . . built Hesebon and Eleale
34 14 tribe of the c. . . . by their families
Josu 4 12 the children of Ruben . . . went armed
13 15 Moses gave a possession to the c. . . .
23 Jordan was the border of the c. . . .
22 9 c. . . . and the children of Gad. 34
11 the c. . . . and of Gad. 15, 21
25 border between us and you, O ye c. . . .
30 the children of Ruben and Gad. 32
sons of Ruben Gen 46 9 the s. . . . Henoch and
Exod 6 14 s. . . . firstborn of Israel. 1 Pa 5:1, 3
Num 2 10 in the camp of the s. . . . on the south
7 30 the prince of the s. . . . , Elisur the
10 18 the s. . . . also marched by their
32 1 s. . . . and Gad had many flocks of
1 Pa 5 18 the sons of Ruben and of Gad. 12:37
Rubenite 1 Pa 11 42 Adina the son of Siza a R.
Rubenites Josu 1 12 he said to the Rubenites
Josu 12 6 their land in possession to the R.
13 23 this is the possession of the Rubenites
22 1 same time Josue called the Rubenites
1 Pa 11 42 Adina . . . the prince of the Rubenites
26 32 made them rulers over the Rubenites
27 16 over the Rubenites, Eliezer the son of
rudder Acts 27 40 loosing withal the r. bands
ruddy 1 K 16 12 was r. and beautiful to behold
1 K 17 42 [David] was a young man, ruddy, and
Cant 5 10 my beloved is white and ruddy, chosen
Lam 4 7 more ruddy than the old ivory, fairer
rude 2 C 11 6 although I be rude in speech, yet
rue Luke 11 42 you tithe mint and rue and every
Rufus Mark 15 21 the father of Alexander and of R.
Rom 16 13 salute Rufus, elect in the Lord, and
rugged Eccu 32 25 trust not thyself to a r. way
ruin Exod 34 12 of that land, which may be thy r.
Deut 7 16 their gods, lest they be thy ruin
Judg 2 3 and their gods may be your ruin. And
8 27 it became a ruin to Gedeon and to all
2 K 15 14 overtake us and bring ruin upon us
4 K 19 25 should be turned to heaps of ruin
2 Pa 28 23 they were the ruin of him and of all
Jdth 13 25 but hast prevented our ruin in the
Esth 14 11 that are not, lest they laugh at our ruin
Ps 51 6 thou hast loved all the words of ruin
Prov 13 14 decline from the ruin of death. 14:27
17 5 that rejoiceth at another man's ruin
19 that exalteth his door, seeketh ruin
18 7 his lips are the ruin of his soul
20 25 is ruin to a man to devour holy ones
24 17 in his ruin let not thy heart rejoice
22 who knoweth the ruin of both? These
26 28 and a slippery mouth worketh ruin
29 8 corrupt men bring a city to ruin: but
Eccu 1 28 wrath of his high spirits is his ruin
5 15 the tongue of the fool is his ruin
9 16 knowest not what his ruin shall be
10 3 unwise king shall be ruin of his people
15 and it shall ruin him in the end
13 16 thou walkest in danger of thy ruin

31 6 the beauty thereof hath been their ruin
32 25 go not in the way of ruin, and thou
Isa 3 6 and let this ruin be under thy hand
8 14 a ruin to the inhabitants of Jerusalem
23 13 thereof, they have brought it to ruin
25 2 to a heap, the strong city to ruin
26 19 of giants thou shalt pull down into r.
Bar 4 31 they that have rejoiced at thy ruin
33 as she rejoiced at thy ruin and was
Eze 18 30 and iniquity shall not be your ruin
27 27 heart of the sea in the day of thy ruin
32 10 his own life, in the day of their ruin
Osee 9 8 the prophet is become a snare of ruin
Abdi 13 of my people in the day of their ruin
Soph 1 3 and the ungodly shall meet with ruin
1 Ma 2 7 I born to see the ruin of my people and the ruin of the holy city
Luke 6 49 and the ruin of that house was great
ruined Prov 28 12 when the wicked reign, men are r.
Isa 3 8 Jerusalem is ruined, and Juda is fallen
ruinous Isa 17 1 shall be as a r. heap of stones
Eze 33 24 that dwell in these ruinous places
27 they that dwell in the ruinous places
36 4 to desolate places and ruinous walls
10 the ruinous places shall be repaired
33 and shall repair the ruinous places
ruins Lev 26 30 you shall fall among r. of your
Ps 109 6 he shall fill ruins: he shall crush the
Eccu 31 38 quarrels and wrath and many ruins
Isa 51 3 and will comfort all the ruins thereof
61 4 shall raise up ancient ruins and shall
64 11 our lovely things are turned into ruins
Eze 21 15 in heart, and that multiplieth ruins
31 13 fowls of the air dwelt upon his ruins
Acts 15 16 and the ruins thereof I will rebuild
rule Gen 1 16 a greater light to rule the day
Gen 1 16 and a lesser light to rule the night
18 to rule the day and the night and to
28 and rule over the fishes of the sea
Num 16 13 except thou rule also like a lord over
24 19 of Jacob shall he come that shall rule
Josu 7 21 of silver, and a golden rule of 50 sicles
24 and the garments and the golden rule
Judg 8 22 said to Gedeon: Rule thou over us
23 I will not rule over you, neither shall my son rule over you, but the Lord shall rule over you
9 2 that 70 men . . . should rule over you
2 or that one man should rule over you
15 11 that the Philistines rule over us
3 K 6 35 golden plates in square work by rule
7 9 sawed by a certain rule and measure
1 Pa 22 12 that thou mayest be able to rule Israel
Ps 2 9 thou shalt rule them with a rod of iron
9 5 he shall rule over all his enemies
27 9 and rule them and exalt them forever
47 15 and ever: he shall rule us for evermore
58 14 shall know that God will rule Jacob
71 8 and he shall rule from sea to sea
102 19 and his kingdom shall rule over all
109 2 rule thou in the midst of thy enemies
135 8 the sun to rule the day: for his mercy
9 moon and the stars to rule the night
Prov 8 16 by me princes rule, and the mighty
12 24 hand of the valiant shall bear rule
17 2 servant shall rule over foolish sons
19 10 for servant to have rule over princes
29 2 when the wicked shall bear rule, the
Wisd 3 8 shall judge nations and r. over people
6 3 give ear, you that rule the people and
6 shall be for them that bear rule. For
23 all ye that bear rule over peoples
13 2 to be the gods that rule the world
Eccu 24 9 in every nation I have had chief rule
44 3 as have borne rule in their dominions
47 23 of Ephraim a rebellious kingdom to rule
Isa 3 4 the effeminate shall rule over them
11 14 shall be under the rule of their hand
19 4 a strong king shall rule over them
28 14 scornful men, who rule over my people
32 1 and princes shall rule in judgment
40 10 with strength, and his arm shall rule
41 2 sight, and he shall rule over kings
44 13 carpenter hath stretched out his rule
52 5 they that rule over them treat them
54 5 that made thee shall rule over thee
63 19 when thou didst not rule over us and
Jer 30 8 strangers shall no more rule over him
Bar 3 16 they that rule over the beasts and
Eze 19 11 make scepters for them that bear rule
29 15 shall rule no more over the nations
34 27 the hand of those that rule over them
Dan 2 39 which shall rule over all the world
11 3 shall rule with great power. 5
Joel 2 17 that the heathen should rule over them
Zach 6 13 shall sit and rule upon his throne
1 Ma 6 37 above: and an Indian to rule the beast
8 16 year, to rule over all their country
2 Ma 4 10 he had gotten the rule into his hands
Mat 2 6 the captain that shall rule my people
Mark 10 42 you know that they who seem to rule
Acts 20 28 bishops, to rule church of God, which
Rom 12 6 to be used according to rule of faith
15 12 he that shall rise up to rule Gentiles
2 C 10 13 according to the measure of the rule
15 magnified in you according to our rule
16 not to glory in another man's rule, in
Gal 6 16 and whosoever shall follow this rule
Phil 3 16 let us also continue in the same rule
1 Tim 3 5 know not how to rule his own house
12 who rule well their children, and their
5 17 the priests that rule well, be esteemed
Apoc 2 27 rule them with a rod of iron. 19:15
7 17 shall rule them and shall lead them to
12 5 who was to rule all nations with an
ruled Gen 36 30 that ruled in the land of Seir
Gen 36 31 kings that ruled in the land of Edom
Ruth 1 1 when the judges ruled, there came a
2 K 3 6 the son of Ner ruled the house of Saul
Prov 13 10 with counsel, are ruled by wisdom
Isa 3 12 and women have ruled over them. O my
Lam 5 8 servants have ruled over us: there was
Eze 34 4 but you ruled over them with rigor
Dan 5 21 he knew that the most High ruled in
11 4 to his power with which he ruled. For
1 Ma 7 8 that ruled beyond the great river in
ruler Gen 24 2 who was ruler over all he had
Gen 41 33 make him ruler over the land of Egypt
45 26 he is ruler in all the land of Egypt
49 10 nor a ruler from his thigh, till he come
Num 14 12 thee I will make a ruler over a great
Judg 9 28 made Zebul his servant ruler over the
30 Zebul the ruler of the city, hearing
10 1 there arose a ruler in Israel, Thola
1 K 9 16 thou shalt anoint him to be ruler over
2 K 6 21 commanded me to be r. over the people
7 8 to be ruler over my people Israel
23 3 the ruler of men, the just ruler in
3 K 1 35 will appoint him to be r. over Israel
1 Pa 11 2 and thou shalt be ruler over them
15 27 Chonenias the ruler of the prophecy
17 7 be r. of my people Israel. 2 Pa 6:5
27 16 Eliezer the son of Zechri was ruler
2 Pa 7 18 of thy stock to be ruler in Israel
11 22 the chief ruler over all his brethren
19 11 who is ruler in the house of Juda
2 Es 7 2 Hananias r. of the house of Jerusalem

11 9 Joel the son of Zechri their ruler
14 their ruler Zabdiel son of the mighty
Esth 15 5 called upon God the ruler and Savior
Ps 104 20 released him: the ruler of the people
21 house, and ruler of all his possession
Eccu 10 2 what manner of man the ruler of a city
4 will raise up a profitable ruler over
17 14 over every nation he set a ruler. And
23 1 father, and sovereign ruler of my life
32 1 they made thee ruler? Be not lifted
37 21 tongue is continually the ruler of them
49 17 the ruler of his brethren, the stay of
Jer 40 11 the son of Saphan ruler over them
51 46 iniquity in the land, and r. upon r.
Mich 5 2 unto me that is to be the r. in Israel
Haba 1 14 as the creeping things that have no r.
1 Ma 2 17 said to Mathathias: Thou art a ruler
55 Jesus . . . was made ruler in Israel
11 57 I appoint thee r. over the four cities
2 Ma 9 19 Antiochus king and ruler wisheth much
13 3 that he should be appointed chief ruler
Isa 3 6 thou hast a garment, be thou our ruler
7 make me not ruler of the people. For
16 1 the lamb, the ruler of the earth, from
Jer 29 26 shouldst be ruler in house of the Lord
Mat 9 18 a certain ruler came up and adored him
23 was come into the house of the ruler
Mark 5 35 from the r. of the synagogue's house
36 saith to the ruler of the synagogue
38 house of the ruler of the synagogue
Luke 8 41 and he was a ruler of the synagogue
49 cometh one to the r. of the synagogue
13 14 ruler of the synagogue, being angry
18 18 a certain ruler asked him, saying
John 3 1 Nicodemus, a ruler of the Jews. This
4 46 certain ruler whose son was sick at
49 the ruler saith to him: Lord, come
Acts 18 8 Crispus, the ruler of the synagogue
17 Sosthenes, the ruler of the synagogue
Jude 4 denying the only sovereign Ruler, and
rulers Gen 47 6 make them rulers over my cattle
Exod 16 22 r. of the multitude came and told Moses
18 21 appoint of them rulers of thousands
25 he appointed them rulers of the people, rulers over thousands
34 31 Aaron and the r. of the congregation
Num 7 2 rulers of them who had been numbered
13 3 one of every tribe, of the rulers
Deut 1 13 that I may appoint them your rulers
15 and appointed them rulers, tribunes
4 K 10 5 rulers of the city and the ancients
1 Pa 21 2 said to Joab and to r. of the people
26 32 king David made them rulers over the
27 31 rulers of the substance of king David
2 Pa 1 2 rulers and to the judges of all Israel
8 9 rulers of his chariots and horsemen
29 20 assembled all the rulers of the city
35 8 rulers of the house of the Lord, gave
1 Es 10 14 let rulers be appointed in all the
2 Es 4 16 mail, and the rulers were behind them
12 43 rulers of the city might bring them
Esth 1 22 that the husbands should be rulers
8 9 who were rulers over the 127 provinces
Job 29 10 the rulers held their peace, and their
34 18 apostate: who calleth rulers ungodly
Eccu 10 3 inhabited through prudence of the r.
33 19 with your ears, ye rulers of the church
Isa 1 10 word of the Lord, ye rulers of Sodom
13 2 and let the rulers go into the gates
32 8 and he shall stand above the rulers
49 7 is abhorred, to the servant of rulers
Jer 33 26 to be rulers of the seed of Abraham
50 21 go up against the land of the rulers
51 23 I will break in pieces captains and r.
28 their captains and all their rulers and
57 her captains and her rulers and her
Eze 19 14 no strong rod, to be a scepter of r.
23 6 princes and rulers, beautiful youths
12 the princes and rulers that came to her
23 all the captains and r., the princes
Dan 3 2 the judges, the captains, the rulers. 3
1 Ma 1 53 he appointed rulers over the people
14 42 should appoint rulers over their works
2 Ma 10 21 he assembled the rulers of the people
Mark 5 22 cometh one of the r. of the synagogue
Luke 19 47 r. of the people sought to destroy
23 35 the rulers with them derided him
John 7 26 have the r. known for a truth that this
32 the rulers and Pharisees sent ministers
48 hath any one of the rulers believed
Acts 3 17 through ignorance, as did also your r.
13 15 rulers of the synagogue sent to them
27 and the rulers thereof, not knowing him
14 5 assault made by . . . Jews with their r.
16 19 them into the marketplace to the rulers
17 6 Jason and certain brethren to the r.
8 stirred up the people, and the rulers
19 31 some also of the rulers of Asia, who
Eph 6 12 against the rulers of the world of this
rulest 2 Pa 20 6 God in heaven and r. over all
Ps 79 2 give ear, O thou that rulest Israel
88 10 thou rulest the power of the sea: and
ruleth Ps 22 1 Lord r. me: and I shall want
Ps 65 7 who by his power ruleth forever: his
Prov 16 32 he that r. his spirit, than he that
22 7 the rich ruleth over the poor: and the
Ecce 8 9 ruleth over another to his own hurt
Dan 4 14 most High ruleth in the kingdom of. 29
22 most High r. over the kingdom of men
Rom 12 8 he that ruleth, with carefulness; he
1 Tim 3 4 one that r. well his own house, having
ruling Eccu 44 4 and r. over the present people
Ruma Josu 15 52 Arab and Ruma and Esaan and
Judg 9 41 Abimelech sat down in Ruma: but Zebul
4 K 23 36 Zebida the daughter of Phadaia of Ruma
ruminate Cant 7 9 for his lips and his teeth to r.
rumor 2 K 13 30 a rumor came to David, saying
Jer 49 14 have heard a r. from the Lord. Abdi 1
51 46 rumor that shall be heard in the land
46 a rumor shall come in one year, and after this year another rumor
Eze 7 26 upon trouble, and rumor upon rumor
2 Ma 4 39 and the rumor of it was spread abroad
5 5 there was gone forth a false rumor
Luke 7 17 and this rumor of him went forth
rumors Mat 24 6 wars and r. of wars. Mark 13:7
rump Exod 29 22 the fat of the ram and the rump
Lev 3 9 the whole rump with the kidneys
7 3 they shall offer thereof the rump and
8 25 the rump and all the fat that covereth
9 19 the bullock and the rump of the
run Gen 31 27 wouldst thou run away privately
Gen 49 22 daughters run to and fro upon the wall
Lev 1 15 the blood run down upon the brim of
15 28 if the blood stop and cease to run
Num 16 47 had run to the midst of the multitude
Deut 33 26 the clouds run hither and thither
Josu 3 13 that are beneath shall run down and
Judg 8 21 do thou rise and run upon us: because
15 5 that they might run about hither and
1 K 8 11 footmen to run before his chariots
17 17 and run to the camp to thy brethren
20 6 that he might run to Bethlehem his
26 8 I will run him through with my spear
2 K 15 1 and 50 men to run before him [Absalom]
18 19 I will run and tell the king, that

22 22 why might not I also run after Chusai
22 Joab said to him: Why wilt thou run
23 he answered: But what if I run? And
23 said to him: Run. Then Achimaas running
22 30 in thee I will run girded: in my God I
3 K 1 5 and 50 men to run before him [Adonias]
18 35 and the water run round about the altar
20 39 and when a certain man was run away
4 K 4 22 that I may run to the man of God and
5 20 will run after him and take something
7 4 let us run over to the camp of the
2 Es 4 20 the trumpet, run all thither unto us
Tob 11 10 began to run stumbling with his feet
Jdth 14 3 the watchmen must needs run to awake
4 when the captains of them shall run to
Job 15 26 he hath run against him with his neck
34 9 not please God, although he run with
40 18 that the Jordan may run into his mouth
Ps 18 6 hath rejoiced as a giant to run the way
49 18 see a thief thou didst run with him
58 5 without iniquity have I run, and
77 16 and made streams run down as rivers
118 32 I have run the way of thy commandments
147 18 shall blow, and the waters shall run
Prov 1 16 their feet run to evil and make haste
3 10 thy presses shall run over with wine
6 3 run about, make haste, stir up thy
18 that are swift to run into mischief
Ecce 1 7 all the rivers run into the sea, yet
Cant 1 3 we will run after thee to the odor of
4 15 which run with a strong stream from
Wisd 3 7 just shall shine and shall run to and
5 23 and the rivers shall run together in a
16 29 shall run off as unprofitable water
Eccu 11 10 if thou run before, thou shalt not
32 15 but be first to run home to thy house
33 32 hurt him unjustly, he will run away
35 18 do not the widow's tears run down
Isa 1 23 love bribes, they run after rewards
10 18 and he shall run away through fear
40 31 they shall run and not be weary, they
55 5 that knew not thee shall run to thee
59 7 their feet run to evil and make haste
Jer 9 18 and our eyelids run down with waters
13 17 my eyes shall run down with tears
18 14 waters that gush out and run down
49 19 make him run suddenly upon her. 50:44
Lam 1 16 weep, and my eyes run down with water
2 18 let tears run down like a torrent day
3 48 my eye hath run down with streams
Eze 7 17 and all knees shall run with water
21 7 and water shall run down every knee
22 27 run after gains through covetousness
24 16 neither shall thy tears run down. Sigh
32 14 cause their rivers to run like oil
Joel 2 4 and they shall run like horsemen. They
7 they shall run like valiant men: like
9 they shall run upon the wall, they
3 13 the press is full, the fats run over
Amos 6 13 can horses run upon the rocks, or can
8 8 and run down as the river of Egypt
9 5 shall run down as the river of Egypt
Mich 1 4 waters that run down a steep place
Haba 2 2 he that readeth it may run over it
Zach 2 4 run, speak to this young man, saying
4 10 that run to and fro through the whole
6 7 sought to go and to run to and fro
2 Ma 12 16 seemed to run with the blood of the
Acts 27 41 seas met, they run the ship aground; and
1 C 9 24 they that run in race all run indeed
24 the prize? So run that you may obtain
26 so run, not as at an uncertainty: I so
Gal 2 2 perhaps I should run, or had run in vain
5 7 you did run well, who hath hindered you
Phil 2 16 because I have not run in vain, nor
2 Th 3 1 that the word of God may run, and may be
Heb 12 1 let us run by patience to the fight
1 P 4 4 strange, that you run not with them
runner 2 K 2 18 Asael was a most swift runner
Prov 24 34 poverty shall come to thee as a runner
Jer 2 23 as a swift runner pursuing his course
runnest Prov 4 12 when thou r. thou shalt not
runneth 1 Es 8 15 river which r. down to Ahava
Ps 147 15 to the earth: his word runneth swiftly
Prov 10 4 runneth after birds that fly away
18 10 the just r. to it and shall be exalted
Wisd 5 9 shadow, and like a post that r. on
Mat 9 17 break, and the wine runneth out, and
Rom 9 16 nor of him that runneth, but of God that
running Exod 9 23 lightning r. along the ground
Lev 13 12 the leprosy spring out r. about in the
22 4 that suffereth a running of the seed
Josu 7 22 running to his tent, found all hidden
1 K 8 11 and his running footmen to run before
2 K 15 12 the people r. together increased with
18 23 Achimaas r. by a nearer way passed
24 up his eyes saw a man running alone
26 the watchman saw another man running
26 said: I see another man running alone
27 r. of the foremost seemeth to me like the r. of Achimaas
19 41 running together to the king, said
4 K 5 21 when he saw him running after him, he
11 13 Athalia heard the noise of the people r.
2 Pa 23 12 the people r. and praising the king
Tob 10 7 daily running out looked round about
Ps 1 3 is planted near the running waters
57 8 come to nothing, like water r. down
Ecce 11 1 cast thy bread upon the running waters
Wisd 11 7 a fountain of an ever running river
17 17 of water running down with violence
18 the r. that could not be seen of beasts
Isa 30 25 elevated hill rivers of running waters
44 4 as willows beside the running waters
Jer 12 5 been wearied with running with footmen
22 17 oppression and running after evil works
51 31 one running post shall meet another
Eze 1 13 the vision running to and fro in the
Nah 2 4 like lightning running to and fro
3 2 the horse, and of the running chariot
1 Ma 2 24 running upon him he slew him upon the
16 5 there was a running river between them
21 one running before, told John in Gazara
2 Ma 5 2 there were seen horsemen r. in the air
3 by ranks, running one against another
26 r. through the city with armed men
9 2 multitude running together to arms
Mat 27 48 one of them running took a sponge and
28 8 joy, running to tell his disciples
Mark 6 55 running through that whole country
9 14 and running to him, they saluted him
24 when Jesus saw the multitude running
10 17 a certain man running up and kneeling
15 36 one running and filling a sponge with
Luke 6 38 shaken together and running over
11 29 the multitudes r. together, he began
15 20 running to him fell upon his neck
19 4 running before, he climbed up into a
Acts 6 12 running together, they took him and
8 30 Philip r. thither, heard him reading
12 14 running in she told that Peter stood
27 16 and r. under a certain island, that is
Apoc 9 9 and many horses running to battle. And
rupture Lev 21 20 dry scurf in his body, or a r.
rush Jdth 14 2 man take his arms and rush ye out
Job 6 27 you rush in upon the fatherless and

Ps 61 4 how long do you rush in upon a man
Job 8 11 can the rush be green without moisture
Isa 3 5 the people shall rush one upon another
27 6 when they shall rush in unto Jacob
2 Ma 14 41 sought to rush into his house and to
rushed Gen 14 15 rushed upon them in the night
Josu 8 17 the towns open as they had rushed out
Job 1 15 the Sabeans rushed in and took all away
16 15 he hath rushed in upon me like a giant
30 14 they have rushed in upon me, as when
Ps 58 4 the mighty have rushed in upon me
Isa 16 9 voice of the treaders hath rushed in
Jer 48 32 robber hath rushed in upon thy harvest
Dan 13 26 they rushed in by the back door to see
1 Ma 3 23 he rushed suddenly upon them: and
Acts 19 29 they r. with one accord into the theater
rushing Num 24 2 the spirit of God r. upon him
3 K 16 10 Zambri rushing in, struck him [Ela]
Jer 8 6 as a horse rushing to the battle. The
47 3 soldiers, at the rushing of his chariots
2 Ma 11 11 rushing violently upon the enemy like
rust Prov 25 4 take away the rust from silver
Bar 6 11 cannot defend themselves from the rust
23 except a man wipe off the rust, they
Eze 24 6 to the pot whose rust is in it, and its rust is not gone out of it
11 and let the rust of it be consumed
12 the great rust thereof is not gone out
Mat 6 19 where the rust and moth consume and
20 neither the rust nor moth does consume
James 5 3 rust of them shall be for a testimony
rusteth Eccu 12 10 as brass pot his wickedness r.
Ruth Ruth 1 4 was called Orpha, and the other R.
Ruth 1 14 Ruth stuck close to her mother-in-law
18 seeing that Ruth was steadfastly
22 Noemi came with Ruth the Moabitess
2 2 Ruth . . . said to her mother-in-law
8 Booz said to Ruth: Hear me, daughter
21 Ruth said, He also charged me that I
3 9 I am Ruth thy handmaid: spread thy
4 5 thou must take also Ruth the Moabitess
10 and have taken to wife Ruth the
13 Booz therefore took Ruth and married
Mat 1 5 Booz begot Obed of Ruth. And Obed begot

S

Saal 1 Es 10 29 of the sons of Bani . . . Saal and
Saananim Josu 19 33 from Heleph and Elon to S.
Saaph 1 Pa 2 47 sons of Jahaddai . . . Rogom and S.
1 Pa 2 49 S. the father of Madmena begot Sue
Saaphan Eze 8 11 Jezonias the son of Saaphan
Saarim 1 Pa 4 31 and in Bethberai and in S.
Saba Gen 10 7 sons of Regma: Saba and Dadan
Gen 10 28 Jectan begot . . . Saba. 1 Pa 1:22
25 3 Jecsan also begot Saba and Dadan
3 K 10 1 the queen of Saba, having heard of the
4 when the queen of Saba saw all the
13 Solomon gave the queen of S. 2 Pa 9:12
1 Pa 1 9 the sons of Chus: Saba and Hevila
32 the sons of Jecsan, Saba and Dadan
2 Pa 9 1 when the queen of Saba heard of the
9 the queen of Saba gave to king Solomon
Job 6 19 the paths of Thema, the ways of Saba
Ps 71 10 the kings of the Arabians and of Saba
Isa 43 3 atonement, Ethiopia and Saba for thee
60 6 Epha: all they from Saba shall come
Jer 6 20 you bring me frankincense from Saba
Eze 27 22 the sellers of Saba and Reema, they
23 Saba, Assur, and Chelmad sold to thee
38 13 Saba and Dedan and the merchants of
Sabachai 1 Pa 20 4 S. the Husathite slew Saphai
sabacthani Mat 27 46 Eli, Eli, lamma sabacthani
Mark 15 34 Eloi, Eloi, lamma sabacthani? Which
Sabaim 2 Es 7 59 Phochereth who was born of S.
Isa 45 14 merchandise of Ethiopia and of Sabaim
Sabama Num 32 38 children of Ruben built . . . S.
Josu 13 19 Cariathaim and Sabama and Sarathasar
Isa 16 8 have destroyed the vineyard of Sabama
9 the vineyard of Sabama: I will water
Jer 48 32 vineyard of Sabama, I will weep for
Saban Num 32 3 Eleale and Saban and Nebo and
Sabania 2 Es 9 4 Sabania, Bonni, Sarebias, Bani
2 Es 10 12 Zachur, Serebia, Sabania, Odaia
Sabaoth Jer 11 20 Lord of S. who judgest justly
Rom 9 29 unless the Lord of S. had left us a seed
James 5 4 into the ears of the Lord of Sabaoth
Sabarim Josu 7 5 them from gate as far as S.
Eze 47 16 Sabarim, which is between the border
Sabatacha Gen 10 7 Saba and Hevila and S.
Sabath Zach 1 7 eleventh month which is called S.
1 Ma 16 14 month: the same is the month Sabath
Sabatha Gen 10 7 sons of Chus . . . S. 1 Pa 1:9
Sabathaca 1 Pa 1 9 sons of Chus . . . Regma and S.
Sabathai 2 Es 11 16 S. and Jozabed, who were over
sabbath Exod 16 23 tomorrow is the rest of the s.
Exod 16 25 eat it today because it is the sabbath
26 seventh day is the s. 20:10; 31:15
29 the Lord hath given you the sabbath
30 the people kept the sabbath on the
31 13 see that thou keep my sabbath: because
14 keep you my sabbath: for it is holy
16 let the children of Israel keep the s.
35 2 the sabbath and the rest of the Lord
Lev 16 31 it is a sabbath of rest. 23:32
23 3 because it is the rest of the sabbath
3 it is the sabbath of the Lord in all
11 the next day after the sabbath, that it
15 count from the morrow after the sabbath
24 day of the month, you shall keep a s.
39 first day and eighth day shall be a s.
24 8 every sabbath they shall be changed
25 2 observe the rest of the sabbath to the
4 seventh year there shall be a sabbath
26 35 she shall keep a sabbath, and rest in
28 10 which regularly are poured out every s.
Deut 5 12 observe the day of the sabbath, to
14 the seventh is the day of the sabbath
4 K 4 23 today is neither new moon nor sabbath
11 6 third part of you go in on the sabbath
7 all that go forth on the sabbath, keep
9 that went in on the sabbath, with them that went out on the sabbath
16 18 the Musach also for the sabbath, which
1 Pa 9 32 to prepare always new for every s.
2 Pa 23 5 part of you that come to the sabbath
8 came in by the course of the sabbath
8 those who had fulfilled the sabbath
36 21 days of the desolation she kept a s.
2 Es 9 14 madest known to them thy holy sabbath
10 31 not buy them of them on the sabbath
13 15 some treading the presses on the s.
18 wrath upon Israel by violating the s.
19 not open them till after the sabbath
21 time they came no more on the sabbath
Ps 37 1 for a remembrance of the sabbath
92 1 on the day before the sabbath, when
Isa 56 2 keepeth the sabbath from profaning it
6 every one that keepeth the sabbath
58 13 if thou turn away thy foot from the s. . . . and call the s. delightful
66 23 after month, and sabbath after sabbath
Amos 8 5 sabbath [be over], and we shall open
1 Ma 1 45 sacrificed to idols and profaned the s.
48 should forbid the sabbath and the
2 38 they gave them battle on the sabbath

2 Ma 5 25 rested till the holy day of the sabbath
8 26 it was the day before the sabbath
27 they kept the sabbath: blessing the
28 after the s. they divided the spoils
12 38 and kept the sabbath in the same place
Mat 12 1 went through the corn on the sabbath
5 the priests in the temple break the s.
8 Son of man is Lord even of the sabbath
24 20 be not in the winter or on the sabbath
28 1 in the end of the sabbath, when it
Mark 2 23 through the corn fields on the sabbath
27 s. was made for man and not man for s.
28 Son of man is Lord of the sabbath also
6 2 when the s. was come, he began to teach
15 42 that is, the day before the sabbath
16 1 when the s. was past, Mary Magdalen
Luke 6 1 to pass on the second first sabbath
5 Son of man is Lord also of the sabbath
6 another s., that he entered into the
7 watched if he would heal on the s.
13 10 in their synagogue on their sabbath
14 that Jesus had healed on the sabbath
23 54 Parasceve, and the sabbath drew on
John 5 9 walked. And it was the s. that day
10 it is the sabbath; it is not lawful
16 because he did these things on the s.
18 he did not only break the sabbath, but
9 14 it was the s. when Jesus made the clay
16 is not of God, who keepeth not the s.
Acts 1 12 within a sabbath day's journey. And
13 27 the prophets, which are read every s.
42 desired them, that on the next s., they
15 21 where he is read every sabbath. Then
18 4 he reasoned in the synagogue every s.
sabbath day Exod 20 8 thou keep holy the s. d.
Exod 35 3 kindle no fire . . . on the s. day
Num 15 32 man gathering sticks on sabbath day
28 9 on the sabbath day you shall offer
Deut 5 15 that thou shouldst observe the s. day
2 Es 10 31 for use, to sell them on the s. day
13 15 bringing them into Jerusalem on s. day
17 you are doing, profaning the s. day
19 of Jerusalem were at rest on the s. d.
19 none should bring in burthens on s. d.
22 the gates, and to sanctify the s. d.
Ps 91 1 psalm of a canticle on the sabbath day
Jer 17 21 carry no burdens on the sabbath day
22 burdens out of your houses on the s. day
22 do ye any work: sanctify the s. day
24 by the gates of this city on the s. d.
24 if you will sanctify the sabbath day
27 not hearken to me, to sanctify the s. d.
27 by the gates of Jerusalem on the s. d.
Eze 46 1 on the sabbath day it shall be opened
4 prince shall offer to the Lord on s. d.
12 as it is wont to be done on the s. d.
1 Ma 2 32 made war against them on the s. day
34 the king's edict, to profane the s. day
41 up against us to fight on the s. d.
9 34 army over the Jordan on the sabbath day
43 heard it and he came on the sabbath day
2 Ma 6 11 were keeping the sabbath day privately
15 1 upon him with all violence on the s. d.
3 that had commanded the s. d. to be kept
Mat 12 11 same fall into a pit on the s. day
Mark 2 24 why do they on the s. day that which is
Luke 4 16 according to his custom on the s. day
13 14 and be healed; and not on the s. day
15 every one of you on the s. day loose
16 loosed from this bond on the s. day
14 1 on the s. day, to eat bread, that they
3 is it lawful to heal on the s. day
5 immediately draw him out on the s. day
23 56 on the s. day they rested, according
John 7 22 on the s. day you circumcise a man
23 man receive circumcision on the s. day
23 healed the whole man on the s. day
19 31 remain upon the cross on the s. day
31 for that was a great sabbath day
Acts 13 14 entering into . . . on the sabbath day
44 next s. d., the whole city almost came
16 13 upon the sabbath day, we went forth
sabbath days 1 Pa 9 25 came upon their s. d.
Mat 12 2 not lawful to do on the sabbath days
5 on the s. d. the priests in the temple
10 is it lawful to heal on the s. days
12 lawful to do a good deed on the s. days
Mark 1 21 upon the sabbath days going into the
3 2 whether he would heal on the s. days
4 to do good on the sabbath days, or to
Luke 4 31 he taught them on the sabbath days
6 2 which is not lawful on the s. days
9 be lawful on the s. days to do good
Acts 17 2 three s. days he reasoned with them
sabbaths Lev 19 3 keep my sabbaths. 30; 26:2
Lev 23 32 evening you shall celebrate your s.
38 besides the sabbaths of the Lord and
26 34 then shall the land enjoy her sabbaths
35 rest in the sabbaths of her desolation
35 because she did not rest in your s.
43 be left by them, shall enjoy her s.
1 Pa 23 31 in the s. and in the new moons. 2 Pa 2:4; 8:13; 31:3; Eze 46:3
2 Pa 36 21 and the land might keep her sabbaths
2 Es 10 33 continual holocaust on the sabbaths
13 16 and they sold them on the sabbaths
Jdth 8 6 fasted . . . except the sabbaths and
Isa 1 13 the sabbaths . . . I will not abide
56 4 they that shall keep my sabbaths, and
Lam 1 7 her, and have mocked at her sabbaths
2 6 caused feasts and s. to be forgotten
Eze 20 12 I gave them my sabbaths, to be a sign
13 they grievously violated my sabbaths
16 in my statutes, and violated my s.
20 20 sanctify my sabbaths, that they may be
21 and they violated my sabbaths: and I
24 had violated my sabbaths, and their
21 23 and imitating the leisure of sabbaths
22 8 sanctuaries and profaned my sabbaths
26 turned away their eyes from my sabbaths
23 38 same day, and profaned my sabbaths
44 24 all my solemnities and sanctify my s.
45 17 on the new moons and on the sabbaths
Osee 2 11 solemnities, her new moons, her s.
1 Ma 1 41 into mourning, her s. into reproach
10 34 feasts and the s. and the new moons
2 Ma 6 6 neither were the sabbaths kept nor the
Col 2 16 or of the new moon, or of the sabbaths
Sabeans Job 1 15 the S. rushed in and took all
Joel 3 8 they shall sell them to the Sabeans
Sabee Josu 19 2 Bersabee and Sabee and Molada
Saber 1 Pa 2 48 concubine of Caleb bore Saber
Sachacha Josu 15 61 Betharaba, Meddin and S.
Sachar 1 Pa 11 34 Ahiam the son of Sachar an
1 Pa 26 4 Sachar the fourth, Nathanael the fifth
sack Gen 42 27 and one of them opening his sack
Gen 42 28 behold it is in the sack. And they
35 his money tied in the mouth of his s.
44 1 money of every one in top of his sack
2 in the mouth of the younger's sack, put
11 ground, and every man opened his s.
12 he found the cup in Benjamin's sack
sackbut Dan 3 5 the sound . . . of the s. 7, 10, 15
sackcloth Gen 37 34 he put on sackcloth. Esth 4:1
3 K 20 31 let us put sackcloth on our loins
32 they girded sackcloth on their loins

21 27 and fasted and slept in sackcloth
4 K 19 1 and covered himself with sackcloth
2 Es 9 1 came together with fasting and with s.
Esth 4 2 no one clothed with sackcloth might
3 many using sackcloth and ashes for
4 to take away the sackcloth: but he would
Job 16 16 I have sewed sackcloth upon my skin
Ps 29 12 thou hast cut my sackcloth and hast
Eccu 25 24 a bear: and showeth it like sackcloth
Isa 15 3 they are girded with sackcloth: on the
20 2 loose the sackcloth from off thy loins
22 12 to baldness and to girding with s.
37 1 [Ezechias] covered himself with s.
2 ancients of the priests, covered with s.
50 3 will make sackcloth their covering
58 5 and to spread sackcloth and ashes
Jer 6 26 gird thee with sackcloth, O daughter
Bar 4 20 have put upon me the s. of supplication
Dan 9 3 with fasting and sackcloth and ashes
Joel 1 8 lament like a virgin girded with s.
13 lie in s., ye ministers of my God
Amos 8 10 I will bring up s. upon every back
Jon 3 5 proclaimed a fast and put on sackcloth
6 was clothed with s. and sat in ashes
8 let men and beasts be covered with s.
Zach 13 4 shall they be clad with a garment of s.
Mat 11 21 done penance in sackcloth and ashes
Luke 10 13 ago, sitting in sackcloth and ashes
Apoc 6 12 the sun became black as s. of hair
11 3 prophesy 1,260 days, clothed in s.
sackcloths 2 K 3 31 and gird yourselves with s.
4 K 19 2 ancients of the priests covered with s.
sacked 2 Ma 10 37 pillaged and sacked the fortress
sack's Gen 42 27 saw the money in the s. mouth
sacks Gen 42 25 to fill their sacks with wheat and
Gen 42 25 every man's money again in their s.
43 12 carry back what you found in your s.
18 carried back the first time in our s.
21 we opened our sacks and found our money
21 found our money in the mouths of the s.
23 hath given you treasure in your sacks
44 1 fill their sacks with corn, as much as
8 that we found in the top of our sacks
11 they speedily took down their sacks
Josu 9 4 laying old sacks upon their asses, and
sacrament Eph 5 32 this is a great s.; but I
sacred Exod 13 5 celebrate this manner of s. rites
Exod 31 10 their office about the sacred things
39 29 made also the plate of s. veneration
Num 27 11 shall be . . . sacred by a perpetual law
2 Ma 4 48 for the people and the sacred vessels
sacrifice Gen 22 10 the sword, to s. his son
Exod 3 12 offer s. to God upon this mountain
18 to sacrifice unto the Lord. 5:3
5 1 that they may s. to me in the desert
8 let us go and sacrifice to our God
17 let us go and sacrifice to the Lord
7 16 let my people go to sacrifice to me. 8:11, 20; 9:1, 13; 10:3
8 8 I will let the people go to sacrifice
25 and sacrifice to your God in this land
26 we shall s. the abominations of the
27 we will sacrifice to the Lord our God
28 I will let you go to sacrifice to the
29 not letting the people go to sacrifice
10 7 let the men go to sacrifice to the Lord
8 go, sacrifice to the Lord. 24; 12:31
11 men only, and sacrifice to the Lord
12 6 whole multitude . . . shall sacrifice it
21 take a lamb . . . and sacrifice the phase
13 15 I s. to the Lord all that openeth the
23 18 shalt not s. the blood of my victim upon
29 33 that it may be an atoning sacrifice
38 what thou shalt sacrifice upon the altar
42 it is a sacrifice to the Lord, by
34 25 the blood of my sacrifice upon leaven
Lev 1 2 to the Lord a sacrifice of the cattle
2 1 shall offer an oblation of sacrifice
3 remnant of the sacrifice shall be Aaron's
4 thou offerest a s. baked in the oven
7 if the sacrifice be from the gridiron
9 he shall take a memorial out of the s.
11 leaven or honey be burnt in the sacrifice
11 whatsoever sacrifice thou offerest
13 away the salt . . . from thy sacrifice
3 1 sacrifice of peace offerings. 3; 4:10; 7:20; Num 6:18; 7:17, 23, 29
3 shall offer of the s. of peace offerings
6 the sacrifice of peace offering. Num 6:17
9 peace offerings a sacrifice to the Lord
4 4 and shall sacrifice it to the Lord
23 a goat without blemish, s. to the Lord
6 14 this is the law of the sacrifice and
20 ephi of flour for a perpetual sacrifice
23 every s. of the priest shall be consumed
7 1 law of the sacrifice for a trespass
7 as the sacrifice for sin is offered, so
9 every sacrifice of flour that is baked
11 law of the sacrifice of peace offerings
13 leavened bread with the s. of thanks
16 offer a sacrifice or of his own accord
29 let him offer therewith a sacrifice
37 holocaust and of the sacrifice for sin
8 28 for a sweet odor of s. to the Lord
34 rite of the s. might be accomplished
9 4 offering for the sacrifice . . . flour
7 offer sacrifice for thy sin: offer the
17 adding in the sacrifice the libations
10 12 take the sacrifice that is remaining
17 eat in holy place the s. for sin
14 19 and shall offer the sacrifice for sin
32 this is the sacrifice of a leper
17 5 may sacrifice them for peace offerings
7 no more s. their victims to devils
19 5 ye offer in sacrifice a peace offering
23 8 you shall offer sacrifice in fire to
16 you shall offer a new sacrifice to the
Num 4 16 the sacrifice that is always offered
5 8 the ram . . . to be an atoning sacrifice
15 because it is a sacrifice of jealousy
18 on her hands the sacrifice of remembrance
25 from her hand the sacrifice of jealousy
26 to take a handful of the sacrifice of
8 12 thou shalt sacrifice one for sin, and
9 13 because he offered not sacrifice to the
15 4 shall offer a sacrifice of fine flour
6 there shall be a sacrifice of flour
8 a holocaust or a sacrifice of oxen
24 and the sacrifice and libations thereof
18 9 offering and sacrifice . . . shall be for
28 6 most sweet odor of a sacrifice by fire
8 all the rites of the morning sacrifice
9 tempered with oil in sacrifice. 12, 13
29 11 perpetual holocaust with their sacrifice
16 besides . . . the sacrifice and the libation. 19, 22, 25, 28, 31, 34, 38
39 voluntary oblations . . . for sacrifice
Deut 16 2 thou shalt sacrifice the phase to the
17 1 shalt not sacrifice . . . a sheep or an
18 3 whether they s. an ox or a sheep
33 19 shall they s. the victims of justice
Josu 22 23 might lay upon it holocausts and s.
28 not for holocausts nor for sacrifice
Judg 6 18 till I return to thee and bring a s.
26 whereupon thou didst lay the sacrifice
1 K 1 3 to adore and to offer sacrifice to the

4 and Elcana offered sacrifice and gave
21 to offer to the Lord the solemn s.
2 13 whosoever had offered a sacrifice, the
17 they withdrew men from the sacrifice
19 with her husband to offer the solemn s.
29 to eat the firstfruits of every s.
9 12 there is a sacrifice of the people
10 8 mayest . . . sacrifice victims of peace
15 21 to offer sacrifice to the Lord their God
16 2 I am come to sacrifice to the Lord. 5
3 thou shalt call Isai to the sacrifice
5 and come with me to the sacrifice. And
5 and called them to the sacrifice. And
20 29 there is a solemn sacrifice in the city
26 19 up against me, let him accept of s.
2 K 14 17 word of my lord . . . as a sacrifice
15 8 into Jerusalem, I will offer sacrifice
3 K 3 4 he went . . . to Gabaon to sacrifice
8 64 he offered the holocaust and sacrifice
64 to receive the holocaust and sacrifice
11 8 and offered sacrifice to their gods
12 32 to s. to the calves which he had made
18 29 the time was come of offering sacrifice
4 K 10 19 for I have a great s. to offer to Baal
16 12 offered holocausts and his own sacrifice
15 morning holocaust and the evening s.
15 the king's holocaust and his sacrifice
17 35 nor worship them nor s. to them. But
36 adore, and to him shall you sacrifice
23 5 had appointed to s. in the high places
8 high places, where the priests offered s.
1 Pa 15 26 they offered in sacrifice seven oxen
16 29 bring up sacrifice and come ye in his
21 23 and the wheat for the sacrifice: I will
23 29 the sacrifice of fine flour and of
2 Pa 7 5 offered a sacrifice of 22,000 oxen
12 this place to myself for a house of s.
11 16 to s. their victims before the Lord
1 Es 7 19 that are given thee for the sacrifice
9 4 sorrowful until the evening sacrifice
5 at the evening sacrifice I rose up
2 Es 4 2 will they s. and make an end in a day
10 33 and for the continual sacrifice and for
13 9 the vessels of the house of God, the s.
Tob 8 19 up to thee a sacrifice of thy praise
Ps 4 6 offer up the sacrifice of justice
26 6 offered . . . a sacrifice of jubilation
39 7 s. and oblation thou didst not desire
49 14 offer to God the sacrifice of praise
23 sacrifice of praise shall glorify me
50 18 if thou hadst desired sacrifice, I
19 a s. to God is an afflicted spirit
21 thou accept the sacrifice of justice
53 8 I will freely s. to thee, and will give
106 22 let them sacrifice the s. of praise
115 17 sacrifice to thee the s. of praise
140 2 lifting up of my hands, as evening s.
Wisd 14 23 they s. their own children or use
18 9 were offering sacrifice secretly, and
Eccu 7 35 offer . . . the s. of sanctification
31 7 stumblingblock to them that s. to it
34 24 offereth s. of the goods of the poor
35 2 is a wholesome sacrifice to take heed
3 is to offer a propitiatory s. for
4 he that doth mercy, offereth sacrifice
9 the sacrifice of the just is acceptable
15 look not upon an unjust sacrifice, for
45 20 chose him . . . to offer sacrifice to
Isa 1 13 offer s. no more in vain: incense is
57 6 to them, thou hast offered sacrifice
65 3 immolate in gardens and s. upon bricks
66 3 he that killeth a sheep in sacrifice
Jer 11 12 the gods to whom they offer sacrifice
13 altars to offer sacrifice to Baalim
17 to provoke me, offering s. to Baalim
12 3 them together as sheep for a sacrifice
32 29 they offered sacrifice to Baal and
44 3 offer sacrifice and worship other gods
5 and not to sacrifice to strange gods
17 s. to the queen of heaven. 18, 19, 25
21 s. that you offered in the cities of
46 10 there is a sacrifice of the Lord God
Bar 4 7 offering sacrifice to devils, and not
Eze 45 15 of those that Israel feedeth for s.
17 prince shall give . . . the sacrifice
17 he shall offer the sacrifice for sin
24 shall offer the sacrifice of an ephi
25 in regard to . . . the sacrifice and the
46 5 the sacrifice of an ephi for a ram
5 what sacrifice his hand shall allow
7 shall offer in s. an ephi for a calf
11 shall be the s. of an ephi to a calf
11 the s. shall be as his hand shall find
14 he shall offer the s. for it morning
14 sacrifice . . . continual and everlasting
15 he shall offer the lamb and the s.
20 where they shall dress the sacrifice
Dan 2 46 that they should offer in s. to him
3 38 neither is there . . . holocaust or s.
40 so let our s. be made in thy sight
8 11 it took away from him the continual s.
12 strength . . . against the continual s.
13 the vision concerning the continual s.
9 21 at the time of the evening sacrifice
27 the victim and the sacrifice shall fail
11 31 shall take away the continual sacrifice
12 11 when the continual s. shall be taken
Osee 3 4 sit many days . . . without sacrifice
4 13 offered s. upon tops of the mountains
6 6 I desired mercy, and not sacrifice: and
8 13 they shall s. flesh and shall eat it
13 2 to these that say: Sacrifice men, ye
Joel 1 9 sacrifice and libation is cut off. 13
2 14 sacrifice and libation to the Lord
Amos 4 5 offer a sacrifice of praise with leaven
Jon 2 10 voice of praise will s. to thee: I
Haba 1 16 and he will sacrifice to his net
Zach 14 21 all that sacrifice shall come and
Mala 1 8 if you offer the blind for sacrifice
14 offereth in s. that which is feeble
3 4 s. of Juda . . . shall please the Lord
1 Ma 1 54 commanded the cities of Juda to s.
2 15 to compel them . . . to sacrifice and to
22 neither will we s. and transgress the
23 to s. to the idols upon the altar in
25 who compelled them to s., he slew at
4 53 they offered s. according to the law
11 34 to all them that s. in Jerusalem
2 Ma 1 18 when Nehemias offered s. after the
23 while the sacrifice was consuming
26 receive the s. for all thy people Israel
30 sung hymns till the s. was consumed
31 when the s. was consumed, Nehemias
2 9 he offered the s. of the dedication
3 32 s. of health for the recovery of the
35 Heliodorus after he had offered a s.
4 19 silver for the sacrifice of Hercules
20 money . . . to the sacrifice of Hercules
6 21 had commanded of the flesh of the s.
12 43 s. to be offered for the sins of the
Mat 9 13 I will have mercy and not s. 12:7
Luke 2 24 to offer a s., according as it is
Acts 14 12 would have offered s. with the people
Rom 12 1 that you present your bodies a living s.
1 C 10 19 that what is offered in s. to idols, is
20 but the things which the heathens s.

20 they sacrifice to devils, and not to God
Eph 5 2 an oblation and a sacrifice to God for
Phil 2 17 if I be made a victim upon the sacrifice
4 18 an acceptable sacrifice, pleasing to God
Heb 9 26 destruction of sin, by the s. of himself
10 5 sacrifice and oblation thou wouldest not
12 this man offering one sacrifice for sins
26 there is now left no sacrifice for sins
11 4 by faith Abel offered to God a sacrifice
13 15 let us offer the sacrifice of praise
burnt sacrifice Lev 4 35 for a b. s. of the Lord
Lev 6 17 for the burnt s. of the Lord. 7:25
7 5 it is the burnt sacrifice of the Lord
Num 23 17 found him standing by his burnt s.
28 2 burnt sacrifice of most sweet odor
19 shall offer a burnt sacrifice. 29:6
sacrificed Exod 24 5 s. pacific victims of calves
Exod 29 20 and when thou hast sacrificed him
34 15 one call thee to eat of the things s.
Lev 5 15 things that are sacrificed to the Lord
16 27 buck goat, that were sacrificed for sin
22 28 not be s. the same day with their young
27 9 a beast that may be s. to the Lord
11 an unclean beast, which cannot be s.
Deut 15 21 it shall not be sacrificed to the Lord
16 4 any of the flesh of that which was s.
32 17 sacrificed to devils and not to God
1 K 2 15 said to the man that s.: Give me flesh
16 he that s. said to him: Let the fat
6 15 sacrificed victims that day to the Lord
11 15 they sacrificed there victims of peace
15 15 that they might be sacrificed to the
2 K 6 13 he [David] sacrificed an ox and a ram
3 K 3 2 yet the people s. in the high places
3 only he sacrificed in the high places
15 [Solomon] s. victims of peace offerings
8 5 they s. sheep and oxen that could not
63 peace offerings, which he s. to the
4 K 12 3 still s. and burnt incense. 15:36
14 4 the people s. and burnt incense. 15:4
16 4 he s. also and burnt incense. 2 Pa 28:4
22 17 and have sacrificed to strange gods
1 Pa 29 21 and they sacrificed victims to the Lord
2 Pa 5 6 sacrificed rams and oxen without number
7 4 the king and all the people sacrificed
15 11 they sacrificed to the Lord in that day
28 23 s. victims to the gods of Damascus
33 16 s. upon it victims and peace offerings
17 still sacrificed in the high places
22 he sacrificed to all the idols which
34 4 graves of them that had s. to them
25 and have sacrificed to strange gods
35 1 it was sacrificed on the 14th day of
1 Es 4 2 have s. to him since the days of Asor
2 Es 12 42 they s. on that day great sacrifices
Ps 105 37 s. their sons and their daughters to
38 which they s. to the idols of Chanaan
Isa 1 29 idols to which they have sacrificed
65 7 who have s. upon the mountains and
Jer 1 16 and have sacrificed to strange gods
19 4 have s. therein to strange gods whom
13 upon whose roofs they have s. to all
44 15 knew that their wives s. to other gods
23 because you have sacrificed to idols
Bar 6 27 the things that are sacrificed to them
Eze 16 20 hast s. the same to them to be devoured
21 thou hast s. and given my children to
20 28 there they sacrificed their victims
23 39 when they s. their children to their
Osee 11 2 victims to Baalim, and s. to idols
Jon 1 16 and sacrificed victims to the Lord
1 Ma 1 45 s. to idols and profaned the sabbath
58 and s. at the doors of the houses
62 they s. upon the altar of the idol
Mark 14 12 when they sacrificed the pasch, the
Acts 15 29 you abstain from things s. to idols
1 C 5 7 for Christ our pasch is sacrificed
8 1 things that are s. to idols, we know
4 as for meats that are s. to idols, we
7 eat as a thing sacrificed to an idol
10 those things which are sacrificed to
10 28 this has been s. to idols, do not eat
2 Tim 4 6 I am even now ready to be sacrificed
Apoc 2 20 to eat of things sacrificed to idols
sacrifices Gen 31 54 after he had offered s.
Exod 10 25 thou shalt give us also sacrifices
18 12 offered holocausts and s. to God
40 27 the holocaust and the s. upon it
Lev 6 18 concerning the sacrifices of the Lord
7 7 same shall be the law of both these s.
21 21 shall not approach to offer sacrifices
23 19 two lambs . . . for s. of peace offerings
24 9 it is most holy of the sacrifices
Num 7 41 for sacrifices of peace offerings two oxen. 47, 53, 59, 65, 71, 77, 83
88 for s. of peace offerings, oxen 24
10 10 holocausts and the s. of peace offerings
15 14 shall offer s. after the same rite
16 15 respect not their sacrifices: thou
25 2 who called them to their sacrifices
28 3 the sacrifices which you shall offer
20 for the s. of every one three tenths of
28 in the s. of them three tenths of flour
29 3 for their s. three tenths of flour. 9
6 holocaust . . . with the s. thereof
18 sacrifices and libations for every one
21 sacrifices and the libations of every one. 24, 27, 30, 33, 37
Deut 12 14 one of thy tribes shalt thou offer s.
18 1 because they shall eat the sacrifices
Josu 13 14 the sacrifices and victims of the Lord
22 27 victims and s. of peace offerings
29 an altar to offer holocausts and s.
Judg 2 5 and there they offered s. to the Lord
16 23 to offer great s. to Dagon their god
1 K 2 28 of all the s. of the children of Israel
15 22 obedience is better than sacrifices
20 6 are solemn s. there for all his tribe
2 K 15 12 and while he was offering sacrifices
3 K 12 27 if this people go up to offer s. in
15 13 princess in the sacrifices of Priapus
22 44 offered sacrifices . . . in the high
4 K 3 20 when the sacrifices used to be offered
10 24 and they went in to offer sacrifices
16 15 their sacrifices and their libations
2 Pa 7 7 could not hold the holocausts and the s.
32 23 many also brought victims and s. to
1 Es 6 3 place where they may offer sacrifices
7 17 with the sacrifices and libations
2 Es 12 42 they sacrificed on that day great s.
Jdth 4 15 offered the s. to the Lord girded with
Ps 19 4 may he be mindful of all thy sacrifices
49 5 who set his covenant before sacrifices
8 I will not reprove for thy sacrifices
95 8 bring up s. and come into his courts
105 28 and ate the sacrifices of the dead
Prov 16 5 acceptable with God, than to offer s.
21 27 the s. of the wicked are abominable
Ecce 9 2 and to him that despiseth sacrifices
Wisd 12 4 thee by their sorceries and wicked s.
14 15 appointed him rites and sacrifices
23 or use hidden s. or keep watches full
Eccu 34 23 for sins by the multitude of their s.
45 17 his sacrifices were consumed with fire
26 the s. also of the Lord they shall eat
Isa 19 21 and shall worship him with sacrifices

Jer 6 20 nor are your sacrifices pleasing to me
7 21 add your burnt offerings to your s.
22 the matter of burnt offerings and s.
17 26 bringing holocausts and victims and s.
33 18 to offer holocausts and to burn s.
Bar 6 28 menstruous women touch their sacrifices
Osee 4 19 shall be confounded because of their s.
9 4 their s. shall be like the bread of
12 11 were they in Galgal offering sacrifices
Amos 5 25 did you offer victims and s. to me
Mala 3 3 shall offer s. to the Lord in justice
1 Ma 1 47 should forbid holocausts and sacrifices
4 56 sacrifices of salvation and of praise
12 11 remember you in the s. that we offer
2 Ma 1 8 we offered sacrifices and fine flour
21 s. that were laid on, to be sprinkled
33 that were with him had purified the s.
3 3 belonging to the ministry of the s.
6 did not belong to the account of the s.
4 14 neglecting the s., hastened to be
19 it might not be bestowed on the s.
6 7 on the king's birthday to the sacrifices
7 42 there is enough said of the sacrifices
9 16 charges pertaining to the sacrifices
10 3 they offered sacrifices after two years
13 23 being reconciled, offered sacrifices
14 31 that were offering the accustomed s.
Mark 12 33 thing than all holocausts and s.
Luke 13 1 blood Pilate had mingled with their s.
Acts 7 41 and offered sacrifices to the idol
42 did you offer victims and sacrifices
1 C 10 18 are not they, that eat of the sacrifices
Heb 5 1 he may offer up gifts and s. for sins
7 27 to offer s. first for his own sins
8 3 appointed to offer gifts and sacrifices
9 6 accomplishing the offices of sacrifices
9 to which gifts and s. are offered, which
23 themselves with better s. than these
10 1 by the selfsame sacrifices which they
8 s. and oblations and holocausts for sin
11 and often offering the same sacrifices
13 16 by such s. God's favor is obtained
1 P 2 5 to offer up spiritual s., acceptable
sacrificeth Exod 22 20 s. to gods, shall be put
Eccu 34 21 offering of him that s. of a thing
24 is as one that s. the son in the
Isa 66 3 he that s. an ox, is as if he slew
Jer 48 35 high places and that s. to his gods
sacrificing Exod 32 8 adored it and s. victims to
Wisd 12 6 those parents s. with their own hands
Isa 57 5 sacrificing children in the torrents
Jer 17 3 mountains, sacrificing in the field
18 15 s. in vain and stumbling in their
44 8 by s. to other gods in the land of
Acts 14 17 restrained people from s. to them. Now
sacrilege Num 25 18 plague for the s. of Phogor
Acts 19 37 these men, who are neither guilty of s.
Rom 2 22 thou that abhorrest idols, committest s.
sacrileges 2 Ma 4 39 many s. had been committed
sacrilegious 2 Ma 4 38 the s. wretch should be put to
2 Ma 4 42 the s. fellow himself, they slew him
13 6 the s. wretch to be thrown down into
sad Gen 34 3 whereas she was sad, he comforted
Gen 40 6 saw them sad, he asked them, saying
2 Es 2 2 why is thy countenance sad, seeing thou
8 10 holy day of the Lord: and be not sad
Tob 10 3 and he began to be exceeding sad, both
Jdth 7 14 eyes in thirst and sad destruction
Ps 41 6 why art thou sad, O my soul. 42:5
Prov 12 21 just man, it shall not make him sad
25 23 as doth a sad countenance a backbiting
31 6 give strong drink to them that are sad
Wisd 17 4 and sad visions appearing to them
Eccu 22 27 if thou hast opened a sad mouth, fear
Isa 1 5 is sick, and the whole heart is sad
42 4 he shall not be sad nor troublesome
Mat 6 16 be not as the hypocrites, sad. For
14 9 the king was struck sad. Mark 6:26
19 22 had heard this word, he went away sad
26 37 began to grow sorrowful and to be sad
Mark 10 22 who being struck sad at that saying
Luke 24 17 as you walk and are sad? And one of
Phil 2 26 was sad, for that you had heard that he
James 5 13 is any of you sad? Let him pray
sadder Gen 40 7 your countenance s. today than
saddle Lev 15 9 the s. on which he hath sitten
2 K 19 26 spoke to him to saddle me an ass, that
3 K 4 26 horses, and 12,000 for the saddle
13 13 he said to his sons: Saddle me the ass
27 he said to his sons: Saddle me an ass
saddled Gen 22 3 up in the night, s. his ass
2 K 17 23 s. his ass and arose and went home to
3 K 2 40 Semei arose and saddled his ass and
13 13 when they had saddled him, he got up
23 he saddled his ass for the prophet
27 when they had saddled it, and he was
4 K 4 24 she s. an ass and commanded her servant
saddling Num 22 21 and s. his ass went with them
Sadducees Mat 3 7 many of the Pharisees and S.
Mat 16 1 came to him the Pharisees and S.
6 the leaven of the Pharisees and S. 11
12 the doctrine of the Pharisees and S.
22 23 there came to him the S. Mark 12:18
34 hearing that he had silenced the S.
Luke 20 27 came to him some of the Sadducees, who
Acts 4 1 the Sadducees came upon them, being
5 17 which is the heresy of the Sadducees
23 6 one part were S., and other Pharisees
7 dissension between Pharisees and S.
8 S. say that there is no resurrection
sade Ps 118 137 sade. Lam 1:18; 2:18; 3:52, 53, 54; 4:18
sadly 2 K 10 5 men were sadly put to confusion
sadness Esth 16 21 God hath turned this day of s.
Prov 25 20 sadness of a man consumeth the heart
Ecce 7 4 by the s. of the countenance the mind
Eccu 14 2 happy is he that hath had no sadness
25 17 sadness of the heart is every plague
30 22 give not up thy soul to sadness, and
24 and drive away sadness far from thee
25 sadness hath killed many, and there is
38 17 then comfort thyself in thy sadness
19 for of sadness cometh death, and it
21 give not up thy heart to sadness, but
Eze 23 33 with the cup of grief and sadness
1 Ma 6 4 and departed with great sadness and
2 Ma 3 17 the man was so compassed with sadness
Rom 9 2 that I have great sadness, and continual
2 C 9 7 not with sadness, or of necessity: for
Sadoc 2 K 8 17 S. the son of Achitob. 1 Pa 18:16
2 K 15 25 king said to Sadoc: Carry back the ark
29 Sadoc and Abiathar carried back the ark
35 thou hast with thee and S. and Abiathar
35 shalt tell it to Sadoc and Abiathar
36 Achimaas the son of Sadoc. 18:19, 22, 27
17 15 Chusai said to Sadoc and Abiathar the
19 11 king David sent to Sadoc and Abiathar
20 25 Sadoc and Abiathar, priests. 3 K 4:4
4 K 15 33 mother was Jerusa the daughter of Sadoc
1 Pa 6 8 Achitob begot S., and S. begot Achimaas
12 Achitob begot S., and S. begot Sellum
53 Achitob his son, Sadoc his son
9 11 Mosollam the son of Sadoc. 2 Es 11:11
12 28 Sadoc . . . and the house of his father
15 11 David called Sadoc and Abiathar the
24 3 Sadoc of the sons of Eleazar and
31 before David the king and Sadoc

Wisd 4 15 his mercy is with his saints, and that
5 5 God, and their lot is among the saints
18 1 but thy saints had a very great light
Eccu 23 10 meddle not with the names of saints
24 16 my abode is in the full assembly of s.
31 11 church of the s. shall declare his alms
42 17 Lord made the saints to declare all
45 2 he made him like the saints in glory
Isa 26 10 in the land of the saints he hath done
Dan 7 18 the s. of the most high God shall take
21 that horn made war against the saints
22 and gave judgment to the saints of the
22 and the saints obtained the kingdom
25 shall crush the saints of the most High
27 may be given to the people of the s.
8 13 I heard one of the saints speaking
24 the mighty, and the people of the s.
9 24 the saint of saints may be anointed
Osee 11 12 Juda . . . is faithful with the saints
Zach 14 5 shall come, and all the saints with him
1 Ma 7 17 the flesh of thy s., and the blood
Mat 27 52 many bodies of the saints that had
Acts 9 13 hath done to thy saints in Jerusalem
32 visiting all, came to the saints who
41 when he had called the saints and the
26 10 many of the s. did I shut up in prison
18 a lot among s., by faith that is in me
Rom 1 7 the beloved of God, called to be saints
8 27 he asketh for saints according to God
28 to his purpose, are called to be saints
12 13 communicating to necessities of the s.
15 25 Jerusalem, to minister unto the saints
26 contribution for the poor of the saints
31 be acceptable in Jerusalem to the saints
16 2 receive her in the Lord as becometh s.
15 and all the saints that are with them
1 C 1 2 called to be saints, with all that
6 1 before the unjust, and not before saints
2 know you not that the saints shall judge
14 33 I teach in all churches of the saints
16 1 collections that are made for the saints
15 dedicated themselves to ministry of s.
2 C 1 1 with all saints that are in all Achaia
8 4 ministry that is done toward the s. 9:1
9 12 not only supply the want of the saints
13 12 all the saints salute you. Phil 4:22
Eph 1 1 to all the saints who are at Ephesus
15 and of your love towards all the saints
18 glory of his inheritance in the saints
2 19 you are fellow citizens with the saints
3 8 to me, the least of all the saints, is
18 able to comprehend, with all the saints
4 12 for the perfecting of the saints, for
5 3 be named among you, as becometh saints
6 18 all instance and supplication for all s.
Phil 1 1 to all the saints in Christ Jesus, who
Col 1 2 to the saints and faithful brethren in
4 which you have towards all the saints
12 partakers of the lot of the s. in light
26 but now is manifested to his saints, to
1 Th 3 13 our Lord Jesus Christ, with all his s.
2 Th 1 10 he shall come to be glorified in his s.
Philem 5 Lord Jesus, and towards all the saints
7 because the bowels of the saints have
Heb 6 10 ministered, and do minister to the s.
13 24 all your prelates and all the saints
Jude 3 the faith once delivered to the saints
14 Lord cometh with thousands of his s.
Apoc 5 8 odors, which are the prayers of saints
8 3 should offer of the prayers of all s.
4 incense of the prayers of the saints
11 18 the saints and to them that fear thy
13 7 to make war with the saints and to
10 patience and the faith of the saints
14 12 here is the patience of the saints
16 6 they have shed the blood of saints and
17 6 drunk with the blood of the saints and
18 24 the blood of prophets and of saints
19 8 fine linen are the justifications of s.
20 8 encompassed the camp of the saints and

sake Mat 5 10 suffer persecution for justice' sake
Mat 5 11 evil against you, untruly, for my sake
10 18 and before kings for my sake, for a
22 hated by all men for my name's sake. Mark 13:13; Luke 21:17
16 25 lose his life for my sake. Mark 8:35; Luke 9:24
19 29 children or lands for my name's sake
24 9 by all nations for my name's sake
22 for the sake of the elect those days
Mark 6 17 for the sake of Herodias the wife of
10 29 for my sake and for the gospel, who
13 9 governors and kings for my sake, for a
20 but for the sake of the elect which
Luke 6 22 as evil, for the Son of man's sake
18 29 for the kingdom of God's sake, who
21 12 and governors, for my name's sake
John 12 9 they came, not for Jesus' sake only
14 12 believe for the very works' sake. Amen
15 21 will do to you for my name's sake
Acts 9 16 things he must suffer for my name's sake
27 34 take some meat for your health's sake
Rom 8 36 for thy sake we are put to death all the
11 28 they are enemies for your sake: but as
28 they are most dear for sake of fathers
13 5 for wrath, but also for conscience' sake
1 C 4 10 we are fools for Christ's sake, but you
9 23 I do all things for the gospel's sake
10 25 asking no questions for conscience' s. 27
28 do not eat of it for his sake that told
28 that told it, and for conscience' sake
2 C 4 11 delivered unto death for Jesus' sake
7 12 it was not for his sake that did wrong
1 Th 5 13 in charity, for their word's sake. Have
1 Tim 5 23 use a little wine for thy stomach's sake
2 Tim 2 10 I endure all things for the sake of the
Titus 1 11 not for filthy lucre's sake. 5:2
Philem 9 for charity sake I rather beseech
1 P 2 13 to every human creature for God's sake
3 14 you suffer anything for justice' sake
2 P 3 9 but dealeth patiently for your sake
1 J 2 12 are forgiven you for his name's sake
2 J 2 for the sake of the truth which
Jude 16 admiring persons for gain's sake. But

sakes John 11 15 I am glad, for your sakes, that I was
John 12 30 not because of me, but for your sakes
1 C 4 6 to myself and to Apollo, for your sakes
9 10 or doth he say this indeed for your s.
10 these things are written for our sakes
2 C 2 10 for your sakes have I done it in person
4 15 for all things are for your sakes; that
8 9 being rich he became poor, for your s.
1 Th 1 5 we have been among you for your sakes

Salaboni 2 K 23 32 Eliaba of Salaboni. The sons

Salabonite 1 Pa 11 32 Eliaba a Salabonite, the

Salai 3 K 22 42 mother was Azuba daughter of S.

Salamiel Num 1 6 Salamiel the son of Surisaddai. 2:12; 7:36, 41; 10:19

Salamina Acts 13 5 when they were come to S. they

Salathi 1 Pa 12 20 there fled to him . . . Salathi

Salathiel 1 Pa 3 17 of Jechonias were Asir, S.
1 Es 3 2 Zorobabel the son of S. 8; 5:2; 2 Es 12:1; Agge 1:1, 12, 14; 2:3, 24
Jdth 8 1 Nathanias the son of Salathiel, the
Mat 1 12 Jechonias begot S. and S. begot Zorobabel
Luke 3 27 Zorobabel, who was of Salathiel, who

sale Lev 25 38 after the sale he may be redeemed
Deut 28 68 thou be set to sale to thy enemies
2 Ma 8 34 merchants to the sale of the Jews
11 3 to set the high priesthood to sale
Sale Gen 10 24 Sale, of whom was born Heber. And
Gen 11 12 Arphaxad lived 35 years and begot Sale
13 Arphaxad lived after he begot Sale
14 Sale also lived thirty years and begot
15 Sale lived after he begot Heber 403
1 Pa 1 18 Arphaxad begot S., and S. begot Heber
24 Sem, Arphaxad, Sale, Heber, Phaleg
Luke 3 35 Heber, who was of Sale, who was of
Salebim Judg 1 35 he dwelt . . . in Aialon and S.
3 K 4 9 Bendecar, in Macces and in Salebim
Salecha Josu 12 4 in S. and in all Basan unto
Josu 13 11 Hermon and all Basan as far as S.
Saled 1 Pa 2 30 sons of Nadab were S. and Apphaim. And S. died without children
Salem Gen 14 18 Mechisedech the king of Salem
Gen 33 18 he [Jacob] passed over to Salem
Heb 7 1 this Melchisedech was king of Salem
2 and then also king of Salem, that is
Salemoth 1 Pa 24 22 the son of Isaar Salemoth, and the son of Salemoth Johath
Saleph Gen 10 26 Jectan begot . . . S. 1 Pa 1:20
Salim 1 K 9 4 passed also through land of S.
John 3 23 John also was baptizing near Salim
Salisa 1 K 9 4 and through the land of Salisa
Sallem Gen 46 24 Guni and Jeser and Sallem
sallied Judg 20 25 children of Benjamin s. forth
1 Ma 6 31 they sallied forth and burnt them with
9 67 sallied out of the city and burnt the
Salma 1 Pa 2 11 Nahasson begot Salma, the father
1 Pa 2 51 Salma the father of Bethlehem, Hariph
54 the sons of Salma, Bethlehem and
Salmana Judg 8 5 that we may pursue Zebee and S.
Judg 8 6 palms of the hands of Zebee and S.
7 shall have delivered Zebee and Salmana
10 Zebee and Salmana were resting with all
12 Zebee and Salmana fled, and Gedeon
15 behold Zebee and Salmana, concerning
15 the hands of Zebee and Salmana are
18 he said to Zebee and Salmana: What
21 Zebee and Salmana said: Do thou rise
21 Gedeon rose up and slew Zebee and S.
Ps 82 12 make their princes like . . . Salmana
Osee 10 14 destroyed as Salmana was destroyed
Salmanasar 4 K 17 3 against him came up S., king
4 K 18 9 Salmanasar king of the Assyrians came
Tob 1 2 made captive in the days of Salmanasar
13 in the sight of Salmanasar the king
18 Salmanasar the king being dead, when
Salmias 1 Es 10 39 Salmias and Nathan and Adaias
Salmon Ruth 4 20 Nahasson begot S., S. begot Booz
Mat 1 4 Naasson begot S. and S. begot Booz
Luke 3 32 Booz, who was of Salmon, who was of
Salmona Num 33 41 mount Hor, and camped in S.
Salmone Acts 27 7 we sailed near Crete by S.
Salo 1 Pa 9 7 Salo the son of Mosollam, the son
Salom Bar 1 7 son of Helcias the son of Salom
Salome Mark 15 40 among whom was . . . and Salome
Mark 16 1 Mary the mother of James, and Salome
Salomi Num 34 27 of Aser, Ahiud the son of S.
1 Ma 2 26 Phinees did by Samri the son of Salomi
Salomith 1 Pa 3 19 Hananias, and S. their sister
1 Pa 23 9 sons of Semei: Salomith and Hosiel
18 sons of Isaar: Salomith the first
2 Pa 11 20 and Ethai and Ziza and Salomith
Salphaad Num 26 33 Hepher was the father of S.
Num 27 1 then came the daughters of Salphaad
6 the daughters of Salphaad demand a just
36 2 shouldst give to the daughters of S.
6 touching the daughters of Salphaad
10 daughters of S. did as was commanded
Josu 17 3 Salphaad . . . had no sons, but only
1 Pa 7 15 of second was S., and S. had daughters
salt Gen 14 3 vale, which now is the salt sea
Gen 19 26 was turned into a statue of salt
Lev 2 13 thou shalt season it with salt, neither
13 neither shalt thou take away the salt
13 all thy oblations thou shalt offer salt
18 19 it is a covenant of salt forever before
Deut 3 17 which is the most salt sea. Josu 12:3
29 23 brimstone and the heat of salt, so
Josu 15 2 was from the top of the most salt sea
5 the most s. sea even to the end of the
62 and Nebsan and the city of salt and
16 8 out thereof are at the most salt sea
18 19 towards the north of the most salt sea
Judg 9 45 so that he sowed salt in it. And when
4 K 2 20 me a new vessel, and put salt into it
21 and cast the salt into it, and said
2 Pa 13 5 and to his sons by a covenant of salt
1 Es 4 14 remembering the salt that we have eaten
6 9 wheat, salt, wine, and oil according
7 22 bates of oil and salt without measure
Job 6 6 eaten that is not seasoned with salt
Wisd 10 7 standing pillar of salt is a monument
Eccu 22 18 salt and a mass of iron is easier to
39 31 salt, milk, and bread of flour, and
43 21 he shall pour frost as salt upon the
Jer 17 6 in dryness is the desert in a salt land
Eze 16 4 nor salted with salt nor swaddled with
43 24 the priests shall put salt upon them
Soph 2 9 the dryness of thorns and heaps of salt
1 Ma 10 29 I release you from the customs of salt
Mat 5 13 you are the salt of the earth. But if
13 if the s. lose its savor. Luke 14:34
Mark 9 48 every victim shall be salted with salt
49 s. is good. But if the s. Luke 14:34
49 have salt in you, and have peace among
Col 4 6 be always in grace seasoned with salt
James 3 12 neither can the salt water yield sweet
salted Tob 6 6 the rest they s. as much as might
Eze 16 4 nor salted with salt nor swaddled
Mat 5 14 wherewith shall it be salted? It is
Mark 9 48 every one shall be salted with fire
48 every victim shall be salted with salt
saltpans 1 Ma 11 35 the s. also and the crowns
saltpits 2 K 8 13 Syria in valley of the saltpits
4 K 14 7 slew of Edom in valley of the saltpits
1 Pa 18 12 Edomites in the vale of the saltpits
2 Pa 25 11 went to the vale of saltpits and slew
Ps 59 2 of Edom in the vale of the saltpits
Eze 47 11 they shall be turned into saltpits
Saltus 1 Pa 20 5 Adeodatus the son of Saltus
Salu Num 25 14 Zambri the son of Salu, a prince
Salumith Lev 24 11 his mother was called Salumith
Salusa 1 Pa 7 37 Salusa and Jethrau and Bera
salutation Luke 1 29 what manner of s. this should
Luke 1 41 when Elizabeth heard the s. of Mary
44 as soon as the voice of thy s. sounded
1 C 16 21 salutation of me Paul, with my own hand
Col 4 18 s. of Paul with my own hand. 2 Th 3:17
salutations Mat 23 7 salutations in the market place. Luke 11:43; 20:46
salute 1 K 10 4 they will s. thee and will give
1 K 13 10 Saul went forth to meet him and s. him
25 5 salute him in my name with peace. And
14 out of the wilderness to s. our master
2 K 8 10 his son to king David to s. him and to
15 5 when any man came to him to salute him
4 K 4 29 s. him not; and if any man s. thee
10 13 down to salute the sons of the king
Eccu 22 31 not be ashamed to salute a friend
41 25 of silence before them that s. thee

1 Ma 7 33 people came out to salute him peaceably
12 17 to go also to you and to s. you and
Mat 5 47 if you salute your brethren only, what
10 12 when you come into the house, salute
Mark 15 18 they began to salute him: Hail, king
Luke 10 4 shoes; and salute no man by the way
Acts 25 13 came down to Caesarea to s. Festus. And
Rom 16 3 salute Prisca and Aquila. 2 Tim 4:19
5 salute Epenetus, my beloved: who is the
6 salute Mary, who hath labored much among
7 s. Andronicus and Junias, my kinsmen and
8 salute Ampliatus, most beloved to me in
9 s. Urbanus, our helper in Christ Jesus
10 salute Apelles, approved in Christ
11 salute them that are of Aristobulus'
11 salute Herodian, my kinsman. Salute
11 salute them that are of Narcissus'
12 salute Tryphaena and Tryphosa, who labor
12 salute Persis, the dearly beloved, who
13 salute Rufus, elect in the Lord, and his
14 salute Asycritus, Phlegon, Hermas
15 salute Philologus and Julia, Nereus and
16 salute one another with an holy kiss. 1 C 16:20; 2 C 13:12; 1 P 5:14
16 all the churches of Christ salute you
22 Tertius, who wrote this epistle, salute
1 C 16 19 the churches of Asia salute you. Aquila
19 Aquila and Priscilla salute you much
20 all the brethren salute you. Salute one
2 C 13 12 a holy kiss. All the saints salute you
Phil 4 21 salute ye every saint in Christ Jesus
22 brethren who are with me, salute you
22 all the saints salute you; especially
Col 4 15 salute the brethren who are at Laodicea
1 Th 5 26 salute all the brethren with a holy kiss
2 Tim 4 21 Claudia and all the brethren, salute
Titus 3 15 all that are with me salute thee: salute them that love us in the faith
Philem 23 there salute thee Epaphras, my fellow
Heb 13 24 salute all your prelates, and all the
24 the brethren from Italy salute you
2 J 13 children of thy sister Elect s. thee
3 J 14 peace be to thee. Our friends s. thee. Salute the friends by name
saluted Exod 18 7 s. one another with words of
Judg 18 15 they saluted him with words of peace
1 K 30 21 coming to the people, s. them peaceably
Tob 5 6 saluted him and said: From whence art
11 so going in he saluted him and said
1 Ma 7 29 they saluted one another peaceably
11 6 they s. one another, and they lodged
Mark 9 14 and running to him, they saluted him
12 38 and to be saluted in the marketplace
Luke 1 40 the house of Zachary and s. Elizabeth
Acts 18 22 he went up to Jerusalem, and s. church
21 19 whom when he had saluted, he related
saluteth Rom 16 21 Timothy, my fellow laborer, s.
Rom 16 23 my host, and the whole church, s. you
23 saluteth you, and Quartus, a brother
Col 4 10 my fellow prisoner, saluteth you, and
12 Epaphras saluteth you, who is one of you
14 Luke, the most dear physician, saluteth
1 P 5 13 church that is in Babylon . . . s. you
saluting Gen 43 27 he courteously s. them again
Acts 21 7 saluting the brethren, we abode one day
Heb 11 13 beholding them afar off, and s. them
salvation Gen 49 18 I will look for thy salvation
Exod 15 2 he is become salvation to me: he is
1 K 2 1 because I have joyed in thy salvation
11 13 Lord this day hath wrought salvation
14 45 who hath wrought this great salvation
19 5 Lord wrought great s. for all Israel
2 K 22 3 my shield and the horn of my salvation
36 thou hast given me the shield of my s.
46 God of my salvation shall be exalted
51 giving great salvation to his king and
23 5 he is all my salvation and all my will
1 Pa 16 23 show forth from day to day his salvation
2 Pa 6 41 let thy priests . . . put on salvation
Esth 13 13 for the salvation of Israel have kissed
Ps 3 3 there is no salvation for him in his
9 s. is of the Lord: and the blessing
9 16 I will rejoice in thy s.: the Gentiles
12 6 heart shall rejoice in thy salvation
13 7 who shall give out of Sion the s. of
17 3 horn of my salvation and my support
36 hast given me the protection of thy s.
47 let the God of my salvation be exalted
19 6 we will rejoice in thy s. and in the
7 the s. of his right hand is in powers
20 2 in thy s. he shall rejoice exceedingly
6 his glory is great in thy salvation
21 2 far from my s. are the words of my sins
26 1 the Lord is my light and my salvation
27 8 the protector of the s. of his anointed
34 3 say to my soul: I am thy salvation
9 and shall be delighted in his salvation
36 39 salvation of the just is from the Lord
37 23 my help, O Lord, the God of my salvation
39 11 I have declared thy truth and thy s.
17 let such as love thy salvation say
41 6 the s. of my countenance. 12; 42:6
49 23 I will show him the salvation of God
50 14 restore unto me the joy of thy s., and
16 O God, thou God of my salvation: and
52 7 out of Sion the salvation of Israel
59 13 from trouble: for vain is the s. of man
61 2 to God? for from him is my salvation
8 in God is my salvation and my glory
66 3 way upon earth: thy s. in all nations
67 20 God of our s. will make our journey
21 our God is the God of salvation: and
68 14 hear me, in the truth of thy salvation
30 thy salvation, O God, hath set me up
69 5 let such as love thy salvation say
70 15 thy justice: thy s. all the day long
73 12 hath wrought s. in midst of the earth
77 22 not in God: and trusted not in his s.
84 8 thy mercy: and grant us thy salvation
10 his s. is near to them that fear him
87 2 O Lord, the God of my salvation: I
88 27 my God, and the support of my salvation
90 16 of days: I will show him my salvation
95 2 show forth his salvation from day to day
97 1 his right hand hath wrought for him s.
2 the Lord hath made known his salvation
3 have seen the salvation of our God
105 4 of thy people: visit us with thy s.
115 13 I will take the chalice of salvation
117 14 and my praise: and he is become my s.
15 voice of rejoicing and of salvation
21 heard me: and art become my salvation. 28
118 41 thy salvation according to thy word
81 my soul hath fainted after thy s.: and
123 eyes have fainted after thy salvation
155 s. is far from sinners: because they
166 I looked for thy salvation, O Lord
174 I have longed for thy s., O Lord; and
131 16 I will clothe her priests with s.: and
139 8 Lord, the strength of my salvation
143 10 who givest salvation to kings: who
145 3 children of men, in whom there is no s.
149 4 he will exalt the meek unto salvation
Prov 2 7 he will keep the s. of the righteous
8 35 and shall have salvation from the Lord
Wisd 5 2 the suddenness of their unexpected s.

16 6 having a sign of salvation to put them
18 7 thy people received the s. of the just
Eccu 1 22 filling up peace and the fruit of s.
4 28 refrain not to speak in the time of s.
13 18 thy life, and call upon him for thy s.
39 23 and there is no diminishing of his s.
Isa 12 2 and my praise, and he is become my s.
25 9 shall rejoice and be joyful in his s.
26 18 we have not wrought s. on the earth
33 2 our salvation in the time of trouble
6 riches of s., wisdom and knowledge
37 32 remnant, and salvation from mount Sion
45 17 saved in the Lord with an eternal s.
46 12 my s. shall not tarry. I will give s. in
49 6 that thou mayst be my salvation even
8 in the day of s. I have helped thee
51 6 my s. shall be forever, and my. 8
52 7 of him . . . that preacheth salvation
10 shall see the salvation of our God
56 1 my s. is near to come, and my justice
59 11 for salvation, and it is far from us
16 his own arm brought salvation to him
17 a helmet of salvation upon his head
60 18 s. shall possess thy walls, and praise
61 10 hath clothed me with the garments of s.
Jer 3 23 in the Lord our God is the s. of Israel
Lam 3 26 to wait with silence for the s. of God
Bar 4 24 so shall they also shortly see your s.
29 you everlasting joy again with your s.
Joel 2 32 and in Jerusalem shall be salvation
Abdi 17 in mount Sion shall be s., and it shall
Jon 2 10 whatsoever I have vowed for my s. to the
Mich 6 9 s. shall be to them that fear thy name
Haba 3 8 horses: and thy chariots are salvation
13 wentest forth for the s. of thy people
13 of thy people: for s. with thy Christ
1 Ma 3 6 and salvation prospered in his hand
4 56 sacrifices of salvation and of praise
5 62 men by whom s. was brought to Israel
Luke 1 69 hath raised up an horn of s. to us in
71 s. from our enemies and from the hand
77 to give knowledge of s. to his people
2 30 because my eyes have seen thy s. which
3 16 all flesh shall see the s. of God
19 9 this day is s. come to this house
John 4 22 we know; for salvation is of the Jews
Acts 4 12 neither is there s. in any other. For
13 26 to you the word of this s. is sent
47 thou mayest be for s. unto the utmost
16 17 who preach unto you the way of s.
28 28 this s. of God is sent to the Gentiles
Rom 1 16 for it is power of God unto salvation
10 1 to God, is for them unto salvation. For
10 with mouth, confession is made unto s.
11 11 by their offence, s. is come to Gentiles
13 11 now our salvation is nearer than when we
2 C 1 6 it is for your exhortation and salvation
6 2 in day of salvation have I helped thee
2 behold, now is the day of salvation
7 10 worketh penance, steadfast unto s.; but
Eph 1 13 of truth, the gospel of your salvation
6 17 take unto you the helmet of salvation
Phil 1 19 this shall fall out to me unto salvation
28 perdition, but to you of s., and this
2 12 with fear and trembling work out your s.
5 8 and for a helmet the hope of salvation
9 wrath, but unto the purchasing of s. by
2 Th 2 12 chosen you firstfruits unto salvation
2 Tim 2 10 that they also may obtain the salvation
3 15 which can instruct thee to salvation
Heb 1 14 who shall receive the inheritance of s.
2 3 we escape if we neglect so great s.
10 to perfect the author of their salvation
5 9 obey him, the cause of eternal salvation
6 9 nearer to salvation; though we speak
9 28 to them that expect him unto salvation
1 P 1 5 are kept by faith unto s., ready to
9 your faith, even the s. of your souls
10 of which s. the prophets have inquired
2 2 thereby you may grow unto salvation
2 P 3 15 longsuffering of our Lord, salvation
Jude 3 unto you concerning your common s.
Apoc 7 10 s. to our God, who sitteth upon the
12 10 now is come s. and strength and the
19 1 s. and glory and power is to our God
Sama Josu 15 26 Amam, Sama and Molada, and
1 Pa 3 18 and Jecemia, Sama, and Nadabia
8 13 Baria and Sama were heads of their
Samaa 2 K 21 21 Jonathan the son of Samaa the
1 Pa 6 30 Oza his son, Samaa his son, Haggia
39 son of Barachias, the son of Samaa
8 32 Macelloth begot Samaa: and they dwelt
12 3 Ahiezer and Joas the sons of Samaa
20 7 Jonathan the son of Samaa the brother
Samaan 1 Pa 9 38 Macelloth begot Samaan: these
Samachias 1 Pa 26 7 valiant men: and Eliu and S.
Samad 1 Pa 8 12 were Heber and Missam and S.
Samaia 1 Pa 4 37 the son of Semri the son of S.
1 Pa 5 4 sons of Joel: Samaia his son, Gog his
2 Es 6 10 I went into the house of Samaia the
Samaias 1 Pa 12 4 and S. of Gabaon, the stoutest
1 Es 8 13 and Samaias, and with them 60 men
Samaoth 1 Pa 27 8 the fifth captain . . . was S.
Samaraim Josu 18 22 Betharaba and S. and Bethel
Samareth 1 Pa 8 21 and S. the sons of Semei
Samaria 3 K 13 32 that are in the cities of S.
3 K 16 24 he bought the hill of Samaria of Semer
24 called the city which he built Samaria
28 and Amri . . . was buried in Samaria
29 reigned over Israel in Samaria. 4 K 3:1; 10:36; 13:1, 10
32 temple of Baal which he had built in S.
18 2 there was a grievous famine in Samaria
20 1 he [Benadad] fought against Samaria
10 if the dust of Samaria shall suffice
17 there are men come out of Samaria
34 in Damascus, as my father made in S.
43 to hear, and raging came into Samaria
21 1 near the palace of Achab king of S.
18 to meet Achab . . . who is in Samaria
22 10 by the entrance of the gate of Samaria
37 king died and was carried into Samaria
37 and they buried the king in Samaria
38 washed his chariot in pool of Samaria
52 began to reign over Israel in Samaria
4 K 1 2 upper chamber which he had in Samaria
3 to meet messengers of king of Samaria
2 25 from thence he returned to Samaria
3 6 Joram went out that day from Samaria
5 3 with the prophet that is in Samaria
6 19 so he [Eliseus] led them into Samaria
20 when they were come into S., Eliseus
20 themselves to be in midst of Samaria
24 Benadad . . . went up and besieged S.
25 there was a great famine in Samaria
7 1 shall be sold . . . in the gate of S.
18 time tomorrow in the gate of Samaria
10 1 Achab had seventy sons in Samaria
1 Jehu wrote letters and sent to Samaria
12 he [Jehu] arose and went to Samaria
17 brought him [Jonadab] into Samaria
17 all that were left of Achab in Samaria
35 and they buried him [Jehu] in Samaria
13 6 there still remained a grove in S.
9 they buried him [Joachaz] in Samaria
13 Joas was buried in Samaria. 14:16

14 14 and hostages and returned to Samaria
23 son of Joas king of Israel in Samaria
15 8 son of Jeroboam over Israel in Samaria
13 Sellum . . . reigned one month in S.
14 he came into Samaria and struck Sellum . . . in Samaria
17 reigned Manahem . . . ten years in S.
23 reigned Phaceia . . . in S. two years
25 and smote him [Phaceia] in Samaria
27 reigned Phacee . . . over Israel in S.
17 1 Osee the son of Ela reigned in Samaria
5 going up to Samaria, he besieged it
6 the king of the Assyrians took Samaria
24 placed them in the cities of Samaria
24 and they possessed Samaria and dwelt
26 made to dwell in the cities of Samaria
28 been carried away captive from Samaria
33 out of which they were brought to S.
18 9 king of the Assyrians came up to S.
10 after three years . . . S. was taken
34 have they delivered S. out of my hand
21 13 over Jerusalem the line of Samaria
23 18 the prophet that came out of Samaria
19 which were in the cities of Samaria
1 Pa 12 5 Samaria and Saphatia the Haruphite
2 Pa 18 2 down to him after some years to S.
9 in the open court by gate of Samaria
22 9 took him [Ochozias] lying hid in S.
25 13 cities of Juda, from S. to Beth-horon
24 of the hostages, he brought back to S.
28 8 booty: and they brought it to Samaria
9 to meet the army that came to Samaria
15 brethren, and they returned to Samaria
1 Es 4 10 made to dwell in the cities of Samaria
17 sent words to . . . inhabitants of Samaria
Jdth 1 9 to all that were in Samaria and beyond
4 3 they sent into all Samaria round about
Isa 7 9 and the head of S. the son of Romelia
8 4 spoils of Samaria shall be taken away
9 9 shall know, and the inhabitants of S.
10 9 Arphad? Is not Samaria as Damascus
10 their idols of Jerusalem and of Samaria
11 as I have done to S. and her idols
36 19 have they delivered S. out of my hand
Jer 23 13 I have seen folly in the prophets of S.
31 5 vineyards in the mountains of Samaria
41 5 and from Samaria, fourscore men
Eze 16 46 thy elder sister is Samaria, she and
51 Samaria committed not half thy sins
53 by bringing back S. and her daughters
55 Samaria and her daughters shall return
23 4 S. is Oolla, and Jerusalem is Ooliba
33 with the cup of thy sister Samaria
Osee 7 1 was discovered, and wickedness of S.
8 6 calf of S. shall be turned to spiders'
10 5 inhabitants of S. have worshipped the
7 Samaria hath made her king to pass
14 1 let Samaria perish, because she hath
Amos 3 9 assemble yourselves upon mountains of S.
12 of Israel be taken out that dwell in S.
4 1 that are in the mountains of Samaria
6 1 that have confidence in mountain of S.
8 14 that swear by the sin of Samaria
Abdi 19 Ephraim and the country of Samaria
Mich 1 1 he saw concerning S. and Jerusalem
5 wickedness of Jacob? Is it not Samaria
6 I will make Samaria as a heap of stones
1 Ma 3 10 army from S. to make war against Israel
5 66 aliens, and he went through Samaria
10 30 cities that are added thereto out of S.
38 to Judea out of the country of Samaria
11 28 free from tribute . . . and Samaria
34 which are added to Judea, out of S.
2 Ma 15 1 that Judas was in the places of S.
Luke 17 11 through the midst of S. and Galilee
John 4 4 he was of necessity to pass through S.
5 he cometh therefore to a city of S.
7 there cometh a woman of Samaria to
Acts 1 8 and in all Judea and Samaria and even
8 1 through the countries of Judea and S.
5 Philip going down to the city of S.
9 seducing the people of Samaria, giving
14 heard that S. had received the word
9 31 had peace throughout . . . and Samaria
15 3 passed through Phenice, and Samaria

Samarias 1 Es 10 32 Benjamin, Maloch, S. And of

Samaritan Luke 10 33 S. being on his journey, came
Luke 17 16 thanks: and this was a Samaritan
John 4 9 S. woman saith to him: How dost thou
9 to drink, who am a Samaritan woman
8 48 that thou art a S. and hast a devil

Samaritans 4 K 18 29 places, which the S. had made
2 Es 4 2 brethren and the multitude of the S.
Mat 10 5 into the city of the S. . . . enter ye not
Luke 9 52 into city of the S. to prepare for the
John 4 9 Jews do not communicate with the S.
39 many of the Samaritans believed in him
40 when the S. were come to him, they
Acts 8 25 gospel to many countries of the S.

Samarite Gen 10 18 Chanaan begot . . . the S. 1 Pa 1:16

samech Ps 118 113 samech. Lam 1:15; 2:15; 3:43, 44, 45; 4:15

Samgar Judg 3 31 Samgar the son of Anath. 5:6

Samir Josu 15 48 in the mountain Samir and Jether
Judg 10 1 who dwelt in Samir of mount Ephraim
2 [Thola] died and was buried in Samir
1 Pa 24 24 the son of Micha, Samir. The brother

Samma Gen 36 13 sons of Rahuel . . . S. 17; 1 Pa 1:37
1 K 16 9 and Isai brought Samma, and he said
17 13 his three sons . . . the third Samma
1 Pa 2 43 sons of Hebron . . . Recem and Samma
44 S. begot Raham, the father of Jercaam
5 8 Azaz the son of Samma, the son of Joel
7 37 Samma and Salusa and Jethran and
11 44 Samma and Jehiel the sons of Hotham

Sammaa 1 Pa 6 30 Oza his son, Sammaa his son

Sammai 1 Pa 2 44 Recem begot Sammai. The son of S.
1 Pa 4 17 he begot Mariam and Sammai and

Sammoth 1 Pa 11 27 valiant men . . . S. an Arorite

Sammua Num 13 5 of Ruben, S. the son of Zechur
2 Es 12 18 of Belga, Sammua: of Semaia, Jonathan

Samos Acts 20 15 next day we arrived at Samos

Samothracia Acts 16 11 with straight course to S.

Samri 2 Pa 29 13 sons of Elisaphan, S. and Jahiel

Samsai 1 Es 4 9 Reum Beelteem and S. the scribe
1 Es 4 17 sent word to . . . Samsai the scribe
23 was read before . . . Samsai the scribe

Samsari 1 Pa 8 26 and Samsari . . . sons of Jeroham

Samson Judg 13 24 bore a son and called his name S.
Judg 14 1 S. went down to Thamnatha, and seeing
3 Samson said to his father: Take this
5 Samson went down with his father and
6 spirit of the Lord came upon Samson
10 and made a feast for his son Samson
12 Samson said to them: I will propose
15 they said to the wife of Samson: Soothe
16 she wept before Samson and complained
15 1 Samson came, meaning to visit his wife
3 Samson answered him: From this day I
6 done this thing? And it was answered: S.
7 Samson said to them. Although you have
10 we are come to bind Samson and to
11 said to Samson: Knowest thou not that
12 Samson said to them: Swear to me and
16 2 that Samson was come into the city
3 Samson slept till midnight, and then

6 and Dalila said to Samson: Tell me
7 Samson answered her: If I shall be
9 the Philistines are upon thee, Samson. 12, 14, 20
13 Samson answered her: If thou plattest
23 our god hath delivered our enemy Samson
25 commanded that Samson should be called
Heb 11 32 Samson, Jephthe, David, Samuel and the
Samson's Judg 16 27 were beholding Samson's play
Samua 2 K 5 14 Samua and Sobab and Nathan and
1 Pa 14 4 born to him in Jerusalem: Samua and
2 Es 11 17 Abda the son of S., the son of Galal
Samuel Num 34 20 of the tribe of Simeon, Samuel
1 K 1 20 a son, and called his name Samuel
2 18 Samuel ministered before the face of
21 child S. became great before the Lord
26 the child Samuel advanced and grew
3 1 the child Samuel ministered to the Lord
3 Samuel slept in the temple of the Lord
4 Lord called Samuel. And he answered
6 and the Lord called Samuel again. And
6 Samuel arose and went to Heli and said
7 now Samuel did not yet know the Lord
8 Lord called Samuel again the third time
9 he said to Samuel: Go and sleep: and if
9 Samuel went and slept in his place
10 and he called . . . Samuel, Samuel. And
10 Samuel said: Speak, Lord, for thy
11 Lord said to Samuel: behold I do a
15 Samuel slept till morning, and opened
15 S. feared to tell the vision to Heli
16 Heli called Samuel and said: Samuel
18 so Samuel told him all the words, and
19 Samuel grew and the Lord was with him
20 knew that Samuel was a faithful prophet
21 the Lord revealed himself to Samuel
21 word of S. came to pass to all Israel
7 3 Samuel spoke to all the house of Israel
5 Samuel said: Gather all Israel to
6 Samuel judged the children of Israel
8 they said to Samuel: Cease not to cry
9 Samuel took a sucking lamb and offered
9 Samuel cried to the Lord for Israel
10 when Samuel was offering the holocaust
12 S. took a stone and laid it between
13 against Philistines all the days of S.
15 S. judged Israel all the days of his life
8 1 it came to pass when Samuel was old
4 ancients . . . came to Samuel to Ramatha
6 was displeasing in the eyes of Samuel
6 judge us. And S. prayed to the Lord
7 the Lord said to Samuel: Hearken to the
10 Samuel told all the words of the Lord
19 would not hear the voice of Samuel
21 Samuel heard all the words of the people
22 the Lord said to Samuel: Hearken to
22 and Samuel said to the men of Israel
9 14 S. was coming out over against them
15 the Lord had revealed to ear of Samuel
17 when Samuel saw Saul, the Lord said
18 Saul came to S. in the midst of the
19 Samuel answered Saul, saying: I am the
22 Samuel taking Saul and his servant
23 S. said to the cook: Bring the portion
24 S. said: Behold what is left, set it
24 and Saul ate with Samuel that day
26 S. called Saul on the top of the house
26 both of them, to wit, he and Samuel
27 S. said to Saul: Speak to the servant
10 1 S. took a little vial of oil and poured
9 had turned his back to go from Samuel
14 and not finding them we went to Samuel
15 tell me what Samuel said to thee. And
16 the kingdom of which Samuel had spoken
17 and Samuel called together the people
20 Samuel brought to him all the tribes
24 Samuel said to all the people: Surely
25 Samuel told the people the law of
25 and Samuel sent away all the people
11 7 come forth and follow Saul and Samuel
12 people said to Samuel: Who is he that
14 Samuel said to the people: Come and
12 1 S. said to all Israel: Behold I have
6 S. said to the people: It is the Lord
11 Jephte and Samuel, and delivered you
18 Samuel cried unto the Lord, and the
19 people greatly feared the Lord and S.
19 all the people said to Samuel: Pray for
20 Samuel said to the people: Fear not, you
13 8 according to the appointment of Samuel
8 Samuel came not to Galgal, and the
10 Samuel came; and Saul went forth to meet
11 Samuel said to him: What hast thou done
13 Samuel said to Saul: Thou hast done
15 Samuel arose and went up from Galgal
15 1 Samuel said to Saul: The Lord sent me
10 the word of the Lord came to Samuel
11 Samuel was grieved, and he cried unto
12 when Samuel rose early, to go to Saul
12 it was told Samuel that Saul was come
12 to Galgal. And Samuel came to Saul
13 when S. was come to Saul, Saul said
14 S. said: What meaneth then this bleating
16 Samuel said to Saul: Suffer me, and
17 Samuel said: When thou wast a little
20 Saul said to S.: Yea I have hearkened
22 and Samuel said: Doth the Lord desire
24 and Saul said to Samuel: I have sinned
26 Samuel said to Saul: I will not return
27 Samuel turned about to go away: but
28 Samuel said to him: The Lord hath rent
31 so Samuel turned again after Saul
32 Samuel said: Bring hither to me Agag
33 S. said: As thy sword hath made women
33 Samuel hewed him in pieces before the
34 S. departed to Ramatha: but Saul
35 Samuel saw Saul no more till the day
35 nevertheless Samuel mourned for Saul
16 1 the Lord said to Samuel: How long wilt
2 Samuel said: How shall I go? for Saul
4 Samuel did as the Lord had said to him
7 Lord said to Samuel: Look not on his
8 brought him [Abinadab] before Samuel
10 brought his seven sons before Samuel
10 Samuel said to Isai: The Lord hath not
11 S. said to Isai: Are here all thy sons
11 S. said to Isai: Send and fetch him
13 then Samuel took the horn of oil and
13 and Samuel rose up and went to Ramatha
19 18 escaped and came to Samuel in Ramatha
18 he and Samuel went and dwelt in Najoth
20 S. presiding over them, the spirit of
22 in what place are Samuel and David
24 prophesied with the rest before Samuel
25 1 Samuel died, and all Israel was gathered
28 3 Samuel was dead, and all Israel mourned
11 and he [Saul] said: Bring me up Samuel
12 when the woman saw Samuel, she cried
14 and Saul understood that it was Samuel
15 Samuel said to Saul: Why hast thou
16 Samuel said: Why askest thou me, seeing
20 was frightened with the words of Samuel
1 Pa 6 28 the sons of Samuel: The firstborn
33 the son of Joel, the son of Samuel
7 2 and Samuel, chiefs of the houses of
9 22 David and Samuel the seer appointed

13 3 I have commanded my s. one and have
23 18 and her hire shall be s. to the Lord
30 29 as in the night of the s. solemnity
66 17 were s. and thought themselves clean
Jer 1 5 camest forth out of the womb, I s. thee
Eze 20 41 and I will be sanctified in you in
28 22 in her, and shall be sanctified in
25 I will be s. in them before the
36 23 when I shall be s. in you before their
38 16 when I shall be sanctified in thee
23 will be magnified and I will be s.
39 27 and shall be sanctified in them in the
46 20 outward court, and the people be s.
48 14 because they are sanctified to the Lord
Soph 1 7 a victim, he hath sanctified his guests
Agge 2 13 if a man carry s. flesh in the skirt
13 wine or oil or any meat: shall it be s.
Zach 2 12 Juda his portion in the s. land: and
8 3 of the Lord of hosts, the s. mountain
14 21 caldron . . . shall be s. to the Lord
1 Ma 4 48 they s. the temple and the courts
2 Ma 2 8 that the place might be s. to the great
15 2 but give honor to the day that is s.
John 10 36 him whom the Father hath sanctified
17 19 they also may be sanctified in truth
Acts 20 32 to give an inheritance among all the s.
Rom 15 16 acceptable and s. in the Holy Ghost. I
1 C 1 2 Corinth, to them that are s. in Christ
6 11 you are washed, but you are sanctified
7 14 the unbelieving husband is sanctified
14 wife is sanctified by believing husband
1 Tim 4 5 it is sanctified by the word of God and
2 Tim 2 21 sanctified and profitable to the Lord
Heb 2 11 he that sanctifieth and they who are s.
10 10 we are s. by the oblation of the body of
14 perfected forever them that are s.
29 by which he was s., and hath offered
Apoc 22 11 that is holy, let him be s. still
sanctifier Eze 37 28 am the Lord the s. of Israel
sanctifieth Mat 23 17 temple that s. the gold
Mat 23 19 or the altar that sanctifieth the gift
Heb 2 11 he that s. and they who are sanctified
1 J 3 3 that hath this hope in him, s. himself
sanctify Exod 13 2 s. unto me every firstborn
Exod 19 10 sanctify them today and tomorrow and
23 limits about the mount, and sanctify it
28 41 and shalt sanctify them, that they
29 24 shalt s. them elevating before the Lord
26 thou shalt sanctify it before the Lord
27 shalt s. both the consecrated breast
36 and shalt anoint it to sanctify it
37 shalt thou expiate the altar and s. it
44 I will sanctify also the tabernacle
30 29 thou shalt sanctify all, and they shall
30 and his sons, and shalt s. them, that
31 13 am the Lord who s. you. Lev 20:8; 22:32
Lev 16 19 times let him expiate and sanctify it
20 7 sanctify yourselves and be ye holy
21 8 am holy, the Lord, who sanctify them
15 for I am the Lord who sanctify him
23 I am the Lord who sanctify them. 22:9, 16; Eze 20:12
23 11 be acceptable for you and shall s. it
25 10 thou shalt sanctify the fiftieth year
27 14 vow his house and sanctify it to the
26 to the Lord, no man may s. and vow
Num 6 11 he shall sanctify his head that day
20 12 to s. me before the children of Israel
27 14 neither would you s. me before them
Deut 5 12 day of the sabbath, to sanctify it
15 19 and thy sheep, thou shalt s. to the
32 51 you did not s. me among the children
Josu 7 13 sanctify the people and say to them
2 Pa 29 16 into the temple of the Lord to s. it
2 Es 13 22 gates and to sanctify the sabbath day
Eccu 2 20 in his sight will s. their souls
35 11 and sanctify thy tithes with joy
Isa 8 13 sanctify the Lord of hosts himself
29 23 they shall s. the Holy One of Jacob
42 21 the Lord was willing to sanctify him
Jer 17 22 s. the sabbath day, as I commanded
24 if you will sanctify the sabbath day
27 to sanctify the sabbath day, and not
Eze 20 20 sanctify my sabbaths, that they may
36 23 and I will sanctify my great name
44 19 not s. the people with their vestments
24 solemnites and sanctify my sabbaths
Joel 1 14 sanctify ye a fast, call an assembly
2 15 s. a fast, call a solemn assembly
16 sanctify the church, assemble the
Zach 7 3 or must I s. myself as I have now
1 25 the fathers and didst sanctify them
2 Ma 26 preserve thy own portion and s. it
John 17 17 s. them in truth. Thy word is truth
19 for them do I sanctify myself, that
Acts 21 24 take these, and s. thyself with them
Eph 5 26 he might sanctify it, cleansing it by
1 Th 5 23 himself sanctify you in all things; that
Heb 9 13 sprinkled, sanctify such as are defiled
13 12 that he might s. the people by his own
1 P 3 15 but s. the Lord Christ in your hearts
sanctifying Isa 29 23 midst of him, s. my name
Rom 15 16 sanctifying the gospel of God, that the
sanctuaries Lev 26 31 will make your s. desolate
Isa 16 12 he shall go in to his sanctuaries to
Jer 51 51 strangers are come upon the s. of the
Eze 22 8 thou hast despised my sanctuaries and
26 law, and have defiled my sanctuaries
28 18 thou hast defiled thy sanctuaries by
Amos 7 9 sanctuaries of Israel shall be laid
sanctuary Exod 15 17 thy s., O Lord, which thy
Exod 25 8 they shall make me a sanctuary, and I
26 33 the s. and the holy of holies shall
28 29 when he shall enter into the sanctuary
35 he goeth in and cometh out of the s.
43 to minister in the sanctuary. 29:30
30 24 by the weight of the sanctuary. Num 7:25, 43, 61, 85, 86; 18:16
31 11 and the incense of spices in the s.
36 1 necessary for the uses of the sanctuary
6 offer any more for the work of the s.
38 24 that was spent in the work of the s.
24 according to the standard of the s.
26 were cast the sockets of the sanctuary
39 41 Aaron and his sons used in the s.
Lev 4 6 sprinkle . . . before veil of the s.
5 15 according to the weight of the s. Num 3:47, 50; 7:13, 19, 31, 49, 55, 67, 73, 79
6 30 to make atonement in the sanctuary
10 4 away your brethren from before the s.
18 you ought to have eaten it in the s.
12 4 neither shall she enter into the s.
16 2 that he enter not at all into the s.
16 expiate the s. from the uncleanness
17 when the high priest goeth into the s.
20 after he hath cleansed the sanctuary
23 when he entered into the sanctuary
27 whose blood was carried into the s.
33 and he shall expiate the sanctuary
19 30 reverence my sanctuary. 26:2
20 3 to Moloch, and hath defiled my s.
21 12 lest he defile the sanctuary of the Lord
22 loaves that are offered in the sanctuary
23 and he must not defile my sanctuary
22 9 not fall into sin and . . . die in the s.
14 shall give it to the priest into the s.

27 3 after the weight of the s. Num 7:37
25 made according to the sicle of the s.
Num 3 28 they shall have the guard of the s.
31 the altars and the vessels of the s.
32 them that watch for the guard of the s.
38 having the custody of the sanctuary
4 12 wherewith they minister in the s.
15 and his sons have wrapped up the s.
15 shall not touch the vessels of the s.
16 of all the vessels that are in the s.
20 see the things that are in the sanctuary
5 10 whatsoever is offered into the sanctuary
7 9 because they serve in the sanctuary
8 19 presume to approach unto my sanctuary
10 21 Caathites also marched carrying the s.
18 1 shall bear the iniquity of the sanctuary
3 shall not come nigh the vessels of the s.
5 watch ye in the charge of the s. and
10 thou shalt eat it in the sanctuary
19 all the firstfruits of the sanctuary
19 20 because he hath profaned the sanctuary
28 7 part of a hin for every lamb in the s.
Deut 26 15 look from thy sanctuary and thy
Josu 24 26 the oak that was in the s. of Lord
3 K 8 4 and all the vessels of the sanctuary
8 were seen without in the sanctuary
10 the priests were come out of the s.
1 Pa 9 29 had the instruments of the sanctuary
22 19 and build a sanctuary to the Lord
23 28 place of purification and in the s.
32 keep . . . ceremonies of the sanctuary
24 5 princes of the s. and princes of God
28 10 to build the house of the sanctuary
2 Pa 5 5 carried the vessels of the sanctuary
11 priests were come out of the sanctuary
20 8 built in it a sanctuary to thy name
26 18 go out of the sanctuary, do not despise
29 5 take away all filth out of the sanctuary
7 nor offered holocausts in the sanctuary
21 they offered . . . for the sanctuary
30 8 and come to his sanctuary which he
35 3 put the ark in the sanctuary of the
5 serve ye in the sanctuary by the
36 17 with the sword in the house of his s.
Jdth 9 11 promise themselves to violate the s.
16 24 joyful in the sight of the sanctuary
Ps 19 3 may he send thee help from the sanctuary
55 1 removed at a distance from the sanctuary
62 3 in the sanctuary have I come before thee
67 25 of my king who is in his sanctuary
72 17 until I go into the sanctuary of God
73 3 hath done wickedly in the sanctuary
7 they have set fire to thy sanctuary
77 54 them into the mountain of his s.: the
69 he built his sanctuary as of unicorns
82 13 let us possess the sanctuary of God
88 40 thou hast profaned his sanctuary on
101 20 hath looked forth from his high s.
113 2 Judea was made his sanctuary, Israel
Eccu 45 30 to be the prince of the sanctuary
47 15 and prepare a sanctuary forever
Isa 60 13 to beautify the place of my sanctuary
63 18 our enemies have trodden down thy s.
64 10 the city of thy s. is become a desert
Lam 1 10 seen the Gentiles enter into her s.
2 7 he hath cursed his sanctuary: he hath
20 and the prophet be slain in the s.
4 1 the stones of the s. are scattered
Eze 5 11 because thou hast violated my sanctuary
7 24 and they shall possess their sanctuary
8 6 that I should depart far off from my s.
9 6 kill him not, and begin ye at my s.
11 16 I will be to them a little sanctuary
23 38 they polluted my s. on the same day
39 went into my sanctuary the same day
24 21 behold I will profane my sanctuary
25 3 hast said: Ha, ha, upon my sanctuary
37 26 will set my s. in the midst of them
28 when my s. shall be in the midst of them
41 21 the face of the s., sight to sight
23 two doors in the temple and in the s.
42 20 between s. and the place of the people
43 21 burn him . . . without the sanctuary
44 1 way of the gate of the outward s.
5 with all the goings out of the sanctuary
7 strangers . . . to be in my sanctuary
8 have not kept the ordinances of my s.
8 keepers of my charge in my sanctuary
9 no stranger . . . shall enter into my s.
11 shall be officers in my sanctuary
15 who kept the ceremonies of my s.
16 they shall enter into my sanctuary
19 in the store chamber of the sanctuary
27 in the day that he goeth into the s.
27 to minister unto me in the sanctuary
45 2 for the s. on every side 500 by 500
4 for the priests the ministers of the s.
4 for the holy place of the sanctuary
6 according to the separation of the s. 7
7 over against the separation of the s.
18 and thou shalt expiate the sanctuary
46 19 into the chambers of the sanctuary
47 12 waters thereof shall issue out of the s.
48 8 the s. shall be in the midst thereof
10 shall be the firstfruits of the s.
10 s. of the Lord shall be in the midst
11 the sanctuary shall be for the priests
18 the firstfruits of the s. 20, 21
21 s. of the temple shall be in the midst
Dan 8 11 cast down the place of his sanctuary
13 s. and the strength be trodden under
14 and the sanctuary shall be cleansed
9 17 show thy face upon thy sanctuary
26 shall destroy the city and the s.
11 30 indignation against covenant of the s.
30 that have forsaken covenant of the s.
31 they shall defile the s. of strength
Amos 7 13 because it is the king's sanctuary
Soph 3 4 her priests have polluted the sanctuary
1 Ma 1 23 he proudly entered into the sanctuary
38 a place to lie in wait against the s.
39 shed innocent blood round about the s.
41 her sanctuary was desolate like a
2 12 our sanctuary . . . is laid waste
3 43 let us fight for our people and our s.
45 and the sanctuary was trodden down
58 against us to destroy us and our s.
4 38 and they saw the sanctuary desolate
5 1 heard that the altar and the s. were
6 7 compassed about the s. with high walls
51 turned his army against the sanctuary
7 42 that he hath spoken ill against the s.
9 54 walls of inner court of s. to be thrown
13 3 have fought for the laws and the s.
6 I will avenge then my nation and the s.
14 15 he glorified the s. and multiplied
36 profaned all places round about the s.
42 that he should have the charge of the s.
48 be set up within the compass of the s.
2 Ma 2 17 rendered . . . the priesthood and the s.
4 34 him to come forth out of the s., and
Heb 9 1 divine service, and a worldly sanctuary

sand Gen 22 17 as the sand that is by the sea
Exod 2 12 the Egyptian and hid him in the sand
Josu 11 4 a people exceeding numerous as the s.
Judg 7 12 camels also were innumerable as the s.

1 K 13 5 like sand on the seashore for number
3 K 4 29 largeness of heart as the sand that
Ps 138 18 they shall be multiplied above the sand
Prov 27 3 a stone is heavy, and sand weighty
Wisd 7 9 in comparison of her, is as a little s.
Eccu 18 8 as a pebble of the sand, so are a few
22 18 sand and salt and a mass of iron is
Isa 48 29 thy seed had been as the sand, and the
Jer 5 22 I have set the sand a bound for the
9 11 will make Jerusalem to be heaps of sand
Eze 47 8 issue forth toward the hillocks of sand
Dan 3 36 as the sand that is on the seashore
1 Ma 11 1 army, like the sand that lieth upon
Mat 7 26 that built his house upon the sand
Heb 11 12 as the sand which is by the seashore
sand of the sea Gen 32 12 my seed like the s. . . .
Gen 41 49 wheat, that it was equal to the s. . . .
2 K 17 11 the s. . . . which cannot be numbered
3 K 4 20 as the sand of the sea in multitude
Job 6 3 as the s. . . . this would appear
Ps 77 27 feathered fowls like as the s. . . .
Eccu 1 2 who hath numbered the sand of the sea
Isa 10 22 people, O Israel, shall be as the s. . . .
Jer 15 8 are multiplied to me above the s. . . .
33 22 nor the sand of the sea be measured
Osee 1 10 children of Israel shall be as s. . . .
Rom 9 27 children of Israel be as sand of the sea
Apoc 12 18 and he stood upon the sand of the sea
20 7 the number of whom is as the s. . . .
sandals Jdth 10 3 put s. on her feet and took
Jdth 16 11 her s. ravished his eyes, her beauty
Mark 6 9 but to be shod with sandals, and that
Acts 12 8 gird thyself and put on thy sandals
sands Deut 33 19 the hidden treasurers of the s.
sandy Eccu 25 27 as the climbing of a sandy way
sang Ps 105 12 words: and they sang his praises
Sanir Deut 3 9 call Sarion, and the Amorrhites S.
1 Pa 5 23 Basan unto Baal, Hermon, and Sanir
Cant 4 8 from the top of Sanir and Hermon, from
Eze 27 5 with fir trees of Sanir they have built
Saph 2 K 21 18 then Sobochai of Husathi slew S.
Saphai 1 Pa 20 4 Sabachai the Husathite slew S.
Saphan 4 K 22 3 king sent S. the son of Assia
4 K 22 8 Helcias the high priest said to Saphan
8 and Helcias gave the book to Saphan
9 Saphan the scribe came to the king
10 and Saphan the scribe told the king
10 when S. had read it before the king
12 the son of S. . . . and S. the scribe
14 and Saphan and Asaia went to Holda
25 22 Ahicam the son of Saphan. 2 Pa 34:20; Jer 26:24; 39:14; 40:5, 9, 11; 41:2; 43:6
1 Pa 5 12 and Saphan the second: and Janai
7 15 wives for his sons Happhim and S.
2 Pa 34 8 he sent Saphan the son of Eselias and
15 [Helcias] said to Saphan the scribe
20 Saphan the scribe and Asaa the king's
Jer 29 3 the hand of Elasa the son of Saphan
36 10 Gamarias the son of Saphan. 11, 12
Saphat Num 13 6 of Simeon, S. the son of Huri
3 K 19 16 Eliseus the son of Saphat. 19; 4 K 3:11; 6:31
1 Pa 3 22 Naaria and Saphat, six in number
5 12 and Janai and Saphat in Basan. And
27 29 over the oxen in the valleys, Saphat
Saphathia 2 K 3 4 fifth S. the son of Abital
Saphatia 1 Pa 12 5 and Saphatia the Haruphite
1 Es 2 57 children of S., the children of Hatil
8 8 of the sons of Saphatia, Zebedia
2 Es 7 59 children of Saphatia, the children
Saphatias 1 Pa 3 3 the fifth S. of Abital
1 Pa 9 8 Mosallam the son of Saphatias the son
27 16 over the Simeonites, Saphatias the son
2 Pa 21 2 S., all these were sons of Josaphat
2 Es 11 4 Amarias the son of Saphatias, the son
Jer 38 1 Saphatias the son of Mathan, and
Saphira Acts 5 1 Ananias, with S. his wife, sold
Saphon Josu 13 27 Bethnemra and Socoth and Saphon
sapphire Exod 24 10 as it were a work of s. stone
Exod 28 18 carbuncle, a s., and a jasper. 39:11
Tob 13 21 gates of Jerusalem shall be built of s.
Job 28 16 precious stone sardonyx or the s.
Lam 4 7 than the old ivory, fairer than the s.
Eze 1 26 as the appearance of the sapphire stone
10 1 over them as it were the sapphire stone
28 13 the onyx and the beryl and the sapphire
Apoc 21 19 was jasper: the second, sapphire: the
sapphires Job 28 6 stones of it are the place of s.
Cant 5 14 his belly as of ivory, set with s.
Isa 54 11 will lay thy foundations with s.
Sara Gen 17 15 shalt not call Sarai, but Sara
Gen 17 17 shall Sara that is 90 years old bring
19 Sara thy wife shall bear thee a son
21 Isaac, whom Sara shall bring forth
18 6 Abraham made haste into the tent to S.
9 said to him: Where is Sara thy wife
10 and Sara thy wife shall have a son
10 which when Sara heard, she laughed
11 ceased to be with Sara after manner of
13 why did Sara laugh, saying: Shall I
14 Sara shall have a son. Sara denied saying: I did not laugh
20 2 said of Sara his wife: She is my sister
14 and restored to him Sara his wife
16 to Sara he said: Behold I have given
18 house of Abimelech on account of Sara
21 1 and the Lord visited Sara as he had
3 his son, whom Sara bore him, Isaac
6 Sara said: God hath made a laughter
7 should hear that S. gave suck to a son
9 when Sara had seen the son of Agar
12 in all that Sara hath said to thee
23 1 Sara lived 127 years. And she died
19 Abraham buried Sara his wife in a
24 36 Sara my master's wife hath borne my
67 who brought her into the tent of Sara
25 10 there was he buried, and Sara his wife
46 17 and Beria and Sara their sister. The
49 31 they buried him and Sara his wife
Num 26 46 name of the daughter of Aser was Sara
1 Pa 7 24 and his daughter was Sara, who built
30 children of Aser . . . Sara, Jessui and Baria and Sara their sister
Tob 3 7 Sara daughter of Roguel in Rages
6 11 he hath a daughter named Sara, but he
7 8 his wife and Sara their daughter wept
10 promise to give me Sara thy daughter
19 brought Sara her daughter in thither
8 4 Sara, arise, and let us pray to God
10 Sara also said: Have mercy on us
10 10 he delivered Sara unto him, and half
11 18 after seven days Sara his son's wife
12 14 to deliver Sara thy son's wife from
Isa 51 2 your father and to Sara that bore you
Rom 4 19 years old, nor the dead womb of Sara
9 9 will I come; and Sara shall have a son
Heb 11 11 by faith also Sara herself, being barren
1 P 3 6 as Sara obeyed Abraham, calling him
Saraa Josu 19 41 border of their possession was S.
Josu 19 50 city which he asked for, Thamnath Saraa
Judg 13 2 now there was a certain man of Saraa
25 camp of Dan, between Saraa and Esthaol
16 31 buried it between Saraa and Esthaol
18 2 stock and family from S. and Esthaol
8 they returned to their brethren in Saraa
11 from Saraa and Esthaol, 600 men

2 Pa 11 10 Saraa also and Aialon and Hebron
2 Es 11 29 some dwelt . . . at Remmon and at S.
Sarabias 1 Es 8 18 S. and his sons and his brethren
1 Es 8 24 chief of the priests, Sarabias and
Sarai Gen 11 29 name of Abram's wife was Sarai
Gen 11 30 Sarai was barren and had no children
31 and Sarai his daughter-in-law the wife
12 5 he took Sarai his wife, and Lot his
11 he said to Sarai his wife: I know that
17 grievous stripes for S., Abram's wife
16 1 Sarai the wife of Abram had brought
5 and Sarai said to Abram: Thou dost
6 when Sarai afflicted her, she ran away
8 Agar, handmaid of Sarai, whence comest
8 I flee from the face of Sarai, my
17 15 S. thy wife thou shalt not call S.
1 Pa 2 54 half of the place of rest of Sarai
1 Es 10 40 Sarai, Ezrel, and Selemiau, Semeria
Saraia 4 K 25 23 and Saraia the son of Thanehumeth
1 Pa 4 13 of Cenez were Othoniel and Saraia
14 Saraia begot Joab the father of the
35 son of Sosabia the son of Saraia
1 Es 2 2 Jorobabel, Josue, Nehemia, Saraia
2 Es 11 11 Saraia the son of Helcias, the son of
12 1 Saraia, Jeremias, Esdras, Amaria
12 of Saraia, Maraia: of Jeremias, Hanania
Saraias 2 K 8 17 and Saraias was the scribe
1 Pa 6 14 Azarias begot S., and S. begot Josedec
1 Es 7 1 Esdras the son of Saraias, the son of
2 Es 10 2 Saraias, Azarias, Jeremias, Pheshur
Jer 36 26 S. the son of Ezriel, and Selemias the
51 59 that Jeremias the prophet commanded S.
59 Saraias was chief over the prophecy
61 Jeremias said to S.: When thou shalt
52 24 the general took S. the chief priest
Saraim Josu 15 36 Saraim and Adithaim and Gedera
1 K 17 53 fell of the Philistines in the way of S.
Saraites 1 Pa 2 53 of them came the Saraites
Sarar 2 K 23 33 Aliam the son of S. the Arorite
Sara's Gen 25 12 Agar the Egyptian, S. servant
Sarasar 4 K 19 37 Adramelech and Sarasar his sons slew him. Isa 37:38
Zach 7 2 when Sarasar and Rogommelech and
Sarathasar Josu 13 19 and S. in the mountain of
Sarathi 1 Pa 4 2 these are the families of Sarathi
sardine Apoc 4 3 the jasper and s. stone; and
Sardis Apoc 1 11 and to Thyatira and to Sardis
Apoc 4 1 to the angel of the church of Sardis
4 but thou hast a few names in Sardis
sardius Exod 28 17 first row shall be a s. stone
Exod 39 10 was a sardius, a topaz, an emerald
Eze 28 13 thy covering: the sardius, the topaz
Apoc 21 20 the sixth, sardius: the seventh
sardonyx Job 28 16 the most precious stone s.
Apoc 21 20 the fifth, sardonyx: the sixth
Sarea Josu 15 33 Estaol and Sarea and Asena and
Sareas Jer 40 8 S. the son of Thanehumeth, and
Sarebia 2 Es 12 8 Sarebia, Juda, Mathanias, they
Sarebias 2 Es 9 4 Sarebias, Bani, and Chanani
Sared Gen 46 14 sons of Zabulon: Sared and Elon
Num 26 26 Sared, of whom is the family of the
Sareda 3 K 11 26 son of Nabat an Ephrathite of S.
Saredatha 2 Pa 4 17 ground between Sochot and S.
Saredites Num 26 26 is the family of the S.
Sarephta 3 K 17 9 and go to S. of the Sidonians
3 K 17 10 he [Elias] arose and went to Sarephta
Sarepta Abdi 20 of the Chanaanites even to S.
Luke 4 26 was Elias sent, but to Sarepta of
Sares 1 Pa 7 16 name of his brother was Sares
Sargon Isa 20 1 S. the king of the Assyrians
Saria 1 Pa 8 38 Ismahel, Saria, Obdia. 9:44
Sarid Josu 10 19 of their possession was unto S.
Josu 19 12 and it returneth from Sarid eastward
Sarion Deut 3 9 which the Sidonians call Sarion
Sarohen Josu 19 6 and Bethlebaoth and Sarohen
Saron Josu 12 18 one, the king of Saron one
1 Pa 5 16 and in all the suburbs of Saron, unto
27 29 over the herds that fed in Saron was
Isa 33 9 Saron is become as a desert: and Basan
35 2 the beauty of Carmel and Saron, they
Acts 9 35 at Lydda and Saron, saw him: who were
Saronite 1 Pa 27 29 over the herds . . . Setrai a S.
Sarsachim Jer 39 3 Sereser, Semegarnabu, S.
Sarthan Josu 3 16 called Adom, to the place of S.
3 K 7 46 ground between Socoth and Sarthan
Sarthana 3 K 4 12 all Bethsan, which is by S.
Sarua 3 K 11 26 whose mother was named Sarua
Sarug Gen 11 20 Reu lived 32 years and begot Sarug
Gen 11 21 and Reu lived after he begot Sarug
22 Sarug lived 30 years and begot Nachor
23 and Sarug lived after he begot Nachor
Luke 3 35 Nachor, who was of Sarug, who was of
Sarvia 1 K 26 6 Abisai the son of S. 2 K 16:9; 18:2; 19:21; 21:17; 1 Pa 18:12
2 K 2 13 Joab the son of S. 8:16; 14:1; 23:18, 37; 3 K 1:7; 2:5, 22; 1 Pa 11:6, 39; 18:15; 26:28; 27:24
18 were the three sons of Sarvia there
3 39 the sons of Sarvia are too hard for me
16 10 do with you, ye sons of Sarvia. 19:22
17 25 Abigail . . . the sister of Sarvia
1 Pa 2 16 their sisters were Sarvia and Abigail
16 the sons of Sarvia: Abisai, Joab, and
Sassabasar 1 Es 1 8 to S. the prince of Juda
1 Es 1 11 these Sassabasar brought with them
5 14 they were delivered to one Sassabasar
16 then came this same S. and laid the
sat Mat 4 16 the people that sat in darkness hath
Mat 4 16 that sat in the region of the shadow
9 10 sat down with Jesus and his disciples
13 1 out of the house, sat by the seaside
2 he went up into a boat and sat: and all
14 9 for them that sat with him at table
15 29 going up into a mountain, he sat there
26 20 he sat down with his twelve disciples
55 I sat daily with you, teaching in the
58 going in, he sat with the servants
69 Peter sat without in the court: and
27 36 and they sat and watched him. And they
28 2 rolled back the stone, and sat upon it
Mark 2 15 as he sat at table in his house, many
15 sat down together with Jesus and his
3 32 the multitude sat about him; and they
34 about on them who sat about him, he
4 1 went up into a ship and sat in the sea
6 40 they sat down in ranks, by hundreds
10 46 sat by the wayside begging. Who when
11 2 tied, upon which no man yet hath sat
7 garments on him, and he sat upon him
13 3 and as he sat on the mount of Olivet
14 54 he sat with the servants at the fire
Luke 4 20 restored it to the minister and sat
5 17 as he sat teaching, that there were
7 15 he that was dead sat up, and began
36 of the Pharisee, and sat down to meat
37 when she knew that he sat at meat in
49 that sat at meat with him began to
11 37 he going in, sat down to eat. And the
14 15 when one of them that sat at table
18 35 blind man sat by the wayside begging
22 14 he sat down, and the twelve apostles
John 4 6 with his journey, sat thus on the well
6 3 and there he sat with his disciples
10 the men therefore sat down, in number
9 8 is not this he that sat and begged
11 20 went to meet him: but Mary sat at home

12 14 Jesus found a young ass, and sat upon
19 13 and sat down in the judgment seat in
Acts 2 3 fire, and it sat upon every one of them
3 10 who sat begging alms at the Beautiful
6 15 all that sat in the council, looking
9 40 her eyes; and seeing Peter, she sat up
12 21 [Herod] sat in the judgment seat, and
13 14 into the synagogue . . . they sat down
14 7 and there sat a certain man at Lystra
25 6 the next day he sat in judgment seat
26 30 Bernice, and they sat with them. And
1 C 10 7 the people sat down to eat and drink
Apoc 4 3 he that sat was to the sight like the
5 1 of him that sat on the throne, a book
7 hand of him that sat on the throne
6 2 he that sat on him had a bow, and there
4 to him that sat thereon it was given
5 he that sat on him had a pair of scales
8 he that sat upon him, his name was
9 17 they that sat on them had breastplates
14 15 to him that sat upon the cloud: Thrust
16 he that sat on the cloud thrust his
19 11 and he that sat upon him was called
19 war with him that sat upon the horse
20 4 I saw seats: and they sat upon them
21 5 and he that sat on the throne, said
Satan Job 1 6 S. also was present among them. And
Job 1 9 S. answering, said: Doth Job fear God
12 the Lord said to S. 2:2, 3, 6; Zach 3:2
12 S. went forth from the presence. 2:7
2 1 and Satan came among them and stood
4 Satan answered and said: Skin for skin
2 K 19 22 why are you a satan this day to me
1 Pa 21 1 Satan rose up against Israel: and moved
Zach 3 1 Satan stood on his right hand to be
2 the Lord rebuke thee, O Satan: and the
Mat 4 10 Jesus saith to him: Begone, Satan
12 26 if Satan cast out Satan, he is divided
16 23 go behind me, Satan. Mark 8:33
Mark 1 13 and was tempted by Satan; and he was
3 23 how can Satan cast out Satan? And if
26 if Satan be risen up against himself
4 15 Satan cometh and taketh away the word
Luke 10 18 I saw Satan like lightning falling
11 18 if Satan also be divided against
13 16 whom Satan hath bound, lo, these
22 3 Satan entered into Judas, who was
31 Satan hath desired to have you, that
13 27 after the morsel, S. entered into him
Acts 5 3 why hath Satan tempted thy heart that
26 18 converted from . . . power of Satan to God
Rom 16 20 the God of peace crush Satan under your
1 C 5 5 to deliver such a one to Satan for the
7 5 Satan tempt you for your incontinency
2 C 2 11 that we be not overreached by Satan. For
11 14 no wonder: for S. himself transformeth
12 7 my flesh, an angel of Satan, to buffet
1 Th 2 18 and again: but Satan hath hindered us
2 Th 2 9 is according to the working of Satan
1 Tim 1 20 whom I have delivered up to Satan, that
5 15 some are already turned aside after S.
Apoc 2 9 are not, but are the synagogue of Satan
13 dwellest, where the seat of Satan is
13 slain among you, where Satan dwelleth
24 who have not known the depths of Satan
3 9 I will bring of the synagogue of Satan
12 9 who is called the devil and Satan, who
20 2 old serpent, which is the devil and S.
7 Satan shall be loosed out of his prison
satisfaction 2 K 19 7 speak to the s. of thy
1 Es 5 5 and then they should give satisfaction
Prov 6 35 nor will he accept for satisfaction
Acts 17 9 having taken s. of Jason and of the
19 33 would have given the people s. . . . But
satisfied Lev 10 20 when Moses had heard he was s.
Num 20 6 that being s., they may cease to murmur
Josu 22 30 had heard this, they were satisfied
Judg 19 25 they would not be s. with his words
4 K 14 11 but Amasias did not rest satisfied
Ps 16 15 I shall be s. when thy glory shall
106 9 he hath s. the empty soul and hath
Prov 12 11 tilleth his land shall be s. with bread
18 20 of a man's mouth shall his belly be s.
27 20 so the eyes of men are never satisfied
30 15 three things that never are satisfied
16 the earth which is not s. with water
Ecce 4 8 neither are his eyes s. with riches
5 9 covetous man shall not be s. with money
Eccu 12 16 he will not be satisfied with blood
14 9 he will not be s. till he consume his
Jer 50 19 his soul shall be s. in mount Ephraim
Lam 5 6 that we might be satisfied with bread
Bar 6 58 owner thereof will be well satisfied
Eze 16 28 because thou wast not yet satisfied
29 and neither so wast thou satisfied
Dan 13 32 they might be satisfied with her beauty
Haba 2 5 he is never satisfied: but will gather
satisfieth Ps 102 5 who s. thy desire with good
satisfy Jdth 7 11 enough to s. them, no not for
Judg 19 24 humble them and s. your lust: only I
Job 38 39 and satisfy the appetite of her whelps
Ps 131 15 widow: I will s. her poor with bread
Wisd 16 3 was necessary to satisfy their desire
19 12 to satisfy their desire, the quail came
Isa 55 2 for that which doth not satisfy you
58 10 and shalt satisfy the afflicted soul
Eze 7 19 they shall not satisfy their soul
21 17 together, and will s. my indignation
2 Ma 2 28 seek to satisfy the will of others
Mark 15 15 being willing to satisfy the people
1 P 3 15 ready always to satisfy every one
satisfying Eze 25 15 and satisfying old enmities
sattest Eze 23 41 thou s. on a very fine bed and
1 Ma 10 55 s. in the throne of their kingdom
Saul Acts 7 57 young man whose name was Saul
Acts 7 59 and Saul was consenting to his death
8 3 but Saul made havock of the church
9 1 Saul as yet breathing out threatenings
4 S. why persecutest thou me. 22:7; 26:14
8 Saul arose from the ground; and when
11 one named Saul of Tarsus. For behold he
17 Saul, the Lord Jesus hath sent me, he
22 Saul increased much more in strength
24 laying in wait was made known to Saul
11 25 Barnabas went to Tarsus to seek Saul
30 by the hands of Barnabas and Saul
12 25 Saul returned from Jerusalem, having
13 1 brother of Herod the tetrarch, and S.
7 sending for Barnabas and S., desired
9 then Saul, otherwise Paul, filled with
21 and God gave them Saul the son of Cis
22 13 said to me: Brother Saul, look up. And
house of Saul 2 K 3 1 war between h. . . . and the
2 K 3 6 war between h. . . . and the house of
8 who have shown mercy to the h. . . . thy
10 kingdom be translated from the h. . . .
9 1 any one, think you, left of the h. . . .
2 was of the h. . . . a servant named Siba
3 is there any one left of the h. . . .
16 5 a man of the kindred of the h. . . .
8 repaid thee for all the blood of h. . . .
19 17 and Siba the servant of the h. . . . : and
1 Pa 12 29 great part of them followed the h. . . .
servants of Saul 1 K 16 15 s. . . . said to him
1 K 17 8 not I a Philistine and you the s. . . .
18 23 s. . . . spoke all these words in the

24 the s. . . . told him, saying: Such words
21 7 a certain man of the s. . . . was there
22 9 and was the chief among the s. . . .
Saulites Num 26 13 of him is the family of the S.
Saul's 1 K 9 3 asses of Cis, S. father, were lost
1 K 10 14 Saul's uncle said to him and to his
14 50 the name of Saul's wife was Achinoam
18 5 especially in eyes of Saul's servants
20 25 Abner sat by Saul's side, and David's
21 7 Edomite, the chiefest of S. herdsmen
24 5 cut off the hem of Saul's robe. 6
26 12 cup of water which was at Saul's head
31 9 they cut off Saul's head and stripped
2 K 1 2 a man who came out of Saul's camp with
2 8 Abner . . . general of Saul's army, took
Saura 1 Ma 6 43 Eleazar the son of Saura saw
savage 2 Ma 4 25 the rage of a savage beast
save Gen 19 17 save thy life: look not back
Gen 19 17 save thyself in the mountain, lest thou
34 that we may save seed of our father
50 20 you see, and might save many people
Exod 1 18 that you would save the men children
22 of the female, ye shall save alive
22 20 sacrificeth . . . save only to the Lord
Num 31 18 that are virgins save for yourselves
Josu 2 13 that you will save my father and mother
10 6 come up quickly and save us and bring
22 22 let him not save us, but punish us
Judg 6 36 if thou wilt save Israel by my hand
7 7 by the 300 men . . . I will save you
21 11 kill, but the virgins you shall save
1 K 4 3 that it may save us from the hand of
7 8 that he may save us out of the hand of
9 16 he shall save my people out of the
10 24 God save the king. 4 K 11:12; 2 Pa 23:11
27 shall this fellow be able to save us
14 6 because it is easy for the Lord to save
19 11 unless thou save thyself this night
23 2 the Philistines and shalt save Ceila
2 K 3 18 by the hand of . . . David I will save
8 2 to put to death, and one to save alive
14 4 worshipped and said: Save me, O king
16 16 God save thee, O king. 18:28
18 5 saying: Save me the boy Absalom. 12
20 9 Joab said to Amasa: God save thee, my
22 28 and the poor people thou wilt save
42 cry, and there shall be none to save
44 wilt save me from the contradictions
3 K 1 12 take my counsel, and save thy life
25 and saying: God save king Adonias
34 God save king Solomon. 39
18 5 can find grass and save the horses and
20 31 Israel: perhaps he will save our lives
4 K 6 26 woman cried out . . . Save me, my lord
27 if the Lord doth not save thee, how can I save thee
7 7 and fled, desiring to save their lives
16 7 save me out of the hand of the king
19 19 Lord our God, save us from his hand
34 will protect this city and will save it
1 Pa 4 10 and save me from being oppressed by evil
16 35 say ye: Save us, O God our savior
2 Pa 20 9 and thou wilt hear us, and save us
2 Es 6 11 would go into temple to save his life
9 27 to save them from the hands of their
Tob 13 5 and he will save us for his own mercy
Jdth 15 1 they thought only to save themselves
Job 5 15 he shall save the needy from the sword
30 24 if they shall fall down thou wilt save
40 9 that thy right hand is able to save thee
Ps 3 7 arise, O Lord; save me, O my God. For
6 5 save me for thy mercy's sake. For there
7 2 save me from all them that persecute me
3 is no one to redeem me nor to save
11 2 save me, O Lord, for there is now no
17 28 thou wilt save the humble people; but
42 cried, but there was none to save them
19 9 O Lord, save the king; and hear us in
21 9 let him deliver him: let him save him
22 save me from the lion's mouth: and my
27 9 save, O Lord, thy people, and bless
30 3 and a house of refuge to save me
17 upon thy servant: save me in thy mercy
33 19 and he will save the humble of spirit
36 40 them from the wicked, and save them
43 4 neither did their own arm save them
7 my bow: neither shall my sword save me
53 3 save me, O God, by thy name, and judge
54 17 cried to God: and the Lord will save me
55 8 for nothing shalt thou save them: in
58 3 and save me from bloody men. For behold
59 7 save me with thy right hand and hear
68 2 save me, O God: for the waters are come
19 save me because of my enemies. Thou
36 God will save Sion, and the cities of
70 2 incline thy ear unto me and save me
71 4 he shall save the children of the poor
13 he shall save the souls of the poor
75 10 to save all the meek of the earth. For
79 3 stir up thy might, and come to save us
85 2 save thy servant . . . that trusteth in
16 and save the son of thy handmaid. Show
105 47 save us, O Lord our God: and gather
107 7 save with thy right hand and hear me
108 26 save me according to thy mercy. And let
31 poor, to save my soul from persecutors
117 25 Lord, save me: O Lord, give good success
118 94 I am thine, save thou me; for I have
146 I cried unto thee, save me: that I may
173 let thy hand be with me to save me
144 19 he will hear their prayer and save them
Ecce 8 8 neither shall wickedness s. the wicked
Wisd 14 4 showing that thou art able to save
Isa 25 9 waited for him, and he will save us
33 22 the Lord is our king: he will save us
35 4 himself will come and will save you
37 20 Lord our God, save us out of his hand
35 protect this city and will save it
38 20 Lord, save me, and we will sing our
44 20 he will not save his soul nor say
45 20 and pray to a god that cannot save
46 2 they could not save him that carried
4 I will bear: I will carry and will save
7 he shall not save them from tribulation
47 13 let now the astrologers . . . save thee
15 way, there is none that can save thee
49 25 thee, and thy children I will save
26 that I am the Lord that save thee
59 1 not shortened that it cannot save
63 1 justice, and am a defender to save
Jer 11 12 they shall not save them in the time
14 9 as a mighty man that cannot save? But
15 20 I am with thee to save thee and to
17 14 save me, and I shall be saved: for thou
25 35 leaders of the flock to save themselves
30 10 I will save thee from a country afar
11 with thee, saith the Lord, to save thee
31 7 and say: Save, O Lord, thy people
42 11 for I am with you to save you and to
45 5 thee thy life and save thee in all
46 27 behold I will save thee from afar off
48 6 flee, save your lives: and be as heath
51 6 and let every one save his own life
45 that every man may save his life from
Lam 4 17 a nation that was not able to save
Bar 4 22 in the Eternal that he will save you

6 14 but cannot save himself from war or
35 nor save the weak from the mighty
49 from war nor save themselves from evils
Eze 13 19 and to save souls alive which should
18 27 justice: he shall save his soul alive
33 5 to himself, he shall save his life
34 22 I will save my flock, and it shall
36 29 and I will save you from all your
37 23 I will save them out of all the places
Dan 3 17 is able to save us from the furnace
96 there is no other God that can save
6 14 till sunset he labored to save him
Osee 1 7 I will save them by the Lord their God
7 I will not save them by bow nor by
13 10 let him save thee in all thy cities
14 4 Assyria shall not save us, we will not
Amos 2 14 neither shall the strong save his
Mich 6 14 shalt take hold, but shalt not save
14 those whom thou shalt save, I will
Haba 1 2 I cry . . . and thou wilt not save
Soph 3 17 he will save: he will rejoice over
19 and I will save her that halteth
Zach 8 7 I will save my people from the land
13 so will I save you, and you shall be
9 16 their God will save them in that day
10 6 I will . . . save the house of Joseph
12 7 the Lord shall save the tabernacles
1 Ma 9 9 let us save our lives now and return
10 83 idol's temple, there to save themselves
2 Ma 7 25 with the young man to save his life
11 6 would send a good angel to save Israel
Mat 1 21 he shall save his people from their
8 25 saying: Lord, save us, we perish. And
13 57 honor, save in his own country and in
14 30 he cried out, saying: Lord, save me
16 25 he that will save his life, shall lose it. Mark 8:35; Luke 9:24
18 11 is come to save that which was lost
27 40 save thy own self: if thou be the Son
42 himself he cannot save. Mark 15:31
Mark 3 4 to s. life, or to destroy. Luke 6:9
8 35 my sake and the gospel, shall save it
15 30 save thyself, coming down from the
Luke 9 24 his life for my sake, shall save it
56 came not to destroy souls, but to save
17 33 whosoever shall seek to save his life
19 10 Son of man is come to seek and to s.
23 35 let him save himself, if he be Christ
37 be the king of the Jews, save thyself
39 if thou be Christ, save thyself and us
John 12 27 say? Father, save me from this hour
47 judge the world, but to save the world
Acts 2 40 save yourselves from this perverse
7 25 that God by his hand would save them
20 23 there: save that the Holy Ghost in every
27 43 the centurion, willing to save Paul
43 and save themselves, and get to land
Rom 11 14 my flesh, and may save some of them. For
1 C 1 21 our preaching, to save them that believe
7 16 whether thou shalt save thy husband? Or
16 O man, whether thou shalt save thy wife
9 22 all things to all men, that I might save
2 C 11 24 did I receive forty stripes, save one
Gal 6 14 save in the cross of our Lord Jesus
1 Tim 1 15 Jesus came into this world to s. sinners
4 16 in doing this thou shalt both s. thyself
Heb 5 7 was able to save him from death, was
7 25 he is able also to save forever them
James 1 21 word, which is able to save your souls
2 14 shall faith be able to save him? And
5 15 prayer of faith shall save the sick
20 shall save his soul from death, and
Jude 23 others save, pulling them out of the

Save Gen 14 5 the Emim in Save of Cariathaim
Gen 14 17 that were with him in the vale of Save
saved Gen 7 3 that seed may be saved upon the
Gen 19 20 little one, and I shall be saved in it
22 make haste and be saved there because
32 30 face to face, and my soul has been s.
Exod 1 17 but saved the men children. And the
Num 31 15 why have you saved the women? Are not
Deut 19 4 that fleeth, whose life is to be saved
20 11 people that are therein shall be saved
33 29 O people, that art saved by the Lord
Josu 6 25 Josue saved Rahab the harlot and her
8 22 not one of so great a multitude was s.
9 20 let their lives be saved, lest the
Judg 5 13 the remnants of the people are saved
8 19 if you had saved them, I would not
1 K 10 19 your God, who only hath saved you
14 23 and the Lord saved Israel that day
22 23 with me [David] thou shalt be saved
23 5 David saved the inhabitants of Ceila
25 26 hath saved thy hand to thee: and now
27 1 to be s. in the land of the Philistines
11 David saved neither man nor woman
2 K 19 5 thy servants, that have saved thy life
9 s. us out of hand of the Philistines
22 4 and I shall be saved from my enemies
4 K 14 27 he saved them by the hand of Jeroboam
19 31 which shall be saved out of mount Sion
2 Pa 32 22 and the Lord saved Ezechias and the
1 Es 9 13 seeing that thou our God hast saved us
14 not to leave us a remnant to be saved
15 for we remain yet to be saved as at
Tob 11 17 chastised me and thou hast saved me
Jdth 10 15 thou hast saved thy life by taking this
Job 22 29 bow down his eyes, he shall be saved
30 innocent shall be saved, and he shall be saved by the cleanness of
Ps 17 4 and I shall be saved from my enemies
20 he saved me because he was well pleased
19 7 that the Lord hath saved his anointed
21 6 they cried to thee, and they were saved
29 4 hast saved me from them that go down
30 8 hast saved my soul out of distresses
32 16 the king is not saved by a great army
16 nor shall the giant be saved by his own
17 safety: neither shall he be saved by
33 7 and saved him out of all his troubles
43 8 hast saved us from them that afflict us
54 9 I waited for him that hath saved me
69 1 to remembrance that the Lord saved him
79 4 show us thy face, and we shall be s. 8
20 show thy face, and we shall be saved
105 8 he saved them for his own name's sake
10 he saved them from the hand of them
21 they forgot God, who saved them, who
118 117 help me, and I shall be saved: and I
137 7 and thy right hand hath saved me. The
Prov 11 21 but the seed of the just shall be saved
28 18 that walketh uprightly, shall be saved
26 that walketh wisely, he shall be saved
Wisd 14 5 passing over the sea by ship are s.
18 5 one child being cast forth and saved
Eccu 3 2 and so do that you may be saved. For
51 16 thou hast saved me from destruction
Isa 30 15 return and be quiet, you shall be saved
37 31 which shall be s. of the house of Juda
43 12 I have declared and have saved. I
45 17 Israel is saved in the Lord with an
20 together, ye that are s. of the Gentiles
22 converted to me, and you shall be s.
63 5 my own arm hath saved for me, and my
9 the angel of his presence saved them
64 5 been always, and we shall be saved

66 19 will send of them that shall be saved
Jer 4 14 Jerusalem, that thou mayst be saved
8 20 summer is ended, and we are not s.
17 14 save me, and I shall be saved: for
23 6 in those days shall Juda be s. 33:16
30 7 Jacob, but he shall be saved out of it
39 18 but thy life shall be saved for thee
Bar 6 54 indeed will flee away and be saved
Eze 6 9 that are saved of you shall remember
14 22 left in it some that shall be saved
17 15 hath done thus prosper or be saved
Dan 3 88 and saved us out of the hand of death
88 saved us out of the midst of the fire
11 41 these only shall be saved out of his
12 1 that time shall thy people be saved
13 62 and innocent blood was s. in that day
Joel 2 32 upon the name of the Lord shall be s.
1 Ma 4 9 our fathers were saved in the Red Sea
9 21 fallen that saved the people of Israel
Mat 10 22 the end, he shall be saved. 13:13; 24:13
19 25 who then can be s. Mark 10:26; Luke 18:26
27 42 he saved others. Mark 15:31; Luke 23:35
Mark 13 20 no flesh should be saved: but for the
16 16 believeth and is baptized, shall be s.
Luke 8 12 lest believing they should be saved
13 23 Lord, are they few that are saved
John 3 17 that the world may be saved by him
5 34 these things, that you may be saved
10 9 if any man enter in, he shall be saved
Acts 2 21 name of the Lord, shall be s. Rom 10:13
47 daily together such as should be saved
4 12 given to men, whereby we must be saved
11 14 thou shalt be saved, and all thy house
15 1 manner of Moses, you cannot be saved
11 we believe to be saved, in like manner
16 30 must I do, that I may be saved? But
31 thou shalt be saved, and thy house
27 20 hope of our being s. was now taken away
31 stay in the ship, you cannot be saved
Rom 5 9 shall we be s. from wrath through him
10 reconciled, shall we be s. by his life
8 24 for we are saved by hope. But hope that
9 27 of the sea, a remnant shall be saved
10 9 him up from dead, thou shalt be saved
11 5 there is a remnant saved according to
26 and so all Israel should be saved, as
1 C 1 18 to them that are saved, that is, to us
3 15 he himself shall be saved, yet so as by
5 5 that the spirit may be saved in the day
10 33 but to many, that they may be saved. Be
15 2 by which also you are saved, if you
2 C 2 15 in them that are s., and in them that
Eph 2 5 Christ, by whose grace you are saved
8 by grace you are saved through faith
1 Th 2 16 the Gentiles, that they may be saved
2 Th 2 10 the truth, that they might be saved
1 Tim 2 4 who will have all men to be saved, and
15 she shall be saved through childbearing
Titus 3 5 he s. us, by the laver of regeneration
James 5 16 for another, that you may be saved
1 P 3 20 eight souls, were saved by water
4 18 if the just man shall scarcely be saved
Jude 5 having saved the people out of the land
savest Tob 13 2 for thou scourgest and thou s.
Ps 16 7 who savest them that trust in thee
Eccu 51 12 savest them out of the hands of the
saveth 1 K 17 47 that the Lord s. not with sword
Job 36 6 but he saveth not the wicked, and he
Ps 7 11 who saveth the upright of heart. God
Eccu 34 15 their hope is on him that saveth them
Dan 13 60 who saveth them that trust in him
1 P 3 21 of the like form, now saveth you also
saving Gen 9 4 s. that flesh with blood you shall
Gen 19 19 hast shown to me, in saving my life
Exod 12 27 the Egyptians, and saving our houses
Ps 43 5 who commandest the saving of Jacob
Eccu 46 2 great for the saving the elect of God
Isa 31 5 delivering, passing over and saving
2 Ma 12 25 for the saving of their brethren. Then
Gal 1 19 saving James the brother of the Lord
Heb 10 39 but of faith to the saving of the soul
11 7 ark for the saving of his house, by the
savior Gen 41 45 called . . . The savior of the world
Deut 32 15 him and departed from God his savior
Judg 3 9 Lord, who raised them up a savior. 15
1 K 14 39 Lord liveth who is the savior of Israel
2 K 22 2 my rock and my strength . . . and my s.
3 my savior, thou wilt deliver me from
4 K 13 5 the Lord gave Israel a savior, and they
1 Pa 16 35 say ye: Save us, O God our savior: and
Esth 15 5 upon God the ruler and Savior of all
Job 13 16 he shall be my savior: for no hypocrite
Ps 23 5 Lord, and mercy from God his Savior
24 5 thou art God my Savior; and on thee
26 9 not thou despise me, O God my Savior
61 3 for he is my God and my savior. 7
64 6 hear us, O God our savior, who art the
78 9 help us, O God, our savior: and for
84 5 convert us, O God our savior: and turn
94 1 let us joyfully sing to God our savior
Wisd 16 7 he saw, by thee the Savior of all
Eccu 51 1 I will praise thee, O God my Savior
Isa 12 2 God is my s., I will deal confidently
17 10 thou hast forgotten God thy savior
19 20 he shall send them a Savior and a
26 1 Sion the city of our strength a savior
43 3 the Holy One of Israel, thy Savior
11 there is no savior besides me. Osee 13:4
45 8 earth be opened, and bud forth a s.
15 hidden God, the God of Israel the s.
21 a just God and a savior, there is none
51 5 near at hand, my savior is gone forth
60 16 shalt know that I am the Lord thy S.
62 1 and her savior be lighted as a lamp
11 thy Savior cometh: behold his reward
63 8 not deny: so he became their savior
Jer 14 8 the Savior thereof in time of trouble
Bar 4 22 come to you from our everlasting S.
Dan 6 27 he is the deliverer and savior, doing
14 42 he is the Savior, working signs and
Mich 7 7 Lord, I will wait for God my Savior
Zach 9 9 will come to thee, the just and savior
1 Ma 4 30 blessed art thou, O Savior of Israel
Luke 1 47 spirit hath rejoiced in God my Savior
2 11 this day is born to you a Savior, who
John 4 42 this is indeed the Savior of the world
Acts 5 31 to be Prince and Savior, to give
13 23 hath raised up to Israel a S., Jesus
Eph 5 23 church. He is the savior of his body
Phil 3 20 whence also we look for the Savior, our
1 Tim 1 1 to commandment of God our S. Titus 1:3
2 3 acceptable in the sight of God our S.
4 10 living God, who is the Savior of all men
2 Tim 1 10 by the illumination of our Savior Jesus
Titus 1 4 and from Christ Jesus our Savior. For
2 10 adorn the doctrine of God our Savior
11 grace of God our Savior hath appeared
13 the great God and our Savior Jesus
3 4 kindness of God our Savior appeared: not
6 through Jesus Christ our Savior: that
2 P 1 1 justice of our God and S. Jesus Christ
11 everlasting kingdom of our Lord and S.
2 20 the knowledge of our Lord and Savior
3 2 the precepts of the Lord and Savior
18 and in the knowledge of our Lord and S.
1 J 4 14 his Son to be the Savior of the world

Jude 25 to the only God our Savior through
savior's Isa 12 3 joy out of the s. fountains
saviors 2 Es 9 27 gavest them s. to save them
Abdi 21 saviors shall come up into mount Sion
savor Gen 8 21 the Lord smelled a sweet savor
Exod 5 21 you have made our savor to stink before
29 18 a most sweet savor of the victim of
25 a most sweet savor in the sight of the
41 have said, for a savor of sweetness
30 34 and onycha, galbanum of sweet savor
35 28 to make the incense of most sweet savor
Lev 1 9 a sweet savor to the Lord. 4:31; Num 15:3, 7
17 most sweet savor to the Lord. 2:2, 9; 3:5; Num 15:10, 24
2 12 the altar for a savor of sweetness
3 16 of the fire and of a most sweet savor
Eccu 38 11 give a sweet savor and a memorial of
45 20 to God, incense and a good savor
Mat 5 13 if the salt lose its s. Luke 14:34
savorest Mat 16 23 thou savorest not the things that are of God. Mark 8:33
savory Gen 27 4 make me savory meat thereof as
Gen 27 17 she gave him the s. meat and delivered
saw Mat 3 16 he saw the Spirit of God descending
Mat 4 18 saw two brothers, Simon who is called
21 he saw other two brethren, James the
8 14 he saw his wife's mother lying and
34 when they saw him, they besought him
9 9 he saw a man sitting in the custom
23 saw the minstrels and the multitude
12 22 healed him, so that he spoke and saw
14 14 coming forth saw a great multitude
17 8 saw no one but only Jesus. And as they
20 3 he saw others standing in the market
34 immediately they saw, and followed him
22 11 he saw there a man who had not on a
26 71 another maid saw him [Peter], and she
Mark 1 10 he saw the heavens opened and the
16 he saw Simon and Andrew his brother
19 he saw James the son of Zebedee and
2 14 he saw Levi the son of Alpheus sitting
3 11 unclean spirits, when they saw him
6 33 they saw them going away, and many knew
34 Jesus going out saw a great multitude
50 they all saw him and were troubled
8 23 he asked him if he saw anything. And
25 so that he saw all things clearly. And
9 7 looking about, they saw no man any
13 he saw a great multitude about them
37 we saw one casting out devils in thy
10 52 he saw, and followed him in the way
11 20 they saw the fig tree dried up from
16 4 they saw the stone rolled back. For
5 they saw a young man sitting on the
Luke 5 2 and saw two ships standing by the
8 when Simon Peter saw, he fell down
20 whose faith when he saw, he said: Man
27 saw a publican named Levi, sitting
8 28 when he saw Jesus, he fell down before
34 which when they that fed them saw
9 32 they saw his glory, and the two men
49 we saw a certain man casting out
10 18 I saw Satan like lightning falling
32 near the place and saw him, passed by
15 20 a great way off, his father saw him
17 14 whom when he saw, he said: Go, show
15 when he saw that he was made clean
18 15 when the disciples saw, they rebuked
43 he saw, and followed him, glorifying
43 when they saw it, gave praise to God
19 5 looking up, he saw him, and said to
7 when all saw it, they murmured, saying
21 1 he saw the rich men cast their gifts
2 and he saw also a certain poor widow
23 48 and saw the things that were done
55 saw the sepulcher, and how his body
24 12 he saw the linen cloths laid by
37 supposed that they saw a spirit. And
John 1 14 we saw his glory, the glory as it were
29 next day, John saw Jesus coming to him
32 I saw the Spirit coming down as a dove
34 I saw, and I gave testimony, that this
39 they came and saw where he abode, and
48 was under the fig tree, I saw thee
50 I saw thee under the fig tree, thou
6 2 they saw the miracles which he did on
22 saw that there was no other ship there
24 saw that Jesus was not there nor his
8 56 see my day: he saw it, and was glad
11 31 when they saw Mary that she rose up
33 when he saw her weeping, and the Jews
12 41 when he saw his glory and spoke of him
19 33 they saw that he was already dead
35 he that saw it, hath given testimony
20 1 she saw the stone taken away from the
5 saw the linen cloths lying. 6
8 sepulcher: and he saw and believed
12 she saw two angels in white, sitting
14 saw Jesus standing, and she knew not
20 were glad when they saw the Lord. He
21 9 they saw hot coals lying, and a fish
20 saw that disciple whom Jesus loved
Acts 3 9 all the people saw him walking and
6 15 saw his face as if it had been the
7 55 saw the glory of God, and Jesus
8 18 when Simon saw that by the imposition
39 and the eunuch saw him no more. And
9 8 he saw nothing. But they leading him by
12 he saw a man named Ananias coming in
35 at Lydda and Saron, saw him: who were
10 3 this man saw in a vision manifestly
11 he saw the heaven opened, and a certain
11 5 I saw in an ecstasy of mind a vision
6 I . . . saw fourfooted creatures of
12 9 [Peter] thought he saw a vision. And
16 when they had opened they saw him
13 36 unto his fathers, and saw corruption
37 raised from the dead, saw no corruption
21 27 Asia, when they saw him in the temple
32 when they saw tribune and the soldiers
22 9 that were with me, saw indeed the light
18 saw him saying unto me: Make haste, and
26 13 at midday, O king, I saw in the way
28 4 and when the barbarians saw the beast
15 whom when Paul saw, he gave thanks to
Gal 1 19 but other of the apostles I saw none
2 14 I saw that they walked not uprightly
Heb 3 9 tempted me, proved and saw my works
11 23 because they saw he was a comely babe
Apoc 1 12 I saw seven golden candlesticks: and
5 1 I saw in the right hand of him that
2 I saw a strong angel, proclaiming with
6 I saw: and behold in the midst of the
6 1 I saw that the Lamb had opened one of
2 I saw; and behold a white horse, and
9 I saw under the altar the souls of them
12 I saw, when he had opened the sixth
7 1 I saw four angels standing on the four
2 I saw another angel. 14:6; 18:1
9 I saw a great multitude which no man
8 2 I saw seven angels standing in the
9 1 I saw a star fall from heaven upon the
17 thus I saw the horses in the vision
10 1 I saw another mighty angel come down
5 whom I saw standing upon the sea and

11 11 great fear fell upon them that saw them
12 in a cloud: and their enemies saw them
12 13 when the dragon saw that he was cast
13 1 I saw a beast coming up out of the sea
2 beast which I saw was like to a leopard
3 I saw one of the heads as it were slain
11 I saw another beast coming up out of
14 14 I saw, and behold a white cloud and
15 1 I saw another sign in heaven, great
2 and I saw as it were a sea of glass
16 13 I saw from the mouth of the dragon
17 3 I saw a woman sitting upon a scarlet
6 I saw the woman drunk with the blood
19 11 I saw heaven opened, and behold a white
17 I saw an angel standing in the sun
19 I saw the beast and the kings of the
20 1 I saw an angel coming down from heaven
4 I saw seats; and they sat upon them
11 I saw a great white throne, and one
12 and I saw the dead, great and small
21 1 I saw a new heaven and a new earth
2 I John saw the holy city, and the new
22 I saw no temple therein. For the Lord
sawed 2 K 12 31 he s. them and drove over them
3 K 7 9 which were sawed by a certain rule
sawest Gen 20 10 what s. thou, that thou hast
1 K 19 5 thou sawest it and didst rejoice. Why
2 K 18 11 if thou sawest him, why didst thou not
2 Es 9 9 thou s. the affliction of our fathers
Dan 2 31 thou O king, sawest, and behold there
34 thus thou sawest, till a stone was
41 thou sawest the feet and the toes
41 thou sawest the iron mixed with. 43
45 as thou sawest that the stone was
4 17 the tree which thou sawest which
8 20 the ram, which thou sawest with horns
13 54 if thou sawest her, tell me under what tree thou sawest them
Apoc 1 20 which thou sawest in my right hand and
17 8 the beast, which thou sawest, was
12 the ten horns which thou sawest. 16
15 the waters which thou sawest where the
18 woman which thou s. in the great city
saws Isa 28 27 gith shall not be thrashed with s.
saying Mark 7 29 for this s. go thy way, the devil
Mark 10 22 who being struck sad at that saying
Luke 1 29 having heard, was troubled at his s.
John 4 37 in this is the saying true: That it is
42 we now believe not for thy saying
6 61 this saying is hard, and who can hear
7 36 what is this saying that he hath said
12 38 that the saying of Isaias the prophet
19 8 Pilate therefore had heard this saying
21 23 this saying therefore went abroad
Acts 6 5 the s. was liked by all the multitude
1 C 15 54 come to pass the saying that is written
1 Tim 1 15 a faithful saying. 3:1; 4:9; 2 Tim 2:11; Titus 3:8
sayings Prov 1 6 the wise and their mysterious s.
Prov 4 20 words, and incline thy ear to my s.
Eccu 6 35 sayings of praise may not escape thee
12 12 words, and be pricked with my sayings
39 2 he will keep the sayings of renowned
Luke 3 4 in the book of the sayings of Isaias
scab Lev 13 6 clean, because it is but a scab
Lev 21 20 a continual scab or a dry scurf in his
22 22 or blisters or a scab or a dry scurf
Deut 28 27 with the scab and with the itch, so
scabbard 2 K 20 8 in a s. made in such manner
Job 20 25 and cometh forth from its scabbard
Jer 47 6 go into thy scabbard, rest and be still
Eze 21 28 O sword, come out of the scabbard
John 18 11 put up thy sword into the scabbard
scaffold 2 Pa 6 13 Solomon had made a brazen s.
scale Jer 5 10 s. the walls thereof and throw
Joel 2 7 like men of war they shall scale
scaled Prov 21 22 the wise man hath s. the city
scales Lev 11 9 all that hath fins and scales
Lev 11 10 whatsoever hath not fins and scales
12 all that have not fins and scales, in
Deut 14 9 all that have fins and scales, you
10 without fins and s., you shall not eat
1 K 17 5 clothed with a coat of mail with scales
Job 41 6 shut close up with scales pressing
Isa 40 12 and weighed the mountains in scales
46 6 and weigh out silver in the scales
Eze 29 4 fish of thy rivers to stick to thy s.
4 all thy fish shall stick to thy scales
Acts 9 18 fell from his eys as it were scales
Apoc 6 5 he that sat on him had a pair of scales
scandal Exod 10 7 how long shall we endure this s.
Exod 23 33 undoubtedly will be a scandal to thee
4 K 23 13 to Chamos the scandal of Moab, and to
Ps 49 20 didst lay a s. against thy mother's son
Prov 22 25 his ways, and take scandal to thy soul
Mat 16 23 thou art a scandal unto me: because
18 7 that man by whom the scandal cometh
Rom 9 33 I lay in Sion a . . . rock of scandal; and
14 13 stumblingblock or s. in your brother's
Gal 5 11 then is the s. of the cross made void
1 P 2 8 stone of stumbling and a rock of s.
1 J 2 10 light, and there is no scandal in him
scandalize Mat 5 29 if thy right eye s. thee
Mat 5 30 if thy right hand scandalize thee, cut
17 26 that we may not s. them, go to the
18 6 s. one of these little ones. Mark 9:41; Luke 17:2
8 if thy hand or thy foot s. thee, cut
9 if thy eye scandalize thee. Mark 9:46
Mark 9 42 if thy hand s. thee, cut it off: it is
44 if thy foot s. thee, cut it off. It
John 6 62 to them: Doth this scandalize you
1 C 8 13 if meat s. my brother, I will never eat
13 eat flesh, lest I should s. my brother
scandalized Eccu 3 28 perverse of heart shall be s.
Mat 11 6 is he that shall not be s. in me
13 21 of the word, he is presently s. And
57 they were s. in his regard. But Jesus
15 12 when they heard this word, were s.
24 10 then shall many be scandalized: and
26 31 all you shall be s. in me this night
33 although all shall be s. Mark 14:29
33 I will never be scandalized. Jesus said
Mark 4 17 for the word, they are presently s.
6 3 they were scandalized in regard of him
14 27 you will all be s. in my regard this
Luke 7 23 is he whosoever shall not be s. in me
John 16 1 to you, that you may not be s. They
Rom 14 21 whereby thy brother is offended or s.
2 C 11 29 who is scandalized, and I am not on fire
scandals Eze 11 18 and shall take away all the s.
Eze 11 21 whose heart walketh after their s.
20 7 let every man cast away the scandals
Mat 13 41 gather out of his kingdom all scandals
18 7 woe to the world because of scandals
7 it must needs be that scandals come
Luke 17 1 impossible that s. should not come
scant Mich 6 10 a scant measure full of wrath
scar Lev 13 19 there appeareth a white scar or
Lev 13 21 and the scar somewhat obscure and be
23 it is but the scar of an ulcer, and the
24 it is healed hath a white or red scar
25 evil of leprosy is broken out in the s.
28 it is only the scar of a burning
14 56 of a scar and of blisters breaking out
22 22 or have a scar or blisters or a scab or

Jer 30 17 I will close up thy scar and will heal
scarce Gen 27 30 Isaac had s. ended his words
2 Pa 9 6 that scarce one half of thy wisdom
Tob 2 8 thou didst scarce escape the sentence
Jdth 15 13 and thirty days were scarce sufficient
Job 26 14 heard scarce a little drop of his word
Prov 6 26 price of a harlot is scarce one loaf
Eccu 21 23 a wise man will scarce laugh low to
29 7 he will scarce pay one half and will
Acts 14 17 they scarce restrained the people from
27 7 and were scarce come over against Gnidus
Rom 5 7 for scarce for a just man will one die
scarcely Eccu 32 10 s. speak in thy own cause
1 P 4 18 if the just man shall scarcely be saved
scarcity Gen 41 30 seven years of so great s.
Gen 41 31 greatness of the scarcity shall destroy
36 land shall not be consumed with s.
54 seven years of scarcity, which Joseph
scarecrow Bar 6 69 a s. in a garden of cucumbers
scared Wisd 17 9 s. with the passing by of beasts
scarlet Gen 38 27 midwife tied a scarlet thread
Gen 38 30 on whose hand was the scarlet thread
Exod 25 4 violet and purple and scarlet. 26:1, 31, 36; 27:16; 28:5, 6, 8, 15, 33; 35:6, 23, 25; 36:8, 35, 37; 38:18, 23; 39:1, 2, 8, 22, 28; 2 Pa 3:14
35 35 blue and purple and scarlet twice
Lev 14 4 cedar wood and s. and hyssop. 49
6 cedar wood and the s. and the hyssop
51 the hyssop and the scarlet. 52
Num 4 8 shall spread over it a cloth of scarlet
19 6 cedar wood and hyssop and scarlet
Josu 2 18 this scarlet cord be a sign, and thou
21 she hung the scarlet cord in the window
7 21 I saw among the spoils a scarlet garment
2 K 1 24 who clothed you with s. in delights
2 Pa 2 7 in purple, in scarlet and in blue, and
14 also, and violet and silk and scarlet
Cant 4 3 thy lips are as a scarlet lace: and
Eccu 45 13 twisted scarlet the work of an artist
Isa 1 18 if your sins be as scarlet, they shall
Jer 4 30 though thou clothest thyself with s.
Lam 4 5 they that were brought up in scarlet
Bar 6 71 and the scarlet which are motheaten
Nah 2 3 the men of the army are clad in scarlet
Mat 27 28 they put a scarlet cloak about him
Heb 9 19 goats, with water and scarlet wool and
Apoc 17 3 sitting upon a scarlet colored beast
4 clothed round about with purple and s.
18 12 fine linen and purple and silk and s.
16 with fine linen and purple and scarlet
scatter Gen 49 7 and will s. them in Israel
Lev 26 33 I will scatter you among the Gentiles
Num 16 37 to s. the fire of one side and the
Deut 4 27 Lord will destroy you and scatter you
28 64 the Lord shall scatter thee among all
3 K 14 15 shall scatter them beyond the river
2 Es 1 8 I will s. you abroad among the nations
Job 40 6 scatter the proud in thy indignation
Ps 58 12 scatter them by thy power; and bring
67 13 s. thou the nations that delight in
105 27 and to scatter them in the countries
143 6 lightning, and thou shalt scatter them
Ecce 3 5 time to s. stones and a time to gather
Isa 24 1 scatter abroad the inhabitants thereof
28 25 s. cummin and put wheat in order
41 16 and the whirlwind shall scatter them
Jer 9 16 I will scatter them among the nations
13 14 I will scatter them every man from
24 and I will scatter them as stubble
15 7 I will scatter them with a fan in
18 17 will I scatter them before the enemy
31 28 to throw down and to s. and to destroy
49 32 I will s. into every wind them that
36 I will s. them into all these winds
Bar 2 29 nations, where I will scatter them
Eze 5 2 third part thou shalt s. in the wind
10 I will s. thy whole remnant into every
12 a third part of thee will I scatter
6 5 I will s. your bones round about your
12 14 troops I will scatter into every wind
20 23 and scatter them through the countries
22 15 and will s. thee among the countries
29 12 I will s. the Egyptians among the
30 23 scatter them through the countries. 26
Dan 4 11 off its leaves, and scatter its fruits
11 24 he shall scatter their spoils and their
Haba 3 14 came out as a whirlwind to scatter me
Zach 1 21 upon the land of Juda to scatter it
Mala 2 3 I will scatter upon your face the dung
scattered Gen 11 4 before we be scattered abroad
Gen 11 8 so the Lord scattered them from that
9 the Lord scattered them abroad upon
Exod 5 12 the people was scattered through all
14 41 the scraping be s. without the city
Num 10 35 let thy enemies be scattered, and let
Deut 28 25 and be s. throughout all the kingdoms
30 1 the Lord thy God shall have s. thee
3 nations into which he scattered thee
Judg 7 12 eastern people lay s. in the valley
9 44 enemies that were s. about the field
1 K 11 11 the rest were scattered, so that two
2 K 18 8 the battle there was s. over the face
22 15 he shot arrows and scattered them
3 K 22 17 I saw all Israel s. upon the hills
4 K 25 5 warriors that were with him were s.
1 Pa 10 7 forsook their cities and were s. up and
2 Pa 18 16 I saw all Israel s. in the mountains
Tob 3 4 nations amongst which thou hast s. us
13 4 because he hath therefore scattered you
14 6 our brethren that are scattered abroad
Jdth 5 23 places wherein they were scattered
Job 4 11 the young lions are scattered abroad
6 17 when they shall be s. they shall perish
Ps 17 15 forth his arrows, and he scattered them
21 15 like water: and all my bones are s.
43 12 hast scattered us among the nations
52 6 God hath s. the bones of them that
58 16 they shall be scattered abroad to eat
67 2 God arise, and let his enemies be s.
88 11 strength thou hast s. thy enemies
91 10 all the workers of iniquity shall be s.
140 7 our bones are s. by the side of hell
Prov 29 18 the people shall be scattered abroad
Wisd 5 15 a smoke that is s. abroad by the wind
11 21 and s. by the breath of thy power
17 3 they were s. under a dark veil of
Eccu 28 16 and s. them from nation to nation
48 16 and were s. through all the earth
Isa 33 3 lifting up thyself the nations are s.
56 8 who gathereth the scattered of Israel
Jer 3 13 thou hast s. thy ways to strangers
10 21 not understood, and all their flock is s.
23 2 you have scattered my flock and driven
30 11 nations among which I have s. thee
31 10 he that s. Israel will gather him
40 7 that were s. through the countries
13 been scattered about in the countries
43 5 to which they had before been s., to
49 5 you shall be s. every one out of one
50 17 Israel is a scattered flock, the lions
52 8 all his companions were scattered from
Lam 4 1 stones of the sanctuary are s. in the
Bar 2 4 people among whom the Lord hath s. us
13 nations, where thou hast scattered us
3 8 hast scattered us to be a reproach

4 37 whom thou sentest away scattered, they
Eze 6 8 when I shall have scattered you through
11 16 I have s. them among the countries
17 countries wherein you are scattered
12 15 and scattered them in the countries
17 21 the residue shall be s. into every
20 34 countries in which you are scattered
41 lands into which you are scattered
28 25 of the people among whom they are s.
29 13 among whom they have been scattered
34 5 my sheep were s. because there was no
5 the beasts of the field, and were s.
6 my flocks were s. upon the face of the
12 the midst of his sheep that were s.
12 places where they have been scattered
21 your horns, till they were s. abroad
36 19 I scattered them among the nations
Joel 3 2 whom they have s. among the nations
Zach 1 19 the horns that have scattered Juda. 21
2 6 I have s. you into the four winds
11 16 nor seek what is s. nor heal what is
13 7 shepherd, and the sheep shall be s.
8 two parts in it shall be scattered and
1 Ma 10 83 and they that were s. about the plain
2 Ma 1 27 gather together our scattered people
Luke 1 51 he hath s. the proud in the conceit of
John 16 32 you shall be s. every man to his own
Acts 5 36 all that believed him were scattered
James 1 1 to the twelve that were s. abroad
scattereth Job 21 18 ashes which the whirlwind s.
Ps 147 16 like wool: scattereth mists like ashes
Prov 20 8 scattereth away all evil with his look
26 a wise king scattereth the wicked
Eccu 43 19 scattereth the snow, and the falling
Mat 12 30 gathereth not with me, s. Luke 11:23
John 10 12 catcheth and scattereth the sheep
scattering 2 K 16 13 stones at him and s. earth
Dan 12 7 s. of the band of the holy people
Scenopegia 2 Ma 1 9 celebrate ye the days of S.
2 Ma 1 18 that you also may keep the day of S.
scent Job 14 9 at the scent of water, it shall
Jer 48 11 in him, and his scent is not changed
scepter Gen 49 10 s. shall not be taken away from
Num 13 12 of the scepter of Manasses, Gaddi
18 2 scepter of thy father, and let them be
24 17 a scepter shall spring up from Israel
Esth 4 11 king shall hold out the golden scepter
5 2 held out toward her the golden scepter
2 and kissed the top of his scepter
8 4 held out the golden scepter with his
14 11 give not, O Lord, thy scepter to them
15 14 come near then, and touch the scepter
15 he took the golden scepter and laid it
Ps 44 7 s. of thy kingdom is s. of uprightness
73 2 the scepter of thy inheritance which
109 2 the Lord will send forth the scepter
Wisd 10 14 brought him the scepter of the kingdom
Isa 9 24 the scepter of their oppressor thou
Jer 51 19 Israel is the scepter of his inheritance
Bar 6 13 this holdeth a scepter as a man, as a
Eze 19 14 no strong rod, to be a s. of rulers
20 37 I will make you subject to my scepter
21 10 thou removest the scepter of my son
13 when it shall overthrow the scepter
Amos 1 5 that holdeth the s. from the house
8 him that holdeth the s. from Ascalon
Zach 10 11 the scepter of Egypt shall depart
Heb 1 8 s. of justice is the s. of thy kingdom
scepters Wisd 6 22 delight be in thrones and s.
Eccu 35 23 and broken the scepters of the unjust
Eze 19 11 make scepters for them that bear rule
30 18 when I shall break there the scepters
Haba 3 14 thou hast cursed his scepters, the head

Sceva Acts 19 14 seven sons of S., a Jew, a chief
schism 1 C 12 25 that there might be no s. in
schisms 1 C 1 10 that there be no s. among you
1 C 11 18 church, there are schisms among you; and
scholar Mala 2 12 both the master and the s.
school Acts 19 9 daily in s. of one Tyrannus
scibboleth Judg 12 6 they asked him: Say then, S.
science Gen 44 15 like me in the s. of divining
Prov 30 3 have not known the science of saints
Eccu 17 6 created in them the s. of the spirit
Dan 1 4 acute in knowledge and instructed in s.
sciniphs Exod 8 16 be s. in all the land of Egypt
Exod 8 17 there came s. on men and on beasts
17 dust of the earth was turned into s.
18 sciniphs as well on men as on beasts
18 to bring forth s. and they could not
Ps 104 31 came divers sorts of flies and sciniphs
scoff Ps 43 14 a scoff and derision to them that
Jer 20 7 all the day, all scoff at me. For I am
Eze 5 15 thou shalt be a reproach and a scoff
scoffed 2 Es 2 19 they s. at us and despised us
2 Es 4 1 he [Sanaballat] scoffed at the Jews
Ps 34 16 they scoffed at me with scorn: they
79 7 and our enemies have scoffed at us
scoffer Prov 22 10 cast out the s., and contention
scoffers 2 P 3 3 there shall come deceitful s.
scorched Mat 13 6 the sun was up they were s.
Mark 4 6 when the sun was risen, it was s.
Apoc 16 8 and men were scorched with great heat
scorn 4 K 19 21 thee and laughed thee to scorn
Job 12 4 simplicity of just man is laughed to s.
22 19 the innocent shall laugh them to scorn
30 1 but now the younger in time scorn me
Ps 21 8 that saw me have laughed me to scorn
34 16 they scoffed at me with scorn: they
78 4 a scorn and derision to them that are
Prov 3 34 he shall scorn the scorners, and to
Wisd 4 18 but the Lord shall laugh them to scorn
Eccu 7 12 laugh no man to scorn in the bitterness
20 18 and how many will laugh him to scorn
Isa 37 22 despised thee and laughed thee to scorn
Eze 23 32 thou shalt be had in derision and scorn
Mat 9 24 they laughed him to scorn. Mark 5:40; Luke 8:53
scorned Wisd 11 15 whom they s. before, when he
scorner Prov 9 7 he that teacheth a s., doth an
Prov 9 8 rebuke not a scorner lest he hate thee
12 if a scorner, thou alone shalt bear the
13 1 he that is a scorner, heareth not
14 6 scorner seeketh wisdom, and findeth
29 20 hath failed, the scorner is consumed
scorners Prov 3 34 he shall scorn the s., and to
13 15 in the way of scorners is a deep pit
19 29 judgments are prepared for scorners
Osee 7 5 stretched out his hand with s.
scorneth Job 39 7 he s. the multitude of the city
Job 39 18 she scorneth the horse and his rider
Prov 19 28 an unjust witness s. judgment: and the
scornful Isa 28 14 the word of the Lord, ye s. men
scorning Job 34 7 who drinketh up s. like water
scorpion Num 34 4 by the ascent of the s. and so
Deut 8 15 the s. and the dipsas, and no water
Josu 15 3 towards the ascent of the scorpion
Judg 1 36 was from the ascent of the scorpion
Eccu 26 10 is as he that taketh hold of a scorpion
Luke 11 12 an egg, will he reach him a scorpion
Apoc 9 5 was as the torment of a scorpion when
scorpions 3 K 12 11 but I will beat you with scorpions. 14; 2 Pa 10:11, 14
Eccu 39 36 teeth of beasts and s. and serpents
Eze 2 6 thou dwellest with scorpions. Fear not
Luke 10 19 to tread upon serpents and scorpions
Apoc 9 3 as the s. of the earth have power; and

10 they had tails like to scorpions, and
scoured Lev 6 28 be of brass, it shall be scoured
scourge Exod 30 12 there shall be no s. among them
Num 25 8 the scourge ceased from the children
2 Pa 6 28 whatsoever scourge or infirmity shall
29 knowing his own scourge and infirmity
Job 4 5 now the scourge is come upon thee
5 21 hidden from the scourge of the tongue
9 23 if he scourge, let him kill at once
23 2 the hand of my scourge is more grievous
Ps 90 10 nor shall the scourge come near thy
Eccu 4 19 and she will scourge him with the
23 12 scourge shall not depart from his house
26 9 with jealous woman is a s. of the tongue
Isa 10 26 shall raise up a scourge against him
19 22 Lord shall strike Egypt with a scourge
28 15 when the overflowing s. shall pass. 18
2 Ma 9 11 being admonished by the scourge of God
Mat 10 17 they will s. you in their synagogues
23 34 some you will s. in your synagogues
Mark 10 34 on him and scourge him and kill him
John 2 15 a scourge of little cords, he drove
Acts 22 25 is it lawful for you to scourge a man
scourged Gen 12 17 Lord s. Pharao and his house
Exod 5 14 were scourged by Pharao's taskmasters
19 20 they both shall be scourged, and they
Ps 72 5 neither shall they be s. like other men
14 and I have been scourged all the day
Prov 19 25 the wicked man being scourged, the fool
Wisd 16 16 were s. by the strength of thy arm
2 Ma 3 26 s. him without ceasing with many
34 and thou having been scourged by God
38 thou shalt receive him again s., if
5 18 had been forthwith scourged and put
Mat 20 19 to be mocked and s. and crucified and
27 26 having scourged Jesus, delivered him
Mark 15 15 up Jesus, when he had s. him, to be
Luke 18 32 and shall be mocked and scourged and
33 after they have scourged him, they
John 19 1 Pilate took Jesus and scourged him
Acts 5 40 apostles, after they had scourged them
22 24 that he should be s. and tortured: to
scourges 2 Pa 10 11 my father beat you with s. 14
Job 19 6 and compassed me with his scourges
Jdth 9 27 us believe that these s. of the Lord
Ps 31 10 many are the scourges of the sinner
34 15 s. were gathered together upon me
37 18 I am ready for scourges: and my sorrow
38 11 remove thy s. from me. The strength
Eccu 23 2 who will set scourges over my thoughts
40 9 famine and affliction and scourges
2 Ma 7 1 were tormented with whips and scourges
scourgest Tob 13 2 for thou s. and thou savest
Wisd 12 22 thou s. our enemies very many ways
scourgeth Heb 12 6 he s. every son whom he
scrape Eze 26 4 I will scrape her dust from her
scraped Lev 14 41 the house be s. on the inside
Lev 14 43 be taken out and the dust scraped off
Job 2 8 and he took a potsherd and scraped the
scraping Lev 14 41 dust of the s. be scattered
screak Amos 2 13 I will s. under you as a wain
Amos 8 3 the hinges of the temple shall screak
screaketh Amos 2 13 as a wain s. that is laden
screech Lev 11 17 you must not eat . . . the s. owl
scribe 2 K 8 17 priests: and Saraias was the s.
2 K 20 25 and Siva was scribe: and Sadoc and
4 K 12 10 king's scribe and the high priest came
18 18 who was over the house, and Sobna the s.
37; 22:3; Isa 36:3, 22; 37:2
22 3 the scribe of the temple of the Lord
8 high priest said to Saphan the scribe
9 Saphan the scribe came to the king
10 and Saphan the scribe told the king
12 Saphan the scribe and Asaia the king's
1 Pa 18 16 were the priests: and Susa, scribe
24 6 Semeias the son of Nathanael the scribe
2 Pa 24 11 the king's scribe and he whom the high
26 11 was under the hand of Jehiel the scribe
34 15 [Helcias] said to Saphan the scribe
20 Saphan the scribe and Asaa the king's
1 Es 4 9 Reum Beelteem and Samsai the scribe
17 king sent word to . . . Samsai the s.
23 Samsai the s. and their counsellors
7 6 he was a ready s. in the law of Moses
11 the scribe instructed in the words
12 to Esdras . . . the most learned scribe
21 Esdras the priest, the s. of the law
2 Es 8 1 they spoke to Esdras the scribe, to
4 Esdras the scribe stood upon a step of
9 Esdras the priest and scribe . . . said
13 gathered together to Esdras the scribe
12 26 days . . . of Esdras the priest and s.
35 and Esdras the scribe before them at
13 13 Selemias the priest and Sadoc the scribe
Eccu 10 5 upon the person of the s. he shall lay
38 25 the wisdom of a scribe cometh by his
Jer 36 10 Gamarias the son of Saphan the scribe
12 princes sat there, Elisama the scribe
20 the chamber of Elisama the scribe. 21
26 to take up Baruch the scribe and
32 Baruch the son of Nerias the scribe
37 14 that was in house of Jonathan the s.
19 not back into house of Jonathan the s.
52 25 a scribe, an officer of the army
Mat 8 19 a certain scribe came and said to him
13 52 every scribe instructed in the kingdom
Mark 12 32 the scribe said to him: Well, Master
1 C 1 20 where is the wise? Where is the scribe
scribes 3 K 4 3 and Ahia, the sons of Sisa, s.
1 Pa 2 55 the families of the scribes that dwell
2 Pa 34 13 burdens for divers uses, were scribes
Esth 3 12 the king's scribes were called in the
8 9 king's s. and secretaries were called
Jer 8 8 pen of the s. hath wrought falsehood
1 Ma 5 42 set the s. of the people by the torrent
7 12 a company of the scribes to require
2 Ma 6 18 Eleazar one of the chief of the scribes
Mat 9 3 of the scribes said within themselves
16 21 from the ancients and scribes and
17 10 scribes say that Elias must come first
23 34 prophets and wise men and scribes: and
26 57 the s. and the ancients were assembled
27 41 with the s. and ancients, mocking, said
Mark 1 22 as one having power, and not as the s.
2 6 were some of the scribes sitting there
3 22 s. who were come down from Jerusalem
7 1 the Pharisees and some of the scribes
5 and scribes asked him: Why do not thy
8 31 by the high priests and the scribes
9 10 why then do the Pharisees and s. say
13 and the scribes disputing with them
12 28 there came one of the scribes that
35 how do the scribes say, that Christ is
38 beware of the scribes. Luke 20:46
14 53 priests and the scribes . . . assembled
15 1 with the ancients and the scribes and
31 mocking, said with the scribes one to
Luke 5 30 Pharisees and s. murmured, saying. 15:2
Acts 4 5 their princes and ancients and s. were
6 12 they stirred up . . . and the scribes
scrip 1 K 17 40 put them into the shepherd's s.
1 K 17 49 put his hand into his scrip and took
4 K 4 42 of barley, and new corn in his scrip
Mat 10 10 nor scrip for your journey, nor two
Mark 6 8 no scrip, no bread, nor money in their
Luke 9 3 neither staff nor scrip nor bread nor

10 4 carry neither purse nor scrip nor
22 35 I sent you without purse and scrip
36 let him take it, and likewise a scrip
scripture Dan 10 21 set down in the s. of truth
Mark 12 10 have you not read this scripture. The
15 28 the s. was fulfilled, which saith
Luke 4 21 this day is fulfilled this s. in your
John 2 22 they believed the s. and the word that
7 38 as the s. saith, Out of his belly
42 doth not the s. say: That Christ
10 35 and the scripture cannot be broken
13 18 that s. may be fulfilled. 17:12
19 24 that s. might be fulfilled. 28, 36
37 another s. saith: They shall look on
20 9 as yet they knew not the scripture
Acts 1 16 the scripture must needs be fulfilled
8 32 the place of the scripture which he
35 Philip . . . beginning at this scripture
Rom 1 2 promised before . . . in holy scripture
4 3 for what saith the s.? Abraham believed
9 17 for the scripture saith to Pharao: To
10 8 what saith the scripture? The word is
11 the s. saith: Whosoever believeth in him
11 2 know you not what the scripture saith
Gal 3 8 the s., foreseeing, that God justifieth
22 scripture hath concluded all under sin
4 30 what saith the scripture? Cast out the
1 Tim 5 18 the scripture saith: Thou shalt not
2 Tim 3 16 all s., inspired of God, is profitable
James 2 23 the s. was fulfilled, saying: Abraham
4 5 that the s. saith in vain: To envy
1 P 2 6 it is said in the scripture: Behold I
2 P 1 20 no prophecy of s. is made by private
scriptures Eccu 44 5 published canticles of the s.
Mat 21 42 have you never read in the Scriptures
22 29 you err, not knowing the Scriptures
26 54 how then shall the s. be fulfilled
56 that the s. of the prophets might be
Mark 12 24 you know not the s. nor the power of
14 49 that the scriptures may be fulfilled
Luke 24 27 he expounded to them in all the s. the
32 in the way, and opened to us the s.
45 that they might understand the s.
John 5 39 search the scriptures, for you think
7 52 search the s. and see that out of
Acts 17 2 days he reasoned with them out of the s.
11 daily searching the s., whether these
18 24 Apollo . . . one mighty in the scriptures
28 showing by the scriptures, that Jesus
Rom 15 4 through patience and comfort of the s.
16 26 now is made manifest by the scriptures
1 C 15 3 died for our sins, according to the s.
4 the third day, according to the s.: and
2 Tim 3 15 thou hast known the holy scriptures
James 2 8 according to the s., Thou shalt love
2 P 3 16 as they do also the other scriptures
scrivener Ps 44 2 my tongue is the pen of a s.
scruple 1 K 25 31 and a scruple of heart to my lord
sculptures 3 K 7 24 two rows cast of chamfered s.
3 K 7 35 having its gravings and divers s.
scurf Lev 21 20 or a dry scurf in his body
Lev 22 22 or blisters or a scab or a dry scurf
scurrility Eph 5 4 s., which is to no purpose
scythes Judg 1 19 had many chariots armed with s.
Judg 4 3 he had 900 chariots set with scythes
13 his 900 chariots armed with scythes
Scythian Col 3 11 barbarian nor S., bond nor free
Scythians 2 Ma 4 47 their cause even before S.
Scythopolis 2 Ma 12 29 thence they departed to S.
Scythopolitans 2 Ma 12 30 that were among the S.
sea Gen 1 22 fill the waters of the sea: and let
Gen 1 22 over the fishes of the sea. 28
9 2 fishes of the sea are delivered into
14 3 woodland vale, which now is the salt sea
Exod 14 2 which is between Magdal and the sea
2 you shall encamp before it upon the sea
16 stretch forth thy hands over the sea. 26
21 stretched forth his hand over the sea
27 stretched forth his hand towards the sea
28 who had come into the sea after them
15 1 rider he hath thrown into the sea. 21
4 his army he hath cast into the sea
10 thy wind blew and the sea covered them
19 his chariots and horsemen into the sea
19 back upon them the waters of the sea
20 11 heaven and earth and the sea and all
23 31 Red Sea to the sea of the Palestines
36 27 that side . . . which looketh to the sea
32 side of the tabernacle towards the sea
Lev 11 9 as well in the sea as in the rivers and
Num 11 22 shall the fishes of the sea be gathered
31 taking quails up beyond the sea
13 30 the Chanaanite abideth by the sea
34 3 most salt sea for its furtherest limits
11 thence . . . eastward to sea of Cenereth
12 shall be closed in by the most salt sea
35 5 toward the sea . . . the same extent
Deut 3 17 borders of Cenereth unto the sea of the desert which is the most salt sea
4 49 unto the sea of the wilderness and
11 24 unto western sea shall be your borders
30 13 nor is it beyond the sea; that thou
13 which of us can cross the sea and bring
33 19 suck as milk the abundance of the sea
23 he shall possess the sea and the south
34 2 land of Juda unto the furthermost sea
Josu 3 16 the sea of the wilderness, which now is called the Dead Sea
9 1 the plains, in the places near the sea
12 3 from the wilderness to sea of Cenereth
3 and to the sea of the wilderness, which is the most salt sea
13 27 uttermost part of the sea of Cenereth
15 2 was from the top of the most salt sea
5 the beginning shall be the most salt sea
5 bay of the sea unto the same river
46 from Accaron even to the sea: all
16 6 the confines go out unto the sea: but
8 towards the sea unto valley of reeds
8 goings out thereof are at most salt sea
17 9 and the outgoings of it are at the sea
10 and the sea is the border of both, and
18 14 thence going round towards the sea
14 this is their coast towards the sea
15 from part of Cariathiarim towards sea
19 towards the north of the most salt sea
19 11 it went up from the sea and from Merala
26 it reacheth to Carmel by the sea and
29 outgoings thereof shall be at the sea
24 6 out of Egypt, and you came to the sea
7 brought the sea upon them, and covered
2 K 22 16 the overflowings of the sea appeared
3 K 5 9 down from Libanus to the sea: and I
9 put them together in floats in the sea
7 23 a molten sea of ten cubits. 2 Pa 4:2
24 for ten cubits going about the sea
25 and the sea was above upon them, and
39 the sea he put on the right side of
44 one sea, and twelve oxen under the sea
9 27 sailors that had knowledge of the sea
10 22 the navy of Hiram by sea to Tharsis
18 43 go up and look toward the sea. And he
44 a little cloud arose out of the sea
22 49 king Josaphat made navies on the sea
4 K 14 25 Emath, unto the sea of the wilderness
16 17 took down the sea from the brazen oxen

25 13 and the bases and the sea of brass
16 two pillars, one sea, and the bases
1 Pa 16 32 let the sea roar, and the fulness
18 8 of which Solomon made the brazen sea
2 Pa 2 16 will convey them in floats by sea
4 3 encompassed the belly of the sea, as
4 sea itself was set upon the 12 oxen
4 and the sea stood upon them: and the
4 hinder parts . . . inward under the sea
6 the sea was for the priests to wash in
10 and he set the sea on the right side
15 one sea and twelve oxen under the sea
20 2 multitude against thee from beyond sea
1 Es 3 7 from Libanus to the sea of Joppe
2 Es 9 11 thou didst divide the sea before them
Tob 8 7 earth and the sea . . . bless thee. Thou
Jdth 2 14 of Mambre, till one comes to the sea
5 12 God of heaven opened the sea to them
12 walked through the bottom of the sea
Esth 10 1 all the islands of the sea tributary
Job 7 12 am I a sea or a whale, that thou hast
9 8 and walketh upon the waves of the sea
11 9 measure of him . . . broader than the sea
12 8 and the fishes of the sea shall tell
14 11 the waters should depart out of the sea
28 14 and the sea saith: It is not with me
36 30 he shall cover also the ends of the sea
38 8 who shut up the sea with doors when
16 hast thou entered into depths of the sea
41 22 he shall make the deep sea to boil
Ps 8 9 the fishes of the sea, that pass through the paths of the sea
32 7 together the waters of the sea as in a
45 3 be removed into the heart of the sea
64 6 of the earth and in the sea afar off
8 who troublest the depth of the sea
65 6 who turneth the sea into dry land
67 23 I will turn them into the depth of sea
68 3 I am come into the depth of the sea
35 praise him; the sea and everything
71 8 he shall rule from sea to sea, and
73 13 by thy strength didst make the sea firm
76 20 thy way is in the sea, and thy paths
77 13 he divided the sea and brought them
53 the sea overwhelmed their enemies
79 12 forth its branches unto the sea, and
88 10 thou rulest the power of the sea: and
13 the north and the sea thou hast created
26 I will set his hand in the sea: and his
92 4 wonderful are the surges of the sea
94 5 for the sea is his, and he made it
95 11 let the sea be moved. 97:7
103 26 this sea dragon which thou hast formed
105 7 provoked to wrath going up to the sea
106 3 from the north and from the sea. They
23 they that go down to the sea in ships
113 3 the sea saw and fled: Jordan was
5 what ailed thee, O thou sea, that thou
134 6 he hath done . . . in earth, in the sea
138 9 dwell in the uttermost parts of the sea
145 6 who made heaven and earth, the sea
Prov 8 29 when he compassed the sea with its
Ecce 1 7 all the rivers run into the sea, yet the sea doth not overflow
Wisd 5 23 the water of the sea shall rage against
10 19 their enemies she drowned in the sea
14 3 thou hast made a way even in the sea
4 though a man went to sea without art
5 passing over the sea by ship are saved
19 12 the quail came up to them from the sea
Eccu 18 8 as a drop of water of the sea are
24 8 have walked in the waves of the sea
39 her thoughts are more vast than the sea
43 and my river came near to a sea: for I
29 23 hath tossed them as a wave of the sea
40 11 all waters shall return to the sea
43 26 let them that sail on the sea, tell
44 23 they should inherit from sea to sea
50 3 they were filled as the sea above
Isa 5 30 that day, like the roaring of the sea
9 1 the way of the sea beyond the Jordan
10 26 and his rod over the sea, and he shall
11 9 as the covering waters of the sea
11 Emath, and from the islands of the sea
14 shoulders of the Philistines by the sea
15 waste the tongue of the sea of Egypt
16 8 are left, they are gone over the sea
17 12 like the multitude of the roaring sea
18 2 that sendeth ambassadors by the sea
19 5 the water of the sea shall be dried up
21 1 the burden of the desert of the sea
23 1 howl, ye ships of the sea. 14
2 merchants of Sidon passing over the sea
4 sea speaketh, even strength of the sea
11 he stretched out his hand over the sea
24 14 shall make a joyful noise from the sea
15 glorify . . . in the islands of the sea
27 1 shall slay the whale that is in the sea
42 10 you that go down to the sea, and all
43 16 the Lord, who made a way in the sea
48 18 thy justice as the waves of the sea
49 12 these from the north and from the sea
50 2 my rebuke I will make the sea a desert
51 10 hast not thou dried up the sea, the
10 who madest the depth of the sea a way
15 Lord thy God, who trouble the sea, and
57 20 the wicked are like the raging sea
60 5 multitude of the sea shall be converted
9 the ships of the sea in the beginning
63 11 he that brought them up out of the sea
66 19 be saved, to the Gentiles into the sea
Jer 5 28 I have set the sand a bound for the sea
6 23 their voice shall roar like the sea
25 22 of the islands that are beyond the sea
27 19 saith the Lord of hosts . . . to the sea
31 35 who stirreth up the sea, and the waves
48 32 thy branches are gone over the sea
32 they are come even to the sea of Jazer
49 23 tidings, they are troubled as in the sea
50 42 their voice shall roar like the sea
51 36 I will make her sea desolate, and will
42 the sea is come up over Babylon: she
52 17 sea of brass that was in the house
20 and the two pillars and one sea and
Lam 2 13 great as the sea is thy destruction
4 3 even the sea monsters have drawn out
Bar 3 30 who hath passed over the sea and found
Eze 1 16 was like the appearance of the sea
26 3 to thee as the waves of the sea rise up
16 all the princes of the sea shall come
17 that dwellest in the sea, renowned city that was strong in the sea
18 islands in the sea shall be troubled
27 3 that dwelleth at the entry of the sea
4 and situate in the heart of the sea
5 have built thee with all sea planks
9 ships of the sea . . . were thy factors
25 the ships of the sea were thy chief
25 glorified exceedingly in heart of the sea
26 broken thee in the heart of the sea
27 shall fall in the heart of the sea
29 all the pilots of the sea shall stand
33 merchandise that went from thee by sea
34 now thou art destroyed by the sea
28 2 chair of God in the heart of the sea
8 that are slain in the heart of the sea

32 2 the dragon that is in the sea: and thou
38 20 fishes of the sea . . . shall be moved
41 12 the way that looked toward the sea
45 7 from side of the sea even to the sea
47 8 these waters . . . shall go into the sea
17 from the sea even to the court of Enan
18 Jordan making the bound to the east sea
20 side toward the sea, is the great sea
20 to Emath: this is the side of the sea
48 1 from the east side thereof to the sea
2 even to the side of the sea. 3–8, 27
8 the east side to the side of the sea
10 toward the sea 10,000 in breadth, and
17 to the sea 250. And the residue in
21 toward the sea . . . unto border of sea
27 from east side to the side of the sea
Dan 7 3 great beasts . . . came up out of the sea
Osee 4 3 fishes of the sea also shall be gathered
11 10 the children of the sea shall fear
Joel 2 20 with his face towards the east sea
20 his hinder part towards the utmost sea
Amos 5 8 that calleth the waters of the sea
8 12 and they shall move from sea to sea
9 3 from my eyes in the depth of the sea
6 who calleth the waters of the sea, and
Jon 1 4 the Lord sent a great wind into the sea
4 a great tempest was raised in the sea
5 cast forth the wares . . . into the sea
9 who made both the sea and the dry land
11 to thee, that the sea may be calm to us
11 to us? For the sea flowed and swelled
12 and cast me into the sea, and the sea shall be calm to you
13 the sea tossed and swelled upon them
15 took Jonas and cast him into the sea, and the sea ceased from raging
2 4 into the deep in the heart of the sea
6 the sea hath covered my head. I went
Mich 7 12 they shall come . . . from sea to sea
19 all our sins into the bottom of the sea
Nah 1 4 he rebuketh the sea and drieth it up
3 8 the sea is its riches, the waters are
Haba 1 14 wilt make men as the fishes of the sea
2 14 as waters covering the sea. Woe to
3 8 was thy . . . indignation in the sea
15 madest a way in the sea for thy horses
Soph 1 3 I will gather . . . the fishes of the sea
Agge 2 7 I will move . . . the sea and the dry land
Zach 9 4 shall strike her strength in the sea
10 his power shall be from sea to sea
10 11 shall pass over the strait of the sea
11 shall strike the waves in the sea
14 8 half of them to the east sea, and half of them to the last sea
1 Ma 4 23 and purple of the sea and great riches
6 29 from the islands of the sea hired troops
8 23 success . . . by sea and by land forever
32 make war against thee by sea and land
13 29 be seen by all that sailed on the sea
14 5 made an entrance to the isles of the sea
34 fortified Joppe which lieth by the sea
15 1 sent letters from the isles of the sea
14 the ships drew near by sea: and they
14 annoyed the city by land and by sea
2 Ma 5 21 now make the sea passable on foot
9 8 to command even the waves of the sea
Mat 4 15 the way of the sea beyond the Jordan
18 his brother, casting a net into the sea
8 24 a great tempest arose in the sea, so
26 he commanded the winds and the sea
27 winds and the sea obey him. Mark 4:40
32 down a steep place into the sea: and
13 47 is like to a net cast into the sea
14 25 to them walking upon the sea. Mark 6:48
26 seeing him walking upon sea. Mark 6:49
17 26 go to the sea, and cast in a hook
18 6 be drowned in the depth of the sea
21 21 take up and cast thyself into the sea
23 15 you go round about the sea and the
Mark 1 16 casting nets into the sea, for they
3 7 retired with his disciples to the sea
4 1 went up into a ship and sat in the sea
39 rebuked the wind and said to the sea
5 1 they came over the strait of the sea
13 was carried headlong into the sea
13 and were stifled in the sea. And they
21 he was nigh unto the sea. And there
9 41 neck, and he were cast into the sea
11 23 thou removed and be cast into the sea
Luke 8 25 commandeth both the winds and the sea
17 2 his neck, and he cast into the sea
6 be thou transplanted into the sea
21 25 roaring of the sea and of the waves
John 6 16 his disciples went down to the sea
17 they went over the sea to Capharnaum
18 the sea arose, by reason of a great
19 they see Jesus walking upon the sea
22 stood on the other side of the sea
25 found him on the other side of the sea
21 1 to the disciples at the sea of Tiberias
7 and cast himself into the sea. But the
Acts 4 24 didst make heaven and earth, the sea
14 14 sea, and all things that are in them
17 14 Paul, to go unto the sea; but Silas
21 7 we having finished the voyage by sea
27 5 and sailing over the sea of Cilicia, and
38 ship, casting the wheat into the sea
40 they committed themselves to the sea
41 part was broken with violence of sea
43 cast themselves first into the sea, and
28 4 who though he hath escaped the sea, yet
29 30 having let down the boat into the sea
1 C 10 1 the cloud, and all passed through sea
2 were baptized, in the cloud, and in sea
2 C 11 25 night and day I was in depth of the sea
26 in perils in the sea, in perils from
James 1 6 is like a wave of the sea, which is
Jude 13 raging waves of the sea, foaming out
Apoc 4 6 a sea of glass, like to crystal; and in
5 13 the earth, and such as are in the sea
7 1 blow upon the earth nor upon the sea
2 given to hurt the earth and the sea
3 hurt not the earth nor the sea nor the
8 8 mountain . . . was cast into the sea
8 the third part of the sea became blood
9 died, which had life in the sea, and
10 2 and he set his right foot upon the sea
5 standing upon the sea and upon the
6 sea and the things which are therein
8 who standeth upon the sea and upon the
13 1 I saw a beast coming up out of the sea
14 7 that made heaven and earth, the sea
15 2 and I saw as it were a sea of glass
2 standing on the sea of glass, having
16 3 angel poured out his vial upon the sea
3 and every living soul died in the sea
18 17 as many as work in the sea, stood afar
19 were made rich that had ships at sea
21 millstone, and cast it into the sea
20 13 the sea gave up the dead that were in
21 1 was gone, and the sea is now no more

great sea Num 34 5 end in the shore of the g. s.
Num 34 6 west side shall begin from the g. s.
7 borders shall begin from the great sea
Josu 1 4 land of the Hethites unto the great sea
5 1 possessed the places near the great sea

9 1 and on the coasts of the great sea
15 4 bounds thereof shall be the great sea
11 is bounded westward with the great sea
47 to torrent of Egypt and the great sea
16 3 countries of it are ended by the g. s.
23 4 east of the Jordan unto the great sea
Ps 103 25 g. s., which stretcheth wide its arms
Eze 47 10 as the fishes of the great sea, a very
15 from the g. s. by the way of Hethalon
19 and the torrent even to the great sea
20 side toward the sea, is the great sea
48 28 inheritance over against the great sea
Dan 7 2 winds . . . strove upon the great sea
midst of the sea Exod 14 16 may go through m. . . .
Exod 14 22 of Israel went in through the m. . . .
23 chariots and horsemen through m. . . .
29 of Israel marched through the m. . . .
15 8 were gathered together in the m. . . .
Num 33 8 they passed through the m. . . . 2 Es 9:11
Prov 23 34 shalt be as one sleeping in the m. . . .
30 19 way of a ship in the midst of the sea
Eze 26 5 drying place for nets in the m. . . .
27 32 which is become silent in the m. . . .
Mat 14 24 the boat in the m. . . . was tossed with
Mark 6 47 the ship was in the midst of the sea
Red Sea; *see* **Red**
sand of the sea; *see* **sand**
seacoast Eze 25 16 destroy the remnant of the s.
Soph 2 5 woe to you that inhabit the seacoast
6 seacoast shall be the resting place of
1 Ma 7 1 a few men into a city of the seacoast
15 11 and he fled along by the seacoast
38 appointed Cendebeus captain of the s.
2 Ma 8 11 to the cities upon the s. to invite
Mat 4 13 dwelt in Capharnaum on the seacoast
Luke 6 17 the seacoast both of Tyre and Sidon
seal Job 9 7 the stars as it were under a seal
Job 38 14 the seal shall be restored as clay
Cant 8 6 put me as a seal upon thy heart, as a
6 put me . . . as a seal upon thy arm
Eccu 22 33 mouth, and a sure seal upon my lips
Isa 8 16 seal the law among my disciples. And I
Eze 28 12 thou wast the seal of resemblance
Dan 8 26 thou therefore seal up the vision
12 4 shut up the words and seal the book
14 10 and seal it with thy own ring: and when
John 3 33 hath set his seal that God is true
Rom 4 11 a seal of justice of the faith, which
1 C 9 2 for you are the seal of my apostleship
2 Tim 2 19 of God standeth firm, having this seal
Apoc 6 3 when he had opened the . . . seal. 5, 7, 9, 12; 8:1
10 4 seal up the things which the seven
20 3 shut him up and set a seal upon him
22 10 seal not the words of the prophecy of
sealed Deut 32 34 and sealed up in my treasures
3 K 21 8 sealed them with his ring and sent
Job 14 17 thou hast sealed up my offences as it
Cant 4 12 garden enclosed, a fountain sealed up
Wisd 2 5 it is fast sealed, and no man returneth
Isa 29 11 as the words of a book that is sealed
11 shall answer: I cannot, for it is s.
Jer 32 10 I wrote it in a book and sealed it
11 deed of the purchase that was sealed
14 deed of the purchase that is sealed up
44 deeds shall be written and sealed
Dan 6 17 which the king sealed with his own
12 9 the words are shut up and sealed until
14 13 having sealed it with the king's ring
John 6 27 for him hath God, the Father, sealed
2 C 1 22 who also hath sealed us, and given the
Eph 4 30 are sealed unto the day of redemption
Apoc 5 1 and without, sealed with seven seals
sealeth Job 37 7 he s. up the hand of all men
sealing Mat 27 66 sepulcher sure, s. the stone
seals Eccu 38 28 he who maketh graven seals and
Jer 32 11 with the seals that were on the outside
Dan 14 16 are the seals whole, Daniel? And he
Apoc 5 1 and without, sealed with seven seals
2 book and to loose the seals thereof
5 and to loose the seven seals thereof
9 to take the book and to open the seals
6 1 had opened one of the seven seals and
seam John 19 23 the coat was without seam, woven
search Gen 31 32 search, and if thou find any of
Gen 31 35 his careful search was in vain. And Jacob
1 K 23 23 I will search him out in all the
2 K 10 3 to search and spy into the city and
3 K 20 6 they shall s. thy house and the houses
4 K 10 23 search and see that there be not any
1 Pa 19 3 to consider and s. and spy out thy land
1 Es 4 15 that search may be made in the books
19 search hath been made, and it is found
5 17 let him search in the king's library
Jdth 5 24 s. if there be any iniquity of theirs
8 33 that you s. not into what I am doing
Job 8 8 s. diligently into the memory of the
10 6 my iniquity, and search after my sins
36 23 who can search out his ways? Or who
Ps 43 22 shall not God search out these things
60 8 his mercy and truth who shall search
63 7 they have failed in their search. Man
108 11 may the usurer search all the substance
118 2 are they that search his testimonies
34 I will search thy law; and I will keep
115 I will s. the commandments of my God
Prov 18 17 his friend cometh and shall search him
25 2 glory of kings to search out the speech
28 11 that is prudent shall search him out
Ecce 1 13 and search out wisely concerning all
6 4 works and search out your thoughts
9 16 that are in heaven, who shall s. out
13 7 conversant among his works, they s.
Eccu 3 22 s. not into things above thy ability
6 28 search for her, and she shall be made
18 3 who shall s. out his glorious acts
24 38 and a weaker shall not search her out
39 3 he will search out the hidden meanings
Isa 34 16 search ye diligently in the book of the
Jer 17 10 I am the Lord who search the heart
Lam 3 40 let us search out ways and seek and
Bar 3 23 that search after the wisdom that is
31 nor that can search out her paths: but
Amos 9 3 I will search and take them away from
Soph 1 12 I will search Jerusalem with lamps
1 Ma 9 26 diligent search after friends of Judas
John 5 39 search the scriptures. 7:52
searched Gen 31 34 when he had s. all the tent
Gen 31 37 and searched all my household stuff
44 12 which when he had searched, beginning
1 Es 6 1 they searched in the library of the
Job 5 27 is even so, as we have searched out
28 11 the depths also of rivers he hath s.
27 declared and prepared and searched it
29 16 I knew not, I s. out most diligently
Ps 63 7 they have searched after iniquities
138 3 my path and my line thou hast s. out
Eccu 1 3 who hath s. out the wisdom of God
42 18 he hath searched out the deep and
Jer 31 37 foundations of the earth searched out
Abdi 6 how have they searched Esau, how have
Soph 1 6 not sought the Lord nor s. after him
1 Ma 3 48 in which the Gentiles searched for the
1 P 1 10 have inquired and diligently searched
searcher Ps 7 10 s. of hearts and reins is God
Prov 25 27 he that is a searcher of majesty, shall

20 sons of Seir . . . S. and Ana. 1 Pa 1:38
24 sons of Sebeon: Aia and Ana. 1 Pa 1:40
24 when he fed the asses of S. his father
29 duke Sobal, duke Sebeon, duke Ana
Sebethai 1 Es 10 15 Mesollam and S., Levites
Sebia 1 Pa 8 9 Jobab and Sebia and Mosa and
2 Pa 24 1 the name of his mother was Sebia of
Sebnia 2 Es 9 5 S. and Phathahia said: Arise
Seboim Gen 10 19 Adama and S. even to Lasa
Gen 14 2 Semeber king of Seboim, and against
8 king of Seboim and the king of Bala
Deut 29 23 Sodom and Gomorrha, Adama and S.
1 K 13 18 above valley of S. towards the desert
2 Es 11 34 Hadid, Seboim, and Neballat, Lod
Osee 11 8 as Adama, shall I set thee as Seboim
Sechem Num 26 31 S., of whom is the family of
Josu 17 2 to the children of Sechem and to the
1 Pa 7 19 sons of Semida were Ahiu and Sechem
Sechemites Num 26 31 is the family of the S.
Sechenia 1 Pa 24 11 the tenth [lot] to Sechenia
Sechenias 1 Pa 3 21 Obdia, whose son was Sechenias. The son of S. was Semeia
2 Pa 31 15 and Semeias and Amarias and S.
1 Es 8 3 of the sons of S., the son of Pharos
5 sons of Sechenias, the son of Ezechiel
10 2 S. the son of Jehiel of the sons of
2 Es 3 29 Semaia the son of S., keeper of the
6 18 he was the son-in-law of Sechenias
Sechia 1 Pa 8 10 Jehus and Sechia and Marma. These
Sechrona Josu 15 11 bendeth to S., and passeth
Second Soph 1 10 gate, and a howling from the S.
4 K 22 14 who dwelt in Jerusalem in the Second
secondly Eccu 23 33 s., she hath offended against
1 C 12 28 first apostles, s. prophets, thirdly
secret Num 5 13 the adultery is s. and cannot be
Deut 27 15 and shall put it in a secret place
29 29 secret things to the Lord our God
Judg 3 19 I have a s. message to thee, O king
22 by the secret parts of nature the
1 K 5 9 they had emerods in their secret parts
19 2 thou shalt abide in a secret place
Tob 12 7 it is good to hide the secret of a king
11 I will not hide the secret from you
Jdth 2 2 to them the secret of his counsel. And
Job 13 10 because in secret you accept his person
20 26 all darkness is hid in his s. places
28 18 wisdom is drawn out of secret places
31 27 and my heart in secret hath rejoiced
Ps 9 9 he lieth in wait in secret like a lion
16 12 as a young lion dwelling in s. places
18 13 from my secret ones cleanse me, O Lord
26 5 in the secret place of his tabernacle
30 21 shalt hide them in the s. of thy face
63 5 to shoot in secret the undefiled. They
80 8 heard thee in the s. place of tempest
138 15 thee, which thou hast made in secret
Prov 21 14 a secret present quencheth anger: and
25 9 discover not the secret to a stranger
31 4 no secret where drunkenness reigneth
Eccu 11 4 and his works are glorious and secret
27 17 that discloseth the secret of a friend
42 1 disclose not the thing that is secret
48 28 and secret things before they came
Isa 24 16 my s. to myself, my s. to myself
45 3 the concealed riches of secret places
19 I have not spoken in secret. 48:16
Jer 13 17 my soul shall weep in secret for your
23 24 shall a man be hid in secret places
Lam 3 10 in wait: as a lion in secret places
Eze 7 22 they shall violate my secret place
28 3 than Daniel: no s. is hid from thee
Dan 2 18 God of heaven concerning this secret
27 secret that the king desireth to know
30 to me also this secret is revealed
47 seeing thou couldst discover this s.
4 6 that no secret is impossible to thee
14 12 made under the table a secret entrance
Amos 3 7 doth nothing without revealing his s.
Haba 3 14 that devoureth the poor man in secret
1 Ma 1 56 into the secret places of fugitives
2 31 were gone away into the secret places
36 them, nor stopped up the secret places
41 that were slain in the secret places
2 Ma 1 16 opening a s. entrance of the temple
Mat 6 4 that thy alms may be in secret, and
4 thy Father who seeth in secret. 6, 18
6 the door, pray to thy Father in secret
18 but to thy Father who is in secret
Mark 4 22 neither was it made secret, but that
Luke 8 17 there is not anything secret that shall
John 7 4 no man that doth anything in secret
10 not openly, but as it were in secret
18 20 and in secret I have spoken nothing
Rom 16 25 which was kept secret from eternity
2 C 12 4 into paradise, and heard secret words
Eph 5 12 things that are done by them in secret
secretaries Esth 8 9 scribes and s. were called
secretary's Jer 36 12 house to the s. chamber
secretly Gen 18 12 she laughed secretly, saying
Gen 24 45 pondered these things s. with myself
Deut 13 6 would persuade thee secretly, saying
27 24 he that secretly killeth his neighbor
28 57 they shall eat them s. for the want
Josu 2 1 sent from Setim two men to spy secretly
1 K 23 9 that Saul s. prepared evil against him
24 5 David arose and s. cut off the hem of
26 5 David arose s. and came to the place
2 K 4 6 they entered into the house secretly
12 12 thou didst it secretly: But I will do
Tob 12 6 then he said to them secretly: bless ye
Jdth 7 7 they were seen secretly to draw water
Job 29 4 youth, when God was s. in my tabernacle
Ecce 10 11 he is nothing better that backbiteth s.
Wisd 18 9 were offering sacrifice secretly and
Jer 9 8 and secretly he lieth in wait for him
37 16 asked him secretly in his house and
Bar 6 9 the priests secretly convey away from
1 Ma 9 60 sent secretly letters to his adherents
Mat 17 18 came the disciples to Jesus secretly
Mark 9 27 his disciples s. asked him: Why could
John 11 28 and called her sister Mary secretly
19 28 but secretly for fear of the Jews
Jude 4 certain men are secretly entered in
secrets Exod 7 11 enchantments and certain s.
Deut 25 11 forth her hand and take him by the s.
Jdth 10 13 that I may tell him their secrets and
Job 11 6 might show thee the secrets of wisdom
Ps 43 22 he knoweth the secrets of the heart
Prov 11 13 that walketh deceitfully, revealeth s.
20 19 meddle not with him that revealeth s.
Wisd 2 22 they knew not the secrets of God nor
Eccu 1 39 God discover thy secrets and cast
4 21 will disclose her secrets to him and
13 14 will examine thee concerning thy s.
14 23 and hath understanding in her secrets
22 27 disclosing of s. or a treacherous wound
27 19 if thou discover his secrets, follow
24 to disclose the secrets of a friend
39 3 conversant in the secrets of parables
10 and in his secrets shall he meditate
Isa 40 23 bringeth searchers of s. to nothing
Jer 49 10 Esau bare, I have revealed his secrets
Dan 5 12 showing of secrets and resolving of
2 Ma 13 21 disclosed the secrets to the enemies
Rom 2 16 day when God shall judge the secrets of
1 C 14 25 secrets of his heart are made manifest

sect Acts 15 5 arose some of the s. of Pharisees
Acts 24 5 author of sedition of sect of Nazarenes
26 5 according to the most sure sect of our
28 22 for as concerning this sect, we know
sects Gal 5 20 quarrels, dissensions, sects
2 P 2 1 who shall bring in sects of perdition
10 willed, they fear not to bring in sects
secular 2 Tim 2 4 himself with s. businesses
Secundus Acts 20 4 Aristarchus, and S., and
secure Judg 7 11 shalt go down more s. to the
Judg 8 11 who were secure and suspected no hurt
18 7 s. and easy, having no man at all to
10 we shall come to a people that is s.
27 to a people that was quiet and secure
2 K 19 33 that thou mayest rest secure with me
1 Pa 4 22 men of Lying and S. and Burning, who
2 Pa 20 20 Lord your God, and you shall be secure
Job 11 18 and being buried thou shalt sleep s.
21 9 their houses are secure and peaceable
Prov 11 15 aware of the snares, shall be secure
15 15 secure mind is like a continual feast
Ecce 8 14 there are wicked men who are so secure
Wisd 6 16 watcheth for her, shall quickly be s.
7 23 assured, secure, having all power
Eccu 4 16 looketh upon her, shall remain secure
Jer 12 5 hast been secure in a land of peace
Bar 6 17 so do the priests secure the doors
Eze 28 26 and they shall dwell therein secure
34 25 wilderness, shall sleep s. in forests
Osee 2 18 land, and I will make them sleep secure
Zach 14 11 but Jerusalem shall sit secure. And
1 Ma 4 61 he fortified it to secure Bethsura
Mat 28 14 we will persuade him and secure you
secured Judg 12 5 s. the fords of the Jordan
securely 1 K 12 11 round about, and you dwelt s.
Jdth 14 5 they are fleeing, go after them s.
Jer 32 37 and will cause them to dwell securely
33 16 and Jerusalem shall dwell securely
49 31 is at ease and that dwelleth securely
Eze 34 28 they shall dwell securely without any
38 8 shall all of them dwell securely in it
11 that are at rest and dwell securely
14 my people of Israel shall dwell s.
39 26 they shall dwell in their land securely
security Isa 4 6 for a s. and covert from the
Isa 32 17 service of justice quietness and s.
Soph 2 15 glorious city that dwelt in security
1 Th 5 3 when they shall say, peace and security
Sedada Num 34 8 as far as the borders of Sedada
Eze 47 15 the way of Hethalon, as men go to S.
Sedecias 3 K 22 11 S. the son of Chanaana made himself horns of iron. 2 Pa 18:10
3 K 22 24 Sedecias . . . struck Micheas. 2 Pa 18:23
4 K 24 17 his stead: and called his name Sedecias
18 Sedecias was one and twenty years old
20 S. revolted from the king of. Jer 52:3
25 4 Sedecias fled by the way that leadeth
7 slew the sons of S. Jer 39:6; 52:10
1 Pa 3 15 the third Sedecias, the fourth Sellum
16 of Joakim was born Jechonias and S.
2 Pa 36 10 made Sedecias his uncle king over Juda
11 Sedecias was one and twenty years old
2 Es 10 1 Sedecias, Saraias, Azarias, Jeremias
Jer 1 3 the eleventh year of Sedecias. 39:2
21 3 thus shall you say to Sedecias: Thus
29 21 to Sedecias the son of Maasias, who
22 the Lord made thee like Sedecias and
32 5 and he shall lead Sedecias to Babylon
36 12 and Sedecias the son of Hananias, and
37 16 Sedecias the king, sending, took him
38 15 Jeremias said to S.: If I shall declare
17 said to Sedecias: Thus saith the Lord
24 S. said to Jeremias: Let no man know
39 5 took S. in the plain of the desert
7 he also put out the eyes of S. 52:11
52 1 Sedecias was one and twenty years old
8 they overtook Sedecias in the desert
Bar 1 1 son of Maasias, the son of Sedecias
8 the silver vessels which Sedecias
king Sedecias 4 K 25 2 eleventh year of k. S. Jer 52:5
Jer 21 1 when king S. sent unto him Phassur
34 8 after that king S. had made a covenant
37 1 king S. the son of Josias reigned
3 king S. sent Juchal the son of Selemias
17 Jeremias said to king S.: In what have
20 king S. commanded that Jeremias should
38 5 king S. said: Behold he is in your
14 king Sedecias sent, and took Jeremias
16 king S. swore to Jeremias, in private
19 king S. said to Jeremias: I am afraid
51 59 when he went with king S. to Babylon
Sedecias king of Juda Jer 21 7 I will give S. . . . and his servants
Jer 24 8 so will I give S. . . . and his princes
27 3 that are come to Jerusalem to S. . . .
12 I spoke to S. . . . according to all
28 1 beginning of reign of S. . . . 49:34
29 3 whom S. . . . sent to Babylon to
32 1 from the Lord in tenth year of S. . . .
3 S. . . . had shut him up, saying: Why
4 S. . . . shall not escape out of the
34 2 go and speak to S. . . . and say to him
4 hear the word of the Lord, O S. . . .
6 spoke all these words to S. . . . And
21 S. . . . and his princes, I will give
39 1 ninth year of Sedecias king of Juda
4 S. . . . and all the men of war saw
44 30 as I delivered S. . . . into the hand
Sedei Bar 1 1 son of Sedecias the son of S.
Sedeur Num 1 5 Elisur the son of S. 7:30, 35
Num 10 18 prince was Helisur the son of S.
sedge-bush Job 8 11 or a s. grow without water
sedges Exod 2 3 laid him in the s. by the
Exod 2 5 when she saw the basket in the sedges
Sedi Bar 1 4 dwelt in Babylonia by the river Sedi
sedition Num 16 42 when there arose a sedition
Num 16 49 had perished in the sedition of Core
20 3 and making sedition they said: Would
26 9 in the sedition of Core, when they
27 3 in the desert, and was not in the s.
Judg 12 1 there arose a sedition in Ephraim
2 Ma 4 30 they of Tharsus and Mallos raised a s.
Mark 15 7 who in the s. had committed murder
Luke 23 19 for a certain s. made in the city and
25 who for murder and sedition had been
Acts 24 5 author of sedition of sect of Nazarenes
seditions 1 Es 4 19 s. and wars have been raised
2 Ma 14 6 nourish wars and raise seditions, and
Luke 21 9 you shall hear of wars and seditions
Acts 24 5 raising seditions among all the Jews
2 C 6 5 in stripes, in prisons, in seditions
12 20 whisperings, swellings, s., be among
seditious Mark 15 7 in prison with some s. men
seduce Exod 22 16 if a man s. a virgin not yet
Mat 24 4 take heed that no man seduce you. For
5 they will seduce many. 11
Mark 13 22 to seduce, if it were possible, even
Rom 16 18 seduce the hearts of the innocent. For
Col 2 18 let no man seduce you, willing in
1 J 2 26 concerning them that seduce you. And
Apoc 2 20 to teach and to seduce my servants, to
20 3 he should no more seduce the nations
7 shall go forth and seduce the nations
seduced 4 K 21 9 but were s. by Manasses to do
2 Pa 33 9 Manasses s. Juda and the inhabitants
2 Es 1 7 we have been seduced by vanity and have

Prov 5 20 why art thou s., my son, by a strange
Luke 21 8 take heed you be not seduced; for many
John 7 47 answered them: Are you also seduced
Rom 7 11 s. me, and by it killed me. Wherefore
1 C 15 33 be not seduced: Evil communications
2 C 11 3 I fear lest, as the serpent seduced Eve
1 Tim 2 14 Adam was not s.; but the woman being **s.**
Apoc 13 14 and he s. them that dwell on the earth
19 20 he s. them who received the character
20 9 the devil, who s. them, was cast into
seducer Mat 27 63 remembered that that s. said
2 J 7 this is a seducer and an antichrist
seducers Wisd 10 12 she defended him from seducers
2 Tim 3 13 evil men and seducers shall grow worse
Titus 1 10 vain talkers and s.: especially they
2 J 7 many s. are gone out into the world
seduceth John 7 12 said: No, but he s. the people
Apoc 12 9 who seduceth the whole world; and he
seducing Acts 8 9 s. the people of Samaria, giving
seduction Jer 14 14 and the s. of their own heart
2 Th 2 10 all the seduction of iniquity to them
see Mat 5 8 clean of heart: for they shall see God
Mat 5 16 that they may see your good works and
7 5 then shalt thou see to cast out the mote
8 4 see thou tell no man: but go, show
9 30 see that no man know this. But they
11 5 blind see, the lame walk. Luke 7:22
7 out into the desert to see. Luke 7:24
8 what went you out to see. 9; Luke 7:25, 26
12 38 master, we would see a sign from thee
13 13 seeing they see not, and hearing they
14 you shall see, and shall not perceive. Acts 28:26
15 should see with their eyes. Acts 28:27
16 blessed are your eyes because they see
17 desired to see the things that you see. Luke 10:24
15 31 speak, the lame walk, the blind see
16 28 till they see the Son of man coming
18 10 see that you despise not one of these
10 always see the face of my Father who
22 11 the king went in to see the guests: and
23 39 you shall not see me henceforth till
24 2 do you see all these things? Amen I
6 see that ye be not troubled. For these
15 shall see the abomination. Mark 13:14
30 they shall see the Son of man coming. Mark 13:26; Luke 21:27
33 when you shall see all these things
25 37 when did we see thee hungry. 44
38 when did we see thee a stranger, and
39 when did we see thee sick or in prison
26 58 servants, that he might see the end
64 see the Son of man sitting. Mark 14:62
27 49 let us see whether Elias will come to
28 1 the other Mary to see the sepulcher
6 see the place where the Lord was laid
7 there you shall see him. Mark 16:7
10 Galilee, there they shall see me. Who
Mark 1 44 see thou tell no one; but go, show
4 12 that seeing they may see and not
5 14 went out to see what was done. Luke 8:35
15 they see him that was troubled with
32 looked about to see her who had done
6 38 how many loaves have you? Go and see
8 18 having eyes, see you not? And having
24 I see men as it were trees, walking
25 and he began to see and was restored
39 till they see kingdom of God. Luke 9:27
10 51 said to him: Rabboni, that I may see
12 15 bring me a penny that I may see it
13 29 you shall see these things. Luke 21:31
15 32 that we may see and believe. John 6:30
36 let us see if Elias come to take him
Luke 2 15 let us see this word that is come to
26 he should not see death before he had
3 6 all flesh shall see the salvation of
6 42 then shalt thou see clearly to take
8 10 that seeing they may not see, and
16 they who come in may see the light
20 stand without, desiring to see thee
9 9 things? And he sought to see him. And
10 23 that see the things which you see
11 33 they that come in may see the light
12 54 when you see a cloud rising from the
55 when ye see the south wind blow, you
13 28 when you shall see Abraham and Isaac
35 you shall not see me till the time
14 18 and I must needs go out and see it
29 all that see it begin to mock him
17 22 to see one day of the Son of man
22 Son of man; and you shall not see it
23 say to you: See here, and see there
18 41 but he said: Lord, that I may see
19 3 he sought to see Jesus who he was
4 tree, that he might see him; for he
20 13 when they see him, they will reverence
21 6 these things which you see, the days
20 when you shall see Jerusalem compassed
29 see the fig tree and all the trees
23 8 desirous for a long time to see him
8 he hoped to see some sign wrought by
24 39 see my hands and feet, that it is I
39 and bones, as you see me to have
John 1 33 upon whom thou shalt see the Spirit
39 he saith to them: Come and see. They
46 Philip saith to him: Come and see
50 things than these shalt thou see
51 you shall see the heaven opened and
3 3 he cannot see the kingdom of God
36 not the Son, shall not see life; but
4 29 see a man who has told me all things
35 up your eyes and see the countries
48 unless you see signs and wonders, you
6 19 they see Jesus walking upon the sea
63 if then you shall see the Son of man
7 3 disciples also may see thy works which
8 51 word, he shall not see death forever
56 rejoiced that he might see my day
9 11 I washed, and I see. 15
19 blind? How then doth he now see? His
25 that whereas I was blind, now I see
39 that they who see not, may see; and
39 and they who see, may become blind
41 have sin: but now you say: We see
11 34 they say to him: Lord, come and see
40 thou shalt see the glory of God? They
12 9 but that they might see Lazarus, whom
19 do you see that we prevail nothing
21 we would see Jesus. Philip cometh and
40 that they should not see with their
14 19 but you see me: because I live, and
16 10 and you shall see me no longer. And
16 and you shall not see me. 17, 19
16 while, and you shall see me. 17, 19
22 I will see you again, and your heart
17 24 that they may see my glory which thou
18 26 did not I see thee in the garden with
20 25 except I shall see in his hands the
27 thy finger hither, and see my hands
Acts 2 17 your young men shall see visions, and
27 suffer thy Holy One to see corruption
31 neither did his flesh see corruption
33 hath poured forth that which you see
7 55 I see the heavens opened, and the Son
8 13 wondered to see the signs and

23 for I see thou art in the gall of
36 see, here is water: what doth hinder
13 35 suffer thy holy one to see corruption
15 36 word of the Lord, to see how they do
19 21 I have been there, I must see Rome also
26 and you see and hear, that this Paul
20 25 shall see my face no more. Wherefore I
38 that they should see his face no more
22 11 I did not see for the brightness of the
14 know his will, and see the Just One
25 24 you see this man, about whom all the
27 10 I see that the voyage beginneth to be
28 20 I desired to see you, and to speak to
Rom 1 11 I long to see you, that I may impart
7 23 but I see another law in my members
8 25 if we hope for that which we see not
11 8 eyes that they should not see; and ears
10 darkened, that they may not see: and
22 see then the goodness and the severity
15 21 shall see, and they that have not heard
24 I hope that as I pass, I shall see you
1 C 16 7 I will not see you now by the way, for
10 if Timothy come, see that he be with you
Gal 1 18 I went to Jerusalem, to see Peter, and I
Eph 3 9 to enlighten all men, that they may see
5 15 see therefore, brethren, how you walk
Phil 1 27 whether I come and see you, or, being
2 23 as I shall see how it will go with me
1 Th 2 17 to see your face with great desire
3 6 desiring to see us as we also to see you
10 praying that we may see your face, and
5 15 see that none render evil for evil to
1 Tim 6 16 whom no man hath seen, nor can see: to
2 Tim 1 4 desiring to see thee, being mindful of
Heb 2 8 see not as yet all things subject to him
3 19 we see they could not enter in because
8 5 see, saith he, that thou make all things
10 25 more as you see the day approaching
11 5 translated, that he should not see death
12 14 without which no man shall see God
25 see that you refuse him not that
13 23 if he come shortly, I will see you
James 2 24 do you see that by works a man is
1 P 1 8 though you see him not, you believe
3 10 that will love life and see good days
1 J 3 2 because we shall see him as he is
17 and shall see his brother in need and
3 J 14 I hope speedily to see thee, and we
Apoc 1 7 every eye shall see him, and they also
12 I turned to see the voice that spoke
3 18 with eyesalve, that thou mayest see
5 4 worthy to open the book nor to see it
6 1 saying: Come and see. 3, 5, 7
6 see thou hurt not the wine and the oil
9 20 which neither can see nor hear nor
11 9 shall see their bodies for three days
16 15 he walk naked and they see his shame
18 7 no widow; and sorrow I shall not see
9 shall see the smoke of her burning
19 10 he saith to me: See thou do it not. 22:9
22 4 they shall see his face: and his name

seed Gen 1 11 green herb, and such as may seed
Gen 1 11 kind, which may have seed in itself
12 such as yieldeth seed according to its
12 seed each one according to its kind
29 have given you every herb bearing seed
29 trees that have in themselves seed
4 25 God hath given me another seed for
7 3 that seed may be saved upon the face
9 9 my covenant with you and with your seed
15 3 but to me thou hast not given seed
19 32 that we may preserve seed of our father
34 that we may save seed of our father
32 12 multiply my seed like the sand of the
38 8 thou mayst raise seed to thy brother
47 19 give us seed, lest for want of tillers
23 take seed and sow the fields that you
24 the other four you shall have for seed
Exod 16 31 and it was like coriander seed white
32 13 I will multiply your seed as the stars
13 I will give to your seed, and you shall
Lev 11 37 if it fall upon seed corn, it shall not
38 if any man pour water upon the seed
12 2 if a woman having received seed shall
15 2 the man that hath an issue of seed
10 under him that hath the issue of seed
16 man from whom the seed of copulation
32 law of him that hath the issue of seed
18 20 nor be defiled with mingling of seed
21 21 whosoever of seed of Aaron the priest
22 4 man of seed of Aaron, that is a leper
4 that suffereth a running of the seed
4 he whose seed goeth from him as in
26 16 you shall sow your seed in vain, which
27 16 according to the measure of the seed
Num 5 2 whosoever hath an issue of seed or is
11 7 the manna was like coriander seed
16 40 one that is not of the seed of Aaron
Deut 11 10 when the seed is sown, waters are
22 9 both the seed which thou hast sown
25 5 her, and raise up seed for his brother
28 38 shalt cast much seed into the ground
Ruth 4 12 of the seed which the Lord shall give
1 K 2 20 the Lord give thee seed of this woman
20 42 between my seed and thy seed forever
24 22 wilt not destroy my seed after me
2 K 3 29 of Joab one that hath an issue of seed
3 K 11 14 Adad the Edomite of the king's seed
39 I will for this afflict the s. of David
4 K 11 1 arose and slew all the royal seed. But
17 20 the Lord cast off all the s. of Israel
25 25 the son of Elisama of the seed royal
1 Pa 16 13 O ye seed of Israel his servants, ye
2 Pa 20 7 and gavest it to the seed of Abraham
1 Es 9 2 they have mingled the holy seed with
2 Es 9 2 s. of the children of Israel separated
Tob 6 22 that in the seed of Abraham thou mayst
9 11 your s. be blessed by the God of Israel
13 20 if there shall remain of my seed, to see
Esth 6 13 if Mardochai be of the s. of the Jews
Job 14 4 clean that is conceived of unclean seed
21 8 their seed continueth before them, a
39 12 that he will render thee the seed and
Ps 21 24 all ye the seed of Jacob, glorify him
25 let all the seed of Israel fear him
31 shall live: and my seed shall serve him
36 28 the seed of the wicked shall perish
68 37 seed of his servants shall possess it
104 6 ye seed of Abraham his servant: ye
Prov 11 21 the seed of the just shall be saved
Wisd 3 16 seed of unlawful bed shall be rooted
7 2 compacted in blood, of the seed of man
10 15 blameless seed from the nation that
12 11 was a cursed seed from the beginning
14 6 left to the world seed of generation
Eccu 10 23 that seed of men shall be honored
23 that seed shall be dishonored which
47 24 will not utterly take away the seed of
Isa 1 4 a wicked seed, ungracious children
9 except Lord of hosts had left us seed
6 13 shall stand therein, shall be a holy s.
14 20 seed of the wicked shall not be named
17 10 plants, and shalt sow strange seed
23 3 the seed of the Nile in many waters
27 6 shall fill face of the world with seed
41 8 chosen, the seed of Abraham, my friend

45 19 I have not said to the seed of Jacob
26 s. of Israel be justified and praised
53 10 he shall see a long-lived seed, and the
55 10 give seed to the sower, and bread to
57 3 seed of the adulterer and of the harlot
4 are not you wicked children, a false s.
59 21 nor out of the mouth of thy seed's s.
61 9 the seed which the Lord hath blessed
11 as the garden causeth her s. to shoot
65 9 I will bring forth a seed out of Jacob
23 they are the seed of the blessed of
66 22 so shall your s. stand, and your name
Jer 2 21 thee a chosen vineyard, all true seed
7 15 your brethren, the whole s. of Ephraim
23 8 hither the seed of the house of Israel
31 27 I will sow . . . with the seed of men and with the seed of beasts
36 then also the s. of Israel shall fail
37 will cast away all the seed of Israel
33 22 so will I multiply the seed of David
26 I will also cast off the seed of Jacob
26 to be rulers of the seed of Abraham
35 7 shall ye build houses nor sow seed
9 nor to have vineyard or field or seed
Eze 17 5 he took of the seed of the land and put it in the ground for seed
13 he shall take one of the king's seed
44 22 virgins of the seed of house of Israel
Dan 1 3 bring in some . . . of the king's seed
2 43 indeed together with the seed of man
9 1 Assuerus of the seed of the Medes
11 6 neither shall her seed stand: and she
13 56 thou seed of Chanaan, and not of Juda
Amos 9 13 treader of grapes him that soweth seed
Agge 2 20 is the seed as yet sprung up? Or hath
Zach 8 12 but there shall be the seed of peace
Mala 2 15 what doth one seek but the seed of God
1 Ma 1 40 she became a stranger to her own seed
5 62 not of the seed of those men by whom
7 14 that is a priest of the seed of Aaron
10 29 and remit . . . the thirds of the seed
Mat 13 19 that received the seed by the wayside
20 received the seed upon stony ground
22 that received the seed among thorns
23 received the seed upon good ground is
24 man that sowed good seed in his field
27 didst thou not sow good seed in thy
38 the good seed are the children of the
31 like to a grain of mustard seed. Luke 13:19; 17:6
17 19 as a grain of mustard seed. Mark 4:31
Mark 4 26 as if a man should cast seed into the
27 and the seed should spring, and grow
12 19 raise up s. to his brother. Luke 20:28
Luke 8 11 the seed is the word of God. And they
John 7 42 Christ cometh of the seed of David
8 33 we are the seed of Abraham and we have
Acts 13 23 this man's seed God according to his
Rom 1 3 who was made to him of seed of David
4 16 the promise might be firm to all seed
9 7 that are the seed of Abraham, children
8 promise, are accounted for the seed. For
29 unless Lord of Sabaoth had left us seed
11 1 and Israelite of the seed of Abraham, of
1 C 15 38 will: and to every seed its proper body
2 C 9 10 he that ministered seed to the sower
10 will multiply your seed, and increase
11 22 they are the seed of Abraham: so am I
Gal 3 19 until the seed should come, to whom he
29 then are you the seed of Abraham, heirs
2 Tim 2 8 again from the dead, of the s. of David
Heb 2 16 of the seed of Abraham he taketh hold
11 11 received strength to conceive seed, even
1 P 1 23 being born again not of corruptible s.
Apoc 12 17 to make war with the rest of her seed

his seed Gen 17 19 and with his seed after him
Gen 38 9 spilled his seed upon the ground lest
46 6 he came into Egypt with all his seed
48 19 and his seed shall grow into nations
Exod 28 43 law forever to Aaron and to his seed
30 21 everlasting law to him and to his seed
Lev 20 3 he hath given of his seed to Moloch
4 that hath given of his seed to Moloch
15 15 be cleansed of the issue of his seed
20 2 give of his seed to the idol Moloch
Num 14 24 round: and his seed shall possess it
24 7 and his seed shall be in many waters
25 13 shall be both to him and his seed
Josu 24 3 of Chanaan, and I multiplied his seed
2 K 4 8 this day of Saul and of his seed
22 51 David his anointed and to his s. Ps 17:51
3 K 2 33 and upon the head of his seed forever
33 to David and his seed and his house
15 29 left not so much as one soul of his s.
2 Es 9 8 to give it to his seed: and thou hast
Esth 10 3 which were for the welfare of his seed
Job 18 19 his seed shall not subsist nor his
Ps 24 13 and his seed shall inherit the land
36 25 forsaken, nor his seed seeking bread
26 and his seed shall be in blessing
88 30 I will make his seed to endure for
37 David: his seed shall endure forever
111 2 his seed shall be mighty upon earth
Eccu 44 23 he would exalt his seed as the stars
45 19 to his seed as the days of heaven
26 which he gave to him and to his seed
30 should be to him and to his seed
31 an inheritance to him and to his seed
46 11 his s. obtained it for an inheritance
47 27 and he left behind him of his seed
Isa 14 29 and his seed shall swallow the bird
Jer 22 28 why are they cast out, he and his seed
30 there shall not be a man of his seed
29 32 visit upon Semeias . . . and upon his s.
33 26 so as not to take any of his seed to
36 31 I will punish him and his seed and his
49 10 his seed is laid waste, and his
Luke 1 55 to Abraham and to his seed forever
8 5 the sower went out to sow his seed
Acts 7 5 possession, and to his seed after him
6 his seed should sojourn in a strange
Rom 4 13 the promise to Abraham, or to his seed
Gal 3 16 were the promises made and to his seed
1 J 3 9 his seed abideth in him, and he cannot

their seed Deut 1 8 give it to them and to t. s.
Deut 4 37 loved thy fathers and chose their seed
10 15 them and chose their seed after them
11 9 to their seed a land which floweth
31 21 take away out of the mouth of their seed
1 Es 2 59 house of their fathers and their seed
2 Es 7 61 their seed, whether they were of Israel
9 31 observed by themselves and by t. s.
Esth 9 27 took upon themselves and their seed
Ps 20 11 their s. from among the children of men
101 29 their seed shall be directed forever
105 27 to cast down t. s. among the nations
Eccu 44 11 good things continue with their seed
12 their seed hath stood in the covenants
13 t. s. and their glory shall not be
Isa 61 9 shall know their s. among the Gentiles
Dan 3 36 that thou wouldst multiply their seed

thy seed Gen 3 15 woman, and thy s. and her s.
Gen 12 7 to thy seed will I give this land
13 15 I will give to thee and to thy seed
16 I will make thy seed as the dust
16 he shall be able to number thy seed

15 5 so shall thy seed be. Abram believed
13 thy seed shall be a stranger in a land
18 to thy seed will I give this land
16 10 I will multiply thy seed. 22:17; 26:4
17 7 me and thee, and between thy seed
7 to be a God to thee and to thy seed
8 will give to thee and to . . . thy seed
9 shalt keep my covenant, and thy seed
10 between me and you, and thy seed after
21 12 in Isaac shall thy seed be called
13 great nation, because he is thy seed
22 17 thy seed shall possess the gates of
18 in thy s. shall all the nations. 26:4
24 7 to thy seed will I give this land: he
60 may thy seed possess the gates of their
26 3 to thy seed I will give all these
24 I will bless thee and multiply thy s.
28 4 of Abraham to thee and to thy seed
13 will give to thee and to thy s. 35:12
14 thy seed shall be as the dust of the
14 thee and in thy seed all the tribes of
48 4 this land to thee and to thy seed
11 God hath showed me thy seed. And when
Exod 33 1 saying: To thy seed I will give it
Lev 18 21 thy seed to be consecrated to the
21 17 of thy seed . . . hath a blemish, he
Deut 28 46 and wonders on thee and on thy seed
59 thy plagues and the plagues of thy s.
30 6 thy heart and the heart of thy seed
19 that both thou and thy seed may live
34 4 saying: I will give it to thy seed
2 K 7 12 will raise up thy seed after. 1 Pa 17:11
4 K 5 27 stick to thee and to thy seed forever
Job 5 25 also that thy seed shall be multiplied
Ps 88 5 thy seed will I settle forever. And
Ecce 11 6 in the morning sow thy seed, and in
Eccu 47 22 and defiled thy seed so as to bring
Isa 17 11 in the morning thy seed shall flourish
30 23 and rain shall be given to thy seed
43 5 I will bring thy seed from the east
44 3 I will pour out my spirit upon thy seed
48 19 thy seed had been as the sand, and the
54 3 thy seed shall inherit the Gentiles
59 21 nor out of the mouth of thy seed nor
Jer 30 10 and thy seed from the land of their
46 27 thy seed out of the land of thy
2 Ma 7 17 he will torment thee and thy seed
Acts 3 25 in thy seed shall all the kindreds of
Rom 4 18 was said to him: So shall thy seed be
9 7 in Isaac shall thy seed be. Heb 11:18
Gal 3 16 of one, And to thy seed, which is Christ
seed's Isa 59 21 of the mouth of thy seed's seed
seeds Lev 19 19 not sow thy field with different s.
Deut 22 9 not sow thy vineyard with divers seeds
Ps 125 6 went and wept, casting their seeds
Mat 13 32 which is the least indeed of all seeds
Mark 4 31 is less than all the seeds that are
Gal 3 16 he saith not, And to his seeds, as of
seedtime Gen 8 22 s. and harvest, cold and heat
seeing Gen 6 2 seeing the daughters of men, that
Gen 6 5 God seeing that the wickedness of men
18 18 seeing he shall become a great and
27 seeing I have once begun. 31
19 1 seeing them, he rose up and went to
24 62 is called Of the living and the seeing
25 11 well named Of the living and seeing
28 6 Esau s. that his father had blessed
29 31 the Lord seeing that he despised Lia
30 1 Rachel, seeing herself without children
37 4 his brethren seeing that he was loved
40 16 seeing that he had wisely interpreted
41 39 seeing God hath shown thee all that
42 21 seeing the anguish of his soul, when
46 29 seeing him, he fell upon his neck and
48 11 I am not deprived of seeing thee
17 Joseph seeing that his father had put
Exod 2 2 and seeing him a goodly child, hid him
6 and seeing within it an infant crying
4 11 who made . . . the seeing and the blind
14 and seeing thee shall be glad at heart
8 15 and Pharao seeing that rest was given
9 34 Pharao s. that the rain and the hail
32 1 seeing that Moses delayed to come down
34 30 seeing the face of Moses horned, were
Num 20 30 multitude seeing that Aaron was dead
22 2 seeing all that Israel had done to the
23 the ass seeing the angel standing in
25 ass seeing him, thrust herself close
Deut 29 22 s. the plagues of that land and the
Josu 7 8 seeing Israel turning their backs to
8 20 seeing the smoke of the city rise up
21 all Israel s. that the city was taken
Judg 3 25 seeing that no man opened the door
6 22 Gedeon seeing that it was the angel
9 43 seeing that the people came out of the
14 1 seeing there a woman of the daughters
16 18 seeing that he had discovered to her
24 the people also seeing this, praised
18 26 Michas seeing that they were stronger
19 25 which the man seeing, brought out his
20 31 seeing their enemies flee, pursued them
36 children of Israel seeing, gave them
41 children of Benjamin seeing, turned
Ruth 1 18 s. that Ruth was steadfastly determined
1 K 5 7 the men of Azotus seeing this kind of
10 11 seeing that he was with the prophets
12 12 seeing that Naas . . . was come against
17 51 Philistines seeing that their champion
26 3 seeing that Saul was come after him
28 16 seeing the Lord has departed from thee
31 7 seeing that the Israelites were fled
2 K 1 7 seeing me, he [Saul] called me. And I
10 6 seeing that they had done an injury to
9 seeing that the battle was prepared
14 seeing that the Syrians were fled, they
15 the Syrians seeing that they had fallen
19 seeing themselves overcome by Israel
17 23 Achitophel seeing that his counsel was
3 K 1 48 to sit on my throne, my eyes seeing it
3 28 s. that the wisdom of God was in him
11 28 Solomon s. him a young man ingenious
12 16 seeing that the king would not hearken
16 18 Zambri seeing that the city was about
4 K 2 15 sons of the prophets . . . s. it, said
9 27 Ochozias . . . seeing this, fled by the
11 1 s. that her son was dead. 2 Pa 22:10
1 Pa 17 27 for seeing thou blessest it, O Lord
19 15 children of Ammon s. that the Syrians
16 the Syrians seeing that they had fallen
21 28 David s. that the Lord had heard him
30 s. the sword of the angel of the Lord
28 10 therefore s. the Lord hath chosen thee
2 Pa 15 9 s. that the Lord his God was with him
1 Es 9 13 seeing that thou our God hast saved us
2 Es 2 2 seeing thou dost not appear to be sick
3 seeing the city of the place of the
Jdth 10 19 Judith seeing Holofernes sitting under
13 29 Achior seeing the head of Holofernes
14 6 Achior seeing the power that the God of
8 watchmen seeing this ran to the tent
14 and seeing the body of Holofernes lying
15 3 the children of Israel s. them fleeing
Job 6 21 now seeing my affliction you are afraid
26 14 seeing we have heard scarce a little
34 31 seeing then I have spoken of God, I
Ps 21 9 save him, seeing he delighteth in him

49 17 seeing thou hast hated discipline and
72 3 seeing the prosperity of sinners. For
Prov 17 16 riches, seeing he cannot buy wisdom
20 12 and the s. eye, the Lord hath made them
27 12 prudent man seeing evil hideth himself
Ecce 1 8 the eye is not filled with seeing
Wisd 12 27 s. with indignation that they suffered
5 2 these seeing it, shall be troubled with
19 8 thy hand, s. thy miracles and wonders
Eccu 15 19 in power, s. all men without ceasing
Isa 56 10 not able to bark, seeing vain things
21 3 I was troubled at the seeing of it. My
Bar 6 50 seeing they are but of wood, and laid
Eze 16 30 seeing thou dost all these the works
18 13 seeing he hath done all these detestable
14 who, seeing all his father's sins
19 5 she seeing herself weakened and that
22 28 seeing vain things and divining lies
Dan 2 47 s. thou couldst discover this secret
13 38 seeing this wickedness, ran up to them
50 seeing God hath given thee the honor
1 Ma 4 21 seeing at the same time Judas and his
6 47 they seeing the strength of the king
11 38 seeing that the land was quiet before
39 s. that all the army murmured against
12 51 seeing that they stood for their lives
13 2 seeing that the people was in dread
14 35 the people seeing the acts of Simon
16 6 the men seeing him, passed over after
2 Ma 2 2 seeing the idols of gold and silver
8 8 seeing that the man gained ground by
14 3 s. that there was no safety for him
9 seeing thou knowest all these things
26 Alcimus seeing the love they had one
Mat 2 10 seeing the star they rejoiced with
3 7 seeing many of the Pharisees and
5 1 seeing the multitude, he went up into
9 8 multitude seeing it, feared and
11 Pharisees s. it, said to his disciples
22 Jesus turning and seeing her, said
36 s. the multitudes, he had compassion
12 2 the Pharisees seeing them, said to him
13 13 seeing they see not, and hearing they
14 s. you shall see, and shall not perceive. Acts 28:26
14 26 s. him walking upon the sea. Mark 6:49
30 seeing the wind strong, he was afraid
15 31 seeing the dumb speak, the lame walk
18 31 fellow servants seeing what was done
21 15 seeing the wonderful things that he
19 s. a certain fig tree by the wayside
20 the disciples seeing it wondered, saying
32 you, seeing it, did not even afterwards
38 husbandmen, seeing the son, said among
26 8 disciples seeing it, had indignation
27 3 seeing that he was condemned, repenting
24 Pilate s. that he prevailed nothing
28 17 seeing him they adored: but some
Mark 2 16 seeing that he ate with publicans and
4 12 that seeing they may see and not
5 6 seeing Jesus afar off, he ran and
22 seeing him, falleth down at his feet
6 48 seeing them laboring in rowing, for
8 33 seeing his disciples, threatened Peter
9 14 presently all the people seeing Jesus
12 28 seeing that he had answered them well
34 seeing that he had answered wisely
14 69 maidservant seeing him, began to say
15 39 seeing that crying out in this manner
Luke 1 12 Zachary seeing him, was troubled and
2 17 seeing, they understood of the word
48 seeing him, they wondered. And his
5 12 full of leprosy, who seeing Jesus
7 39 seeing it, spoke within himself
8 10 that seeing they may not see, and
47 the woman seeing that she was not hid
10 31 same way: and seeing him, passed by
33 seeing him, was moved with compassion
11 17 he seeing their thoughts, said to them
19 41 s. the city, he wept over it, saying
22 49 seeing what would follow, said to him
58 another seeing him, said: Thou also
23 8 Herod seeing Jesus, was very glad
40 seeing thou art under the same
47 the centurion, seeing what was done
John 1 38 turning and seeing them following them
2 18 seeing thou dost these things? Jesus
23 name, seeing his signs which he did
9 7 and washed, and he came seeing. The
11 32 seeing him, she fell down at his feet
Acts 2 15 seeing it is but the third hour of the
4 13 seeing the constancy of Peter and of
14 s. the man also who had been healed
7 31 Moses seeing it, wondered at the sight
34 seeing I have seen the affliction of
8 6 and seeing the miracles which he did
9 7 hearing indeed voice, but seeing no man
40 she opened her eyes; and seeing Peter
12 3 seeing that it pleased the Jews, he
13 11 blind, not seeing the sun for a time
45 Jews s. multitudes, were filled with
14 3 [Paul] s. that he had faith to be
16 19 masters, s. that the hope of their gain
27 seeing the doors of the prison open
17 16 seeing city wholly given to idolatry
23 passing by, and seeing your idols, I
25 seeing it is he who giveth to all life
28 6 expecting long, and seeing that there
1 C 1 21 for seeing that in the wisdom of God
2 C 4 1 therefore, s. we have this ministration
7 8 did repent, seeing that the same epistle
11 18 s. that many glory according to flesh
Phil 2 28 that seeing him again, you may rejoice
2 Th 1 6 seeing it is a just thing with God to
Heb 4 6 seeing then it remaineth that some are
8 4 seeing that there would be others to
11 27 he endured as s. him that is invisible
2 P 3 11 seeing then that all these things are
Apoc 17 8 seeing the beast that was, and is not
18 18 cried, seeing the place of her burning
seek Gen 37 16 he answered: I seek my brethren
Gen 41 57 to seek some relief of their want
Exod 18 15 to me to seek the judgment of God
Lev 13 36 he shall seek no more whether the hair
19 18 seek not revenge nor be mindful of
Num 24 1 had gone before, to seek divination
32 19 neither will we seek anything beyond
Deut 4 29 when thou shalt seek there the Lord
29 if thou seek him with all thy heart
12 30 lest thou seek after their ceremonies
22 2 with thee until thy brother seek them
14 and seek occasions to put her away
23 6 neither shalt thou s. their prosperity
Ruth 3 1 my daughter, I will seek rest for thee
1 K 9 3 arise, go, and seek the asses. And when
10 2 are found which thou wentest to seek
14 to seek the asses; and not finding them
16 16 will seek out a man skilful in playing
23 15 that Saul and his men went to seek him
15 that Saul was come out to seek his life
25 then Saul and his men went to seek him
24 3 went out to seek after David and his
25 26 all they that seek evil to my lord
29 if . . . persecute thee and seek thy life
26 2 to seek David in the wilderness of Ziph
20 king of Israel is come out to s. a flea

27 1 that Saul . . . cease to seek me in all
28 7 seek me a woman that hath a divining
2 K 5 17 they all came to seek David: and when
14 7 and they seek to quench my spark which
3 K 1 2 let us seek for . . . the king a young
2 40 to Achis to Geth to seek his servants
18 10 whither my lord hath not sent to seek
19 10 they seek my life to take it away. 14
4 K 2 16 that can go and seek thy master, lest
6 19 I will show you the man whom you seek
1 Pa 4 39 into Gador . . . to seek pastures for
14 8 went all up to seek him: and David
16 10 heart of them rejoice that seek the Lord
11 seek ye the Lord and his power: seek ye his face evermore
21 3 why doth my lord seek this thing which
22 19 souls, to seek the Lord your God: and
28 8 seek all the commandments of the Lord
9 if thou seek him, thou shalt find him
2 Pa 7 14 and seek out my face and do penance
11 16 gave their heart to seek the Lord
12 14 not prepare his heart to seek the Lord
14 4 and he commanded Juda to seek the Lord
15 2 if you seek him, you shall find him
4 and shall seek him, they shall find him
12 covenant that they should seek the Lord
13 if any one, said he, seek not the Lord
16 12 in his illness he did not seek the Lord
19 3 prepared thy heart to seek the Lord
30 19 who with their whole heart, s. the Lord
31 21 to seek his God with all his heart, and
34 3 he began to seek the God of his father
1 Es 4 2 for we seek your God as ye do; behold
6 21 to seek the Lord the God of Israel, did
7 10 his heart to seek the law of the Lord
8 22 upon all them that seek him in goodness
9 12 and seek not their peace nor their
Tob 4 19 seek counsel always of a wise man
5 4 and seek thee out some faithful man
17 dost thou seek the family of him thou
14 10 seek to do the things that please him
Job 7 21 if thou seek me in the morning, I shall
15 23 when he moveth himself to seek bread
Ps 4 3 you love vanity and seek after lying
9 4 he will not seek him: God is not before
11 hast not forsaken them that seek thee
13 2 be any that understand and seek God
21 27 they shall praise the Lord that s. him
23 6 the generation of them that seek him, of them that seek the face of the God
24 10 to them that seek after his covenant
26 4 this will I seek after: that I may dwell
8 thy face, O Lord, will I still seek
33 11 they that seek the Lord shall not be
15 do good: seek after peace and pursue it
34 4 and ashamed that seek after my soul
36 10 shalt seek his place, and shalt not find
39 15 that seek after my soul to take it away
17 let all that seek thee rejoice and be
52 3 that did understand or did seek God
67 31 who seek to exclude them who are tried
68 7 who seek thee, O God of Israel. Because
33 seek ye God, and your soul shall live
69 3 and ashamed that seek my soul: let them
5 let all that seek thee rejoice and be
70 13 confusion and shame that seek my hurt
24 put to shame that seek evils to me
77 7 of God: and may seek his commandments
82 17 with shame: and they shall seek thy name
104 3 heart of them rejoice that seek the Lord
4 seek ye the Lord, and be strengthened: seek his face ever more
45 justifications, and seek after his law
118 2 that seek him with their whole heart
33 and I will always seek after it. Give
69 I will seek thy commandments with
145 Lord: I will seek thy justifications
176 seek thy servant, because I have not
Prov 2 4 if thou shalt seek her as money and
24 1 seek not to be like evil men, neither
15 nor seek after wickedness in the house
19 wicked, nor seek to be like the ungodly
28 5 they that seek after the Lord, take
29 10 upright: but just men seek his soul
26 many seek the face of the prince: but
Ecce 1 13 to s. and search out wisely concerning
7 1 man to s. the things that are above him
26 seek out wisdom and reason: and to
8 17 and the more he shall labor to seek
Cant 3 2 I will seek him whom my soul loveth
5 17 aside, and we will seek him with thee
Wisd 1 1 and seek him in simplicity of heart
12 s. not death in the error of your life
6 13 and is found by them that seek her. She
15 he that awaketh early to seek her, shall
24 will seek her out from the beginning of
Eccu 2 13 protector to all that seek him in truth
19 will seek after the things that are
3 22 seek not the things that are too high
4 12 protecteth them that seek after her
7 4 seek not of the Lord a pre-eminence
6 seek not to be made a judge, unless
12 12 thy place, and seek to take thy seat
16 25 equity, and will seek to declare wisdom
24 46 will leave it to them that seek wisdom
47 but for all that seek out the truth
28 3 anger, and doth he seek remedy of God
32 18 that will seek him early, shall find
33 18 but for all that seek discipline. Hear
33 knowest not . . . in what way to seek him
39 1 wise man will seek out the wisdom of
40 27 and it needeth not to seek for help
51 19 very end I will seek after her, and
Isa 1 17 seek judgment, relieve the oppressed
8 19 seek of pythons and of diviners, who
19 should not the people seek of their
13 17 who shall not seek silver nor desire
21 12 night; if you seek, seek: return, come
41 12 thou shalt seek them and shalt not find
17 needy and the poor seek for waters
45 19 I have not said . . . Seek me in vain
51 1 you that seek the Lord: look unto
55 6 seek ye the Lord, while he may be found
57 5 who seek your comfort in idols under
58 2 they seek me from day to day and desire
Jer 2 24 that seek her shall not fail: in her
33 to show thy way good to seek my love
4 30 despised thee, they will seek thy life
5 1 and seek in the broad places thereof
11 21 who seek thy life. 22:25; 38:16
19 7 that seek their lives. 9; 46:26
21 7 that seek their life. 34:20; 49:37
23 27 who seek to make my people forget my
29 7 seek the peace of the city, to which
13 you shall seek me, and shall find me
13 when you shall seek me with all your
30 14 and will not seek after thee: for I
17 she that hath none to seek after her
44 30 the hand of them that seek his life
45 5 dost thou seek great things for thyself
5 seek not: for behold I will bring evil
50 4 haste, and shall s. the Lord their God
Lam 1 11 all her people sigh, they seek bread
3 40 let us search our ways and seek and
Bar 4 28 you shall seek him ten times as much
Eze 7 25 they will seek for peace and there

26 they shall seek a vision of the prophet
34 8 my shepherds did not seek after my
11 I myself will seek my sheep and will
16 I will seek that which was lost: and
39 14 to seek out them that were remaining
14 seven months they shall begin to seek
Dan 2 8 that you seek to gain time, since you
3 41 and we fear thee and seek thy face
Osee 2 7 she shall seek them, and shall not
3 5 and shall seek the Lord their God
5 6 they shall go to seek the Lord and
15 until you are consumed and seek my face
10 12 the time to seek the Lord is when he
Amos 5 4 seek ye me, and you shall live. But
5 seek not Bethel, and go not into Galgal
6 seek ye the Lord, and live: lest the
8 seek him that maketh Arcturus and
14 seek ye good, and not evil, that you
Nah 3 7 whence shall I seek a comforter for
11 thou shalt seek help from the enemy
Soph 2 3 seek the Lord, all ye meek of the earth
3 seek the just, seek the meek: if by
Zach 8 21 let us seek the Lord of hosts: I also
22 shall come to seek the Lord of hosts
11 16 nor seek what is scattered nor heal
12 9 I will seek to destroy all the nations
Mala 2 7 they shall seek the law at his mouth
15 what doth one seek, but the seed of
3 1 Lord, whom you seek, and the angel of
2 Ma 1 20 sent some . . . to seek for the fire
2 28 and seek to satisfy the will of others
30 must s. out fit things for the adorning
Mat 2 13 Herod will s. the child to destroy him
6 32 all these things do the heathens seek
33 s. ye . . . first the kingdom. Luke 12:31
7 7 seek, and you shall find. Luke 11:9
18 12 go to seek that which is gone astray
28 5 I know that you seek Jesus who was
Mark 1 37 they said to him: All seek for thee
3 32 and thy brethren without seek for thee
8 12 why doth this generation seek a sign
16 6 you seek Jesus of Nazareth, who was
Luke 12 29 seek not you what you shall eat or
30 do the nations of the world seek
13 24 shall seek to enter, and shall not be
15 8 and seek diligently until she find it
17 33 whosoever shall seek to save his life
19 10 the Son of man is come to seek and
24 5 why seek you the living with the dead
John 1 38 saith to them: What seek you? Who said
5 30 because I seek not my own will, but
44 is from God alone, you do not seek
6 26 you seek me, not because you have seen
7 20 why seek you to kill me? The multitude
25 is not this he whom they seek to kill
34 you shall s. me and shall not find. 36
8 21 I go, and you shall seek me, and you
37 you seek to kill me because my word
40 but now you seek to kill me, a man
50 I seek not my own glory: there is one
13 33 you shall seek me; and as I said to
18 4 and said to them: Whom seek ye? They
7 he asked them: Whom seek ye? And
8 if therefore you seek me, let these
Acts 9 11 seek in the house of Judas, one named
10 19 to him: Behold three men seek thee
21 behold, I am he whom you seek; what
11 25 Barnabas went to Tarsus to seek Saul
15 17 residue of men may seek after the Lord
17 27 they should seek God, if happily they
Rom 2 7 seek glory and honor and incorruption
10 20 I was found by them that did not s. me
11 3 I am left alone, and they seek my life
1 C 1 22 and the Greeks seek after wisdom: but
7 27 bound to a wife? seek not to be loosed
27 thou loosed from wife? seek not a wife
10 24 let no man seek his own, but that which
14 12 seek to abound unto the edifying of the
2 C 12 14 I seek not the things that are yours
13 3 do you seek a proof of Christ that
Gal 1 10 or do I seek to please men? If I yet
2 17 if while we s. to be justified in Christ
Phil 2 21 all seek the things that are their own
4 17 not that I seek the gift, but I seek
Col 3 1 seek the things that are above; where
Heb 11 6 is a rewarder to them that seek him
14 signify that they seek a country. And
13 14 city, but we seek one that is to come
1 P 3 11 let him seek after peace and pursue it
Apoc 9 6 men shall seek death, and shall not

seekest Gen 44 9 be found that which thou s.
Judg 4 22 show thee the man whom thou seekest
2 K 20 19 thou s. to destroy the city [Abela]
3 K 11 22 that thou s. to go to thy own country
John 4 27 what seekest thou? or, why talkest
20 15 why weepest thou? Whom seekest thou

seeketh Deut 18 11 that s. the truth from the dead
1 K 19 2 Saul my father seeketh to kill thee
20 1 thy father, that he seeketh my life
22 23 that s. my life, s. thy life also
24 10 men that say: David seeketh thy hurt
2 K 16 11 forth from my bowels, seeketh my life
4 K 5 7 see how he seeketh occasions against me
Job 39 8 pasture, and s. for every green thing
Ps 36 32 just man, and s. to put him to death
Prov 11 27 he rise early who seeketh good things
27 he that seeketh after evil things
14 6 scorner s. wisdom, and findeth it not
15 14 the heart of the wise s. instruction
17 9 a transgression, seeketh friendships
11 an evil man always seeketh quarrels
16 maketh his house high, s. a downfall
19 he that exalteth his door, seeketh ruin
18 1 to depart from a friend, s. occasions
15 ear of the wise seeketh instruction
27 21 the heart of the wicked s. after evils
21 righteous heart s. after knowledge
Ecce 7 29 the account, which yet my soul seeketh
Eccu 27 1 he that s. to be enriched, turneth
28 1 he that seeketh to revenge himself
32 19 he that s. the law, shall be filled
33 26 hands be idle, and he seeketh liberty
26 under correction, and s. to rest: let
Isa 17 5 as he that seeketh ears in the vale of
40 20 workman seeketh how he may set up an
Jer 5 1 that executeth judgment and s. faith
38 4 this man seeketh not peace to this
Lam 3 25 in him, to the soul that seeketh him
Mat 7 8 he that seeketh, findeth. Luke 11:10
12 39 adulterous generation s. a sign. 16:4
John 4 23 Father also seeketh such to adore him
7 4 himself seeketh to be known openly
18 of himself, seeketh his own glory
18 he that seeketh the glory of him that
20 hast a devil; who seeketh to kill thee
8 50 there is one that seeketh and judgeth
Rom 3 11 there is none that seeketh after God
1 C 13 5 is not ambitious, seeketh not her own

seeking Judg 5 26 s. in his head a place for the
Judg 6 39 seeking a sign in the fleece. I pray
Ps 36 25 just forsaken, not his seed s. bread
103 21 prey, and seeking their meat from God
Ecce 12 9 seeking out, he set forth many parables
Wisd 6 17 seeking such as are worthy of her, and
8 18 I went about seeking, that I might take
13 6 seeking God and desirous to find him

Eccu 3 3 s. the judgment of the mothers, hath
32 12 hear in silence and withal seeking
23 controlled by the things of his own s.
51 29 my entrails were troubled in s. her
Isa 16 5 judging and s. judgment and quickly
Eze 21 21 seeking divination, shuffling arrows
Amos 8 12 go about seeking the word of the Lord
1 Ma 6 18 they were continually s. their hurt
Mat 12 43 he walketh through dry places s. rest
46 stood without, seeking to speak to him
47 thy brethren stand without, s. thee
13 45 is like to a merchant s. good pearls
21 46 s. to lay hands on him, they feared
Luke 2 45 they returned into Jerusalem, s. him
11 24 places without water, seeking rest
54 s. to catch something from his mouth
13 6 he came seeking fruit on it, and
7 I come seeking fruit on this fig tree
John 6 24 came to Capharnaum, seeking for Jesus
Acts 13 8 s. to turn away the proconsul from
Rom 10 3 seeking to establish their own, have not
1 C 10 33 men, not s. that which is profitable to
1 P 5 8 goeth about seeking whom he may devour
seem Gen 21 12 let it not seem grievous to thee
Gen 45 5 let it not seem to you a hard case
Lev 13 34 the evil seem to have stayed in its
Num 11 15 but if it seem unto thee otherwise
Deut 1 17 if anything seem hard to you, refer
Josu 14 7 him word again as to me seemed true
24 15 if it s. evil to you to serve the Lord
1 K 18 23 doth it seem to you a small matter to
24 5 him as it shall seem good in thy eyes
2 K 15 3 thy words seem to me good and just
1 Es 5 17 if it s. good to the king. 2 Es 2:5, 7
7 18 if it seem good to thee and to thy
Job 35 2 doth thy thought seem right to thee
37 24 all that seem to themselves to be wise
Jer 30 11 mayst not seem to thyself innocent
Dan 14 5 doth not Bel seem to thee to be a
Zach 8 6 if it seem hard in the eyes of the
Mark 10 42 you know that they who seem to rule
Luke 22 24 of them should seem to be the greater
1 C 3 18 if any man among you seem to be wise in
11 16 if any man seem to be contentious, we
14 37 if any seem to be prophet, or spiritual
21 22 those that seem to be the more feeble
seemed Gen 19 14 he s. to them to speak as it
Gen 29 20 they seemed but a few days because
Num 11 10 Moses also the thing s. insupportable
13 34 comparison of whom, we s. like locusts
Josu 14 7 brought him word again as to me s. true
Judg 7 13 it seemed to me as if a hearth cake
17 6 which seemed right to himself. 21:24
2 K 3 19 all that seemed good to Israel and to
36 that the king did seemed good in the
7 19 this hath seemed little in thy sight
3 K 7 36 so that they seemed not to be engraven
1 Pa 17 17 even this hath s. little in thy sight
2 Es 7 2 he seemed as a sincere man and one that
13 8 it seemed to me exceeding evil. And I
Tob 10 7 ways by which there seemed any hope he
12 19 I seemed indeed to eat and to drink
Job 32 1 Job, because he seemed just to himself
Ecce 5 17 this therefore hath seemed good to me
9 13 and it seemed to me to be very great
Wisd 3 2 sight of the unwise they seemed to die
Jer 18 4 it seemed good in his eyes to make it
27 5 it to whom it seemed good in my eyes
Dan 3 99 it hath seemed good to me therefore
6 1 it s. good to Darius, and he appointed
13 5 judges that s. to govern the people
1 Ma 1 13 the word seemed good in their eyes
6 43 it seemed to him that the king was
8 26 hath seemed good to the Romans. 28
15 19 seemed good therefore to us to write
20 it hath seemed good to us to receive
2 Ma 3 25 upon him, s. to have armor of gold
9 8 he that seemed to himself to command
12 16 s. to run with the blood of the slain
44 it would have seemed superfluous and
13 23 to all things that seemed reasonable
14 4 which seemed to belong to the temple
Mat 11 26 it seemed good in thy sight. Luke 10:21
Luke 1 3 it seemed good to me also, having
24 11 these words seemed to them as idle
Acts 15 25 hath s. good to us, being assembled
28 it hath s. good to the Holy Ghost and
34 it s. good unto Silas to remain there
16 13 where it s. that there was prayer; and
Gal 2 2 them who seemed to be something. 6
6 to me they that s. to be something added
9 John, who seemed to be pillars, gave to
seemeth Lev 14 35 s. to me that there is plague
Deut 12 8 that which seemeth good to himself
Josu 9 25 as it seemeth good and right unto thee
1 K 1 23 do what seemeth good to thee [Anna]
14 36 do all that seemeth good in thy eyes
40 do what seemeth good in thy eyes. And
2 K 17 11 this seemeth to me to be good counsel
18 4 what seemeth good to you, that will I
27 running of the foremost s. to me like
19 37 do to him whatsoever s. good to thee
24 22 and offer, as it seemeth good to him
2 Pa 10 9 said to them: What seemeth good to you
Job 8 16 he seemeth to have moisture before the
Prov 14 12 there is a way which seemeth just to a
16 25 there is a way that s. to a man right
21 2 every way of a man s. right to himself
28 11 the rich man seemeth to himself wise
2 Ma 15 21 according as it seemeth good to him
Mat 25 29 that also which he seemeth to have
Acts 17 18 he s. to be a setter forth of new gods
25 27 for it s. to me unreasonable to send a
1 C 7 36 but if any man think that he seemeth
Heb 12 11 seemeth not to bring with it joy, but
seeming Judg 20 32 by their s. to flee to bring
seemly Prov 19 10 delicacies are not s. for a fool
Prov 26 1 so glory is not seemly for a fool
Eccu 15 9 praise is not s. in mouth of a sinner
seen Gen 5 24 was seen no more: because God took
Gen 7 1 thee I have seen just before me in
9 22 which when Cham . . . had seen, to wit
16 13 name . . . Thou the God who hast seen me
13 here have I seen the hinder parts of
21 9 when Sara had seen the son of Agar
24 30 when he had seen the earrings and
31 12 I have seen all that Laban hath done
32 30 saying: I have seen God face to face
33 10 for I have seen thy face as if I should
10 if I should have seen the countenance
43 16 when he had seen them, and Benjamin
45 13 all things that you have seen in Egypt
46 30 with joy, because I have seen thy face
Exod 3 7 I have seen the affliction of my people
9 I have seen their affliction wherewith
16 I have seen all that hath befallen
9 24 great bigness, as never before was seen
10 6 number as thy fathers have not seen
13 7 shall not be seen anything leavened
18 14 when his kinsman had seen all things
19 4 you have seen what I have done to the
20 22 you have seen that I have spoken to you
34 3 let not any man be seen throughout all
10 I will do signs such as were never seen
Lev 5 1 because he himself hath seen, or is
13 7 again, after he was seen by the priest

Num	14	14	and art seen face to face, and thy cloud
		22	all the men that have seen my majesty
	23	21	neither is there an image god to be seen
	27	13	when thou shalt have seen it, thou
Deut	1	28	we have seen the sons of the Enacims
		31	in the wilderness, as thou hast seen
	3	21	thy eyes have seen what the Lord your
	4	3	your eyes have seen all that the Lord
		9	the words that thy eyes have seen, and
	9	2	sons of the Enacims, whom thou hast seen
	10	21	terrible things which thy eyes have seen
	11	7	your eyes have seen all the great works
	16	4	no leaven shall be seen in all thy
	29	2	you have seen all the things that the
		3	temptations, which thy eyes have seen
		17	you have seen their abominations and
		28	into a strange land, as it is seen
	34	4	thou hast seen it with thy eyes and
Josu	3	16	like a mountain, were seen afar off
Judg	5	8	spear was not s. among 40,000 of Israel
	6	22	for I have seen the angel of the Lord
	7	13	this manner related what he had seen
	13	22	certainly die, because we have seen God
	18	9	we have seen the land which is exceeding
	19	3	and had seen him, he met him with joy
		30	when every one had seen this, they
Ruth	4	1	when he had seen the kinsman going by
1 K	6	19	because they had seen the ark of the
	12	24	you have seen the great works which he
	14	8	when we shall be seen by them, if they
		29	you have seen yourselves that my eyes
	16	18	behold I have seen a son of Isai the
	17	25	have you seen this man that is come up
	22	6	Saul heard that David was seen and
	23	22	where his foot is, and who hath seen him
	24	11	thy eyes have seen that the Lord hath
	28	13	what hast thou seen? And the woman said
2 K	17	17	they might not be seen nor enter into
	18	21	and tell the king what thou hast seen
3 K	6	18	and no stone could be seen in the wall
	8	8	the ends of them were seen without in
		8	but were not seen farther out, and there
	10	12	such thyine trees . . . nor seen unto this
	18	17	and when he had seen him, he said
	20	13	hast thou seen all this exceeding great
		40	on a sudden he was not to be seen
	21	29	hast thou not seen Achab humbled
4 K	16	10	when he had seen the altar of Damascus
	20	5	thy prayer, and I have seen thy tears
	23	29	slain at Mageddo, when he had seen him
1 Pa	29	17	I have seen with great joy thy people
2 Pa	5	9	ends were seen before the oracle
	9	3	and when she had seen these things
		6	until I came, and my eyes had seen
		11	never were there seen such trees in the
	25	21	themselves to be seen by one another
1 Es	3	12	the ancients that had seen the former
Tob	12	19	and drink, which cannot be seen by men
Jdth	7	7	they were seen secretly to draw water
		16	after we have seen our wives and our
Job	3	16	being conceived have not seen the light
	4	8	I have seen those who work iniquity
	5	3	I have seen a fool with a strong root
	9	25	have fled away and have not seen good
	13	1	my eye hath seen all these things and
	15	17	and I will tell thee what I have seen
	20	7	and they that had seen him, shall say
		9	the eyes that had seen him, shall see
	28	10	his eye hath seen every precious thing
	38	17	hast thou seen the darksome doors
Ps	34	21	well done, our eyes have seen it
		22	thou hast seen, O Lord, be not thou
	36	25	and I have not seen the just forsaken

		35	I have seen the wicked highly exalted
	47	9	as we have heard, so have we seen
	54	10	I have seen iniquity and contradiction
	67	25	they have seen thy goings, O God
	73	9	our signs we have not seen, there is now
	83	8	the God of gods shall be seen in Sion
	89	15	the years in which we have seen evils
	97	3	all the ends of the earth have seen
	101	17	and he shall be seen in his glory
	106	24	these have seen the works of the Lord
	118	96	I have seen an end of all perfection
Prov	22	29	hast thou seen a man swift in his work
	24	32	when I had seen, I laid it up in my
	25	8	which thy eyes have seen, utter not
	26	12	hast thou seen a man wise in his own
	29	20	hast thou seen a man hasty to speak
	31	18	and seen that her traffic is good
Ecce	1	14	I have seen all things that are done
	3	10	I have seen the trouble, which God hath
	4	3	nor hath seen the evils that are done
	5	12	have seen under the sun. 6:1; 9:13; 10:5
	6	5	he hath not seen the sun, nor known the
	10	7	I have seen servants upon horses: and
Cant	3	3	have you seen him whom my soul loveth
Wisd	6	13	is easily seen by them that love her
	13	1	by these good things that are seen
		5	the creator of them may be seen, so as
		7	the things are good which are seen
	17	6	fear of that face, which was not seen
		18	the running that could not be seen
Eccu	1	23	it hath seen and numbered her: but
	16	6	many such things hath my eyes seen
	20	32	treasure that is not seen. 41:17
	34	12	I have seen many things by travelling
	42	15	I will declare the things I have seen
	43	36	we have seen but a few of his works
Isa	6	5	I have seen with my eyes the King the
	9	2	in darkness, have seen a great light
	16	12	when it is seen that Moab is wearied
	38	5	prayer, and I have seen thy tears
	39	4	that are in my house have they seen
	44	16	aha, I am warm, I have seen the fire
	47	3	and thy shame shall be seen: I will
	52	15	it was not told of him, have seen
	53	2	we have seen him, and there was no
	60	2	and his glory shall be seen upon thee
	64	4	the eye hath not seen, O God, besides
	66	8	and who hath seen the like to this
		19	and have not seen my glory. And they
Jer	1	12	thou hast seen well: for I will watch
	3	6	hast thou seen what rebellious Israel
	6	1	evil is seen out of the north, and a
	7	11	I am he: I have seen it, saith the Lord
	12	3	hast known me, thou hast seen me and
	13	27	I have seen thy adulteries and thy
	23	13	I have seen folly in the prophets of
		14	I have seen the likeness of adulterers
		18	hath seen and heard his word? Who hath
	30	6	why then have I seen every man with
	33	24	not seen what this people hath spoken
	41	13	were with Ismahel, had seen Johanan
	44	2	you have seen all this evil that I
	46	5	I have seen them dismayed and turning
Lam	1	7	the enemies have seen her, and have
		8	because they have seen her shame: but
		10	she hath seen the Gentiles enter into
	2	14	thy prophets have seen false and foolish
		14	they have seen for thee false revelations
		16	we have found it, we have seen it
	3	59	thou hast seen, O Lord, their iniquity
		60	thou hast seen all their fury and all
Bar	3	20	young men have seen the light and
		22	neither hath it been seen in Theman

4 10 I have seen the captivity of my people
24 have now seen your captivity from God
6 60 the lightning . . . is easy to be seen
Eze 8 4 vision which I had seen in the plain
15 thou hast seen, O son of man. 17; 47:6
10 15 I had seen by the river Chobar. 22; 43:3
11 24 vision which I had seen was taken up
13 7 have you not seen a vain vision and
8 spoken vain things, and have seen lies
16 50 I took them away as thou hast seen
23 14 when she had seen men painted on the
43 3 the appearance which I had seen when
Dan 4 6 visions of my dreams that I have seen
7 7 other beasts which I had seen before it
8 1 after what I had seen in the beginning
6 which I had seen standing before the
9 21 whom I had seen in the vision at the
Osee 6 10 I have seen a horrible thing in the
Zach 9 8 for now I have seen with my eyes
14 the Lord God shall be seen over them
10 2 the diviners have seen a lie, and the
1 Ma 4 20 the smoke that was seen declared what
21 when they had seen this, they were
9 27 there was no prophet seen in Israel
13 3 and the distresses that we have seen
29 be seen by all that sailed on the seas
15 36 report . . . of all that he had seen
2 Ma 3 36 which he had seen with his own eyes
5 2 were seen horsemen running in the
6 9 death: then was misery to be seen
12 9 of the fire was seen at Jerusalem
Mat 2 9 star which they had seen in the east
4 16 sat in darkness, hath seen great light
6 1 before men, to be seen by them
5 that they may be seen by men: Amen I
9 33 never was the like seen in Israel
11 4 to John what you have heard and seen
13 17 that you see, and have not seen them. Luke 10:24
23 5 works they do for to be seen of men
27 54 having seen the earthquake and the
Mark 2 5 when Jesus had seen their faith, he
5 16 they that had seen it, told them in
7 2 they had seen some of his disciples
9 8 any man what things they had seen
19 when he had seen him, immediately the
11 13 when he had seen afar off a fig tree
14 67 she had seen Peter warming himself
16 11 was alive and had been seen by her
14 who had seen him after he was risen
Luke 1 22 that he had seen a vision in the
2 20 all the things they had heard and seen
26 before he had seen the Christ of the
30 my eyes have seen thy salvation, which
5 26 we have seen wonderful things today
7 13 whom when the Lord had seen, being
22 to John what you have heard and seen
8 36 they also that had seen, told them
9 36 of these things which they had seen
54 James and John, had seen this, they
19 37 for all the mighty works they had seen
22 56 maid had seen sitting at the light
24 23 they had also seen a vision of angels
John 1 18 no man hath seen God at any time: the
3 11 we testify what we have seen, and you
32 what he hath seen and heard, that he
4 45 having seen all the things he had done
5 6 him when Jesus had seen lying, and
37 voice at any time nor seen his shape
6 5 and seen that a very great multitude
14 when they had seen what a miracle
26 not because you have seen miracles
36 also have seen me, and you believe not
46 not that any man hath seen the Father
46 is of God, he hath seen the Father
8 38 that which I have seen with my Father
38 that you have seen with your father
57 and hast thou seen Abraham? Jesus
9 8 who had seen him before that he was a
37 thou hast both seen him; and it is he
11 45 had seen the things that Jesus did
14 7 shall know him, and you have seen him
15 24 they have both seen and hated me and
19 6 and the servants had seen him, they
26 Jesus therefore had seen his mother
20 18 I have seen the Lord, and these things
25 we have seen the Lord. But he said to
29 because thou hast seen me, Thomas
29 that have not seen, and have believed
21 21 him therefore when Peter had seen
Acts 1 11 as you have seen him going into
3 3 when he had seen Peter and John about
16 this man, whom you have seen and known
4 20 things which we have seen and heard
7 24 when he had seen one of them suffer
34 I have seen the affliction of my
44 to the form which he had seen. Which
9 27 told them how he had seen the Lord
10 17 the vision that he had seen should mean
11 13 he told us how he had seen an angel
23 when he [Barnabas] . . . had s. the grace
13 12 when he had seen what was done, believed
31 who was seen for many days, by them
14 10 multitudes had s. what Paul had done
16 10 and as soon as he had seen the vision
40 having s. the brethren, they comforted
21 29 they had seen Trophimus the Ephesian in
22 15 things which thou hast seen and heard
26 16 witness of . . . things which thou hast s.
Rom 1 20 are clearly seen, being understood by
8 24 but hope that is seen, is not hope. For
1 C 2 9 that eye hath not seen, nor ear heard
9 1 have not I seen Christ Jesus our Lord
15 5 and that he was seen by Cephas; and
6 was he seen by more than 500 brethren
7 after that, he was seen by James, then
8 last of all, he was seen also by me, as
2 C 4 18 we look not at things which are seen
18 but at the things which are not seen
18 the things which are seen, are temporal
18 things which are not seen, are eternal
Gal 2 7 they had seen that to me was committed
Phil 1 30 which you have seen in me, and now have
4 9 received and heard and seen in me, these
Col 2 1 have not seen my face in the flesh: that
18 in the things which he hath not seen, in
1 Tim 6 16 whom no man hath seen, nor can see: to
Heb 11 7 those things which as yet were not seen
12 21 so terrible was that which was seen
James 5 11 you have seen the end of the Lord
1 P 1 8 whom having not seen, you love: in
1 J 1 1 which we have seen with our eyes
2 we have seen and do bear witness and
3 which we have seen and have heard
3 6 hath not seen him nor known him
4 12 no man hath seen God at any time. If
14 we have seen and do testify that the
3 J 11 he that doth evil, hath not seen God
Apoc 1 2 Christ, what things soever he hath seen
17 when I had seen him, I fell at his feet
19 the things which thou hast seen and
11 19 ark of his testament was seen in his
12 3 there was seen another sign in heaven
17 6 and I wondered when I had seen her
22 8 who have heard and seen these things
8 after I had heard and seen, I fell

seer 1 K 9 9 in time past was called a seer
1 K 9 9 come, let us go to the seer. For he
11 they said to them: Is the seer here
18 pray thee, where is the house of the s.
19 I am the seer, go up before me to the
2 K 15 27 O seer, return into the city in peace
24 11 Gad the prophet and the seer of David
1 Pa 9 22 David and Samuel the seer appointed
21 9 Lord spoke to Gad the seer of David
25 5 these were the sons of Heman the seer
26 28 all these things that Samuel the seer
29 29 written in the book of Samuel the seer
29 and in the book of Gad the seer
2 Pa 9 29 and in the vision of Addo the seer
12 15 the prophet and of Addo the seer
16 10 and Asa was angry with the seer and
19 2 the son of Hanani the seer met him
29 25 of David the king and of Gad the seer
30 with words of David and Asaph the seer
Amos 7 12 thou seer, go, flee away into the
seers 4 K 17 13 by hand of all the prophets and s.
2 Pa 33 18 words of the seers that spoke to him
Isa 30 10 who say to the seers: See not: and to
sees Eze 33 3 he sees the sword coming upon
seest Gen 13 15 all the land which thou seest
Gen 27 2 thou seest that I am old and know
31 43 all things that thou seest are mine
Lev 10 19 to me what thou seest has happened
Deut 2 30 into thy hands, as now thou seest
4 38 as thou seest at this present day
21 11 seest in the number of the captives
22 1 if thou seest thy brother's ox or his
Judg 9 36 thou seest the shadows of the mountains
4 K 2 19 is very good, as thou, my lord, seest
2 Pa 31 10 this great store, which thou seest
Tob 9 5 thou seest how Raguel hath adjured me
Ps 9 14 thou seest it, for thou considerest
Isa 42 20 thou that seest many things, wilt thou
Jer 1 11 what seest thou, Jeremias. 24:3
13 seest thou? And I said. Zach 4:2; 5:2
7 17 seest thou not what they do in the
20 12 who seest the reins and the heart: let
32 24 all come to pass, as thou thyself seest
Eze 8 12 thou seest, O son of man, what the
40 4 declare all that thou seest, to the
Dan 14 5 seest thou not how much he eateth
Amos 7 8 what seest thou, Amos. 8:2
Mat 7 3 why seest thou the mote. Luke 6:41
3 s. not the beam that is. Luke 6:42
Mark 5 31 thou seest the multitude thronging
13 2 seest thou all these great buildings
Acts 21 20 thou seest, brother, how many thousands
James 2 22 seest thou, that faith did cooperate
Apoc 1 11 what thou seest, write in a book and
seeth Gen 16 13 hinder parts of him that s. me
Gen 16 14 well of him that liveth and seeth me
22 17 name of that place, The Lord seeth
Num 24 16 and seeth the visions of the Almighty
1 K 16 7 man seeth those things that appear
Job 10 4 flesh: or shalt thou see as a man seeth
11 11 when he seeth iniquity, doth he not
42 5 heard thee, but now my eye seeth thee
Prov 24 12 s. into the heart, he understandeth
Ecce 3 13 and seeth good of his labor, this is
5 10 that he s. the riches with his eyes
Eccu 7 12 humbleth and exalteth, God who s. all
13 8 when he seeth thee, he will forsake
23 25 and saying: Who seeth me: Darkness
26 walls cover me and no man seeth me
27 that his eye seeth all things, for
25 10 liveth and s. the fall of his enemies
30 21 he seeth with his eyes and groaneth
39 25 he seeth from eternity to eternity
Isa 28 4 when he that seeth it shall behold
7 they have not known him that seeth
29 15 say: Who seeth us and who knoweth us
47 10 hast said: There is none that seeth me
57 11 I am silent and as one that seeth not
Eze 8 12 for they say: The Lord seeth us not
9 9 the earth, and the Lord seeth not
12 27 the vision that this man seeth is for
Dan 13 20 orchard are shut, and nobody seeth us
2 Ma 9 5 God of Israel, that seeth all things
12 22 presence of God, who seeth all things
Mat 6 4 thy Father who seeth in secret. 6, 18
Mark 5 38 he seeth a tumult, and people weeping
John 5 19 but what he seeth the Father doing
6 40 who seeth the Son and believeth in him
9 21 how he now seeth, we know not; or who
10 12 seeth the wolf coming, and leaveth
11 9 because he seeth the light of this
12 45 that seeth me, seeth him that sent me
14 9 that seeth me seeth the Father also
17 cannot receive because it s. him not
19 and the world seeth me no more. But
Rom 8 24 what a man seeth, why doth he hope for
2 C 12 6 think of me above that which he s. in
1 J 4 20 loveth not his brother, whom he seeth
20 how can he love God, whom he seeth not
seethe Zach 14 21 of them, and shall s. in them
seething Eze 24 5 the s. thereof is boiling hot
Segor Gen 13 10 like Egypt as one comes to Segor
Gen 14 2 the king of Bala, which is Segor. 8
19 22 the name of that city was called Segor
23 the earth and Lot entered into Segor
30 Lot went up out of Segor and abode
30 he [Lot] was afraid to stay in Segor
34 3 the city of palm trees as far as Segor
Isa 15 5 the bars thereof shall flee unto Segor
Jer 48 34 from Segor to Oronaim, as a heifer of
Segub 3 K 16 34 in his youngest son S. he set up
1 Pa 2 21 she bore him Segub. And S. begot Jair
Sehesima Josu 19 22 Thabor and S. and Bethsames
Sehon Num 21 27 let the city of Sehon be built
Num 21 28 a flame from the city of Sehon, and
Deut 2 31 to deliver unto thee S. and his land
32 Sehon came out to meet us with all
31 4 to them as he did to Sehon and Og
Josu 2 10 Jordan: Sehon and Og whom you slew
13 21 dukes of Sehon inhabitants of the land
2 Es 9 22 and they possessed the land of Sehon
Sehon king of Hesebon; *see* **Hesebon**
Sehon king of the Amorrhites; *see* **Amorrhites**
Seir Gen 14 6 Chorreans in the mountains of Seir
Gen 32 3 Esau his brother to the land of Seir
33 14 able, until I come to my lord in Seir
16 that day the way that he came, to Seir
36 20 these are the sons of Seir the Horrite
21 the sons of Seir in the land of Edom
30 Horrites that ruled in the land of Seir
Num 24 18 inheritance of Seir shall come to their
Deut 1 44 slaughter of you from Seir as far as
2 29 of Esau have done that dwell in Seir
4 children of Esau, who dwell in S. 22
8 children of Esau, that dwelt in Seir
12 Horrhites also formerly dwelt in Seir
33 2 Sinai, and from Seir he rose up to us
Josu 11 17 part of mountain that goeth up to Seir
12 7 mount, part of which goeth up into Seir
Judg 5 4 Lord, when thou wentest out of Seir
1 Pa 1 38 sons of Seir: Lotan, Sobal, Sebeon
2 Pa 25 11 slew of the children of Seir 10,000
14 set up the gods of the children of S.
Isa 21 11 calleth to me out of Seir: Watchman
Eze 25 8 Moab and Seir have said: Behold the
mount Seir Eccu 50 28 they that sit on mount S.

Eze 35 2 thy face against mount Seir, and
3 I come against thee, mount Seir, and I
7 I will make mount Seir waste and
15 thou shalt be laid waste, O mount Seir
Seira 4 K 8 21 Joram came to Seira, and all the
Seirath Judg 3 26 and he [Aod] came to Seirath
seize Gen 19 19 lest some evil seize me and I die
1 K 19 14 and Saul sent officers to seize David
Job 3 6 let a darksome whirlwind seize upon it
Ps 7 3 lest at any time he seize upon my soul
Bar 6 4 fear of them should seize upon you
1 Ma 9 60 to seize upon Jonathan and them that
12 40 he sought to seize upon him and to
seized Gen 15 12 and darksome horror s. upon him
Exod 15 15 trembling seized on the stout men of
Deut 33 20 hath seized upon the arm and the top
Judg 3 28 seized upon the fords of the Jordan
16 21 Philistines seized upon him [Samson]
1 Pa 21 30 he was seized with an exceeding great
2 Pa 20 3 Josaphat being seized with fear, betook
2 Es 2 2 I was seized with an exceeding great
Tob 12 16 being seized with fear they fell upon
Jdth 4 2 dread and horror s. upon their minds
3 s. upon all the tops of the mountains
13 29 Achior . . . being s. with a great fear
15 1 being seized with trembling and fear
Job 4 14 fear seized upon me, and trembling
Osee 13 1 when Ephraim spoke, a horror s. Israel
1 Ma 4 21 they were seized with great fear, seeing
7 2 the army seized upon Antiochus and
9 6 and they were seized with great fear
Mark 16 8 a trembling and fear had seized them
Luke 8 29 many times it seized him, and he was
Acts 10 4 being seized with fear, said: What
seizeth Luke 9 39 spirit s. him, and he suddenly
Sela Gen 38 5 also a third, whom she called Sela
Gen 38 11 father's house till S. my son grow up
14 because Sela was grown up, and she
26 because I did not give her to Sela my
46 12 Onan and Sela and Phares and Zara
Num 26 20 Sela of whom is the family of the
Josu 18 28 Sela, Eleph, and Jebus, which is
1 Pa 2 3 the sons of Juda: Her, Onan and Sela
4 21 the sons of Sela the son of Juda
Selahi 2 Pa 20 31 Azuba the daughter of Selahi
Selaites Num 26 20 of whom is family of the S.
Selcha Deut 3 10 Basan as far as S. 1 Pa 5:11
Selebin Josu 19 42 Selebin and Aialon and
Selec 2 K 23 37 Selec of Ammoni, Naharai
1 Pa 11 39 Selec an Ammonite, Naharai a
Selemia 2 Es 3 30 Hanania the son of Selemia
Selemias 1 Pa 26 14 lot of the east fell to S.
2 Es 13 13 we set over the storehouses Selemias
Jer 36 14 son of Nathanias, the son of Selemias
26 S. the son of Abdeel to take up Baruch
37 3 Juchal the son of Selemias. 38:1
12 named Jerias, the son of Selemias
Selemiau 1 Es 10 41 S., Semeria, Sellum, Amaria
Selemith 1 Pa 26 25 Zechri and his son Selemith
1 Pa 26 26 Selemith and his brethren were over
28 they were under the hand of Selemith
Seleph 2 Es 3 30 Hanun the sixth son of Seleph
Selethai 1 Pa 8 20 Elioenai and S. and Elial
Seleucia 1 Ma 11 8 cities by seaside, even to S.
Acts 13 4 being sent by Holy Ghost, went to S.
Seleucus 1 Ma 7 1 Demetrius the son of Seleucus
2 Ma 3 3 S. king of Asia allowed out of his
4 7 after the death of S., when Antiochus
5 18 was sent by king S. to rob the treasury
14 1 Demetrius the son of S. was come up
self Mark 12 33 one's neighbor as one's self
selfsame Gen 7 13 in the s. day Noe and Sem and
Gen 17 26 selfsame day was Abraham circumcised
Job 33 14 repeateth not the selfsame thing the
Ps 4 9 in peace in the selfsame I will sleep
101 28 thou art always the selfsame, and thy
Eze 40 1 in the selfsame day the hand of the
Mat 26 44 third time, saying the selfsame word
27 44 the s. thing the thieves also, that
2 C 3 14 until this present day, the s. veil, in
7 11 behold this selfsame thing, that you
Phil 2 18 for the s. thing do you also rejoice
Heb 1 12 thou art the selfsame, and thy years
10 1 by the s. sacrifices which they offer
selfwill Gen 49 6 in their s. they undermined a
Selim Josu 15 32 Lebaoth and Selim and Aen and
sell Gen 25 31 sell me thy first birthright. He
Gen 47 22 not forced to sell their possessions
Exod 21 7 if any man sell his daughter to be
8 no power to s. her to a foreign nation
16 he that shall steal a man and sell him
35 they shall sell the live ox and shall
22 1 ox or a sheep and kill or sell it
Lev 25 14 when thou shalt sell anything to thy
15 he shall sell to thee according to the
16 sell to thee the time of the fruits
25 impoverished sell his little possession
39 by poverty, sell himself to thee, thou
47 being impoverished sell himself to him
Deut 2 28 sell us meat for money, that we may
14 21 to the stranger . . . or sell it to him
25 thou shalt sell them all and turn
21 14 but thou mayst not sell her for money
Ruth 4 3 will sell a parcel of land that belonged
3 K 10 29 the Hethites and of Syria sell horses
4 K 4 7 go, sell the oil and pay thy creditor
2 Es 5 8 and will you then sell your brethren
10 31 of the land bring in things to sell
31 to sell them on the sabbath day, that
13 15 sell on a day on which it was lawful to sell
Prov 11 26 blessing upon head of them that sell
23 23 buy truth, and so not sell wisdom and
Bar 6 27 to them, their priests sell and abuse
Eze 48 14 and they shall not sell thereof nor
Joel 3 8 and I will sell your sons and your
8 they shall sell them to the Sabeans
Amos 8 5 over, and we shall sell our wares
6 and may sell the refuse of the corn
1 Ma 12 36 that they might neither buy nor sell
2 Ma 5 24 to sell the women and the younger
Mat 19 21 sell what thou hast. Mark 10:21; Luke 18:22
25 9 go ye rather to them that sell and
Luke 12 33 sell what you possess and give alms
22 36 let him sell his coat and buy a sword
Apoc 13 17 and that no man might buy or sell but
Sella Gen 4 19 and the name of the other Sella
Gen 4 22 Sella also brought forth Tubalcain
23 Lamech said to his wives Ada and S.
4 K 12 20 house of Mello in the descent of Sella
Sellai 2 Es 11 8 after him Gebbai, Sellai, 928
2 Es 12 20 of Sellai, Celai: of Amoc, Heber
Sellem Num 26 49 S., of whom is the family of
Sellemites Num 26 49 of whom is family of the S.
seller Isa 24 2 as with the buyer, so with the s.
Eze 7 12 the buyer rejoice: nor the s. mourn
13 the seller shall not return to that
Acts 16 14 woman named Lydia, a s. of purple, of
sellers 2 Es 3 30 of the sellers of small wares
Eze 27 22 the sellers of Saba and Reema, they
Selles 1 Pa 7 35 Jemna and Selles and Amal
selleth Lev 25 29 he that s. a house within the
Mat 13 44 selleth all that he hath and buyeth
selling Gen 47 20 every man s. his possessions
Lev 25 50 from the time of his selling unto
Deut 24 7 and selling him shall take a price
Eccu 27 2 in the midst of selling and buying

12 12 treat not . . . with a buyer of selling
1 Ma 13 49 country, and from buying and selling
Sellum 4 K 15 10 Sellum the son of Jabes. 13, 14
4 K 15 15 the rest of the acts of Sellum and his
22 14 the prophetess wife of S. 2 Pa 34:22
1 Pa 2 40 Sisamoi begot S., S. begot Icamia
3 15 third Sedecias, the fourth Sellum
4 25 Sellum his son, Mapsam his son
6 12 Sadoc begot S., S. begot Helcias
7 13 and Jezer and Sellum, sons of Bala
9 17 the porters were Sellum and Accub
17 their brother Sellum was the prince
19 Sellum the son of Core, the son of
31 Mathathias . . . firstborn of Sellum
2 Pa 28 12 Ezechias the son of Sellum, and Amasa
1 Es 2 42 of the porters: the children of Sellum
7 2 Helcias the son of Sellum, the son of
10 24 of the porters, Sellum and Telem
42 Semeria, Sellum, Amaria, Joseph
2 Es 3 12 to him built Sellum the son of Alohes
15 and the gate of the fountain Sellum
7 46 the porters: the children of Sellum
11 7 children of Benjamin: Sellum the son
12 6 Sellum, Amoc, Helcias, Idaia. These
Jer 22 11 thus saith the Lord to Sellum the son
32 7 Hanameel the son of Sellum thy cousin
35 4 Maasias the son of Sellum, who was
Selmai 2 Es 7 48 of Hagaba, the children of S.
Selmon Judg 9 48 went up into mount Selmon
2 K 23 28 Selmon the Ahohite, Maharai the
Ps 67 15 they shall be whited with snow in S.
Selomith 1 Es 8 10 of the sons of S., the son of
Sem Gen 5 31 Sem, Cham, and Japheth. 6:10; 7:13;
9:18; 10:1; 1 Pa 1:4
Gen 9 23 Sem and Japheth put a cloak upon
26 said: Blessed be the Lord God of Sem
27 and may he dwell in the tents of Sem
10 21 of Sem also, the father of all the
22 the sons of Sem: Elam and Assur
31 these are the children of Sem
11 10 these are the generations of Sem
11 Sem lived after he begot Arphaxad
1 Pa 1 17 the sons of Sem: Elam and Asur and
24 Sem, Arphaxad, Sale, Heber, Phaleg
Eccu 49 19 Seth and Sem obtained glory among men
Luke 3 36 Arphaxad, who was of Sem, who was of
Semaath 4 K 12 21 Josachar the son of Semaath
Semaia 2 Es 3 29 after him built Semaia the
2 Es 6 10 and I went into the house of Semaia
12 18 of Semaia, Jonathan: of Joiarib, Azzi
Semarith 2 Pa 24 26 Jozabad the son of Semarith
Semathites 1 Pa 2 53 Semathites and Maserites
Semeber Gen 14 2 Semeber king of Seboim
Semegarnabu Jer 39 3 Neregel, Sereser, S.
Semei Exod 6 17 sons of Gerson: Lobni and S. 1 Pa 6:17
Num 3 18 the sons of Gerson: Lebni and Semei
2 K 16 5 of the house of Saul named Semei
7 thus said S. when he cursed the king
13 Semei by the hill's side went over
19 16 Semei . . . made haste and went down
18 Semei . . . falling down before the king
21 shall Semei for these words not be
23 king said to Semei: Thou shalt not die
3 K 1 8 Nathan the prophet and Semei and Rei
2 8 hast also with thee S. the son of Gera
36 king also sent and called for Semei
38 Semei said to the king: The saying
38 Semei dwelt in Jerusalem many days
39 servants of Semei ran away to Achis
39 it was told Semei that his servants
40 and Semei arose and saddled his ass
41 was told Solomon that Semei had gone
44 the king said to Semei: Thou knowest
4 18 Semei the son of Ela in Benjamin
1 Pa 2 28 Onam had sons Semei and Jada. And the
28 the sons of Semei. 4:27; 8:21; 23:9, 10
32 the sons of Jada the brother of Semei
3 19 of Phadaia were born Zorobabel and S.
4 26 sons of Masma . . . Semei his son, Zachur
his son, Semei his son
5 4 his son, Gog his son, Semei his son
6 29 Lobni his son, Semei his son, Oza
42 the son of Zamma, the son of Semei
23 7 sons of Gerson were Leedan and Semei
26 6 to Semei his son were born sons, heads
2 Pa 29 14 of the sons of Heman, Jahiel and S.
31 12 and Semei his brother was the second
13 under the hand of Chonenias and Semei
1 Es 10 23 Jozabed and Semei and Celaia, the same
33 Eliphelet, Jermai, Manassa, Semei
38 Jasi and Bani and Bennui, Semei, and
Esth 2 5 Jair the son of Semei. 11:2
Jer 26 20 Urias the son of S. of Cariathiarim
Zach 12 13 the families of Semei apart, and their
Luke 3 26 Mathathias, who was of Semei, who
Semeia 1 Pa 3 22 the son of Sechenias was Semeia
1 Pa 9 14 Semeia the son of Hassub, the son of
16 Semeia the son of Galal, the son of
15 11 Joel, Semeia, Eliel, and Aminadab
1 Es 10 21 Elia and Semeia and Jehiel and Ozias
2 Es 8 4 stood by him Mathathias and Semeia
10 8 Maazia, Belgia, Semeia: these were
11 15 of the Levites, Semeia the son of Hasub
12 6 Semeia and Joiarib, Idaia, Sellum
33 Benjamin and Semeia and Jeremias
34 Jonathan the son of Semeia, the son of
35 and his brethren Semeia and Azareel
41 and Maasia and Semeia and Eleazar
Semeias 3 K 12 22 the word of the Lord came to Semeias.
2 Pa 11:2; 12:7
1 Pa 15 8 of sons of Elisaphan, Semeias the chief
24 6 S. the son of Nathanael the scribe
25 17 the tenth to Semeias, to his sons and
26 4 sons of Obededom, S. the firstborn
7 the sons then of Semeias were Othni
27 27 the dressers of the vineyards, was S.
2 Pa 12 5 Semeias the prophet came to Roboam
15 are written in the books of Semeias
17 8 with them the Levites, Semeias and
29 14 the sons of Idithun, Semeias and Oziel
31 15 Benjamin, Jesue, and Semeias and
35 9 and S. and Nathanael, his brethren
1 Es 8 16 I sent Eliezer and Ariel and Semeias
10 31 Josue, Melchias, Semeias, Simeon
Jer 29 24 to S. the Nehelamite thou shalt say
31 because S. hath prophesied to you
31 saith the Lord to S. the Nehelamite
32 I will visit upon S. the Nehelamite
36 12 the scribe, and Dalaias the son of S.
Semeites Num 3 21 the Lebnites and the Semeites
Semer 3 K 16 24 bought the hill of Samaria of S.
3 K 16 24 built Samaria, after the name of Semer
Semeria 1 Es 10 41 Ezrel, and Selemiau, S.
Semeron Josu 11 1 Madon, and to the king of S.
Josu 12 20 the king of Semeron one, the king
19 15 and Cateth and Naalol and Semeron
2 Pa 13 4 Abia stood upon mount Semeron, which
Semida Num 26 32 S., of whom is the family of the
Josu 17 2 to the children of Semida: these are
1 Pa 7 19 the sons of Semida were Ahiu and
Semidaites Num 26 32 of whom is family of the S.
Semiramoth 1 Pa 15 18 Jaziel and S. and Jahiel
1 Pa 15 20 Oziel and S. and Jehiel and Ani and
16 5 Jahiel and S. and Jehiel and
2 Pa 17 8 S. and Jonathan and Adonias and
Semla Gen 36 36 in his stead, Semla of Masreca

1 Pa 1 47 Semla of Masreca reigned in his stead
48 Semla also died, and Saul of Rohoboth
Semlai 1 Es 2 46 of Hagab, the children of S.
Semma 2 K 23 11 after him was S. the son of Age
2 K 23 25 Semma of Harodi, Elica of Harodi
33 Semma of Orori, Aliam the son of
Semmaa 2 K 13 3 Jonadab the son of Semmaa. 32
Semmaath 2 Pa 24 26 Zabad the son of Semmaath
Semran Num 26 24 S., of whom is the family of
Semranites Num 26 24 of whom is family of the S.
Semri 1 Pa 4 37 Idaia the son of Semri, the son
1 Pa 26 10 of the sons of Merari: Semri the chief
Semron Gen 46 13 Thola and Phua and Job and S.
Sen 1 K 7 12 laid it between Masphath and Sen
Senaa 1 Es 2 35 the children of Senaa. 7:38
senate 1 Ma 8 15 had made themselves a s. house
1 Ma 8 19 entered into the senate house. 12:3
2 Ma 1 10 the senate and Judas, to Aristobolus
11 27 Antiochus to the senate of the Jews
senators Prov 31 23 when he sitteth among the s.
Dan 6 7 s. and judges have consulted together
send Mat 8 31 send us into the herd of swine. And he
Mat 10 16 I send you as sheep in the midst of
34 that I came to send peace upon earth
34 not to send peace, but the sword
11 10 I send my angel before thy face. Mark 1:2; Luke 7:27
13 41 Son of man shall send his angels
23 34 I send to you prophets, and wise men
24 31 he shall send his angels with a
Mark 3 14 that he might send them to preach
5 12 send us into the swine, that we may
6 7 and began to send them two and two
13 27 and then shall he send his angels and
Luke 10 2 that he send laborers into his harvest
3 I send you as lambs among wolves. Carry
11 49 I will send to them prophets and
16 24 send Lazarus, that he may dip the tip
27 send him to my father's house, for
20 13 I will send my beloved son: it may be
24 49 I send the promise of my Father upon
John 12 30 that receiveth whomsoever I send
14 26 whom the Father will send in my name
15 26 whom I will send you from the Father
16 7 but if I go, I will send him to you
17 8 have believed that thou didst send me
20 21 Father hath sent me, I also send you
Acts 3 20 he shall s. him who hath been preached
7 34 come, and I will send thee into Egypt
10 5 now send men to Joppe, and call hither
22 send for thee into his house, and to
32 s. to Joppe, and call hither Simon. 11:13
11 29 purposed to send relief to the brethren
15 22 to send to Antioch, with Paul and
25 men, and to send them unto you, with
22 21 unto Gentiles afar off, will I send thee
24 25 a convenient time, I will send for thee
25 21 to be kept, till I might send him to
25 Augustus, I have determined to send him
26 17 the nations, unto which now I send thee
1 C 16 3 I send to carry your grace to Jerusalem
Phil 2 19 I hope in the Lord Jesus to send Timothy
23 him therefore I hope to send unto you
25 necessary to send to you Epaphroditus
2 Th 2 10 shall send them the operation of error
Titus 3 12 when I shall send to thee Artemas or
13 send forward Zenas, the lawyer, and
Apoc 1 11 and send to the seven churches which
11 10 and shall send gifts one to another
send away Gen 24 56 s. me away, that I may go to
Gen 30 25 send me away that I may return into my
1 K 5 11 send away the ark of the God of Israel
6 3 send it not away empty, but render
8 and send it away that it may go. And
20 13 will send thee away that thou mayest
2 K 3 24 why didst thou send him [Abner] away
11 12 and tomorrow I will send thee away
Job 14 20 his face, and shalt send him away
24 7 they send men away naked, taking away
Eccu 29 12 send him not away empty handed because
Jer 28 16 I will send thee away from off the
Dan 13 21 thou didst send away thy maids from
Mat 14 15 s. a. multitudes, that going. Luke 9:12
15 23 send her away, for she crieth after us
32 I will not send them away fasting
Mark 6 36 send them away, that going into the
8 3 if I shall send them away fasting
send back Gen 43 14 s. back with you your brother
1 K 6 2 how we are to send it back to its place
3 if you send back the ark of the God
Jer 37 19 send me not back into the house of
1 Ma 12 45 send them back to their own houses
send forth Deut 28 8 Lord will s. forth a blessing
Jdth 16 17 thou didst send forth thy spirit, and
Job 20 23 that God may send forth the wrath of
39 3 they cast them and send forth roarings
Ps 42 3 send forth thy light and thy truth
103 30 thou shalt send forth thy spirit, and
109 2 the Lord will send forth the scepter
143 6 send forth lightning, and thou shalt
Eccu 11 32 send forth stinking breath and as
39 19 send forth flowers, as the lily, and
Isa 16 1 send forth, O Lord, the lamb, the
Amos 8 11 I will send forth a famine into the
Mat 9 38 that he send forth laborers into his
12 20 till he send forth judgment unto victory
James 3 11 doth a fountain send forth, out of
sendest Deut 15 13 when thou sendest him out free
4 K 1 6 that thou s. to Beelzebub the god of
Ps 103 10 thou sendest forth springs in the vales
sendeth Ps 147 15 who s. forth his speech to the
Ps 147 17 he sendeth his crystal like morsels
Prov 26 6 that s. words by a foolish messenger
Eccu 24 37 who s. knowledge as the light and
43 14 s. forth swiftly the lightnings of
Isa 18 2 that sendeth ambassadors by the sea
Bar 3 33 he that sendeth forth light, and it
Mark 11 1 he sendeth two of his disciples. 14:13
sending Gen 37 32 s. some to carry it to their
Gen 44 4 Joseph sending for the steward of his
45 23 sending to his father as much money
Exod 23 28 sending out hornets before, that shall
Num 13 4 sending from the desert of Pharan
Josu 2 21 sending them on their way, she hung
5 8 sending, they gathered together all
3 K 2 42 sending he called for him [Semei] and
20 2 and sending messengers to Achab king
1 Pa 21 26 sending fire from heaven upon the altar
1 Es 4 17 king . . . sending greeting and peace
Job 1 4 sending they called their three sisters
Wisd 11 19 or sending forth a stinking smoke
Isa 32 20 sending thither the foot of the ox
Jer 7 25 day to day, rising up early and sending
25 4 rising early and sending, and you have
26 5 sending, and you have not hearkened
29 19 rising by night and sending: and you
35 15 sending and saying: Return ye every
37 16 Sedecias . . . sending, took him: and
44 4 rising early and sending and saying
Mat 2 8 sending them into Bethlehem, said: Go
16 sending killed the men children that
11 2 sending two of his disciples he said
22 7 sending his armies, he destroyed those
Mark 4 36 sending away the multitude, they take
6 27 sending an executioner, he commanded
15 44 sending for the centurion, he asked

Josu 2 1 sent from Setim two men to spy secretly
3 and the king of Jericho sent to Rahab
7 they that were sent, pursued after them
6 17 she hid the messengers whom we sent
22 two men that had been sent for spies
25 whom he had sent to spy out Jericho
7 2 and when Josue sent men from Jericho
22 Josue therefore sent ministers: who
8 3 he sent 30,000 chosen valiant men
10 3 Adonisedec . . . sent to Oham king of
6 but the inhabitants . . . sent to Josue
11 1 he [Jabin] sent to Jobab king of Madon
14 7 sent me from Cadesbarne to view the
11 time when I was sent to view the land
22 13 sent to them into the land of Galaad
24 5 I sent Moses and Aaron, and I struck
9 [Balac] sent and called for Balaam
12 I sent before you hornets: and I drove
Judg 3 15 children of Israel sent presents to
4 6 she [Debbora] sent and called Barac
6 8 sent unto them a prophet, and he spoke
14 know that I have sent thee [Gedeon]
7 22 Lord sent the sword into all the camp
9 23 Lord sent a very evil spirit between
11 14 Jephte again sent word by them and
17 he sent also to the king of Moab, who
28 words of Jephte, which he sent him by
12 9 daughters, whom he sent abroad and
16 18 she [Dalila] sent to the princes of
18 2 children of Dan sent five most valiant
14 had been sent to view the land of Lais
19 29 sent the pieces into all the borders
21 10 they sent 10,000 of the most valiant
1 K 4 4 the people s. to Silo and they brought
5 10 they sent the ark of God into Accaron
11 they sent . . . and gathered together all
11 7 in pieces, and sent them into all the
12 8 and the Lord sent Moses and Aaron
11 the Lord sent Jerobaal and Badan and
20 so Saul sent officers to take David
20 22 in peace for the Lord hath sent thee
29 one of my brethren hath sent for me
21 2 the thing for which thou art sent by me
22 11 the king sent to call for Achimelech
25 5 he sent ten young men and said to them
32 who sent thee this day to meet me and
39 David sent and treated with Abigail
40 David hath sent us to thee [Abigail]
26 4 he [David] sent spies and learned that
30 26 David . . . sent presents of the prey
31 9 sent into the land of the Philistines
2 K 3 15 Isboseth sent and took her [Michol]
8 10 Thou sent Joram his son to king David
10 2 David sent his servants to comfort him
3 thinkest David hath sent comforters
3 rather sent . . . to search and spy into
5 [David] sent to meet them: for the men
6 children of Ammon . . . sent and hired
7 he sent Joab and the whole army of
16 Adarezer sent and fetched the Syrians
11 1 David sent Joab and his servants with
3 king sent and inquired who the woman
5 [Bethsabee] sent and told David and
6 David sent to Joab, saying: Send me
6 Joab sent Urias to David. And Urias
14 sent it by the hand of Urias, writing
18 then Joab sent, and told David all
27 David s. and brought her into his house
12 1 Lord sent Nathan to David, and when
25 sent by the hand of Nathan the prophet
13 7 then David sent home to Thamar, saying
14 2 Joab . . . sent to Thecua and fetched
29 he sent therefore to Joab to send him
29 when he had sent the second time, and
32 I sent to thee beseeching thee to come
15 10 Absalom sent spies into all the tribes
12 Absalom also sent for Achitophel the
18 2 David . . . sent forth a third part of
29 when thy servant Joab s. me thy servant
19 11 David sent to Sadoc . . . saying: Speak
14 they sent to the king, saying: Return
22 17 he sent from on high and took me and
24 13 answer I shall return to him that s. me
15 the Lord sent a pestilence upon Israel
3 K 1 44 hath sent with him Sadoc the priest
53 king Solomon sent and brought him out
2 29 Solomon sent Banaias the son of Joiada
36 the king also sent and called for Semei
5 1 Hiram . . . sent his servants to Solomon
2 Solomon sent to Hiram, saying: Thou
8 Hiram sent to Solomon, saying: I have
14 he sent them to Libanus, 10,000 every
7 13 Solomon s. and brought Hiram from Tyre
9 14 Hiram sent to king Solomon 120 talents
27 Hiram sent his servants in the fleet
12 3 they sent and called him [Jeroboam]. 20
18 Roboam sent Aduram, who was over the
14 6 I am sent to thee with heavy tidings
15 18 his servants: and sent them to Benadad
19 therefore I have sent thee presents of
20 Benadad . . . s. the captains of his army
22 king Asa sent word into all Juda, saying
18 10 whither my lord hath not sent to seek
20 Achab sent to all the children of Israel
19 2 Jezabel sent a messenger to Elias
20 5 saith Benadad, who sent us unto thee
7 he sent to me for my wives and for my
10 [Benadad] sent again and said: Such
17 Benadad sent. And they told him, saying
21 8 letters . . . and s. them to the ancients
11 the letters which she had sent to them
14 they sent to Jezabel, saying: Naboth is
4 K 1 6 and return to the king, that sent you
9 he sent to him [Elias] a captain of
11 he sent to him another captain of fifty
13 he sent a third captain of fifty men
2 2 the Lord hath sent me as far as Bethel
4 because the Lord hath sent me to Jericho
6 Lord hath sent me as far as the Jordan
17 they sent 50 men: and they sought three
3 7 and he sent to Josaphat king of Juda
5 6 know that I have sent to thee Naaman
7 this man hath sent to me, to heal a man
8 he [Eliseus] sent to him, saying: Why
10 Eliseus sent a messenger to him, saying
22 my master hath sent me to thee, saying
6 9 man of God sent to the king of Israel
10 king of Israel sent to the place which
14 he sent thither horses and chariots and
32 sat with him. So he sent a man before
32 murderer hath sent to cut off my head
7 14 the king sent into the camp of the
8 9 Benadad . . . hath s. me to thee, saying
9 19 he sent a second chariot of horses
10 1 Jehu . . . sent to Samaria to the chief
5 the rulers . . . sent to Jehu, saying: We
7 sent them to him [Jehu] to Jezrahel
21 he sent into all the borders of Israel
11 4 Joiada sent and taking the centurions
12 18 sent it to Hazael king of Syria, and he
14 9 king of Israel sent again to Amasias
9 a thistle of Libanus sent to a cedar
19 they sent after him to Lachis and killed
16 8 he sent it for a present to the king
10 king Achaz sent . . . a pattern of it
17 13 as I have sent to you in the hand of my

25 the Lord sent lions among them, which
26 the Lord hath sent lions among them
18 17 king of the Assyrians sent Tharthan
27 hath my master sent me to thy master
19 2 he [Ezechias] sent Eliacim . . . to Isaias
4 hath sent to reproach the living God
16 who hath sent to upbraid . . . the living
20 Isaias . . . sent to Ezechias, saying
22 3 the king sent Saphan . . . the scribe of
15 tell the man that sent you to me
18 who sent you to consult the Lord
23 1 he sent. And all the ancients of Juda
16 he sent and took the bones out of the
24 2 Lord sent against him the rovers of the
2 he sent them against Juda, to destroy
1 Pa 10 9 sent it into their land to be carried
12 19 Philistines taking counsel s. him back
18 10 he sent Adoram his son to king David
19 3 that David . . . hath sent comforters to
5 they sent word to David, who sent to meet
them
6 Hanon . . . sent 1,000 talents of silver
8 when David heard of it, he sent Joab
21 12 what I shall answer him who sent me
14 the Lord sent a pestilence upon Israel
15 he sent an angel to Jerusalem to strike
2 Pa 2 3 he sent also to Hiram king of Tyre
11 king of Tyre sent a letter to Solomon
13 have sent thee my father Hiram, a wise
8 18 Hiram sent him ships by the hands of
10 3 they sent for him and he came with all
18 king Roboam sent Aduram who was over
16 2 [Asa] sent to Benadad king of Syria
3 I have sent thee silver and gold
4 he sent the captains of his armies
17 7 he sent of his princes Benhail and
24 19 he sent prophets to them to bring
23 they sent all the spoils to the king of
25 13 that army which Amasias had sent back
15 against Amasias, sent a prophet to him
17 sent to Joas . . . saying: Come, let us
18 the thistle . . . sent to the cedar in
18 but he [Joas] sent back the messengers
27 they sent and killed him [Amasias] there
28 16 Achaz sent to the . . . Assyrians asking
30 1 Ezechias sent to all Israel and Juda
32 9 Sennacherib . . . sent his servants to
21 the Lord sent an angel, who cut off
31 that were sent to him to inquire of
34 8 he sent Saphan the son of Eselias
22 Helcias and they that were sent with
23 tell the man that sent you to me
26 as to the king of Juda that sent you
36 10 Nabuchodonosor sent and brought him
15 God of their fathers sent to them
1 Es 4 11 copy of the letter which they sent
14 therefore sent and certified the king
17 the king sent word to Reum Beelteem
18 accusation which you have sent to us
5 6 the letter . . . sent to Darius the king
7 the letter which they sent him was
7 14 thou art sent from before the king
8 16 I sent Eliezer and Ariel and Semeias
17 I sent them to Eddo, who is chief in
2 Es 2 6 and it pleased the king, and he sent me
9 the king had sent with me captains of
6 2 Sanaballat . . . sent to me saying: Come
4 they sent to me according to this word
5 Sanaballat sent his servant to me the
8 I sent to them, saying: There is no
12 I understood that God had not sent him
17 letters were sent by the principal men
Tob 3 25 Raphael was sent to heal them both
5 24 money, for which thou hast sent him
8 15 so she sent one of her maidservants
10 6 with whom we sent him is very trusty
12 14 the Lord hath sent me to heal thee
20 that I return to him that sent me
Jdth 1 7 he sent to all that dwelt in Cilicia
11 sent them back empty and rejected them
3 1 sent their ambassadors, who coming
4 3 they sent into all Samaria round about
8 9 she sent to the ancients Chabri and
11 8 that he hath sent word by his prophets
13 Lord hath sent me to tell thee these
17 I am sent to tell these very things to
20 God hath done well who sent thee
15 6 every city sent their chosen young men
Job 1 5 Job sent to them and sanctified them
22 9 thou hast sent widows away empty, and
39 5 who hath sent out the wild ass free
Ps 17 15 and he sent forth his arrows, and he
17 he sent from on high, and took me
56 4 he hath sent from heaven and delivered
4 God hath sent his mercy and his truth
58 1 when Saul sent and watched his house
76 18 the waters: the clouds sent out a sound
77 25 he sent them provisions in abundance
45 he sent amongst them divers sorts of
49 he sent upon them the wrath of his
49 trouble, which he sent by evil angels
104 17 he sent a man before them: Joseph, who
20 the king sent and he released him
26 sent Moses his servant: Aaron the man
28 he sent darkness, and made it obscure
105 15 and sent fulness into their souls
106 20 he sent his word and healed them
110 9 he hath sent redemption to his people
118 136 my eyes have sent forth springs of
134 9 he sent forth signs and wonders in the
Prov 9 3 she hath sent her maids to invite to
10 26 is the sluggard to them that sent him
17 11 cruel angel shall be sent against him
22 21 to answer . . . to them that sent thee
25 13 faithful messenger to him that sent
Cant 1 11 my spikenard sent forth the odor
Wisd 12 25 hast sent a judgment upon them as
16 3 that were shown and sent among them
18 which were sent against the wicked
Eccu 28 27 it shall be sent upon them as a lion
34 6 vision sent forth from the most High
48 20 came up and sent Rabsaces and lifted
Isa 9 8 the Lord sent a word into Jacob and
20 1 when Sargon . . . had sent him, and he
28 2 and sent forth upon a spacious land
36 2 king of the Assyrians sent Rabsaces
12 hath my master sent me to thy master
37 2 he sent Eliacim . . . to Isaias the son
4 sent to blaspheme the living God. 17
21 Isaias . . . sent to Ezechias, saying
43 14 for your sake I sent to Babylon and
48 16 and now the Lord God hath sent me
55 11 in the things for which I sent it
61 1 he hath sent me to preach to the meek
Jer 7 25 I have sent to you all my servants
14 14 falsely in my name: I sent them not
19 14 whither the Lord had sent him to
21 1 king Sedecias sent unto him Phassur
23 32 when I sent them not nor commanded
38 I have sent to you, saying: Say not
24 5 whom I have sent forth out of this
25 4 Lord hath sent to you all his servants
17 drink of it, to which the Lord sent me
26 5 the prophets, whom I sent to you
12 Lord sent me to prophesy concerning
15 the Lord sent me to you to speak all

22 king Joakim sent men into Egypt
27 15 I have not sent them, saith the Lord
28 9 whom the Lord hath sent in truth
15 the Lord hath not sent thee, and thou
29 1 letter which Jeremias the prophet sent
3 whom Sedecias . . . sent to Babylon to
9 my name: and I have not sent them
19 which I sent to them by my servants
20 whom I have sent out from Jerusalem
28 he hath also sent to us in Babylon
31 prophesied to you, and I sent him not
35 15 I have sent to you all my servants
36 14 all the princes sent Judi the son of
21 the king sent Judi that he should
37 3 Sedecias sent Juchal . . . to Jeremias
6 who sent you to inquire of me: Behold
38 14 king Sedecias sent and took Jeremias
39 13 Nabuzardan the general sent, and
14 sent and took Jeremias out of the
40 10 the Chaldeans that are sent to us: but
14 hath sent Ismahel . . . to kill thee
42 9 God of Israel to whom you sent me
20 for you sent me to the Lord our God
21 the things for which he hath sent me
43 1 for which the Lord . . . had sent him
2 our God hath not sent thee, saying
44 4 I sent to you all my servants the
49 14 an ambassador is sent to the nations
Lam 1 13 he hath sent fire into my bones, and
Bar 1 7 they sent it to Jerusalem to Joakim
10 we have sent you money, buy with it
14 this book, which we have sent to you
21 of the prophets whom he sent to us
2 20 because thou hast sent out thy wrath
4 23 I sent you forth with mourning and
6 1 epistle that Jeremias sent to them
59 and sent forth for profitable uses
62 the fire also being sent from above
Eze 2 9 and behold a hand was sent to me
3 5 thou art not sent to a people of a
6 if thou wert sent to them, they would
13 6 whereas the Lord hath not sent them
17 15 and sent ambassadors to Egypt, that
23 40 they sent for men coming from afar
40 to whom they had sent a messenger
31 4 it sent forth its rivulets to all the
Dan 3 2 king sent to call together the nobles
95 hath sent his angel and delivered his
5 24 he hath sent the part of the hand which
6 22 my God hath sent his angel and hath
10 11 upright: for I am sent now to thee
13 29 presently they sent. And she came with
14 36 take the dinner that God hath sent thee
Osee 5 13 and sent to the avenging king: and he
Joel 2 25 my great host which I sent upon you
Amos 4 10 I sent death upon you in the way of
7 10 Amasias . . . sent to Jeroboam king
Abdi 1 he hath sent an ambassador to the
7 they have sent thee out even to the
13 thou shalt not be sent out against
Jon 1 4 the Lord sent a great wind into the sea
Mich 6 4 I sent before thy face Moses and
Agge 1 12 the Lord their God sent him to them
Zach 1 10 the Lord hath sent to walk through
2 8 he hath sent me to the nations that
know that the Lord of hosts sent me
9 know that the Lord of hosts sent me
11 Lord of hosts hath sent me to thee
4 9 Lord of hosts hath sent me to you
6 15 the Lord of hosts sent me to you
7 2 sent to the house of God to entreat
12 words which the Lord of hosts sent
9 11 hast sent forth thy prisoners out
Mala 2 4 know that I sent you this commandment

1 Ma 1 30 the king sent the chief collector
2 15 that were sent from king Antiochus
17 they that were sent from Antiochus
25 man whom king Antiochus had sent
3 27 he sent and gathered the forces of
39 he sent with them 40,000 men and
5 38 and Judas sent men to view the army
47 and Judas sent to them with peaceable
6 12 I sent to destroy the inhabitants of
60 and he sent to them to make peace
7 8 chose Bacchides . . . and he sent him
19 he sent and took many of them that
26 and the king sent Nicanor one of his
27 he sent to Judas and to his brethren
41 that were sent by king Sennacherib
8 10 they sent a general against them and
17 he sent them to Rome to make a league
20 have sent us to you to make alliance
22 tables of brass and sent to Jerusalem
9 1 he sent again Bacchides and Alcimus
35 Jonathan sent his brother a captain
63 sent word to them that were of Judea
70 sent ambassadors to him to make peace
10 3 Demetrius sent a letter to Jonathan
17 wrote a letter and sent it to him
20 he sent him a purple robe and a crown
51 Alexander sent ambassadors to Ptolemee
69 he sent to Jonathan the high priest
89 he sent him a buckle of gold as the
11 9 and he sent ambassadors to Demetrius
17 Alexander's head, and sent it to
41 and Jonathan sent to king Demetrius
42 Demetrius sent to Jonathan, saying: I
44 Jonathan sent him 3,000 valiant men
58 he sent him vessels of gold for his
62 sons . . . and sent them to Jerusalem
12 1 certain men and sent them to Rome
3 Jews have sent us to renew the amity
7 were letters sent long ago to Onias
10 long time passed since you sent to us
16 have sent them to the Romans to renew
19 the letter which he had sent to Onias
26 and he sent spies into their camp
47 of whom he sent 2,000 into Galilee
49 Tryphon sent an army and horsemen
13 11 he sent Jonathan the son of Absalom
17 the money and the children to be sent
18 because he sent not the money and
19 sent the children and the 100 talents
25 and Simon sent and took the bones of
34 sent to king Demetrius, to the end
37 crown and the palm which you sent, we
14 2 he sent one of his princes to take
19 of the letters that the Spartans sent
21 ambassadors that were sent to our
24 Simon sent Numenius to Rome with a
15 17 being sent from Simon the high priest
26 Simon sent to him 2,000 chosen men
28 he sent to him Athenobius one of his
16 18 sent to the king that he should send
19 he sent others to Gazara to kill John
20 and he sent others to take Jerusalem
21 he hath sent men to kill thee also
2 Ma 1 20 that Nehemias should be sent by the
20 he sent some of the posterity of those
3 7 sent him with commission to bring him
37 to be sent yet once more to Jerusalem
4 19 the wicked Jason sent from Jerusalem
20 sent it to the sacrifice of Hercules
21 Apollonius . . . was sent into Egypt to
23 sent Menelaus . . . to carry money to
44 three men were sent from the ancients
5 18 who was sent by king Seleucus to rob

24 he sent that hateful prince Apollonius
6 1 king sent a certain old man of Antioch
23 rather be sent into the other world
8 9 and he with all speed sent Nicanor
11 he sent immediately to the cities upon
11 13 [Lysias] sent to them and promised
17 who were sent from you, delivering
20 these and to them that are sent by me
32 we have sent also Menelaus to speak
34 the Romans also sent them a letter
12 21 he sent the women and children and
43 he sent 12,000 drachms of silver to
13 20 Judas sent necessaries to them that
14 12 he sent Nicanor . . . into Judea: going
19 he sent Posidonius . . . to present
39 sent 500 soldiers to take him. For
Mat 10 5 these twelve Jesus sent: commanding
40 me, receiveth him that sent me
14 10 he sent and beheaded John in the prison
35 they sent into all that country and
15 24 I was not sent but to the sheep that
20 2 he sent them into his vineyard. And
21 1 Jesus sent two disciples, saying to
34 he sent his servants to the husbandmen
36 he sent other servants more than the
37 last of all he sent to them his son
22 3 he sent his servants to call them that
4 again he sent other servants, saying
16 they sent to him their disciples with
23 37 stonest them that are sent unto thee
26 47 sent from the chief priests and the
27 19 his wife sent to him, saying: Have
Mark 3 31 standing without, sent unto him
6 17 had sent and apprehended John and
8 26 he sent him into his house, saying
9 36 receiveth not me, but him that s. me
12 2 he sent to the husbandmen a servant to
4 again he sent to them another servant
5 he sent another, and him they killed
6 he also sent him unto them last of all
13 they sent to him some of the Pharisees
Luke 1 19 and am sent to speak to thee and to
26 Gabriel was sent from God into a city
4 18 he hath sent me to heal the contrite
26 to none of them was Elias sent, but
43 for therefore am I sent. And he was
7 3 he sent unto him the ancients of the
6 centurion sent his friends to him
10 they who were sent, being returned
19 and sent them to Jesus, saying: Art
20 John the Baptist hath sent us to thee
9 2 he sent them to preach the kingdom
48 receiveth him that sent me. For he
52 he sent messengers before his face
10 1 he sent them two and two before his
16 me, despiseth him that sent me. And
13 34 and stonest them that are sent to thee
14 17 he sent his servant at the hour of
15 15 sent him into his farm to feed swine
19 14 they sent an embassage after him
29 he sent two of his disciples, saying
32 they that were sent, went their way
20 10 at the season he sent a servant to the
11 and again he sent another servant
12 he sent the third; and they wounded
20 they sent spies, who would feign
22 8 he sent Peter and John, saying: Go
35 when I sent you without purse and
23 11 garment, and sent him back to Pilate
15 I sent you to him, and behold, nothing
John 1 6 there was a man sent from God, whose
19 when the Jews sent from Jerusalem
22 give an answer to them that sent us
24 that were sent were of the Pharisees
33 he who sent me to baptize with water
3 28 Christ, but that I am sent before him
34 he whom God hath sent, speaketh the
4 34 to do the will of him that sent me
38 I have sent you to reap that in which
5 23 the Father, who hath sent him. Amen
24 and believeth him that sent me, hath
30 but the will of him that sent me. If I
33 you sent to John, and he gave testimony
36 of me, that the Father hath sent me
37 the Father himself who hath sent me
38 whom he hath sent, him you believe not
6 29 you believe in him whom he hath sent
38 but the will of him that sent me
39 the will of the Father who sent me
40 the will of my Father that sent me
44 the Father, who sent me, draw him
58 as the living Father hath sent me
7 16 is not mine, but his that sent me
18 the glory of him that sent him, he is
28 he that sent me is true, whom you
29 I am from him, and he hath sent me
32 rulers and Pharisees sent ministers
33 and then I go to him that sent me
8 16 but I and the Father that sent me
18 Father that sent me giveth testimony
26 he that sent me, is true: and the
29 he that sent me, is with me and he
42 I came not of myself, but he sent me
9 7 of Siloe, which is interpreted, Sent
10 36 the Father hath sanctified and sent
11 3 his sisters therefore sent to him
42 may believe that thou hast sent me
12 44 believe in me, but in him that sent me
45 that seeth me, seeth him that sent me
49 the Father who sent me, he gave me
13 16 apostle greater than he that sent him
20 me, receiveth him that sent me. When
14 24 not mine; but the Father's who sent me
15 21 they know not him that sent me. If I
16 5 and now I go to him that sent me, and
17 3 and Jesus Christ, whom thou hast sent
18 as thou hast sent me into the world
18 I also have sent them into the world
21 may believe that thou hast sent me
23 world may know that thou hast sent me
25 have known that thou hast sent me
18 24 Annas sent him bound to Caiphas the
20 21 as the Father hath sent me, I also
Acts 3 26 his Son, hath sent him to bless you
5 21 s. to the prison to have them brought
7 12 in Egypt, he sent our fathers first
35 him God sent to be prince and redeemer
8 14 they sent unto them Peter and John
9 17 Saul, the Lord Jesus hath sent me, he
38 sent unto him two men, desiring him
10 8 had related all, he sent them to Joppe
17 the men who were sent from Cornelius
20 doubting nothing: for I have s. them
29 no doubt, I came when I was sent for
29 for what cause you have sent for me
33 I sent to thee: and thou hast done
36 God sent the word to the children of
11 11 wherein I was, sent to me from Caesarea
22 they sent Barnabas as far as Antioch
12 11 the Lord hath sent his angel, and hath
13 4 they being sent by the Holy Ghost
15 rulers of the synagogue sent to them
26 the word of this salvation is sent
15 27 we have sent therefore Judas and Silas
33 brethren, unto them that had s. them
16 35 magistrates sent the serjeants, saying

36 magistrates have sent to let you go
19 31 sent unto him, desiring that he would
23 30 I sent him to thee, signifying also to
24 24 sent for Paul, and heard of him faith
28 28 salvation of God is sent to the Gentiles
Rom 10 15 how shall they preach unless they be s.
2 C 8 18 we have sent also with him the brother
22 we have sent with them our brother also
9 3 now I have sent the brethren, that the
12 17 you by any of them whom I sent to you
18 Titus, and I sent with him a brother
Gal 4 4 God sent his Son, made of a woman, made
6 God hath sent the Spirit of his Son into
Eph 6 22 whom I have sent to you for this same
Phil 2 28 I sent him the more speedily: that
4 16 unto Thessalonica also you sent once
18 things you sent, an order of sweetness
Col 4 8 whom I have sent to you for this same
1 Th 3 2 and we sent Timothy, our brother, and
5 sent to know your faith: lest perhaps
2 Th 2 2 nor by epistle, as sent from us, as if
2 Tim 4 12 but Tychicus I have sent to Ephesus
Philem 12 whom I have sent back to thee. And do
Heb 1 14 spirits, sent to minister for them, who
1 P 1 12 the Holy Ghost being sent down from
2 14 or to governors as sent by him for the
1 J 4 9 God hath sent his only begotten Son
10 sent his Son to be a propitiation for
14 that the Father hath sent his Son to
Apoc 5 6 of God, sent forth into all the earth
22 6 sent his angel to show his servants the
16 have sent my angel to testify to you
sent away Gen 21 14 the boy and sent her away
Gen 24 59 so they sent her away, and her nurse
26 29 but with peace have sent thee away
31 Isaac sent them away peaceably to
28 5 when Isaac had sent him away, he took
31 42 now thou hadst sent me away naked
44 3 they were sent away with their asses
45 24 so he sent away his brethren, and at
Josu 8 9 he sent them away, and they went
22 6 Josue blessed them and sent them away
7 when he [Josue] sent them away to
24 28 he sent the people away every one to
Judg 1 26 who being sent away, went into the
2 6 Josue sent away the people, and the
11 38 and he sent her away for two months
1 K 10 25 and Samuel sent away all the people
20 22 for the Lord hath sent thee away. And
2 K 3 2 [David] had now sent him [Abner] away
23 hath sent him [Abner] away, and he is
10 4 to the buttocks and sent them away
3 K 8 66 the eighth day he sent away the people
4 K 5 24 sent the men away, and they departed
1 Pa 8 8 he sent away Husim and Bara his wives
19 4 buttocks to the feet and s. them away
2 Pa 7 10 s. away the people to their dwellings
Tob 5 23 our old age, and sent him away from us
10 10 sent him away safe and joyful from him
Wisd 19 2 had sent them away with great care
Bar 4 11 but I sent them away with weeping and
Dan 13 36 and sent away the maids from her. Then
1 Ma 11 38 sent away all his forces, every man
55 hands which Demetrius had sent away
1 Ma 12 46 as he said: and sent away his army
2 Ma 14 23 but sent away the flocks of the
Mat 13 36 having sent away the multitudes, he
Mark 1 43 him, and forthwith sent him away. And
8 9 about 4,000; and he sent them away
12 3 sent him away empty. Luke 20:10, 11
Luke 8 38 but Jesus sent him away, saying: Return
14 4 healed him and sent him away. And
23 7 he sent him away to Herod, who was
Acts 4 21 they threatening, sent them away, not
9 30 to Caesarea, and sent him away to Tarsus
13 3 their hands upon them, s. them away
17 10 sent away Paul and Silas by night unto
14 immediately brethren sent away Paul
sent letters 4 K 20 12 sent letters and presents to Ezechias. Isa 39:1
2 Es 6 19 Tobias sent letters to put me in fear
Jer 29 25 because thou hast sent letters in thy
1 Ma 1 46 the king sent letters by the hands of
5 10 they sent letters to Judas and his
9 60 sent secretly letters to his adherents
12 2 he sent letters to the Spartans and to
15 1 sent letters from the isles of the sea
16 19 to the tribunes he sent letters to come
sent messengers; *see* **messengers**
sentence Gen 44 10 let it be according to your s.
Exod 21 31 he shall fall under the like sentence
Num 35 25 shall be brought by sentence into the
Deut 17 11 and thou shalt follow their sentence
Josu 11 20 it was the sentence of the Lord that
Judg 19 30 give sentence and decree in common
1 Es 4 21 hear the sentence: Hinder those men
Tob 2 8 scarce escape the sentence of death
Esth 1 15 what s. ought to pass upon Vasthi
16 9 we give s. according to the quality
Job 29 21 that heard me, waited for my sentence
33 3 my lips shall speak a pure sentence
Prov 15 23 a man rejoiceth in the s. of his mouth
Ecce 8 11 because s. is not speedily pronounced
Eccu 41 3 death, thy sentence is welcome to the
5 fear not the s. of death. Remember
5 this s. is from the Lord upon all flesh
Dan 2 9 there is one sentence concerning you
14 inquired concerning the law and the s.
15 why so cruel a sentence was gone forth
4 14 decree by the sentence of the watchers
21 interpretation of the s. of the most
6 8 confirm the s. and sign the decree
13 55 angel of God having received the s.
Luke 23 24 Pilate gave s. that it should be as
Acts 26 10 they were put to death, I brought the s.
sentences Job 38 2 is this that wrappeth up s.
Prov 26 16 than seven men that speak sentences
Dan 8 23 face, and understanding dark s. And
sentest Num 13 28 the land to which thou s. us
Num 24 12 messengers, whom thou sentest to me
1 K 25 25 thy servants, my lord, whom thou s.
Bar 4 37 whom thou sentest away scattered, they
sentiment Phil 2 2 one accord, agreeing in s.
sentinels 1 Ma 12 27 set s. round about the camp
Senua 2 Es 11 9 Judas the son of S. was second
Seon Josu 19 19 Hapharaim and S. and Anaharath
Seor Gen 23 8 Ephron the son of Seor. 25:9
Seorim 1 Pa 24 8 the fourth [lot] to Seorim
separate Gen 30 32 s. all the sheep of divers
Exod 29 27 shoulder that thou didst s. of the ram
Lev 20 25 do you also separate the clean beast
Num 8 14 shalt separate them from the midst of
15 19 you shall separate firstfruits to the
20 you s. firstfruits of your barnfloors
16 21 separate yourselves from among this
24 to s. themselves from the tents of Core
18 29 shall separate for the gifts of the
31 28 shalt separate a portion to the Lord
Deut 14 28 thou shalt separate another tithe of
19 2 shalt separate to thee three cities
7 that thou separate three cities at
1 K 15 32 doth bitter death s. in this manner
1 Es 10 11 s. yourselves from the people of the
Prov 20 3 for a man to s. himself from quarrels
Wisd 1 3 perverse thoughts separate from God
Eccu 6 13 separate thyself from thy enemies and

Isa 56 3 Lord will divide and s. me from his
Jer 15 19 if thou wilt s. the precious from the
Eze 14 7 if he s. himself from me and place
12 the building that was separate and
13 the separate building and the walls
14 the separate place toward the east
42 1 over against the separate building. 10
13 which are before the separate building
45 1 separate ye firstfruits to the Lord
9 separate your confines from my people
Dan 13 51 s. these two far from one another, and
1 Ma 12 36 to separate it from the city, that so
Mat 13 49 shall s. the wicked from among the just
24 51 s. him and appoint his. Luke 12:46
25 32 he shall s. them one from another
Luke 6 22 and when they shall separate you and
Acts 13 2 separate me Saul and Barnabas, for
Rom 8 35 who then shall s. us from love of Christ
39 shall be able to separate us from love
2 C 6 17 go out from among them, and be ye s.
Jude 19 who s. themselves, sensual men, having
separated Gen 13 11 s. one brother from the other
Gen 13 14 after Lot was separated from him
25 6 separated them from Isaac his son
30 35 separated the same day the she goats
40 Jacob separated the flock, and put
40 when the flocks were separated one
Lev 7 34 the shoulder that is s. I have taken
8 25 with the right shoulder he separated
9 21 Aaron separated their breasts and the
10 14 and the shoulder that is separated
13 3 upon his judgment he shall be separated
44 is s. by the judgment of the priest
15 19 of blood, shall be separated seven days
33 that is separated in her monthly times
20 24 have s. you from other people. 26
Num 6 20 breast, which was commanded to be s.
12 14 let her be s. seven days without the
18 24 which I have separated for their uses
31 42 which he had s. for them that had been
35 6 six shall be separated for refuge to
13 that are s. for the refuge of fugitives
36 10 as they were separated by the Lord
Deut 10 8 he s. the tribe of Levi, to carry
26 14 nor separated them for any uncleanness
32 8 when he separated the sons of Adam
Josu 16 9 s. for the children of Ephraim in the
Judg 17 5 he s. also therein a little temple
18 7 being very rich, and living separated
3 K 8 53 thou hast separated them to thyself
4 K 17 21 Jeroboam separated Israel from the Lord
1 Pa 23 13 Aaron was separated to minister in the
25 1 s. for the ministry the sons of Asaph
2 Pa 25 10 then Amasias separated the army that
35 12 they separated them to give them by
1 Es 6 21 had s. themselves from the filthiness
8 24 s. twelve of the chief of the priests
9 1 Levites have not s. themselves from
2 Es 4 19 we are s. on the wall one far from
9 2 separated themselves from every stranger
10 28 that had s. themselves from the people
13 3 they s. every stranger from Israel
30 I separated from them all strangers
Job 41 8 one another fast and shall not be s.
Ps 34 16 they were separated, and repented not
Eze 41 15 which was s. at the back of it: and
42 12 s. towards the east as one entereth
Osee 4 18 their banquet is s., they have gone
Amos 6 3 you that are s. unto the evil day
Zach 14 4 half of the mountain shall be s. to
Acts 19 9 he s. the disciples, disputing daily
Rom 1 1 an apostle, s. unto the gospel of God
Gal 1 15 who s. me from my mother's womb, and
2 12 withdrew and s. himself, fearing them
Heb 7 26 undefiled, separated from sinners and
separateth Prov 16 28 one full of words s. princes
Prov 17 9 he that repeateth it again, s. friends
Mat 25 32 as the shepherd s. the sheep from the
separation Lev 12 2 of the s. of her flowers
Lev 15 21 sitteth on in the days of her s. shall
Num 6 5 all the time of his s. no razor shall
8 all the days of his s. he shall be
12 to the Lord the days of his separation
Isa 7 17 time of the s. of Ephraim from Juda
Eze 42 20 a separation between the sanctuary and
45 7 according to the s. of the sanctuary. 7
7 over against the s. of the sanctuary
Osee 13 15 he shall make a s. between brothers
Luke 12 51 I tell you, no; but separation. For
Sephaath Judg 1 17 Chanaanites that dwelt in S.
Sepham 1 Pa 7 12 S. and Hapham the sons of Hir
Sephama Num 34 10 from the village of Enan unto S.
Num 34 11 from Sephama the bounds shall go down
Sephamoth 1 K 30 28 and that were in Sephamoth
Sephar Gen 10 30 Messa as we go on as far as S.
Sepharvaim 4 K 17 24 from Emuth and from S.
4 K 17 31 that were of Sepharvaim burnt their
31 and Anamelech the gods of Sepharvaim
18 34 where is the god of S. Isa 36:19
19 13 king of the city of S. Isa 37:13
Sephata 2 Pa 14 10 for battle in the vale of S.
Sephatia 1 Es 2 4 the children of Sephatia, 372. 2 Es 7:9
Sephei 1 Pa 4 37 Ziza also the son of Sephei
Sephela 1 Ma 12 38 Simon built Adiada in Sephela
Sepher Num 33 23 camped in the mountain Sepher
Num 33 24 departing from the mountain Sepher
Sephet Tob 1 1 on the right hand the city of S.
Sephi 1 Pa 1 36 Sephi, Gathan, Cenez, and
1 Pa 1 40 Manahath and Ebal, S. and Onam
Sephian Gen 46 16 the sons of Gad: Sephian
Sephim 1 Pa 26 16 to S. and Hosa towards the west
Sepho Gen 36 11 Eliphaz had sons: Theman, Omar, S.
Gen 36 15 duke Omar, duke Sepho, duke Cenez
23 Manahat and Ebal and Sepho and
Sephon Num 26 15 sons of Gad by their kindreds: S.
Sephonites Num 26 15 of him is family of the S.
Sephor Num 22 2 Balac the son of Sephor. 10, 16; Josu 24:9; Judg 11:25
Num 23 18 give ear: hear, thou son of Sephor
Sephora Exod 1 15 one was called S., the other
Exod 2 21 [Moses] took S. his daughter to wife
4 25 Sephora took a very sharp stone and
18 2 he took Sephora the wife of Moses whom
Sephtan Num 34 24 Camuel the son of Sephtan
Sephuphan 1 Pa 8 5 Gera and S. and Huram. These
Septhai 2 Es 8 7 Septhai, Odia, Maasia, Celtia
sepulcher Gen 23 6 from burying thy dead in his s.
Gen 35 20 Jacob erected a pillar over the s.
50 5 thou shalt bury me in my sepulcher
Deut 34 6 no man hath known of his sepulcher
Judg 8 32 buried in the sepulcher of his father
1 K 10 2 find two men by the sepulcher of Rachel
2 K 2 32 buried him in sepulcher of his father
4 12 buried in the s. of Abner in Hebron
17 23 was buried in sepulcher of his father
19 37 buried by the sepulcher of my father
21 14 in the sepulcher of Cis his father
3 K 13 22 not be brought into sepulcher of thy
30 laid his dead body in his own sepulcher
31 in the sepulcher wherein the man of God
14 13 of Jeroboam shall be laid in a s.
4 K 9 28 buried him [Ochozias] in his sepulcher
13 21 cast the body into sepulcher of Eliseus
21 26 and they buried him in his sepulcher
22 20 shalt be gathered to thy sepulcher
23 30 and buried him in his own sepulcher

17 it is the sepulcher of the man of God
2 Pa 16 14 they buried him in his own sepulcher
3 16 over against the sepulcher of David
2 Es 2 5 the city of the sepulcher of my father
Tob 14 12 your mother by me in one sepulcher
Ps 5 11 their throat is an open sepulcher. 13:3
87 12 shall any one in the s. declare thy
Isa 11 10 and his sepulcher shall be glorious
22 16 hast hewed thee out a sepulcher here
Jer 5 16 their quiver is as an open sepulcher
Eze 39 11 will give Gog a noted place for a s.
1 Ma 9 19 buried him in the s. of their fathers
13 27 Simon built over the s. of his father
30 the sepulcher that he made in Modin
2 Ma 5 10 nor being partaker of the s. of his
Mat 27 61 sitting over against the sepulcher
64 command therefore the s. to be guarded
66 made the s. sure, sealing the stone
28 1 and the other Mary to see the sepulcher
8 they went out quickly from the s. with
Mark 15 46 laid him in a s. which was hewed out
46 rolled a stone to the door of the s.
16 2 they come to the s., the sun being
3 stone from the door of the sepulcher
5 entering into the s., they saw a young
8 going out, fled from the sepulcher
Luke 23 53 laid him in a s. that was hewed in
55 saw the s., and how his body was laid
24 1 they came to the s., bringing the
2 found the stone rolled back from the s.
9 going back from the s., they told all
12 Peter rising up, ran to the sepulcher
22 before it was light, were at the s.
24 some of our people went to the s. and
John 11 38 Jesus . . . cometh to the sepulcher
19 41 a new s. wherein no man yet had been
42 because the s. was nigh at hand. And
20 1 it was yet dark, unto the sepulcher
1 saw the stone taken away from the s.
2 taken away the Lord out of the s.
3 and they came to the sepulcher. And
4 and came first to the sepulcher. And
6 went into the s. and saw the linen
8 who came first to the sepulcher: and
11 Mary stood at the s. without, weeping
11 stooped down and looked into the s.
Acts 2 29 his s. is with us to this present day
7 16 the sepulcher that Abraham bought for
13 29 from the tree, they laid him in a s.
Rom 3 13 their throat is an open sepulcher; with
sepulchers Gen 23 6 thy dead in our principal s.
4 K 23 16 the sepulchers that were in the mount
16 took the bones out of the sepulchers
2 Pa 21 20 but not in the s. of the kings. 24:25
26 23 buried him in the field of the royal s.
28 27 the sepulchers of the kings of Israel
32 33 above the sepulchers of sons of David
2 Es 2 3 city of place of the s. of my fathers
Ps 48 12 their sepulchers shall be their houses
67 7 that provoke, that dwell in sepulchers
87 6 like the slain sleeping in the s.
Isa 65 4 that dwell in sepulchers and sleep in
Eze 37 12 will bring you out of your s., O my
13 when I shall have opened your s.
1 Ma 2 70 in the s. of his fathers in Modin
2 Ma 12 39 in the sepulchers of their fathers
Mat 8 28 coming out of the s., exceeding fierce
23 27 you are like to whited sepulchers
29 that build the s. of the prophets and
Luke 8 27 he abide in a house, but in the s.
11 44 you are as s. that appear not, and
48 killed them, and you build their s.
Apoc 11 9 not suffer their bodies to be laid in s.

Ser Josu 29 35 the strong cities are Assedim, Ser
Seraias 4 K 25 18 the general of the army took S.
seraphims Isa 6 2 upon it stood the seraphims
Isa 6 6 one of the seraphims flew to me, and in
Serebia 2 Es 8 7 Josue and Bani and S., Jamin
2 Es 9 5 Hasebnia, Serebia, Oduia, Sebma and
10 12 Zachur, Serebia, Sabania, Odaia
12 24 chief of the Levites were Hasebia, S.
Sereser Jer 39 3 Neregel, S., Semegarnabu
Jer 39 13 Rabsares and Neregel and Sereser
Sereth 1 Pa 4 7 sons of Halaa, Sereth, Isaar
Serezer Jer 39 3 Rabsares, Neregel, Serezer
Sergius Acts 13 7 with the proconsul S. Paulus
seriously Prov 21 12 considereth s. the house of
serjeants Acts 16 35 magistrates sent the s.
Acts 16 38 the s. told these words to magistrates
Seron 1 Ma 3 13 S. captain of the army of Syria
1 Ma 3 23 Seron and his host were overthrown
Seror 1 K 9 1 son of Abiel, the son of Seror
serpent Gen 3 1 the serpent was more subtle
Gen 3 4 serpent said to the woman: No, you
13 the serpent deceived me and I did eat
14 and the Lord God said to the serpent
49 17 Dan be a snake in the way, a s. in the
Exod 4 3 it was turned into a serpent. 7:10
7 9 and it shall be turned into a serpent
15 the rod that was turned into a serpent
Num 21 8 make a brazen serpent and set it up
9 Moses therefore made a brazen serpent
Deut 8 15 was the serpent burning with his breath
4 K 18 4 groves, and broke the brazen serpent
Job 26 13 hand brought forth the winding serpent
Ps 57 5 according to the likeness of a serpent
139 4 sharpened their tongues like a serpent
Prov 30 19 the way of a serpent upon a rock
Ecce 10 8 breaketh a hedge, a s. shall bite him
11 if a serpent bite in silence, he is
Eccu 12 13 pity an enchanter struck by a serpent
21 2 flee from sins as from face of a s.
25 22 no head worse than the head of a s.
Isa 14 29 out of the root of the serpent shall
27 1 shall visit leviathan the bar serpent and leviathan the crooked serpent
Amos 5 19 the wall, and a serpent should bite him
9 3 there will I command the serpent, and
Mat 7 10 a fish, will he reach him a serpent
Luke 11 11 will he for a fish give him a serpent
John 3 14 as Moses lifted up the serpent in the
2 C 11 3 I fear lest, as the serpent seduced Eve
Apoc 12 9 dragon was cast out, that old serpent
14 half a time, from the face of the s.
15 the s. cast out of his mouth after the
20 2 laid hold of the dragon the old serpent
serpent's Isa 65 25 dust shall be the s. food
serpents Exod 7 12 and they were turned into s.
Num 21 5 sent among the people fiery serpents
7 that he may take away these serpents
Deut 32 24 that trail upon the ground and of s.
Jdth 8 25 destroyer, and perished by serpents
Ps 148 10 all cattle: serpents and feathered fowls
Wisd 11 16 being deceived worshipped dumb serpents
16 5 destroyed with the bitings of crooked s.
10 not even the teeth of venomous serpents
17 9 passing by of beasts and hissing of s.
Eccu 10 13 he shall inherit serpents and beasts
39 36 teeth of beasts and scorpions and s.
Isa 13 21 their houses shall be filled with s.
Jer 8 17 I will send among you s., basilisks
Mich 7 17 they shall lick the dust like serpents
Mat 10 16 be ye therefore wise as serpents and
23 33 you serpents, generation of vipers, how
Mark 16 18 they shall take up serpents; and if
Luke 10 19 you power to tread upon serpents and

1 C 10 9 tempted, and perished by the serpents
James 3 7 every nature . . . of birds and of s.
Apoc 9 19 their tails are like to serpents and
Serug 1 Pa 1 26 Serug, Nachor, Thare, Abram
servant Mat 8 13 the servant was healed at the same hour
Mat 10 24 nor the servant above his lord. It is
25 his master, and the servant as his lord
18 26 that servant, falling down, besought
27 the lord of that servant being moved
28 when that servant was gone out, he
32 thou wicked servant, I forgave thee
20 27 first among you, shall be your servant
23 11 greatest among you shall be your s.
24 45 is a faithful and wise servant, whom
46 blessed is that servant, whom when his
48 if that evil servant shall say in his
50 lord of that s. shall come. Luke 12:46
25 21 well done, good and faithful s. 23
26 wicked and slothful servant, thou
30 the unprofitable servant cast ye out
26 51 striking the s. of the high priest, cut
69 there came to him a servant maid
Mark 10 44 first among you, shall be the s. of
12 2 he sent to the husbandmen a servant to
4 again he sent to them another servant
Luke 7 2 the servant of a certain centurion
10 found the s. whole who had been sick
12 43 blessed is that servant whom when his
45 but if that servant shall say in his
47 that servant who knew the will of his
14 21 the s. returning, told these things
22 the s. said: Lord, it is done as thou
23 the lord said to the servant: Go out
16 13 no servant can serve two masters: for
17 7 having a s. plowing or feeding cattle
9 doth he thank that servant for doing
19 17 well done, thou good servant, because
22 I judge thee, thou wicked servant
20 10 he sent a s. to the husbandmen, that
11 and again he sent another servant
22 50 struck s. of the high priest. John 18:10
56 certain servant maid had seen sitting
John 8 34 committeth sin, is the servant of sin
35 the s. abideth not in the house forever
13 16 servant is not greater than his lord
15 15 the s. knoweth not what his lord doth
20 servant is not greater than his master
18 10 the name of the servant was Malchus
Rom 1 1 Paul, a servant of Jesus Christ, called
14 4 thou that judgest another man's servant
1 C 9 19 I made myself the servant of all, that
Gal 1 10 I should not be the servant of Christ
4 1 he differeth nothing from a s., though
7 now he is not a servant, but a son. And
Phil 2 7 taking the form of a servant, being made
Col 1 7 Epaphras, our most beloved fellow s.
4 7 minister and fellow servant in the Lord
12 servant of Christ Jesus, who is always
2 Tim 2 24 the s. of the Lord must not wrangle: but
Titus 1 1 Paul, a servant of God, and an apostle
Philem 16 not now as a servant, but instead of a servant, a most dear brother
Heb 3 5 as a servant, for a testimony of those
James 1 1 James the servant of God and of our
2 P 1 1 servant and apostle of Jesus Christ
Jude 1 Jude, the servant of Jesus Christ, and
his servant Mat 18 29 his fellow s. falling down besought
Luke 1 54 he hath received Israel his servant
69 to us, in the house of David his s.
7 3 him to come and heal his servant
14 17 he sent his servant at the hour of
21 said to his servant: Go out quickly
Apoc 1 1 sending by his angel to his s. John
my servant Mat 8 6 my servant lieth at home sick of the
Mat 8 8 and my s. shall be healed. Luke 7:7
9 to my servant, Do this. Luke 7:8
12 18 behold my s. whom I have chosen, my
thy servant Mat 18 33 compassion also on thy fellow servant
Luke 2 29 now dost thou dismiss thy servant
Acts 4 25 mouth of our father, David, thy s.
Apoc 19 10 I am thy fellow servant, and of. 22:9
servant's 2 K 13 24 behold thy s. sheep are shorn
3 K 11 34 for David my s. sake. 4 K 19:34; 20:6
4 K 8 19 for David his servant's sake, as he
1 Pa 17 19 O Lord, for thy servant's sake
servants Mat 13 27 the s. of the goodman of the house
Mat 13 28 the s. said to him: Wilt thou that we
21 36 he sent other servants more than the
22 4 again he sent other servants, saying
25 19 the lord of those servants came and
26 58 he sat with the servants. Mark 14:54
Mark 14 65 the servants struck him with the palms
Luke 12 37 blessed are those servants. 38
15 17 how many hired servants in my father's
19 make me as one of thy hired servants
26 and he called one of the servants and
17 10 we are unprofitable servants; we have
19 13 calling his ten s., he gave them ten
John 15 15 I will not now call you servants: for
18 3 and servants from the chief priests
12 tribune and the servants of the Jews
18 the s. and ministers stood at a fire
22 one of the servants standing by, gave
26 one of the servants of the high priest
36 my servants would certainly strive that
19 6 and the servants had seen him, they
Acts 2 18 upon my servants indeed, and upon my
4 29 grant unto thy servants that with all
16 17 men are s. of the most high God, who
Rom 6 16 you yield yourselves servants to obey
17 that you were the s. of sin, but have
18 we have been made servants of justice
20 for when you were the servants of sin
22 become servants to God, you have your
2 C 4 5 ourselves your servants through Jesus
Eph 6 5 servants, be obedient to them that are
6 as the servants of Christ doing the will
Phil 1 1 Paul and Timothy, the servants of Jesus
Col 3 22 servants, obey in all things your
4 1 do to your s. that which is just and
1 Tim 6 1 whosoever are servants under the yoke
Titus 2 9 exhort servants to be obedient to their
1 P 2 16 for malice, but as the servants of God
18 servants, be subject to your masters
Apoc 2 20 to teach and to seduce my servants, to
6 11 till their fellow servants and their
7 3 till we sign the servants of our God
11 18 reward to thy servants the prophets
his servants Mat 14 2 said to his servants: This is John
Mat 18 23 who would take an account of his s.
28 he found one of his fellow servants
31 his fellow s. seeing what was done
21 34 he sent his servants to the husbandmen
35 the husbandmen laying hands on his s.
22 3 he sent his servants to call them that
6 the rest laid hands on his servants
8 then he saith to his servants: The
10 his servants going forth into the ways
24 49 begin to strike his fellow servants
25 14 called his servants and delivered to
Mark 13 34 gave authority to his servants over
Luke 15 22 the father said to his servants: Bring
19 15 commanded his servants to be called
John 4 51 going down, his servants met him; and
Acts 10 7 he called two of his household s., and

Rom	6	16	obey, his servants you are whom you obey
Apoc	1	1	to make known to his s. the things
	10	7	hath declared to his s. the prophets
	19	2	and hath revenged the blood of his s.
		5	give praise to our God, all ye his s.
	22	3	in it, and his servants shall serve him
		6	sent his angel to show his servants
serve Gen	15	14	the nation which they shall s.
Gen	20	16	this shall serve thee for a covering
	25	23	and the elder shall serve the younger
	27	29	let peoples s. thee, and tribes worship
		40	the sword and shalt serve thy brother
	29	15	shalt thou s. me without wages? Tell
		18	I will serve thee seven years for Rachel
		25	did not I serve thee for Rachel? Why
	47	25	upon us, and we will gladly s. the king
Exod	4	23	let my son go, that he may serve me
	14	12	from us that we may serve the Egyptians
		12	it was much better to serve them than
	20	5	thou shalt not adore them nor s. them
	23	24	not adore their gods nor serve them
		25	you shall serve the Lord your God, that
		33	against me, if thou serve their gods
Lev	26	13	that you should not serve them, and
Num	7	5	s. in the ministry of the tabernacle
		9	because they serve in the sanctuary
	8	11	that they may serve in his ministry
		15	tabernacle of the covenant to s. me
		19	to s. me for Israel in the tabernacle
		25	of their age, they shall cease to serve
	16	9	that you should s. him in the service
	18	6	to serve in the ministries of the
		21	the ministry wherewith they serve me
		23	only the sons of Levi may serve me in
		31	wherewith you serve in the tabernacle
Deut	4	19	by error thou adore and serve them
		28	you shall serve gods that were framed
	5	9	and thou shalt not serve them. For I
		15	remember that thou also didst serve in
	6	13	Lord thy God, and shalt serve him only
	7	4	that he may rather serve strange gods
		16	neither shalt thou serve their gods
	8	19	strange gods, and s. and adore them
	10	12	s. the Lord thy God with all thy heart
		20	the Lord thy God and serve him only
	11	13	serve him with all your heart and with
		16	serve strange gods. 13:6, 13; 17:3; 28:36, 64; Josu 24:16, 20; 1 K 26:19; 2 Pa 7:19; Bar 1:22
	13	2	knowest not, and let us serve them
		4	him you shall serve, and to him you
	15	17	he shall serve thee forever: thou shalt
	20	11	and shall serve thee paying tribute
	28	47	because thou didst not serve the Lord
		48	thou shalt serve thy enemy, whom the
	29	18	to go and s. the gods of those nations
	30	17	thou adore strange gods and serve them
	31	20	after strange gods, and will s. them
Josu	9	21	to serve the whole multitude in hewing
	22	5	serve him with all your heart and with
		27	that we may serve the Lord and that
	23	7	gods, and serve them and adore them
	24	14	fear the Lord and serve him with a
		14	and in Egypt, and serve the Lord
		15	if it seem evil to you to s. the Lord
		15	whom you would rather serve, whether
		15	and my house we will serve the Lord
		18	we will serve the Lord, for he is our
		19	you will not be able to serve the Lord
		21	thou sayest, but we will serve the Lord
		22	have chosen you the Lord to serve him
		24	we will serve the Lord our God, and we
Judg	9	28	what is Sichem, that we should s. him
		28	Sichem? Why then shall we serve him
		38	who is Abimelech that we shall serve
	10	6	they left the Lord and did not s. him
1 K	7	3	unto the Lord, and serve him only and
	11	1	covenant with us and we will s. thee
	12	10	of our enemies, and we will serve thee
		14	if you will fear the Lord and s. him
		20	serve the Lord with all your heart
		24	fear the Lord and serve him in truth
	17	9	you shall be servants and shall serve us
2 K	8	2	Moab was made to s. David under tribute
		14	and all Edom was made to serve David
	16	19	whom shall I serve? Is it not the
		19	served thy father, so will I serve thee
	22	44	people which I know not, shall serve me
3 K	12	4	he put upon us, and we will serve thee
4 K	4	1	to take away my two sons to serve him
	25	24	be not afraid to serve the Chaldees
		24	serve the king of Babylon. Jer 25:11; 27:17; 40:9; Bar 2:21, 22
1 Pa	9	33	that they might serve continually day
	18	6	that Syria also should serve him and
		13	that Edom should serve David: and the
	28	9	serve him with a perfect heart and a
2 Pa	8	9	set not to serve in the king's works
	10	4	of the burden, that we may serve thee
	12	8	yet they shall serve him that they may
	30	8	serve the Lord the God of your fathers
	33	16	he commanded Juda to serve the Lord
	34	33	were left in Israel, to serve the Lord
	35	5	s. ye in the sanctuary by the families
Tob	6	6	they salted as much as might serve them
	14	10	serve the Lord in truth and seek to do
Jdth	3	2	it is better for us to live and serve
	11	1	was willing to serve Nabuchodonosor
		5	not only men serve him through thee
	16	17	let all thy creatures serve thee
Job	4	18	they that serve him are not steadfast
	21	15	who is the Almighty, that we should s.
	39	9	shall the rhinoceros be willing to s.
Ps	2	11	s. ye the Lord with fear: and rejoice
	21	31	shall live: and my seed shall s. him
	71	11	adore him: all nations shall serve him
	99	2	serve the Lord with gladness. Come
	101	23	together, and kings, to serve the Lord
	118	91	day goeth on: for all things serve thee
Prov	11	29	and the fool shall serve the wise
Ecce	2	8	and vessels to serve to pour out wine
Wisd	15	7	likewise such as serve to the contrary
Eccu	3	8	and will serve them as his masters
	4	15	they that serve her, shall be servants
	8	10	and to serve great men without blame
	10	28	free shall s. a servant that is wise
	39	4	he shall serve among great men and
Isa	14	3	wherewith thou didst serve before
	19	23	the Egyptians shall serve the Assyrian
	43	23	not caused thee to serve with oblation
		24	hast made me to serve with thy sins
	60	12	the kingdom that will not serve thee
Jer	2	20	thou saidst: I will not serve. For on
	5	19	so shall you serve strangers in a land
	11	10	after strange gods to s. them. 13:10
	16	13	and there you shall serve strange gods
	17	4	I will make thee serve thy enemies in
	25	6	gods to serve them and adore them
	27	6	field I have given him to serve him
		7	all nations shall serve him and his
		8	that will not serve Nabuchodonosor
		9	not serve the king of Babylon. 13, 14
		11	king of Babylon, and shall serve him
		12	of the king of Babylon and serve him
	28	14	nations, to serve Nabuchodonosor king
		14	they shall serve him: moreover also

30 9 they shall serve the Lord their God
34 14 so he shall serve thee six years
40 9 fear not to serve the Chaldeans: dwell
Bar 1 12 may serve them many days and may find
Eze 20 39 after your idols, and serve them. But
40 shall all the house of Israel serve me
48 18 bread to them that serve the city
19 that serve the city shall serve it out of all the
Dan 3 95 that they might not serve nor adore
7 14 tribes and tongues shall serve him
27 all kings shall serve him and shall
Soph 3 9 and may serve him with one shoulder
Zach 9 8 with them that serve me in war, going
1 Ma 6 23 we determined to serve thy father and
11 42 nation, when opportunity shall serve
Mat 4 10 him only shalt thou serve. Luke 4:8
6 24 no man can serve two masters. For
24 you cannot s. God and mammon. Luke 10:13
Luke 1 74 we may serve him without fear, in
10 40 my sister hath left me alone to serve
15 29 for so many years do I serve thee
16 13 no servant can serve two masters: for
17 8 serve me whilst I eat and drink, and
Acts 6 2 leave the word of God and serve tables
7 7 the nation which they shall serve will
7 out, and shall serve me in this place
42 gave them up to s. the host of heaven
24 14 so do I serve the Father and my God
27 23 God, whose I am, and whom I serve, stood
Rom 1 9 for God is my witness, whom I serve in
6 6 to end that we may serve sin no longer
19 yielded your members to s. uncleanness
19 now yield your members to serve justice
7 6 that we should s. in newness of spirit
25 I myself, with mind serve the law of God
9 12 her: The elder shall serve the younger
16 18 they that are such, serve not Christ
1 C 9 13 they that serve the altar, partake with
Gal 4 9 elements, which you desire to s. again
5 13 by charity of the spirit s. one another
Phil 3 3 circumcision, who in spirit serve God
Col 3 24 inheritance. Serve ye the Lord Christ
1 Th 1 9 idols, to serve the living and true God
1 Tim 6 2 but serve them the rather, because they
2 Tim 1 3 whom I serve from my forefathers with
Heb 8 5 who serve unto the example and shadow
9 14 from dead works, to serve the living God
12 28 let us serve, pleasing God, with fear
13 10 no power to eat who s. the tabernacle
Apoc 7 15 they serve him day and night in his
22 3 in it, and his servants shall serve him
served Gen 14 4 they had served Chodorlahomor
Gen 29 20 Jacob served seven years for Rachel
30 served with him other seven years
30 26 for whom I have served thee, that I
29 thou knowest how I have served thee
31 6 you know that I have served your father
41 in this manner have I served thee
40 4 them to Joseph and he served them
Lev 25 53 allowed for which he served before
Num 22 29 deserved it, and hast served me ill
Deut 15 12 hath served thee six years. 18
29 26 s. strange gods. Josu 23:16; 24:2; 1 K 8:8
Josu 24 14 gods which your fathers served. 15
31 Israel served the Lord all the days of
Judg 2 7 they served the Lord all his days
11 did evil . . . and they served Baalim
3 6 their sons, and they served their gods
7 forgot their God and served Baalim
8 they served him eight years. And they
14 the children of Israel served Eglon
10 6 served idols, Baalim and Astaroth
10 the Lord our God, and have s. Baalim
16 of strange gods and served the Lord
1 K 4 9 to the Hebrews as they have s. you
7 4 and Astaroth, and served the Lord only
12 10 and have served Baalim and Astaroth
2 K 8 6 and Syria served David under tribute
9 12 of the house of Siba served Miphiboseth
10 19 made peace with Israel: and served them
16 19 as I have served thy father, so will I
3 K 1 4 she slept with the king and served him
4 21 they brought him presents and s. him
16 31 he [Achab] went and served Baal and
22 54 he s. also Baal, and worshipped him
4 K 4 13 hast diligently s. us in all things
17 16 host of heaven: and they served Baal
33 they s. also their own gods according
41 nevertheless served also their idols
18 7 king of the Assyrians and s. him not
1 Pa 19 9 they went over to David and served him
21 3 the host of heaven, and served them
21 s. abominations which his father had s.
27 1 and officers, that served the king
2 Pa 22 8 brethren of Ochozias, who served him
24 18 and served groves and idols, and wrath
33 22 his father had made, and served them
36 20 and there served the king and his sons
2 Es 9 35 have not served thee in their kingdoms
Ps 17 45 people which I knew not, hath served me
80 7 his hands had served in baskets. Thou
100 6 walked in the perfect way, he served me
105 36 their works: and served their idols
Eccu 25 11 hath not s. such as are unworthy of
Isa 44 15 it hath served men for fuel: he took
Jer 5 19 have forsaken me and s. a strange god
8 2 have loved and whom they have served
16 11 went after strange gods and served them
22 9 adored strange gods and served them
25 14 they have served them, whereas they
Bar 4 32 the cities which thy children have s.
Osee 12 12 Israel served for a wife and was a
Zach 2 9 a prey to those that served them
1 Ma 12 1 Jonathan saw that the time served him
John 12 2 him a supper there: and Martha served
Acts 13 36 when he had served in his generation
43 Jews, and of strangers who served God
17 4 of those that s. God, and of Gentiles
17 Jews, and with them that served God
25 is he s. with men's hands, as though
Rom 1 25 worshipped and s. the creature rather
Gal 4 8 not knowing God, you served them, who
Phil 2 22 so hath he served with me in the gospel
server John 9 31 but if a man be a s. of God
1 C 5 11 a server of idols, or a railer, or a
servers 1 C 5 10 extortioners, or the s. of idols
Apoc 22 15 murderers and servers of idols and
servest Dan 6 16 thy God, whom thou always s.
Dan 6 20 thy God, whom thou servest always
serveth Mala 3 14 laboreth in vain that s. God
Mala 3 17 man spareth his son that serveth him
18 between him that s. God, and him that s. him not
Luke 22 26 that is the leader, as he that serveth
27 sitteth at table, or he that serveth
27 the midst of you as he that serveth
Rom 14 18 for he that in this serveth Christ
1 C 9 7 who serveth as a soldier at any time
Heb 9 9 make him perfect that serveth, only in
service Gen 29 27 the s. that thou shalt render
Gen 30 26 knowest the s. that I have rendered
40 13 Pharao will remember thy service and
44 33 in the s. of my lord, and let the boy
Exod 1 14 and brick and with all manner of s.
10 26 are necessary for the s. of the Lord
26 what is the meaning of this service

43 this is the service of the phase: no
25 9 all the vessels for the s. 1 Pa 23:26
30 28 furniture that belongeth to the service
35 21 whatsoever was necessary to the service
Lev 24 3 by a perpetual service and rite in your
25 39 not oppress him with the service of
Num 3 7 appertaineth to the s. of the multitude
10 and his sons over the s. of priesthood
36 things that pertain to this kind of s.
4 4 this is the service of the sons of Caath
16 pertaineth to the s. of the tabernacle
28 the s. of the family of the Gersonites
30 ministry and to the s. of the covenant
7 8 according to their offices and service
16 9 serve him in the s. of the tabernacle
18 7 that pertain to the service of the altar
Deut 4 19 created for the s. of all the nations
Josu 9 27 should be in the s. of all the people
3 K 12 4 take off a little of the grievous s.
1 Pa 9 19 were over the works of the service
23 28 the service of the house of. 25:6; 28:20; 2 Pa 29:35
26 8 their brethren, most able men for s.
30 and for the service of the king
32 for all the s. of God and the king
28 13 for all the vessels of the service
2 Pa 12 8 difference between my s. and the s. of a kingdom of the earth
31 21 in all the service of the ministry
35 15 depart one moment from their service
16 all the service of the Lord was duly
1 Es 8 20 gave for the service of the Levites
Jdth 3 6 use our service as it shall please thee
5 11 and bring them back to their service
8 16 in an humble spirit in his service
Ps 103 14 and herb for the service of men. That
146 8 and herbs for the service of men. Who
Wisd 15 7 fashioneth every vessel for our s.
Eccu 2 1 when thou comest to the service of God
5 1 of no service in the time of vengeance
50 15 finishing his service, on the altar
Isa 32 17 and the service of justice quietness
Eze 27 9 for the s. of thy various furniture
29 18 made his army to undergo hard service
18 for the service that he rendered me
20 for the service that he hath done me
44 14 doorkeepers of the house, for all the s.
Osee 2 8 they have used in the service of Baal
1 Ma 1 45 many of Israel consented to his s.
2 19 from the s. of the law of his fathers
11 58 he sent him vessels of gold for his s.
Luke 19 31 the Lord hath need of his service
John 16 2 will think that he doth a s. to God
Rom 9 4 and the s. of God, and the promises
12 1 pleasing unto God, your reasonable s.
15 31 that the oblation of my service may be
1 C 10 14 fly from the service of idols. I speak
Phil 2 17 the sacrifice and service of your faith
30 part was wanting towards my service
Col 3 5 which is the service of idols. For which
Heb 9 1 also justifications of divine service
services Num 8 22 to do their s. before Aaron
2 Pa 24 17 and he was soothed by their services
Esth 16 13 by whose fidelity and good services
servile Lev 23 7 do no servile work therein. 8, 21, 28, 35, 36; Num 28:26; 29:1, 7, 12, 35
Num 28 18 you shall not do any servile work
serving Exod 14 5 we let Israel go from s. us
Num 3 8 tabernacle, s. in the ministry thereof
Judg 2 13 forsaking him and s. Baal and Astaroth
19 following strange gods, serving them
1 Pa 25 1 number s. in their appointed office
Wisd 14 21 men serving either their affection or
16 21 serving every man's will, it was turned
24 the creature s. thee the Creator, is
Luke 2 37 fasting and prayers s. night and day
10 40 Martha was busy about much serving
Acts 20 19 serving the Lord with all humility, and
26 7 our 12 tribes, serving night and day
Rom 12 11 in spirit fervent. Serving the Lord
13 6 ministers of God, s. unto this purpose
Gal 4 3 were s. under the elements of the world
Eph 5 5 person, which is a serving of idols
6 6 not serving to the eye. Col 3:22
7 with a good will serving, as to the Lord
servitude 2 Pa 10 4 who laid upon us a heavy s.
1 Ma 8 18 oppressed the kingdom of Israel with s.
Rom 8 21 delivered from the s. of corruption
1 C 7 15 brother or sister is not under servitude
Gal 2 4 that they might bring us into servitude
Heb 2 15 all their lifetime subject to servitude
Sesac 3 K 11 40 arose and fled into Egypt to S.
3 K 14 25 Sesac king of Egypt came. 2 Pa 12:2
1 Pa 8 14 Ahio and Sesac and Jerimoth and
25 Jephdaia and Phanuel the sons of S.
2 Pa 12 5 I have left you in the hand of Sesac
5 together in Jerusalem, fleeing from S.
7 upon Jerusalem by the hand of Sesac
9 so Sesac . . . departed from Jerusalem
Jer 25 26 king of Sesac shall drink after them
Sesach Jer 51 41 how is Sesach taken, and the
Sesai Josu 15 14 sons of Enac, Sesai and Ahiman
Judg 1 10 slew Sesai and Ahiman and Tholmai
Sesan 1 Pa 2 31 Jesi begot S. And S. begot Oholai
set Mat 4 5 set him upon the pinnacle. Luke 4:9
Mat 5 1 when he was set down, his disciples
10 35 I came to set a man at variance against
18 2 set him in the midst of them. Mark 9:35
25 33 he shall set the sheep on his right
Mark 4 21 and not to be set on a candlestick
6 53 of Genezareth, and set to the shore
Luke 2 34 this child is set for the fall and
4 19 to set at liberty them that are
9 47 took a child and set him by him. And
51 set his face to go to Jerusalem. And
12 44 he will set him over all that he
19 35 on the colt, they set Jesus thereon
23 11 Herod with his army set him at nought
John 2 6 there were set there six waterpots
3 33 hath set his seal that God is true
6 11 distributed to them that were set down
8 3 they set her in the midst and said to
13 12 being set down again, he said to them
19 29 was a vessel set there full of vinegar
Acts 5 27 they set them before the council. And
13 47 I have set thee to be light of Gentiles
15 16 I will rebuild, and I will set it up
17 5 making tumult, set city in an uproar
6 they that set the city in an uproar
18 10 no man shall set upon thee, to hurt
19 27 craft is in danger to be set at nought
21 1 being parted from them, we set sail, we
23 24 provide beasts, that they may set Paul
26 32 this man might have been set at liberty
28 10 when we were to set sail, they laded us
1 C 6 4 set them to judge, who are the most
11 34 rest I will set in order, when I come
12 18 God hath set the members every one of
28 God indeed hath set some in the church
Gal 3 19 it was set because of transgressions
Phil 1 16 I am set for the defence of the gospel
Titus 1 5 thou shouldest set in order the things
Heb 2 7 hast set him over the works of thy hands
8 1 who is set on the right hand of the
13 23 our brother Timothy is set at liberty
1 P 2 8 believe, whereunto also they are set

Apoc 3 21 and am set down with my Father in his
4 2 a throne set in heaven, and upon the
10 2 and he set his right foot upon the sea
20 3 shut him up and set a seal upon him
set before Mark 6 41 to his disciples to set before them
Mark 8 6 his disciples for to set before them
6 and they set them before the people
7 commanded them to be set before them
Luke 9 16 disciples to set before the multitude
10 8 eat such things as are set before you
11 6 I have not what to set before him
Acts 6 6 these they set before the apostles
22 30 bringing forth Paul, he set him before
1 C 10 27 eat of anything that is set before you
Heb 6 18 to hold fast the hope set before us
12 2 having joy set before him, endured the
set forth Luke 1 1 many have taken in hand to set forth
Acts 21 2 Phenice, we went aboard, and set forth
1 C 4 9 for I think that God hath set forth us
Gal 3 1 eyes Jesus Christ hath been set forth
set in array Josu 8 14 set it in battle a. toward
Judg 20 22 Israel . . . set their army in array
33 set their army in battle array in the
Seth Gen 4 25 a son and called his name Seth
Gen 4 26 to Seth also was born a son, whom
5 3 and likeness, and called his name Seth
4 the days of Adam, after he begot Seth
6 Seth also lived 105 years and begot
7 and Seth lived after he begot Enos
8 all the days of Seth were 912 years
Num 24 17 shall waste all the children of Seth
1 Pa 1 1 Adam, Seth, Enos, Cainan, Malaleel
Eccu 49 19 Seth and Sem obtained glory among men
Luke 3 38 Henos, who was of Seth, who was of
Sethar Esth 1 14 nearest him were Charsena and S.
Sethri Exod 6 22 Mizael and Elizapham and Sethri
setim wood Exod 25 5 violet skins and s. wood
Exod 25 10 frame an ark of setim wood, the
13 shalt make bars also of setim wood
23 shalt make a table also of setim wood
28 the bars also . . . make of setim wood
26 15 boards of the tabernacle . . . of s. w.
26 shalt make also five bars of s. wood
32 hang it up before four pillars of s. w.
27 1 make also an altar of setim wood
6 two bars for the altar of setim wood
30 1 an altar to burn incense, of setim wood
5 shalt make the bars also of setim wood
35 7 and violet colored skins, setim wood
24 to the Lord, and s. w. for divers uses
36 20 made also the boards . . . of setim wood
31 he made also bars of setim wood. 37:4
36 four pillars of setim wood, which with
37 1 Beseleel made also the ark of s. w.
10 he made also the table of setim wood
15 bars themselves . . . of setim wood. 28
25 made also the altar . . . of setim wood
38 1 the altar of holocaust of setim wood
6 and he made the bars of setim wood
Deut 10 3 and I made an ark of setim wood. And
Setim Josu 2 1 sent from Setim two men to spy
Josu 3 1 they departed from Setim and came to
Mich 6 5 answered him from Setim to Galgal
Setrai 1 Pa 27 29 and over the herds . . . was Setrai
setter Acts 17 18 to be a s. forth of new gods
settest Eze 16 18 s. my oil and my sweet incense
Abdi 3 and settest up thy throne on high
setteth Job 5 11 who s. up the humble on high
Job 39 18 she setteth up her wings on high: she
40 12 he setteth up his tail like a cedar
Ps 17 34 and who setteth me upon high places
144 14 and setteth up all that are cast down
Prov 17 27 he that setteth bounds to his words
29 4 a just king setteth up the land: a
Eccu 10 10 setteth even his own soul to sale
27 29 he that s. a stone for his neighbor
38 31 he setteth his mind to finish his work
Jer 30 21 that s. his heart to approach to me
43 3 Baruch . . . setteth thee on against us
Luke 8 16 setteth it upon a candlestick that
12 42 whom his lord setteth over his family
John 2 10 at first setteth forth good wine, and
Settim Num 25 1 Israel at that time abode in S.
setting Gen 15 12 when the sun was setting, a deep
Exod 17 1 setting forward from the desert of Sin
40 21 setting there in order the loaves of
Num 10 21 came to the place of setting it up
21 10 setting forwards camped in Oboth. And
24 1 setting his face towards the desert
Deut 11 30 way that goeth to the s. of the sun
Judg 15 5 setting them on fire he let the foxes
16 2 setting guards at the gate of the city
2 K 22 34 and setting me upon my high places
3 K 2 34 Banaias . . . setting upon him slew him
1 Es 4 12 setting up the ramparts thereof and
Jdth 6 10 setting him in the midst of the people
Ps 106 3 rising and from the setting of the sun
Wisd 13 15 setting it in a wall and fastening it
Jer 5 26 setting snares and traps to catch men
Bar 5 5 from the rising to the setting sun
2 Ma 4 15 setting nought by the honors of their
8 17 s. before their eyes the injury they
Mat 27 66 sealing the stone and setting guards
Luke 10 34 setting him upon his own beast
Acts 4 7 setting them in the midst, they said
Eph 1 20 dead, and s. him on his right hand
Heb 7 18 is indeed a setting aside of the former
9 2 the table, and the setting forth of
settle 1 Pa 17 14 I will settle him in my house
Ps 88 5 thy seed will I settle forever. And I
Eze 36 11 I will settle you as from the beginning
1 Ma 3 36 he should settle strangers to dwell
settled Ps 4 10 singularly hast s. me in hope
Eccu 42 17 the Lord Almighty hath firmly settled
Soph 1 12 men that are settled on their lees
2 Ma 4 6 that matters should be s. in peace
Col 1 23 continue in the faith, grounded and s.
settlements Josu 22 8 you return to your s. with
sevenfold Gen 4 15 Cain, shall be punished s.
Gen 4 24 sevenfold vengeance shall be taken
24 for Lamech seventy times sevenfold
Ps 78 12 render to our neighbors sevenfold in
Prov 6 31 and if he be taken he shall restore s.
7 3 thou shalt not reap them sevenfold
20 12 small price, and restoreth the same s.
14 do thee no good: for his eyes are s.
40 8 and upon sinners are sevenfold more
Isa 30 26 light of the sun shall be sevenfold
several Exod 39 14 each one with its several name
Apoc 21 21 and every s. gate was of one s. pearl
severe Wisd 5 21 sharpen his s. wrath for a spear
Wisd 6 6 most severe judgment shall be for them
11 11 as a severe king, thou didst examine
Isa 27 8 he hath meditated with his s. spirit
severely 2 C 13 10 present, I may not deal more s.
severity Rom 11 22 see . . . the s. of God
Rom 11 22 towards them indeed that are fallen, **s.**
sew Ecce 3 7 a time to rend and a time to sew
Eze 13 18 that sew cushions under every elbow
sewed Gen 3 7 they sewed together fig leaves
Josu 9 4 wine bottles rent and sewed up again
Job 16 16 I have sewed sackcloth upon my skin
Eze 16 16 made thee high places sewed together
seweth Mark 2 21 no man s. a piece of raw cloth
sex Gen 6 19 bring two . . . of the male sex
Gen 34 15 the male **sex** among you be circumcised

Exod 1 22 whatsoever shall be born of male sex
13 12 whatsoever thou shalt have of male sex
15 that openeth the womb of the male sex
Num 1 2 as many as are of the male sex, from
20 all that were of the male sex. 22
3 22 were numbered, people of the male sex
28 all of the male sex from one month
40 number the firstborn of the male sex
31 17 kill all that are of the male sex
35 and 32,000 persons of the female sex
Deut 7 14 be barren among you of either sex
15 19 thy God whatsoever is of the male sex
20 13 all that are therein of the male sex
sexes Judg 16 27 3,000 persons of both sexes
2 Pa 31 18 and to their children of both sexes
sextary Lev 14 10 sacrifice, and a s. of oil apart
Lev 14 12 a trespass offering with the s. of oil
15 he shall pour of the sextary of oil
21 for a sacrifice and a sextary of oil
24 for trespass and the sextary of oil
19 36 the bushel just and the sextary equal
shade Job 7 2 as a servant longeth for the shade
Isa 4 6 there shall be a tabernacle for a shade
shades Job 40 17 the shades cover his shadow, the
shadow Gen 19 8 come in under the s. of my roof
Judg 9 15 come ye and rest under my shadow: but
3 K 19 5 slept in the shadow of the juniper tree
4 K 20 9 wilt thou that the shadow go forward
10 easy matter for the s. to go forward
11 and he brought the shadow ten degrees
1 Pa 29 15 our days upon earth are as a shadow
Job 8 9 our days upon earth are but a shadow
14 2 and fleeth as a shadow and never
40 16 he sleepeth under the shadow; in the
17 shades cover his shadow, the willows
Ps 16 8 protect me under the s. of thy wings
56 2 in the shadow of thy wings will I hope
79 11 the shadow of it covered the hills
101 12 my days have declined like a shadow
108 23 I am taken away like the shadow when
143 4 vanity: his days pass away like a s.
Ecce 7 1 the time that passeth like a shadow
8 13 as a shadow let them pass away that
Cant 2 3 I sat down under his shadow, whom I
Wisd 2 5 our time is as the passing of a shadow
5 9 those things are passed away like a s.
15 4 deceived us, nor the s. of a picture
Eccu 34 2 like to him that catcheth at a shadow
Isa 16 3 make thy shadow as the night in the
25 4 the whirlwind, a shadow from the heat
30 2 and trusting in the shadow of Egypt
3 confidence of the s. of Egypt to your
32 2 the shadow of a rock that standeth out
34 15 cherished them in the shadow thereof
38 8 I will bring again the s. of the lines
49 2 in s. of his hand he hath protected me
51 16 protected thee in the s. of my hand
Jer 48 45 snare stood in the shadow of Hesebon
Lam 4 20 under thy shadow we shall live among
Bar 1 12 under the shadow of Nabuchodonosor . . .
and under the shadow of Balthasar
Eze 17 23 its nest under the s. of the branches
31 6 when he had spread forth his shadow
6 of many nations dwelt under his shadow
12 of the earth shall depart from his s.
17 shall sit down under his shadow in the
Osee 4 13 because the shadow thereof was good
14 8 be converted that sit under his shadow
Jon 4 5 and he sat under it in the shadow till
6 to be a shadow over his head and to
Mark 4 32 may dwell under the shadow thereof
Acts 5 15 that when Peter came, his shadow at
Col 2 17 which are a shadow of things to come
Heb 8 5 who serve unto the example and shadow
10 1 law having a shadow of the good things
James 1 17 is no change nor shadow of alteration
shadow of death Job 3 5 the s. . . . cover it
Job 10 22 where the shadow of death . . . dwelleth
12 22 bringeth up to light the shadow of d.
24 17 it is to them the shadow of death
28 3 he considereth . . . the shadow of death
34 22 and there is no shadow of death where
Ps 22 4 in the midst of the shadow of death
43 20 the shadow of death hath covered us
87 7 laid me . . . in the shadow of death
106 10 sat in darkness and in the s. . . .
14 out of darkness and the shadow of death
Isa 9 2 in the region of the shadow of death
Jer 13 16 he will turn it into the s. of death
Mat 4 16 in the region of the shadow of death
Luke 1 79 that sit in . . . the shadow of death
shadows Judg 9 36 seest the s. of the mountains
Cant 2 17 the daybreak and the s. retire. 4:6
Jer 6 4 the s. of the evening are grown longer
shady Deut 12 2 under every shady tree. 4 K 17:10
Ps 117 27 appoint a solemn day, with shady boughs
Eze 20 28 every high hill and every shady tree
shaft Exod 25 31 the s. thereof and the branches
Exod 25 33 that are to come out from the shaft
35 make six coming forth out of one shaft
37 17 from the shaft whereof its branches
19 out from the shaft of the candlestick
20 in the shaft itself were four cups
21 six branches going out from one shaft
Num 8 4 gold, both the shaft in the middle
2 K 21 19 the shaft of whose spear was like a
shafts Wisd 5 22 shafts of lightning shall go
shake Gen 27 40 shalt s. off and loose his yoke
Judg 16 20 I will go out . . . and shake myself
2 Es 5 13 may God shake every man that shall not
Ps 28 8 Lord shall shake the desert of Cades
Wisd 4 19 shall shake them from the foundations
Eccu 12 19 he will shake his head and clap his
13 8 forsake thee and s. his head at thee
22 2 that toucheth him will shake his hands
Isa 10 32 he shall shake his hand against the
52 2 shake thyself from the dust, arise, sit
Jer 51 38 they shall shake their manes like young
Eze 26 10 thy walls shall shake at the noise
15 shall not the islands shake at the
Dan 4 11 shake off its leaves and scatter its
Mat 10 14 s. off dust from your feet. Mark 6:11
Luke 6 48 house, and it could not shake it; for
9 5 shake off even the dust of your feet
shaked Ps 108 25 saw me and they s. their heads
shaken 2 K 22 8 mountains were moved and shaken
3 K 14 15 Israel as a reed is shaken in the water
2 Es 5 13 thus may he be shaken out and become
Job 38 13 hast thou shaken the ungodly out of it
Ps 108 23 I am shaken off as locusts. My knees
126 4 children of them that have been shaken
Wisd 4 4 they shall be shaken with the wind and
Eccu 13 25 when a rich man is shaken, he is kept
16 19 they shall be shaken with trembling
43 17 at his sight shall the mountains be s.
Isa 18 5 left shall be cut away and shaken out
24 13 should be shaken out of the olive tree
18 foundations of the earth shall be s.
20 with shaking shall the earth be shaken
33 9 and Basan and Carmel are shaken. Now
Nah 3 12 if they be shaken, they shall fall into
Mat 11 7 a reed s. with the wind. Luke 7:24
Luke 6 38 pressed down and shaken together and
Acts 16 26 foundations of the prison were shaken
Apoc 6 13 figs when it is shaken by a great wind
shaketh Job 9 6 s. the earth out of her place

Job 41 20 him to scorn who shaketh the spear
Ps 28 8 voice of the Lord shaketh the desert
Isa 33 15 and shaketh his hands from all bribes
shaking Job 38 13 extremities of earth s. them
Ps 43 15 a shaking of the head among the people
Isa 17 6 and as the shaking of the olive tree
24 20 with shaking shall the earth be shaken
2 Ma 11 8 with golden armor, shaking a spear
Acts 13 51 shaking off the dust of their feet
28 5 he indeed s. off the beast into the fire
shakings 2 Ma 5 3 with the shakings of shields
shambles 1 C 10 25 whatsoever is sold in the s.
shame Exod 32 25 occasion of the s. of the filth
Lev 18 15 neither shalt thou discover her shame
17 daughter's daughter to discover her s.
20 17 and she behold her brother's shame
19 hath uncovered shame of his own flesh
20 uncover the shame of his near akin
Ruth 2 16 that she may gather them without shame
2 K 13 13 I shall not be able to bear my shame
Job 6 20 unto men, and are covered with shame
Ps 34 26 them be clothed with confusion and s.
43 8 hast put them to shame that hate us
10 hast cast us off and put us to shame
16 all the day long my shame is before me
68 8 reproach; shame hath covered my face
20 knowest . . . my confusion and my shame
69 4 presently turned away blushing for s.
4 blush for shame that desire evils to me
70 13 them be covered with confusion and s.
24 put to shame that seek evils to me
82 17 fill their faces with shame; and they
108 29 that detract me be clothed with shame
118 31 testimonies, O Lord: put me not to s.
Prov 6 33 he gathereth to himself shame and
13 18 shame to him that refuseth instruction
29 15 his own will bringeth his mother to s.
Eccu 3 12 father: for his s. is no glory to thee
4 25 a shame that bringeth sin, and there is a shame that bringeth glory
6 1 evil man shall inherit reproach and s.
13 8 he will shame thee by his meats till
26 11 her reproach and shame shall not be hid
29 18 he that hath lost shame, will leave
22 when he hath lost all shame he shall
27 clothing, and a house to cover shame
41 19 have a shame of these things I am
42 14 a woman bringing shame and reproach
Isa 20 4 buttocks uncovered to the s. of Egypt
22 18 the shame of the house of thy Lord
30 3 confidence of shadow of Egypt to your s.
47 2 uncover thy shame, strip thy shoulder
3 discovered, and thy s. shall be seen
54 4 for thou shalt not be put to shame
4 shalt forget the shame of thy youth
61 7 for your double confusion and shame
Jer 3 25 our shame shall cover us because we
10 17 gather up thy shame out of the land
13 26 thy face, and thy shame hath appeared
23 40 reproach upon you, and a perpetual s.
51 51 reproach: shame hath covered our faces
Lam 1 8 because they have seen her shame: but
Eze 7 18 and shame shall be upon every face
16 36 and thy shame [hath been] discovered
37 will discover thy shame in their sight
52 be thou also confounded and bear thy s.
54 that thou mayest bear thy shame and
32 24 borne their s. with them that. 25, 30
36 6 you have borne the s. of the Gentiles
7 shall themselves bear their shame. But
15 to hear in thee the s. of the nations
44 13 but they shall bear their shame and
Dan 3 33 we are become a shame and reproach to
Osee 2 5 that conceived them is covered with s.
4 7 I will change their glory into shame
18 have loved to bring shame upon them
10 6 s. shall fall upon Ephraim, and Israel
Mich 1 11 Beautiful place, covered with thy s.
7 10 she shall be covered with shame, who
Nah 3 5 I will discover thy shame to thy face
5 will show . . . thy shame to kingdoms
Haba 2 16 art filled with shame instead of glory
Soph 3 5 the wicked man hath not known shame
Luke 14 9 thou begin with shame to take the
1 C 4 35 it is shame for woman to speak in church
6 5 I speak to your shame. 15:34
11 6 if it be a shame to a woman to be shorn
14 nourish his hair, it is a shame unto him
22 and put them to shame that have not
2 C 7 14 I have not been put to shame; but as we
Eph 5 12 secret, it is a shame even to speak of
Phil 3 19 and whose glory is in their shame; who
Heb 12 2 endured the cross, despising the shame
Apoc 3 18 shame of thy nakedness may not appear
16 15 he walk naked and they see his shame
shamed 2 K 19 5 thou hast s. this day the faces
shamefaced Eccu 26 19 s. woman is grace upon grace
shamefacedness Eccu 20 24 his own soul through s.
Eccu 32 14 before s. goeth favor: and for thy
41 20 it is not good to keep all s.: and all
shameful 2 Pa 24 24 they executed s. judgments
Jdth 12 11 for it is looked upon as shameful among
Wisd 2 20 let us condemn him to a most s. death
Eccu 45 29 stood up in the s. fall of the people
Haba 2 16 s. vomiting shall be on thy glory
Rom 1 26 God delivered them up to s. affections
shamefully Deut 25 3 thy brother depart s. torn
2 Ma 8 17 the city, which had been s. abused
11 12 Lysias himself fled away shamefully
1 Th 2 2 been shamefully treated, as you know
shameless 1 K 20 30 the confusion of thy s. mother
Eccu 23 6 me not over to a s. and foolish mind
42 11 sure watch over a shameless daughter
Isa 33 19 the s. people thou shalt not see, the
Eze 16 30 the works of a shameless prostitute
Dan 8 23 there shall arise a king of a s. face
shameth Prov 28 7 feedeth gluttons, s. his father
Eccu 22 5 she that is bold s. both her father
shape Wisd 18 1 indeed, but did not see their s.
Dan 4 33 and my shape returned to me: and my
Mark 16 12 he appeared in another shape to two
Luke 3 21 descended in a bodily shape as a dove
9 29 shape of his countenance was altered
John 5 37 voice at any time nor seen his shape
James 1 11 beauty of the shape thereof perished
shapes Apoc 9 7 s. of the locusts were like
share Exod 29 26 and it shall fall to thy share
Exod 29 28 they shall fall to Aaron's share and
Deut 2 35 cattle which came to the share of them
1 Ma 10 30 which is my share, I leave to you from
shared Exod 18 22 burden being s. out unto others
Jer 12 14 that I have shared out to my people
shares Gen 14 24 shares of the men that came with
Gen 14 24 Mambre: these shall take their shares
1 K 13 21 their shares and their spades and their
sharp Exod 4 25 Sephora took a very sharp stone
Ps 44 6 thy arrows are sharp: under thee shall
51 4 as a sharp razor, thou hast wrought
56 5 arrows, and their tongue a sharp sword
90 3 the hunters: and from the sharp word
119 4 the sharp arrows of the mighty, with
Prov 5 4 sharp as a two-edged sword. Her feet
25 18 like a dart and a sword and a s. arrow
Wisd 18 16 with a sharp sword carrying thy
Isa 5 28 their arrows are sharp and all their
49 2 hath made my mouth like a sharp sword

Eze 5 1 take thee a sharp knife that shaveth
21 15 have set the dread of the sharp sword
Apoc 1 16 came out a sharp two-edged sword: and
2 12 that hath the sharp two-edged sword
14 14 in his hand a sharp sickle. And another
17 he also having a sharp sickle. And
18 to him that had the sharp sickle
18 thrust in thy sharp sickle and gather
19 the angel thrust in his sharp sickle
19 15 proceedeth a sharp two-edged sword
sharpen 1 K 13 20 to s. every man his plowshare
Wisd 5 21 he will sharpen his severe wrath for a
Jer 51 11 sharpen the arrows, fill the quivers
sharpened Ps 139 4 they have s. their tongues
Ecce 10 10 with much labor it shall be sharpened
Eze 21 9 the sword is sharpened and furbished
10 it is sharpened to kill victims: it is
11 this sword is s. and it is furbished
16 be thou sharpened, go to the right
sharpeneth Prov 27 17 iron sharpeneth iron, so a man sharpeneth the countenance of
sharply Judg 8 1 they chid him [Gedeon] sharply
Titus 1 13 rebuke them sharply, that they may be
shave Lev 14 8 shall s. all the hair of his body
Lev 14 9 he shall shave the hair of his head
19 27 hair roundwise: nor shave your beard
21 5 neither shall they shave their head
Num 6 9 he shall shave it forthwith on the
8 7 let them shave all the hairs of their
Deut 21 12 she shall shave her hair and pare her
Isa 7 20 Lord shall shave with a razor that is
Eze 27 31 and they shall shave themselves bald
44 20 neither shall they shave their heads
Acts 21 24 them, that they may shave their heads
shaved Gen 41 14 s. him, and changing his apparel
Num 6 18 hair of consecration of Nazarite be s.
Judg 16 19 a barber, and shaved his seven locks
2 K 10 4 shaved off the one half of their beards
1 Pa 19 4 Hanon shaved the heads and beards of
2 Es 13 25 some of them, and shaved off their hair
shaven Lev 13 33 the man shall be s. all but the
Num 6 19 Nazarite, after his head is shaven
Judg 16 17 if my head be shaven, my strength
Job 1 20 having shaven his head fell down upon
Isa 15 2 baldness, and every beard shall be s.
Jer 41 5 fourscore men, with their beards s.
48 37 bald, and every beard shall be shaven
Bar 6 30 and their heads and beards shaven and
1 C 11 5 for it is all one as if she were shaven
shaveth Eze 5 1 sharp knife that s. the hair
she Lev 4 28 he shall offer a she goat without
Lev 5 6 an ewe lamb or a she goat, and the
Num 15 27 he shall offer a she goat of a year old
Job 1 3 his possession was . . . 500 she asses
sheaf Gen 37 7 my sheaf arose as it were, and
Gen 37 7 about, bowed down before my sheaf
Lev 23 11 who shall lift up the sheaf before the
12 same day that the sheaf is consecrated
15 sabbath wherein you offered the sheaf
Deut 24 19 field, and hast forgot and left a sheaf
shear Gen 31 19 Laban was gone to shear his sheep
Gen 38 13 come up to Thamnas to shear his sheep
Deut 15 19 thou shalt not shear the firstlings
shearer Isa 53 7 dumb as a lamb before his s.
Acts 8 32 lamb without voice before his shearer
shearers Gen 38 12 to the shearers of his sheep
1 K 25 11 which I have killed for my shearers
shearing Deut 18 4 a part of the wool from the s.
1 K 25 2 he was shearing his sheep in Carmel
4 that Nabal was shearing his sheep, he
7 with us in the desert were shearing
sheath 1 K 17 51 sword, and drew it out of the s.
1 Pa 21 27 put up his sword again into the sheath
Eze 21 3 draw forth my sword out of its sheath
4 shall my sword go forth out of its s.
5 have drawn my sword out of its sheath
30 return into thy sheath. I will judge
sheaves Gen 37 7 I thought we were binding s. in
Gen 37 7 your sheaves standing about, bowed
41 47 the corn being bound up into sheaves
Lev 23 10 you shall bring sheaves of ears, the
Ruth 3 7 he went to sleep by the heap of sheaves
2 Es 13 15 on the sabbath, and carrying sheaves
Jdth 8 2 standing over them that bound sheaves
Ps 125 7 with joyfulness, carrying their sheaves
128 7 nor he that gathereth s. his bosom
shed Gen 9 6 his blood shall be shed: for man was
Lev 14 17 blood that was shed for trespass. 28
Num 26 1 after the blood of the guilty was shed
Deut 19 6 kinsman of him whose blood was shed. 12
10 that innocent blood may not be shed
21 9 the innocent's blood that was shed
22 8 lest blood be shed in thy house and
Josu 20 9 to revenge the blood that was shed
1 K 26 20 let not my blood be shed upon the
2 K 20 10 and shed out his bowels to the ground
3 K 2 31 blood which hath been shed by Joab
4 K 24 4 for the innocent blood that he shed
Ps 78 10 of thy servants which hath been shed
Eccu 38 16 my son, shed tears over the dead and
Jer 9 18 let our eyes shed tears and our eyelids
14 17 let my eyes shed down tears night and
Eze 22 4 in thy blood which thou hast shed
13 blood that hath been shed in the midst
24 7 she hath shed it upon the smooth rock
7 she hath not shed it upon the ground
36 18 for the blood which they had shed upon
1 Ma 7 17 they have shed round about Jerusalem
2 Ma 4 37 and being moved to pity, shed tears
Mat 23 35 just blood that hath been shed upon the
26 28 which shall be s. for many. Mark 14:24
Luke 11 50 which was shed from the foundation
22 20 my blood, which shall be shed for you
Acts 22 20 blood of Stephen thy witness was shed
Apoc 16 6 they have shed the blood of saints and
shed blood Gen 9 6 whosoever shall s. man's b.
Gen 37 22 not take away his life nor s. his b.
Lev 17 4 guilty of blood: as if he had s. blood
Num 35 6 who hath shed blood may flee to them
11 who have shed blood against their will
15 who hath shed blood against his will
33 that hath shed the blood of another
Deut 21 7 our hands did not shed this blood nor
1 K 25 31 that thou hast shed innocent blood or
3 K 2 5 and shed the blood of war in peace
4 K 21 16 shed also very much innocent blood
1 Pa 22 8 hast shed much blood and fought many
28 3 art a man of war and hast shed blood
Ps 13 3 their feet are swift to shed blood
105 38 they shed innocent blood: the blood of
Prov 1 16 to evil and make haste to shed blood
6 17 hands that shed innocent blood, a heart
Isa 59 7 and make haste to shed innocent blood
Jer 7 6 shed not innocent blood in this. 22:3
26 15 you will shed innocent blood against
Lam 4 13 have shed the blood of the just in
Eze 16 38 and they that shed blood are judged
22 6 employed his arm in thee to shed blood
9 have been in thee to shed blood and
12 have taken gifts in thee to shed blood
27 wolves ravening the prey to shed blood
24 8 I have shed her blood upon the smooth
33 25 that shed blood: shall you possess the
Joel 3 19 have shed innocent blood in their land
1 Ma 1 39 they shed innocent blood round about
2 Ma 1 8 burnt the gate, and s. innocent blood

Rom 3 15 their feet swift to shed blood
shedder Eze 18 10 son that is . . . a s. of blood
shedders Eze 23 45 and as s. of blood are judged
sheddeth Eccu 28 13 a hasty quarrel s. blood and
Eccu 34 27 he that sheddeth blood and he that
Eze 22 3 this is the city that sheddeth blood
shedding Judg 9 24 s. of their blood upon Abimelech
1 K 1 10 prayed to the Lord, s. many tears
1 Pa 22 8 after shedding so much blood before me
Eccu 27 16 of the proud is the s. of blood
Jer 22 17 and upon shedding innocent blood and
Heb 9 22 without shedding of blood there is no
11 28 pasch, and the shedding of the blood
sheep Gen 12 16 he [Abram] had sheep and oxen
Gen 20 14 Abimelech took sheep and oxen and
21 27 Abraham took sheep and oxen and gave
24 35 and he hath given him sheep and oxen
26 14 he had possessions of sheep and of
29 3 all the sheep were gathered together
3 after the sheep were watered, to put it
7 first give the sheep drink and so
9 Rachel came with her father's sheep
10 and that they were the sheep of Laban
30 31 I will feed and keep thy sheep again
32 separate all the sheep of divers colors
32 of divers colors, as well among the s.
33 among the sheep as among the goats
35 the she goats and the sheep and the
39 the sheep beheld the rods and brought
31 8 all the sheep brought forth speckled
19 Laban was gone to shear his sheep
32 5 I have oxen and asses and sheep and
7 flocks and the sheep and the oxen
33 13 have with me tender children and sheep
34 28 they took their sheep and their herds
37 13 thy brethren feed the sheep in Sichem
38 12 to Thamnas to the shearers of his s.
13 come up to Thamnas to shear his sheep
45 10 thy sons' sons, thy sheep, and thy
47 1 sheep and their herds and all that
17 in exchange for their horses and sheep
Exod 2 17 defending the maids, watered their s.
19 with us, and gave the sheep to drink
3 1 Moses fed the sheep of Jethro his
9 3 grievous murrain upon thy . . . sheep
10 9 with our sheep and herds: for it is the
24 let your sheep only and herds remain
12 32 your sheep and herds take along with
38 went up also with them s. and herds
13 13 of an ass thou shalt change for a s.
20 24 peace offerings, your sheep and oxen
22 1 if any man steal an ox or a sheep and
1 oxen for one ox, and four s. for one s.
4 ass or sheep: he shall restore double
9 fraud, either in ox or in ass or sheep
10 if a man deliver ass, ox, sheep or any
30 firstborn of thy oxen also and sheep
34 3 oxen nor the s. feed over against it
19 of oxen and of sheep, it shall be mine
20 of an ass thou shalt redeem with a s.
Lev 1 2 offering victims of oxen and sheep, if
10 a holocaust of sheep or of goats, he
7 23 the fat of a sheep and of an ox and
17 3 if he kill an ox or a sheep or a goat
22 19 of the beeves or of the sheep or of
21 whether of beeves or of sheep, shall
23 or a sheep that hath the ear and the
27 a sheep or a goat is brought forth
28 it be a cow or a sheep, they shall not
27 26 bullock or sheep, they are the Lord's
32 of all the tithes of oxen and sheep
Num 11 22 shall multitude of sheep and oxen be
15 3 unto the Lord, of oxen or of sheep
18 17 the firstling of a cow and of a sheep
22 40 when Balac had killed oxen and sheep
27 17 as sheep without a shepherd. 2 Pa 18:16
31 28 persons as of oxen and asses and sheep
30 take the fiftieth head of . . . sheep
32 had taken, was 675,000 sheep, 72,000
36 in the battle, to wit, 337,500 sheep
37 of the Lord were reckoned 675 sheep
43 out of the 337,500 sheep . . . Moses took
32 24 folds and stalls for your sheep and
Deut 12 6 firstborn of your herds and your sheep
14 4 that you shall eat, the ox and the s.
23 firstborn of thy herds and thy sheep
26 of the herds or of sheep, wine also
15 19 that come of thy herd and thy sheep
19 not shear the firstlings of thy sheep
16 2 phase to the Lord thy God, of sheep
17 1 s. or an ox wherein there is blemish
18 3 whether they sacrifice an ox or a sheep
4 wool from the shearing of their sheep
22 1 brother's ox or his sheep go astray
28 4 thy herds, and the folds of thy sheep
31 may thy sheep be given to thy enemies
32 14 milk of the sheep with the fat of lambs
Josu 6 21 sheep and the asses they slew with the
7 24 oxen and asses and sheep, the tent
Judg 6 4 of life, nor sheep nor oxen nor asses
1 K 14 32 they took sheep and oxen and calves
15 3 suckling, ox and sheep, camel and ass
15 the people spared the best of the sheep
21 people took of the spoils s. and oxen
16 11 yet a young one, who keepeth the sheep
17 28 why didst thou leave those few sheep
34 thy servant kept his father's sheep
22 19 sheep with the edge of the sword
25 2 and he had three thousand sheep and
2 he was shearing his sheep in Carmel
4 that Nabal was shearing his sheep, he
16 we were with them keeping the sheep
18 wine and five sheep ready dressed
27 9 and took away the sheep and the oxen
2 K 7 8 from following the sheep to be ruler
12 2 the rich man had exceeding many sheep
4 he spared to take of his own sheep
13 23 that the sheep of Absalom were shorn
24 behold thy servant's sheep are shorn
17 29 and butter and sheep and fat calves
24 17 these that are the sheep, what have
3 K 8 5 they sacrificed sheep and oxen that
63 to the Lord, 22,000 oxen and 120,000 s.
22 17 s. that have no shepherd. Jdth 11:15
4 K 3 4 Mesa, king of Moab, nourished many s.
5 26 to buy oliveyards and vineyards and s.
1 Pa 5 21 of camels 50,000 and of sheep 250,000
12 40 and oxen and sheep in abundance, for
27 31 over the sheep, Jaziz an Agarene
2 Pa 18 2 Achab at his coming killed sheep and
29 33 to the Lord 600 oxen and 3,000 sheep
30 24 thousand bullocks and 10,000 sheep
24 thousand bullocks and 7,000 sheep
31 6 brought in the tithes of oxen and s.
2 Es 10 36 firstlings of our oxen and of our sheep
Tob 7 9 Raguel commanded a sheep to be killed
Job 1 3 and his possession was 7,000 sheep
16 striking the sheep and the servants
31 20 not warmed with the fleece of my sheep
42 12 he had 14,000 sheep and 6,000 camels
Ps 8 8 under his feet, all sheep and oxen
43 12 hast given us up like sheep to be eaten
22 are counted as sheep for the slaughter
48 15 they are laid in hell like sheep: death
73 1 against the sheep of thy pasture
76 21 hast conducted thy people like sheep

77 52 he took away his own people as sheep
78 13 thy people and the s. of thy pasture
79 2 thou that leadest Joseph like a sheep
94 7 his pasture and the sheep of his hand
99 3 his people and the sheep of his pasture
106 41 made him families like a flock of sheep
118 176 I have gone astray like a sheep that
143 13 their s. fruitful in young, abounding
Cant 6 5 thy teeth as a flock of sheep, which
Jer 12 3 them together as sheep for a sacrifice
23 1 that destroy and tear the sheep of my
Isa 7 21 shall nourish a young cow and two sheep
11 6 lion and the sheep shall abide together
13 14 as a doe fleeing away, and as a sheep
53 6 all we like sheep have gone astray
7 shall be led as a s. to the slaughter
66 3 he that killeth a sheep in sacrifice
Eze 34 5 my sheep were scattered, because there
6 my s. have wandered in every mountain
8 my sheep are become a prey to all the
11 behold I myself will seek my sheep and
12 when he shall be in the midst of his s.
12 scattered, so will I visit my sheep
15 I will feed my sheep: and I will cause
19 my sheep were fed with that which you
Dan 14 2 forty sheep and sixty vessels of wine
31 two carcasses every day, and two sheep
Jon 3 7 oxen nor sheep, taste anything: let
Mich 2 12 as the sheep in the midst of the
Zach 13 7 and the sheep shall be scattered: and
Mat 7 15 come to you in the clothing of sheep
9 36 lying like sheep that have no shepherd
10 6 to the lost s. of the house of Israel
16 I send you as sheep in the midst of
12 11 that hath one sheep: and if the same
12 how much better is a man than a sheep
15 24 to the sheep that are lost of the
18 12 if a man have an hundred sheep, and
25 32 separateth the sheep from the goats
33 he shall set the sheep on his right
26 31 sheep of the flock shall be dispersed
Mark 6 34 they were as sheep not having a
14 27 and the sheep shall be dispersed. But
Luke 15 4 that hath an hundred sheep: and if
6 I have found my sheep that was lost
John 2 14 that sold oxen and sheep and doves
15 the sheep also and the oxen and the
10 2 by the door is the shepherd of the s.
3 the sheep hear his voice: and he
3 and he calleth his own sheep by name
4 when he hath let out his own sheep
4 the sheep follow him, because they
7 I am the door of the sheep. All others
8 robbers: and the sheep heard them not
11 shepherd giveth his life for his s.
12 whose own the sheep are not, seeth
12 and leaveth the sheep and flieth
12 wolf catcheth and scattereth the s.
13 and he hath no care for the sheep
15 and I lay down my life for my sheep
16 other sheep I have that are not of
26 because you are not of my sheep. My sheep hear my voice
21 17 he said to him: Feed my sheep
Acts 8 32 was led as a sheep to the slaughter
Rom 8 36 accounted as sheep for the slaughter
Heb 13 20 the great pastor of the sheep, our
1 P 2 25 for you were as sheep going astray
Apoc 18 13 and sheep and horses and chariots and
flocks of sheep; *see* **flocks**
sheepcotes 1 K 24 4 and he came to the s. which
2 Pa 14 15 and they destroyed the sheepcotes
Eze 25 4 shall place their sheepcotes in thee
Mich 2 12 as the sheep in the midst of the s.
sheepfold John 10 1 not by the door into the s.
sheepfolds Num 32 16 we will make s. and stalls
sheepskins Heb 11 37 they wandered about in s.
sheet Acts 10 11 linen s. let down by four corners
Acts 11 5 descending, as it were a great sheet
shelter Josu 10 19 to s. themselves in their cities
Eccu 14 26 shall set his children under her s.
shepherd Gen 4 2 Abel was a shepherd, and Cain
Gen 38 12 the Odollamite the s. of his flock
20 and Juda sent a kid by his shepherd
Num 27 17 sheep without a shepherd. 2 Pa 18:16
3 K 22 17 sheep that have no shepherd. Jdth 11:15
Ecce 12 11 of masters are given from one shepherd
Wisd 17 16 any one were a husbandman or a s.
Eccu 18 13 correcteth, as shepherd doth his flock
Isa 40 11 he shall feed his flock like a shepherd
44 28 who say to Cyrus: Thou art my shepherd
49 10 merciful to them, shall be their s.
Jer 31 10 will keep him as the s. doth his flock
43 12 as a shepherd putteth on his garment
49 19 that s. that can withstand my. 50:44
51 23 I will break in pieces the shepherd
Eze 34 5 because there was no shepherd. 8
12 as the shepherd visiteth his flock
23 I will set up one shepherd over them
23 them and he shall be their shepherd
37 24 them, and they shall have one shepherd
Amos 3 12 as if a s. should get out of the lion's
Zach 10 2 be afflicted, because they have no s.
11 15 the instruments of a foolish shepherd
16 I will raise up a shepherd in the land
17 s. and idol, that forsaketh the flock
13 7 awake, O sword, against my shepherd
7 strike the shepherd, and the sheep
Mat 9 36 lying like sheep that have no shepherd
25 32 as the s. separateth the sheep from
26 31 I will strike the shepherd. Mark 14:27
Mark 6 34 they were as sheep not having a s.
John 10 2 in by the door is the s. of the sheep
11 I am the good s. The good s. giveth
12 he that is not the shepherd, whose
14 I am the good shepherd; and I know
16 shall be one fold and one shepherd
1 P 2 25 the shepherd and bishop of your souls
shepherd's Lev 27 32 that pass under the s. rod
1 K 17 40 and put them into the shepherd's scrip
Isa 38 12 away from me, as a shepherd's tent
shepherds Gen 29 4 he [Jacob] said to the s.
Gen 46 32 the men are shepherds, and their
34 Egyptians have all s. in abomination
34 we thy servants are shepherds. 47:3
Exod 2 17 shepherds came and drove them away
19 delivered us from the hands of the s.
1 K 25 7 thy s. that were with us in the desert
Cant 1 7 kids beside the tents of the shepherds
Isa 13 20 nor shall shepherds rest there. But
31 4 when a multitude of s. shall come
56 11 the s. themselves knew no understanding
63 11 the sea with the shepherds of his flock
Jer 6 3 s. shall come to her with their flocks
25 34 howl, ye shepherds, and cry: and
35 the shepherds shall have no way to flee
36 a voice of the cry of the shepherds
50 6 their s. have caused them to go astray
Eze 34 2 prophesy concerning the s. of Israel
2 say to the shepherds: Thus saith the
2 woe to the shepherds of Israel, that
2 should not the flocks be fed by the s.
7 ye shepherds, hear the word of the. 9
8 my s. did not seek after my flock
8 but the shepherds fed themselves, and
10 I myself come upon the shepherds, I

Prov 4 18 the path of the just as a shining light
Eccu 26 22 as the lamp shining upon the holy
43 4 s. with his beams, he blindeth the
9 shining gloriously in the firmament of
Eze 1 27 the resemblance of fire s. round about
Joel 2 10 the stars have withdrawn their s. 3:15
Nah 3 3 and of the shining sword and of the
Mark 9 2 and his garments became shining and
Luke 24 4 two men stood by them, in s. apparel
John 5 35 he was a burning and a shining light
Acts 26 13 s. round about me, and them that were
ship Prov 30 19 way of a ship in the midst of the
Prov 31 14 she is like the merchant's ship, she
Wisd 5 10 a ship that passeth through the waves
14 5 passing over the sea by ship are saved
Eccu 33 2 dashed in pieces as a ship in a storm
Isa 30 17 till you be left as the mast of a ship
33 21 no ship with oars shall pass by it
Jon 1 3 found a ship going to Tharsis: and he
4 the ship was in danger to be broken
5 forth the wares that were in the ship
5 down into the inner part of the ship
1 Ma 15 37 Tryphon fled away by ship to Orthosias
Mat 4 21 in a ship with Zebedee their father
Mark 1 19 were mending their nets in the ship
20 their father Zebedee in the ship with
3 9 that a small ship should wait on him
4 1 so that he went up into a ship and sat
36 take him even as he was in the ship
37 and the waves beat into the ship, so
37 so that the ship was filled. And he
38 he was in the hinder part of the ship
5 2 as he went out of the ship, immediately
18 when he went up into the ship, he that
21 Jesus had passed again in the ship
6 32 going up into a ship, they went into a
45 disciples to go up into the ship, that
47 the ship was in the midst of the sea
51 and he went up to them into the ship
54 when they were gone out of the ship
8 10 going up into a ship with his disciples
13 he went up again into the ship and
14 but one loaf with them in the ship
Luke 5 3 taught the multitudes out of the ship
7 partners that were in the other ship
8 22 he went into a little ship with his
37 going up into the ship, returned
John 6 17 when they had gone up into a ship
19 and drawing nigh to the ship, and they
21 to take him into the ship; and presently the ship was at the land
22 saw that there was no other ship there
22 Jesus had not entered into the ship
21 3 went forth and entered into the ship
6 the net on the right side of the ship
8 the other disciples came in the ship
Acts 20 13 going aboard the ship, sailed to Assos
38 they brought him on his way to the ship
21 2 we had found s. sailing over to Phenice
3 there the ship was to unlade her burden
6 we took ship; and they returned home
27 2 going on board a ship of Adrumetum, we
6 the centurion finding ship of Alexandria
10 not only of the lading and ship, but
11 master of ship, more than those things
15 when ship was caught, and could not bear
15 giving up the ship to the winds, we
17 helps, undergirding ship, and fearing
18 the next day they lightened the ship
19 their own hands tackling of the ship
22 life among you, but only of the ship
30 shipmen sought to fly out of the ship
30 cast anchors out of forepart of the ship
31 stay in the ship, you cannot be saved
37 meat. And we were in all in the ship
38 they lightened the s., casting the wheat
39 minded, if they could, to thrust in ship
41 seas met, they run the ship aground; and
44 on those things that belonged to the s.
28 11 we sailed in a ship of Alexandria, that
shipmaster Jon 1 6 the s. came to him and said
Apoc 18 17 every shipmaster, and all that sail
shipmen Acts 27 27 s. deemed that they discovered
Acts 27 30 as the s. sought to fly out of the ship
shipping John 6 24 they took shipping and came
ships Gen 49 13 in the road of ships, reaching
Deut 28 68 bring thee again with ships into Egypt
Judg 5 17 and Dan applied himself to ships
3 K 22 49 the ships were broken in Asiongaber
50 go with thy servants in the ships
2 Pa 8 18 Hiram sent him ships by the hands
9 21 the king's ships went to Tharsis with
20 36 was partner with him in making ships
36 and they made the ships in Asiongaber
37 the ships are broken and they could
Job 9 26 passed by as ships carrying fruits
Ps 47 8 shalt break in pieces the s. of Tharsis
103 26 and great. There the ships shall go
106 23 they that go down to the sea in ships
Isa 2 16 and upon all the ships of Tharsis
23 1 howl, ye ships of the sea, for. 14
43 14 the Chaldeans glorying in their ships
60 9 the ships of the sea in the beginning
Eze 26 18 now shall the ships be astonished
27 9 all the ships of the sea and their
25 the ships of the sea were thy chief
29 shall come down from their ships: the
30 9 in ships to destroy the confidence of
1 Ma 1 18 horsemen and a great number of ships
8 26 wheat or arms or money or ships. 28
11 1 together an army . . . and many ships
13 29 ships carved, which might be seen by
15 3 great army, and have built ships of war
14 and the ships drew near by sea: and
2 Ma 12 9 set the haven on fire with the ships
Mark 4 36 and there were other ships with him
Luke 5 2 saw two ships standing by the lake
3 going into one of the ships that was
7 they came and filled both the ships
11 having brought their ships to land
John 6 23 other ships came in from Tiberias
James 3 4 behold also ships, whereas they are
Apoc 8 9 third part of the ships was destroyed
18 19 were made rich that had ships at sea
shipwreck 2 C 11 25 thrice I suffered shipwreck
1 Tim 1 19 some rejecting have made shipwreck
shirts Judg 14 12 I will give you thirty shirts
Judg 14 13 you shall give me thirty shirts and
shocked 2 Ma 6 12 that they be not s. by these
shod 2 Pa 28 15 when they had clothed and s. them
Eze 16 10 shod thee with violet colored shoes
Mark 6 9 but to be shod with sandals, and that
Eph 6 15 s. with the preparation of the gospel
shoe Gen 14 23 woof thread unto the shoe latchet
Deut 25 9 shall take off his shoe from his foot
33 25 his shoe shall be iron and brass. As
Ruth 4 7 the man put off his shoe and gave it
8 said to his kinsman: Put off thy shoe
Ps 59 10 into Edom will I stretch out my shoe
107 10 over Edom I will stretch out my shoe
Eccu 46 22 money or anything else, even to a shoe
John 1 27 latchet of whose shoe I am not worthy
shoes Exod 3 5 put off the shoes from thy feet
Exod 12 11 you shall have shoes on your feet
Deut 29 5 neither are shoes of your feet consumed
Josu 5 16 loose, saith he, thy shoes from off

9 5 very old shoes, which for a show of age
13 and the shoes we have on our feet
3 K 2 5 and in his shoes that were on his feet
Cant 7 1 how beautiful are thy steps in shoes
Isa 3 18 will take away the ornaments of shoes
5 27 nor latchet of their shoes be broken
11 15 men may pass through it in their shoes
20 2 and take off thy shoes from thy feet
Eze 16 10 and shod thee with violet colored shoes
24 17 thy shoes on thy feet, and cover not
23 on your heads, and shoes on your feet
Dan 3 21 and their shoes and their garments
Amos 2 6 and the poor man for a pair of shoes
8 6 and the poor for a pair of shoes
Mat 3 11 whose shoes I am not worthy to bear
10 10 nor two coats nor shoes nor a staff
Mark 1 7 latchet of whose s. I am not. Luke 3:16
10 4 carry neither purse nor scrip nor s.
15 22 on his hand, and shoes on his feet
22 35 you without purse and scrip and shoes
Acts 7 33 loose the shoes from thy feet, for the
13 25 s. of his feet I am not worthy to loose
shone Ps 96 4 his lightnings have shone forth
Ps 117 27 Lord is God, and he hath shone upon us
Eccu 50 6 he shone in his days as the morning
Eze 43 2 and the earth shone with his majesty
1 Ma 6 39 when the sun shone upon the shields
39 and they shone like lamps of fire
2 Ma 1 22 the time came that the sun shone out
Luke 2 9 brightness of God s. round about them
Acts 22 6 suddenly from heaven there s. round
shook Judg 16 30 he had strongly s. the pillars
2 K 22 8 earth shook and trembled. Ps 17:8; 76:19
2 Es 5 13 I shook my lap and said: So may God
Job 1 19 shook the four corners of the house
Isa 14 16 this the man . . . that shook kingdoms
Eze 31 16 I shook the nations with the sound
Amos 9 1 hinges, and let the lintels be shook
1 Ma 9 13 the earth shook at the noise of the
Acts 18 6 he shook his garments, and said to them
shoot 1 K 20 20 I will shoot three arrows near
1 K 20 20 will shoot as if I were exercising
36 fetch me the arrows which I shoot
4 K 13 17 Eliseus said: Shoot an arrow. And he
19 32 this city, nor shoot an arrow into it
2 Pa 26 15 to shoot arrows and great stones: and
Job 8 16 his rising his blossom shall s. forth
Ps 10 3 to shoot in the dark the upright of
63 5 thing, to shoot in secret the undefiled
6 they will shoot at him on a sudden
77 9 who bend and shoot with the bow: they
143 6 shoot out thy arrows, and thou shalt
Isa 37 33 this city nor shoot an arrow into it
61 11 causeth her seed to shoot forth: so
Jer 46 9 Lydians, that take, and shoot arrows
Eze 17 23 it shall shoot forth into branches
31 14 nor shoot up their tops among the
36 8 shoot ye forth your branches and
Osee 14 6 his root shall shoot forth as that
1 Ma 6 51 pieces to shoot arrows and slings
Luke 21 30 when they now shoot forth their fruit
shooteth Prov 26 18 as he is guilty that s. arrows
Mark 4 32 shooteth out great branches, so that
shooting 3 K 22 34 bent his bow, s. at a venture
1 Pa 12 2 with slings, and shooting arrows
Wisd 11 19 s. horrible sparks out of their eyes
Amos 7 1 of the shooting up of the latter rain
shore Num 34 5 in the shore of the great sea
3 K 9 26 by Ailath on the shore of the Red Sea
Eze 47 11 on the shore thereof and in the fenny
Mat 13 2 all the multitude stood on the shore
48 sitting by the shore, they chose out
Mark 6 53 of Genezareth, and set to the shore
John 21 4 Jesus stood on the shore: yet the
Acts 21 5 kneeled down on the shore, and we prayed
27 39 discovered certain creek that had a s.
40 to the wind, they made towards shore
28 13 compassing by the shore, we came to
sea shore; *see* **seashore**
shorn 2 K 13 23 the sheep of Absalom were shorn in
2 K 13 24 thy servant's sheep are shorn. Let the
Cant 4 2 as flocks of sheep, that are shorn
Acts 18 18 having shorn his head in Cenchrae: for
1 C 11 6 woman be not covered, let her be shorn
6 if it be a shame to a woman to be shorn
short Deut 30 18 shalt remain but a short time in
Jdth 7 17 that our end may be short by the edge
Job 14 1 living for a short time, is filled
5 the days of man are short, and the
16 23 short years pass away and I am walking
20 5 that the praise of the wicked is short
Ps 2 13 wrath shall be kindled in a short time
Wisd 2 1 time of our life is short and tedious
4 13 being made perfect in a short space, he
9 5 I am . . . a weak man and of short time
5 falling short of the understanding
15 9 nor that his life is short, but he
16 3 after suffering want for a short time
6 they were troubled for a short time
Eccu 10 11 all power is of short life. A long
12 physician cutteth off a short sickness
25 26 all malice is short to the malice of
32 11 asked twice, let thy answer be short
Isa 3 22 changes of apparel and short cloaks
28 20 a short covering cannot cover both
22 and a cutting short upon all the earth
30 20 give you spare bread and short water
Jer 27 16 shall not in a short time be brought
Dan 7 1 relating the sum of it in short, he
1 Ma 7 50 of Juda was quiet for a short time
2 Ma 2 33 and to be short in the story itself
7 36 having now undergone a short pain
11 1 a short time after this Lysias the
Rom 9 28 shall finish his word, and cut it short
28 a short word shall the Lord make upon
1 C 7 29 I say, brethren; the time is short; it
2 C 12 11 for I have no way come short of them
1 Th 2 17 taken away from you for a short time
Apoc 12 12 knowing that he hath but a short time
17 10 is come, he must remain a short time
shorten Eccu 30 26 envy and anger s. a man's days
shortened Job 17 1 my days shall be s., and only
Ps 88 46 thou hast s. the days of his time: thou
Prov 10 27 and the years of the wicked shall be s.
Isa 50 2 is my hand s. and become little, that
59 1 the hand of the Lord is not shortened
Dan 9 24 seventy weeks are shortened upon thy
Mat 24 22 unless those days had been shortened
22 of the elect those days shall be s.
Mark 13 20 unless the Lord had shortened the days
20 chosen, he hath shortened the days
short-lived Ecce 10 1 than a small and s. folly
shortly Job 10 20 fewness of my days be ended s.
Ps 36 2 they shall shortly wither away as grass
Wisd 14 14 be found to come shortly to an end
Bar 4 24 shall they also s. see your salvation
Eze 7 8 shortly I will pour out my wrath upon
2 Ma 2 18 will shortly have mercy upon us and·
Acts 25 4 he himself would very s. depart thither
1 C 4 19 I will come to you shortly, if the Lord
Phil 2 19 to send Timothy unto you shortly, that
24 I myself also shall come to you shortly
1 Tim 3 14 hoping that I shall come to thee s.
Heb 13 23 with whom, if he come shortly, I will
Apoc 1 1 the things which must s. come to pass
22 6 the things which must be done shortly

shot Exod 19 13 shall be shot through with arrows
1 K 20 36 he shot another arrow beyond the boy
37 of the arrow which Jonathan had shot
2 K 11 24 the archers shot their arrows at thy
22 15 he shot arrows and scattered them
4 K 9 24 and shot Joram between the shoulders
13 17 said: Shoot an arrow. And he shot
2 Pa 18 33 of the people s. an arrow at a venture
Wisd 5 12 as when an arrow is shot at a mark
22 they shall be shot out and shall fly to
Lam 3 13 he hath shot into my reins the
Eze 17 6 into branches, and shot forth sprigs
9 all the branches it hath shot forth
31 10 and shot up his top green and thick
Mark 4 5 and it shot up immediately, because
shoulder Gen 21 14 Abraham . . . put it upon her s.
Gen 24 15 having a pitcher on her shoulder: an
45 a pitcher, which she carried on her s.
46 let down the pitcher from her shoulder
49 15 and he bowed his shoulder to carry
Exod 29 22 fat that is upon them, and the right s.
27 s. that thou didst separate of the ram
Lev 7 32 right shoulder also of the victims of
33 he shall have the right shoulder also
34 the s. that is separated I have taken
8 25 with the right shoulder, he separated
26 them upon the fat, and the right s.
10 14 the s. that is separated you shall eat
15 the shoulder and the breast and the
Num 6 19 take the boiled shoulder of the ram
20 to be separated, and the shoulder
18 18 the right shoulder shall be thine
Deut 18 3 shall give to the priest the shoulder
Judg 9 48 laying it on his s. and carrying it
1 K 9 24 cook took up the shoulder and set it
2 Es 9 29 and they withdrew the shoulder and
Job 31 22 let my shoulder fall from its joint
36 that I may carry it on my shoulder
Eccu 6 26 bow down thy shoulder and bear her
Isa 9 4 the rod of their shoulder, and the
6 the government is upon his shoulder
10 27 shall be taken away from off thy s.
14 25 his burden shall be taken off their s.
22 22 key of the house of David upon his s.
47 2 uncover thy shame, strip thy shoulder
Bar 2 21 bow down your shoulder and your neck
Eze 24 4 good piece, the thigh and the shoulder
25 9 I will open the shoulder of Moab from
29 7 didst break and rent all their shoulder
18 bald, and every shoulder was peeled
Soph 3 9 and may serve him with one shoulder
Zach 7 11 they turned away the s. to depart
Mala 2 3 I will cast the shoulder to you, and
2 Ma 12 35 cut off his shoulder: and so Gorgias
15 30 hand with the s. should be cut off
shoulders Gen 9 23 put a cloak upon their s.
Exod 12 34 cloaks, put it on their shoulders
28 12 names before the Lord upon both s.
Lev 9 21 the right shoulders, elevating them
Num 7 9 carry the burdens upon their own s.
Deut 32 11 taken him and carried him on his s.
33 12 between his shoulders shall be rest
Josu 4 5 every man a stone on your shoulders
Judg 16 3 laying them on his shoulders, carried
1 K 9 2 from his s. and upward he appeared
10 23 of the people from the s. and upward
17 6 buckler of brass covered his shoulders
4 K 9 24 and shot Joram between the shoulders
1 Pa 15 15 upon their shoulders, with the staves
2 Pa 2 18 to carry burdens on their shoulders
18 33 between the neck and the shoulders
Ps 90 4 will overshadow thee with his shoulders
Eccu 7 35 offer to the Lord the gift of thy s.
Isa 11 14 fly upon the s. of the Philistines
30 6 carry their riches upon s. of beasts
46 7 they bear him on their shoulders and
49 22 and carry thy daughters upon their s.
Bar 6 3 of stone and of wood borne upon s.
25 use of feet they are carried upon s.
Eze 12 6 shalt be carried out upon men's s.
7 and was carried on men's shoulders
12 prince . . . shall be carried on s.
34 21 you thrusted with sides and shoulders
Mat 23 4 and lay them on men's shoulders; but
Luke 15 5 found it, lay it upon his shoulders
shout Exod 32 18 shout of men compelling to flee
Josu 6 5 all the people shall shout together
10 you shall not shout . . . until the day
10 I shall say to you: Cry and shout
16 shout, for the Lord hath delivered
20 all the people making a shout, and the
Judg 18 23 and began to shout out after them
1 K 4 5 all Israel shouted with a great shout
6 Philistines heard the noise of the s.
6 what is this noise of a great shout
1 Es 3 11 the people shouted with a great shout
13 the people shouted with a loud shout
13 distinguish the voice of the s. of joy
Ps 46 2 shout unto God with the voice of joy
64 14 they shall shout, yea they shall sing
65 1 shout with joy to God all the earth
Isa 42 13 zeal: he shall shout and cry: he shall
44 23 shout with joy, ye ends of the earth
Jer 25 30 shout as it were of them that tread
31 7 shout ye, and sing, and say: Save
50 15 shout against her, she hath everywhere
51 14 shall lift up a joyful shout against
Soph 3 14 shout, O Israel: be glad and rejoice
Zach 9 9 shout for joy, O daughter of Jerusalem
2 Ma 15 29 making a shout and a great noise, they
shouted Judg 7 24 all Ephraim s. and took the
1 K 4 5 all Israel shouted with a great shout
14 20 people that were with him s. together
17 20 out to fight and shouted for the battle
52 s. and pursued after the Philistines
2 Pa 13 15 and all the men of Juda shouted: and
15 they shouted, God terrified Jeroboam
1 Es 3 11 the people shouted with a great shout
13 the people shouted with a loud shout
Eccu 50 18 then the sons of Aaron shouted, they
shouting Exod 32 17 the noise of the people s.
Josu 8 16 they s. together and encouraging one
Judg 7 23 men of Israel shouting from Nephtali
10 17 children of Ammon shouting together
15 14 Philistines shouting went to meet him
2 K 6 15 the ark . . . with joyful s. 1 Pa 15:28
2 Pa 15 14 with a loud voice with joyful shouting
1 Es 3 12 shouting for joy, lifted up their voice
Jdth 14 7 went out with a great noise and s.
15 3 they went down . . . shouting after them
Job 39 25 of the captains, and the s. of the army
Isa 16 10 there shall be no rejoicing nor s.
Amos 1 14 with shouting in the day of battle
shovels Num 4 14 forks, pothooks and shovels
3 K 7 40 Hiram made caldrons and shovels
45 caldrons and the shovels and the basins
shower Deut 32 2 dew as a shower upon the herb
Job 29 23 opened their mouth as for a latter s.
37 6 winter rain, and the s. of his strength
Prov 28 3 is like a violent s., which bringeth
Eccu 43 20 the heart is astonished at the shower
Eze 13 11 there shall be an overflowing s. 13
Dan 3 64 every shower and dew, bless ye the
Luke 12 54 presently you say: A shower is coming
showers Job 24 8 with the s. of the mountains
Job 36 27 and poureth out showers like floods

38 25 who gave a course to violent showers
Ps 64 11 shall spring up and rejoice in its s.
71 6 showers falling gently upon the earth
77 44 rivers into blood, and their showers
Eccu 39 9 the words of his wisdom as showers
Jer 3 3 therefore the showers were withholden
14 22 or can the heavens give showers? Art
Eze 34 26 there shall be showers of blessing
Zach 10 1 and will give them showers of rain
shrank Gen 32 25 his thigh, and forthwith it s.
Gen 32 32 the sinew, that shrank in Jacob's thigh
32 sinew of his thigh, and it shrank
shred 4 K 4 39 he shred them into the pot of
shrew Lev 11 30 the shrew and the chameleon
shrink Ecce 12 6 the golden fillet shrink back
shrub Isa 55 13 instead of the s., shall come up
shrubs Isa 7 19 upon all places set with shrubs
1 Ma 4 38 shrubs growing up in the courts as in
shuffling Eze 21 21 seeking divination, s. arrows
shun 2 Tim 2 16 shun profane and vain babblings
shunned 2 K 19 3 the people s. the going into
shut Gen 7 16 Lord shut him in on the outside
Gen 19 6 Lot went out to them and shut the door
10 in Lot unto them, and shut the door
Exod 14 3 the land, the desert hath shut them in
Lev 14 46 into the house when it is shut, shall
Josu 2 7 gone out, the gate was presently shut
Judg 3 24 saw the doors of the parlor shut, and
9 51 having shut and strongly barred the
2 K 13 17 from me: and s. the door after her. 18
4 K 4 4 shut thy door, when thou art within
5 so the woman . . . shut the door upon her
21 and shut the door: and going out, she
33 he [Eliseus] shut the door upon him
6 32 shut the door and suffer him not to
2 Es 6 10 let us shut the doors of the temple
7 3 the gates were shut and barred: and I
13 19 they shut the gates, and I commanded
Tob 6 17 as to shut out God from themselves
8 18 and hast shut out from us the enemy
Jdth 13 1 Vagao shut the chamber doors and went
Job 41 6 shut close up with scales pressing
Ps 68 16 let not the pit shut her mouth upon me
Ecce 12 4 they shall shut the doors in the street
Eccu 4 36 and shut when thou shouldst give
30 18 are hidden in a mouth that is shut
Isa 6 10 and shut their eyes: lest they see
22 22 he shall open, and none shall shut: and he
shall shut, and none shall open
26 20 shut thy doors upon thee, hide thyself
45 1 him, and the gates shall not be shut
52 15 kings shall shut their mouth at him
60 11 they shall not be shut day nor night
Lam 3 8 entreat, he hath shut out my prayer
Eze 41 16 the windows were shut over the doors
44 1 way of the gate . . . and it was shut
2 this gate shall be shut, it shall
2 entered in by it, and it shall be shut
46 1 shall be shut the six days, on which
2 gate shall not be shut till the evening
12 gate shall be shut after he is gone
Dan 13 17 shut the doors of the orchard. 18, 36
20 the doors of the orchard are shut, and
14 10 shut the door fast, and seal it with
13 they shut the door and having sealed
Mala 1 10 among you, that will shut the doors
1 Ma 5 47 were in the city, shut themselves in
10 75 but they shut him out of the city
11 61 they that were in Gaza shut him out
12 48 they of Ptolemais shut the gates
2 Ma 1 15 they shut the temple, when Antiochus
Mat 6 6 having shut the door, pray to thy
13 15 their eyes they have shut. Acts 28:27
23 13 you shut the kingdom of heaven against
25 10 to the marriage, and the door was shut
Luke 11 7 the door is now shut, and my children
13 25 be gone in and shall shut the door
John 20 19 and the doors were shut, where the
26 Jesus cometh, the doors being shut
Acts 5 23 the prison indeed we found shut with
21 30 and immediately the doors were shut. And
Apoc 3 8 a door opened, which no man can shut
11 6 these have power to shut heaven, that
20 3 shut him up and set a seal upon him
21 25 the gates thereof shall not be shut
shut up Gen 8 2 gates of heaven were shut up
Gen 39 20 and he [Joseph] was there shut up
Exod 14 27 the Lord shut them up in the middle
21 29 his master, and he did not shut him up
Lev 13 4 the priest shall shut him up seven days
5 shall shut him up again other 7 days
11 and shall not shut him up, because
21 shall shut him up seven days. 26, 31
33 he shall be shut up other seven days
50 shall shut it up seven days: and on
54 he shall shut it up other seven days
14 38 and forthwith shut it up seven days
Deut 11 17 the Lord being angry shut up heaven
32 30 them and the Lord had shut them up
36 that they who were shut up have also
Josu 6 1 Jericho was close shut up and fenced
10 18 set careful men to keep them shut up
1 K 1 5 the Lord had shut up her womb. 6
6 7 and shut up their calves at home. 10
23 7 he is shut up, being come into a city
26 8 God hath shut up thy enemy this day
2 K 18 28 who hath shut up the men that have
20 3 they were shut up unto the day of their
3 K 8 35 if heaven shall be shut up and there
14 10 him that is shut up and the last. 21:21
4 K 9 8 him that is shut up, and the meanest
14 26 even to them that were shut up in
19 24 dried up . . . all the shut up waters
25 2 the city was shut up and besieged till
2 Pa 6 26 if the heavens be shut up and there
7 13 if I shut up heaven and there fall no
28 24 shut up the doors of the temple of God
29 7 they have shut up the doors that were
Jdth 5 1 had shut up the ways of the mountains
8 5 in which she abode shut up with her
Job 3 10 it shut not up the doors of the womb
12 14 if he shut up a man, there is none that
16 12 God hath shut me up with the unjust man
38 8 who shut up the sea with doors, when
Ps 16 10 have shut up their fat: their mouth
30 9 thou hast not shut me up in the hands
34 3 shut up the way against them that
76 10 will he in his anger shut up his
77 50 and their cattle he shut up in death
62 he shut up his people under the sword
Wisd 17 2 shut up in their houses, lay there
15 he was kept shut up in prison without
18 4 who kept thy children shut up, by whom
Eccu 29 15 shut up alms in the heart of the poor
42 7 shut up and deliver all things in
48 3 he shut up the heaven and he brought
Isa 24 10 every house is shut up, no man cometh
22 they shall be shut up there in prison
29 10 he will shut up your eyes, he will
37 25 foot, all the rivers shut up in banks
61 1 deliverance to them that are shut up
Jer 13 19 cities of the south are shut up, and
20 9 a burning fire, shut up in my bones
32 2 Jeremias . . . was shut up in the court
3 Sedecias . . . had shut him up, saying
33 1 was yet shut up in the court. 39:15

36 5 I am shut up and cannot go into the
Lam 3 9 he hath shut up my ways with square
Eze 3 24 shut thyself up in the midst of thy
35 5 hast shut up the children of Israel
Dan 6 22 hath shut up the mouths of the lions
12 4 shut up the words and seal the book
9 the words are shut up and sealed until
Amos 1 6 captivity to shut them up in Edom
9 they have shut up an entire captivity
Abdi 14 shalt not shut up them that remain
Jon 2 7 the bars of the earth have shut me up
1 Ma 3 18 to be shut up in the hands of a few
4 31 shut up this army in the hands of thy
5 5 they were shut up by him in towers
26 many of them were shut up in Barasa
27 they were kept shut up in the rest
6 18 had shut up the Israelites round about
49 had no victuals, being shut up there
11 65 it many days and shut them up. And
15 25 he shut up Tryphon, that he could
2 Ma 3 19 the virgins also that were shut up
5 8 having been shut up by Aretas the
Luke 3 20 above all, and shut up John in prison
4 25 when heaven was shut up three years
Acts 26 10 many of saints did I shut up in prison
Gal 3 23 we were kept under the law shut up, unto
1 J 3 17 and shall shut up his bowels from him
shutteth Job 9 7 s. up the stars as it were
Isa 33 15 s. his eyes that he may see no evil
Apoc 3 7 he that openeth, and no man shutteth; shutteth, and no man openeth
shutting Josu 2 5 at the time of s. the gate
Judg 3 23 shutting the doors of the parlor and
16 21 s. him up in prison made him grind
Eze 7 23 make a shutting up: for the land is
Sia 1 Es 2 44 of Ceros, the children of Sia
Siaa 2 Es 7 48 Nathinites . . . children of Siaa
Siaha 2 Es 11 21 that dwelt in Ophel and Siaha
Siba 2 K 9 2 of house of Saul, a servant named S.
2 K 9 2 art thou Siba? And he answered: I am Siba
3 Siba said to the king: There is a son
4 Siba said to the king: Behold he is
9 king called Siba the servant of Saul
10 Siba had 15 sons and 20 servants
11 Siba said to the king: As thou my lord
12 kindred of the house of Siba served
16 1 Siba the servant of Miphiboseth came
2 the king said to Siba: What mean these
2 Siba answered: The asses are for the
3 Siba answered the king: He remained
4 Siba said: I beseech thee let me find
4 the king said to Siba: I give thee
19 17 thousand men of Benjamin and Siba
29 thou and Siba divide the possessions
Siban Esth 8 9 third month which is called Siban
sibboleth Judg 12 6 he answered, Sibboleth
Siceleg Josu 15 31 S. and Medemena and Sensenna
Josu 19 5 S. and Bethmarchaboth and Hasersusa
1 K 27 6 then Achis gave him Siceleg that day
30 1 David and his men were come to Siceleg
1 invasion on the south side upon Siceleg
1 smitten Siceleg and burnt it with fire
14 Caleb, and we burnt Siceleg with fire
26 David came to Siceleg and sent presents
2 K 1 1 abode two days in Siceleg. And on the
4 10 I apprehended and slew him in Siceleg
1 Pa 4 30 in Bathuel and in Horma and in S.
12 1 they that came to David to Siceleg
20 when he went back to Siceleg, there
2 Es 11 28 at Siceleg and at Mochona and in the
Sichar John 4 5 of Samaria, which is called S.
Sichem Gen 12 6 the country into the place of S.
Gen 33 19 children of Hemor, the father of Sichem
34 2 Sichem the son of Hemor the Hevite
6 when Hemor the father of Sichem, was
8 soul of my son Sichem has a longing
11 S. also said to her father and to her
13 the sons of Jacob answered Sichem and
18 their offer pleased Hemor and Sichem
25 they killed also Hemor and Sichem
35 4 tree, that is behind the city of Sichem
37 12 and when his brethren abode in Sichem
14 the vale of Hebron, he came to Sichem
Josu 17 7 Machmethath which looketh towards S.
20 7 Nephtali, and Sichem in mount Ephraim
21 21 Sichem one of the cities of refuge
24 1 all the tribes of Israel in Sichem and
25 commandments and judgments in Sichem
32 out of Egypt, they buried in Sichem
32 of the sons of Hemor the father of S.
Judg 8 31 his concubine, that he had in Sichem
9 1 went to Sichem to his mother's brethren
2 speak to all the men of S.: whether
3 spoke of him to all the men of Sichem
6 all the men of Sichem were gathered
6 king by the oak that stood in Sichem
7 hear me, ye men of Sichem, so may
18 king over the inhabitants of Sichem
20 let fire come out from men of Sichem
20 and consume the inhabitants of Sichem
23 Abimelech and the inhabitants of S.
26 the inhabitants of S. taking courage
26 his brethren went over to Sichem
28 who is Abimelech and what is Sichem
28 the men of Emor the father of Sichem
31 Gaal the son of Obed is come into S.
34 laid ambushes near S. in four places
39 in the sight of the people of Sichem
46 they who dwelt in the tower of Sichem
47 that the men of the tower of Sichem
49 of the inhabitants of the tower of S.
21 19 way that goeth from Bethel to Sichem
3 K 12 1 and Roboam went to Sichem. 2 Pa 10:1
25 Jeroboam built Sichem in mount Ephraim
1 Pa 6 67 they gave the cities of refuge Sichem
7 28 Sichem also with her daughters, as far
Ps 59 8 rejoice and I will divide S. 107:8
Eccu 50 28 the foolish people that dwell in Sichem
Jer 41 5 there came some from Sichem and from
Osee 6 9 in the way those that pass out of S.
Acts 7 16 they were translated into Sichem and
16 the sons of Hemor, the son of Sichem
Sichemites Gen 33 18 to Salem, a city of the S.
Judg 9 24 upon the rest of princes of the S.
57 the Sichemites also were rewarded
Sichem's Gen 34 26 sister Dina, out of S. house
sick Gen 48 1 told Joseph that his father was s.
1 K 19 14 and it was answered that he was sick
30 13 I began to be sick three days ago
2 K 13 2 that he fell sick for the love of her
5 upon thy bed, and feign thyself sick
6 lay down and made as if he were sick
3 K 14 1 Abia the son of Jeroboam fell sick
5 thee concerning her son that is sick
17 17 the son of the woman . . . fell sick
4 K 1 2 and was sick: and he sent messengers
8 7 and Benadad king of Syria was sick
29 in Jezrahel because he was sick there
9 16 into Jezrahel: for Joram was sick there
13 14 Eliseus was sick of the illness whereof
20 1 Ezechias was sick unto death: and
12 had heard that Ezechias had been sick
2 Pa 16 12 Asa fell sick in the nine and thirtieth
21 15 thou shalt be sick of a very grievous
22 6 in Jezrahel where he [Joram] lay sick
32 24 in those days Ezechias was s. even to

2 Es 2 2 seeing thou dost not appear to be sick
Wisd 17 8 were sick themselves of a fear worthy
8 fears and troubled from a sick soul
Eccu 7 39 be not slow to visit the sick: for by
18 21 humble thyself before thou art sick
Isa 1 5 the whole head is sick, and the whole
38 1 days Ezechias was sick even to death
9 king of Juda, when he had been sick
39 1 he had heard that he had been sick
Bar 6 27 give nothing of it either to the sick
Eze 34 4 which was sick you have not healed
Dan 8 27 languished and was sick for some days
Mala 1 8 if you offer the lame and the sick
13 in of rapine the lame and the sick
1 Ma 6 8 his bed, and fell sick for grief
Mat 4 24 they presented to him all sick people
8 6 lieth at home sick of the palsy, and
14 wife's mother lying and sick of a fever
16 and all that were sick he healed
9 2 brought to him one sick of the palsy
2 said to the man sick of the palsy. 6
10 8 heal the sick, raise the dead, cleanse
14 14 compassion on them and healed their sick
25 36 covered me: sick, and you visited me
39 when did we see thee sick or in prison
43 sick and in prison, and you did not
44 stranger or naked or sick or in prison
Mark 2 3 to him, bringing one sick of the palsy
4 wherein the man sick of the palsy lay
5 he saith to the sick of the palsy. 10; Luke 5:24
9 easier, to say to the sick of the palsy
17 of a physician, but they that are sick
6 5 that he cured a few that were sick
13 anointed with oil many that were sick
55 about in beds those that were sick
16 18 shall lay their hands upon the sick
Luke 4 40 they that had any sick with divers
5 31 physician; but they that are sick
7 2 who was dear to him, being sick, was
10 the servant whole who had been sick
9 2 kingdom of God, and to heal the sick
10 9 heal the sick that are therein and
John 4 46 certain ruler whose son was sick at
5 3 in these lay a great multitude of sick
11 1 was a certain man sick, named Lazarus
2 whose brother Lazarus was sick. His
3 behold, he whom thou lovest is sick
6 heard therefore that he was sick, he
Acts 5 15 brought forth the s. into the streets
16 bring sick persons and such as were
9 37 in those days that she was sick, and
19 12 there were brought from his body to s.
28 8 father of Publius lay sick of a fever
Phil 2 26 for that you had heard that he was sick
27 indeed he was sick, nigh unto death; but
1 Tim 6 4 sick about questions and strifes of
2 Tim 4 20 and Trophimus I left sick at Miletus
James 5 14 is any man sick among you? Let him
15 prayer of faith shall save the s. man
sickle Deut 23 25 but not reap them with a sickle
Deut 16 9 didst put the sickle to the corn
Jer 50 16 him that holdeth the sickle in the
Mark 4 29 immediately he putteth in the sickle
Apoc 14 14 and in his hand a sharp sickle. And
15 thrust in thy sickle and reap, because
16 thrust his sickle into the earth, and
17 he also having a sharp sickle. And
18 to him that had the sharp sickle
18 thrust in thy sharp sickle and gather
19 the angel thrust in his sharp sickle
sickles Isa 2 4 and their spears into sickles
Joel 3 13 put ye in the sickles, for the harvest

sickness Exod 23 25 and may take away s. from
Deut 7 15 Lord will take away from thee all s.
3 K 17 17 and the sickness was very grievous
Ps 40 4 hast turned all his couch in his s.
Eccu 10 11 a long sickness is troublesome to the
12 physician cutteth off a short sickness
18 20 before sickness take a medicine, and
21 in time of s. show thy conversation
30 17 everlasting rest, than continual s.
31 2 a grievous s. maketh the soul sober
25 shalt not bring sickness upon thy body
37 33 in many meats there will be sickness
38 9 in thy sickness neglect not thyself
Isa 38 9 and was recovered of his sickness
Osee 5 13 Ephraim saw his sickness, and Juda his
2 Ma 9 22 great hope to escape the sickness
Mat 4 23 healing all manner of sickness and
John 11 4 this sickness is not unto death, but
sicknesses Mark 3 15 gave them power to heal s.
sicle Exod 30 13 a sicle hath twenty obols. Lev 27:25; Num 3:47; 18:16; Eze 45:12
Exod 30 13 every one give . . . half a sicle
13 half a sicle shall be offered to the
15 rich man shall not add to half a sicle
Lev 27 25 according to the sicle of the sanctuary
1 K 9 8 the fourth part of a sicle of silver
2 Es 10 32 to give the third part of a sicle
Amos 8 5 that we may . . . increase the sicle
sicles Gen 24 22 golden earrings, weighing two sicles
Gen 24 22 many bracelets of ten sicles weight
Exod 30 23 principal and chosen myrrh 500 sicles, and of cinnamon . . . 250 sicles
38 24 gold that was spent . . . 730 sicles
29 brass also 72,000 talents and 400 sicles
Lev 5 15 that may be bought for two sicles
27 5 a man shall give 20 sicles: a woman
6 for a male shall be given five sicles
7 old or upward, shall give 15 sicles
Num 3 47 shalt take five sicles for every head
50 Moses took the money . . . 1,366 sicles
7 13 a silver dish weighing 130 sicles. 19, 25, 31, 37, 43, 49, 55, 61, 67, 73, 79
13 a silver bowl of seventy sicles. 19, 25, 31, 37, 43, 49, 55, 61, 67, 73, 79
14 a little mortar of ten sicles of gold
20 mortar of gold weighing ten sicles. 26, 38, 44, 50, 56, 62, 68, 74, 80
85 each bowl seventy sicles: that is
85 vessels of silver together 2,400 s.
86 mortars of gold . . . weighing ten s.
86 that is in all 120 sicles of gold
31 52 in weight 16,750 sicles, from the
Josu 7 21 of silver, and a golden rule of 50 s.
Judg 8 26 requested, was 1,700 sicles of gold
1 K 17 5 coat of mail was 5,000 sicles of brass
7 head of his spear weighed 600 sicles
2 K 14 26 the hair of his head at 200 sicles
3 K 10 16 allowed 600 s. of gold for the plates
1 Pa 21 25 David gave . . . 600 sicles of gold
2 Pa 3 9 weight of every nail was fifty sicles
2 Es 5 15 took . . . in money every day 40 sicles
Eze 45 12 now 20 sicles, and 5 and 20 sicles, and 15 sicles make a man
sicles of silver Gen 23 15 is worth 400 s. . . .
Gen 23 16 400 s. . . . of common current money
Exod 21 32 he shall give 30 s. . . . to their master
Lev 27 3 sixty years old, shall give s. . . .
16 of barley, let it be sold for 50 s. . . .
Num 7 85 each dish weighing 130 s. . . . , and
18 16 shall be after one month for 5 s. . . .
Deut 22 19 condemning him besides in 100 s. . . .
29 to the father of the maid 50 s. . . .
Josu 7 21 and 200 s. . . . and a golden rule of

2 K 18 11 I would have given thee ten s. . . .
24 24 the floor and the oxen for 50 s. . . .
3 K 10 29 chariot . . . for 600 sicles of silver
4 K 15 20 of the Assyrians, each man 500 s. . . .
1 Ma 10 40 and I give every year 15,000 s. . . .
42 the 5,000 s. . . . which they received
Sicyon 1 Ma 15 23 things were written to . . . S.
side Gen 6 16 of ark thou shalt set in the s.
Exod 6 20 Jochabed his aunt by the father's side
12 7 and put it upon both the side posts
26 20 second side also of the tabernacle
32 26 if any man be on the Lord's side let
36 25 at that side also of the tabernacle
27 at that side of the tabernacle which
38 12 on that side that looketh to the west
Lev 1 11 immolate it at the side of the altar
5 9 he shall sprinkle the side of the altar
Deut 31 26 book and put it in the side of the ark
Josu 1 14 Moses gave you on this s. of the Jordan
8 5 will approach on the contrary side
12 9 Hai, which is on the side of Bethel
15 8 on the side of the Jebusite towards
10 and passeth by the side of mount Jarim
11 to a part of Accaron at the side: and
18 12 by the side of Jericho on the north s.
16 by the s. of the Jebusite to the south
23 13 and a stumblingblock at your side
Judg 11 18 went round the land of Edom at the s.
19 1 who dwelt on the side of mount Ephraim
18 which is on the side of mount Ephraim
Ruth 2 14 so she sat at the side of the reapers
1 K 6 8 shall put into a little box at the side
15 little box that was at the side of it
20 22 the arrows are on this side of thee
25 Abner sat by Saul's side, and David's
23 26 Saul went on this side of the mountain
2 K 2 16 his sword into side of his adversary
13 34 by a by-way on side of the mountain
16 13 Semei by the hill's side went over
20 10 and he [Joab] struck him in the side
21 14 in the land of Benjamin, in the side
3 K 1 7 priest, who furthered Adonias's side
3 20 she took my child from my side while
6 8 the door for the middle side was on
15 17 of the side of Asa king of Juda. Then
4 K 16 14 and he set it at the side of the altar
2 Pa 26 9 the rest in the same side of the wall
1 Es 4 10 the countries of this side of the river
11 that are on this side of the river
16 no possession on this side of the river
2 Es 12 37 gave thanks went on the opposite side
Jdth 6 9 out of way by the side of the mountain
Job 1 19 a sudden from the side of the desert
Ps 90 7 a thousand shall fall at thy side
140 7 our bones are scattered by side of hell
Prov 3 26 the Lord will be at thy side and will
Wisd 2 25 they follow him that are of his side
Eccu 17 25 go to the side of the holy age with
42 5 to make side of a wicked slave to bleed
Isa 60 4 thy daughters shall rise up at thy side
Jer 20 10 my familiars, and continued at my side
Eze 4 9 days that thou shalt lie upon thy side
40 40 on the outward side, which goeth up
44 side of gate that looketh to the north
44 one at the side of the east gate
41 5 and the breadth of every side chamber
9 the wall for the side chamber without
9 thickness of wall for the side chamber
45 7 from the side of the sea even to the
7 from side of the east even to the east
46 19 by entry that was at side of the gate
47 20 the side toward the sea, is the great
20 Emath, this is the side of the sea
48 2 from the east side even to the side of the sea.
3, 4, 5, 6, 7, 8, 27
Dan 12 5 one on this side upon the bank of
5 another on that side, on the other bank
1 Ma 9 13 on Judas' side . . . also cried out
49 there fell of Bacchides' side that day
11 70 all that were on Jonathan's side fled
John 19 34 with a spear opened his side, and
20 20 showed them his hands and his side
25 and put my hand into his side, I will
27 thy hand, and put it into my side
Acts 12 7 striking Peter on the side, raised
16 13 forth without the gate by a river side
each side Exod 28 27 set on each side of the ephod
Exod 37 27 two golden rings . . . at each side
3 K 6 34 doors of fir tree, one of each side
Jdth 1 2 each side was extended the space of
Eze 16 16 high places sewed together on each side
John 19 18 two others, one on each side, and
east side; *see* **east**
either side Exod 39 4 in the tip on either side
Exod 39 16 rings on either side of the rational
3 K 10 19 two hands on e. s. holding the seat
Judg 20 16 by the stone's going on either side
Jdth 5 12 waters . . . firm as a wall on e. s.
2 Ma 3 26 who stood by him on either side and
1 Tim 5 21 nothing by declining to either side
every side Num 11 31 on every side of the camp
Num 35 4 outward, a thousand paces on every side
Judg 7 18 blow the trumpets on every side of
20 34 death threatened them on every side
2 K 7 1 Lord had given him rest on every side
3 K 4 24 he had peace on every side round about
1 Pa 21 13 I am on every side in a great strait
2 Pa 15 5 but terrors on every side among all
32 22 and gave them treasures on every side
Esth 1 6 and there were hung up on every side
18 11 fears shall terrify him on every side
Job 15 22 round about for the sword on every side
19 10 he hath destroyed me on every side
Eccu 46 6 enemies assaulted him on every side
19 enemies who beset him on every side
47 8 he destroyed the enemies on every side
51 10 they compassed me on every side and
Jer 6 25 the enemy, and fear is on every side
20 3 name Phassur, but fear on every side
10 terror on every side: persecute him
51 2 they are come upon her on every side
Bar 6 17 the gates are made sure on every side
Eze 17 33 gifts to come to thee from every side
37 together against thee on every side
19 8 come together against him on every side
23 24 be armed against thee on every side
28 24 nor a thorn causing pain on every side
36 3 and trodden under foot on every side
37 2 me about through them on every side
21 and I will gather them on every side
39 17 come together from every side to my
40 14 the court of the gate on every side
16 were within the gate on every side
41 5 round about the house on every side. 10
42 15 he measured it on every side round
20 measured the wall thereof on every side
45 2 shall be for the sanctuary on every s.
48 21 shall be for the prince on every side
Dan 13 22 said: I am straitened on every side
1 Ma 12 13 many troubles and wars on every side
2 Ma 8 25 and they pursued them on every side
10 30 covered him on every side with their
13 5 having a heap of ashes on every side
Luke 19 43 round and straiten thee on every side
left side Josu 19 27 out to the l. s. of Cabul
2 K 16 6 right, and on the l. s. of the king

4 K 11 11 unto the left side of the altar and
2 Pa 23 10 to the left side of the temple before
Eze 1 10 the face of an ox on the left side
4 4 thou shalt sleep upon thy left side
Zach 4 3 the other upon the left side thereof
11 the candlestick, and upon the left side
north side; *see* **north**
on this side and on that side Eze 40 10 three on this side and three on that side. 21
Eze 40 12 little chambers were six cubits o. . . .
26 palm trees, one on this side, and another on that side
34 palm trees in the front thereof o. . . .
39 tables on this s. and . . . on that s. 41
48 on this side and five cubits on that s.
49 pillars . . . on this s. and another on that s.
41 1 on this side and six cubits on that s.
2 on this s. and five cubits on that s.
26 representation of palm trees o. . . .
1 Ma 6 38 rest of the horsemen he placed o. . . .
45 the left, and they fell by him o. . . .
9 45 and the water of the Jordan o. . . .
one side Exod 25 12 two rings be on the one side
Exod 25 32 branches . . . three out of the one side
26 13 shall hang down a cubit on the one side
26 boards on one side of the tabernacle
27 9 shall be hangings . . . for one side
14 for one side hangings of 15 cubits
36 31 to hold together the boards of one side
37 8 one cherub in the top of one side
18 three branches on one side, and three
38 14 were on one side with three pillars
Num 16 37 scatter the fire of one side and the
1 K 14 4 steep cliffs like teeth on the one s.
40 be you on one side, and I with Jonathan
17 3 stood on a mountain on the one side
2 K 2 13 the one on the one side of the pool
3 K 10 20 the six steps on the one side and on
1 Pa 13 9 had made it lean a little on one side
Eze 4 8 not turn thyself from one side to the
41 19 was toward the palm tree on one side
45 7 for the prince also on the one side
Dan 7 5 beast like a bear stood up on one side
1 Ma 9 17 fell many wounded of the one side and
other side Gen 45 27 on the other side, told the
Exod 26 13 cubit . . . and another on the other s.
27 and five others on the other side
27 15 other side . . . hangings of 15 cubits
36 32 to hold together the boards of other s.
37 8 other cherub in top of the other side
38 15 on the other side . . . were hangings
Josu 24 2 dwelt of old on other side of the river
Judg 7 5 their knees, shall be on the other s.
11 18 camped on the other side of the Arnon
1 K 14 1 which is on other side of yonder place
40 with Jonathan my son will be on o. s.
17 3 Israel stood on mountain on other side
26 13 when David was gone over to other side
2 K 2 13 pool, and the other on the other side
3 K 20 27 went out on the other side and camped
1 Pa 12 37 and on the other side of the Jordan
Wisd 18 10 on the other side there sounded an ill
19 20 on the other side, the flames wasted
Eccu 37 11 then stand on the other side to see
Eze 40 40 at the other side . . . were two tables
41 19 toward the palm tree on the other side
45 7 on the one side and on the other side
1 Ma 5 41 camp on the other side of the river
2 Ma 10 28 the other side making their rage their
Mat 8 28 he was come on the o. s. of the water
Mark 4 35 let us pass over to the other side
8 13 passed to the other side of the water
Luke 8 22 over to the other side of the lake
John 6 22 stood on the other side of the sea
25 found him on the other side of the sea
Acts 15 2 certain others of other side, should
right side 2 K 24 5 Aroer to the r. s. of the
3 K 7 39 five on the right side of the temple
39 the sea he put on the right side
4 K 11 11 from the right side of the temple
23 13 on right side of the Mount of Offence
2 Pa 4 8 five on the right side, and five on
10 and he set the sea on the right side
23 10 from the right side of the temple
Eze 1 10 the face of a lion on the right side
4 6 shalt sleep again upon thy right side
10 3 the cherubims stood on the right side
47 1 the waters came down to the right side
2 there ran out waters on the right side
Zach 4 3 one upon the right side of the lamp
11 upon the right side of the candlestick
9 14 stronger part . . . was on the right s.
Mark 16 5 young man sitting on the right side
Luke 1 11 standing on the right side of the altar
John 21 6 cast the net on the right side of the
sea side; *see* **seaside**
side chambers; *see* **chambers**
south side; *see* **south**
west side; *see* **west**
Side 1 Ma 15 23 same things were written . . . to S.
sides Exod 25 14 rings that are in the sides of
Exod 25 18 cherubims . . . on the two sides of the
32 six branches shall come out of the s.
26 4 loops of violet in the sides and tops
17 in sides of the boards shall be made
36 24 board on the two sides of the corners
24 where the mortises of the sides end in
37 5 rings that were at the sides of the ark
7 on the two sides of the propitiatory
18 six on the two sides: three branches
26 its grates and the sides and the horns
38 7 stood out in the sides of the altar
39 7 he set them in the sides of the ephod
Num 22 27 angry beat her sides more vehemently
33 55 in your eyes, and spears in your sides
Josu 6 9 sound of trumpets was heard on all s.
3 K 6 5 oracle, and he made sides round about
7 30 at the four sides were undersetters
18 21 how long do you halt between two sides
Jdth 6 4 soldiers shall pass through thy sides
13 28 I will command thy sides to be pierced
Job 15 27 and the fat hangeth down on his sides
31 20 if his sides have not blessed me
Ps 47 3 Sion founded, on the sides of the north
127 3 vine, on the sides of thy house. Thy
Eccu 30 12 beat his sides while he is a child
Isa 14 13 the covenant in the sides of the north
Eze 1 8 under their wings on their four sides
8 had faces and wings on the four sides
16 57 thee, that encompass thee on all sides
28 23 being slain by the sword on all sides
34 21 you thrusted with sides and shoulders
40 41 at the s. of the gate were eight tables
41 2 sides of the gate five cubits on this
6 through the wall of the house in the s.
16 galleries round about on three sides
26 palm trees . . . in the s. of the porch
26 according to the sides of the house
43 16 cubits broad, foursquare with equal s.
1 Ma 9 12 the legion drew near on two sides
Mark 1 45 and they flocked to him from all sides
Apoc 22 2 and on both sides of the river was the
both sides Exod 17 12 stayed up his hands on b. s.
Exod 25 20 them cover both sides of propitiatory
26 5 shall have fifty loops on both sides
13 fencing both sides of the tabernacle

7 10 and wisdom in the sight of Pharao
31 Moses seeing it, wondered at the sight
9 9 he was there three days, without sight
12 him, that he might receive his sight
17 mayest receive thy sight, and be filled
18 he received his sight; and rising up
10 33 all we are present in thy sight, to
27 35 gave thanks to God in the s. of them all
Rom 12 17 of God, but also in the sight of all men
2 C 5 7 for we walk by faith, and not by sight
8 24 to them, in the sight of the churches
1 Th 2 17 away from you for a short time, in s.
2 P 2 8 for in sight and hearing he was just
3 J 6 thy charity in the sight of the church
Apoc 4 3 he that sat was to the sight like the
3 throne, in sight like unto emerald
6 in the sight of the throne was, as it
7 9 the throne and in sight of the Lamb
13 13 unto the earth in the sight of men
14 him to do in the sight of the beast
14 10 in the sight of the holy angels and in the sight of the Lamb
15 4 come and shall adore in thy sight
in his sight 1 C 1 29 that no flesh should glory in his sight
Eph 1 4 be holy and unspotted in his sight in
Heb 4 13 any creature invisible in his sight: but
13 21 which is well pleasing in his sight
1 J 3 19 in his sight shall persuade our hearts
22 those things which are pleasing i. . . .
Apoc 13 12 the power of the former beast i. . . .
in the sight of God Acts 4 19 if it be just i. . . . to hear you rather
Acts 8 21 for thy heart is not right i. . . . Do
10 4 alms are ascended for memorial i. . . .
31 alms are had in remembrance i. . . .
Rom 12 17 good things, not only i. . . . , but also
2 C 4 2 to every man's conscience, i. . . . And
1 Tim 2 3 good and acceptable in the sight of God
1 P 3 4 a meek spirit, which is rich i. . . .
Apoc 11 16 who sit on their seats i. . . . , fell
in thy sight Ps 118 168 because all my ways are in thy sight
Ps 118 169 supplication, O Lord, come near i. . . .
140 2 prayer be directed as incense i. . . .
142 2 i. . . . no man living shall be justified
Wisd 12 14 shall king nor tyrant i. . . . inquire
Isa 38 3 have done that which is good i. . . .
Jer 17 16 out of my lips, hath been right i. . . .
18 20 I have stood i. . . . to speak good for
37 19 let my petition be accepted i. . . .
39 16 and they shall be accomplished i. . . .
Bar 2 19 our prayers, and beg mercy i. . . .
Dan 3 40 so let our sacrifice be made i. . . .
Mat 11 26 seemed good in thy s. Luke 10:21
Acts 10 33 all we are present in thy sight, to hear
Apoc 15 4 come and shall adore in thy sight
sightliness Isa 53 2 him, and there was no s.
sign Gen 9 12 this is the sign of the covenant
Gen 9 13 it shall be the sign of a covenant
17 this shall be the sign of the covenant
17 11 may be for a sign of the covenant
Exod 3 12 have for a sign that I have sent thee
4 8 will believe the word of the latter s.
8 nor hear the voice of the former sign
8 23 people: tomorrow shall this sign be
12 13 the blood shall be unto you for a sign
13 9 and it shall be a sign in thy hand
16 it shall be as a sign in thy hand and
31 13 because it is a sign between me and you
17 children of Israel and a perpetual sign
Num 21 8 serpent, and set it up for a sign. 9
Deut 6 8 shalt bind them as a sign on thy hand
11 18 hang them for a sign on your hands
13 1 and he foretell a sign and a wonder
18 22 shalt have this sign: Whatsoever
Josu 2 18 scarlet cord be a sign, and thou lie
4 6 that it may be a sign among you: and
Judg 6 17 a sign that it is thou that speakest
39 more, seeking a sign in the fleece
20 38 children of Israel had given a sign
1 K 2 34 this shall be a sign to the. 10:1
14 10 our hands, this shall be a sign unto us
41 give a sign by which we may know what
3 K 13 3 and he gave a sign the same day, saying
3 this shall be the sign that the Lord
5 sign which the man of God had given
20 33 the man took this for a sign: and in
4 K 19 29 O Ezechias, this shall be a sign: Eat
20 8 what shall be the sign that the Lord
9 this shall be the sign from the Lord
2 Pa 32 24 heard him [Ezechias] and gave him **a s.**
2 Es 9 38 our Levites and our priests sign it
Esth 8 4 the sign of clemency: and she arose
14 16 that I abominate the sign of my price
Wisd 16 6 having a sign of salvation to put them
Eccu 43 6 declaration of times and a sign of the
7 moon is the sign of the festival day
Isa 5 26 he will lift up a sign to the nations
7 11 ask thee a sign of the Lord thy God
14 the Lord himself shall give you a sign
8 18 whom Lord hath given me for a sign
18 3 when the sign shall be lifted up on
19 20 it shall be for a sign and for a
20 3 be a sign and a wonder of three years
37 30 to thee this shall be a sign: Eat
38 7 this shall be a sign to thee from the
22 what shall be the sign that I shall go
55 13 shall be named for an everlasting sign
66 19 I will set a sign among them, and I
Jer 44 29 this shall be a sign to you, saith the
Eze 4 3 it is a sign to the house of Israel
12 6 I have set thee for a sign of things
11 I am a sign of things to come to you
16 25 hast set up a sign of thy prostitution
20 12 sabbaths, to be a sign between me and
20 that they may be a sign between me and
24 24 for a sign of things to come. 27
39 15 they shall set up a sign by it till the
Dan 6 8 confirm the sentence and s. the decree
2 Ma 15 35 might be an evident and manifest sign
Mat 12 38 master, we would see a sign from thee
39 a sign shall not be given, but the sign of Jonas. 16:4; Luke 11:29
16 1 asked him to show them a sign from
24 3 what shall be the sign of thy coming
30 appear the sign of the Son of man in
26 48 that betrayed him, gave them a sign
Mark 8 11 asking him a sign from heaven, tempting
12 why doth this generation seek a sign
12 a sign shall not be given to this
13 4 what shall be the sign when all these
14 44 betrayed him, had given them a sign
Luke 2 12 this shall be a sign unto you. You
34 for a sign which shall be contradicted
11 16 asked of him a sign from heaven. But
29 it asketh a sign, and a sign shall not
30 as Jonas was a sign to the Ninivites
21 7 what shall be the sign when they shall
23 8 he hoped to see some sign wrought by
John 2 18 what sign dost thou show. 6:30
10 41 and they said: John indeed did no sign
Acts 24 10 governor making a sign to him to speak
28 11 ship . . . whose sign was the Castors. And
Rom 4 11 he received the sign of circumcision
1 C 14 22 tongues are for a sign, not to believers

2 Th 3 17 which is the sign in every epistle. So
Apos 7 2 having the sign of the living God; and
3 till we sign the servants of our God
9 4 not the sign of God on their foreheads
12 1 great sign appeared in heaven; a woman
3 there was seen another sign in heaven
15 1 I saw another sign in heaven, great
signals 1 Ma 7 45 the trumpets after them with s.
signed Ps 4 7 countenance . . . is s. upon us
Eph 1 13 you were signed with the holy Spirit of
Apoc 7 4 heard the number of them that were s.
4 144,000 were signed, of every tribe
5 of the tribe of . . . 12,000 s. 6, 7, 8
signet Eccu 17 18 alms of a man is as a signet
Eccu 32 8 as a signet of an emerald in a work of
49 13 he was as a signet on the right hand
Agge 2 24 and will make thee as a signet, for I
signification Eccu 1 31 is the s. of discipline
signified 2 Ma 2 1 the fire, as it hath been s.
2 Ma 11 17 those things which were s. by them
Acts 11 28 Agabus . . . signified by the Spirit
1 C 1 11 for it hath been signified unto me, my
2 P 1 14 Lord Jesus Christ also hath s. to me
Apoc 1 1 signified, sending by his angel to his
signifieth Exod 16 15 manhu! which s.: What is this
Heb 12 27 he s. the translation of the moveable
signify 3 K 5 9 place which thou shalt s. to me
1 Ma 12 7 to signify that you are our brethren
2 Ma 1 18 it necessary to signify it to you
Acts 23 15 signify to tribune, that he bring him
25 27 not to s. the things laid to his charge
Heb 11 14 they that say these things do signify
1 P 1 11 Spirit of Christ in them did signify
signifying 2 Ma 14 27 s. that he was greatly
John 12 33 s. what death he should die. 18:32
21 19 s. by what death he should glorify God
Acts 23 30 s. also to his accusers to plead before
Heb 9 8 the Holy Ghost s. this, that the way
signs Gen 1 14 let them be for signs and for
Exod 4 9 will not even believe these two signs
17 wherewith thou shalt do the signs
28 and the signs that he had commanded
30 he wrought the signs before the people
7 3 shall multiply my signs and wonders
10 1 that I may work these my signs in him
2 and wrought my signs amongst them
11 9 that many signs may be done in the
34 10 I will do signs such as were never
Num 14 11 all the signs that I have wrought
22 and the signs that I have done in Egypt
Deut 4 34 by temptations, signs, and wonders
6 22 wrought signs and wonders great and
7 19 eyes saw, and the signs and wonders
11 3 the signs and works which he did in
26 8 great terror, with s. and wonders
28 46 they shall be as signs and wonders
29 3 seen, those mighty signs and wonders
34 11 the signs and wonders, which he sent
Josu 24 5 struck Egypt with many s. and wonders
17 and did very great signs in our sight
1 K 10 7 these signs shall happen to thee, do
4 K 23 5 to the moon and to the twelve signs
1 Pa 16 12 signs and the judgments of his mouth
2 Es 9 10 showedst signs and wonders upon Pharao
Esth 10 9 hath wrought great signs and wonders
Ps 64 9 shall be afraid at thy signs: thou shalt
73 4 have set up their ensigns for signs
9 our signs we have not seen, there is
77 43 how he wrought his signs in Egypt, and
104 27 he gave them power to show his signs
134 9 he sent forth signs and wonders in
Wisd 8 8 she knoweth signs and wonders before
10 16 against dreadful kings in wonders and s.
19 12 not without foregoing signs by the
Eccu 36 6 renew thy signs, and work new miracles
42 19 hath beheld the signs of the world
Jer 10 2 be not afraid of the signs of heaven
32 20 who hast set signs and wonders in the
21 out of the land of Egypt with signs
Bar 2 11 with signs and with wonders and with
6 66 neither do they show s. in the heaven
Dan 3 99 the most high God hath wrought signs
100 good to me therefore to publish his s.
6 27 doing signs and wonders in heaven and
Dan 14 42 the Savior, working signs and wonders
2 Ma 14 15 protected his portion by evident signs
Mat 16 3 you not know the signs of the times
24 24 shall show great signs and wonders
Mark 13 22 they shall show signs and wonders, to
16 17 these signs shall follow them that
20 confirming the word with signs that
Luke 1 22 he made signs to them and remained
62 they made signs to his father, how he
21 11 heaven; and there shall be great signs
25 and there shall be signs in the sun
John 2 23 seeing his signs which he did
3 2 no man can do these signs which thou
4 48 unless you see signs and wonders, you
20 30 many other signs also did Jesus in the
Acts 2 19 above, and signs on the earth beneath
22 by miracles and wonders and signs
43 many wonders also and signs were done
4 30 forth thy hand to cures and signs and
5 12 were many signs and wonders wrought
6 8 did great wonders and signs among the
7 36 doing wonders and signs in the land
8 13 Simon . . . wondered to see the signs
14 3 granting signs and wonders to be done
15 12 signs and wonders God had wrought
Rom 15 19 by the virtue of signs and wonders, in
1 C 1 22 both the Jews require s., and the Greeks
2 C 12 12 yet the signs of my apostleship have
12 in signs, and wonders, and mighty deeds
2 Th 2 9 in all power and signs and lying wonders
Heb 2 4 bearing them witness by s. and wonders
Apoc 13 13 he did great signs, so that he made
14 the signs which were given him to do
16 14 the spirits of devils working signs
19 20 wrought signs before him, wherewith he
Sihor Josu 19 26 by the sea and S. and Labanath
1 Pa 13 5 all Israel from Sihor of Egypt even
Silas Acts 15 22 S., chief men among the brethren
Acts 15 27 we have sent therefore Judas and Silas
32 Judas and Silas, being prophets also
34 it seemed good unto S. to remain there
40 Paul choosing Silas, departed, being
16 19 gone, apprehending Paul and Silas
25 at midnight, Paul and Silas praying
29 fell down at the feet of Paul and Silas
17 4 were associated to Paul and Silas; and
10 sent away Paul and Silas by night unto
14 but Silas and Timothy remained there
15 commandment from him to Silas and
18 5 when Silas and Timothy were come from
silence Gen 24 21 he musing beheld her with s.
Judg 3 19 he commanded silence: and all being
4 21 going in softly and with silence, she
16 2 watching there all the night in silence
2 Es 8 7 made silence among the people to hear
Jdth 13 6 and the motion of her lips in silence
16 and commanded silence to be made
Esth 7 4 and I would have mourned in silence
14 16 wear it not in the days of my silence
Job 3 26 have I not kept silence? Have I not
Ps 38 3 kept silence from good things: and my
49 3 shall come, and shall not keep silence

Prov 26 10 and he that putteth a fool to silence
Ecce 3 7 a time to keep s. and a time to speak
9 17 words of the wise are heard in silence
10 11 if a serpent bite in silence, he is
Wisd 18 14 while all things were in quiet silence
Eccu 32 9 hear in silence and for thy reverence
12 hear in silence and withal seeking
41 25 of silence before them that salute thee
Isa 8 6 waters of Siloe, that go with silence
30 15 in s. and in hope shall your strength
42 14 I have kept s., I have been patient
62 7 give them no silence till he establish
Jer 8 14 Lord our God hath put us to silence
48 2 shalt thou in silence hold thy peace
Lam 3 26 it is good to wait with silence for
Eze 24 17 sigh in silence, make no mourning for
Amos 5 13 the prudent shall keep silence at that
8 3 silence shall be cast in every place
Haba 2 20 let all the earth keep silence before
Acts 13 16 and with his hand bespeaking silence
19 33 beckoning with his hand for s., would
21 40 a great s. being made, he spoke unto
22 2 tongue, they kept the more silence
1 C 14 34 let women keep silence in the churches
2 Th 3 12 working with silence, they would eat
1 Tim 2 11 let the women learn in silence, with all
12 authority over the man: but to be in s.
1 P 2 15 you may put to silence the ignorance
Apoc 8 1 s. in heaven as it were for half an
silenced Job 39 32 contendeth with God be so easily s.
Mat 22 34 that he had silenced the Sadducees
silent Deut 18 21 if in s. thought thou answer
1 K 2 9 the wicked shall be silent in darkness
2 K 19 10 how long are you s., and bring not back
Ps 27 1 be not thou silent to me, lest if thou be silent to me, I become
31 3 because I was silent, my bones grew old
34 22 thou hast seen, O Lord, be not thou s.
38 13 be not silent: for I am a stranger with
49 21 things hast thou done, and I was silent
108 2 be not thou silent in my praise: for
Eccu 21 31 silent and wise man shall be honored
26 18 such is a wise and silent woman and
Isa 15 1 Ar of Moab is laid waste, it is silent
1 destroyed in the night, it is silent
23 2 be s., you that dwell in the island
24 8 is ended, the melody of the harp is s.
47 5 sit thou silent, and get thee into
57 11 I am silent and as one that seeth not
65 6 I will not be silent, but I will render
Jer 8 14 fenced city, and let us be silent there
25 37 the fields of peace have been silent
49 26 all the men of war shall be silent
51 6 be not silent upon her iniquity: for it
Eze 24 27 speak, and shalt be silent no more
27 32 is like Tyre, which is become silent
33 22 being opened, I was silent no more
Osee 4 5 I have made thy mother to be silent
6 my people have been silent because
Soph 1 7 be silent before the face of the Lord
3 17 he will be silent in his love, he will
Zach 2 13 let all flesh be silent at the presence
Mat 22 12 a wedding garment? But he was silent
silently Dan 4 16 s. to think within himself
silk Gen 41 42 he put upon him a robe of silk
2 Pa 2 14 also and violet and silk and scarlet
3 14 of violet, purple, scarlet and silk
Esth 1 6 hangings, fastened with cords of silk
8 15 clothed with a cloak of silk and purple
Eze 27 16 they set forth . . . fine linen and silk
1 Ma 4 23 and blue silk, and purple of the sea
Apoc 18 12 and fine linen and purple and silk and
silly 2 Es 4 2 what are the silly Jews doing
2 Tim 3 6 lead captive silly women laden with sins
Silo Josu 18 8 lots for you before the Lord in Silo
Josu 18 9 returned to Josue, to the camp in Silo
10 he cast lots before the Lord in Silo
21 2 they spoke to them in Silo in the land
22 9 parted from children of Israel in Silo
12 they all assembled in Silo, to go up
Judg 18 31 time that the house of God was in Silo
20 18 to the house of God, that is, to Silo
21 2 all came to the house of God in Silo
9 in Silo, no one of them was found there
12 they brought them to the camp in Silo
19 a yearly solemnity of the Lord in Silo
21 when you shall see the daughters of S.
1 K 1 3 sacrifice to the Lord of hosts in Silo
9 after she had eaten and drunk in Silo
24 him to the house of the Lord in Silo
2 14 they to all Israel that came to Silo
3 21 Lord revealed himself to Samuel in S.
21 and the Lord again appeared in Silo
4 3 fetch unto us the ark . . . from Silo
4 people sent to Silo, and they brought
12 out of the army and came to Silo the
14 3 of Heli the priest of the Lord in Silo
3 K 2 27 spoke concerning house of Heli in Silo
14 2 go to Silo where Ahias the prophet is
Ps 77 60 he put away the tabernacle of Silo
Jer 7 12 go ye to my place in Silo, where my
14 as I did to Silo. And I will cast
26 6 I will make this house like Silo: and
9 this house shall be like Silo: and this
41 5 came some from Sichem and from Silo
Siloe 2 Es 3 15 and the walls of the pool of S.
Isa 8 6 hath cast away the waters of Siloe
Luke 13 4 upon whom the tower fell in Siloe
John 9 7 go, wash in the pool of Siloe, which
11 go to the pool of Siloe and wash
Siloni 1 Pa 9 5 of Siloni: Asaia the firstborn
Silonite 3 K 11 29 prophet Ahias the Silonite
3 K 12 15 in the hand of Ahias the S. 15:29
2 Pa 9 29 in the books of Ahias the Silonite
10 15 spoken by the hand of Ahias the S.
2 Es 11 5 Zacharias the son of the Silonite
silver Gen 13 2 in possession of gold and silver
Gen 24 35 sheep and oxen, silver and gold
44 8 out of thy lord's house steal gold or s.
Exod 20 23 you shall not make gods of silver nor
25 3 things you must take; gold and silver
26 25 and their silver sockets sixteen
27 10 with their engraving shall be of silver
11 their heads with their engraving of s.
17 be garnished with plates of s., s. heads
31 4 be artificially made of gold and silver
35 5 offer them to the Lord: gold and silver
24 metal of silver and brass, they offered
32 to work in gold and silver and brass
36 30 and they had sixteen sockets of silver
34 casting for them sockets of silver. 36
38 10 graving of the work, of silver. 12
17 heads with all their gravings of silver
17 the pillars of the court also with silver
19 and their heads and gravings of silver
28 which also he overlaid with silver
Num 7 13 a silver dish weighing 130 sicles. 19, 25, 31, 37, 43, 49, 55, 61, 67, 73, 79
13 a silver bowl of 70 sicles. 19, 25, 31, 37, 43, 49, 55, 61, 67, 73, 79
84 twelve dishes of silver: twelve s. bowls
85 putting all the vessels of s. together
10 2 make thee trumpets of beaten silver
22 18 would give me his house full of s. 24:13
31 22 gold and silver and brass and iron
Deut 7 25 thou shalt not covet the silver and gold

8 13 plenty of gold and of silver and of all
17 17 nor immense sums of silver and gold
29 17 idols, wood and stone, silver and gold
Josu 6 19 whatsoever gold or s. there shall be
24 therein; except the gold and silver
7 21 the silver I covered with the earth
22 the same place together with the silver
24 silver and the garments and the golden
22 8 with silver and gold, brass and iron
Judg 9 4 they gave him 70 weight of silver
17 3 I have consecrated and vowed this silver
1 K 2 36 shall offer a piece of silver and a roll
9 8 the fourth part of a sicle of silver
2 K 8 10 vessels of s. and vessels of brass
11 silver and gold that he had dedicated
21 4 we have no contest about s. and gold
3 K 7 51 brought in . . . the s. and the gold
10 21 there was no s. nor was any account
22 brought from thence gold and silver
27 made s. to be as plentiful in Jerusalem
15 15 he brought in . . . silver and gold and
18 then Asa took all the silver and gold
19 sent thee presents of silver and gold
20 3 thy silver and thy gold is mine: and
5 thy silver and thy gold and thy wives
7 my children, and for my silver and gold
39 or thou shalt pay a talent of silver
4 K 5 22 give them a talent of silver, and two
7 8 they took from thence silver and gold
12 13 not made . . . vessel of gold and silver
18 and all the silver that could be found
14 14 he [Joas] took all the gold and silver
16 8 gathered together the silver and gold
18 15 Ezechias gave all the silver that was
20 13 showed them . . . the gold and the s.
23 35 Joakim gave the silver and the gold
35 exacted both the silver and the gold
25 15 and such as were of silver in silver
1 Pa 18 11 all the vessels of gold and silver and
11 s. and gold which he had taken from
22 14 and of silver a million of talents
16 in gold and in silver and in. 2 Pa 2:7, 14
28 14 silver by weight according to the
15 he gave silver by weight for the silver candlesticks
16 also silver for other tables of silver
17 for lions of silver he set aside a different weight of silver
29 2 and silver for vessels of silver, brass
3 gold and s. for the temple of my God
5 s. for wheresoever . . . need of silver
7 of silver 10,000 talents: and of brass
2 Pa 1 15 the king made silver and gold to be
5 1 had vowed, the silver and the gold and
9 14 who brought gold and silver to Solomon
20 no account was made of silver in those
21 they brought thence gold and silver
24 presents, vessels of silver and of gold
27 silver as plentiful in Jerusalem as
15 18 into house of the Lord, gold and s.
16 2 then Asa brought out silver and gold
3 wherefore I have sent thee silver and
17 11 brought presents . . . and tribute in s.
21 3 gave them great gifts of silver and
24 14 and other vessels of gold and silver
25 24 he [Joas] took all the gold and silver
32 27 great treasures of silver and of gold
34 17 they have gathered together the silver
1 Es 1 4 help him . . . with silver and gold and
9 bowls of gold, a thousand bowls of silver
10 silver cups of a second sort, 410
11 the vessels of gold and silver, 5,400
2 69 they gave . . . 5,000 pounds of silver
5 14 the vessels also of gold and silver
6 5 let the golden and s. vessels of the
7 15 to carry the silver and gold which the
16 silver and gold that thou shalt find
18 with the rest of the silver and gold
8 25 I weighed unto them the silver and gold
26 and a hundred vessels of silver and a
28 are holy, and the silver and gold
30 received the weight of the silver and
33 the s. and the gold . . . were weighed
2 Es 7 71 of gold, and 2,200 pounds of silver
72 of gold, and 2,000 pounds of silver
Jdth 2 10 gold and silver he took out of the
15 14 they gave to Judith in gold and silver
Esth 1 6 the beds also were of gold and silver
Job 3 15 and fill their houses with silver
22 25 s. shall be heaped together for thee
27 16 if he shall heap together s. as earth
17 the innocent shall divide the silver
28 1 silver hath beginnings of its veins
15 neither shall s. be weighed in exchange
Ps 11 7 as silver tried by the fire, purged from
65 10 hast tried us by fire, as s. is tried
67 14 as wings of a dove covered with silver
31 to exclude them who are tried with s.
104 37 brought them out with silver and gold
113 4 idols of the Gentiles are s. 134:15
118 72 above thousands of gold and silver
Prov 3 14 better than the merchandise of silver
8 19 and my blossom than choice silver
10 20 tongue of the just is as choice silver
16 16 for it is more precious than silver
17 3 as silver is tried by fire, and gold
22 1 good favor is above silver and gold
25 4 take away the rust from silver, and
11 is like apples of gold on beds of s.
26 23 earthen vessel adorned with s. dross
27 21 as silver is tried in the fining-pot
Ecce 2 8 I heaped together for myself silver and
12 6 before the silver cord be broken and
Cant 1 10 chains of gold, inlaid with silver
3 10 the pillars thereof he made of silver
8 9 let us build upon it bulwarks of s.
Wisd 7 9 s. in respect to her shall be counted
13 10 of the hands of men, gold and silver
Eccu 2 5 gold and silver are tried in the fire
6 15 no weight of gold and silver is able
8 3 gold and silver hath destroyed many
26 23 as golden pillars upon bases of silver
28 29 melt down thy gold and silver, and
30 15 is better than all gold and silver
40 25 gold and s. make the feet stand sure
47 20 and didst multiply silver as lead
51 33 buy her for yourselves without silver
Isa 1 22 thy silver is turned into dross: thy
2 7 their land is filled with s. and gold
20 shall cast away his idols of s. 31:7
13 17 shall not seek silver nor desire gold
30 22 plates of thy graven things of silver
39 2 the storehouses . . . of the silver and
40 19 or the silversmith with plates of s.
46 6 and weigh out silver in the scales
48 10 I have refined thee, but not as silver
60 9 their silver and their gold with them
17 for iron I will bring silver, and for
Jer 6 30 call them reprobate silver, for the
10 4 he hath decked it with silver and gold
9 silver spread into plates is brought
52 19 as many as were of silver, in silver
Bar 1 8 the silver vessels which Sedecias
3 18 that hoard up silver and gold wherein

18 who work in silver and are solicitous
6 3 in Babylon gods of gold and of silver
7 laid over with gold and s. 50, 56, 70
9 convey away from them gold and silver
29 set offerings before the gods of silver
38 their gods . . . of gold and of silver
54 house of these gods of wood and of s.
57 shall take from them the gold and s.
69 so are their gods of wood and of s.
Eze 7 19 their silver shall be cast forth and
19 their s. and their gold shall not be
16 13 thou wast adorned with gold and silver
17 vessels, of my gold and my silver
22 18 they are become the dross of silver
20 as they gather silver and brass and
22 as silver is melted in the midst of
27 12 riches, with silver, iron, tin, and
28 4 gotten gold and s. into thy treasures
38 13 to take a prey, to take silver and gold
Dan 2 32 but the breast and the arms of silver
35 silver and the gold broken to pieces
39 kingdom, inferior to thee, of silver
45 broke in pieces . . . the silver and the
5 2 should bring the vessels of gold and s.
3 the golden and silver vessels brought
4 praised their gods of gold and of s.
23 hast praised the gods of silver and of
11 8 precious vessels of gold and silver
38 he shall worship with gold and silver
43 over the treasures of gold and of s.
Osee 2 8 and multiplied her silver and gold
8 4 of their s. and their gold they have
9 6 nettles shall inherit their beloved s.
13 2 a molten thing of their silver as the
Joel 3 5 you have taken away my silver and my
Amos 2 6 he hath sold the just man for silver
Nah 2 9 take ye the spoil of the silver, take
Haba 2 19 it is laid over with gold and silver
Soph 1 11 are cut off that were wrapped up in s.
41 neither shall their silver . . . be able
Agge 2 9 the s. is mine, and the gold is mine
Zach 6 11 and thou shalt take gold and silver
9 3 and heaped together silver as earth
13 9 will refine them as silver is refined
14 14 be gathered together, gold and silver
Mala 3 3 shall sit refining and cleansing the s.
3 shall refine them as gold and as s.
1 Ma 1 24 he took the silver and gold and the
2 18 shall be . . . enriched with gold and s.
3 41 they took silver and gold in abundance
4 23 and they got much gold and s. and blue
6 1 Elymais . . . abounding in s. and gold
12 away all the spoils of gold and of s.
8 3 under their power the mines of s. and
10 60 he gave them much silver and gold and
11 24 he took gold and silver and raiment
15 26 Simon sent . . . silver also and gold
32 his magnificence in gold and silver
16 11 he had abundance of silver and gold
19 that he would give them silver and gold
2 Ma 2 2 seeing the idols of gold and silver
4 19 to carry 300 didrachmas of silver for
12 43 he sent 12,000 drachms of silver to
Mat 10 9 do not possess gold nor silver nor
Acts 3 6 silver and gold I have none; but what
17 29 divinity to be like unto gold or s.
19 24 a silversmith, who made silver temples
20 33 I have not coveted any man's s., gold
1 C 3 12 build upon this foundation, gold, silver
2 Tim 2 20 not only vessels of gold and of silver
James 5 3 your gold and silver is cankered: and
1 P 1 18 corruptible things as gold or silver
Apoc 9 20 idols of gold and silver and brass and
18 12 merchandise of gold and silver and

pieces of silver Gen 20 16 given thy brother a thousand pieces of silver
Gen 37 28 him to the Ismaelites for 20 p. . . .
45 22 to Benjamin he gave 300 p. . . . with
Judg 16 5 give thee every one of us 1,100 p. . . .
17 2 the 1,100 p. . . . which thou hadst put
4 she took 200 p. . . . and gave them to
10 give thee every year ten p. . . . and a
2 K 18 12 down in my hands a thousand p. . . .
4 K 6 25 of an ass was sold for fourscore p. . . .
25 cabe of pigeon's dung for 5 p. . . .
2 Pa 1 17 chariot of four horses for 600 p. . . .
Cant 8 11 for the fruit thereof a thousand p. . . .
Isa 7 23 thousand vines at a thousand p. . . .
Jer 32 9 money, seven staters and ten p. . . .
Osee 3 2 I bought her to me for fifteen p. . . .
Zach 11 12 they weighed for my wages thirty p. . . .
13 I took the thirty p. . . . and I cast
Mat 26 15 appointed him thirty pieces of silver
27 3 brought back the 30 pieces of silver
5 casting down the pieces of silver in
6 having taken the pieces of silver, said
9 they took the 30 pieces of silver, the
Acts 19 19 the money to be 50,000 pieces of silver

sicles of silver; ***see*** **sicles**
sockets of silver; ***see*** **sockets**
talents of silver; ***see*** **talents**
vessels of silver and gold; ***see*** **vessels**

silversmith Judg 17 4 gave them to the s. to make
Isa 40 19 the silversmith with plates of silver
Acts 19 24 Demetrius, a s., who made silver temples

silversmiths Wisd 15 9 with the goldsmiths and s.

Simeon Gen 29 33 she called his name Simeon
Gen 34 25 Simeon and Levi . . . slew all the men
30 Jacob said to Simeon and Levi: You have
35 23 Ruben the firstborn and Simeon and
42 25 taking Simeon and binding him in their
36 S. is kept in bonds, and Benjamin
43 23 and he brought Simeon out to them
46 10 sons of Simeon: Jamuel and. Exod 6:15
48 5 shall be reputed to me as Ruben and S.
49 5 Simeon and Levi brethren: vessels of
Exod 1 2 Ruben, Simeon, Levi, Juda, Issachar
6 15 these are the families of Simeon. And
Num 1 6 of Simeon, Salamiel the son of
26 14 the families of the stock of Simeon
Deut 27 12 upon mount Garizim . . . Simeon, Levi
Josu 19 1 lot came forth for the children of S.
8 the inheritance of the children of S.
9 children of S. had their possession in
21 4 out of the tribes of Juda and of S.
9 of the children of Juda and of Simeon
Judg 1 3 and Juda said to Simeon his brother
3 and Simeon went with him [Juda]. And
17 Juda went with Simeon his brother
1 Pa 2 1 sons of Israel: Ruben, Simeon, Levi
4 42 some also of the children of Simeon
2 Pa 15 9 of Ephraim and Manasses and Simeon
34 6 of Manasses and of Ephraim and of S.
1 Es 10 31 Josue, Melchias, Semeias, Simeon
Jdth 8 1 Salathiel the son of Simeon the son of
9 2 Lord God of my father Simeon, who
Eze 48 24 to the west side one portion for Simeon
25 by the border of Simeon from the east
33 the gate of Simeon one, the gate of
1 Ma 2 1 son of John, the son of Simeon
Luke 2 25 was a man in Jerusalem named Simeon
34 Simeon blessed them and said to Mary
3 30 Levi, who was of Simeon, who was of

sons of Simeon Num 1 22 of the s. . . . by their

Num 7 36 fifth day the prince of the s. . . .
26 12 s. . . . by their kindreds: Namuel, of
1 Pa 4 24 sons of Simeon: Namuel and Jamin
6 25 out of the tribe of the sons of Simeon
12 25 of the s. . . . valiant men for war
tribe of Simeon Num 2 12 camped they of the t. . . .
Num 10 19 in the t. . . . the prince was Salamiel
13 6 of the t. . . . , Saphat the son of Huri
25 14 a prince of the kindred and t. . . .
34 20 of the t. . . . , Samuel the son of
Jdth 6 11 Ozias the son of Micha of the t. . . .
Apoc 7 7 of the tribe of Simeon, 12,000 signed
Simeonites 1 Pa 27 16 over the S., Saphatias the
Simeron 1 Pa 7 1 sons of Issachar . . . Simeron
similitude Deut 4 15 you saw not any s. in the
Deut 4 16 you might make a graven similitude
17 the s. of any beasts that are upon
25 deceived, make to yourselves any s.
Ps 143 12 round about after the s. of a temple
Luke 4 23 you will say to me this similitude
5 36 he spoke a s. to them. 6:39; 12:16; 21:29
8 4 cities unto him, he spoke by a s.
Rom 5 14 sinned after the s. of the transgression
Heb 7 15 if according to the s. of Melchisedech
similitudes Osee 12 10 used s. by the ministry of
Simmaa 1 Pa 2 13 second Abinadab, the third S.
1 Pa 3 5 Simmaa and Sobab and Nathan and
Simon 1 Pa 4 20 the sons also of Simon, Amnon
Eccu 50 1 Simon the high priest, the son of Onias
1 Ma 2 3 and Simon, who was surnamed Thasi
65 your brother Simon is a man of counsel
5 17 Judas said to Simon his brother: Choose
20 now 3,000 men were allotted to Simon
21 Simon went into Galilee and fought
55 and Simon his brother in Galilee
9 19 Jonathan and Simon took Judas their
33 Jonathan and Simon his brother knew it
37 was told Jonathan and S. his brother
62 and Simon . . . retired into Bethbessen
65 Jonathan left his brother S. in the
67 Simon . . . sallied out of the city and
10 74 Simon his brother met him to help him
82 S. drew forth his army and attacked
11 59 he made his brother Simon governor
64 left his brother Simon in the country
65 and Simon encamped against Bethsura
12 33 Simon . . . came as far as Ascalon
38 and Simon built Adiada in Sephela
13 1 S. heard that Tryphon was gathering
13 Simon pitched in Addus over against
14 Tryphon understood that S. was risen
17 Simon knew that he spoke deceitfully
20 Simon and his army marched to every
25 Simon . . . took the bones of Jonathan
27 Simon built over the sepulcher of his
33 S. built up the strongholds of Judea
34 S. chose men and sent to king Demetrius
36 king Demetrius to Simon the high priest
42 first year of Simon the high priest
43 Simon besieged Gaza and camped round
45 beseeching Simon to grant them peace
47 S. being moved, did not destroy them
50 and they cried to Simon for peace
54 S. saw that John his son was a valiant
14 4 was at rest all the days of Simon
17 Simon his brother was made high priest
20 of the Spartans to S. the high priest
23 we have written a copy of them to S.
24 Simon sent Numenius to Rome with a
25 what thanks shall we give to Simon
27 third year under Simon the high priest
29 Simon the son of Mathathias of the
32 S. resisted and fought for his nation
35 the people seeing the acts of Simon
46 pleased all the people to establish S.
47 Simon accepted thereof and was well
49 that Simon and his sons may have it
15 1 sent letters . . . to Simon the priest
2 king Antiochus to Simon the high priest
17 being sent from Simon the high priest
21 deliver them to Simon the high priest
24 they wrote a copy thereof to Simon
26 Simon sent to him 2,000 chosen men
32 and saw the glory of Simon and his
33 Simon answered . . . We have neither
36 of the glory of Simon and of all that
16 1 told Simon his father what Cendebeus
2 and Simon called his two eldest sons
13 he purposed treachery against Simon
14 Simon, as he was going through the
16 when Simon and his sons had drunk
2 Ma 3 4 one Simon of the tribe of Benjamin
11 which wicked S. had given intelligence
4 1 Simon . . . who was the betrayer of
4 which increased the malice of Simon
6 that Simon would cease from his folly
23 Menelaus brother of the aforesaid Simon
8 22 captains . . . Simon and Joseph and
10 19 Machabeus left Simon and Joseph and
20 that were with Simon, being led with
14 17 S. the brother of Judas had joined
Mat 4 18 Simon who is called Peter. 10:2
10 4 Simon the Cananean, and Judas
13 55 his brethren James and Joseph and S.
16 17 blessed art thou, Simon Bar-Jona
17 24 what is thy opinion, Simon? The kings
26 6 in the house of S. the leper. Mark 14:3
27 32 found a man of Cyrene, named Simon
Mark 1 16 he saw Simon and Andrew his brother
29 they came into the house of Simon
36 Simon and they that were with him
3 16 to Simon he gave the name Peter: and
18 Thaddeus and Simon the Cananean: and
6 3 brother of . . . and Jude and Simon
14 37 Simon, sleepest thou? Couldst thou not
15 21 they forced one Simon a Cyrenian who
Luke 5 4 he said to Simon: Launch out into the
5 Simon answering said to him: Master
10 Jesus saith to Simon: Fear not: from
6 14 Simon, whom he surnamed Peter, and
15 and Simon who is called Zelotes, and
7 40 Simon, I have somewhat to say to thee
43 Simon answering, said: I suppose that
44 he said to Simon: Dost thou see this
22 31 S., S., behold Satan hath desired to
23 26 they laid hold of one Simon of Cyrene
24 34 risen indeed and hath appeared to S.
John 1 41 he findeth first his brother Simon
42 thou art Simon the son of Jona: thou
6 72 Judas Iscariot, the son of S. 13:2, 26
21 15 S. son of John, lovest thou me. 16, 17
Acts 1 13 where abode . . . Simon Zelotes and
8 9 a certain man named Simon, who before
13 then Simon himself believed also and
18 when Simon saw that by the imposition
24 Simon answering said: Pray you for me
9 43 with one Simon a tanner. 10:6
10 5 call hither one Simon. 32; 11:13
18 asked, if Simon, . . . were lodged there
32 he lodgeth in the house of S. a tanner
13 1 S. who was called Niger, and Lucius
15 14 S. hath related how God first visited
Simon Peter Mat 16 16 S. P. answered and said
Luke 5 8 which when S. P. saw, he fell down
9 20 S. P. answering, said: The Christ of
John 1 40 Andrew the brother of Simon Peter. 6:8

6 69 Simon Peter answered him: Lord, to
13 6 he cometh therefore to Simon Peter
9 S. P. saith to him: Lord, not only my
24 S. P. therefore beckoned to him and
36 S. P. saith to him: Lord, whither
18 10 then S. P., having a sword, drew it
15 Simon Peter followed Jesus, and so did
25 S. P. was standing and warming himself
20 2 she ran therefore and cometh to S. P.
6 then cometh S. P., following him, and
21 2 there were together S. P. and Thomas
3 S. P. saith to them: I go a fishing
7 S. P. when he heard that it was the
11 S. P. went up and drew the net to
15 Jesus saith to Simon Peter: Simon, son
2 P 1 1 Simon Peter, servant and apostle of
Simon's 1 Ma 14 40 had received S. ambassadors
2 Ma 4 3 murders . . . by some of Simon's friends
Mark 1 30 Simon's wife's mother lay in a fit of
Luke 4 38 went into Simon's house. And Simon's wife's mother was taken with
5 3 into one of the ships that was Simon's
10 who were Simon's partners. And Jesus
Acts 10 17 inquiring for Simon's house, stood at
simple Job 1 1 that man was simple and upright
Job 1 8 simple and upright man and fearing God
2 3 a man simple and upright and fearing
8 20 God will not cast away the simple nor
9 21 although I should be simple, even this
Prov 2 21 and the simple shall continue in it
3 32 his communication is with the simple
22 3 the simple passed on and suffered loss
26 22 of a talebearer are as it were simple
Mat 10 16 wise as serpents and simple as doves
Rom 16 19 to be wise in good, and simple in evil
simplicity Gen 20 5 in the s. of my heart and
2 K 15 11 going with simpilcity of heart and
3 K 9 4 as thy father walked, in s. of heart
1 Pa 29 17 I also in the simplicity of my heart
17 provest hearts and lovest simplicity
Job 2 9 dost thou still continue in thy s.
12 4 s. of the just man is laughed to scorn
31 6 just balance, and let God know my s.
Prov 2 7 and protect them that walk in s.
11 3 simplicity of the just shall guide them
19 1 the poor man, that walketh in his s.
20 7 the just that walketh in his simplicity
28 6 better is poor man walking in his s.
Wisd 1 1 and seek him in simplicity of heart
Acts 2 46 their meat with gladness and s. of
Rom 12 8 he that giveth, with simplicity; he that
2 C 1 12 in s. of heart and sincerity of God, and
8 2 abounded unto the riches of their s.
9 11 you may abound unto all simplicity, which
13 for the s. of your communicating unto
11 3 fall from simplicity that is in Christ
Eph 6 5 in the s. of your heart, as to Christ
Col 3 22 but in simplicity of heart, fearing God
sin Mat 12 31 every sin and blasphemy shall be
Mark 3 29 shall be guilty of an everlasting sin
Luke 17 3 if thy brother sin against thee
4 if he sin against thee seven times
John 1 29 who taketh away the sin of the world
5 14 behold thou art made whole: sin no more
8 7 he that is without sin among you, let
11 go, and now sin no more. Again
21 you shall die in your sin. 24
34 committeth sin, is the servant of sin
46 which of you shall convince me of sin
9 41 were blind, you should not have sin
41 you say: We see. Your sin remaineth
15 22 they would not have sin; but now. 24
16 8 he will convince the world of sin and
9 of sin: because they believed not in
19 11 me to thee, hath the greater sin
Acts 7 59 Lord, lay not this sin to their charge
Rom 3 9 Greeks, that they are all under sin. As
20 for by the law is the knowledge of sin
4 8 men to whom Lord hath not imputed sin
5 12 as by one man sin entered into this
12 and by sin death; and so death passed
13 until the law sin was in the world; but
13 sin was not imputed, when law was not
16 as it was by one sin, so also is gift
20 law entered in, that sin might abound
20 and where sin abounded, grace did more
21 that as sin hath reigned to death; so
6 1 then? shall we continue in sin, that
2 for we that are dead to sin, how shall
6 that the body of sin may be destroyed
6 to end that we may serve sin no longer
7 he that is dead is justified from sin
10 in that he died to sin, he died once
11 also reckon, that you are dead to sin
12 let not sin therefore reign in your
13 as instruments of iniquity unto sin
14 for sin shall not have dominion over
15 what then? Shall we sin, because we are
16 whether it be of sin unto death, or of
17 that you were the servants of sin, but
18 being then freed from sin, we have been
20 for when you were the servants of sin
22 but now being made free from sin, and
23 for the wages of sin is death. But the
7 7 is the law sin? God forbid. But I do not
7 but I do not know sin, but by the law
8 sin taking occasion by commandment. 11
8 for without the law sin was dead. And I
9 when the commandment came, sin revived
13 but sin, that it may appear sin, by
13 in me; that sin, by the commandment
14 but I am carnal, sold under sin. For
17 no more I that do it, but sin. 20
23 and captivating me in the law of sin
25 God; but with the flesh, the law of sin
8 2 delivered me from the law of sin and of
3 in likeness of sinful flesh and of sin
3 of sin, hath condemned sin in the flesh
10 body indeed is dead, because of sin; but
14 23 for all that is not of faith is sin. Now
1 C 6 18 every sin that a man doth, is without
8 12 when you sin thus against the brethren
12 weak conscience, you sin against Christ
15 34 awake, ye just, and sin not. For some
56 now the sting of death is sin: and the
56 is sin: and the power of sin is the law
2 C 5 21 him, who knew no sin, he hath made sin
Gal 2 17 is Christ then the minister of sin? God
3 22 scripture hath concluded all under sin
Eph 4 26 be angry, and sin not. Let not the sun
2 Th 2 3 first, and the man of sin be revealed
1 Tim 5 20 them that sin reprove before all: that
Heb 3 13 hardened through deceitfulness of sin
4 15 all things like as we are, without sin
9 26 appeared for the destruction of sin, by
28 he shall appear without sin to them that
10 2 have no conscience of sin any longer
4 oxen and goats sin should be taken away
6 holocausts for sin did not please thee
8 oblations and holocausts for sin thou
18 there is no more an oblation for sin
26 for if we sin wilfully after having
11 25 to have the pleasure of sin for a time
12 1 laying aside every weight and sin
4 unto blood, striving against sin. And
13 11 into holies by the high priest for sin

James 1 15 hath conceived, it bringeth forth sin
15 sin, when it is completed, begetteth
2 9 respect to persons, you commit sin
4 17 good, and doth it not, to him it is sin
1 P 2 20 if committing sin and being buffeted
22 who did no sin, neither was guile found
2 P 1 10 doing these things, you shall not sin
2 14 eyes full of adultery and of sin that
1 J 1 7 his Son cleanseth us from all sin
8 if we say that we have no sin, we
2 1 write to you, that you may not sin
1 if any man sin, we have an advocate
3 4 whosoever committeth sin committeth
4 also iniquity; and sin is iniquity
5 our sins, and in him there is no sin
8 that committeth sin is of the devil
9 is born of God, committeth not sin
5 16 he that knoweth his brother to sin a sin which is not to death
16 there is a sin unto death. 17
17 all iniquity is sin. And there is a
Jude 24 is able to preserve you without sin
Sin Exod 16 1 came into the desert of Sin. Num 20:1; 33:36
Exod 17 1 setting forward from the desert of Sin
Num 13 22 viewed the land from the desert of Sin
27 14 Cades of the desert of Sin. Deut 32:51
14 you offended me in the desert of Sin
33 11 Sea, they camped in the desert of Sin
34 3 shall begin from the wilderness of Sin
Josu 15 1 Edom, to the desert of Sin southward
Sina Josu 15 3 passeth on to Sina: and ascendeth
Ps 67 9 at the presence of the God of Sina
18 the Lord is among them in Sina in
Eccu 48 7 who heardest judgment in Sina, and
Gal 4 25 Sina is a mountain in Arabia, which hath
mount Sina Jdth 5 14 abode in deserts of m. S.
Acts 7 30 to him in the desert of mount Sina
38 angel who spoke to him on mount Sina
Gal 4 24 one from mount Sina, engendering unto
Sinai Exod 16 1 Sin, which is between Elim and S.
Exod 19 1 they came into the wilderness of Sinai
2 coming to the desert of S., they camped
24 16 the glory of the Lord dwelt upon Sinai
Lev 7 38 to the Lord in the desert of Sinai
Num 1 1 spoke to Moses in the desert of Sinai. 3:14; 9:1
19 they were numbered in the desert of S.
3 4 offered strange fire . . . in desert of S.
10 12 by their troops from the desert of S.
26 64 were numbered . . . in the desert of S.
33 15 they camped in the desert of Sinai
16 departing also from the desert of Sinai
Deut 33 2 Lord came from Sinai, and from Seir
Judg 5 5 Sinai before the face of Lord the God
mount Sinai Exod 19 11 down in the sight of all the people upon mount Sinai
Exod 19 18 and all mount Sinai was on a smoke
20 the Lord came down upon mount Sinai
23 the people cannot come up to mount S.
31 18 he had ended these words in mount S.
34 2 mayst forthwith go up into mount Sinai
4 early he went up into the mount Sinai
29 when Moses came down from the m. S.
32 that he had heard of the Lord in m. S.
Lev 7 38 the Lord appointed to Moses in m. S.
25 1 Lord spoke to Moses in m. S. Num 3:1
26 45 in mount Sinai by the hand of Moses
27 34 for the children of Israel in m. S.
Num 28 6 holocaust which you offered in m. S.
2 Es 9 13 thou camest down also to mount Sinai
sincere Gen 20 6 thou didst it with a s. heart
Josu 24 14 serve him with . . . most sincere heart
2 Es 7 2 seemed as a sincere man and one that
Phil 1 10 you may be sincere and without offence
2 15 that you may be blameless and sincere
20 who with sincere affection is solicitous
4 3 my s. companion, help those women
1 P 1 22 from a sincere heart love one another
2 P 3 1 by way of admonition your sincere mind
sincerely Judg 11 9 if you be come to me s., that
Tob 3 5 have not walked sincerely before thee
Prov 10 9 that walketh s., walketh confidently
11 20 his will is in them that walk sincerely
Phil 1 17 some . . . preach Christ not sincerely
sincerity 1 C 5 8 the unleavened bread of s.
2 C 1 12 in simplicity of heart and s. of God
2 17 but with sincerity, but as from God
sinew Gen 32 25 touched the sinew of his thigh
Gen 32 32 unto this day eat not the sinew
32 because he touched the s. of his thigh
Isa 48 4 and thy neck is as an iron sinew
sinews Judg 16 7 cords made of sinews not yet dry
Job 10 11 put me together with bones and sinews
40 12 the sinews of his testicles are wrapped
Eze 37 6 I will lay sinews upon you and will
8 the s. and the flesh came up upon them
sinful Num 32 14 increase and offspring of s. men
Tob 13 7 shown his majesty toward a sinful nation
Eccu 10 26 not magnify a sinful man that is rich
11 34 a sinful man lieth in wait for blood
27 33 sinful man shall be subject to them
28 11 a sinful man will trouble his friends
32 21 a sinful man will flee reproof and
Isa 1 4 woe to the sinful nation, a people
Amos 9 8 are upon the sinful kingdom and I will
1 Ma 1 36 and they placed there a sinful nation
2 62 fear not the words of a sinful man
2 Ma 4 19 Jason sent from Jerusalem sinful men to
Mark 8 38 this adulterous and sinful generation
Luke 5 8 for I am a sinful man, O Lord. For he
24 7 delivered into the hands of sinful men
Rom 7 13 might become sinful above measure. For
8 3 in likeness of sinful flesh and of sin
sing Exod 15 1 let us sing to the Lord. 21
Deut 31 19 know it by heart, and sing it by mouth
Judg 5 3 it is I, that will sing to the Lord
3 I will sing to the Lord the God of
1 K 21 11 did they not sing to him [David]
2 K 22 50 thanks . . . and will sing to thy name
1 Pa 16 9 sing to him, yea, sing praises to him
23 sing ye to the Lord, all the earth
42 musical instruments to sing praises to
23 5 instruments which he had made to s. with
30 to give thanks and to sing praises to
25 6 were distributed to sing in the temple
2 Pa 20 22 and when they began to sing praises
29 27 they began to sing praises to the Lord
31 2 to minister and to praise and to sing
Tob 12 18 bless ye him and sing praises to him
Jdth 16 2 sing ye to the Lord with cymbals, tune
15 let us sing a hymn to the Lord, let
15 let us sing a new hymn to our God
Ps 7 18 and will sing to the name of the Lord
9 3 I will sing to thy name, O thou most
12 sing ye to the Lord, who dwelleth in
12 6 I will sing to the Lord who giveth me
6 I will sing to the name of the Lord
17 50 and I will sing a psalm to thy name
20 14 we will sing and praise thy power
26 6 I will sing and recite a psalm to the
29 5 sing to the Lord, O ye his saints: and
13 that my glory may sing to thee, and I
32 2 harp: sing to him with psaltery

3 sing to him a new canticle, sing well
46 7 sing praises to our God, sing ye: sing praises to our king, sing ye
8 king of all the earth: sing ye wisely
56 8 I will sing, and rehearse a psalm
10 I will sing a psalm to thee among the
58 17 will sing thy strength: and will extol
18 unto thee, O my helper, will I sing
60 9 so will I sing a psalm to thy name
64 14 shout, yea they shall sing a hymn
65 2 sing ye a psalm to his name; give
4 and sing to thee: let it sing a psalm
67 5 sing ye to God, sing a psalm to his
33 sing to God, ye kingdoms of the earth: sing ye to the Lord
33 sing ye to God, who mounteth above the
70 6 of thee shall I continually sing: I am
8 with praise, that I may sing thy glory
22 I will sing to thee with the harp
23 rejoice, when I shall sing to thee
74 10 I will sing to the God of Jacob. And
80 2 helper: sing aloud to the God of Jacob
88 2 the mercies of the Lord I will sing
91 2 and to sing to thy name, O most High
94 1 let us joyfully sing to God our savior
95 1 sing ye to the Lord a new canticle: sing to the Lord, all the earth
2 sing ye to the Lord and bless his name
97 1 sing ye to the Lord a new canticle
4 s. joyfully to God, all the earth. 99:2
4 earth: make melody, rejoice and sing
5 sing praise to the Lord on the harp
100 1 mercy and judgment I will sing to thee
1 I will sing, and I will understand in
103 33 I will sing to the Lord as long as I
33 I will sing praise to my God while I
104 2 sing to him, yea sing praises to him
107 2 I will sing and will give praise with
4 I will sing unto thee among the nations
134 3 sing ye to his name, for it is sweet
136 3 sing ye to us a hymn of the songs of
4 how shall we sing the song of the Lord
137 1 I will sing praise to thee in the
5 let them sing in the ways of the Lord
143 9 I will sing a new canticle: on the
9 strings I will sing praises to thee
145 2 I will sing to my God as long as I
146 7 sing ye to the Lord with praise: sing to our God upon the harp
149 1 sing ye to the Lord a new canticle
3 let them sing to him with the timbrel
Isa 5 1 I will sing to my beloved the canticle
12 5 sing ye to the Lord for he hath done
23 16 sing well, sing many a song, that thou
38 20 we will sing our psalms all the days
42 10 sing ye to the Lord a new song, his
54 1 sing forth praise and make a joyful
55 12 hills shall sing praise before you
Jer 20 13 sing ye to the Lord, praise the Lord
31 7 and sing and say: Save, O Lord, thy
48 33 treader of the grapes shall not sing
Eze 32 18 sing a mournful song for the multitude
Osee 2 15 she shall sing there according to
Amos 6 5 sing to the sound of the psaltery
Zach 2 10 sing praise, and rejoice, O daughter
Rom 15 9 Gentiles, and will sing to thy name
1 C 14 15 I will sing with the spirit, I will s.
James 5 13 is he cheerful in mind? Let him sing
singed Dan 3 94 hair of their head had been s.
singer 1 Pa 6 33 of the sons of Caath, Hemam a s.
singers Exod 32 18 I hear the voice of singers
3 K 10 12 and citterns and harps for singers
4 K 11 14 the singers and the trumpets near him
1 Pa 15 16 some of their brethren to be singers
19 the singers, Heman, Asaph, and Ethan
27 and Chonenias . . . among the singers
23 5 as many singers singing to the Lord
2 Pa 29 28 s. and trumpeters were in their office
35 15 the singers the sons of Asaph stood
1 Es 7 24 the singers and the porters and the
2 Es 12 41 the singers sung loud, and Jezraia was
45 from beginning there were chief singers
Ps 67 26 princes went before joined with s.
Eccu 47 11 and he set singers before the altar
50 20 the singers lifted up their voices
Lam 5 14 young men from the choir of the s.
singeth Prov 25 20 s. songs to a very evil heart
singing Judg 9 27 s. and dancing they went into
Judg 15 17 when he had ended these words singing
1 K 18 6 singing and dancing to meet king Saul
2 K 19 35 the voice of s. men and s. women
1 Pa 2 55 singing and making melody and abiding
6 31 whom David set over the singing men
32 and they ministered . . . with singing
15 27 carried the ark, and the s. men
16 35 and may rejoice in singing thy praises
23 5 as many singers singing to the Lord
2 Pa 7 6 singing the hymns of David by their
23 18 with joy and singing, according to
35 25 lamentations for Josias all the s. men
1 Es 2 65 among them s. men and s. women 200
2 Es 7 67 among them s. men and s. women 245
12 27 rejoice with thanksgiving and with s.
Ecce 2 8 I made me singing men and singing women
Wisd 18 9 singing now the praises of the fathers
Isa 27 2 there shall be singing to the vineyard
51 11 shall come into Sion, singing praises
Haba 3 19 upon my high places singing psalms
Soph 2 14 voice of the singing bird in the window
2 Ma 12 37 singing hymns with a loud voice, he
Eph 5 19 s. and making melody in your hearts to
Col 3 16 singing in grace in your hearts to God
Apoc 15 3 singing the canticle of Moses, the
single Mat 6 22 if thy eye be single. Luke 11:34
singular Ps 79 14 s. wild beast hath devoured it
Wisd 14 18 the s. diligence also of the artificer
singularly Ps 4 10 Lord, s. hast settled me in
Sinite Gen 10 17 Chanaan begot . . . the S. 1 Pa 1:15
sink Jdth 6 5 let not thy countenance sink and
Jer 51 64 thus shall Babylon sink, and she shall
Mat 14 30 when he began to sink, he cried out
sinking Luke 5 7 so that they were almost sinking
sinned Mat 27 4 I have sinned in betraying innocent
Luke 15 18 I have sinned against heaven. 21
John 9 2 who hath sinned, this man or his
3 neither hath this man sinned, nor his
Rom 2 12 whosoever have sinned without the law
12 and whosoever have sinned in the law
3 23 all have s., and do need glory of God
5 12 upon all men, in whom all have sinned
14 even over them also who have not sinned
1 C 7 28 if thou take wife, thou hast not sinned
28 if a virgin marry, she hath not sinned
2 C 12 21 I mourn many of them that sinned before
13 2 now absent, to them that sinned before
Heb 3 17 was it not with them that sinned, whose
2 P 2 4 if God spared not the angels that s.
1 J 1 10 if we say that we have not sinned, we
sinner Ps 9 3 s. is praised in the desires of
Ps 9 4 the sinner hath provoked the Lord
15 break thou the arm of the sinner and
17 the sinner hath been caught in the
31 10 many are the scourges of the sinner
35 12 let not the hand of the sinner move me

36 21 the sinner shall borrow, and not pay
38 2 when the sinner stood against me. I
49 16 to the sinner God hath said: Why dost
54 4 at the tribulation of the sinner. For
57 11 shall wash his hands in blood of the s.
70 4 my God, out of hand of the sinner
81 4 needy out of the hand of the sinner
96 10 them out of the hand of the sinner
108 6 set thou the sinner over him: and may
140 5 not oil of the sinner fatten my head
Prov 11 31 how much more the wicked and the s.
13 6 wickedness overthroweth the sinner
22 substance of s. is kept for the just
Ecce 2 26 to the sinner he hath given vexation
7 27 that is a s. shall be caught by her
8 12 though a sinner do evil a hundred times
9 2 as the good is, so also is the sinner
Eccu 1 32 worship of God is abomination to a s.
2 14 sinner that goeth on the earth two ways
3 29 and the sinner will add sin to sin
5 11 every sinner proved by a double tongue
6 1 so shall every sinner that is envious
9 16 envy not glory and riches of a sinner
12 4 to the merciful, and uphold not the s.
5 give to the good, and receive not a s.
13 21 the lamb, so the s. with the just
15 9 praise is not seemly in mouth of a s.
16 14 sinner shall not escape in his rapines
21 7 reproved walketh in the trace of a s.
23 8 a sinner is caught in his own vanity
27 3 sin shall be destroyed with the sinner
29 20 the sinner and the unclean fleeth from
21 s. atributeth to himself the goods
25 s. that transgresseth the commandment
33 15 so also is the s. against a just man
Isa 65 20 the sinner being a hundred years old
Eze 18 23 is it my will that a sinner should die
Zach 13 1 for the washing of the sinner and of
1 Ma 2 48 they yielded not the horn to the sinner
13 4 mind of Antiochus against the sinner
Luke 7 37 a woman that was in the city, a sinner
39 toucheth him, that she is a sinner
15 7 one sinner that doth penance, more
10 of God upon one sinner doing penance
18 13 O God, be merciful to me a sinner
19 7 a guest with a man that was a sinner
John 9 16 how can a man that is a sinner do such
24 we know that this man is a sinner
25 if he be a sinner, I know not: one
Rom 3 7 why am I also yet judged as a sinner
James 5 20 causeth a sinner to be converted from
1 P 4 18 where shall the ungodly and the sinner
sinners Gen 13 13 of Sodom were very wicked and s.
Num 16 38 are sanctified in the deaths of the s.
1 K 15 18 go, and kill the sinners of Amalec, and
Tob 13 8 be converted therefore, ye sinners
Ps 1 1 nor stood in the way of s., nor sat
5 nor sinners in the council of the just
3 8 thou hast broken the teeth of sinners
7 10 wickedness of s. shall be brought to
10 7 he shall rain snares upon sinners
24 8 he will give a law to s. in the way
36 34 when the s. shall perish, thou shalt
72 3 the wicked, seeing the prosperity of s.
12 behold these are sinners; and yet
74 5 to the sinners: Lift not up the horn
9 all the s. of the earth shall drink
11 I will break all the horns of sinners
83 11 than to dwell in the tabernacles of s.
93 3 how long shall sinners, O Lord: how long shall sinners glory
103 35 let s. be consumed out of the earth
118 110 sinners have laid a snare for me: but
119 all the s. of the earth prevaricators
155 salvation is far from sinners: because
124 3 Lord will not leave the rod of sinners
128 4 who is just will cut the necks of s.
145 9 the ways of sinners he will destroy
Prov 1 10 if s. shall entice thee, consent not
13 21 evil pursueth sinners: and to the just
23 17 let not thy heart envy sinners: but be
Wisd 4 10 living among sinners he was translated
5 14 things as these the s. said in hell
10 13 was sold: but delivered him from s.
14 31 vengeance of sinners always punisheth
19 12 punishments came upon the sinners
Eccu 1 26 to sinners wisdom is an abomination
5 7 his wrath looketh upon sinners
8 13 kindle not the coals of sinners by
11 9 and sit not in judgment with sinners
16 error and darkness are created with s.
22 abide not in the works of sinners. But
12 3 the Highest hateth s., and hath mercy
4 vengeance to the ungodly and to s. and
7 the Highest also hateth s., and will
16 7 in the congregation of sinners a fire
19 19 the device of sinners is not prudence
21 10 congregation of s. is like tow heaped
11 way of s. is made plain with stones
25 26 let the lot of sinners fall upon her
27 14 the discourse of sinners is hateful
39 29 to sinners they are stumblingblocks
32 so to the sinners and the ungodly
40 8 and upon sinners are sevenfold more
41 8 children of sinners become children of
9 inheritance of the children of sinners
49 4 in the days of sinners he strengthened
Isa 1 28 he shall destroy the wicked and the s.
13 9 to destroy the s. thereof out of it
33 14 the s. in Sion are afraid, trembling
Amos 9 10 the sinners of my people shall fall
1 Ma 2 44 and slew the sinners in their wrath
2 Ma 6 13 when sinners are not suffered to go on
Mat 9 10 many publicans and sinners came and
11 eat with publicans and s. Mark 2:16
13 am not come to call the just, but s.
11 19 friend of publicans and s. Luke 7:34
26 45 betrayed into hands of s. Mark 14:41
Mark 2 15 many publicans and sinners sat down
16 and drink with publicans and sinners
17 not to call the just, but s. Luke 5:32
Luke 5 30 eat and drink with publicans and s.
6 32 sinners also love those that love them
33 to you? For sinners also do this
34 sinners also lend to sinners, for to
13 2 that these Galileans were sinners
15 1 publicans and s. drew near unto him
2 this man receiveth s. and eateth with
John 9 31 we know that God doth not hear sinners
Rom 5 8 because when as yet we were sinners
19 many were made sinners; so also by the
Gal 2 15 Jews, and not of the Gentiles sinners
17 we ourselves also are found sinners; is
1 Tim 1 9 for the ungodly and for sinners, for
15 Jesus came into this world to save s.
Heb 7 26 undefiled, separated from sinners and
12 3 endured such opposition from sinners
James 4 8 cleanse you hands, ye sinners: and
Jude 15 which ungodly sinners have spoken
sinneth 1 C 6 18 fornication, sinneth against his own
1 C 7 36 he will; he sinneth not, if she marry
Titus 3 11 such an one, is subverted, and sinneth
1 J 3 6 whosoever abideth in him, sinneth not
6 whosoever s., hath not seen him nor
8 the devil sinneth from the beginning
5 16 to him who sinneth not to death. There

18 whosoever is born of God, sinneth not
sins Mat 9 2 son, thy sins are forgiven thee. 5; Mark 2:5, 9; Luke 5:20, 23; 7:48
Mat 9 6 hath power on earth to forgive sins. Mark 2:10; Luke 5:24
26 28 shed for many unto remission of sins
Mark 1 4 of penance, unto remission of sins
2 7 who can forgive sins but God. Luke 5:21
3 28 all sins shall be forgiven unto the
Luke 7 49 who is this that forgiveth sins also
24 47 remission of sins should be preached
John 9 34 thou wast wholly born in sins, and
20 23 whose sins you shall forgive, they are
23 whose sins you shall retain, they are
Acts 5 31 to give . . . remission of sins. And we
10 43 remission of sins, who believe in him
13 38 forgiveness of sins is preached to you
22 16 and be baptized, and wash away thy sins
26 18 that they may receive forgiveness of s.
Rom 3 25 justice, for remission of former sins
4 7 are forgiven, and whose sins are covered
7 5 passions of sins, which were by the law
Eph 1 7 his blood, the remission of s. Col 1:14
2 5 even when we were dead in sins, hath
1 Tim 5 22 neither be partaker of other men's sins
24 some men's sins are manifest, going
2 Tim 3 6 lead captive silly women laden with s.
Heb 1 3 making purgation of sins, sitteth on
2 17 propitiation for the sins of the people
5 1 offer up gifts and sacrifices for sins
3 so also for himself, to offer for sins
7 27 offer sacrifices first for his own sins
9 28 offered once to exhaust the s. of many
10 3 made a commemoration of sins every year
11 which can never take away sins. But
12 this man offering one sacrifice for sins
26 there is now left no sacrifice for sins
James 5 15 and if he be in sins, they shall be
20 and shall cover a multitude of sins
1 P 2 24 that we, being dead to sins, should
4 1 in the flesh, hath ceased from sins
8 charity covereth a multitude of sins
2 P 1 9 that he was purged from his old sins
Apoc 18 4 that ye be not partakers of her sins
5 her sins have reached unto heaven, and
our sins Luke 11 4 forgive us our sins, for we also
Rom 4 27 who was delivered up for our sins
1 C 15 3 how that Christ died for our sins
Gal 1 4 who gave himself for our sins, that he
1 P 2 25 bore our sins in his body upon the tree
3 18 Christ also died once for our sins
1 J 1 9 if we confess our sins, he is faithful
9 to forgive us our sins and to cleanse
2 2 he is the propitiation for our sins
3 5 he appeared to take away our sins
4 10 Son to be a propitiation for our sins
Apoc 1 5 washed us from our sins in his own
their sins Mat 1 21 shall save his people from their sins
Mat 3 6 Jordan, confessing their sins. Mark 1:5
Mark 4 12 and their sins should be forgiven them
Luke 1 77 unto the remission of their sins
Rom 11 27 when I shall take away their sins. As
2 C 5 19 not imputing to them their sins; and he
1 Th 2 16 saved, to fill up their sins always: for
Heb 8 12 to their iniquities and their sins I
10 17 their s. and iniquities I will remember
your sins Mark 11 25 in heaven, may forgive you your sins
Mark 11 26 your Father . . . forgive you your sins
John 8 24 that you shall die in your sins. For
Acts 2 38 for the remission of your sins: and
3 19 that your sins may be blotted out
1 C 15 17 if vain, for you are yet in your sins
Eph 2 1 you were dead in your offences and sins
Col 2 13 you were dead in your sins. Eph 2:1
James 5 16 confess therefore your sins one to
1 J 2 12 because your sins are forgiven you
Sion 2 K 5 7 David took the castle of S. 1 Pa 11:5
3 K 8 1 of city of David, that is, out of S.
2 Pa 5 2 the city of David, which is Sion
Ps 2 6 I am appointed king by him over Sion
9 12 sing ye to the Lord, who dwelleth in S.
13 7 who shall give out of S. the salvation
19 3 and defend thee out of Sion. May he
47 13 surround Sion and encompass her: Tell
49 2 out of S. the loveliness of his beauty
50 20 deal favorably . . . with Sion; that the
52 7 who will give out of S. the salvation
64 2 a hymn, O God, becometh thee in Sion
68 36 God will save Sion and the cities of
75 3 place is in peace: and his abode in Sion
83 8 the God of gods shall be seen in Sion
86 2 the Lord loveth the gates of Sion
5 shall not Sion say: This man and that
96 8 Sion heard, and was glad. And the
98 2 the Lord is great in Sion, and high
101 14 shalt arise and have mercy on Sion
17 the Lord hath built up Sion: and he
22 declare the name of the Lord in Sion
109 2 the scepter of thy power out of Sion
125 1 brought back the captivity of Sion
127 5 may the Lord bless thee out of Sion
128 5 and turned back that hate Sion. Let
131 13 the Lord hath chosen Sion: he hath
133 3 may the Lord out of Sion bless thee
134 21 blessed be the Lord out of Sion, who
136 1 and wept: when we remembered Sion
3 to us a hymn of the songs of Sion
145 10 thy God, O Sion, unto generation and
147 12 Jerusalem: praise thy God, O Sion
149 2 let the children of Sion be joyful
Cant 3 11 go forth, ye daughters of Sion, and
Eccu 24 15 so was I established in Sion, and in
36 16 fill Sion with thy unspeakable words
48 20 he stretched out his hand against Sion
27 and comforted the mourners in Sion
Isa 1 27 Sion shall be redeemed in judgment and
2 3 the law shall come forth from Sion
3 16 the daughters of Sion are haughty and
17 crown of head of the daughters of Sion
4 3 every one that shall be left in Sion
4 wash away filth of the daughters of S.
10 24 my people that dwellest in Sion, be not
12 6 and praise, O thou habitation of Sion
14 32 that the Lord hath founded Sion and
26 1 Sion the city of our strength a savior
28 16 lay a stone in the foundations of Sion
30 19 people of S. shall dwell in Jerusalem
31 9 Lord hath said it, whose fire is in S.
33 5 he hath filled Sion with judgment and
14 the sinners in S. are afraid, trembling
20 look upon S. the city of our solemnity
34 8 of recompenses of the judgment of S.
35 10 and shall come into Sion with praise
40 9 thou that bringest good tidings to Sion
41 27 the first shall say to Sion: Behold
46 12 I will give salvation in Sion, and my
49 14 Sion said: The Lord hath forsaken me
51 3 the Lord therefore will comfort Sion
11 shall return and shall come into Sion
16 say to Sion: Thou art my people
52 1 arise, put on thy strength, O Sion
7 saith to Sion: Thy God shall reign
8 when the Lord shall convert Sion
59 20 there shall come a redeemer to Sion
60 14 the Sion of the Holy One of Israel

21 3 and for a maiden sister, who hath had
Num 6 7 or for his sister, when they die
25 18 idol Phogar and Cozbi their sister
26 59 Aaron and Moses and Mary their s.
Deut 27 22 cursed be he that lieth with his s.
Judg 15 2 but she hath a sister, who is younger
2 K 13 1 Amnon . . . loved the sister of Absalom
4 Thamar the s. of my brother Absalom
20 s., hold thy peace, he is thy brother
22 he had ravished his sister Thamar
32 from the day that he ravished his s.
17 25 daughter of Naas, the sister of Sarvia
3 K 11 19 the own sister of his wife Taphnes
20 the sister of Taphnes bore him his son
4 K 11 2 Josaba . . . sister of Ochozias, took
1 Pa 1 39 and the sister of Lotan was Thamna
3 9 and they had a sister Thamar. And
19 Zorobabel begot . . . Salomith their s.
4 3 name of their sister was Asalelphuni
19 his wife Odaia the sister of Naham
7 15 and he had a sister named Maacha
18 his sister named Queen bore Goodlyman
30 Jessui and Baria and Sara their sister
32 and Hatham and Suaa their sister
2 Pa 22 11 now Josabeth . . . sister of Ochozias
Cant 8 8 our s. is little and hath no breasts
8 what shall we do to our sister in the
Jer 3 7 and her treacherous sister Juda saw
8 treacherous sister Juda was not afraid
10 treacherous s. Juda hath not returned
22 18 alas, my brother, and alas, sister
Eze 16 45 thou art the sister of thy sisters
46 thy elder sister is Samaria, she and
46 thy younger s. that dwelleth at thy
48 thy sister Sodom herself and her
49 this was the iniquity of Sodom thy s.
55 thy sister Dodom and her daughters
56 Sodom thy s. was not heard of in thy
22 11 the brother hath oppressed his sister
23 4 elder, and Ooliba her younger sister
11 and when her sister Ooliba saw this
11 beyond the fornication of her sister
18 as my soul was alienated from her s.
31 hast walked in the way of thy sister
33 with the cup of thy sister Samaria
44 25 son and daughter, and brother and s.
Osee 2 1 to your sister: Thou hast obtained
Mat 12 50 he is my brother and sister and mother
Luke 10 39 she had a sister called Mary, who
John 11 1 the town of Mary and Martha her sister
5 Jesus loved Martha and her sister Mary
28 went and called her sister Mary
39 Martha, the s. of him that was dead
19 25 his mother and his mother's sister
Rom 16 1 I commend to you Phebe, our sister, who
15 Nereus and his sister, and Olympias; and
1 C 7 15 brother or sister is not under servitude
9 5 power to carry about a woman, a sister
Philem 2 and to Appia, our dearest sister, and
James 2 15 and if a brother or sister be naked
2 J 13 children of thy s. Elect salute thee
my sister Gen 12 13 that thou art my sister
Gen 20 2 of Sara his wife: She is my sister
5 did not he say to me: She is my sister
12 otherwise also she is truly my sister
26 7 [Isaac] answered: She is my sister
30 8 God hath compared me with my sister
2 K 13 5 let my sister Thamar, I pray thee, come
6 let my sister Thamar come and make
11 and said: Come lie with me, my sister
Tob 8 9 do I take my sister to wife, but only
Job 17 14 to worms, my mother and my sister
Prov 7 4 say to wisdom: Thou art my sister
Cant 4 9 thou hast wounded my heart, my sister
10 beautiful are thy breasts, my sister
12 my sister, my spouse, is a garden
5 1 I am come into my garden, O my sister
2 open to me, my sister, my love
Mark 3 35 he is my brother and my sister and
Luke 10 40 Lord, hast thou no care that my sister
sister's Gen 24 30 and bracelets in his s. hands
Gen 29 13 that Jacob his sister's son was come
Eze 23 32 thou shalt drink thy sister's cup
Acts 23 16 when Paul's sister's son had heard, of
sisters Josu 2 13 will save . . . my brethren and s.
1 Pa 2 16 their sisters were Sarvia and Abigail
Job 1 4 they called their three sisters to eat
42 11 came to him, and all his sisters
Eze 16 45 thou art the sister of thy sisters
51 and hast justified thy sisters by all
52 hast surpassed thy s. with thy sins
52 thou that hast justified thy sisters
61 when thou shalt receive thy sisters
Mat 13 56 his sisters, are they not all with us
19 29 left house or brethren or s. Mark 10:29
Mark 6 3 are not also his sisters here with us
10 30 houses and brethren and sisters and
Luke 14 26 and hate not his . . . sisters, yea
John 11 3 his sisters therefore sent to him
1 Tim 5 2 young women, as sisters, in all chastity
sit Mat 8 11 and shall sit down with Abraham and
Mat 14 19 commanded the multitudes to sit down
15 35 multitude to sit down upon the ground
19 28 shall sit on the seat of his majesty
28 you also shall sit on twelve seats
20 21 may sit, the one of thy right hand
23 to sit on my right or left hand is not
21 7 upon them, and made him sit thereon
22 44 sit on my right hand until I make. Mark 12:36; Luke 20:42; Acts 2:34; Heb 1:13
25 31 shall he sit upon the seat of his
26 36 sit you here till I go yonder and
Mark 6 39 they should make them all sit down by
10 37 grant to us, that we may sit, one on
40 but to sit on my right hand or on my
12 39 and to sit in the first chairs in the
14 32 sit you here, while I pray. And he
Luke 1 79 enlighten them that sit in darkness
9 14 make them sit down by fifties in a
15 did so; and made them all sit down
12 37 and make them sit down to meat, and
13 29 shall sit down in the kingdom of God
14 8 sit not down in the first place, lest
10 sit down in the lowest place; that
10 before them that sit at table with thee
28 doth not first sit down and reckon
31 doth not first sit down and think
16 6 take thy bill and sit down quickly
17 7 immediately go, sit down to meat: and
21 35 all that sit upon the face of the
22 30 may sit upon thrones, judging the
John 6 10 make the men sit down. Now there was
Acts 2 30 one should sit upon his throne
8 31 he would come up and sit with him
1 C 8 10 sit at meat in the idol's temple, shall
Eph 2 6 made us sit together in heavenly places
James 2 3 sit thou here well; but say to the
3 thou there, or sit under my footstool
Apoc 3 21 will give to sit with me in my throne
11 16 who sit on their seats in the sight of
14 6 unto them that sit upon the earth and
18 7 saith in her heart: I sit a queen, and
19 18 horses, and of them that sit on them
sitten Mat 23 2 have sitten on chair of Moses
Luke 19 30 on which no man ever hath sitten
sitteth Mat 23 22 by him that sitteth thereon

Mark 16 19 s. on the right hand of God. Heb 10:12
Luke 22 27 he that sitteth at table, or he that
27 is not he that sitteth at table? But
2 Th 2 4 so that he sitteth in the temple of God
Heb 1 3 sitteth on the right hand of the majesty
12 2 s. on the right hand of the throne of
Apoc 4 9 that s. on the throne. 10; 5:13; 6:16; 7:10, 15; 19:4
17 1 harlot, who sitteth upon many waters
9 mountains, upon which the woman s.
sitting Mat 9 9 saw a man s. in the custom
Mat 9 10 as he was sitting at meat in the house
11 16 children s. in market place. Luke 7:32
13 48 sitting by the shore, they chose out
20 30 two blind men sitting by the wayside
21 5 sitting upon an ass, and a colt the
24 3 when he was sitting on mount Olivet
26 64 s. on the right hand of the power of God. Mark 14:62; Luke 22:69
27 19 as he was sitting in the place of
61 sitting over against the sepulcher. And
Mark 2 6 were some of the scribes sitting there
14 sitting by the receipt of custom; and
5 15 sitting, clothed, and well in his wits
12 41 Jesus s. over against the treasury
16 5 young man sitting on the right side
Luke 2 46 sitting in the midst of the doctors
5 3 s. he taught the multitudes out of
17 and doctors of the law sitting by
27 Levi, s. at the receipt of custom
8 35 sitting at his feet, clothed, and
10 13 ago, sitting in sackcloth and ashes
39 sitting also at the Lord's feet, heard
John 2 14 and the changers of money sitting
8 2 and sitting down he taught them
12 15 king cometh, sitting on an ass's colt
Acts 2 2 the whole house where they were sitting
8 28 sitting in his chariot and reading
16 13 sitting down, we spoke to the women
20 9 Eutychus, sitting on the window, being
25 17 on day following, s. in judgment seat
1 C 14 30 if anything be revealed to another s.
Col 3 1 where Christ is sitting at the right
Apoc 4 2 and upon the throne one sitting. And
4 four and twenty ancients sitting
14 14 one sitting like to the Son of man
17 3 I saw a woman sitting upon a scarlet
20 11 white throne, and one sitting upon it
situate Num 22 1 against where Jericho is s.
Num 22 36 s. in the uttermost borders of Arnon
Deut 2 36 a town that is situate in a valley
3 10 cities that are situate in the plain
4 43 s. in the plains of tribe of Ruben
48 Aroer, which is s. upon the bank of
Josu 17 16 are situate Bethsan with its towns
24 30 Thamnathsare, which is s. in mount
Judg 21 19 Silo, which is s. on the north of the
Tob 5 8 Rages . . . which is situate in the
Jdth 7 9 because it is situate in the mountains
Eze 27 4 and situate in the heart of the sea
1 Ma 5 46 was a great city situate in the way
situated Gen 25 9 was s. in the field of Ephron
Gen 50 10 which is situated beyond the Jordan
situation 4 K 2 19 s. of this city is very good
Siva 2 K 20 25 Siva was scribe: and Sadoc
Sivan Bar 1 8 the tenth day of the month Sivan
sixtyfold Mat 13 8 some s., and some thirtyfold
Siza 1 Pa 11 42 Adina the son of Siza a Rubenite
size Exod 36 9 the curtains were of the same s.
Eze 1 18 the wheels had also a size and a
skies Dan 4 17 whose height reached to the skies
skilful Gen 25 27 Esau became a skilful hunter
Exod 1 19 are skilful in the office of a midwife
31 6 wisdom in the heart of every s. man
35 25 the skilful women also gave such things
36 2 every skilful man, to whom the Lord
1 K 16 16 a man skilful in playing on the harp
18 a s. player and one of great strength
1 Pa 15 22 for he [Chonenias] was very skilful
22 15 and of all trades the most skilful
2 Pa 2 7 s. man that knoweth how to work in gold
8 servants are skilful in cutting timber
13 father Hiram, a wise and most s. man
8 18 and s. mariners and they went with
34 12 Levites skilful to play on instruments
2 Es 7 65 stood up a priest learned and skilful
Ecce 9 11 to the learned nor favor to the skilful
Cant 7 1 made by the hand of a skilful workman
Eccu 37 22 a skilful man hath taught many and
Isa 3 3 and the skilful in eloquent speech
40 20 the s. workman seeketh how he may set
Dan 1 4 and skilful in all wisdom, acute in
Amos 5 16 such as are skilful in lamentation
skilfully Wisd 13 11 and s. taken off all the bark
skilfulness Ps 77 72 conduct them by s. of his
skill 3 K 5 6 a man that has skill to hew wood
3 K 7 14 and skill to work all work in brass
2 Pa 2 7 and that hath skill in engraving, with
16 12 rather trusted in the s. of physicians
Jdth 5 27 and without skill in the art of war
Wisd 7 16 and the knowledge and skill of works
13 13 by the skill of his art fashioneth it
14 2 the workman built it by his skill
Eccu 38 3 skill of the physician shall lift up
44 5 by their skill sought out musical tunes
skin Gen 25 25 was red and hairy like a skin
Lev 4 11 but the skin and all the flesh with
7 8 holocaust, shall have the skin thereof
8 17 the calf with the skin, and the flesh
13 2 in whose skin or flesh shall arise a
3 and if he see the leprosy in his skin
3 leprosy appears lower than the skin
4 be a shining whiteness in the skin
5 and hath not spread itself in the skin
6 obscure, and not spread in the skin
10 shall be a white color in the skin
11 leprosy, and grown into the skin. The
12 spring out running about in the skin, and cover all the skin
18 an ulcer in the flesh and the skin
24 also and skin that hath been burnt
25 thereof is lower than the other skin
27 leprosy be grown farther in the skin
35 the spot spread again in the skin, he
38 if a whiteness appear in the skin
39 darkish whiteness shineth in the skin
48 whatsoever is made of a skin, if it be
15 17 the garment or skin that he weareth
Num 19 5 delivering up to the fire her skin
13 and put a goat's skin with the hair
16 the bed and a goat's skin at its head
Tob 11 14 a white skin began to come out of his eyes, like the skin of an egg
Job 2 4 skin for skin, and all that a man hath
7 5 my skin is withered and drawn together
10 11 hast clothed me with skin and flesh
16 16 I have sewed sackcloth upon my skin
18 13 let it devour the beauty of his skin
19 20 my bone hath cleaved to my skin, and
26 I shall be clothed again with my skin
30 30 my skin is become black upon me, and
40 26 wilt thou fill nets with his skin
Jer 13 23 if the Ethiopian can change his skin
Lam 3 4 my skin and my flesh he hath made old
4 8 their skin hath stuck to their bones
5 10 our skin was burnt as an oven by

23 5 and made a great slaughter of them
Esth 9 5 so the Jews made a great slaughter
1 Ma 1 25 he made a great slaughter of men, and
5 3 he [Judas] made a great s. of them
34 they made a great slaughter of them
2 Ma 8 6 he made no small s. of the enemies
12 16 he made an unspeakable slaughter
slave Deut 24 18 that thou wast a slave in Egypt
Ps 104 17 Joseph, who was sold for a slave. They
Prov 29 19 slave will not be corrected by words
30 22 by a slave when he reigneth: by a
Eccu 23 11 as a slave daily put to the question
33 25 and correction and work for a slave
27 and continual labors bow a slave
28 and fetters are for a malicious slave
42 5 to make the side of a wicked slave to
Jer 2 14 is Israel a bondman or a homeborn s.
1 Ma 2 11 she that was free is made a slave
2 P 2 19 of the same also he is the slave. For
slavery Jdth 3 2 or suffer the miseries of s.
slaves Gen 43 18 by violence make slaves of us
Jdth 5 10 and made slaves of them to labor in
Eze 27 13 they brought to thy people slaves and
Mich 6 4 delivered thee out of the house of s.
1 Ma 3 41 to buy the children of Israel for s.
2 Ma 1 27 deliver them that are slaves to the
8 11 to buy up the Jewish s., promising
11 should have ninety s. for one talent
John 8 33 we have never been slaves to any man
Titus 3 3 slaves to divers desires and pleasures
2 P 2 19 themselves are the slaves of corruption
Apoc 18 13 and horses and chariots and slaves and
slay 1 Ma 9 66 he began to slay and to increase
2 Ma 5 12 to go up into the houses to slay
slayer Eze 21 11 it may be in the hand of the s.
slayers Judg 20 37 turned their backs to the s.
sleds 1 Pa 20 3 and made harrows and sleds and
sleep Gen 2 21 God cast a deep sleep upon Adam
Gen 15 12 a deep sleep fell upon Abram and a
28 12 and he saw in his sleep a ladder
16 when Jacob awaked out of sleep, he
30 15 he shall sleep with thee this night
31 10 saw in my sleep that the males which
11 angel of God said to me in my sleep
40 and sleep departed from my eyes
45 26 he awaked as it were out of a deep s.
47 30 but I will sleep with my fathers, and
Exod 22 27 neither hath he any other to sleep in
Lev 15 24 every bed on which he shall sleep
26 6 you shall sleep, and there shall be
Deut 21 13 in unto her and shalt sleep with her
24 13 that he may sleep in his own raiment
28 30 take a wife, and another s. with her
31 16 thou shalt sleep with thy fathers
Judg 4 21 so passing from deep sleep to death
16 14 awaking out of his sleep he drew out
19 she made him sleep upon her knees
20 awaking from sleep, he said in his mind
Ruth 3 4 when he shall go to sleep, mark the
7 he went to s. by the heap of sheaves
13 sleep till the morning. So she slept
1 K 3 5 I did not call; go back and sleep
6 not call thee, my son; return and sleep
9 he said to Samuel: Go and sleep: and
26 12 s. from the Lord was fallen upon them
2 K 7 12 and thou shalt sleep with thy fathers
11 11 to drink, and to sleep with my wife
3 K 1 2 sleep in his bosom and warm our lord
3 19 for in her sleep she overlaid him
Esth 6 1 that night the king passed without s.
Job 3 13 and should have rest in my sleep. With
4 13 when deep sleep is wont to hold men
7 4 if I lie down to sleep, I shall say
21 behold now I shall sleep in the dust
11 18 being buried thou shalt sleep secure
14 12 not awake nor rise up out of his sleep
20 11 they shall sleep with him in the dust
21 26 they shall sleep together in the dust
27 19 the rich man when he shall sleep shall
30 17 they that feed upon me do not sleep
33 15 night when deep sleep falleth upon men
38 37 can make the harmony of heaven to sleep
Ps 4 9 in peace in the selfsame I will sleep
12 4 my eyes that I never sleep in death
67 14 if you sleep among the midst of lots
75 6 they have slept their sleep; and all
77 65 Lord was awaked as one out of sleep
120 4 he shall neither slumber nor sleep
126 2 when he shall give s. to his beloved
131 4 if I shall give sleep to my eyes, or
Prov 3 24 if thou sleep, thou shalt not fear
24 rest, and thy sleep shall be sweet
4 16 they s. not except they have done evil
16 their sleep is taken away unless they
6 4 give not sleep to thy eyes, neither
9 how long wilt thou sleep, O sluggard
9 when wilt thou rise out of thy sleep
10 thou wilt sleep a little, thou wilt
10 wilt fold thy hands a little to sleep
19 15 slothfulness casteth into a deep sleep
20 13 love not sleep, lest poverty oppress
24 33 thou wilt sleep a little, said I, thou
Ecce 5 11 sleep is sweet to a laboring man
11 of the rich will not suffer them to s.
8 16 that day and night take no sleep with
Cant 5 2 I sleep, and my heart watcheth: the
Wisd 7 2 and the pleasure of sleep concurring
17 13 and deepest hell, slept the same sleep
Eccu 13 17 see as it were in sleep, and thou
22 8 that waketh a man out of a deep sleep
24 45 will behold all that sleep, and will
31 1 thought thereof driveth away sleep
24 wholesome sleep with a moderate man
24 he shall sleep till morning and his
40 5 s. of the night changeth his knowledge
6 in s. as in the day of keeping watch
42 9 the care for her taketh away his sleep
Isa 5 27 they shall not slumber nor sleep
21 13 in the forest at evening you shall s.
29 10 mingled for you the spirit of a deep s.
43 17 they lay down to sleep together and
50 11 my hand, you shall sleep in sorrows
51 17 to the bottom of the cup of dead sleep
22 out of thy hand the cup of dead sleep
65 4 sleep in the temple of idols: that eat
Jer 3 25 we shall sleep in our confusion and
31 26 was as it were awaked out of a sleep
26 I saw, and my sleep was sweet to me
51 39 slumber and sleep an everlasting s.
57 they shall sleep an everlasting sleep
Eze 4 4 thou shalt sleep upon thy left side
4 days that thou shalt sleep upon it
6 thou shalt sleep again upon thy right
31 18 thou shalt sleep in the midst of the
32 19 down and sleep with the uncircumcised
27 they shall not sleep with the brave
28 shalt sleep with them that are slain
34 25 shall sleep secure in the forests
Dan 6 18 and even sleep departed from him. Then
12 2 that sleep in the dust of the earth
Osee 2 18 and I will make them sleep secure
Amos 6 4 you that sleep upon beds of ivory
Jon 1 5 of the ship and fell into a deep sleep
Zach 4 1 as a man that is wakened out of his s.
1 Ma 6 10 sleep is gone from my eyes and I
Mat 1 20 appeared to him in his sleep, saying

24 Joseph rising up from sleep, did as
2 12 having received an answer in sleep
13 appeared in sleep to Joseph. 19
22 being warned in sleep, retired into the
26 45 s. ye now and take your rest. Mark 14:41
Mark 4 27 and should sleep, and rise, night and
Luke 9 32 were with him were heavy with sleep
22 46 why sleep you? Arise, pray, lest you
John 11 11 I go that I may awake him out of sleep
12 Lord, if he sleep, he shall do well
13 thought that he spoke of the repose of s.
Acts 16 27 keeper of prison, awaking out of sleep
20 9 being oppressed with a deep sleep, as
9 occasion of his s. fell from third loft
Rom 13 11 is now hour for us to rise from sleep
1 C 11 30 and weak among you, and many sleep. But
15 20 dead, the firstfruits of them that sleep
1 Th 5 6 let us not sleep, as others do; but let
7 they had sleep, sleep in the night, and
10 that, whether we watch or sleep, we may
sleepest Gen 28 13 land wherein thou s. I will
Ps 43 23 arise, why sleepest thou, O Lord? Arise
Prov 6 22 when thou sleepest, let them keep thee
Mark 14 37 Simon, sleepest thou? Couldst thou not
Eph 5 14 rise thou that sleepest, and arise from
sleepeth Lev 14 47 that s. in it and eateth any
Lev 15 4 every bed on which he sleepeth shall
21 and everything that she sleepeth on
26 every bed on which she sleepeth and
33 and of the man that sleepeth with her
Ruth 3 4 mark the place wherein he sleepeth
3 K 1 21 when my lord the king s. with his
Job 40 16 he sleepeth under the shadow in the
Ps 40 9 shall he that s. rise again no more
Mich 7 5 from her that sleepeth in thy bosom
Mat 9 24 the girl is not dead, but sleepeth
Mark 5 39 the damsel is not dead, but sleepeth
Luke 8 52 the maid is not dead, but sleepeth
John 11 11 Lazarus our friend sleepeth; but I go
sleeping Deut 6 7 on thy journey, s. and rising
1 K 26 5 Saul sleeping in a tent, and the rest
7 found Saul lying and s. in the tent
7 Abner and the people s. round about
2 K 4 5 he was sleeping upon his bed at noon
7 he was s. upon his bed in a parlor, and
12 3 of his cup and sleeping in his bosom
Tob 2 11 as he was sleeping, hot dung out of
8 15 safe and sound, sleeping both together
Jdth 14 13 he thought that he was s. with Judith
Job 33 15 and they are sleeping in their beds
Ps 87 6 like the slain s. in the sepulchers
Prov 23 34 as one sleeping in the midst of the sea
Eccu 31 22 in sleeping thou shalt not be uneasy
Isa 56 10 dogs . . . sleeping and loving dreams
Mat 26 43 again, and findeth them sleeping: for
Mark 4 38 part of the ship, s. upon a pillow
13 36 coming on a sudden, he find you s.
14 37 he cometh and findeth them sleeping
Luke 22 45 he found them sleeping for sorrow
Acts 12 6 Peter was sleeping between 2 soldiers
slept Gen 28 11 s. in the same place. And he
Gen 30 16 he [Jacob] slept with her that night
32 13 when he had slept there that night
35 22 Ruben went and slept with Bala, the
41 5 he s. again and dreamed another dream
Num 5 13 shall have slept with another man
19 if another man hath not s. with thee
24 9 lying down he hath slept as a lion
Judg 16 3 Samson slept till midnight, and then
Ruth 3 14 so she slept at his feet till the
1 K 3 3 Samuel slept in the temple of the Lord
5 back and sleep. And he went and slept
9 so Samuel went and slept in his place
15 Samuel slept till morning, and opened
9 25 on the top of the house, and he slept
26 5 beheld the place wherein Saul slept
2 K 11 4 she came in to him, and he s. with her
9 Urias slept before the gate of the
13 [Urias] slept on his couch with the
12 24 unto her and slept with her [Bethsabee]
3 K 1 4 she slept with the king and served him
2 10 slept with his fathers. 11:21, 43; 14:20, 31; 15:8, 24; 16:6, 28; 22:40, 51; 4 K 8:24; 10:35; 13:9, 13; 14:6, 22, 29; 15:7, 22, 38; 16:20; 20:21; 21:18; 2 Pa 9:31; 12:16; 14:1; 16:13; 21:1; 26:2, 23; 27:9; 28:27; 32:33; 33:20
19 5 slept in the shadow of the juniper tree
21 27 Achab fasted and slept in sackcloth
Tob 2 10 cast himself down by the wall and s.
Ps 3 6 I have slept and have taken my rest
56 5 of the young lions. I slept troubled
75 6 they have slept their sleep; and all
Wisd 17 13 and deepest hell, slept the same sleep
Eccu 46 23 after this he slept, and he made known
Isa 14 8 since thou hast slept, there hath none
18 have all of them slept in glory, every
51 20 have slept at the head of all the
Eze 32 21 and slept uncircumcised, slain by
29 have slept with the uncircumcised
30 who slept uncircumcised with them
32 slept in midst of the uncircumcised
Osee 7 6 he slept all the night baking them
Mat 25 5 tarrying, they all slumbered and slept
27 52 of the saints that had slept arose
Luke 8 23 when they were sailing, he slept
Acts 13 36 according to the will of God, slept
1 Th 4 13 so them who have slept through Jesus
14 shall not prevent them who have slept
2 P 3 4 since the time that the fathers slept
slew Luke 13 4 tower fell in Siloe and slew them
slewest 1 K 21 9 the Philistine whom thou s.
slid 2 K 22 11 slid upon the wings of the wind
slide Deut 32 35 due time, that their foot may s.
slight Deut 22 4 shalt not s. it, but shalt lift
Ps 9 1 why dost thou slight us in our wants
Eccu 26 14 and wonder not if she slight thee
slighted Deut 9 23 you s. the commandment of the
Ps 21 25 he hath not slighted nor despised the
Ecce 9 16 then is the wisdom of the poor man s.
Dan 3 12 these men, O king, have s. thy decree
slighteth Deut 21 18 being corrected, s. obedience
Deut 21 20 he slighteth hearing our admonitions
slighting 3 K 20 43 to his house, s. to hear
slime Gen 2 7 formed man of the s. of the earth
Gen 11 3 they had . . . slime instead of mortar
14 10 woodland vale had many pits of slime
Exod 2 3 and daubed it with slime and pitch
Tob 8 8 madest Adam of the slime of the earth
sling 1 K 17 40 and he took a sling in his hand
1 K 17 49 a stone, and cast it with the sling
50 Philistine, with a sling and a stone
25 29 the violence and whirling of a sling
Job 41 19 stones of the sling are to him like
Eccu 47 5 with the stone in the sling he beat
Zach 9 15 and subdue with the stones of the s.
slingers 4 K 3 25 the city was beset by the s.
Jdth 6 8 the slingers came out against them
1 Ma 9 11 the s. and the archers went before the
slinging Judg 20 16 s. stones so sure that they
slings 1 Pa 12 2 in hurling stones with slings
2 Pa 26 14 and bows and slings to cast stones
1 Ma 6 20 they made battering slings and engines
51 and he set up there battering slings
51 and pieces to shoot arrows, and slings
slip Deut 22 8 if any one slip and fall down

3 K 20 39 if he shall slip away, thy life shall
Wisd 10 8 they did not only slip in this, that
Eccu 28 30 lest thou slip with thy tongue and
Heb 2 1 lest perhaps we should let them slip
slipped Deut 19 5 cutting down the tree the axe s.
Ps 72 2 moved: my steps had well nigh slipped
Eccu 14 1 man that hath not slipped by a word
25 11 that hath not slipped with his tongue
Lam 4 18 our steps have slipped in the way
1 Ma 9 7 Judas saw that his army slipped away
slippery Ps 34 6 their way become dark and s.
Prov 26 28 and a slippery mouth worketh ruin
Jer 23 12 shall be as a slippery way in the dark
38 22 in the mire and in a slippery place
slippeth Eccu 19 16 one that s. with the tongue
slipping Deut 19 5 the iron s. from the handle
Eccu 20 20 the slipping of a false tongue is as
slips Wisd 4 3 bastard s. shall not take deep
slipt 1 K 13 8 the people slipt away from him
1 K 13 11 I saw that the people slipt from me
19 10 David slipt away out of the presence
21 13 and slipt down between their hands
sloth Eccu 18 27 the days of sins will beware of s.
slothful Prov 10 4 s. hand hath wrought poverty
Prov 12 24 that which is s. shall be under tribute
15 19 the way of the slothful is as a hedge
18 8 fear casteth down the slothful: and the
19 24 the s. hideth his hand under. 26:15
21 25 desires kill the slothful: for his
22 13 s. man saith: There is lion. 26:13
24 30 I passed by the field of the s. man
26 14 so doth the slothful upon his bed
Mat 25 26 wicked and slothful servant, thou
Rom 12 11 in carefulness not slothful. In spirit
Titus 1 12 always liars, evil beasts, s. bellies
Heb 6 12 you become not s., but followers of
slothfulness Prov 19 15 s. casteth into a deep
Ecce 10 18 by s. a building shall be brought down
slow Judg 5 28 why are feet of his horses so s.
Wisd 15 15 they are slow to walk. For man made
Eccu 7 39 be not slow to visit the sick: for
14 12 remember that death is not slow, and
51 32 why are ye slow? And what do you say
Luke 24 25 O foolish and slow of heart to believe
James 1 19 but slow to speak and slow to anger
slowly Acts 27 7 for many days we had sailed s.
slowness Exod 4 10 I have more . . . s. of tongue
sluggard Prov 6 6 go to the ant, thou sluggard
Prov 6 9 how long wilt thou sleep, O sluggard
10 26 so is the sluggard to them that sent
13 4 the sluggard willeth and willeth not
20 4 of the cold the sluggard would not plow
21 5 but every sluggard is always in want
26 16 sluggard is wiser in his own conceit
Eccu 22 1 sluggard is pelted with a dirty stone
2 s. is pelted with the dung of oxen
slumber Ps 120 3 neither let him s. that keepeth
Ps 120 4 he shall neither slumber nor sleep
131 4 to my eyes, or slumber to my eyelids
Prov 6 4 eyes, neither let thy eyelids slumber
10 thou wilt slumber a little. 24:33
Isa 5 27 they shall not s. nor sleep, neither
Jer 51 39 make them drunk, that they may slumber
slumbered Ps 75 7 they have all s. that mounted
Ps 118 28 my soul hath s. through heaviness
Nah 3 18 thy shepherds have slumbered, O king
Mat 25 5 tarrying, they all slumbered and slept
slumbereth 2 P 2 3 and their perdition s. not
small Gen 30 15 dost thou think it a s. matter
Exod 16 14 it appeared in the wilderness small
30 36 hast beaten all into very small powder
39 3 and drew them small into threads, that
Lev 2 14 at the fire, and break it s. like meal
16 part of the corn broken small and
Num 16 9 is it a s. thing unto you. Josu 22:17
13 is it a small matter to thee that thou
Deut 9 21 pieces, until it was as small as dust
33 6 and not die and be he small in number
1 K 5 9 men of every city, both s. and great
18 23 s. matter to be the king's son-in-law
23 I am a poor man and of small ability
30 19 was nothing missing small or great
2 K 17 13 not be found so much as one small stone
22 43 I shall beat them as small as the dust
3 K 2 20 I desire one small petition of thee
7 8 midst of the porch was a small house
22 31 not fight against any, small or great
4 K 3 18 this is a small thing in the sight of
2 Pa 18 26 him bread and water in a s. quantity
30 fight ye not with small or great, but
35 7 of other small cattle thirty thousand
8 two thousand six hundred small cattle
9 five thousand small cattle and 500 oxen
36 18 all the vessels . . . great and small
2 Es 3 30 and of the sellers of small wares
Job 3 19 the small and great are there, and
8 7 if thy former things were small, thy
Ps 17 43 I shall beat them as small as the dust
Ecce 10 1 than a small and short-lived folly
Eccu 5 18 justify alike the small and the great
11 3 the bee is small among flying things
18 32 assemblies, be they ever so small
19 1 that contemneth small things, shall
20 12 that buyeth much for a small price
48 17 and there was left but a small people
Isa 7 13 is it a small thing for you to be
16 14 and it shall be left small and feeble
28 28 but bread corn shall be broken small
29 5 fan thee, shall be like small dust
30 14 and it shall be broken small, as the
49 6 it is a small thing that thou shouldst
54 7 for a small moment have I forsaken thee
Eze 16 20 is thy fornication small? Thou hast
43 8 but a small wall between me and them
Dan 11 23 shall overcome with a small people
34 shall be relieved with a small help
Abdi 2 I have made thee small among the
1 Ma 3 16 to meet him with a small company
18 multitude or with a small company
29 the tributes of the country were small
6 57 and our provision of victuals is small
2 Ma 1 15 he with a small company had entered
3 14 was no small terror throughout the
8 6 made no small slaughter of the enemies
Mark 3 9 that a small ship should wait on him
Acts 12 18 was no small stir among the soldiers
14 27 they abode no s. time with disciples
15 2 Barnabas had no small contest with them
19 23 there arose no small disturbance about
24 brought no small gain to the craftsmen
26 22 witnessing both to small and great
27 20 no small storm lay on us, all hope of
28 1 barbarians showed us no small courtesy
1 C 4 3 it is a very small thing to be judged
James 3 4 are they turned about with a small helm
5 how small a fire kindleth a great wood
Apoc 20 12 and I saw the dead, great and small
small number; *see* **number**
smallest Isa 40 15 as the s. grain of a balance
1 C 6 2 are you unworthy to judge the s. matters
smell Gen 27 27 fragrant smell of his garments
Gen 27 27 the smell of my son is as the smell of a plentiful field
Exod 30 38 to enjoy the smell thereof, he shall
Deut 4 28 neither see nor hear nor eat nor s.
Ps 113 6 hear not: they have noses and s. not

1 K 28 9 dost thou lay a snare for my life
Ps 9 16 taken in the very snare which they hid
24 15 he shall pluck my feet out of the s.
30 5 thou wilt bring me out of this snare
34 8 let the snare which he knoweth not
8 into that very snare let them fall
56 7 they prepared a snare for my feet; and
68 23 let their table become as a snare
90 3 me from the snare of the hunters: and
118 110 sinners have laid a snare for me: but
123 7 as a sparrow out of the snare of the
7 snare is broken, and we are delivered
139 6 have stretched out cords for a snare
140 9 keep me from the snare, which they
141 4 walked, they have hidden a s. for me
Prov 7 23 as if bird should make haste to the s.
29 6 a snare shall entangle the wicked man
Ecce 7 27 is the hunter's snare, and her heart is
9 12 as birds are caught with the snare
Wisd 14 11 and a snare to the feet of the unwise
Eccu 11 32 the cage, and as the roe into the snare
27 22 as a roe escaped out of the snare
29 he that layeth a snare for another
32 they shall perish in a snare that are
37 7 with him that layeth a snare for thee
51 3 from the snare of an unjust tongue
Isa 8 14 a snare and a ruin to the inhabitants
24 17 the pit and the snare are upon thee
18 shall be taken in the snare. Jer 48:44
Jer 48 43 and the pit and the snare come upon
45 they that fled from the snare stood
50 24 I have caused thee to fall into a s.
Lam 3 47 is become to us a fear and a snare
Osee 5 1 because you have been a snare to them
9 8 the prophet is become a snare of ruin
Amos 3 5 will the bird fall into the snare
5 shall the snare be taken up from the
1 Ma 1 37 there: and they became a great snare
5 4 who were a snare and a stumblingblock
Luke 21 35 as a snare shall it come upon all
Rom 11 9 let their table be made a snare, and a
1 C 7 35 not to cast a snare upon you; but for
1 Tim 3 7 into reproach and the snare of the devil
6 9 into the snare of the devil and into many
2 P 2 12 naturally tending to the snare and to
snared Isa 8 15 and shall be snared and taken
Isa 28 13 and be broken and snared and taken
51 20 ways, as the wild ox that is snared
snares 2 K 22 6 s. of death prevented me. Ps 17:6
3 K 20 7 and see that he layeth snares for us
Job 22 10 therefore art thou surrounded with s.
Ps 10 7 he shall rain snares upon sinners: fire
63 6 they have talked of hiding snares
Prov 1 11 let us hide snares for the innocent
11 6 unjust shall be caught in their own s.
15 but he that is aware of the snares
21 6 shall stumble upon the snares of death
Eccu 9 3 many: lest thou fall into her snares
20 thou art going in the midst of snares
11 31 many are the snares of the deceitful
Jer 5 26 setting snares and traps to catch men
18 22 and have hid snares for my feet. But
Osee 7 6 oven, when he laid snares for them
Abdi 7 eat with thee shall lay s. under thee
Mark 6 19 now Herodias laid snares for him: and
2 Tim 2 26 may recover themselves from the snares
snatch Job 27 21 shall snatch him from his place
Ps 49 22 lest he snatch you away, and there be
John 10 29 no one can snatch them out of the hand
snatched Job 30 5 who s. up these things out of
sneezing Job 41 9 his s. is like the shining of
snorteth Prov 10 5 he that s. in the summer, is
snorting Jer 8 16 the s. of his horses was heard
snout Prov 11 22 golden ring in a swine's snout
snow Exod 4 6 brought it forth leprous as snow
Num 12 10 Mary appeared white as snow with a
2 K 23 20 of a pit in the time of s. 1 Pa 11:22
4 K 5 27 out from him a leper as white as snow
Job 6 16 frost, the snow shall fall upon them
9 30 washed as it were with snow waters
24 19 let him pass from the snow waters to
37 6 he commandeth the snow to go down upon
38 22 entered into storehouses of the snow
Ps 50 9 and I shall be made whiter than snow
67 15 they shall be whited with snow in
147 16 who giveth snow like wool: scattereth
148 8 fire, hail, snow, ice, stormy winds
Prov 25 13 as the cold of snow in time of harvest
26 1 as snow in summer, and rain in harvest
31 21 not fear for her house in cold of snow
Wisd 16 22 snow and ice endured the force of fire
Eccu 43 14 he maketh the snow to fall apace and
19 he scattereth snow, and the falling
Isa 1 18 they shall be made as white as snow
55 10 as the rain and the snow come down
Jer 18 14 shall the snow of Libanus fail from
Lam 4 7 her Nazarites were whiter than snow
Dan 3 70 ye ice and snow, bless the Lord: praise
7 9 his garment was white as snow, and the
1 Ma 13 22 but there fell a very great snow, and
Mat 17 2 and his garments became white as snow
28 3 as lightning, and his raiment as snow
Mark 9 2 shining and exceeding white as snow
Apoc 1 14 were white as white wool and as snow
snows Zach 10 1 the Lord will make snows and will
snuffed Jer 2 24 snuffed up the wind of his love
Jer 14 6 they snuffed up the wind like dragons
snuffers Exod 25 38 the s. also, and where the
Exod 37 23 also the seven lamps with their s.
Num 4 9 the snuffers and all the oil vessels
snuffings Exod 25 38 where the s. shall be put out
Exod 37 23 vessels where the s. were to be put
so 2 K 3 9 so do God to Abner and more also unless
2 K 3 35 David swore, saying: So do God to me
19 13 so do God to me and add more, if thou
Jer 28 6 prophet said: Amen, the Lord do so
so and so Ruth 1 17 the Lord do so and so to me
1 K 3 17 do so and so to thee and add so and so
14 44 may God do so and so to me. 4 K 6:31
20 13 may the Lord do so and so to Jonathan
25 22 may God do so and so and add more to
3 K 2 23 so and so may God do to me, and add
so be it Josu 2 21 as you have spoken, so be it
1 Es 10 12 thy word unto us, so be it done
Jdth 10 9 all with one voice: so be it, so be it
13 26 people said: So be it, so be it. 15:12
Ps 40 14 eternity to eternity. So be it. So be it
71 19 with his majesty. So be it. So be it
88 53 Lord for evermore. So be it. So be it
105 48 all the people say: So be it, so be it
soak Isa 55 10 soak the earth and water it and
soaked Isa 34 7 land shall be soaked with blood
Soam 1 Pa 24 27 of Merari: Oziau and Soam and
Soar Exod 6 15 and Ahod and Jachin and Soar and
Soba 1 K 14 47 kings of Soba and the Philistines
2 K 10 6 of Rohob and the Syrians of Soba
8 but the Syrians of Soba and of Rohob
23 36 Igaal the son of Nathan of Soba, Bonni
3 K 11 24 when David slew them of Soba: and
1 Pa 19 6 out of Syria Maacha and out of Soba
king of Soba 2 K 8 3 the son of Rohob k. . . . 12
2 K 8 5 to succor Adarezer the king of Soba
3 K 11 23 his master Adarezer the king of Soba
1 Pa 18 3 defeated also Adarezer the king of Soba
5 to help Adarezer king of Soba: and
9 all the army of Adarezer king of Soba

50 40 as the Lord overthrew Sodom and
Lam 4 6 is made greater than the sin of Sodom
Eze 16 46 dwelleth at thy right hand is Sodom
48 sister Sodom herself and her daughter
49 this was the iniquity of Sodom thy
53 and restore them by bringing back Sodom
55 thy sister S. and her daughters shall
56 Sodom thy sister was not heard of in
Amos 4 11 as God destroyed Sodom and Gomorrha
Soph 2 9 Moab shall be as Sodom, and the
Mat 10 15 more tolerable for the land of S. 24
11 23 if in Sodom had been wrought the
Luke 10 12 more tolerable at that day for Sodom
17 29 the day that Lot went out of Sodom
Rom 9 29 we had been made as Sodom, and we had
Jdth 1 7 as S. and Gomorrha and the neighboring
Apoc 11 8 is called spiritually Sodom and Egypt
king of Sodom Gen 14 2 war against Bara k. . . .
Gen 14 8 the k. . . . and the king of. 10
17 the k. . . . went out to meet him, after
21 the k. . . . said to Abram: Give me
Sodomites Gen 14 11 all the substance of the S.
2 P 2 6 reducing the cities of the Sodomites
soft Prov 25 15 soft tongue shall break hardness
Wisd 2 3 shall be poured abroad as soft air, and
Mat 11 8 man clothed in s. garments. Luke 7:25
softened 2 Pa 34 27 and thy heart was softened
Job 23 16 God hath softened my heart, and the
softeneth Prov 2 16 stranger, who s. her words
softly Gen 33 14 I will follow softly after him
Judg 4 21 going in softly and with silence, she
Ruth 3 7 she came softly and uncovering his
Tob 11 3 let the family follow softly after us
Soha 2 Es 7 47 Nathinites: the children of Soha
Sohar Gen 46 10 Ahod and Jachin and Sohar and
Sohoria 1 Pa 8 26 Samsari and S. and Otholia
soil Num 32 4 fertile soil for the feeding of
sojourn Gen 12 10 down into Egypt to s. there
Gen 26 3 sojourn in it, and I will be with thee
47 4 we are come to sojourn in thy land
Lev 17 8 who s. among you. 12, 13; 25:45
10 that sojourn among them. Num 15:26
25 6 the strangers that sojourn with thee
Judg 17 8 desired to sojourn wheresoever he
Ruth 1 1 went to sojourn in the land of Moab
4 K 8 1 and s. wheresoever thou canst find
Isa 23 7 shall carry her afar off to sojourn
52 4 down into Egypt . . . to sojourn there
Jer 44 14 gone to sojourn in the land of Egypt
Eze 20 38 out of the land where they sojourn
Acts 7 6 his seed should sojourn in a strange
sojourned Gen 20 1 and sojourned in Gerara
Gen 32 4 I have sojourned with Laban and
35 27 wherein Abraham and Isaac sojourned
36 7 the land in which they sojourned able
37 1 Chanaan wherein his father sojourned
Deut 26 5 down into Egypt and sojourned there
4 K 8 2 she s. in the land of the Philistines
Eccu 16 9 spared not the place where Lot s.
sojourner Gen 21 34 a s. in the land of the
Gen 23 4 I am a stranger and s. among you
Lev 22 10 s. of the priests or a hired servant
40 he shall be as a hireling and a s.
47 if the hand of a stranger or a s.
Num 9 14 the sojourner also and the stranger
Ps 38 13 a sojourner as all my fathers were
104 23 was a sojourner in the land of Cham
118 19 I am a sojourner on the earth: hide
119 6 my soul hath been long a sojourner
sojourners Lev 25 23 you are strangers and s.
Num 35 15 of Israel as for strangers and s.
2 K 4 3 were sojourners there until that time
1 Pa 16 19 number: very few and sojourners in it
29 15 for we are sojourners before thee and
Ps 104 12 yea very few, and sojourners therein
Jer 41 17 and sat as sojourners in Chamaam
Acts 13 17 when they were s. in the land of Egypt
sojourneth Exod 12 49 proselyte that s. with you
Lev 16 29 a stranger that sojourneth among you
18 26 stranger that sojourneth among you
sojourning Ps 119 5 that my s. is prolonged
Wisd 19 10 done in the time of their sojourning
1 P 1 17 during the time of your s. here
sojournment Gen 17 8 thy seed the land of thy s.
Gen 28 4 mayst possess the land of thy s.
Ruth 1 7 out of the place of her sojournment
22 from the land of her sojournment: and
Eccu 16 15 according to wisdom of his sojournment
sold Gen 25 33 and sold his first birthright
Gen 25 34 of having sold his first birthright
31 15 hath he not . . . sold us and eaten up
37 27 that he be sold to the Ismaelites
28 sold him [Joseph] to the Ismaelites
36 the Madianites sold Joseph in Egypt
41 56 the barns and sold to the Egyptians
42 1 hearing that food was sold in Egypt
2 I have heard that wheat is sold in
6 corn was sold by his direction to the
45 4 your brother whom you sold into Egypt
5 that you sold me into these countries
Exod 22 3 if he have not . . . he shall be sold
Lev 25 23 the land also shall not be sold forever
25 he may redeem what he had sold. But
27 counted from that time when he sold it
28 that is sold shall return to the owner
31 it shall be sold according to the same
34 but let not their suburbs be sold
42 let them not be sold as bondmen
50 counting the money that he was s. for
27 14 shall be sold according to the price
16 let it be sold for fifty sicles of
20 if . . . it be sold to any other man
24 to the former owner, who had sold it
27 shall be sold to another for how much
28 devoted to the Lord . . . not be sold
Deut 15 12 or Hebrew woman is sold to thee, and
32 30 because their God had sold them, and
Judg 2 14 and sold them to their enemies that
3 K 10 15 and they that sold by retail, and
21 20 because thou art sold to do evil in
25 Achab, who was sold to do evil in the
4 K 6 25 till the head of an ass was sold for
7 1 fine flour shall be sold for a stater
16 bushel of fine flour was sold for a
Josu 5 8 Jews, that were sold to the Gentiles
13 16 they sold them on the sabbaths to the
20 and they that sold all kinds of wares
Jdth 7 13 God hath sold us into their hands
Ps 43 13 thou hast sold thy people for no price
104 17 them. Joseph, who was sold for a slave
Prov 31 24 she made fine linen and sold it, and
Wisd 10 13 forsook not the just when he was sold
Isa 42 19 who is blind, but he that is sold
50 1 is my creditor, to whom I sold you
1 you are sold for your iniquities, and
52 3 you were sold gratis, and you shall
Jer 34 14 Hebrew, who hath been sold to thee
Bar 4 6 you have been sold to the Gentiles
Eze 7 13 return to that which he hath sold
27 23 Saba, Assur and Chelmad sold to thee
Joel 3 3 and the girl they have sold for wine
6 you have sold to the children of the
7 the place wherein you have sold them
Amos 2 6 he hath sold the just man for silver
Nah 3 4 sold nations through her fornications
Zach 11 5 and repented not, and they sold them

1 Ma 1 16 heathens, and were sold to do evil
2 Ma 4 32 others he had sold at Tyre and in the
5 14 were made prisoners, and as many sold
8 14 others sold all that they had left
14 who had sold them before he came near
10 21 they had sold their brethren for money
Mat 10 29 two sparrows sold for a farthing
13 46 went his way and sold all that he had
18 25 lord commanded that he should be sold
21 12 cast out all them that sold. Mark 11:15; Luke 19:45
12 chairs of them that s. doves. Mark 11:15
26 9 this might have been sold for much
Mark 14 5 this ointment might have been sold for
Luke 12 6 are not five sparrows sold for two
17 28 they bought and sold, they planted
John 2 14 he found in the temple them that sold
16 to them that sold doves he said: Take
12 5 why was not this ointment sold for
Acts 2 45 their possessions and goods they sold
4 34 sold them and brought the price of the
34 the price of the things they sold and
37 having land, sold it and brought the
5 1 Ananias . . . sold a piece of land, and
4 after it was sold, was it not in thy
8 whether you sold the land for so much
7 9 sold Joseph into Egypt; and God was
Rom 7 14 spiritual; but I am carnal, sold under
1 C 10 25 whatsoever is s. in the shambles, eat
Heb 12 16 for one mess sold his first birthright
soldering Isa 41 7 saying: It is ready for s.
soldier Nah 2 7 the soldier is led away captive
2 Ma 8 9 also with him Gorgias, a good soldier
John 19 23 four parts, to every soldier a part
Acts 10 7 two of his household servants, and a s.
28 16 by himself, with a soldier that kept him
1 C 9 7 who serveth as a soldier at any time
Phil 2 25 fellow laborer, and fellow soldier, but
2 Tim 2 3 labor as a good soldier of Christ Jesus
4 Jesus. No man, being a soldier to God
Philem 2 to Archippus, our fellow soldier, and
soldiers Gen 26 26 Phicol chief captain of his s.
Gen 37 36 eunuch of Pharao, captain of the s.
40 3 prison of the commander of the s.
41 10 prison of the captain of the soldiers
12 servant to the same captain of the s.
Josu 8 10 he mustered his soldiers, and went up
10 27 commanded the s. to take them down
Judg 20 44 were 18,000 men, all most valiant s.
1 K 18 5 Saul set him over the soldiers, and he
2 K 24 4 captains of the soldiers went out
3 K 20 25 and make up the number of soldiers
4 K 10 25 Jehu commanded his s. and captains
25 the soldiers and captains slew them
11 4 taking the centurions and the soldiers
25 19 who exercised the young soldiers of
23 the captains of the s. had heard this
26 captains of the soldiers, rising up
1 Pa 12 14 was captain over a hundred soldiers
2 Pa 17 2 he placed numbers of soldiers in all
25 9 I have given to the soldiers of Israel
28 14 so the soldiers left the spoils and
32 6 appointed captains of the soldiers
2 Es 2 9 king had sent with me captains of s.
Jdth 6 4 the sword of my soldiers shall pass
Job 25 3 is there any numbering of his soldiers
Jer 41 3 that were found there, and the soldiers
16 all the captains of the soldiers that
43 4 captains of the soldiers and all the
5 captains of the soldiers took all the
47 3 the marching of arms and of his s.
52 25 who exercised the young soldiers
Eze 27 10 Lydians and the Libyans were thy s.
1 Ma 4 35 he went to Antioch and chose soldiers
5 56 Azarias captain of the s. heard of the
11 3 he put garrisons of s. in every city
40 done, and how his soldiers hated him
2 Ma 5 2 armed with spears, like bands of s.
12 commanded the s. to kill, and not to
11 4 in the multitude of his foot soldiers
12 37 he put Gorgias' soldiers to flight
14 39 sent five hundred soldiers to take him
Mat 8 9 having under me s.; and I say. Luke 7:8
27 27 s. of the governor taking Jesus into
28 12 gave a great sum of money to the s.
Mark 15 16 the s. led him away into the court of
Luke 3 14 and the soldiers also asked him
23 36 the soldiers also mocked him, coming
John 18 3 having received a band of soldiers and
19 2 the s. platting a crown of thorns, put
23 the soldiers therefore, when they had
24 the soldiers indeed did these things
32 the soldiers therefore came; and they
34 but one of the soldiers with a spear
Acts 12 4 delivering him to 4 files of soldiers
6 Peter was sleeping between 2 soldiers
18 was no small stir among the soldiers
21 32 who, forthwith taking with him soldiers
32 when they saw tribune and soldiers they
35 it fell out that he was carried by s.
23 10 commanded the soldiers to go down, and
23 make ready 200 soldiers to go as far as
31 the s., acccording as it was commanded
27 31 Paul said to centurion, and to soldiers
32 soldiers cut off the ropes of the boat
soldiers' Acts 27 42 the s. counsel was, that they
sole Deut 28 35 be thou incurable from the sole
Deut 28 65 be any rest for the sole of thy foot
Josu 1 3 every place that the sole of your foot
2 K 14 25 from the sole of the foot to the crown
Job 2 7 from the sole of the feet even to
18 9 sole of his foot shall be held in a
Isa 1 6 from the sole of the foot unto the
37 25 have dried up with the sole of my foot
Eze 1 7 the sole of their foot was like the sole of a calf's foot
Mala 4 3 shall be ashes under the sole of your
solemn Exod 12 16 first day shall be holy and s.
Lev 23 8 the seventh day shall be more solemn
Num 28 17 on the fifteenth day the solemn feast
1 K 1 21 to offer to the Lord the s. sacrifice
2 19 went up . . . to offer the s. sacrifice
20 6 because there are solemn sacrifices
29 there is a solemn sacrifice in the city
3 K 8 65 made at the same time a solemn feast
2 Pa 5 3 in the solemn day of the seventh month
7 9 eighth day a s. assembly. 2 Es 8:18
Ps 117 27 appoint a solemn day, with shady boughs
Eccu 47 12 and set in order the solemn times
Lam 1 4 none that come to the solemn feast
Eze 36 38 of Jerusalem in her solemn feasts
45 25 seventh month . . . in the solemn feast
46 9 before the Lord in the solemn feasts
Lam 2 7 as in the day of a solemn feast
Joel 2 15 sanctify a fast, call a s. assembly
Osee 9 5 what will you do in the solemn day
1 Ma 10 34 three days before the s. day and three days after the s. day
2 Ma 6 6 nor the solemn days of the fathers
Mat 27 15 upon the solemn day the governor was
Luke 2 41 at the solemn day of the pasch, and
most solemn Lev 23 7 first day shall be m. s.
Lev 23 21 you shall call this day most solemn
27 of atonement, it shall be most solemn
35 first day shall be called most solemn
36 eighth day also shall be most solemn

37 37 which you shall call most solemn
Num 28 25 seventh day also shall be most solemn
29 35 the eighth day, which is most solemn
solemnities Num 15 3 in your s. burning a sweet
Num 29 39 shall you offer to the Lord in your s.
1 Pa 23 31 new moons and the rest of the s.
2 Pa 2 4 on the new moons and the s. of the
31 3 new moons and the other solemnities
1 Es 3 5 on all the solemnities of the Lord
Isa 1 14 hateth your new moons and your s.
29 1 added to year: the s. are at an end
Eze 44 24 my laws and my ordinances in all my s.
45 17 all the s. of the house of Israel
46 11 in the s. there shall be the sacrifice
Osee 2 11 mirth to cease, her s., her new moons
Zach 8 19 joy and gladness and great solemnities
Mala 2 3 upon your face the dung of your s.
solemnity Exod 10 9 it is the s. of the Lord
Exod 12 16 day shall be kept with like solemnity
13 6 seventh day shall be the s. of the Lord
23 18 neither shall the fat of my s. remain
32 5 tomorrow is the solemnity of the Lord
34 25 victim of the solemnity of the Phase
Lev 23 6 the solemnity of the unleavened bread
41 keep the solemnity thereof seven days
Num 29 12 celebrate a s. to the Lord seven days
Deut 16 13 celebrate the s. also of tabernacles
Judg 21 19 a yearly solemnity of the Lord in Silo
2 Pa 7 8 and Solomon kept the s. at that time
9 celebrated the solemnity seven days
30 13 the solemnity of the unleavened bread
22 during the seven days of the solemnity
26 was a great solemnity in Jerusalem
35 7 that were found there in the solemnity
2 Es 8 18 they kept the solemnity seven days
Esth 9 23 undertook to observe with solemnity
27 to pass these days without solemnity
16 24 that will not be partaker of this s.
Ps 73 4 boasts, in the midst of thy solemnity
80 4 on the noted day of your solemnity
Isa 30 29 as in the night of the sanctified s.
33 20 look upon Sion the city of our s.
Eze 45 21 you shall observe the s. of the pasch
23 in the s. of the seven days he shall
2 Ma 15 36 to let this day pass without solemnity
soles Josu 3 13 s. of their feet in the waters
3 K 5 3 put them under the soles of his feet
4 K 19 24 dried up with the soles of my feet
Eccu 26 23 upon the soles of a steady woman. As
Jer 13 22 the soles of thy feet are defiled
Eze 43 7 the place of the soles of my feet
Acts 3 7 his feet and soles received strength
soliciting Deut 24 7 man be found s. his brother
solicitous 1 K 9 20 as for the asses . . . be not s.
Tob 10 1 Tobias his father was s., saying: Why
Prov 11 7 expectation of the s. shall perish
Ecce 2 19 with which I have labored and been s.
Isa 57 11 for whom hast thou been solicitous
Jer 17 8 time of drought it shall not be s.
Bar 3 18 who work in silver and are s., and
Mich 6 8 mercy, and to walk s. with thy God
Mat 6 25 be not s. for your life. Luke 12:22
28 for raiment why are you solicitous
31 be not s. therefore, saying, What shall
34 be not therefore s. for tomorrow
34 the morrow will be s. for itself
Luke 12 11 be not s. how or what you shall answer
26 why are you solicitous for the rest
1 C 7 32 is solicitous for things that belong to
33 wife, is s. for the things of the world
Phil 2 20 who with sincere affection is s. for you
4 6 be nothing s.; but in everything, by
Col 4 12 who is always s. for you in prayers
solicitude Ecce 2 26 a fruitless s. of the mind
1 C 7 32 I would have you to be without s. He
2 C 11 28 instance, the s. for all the churches
solid Exod 38 7 the altar itself was not solid
Eccu 26 24 foundations upon a solid rock, so
solids 1 Pa 29 7 gold, 5,000 talents and 10,000 s.
1 Es 2 69 they gave . . . 61,000 solids of gold
8 27 cups of gold of a thousand solids
solitary Job 3 7 let that night be s. and not
Lam 1 1 how doth the city sit s. that
3 28 he shall sit solitary and hold his
solitudes Job 3 14 build themselves solitudes
Solomon Mat 1 6 David the king begot Solomon of her
Mat 1 7 Solomon begot Roboam. And Roboam begot
6 29 even S. in all his glory. Luke 12:27
12 42 to hear the wisdom of S. Luke 11:31
42 behold a greater than Solomon here
Luke 11 31 and behold more than Solomon here
Acts 7 47 but Solomon built him a house. Yet
Solomon's 3 K 4 27 also for king S. table, with
3 K 9 16 dowry to his daughter, Solomon's wife
10 24 all the earth desired to see S. face
1 Pa 3 10 Solomon's son was Roboam: whose son
2 Pa 8 6 the strong cities that were Solomon's
10 chief captains of king Solomon's army
18 they went with S. servants to Ophir
John 10 23 in the temple, in Solomon's porch. The
Acts 3 11 the porch which is called Solomon's
5 12 all with one accord in Solomon's porch
solution Dan 2 24 I will tell the s. to the king
solutions Wisd 8 8 s. of arguments: she knoweth
somebody Luke 8 46 Jesus said: S. hath touched me
Acts 5 36 affirming himself to be somebody, to
Somer 4 K 12 21 Jozabad the son of Somer his
1 Pa 6 46 the son of Boni the son of Somer
7 32 Heber begot Jephlat and Somer and
34 the sons of Somer: Ahi and Roaga
something Gen 24 10 carrying s. of all his goods
Gen 27 3 thou hast taken something by hunting
Lev 13 2 a blister or as it were s. shining
Josu 7 1 Achan . . . took s. of the anathema
4 K 4 39 he found something like a wild vine
5 20 after him and take something of him
15 13 by our doing something against the law
2 Pa 5 9 because they were something longer
10 4 and ease something of the burden
Job 32 12 long as I thought you said something
Eccu 23 22 quenched, till it devour something
Mich 3 5 if a man give not s. into their mouth
Mat 20 20 adoring and asking something of him
Mark 5 43 that s. should be given her to eat
Luke 11 54 seeking to catch s. from his mouth
John 13 29 he should give something to the poor
Acts 3 5 so hoping that he should receive s.
21 37 may I speak s. to thee? Who said: Canst
23 15 as if you meant to know s. more certain
17 to tribune, for he hath s. to tell him
18 thee, who hath something to say to thee
20 as if they meant to inquire something
Gal 2 2 them who seemed to be something. 6
6 to me they that seemed to be s. added
6 3 if any man think himself to be something
Eph 4 28 that he may have something to give to
Heb 8 3 he also should have something to offer
sometime Job 3 18 s. bound together without
Job 19 19 that were sometime my counsellors
Col 1 21 whereas you were sometime alienated
sometimes 2 K 11 25 s. one, s. another is consumed
Ecce 4 14 s. a man cometh forth to a kingdom
8 9 sometimes one man ruleth over another
Wisd 17 14 were s. molested with the fear of
14 s. fainted away, their soul failing
Eccu 34 13 s. I have been in danger of death

37 18 soul of a holy man discovereth s. true
2 Ma 15 40 to use s. the one, and s. the other
somewhat Gen 42 7 s. roughly, asking them
Lev 13 6 the leprosy be somewhat obscure. 26
19 appeareth a white scar, or s. red
21 former color, and the scar s. obscure
56 place of the leprosy be somewhat dark
Luke 7 40 Simon, I have somewhat to say to thee
Acts 10 10 he was desirous to taste somewhat. And
2 C 5 12 that you may have somewhat to answer
10 8 if also I should boast somewhat more of
Apoc 2 4 I have s. against thee, because thou
Somorias 2 Pa 11 19 bore him sons Jehus and S.
Son of God Wisd 2 13 calleth himself son of God
Wisd 2 18 if he be the true son of God, he will
Dan 3 92 form of the fourth is like the Son of God
Mat 4 3 if thou be the Son of God. 6; 27:40; Luke 4:3, 9
8 29 to do with thee, Jesus Son of God
14 33 thou art the Son of God. Mark 3:12; Luke 4:41; John 1:49
26 63 if thou be the Christ the Son of God
27 43 said: I am the Son of God. John 10:36
54 saying: Indeed this was the Son of God
Mark 1 1 gospel of Jesus Christ, the Son of God
15 39 indeed this man was the Son of God
Luke 1 35 of thee shall be called the Son of God
22 70 art thou then the Son of God? Who said
John 1 34 testimony that this is the Son of God
3 18 name of the only begotten Son of God
5 25 shall hear the voice of the S. . . . 28
6 70 thou art the Christ, the Son of God
9 35 dost thou believe in the Son of God
11 4 the Son of God may be glorified by it
19 7 he made himself the Son of God
20 31 that Jesus is the Christ, the S. . . .
Acts 8 37 that Jesus Christ is the Son of God
9 20 preached . . . that he is the Son of God
Rom 1 4 was predestinated the Son of God in
2 C 1 19 for the Son of God, Jesus Christ who was
Gal 2 20 I live in the faith of the Son of God
Eph 4 13 and of the knowledge of the Son of God
Heb 4 14 Jesus the Son of God: let us hold fast
5 8 whereas indeed he was the Son of God
6 6 again to themselves the Son of God, and
7 3 likened unto the Son of God, continueth
10 29 hath trodden under foot the Son of God
1 J 3 8 for this purpose the S. . . . appeared
4 15 confess that Jesus is the Son of God
5 5 believeth that Jesus is the Son of God
10 he that believeth in the Son of God
13 believe in the name of the Son of God
20 we know that the Son of God is come
Apoc 2 18 saith the Son of God, who hath his eyes
son of man Num 23 19 nor as the son of man
Job 16 22 as the son of man is judged with his
35 8 thy justice may help the son of man
Ps 8 5 or the son of man that thou visitest
79 16 son of man whom thou hast confirmed. 18
143 3 son of man, that thou makest account
Eccu 17 29 because the son of man is not immortal
Isa 51 12 son of man, who shall wither away
56 2 son of man that shall lay hold on this
Jer 49 18 there shall no son of man inhabit it
33 abide there nor son of man inhabit it
50 40 neither shall the son of man inhabit it
51 43 dwell nor son of man pass through it
Eze 2 1 he said to me: Son of man, stand upon
3 son of man, I send thee to the children
6 and thou, O son of man, fear not
8 thou, O son of man, hear all that I say
3 1 son of man, eat all that thou shalt
3 son of man, thy belly shall eat, and
4 son of man, go to the house of Israel
10 son of man, receive in thy heart and
17 s. . . . , I have made thee a watchman. 33:7
25 son of man, behold they shall put bands
4 1 thou, O son of man, take thee a tile
16 son of man: Behold, I will break in
5 1 son of man, take thee a sharp knife
6 2 son of man, set thy face towards. 21:2
7 2 son of man, thus saith the Lord God
8 5 son of man, lift up thy eyes towards
6 son of man, dost thou see, thinkest
8 son of man, dig in the wall. And when
12 thou hast seen, O s. . . . 15, 17; 47:6
11 2 s. . . . , these are the men that study
4 prophesy, thou son of man. And the
15 s. . . . , thy brethren, thy brethren
12 2 son of man, thou dwellest in the midst
3 s. . . . , prepare thee all necessaries
9 s. . . . , hath not the house of Israel
18 son of man, eat thy bread in trouble
22 son of man, what is this proverb
27 son of man, behold the house of Israel
13 2 son of man, prophesy thou against the
17 son of man, set thy face against. 20:46; 25:2; 28:21; 29:2; 35:2; 38:1
14 3 son of man, these men have placed
13 son of man, when a land shall sin
15 2 son of man, what shall be made of the
16 2 son of man, make known to Jerusalem
17 2 son of man, put forth a riddle and
20 3 son of man, speak to the ancients of
4 if thou judgest, O son of man, declare
27 speak to house of Israel. O son of man
21 6 son of man, mourn with the breaking
9 son of man, prophesy. 28; 30:2; 38:14
12 cry and howl, O son of man, for this
14 son of man, prophesy, and strike thy
19 thou son of man, set these two ways
22 2 thou son of man, dost thou not judge
18 son of man, the house of Israel is
24 son of man, say to her: Thou art a
23 2 son of man, there were two women
36 son of man, dost thou judge Oolla
24 2 son of man, write thee the name of
16 son of man, behold I take from thee
25 son of man, behold in the day wherein
26 2 son of man, because Tyre hath said
27 2 s. . . . , take up a lamentation. 28:11; 32:2
28 2 son of man, say to the prince of Tyre
29 18 son of man, Nabuchodonosor . . . hath
30 21 son of man, I have broken the arm
31 2 son of man, speak to Pharao king of
32 18 son of man, sing a mournful song for
33 2 son of man, speak to the children of
10 son of man, say to the house of Israel
12 s. . . . , say to the children of thy
24 son of man, they that dwell in these
30 son of man: the children of thy people
34 2 son of man, prophesy concerning the
36 1 son of man, prophesy to the mountains
17 son of man, when the house of Israel
37 3 son of man, dost thou think these bones
9 to the spirit, prophesy, O son of man
11 son of man: All these bones are the
16 son of man, take thee a stick: and
39 1 son of man, prophesy against Gog
17 son of man . . . say to every fowl and
40 4 son of man, see with thy eyes and hear
43 7 son of man, the place of my throne
10 son of man, show to the house of Israel
18 son of man, thus saith the Lord God
44 5 son of man, attend with thy heart
Dan 7 13 one like the s. . . . came with the

8 17 understand, O son of man, for in the
10 16 likeness of a s. . . . touched my lips
Mat 8 20 S. . . . hath not where to lay. Luke 9:58
9 6 S. . . . hath power on earth to forgive sins. Mark 2:10; Luke 5:24
10 23 of Israel, till the Son of man come
11 19 the S. . . . came eating and drinking, and
12 8 Son of man is Lord even of the sabbath. Mark 2:28; Luke 6:5
32 speak word against the S. . . . Luke 12:10
40 so shall the Son of man be in the
13 37 soweth the good seed, is Son of man
41 Son of man shall send his angels
16 13 whom do men say that the Son of man is
27 Son of man shall come in the glory of
28 till they see the Son of man coming
17 9 till the S. . . . be risen. Mark 9:8
12 the Son of man shall suffer from them
21 Son of man shall be betrayed. 20:18; 26:45; Mark 9:30; 10:33; 14:41
18 11 the Son of man is come to save that
19 28 when the Son of man shall sit on the
20 28 Son of man is not come to be ministered. Mark 10:45
24 27 also the coming of the S. . . . 37, 39
30 appear the sign of the Son of man in
30 they shall see the S. . . . Mark 13:26
44 know not the Son of man will come
25 31 when the Son of man shall come in his
26 2 S. . . . shall be delivered. Luke 9:44
24 S. . . . indeed goeth. Mark 14:21; Luke 22:22
24 by whom the Son of man shall be betrayed. Mark 14:21
64 you shall see the Son of man sitting
Mark 8 31 S. . . . must suffer. Mark 9:11; Luke 9:22
38 the Son of man also will be ashamed of
14 62 you shall see the Son of man sitting
Luke 7 34 the Son of man is come eating and
9 26 of him the Son of man shall be ashamed
56 Son of man came not to destroy souls
11 30 so shall the Son of man also be to
12 8 him shall the Son of man also confess
40 think not, the Son of man will come
17 22 to see one day of the Son of man; and
24 so shall the Son of man be in his day
26 be also in the days of the Son of man
30 when the Son of man shall be revealed
18 8 the Son of man when he cometh, shall
31 prophets concerning the Son of man
19 10 the Son of man is come to seek and
21 27 they shall see the Son of man coming
36 and to stand before the Son of man
22 48 dost thou betray the Son of man with
69 the Son of man shall be sitting on the
24 7 the Son of man must be delivered into
John 1 51 and descending upon the Son of man
3 13 the Son of man who is in heaven. And
14 so must the Son of man be lifted up
5 27 because he is the Son of man. Wonder
6 27 which the Son of man will give you
54 you eat the flesh of the Son of man
63 see the Son of man ascend up where he
8 28 shall have lifted up the Son of man
12 23 that the Son of man should be glorified
34 the Son of man must be lifted up
34 be lifted up? Who is this Son of man
13 31 now is the Son of man glorified, and
Acts 7 55 Son of man standing on the right hand
Heb 2 6 or the son of man, that thou visitest
Apoc 1 13 one like to the Son of man, clothed
14 14 one sitting like to the Son of man
song Exod 15 21 and she began the song to them
Num 21 17 then Israel sung this song: Let the
Deut 31 19 this s. may be unto me for a testimony
1 Pa 15 21 sung a song of victory for the octave
25 7 that taught the song of the Lord, all
Job 30 9 now I am turned into their song, and
Ps 39 4 canticle into my mouth, a song to our
68 13 they that drank wine made me their song
118 54 justifications were the subject of my s.
136 4 how shall we sing the song of the Lord
Isa 23 15 shall be unto Tyre as song of a harlot
16 sing well, sing many a song, that thou
24 9 they shall not drink wine with a song
30 29 you shall have a song as in the night
42 10 sing ye to the Lord a new song, his
Lam 3 14 people, their song all the day long
63 and their rising up, I am their song
Eze 27 32 they shall take up a mournful song
32 18 son of man, sing a mournful song for
33 31 they turn them into a song of their
32 thou art to them as a musical song
Mich 2 4 a song shall be sung with melody by
songs Gen 31 27 on the way with joy and with s.
Job 35 10 who hath given songs in the night? Who
Ps 136 3 sing . . . a hymn of the songs of Sion
3 required of us the words of songs. And
Prov 25 20 that singeth songs to a very evil heart
Eze 26 13 the multitude of thy songs to cease
Amos 5 23 take away from me the tumult of thy s.
8 10 and all your songs into lamentation
2 Ma 15 25 came forward with trumpets and songs
son-in-law Gen 19 12 any of thine? S. or sons
Gen 30 36 journey betwixt himself and his s.
Judg 15 6 Samson the s. of the Thamnathite
19 4 the son-in-law tarried in the house
6 father of young woman said to his s.
10 his s. would not consent to his words
1 K 18 18 that I should be son-in-law of the king
21 thou shalt be my son-in-law this day
22 therefore be the king's son-in-law
23 a small matter to be the king's s.
26 the eyes of David to be the king's s.
27 that he might be his son-in-law. Saul
22 14 David, who is the king's son-in-law
4 K 8 27 the son-in-law of the house of Achab
2 Es 6 18 he was the son-in-law of Sechenias
13 28 was s. to Sanaballat the Horonite
Tob 10 8 Raguel said to his son-in-law: Stay
1 Ma 10 54 daughter to wife, and I will be the s.
16 12 he was son-in-law of the high priest
son's Gen 11 31 Lot the son of Aran, his s. son
Gen 27 31 father and eat of thy son's venison
30 14 give me part of thy son's mandrakes
15 unless thou take also my s. mandrakes
16 I have hired thee for my s. mandrakes
37 32 whether it be thy son's coat, or not
33 it is my s. coat, an evil wild beast
Lev 18 10 not uncover nakedness of s. daughter
15 because she is thy son's wife, neither
17 thou shalt not take her son's daughter
Judg 8 22 over us, and thy son and thy son's son
3 K 11 35 away the kingdom out of his son's hand
21 29 in his son's days will I bring the evil
Tob 11 18 Sara his son's wife . . . arrived safe
12 14 to deliver Sara thy son's wife from
Jer 27 7 serve him and his son and his son's son
sons and daughters Gen 5 4 he begot s. and d.
Gen 5 7 lived . . . years, and begot s. and d. 10, 13, 16, 19, 22, 26, 30; 11:11, 13, 15, 17, 19, 21, 23, 25
31 55 in the night and kissed his s. and d.
46 15 all the souls of her s. and d., 33
Exod 3 22 you shall put them on your s. and d.
10 9 our young and old, with our s. and d.

21 4 a wife, and she hath borne s. and d.
32 2 ears of your wives and your s. and d.
Lev 10 14 thou and thy s. and thy d. with thee
26 29 eat the flesh of your s. and of your d.
Num 18 11 to thee and to thy s. and to thy d. and
19 have given to thee and to thy s. and d.
Deut 12 12 you and your s. and your d., your
31 Lord abhorreth, offering their s. and d.
28 32 thy s. and thy d. be given to another
41 shalt beget s. and d. and shalt not
53 and the flesh of thy s. and of thy d.
32 19 because his own s. and d. provoked him
Josu 7 24 took Achan . . . his s. also and his d.
1 K 1 4 and to all her s. and d. portions: but
30 6 was bitterly grieved for his s. and d.
2 K 5 13 were born to David other s. also and d.
19 5 and the lives of thy s. and of thy d.
4 K 17 17 and consecrated their s. and their d.
1 Pa 14 3 in Jerusalem; and he begot s. and d.
2 Pa 24 3 two wives, by whom he had s. and d.
2 Es 4 14 for your brethren, your s. and your d.
5 2 our s. and our d. are very many: let
5 we bring into bondage our s. and our d.
10 28 their wives, their s. and their d. All
Job 1 13 his s. and d. were eating and drinking
18 thy s. and d. were eating and drinking
Ps 105 37 sacrificed their s. and their d. to
Wisd 9 7 people, and a judge of thy s. and d.
Isa 56 5 place, and a name better than s. and d.
Jer 3 24 devoured . . . their s. and their d.
5 17 they shall devour thy s. and thy d.
7 31 to burn their s. and their d. in the
11 22 their s. and their d. shall die by
14 16 their wives, their sons and their d.
16 2 neither shalt thou have s. and d. in
3 saith the Lord concerning the s. and d.
29 6 take ye wives and beget s. and d.: and
6 and let them bear s. and d.: and be ye
32 35 to consecrate their s. and their d.
48 46 thy s. and thy d. are taken captives
Bar 4 14 remember the captivity of my s. and d.
Eze 14 22 who shall bring away their s. and d.
16 20 thou hast taken thy s. and thy d.
23 4 I took them and they bore s. and d.
10 her disgrace, took away her s. and d.
25 they shall take thy s. and thy d. and
47 they shall kill their s. and d.: and
24 21 your s. and your d. whom you have left
25 their souls rest, their s. and their d.
Joel 2 28 and your s. and your d. shall prophesy
3 8 I will sell your s. and your d. by the
Amos 7 17 thy s. and thy d. shall fall by the
sons' Gen 45 10 and thy sons and thy sons' sons
Gen 46 26 thigh, besides his sons' wives. 66
Exod 29 28 shall fall to Aaron's share and his s.
Lev 2 3 be Aaron's and his s. 10; 7:31; 24:9
sons-in-law Gen 19 14 out and spoke to his s.
sooner Exod 2 18 why are ye come s. than usual
2 K 2 27 if thou hadst spoke sooner, even in the
Heb 13 19 I may be restored to you the sooner
soothe Judg 14 15 s. thy husband and persuade him
2 Pa 10 7 thou please this people and s. them
soothed 2 Pa 24 17 he was s. by their services
soothsayer Num 22 5 Balaam . . . a s. who dwelt
Josu 13 22 Balaam also son of Beor the s.
Prov 23 7 like a s. and diviner, he thinketh
soothsayers Lev 19 31 neither ask anything of s.
Lev 20 6 shall go aside after magicians and s.
Deut 18 10 that consulteth s. or observeth dreams
14 hearken to soothsayers and diviners
1 K 28 3 put away all the magicians and s.
9 hath rooted out the magicians and s.
4 K 21 6 multiplied s. to do evil before the
23 5 he destroyed the s. whom the kings
24 the diviners by spirits and s. and the
Isa 2 6 and have had s. as the Philistines
19 3 their diviners and their wizards and s.
44 25 and make the soothsayers mad. That
Jer 27 9 hearken not to your . . . soothsayers
Dan 2 27 or the s. can declare to the king
4 4 the Chaldeans, and the s. 5:7
5 11 men, enchanters, Chaldeans and s.
soothsaying Num 23 23 there is no s. in Jacob
soothsayings 4 K 17 17 to divinations and s.
Sopater Acts 20 4 there accompanied him Sopater
Sophach 1 Pa 19 16 Sophach, general of army. 18
Sophan Num 32 35 the sons of Gad built . . . Sophan
Sophar Job 2 11 S. the Naamathite. 11:1; 20:1; 42:9
Sopher 4 K 25 19 Sopher the captain of the army
Sopheret 1 Es 2 55 the children of Sopheret, the
Sophereth 2 Es 7 57 Nathinites . . . children of S.
sophistically Eccu 37 23 he that speaketh s. is
Sophonias 4 K 25 18 took . . . S. the second priest
1 Pa 6 36 Azarias the son of Sophonias, the son
Jer 21 1 Sophonias the son of Naasias the priest. 29:25; 37:3
29 29 Sophonias the priest read this letter
52 24 chief priest, and S. the second priest
Soph 1 1 word of the Lord that came to S.
Zach 6 10 into the house of Josias the son of S.
14 Idaias, and to Hem the son of S.
sorcerers Jer 27 9 hearken not to your . . . s.
Mala 3 5 will be a speedy witness against s.
Apoc 21 8 sorcerers and idolaters and all liars
22 15 without are dogs and sorcerers and
sorceress Isa 57 3 hither, you sons of the s.
sorceries 4 K 9 22 her many s. are in their
Wisd 12 4 did works hateful to thee by their s.
Isa 47 9 the multitude of thy sorceries. 12
Mich 5 11 I will take away s. out of thy hand
Apoc 9 21 murders nor from their sorceries nor
sore Lev 13 28 it is the sore of a burning
Deut 28 35 Lord strike thee with a very sore ulcer
Mat 27 54 were sore afraid, saying: Indeed this
Apoc 16 2 there fell a sore and grievous wound
Sorec Judg 16 4 who dwelt in the valley of Sorec
sores Isa 1 6 wounds and bruises and swelling sores
Ps 37 6 my s. are putrified and corrupted
Luke 16 20 who lay at his gate full of sores
21 the dogs came and licked his sores
Sori 1 Pa 25 3 Godolias, Sori, Jeseias, and
sorrow Gen 3 16 in s. shalt thou bring forth
Gen 6 6 being touched inwardly with sorrow
37 35 to comfort their father in his sorrow
42 38 my gray hairs with s. to hell. 44:29
44 31 his gray hairs with sorrow unto hell
49 3 Ruben . . . the beginning of my sorrow
67 her so much, that it moderated the s.
Exod 3 8 knowing their sorrow, I am come down
1 K 1 5 to Anna he gave one portion with s.
16 but of the abundance of my sorrow and
1 Pa 4 9 saying: Because I bore him with sorrow
Tob 6 15 their old age with sorrow to hell
Esth 9 22 their mourning and sorrow was turned
Job 5 6 s. doth not spring out of the ground
6 3 therefore my words are full of sorrow
10 afflicting me with sorrow, he spare not
9 27 face, and am tormented with sorrow
10 20 that I may lament my sorrow a little
15 35 he hath conceived sorrow and hath
16 8 but now my sorrow hath oppressed me
20 10 his hands shall render to him his s.
22 and every sorrow shall fall upon him
21 19 God shall lay up the s. of the father
33 19 he rebuketh also by sorrow in the bed
Ps 7 15 he hath conceived sorrow and brought

17 his sorrow shall be turned on his own
9 7 under his tongue are labor and sorrow
14 for thou considerest labor and sorrow
12 2 soul, sorrow in my heart all the day
37 18 my sorrow is continually before me
38 3 things: and my sorrow was renewed
40 4 the Lord help him on his bed of sorrow
59 5 hast made us drink the wine of sorrow
89 10 what is more of them is labor and s.
106 39 through the trouble of evils and sorrow
114 3 I met with trouble and sorrow: and I
126 2 sitten, you that eat the bread of s.
Prov 10 1 foolish son is the sorrow of his mother
10 winketh with the eye shall cause s.
14 13 laughter shall be mingled with sorrow
17 25 sorrow of the mother that bore him
31 7 and remember their sorrow no more
Ecce 5 15 in many cares and in misery and s.
Wisd 4 19 they shall be in s., and their memory
10 9 wisdom hath delivered from sorrow
Eccu 2 4 and in thy sorrow endure, and in thy
11 11 maketh haste and is in sorrow and is
27 32 s. shall consume them before they die
30 10 laugh not with him lest thou have s.
12 and so be a sorrow of heart to thee
38 19 s. of the heart boweth down the neck
20 in withdrawing aside sorrow remaineth
Isa 29 2 it shall be in sorrow and mourning
35 10 s. and mourning shall flee. 51:11
65 14 and you shall cry for sorrow of heart
Jer 8 18 my sorrow is above sorrow, my heart
15 18 why is my sorrow become perpetual
20 18 out of the womb, to see labor and s.
30 15 thy affliction? Thy sorrow is incurable
31 13 and make them joyful after their sorrow
45 3 Lord hath added sorrow to my sorrow
Lam 1 12 see if there be any s. like to my s.
13 wasted with sorrow all the day long
18 all ye people, and see my sorrow: my
Eze 7 27 the prince shall be clothed with sorrow
12 18 drink thy water in hurry and sorrow
23 33 shalt be filled with drunkenness and s.
Mich 4 9 s. hath taken thee as a woman in labor
1 Ma 6 11 into what floods of sorrow, wherein
2 Ma 3 16 declared the inward s. of his mind
17 him, what sorrow he had in his heart
9 9 whilst he lived in sorrow and pain
Luke 22 45 he found them sleeping for sorrow
John 16 6 to you, sorrow hath filled your heart
20 your sorrow shall be turned into joy
21 a woman, when she is in labor, hath s.
22 so also you now indeed have sorrow
Rom 9 2 I have great sadness, and continual s.
2 C 2 1 not to come to you again in sorrow. For
3 when I come, have sorrow upon sorrow
7 be swallowed up with overmuch sorrow
7 10 for the sorrow that is according to God
10 the sorrow of the world worketh death
Phil 2 27 lest I should have sorrow upon sorrow
28 rejoice, and I may be without sorrow
Heb 12 11 not to bring with it joy, but sorrow
James 4 9 mourning, and your joy into sorrow
Apoc 18 7 so much torment and sorrow give ye to
7 no widow; and sorrow I shall not see
21 4 nor sorrow shall be any more, for the
sorrowful Lev 10 19 ceremonies, having a s. heart
1 Es 9 4 I sat s. until the evening sacrifice
2 Es 2 3 why should not my countenance be s.
8 11 the day is holy, and be not sorrowful
Ps 34 14 as one mourning and s. so was I humbled
37 7 I walked sorrowful all the day long
42 2 why do I go sorrowful whilst my enemy
68 30 but I am poor and sorrowful: thy
Prov 17 22 a sorrowful spirit drieth up the bones
Eccu 30 5 and when he died he was not sorrowful
9 with him, and he shall make thee s.
Jer 8 21 I am afflicted and made sorrowful
Lam 1 22 sighs are many, and my heart is s.
5 17 therefore is our heart sorrowful
Bar 2 18 the soul that is s. for the greatness
Zach 9 5 Ascalon . . . shall be very sorrowful
Mala 3 14 and that we have walked sorrowful
Mat 26 37 began to grow sorrowful and to be sad
38 soul is s. even unto death. Mark 14:34
Mark 10 22 went away s.: for he had great
14 19 they began to be s. and to say to him
Luke 18 23 having heard these things, became s.
24 Jesus seeing him become s., said: How
John 16 20 you shall be made sorrowful, but your
2 C 2 2 if I make you sorrowful, who is he then
2 but the same who is made sorrowful by me
4 not that you should be made sorrowful
6 10 as sorrowful, yet always rejoicing; as
7 8 although I made you s. by my epistle
8 but for a time, did make you sorrowful
9 not because you were made sorrowful; but
9 you were made sorrowful unto penance
9 you were made s. according to God. 11
1 Th 4 12 asleep, that you be not sorrowful, even
1 P 1 6 made sorrowful in divers temptations
sorrowing Luke 2 48 and I have sought thee s.
sorrows Gen 3 16 I will multiply thy sorrows
Exod 15 14 sorrows took hold on the inhabitants
Job 4 8 who work iniquity and sow sorrows
7 4 be filled with s. even till darkness
21 17 shall distribute the s. of his wrath
30 17 night my bone is pierced with sorrows
Ps 17 5 the sorrows of death surrounded me
6 the sorrows of hell encompassed me
93 19 according to multitude of my sorrows
114 3 sorrows of death have compassed me
Ecce 2 23 all his days are full of sorrows and
Eccu 3 29 wicked heart shall be laden with s.
14 15 to divide by lot thy sorrows and labors
Isa 50 11 my hand, you shall sleep in sorrows
53 3 a man of sorrows, and acquainted with
4 infirmities and carried our sorrows
Jer 13 21 shall not sorrows lay hold on thee
22 23 mourned when sorrows came upon thee
49 24 anguish and sorrows have taken her
Osee 13 13 the s. of a woman in labor shall come
Mat 24 8 these are the beginnings of sorrows
Mark 13 8 these things are the beginning of s.
Acts 2 24 having loosed the sorrows of hell, as
1 Tim 6 10 entangled themselves in many sorrows
1 P 2 19 a man endure s., suffering wrongfully
sorry Judg 21 15 all Israel was very sorry and
Ps 4 5 be sorry for them upon your beds
Eccu 13 6 and he will not be sorry for thee
37 16 in the dark, will be sorry for thee
Isa 23 5 will be sorry when they shall hear
51 19 shall be sorry for thee? Desolation
1 Ma 10 22 Demetrius . . . was exceeding sorry
14 16 was dead: and they were very sorry
sort Gen 6 19 bring two of a sort into the ark
Gen 6 20 two of every sort shall go in with
Num 13 19 view the land, of what sort it is: and
3 K 17 20 with whom I am after a sort maintained
4 K 24 14 none were left but the poor sort of
2 Pa 2 14 knoweth to grave all sort of graving
1 Es 1 10 silver cups of a second sort
Jdth 5 3 what are their cities, and of what sort
Jer 52 15 of the rest of the common sort who
2 Ma 5 24 to sell the women and the younger sort
Acts 17 5 some wicked men of the vulgar sort, and
Rom 15 15 more boldly in some sort, as it were

1 C 3 13 every man's word, of what sort it is
2 Tim 3 6 for of these sort are they who creep
Heb 10 33 of them that were used in such sort. For
sorts Lev 19 19 a garment that is woven of two s.
2 Pa 32 5 and made all sorts of arms and shields
Ps 77 45 amongst them divers sorts of flies
104 31 there came divers sorts of flies and
Eccu 23 21 two sorts of men multiply sins, and
25 3 three sorts my soul hateth, and I am
26 28 two sorts of callings have appeared
Eze 47 10 there shall be many sorts of the fishes
2 Ma 5 3 armor and of harnesses of all sorts
Sosipater 2 Ma 12 19 and S., who were captains
2 Ma 12 24 hands of the band of Dositheus and S.
Rom 16 21 Lucius and Jason and S., my kinsmen
Sosthenes Acts 18 17 laying hold on S., the ruler
1 C 1 1 will of God, and Sosthenes a brother
Sostratus 2 Ma 4 27 S. the governor of the castle
2 Ma 4 29 S. was made governor of the Cyprians
Sotai 1 Es 2 55 children of Sotai, the children
Sothai 2 Es 7 57 Nathinites . . . children of S.
sought Gen 27 20 what I sought came quickly in my
Gen 37 15 in the field, and asked what he s.
Exod 2 15 and Pharao . . . sought to kill Moses
4 19 they are all dead that sought thy life
Lev 10 16 when Moses sought for the buck goat
Josu 2 22 having sought them through all the way
Judg 14 4 s. an occasion against the Philistines
18 1 tribe of Dan s. them an inheritance
1 K 10 21 they sought him [Saul] therefore, and
13 14 the Lord hath s. him a man according
14 4 by which Jonathan sought to go over
17 when they had sought, it was found
23 14 Saul sought him always; but the Lord
27 4 he [Saul] sought no more after him
2 K 3 8 hast thou sought . . . to charge me
17 you s. for David that he might reign
4 8 of Isboseth . . . who sought thy life
17 20 they that sought them, when they found
21 2 Saul sought to slay them out of zeal
3 K 1 3 so they s. a beautiful young woman in
11 40 Solomon . . . sought to kill Jeroboam
4 K 2 17 they s. three days but found him not
1 Pa 13 3 we sought it not in the days of Saul
2 Pa 1 5 Solomon and all the assembly sought it
11 23 and he [Roboam] sought many wives
14 7 because we have sought the Lord the God
15 15 with all their will they sought him
22 9 and he sought for Ochozias himself
9 of Josaphat who had sought the Lord
26 5 s. the Lord in the days of Zacharias
5 and as long as he sought the Lord, he
1 Es 2 62 they s. the writing of their genealogy
8 15 I sought among the people and among
2 Es 2 10 sought the prosperity of the children
7 64 these s. their writing in the record
12 27 they s. the Levites out of all their
Ps 9 15 his sin shall be s. and shall not be
26 8 my face hath sought thee: thy face
33 5 I sought the Lord, and he heard me
36 36 I s. him and his place was not found
37 13 they that sought my soul used violence
13 they that sought evils to me spoke vain
53 5 the mighty have sought after my soul
62 10 but they have sought my soul in vain
76 3 in the day of my trouble I sought God
77 34 when he slew them, then they sought him
85 14 assembly of the mighty have s. my soul
110 2 sought out according to all his wills
118 10 whole heart have I sought after thee
22 I have s. after thy testimonies. 45
56 I sought after thy justifications
94 for I have sought thy justifications
100 because I have sought thy commandments
129 therefore my soul hath sought them
155 they have not sought thy justifications
121 8 I have sought good things for thee
Prov 31 13 she hath sought wool and flax, and hath
Ecce 12 10 he sought profitable words, and wrote
Cant 3 1 I sought him whom my soul loveth: I
1 s. him, and I found him not. 2; 5:6
Wisd 8 2 and have sought her out from my youth
19 16 sought the passage of his own door
Eccu 21 20 mouth of the prudent is sought after
24 11 I sought rest and I shall abide in
34 14 that fear God, is sought after and
36 2 nations that have not s. after thee
39 26 all things shall be s. in their time
28 nations, that have not s. after him
44 5 such as by their skill sought out
5 s. out musical tunes and published
47 31 and they sought out all iniquities
51 5 the hands of them that sought my life
18 I s. for wisdom openly in my prayer
20 from my youth up I sought after her
Isa 9 13 have not s. after the Lord of hosts
26 16 Lord, they have sought after thee in
31 1 and have not sought after the Lord
34 16 one hath not sought for the other
38 10 I sought for the residue of my years
62 12 a city sought after, and not forsaken
63 5 I sought, and there was none to give
65 1 they have sought me that before asked
1 they have found me that sought me not
19 for my people that have sought me
Jer 8 2 and whom they have sought and adored
10 21 have not sought the Lord: therefore
26 21 the king sought to put him to death
44 30 his enemy, and that sought his life
50 20 iniquity of Israel shall be sought for
Lam 1 19 while they sought their food, to
Eze 22 30 I sought among them for a man that
25 12 and hath sought revenge of them
26 21 if thou be sought for, thou shalt
34 4 neither have you s. that which was
6 and there was none that sought them
Dan 2 13 his companions were sought for, to be
4 33 my magistrates sought for me, and I
6 4 the governors sought to find occasion
8 15 saw the vision and sought the meaning
Osee 7 10 nor have they sought him in all these
Abdi 6 have they s. out his hidden things
Soph 1 6 that have not sought the Lord nor
Zach 6 7 went out and sought to go and to run
1 Ma 2 29 then many that sought after judgment
3 5 pursued the wicked and sought them out
4 5 and he sought them in the mountains
6 3 sought to take the city and to pillage
56 that he sought to take upon him the
7 13 and they sought peace of them. For
9 26 they sought out and made diligent
32 and Bacchides . . . sought to kill him
11 1 and he sought to get the kingdom of
10 for he hath sought to kill me. And he
12 40 he sought to seize upon him and to
53 heathens . . . sought to destroy them
14 4 and he sought the good of his nation
14 he sought the law, and took away every
35 he sought . . . to advance his people
16 22 knew that they sought to make him away
2 Ma 4 7 Jason . . . sought the high priesthood
13 21 he was sought out and taken up and
14 32 where the man was whom he sought
41 multitude s. to rush into his house
Mat 2 20 they are dead that sought the life of
26 16 s. opportunity to betray him. Luke 22:6

59 the whole council sought false witness
Mark 11 18 sought how they might destroy him
12 12 they s. to lay hands on him. Luke 20:19
14 1 sought how they might by some wile lay
11 he sought how he might conveniently
55 sought for evidence against Jesus
Luke 2 44 sought him among their kinsfolks and
48 thy father and I have sought thee
49 how is it that you sought me? Did you
4 42 multitudes sought him and came unto
5 18 they sought means to bring him in
6 19 multitude sought to touch him, for
9 9 things? And he sought to see him
19 3 he sought to see Jesus who he was
47 rulers of the people s. to destroy him
22 2 sought how they might put Jesus to
John 5 18 the Jews sought the more to kill him
7 1 because the Jews sought to kill him
11 the Jews therefore sought him on the
30 they sought therefore to apprehend
10 39 they sought therefore to take him
11 8 the Jews but now sought to stone thee
56 they sought therefore for Jesus; and
19 12 Pilate sought to release him. But the
Acts 9 29 Greeks; but they sought to kill him
12 19 when Herod had sought for him, and
13 11 [Elymas] sought some one to lead him
16 10 immediately we s. to go into Macedonia
17 5 s. to bring them out unto the people
27 30 as the shipmen s. to fly out of the ship
Rom 9 32 because they sought it not by faith, but
11 7 that which Israel sought, he hath not
1 Th 2 6 nor sought we glory of men, neither of
2 Tim 1 17 he carefully sought me, and found me
Heb 8 7 a place have been sought for a second
12 17 although with tears he had sought it
soul Gen 2 7 man became a living soul. And the
Gen 17 14 that soul shall be destroyed out of his
34 8 soul of my son Sichem has a longing
36 6 Esau took . . . every soul of his house
Exod 12 15 that soul shall perish out of Israel
Lev 4 2 the soul that sinneth through ignorance
7 18 whatsoever soul shall defile itself with
17 11 may be for an expiation of the soul
12 no soul of you nor of the strangers
15 the soul that eateth that which died of
18 29 every soul that shall commit any of
19 8 that soul shall perish from among his
20 6 soul that shall go aside after magicians
6 I will set my face against that soul and
23 29 every soul that is not afflicted on this
30 every soul that shall do any work
Num 9 6 by occasion of the soul of a man. 7
13 that soul shall be cut off from among
15 27 but if one soul shall sin ignorantly
30 soul that committeth anything through
31 28 one soul of 500 as well of persons
Deut 12 23 for the blood is for the soul: and
23 must not eat the soul with the flesh
28 65 and a soul consumed with pensiveness
Josu 10 32 sword, and every soul that was in it
1 K 18 1 the soul of Jonathan was knit with the soul of David
25 29 the soul of my lord shall be kept as
30 6 soul of every man was bitterly grieved
2 K 5 8 the lame that hated the soul of David
14 14 neither will God have a soul to perish
3 K 15 29 left not so much as one s. of his seed
17 21 let the soul of this child . . . return
22 soul of the child returned into him
4 K 12 4 which is offered for the price of a s.
Tob 4 11 not suffer the s. to go into darkness
Job 3 20 to them that are in bitterness of soul
11 20 their hope the abomination of the soul
12 10 in whose hand is the soul of every
21 25 another dieth in bitterness of soul
24 12 the soul of the wounded hath cried out
31 39 have afflicted the soul of the tillers
Ps 85 4 give joy to the soul of thy servant
93 21 will hunt after the soul of the just
106 9 he hath satisfied the empty soul and hath filled the hungry soul
Prov 6 26 catcheth the precious soul of a man
10 3 Lord will not afflict soul of the just
11 25 soul which blesseth, shall be made fat
13 2 the soul of transgressors is wicked
4 soul of them that work shall be made
12 hope that is deferred afflicteth the s.
19 is accomplished, delighteth the soul
15 30 light of the eyes rejoiceth the soul
16 1 is the part of man to prepare the soul
24 as a honeycomb: sweet to the soul
26 the soul of him that laboreth
19 2 where there is no knowledge of the soul
15 and an idle soul shall suffer hunger
21 10 the soul of the wicked desireth evil
25 25 as cold water to a thirsty soul, so is
27 7 a soul that is full shall tread upon
7 soul that is hungry shall take even
9 of a friend are sweet to the soul
Wisd 1 4 will not enter into a malicious soul
11 mouth that belieth, killeth the soul
8 19 child and had received a good soul
9 15 corruptible body is a load upon the s.
10 7 is a monument of an incredulous soul
16 entered into the soul of the servant
15 11 him that inspired into him the soul
16 14 neither shall he call back the soul
17 8 fears and troubles from a sick soul
Eccu 4 2 despise not the hungry soul: and
6 4 wicked s. shall destroy him that hath
16 31 soul of every living thing hath shown
23 22 a hot soul is a burning fire, it will
26 18 so much worth as a well instructed soul
20 no price is worthy of a continent soul
27 24 leaveth no hope to an unhappy soul
30 15 health of the soul in holiness of
31 2 grievous sickness maketh the s. sober
36 wine . . . is the joy of the soul and
39 wine . . . is bitterness of the soul
34 17 soul of him that feareth the Lord is
20 raiseth up the soul and enlighteneth
37 16 whose soul is according to thy own soul
18 the soul of a holy man discovereth
31 every kind pleaseth not every soul
49 19 above every soul Adam in the beginning
Isa 10 18 consumed from the s. even to the flesh
26 8 remembrance are the desire of the soul
32 6 to make empty the soul of the hungry
49 7 Holy One to the soul that is despised
58 10 and shalt satisfy the afflicted soul
Jer 4 10 the sword reaching even to the soul
20 13 he hath delivered the soul of the poor
31 14 I will fill the soul of the priests
25 for I have inebriated the weary soul
25 and I have filled every hungry soul
38 16 as Lord liveth, that made us this soul
43 6 every s. which Nabuzardan . . . had left
Lam 1 11 things for food to relieve the soul
3 25 in him, to the soul that seeketh him
Bar 2 18 the soul that is sorrowful for the
18 hungry soul giveth glory and justice
3 1 the s. in anguish . . . crieth to thee
Eze 18 4 as the soul of the father, so also the soul of the son is mine
4 s. that sinneth, the same shall die. 20

27 31 weep for thee with bitterness of soul
33 6 and the sword come and cut off a soul
Jon 2 6 compassed me about even to the soul
Agge 2 14 that is unclean by occasion of a soul
1 Ma 10 33 every soul of the Jews that hath been
2 Ma 6 30 but in soul am well content to suffer
7 22 I neither gave you breath nor soul
Mat 10 28 and are not able to kill the soul: but
28 can destroy both soul and body in hell
Mark 12 33 with the whole soul and with the whole
Luke 12 19 soul, thou hast much goods laid up
Acts 2 43 and fear came upon every soul: many
3 23 every soul which will not hear that
4 32 had but one heart and one soul: neither
27 44 pass, that every soul got safe to land
Rom 2 9 anguish upon every soul of man that
13 1 let every s. be subject to higher powers
1 C 15 45 man Adam was made into a living soul
1 Th 5 23 your whole spirit and soul and body, may
Heb 4 12 unto the division of the soul and spirit
6 19 as an anchor of the soul, sure and firm
10 39 but of faith to the saving of the soul
1 P 2 11 desires which was against the soul
2 P 2 8 vexed the just soul with unjust works

every living soul; *see* **living**

her soul Gen 35 18 her soul was departing for pain
Num 30 4 oath wherewith she hath bound her soul
7 shall bind her soul by an oath: the day
9 words wherewith she had bound her soul
14 by oath, to afflict her soul by fasting
4 K 4 27 her alone for her soul is in anguish
Isa 5 14 therefore hath hell enlarged her soul
Jer 3 11 rebellious Israel hath justified her s.
15 9 her soul hath fainted away: her sun
Eze 23 17 and her soul was glutted with them

his soul Gen 34 3 his s. was fast knit unto her
Gen 42 21 seeing the anguish of his soul, when
Exod 12 19 his s. shall perish out of the assembly
31 14 his soul shall perish out of the midst. Num 19:20
Lev 17 10 I will set my face against his soul
27 2 promised his soul to God, shall give
Judg 16 16 his soul fainted away and was wearied
1 K 18 1 and Jonathan loved him as his own soul
3 for he loved him as his own s. 20:17
3 K 19 4 requested for his s. that he might die
4 K 23 25 and with all his soul. 2 Pa 34:31
Tob 1 12 he kept his soul and never was defiled
9 4 one day more, his soul will be afflicted
Jdth 13 29 the earth, and his soul swooned away
16 11 her beauty made his soul her captive
Job 14 22 and his soul shall mourn over him
23 13 and whatsoever his soul hath desired
27 8 if . . . God deliver not his soul? Will
31 30 to sin, by wishing a curse to his soul
33 18 rescuing his soul from corruption: and
20 to his soul the meat which before he
22 his soul hath drawn near to corruption
28 he hath delivered his soul from going
Ps 9 3 is praised in the desires of his soul
10 6 that loveth iniquity hateth his own s.
23 4 who hath not taken his soul in vain
24 13 his soul shall dwell in good things
38 12 thou hast made his soul to waste away
48 9 nor price of the redemption of his s.
19 in his life time his s. will be blessed
88 49 deliver his soul from the hand of hell
104 18 the iron pierced his soul until his
Prov 6 16 and the seventh his soul detesteth
30 he stealeth to fill his hungry soul
32 adulterer . . . shall destroy his own s.
8 36 sin against me, shall hurt his own soul
11 17 merciful man doth good to his own soul
13 3 keepeth his mouth, keepeth his soul
25 the just eateth and filleth his soul
14 10 knoweth the bitterness of his own s.
15 32 instruction, despiseth his own soul
16 17 that keepeth his soul keepeth his way
18 7 his lips are the ruin of his soul
19 8 possesseth a mind, loveth his own soul
16 commandment, keepeth his own soul
20 2 sinneth against his own soul. It is
21 23 tongue, keepeth his soul from distress
22 5 that keepeth his own soul departeth
23 afflict them that have afflicted his s.
23 14 shalt . . . deliver his soul from hell
25 13 sent him, for he refresheth his soul
29 10 upright: but just men seek his soul
24 with a thief, hateth his own soul
Ecce 2 24 to show his soul good things of his
6 2 his soul wanteth nothing of all that
3 and his soul make no use of the goods
7 mouth, but his soul shall not be filled
Wisd 4 11 understanding, or deceit beguile his s.
14 his soul pleased God: therefore he
Eccu 4 6 curseth thee in bitterness of his soul
19 try him by her laws, and trust his s.
7 12 scorn in the bitterness of his soul
10 10 setteth even his own soul to sale
32 him that sinneth against his own soul
32 him that dishonoreth his own soul
14 4 together by wronging his own soul
8 his face, and despiseth his own soul
9 satisfied till he consume his own soul
19 3 his soul shall be taken away out of
4 that sinneth against his own soul. 6
20 8 useth many words shall hurt his own s.
24 there is that will destroy his own s.
21 30 curseth the devil, he curseth his own s.
31 talebearer shall defile his own soul
23 25 despising his own soul and saying
27 22 the snare: because his soul is wounded
31 24 his soul shall be delighted with him
37 21 yet is unprofitable to his own soul
22 many, and is sweet to his own soul
25 wise man that is wise to his own soul
40 30 feedeth his s. with another man's meat
45 29 in goodness and readiness of his soul
Isa 15 4 Moab kneel, his soul shall howl to
29 8 when he is awake, his soul is empty
8 faint with thirst, and his s. is empty
44 20 he will not save his soul nor say
53 11 because his soul hath labored, he
12 he hath delivered his soul unto death
58 5 for a man to afflict his s. for a day
Jer 50 19 his soul shall be satisfied in mount
Eze 18 27 justice: he shall save his soul alive
Amos 6 8 Lord God hath sworn by his own soul
Jon 4 8 desired for his soul that he might die
Mich 7 3 hath uttered the desire of his soul
Haba 2 4 his soul shall not be right in himself
2 Ma 3 1 and the hatred his soul had of evil
Mat 16 26 suffer the loss of his own s. Mark 8:36
26 exchange shall a man give for his soul
Mark 8 37 give in exchange for his soul? For
Acts 20 10 be not troubled, for his soul is in him
James 5 20 shall save his soul from death, and

my soul Gen 12 13 that my soul may live for thy
Gen 19 20 not a little one, and my soul shall live
27 4 my soul may bless thee. 25
32 30 to face, and my soul has been saved
49 6 let not my soul go into their counsel
Exod 15 9 the spoils, my soul shall have its fill
Lev 26 11 my soul shall not cast you off. I will
30 your idols, and my soul shall abhor you
Num 23 10 let my soul die the death of the just

Judg 5 21 tread thou, my soul, upon the strong
1 K 1 15 have poured out my s. before the Lord
2 35 do according to my heart and my soul
4 9 delivered my soul out of all. 3 K 1:29
Tob 3 16 have kept my soul clean from all lust
4 3 when God shall take my soul, thou shalt
13 9 and I and my soul will rejoice in him
19 my soul, bless thou the Lord because
Job 6 7 which before my soul would not touch
7 11 will talk with the bitterness of my s.
15 so that my soul rather chooseth hanging
9 21 even this my soul shall be ignorant of
10 1 my soul is weary of my life, I will
1 will speak in the bitterness of my s.
13 14 teeth, and carry my soul in my hands
16 4 would God your soul were for my soul
19 2 how long do you afflict my soul and
27 2 who hath brought my soul to bitterness
30 16 my soul fadeth within myself, and the
25 my soul had compassion on the poor
Ps 3 3 many say to my soul: There is no
6 4 my soul is troubled exceedingly; but
5 O Lord, and deliver my soul: O save me
7 3 lest at any time he seize upon my soul
6 let the enemy pursue my soul and
10 2 how then do you say to my soul: Get
12 2 how long shall I take counsels in my s.
15 10 thou wilt not leave my soul in hell
16 9 my enemies have surrounded my soul
13 deliver my soul from the wicked one
21 21 deliver, O God, my soul from the sword
31 to him my soul shall live: and my seed
22 3 he hath converted my soul. He hath
24 1 thee, O Lord, have I lifted up my soul
20 keep thou my soul and deliver me: I
25 9 take not away my soul, O God, with the
29 4 brought forth, O Lord, my s. from hell
30 8 hast saved my soul out of distresses
10 my eye is troubled with wrath, my soul
33 3 in the Lord shall my soul be praised
34 3 say to my soul: I am thy salvation
4 and ashamed that seek after my soul
7 they have upbraided my soul. Let the
9 my soul shall rejoice in the Lord
12 good: to the depriving me of my soul
13 I humbled my soul with fasting; and
17 rescue thou my soul from their malice
37 13 they that sought my soul used violence
39 15 that seek after my soul to take it away
40 5 heal my soul, for I have sinned against
41 2 so my soul panteth after thee, O God
3 my soul hath thirsted after the strong
5 and poured out my soul in me: for I
6 why art thou sad, O my soul. 42:5
7 my soul is troubled within myself
12 why art thou cast down, O my soul
48 16 God will redeem my soul from the
53 5 the mighty have sought after my soul
6 the Lord is the protector of my soul
54 19 he shall redeem my soul in peace
55 7 as they have waited for my soul, for
13 thou hast delivered my soul from death
56 2 on me: for my soul trusteth in thee
5 hath delivered my soul from the midst
7 they bowed down my soul. They dug a
58 4 behold they have caught my soul: the
61 2 shall not my soul be subject to God
6 be thou, O my soul, subject to God
62 2 for thee my soul hath thirsted: for
6 let my soul be filled as with marrow
9 my soul hath stuck close to thee: thy
10 but they have sought my soul in vain
63 2 deliver my soul from the fear of the
65 9 who hath set my soul to live: and
16 great things he hath done for my soul
68 2 waters are come in even unto my soul
11 I covered my soul in fasting: and it
19 attend to my soul, and deliver it
69 3 them be ashamed that seek my soul
70 10 that watched my soul have consulted
13 come to nothing that detract my soul
23 and my soul which thou hast redeemed
76 3 my soul refused to be comforted: I
83 3 my soul longeth and fainteth for the
85 2 preserve my soul, for I am holy: save
4 to thee, O Lord, I have lifted up my s.
13 delivered my s. out of the lower hell
14 assembly of mighty have sought my soul
87 4 my soul is filled with evils: and my
93 17 my soul had almost dwelt in hell. If
19 thy comforts have given joy to my soul
102 1 bless the Lord, O my soul. 2; 103:1
22 my soul, bless thou the Lord. 103:35
108 20 and who speak evils against my soul
31 to save my soul from persecutors
114 4 O Lord, deliver my soul. The Lord is
7 turn, O my soul, into thy rest: for
8 he hath delivered my soul from death
118 20 my soul hath coveted to long for thy
25 my soul hath cleaved to the pavement
28 my soul hath slumbered through
81 my s. hath fainted after thy salvation
109 my soul is continually in my hands
129 therefore my soul hath sought them
167 my soul hath kept thy testimonies
175 my soul shall live and shall praise
119 2 deliver my soul from wicked lips and
6 my soul hath been long a sojourner
129 4 my soul hath relied on his word: my
5 my soul hath hoped in the Lord. From
130 2 humbly minded, but exalted my soul
2 his mother, so reward in my soul
137 3 shalt multiply strength in my soul
138 14 works, and my soul knoweth right well
140 8 I put my trust, take not away my soul
141 5 is no one that hath regard to my soul
8 bring my soul out of prison, that I
142 3 for the enemy hath persecuted my soul
6 my soul is as earth without water unto
8 for I have lifted up my soul to thee
11 thou wilt bring my soul out of trouble
12 cut off all them that afflict my soul
145 2 praise the Lord, O my soul, in my
Ecce 4 8 and defraud my soul of good things
7 29 account, which yet my soul seeketh
Cant 1 6 whom my soul loveth. 3:1, 2, 3, 4
5 6 my soul melted when he spoke: I sought
6 11 my soul troubled me for the chariots
Eccu 16 17 what is my soul in such an immense
25 3 three sorts my soul hateth, and I am
50 27 two nations which my soul abhorreth
51 8 my soul shall praise the Lord even to
25 my soul hath wrestled for her, and in
27 I directed my soul to her, and in
Isa 1 14 my soul hateth your new moons and
26 9 my soul hath desired thee in the night
38 15 my years in the bitterness of my soul
17 thou hast delivered my soul that it
42 1 my elect, my soul delighteth in him
61 10 and my soul shall be joyful in my God
Jer 4 19 my soul hath heard the sound of the
31 woe is me, for my soul hath fainted
5 9 shall not my soul take revenge. 29
6 8 lest my soul depart from thee, lest I
9 9 shall not my soul be revenged on such
12 7 my dear soul into hand of her enemies

13 17 my soul shall weep in secret for your
15 1 my soul is not towards this people
18 20 they have digged a pit for my soul
32 41 will plant them . . . with all my soul
Lam 1 16 the relief of my soul, is far from me
3 17 my soul is removed far off from peace
20 and my soul shall languish within me
24 the Lord is my portion, said my soul
51 my eye hath wasted my soul because
58 judged, O Lord, the cause of my soul
Eze 4 14 behold my soul hath not been defiled
23 18 my soul was alienated from her
Jon 2 8 when my soul was in distress within
Mich 6 7 fruit of my body for the sin of my s.
7 1 my soul desired the firstripe figs
Zach 11 8 my soul was straitened in their regard
Mat 12 18 in whom my soul hath been well pleased
26 38 my soul is sorrowful. Mark 14:34
Luke 1 46 my soul doth magnify the Lord. And my
12 19 I will say to my soul: Soul, thou
John 12 27 now is my soul troubled. And what
Acts 2 27 thou wilt not leave my soul in hell
2 C 1 23 I call God to witness upon my soul, that
Heb 10 38 himself, he shall not please my soul
our soul Num 11 6 our soul is dry, our eyes behold
Num 21 5 our soul now loatheth this very light
Ps 32 20 our soul waiteth for the Lord: for he
43 25 our soul is humbled down to the dust
122 4 our soul is greatly filled: we are a
123 5 our soul hath passed through a torrent
5 perhaps our soul had passed through a
7 our soul hath been delivered as a
their soul 3 K 2 4 their heart and with all their s. 8:48; 4 K 23:3; 2 Pa 6:38; 15:12
Tob 12 10 iniquity, are enemies to their own s.
Jdth 8 21 their very s. resteth upon you: comfort
Job 36 14 their soul shall die in a storm, and
Ps 106 5 thirsty: their soul fainted in them
18 their soul abhorred all manner of meat
26 their soul pined away with evils
Wisd 17 14 fainted away, their soul failing them
Eccu 38 39 work of their craft, applying their s.
Isa 66 3 their soul is delighted in their
Jer 31 12 their soul shall be as a watered garden
Eze 7 19 they shall not satisfy their soul
Osee 9 4 their bread is life for their soul
Zach 11 8 their soul also varied in my regard
thy soul Gen 27 19 that thy soul may bless me. 31
Deut 4 9 keep thyself and thy soul carefully
29 and all the affliction of thy soul
6 5 love the Lord . . . with thy whole soul
10 12 serve the Lord . . . with all thy soul
12 20 eat the flesh that thy soul desireth
13 6 friend, whom thou lovest as thy own soul
14 26 buy . . . all that thy soul desireth
26 16 and fulfil them . . . with all thy soul
30 2 return to him . . . with all thy soul
6 thou mayst love . . . with all thy soul
10 return to Lord . . . with all thy soul
Ruth 4 15 shouldst have one to comfort thy soul
1 K 1 26 as thy soul liveth. 17:55; 4 K 2:4, 6; Jdth 12:4
2 16 then take as much as thy soul desireth
33 eyes may faint and thy soul be spent
20 3 the Lord liveth and thy soul liveth. 25:26; 4 K 4:30
4 whatsoever thy soul shall say to me
23 20 as thy soul hath desired to come down
2 K 3 21 reign over all as thy soul desireth. 3 K 11:37
11 11 by the welfare of thy soul I will not
14 19 by the health of thy soul, my lord
3 K 21 5 the matter that thy soul is so grieved
4 K 2 2 as thy soul liveth, I will not leave
Job 18 4 detroyest thy soul in thy fury
Ps 120 7 all evil: may the Lord keep thy soul
Prov 2 10 heart, and knowledge please thy soul
3 22 and there shall be life to thy soul
19 18 to the killing of him set not thy soul
22 25 his ways and take scandal to thy soul
23 2 thou have thy soul in thy own power
24 12 nothing deceiveth keeper of thy soul
14 the doctrine of wisdom to thy soul
29 17 and shall give delight to thy soul
Eccu 1 38 fall, and bring dishonor upon thy soul
2 1 and prepare thy soul for temptation
4 7 humble thy soul to the ancient and bow
9 and be not fainthearted in thy soul
24 for thy soul be not ashamed to say the
26 own person nor against thy soul a lie
33 strive for justice for thy soul, and
6 2 extol not thyself in thoughts of thy s.
7 23 servant be dear to thee as thy own s.
28 if thou hast wife according to thy s.
31 with all thy soul fear the Lord and
33 honor God with all thy soul and give
9 2 give not power of thy soul to a woman
6 give not thy soul to harlots in any
10 31 my son, keep thy soul in meekness
14 16 give and take, and justify thy soul
18 23 before prayer prepare thy soul: and be
31 if thou give to thy soul her desires
30 22 give not up thy soul to sadness, and
24 have pity on thy own soul, pleasing
32 25 thou set a stumblingblock to thy soul
27 in every work of thine regard thy soul
33 31 let him be to thee as thy own soul
31 in blood of thy s. thou hast gotten him
37 16 whose soul is according to thy own s.
30 prove thy soul in thy life: and if it
47 16 wisdom, and thy soul covered the earth
Isa 51 23 and have said to thy soul: Bow down
58 10 shalt pour out thy soul to the hungry
11 and will fill thy soul with brightness
Jer 14 19 Juda, or hath thy soul abhorred Sion
38 17 thy soul shall live, and this city shall
20 well with thee, and thy s. shall live
Eze 3 19 thou hast delivered thy soul. 21
16 5 in the abjection of thy soul, in the
23 22 with whom thy soul hath been glutted. 28
33 9 but thou hast delivered thy soul. Thou
Haba 2 10 many people, and thy soul hath sinned
Mat 22 37 whole heart and with thy whole soul. Mark 12:30; Luke 10:27
Luke 2 35 and thy own soul a sword shall pierce
12 20 do they require thy soul of thee
3 J 2 fare well as thy s. doth prosperously
Apoc 18 14 the fruits of the desire of thy soul
your soul Gen 23 8 if it please your soul that
Deut 11 13 and serve him . . . with all your soul
13 3 you love him . . . with all your soul
Josu 22 5 all your heart and with all your soul
Job 16 4 would God your soul were for my soul
Ps 68 33 seek ye God, and your soul shall live
Eccu 51 34 and let your soul receive discipline
37 let your soul rejoice in his mercy
Isa 55 2 your s. shall be delighted in fatness
3 hear and your soul shall live, and I
Eze 24 21 and for which your soul feareth
souls Gen 12 5 the souls which they had gotten
Gen 46 15 the souls of her sons . . . thirty-three
18 these she bore to Jacob, sixteen souls
22 sons of Rachel . . . all the souls. 14
25 sons of Bala . . . all the souls, seven
26 all the souls that went with Jacob
27 the sons of Joseph . . . two souls
27 souls of the house of Jacob . . . were 70

Exod 1 5 souls that came out of Jacob's thigh
12 4 according to the number of souls which
16 16 number of your s. that dwell in a tent
30 12 shall give a price for their souls
16 he may be merciful to their souls
Lev 11 43 do not defile your souls nor touch
44 defile not your s. by any creeping thing
16 29 you shall afflict your souls. 31; 23:27, 32; Num 29:7
17 11 atonement with it upon altar for your s.
20 25 defile not your souls with beasts
Num 31 40 to the portion of the Lord, 32 souls
Deut 4 15 keep therefore your souls carefully
10 22 in seventy souls thy fathers went down
Josu 2 13 and deliver our souls from death. They
10 35 put to the sword all the s. that were
37 and all the souls that dwelt in it
11 11 cut off all the souls that abode there
1 K 22 22 death of all the souls of thy father's
25 29 souls of thy enemies shall be whirled
1 Pa 5 21 they took . . . of men 100,000 souls
22 19 give therefore your hearts and your s.
Jdth 4 7 they humbled their souls in fasting
8 16 let us humble our souls before him
11 5 for chastising of all straying souls
Job 33 30 may withdraw their s. from corruption
Ps 18 8 law of the Lord . . . converting souls
32 19 to deliver their souls from death: and
33 23 will redeem the souls of his servants
71 13 he shall save the souls of the poor
14 he shall redeem their souls from
73 19 beasts the souls that confess to thee
19 forget not to the end the s. of thy
77 50 he spared not their souls from death
96 10 Lord preserveth the s. of his saints
105 15 and sent fulness into their souls
Prov 1 18 practise deceits against their own s.
19 destroy the souls of the possessors
7 10 woman . . . prepared to deceive souls
11 30 and he that gaineth souls, is wise
13 13 deceitful souls go astray in sins
14 25 a faithful witness delivereth souls
18 8 souls of the effeminate shall be hungry
22 9 carrieth away the s. of the receivers
Wisd 2 22 nor esteemed the honor of holy souls
3 1 souls of the just are in the hand of
13 fruit in the visitation of holy souls
7 27 conveyeth herself into holy souls
11 27 they are thine, O Lord, who lovest s.
12 6 parents sacrificing . . . helpless s.
14 11 and a temptation to the souls of men
17 1 therefore undisciplined s. have erred
Eccu 2 20 in his sight will sanctify their souls
21 3 teeth of a lion, killing the souls of
30 7 for the souls of his sons he shall bind
51 32 your souls are exceeding thirsty. I
Isa 3 9 woe to their s., for evils are rendered
58 3 have we humbled our souls, and thou
Jer 2 34 the blood of the souls of the poor
6 16 shall find refreshment for your souls
17 21 take heed to your souls, and carry no
26 19 are doing a great evil against our s.
37 8 deceive not your souls, saying: The
42 20 for you have deceived your own souls
44 7 this great evil against your own souls
52 29 Nabuchodonosor, 832 s. from Jerusalem
30 carried away of the Jews 745 souls
30 so all the souls were 4,600. And it
Lam 1 19 sought their food to relieve their s.
2 12 when they breathed out their souls
Bar 6 6 will demand an account of your souls
Eze 13 18 and make pillows . . . to catch souls
18 when they caught the s. of my people
18 they gave life to their souls. And
19 to kill souls which should not die
19 to save s. alive which should not live
20 wherewith you catch flying souls: and
20 I will let go the souls that you catch, the souls that should fly
14 14 they shall deliver their own souls
20 they shall only deliver their own s.
17 17 and build forts, to cut off many souls
18 4 all souls are mine: as the soul of the
22 25 the prey, they have devoured souls
27 to shed blood and to destroy souls
24 25 their eyes, upon which their souls rest
Dan 3 86 ye spirits and souls of the just, bless
Osee 4 8 lift up their s. to their iniquity
1 Ma 1 51 let their souls be defiled with all
Mat 11 29 and you shall find rest to your souls
Luke 9 56 Son of man came not to destroy souls
21 19 patience you shall possess your s.
John 10 24 how long dost thou hold our souls in
Acts 2 41 added in that day about 3,000 souls
7 14 and all his kindred, 75 souls. So
14 21 confirming the souls of the disciples
15 24 with words, subverting your souls; to
27 37 we were in all in ship, 276 souls. And
2 C 12 15 spend and be spent myself for your s.
1 Th 2 8 gospel of God, but also our own souls
Heb 13 17 to render an account of your souls
James 1 21 word, which is able to save your souls
1 P 1 9 faith, even the salvation of your s.
22 purifying your souls in the obedience
2 25 the shepherd and bishop of your souls
3 20 wherein a few, that is, eight souls
4 19 commend their souls in good deeds to
2 P 2 14 alluring unstable souls, having their
Apoc 6 9 the souls of them that were slain for
18 13 chariots and slaves and souls of men
20 4 the souls of them that were beheaded

sound Exod 19 13 the trumpet shall begin to sound
Exod 19 19 sound of the trumpet grew by degrees
20 18 noises, and sound of the trumpet
28 35 that the sound may be heard when he
Lev 13 56 and divide it from that which is sound
23 24 memorial, with the s. of trumpets
25 9 shalt sound the trumpet in the seventh
26 36 sound of a flying leaf shall terrify
Num 10 3 when thou shalt sound the trumpets
4 if thou sound but once, the princes
5 if the sound of the trumpets be longer
6 when the trumpets shall sound for a
7 sound of the trumpets shall be plain
7 they shall not make a broken sound
8 sons of Aaron . . . shall s. the trumpets
9 you shall s. aloud with the trumpets
10 sound the trumpets over the holocausts
23 21 the sound of the victory of the king
31 6 delivered to him . . . the trumpets to s.
Deut 12 15 sound and without blemish, such as
Josu 6 4 the priests shall sound the trumpets
5 shall s. in your ears, all the people
9 the sound of the trumpets was heard
20 when the voice and the sound thundered
Judg 7 18 when the trumpet shall s. in my hand
19 they began to sound their trumpets
2 K 5 24 when thou shalt hear the sound of one
6 15 brought the ark . . . with s. of trumpet
15 10 you shall hear the sound of the trumpet
3 K 1 34 you shall sound the trumpet and shall
41 Joab also hearing sound of the trumpet
14 6 Ahias heard the sound of her feet
18 41 there is a sound of abundance of rain
4 K 6 32 s. of his master's feet is behind him
1 Pa 14 15 shalt hear the sound of one going in

15 28 sounding with the sound of the cornet
16 6 to sound the trumpet continually before
2 Pa 5 13 the sound was heard afar off, so that
13 12 and his priests who sound with trumpets
14 priests began to s. with the trumpets
15 14 with s. of trumpet and s. of cornets
29 27 to sound with trumpets and divers
2 Es 4 20 you shall hear the sound of the trumpet
Tob 6 21 that sound children may be born of you
8 15 and found them safe and sound, sleeping
Job 6 30 neither shall folly sound in my mouth
15 21 sound of dread is always in his ears
21 12 and rejoice at the sound of the organ
34 35 and his words sound not discipline
37 2 the sound that cometh out of his mouth
Ps 18 5 their sound hath gone forth into all
46 6 the Lord with the sound of trumpet
76 18 waters, the clouds sent out a sound
97 6 with long trumpets and sound of cornet
150 3 praise him with sound of trumpet
Cant 2 14 let thy voice sound in my ears: for
Wisd 5 11 only the sound of the wings beating
19 17 is changed, yet all keep their sound
17 the sound of the quality is changed
Eccu 30 14 better is a poor man who is sound
15 a sound body, than immense revenues
31 24 sound and wholesome sleep with a
45 11 as he went there might be a sound
50 20 sound of sweet melody was increased
Isa 13 4 the noise of the sound of kings, of
16 11 my bowels shall sound like a harp for
18 3 you shall hear the s. of the trumpet
Jer 4 5 sound with the trumpet in the land
19 hath heard the sound of the trumpet
21 long shall I hear s. of the trumpet
6 1 sound the trumpet in Thecua and set
17 hearken ye to the sound of the trumpet
8 16 was moved at the s. of the neighing
10 22 the sound of a noise cometh, a great
25 10 from them . . . the sound of the mill
42 14 nor hear the sound of the trumpet
46 22 her voice shall sound like brass, for
48 36 my heart shall sound from Moab like
36 my heart shall sound like pipes from
51 27 s. with the trumpet among the nations
Eze 10 5 sound of the wings of the cherubims
26 13 s. of thy harps shall be heard no more
15 islands shake at the sound of thy fall
27 28 at the sound of the cry of thy pilots
31 16 shook the nations with the s. of his
33 3 sound the trumpet and tell the people
4 that heareth the sound of the trumpet
5 he heard the sound of the trumpet
6 sword coming, and s. not the trumpet
Dan 3 5 shall hear the s. of the trumpet. 10, 15
7 when all the people heard the sound of
Joel 2 1 sound an alarm in my holy mountain
Amos 2 2 noise, with the sound of the trumpet
3 6 shall the trumpet sound in a city
6 5 that sing to the sound of the psaltery
Zach 9 14 the Lord God will sound the trumpet
Mat 6 2 sound not a trumpet before thee, as
Acts 2 2 there came a sound from heaven, as of
Rom 10 18 yes, verily, their sound hath gone forth
1 C 14 7 even things without life that give sound
8 if the trumpet give an uncertain sound
15 52 for the trumpet shall sound, and the
1 Tim 1 10 other thing is contrary to s. doctrine
6 3 consent not to the sound words of our
2 Tim 1 13 hold the form of sound words, which thou
4 3 when they will not endure sound doctrine
Titus 1 9 be able to exhort in sound doctrine
13 that they may be sound in the faith
2 1 speak thou the things that become sound
2 sound in faith, in love, in patience
8 sound word that cannot be blamed: that
Heb 12 19 s. of a trumpet and the voice of words
Apoc 1 15 his voice as the sound of many waters
8 6 prepared themselves to s. the trumpet
13 angels who are yet to s. the trumpet
10 7 when he shall begin to s. the trumpet
18 22 the sound of the mill shall be heard no

sounded Exod 19 16 the noise of the trumpet s.
Josu 6 16 the priests sounded with the trumpets
Judg 3 27 s. the trumpet in mount Ephraim: and
6 34 Gedeon, and he sounded the trumpet
7 20 when they sounded their trumpets in
22 persisted sounding the trumpets. And
1 K 13 3 Saul s. the trumpet over all the land
2 K 2 28 Joab s. the trumpet, and all the army
18 16 Joab sounded the trumpet and kept back
20 1 he [Seba] sounded the trumpet and said
22 he [Joab] sounded the trumpet and they
3 K 1 39 they s. the trumpet, and all the people
4 K 9 13 they s. the trumpet and said: Jehu is
1 Pa 15 19 and Ethan, s. with cymbals of brass
24 sounded with trumpets before the ark
16 5 and Asaph sounded with cymbals: but
42 Heman and Idithun sounded the trumpet
2 Pa 5 12 sounded with cymbals and psalteries
13 so when they all sounded together
7 6 the priests sounded the trumpets before
2 Es 4 18 they built and sounded with a trumpet
Wisd 18 10 sounded an ill according cry of the
Eccu 50 18 they sounded with beaten trumpets
1 Ma 3 54 then they sounded with trumpets and
4 13 were with Judas sounded the trumpet
40 and they s. with the trumpets of alarm
5 33 they sounded their trumpets and cried
6 33 battle, and they sounded the trumpets
7 45 they sounded the trumpets after them
9 12 sides, and they sounded the trumpets
16 8 and they sounded the holy trumpets
Luke 1 44 voice of thy salutation s. in my ears
Apoc 8 7 angel s. the trumpet. 8, 10, 12; 9:1, 13; 11:15

soundeth 1 K 15 14 which s. in my ears, and the
Job 39 24 when the noise of the trumpet soundeth

sounding Num 10 6 at the second s. and like noise
Num 29 1 it is the day of the sounding and of
Josu 6 13 walking and sounding the trumpets
20 making a shout, and the trumpets s.
Judg 7 22 the 300 . . . persisted s. the trumpets
4 K 11 14 rejoicing and sounding the. 2 Pa 23:13
1 Pa 15 28 sounding with the sound of the cornets
2 Pa 5 12 with them 120 priests s. with trumpets
Jdth 15 3 they went down sounding with trumpets
Job 28 26 rain, and a way for the sounding storms
Ps 150 5 praise him on high sounding cymbals
Acts 27 28 who also sounding, found 20 fathoms; and
1 C 13 1 I am become as sounding brass, or a

soundness Prov 14 30 s. of heart is life of the
Isa 1 6 there is no soundness therein: wounds
Acts 3 16 hath given him perfect soundness in

sounds 1 C 14 7 except they give distinction of s.

sour Wisd 4 5 be unprofitable and sour to eat
Jer 31 29 the fathers have eaten a sour grape
30 that shall eat the sour grape, his
Eze 18 2 the fathers have eaten sour grapes

source 2 Pa 32 30 stopped the upper source of the

sources Ps 106 33 s. of waters into dry ground

south Gen 12 9 Abram went forward . . . to the s.
Gen 13 1 and Lot with him, into the south. And he
3 from the south to Bethel to the place
14 to the north and to the south, to the
20 1 from thence to the south country and

24 62 he [Isaac] dwelt in the south country
28 14 shalt spread abroad . . . to the south
Num 13 30 Amalec dwelleth in the south, the
21 1 Arad . . . who dwelt towards the s. 23:40
34 4 toward the south as far as Cadesbarne
35 5 toward the south . . . shall be 2,000 cubits
Deut 1 7 hills and the vales towards the south
3 27 cast thy eyes round . . . to the south
33 23 he shall possess the sea and the south
34 3 furthermost sea, and the south part
Josu 10 40 of the hills and of the south. 11:16
12 8 in the south was the Hethite and the
15 1 to the uttermost part of the south coast
2 bay thereof that looketh to the south
4 shall be the limit of the south coast
8 side of the Jebusite towards the south
21 by the borders of Edom to the south
17 10 possession of Ephraim is on the south
18 13 on the south of the nether Beth-horon
16 by side of the Jebusite to the south
19 salt sea at the s. end of the Jordan
19 8 Baalath Beer Ramath to the s. quarter
Judg 1 9 dwelt in the mountains and in the s.
21 19 on the south of the town of Lebona
1 K 10 2 in the borders of Benjamin to the s.
14 5 other to the south over against Gabaa
20 41 his place, which was towards the south
27 10 against the south of Juda and against the south of Jerameel and against the south of Ceni
30 14 invasion . . . upon the south of Caleb
27 and that were in Ramoth to the south
2 K 24 7 they came to the south of Juda into
3 K 7 25 three towards the south and three
1 Pa 26 15 to Obededom . . . that towards the south
17 towards the south likewise four a day
2 Pa 4 4 other three toward the south, and the
10 over against the east toward the south
28 18 Philistines . . . to the south of Juda
Jdth 2 13 and on the south of the land of Cellon
15 of Japheth, which are towards the south
Job 9 9 Hyades and the inner parts of the s.
37 17 hot, when the south wind blows upon
39 26 spreading her wings to the south? Will
Ps 77 26 he removed the south wind from heaven
125 4 captivity, O Lord, as a stream in the s.
Ecce 1 6 again, maketh his round by the south
11 3 if the tree fall to the south or to
Cant 4 16 O north wind, and come, O south wind
Eccu 43 17 at his will the south wind shall blow
Isa 21 1 as whirlwinds come from the south, it
14 you that inhabit the land of the south
30 6 the burden of the beasts of the south
43 6 to the south: Keep not back: bring my
49 12 sea, and these from the south country
Jer 13 19 the cities of the south are shut up
17 26 and from the south, bringing holocausts
32 44 cities that are towards the s. 33:13
Eze 20 46 thy face against the way of the south
46 drop towards the south and prophesy against the forest of the south field
47 say to the south forest: Hear the word
47 from the s. even to the north. 21:4
25 13 and will make it desolate from the s.
27 26 the south wind hath broken thee in
40 2 of a city, bending towards the south
24 brought me out to the way of the south
24 behold the gate that looked to the s.
27 gate of inner court towards the south
27 from gate to gate towards the south
28 into the inner court at the s. gate
44 their prospect was towards the south
45 chamber which looketh toward the south
41 11 and another door was toward the south
42 12 chambers that were towards the south
13 chambers of the s., which are before
18 towards the south he measured 500
46 9 by the way of the south gate
47 1 temple to the south part of the altar
48 10 toward the south 5 and 20 thousand
17 and the suburbs . . . to the south 250
Dan 8 4 with his horns . . . against the south
9 and it became great against the south
11 5 king of the s. shall be strengthened
6 daughter of king of the s. shall come
9 the king of the south shall enter into
11 the king of the south being provoked
14 shall rise up against king of the s.
15 arms of the south shall not withstand
25 stirred up against the king of the s.
25 king of the south shall be stirred up
29 return, and he shall come to the s.
40 king of the s. shall fight against him
Abdi 9 thy valiant men of the south shall be
19 they that are toward the south shall
20 shall possess the cities of the south
Haba 3 3 God will come from the south, and the
Zach 6 6 grisled went forth to land of the s.
7 7 there were inhabitants towards the s.
9 14 and go in the whirlwind of the south
14 4 north, and halt thereof to the south
10 to Remmon to the south of Jerusalem
1 Ma 5 65 Judas . . . in the land toward the s.
Mat 12 42 queen of the s. shall rise. Luke 11:31
55 when ye see the south wind blow, you
13 29 the west and the north and the south
Acts 8 26 go towards the south to the way that
27 13 south wind gently blowing, thinking that
28 13 the south wind blowing, we came the
Apoc 21 13 on the south, three gates: and on the

south side Exod 26 18 twenty shall be in the s. s.
Exod 26 35 candlestick in the south side of the
27 9 in the south side . . . shall be hangings
36 23 twenty were at the s. side southward
38 9 in south side whereof were hangings
40 22 over against the table on the south side
Num 2 10 in the camp . . . on the south side, the
3 29 and shall camp on the south side. And
8 2 candlestick be set up on the south side
10 6 on south side shall take up their tents
13 18 go you up by the south side. And when
23 they went up at the south side and
34 3 s. side shall begin from the wilderness
4 limits shall go round on the south side
Josu 11 2 over against the south side of Ceneroth
13 2 on the south side that lieth under
4 and on the south side are the Hevites
15 7 on the south side of the torrent: and
18 5 Juda be in his bounds on the s. side
15 on the south side the border goeth out
Judg 1 16 which is at the south side of Arad
1 K 30 1 invasion on the s. side upon Siceleg
14 invasion on the s. side of Cerethi
Jdth 7 6 without the city on the south side
Eze 47 19 the south side southward is from Thamar
19 this is the south side southward
48 16 on the south side 4,500; and on the
28 border of Gad, the south side southward
33 at the south side, thou shalt measure
1 Ma 3 57 pitched on the south side of Emmaus

southern Josu 15 19 given me a s. and dry land

southward Exod 26 18 shall be in the south side s.
Exod 27 9 the south side whereof southward
36 23 of which 20 were at the south side s.
Josu 15 1 Edom, to the desert of sin southward
18 13 and passing along southward by Luza

19 34 passeth along to Zabulon southward
3 K 7 39 temple over against the east southward
Eze 47 19 south side southward is from Thamar
19 and this is the south side southward
48 28 the border of Gad, the south side s.
southwest Josu 18 14 towards Beth-horon to the s.
Ps 77 26 his power brought in the s. wind
Acts 27 12 looking towards southwest and northwest
sovereign Eccu 15 10 the s. Lord will give praise
Eccu 23 1 sovereign ruler of my life, leave me
46 6 called upon the most high Sovereign
Isa 3 1 the s. the Lord of hosts shall take
10 16 the s. Lord . . . shall send leanness
33 the s. Lord of hosts shall break the
51 22 thus saith thy Sovereign the Lord
Jude 4 denying the only sovereign Ruler, and
sovereignty Judg 5 11 gates and obtained the s.
sow Gen 47 23 take seed and sow the fields, that
Exod 23 10 six years thou shalt sow thy ground
Lev 19 19 not sow thy field with different seeds
25 3 six years thou shalt sow thy field
4 shalt not sow thy field nor prune
11 you shall not sow nor reap the things
20 if we sow not nor gather our fruits
22 and the eighth year you shall sow
26 16 you shall sow your seed in vain, which
Deut 22 9 thou shalt not sow thy vineyard with
4 K 19 29 in the third year sow and reap: plant
Job 4 8 who work iniquity and sow sorrows and
31 8 then let me sow and let another eat
Ps 125 5 they that sow in tears shall reap in
Ecce 11 4 that observeth the wind, shall not sow
6 in the morning sow thy seed, and in the
Eccu 7 3 son, sow not evils in the furrows of
Isa 17 10 plants, and shalt sow strange seed
28 24 plow all the day to sow, shall he
25 will he not . . . sow gith and scatter
30 23 wheresoever thou shalt sow in the land
32 20 blessed are ye that s. upon all waters
37 30 in the third year sow and reap and
Jer 4 3 ground, and sow not upon thorns
31 27 I will sow the house of Israel and
35 7 shall ye build houses nor sow seed
Osee 2 23 I will sow her unto me in the earth
8 7 shall sow wind, and reap a whirlwind
10 12 sow for yourselves in justice and
Mich 6 15 thou shalt sow, but shalt not reap
Zach 10 9 and I will sow them among peoples
Mat 6 26 they neither sow nor do they reap nor
13 3 the sower went forth to sow. Mark 4:3; Luke 8:5
27 didst thou not sow good seed in thy
25 26 knewest that I reap where I sow not
Luke 12 24 for they sow not neither do they reap
19 21 reapest that which thou didst not sow
22 and reaping that which I did not sow
Gal 6 8 for what things a man shall sow, those
2 P 2 22 the sow that was washed, to her
sowed Gen 26 12 Isaac s. in that land, and he
Lev 27 16 if the ground be sowed with 30 bushels
Num 20 5 wretched place which cannot be sowed
Judg 9 45 so that he sowed salt in it. And when
Ps 106 37 they sowed fields and planted vineyards
Agge 1 6 you have sowed much and brought in
Mat 13 24 a man that sowed good seed in his
31 a man took and sowed in his field
39 enemy that sowed them is the devil
Mark 3 4 whilst he sowed, some fell. Luke 8:5
sower Isa 55 10 and give seed to the sower and
Jer 50 16 destroy the sower out of Babylon and
Mat 13 3 the sower went forth to sow. Mark 4:3; Luke 8:5
18 hear you . . . the parable of the sower
Acts 17 18 what is it, that this word s. would say
2 C 9 10 he that ministereth seed to the sower
sowest 1 C 15 36 which thou s. is not quickened
1 C 15 37 that which thou s., thou s. not the body
soweth Prov 6 14 and at all times he s. discord
Prov 6 19 that soweth discord among brethren
11 18 to him that soweth justice, there is
22 8 he that s. iniquity shall reap evils
Eccu 6 19 to her as one that ploweth and soweth
Amos 9 13 treader of grapes him that s. seed
Mat 13 4 whilst he soweth, some fell by the
37 he that s. the good seed, is the Son
Mark 4 14 he that soweth, soweth the word. And
John 4 36 he that soweth and he that reapeth
37 it is one man that soweth, and it is
2 C 9 6 he who s. sparingly, shall also reap
6 he who s. in blessings, shall also reap
Gal 6 8 he that soweth in his flesh, of flesh
8 he that soweth in the spirit, of spirit
sowing Lev 26 5 shall reach unto the sowing time
sown Exod 23 16 whatsoever thou hast sown in the
Deut 11 10 when the seed is sown, waters are
21 4 valley, that never was plowed nor sown
22 9 lest both the seed which thou hast sown
29 23 so that it cannot be sown any more
Judg 6 3 when Israel had sown, Madian and
Eccu 40 22 more than these green sown fields
Isa 19 7 everything sown by the water shall be
40 24 stock was neither planted nor sown
Jer 2 2 the desert, in a land that is not sown
12 13 they have sown wheat and reaped thorns
Eze 36 9 you, and you shall be plowed and sown
Nah 1 14 no more of thy name shall be sown
Mat 13 19 that which was sown in his heart
25 24 thou reapest where thou hast not sown
Mark 4 15 the wayside, where the word is sown
15 the word that was sown in their hearts
16 that are sown on the stony ground: who
18 there are who are sown among thorns
20 who are sown upon good ground, who
31 mustard seed: which when it is sown in
32 when it is sown, it groweth up and
1 C 9 11 we have sown unto you spiritual things
15 42 it is sown in corruption, it shall rise
43 it is sown in dishonor, it shall rise
43 sown in weakness, it shall rise in power
44 it is sown a natural body, it shall rise
James 3 18 the fruit of justice is sown in peace
space Gen 30 36 he set the space of three days'
Gen 32 16 be a space between drove and drove
Num 11 31 for the space of one day's journey
Josu 3 4 you and ark the s. of 2,000 cubits
10 13 hasted not to go down the s. of one day
1 K 26 13 and a good space was between them
3 K 7 5 with equal space between the pillars
2 Pa 20 24 for a great space, full of dead bodies
Jdth 1 2 side was extended the space of 20 feet
Job 26 7 out the north over the empty space
Wisd 4 13 being made perfect in a short space
Eze 41 8 measure of a reed the space of six
2 Ma 5 2 space of forty days there were seen
14 slain in the space of three whole days
7 20 seven sons slain in space of one day
11 5 space of five furlongs from Jerusalem
14 1 after the space of three years, Judas
Luke 4 2 desert, for the space of forty days
22 59 after the space, as it were of one
Acts 5 7 about the space of three hours after
13 18 for the space of forty years endured
19 8 he spoke boldly for the s. of 3 months
10 this continued for the space of 2 years
34 for the space of about 2 hours, cried
spaces 3 K 7 31 spaces between the pillars were

spacious Exod 3 8 into a good and spacious land
Judg 18 10 that is secure, into a spacious country
1 Pa 4 40 country spacious and quiet and fruitful
Ps 30 9 hast set my feet in a spacious place
Isa 22 18 thee . . . into a large and s. country
28 2 and sent forth upon a spacious land
33 21 rivers, very broad and spacious streams
Osee 4 16 feed them, as a lamb in a s. place
spade 1 K 13 20 to sharpen every man . . . his s.
spades 1 K 13 21 their spades and their forks
Joel 3 10 into swords, and your s. into spears
Mich 4 3 plowshares, and their spears into s.
Spain 1 Ma 8 3 they had done in the land of S.
Rom 15 24 begin to take my journey into Spain, I
28 I will come by you into Spain. And I
span Exod 28 16 it shall be the measure of a span
Exod 39 9 double, of the measure of a span
1 K 17 4 whose height was six cubits and a span
Lam 2 20 fruit, their children of a span long
spare Gen 18 24 wilt thou not spare that place
Gen 18 26 I will spare the whole place for their
Deut 7 16 thy eye shall not spare them, neither
13 8 neither let thy eye spare him to pity
1 K 15 3 spare him not nor covet anything that
29 the triumpher in Israel will not spare
2 K 18 16 Joab . . . willing to s. the multitude
4 K 1 14 now I beseech thee to spare my life
7 4 if they spare us, we shall live: but
2 Es 13 22 spare me according to the multitude of
Jdth 2 6 thy eye shall not spare any kingdom
Job 6 10 afflicting me with sorrow he spare not
7 11 wherefore I will not spare my mouth
16 spare me, for my days are nothing
19 how long wilt thou not spare me nor
9 28 that thou didst not spare the offender
14 16 numbered my steps, but spare my sins
20 13 he will spare it and not leave it and
27 22 shall cast upon him, and shall not s.
41 3 I will not spare him, nor his mighty
Ps 18 14 from those of others spare thy servant
71 13 he shall spare the poor and needy
Prov 6 34 and rage of the husband will not spare
Wisd 2 10 not spare the widow nor honor the
Eccu 13 15 he will not spare to do thee hurt
23 2 heart, that they spare me not in their
Isa 9 19 fire: no man shall spare his brother
13 18 their eye shall not spare their sons
27 11 he that formed it shall not spare it
30 20 the Lord will give you spare bread and
54 2 spare not: lengthen thy cords and
Jer 13 14 will not spare, and I will not pardon
21 7 moved to pity, nor spare them nor
46 28 neither will I spare thee as if thou
50 14 fight against her, spare not arrows
51 3 spare not her young men, destroy all
Eze 5 11 and my eye shall not spare and I will
7 4 and my eye shall not spare thee, and
9 my eye shall not spare, neither will I
8 18 my eye shall not spare them, neither
9 5 let not your eyes spare, nor be ye
10 neither shall my eye spare nor will I
24 14 I will not pass by nor spare nor be
Joel 2 17 spare, O Lord, spare thy people: and
Jon 4 11 shall not I spare Ninive, that great
Haba 1 17 will not spare continually to slay
Zach 11 6 will no more spare the inhabitants
Mala 3 17 I will spare them as a man spareth
1 Ma 13 5 far be it from me to s. my life in
2 Ma 5 12 not to spare any that came in their
Rom 11 21 fear lest perhaps he also spare not thee
1 C 7 28 of the flesh. But I spare you. This
2 C 1 23 that to spare you, I came not any more
13 2 that if I come again, I will not spare
spared Gen 19 16 because the Lord spared him
Gen 22 12 not spared thy only begotten son. 16
Num 16 9 hath spared you from all the people
1 K 15 9 and Saul and the people spared Agag
15 the people s. the best of the sheep
24 11 but my eye hath spared thee [Saul]
2 K 12 4 spared to take of his own sheep and
21 7 the king spared Miphiboseth the son
4 K 5 20 my master hath s. Naaman this Syrian
2 Pa 36 15 because he spared his people and his
Jdth 13 25 for that thou hast not spared thy life
Job 10 14 if . . . thou hast spared me for an hour
16 14 wounded my loins, he hath not spared
Ps 77 50 he spared not their souls from death
Eccu 16 9 and he spared not the place where Lot
Lam 2 2 down headlong, and hath not spared
17 hath destroyed, and hath not spared
3 43 thou hast killed and hast not spared
Eze 20 14 I spared them for the sake of my name
17 yet my eye spared them, so that I
Joel 2 18 his land, and hath spared his people
Zach 11 5 and their shepherds spared them not
Acts 20 27 I have not spared to declare unto you
Rom 8 32 that spared not even his own Son, but
11 21 if God hath not s. the natural branches
2 P 2 4 if God spared not the angels that
5 and spared not the original world, but
sparedst Wisd 12 8 even those thou s. as men
sparest Wisd 11 27 but thou sparest all: because
spareth Prov 13 24 spareth the rod hateth his son
Mala 3 17 as a man s. his son that serveth him
sparing Job 16 6 would move my lips, as s. you
Isa 30 18 shall he be exalted sparing you
Acts 20 29 enter in among you, not s. the flock
Col 2 23 not sparing the body; not in any honor
sparingly Eccu 11 18 that is enriched by living s.
2 C 9 6 who soweth s., shall also reap sparingly
spark 2 K 14 7 seek to quench my spark which is
Wisd 2 2 and speech a spark to move our heart
Eccu 11 34 of one spark cometh a great fire, and
28 14 if thou blow the spark, it shall burn
42 23 what we can know is but as a spark
Isa 1 31 of tow, and your work as a spark
sparkled Eze 1 7 they s. like the appearance
sparks Wisd 3 7 and fro like s. among the reeds
Wisd 11 19 horrible sparks out of their eyes
sparrow Lev 14 6 in the blood of the s. 51
Lev 14 7 he shall let go the living sparrow
50 having immolated one sparrow in an
51 the scarlet and the living sparrow
52 as well with the blood of the sparrow
52 water, and with the living sparrow
53 and when he hath let go the sparrow
Ps 10 2 from hence to the mountain like a s.
83 4 sparrow hath found herself a house
101 8 as a sparrow all alone on the housetop
123 7 as a sparrow out of the snare of the
Prov 26 2 and a sparrow going here or there
sparrows Lev 14 4 offer for himself two living s.
Lev 14 5 one of the sparrows to be immolated
49 he shall take two sparrows and cedar
Ps 103 17 the sparrows shall make their nests
Mat 10 29 are not two sparrows sold for a
31 better are you than many sparrows
Luke 12 6 are not five sparrows sold for two
7 you are of more value than many s.
Sparta 1 Ma 14 16 heard at Rome and as far as S.
Spartans 1 Ma 12 2 and he sent letters to the S.
1 Ma 12 5 letters which Jonathan wrote to the S.
6 to the S., their brethren, greeting
21 is found in writing concerning the S.
14 19 copy of the letters that the S. sent
20 princes and the cities of the Spartans

23 be a memorial to the people of the S.
15 23 to Lampsacus and to the Spartans
spat John 9 6 he spat on the ground and made
speak Mat 5 11 and speak all that is evil against you
Mat 6 7 speak not much, as the heathens. For
10 19 take no thought how or what to speak
19 given you in that hour what to speak
20 it is not you that speak, but the
27 in the dark, speak ye in the light: and
12 32 shall speak a word against the Son of
32 that shall speak against the Holy Ghost
34 how can you speak good things, whereas
36 every idle word that men shall speak
46 stood without, seeking to speak to him
13 13 therefore do I s. to them in parables
34 he did not speak to them. Mark 4:34
15 31 seeing the dumb speak, the lame walk
Mark 1 25 speak no more, and go out of the man
34 suffered them not to speak. Luke 4:41
2 7 why doth this man speak thus? He
7 37 deaf to hear and the dumb to speak
9 38 my name, and can soon speak ill of me
12 1 he began to speak to them in parables
13 11 beforehand what you shall speak; but
11 given you in that hour, that speak ye
11 it is not you that speak, but the
14 71 I know not this man of whom you speak
16 17 they shall speak with new tongues
Luke 1 19 and am sent to speak to thee and to
20 shalt not be able to speak until the
22 came out, he could not speak to them
5 4 when he had ceased to speak, he said
7 15 was dead, sat up, and began to speak
24 s. to the multitudes concerning John
10 40 speak to her therefore, that she help
12 13 speak to my brother that he divide
41 Lord, dost thou speak this parable to
20 9 he began to speak to the people this
John 1 37 the two disciples heard him speak, and
3 11 we speak what we know, and we testify
12 if I shall s. to you heavenly things
7 17 of God, or whether I speak of myself
46 never did man speak like this man
8 25 beginning, who also speak unto you
26 many things I have to speak and to
26 these same I speak in the world. And
28 hath taught me, these things I speak
38 I speak that which I have seen with
9 21 he is of age, let him speak for himself
10 25 I speak to you, and you believe not
12 49 what I should say and what I should s.
50 things therefore that I speak, even as
50 as the Father said unto me, so do I s.
13 18 I speak not of you all: I know whom
14 10 that I s. to you, I s. not of myself
30 I will not now speak many things with
16 13 for he shall not speak of himself
13 he shall hear, he shall speak; and the
25 will no more speak to you in proverbs
17 13 these things I speak in the world
Acts 2 4 began to speak with divers tongues
4 as the Holy Ghost gave them to speak
6 heard them speak in his own tongue
7 are not all these that speak, Galileans
11 we have heard them speak in our own
29 speak to you of the patriarch David
3 22 whatsoever he shall speak to you. And
4 17 that they speak no more in this name
18 they charged them not to speak at all
20 we cannot but speak the things which
29 all confidence they may s. thy word
5 20 go and standing speak in the temple
40 not speak at all in the name of Jesus
6 11 heard him speak words of blasphemy
13 to speak words against the holy place
8 34 of whom doth the prophet speak this
11 14 who shall speak to thee words, whereby
15 when I had begun to s., the Holy Ghost
13 15 exhortation to make to the people, s.
42 they would s. unto them these words
46 behoved us first to s. the word of God
18 9 do not fear, but s.; and hold not thy
26 this man therefore began to s. in the
21 37 may I s. something to thee? Who said
37 who said: Canst thou speak Greek? Art
39 beseech thee, suffer me to s. to people
23 5 thou shalt not speak evil of the prince
24 10 governor making a sign to him to speak
26 1 thou art permitted to s. for thyself
25 I speak words of truth and soberness
26 to whom also I speak with confidence
28 20 I desired to see you, and to s. to you
21 hither, relate or s. any evil of thee
25 well did Holy Ghost speak to our fathers
Rom 3 6 I speak according to man. God forbid
6 19 I speak an human thing, because of the
7 1 I speak to them that know the law, that
9 1 I speak the truth in Christ, I lie not
15 18 I dare not to s. of any of those things
1 C 1 10 that you all speak the same thing, and
2 6 we speak wisdom among the perfect: yet
7 we speak wisdom of God in a mystery
13 which things also we speak, not in the
3 1 I, brethren, could not speak to you as
6 5 I speak to your shame. Is it so that
7 6 but I speak this by indulgence, not by
12 for to the rest I speak, not the Lord
35 and this I speak for your profit: not
10 15 idols. I speak as to wise men: judge ye
12 30 do all s. with tongues? Do all interpret
13 1 if I speak with the tongues of men, and
14 5 have you all to speak with tongues, but
6 unless I s. to you either in revelation
11 be to him to whom I speak a barbarian
18 I thank my God I speak with all your
19 I had rather speak five words with my
21 other tongues and other lips I will s.
23 one place, and all speak with tongues
27 if any speak with a tongue, let it be
28 church, and speak to himself and to God
29 let the prophets speak, two or three
34 for it is not permitted them to speak
35 it is a shame for woman to s. in church
39 and forbid not to speak with tongues
15 34 of God, I speak it to your shame. But
2 C 2 17 from God, before God, in Christ we speak
4 13 believe, for which cause we speak also
6 13 I speak as to my children, be you also
8 8 I speak not as commanding; but by the
11 17 I speak, I speak not according to God
21 I speak according to dishonor, as if we
21 if any man dare, I speak foolishly, I
23 I speak as one less wise: I am more; in
12 19 we speak before God in Christ; but all
Gal 3 15 I speak after the manner of man, yet
Eph 4 25 putting away lying, speak ye the truth
5 12 secret, it is a shame even to speak of
32 but I speak in Christ and in the church
6 20 be bold to speak according as I ought
Phil 1 14 to speak the word of God without fear
4 11 I speak not as it were for want. For I
Col 4 3 speech to speak the mystery of Christ
4 make it manifest as I ought to speak
1 Th 1 8 so that we need not to speak anything
2 2 to speak unto you the gospel of God in
4 even so we speak, not as pleasing men

16 16 prohibiting us to speak to the Gentiles
1 Tim 5 14 occasion to the adversary to s. evil
Titus 2 1 speak thou the things that become sound
15 these things s., and exhort and rebuke
3 2 to speak evil of no man, not to be
Heb 2 5 the world to come, whereof we speak
6 9 nearer to salvation; though we s. thus
9 5 is not needful to s. now particularly
James 1 19 but slow to speak and slow to anger
2 12 so speak ye, and so do, as being to
1 P 2 12 they speak against you as evildoers
3 10 and his lips that they speak no guile
16 whereas they speak evil of you, they
4 11 if any man s., let him s. as the words
1 J 4 5 of the world they speak, and the world
2 J 12 be with you, and speak face to face
3 J 14 and we will speak mouth to mouth
Apoc 13 15 that the image of the beast should s.
speaker Job 16 9 false s. riseth up against my
Wisd 1 6 will not acquit the evil speaker
Mat 22 16 know that thou art a true s. Mark 12:14
Acts 14 11 Mercury; because he was chief speaker
speakers Job 12 20 the speech of the true s.
Eccu 23 8 the evil speakers shall fall thereby
speakest Num 32 27 to the war, as thou, my lord, s.
Judg 6 17 sign that it is thou that s. to me
2 K 6 22 with the handmaids of whom thou s.
19 29 why s. thou [Miphiboseth] any more
4 K 6 12 that thou speakest in thy privy chamber
Job 15 3 thou s. that which is not good for thee
Wisd 12 2 admonishest them and speakest to them
Isa 40 27 and speakest, O Israel: My way is hid
Mat 13 10 why s. thou to them in parables? Who
Luke 20 21 that thou s. and teachest rightly
John 16 29 thou s. plainly, and s. no proverb
19 10 speakest thou not to me? Knowest thou
Acts 17 19 this new doctrine is, which thou s. of
speaketh Gen 45 12 it is my mouth that s. to you
Deut 5 26 who s. out of the midst of the fire
Job 11 2 shall not he that s. much, hear also
33 14 God s. once, and repeateth not the
Ps 11 4 the tongue that speaketh proud things
14 3 he that speaketh truth in his heart
100 7 that s. unjust things did not prosper
Prov 2 12 from the man that s. perverse things
6 13 with the foot, s. with the finger
8 3 in the very doors she speaketh, saying
12 17 he that speaketh that which he knoweth
13 13 whosoever s. ill of anything, bindeth
16 13 that s. right things shall be loved
19 5 he that speaketh lies shall not escape
9 he that speaketh lies shall perish
29 5 that s. to his friend with flattering
Cant 2 10 my beloved speaketh to me: Arise
Wisd 1 8 he that s. unjust things cannot be hid
Eccu 12 15 an enemy s. sweetly with his lips
22 9 he speaketh with one that is asleep
27 8 praise not a man before he speaketh
37 23 he that speaketh sophistically is
Isa 8 12 that this people s. is a conspiracy
23 4 O Sidon: for the sea speaketh, even
32 7 when the poor man speaketh judgment
33 15 that walketh in justices and s. truth
Jer 8 6 no man speaketh what is good, there
9 8 one speaketh peace with his friend
Amos 5 10 abhorred him that speaketh perfectly
Mat 10 20 Spirit of your Father that speaketh
12 34 abundance of the heart the mouth speaketh. Luke 6:45
Luke 5 21 who is this who s. blasphemies? Who
12 10 s. a word against the Son of man
John 3 31 he is, and of the earth he speaketh
34 hath sent, speaketh the words of God
7 18 he that s. of himself, seeketh his own
26 he s. openly, and they say nothing
8 44 when he s. a lie, he s. of his own
13 24 who is it of whom he speaketh? He
16 18 we know not what he speaketh. And
19 12 himself a king, s. against Caesar
Rom 3 19 things soever the law s., it s. to them
10 6 justice which is of faith, speaketh thus
1 C 14 2 he that s. in a tongue, s. not unto
2 yet by the Spirit he speaketh mysteries
3 he that prophesieth, speaketh to men
4 he that s. in tongue, edifieth himself
5 than he that speaketh with tongues
11 and he that speaketh, a barbarian to me
13 he that s. by a tongue, let him pray
2 C 13 3 seek a proof of Christ that s. in me
Heb 11 4 and by it he being dead yet speaketh
12 5 which s. to you, as unto children
24 which s. better than that of Abel
25 see that you refuse him not that s.
25 from him that s. to us from heaven
Jude 16 and their mouth speaketh proud things
speaking Gen 17 22 left off speaking with him
Gen 18 33 after he had left speaking to Abraham
29 9 they were yet speaking, and behold
Exod 19 9 that the people may hear me speaking
34 33 having done speaking, he put a veil
Num 7 89 heard the voice of one speaking to him
13 27 speaking to them and to all the
14 36 speaking ill of the land that it was
16 5 speaking to Core and all the multitude
20 the Lord speaking to Moses and Aaron
31 as he had made an end of s., the earth
21 5 speaking against God and Moses, they
23 4 Balaam s. to him, said: I have erected
Deut 4 33 speaking out of the midst of fire, as
5 24 that God s. with man, man hath lived
20 9 their peace and have made an end of s.
32 45 these words, speaking to all Israel
Josu 9 21 as they were s. these things, Josue
1 K 17 28 when he was speaking with others, he
18 1 had made an end of speaking to Saul
24 17 an end of speaking these words to Saul
2 K 13 36 and when he made an end of speaking
3 K 1 14 while thou art yet s. there with the
22 as she was yet s. with the king, Nathan
4 K 6 33 while he was yet speaking to them, the
2 Pa 10 16 the people upon the king's s. roughly
36 12 Jeremias the prophet speaking to him
Tob 7 6 when he was speaking many good things
Jdth 6 1 pass when they had left off speaking
Job 1 16 he was yet speaking. 17, 18
6 29 speaking that which is just, judge ye
7 13 relieved s. with myself on my couch
15 2 as if he were speaking in the wind
32 4 Eliu waited while Job was speaking
15 answered no more and they left off s.
33 23 if there shall be an angel s. for him
Ps 33 14 keep . . . thy lips from speaking guile
34 20 and s. in the anger of the earth they
Prov 25 28 cannot refrain his own spirit in s.
Ecce 2 15 speaking with my own mind, I perceived
Isa 19 18 speaking the language of Chanaan and
65 24 as they are yet speaking, I will hear
Jer 7 13 spoken to you, rising up early, and s.
20 8 for I am speaking now this long time
25 3 rising before day, and speaking, and
26 7 heard Jeremias speaking these words
8 an end of s. all that the Lord had
35 14 to you, rising early and speaking
38 4 s. to them according to these words
43 1 Jeremias had made an end of speaking
Eze 2 2 my feet: and I heard him s. to me

10 5 as the voice of God Almighty speaking
43 6 I heard one speaking to me out of the
Dan 2 20 speaking he said: Blessed be the name
7 8 and a mouth speaking great things. 20
8 13 I heard one of the saints speaking
13 I know not to whom that was speaking
9 20 while I was yet s. and praying and
21 I was yet speaking in prayer, behold
10 15 and when he was s. such words to me
Osee 1 2 beginning of the Lord's s. by Osee
1 Ma 2 23 as he left off speaking these words
3 23 as he had made an end of speaking
23 soon as he had made an end of speaking
4 19 as Judas was speaking these words
2 Ma 7 30 while she was yet speaking these words
15 9 speaking to them out of the law and
Mat 6 7 they think that in their much speaking
9 18 as he was speaking. Luke 11:37
12 46 as he was yet s. 17:5; Luke 8:49; 22:47, 60
Mark 5 35 while he was yet speaking. 14:43
Luke 7 32 speaking one to another, and saying
24 36 whilst they were s. these things, Jesus
John 4 26 I am he, who am speaking with thee
Acts 1 3 and speaking of the kingdom of God
4 1 as they were s. to the people, the
7 44 s. to Moses, that he should make it
10 44 Peter was yet speaking these words
46 they heard them speaking with tongues
11 19 s. the word to none, but to the Jews
13 43 s. to them, persuaded them to continue
14 8 this same heard Paul s. Who looking
17 s. these things, they scarce restrained
19 9 speaking evil of the way of the Lord
20 30 shall arise men s. perverse things, to
26 14 voice s. to me in the Hebrew tongue
28 25 Paul speaking this one word: Well did
1 C 12 3 no man, speaking by the Spirit of God
14 6 if I come to you speaking with tongues
9 for you shall be speaking into the air
Eph 5 19 speaking to yourselves in psalms, and
1 Tim 4 2 speaking lies in hypocrisy, and having
5 13 speaking things which they ought not
1 P 4 4 speaking evil of you. Who shall render
2 P 2 16 speaking with a man's voice, forbade
18 s. proud words of vanity, they allure
3 16 epistles, s. in them of these things
Apoc 4 1 of a trumpet speaking with me, said
10 8 s. to me and saying: Go, and take the
13 5 to him a mouth speaking great things
spear Judg 5 8 a shield and spear was not seen
1 K 13 22 there was neither sword nor spear found
17 7 staff of his spear was like a weaver's
7 head of his spear weighed 600 sicles
47 Lord saveth not with sword and spear
18 10 held a spear in his hand. 19:9
19 10 the spear missed him and was fastened
10 to nail David to the wall with his s.
20 33 Saul caught up a spear to strike him
21 8 hast thou here at hand a spear or a
22 6 Saul . . . having his spear in his hand
26 7 spear fixed in the ground at his head
8 I will run him through with my spear
11 take the spear, which is at his head
12 David took the spear and cup of water
16 now where is the king's spear and the
22 behold the king's spear: let one of
2 K 1 6 Gelboe, and Saul leaned upon his spear
2 23 Abner struck him with his spear with
21 16 iron of whose spear weighed 300 ounces
19 the shaft of whose spear was like a
23 18 his spear against 300. 1 Pa 11:11, 20
21 slew him with his own s. 1 Pa 11:23
21 a sight, having a spear in his hand

21 forced the spear out of the hand of the
1 Pa 11 23 who had a spear like a weaver's beam
23 with a staff and plucked away the s.
12 8 warriors, holding shield and spear
24 sons of Juda bearing shield and spear
34 furnished with shield and spear. Of
20 5 staff of whose s. was like a weaver's
2 Pa 9 15 of gold, which went to every spear
25 5 and could hold the spear and shield
Jdth 11 2 never would have lifted up my spear
Job 39 23 the spear and shield shall glitter
41 17 shall not be able to hold, nor a spear
20 him to scorn who shaketh the spear
Wisd 5 21 will sharpen his severe wrath for a s.
Eccu 29 16 the mighty, and better than the spear
Nah 3 3 the noise . . . of the glittering spear
Haba 3 11 in the brightness of thy glittering s.
2 Ma 11 8 with golden armor, shaking a spear
15 11 not with defence of shield and spear
John 19 34 but one of the soldiers with a spear
spearmen Acts 23 23 200 s. for the third hour
spears Num 33 55 in your eyes, and s. in your sides
1 K 13 19 Hebrews should make them swords or s.
4 K 11 10 and he [Joiada] gave them the spears
2 Pa 9 15 king Solomon made 200 golden spears
11 12 he made an armory of shields and spears
14 8 of men that bore shields and spears
23 9 gave to the captains the spears and the
26 14 for the whole army, shields and spears
2 Es 4 13 with their swords and spears and bows
16 ready for to fight, with spears and
21 hold our spears from the rising of the
Jdth 7 8 trust not in their spears nor in their
9 9 their arrows, and glory in their spears
Isa 2 4 plowshares, and their s. into sickles
Jer 46 4 furbish the spears, put on coats of
Eze 38 4 armed with s. and shields and swords
39 9 the spears, the bows, and the arrows
Joel 3 10 into swords, and your spades into s.
Mich 4 3 plowshares, and their s. into spades
5 6 the land of Nemrod with the spears
2 Ma 5 2 in gilded raiment and armed with spears
special Mala 3 17 they shall be my s. possession
2 Ma 4 11 had been decreed of special favor
8 9 Nicanor . . . one of his s. friends
Acts 10 24 called . . . his kinsmen and s. friends
specify 1 Ma 12 7 copy here underwritten doth s.
speck Tob 6 9 in which there is a white speck
speckled Gen 30 32 sheep of divers colors, and s.
Gen 30 39 brought forth spotted . . . and speckled
31 8 the speckled shall be thy wages: all
10 divers colors and spotted and s. 12
39 8 all the sheep brought forth speckled
Jer 12 9 inheritance to me as a speckled bird
Zach 1 8 horses, red, speckled, and white
spectacle 1 C 4 9 we are made a s. to the world
speech Gen 4 23 of Lamech, hearken to my speech
Gen 11 1 one tongue and of the same speech
7 may not understand one another's speech
31 50 none is witness of our speech but God
1 K 25 32 to meet me, and blessed be thy speech
Deut 32 2 let my speech distil as the dew, as a
2 K 14 20 come about with this form of speech
2 Es 13 24 spoke half in the speech of Azotus
Jdth 8 21 comfort their hearts by your speech
Job 5 8 Lord, and address my speech to God
10 1 I will let go my speech against myself
12 20 changeth the s. of the true speakers
13 17 hear ye my speech, and receive with
29 22 and my speech dropped upon them. They
Ps 18 3 day to day uttereth speech, and night
55 11 in the Lord will I praise his speech
103 34 let my speech be acceptable to him

138 4 for there is no speech in my tongue
147 15 sendeth forth his speech to the earth
Prov 13 3 he that hath no guard on his speech
23 9 will despise the instruction of thy s.
25 2 glory of kings to search out the speech
Ecce 7 9 better is the end of a speech than
Cant 4 3 scarlet lace: and thy speech sweet
Wisd 1 11 obscure speech shall not go for nought
2 2 and speech a spark to move our heart
3 18 nor speech of comfort in day of trial
Eccu 9 24 praised . . . for wisdom of his speech
20 5 that is hateful, that is bold in speech
23 15 also another speech opposite to death
17 mouth be accustomed to indiscreet s.
32 16 a mind, but not in sin or proud speech
Isa 3 3 and the skilful in eloquent speech
28 11 with the speech of lips, and with
23 hearken, and hear my speech. Shall the
29 4 thy s. shall be heard out of the ground
4 out of the ground thy s. shall mutter
32 9 confident daughters, give ear to my s.
33 19 not see, the people of profound speech
Eze 3 5 not sent to a people of a profound s.
6 nor to many nations of a strange speech
21 2 let thy s. fly towards the holy places
Haba 2 6 and a dark speech concerning him: and
2 Ma 2 32 to pursue brevity of speech and to
15 12 manners, and graceful in his speech
40 if the speech be always nicely framed
Mat 5 37 let your s. be yea, yea. James 5:12
22 15 how to insnare him in his speech. And
26 73 even thy speech doth discover thee
Luke 4 32 for his speech was with power. And
John 8 43 why do you not know my speech? Because
Acts 20 7 he continued his speech until midnight
1 C 1 17 not in wisdom of speech, lest the cross
2 1 came not in loftiness of speech or of
4 my s. and my preaching was not in the
4 19 not the s. of them that are puffed up
20 the kingdom of God is not in speech, but
14 9 except you utter by the tongue plain s.
2 C 10 10 is weak, and his speech contemptible
11 6 for although I be rude in speech, yet
Eph 4 29 let no evil s. proceed from your mouth
6 19 for me, that speech may be given me
Col 3 8 filthy speech out of your mouth. Lie
4 3 God may open unto us a door of speech
6 let your speech be always in grace
1 Th 2 5 time, the speech of flattery, as you
2 Tim 2 17 their speech spreadeth like a canker
Heb 4 13 open to his eyes, to whom our speech is
Jude 9 against him the judgment of railing s.
speeches Job 6 26 you dress up s. only to rebuke
Job 33 1 hear therefore, O Job, my speeches
34 37 provoke God to judgment with his s.
Ps 18 4 there are no speeches nor languages
Wisd 8 8 she knoweth the subtilties of speeches
Eccu 36 21 the wise heart [tasteth] false s.
41 28 be ashamed of upbraiding speeches
2 Ma 2 3 with other such like s. he exhorted
15 11 with very good s. and exhortations
Rom 16 18 by pleasing s. and good words, seduce
1 C 12 10 to another, interpretation of speeches
28 kinds of tongues, interpretations of s.
speechless Wisd 4 19 burst them puffed up and s.
2 Ma 3 29 by the power of God lay speechless
speed Gen 24 61 with s. returned to his master
Gen 32 6 he cometh with speed to meet thee
45 19 make haste to come with all speed
Num 23 4 and when he was gone with speed
2 Pa 24 5 do this with speed; but the Levites
Isa 5 26 they shall come with speed swiftly
8 1 take away the spoils with speed
2 Ma 8 9 and he with all speed sent Nicanor
Acts 17 15 they should come to him with all speed
2 J 10 house nor say to him, God speed you
11 that saith unto him, God speed you
speedily Gen 24 46 she s. let down the pitcher
Gen 41 32 cometh to pass and is fulfilled s.
44 11 they speedily took down their sacks
Exod 12 33 to go forth out of the land speedily
Num 20 19 the price, only let us pass speedily
Josu 23 16 indignation . . . quickly and speedily
1 K 20 38 make haste speedily, stand out. And
2 Pa 30 10 the posts went speedily from city to
35 13 they distributed them speedily among all
Ps 6 11 let them . . . be ashamed very speedily
68 18 I am in trouble, hear me speedily
78 8 let thy mercies speedily prevent us
101 3 shall call upon thee, hear me speedily
142 7 hear me speedily, O Lord: my spirit
Ecce 8 11 because sentence is not s. pronounced
Wisd 2 6 let us speedily use the creatures as
6 6 horribly and speedily will he appear to
Eccu 20 20 fall of the wicked shall come speedily
21 6 judgment shall come for him speedily
Isa 58 8 and thy health shall speedily arise
Jer 36 29 king of Babylon shall come speedily
49 30 get away speedily, sit in deep holes
1 Ma 6 27 unless thou speedily prevent them
2 Ma 7 27 calling upon God to be s. merciful
John 11 31 that she rose up speedily and went out
Rom 16 20 crush Satan under your feet speedily
Phil 2 28 I sent him the more speedily: that
3 J 14 I hope speedily to see thee, and we
speedy Eccu 43 24 is the speedy coming of a cloud
Soph 1 18 shall make even a speedy destruction
Mala 3 5 and will be a speedy witness against
spend Deut 32 23 will spend my arrows among them
Judg 19 9 today also, and spend the day in mirth
1 Es 7 20 thou shalt have occasion to spend, it
Jdth 12 4 thy handmaid shall not spend all these
Job 21 13 they spend their days in wealth and
Prov 21 20 and the foolish man shall spend it
Isa 55 2 why do you spend money for that which
Luke 10 35 thou shalt spend over and above, I
1 C 16 6 I shall abide, or even spend the winter
2 C 12 15 I most gladly will spend and be spent
James 4 13 city, and there we will spend a year
spent Gen 21 15 the water in the bottle was s.
Gen 24 63 field, the day being now well spent
35 29 being spent with age he [Isaac] died
47 18 how that our money is spent and our
50 10 lamentation, they s. full seven days
Exod 18 18 thou art spent with foolish labor
38 24 the gold that was spent in the work
Lev 26 20 your labor shall be spent in vain
Deut 25 18 when thou wast spent with hunger and
26 14 nor spent anything of them in funerals
Judg 19 11 near Jebus, and the day was far s.
Ruth 1 12 I am now spent with age and not fit
1 K 2 33 eyes may faint and thy soul be spent
9 7 the bread is spent in our bags: and we
Ps 89 9 all our days are spent: and in thy
Prov 5 11 when thou shalt have spent thy flesh
Isa 49 4 I have spent my strength without cause
Jer 20 18 my days should be spent in confusion
37 20 till all the bread in the city were s.
Dan 14 2 there were spent upon him every day
1 Ma 7 48 they spent that day with great joy
Mark 5 26 had spent all that she had, and was
6 35 the day was now far spent. Luke 24:29
Luke 15 14 after he had spent all, there came
Acts 15 33 after they had spent some time there
18 23 after he had spent some time there
20 3 when he had spent 3 months, the Jews laid

27 9 and when much time was spent, and when
2 C 12 15 I most gladly will spend and be spent
spiced Cant 8 2 will give thee a cup of s. wine
spices Gen 37 25 carrying spices and balm and
Exod 25 6 oil to make light: spices for ointment
30 23 take s. of principal and chosen myrrh
34 take unto thee spices, stacte, and
31 11 oil of unction and incense of s. 35:15
35 28 and spices and oil for the lights
37 29 and incense of the purest spices
39 37 ointment and the incense of spices
Lev 40 25 burnt upon it the incense of spices
3 K 10 2 and camels that carried spices and an
10 and of spices a very great store and
10 no more such abundance of spices as
25 armor and spices and horses. 2 Pa 9:24
4 K 20 13 the house of his aromatical spices
1 Pa 9 29 wine and oil and frankincense and s.
30 made the ointments of the spices. And
2 Pa 2 4 and to perfume with aromatical spices
9 1 riches, and camels, which carried s.
9 there were no such spices as these
9 of gold, and spices in great abundance
16 14 laid him on his bed full of spices
32 27 of precious stones, of spices, and of
Esth 2 14 used certain perfumes and sweet spices
Cant 3 6 as pillar of smoke of aromatical spices
4 10 thy ointments above all aromatical s.
16 let the aromatical spices thereof flow
5 1 my myrrh, with my aromatical spices
13 cheeks are as beds of aromatical spices
6 1 to the bed of aromatical spices
8 14 upon the mountains of aromatical spices
Isa 39 2 storehouses of his aromatical spices
Eze 27 22 with all the best spices and precious
Mark 16 1 bought sweet spices, that coming, they
Luke 23 56 they prepared spices and ointments
24 1 bringing the spices which they had prepared
John 19 40 bound it in linen cloths, with the s.
spider Ps 38 12 his soul to waste away like a s.
Ps 89 9 our years shall be considered as a s.
spider's Job 8 14 trust shall be like the s. web
spiders Isa 59 5 and have woven the webs of s.
spiders' Osee 8 6 be turned to spiders' webs
spies Gen 42 9 he said to them: You are spies
Gen 42 14 this is it that I said: You are spies
16 by the health of Pharao you are spies
30 took us to be spies of the country
34 that I may know you are not spies
Num 21 1 Israel was come by the way of the s.
Josu 2 3 for they are spies, and are come to
23 the spies returned and came down from
6 22 the two men that had been sent for s.
1 K 26 4 he [David] sent spies and learned
2 K 15 10 Absalom sent spies into all the tribes
1 Ma 12 26 he sent spies into their camp, and
Luke 20 20 spies who should feign themselves just
Heb 11 31 receiving the spies with peace. And what
spikenard Cant 1 11 my s. sent forth the odor
Cant 4 13 of the orchard. Cypress with spikenard
14 spikenard and saffron, sweet cane
Mark 14 3 box of ointment of precious spikenard
John 12 3 pound of ointment of right spikenard
spilled Gen 38 9 s. his seed upon the ground
Mark 2 22 the wine will be spilled, and the
Luke 5 37 the bottles, and it will be spilled
spin Mat 6 28 neither do they spin. Luke 12:27
spindle Prov 31 19 have taken hold of the s.
spirit Exod 6 9 to him, for anguish of spirit
Exod 28 3 I have filled with the spirit of wisdom
Lev 20 27 there is a pythonical or divining spirit
Num 5 14 if the spirit of jealousy stir up the
30 husband stirred up by spirit of jealousy
11 25 away of the spirit that was in Moses
25 when the spirit had rested on them
26 Medad, upon whom the spirit rested
14 24 Caleb, who being full of another spirit
Deut 34 9 Josue . . . was filled with s. of wisdom
Josu 2 11 neither did there remain any s. in us
5 1 and there remained no spirit in them
Judg 8 3 had said this, their s. was appeased
9 23 Lord sent a very evil spirit between
1 K 16 14 evil spirit from the Lord troubled him
15 an evil spirit from God troubleth thee
16 when the evil spirit . . . is upon thee
23 whensoever the evil s. from the Lord
23 for the evil spirit departed from him
18 10 evil spirit from God came upon Saul
19 9 evil s. from the Lord came upon Saul
28 7 a woman that hath a divining spirit
8 divine to me by thy divining spirit
2 K 13 21 not afflict spirit of his son Amnon
22 16 at the blast of the spirit of his wrath
3 K 10 5 she had no longer any spirit in her
22 21 there came forth a spirit and stood
22 lying spirit in the mouth of all. 23
4 K 2 9 that in me may be thy double spirit
15 s. of Elias hath rested upon Eliseus
19 7 I will send a spirit upon him, and he
1 Pa 5 26 stirred up the spirit of Phul king of
26 s. of Thelgathphalnasar king of Assur
12 18 the spirit came upon Amasai the chief
2 Pa 9 4 there was no more spirit in her, she
18 20 there came forth a spirit, and stood
21 I will go out and be a lying spirit
22 the Lord hath put a spirit of lying
21 16 against Joram the s. of the Philistines
1 Es 1 1 Lord stirred up the spirit of Cyrus
5 whose spirit God had raised up, to go
Tob 10 9 and their s. is grievously afflicted
12 3 he chased from her the evil spirit
Jdth 8 16 continuing in an humble spirit in his
Esth 15 11 and God changed the king's spirit
Job 4 9 consumed by the spirit of his wrath
15 when a spirit passed before me, the
12 10 and the spirit of all flesh of man
20 3 spirit of my understanding shall answer
32 8 as I see, there is a spirit in men
18 the spirit of my bowels straiteneth me
Ps 17 16 at the blast of the s. of thy wrath
31 2 and in whose spirit there is no guile
32 6 power of them by the spirit of his mouth
33 19 and he will save the humble of spirit
50 12 renew a right spirit within my bowels
14 strengthen me with a perfect spirit
19 a sacrifice to God is an afflicted s.
54 9 saved me from pusillanimity of spirit
75 13 who taketh away the spirit of princes
77 8 whose spirit was not faithful to God
102 16 the spirit shall pass in him, and he
150 5 of joy: let every spirit praise the Lord
Prov 15 4 is immoderate, shall crush the spirit
13 by grief of mind the s. is cast down
16 18 the spirit is lifted up before a fall
17 22 a sorrowful spirit drieth up the bones
27 of understanding is of a precious s.
18 14 s. of a man upholdeth his infirmity
14 s. that is easily angered, who can bear
20 27 s. of a man is the lamp of the Lord
29 23 glory shall uphold the humble of spirit
Ecce 1 6 the spirit goeth forward surveying all
14 vanity and vexation of spirit. 2:17; 4:16
17 labor and vexation of spirit. 2:22
3 21 if the spirit of the children of Adam
21 if the spirit of the beasts descend

6 9 is vanity and presumption of spirit
8 8 not in man's power to stop the spirit
10 4 if the spirit of him that hath power
11 5 knowest not what is the way of the s.
12 7 and the spirit return to God, who gave
Wisd 1 5 Holy Spirit of discipline will flee
6 the spirit of wisdom is benevolent
2 3 our spirit shall be poured abroad as
5 3 and groaning for anguish of spirit
7 7 and the spirit of wisdom came upon me
22 in her is the spirit of understanding
9 17 and send thy Holy Spirit from above
15 11 that breathed into him a living spirit
16 14 when the spirit is gone forth, it shall
Eccu 7 19 humble thy spirit very much: for the
15 5 shall fill him with the s. of wisdom
16 25 whilst with equity of s. I tell thee
17 6 created in them the science of the s.
34 14 the spirit of those that fear God is
39 8 him with the spirit of understanding
48 27 with a great spirit he saw the things
Isa 4 4 by the spirit of judgment and by the spirit of burning
11 2 the spirit of wisdom and of understanding, the spirit of counsel and of fortitude, the spirit of knowledge and of godliness
3 be filled with the spirit of the fear
19 3 the spirit of Egypt shall be broken
14 mingled . . . the spirit of giddiness
28 6 spirit of judgment to him that sitteth
29 10 mingled for you the s. of a deep sleep
24 they that erred in spirit, shall know
31 3 their horses, flesh, and not spirit
32 15 until the spirit be poured upon us
37 7 I will send a spirit upon him, and he
42 5 and spirit to them that tread thereon
54 6 woman forsaken and mourning in spirit
57 15 with a contrite and humble spirit, to revive the spirit of the humble
16 the spirit shall go forth from my face
61 3 garment of praise for the s. of grief
63 10 afflicted the spirit of his Holy One
11 midst of them the s. of his Holy One
65 14 you . . . shall howl for grief of spirit
66 2 to him that is . . . of a contrite spirit
Jer 10 14 is false and there is no spirit in them
51 11 raised up spirit of kings of the Medes
Bar 2 17 s. is taken away from their bowels
3 1 and the troubled spirit crieth to thee
Eze 1 12 whither impulse of the s. was to go
20 whithersoever the spirit went, thither as the spirit went the wheels
20 the s. of life was in the wheels. 21
2 2 and the spirit entered into me after
3 12 the spirit took me up, and I heard
14 the spirit also lifted me. 8:3; 11:1, 24; 43:5
14 away . . . in the indignation of my spirit
24 the spirit entered into me and set me
10 17 up: for the spirit of life was in them
11 19 will put a new spirit in their bowels
13 3 prophets that follow their own spirit
18 31 yourselves a new heart and a new spirit
21 7 feeble, and every spirit shall faint
36 26 heart, and put a new spirit within you
37 5 I will send spirit into you, and you
6 I will give you spirit and you shall
8 them, but there was no spirit in them
9 he said to me: Prophesy to the spirit
9 say to the spirit: Thus saith the Lord
9 come, spirit, from the four winds
10 the s. came into them, and they lived
Dan 3 39 in a contrite heart and humble spirit
4 5 the spirit of the holy gods. 6, 15; 5:11
5 12 greater spirit . . . were found in him
14 that thou hast the spirit of the gods
13 45 raised up the holy s. of a young boy
Osee 4 12 s. of fornication hath deceived them
5 4 spirit of fornication is in the midst
Mich 2 11 I were not a man that hath the spirit
Haba 2 19 there is no s. in the bowels thereof
Agge 1 14 Lord stirred up the s. of Zorobabel
14 Lord stirred up . . . the spirit of Jesus
14 the spirit of all the rest of the people
Zach 12 1 and formeth the spirit of man in him
10 I will pour out . . . the spirit of grace
Mala 2 15 keep then your s., and despise not. 16
1 Ma 13 7 the spirit of the people was enkindled
2 Ma 3 24 the spirit of the almighty God gave a
14 46 calling upon the Lord of life and spirit
Mat 4 1 Jesus was led by the spirit into the
5 3 blessed are the poor in spirit: for
10 20 the Spirit of your Father that speaketh
12 31 blasphemy of the Spirit shall not be
22 43 how then doth David in spirit call him
26 41 the s. indeed is willing. Mark 14:38
Mark 1 10 and the Spirit as a dove descending
12 Spirit drove him out into the desert
8 12 sighing deeply in spirit, he saith
9 16 my son to thee, having a dumb spirit
19 the spirit troubled him; and being
24 deaf and dumb spirit, I command thee
Luke 1 17 in the spirit and power of Elias; that
80 grew and was strengthened in spirit
2 27 he came by the Spirit into the temple
4 1 was led by the Spirit into the desert
14 Jesus returned in the power of the s.
8 55 her spirit returned, and she arose
9 39 a spirit seizeth him, and he suddenly
55 you know not of what spirit you are
11 13 give the good Spirit to them that ask
13 11 woman who had a spirit of infirmity
24 37 supposed that they saw a spirit. And
39 a spirit hath not flesh and bones, as
John 1 33 shalt see the Spirit descending and
3 6 which is born of the Spirit is spirit
8 the Spirit breatheth where he will
8 is every one that is born of the Spirit
34 God doth not give the S. by measure
4 23 shall adore the Father in spirit and
24 God is a spirit; and they that adore
24 must adore him in spirit and in truth
6 64 it is the spirit that quickeneth: the
64 I have spoken to you, are spirit and
7 39 this he said of the Spirit which they
39 for as yet the Spirit was not given
11 33 groaned in the spirit and troubled
13 21 these things, he was troubled in s.
14 17 the Spirit of truth, whom the world
15 26 the Spirit of truth, who proceedeth
16 13 when he, the Spirit of truth, is come
Acts 6 10 to resist the wisdom and the spirit
8 29 the Spirit said to Philip: Go near and
10 19 Spirit said to him: Behold three men
11 12 S. said to me, that I should go with
28 Agabus . . . signified by the S., that
16 7 the Spirit of Jesus suffered them not
16 girl, having a pythonical s., met us
18 said to the spirit: I command thee, in
18 25 being fervent in spirit, spoke, and
19 15 the wicked spirit, answering, said to
16 the man in whom the wicked spirit was
21 Paul purposed in the spirit, when he had
20 22 now, behold, being bound in the spirit
21 4 who said to Paul through the Spirit
23 8 no resurrection, neither angel, nor s.
9 what if a spirit hath spoken to him, or

Rom 1 4 according to spirit of sanctification
2 29 circumcision is that . . . in the spirit
7 6 we should serve in newness of spirit
8 2 flesh. For the law of the spirit of life
4 to flesh, but according to the spirit
5 they that are according to the spirit
5 mind the things that are of the spirit
6 wisdom of the spirit is life and peace
9 you are not in the flesh, but in spirit
9 if any man have not the Spirit of Christ
10 spirit liveth, because of justification
11 if the S. of him that raised up Jesus
13 if by the Spirit you mortify the deeds
15 for you have not received the spirit of
15 received the spirit of adoption of sons
16 the Spirit himself giveth testimony to
16 himself giveth testimony to our spirit
23 who have the firstfruits of the Spirit
26 likewise the Spirit also helpeth our
26 the Spirit himself asketh for us with
27 knoweth what the S. desireth; because
11 8 God hath given them s. of insensibility
12 11 in spirit fervent. Serving the Lord
1 C 2 4 but in showing of the Spirit and power
10 for the Spirit searcheth all things, yea
11 but the spirit of a man that is in him
12 we have received not s. of this world
12 world, but the Spirit that is of God
13 wisdom; but in doctrine of the Spirit
4 21 charity, and in the spirit of meekness
5 3 absent in body, but present in s., have
5 that the spirit may be saved in the day
6 11 Jesus Christ, and the Spirit of our God
7 34 may be holy both in body and in spirit
11 8 to one indeed, by the Spirit, is given
12 4 diversities of graces, but same Spirit
7 manifestation of the Spirit is given to
8 knowledge, according to the same Spirit
9 to another, faith in the same spirit
14 2 yet by the Spirit he speaketh mysteries
15 I will pray with the spirit, I will pray
15 will sing with the spirit, I will sing
16 thou shalt bless with the spirit, how
15 45 the last Adam into a quickening spirit
2 C 1 22 given pledge of the Spirit in our hearts
3 3 written not with ink, but with Spirit
6 not in the letter, but in the spirit
6 letter killeth, but the s. quickeneth
8 ministration of s. be rather in glory
17 now the Lord is a Spirit. And where the
4 13 having the same spirit of faith, as it
5 5 who hath given us the pledge of the S.
7 1 defilement of the flesh and of the s.
11 4 or if you receive another Spirit, whom
12 18 did we not walk with the same spirit
Gal 3 2 did you receive the Spirit by the works
3 you began in the Spirit, you would now
5 he therefore who giveth to you the S.
14 that we may receive the promise of S.
4 6 God hath sent the Spirit of his Son into
29 persecuted him that was after the spirit
5 5 we in spirit, by faith, wait for hope
13 by charity of the s. serve one another
16 walk in the spirit, and you shall not
17 the flesh lusteth against the spirit: and the spirit against the flesh
18 but if you are led by the spirit, you
22 but the fruit of the Spirit is, charity
25 if we live in the Spirit, let us also walk in the Spirit
6 1 instruct such a one in s. of meekness
8 soweth in the s., of s. shall reap life
18 Jesus Christ be with your s., brethren
Eph 1 13 signed with the holy Spirit of promise
17 may give unto you the spirit of wisdom
2 2 spirit that now worketh on the children
22 into an habitation of God in the Spirit
3 5 holy apostles and prophets in the Spirit
4 3 careful to keep the unity of the Spirit
23 be renewed in the spirit of your mind
5 18 but be ye filled with the holy Spirit
6 17 salvation, and the sword of the Spirit
18 praying at all times in the spirit; and
Phil 1 19 supply of the Spirit of Jesus Christ
2 1 if any society of the spirit, if any
3 3 circumcision, who in spirit serve God
4 23 Lord Jesus Christ be with your spirit
Col 1 8 manifested to us your love in the spirit
2 5 in body, yet in spirit I am with you
1 Th 4 8 who also hath given his holy Spirit in
5 19 extinguish not the spirit. Despise not
23 your whole spirit and soul and body, may
2 Th 2 2 neither by spirit, nor by word, nor by
8 Lord Jesus shall kill with the spirit
12 in sanctification of the spirit, and
1 Tim 3 16 the flesh, was justified in the spirit
4 1 now the Spirit manifestly saith, that
2 Tim 1 7 God hath not given us the spirit of fear
Philem 25 our Lord Jesus Christ be with your s.
Heb 4 12 unto the division of the soul and spirit
10 29 offered an affront to the S. of grace
James 2 26 the body without the spirit is dead
4 5 to envy doth the spirit covet which
1 P 1 2 unto the sanctification of the Spirit
11 Spirit of Christ in them did signify
3 4 a quiet and a meek spirit, which is
18 in the flesh, but enlivened in the s.
4 6 may live according to God in the Spirit
1 J 3 24 by the Spirit which he hath given us
4 1 believe not every spirit, but try the
2 every s. which confesseth that Jesus
3 every spirit that dissolveth Jesus
6 the s. of truth and the s. of error
5 6 it is the Spirit which testifieth
8 the spirit and the water and the blood
Jude 19 sensual men, having not the Spirit
Apoc 1 10 I was in the spirit on the Lord's day
2 7 what the Spirit saith to the churches. **11, 17, 29; 3:6, 13, 22**
4 2 I was in the spirit: and behold there
11 11 spirit of life from God entered into
14 13 now, saith the Spirit, that they may
17 3 took me away in spirit into the desert
19 10 of Jesus is the spirit of prophecy
21 10 he took me up in spirit to a great and
22 17 the spirit and the bride say: Come

his spirit Gen 45 27 he had sent, his s. revived
Num 11 29 that the Lord would give them his s.
Deut 2 30 God had hardened his spirit and fixed
Judg 15 19 drank them, he refreshed his spirit
1 K 30 12 his s. returned and he was refreshed
Job 26 13 his spirit hath adorned the heavens
34 14 he shall draw his spirit and breath
Ps 105 33 because they exasperated his spirit
145 4 his spirit shall go forth and he shall
Prov 16 32 he that ruleth his spirit than he
25 28 cannot refrain his own s. in speaking
Eccu 38 24 comfort him in the departing of his s.
48 13 his spirit was filled up in Eliseus
Isa 11 15 over the river in the strength of his s.
27 8 hath meditated with his severe spirit
34 16 his spirit it hath gathered them
48 16 Lord God hath sent me, and his spirit
Dan 2 1 had a dream, and his s. was terrified
5 20 and his spirit hardened unto pride
14 35 over the den in the force of his spirit

Zach 7 12 sent in his s. by the hand of the
Haba 1 11 then shall his spirit be changed and
Mala 2 15 and she is the residue of his spirit
Mark 2 8 Jesus presently knowing in his spirit
Acts 17 16 his spirit was stirred within him
Rom 8 11 because of his Spirit that dwelleth in
1 C 2 10 to us God hath revealed them, by his S.
2 C 7 13 because his spirit was refreshed by you
Eph 3 16 glory, to be strengthened by his Spirit
1 P 4 14 that which is his Spirit, resteth upon
1 J 4 13 because he hath given us of his spirit
my spirit Gen 6 3 my s. shall not remain in man
Tob 3 6 command my s. to be received in peace
Job 6 4 the rage whereof drinketh up my spirit
7 11 I will speak in the affliction of my s.
9 18 he alloweth not my spirit to rest
10 12 thy visitation hath preserved my spirit
17 1 my spirit shall be wasted, my days
Ps 30 6 into thy hands I commend my spirit
76 4 and my spirit swooned away. My eyes
7 I was exercised and I swept my spirit
141 4 when my spirit failed me, then thou
142 4 and my spirit is in anguish within me
7 my spirit hath fainted away. Turn not
Prov 1 23 behold I will utter my spirit to you
Eccu 24 27 for my spirit is sweet above honey, and
25 1 with three things my spirit is pleased
Isa 26 9 with my spirit within me in the morning
30 1 would begin a web, and not by my spirit
38 16 life of my spirit be in such things
42 1 I have given my spirit upon him, he
44 3 I will pour out my spirit upon thy seed
59 21 my spirit that is in thee, and my
Eze 36 27 I will put my s. in the midst of you
37 14 and shall have put my spirit in you
39 29 I have poured out my spirit upon all
Dan 7 15 my spirit trembled, I Daniel was
Joel 2 28 I will pour out my s. upon all flesh
29 in those days I will pour forth my s.
Agge 2 6 my spirit shall be in the midst of you
Zach 4 6 not with an army . . . but by my spirit
6 8 quieted my s. in the land of the north
Mat 12 18 I will put my spirit upon him, and he
Luke 1 47 my spirit hath rejoiced in God my
23 46 into thy hands I commend my spirit
Acts 2 17 I will pour out of my Spirit upon all
18 will I pour out . . . of my spirit, and
7 58 saying: Lord Jesus, receive my spirit
Rom 1 9 God . . . whom I serve in my spirit in the
1 C 5 4 my s., with the power of our Lord Jesus
14 14 if I pray in a tongue, my spirit prayeth
16 18 have refreshed both my spirit and yours
2 C 2 13 I had no rest in my spirit, because I
one spirit 1 C 6 17 joined to Lord, is one s.
1 C 12 9 another, grace of healing in one Spirit
11 all these things one and the same Spirit
13 in one Spirit were we all baptized into
13 in one Spirit we have all been made to
Eph 2 18 access both in one Spirit to the Father
4 4 one body and one Spirit; as you are
Phil 1 27 that you stand fast in one spirit, with
spirit of God Gen 41 38 another man, that is full of the s. . . .
Exod 31 3 filled him with the s. . . . , with. 35:31
Num 24 2 s. . . . rushing upon him, he took up
2 Pa 15 1 s. . . . came upon Azarias the son of
24 20 spirit of God then came upon Zacharias
Job 27 3 and the spirit of God in my nostrils
33 4 s. . . . made me, and the breath of
Eze 11 24 brought me . . . by the spirit of God
Dan 6 3 a greater spirit of God was in him
Mat 3 16 he saw the Spirit of God descending
12 28 if I by the Spirit of God cast out
Rom 8 9 so be that the Spirit of God dwell in
14 whosoever are led by the Spirit of God
1 C 2 11 no man knoweth, but the Spirit of God
14 these things that are of the S. of God
3 16 that the Spirit of God dwelleth in you
7 40 I think that I also have the s. of God
12 3 no man, speaking by the Spirit of God
Eph 4 30 and grieve not the holy Spirit of God
1 J 4 2 by this is the Spirit of God known
spirit of the Lord Judg 3 10 s. . . . was in him
Judg 6 34 s. . . . came upon Gedeon, and he sounded
11 29 s. . . . came upon Jephte, and going
13 25 s. . . . began to be with him in the
14 6 s. . . . came upon Samson, and he tore
19 s. . . . came upon him, and he went
15 14 s. . . . came strongly upon him: and as
1 K 10 6 s. . . . shall come upon thee, and thou
10 s. . . . came upon him, and he prophesied
11 6 s. . . . came upon Saul, when he had
16 13 s. . . . came upon David from that day
14 s. . . . departed from Saul, and an evil
19 20 s. . . . came also upon them, and they
23 s. . . . came upon him also, and he
2 K 23 2 s. . . . hath spoken by me and his word
3 K 18 12 s. . . . will carry thee into a place that
22 24 hath then the s. . . . left me, and spoken
4 K 2 16 perhaps s. . . . hath taken him up and
2 Pa 18 23 which way went the s. . . . from me
20 14 upon whom the spirit of the Lord came
Wisd 1 7 the s. . . . hath filled the whole world
Isa 11 2 spirit of the Lord shall rest upon him
40 7 because the s. . . . hath blown upon it
13 who hath forwarded the s. . . . ? Or
59 19 stream, which the s. . . . driveth on
61 1 s. . . . is upon me, because the Lord
63 14 the spirit of the Lord was their leader
Eze 11 5 s. . . . fell upon me and said to me
37 1 and brought me forth in the s. . . .
Mich 2 7 is the spirit of the Lord straitened
3 8 filled with the strength of the s. . . .
Luke 4 18 the Spirit of the Lord is upon me
Acts 5 9 have you agreed to tempt the S. . . .
8 39 the S. . . . took away Philip; and the
2 C 3 17 where the S. . . . is, there is liberty
18 from glory to glory, as by the S. . . .
thy spirit Num 11 17 I will take of thy spirit
2 Es 9 20 and thou gavest them thy good spirit
30 didst testify against them by thy s.
Jdth 16 17 thou didst send forth thy spirit, and
Job 15 13 why doth thy spirit swell against God
Ps 50 13 and take not thy holy spirit from me
103 30 shalt send forth thy s., and they
138 7 whither shall I go from thy spirit
142 10 thy good spirit shall lead me into the
Wisd 12 1 how good and sweet is thy spirit
2 Tim 4 22 Lord Jesus Christ be with thy spirit
unclean spirit Zach 13 2 prophets and the u. s.
Mat 12 43 when an u. s. it gone out. Luke 11:24
Mark 1 23 a man with an unclean s. Mark 5:2
26 the u. s. tearing him and crying out
3 30 because they said: He hath an u. s.
5 8 go out of the man thou unclean spirit
7 25 whose daughter had an unclean spirit
9 24 he threatened the u. s., saying to him
Luke 8 29 commanded the u. s. to go out of the
9 43 Jesus rebuked the unclean spirit and
Apoc 18 2 and the hold of every unclean spirit
spirits Num 16 22 God of the s. of all flesh. 27:16
Deut 18 11 one that consulteth pythonic spirits
4 K 23 24 the diviners by spirits and soothsayers
Jdth 13 30 after he had recovered his spirits
Ps 103 4 who makest thy angels spirits: and
Prov 16 2 the Lord is the weigher of spirits

Wisd 7 23 containing all spirits, intelligible
Eccu 1 28 wrath of his high spirits is his ruin
39 33 spirits that are created for vengeance
Dan 3 65 ye spirits of God, bless the Lord
86 ye spirits and souls of the just, bless
Mat 8 16 he cast out the spirits with his word
12 45 taketh with him 7 other s. Luke 11:26
Mark 5 12 the spirits besought him, saying: Send
Luke 7 21 diseases and hurts, and evil spirits
8 2 who had been healed of evil spirits
10 20 that spirits are subject unto you
Acts 19 12 the wicked spirits went out of them
13 invoke over them that had evil spirits
1 C 12 10 to another, the discerning of spirits
14 12 as you are zealous of spirits, seek to
32 the spirits of the prophets are subject
Eph 6 12 against the spirits of wickedness in
1 Tim 4 1 faith, giving heed to spirits of error
Heb 1 7 he that maketh his angels spirits, and
14 they not all ministering spirits, sent
12 9 obey the Father of spirits and live
23 to the spirits of the just made perfect
1 P 3 19 to those spirits that were in prison
1 J 4 1 but try the spirits if they be of God
Apoc 1 4 seven s. which are before his throne
3 1 he that hath the seven spirits of God
4 5 which are the seven s. of God. 5:6
16 14 they are the spirits of devils working
22 6 God of the spirits of the prophets

unclean spirits Mat 10 1 gave them power over unclean spirits. Mark 6:7
Mark 1 27 he commandeth the u. s. Luke 4:36
3 11 the u. s., when they saw him, fell
5 13 the u. s. going out, entered into the
6 18 that were troubled with u. spirits
Acts 5 16 such as were troubled with u. spirits
8 7 many of them who had unclean spirits
Apoc 16 13 three unclean spirits like frogs. For

spiritual Osee 9 7 foolish, the s. man was mad
Rom 1 11 I may impart unto you some s. grace
7 14 for we know that the law is spiritual
15 27 partakers of their s. things, they ought
1 C 2 13 comparing s. things with spiritual. But
15 the spiritual man judgeth all things
3 1 could not speak to you as unto s., but
9 11 we have sown unto you spiritual things
10 3 and did all eat the same spiritual food
4 and all drank the same spiritual drink
4 they drank of the spiritual rock that
12 1 concerning s. things, my brethren, I
14 1 after charity, be zealous for s. gifts
37 if any seem to be prophet, or spiritual
15 44 natural body, it shall rise a s. body
44 natural body, there is also a s. body
46 not first which is spiritual, but that
46 afterwards that which is spiritual. The
Gal 6 1 you, who are s., instruct such a one in
Eph 1 3 hath blessed us with spiritual blessings
5 19 hymns, and s. canticles. Col 3:16
Col 1 9 in all wisdom, and s. understanding
1 P 2 5 a s. house, a holy priesthood, to
5 to offer up s. sacrifices, acceptable

spiritually 1 C 2 14 because it is s. examined
Apoc 11 8 is called spiritually Sodom and Egypt

spit Deut 25 9 and spit in his face and say
Job 30 10 are not afraid to spit in my face
Eccu 28 14 thou spit upon it, it shall be quenched
Isa 50 6 them that rebuked me and spit upon me
Mat 26 67 then did they spit in his face and
Mark 10 34 they shall mock him and spit on him
14 65 some began to spit on him and to cover
15 19 with a reed; and they did spit on him
Luke 18 32 be mocked and scourged and spit upon

spitten Num 12 14 if father had s. upon her face

spitting Mat 27 30 s. upon him, they took the reed
Mark 7 33 and spitting, he touched his tongue
8 23 spitting upon his eyes, laying his

spittle Lev 15 8 cast his s. upon him that is
Judg 16 9 a thread of tow twined with spittle
1 K 21 13 his spittle ran down upon his beard
Job 7 19 nor suffer me to swallow down my s.
John 9 6 ground, and made clay of the spittle

spoil Gen 49 27 in the evening shall divide the s.
Exod 3 22 and daughters, and shall spoil Egypt
Num 31 20 of all the spoil, every garment or
27 thou shalt divide the spoil equally
32 the spoil which the army had taken
Deut 20 19 neither shalt thou spoil the country
Josu 11 14 divided among themselves all the spoil
4 K 21 14 they shall become a prey and a spoil
2 Pa 25 13 killed 3,000, took away much spoil
1 Es 9 7 and to spoil and to confusion of face
Tob 3 4 therefore are we delivered to spoil
Jdth 5 18 they were given to spoil and to the
Esth 3 13 and to make a spoil of their goods
8 11 all their houses, and to take their s.
Ps 118 162 as one that hath found great spoil
Prov 24 15 house of the just, nor spoil his rest
Ecce 10 1 dying flies spoil the sweetness of the
Isa 3 14 the spoil of the poor is in your house
33 23 divided: the lame shall take the spoil
42 22 a spoil, and there is none that saith
24 who hath given Jacob for a spoil, and
Jer 6 7 violence and s. shall be heard in her
15 13 thy treasures I will give unto spoil
17 3 and all thy treasures to the spoil
21 9 his life shall be to him as a spoil
49 32 and their camels shall be for a spoil
50 37 treasures, and they shall be made a s.
Eze 7 21 into the hands of strangers for spoil
25 7 deliver thee to be the spoil of nations
26 5 she shall be a spoil to the nations
12 shall make a spoil of thy merchandise
34 8 as my flocks have been made a spoil
22 flock, and it shall be no more a spoil
28 they shall be no more for a spoil
Dan 11 33 by fire and by captivity and by spoil
Nah 2 9 take ye the spoil of the silver, take the spoil of the gold
Haba 2 7 and thou shalt be a spoil to them
8 left of the people shall spoil thee
Soph 2 9 remnant of my people shall make a spoil
Mala 3 11 he shall not spoil the fruit of your
1 Ma 13 34 for all that Tryphon did was to spoil

spoiled 1 K 14 48 the hand of them that s. them
2 K 11 1 and they spoiled the children of Ammon
Eccu 36 27 no hedge, the possession shall be s.
Isa 17 14 and the lot of them that spoiled us
18 2 whose land the rivers have spoiled. 7
24 3 waste, and it shall be utterly spoiled
33 1 end of spoiling, thou shalt be spoiled
1 shalt not thou thyself also be spoiled
Jer 4 30 when thou art spoiled what wilt thou
5 6 wolf in the evening hath spoiled them
Eze 36 4 that are forsaken, that are spoiled
Amos 3 11 thee, and thy houses shall be spoiled
Mich 2 4 say: We are laid waste and spoiled
Haba 2 8 thou hast spoiled many nations, all
Zach 11 3 because the pride of the Jordan is s.
1 Ma 6 24 and have spoiled our inheritances
8 10 spoiled them and took possession of
2 Ma 9 16 temple also which before he had spoiled

spoiler Isa 21 2 he that is a spoiler, spoileth
Jer 15 8 upon them . . . a spoiler at noonday
48 8 the spoiler shall come upon every city
18 the spoiler of Moab is come up to thee

51 56 because the spoiler is come upon her
spoilers 4 K 17 20 delivered them into hand of s.
Jer 12 12 the s. are come upon all the ways
51 48 spoilers shall come to her from north
53 there should come spoilers upon her
Nah 2 2 the spoilers have laid them waste
spoilest Isa 33 1 woe to thee that s., shalt not
spoileth Isa 21 2 and he that is a spoiler, s.
spoiling Isa 33 1 shalt have made an end of s.
spoils Exod 15 9 I will divide the spoils, my
Num 21 1 overcoming them carried off their s.
Deut 2 35 spoils of the cities which we took
3 7 s. of the cities we took for our prey
20 14 shalt eat the spoils of thy enemies
Josu 7 21 I saw among the s. a scarlet garment
8 2 s. and all the cattle you shall take
Judg 5 19 Mageddo and yet they took no spoils
30 perhaps he is now dividing the spoils
8 24 give me the earlets of your spoils
25 cast upon it the earlets of the s.
9 25 taking spoils of all that passed by
1 K 14 32 falling upon the spoils, they took
15 12 out of the choicest of the spoils which
21 the people took of the spoils sheep
30 16 and the spoils which they had taken
19 was nothing missing . . . of the spoils
2 K 2 21 one of young men take thee his spoils
8 12 of the spoils of Adarezer the son of
12 30 spoils of the city . . . he carried away
23 10 returned to take spoils of them that
4 K 3 23 one another: go now, Moab, to the s.
1 Pa 10 8 the Philistines taking away the spoils
26 27 the wars, and the spoils won in battles
2 Pa 14 13 and they took abundance of spoils
15 11 sacrificed . . . of the spoils and of
20 25 to take away the spoils of the dead
25 nor in three days take away the spoils
24 23 all the spoils to the king of Damascus
28 14 so the soldiers left the spoils and all
15 and with the spoils clothed all them
Jdth 9 3 and all their spoils to be divided
15 7 took away the s. which the Assyrians
8 all were made rich by their spoils
13 gather up the spoils of the Assyrians
Esth 9 10 they would not touch the spoils of their
Ps 67 13 beauty of the house shall divide spoils
Prov 1 13 we shall fill our houses with spoils
16 19 than to divide spoils with the proud
31 11 and he shall have no need of spoils
Isa 8 1 take away the s. with speed, quickly
3 hasten to take away the spoils: make
4 spoils of Samaria shall be taken away
9 3 a prey, when they divide the spoils
5 every violent taking of s., with tumult
10 6 to take away the s. and to lay hold on
13 have taken the spoils of the princes
33 4 your spoils shall be gathered together
23 the spoils of much prey be divided
53 12 shall divide the spoils of the strong
Eze 29 19 for a prey and rifle the spoils thereof
38 12 to take spoils and lay hold on the prey
13 art thou come to take spoils? Behold
13 and substance, and to take rich spoils
Dan 11 24 he shall scatter their spoils and
Mich 4 13 shalt immolate the spoils of them to
Zach 14 1 thy s. shall be divided in the midst
1 Ma 1 36 gathered together the s. of Jerusalem
2 10 her kingdom and gotten of her spoils
3 12 he took their spoils, and Judas took the
20 and our children, and to take our s.
4 17 be not greedy of the spoils: for there
18 you shall take the spoils afterwards
23 Judas returned to take the spoils
5 13 captives, and taken their spoils
28 and took all their spoils and burnt it
6 6 store of spoils which they had gotten
12 also I took away all the spoils of gold
9 40 mountains, and they took all their s.
10 87 with his people, having many spoils
11 48 fire to the city, and got many spoils
51 returned to Jerusalem with many spoils
2 Ma 8 27 together their arms and their spoils
28 they divided the spoils to the feeble
30 they divided amongst them many spoils
31 residue of their spoils they carried to
Luke 11 22 trusted, and will distribute his s.
took the spoils 1 Pa 20 2 took also the s. of the city
Wisd 10 19 the just took the spoils of the wicked
1 Ma 1 3 and took the spoils of many nations
20 he took the spoils of the land of Egypt
33 he took the s. of the city and burnt
5 22 he [Simon] took the spoils of them
35 took the spoils thereof and burnt it
51 he razed the city and took the spoils
68 he took the spoils of the cities and
7 47 they took the spoils of them for a
10 84 took the spoils of them and the temple
11 61 suburbs round about and took the s.
12 31 defeated them and took the spoils of
spokes 3 K 7 33 spokes and strakes and naves
sponge Mat 27 48 took a s. and filled it with
Mark 15 36 one running and filling a sponge with
John 19 29 putting a sponge full of vinegar about
sport Prov 10 23 mischief as it were for sport
sporting 2 P 2 13 s. themselves to excess
spot Lev 13 31 if he perceive the place of the s.
Lev 13 32 if the spot be not grown, and the hair
33 shaven all but the place of the spot
35 the spot spread again in the skin, he
37 if the spot be stayed, and the hair be
49 it be infected with a white or red spot
57 places that before were without spot
14 56 blisters breaking out, of a shining s.
Deut 18 13 shalt be . . . without spot before the
2 K 2 23 he [Asae] died upon the spot; and all
Job 11 15 thou lift up thy face without spot
15 14 man that he should be without spot
31 7 if a spot hath cleaved to my hands
Ps 18 14 then shall I be without spot: and I
Cant 4 7 my love, and there is not a spot in thee
Wisd 13 14 covering every spot that is in it
Eph 5 27 a glorious church, not having spot or
1 Tim 6 14 thou keep the commandment without spot
Apoc 14 5 without spot before the throne of God
spotless Ps 17 24 I shall be s. with him: and
Wisd 4 9 gray hairs. And a s. life is old age
Jude 24 to present you spotless before the
spots Lev 14 44 walls full of s., it is a lasting
2 P 2 13 stains and spots, sporting themselves
Jude 12 these are spots in their banquets
spotted Gen 30 32 all that is brown and s. and
Gen 30 33 not of divers colors and spotted
35 rams of divers colors and spotted
39 brought forth spotted and of divers
31 10 were of divers colors and spotted
12 are of divers colors, spotted and
Lev 13 15 if it be spotted with leprosy, is
Jude 23 hating also the spotted garment which
spouse Exod 4 25 a bloody s. art thou to me. 26
Cant 4 8 come from Libanus, my spouse, come
9 wounded my heart, my sister, my spouse
10 thy breasts, my sister, my spouse
11 thy lips, my spouse, as a dropping
12 my spouse is a garden enclosed, a
5 1 into my garden, O my sister, my spouse
Wisd 8 2 have desired to take her for my spouse

spouses Osee 4 13 your s. shall be adulteresses
Osee 4 14 I will not visit . . . upon your spouses
spread Gen 9 19 all mankind s. over the whole
Gen 10 18 of the Chanaanites were spread abroad
28 14 thou shalt spread abroad to the west
Exod 40 17 spread the roof over the tabernacle
Lev 13 5 hath not spread itself in the skin
6 obscure and not spread in the skin
22 if it spread, he shall judge him to
35 the spot spread again in the skin he
55 nor yet the leprosy spread, he shall
14 39 if he find that the leprosy is spread
48 that the leprosy is not spread in the
Num 4 6 shall spread over it a cloth. 8
11 spread over it a cover of violet. 12
Deut 22 17 they shall spread the cloth before
32 11 he spread his wings and hath taken
Judg 15 9 Jawbone, where their army was spread
19 27 with her hands spread on the threshold
Ruth 1 19 the report was quickly spread among all
3 9 spread thy coverlet over thy servant
15 spread thy mantle wherewith thou art
15 and when she spread it and held it
1 K 30 16 were lying spread upon all the ground
2 K 5 22 s. themselves in the valley of Raphaim
16 22 so they spread a tent for Absalom on
17 19 s. a covering over the mouth of the
21 10 took haircloth and spread it under her
22 43 I shall crush them and spread them
3 K 8 7 the cherubims spread forth their wings
22 spread forth his hands towards heaven
38 shall s. forth his hands in this house
54 had spread his hands towards heaven
4 K 8 15 spread it upon his face; and he died
19 14 s. it before the Lord, and he prayed
1 Pa 14 9 the Philistines came and s. themselves
13 spread themselves abroad in the valley
2 Pa 3 13 wings of the two cherubims were spread
5 8 so that the cherubims s. their wings
6 29 pray and shall spread forth his hands
25 13 spread themselves among the cities of
26 8 his name was spread abroad even to the
28 18 the Philistines also spread themselves
1 Es 9 5 and spread out my hands to the Lord
Job 11 13 heart and hast spread thy hands to him
36 29 if he will s. out clouds as his tent
37 11 the clouds spread their light: which
38 24 by what way is the light spread, and
Ps 43 21 if we have spread forth our hands to a
104 39 he spread a cloud for their protection
Prov 1 17 a net is spread in vain before the eyes
23 32 will s. abroad poison like a basilisk
Wisd 17 20 over them only was s. a heavy night
Isa 19 8 they that spread nets upon the waters
33 23 shalt not be able to spread the flag
37 14 and Ezechias spread it before the Lord
58 5 and to spread sackcloth and ashes
65 2 I have spread forth my hands all the
Jer 8 2 shall spread them abroad to the sun
10 9 silver spread into plates is brought
49 22 he shall spread his wings over Bosra
50 11 you are spread abroad as calves upon
Lam 1 13 he hath spread a net for my feet, he
17 Sion hath s. forth her hands, there
Eze 2 9 and he spread it before me, and it
12 13 I will spread my net over him, and he
16 8 and I spread my garment over thee
17 20 I will spread my net over him and
19 8 and they spread their net over him
27 7 thy sail, to be spread on thy mast
31 6 when he had spread forth his shadow
32 3 I will spread out my net over thee
23 spread terror in the land of the living
25 they spread their terror in the. 26
32 I have spread my terror in the land
Osee 5 1 over, and a net spread upon Thabor
7 9 gray hairs also are spread about upon
12 I will spread my net upon them: I
14 7 his branches shall spread, and his
Joel 2 2 the morning spread upon the mountains
Nah 3 16 the bruchus hath spread himself and
Haba 1 8 their horsemen shall be spread abroad
2 Ma 4 39 and the humor of it was spread abroad
8 7 fame of his valor and spread abroad
Mat 9 31 spread his fame abroad in all that
21 8 s. their garments in the way. Mark 11:8
28 15 this word was spread abroad among the
Mark 1 28 the fame of him was spread forthwith
Luke 19 36 they spread their clothes underneath
John 9 6 and spread the clay upon his eyes
Acts 4 17 that it may be no farther spread among
Rom 10 21 I s. my hands to a people that believeth
1 Th 1 8 from you was spread abroad the word of
spreadeth Job 9 8 who alone s. out the heavens
Job 26 9 throne, and spreadeth his cloud over it
Prov 29 5 words, spreadeth a net for his feet
Isa 6 13 as an oak that spreadeth its branches
40 22 and s. them out as a tent to dwell in
Jer 17 8 that s. out its roots towards moisture
Haba 1 17 he spreadeth his net and will not
2 Tim 2 17 their speech spreadeth like a canker
spreading Exod 25 20 s. their wings and. 37:9
Num 17 8 s. the leaves, were formed into almonds
Judg 8 25 s. a mantle on the ground, they cast
1 Pa 28 18 of the cherubims spreading their wings
Job 39 26 spreading her wings to the south
Wisd 17 17 among the spreading branches of trees
Jer 4 31 of Sion, dying away, s. her hands
Eze 17 6 grew into a s. vine of low stature
31 7 and for the spreading of his branches
sprigs Isa 18 5 the sprigs thereof shall be cut off
Eze 17 6 branches, and shot forth sprigs
spring Gen 2 6 a spring rose out of the earth
Gen 17 16 kings of people shall spring from him
19 25 all things that spring from the earth
24 13 I stand nigh the spring of water, and
16 she went down to the s. and filled her
30 stood by the camels and near to the s.
Exod 10 5 all the trees that spring in the fields
Lev 13 12 if the leprosy spring out running
Num 21 17 this song: Let the well spring out
24 17 a scepter shall spring up from Israel
Deut 16 1 month of new corn . . . first of the s.
Judg 15 19 the Spring of him that invoked from
4 K 2 21 he went out to the spring of the waters
19 29 such things as spring of themselves
Jdth 7 10 about a hundred men at every spring
Job 5 6 sorrow doth not s. out of the ground
8 19 that others may spring again out of
14 9 at the scent of water, it shall spring
31 12 and rooteth up all things that spring
Ps 64 11 it shall spring up and rejoice in its
71 7 in his days shall justice spring up
73 17 summer and the s. were formed by thee
91 8 when the wicked shall s. up as grass
Prov 11 28 the just shall s. up as a green leaf
25 26 is as . . . and a corrupted spring
Ecce 11 6 knowest not which may rather s. up
Eccu 46 14 their bones spring up out of their
49 12 bones of the twelve prophets spring up
50 8 of roses in the days of the spring
Isa 15 6 withered away, the spring is faded
37 30 eat . . . things that s. of themselves
42 5 and the things that spring out of it
9 before they spring forth, I will make
43 19 now they shall spring forth, verily

44 4 they shall spring up among the herbs
45 8 and let justice spring up together
55 10 make it to spring and give seed to the
61 11 Lord God make justice to spring forth
Jer 33 15 bud of justice to spring forth unto
51 36 desolate, and will dry up her spring
Dan 3 76 ye things that spring up in the earth
Osee 10 4 judgment shall spring up as bitterness
14 6 Israel shall spring as the lily, and
Haba 3 17 there shall be no spring in the vines
Zach 6 12 under him shall he spring up and shall
Mark 4 27 and the seed should spring, and grow
springeth 2 K 23 4 the grass s. out of the earth
2 K 23 5 ought thereof that springeth not up
Eccu 14 18 leaf that s. out on a green tree
springing Wisd 19 7 of the great deep a s. field
Jer 2 31 Israel, or a lateward springing land
Zach 9 17 the elect, and wine s. forth virgins
John 4 14 springing up into life everlasting
Heb 12 15 any root of bitterness springing up
springs 4 K 3 19 shall stop up all the s. of
4 K 3 25 they stopt up all the springs of waters
2 Pa 32 3 to stop up the heads of the springs
4 and they stopped up all the springs
Jdth 7 7 were springs not far from the walls
9 set guards at the springs that they
Ps 103 10 sendest forth springs in the vales
106 35 and a dry land into water springs
118 136 my eyes have sent forth s. of water
Isa 35 7 thirsty land [shall become] springs of
Osee 13 15 it shall dry up his springs and shall
Joel 1 20 the springs of waters are dried up
springtime Gen 35 16 he came in the s. to the
Gen 48 7 Rachel died . . . and it was springtime
Exod 34 18 springtime thou camest out from Egypt
4 K 5 19 departed from him in the springtime
sprinkle Exod 9 8 let Moses sprinkle it in the air
Exod 12 22 and sprinkle the transom of the door
29 21 shalt sprinkle Aaron and his vesture
Lev 4 6 he shall sprinkle with it seven times
17 sprinkle it seven times before the veil
5 9 shall sprinkle the side of the altar
14 7 shall s. him that is to be cleansed
16 and s. it before the Lord seven times
27 he shall sprinkle it seven times
51 shall sprinkle the house seven times
16 14 sprinkle with his finger seven times
15 may sprinkle it over against the oracle
Num 19 4 shall sprinkle it over against the door
18 shall sprinkle therewith all the tent
Ps 50 9 thou shalt sprinkle me with hyssop
Isa 32 15 he shall sprinkle many nations, kings
Jer 6 26 and sprinkle thee with ashes: make
25 34 sprinkle yourselves with ashes, ye
Mich 1 10 sprinkle yourselves with dust. And
sprinkle Exod 9 8 let Moses sprinkle it in the air
Exod 24 8 blood and sprinkled it upon the people
Lev 6 27 if a garment be s. with the blood
8 11 and sprinkled the altar seven times
30 he sprinkled Aaron and his vestments
Num 8 7 let them be sprinkled with the water
19 12 shall be sprinkled with this water
12 if he were not s. on the third day
13 and is not s. with this mixture, shall
13 not s. with the water of expiation
20 not s. with the water of purification
21 he also that sprinkled the water
4 K 9 33 the wall was sprinkled with her blood
2 Pa 29 24 sprinkled their blood before the altar
35 11 the priests sprinkled the blood with
Job 2 12 they sprinkled dust upon their heads
18 15 let brimstone be sprinkled in his tent
Isa 63 3 their blood is s. upon my garments
Lam 2 10 they have s. their heads with dust
Eze 27 30 heads, and shall be s. with ashes
Dan 4 20 let it be s. with the dew of heaven
2 Ma 1 21 be sprinkled with the same water
Heb 9 13 the ashes of an heifer being sprinkled
19 sprinkled both the book itself and all
21 in like manner, he sprinkled with blood
10 22 having our hearts sprinkled from an evil
Apoc 19 13 clothed with a garment s. with blood
sprinkling Lev 16 19 s. with his finger seven times
3 K 20 38 disguised himself by s. dust on his
2 Ma 10 25 sprinkling earth upon their heads and
Heb 12 24 to the s. of blood which speaketh
1 P 1 2 and s. of the blood of Jesus Christ
sprout Job 14 7 again, and the boughs thereof s.
sprung Gen 2 5 plant of the field before it s.
Gen 41 6 seven other ears spurng up thin and
23 other seven . . . sprung of the stock
Exod 1 7 increased and s. up into multitudes
Ps 84 12 truth is sprung out of the earth: and
Prov 8 24 fountains of waters as yet sprung out
Eze 17 6 and it sprung up and grew into a
Dan 7 8 horn sprung out of the midst of them
Joel 2 22 places of the wilderness are sprung
Agge 2 20 is the seed as yet sprung up? Or
Mat 4 16 shadow of death, light is sprung up
13 5 and they sprung up immediately
26 when the blade was sprung up, and had
Luke 8 6 and as soon as it was sprung up, it
8 being sprung up, yielded fruit a
Heb 7 14 evident that our Lord s. out of Juda: in
11 12 there sprung even from one, and him as
spun Exod 35 25 gave such things as they had spun
spy Num 13 26 they that went to spy out the land
Josu 2 1 from Setim two men to spy secretly
2 there are men come . . . to spy the land
6 25 whom he had sent to spy out Jericho
Judg 18 2 to spy out the land and to view it
2 K 10 3 to search and spy into the city and
1 Pa 19 3 to consider and search and spy out
Eccu 8 14 lest he sit as a spy to entrap thee
11 32 as a spy that looketh on the fall
Gal 2 4 who came in privately to spy our liberty
squander Prov 29 3 shall s. away his substance
Eccu 14 4 will squander away his goods in rioting
square Exod 38 1 of setim wood, five cubits s.
3 K 5 17 of the temple and should square them
6 35 golden plates in square work by rule
7 5 over the pillars were square beams
31 spaces between the pillars were square
Jdth 1 2 on the square of them, each side was
Isa 9 10 but we will build with square stones
Lam 3 9 shut up my ways with square stones
Eze 40 42 tables . . . were made of square stones
Amos 5 11 shall build houses with square stone
1 Ma 10 11 with square stones for fortification
squared Jdth 1 2 of stones squared and hewed
squeezeth Prov 30 33 he that strongly s. the paps
stab 2 K 2 22 lest I be obliged to stab thee to
2 K 18 11 why didst thou not stab him [Absalom]
stabbed 2 K 4 6 s. him in the groin and fled
Jdth 5 28 then shall he with them be stabbed
6 4 and thou shalt be stabbed and fall
Jer 18 21 let their young men be stabbed with
Eze 23 47 let them be stabbed with their swords
stable Eze 25 5 make Rabbath a s. for camels
stables 2 Pa 9 25 40,000 horses in the stables
Stachys Rom 16 9 and Stachys, my beloved. Salute
stacks Exod 22 6 if a fire . . . catch s. of corn
stacte Exod 30 34 take unto thee spices, stacte
Ps 44 9 myrrh and stacte and cassia perfume
Eze 27 19 stacte and calamus were in thy market
staff Gen 32 10 with my s. I passed over this

Gen 38 18 staff which thou holdest in thy hand
25 whose ring and bracelet and s. this is
Exod 21 19 and walk abroad upon his staff, he that
Lev 26 26 have broken the staff of your bread
Num 22 27 her sides more vehemently with a s.
1 K 17 7 staff of his spear was like a weaver's
40 he took his staff, which he had always
43 that thou comest to me with a staff
2 K 23 7 with iron and with the s. of a lance
4 K 4 29 take my staff in thy hand and go
29 lay my staff upon the face of the child
31 laid the s. upon the face of the child
18 21 trust in Egypt a s. of a broken reed
1 Pa 11 23 and he went down to him with a staff
20 5 s. of whose spear was like a weaver's
Tob 5 23 hast taken the staff of our old age
10 4 of our eyes, the staff of our old age
Ps 22 4 and thy staff, they have comforted me
Isa 10 5 he is the rod and the staff of my anger
15 a staff exalt itself, which is but wood
24 he shall lift up his staff over thee
14 5 Lord hath broken the s. of the wicked
28 27 cummin [shall be beaten] with a staff
36 6 thou trustest upon this broken staff
Jer 48 17 how is the strong staff broken, the
Eze 4 16 will break in pieces the staff of bread
5 16 will break among you the staff of bread
14 13 will break the s. of the bread thereof
29 6 thou hast been a staff of a reed
Osee 4 12 their staff hath declared unto them
Zach 8 4 every man with his staff in his hand
Mat 10 10 nor two coats nor shoes nor a staff
Mark 6 8 nothing for the way, but a staff only
Luke 9 3 neither staff nor scrip nor bread nor
stagger Job 12 25 he shall make them s. like men
Ecce 12 3 the strong men shall stagger and the
Isa 29 9 astonished and wonder, waver and s.
9 stagger, and not with drunkenness. For
Mat 21 21 if you shall have faith and stagger not
Mark 11 23 not stagger in his heart, but believe
staggered Jer 51 7 and therefore they have s.
Rom 4 20 in the promise also of God he s. not
staggering Job 4 4 confirmed them that were s.
Isa 28 1 the fat valley, staggering with wine
stags Ps 28 9 voice of the Lord prepareth the s.
stain Josu 22 17 stain of that crime remaineth
Eccu 33 24 let no stain sully thy glory. In the
1 Ma 9 10 brethren and let us not stain our glory
2 Ma 6 25 a stain and a curse upon my old age
stained Num 35 33 is s. with the blood of the
Eccu 34 21 the offering of him . . . is stained
47 22 thou hast stained thy glory and defiled
Isa 63 3 and I have stained all my apparel. For
Jer 2 22 thou art stained in thy iniquity before
stains 2 P 2 13 stains and spots, sporting
stairs 3 K 6 8 by winding s. they went up to
2 Pa 9 11 of the thyine trees stairs in house of
2 Es 12 36 by the stairs of the city of David
Eze 41 7 going up by winding stairs, and it led
Acts 21 35 when he was come to stairs, it fell out
40 Paul standing on the stairs, beckoned
stake Eccu 27 2 a s. sticketh fast in the midst
Eccu 37 10 lest he thrust a stake into the ground
stakes Josu 23 13 and s. in your eyes till he take
Job 40 19 bore through his nostrils with stakes
Isa 54 2 thy cords, and strengthen thy stakes
stalk Gen 41 5 ears of corn came up upon one s.
Gen 41 22 seven ears of corn grew upon one s.
Osee 8 7 there is no standing stalk in it
stalks Josu 2 6 covered them with the s. of flax
stallion Eccu 33 6 a mocker, is like a s. horse
stallions Jer 5 8 as amorous horses and s.
stalls Num 32 16 we will make sheepfolds and s.
Num 32 24 folds and stalls for your sheep and
3 K 4 26 had 40,000 stalls of chariot horses
2 Pa 32 28 stalls for all beasts and folds for
Haba 3 17 there shall be no herd in the stalls
stammerers Isa 32 4 tongue of s. shall speak
stamp Eze 6 11 and stamp with thy foot and say
stamped Eze 25 6 hands, and s. with thy foot
Dan 7 19 the rest he s. upon with his feet
8 7 on the ground, he stamped upon him
stand Mat 6 5 that love to stand and pray in the
Mat 12 25 divided against itself shall not stand
26 how then shall his kingdom s. Luke 11:18
47 and thy brethren s. without. Luke 8:20
16 28 some of them that s. here. Mark 8:39
20 6 why stand you here all the day idle
Mark 3 3 withered hand: Stand up in the midst
24 that kingdom cannot stand. And if a
25 that house cannot stand. And if Satan
26 he is divided and cannot stand, but
11 25 when you shall stand to pray, forgive
13 9 you shall stand before governors and
Luke 1 19 I am Gabriel, who stand before God
6 8 arise, and stand forth in the midst
13 25 you shall begin to stand without and
21 36 and to stand before the Son of man
John 11 42 because of the people who stand about
Acts 1 11 why stand you looking up to heaven
8 38 commanded the chariot to stand still
14 9 s. upright on thy feet. And he leaped
25 10 I stand at Caesar's judgment seat, where
26 6 fathers, do I stand subject to judgment
16 rise up, and stand upon thy feet: for
22 I s. unto this day, witnessing both to
Rom 5 2 we stand, and glory in hope of the glory
9 11 God, according to election, might stand
14 4 shall s.: for God is able to make him s.
10 we shall all s. before the judgment seat
1 C 2 5 faith might not s. on the wisdom of men
10 12 he that thinketh himself to s., let him
15 1 have received, and wherein you stand
16 13 watch ye, stand fast in the faith, do
2 C 1 23 helpers of your joy: for in faith you s.
13 1 three witnesses shall every word stand
Gal 5 1 stand fast, and be not held again under
Eph 6 11 that you may be able to stand against
13 day, and to stand in all things perfect
14 stand therefore, having your loins girt
Phil 1 27 that you stand fast in one spirit, with
4 1 so stand fast in the Lord, my dearly
Col 4 12 that you may stand perfect, and full in
1 Th 3 8 now we live, if you stand in the Lord
2 Th 2 14 stand fast; and hold the traditions
James 2 3 stand thou there, or sit under my
1 P 5 12 true grace of God, wherein you stand
Apoc 3 20 I stand at the gate and knock. If any
6 17 is come, and who shall be able to stand
11 4 that stand before the Lord of the earth
18 15 shall stand afar off from her, for
standard Exod 30 13 according to s. of the temple
Exod 38 24 according to the s. of the sanctuary
Isa 11 12 shall set up a s. unto the nations
49 22 will set up my standard to the people
62 10 lift up the standard to the people
Jer 4 6 set up the s. in Sion. Strengthen
6 1 set up the standard over Bethacarem
50 2 and publish it, lift up a standard
51 12 upon walls of Babylon set up the s.
27 set ye up a standard in the land
standards Num 2 2 by their troops, ensigns, and s.
standers-by Mark 14 69 began to say to the s.
Mark 15 35 some of the standers-by hearing, said
standest Acts 7 33 place wherein thou s. is holy
Rom 11 20 thou s. by faith: be not highminded, but

standeth John 3 29 who standeth and heareth him
Acts 4 10 this man s. here before you whole
Rom 14 4 to his own lord he standeth or falleth
2 Tim 2 19 the sure foundation of God standeth firm
Heb 10 11 priest indeed standeth daily ministering
James 5 9 the judge standeth before the door
Apoc 10 8 from hand of the angel who standeth
standing Mat 20 3 others s. in the market place
Mat 20 6 went out and found others standing
24 15 standing in the holy place: he that
Mark 3 31 s. without, sent unto him, calling him
10 49 Jesus, standing still, commanded him
13 14 desolation, s. where it ought not: he
Luke 1 11 angel of the Lord, s. on the right
4 39 standing over her, he commanded the
5 2 saw two ships standing by the lake
7 38 standing behind at his feet, she
9 27 there are some standing here that
18 11 the Pharisee s., prayed thus with
13 the publican, s. afar off, would not
40 Jesus s., commanded him to be brought
19 8 Zacheus standing, said to the Lord
32 found the colt standing as he had said
John 5 13 from the multitude s. in the place
11 56 with another, standing in the temple
18 18 Peter also, s. and warming himself
22 one of the servants standing by, gave
25 Peter was standing and warming himself
19 26 the disciple standing whom he loved
20 14 saw Jesus standing, and she knew not
Acts 2 14 Peter standing up with the eleven
4 14 been healed, standing with them, they
5 20 go and standing speak in the temple
23 the keepers standing before the doors
25 are in the temple s. and teaching the
7 55 Jesus s. on the right hand of God
11 13 seen an angel in his house, standing
16 9 man of Macedonia s. and beseeching him
17 22 Paul s. in the midst of the Areopagus
22 13 coming to me, and standing by me, said
23 11 Lord standing by him, said: Be constant
24 20 iniquity, when s. before the council
21 that I cried, s. among them, concerning
27 21 Paul s. forth in the midst of them, said
Heb 9 8 the former tabernacle was yet standing
Apoc 5 6 a Lamb standing as it were slain
7 1 angels s. on the four corners of the
9 s. before the throne and in sight of
8 2 seven angels s. in the presence of God
10 5 s. upon the sea and upon the earth
15 2 standing on the sea of glass, having
18 10 s. afar off for fear of her torments
19 17 I saw an angel standing in the sun
20 12 standing in the presence of the throne
star Num 24 17 a star shall rise out of Jacob
Job 11 17 thou shalt rise as the day star. And
38 32 canst thou bring forth the day star
32 and make the evening star to rise
Ps 109 3 before the day star I begot thee. The
Eccu 50 6 shone in his days as the morning star
Amos 5 26 star of your god, which you made to
Mat 2 2 we have seen his star in the east and
7 the time of the star which appeared to
9 the star which they had seen in the
10 seeing the star they rejoiced with
Acts 7 43 and the star of your god Rempham
1 C 15 41 for star differeth from star in glory
2 P 1 19 and the day star arise in your hearts
Apoc 2 28 and I will give him the morning star
8 10 a great star fell from heaven, burning
11 name of the star is called Wormwood
9 1 I saw a star fall from heaven upon the
22 16 the bright and morning star. And the
stare Job 15 12 why dost thou s. with thy eyes
stared Ps 21 18 they have looked and s. upon me
stars Gen 1 16 to rule the night: and the stars
Gen 15 5 number the stars if thou canst. And he
37 9 moon and eleven stars worshipping me
Judg 5 20 the stars remaining in their order and
2 Es 4 21 of the morning till the stars appear
Job 3 9 let the stars be darkened with the mist
9 7 shutteth up the s. as it were under a
22 12 elevated above the height of the stars
25 5 and the stars are not pure in his sight
38 7 when the morning stars praised me
31 able to join together the shining s.
Ps 8 4 and the stars which thou hast founded
135 9 moon and the stars to rule the night
146 4 who telleth the number of the stars
148 3 praise him, all ye stars and light
Ecce 12 2 the moon and the stars be darkened
Wisd 7 19 year and the dispositions of the stars
29 and above all the order of the stars
10 17 and for the light of stars by night
13 2 swift air or the circle of the stars
17 5 bright flames of the stars enlighten
Eccu 43 10 the glory of the stars is the beauty
44 23 he would exalt his seed as the stars
Isa 14 13 I will exalt my throne above the stars
47 13 that gazed at the stars and counted
Jer 31 35 the order of the moon and of the stars
Bar 3 34 the stars have given light in their
6 59 the stars being bright, and sent forth
Eze 32 7 I will make the stars thereof dark
Dan 8 10 down of the strength and of the stars
12 3 instruct many to justice, as stars
Joel 2 10 the stars have withdrawn their. 3:15
Abdi 4 thou set thy nest among the stars
Mat 24 29 the stars shall fall from heaven and
Luke 21 25 signs in the sun . . . and in the stars
Acts 27 20 when neither sun nor stars appeared for
1 C 15 41 glory of the stars. For star differeth
Jdth 1 13 wandering stars, to whom the storm of
Apoc 1 16 he had in his right hand seven stars
20 the mystery of the seven stars, which
20 the seven stars are the angels of the
2 1 who holdeth the 7 stars in his right
3 1 spirits of God and the seven stars
6 13 the stars from heaven fell upon the
8 12 moon, and the third part of the stars
12 1 on her head a crown of twelve stars
stars of heaven Gen 22 17 multiply thy seed as the stars of heaven. 26:4
Exod 32 13 will multiply your seed as the s. . . .
Deut 1 10 and you are this day as the s. . . . for
4 19 sun and the moon and all the s. . . .
10 22 God hath multiplied thee as the s. . . .
28 62 number who before were as the s. . . .
1 Pa 27 23 would multiply Israel like the s. . . .
2 Es 9 23 multiply their children as the s. . . .
Isa 13 10 the s. . . . and their brightness shall not
Jer 33 22 as the s. . . . cannot be numbered nor
Dan 3 36 multiply their seed as the s. . . .
63 ye stars of heaven, bless the Lord
Nah 3 16 thy merchandises above the s. . . .
2 Ma 9 10 he could reach to the stars of heaven
Mark 13 25 the stars of heaven shall be falling
Heb 11 12 as the stars of heaven in multitude, and
Apoc 12 4 the third part of the stars of heaven
state Judg 20 27 of him concerning their state
2 Pa 24 13 house of the Lord in its former state
Job 14 2 never continueth in the same state
Eccu 38 39 shall strengthen the s. of the world
Eze 16 55 shall return to their ancient state
55 shall return to your ancient state
Amos 6 1 in with state into the house of Israel

2 Ma 14 10 not possible that the state should be
Mat 12 45 the last state of that man is made
Luke 11 26 the last state of that man becomes
Phil 4 11 I have learned, in whatsoever s. I am
2 P 2 20 their latter state is become unto them
stately Jdth 2 14 and he forced all s. cities
stater 4 K 7 1 flour shall be sold for a stater
4 K 7 1 two bushels of barley for a stater. 16
16 bushel of fine flour was sold for a s.
18 a bushel of fine flour for a stater
18 two bushels of barley shall be for a s.
Mat 17 26 thou shalt find a stater: take that
staters Jer 32 9 I weighed him the money, 7 s.
Eze 4 10 shall be in weight 20 staters a day
station Eccu 33 12 and turned them from their s.
Isa 22 19 I will drive thee out from thy station
Dan 2 48 king advanced Daniel to a high station
1 Tim 2 2 for all that are in high station: that
statuary Zach 11 13 cast it to the s., a handsome
Zach 11 13 into the house of the Lord to the s.
statue Gen 19 26 was turned into a statue of salt
Deut 16 22 make nor set up to thyself a statue
4 K 10 26 brought the statue out of Baal's temple
2 Pa 33 7 a molten statue in the house of God
Isa 40 19 hath the workman cast a graven statue
Dan 2 31 there was as it were a great statue
31 this statue, which was great and high
32 head of this statue was of fine gold
34 it struck the statue upon the feet
35 but the stone that struck the statue
3 1 Nabuchodonosor made a statue of gold
2 s. which king Nabuchodonosor had. 7
3 they stood before the statue which king
5 s. which king Nabuchodonosor hath set
10 himself and adore the golden statue
12 statue which thou hast set up. 18
14 the golden statue that I have set up
15 and adore the statue which I have made
statues Exod 23 24 break their s. 34:13; Deut 7:5
Num 33 52 break in pieces their statues and waste
Deut 12 3 break down their statues, burn their
3 K 14 23 they also built them altars and statues
4 K 3 2 he took away the statues of Baal which
17 10 they made them statues and groves on
18 4 broke the s. in pieces and cut down
23 14 and he broke in pieces the statues
2 Pa 14 3 broke the statues and cut down the
28 2 moreover also he cast s. for Baalim
33 19 and set up groves and statues before
Wisd 14 16 s. were worshipped by the commandment
Jer 43 13 he shall break the statues of the house
Eze 26 11 thy famous statues shall fall to the
Mich 5 12 destroy thy graven things and thy s.
1 Ma 5 68 he burnt the statues of their gods
stature Deut 2 21 great and many and of tall s.
1 K 16 7 nor on the height of his stature
2 K 21 20 where there was a man of great stature
1 Pa 11 23 whose stature was of five cubits and
20 6 a man of great stature, whose fingers
Cant 7 7 thy stature is like to a palm tree
Isa 10 33 the tall of stature shall be cut down
45 14 men of stature shall come over to thee
Bar 3 26 of great stature, expert in war. The
Eze 17 6 grew into spreading vine of low stature
19 11 her s. was exalted among the branches
31 3 full of leaves, of a high stature, and
Dan 2 31 which was great and high, tall of s.
Mat 6 27 add to his s. one cubit. Luke 12:25
Luke 19 3 crowd, because he was low of stature
statute 1 K 30 25 and since was made a statute
2 Ma 10 8 they ordained by a common statute and
statutes Deut 4 5 I have taught you statutes
3 K 6 12 if thou wilt walk in my statutes and
8 61 that we may walk in his statutes and
Ps 118 86 all thy statutes are truth: they have
Eze 20 11 I gave them my statutes and I showed
13 they walked not in my statutes, and
16 walked not in my s. and violated
18 walk not in the s. of your fathers
19 walk ye in my statutes, and observe
24 had cast off my s. and had violated
25 I also gave them s. that were not good
Mich 6 16 thou hast kept the statutes of Amri
staves Exod 12 11 holding staves in your hands
Exod 35 12 ark and the staves, the propitiatory
Num 21 18 of the lawgiver and with their staves
3 K 8 7 covered the ark and the staves thereof
8 whereas the staves stood out, the ends
1 Pa 15 15 upon their shoulders, with the staves
2 Pa 5 8 covered the ark itself and its staves
9 ends of the staves wherewith the ark
Mark 14 43 multitude with swords and staves from
48 with swords and staves to apprehend
stay Gen 19 17 neither s. thou in all the country
Gen 19 30 he [Lot] was afraid to stay in Segor
22 5 stay you here with the ass: I and the
24 55 let the maid stay at least ten days
56 stay me not, said he, because the Lord
26 2 stay in the land that I shall tell thee
29 19 than to another man; stay with me
33 15 may stay to accompany thee in the way
44 33 I . . . will stay instead of the boy
47 1 behold they stay in the land of Gessen
Exod 9 28 and that you may stay here no longer
12 39 not suffering them to make any stay
16 29 let each man stay at home, and let
Lev 13 23 if it stay in its place, it is but the
28 if the whiteness stay in its place
Num 9 8 stay that I may consult the Lord what
22 19 I pray you to stay here this night also
31 19 and stay without the camp seven days
Josu 6 23 made them to stay without the camp
10 19 stay you not, but pursue after the
Judg 17 10 Michas said: Stay with me, and be
19 6 I beseech thee to stay here today
7 and made him stay with him. But
20 I beseech thee stay not in the street
1 K 1 23 and stay till thou wean him [Samuel]
14 9 stay till we come to you: let us stand
23 13 uncertain where they should stay
2 K 10 5 stay at Jericho till your beards be
22 19 affliction, and the Lord became my stay
4 K 2 2 Elias said to Eliseus: Stay thou here
4 and Elias said to Eliseus: Stay here
6 Elias said to him: Stay here because
7 3 what mean we to stay here till we die
9 3 and flee, and shalt not stay there
15 20 turned back and did not stay in the
25 24 stay in the land and serve the king of
1 Pa 19 5 ordered them to stay at Jericho till
29 15 as a shadow, and there is no stay
2 Pa 25 19 stay at home, why dost thou provoke
2 Es 4 22 let every one with his servant stay in
13 21 why stay you before the wall? If you
Tob 4 15 let not the wages . . . stay with thee
5 9 stay for me, I beseech thee, till I
9 4 if I stay one day more, his soul will
10 1 but as Tobias made longer stay upon
8 stay here and I will send a messenger
14 12 children, hear me and do not stay here
Job 31 32 the stranger did not stay without my
39 9 serve thee or will he stay at thy crib
Prov 28 17 even to the pit, no man will stay him
Cant 2 5 stay me up with flowers, compass me
Eccu 3 34 time of his fall he shall find a sure s.
11 22 trust in God and stay in thy place

34 19 powerful protector and strong stay
49 17 of his brethren, the stay of the people
Isa 19 13 Egypt, the stay of the people thereof
Jer 4 6 strengthen yourselves, stay not
40 4 come with me to Babylon, stay here
1 Ma 5 42 suffer no man to stay behind: but
2 Ma 7 17 stay patiently a while, and thou shalt
30 said: For whom do you stay? I will
Mat 26 38 stay you here, and watch. Mark 14:34
Mark 15 36 stay, let us see if Elias come to take
Luke 24 29 stay with us, because it is towards
49 stay you in the city till you be
Acts 27 31 except these s. in ship, you cannot be
stayed Gen 8 12 he stayed yet other seven days
Exod 17 12 Aaron and Hur stayed up his hands on
Lev 13 34 evil seem to have stayed in its place
37 if the spot be stayed, and the hair be
Num 9 20 as the cloud stayed over the tabernacle
22 8 while they stayed with Balaam, God
35 28 fugitive ought to have s. in the city
Deut 1 6 you have stayed long enough in this
Josu 2 22 mountains, and stayed there three days
7 7 would God, we had stayed beyond the
8 9 Josue stayed that night in the midst
1 K 1 23 so the woman stayed at home and gave
30 9 and some being weary stayed there
10 for 200 stayed, who being weary could
21 who being weary had stayed and were not
2 K 17 17 and Achimaas s. by the fountain Rogel
24 25 and the plague was stayed from Israel
1 Pa 20 1 but David stayed at Jerusalem, when
1 Es 8 15 we s. there three days, and I sought
32 to Jerusalem and we s. there three days
2 Es 13 20 stayed without Jerusalem once or twice
Tob 11 14 and he stayed about half an hour
Jdth 3 15 and stayed there for thirty days, in
Wisd 18 23 stood between and stayed the assault
Eze 10 16 the wheels stayed not behind, but were
Agge 1 10 were stayed from giving dew, and the
1 Ma 6 53 such as had stayed in Judea of them
Mat 3 14 but John stayed him, saying: I ought
Luke 4 42 they stayed him that he should not
John 1 39 and they stayed with him that day
7 9 he himself stayed in Galilee. But
Acts 18 11 he stayed there a year and 6 months
18 Paul, when he had s. yet many days
20 5 these going before, s. for us at Troas
16 lest he should be s. any time in Asia
stayeth Eccu 14 23 that traceth and s. in her ways
stead Exod 4 16 he shall speak in thy s. to the
Exod 29 30 be appointed high priest in his stead
Lev 16 32 office of priesthood in his father's s.
Deut 2 21 he made them to dwell in their stead
23 destroyed them and dwelt in their s.
2 K 16 8 hast usurped the kingdom in his stead
17 25 Absalom appointed Amasa in Joab's stead
20 11 he that would have been in Joab's stead
3 K 1 30 he shall sit upon my throne in my stead
35 throne, and he shall reign in my stead
20 24 army, and put captains in their stead
4 K 23 30 made him king in his father's stead
24 17 Matthanias his uncle in his stead
1 Pa 4 43 and they dwelt there in their stead
5 10 dwelt in their tents in their stead
22 dwelt in their stead till the captivity
2 Pa 1 8 and hast made me king in his stead
33 25 made Josias his son king in his stead
36 4 Eliakim his brother king in his stead
Job 34 24 shall make others to stand in their s.
Eccu 10 17 hath set up the meek in their stead
1 Ma 3 1 called Machabeus, rose up in his stead
9 30 to be our prince and captain in his s.
Philem 13 in thy stead he might have ministered to

reigned in his stead; *see* **reigned**
steadfast Job 4 18 that serve him are not s.
Job 11 15 thou shalt be s. and shalt not fear
Prov 12 19 lip of truth shall be steadfast forever
Wisd 7 23 s., assured, secure, having all power
Eccu 5 12 be s. in the way of the Lord and in
6 11 a friend if he continue steadfast
11 21 s. in thy covenant and be conversant
1 C 7 37 determined being s. in his heart, having
15 58 brethren, be ye steadfast and unmoveable
2 C 1 7 that our hope for you may be steadfast
7 10 worketh penance, s. unto salvation; but
Heb 2 2 spoken by angels, became steadfast, and
steadfastly Ruth 1 18 that Ruth was s. determined
Luke 9 51 he s. set his face to go to Jerusalem
Acts 7 55 looking up s. to heaven, saw the glory
2 C 3 7 children of Israel could not s. behold
13 children of Israel might not s. look
steadfastness Eccu 4 29 s. in the works of justice
Col 2 5 the s. of your faith which is in Christ
2 P 3 17 you fall from your own steadfastness
steady Eccu 10 1 of prudent man shall be steady
Eccu 26 23 feet upon the soles of a steady woman
37 20 steady counsel before every action
steal Gen 44 8 should s. out of thy lord's house
Exod 20 15 thou shalt not steal. Deut 5:19
21 16 he that shall steal a man and sell him
22 1 if any man steal an ox or a sheep
Lev 19 11 you shall not steal. You shall not lie
Deut 15 9 a wicked thought steal in upon thee
Jer 7 9 to steal, to murder, to commit adultery
23 30 who steal my words every one from his
Prov 30 9 being compelled by poverty, I should s.
Osee 7 1 and the thief is come in to steal
Mat 6 19 where thieves break through and steal
20 thieves do not break through nor steal
19 18 thou shalt not s. Luke 18:20; Rom 13:9
27 64 disciples come and steal him away
Mark 10 19 do not kill, do not steal, bear not
John 10 10 the thief cometh not, but for to steal
Rom 2 21 that preachest that men should not steal
Eph 4 28 he that stole, let him now steal no more
stealest Rom 2 21 that men should not steal, s.
stealeth Prov 6 30 for he s. to fill his hungry soul
Prov 28 24 he that s. anything from his father or
stealth Exod 22 12 if it were taken away by s.
Job 4 12 my ears by stealth as it were received
steep 1 K 14 4 s. cliffs like teeth on the one
2 Pa 25 12 brought to the steep of a certain rock
Jdth 7 8 the s. hills and precipices guard them
Mich 1 4 as waters that run down a steep place
2 Ma 13 5 this had a prospect steep down. From
14 46 standing upon a steep rock, when he
Mat 8 32 violently down a steep place. Luke 8:33
stellio Prov 30 28 s. supporteth itself on hands
stello Lev 11 30 s. and the lizard and the mole
stench Isa 3 24 a sweet smell there shall be s.
Joel 2 20 his s. shall ascend, and his rottenness
Amos 4 10 I made the stench of your camp to come
2 Ma 9 10 to carry, for the intolerable stench
12 could not now abide his own stench
step Deut 2 5 so much as the step of one foot
1 K 20 3 but one step . . . between me and death
4 K 23 3 king stood upon the step: and made a
2 Pa 23 13 saw the king standing upon the step
2 Es 8 4 Esdras . . . stood upon a step of wood
9 4 stood up upon the step of the Levites
Job 18 7 s. of his strength shall be straitened
31 7 if my step hath turned out of the way
37 at every step of mine I would pronounce
Stephanas 1 C 16 15 you know the house of S.
1 C 16 17 I rejoice in the presence of Stephanas
Stephanus 1 C 1 16 baptized also household of S.

Stephen Acts 6 5 chose S., a man full of faith
Acts 6 8 Stephen, full of grace and fortitude
9 and Asia, disputing with Stephen
7 58 they stoned Stephen, invoking and
11 19 persecution that arose on occasion of S.
22 20 when the blood of Stephen thy witness
Stephen's Acts 8 2 took order for S. funeral
stepmother Lev 20 11 if a man lie with his s.
steps Exod 14 9 the Egyptians followed the steps
Exod 20 26 shalt not go up by steps unto my altar
Josu 22 29 Lord, and leave off following his steps
Judg 5 15 and followed the steps of Barac, who
16 26 he said to the lad that guided his s.
Ruth 2 7 following the steps of the reapers
2 K 22 37 thou shalt enlarge my steps under me
3 K 10 19 it had six steps: and the top of the
20 little lions stood upon the six steps
4 K 18 6 and departed not from his steps, but
2 Pa 9 18 and six steps to go up to the throne
19 little lions standing upon the steps
2 Es 3 15 steps that go down from city of David
Tob 14 12 direct your steps to depart hence: for
Esth 13 13 have kissed even the steps of his feet
Job 6 18 the paths of their steps are entangled
11 7 thou wilt comprehend the steps of God
13 27 hast considered the steps of my feet
14 16 thou indeed hast numbered my steps
23 11 my foot hath followed his steps, I
31 4 my ways and number all my steps
34 21 and he considereth all their steps
Ps 17 37 thou hast enlarged my steps under me
36 23 shall the steps of a man be directed
31 and his steps shall not be supplanted
39 3 upon a rock and directed my steps
43 19 neither hast thou turned aside our s.
58 5 have I run and directed my steps
72 2 moved: my steps had well nigh slipped
83 6 he hath disposed to ascend by steps
84 14 and shall set his steps in the way
118 133 direct my steps according to thy word
139 5 have proposed to supplant my steps
Prov 2 15 are perverse, and their steps infamous
3 6 on him, and he will direct thy steps
4 12 thy steps shall not be straitened
25 let thy eyelids go before thy steps
5 5 and her steps go in as far as hell
6 path of life, her steps are wandering
21 of man, and considereth all his steps
14 15 the discreet man considereth his steps
15 21 the wise man maketh straight his steps
16 9 but the Lord must direct his steps
19 3 folly of a man supplanteth his steps
20 24 the steps of man are guided by the Lord
Cant 1 7 follow after the steps of the flocks
7 1 how beautiful are thy steps in shoes
Eccu 1 7 understood the multiplicity of her s.
6 36 let thy foot wear the s. of his doors
50 31 the light of God guideth his steps
Isa 3 12 thee and destroy the way of thy steps
26 6 feet of the poor, the steps of the needy
59 8 there is no judgment in their steps
60 14 shall worship the steps of thy feet
Jer 10 23 a man to walk and to direct his steps
Lam 4 18 our steps have slipped in the way
Eze 40 6 east, and he went up the steps thereof
22 they went up to it by seven steps
26 there were seven steps to go up to it
31 were eight steps to go up to it. 49
34 the going up thereof was by eight steps
37 the going up to it was by eight steps
43 17 and its steps turned toward the east
Rom 4 12 that follow the steps of the faithful
2 C 12 18 spirit? did we not in the same steps
Heb 12 13 make straight steps with your feet
1 P 2 21 that you should follow his steps. Who
stept 1 K 18 11 David stept aside out of his
stern Prov 23 34 asleep when the stern is lost
2 Ma 14 30 that Nicanor was more stern to him
Acts 27 29 they cast four anchors out of the stern
stew Eze 16 24 didst also build thee a common s.
steward Gen 15 2 the son of the s. of my house
Gen 43 16 he commanded the steward of his house
19 going up to the steward of the house
44 1 Joseph commanded the steward of his
Mat 20 8 Lord of the vineyard saith to his s.
Luke 8 3 Joanna the wife of Chusa, Herod's s.
12 42 is the faithful and wise steward
16 1 a certain rich man who had a steward
2 now thou canst be steward no longer
3 the s. said within himself: What shall
8 the Lord commended the unjust steward
John 2 8 carry to the chief steward of the
9 when the chief steward had tasted the
9 chief steward calleth the bridegroom
Titus 1 7 as the steward of God: not proud, not
stewards 1 P 4 10 good s. of the manifold grace
stewardship Luke 16 2 give an account of thy s.
Luke 16 3 my lord taketh away from me the s.
4 when I shall be removed from the s.
stews Eze 16 39 they shall . . . throw down thy s.
Joel 3 3 the boy they have put in the stews
Stharbuzanai 1 Es 5 3 S. and their counsellors
1 Es 5 6 S. and his counsellors . . . sent to Darius
6 6 S. and your counsellors . . . depart for
13 S. and his counsellors diligently
Sthur Num 13 14 of Aser, Sthur the son of Michael
stibic 4 K 9 30 painted her face with s. stone
Jer 4 30 paintest thy eyes with stibic stone
stick Lev 5 8 so that it stick to the neck
Deut 13 17 of that anathema stick to thy hand
28 60 and they shall stick fast to thee
4 K 5 27 leprosy of Naaman shall also s. to thee
Job 41 8 they stick one to another and they hold
Ps 68 3 I stick fast in the mire of the deep
15 of the mire, that I may not stick fast
93 20 doth the seat of iniquity stick to thee
Eccu 27 2 selling and buying, sin shall s. fast
Eze 3 26 I will make thy tongue stick fast to
29 4 fish of thy rivers to s. to thy scales
5 thy fish shall stick to thy scales
37 16 take thee a stick: and write upon it
16 take another stick and write upon it
16 for Joseph, the stick of Ephraim, and
17 join them one to the other into one s.
19 behold I will take the stick of Joseph
19 them together with the stick of Juda
19 Juda, and will make them one stick
Dan 2 43 they shall not stick fast one to
sticketh Eccu 19 12 as an arrow that s. in a man's
Eccu 27 2 as a stake s. fast in the midst of the
Jer 13 11 as the girdle sticketh close to the
sticking Gen 22 13 the briers s. fast by the horns
2 K 18 14 panted for life, sticking on the oak
Acts 27 41 forepart indeed, sticking fast, remained
sticks Num 15 32 man gathering s. on sabbath day
3 K 17 10 he saw the widow woman gathering s.
12 I am gathering two sticks that I may go
Eze 37 20 the sticks whereon thou hast written
Dan 3 46 to heat the furnace with . . . dry sticks
Acts 28 3 had gathered together a bundle of s.
stiff Exod 15 15 inhabitants of Chanaan became s.
Deut 31 27 thy obstinacy and thy most stiff neck
2 K 23 10 till his hand was weary and grew stiff
Prov 29 1 that with a stiff neck despiseth him
Eccu 33 27 yoke and the thong bend a stiff neck
Bar 2 30 for they are a people of a stiff neck

33 away themselves from their stiff neck
stiffen Deut 10 16 heart, and s. your neck no more
stiffnecked Exod 32 9 this people is s. Deut 9:13
Exod 33 3 thou art a stiffnecked people. 5
34 9 wilt go with us, for it is a s. people
Deut 9 6 thou art a very stiffnecked people
Eccu 16 11 if one had been s., it is a wonder
Acts 7 51 you s. and uncircumcised in heart and
stifled Mark 5 13 and were stifled in the sea
Luke 8 33 place into the lake, and were stifled
still Mark 4 39 said to the sea: Peace, be still. And
Mark 8 17 have you still your heart blinded
10 49 Jesus, standing still, commanded him
15 5 but Jesus still answered nothing; so
John 11 6 he still remained in the same place
30 he was still in that place where
Acts 8 38 commanded the chariot to stand still
Phil 1 24 to abide still in the flesh, is needful
1 Tim 5 23 do not still drink water, but use a
Apoc 22 11 let him hurt still . . . be filthy still . . . be justified still . . . be sanctified s.
sting 1 C 15 55 victory? O death, where is thy s.
1 C 15 56 now the sting of death is sin: and the
2 C 12 7 there was given me a sting of my flesh
stinging Jer 51 27 the horse as the s. locust
stings Apoc 9 10 were stings in their tails
stink Exod 5 21 have made our savor to s. before
Isa 34 3 out of their carcasses shall rise a s.
stinketh John 11 39 Lord by this time he s., for
stinking Wisd 11 19 or sending forth a s. smoke
Eccu 11 32 bowels send forth stinking breath
Eze 32 6 water the earth with thy s. blood
stipulations Jer 32 11 that was sealed, and the s.
stir Num 5 14 if the spirit of jealousy stir up
Deut 2 5 heed that you stir not against them
1 K 26 19 if the Lord stir thee up against me
Jdth 8 12 but rather that may stir up wrath
Job 41 1 I will not stir him up, like one that
Ps 79 3 stir up thy might, and come to save us
Prov 6 3 about, make haste, stir up thy friend
Cant 2 7 that you stir not up nor make the
3 5 that you stir not up, nor awake my. 8:4
Isa 42 13 as a man of war shall he stir up zeal
46 7 and shall not stir out of his place
Dan 11 2 he shall stir up all against the
1 Ma 6 38 with trumpets to stir up the army
2 Ma 15 17 and proper to stir up the courage
Acts 12 18 was no small stir among the soldiers
2 Tim 1 6 that thou stir up the grace of God which
2 P 1 13 to stir you up by putting you in
3 1 I stir up by the way of admonition
stirred Num 5 30 husband s. up by the spirit of
Deut 32 16 and stirred him up to anger with their
Josu 9 20 lest wrath of the Lord be stirred up
2 K 24 1 stirred up David among them, saying
1 Pa 5 26 God of Israel s. up the spirit of Phul
2 Pa 21 16 the Lord stirred up against Joram the
29 8 the wrath of the Lord hath been s. up
36 22 the Lord stirred up the heart of Cyrus
1 Es 1 1 Lord stirred up the spirit of Cyrus
Prov 15 18 patient appeaseth those that are s. up
29 22 he that is easily stirred up to wrath
Isa 14 9 it stirred up the giants for thee
Dan 11 10 and he shall return and be stirred up
25 his heart shall be stirred up against
25 the king of the south shall be s. up
Osee 11 8 within me, my repentance is stirred up
14 1 she hath s. up her God to bitterness
Haba 2 7 be stirred up that shall tear thee
Agge 1 14 the Lord s. up the spirit of Zorobabel
1 Ma 3 49 s. up the Nazarites that had fulfilled
2 Ma 13 4 King of kings stirred up the mind of
Acts 6 12 they stirred up the people. 17:8
13 50 Jews stirred up religious . . . women
14 2 Jews s. up and incensed the minds of
17 16 his spirit was stirred within him
21 27 s. up all the people, and laid hands
stirreth Prov 10 12 hatred s. up strifes, and
Prov 15 1 but a harsh word stirreth up fury. The
18 a passionate man stirreth up strifes
16 28 a perverse man stirreth up quarrels
26 21 so an angry man stirreth up strife
28 25 puffeth up himself, s. up quarrels
Jer 31 35 who stirreth up the sea, and the waves
Luke 23 5 he stirreth up the people, teaching
stirring Acts 17 13 s. up and troubling the
stock Gen 17 12 whosoever is not of your stock
Gen 21 23 me nor my posterity nor stock
27 46 if Jacob take a wife of the stock of
28 1 take not a wife of the s. of Chanaan
41 23 thin and blasted, sprung of the stock
Lev 21 15 he shall not mingle the stock of his
Num 2 4 sum of the fighting men of his stock
8 the army of fighting men of his stock
23 10 know the number of the stock of Israel
24 22 and thou be chosen of the stock of Cin
26 7 the families of the stock of Ruben
14 the families of the stock of Simeon
36 1 of the stock of the children of Joseph
Josu 11 22 left not any of the s. of the Enacims
Judg 18 2 sent five most valiant men of their s.
2 K 21 5 not so much as one left of his stock
1 Pa 9 28 some of their stock had the charge
20 6 also was born of the stock of Rapha
2 Pa 7 18 shall not fail thee a man of thy stock
8 7 that were not of the stock of Israel
Job 14 8 and its stock be dead in the dust
Ps 77 48 to the hail, and their stock to the fire
Eccu 47 25 Jacob, and to David of the same stock
Isa 40 24 their s. was neither planted nor sown
44 3 seed, and my blessing upon thy stock
19 I fall down before the s. of a tree
Jer 2 27 saying to a stock: Thou art my father
1 Ma 12 21 that they are of the stock of Abraham
2 Ma 1 10 of the stock of the anointed priests
7 7 the next to make him a mocking stock
10 the third was made a mocking stock
Acts 13 26 children of the stock of Abraham, and
Phil 3 5 of the stock of Israel, of the tribe of
Apoc 22 16 I am the root and stock of David, the
stocks Job 13 27 put my feet in the s. 33:11
Jer 3 9 the harlot with stones and with stocks
20 2 prophet, and put him in the stocks
3 Phassur brought Jeremias out of the s.
29 26 to put him in the s. and into prison
Eze 20 32 earth, to worship stocks and stones
Osee 4 12 my people have consulted their stocks
Acts 16 24 and made their feet fast in the stocks
Stoics Acts 17 18 Epicureans and of the Stoics
stole Gen 31 19 Rachel s. away her father's idols
Gen 44 17 he that stole the cup, he shall be
Exod 22 4 if that which he stole be found with
4 K 11 2 s. him from among the king's. 2 Pa 22:11
Mat 28 13 stole him away when we were asleep
Eph 4 28 he that stole, let him now steal no more
stolen Gen 27 36 he hath stolen away my blessing
Gen 31 30 why hast thou s. away my gods? Jacob
32 knew not that Rachel had s. the idols
40 15 I was stolen away out of the land of
44 5 the cup which you have stolen is that
Exod 22 7 and they be stolen away from him that
Josu 7 11 have s. and lied, and have hidden it
2 K 19 41 the men of Juda stolen thee away and
21 12 had s. them from the street of Bethsan
Tob 2 21 take heed lest perhaps it be stolen
Prov 6 30 not so great when a man hath stolen

9 17 stolen waters are sweeter, and hidden
Abdi 5 would they not have stolen till they
2 Ma 4 32 having stolen certain vessels of gold
stomach Judg 19 5 bread, and strengthen thy stomach
3 K 22 34 between the lungs and the stomach. But
Job 15 2 and fill his stomach with burning heat
stomacher Isa 3 24 instead of a s., haircloth
Jer 2 32 or a bride her stomacher? But my
stomach's 1 Tim 5 23 a little wine for thy s. sake
stone Gen 2 12 found bdellium and the onyx stone
Gen 28 18 took the stone which he had laid under
22 this stone, which I have set up
29 2 mouth thereof was closed with a great s.
3 custom . . . to roll away the stone
8 we remove the stone from the well's
10 he removed the s. wherewith the well
31 13 Bethel, where thou didst anoint the s.
45 Jacob took a stone and set it up for
51 and the stone which I have set up
52 and the stone, be they for a testimony
35 14 but he set up a monument of stone
49 24 came forth a pastor, the stone of Israel
Exod 4 25 Sephora took a very sharp stone and
7 19 both in vessels of wood and of stone
8 26 in their presence, they will stone us
15 5 they are sunk to the bottom like a stone
16 let them become unmoveable as a stone
17 4 a little more and they will stone me
12 they took a stone, and put under him
20 25 and if thou make an altar of stone
21 18 one strike his neighbor with a stone
24 10 as it were a work of sapphire stone
28 10 six names on one stone, and the
17 sardius s. and a topaz and an emerald
21 each stone with the name of one
31 18 gave to Moses two stone tables of
Lev 20 2 the people of the land shall stone him
27 let them die: they shall stone them
24 14 and let all the people stone him
26 1 nor set up a remarkable stone in
Num 15 35 die, let all the multitude stone him
35 17 if he throw a stone, and he that is
Deut 4 28 wood and stone, that neither see nor
21 21 the people of the city shall stone him
22 21 the men of the city shall stone her to
28 36 serve strange gods, wood and stone
64 serve strange goods . . . wood and stone
29 17 their idols, wood and stone, silver and
32 13 rock, and oil out of the hardest stone
Josu 4 5 carry from thence every man a stone
5 2 make thee knives of s., and circumcise
15 6 going up to the stone of Boen the
18 18 Abenboen, that is, the stone of Boen
24 26 he took a great stone and set it under
27 this stone shall be a testimony unto
Judg 9 5 seventy men upon one stone. 18
1 K 4 1 camped by the Stone of help. And the
5 1 it from the Stone of help into Azotus
6 14 there was a great s., and they cut in
15 and they put them upon the great stone
18 to the great Abel (the stone) whereon
7 12 Samuel took a stone and laid it between
12 he called the place, the Stone of help
14 33 roll here to me now a great stone
34 slay them upon this stone and eat
17 49 hand into his scrip and took a stone
49 and the stone was fixed in his forehead
50 Philistine, with a sling and a stone
20 19 beside the stone, which is called Ezel
25 37 and he [Nabal] became as a stone
30 6 for the people had a mind to stone him
2 K 17 13 not be found so much as one small stone
20 8 at the great stone which is in Gabaon

3 K 1 9 Adonias . . . by the stone of Zoheleth
6 18 no s. could be seen in the wall at all
21 10 carry him [Naboth] out and stone him
4 K 9 30 painted her face with stibic stone and
16 17 and put it upon a pavement of stone
19 18 works of men's hands of wood and stone
2 Pa 7 3 upon the stone pavement, they adored
2 Es 4 3 he will leap over their stone wall
9 11 depth, as a stone into mighty waters
Job 19 24 graven with an instrument in flint s.
28 2 stone melted with heat is turned into
3 the stone also that is in the dark
16 with the most precious stone sardonyx
38 6 or who laid the corner stone thereof
30 the waters are hardened like a stone
41 15 his heart shall be as hard as a stone
Ps 90 12 lest thou dash thy foot against a stone
117 22 stone which the builders rejected; the
Prov 8 19 better than gold and the precious stone
24 31 and the stone wall was broken down
26 8 as he that casteth a stone into the
27 he that rolleth a s., it shall return
27 3 a stone is heavy, and sand weighty
Wisd 5 23 upon them from the stone casting wrath
7 9 did I compare with her any precious s.
11 4 of their thirst out of the hard stone
13 10 called gods . . . an unprofitable stone
Eccu 6 22 be to them as a mighty stone of trial
22 1 sluggard is pelted with a dirty stone
25 he that flingeth a s. at birds, shall
27 28 if one cast a stone on high, it will
29 that setteth a stone for his neighbor
29 13 hide it not under a stone to be lost
47 5 with the stone in the sling he beat
50 10 adorned with every precious stone. As
Isa 8 14 a stone of stumbling and a rock of
28 16 I will lay a stone in the foundations of Sion, a tried stone, a corner stone, a precious stone
37 19 works of men's hands, of wood and stone
Jer 2 27 to a stone: Thou hast begotten me
4 30 paintest thy eyes with stibic stone
51 26 not take of thee a stone for the corner nor a stone for foundations
63 thou shalt tie a stone to it and shalt
Lam 3 53 and they have laid a stone over me
Bar 6 3 gods of gold and of silver and of stone
38 gods of wood and of stone and. 56
Eze 1 26 as the appearance of the sapphire stone
10 1 over them as it were the sapphire stone
9 to the sight like the chrysolite stone
16 40 and they shall stone thee with stones
23 47 let the people stone them with stones
28 13 every precious stone was thy covering
40 17 and a pavement of stone in the court
42 3 outward court that was paved with stone
Dan 2 34 till a stone was cut out of a mountain
35 the stone that struck the statue became
45 sawest that the stone was cut out of
5 4 and praised their gods . . . of stone
23 hast praised the gods . . . of stone
6 17 a stone was brought and laid upon the
Amos 5 11 you shall build houses with square s.
9 9 there shall not a little stone fall to
Haba 2 11 the stone shall cry out of the wall
19 saith . . . to the dumb stone: Arise
Agge 2 16 before there was a s. laid upon a stone
Zach 3 9 the s. that I have laid before Jesus
9 upon one stone there are seven eyes
4 7 and he shall bring out the chief stone
7 12 made their heart as the adamant stone
12 3 I will make Jerusalem a burdensome stone
1 Ma 2 36 neither did they cast a stone at them
10 73 in the plain, where there is no stone

13 27 a building lofty . . . of polished stone
Mat 4 6 dash thy foot against a s. Luke 4:11
7 9 ask bread, will he reach him a stone
21 42 the stone which the builders rejected. Mark 12:10; Luke 20:17; 1 P 2:7
44 whosoever shall fall on this stone
24 2 not be left here a s. upon a s. Mark 13:2; Luke 21:6
27 60 he rolled a great stone to the door of
66 the sepulcher sure, sealing the stone
28 2 rolled back the stone, and sat upon it
Mark 15 46 he rolled a stone to the door of the
16 3 who shall roll us back the stone from
4 they saw the stone rolled back. For
Luke 4 3 say to this stone that it be made
11 11 bread, will he give him a stone? Or
19 44 leave in thee a stone upon a stone
20 6 the whole people will stone us: for
18 whosoever shall fall upon that stone
23 53 in a sepulcher that was hewed in stone
24 2 and they found the stone rolled back
John 2 6 set there six waterpots of stone
8 5 commanded us to stone such a one
7 let him first cast a stone at her
10 31 Jews then took up stones to stone him
32 for which of those works do you s. me
33 for a good work we stone thee not, but
11 8 the Jews but now sought to stone thee
38 a cave; and a stone was laid over it
41 they took therefore the stone away
20 1 she saw the stone taken away from the
Acts 4 11 is the stone which was rejected by you
14 5 use them contumeliously, and to s. them
17 29 be like unto gold, or silver, or stone
Eph 2 20 Jesus Christ . . . being chief corner s.
1 P 2 4 upon whom coming, as to a living stone
6 I lay in Sion, a chief corner stone
8 a stone of stumbling, and a rock of
Apoc 4 3 like the jasper and the sardine stone
9 20 idols of . . . brass and stone and wood
18 12 all manner of vessels of precious stone
21 and a mighty angel took up a stone
21 11 light thereof was like to a precious s.
11 as to the jasper stone, even as crystal
18 wall thereof was of jasper stone: but
tables of stone Exod 24 12 will give thee t. . . .
Exod 34 1 hew thee two t. . . . like unto the
4 he cut out two t. . . . , such as had been
Deut 4 13 ten words that he wrote in two t. . . .
5 22 he wrote them in two t. . . . which he
9 9 into the mount to receive the t. . . .
10 the Lord gave me two t. . . . written
10 1 hew thee two t. . . . like the former
3 when I had hewn two t. . . . like the
3 K 8 9 was nothing else but the two t. . . .
2 C 3 3 not in tables of stone, but in fleshly
stonecutters 1 Pa 22 2 appointed s. to hew stones
2 Pa 24 12 they hired with it stonecutters and
stoned Exod 19 13 he shall be stoned to death or
Exod 21 28 and they die, he shall be stoned
29 the ox shall be stoned, and his owner
32 master, and the ox shall be stoned
Lev 24 23 blasphemed . . . and they stoned him
Num 14 10 cried out and would have stoned them
15 36 had brought him out, they stoned him
Deut 13 10 with stones shall he be stoned to death
17 5 gates of thy city, and they shall be s.
22 24 gate of that city, and they shall be s.
Josu 7 25 all Israel stoned him: and all things
3 K 12 18 all Israel stoned him [Aduram] and he
21 13 without the city and s. him to death
14 saying: Naboth is stoned and is dead
15 when Jezabel heard that Naboth was s.
2 Pa 10 18 children of Israel s. him and he died
24 21 against him and stoned him [Zacharias]
Mich 4 11 they say: Let her be stoned, and let
Mat 21 35 beat one and killed another and stoned
Acts 5 26 the people, lest they should be stoned
7 57 without the city, they stoned him; and
58 they stoned Stephen, invoking and
2 C 11 25 once I was stoned, thrice I suffered
Heb 11 37 they were stoned, they were cut asunder
12 20 shall touch the mount, it shall be s.
stone's Judg 20 16 by the s. going on either side
Luke 22 41 away from them a stone's cast; and
stones Gen 11 3 they had brick instead of stones
Gen 28 11 he took of the stones that lay there
31 46 they gathering stones together, made
46 said to his brethren: Bring hither s.
Exod 20 25 thou shalt not build it of hewn stones
25 7 onyx s. and precious s. to adorn the
28 9 and thou shalt take two onyx stones
17 shalt set in it four rows of stones
35 9 onyx s. and precious s. for the adorning
27 princes offered onyx s. and precious s.
33 engraving s. and in carpenters' work
39 6 he prepared also two onyx stones, fast
14 the twelve stones were engraved with
Lev 14 40 stones wherein the leprosy is, be taken
42 other stones be laid in the place of
43 after the stones be taken out and the
45 and shall cast the stones and timber
Deut 8 9 where the stones are iron, and out of
13 10 with s. shall he be stoned to death
27 2 thou shalt set up great stones and
4 set up the stones which I command
5 of stones which iron hath not touched
6 of stones not fashioned nor polished
8 thou shalt write upon the stones all
Josu 4 3 twelve very hard stones, which you
6 saying: What mean these stones? You
7 were these stones set for a monument
8 channel of the Jordan twelve stones
9 Josue put other twelve s. in the midst
20 the 12 stones which they had taken out
21 shall say to them: What mean these s.
7 26 upon him [Achan] a great heap of s.
8 29 heaping upon it a great heap of stones
31 an altar of unhewn stones which iron
32 he wrote upon stones the Deuteronomy
10 11 Lord cast down upon them great stones
18 roll great stones to mouth of the cave
27 put great stones at the mouth thereof
Judg 20 16 slinging stones so sure that they could
1 K 17 40 chose him five smooth stones out of
2 K 16 6 he threw stones at David and at all the
13 casting s. at him and scattering earth
18 17 laid an exceeding great heap of stones
3 K 5 15 and 80,000 to hew stones. 2 Pa 2:2, 18
17 should bring great stones, costly s.
18 the Giblians prepared timber and stones
6 7 built of stones hewed and made ready
36 with three rows of polished stones
7 9 all of costly stones, which were sawed
10 the foundations were of costly stones
10 great stones of 10 cubits or 8 cubits
11 and above there were costly stones
12 with three rows of hewed stones, and
10 27 to be as plentiful in Jerusalem as s.
15 22 they took away the stones from Rama
18 31 he took twelve stones according to
32 and he built with the stones an altar
38 holocaust and the wood and the stones
4 K 3 19 goodly field you shall cover with s.
12 12 repairs: and to them that cut stones
12 to buy timber and stones to be hewed

22 6 bought, and stones out of the quarries
1 Pa 12 2 using either hand in hurling stones
22 2 he appointed stonecutters to hew stones
14 timber also and stones I have prepared
15 workmen in abundance, hewers of stones
29 2 onyx stones and stones like alabaster
8 all they that had stones, gave them
2 Pa 1 15 and gold to be in Jerusalem as stones
9 27 silver as plentiful in Jerusalem as s.
16 6 they carried away from Rama the stones
26 14 and bows and slings to cast stones
15 to shoot arrows and great stones: and
34 11 to buy stones out of the quarries and
1 Es 3 7 they gave money to hewers of stones
5 8 are building with unpolished stones
6 4 three rows of unpolished stones and
2 Es 4 2 are they able to raise stones out of
Tob 13 22 be paved with white and clean stones
Jdth 1 2 of stones squared and hewed: he made
Job 5 23 a covenant with the stones of the lands
6 12 my strength is not the strength of s.
8 17 shall be thick upon a heap of stones
17 and among the stones he shall abide
14 19 waters wear away the stones, and
24 8 having no covering embrace the stones
28 6 stones of it are the place of sapphires
41 19 s. of the sling are to him like stubble
Ps 101 15 s. thereof have pleased thy servants
Ecce 10 9 he that removeth stones, shall be hurt
Wisd 14 21 gave the incommunicable name to stones
17 18 mighty noise of stones tumbling down
18 24 in the four rows of the s. the glory
Eccu 21 9 as he that gathereth himself stones
11 way of sinners is made plain with s.
27 2 in the midst of the joining of stones
32 25 shalt not stumble against the stones
Isa 2 21 shall go . . . into the holes of stones
5 2 picked the s. out of it and planted it
9 10 but we will build with square stones
17 1 shall be as a ruinous heap of stones
27 9 shall have made all the s. of the altar, as burnt s. broken in pieces
54 11 I will lay thy stones in order and
12 thy gates of graven stones, and all thy borders of desirable stones
60 17 for wood brass, and for stones iron
62 10 make the road plain, pick out the s.
Jer 3 9 played the harlot with stones and with
26 18 Jerusalem shall be a heap of stones
43 9 take great stones in thy hand and thou
10 I will set his throne over these stones
50 26 take the stones out of the way and
Lam 3 9 shut up my ways with square stones
4 1 stones of the sanctuary are scattered
Bar 6 38 and of silver, are like the stones that
42 sit in the ways, burning olive stones
Eze 16 40 they shall stone thee with stones
20 32 earth, to worship stocks and stones
23 47 let the people stone them with stones
26 12 they shall lay thy s. and thy timber
28 14 walked in the midst of the s. of fire
40 42 tables . . . were made of square stones
Mich 1 6 I will make Samaria as a heap of stones
6 I will bring down the stones thereof
3 12 Jerusalem shall be as a heap of stones
Zach 5 4 the timber thereof and the s. thereof
9 15 subdue with the stones of the sling
16 holy s. shall be lifted up over his
1 Ma 4 43 took away the s. that had been defiled
46 they laid up the stones in the mountain
47 they took whole stones according to
5 47 and stopped up the gates with stones
6 51 engines to cast stones and javelins
10 11 with square stones for fortification
2 Ma 1 16 they cast stones and slew the leader
31 to be poured out upon the great stones
4 41 some caught up s., some strong clubs
10 3 taking fire out of the fiery stones
Mat 3 9 God is able of these stones. Luke 3:8
4 3 command that these stones be made bread
Mark 5 5 crying and cutting himself with stones
13 1 Master, behold what manner of stones
Luke 19 40 hold their peace, the stones will cry
21 5 it was adorned with goodly stones and
John 8 59 they took up stones therefore to
10 31 the Jews then took up stones to stone
2 C 3 7 engraven with letters upon stones, was
1 P 2 5 be you also as living stones built up

precious stones; *see* **precious**

stonest Mat 23 37 s. them that are. Luke 13:34

stoning Acts 14 18 s. Paul, drew him out of the

stony Deut 21 4 her into a rough and s. valley
Job 39 28 among cragged flints and stony hills
Ps 113 8 stony hill into fountains of waters
Eze 11 19 I will take away the s. heart. 36:26
Mat 13 5 other some fell upon s. ground. Mark 4:5
20 received the seed upon stony ground
Mark 4 16 that are sown on the stony ground: who

stood Mat 2 9 until it came and stood over where the
Mat 12 46 mother and his brethren stood without
13 2 all the multitude stood on the shore
20 32 Jesus stood and called them, and said
27 11 and Jesus stood before the governor
47 some that stood there and heard, said
Mark 11 5 some of them that stood there said to
14 47 one of them that stood by, drawing a
70 they that stood by said again to Peter
15 39 centurion who stood over against him
Luke 2 9 an angel of the Lord stood by them
5 1 he stood by the lake of Genesareth
6 8 the midst. And rising he stood forth
17 he stood in a plain place, and the
7 14 and they that carried it stood still
9 32 and the two men that stood with him
10 25 lawyer stood up, tempting him and
40 who stood and said: Lord, hast thou
12 1 when great multitudes stood about him
17 12 that were lepers, who stood afar off
23 10 chief priests and the scribes stood by
35 the people stood beholding, and the
49 stood afar off, beholding these things
24 4 two men stood by them, in shining
36 Jesus stood in the midst of them and
John 1 26 hath stood one in the midst of you
35 John stood, and two of his disciples
6 22 that s. on the other side of the sea
7 37 Jesus stood and cried, saying: If any
8 44 he stood not in the truth; because
12 29 that stood and heard, said that it
18 5 Judas also . . . stood with them. As
16 but Peter stood at the door without
18 stood at a fire of coals, because it
19 25 there stood by the cross of Jesus, his
20 11 Mary stood at the sepulcher without
19 Jesus came and stood in the midst
26 stood in the midst and said: Peace be
21 4 Jesus stood on the shore: yet the
Acts 1 10 behold two men stood by them in white
3 8 he leaping up, stood and walked and
4 26 the kings of the earth stood up and
9 7 stood amazed, hearing indeed a voice
39 widows stood about him weeping, and
10 17 for Simon's house, stood at the gate
30 a man stood before me in white apparel
12 7 an angel of the Lord stood by him: and
14 she told that Peter s. before the gate

14 19 disciples s. round about him, he rose
22 20 I stood by and consented and kept the
25 Paul saith to centurion that stood by
23 2 commanded them that s. by him to strike
4 they that stood by said: Dost thou
25 7 the Jews stood about him, who were come
18 when the accusers s. up, they brought
27 23 whom I serve, stood by me this night
2 Tim 4 16 at my first answer no man stood with me
17 Lord stood by me, and strengthened me
Apoc 7 11 the angels stood round about the throne
8 3 angel came and stood before the altar
11 11 they stood upon their feet, and great
12 4 the dragon stood before the woman who
18 and he stood upon the sand of the sea
14 1 a lamb stood upon mount Sion, and with
18 17 as work in the sea, stood afar off
stoodest Abdi 11 day when thou s. against him
stool 1 K 1 9 Heli the priest sitting upon a s.
1 K 4 13 Heli sat upon a stool over against the
18 he fell from his stool backwards by
4 K 4 10 a table and a stool and a candlestick
stoop Job 9 13 under whom they s. that bear up
Isa 2 11 haughtiness of men shall be made to s.
Mark 1 7 am not worthy to stoop down and loose
stooped 2 Pa 36 17 or even him that s. for age
John 20 5 when he stooped down, he saw the linen
11 she stooped down, and looked into the
stooping Luke 24 12 s. down, he saw the linen
John 8 8 again stooping down, he wrote on the
stop Lev 15 28 if the blood stop and cease to
2 K 20 12 passed might not stop on his account
4 K 3 19 shall s. up all the springs of waters
1 Pa 21 15 it is enough, now stop thy hand. And
2 Pa 32 3 to stop up the heads of the springs
Jdth 7 24 he will put a stop to his indignation
Job 38 31 canst thou stop the turning about of
Ps 106 42 and all iniquity shall stop her mouth
Ecce 8 8 not in man's power to stop the spirit
Osee 2 6 I will stop it up with a wall, and she
stopped Gen 26 15 s. up at that time all the wells
Gen 26 18 the Palestines had of old stopped up
Num 24 3 whose eye is stopped up. 15
1 K 24 8 David stopped his men with his words
2 Pa 32 4 they stopped up all the springs and
30 that stopped the upper source of the
Jdth 16 5 his multitude stopped up the torrents
10 11 and stopped her, saying: Whence comest
Ps 62 12 mouth is stopped of them that speak
Eccu 46 5 was not the sun stopped in his anger
Dan 10 17 in me, moreover, my breath is stopped
Zach 7 11 they stopped their ears, not to hear
1 Ma 2 36 them, nor stopped up the secret places
5 47 and stopped up the gates with stones
9 55 his mouth was stopped and he was
2 Ma 2 5 Jeremias . . . and so stopped the door
Luke 8 44 the issue of her blood stopped. And
Acts 7 56 stopped their ears, and with one
Rom 3 19 that every mouth may be stopped, and all
Heb 11 33 promises, stopped the mouths of lions
stoppeth Ps 57 5 the deaf asp that stoppeth her ears
Prov 21 13 that s. his ear against the cry of
Isa 33 15 stoppeth his ears lest he hear blood
stopping 2 K 20 11 s. at the dead body of Amasa
2 Ma 9 4 without stopping in his journey, the
stopt 4 K 3 25 s. up all the springs of waters
storax Gen 43 11 storax, myrrh, turpentine
Eccu 24 21 and I perfumed my dwelling as storax
store Gen 24 25 we have good store of both straw
Lev 25 22 new grow up, you shall eat the old store
26 10 shall eat the oldest of the old store
3 K 10 10 and of spices a very great store
4 K 20 17 that thy fathers have laid up in store
1 Pa 29 16 all this store that we have prepared
2 Pa 31 10 that which is left is this great store
2 Es 5 18 ten days I gave store of divers wines
Isa 23 18 shall not be kept in store nor laid up
39 6 that thy fathers have laid up in store
Eze 42 5 where were the store chambers lower
44 19 lay them up in the store chamber
45 5 they shall possess 20 store chambers
1 Ma 6 6 store of spoils which they had gotten
2 Ma 3 6 the common store was infinite, which
1 Tim 6 19 to lay up in store for themselves a good
2 P 3 7 by the same word are kept in store
stored Deut 32 34 are not these things s. up with
1 Ma 1 36 they stored up armor and victuals
6 53 all that which had been stored up
13 33 he s. up victuals in the fortresses
James 5 3 you have stored up to yourselves wrath
storehouse 2 Es 10 37 s. of our God and the tithes
2 Es 13 7 to make him a storehouse in the courts
8 of the house of Tobias out of the s.
Jer 38 11 king's house that was under the s.
Mala 3 10 bring all the tithes into the s.
Luke 12 24 neither have they storehouse nor barn
storehouses Deut 28 8 a blessing upon thy s.
2 Pa 11 11 he put in them governors and s. of
31 11 Ezechias commanded to prepare s. in
32 28 storehouses also of corn, of wine
2 Es 12 43 over the storehouses of the treasure
13 9 and they cleansed the storehouses
12 wine and the oil into the storehouses
13 we set over the storehouses Selemias
Job 38 22 entered into storehouses of the snow
Ps 32 7 laying up the depths in storehouses
143 13 their s. full, flowing out of this into
Eccu 1 21 increase and the s. with her treasures
Isa 39 2 he showed them the storehouses of his
2 all the storehouses of his furniture
Joel 1 17 the s. are broken down: because the
storeroom 2 Es 10 38 to the s. into the treasure
2 Es 13 5 and he made him a great s., where
storerooms Prov 24 4 by instruction the s. shall
Cant 1 3 the king hath brought me into his s.
stores Gen 47 22 was given out of the public s.
Deut 28 5 be thy barns and blessed thy stores
17 be thy barn, and cursed thy stores
1 Pa 27 25 over those stores which were in cities
Job 24 11 their rest at noon among the stores
Ps 16 14 belly is filled from thy hidden s.
134 7 bringeth forth winds out of his stores
Jer 41 8 we have stores in the field, of wheat
storest Tob 4 10 s. up to thyself a good reward
storeth Ps 38 7 he s. up: and he knoweth not
stories Gen 6 16 and third s. shalt thou make it
Eze 42 6 they were of three stories and had not
storing Amos 3 10 s. up iniquities and robberies
stork Deut 14 16 heron and the swan and the stork
Jer 8 7 and the stork have observed the time
storm Tob 3 22 after a s. thou makest a calm
Job 36 14 their soul shall die in a storm and
Ps 54 9 from pusillanimity of spirit and a s.
106 25 arose a storm of wind: and the waves
29 he turned the storm into a breeze
Wisd 5 15 froth which is dispersed by the storm
Eccu 16 21 storm, which no eye of man shall see
32 14 before a storm goeth lightning: and
33 2 dashed in pieces as a ship in a storm
43 18 so doth the northern storm and the
Isa 28 2 mighty and strong, as a storm of hail
32 2 wind, and hideth himself from a storm
Jer 30 23 his fury going forth, a violent storm
Eze 27 35 their kings being struck with the s.
38 9 shalt go up and come like a storm
Mat 16 3 there will be a storm, for the sky

Mark 4 37 there arose a great storm of wind
Luke 8 23 there came down a storm of wind upon
Acts 27 20 no small storm lay on us, all hope of
Heb 12 18 a whirlwind and darkness and storm
Jude 13 storm of darkness is reserved forever
storms Job 28 26 a way for the sounding storms
Ps 10 7 storms of winds shall be the portion
stormy Ps 148 8 ice, s. winds, which fulfil his
Eze 13 11 and a stormy wind to throw it down
story 2 Ma 2 33 to be short in the story itself
stout Gen 10 9 he was a stout hunter before
Gen 10 9 even as Nemrod the stout hunter before
Exod 15 15 seized on the stout men of Moab: all
2 Pa 32 21 angel, who cut off all the stout men
Prov 24 5 and a knowing man, stout and valiant
Isa 5 22 wine, and stout men at drunkenness
Jer 48 14 are valiant and stout men in battle
Amos 2 16 the stout of heart among the valiant
1 Ma 9 14 all the stout of heart came together
2 Ma 12 27 stout young men standing upon the walls
stoutest Judg 5 22 s. of the enemies fled amain
1 Pa 12 4 Samaias . . . stoutest among the thirty
1 Ma 2 42 the Assideans, the stoutest of Israel
stoutly Judg 9 52 coming near the tower, fought s.
straggling Judg 20 45 as they were s. and going
straight Gen 24 27 hath brought me the s. way. 48
Deut 28 29 dark, and not make straight thy ways
1 K 6 12 the kine took the straight way that
Prov 4 25 let thy eyes look straight on, and let
26 make straight the path for thy feet
27 but he will make thy courses straight
14 15 and his way shall be made straight
15 21 the wise man maketh straight his steps
Eccu 4 20 and make a straight way to him and
Isa 35 8 this shall be unto you a straight way
40 3 make straight in the wilderness the
4 and the crooked shall become straight
42 16 will make . . . crooked things straight
Eze 1 7 their feet were straight feet, and the
9 but every one went straight forward
12 every one of them went straight forward
23 were their wings straight, the one
10 22 impulse of every one to go s. forward
47 20 straight on, till thou come to Emath
Mat 3 3 make s. his paths. Mark 1:3; Luke 3:4
Luke 3 5 and the crooked shall be made straight
13 13 she was made straight, and glorified
John 1 23 make straight the way of the Lord
Acts 16 11 we came with s. course to Samothracia
21 1 we came with a straight course to Coos
Heb 12 13 make straight steps with your feet
straightway Mark 15 1 s. in the morning the chief
strain Mat 23 24 who s. out a gnat, and swallow
straineth Prov 30 33 to bring out milk, s. out butter
strait Exod 28 4 a tunick and a s. linen garment
Lev 8 7 priest with the strait linen garment
2 K 24 14 said to Gad: I am in a great strait
4 K 6 1 we dwell . . . is too strait for us
1 Pa 21 13 I am on every side in a great strait
Isa 28 22 lest your bonds be tied strait. For
49 20 the place is too straight for me, make
Zach 10 11 shall pass over the strait of the sea
Mat 7 14 strait is the way that leadeth to life
Mark 5 1 they came over the strait of the sea
21 again in the ship over the strait, a
Acts 9 11 go into the street that is called Strait
straiten Ps 34 5 let the angel of the Lord s. them
Eccu 16 28 any of them straiten his neighbor at
Jer 19 9 seek their lives, shall straiten them
Luke 19 43 round, and straiten thee on every side
straitened Exod 14 3 they are s. in the land, the
Judg 1 34 the Amorrhite s. the children of Dan
1 K 13 6 the men of Israel saw that they were s.
2 K 22 46 shall be straitened in their distresses
Job 18 7 the step of his strength shall be s.
20 22 when he shall be filled, he shall be s.
Prov 4 12 thy steps shall not be straitened, and
Isa 28 20 the bed is straitened, so that one must
Dan 13 22 I am s. on every side: for if I do
Mich 2 7 is the spirit of the Lord straitened
Zach 11 8 and my soul was s. in their regard
1 Ma 13 49 and they were straitened with hunger
Luke 12 50 how am I s. until it be accomplished
2 C 4 8 we are straitened, but are not destitute
6 12 you are not straitened in us, but in
12 in your own bowels you are straitened
Phil 1 23 but I am straitened between two: having
straiteneth Job 32 18 spirit of my bowels s. me
straitness Dan 9 25 the walls in s. of times
2 Ma 12 21 at by reason of the s. of the places
straits Lam 1 3 taken her in the midst of s.
strakes 3 K 7 33 and s. and naves were all cast
strange Lev 10 1 offering before the Lord s. fire
Lev 16 1 slain upon their offering strange fire
Num 3 4 when they offered strange fire before
26 61 when they had offered the strange fire
Deut 29 28 hath thrown them into a strange land
3 K 11 1 king Solomon loved many strange women
4 K 19 24 I have drunk strange waters and have
2 Es 13 27 against our God and marry s. women
Tob 10 4 did we send thee to go to a s. country
Jdth 5 22 were led away captive into a s. land
Ps 17 46 strange children have faded away and
136 4 how shall we sing . . . in a s. land
143 7 waters from the hand of s. children
11 me out of the hand of s. children
Prov 2 16 mayst be delivered from the s. women
5 20 thou seduced, my son, by a s. woman
21 8 the perverse way of a man is strange
22 14 the mouth of a s. woman is a deep pit
23 27 and a strange woman is a narrow pit
33 thy eyes shall behold strange women
Wisd 16 16 being persecuted by strange waters
Eccu 29 24 have wandered in strange countries
32 22 s. and proud man will not dread fear
36 3 lift up thy hand over the s. nations
39 5 he shall pass into strange countries
49 7 and their glory to a strange nation
Isa 2 6 and have adhered to strange children
17 10 good plants and shalt sow strange seed
28 21 he may do his work, his strange work
21 his work is strange to him. And now
43 12 there was no strange one among you
Jer 2 21 good for nothing, O strange vineyard
8 19 with their idols and strange vanities
22 26 that bore thee, into a strange country
Bar 4 3 nor thy dignity to a strange nation
15 a wicked nation, and of a s. tongue
Eze 3 6 nor to many nations of a s. speech
Soph 1 8 such as are clothed with s. apparel
1 Ma 6 13 I perish with great grief in a s. land
2 Ma 5 9 perished in a strange land, going to
9 28 died a miserable death in a s. country
Mat 21 33 and went into a strange country. And
Acts 7 6 should sojourn in a strange country
Heb 13 9 be not led away with various and s.
1 P 4 4 they think it strange that you run not
12 think not strange the burning heat
strange god; *see* **god**
strange gods; *see* **gods**
stranger Gen 15 13 thy seed shall be a stranger
Gen 19 9 thou camest in, said they, as a s.
21 23 land wherein thou hast lived a stranger
23 4 am a stranger and sojourner among you
45 1 and no s. be present at their knowing
Exod 2 22 I have been a s. in a foreign. 18:3

12 19 whether he be a stranger or born in
45 the s. and the hireling shall not eat
48 any s. be willing to dwell among you
20 10 nor thy beast nor the s. that is
22 21 thou shalt not molest a s. 23:9
23 12 and the stranger may be refreshed
29 33 a s. shall not eat of them, because they
30 33 and shall give thereof to a stranger
Lev 16 29 stranger that sojourneth among you. 18:26
17 15 be one of your own country or a s.
19 33 if a stranger dwell in your land and
22 10 no s. shall eat of the sanctified things
13 no stranger hath leave to eat of them
25 to your God from the hand of a s.
24 16 whether he be a native or a stranger
22 whether he be a stranger or a native
25 35 receive him as a stranger and sojourner
47 if the hand of a s. or a sojourner
Num 1 51 what s. soever cometh to it, shall be
3 10 the s. that approacheth to minister
38 what stranger soever cometh unto it
9 14 the stranger . . . shall make the phase
14 for the stranger and for him that was
15 30 he be born in the land or a stranger
16 40 s. or any one that is not of the seed
18 4 a s. shall not join himself with you
7 if any stranger shall approach, he
Deut 1 16 whether . . . of your country or a s.
5 14 nor the s. that is within thy gates
10 18 loveth the s. and giveth him food
14 21 give it to the s. that is within thy
29 s. and the fatherless and the widow. 16:11, 14; 24:19, 20, 21; 26:12, 13; 27:19; Jer 14:8; 22:3
15 3 foreigner or s. thou mayst exact it
23 7 because thou wast a s. in his land
20 shalt not lend . . . but to the s.
24 14 whether he be thy brother or a stranger
17 not pervert the judgment of the s.
26 11 Levite and the s. that is with thee
28 43 s. that liveth with thee in the land
Josu 8 33 both the stranger and he that was born
Judg 19 16 and dwelt as a stranger in Gabaa; but
2 K 1 13 I am the son of a stranger of Amalec
12 4 and when a certain stranger was come
4 to make a feast for that stranger who
15 19 with the king, for thou art a stranger
22 45 the sons of the stranger will resist
3 K 8 41 the stranger, who is not of thy people
43 for which that s. shall call upon thee
2 Pa 6 32 if the stranger also, who is not of
33 do all that which that stranger shall
2 Es 9 2 separated themselves from every s.
13 3 they separated every s. from Israel
Esth 14 15 abhor the bed . . . of every stranger
16 10 was received being a stranger by us
Job 15 19 no stranger hath passed among them
19 15 maidservants have counted me as a s.
31 32 the stranger did not stay without
Ps 38 13 be not silent: for I am a s. with thee
68 9 I am become a stranger to my brethren
93 6 have slain the widow and the stranger
Prov 2 16 the stranger, who softeneth her words
6 1 hast engaged fast thy hand to a s.
24 from the flattering tongue of the s.
7 5 the stranger who sweeteneth her words
11 15 with evil, that is surety for a stranger
14 10 the stranger shall not intermeddle
20 16 garment of him that is surety for a s.
25 9 discover not the secret to a stranger
27 2 own mouth: a s., and not thy own lips
13 that hath been surety for a stranger
Ecce 6 2 but a stranger shall eat it up. This
Eccu 8 21 before a s. do no matter of counsel
11 36 receive a stranger in, and he shall
29 30 where a man is a stranger, he shall
32 go, stranger, and furnish the table
45 16 no s. was ever clothed with them
Isa 14 1 the stranger shall be joined with them
54 15 he that was a stranger to thee before
56 3 and let not the son of the stranger
6 children of the stranger that adhere
Jer 7 6 if you oppress not the stranger, the
14 8 why wilt thou be a stranger in the land
22 3 afflict not the s., the fatherless
Eze 14 7 every stranger among the proselytes
22 7 they have oppressed the stranger in
29 they oppressed the stranger by calumny
44 9 no stranger uncircumcised in heart
9 no stranger that is in the midst of
47 23 in what tribe soever the s. shall be
Zach 7 10 oppress not the widow . . . and the s.
Mala 3 5 oppress the s. and have not feared me
1 Ma 1 40 she became a stranger to her own seed
Mat 25 35 I was a stranger and you took me. 43
38 when did we see thee a stranger. 44
Luke 17 18 give glory to God, but this stranger
24 18 art thou only a stranger in Jerusalem
John 10 5 a stranger they follow not, but fly
Acts 7 29 was a stranger in the land of Madian

strangers Gen 17 27 and s. were circumcised with
Gen 31 15 hath he not counted us as strangers
42 7 he spoke as it were to strangers
Exod 6 4 land . . . wherein they were strangers
22 21 also were strangers in land of Egypt. 23:9; Lev 19:34; Deut 10:19
Lev 17 8 the strangers who sojourn among you
10 strangers that sojourn among them. 12, 13; 25:45
19 10 to the poor and the strangers to take
20 2 or of the strangers . . . give of his seed
22 18 of the strangers who dwell with you
23 22 leave them for the poor and for the s.
25 6 and to the s. that sojourn with thee
23 you are strangers and sojourners with
Num 15 13 and the s. shall offer sacrifices
15 and for them who are s. in the land
26 and the s. that sojourn among them
29 whether they be natives or strangers
19 10 s. that dwell among them shall observe
35 15 for the children of Israel as for s.
Deut 10 19 and do you therefore love strangers
29 22 and the s. that shall come from afar
31 12 and s. that are within thy gates
Josu 8 35 with the women and children and s.
20 9 for the s. that dwelt among them
2 K 22 46 the strangers are melted away, and
3 K 11 8 for all his wives that were strangers
1 Pa 29 15 we are sojourners before thee and s.
2 Pa 15 9 the strangers with them of Ephraim
2 Es 13 30 I separated from them all strangers
Tob 1 7 all his tithes to the proselytes and s.
Jdth 9 2 to execute vengeance against strangers
Job 19 13 my acquaintance like s. have departed
Ps 17 46 the children that are s. have lied
48 11 shall leave their riches to strangers
53 5 strangers have risen up against me
108 11 let strangers plunder his labors
145 9 the Lord keepeth the strangers, he
Prov 5 9 give not thy honor to strangers, and
10 lest s. be filled with thy strength
17 neither let strangers be partakers
20 16 take a pledge from him for strangers
27 13 take from him a pledge for strangers
Wisd 19 13 others indeed received not strangers
14 against their will received the s.

Eccu 45 22 and strangers stood up against him
Isa 1 7 your country s. devour before your
5 17 s. shall eat the deserts turned into
25 2 the house of strangers, to be no city
5 shalt bring down the tumult of s.
60 10 children of s. shall build up thy walls
61 5 strangers shall stand and shall feed
5 sons of s. shall be your husbandmen
62 8 sons of the s. shall not drink thy wine
Jer 2 25 I have loved strangers, and I will
3 13 hast scattered thy ways to strangers
5 19 so shall you serve s. in a land that
8 10 will I give their women to strangers
30 8 strangers shall no more rule over him
35 7 face of the earth, in which you are s.
51 51 s. are come upon the sanctuaries
Lam 5 2 our houses [are turned] to strangers
Eze 7 21 into the hands of strangers for spoil
16 32 as an adulteress that bringeth in s.
28 7 I will bring upon thee strangers
10 shalt die . . . by the hand of strangers
30 12 all that is therein by the hands of s.
31 12 s. and the most cruel of the nations
44 7 brought in s. uncircumcised in heart
47 22 inheritance to you and to the strangers
Dan 11 4 be rent in pieces, even for strangers
Osee 5 7 have begotten children that are s.
7 9 strangers have devoured his strength
8 7 if it should yield, s. shall eat it
Joel 3 17 strangers shall pass through it no more
Abdi 11 when s. carried away his army captive
1 Ma 1 40 the city was made the habitation of s.
2 8 are come into the hands of strangers
3 36 and that he should settle strangers
41 Syria and of the land of the strangers
45 the children of s. were in the castle
4 12 the strangers lifted up their eyes
22 all fled away into the land of the s.
26 such of the s. as escaped, went and
30 didst deliver up the camp of the s.
5 15 all Galilee is filled with strangers
68 to Azotus into land of the strangers
10 12 the s. that were in the strongholds
11 68 army of the s. met him in the plain
12 10 lest we should become strangers to you
2 Ma 10 5 temple had been polluted by the s.
14 taking with him the s., often fought
Mat 17 24 of their own children, or of strangers
25 he [Peter] said: Of strangers. Jesus
27 7 to be a burying place for strangers
John 10 5 they know not the voice of strangers
Acts 2 10 about Cyrene, and strangers of Rome
13 43 Jews, and of strangers who served God
17 21 the Athenians, and s. that were there
Eph 2 12 strangers to the testament, having no
19 you are no more strangers and foreigners
11 13 are pilgrims and strangers on the earth
1 P 1 1 to the s. dispersed through Pontus
2 11 you as s. and pilgrims, to refrain
3 J 5 for the brethren, and that for s.
strangled 1 K 17 35 and I s. and killed them. For
Acts 15 20 refrain from things strangled. 21:25
29 from things s., and from fornication
straw Gen 24 25 good store of both s. and hay
Gen 24 32 the camels, and gave straw and hay
Exod 5 7 you shall give straw no more to the
7 but let them go and gather straw
10 thus saith Pharao, I allow you no straw
12 all the land of Egypt to gather straw
13 wont to do when straw was given you
16 straw is not given us, and bricks are
18 straw shall not be given you, and you
Judg 19 19 we have straw and hay for provender

3 K 4 28 they brought barley also and straw
Job 13 25 power, and thou pursuest a dry straw
41 18 he shall esteem iron as straw, and
Isa 11 7 the lion shall eat straw like the ox
25 10 as straw is broken in pieces with the
65 25 the lion and the ox shall eat straw
Eze 13 10 they daubed it with dirt without straw
stray Exod 23 2 most part, to stray from the truth
Ps 118 10 let me not stray from thy commandments
strayed Exod 32 8 quickly strayed from the way
straying Jdth 11 5 for chastising of all s. souls
stream Ps 45 5 s. of the river maketh the city
Ps 125 4 captivity, O Lord, as a s. in the south
Prov 18 4 fountain of wisdom as an overflowing s.
Cant 4 15 which run with a strong stream from
Eccu 4 32 not strive against the s. of the river
Isa 59 19 when he shall come as a violent stream
Dan 7 10 a swift stream of fire issued forth
2 Ma 14 45 his blood ran down with a great stream
Luke 6 48 the stream beat vehemently. 49
streams Exod 7 19 their rivers and s. and pools
Exod 8 5 stretch forth thy hand upon the streams
Num 13 30 and near the streams of the Jordan
21 14 so will he do in the streams of Arnon
Deut 8 15 brought forth s. out of the hardest
Job 20 17 let him not see the s. of the river
Ps 64 11 fill up plentifully the streams thereof
77 16 and made streams run down as rivers
20 gushed out, and the s. overflowed
Prov 5 15 and the streams of thy own well
Cant 5 12 and sit beside the plentiful streams
Isa 11 15 shall strike it in the seven streams
19 6 s. of the banks shall be diminished
33 21 very broad and spacious s.: no ship
34 9 s. thereof shall be turned into pitch
35 6 in the desert, and s. in the wilderness
44 3 ground, and streams upon the dry land
Jer 46 7 his streams swell like those of rivers
Lam 3 48 hath run down with streams of water
Eze 31 4 s. thereof ran round about his roots
32 2 and didst trample upon their streams
street Gen 19 2 no, but we will abide in the s.
Judg 19 15 they sat in the street of the city
17 sitting with his bundles in the street
20 I beseech thee, stay not in the street
2 K 21 12 stolen them from the street of Bethsan
2 Pa 29 4 and assembled them in the east street
32 6 all together in the street of the gate
1 Es 10 9 sat in the street of the house of God
2 Es 3 8 unto the wall of the broad street
9 Hur, lord of the street of Jerusalem
11 built half the street and the tower
12 lord of half the street of Jerusalem
14 lord of the street of Bethacharam
15 built, lord of the street of Maspha
16 lord of half the street of Bethsur
17 lord of half the street of Ceila
17 built Hasebias . . . in his own street
8 1 street which is before the water gate
3 street that was before the water gate
16 and in the street of the water gate
16 in the street of the gate of Ephraim
Tob 2 3 children of Israel lay slain in the s.
Esth 4 1 cried with a loud voice in the street
6 was standing in the street of the city
6 9 going through the street of the city
11 arraying Mardochai in the street
Job 29 7 in the street they prepared me a chair
Prov 7 8 passeth through the s. by the corner
Ecce 12 4 they shall shut the doors in the street
5 mourners shall go round about in the s.
Isa 59 14 truth hath fallen down in the street
Lam 4 1 scattered in the top of every street

Eze 16 24 a brothel house in every street
31 hast made thy high place in every s.
Dan 9 25 and the street shall be built again
Amos 5 16 in every street there shall be wailing
Nah 3 10 dashed in pieces at top of every s.
Acts 9 11 go into the street that is called Strait
12 10 they passed on through one street: and
Apoc 21 21 the street of the city was pure gold
22 2 in the midst of the street thereof and
streets Gen 10 11 built Ninive and the s. of the
Deut 13 16 gather together in the midst of the s.
2 K 1 20 publish it not in streets of Ascalon
22 43 abroad like the mire of the streets
3 K 20 34 do thou make thee streets in Damascus
Tob 13 22 its streets shall be paved with white
22 alleluia shall be sung in its streets
Job 18 17 let not his name be renowned in the s.
Ps 17 43 to nought, like the dirt in the s.
54 12 deceit have not departed from its s.
143 14 nor crying out in their streets. They
Prov 1 20 she uttereth her voice in the streets
5 16 and in the streets divide thy waters
7 12 now abroad, now in the streets, now
22 13 I shall be slain in midst of the s.
Cant 3 2 in the s. and the broad ways I will
Eccu 9 7 nor wander up and down in the streets
23 30 shall be punished in the streets of
24 19 a plane tree by the water in the s.
49 8 made the streets thereof desolate
Isa 5 25 as dung in the midst of the streets
10 6 them down like the mire of the streets
15 3 in their streets they are girded with
3 and in their streets all shall howl
24 11 shall be a crying for wine in the s.
Jer 9 21 destroy . . . the young men from the s.
48 38 housetops of Moab and in the streets
49 26 young men shall fall in her s. 50:30
Lam 2 11 fainted away in the streets of the city
12 as the wounded in the s. of the city
19 for hunger at the top of all the s.
4 5 fed delicately have died in the s.
8 they are not known in the streets
14 have wandered as blind men in the s.
18 have slipped in the way of our streets
Eze 11 6 filled the s. thereof with the slain
26 11 he shall tread down all thy streets
28 23 pestilence, and blood in her streets
Mich 7 10 under foot as the mire of the streets
Nah 2 4 jostle one against another in the s.
Zach 8 5 s. of the city shall be full of boys
5 boys and girls playing in the streets
9 3 and gold as the mire of the streets
1 Ma 1 58 doors of the houses and in the streets
2 9 her old men are murdered in the s.
14 9 the ancient men sat all in the streets
2 Ma 3 19 the women . . . came together in the s.
10 2 the heathens had set up in the s.
Mat 6 2 do in the synagogues and in the streets
5 synagogues and corners of the streets
12 19 any man hear his voice in the streets
Mark 6 56 they laid the sick in the streets and
Luke 10 10 going forth into the streets thereof
13 26 and thou hast taught in our streets
14 21 go out quickly into the streets and
Acts 5 15 brought forth the sick into the s.
Apoc 11 8 their bodies shall lie in the streets
streets of Jerusalem; *see* **Jerusalem**
strength Exod 15 6 right hand . . . is magnified in s.
Num 14 17 let the s. of the Lord be magnified
23 22 whose s. is like to the rhinoceros. 24:8
Deut 8 17 strength of my own hand have achieved
18 thy God, that he hath given thee s.
28 32 may there be no strength in thy hand
Josu 2 9 inhabitants of the land have lost all s.
14 11 the strength of that time continueth
17 17 art a great people and of great strength
Judg 8 21 strength of a man is according to his age
16 6 wherein thy greatest strength lieth
1 K 2 4 and the weak are girt with strength
16 18 skilful player and one of great strength
28 20 and there was no strength in him [Saul]
22 thou mayest eat and recover strength
2 K 22 33 God who hath girded me with strength
40 thou hast girded me with strength to
3 K 1 8 s. of David's army was not with Adonias
19 8 and walked in the strength of that food
4 K 6 14 sent thither . . . the s. of an army
19 3 the woman in travail hath not strength
1 Pa 8 40 valiant men and archers of great s.
16 27 before him: s. and joy in his place
20 1 an army and the strength of the troops
2 Pa 16 9 eyes of the Lord . . . give strength to
20 6 in thy hand is strength and power, and
12 as for us we have not strength enough
25 8 consist in the strength of the army
2 Es 4 10 the strength of the bearer of burdens
8 10 the joy of the Lord is our strength
Jdth 9 16 nor is thy pleasure in the s. of horses
Esth 14 8 attributing the strength of their hands
10 may . . . praise the strength of idols
Job 3 17 there the wearied in s. are at rest
6 12 my s. is not the strength of stones
9 4 he is wise in heart and mighty in s.
19 if s. be demanded, he is most strong
12 13 with him is wisdom and strength, he
16 with him is strength and wisdom, he
22 8 in the s. of thy arm thou didst possess
23 6 should contend with me with much s.
26 2 the arm of him that has no strength
30 2 s. of whose hands was to me as nothing
36 19 and all the mighty of strength
37 23 he is great in s. and in judgment
39 19 wilt thou give strength to the horse
41 13 in his neck strength shall dwell, and
Ps 17 33 God who hath girt me with strength
40 thou hast girded me with strength
27 8 the Lord is the strength of his people
28 10 Lord will give strength to his people
29 8 thou gavest strength to my beauty
38 11 strength of thy hand hath made me faint
45 2 our God is our refuge and strength
47 14 set your hearts on her strength: and
59 9 Ephraim is the strength of my head
60 4 a tower of s. against the face of the
67 7 bringeth out them that were bound in s.
36 will give power and s. to his people
70 3 thou unto me . . . a place of strength
72 4 nor is there strength in their stripes
92 1 the Lord is clothed with strength and
102 20 you that are mighty in strength and
117 16 hand of the Lord hath wrought strength
137 3 thou shalt multiply strength in my soul
139 8 Lord, the strength of my salvation
146 10 not delight in strength of the horse
Prov 8 14 prudence is mine, strength is mine
10 29 s. of the upright is the way of the Lord
14 4 the strength of the ox is manifest
26 in fear of the Lord is confidence of s.
15 5 abundant justice there is greatest s.
6 the house of the just is very much s.
21 22 cast down the s. of the confidence
24 12 if thou say: I have not strength enough
31 17 she hath girded her loins with strength
25 strength and beauty are her clothing
Ecce 7 8 shall destroy the strength of his heart
9 16 wisdom is better than s. Wisd 6:1

Wisd 2 11 let our strength be the law of justice
6 4 strength [is given] by the most High
11 22 who shall resist the s. of thy arm
16 16 scourged by the strength of thy arm
23 did even forget its own strength. For
24 abateth its strength for the benefit
18 22 overcame . . . not by strength of body
Eccu 7 6 unless thou have s. enough to extirpate
17 2 clothed him with strength according to
31 40 lessening strength and causing wounds
38 19 it overwhelmeth the strength, and the
40 26 riches and strength lift up the heart
41 3 to him whose strength faileth: who is
43 34 exalt him, put forth all your strength
44 4 by the strength of wisdom instructing
46 11 the Lord gave strength also to Caleb
47 6 and he gave strength in his right hand
Isa 1 31 your s. shall be as the ashes of tow
3 1 the whole strength of bread and the whole strength of water
8 4 strength of Damascus and the spoils of
10 13 by the strength of my own hand I have
14 hath found the strength of the people
11 15 over the river in the s. of his spirit
23 4 speaketh, even the strength of the sea
14 of the sea, for your s. is laid waste
25 4 hast been a s. to the poor, a s. to the
26 1 Sion the city of our strength a savior
28 6 strength to them that return out of the
30 2 hoping for help in the s. of Pharao
3 s. of Pharao shall be to your confusion
15 silence and in hope shall your s. be
33 23 they shall be of no strength: thy mast
36 5 with what counsel or strength dost thou
37 3 there is not strength to bring forth
40 9 lift up thy voice with strength, thou
10 the Lord God shall come with strength
29 he that giveth strength to the weary
41 1 let . . . the nations take new strength
44 12 wrought with the strength of his arm
50 2 is there no strength in me to deliver
51 9 put on strength, O thou arm of the Lord
60 5 s. of the Gentiles shall come to thee
11 that s. of the Gentiles may be brought
Jer 48 30 strength thereof is not according to it
51 53 and establish her strength on high
Lam 1 6 they are gone away without strength
Bar 1 12 that the Lord may give us strength
3 14 learn where is wisdom, where is strength
Eze 28 5 thou hast increased thy strength: and
30 15 upon Pelusium the strength of Egypt
21 that it might recover s. and hold
33 28 the proud strength thereof shall fail
Dan 2 23 thou hast given me wisdom and strength
37 hath given thee a kingdom and strength
4 27 by the strength of my power and in
8 9 against the east and against the s.
10 magnified even unto the s. of heaven
10 it threw down of the s. and of the
11 magnified even to the prince of the s.
12 strength was given him against the
13 and the strength be trodden under foot
10 1 Baltassar, a true word and great s.
8 and there remained no strength in me
8 I fainted away and retained no strength
16 and no strength hath remained in me
17 no s. remaineth in me, moreover
11 6 she shall not obtain the strength of
15 to resist, and they shall not have s.
31 they shall defile the sanctuary of s.
Joel 3 16 the strength of the children of Israel
Amos 6 14 taken unto us horns by our own strength
Mich 3 8 I am filled with the s. of the spirit
5 4 shall . . . feed in the s. of the Lord
Nah 1 7 the Lord is good and giveth strength
3 9 Ethiopia and Egypt were the s. thereof
Soph 2 14 upper post, for I will consume her s.
Agge 2 23 the s. of the kingdom of the Gentiles
Zach 9 4 and shall strike her s. in the sea
1 Ma 2 49 now hath pride . . . gotten strength
61 none that trust in him fail in strength
3 19 the army, but s. cometh from heaven
35 to destroy . . . the strength of Israel
6 47 they seeing the strength of the king
62 Sion, and saw the strength of the place
10 71 for with me is the strength of war
2 Ma 10 34 trusting to the strength of the place
12 14 trusting in the strength of the walls
28 breaketh the strength of the enemies
Mark 12 33 whole soul and with the whole strength
Acts 3 7 his feet and soles received strength
12 as if by our strength or power we had
9 22 Saul increased much more in strength
2 C 1 8 were pressed out of measure above our s.
Heb 9 17 otherwise it is as yet of no strength
11 11 received strength to conceive seed, even
34 recovered s. from weakness, became
2 P 2 11 angels who are greater in strength and
Apoc 3 8 thou hast a little strength, and hast
5 12 power and divinity and wisdom and s.
7 12 power and strength to our God forever
12 10 now is come salvation and s. and the

his strength Deut 33 11 bless, O Lord, his strength
Judg 15 19 spirit and recovered his strength
16 5 of him wherein his great strength lieth
9 was not known wherein his s. lay
19 immediately his s. departed from him
1 K 2 9 no man shall prevail by his own s. The
3 K 15 23 all the acts of Asa and all his s.
4 K 10 34 acts of Jehu . . . and his strength
23 25 all his soul and with all his strength
1 Es 8 22 his power and strength and wrath upon
Jdth 4 12 Amalec that trusted in his own strength
16 5 north in the multitude of his strength
Esth 10 2 his s. and his empire and the dignity
Job 18 7 step of his strength shall be straitened
12 let his strength be wasted with famine
36 22 God is high in his strength, and none
37 6 winter rain, and the shower of his s.
39 11 thou have confidence in his great s.
40 11 his strength is in his loins, and his
Ps 32 16 giant be saved by his own great s.
17 be saved by the abundance of his s.
45 4 the mountains were troubled with his s.
88 41 thou hast made his strength fear
101 24 answered him in the way of his strength
Prov 10 15 substance of rich man is the city of his strength. 18:11
Eccu 34 18 doth he look, and who is his strength
38 33 boweth down his s. before his feet
46 11 his s. continued even to his old age
Isa 16 6 his indignation is more than his s.
31 9 his s. shall pass away with dread
40 26 by the greatness of his might and s.
62 8 his right hand and by the arm of his s.
63 1 walking in the greatness of his strength
Jer 9 23 let not the strong man glory in his s.
Eze 38 6 northern parts and all his strength
Dan 8 6 ran towards him in the force of his s.
22 of his nation, but not with his s.
11 25 his s. and his heart shall be stirred
Osee 7 9 strangers have devoured his strength
12 3 by his s. he had success with an angel
Amos 2 14 the valiant shall not possess his s.
Haba 1 11 fall: this is his strength of his god
3 4 in his hands: there is his s. hid

Apoc 13 2 the dragon gave him his own strength
my strength Gen 49 3 firstborn, thou art my s.
Exod 15 2 the Lord is my strength and my praise
Judg 7 2 say: I was delivered by my own strength
16 17 my strength shall depart from me
28 restore to me now my former strength
2 K 22 2 the Lord is my rock and my strength
Job 6 11 what is my strength, that I can hold
12 my s. is not the s. of stones, nor is
31 24 if I have thought gold my strength
Ps 17 2 I will love thee, O Lord, my strength
21 16 my s. is dried up like a potsherd
30 4 thou art my strength and my refuge
11 my s. is weakened through poverty
37 11 my strength hath left me, and the
42 2 thou art God my strength: why hast
58 10 I will keep my strength to thee: for
70 9 when my strength shall fail, do not
117 14 Lord is my s. and my. Isa 12:2
Isa 27 5 or rather shall it take hold of my s.
33 13 you that are near know my strength
49 4 I have spent my strength without cause
5 my God is made my strength. And he
Jer 16 19 O Lord, my might and my strength
Lam 1 14 put upon my neck: my s. is weakened
Haba 3 19 the Lord God is my strength: and he
their strength Judg 20 22 Israel trusting in t. s.
Jdth 6 15 and glory in their own strength. So
Ps 48 7 they that trust in their own strength
77 61 delivered their strength into captivity
88 18 thou art the glory of their strength
Prov 20 29 the joy of young men is their strength
Eccu 16 8 were destroyed trusting to their own s.
Isa 40 31 hope in the Lord shall renew their s.
63 6 brought down their s. to the earth
Jer 23 10 is become evil, and their s. unlike
49 35 the bow of Elam, and their chief s.
51 30 their strength hath failed and they
Eze 24 25 I will take away from them their s.
32 30 fearing and confounded in their s.
Dan 3 44 thy might, and let their s. be broken
Joel 2 22 and the vine have yielded their s.
Jon 3 8 and cry to the Lord with all their s.
Mich 4 13 and their strength to the Lord of the
7 16 and shall be confounded at all their s.
Nah 2 10 all the loins lose their strength
Soph 1 13 their strength shall become a booty
1 Ma 4 32 cause the boldness of their s. to
Apoc 17 13 their s. and power they shall deliver
thy strength Exod 15 13 in thy s. thou hast carried
Exod 18 18 the business is above thy strength
Deut 3 24 or to be compared to thy strength
6 5 soul and with thy whole strength
9 29 hast brought out by thy great strength
Judg 6 14 go in this thy strength, and thou shalt
16 15 me wherein thy great strength lieth
2 Pa 6 41 thou and the ark of thy strength: let
2 Es 1 10 whom thou hast redeemed by thy great s.
Ps 20 2 in thy strength, O Lord, the king shall
14 be thou exalted, O Lord, in thy own s.
53 3 thy name, and judge me in thy strength
58 17 I will sing thy strength: and will extol
64 7 who preparest the mountains by thy s.
65 3 in the multitude of thy s. thy enemies
67 29 command thy strength, O God: confirm
73 13 by thy s. didst make the sea firm
88 11 with the arm of thy strength thou hast
109 3 principality in the day of thy strength
121 7 let peace be in thy strength: and
Prov 5 10 lest strangers be filled with thy s.
24 10 distress, thy s. shall be diminished
Eccu 3 15 despise him not when thou art in thy s.
5 2 follow not in thy strength the desires
6 2 lest thy strength be quashed by folly
7 32 with all thy s. love him that made
9 2 to a woman, lest she enter upon thy s.
Isa 52 1 arise, put on thy strength, O Sion
63 15 where is thy zeal and thy strength
Jer 17 3 I will give thy strength and all thy
Eze 28 5 and thy heart is lifted up with thy s.
Amos 3 11 thy strength shall be taken away
Mark 12 30 whole mind and with thy whole strength
Luke 10 27 thy whole soul and with all thy s.
strengthen Gen 18 5 and strengthen ye your heart
Deut 3 28 Josue, and encourage and s. him
Judg 19 5 little bread and strengthen thy stomach
3 K 20 22 s. thyself and know and see what thou
Jdth 8 31 pray that God may strengthen my design
9 18 strengthen the resolution in my heart
10 8 may he strengthen all the counsel of
13 7 strengthen me, O Lord God of Israel
9 strengthen me, O Lord God, at this hour
Job 16 6 I would s. you with my mouth and would
Ps 50 14 and strengthen me with a perfect spirit
88 22 help him: and my arm shall s. him
103 15 that bread may strengthen man's heart
118 28 strengthen thou me in thy words. Remove
Prov 15 25 and will s. the borders of the widow
Eccu 4 20 she will s. him and make a straight
38 39 they shall s. the state of the world
Isa 8 9 s. yourselves and be overcome, gird
9 7 kingdom; to establish it and s. it
22 21 robe, and will s. him with thy girdle
35 3 s. ye the feeble hands, and confirm
54 2 lengthen thy cords and s. thy stakes
Jer 4 6 strengthen yourselves, stay not: for
6 1 s. yourselves, ye sons of Benjamin
51 12 the standard, strengthen the watch
Eze 30 24 I will s. the arms of the king of. 25
34 16 I will strengthen that which was weak
Nah 2 1 strengthen thy power exceedingly. For
Zach 10 6 I will strengthen the house of Juda
12 I will strengthen them in the Lord
1 Ma 6 18 their hurt, and to s. the Gentiles
10 23 friendship of the Jews to s. himself
2 Ma 15 17 and s. the hearts of the young men
Rom 1 11 unto you some spiritual grace, to s. you
2 Th 3 3 who will s. and keep you from evil
James 5 8 patient, and strengthen your hearts
Apoc 3 2 and strengthen the things that remain
strengthened Gen 48 2 being s. he sat on his bed
Gen 49 26 the blessings of thy father are s.
Judg 3 12 who s. against them Eglon king of Moab
7 11 then shall thy hands be strengthened
1 K 23 16 the wood, and s. his hands in God
2 K 2 7 let your hands be s. and be ye men of
16 21 father, their hands may be s. with thee
3 K 2 12 and his kingdom was s. exceedingly
2 Pa 1 1 and Solomon . . . was s. in his kingdom
11 17 they strengthened the kingdom of Juda
12 1 when the kingdom of Roboam was s. and
13 Roboam therefore was s. in Jerusalem
13 18 children of Juda were exceedingly s.
21 Abia, being s. in his kingdom, took
25 3 when he saw himself s. in his kingdom
26 15 the Lord helped him and had s. him
27 6 Joatham was strengthened because he
1 Es 7 28 I being s. by the hand of the Lord my
9 12 that you may be s. and may eat the
2 Es 2 18 their hands were strengthened in good
6 9 wherefore I s. my hands the more. And
Jdth 15 11 and thy heart has been strengthened
11 the hand of the Lord hath s. thee and
Job 4 3 thou hast strengthened the weary hands
4 thou hast s. the trembling knees
14 20 thou hast s. him for a little while

15 25 hath s. himself against the Almighty
21 7 are they advanced and s. with riches
Ps 9 20 arise, O Lord, let not man be s.: let
30 25 ye manfully, and let your heart be s.
102 11 he hath s. his mercy towards them that
104 4 seek ye the Lord, and be strengthened
24 strengthened them over their enemies
111 8 his heart is s., he shall not be moved
147 13 he hath s. the bolts of thy gates, he
Prov 12 3 men shall not be s. by wickedness: and
20 18 designs are strengthened by counsels
28 his throne is strengthened by clemency
24 3 by prudence it shall be strengthened
30 1 who being s. by God, abiding with him
31 17 with strength, and hath s. her arm
Ecce 7 20 wisdom hath strengthened the wise more
Eccu 17 20 he hath s. them that were fainting
49 4 in the days of sinners he s. godliness
12 they s. Jacob and redeemed themselves
Isa 41 7 he strengthened it with nails, that it
10 I have s. thee and have helped thee
Jer 5 6 their rebellions are strengthened. How
9 3 they have s. themselves upon the earth
23 14 they s. the hands of the wicked, that
Eze 7 13 shall man be s. in the iniquity of his
13 22 and have s. the hands of the wicked
34 4 the weak you have not strengthened
Dan 8 24 his power shall be strengthened, but
10 18 touched me again and strengthened me
19 speak, O my lord, for thou hast s. me
11 1 up that he might be s. and confirmed
5 and the king of the south shall be s.
6 that strengthened her in these times
Osee 7 15 have chastised them and s. their arms
12 4 prevailed over the angel and was s.
Zach 8 9 let your hands be s., you that hear
13 fear not, let your hands be s. For
12 5 let the inhabitants . . . be s. for me
1 Ma 14 14 he s. all those of his people that
Luke 1 80 the child grew and was s. in spirit
Acts 3 16 hath his name s.; and the faith which
9 19 when he had taken meat, he was s.
Rom 4 20 but was s. in faith, giving glory to God
1 C 16 13 fast in faith, do manfully, and be s.
Eph 3 16 glory, to be strengthened by his Spirit
6 10 finally, brethren, be s. in the Lord
Col 1 11 s. with all might, according to power
1 Tim 1 12 I give him thanks who hath s. me, even
2 Tim 4 17 Lord stood by me, and strengthened me

strengtheneth Ps 36 17 but the Lord s. the just
Phil 4 13 I can do all things in him who s. me

strengthening Judg 19 8 meat, and s. thyself
Eze 3 14 hand of the Lord was with me, s. me
Luke 22 43 angel from heaven strengthening him

stretch 4 K 21 13 I will s. over Jerusalem the
2 C 10 14 we s. not ourselves beyond our measure

stretch forth Exod 3 20 I will s. forth my hand. Jer 6:12; Eze 6:14; 14:9, 13; 25:7, 13, 16; 35:2
Exod 7 19 stretch forth thy hand upon the waters
8 5 stretch forth thy hand upon the streams
16 s. forth thy rod and strike the dust
9 22 stretch forth thy hand towards heaven
29 I will stretch forth my hands to the
10 12 stretch forth thy hand upon the land
21 stretch forth thy hand towards heaven
14 16 stretch forth thy hands over the sea
26 stretch forth thy hand over the sea
Job 1 11 but stretch forth thy hand a little
Ps 124 3 that the just may not s. forth their
Eccu 15 17 s. forth thy hand to which thou wilt
Isa 1 15 and when you stretch forth your hands
25 11 he shall stretch forth his hands under
Jer 10 20 is none to stretch forth my tent
48 40 shall stretch forth his wings to Moab
1 Ma 12 42 durst not s. forth his hand against him
14 31 to s. forth their hands against their
Luke 6 10 stretch forth thy hand. Mark 3:5
22 53 you did not stretch forth your hands
John 21 18 thou shalt stretch forth thy hands

stretch out Exod 9 15 I will s. out my hand to
Ps 59 10 into Edom I will stretch out my shoe
67 32 Ethiopia shall soon s. out her hands
107 10 over Edom I will stretch out my shoe
Eccu 7 36 stretch out thy hand to the poor
31 16 stretch not out thy hand first, lest
Isa 44 24 that alone stretch out the heavens
54 2 stretch out the skins of thy tabernacle
58 9 and cease to stretch out the finger
Jer 15 6 and I will s. out my hand against thee
51 25 I will stretch out my hand upon. Eze 16:27; 25:7; Soph 1:4
Soph 2 13 he will stretch out his hand upon the
1 Ma 12 39 and to s. out his hand against king

stretched 3 K 17 21 he s. and measured himself
Job 38 5 who hath stretched the line upon it
Eze 1 11 and their wings were stretched upward
Zach 1 16 the building line shall be stretched

stretched forth Exod 7 5 who have s. f. my hand
Exod 8 6 Aaron stretched forth his hand. 17
9 23 Moses stretched forth his rod. 10:13
33 he stretched forth his hands to the Lord
10 22 Moses stretched forth his hand
14 21 when Moses had s. forth his hand. 27
3 K 6 27 cherubims s. f. their wings, and
13 4 he s. forth his hand from the altar
4 his hand which he s. forth against him
2 Pa 6 12 of Israel and stretched forth his hands
Job 28 9 he hath s. forth his hand to the flint
Ps 54 21 hath stretched forth his hand to repay
79 12 it s. forth its branches unto the sea
137 7 s. forth thy hand against the wrath
142 6 I stretched forth my hands to thee
Eccu 50 16 s. forth his hand to make a libation
51 26 I stretched forth my hands on high
Isa 45 12 my hand stretched forth the heavens
Eze 17 7 stretched forth her branches to him
30 25 he shall have s. it forth upon the
1 Ma 9 47 Jonathan s. forth his hand to strike
2 Ma 15 15 Jeremias s. forth his right hand
Mat 12 13 he s. it forth. Mark 3:5; Luke 6:10
Mark 1 41 s. forth his hand; and touching him
Acts 12 1 the king stretched forth his hands

stretched out Josu 8 26 which he had s. out on
2 K 24 16 angel of the Lord had s. out his hand
Job 15 25 he hath s. out his hand against God
26 7 he s. out the north over the empty
Ps 87 10 I stretched out my hands to thee
139 6 they have s. out cords for a snare
Prov 1 24 I s. out my hand, and there was none
31 20 stretched out her hands to the poor
Eccu 4 36 let not thy hand be stretched out to
24 22 I have stretched out my branches as
46 3 and s. out swords against the cities
48 20 stretched out his hand against Sion
Isa 3 16 have walked with stretched out necks
5 25 and he hath s. out his hand upon them
25 but his hand is stretched out still. 9:12, 17, 21; 10:4
14 26 this is the hand that is stretched out
27 his hand is stretched out: and who
23 11 he s. out his hand over the sea, he
34 11 a line shall be stretched out upon it
42 5 created the heavens and s. them out
44 13 the carpenter hath s. out his rule
51 13 who stretched out the heavens and

Jer 51 15 s. out the heavens by his understanding
Lam 2 8 he hath stretched out his line and
Eze 1 22 and stretched out over their heads
4 7 and thy arm shall be stretched out
10 7 one cherub stretched out his arm from
28 14 cherub stretched out and protecting
37 8 the skin was stretched out over them
Osee 7 5 wine: he s. out his hand with scorners
1 Ma 7 47 which he had proudly stretched out and
2 Ma 7 10 and courageously s. out his hands: and
14 32 he s. out his hand to the temple and
15 32 hand, which he had stretched out
stretched out arm; *see* **arm**
stretchedst Exod 15 12 thou s. forth thy hand
stretchest Job 30 24 thou s. not forth thy hand
Ps 103 2 who s. out the heaven like a pavilion
stretcheth Ps 103 25 sea which s. wide its arms
Isa 25 11 stretcheth forth his hands to swim
40 22 he that s. out the heavens as nothing
Jer 10 12 s. out the heavens by his knowledge
Zach 12 1 who stretcheth forth the heavens and
stretching Gen 48 14 he s. forth his right hand
Lev 9 22 s. forth his hands to the people, he
Eccu 14 13 s. out thy hand give to the poor
Isa 8 8 the s. out of his wings shall fill the
2 Ma 14 34 the priests s. forth their hands to
15 21 stretching out his hands to heaven
Mat 8 3 Jesus s. forth his hand. 12:49; 14:31; Luke 5:13
26 51 s. forth his hand, drew out his sword
Acts 4 30 by s. forth thy hand to cures and
26 1 Paul s. forth his hand, began to make
Phil 3 13 s. forth myself to those that are before
strew Job 41 21 he shall strew gold under him
strewed Exod 32 20 which he strewed into water
1 K 4 12 rent and his head strewed with dust
2 K 1 2 rent, and dust strewed on his head
2 Pa 34 4 strewed the fragments upon the graves
Isa 14 11 under thee shall the moth be strewed
Mat 21 8 and s. them in the way. Mark 11:8
25 24 gatherest where thou hast not strewed
26 and gather where I have not strewed
strict Eccu 26 13 on a daughter . . . set a s. watch
strictly 2 Ma 10 12 determined to be s. just to
Mat 9 30 Jesus s. charged them. Mark 3:12; 8:30
Mark 1 43 clean. And he strictly charged him
5 43 he charged them s. that no man should
Luke 9 21 he strictly charging them, commanded
strife Gen 13 7 arose a s. between the herdsmen
Judg 5 15 was found a s. of courageous men. 16
12 2 I and my people were at great strife
2 K 19 9 all the people were at strife in all
Prov 17 1 than house full of victims with strife
18 6 lips of a fool intermeddle with strife
26 21 so an angry man stirreth up strife
30 33 provoketh wrath bringeth forth strife
Eccu 6 9 that will disclose hatred and strife
28 10 refrain from strife, and thou shalt
11 a passionate man kindleth a strife
40 4 fear of death, continual anger, and s.
9 strife and sword . . . for the wicked
Isa 58 4 behold you fast for debates and strife
Jer 15 10 why hast thou borne me a man of strife
Luke 22 24 there was also a strife amongst them
Acts 7 26 to them when they were at strife
strifes Prov 10 12 hatred stirreth up strifes: and
Prov 15 18 a passionate man stirreth up strifes
1 Tim 6 4 sick about questions and s. of words
2 Tim 2 23 knowing that they beget strifes. But
strike Exod 3 20 will strike Egypt with all my
Exod 7 17 I will strike with the rod that is in
8 2 I will strike all thy coasts with frogs
16 rod, and strike the dust of the earth
9 15 to strike thee and thy people with
12 13 when I shall strike the land of Egypt
17 5 wherewith thou didst strike the river
6 thou shalt strike the rock, and water
19 22 be sanctified, lest he strike them
21 18 one strike his neighbor with a stone
22 if . . . one strike a woman with child
26 man strike the eye of his manservant
27 also if he strike out a tooth of his
22 24 and I will strike you with the sword
32 32 strike me out of the book that thou
33 him will I strike out of my book: but
Lev 26 24 will strike you seven times for your
Num 14 12 will s. them therefore with pestilence
24 17 and shall strike the chiefs of Moab
35 16 if any man strike with iron, and he
21 strike him with his hand, and he die
Deut 19 11 and rise and strike him, and he die
21 4 shall strike off the head of the heifer
28 27 Lord s. thee with the ulcer of Egypt
28 the Lord strike thee with madness and
35 the Lord strike thee with a very sore
32 39 I will s. and I will heal: and there
33 11 strike the backs of his enemies and let
1 K 20 33 Saul caught up a spear to strike him
26 10 unless the Lord shall strike him or
2 K 5 8 whosoever should strike the Jebusites
24 to strike the army of the Philistines
13 28 when I shall say to you: Strike him
20 8 out with the least motion and strike
3 K 14 14 shall strike Israel as a reed is shaken
20 35 strike me. But he would not strike
37 said to him: Strike me. And he struck
22 34 chanced to strike the king of Israel
4 K 6 18 strike, I beseech thee, this people with
9 27 said: Strike him also in his chariot
13 17 thou shalt strike the Syrians in Aphec
18 strike with an arrow upon the ground
1 Pa 11 6 whosoever shall first s. the Jebusites
14 15 to strike the army of the Philistines
21 15 he sent an angel to Jerusalem to s. it
2 Pa 21 14 Lord will s. thee with a great plague
Jdth 9 13 do thou strike him by the graces of
16 8 neither did the sons of Titan s. him
Prov 17 26 nor to strike the prince, who judgeth
23 13 thou s. him with the rod, he shall not
Eccu 43 18 of his thunder shall strike the earth
Isa 1 5 for what shall I strike you any more
2 19 he shall rise up to s. the earth. 21
10 24 he shall strike thee with his rod
11 4 he shall strike the earth with the
15 shall strike it in the seven streams
19 22 Lord shall strike Egypt with a scourge
27 12 the Lord will strike from the channel
49 10 shall the heat nor the sun strike them
58 4 and strike with the fist wickedly. Do
Jer 18 18 and let us strike him with the tongue
20 4 and shall strike them with the sword
21 6 I will s. the inhabitants of this city
7 he shall strike them with the edge of
13 you say: Who shall strike us? and who
43 11 he shall . . . strike the land of Egypt
46 13 come and strike the land of Egypt
Eze 6 11 strike with thy hand, and stamp with
7 9 know that I am the Lord that strike
9 5 after him through the city and strike
21 12 strike therefore upon thy thigh because
14 and strike thy hands together and
Osee 6 2 he will strike, and he will cure us
7 12 I will s. them as their congregation
Amos 3 15 I will strike the winter house with
6 12 he will strike the greater houses
9 1 strike the hinges, and let the lintels

Mich 5 1 with a rod shall they strike the cheek
6 13 began to strike thee with desolation
Zach 9 4 shall strike her strength in the sea
10 11 and shall strike the waves in the sea
12 4 will s. every horse with astonishment
4 will strike every horse of the nations
13 7 strike the shepherd, and the sheep
14 12 plague wherewith the Lord shall strike
18 wherewith the Lord will strike all
Mala 4 6 lest I come and strike the earth
1 Ma 4 2 of the Jews and strike them suddenly
32 strike them with fear and cause the
9 47 forth his hand to strike Bacchides
Mat 5 39 if one strike thee on thy right cheek
24 49 begin to strike his fellow servants
26 31 I will strike the shepherd. Mark 14:27
Luke 12 45 shall begin to strike the menservants
22 49 Lord, shall we strike with the sword
Acts 23 2 stood by him to strike him on the mouth
3 God shall strike thee, thou whited wall
2 C 11 20 lifted up, if a man strike you on face
Apoc 11 6 to strike the earth with all plagues
19 15 that with it he may strike the nations
striker Num 35 21 s. shall be guilty of murder
1 Tim 3 3 not given to wine, no s., but modest
Titus 1 7 no striker, not greedy of filthy lucre
strikers Isa 50 6 I have given my body to the s.
strikest Exod 2 13 why strikest thou thy neighbor
Num 22 28 why strikest thou me, lo, now this
John 18 23 but if well, why strikest thou me
striketh Exod 21 12 he that s. a man with a will
Exod 21 15 he that striketh his father or mother
20 he that striketh his bondman or
Lev 24 17 he that striketh and killeth a man
21 he that striketh a beast, shall render
21 that striketh a man shall be punished
Job 5 18 he striketh, and his hands shall heal
Prov 27 22 when a pestle s. upon sodden barley
Isa 10 20 no more upon him that striketh them
Lam 3 30 his cheek to him that striketh him
2 Ma 3 39 he s. and destroyeth them that come
Luke 6 29 that striketh thee on the one cheek
Apoc 9 5 of a scorpion when he striketh a man
striking Exod 2 11 Egyptian s. one of the Hebrews
Exod 12 23 will pass through s. the Egyptians
27 striking the Egyptians, and saving our
Judg 4 21 striking it with the hammer, drove
2 K 6 8 place was called: The striking of Oza
18 15 of Joab, ran up, and s. him slew him
21 17 and striking the Philistine killed him
24 17 when he saw the angel s. the people
1 Pa 21 15 as he was striking it, the Lord beheld
Job 1 16 striking the sheep and the servants
Prov 19 29 and s. hammers for the bodies of fools
Isa 41 7 coppersmith striking with the hammer
Eze 3 13 creatures striking one against another
Mat 26 51 s. the servant of the high priest, cut
Luke 23 48 done, returned striking their breasts
Acts 7 24 s. the Egyptian, he avenged him who
12 7 he striking Peter on the side, raised
string Mark 7 35 string of his tongue was loosed
strings Deut 22 12 thou shalt make s. in the hem
Ps 32 2 instrument of ten strings. 91:4; 143:9
150 4 praise him with strings and organs
strip Judg 14 15 the wedding on purpose to s. us
1 K 31 8 the Philistines came to strip the slain
Ps 34 10 and the poor from them that strip him
Isa 24 1 waste the earth and shall strip it
32 11 strip you, and be confounded, gird
47 2 uncover thy shame, strip thy shoulder
Eze 16 39 they shall strip thee of thy garments
17 9 and strip off its fruit and dry up
23 36 they shall strip thee of thy garments
Osee 2 3 lest I strip her naked and set her
stripe Exod 21 25 wound for wound, stripe for s.
stripes Gen 12 17 his house with most grievous s.
Deut 25 2 that the offender be worthy of stripes
2 K 7 14 with the stripes of the children of men
Ps 72 4 nor is there strength in their stripes
88 33 will visit . . . their sins with stripes
Prov 17 10 than a hundred stripes with a fool
20 30 and stripes in the more inward parts
Eccu 22 6 stripes and instruction of wisdom are
Isa 16 7 the brick walls, tell ye their stripes
Jer 6 7 and stripes are continually before me
2 Ma 3 26 him without ceasing with many stripes
6 30 was now ready to die with the stripes
7 37 by torments and s. mayst confess that
Luke 12 47 shall be beaten with many stripes
48 did things worthy of stripes, shall be beaten with few stripes
Acts 16 23 they had laid many stripes upon them
33 washed their stripes, and himself was
2 C 6 5 in stripes, in prisons, in seditions
11 23 in s. above measure, in deaths often
24 five times did I receive forty stripes
Heb 11 36 had trial of mockeries and stripes
1 P 2 24 by whose stripes you were healed. For
stripling Gen 4 23 and a s. to my own bruising
stripped Exod 12 36 they stripped the Egyptians
Exod 32 25 Aaron had stripped them by occasion of
Num 20 26 when thou hast stripped the father
28 when he had stripped Aaron of his
1 K 18 4 Jonathan stripped himself of the coat
19 24 he [Saul] stripped himself also of his
31 9 and stripped him [Saul] of his armor
1 Pa 10 9 when they had stripped him and cut off
2 Pa 28 19 he had stripped it of help and
21 Achaz stripped the house of the Lord
2 Es 4 23 s. himself when he was to be washed
Jdth 2 16 and stripped them of all their riches
Job 14 10 when he shall be dead and stripped and
19 9 he hath stripped me of my glory, and
20 19 because he broke in and s. the poor
22 6 stripped the naked of their clothing
24 9 and stripped the poor common people
Isa 3 12 their oppressors have stripped them
Jer 17 4 be left stripped of thy inheritance
Bar 6 17 locks lest they be stripped by thieves
Joel 1 7 he hath stripped it bare and cast it
Mich 1 8 I will go stripped and naked: I will
2 Ma 4 38 Andronicus to be s. of his purple and
Luke 10 30 who also stripped him, and having
Heb 10 34 joy the being stripped of your own goods
stripping Mat 27 28 s. him, they put a scarlet
Col 3 9 stripping yourselves of the old man
stript Gen 37 23 stript him of his outside coat
strive Job 33 13 dost thou strive against him
Prov 3 30 s. not against a man without cause
Eccu 4 32 do not strive against the stream of
33 strive for justice for thy soul and
8 1 strive not with a powerful man, lest
4 strive not with a man that is full
9 13 strive not with her over wine; and
11 9 s. not in a matter which doth not
Isa 41 11 shall perish that strive against thee
Luke 13 24 strive to enter by the narrow gate
John 18 36 my servants would certainly s. that
2 Tim 2 5 not crowned, except he strive lawfully
striveth Wisd 15 9 he s. with the goldsmiths and
1 C 9 25 and every one that striveth for mastery
2 Tim 2 5 he also that striveth for the mastery
striving Col 1 29 s. according to his working
Heb 12 4 resisted unto blood, s. against sin
strivings Titus 3 9 contentions and s. about the
stroke Lev 13 2 that is, the s. of the leprosy

15 14 spirit of the Lord came s. upon him
16 30 when he had strongly shook the pillars
Prov 30 33 he that strongly squeezeth the paps
Isa 30 32 passage of the rod shall be s. grounded
1 Ma 5 46 city situate in the way, s. fortified
strove Gen 26 20 herdsmen of Gerara s. against
Num 20 13 where the children of Israel strove
Deut 9 7 hast always strove against the Lord
Judg 11 25 canst show that he s. against Israel
3 K 3 22 in this manner they s. before the king
Dan 7 2 winds . . . s. upon the great sea. And
2 Ma 3 4 s. in opposition to the high priest
John 6 53 the Jews therefore s. among themselves
Acts 23 9 some of the Pharisees rising up, strove
struck Gen 19 11 without, they s. with blindness
Gen 27 33 Isaac was struck with fear and
41 8 being struck with fear, he sent to all
45 3 being struck with exceeding great fear
Exod 7 20 rod he struck the water of the river
25 after that the Lord struck the river
8 17 and he struck the dust of the earth
20 18 struck with fear, they stood afar off
21 19 he that struck him shall be quit, yet
32 35 the Lord therefore struck the people
Num 3 13 since I s. the firstborn in the land
11 33 s. them with an exceeding great plague
14 37 and were s. in the sight of the Lord
20 11 struck the rock twice with the rod
21 8 whosoever being struck shall look on it
35 16 with iron, and he die that was struck
17 a stone, and he that is struck die
18 if he that is struck with wood die
18 by the blood of him that struck him
24 between him that struck and the next of
27 be struck by him that is the avenger
Deut 19 5 slipping from the handle s. his friend
Josu 7 5 heart of the people was s. with fear
10 26 Josue struck and slew them and hanged
24 5 I struck Egypt with many signs and
Judg 3 22 left it in his body as he had s. it in
4 15 the Lord struck a terror into Sisara
5 26 hammer, and she struck Sisara, seeking
7 13 when it was come to a tent it struck it
1 K 4 8 these are the gods that struck Egypt
6 6 did not he, after he was struck, then
17 35 I pursued after them and struck them
49 struck the Philistine in the forehead
50 and he struck and slew the Philistine
24 6 David's heart struck him because he
25 38 the Lord struck Nabal, and he died
31 4 he was struck with exceeding great fear
2 K 1 15 and he struck him so that he died
2 23 Abner struck him with his spear with a
4 7 they s. him and killed him [Isboseth]
6 7 he struck him [Oza] for his rashness
8 grieved because the Lord had s. Oza
12 15 the Lord also s. the child which the
20 10 [Joab] struck him [Amasa] in the side
24 10 David's heart struck him after the
3 K 2 46 [Banaias] . . . struck him and he died
16 10 Zambri rushing in, struck him [Ela]
20 37 and he struck him and wounded him
22 24 Sedecias . . . s. Micheas on the cheek
4 K 2 8 took his mantle . . . and s. the waters
14 he struck the waters with the mantle of
6 18 the Lord struck them with blindness
9 27 they struck him [Ochozias] in the going
12 21 servant struck him [Joas] and he died
13 18 he struck three times and stood still
15 5 the Lord struck the king, so that he
10 struck him publicly and killed him
14 he came into Samaria and struck Sellum
30 struck him [Phacee] and slew him
1 Pa 10 4 would not for he was struck with fear
13 10 the Lord was angry with Oza and s. him
15 13 lest as the Lord at first struck us
21 7 he struck Israel. And David said
2 Pa 13 20 Lord struck him [Jeroboam] and he died
18 23 Sedecias . . . came and struck Micheas
33 arrow . . . and struck the king of Israel
21 18 besides all this the Lord struck him
28 23 to the gods of Damascus that struck him
Jdth 5 10 and he struck the whole land of Egypt
13 10 and she struck twice upon his neck
16 7 but the almighty Lord hath struck him
Job 2 7 struck Job with a very grievous ulcer
16 11 they have struck me on the cheek
26 12 his wisdom has struck the proud one
34 26 he hath struck them, as being wicked
Ps 3 8 thou hast struck all them who are my
77 15 he struck the rock in the wilderness
20 he struck the rock, and the waters
Cant 5 7 found me: they s. me and wounded me
Wisd 17 6 being struck with the fear of that
19 16 but they were struck with blindness
Eccu 12 13 pity and enchanter struck by a serpent
Isa 5 25 his hand upon them and struck them
9 13 returned to him who hath struck them
14 6 that struck the people in wrath with
29 rod of him that struck thee is broken
27 7 hath he struck him according to the stroke of him that struck him
30 31 shall fear being struck with the rod
51 9 hast not thou struck the proud one
53 4 as one struck by God and afflicted
8 of my people have I struck him. And
57 17 I was angry and I struck him: I hid
60 10 for in my wrath have I struck thee
Jer 2 30 in vain have I struck your children
5 3 thou hast struck them, and they have
14 19 why then hast thou struck us, so
20 2 Phassur struck Jeremias the prophet
31 19 didst show unto me, I struck my thigh
41 2 with him, and they struck Godolias
52 27 the king of Babylon struck them and
Lam 3 43 in thy wrath, and hast struck us
Eze 27 35 their kings being struck with the
32 15 shall have struck all the inhabitants
34 21 struck all the weak cattle with your
Dan 2 34 and it struck the statue upon the feet
35 but the stone that struck the statue
5 6 his knees struck one against the other
8 7 struck the ram: and broke his two
11 30 he shall be struck and shall return
Osee 9 16 Ephraim is struck, their root is
Amos 4 9 I struck you with a burning wind and
Jon 4 7 it struck the ivy and it withered
Nah 1 13 his rod with which he struck thy back
Agge 2 18 I struck you with a blasting wind and
1 Ma 1 32 and struck it with a great slaughter
6 8 words, that he was struck with fear
9 55 at that time Alcimus was struck: and
66 struck Odares and his brethren and
10 8 and they were struck with great fear
12 28 they were struck with fear and dread
13 43 and he struck one tower and took it
2 Ma 3 24 were struck with fainting and dread
25 ran fiercely and struck Heliodorus
4 42 and some struck down to the ground
9 5 struck him with an incurable and
28 blasphemer, being grievously struck
12 22 the enemies were struck with fear
14 41 he struck himself with his sword
Mat 14 9 the king was struck sad. Mark 6:26
26 67 struck his face with the palms of their
68 O Christ, who is he that struck thee

27 30 they took the reed and struck his head
28 4 the guards were struck with terror
Mark 9 5 for they were struck with fear. And
14 were astonished and struck with fear
10 22 who being struck sad at that saying
14 47 struck a servant of the chief priest
65 struck him with the palms of their
15 19 and they struck his head with a reed
Luke 18 13 but struck his breast, saying: O God
22 50 s. servant of high priest. John 18:10
63 held him, mocked him and struck him
64 prophesy, who is it that struck thee
Acts 12 23 an angel of the Lord s. him, because
23 3 to the law commandest me to be struck
struckest Haba 3 13 thou s. the head of the house
struggled Gen 25 22 children struggled in her womb
strumpet Gen 34 31 they abuse our sister as a s.
Lev 19 29 make not thy daughter a common s.
Deut 23 18 shalt not offer the hire of a strumpet
stubble Exod 15 7 which hath devoured them like s.
Job 41 19 stones of the sling are to him like s.
20 as stubble will he esteem the hammer
Ps 82 14 wheel: and as stubble before the wind
Isa 5 24 tongue of the fire devoureth the s.
33 11 heat, you shall bring forth stubble
40 24 whirlwind shall take them away as s.
41 2 sword, as stubble driven by the wind
47 14 they are as s., fire hath burnt them
Jer 13 24 I will scatter them as stubble, which
Joel 2 5 flame of fire devouring the stubble
Abdi 18 the house of Esau [shall be] stubble
Nah 1 10 they shall be consumed as stubble
Mala 4 1 all that do wickedly shall be stubble
1 C 3 12 precious stones, wood, hay, stubble
stubborn Gen 49 7 their fury, because it was s.
Deut 21 18 if a man have a s. and unruly son
20 this our son is rebellious and s.
Judg 2 19 the stubborn way by which they were
Prov 29 21 afterwards shall find him stubborn
Eccu 30 8 a horse not broken becometh stubborn
12 a child, lest he grow stubborn and
Isa 48 4 for I knew that thou art stubborn
Jer 8 5 turned away with a s. revolting? They
2 Tim 3 4 traitors, s., puffed up and lovers of
stubbornness Lev 26 19 break the pride of your s.
Deut 9 27 look not on the s. of this people
stuck Ruth 1 14 stuck close to her mother-in-law
2 K 18 9 Absalom . . . his head stuck in the oak
20 2 the men of Juda stuck to their king
4 K 3 3 he stuck to the sins of Jeroboam the
18 6 stuck to the Lord and departed not
Ps 9 16 the Gentiles have stuck fast in the
62 9 my soul hath stuck close to thee: thy
118 31 I have stuck to thy testimonies, O Lord
Lam 4 4 hath stuck to the roof of his mouth
8 their skin hath stuck to their bones
studied Ps 37 13 and s. deceits all the day long
Ps 72 16 I studied that I might know this thing
studieth Prov 15 28 mind of the just s. obedience
Prov 17 19 he that s. discords, loveth quarrels
24 2 because their mind studieth robberies
studious 2 Ma 2 26 for the s. that they may more
study Prov 23 30 and s. to drink off their cups
Prov 27 11 study wisdom, my son, and make my heart
Ecce 2 15 myself more to the study of wisdom
12 12 much s. is an affliction of the flesh
Eze 11 2 these are the men that study iniquity
2 Tim 2 15 study to present thyself approved unto
studying Eccu 44 6 in virtue, s. beautifulness
2 Ma 2 29 plan proposed, studying to be brief
stuff Gen 31 37 had searched all my household stuff
Gen 45 20 leave nothing of your household stuff
2 Pa 20 25 they found . . . stuff of various kinds
Jdth 15 14 to Judith . . . all household stuff
stumble Prov 3 23 and thy foot shall not stumble
Prov 19 2 that is hasty with his feet shall s.
21 6 shall stumble upon the snares of death
Eccu 13 29 and if he s., they will overthrow him
27 29 for his neighbor, shall s. upon it
32 25 thou shalt not s. against the stones
37 16 when thou shalt stumble in the dark
Isa 8 15 very many of them shall stumble and
Jer 13 16 before your feet stumble upon the dark
31 9 they shall not stumble in it: for I am
Dan 11 19 he shall stumble and fall and shall
Nah 2 5 men, they shall stumble in their march
Mala 2 8 and have caused many to stumble at
1 P 2 8 to them who stumble at the word
stumbled 1 K 21 13 [David] s. against the doors
Isa 59 10 we have s. at noonday as in darkness
Jer 46 12 the strong hath stumbled against the
Rom 9 32 for they s. at the stumblingstone. As
11 11 have they so s., that they should fall
stumbleth Isa 63 13 in the wilderness that s. not
John 11 9 man walk in the day, he stumbleth not
10 if he walk in the night, he stumbleth
stumbling Tob 11 10 rising up, began to run s.
Eccu 34 20 a preservation from stumbling and a
Isa 8 14 stone of s. and for a rock of offence
Jer 18 15 s. in their ways, in ancient paths
1 P 2 8 a stone of stumbling, and a rock of
stumblingblock Lev 19 14 nor put a s. before the
Josu 23 13 s. at your sides, and stakes in your
1 K 18 21 that she may be a s. to him [David]
Ps 48 14 this way of theirs is a s. to them
68 23 let their table become as . . . a s.
105 36 idols, and it became a s. to them
118 165 thy law, and to them there is no s.
139 6 have laid for me a s. by the wayside
Prov 4 12 thou runnest thou shalt not meet a s.
Eccu 1 37 and let not thy lips be a s. to thee
7 6 powerful and lay a s. for thy integrity
9 5 maiden lest her beauty be a s. to thee
27 26 and on thy words he will lay a s.
31 7 gold is a s. to them that sacrifice to
40 of drunkenness is the s. of the fool
32 19 deceitfully, shall meet with a s.
25 way, lest thou set a s. to thy soul
Eze 3 20 I will lay a s. before him, he shall
7 19 it hath been the s. of their iniquity
14 3 their face the s. of their iniquity
4 s. of his iniquity before his face. 7
28 24 house of Israel shall have no more a s.
44 12 s. of iniquity to the house of Israel
1 Ma 5 4 were a snare and a s. to the people
Rom 11 9 let their table be made . . . trap and s.
14 13 put not s. or scandal in your brother's
1 C 1 23 unto Jews indeed a stumblingblock, and
8 9 liberty become stumblingblock to weak
Apoc 2 14 taught Balac to cast a s. before the
stumblingblocks Ps 140 9 s. of them that work
Eccu 39 29 to sinners they are s. in his wrath
Isa 57 14 take away the s. out of the way of my
Jer 4 1 if thou wilt take away thy s. out of
stumblingstone Rom 9 32 stumbled at the s.
Rom 9 33 I lay in Sion a s. and a rock of scandal
stump 1 K 5 5 only the stump of Dagon remained
Dan 4 12 leave the stump of its roots in the
20 the stump of the roots thereof. 23
stupefied Nah 2 3 the drivers are stupefied
stupid Ecce 7 17 is necessary, lest thou become s.
Sua 4 K 17 4 messengers to Sua the king of Egypt
1 Pa 4 11 Caleb the brother of Sua begot Mahir
Suaa 1 Pa 7 32 Heber begot . . . Suaa their sister
Sual 1 K 13 17 the way of Ephra to the land of S.
1 Pa 7 36 sons of Supha: Sue, Hernapher, and S.

Suar Num 1 8 Nathanael the son of Suar. 2:5; 7:18, 23; 10:15
Suba 2 Pa 8 3 he went also into Emath Suba and
Subael 1 Pa 24 20 was of the sons of Amram, Subael
1 Pa 24 20 and of the sons of Subael, Jehedeia
25 20 the thirteenth to Subael, to his sons
26 24 Subael . . . chief over the treasures
subdue Gen 1 28 fill the earth, and subdue it
Isa 14 2 and shall subdue their oppressors. And
45 1 to subdue nations before his face and
Zach 9 15 and subdue with the stones of the sling
1 Ma 4 28 horsemen, that he might subdue them
6 27 thou shalt not be able to subdue them
Phil 3 21 able to subdue all things unto himself
subdued Deut 25 19 shall have s. all the nations
Josu 17 13 they subdued the Chanaanites and
18 1 and the land was subdued before them
23 1 the nations round about being subdued
2 K 8 11 all the nations which he had subdued
Ps 17 40 hast s. under me them that rose up
46 4 he hath subdued the people under us
Wisd 18 22 he subdued him that punished them
1 Ma 1 5 he s. countries of nations and princes
5 44 and Carnaim was subdued, and could
1 C 15 28 all things shall be subdued unto him
subduest Ps 17 48 subduest the people under me
subdueth Ps 143 2 subdueth my people under me
Dan 2 40 into pieces and subdueth all things
subject Gen 37 8 shall we be s. to thy dominion
Exod 21 21 shall not be subject to the punishment
Lev 15 3 shall he be judged subject to this evil
25 long as she is subject to this disease
26 17 shall be made subject to them that hate
Num 32 29 if . . . the land be made subject to you
1 Pa 29 24 and were subject to Solomon the king
2 Pa 21 8 revolted from being subject to Juda
Jdth 3 2 and be subject to thee, than to die
4 let all we have be subject to thy law
Esth 9 16 which were s. to the king's dominion
13 1 provinces, that are subject to his empire
Ps 36 7 be subject to the Lord and pray to him
59 10 to me the foreigners are made subject
61 2 shall not my soul be subject to God
6 but be thou, O my soul, subject to God
118 54 thy justifications were s. of my song
Prov 18 1 he shall ever be subject to reproach
Ecce 3 19 all things are subject to vanity. And
5 8 reigneth over all the land s. to him
Wisd 1 4 nor dwell in a body subject to sins
8 14 and nations shall be subject to me
Eze 20 37 will make you subject to my scepter
36 3 are become the subject of the talk
2 Ma 9 12 it is just to be subject to God, and
Mat 8 9 I also am man s. to authority. Luke 7:8
Luke 2 51 to Nazareth and was subject to them
10 17 the devils also are subject to us in
20 that spirits are subject unto you
Acts 26 6 fathers, do I stand subject to judgment
Rom 3 19 all the world may be made subject to God
8 7 for it is not subject to the law of God
20 creature was made subject to vanity
20 reason of him that made it s., in hope
13 1 let every soul be s. to higher powers
5 wherefore be subject of necessity, not
1 C 14 32 of the prophets are s. to the prophets
34 but to be subject, as also the law saith
15 28 then Son also himself shall be subject
16 16 that you also be subject to such, and
Eph 5 21 being subject one to another, in fear
22 let women be subject to their husbands
24 as the church is subject to Christ, so
Col 3 18 wives, be subject to your husbands
Titus 1 7 not proud, not subject to anger, not
3 1 admonish them to be subject to princes
Heb 2 8 he left nothing not subject to him. But
8 see not as yet all things subject to him
15 all their lifetime subject to servitude
13 17 obey your prelates, and be s. to them
James 4 7 be subject therefore to God, but
1 P 2 13 be ye subject therefore to every human
18 servants, be subject to your masters
3 1 let wives be subject to their husbands
22 and virtues being made subject to him
5 5 young men, be subject to the ancients
subjected Ps 8 8 thou hast s. all things under
Eph 1 22 he hath s. all things under his feet
Heb 2 5 God hath not s. unto angels the world
8 thou hast s. all things under his feet
8 in that he hath subjected all things to
subjection Wisd 15 14 people that hold them in s.
Eccu 47 21 thou wast brought under subjection
Jer 34 11 let go free, and brought them into s.
16 you have brought them into subjection
2 Ma 13 11 again in s. to blasphemous nations
1 C 9 27 I chastise my body, and bring it into s.
Gal 2 5 to whom we yielded not by subjection, no
1 Tim 2 11 learn in silence, with all subjection
3 4 having his children in subjection with
1 P 3 5 bring in s. to their own husbands: as
subjects Esth 13 2 to govern my s. with clemency
Esth 16 3 endeavor to oppress the king's subjects
2 Ma 9 19 to his very good subjects the Jews
submit Exod 10 3 how long refusest thou to s. to
Job 22 21 submit thyself then to him, and be at
Eccu 4 31 s. not thyself to every man for sin
51 34 submit your neck to the yoke, and let
submitted Rom 10 3 not s. themselves to the
submitteth Eccu 19 24 there is one that s. himself
suborn 3 K 21 10 s. two men, sons of Belial
suborned Acts 6 11 then they suborned men to say
subscribe Isa 44 5 another shall s. with his
subscribed Jer 32 12 that s. the book of the
subscribers 2 Es 10 1 and the s. were Nehemias
subsist Job 18 19 his seed shall not s. nor his
subsistence 2 Ma 3 10 for the s. of the widows
substance Gen 7 4 and I will destroy every s.
Gen 7 23 he destroyed all the s. that was upon
12 5 all the s. which they had gathered
13 6 their s. was great and they could not
14 11 they took all the s. of the Sodomites
16 [Abram] brought back all the substance
15 14 they shall come out with great s. And
31 9 God hath taken your father's substance
37 what hast thou found of all the s.
34 23 their s. and cattle and all that they
Num 16 32 them with their tents and all their s.
32 1 their substance in beasts was infinite
Deut 11 6 households and tents and all their s.
Josu 22 8 with much s. and riches you return
1 Pa 27 31 rulers of the substance of king David
28 1 who had the charge over the substance
2 Pa 21 14 children and thy wives and all thy s.
17 they carried away all the substance
32 29 Lord had given him very much substance
35 7 all these were of the king's substance
1 Es 8 21 for our children and for all our s.
Tob 4 7 give alms out of thy substance, and
Esth 9 15 men: but they took not their substance
Job 6 22 to me, and give me of your substance
Ps 16 14 their little ones the rest of their s.
38 6 my substance is as nothing before thee
8 Lord? And my substance is with thee
88 48 remember what my substance is: for
108 11 may the usurer search all his substance
138 15 my s. in the lower parts of the earth
Prov 1 13 we shall find all precious substance

3 9 honor the Lord with thy substance and
6 31 shall give up all the s. of his house
10 15 s. of rich man is city of his. 18:11
12 27 s. of just man shall be precious gold
13 11 s. got in haste shall be diminished
22 s. of the sinner is kept for the just
29 3 shall squander away his substance
31 3 give not thy substance to women, and
Ecce 5 18 God hath given riches and s. 6:2
6 3 no use of the goods of his substance
Cant 8 7 all the substance of his house for love
Wisd 13 17 inquiring concerning his substance
Eccu 21 5 s. of the proud shall be rooted out
38 20 s. of the poor is according to his
Jer 20 5 I will give all the s. of this city
Eze 38 13 to carry away goods and substance
Luke 8 3 ministered to him of their substance
43 bestowed all her s. on physicians
15 12 give me the portion of substance that
Heb 10 34 have a better and a lasting substance
11 1 now faith is the substance of things
1 J 3 17 he that hath the substance of this
his substance Gen 14 12 dwelt in Sodom, and his s.
Gen 14 16 Lot his brother with his substance
31 1 enriched by his s. is become great
18 he took all his substance and flocks
36 6 and every soul of his house and his s.
39 5 and multiplied all his substance
Deut 21 16 to divide his substance among his sons
Josu 7 15 burnt with fire with all his s.
2 Pa 31 3 of his proper substance the holocaust
1 Es 10 8 his substance should be taken away
Tob 1 22 to be and took away all his s.
25 all his substance was restored to him
6 12 all his substance is due to thee, and
10 10 and half of all his s. in menservants
15 29 neither shall his substance continue
Job 1 10 and all his substance round about
Luke 15 12 he divided unto them his substance
13 there wasted his substance, living
30 who hath devoured his s. with harlots
Heb 1 3 glory, and the figure of his substance
3 14 hold the beginning of his substance firm
subtile Wisd 7 22 s. eloquent, active, undefiled
Wisd 7 23 all spirits, intelligible, pure, subtile
subtilties Eccu 39 2 withal into the s. of parables
subtilty Prov 1 4 to give s. to little ones, to
Prov 8 5 O little ones, understand subtilty
Mat 26 4 that by s. they might apprehend Jesus
2 C 11 3 serpent seduced Eve by his subtilty, so
subtle Gen 3 1 the serpent was more s. than any
Eccu 19 20 there is a subtle wickedness and the
37 21 there is a man that is subtle and a
subtlety Eccu 34 11 surprised, shall abound with s.
Subuel 1 Pa 23 16 the sons of Gersom: S. the first
1 Pa 25 4 sons of Heman . . . Subuel and Jerimoth
suburbs Lev 25 34 let not their s. be sold because
Num 35 3 cities to dwell in, and their suburbs. Josu 14:4
3 suburbs may be for their cattle and
4 which s. shall reach from the walls
5 in the midst, and the suburbs without
7 the cities . . . with their suburbs. Josu 21:19, 26, 33
Deut 32 32 vineyard . . . of suburbs of Gomorrha
Josu 21 2 and their suburbs to feed our cattle
3 gave out . . . cities and their suburbs
8 to the Levites the cities and their s. 1 Pa 6:64
11 and the suburbs thereof. 13, 21; 1 Pa 6:55, 57
16 and . . . , with their suburbs. 18, 22, 24, 25, 27, 29, 31, 32; 1 Pa 6:58, 59
35 four cities with their suburbs. 36, 37
1 Pa 5 16 and in all the suburbs of Saron unto
6 60 *N.* and its suburbs. 70, 71, 72, 73, 75, 76, 77, 79, 80
60 *N.* with its suburbs. 67, 68, 69, 71, 72, 73, 74, 75, 76, 77, 78, 79, 80, 81
9 16 who dwelt in the suburbs of Netophati
13 2 that dwell in the s. of the cities
2 Pa 11 14 leaving their s. and their possessions
31 19 and in the suburbs of each city
Isa 16 8 the suburbs of Hesebon are desolate
Eze 45 2 fifty cubits for the suburbs thereof
48 15 for the city for dwelling and for s.
17 s. of the city shall be to the north
1 Ma 11 4 showed him . . . Azotus and the suburbs
61 besieged it and burnt all the suburbs
subvert Titus 1 11 reproved, who s. whole houses
subverted 2 Tim 2 18 have s. the faith of some
Titus 3 11 such an one, is subverted, and sinneth
subverting Acts 15 24 with words, s. your souls
2 Tim 2 14 profit, but to the s. of the hearers
succeed Num 14 41 shall not s. prosperously with
Num 27 6 let them succeed him in his inheritance
9 no daughter, his brethren shall s. him
28 14 month, as they succeed one another
2 Pa 18 14 go up, for all shall s. prosperously
Job 20 2 various thoughts s. one another in me
20 believe . . . and all things shall s.
23 8 were accustomed to s. one another
Dan 11 28 he shall succeed and shall return
30 of the sanctuary, and he shall succeed
32 know their God shall prevail and s.
succeeded Gen 36 38 Balanan . . . s. to the kingdom
Deut 10 6 Eleazar his son succeeded him in the
Josu 5 7 children of these s. in the place of
14 4 their place s. the children of Joseph
Judg 10 3 to him succeeded Jair the Galaadite
12 11 to him s. Ahialon a Zabulonite: and
Dan 5 31 Darius . . . succeeded to the kingdom
1 Ma 4 27 because things had not s. in Israel
2 Ma 8 8 part succeeded prosperously with him
succeededeth Lev 6 22 rightfully s. his father
succeeding 2 Ma 4 29 Lysimachus his brother s.
success 2 Pa 18 12 and speak thou also good s.
Ps 117 25 save me: O Lord, give good success
Eccu 3 28 goeth two ways shall not have success
32 in works of justice shall have success
11 17 his advancement shall have success
20 9 there is success in evil things to a
Jer 32 5 you shall have no s. And Jeremias
1 Ma 3 19 the s. of war is not in the multitude
5 56 heard of the good success and the
8 23 good success be to the Romans and
2 Ma 10 7 for him that had given them good s.
23 having good success in arms and in all
28 Lord for a surety of victory and s.
13 16 they went off with good success. Now
successful Dan 8 25 craft shall be s. in his
succession Deut 18 8 city, by s. from his fathers
Jdth 14 6 with all the succession of his kindred
successions Exod 27 21 throughout their s. among
Exod 30 21 law to him and to his seed by s. and
successively 2 K 21 1 David for three years s.
successor Ruth 4 14 thy family to want a s.
Eccu 46 1 Jesus . . . who was successor of Moses
2 Ma 14 26 he meant to make Judas . . . his s.
Acts 24 27 Felix had for successor Portius Festus
successors Eccu 48 8 madest prophets s. after
succor Josu 10 6 save us, and bring us succor
Josu 10 33 Horam . . . came up to succor Lachis
Judg 18 28 no man at all who brought them any s.
2 K 8 5 Syrians . . . came to succor Adarezer
18 3 thou shouldst be in the city to s. us
Eccu 51 10 I looked for the succor of men, and
2 Ma 11 7 exhorted . . . to succor their brethren

Heb 2 18 able to s. them also that are tempted
succors Wisd 17 11 but a yielding up of the s.
Dan 11 25 with many and very strong succors
1 Ma 3 15 went up with him, strong succors, to
14 1 went into Media to get him succors
suck Gen 21 7 should hear that Sara gave suck
Deut 32 13 that he might suck honey out of the
33 19 who shall suck as milk the abundance
1 K 1 23 stayed at home and gave her son suck
3 K 3 21 in the morning to give my child suck
Job 20 16 he shall suck the head of asps and
39 30 her young ones shall suck up blood
Isa 60 16 shalt suck the milk of the Gentiles
66 11 that you may suck and be filled with
12 glory of the Gentiles that you shall s.
Lam 4 3 they have given suck to their young
Joel 2 16 ones and them that suck at the breasts
2 Ma 7 27 and gave thee suck three years and
Mat 24 19 that give suck in those days. Mark 13:17; Luke 21:23
Luke 11 27 and the paps that gave thee suck
23 29 and the paps that have not given suck
sucking Deut 32 25 s. child with the man in years
1 K 7 9 Samuel took a sucking lamb and offered
Cant 8 1 sucking the breasts of my mother, that
Isa 11 8 the sucking child shall play on the
Lam 4 4 the tongue of the sucking child hath
suckled Job 3 12 knees? Why s. at the breasts
suckling 1 K 6 10 two kine that had s. calves
1 K 15 3 slay . . . child and suckling, ox and
Jer 44 7 should die of you . . . child and s.
sucklings 1 K 22 19 and women, children and s.
Ps 8 3 out of the mouth of infants and s.
Lam 2 11 when the . . . sucklings fainted away
Mat 21 16 out of the mouth of infants and of s.
sudden Josu 11 7 to the waters of Meron on a s.
Judg 20 37 that were in ambush arose on a sudden
21 21 come ye on a s. out of the vineyards
1 K 4 19 her pains came upon her on a sudden
3 K 20 40 on a sudden he was not to be seen. And
Job 1 19 a violent wind came on a sudden from
9 12 if he examine on a sudden, who shall
10 8 thus cast me down headlong on a sudden
16 13 am all on a sudden broken to pieces
22 10 snares and sudden fear troubleth thee
37 21 the air on a sudden shall be thickened
Ps 63 6 they will shoot at him on a sudden
Prov 1 27 when sudden calamity shall fall on you
3 25 be not afraid of sudden fear, nor of
Wisd 17 6 there appeared to them a sudden fire
14 s. and unlooked-for fear was come upon
19 16 they were covered with sudden darkness
Eccu 5 9 for his wrath shall come on a sudden
11 23 on a sudden to make the poor man rich
Isa 30 13 destruction thereof shall come on a s.
Jer 4 20 my tents are destroyed on a sudden
15 8 a terror on a sudden upon the cities
Eze 26 16 shall wonder at thy sudden fall. And
32 10 they shall be astonished on a sudden
2 Ma 14 17 the sudden coming of the adversaries
Mark 13 36 lest coming on a sudden, he find you
1 Th 5 3 then shall s. destruction come upon
suddenly Num 6 9 if any man die s. before him
Josu 10 9 so Josue . . . came upon them suddenly
2 Pa 29 36 doing this thing was taken suddenly
Job 7 18 and thou provest him suddenly. How
24 17 if the morning suddenly appear, it is
26 12 the seas are suddenly gathered together
34 20 they shall suddenly die, and the people
Ps 72 19 they have suddenly ceased to be: they
Prov 6 15 and he shall suddenly be destroyed
24 22 their destruction shall rise suddenly
29 1 shall suddenly be destroyed: and health
Ecce 9 12 when it shall suddenly come upon them
Wisd 17 16 in the field and was s. overtaken, he
Isa 27 3 I will suddenly give it to drink: lest
29 6 and it shall be at an instant suddenly
40 24 suddenly he hath blown upon them, and
47 9 shall come upon thee s. in one day
11 misery shall come upon thee suddenly
48 3 I did them s. and they came to pass
60 22 the Lord will suddenly do this thing
Jer 6 26 the destroyer shall s. come upon us
18 7 I will s. speak against a nation and
9 and I will suddenly speak of a nation
22 shalt bring the robber upon them s.
49 19 I will make him run s. upon her. 50:44
51 8 Babylon is s. fallen and destroyed: howl
Haba 2 7 shall they not rise up suddenly that
1 Ma 1 32 he fell upon the city suddenly and
3 23 he rushed s. upon them: and Seron
4 2 they might . . . strike them suddenly
5 28 suddenly turned their march into the
2 Ma 3 27 and Heliodorus s. fell to the ground
5 5 Jason . . . suddenly assaulted the city
14 22 mischief might be s. practised by
Luke 2 13 suddenly there was with the angel a
9 39 and he s. crieth out, and he throweth
21 34 and that day come upon you suddenly
Acts 2 2 s. there came a sound from heaven, as
9 3 and suddenly a light from heaven shined
16 26 s. there was a great earthquake, so
22 6 s. from heaven there shone round about
28 6 and that he would s. fall down and die
suddenness Wisd 5 2 the s. of their unexpected
Sue Gen 25 2 who bore him . . . Jesboc and Sue
Gen 38 2 daughter of a man of Chanaan, called S.
12 daughter of Sue the wife of Juda died
1 Pa 1 32 Madan, Madian, Jesboc, and Sue
2 3 the Chanaanitess the daughter of Sue
49 begot Sue the father of Machbena
7 36 sons of Supha: Sue, Hernapher, and
suffer Gen 38 16 said: Suffer me to lie with thee
Gen 38 17 I will suffer what thou wilt, if thou
42 21 we deserve to suffer these things
Exod 12 23 not suffer the destroyer to come into
22 18 wizards thou shalt not suffer to live
23 11 seventh year . . . suffer it to rest
Lev 24 20 the like shall he be compelled to s.
Num 16 40 lest he should suffer as Core suffered
Deut 20 16 thou shalt suffer none at all to live
22 26 the damsel shall s. nothing: neither
26 his life, so also did the damsel suffer
24 19 suffer the stranger . . . to take it
28 29 mayst thou at all times suffer wrong
33 mayst thou always suffer oppression
Josu 10 19 not s. them . . . to shelter themselves
Judg 9 41 would not suffer them to abide in it
11 17 suffer me to pass through thy land. 19
15 1 her father would not suffer him, saying
16 26 suffer me to touch the pillars which
1 K 15 16 suffer me [Samuel] and I will tell thee
4 K 6 32 door, and suffer him not to come in
Tob 4 11 will not suffer the soul to go into
7 12 they know that we suffer great famine
14 never suffer pride to reign in thy mind
Jdth 3 2 or suffer the miseries of slavery. All
8 26 ourselves for these things which we s.
Job 6 2 calamity that I suffer were weighed
7 19 nor s. me to swallow down my spittle
10 14 why dost thou not s. me to be clean
20 suffer me . . . that I may lament my
20 18 of his devices so also shall he suffer
21 3 suffer me, and I will speak, and after
24 11 having trodden the winepresses suffer
12 God doth not s. it to pass unrevenged

36 2 s. me a little and I will show thee
Ps 9 14 humiliation which I s. from my enemies
54 23 he shall not suffer the just to waver
58 7 shall suffer hunger like dogs. 15
88 34 nor will I suffer my truth to fail
102 6 and judgment for all that suffer wrong
120 3 may he not suffer thy foot to be moved
145 7 judgment for them that suffer wrong
Prov 19 15 and an idle soul shall suffer hunger
19 he that is impatient, shall s. damage
28 27 that despiseth . . . shall s. indigence
Ecce 5 11 of the rich will not s. them to sleep
Wisd 14 10 that made it, shall suffer torments
18 1 did not suffer the same things, they
Eccu 23 1 counsel: nor suffer me to fall by them
19 lest . . . infatuated and s. reproach
Isa 38 14 I suffer violence, answer thou for me
Jer 42 14 sound of the trumpet, nor suffer hunger
Bar 4 25 suffer patiently the wrath that is come
Dan 14 11 hath eaten up all, we will suffer death
Amos 3 9 that s. oppression in the inner rooms
Soph 3 18 mayest no more suffer reproach for
1 Ma 5 42 suffer no man to stay behind: but let
7 38 s. them not to continue any longer
12 40 fearing lest Jonathan would not s. him
2 Ma 4 48 did soon suffer unjust punishment
6 15 so as to suffer our sins to come to
28 if . . . I suffer an honorable death
30 I suffer grievous pains in body: but in
30 in soul am well content to suffer these
7 18 we suffer these things for ourselves
32 for we suffer thus for our sins. And
12 2 would not suffer them to live in peace
13 11 not suffer the people, that had of late
14 6 will not s. the realm to be in peace
42 to suffer abuses unbecoming his noble
Mat 3 15 suffer it to be so now. For so it
5 10 that suffer persecution for justice'
8 21 s. me first to go and bury. Luke 9:59
13 30 suffer both to grow until the harvest
16 21 to Jerusalem and suffer many things
26 s. the loss of his own soul. Mark 8:36
17 12 the Son of man shall suffer from them
16 how long shall I suffer you. Mark 9:18
19 14 suffer the little children. Mark 10:14
23 13 are going in, you suffer not to enter
24 43 s. his house to be broken. Luke 12:39
Mark 7 12 you suffer him not to do anything for
27 suffer first the children to be filled
8 31 Son of man must s. many things. Luke 9:2
9 11 he must s. many things. Luke 17:25
Luke 8 32 that he would suffer them to enter
9 41 shall I be with you and suffer you
18 16 suffer children to come to me, and
22 15 this pasch with you before I suffer
51 suffer ye thus far. And when he had
24 46 and thus it behoved Christ to suffer
Acts 2 27 nor s. thy Holy One to see corruption
3 18 that his Christ should suffer, he hath
5 41 to s. reproach for the name of Jesus
7 24 he had seen one of them suffer wrong
9 16 things he must suffer for my name's sake
13 35 thou shalt not s. thy holy one to see
17 3 Christ was to suffer, and to rise again
21 39 I beseech thee, s. me to speak to people
26 23 Christ should suffer, and that he should
28 4 yet vengeance doth not s. him to live
Rom 8 17 if we s. with him, that we may be also
1 C 3 15 if any man's work burn, he shall suffer
4 12 we are persecuted, and we suffer it
6 7 do you not rather suffer yourselves to
10 13 who will not s. you to be tempted above
12 26 one member s. anything, all members s.
2 C 1 6 the same sufferings which we also suffer
4 8 in all things we suffer tribulation, but
9 we s. persecution, but are not forsaken
7 9 you might suffer damage by us in nothing
11 19 also. For you gladly suffer the foolish
20 you s. if a man bring you into bondage
Gal 5 11 why do I yet suffer persecution? Then
6 12 they may not suffer the persecution of
Phil 1 29 to believe in him, but also to s. for
4 12 both to abound, and to suffer need. I
1 Th 3 4 we foretold you that we should suffer
2 Th 1 5 kingdom of God, for which also you s.
1 Tim 2 12 but I suffer not a woman to teach, nor
5 10 ministered to them that s. tribulation
2 Tim 1 12 which cause I also suffer these things
2 12 if we suffer, we shall also reign with
3 12 in Christ Jesus, shall s. persecution
Heb 13 22 that you s. this word of consolation
1 P 2 20 but if doing well you suffer patiently
3 14 but if also you suffer anything for
17 doing well . . . to suffer, than doing
4 15 let none of you suffer as a murderer
19 that s. according to the will of God
Apoc 2 10 of those things which thou shalt suffer
11 9 not suffer their bodies to be laid in

suffered Gen 20 6 I s. thee not to touch her
Gen 31 7 God hath not suffered him to hurt me
28 not suffered me to kiss my sons and
50 15 should remember the wrong he suffered
Num 15 40 lest he should suffer as Core suffered
Judg 3 28 they suffered no man to pass over
11 20 s. him not to pass through his borders
Ruth 4 14 hath not s. thy family to want a
1 K 24 8 suffered them not to rise against Saul
2 K 21 16 s. neither the birds to tear them by
1 Pa 16 21 he suffered no man to do them wrong
19 5 for they had suffered a great affront
Tob 4 4 how great perils she suffered for thee
Jdth 13 20 Lord hath not s. his handmaid to be
Job 16 18 these things I have suffered without
Ps 33 11 rich have wanted, and have s. hunger
65 9 hath not suffered my feet to be moved
104 14 he suffered no man to hurt them: and
106 38 their cattle he s. not to decrease
Prov 22 3 the simple passed on and suffered loss
27 12 little ones passing on have s. losses
Ecce 8 8 neither is he suffered to rest when war
Wisd 3 4 in the sight of men they s. torments
12 27 they s. by those very things which
18 11 common man s. in like manner as the
11 the servant s. the same punishment as
19 not know why they suffered these evils
19 12 they s. justly according to their own
Eccu 38 16 as if thou hadst s. some great harm
Jer 15 15 for thy sake I have suffered reproach
1 Ma 15 14 and s. none to come in or to go out
2 Ma 6 13 when sinners are not s. to go on in
11 13 considering . . . the loss he had s.
Mat 3 15 all justice. Then he suffered him
27 19 I have s. many things this day in a
Mark 1 34 he s. them not to speak. Luke 4:41
5 26 had s. many things from many physicians
11 16 he suffered not that any man should
Luke 8 32 into them. And he suffered them
51 he s. not any man to go in with him
13 2 because they suffered such things? No
24 26 ought not Christ to have suffered
Acts 7 24 avenged him who suffered the injury
14 15 in times past s. all nations to walk
16 7 the Spirit of Jesus suffered them not
19 30 people, the disciples suffered him not
28 5 beast into the fire, suffered no harm
16 Paul was suffered to dwell by himself

2 C 7 5 no rest, but we suffered all tribulation
12 did wrong, nor for him that s. it; but
11 25 thrice I suffered shipwreck, a night
Gal 3 4 have you s. so great things in vain
Phil 3 8 for whom I have suffered the loss of
1 Th 2 2 having suffered many things before, and
14 you also have suffered the same things
Heb 2 18 in that, wherein he himself hath s. and
5 8 obedience by things which he suffered
7 23 by reason of death they were not s. to
9 26 he ought to have suffered often from
13 12 Jesus . . . suffered without the gate
1 P 2 21 Christ also s. for us, leaving you an
23 when he suffered, he threatened not
4 1 Christ therefore having s. in the flesh
1 that hath s. in the flesh, hath ceased
5 10 after you have suffered a little, will
sufferest 1 K 28 18 to thee what thou s. this day
Apoc 2 20 thou sufferest the woman Jezabel, who
suffereth Lev 15 13 if he who s. this disease be
Lev 22 4 or that suffereth a running of the seed
Prov 17 14 before he s. reproach he forsaketh
Eccu 4 9 deliver him that s. wrong out of the
2 Ma 14 8 all our nation s. much from the
Mat 11 12 kingdom of heaven suffereth violence
17 14 he is a lunatic and suffereth much
Eph 4 28 something to give to him that s. need
suffering Exod 12 39 not s. them to make any stay
Job 19 7 I shall cry s. violence, and no one
Wisd 16 3 after suffering want for a short time
Lam 3 39 murmured, man suffering for his sins
Haba 1 2 shall I cry out to thee s. violence
2 Ma 7 5 while he was s. therein long torments
Acts 27 7 the wind not suffering us, we sailed
Heb 2 9 angels, for the suffering of death
James 5 10 an example of s. evil, of labor and
1 P 2 19 a man endure sorrows, s. wrongfully
Jude 7 s. the punishment of eternal fire. In
sufferings Rom 8 18 I reckon that the s. of this
2 C 1 5 as the sufferings of Christ abound in us
6 the same sufferings which we also suffer
7 as you are partakers of the sufferings
Phil 3 10 fellowship of his sufferings, being made
Col 1 24 who now rejoice in my sufferings for
24 things that are wanting of s. of Christ
1 P 1 11 when it foretold those s. that are in
4 13 if you partake of the s. of Christ
5 1 and a witness of the s. of Christ
suffice Exod 12 4 less than may s. to eat the lamb
Exod 16 21 as much as might suffice to eat: and
36 7 the things that were offered did s.
Num 11 22 that it may suffice for their food
3 K 20 10 if the dust of Samaria shall s. for
Eze 44 6 let all your wicked doings s. you, O
45 9 let it suffice you, O princes of Israel
2 Ma 6 17 let this suffice in a few words for
sufficiency Lev 12 8 if her hand find not s.
2 C 3 5 as of ourselves; but our s. is from God
9 8 having all s. in all things, may abound
sufficient Exod 16 4 gather what is s. for every
Tob 5 25 for our poverty was sufficient for us
12 3 what can we give him s. for these
Jdth 2 8 provisions sufficient for the armies
15 13 and thirty days were scarce sufficient
Prov 25 16 found honey, eat what is s. for thee
Wisd 18 12 neither were the living s. to bury them
Eccu 11 26 say not: I am sufficient for myself: and
31 22 how sufficient is a little wine for a
Isa 40 16 beasts thereof s. for a burnt offering
2 Ma 10 19 in sufficient number to besiege them
Mat 6 34 sufficient for the day is the evil
John 6 7 him: 200 pennyworth of bread is not s.
2 C 2 6 this rebuke is sufficient, which is
16 for these things who is so sufficient
3 5 not that we are sufficient to think
12 9 to me: My grace is sufficient for thee
1 Tim 5 16 that there may be sufficient for them
1 P 4 3 time past is s. to have fulfilled the
suffocatest Eze 36 13 and one that s. thy nation
suggest Job 13 12 whatsoever my mind shall s. to
suggested Gen 44 22 we s. to my lord: The boy
Exod 18 24 things that he had suggested unto him
Dan 6 6 craftily suggested to the king and
suggesting 2 Ma 13 4 Lysias s. that he was the
suggestion 2 Ma 6 8 by the s. of the Ptolemeans
suggestions Esth 16 7 by the evil s. of certain
Suham Num 26 42 the sons of Dan . . . Suham
Suhamites Num 26 42 is the family of the S.
Num 26 43 all were Suhamites, whose number was
Suhite Job 2 11 Baldad the Suhite. 8:1; 18:1; 25:1; 42:9
suit Judg 17 10 and a double suit of apparel and
suitable Judg 9 16 a s. return for the benefits
Sulamitess Cant 6 12 return, O Sulamitess: return
Cant 7 1 what shalt thou see in the Sulamitess
sully Eccu 33 24 let no stain sully thy glory. In
sum Exod 30 12 the sum of the children of Israel. Num 26:2, 51
Num 1 2 take the sum of all the congregation
49 neither shalt thou put down the sum
2 4 the sum of the fighting men . . . 74,600
3 40 firstborn . . . thou shalt take the sum
4 2 take the sum of the sons of Caath
22 take the sum of the sons of Gerson
31 26 the sum of the things that were taken
2 K 24 9 the sum of the number of the people
3 K 9 15 this is the sum of the expenses which
1 Pa 4 27 to the sum of the children of Juda
9 1 sum of them was written in the book
2 Pa 9 14 beside the sum which the deputies of
15 the sum of six hundred pieces of gold
24 11 was gathered an immense sum of money
27 concerning his sons and the s. of money
Tob 1 17 he gave him the aforesaid sum of money
4 22 and receive of him the foresaid sum
Eccu 43 29 the sum of our words is, He is all
51 36 receive ye discipline as a great sum
Dan 7 1 relating the sum of it in short, he
Mat 28 12 a great sum of money to the soldiers
Acts 7 16 Abraham bought for a sum of money of
22 28 being free of this city with a great sum
Heb 8 1 this is the sum: We have such an high
summer Gen 8 22 cold and heat, summer and winter
Judg 3 20 he was sitting in a summer parlor alone
24 is easing nature in his summer parlor
Ps 73 17 s. and the spring were formed by thee
Prov 6 8 her meat for herself in the summer
10 5 he that snorteth in the summer is the
20 4 he shall beg therefore in the summer
26 1 as snow in summer, and rain in harvest
Eccu 50 8 frankincense in the time of summer
Isa 18 6 the fowls shall be upon them all the s.
Jer 8 20 harvest is past, the summer is ended
Amos 3 15 winter house with the summer house
Zach 14 8 they shall be in summer and in winter
Mat 24 32 you know that s. is nigh. Luke 21:30
Mark 13 28 you know that summer is very near
summer's Dan 2 35 chaff of a s. thrashingfloor
sumptuous Eccu 29 28 s. cheer abroad in another
sumptuously Luke 16 19 and feasted s. every day
sums Deut 17 17 immense sums of silver and gold
2 Ma 1 14 that he might receive great sums of
3 6 was full of immense sums of money, and
10 told him that these were sums deposited
sun Gen 15 12 when the sun was setting, a deep
Gen 15 17 when the sun was set, there arose
19 23 the sun was risen upon the earth

	32	31	immediately the sun rose upon him
	37	9	I saw in a dream, as it were the sun
Exod	16	21	after the sun grew hot, it melted
	22	3	if he did this when the sun is risen
Lev	11	25	shall be unclean until the sun set
	22	7	the sun is down, then being purified
Num	25	4	hang them up on gibbets against the sun
Deut	4	19	thou see the sun and the moon
		47	Jordan towards the rising of the sun
	11	30	that goeth to the setting of the sun
	16	6	evening at the going down of the sun
	17	3	and adore them, the sun and the moon
	24	13	before the going down of the sun. 15
	33	14	of the fruits brought forth by the sun
Josu	1	4	toward the going down of the sun
		15	the Jordan, toward the rising of the sun
	8	29	and the going down of the sun. Then
	10	12	move not, O sun, toward Gabaon, nor
		13	the sun and moon stood still, till the
		13	the sun stood still in the midst of
		27	when sun was down, he commanded the
	12	1	towards the rising of the sun, from
	15	7	that are called the fountain of the sun
	18	17	is to say, the fountain of the sun
	19	34	towards the rising of the sun. And the
		41	Hirsemes, that is, the city of the sun
Judg	8	13	returning from battle before sun rising
	9	33	at sun rising set upon the city. And
	14	18	on seventh day before the sun went down
	19	14	and the sun went down upon them when
1 K	11	9	tomorrow, when the sun shall be hot
2 K	2	24	pursued after Abner, the sun went down
	12	11	with thy wives in sight of this sun
		12	all Israel, and in the sight of the sun
	23	4	of the morning, when the sun riseth
3 K	22	36	all the army before the sun set, saying
4 K	3	22	the sun being now up and shining
	23	5	burnt incense to Baal and to the sun
		11	kings of Juda had given to the sun
		11	and he burnt the chariots of the sun
1 Pa	4	22	and he that made the sun to stand
2 Es	7	3	be opened till the sun be hot. And
Tob	2	4	after the sun was down, he might bury
		7	when sun was down, he went and buried
Jdth	14	2	as soon as the sun shall rise, let
Esth	10	6	turned into a light and into the sun
	11	11	the light and the sun rose up, and
Job	8	16	to have moisture before the sun cometh
	9	7	commandeth the sun, and it riseth not
	31	26	if I beheld the sun when it shined
	41	21	beams of the sun shall be under him
Ps	18	6	he hath set his tabernacle in the sun
	49	1	from the rising of the sun to the
	57	9	they shall not see the sun. Before
	71	5	he shall continue with the sun and
		17	his name continueth before the sun
	73	16	made the morning light and the sun
	88	38	and his throne as the sun before me
	103	19	the sun knoweth his going down. Thou
		22	the sun ariseth, and they are gathered
	106	3	and from the setting of the sun, from
	112	3	from the rising of the sun unto the
	120	6	the sun shall not burn thee by day
	135	8	the sun to rule the day: for his mercy
	148	3	praise ye him, O sun and moon: praise
Ecce	1	3	labor that he taketh under the sun
		5	the sun riseth and goeth down, and
		10	nothing under the sun is new, neither
		13	things that are done under the sun. 14
	2	3	what they ought to do under the sun
		11	nothing was lasting under the sun
		17	saw that all things under sun are evil
		18	I had earnestly labored under the sun
		20	laboring any more under the sun. For
		22	he hath been tormented under the sun
	3	16	I saw under the sun in the place of
	4	1	oppressions that are done under the sun
		3	the evils that are done under the sun
		7	found also another vanity under the sun
		15	all men living, that walk under the sun
	5	12	evil which I have seen under the sun
		17	he hath labored under the sun, all
	6	1	evil which I have seen under the sun
		5	he hath not seen the sun nor known
	7	1	what shall be after him under the sun
		12	more advantage to them that see the sun
	8	9	the works that are done under the sun
		15	was no good for a man under the sun
		15	which God hath given him under the sun
		17	of God that are done under the sun
	9	3	all things that are done under the sun
		6	in the work that is done under the sun
		9	which are given to thee under the sun
		9	wherewith thou laborest under the sun
		11	I saw that under the sun, the race
		13	I have seen under the sun. 10:5
	11	7	delightful for the eyes to see the sun
	12	2	before the sun and the light and the
Cant	1	5	the sun hath altered my color: the sons
	6	9	fair as the moon, bright as the sun
Wisd	2	3	is driven away by the beams of the sun
	5	6	sun of understanding hath not risen
	7	29	she is more beautiful than the sun
	13	2	or the sun and moon to be the gods
	16	28	we ought to prevent the sun to bless
	18	3	thou gavest them a harmless sun
Eccu	17	16	and all their works are as the sun
		30	what is brighter than the sun; yet
	23	28	Lord are far brighter than the sun
	26	21	as the sun when it riseth to the world
	27	12	continueth in wisdom as the sun: but a
	33	7	another year, when all come of the sun
		8	the sun being made, and keeping his
	34	19	and a cover from the sun at noon
	42	16	the sun giving light hath looked upon
	43	2	the sun when he appeareth showing
		4	the sun three times as much, burneth
	46	5	was not the sun stopped in his anger
	50	7	as the sun when it shineth, so did
Isa	13	10	the sun shall be darkened in his rising
	19	18	one shall be called the city of the sun
	24	23	blush, and the sun shall be ashamed
	30	26	shall be as the light of the sun
		26	light of the sun shall be sevenfold
	38	8	by which it is gone down in the sun dial of Achaz with the sun
		8	and the sun returned ten lines by the
	41	25	shall come from the rising of the sun
	45	6	who are from the rising of the sun
	49	10	neither shall . . . the sun strike them
	59	19	from the rising of the sun, his glory
	60	19	no more have the sun for thy light
		20	thy sun shall go down no more, and
Jer	8	2	shall spread them abroad to the sun
	15	9	her sun is gone down, while it was yet
	31	35	giveth the sun for the light of the
	43	13	the statues of the house of the sun
Bar	2	25	are cast out to the heat of the sun
	5	5	from the rising to the setting sun
	6	59	the sun and the moon and the stars
		66	nor shine as the sun nor give light as
Eze	8	16	adored towards the rising of the sun
	11	1	looketh towards the rising of the sun
	32	7	I will cover the sun with a cloud
Dan	3	62	O ye sun and moon, bless the Lord
Joel	2	10	the sun and moon are darkened. 3:15

31 the sun shall be turned into darkness
Amos 8 9 that the sun shall go down at midday
Jon 4 8 when the sun was risen, the Lord
8 the sun beat upon the head of Jonas
Mich 3 6 the sun shall go down upon the prophets
Nah 3 17 the sun arose, and they flew away
Haba 3 11 the sun and the moon stood still
Zach 8 7 from land of the going down of the sun
Mala 1 11 from the rising of the sun even to the
4 2 sun of justice shall arise, and health
1 Ma 6 39 when the sun shone upon the shields
10 50 was hard fought till the sun went down
12 27 when sun was set, Jonathan commanded
2 Ma 1 22 the time came that the sun shone out
10 28 soon as the sun was risen both sides
Mat 5 45 maketh his sun to rise upon the good
13 6 when the sun was up they were scorched
43 then shall the just shine as the sun
17 2 his face did shine as the sun: and his
24 29 the sun shall be darkened. Mark 13:24
Mark 4 6 when the sun was risen, it was
16 2 the sepulcher, the sun being now risen
Luke 4 40 when the sun was down, all they that
21 25 and there shall be signs in the sun
23 45 the sun was darkened, and the veil
Acts 2 20 the sun shall be turned into darkness
13 11 blind, not seeing the sun for a time
26 13 above the brightness of the sun, shining
27 20 when neither sun nor stars appeared for
1 C 15 41 one is the glory of the sun, another the
Eph 4 26 let not the sun go down upon your anger
James 1 11 the sun rose with a burning heat and
Apoc 1 16 face was as the sun shineth in his power
6 12 the sun became black as sackcloth of
7 2 ascending from the rising of the sun
16 neither shall the sun fall on them nor
8 12 the third part of the sun was smitten
9 2 the sun and the air were darkened with
10 1 his face was as the sun, and his feet
12 1 a woman clothed with the sun, and the
16 8 poured out his vial upon the sun, and
12 the kings from the rising of the sun
19 17 I saw an angel standing in the sun
21 23 the city hath no need of the sun nor
22 5 nor the light of the sun, because the
Sunam 1 K 28 4 came and camped in Sunam: and
4 K 4 8 a day when Eliseus passed by Sunam
Sunamitess 3 K 1 3 and they found Abisag a S.
3 K 1 15 Abisag the Sunamitess ministered to him
2 17 give me Abisag the Sunamitess to wife
21 let Abisag the Sunamitess be given
22 why dost thou ask Abisag the S. for
4 K 4 12 call this Sunamitess. And. 36
25 to Giezi his servant: Behold that S.
sunbeam Wisd 16 27 being warmed with a little s.
sunder Ps 106 14 and broke their bonds in sunder
sundry Heb 1 1 who at s. times and in divers
Sunem Josu 19 18 Jezrael and Casaloth and Sunem
sung Exod 15 1 then Moses . . . sung this canticle
Num 21 17 Israel sung this song: Let the well
17 they sung thereto: The well, which
Judg 5 1 Debbora and Barac . . . sung, and said
1 K 18 7 and the women sung as they played
29 5 David to whom they sung in their dances
1 Pa 15 20 sung mysteries upon psalteries. And
21 s. a song of victory for the octave
1 Es 3 11 they sung together hymns and praise to
2 Es 12 41 the singers sung loud, and Jerzaia was
Tob 13 22 and Alleluia shall be sung in its streets
Jdth 16 1 Judith sung this canticle to the Lord
Job 36 24 work, concerning which men have sung
Ps 7 1 psalm of David which he sung to the
Wisd 10 20 and they sung to thy holy name, O Lord
Isa 26 1 this canticle be sung in the land of
Eze 33 32 song which is sung with a sweet and
Mich 2 4 a song shall be sung with melody by
1 Ma 4 24 they sung a hymn and blessed God in
2 Ma 1 30 priests sung hymns till the sacrifice
Apoc 5 9 they sung a new canticle, saying: Thou
14 3 they sung as it were a new canticle
Suni Gen 46 16 sons of Gad: . . . Suni. Num 26:15
Sunites Num 26 15 of him is family of the S.
sunk Exod 15 5 they are sunk to the bottom like
Exod 15 10 they sunk as lead in the mighty waters
Jer 38 6 and Jeremias sunk into the mire. Now
Lam 2 9 her gates are sunk into the ground
sunset Gen 28 11 would rest in it after sunset
Exod 17 12 his hands were not weary until sunset
22 26 shalt give it him again before sunset
Deut 23 11 after sunset he shall return into the
2 K 3 35 bread or anything else before sunset
2 Pa 18 34 until the evening, and died at the s.
Dan 6 14 till sunset he labored to save him
sunset Mark 1 32 after sunset, they brought to him
sup Abdi 16 they shall drink and sup up and
Apoc 3 20 and will sup with him, and he with me
superabounded Eph 1 8 s. in us in all wisdom and
superfluous Ecce 2 26 given vexation and s. care
2 Ma 12 44 s. and vain to pray for the dead
2 C 9 1 it is superfluous for me to write unto
superior Job 31 21 I saw myself s. in the gate
superiority Eccu 25 30 a woman, if she have s.
supernal Phil 3 14 the prize of the s. vocation
superscription Luke 23 38 was also a s. written.
superstition Acts 25 19 questions of their own s.
Col 2 23 show of wisdom in s. and humility, and
superstitious Acts 17 22 things you are too s.
supersubstantial Mat 6 11 this day our s. bread
Suph 1 K 1 1 Thohu the son of Suph. 1 Pa 6:35
1 K 9 5 when they were come to the land of S.
Supha 1 Pa 7 35 sons of Helem his brother: Supha
1 Pa 7 36 the sons of Supha: Sue, Hernapher
Supham Num 26 39 sons of Benjamin . . . Supham
Suphamites Num 26 39 is the family of the S.
supped Tob 8 1 after they had s. they brought
Luke 22 20 chalice also, after he had s. 1 C 11:35
supper Jdth 6 19 made him [Achior] a great supper
Jdth 12 10 Holofernes made a s. for his servants
Dan 6 18 laid himself down without taking supper
Mat 26 26 whilst they were at supper, Jesus took
Mark 6 21 Herod made a supper for his birthday
Luke 14 12 when thou makest a dinner or a supper
16 a certain man made a great supper
17 sent his servant at the hour of supper
24 were invited, shall taste of my supper
17 8 make ready my supper and gird thyself
John 12 2 made him a supper there: and Martha
13 2 when supper was done, the devil having
4 he riseth from supper and layeth aside
21 20 also leaned on his breast at supper
1 C 11 20 it is not now to eat the Lord's supper
21 one taketh before his own supper to eat
Apoc 19 9 that are called to the marriage supper
17 together to the great supper of God
suppers Mark 12 39 have the highest places at s.
supplant Ps 16 13 O Lord, disappoint and s. him
Ps 139 5 who have proposed to supplant my steps
Jer 9 4 every brother will utterly supplant
supplanted Gen 27 36 hath s. me lo this second
Ps 36 31 and his steps shall not be supplanted
40 10 ate my bread, hath greatly supplanted
Isa 29 21 s. him that reproved them in the gate
Osee 6 8 Galaad is supplanted with blood
12 3 in the womb he supplanted his brother
supplanteth Prov 19 3 folly of a man s. his steps
supplicants Soph 3 10 my s. the children of my

supplication 3 K 8 30 mayest hearken to the s.
3 K 8 37 supplication to thee in their captivity
52 open to the supplication of thy servant
54 end of praying all this prayer and s.
9 3 heard thy prayer and thy supplication
2 Pa 6 19 the prayer of thy servant and his s.
7 14 being converted, shall make s. to me
20 4 all came out of their cities to make s.
Jdth 9 17 hear me a poor wretch, making s. to
Esth 13 17 hear my supplication, and be merciful
18 with like mind and supplication cried
Job 9 15 would make supplication to my judge
41 3 words, and framed to make supplication
Ps 6 10 the Lord hath heard my supplication
16 1 attend to my s. Give ear unto my
21 25 nor despised the s. of the poor man
27 2 hear, O Lord, the voice of my s. when
6 hath heard the voice of my supplication
29 9 will make supplication to my God
38 13 hear my prayer, O Lord, and my s.
54 2 my prayer, and despise not my s.: be
60 2 hear, O God, my s.: be attentive to
63 2 when I make s. to thee: deliver my
65 19 hath attended to the voice of my s.
101 1 poured out his supplication before the
118 169 let my supplication, O Lord, come near
129 2 attentive to voice of my supplication
139 7 hear, O Lord, the voice of my s.
141 2 with my voice I made s. to the Lord
7 attend to my supplication: for I am
142 1 my prayer: give ear to my supplication
Wisd 13 18 for health he maketh supplication to
18 21 and by incense making supplication
Eccu 39 7 and will make supplication for his sins
Isa 45 44 and shall make supplication to thee
Jer 7 16 nor take to thee praise and s. for them
36 7 if so be they may present their s.
38 26 I presented my s. before the king that
42 2 let our supplication fall before thee
Bar 4 20 have put upon me the sackcloth of s.
Dan 6 11 found Daniel praying and making s.
9 3 to pray and make s. with fasting and
17 hear the supplication of thy servant
Osee 12 4 he wept and made supplication to him
1 Ma 7 37 it might be a house of prayer and s.
11 49 making s. and saying: Grant us peace
62 the men of Gaza made s. to Jonathan
2 Ma 3 18 praying and making public supplication
20 their hands towards heaven, made s.
8 29 and they had all made a common s., they
9 18 wrote to the Jews in the manner of a s.
14 15 made s. to him who chose his people
Eph 6 18 by all prayer and s. praying at all
18 with all instance and s. for all saints
Phil 1 4 always in all my prayers making s. for
4 6 in everything, by prayer and s., with
supplications 3 K 8 28 have regard to . . . his s.
3 K 8 33 and make supplications to thee in this
45 hear thou . . . their s. 49; 2 Pa 6:35
Job 40 22 will he make many supplications to thee
Prov 18 23 the poor will speak with supplications
Jer 42 9 to present your supplications before
Dan 9 20 presenting my s. in the sight of my God
1 Tim 2 1 that s., prayers, intercessions and
5 5 continue in s. and prayers night and day
Heb 5 7 offering up prayers and supplications
supplied Jdth 7 6 fountain which s. them with
Eze 27 12 thy merchants supplied thy fairs with
1 C 16 17 wanting on your part, they have supplied
2 C 11 9 brethren s. who came from Macedonia
Col 2 19 being supplied with nourishment and
supplieth Eph 4 16 by what every joint supplieth
supply 2 C 8 14 let your abundance supply their want
2 C 8 14 their abundance also may s. your want
9 12 this office doth not only supply want
Phil 1 19 supply of the Spirit of Jesus Christ
4 19 and may my God supply all your want
support Judg 16 26 pillars which s. the whole house
1 Es 6 3 may s. the height of threescore cubits
Ps 17 3 horn of my salvation and my support
41 10 I will say to God: Thou art my support
58 17 thou art become my support and my
88 27 God, and the support of my salvation
104 16 he broke in pieces all the s. of bread
143 2 refuge: my support and my deliverer
145 9 he will support the fatherless and the
Eccu 3 14 son, support the old age of thy father
49 17 Joseph . . . the support of his family
1 Ma 3 43 to them and were a support to them
Acts 20 35 so laboring you ought to s. the weak
1 Th 5 14 support the weak, be patient towards all
supported Ps 117 13 fall: but the Lord s. me
Ecce 4 10 one fall, he shall be s. by the other
Isa 59 16 and his own justice supported him. He
supporteth Prov 30 28 stellio s. itself on hands
supporting Eph 4 2 s. one another in charity
suppose Gen 31 30 s. thou didst desire to go to
Jdth 7 9 they suppose . . . to be impregnable
Luke 7 43 I s. that he to whom he forgave most
Acts 2 15 these are not drunk as you suppose
17 29 not s. the divinity to be like unto gold
2 C 11 5 I s. that I have done nothing less than
supposed Bar 6 39 be s. or to be said, that they
Bar 6 55 how then can it be s. or admitted that
Luke 3 23 being, as it was supposed, the son
24 37 frightened, s. that they saw a spirit
Acts 21 29 whom they s. that Paul had brought into
28 6 s. that he would begin to swell up, and
supposing 2 Ma 4 32 Menelaus s. that he had found
Acts 16 27 s. that the prisoners had been fled
Phil 1 17 s. that they raise affliction to my
1 Tim 6 5 truth, supposing again to be godliness
suppresseth Prov 18 18 the lot s. contentions and
Sur Gen 16 7 in the way to Sur in the desert
Gen 20 1 Abraham . . . dwelt between Cades and Sur
25 18 he dwelt from Hevila as far as Sur
Exod 15 22 went forth into the wilderness of Sur
Num 25 15 was called Cozbi the daughter of Sur
31 8 Recem and Sur and Hur. Josu 13:21
1 K 15 7 from Hevila, until thou comest to Sur
27 8 of the countries, as men go to Sur
4 K 11 6 let a third part be at the gate of Sur
1 Pa 8 30 and Sur and Cis and Baal. 9:36
sure Gen 23 18 was made sure to Abraham for a
Gen 23 20 the field was made sure to Abraham
Judg 20 16 slinging stones so s. that they could
Ruth 4 7 that the grant might be sure, the man
Tob 3 21 one is sure of that worshippeth thee
Ps 68 3 the deep: and there is no sure standing
Wisd 7 22 spirit of understanding: holy . . . sure
14 3 and a most sure path among the waves
Eccu 3 34 of his fall he shall find a sure stay
22 33 mouth, and a sure seal upon my lips
40 25 and silver make the feet stand sure
42 6 sure keeping is good over a wicked
11 sure watch over a shameless daughter
Isa 22 23 fasten him as a peg in a sure place
25 that was fastened in the sure place
33 16 bread is given him, his waters are s.
Jer 33 3 show thee great things and sure things
Bar 6 17 the gates are made sure on every side
2 Ma 3 22 and sure for those that had committed
14 43 missed of giving himself a sure wound
Mat 27 66 made the sepulcher sure, sealing the
Acts 26 5 according to the most sure sect of our
Rom 8 38 for I am sure that neither death, nor

2 Tim 2 19 the sure foundation of God standeth firm
Heb 6 19 as an anchor of the soul, sure and firm
2 P 1 10 you may make sure your calling and
surely Gen 20 7 know that thou shalt surely die
Gen 26 11 man's wife shall s. be put to death
38 23 surely she cannot charge us with a lie
1 K 10 24 surely you see him whom the Lord hath
14 39 by Jonathan . . . he shall surely die
24 21 I know that thou shalt surely be king
25 28 the Lord will surely make for my lord
30 8 thou shalt surely overtake them and
2 K 2 6 the Lord surely will render you mercy
5 19 I will surely deliver the Philistines
9 7 I will s. show thee mercy for Jonathan
12 14 that is born to thee, shall surely die
4 K 1 4 thou [Ochozias] shalt surely die. 6, 16
5 13 surely thou shouldst have done it: how
8 10 hath shown me that he shall surely die
18 30 the Lord will surely deliver us, and
2 Es 13 26 surely among many nations there was not
Jdth 5 24 their God will surely deliver them to
Job 21 27 surely I know your thoughts and your
39 32 surely he that reproveth God, ought
Ps 38 7 surely man passeth as an image: yea
12 surely in vain is any man disquieted
84 10 surely his salvation is near to them
Prov 23 30 s. they that pass their time in wine
Eccu 5 3 for God will surely take revenge. Say
14 12 covenant of this world shall s. die
28 1 will s. keep his sins in remembrance
Isa 14 24 surely as I have thought, so shall it
22 14 s. this iniquity shall not be forgiven
30 19 he will surely have pity on thee: at
36 15 the Lord will surely deliver us and
40 24 s. their stock was neither planted nor
53 4 surely he hath borne our infirmities
62 8 surely I will no more give thy corn
63 8 surely that are my people, children
Jer 16 19 surely our fathers have possessed lies
22 6 surely I will make thee a wilderness
31 20 surely Ephraim is an honorable son to
20 son to me, surely he is a tender child
33 26 surely I will also cast off the seed
34 3 but thou shalt surely be taken, and
37 8 the Chaldeans shall surely depart and
38 3 this city shall surely be delivered
49 20 surely the little ones of the flock
50 45 surely the little ones of the flocks
51 56 strong revenger, will surely repay
Bar 3 13 thou hadst s. dwelt in peace forever
Eze 3 18 to the wicked, Thou shalt surely die
8 12 surely thou seest, O son of man, what
15 surely thou hast seen. 17; 47:6
18 9 he is just, he shall surely live, saith
13 he shall surely die, his blood shall
28 he hath wrought, he shall surely live
33 8 O wicked man, thou shalt surely die
13 to the just that he shall surely live
14 to the wicked: Thou shalt surely die
15 he shall surely live, and shall not
16 judgment and justice, he shall s. live
Osee 5 9 have shown that which shall surely be
Amos 8 7 surely I will never forget all their
Haba 2 3 it shall surely come, and it shall
3 9 thou wilt surely take up thy bow
Soph 3 7 I said: Surely thou wilt fear me, thou
Mala 2 17 surely where is the God of judgment
Mat 26 73 s. thou also art one of them. Mark 14:70
Luke 7 39 would know surely who and what manner
12 39 he would surely watch and would not
Apoc 22 20 surely, I come quickly: Amen
sureties Prov 22 26 offer themselves s. for debts
surety Prov 6 1 thou be surety for thy friend
Prov 11 15 with evil, that is s. for a stranger
17 18 hands when he is surety for his friend
20 16 garment of him that is surety for a
27 13 that hath been surety for a stranger
Eccu 8 16 be not surety above thy power: and if
16 if thou be surety, think as if thou
29 18 a good man is surety for his neighbor
19 forget not the kindness of thy surety
20 and the unclean fleeth from his surety
21 attributeth to himself goods of his s.
22 a man is surety for his neighbor
2 Ma 10 28 Lord for a s. of victory and success
Heb 7 22 made a surety of a better testament. And
suretyship Eccu 29 23 evil s. hath undone many
Eccu 29 25 shall fall into an evil suretyship
surface Gen 2 6 watering all the s. of the earth
Job 38 30 the surface of the deep is congealed
Isa 28 25 when he hath made plain the surface
Eze 17 5 planted it on the surface of the earth
Dan 5 5 upon the surface of the wall of the
surfeited Ps 77 65 that hath been s. with wine
surfeiting Eccu 37 34 by s. many have perished
Zach 12 2 a lintel of s. to all the people round
Luke 21 34 your hearts be overcharged with s.
surges Ps 92 4 wonderful are the s. of the sea
Suriel Num 3 35 prince S. the son of Abihaiel
Surisaddai Num 1 6 Salamiel the son of Surisaddai. 2:12; 7:36, 41; 10:19
surname Eccu 47 19 surname is, God of Israel
Isa 44 5 surname himself by the name of Israel
surnamed Gen 35 6 Luza . . . surnamed Bethel
4 K 17 34 children of Jacob, whom he s. Israel
Dan 10 1 was revealed to Daniel, s. Baltassar
1 Ma 2 2 sons: John who was surnamed Gaddis
3 and Simon who was surnamed Thasi
5 and Eleazar who was surnamed Abaron
5 and Jonathan who was surnamed Apphus
10 1 Alexander . . . s. the Illustrious came
Luke 6 14 Simon, whom he surnamed Peter, and
22 3 Judas, who was surnamed Iscariot
Acts 1 23 Joseph . . . who was surnamed Justus
4 36 who by the apostles was s. Barnabas
10 5 Simon, who is s. Peter. 18, 32; 11:13
12 12 John, who was surnamed Mark. 25
15 22 Judas, who was surnamed Barsabas, and
37 with them John also, that was s. Mark
surpass Deut 7 7 not because you s. all nations
surpassed Ruth 3 10 thy latter kindness has s.
3 K 4 30 wisdom of Solomon s. the wisdom of all
Prov 31 29 riches: thou hast surpassed them all
Ecce 2 9 I surpassed in riches all that were
Eze 5 7 because you have s. the Gentiles that
16 51 hast surpassed them with thy crimes
52 that hast s. thy sisters with thy sins
surpasseth 1 Pa 22 14 the abundance s. all account
Eph 3 19 charity of Christ, which s. all knowledge
Phil 4 7 the peace of God, which surpasseth all
surprised Eccu 5 14 thou be s. in an unskillful
Eccu 34 11 he that hath been s., shall abound
Jer 51 41 the renowned one of all the earth s.
surround Josu 7 9 will s. us and cut off our name
Job 15 24 distress shall s. him as a king that
Ps 7 8 a congregation of people shall s. thee
31 7 deliver me from them that surround me
47 13 surround Sion and encompass her: tell
54 11 day and night shall iniquity s. it
surrounded Josu 8 22 enemies who were s. by them
Josu 10 34 passed from Lachis to Eglon and s. it
Judg 9 50 which he s. and besieged with his army
16 2 they surrounded him [Samson], setting
2 K 22 5 the pangs of death have surrounded me
4 K 8 21 defeated the Edomites that had s. him
24 10 and the city was s. with their forts

25 1 army against Jerusalem: and they s. it
2 Pa 18 31 and they surrounded him to attack him
21 9 the Edomites who had surrounded him
Job 3 23 God hath surrounded him with darkness
22 10 therefore art thou s. with snares and
Ps 16 9 my enemies have surrounded my soul
11 cast me forth and now they have s. me
17 5 the sorrows of death surrounded me
21 13 many calves have s. me: fat bulls have
39 13 evils without number have surrounded me
Ps 44 10 gilded clothing, surrounded with variety
117 12 they surrounded me like bees and they
Cant 3 7 threescore . . . s. the bed of Solomon
Eccu 51 6 oppression of the flame which s. me
1 Ma 10 80 they s. his army and cast darts at
surrounding Judg 9 49 s. the fort, they set it on
Ps 3 7 not fear thousands of the people s. me
117 11 s. me they compassed me about: and in
surrounds Heb 12 1 weight and sin which s. us
surveyed 1 Pa 21 5 number of them, whom he had s.
Ecce 7 26 have surveyed all things with my mind
surveying Josu 18 9 s. it, divided it into seven
Ecce 1 6 forward surveying all places round about
Susa 1 Pa 18 16 were the priests: and Susa, scribe
2 Es 1 1 I was in the castle of Susa. Dan 8:2
Susagaz Esth 2 14 under the hand of S. the eunuch
Susan Esth 1 2 the city Susan was the capital
Esth 1 5 all the people that were found in Susan
2 4 let them bring them to the city of S.
5 was a man in the city of Susan, a Jew
8 beautiful virgins were brought to Susan
3 15 edict was hung up in Susan. 8:14; 9:14
4 8 edict which was hanging up in Susan
16 Jews whom thou shalt find in Susan
9 6 in Susan they killed five hundred men
11 number of them that were killed in S.
12 killed 500 men in the city of Susan
13 to do tomorrow in Susan as they have
15 they killed in Susan three hundred men
18 that were killing in the city of Susan
11 3 a Jew who dwelt in the city of Susan
16 18 before the gates of this city Susan
Susanechites 1 Es 4 9 Beelteem and . . . the S.
Susanna Dan 13 7 S. went in and walked in her
Dan 13 22 S. sighed and said: I am straitened
24 Susanna cried out with a loud. 42
27 never . . . any such word said of S.
28 full of wicked device against Susanna
29 send to Susanna daughter of Helcias
31 Susanna was exceeding delicate and
63 praised God for their daughter S.
Luke 8 3 Susanna and many others who ministered
Susi Num 13 12 of Manasses, Gaddi the son of S.
suspect 1 K 22 15 let not the king s. such a thing
Ps 67 17 why suspect, ye curdled mountains? A
Eccu 9 18 shalt not suspect the fear of death
2 Ma 3 32 the king might perhaps suspect that
suspected Judg 8 11 were secure and s. no hurt
2 K 17 29 for they s. that the people were faint
3 K 22 32 they s. that he was the king of Israel
Tob 8 17 it hath not happened as we suspected
Eccu 23 30 and where he s. not, he shall be taken
2 Ma 4 34 and, though he were suspected by him
5 11 king s. that the Jews would forsake
suspecteth Job 15 21 peace, he always s. treason
suspecting 2 Ma 12 4 s. nothing, because of the
suspense Tob 7 11 as he was in s. and gave no
John 10 24 dost thou hold our souls in suspense
suspicion Num 5 14 or is charged with false s.
Eccu 3 26 the s. of them hath deceived many
Dan 6 4 they could find no cause nor suspicion
4 no fault nor suspicion was found in
suspicions 1 Tim 6 4 blasphemies, evil suspicions

sustain Num 22 3 not able to sustain his assault
Ps 54 23 upon the Lord, and he shall sustain
2 Ma 10 18 manner of provision to sustain a siege
Mat 6 24 or he will sustain the one and despise
sustenance Judg 6 4 all in Israel for s. of life
2 K 19 32 he provided the king with sustenance
Wisd 16 21 thy sustenance showed thy sweetness
Suthala Num 26 35 of Ephraim . . . S. 1 Pa 7:20
Num 26 36 son of Suthala was Heran, of whom
1 Pa 7 21 Zabad, and his son Suthala, and his son
Suthalaites Num 26 35 is the family of the S.
swaddled Eze 16 4 with salt, nor s. with clouts
swaddling Job 38 9 it in a mist as in s. bands
Wisd 7 4 I was nursed in swaddling clothes and
Luke 2 7 wrapped him up in swaddling clothes
12 find the infant wrapped in s. clothes
swallow Num 16 30 if the earth . . . s. them down
Num 16 34 lest perhaps the earth s. us up also
Job 7 19 nor suffer me to s. down my spittle
8 18 if one swallow him up out of his place
Ps 68 16 drown me nor the deep swallow me up
Prov 1 12 let us swallow him up alive like hell
Isa 14 29 and his seed shall swallow the bird
38 14 I will cry like a young swallow, I will
42 14 I will destroy and swallow up at once
Jer 8 7 the swallow and the stork have observed
Lam 2 16 have said: We will swallow her up
Jon 2 1 a great fish to swallow up Jonas: and
Mat 23 24 strain out a gnat, and swallow a camel
swallowed Exod 15 12 and the earth s. them. In
Num 11 2 and the fire was swallowed up. And
26 10 opening her mouth, swallowed up Core
Deut 11 6 swallowed up with their households
2 K 17 16 lest the king be s. up, and all the
Job 20 15 the riches which he hath s., he shall
37 20 man shall speak, he shall be s. up
Ps 34 25 neither let them say: We have s. him
105 17 earth opened and swallowed up Dathan
106 27 and all their wisdom was swallowed up
123 3 perhaps they had swallowed us up alive
4 perhaps the waters had swallowed us up
140 6 falling upon the rock have been s. up
Isa 28 7 they are swallowed up with wine, they
49 19 that s. thee up shall be chased far
Jer 51 34 hath swallowed me up like a dragon
44 his mouth that which he had s. down
Osee 8 8 Israel is swallowed up: now is he
1 C 15 54 death is s. up in victory. O death where
2 C 2 7 be swallowed up with overmuch sorrow
5 4 that which is mortal may be s. up by life
Heb 11 29 the Egyptians attempting, were s. up
Apoc 12 16 and s. up the river which the dragon
swalloweth Job 39 24 and raging he s. the ground
Ps 57 10 he s. them up, as alive, in his wrath
swallowing 1 P 3 22 s. down death, that we might
swallow's Tob 2 11 hot dung out of a s. nest
swallows Bar 6 21 s. and other birds fly upon
swam 4 K 6 6 it in thither: and the iron swam
Wisd 19 18 the things before swam in the water
1 Ma 9 48 and swam over the Jordan to them
swan Lev 11 18 the swan and the bittern and
Deut 14 16 the heron and the swan and the stork
swarm Exod 8 24 a very grievous swarm of flies
Judg 14 8 swarm of bees in the mouth of the lion
Nah 3 17 locusts which swarm on the hedges
Haba 3 16 into my bones and swarm under me
2 Ma 1 12 he made numbers of men swarm out of
swarmed 2 Ma 9 9 worms s. out of the body of
swathed Eze 30 21 s. with linen, that it might
swear Gen 21 24 swear therefore by God that thou
Gen 21 24 and Abraham said: I will swear. And he
31 because there both of them did swear
24 3 that I may make thee swear by the

37 my master made me swear, saying
25 33 Jacob said: Swear therefore to me
47 31 he [Jacob] said: Swear then to me
50 5 my father made me swear to him, saying
6 father according as he made thee swear
24 he [Joseph] made them swear to him
Exod 22 8 shall swear that he did not lay his
23 13 name of strange gods you shall not s.
Lev 6 3 denying it, shall also swear falsely
19 12 thou shalt not swear falsely by my name
Deut 6 13 thou shalt swear by his name. 10:20
26 15 as thou didst swear to our fathers
Josu 2 12 swear ye to me by the Lord, that as I
17 oath, which thou hast made us s. 20
23 7 you should swear by the name of their
Judg 15 12 swear to me and promise me that you
17 2 concerning which thou didst swear in
1 K 24 22 swear to me by the Lord that thou wilt
30 15 swear to me by God that thou wilt not
2 K 19 7 I swear to thee by the Lord, that if
3 K 1 13 swear to me thy handmaid, saying
17 thou didst s. to thy handmaid by the
51 let king Solomon swear to me this day
2 Pa 6 22 come to swear against him and bind
36 13 Nabuchodonosor, who had made him s. by
1 Es 10 5 to swear that they would do according
2 Es 10 29 they came to promise and swear that
13 25 made them swear by God that they would
Ps 62 12 they shall be praised that s. by him
88 50 to what thou didst swear to David in
Ps 101 9 that praised me did swear against me
Wisd 14 29 though they swear amiss, they look not
31 of them by whom they swear, but the
Eccu 23 14 if he swear in vain, he shall not be
Isa 45 24 to me, and every tongue shall swear
48 1 you who swear by the name of the Lord
65 16 in the earth, shall swear by God, amen
Jer 4 2 thou shalt swear: As the Lord liveth
5 2 liveth; this also they will s. falsely
7 and swear by them that are not gods
7 9 to swear falsely, to offer to Baalim
12 16 to swear by my name: The Lord liveth
16 have taught my people to swear by Baal
22 5 I swear by myself, saith the Lord
32 22 which thou didst s. to their fathers
Osee 4 15 and do not swear: The Lord liveth
Amos 8 14 they that swear by the sin of Samaria
Soph 1 5 s. by the Lord and s. by Melchom
Mat 5 34 but I say to you not to swear at all
36 neither shalt thou swear by the head
23 16 whosoever shall swear by the temple. 21
16 he that shall swear by the gold of the
18 whosoever shall swear by the altar
18 shall swear by the gift that is upon it
26 74 he began to curse and to s. Mark 14:71
Heb 3 18 to whom did he swear, that they should
6 13 had no one greater by whom he might s.
16 men swear by one greater than themselves
James 5 12 swear not, neither by heaven nor by
swearers Mala 3 5 witness against . . . false s.
sweareth Lev 5 4 person that s. and uttereth
Ps 14 4 he that sweareth to his neighbor and
Ecce 9 2 the perjured, so he also that s. truth
Eccu 23 11 so everyone that sweareth and nameth
12 a man that s. much, shall be filled
27 15 the speech that s. much shall make the
Isa 65 16 he that sweareth in the earth, shall
Zach 5 4 that sweareth . . . shall be judged by
4 him that sweareth falsely by my name
Mat 23 20 that s. by the altar, s. by it and by
21 s. by it and by him that dwelleth in it
22 he that s. by heaven, s. by the throne
swearing Gen 47 31 as he was s., Israel adored
Eccu 23 9 not thy mouth be accustomed to swearing
Isa 19 18 Chanaan, and s. by the Lord of hosts
sweat Gen 3 19 in the sweat of thy face shalt thou
Eccu 34 26 taketh away the bread gotten by sweat
Eze 44 18 girded with anything that causeth s.
2 Ma 2 27 a business full of watching and sweat
Luke 22 44 his sweat became as drops of blood
sweep 3 K 14 10 I will sweep away the remnant of
Isa 14 23 I will sweep it and wear it out with
Luke 15 8 candle and sweep the house and seek
sweet Gen 8 21 Lord smelled a sweet savor, and said
Gen 34 3 sad, he comforted her with sweet words
Exod 30 7 shall burn sweet smelling incense upon
34 onycha, galbanum of sweet savor
Lev 1 9 a sweet savor to the Lord. 2:9; 4:31; Num 15:7
4 7 horns of the altar of the s. incense
8 28 for a sweet odor of sacrifice to the
17 6 the fat for a sweet odor to the Lord
26 31 will receive no more your sweet odors
Num 4 16 the sweet incense and the sacrifice
15 3 burning a sweet savor unto the Lord
2 K 19 35 are my senses quick to discern sweet
2 Es 8 10 go, eat fat meats and drink sweet wine
Jdth 5 15 there bitter fountains were made sweet
Job 20 12 when evil shall be sweet in his mouth
Ps 24 8 the Lord is sweet and righteous
33 9 taste, and see that the Lord is sweet
85 5 art sweet and mild: and plenteous in
99 5 the Lord is sweet, his mercy endureth
108 21 sake: because thy mercy is sweet
118 103 how sweet are thy words to my palate
134 3 sing ye to his name, for it is sweet
144 9 Lord is sweet to all: and his tender
Prov 3 24 shalt rest, and thy sleep shall be s.
16 21 he that is sweet in words shall attain
24 s. to the soul, and health to the bones
20 17 the bread of lying is sweet to a man
27 7 hungry shall take even bitter for s.
9 counsels of a friend are sweet to the
Ecce 5 11 sleep is sweet to a laboring man
11 7 light is sweet and it is delightful
Cant 1 2 smelling sweet of the best ointments
3 and his fruit was sweet to my palate
13 vines in flower yield their s. smell
14 thy voice is sweet and thy face comely
4 3 a scarlet lace: and thy speech sweet
10 the sweet smell of thy ointments above
14 saffron, sweet cane and cinnamon, with
6 3 sweet and comely as Jerusalem: terrible
Wisd 7 22 sure, sweet, loving that which is good
12 1 how good and sweet is thy spirit
Eccu 6 5 a sweet word multiplieth friends and
23 24 is a fornicator, all bread is sweet
24 20 I gave a sweet smell like cinnamon
20 I yielded a sweet odor like the best
27 for my spirit is sweet above honey
37 22 many, and is sweet to his own soul
38 5 was not bitter water made sweet with
7 shall make sweet confections and shall
11 give a sweet savor and a memorial
39 18 give ye a sweet odor as frankincense
40 18 life of a laborer . . . shall be sweet
21 and the psaltery make a sweet melody
32 begging will be sweet in the mouth of
47 11 by their voices he made sweet melody
49 1 like the composition of a sweet smell
2 his remembrance shall be sweet as
50 20 sound of sweet melody was increased
Isa 3 20 tablets and sweet balls and earrings
24 instead of a sweet smell there shall
5 20 put bitter for s., and s. for bitter
39 2 the storehouses of . . . the sweet odors

43 24 thou hast bought me no sweet cane
Jer 31 26 I saw, and my sleep was sweet to me
Eze 3 3 and it was sweet as honey in my mouth
16 18 settest my oil and my sweet incense
19 hast set before them for a sweet odor
20 28 there they set their sweet odors and
33 32 sung with a sweet and agreeable voice
Mat 11 30 my yoke is sweet and my burden light
Mark 16 1 bought sweet spices, that coming, they
James 3 11 the same hole, sweet and bitter water
12 neither can the salt water yield sweet
1 P 2 3 you have tasted that the Lord is sweet
Apoc 10 9 in thy mouth it shall be s. as honey
10 it was in my mouth sweet as honey: and
most sweet Exod 29 18 a m. s. savor of the victim
Exod 29 25 most sweet savor in sight of the Lord
35 8 make ointment and most sweet incense
28 to make the incense of most sweet savor
Lev 1 13 most sweet savor to the Lord. 17; 2:2; 3:5; Num 15:10, 24
3 16 of the fire and of a most sweet savor
6 15 most sweet odor to the Lord. 22; 8:21; 23:22; Num 18:17; 28:24, 27; 29:2, 13, 36; 28:8
23 13 most sweet odor: libations also of
Num 28 2 burnt sacrifice of most sweet odor
6 for a most sweet odor of a sacrifice
13 it is a holocaust of most sweet odor
29 8 to the Lord for a most sweet odor
Prov 24 13 the honeycomb most sweet to thy throat
Cant 5 16 his throat most sweet, and he is all
sweeten Eccu 27 26 he will s. his mouth and will
sweeteneth Prov 7 5 the stranger who s. her words
sweeter Judg 14 18 to him: What is s. than honey
Ps 18 11 sweeter than honey and the honeycomb
Prov 9 17 stolen waters are sweeter, and hidden
Eccu 23 37 nothing s. than to have regard to the
sweetly Wisd 8 1 mightily, and ordereth all things s.
Eccu 12 15 enemy speaketh s. with his lips, but
sweetmeats Ps 54 15 didst take s. together with
sweetness Exod 15 25 waters, they were turned into s.
Exod 29 41 for a savor of sweetness. Lev 2:12
Judg 9 11 can I leave my sweetness and my
14 14 out of the strong came forth sweetness
Job 24 20 may worms be his sweetness: let him
Ps 20 4 prevented him with blessings of s.
30 20 how great is the multitude of thy s.
67 11 in thy s., O God, thou hast provided
144 7 the memory of the abundance of thy s.
Ecce 10 1 dying flies spoil s. of the ointment
Wisd 16 20 and the sweetness of every taste
21 showed thy sweetness to thy children
Eccu 4 13 watch for her, shall embrace her s.
11 3 her fruit hath the chiefest sweetness
35 8 is an odor of sweetness in the sight
Eze 20 41 I will accept of you for an odor of s.
Joel 3 18 mountains shall drop down s. Amos 9:13
2 C 6 6 in sweetness, in the Holy Ghost, in
Eph 5 2 sacrifice to God for odor of sweetness
Phil 4 18 things you sent, an odor of sweetness
sweetsmelling Exod 25 6 spices . . . for s. incense
Eccu 59 8 as the s. frankincense in the time of
Jer 6 20 and the s. cane from a far country
Bar 5 8 every s. tree have overshadowed Israel
Eze 6 13 where they burnt s. frankincense
swell Num 5 21 may thy belly swell and burst
Num 5 22 may thy womb swell and thy thigh rot
Deut 17 13 that no one afterwards swell with pride
Job 15 13 why doth thy spirit swell against God
Isa 51 15 the sea, and the waves thereof swell
Jer 5 22 they shall swell, and shall not pass
46 7 his streams swell like those of rivers
Acts 28 6 supposed that he would begin to s. up
swelled Judg 8 3 with which they s. against him
Jon 1 11 to us? For the sea flowed and swelled
13 the sea tossed and swelled upon them
swelling Exod 9 9 be boils and swelling blains
Exod 9 10 there came boils with swelling blains
Num 5 27 her belly swelling, her thigh shall rot
17 8 that the buds swelling it had bloomed
Deut 1 43 swelling with pride, you went up into
Josu 3 16 waters . . . swelling up like a mountain
Job 31 23 feared God as waves swelling over me
38 11 thou shalt break thy swelling waves
Prov 26 23 s. lips joined with a corrupt heart
Isa 1 6 wounds and bruises and swelling sores
Jer 12 5 wilt thou do in the s. of the Jordan
49 19 lion from the s. of the Jordan. 50:44
2 Ma 9 4 swelling with anger he thought to
swellings 2 C 12 20 whisperings, s., seditions
swept 3 K 14 10 as dung is swept away till all
Ps 76 7 I was exercised and I swept my spirit
Mat 12 44 findeth it empty, swept, and garnished
Luke 11 25 he findeth it swept and garnished
swift 2 K 2 18 Asael was a most swift runner
1 Pa 12 8 they were swift like the roebucks on
Ps 13 3 their feet are swift to shed blood
Prov 6 18 feet that are s. to run into mischief
22 29 hast thou seen a man swift in his work
Ecce 9 11 the race is not to the swift, nor the
Wisd 13 2 the fire or the wind or the swift air
Eccu 11 24 in a swift hour his blessing beareth
18 26 all these are swift in the eyes of
Isa 18 2 go, ye swift angels, to a nation rent
19 1 Lord will ascend upon a swift cloud
30 16 and we will mount upon swift ones
Jer 2 23 as a swift runner pursuing his course
46 6 let not the swift flee away, nor the
Dan 7 10 a swift stream of fire issued forth
Amos 2 14 and flight shall perish from the swift
Haba 1 6 Chaldeans, a bitter and swift nation
Soph 1 14 it is near and exceeding swift: the
Rom 3 15 their feet swift to shed blood
James 1 19 let every man be swift to hear, but
2 P 2 1 upon themselves swift destruction
swifter 2 K 1 23 they were swifter than eagles
Job 9 25 my days have been swifter than a post
Isa 30 16 shall they be swifter that shall pursue
Jer 4 13 his horses are swifter than eagles
Lam 4 19 our persecutors were swifter than
Haba 1 8 and swifter than evening wolves: and
swiftly Deut 28 49 like an eagle that flyeth s.
Job 6 15 as the torrent that passeth swiftly
7 6 my days have passed more swiftly than
Ps 44 2 pen of a scrivener that writeth swiftly
147 15 to the earth: his word runneth swiftly
Eccu 43 14 sendeth forth s. the lightnings of his
Isa 5 26 they shall come with speed swiftly
Jer 48 16 thereof shall come on exceeding s.
Dan 9 21 flying swiftly touched me at the time
swim Isa 25 11 stretcheth forth his hands to swim
Acts 27 43 who could swim, should cast themselves
swimmeth Isa 25 11 as he that s. stretcheth forth
swimming Acts 27 42 lest any of them, s. out
swine Lev 11 7 swine, which though it divideth
Deut 14 8 the swine also . . . shall be unclean
Mat 7 6 neither cast ye your pearls before s.
8 30 an herd of many s. feeding. Luke 8:32
31 send us into the herd of swine. And he
32 they going out, went into the swine
Mark 5 11 a great herd of swine, feeding. And
12 send us into the swine, that we may
13 entered into the swine. Luke 8:33
16 told them . . . and concerning the swine
Luke 15 15 sent him into his farm to feed swine
16 with the husks the swine did eat; and

swine's Prov 11 22 a golden ring in a s. snout
Isa 65 4 that eat s. flesh, and profane broth
66 3 as if he should offer swine's blood
17 they that did eat swine's flesh and
1 Ma 1 50 and swine's flesh to be immolated and
2 Ma 6 18 to open his mouth to eat swine's flesh
7 1 compelled by the king to eat s. flesh
swollen Job 16 17 my face is s. with weeping
swoon Esth 15 18 down again, and was almost in a s.
Wisd 17 18 these things made them to swoon for
swooned Jdth 13 29 and his soul swooned away
Ps 76 4 was exercised and my spirit swooned
sword Gen 3 24 cherubims, and a flaming s.
Gen 22 6 carried in his hands fire and a sword
10 took the sword, to sacrifice his son
27 40 thou shalt live by the sword
31 26 as captives taken with the sword
48 22 which I took . . . with my sword and bow
Exod 5 3 a pestilence of the sword fall upon us
21 you have given him a sword to kill us
15 9 I will draw my sword, my hand shall
18 4 delivered me from the sword of Pharao
22 24 I will strike you with the sword
Lev 26 6 the sword shall not pass through your
25 I will bring in upon you the sword
33 I will draw out the sword after you
36 shall flee as it were from the sword
Num 14 3 into this land, lest we fall by the s.
43 by their sword you shall fall because
22 23 standing in the way with a drawn s. 31
29 I would I had a sword that I might
31 8 Balaam . . . they killed with the sword
Deut 32 25 the sword shall lay them waste, and
42 blood, and my sword shall devour flesh
33 29 thy help, and the sword of thy glory
Josu 5 13 against him, holding a drawn sword
8 24 falling by the sword in the same
10 32 and put it [Lachis] to the sword
35 put to the sword all the souls that were
37 putting to the sword all that he found
11 10 slew the king thereof with the sword
12 put to the sword and destroyed all the
13 22 children of Israel slew with the sword
19 47 put it to the sword and possessed it
24 12 not with thy sword nor with thy bow
Judg 1 8 took it and put it to the sword
3 16 he made himself a two-edged sword
7 14 nothing else but the sword of Gedeon
20 the sword of the Lord and of Gedeon
22 Lord sent the sword into all the camp
8 10 and 120,000 warriors that drew the sword
9 54 draw thy sword and kill me. 1 K 31:4; 1 Pa 10:4
19 29 took a sword and divided the dead body
20 15 thousand men that drew the sword
25 to kill 18,000 men that drew the sword
35 all fighting men and that drew the s.
48 all the remains of the city to the s.
21 10 inhabitants of Jabes Galaad to the s.
1 K 13 22 there was neither sword nor spear found
14 20 every man's sword was turned upon his
15 33 as thy sword hath made women childless
17 45 thou comest to me with a sword; but I
47 Lord saveth not with sword and spear
50 as David had no sword in his hand
21 8 here at hand a spear or a sword? For I brought not my own sword
9 here is the sword of Goliath the
22 10 and gave him the sword of Goliath
13 hast given him bread and a sword
2 K 1 12 because they were fallen by the sword
22 sword of Saul did not return empty
2 26 shall thy sword rage unto utter
3 29 distaff, or that falleth by the sword
11 25 sometimes another is consumed by sword
12 9 hast killed Urias . . . with the sword
9 with the sword of children of Ammon
10 s. shall never depart from thy house
18 8 than whom the sword devoured that
20 8 was girded with a sword hanging down
10 Amasa did not take notice of the sword
21 16 being girded with a new sword, attempted
23 10 weary, and grew stiff with the sword
24 9 valiant men that drew the sword
3 K 1 51 will not kill his servant with the s.
2 8 I will not kill thee with a sword
32 slew them with the sword, my father
3 24 king therefore said: Bring me a sword
24 when they had brought a sword before
19 1 slain all the prophets with the sword
10 have slain thy prophets with the s. 14
17 whosoever shall escape sword of Hazael
17 whosoever shall escape sword of Jehu
4 K 3 23 they said: It is the blood of the sword
26 with him 700 men that drew the sword
6 22 thou didst not take them with thy sword
8 12 their young men thou wilt kill with s.
11 15 let him be slain with the sword. For
20 Athalia was slain with s. 2 Pa 23:21
19 37 sons slew him with the s. 2 Pa 32:21; Isa 37:38
1 Pa 21 5 be 1,100,000 men that drew the sword
12 not be able to escape their sword
12 days to have the sword of the Lord
16 with a drawn sword in his hand, turned
30 seeing the sword of the angel of Lord
2 Pa 20 9 fall upon us, the sword of judgment
21 4 slew all his brethren with the sword
23 14 let her be killed with the sword. For
29 9 our fathers are fallen by the sword
36 17 he slew their young men with the sword
20 whosoever escaped the sword, was led
1 Es 9 7 have been delivered . . . to the sword
2 Es 4 17 and with the other he held a sword
18 was girded with a sword about his reins
Jdth 4 12 not by fighting with the sword, but by
5 16 went in . . . without shield and sword
18 they were given to spoil and to the s.
28 he with them be stabbed with the sword
6 3 shalt die with them by the sword
4 the sword of my soldiers shall pass
6 punishment they deserve from my sword
7 9 thou shalt destroy them without sword
8 19 given up to their enemies, to the sword
9 2 gavest him a s. to execute vengeance
11 and to beat down with their sword
13 28 thy sides to be pierced with a sword
16 6 and kill my young men with the sword
11 with a sword she cut off his head
Esth 16 24 perish by the sword and by fire
Job 1 15 and slew the servants with the sword
17 have slain the servants with the sword
5 15 the needy from the sword of their mouth
20 in battle, from the hand of the sword
15 22 looking round about for the sword
19 29 flee then from the face of the sword
29 the sword is the revenger of iniquities
20 25 the sword is drawn out, and cometh
27 14 his sons . . . shall be for the sword
33 18 and his life from passing to the sword
36 12 hear not, they shall pass by the sword
39 22 he turneth not his back to the sword
41 17 when a sword shall lay at him, it
Ps 16 13 thy sword from the enemies of thy hand
21 21 deliver, O God, my soul from the sword
34 3 bring out the sword, and shut up the

36 14 the wicked have drawn out the sword
15 let their sword enter into their own
43 4 they got not . . . by their own sword
7 bow: neither shall my sword save me
44 4 gird thy sword upon thy thigh, O thou
56 5 arrows, and their tongue a sharp sword
58 8 mouth, and a sword is in their lips
62 11 delivered into the hands of the sword
63 4 have whetted their tongues like a sword
75 4 broken the powers of . . . the sword
77 62 he shut up his people under the sword
64 their priests fell by the sword: and
88 44 hast turned away the help of his sword
143 10 servant David from the malicious sword
Prov 5 4 her end . . . sharp as a two-edged sword
12 18 pricked as it were with s. of conscience
25 18 is like a dart and a sword and a sharp
Cant 3 8 every man's sword upon his thigh
Wisd 18 16 with a sharp sword carrying thy
Eccu 21 4 all iniquity is like a two-edged sword
22 26 thou hast drawn a sword at a friend
26 27 hath prepared such an one for the sword
39 36 the sword taking vengeance upon the
40 9 strife and sword . . . for the wicked
Isa 1 20 the sword shall devour you because
2 4 nation shall not lift up s. against
14 19 among them that were slain by the sword
21 15 from the sword that hung over them
22 2 thy slain are not slain by the sword
27 1 and strong sword shall visit leviathan
31 8 shall flee not at the face of the sword
8 sword not of a man shall devour him
34 5 my sword is inebriated in heaven
6 sword of the Lord is filled with blood
49 2 hath made my mouth like a sharp sword
51 19 and the sword, who shall comfort thee
65 12 I will number you in the sword, and
Jer 2 30 your sword hath devoured your prophets
4 10 the sword reaching even to the soul
5 12 we shall not see the sword and famine
17 with the sword they shall destroy thy
6 25 s. of enemy and fear is on every side
9 16 I will send the sword after them
11 22 their young men shall die by the sword
12 12 the sword of the Lord shall devour
14 12 for I will consume them by the sword
13 you shall not see the sword, and there
15 s. and famine shall not be in this
15 by s. and famine shall those prophets
16 because of the famine and the sword
18 fields, behold the slain with the sword
15 2 such as are for the sword, to the sword
3 the sword to kill, and the dogs to tear
9 residue . . . I will give up to the sword
16 4 they shall be consumed with the sword
18 21 bring them into the hands of the sword
21 their young men be stabbed with the s.
19 7 I will destroy them with the sword
20 4 and shall strike them with the sword
21 7 such as are left . . . from the sword
9 this city, shall die by the s. 38:2
24 10 I will send among them the sword and
25 16 shall . . . be mad because of the sword
27 and rise no more, because of the sword
29 I will call for the sword upon all the
31 wicked I have delivered up to the sword
26 23 he slew him [Urias] with the sword
27 8 will visit upon that nation with the s.
13 why will you die . . . by the sword
29 17 I will send upon them the sword and
18 I will persecute them with the sword
31 2 were left and escaped from the sword
32 24 by the sword and the famine and the
36 shall be delivered . . . by the sword
33 4 and to the bulwarks and to the sword
34 4 thou shalt not die by the sword. But
17 a liberty for you . . . to the sword
39 18 thou shalt not fall by the sword
41 2 they struck Godolias . . . with the sword
42 16 sword which you fear, shall overtake
17 to dwell there, shall die by the s.
22 certainly that you shall die by the s.
43 11 such as are for the sword, to the sword
44 12 they shall be consumed . . . by the sword
13 as I have visited Jerusalem by the s.
18 we . . . have been consumed by the sword
27 shall be consumed by the sword and
28 a few men that shall flee from the sword
46 10 sword shall devour and shall be filled
14 sword shall devour all round about thee
16 nativity, from the sword of the dove
47 6 thou sword of the Lord, how long wilt
48 2 and the sword shall follow thee. A
49 37 I will send the sword after them
50 16 for fear of the sword of the dove
35 a sword is upon the Chaldeans, saith
36 a sword upon her diviners, and they
36 a sword upon her valiant ones, and they
37 a sword upon their horses, and upon
37 a sword upon her treasures, and they
51 50 you that have escaped the sword, come
Lam 1 20 abroad the sword destroyeth, and at
2 21 my young men are fallen by the sword
4 9 better with them that were slain by s.
5 9 because of the sword in the desert
Bar 2 25 pains, by famine, and by the sword
6 14 and this hath in his hand a sword
Eze 5 2 I will draw out the sword after. 12
17 I will bring in the sword upon thee
6 3 I will bring upon you the sword and
8 some that shall escape the sword among
12 he that is near shall fall by the sword
7 15 the sword without: and the pestilence
15 is in the field shall die by the sword
11 8 you have feared the sword, and I will bring the sword upon you
12 14 I will draw out the sword after them
16 leave a few men of them from the sword
14 17 if I bring the sword upon that land, and say to the sword
21 judgments, the sword and the famine and
21 3 I will draw forth my sword out of its
4 shall my s. go forth out of its sheath
5 that I the Lord have drawn my sword
9 sword is sharpened and furbished. 11
12 this sword is upon my people, it is
12 they are delivered up to the sword
14 let the sword be doubled, and let the sword of the slain be tripled
14 this is the sword of a great slaughter
15 I have set the dread of the sharp sword, the sword that is furbished
19 for s. of the king of Babylon to come
20 that the sword may come to Rabbath
28 O sword, come out of the scabbard
23 10 and slew her with the sword: and they
26 6 daughters . . . shall be slain by the s.
8 daughters . . . he will kill with the s.
11 thy people he shall kill with the sword
28 23 they shall fall being slain by the sword
29 8 behold I will bring the sword upon thee
10 desolate, and wasted by the sword, from
30 4 and the sword shall come upon Egypt
21 might recover strength and hold the s.
22 I will cause the sword to fall out of
24 and will put my sword in his hand

25 when I shall have given my sword into
31 17 them that are slain by the sword. 18
32 10 when my sword shall begin to fly upon
11 sword of the king of Babylon shall come
20 midst of them that are slain with the s.
20 the sword is given, they have drawn her
21 slept uncircumcised, slain by the sword
22 slain, and that fell by the sword
23 them slain, and fallen by the s. 24
25 are uncircumcised and slain by the sword
26 and slain, and fallen by the sword
28 that are slain by the sword. 29, 30, 32
31 multitude, which was slain by the sword
33 2 when I bring the sword upon a land
3 he see the sword coming upon the land
4 if the sword come and cut him off
6 if the watchman see the sword coming
6 and the sword come and cut off a soul
35 5 children of Israel in hands of the sword
8 shall fall that are slain with the s.
38 8 land that is returned from the sword
21 I will call in the sword against him
21 s. shall be pointed against his brother
39 23 enemies and they fell all by the sword
Dan 13 59 angel of the Lord waiteth with a sword
14 25 I will kill this dragon without sword
Osee 1 7 I will not save them by bow nor by sword
2 18 I will destroy the bow and the sword
11 6 the sword hath begun in his cities
14 1 let them perish by the sword, let their
Amos 1 11 hath pursued his brother with the sword
4 10 I slew your young men with the sword
7 9 against house of Jeroboam with the s.
11 Jeroboam shall die by the sword, and
9 1 will slay the last of them with the s.
4 there will I command the sword, and it
Mich 4 3 nation shall not take s. against nation
5 6 shall feed land of Assyria with the s.
6 14 shalt save, I will give up to the s.
Nah 2 13 the sword shall devour thy young lions
3 3 the noise . . . of the shining sword
15 thou shalt perish by the sword, it shall
Soph 2 12 also shall be slain with my sword
Agge 2 23 every one by the sword of his brother
Zach 9 13 make thee as the sword of the mighty
11 17 the sword upon his arm and upon his
13 7 awake, O sword, against my shepherd
1 Ma 2 9 her young men are fallen by the sword
3 12 Judas took the sword of Apollonius and
4 15 the hindmost of them fell by the sword
33 cast them down with s. of them that
7 46 they were all slain with the sword, and
8 23 far be the sword and enemy from them
9 73 so the sword ceased from Israel: and
10 85 so they that were slain by the sword
12 48 in with him they slew with the sword
2 Ma 12 6 slew with the sword them that escaped
14 18 afraid to try the matter by the sword
15 15 gave to Judas a sword of gold, saying
16 take this holy sword a gift from God
Mat 10 34 not to send peace, but the sword
26 52 put up again thy sword into its place
52 take the s. shall perish with the s.
Mark 14 47 drawing a sword, struck a servant of
Luke 2 35 and thy own soul a sword shall pierce
22 36 let him sell his coat and buy a sword
49 Lord, shall we strike with the sword
John 18 10 Simon Peter, having a sword, drew it
11 put up thy sword into the scabbard
Acts 12 2 killed James . . . with the sword. And
Rom 8 35 danger? or persecution? or the sword
13 4 for he beareth not the sword in vain
Eph 6 17 salvation, and the sword of the Spirit
Heb 11 37 they were put to death by the sword
Apoc 1 16 came out a sharp two-edged sword: and
2 12 that hath the sharp two-edged sword
16 against them with the s. of my mouth
6 4 a great sword was given to him. And
8 to kill with sword, with famine, and
13 10 he that shall kill by the sword, must
10 must be killed by the sword. Here is
14 which had the wound by the sword and
19 15 proceedeth a sharp two-edged sword
21 the rest were slain by the sword of him
edge of the sword; ***see*** **edge**
fall by the sword Lev 26 8 enemies shall fall before you by the sword
Num 14 3 lest we fall by the sword, and our
4 K 19 7 I will make him fall by the sword in his
Isa 3 25 fairest men also shall fall by the sword
13 15 to their aid, shall fall by the sword
31 8 the Assyrian shall fall by the sword
37 7 will cause him to fall by the sword
Jer 20 4 they shall fall by the sword of their
39 18 and thou shalt not fall by the sword
44 12 they shall fall by the sword and by
Eze 5 12 a third part of thee shall fall by the s.
6 11 they shall fall by the sword, by the
12 that is near, shall fall by the sword
11 10 you shall fall by the sword: I will
17 21 his bands shall fall by the sword
23 25 what remains shall fall by the sword
24 21 you have left, shall fall by the sword
25 13 are in Dedan shall fall by the sword
30 5 shall fall with them by the sword
6 shall they fall in it by the sword
17 of Bubastus shall fall by the sword
33 27 ruinous places, shall fall by the sword
Dan 11 33 they shall fall by the sword and by
Osee 7 16 their princes shall fall by the sword
Amos 7 17 thy daughters shall fall by the sword
9 10 sinners . . . shall fall by the sword
1 Ma 7 38 and let them fall by the sword
his sword Exod 32 27 man his s. upon his thigh
Judg 8 20 drew not his sword; for he was afraid
1 K 17 39 David having girded his sword upon his
51 took his sword and drew it out of the
18 4 rest of his garments, even to his s.
22 19 he smote with the edge of his sword
25 13 let every man gird on his sword. And
13 and they girded on every man his sword
13 David also girded on his sword: and
31 4 Saul took his sword and. 1 Pa 10:4
5 he also fell upon his s. 1 Pa 10:5
2 K 2 16 his s. into the side of his adversary
1 Pa 21 27 put up his sword again into the sheath
Jdth 9 12 pride may be cut off with his own s.
13 8 and loosed his sword that hung tied
Job 40 14 who made him, he will apply his s.
Ps 7 13 he will brandish his sword: he hath
Isa 41 2 shall give them as the dust to his s.
66 16 shall judge by fire and by his sword
Jer 48 10 that withholdeth his sword from blood
1 Ma 3 3 and protected the camp with his sword
2 Ma 14 41 taken, he struck himself with his s.
Mat 26 51 forth his hand, drew out his sword
Acts 16 27 drawing his sword, would have killed
swords Gen 34 25 brothers of Dina, taking their s.
Josu 10 11 hailstones than were slain by the s.
Judg 20 17 were found 400,000 that drew swords
1 K 13 19 lest the Hebrews should make them s.
1 Pa 5 18 bearing shields and s., and banding
2 Pa 23 10 he set all the people with swords in
2 Es 4 13 I set the people . . . with their swords
Ps 9 7 the swords of the enemy have failed
149 6 and two-edged swords in their hands

Prov 22 5 and swords are in way of the perverse
30 14 generation that for teeth hath swords
Cant 3 8 all holding swords, and most expert
Eccu 46 3 stretched out swords against the cities
Isa 2 4 shall turn their s. into plowshares
21 15 they are fled from before the swords
Eze 16 40 and shall slay thee with their swords
23 47 let them be stabbed with their swords
28 7 they shall draw their swords against
30 11 they shall draw their swords upon Egypt
32 12 by s. of the mighty I will overthrow
27 laid their swords under their heads
33 26 you stood on your swords, you have
38 4 armed with spears and shields and s.
Joel 3 10 cut your plowshares into swords
Mich 4 3 shall beat their s. into plowshares
1 Ma 4 6 only, who neither had armor nor swords
2 Ma 5 3 with drawn swords, and casting of darts
12 22 wounded with strokes of their own s.
Mat 26 47 great multitude with swords and clubs
55 as it were to a robber with swords and
Mark 14 43 multitude with swords and staves from
48 with swords and staves to apprehend
Luke 22 38 said: Lord, behold here are two swords
52 are ye come . . . with swords and clubs
swore Gen 24 7 swore to me, saying: To thy seed
Gen 24 9 lord, and swore to him upon this word
25 33 Esau swore to him, and sold his first
26 3 which I swore to Abraham. Exod 33:1; Deut 34:4
31 morning, they swore one to another
31 53 Jacob swore by the fear of his father
50 23 the land which he swore to Abraham
Exod 2 21 Moses s. that he would dwell with him
13 5 swore to thy fathers. Deut 4:31; 6:10; 7:12, 13; 8:18; 13:17; 19:8; 27:3; 29:13
11 as he swore to thee and thy fathers
Num 14 23 for which I swore to their fathers. Deut 10:11; 31:20; Josu 1:6
30 5 whatsoever she promised and swore
32 10 he swore in his anger, saying: If
Deut 1 8 Lord swore to your fathers. 8:1
34 he was angry and swore and said: Not
4 21 he swore that I should not pass over
6 18 the Lord swore to thy fathers. 11:21; 28:11; 30:20
23 which he swore to our fathers. 26:3
7 8 oath which he swore to your fathers
28 9 as he swore to thee: If thou keep
31 7 which the Lord swore he would give
Josu 9 15 princes also of the multitude s. to them
14 9 Moses swore in that day, saying: The
Judg 2 1 I swore to your fathers. Jer 11:5
1 K 19 6 Saul . . . swore: As the Lord liveth he
20 3 he [Jonathan] swore again to David
17 Jonathan swore again to David because
24 23 David swore to Saul. So Saul went
28 10 and Saul swore unto her by the Lord
30 15 and David swore to him. And when he
2 K 3 35 David swore, saying: So do God to me
19 23 shalt not die. And he swore unto him
21 17 then David's men s. unto him, saying
3 K 1 29 the king swore and said: As the Lord
30 even as I swore to thee by the Lord
2 8 I s. to him . . . I will not kill thee
23 Solomon swore . . . So and so may God
4 K 25 24 Godolias s. to them and to their men
2 Pa 15 14 they s. to the Lord with a loud voice
15 for with all their heart they swore
1 Es 10 5 according to this word, and they s.
Jdth 1 12 swore by his throne and kingdom
Ps 94 11 swore in my wrath that they shall not
131 2 how he swore to the Lord, he vowed
Isa 54 9 days of Noe, to whom I swore, that I
Jer 38 16 Sedecias swore to Jeremias, in private
40 9 Godolias . . . s. to them and to their
Eze 16 8 I swore to thee and I entered into
1 Ma 6 61 king and the princes swore to them
7 35 swore in anger, saying: Unless Judas
9 71 swore that he would do him no harm
2 Ma 13 23 he swore to all things that seemed
14 22 swore unto him that they knew not
33 swore, saying: Unless you deliver
Mark 6 23 he swore to her: Whatsoever thou shalt
Luke 1 73 the oath which he swore to Abraham our
Heb 6 13 whom he might swear, swore by himself
Apoc 10 6 he swore by him that liveth forever
sworest Exod 32 13 to whom thou s. by thy own self
sworn Gen 22 16 by my own self have I sworn
Num 11 12 which thou hast s. to their fathers
14 16 into the land for which he had sworn
17 as thou hast sworn, saying: The Lord
Deut 2 14 of the camp, as the Lord had sworn
Josu 5 6 to whom he had sworn before, that he
9 18 the princes of the multitude had sworn
19 we have sworn to them in the name of
21 41 the land that he had sworn to give
Judg 2 15 said, and as he had sworn to them
21 1 children of Israel had also sworn in
7 s. not to give our daughters to them
1 K 3 14 have I sworn to the house of Heli
12 22 Lord hath sworn to make you his people
20 42 and let all stand that we have sworn
2 K 3 9 as the Lord hath sworn to David, so I
21 2 the children of Israel had s. to them
2 Es 6 18 there were many in Judea sworn to him
Ps 23 4 nor sworn deceitfully to his neighbor
88 4 I have sworn to David my servant: Thy
36 once I have sworn by my holiness: I
109 4 Lord hath s. and he will not repent
118 106 I have sworn and am determined to keep
131 11 the Lord hath sworn truth to David
Wisd 12 21 to whose parents thou hast sworn and
14 30 heed to idols, and have s. unjustly
Isa 14 24 the Lord of hosts hath sworn, saying
45 23 I have sworn by myself, the word of
54 9 so have I sworn not to be angry with
62 8 the Lord hath sworn by his right hand
Jer 44 26 I have sworn by my great name, saith
49 13 I have sworn by myself, saith the Lord
51 14 Lord of hosts hath sworn by himself
Dan 12 7 had sworn, by him that liveth forever
Amos 4 2 Lord God hath sworn by his holiness
6 8 Lord God hath sworn by his own soul
8 7 Lord hath sworn against the pride of
Mich 7 20 which thou hast sworn to our fathers
Acts 2 30 knew that God hath sworn to him with
Heb 3 11 as I have sworn in my wrath. 4:3
7 21 Lord hath sworn, and he will not repent
sycamore Luke 19 4 he climbed up into a s. tree
sycamores 3 K 10 27 as common as s. 2 Pa 9:27
2 Pa 1 15 cedar trees as sycamores, which grow
Isa 9 10 they have cut down the sycamores, but
Syene Eze 29 10 from the tower of Syene. 30:6
Sylvanus 2 C 1 19 by me, and S. and Timothy
1 Th 1 1 Paul and S. and Timothy. 2 Th 1:1
1 Pa 5 12 by Sylvanus, a faithful brother unto
symphony Dan 3 5 psaltery and of the s. 7, 10
synagogue Num 4 34 the princes of the s. 31:13
Num 16 2 leading men of the synagogue, and
Mark 1 21 going into the s., he taught them
23 in their s. a man with an unclean
29 going out of the synagogue, they came
3 1 he entered again into the synagogue
5 22 cometh one of the rulers of the s.
36 saith to the ruler of the synagogue

15 the Syrians seeing that they had fallen
16 Adarezer sent and fetched the Syrians
17 the Syrians set themselves in array
18 and the Syrians fled before Israel
19 all the Syrians were afraid to help
3 K 20 20 the Syrians fled, and Israel pursued
21 slew the Syrians with a great slaughter
26 Benadad mustered the Syrians and
27 of goats but the S. filled the land
28 the Syrians have said: The Lord is
29 children of Israel slew of the Syrians
22 35 stood in his chariot against the S.
4 K 6 9 for the Syrians are there in ambush
7 4 let us run over to camp of the Syrians
5 to first part of the camp of the S.
10 we went to the camp of the Syrians
12 I tell you what the Syrians have done
14 king sent into the camp of the Syrians
15 Syrians had cast away in their fright
16 pillaged the camp of the Syrians: and
8 28 the Syrians wounded Joram. 2 Pa 22:5
29 Syrians had wounded him in Ramoth when
9 15 for the Syrians had wounded him when
13 17 thou shalt strike the Syrians in Aphec
1 Pa 18 5 Syrians of Damascus came also to help
19 10 Israel, and marched against the Syrians
12 if the Syrians be too strong for me
14 went against the Syrians to the battle
16 the Syrians seeing that they had fallen
16 the Syrians that were beyond the river
2 Pa 18 34 in his chariot against the Syrians
24 24 a very small number of the Syrians
Isa 9 12 the Syrians from the east, and the
Amos 9 7 and the Syrians out of Cyrene? Behold
Syrophenician Mark 7 26 was a Gentile, a S. born

T

Tabbaoth 1 Es 2 43 the children of Tabbaoth
Tabee Gen 22 24 his concubine, named Roma, bore T.
Tabeel Isa 7 6 and make the son of T. king
Tabelias 1 Pa 26 11 T. the third, Zacharias the
tabernacle Exod 16 34 Aaron put it in the t. to be
Exod 25 9 according to all the likeness of the t.
26 1 thou shalt make the t. in this manner
6 joined, that it may be made one t.
7 to cover the top of the tabernacle
12 cover the back parts of the tabernacle
13 curtains, fencing both sides of the t.
15 make also the boards of the tabernacle
20 in the second side also of the t.
22 on the west side of the tabernacle
23 in the corners at the back of the t.
26 boards on one side of the tabernacle
30 and thou shalt rear up the tabernacle
35 candlestick in south side of the t.
36 a hanging in the entrance of the t.
27 9 make also the court of the tabernacle
19 all the vessels of the t. for all uses
33 7 Moses also taking the t., pitched it
8 when Moses went forth to the tabernacle
8 back of Moses till he went into the t.
11 Josue . . . departed not from the t.
35 11 t. and the roof thereof, and the cover
18 the pins of the t. and of the court
36 8 to accomplish the work of the tabernacle
13 and they might be made one tabernacle
14 to cover the roof of the tabernacle
19 he made also a cover for the tabernacle
20 he made also the boards of the t. of
22 for all the boards of the tabernacle
25 at that side also of the t. that
27 side of the tabernacle which looketh
28 two others at each corner of t. behind
31 boards of one side of the tabernacle
32 bars at the west side of the tabernacle
37 hanging in the entry of the tabernacle
38 15 he made the entry of the tabernacle
20 pins also of the t. and of the court
39 31 all the work of the t. and of the roof
32 they offered the t. and the roof and
38 the hanging in the entry of the t.
40 to be made for the ministry of the t.
40 5 put the hanging in the entry of the t.
7 the laver between the altar and the t.
9 anoint the tabernacle with its vessels
15 of the second year, the t. was set up
17 spread the roof over the tabernacle
19 he had brought the ark into the t.
20 he set the table in the tabernacle
31 he set up the court round about the t.
34 time the cloud removed from the t.
36 the cloud of the Lord hung over the t.
Lev 4 7 altar of holocaust in entry of the t.
6 16 the holy place of the court of the t.
26 place, in the court of the tabernacle
8 10 with which he anointed the tabernacle
35 shall you remain in the tabernacle
15 31 when they shall have defiled my t.
16 17 let no man be in the t. when the
20 hath cleansed the sanctuary and the t.
26 11 I will set my t. in the midst of you
Num 1 50 they shall carry the tabernacle and all
50 shall encamp round about the tabernacle
51 the Levites shall take down the t.
53 their tents round about the tabernacle
3 8 let them keep the vessels of the t.
23 these shall pitch behind the tabernacle
26 the t. itself and the cover thereof
26 in the entry of the court of the t. and
26 cords of the t. and all the furniture
36 custody shall be the boards of the t.
4 16 pertaineth to the service of the t.
25 to carry the curtains of the tabernacle
26 veil in the entry that is before the t.
31 they shall carry the boards of the t.
47 that go into the ministry of the t.
5 17 little earth of the pavement of the t.
7 1 day that Moses had finished the t.
3 and they offered them before the t.
5 to serve in the ministry of the t.
9 15 day that the tabernacle was reared up
15 the evening there was over the t.
17 the cloud that covered the tabernacle
18 at his commandment they pitched the t.
18 days that the cloud abode over the t.
20 soever as the cloud stayed over the t.
21 at break of day left the tabernacle
22 if it remained over the tabernacle
10 17 and the tabernacle was taken down
21 so long was the tabernacle carried
11 24 made them to stand about the tabernacle
26 but were not gone forth to the t.
12 5 stood in the entry of the t. calling
10 the cloud also that was over the t.
16 9 serve him in the service of the t.
17 13 whosoever approacheth to the t.
18 3 about all the works of the tabernacle
4 and watch in the charge of the t.
6 to serve in the ministries of the t.
22 may not approach any more to the t.
23 sons of Levi may serve me in the t.
19 13 shall profane the t. of the Lord, and
31 30 that watch in the charge of the t. of
47 Levites that watched in the tabernacle
Deut 31 15 cloud which stood in entry of the t.

Josu 22 19 to the land wherein is the tabernacle
1 K 21 7 was there that day, with in the t. of
2 K 6 17 in its place in the midst of the t.
7 6 but have walked in a t. and in a tent
3 K 1 39 priest took a horn of oil out of the t.
2 28 and Joab fled into the tabernacle of
29 that Joab was fled into the tabernacle
8 4 the vessels . . . that were in the t.
1 Pa 6 48 for all the ministry of the tabernacle
9 19 keepers of the gates of the tabernacle
23 and the tabernacle by their turns. In
15 1 ark of God and pitched a t. for it
16 39 the t. of the Lord in the high place
17 5 been always changing places in a t.
21 29 t. of the Lord which Moses made in the
23 26 the Levites to carry any more the t.
2 Pa 1 4 he had pitched a tabernacle for it
5 the altar . . . was there before the t.
5 5 with all the furniture of the t. And
5 the vessels . . . which were in the t.
29 6 their faces from the t. of the Lord
1 Es 7 15 of Israel, whose t. is in Jerusalem
Jdth 13 31 thou by thy God in every t. of Jacob
Job 19 12 and have besieged my t. round about
29 4 when God was secretly in my tabernacle
31 31 if men of my tabernacle have not said
Ps 28 1 at the finishing of the tabernacle
41 5 into the place of the wonderful t.
77 60 he put away the tabernacle of Silo
67 he rejected the tabernacle of Joseph
131 3 if I shall enter into the tabernacle
5 a t. for the God of Jacob. Behold we
Eccu 24 12 that made me, rested in my tabernacle
Isa 4 6 there shall be a tabernacle for a shade
16 5 upon it in truth in the t. of David
22 15 thee in to him that dwelleth in the t.
33 20 a tabernacle that cannot be removed
Jer 10 20 my tabernacle is laid waste, all my
Lam 2 4 in the t. of the daughter of Sion, he
Eze 37 27 my tabernacle shall be with them: and
41 1 on that side, the breadth of the t.
Amos 5 26 carried a tabernacle for your Moloch
9 11 I will raise up the t. of David that
2 Ma 2 4 the t. and the ark should accompany
5 carried in thither the t. and the ark
Acts 7 43 you took unto you the t. of Moloch
46 desired to find a t. for the God of
15 16 I will return, and will rebuild the t.
2 C 5 4 we also, who are in this t., do groan
Heb 8 2 a minister of . . . the true tabernacle
5 when he was to finish the tabernacle
9 2 for there was a tabernacle made the
3 after the second veil, the tabernacle
6 into the first t. the priests indeed
8 the former tabernacle was yet standing
11 by a greater and more perfect tabernacle
21 the tabernacle also and all the vessels
13 10 have no power to eat who serve the t.
2 P 1 13 as long as I am in this t., to stir
14 the laying away of this my t. is at
Apoc 21 3 behold the tabernacle of God with men
door of the tabernacle; *see* **door**
his tabernacle Josu 22 29 erected before his t.
2 K 15 25 he will show me it, and his tabernacle
Tob 13 12 may rebuild his tabernacle in thee
Job 18 6 the light shall be dark in his t. and
14 his confidence be rooted out of his t.
15 let the companions . . . dwell in his t.
20 26 shall be afflicted when left in his t.
Ps 18 6 he hath set his tabernacle in the sun
26 5 he hath hidden me in his tabernacle
5 in the secret place of his tabernacle
6 have offered up in his t. a sacrifice
45 5 most High hath sanctified his own t.
77 60 Silo, his t. where he dwelt among men
131 7 we will go in to his tabernacle: we
Lam 2 6 he hath thrown down his tabernacle
Dan 11 45 and he shall fix his tabernacle Apadno
Apoc 13 6 to blaspheme his name and his t. and
tabernacle of the covenant Exod 31 7 the t. . . . and the ark of the testimony
Exod 33 7 called the name thereof, The t. . . .
7 went forth to the t. . . . without the
9 and when he was gone into the t. . . .
40 30 when they went into the t. . . . , and
33 neither could Moses go into t. . . .
Lev 24 3 veil of the testimony, in the t. . . .
Num 1 1 in the desert of Sinai in the t. . . .
2 2 their kindreds, round about the t. . . .
3 25 and their charge shall be in the t. . . .
26 drawn before the doors of the t. . . .
38 before tabernacle of the covenant . . . Moses and Aaron camp before the t. . . .
4 3 in to stand and to minister in t. . . .
5 and his sons shall go into the t. . . .
15 of the sons of Caath; in the t. . . .
23 that go in and minister in the t. . . .
25 that hangeth in the entry of the t. . . .
28 family of the Gersonites in the t. . . .
33 Merarites and their ministry in t. . . .
35 that go in to the ministry of t. . . .
37 people of Caath that go in to t. . . .
39 all that go in to minister in t. . . .
43 go in to fulfil the rites of the t. . . .
6 13 bring him to the door of the t. . . .
18 shaved off before the door of t. . . .
7 89 and when Moses entered into the t. . . .
8 9 bring the Levites before the t. . . .
15 afterwards they shall enter into t. . . .
19 to serve me for Israel in the t. . . .
22 purified they might go into the t. . . .
24 shall go in to minister in the t. . . .
26 ministers of their brethren in t. . . .
10 3 unto thee to the door of the t. . . .
11 the cloud was taken up from the t. . . .
11 16 bring them to the door of the t. . . .
12 4 come out you three only to the t. . . .
14 10 of the Lord appeared over the t. . . .
16 43 Moses and Aaron fled to the t. . . .
50 returned to Moses to door of the t. . . .
17 4 thou shalt lay them up in the t. . . .
18 21 wherewith they serve me in the t. . . .
20 6 went into the t. . . . and fell flat
27 2 at the door of the t. . . . and said
3 K 8 4 carried ark of the Lord and the t. . . .
1 Pa 23 32 keep the observances of the t. . . .
2 Pa 1 3 place of Gabaon, where was the t. . . .
6 the brazen altar before the t. . . .
13 Gabaon to Jerusalem before the t. . . .
tabernacle of the testimony Exod 27 21 that a lamp may burn always in the t. . . .
Exod 28 43 when they shall go in to the t. . . .
29 10 present also the calf before the t. . . .
30 and that shall enter into the t. . . .
32 in the entry of the t. . . . 38:30; Lev 3:2, 8, 13; 40:26
42 the door of the t. . . . 40:12; Lev 4:18; 12:6; 14:11, 23; 15:14, 29; 16:7; 17:5, 6, 9; 19:21; Josu 19:51
44 I will sanctify also the t. . . . with
30 16 deliver unto the uses of the t. . . .
18 set it between the t. . . . and the altar
20 when they are going into the t. . . .
26 therewith thou shalt anoint the t. . . .
36 thou shalt set of it before the t. . . .
35 21 mind, to make the work of the t. . . .

38 21 these are the instruments of the t. . . .
40 2 the month, thou shalt set up the t. . . .
20 and he set the table in the t. . . .
22 set the candlestick also in the t. . . .
28 laver between the t. . . . and the altar
32 the cloud covered the t. . . . , and the
Lev 1 1 Moses and spoke to him from the t. . . .
4 5 the calf and carry it into the t. . . .
7 altar . . . which is in the t. . . .
16 shall carry of the blood into t. . . .
18 altar that is before the Lord in t. . . .
6 30 of which is carried into the t. . . .
9 23 Moses and Aaron went into the t. . . .
10 9 sons, when you enter into the t. . . .
16 16 to this rite shall he do to the t. . . .
23 Aaron shall return into the t. . . . , and
33 expiate the sanctuary and the t. . . .
Num 1 50 appoint them over the t. . . . and all
53 shall keep watch and guard the t. . . .
2 17 t. . . . shall be carried by the officers
3 7 service of the multitude before t. . . .
17 7 laid them up before the Lord in t. . . .
10 carry back the rod of Aaron into t. . . .
18 2 thy sons shall minister in the t. . . .
31 wherewith you serve in the t. . . .
31 54 they brought into the t. . . . for a
Deut 31 14 call Josue and stand ye in the t. . . .
14 and Josue went and stood in the t. . . .
Josu 18 1 Silo, and there they set up the t. . . .
1 Pa 6 32 and they ministered before the t. . . .
9 21 was porter of the gate of the t. . . .
2 Pa 24 6 multitude of Israel to bring into t. . . .
Acts 7 44 the t. . . . was with our fathers in the
Apoc 15 5 the temple of the t. . . . in heaven
thy tabernacle Job 5 24 that thy t. is in peace
Job 11 14 let not injustice remain in thy t.
22 23 shalt put away iniquity far from thy t.
Ps 14 1 who shall dwell in thy tabernacle
30 21 thou shalt protect them in thy t.
60 5 in thy tabernacle I shall dwell forever
Wisd 9 8 a resemblance of thy holy tabernacle
tabernacles Exod 1 11 built for Pharao cities of t.
Lev 23 34 shall be kept the feast of tabernacles
42 of the race of Israel shall dwell in t.
43 the children of Israel to dwell in t.
Num 24 5 how beautiful are thy t., O Jacob
6 as t. which the Lord hath pitched, as
Deut 16 13 celebrate the solemnity also of t.
16 and in the feast of t. 2 Pa 8:13
31 10 the feast of t., when all Israel come
33 18 thy going out; and Issachar in thy t.
1 Es 3 4 they kept the feast of t., as it is
2 Es 8 14 children of Israel should dwell in t.
15 branches of thick trees, to make t.
16 and they made themselves tabernacles
17 the captivity, made t. and dwelt in t.
Job 12 6 the tabernacles of robbers abound and
15 34 fire shall devour their tabernacles
18 21 these then are the t. of the wicked
Ps 42 3 brought me . . . into thy tabernacles
59 8 I will mete out the vale of t. 107:8
68 26 let there be none to dwell in their t.
77 51 of all their labor in the t. of Cham
55 tribes of Israel to dwell in their t.
82 7 the tabernacles of the Edomites and
83 2 how lovely are thy t., O Lord of hosts
11 than to dwell in the t. of sinners
86 2 above all the tabernacles of Sion
117 15 is in the tabernacles of the just
Prov 14 11 tabernacles of the just shall flourish
Isa 32 18 and in the tabernacles of confidence
54 2 and stretch out the skins of thy t.
Osee 9 6 the bur shall be in their tabernacles
12 9 will yet cause thee to dwell in t.
Zach 12 7 Lord shall save the tabernacles of Juda
14 16 keep the feast of tabernacles. 18, 19
Mala 2 12 and the scholar, out of the t. of Jacob
1 Ma 10 21 at the feast day of the tabernacles
2 Ma 10 6 after the manner of the feast of the t.
6 they had kept the feast of the t. when
Mat 17 4 make here three t. Mark 9:4; Luke 9:33
John 7 2 the Jews' feast of t. was at hand
Tabitha Acts 9 36 certain disciple named Tabitha
Acts 9 40 he said: Tabitha, arise. And she opened
table Gen 43 31 and said: Set bread on the table
Exod 25 23 shalt make a table also of setim wood
26 in the four corners of the same table
27 the table may be carried. The bars
28 them with gold to bear up the table
30 thou shalt set upon the table loaves
26 35 the table without the veil: and over
35 over against the table the candlestick
35 the table shall stand in the north side
30 27 table with the vessels thereof. 39:35
31 8 and the table and the vessels thereof
35 13 table with the bars and the vessels
37 10 he made also the table of setim wood
13 in four corners at each foot of the t.
14 them, that the table might be carried
16 vessels for the divers uses of the t.
40 4 thou shalt bring in the table, and set
22 over against the table on the south
Lev 24 6 upon the most clean table before the
Num 3 31 they shall keep the ark and the table
4 7 wrap up also the table of proposition
8 2 towards the table of the loaves of
Judg 1 7 the leavings of the meat under my table
1 K 20 29 he came not to the king's t. Then Saul
34 Jonathan rose from table in great anger
2 K 9 7 thou shalt eat bread at my table always
10 shall always eat bread at my table
11 and Miphiboseth shall eat at my table
13 he ate always of the king's table
19 28 servant among the guests at thy table
3 K 2 7 Galaadite, and let him eat at thy t.
4 27 necessaries also for king Solomon's t.
7 48 altar of gold and the table of gold
10 5 meat of his table, and the apartments
13 20 as they sat at table, the word of the
18 19 who eat at Jezabel's table. Achab
4 K 4 10 a table and a stool and a candlestick
2 Pa 9 4 meats of his table, and the dwelling
13 11 are set forth on a most clean table
29 18 t. of proposition with all its vessels
2 Es 5 17 to number of 150 men were at my table
Tob 2 3 leaped up from his place at the table
9 8 he found Tobias sitting at the table
Jdth 12 1 should be given her from his own table
Esth 1 8 set over every table one of his nobles
14 17 that I have not eaten at Aman's table
Job 36 16 rest of thy t. shall be full of fatness
Ps 22 5 thou hast prepared a table before me
68 23 let their table become as a snare
77 19 can God furnish a t. in the wilderness
20 or provide a table for his people
127 3 as olive plants, round about thy table
Prov 9 2 mingled her wine and set forth her t.
Eccu 6 10 is a friend a companion at the table
14 10 be needy and pensive at his own table
29 32 go, stranger, and furnish the table
31 12 art thou set at a great table? Be not
40 30 that looketh toward another man's table
Isa 21 5 prepare the table, behold in the
65 11 that set a table for fortune and offer
Jer 17 1 it is graven upon table of their heart
Eze 23 41 and a table was decked before thee

39 20 you shall be filled at my table with
41 22 this is the table before the Lord. And
44 16 and they shall come near to my table
Dan 1 8 would not be defiled with the king's t.
11 27 they shall speak lies at one table
14 12 they had made under the table a secret
17 door, the king looked upon the table
20 consumed the things that were on the t.
Mala 1 7 the table of the Lord is contemptible
12 say: The table of the Lord is defiled
1 Ma 1 23 table of proposition, and the pouring
4 49 incense and the table into the temple
51 they set the loaves upon the table
Mat 14 9 for them that sat with him at table
15 27 fall from the table of their masters
26 7 poured it on his head as he was at t.
Mark 2 15 as he sat at table in his house, many
6 22 Herod and them that were at table with
26 of them that were with him at table
7 28 the whelps also eat under the table
14 18 when they were at table and eating
16 14 to the eleven as they were at table
Luke 1 63 demanding a writing table, he wrote
5 29 others, that were at table with them
14 7 they chose the first seats at the t.
10 before them that sit at table with
15 when one of them that sat at table
16 21 that fell from the rich man's table
22 21 betrayeth me is with me on the table
27 he that sitteth at table, or he that
27 is not he that sitteth at table? But
30 you may eat and drink at my table in
24 30 whilst he was at table with them, he
John 12 2 was one of them that were at table
13 28 no man at the table knew to what
Acts 16 34 he laid table for them, and rejoiced
Rom 11 9 let their table be made a snare, and a
1 C 10 21 not be partakers of the table of Lord
21 of the Lord, and of the table of devils
Heb 9 2 wherein were the candlesticks and the t.
tables Exod 32 16 of God was graven in the t.
Exod 32 19 he threw the tables out of his hand
34 1 the words which were in the tables
4 carrying with him the tables. And when
28 he wrote upon the tables the ten words
Deut 9 17 I cast the tables out of my hands
10 2 I will write on the tables the words
4 he wrote in the tables, according as
5 down and put the tables into the ark
4 K 21 13 as tables are wont to be effaced, and
1 Pa 28 16 gold for the t. of proposition, according to the diversity of the t.
16 also silver for other tables of silver
2 Pa 4 8 moreover also ten tables: and he set
19 the golden altar and the tables upon
Prov 3 3 write them in the tables of thy heart
7 3 write it upon the tables of thy heart
Isa 28 8 all tables were full of vomit and filth
Eze 40 41 four tables were on this side, and four tables on that side
41 at the sides of the gate were eight t.
42 and the four tables for the holocausts
43 upon the tables was the flesh of the
Haba 2 2 vision, and make it plain upon tables
1 Ma 8 22 graven in tables of brass, and sent
14 18 they wrote to him in tables of brass
26 and registered it in tables of brass
48 should be put in tables of brass
Mat 21 12 the t. of the moneychangers. Mark 11:15
John 2 15 out, and the tables he overthrew. And
Acts 6 2 leave the word of God and serve tables
2 C 3 3 but in the fleshly tables of the heart
Heb 9 4 and the tables of the testament. And

tables of stone; *see* **stone**
two tables Exod 31 18 gave to Moses two stone **t.**
Exod 32 15 carrying the two t. of the testimony
34 1 hew thee two t. of stone. Deut 10:1
4 then he cut out two tables of stone
29 he held the two tables of the testimony
Deut 4 13 that he wrote in two tables of stone
5 22 he wrote them in two tables of stone
9 10 Lord gave me two tables of stone. 11
15 held the two tables of the covenant
10 3 when I had hewn two tables of stone
3 K 8 9 nothing else but the two tables
2 Pa 5 10 the two tables which Moses put there
Eze 40 39 in porch of the gate were two tables
40 toward the north, were two tables
40 before porch of the gate were two t.
tablets Exod 35 22 earrings, rings, and tablets
Num 31 50 in the booty, in garters and tablets
Isa 3 20 tablets and sweet balls and earrings
Tabremon 3 K 15 18 sent them to Benadad son of **T.**
tackling Acts 27 19 with their own hands the t.
tacklings Isa 33 23 thy t. are loosed, and they
Tahas Gen 22 24 Roma bore . . . Tahas and Maacha
tail Exod 4 4 out thy hand and take it by the t.
Lev 22 23 that hath the ear and the tail cut off
Deut 28 13 make thee the head and not the tail
44 the head, and thou shalt be the tail
Judg 15 4 and coupled them tail to tail, and
Tob 11 9 by his fawning and wagging his tail
Job 40 12 he setteth up his tail like a cedar
Isa 9 14 shall destroy . . . the head and the tail
15 that teacheth lies, he is the tail
19 15 no work for Egypt, to make head or tail
Apoc 12 4 and his tail drew the third part of
tails Isa 7 4 the two t. of these firebrands
Judg 15 4 fastened torches between the tails
Apoc 9 10 they had tails like to scorpions, and
10 were stings in their tails; and their
19 is in their mouths and in their tails
19 their tails are like to serpents and
tale Eccu 22 6 tale out of time is like music in
talebearer Prov 26 20 when the t. is taken away
Prov 26 22 words of a t. are as it were simple
Eccu 21 31 talebearer shall defile his own soul
talent Exod 25 39 weight of candlestick . . . a t.
Exod 37 24 vessels thereof weighed a t. of gold
38 27 one t. being reckoned for every socket
2 K 12 30 weight of which was a talent of gold
3 K 20 39 or thou shalt pay a talent of silver
4 K 5 22 give them a talent of silver, and two
23 33 silver, and a talent of gold. 2 Pa 36:3
1 Pa 20 2 found in it a talent weight of gold
Zach 5 7 behold a talent of lead was carried
2 Ma 8 11 should have 90 slaves for one talent
Mat 25 24 he that had received the one talent
25 went and hid thy talent in the earth
28 take ye away therefore the talent
Apoc 16 21 great hail, like a talent, came down
talents Exod 38 24 offered in gifts was 9 and 20 t.
Exod 38 27 hundred sockets were made of 100 t.
29 were offered of brass 72,000 talents
4 K 5 23 is better that thou take two talents
1 Pa 22 14 of gold 100,000 talents, and of silver **a** million of talents
29 7 of gold 5,000 talents . . . of silver 10,000 talents, and of brass 18,000 t.
2 Pa 3 8 amounting to about six hundred talents
25 9 what will then become of the 100 t.
Esth 3 9 I will pay ten thousand talents to thy
1 Ma 11 28 he promised him three hundred talents
13 19 sent the children and the hundred t.
15 31 tributes of the cities other 500 t.
35 for these we will give a hundred **t.**

2 Ma 4 8 out of other revenues fourscore t.
5 21 taken away out of the temple 1,800 t.
8 10 for the king the tribute of 2,000 t.
Mat 18 24 that owed him ten thousand talents
25 15 to one he gave five talents, and to
16 he that had received the five t. 20
20 coming, brought other five talents
20 thou didst deliver to me five talents
22 that had received the two talents came
22 thou deliveredst two talents to me
28 and give it him that hath ten talents
talents of gold 3 K 9 14 King Solomon 120 t. . . .
3 K 9 28 they brought . . . 420 talents of gold
10 10 she gave the king 120 t. . . . 2 Pa 9:9
14 every year was 666 t. . . . 2 Pa 9:13
4 K 18 14 a tax . . . of silver and 30 t. of g.
1 Pa 29 4 3,000 t. . . . of the gold of Ophir
2 Pa 8 18 they took thence 450 talents of gold
talents of silver Exod 38 26 moreover 100 t. . . .
3 K 16 24 hill of Samaria of Semer for 2 t. . . .
4 K 5 5 departed and took with him 10 t. . . .
23 and bound two t. of silver in two bags
15 19 gave Phul a thousand talents of silver
18 14 a tax . . . of 300 talents of silver
23 33 fine . . . of a hundred t. of silver
1 Pa 19 6 sent 1,000 t. . . . to hire them chariots
29 4 and 7,000 t. of refined silver to
2 Pa 25 6 100,000 valiant men for 100 t. . . .
27 5 gave him at that time 100 t. . . .
36 3 condemned the land in 100 t. of silver
1 Es 7 22 give it without delay, unto 100 t. . . .
8 26 I weighed to their hands 650 t. . . .
Tob 1 16 and had ten t. . . . of that with which
4 21 I lent ten t. . . . while thou wast yet
1 Ma 13 16 now send 100 t. . . . and his two sons
15 31 if not, give me for them 500 t. . . .
2 Ma 3 11 the whole was 400 talents of silver
4 8 promising him 360 talents of silver
24 offering more than Jason by 300 t. . . .
tales Luke 24 11 words seemed to them as idle t.
talitha Mark 5 41 he saith to her: Talitha cumi
talk 2 K 19 11 t. of all Israel was come to the
Job 7 11 I will talk with the bitterness of my
11 2 shall a man full of talk be justified
Prov 6 22 and when thou awakest, talk with them
Ecce 10 13 end of his talk is a mischievous error
Wisd 8 12 if I talk much they shall lay their
Eccu 13 14 for by much talk he will sift thee
22 14 talk not much with a fool, and go not
38 26 talk is about the offspring of bulls
Eze 33 30 that talk of thee by the walls and in
36 3 and are become the subject of the talk
talkative Prov 7 10 to deceive souls; t. and
talked Gen 42 21 t. one to another: We deserve
Gen 50 15 afraid, and talked one with another
1 K 17 23 as he t. with them, that baseborn man
4 K 8 4 king talked with Giezi, the servant
Ps 58 13 their . . . lying they shall be t. of
63 6 they have talked of hiding snares; they
Luke 4 36 they talked among themselves, saying
6 11 and they talked one with another
24 14 they talked together of all these
15 while they talked and reasoned with
John 4 27 wondered that he t. with the woman
Acts 20 11 having t. a long time to them, until
talkers Titus 1 10 t. and seducers: especially
talkest John 4 27 why talkest thou with her
talketh John 9 37 it is he that t. with thee
talking Gen 27 6 I heard thy father t. with Esau
3 K 18 27 perhaps he is talking or is in an inn
4 K 2 11 went on, walking and talking together
Eccu 21 19 the talking of a fool is like a burden
Mat 17 3 Moses and Elias talking with him. And
Mark 9 3 and they were talking with Jesus. And
Luke 9 30 behold two men were talking with him
Acts 10 27 talking with him, he went in, and
Eph 5 4 foolish talking, or scurrility, which is
tall Num 13 33 we beheld are of a tall stature
Deut 2 10 a people great and strong, and so tall
21 great and many, and of tall stature
9 2 a people great and tall, the sons of
4 K 19 23 have cut down its tall cedars and its
Jdth 16 8 nor t. giants oppose themselves to him
Isa 2 13 upon all the tall and lofty cedars of
37 24 I will cut down its tall cedars and
Dan 2 31 which was great and high, t. of stature
taller Deut 1 28 very great and taller than we
tamaric Jer 17 6 shall be like t. in the desert
tame Mark 5 4 pieces, and no one could t. him
James 3 8 but the tongue no man can tame, an
tamed James 3 7 is t. and hath been t. by the
Tanis Num 13 23 was built seven years before T.
Ps 77 12 land of Egypt, in the field of Tanis
43 and his wonders in the field of Tanis
Isa 19 11 princes of Tanis are become fools. 13
30 4 for thy princes were in Tanis, and thy
tanner Acts 9 43 in Joppe, with one Simon a t.
Acts 10 6 he lodgeth with one Simon a tanner
32 he lodgeth in the house of Simon a t.
tapestry Exod 35 35 to do carpenters' work and t.
Exod 38 23 and worker in tapestry and embroidery
2 K 17 28 brought him beds and tapestry and
Prov 7 16 have covered it with painted tapestry
31 22 made for herself clothing of tapestry
Eze 27 20 thy merchants in tapestry for seats
Tapheth 3 K 4 11 had T. the daughter of Solomon
Taphnes 3 K 11 19 the own sister of his wife T.
3 K 11 20 the sister of Taphnes bore him his son
20 T. brought him up in house of Pharao
Jer 2 16 and of Taphnes have defloured thee
Taphnis Jer 43 7 they came as far as Taphnis
Jer 43 8 of the Lord came to Jeremias in T.
9 the gate of Pharao's house in Taphnis
44 1 dwelling in Magdal and in Taphnis and
46 14 let it be known in Memphis and in T.
Eze 30 14 Phatures and will make a fire in T.
18 in Taphnis the day shall be darkened
Taphsar Jer 51 27 number T. against her, bring
Taphua Josu 12 17 the king of Taphua one, the
Josu 15 34 Engannim and Taphua and Enaim and
16 8 from Taphua it passeth on towards the
17 7 inhabitants of the fountain of Taphua
8 lot of Manasses took in land of Taphua
target 3 K 10 17 pounds of gold covering one t.
targets 3 K 10 17 three hundred t. of fine gold
2 Pa 23 9 the shields, and targets of king David
tarried Num 9 21 if the cloud t. from evening
Judg 19 4 the son-in-law tarried in the house
2 K 11 12 Urias t. in Jerusalem that day and the
15 29 into Jerusalem, and they tarried there
20 5 but he tarried beyond the set time
Luke 1 21 that he tarried so long in the temple
Acts 21 4 finding disciples, we t. there 7 days
10 we t. there for some days, there came
25 5 having tarried among them no more than
14 as they t. there many days, Festus told
28 12 Syracusa, we tarried there three days
Gal 1 18 Peter, and I tarried with him 15 days
tarriest Acts 22 16 why t. thou? Rise up, and be
tarrieth Mich 5 7 nor t. for the children of men
tarry Lev 14 8 that he t. without his own tent
Num 22 8 tarry here this night and I will answer
Judg 19 9 tarry with me today also, and spend
1 K 22 3 father and my mother tarry with you
2 K 11 12 said to Urias: Tarry here today, and
17 16 tarry not this night in the plains of

19 7 there will not tarry with thee so much
Tob 10 1 why thinkest thou doth my son tarry
Eccu 7 18 wrath, for it will not tarry long
17 26 tarry not in the error of the ungodly
42 12 and tarry not among women. For from
Isa 46 12 my salvation shall not tarry. I will
John 4 40 they desired that he would tarry there
Acts 10 48 they desired him to tarry with them
18 20 desired him, that he would t. a longer
28 14 we were desired to tarry with them seven
1 C 16 8 I will tarry at Ephesus until Pentecost
1 Tim 3 15 if I tarry long, that thou mayest know
tarrying Mat 25 5 the bridegroom t., they all
Tarsus Acts 9 11 one named Saul of Tarsus. For
Acts 9 30 to Caesarea, and sent him away to Tarsus
11 25 Barnabas went to Tarsus to seek Saul
21 39 Paul said to him: I am a Jew of Tarsus
22 3 I am a Jew, born at Tarsus in Cilicia
task Exod 5 8 lay upon them the task of bricks
Exod 5 14 have you not made up the task of bricks
2 Ma 2 27 we have taken in hand no easy task
taskmasters Exod 5 6 and the t. of the people
Exod 5 10 t. went out and said to the people
14 were scourged by Pharao's taskmasters
taste Exod 16 31 t. thereof like to flour with
Num 11 8 cakes thereof of the taste of bread
Judg 19 5 t. first a little bread and strengthen
1 K 14 43 I did but taste a little honey with
2 K 3 35 if I t. bread or anything else before
Job 6 6 can a man taste that which when tasted
12 11 palate of him that eateth, the taste
34 3 the mouth discerneth meats by the taste
Ps 33 9 taste, and see that the Lord is sweet
Wisd 16 2 desire of delicious food, of a new t.
20 and the sweetness of every taste. For
Jer 48 11 therefore his t. hath remained in him
Jon 3 7 beasts, oxen nor sheep taste anything
2 Ma 13 18 taken a taste of the hardiness of the
Mat 16 28 not t. death till they see. Mark 8:39; Luke 9:27
Luke 14 24 were invited, shall taste of my supper
John 8 52 word, he shall not taste death forever
Acts 10 10 he was desirous to taste somewhat. And
Col 2 21 touch not, taste not, handle not: which
Heb 2 9 of God he might taste death for all
tasted Exod 22 31 flesh that beasts have t. of
1 K 14 24 so none of the people tasted any food
29 because I tasted a little of this honey
2 K 17 20 after they had tasted a little water
4 K 4 40 when they had tasted of the pottage
Job 6 6 that which when tasted bringeth death
Prov 31 18 hath tasted and seen that her traffic
Wisd 16 3 want for a short time, t. a new meat
Mat 27 34 when he had t., he would not drink
John 2 9 when the chief steward had tasted the
Heb 6 4 have tasted also the heavenly gift, and
5 have moreover tasted the good word of
1 P 2 3 if so be you have t. that the Lord is
tasteth Eccu 36 21 the palate tasteth venison and
tasting Acts 20 11 and breaking bread and t.
tattlers 1 Tim 5 13 not only idle, but t. also
tau Ps 118 169 tau. Let my supplication, O Lord
taught Deut 4 5 I have taught you statutes and
Deut 31 22 and taught it to the children of Israel
32 10 he led him about and taught him: and
4 K 12 2 the days that Joiada . . . taught him
17 28 t. them how they should worship the
1 Pa 25 7 brethren, that t. the song of the Lord
2 Pa 8 10 were 250, who taught the people. And
17 9 and they taught the people in Juda
2 Es 8 12 the words that he had taught them
Tob 1 10 from his infancy he t. him to fear God
Job 4 3 behold thou hast taught many, and thou
15 5 thy iniquity hath taught thy mouth
Ps 70 17 thou hast taught me, O God, from my
Prov 4 4 he taught me and said: Let thy heart
5 13 not heard the voice of them that t. me
Ecce 12 9 he taught the people and declared the
Wisd 7 21 is the worker of all things, taught me
12 19 hast taught thy people by such works
Eccu 18 18 a gift of one ill taught consumeth
21 14 not wise in good, will not be taught
26 but he that is well taught will stand
22 3 a son ill taught is the confusion of
31 22 a little wine for a man well taught
33 29 for idleness hath taught much evil
37 22 a skilful man hath taught many, and
40 31 a man, well instructed and taught
Isa 8 11 as he hath taught me, with a strong
40 13 his counsellor and hath taught him
14 and taught him the path of justice and taught him knowledge
54 13 all thy children shall be taught of
Jer 2 33 also taught thy malices to be thy ways
9 5 have taught their tongue to speak lies
14 Baalim, which their fathers t. them
12 16 if they will be taught and will learn
16 as they have taught my people to swear
13 21 thou hast taught them against thee
32 33 when I taught them early in the morning
Osee 10 11 heifer taught to love to tread out corn
Mich 3 11 and her priests have taught for hire
Mat 5 2 opening his mouth, he taught them
13 54 he taught them in their synagogues
28 15 taking the money, did as they were t.
Mark 1 21 into the synagogue, he taught them
2 13 came to him, and he taught them. And
4 2 he taught them many things in parables
6 30 things that they had done and taught
9 30 he taught his disciples and said to
10 1 was accustomed, he taught them again
11 17 he taught, saying to them: Is it not
Luke 4 15 and he taught in their synagogues and
31 he taught them on the sabbath days
5 3 he t. the multitudes out of the ship
6 6 he entered into the synagogue and t.
11 1 as John also taught his disciples
13 26 and thou hast taught in our streets
John 6 45 and they shall all be taught of God
7 14 Jesus went up into the temple and t.
8 2 sitting down he taught them. And the
28 but as the Father hath taught me
18 20 I have always taught in the synagogue
Acts 4 2 being grieved that they t. the people
5 21 entered into the temple and taught
11 26 they taught a great multitude, so
14 20 when they . . . had taught many, they
15 1 coming down from Judea, t. the brethren
18 25 spoke, and taught diligently the things
20 20 preached it to you, and t. you publicly
22 3 t. according to the truth of the law
Eph 4 21 him, and have been taught in him, as the
Heb 5 12 you have need to be taught again what
1 J 2 27 as it hath taught you, abide in him
Apoc 2 14 taught Balac to cast a stumblingblock
Taverns Acts 28 15 Appii Forum, and Three Taverns
tax 4 K 15 20 and Manahem laid a tax upon Israel
4 K 18 14 the king of the Assyrians put a tax
taxed 4 K 23 35 after he had taxed the land for
1 Ma 13 39 and if any other thing were taxed in
39 in Jerusalem, now let it not be taxed
taxes 2 Ma 4 28 appertained the gathering of the t.
teach Exod 4 12 will t. thee what thou shalt speak
Exod 24 12 written: that thou mayst teach them
Lev 10 11 may teach the children of Israel all
15 31 you shall teach therefore the children

Deut 1 15 who might teach you all things. And
4 1 and judgments which I teach thee
9 thou shalt teach them to thy sons and
10 and may teach their children. And you
14 that I should teach you the ceremonies
36 hear his voice, that he might t. thee
5 31 which thou shalt teach them, that they
6 1 God commanded that I should teach you
11 19 teach your children that they meditate
17 10 what they shall teach thee, according
20 18 lest they teach you to do all the
24 8 of the Levitical race shall teach thee
31 19 canticle, and teach the children of
Josu 4 22 you shall teach them and say: Israel
Judg 13 8 again and teach us what we ought to do
1 K 12 23 I will t. you the good and right way
2 K 1 18 they should teach the children of Juda
4 K 17 27 let him teach them the ordinances of
1 Pa 22 13 the Lord commanded Moses to t. Israel
26 29 over Israel to t. them and judge them
2 Pa 6 27 teach them the good way in which they
17 7 Micheas, to teach in cities of Juda
1 Es 7 10 to teach in Israel the commandments
25 yea and the ignorant teach ye freely
2 Es 9 20 gavest them thy good Spirit to t. them
Job 6 24 teach me, and I will hold my peace
8 10 they shall teach thee: they shall speak
12 7 the beasts, and they shall teach thee
21 22 shall any one teach God knowledge, who
26 4 whom hast thou desired to teach? Was
27 11 I will teach you by the hand of God
32 7 a multitude of years would t. wisdom
33 33 peace, and I will teach thee wisdom
34 32 if I have erred, teach thou me: if I
Ps 17 36 thy discipline, the same shall t. me
24 4 thy ways to me, and teach me thy paths
5 direct me in thy truth and teach me
9 he will teach the meek his ways all
33 12 I will teach you the fear of the Lord
50 15 I will teach the unjust thy ways: and
93 12 and shalt teach him out of thy law
104 22 himself and teach his ancients wisdom
118 12 teach me thy justifications. 26, 64, 68, 124, 135, 171
66 teach me goodness and discipline and
108 and teach me thy judgments. My soul
131 12 testimonies which I shall teach them
142 10 teach me to do thy will, for thou art
Prov 9 9 teach a just man, and he shall make
10 21 the lips of the just teach many: but
Cant 8 2 there thou shalt teach me, and I will
Eccu 45 6 that he might teach Jacob his covenant
21 he should teach Jacob his testimonies
Isa 2 3 he will teach us his ways, and we will
27 11 women shall come and teach it: for
28 9 whom shall he teach knowledge? And
26 in judgment: his God will teach him
48 17 God that teach thee profitable things
Jer 9 20 and teach your daughters wailing: and
31 34 they shall teach no more every man
Eze 44 23 they shall t. my people the difference
Dan 1 4 that he might teach them the learning
9 22 I am now come forth to teach thee and
10 14 I am come to teach thee what things
11 33 learned among the people shall t. many
Osee 10 12 shall come that shall teach you justice
Mich 4 2 he will teach us of his ways, and we
Haba 2 19 the dumb stone: Arise: can it teach
Mat 5 19 and shall so teach men, shall be called
19 he that shall do and teach, he shall be
11 1 to teach and preach in their cities
28 19 going therefore, teach ye all nations
Mark 4 1 he began to teach by the seaside; and
6 2 he began to teach in the synagogue
34 he began to teach them many things
8 31 he began to teach them that the Son
Luke 11 1 Lord, teach us to pray, as John also
12 12 the Holy Ghost shall teach you in the
John 7 35 among the Gentiles and t. the Gentiles
9 34 born in sins, and dost thou teach us
14 26 he will teach you all things and bring
16 13 is come, he will teach you all truth
Acts 1 1 which Jesus began to do and to teach
4 18 nor teach in the name of Jesus. But
5 28 that you should not teach in this name
42 to teach and preach Christ Jesus. And
1 C 4 17 as I teach everywhere in every church
7 17 walk: and so in all churches I teach
11 14 doth not even nature itself teach you
14 33 I teach in all churches of the saints
1 Tim 1 3 charge some not to teach otherwise, not
2 12 but I suffer not a woman to teach, nor
4 11 these things command and teach. Let no
6 2 benefit. These things teach and exhort
3 if any man teach otherwise, and consent
2 Tim 2 2 who shall be fit to teach others also
24 be mild towards all men, apt to teach
3 16 is profitable to teach, to reprove, to
Titus 2 4 they may teach the young women to be
Heb 8 11 and they shall not teach every man his
1 J 2 27 you have no need that any man t. you
Apoc 2 20 to teach and to seduce my servants, to

teacher Deut 33 21 in his portion the teacher was
2 Pa 15 3 without a priest a teacher and without
Eccu 37 21 that is subtle and a teacher of many
Isa 30 20 will not cause thy teacher to flee
20 and thy eyes shall see thy teacher
33 18 where is the teacher of little ones
Osee 5 2 I am the teacher of them all. I know
Joel 2 23 hath given you a teacher of justice
John 3 2 thou art come a teacher from God; for
Rom 2 20 a teacher of infants, having the form
1 Tim 3 2 chaste, given to hospitality, a teacher
2 Tim 1 11 an apostle and teacher of the Gentiles

teachers 1 Pa 25 7 all the teachers, were 288
Ps 118 99 I have understood more than all my t.
Isa 43 27 thy teachers have transgressed against
1 Tim 1 7 desiring to be teachers of the law
2 Tim 4 3 they will heap to themselves teachers
2 P 2 1 shall be among you lying teachers

teachest Mat 22 16 t. the way of God in truth. Mark 12:14; Luke 20:21
Luke 20 21 that thou speakest and t. rightly
Acts 21 21 that thou t. those Jews, who are among
Rom 2 21 that teachest another, t. not thyself

teacheth 2 K 22 35 t. my hands to war. Ps 17:35
Job 35 11 who t. us more than the beasts of the
Ps 93 10 he that teacheth man knowledge? The
143 1 who teacheth my hands to fight, and my
Prov 9 7 he that t. a scorner, doth an injury
Wisd 8 4 is she that t. the knowledge of God
7 she teacheth temperance and prudence
Eccu 18 13 he hath mercy and teacheth and
22 7 he that teacheth a fool is like one
30 3 he that t. his son, maketh his enemy
Isa 9 15 and the prophet that teacheth lies
Acts 21 28 this is the man that t. all men every
Rom 12 7 ministering; or he that t., in doctrine
1 J 2 27 as his unction t. you of all things

teaching Job 33 16 t. instructeth them in what
Eze 29 16 to the house of Israel, t. iniquity
Mat 4 23 teaching in their synagogues. 9:35
7 29 t. them as one having power. Mark 1:22
15 9 t. doctrines and commandments of men
21 23 there came to him as he was teaching
26 55 daily with you, teaching in the temple

Amos 4 6 I also have given you dulness of teeth
Mich 3 5 bite with their teeth and preach peace
Zach 9 7 his abominations from between his teeth
Mat 8 12 weeping and gnashing of t. 13:42, 50; 22:13; 24:51; 25:30; Luke 13:28
Mark 9 17 he foameth and gnasheth with the teeth
Acts 7 54 they gnashed with the teeth at him
Apoc 9 8 their teeth were as lions: and they
Tehinna 1 Pa 4 12 T. father of the city of Naas
Telem Josu 15 24 Ziph and Telem and Baloth
1 Es 10 24 of the porters, Sellum and Telem
tellers Deut 18 11 pythonic spirits or fortune t.
Bar 3 23 tellers of fables and searchers of
Telmela 2 Es 7 61 they that came up from Telmela
Telmon 1 Pa 9 17 the porters were . . . T. 2 Es 11:19
1 Es 2 42 the children of Telmon. 2 Es 7:46
2 Es 12 25 Telmon . . . were keepers of the gates
temper Gen 18 6 t. together three measures of
temperance Wisd 8 7 she teacheth t. and prudence
temperate Eccu 37 34 that is t. shall prolong life
tempered Exod 29 40 of flour t. with beaten oil
Exod 30 35 incense . . . well tempered together
Lev 7 12 cakes tempered and mingled with oil
Num 15 4 t. with the fourth part of a hin of oil
6 t. with the third part of a hin of oil
9 flour tempered with half a hin of oil
28 5 shall be tempered with the purest oil
2 K 13 8 she [Thamar] took meal and tempered
1 C 12 24 God hath tempered the body together
tempered with oil; *see* **oil**
tempering Wisd 15 7 the potter also t. soft earth
Eze 13 11 to them that daub without tempering
15 them that daub it without t. the mortar
22 28 have daubed them without t. the mortar
tempest Job 27 20 a t. shall oppress him in the
Ps 49 3 mighty tempest shall be round about
Job 37 9 out of the inner parts shall a t. come
Ps 68 3 a tempest hath overwhelmed me. I have
16 let not the tempest of water drown me
80 8 heard thee in the secret place of t.
82 16 so shalt thou pursue them with thy t.
Prov 1 27 destruction, as a t., shall be at hand
10 25 as a tempest that passeth, so the
Isa 5 28 their wheels like the violence of a t.
17 13 as a whirlwind before a tempest. In
29 6 with a great noise of whirlwind and t.
54 11 poor little one, tossed with tempest
Jer 4 13 and his chariots as a tempest: his horses
23 19 and a tempest shall break out and come
Dan 11 40 shall come against him like a tempest
Jon 1 4 a great tempest was raised in the sea
12 for my sake this great t. is upon you
Nah 1 3 the Lord's ways are in a tempest, and
Mat 8 24 a great tempest arose in the sea, so
Acts 27 18 we being mightily tossed with the t.
tempestuous Acts 27 14 arose against it a t. wind
temple Exod 30 13 according to standard of the t.
Deut 3 29 over against the temple of Phogor. 4:46
Judg 9 4 silver out of temple of Baalberith
27 went into the temple of their god. 46
17 5 also therein a little temple for the god
1 K 2 29 I commanded to be offered in the temple
32 shalt see thy rival in the temple, in
5 2 brought it into the temple of Dagon
5 nor any that go into the temple tread
31 10 put his armor in temple of Astaroth
2 K 5 8 the lame shall not come into the temple
3 K 3 2 for there was no temple built to the
5 5 I purpose to build a temple to the name
17 for the foundation of the temple, and
6 3 there was a porch before the temple
3 measure of the breadth of the temple
3 before the face of the temple. And he
4 he made in the temple oblique windows
5 upon wall of the temple he built floors
5 round about the temple and the oracle
6 not be fastened in walls of the temple
16 cedar at the hinder part of the temple
17 temple itself . . . was forty cubits long
22 nothing in the t. that was not covered
27 cherubims in midst of the inner temple
27 the other wings in midst of the temple
29 walls of temple round about he carved
33 he made in the entrance of the temple
7 21 two pillars in the porch of the temple
39 five on the right side of the temple
39 sea he put on right side of the temple
50 for the doors of the house of the temple
8 6 into the oracle of the temple, into
48 temple which I have built to thy name
9 7 the temple which I have sanctified
25 and the temple was finished. And king
11 7 Solomon built a temple for Chamos the
16 32 an altar for Baal in the temple of Baal
4 K 5 18 master goeth into temple of Remmon
18 if I bow down in temple of Remmon when
10 21 went into the temple of Baal. 11:18
23 went to the temple of Baal and said
25 went into the city of the temple of Baal
26 brought the statue out of Baal's temple
27 they destroyed also the temple of Baal
11 8 shall enter the precinct of the temple
11 from the right side of the temple, unto
11 left side of altar and of the temple
15 without the precinct of the t. 2 Pa 23:14
12 6 did not make the repairs of the temple
7 why do you not repair the temple? Take
7 restore it for repairing of the temple
16 14 he removed from the face of the temple
18 which he had built in the temple: and
19 37 was worshipping in temple of Nesroch
21 7 in this temple . . . I will put my name
22 4 which the doorkeepers of the temple
5 to repair the temple. That is, to
1 Pa 9 33 dwelt in the chambers, by the temple
10 10 dedicated in the temple of their god
10 fastened up in the temple of Dagon
28 11 description of porch and of the temple
29 4 to overlay the walls of the temple
2 Pa 3 6 he paved also the floor of the temple
8 according to the breadth of the temple
15 before the doors of the temple two
17 pillars he put at entrance of the temple
4 7 he set them in the temple, five on. 8
22 graved the doors of the inner temple
22 doors of temple without were of gold
5 7 that is, to the oracle of the temple
6 13 had set it up in the midst of the temple
23 7 if any other come into the temple, let
10 from the right side of the temple
10 to the left side of the temple, before
10 before the altar and the temple, round
24 7 and adorned the temple of Baal with
14 with it were made vessels for the temple
29 17 they purified the temple in eight days
19 and all the furniture of the temple
34 10 to repair the temple, and mend all
35 3 put the ark in sanctuary of the temple
20 after that Josias had repaired the t.
36 18 and the treasures of the temple and of
1 Es 1 7 had put them in the temple of his god
3 8 second year of their coming to the t.
12 ancients that had seen the former temple
12 foundation of this t. before their eyes
4 1 heard that . . . were building a temple
5 11 we are building a temple that was built

		14	Nabuchodonosor had taken out of temple
		14	brought them to the temple of Babylon
		14	brought out of the temple of Babylon
		15	put them in the t. that is in Jerusalem
	6	5	took out of the temple of Jerusalem
		5	carried back to the temple of Jerusalem
2 Es	3	27	built . . . unto the wall of the temple
	6	10	house of God in the midst of the temple
		10	let us shut the doors of the temple
		11	would go into temple to save his life
	11	12	brethren that do the works of the t.
Ps	44	16	be brought into the temple of the king
	143	12	after the similitude of a temple
Wisd	9	8	hast commanded me to build a temple
Eccu	45	11	that might be heard in the temple for
	50	1	and in his days fortified the temple
		2	the height of the temple was founded
		2	building and high walls of the temple
	51	19	I prayed for her before the temple
Isa	6	1	his train filled the temple. Upon
	22	15	to Sobna who is over the temple: and
	37	38	worshipping in the temple of Nesroch
	44	28	to the temple: Thy foundations shall be
	65	4	and sleep in the temple of idols: that
	66	6	a voice from the temple, the voice of
Jer	30	18	place, and the temple shall be founded
Bar	1	8	which had been taken away out of the t.
	2	26	thou hast made the temple, in which
Eze	10	18	went forth from threshold of the temple
	40	45	that watch in the wards of the temple
		47	altar that was before face of the temple
		48	brought me into the porch of the temple
	41	1	he brought me into the temple, and he
		4	before the face of the temple: and
		6	not to touch the wall of the temple
		7	it led into the upper loft of the temple
		7	temple broader in the higher parts
		15	inner t. and the porches of the court
		20	palm trees wrought in wall of the temple
		23	there were two doors in the temple
		25	also wrought in the doors of the temple
	42	8	the length before the face of the temple
	43	4	majesty of the Lord went into the temple
		10	show to the house of Israel the temple
	44	5	mark well the ways of the temple, with
	45	3	shall be the t. and the holy of holies
	47	1	came down to the right side of the t.
	48	21	sanctuary of t. shall be in the midst
Dan	5	2	had brought away out of the temple. 3
	9	27	in the t. the abomination of desolation
	14	9	king went with Daniel into t. of Bel
		13	he sifted them all over the temple
		21	who destroyed him and his temple. And
Osee	10	5	the wardens of its temple that rejoiced
Amos	8	3	the hinges of the temple shall screak
Mich	3	12	mountain of the t. as the high places
Nah	2	6	the t. is thrown down to the ground
Zach	6	12	shall build a temple to the Lord. 13
	8	9	founded, that the temple might be built
1 Ma	1	23	golden ornament that was before the t.
	2	8	her t. is become as a man without honor
	4	38	chambers joining to the t. thrown down
		46	stones in the mountain of the temple
		48	the things that were within the temple
		48	they sanctified the t. and the courts
		49	brought in . . . the table into the temple
		50	and they gave light in the temple. And
		57	they adorned the front of the temple
	5	43	fled to the temple that was in Carnaim
		44	and the temple he burnt with fire with
	6	2	was in it a temple exceeding rich: and
	7	36	before the face of the altar and the t.
	10	43	whosoever shall flee into the temple
		83	into Bethdagon their idol's temple
		84	took the spoils . . . and the t. of Dagon
	11	4	they showed him the temple of Dagon
	13	53	he fortified the mountain of the temple
	15	9	we will glorify . . . the t. with great
	16	20	others to take . . . the mountain of the t.
2 Ma	1	13	he fell in the temple of Nanea, being
		15	had entered into the compass of the t.
		15	they shut the temple, when Antiochus
		16	opening a secret entrance of the temple
		18	to keep the purification of the temple
		18	after the temple and the altar was built
		34	the king . . . made a temple for it that
	2	9	dedication, and of the finishing of t.
		20	the purification of the great temple
		23	most renowned temple in all the world
	3	2	glorified the t. with very great gifts
		4	who was appointed overseer of the t.
		12	who had trusted to the place and temple
		30	the temple . . . was filled with joy and
	4	14	despising the temple and neglecting
		32	certain vessels of gold out of the t.
		39	committed by Lysimachus in the temple
	5	15	he presumed also to enter into the t.
		21	taken away out of the t. 1800 talents
	6	2	to defile the t. that was in Jerusalem
		2	to call it the t. of Jupiter Olympius
		4	the temple was full of the riot and
	8	2	and would have pity on the temple
	9	2	and attempted to rob the temple and
	10	1	recovered the temple and the city again
		3	having purified the temple, they made
		5	day that the temple had been polluted
	11	3	and to make a gain of the temple, as
		25	that the t. should be restored to them
	13	14	even to death, for the laws, the temple
		23	honored the temple and left gifts
	14	4	boughs which seemed to belong to the t.
		13	Alcimus the high priest of the great t.
		32	he stretched out his hand to the temple
		33	I will dedicate this temple to Bacchus
		35	wast pleased that the temple of thy
	15	17	holy city and the temple were in danger
		18	fear was for the holiness of the temple
		33	to be hanged up over against the temple
Mat	4	5	set him upon pinnacle of t. Luke 4:9
	12	5	the priests in the temple break the
		6	is here a greater than the temple
	21	12	that sold and bought in t. Mark 11:15
		14	to him the blind and the lame in the t.
		15	and the children crying in the temple
		23	when he was come into the temple
	23	16	whosoever shall swear by the temple. 21
		16	shall swear by the gold of the temple
		17	is greater, the gold or the temple that
		35	killed between the temple and the altar
	24	1	Jesus being come out of the temple
		1	to show him the buildings of the temple
	26	55	daily with you, teaching in the temple
	27	5	the pieces of silver in the temple, he
		51	veil of the temple was rent. Mark 15:38; Luke 23:45
Mark	11	11	entered into Jerusalem, into the t.
		15	when he was entered into the temple
		16	should carry a vessel through the t.
		27	and when he was walking in the temple
	12	35	teaching in the temple: How do the
	13	1	as he was going out of the temple
		3	mount of Olivet over against the t.
	14	49	I was daily with you in the temple
		58	I will destroy this temple made with
Luke	1	21	that he tarried so long in the temple
		22	that he had seen a vision in the t.

2 27 he came by the Spirit into the temple
37 who departed not from the temple, by
46 they found him in the temple, sitting
11 51 slain between the altar and the t.
18 10 two men went up into the temple to
19 45 entering into the temple, he began to
47 he was teaching daily in the temple
20 1 he was teaching the people in the t.
21 5 some saying of the temple, that it
37 daytime he was teaching in the temple
38 in the morning to him in the temple
22 52 and magistrates of the temple, and
53 I was daily with you in the temple
24 53 and they were always in the temple
John 2 14 he found in the temple them that sold
15 he drove them all out of the temple
19 destroy this temple, and in three days
20 years was this temple in building; and
21 he spoke of the temple of his body
5 14 Jesus findeth him in the temple and
7 14 Jesus went up into the temple and
28 Jesus therefore cried out in the t.
8 2 he came again into the temple and all
20 treasury, teaching in the temple: and
59 hid himself and went out of the temple
10 23 and Jesus walked in the temple, in
11 56 with another, standing in the temple
18 20 taught in the synagogue and in the t.
Acts 2 46 daily with one accord in the temple
3 1 Peter and John went up into the temple
2 alms of them that went into the temple
3 and John about to go into the temple
8 and went in with them into the temple
10 alms at the Beautiful gate of the temple
4 1 the priests and the officer of the temple
5 20 go and standing speak in the temple
21 in the morning entered into the temple
24 when the officer of the temple and the
25 are in the t. standing and teaching
42 every day they ceased not in the t.
19 27 the t. of great Diana shall be reputed
21 26 purified with them, entered into the t.
27 when they saw him in the t., stirred up
28 hath brought in Gentiles into the t.
29 supposed that Paul had brought into t.
30 taking Paul, they drew him out of temple
22 17 praying in the t., that I was in trance
24 6 hath gone about to profane the temple
12 neither in the temple did they find me
18 I was found purified in the t.: neither
25 8 against law of Jews, nor against the t.
26 21 for this cause Jews, when I was in t.
1 C 6 19 your members are t. of the Holy Ghost
8 10 sit at meat in the idol's temple, shall
2 C 6 16 you are the temple of the living God; as
Apoc 3 12 I will make him a pillar in the temple
11 2 the court which is without the temple
14 15 another angel came out from the t. 17
15 5 t. of the tabernacle of the testimony
6 the seven angels came out of the temple
8 the temple was filled with smoke from
8 no man was able to enter into the t.
16 1 I heard a great voice out of the t.
17 came a great voice out of the temple
21 22 I saw no temple therein. For the Lord
22 the Lord God Almighty is the temple

his temple 2 K 22 7 hear my voice out of his t.
2 Pa 36 7 the Lord, and put them in his temple
Ps 10 5 the Lord is in his holy temple, the
17 7 he heard my voice from his holy temple
26 4 of the Lord and may visit his temple
28 9 in his temple all shall speak his glory
Jer 50 28 Lord our God, the revenge of his t.
51 11 the Lord, the vengeance of his temple
Mich 1 2 to you, the Lord from his holy temple
Haba 2 20 the Lord is in his holy temple: let all
Mala 3 1 you desire, shall come to his temple
Apoc 7 15 serve him day and night in his temple
11 19 ark of his testament was seen in his t.

holy temple Eccu 49 14 and set up a holy temple
Ps 5 8 will worship towards thy holy t. 137:2
17 7 he heard my voice from his holy temple
27 2 when I lift up my hands to thy holy t.
78 1 they have defiled thy holy temple
Dan 3 53 blessed . . . in the holy t. of thy glory
Jon 2 5 yet I shall see thy holy temple again
8 may come to thee, unto thy holy temple
Mich 1 2 to you, the Lord from his holy temple
Haba 2 20 the Lord is in his holy temple: let all
Eph 2 21 groweth up into an holy temple in Lord

temple of Baal; *see* **Baal**

temple of God 1 Pa 29 3 silver for the t. . . .
2 Pa 24 5 money to repair the temple of your God
28 24 shut up the doors of the t. . . . and
1 Es 1 4 which they offer freely to the t. . . .
3 6 the temple of God was not yet founded
9 that did the work in the temple of God
5 2 and began to build the temple of God
14 vessels also . . . of the t. of God
16 laid foundations of the temple of God
6 5 silver vessels of the temple of God
5 also were placed in the temple of God
7 let that temple of God be built by
7 17 upon the altar of the t. of your God
10 1 and lying before the temple of God
Wisd 3 14 acceptable lot in the temple of God
Eccu 50 7 so did he shine in the temple of God
1 Ma 1 47 atonements to be made in the t. . . .
2 Ma 14 33 I will lay this temple of God even
Mat 21 12 Jesus went into the temple of God
26 61 I am able to destroy the t. of God and
27 40 that destroyest the t. . . . Mark 15:29
1 C 3 16 know you not, that you are the t. . . .
17 if any man violate the temple of God
17 the temple of God is holy, which you
2 C 6 16 what agreement hath the temple of God
2 Th 2 4 so that he sitteth in the temple of God
Apoc 11 1 measure the temple of God and the altar
19 the temple of God was opened in heaven

temple of the Lord 1 K 1 9 upon a stool before the door of the temple of the Lord
1 K 1 7 returned that they went up to t. . . .
3 3 Samuel slept in t. . . . where the ark
3 K 8 63 children of Israel dedicated the t. . . .
7 40 work of king Solomon in the t. . . . The
4 K 11 4 brought them in to him into the t. . . .
13 going in to the people into the t. . . .
15 let her not be slain in the t. . . . And
12 4 which is brought into the t. . . . by
4 free heart they bring into the t. . . .
4 things, which is brought into t. . . .
9 money that was brought to the t. . . . 13
13 for the t. . . . , bowls or fleshhooks
14 that the t. . . . might be repaired. And
16 for sins they brought not into t. . . .
18 be found in the treasures of the t. . . .
16 14 altar and from the place of the t. . . .
18 from without he turned into the t. . . .
18 16 Ezechias broke the doors of the t. . . .
20 5 third day thou shalt go up to t. . . .
8 and that I shall go up to the t. . . .
21 5 heaven in the two courts of the t. . . .
7 grave, which he had made in the t. . . .
22 3 the scribe of the t. . . . , saying to him
4 which is brought into the t. . . . , which
5 it to those that work in the t. . . .

6 the quarries to repair the t. . . . But
9 overseers of the works of the t. . . .
23 2 and the king went up to the t. . . .
4 to cast out of t. . . . all the vessels
11 sun, at the entering in of the t. . . .
12 made in the two courts of the t. . . .
24 the priest had found in the t. . . .
24 13 king of Israel had made in the t. . . .
25 13 pillars of brass that were in t. . . .
16 which Solomon had made in the t. . . .
1 Pa 9 27 their watches round about the t. . . .
23 28 works of the ministry of the t. . . .
25 6 were distributed to sing in the t. . . .
26 27 building and furniture of the t. . . .
28 13 vessels of the service of the t. . . .
2 Pa 7 2 could priests enter into the t. . . .
2 majesty of Lord had filled the t. . . .
7 middle of the court before the t. . . .
23 12 came in to the people, into the t. . . .
24 7 that had been dedicated in the t. . . .
18 they forsook the t. . . . the God of
26 16 going into the t. . . . he had a mind
27 2 he [Joatham] entered not into t. . . .
29 16 and the priests went into the t. . . .
17 they came into the porch of the t. . . .
31 16 upward, to all that went into t. . . .
34 8 had cleansed the land and the t. . . .
14 that had been brought into the t. . . .
1 Es 1 5 go up to build the t. . . . which was in
7 brought forth the vessels of the t. . . .
2 68 fathers, when they came to the t. . . .
3 10 laid the foundations of the t. . . .
11 because the foundations of the t. . . .
Tob 1 6 and went to Jerusalem and to the t. . . .
Jdth 4 2 same to Jerusalem and to the t. . . .
8 to lie prostrate before the t. . . .
Jer 7 4 saying: The t. . . . , the t. . . . , it is the t. . . .
24 1 full of figs, set before the t. . . .
Bar 1 8 when he received vessels of the t. . . .
14 to be read in the temple of the Lord
Eze 8 16 at the door of the temple of the Lord
16 having their backs towards the t. . . .
Agge 2 16 stone laid upon a stone, in the t. . . .
19 foundations of the t. . . . were laid
Zach 6 14 a memorial in the temple of the Lord
15 come and shall build in the t. . . .

thy temple Esth 14 9 extinguish glory of thy t.
Ps 5 8 will worship towards thy holy t. 137:2
27 2 when I lift up my hands to thy holy t.
47 10 mercy, O God, in the midst of thy t.
64 5 holy is thy t., wonderful in justice
67 30 from thy temple in Jerusalem, kings
78 1 they have defiled thy holy temple
Jon 2 5 yet I shall see thy holy temple again
8 may come to thee, unto thy holy temple

temples Judg 4 21 nail upon the t. of his head
Judg 4 22 and the nail fastened in his temples
5 26 strongly piercing through his temples
1 K 31 9 to publish it in the t. of their idols
3 K 12 31 he made temples in the high places
13 32 against all the t. of the high places
4 K 17 29 in the temples of the high places. 32
23 19 all the t. of the high places, which
1 Pa 10 9 and shown in the temples of the idols
2 Pa 14 5 cities of Juda the altars and temples
34 7 had demolished all profane temples
Jdth 4 2 done to other cities and their temples
Ps 131 5 my eyelids, or rest to my temples
Isa 13 22 and sirens in the temples of pleasure
17 8 wrought, such as groves and temples
27 9 the groves and temples shall not stand
Jer 43 12 fire in the t. of the gods of Egypt
13 t. of the gods of Egypt he shall burn
Bar 6 30 priests sit in their temples, having
Eze 6 6 and your temples shall be destroyed
Osee 8 14 forgotten his Maker and hath built t.
Joel 3 5 you have carried into your temples
Soph 1 4 names of the wardens of the temples
1 Ma 1 50 commanded altars to be built, and t.
2 Ma 10 2 the streets, as also the t. of the
11 3 of the other temples of the Gentiles
Acts 17 24 dwelleth not in t. made with hands
19 24 a silversmith, who made silver temples

temporal 2 C 4 18 things which are seen, are t.

tempt Exod 17 2 wherefore do you tempt the Lord
Deut 6 16 thou shalt not tempt the Lord thy God
Jdth 8 11 and who are you that tempt the Lord
Wisd 1 2 he is found by them that tempt him not
Isa 7 12 not ask, and I will not tempt the Lord
Mat 4 7 thou shalt not t. the Lord. Luke 4:12
22 18 why do you tempt me, ye hypocrites
Mark 12 15 why tempt you me? Bring me a penny
Luke 20 23 why tempt you me? Show me a penny
Acts 5 9 why have you agreed to tempt the
15 10 why tempt you God to put a yoke upon
1 C 7 5 Satan tempt you for your incontinency
10 9 neither let us tempt Christ: as some

temptation Exod 17 7 the name of that place T.
Deut 6 16 thou temptedst him in the place of t.
9 22 at the place of t., and at the graves
33 8 whom thou hast proved in the t. and
Tob 12 13 necessary that t. should prove thee
Ps 17 30 I shall be delivered from temptation
94 9 the day of temptation in the wilderness
Wisd 14 11 a temptation to the souls of men and
Eccu 2 1 and prepare thy soul for temptation
4 18 she walketh with him in temptation
33 1 but in temptation God will keep him
44 21 in temptation he was found faithful
1 Ma 2 52 was not Abraham found faithful in t.
Mat 6 13 lead us not into temptation. Luke 11:4
26 41 that ye enter not into t. Mark 14:38
Luke 4 13 and all the t. being ended, the devil
8 13 in time of temptation they fall away
22 40 pray, lest ye enter into t. 46
1 C 10 13 let no temptation take hold on you, but
13 will make also with temptation issue
Gal 4 13 to you . . . : and your t. in my flesh, you
1 Tim 6 9 fall into temptation and into the snare
Heb 3 8 in the day of temptation in the desert
James 1 12 blessed is the man that endureth t.
2 P 2 9 how to deliver the godly from t.
Apoc 3 10 keep thee from the hour of temptation

temptations Deut 4 34 the midst of nations by t.
Deut 29 3 temptations which thy eyes have seen
Luke 22 28 have continued with me in my t.
Acts 20 19 serving Lord . . . with tears, and t.
James 1 2 joy, when you shall fall into divers t.
1 P 1 6 made sorrowful in divers temptations

tempted Gen 22 1 God t. Abraham, and said to him
Exod 17 7 for that they tempted the Lord, saying
Num 14 22 have tempted me now ten times and have
2 Pa 32 31 God left him that he might be tempted
Jdth 8 21 how our fathers were tempted that they
22 how our father Abraham was tempted and
Ps 34 16 they tempted me, they scoffed at me
77 18 they tempted God in their hearts, by
41 and they turned back and tempted God
56 they t. and provoked the most high God
94 9 where your fathers tempted me, they
105 14 they t. God in the place without water
Prov 30 9 being filled, I should be t. to deny
Mala 3 15 and they have t. God and are preserved
Mat 4 1 desert, to be tempted by the devil
Mark 1 13 and was tempted by Satan; and he was

Luke 4 2 and was tempted by the devil. And he
Acts 5 3 why hath Satan tempted thy heart that
1 C 10 9 as some of them tempted, and perished
13 who will not suffer you to be t. above
Gal 6 1 thyself, lest thou also be tempted
1 Th 3 5 he that tempteth should have t. you
Heb 2 18 himself hath suffered and been tempted
18 able to succor them also that are t.
3 9 where your fathers tempted me, proved
4 15 one tempted in all things like as we are
11 37 they were t., they were put to death
James 1 13 let no man, when he is tempted, say that he is tempted by God
14 man is t. by his own concupiscence
temptedst Deut 6 16 as thou t. him in the place
tempter Mat 4 3 t. coming said to him: If thou
James 1 13 God is not a tempter of evils, and he
tempteth Eccu 18 23 be not as a man that t. God
1 Th 3 5 lest perhaps he that tempteth should
James 1 13 of evils, and he tempteth no man. But
tempting Mat 16 1 Pharisees and Sadducees t.: and
Mat 19 3 came to him the Pharisees t. him and
22 35 asked him, tempting him: Master, which
Mark 8 11 a sign from heaven, tempting him
10 2 to put away his wife? tempting him
Luke 10 25 lawyer stood up, t. him and saying
11 16 tempting, asked of him a sign from
John 8 6 this they said tempting him, that
tender Gen 18 7 took from thence a calf very t.
Gen 33 13 that I have with me tender children
Deut 28 56 the tender and delicate woman that
2 K 3 39 yet am tender, though anointed king
23 8 was like the most tender little worm
1 Pa 22 5 Solomon my son is very young and tender
29 1 Solomon . . . is as yet young and tender
2 Es 9 27 the multitude of thy tender mercies. 13:22; Ps 50:3; 68:17; Dan 9:18
Ps 39 12 withhold not thou . . . thy t. mercies
Prov 4 3 I also was my father's son, tender and
Isa 47 1 no more be called delicate and tender
53 2 and he shall grow up as a tender plant
63 7 I will remember the tender mercies of
Jer 31 20 son to me, surely he is a tender child
Eze 17 22 I will crop off a tender twig from the
Mat 24 32 branch thereof is now t. Mark 13:28
tenderly Gen 44 20 his father loveth him tenderly
tenderness Deut 28 56 for overmuch niceness and t.
Esth 15 6 as if for delicateness and overmuch t.
tending 2 P 2 12 naturally t. to the snare and
tenor 3 K 21 9 this was the tenor of the letters
tens Exod 18 21 rulers . . . of fifties and of tens
Exod 18 25 over fifties and over tens. Deut 1:15; 1 Ma 3:55
tent Gen 9 21 Noe . . . was uncovered in his tent
Gen 12 8 there pitched his tent, having Bethel
13 3 where before he had pitched his tent
18 Abram removing his tent came and dwelt
18 1 he was sitting at the door of his tent
2 to meet them from the door of his tent
6 Abraham made haste into the tent to
9 he answered: Lo, she is in the tent
10 she laughed behind the door of the tent
24 67 who brought her into the tent of Sara
26 25 name of the Lord, and pitched his tent
31 25 had pitched his tent in the mountain
25 his tent in the same mount of Galaad
33 so Laban went into the tent of Jacob
33 when he was entered into Rachel's tent
34 and when he had searched all the tent
35 21 pitched his t. beyond the Flock tower
Exod 16 16 number of your souls that dwell in a t.
18 7 when he was come into the tent, Moses
Lev 14 8 tarry without his own tent seven days
Num 11 10 weeping . . . every one at door of his t.
19 14 the law of a man that dieth in a tent
14 all that go into his tent and all the
18 shall sprinkle therewith all the tent
Josu 7 21 in the ground in the midst of my tent
22 running to his tent, found all hidden
23 and taking them away out of the tent
24 sheep, the tent also and all the goods
Judg 4 17 Sisara fleeing came to tent of Jahel
18 went in to her tent, and being covered
20 stand before the door of the tent, and
21 Jahel Haber's wife took a nail of the t.
22 and when he came into her tent, he saw
5 24 and blessed be she [Jahel] in her tent
7 13 when it was come to a tent it struck it
1 K 17 54 but his armor he put in his tent. Now
26 5 Saul sleeping in a tent, and the rest
7 found Saul lying and sleeping in the t.
2 K 7 6 walked in a tabernacle and in a tent
16 22 so they spread a tent for Absalom on
4 K 7 8 went into one tent and ate and drank
8 came again and went into another tent
1 Pa 16 1 tent which David had pitched for it
17 5 in a tabernacle and in a tent, abiding
Jdth 10 16 brought her to the tent of Holofernes
12 4 his servants brought her into the tent
9 going in, she remained pure in the t.
14 4 shall run to the tent of Holofernes and
9 they that were in the tent came and
15 and he went into the tent of Judith
Job 18 15 let brimstone be sprinkled in his tent
36 29 if he will spread out clouds as his t.
Eccu 14 25 shall set up his tent nigh unto her
Isa 24 20 he removed as the tent of one night
38 12 rolled away from me, as a shepherd's t.
40 22 spreadeth them out as a tent to dwell
54 2 enlarge the place of thy tent, and
Jer 10 20 there is none to stretch forth my tent
37 9 shall rise up, every man from his tent
Lam 2 6 he hath destroyed his tent as a garden
tenths Lev 14 10 three tenths of flour tempered with oil. Num 28:12, 20, 28; 29:3, 9, 14
Lev 23 13 two tenths of flour tempered with oil. Num 28:9, 12
17 of two tenths of flour leavened, which
24 5 two tenths shall be in every loaf: and
Num 15 6 be a sacrifice of flour of two tenths
9 three t. of flour tempered with half
28 20 calf, and two tenths to every ram
29 3 to every calf, two tenths to a ram. 9
14 two tenths to each ram, being two rams
1 Ma 10 31 the tenths and tributes be for itself
tentmakers Acts 18 3 now they were t. by trade
tents Gen 4 20 father of such as dwell in tents
Gen 9 27 and may he dwell in the tents of Sem
13 5 sheep and herds of beasts and tents
16 12 pitch his tents over against all his
25 27 but Jacob a plain man dwelt in tents
33 17 having built a house and pitched tents
17 name of the place Socoth, that is, T.
19 field, in which he pitched his tents
Exod 19 2 pitched their tents over against the
33 10 worshipped at the doors of their tents
Num 1 53 the Levites shall pitch their tents
2 3 on the east Juda shall pitch his tents
27 the tribe of Aser pitched their tents
9 20 they pitched their tents, and at his
21 and a night, they took down their tents
23 word of the Lord they pitched their t.
10 6 on south side shall take up their t.
13 1 pitched their tents in desert of Pharan
16 24 themselves from the tents of Core and
26 depart from the tents of these wicked

27 when they were departed from their t.
32 devoured them with their tents and all
21 11 they pitched their tents in Jeabarim
24 2 he saw Israel abiding in their tents
5 how beautiful . . . thy tents, O Israel
33 10 they pitched their tents by the Red Sea
14 they pitched their tents in Raphidim
28 and pitched their tents in Methca
45 they pitched their tents in Dibongab
Deut 1 27 you murmured in your tents and said
33 wherein you should pitch your tents
5 30 say to them: Return into your tents
11 6 up with their households and tents
Josu 3 14 so the people went out of their tents
4 3 where you shall pitch your tents this
Judg 4 11 had pitched his tents unto the valley
6 4 pitching their tents among them, wasted
5 all their flocks came with their tents
7 8 rest of multitude to depart to their t.
8 11 by the way of them that dwelt in tents
10 17 pitched their tents in Galaad: against
20 8 we will not return to our tents, neither
2 K 11 11 Israel and Juda dwell in tents, and my
4 K 7 7 left their tents and their horses and
10 and asses tied, and the tents standing
8 21 but the people fled into their tents
1 Pa 2 55 making melody, and abiding in tents
4 41 they beat down their tents and slew
5 10 dwelt in their tents in their stead
Ps 105 25 and they murmured in their tents: they
Cant 1 4 as the tents of Cedar, as the curtains
7 kids beside the tents of the shepherds
Wisd 11 2 in desert places they pitched their t.
Isa 13 20 neither shall the Arabian pitch his t.
Jer 4 20 my tents are destroyed on a sudden
6 3 have pitched their tents against her
35 7 you shall dwell in tents all your days
10 we have dwelt in tents and have been
49 29 they shall take their tents and their
Eze 25 4 and shall set up their tents in thee
Haba 3 7 I saw the tents of Ethiopia for their
Zach 14 15 beasts, that shall be in those tents
1 Ma 4 29 and pitched their tents in Bethoron
5 39 pitched their tents beyond the torrent
6 48 pitched their tents against Judea and
9 5 Judas had pitched his tents in Laisa
66 children of Phaseron in their tents
10 75 they pitched their tents near Joppe
2 Ma 12 12 hands, they departed to their tents
Terebinth 1 K 17 2 came to the valley of T. and
1 K 17 19 were in the valley of T. fighting
21 9 thou slewest in the valley of Terebinth
termeth Rom 4 6 as David also t. blessedness
terminated Josu 19 47 Joppe, and is t. there
terrestrial 1 C 15 40 there are . . . bodies t.
1 C 15 40 glory of celestial, and another of t.
terrible Gen 28 17 how terrible is this place
Exod 15 11 t. and praiseworthy, doing wonders
19 18 of a furnace: and all the mount was t.
34 10 may see the terrible work of the Lord
Deut 1 19 through the t. and vast wilderness
7 21 midst of thee, a God mighty and t.
8 15 leader in the great and t. wilderness
10 17 a great God and mighty and terrible
21 for thee these great and t. things
28 58 fear his glorious and terrible name
2 K 7 23 do for them great and terrible things
2 Es 1 5 God of heaven, strong, great, and t.
4 14 remember the Lord who is great and t.
9 32 our God, great, strong, and terrible
Job 16 10 my enemy hath beheld me with t. eyes
20 25 the t. ones shall go and come upon him
41 5 his teeth are terrible round about
Ps 46 3 Lord is high, terrible: a great king
65 3 how terrible are thy works, O Lord
5 is t. in his counsels over the sons
75 8 thou art t., and who shall resist thee
12 to him that is t. even to him who
13 to the t. with the kings of the earth
88 8 t. above all them that are about him
98 3 great name: for it is terrible and holy
105 22 terrible things in the Red Sea. And
110 9 holy and terrible is his name: the fear
144 6 shall speak of the might of thy t. acts
Cant 6 3 terrible as an army set in array. 9
Wisd 5 2 shall be troubled with t. fear, and
23 rivers shall run together in t. manner
8 15 t. kings hearing shall be afraid of me
17 9 though no t. thing disturbed them: yet
Eccu 9 25 man full of tongue is t. in his city
43 31 the Lord is t. and exceeding great
Isa 18 2 a terrible people, after which. 7
21 1 from the desert from a terrible land
Eze 1 22 appearance of crystal t. to behold
Dan 2 31 thee and the look thereof was terrible
7 7 fourth beast, terrible and wonderful
19 different from all and exceeding t.
9 4 Lord God, great and t., who keepest
Joel 2 11 day of the Lord is great and very t.
Haba 1 7 they are dreadful and terrible from
Soph 2 11 the Lord shall be terrible upon them
2 Ma 3 25 a horse with a terrible rider upon
Heb 12 21 so terrible was that which was seen
terrified Exod 20 18 being t. and struck with fear
Deut 1 28 the messengers have t. our hearts
28 67 thy heart, wherewith thou shalt be t.
1 K 7 10 upon the Philistines and terrified them
2 Pa 14 12 and the Lord terrified the Ethiopians
Job 31 34 if . . . contempt of kinsmen hath t. me
Dan 2 1 dream, and his spirit was terrified
Luke 21 9 wars and seditions, be not terrified
Acts 7 32 Moses being t., durst not behold. And
24 25 Felix being t., answered: For this time
Phil 1 27 in nothing be ye t. by the adversaries
2 Th 2 2 moved from your sense, nor be terrified
terrify Lev 26 36 of a flying leaf shall t. them
Job 7 14 me with dreams and t. me with visions
9 34 and let not his fear terrify me. I will
13 21 far from me and let not thy dread t. me
15 24 tribulation shall terrify him, and
18 11 fears shall terrify him on every side
33 7 yet let not my wonder terrify thee
Jer 46 27 there shall be none to terrify him
50 34 to terrify the land and to disquiet
Lam 2 22 that should terrify me round about and
Haba 2 17 the ravaging of beasts shall t. them
2 C 10 9 thought as it were to t. you by epistles
terrifying Eccu 4 35 t. them of thy household
terror Gen 35 5 terror of God fell upon all the
Deut 26 8 with great terror, with signs and
28 34 and be astonished at the t. of those
32 25 shall lay them waste, and terror within
Judg 4 15 the Lord struck a terror into Sisara
Esth 13 2 might live quietly without any terror
Job 25 2 power and terror are with him, who
37 2 hear ye attentively the t. of his voice
39 20 the glory of his nostrils is terror
Ps 90 5 not be afraid of the t. of the night
Prov 1 33 hear me, shall rest without terror
Isa 10 33 shall break the earthen vessel with t.
19 17 land of Juda shall be a terror to Egypt
30 30 and shall show the terror of his arm
54 14 from terror, for it shall not come
Jer 15 8 I have cast a terror on a sudden upon
17 17 be not thou a terror unto me, thou
20 10 terror on every side. Persecute him

30 5 we have heard a voice of terror: there
32 21 and with great terror. And hast given
46 5 looked not back: terror was round about
Eze 26 18 be astonished in the day of the terror
30 13 I will cause a t. in the land of Egypt
32 23 they that heretofore spread terror in
24 their t. in land of the living. 25, 26
27 they were the terror of the mighty
32 spread my t. in the land of the living
34 28 shall dwell securely without any terror
Dan 10 7 exceeding great terror fell upon them
2 Ma 3 14 no small t. throughout the whole city
Mat 28 4 the guards were struck with terror
Rom 13 3 princes are not a terror to good work
terrors 1 Pa 17 21 by his greatness and t. cast
2 Pa 15 5 but terrors on every side among all
Job 6 4 the terrors of the Lord war against me
Ps 87 17 and thy terrors have troubled me. They
Luke 21 11 and famines and terrors from heaven
Tertius Rom 16 22 I T., who wrote this epistle.
Tertullus Acts 24 1 ancients, and one T. an orator
Acts 24 2 T. began to accuse him, saying: Whereas
testament Exod 30 26 anoint . . . the ark of the t.
Num 14 44 ark of the testament . . . departed not
Ps 104 10 to Israel for an everlasting testament
Eccu 16 22 the testament is far from some, and
45 19 was made to him for an everlasting t.
Zach 9 11 by the blood of thy t. hast sent forth
Mala 3 1 the angel of the t., whom you desire
1 Ma 1 60 books of the t. of the Lord were found
2 27 maintaineth the t., let him follow me
Mat 26 28 is my blood of the new t. Mark 14:24
Luke 1 72 and to remember his holy testament
22 20 new testament in my blood. 1 C 11:25
Acts 3 25 the t. which God made to our fathers
Rom 9 4 to whom belongeth . . . the testament and
2 C 3 6 made us fit ministers of new testament
14 veil, in reading of the old testament
Gal 3 15 yet man's testament, if it be confirmed
17 I say, that the t. which was confirmed
Eph 2 12 strangers to the testament, having no
Heb 7 22 made a surety of a better testament
8 6 he is mediator of a better testament
8 unto the house of Juda, a new testament
9 according to the t. which I made to
9 they continued not in my testament: and
10 this is the t. which I will make. 10:16
9 4 ark of the t. covered about on every
4 and the tables of the testament. And
15 he is the mediator of the new testament
15 which were under the former testament
16 where there is a testament, the death
17 testament is of force, after men are
20 this is the blood of the t., which God
10 29 esteemed the blood of the t. unclean
12 24 to Jesus the mediator of the new t.
13 20 in the blood of the everlasting t.
Apoc 11 19 ark of his t. was seen in his temple
testaments Gal 4 24 for these are the two t.
testator Heb 9 15 t. must of necessity come in
Heb 9 17 no strength, whilst the testator liveth
testicles Lev 22 24 beast that hath the t. bruised
Deut 23 1 whose testicles are broken or cut away
Job 40 12 the sinews of his testicles are wrapped
testified 4 K 17 13 the Lord t. to them in Israel
4 K 17 15 testimonies which he t. against them
2 Pa 24 19 they would not give ear when they t.
2 Es 9 34 which thou hast testified among them
Isa 59 12 and our sins have testified against us
Jer 14 7 if our iniquities have t. against us
2 Ma 3 36 and he t. to all men the works of the
John 13 21 he t. and said: Amen, amen I say to
Acts 8 25 having t. and preached the word of the
23 11 as thou hast t. of me in Jerusalem, so
1 Th 2 12 we testified to everyone of you, that
4 6 as we have told you before, and have t.
Heb 2 6 one in a certain place hath testified
1 J 5 9 because he hath testified of his Son
10 which God hath testified of his Son
testifieth John 3 32 seen and heard, that he t.
Heb 7 17 for he testifieth: Thou art a priest
1 J 5 6 Spirit which t., that Christ is the
testify Deut 32 46 words, which I t. to you this
1 K 8 9 but yet testify to them and foretell
2 Es 9 30 didst t. against them by thy spirit
Ps 49 7 I will testify to thee: I am God, thy
80 9 O my people, and I will t. to thee
Jer 6 10 and to whom shall I testify, that he
Amos 3 13 hear ye, and t. in the house of Jacob
Luke 16 28 that he may t. unto them, lest they
John 3 11 we testify what we have seen, and you
Acts 2 40 did he testify and exhort them, saying
10 42 testify that it is he who was appointed
20 24 I received from the Lord Jesus, to t.
Gal 5 3 I t. again to every man circumcising
Eph 4 17 I say and testify in the Lord: That
Heb 10 15 the Holy Ghost also doth testify this
1 J 4 14 we have seen and do testify that the
Apoc 22 16 have sent my angel to testify to you
18 I testify to every one that heareth the
testifying 2 Ma 12 30 t. that they were used
Acts 18 5 Paul was earnest in preaching, t. to
20 21 t. both to Jews and Gentiles penance
28 23 t. the kingdom of God, and persuading
1 P 5 12 t. that this is the true grace of God
testimonies Deut 4 45 these are the t. and
Deut 6 17 the t. and ceremonies which he hath
20 what mean these t. and ceremonies
3 K 2 3 his precepts and judgments and t.
4 K 17 15 the t. which he testified against them
23 3 to keep his commandments and his t.
1 Pa 29 19 may keep thy commandments and thy t.
2 Pa 34 31 and keep his commandments and t. and
2 Es 9 34 thy t. which thou hast testified among
Ps 24 10 that seek after his covenant and his t.
77 56 high God: and they kept not his t.
92 5 thy t. are become exceedingly credible
98 7 they kept his testimonies and the
118 2 blessed are they that search his t.
14 been delighted in the way of thy t.
22 I have sought after thy testimonies
24 thy testimonies are my meditation. 99
31 I have stuck to thy testimonies, O Lord
36 incline my heart into thy testimonies
46 spoke of thy testimonies before kings
59 turned my feet unto thy testimonies
79 and they that know thy testimonies
88 I shall keep the t. of thy mouth
95 but I have understood thy testimonies
111 I have purchased thy testimonies for
119 therefore have I loved thy testimonies
125 that I may know thy testimonies. It is
129 thy t. are wonderful: therefore my
138 hast commanded justice thy testimonies
144 thy testimonies are justice forever
152 from the beginning concerning thy t.
157 have not declined from thy testimonies
167 my soul hath kept thy t.: and hath
168 have kept thy commandments and thy t.
131 12 these my t. which I shall teach them
Eccu 45 21 he should teach Jacob his testimonies
Jer 44 23 in his commandments and in his t.
Mat 15 19 come forth . . . thefts, false t.
27 13 how great t. they allege against thee
testimony Gen 21 30 that they may be a t. for me
Gen 31 44 for a testimony between me and thee

47 called it . . . The hillock of testimony
52 and the stone, be they for a testimony
Exod 25 21 in which thou shalt put the testimony
27 21 veil that hangs before the testimony
30 6 propitiatory wherewith the t. is
31 18 gave to Moses two stone tables of t.
32 15 carrying the two tables of the t. in
34 29 he held the two tables of the testimony
39 31 the roof of the testimony was finished
40 18 and he put the testimony in the ark
27 of holocaust in the entry of the t.
Lev 1 3 at the door of the testimony, to make
4 4 shall bring it to door of the testimony
16 13 the oracle, which is over the testimony
24 3 without the veil of the testimony in
40 24 altar of gold under the roof of the t.
Num 4 30 the service of the covenant of the t.
6 10 in the entry of the covenant of the t.
17 4 tabernacle of the covenant before the t.
Deut 31 19 and this song may be unto me for a t.
21 canticle shall answer them for a t.
26 it may be there for a t. against thee
Josu 22 27 for a testimony between us and you. 28
34 which they had built, Our testimony
24 27 this stone shall be a t. unto you that
Ruth 4 7 was a testimony of cession of right
4 K 11 12 the diadem upon him, and the testimony
2 Pa 23 11 the crown upon him, and the testimony
Jdth 13 27 God of Israel, to whom thou gavest t.
Ps 18 8 the testimony of the Lord is faithful
77 5 and he set up a testimony in Jacob
79 1 a t. for Asaph, a psalm. Give ear
80 6 ordained it for a testimony in Joseph
121 4 the testimony in Israel, to praise
Wisd 10 7 whose land for a t. of their wickedness
Eccu 31 28 the testimony of his truth is faithful
29 testimony of his niggardliness is true
36 17 give t. to them that are thy creatures
Isa 8 16 bind up the testimony, seal the law
20 to the law rather, and to the t. And
19 20 it shall be for a sign and for a t.
30 8 shall be in the latter days for a t.
Mat 8 4 commanded for a testimony to them. Mark 1:44; Luke 5:14
10 18 for a t. to them and to the Gentiles
24 14 world, for a testimony to all nations
Mark 6 11 dust from your feet for a t. Luke 9:5
13 9 for my sake for a testimony unto them
Luke 4 22 and all gave testimony to him: and
21 13 and it shall happen unto you for a t.
22 71 what need we any further testimony
John 1 7 give testimony of the light. 8
19 this is the t. of John, when the Jews
32 John gave t., saying: I saw the Spirit
34 I gave t. that this is the Son of God
2 25 that any should give testimony of man
3 11 and you receive not our t. If I have
32 and no man receiveth his testimony. He
33 he that hath received his testimony
4 39 word of the woman giving testimony
44 himself gave t. that a prophet hath
5 33 and he gave testimony to the truth
34 I receive not t. from man: but I saw
36 give t. to me, that the Father hath
37 hath given testimony of me: neither
39 the same are they that give t. of me
7 7 because I give testimony of it, that
8 13 thou givest testimony of thyself: thy
13 of thyself: thy testimony is not true
14 I give t. of myself, my t. is true
17 that the testimony of two men is true
18 I am one that give testimony of myself
18 Father that sent me giveth testimony
10 25 Father, they give testimony of me
12 17 multitude therefore gave testimony
15 26 he shall give testimony of me. And
27 you shall give t. because you are with
18 23 give testimony of the evil; but if
37 I should give testimony to the truth
19 35 hath given t., and his t. is true. And
21 24 who giveth testimony of these things
24 we know that his testimony is true
Acts 4 33 give t. of the resurrection of Jesus
10 22 good testimony from all the nation
43 all the prophets give testimony, that
13 22 to whom giving testimony, he said: I
14 3 who gave t. to the word of his grace
16 he left not himself without testimony
15 8 and God, who knoweth hearts, gave t.
16 2 and Iconium, gave a good testimony. Him
22 12 having t. of all the Jews who dwelt
18 will not receive thy t. concerning me
26 5 beginning, if they will give testimony
Rom 8 16 Spirit himself giveth t. to our spirit
1 C 1 6 as the t. of Christ was confirmed in
2 1 wisdom, declaring unto you t. of Christ
15 15 we have given testimony against God
2 C 1 12 glory is this, the t. of our conscience
Col 4 13 I bear him t. that he hath much labor
2 Th 1 10 because our t. was believed upon you in
1 Tim 2 6 a redemption for all, a t. in due times
3 7 he must have a good testimony of them
5 10 having t. for her good works, if she
6 13 who gave testimony under Pontius Pilate
2 Tim 1 8 be not thou therefore ashamed of the t.
Titus 1 13 this testimony is true. Wherefore rebuke
Heb 3 5 for a testimony of those things which
11 2 by this the ancients obtained a t. By
4 by which he obtained a testimony that
4 God giving testimony to his gifts; and
5 before his translation he had t. that
39 approved by the t. of faith, received
James 5 3 rust of them shall be for a testimony
1 J 5 7 three who give t. in heaven, the Father
8 three that give testimony on earth
9 if we receive the t. of men, the t. of God is greater
9 this is the t. of God, which is greater
10 hath the testimony of God in himself
10 t. which God hath testified of his Son
11 the t., that God hath given to us
3 J 3 gave testimony to the truth in thee
6 have given testimony to thy charity
12 to Demetrius testimony is given by all
12 we also give testimony: and thou knowest that our testimony is true
Apoc 1 2 who hath given t. to the word of God
2 and the t. of Jesus Christ, what things
9 word of God and for the t. of Jesus
6 9 and for the testimony which they held
11 7 when they shall have finished their t.
12 11 of the Lamb and by the word of the t.
17 and have the testimony of Jesus Christ
19 10 thy brethren, who have the t. of Jesus
10 t. of Jesus is the spirit of prophecy
20 4 that were beheaded for the t. of Jesus
22 20 he that giveth t. of these things

ark of the testimony; *see* **ark**

tabernacle of the testimony; *see* **tabernacle**

teth Ps 118 65 teth. Lam 1:9; 2:9; 3:25, 26, 27; 4:9

tetrarch Mat 14 1 Herod the t. heard the fame
Luke 3 1 and Herod being tetrarch of Galilee
1 Philip his brother tetrarch of Iturea
1 and Lysanias tetrarch of Abilina
19 Herod the t., when he was reproved
9 7 Herod, the tetrarch, heard of all

Acts 13 1 foster brother of Herod the tetrarch
Thaan 1 Pa 7 25 Thale, of whom was born Thaan
Thabeel 1 Es 4 7 Thabeel . . . wrote to Artaxerxes
Thabor Josu 19 22 the border thereof cometh to T.
Judg 4 6 lead an army to mount Thabor, and thou
12 Barac . . . was gone up to mount Thabor
14 Barac went down from mount Thabor, and
8 18 were they whom you slew in Thabor
1 K 10 3 and shalt come to the oak of Thabor
1 Pa 6 77 out of the tribe of Zabulon . . . Thabor
Ps 88 13 Thabor and Hermon shall rejoice
Jer 46 18 as Thabor is among the mountains, and
Osee 5 1 watched over, and a net spread upon T.
Thacasin Josu 19 13 east side of Gethhepher and T.
Thadal Gen 14 1 Thadal king of nations made war
Gen 14 9 against . . . Thadal king of nations
Thaddeus Mat 10 3 James son of Alpheus, and T.
Mark 3 18 James of Alpheus and Thaddeus and
Thahath Num 33 26 from Maceloth they came to T.
Num 33 27 removing from Thahath they camped in
1 Pa 6 24 Asir his son, Thahath his son, Uriel
37 Sophonias the son of Thahath, the son
7 20 T. his son, Elada his son, T. his son
Thalassa Acts 27 8 nigh to which was city of T.
Thalassar Isa 37 12 of Eden, that were in T.
Thale 1 Pa 7 25 Rapha was his son . . . and Thale
Thamar Gen 38 6 a wife . . . whose name was Thamar
Gen 38 11 said to Thamar his daughter-in-law
13 was told Thamar that her father-in-law
24 T. thy daughter-in-law hath played the
Ruth 4 12 of Phares whom Thamar bore unto Juda
2 K 13 1 beautiful, and her name was Thamar
4 I am in love with Thamar the sister of
5 let my sister Thamar, I pray thee, come
6 let my sister Thamar come and make
7 David sent home to Thamar, saying
8 Thamar came to the house of Amnon
10 Amnon said to Thamar: Bring the mess
10 and Thamar took the little messes
20 so Thamar remained pining away in the
22 he had ravished his sister Thamar
32 day that he ravished his sister Thamar
14 27 one daughter, whose name was Thamar
1 Pa 2 4 Thamar his daughter-in-law bore him
3 9 concubines and they had a sister Thamar
Eze 47 19 the south side southward is from Thamar
48 28 the border shall be from Thamar, even
Mat 1 3 Judas begot Phares and Zara of Thamar
Thamna Gen 36 12 Thamna was the concubine of Eliphaz
Gen 36 22 the sister of Lotan was T. 1 Pa 1:39
40 duke Thamna, duke Alva. 1 Pa 1:51
Josu 15 10 Bethsames and passeth into Thamna
57 Accain, Gabaa, and Thamna: ten cities
1 Pa 1 36 Gathan, Cenez, and by T., Amalec
Thamnan 2 Pa 28 18 Socho and T. and Gamzo, with
Thamnas Gen 38 12 to T. to the shearers of his
Gen 38 13 her father-in-law was come up to T.
14 in the cross way that leadeth to T.
Thamnata 1 Ma 9 50 T. and Phara and Thopo, with
Thamnatha Judg 14 1 then Samson went down to T.
Judg 14 2 I saw a woman in Thamnatha of the
5 down with his father and mother to T.
Thamnathite Judg 15 6 Samson son-in-law of the T.
Thamnath Saraa Josu 19 50 which he asked for, T. S.
Thamnathsare Josu 24 30 in the border of his possession
in Thamnathsare. Judg 2:9
Thanac Josu 21 25 the half tribe of Manasses, T.
Judg 1 27 did not destroy Bethsand and Thanac
3 K 4 12 who governed Thanac and Mageddo and
Thanach Judg 5 19 kings of Chanaan fought in T.
1 Pa 7 29 Thanach and her daughters, Mageddo
Thanath-selo Josu 16 6 eastward into Thanath-selo
Thanehumeth 4 K 25 23 and Saraia the son of T.
Jer 40 8 and Sareas the son of Thanehumeth
thank Luke 17 9 doth he thank that servant for
1 C 14 18 I thank my God I speak with all your
thankful Col 3 15 one body: and be ye thankful
thanks Lev 7 13 bread with the sacrifice of t.
2 K 8 10 with him and to return him thanks
22 50 therefore will I give thanks to thee
1 Pa 23 30 to give thanks and to sing praises
25 3 to give thanks and to praise the Lord
29 13 our God we give thanks to thee and
2 Es 12 24 to praise and to give thanks according
37 second choir of them that gave thanks
45 with canticles, and give thanks to God
Tob 2 14 giving thanks to God all the days of
11 7 giving thanks to him, go to thy father
12 had adored God and given him thanks
Esth 16 4 not to return thanks for benefits
Ps 34 18 will give t. to thee. 78:13; Isa 12:1
105 47 we may give thanks to thy holy name
108 30 I will give great thanks to the Lord
Wisd 18 2 before had been wronged, gave thanks
Eccu 12 1 shall be much thanks for thy good deeds
17 27 give thanks whilst thou art living
27 and in health thou shalt give thanks
20 17 shall be no thanks for his good deeds
35 4 he shall return thanks, that offereth
37 12 nor with envious man of giving thanks
47 9 works he gave thanks to the holy one
51 17 I will give thanks and praise thee
Dan 2 23 God of our fathers, I give thanks and
3 89 give thanks to the Lord, because he is
90 praise him and give him thanks because
6 10 adored and gave thanks before his God
1 Ma 14 25 what thanks shall we give to Simon
2 Ma 1 11 we give him great thanks forasmuch
3 33 give t. to Onias the priest: because
35 given t. to Onias, taking his troops
9 20 your mind, we give very great thanks
12 31 they gave them thanks exhorting them
Mat 15 36 giving thanks, he brake, and gave to
26 27 taking the chalice, he gave thanks
Mark 8 6 giving thanks, he broke and gave to
14 23 having taken the chalice, giving t.
Luke 6 32 what thanks are to you. 33, 34
17 16 before his feet, giving thanks: and
18 11 I give thee thanks. John 11:41
22 17 gave t. and said: Take, and divide it
19 he gave thanks and brake: and gave
John 6 11 when he had given t., he distributed
23 eaten bread, the Lord giving t.
Acts 27 35 he gave thanks to God. 28:15
Rom 1 8 I give thanks to my God. 1 C 1:4; Phil 1:3; Philem 4
21 glorified him as God, or given thanks
6 17 thanks be to God. 1 C 15:57; 2 C 2:14; 8:16; 9:15
14 6 to the Lord: for he giveth thanks to God
6 eateth not, and giveth thanks to God
16 4 to whom not I only give thanks, but
1 C 1 14 I give God thanks, that I baptized none
10 30 of, for that for which I give thanks
11 24 giving thanks, broke, and said: Take ye
14 17 for thou indeed givest thanks well, but
2 C 1 11 t. may be given by many in our behalf
Eph 1 16 cease not to give thanks for you, making
5 4 purpose; but rather giving of thanks
20 giving thanks always for all things, in
Col 1 3 we give thanks to God. 1 Th 1:2; 2:13
12 giving thanks to God the Father, who
3 17 giving thanks to God and the Father
1 Th 3 9 what thanks can we return to God for you
5 18 in all things give thanks; for this is
2 Th 1 3 we are bound to give thanks always to

2 12 we ought to give thanks to God always
1 Tim 1 12 I give him thanks who hath strengthened
2 Tim 1 3 I give thanks to God, whom I serve from
Apoc 11 17 we give thee thanks, O Lord God
thanksgiving Lev 7 12 if the oblation be for t.
Lev 22 29 if you immolate a victim for t. to
2 Es 12 27 and to rejoice with t. and with singing
43 bring them in by them in honor of t.
Ps 94 2 us come before his presence with t.
Eccu 51 15 continually and will praise it with t.
Isa 51 3 therein t. and the voice of praise
1 Ma 13 51 with t. and branches of palm trees
2 Ma 10 38 they blessed the Lord with hymns and t.
Acts 24 3 most excellent Felix, with all t.
1 C 10 30 if I partake with t., why am I evil
2 C 4 15 may abound in t. unto the glory of God
9 11 which worketh through us t. to God
Phil 4 6 with t., let your petitions be made
Col 2 7 learned, abounding in him in t. Beware
4 2 prayer; watching in it with thanksgiving
1 Tim 4 3 hath created to be received with t. by
4 be rejected that is received with t.
Apoc 7 12 and glory and wisdom and thanksgiving
thanksgivings 2 C 9 12 by many t. in the Lord
1 Tim 2 1 and thanksgivings be made for all men
thankworthy 1 P 2 19 this is thankworthy. 20
Thaphsa 3 K 4 24 from Thaphsa to Gazan, and all
Thaphua 1 Pa 2 43 sons of Hebron, Core and T.
Thapsa 4 K 15 16 then Manahem destroyed Thapsa
Thara Esth 12 1 Bagatha and T. the king's eunuchs
Tharaa 1 Pa 8 35 sons of Micha . . . Tharaa. 9:41
Tharaca Isa 37 9 about T. the king of Ethiopia
Tharana 1 Pa 2 48 concubine of Caleb bore . . . T.
Thare Gen 11 24 and Nachor . . . begot Thare. And
Gen 11 25 and Nachor lived after he begot Thare
26 Thare lived seventy years and begot
27 generations of Thare: T. begot Abram
28 and Aran died before Thare his father
31 Thare took Abram his son, and Lot the
Num 33 27 from Thahath they camped in Thare. And
Josu 24 2 T. the father of Abraham and Nachor
1 Pa 1 26 Thare, Abram, this is Abraham. And
Luke 3 34 Abraham, who was of Thare, who was of
Tharela Josu 18 27 Recem, Jarephel, and Tharela
Thares Esth 2 21 and T., two of the king's eunuchs
Esth 6 2 the treason of Bagathan and Thares
Tharseas 2 Ma 3 5 Apollonius the son of Tharseas
Tharsis Gen 10 4 sons of Javan: Elisa and Tharsis. 1 Pa 1:7
3 K 10 22 with the navy of Hiram by sea to T.
1 Pa 7 10 and Zethan and Tharsis and Ahisahar
2 Pa 9 21 the king's ships went to Tharsis with
20 36 him in making ships to go to Tharsis
37 broken, and they could not go to T.
Jdth 2 13 pillaged all the children of Tharsis
Esth 1 14 Tharsis and Mares and Marsana and
Ps 47 8 shalt break in pieces the ships of T.
71 10 the kings of Tharsis and the islands
Isa 2 16 upon all the ships of Tharsis and upon
Jer 10 9 brought from T., and gold from Ophaz
Eze 38 13 and Dedan and the merchants of Tharsis
Jon 1 3 Jonas rose up to flee into Tharsis
3 found a ship going to Tharsis: and he
3 to go with them to Tharsis from the
4 2 therefore I went before to flee into T.
Tharsus 2 Ma 4 30 they of T. and Mallos raised
Tharthac 4 K 17 31 Hevites made Nebahaz and T.
Tharthan 4 K 18 17 king of the Assyrians sent T.
Isa 20 1 in the year that Tharthan entered
Thasi 1 Ma 2 3 and Simon who was surnamed Thasi
Thathanai 1 Es 5 3 T. who was governor beyond the
1 Es 5 6 T. governor of the country. 6:6, 13
thau Lam 1 22 thau. 2:22; 3:64, 65, 66; 4:22
Eze 9 4 mark Thau upon the foreheads of the
6 upon whomsoever you shall see Thau
theater Acts 19 29 rushed with one accord into t.
Acts 19 31 he would not venture himself into the t.
Thebath 1 Pa 18 8 out of T. and Chun, cities
Thebes Judg 9 50 thence came to the town of T.
2 K 11 21 and slew him [Abimelech] in Thebes
Thebni 3 K 16 22 the people that followed Thebni
3 K 16 22 and Thebni died, and Amri reigned. In
Thecel Dan 5 25 is written: Mane, Thecel, Phares
Dan 5 27 Thecel: thou art weighed in the balance
Thecua 2 K 14 2 sent to Thecua and fetched from
2 K 14 4 when the woman of Thecua was come in
9 the woman of Thecua said to the king
23 26 of Phalti, Hira the son of Acces of T.
4 K 22 14 the wife of Sellum the son of Thecua
1 Pa 2 24 bore him Ashur the father of Thecua
4 5 Assur the father of T. had two wives
2 Pa 20 20 went out through the desert of Thecua
1 Es 10 15 Jaasia the son of T. were appointed
Jer 6 1 sound the trumpet in Thecua and set
Amos 1 1 who was among the herdsmen of Thecua
1 Ma 9 33 they fled into the desert of Thecua
Thecuath 2 Pa 34 22 Sellum the son of Thecuath
Thecue 2 Pa 11 6 he [Roboam] built . . . Thecue
Thecuite 1 Pa 11 28 the son of Acces a T. 27:9
Thecuites 2 Es 3 5 and next to them the T. built
2 Es 3 27 the Thecuites built another measure
theft Gen 30 33 the goats, shall accuse me of theft
Gen 31 32 whereas thou chargest me with theft
39 whatsoever was lost by theft, thou
Exod 22 3 to make restitution for the theft
1 Pa 2 7 sinned by the theft of the anathema
Tob 2 21 touch anything that cometh by theft
Wisd 14 25 mingled together, blood, murder, theft
Eccu 41 24 of theft and of the truth of God and
Osee 4 2 theft and adultery have overflowed
thefts Mat 15 19 come forth . . . fornications, t.
Mark 7 22 fornications, murders, thefts
Apoc 9 21 their fornication nor from their thefts
Theglathphalasar 4 K 15 29 T. king of Assyria
4 K 16 7 and Achaz sent messengers to T., king
10 king Achaz went to Damascus to meet T.
Thehen Num 26 35 T., of whom is the family of
Thehenites Num 26 35 is the family of the T.
Thelassar 4 K 19 12 of Eden that were in T.
Thelgathphalnasar 1 Pa 5 6 T. king of the Assyrians. 2 Pa 28:20
1 Pa 5 26 and the spirit of T. king of Assur
Thelharsa 1 Es 2 59 Thelmela, T., Cherub. 2 Es 7:61
Thelmela 1 Es 2 59 are they that came up from T.
Thema Gen 25 15 Hadar and Thema and Jethur and
1 Pa 1 30 Hadad and Thema, Jetur, Naphis, Cedma
1 Es 2 53 the children of Thema. 2 Es 7:55
Job 6 19 consider the paths of Thema, the ways
Jer 25 23 Dedan and Thema and Buz and all that
Theman Gen 36 11 Eliphaz had sons: Theman, Omar
Gen 36 15 duke T., duke Omar, duke Sepho, duke
42 duke Cenez, duke T., duke. 1 Pa 1:53
1 Pa 1 36 sons of Eliphaz: Theman, Omar, Sephi
Jer 49 7 is wisdom no more in Theman? Counsel
20 thought concerning the inhabitants of
Bar 3 22 neither hath it been seen in Theman
23 merchants of Merrha and of Theman, and
Amos 1 12 I will send a fire into Theman: and
Themani 1 Pa 4 6 Naara bore him . . . Themani
Themanite Job 2 11 Eliphaz the Themanite. 4:1; 15:1; 22:1; 42:7, 9
Themanites Gen 36 34 the land of the T. 1 Pa 1:45
Themna Josu 10 43 Jethela, Elon and T. and Acron
Thenac Josu 12 21 the king of Thenac one, the
Josu 17 11 inhabitants of Thenac with the villages
Theodas Acts 5 36 before these days rose up T.

23 21 do not think him one to be contemned
Deut 4 39 think in thy heart that the Lord he is
32 7 think upon every generation: ask thy
Josu 8 6 they will think that we flee as before
22 19 if you t. the land of your possession
1 K 25 17 consider and think what thou hast to
2 K 9 1 is there any one, think you, left of
13 32 let not my lord the king think that all
3 K 21 2 if thou think it more convenient for
2 Pa 25 8 if thou think that battles consist in
2 Es 6 6 that thou and the Jews think to rebel
Tob 3 3 Lord, think of me and take not revenge
Jdth 6 5 but if thou think thy prophecy true
10 18 that we should not think it worth our
Job 11 17 when thou shalt think thyself consumed
14 3 dost thou think it meet to open thy
22 11 didst thou t. that thou shouldst not
12 dost not thou think that God is higher
31 1 not so much as think upon a virgin
Ps 37 19 iniquity: and I will think for my sin
118 16 I will think of thy justifications
Prov 3 6 think on him, and he will direct thy
12 20 heart of them that think evil things
28 5 evil men think not on judgment: but
Wisd 1 1 think of the Lord is goodness and seek
6 16 to think therefore upon her is
9 13 who can think what the will of God is
12 22 we judge we may think on thy goodness
Eccu 3 22 commanded thee, think on them always
8 16 think as if thou wert to pay it
11 5 whom no man would think on, hath worn
14 22 shall think of the all-seeing eye of
21 20 they will think upon his words in their
27 13 be continually among men that think
34 9 shall think of many things: and he
Isa 10 8 and his heart shall not think so: but
29 16 as if the clay should think against
Jer 23 23 am I, think ye, a God at hand, saith
26 3 the evil that I think to do unto them
29 11 for I know the thoughts that I think
Lam 3 21 these things I shall think over in my
Bar 3 5 but think upon thy hand and upon thy
Eze 37 3 dost thou think these bones shall live
Dan 2 29 didst begin to think in thy bed, what
4 16 began silently to think within himself
7 25 he shall think himself able to change
9 13 our iniquities, and think on thy truth
Jon 1 6 if so be that God will think of us
4 4 dost thou think thou hast reason to. 9
Mala 3 2 able to think of the day of his coming
16 fear the Lord and think on his name
2 Ma 6 24 might think that Eleazar, at the age
7 16 think not that our nation is forsaken
19 do not think that thou shalt escape
Mat 3 9 think not to say within yourselves
5 17 do not think that I am come to destroy
6 7 they think that in their much speaking
9 4 why do you think evil in your hearts
10 34 do not think that I came to send peace
16 8 why do you think within yourselves
18 12 what think you? If a man have an
21 28 what think you? A certain man had two
22 17 what dost thou think, is it lawful to
42 what think you of Christ? Whose son is
26 66 the blasphemy: what think you. Mark 14:64
Mark 2 8 why think you these things in your
Luke 1 66 what an one, think ye, shall this
5 21 began to think, saying: Who is this
22 what is it you think in your hearts
7 7 neither did I think myself worthy to
8 25 who is this, think you, that he
12 40 at what hour you think not, the Son of
51 think ye that I am come to give peace
13 2 think you that these Galileans were
4 think you that they also were debtors
14 31 and think whether he be able, with
17 10 thank that servant . . . ? I think not
18 8 shall he find, think you, faith on
John 5 39 for you think in them to have life
45 think not that I will accuse you to
11 56 what think you that he is not come to
16 2 will think that he doth a service to
21 25 the world itself, I think, would not
Acts 13 25 I am not he, whom you t. me to be: but
26 2 I think myself happy, O king Agrippa
9 I indeed did formerly t., that I ought
1 C 4 9 I t. that God hath set forth us apostles
7 26 I think therefore that this is good for
36 but if any man think that he seemeth
40 I think that I also have spirit of God
8 2 and if any man think that he knoweth
12 23 such as we think to be less honorable
2 C 3 5 not that we are sufficient to think
10 7 he is Christ's, let him think this again
11 let such a one think this, that such as
11 16 again, let no man think me to be foolish
12 6 lest any man should think of me above
19 steps? Of old, think you that we excuse
Gal 6 3 if any man think himself to be something
Phil 1 7 as it is meet for me to think this for
4 8 praise of discipline, t. on these things
10 as you did also think; but you were
Heb 10 29 how much more, do you think he deserveth
12 3 think diligently upon him that endured
James 1 7 think that he shall receive anything
26 any man think himself to be religious
1 P 4 4 they think it strange that you run not
12 think not strange the burning heat
5 12 faithful brother unto you, as I think
2 P 1 13 I think it meet as long as I am in
thinkest Gen 17 17 shall a son, t. thou, be born
2 K 10 3 thinkest thou that for the honor of
1 Pa 19 3 thou thinkest perhaps that David to do
Tob 10 1 why thinkest thou doth my son tarry
2 is Gabelus dead, thinkest thou, and no
Job 13 24 thy face, and thinkest me thy enemy
14 14 shall man that is dead, thinkest thou
17 16 t. thou that there at least I shall
Ecce 7 11 say not: What t. thou is the cause that
Jer 37 16 thinkest thou, any word from the Lord
Eze 8 6 dost thou see, thinkest thou, what
Dan 2 26 thinkest thou indeed that thou canst
6 20 been able, thinkest thou, to deliver
Mat 18 1 who thinkest thou is the greater in
24 45 who, thinkest thou, is a faithful and
26 53 thinkest thou that I cannot ask my
Mark 4 40 who is this, thinkest thou, that both
Luke 12 42 who, thinkest thou, is the faithful
Rom 2 3 t. thou this, O man, that judgest them
Acts 8 30 t. thou that thou understandest what
28 22 we desire to hear of thee what thou t.
thinketh 1 K 23 22 t. of me, that I lie craftily
Job 11 12 and thinketh himself born free like a
Prov 23 7 he thinketh that which he knoweth not
Ecce 7 3 the living thinketh what is to come
Eccu 16 23 wanteth understanding, t. vain things
23 and erring man thinketh foolish things
Haba 2 9 thinketh he may be delivered out of
Luke 8 18 that also which he thinketh he hath
1 C 7 34 virgin t. on the things of the Lord
34 she that is married t. on the things of
10 12 he that t. himself to stand, let him
13 5 is not provoked to anger, t. no evil
Phil 3 4 if any other t. he may have confidence
thinking Gen 26 7 t. lest perhaps they would kill
Gen 31 52 pass beyond it, thinking harm to me

Exod 13 17 thinking lest perhaps they would repent
Judg 19 28 he thinking she was taking her rest
1 K 10 2 thy father t. no more of the asses
18 11 thinking to nail David to the wall
2 Es 6 9 t. that our hands would cease from the
Job 15 12 as if they were thinking great things
22 18 whose way of thinking be far from me
Wisd 8 17 thinking these things with myself and
12 15 t. it not agreeable to thy power to
Eccu 31 2 the thinking beforehand turneth away
1 Ma 5 61 thinking that they should do manfully
2 Ma 5 6 thinking they had been enemies and
21 thinking through pride that he might
7 24 Antiochus thinking himself despised
11 2 thinking to take the city and make it
12 12 Judas t. that they might be profitable
43 of the dead, t. well and religiously
14 14 thinking the miseries and calamities
Mark 2 6 sitting there and t. in their hearts
Luke 2 44 thinking that he was in the company
3 15 were thinking in their hearts of John
11 38 t. within himself, why he was not
John 20 15 she thinking that it was the gardener
Acts 10 19 as Peter was thinking of the vision
14 18 out of city, thinking him to be dead
27 13 t. that they had obtained their purpose
thinner Lev 13 30 hair yellow and t. than usual
Thiras Gen 10 2 and Mosoch and Thiras. 1 Pa 1:5
thirdly Eccu 23 33 thirdly, she hath fornicated
1 C 12 28 secondly prophets, thirdly doctors
thirds 1 Ma 10 29 and the thirds of the seed
Thiria 1 Pa 4 16 Ziph and Zipha, Thiria, and
thirst Exod 17 3 to children and our beasts with t.
Deut 28 48 serve thy enemy . . . in hunger and t.
Judg 15 18 behold I die for thirst, and shall fall
2 K 17 29 were faint with hunger and thirst in
2 Pa 32 11 give you up to die by hunger and thirst
2 Es 9 15 for them out of the rock in their t.
20 thou gavest them water for their thirst
Jdth 7 14 cast down before their eyes in thirst
17 is made longer by the drought of thirst
16 13 lowly ones appeared, parched with t.
Job 18 9 and thirst shall burn against him
24 11 trodden the winepresses suffer thirst
Ps 61 5 cast away my price; I ran in thirst
68 22 in my thirst they gave me vinegar to
103 11 wild asses shall expect in their thirst
Prov 25 21 if he thirst, give him water to drink
Wisd 11 4 a refreshment of their thirst out of
9 showing by the thirst that was then
Eccu 24 29 they that drink me, shall yet thirst
Isa 5 13 their multitude were dried up with t.
25 5 tumult of strangers, as heat in thirst
29 8 he is awake, is yet faint with thirst
41 17 their tongue hath been dry with thirst
49 10 they shall not hunger nor thirst
50 2 want of water and shall die for thirst
55 1 you that thirst, come to the waters
Jer 2 25 being bare, and thy throat from thirst
48 18 and sit in thirst, O dwelling of the
Lam 4 4 stuck to the roof of his mouth for t.
Amos 8 11 nor a thirst of water, but of hearing
13 the young men shall faint for thirst
Mat 5 6 blessed are they that hunger and thirst
John 4 13 drinketh of this water, shall thirst
13 will give him, shall not thirst forever
15 give me this water, that I may not t.
6 35 that believeth in me shall never t.
7 37 if any man thirst, let him come to me
19 28 said: I thirst. Now there was a vessel
Rom 12 20 if he thirst, give him to drink. For
1 C 4 11 unto this hour we both hunger and thirst
2 C 11 27 in much watchings, in hunger and thirst
Apoc 7 16 they shall no more hunger nor thirst
thirsted Ps 41 3 my soul hath t. after the
Ps 62 2 for thee my soul hath thirsted: for
Isa 48 21 they thirsted not in the desert when
thirsteth Joel 1 20 garden bed that t. after rain
Apoc 21 6 to him that thirsteth, I will give of
22 17 he that thirsteth, let him come: and
thirsting Wisd 11 15 their t. being unlike to that
thirsty Exod 17 3 the people were thirsty there
Deut 29 19 the drunken may consume the thirsty
Judg 4 19 a little water, for I am very thirsty
15 18 being very thirsty, he cried to the
Ruth 2 9 if thou art thirsty, go to the vessels
Job 5 5 the thirsty shall drink up his riches
Ps 106 5 they were hungry and thirsty: their
Wisd 11 4 they were thirsty and they called upon
Eccu 26 15 open her mouth as a thirsty traveller
51 32 your souls are exceeding thirsty. I
Isa 21 14 meeting the thirsty, bring him water
29 8 as he that is thirsty dreameth and
32 6 and take away drink from the thirsty
35 7 and the thirsty land springs of water
44 3 pour out waters upon the thirsty ground
53 2 and as a root out of a thirsty ground
65 13 shall drink, and you shall be thirsty
Mat 25 35 I was thirsty, and you gave me to drink
37 thirsty, and gave thee drink? And
42 I was thirsty, and you gave me not to
44 when did we see thee hungry or thirsty
thirtyfold Mat 13 8 some sixtyfold, and some t.
thistle 4 K 14 9 t. of Libanus sent to a cedar
4 K 14 9 Libanus, passed and trod down the t.
2 Pa 25 18 the thistle that is in Libanus sent
18 the beasts . . . trod down the thistle
Isa 34 13 the thistle in the fortresses thereof
Osee 10 8 the bur and the thistle shall grow up
thistles Gen 3 18 thorns and t. shall it bring
Job 31 40 let thistles grow up to me instead of
Eccu 43 21 shall become like the tops of thistles
Mat 7 16 grapes of thorns, or figs of thistles
Thobadonias 2 Pa 17 8 Adonias and Tobias and T.
Thochen 1 Pa 4 32 and T. and Asan, five cities
Thogorma Gen 10 3 and Riphath and T. 1 Pa 1:6
Eze 27 14 from the house of T. they brought horses
38 6 house of Thogorma, the northern parts
Thohu 1 K 1 1 son of Eliu the son of Thohu
1 Pa 6 34 the son of Eliel the son of Thohu
Thola Gen 46 13 the sons of Issachar: Thola and Phua. 1 Pa 7:1
Num 26 23 Thola, of whom is the family of the
Judg 10 1 there arose a ruler in Israel, Thola
1 Pa 7 2 the sons of Thola: Ozi and Raphaia
2 of the posterity of T. were numbered
Tholad 1 Pa 4 29 in Bala and in Asom and in T.
Tholaites Num 26 23 is the family of the T.
Tholmai Num 13 23 were Achiman and Sisai and T.
Josu 15 14 Ahirman and T. of the race of Enac
Judg 1 10 slew Sesai and Ahiman and Tholmai: and
2 K 3 3 Maacha daughter of T. king of Gessur
Tholomai 2 K 13 37 Absalom fled and went to T.
Thomas Mat 10 3 T. and Matthew the publican
Mark 3 18 and Matthew and Thomas and James of
Luke 6 15 Matthew and Thomas, James the son of
John 11 16 Thomas . . . who is called Didymus
14 5 Thomas saith to him: Lord, we know
20 24 Thomas, one of the twelve, who is
26 were within, and Thomas with them
27 then he saith to Thomas: Put in thy
28 Thomas answered and said to him: My
29 because thou hast seen me, Thomas
21 2 there were together Simon Peter and T.
Acts 1 13 where abode . . . Philip and Thomas
thong Job 39 10 the rhinoceros with thy thong to

Osee 7 14 they have thought upon wheat and wine
Amos 6 5 thought themselves to have instruments
Zach 1 6 the Lord of hosts thought to do to us
8 15 I have thought in these days to do good
1 Ma 2 63 and his thought is come to nothing
5 2 they thought to destroy the generation
2 Ma 1 18 we thought it necessary to signify it
6 29 they t. were uttered out of arrogancy
7 21 joining a man's heart to a woman's t.
9 4 he thought to revenge upon the Jews
10 the man that thought a little before
21 I thought it necessary to take care
11 36 as he thought should be referred to
12 46 holy and wholesome thought to pray for
14 40 he t. by insnaring him to hurt the
15 6 thought to set up a public monument
Mat 1 20 but while he thought on these things
6 27 which of you by taking t. Luke 12:25
10 19 take no thought how or what to speak
16 7 they t. within themselves. 21:25; Mark 11:31; Luke 20:5, 14
20 10 thought that they should receive more
Mark 2 8 that they so thought within themselves
6 49 the sea, thought it was an apparition
Luke 1 29 thought with herself what manner of
9 46 there entered a thought into them
12 17 he thought within himself, saying
19 11 they thought that the kingdom of God
John 11 13 they t. that he spoke of the repose of
12 10 chief priests thought to kill Lazarus
13 29 some thought, because Judas had the
Acts 5 33 and they thought to put them to death
7 25 he t. that his brethren understood
8 20 hast thought that the gift of God may
22 perhaps this thought of thy heart may
12 9 [Peter] thought he saw a vision. And
25 18 of things which I thought ill of: but
26 8 why should it be t. a thing incredible
1 C 13 11 understood as a child, I t. as a child
2 C 9 5 I t. it necessary to desire the brethren
10 2 I am thought to be bold, against some
9 that I may not be thought as it were to
Phil 2 6 t. it not robbery to be equal with God
25 I have thought it necessary to send to
4 10 that now at length your thought for me
1 Th 3 1 we t. it good to remain at Athens alone
Heb 4 1 you should be thought to be wanting
1 P 4 1 be you also armed with the same thought
thoughtest Ps 49 21 t. unjustly that I should be
thoughtful Mark 13 11 be not t. beforehand what
thoughts Num 15 39 and not follow their own t.
Deut 31 21 I know their thoughts, and what they
1 K 2 3 to him are thoughts prepared. The bow
1 Pa 28 9 and understandeth all the t. of minds
Jdth 2 3 his thoughts were to bring all the
Job 12 5 lamp despised in the t. of the rich
17 11 my thoughts are dissipated, tormenting
20 2 various thoughts succeed one another
21 27 surely I know your thoughts and your
Ps 32 11 t. of his heart to all generations
39 6 in thy t. there is no one like to thee
55 6 all their thoughts were against me
91 6 works. Thy thoughts are exceeding deep
93 11 the Lord knoweth the thoughts of men
138 3 thou hast understood my thoughts afar
145 4 in that day all their t. shall perish
Prov 5 2 that thou mayest keep thoughts, and
8 12 and am present in learned thoughts
12 5 the thoughts of the just are judgments
15 26 evil thoughts are an abomination to the
16 3 and thy thoughts shall be directed
19 21 there are many thoughts in the heart
21 5 the thoughts of the industrious always
22 20 of ways, in thoughts and knowledge
Wisd 1 3 perverse thoughts separate from God
5 thoughts that are without understanding
9 made into the thoughts of the ungodly
2 14 he is become a censurer of our thoughts
6 4 your works, and search out your t.
7 15 to conceive t. worthy of those things
9 14 the thoughts of mortal men are fearful
Eccu 6 2 extol not thyself in the t. of thy soul
37 let thy thoughts be upon the precepts
23 2 who will set scourges over my thoughts
24 39 her thoughts are more vast than the sea
27 5 perplexity of a man in his thoughts
33 5 his t. are like a rolling axletree
40 2 their thoughts and fears of the heart
Isa 55 7 way, and the unjust man his thoughts
8 for my thoughts are not your thoughts
9 and my thoughts above your thoughts
59 7 their t. are unprofitable t.: wasting
65 2 way that is not good after their own t.
66 18 I know their works and their thoughts
Jer 4 4 because of the wickedness of your t.
14 how long shall hurtful t. abide in thee
6 19 the fruits of their own t.: because
18 12 we will go after our own thoughts and
29 11 the thoughts that I think towards you, saith the Lord, thoughts of peace
49 20 his t. which he hath thought. 50:45
Lam 3 60 and all their thoughts against me
Eze 11 5 for I know the thoughts of your heart
Dan 2 30 mightest know the thoughts of thy mind
4 2 my t. in my bed, and the visions of
16 and his thoughts troubled him. 5:6
5 10 let not thy thoughts trouble thee
7 28 was much troubled with my thoughts
Osee 5 4 will not set their thoughts to return
Mich 2 7 straitened, or are these his thoughts
4 12 they have not known the t. of the Lord
Soph 3 7 rose early and corrupted all their t.
Zach 1 4 ways and from your wicked thoughts
Mat 9 4 Jesus seeing their thoughts, said
12 25 Jesus knowing their thoughts, said to
15 19 from the heart come forth evil t.
Mark 7 21 proceed evil thoughts, adulteries
Luke 2 35 many hearts, thoughts may be revealed
5 22 when Jesus knew their thoughts
6 8 but he knew their thoughts; and said
9 47 Jesus seeing the thoughts of their
11 17 he seeing their thoughts, said to them
24 38 why do thoughts arise in your hearts
Rom 1 21 became vain in their thoughts, and their
2 15 their t. between themselves accusing, or
14 1 unto you: not in disputes about thoughts
1 C 3 20 the Lord knoweth the t. of the wise
Eph 2 3 will of the flesh and of our thoughts
Heb 4 12 is a discerner of the t. and intents of
James 2 4 are become judges of unjust thoughts
thousands Gen 24 60 thou increase to t. of t.
Exod 18 21 appoint of them rulers of thousands
25 rulers over t. and over hundreds and
20 6 showing mercy unto t. to them that
34 7 who keepest mercy unto thousands
Deut 1 11 add to this number many thousands and
33 2 and with him thousands of saints. In
17 and these the thousands of Manasses
1 K 18 7 slew his t., and David his ten t. 29:5
8 they have given David ten thousands
21 11 hath slain his t., and David his ten t.
23 23 search him out in all the t. of Juda
29 2 with their hundreds and their thousands
2 K 18 1 captains of thousands. 1 Pa 12:20; 27:1; 29:6; 2 Pa 1:2; 25:5
4 their troops, by hundreds and by t.

1 Pa 13 1 with the captains of thousands and of
15 25 the captains over t. 26:26; 28:1
Job 33 23 speaking for him, one among thousands
Ps 3 7 I will not fear thousands of the people
67 18 chariot of God is attended by ten t.; t. of them that rejoice
83 11 better is one day in thy courts above t.
118 72 above thousands of gold and silver
Cant 5 10 is white and ruddy, chosen out of t.
Jer 32 18 thou showest mercy unto thousands
Dan 3 40 bullocks, and as in t. of fat lambs
7 10 before him: t. of t. ministered to him
11 12 and he shall cast down many thousands
Mich 5 2 little one among the thousands of Juda
6 7 the Lord be appeased with t. of rams
7 with many thousands of fat he goats
1 Ma 3 55 captains over the people, over t.
2 Ma 11 4 soldiers and the t. of his horsemen
Acts 21 20 how many t. there are among the Jews
Heb 12 22 company of many thousands of angels
Jude 14 Lord cometh with t. of his saints
Apoc 5 11 the number of them was t. of t., saying
Thracians 2 Ma 12 35 horseman of the T. came upon
thrash Isa 28 28 thrasher shall not t. it forever
Isa 41 15 thou shalt thrash the mountains and
thrashed Isa 28 27 gith shall not be t. with saws
Amos 1 3 they have t. Galaad with iron wains
thrasher Isa 28 28 t. shall not thrash it forever
thrasheth 1 C 9 10 he that t., in hope to receive
thrashing 4 K 13 7 dust by t. in the barnfloor
1 Pa 21 20 at that time he was thrashing wheat
Isa 21 10 O my thrashing, and the children of my
41 15 have made thee as a new thrashing wain
Jer 51 33 this is the time of her thrashing: yet
thrashingfloor 2 K 24 16 was by the t. of Areuna
2 K 24 18 altar to the Lord in the t. of Areuna
21 to buy the t. of thee and build an
1 Pa 21 15 stood by the t. of Ornan the Jebusite
18 in the t. of Ornan. 28; 2 Pa 3:1
21 went out of the t. to meet him [David]
22 give me this place of thy t. that I
Jer 51 33 the daughter of Babylon is like a t.
Dan 2 35 became like the chaff of a summer's t.
thread Gen 14 23 from the very woof thread unto
Gen 38 27 whereon the midwife tied a scarlet t.
30 on whose hand was the scarlet thread
Judg 16 9 as a man would break a thread of tow
threads Exod 39 3 and drew them small into t.
Judg 16 12 broke the bands like threads of webs
threaten Jdth 8 15 for God will not t. like man
Ps 102 9 be angry: nor will he threaten forever
Eccu 19 17 thy neighbor before thou threaten him
Acts 4 17 let us threaten them that they speak
threatened Eze 20 21 t. to pour out my indignation
Jdth 13 28 threatened thee with death, saying
2 Pa 26 19 Onias was angry and . . . t. the priests
Judg 20 34 present death t. them on every side
Josu 23 15 upon you all the evils he hath t.
9 25 not destroy you as he had threatened
Mark 1 25 Jesus threatened him, saying: Speak no
8 33 t. Peter, saying: Go behind me, Satan
9 24 he t. the unclean spirit, saying to
1 P 2 23 when he suffered, he threatened not
threateneth Gen 27 42 thy brother t. to kill thee
threatening Job 16 10 t. me he hath gnashed with
Isa 30 30 in the threatening of wrath, and the
Jer 10 10 not be able to abide his threatening
Acts 4 21 they t., sent them away, not finding
threatenings Acts 4 29 behold their t. and grant
Acts 9 1 Saul as yet breathing out threatenings
Eph 6 9 to them, forbearing t., knowing that
threats Eccu 22 30 and threats, before blood
Jer 15 17 because thou hast filled me with t.

threefold Ecce 4 12 t. cord is not easily broken
threescore Acts 27 37 two hundred, threescore and sixteen souls
1 Tim 5 9 a widow be chosen of no less than t.
thresh Judg 8 7 I will t. your flesh with the
threshing Lev 26 5 the t. of your harvest shall
Judg 6 11 when Gedeon his son was threshing
Ruth 2 17 t. what she had gleaned, she found
threshingfloor Gen 50 10 came to the t. of Atad
Ruth 3 2 night he winnoweth barley in the t.
threshold Judg 19 27 her hands spread on the t.
1 K 5 4 of his hands were cut off upon the t.
5 tread on the t. of Dagon in Azotus
3 K 14 17 when she was coming in to the threshold
Eze 9 3 to the t. of the house. And he called
10 4 above the cherub, to the t. of the
18 went forth from the t. of the temple
40 6 he measured the breadth of the t. 11
6 one threshold was one reed broad
8 threshold of the gate by the porch
41 16 over against the t. of every one
21 the t. was foursquare, and the face of
43 8 they who have set their t. by my t.
46 2 he shall stand at the t. of the gate
2 he shall adore upon the t. of the gate
47 1 waters issued out from under the t.
Soph 1 9 that entereth arrogantly over the t.
2 14 and the urchin shall lodge in the t.
thresholds Eze 41 16 t. and the oblique windows
threw Exod 32 19 threw the tables out of his hand
Deut 9 21 as dust, I threw it into the torrent
Josu 7 23 and threw them down before the Lord
8 29 threw it in the very entrance of the
Judg 15 17 he threw the jawbone out of his hand
1 K 18 11 threw it, thinking to nail David to
2 K 16 6 [Semei] threw stones at David and at
4 K 9 33 they threw her [Jezabel] down, and the
2 Es 9 26 and threw thy law behind their backs
Jer 39 8 they threw down the wall of Jerusalem
Dan 8 10 it threw down of the strength and of
1 Ma 1 33 threw down the houses thereof and the
2 45 they threw down the altars: and they
4 45 had defiled it; so they threw it down
5 43 t. away their weapons and fled. 7:44
68 and he threw down their altars and
7 19 killed and threw them into a great pit
8 10 and threw down their walls and brought
11 51 and they threw down their arms and
2 Ma 1 16 their heads, they threw them forth
4 41 and some threw ashes upon Lysimachus
6 10 they threw down headlong from the walls
10 2 he threw down the altars which the
12 15 threw down the walls of Jericho in the
14 43 manfully t. himself down to the crowd
Luke 9 42 devil threw him down and tore him
Acts 22 23 as they cried out and threw off their
threwest 2 Es 9 11 persecutors thou t. into the
thrice Exod 23 17 t. a year shall all thy males
Exod 34 24 sight of the Lord thy God t. in a year
1 K 20 41 on his face to the ground, adored t.
Eccu 13 8 have drawn thee dry twice or thrice
48 3 brought down fire from heaven thrice
Mat 26 34 cock crow, thou wilt deny me thrice. 75; Mark 14:30; Luke 22:61
14 72 crow twice, thou shalt thrice deny me
Luke 22 34 till thou thrice deniest that thou
John 13 38 not crow, till thou deny me thrice
Acts 10 16 this was done thrice; and presently
2 C 11 25 thrice was I beaten with rods, once I
25 thrice I suffered shipwreck, a night and
12 8 for which thing thrice I besought Lord
Apoc 6 6 thrice two pounds of barley for a penny
thrive Wisd 4 3 brood of the wicked shall not t.

throat Lev 1 16 crop of the throat and the
1 K 17 35 and I caught them by the throat, and I
Job 20 13 not leave it and will hide it in his t.
29 10 their tongue cleaved to their throat
Ps 5 11 their t. is an open sepulcher. 13:3
113 7 shall they cry out through their t.
Prov 5 3 and her throat is smoother than oil
23 2 put a knife to thy throat, if it be so
24 13 the honeycomb most sweet to thy throat
Cant 5 16 his throat most sweet, and he is all
7 9 thy throat like the best wine, worthy
Jer 2 25 from being bare, and thy t. from thirst
Osee 8 1 let there be a trumpet in thy throat
Rom 3 13 their throat is an open sepulcher; with
throne Gen 41 40 only in the kingly t. will I be
Exod 17 16 the hand of the throne of the Lord
Deut 17 18 after he is raised to the throne of
1 K 2 8 with princes, and hold the t. of glory
2 K 3 10 throne of David be set up over Israel
7 13 I will establish throne of his kingdom
3 K 1 13 he shall sit on my throne. 17, 30, 35
24 after me, and let him sit upon my t.
27 who should sit on the throne of my lord
37 higher than the throne of my lord king
46 Solomon sitteth upon the throne of the
48 given this day one to sit on my throne
2 12 Solomon sat upon the throne of his
19 and a throne was set for king's mother
24 placed me upon the throne of David
45 throne of David shall be established
5 5 whom I will set upon the t. in thy
7 7 he made also the porch of the throne
9 5 I will establish the t. of thy kingdom
10 18 also made a great throne of ivory: and
19 the top of the throne was round behind
4 K 10 3 set him on his father's t. and fight
11 19 and he sat on the throne of the kings
25 28 set his t. above the t. of the kings
1 Pa 22 10 I will establish the throne of his
28 5 Solomon my son, to sit upon the throne
29 23 and Solomon sat on throne of the Lord
2 Pa 7 18 I will raise up the t. of thy kingdom
9 17 king also made a great throne of ivory
18 and six steps to go up to the throne
19 was not such a throne in any kingdom
23 20 house and set him on the royal throne
Esth 1 2 when he sat on the t. of his kingdom
Job 36 7 he placeth kings on the throne forever
Ps 9 5 thou hast sat on the throne, who
10 5 temple, the Lord's throne is in heaven
Prov 16 12 the throne is established by justice
20 8 that sitteth on the throne of judgment
Wisd 9 10 and from the throne of thy majesty
12 be worthy of the throne of my father
Eccu 11 5 many tyrants have sat on the throne
24 7 my throne is in a pillar of a cloud
34 sitting on the throne of glory forever
40 3 from him that sitteth on a glorious t.
47 13 kingdom and a t. of glory in Israel
Isa 6 1 I saw the Lord sitting upon a throne
9 7 he shall sit upon the throne of David
14 13 I will exalt my throne above the stars
16 5 a throne shall be prepared in mercy
22 23 and he shall be for a throne of glory
47 1 no throne for daughter of the Chaldeans
66 1 heaven is my throne, and the earth my
Jer 3 17 shall be called the throne of the Lord
14 21 not disgrace in us the t. of thy glory
17 12 high and glorious t. from the beginning
25 sitting upon the throne of David and
22 2 that sittest upon the throne of David
30 that shall sit upon the throne of David
29 16 that sitteth upon the throne of David
33 17 to sit upon t. of the house of Israel
36 30 none to sit upon the throne of David
49 38 I will set my t. in Elam and destroy
Eze 1 26 was the likeness of a throne, as the
26 upon the likeness of the throne, was
10 1 the appearance of the likeness of a t.
43 7 the place of my throne and the place
Dan 3 54 blessed art thou on the throne of thy
5 20 he was put down from the throne of his
7 9 his t. like flames of fire: the wheels
Amos 6 3 that approach to the throne of iniquity
Agge 2 23 I will overthrow the throne of kingdoms
1 Ma 2 57 David by his mercy obtained the throne
7 4 Demetrius sat upon t. of his kingdom
10 52 am set in the throne of my ancestors
53 we are placed in the t. of his kingdom
55 sattest in the throne of their kingdom
11 52 Demetrius sat in the t. of his kingdom
Mat 5 34 heaven, for it is the throne of God
23 22 sweareth by the throne of God and by
Luke 1 32 shall give unto him the t. of David
Acts 7 49 heaven is my throne, and the earth my
Heb 4 16 with confidence to the throne of grace
8 1 who is set on the right hand of the t.
12 2 on the right hand of the throne of God
Apoc 3 21 will give to sit with me in my throne
4 2 a throne set in heaven, and upon the throne one sitting
3 was a rainbow round about the throne
4 about the throne were four and twenty
5 from the throne proceeded lightnings
5 seven lamps burning before the throne
6 in the sight of the throne was, as it
6 in the midst of the throne and. 5:6
6 and round about the throne were four
9 him that sitteth on the t. 10; 5:13; 6:16
10 cast their crowns before the throne
5 1 of him that sat on the throne, a book
7 hand of him that sat on the throne
11 of many angels round about the throne
7 9 standing before the throne and in sight
10 our God, who sitteth upon the throne
11 the angels stood round about the throne
11 they fell down before the throne upon
15 they are before the throne of God and
15 that sitteth on the throne shall dwell
17 Lamb, which is in midst of the throne
8 3 altar which is before the throne of God
14 3 a new canticle before the throne and
5 without spot before the throne of God
16 17 out of the temple from the throne
19 4 adored God that sitteth upon the throne
5 and a voice came out from the throne
20 11 I saw a great white throne, and one
12 standing in the presence of the throne
21 3 I heard a great voice from the throne
5 and he that sat on the throne, said
22 1 proceeding from the throne of God
3 the throne of God and of the Lamb
his throne Exod 11 5 Pharao, who sitteth on his t.
Exod 12 29 firstborn of Pharao who sat on his t.
Judg 3 20 he forthwith rose up from his throne
2 K 14 9 may the king and his t. be guiltless
3 K 1 37 make his throne higher than the throne
2 19 to her and sat down upon his throne
33 and to his throne be peace forever
3 6 given him a son to sit on his throne
16 11 when he was king and sat upon his t.
22 10 sat each on his throne clothed with
19 I saw the Lord sitting on his throne
4 K 13 13 fathers: and Jeroboam sat upon his t.
25 28 set his t. above the t. of the kings
1 Pa 17 12 I will establish his throne forever

14 14 his throne shall be most firm forever
2 Pa 9 7 been pleased to set thee on his throne
18 18 I saw the Lord sitting on his throne
Jdth 1 12 swore by his throne and kingdom that
Esth 3 1 set his throne above all the princes
5 1 he sat upon his throne in the hall of
15 9 where he sat upon his royal throne
11 and in fear he leaped from his throne
Job 23 3 find him and come even to his throne
26 9 he withholdeth the face of his throne
Ps 9 8 hath prepared his throne in judgment
26 9 nations: God sitteth on his holy throne
88 30 and his throne as the days of heaven
38 his throne as the sun before me: and
45 hast cast his throne down to ground
96 2 are the establishment of his throne
102 19 Lord hath prepared his t. in heaven
Prov 20 28 his throne is strengthened by clemency
25 5 his throne shall be established with
29 14 his throne shall be established forever
Eccu 1 8 who sitteth upon his throne and is the
Jer 1 15 shall set every one his throne in the
13 13 of race of David that sit upon his t.
22 4 sitting upon his throne, and riding
33 21 not have a son to reign upon his throne
43 10 I will set his throne over these stones
10 he shall set his throne over them
52 32 he set his throne above the thrones
Jon 3 6 he rose up out of his throne and cast
Zach 6 13 shall sit, and rule upon his throne
13 he shall be a priest upon his throne
Acts 2 30 one should sit upon his throne
Apoc 1 4 seven spirits which are before his t.
3 21 set down with my Father in his throne
12 5 was taken up to God and to his throne
throne of Israel 3 K 2 4 from thee a man on t. . . .
3 K 8 20 and sit upon the t. . . . as the Lord
25 man in my sight to sit on the t. . . .
9 5 fail a man of thy race upon the t. . . .
10 9 and who hath set thee upon the t. . . .
4 K 10 30 thy children shall sit upon the t. . . .
15 12 generation shall sit upon the t. . . .
2 Pa 6 10 and sit upon the t. . . . as the Lord
16 man in my sight to sit upon the t. . . .
thy throne 2 K 7 16 thy t. shall be firm forever
3 K 1 20 tell them who shall sit on thy throne
47 make his throne greater than thy throne
8 13 to be thy most firm throne forever
49 heaven, in the firmament of thy throne
Ps 44 7 thy throne, O God, is forever and
88 5 and I will build up thy throne unto
15 are the preparation of thy throne
92 2 thy throne is prepared from of old
131 11 of thy womb I will set upon thy throne
12 for evermore shall sit upon thy throne
Wisd 9 4 give me wisdom, that sitteth by thy t.
18 15 from heaven from thy royal throne
Lam 5 19 thy t. from generation to generation
Abdi 3 and settest up thy throne on high
Heb 1 8 thy throne, O God, is forever and ever
thrones 2 Pa 18 9 both sat on their t., clothed
Wisd 5 24 shall overthrow the t. of the mighty
6 22 if then your delight be in thrones
7 8 I preferred her before kingdoms and t.
Eccu 10 17 overturned the thrones of proud princes
Isa 14 9 are risen up from their thrones, all
Jer 52 32 above the thrones of the kings that
Eze 26 16 shall come down from their thrones
Dan 7 9 I beheld till thrones were placed and
Luke 22 30 may sit upon thrones, judging the
Col 1 16 whether thrones, or dominations, or
throng 2 Ma 14 46 he cast them upon the throng
Mark 3 9 lest they should throng him. For he
Luke 8 45 the multitudes throng and press thee
thronged Mark 5 24 followed him, and they t. him
Luke 8 42 he was thronged by the multitudes
thronging Mark 5 31 seest the multitude t. thee
throttled Mat 18 28 laying hold of him, he t. him
throughout Gen 13 10 which was watered throughout
Exod 34 3 maybe seen throughout all the mount
36 22 two mortises throughout every board
2 Pa 3 5 with plates of fine gold throughout
Ps 44 18 remember thy name t. all generations
71 5 before the moon t. all generations
Jer 12 9 it as a bird dyed throughout? Come
1 Ma 1 57 they built altars t. all the cities
Mat 4 24 his fame went throughout all Syria
Luke 7 17 of him went forth throughout all Judea
17 and t. all the country round about
John 19 23 woven from the top throughout. They
throw Num 35 17 if he throw a stone, and he that
Judg 2 2 but should throw down their altars
2 K 20 15 with Joab, labored to t. down the walls
19 why wilt thou t. down the inheritance
20 I do not throw down nor destroy. The
4 K 9 33 said to them: Throw her down headlong
Job 18 2 how long will you throw out words
Ecce 10 12 lips of a fool shall throw him down
Eccu 12 15 lieth in wait, to throw thee into a pit
Jer 5 10 walls thereof and throw them down
31 28 and to throw down and to scatter and
51 63 shalt throw it into the midst of the
Eze 6 4 I will throw down your altars and your
13 11 and a stormy wind to throw it down
16 39 they shall . . . throw down thy stews
32 4 and I will throw thee out on the land
Mich 5 11 will throw down all thy strongholds
Mala 1 4 shall build up, and I will throw down
1 Ma 6 62 gave commandment to throw down the wall
throweth Luke 9 39 he t. him down and teareth him
thrown Exod 15 1 rider he hath t. into the sea. 21
Deut 29 28 hath thrown them into a strange land
2 K 11 20 knew you not that many darts are t.
20 21 his head shall be thrown to thee from
3 K 19 10 they have thrown down thy altars, they
Ps 101 11 lifted me up thou hast thrown me down
Wisd 11 15 when he was thrown out at the time
18 18 one thrown here, another there, half
Isa 9 16 blessed, shall be thrown down headlong
14 31 O city, all Philistia is thrown down
50 15 her walls are thrown down, for it is
Lam 2 6 he hath thrown down his tabernacle
Eze 6 6 the high places shall be thrown down
38 20 the mountains shall be thrown down
Amos 7 9 places of the idol shall be t. down
Nah 2 6 temple is thrown down to the ground
1 Ma 4 38 joining to the temple are thrown down
6 7 they had thrown down the abomination
9 54 of the sanctuary to be thrown down
2 Ma 12 22 they were often thrown down by their
13 6 wretch to be thrown down into the ashes
Mark 9 19 being thrown down upon the ground, he
13 2 stone that shall not be t. Luke 21:6
Luke 4 35 when the devil had thrown him into
Apoc 12 9 his angels were thrown down with him
18 21 Babylon, that great city, be thrown down
thrust Gen 26 27 and have thrust out from you
Exod 11 1 he shall let you go and thrust you out
Num 22 25 thrust herself close to the wall and
25 8 thrust both of them through together
Judg 3 21 t. it into his belly with such force
11 2 they were grown up, thrust out Jephte
16 19 him away and thrust him from her
1 K 2 14 thrust it into the kettle or into the
2 K 2 16 thrust his sword into the side of his
23 in the groin and thrust him through

34 10 till, trade, and possess it. Sichem
21 let them trade in the land and till it
21 large and wide wanteth men to till it
2 K 9 10 and thy servants shall till the land
Prov 24 27 and diligently till thy ground: that
Isa 30 24 the ass colts that till the ground
Jer 27 11 they shall till it and dwell in it
tillage 1 Pa 27 26 and over the t. and the
Prov 13 23 much food is in the tillage of fathers
tilled 1 Pa 27 26 husbandmen, who t. the ground
Eze 36 34 and the desolate land shall be tilled
Amos 9 13 sweetness, and every hill shall be t.
1 Ma 14 8 every man tilled his land with peace
Heb 6 7 herbs meet for them by whom it is t.
tillers Gen 47 19 for want of t. the land be turned
Job 31 39 afflicted the soul of the tillers
tilleth Prov 12 11 t. his land shall be satisfied
Prov 28 18 that t. his ground, shall be filled
Eccu 20 30 he that tilleth his land shall make
timber Gen 6 14 make thee an ark of t. planks
Lev 14 45 and shall cast the stones and timber
3 K 5 18 the Giblians prepared timber and stones
6 10 covered the house with timber of cedar
15 22 stones from Rama and the timber thereof
4 K 6 2 every man a piece of timber, that we
5 happened as one was felling some timber
12 12 and to buy timber and stones to be
22 6 that timber may be bought, and stones
1 Pa 22 14 timber also and stones I have prepared
2 Pa 2 8 skilful in cutting timber in Libanus
9 to provide me timber in abundance
14 in iron and in marble and in timber
16 6 the timber that Baasa had prepared for
34 11 t. for the couplings of the building
1 Es 5 8 stones, and timber, is laid in the walls
6 4 stones, and so rows of new timber
2 Es 2 8 to give me timber that I may cover the
Eze 26 12 they shall lay thy stones and thy timber
Haba 2 11 the timber that is between the joints
Agge 1 8 bring timber and build the house: and
Zach 5 4 shall consume it, with the t. thereof
timbrel Exod 15 20 took a t. in her hand and
1 K 10 5 with a psaltery and a timbrel and a
Job 21 12 they take the timbrel and the harp
Ps 80 3 take a psalm and bring hither the t.
149 3 let them sing to him with the timbrel
150 4 praise him with timbrel and choir
Isa 5 12 harp, and the lyre, and the timbrel
timbrels Gen 31 27 and songs, and with timbrels
Exod 15 20 went forth after her with timbrels
Judg 11 34 his only daughter met him with timbrels
1 K 18 6 to meet king Saul, with timbrels of joy
2 K 6 5 on harps and lutes and timbrels and
1 Pa 13 8 with psalteries and timbrels, harps, and
Jdth 3 10 and lights, and dances, timbrels and flutes
16 2 begin ye to the Lord with timbrels, sing
Ps 67 26 of young damsels playing on timbrels
Isa 24 8 the mirth of timbrels hath ceased, the
30 32 to rest upon him with timbrels and harps
Jer 31 4 shalt again be adorned with thy t.
1 Ma 9 39 to meet them with timbrels, and musical
Timeus Mark 10 46 Bartimeus . . . the son of Timeus
Timon Acts 6 5 and T. and Parmenas and Nicolas
timorous Judg 7 3 whosoever is fearful and t.
Timotheus 1 Ma 5 6 and T. was their captain: and
1 Ma 5 11 Timotheus is the captain of their host
34 the host of T. understood that it was
37 T. gathered another army and camped
40 T. said to the captains of his army
2 Ma 8 30 that were with T. and Bacchides who
32 Philarches who was with Timotheus
9 3 of what had happened to Nicanor and T.
10 24 T. who before had been overcome by the
32 Timotheus fled into Gazara a stronghold
37 they killed T., who was found hid in
12 2 that were behind, namely, Timotheus and
10 and were marching towards Timotheus
18 as for Timotheus, they found him not
19 slew them that were left by T. in the
20 Machabeus . . . went forth against T.
21 when T. had knowledge of the coming of
24 T. himself fell into the hands of the
Timothy Acts 16 1 certain disciple there named T.
Acts 17 14 but Silas and Timothy remained there
15 commandment from him to Silas and T.
18 5 when Silas and Timothy were come from
19 22 two of them that ministered to him, T.
20 4 Secundus, and Gaius of Derbe, and T.
Rom 16 21 Timothy, my fellow laborer, saluteth you
1 C 4 17 for this cause have I sent to you T.
16 10 if Timothy come, see that he be with you
2 C 1 1 will of God, and Timothy our brother
19 us, by me, and Sylvanus, and Timothy
Phil 1 1 Paul and Timothy, the servants of Jesus
2 19 I hope in the Lord Jesus to send Timothy
Col 1 1 the will of God, and Timothy, a brother
1 Th 1 1 Paul and Sylvanus and Timothy. 2 Th 1:1
3 2 and we sent Timothy, our brother, and
6 when Timothy came to us from you, and
1 Tim 1 2 to Timothy, his beloved son in faith
18 precept I commend to thee, O son Timothy
6 20 O Timothy, keep that which is committed
2 Tim 1 2 to Timothy my dearly beloved son, grace
Philem 1 Timothy, a brother: to Philemon, our
Heb 13 23 our brother Timothy is set at liberty
tin Num 31 22 tin, and all that may pass through
Isa 1 25 I will take away all thy tin. And I
Eze 22 18 all these are brass and tin and iron
20 as they gather silver and brass and tin
27 12 riches, with silver, iron, tin, and lead
Zach 4 10 shall see the tin plummet in the hand
tingle 1 K 3 11 his ears shall t. 4 K 21:12; Jer 19:2
tinkling 1 C 13 1 as sounding brass or t. cymbal
tip Exod 29 20 upon the tip of the right ear. Lev 14:14, 17, 25
Lev 8 23 touched the tip of Aaron's right ear
24 he had touched the tip of the right ear
14 28 shall touch the tip of the right ear
Judg 6 21 angel of Lord put forth tip of the rod
Amos 3 12 of lion's mouth two legs or tip of ear
Luke 16 24 that he may dip the tip of his finger
tire Eze 24 17 let the tire of thy head be upon
tired Jdth 7 22 cries, and t. with these weepings
Titan Jdth 16 8 did the sons of Titan strike him
tithe Deut 14 23 the tithe of thy corn, and thy
Deut 14 28 thou shalt separate another tithe
1 K 8 17 your flocks also he will tithe, and you
2 Pa 31 5 brought the tithe of all things which
2 Es 10 38 shall offer the tithe of their tithes
13 12 all Juda brought the tithe of the corn
Mat 23 23 because you tithe mint. Luke 11:42
tithes Gen 14 20 he gave him the tithes of all
Gen 28 22 to me, I will offer tithes to thee
Exod 22 29 shalt not delay to pay thy tithes and
Lev 27 30 all tithes of the land, whether of corn
32 of all the tithes of oxen, and sheep
Num 18 21 to the sons of Levi all the tithes
24 content with the oblation or tithes
26 receive of the children of Israel the t.
28 things of which you receive tithes
29 things that you shall offer of the t.
30 better things of the tithes, and shall
Deut 12 6 t. and firstfruits of your hands. 11
17 not eat in thy towns the tithes of thy
14 22 thou shalt set aside the tithes of all
26 12 in the third year of tithes thou shalt

today Gen 24 42 I came t. to the well of water
Gen 40 7 why is your countenance sadder today
Exod 5 14 task of bricks both yesterday and today
16 25 Moses said: Eat it today because it is
25 t. it shall not be found in the field
19 10 sanctify them t. and tomorrow, and let
Lev 9 4 oil; for t. the Lord will appear to you
Josu 22 18 you have forsaken the Lord today, and
Judg 19 6 I beseech thee to stay here today
9 tarry with me today also and spend
Ruth 2 19 where hast thou gleaned today, and
1 K 2 16 the fat first be burnt today according
4 3 why hath the Lord defeated us today
9 12 he came today into the city, for there
12 is a sacrifice of the people today
13 go up, for today you shall find him
19 that you may eat with me today, and I
12 17 is it not wheat harvest today? I will
14 38 by whom this sin hath happened today
41 thou answerest not thy servant today
20 27 to meat neither yesterday nor today
22 15 did I begin today to consult the Lord
25 33 kept me today from coming to blood
27 10 whom hast thou gone against today
2 K 6 20 how glorious was king of Israel today
11 12 tarry here today, and tomorrow I will
15 20 today shalt thou be forced to go forth
16 3 today will the house of Israel restore
3 K 1 25 he is gone down today and hath killed
12 7 if thou wilt yield to this people today
4 K 4 23 today is neither new moon nor sabbath
6 28 give thy son that we may eat him today
1 Pa 29 5 let him fill his hand today, and offer
Tob 8 4 let us pray to God today and tomorrow
Esth 9 13 to do tomorrow in Susan as . . . today
Ps 94 8 today if you shall hear his voice
Eccu 10 12 a king is today, and tomorrow he shall
20 16 today a man lendeth, and tomorrow he
39 23 yesterday for me, and today for thee
Isa 56 12 it shall be as today, so also tomorrow
Jer 34 15 you turned today, and did that which
Eze 24 2 set himself against Jerusalem today
Osee 4 5 and thou shalt fall today, and the
Zach 9 12 will render thee double as I declare t.
1 Ma 2 63 today he is lifted up, and tomorrow he
3 17 we are ready to faint with fasting t.
5 32 fight ye today for your brethren
7 42 destroy this army in our sight today
Mat 6 30 grass of the field, which is today and
16 3 today there will be a storm, for the
21 28 son, go work today in my vineyard. And
Mark 14 30 today, even in this night, before the
Luke 5 26 we have seen wonderful things today
12 28 the grass that is today in the field
13 32 and do cures today and tomorrow, and
33 I must walk today and tomorrow, and
24 21 today is the third day since these
Heb 1 5 thou art my Son, today have I begotten
3 7 t. if you shall hear his voice. 15; 4:7
13 whilst it is called today, that none of
4 7 today, after so long a time, as it is
13 8 Jesus Christ yesterday and today and
James 4 13 today or tomorrow we will go into
toe Lev 8 23 great toe of his right foot. 14:14, 17, 25, 28
toil Gen 3 17 with labor and toil shalt thou eat
1 Th 2 9 our labor and toil: working night and
2 Th 3 8 in labor and in toil we worked night and
token Gen 41 32 it is a token of the certainty
Num 17 10 that it may be kept there for a token
Josu 2 12 and give me a true token, that you
Tob 5 2 what token shall I give him? Nor did I
Ps 85 17 show me a token for good: that they
Eccu 13 32 the token of a good heart, and a good
2 Ma 6 13 it is a token of great goodness when
tokens Deut 22 15 bring with them the tokens of her
Deut 22 17 the tokens of my daughter's virginity
Wisd 2 9 let us everywhere leave tokens of joy
Isa 44 25 that make void the tokens of diviners
toes Exod 29 20 upon the thumbs and great toes
Lev 8 24 and the great toes of their right feet
Judg 1 6 him, and cut off his fingers and toes
7 having their fingers and toes cut off
2 K 21 20 and six toes on each foot, four and
1 Pa 20 6 fingers and toes were four and twenty
Dan 2 41 thou sawest the feet and the toes
42 the toes of the feet were part of iron
tolerable Mat 10 15 t. for the land of Sodom. 11:24
Mat 11 22 more t. for Tyre and Sidon. Luke 10:14
Luke 10 12 more tolerable at that day for Sodom
toll 1 Es 4 13 they will not pay tribute nor toll
1 Es 4 20 and have received tribute and toll
7 24 no authority to impose toll or tribute
Tolmai 1 Pa 3 28 Maacha the daughter of Tolmai
tomb 2 Pa 34 2 be brought to thy tomb in peace
Mark 6 29 took his body and laid it in a tomb
tombs Mat 27 53 coming out of the t. after his
Mark 5 3 who had his dwelling in the tombs and
tomorrow Gen 30 33 justice shall answer for me t.
Exod 8 10 he [Pharao] answered: Tomorrow. But he
23 thy people: tomorrow shall this sign be
29 from his servants and from his people t.
9 5 tomorrow will the Lord do this thing
18 I will cause it to rain tomorrow at this
10 4 I will bring in tomorrow the locust
13 14 thy son shall ask thee t. Deut 6:20
16 23 tomorrow is the rest of the sabbath
17 9 t. I will stand on the top of the hill
19 10 sanctify them today and tomorrow, and
32 5 tomorrow is the solemnity of the Lord
Num 11 18 tomorrow you shall eat flesh: for I have
14 25 tomorrow remove the camp, and return
16 7 putting fire in them tomorrow, put
16 stand apart before the Lord tomorrow
Josu 3 5 tomorrow the Lord will do wonders among
4 6 your children shall ask you tomorrow
21 shall ask their fathers tomorrow and
7 13 be ye sanctified against tomorrow
11 6 tomorrow at this same hour I will
22 18 tomorrow his wrath will rage against
24 tomorrow your children will say to our
27 that your children t. may not say to
Judg 6 31 let him die before tomorrow light appear
19 9 and tomorrow thou shalt depart, that
20 28 tomorrow I will deliver them into your
1 K 9 16 tomorrow about this same hour I will
11 9 tomorrow, when the sun shall be hot
19 11 this night, tomorrow thou wilt die
20 5 behold tomorrow is the new moon, and I
12 discover my father's mind tomorrow
18 tomorrow is the new moon, and thou
19 thy seat will be empty till after t.
28 19 t. thou and thy sons shall be with me
2 K 11 12 tomorrow I will send thee away. Urias
3 K 19 2 if by this hour tomorrow I make not
20 6 tomorrow . . . I will send my servants
4 K 6 28 we will eat my son tomorrow. So we
7 1 tomorrow about this time a bushel of
18 at this very time tomorrow in the gate
10 6 and come to me to Jezrahel by tomorrow
2 Pa 20 16 tomorrow you shall go down against them
17 tomorrow you shall go out against them
Tob 8 4 let us pray to God today and tomorrow
Esth 5 8 tomorrow I will open my mind to the king
12 with her I am also to dine tomorrow
9 13 be granted to the Jews to do tomorrow
Prov 3 28 tomorrow I will give to thee: when

27 1 boast not for tomorrow, for thou
Eccu 10 12 king is today, and tomorrow he shall die
Isa 22 13 and drink; for tomorrow we shall die
56 12 it shall be as today, so also tomorrow
1 Ma 2 63 and tomorrow he shall not be found
Mat 6 30 t. is cast into the oven. Luke 12:28
34 be not therefore solicitous for t.
Luke 13 32 and do cures today and tomorrow, and
33 I must walk today and tomorrow, and
Acts 23 20 that thou wouldst bring forth Paul t.
25 22 tomorrow, said he, thou shalt hear him
1 C 15 32 eat and drink, for tomorrow we shall die
James 4 13 today or tomorrow we will go into
tongs Exod 27 3 tongs and fleshhooks and firepans
Exod 38 3 divers vessels of brass, cauldrons, tongs
Num 4 9 candlestick with the lamps and tongs
2 Pa 4 21 and lamps and golden tongs: all were
Isa 6 6 which he had taken with the tongs
tongue Gen 10 5 every one according to his tongue
Gen 11 1 the earth was of one tongue, and of
6 it is one people, and all have one t.
7 go down and there confound their t.
41 45 called him in the Egyptian tongue
Exod 4 10 more impediment and slowness of t.
Deut 28 49 whose tongue thou canst not understand
Josu 10 21 no man durst move his tongue against
2 K 23 2 by me and his word by my tongue. The
4 K 18 26 we understand that tongue: and speak
2 Pa 32 18 with a loud voice, in the Jews' tongue
1 Es 4 7 and was read in the Syrian tongue
Job 5 21 hidden from the scourge of the tongue
6 30 you shall not find iniquity in my tongue
15 5 imitatest the tongue of blasphemers
20 12 mouth, he will hide it under his tongue
16 and the viper's tongue shall kill him
27 4 neither shall my tongue contrive lying
29 10 their tongue cleaved to their throat
33 2 let my tongue speak within my jaws
40 20 canst thou tie his tongue with a cord
Ps 9 7 under his tongue are labor and sorrow
11 4 the tongue that speaketh proud things
5 have said: We will magnify our tongue
14 3 who hath not used deceit in his tongue
15 9 and my tongue hath rejoiced: moreover
21 16 my tongue hath cleaved to my jaws
33 14 keep thy tongue from evil, and thy lips
34 28 my tongue shall meditate thy justice
36 30 his tongue shall speak judgment. The
38 2 ways: that I sin not with my tongue
5 I spoke with my tongue: O Lord, make
44 2 my tongue is the pen of a scrivener
49 19 evils, and thy tongue framed deceits
50 16 my tongue shall extol thy justice
51 4 thy tongue hath devised injustice
6 loved all words of ruin, O deceitful t.
56 5 arrows, and their tongue a sharp sword
65 17 mouth: I extolled him with my tongue
67 24 tongue of thy dogs be red with the same
70 24 my tongue shall meditate on thy justice
72 9 their t. hath passed through the earth
77 36 with their tongue they lied unto him
80 6 he heard a tongue which he knew not
118 172 my tongue shall pronounce thy word
119 2 from wicked lips and a deceitful tongue
3 be added to thee, to a deceitful tongue
125 2 with gladness; and our tongue with joy
136 6 let my tongue cleave to my jaws, if I
138 4 for there is no speech in my tongue
139 12 a man full of tongue shall not be
Prov 6 17 haughty eyes, a lying tongue, hands that
24 from the flattering t. of the stranger
8 13 I hate . . . mouth with a double tongue
10 20 tongue of the just is as choice silver
31 the tongue of the perverse shall perish
12 18 but the tongue of the wise is health
19 hasty witness, frameth a lying tongue
15 2 tongue of the wise adorneth knowledge
4 a peaceable tongue is a tree of life
16 1 soul: and of the Lord to govern the t.
17 4 evil man obeyeth an unjust tongue
20 he that perverteth his tongue, shall
21 6 gathereth treasures by a lying tongue
23 that keepeth his mouth and his tongue
25 15 a soft tongue shall break hardness
23 doth a sad countenance a backbiting t.
26 28 a deceitful tongue loveth not truth
28 23 by a flattering tongue deceiveth him
31 26 the law of clemency is on her tongue
Cant 4 11 honey and milk are under thy tongue
Wisd 1 6 of his heart and a hearer of his tongue
11 refrain your tongue from detraction
Eccu 4 29 by the tongue wisdom is discerned
34 be not hasty in thy tongue: and slack
5 11 every sinner proved by a double tongue
15 the tongue of the fool is his ruin
16 whisperer, and be not taken in thy t.
6 5 a gracious t. in a good man aboundeth
8 4 strive not with man that is full of t.
9 25 a man full of tongue is terrible in
17 5 he gave them counsel and a tongue
19 16 is one that slippeth with the tongue
17 that hath not offended with his tongue
20 18 that eat his bread are of a false tongue
20 slipping of a false tongue is as one
21 8 he that is mighty by a bold tongue
22 33 them, and that my t. destroy me not
25 9 I will utter to men with my tongue
11 that hath not slipped with his tongue
27 so is a wife full of tongue to quiet
26 9 with a jealous woman is a scourge of t.
28 13 t. that beareth witness bringeth death
16 t. of a third person hath disquieted
19 tongue of a third person hath cast out
21 stroke of the t. will break the bones
22 as have perished by their own tongue
23 that is defended from a wicked tongue
28 hear not a wicked tongue, and make
30 take heed lest thou slip with thy tongue
36 25 if she have a tongue that can cure
37 21 tongue is continually the ruler of them
40 21 a pleasant tongue is above them both
51 3 from the snare of an unjust tongue
7 from an unclean tongue and from lying
7 king, and from a slanderous tongue
30 hath given me a tongue for my reward
Isa 3 8 their t. and their devices are against
5 24 as t. of the fire devoureth the stubble
11 15 waste the tongue of the sea of Egypt
28 11 with another tongue he will speak
30 27 his tongue as a devouring fire. His
32 4 t. of stammerers shall speak readily
33 19 not understand the eloquence of his t.
35 6 the tongue of the dumb shall be free
36 11 speak to thy servants in the Syrian t.
41 17 their tongue hath been dry with thirst
45 24 to me, and every tongue shall swear
50 4 the Lord hath given me a learned tongue
54 17 every tongue that resisteth thee in
57 4 your mouth wide, and put out your t.
59 3 lies, and your tongue uttereth iniquity
Jer 9 3 they have bent their tongue, as a bow
5 have taught their tongue to speak lies
8 their tongue is a piercing arrow, it
18 18 let us strike him with the tongue, and
Lam 4 4 t. of the sucking child hath stuck to
Bar 4 15 wicked nation, and of a strange tongue

6 7 their tongue that is polished by the
Eze 3 5 of an unknown tongue, but to the house
6 strange speech and of an unknown t.
26 I will make thy tongue stick fast to
Dan 1 4 might teach them . . . t. of the Chaldeans
3 96 that every people, tribe, and tongue
Osee 7 16 the sword, for the rage of their tongue
Mich 6 12 their t. was deceitful in their mouth
Soph 3 13 nor shall a deceitful tongue be found
Zach 14 12 their tongue shall consume away in
2 Ma 7 3 commanded to cut out the t. of him that
10 he quickly put forth his tongue, and
15 33 that the tongue of the wicked Nicanor
Mark 7 33 and spitting, he touched his tongue
35 the string of his tongue was loosed
Luke 1 64 mouth was opened, and his t. loosed
16 24 finger in water, to cool my tongue
Acts 1 19 was called in their tongue, Haceldama
2 6 heard them speak in his own tongue
8 have we heard every man our own t.
26 been glad, and my tongue hath rejoiced
14 10 lifted up their voice in Lycaonian t.
21 40 spoke unto them in the Hebrew t. 22:2
26 14 voice speaking to me in the Hebrew t.
Rom 14 11 and every tongue shall confess to God
1 C 14 2 he that speaketh in a tongue. 4
9 except you utter by the t. plain speech
13 he that speaketh by a t., let him pray
14 if I pray in a tongue, my spirit prayeth
19 you also; than 10,000 words in a tongue
26 hath a tongue, hath an interpretation
27 if any speak with a tongue, let it be
Phil 2 11 that every tongue should confess that
James 1 26 not bridling his tongue, but deceiving
3 5 the tongue is indeed a little member
6 the tongue is a fire, a world of
6 tongue is placed among our members
8 but the tongue no man can tame, an
1 Pa 3 10 let him refrain his tongue from evil
1 J 3 18 let us not love in word nor in tongue
Apoc 5 9 out of every tribe and tongue and
13 7 over every tribe and people and tongue
14 6 over every nation and tribe and tongue
tongued Prov 18 8 words of the double tongued
Eccu 5 17 mark of disgrace upon the double t.
28 15 the double tongued is accursed: for he
1 Tim 3 8 not double t., not given to much wine
tongues Gen 10 20 Cham in their kindreds and t.
Gen 10 31 according to their kindreds and tongues
Judg 7 5 that shall lap the water with their t.
Ps 5 11 they dealt deceitfully with their t.
13 3 with their t. they acted deceitfully
30 21 from the contradiction of tongues
54 10 and divide their tongues: for I have
63 4 have whetted their tongues like a sword
9 their tongues against them are made weak
108 3 spoken against me with deceitful tongues
139 4 they have sharpened their tongues
Wisd 10 21 made the tongues of infants eloquent
Isa 66 18 them together with all nations and t.
Jer 23 31 who use their tongues, and say: The
Dan 3 98 to all peoples, nations, and tongues
7 14 all peoples, tribes and t. shall serve
Mark 16 17 they shall speak with new tongues
Acts 2 3 parted tongues as it were of fire, and
4 began to speak with divers tongues
11 heard them speak in our own tongues
10 46 they heard them speaking with tongues
19 6 they spoke with tongues and prophesied
Rom 3 13 their t. they have dealt deceitfully
1 C 12 10 to another, diverse kinds of tongues
28 helps, governments, kinds of tongues
30 do all speak with t.? Do all interpret
13 1 if I speak with the tongues of men, and
8 tongues shall cease, or knowledge shall
14 5 have you all to speak with tongues, but
5 than he that speaketh with tongues
6 if I come to you speaking with tongues
10 so many kinds of tongues in this world
18 I thank my God I speak with all your t.
21 in other t. and other lips I will speak
22 tongues are for a sign, not to believers
23 one place, and all speak with tongues
39 and forbid not to speak with tongues
Apoc 7 9 and tribes and peoples and tongues
10 11 and peoples and tongues and kings
11 9 they of the tribes and peoples and t.
16 10 and they gnawed their tongues for pain
17 15 are peoples and nations and tongues
tonight Gen 19 34 him drink wine also tonight
too Gen 39 19 giving too much credit to his wife's
Exod 36 7 offered did suffice and were too much
Lev 11 6 for that too cheweth the cud, but
Num 11 14 people, because it is too heavy for me
16 7 you take too much upon you, ye sons of
Deut 19 6 if the way be too long and take away the
tool Exod 20 25 if thou lift up a tool upon it
3 K 6 7 nor any tool of iron heard in the house
tooth Exod 21 24 eye for eye, t. for t. Deut 19:21
Exod 21 27 also if he strike out a tooth of his
Lev 24 20 tooth for tooth, shall he restore
Judg 15 19 opened a great tooth in jaw of the ass
Prov 25 19 is like a rotten tooth and weary foot
Mat 5 38 eye for an eye, and a tooth for a tooth
top Gen 6 16 in a cubit shalt thou finish the top
Gen 11 4 the top whereof may reach to heaven
28 12 the top thereof touching heaven: the
18 title, pouring oil upon the top of it
44 1 money of every one in top of his sack
8 that we found in the top of our sacks
Exod 17 9 I will stand on the top of the hill
10 Hur went up upon the top of the hill
19 20 Sinai, in the very top of the mount
20 he called Moses unto the top thereof
24 17 a burning fire upon the top of the mount
26 7 to cover the top of the tabernacle
24 joined together from beneath unto top
28 7 two edges joined in top on both sides
23 in the two ends at top of the rational
26 which thou shalt put in the top parts
34 2 stand with me upon the top of the mount
36 29 were joined from beneath unto the top
37 8 one cherub in the top of one side
8 other cherub in top of the other side
38 5 at four ends of the net at the top
39 4 one to the other in the top on either
Num 14 40 went up to the top of the mountain. 44
20 29 Aaron being dead in top of the mountain
21 20 to the top of Phasga, which looked
23 14 place, upon top of mount Phasga, Balaam
28 brought him upon the top of mount Phogor
28 35 from sole of foot to top of the head
Deut 3 27 go up to the top of Phasga, and cast
33 20 seized upon arm and top of the head
34 1 to the top of Phasga over against Jericho
Josu 15 2 beginning was from top of most salt sea
8 ascending to the top of the mountain
9 it passeth on from top of the mountain
Judg 6 26 to the Lord thy God in top of this rock
9 7 stood on top of mount Garizim: and
25 against him on the top of the mountains
16 3 carried them to the top of the hill
1 K 9 25 he spoke with Saul upon top of the house
25 a bed for Saul on the top of the house
26 Samuel called Saul on the top of house
26 13 stood on the top of the hill afar off

2 K 2 25 body, they stood on the top of a hill
15 32 David was come to top of the mountain
16 22 tent for Absalom on top of the house
18 24 watchman that was on the top of gate
3 K 6 15 to the top of the walls and to the roofs
16 of the temple, from floor to the top
7 7 cedar wood from the floor to the top
9 from foundation to top of the walls
18 the chapiters, that were upon the top
19 that were upon the top of the pillars
20 other chapiters in top of the pillars
31 within: was in the top of the chapiter
35 in top of the base there was a round
41 that were upon the top of the pillars
10 19 the top of the throne was round behind
18 42 Elias went up to the top of Carmel
4 K 1 9 as he was sitting on the top of a hill
12 9 took a chest and bored a hole in the top
19 23 to the top of Libanus, and have cut down
23 12 the top of the upper chamber of Achaz
2 Pa 25 12 cast them down headlong from the top
2 Es 8 16 every man on the top of his house
Tob 11 5 beside the way daily on the top of a hill
Esth 5 2 and kissed the top of his scepter. And
Jdth 7 3 they came by the hillside to the top
Job 2 7 of the foot even to the top of his head
Ps 73 5 in the going out and on the highest top
Prov 8 2 standing in the top of the highest
Cant 4 8 shalt be crowned from the top of Amana
8 from the top of Sanir and Hermon, from
Eccu 40 15 as unclean roots upon the top of a rock
Isa 1 6 from sole of foot unto the top of head
2 2 shall be prepared on top of mountains
17 6 or three berries in the top of a bough, or four or five upon the top of the tree
30 17 mast of ship on the top of a mountain
37 23 the mountains, to the top of Libanus
24 and will enter to the top of its height
42 11 shall cry from the top of the mountains
Lam 2 19 for hunger at the top of all the streets
4 1 scattered in the top of every street
Eze 17 4 he cropped off the top of the twigs
22 tender twig from the top of the branches
31 3 his top was elevated among the thick
8 the fir trees did not equal his top
10 and shot up his top green and thick
43 12 the house upon the top of the mountain
Dan 11 45 he shall come even to the top thereof
14 35 Lord took him by the top of his head
Osee 9 10 of the fig tree in the top thereof
Amos 1 2 the top of Carmel is withered. Thus
9 3 though they be hid in the top of Carmel
Mich 4 1 be prepared in the top of mountains
Nah 3 10 dashed in pieces at top of every street
Zach 4 2 and its lamp upon the top of it: and
2 lights that were upon the top thereof
2 Ma 15 35 Nicanor's head in the top of the castle
Mat 27 51 from the top even to bottom. Mark 15:38
John 19 23 woven from the top throughout. They
Heb 11 21 Joseph, and adored the top of his rod
topaz Exod 28 17 a sardius stone and a topaz
Exod 39 10 was a sardius, a topaz, an emerald
Job 28 19 topaz of Ethiopia shall not be equal
Ps 118 127 thy commandments above gold and the t.
Eze 28 13 thy covering: the sardius, the topaz
Apoc 21 20 the ninth, a topaz: the tenth, a
Topheth 4 K 23 10 he defiled T., which is in the
Isa 30 33 Topheth is prepared from yesterday
Jer 7 31 have built the high places of Topheth
32 it shall no more be called Topheth
32 they shall bury in Topheth because
19 6 this place shall no more be called T.
11 and they shall be buried in Topheth
12 and I will make this city as Topheth
13 shall be unclean as the place of Topheth
14 then Jeremias came from T., whither
tops Gen 8 5 the tops of the mountains appeared
Exod 26 4 loops of violet in the sides and tops
Num 23 9 I shall see him from the tops of rocks
Deut 33 15 of the tops of the ancient mountains
2 K 5 8 to the gutters of the tops of houses
24 one going in the tops of the pear trees
3 K 7 16 to be set upon the tops of the pillars
22 upon tops of pillars he made lily work
42 which were upon the tops of the pillars
4 K 19 26 the green herb on the tops of houses
1 Pa 14 15 one going in the tops of the pear trees
Jdth 4 3 seized upon all the t. of the mountains
Job 24 24 as the tops of the ears of corn shall
Ps 71 16 on the earth on the tops of mountains
128 6 be as grass upon the tops of houses
Eccu 43 21 shall become like the tops of thistles
Isa 15 3 sackcloth: on the tops of their houses
Eze 6 13 hill, and on all the tops of mountains
31 14 nor shoot up their tops among the thick
Osee 4 13 offered sacrifice upon the tops of the
Joel 2 5 chariots upon the tops of mountains
Soph 1 5 hosts of heaven upon the t. of houses
torch Eccu 48 1 his word burnt like a torch
2 Ma 4 22 and came in with torch lights and with
Apoc 8 10 burning as it were a torch, and it fell
torches Judg 15 4 fastened t. between the tails
Job 41 10 lamps, like torches of lighted fire
Nah 2 4 their looks are like t., like lightning
John 18 3 cometh thither with lanterns and t.
tore Judg 8 16 and tore them with the same and cut
Judg 14 6 he tore the lion as he would have torn
4 K 2 24 and tore of them two and forty boys
Luke 9 42 the devil threw him down and t. him
torment Wisd 3 1 t. of death shall not touch them
Wisd 17 12 that cause which bringeth the torment
1 Ma 9 56 Alcimus died at that time in great t.
2 Ma 6 19 went forward voluntarily to the torment
7 17 he will torment thee and thy seed
Mat 8 29 hither to torment us before the time
Mark 5 7 I adjure thee . . . that thou t. me not
Luke 8 28 I beseech thee, do not torment me
Apoc 9 5 they should torment them five months
5 their t. was as the t. of a scorpion
18 7 so much torment and sorrow give ye to
tormented Job 9 27 my face, and am t. with sorrow
Ecce 2 22 with which he hath been tormented under
Wisd 6 7 the mighty shall be mightily tormented
11 10 wicked were judged with wrath and t.
12 absent or present, they were t. alike
17 sinneth, by the same also he is t.
12 23 hast also greatly tormented them who
2 Ma 7 1 they were tormented with whips and
13 dead, they t. the fourth in the like
15 brought the fifth, they t. him. But
9 6 he had t. the bowels of others with
Mat 8 6 palsy, and is grievously tormented
Luke 16 24 for I am tormented in this flame
25 now he is comforted, and thou art t.
2 P 2 9 unto the day of judgment to be t.
Apoc 11 10 these two prophets t. them that dwelt
14 10 shall be t. with fire and brimstone
18 10 the false prophet shall be tormented
tormentest Job 10 16 thou t. me wonderfully
tormenting Job 17 11 are dissipated, t. my heart
tormentor 2 Ma 7 29 thou shalt not fear this t.
torments Jdth 6 13 to be put to death by diverse t.
Wisd 3 4 in sight of men they suffered torments
14 10 with him that made it, shall suffer t.
19 4 what was wanting to their torments
Eccu 39 33 in their fury they lay on grievous t.

15 5 if any man touch his bed, he shall wash
11 every person whom such a one shall t.
12 if he touch a vessel of earth it shall
23 shall touch any vessel on which she
Num 4 15 they shall not touch the vessels of the
16 26 touch nothing of theirs, lest you be
19 16 if any man in the field t. the corpse
21 every one that shall touch the waters
Deut 14 8 their carcasses you shall not touch
Josu 2 19 upon our head if any man touch them
6 18 lest you touch ought of those things
9 19 and therefore we may not touch them
Judg 13 5 and no razor shall touch his head
15 26 suffer me to touch the pillars which
2 K 14 10 and he shall not touch thee any more
23 7 if a man will touch them, he must be
1 Pa 16 22 touch not my anointed and do no evil to
Tob 2 21 or to t. anything that cometh by theft
Jdth 11 12 which God forbade them to touch, in
12 things which they ought not to touch
Job 1 11 touch all that he hath, and see if he
2 5 and touch his bone and his flesh, and
5 19 in the seventh, evil shall not t. thee
6 7 which before my soul would not touch
20 6 heaven, and his head touch the clouds
Ps 104 15 t. ye not my anointed: and do no evil
143 5 touch the mountains, and they shall
Prov 6 29 not be clean when he shall touch her
23 10 touch not the bounds of little ones
Cant 5 4 my bowels were moved at his touch
Wisd 3 1 torment of death shall not touch them
Isa 52 11 touch no unclean thing: go out of the
Jer 12 14 that touch the inheritance that I
Lam 4 15 depart, get ye hence, touch not: for
Bar 6 28 menstruous women t. their sacrifices
Eze 17 10 when the burning wind shall touch it
41 6 not to touch the wall of the temple
Agge 2 13 and touch with his skirt, bread or
14 touch any of all these, shall it be
Mat 9 21 I shall t. only his garment. Mark 5:28
14 36 they might t. but the hem. Mark 6:56
Mark 3 10 they pressed upon him for to touch him
8 22 besought him that he would touch him
10 13 children, that he might touch them
Luke 6 19 multitude sought to touch him, for
11 46 yourselves touch not the packs with
18 15 infants, that he might touch them
John 20 17 do not touch me, for I am not yet
1 C 7 1 is good for a man not to touch a woman
2 C 6 17 Lord, and touch not the unclean thing
Col 2 21 touch not, taste not, handle not: which
Heb 11 28 the firstborn, might not touch them. By
12 20 so much as a beast shall t. the mount
touched Gen 6 6 being t. inwardly with sorrow
Gen 20 4 Abimelech had not touched her, and he
26 29 have touched nothing of thine, nor have
32 25 he touched the sinew of his thigh. 32
Exod 4 25 her son, and touched his feet and said
Lev 7 19 that hath touched any unclean thing
21 that hath touched the uncleanness of man
8 15 he touched the horns of the altar. 9:9
23 touched the tip of Aaron's right ear
24 had touched the tip of the right ear of
11 38 it be touched by the carcasses, it shall
Num 31 19 killed a man or t. one that is killed
Deut 27 5 stones which iron hath not t. Josu 8:31
30 1 thou shalt be t. with repentance of thy
Judg 6 5 camels, wasting whatsoever they touched
21 t. the flesh and the unleavened loaves
10 16 he was touched with their miseries
1 K 6 9 that it is not his hand hath touched us
10 26 of the army, whose hearts God had t.
3 K 6 27 wing of one t. one wall, and the wing of
the other cherub t. the other wall
27 of the temple touched one another
19 5 an angel of the Lord touched him and
7 came again the second time and t. him
4 K 5 11 t. with his hand the place of leprosy
13 21 when it had t. the bones of Eliseus
1 Pa 13 10 him, because he had touched the ark
2 Pa 3 12 and t. the wing of the other cherub
Job 4 5 it hath t. thee, and thou art troubled
19 21 the hand of the Lord hath touched me
Wisd 18 20 touched by an assault of death and
Isa 6 7 he touched my mouth and said: Behold
7 behold this hath touched thy lips and
9 1 land of Nephtali was lightly touched
Jer 1 9 forth his hand and touched my mouth
4 18 because it hath touched thy heart. My
Dan 3 50 the fire touched them not at all, nor
8 5 and he touched not the ground and
18 he touched me and set me upright, and
9 21 flying swiftly touched me at the time
10 10 and behold a hand t. me and lifted me
16 of a son of man touched my lips: then
18 that looked like a man touched me again
Osee 4 2 overflowed, and blood hath t. blood
Mich 1 9 it hath t. the gate of my people even
Mat 8 3 forth his hand, touched him. Luke 5:13
15 he touched her hand, and the fever
9 20 and touched the hem of his garment
9 he touched their eyes. 20:34
14 36 as many as touched were made whole
17 7 Jesus came and touched them: and said
Mark 5 27 behind him and touched his garment
30 said: Who hath touched my garments
31 and sayest thou who hath touched me
6 56 as many as touched him were made whole
7 33 and spitting, he touched his tongue
Luke 7 14 he came near and touched the bier
8 44 and touched the hem of his garment
45 Jesus said: Who is it that touched me
45 and dost thou say, Who touched me
46 Jesus said: Somebody hath touched me
47 for what cause she had touched him
22 51 when he had touched his ear, he healed
Heb 12 18 not come to a mountain that might be t.
toucheth Exod 19 12 every one that t. the mount
Lev 5 2 whosoever toucheth any unclean thing
6 18 that toucheth them shall be sanctified
11 26 he that toucheth it, shall be defiled
31 he that toucheth their carcasses. 36
39 he that toucheth the carcass thereof
15 7 he that toucheth his flesh, shall wash
20 every one that toucheth her, shall be
22 he that toucheth her bed shall wash
27 whosoever toucheth them shall wash his
22 4 he that toucheth anything unclean
5 he that toucheth a creeping thing
Num 19 11 that toucheth the corpse of a man. 19:13
22 whatsoever a person t. who is unclean
22 person that t. any of these things
Ps 103 32 he t. the mountains, and they smoke
Eccu 13 1 he that t. pitch, shall be defiled
22 2 everyone that toucheth him will shake
34 30 if he t. him again, what doth his
Amos 9 5 is he who toucheth the earth and it
Zach 2 8 that t. you, t. the apple of my eye
Luke 7 39 of woman this is that toucheth him
1 J 5 18 and the wicked one toucheth him not
touching Gen 28 12 the top thereof touching heaven
Lev 4 25 t. therewith the horns of the altar
13 59 law touching the leprosy of any woolen
22 5 thing, the touching of which is defiling
Num 4 19 not die, by t. the holies of holies
8 22 commanded Moses touching the Levites

27 order the Levites touching their charge
19 18 that are defiled with t. any such thing
36 6 the Lord t. the daughters of Salphaad
Eccu 34 30 washeth himself after t. the dead, if
37 12 touching her of whom she is jealous
Jer 1 16 against them, t. all their wickedness
2 Ma 11 36 touching such things as he thought
Mark 1 41 t. him, saith to him: I will. Be thou
Acts 5 35 intend to do as touching these men
11 22 church that was at Jerusalem, t. these
21 25 as t. the Gentiles that believe, we
23 15 something more certain t. him. 20
26 2 t. all the things whereof I am accused
Rom 11 28 but as t. the election, they are most
1 C 16 12 touching our brother Apollo, I give you
Col 4 10 Barnabas, t. whom you have received
1 Th 4 9 as touching the charity of brotherhood
tow Judg 16 9 a man would break a thread of tow
Eccu 21 10 congregation of sinners is like tow
Isa 1 31 your strength shall be as ashes of tow
Dan 3 46 brimstone, and tow, and pitch, and dry
towel John 13 4 having taken a t. girded himself
John 13 5 and to wipe them with the towel
tower Gen 11 4 let us make a city and a tower
Gen 11 5 came down to see the city and the tower
35 21 pitched his tent beyond the Flock tower
Judg 8 9 in peace, I will destroy this tower
17 he demolished the tower of Phanuel
9 46 who dwelt in the t. of Sichem had heard
47 that the men of the tower of Sichem
49 of the inhabitants of the t. of Sichem
51 upon the battlements of the tower to
51 in the mist of the city a high tower
52 Abimelech coming near the tower, fought
4 K 9 17 that stood upon the tower of Jezrahel
15 25 in the tower of the king's house, near
17 9 from the tower of the watchmen. 18:8
2 Pa 20 24 when Juda came to the watch tower, that
2 Es 2 8 that I may cover the gates of the tower
3 1 even unto the tower of a hundred cubits
1 sanctified it unto the t. of Hananeel
11 the street and the tower of the furnaces
25 over against the bending and the tower
26 the east, and the tower that stood out
27 from the great tower that standeth out
12 37 and upon the tower of the furnaces
38 above fish gate and tower of Hananeel
38 and the tower of Emath and even to the
Ps 60 4 t. of strength against face of the enemy
Prov 9 3 sent her maids to invite to the tower
18 10 the name of the Lord is a strong tower
Cant 4 4 thy neck is as the tower of David
7 4 thy neck as a tower of ivory. Thy eyes
4 thy nose is as the tower of Libanus
8 10 my breasts are as a tower since I am
Isa 2 15 and upon every high tower and every
5 2 built a tower in the midst thereof
30 25 of many, when the tower shall fall
Jer 31 38 from the tower of Hanameel even to the
Eze 29 10 from the tower of Syene. 30:6
Mich 4 8 thou, O cloudy tower of the flock
Haba 2 1 fix my foot upon the tower: and I
Zach 14 10 from the tower of Hananeel even to
1 Ma 13 43 and he struck one tower and took it
2 Ma 13 5 in that place a tower fifty cubits high
Mat 21 33 dug in it a press and built a tower and
Mark 12 1 and built a tower, and let it out to
Luke 13 4 upon whom the tower fell in Siloe
14 28 having a mind to build a tower, doth
towers 2 Pa 14 7 fortify them with t. and gates
2 Pa 17 12 he built in Juda houses like towers
26 9 and Ozias built towers in Jerusalem
10 and he built towers in the wilderness
15 which he placed in the towers and in
27 4 and castles and towers in the forests
32 5 broken down, and built towers upon it
36 19 burnt all the towers and whatsoever
Jdth 1 2 towers thereof he made 100 cubits high
3 according to the height of the towers
Ps 47 13 encompass her: tell ye in her towers
121 7 strength: and abundance in thy towers
Lam 2 7 hath delivered the walls of the towers
Eze 26 4 walls of Tyre, and destroy the towers
9 shall destroy thy towers with his arms
27 11 Pygmeans also that were in thy towers
Soph 3 6 their towers are beaten down: I have
1 Ma 4 60 strong t. round about lest the Gentiles
5 5 they were shut up by him in towers
5 and burnt their towers with fire and
65 he burnt the walls thereof and the t.
6 37 there were strong wooden towers which
13 33 fortifying them with high towers and
16 10 they fled even to the towers that were
2 Ma 10 18 some were fled into very strong towers
20 money by some that were in the towers
22 and forthwith took the two towers
36 to set fire to the towers and the gates
town Gen 24 11 made camels lie down without the t.
Gen 33 18 Syria: and he [Jacob] dwelt by the town
44 13 their asses again, returned into the t.
Lev 14 45 all the dust without the town into an
Num 22 36 to meet him in a town of the Moabites
34 4 shall go out to the town called Adar and
Deut 2 36 a town that is situate in a valley, as
3 4 there was not a town that escaped us
Josu 7 2 on the east side of the town of Bethel
8 1 men, arise and go up to the town of Hai
10 2 cities, and greater than the town of Hai
13 17 Bamothbaal, and the town of Baalmaon
18 24 the town Emona and Ophni and Gabee
Judg 6 28 when the men of that town were risen
9 20 of Sichem and the town of Mello: and
20 of Sichem and from the town of Mello
50 thence came to the town of Thebes
14 5 were come to the vineyards of the town
19 12 will not go into town of an other nation
21 19 on the south of the town of Lebona
1 K 9 25 from the high place into the town, and
4 K 14 11 one another in Bethsames a town in Juda
Esth 9 2 together in every city and town and
Haba 2 12 to him that buildeth a town with blood
2 Ma 14 16 and went to the town of Dessau to meet
Mat 10 11 city or town you shall enter, inquire
Mark 8 23 hand, he led him out of the town; and
26 if thou enter into the town, tell
Luke 5 17 were come out of every town of Galilee
9 56 and they went into another town. And
10 38 he entered into a certain town. 17:12
19 30 go into the town which is over against
24 13 to a town which was sixty furlongs
28 they drew nigh to the town whither
John 7 42 Bethlehem the town where David was
11 1 the town of Mary and Martha her sister
30 Jesus was not yet come into the town
Acts 19 35 when the town clerk had appeased the
towns Gen 13 12 Lot abode in the towns that were
Gen 25 16 their names by their castles and t.
Num 35 3 that they may abide in the towns and
8 each shall give towns to the Levites
Deut 3 5 innumerable towns that had no walls
14 Havoth Jair . . . t. of Jair. Judg 10:4
12 17 mayst not eat in thy towns the tithes
21 commanded thee, and shalt eat in thy t.
Josu 8 17 leaving the t. open as they had rushed
10 37 and all towns of that country and all
39 the towns round about he destroyed

13 30 which are in Basan, threescore towns
15 9 reacheth to towns of mount Ephron: and
45 Accaron with the towns and villages
47 Gaza with its towns and villages, even
47 Azotus with its towns and villages
17 11 inhabitants of Dor, with the towns
16 are situate Bethsan with its towns
2 K 2 3 and they abode in the towns of Hebron
3 K 4 13 Galaad he had the towns of Jair the
9 19 all the towns that belonged to himself
12 to see the towns which Solomon had
1 Pa 2 23 Gessur and Aram the towns of Jair and
4 32 their towns also were Etam and Aen
5 16 in Basan and in the towns thereof and
6 54 dwelling places by the t. and confines
9 22 were registered in their proper towns
2 Pa 26 6 and he [Ozias] built towns in Azotus
Jdth 4 4 they compassed their towns with walls
Esth 4 3 in all provinces, towns, and places
9 19 those Jews that dwelt in towns not
1 Ma 5 8 he took the city of Gazer and her towns
65 he took Chebron and her towns: and he
7 46 forth out of all the towns of Judea
2 Ma 8 1 went privately into the towns: and
6 coming unawares upon the towns and
Mat 9 35 Jesus went about all the cities and t.
14 15 going into the towns, they may buy
Mark 1 38 into the neighboring towns and cities
6 36 going into the next villages and towns
56 he entered, into towns or into villages
8 27 into the towns of Caesarea Philippi
Luke 8 1 travelled through the cities and towns
9 6 they went about through the towns
12 into the towns and villages round
13 22 he went through the cities and towns
trace Wisd 2 3 pass away as the trace of a cloud
Wisd 5 10 is gone by, the trace cannot be found
Eccu 21 7 walketh in the trace of a sinner: and
traces Eccu 42 19 revealeth the t. of hidden things
traceth Eccu 14 23 after her as one that traceth
Trachonitis Luke 3 1 Iturea and the country of T.
trade Gen 34 10 till, trade, and possess it
Gen 34 21 let them trade in the land and till it
Luke 19 13 and said to them: Trade till I come
Acts 18 3 and because he was of the same trade
3 now they were tentmakers by trade. And
19 25 you know that our gain is by this trade
traded Mat 25 16 traded with the same and gained
traders Isa 23 8 her t. the nobles of the earth
trades 1 Pa 22 15 of all trades the most skilful
trading Luke 19 15 much every man had gained by t.
tradition Mat 15 2 thy disciples transgress the t.
Mat 15 3 the commandment of God for your t. 6
Mark 7 3 holding the tradition of the ancients
5 according to the t. of the ancients
8 you hold the tradition of men, the
9 that you may keep your own tradition
13 the word of God by your own tradition
Col 2 8 vain deceit; according to the t. of man
2 Th 3 6 tradition which they have received of us
1 P 1 18 conversation of the t. of your fathers
traditions Acts 6 14 shall change the t. which
Gal 1 14 zealous for the traditions of my fathers
2 Th 2 14 hold the t. which you have learned
traffic Prov 31 18 and seen that her t. is good
Eccu 37 12 nor with a merchant about traffic nor
Isa 23 17 will bring her back again to her t.
Eze 27 15 many islands were the t. of thy hand
28 5 by thy traffic, thou hast increased thy
18 and by the iniquity of thy traffic
John 2 16 house of my Father a house of traffic
James 4 13 and will traffic and make our gain
trail Deut 32 24 creatures that t. upon the ground
traileth Lev 11 42 many feet, or t. on the earth
train Gen 50 9 in his t., chariots and horsemen
3 K 10 2 entering into Jerusalem with great t.
4 K 5 15 to the man of God with all his train
2 Pa 10 8 brought up with him and were in his t.
Esth 15 7 bearing up her train flowing on ground
Isa 6 1 elevated: his train filled the temple
trained Deut 8 5 so the Lord thy God hath t. thee
Judg 3 2 their enemies, and to be t. up to war
1 Pa 5 18 bending the bow and t. up to battles
1 Ma 4 7 them, and these were trained up to war
6 30 and 32 elephants trained to battle
traineth Deut 8 5 that as a man t. up his son
traitor 1 K 22 13 continuing a traitor to this day
Esth 8 5 the former letters of Aman the traitor
2 Ma 3 38 if thou hast any enemy or traitor to
4 2 he presumed to call him a traitor to the
5 15 Menelaus, that traitor to the laws
10 13 and being oftentimes called traitor
14 26 who was a traitor to the kingdom, his
Luke 6 16 Judas Iscariot, who was the traitor
traitors Esth 16 23 they that are traitors to their
2 Ma 10 22 so he put these traitors to death and
2 Tim 3 4 traitors, stubborn, puffed up, and
trample Ps 90 13 shalt t. under foot the lion
Eze 32 2 and didst trample upon their streams
Mat 7 6 lest perhaps they trample them under
trampled Isa 63 3 t. on them in my indignation
trance Acts 22 17 in temple, that I was in a t.
tranquillity Wisd 12 18 of power judgest with t.
transfer 1 Pa 19 23 t. to him the kingdom of Saul
transferred Num 36 3 being t. to another tribe
3 K 2 15 the kingdom is t. and is become my
1 Pa 10 14 and transferred his kingdom to David
1 C 4 6 a figure t. to myself and to Apollo, for
transfigured Mat 17 2 was t. before them. Mark 9:1
transformed Wisd 16 25 it was t. into all things
2 C 3 18 are t. into the same image from glory
11 15 t. as the ministers of justice, whose
transformeth 2 C 11 14 t. himself into angel of
transforming 2 C 11 13 t. themselves into apostles
transgress Num 14 41 why t. you the word of Lord
Num 31 16 made you transgress against the Lord by
Deut 17 2 thy God, and transgress his covenant
Josu 22 20 did not Achan son of Zare transgress
1 K 2 24 you make the people of the Lord to t.
2 Pa 21 11 commit fornication and Juda to t. And
24 20 why transgress you the commandment of
2 Es 1 8 if you shall transgress, I will scatter
13 27 great evil to transgress against our God
Tob 4 6 nor transgress the commandments of the
Eccu 7 20 do not t. against thy friend deferring
39 37 they shall not transgress his word
Isa 48 8 I know that transgressing thou wilt t.
Jer 12 1 well with all them that transgress
Eze 14 13 against me, so as to t. grievously
Dan 6 8 nor any man be allowed to t. it. So
1 Ma 2 22 and transgress the commandments of our
2 Ma 7 2 rather than to t. the laws of God
Mat 15 2 why do thy disciples t. the tradition
3 why do you also t. the commandment of
transgressed Lev 26 40 have t. against me. Osee 7:13
Num 5 6 by negligence shall have transgressed
Deut 26 13 I have not t. thy commandments nor
Josu 7 1 children of Israel t. the commandment
11 Israel hath sinned and t. my covenant
15 because he hath t. the covenant of the
23 16 when you shall have t. the covenant
1 K 14 33 you have t.: roll here to me now a
15 24 I [Saul] have t. the commandment of
3 K 8 50 by which they have t. against thee
4 K 18 12 Lord their God, but t. his covenant
1 Pa 10 13 because he t. commandment of the Lord

Ps 7 6 and tread down my life on the earth
Prov 27 7 is full shall tread upon the honeycomb
Isa 10 7 to tread them down like the mire of
14 25 upon my mountains t. him under foot
16 10 he shall not tread out wine in the
10 that was wont to tread it out: the voice
26 6 the foot shall tread it down, the feet
42 5 and spirit to them that tread thereon
63 2 theirs that tread in the winepress
Jer 25 30 as it were of them that tread grapes
50 26 forth that shall tread her down: take
Eze 26 11 he shall tread down all thy streets
34 18 also tread down with your feet the
Dan 7 23 whole earth, and shall tread it down
Osee 10 11 taught to love to tread out corn but
Mich 1 3 will tread upon the high places of the
4 13 and tread, O daughter of Sion: for I
5 6 when he shall tread in our borders
8 when he shall go through and tread
6 15 thou shalt tread the olives, but shalt
Nah 3 14 go into the clay and tread, work it
Haba 3 12 thou wilt tread the earth under foot
Mala 4 3 you shall tread down the wicked when
1 Ma 4 60 and tread it down as they did before
14 31 their enemies desired to tread down
Luke 10 19 I have given you power to tread upon
Apoc 11 2 the holy city they shall tread under
treader Jer 48 33 t. of the grapes shall not sing
Amos 9 13 the t. of grapes him that soweth seed
treaders Isa 16 9 voice of the t. hath rushed in
Isa 16 10 voice of the treaders I have taken away
treadest Deut 28 23 the ground thou t. on, of iron
treadeth Deut 25 4 not muzzle the ox that t. out
Isa 59 8 that t. in them, knoweth no peace
1 C 9 9 ox that t. out the corn. 1 Tim 5:18
Apoc 19 15 he t. the winepress of the fierceness
treading Judg 9 27 and treading down the grapes
2 Es 13 15 some t. the presses on the sabbath
Isa 22 5 it is a day of slaughter and of t. down
41 25 dirt, and as the potter treading clay
Dan 7 7 treading down the rest with its feet
Zach 10 5 t. under foot the mire of the ways
treason 2 Pa 23 13 rent her garments and said: T.
Esth 6 2 discovered the treason of Bagathan
16 14 he might work treason against us left
Job 15 21 is peace, he always suspecteth treason
Jer 29 32 hath spoken treason against the Lord
treasure Gen 43 23 your father hath given you t.
Gen 47 14 brought it into the king's treasure
Num 20 6 open to them thy treasure, a fountain
Deut 28 12 Lord will open his excellent treasure
1 Es 8 29 into the treasure of house of the Lord
2 Es 7 70 Athersatha gave into the treasure
71 gave to the treasure of the work, twenty
10 38 to the storeroom into the treasure house
12 43 men over the storehouses of the treasure
Job 3 21 not, as they that dig for a treasure
Prov 2 4 shalt dig for her as for a treasure
21 20 there is a treasure to be desired and
Wisd 7 14 she is an infinite treasure to men
Eccu 3 5 is as one that layeth up a treasure
6 14 that hath found him, hath found a t.
15 6 shall heap upon him a treasure of joy
20 32 and treasure that is not seen: what
29 14 place thy treasure in the commandments
30 23 a never failing treasure of holiness
40 18 and in it thou shalt find a treasure
41 17 treasure that is not seen, what profit
Isa 33 6 the fear of the Lord is his treasure
Jer 35 4 was by the treasure house of the princes
4 above the treasure of Maasias the son
4 to treasure house of the sons of Hanan
Dan 1 2 vessels he brought into the t. house
Osee 13 15 he shall carry off the t. of every
Mat 6 21 where thy t. is, there is thy heart
12 35 good man out of a good t. Luke 6:45
35 evil man out of an evil t. Luke 6:45
13 44 is like unto a t. hidden in a field
52 forth out of his t. new things and old
19 21 thou shalt have t. in heaven. Mark 10:21; Luke 18:22
Luke 12 21 so is he that layeth up treasure for
33 a treasure in heaven which faileth not
34 where your t. is, there will your
2 C 4 7 we have this t. in earthen vessels, that
Heb 11 26 greater riches than the treasure of the
treasurer Rom 16 23 Erastus, the t. of the city
treasurers Esth 3 9 pay 10,000 talents to thy t.
treasures Deut 32 34 me, and sealed up in my t.
Deut 33 19 and the hidden treasures of the sands
Josu 6 19 to the Lord, laid up in his treasures
3 K 7 51 t. of the house of the Lord. 14:26; 15:18; 4 K 24:13; 1 Pa 26:22; 28:12; 29:8; 2 Pa 12:9; 16:2
15 18 the t. of the king's house. 4 K 24:13; 2 Pa 25:24
4 K 12 18 be found in the treasures of the temple
20 13 and all that he had in his treasures
15 there is nothing among my treasures
1 Pa 9 26 were over the chambers and treasures
26 20 the t. of the house of God. 2 Pa 5:1
24 son of Moses, was chief over the t.
26 over the treasures of the holy things
28 11 and of the temple and of the treasures
12 the treasures of the consecrated things
2 Pa 8 15 and as to the keeping of the treasures
32 22 and gave them treasures on every side
27 he gathered himself great treasures
36 18 and the treasures of the temple and of
Tob 12 8 more than to lay up treasures of gold
Jdth 12 1 she should go in where his t. were laid
Job 38 22 hast thou beheld the t. of the hail
Prov 8 21 love me, and may fill their treasures
Prov 10 2 t. of wickedness shall profit nothing
15 16 than great treasures without content
21 6 gathereth treasures by a lying tongue
Eccu 1 21 increase, and the storehouses with her t.
26 in the t. of wisdom is understanding
31 in the t. of wisdom is the signification
35 meekness: and he will fill up his t.
4 21 will heap upon him t. of knowledge and
31 8 nor put his trust in money nor in t.
41 15 more than a thousand t. precious and
43 15 through this are the treasures opened
Isa 2 7 there is no end of their treasures
30 6 their t. upon the bunches of camels
39 2 all things that were found in his t.
4 which I have not shown them in my t.
45 3 I will give thee hidden treasures and
Jer 10 13 bringeth forth the wind out of his t.
15 13 thy treasures I will give unto spoil
17 3 all thy treasures to the spoil and thy
20 5 all the treasures of the kings of Juda
35 2 into one of the chambers of the t.
48 7 trusted in thy bulwarks and in thy t.
49 4 daughter, that hast trusted in thy t.
50 37 a sword upon her treasures and they shall
51 13 rich in treasures, thy end is come
16 brought forth the wind out of his t.
Bar 3 15 who hath gone in to her t.? Where are
Eze 27 27 thy t., and thy manifold furniture, thy
28 4 hast gotten gold and silver into thy t.
Dan 11 43 he shall have power over the treasures
Mich 6 10 the t. of iniquity and a scant measure
1 Ma 1 24 he took the hidden treasures which he
3 29 perceived that money of his t. failed

Mat 2 11 opening their treasures, they offered
6 19 lay not up to yourselves t. on earth
20 lay up to yourselves t. in heaven
Acts 8 27 who had charge over all her treasures
Col 2 3 in whom are hid all the t. of wisdom
king's treasures 3 K 14 26 the k. . . . , and carried all off
4 K 14 14 in the k. . . . , and hostages and returned
16 8 in the k. . . . , he sent it for a present
18 15 in the k. . . . At that time Ezechias broke
1 Pa 27 25 over the king's treasures was Azmoth
2 Pa 16 2 of the k. . . . and sent to Benadad king
Esth 4 7 to pay money into the king's treasures
treasurest Rom 2 5 thou t. up to thyself wrath
treasury Josu 6 24 into the t. of the Lord. But
1 Es 7 20 it shall be given out of the treasury
2 Es 3 30 son of Barachias against his treasury
10 39 to the treasury the firstfruits of corn
13 4 who was set over the treasury of the house
Jer 36 10 in the t. of Gamarias the son of Saphan
1 Ma 3 28 he opened his t. and gave out pay to
14 49 a copy thereof should be put in the t.
2 Ma 3 6 t. in Jerusalem was full of immense sums
23 place with his guard about the treasury
28 all his guard into the aforesaid t.
40 the keeping of the treasury fell out in
4 42 himself, they slew him beside the t.
5 18 was sent by king Seleucus to rob the t.
Mark 12 41 Jesus sitting over against the t.
41 how the people cast money into the t.
43 than all they who have cast into the t.
Luke 21 1 men cast their gifts into the treasury
John 8 20 words Jesus spoke in the treasury
treat Prov 25 9 treat thy cause with thy friend
Eccu 9 21 and treat with the wise and prudent
30 31 treat him as a brother: because in
37 12 treat not with a man without religion
Isa 52 5 rule over them treat them unjustly
1 Ma 15 28 of his friends to t. with him, saying
2 Ma 1 28 that treat us injuriously with pride
4 21 Egypt to treat with the nobles of king
Mark 9 32 what did you treat of in the way
Acts 7 6 bondage, and treat them evil 400 years
Phil 2 29 Lord; and t. with honor such as he is
treated 1 K 25 39 David sent and t. with Abigail
3 K 4 33 he treated about trees from the cedar
2 Pa 10 8 and began to treat with the young men
Jdth 10 16 he will treat thee well and thou wilt
Ps 91 15 old age: and shall be well treated
Eccu 49 9 they t. him evil, who was consecrated
1 Ma 11 26 the king t. him as his predecessors
14 9 t. together of the good things of the
2 Ma 2 9 he t. wisdom in a magnificent manner
9 28 as he himself had treated others, died
12 30 they had treated them with humanity
13 22 king treated with them that were in
Mat 22 6 having treated them contumeliously
Acts 24 25 as he treated of justice, and chastity
1 Th 2 2 been shamefully treated, as you know
treating Luke 20 11 treating him reproachfully
Acts 27 3 Julius t. Paul courteously, permitted
treatise Acts 1 1 the former treatise, I made
tree Gen 1 11 fruit tree yielding fruit after its
Gen 1 12 tree that beareth fruit, having seed
2 9 the tree of knowledge of good and evil
9 tree of life also in midst of paradise
16 of every t. of paradise thou shalt eat
17 of the t. of knowledge of good and evil
3 1 that you should not eat of every tree
3 tree which is in the midst of paradise
6 woman saw that the tree was good to eat
11 thou hast eaten of the tree whereof I
12 gave me of the tree, and I did eat
17 eaten of the tree whereof I commanded
22 take also of the tree of life and eat
24 to keep the way of the tree of life
18 4 ye your feet, and rest ye under the tree
8 but he stood by them under the tree
35 4 he buried them under the turpentine tree
Exod 9 25 and it broke every tree in the country
15 25 he showed him [Moses] a tree, which when
Lev 23 40 first day fruits of the fairest tree
Deut 12 2 under every shady tree. 4 K 17:10
16 21 no grave, nor any tree near the altar of
19 5 in cutting down the tree the axe slipped
20 19 for it is a tree, and not a man, neither
21 23 his body shall not remain upon the tree
23 accursed of God that hangeth on a tree
22 6 by the way, a bird's nest in a tree
Judg 9 48 axe, he cut down the bough of a tree
1 K 14 2 pomegranate tree, which was in Magron
3 K 6 34 and two doors of fir tree, one of each
13 14 him sitting under a turpentine tree
14 23 and under every green tree. 4 K 16:4; 2 Pa 28:4; Isa 57:5; Jer 2:20; 3:6, 13
19 4 was there, and sat under a juniper tree
5 slept in the shadow of the juniper tree
4 K 3 19 and shall cut down every fruitful tree
14 9 thistle of Libanus sent to a cedar tree
2 Es 10 35 firstfruits of all fruit of every tree
37 fruit of every tree, of the vintage also
Jdth 6 9 they tied Achior to a tree hand and foot
Job 14 7 a tree hath hope; if it be cut, it
19 10 as from a tree that is plucked up. His
24 20 broken in pieces as an unfruitful tree
Ps 1 3 he shall be like a tree which is planted
Prov 3 18 she is a tree of life to them that lay
11 30 fruit of the just man is a tree of life
13 12 desire when it cometh is a tree of life
15 4 a peaceable tongue is a tree of life
Ecce 11 3 if the tree fall to the south or to the
12 5 almond tree shall flourish, the locust
5 and the caper tree shall be destroyed
Cant 2 3 as the apple tree among the trees of
8 5 under the apple tree I raised thee up
Wisd 13 11 hath cut down a tree proper for his use
Eccu 6 3 and thou be left as a dry tree in the
14 18 leaf that springeth out on a green tree
24 17 as a cypress tree on mount Sion. I was
19 as a plane tree by the water in the
22 my branches as the turpentine tree
27 7 dressing of a tree showeth the fruit
50 11 a cypress tree rearing itself on high
Isa 6 13 be made a show as a turpentine tree
17 6 four or five upon the top of the tree
41 19 I will set in the desert the fir tree, the elm, and the box tree
44 14 he hath planted the pine tree which the
19 shall I fall down before stock of a t.
23 O forest, and every tree therein: for
55 13 shall come up the fir tree and instead
13 nettle, shall come up the myrtle tree
56 3 eunuch say: Behold I am a dry tree
60 13 shall come to thee, the fir tree and the box tree and the pine tree
65 22 as the days of a tree, so shall be the
Jer 10 3 hath cut a tree out of the forest with
17 8 he shall be as a tree that is planted
Bar 5 8 sweet-smelling tree have overshadowed
Eze 6 13 and under every woody tree and under
15 6 as the vine tree among the trees of
17 24 I the Lord have brought down the high tree and exalted the low tree
24 dried up the green tree and have caused the dry tree to flourish
20 28 every high hill and every shady tree

47 and will burn in thee every green tree and every dry tree
21 10 my son, thou hast cut down every tree
31 8 no tree in the paradise of God was like
34 27 tree of the field shall yield its fruit
36 30 I will multiply the fruit of the tree
Dan 4 7 behold a tree in the midst of the earth
8 the tree was great and strong: and the
11 cut down the tree and chop off the
17 the tree which thou sawest which was
20 cut down the tree and destroy it, but
23 the roots thereof, that is, of the tree
13 54 tell me under what t. thou sawest them
54 together. He said: Under a mastic tree
58 under what tree didst thou take them
58 and he answered: Under a holm tree
Osee 4 13 poplar and the turpentine tree, because
14 9 make him flourish like a green fir tree
Joel 1 12 hath languished: the pomegranate tree
12 the apple tree and all the trees of the
2 22 the tree hath brought forth its fruit
Zach 11 2 howl, thou fir tree, for the cedar is
Mat 3 10 every tree therefore that doth not
7 17 good tree bringeth forth good fruit
17 evil tree bringeth forth evil fruit
18 a good tree cannot bring forth evil
18 neither can an evil tree bring forth
19 t. that bringeth not forth. Luke 3:9
12 33 either make the tree good and its
33 make the tree evil and its fruit evil
33 for by the fruit the tree is known
13 32 than all herbs, and becometh a tree
Luke 6 43 nor an evil tree that bringeth forth
44 for every tree is known by its fruit
13 19 and it grew and became a great tree
17 6 you might say to this mulberry tree
19 4 he climbed up into a sycamore tree
Acts 5 30 hanging him upon a tree. 10:39
13 29 taking him down from the tree, they
Gal 3 13 cursed is every one that hangeth on t.
1 P 2 24 bore our sins in his body upon the tree
Apoc 2 7 I will give to eat of the tree of life
7 1 nor upon the sea nor on any tree. And
9 4 nor any green thing nor any tree: but
22 2 was the tree of life, bearing twelve
2 leaves of the tree were for the healing
14 may have a right to the tree of life

fig tree; *see* **fig**
olive tree; *see* **olive**
palm tree; *see* **palm**

trees Gen 1 29 t. that have in themselves seed
Gen 2 9 brought forth of ground all manner of t.
3 2 the fruit of the t. that are in paradise
8 Lord God, amidst the trees of paradise
21 15 she cast the boy under one of the trees
23 17 all the trees thereof in all its limits
30 37 of almond and of plane trees and pilled
Exod 10 5 they shall feed upon all the trees
15 what fruits soever were on the trees
15 not anything that was green on the t.
Lev 19 23 shall have planted in it fruit trees
23 40 boughs of thick trees and willows of the
26 4 the trees shall be filled with fruit
20 increase, nor the t. yield their fruit
27 30 of the fruits of trees are the Lord's
Num 13 21 fat or barren, woody or without trees
Deut 8 8 barley and vineyards wherein fig trees
20 19 thou shalt not cut down the trees
20 there be any t. that are not fruitful
24 20 have gathered the fruit of thy olive t.
20 whatsoever remaineth on the trees
28 40 thou shalt have olive trees in all thy
42 the blast shall consume all the trees
Judg 9 9 come to be promoted among the trees
8 trees went to anoint a king over them
10 the t. said to the fig tree: Come thou
11 to be promoted among the other trees
12 the trees said to the vine: Come thou
13 and be promoted among the other trees
14 all the trees said to the bramble: Come
49 they cut down boughs from the trees
2 K 5 23 over against the pear t. 1 Pa 14:14
24 in the tops of the pear t. 1 Pa 14:15
3 K 4 33 and he treated about trees from the
5 8 concerning cedar trees and fir trees
10 gave Solomon cedar trees and fir trees
9 11 Solomon with cedar trees and fir trees
10 11 from Ophir great plenty of thyine trees
12 king made of the thyine trees the rails
12 there were no such thyine trees as these
4 K 3 25 cut down all the trees that bore fruit
19 23 its tall cedars and its choice fir trees
1 Pa 16 33 shall the trees of the wood give praise
2 Pa 2 8 fir trees and pine trees from Libanus
10 men that are to cut down the trees, for
16 we will cut down as many trees out of
9 10 brought gold of Ophir and thyine trees
11 the king made of the thyine trees stairs
11 seen such trees in the land of Juda
2 Es 8 15 of palm, and branches of thick trees
9 25 fruit trees in abundance: and they ate
Jdth 2 17 trees and vineyards to be cut down
Esth 7 7 banquet into the garden set with trees
8 back out of the garden set with trees
Job 30 4 they ate grass and barks of trees and
Ps 51 10 as a fruitful olive tree in house of God
73 5 as with axes in a wood of trees, they
77 47 and their mulberry trees with hoarfrost
95 12 shall all the trees of the woods rejoice
103 16 the trees of the field shall be filled
104 33 and their fig trees: and he broke in pieces the trees of their coasts
148 9 hills, fruitful trees and all cedars
Ecce 2 5 and set them with trees of all kinds
6 therewith the wood of the young trees
10 9 that cutteth trees, shall be wounded
Cant 1 16 of cedar, our rafters of cypress trees
2 3 apple tree among the trees of the woods
4 14 with all the trees of Libanus, myrrh
5 1 and eat the fruit of his apple trees
Wisd 10 7 the trees bear fruits that ripen not
17 17 among the spreading branches of trees
Isa 7 2 as the trees of the woods are moved
10 19 that remain of the trees of his forest
14 8 the fir trees also have rejoiced over
37 24 tall cedars and its choice fir trees
44 14 that stood among the trees of the forest
55 12 all the trees of the country shall clap
Jer 6 6 hew down her trees, cast up a trench
7 20 upon the trees of the field and upon the
17 2 their green t. upon the high mountains
Eze 15 2 out of all the t. of the woods that are among the t. of the forests
6 vine tree among the trees of the forests
17 24 all the trees of the country shall know
27 5 with fir trees of Sanir they have built
31 4 sent forth its rivulets to all the t.
5 his height exalted above all the trees
8 the fir trees did not equal his top
8 neither were the plane t. to be compared
9 all the trees of pleasure, that were
14 none of the t. by the waters shall exalt
15 all the trees of the field trembled
16 all the trees of pleasure, the choice
18 and lofty among the trees of pleasure
18 brought down with the t. of pleasure

47 7 on bank of torrent were very many trees
12 shall grow all trees that bear fruit
Osee 2 12 will destroy her vines and her fig t.
Joel 1 12 all the t. of the field are withered
19 the flame hath burnt all the trees
Nah 3 12 thy strongholds shall be like fig trees
Zach 1 8 stood among the myrtle trees. 10, 11
4 3 and two olive trees over it: one upon
11 what are these two olive trees upon
1 Ma 10 30 and the half of the fruit of trees
11 34 fruits of the land and of the trees
14 8 t. of the fields [yielded] their fruit
Mat 3 10 axe is laid to root of the t. Luke 3:9
21 8 others cut boughs from the t. Mark 11:8
Mark 8 24 I see men as it were trees, walking
21 29 see the fig tree and all the trees
Jude 12 trees of the autumn, unfruitful, twice
Apoc 7 3 hurt not the earth . . . nor the trees
8 7 third part of the trees was burnt up
11 4 these are the two olive trees and the
cedar trees; *see* **cedar**
palm trees; *see* **palm**
tremble Deut 2 25 thy name they may fear and t.
Job 9 6 place, and the pillars thereof tremble
26 11 the pillars of heaven tremble and dread
Ps 103 32 upon the earth, and maketh it tremble
Ecce 12 3 when the keepers of the house shall t.
Eccu 34 16 feareth the Lord shall t. at nothing
Isa 19 17 that shall remember it shall tremble
54 10 be moved, and the hills shall tremble
64 2 nations might tremble at thy presence
66 5 the Lord, you that tremble at his word
Jer 10 10 at his wrath the earth shall tremble
Joel 2 1 the inhabitants of the land tremble
Amos 8 8 shall not the land tremble for this
Nah 1 5 the mountains tremble at him and the
Heb 12 21 Moses said: I am frighted, and tremble
James 2 19 the devils also believe and tremble
trembled Judg 5 4 the earth t., and the heavens
1 K 14 15 the earth trembled and it happened as a
2 K 22 8 the earth shook and t. Ps 17:8; 76:19
4 K 19 26 they trembled and were confounded
Ps 13 5 there have they trembled for fear. 52:6
45 7 he uttered his voice, the earth trembled
75 9 the earth trembled and was still, when
96 4 the world: the earth saw and trembled
Eccu 26 5 at the fourth my face hath trembled
48 21 then their hearts and hands trembled
Isa 37 27 they trembled and were confounded: they
Jer 4 24 mountains, and behold they trembled
48 1 strong city is confounded and hath t.
Eze 31 15 all the trees of the field trembled
Dan 5 19 trembled and were afraid of him: whom
7 15 my spirit t., I Daniel was affrighted
Joel 2 10 at their presence the earth hath t.
Haba 3 16 troubled: my lips trembled at the voice
1 Ma 2 24 his reins trembled, and his wrath was
trembleth Job 37 1 at this my heart trembleth
Isa 66 2 spirit, and that t. at my words? He
trembling Gen 28 17 t. he said: How terrible
Exod 15 15 trembling seized on stout men of Moab
1 K 15 32 was presented to him very fat and t.
1 Es 10 9 trembling because of the sin and rain
Tob 13 6 with fear and trembling give ye glory
Jdth 15 1 being seized with trembling and fear
Job 4 4 thou hast strengthened the t. knees
14 fear seized upon me, and trembling
21 6 and trembling taketh hold on my flesh
Ps 2 11 and rejoice unto him with trembling
47 7 trembling took hold of them. There
54 6 fear and trembling are come upon me
Eccu 16 19 they shall be shaken with trembling
Isa 24 19 with trembling shall the earth be moved
33 14 t. hath seized upon the hypocrites
Bar 3 33 it, and it obeyeth him with trembling
Jer 49 24 trembling hath seized on her: anguish
Eze 7 16 them t., every one for his iniquity
Dan 8 17 I fell on my face trembling, and he
10 11 this word to me, I stood trembling
1 Ma 7 18 fear and t. fell upon all the people
Mark 5 33 but the woman fearing and trembling
16 8 a trembling and fear had seized them
Luke 8 47 came t. and fell down before his feet
Acts 9 6 he trembling and astonished, said: Lord
16 29 calling for a light, he went in and t.
1 C 2 3 I was with you . . . in much trembling
2 C 7 15 with fear and trembling you received him
Eph 6 5 to the flesh, with fear and trembling
Phil 2 12 with fear and trembling work out your
trench 3 K 18 32 and he made a trench for water
3 K 18 35 and the trench was filled with water
38 licked up the water that was in trench
4 K 19 32 nor cast a trench about it. Isa 37:33
Isa 29 2 I will make a trench about Ariel and it
Jer 6 6 cast up a trench about Jerusalem: this
Eze 43 13 and this was the trench of the altar
Luke 19 43 enemies shall cast a trench about thee
trespass Exod 32 31 either forgive them this t.
Lev 6 17 which is offered for sin and for t.
7 1 the law of the sacrifice for a trespass
2 victim also for a t. shall be slain
5 burnt sacrifice of the Lord for a t.
7 sin is offered, so is also that for a t.
37 the sacrifice for sin and for trespass
14 12 offer it for a trespass offering with
13 victim for a t. offering pertaineth to
14 that was immolated for trespass, shall
17 the blood that was shed for t. 28
21 a lamb for an offering for trespass
24 priest receiving the lamb for trespass
31 pigeon, one for trespass and the other
19 21 for his trespass he shall offer a ram
22 16 bear the iniquity of their trespass
Num 18 9 rendered to me for sin and for trespass
Judg 11 27 therefore I do not t. against thee, but
3 K 8 31 if any man t. against his neighbor and
4 K 12 16 money for t., and the money for sins
Eze 40 39 t. offering might be slain thereon
42 13 the offering for sin and for trespass
44 29 victim both for sin and for trespass
46 20 the sin offering and the t. offering
trespassed Lev 5 19 because by mistake he t.
Deut 32 51 because you [Moses] t. against me in
Dan 3 29 and we have trespassed in all things
trial Tob 2 12 t. the Lord therefore permitted
Tob 3 21 his life, if it be under t., shall be
Wisd 3 18 nor speech of comfort in day of trial
4 6 against their parents in their trial
Eccu 4 19 bring upon him fear and dread trial
6 22 to them as a mighty stone of trial
27 6 trial of affliction [trieth] just men
8 speaketh, for this is the trial of men
Rom 5 4 and patience trial; and trial hope; and
Heb 11 36 others had trial of mockeries and
1 P 1 7 that the trial of your faith, much
trials Jdth 8 24 not receive the t. with the fear
tribulation 4 K 19 3 this day is a day of t.
2 Es 9 27 in time of their tribulation they cried
37 will, and we are in great tribulation
Tob 3 13 in the time of tribulation forgivest
21 if it be under t., it shall be delivered
Jdth 13 25 distress and tribulation of thy people
Esth 11 8 was a day of darkness and danger, of t.
14 12 show thyself to us in the time of our t.
Job 15 24 t. shall terrify him and distress shall
36 19 lay down thy greatness without t. and

Ps 9 10 a helper in due time in tribulation
19 2 Lord hear thee in the day of tribulation
21 12 trbulation is very near: for there is
54 4 at the tribulation of the sinner. For
90 15 I am with him in tribulation, I will
105 44 he saw when they were in tribulation
106 6 they cried to the Lord in their t.
137 7 if I shall walk in midst of tribulation
Prov 1 27 when t. and distress shall come upon you
Eccu 2 13 will forgive sins in day of tribulation
Isa 5 30 and behold darkness of tribulation
22 18 will crown thee with a crown of t.
26 16 in the t. of murmuring thy instruction
37 3 this day is a day of tribulation and
46 7 he shall not save them from tribulation
Jer 15 11 and in the time of t. against the enemy
16 19 my refuge in the day of tribulation
30 7 it is the time of tribulation to Jacob
Amos 3 11 the land shall be in tribulation and
Abdi 14 remain of him in the day of tribulation
Haba 3 16 that I may rest in the day of t.: that
Soph 1 14 the mighty man shall there meet with t.
15 a day of tribulation and distress, a day
Zach 8 10 to him that went out, because of the t.
1 Ma 6 11 into how much tribulation am I come
9 27 there was a great tribulation in Israel
Mat 13 21 when there ariseth t. and persecution
24 21 there shall be then great tribulation
29 after the t. of those days, the sun
Mark 4 17 when t. and persecution ariseth for
13 24 after that t., the sun shall be
Acts 7 11 and great t.; and our fathers found
Rom 2 9 t. and anguish upon every soul of man
5 3 knowing that t. worketh patience; and
8 35 Christ? Shall tribulation? or distress
12 12 hope. Patient in t. Instant in prayer
1 C 7 28 such shall have t. of the flesh. But I
2 C 1 4 who comforteth us in all our tribulation
6 now whether we be in t., it is for your
8 have you ignorant, brethren, of our t.
4 8 in all things we suffer t., but are not
17 momentary and light of our t., worketh
6 4 of God, in much patience, in tribulation
7 4 abound with joy in all our tribulation
5 no rest, but we suffered all tribulation
8 2 that in much experience of tribulation
Phil 4 14 done well in communicating to my t. And
1 Th 1 6 receiving the word in much tribulation
3 7 in all our necessity and tribulation
2 Th 1 6 just thing with God to repay tribulation
1 Tim 5 10 have ministered to them that suffer t.
James 1 27 the fatherless and widows in their t.
Apoc 1 9 your partner in t. and in the kingdom
2 9 I know thy t. and thy poverty, but thou
10 and you shall have tribulation ten days
22 with her shall be in very great t.
7 14 who are come out of great tribulation
tribulations 1 K 10 19 all your evils and your t.
Jdth 8 22 [Abraham] being proved by many t., was
23 passed through many tribulations, was
Ps 24 22 deliver Israel, O God, from all his t.
Mark 13 19 such t. as were not from the beginning
Acts 7 10 and delivered him out of all his t.
14 21 that through many t. we must enter
Rom 5 3 we glory also in tribulations, knowing
Eph 3 13 I pray you not to faint at my t. for you
1 Th 3 3 that no man should be moved in these t.
4 foretold you that we should suffer t.
2 Th 1 4 in all your persecutions and t., which
Heb 10 33 by reproaches and t., were made a
tribunal 4 K 11 14 saw the king standing upon a t.
2 Pa 34 31 standing up in his tribunal, he made
tribune 1 K 17 18 ten little cheeses to the t.
John 18 12 then the band and the tribune and the
Acts 21 31 it was told the tribune of the band
32 when they saw tribune and soldiers they
33 then tribune coming near, took him, and
37 he saith to the tribune: May I speak
22 24 t. commanded him to be brought into the
26 to the tribune, and told him, saying
27 the tribune coming, said to him: Tell me
28 the t. answered: I obtained the being
29 t. also was afraid after he understood
23 10 t. fearing lest Paul should be pulled in
15 signify to tribune, that he bring him
17 bring this young man to the tribune, for
18 he taking him, brought him to the t.
19 t. taking him by the hand, went aside
22 t. therefore dismissed the young man
24 7 Lysias the tribune coming upon us, with
22 when Lysias the tribune shall come down
tribunes Num 31 14 officers of the army, the t.
Num 31 48 t. and centurions were come to Moses
52 from the tribunes and from centurions
Deut 1 15 and appointed them rulers, tribunes
1 K 8 12 will appoint of them to be his tribunes
22 7 make you all tribunes and centurions
Jdth 14 11 when his captains and tribunes were come
1 Ma 16 19 to the tribunes he sent letters to come
Mark 6 21 for the princes and tribunes and chief
Acts 25 23 entered into hall of audience, with t.
Apoc 6 15 princes and the tribunes and the rich
19 18 flesh of kings and the flesh of tribunes
tributaries Josu 17 13 and made them their t.
Judg 1 28 he made them tributaries and would
30 them, and became their tributaries
33 Bethsamites and Bethanites were t.
2 Pa 8 8 Solomon made to be the tributaries
Isa 31 8 his young men shall be tributaries
1 Ma 1 5 and they became tributaries to him
tributary Judg 1 35 and he became t. to him
3 K 9 21 Solomon made tributary unto this day
Lam 1 1 princes of provinces made tributary
tribute Gen 49 15 became a servant under tribute
Deut 20 11 and shall serve thee paying tribute
Josu 16 10 of Ephraim until this day paying t.
1 K 17 25 his father's house free from tribute
2 K 8 1 and David took the bridle of tribute
2 Moab was made to serve David under t.
6 and Syria served David under tribute
3 K 4 6 Adoniram the son of Abda over the t.
12 18 Aduram, who was over the tribute: and
4 K 17 3 because his servant, and paid him t.
4 that he might not pay tribute to the
2 Pa 17 11 presents to Josaphat and t. in silver
1 Es 4 13 they will not pay tribute nor toll
20 and have received tribute and toll
6 8 tribute that is paid out of the country
7 24 no authority to impose toll or tribute
2 Es 5 4 let us borrow money for the king's t.
Prov 12 24 which is slothful, shall be under t.
Isa 14 4 to nothing, the tribute hath ceased
1 Ma 8 2 them, and brought them under tribute
4 the rest pay them tribute every year
7 reign after him, should pay a great t.
11 28 that he would make Judea free from t.
2 Ma 8 10 for the king the t. of 2,000 talents
36 that had promised to levy the tribute
Mat 17 24 of whom do they receive tribute or
22 17 is it lawful to give t. to Caesar. Mark 12:14; Luke 20:22
19 show me the coin of the tribute. And
Luke 23 2 forbidding to give tribute to Caesar
Rom 13 6 for therefore also you pay tribute. For
7 tribute, to whom tribute is due: custom
tributes 2 K 20 24 but Aduram over the tributes

3 K 10 15 brought him that were over the tributes
11 28 made him chief over the tributes of all
12 18 Aduram, who was over the tributes
1 Ma 1 30 sent the chief collector of his tributes
3 29 that the t. of the country were small
31 to take tributes of the countries
10 29 I free you and all the Jews from t.
31 let the tenths and t. be for itself
33 that all be discharged from tributes
11 35 to us of the tithes and of the tributes
15 30 the tributes of the places whereof you
31 the t. of the cities other 500 talents
16 18 him the country, and their cities and t.
trickling Luke 22 44 blood, t. down upon the ground
tried Gen 48 17 t. to lift it from Ephraim's head
2 K 22 31 the word of the Lord is tried by fire
Job 23 10 and has tried me as gold that passeth
34 36 let Job be tried even to the end
Ps 11 7 pure words, as silver tried by the fire
16 3 it by night, thou hast tried me by fire
17 31 the words of the Lord are fire tried
65 10 hast tried us by fire, as silver is t.
67 31 who seek to exclude them that are tried
Prov 17 3 as silver is tried by fire, and gold
27 21 as silver is tried in the fining-pot
21 a man is tried by the mouth of him that
30 5 every word of God is fire tried: he is
Ecce 7 24 I have tried all things in wisdom
Wisd 1 3 his power, when it is tried, reproveth
3 5 God hath tried them and found them
11 10 when they were tried and chastised
Eccu 2 5 gold and silver are tried in the fire
31 10 who hath been tried thereby and made
34 9 doth he know, that hath not been tried
11 he that hath not been tried, what
Isa 28 16 tried stone, a corner stone, a precious
Eze 21 13 it is tried: and that when it shall
Dan 1 14 these words, he tried them for ten days
11 35 shall fall that they may be tried
12 10 white, and shall be tried as fire
Zach 13 9 I will try them as gold is tried. They
Heb 11 17 Abraham, when he was t., offered Isaac
1 P 1 7 than gold which is tried by the fire
Apoc 2 2 thou hast tried them who say they are
10 you into prison that you may be tried
3 18 buy of me gold fire tried, that thou
trier Jer 6 27 for a strong t. among my people
triest Jer 11 20 and t. the reins and the hearts
trieth Deut 13 3 the Lord your God trieth you
Job 34 3 the ear trieth words, and the mouth
Ps 10 6 the Lord trieth the just and the wicked
Prov 17 3 furnace: so the Lord t. the hearts
Eccu 27 6 the furnace trieth the potter's vessels
31 31 fire trieth hard iron: so wine drunk
triflers Wisd 2 16 we are esteemed by him as t.
Soph 3 18 the t. that were departed from the law
trimmed 2 K 19 24 his feet nor t. his beard
Mat 25 7 virgins arose and trimmed their lamps
triple Eze 42 3 gallery joined to a t. gallery
tripled Eze 21 14 let the sword of the slain be t.
Tripolis 2 Ma 14 1 by the haven of T. to places
triumph 2 K 1 20 daughters of uncircumcised t.
Ps 139 9 not thou forsake me lest they should t.
Eze 22 5 far from thee shall triumph over thee
Haba 1 10 their prince shall t. over kings and
2 C 2 14 God, who always maketh us to triumph
triumphant 1 K 15 12 erected for himself a t. arch
triumphed Jdth 5 17 was no one that t. over this
triumpher 1 K 15 29 t. in Israel will not spare
triumpheth Wisd 4 2 it triumpheth crowned forever
triumphing Col 2 15 t. over them in himself. Let
Troas Acts 16 8 through Mysia, they went down to T.
Acts 16 11 and sailing from Troas, we came with
20 5 these going before, stayed for us at T.
6 came to them to T. in five days, where
2 C 2 12 when I was come to Troas for the gospel
2 Tim 4 13 the cloak that I left at Troas, with
trod 4 K 7 20 the people t. upon him in the gate
4 K 9 33 the hoofs of the horses trod upon her
14 9 and t. down the thistle. 2 Pa 25:18
Ps 56 4 made them a reproach that trod upon me
Isa 16 4 failed, that trod the earth under foot
Dan 8 10 of the stars, and trod upon them. And
Luke 12 1 so that they trod one upon another
trodden Deut 1 36 the land that he hath t. upon
Josu 14 9 land which thy foot hath trodden upon
Job 22 15 ages, which wicked men have trodden
24 11 after having t. the winepresses suffer
28 8 of the merchants have not trodden it
Ps 55 2 for man hath trodden me under foot
3 my enemies have t. on me all the day
Eccu 9 10 harlot, shall be t. upon as dung in the
24 11 I have t. under my feet the hearts
Isa 5 5 thereof, and it shall be trodden down
18 2 expecting and trodden under foot. 7
25 10 Moab shall be t. down under him, as
28 3 of Ephraim shall be trodden under feet
18 pass, you shall be trodden down by it
63 3 I have trodden the winepress alone
3 have trodden them down in my wrath
6 I have trodden down the people in my
18 enemies have t. down thy sanctuary
Jer 12 10 they have trodden my portion under
18 15 to walk by them, in a way not trodden
Lam 1 15 the Lord hath trodden the winepress
Eze 16 6 t. under foot in thy own blood. 22
34 19 which you had trodden with your feet
36 3 been desolate and trodden under foot
Dan 8 13 and the strength be t. under foot
Mich 7 10 now shall she be trodden under foot
1 Ma 3 45 the sanctuary was trodden down: and
51 for thy holies are trodden down and
2 Ma 8 2 people that was trodden down by all
Mat 5 13 out, and to be trodden on by men
Luke 8 5 it was trodden down, and the fowls
21 24 Jerusalem shall be trodden down by the
Heb 10 29 hath trodden under foot the Son of God
Apoc 14 20 the press was trodden without the city
Troglodites 2 Pa 12 3 to wit, Libyans and T.
troop Judg 9 37 one troop cometh by the way that
2 K 23 11 were gathered together in a troop: for
4 K 9 17 saw the troop of Jehu coming, and said
17 and said: I see a troop. And Joram
Isa 14 31 is none that shall escape his troop
troops Exod 40 34 Israel went forward by their t.
Num 1 3 you shall number them by their troops
52 shall camp every man by his troops
2 2 Israel shall camp by their troops
9 they by their troops shall march first
16 camp of Ruben were 151,450 by their t.
17 officers of the Levites and their troops
24 camp of Ephraim were 108,100 by their t.
32 divided according to . . . their troops
34 they camped by their t., and marched
10 12 marched by their troops from the desert
14 the sons of Juda by their troops: whose
18 marched by their troops and ranks whose
22 moved their camp by their t. in whose
25 marched the sons of Dan by their troops
28 of the children of Israel by their t.
33 1 who went out of Egypt by their troops
Josu 4 13 and 40,000 fighting men by their troops
11 4 they all came out with their troops
Judg 8 10 of all the troops of the eastern people
1 K 17 1 Philistines gathering together their t.
29 1 troops of the Philistines were gathered

2 K 18 4 the people went forth by their troops
4 K 25 10 which was with the commander of the t.
1 Pa 20 1 an army and the strength of the troops
Jdth 3 15 all the troops of his army to be united
7 2 in his troops 120,000 footmen and
Job 1 17 the Chaldeans made three t. and have
19 12 his troops have come together and have
Isa 13 4 hath given charge to the troops of war
Eze 12 14 his guards and his t. I will scatter
1 Ma 6 29 from the islands of the sea hired t.
33 made his troops march on fiercely
7 20 and left with him troops to help him
9 11 the horsemen were divided into two t.
11 38 all the troops of his fathers hated him
12 43 he commanded his troops to obey him
15 12 him, and his troops had forsaken him
2 Ma 3 35 taking his troops with him, returned
10 24 together a multitude of foreign t.
Trophimus Acts 20 4 of Asia, Tychicus and T.
Acts 21 29 they had seen Trophimus the Ephesian in
2 Tim 4 20 and Trophimus I left sick at Miletus
trouble Deut 23 16 cities: give him no trouble
Josu 7 25 the Lord trouble thee this day. And all
1 K 25 15 very good to us, and gave us no trouble
3 K 2 26 hast endured trouble in all the troubles
2 Pa 15 6 the Lord will trouble them with all
29 8 and he hath delivered them to trouble
Tob 7 20 for the trouble thou hast undergone
Job 13 11 shall move himself, he shall t. you
16 3 is it any trouble to thee to speak
Ps 2 5 in his anger, and t. them in his rage
9 1 in our wants, in the time of trouble
12 5 they that trouble me will rejoice when
20 10 Lord shall trouble them in his wrath
26 2 my enemies that trouble me, have
12 to the will of them that trouble me
31 7 from the t. which hath encompassed me
36 39 their protector in the time of trouble
41 6 my soul: and why dost thou trouble me
11 my enemies who t. me have reproached
43 24 and forgettest our want and our trouble
49 15 call upon me in the day of trouble
53 9 hast delivered me out of all trouble
58 17 my refuge, in the day of my trouble
59 13 give us help from trouble: for vain
65 14 hath spoken, when I was in trouble
68 18 for I am in trouble, hear me speedily
76 3 in the day of my trouble I sought God
77 49 indignation and wrath and t., which
82 16 and shalt trouble them in thy wrath
85 7 called upon thee in day of my trouble
101 3 in the day when I am in trouble, incline
106 39 afflicted through the trouble of evils
107 13 grant us help from trouble: for vain
114 3 I met with trouble and sorrow: and I
117 5 in my trouble I called upon the Lord
118 143 trouble and anguish have found me: thy
119 1 in my trouble I cried to the Lord: and
141 3 before him I declare my trouble: when
142 11 thou wilt bring my soul out of trouble
143 6 thy arrows, and thou shalt trouble them
Prov 15 6 in the fruits of the wicked is trouble
25 19 unfaithful man in the time of trouble
Ecce 3 10 seen the trouble which God hath given
Eccu 6 8 will not abide in day of thy trouble
22 15 him, that thou mayst not have trouble
29 in the time of his trouble continue
28 11 a sinful man will trouble his friends
29 4 given trouble to them that helped them
37 4 in time of trouble he will be against
40 4 wrath, envy, trouble, unquietness
24 brethren are a help in the time of t.
51 14 not leave me in the day of my trouble
Isa 8 22 behold trouble and darkness, weakness
13 13 for this I will trouble the heaven
17 14 evening, behold there shall be trouble
30 6 in a land of trouble and distress, from
33 2 our salvation in the time of trouble
36 18 neither let Ezechias trouble you, saying
51 15 Lord thy God, who trouble the sea and
65 23 in vain, nor bring forth in trouble
Jer 14 8 the Savior thereof in time of trouble
19 time of healing, and behold trouble
Eze 7 26 trouble shall come upon trouble, and
12 18 eat thy bread in trouble and drink thy
32 2 didst t. the waters with thy feet
13 the foot of man shall t. them no more
13 shall the hoof of beasts trouble them
Dan 4 16 the interpretation thereof trouble thee
5 10 ever: let not thy thoughts trouble thee
6 2 and the king might have no trouble
11 44 out of the north shall trouble him
Amos 1 14 with a whirlwind in the day of trouble
Nah 1 7 giveth strength in the day of trouble
1 Ma 5 16 for their brethren that were in trouble
10 63 that no man trouble him for any manner
11 53 but gave him [Jonathan] great trouble
13 5 to spare my life in any time of trouble
2 Ma 1 7 in the t. and violence that came upon us
3 30 a little before was full of fear and t.
10 30 with blindness and filled with trouble
Mat 26 10 why do you trouble this woman? For she
Mark 5 35 why dost thou trouble the master any
Luke 7 6 Lord, trouble not thyself; for I am
8 49 thy daughter is dead, trouble him not
11 7 trouble me not, the door is now shut
Gal 1 7 only there are some that trouble you
5 12 they were even cut off, who trouble you
2 Th 1 6 tribulation to them that trouble you
troubled Gen 34 30 you have troubled me and made
Gen 42 28 they were astonished and troubled
Exod 15 15 then were the princes of Edom troubled
Josu 6 18 camp of Israel be under sin and be t.
7 3 why should all the people be troubled
25 because thou hast t. us, the Lord
10 10 the Lord troubled them at the sight of
13 3 from the troubled river that watereth
Judg 7 21 all the camp was t., and crying out
Ruth 3 8 the man was afraid and troubled: and he
1 K 1 6 her rival also afflicted her and t. her
14 29 my father hath troubled the land: you
16 14 an evil spirit from the Lord t. him
28 21 for he [Saul] was very much troubled
2 K 4 1 weakened, and all Israel was troubled
3 K 18 18 I have troubled Israel, but thou and
4 K 6 11 heart of the king of Syria was t. for
8 11 and was troubled so far as to blush
1 Pa 2 7 Achar, who troubled Israel and sinned
13 11 David was t. because Lord had divided
1 Es 4 4 Juda, and troubled them in building
Tob 10 6 hold thy peace and be not troubled
12 16 they were troubled and being seized with
Jdth 8 17 as our heart is troubled by their pride
14 17 their minds were troubled exceedingly
16 30 there was none that troubled Israel
Job 4 5 it hath touched thee, and thou art t.
21 4 not have just reason to be troubled
23 15 therefore I am troubled at his presence
16 and the Almighty hath troubled me
34 20 the people shall be t. at midnight
Ps 6 3 heal me, O Lord, for my bones are t.
4 and my soul is troubled exceedingly
8 my eye is troubled through indignation
11 be ashamed and be very much troubled
17 5 the torrents of iniquity troubled me
8 the foundations of the mountains were t.

15 he multiplied lightnings, and t. them
29 8 thy face from me, and I became troubled
30 10 my eye is troubled with wrath, my
37 11 my heart is t., my strength hath left
41 7 my soul is troubled within myself
45 3 not fear, when the earth shall be t.
4 their waters roared and were troubled
4 the mountains were t. with his strength
7 nations were t., and kingdoms were bowed
47 6 they were troubled, they were moved
54 3 I am grieved in my exercise; and am t.
5 my heart is troubled within me. 108:22
56 5 midst of the young lions, I slept t.
59 4 hast moved the earth and hast t. it
63 9 all that saw them were troubled; and
64 8 the Gentiles shall be troubled, and they
67 5 the wicked shall be t. at his presence
75 6 all the foolish of heart were troubled
76 5 watches: I was troubled and I spoke not
17 afraid, and the depths were troubled
80 15 laid my hand on them that troubled them
82 18 let them be ashamed and troubled
87 16 being exalted have been humbled and t.
17 and thy terrors have troubled me
89 7 and are troubled in thy indignation
103 29 away thy face, they shall be troubled
106 27 they were troubled and reeled like a
118 60 I am ready and am not troubled: that
142 4 me: my heart within me is troubled
Prov 25 26 as a fountain troubled with the foot
Cant 6 11 my soul troubled me for the chariots
Wisd 5 2 shall be troubled with terrible fear
16 6 they were troubled for a short time
17 3 t. with exceeding great astonishment
4 for noises coming down troubled them
10 a t. conscience always forecasteth
18 17 visions of evil dreams troubled them
19 the visions that t. them foreshowed
Eccu 28 15 for he hath t. many that were at peace
30 7 at every cry his bowels shall be t.
40 7 he is t. in the vision of his heart
51 29 my entrails were t. in seeking her
Isa 5 25 the mountains were troubled and their
9 19 the land is troubled, and the people
14 16 is this the man that t. the earth
21 3 I was troubled at the seeing of it
23 11 over the sea, he troubled kingdoms
32 10 you that are confident shall be t.
11 be troubled, ye confident ones: strip
44 8 fear ye not, neither be ye troubled
63 9 in all their affliction he was not t.
Jer 2 18 Egypt, to drink the troubled water
4 19 senses of my heart are troubled within
24 trembled: and all the hills were t.
17 16 I am not troubled, following thee for
25 16 they shall drink and be troubled and
31 20 therefore are my bowels troubled for
33 9 they shall fear and be troubled for all
49 23 tidings, they are troubled as in the sea
51 29 in a commotion and shall be troubled
Lam 1 20 in distress, my bowels are troubled
2 11 my bowels are troubled: my liver is
Bar 3 1 the troubled spirit crieth to thee
Eze 7 27 people of the land shall be troubled
26 18 islands in the sea shall be troubled
27 28 thy fleets shall be troubled at sound
34 18 you troubled the rest with your feet
19 and they drank what your feet had t.
Dan 2 3 being troubled in mind I know not
3 50 touched them not at all nor t. them
4 2 and the visions of my head troubled me
16 and his thoughts troubled him. 5:6
5 9 king Baltasar was much troubled and his nobles also were troubled. Then
7 15 the visions of my head troubled me
28 was much troubled with my thoughts
Jon 4 1 Jonas was exceedingly troubled and was
Mich 7 3 his soul, and they have troubled it
Haba 3 7 of the land of Madian shall be t.
16 heard and my bowels were troubled
1 Ma 3 5 that t. his people he burnt with fire
6 workers of iniquity were troubled: and
10 67 heard of it and was much troubled
12 44 why hast thou troubled all the people
2 Ma 9 24 was left, might not be t. Moreover
Mat 2 3 king Herod hearing this, was troubled
9 20 woman who was troubled with an issue
14 26 walking upon the sea, were troubled
15 22 my daughter is grievously t. by a devil
17 22 and they were troubled exceedingly
24 6 see that ye be not troubled. For these
26 22 they being very much troubled, began
Mark 1 34 that were t. with divers diseases; and
5 15 see him that was t. with the devil
18 he that had been t. with the devil
6 50 for they all saw him and were troubled
9 19 the spirit troubled him; and being
Luke 1 12 Zachary seeing him, was troubled and
29 who having heard, was t. at his saying
6 18 were t. with unclean spirits. Acts 5:16
10 41 and art troubled about many things
24 37 they being troubled and frightened
38 why are you troubled, and why do
John 5 7 I have no man, when the water is t.
11 33 groaned in the spirit and t. himself
12 27 now is my soul troubled. And what
13 21 these things, he was troubled in spirit
14 1 let not your heart be troubled. 27
Acts 15 24 t. you with words, subverting your souls
20 10 be not troubled, for his soul is in him
2 Th 1 7 to you who are troubled, rest with us
1 P 3 14 afraid of their fear, and be not t.
troubles 3 K 2 26 in all the t. my father endured
Tob 13 19 Jerusalem his city from all her troubles
Job 5 19 in six troubles he shall deliver thee
Ps 24 17 troubles of my heart are multiplied
33 5 he delivered me from all my troubles
7 and saved him out of all his troubles
18 delivered them out of all their troubles
45 2 a helper in troubles which have found
70 20 how great troubles hast thou shown me
Wisd 17 8 promised to drive away fears and t.
1 Ma 12 13 we have had many troubles and wars
troublesome Judg 14 17 as she was t. to him, he
Job 16 2 you are all troublesome comforters
Ps 34 13 when they were t. to me, I was clothed
54 4 in wrath they were troublesome to me
Eccu 10 11 long sickness is t. to the physician
13 13 be not t. to him, lest thou be put
Isa 1 14 they are become t. to me, I am weary
42 4 he shall not be sad nor troublesome
1 Ma 12 14 we would not be troublesome to you
Luke 18 5 because this widow is t. to me, I will
Gal 6 17 let no man be troublesome to me; for I
troublest 3 K 18 17 art thou he that t. Israel
Ps 64 8 who troublest the depth of the sea
troubleth 1 K 16 15 evil spirit from God t. thee
Job 22 10 snares, and sudden fear troubleth thee
Prov 11 29 troubleth his own house. 15:27
Ecce 7 8 oppression troubleth the wise and shall
Gal 5 10 he that t. you, shall bear the judgment
troubling Acts 17 13 stirring up and t. multitude
troughs Exod 2 16 when the troughs were filled
Gen 24 20 pouring out the pitcher into the troughs
30 38 he put them in the troughs where
40 put the rods in the troughs. 41

trowel Amos 7 7 in his hand a mason's trowel
Amos 7 8 I said: A mason's trowel. And the Lord
8 I will lay down the trowel in the midst
true Gen 42 16 proved, whether it be t. or false
Gen 42 20 that I may find your words to be true
Exod 34 6 patient and of much compassion and t.
Deut 17 4 diligently, and found it to be true
22 20 if what he charged her with be true
25 15 thy bushel shall be equal and true
15 shalt have a just and a true weight
Josu 2 12 me a true token, that you will save
14 7 him word again as to me seemed true
2 K 7 28 art God, and thy words shall be true
3 K 10 6 the report is true which I heard in
17 24 word of the Lord in thy mouth is true
22 16 tell me nothing but that which is true
2 Pa 9 5 the word is true which I heard in my
15 3 without true God and without a priest
Jdth 6 5 but if thou think thy prophecy true
8 28 things which thou hast spoken are t.
Job 12 20 changeth the speech of the t. speakers
Ps 18 10 judgments of the Lord are t., justified
85 15 patient and of much mercy, and true
Wisd 1 6 and he is a true searcher of his heart
2 17 let us see then if his words be true
18 if he be the true son of God, he will
5 19 will take true judgment instead of a
6 18 is the most true desire of discipline
7 17 true knowledge of the things that are
12 27 they acknowledged him the true God
15 1 thou, our God, art gracious and true
Eccu 5 13 and return a true answer with wisdom
25 12 he that findeth a true friend and
31 29 testimony of his niggardliness is t.
37 18 discovereth sometimes true things
20 let the true word go before thee
Jer 2 21 a chosen vineyard, all true seed: how
10 10 but the Lord is the true God: he is
14 13 will give you true peace in this place
Eze 18 8 hath executed true judgment between
Dan 2 9 you also give a true interpretation
45 dream is true, and the interpretation
3 14 said: Is it true, O Sidrach, Misach and
27 and all thy works are true, and thy
27 ways right, and all thy judgments true
28 hast executed true judgments in all
31 to us, thou hast done in true judgment
91 the king, and said: True, O king. He
4 34 because all his works are true and his
6 12 the word is true according to the decree
8 26 vision . . . which was told, is true
10 1 a true word and great strength: and
Zach 7 9 judge ye true judgment and show ye
Mat 22 16 thou art a true speaker. Mark 12:14
Luke 16 11 trust you with that which is the true
John 1 9 that was the true light, which
3 33 hath set his seal that God is true
4 23 when the true adorers shall adore the
37 in this is the saying true: That it is
5 31 of myself, my witness is not true
32 which he witnesseth of me is true
6 32 my Father giveth you the true bread
7 18 he is true, and there is no injustice
28 he that sent me is true. 8:26
8 13 of thyself: thy testimony is not true
14 my testimony is true. 16
17 that the testimony of two men is true
10 42 John said of this man, were true
15 1 I am the true vine; and my Father is
17 3 they may know thee, the only true God
19 35 and his testimony is true. And he
35 and he knoweth that he saith true
21 24 we know that his testimony is true
Acts 12 9 he knew not that it was true which
Rom 3 4 but God is true; and every man a liar
2 C 6 8 as deceivers, and yet true; as unknown
Phil 4 8 whatsoever things are true, whatsoever
1 Th 1 9 idols, to serve the living and true God
1 Tim 6 19 that they may lay hold on the true life
Titus 1 13 testimony is true. Wherefore rebuke
Heb 8 2 a minister of . . . the true tabernacle
9 24 with hands, the patterns of the true
10 22 let us draw near with a true heart in
1 P 5 12 that this is the true grace of God
2 P 2 22 that of the true proverb has happened
1 J 2 8 which thing is true both in him and
8 passed, and the true light now shineth
5 20 that we may know the true God and may
20 true God, and may be in his true Son
20 this is the true God and life eternal
3 J 12 knowest that our testimony is true
Apoc 3 7 saith the Holy One and the true one
14 Amen, the faithful and true witness
6 10 how long, O Lord, holy and true, dost
15 3 just and true are thy ways, O King of
16 7 true and just are thy judgments. And
19 2 true and just are his judgments, who
9 to me: These words of God are true
11 sat upon him was called faithful and t.
21 5 words are most faithful and t. 22:6
truest Eze 43 13 of the altar by the truest cubit
truly Gen 20 12 also she is truly my sister, the
1 K 20 3 but t. as the Lord liveth and thy soul
21 5 truly, as to what concerneth women
25 21 truly in vain have I kept all that
26 25 David: and truly doing thou shalt do
Jdth 8 21 whether they worshipped their God t.
Eccu 42 1 shalt thou be truly without confusion
Isa 59 4 is there any one that judgeth truly
Jer 3 23 t. in the Lord our God is salvation
10 19 truly this is my own evil, and I will
Luke 11 48 t. you bear witness that you consent
John 4 18 thy husband. This thou hast said truly
Heb 11 15 truly if they had been mindful of that
trumpet Exod 19 13 when the t. shall begin to sound
Exod 19 16 noise of the trumpet sounded exceeding
19 the sound of the trumpet grew by degrees
20 18 flames, and the sound of the trumpet
Lev 25 9 sound the trumpet in seventh month, the
Num 10 6 second sounding and like noise of the t.
Josu 6 5 when the voice of the trumpet shall give
Judg 3 27 he sounded the t. in mount Ephraim
6 34 and he [Gedeon] sounded the trumpet
7 18 when the trumpet shall sound in my hand
1 K 13 3 Saul sounded trumpet over all the land
2 K 2 28 Joab sounded the trumpet. 18:16
6 15 joyful shouting, and with sound of t.
15 10 you shall hear the sound of the trumpet
20 1 he [Seba] sounded the trumpet and said
22 and he [Joab] sounded the trumpet and
3 K 1 34 you shall sound the trumpet and shall
39 they sounded the trumpet. 4 K 9:13
41 Joab also hearing sound of the trumpet
1 Pa 16 6 to sound the trumpet continually before
42 Heman and Idithun sounded the trumpet
2 Pa 15 14 shouting, and with sound of trumpet
2 Es 4 18 built, and sounded with a trumpet by me
20 you shall hear the sound of the trumpet
Job 39 24 when the noise of the trumpet soundeth
25 when he heareth the trumpet, he saith
Ps 46 6 the Lord with the sound of trumpet
80 4 blow up the trumpet on the new moon
150 3 praise him with sound of trumpet: praise
Isa 18 3 you shall hear the sound of the trumpet
27 13 noise shall be made with a great t.
58 1 not, lift up thy voice like a trumpet

Jer 4 5 and sound with the trumpet in the land
19 the sound of the t. Eze 33:5; Dan 3:7
21 how long shall I hear sound of the t.
6 1 sound the trumpet in Thecua, and set
17 hearken ye to the sound of the trumpet
42 14 nor hear the sound of the trumpet
51 27 sound with the trumpet among the nations
Eze 7 14 blow the trumpet let all be made ready
33 3 sound the trumpet and tell the people
4 that heareth the sound of the trumpet
6 coming, sound not the trumpet: and
Dan 3 5 shall hear the sound of the t. 10, 15
Osee 5 8 the cornet in Gabaa, the trumpet in Rama
8 1 let there be a trumpet in thy throat
Joel 2 1 blow ye the trumpet in Sion, sound an
15 blow the trumpet in Sion, sanctify
Amos 2 2 with a noise, with the sound of trumpet
3 6 shall the trumpet sound in a city, and
Soph 1 15 a day of the trumpet and alarm against
Zach 9 14 the Lord God will sound the trumpet
1 Ma 4 13 that were with Judas sounded the trumpet
5 31 went up to heaven like a trumpet and
Mat 6 2 sound not a trumpet before thee, as
24 31 he shall send his angels with a t.
1 C 14 8 if the trumpet give an uncertain sound
15 52 at the last trumpet: for the trumpet
52 for the trumpet shall sound, and the
1 Th 4 15 and with the trumpet of God: and the
Heb 12 19 sound of a t. and the voice of words
Apoc 1 10 behind me a great voice as of a trumpet
4 1 of a trumpet speaking with me, said
8 6 prepared themselves to sound the t.
7 angel sounded the t. 8, 10, 12; 9:1, 13; 11:15
13 angels who are yet to sound the t.
9 14 the sixth angel, who had the trumpet
10 7 when he shall begin to sound the t.
18 22 that play on the pipe and on the t.
trumpeters 2 Pa 29 28 the t. were in their office
trumpets Lev 23 24 with the sound of trumpets
Num 10 2 make thee two trumpets of beaten silver
3 when thou shalt sound the trumpets, all
5 if the sound of the trumpets be longer
6 when the trumpets shall sound for a
7 the sound of the trumpets shall be plain
8 sons of Aaron the priest shall sound t.
9 you shall sound aloud with the trumpets
10 sound the trumpets over the holocausts
29 1 the day of the sounding and of trumpets
31 6 holy vessels, and the trumpets to sound
Josu 6 4 the priests shall take the seven t.
4 the priests shall sound the trumpets
6 let 7 other priests take the 7 trumpets
8 the seven priests blew the seven t.
9 the sound of the trumpets was heard
13 seven of them [took] seven trumpets
13 walking and sounding the trumpets
13 followed the ark, and they blew the t.
16 priests sounded with the trumpets. 1 Pa 15:24; 2 Pa 7:6
20 a shout, and the trumpets sounding
Judg 7 8 taking victuals and trumpets according
16 and gave them trumpets in their hands
18 do you also blow the trumpets on every
19 alarmed, they began to sound their t.
20 with their right hands the trumpets
20 when they sounded their trumpets
22 persisted sounding the trumpets. And
4 K 11 14 the singers and the trumpets near him
14 rejoicing and sounding the trumpets
12 13 or fleshhooks, or censers, or trumpets
1 Pa 13 8 timbrels and cymbals and trumpets, and
15 28 with trumpets and cymbals and psalteries
2 Pa 5 12 twenty priests, sounding with trumpets
13 sounded together both with trumpets
13 12 his priests who sound with trumpets
14 to sound with the trumpets. 29:27
20 28 with psalteries and harps and trumpets
23 13 rejoicing and sounding with trumpets
29 26 David, and the priests with trumpets
1 Es 3 10 priests stood in their ornaments with t.
2 Es 12 34 of the sons of the priests with trumpets
40 Elioenai, Zacharia, Hanania with t.
Jdth 15 3 they went down sounding with trumpets
Ps 97 6 with long trumpets and sound of cornet
Eccu 50 18 they sounded with beaten trumpets and
1 Ma 3 54 they sounded with trumpets. 4:40
6 33 they sounded the t. 7:45; 9:12
38 wings, with trumpets to stir up the army
16 8 and they sounded the holy trumpets: and
2 Ma 15 25 came forward with trumpets and songs
Apoc 8 2 there were given to them seven trumpets
6 the 7 angels who had the 7 trumpets
trust Gen 44 32 servant, who took him into my trust
Lev 6 2 which was committed to his trust; or
Deut 28 66 neither shalt thou trust thy life
2 K 22 3 God is my strong one, in him will I t.
31 is the shield of all that trust in him
4 K 18 20 on whom dost thou trust, that thou
21 dost thou trust in Egypt a staff of a
21 to all that trust in him. Isa 36:6
22 we trust in the Lord. Isa 36:7
24 dost thou trust in Egypt for chariots
30 neither let him make you t. in the Lord
22 7 have it in their power and in their t.
1 Pa 9 22 Samuel the seer appointed in their t.
2 Pa 16 9 who with a perfect heart trust in him
32 10 in whom do you t., that you sit still
Jdth 6 15 thou forsakest not them that t. on thee
7 8 of Israel trust not in their spears nor
20 and deliver not them that trust in thee
9 9 who trust in their multitude and in
Job 8 14 his trust shall be like the spider's web
13 15 should kill me, I will trust in him
24 22 standeth up, he shall not t. to his life
39 12 wilt thou trust him that he will render
Ps 2 13 blessed are all they that trust in him
4 6 sacrifice of justice, and t. in the Lord
7 2 in thee have I put my trust. 140:8
10 2 in the Lord I put my trust: how then
15 1 I have put my trust in thee. 30:15; 54:24; 55:4
16 7 who savest them that trust in thee
17 3 helper, and in him will I put my trust
31 is the protector of all that t. in him
19 8 some trust in chariots, and some in
24 2 in thee, O my God, I put my trust
25 1 and I have put my trust in the Lord
33 23 of them that t. in him shall offend
35 8 their t. under the covert of thy wings
36 3 trust in the Lord and do good and dwell
5 thy way to the Lord, and trust in him
39 5 whose trust is in the name of the Lord
43 7 I will not t. in my bow: neither shall
48 7 they that trust in their own strength
55 5 in God I have put my trust: I will not
61 9 trust in him, all ye congregation of
11 trust not in iniquity, and cover not
90 2 my God, in him will I trust. For he
4 and under his wings thou shalt trust
113 8 them: and all such as trust in them
117 9 it is good to trust in the Lord, rather than to trust in princes
124 1 that t. in the Lord shall be as mount
145 2 put not your trust in princes: in the
Prov 22 19 that thy trust may be in the Lord
25 19 to trust to an unfaithful man in the

26 25 when he shall speak low, trust him not
Wisd 3 9 that trust in him shall understand the
14 5 men also trust their lives even to a
29 whilst they trust in idols, which are
15 6 to have no better things to trust in
16 24 benefit of them that trust in thee
Eccu 2 6 direct thy way, and trust in him. Keep
4 17 if he trust to her, he shall inherit
19 try him by her laws and trust his soul
7 28 to her that is hateful, t. not thyself
11 22 trust in God and stay in thy place
12 10 never trust thy enemy; for as a brass
16 2 trust not to their life and respect not
31 8 nor put his trust in money nor in
32 25 trust not thyself to a rugged way, lest
34 7 failed that put their trust in them
36 28 who will trust him that hath no rest
38 35 all these trust to their hands and
Isa 36 5 on whom dost thou trust, that thou art
9 if thou trust in Egypt, in chariots
15 not Ezechias make you trust in the Lord
42 17 confounded, that trust in a graven thing
57 13 that putteth his trust in me, shall
59 4 but they trust in a mere nothing and
Jer 2 37 the Lord hath destroyed thy trust and
7 4 trust not in lying words, saying: The
8 you put your trust in lying words, which
14 called upon, and in which you trust
9 4 let him not trust in any brother of his
28 15 made this people to trust in a lie
29 31 and hath caused you to trust in a lie
39 18 because thou hast put thy trust in me
46 25 Pharao, and upon them that trust in him
Bar 1 16 not believed him nor put our t. in him
3 18 silver and gold, wherein men trust
Dan 3 40 no confusion to them that t. in thee
13 60 who saveth them that trust in him
Mich 7 5 and trust not in a prince: keep the
1 Ma 10 37 of the kingdom, that are of trust
2 Ma 8 18 they trust in their weapons and in
18 we trust in the Almighty Lord, who
9 27 for I trust that he will behave with
Mark 10 24 hard is it for them that t. in riches
Luke 16 11 will t. you with that which is the
John 2 24 Jesus did not trust himself unto them
5 45 accuseth you, Moses, in whom you trust
1 C 16 7 I trust that I shall abide with you some
2 C 1 9 that we should not trust in ourselves
10 we trust that he will yet also deliver
5 11 I trust also that in your consciences
10 7 if any man trust to himself, that he is
13 6 I trust that you shall know that we are
Phil 2 24 I trust in the Lord, that I myself also
1 Tim 1 11 which hath been committed to my trust
5 5 let her trust in God, and continue in
6 17 nor to t. in the uncertainty of riches
20 keep that which is committed to thy t.
2 Tim 1 14 keep the good thing committed to thy t.
Heb 2 13 I will put my trust in him. And again
6 9 we trust better things of you, and
13 18 we trust we have a good conscience
1 P 1 13 trust perfectly in the grace which is
trusted Deut 32 37 are their gods, in whom they t.
4 K 18 5 [Ezechias] trusted in the Lord the God
1 Pa 10 14 and trusted not in the Lord: therefore
2 Pa 13 18 because they had trusted in the Lord
16 12 rather t. in the skill of physicians
17 3 and [Josaphat] trusted not in Baalim
Jdth 4 12 Amalec that trusted in his own strength
Ps 12 6 but I have trusted in thy mercy. My
32 21 and in his holy name we have trusted
40 10 the man of my peace, in whom I trusted
51 9 trusted in the abundance of his riches
77 22 and trusted not in his salvation. And
118 42 that I have trusted in thy words. And
Wisd 18 6 knowing what oaths they had trusted to
Isa 30 12 have trusted in oppression and tumult
31 1 have not trusted in the Holy One of
47 10 thou hast trusted in thy wickedness
Jer 13 25 forgotten me, and hast t. in falsehood
15 18 deceitful waters that cannot be t.
48 7 thou hast trusted in thy bulwarks
13 ashamed of Bethel, in which they t.
49 4 that hast trusted in thy treasures
Osee 10 13 because thou hast trusted in thy ways
Haba 2 18 t. in a thing of his own forging, to
Soph 3 2 she hath not trusted in the Lord, she
1 Ma 10 78 of horsemen, and he trusted in them
2 Ma 3 12 who had trusted to the place and temple
15 7 trusted with all hope that God would
Mat 27 43 he trusted in God; let him now deliver
Luke 11 22 away all his armor wherein he trusted
18 9 to some who trusted in themselves as
1 P 3 5 holy women also, who trusted in God
trustedst Deut 28 52 wherein thou t. in all thy
2 Pa 16 8 yet because thou trustedst in the Lord
trustest 4 K 18 19 what this confidence wherein thou trustest. Isa 36:4
4 K 19 10 thy God deceive thee, in whom thou trustest. Isa 37:10
Isa 36 6 thou trustest upon this broken staff
Jer 5 17 strong cities, wherein thou trustest
1 Ma 7 7 send some man whom thou trustest and
10 71 if thou trustest in thy forces, come
trusteth Job 40 18 he t. that the Jordan may run
Ps 56 2 on me: for my soul trusteth in thee
83 13 blessed is man that trusteth in thee
85 2 servant, O my God, that t. in thee
134 18 and every one that trusteth in them
Prov 10 4 he that t. to lies feedeth the winds
11 28 that trusteth in his riches shall fall
12 2 that t. in his own devices doth wickedly
16 20 he that trusteth in the Lord is blessed
28 25 that t. in the Lord, shall be healed
26 he that t. in his own heart, is a fool
29 25 that t. in the Lord, shall be set on
31 11 heart of her husband trusteth in her
Eccu 32 28 he that trusteth in him, shall fare
Jer 17 5 cursed be the man that t. in man and
7 blessed be the man that t. in the Lord
trusting Judg 20 22 Israel t. in their strength
Jdth 9 6 trusting in their chariots and in their
Prov 17 12 than a fool trusting in his own folly
Eccu 16 8 were destroyed t. to their own strength
19 10 trusting that it will not burst thee
Isa 30 2 and trusting in the shadow of Egypt
31 1 to Egypt for help, trusting in horses
Eze 16 15 trusting in thy beauty, thou playedst
33 13 t. in his justice, commit iniquity
13 he, t. in his justice, commit iniquity
2 Ma 7 40 died undefiled, wholly t. in the Lord
10 34 within, t. to the strength of the place
11 4 and t. in the multitude of his foot
12 14 t. in the strength of the walls and
Philem 21 t. in thy obedience, I have written to
trusty Tob 10 6 with whom we sent him is very t.
truth Gen 24 27 not taken away his mercy and t.
Gen 24 49 if you do according to mercy and truth
32 10 of thy truth which thou hast fulfilled
40 22 that the truth of the interpreter might
47 29 shalt show me this kindness and truth
Exod 18 21 whom there is t. and that hate avarice
23 2 of the most part, to stray from the t.
28 30 in rational of judgment doctrine and t.
Lev 8 8 rational, on which was Doctrine and T.
Deut 13 14 the truth of the thing by looking well

17 9 shall show thee the t. of the judgment
18 11 that seeketh the truth from the dead
31 17 in t. it is because God is not with me
Josu 2 14 land, we will show thee mercy and truth
Judg 16 17 opening the truth of the thing, he said
1 K 12 24 fear the Lord and serve him in truth
2 K 2 6 surely will render you mercy and truth
15 20 Lord will show thee mercy and truth
20 19 am not I she that answer t. in Israel
3 K 2 4 ways, and shall walk before me in truth
3 6 walked before thee in truth. 4 K 20:3
4 K 5 15 in truth I know there is no other God
19 17 of a t., O Lord, the kings of Assyrians
20 19 let peace and truth be in my days
2 Pa 18 15 to say nothing but the truth to me
31 20 that which was good, and right and truth
32 1 after these things and this truth
2 Es 9 13 right judgments and the law of truth
33 because thou hast done truth, but we
Tob 1 2 captivity, forsook not the way of truth
3 2 and all thy ways mercy and truth and
12 11 I discover then the truth unto you
14 10 serve the Lord in truth and seek to do
11 and bless him at all times in truth
Jdth 5 5 I will tell the truth in thy sight
Esth 9 30 should have peace and receive truth
Job 6 25 why have you detracted the words of t.
21 34 answer is shown to be repugnant to t.
Ps 5 10 for there is no truth in their mouth
14 3 he that speaketh truth in his heart
24 5 direct me in thy truth and teach me
10 ways of the Lord are mercy and truth
25 3 and I am well pleased with thy truth
29 10 confess to thee, or declare thy truth
30 6 redeemed me, O Lord, the God of truth
24 the Lord will require truth and will
35 6 thy truth reacheth even to the clouds
39 11 heart: I have declared thy truth and
11 not concealed thy mercy and thy truth
12 and thy truth have always upheld me
42 3 send forth thy light and thy truth
44 5 because of t. and meekness and justice
50 8 thou hast loved truth: the uncertain
53 7 enemies; and cut them off in thy truth
56 4 God hath sent his mercy and his truth
11 heavens; and thy t. unto the clouds
60 8 his mercy and truth who shall search
68 14 hear me, in the truth of thy salvation
70 22 I will also confess to thee thy truth
83 12 God loveth mercy and truth: the Lord
84 11 mercy and truth have met each other
12 truth is sprung out of the earth: and
85 11 and I will walk in thy truth: let my
87 12 mercy: and thy truth in destruction
88 2 I will show forth thy truth with my
3 thy truth shall be prepared in them
6 thy truth in the church of the saints
9 Lord, and thy truth is round about thee
15 mercy and t. shall go before thy face
25 my truth and my mercy shall be with him
34 nor will I suffer my truth to fail
50 those didst swear to David in thy truth
90 5 his truth shall compass thee with a
91 3 morning, and thy truth in the night
95 13 with justice, and the people with his t.
97 3 remembered his mercy and his truth
99 5 his truth to generation and generation
107 5 thy truth even unto the clouds. Be thou
110 7 works of his hands are t. and judgment
8 ever and ever, made in truth and equity
116 2 truth of the Lord remaineth forever
118 30 I have chosen the way of truth: thy
43 take not thou the word of truth utterly
75 and in thy truth thou hast humbled me
86 all thy statutes are truth: they have
90 thy truth unto all generations: thou
138 testimonies: and thy truth exceedingly
142 justice forever: and thy law is the t.
151 O Lord: and all thy ways are truth
160 the beginning of thy words is truth
131 11 the Lord hath sworn truth to David
137 2 for thy mercy and for thy truth: for
142 1 ear to my supplication in thy truth
144 18 to all that call upon him in truth
145 7 who keepeth truth forever: who
Prov 3 3 let not mercy and truth leave thee
8 7 my mouth shall meditate truth and my
12 19 the lip of truth shall be steadfast
14 22 mercy and truth prepare good things
16 6 by mercy and t. iniquity is redeemed
18 5 to decline from the truth of judgment
20 28 mercy and truth preserve the king and
22 21 words of truth, to answer out of these
23 23 buy truth, and do not sell wisdom
26 28 a deceitful tongue loveth not truth
28 21 for morsel of bread forsaketh the truth
29 14 the king that judgeth the poor in truth
Ecce 9 2 perjured, so he also that sweareth t.
12 10 words most right and full of truth
Wisd 3 9 trust in him, shall understand the t.
5 6 we have erred from the way of truth
6 24 light, and will not pass over the truth
Eccu 2 13 protector to all that seek him in truth
4 24 soul be not ashamed to say the truth
30 in nowise speak against the truth, but
5 12 Lord, and in truth of thy judgment
15 8 that speak t. shall be found with her
16 25 I show forth in truth his knowledge
17 20 hath appointed to them the lot of truth
18 29 have understood truth and justice and
19 23 uttereth an exact word telling the t.
24 25 is all grace of the way and of the t.
32 most High, and the knowledge of truth
47 but for all that seek out the truth
27 10 t. will return to them that practice
31 28 the testimony of his truth is faithful
34 4 what t. can come from that which is
22 that wait upon him in the way of truth
37 19 that he may direct thy way in truth
41 24 of theft and of the truth of God and
45 12 man, endued with judgment and truth
Isa 10 20 they shall lean upon the Lord . . . in t.
16 5 one shall sit upon it in truth in the
26 2 the just nation, that keepeth the truth
33 15 walketh in justices and speaketh truth
37 18 of a truth, O Lord, the kings of the
38 3 how I have walked before thee in truth
18 down into the pit, look for thy truth
19 shall make thy t. known to the children
39 8 only let peace and truth be in my days
42 3 shall bring forth judgment unto truth
43 9 justified and hear and say: It is truth
48 1 Israel, but not in truth nor in justice
59 14 truth hath fallen down in the street
15 truth hath been forgotten: and he that
61 8 I will make their work in truth and I
Jer 4 2 as the Lord liveth, in truth and in
5 3 O Lord, thy eyes are upon truth: thou
9 3 as a bow, for lies, and not for truth
5 they will not speak the truth: for they
23 28 let him speak my word with truth
26 15 in truth the Lord sent me to you, to
28 9 known, whom the Lord hath sent in truth
32 41 I will plant them in this land in truth
33 6 to them the prayer of peace and truth
42 5 Lord be witness between us of truth

49 20 of a truth they shall destroy them
50 45 of a truth their habitation shall be
Bar 4 13 they entered by the paths of his truth
Eze 18 9 and kept my judgments, to do truth: he
Dan 3 28 according to truth and judgment, thou
7 16 asked the truth of him concerning all
8 12 truth shall be cast down on the ground
9 13 our iniquities, and think on thy truth
10 21 is set down in the scripture of truth
11 2 now I will show thee the truth. Behold
13 48 or knowledge of the truth, you have
Osee 4 1 there is no t., and there is no mercy
Mich 7 20 thou wilt perform the truth to Jacob
Zach 8 3 shall be called The city of truth
8 will be their God in t. and in justice
16 speak ye t. every one to his neighbor
16 judge ye truth and judgment of peace
19 solemnities: only love ye t. and peace
Mala 2 6 the law of truth was in his mouth
1 Ma 7 18 is no truth nor justice among them
2 Ma 7 6 the Lord God will look upon the truth
Mat 22 16 teachest the way of God in truth. Mark 12:14; Luke 20:21
Mark 5 33 before him and told him all the truth
12 32 well, Master, thou hast said in truth
Luke 9 27 but I tell you of a truth: There are
22 59 of a truth, this man was also with him
John 1 14 among us . . . full of grace and truth
3 21 he that doth truth, cometh to the
4 23 adore the Father in spirit and in t.
24 must adore him in spirit and in truth
5 33 and he gave testimony to the truth
6 14 this is of a truth the prophet that is
7 26 have the rulers known for a truth that
8 32 you shall know the truth, and the truth shall make you free
40 a man who have spoken the truth to you
44 he stood not in the truth; because truth is not in him
45 if I say the truth, you believe me not
46 if I say the truth to you, why do
14 6 I am the way and the truth and the
17 the spirit of truth, whom the world
15 26 the Spirit of truth, who proceedeth
16 7 I tell you the truth: it is expedient
13 when he, the Spirit of truth, is come
13 is come, he will teach you all truth
17 17 sanctify them in t. Thy word is t.
19 they also may be sanctified in truth
18 37 I should give testimony to the truth
37 that is of the truth, heareth my voice
38 Pilate saith to him: What is truth
Acts 4 27 of a truth there assembled together in
22 3 taught according to truth of the law
26 25 I speak words of truth and soberness
Rom 1 18 that detain the t. of God in injustice
25 who changed the truth of God into a lie
2 2 the judgment of God is, according to t.
8 who obey not the truth, but give credit
20 form of knowledge and of truth in law
3 7 if the truth of God hath more abounded
9 1 I speak the truth in Christ, I lie not
15 8 minister of the circumcision for truth
1 C 5 8 unleavened bread of sincerity and truth
13 6 iniquity, but rejoiceth with the truth
2 C 4 2 by manifestation of truth commending
6 7 in word of truth, in the power of God
7 14 have spoken all things to you in truth
14 that was made to Titus is found a truth
11 10 the truth of Christ is in me, that this
12 6 not be foolish; for I will say the truth
13 8 nothing against truth; but for the truth
Gal 2 5 that truth of the gospel might continue
14 uprightly unto the truth of the gospel
3 1 that you should not obey the truth. 5:7
4 16 your enemy, because I tell you the truth
Eph 1 13 after you had heard the word of truth
4 15 but doing the truth in charity, we may
21 taught in him, as the truth is in Jesus
24 created in justice and holiness of truth
25 putting away lying, speak ye the truth
5 9 is in all goodness and justice and truth
6 14 having your loins girt about with truth
Phil 1 18 whether by occasion, or by truth, Christ
Col 1 5 you have heard in the word of the truth
6 heard and knew the grace of God in truth
2 Th 2 10 receive not the love of the truth, that
11 judged who have not believed the truth
12 sanctification of spirit, and faith of t.
1 Tim 2 4 to come to the knowledge of the truth
7 an apostle, I say the truth, I lie not
7 doctor of the Gentiles in faith and t.
3 15 God, the pillar and ground of the truth
4 3 and by them that have known the truth
6 5 are destitute of the truth, supposing
2 Tim 2 15 rightly handling the word of truth. But
18 who have erred from the truth, saying
25 admonishing them that resist the truth
25 give them repentance to know the truth
3 7 attaining to the knowledge of the truth
8 Moses, so these also resist the truth
4 4 turn away their hearing from the truth
Titus 1 1 God and the acknowledging of the truth
14 who turn themselves away from the truth
Heb 10 26 after having the knowledge of the truth
James 1 18 he begotten us by the word of truth
3 14 and be not liars against the truth
5 19 if any of you err from the truth, and
2 P 1 12 and are confirmed in the present truth
2 2 way of truth shall be evil spoken of
1 J 1 6 we lie, and do not the truth. But if
8 ourselves, and the truth is not in us
2 4 is a liar, and the truth is not in him
21 as to them that know not the truth
21 and that no lie is of the truth. Who
27 of all things, and is truth and is no
3 18 nor in tongue, but in deed and in t.
19 in this we know that we are of the t.
4 6 by this we know the spirit of truth
5 6 testifieth, that Christ is the truth
2 J 1 children, whom I love in the truth
1 all they that have known the truth
2 sake of the t. which dwelleth in us
3 of the Father; in truth and charity
4 of thy children walking in truth, as
3 J 1 beloved Gaius, whom I love in truth
3 gave testimony to the truth in thee
3 even as thou walkest in the truth
4 to hear that my children walk in truth
8 we may be fellow helpers of the truth
12 given by all, and by the truth itself
truth's Ps 113 2 thy mercy and for thy t. sake
truths Job 13 17 receive with you ears hidden t.
Ps 11 2 saint: t. are decayed from among the
try Judg 2 22 that through them I may try Israel
Judg 3 4 he left them, that he might try Israel
6 39 if I try once more, seeking a sign
7 4 to the waters, and there I will try them
1 K 17 39 began to try if he could walk in armor
3 K 10 1 to try him with hard questions. 2 Pa 9:1
Ps 25 2 prove me, O Lord, and try me: burn my
Wisd 2 19 know his meekness and try his patience
11 11 thou didst admonish and try them as a
Eccu 4 19 till she try him by her laws and trust
6 7 try him before thou takest him and
39 5 he shall try good and evil among men

Jer 9 7 behold I will melt, and try them: for
Dan 1 12 try, I beseech thee, thy servants
Zach 13 9 I will try them as gold is tried. They
Mala 3 10 and try me in this, saith the Lord
1 Ma 10 71 and there let us try one another: for
2 Ma 14 18 afraid to try the matter by the sword
Luke 14 19 yoke of oxen, and I go to try them
John 6 6 this he said to try him; for he
1 C 3 13 and the fire shall try every man's work
2 C 13 5 try your own selves if you be in faith
1 P 4 12 the burning heat which is to try you
1 J 4 1 but try the spirits if they be of God
Apoc 3 10 to try them that dwell upon the earth
trying James 1 3 knowing that the t. of your
Tryphaena Rom 16 12 salute Tryphaena and Tryphosa
Tryphon 1 Ma 11 39 there was one T. who had been
1 Ma 11 54 T. returned, and with him Antiochus
56 Tryphon took the elephants and made
12 39 when T. had conceived a design to make
42 when T. saw that Jonathan came with
49 T. sent army and horsemen into Galilee
13 1 Simon heard that T. was gathering
12 Tryphon removed from Ptolemais with a
14 T. understood that Simon was risen up
20 Tryphon entered within the country
21 in the castle, sent messengers to T.
22 Tryphon made ready all his horsemen
24 and T. returned and went into his own
31 Tryphon when he was upon a journey
34 for all that Tryphon did was to spoil
14 1 to get him succors to fight against T.
15 10 so that few were left with Tryphon
25 he shut up Tryphon, that he could not
37 Tryphon fled away by ship to Orthosias
39 the king himself pursued after Tryphon
Tryphosa Rom 16 12 salute Tryphaena and Tryphosa
Tubalcain Gen 4 22 Sella also brought forth T.
Gen 4 22 and the sister of Tubalcain was Noema
Tubianites 2 Ma 12 17 the Jews that are called T.
Tubin 1 Ma 5 13 that were in the places of T.
tumbling Wisd 17 18 the noise of stones t. down or
tumult Num 16 42 sedition and the tumult increased
2 K 18 29 I saw a great tumult, O king, when thy
Job 3 17 there the wicked cease from tumult
Wisd 1 10 tumult of murmuring shall not be hid
Isa 3 5 the child shall make a tumult against
9 5 violent taking of spoils, with tumult
17 12 tumult of crowds, like the noise of many
25 5 shalt bring down the t. of strangers
30 12 have trusted in oppression and tumult
52 12 for you shall not go out in a tumult
Jer 46 17 of Egypt, a tumult time hath brought
25 I will visit upon the t. of Alexandria
48 45 crown of the head of the children of t.
Eze 23 46 deliver them over to tumult and rapine
Osee 10 14 a tumult shall arise among thy people
Amos 5 23 take away from me the t. of thy songs
Mich 1 13 a tumult of chariots hath astonished
2 12 they shall make a tumult by reason of
Zach 14 13 in that day there shall be a great t.
1 Ma 9 39 behold a tumult and great preparation
2 Ma 13 16 with exceeding great fear and tumult
Mat 26 5 lest perhaps there should be a tumult
27 24 but that rather a tumult was made
Mark 5 38 he seeth a tumult, and people weeping
14 2 lest there should be a t. among the
Acts 17 5 making t., set the city in an uproar
20 1 after the t. was ceased, Paul calling
21 34 he could not know certainty for the t.
38 who before these days didst raise a t.
24 18 neither with multitude, nor with tumult
tumults Esth 11 5 behold there were voices and t.
Wisd 14 25 and unfaithfulness tumults and perjury

tune Josu 6 5 shall give a longer and broken tune
Jdth 16 2 tune unto him a new psalm, extol and
Jer 48 33 not sing the accustomed cheerful tune
tunes 1 Pa 15 22 prophecy, to give out the tunes
Eccu 44 5 by their skill sought out musical tunes
tunick Exod 28 4 rational and an ephod, a tunick
Exod 28 31 made the t. of the ephod all of violet
33 at the feet of the same tunick round
39 thou shalt gird the t. with fine linen
29 5 with the linen garment and the tunick
39 20 they made also the tunick of the ephod
23 at the bottom of the tunick round about
Lev 6 10 priest shall be vested with the tunick
8 7 putting on him the violet tunick and
16 4 he shall be vested with a linen tunick
tunicks Exod 28 40 thou shalt prepare linen t.
Exod 29 8 shalt put on them the linen tunicks
39 25 they made also fine linen tunicks with
Lev 8 13 sons, he vested them with linen tunicks
10 5 as they lay, vested with linen tunicks
turbans Eze 23 15 with dyed t. on their heads
turnings 3 K 6 18 turnings and joints thereof
turns 3 K 5 14 ten thousand every month by turns
1 Pa 9 18 sons of Levi waited by their turns
19 their families in turns were keepers
23 and the tabernacle by their turns
2 Es 4 22 let us take our turns in the night
turpentine Gen 35 4 buried them under the t. tree
Gen 43 11 storax, myrrh, turpentine and almonds
3 K 13 14 found him sitting under a turpentine
Eccu 24 22 my branches as the turpentine tree
Isa 6 13 shall be made a show as a t. tree
Osee 4 13 t. tree, because the shadow thereof was
turtle Gen 15 9 a turtle also and a pigeon
Lev 12 6 a young pigeon or a turtle for sin
14 30 he shall offer a turtle or young pigeon
Ps 83 4 the turtle a nest for herself where
Cant 2 12 the voice of the turtle is heard in our
Jer 8 7 the turtle . . . have observe the time
turtledove's Cant 1 9 are beautiful as the t.
turtledoves Luke 2 24 pair of t. or two young
turtles Lev 1 14 to the Lord be of birds, of t.
Lev 5 7 two turtles or two young pigeons. 11; 12:8; 14:22; 15:14, 29; Num 6:10
tutors 4 K 10 5 and the tutors sent to Jehu
Gal 4 2 but is under tutors and governors until
twice Exod 16 22 sixth day they gathered t. as much
Num 19 6 wood, and hyssop, and scarlet t. dyed
20 11 struck the rock t. with the rod, there
1 K 18 11 stept aside out of his presence twice
3 K 11 9 Israel, who had appeared to him twice
4 K 6 10 well to himself there not once nor t.
2 Es 13 20 stayed without Jerusalem once or twice
Jdth 13 10 and she struck twice upon his neck
Job 42 10 the Lord gave Job twice as much as he
Eccu 12 7 shalt receive t. as much evil for all
13 8 drawn thee dry twice or thrice and at
32 11 if thou be asked t., let thy answer
Eze 41 6 one by another, were t. thirty-three
1 Ma 10 72 thy fathers have t. been put to flight
Mark 14 30 before the cock crow twice. 72
Luke 18 12 I fast twice in a week: I give tithes
Jude 12 twice dead, plucked up by the roots
violet and purple and scarlet twice dyed; *see* **violet**
twig Eze 17 22 I will crop off a tender t. from
twigs Eze 17 4 he cropped off the top of the t.
twined Judg 16 9 thread of tow t. with spittle
twinkling 1 C 15 52 moment, in the t. of an eye
twins Gen 25 24 twins were found in her womb
Gen 38 27 there appeared t. in her womb: and in
Cant 4 2 up from the washing, all with twins
5 like two young roes that are t. 7:3
6 5 from the washing, all with twins and

twist Lev 5 8 twist back the head of it to the
twisted Exod 36 8 curtains of twisted fine linen
Exod 38 16 court were woven with twisted linen
39 3 they might be twisted with the woof
Eccu 45 13 of t. scarlet the work of an artist
fine twisted linen; *see* **linen**
twisting Lev 1 15 t. back the neck, and breaking
two-edged Judg 3 16 he made himself a t. sword
Ps 149 6 and two-edged swords in their hands
Prov 5 4 wormwood, and sharp as a t. sword
Eccu 21 4 iniquity is like a two-edged sword
Heb 4 12 more piercing than any two-edged sword
Apoc 1 16 came out a sharp two-edged sword: and
2 12 that hath the sharp two-edged sword
19 15 proceedeth a sharp two-edged sword
twofold Mat 23 15 child of hell t. more than
Tychicus Acts 20 4 and of Asia, T. and Trophimus
Eph 6 21 Tychicus, my dearest brother. Col 4:7
2 Tim 4 12 but Tychicus I have sent to Ephesus
Titus 3 12 when I shall send to thee Artemas or T.
tying Judg 16 13 tying them round about a nail
Tyrannus 2 Ma 4 40 violence, one T. being captain
Acts 19 9 daily in the school of one Tyrannus
tyranny 3 K 16 20 of his conspiracy and tyranny
Job 15 20 number of the years of his tyranny
Wisd 16 4 come upon them that exercised tyranny
tyrant Job 34 19 nor hath regarded the tyrant
Wisd 12 14 nor tyrant in thy sight inquire about
2 Ma 4 25 but having the mind of a cruel tyrant
7 27 mocking the cruel tyrant, she said
tyrants Job 35 9 for the violence of the arm of t.
Wisd 14 16 were worshipped by commandment of t.
Eccu 11 5 many tyrants have sat on the throne
Tyre Josu 19 29 Horma to the strong city of Tyre
2 K 24 7 they passed near the walls of Tyre
3 K 7 13 sent, and brought Hiram from Tyre
9 12 Hiram came out of Tyre, to see the
Ps 44 13 the daughters of Tyre with gifts, yea
82 8 Philistines, with the inhabitants of T.
86 4 behold the foreigners, and Tyre and
Isa 23 1 the burden of Tyre. Howl, ye ships
5 sorry when they shall hear of Tyre
8 who hath taken this counsel against T.
15 that thou, O Tyre, shalt be forgotten
15 shall be unto T. as song of a harlot
17 that the Lord will visit Tyre, and will
Jer 25 22 all the kings of Tyre and all the kings
47 4 Tyre and Sidon shall be destroyed
Eze 26 2 because Tyre hath said of Jerusalem
3 behold I come against thee, O Tyre
4 they shall break down the walls of Tyre
7 will bring against Tyre Nabuchodonosor
15 thus saith the Lord God to Tyre: Shall
27 2 man, take up a lamentation for Tyre
3 say to Tyre that dwelleth at the entry
3 O Tyre, thou hast said: I am of perfect
8 thy wise men, O Tyre, were thy pilots
32 what city is like Tyre, which is become
28 2 say to the prince of Tyre: Thus saith
29 18 to undergo hard service against Tyre
18 no reward given him nor his army for T.
Osee 9 13 Ephraim, as I saw, was a Tyre founded
Joel 3 4 what have you to do with me, O Tyre
Amos 1 9 for three crimes of Tyre, and for four
10 I will send a fire upon the wall of Tyre
Zach 9 2 the borders thereof and Tyre and Sidon
3 Tyre hath built herself a stronghold
1 Ma 5 15 of Tyre and of Sidon were assembled
11 59 governor from the borders of Tyre
2 Ma 4 18 used every fifth year was kept at Tyre
32 and others he had sold at Tyre and in
44 when the king was come to Tyre, three
Mat 11 21 if in Tyre and Sidon. Luke 10:13
22 be more tolerable for Tyre. Luke 10:14
15 21 retired into the coasts of Tyre and
Mark 3 8 they about Tyre and Sidon, a great
7 24 went into the coasts of Tyre and Sidon
31 going out of the coasts of Tyre, he
Luke 6 17 the seacoast both of Tyre and Sidon
Acts 21 3 we sailed into Syria, and came to Tyre
7 voyage by sea, from Tyre came down to
king of Tyre 2 K 5 11 Hiram k. . . . sent messengers. 1 Pa 14:1
3 K 5 1 Hiram king of Tyre sent his servants
9 11 Hiram the king of Tyre furnishing
2 Pa 2 3 he sent also to Hiram king of Tyre
11 Hiram king of Tyre sent a letter to
Jer 27 3 children of Ammon, and to the k. . . .
Eze 28 11 a lamentation upon the king of Tyre
Tyrian 3 K 7 14 whose father was a T. 2 Pa 2:14
Tyrians 1 Pa 22 4 Tyrians brought to David
1 Es 3 7 drink and oil to the Sidonians and T.
2 Es 13 16 some Tyrians also dwelt there, who
Eccu 46 21 he crushed the princes of the Tyrians
2 Ma 4 49 the T. being moved with indignation
Acts 12 20 he was angry with the Tyrians and the
tying Gen 49 11 tying his foal to the vineyard
Exod 12 34 and tying it in their cloaks, put it on

U

Ubil 1 Pa 27 30 over the camels, U. an Ishmahelite
udder Lev 22 27 shall be seven days under the u.
Uel 1 Es 10 34 sons of Bani, Maaddi, Amram, and U.
Ulai Dan 8 2 that I was over the gate of Ulai
Dan 8 16 heard the voice of a man between Ulai
Ulam 1 Pa 7 16 Sares: his sons were Ulam and Recen
1 Pa 7 17 the son of Ulam, Baden. These are
8 39 his brothers, were Ulam the firstborn
40 sons of Ulam were most valiant men
ulcer Lev 13 18 when also there has been an ulcer
Lev 13 19 in the place of the u. there appeareth
20 plague of leprosy is broken out in u.
23 it is but the scar of an ulcer and the
Deut 28 27 strike thee with the ulcer of Egypt
35 Lord strike thee with a very sore ulcer
Job 2 7 struck Job with a very grievous ulcer
unable Num 11 23 is the hand of the Lord unable
Wisd 11 18 was not unable to send upon them a
12 9 not that thou wast unable to bring
13 16 knowing that it is u. to help itself
19 him that is unable to do anything
unaccountable Prov 5 6 steps are wandering and u.
unaccustomed Jer 31 18 bullock u. to the yoke
unadvisedly 1 Ma 5 67 went out u. to fight
unanimous Eccu 6 12 shalt have u. friendship
unanimously Wisd 18 9 they u. ordered a law
unarmed Jdth 5 27 men unarmed and without force
unawares Josu 20 3 shall kill a person unawares
Josu 20 5 because he slew his neighbor unawares
9 whosoever had killed a person unawares
2 Ma 8 6 coming unawares upon the towns and
Gal 2 4 false brethren unawares brought in, who
unbecoming 2 Ma 14 42 abuses u. his noble birth
unbelief Mat 13 58 miracles there because of their u.
Mat 17 19 because of your u. For, amen I say to
Mark 6 6 he wondered because of their unbelief
9 23 I do believe, Lord: help my unbelief
Rom 3 3 shall their u. make faith of God without
11 20 because of unbelief they were broken off
23 if they abide not still in u., shall be
30 have obtained mercy, through their u.
32 for God hath concluded all in unbelief
Eph 2 2 now worketh on the children of unbelief
5 6 anger of God upon the children of u.
Col 3 6 cometh upon the children of unbelief

1 Tim 1 13 because I did it ignorantly in unbelief
Heb 3 12 in any of you an evil heart of unbelief
19 could not enter in, because of unbelief
4 6 did not enter because of unbelief: again
11 fall into the same example of unbelief
unbeliever 1 C 7 15 if the u. depart, let him
2 C 6 15 what part hath the faithful with the u.
unbelievers Jdth 13 27 hath cut off head of all u.
Eze 2 6 thou art among u. and destroyers and
Luke 12 46 him his portion with unbelievers. And
Rom 15 31 I may be delivered from the u. that are
1 C 6 6 brother, and that before unbelievers
14 22 sign, not to believers, but to u.; but
22 prophecies not to u., but to believers
2 C 4 4 hath blinded the minds of unbelievers
6 14 bear not the yoke with unbelievers. For
Titus 1 15 and to unbelievers, nothing is clean
Heb 11 31 perished not with the u., receiving
unbelieving Eccu 16 7 in an u. nation wrath shall
Isa 65 2 hands all the day to an u. people who
Haba 2 4 he that is unbelieving, his soul shall
Mat 17 16 u. and perverse generation, how long
Acts 14 2 the u. Jews stirred up and incensed
1 C 7 14 the unbelieving husband is sanctified
14 u. wife is sanctified by the believing
Apoc 21 8 fearful and u. and the abominable and
unburied 2 Ma 5 10 that had cast out many u.
2 Ma 5 10 both unlamented and unburied, neither
uncertain 1 K 23 13 u. where they should stay
Job 15 20 number of the years of his tyranny is u.
Ps 50 8 the u. and hidden things of thy wisdom
Ecce 9 2 all things are kept uncertain for the
Wisd 9 14 fearful, and our counsels uncertain
1 C 14 8 if the trumpet give an uncertain sound
uncertainty 1 C 9 26 so run, not as at an u.
1 Tim 6 17 nor to trust in the u. of riches, but
unchangeable Job 15 15 among his saints none is u.
unchaste Apoc 22 15 sorcerers and u. and murderers
uncircumcised Gen 34 14 sister to one that is u.
Exod 6 12 I am of uncircumcised lips. 30
12 48 if any man be u., he shall not eat
Lev 26 41 until their u. mind be ashamed: then
Josu 5 6 that were born in the desert . . . were u.
7 they were u. even as they were born
Judg 14 3 wife of the Philistines, who are u.
15 18 shall fall into the hands of the u.
1 K 14 6 let us go over to garrison of these u.
17 26 who is this uncircumcised Philistine. 36
36 this u. Philistine shall be also as one
31 4 lest these u. come. 1 Pa 10:4
2 K 1 20 lest the daughters of the u. triumph
Esth 14 15 and abhor the bed of the uncircumcised
Isa 52 1 the u. and unclean shall no more pass
Jer 6 10 their ears are u., and they cannot
9 26 all the house of Israel are u. in
26 all the nations are u. in the flesh
Eze 28 10 thou shalt die the death of the u.
31 18 thou shalt sleep in the midst of the u.
32 19 go down and sleep with the u. They
21 helpers, and slept uncircumcised, slain
24 went down u. to the lowest parts of
25 all these are u. and slain by the
26 all of them uncircumcised and slain
27 with them that fell uncircumcised, that
28 be broken in the midst of the u. and
29 have slept with the uncircumcised and
30 slept u. with them that are slain by
32 hath slept in the midst of the u. with
44 7 strangers u. in heart and u. in flesh. 9
1 Ma 1 51 leave their children uncircumcised
2 46 found in confines of Israel that were u.
Acts 7 51 you stiffnecked and u. in heart and
11 3 why didst thou go in to man u., and
Rom 2 26 if, then, the u. keep the justices of
4 11 which he had, being u.; that he might be
11 all them that believe, being u., that
uncircumcision Rom 2 25 thy circumcision is made u.
Rom 2 26 this u. be counted for circumcision? And
27 is u., if it fulfil the law, judge thee
3 30 circumcision by faith, and u. through
4 9 circumcision only, or in the u. also
10 when he was in circumcision, or in u.
10 not in circumcision, but in u. And he
12 that is in the u. of our father Abraham
1 C 7 18 let him not procure uncircumcision. Is
18 is any man called in uncircumcision? Let
19 circumcision is nothing, and u. is
Gal 2 7 to me was committed the gospel of the u.
5 6 Jesus . . . availeth anything nor u. 6:15
Eph 2 11 who are called u. by that which is
Col 2 13 dead in your sins, and the u. of your
3 11 Gentile nor Jew, circumcision nor u.
uncle Gen 28 2 of the daughters of Laban thy u.
Gen 29 10 they were the sheep of Laban his uncle
Lev 10 4 the sons of Oziel, the uncle of Aaron
20 20 with wife of his u. by the father, or of his u. by the mother
25 49 redeem him; either his u. or his uncle's
Num 36 11 were married to the sons of their uncle
Judg 10 1 son of Phua, the uncle of Abimelech
1 K 10 14 Saul's uncle said to him and to his
15 his uncle said to him [Saul]: Tell me
16 Saul said to his uncle: He told us
4 K 24 17 he appointed Matthanias his uncle in his
1 Pa 11 26 Joab, and Elchanan the son of his uncle
27 32 Jonathan, David's uncle, a counsellor
2 Pa 36 10 made Sedecias his uncle king over Juda
Esth 8 1 confessed to him that he was her uncle
unclean Gen 7 3 of the beasts that are u. two
Gen 7 8 beasts clean and unclean, and of fowls
Lev 5 2 whosoever toucheth any unclean thing
7 19 that hath touched any unclean thing
10 10 and unholy between unclean and clean
11 4 shall reckon it among the unclean
5 the cherogrillus . . . is unclean. The
8 because they are unclean to you. These
12 scales, in the waters, shall be unclean
24 shall be unclean until the evening. 11:28, 31, 32, 39, 40; 14:46; 15:5, 6 7, 8, 10, 11, 16, 17, 18, 20, 22, 27; 22:6; Num 19:7, 8, 10, 19, 21, 22
25 shall be unclean until the sunset
26 nor cheweth the cud, shall be unclean
27 which go on all four, shall be unclean
28 all these things are unclean to you
29 shall be reckoned among unclean things
34 out of any such vessel, shall be unclean
35 be destroyed, and shall be unclean
35 dead beasts shall fall, it shall be u.
43 nor touch aught thereof, lest you be u.
47 differences of the clean and unclean
12 2 shall be unclean seven days. 19:14, 16; Lev 15:24
5 child, she shall be unclean two weeks
13 11 shall declare him u. 20, 25, 27
11 he is evidently unclean. 36
15 shall be reckoned among the unclean
15 if it be spotted with leprosy, is u.
30 he shall declare them unclean, because
45 shall cry out that he is defiled and u.
46 time that he is a leper and unclean
51 he shall judge the garment unclean
55 he shall judge it unclean and shall
59 to be cleansed or pronounced unclean
14 36 lest all things become unclean that are
40 without the city into u. place. 41, 45

44 leprosy, and the house is unclean
57 be known when a thing is clean or u.
15 2 hath an issue of seed, shall be u.
4 on which he sleepeth, shall be unclean
9 on which he hath sitten shall be u.
25 subject to this disease shall be unclean
19 23 that comes forth shall be u. to you
20 25 separate the clean beast from the u.
25 and the clean fowl from the unclean
25 which I have shown you to be unclean
21 4 anything that may make him unclean
22 4 he that toucheth anything unclean
5 toucheth creeping thing or any u. thing
27 11 an u. beast, which cannot be sacrificed
27 if it be an u. beast, he that offereth
Num 6 7 neither shall he make himself unclean
9 6 u. by occasion of the soul of a man. 7
10 u. by occasion of one that is dead
18 15 every beast that is unclean thou shalt
19 11 and is therefore unclean seven days
13 he shall be unclean and his uncleanness
15 nor binding over it, shall be unclean
19 that is clean shall purify the unclean
22 whatsoever a person toucheth who is u., he shall make it unclean
Deut 12 15 whether it be unclean, that is to say
22 both the clean and unclean shall eat
14 3 eat not the things that are unclean
7 the hoof, they shall be unclean to you
8 cheweth not the cud, shall be unclean
10 not eat, because they are unclean
12 the unclean eat not: to wit, the eagle
19 hath little wings, shall be unclean
15 22 the clean and the unclean shall eat them
21 5 is clean or unclean should be judged
Josu 22 19 land of your possession to be unclean
Judg 13 4 drink, and eat not any unclean thing
7 nor eat any unclean thing. 14
2 Pa 23 19 that none who was unclean in anything
1 Es 9 11 which you go to possess, is an u. land
Job 14 4 clean that is conceived of unclean seed
Ecce 9 2 to the clean and to the unclean, to him
Eccu 29 20 sinner and the u. fleeth from his surety
34 4 what can be made clean by the unclean
40 15 as u. roots upon the top of a rock
51 7 from an unclean tongue and from lying
Isa 6 5 because I am a man of unclean lips
5 of a people that hath unclean lips
35 8 the unclean shall not pass over it
52 1 unclean shall no more pass through thee
11 touch no unclean thing: go out of the
64 6 and we are all become as one unclean
65 5 not near me, because thou art unclean
Lam 2 2 he hath made the kingdom unclean and
Eze 4 14 no unclean flesh hath entered into
Jer 19 13 shall be u. as the place of Topheth
22 24 thou art a land that is unclean and
44 23 to discern between clean and unclean
25 for whom they may become unclean. And
Osee 8 8 among the nations like an u. vessel
9 3 hath eaten u. things among the Assyrians
Agge 2 14 if one that is u. by occasion of a
Zach 13 1 of the sinner and of the unclean woman
1 Ma 1 50 to be immolated, and unclean beasts
65 that they would not eat u. things
65 die than to be defiled with u. meats
4 43 had been defiled into an u. place
Luke 4 33 was a man who had an unclean devil
Acts 10 14 anything that is common and unclean
28 to me, to call no man common or unclean
11 8 nothing common or u. hath ever entered
Rom 14 14 that nothing is unclean of itself; but
14 anything to be u., to him it is unclean
1 C 7 14 otherwise your children should be u.
2 C 6 17 Lord, and touch not the unclean thing
Eph 5 5 understand, that no fornicator, or u.
Heb 10 29 esteemed the blood of the testament u.
Apoc 18 2 the hold of every u. and hateful bird
unclean spirit; *see* **spirit**
unclean spirits; *see* **spirits**
uncleanness Lev 5 2 forgetteth his u., he is
Lev 5 3 and touch anything of the u. of man
3 u. wherewith he is wont to be defiled
7 21 that hath touched the uncleanness of man
13 8 shall be condemned of uncleanness. If the
15 30 Lord, and for the issue of her u.
31 to take heed of uncleanness, that they
16 16 from the u. of the children of Israel. 19
21 1 let not a priest incur an uncleanness
22 3 in whom there is u., shall perish
Num 19 13 his uncleanness shall remain upon him
Deut 7 26 abhor it as uncleanness and filth because
23 14 let no uncleanness appear therein lest
24 1 find not favor in his eyes, for some u.
26 14 nor separated them for any uncleanness
2 K 11 4 she was purified from her uncleanness
2 Pa 29 16 and brought out all the uncleanness
1 Es 9 11 according to the u. of the people and
Jdth 9 2 who had defiled by their uncleanness
Wisd 14 26 the irregularity of adultery and u.
Isa 30 22 as the u. of a menstruous woman. Thou
Eze 7 20 I have made it an uncleanness to them
22 10 humbled the u. of the menstruous woman
15 I will put an end to thy uncleanness
23 7 defiled herself with the u. of all them
24 13 thy uncleanness is execrable: because I
36 17 like the u. of a menstruous woman
39 24 dealt with them according to their u.
Mich 2 10 for that u. of the land, it shall be
1 Ma 13 48 having cast out of it all u., he placed
14 7 took away all uncleanness out of it
Mat 23 25 you are full of rapine and uncleanness
Rom 1 24 to the desires of their heart, unto u.
6 19 have yielded your members to serve u.
2 C 12 21 and have not done penance for the u.
Gal 5 19 which are fornication, u., immodesty
Eph 4 19 unto the working of all uncleanness
5 3 fornication and all u., or covetousness
Col 3 5 upon the earth; fornication, u., lust
1 Th 2 3 error, nor of uncleanness, nor in deceit
4 7 for God hath not called us unto u., but
James 1 21 casting away all u. and abundance of
2 P 2 10 after the flesh in the lust of u.
uncleannesses 4 K 23 24 of the idols, and the u.
Eze 14 3 have placed their u. in their hearts
4 that shall place his u. in his heart
4 according to the multitude of his u.
33 25 up your eyes to your uncleannesses
36 29 and I will save you from all your u.
1 Ma 1 51 let their souls be defiled with all u.
13 50 and cleansed the castle from u. and
uncle's Lev 25 49 either his uncle or his u. son
1 Pa 11 12 after him was Eleazar his uncle's son
Jer 32 8 Hanameel my uncle's son. 9, 12
uncles Num 27 11 if he have no u. by the father
unclothed 2 C 5 4 because we would not be u.
uncomely 1 C 12 23 those that are our u. parts
uncondemned Acts 16 37 beaten us publicly, u., men
Acts 22 25 scourge a man that is a Roman, and u.
uncover Lev 10 6 u. not your heads, and rend not
Lev 18 6 of kin to him, to uncover her nakedness
7 not uncover the nakedness of thy father
7 mother, thou shalt not u. her nakedness
8 not u. nakedness of thy father's wife
9 not u. the nakedness of thy sister
10 not u. nakedness of thy son's daughter

11 not uncover the nakedness of thy father's wife's daughter
12 not u. nakedness of thy father's sister
13 not u. nakedness of thy mother's sister
14 not u. nakedness of thy father's brother
15 not u. nakedness of thy daughter-in-law
16 not u. nakedness of thy brother's wife
17 not uncover the nakedness of thy wife
19 neither shalt thou u. her nakedness
20 18 in her flowers u. her nakedness
19 not u. the nakedness of thy aunt and
20 uncover the shame of his near akin, both
21 10 shall not uncover his head, he shall not
Num 5 18 he shall uncover her head and shall put
Isa 47 2 uncover thy shame, strip thy shoulder
uncovered Gen 9 21 and was u. in his tent. Which
Gen 9 22 that his father's nakedness was u.
Lev 20 19 hath u. the shame of his own flesh
21 hath uncovered his brother's nakedness
Jdth 9 2 and uncovered the virgin unto confusion
Isa 20 4 with their buttocks uncovered to the
Dan 13 32 commanded that her face should be u.
Mark 2 4 they uncovered the roof where he was
1 C 11 13 a woman, to pray unto God uncovered
uncovereth Deut 27 20 father's wife, and u. his bed
uncovering Ruth 3 7 u. his feet, laid herself down
2 K 6 20 u. himself before the handmaids of his
unction Lev 10 7 oil of the holy u. is on you
Lev 21 12 oil of the holy unction of his God is
Exod 40 13 that the unction of them may prosper
1 J 2 20 you have the unction from the Holy One
27 the unction which you have received
27 as his unction teacheth you of all
oil of unction; *see* **oil**
undefiled Ps 17 31 as for my God, his way is u.
Ps 36 18 Lord knoweth days of the undefiled
63 5 to shoot in secret the undefiled. They
118 1 blessed are the undefiled in the way
80 my heart be u. in thy justifications
Cant 5 2 my love, my dove, my undefiled: for
Wisd 3 13 happy is the barren and the undefiled
4 2 winning the reward of u. conflicts
7 22 subtile, eloquent, active, undefiled
8 20 more good, I came to a body undefiled
14 24 neither keep life, nor marriage u.
2 Ma 7 40 so this man also died undefiled, wholly
14 36 keep this house forever undefiled
15 34 hath kept his own place undefiled
2 C 7 11 showed yourselves to be u. in the matter
Heb 7 26 undefiled, separated from sinners and
13 4 honorable in all, and the bed u.
James 1 27 religion clean and u. before God and
1 P 1 4 an inheritance incorruptible and u.
19 as of a lamb unspotted and undefiled
undergirding Acts 27 17 u. the ship and fearing
undergo Eze 29 18 his army to u. hard service
2 Ma 2 28 many, we willingly undergo the labor
undergone Tob 7 20 for the trouble thou hast u.
2 Ma 7 36 having now undergone a short pain, are
undermine Eccu 12 18 help thee, will u. thy feet
undermined Gen 49 6 in their selfwill they u. a
2 Ma 4 26 u. his own brother, being himself u.
undermining Exod 22 2 breaking open house or u. it
underneath Exod 40 18 in the ark, thrusting bars u.
Deut 33 27 underneath are the everlasting arms
3 K 6 6 the floor that was u. was five cubits
2 Pa 32 30 waters of Gihon and turned them away u.
Luke 19 36 they spread their clothes underneath
undersetters 3 K 7 30 at the four sides were u.
3 K 7 34 four u. that were at every corner of
understand Gen 11 7 they may not u. one another's
Gen 24 14 by this I shall understand that thou
Lev 4 14 afterwards shall understand their sin
5 17 guilty of sin, understand his iniquity
Deut 28 49 whose tongue thou canst not understand
29 4 Lord hath not given you a heart to u.
9 that you may understand all that you do
32 29 O that they would be wise and would u.
Josu 1 7 mayst u. all things which thou dost
8 then shalt thou direct thy way and u.
22 22 he knoweth and Israel also shall u.
Ruth 4 4 I would have thee to understand this
2 K 14 20 of God, to u. all things upon earth
3 K 2 3 that thou mayest u. all thou dost, and
4 K 18 26 in Syriac, for we u. that tongue and
1 Pa 28 19 I might u. all the works of the pattern
1 Es 7 24 we give you also to u. concerning all
2 Es 4 11 enemies said: Let them not know nor u.
8 2 and all those that could understand. 3
10 29 that could u., promising for their
Job 9 11 if he depart I shall not understand
11 6 thou mightest u. that he exacteth much
14 21 to honor or dishonor, he shall not u.
15 9 what dost thou u. that we know not
18 2 understand first, and so let us speak
19 6 u. that God hath not afflicted me with
23 5 me, and u. what he would say to me
8 if to the west, I shall not u. him
32 9 neither do the ancients u. judgment
34 27 and would not understand all his ways
38 20 u. the paths of the house thereof
Ps 2 10 O ye kings, u.: receive instruction
5 2 Lord, to my words, understand my cry
13 2 to see if there be any that understand
18 13 who can u. sins? From my secret ones
35 4 he would not u. that he might do well
48 13 man when he was in honor did not u. 21
49 22 u. these things, you that forget God
52 3 to see if there were any that did u.
63 10 the works of God: and u. his doings
72 17 and u. concerning their last ends. But
91 7 nor will the fool u. these things
93 7 see: neither shall the God of Jacob u.
8 u., ye senseless among the people: and
100 2 I will u. in the unspotted way, when
106 43 and will u. the mercies of the Lord
118 27 me to u. the way of thy justifications
Prov 1 3 to understand the words of prudence
6 he shall understand a parable and the
2 5 then shalt thou u. the fear of the Lord
9 then shalt thou u. justice and judgment
8 5 O little ones, understand subtility
9 they are right to them that understand
14 8 wisdom of discreet man is to u. his way
19 25 rebuke a wise man he will u. discipline
20 24 who is the man that can u. his own way
Ecce 8 16 and to understand the distraction that
9 1 that I might carefully understand them
Wisd 3 9 that trust in him shall u. the truth
4 14 the people see this, and understand not
17 shall not u. what God hath designed for
6 2 hear, therefore, ye kings, and u.: learn
13 1 seen, could not understand him that is
4 let them u. by them that he that made
Eccu 5 13 to hear the word, that thou mayst u.
16 21 his ways who shall understand and the
38 38 of judgment they shall not understand
Isa 6 9 hearing, hear, and understand not: and
10 their ears, and u. with their heart
28 9 whom shall he make to u. the hearing
19 vexation alone shall make you understand
32 4 heart of fools shall u. knowledge
33 19 not u. the eloquence of his tongue
36 11 in the Syrian tongue: for we u. it
41 20 consider and understand together that
43 10 and understand that I myself am

44 9 that they do not see nor understand
18 they may not u. with their heart
52 13 my servant shall understand, he shall
Jer 5 15 know nor understand what they say
9 12 the wise man that may u. this and to
23 20 days you shall understand his counsel
26 15 and u., that if you put me to death
Bar 2 31 give them a heart, and they shall u.
Eze 3 6 whose words thou canst not u.: and if
Dan 8 16 make this man to u. the vision. And he
17 understand, O son of man, for in the
9 22 to teach thee, that thou mightest u.
23 thou mark the word and u. the vision
10 11 u. the words that I speak to thee
12 didst set thy heart to understand
12 10 none of the wicked shall understand
10 but the learned shall understand. And
Osee 4 14 that doth not u. shall be beaten. If
14 10 and he shall understand these things
Mat 13 13 hear not, neither do they understand
14 shall hear, and shall not u. Acts 28:26
15 and u. with their heart. Acts 28:27
15 10 hear ye and understand. Not that which
17 do you not u., that whatsoever entereth
16 9 do you not yet understand, neither
11 why do you not u. that it was not
24 15 he that readeth let him u. Mark 13:14
Mark 4 12 they may hear and not understand: lest
7 14 and understand. There is nothing from
18 u. you not that everything from without
8 17 do you not yet know nor understand
21 how do you not yet understand? And
14 68 I neither know nor u. what thou sayest
Luke 8 10 and hearing may not understand. Now
24 45 that they might u. the scriptures. And
John 12 40 eyes, nor understand with their heart
Acts 24 11 thou mayest u., that there are yet but
Rom 1 32 known the justice of God, did not u.
7 15 for that which I work, I understand not
15 21 and they that have not heard shall u.
1 C 2 14 is foolishness to him, and he cannot u.
12 3 I give you to understand, that no man
16 12 I give you to u., that I much entreated
Gal 1 11 I give you to understand, brethren, that
Eph 3 4 as you reading, may u. my knowledge in
20 more abundantly than we desire or u.
5 5 for know you this and understand, that
2 Tim 2 7 understand what I say: for the Lord will
Heb 11 3 by faith we understand that the world
understandest Isa 29 16 fashioned it: Thou u. not
Acts 8 30 thinkest thou that thou u. what thou
understandeth Lev 5 4 afterwards u. his offence
1 Pa 28 9 understandeth all the thoughts of minds
Job 4 20 because no one u., they shall perish
28 23 God u. the way of it and he knoweth
Ps 32 15 them: who understandeth all their works
Prov 1 5 he that u., shall possess governments
17 8 he turneth himself, he u. wisely
24 12 he that seeth into the heart, he u.
29 19 he u. what thou sayest, and will not
Ecce 8 5 the heart of a wise man understandeth
Wisd 9 11 she knoweth and u. all things and shall
Eccu 23 27 he u. not that his eye seeth all things
Isa 57 1 because there is none that u.; for the
Jer 9 24 glory in this, that he u. and knoweth
Mat 13 19 word of the kingdom and u. it not
23 he that heareth the word and u. and
Rom 3 11 there is none that u., there is none
understanding Exod 31 3 filled him with wisdom and u. 35:31
Exod 36 1 to whom the Lord gave wisdom and u.
Deut 1 13 among you wise and understanding men
4 6 this is your wisdom and understanding
6 behold a wise and understanding people
2 K 14 1 u. that the king's heart was turned to
3 K 3 9 to thy servant an u. heart, to judge
12 and have given thee a wise and u. heart
4 29 and God gave to Solomon wisdom and u.
7 14 full of wisdom and u. and skill to work
1 Pa 12 32 sons of Issachar men of understanding
19 10 Joab u. that the battle was set against
22 12 Lord also give thee wisdom and u., that
30 22 that had good u. concerning the Lord
2 Pa 2 12 endued with understanding and prudence
Tob 6 17 horse and mule, which have not u., over
Job 12 13 and strength, he hath counsel and u.
17 4 thou hast set their heart far from u.
20 3 the spirit of my u. shall answer for me
28 12 where is place of understanding. 20
28 to depart from evil, is understanding
32 8 inspiration of the Almighty giveth u.
34 10 ye men of understanding, hear me: for
16 if then thou hast u., hear what is said
34 let men of understanding speak to me
38 4 tell me if thou hast understanding
36 or who gave the cock understanding
39 17 neither hath he given her understanding
Ps 15 7 bless the Lord, who hath given me u.
31 1 to David himself, understanding. Blessed
8 I will give thee u., and I will instruct
9 horse and the mule, who have no u.
41 1 understanding for the sons of Core
43 1 end, for the sons of Core, to give u.
44 1 for the sons of Core, for understanding
48 4 meditation of my heart understanding
51 1 understanding for David. 53:1; 54:1; 141:1
73 1 understanding for Asaph. 77:1
87 1 to answer u. of Eman the Ezrahite
88 1 of understanding, for Ethan the Ezrahite
110 10 a good understanding to all that do it
118 34 give me u., and I will search thy law
73 give me understanding, and I will learn
100 I have had understanding above ancients
104 by the commandments I have had u.
125 servant: give me u. that I may know thy
130 giveth understanding to little ones
144 give me understanding, and I shall live
169 sight: give me u. according to thy word
135 5 who made the heavens in understanding
Prov 1 4 ones, to the young man knowledge and u.
3 4 shalt find grace and good understanding
10 21 shall die in the want of understanding
15 32 that yieldeth to reproof possesseth u.
17 27 the man of u. is of a precious spirit
28 close his lips, a man of understanding
23 23 not sell wisdom and instruction and u.
Wisd 1 5 from thoughts that are without u. and
4 8 the understanding of a man is gray hairs
11 lest wickedness should alter his u.
5 6 the sun of u. hath not risen upon us
6 16 upon her is perfect u.: and he that
7 7 I wished, and understanding was given me
22 in her is the spirit of understanding
9 5 falling short of the u. of judgment
12 24 after the manner of children without u.
Eccu 1 4 the u. of prudence from everlasting
24 distribute knowledge and understanding
26 in the treasures of wisdom is u. and
30 a good u. will hide his words for a
2 2 receive the words of understanding
3 15 if his understanding fail, have patience
25 are shown to thee above the u. of men
32 wise heart, which hath u. will abstain
4 21 treasures of knowledge and u. of justice
29 is discerned: and u. and knowledge
5 14 if thou have understanding, answer

6 36 if thou see a man of understanding, go
8 10 shalt learn wisdom and instruction of u.
12 of them thou shalt learn understanding
14 23 and hath understanding in her secrets
15 3 with the bread of life and u. she shall
5 him with the spirit of wisdom and u.
16 23 that wanteth u. thinketh vain things
24 learn the discipline of understanding
17 5 filled them with the knowledge of u.
18 28 every man of u. knoweth wisdom and
29 that were of good understanding in words
19 21 that hath less wisdom and wanteth u.
21 than he that aboundeth in understanding
20 19 he doth not distribute with right u.
21 12 keepeth justice shall get the u. thereof
13 perfection of fear of God is . . . u.
15 there is no u. where there is bitterness
22 10 weep for the fool, for his u. faileth
24 36 who maketh understanding to abound
25 7 comely is wisdom for aged, and u.
29 34 grievous to a man of understanding
31 2 thinking beforehand turneth away the u.
32 22 a man of counsel will not neglect u.
33 3 a man of u. is faithful to the law
34 1 hopes of a man that is void of u. are
9 learned many things, shall show forth u.
37 25 the fruit of his u. is commendable
26 fruits of his understanding are faithful
39 8 will fill him with the spirit of u.
Isa 11 2 spirit of wisdom and of understanding
29 14 u. of their prudent men shall be hid
24 that erred in spirit, shall know u.
40 14 showed him the way of understanding
56 11 the shepherds themselves knew no u.
Jer 5 21 hear, O foolish people, and without u.
51 15 stretched out the heavens by his u.
Bar 3 14 wisdom, where is strength, where is u.
23 searchers of prudence and understanding
32 and hath found her out with his u.
Eze 28 4 thy u. thou hast made thyself strong
Dan 1 17 gave knowledge and u. in every book
17 the u. also of all visions and dreams
20 in all matters of wisdom and u., that
2 21 and knowledge to them that have u.
5 12 understanding and interpretation of
14 and u. and wisdom are found in thee
8 23 shameless face and u. dark sentences
10 1 for there is need of u. in a vision
Osee 4 11 wine, and drunkenness take away the u.
Abdi 8 and u. out of the mount of Esau? And
2 Ma 11 13 as he was a man of understanding
Mat 15 16 are you also yet without understanding
Mark 12 33 heart and with the whole u. and with
Luke 24 45 then he opened their u., that they
Acts 4 13 u. that they were illiterate and
14 6 they u. it, fled to Lystra and Derbe
23 27 with an army, u. that he is a Roman
1 C 14 14 prayeth, but my u. is without fruit
15 I will pray also with the understanding
15 I will sing also with the understanding
19 had rather speak five words with my u.
2 C 10 5 bringing into captivity every u. unto
Eph 4 18 mind, having their u. darkened, being
5 17 understanding what is the will of God
Phil 1 9 more abound in knowledge, and in all u.
4 7 peace of God, which surpasseth all u.
Col 1 9 in all wisdom, and spiritual u.: that
2 2 riches of fulness of understanding
1 Tim 1 7 u. neither the things they say, nor
2 Tim 2 7 the Lord will give thee in all things u.
2 P 1 20 u. this first, that no prophecy of
1 J 5 20 he hath given us understanding that
Apoc 13 18 he that hath u., let him count the

17 9 and here is the u. that hath wisdom
understandings Ps 52 1 understandings to David
understood Gen 8 11 u. that the waters were ceased
Gen 42 23 they knew not that Joseph understood
Judg 13 21 Manue u. that it was an angel of the
20 34 u. not that present death threatened
1 K 3 9 then Heli u. that the Lord called the
4 6 u. that the ark of the Lord was come
18 28 Saul saw and u. that the Lord was with
20 33 Jonathan u. that it was determined by
23 9 David u. that Saul secretly prepared
28 14 and Saul understood that it was Samuel
2 K 3 37 u. that day that it was not the king's
12 19 he [David] u. that the child was dead
14 22 thy servant hath u. that I have found
2 Pa 26 5 Zacharias that understood and saw God
2 Es 6 12 I u. that God had not sent him, but
8 8 and they understood when it was read
8 distinctly and plainly to be understood
12 they u. the words that he had taught
13 7 I u. the evil that Eliasib had done for
Job 13 1 heard them, and I have u. them all
Ps 27 5 they have not u. the works of the Lord
81 5 they have not known nor understood
105 7 our fathers u. not thy wonders in Egypt
118 95 but I have understood thy testimonies
99 I have u. more than all my teachers
138 3 thou hast u. my thoughts afar off
Prov 30 32 if he had u., he would have laid his
Ecce 8 17 and I understood that man can find no
Eccu 1 7 hath u. the multiplicity of her steps
3 31 heart of the wise is u. in wisdom
16 20 and every heart is understood by him
18 29 have understood truth and justice and
19 13 a friend, lest he may not have u. and
23 31 he u. not the fear of the Lord. So
Isa 1 3 and my people hath not understood
10 13 by my own wisdom I have understood
40 21 have you not u. the foundations of
42 25 and set him on fire, and he u. not
44 18 they have not known nor understood
Jer 10 21 therefore have they not understood
20 11 have not u. the everlasting reproach
32 8 I u. that this was the word of Lord
Bar 3 21 nor have they u. the paths thereof
Eze 10 20 I understood that they were cherubims
Dan 8 5 I understood: and behold a he goat
9 2 I Daniel u. by books the number of the
10 1 and he understood the word: for there is
12 8 I heard, and understood not. And I
Mich 4 12 and have not understood his counsel
Zach 11 11 u. that it is the word of the Lord
1 Ma 3 11 Judas u. it, and went forth to meet
5 34 understood that it was Machabeus and
6 17 Lysias u. that the king was dead and
9 34 Bacchides u. it and he came himself
12 50 when they u. that Jonathan and all
13 14 when Tryphon u. that Simon was risen
2 Ma 4 21 and Antiochus u. that he was wholly
33 when Onias u. most certainly, he
11 6 him, u. that the strongholds were
12 8 when he u. that the men of Jamnia
13 1 Judas u. that Antiochus Eupator was
10 when Judas u., he commanded the people
23 when he u. that Philip, who had
14 1 u. that Demetrius the son of Seleucus
15 1 when Nicanor u. that Judas was in
28 they u. that Nicanor was slain in his
Mat 13 51 have ye u. all these things? They say
16 12 they u. that he said not that they
17 13 the disciples u. that he had spoken to
Mark 6 52 for they u. not concerning the loaves
9 31 but they understood not the word, and

15 45 when he had u. it by the centurion
Luke 1 22 they u. that he had seen a vision in
2 17 they u. of the word that had been
50 they u. not the word that he spoke
9 45 but they understood not this word
18 34 they understood none of these things
34 they u. not the things that were said
23 7 when he u. that he was of Herod's
John 4 1 when Jesus therefore u. that the
8 27 u. not that he called God his Father
10 6 but they u. not what he spoke to them
Acts 7 25 he thought that his brethren u. that
25 would save them; but they u. it not
22 29 tribune also was afraid after he u.
23 34 and understood that he was of Cilicia
Rom 1 20 are clearly seen, being u. by the things
1 C 13 11 I spoke as a child, I understood as a
2 P 3 16 certain things hard to be understood
undertake 2 Ma 2 25 desire to u. the narrations
undertaketh Eccu 29 25 he that u. many things
undertaking 2 Ma 2 27 in u. this work of abridging
underwritten 1 Ma 12 7 copy here u. doth specify
undisciplined Wisd 17 1 u. souls have erred
undo Isa 58 6 undo the bundles that oppress, let
undone Exod 10 7 dost thou not see that Egypt is u.
Num 21 29 thou art undone, O people of Chamos
Josu 11 15 he left not one thing undone of all
Eccu 28 18 forces of people and u. strong nations
29 23 evil suretyship hath u. many of good
Jer 49 24 Damascus is undone, she is put to flight
Mat 23 23 done, and not to leave those undone
Luke 11 42 and not to leave the other undone
undoubtedly Exod 23 33 u. will be a scandal to thee
Lev 13 43 shall condemn him undoubtedly of leprosy
Ruth 3 13 I will undoubtedly take thee as the
2 Ma 3 38 is u. in that place a certain power
Acts 28 4 undoubtedly this man is a murderer
1 C 15 27 u., he is excepted, who put all things
uneasy Tob 5 18 lest I should make thee uneasy
Eccu 31 22 thou shalt not be uneasy with it
unexpected Wisd 5 2 of their u. salvation. Saying
unexperienced 2 Pa 13 7 for Roboam was u. and of
unfaithful Deut 32 20 generation and u. children
Prov 25 19 to trust to an u. man in the time of
Ecce 5 3 an u. and foolish promise displeaseth
Eccu 23 33 she hath been u. to the law of the
Isa 21 2 he that is u. dealeth unfaithfully
unfaithfully Isa 21 2 is unfaithful dealeth u.
unfaithfulness Wisd 14 25 corruption and u., tumults
unfeigned Wisd 18 16 carrying thy u. commandment
2 C 6 6 in the Holy Ghost, in charity unfeigned
1 Tim 1 5 good conscience, and an unfeigned faith
2 Tim 1 5 that faith which is in thee unfeigned
unfenced Gen 42 12 to consider the unfenced parts
unfolded Luke 4 17 as he u. the book he found
unfruitful Job 24 20 in pieces as an u. tree
Eph 5 11 no fellowship with the unfruitful works
Titus 3 14 necessary uses: that they be not u.
2 P 1 8 nor u. in the knowledge of our Lord
Jude 12 trees of the autumn, u., twice dead
ungirded 3 K 20 11 boast himself as the ungirded
ungodliness Rom 1 18 against all u. and injustice
Rom 11 26 shall turn away ungodliness from Jacob
2 Tim 2 16 for they grow much towards ungodliness
Titus 2 12 denying u. and worldly desires, we
Jude 15 all the works of their ungodliness
18 according to their own desires in u.
ungodly 2 Pa 19 2 thou helpest u. and thou art
Job 27 7 let my enemy be as the ungodly, and my
34 18 an apostate: who calleth rulers ungodly
38 13 hast thou shaken the ungodly out of it
Ps 1 1 walked in the counsel of the ungodly
Prov 24 19 wicked: nor seek to be like the ungodly
Wisd 1 9 into the thoughts of the ungodly: and
Eccu 7 19 vengeance on the flesh of the ungodly
11 11 there is an u. man that laboreth, and
12 4 God will repay vengeance to the ungodly
6 give not to the ungodly: hold back thy
7 will repay vengeance to the ungodly
13 30 is very wicked in the mouth of the u.
16 1 rejoice not in ungodly children, if they
3 God, than a thousand ungodly children
5 tribe of the u. shall become desolate
17 26 tarry not in the error of the ungodly
21 30 while the ungodly curseth the devil
22 5 will not be inferior to the ungodly
13 an ungodly man all the days of their life
37 13 nor with the ungodly of piety, nor with
39 32 so to the sinners and the ungodly they
36 taking vengeance upon the ungodly unto
40 15 offspring of the u. shall not bring
41 8 converse near the houses of the ungodly
10 will complain of an ungodly father
11 woe to you, ungodly men, who have
13 so the ungodly shall from malediction
14 name of the ungodly shall be blotted out
42 2 of judgment to justify the ungodly
Isa 53 9 he shall give the ungodly for his burial
Soph 1 3 the ungodly shall meet with ruin: and
1 Ma 7 5 to him the wicked and ungodly men of
Rom 4 5 believeth in him that justifieth the u.
5 6 to the time, die for the ungodly? For
1 Tim 1 9 for the ungodly, and for sinners, for
1 P 4 18 where shall the u. and the sinner
2 P 2 5 flood upon the world of the ungodly
3 7 and perdition of the ungodly men
Jude 4 ungodly men, turning the grace of our
15 to reprove all the ungodly for all the
15 whereby they have done ungodly and
15 which ungodly sinners have spoken
ungracious Isa 1 4 a wicked seed, u. children
ungrateful 2 Tim 3 2 disobedient to parents, u.
unhappiness Ps 13 3 and u. in their ways: and the
unhappy 1 K 1 15 I am an exceeding unhappy woman
Prov 19 26 away his mother, is infamous and u.
Wisd 3 11 rejecteth wisdom and discipline is u.
13 10 u. are they, and their hope is among
15 14 are foolish and unhappy and proud
Eccu 27 24 leaveth no hope to an unhappy soul
2 Ma 8 35 being rendered very unhappy by the
15 3 that unhappy man asked if there were
Rom 7 24 unhappy man that I am, who shall deliver
unharnessed Gen 24 32 he unharnessed the camels
unheard of 2 Ma 4 13 u. wickedness of Jason
unhewn Josu 8 31 an altar of unhewn stones which
unholy Lev 10 10 to discern between holy and u.
unicorn Ps 91 11 exalted like that of the unicorn
unicorns Ps 21 22 my lowness from horns of the u.
Ps 28 6 and as the beloved son of unicorns
77 69 he built his sanctuary as of unicorns
Isa 34 7 the unicorns shall go down with them
uninhabitable Jer 51 29 Babylon desert and u.
uninhabited Lev 16 22 iniquities into an u. land
Jer 2 6 through a land u. and unpassable, through
6 8 lest I make thee desolate, a land u.
46 19 and shall be forsaken and uninhabited
48 9 cities thereof shall be desolate and u.
51 43 a land u. and desolate, a land wherein
united Jdth 3 15 troops of his army to be united
Jdth 15 4 because the Assyrians were not united
unity Ps 132 1 brethren to dwell together in u.
Eph 4 3 careful to keep the unity of the Spirit
13 until we all meet into the u. of faith
unjust Lev 19 15 shalt not do that which is u.
Lev 19 35 do not any unjust thing in judgment
Judg 11 27 by declaring an unjust war against me

Job 21 27 your u. judgments against me. For you
Ps 5 6 nor shall the u. abide before thy eyes
9 3 his soul: and the unjust man is blessed
17 49 from the u. man thou wilt deliver me
24 4 be confounded that act unjust things
19 and have hated me with an unjust hatred
25 4 will I go in with the doers of u. things
26 12 unjust witnesses have risen up against
34 11 unjust witnesses rising up have asked
35 2 the unjust hath said within himself
36 7 his way: the man who doth unjust things
28 unjust shall be punished, and the seed
38 the unjust shall be destroyed together
40 9 they determined against me an u. word
42 1 deliver me from u. and deceitful man
50 15 I will teach the unjust thy ways: and
70 4 transgressor of the law and of the u.
100 3 not set before my eyes any unjust thing
7 that speaketh u. things did not prosper
103 35 the unjust, so that they be no more
118 113 I have hated the unjust: and have loved
118 judgments: for their thought is unjust
139 2 man: rescue me from the unjust man
Prov 11 6 u. shall be caught in their own snares
17 4 the evil man obeyeth an unjust tongue
19 28 an unjust witness scorneth judgment
21 18 unjust [is delivered] for the righteous
22 12 the words of the unjust are overthrown
Wisd 1 8 that speaketh u. things cannot be hid
4 16 soon ended, the long life of the unjust
10 3 when the unjust went away from her
11 7 thou gavest human blood to the unjust
14 31 punisheth the transgression of the u.
16 24 is made fierce against the unjust for
18 7 the just, and destruction of the unjust
Eccu 5 1 not thy heart upon unjust possessions
7 2 depart from the unjust, and evils shall
9 17 not pleased with wrong done by the u.
19 22 subtilty, and the same is unjust
20 3 by violence executeth u. judgment
28 26 shall possess the ways of the u.: and
34 21 mockeries of the u. are not acceptable
23 respect to the oblations of the unjust
35 15 look not upon an unjust sacrifice
23 and broken the scepters of the unjust
40 13 riches of the unjust shall be dried up
51 3 from the snare of an unjust tongue
7 lying words and from an unjust king
Isa 55 7 unjust man [forsake] his thoughts, and
Eze 33 15 and do no unjust thing: he shall surely
17 whereas their own way is unjust. For
Dan 3 32 hands of our enemies that are unjust
13 53 in judging u. judgments, oppressing
Haba 1 13 upon them that do unjust things and
1 Ma 14 14 took away every unjust and wicked man
2 Ma 3 4 to bring about some unjust thing in the
4 35 the unjust murder of so great a man
36 complaining of the u. murder of Onias
48 did soon suffer unjust punishment
8 4 most u. deaths of innocent children
Mat 5 45 raineth upon the just and the unjust
Luke 16 8 the Lord commended the unjust steward
10 unjust in that which is little, is unjust also in that which
11 not been faithful in the unjust mammon
18 6 hear what the unjust judge saith. And
11 the rest of men, extortioners, unjust
Acts 24 15 resurrection of the just and unjust. And
Rom 3 5 is God unjust, who executeth wrath? I
1 C 6 1 go to be judged before the unjust, and
9 know you not that the unjust shall not
1 Tim 1 9 for the just man, but for the unjust
Heb 6 10 God is not unjust, that he should forget
James 2 4 are become judges of unjust thoughts
1 P 3 18 for our sins, the just for the unjust
2 P 2 8 vexed the just soul with unjust works
9 to reserve the unjust unto the day of
unjustly Exod 5 16 thy people is u. dealt withal
Lev 19 15 that which is unjust, nor judge unjustly
Judg 9 20 if unjustly, let fire come out from him
2 K 21 5 man that crushed us and oppressed us u.
3 K 8 47 we have sinned, we have done unjustly
2 Pa 6 37 we have done wickedly, we have dealt u.
Jdth 7 19 we have done unjustly, we have committed
Ps 49 21 thoughtest u. that I should be like to
81 2 how long will you judge unjustly: and
105 6 we have acted unjustly, we have wrought
118 78 they have done unjustly towards me: but
86 they have persecuted me unjustly, do
Prov 2 22 they that do u. shall be taken away
Wisd 12 13 thou dost not give judgment unjustly
23 have lived foolishly and unjustly, by
14 28 prophesy lies or they live unjustly
30 and have sworn unjustly, in guile
Eccu 5 10 not anxious for goods unjustly gotten
30 32 if thou hurt him unjustly, he will
Isa 52 5 rule over them treat them unjustly
Jer 22 3 nor oppress them unjustly: and shed
Bar 2 12 wickedly, we have acted unjustly, O Lord
Joel 3 19 because they have done unjustly against
Soph 3 4 they have acted u. against the law
1 Ma 15 33 which was for some time u. possessed
2 Ma 8 17 the injury they had u. done to the
1 P 2 23 to him that judged him unjustly. Who
unknown Gen 31 31 that I departed unknown to thee
Wisd 11 19 u. beasts of a new kind, full of rage
19 13 received not strangers u. to them, but
Eccu 19 24 if he did not see that which is u.
Eze 3 5 speech, and of an unknown tongue. 6
2 Ma 1 19 that the place was unknown to all men
2 7 the place shall be u., till God gather
Acts 17 23 written: To the unknown God. What
2 C 6 8 yet true; as unknown, and yet known; as
Gal 1 22 I was unknown by face to the churches
unlade Acts 21 3 the ship was to unlade her burden
unlamented 2 Ma 5 10 both unlamented and unburied
unlawful Gen 34 14 which with us is unlawful
Gen 43 32 unlawful for the Egyptians to eat with
Lev 20 21 brother's wife, doth an unlawful thing
Wisd 3 16 seed of the u. bed shall be rooted out
4 6 children that are born of u. beds are
2 Ma 4 14 and of the unlawful allowance thereof
6 5 altar also was filled with u. things
20 any u. things for the love of life
1 P 4 3 and unlawful worshipping of idols
unlearned 1 Pa 25 8 learned and the u. together
Ecce 2 16 dieth in like manner as the unlearned
Eccu 6 21 very unpleasant is wisdom to the u.
51 31 draw near to me, ye u., and gather
1 C 14 16 shall he that holdeth place of the u.
23 there come in u. persons or infidels
24 one that believeth not, or an u. person
2 Tim 2 23 avoid foolish and unlearned questions
2 P 3 16 which the unlearned and unstable wrest
unleavened Exod 12 39 and they made earth cakes u.
Lev 2 4 unleavened wafers, anointed with oil
7 12 tempered with oil, and unleavened wafers
Num 6 19 one u. cake . . . and one u. wafer
Judg 6 19 made u. loaves of a measure of flour
20 take the flesh and the unleavened loaves
21 touched the flesh and the u. loaves
21 consumed the flesh and the u. loaves
1 Pa 23 29 of the u. cakes and of the frying pan
1 C 5 7 be a new paste, as you are unleavened
unleavened bread; *see* **bread**
unlike Prov 15 7 heart of fools shall be unlike

Wisd 11 15 their thirsting being unlike to that
Jer 23 10 become evil, and their strength unlike
Dan 7 7 it was unlike to the other beasts which
unlooked-for Wisd 11 8 to thine abundant water u.
Wisd 17 14 unlooked-for fear was come upon them
18 17 and fears unlooked-for came upon them
unmarried 1 C 7 8 I say to u. and to widows
1 C 7 11 if she depart, that she remain u., or
34 the u. woman and the virgin thinketh
unmerciful Jer 50 42 they are cruel and unmerciful
2 Tim 3 3 slanderers, incontinent, unmerciful
unmindful Eccu 11 27 good things be not u. of evils
Eccu 11 27 evils be not unmindful of good things
37 6 be not unmindful of him in thy riches
unmoveable Exod 15 16 let them become u. as a stone
Acts 27 41 sticking fast, remained u.: but hinder
1 C 15 58 brethren, be ye steadfast and unmoveable
unnecessary Eccu 3 24 in u. matters be not over
unpassable Jer 2 6 a land uninhabited and u.
Jer 50 12 nations, a wilderness unpassable and dry
Joel 2 20 I will drive him into a land u. and
unpleasant Eccu 6 21 u. is wisdom to the unlearned
unpolished 1 Es 5 8 are building with u. stones
1 Es 6 4 three rows of unpolished stones and
unprepared 2 C 9 4 with me, and find you u., we
unprofitable Job 15 16 is man abominable and u.
Ps 13 3 are become unprofitable together. 52:4
Prov 6 12 a man that is an apostate, an u. man
Wisd 3 11 labors without fruit and their works u.
4 5 their fruits shall be u. and sour to eat
13 10 an u. stone the work of an ancient
18 for help calleth upon that which is u.
16 29 shall run off as unprofitable water
Eccu 15 22 multitude of faithless and u. children
37 21 yet is unprofitable to his own soul
Isa 14 19 as an unprofitable branch defiled and
59 6 their works are unprofitable works
7 their thoughts are u. thoughts: wasting
Osee 10 4 you speak words of an u. vision and
Amos 5 5 into captivity, and Bethel shall be u.
Mich 2 1 you that devise that which is u.
Zach 10 2 the idols have spoken what was u. and
Mat 25 30 the unprofitable servant cast ye out
Luke 17 10 we are unprofitable servants; we have
Rom 3 12 they are become u. together: there is
1 Tim 6 9 into many u. and hurtful desires, which
Titus 3 9 law. For they are unprofitable and vain
Philem 11 who hath been heretofore u. to thee
unprofitableness Heb 7 18 because of weakness and u.
unpunished Deut 5 11 he shall not be unpunished
Prov 17 5 at another man's ruin, shall not be u.
19 5 false witness shall not be unpunished. 9
Eccu 7 8 for even in one thou shalt not be u.
16 11 it is a wonder if he had escaped u.
2 Ma 4 17 the laws of God doth not pass u.: but
7 19 that thou shalt escape unpunished, for
unquenchable Mat 3 12 he will burn with u. fire. Luke 3:17
Mark 9 42 go into hell, into unquenchable fire
44 to be cast into the hell of u. fire
unquiet 1 Th 5 14 rebuke the unquiet, comfort the
James 3 8 an unquiet evil, full of deadly poison
unquietness Eccu 40 4 wrath, envy, trouble, u.
unreasonable Acts 25 27 it seemeth to me u. to send
unrevenged Job 24 12 doth not suffer it to pass u.
unruly Deut 21 18 have a stubborn and unruly son
Titus 1 6 children, not accused of riot, or unruly
unsatiable Ps 100 5 had a proud eye and an u. heart
unsavory Job 6 6 can an unsavory thing be eaten
Mark 9 49 if the salt become unsavory, wherewith
unsearchable Job 5 9 u. and wonderful things
Job 37 5 that doth great and unsearchable things
Prov 25 3 and the heart of kings is unsearchable
Jer 17 9 heart is perverse above all things and u.
Bar 3 18 and their works are unsearchable. They
Rom 11 33 and how u. his ways! For who hath known
Eph 3 8 Gentiles, the u. riches of Christ, and
unseemly Prov 26 7 parable is u. in the mouth of
unshod Deut 25 10 Israel, the house of the unshod
unskilful Job 38 2 up sentences in u. words
Eccu 5 14 thou be surprised in an u. word and
Heb 5 13 is unskilful in the word of justice: for
unspeakable Eccu 36 16 fill Sion with thy u. words
2 Ma 12 16 he made an unspeakable slaughter, so
Rom 8 26 asketh for us with u. groanings. And he
2 C 9 15 thanks be to God for his u. gift. Now
1 P 1 8 shall rejoice with joy unspeakable
unspotted Job 22 3 thou give him if thy way be u.
Job 33 9 I am u., and there is no iniquity in me
Ps 18 8 the law of the Lord is u., converting
100 2 I will understand in the u. way, when
Wisd 7 26 and the u. mirror of God's majesty
Eph 1 4 that we should be holy and unspotted in
Col 1 22 to present you holy and unspotted, and
Heb 9 14 offered himself u. unto God, cleanse
James 1 27 keep one's self u. from this world
1 P 1 19 as of a lamb unspotted and undefiled
2 P 3 14 may be found before him unspotted and
unstable Lam 1 8 therefore is she become u.
2 P 2 14 alluring unstable souls, having their
3 16 which the unlearned and unstable wrest
unsteady Prov 11 18 the wicked maketh an u. work
Ecce 9 9 all the days of thy unsteady life
unstopped Isa 35 5 ears of the deaf shall be u.
unsufferable Mala 3 13 your words have been u.
untempered Eze 13 14 daubed with untempered mortar
unthankful Wisd 16 29 the hope of the u. shall melt
Eccu 29 21 he that is of an u. mind will leave
31 and feed and give drink to the u.
Luke 6 35 he is kind to the unthankful, and to
untilled Eze 36 35 this land that was untilled is
untimely Job 3 16 as a hidden u. birth I should
Ecce 6 3 that the untimely born is better than he
untouched 4 K 23 18 were left u. with the bones
untruly Mat 5 11 is evil against you, untruly
unwary Prov 23 28 whom she shall see unwary, she
unwashed Mat 15 20 to eat with u. hands doth not
Mark 7 2 common, that is, with unwashed hands
unwillingly Deut 4 42 should kill his neighbor u.
1 Pa 21 6 Joab u. executed the king's orders
Eccu 14 7 he doth it ignorantly and u.: and
unwise Prov 1 22 the unwise hate knowledge? Turn
Prov 8 5 subtilty and ye unwise, take notice
9 4 to the unwise she said: Come, eat my
19 1 that is perverse in his lips and unwise
Wisd 1 3 when it is tried, reproveth the unwise
3 2 in sight of the unwise they seemed to die
5 21 shall fight with him against the unwise
14 11 and a snare to the feet of the unwise
Eccu 6 21 the unwise will not continue with her
10 3 an unwise king shall be the ruin of
20 21 continually in the mouth of the unwise
24 by occasion of an unwise person he
21 21 knowledge of the unwise is as words
28 lips of the u. will be telling foolish
27 13 in the midst of the unwise keep in
40 32 begging will be sweet in mouth of the u.
42 8 be not ashamed to inform the unwise
Osee 13 13 he is an unwise son: for now he shall
Rom 1 14 to wise and to unwise, I am a debtor: so
Eph 5 15 walk circumspectly: not as unwise, but
17 evil. Wherefore become not unwise, but
Titus 3 3 we ourselves also were some time unwise
2 P 3 17 led aside by the error of the unwise
unwisely Job 42 3 therefore I have spoken u.
unworthily 2 Ma 5 16 he u. handled and profaned

1 C 11 27 drink the chalice of the Lord unworthily
29 he that eateth and drinketh unworthily
unworthy Tob 3 19 and either I was u. of them or
Job 30 2 they were thought u. of life itself
Eccu 25 11 not served such as are unworthy of
Dan 11 20 vile and unworthy of kingly honor: and
Acts 13 46 judge yourselves u. of eternal life
1 C 6 2 are you u. to judge the smallest matters
up and down 1 K 23 13 from Ceila, wandered u. . . .
1 Pa 10 7 cities, and were scattered up and down
Eccu 9 7 nor wander up and down in the streets
upbraid Lev 19 33 abide among you, do not upbraid
4 K 19 16 sent to upbraid unto us the living God
1 Es 6 13 might have some evil to u. me withal
Prov 25 10 heard it, and cease not to upbraid thee
Eccu 18 18 a fool will upbraid bitterly: and a
20 15 will give a few things, and upbraid much
41 28 after thou hast given, upbraid not
Mat 11 20 to upbraid the cities wherein were
upbraided Judg 8 15 concerning whom you u. me
1 K 1 6 insomuch that she upbraided her, that
Tob 2 23 other such like words she upbraided him
Ps 34 7 without cause they have u. my soul. Let
Mark 16 14 he u. them with their incredulity and
upbraider 2 Ma 7 24 despising the voice of the u.
upbraideth Prov 14 31 poor, upbraideth his Maker
Wisd 2 12 u. us with transgressions of the law
Eccu 22 25 so he that u. his friend, breaketh
Bar 6 43 she upbraideth her neighbor, that she
James 1 5 to all men abundantly, and u. not
upbraiding Eccu 22 27 reconciliation: except u.
Eccu 29 34 the upbraiding of houseroom and the
41 28 be ashamed of u. speeches before friends
upheld Ps 29 2 thou hast upheld me: and hast not
Ps 39 12 and thy truth have always upheld me
40 13 thou hast upheld me by reason of my
Isa 41 10 right hand of my just one hath u. thee
uphold 4 K 12 12 expenses to uphold the house
2 Pa 24 12 brass, to u. what began to be falling
Ps 118 116 uphold me according to thy word, and I
122 uphold thy servant unto good: let not
Prov 29 23 glory shall uphold the humble of spirit
Eccu 12 4 to be merciful and uphold not the sinner
Isa 42 1 my servant, I will uphold him: my elect
50 4 know how to uphold by word him that is
51 18 none that can uphold her among all the
Eze 30 6 also that uphold Egypt shall fall and
upholdeth Prov 18 14 of a man u. his infirmity
upholding Wisd 6 26 king is the u. of the people
Heb 1 3 and u. all things by the word of his
upper Exod 12 7 on the upper door posts of the
Exod 39 21 for the head in the upper part at middle
Deut 24 6 take the nether nor the u. millstone
Josu 15 19 the u. and nether watery ground. Judg 1:15
16 5 Ataroth-addar unto Beth-horon the upper
3 K 17 19 and carried him into the upper chamber
23 brought him down from the upper chamber
4 K 1 2 through the lattices of his u. chamber
18 17 conduit of the upper pool. Isa 7:2; 36:2
1 Pa 7 24 built Bethoron, the nether and the u.
28 11 of u. floor and of the inner chambers
2 Pa 3 9 u. chambers also he overlaid with gold
8 5 he built Beth-horon the upper and
23 20 and brought him through the upper gate
32 30 that stopped the u. source of the waters
Tob 1 1 which is in the upper parts of Galilee
8 3 bound him in the desert of upper Egypt
Jdth 8 5 a private chamber in the upper part of
Ps 103 13 waterest the hills from thy upper rooms
Jer 20 2 were in the upper gate of Benjamin
36 10 in the upper court, in the entry of
Eze 9 2 came from the way of the upper gate
41 7 into the upper loft of the temple
20 even to the upper parts of the gate
Dan 6 10 the windows in his upper chamber towards
Soph 2 14 the raven on the upper post, for I will
Acts 1 13 they went up into an upper room, where
9 37 they laid her in an upper chamber
39 brought him into the upper chamber
19 1 passed through the upper coasts, came
20 8 number of lamps in the upper chamber
uppermost Gen 40 17 in one basket which was u.
Bar 2 5 we are brought under, and are not u.
Luke 11 43 you love the uppermost seats in the
upright Exod 26 15 of the tabernacle standing u.
Lev 26 13 your necks, that you might go upright
1 K 29 6 thou art upright and good in my sight
3 K 3 6 an u. heart with thee: and thou hast
2 Pa 3 13 and they stood upright on their feet
Job 1 1 and that man was simple and upright
8 a simple and upright man and fearing God
2 3 a man simple and upright and fearing
8 6 if thou wilt walk clean and upright
33 3 my words are from my upright heart
Ps 7 11 Lord: who saveth upright of heart
10 3 to shoot in the dark the u. of heart
19 9 but we are risen and are set upright
24 21 the innocent and the u. have adhered to
32 1 O ye just: praise becometh the upright
36 14 and needy, to kill the upright of heart
63 11 all the u. in heart shall be praised
93 15 are near it are all the upright of heart
139 14 u. shall dwell with thy countenance
Prov 2 21 they that are upright shall dwell in
10 29 strength of upright is way of the Lord
11 5 justice of the upright shall make his
28 10 and the upright shall possess his goods
29 10 bloodthirsty men hate the upright
Wisd 9 3 execute justice with an upright heart
Eccu 27 15 the hair of the head stand upright
Bar 6 26 if a man set them upright, will they
Dan 8 18 and he touched me and set me upright
10 11 stand upright: for I am sent now to
11 17 he shall make upright conditions with
Mich 7 2 there is none upright among men: they
Acts 14 9 stand u. on thy feet. And he leaped
uprightly Prov 28 18 he that walketh u., shall be
Mich 2 7 good to him that walketh uprightly
Gal 2 14 when I saw that they walked not u. unto
uprightness Deut 9 5 the uprightness of thy heart
3 K 9 4 in simplicity of heart and in u.: and
Job 33 23 among thousands, to declare man's u.
Ps 44 7 scepter of thy kingdom is scepter of u.
118 7 I will praise thee with u. of heart
Isa 57 2 that hath walked in his uprightness
uproar 1 K 4 14 what meaneth the noise of this u.
1 K 14 19 there arose a great uproar in the camp
3 K 1 41 this noise of the city in an uproar
Isa 14 9 hell below was in an uproar to meet
1 Ma 13 44 there was a great uproar in the city
Acts 17 5 set the city in an uproar. 6
19 40 called in question for this day's uproar
21 30 the whole city was in an uproar: and the
upside Lam 3 9 he hath turned my paths u. down
upward Num 1 3 from 20 years old and upward. 18, 20, 22, 24, 26, 28, 30, 32, 34, 36, 38, 40, 42, 45; 14:29; 25:4; 26:2; 32:11; 1 Pa 23:24, 27; 2 Pa 31:17; 1 Es 3:8
Num 3 15 every male from one month and upward. 22, 28, 34, 39, 40, 43; 26:62
4 3 from thirty years old and upward. 23, 30, 35, 39, 43, 47
1 K 9 2 from his shoulders and u. he appeared
10 23 of the people from the shoulders and u.
4 K 19 30 root downward, and bear fruit upward
2 Pa 31 16 males from three years old and upward

2 Es 3 28 u. from horse gate the priests built
Ecce 3 21 spirit of the children of Adam ascend u.
Isa 37 31 downward, and shall bear fruit upward
38 14 my eyes are weakened looking upward
Eze 1 11 their wings were stretched upward
27 from his loins and upward. 8:2
43 15 from the Ariel upward were four horns
Agge 2 16 from this day and upward, before there
upwards Exod 30 14 from 20 years and upwards, shall
Exod 38 25 from twenty years old and u. 2 Pa 25:5
Num 8 24 from 25 years old and upwards, they
1 Pa 23 3 from the age of 30 years and upwards
Isa 8 21 king and their God and look upwards
Luke 13 11 neither could she look upwards at all
Ur Gen 11 28 of his nativity in Ur of the Chaldees
Gen 11 31 brought them out of Ur of the Chaldees
15 7 Lord who brought thee out from Ur
1 Pa 11 35 Eliphal the son of Ur, Hepher a
Urai 1 Pa 7 7 Ozi and Ozial and Jerimoth and Urai
Urbanus Rom 16 9 salute U. our helper in Christ
urchin Soph 2 14 bittern and the u. shall lodge
urge Luke 11 53 lawyers began violently to u. him
urged 2 Ma 10 19 those expeditions which urged
urgent Dan 3 22 the king's commandment was urgent
urging 2 Ma 9 4 judgment of heaven u. him forward
Uri Exod 31 2 Beseleel the son of Uri. 35:30; 38:22; 2 Pa 1:5
3 K 4 19 Gaber the son of Uri, in the land of
1 Pa 2 20 Hur begot Uri; and Uri begot Bezeleel
1 Es 10 24 the porters, Sellum and Telem and Uri
Uria 2 Es 8 4 stood by him . . . Ania and Uria
Urias 2 K 11 3 the wife of Urias the Hethite
2 K 11 6 send me Urias the Hethite. And Joab sent Urias to David
7 and Urias came to David. And David
8 David said to Urias: Go into thy house
8 Urias went out from the king's house
9 Urias slept before gate of king's house
10 David said to Urias: Didst thou not come
10 that said: Urias went not to his house
11 Urias said to David: The ark of God
12 David said to Urias: Tarry here today
12 Urias tarried in Jerusalem that day
14 Joab: and sent it by the hand of Urias
15 set ye Urias in the front of the battle
16 he put Urias in the place where he
17 and Urias the Hethite was killed also
21 thy servant U. the Hethite is also slain
24 servant Urias the Hethite is also dead
26 heard that Urias her husband was dead
12 9 thou hast killed Urias the Hethite
10 hast taken the wife of U. the Hethite
15 which the wife of Urias had borne
23 39 Urias the Hethite, thirty and seven in
3 K 15 5 except the matter of Urias the Hethite
4 K 16 10 king Achaz sent to Urias the priest
1 Pa 11 41 Urias a Hethite, Zabad the son of
2 Es 3 3 Marimuth the son of Urias the son of
21 Merimuth the son of Urias the son of
Jer 26 20 Urias the son of Semei of Cariathiarim
21 Urias heard it and was afraid and fled
23 they brought Urias out of Egypt: and
Mat 1 6 of her that had been the wife of Urias
Urias the priest 4 K 16 10 Achaz sent to U. . . .
4 K 16 11 and Urias the priest built an altar
11 so did Urias the priest until king Achaz
15 king Achaz commanded Urias the priest
16 Urias the priest did according to all
1 Es 8 33 Meremoth the son of Urias the priest
Isa 8 2 faithful witnesses, U. . . . and
Uriel 1 Pa 6 24 sons of Caath . . . Uriel his son
1 Pa 15 5 Uriel was the chief and his brethren
11 the Levites, Uriel, Asaia, Joel, Semeia
2 Pa 13 2 Michaia the daughter of Uriel of Gabaa
urine 4 K18 27 drink their u. with you. Isa 36:12
urn Esth 3 7 the lot was cast into an urn. 9:26
Us Gen 10 23 sons of Aram: Us and Hull
Usal 1 Pa 1 21 Jectan begot . . . Usal and Decla
use Gen 16 6 hand, use her as it pleaseth thee
Exod 28 43 Aaron and his sons shall use them when
29 29 holy vesture, which Aaron shall use
38 30 vessels that belong to the use thereof
Lev 23 20 before Lord, they shall fall to his use
Num 4 14 vessels that they use in the ministry
18 13 brought to Lord, shall be for thy use
18 the flesh shall fall to thy use, as the
31 12 things for use they carried to the camp
20 vessel, or anything made for use, of
Deut 22 5 neither shall a man use woman's apparel
Josu 5 12 the children of Israel use that food
7 1 took to their own use of the anathema
Judg 9 9 which both gods and men make use of
8 26 kings of Madian were wont to use and
19 19 bread and wine for the use of myself and
21 17 we must use all care, and provide with
Ruth 4 6 do thou make use of my privilege, which
1 K 23 22 use all diligence and curiously inquire
2 Es 10 31 in things to sell, or anything for use
33 for every use of the house of our God
Tob 12 19 but I use an invisible meat and drink
Jdth 3 6 use our service as it shall please thee
11 12 these have they purposed to make use of
Esth 2 3 other things necessary for their use
Ecce 6 3 and his soul make no use of the goods
Wisd 2 6 let us speedily use the creatures
7 14 they that use, become the friends of God
13 11 hath cut down a tree proper for his use
14 23 own children, or use hidden sacrifices
15 7 but what is the use of these vessels
15 neither have the use of eyes to see
16 11 they might not be able to use thy help
Eccu 9 4 use not much the company of her that
13 5 if thou give, he will make use of thee
31 19 use as a frugal man the things that
42 24 for every use all things obey him
Jer 13 7 so that it [girdle] was fit for no use
10 this girdle which is fit for no use
23 31 who use their tongues, and say: The
Bar 6 25 having not the use of feet, they are
Eze 16 44 proverb, shall use this against thee
18 2 you use among you this parable as a
Nah 3 4 and that made use of witchcraft, that
2 Ma 4 40 Lysimachus . . . began to use violence
11 31 Jews may use their own kind of meats
15 40 pleasant to use sometimes the one
Acts 14 5 rulers, to use them contumeliously, and
Rom 1 26 natural u. into that u. which is against
27 leaving the natural use of the women
1 C 7 21 thou mayest be made free, use it rather
31 they that use this world, as if they
2 C 1 17 I was thus minded, did I use lightness
3 12 such hope, we use much confidence: and
5 11 we use persuasion to men; but to God we
Phil 4 16 also you sent once and again for my use
Col 2 22 are unto destruction by the very use
1 Th 4 11 that you use your endeavor to be quiet
1 Tim 1 8 law is good, if a man use it lawfully
2 12 nor to use authority over the man; but
5 23 use a little wine for thy stomach's sake
used Gen 12 13 that I may be well used for thee
Gen 12 16 they used Abram well for her sake. And
Exod 14 31 mighty hand that the Lord had used
35 19 vestments that are to be used in the
39 41 Aaron and his sons u. in the sanctuary
Josu 6 4 trumpets, which are used in jubilee. 13
Judg 3 15 who used the left hand as well as the

14 10 Samson: for so the young men used to do
1 K 17 39 I cannot go thus for I am not used to
2 K 13 18 virgins, used such kind of garments
20 18 a saying was used in the old proverb
3 K 7 23 wheels as are u. to be made in chariot
4 K 3 20 when the sacrifices used to be offered
21 6 he used divination and observed omens
1 Pa 12 15 when it is used to flow over its banks
Ps 14 3 who hath not used deceit in his tongue
37 13 they that sought my soul used violence
Jer 52 18 that had been used in the ministry
Eze 22 29 people of the land have used oppression
Osee 2 8 have used in the service of Baal
12 10 I have used similitudes by the ministry
2 Ma 4 18 game that was used every fifth year
12 30 that they were used kindly by them
Mat 21 5 foal of her that is used to the yoke
Mark 2 18 John and of the Pharisees used to fast
12 4 the head, and used him reproachfully
Acts 27 17 which being taken up, they used helps
Rom 12 6 to be used according to rule of faith
1 C 7 31 use this world, as if they used it not
9 12 have not used this power: but we bear
15 but I have used none of these things
1 Th 2 5 have we u. at any time the speech of
Heb 10 33 of them that were used in such sort. For
2 P 2 16 the dumb beast used to the yoke, which
useful Tob 6 5 are necessary for u. medicines
Eze 15 4 ashes: shall it be useful for any work
useless Jer 48 38 have broken Moab as an u. vessel
Bar 6 15 when it is broken becometh useless
uses Exod 27 3 make for the uses thereof pans
Exod 27 19 vessels of the tabernacle for all uses
30 16 deliver unto the uses of the tabernacle
37 such a composition for your own uses
35 24 Lord, and setim wood for divers uses
36 1 necessary for the uses of the sanctuary
37 16 for the divers uses of the table, dishes
38 3 for the uses thereof, he prepared divers
Lev 7 24 beasts, you shall have for divers uses
Num 18 24 which I have separated for their uses
Deut 20 20 but wild, and fit for other uses
4 K 12 18 kings of Juda had dedicated to holy u.
1 Pa 28 14 the diversity of the vessels and uses
2 Pa 15 18 gold and silver and vessels of divers u.
34 13 that carried burdens for divers uses
Wisd 13 11 vessel profitable for the common uses
15 7 vessels that are for clean uses and
Bar 6 15 that a man uses, when it is broken
59 and sent forth for profitable uses, are
Titus 3 14 excel in good works for necessary uses
useth Wisd 13 12 u. the chips of his work to dress
Eccu 20 8 he that useth many words shall hurt
Eze 16 44 that useth a common proverb shall use
18 24 which the wicked man useth to work
Luke 16 16 every one useth violence towards it
using 1 Pa 12 2 the bow and using either hand
1 P 4 9 using hospitality one towards another
usual Gen 40 7 countenance sadder today than u.
Exod 2 18 why are ye come sooner than usual
Lev 13 30 the hair yellow and thinner than usual
Judg 15 1 would have gone into her chamber as u.
2 Pa 15 12 he went in to confirm as u. the covenant
Eccu 23 10 let not the naming of God be usual
2 Ma 14 30 when they met together as usual he
usurer Ps 108 11 the u. search all his substance
usuries Exod 22 25 nor oppress them with usuries
Ps 71 14 he shall redeem their souls from u.
usurped 2 K 16 8 thou hast u. the kingdom in his
1 Ma 15 3 have u. the kingdom of our fathers
usury Lev 25 36 take not usury of him nor more
Lev 25 37 not give him thy money upon usury
Deut 23 19 not lend to thy brother money to usury
20 lend that which he wanteth without u.
2 Es 5 7 do you every one exact usury of your
Ps 14 5 hath not put out his money to usury
54 12 usury and deceit have not departed
Prov 28 8 that heapeth together riches by usury
Jer 15 10 I have not lent on usury, neither hath
10 neither hath any man lent to me on usury
Eze 18 8 hath not lent upon usury, nor taken
13 that giveth upon usury and that taketh
17 hath not taken usury and increase
22 12 thou hast taken usury and increase
Mat 25 27 have received my own with usury. Take
Luke 19 23 I might have exacted it with usury
Uthai 1 Es 8 14 the sons of Begui, U. and Zachur
utmost Exod 13 20 in the u. coasts of wilderness
Ps 2 8 u. parts of earth for thy possession
Joel 2 20 hinder part towards the utmost sea
1 Ma 3 9 to the utmost part of the earth and
Mat 24 31 heavens to the utmost bounds of them
Acts 13 47 salvation unto the u. part of the earth
utter Lev 5 1 if he do not u. it, he shall bear
Num 24 13 to utter anything of my own head either
Josu 2 20 betray us and utter this word abroad
Judg 5 12 Debbora, arise, arise, and u. a canticle
2 K 2 26 shall thy sword rage unto u. destruction
4 K 13 19 smitten Syria even to utter destruction
2 Pa 14 13 Ethiopians fell even to u. destruction
1 Es 9 14 angry with us unto utter destruction
Job 6 26 rebuke, and you utter words to the wind
8 10 and utter words out of their hearts
15 13 to utter such words out of thy mouth
Ps 77 2 I will utter propositions from the
93 4 shall they utter and speak iniquity
118 171 my lips shall utter a hymn, when thou
Prov 1 23 behold I will utter my spirit to you
23 33 thy heart shall utter perverse things
25 8 seen, utter not hastily in a quarrel
Ecce 5 1 hasty to utter a word before God. For
Wisd 3 3 going away from us for utter destruction
Eccu 25 9 the tenth I will utter to men with
Jer 5 18 not bring you to utter destruction
25 30 shall utter his voice from his holy
Eze 5 17 evil beasts unto utter destruction
Joel 3 16 u. his voice from Jerusalem. Amos 1:2
Nah 1 8 he will make an utter end. 9
1 Ma 5 5 and devoted them to utter destruction
Mat 13 35 I will utter things hidden from the
1 C 14 9 except you u. by the tongue plain speech
2 C 12 4 which it is not granted to man to utter
utterance 1 C 1 5 in all u. and in all knowledge
uttered Jdth 8 24 but uttered their impatience
Ps 18 3 day to day uttereth speech, and night
44 2 my heart hath uttered a good word: I
45 7 he uttered his voice, the earth trembled
65 14 my vows, which my lips have uttered
Prov 1 20 she uttereth her voice in the streets
21 gates of the city she u. her words
6 19 a deceitful witness that uttereth lies
10 18 he that uttereth reproach is foolish
32 mouth of the wicked u. perverse things
14 5 but a deceitful witness uttereth a lie
25 and the double dealer uttereth lies
26 2 a curse uttered without cause shall
29 11 a fool uttereth all his mind: a wise
Wisd 7 3 the first voice which I u. was crying
Eccu 19 23 one that uttereth an exact word telling
22 9 asleep, who uttereth wisdom to a fool
Isa 59 3 lies, and your tongue uttereth iniquity
13 have conceived and u. from the heart
Jer 48 34 to Jasa, they have uttered their voice
Joel 2 11 the Lord hath uttered his voice before
Mich 7 3 hath uttered the desire of his soul
2 Ma 6 29 they thought were u. out of arrogancy

Luke 9 36 whilst the voice was uttered, Jesus
Heb 5 11 and hard to be intelligibly uttered
Apoc 10 3 seven thunders uttered their voices
4 when the seven thunders had uttered
uttereth Lev 5 4 sweareth and u. with his lips
Jer 51 16 when he uttereth his voice the waters
uttering 2 Ma 12 14 u. such words as were not to
utterly Num 17 13 to a man to be u. destroyed
Num 21 2 I will utterly destroy their cities
Deut 3 3 and we utterly destroyed them. 6
7 2 thou shalt utterly destroy them. Thou
23 slay them until they be u. destroyed
26 shalt utterly abhor it as uncleanness
8 19 thee that thou shalt utterly perish
29 21 u. destroy him out of all the tribes of
Josu 10 20 and almost utterly consumed, they that
11 11 utterly destroyed all and burned the
Judg 4 16 multitude of enemies was u. destroyed
1 K 15 3 and utterly destroy all that he hath
18 until thou hast utterly destroyed them
3 K 15 29 seed, till he had utterly destroyed him
18 5 that the beasts may not utterly perish
4 K 13 23 not destroy them nor utterly cast them
1 Pa 4 41 utterly destroyed them unto this day
2 Pa 12 12 and they were not utterly destroyed
31 1 till they had utterly destroyed them
2 Es 9 31 thou didst not utterly consume them
Ps 118 8 do not thou utterly forsake me. By what
43 word of truth utterly out of my mouth
Prov 30 18 the fourth I am utterly ignorant of
Wisd 4 19 and they shall be utterly laid waste
Eccu 10 16 wicked, and hath utterly destroyed them
47 24 he will not utterly take away the seed
Isa 2 18 and idols shall be utterly destroyed
24 3 waste, and it shall be utterly spoiled
Jer 4 27 but yet I will not utterly destroy
5 10 them down, but do not utterly destroy
9 4 every brother will utterly supplant
12 17 I will utterly pluck out and destroy
14 19 thou utterly cast away Juda or hath
30 11 I will utterly consume all the nations
11 I will not utterly consume thee: but I
51 58 of Babylon shall be u. broken down
64 and she shall be utterly destroyed
Lam 5 22 but thou hast utterly rejected us, thou
Eze 9 6 utterly destroy old and young, maidens
29 10 the land of Egypt utterly desolate
Osee 1 6 Israel, but I will utterly forget them
Amos 9 8 I will not u. destroy the house of
Nah 1 15 through thee again, he is u. cut off
Zach 11 17 his right eye shall be u. darkened
1 Ma 3 42 destroy the people and u. abolish
2 Ma 8 18 at a beck can utterly destroy both
9 15 would utterly destroy them with their
uttermost Gen 31 6 to the uttermost of my power
Num 11 1 that were at the u. part of the camp
20 16 which is in the u. of thy borders, and
22 36 situate in the u. borders of Arnon
39 was in the u. borders of his kingdom
41 he beheld the u. part of the people
33 6 is in the u. borders of the wilderness
37 in the u. borders of the land of Edom
Deut 28 49 from the uttermost ends of the earth
Josu 13 27 the u. part of the sea of Cenereth
15 1 to the uttermost part of the south
21 from the u. parts of children of Juda
1 K 14 2 Saul abode in the u. part of Gabaa
2 Es 1 9 led away to the u. parts of the world
Ps 64 9 they that dwell in the uttermost borders
138 9 and dwell in the u. parts of the sea
Prov 31 10 from the u. coasts is the price of her
Isa 7 18 in the u. parts of the rivers of Egypt
Jer 50 26 ye against her from the u. borders
Mark 13 27 of the earth to the u. part of heaven
Acts 1 8 even to the uttermost part of the earth
Uzal Gen 10 27 Jectan begot . . . Aduram and Uzal

V

vagabond Gen 4 12 fugitive and a v. shalt thou
Gen 4 14 I shall be a vagabond and a fugitive
vagabonds Judg 9 4 men that were needy, and v.
Ps 108 10 his children be carried about vagabonds
Vagao Jdth 12 10 said to Vagao his eunuch: Go and
Jdth 12 12 then Vagao went in to Judith and said
13 1 and Vagao shut the chamber doors
14 13 Vagao going into his chamber, stood
vah Mat 27 40 vah, thou that destroyest. Mark 15:29
vain Gen 31 35 his careful search was in vain
Exod 20 7 name of Lord thy God in vain. Deut 5:11
Lev 26 16 you shall sow your seed in vain, which
20 your labor shall be spent in vain, the
Deut 5 11 that taketh his name upon a vain thing
32 47 they are not commanded you in vain, but
Josu 7 3 all the people be troubled in vain
1 K 12 21 and turn not aside after vain things
21 nor deliver you, because they are vain
25 21 in vain have I kept all that belonged
2 Pa 13 7 and there were gathered to him vain men
32 15 nor delude you with a vain persuasion
Job 1 9 doth Job fear God in vain? Hast not
6 18 they shall walk in v. and shall perish
9 29 wicked, why have I labored in vain? If
11 12 a vain man is lifted up into pride and
12 24 deceiveth them that they walk in vain
21 34 how then do ye comfort me in vain
27 12 why do you speak vain things without
35 13 God therefore will not hear in vain
16 therefore Job openeth his mouth in vain
39 16 she hath labored in vain, no fear
Ps 2 1 and the people devised vain things
5 10 in their mouth: their heart is vain
11 3 they have spoken vain things every one
23 4 who hath not taken his soul in vain
32 17 vain is the horse for safety: neither
37 13 sought evils to me spoke vain things
38 7 yea, and he is disquieted in vain. He
12 surely in vain is any man disquieted
40 7 came in to see me, he spoke vain things
59 13 trouble: for v. is the salvation of man
61 10 but vain are the sons of men, the sons
62 10 they have sought my soul in vain, they
72 13 then have I in vain justified my heart
88 48 made all the children of men in vain
93 11 thoughts of men, that they are vain
107 13 trouble: for vain is the help of man
126 1 house, they labor in v. that build it
1 he watcheth in vain that keepeth it
2 it is vain for you to rise before light
138 20 they shall receive thy cities in vain
Prov 1 17 a net is spread in vain before the eyes
12 8 he that is vain and foolish, shall be
21 6 by a lying tongue, is vain and foolish
26 7 as a lame man hath fair legs in vain
31 30 favor is deceitful, and beauty is vain
Ecce 2 11 the labors wherein I had labored in vain
19 solicitous: is there anything so vain
6 4 he came in vain and goeth to darkness
8 14 just: but this also I judge most vain
11 10 for youth and pleasure are vain
Wisd 3 11 their hope is vain, and their labors
13 1 all men are vain, in whom there is
15 8 of the same clay by a vain labor he
9 it a glory to make vain things. For
10 is ashes, and his hope vain earth
Eccu 16 23 thinketh vain things: and the foolish

20 21 without grace is as a vain fable, it
23 14 if he swear in vain, he shall not be
34 1 are vain and deceitful: and dreams lift
Isa 1 13 offer sacrifice no more in vain
29 21 and declined in vain from the just
30 7 Egypt shall help in vain, and to no
41 29 in the wrong, and their works are vain
45 18 he did not create it in vain: he formed
19 seek me in vain. I am the Lord that
49 4 I have labored in vain, I have spent my strength . . . in vain
56 10 not able to bark, seeing vain things
65 23 my elect shall not labor in vain nor
Jer 2 5 after vanity and are become vain. And
30 in vain have I struck your children
4 30 thou shalt dress thyself out in vain
6 29 the founder hath melted in vain: for
10 3 the laws of the people are vain: for the
15 they are vain things, and a ridiculous
18 15 have forgotten me, sacrificing in vain
46 11 in vain dost thou multiply medicines
50 9 a destroyer, shall not return in vain
51 18 they are vain works, and worthy to be
Lam 4 17 expecting help for us in vain, when
Eze 6 10 I the Lord have not spoken in vain
12 24 shall be no more any vain visions nor
13 6 Lord. They see vain things and they
7 have you not seen a vain vision and
8 because you have spoken vain things
9 the prophets that see vain things and
23 you shall not see vain things nor divine
21 23 as one consulting the oracle in vain
29 they see vain things in thy regard
22 28 seeing vain things and divining lies
Osee 12 11 in vain were they in Galgal offering
Jon 2 9 they that are vain observe vanities
Haba 2 13 the nations in v., and they shall faint
Zach 10 2 they comforted in vain: therefore they
Mala 3 14 he laboreth in vain that serveth God
1 Ma 9 68 and his enterprise was in vain. And
2 Ma 7 34 be not lifted up . . . with vain hopes
12 44 and vain to pray for the dead. And
Mat 15 9 in vain do they worship me. Mark 7:7
Acts 4 25 and the people meditate vain things
14 14 to be converted from these vain things
Rom 1 21 became vain in their thoughts, and their
13 4 for he beareth not the sword in vain
1 C 3 20 thoughts of the wise, that they are vain
15 2 you, unless you have believed in vain
14 preaching v., and your faith is also v.
17 not risen again, your faith is vain, for
58 knowing that your labor is not in vain
2 C 6 1 you receive not the grace of God in vain
Gal 2 2 perhaps I should run, or had run in vain
21 be by the law, then Christ died in vain
3 4 great things in vain? If it be yet in v.
4 11 lest perhaps I have labored in vain
5 26 let us not be made desirous of v. glory
Eph 5 6 let no man deceive you with vain words
Phil 2 3 through contention, neither by v. glory
16 not run in vain, nor labored in vain
Col 2 8 cheat you by philosophy and vain deceit
18 in vain puffed up by the sense of his
1 Th 2 1 in unto you, that it was not in vain
3 5 and our labor should be made vain
1 Tim 1 6 are turned aside unto vain babbling
2 Tim 2 16 but shun profane and vain babblings: for
Titus 1 10 vain talkers, and seducers: especially
3 9 law. For they are unprofitable and vain
James 1 26 this man's religion is vain. Religion
2 20 wilt thou know, O vain man, that faith
4 5 think that the scripture saith in vain
1 P 1 18 vain conversation of the tradition

vainly 4 K 17 15 followed vanities and acted v.
Job 15 31 not believe, being v. deceived by error
Ecce 2 2 I said: why art thou vainly deceived
vale Gen 12 6 Sichem as far as the noble vale
Gen 13 18 came and dwelt by the vale of Mambre
14 3 came together into the woodland vale
8 in battle array in the woodland vale
10 woodland vale had many pits of slime
13 who dwelt in the vale of Mambre the
17 vale of Save, which is the king's vale
18 1 appeared to him in the vale of Mambre
37 14 being sent from the vale of Hebron
2 K 24 5 which is in the vale of Gad. And by
1 Pa 14 9 spread themselves in vale of Raphaim
18 12 Edomites in the vale of the saltpits
2 Pa 14 10 array for battle in the vale of Sephata
25 11 went to the vale of saltpits and slew
Ps 59 2 of Edom, in the vale of the saltpits
8 mete out the v. of tabernacles. 107:8
83 7 to ascend by steps, in the v. of tears
Isa 17 5 seeketh ears in the vale of Raphaim
Vale Casis Josu 18 21 Jericho and Bethhagla and V.
vales Deut 1 7 and the vales towards the south
Ps 64 14 and the vales shall abound with corn
103 10 sendest forth springs in the vales
valiant Deut 31 7 take courage and be valiant. 23
Josu 1 7 take courage . . . and be very valiant
Judg 5 13 the Lord hath fought among the v. ones
1 K 9 1 of a man of Jemini valiant and strong
2 K 1 19 how are the valiant fallen. 25, 27
21 was cast away the shield of the valiant
22 from the fat of the valiant, the arrow
2 16 was called; The field of the valiant
15 18 and all the Gethites, valiant warriors
17 8 that they are very valiant and bitter
10 that all who are with him are valiant
22 26 wilt be holy: and with the v. perfect
1 Pa 11 24 who was renowned among the three v.
2 Pa 17 17 after him was Eliada valiant in battle
Prov 12 24 hand of the valiant shall bear rule
16 32 patient man is better than the valiant
24 5 and a knowing man, stout and valiant
31 10 who shall find a valiant woman? Far
Wisd 8 15 I shall be found good, and v. in war
Eccu 28 19 hath cast out valiant women and hath
46 1 v. in war was Jesus the son of Nave
Isa 3 1 from Juda the valiant and the strong
Jer 5 16 they are all valiant. And they shall
48 14 how do you say: We are valiant and
Amos 2 14 the v. shall not possess his strength
16 stout of heart among the v. shall flee
1 Ma 2 66 v. and strong from his youth up, let
Heb 11 34 became valiant in battle, put to flight
most valiant Josu 10 2 its fighting men were m. v.
Judg 6 12 Lord is with thee, O most valiant of men
11 1 Jephte . . . a most valiant man and a
20 44 were 18,000 men, all most v. soldiers
46 fighting men, most valiant for war
1 Pa 7 7 sons of Bela . . . most valiant warriors
40 choice and most valiant captains of
11 19 these things did the three most valiant
12 1 were most v. and excellent warriors
2 Pa 13 3 were also chosen and most v. for war
2 Ma 12 42 most valiant Judas exhorted the
See also **valiant men**
valiant man Judg 11 1 a most v. man and a
1 K 14 52 whomsoever Saul saw to be a valiant man
18 17 be a v. man and fight the battles of
2 K 17 10 the most v. man whose heart is as the
10 know thy father to be a valiant man
23 20 son of Joiada a most v. man. 1 Pa 11:22
3 K 1 42 because thou art a v. man and bringest
11 28 Jeroboam was a valiant and mighty man

4 K 5 1 he was a valiant man and rich, but a
1 Ma 13 54 his son was a valiant man for war
2 Ma 12 35 one of Bacenor's band, a valiant man
valiant men Josu 6 2 Jericho and the king thereof and all the valiant men
Josu 8 3 and he sent 30,000 chosen valiant men
10 7 warriors with him, most valiant men
Judg 3 29 about 10,000, all strong and valiant men
5 7 the valiant men ceased, and rested
23 came not . . . to help his most v. men
18 2 children of Dan sent five most v. men
17 the 600 valiant men waiting not far
20 16 who were 7,000 most v. men, fighting
21 10 they sent 10,000 of the most v. men
1 K 31 12 all the most v. men arose and walked
2 K 13 28 take courage, and be valiant men. And
20 7 all the v. men went out of Jerusalem
23 8 the names of the valiant men of David
9 Eleazar . . . one of the three v. men
16 the three valiant men broke through
23 was renowned among the three v. men
24 9 were found of Israel 800,000 v. men
3 K 1 10 all the valiant men . . . he invited not
1 Pa 5 24 v. and powerful men and famous chiefs
7 2 of Thola . . . 220,600 most valiant men
4 six and 30,000 most v. men ready for
5 of Issachar . . . 87,000 most v. men
9 most valiant men for war, 20,200. And
11 valiant men, 17,200 fit to go out to
2 Pa 13 3 400,000 most valiant and chosen men
Cant 4 4 upon it, all the armor of valiant men
Jer 41 16 valiant men for war, and the women
46 9 let the valiant men come forth
15 why are thy valiant men come to nothing
48 41 the heart of the valiant men of Moab
50 27 destroy all her valiant men, let them
51 30 valiant men of Babylon have forborne
56 her valiant men are taken, and their
57 her rulers and her valiant men: and
Joel 2 7 they shall run like valiant men: like
Abdi 9 thy valiant men of the south shall be
Nah 2 5 he will muster up his valiant men
Zach 10 7 shall be as the valiant men of Ephraim
1 Ma 3 58 gird yourselves and be valiant men
4 3 rose up, he and the valiant men, to
6 37 upon every one thirty-two valiant men
11 44 Jonathan sent him 3,000 valiant men
14 32 armed the valiant men of his nation
2 Ma 13 15 with most valiant chosen young men
valiant ones Judg 5 13 fought among the v. ones
Cant 3 7 threescore v. ones of the most v. of
Isa 3 25 sword, and thy valiant ones in battle
Jer 46 5 their backs, their valiant ones slain
49 22 heart of the valiant ones of Edom
50 36 sword upon her valiant ones, and they
valiantly Josu 8 20 turned back most v. against
Eccu 48 25 walked valiantly in the way of David
1 Ma 2 46 they did valiantly. And they pursued
valley Num 21 20 is a v. in the country of Moab
Num 32 9 far as the v. of the cluster. Deut 1:24
Deut 2 36 a town that is situate in a valley
3 29 we abode in the valley over against
4 46 in the valley over against the temple
11 30 the v. that reacheth and entereth far
21 4 bring her into a rough and stony valley
6 heifer that was killed in the valley
34 7 in the valley of the land of Moab
Josu 7 24 brought them to the valley of Achor
26 place was called the Valley of Achor
8 11 between which and them there was a v.
13 and stood in the midst of the valley
10 12 O moon, toward the valley of Ajalon
12 2 and of the middle part in the valley
13 9 Arnon and in the midst of the valley
16 in midst of valley of the same torrent
19 Sarathasar in the mountain of the v.
27 in the valley Betharan and Bethnemra
15 7 borders of Debara from valley of Achor
8 up by the valley of the son of Ennom
8 in the end of the valley of Raphaim
16 8 towards the sea into the v. of reeds
17 9 goeth down to the valley of the reeds
16 and Jezrael in the midst of the valley
18 16 the valley of the children of Ennom
16 furthermost part of the v. of Raphaim
16 [Geennom] that is the valley of Ennom
19 14 thereof are the valley of Jephtahel
27 and to the valley of Jephthael
Judg 1 19 to destroy the inhabitants of the v.
4 11 unto the valley which is called Sennim
6 33 camped in the valley of Jezrael. But
7 1 in valley on north side of high hill
8 camp of Madian was beneath him in the v.
12 people lay scattered in the valley as
16 4 woman who dwelt in the v. of Sorec
1 K 6 13 were reaping wheat in the valley: and
13 18 above the valley of Seboim towards the
17 2 came to the valley of Terebinth, and
3 and there was a valley between them
19 were in the v. of Terebinth fighting
52 Philistines till they came to the valley
21 9 thou slewest in the valley of Terebinth
31 7 men of Israel that were beyond the v.
2 K 2 24 aqueduct that lieth over against the v.
5 18 spread themselves in v. of Raphaim. 22
8 13 Syria in the v. of the saltpits
18 18 pillar, which is in the king's valley
23 13 camp . . . was in the v. of the giants
4 K 2 16 upon some mountain or into some valley
14 7 slew of Edom in valley of the saltpits
23 4 burnt them . . . in the valley of Cedron
6 without Jerusalem to valley of Cedron
10 Topheth which is in the valley of the son of Ennom. Jer 7:31
1 Pa 4 14 Joab father of the Valley of artificers
11 15 Philistines encamped in v. of Raphaim
14 13 spread themselves abroad in the valley
2 Pa 20 26 were assembled in valley of Blessing
26 called that place the v. of Blessing
26 9 towers . . . over the gate of the valley
28 3 burnt incense in the valley of Benennom
33 6 through the fire in valley of Benennom
14 on west side of Gihon in the valley
2 Es 2 13 out by night by the gate of the valley
15 I came to the gate of the valley
3 13 the gate of the valley Hanun built
11 30 from Bersabee unto the valley of Ennom
35 Lod and Ono the valley of craftsmen
Jdth 12 7 into the valley of Bethulia, and washed
13 12 having compassed the valley, they came
Isa 22 1 the burden of the valley of vision
5 in the valley of vision, searching the
28 1 were on the head of the fat valley
4 who is on the head of the fat valley
21 as in the valley which is in Gabaon
40 4 every valley shall be exalted, and
65 10 v. of Achor into place for the herds
Jer 2 23 see thy ways in the valley, know what
7 32 nor the v. of the son of Ennom, but the v. of slaughter. 19:6
19 2 forth into the v. of the son of Ennom
21 13 that dwellest in a valley upon a rock
31 40 the whole valley of dead bodies and of
32 35 which are in the v. of the son of Ennom
47 5 peace with the remnant of their valley
49 4 thy v. hath flowed away, O delicate

Eze 31 12 his boughs shall fall in every valley
39 11 the valley of the passengers on the east
11 valley of the multitude of Gog. 15
Osee 1 5 bow of Israel in the v. of Jezrahel
2 15 valley of Achor for an opening of hope
Joel 3 2 them down into the valley of Josaphat
13 come up into the valley of Josaphat
14 nations in the valley of destruction
14 is near in the valley of destruction
Mich 1 6 the stones thereof into the valley
Zach 14 5 you shall flee to the valley of those
5 v. of the mountains shall be joined
2 Ma 1 19 fire from the altar, and hid it in a v.
Luke 3 5 every valley shall be filled; and
valleys Num 14 25 the Chanaanite dwell in the v.
Num 24 6 as woody valleys, as watered gardens
3 K 18 5 into all valleys, to see if we can
20 28 hills, but is not God of the valleys
1 Pa 12 15 put to flight all that dwell in the v.
27 29 over the oxen in the valleys, Saphat
Jdth 16 5 and their horses covered the valleys
Job 6 15 that passeth swiftly by the valleys
30 5 snatched up these things out of the v.
39 10 will he break the clods of the valleys
Cant 2 1 the field, and the lily of the valleys
6 10 to see the fruits of the valleys and
Isa 7 19 them rest in the torrents of the v.
22 7 thy choice v. shall be full of chariots
Jer 48 8 the v. shall perish, and the plains
49 4 why gloriest thou in the valleys? Thy
Bar 5 7 and to fill up the valleys to make them
Eze 6 3 to the rocks and the valleys: Behold
7 16 in the mountains like doves of the v.
32 6 the valleys shall be filled with thee
35 8 slain: in thy hills and in thy valleys
36 4 hills, to the brooks and to the valleys
6 hills, the ridges and to the valleys
Mich 1 4 v. shall be cleft, as wax before the
valor 2 K 2 7 strengthened and be ye men of v.
4 K 13 8 all that he did and his valor. 12; 14:15, 28
1 Pa 12 30 men of great valor renowned in their
26 6 for they were men of great valor
29 30 and of all his reign and his valor
1 Ma 9 11 in the front were all men of valor
2 Ma 8 7 the fame of his valor was spread
10 28 having with their valor the Lord for a
14 18 hearing of the v. of Judas' companions
15 17 that valor might decide the matter
valuable Judg 18 21 the cattle and all that was v.
Luke 12 24 how much are you more v. than they
value Lev 25 27 the value of the fruits shall be
Lev 27 8 as much as he shall value him at and
Mat 6 26 are not you of much more value than
Luke 12 7 you are of more v. than many sparrows
Vania 1 Es 10 36 of the sons of Bani . . . Vania
vanish Ps 36 20 come to nothing and vanish like
Ps 67 3 let them vanish away: as wax melteth
Isa 51 6 the heavens shall vanish like smoke
James 4 15 while, and afterwards shall vanish
vanished Judg 6 21 angel of the Lord v. out of
Ps 101 4 my days are vanished like smoke and
Luke 24 31 and he vanished out of their sight. And
vanisheth Ps 67 2 as smoke v., so let them vanish
vanities Deut 32 21 have angered me with their v.
3 K 16 13 the God of Israel with their vanities
26 God of Israel to anger with their v.
4 K 17 15 and they followed v. and acted vainly
Ps 30 7 hast hated them that regard vanities
39 5 who hath not had regard to vanities
Ecce 1 2 vanity of v., said Ecclesiastes. 12:8
5 6 many dreams, there are many vanities
Isa 59 4 trust in a mere nothing and speak v.
Jer 8 19 with their idols and strange vanities
Jon 2 9 they that are vain observe vanities
vanity 2 Es 1 7 we have been seduced by vanity
Job 11 11 for he knoweth the vanity of men
31 5 if I have walked in vanity, and my
Ps 4 3 why do you love vanity, and seek
25 4 I have not sat with the council of v.
51 9 his riches: and prevailed in his vanity
61 10 that by v. they may together deceive
77 33 their days were consumed in vanity
118 37 eyes that they may not behold vanity
143 4 man is like to vanity: his days pass
8 whose mouth hath spoken vanity. 11
Prov 30 8 remove far from me vanity, and lying
Ecce 1 2 v. of vanities, said Ecclesiastes. 12:8
2 vanity of vanities, and all is vanity
14 all is vanity and vexation of spirit
2 1 and I saw that this also was vanity
11 I saw in all things v. and vexation
15 I perceived that this also was vanity
17 and all vanity and vexation of spirit
21 this also is v. 26; 4:16; 5:9; 6:9; 7:7; 8:10
23 not rest in mind? And is not this vanity
3 19 all things are subject to vanity
4 4 in this also there is v. and fruitless
7 found also another vanity under the sun
8 in this also is vanity and a grievous
6 2 this is vanity and a great misery. If
11 many words that have much vanity in
7 16 also I saw in the days of my vanity
8 14 there is also another vanity, which is
9 9 under the sun all the time of thy v.
11 8 things past shall be accused of vanity
12 8 all things are vanity. And whereas
Wisd 4 12 the bewitching of vanity obscureth
14 14 by the vanity of men they came into
Eccu 3 26 hath detained their minds in vanity
17 29 are delighted with the vanity of evil
23 8 a sinner is caught in his own vanity
34 5 the dreams of evildoers are vanity
Isa 5 18 that drew iniquity with cords of vanity
24 10 the city of vanity is broken down
40 17 counted to him as nothing, and vanity
23 made the judges of the earth as vanity
41 29 vain: their idols are wind and vanity
Jer 2 5 from me, and have walked after vanity
10 8 the doctrine of their vanity is wood
16 19 a vanity which hath not profited them
Zach 10 2 and the dreamers have spoken vanity
Rom 8 20 creature was made subject to vanity
Eph 4 17 walk in the vanity of their mind, having
2 P 2 18 speaking proud words of vanity, they
vapor Lev 16 13 v. thereof may cover the oracle
Wisd 7 25 she is a vapor of the power of God
11 19 breathing out a fiery vapor or sending
Eccu 22 30 as the vapor of a chimney and the
38 29 vapor of the fire wasteth his flesh
Joel 2 30 and fire and vapor of smoke. Acts 2:19
James 4 14 it is a vapor which appeareth for a
vapors Eccu 43 4 breathing out fiery vapors
Vapsi Num 13 15 of Nephtali, Nahabi the son of V.
variance Mat 10 35 set a man at v. against his
varied Exod 36 8 with varied work and the art of
Zach 11 8 their soul also varied in my regard
varieth Eccu 38 28 by . . . diligence v. the figure
varieties Ps 44 15 clothed round about with v.
variety Exod 26 31 embroidered work and goodly v.
Exod 28 8 variety of the work shall be of gold
31 5 precious stones and variety of wood
Josu 22 8 brass and iron, and variety of raiment
Esth 1 6 with painting of wonderful variety
Ps 44 10 gilded clothing; surrounded with variety
Eccu 43 27 wonderful works: a variety of beasts
Eze 17 3 full of feathers and of variety

venomous Wisd 16 10 even the teeth of v. serpents
vent Job 32 19 is as new wine which wanteth vent
venture 3 K 22 34 shooting at a v., and chanced
2 Pa 18 33 shot an arrow at a venture and struck
Acts 19 31 he would not v. himself into theater
verdure Isa 35 7 rise up the v. of the reed and
verily Gen 16 13 v. here have I seen the hinder
Ps 54 13 I would verily have borne with it. And
Isa 43 19 forth, verily you shall know them
45 15 verily thou art a hidden God, the God
49 25 yea verily, even the captivity shall
Eze 18 19 verily, because the son hath wrought
20 30 verily, you are defiled in the way
Dan 2 47 verily your God is the God of gods
Mich 6 8 verily, to do judgment and to love
Luke 12 44 verily I say to you. 21:3
Rom 10 18 yes, verily, their sound hath gone forth
Gal 3 21 verily justice should have been by law
verity Luke 1 4 that thou mayest know the verity
vermilion Wisd 13 14 laying it over with vermilion
Jer 22 14 cedar, and painteth them with vermilion
verses Ps 4 1 unto the end, in v. 6:1; 53:1; 54:1
very Mat 10 30 the very hairs of your head are all numbered. Luke 12:7
Luke 10 11 even the very dust of your city that
13 1 there were present at that very time
John 14 12 believe for the very works' sake. Amen
17 8 have known in very deed that I came
Acts 10 34 said: In very deed I perceive, that
12 11 now I know in very deed, that the Lord
Phil 1 6 being confident of this very thing, that
Col 2 22 are unto destruction by the very use
Heb 10 1 not the very image of the things; by the
1 J 2 5 in him in very deed the charity of God
vessel Exod 16 33 take a v. and put manna into it
Exod 22 7 if a man deliver money or any vessel
35 22 every vessel of gold was set aside
Lev 6 28 vessel, wherein it was sodden, shall
28 vessel be of brass, it shall be scoured
11 32 defiled, whether it be a vessel of wood
33 earthen vessel into which any of these
34 if water from such a vessel be poured
34 that is drunk out of any such vessel
14 5 to be immolated in an earthen vessel
50 immolated one sparrow in an earthen v.
15 12 if he touch a vessel of earth it shall
12 if a vessel of wood, it shall be washed
23 touch any vessel on which she sitteth
26 every vessel on which she sitteth
Num 5 17 shall take holy water in an earthen v.
19 15 vessel that hath no cover nor binding
17 pour living waters upon them into a v.
31 20 of all the spoil, every garment or v.
Judg 6 38 fleece, he filled a vessel with the dew
2 K 16 1 cakes of figs, and a vessel of wine
3 K 17 10 give me a little water in a vessel
19 6 a hearth cake and a vessel of water
4 K 2 20 bring me a new vessel, and put salt
4 6 said to her son: Bring me yet a vessel
12 13 or any vessel of gold and silver
1 Pa 28 14 gold by weight for every vessel for
Jdth 10 5 wine to carry, and a vessel of oil
Ps 2 9 them in pieces like a potter's vessel
30 13 I am become as a v. that is destroyed
32 7 the waters of the sea, as in a vessel
77 13 made the waters to stand as in a vessel
Prov 20 15 lips of knowledge are a precious vessel
25 4 shall come forth a most pure vessel
26 23 like an earthen vessel adorned with
Wisd 13 11 formeth a vessel profitable for the
14 6 hope of the world fleeing to a vessel
15 7 fashioneth every vessel for our service
Eccu 21 17 heart of a fool is like a broken vessel
38 30 the pattern of the vessel he maketh
50 10 as a massy vessel of gold, adorned
Isa 10 33 shall break the earthen v. with terror
22 24 kinds of vessels, every little vessel
30 14 as the potter's vessel is broken all
66 20 should bring an offering in a clean v.
Jer 18 4 vessel was broken which he was making
4 and turning he made another vessel
19 11 as the potter's vessel is broken, which
22 28 Jechonias an earthen and a broken v.
28 is he a vessel wherein is no pleasure
32 14 and put them in an earthen vessel, that
48 11 hath not been poured out from v. to v.
38 I have broken Moab as an useless vessel
51 34 he hath made me as an empty vessel
Bar 6 15 as a vessel that a man uses when it is
58 else a profitable vessel in the house
Eze 4 9 put them in one vessel, and make thee
15 3 of it for any vessel to hang thereon
Osee 8 8 among the nations like an unclean v.
13 15 the treasure of every desirable vessel
Zach 5 6 he said: This is a vessel going forth
7 a woman sitting in the midst of the v.
8 he cast her into the midst of the v.
9 they lifted up the vessel between the
10 whither do these carry the vessel? And
Mark 11 16 any man should carry a vessel through
Luke 8 16 covereth it with a vessel or putteth
John 19 29 was a vessel set there full of vinegar
Acts 9 15 this man is to me a vessel of election
10 11 a certain vessel descending. 11:5
16 the vessel was taken up into heaven
Rom 9 21 of the same lump, to make one vessel
1 Th 4 4 you should know how to possess his v.
2 Tim 2 21 these, he shall be a vessel unto honor
1 P 3 7 to the female as to the weaker vessel
Apoc 2 27 as the v. of a potter they shall be
vessels Gen 43 11 fruits of the land in your v.
Gen 49 5 Simeon and Levi brethren: vessels of
Exod 7 19 both in v. of wood and of stone. And
25 9 all the vessels for the service thereof
27 3 all its vessels thou shalt make of brass
19 vessels of the tabernacle for all uses
30 27 the table with the v. thereof. 39:35
31 7 and all the vessels of the tabernacle
8 the table and the vessels thereof, the
8 candlestick with the v. thereof. 35:24
9 of the holocaust and of all their v.
35 13 the bars and the vessels. 16; 39:39
14 the vessels thereof and the lamps and
37 16 vessels for the divers uses of the table
23 v. where the snuffings were to be put
38 3 for uses thereof he prepared divers v.
30 vessels that belong to the use thereof
40 nothing was wanting of the vessels that
40 9 anoint the tabernacle with its vessels
10 altar of holocaust and all its vessels
Lev 8 11 he anointed it and all the v. thereof
Num 1 50 tabernacle of testimony and all the v.
3 8 let them keep the v. of the tabernacle
31 shall keep . . . vessels of the sanctuary
4 9 the snuffers and all the oil vessels
12 all the v. wherewith they minister
14 shall put it with all the vessels that
14 they shall cover all the vessels of the
15 wrapped up the sanctuary and the v.
15 shall not touch the v. of the sanctuary
16 all the v. that are in the sanctuary
26 cords and the vessels of the ministry
32 shall receive by account all the vessels
7 1 sanctified it with all its v., the altar likewise and all the v. thereof
85 putting all the v. of silver together

18 3 they shall not come nigh the vessels of
19 14 vessels that are there, shall be unclean
31 6 he delivered to him the holy vessels
Josu 6 19 vessels of brass and iron, let it be
24 vessels of brass and iron, which they
Ruth 2 9 if thou art thirsty, go to the vessels
1 K 17 22 David leaving v. which he had brought
21 5 the vessels of the young men were holy
5 also be sanctified this day in the v.
25 18 took 200 loaves and 2 v. of wine and
2 K 8 10 gold and v. of silver and v. of brass
17 28 beds and tapestry and earthen v.
3 K 7 45 all the vessels that Hiram made for
47 and Solomon placed all the vessels
48 Solomon made all the vessels for the
51 the silver and the gold and the vessels
8 4 and all the vessels of the sanctuary
10 21 vessels out of which king Solomon drank
15 15 the Lord, silver and gold, and vessels
4 K 4 3 borrow of all thy neighbors empty v.
4 pour out thereof into all those vessels
5 brought her the vessels, and she poured
6 when the vessels were full, she said
7 15 was full of garments and vessels, which
14 14 the gold and silver and all the vessels
20 13 house of his vessels and all that he
23 4 vessels that had been made for Baal
25 14 took away . . . all the vessels of brass
1 Pa 9 28 had the charge of the vessels for the
28 the vessels were both brought in and
18 8 and the pillars and the v. of brass
22 19 the vessels consecrated to the Lord
23 26 all the vessels for the service thereof
26 20 Achias was over . . . the holy vessels
28 13 for all the vessels of the service
14 the diversity of the vessels and uses
29 2 and silver for vessels of silver
2 Pa 4 16 the vessels did Hiram his father make
18 multitude of vessels was innumerable
19 Solomon made all the v. for the house
22 the vessels also for the perfumes and
5 1 and all the vessels he put among the
5 carried the vessels of the sanctuary
9 20 vessels of the king's table were of gold
20 v. of the house of forest of Libanus
15 18 and silver and vessels of divers uses
20 25 and garments and most precious vessels
24 14 with it were made vessels for the temple
25 24 he [Joas] took . . . all the vessels
28 24 Achaz having taken away all the vessels
29 18 we have sanctified . . . the v. thereof
18 the table of proposition with all its v.
32 27 vessels of great price. Storehouses also
36 7 he carried also thither the vessels
10 the most precious vessels of the house
18 all the vessels of the house of the Lord
1 Es 1 7 king Cyrus brought forth the vessels
10 other vessels a thousand. All the vessels
5 15 take these vessels, and go and put them
6 5 let the golden and silver vessels of
7 19 the vessels also, that are given thee
8 25 the vessels consecrated for the house of
26 and a hundred vessels of silver and a
27 two vessels of the best shining brass
28 Lord, and the vessels are holy, and
30 the vessels, to carry them to Jerusalem
33 and the vessels were weighed in the
2 Es 10 39 the sanctified vessels shall be there
13 5 frankincense and vessels and the tithes
8 forth the v. of the house of Tobias
9 I brought thither again the vessels
Esth 1 7 the meats were brought in divers vessels
Job 32 19 vent, which bursteth the new vessels
Ecce 2 8 and vessels to serve to pour out wine
Wisd 15 7 maketh both v. that are for clean uses
7 but what is the use of these vessels
13 maketh brittle vessels and graven gods
Eccu 27 6 the furnace trieth the potter's vessels
Isa 18 2 in vessels of bulrushes upon the waters
22 24 father's house, divers kinds of vessels
24 from the vessels of cups even to every
32 7 vessels of the deceitful are most wicked
52 11 you that carry the vessels of the Lord
65 4 profane broth is in their vessels. That
Jer 14 3 they carried back their vessels empty
25 34 you shall fall like precious vessels
27 16 v. of the Lord shall now in a short time
18 v. which were left in house of the Lord
19 rest of the v. that remain in this city
21 to the v. that are left in the house
28 3 all the vessels of the house of the Lord
6 that the vessels may be brought again
40 10 and the oil, and lay it up in your v.
48 12 him down, and shall empty his vessels
49 29 all their vessels and their camels: and
52 18 v. that had been used in the ministry
20 no weight of the brass of all these v.
Lam 4 2 how are they esteemed as earthen vessels
Bar 1 8 when he received the v. of the temple
8 silver vessels which Sedecias . . . had
Eze 16 17 thou tookest thy beautiful vessels, of
39 shall take away the v. of thy beauty
27 13 to thy people slaves and v. of brass
40 42 tables . . . to lay the vessels upon in
Dan 1 2 part of the vessels of the house of God
2 v. he brought into the treasure house
5 3 were the golden and silver v. brought
23 the v. of his house have been brought
14 2 forty sheep and sixty vessels of wine
Agge 2 17 into the press, to press out fifty v.
1 Ma 1 23 candlestick of light and all the v.
23 of proposition and the pouring vessels
24 silver and gold and the precious v.
2 9 the v. of her glory are carried away
4 49 they made new holy v. and brought
14 15 multiplied the v. of the holy places
2 Ma 4 48 for the people and the sacred vessels
5 16 taking in his wicked hands, the holy v.
9 16 and to multiply the holy vessels, and
Mat 13 48 they chose out the good into vessels
25 4 but the wise took oil in their vessels
Mark 7 4 pots and of brazen vessels and of beds
Rom 9 22 endured with much patience v. of wrath
23 show riches of his glory on v. of mercy
2 C 4 7 we have this treasure in earthen vessels
Heb 9 21 the tabernacle also and all the vessels
2 Tim 2 20 not only vessels of gold and of silver
Apoc 18 12 all manner of vessels of ivory and all
12 all manner of vessels of precious stone
vessels of gold 2 K 8 10 in his hand were v. . . .
4 K 24 13 and he cut in pieces all the v. of gold
1 Pa 18 11 all the v. . . . and silver and brass
2 Pa 24 14 bowls and other v. . . . and silver
1 Es 1 11 all the v. . . . and silver, 5,400
2 Tim 2 20 not only v. . . . and of silver, but
vessels of silver and gold Gen 24 53 bring forth **v. . . .** and garments
Exod 3 22 of her that is in her house v. . . .
12 35 they asked of the Egyptians v. . . .
3 K 10 25 brought him presents, v. . . . , garments
1 Es 1 6 helped their hands with v. . . . , with
vest Exod 28 41 thou shalt vest Aaron thy brother
Num 20 26 thou shalt vest therewith Eleazar his
vested Exod 28 35 Aaron shall be vested with it
Lev 6 10 priest shall be vested with the tunick
8 7 he vested the high priest with the

13 he vested them with linen tunicks
10 5 as they lay, vested with linen tunicks
16 4 he shall be vested with a linen tunick
32 he shall be vested with the linen robe
21 10 hath been v. with the holy vestments
Num 20 28 he vested Eleazar his son with them
vestment 1 Ma 10 21 Jonathan put on the holy v.
vestments Exod 28 3 that they may make Aaron's v.
Exod 28 4 these shall be the vestments that they
4 they shall make the holy vestments
29 5 shalt clothe Aaron with his vestments
21 and his vesture, his sons and their v.
21 after they and their vestments are
31 10 holy v. in the ministry for Aaron
35 19 v. that are to be used in the ministry
21 necessary . . . to the holy vestments
39 1 the vestments for Aaron to wear when
41 the vestments also which the priests
40 13 shalt put on them the holy vestments
Lev 6 11 shall put off his former vestments
8 2 take Aaron with his sons, their v.
30 and his v. and his sons and their v.
31 had sanctified them in their vestments
16 4 these are holy vestments: all which
23 putting off the v. which he had on
32 with the linen robe and the holy v.
21 10 who hath been vested with the holy v.
Num 20 28 had stripped Aaron of his vestments
Eze 42 14 there they shall lay their vestments
44 19 not sanctify the people with their v.
2 Ma 3 15 before the altar in their priests' v.
vesture Exod 28 2 make a holy vesture for Aaron
Exod 29 21 shalt sprinkle Aaron and his vesture
29 the holy vesture which Aaron shall use
35 19 the vesture of Aaron the high priest
Num 20 26 hast stripped the father of his vesture
Ps 21 19 and upon my vesture they cast lots
101 27 as a vesture thou shalt change them
Eccu 50 12 he honored the vesture of holiness
Mat 27 35 and upon my vesture they cast lots
John 19 24 and upon my vesture they have cast lot
Heb 1 12 as a vesture shalt thou change them, and
vetches Isa 28 25 wheat in order . . . and vetches
vex Deut 32 21 will vex them with a foolish nation
vexation Ecce 1 14 vanity and vexation of spirit. 2:17; 4:16
Ecce 1 17 labor and vexation of spirit. 2:22
2 11 all things vanity and vexation of mind
26 to the sinner he hath given vexation
4 6 hands full with labor and v. of mind
8 is vanity and a grievous vexation
Isa 14 3 rest from thy labor and from thy v.
28 19 v. alone shall make you understand
Jer 24 9 I will deliver them up to vexation
vexed 2 P 2 8 v. the just soul with unjust
vial 1 K 10 1 Samuel took a little vial of oil
Apoc 16 2 poured out his v. 3, 4, 8, 10, 12, 17
vials 1 Ma 1 23 pouring vessels and the vials
Apoc 5 8 golden vials full of odors, which are
15 7 golden vials full of the wrath of God
16 1 go and pour out the seven vials
17 1 angels, who had the seven vials, and
21 9 vials full of the seven last plagues
vices Job 20 11 filled with the v. of his youth
Gal 5 24 flesh, with the vices and concupiscences
victim Gen 22 7 where is the victim for the
Gen 22 8 God will provide himself a victim for
Exod 12 27 the victim of the passage of the Lord
23 18 not sacrifice blood of my victim upon
29 18 a most sweet savor of the victim
36 hast offered the victim of expiation
30 9 composition nor oblation, and victim
34 25 in the morning anything of the victim
Lev 1 4 his hand upon the head of the v. 4:29
6 when they have flayed the victim, they
3 8 his hand upon the head of his victim
9 offer of the victim of peace offerings
4 25 his finger in the blood of the victim
32 if he offer of the flock a victim for
6 25 this is the law of the victim for sin
30 for the victim that is slain for sin
7 2 the victim also for a trespass shall be
8 that offereth the victim of holocaust
14 shall pour out the blood of the victim
18 any man eat of the flesh of the victim
29 offereth a v. of peace offerings. 22:21
30 hold in his hands the fat of the victim
9 7 when thou hast slain the people's v.
12 he immolated also the v. of holocaust
13 the victim being cut into pieces, they
10 19 hath been offered the victim for sin
14 13 where the victim for sin is wont to be
13 v. for a trespass offering pertaineth
14 priest taking of the blood of the v.
17 8 that offereth a holocaust or a victim
22 29 if you immolate a v. for thanksgiving
Num 6 14 ram . . . for a victim of peace offering
15 3 to the Lord for a holocaust or a v.
4 whosoever immolateth the victim, shall
5 libations for the holocaust or for the v.
19 2 this is the observance of the victim
28 14 that are to be poured out for every v.
1 K 9 13 because he blesseth the victim and
4 K 5 17 not henceforth offer holocaust or v.
16 15 blood of the victim thou shalt pour out
Prov 7 22 followeth her as an ox led to be victim
Wisd 3 6 as a victim of a holocaust he hath
Isa 34 6 there is a victim of the Lord in Bosra
Jer 11 19 lamb, that is carried to be a victim
Eze 39 17 together from every side to my victim
17 great v. upon the mountains of Israel
19 till you be drunk of the victim which
40 42 in which holocaust and the v. is slain
44 29 they shall eat the victim both for sin
Dan 9 27 the victim and the sacrifice shall fail
Soph 1 7 for the Lord hath prepared a victim
8 in the day of the victim of the Lord
Mark 9 48 every victim shall be salted with salt
Phil 2 17 if I be made a victim upon the sacrifice
victims Gen 43 16 kill v. and prepare a feast
Gen 46 1 killing victims there to the God of his
Exod 24 5 sacrificed pacific victims of calves
29 28 the beginnings of their peace victims
32 6 they offered holocausts and peace v.
8 adored it and sacrificing victims to it
Lev 1 2 offering victims of oxen and sheep
4 33 place where the victims of holocausts
9 22 the victims for sin and the holocausts
17 5 shall bring to the priest their victims
7 no more sacrifice their v. to devils
Deut 12 6 in that place your holocausts and v.
11 victims and tithes and firstfruits of
27 the blood of thy victims thou shalt pour
18 3 from them that offer victims: whether
27 7 shalt immolate peace victims and eat
32 38 of whose victims they ate the fat
33 19 there shall they sacrifice v. of justice
Josu 13 14 sacrifices and victims of the Lord God
22 26 not for holocausts, nor to offer v.
27 a right to offer both holocausts and v.
29 to offer holocausts and sacrifices and v.
Judg 21 4 holocausts and victims of peace, and
1 K 2 29 why have you kicked away my victims
3 14 shall not be expiated with victims
6 15 offered holocausts and sacrificed v.
10 8 oblation and sacrifice victims of peace

11 15 they sacrificed there victims of peace
15 22 doth the Lord desire holocausts and v.
2 K 6 12 David seven choirs and calves for v.
3 K 3 4 a thousand victims for holocausts did
8 62 and all Israel with him offered victims
1 Pa 21 28 Jebusite, forthwith offered victims
29 21 sacrificed v. to the Lord. Jon 1:16
2 Pa 1 6 offered upon it a thousand victims
5 6 so great was multitude of the victims
7 1 consumed the holocausts and the victims
4 people sacrificed v. before the Lord
9 4 victims which he offered in the house
11 16 to sacrifice their victims before Lord
28 23 sacrificed v. to the gods of Damascus
23 and I will appease them with victims
29 31 come and offer victims and praises
31 and all the multitude offered victims
32 23 many also brought victims and sacrifices
33 16 Lord, and sacrificed upon it victims
Prov 7 14 I vowed victims for prosperity, this day
9 2 she hath slain her victims, mingled
15 8 victims of the wicked are abominable
17 1 than house full of victims with strife
21 3 pleaseth the Lord more than victims
Ecce 4 17 obedience, than the victims of fools
9 2 unclean, to him that offereth victims
Isa 1 11 you offer me the multitude of your v.
43 23 nor hast thou glorified me with thy v.
24 filled me with the fat of thy victims
56 7 and their victims shall please me upon
57 7 hast gone up thither to offer victims
Jer 14 12 if they offer holocausts and victims
17 26 bringing holocausts and victims and
33 18 to burn sacrifices and to kill victims
Eze 20 28 and there they sacrificed their victims
21 10 it is sharpened to kill victims: it is
40 41 tables, upon which they slew the v.
44 11 holocausts and the v. of the people
46 24 shall boil the victims of the people
Dan 2 46 in sacrifice to him victims and incense
Osee 5 2 have turned aside victims into the depth
8 13 they shall offer victims, they shall
11 2 they offered victims to Baalim, and
Amos 4 4 bring in the morning your victims
5 25 did you offer victims and sacrifices
Haba 1 16 will he offer victims to his drag
Acts 7 42 did you offer victims and sacrifices
victims of peace offerings Lev 4 26 as is wont to be done
with the v. . . .
Lev 4 31 is wont to be taken away of the v. . . .
7 34 children of Israel, from off their v. . . .
37 for consecration, and the v. . . . : which
10 14 for thee and thy children, of the v. . . .
Num 7 35 a buck goat for sin: and for v. . . . two
15 8 of oxen, to fulfil thy vow or for v. . . .
29 39 sacrifice, for libation and for v. . . .
Josu 8 31 holocausts to Lord and immolated v. . . .
22 23 it holocausts and sacrifice and v. . . .
Judg 20 26 offered to him holocausts and v. . . . and
3 K 3 15 offered holocausts and sacrificed v. . . .
8 63 Solomon slew v. . . . which he sacrificed
9 25 every year holocausts and v. . . . upon
2 Pa 30 22 days of solemnity, immolating v. . . .
35 13 the v. . . . they boiled in caldrons, and
victories 2 Pa 26 8 of Egypt for his frequent v.
victorious Wisd 10 20 with one accord thy v. hand
victory Num 23 21 the sound of the v. of the king
Judg 4 9 the v. shall not be attributed to thee
11 36 since the v. hath been granted to thee
15 18 victory into the hand of thy servant
2 K 12 28 the victory be ascribed to my name
19 2 v. of that day was turned into mourning
23 10 and the Lord wrought a great victory
12 and the Lord gave a great victory
1 Pa 15 21 sung a song of victory for the octave
29 11 power and glory and victory: and to
Jdth 13 20 rejoicing for his victory, for my escape
16 22 all the people after the victory came
24 the joy of this victory was celebrated
31 the day of the festivity of this victory
Job 23 7 and let my judgment come to victory
Prov 21 28 an obedient man shall speak of victory
22 9 shall purchase victory and honor: but
2 Ma 8 33 when they kept the feast of the victory
10 28 Lord for a surety of victory and success
38 in Israel, and given them the victory
12 11 by the help of God they got the v.
13 15 for a watchword, the victory of God
15 6 monument of his victory over Judas
8 to hope for victory from the Almighty
21 who giveth v. to them that are worthy
Mat 12 20 till he send forth judgment unto v.
1 C 15 54 death is swallowed up in v. O death
55 O death, where is thy victory? O death
57 to God, who hath given us the victory
1 J 5 4 this is the victory which overcometh
victuals Gen 14 11 all their v. and went their way
Josu 1 11 prepare you victuals: for after the
9 11 take with you victuals for a long way
14 they took therefore of their victuals
Judg 7 8 taking victuals and trumpets according
17 10 double suit of apparel and thy victuals
20 10 to bring victuals for the army, that we
1 K 22 10 Lord for him, and gave him [David] v.
3 K 4 7 who provided victuals for the king
11 18 appointed him v. and assigned him land
20 27 taking victuals went out on other side
2 Pa 31 8 victuals were given faithfully out
Prov 31 15 household and victuals to her maidens
Jer 40 5 general of the army gave him victuals
1 Ma 1 36 they stored up armor and victuals
6 49 because they had no victuals, being
53 there were no victuals in the city
57 our provision of victuals is small
9 52 garrisons in them and provisions of v.
13 21 through the desert, and send them v.
33 he stored up victuals in the fortresses
14 10 he provided victuals for the cities
2 Ma 12 14 the provision of victuals, behaved in
Mat 14 15 they may buy themselves victuals
Luke 9 12 they may lodge and get victuals; for
view Gen 42 9 come to view the weaker parts
Lev 13 10 to the priest, and he shall view him
13 the priest shall view him. 17
25 the priest shall view it and if he see
27 on the seventh day he shall view him
39 the priest shall view them. If he find
14 36 he shall go in to view the leprosy
Num 13 3 send men to view the land of Chanaan
17 whom Moses sent to view the land: and
18 and Moses sent them to view the land of
19 view the land, of what sort it is
14 36 whom Moses had sent to view the land
38 all them that had gone to view the land
21 32 Moses sent some to take a view of Jazer
27 12 view from thence the land which I will
32 8 I sent from Cadesbarne to view the land
Deut 1 22 let us send men who may view the land
Josu 2 1 view the land and the city of Jericho
3 spies and are come to v. all the land
7 2 go up and view the country: and they
14 7 from Cadesbarne, to view the land and
11 when I was sent to view the land
Judg 18 2 out the land and to view it diligently
2 said to them: Go and view the land
14 had been sent to view the land of Lais

1 Ma 5 38 Judas sent men to view the army: and
2 Ma 4 5 but with a view to the common good
Acts 7 31 as he drew near to view it, the voice
viewed Num 13 22 they v. the land from the desert
Num 13 33 ill of the land, which they had viewed
33 the land which we have viewed before the
14 6 themselves also had viewed the land
34 forty days wherein you viewed the land
32 9 having viewed all the country, they
Deut 1 24 having v. the land, taking of fruits
Josu 7 2 fulfilled his command and viewed Hai
2 Es 2 13 I v. the wall of Jerusalem which was
15 torrent, and viewed the wall and going
Mark 11 11 having viewed all things round about
vigilant 2 Tim 4 5 be thou v., labor in all things
vigor 4 K 9 22 her many sorceries are in their v.
Acts 18 28 with much v. he convinced the Jews
vigorous 2 Ma 12 27 walls made a v. resistance
vigorously Judg 20 39 they fled and pursued them v.
2 K 11 23 we v. charged and pursued them even to
vile Lev 21 7 to wife a harlot or a vile prostitute
1 K 15 9 everything that was vile and good for
Job 18 3 as beasts and counted vile before you
Jer 15 19 separate the precious from the vile
Lam 1 11 and consider, for I am become vile
Bar 6 25 declaring to men how vile they are
Dan 11 20 stand up in his place one most vile
vilest Wisd 15 18 worship also the v. creatures
village Lev 25 31 if the house be in a village
Num 34 9 Zephrona, and the village of Enan
10 from the village of Enan unto Sephama
Deut 2 36 not a village or city that escaped
1 K 6 18 to the village that was without wall
Mat 21 2 go ye into the village. Mark 11:2
villages Exod 8 13 of houses, and out of the v.
Num 21 25 and in the villages thereof. Judg 11:26; 2 Es 11:25, 27, 28, 30, 31
32 and they took the villages of it and
31 10 their villages and castles they burned
32 41 the son of Manasses went and took the v.
41 Jair, that is to say villages of Jair
42 Canath and the v. thereof. 1 Pa 2:23
Josu 13 17 and Hesebon and all their villages
23 their kindreds, of cities and villages
28 by their families, their cities and v.
30 and all the villages of Jair which are
15 32 all the cities 29, and their villages
36 cities and their villages. 41, 44, 51, 54, 57, 59, 60, 62; 18:24, 28; 19:6, 7, 15, 16, 22, 23, 30, 31, 38, 39, 48
45 Accaron with the towns and villages
46 towards Azotus and the villages thereof
47 Azotus with its towns and villages
47 Gaza with its towns and villages, even
16 9 there were cities with their villages
17 11 Bethsan and its v., and Jeblaam with its v.
11 inhabitants of Thenac with the villages
11 inhabitants also of Endor with the v.
11 inhabitants of Mageddo with their v.
19 8 all villages round about these cities
21 12 but the fields and the villages thereof
Judg 1 27 Bethsan and Thanac with their villages
27 Jeblaam and Mageddo with their villages
11 26 in Aroer and its villages and in all
20 48 and villages of Benjamin were consumed
1 K 5 6 in the villages and fields in the midst
1 Pa 4 33 all their v. round about these cities
6 56 the villages to Caleb son of Jephone
9 25 their brethren dwelt in villages and
27 25 the v. and in the castles was Jonathan
2 Pa 28 18 Thamnan and Gamzo with their villages
2 Es 6 2 make a league together in the villages
11 30 Zanoa, Odollam, and in their villages
12 28 and out of the villages of Nethuphati
29 had built themselves v. round about
Esth 9 19 in towns not walled and in villages
Cant 7 11 the field, let us abide in the villages
Mark 6 6 he went through the villages round
36 that going into the next villages and
56 into towns or into villages or cities
Luke 8 34 told it in the city and in the v.
9 12 into the towns and v. round about
vine Gen 40 9 his dream: I saw before me a vine
Gen 49 11 his ass, O my son to the vine.˙He shall
Judg 9 12 the trees said to the vine: Come thou
13 14 eat nothing that cometh of the vine
3 K 4 25 every one under his vine and under his
4 K 4 39 he found something like a wild vine
Job 15 33 he shall be blasted as a vine when
Ps 127 3 thy wife as a fruitful vine on the sides
Cant 7 8 shall be as the clusters of the vine
Eccu 24 23 as the vine I have brought forth a
Isa 24 7 mourned, the vine hath languished away
34 4 down as the leaf falleth from the vine
36 16 eat ye every one of his vine and every
Jer 6 9 the remains of Israel, as in a vine
Eze 15 2 what shall be made of wood of the vine
6 as the vine tree among the trees of
17 6 grew into spreading vine of low stature
6 it became a vine, and grew into branches
7 this vine, bending as it were her roots
8 that it might become a large vine
19 10 thy mother is like a vine in thy blood
Osee 10 1 Israel a vine full of branches the fruit
14 8 wheat, and they shall blossom as a vine
Joel 2 22 and the vine have yielded their strength
Mich 4 4 every man shall sit under his vine
Nah 2 2 and have marred their vine branches
Agge 2 20 as yet sprung up? or hath the vine
Zach 3 10 his friend under the vine and under
8 12 the vine shall yield her fruit and the
Mala 3 11 neither shall v. in the field be barren
1 Ma 14 12 every man sat under his vine and under
Mat 26 29 henceforth of this fruit of the vine
Mark 14 25 no more of the fruit of the vine until
Luke 22 18 I will not drink of the fruit of the v.
John 15 1 I am the true vine; and my Father is
4 unless it abide in the vine, so
5 I am the vine; you the branches: he
James 3 12 bear grapes; or the vine, figs? So
vinedressers Jer 52 16 general left some for v.
Osee 2 15 I will give her vinedressers out of the
Joel 1 11 the v. have howled for the wheat and
vinegar Num 6 3 they shall not drink v. of wine
Ruth 2 14 bread, and dip thy morsel in the vinegar
Ps 68 22 in my thirst they gave me vinegar to
Prov 10 26 as vinegar to the teeth and smoke to
25 20 as vinegar upon niter, so is he that
Mat 27 48 a sponge and filled it with vinegar
Mark 15 36 and filling a sponge with vinegar and
Luke 23 36 coming to him, and offering him v.
John 19 29 was a vessel set there full of vinegar
29 a sponge full of vinegar about hyssop
30 when he had taken the vinegar, said
vines Lev 25 11 gather firstfruits of the vines
Num 20 5 sowed nor bringeth forth figs nor v.
Deut 32 32 their vines are of vineyard of Sodom
4 K 25 12 the land he left some dressers of vines
2 Pa 26 10 also vineyards and dressers of vines
Cant 2 13 the vines in flower yield their sweet
15 little foxes that destroy the vines
Isa 5 2 and planted it with the choicest vines
7 23 where there were a thousand vines at a
61 5 husbandmen and dressers of your vines
Jer 8 13 there is no grape on the vines and
Osee 2 12 I will destroy her vines and her fig

Haba 3 17 there shall be no spring in the vines
vineyard Gen 9 20 till the ground and planted v.
Gen 49 11 tying his foal to the vineyard and his
Exod 22 5 if any man hurt a field or a vineyard
5 he hath in his own field or in his v.
23 11 so shalt thou do with thy vineyard and
Lev 19 10 grapes that fall down in thy vineyard
25 3 six years thou shalt prune thy vineyard
4 sow thy field nor prune thy vineyard
Num 6 4 eat nothing that cometh of the vineyard
Deut 20 6 what man is there that hath planted a v.
22 9 not sow thy vineyard with divers seeds
9 and fruit of the vineyard be sanctified
23 24 going into thy neighbor's vineyard, thou
24 21 thou make the vintage of thy vineyard
28 30 thou plant a vineyard and not gather
39 thou shalt plant a vineyard and dig it
32 32 their vines are of vineyard of Sodom
3 K 21 1 had at that time a vineyard near the
2 to Naboth, saying; Give me thy vineyard
2 I will give thee for it a better v.
6 give me thy vineyard and take money
6 I will give thee a better vineyard
6 said: I will not give thee my vineyard
7 I will give thee the vineyard of Naboth
15 take possession of vineyard of Naboth
16 went down to the vineyard of Naboth
18 he is going down to vineyard of Naboth
4 K 18 31 shall eat of his own vineyard and of his
Job 24 6 gather the vintage of his vineyard
Ps 79 9 hast brought a vineyard out of Egypt
15 and see, and visit this vineyard: and
Prov 24 30 by the vineyard of the foolish man
31 16 her hands she hath planted a vineyard
Cant 1 5 my vineyard I have not kept. Show me
2 15 vines: for our vineyard hath flourished
6 10 to look if the vineyard had flourished
7 12 let us see if the vineyard flourish
8 11 the peaceable had a vineyard in that
12 my vineyard is before me. A thousand
Isa 1 8 shall be left as a covert in a vineyard
3 14 for you have devoured the vineyard
5 1 canticle of my cousin concerning his v.
1 my beloved had a vineyard on a hill
3 judge between me and my vineyard. What
4 that I ought to do more to my vineyard
5 I will show you what I will do to my v.
7 v. of Lord of hosts is house of Israel
10 ten acres of v. shall yield one little
16 8 have destroyed the vineyard of Sabama
9 weeping of Jazer the v. of Sabama
27 2 be singing to the vineyard of pure wine
32 12 country, for the fruitful vineyard
Jer 2 21 yet I planted thee a chosen vineyard
21 good for nothing, O strange vineyard
12 10 many pastors have destroyed my vineyard
35 9 nor to have vineyard or field or seed
48 32 vineyard of Sabama, I will weep for thee
Joel 1 7 he hath laid my vineyard waste and
12 the vineyard is confounded and the fig
Mich 1 6 stones in the field when a v. is planted
Mat 20 1 to hire laborers into his vineyard
2 he sent them into his vineyard. And
4 go you also into my vineyard. 7
8 the lord of the v. saith to his steward
21 28 son, go work today in my vineyard. And
33 planted a vineyard and made a hedge
39 cast him forth out of the v. Mark 12:8
40 lord of the vineyard shall come, what
41 will let out his vineyard to other
Mark 12 1 a certain man planted a v. Luke 20:9
2 to receive . . . of the fruit of the v.
9 will the lord of the v. Luke 20:15
9 will give the v. to others. Luke 20:16
Luke 13 6 a fig tree planted in his vineyard
7 said to the dresser of the v.: Behold
20 10 should give him of the fruit of the v.
13 the lord of the vineyard said: What
15 casting him out of the v., they killed
1 C 9 7 who planteth vineyard, and eateth not
Apoc 14 18 clusters of the vineyard of the earth
19 and gathered the vineyard of the earth
vineyards Num 16 14 possessions of fields and v.
Num 20 17 through the vineyards, we will not drink
21 22 aside into the fields or the vineyards
22 24 wherewith the vineyards were enclosed
Deut 6 11 didst not dig vineyards and oliveyards
8 8 a land of wheat and barley and vineyards
Josu 24 13 v. and oliveyards, which you planted not
Judg 9 27 wasting the vineyards and treading down
11 33 Abel, which is set with vineyards, with
14 5 when they were come to the vineyards of
15 5 the flame consumed also the vineyards
21 20 go and lie hid in the vineyards, and
21 come ye on a sudden out of the vineyards
1 K 8 14 he will take your fields and your v.
15 and of the revenues of your vineyards
22 7 give every one of you fields and v.
4 K 5 26 to buy oliveyards and v. and sheep
18 32 a land of bread and vineyards a land of
19 29 plant vineyards and eat the fruit of
1 Pa 27 27 over the dressers of the vineyards
2 Pa 26 10 he had also vineyards and dressers of
2 Es 5 3 mortgage our lands and our vineyards
4 let us give up our fields and vineyards
5 and our vineyards other men possess
11 this day their fields and their v.
9 25 cisterns made by others, vineyards
Jdth 2 17 trees and vineyards to be cut down
Job 24 18 let him not walk by the way of the v.
Ps 77 47 he destroyed their vineyards. 104:33
106 37 they sowed fields and planted vineyards
Ecce 2 4 I built me houses and planted v.
Cant 1 5 made me the keeper in the vineyards
13 is to me, in the vineyards of Engaddi
7 12 let us get up early to the vineyards
Isa 16 10 no rejoicing nor shouting in the v.
36 17 of wine, a land of bread and vineyards
37 30 plant vineyards and eat the fruit of
65 21 they shall plant vineyards. Amos 9:14; Soph 1:13
Jer 5 17 they shall eat thy vineyards and thy
31 5 thou shalt yet plant vineyards in the
32 15 and vineyards shall be possessed again
35 7 nor sow seed nor plant vineyards
39 10 he gave them vineyards and cisterns
Amos 4 9 eaten up your many gardens and your v.
5 11 you shall plant most delightful v.
17 in all vineyards there shall be wailing
1 Ma 3 56 were planting v. or were fearful that
vintage Lev 25 5 grapes of firstfruits as a v.
Lev 26 5 shall reach unto the v. and the v. shall reach unto
Deut 7 13 corn and thy vintage, thy oil and thy
24 21 thou make the v. of thy vineyard
28 30 and not gather the vintage thereof
2 Es 10 37 the v. also and of oil to the priests
Job 24 6 gather the vintage of his vineyard
Eccu 24 37 as Gehon in the time of the vintage
Isa 16 9 hath rushed in upon thy vintage and upon
24 7 the vintage hath mourned, the vine hath
13 or grapes when the vintage is ended
32 10 the vintage is at an end, the gathering
Jer 31 5 shall not gather the v. before the time
40 10 gather ye the vintage and the harvest
48 32 rushed in upon thy harvest and thy v.

Lam 1 12 he hath made a vintage of me, as the
22 v. of them, as thou hast made v. of me
Mich 7 1 gleaneth in autumn the grapes of the v.
vintages Judg 8 2 better than the v. of Abiezer
violate Jdth 9 11 to v. thy sanctuary and defile
Eze 7 22 they shall violate my secret place
Dan 6 12 Persians, which it is not lawful to v.
1 C 3 17 if any man violate the temple of God
violated Eze 5 11 thou hast v. my sanctuary
Eze 13 19 they violated me among my people for a
20 9 that it might not be v. before the
13 violated my sabbaths. 16, 21, 24
22 that it might not be violated before
Osee 8 1 covenant and have violated my law
Acts 21 28 temple, and hath v. this holy place. For
violating 2 Es 13 18 upon Israel by v. sabbath
Mala 2 10 v. the covenant of our fathers? Juda
violence Gen 43 18 by violence make slaves of us
Lev 19 13 neighbor, nor oppress him by violence
Deut 28 29 be oppressed with violence and mayst
Judg 8 1 him sharply and almost offered v.
1 K 25 29 as with the v. and whirling of a sling
Job 5 5 armed man shall take him by violence
19 7 I shall cry suffering violence, and no
22 11 covered with v. of overflowing waters
24 6 whom by v. they have oppressed. They
27 8 if through covetousness he take by v.
35 9 for the violence of the arm of tyrants
Ps 37 13 they that sought my soul used violence
Prov 22 22 do no violence to the poor, because he
27 4 who can bear the v. of one provoked
28 17 doth violence to the blood of a person
Ecce 4 1 were not able to resist their violence
Wisd 17 17 fall of water running down with v.
Eccu 20 3 that by v. executeth unjust judgment
22 22 shall not resist against the v. of fear
Isa 5 28 their wheels like the v. of a tempest
Jer 6 7 violence and spoil shall be heard in her
10 2 violence to the cause of the humble
21 12 deliver him that is oppressed by v.
28 2 as the v. of many waters overflowing
38 14 I suffer violence, answer thou for me
Eze 18 7 hath taken nothing away by violence
12 poor, that taketh away by violence
16 nor taken away with violence but hath
18 and offered violence to his brother
46 18 take of the people's inheritance by v.
Mich 2 2 coveted fields, and taken them by v.
Nah 3 1 city of blood, all full of lies and v.
Haba 1 2 shall I cry out to thee suffering v.
1 Ma 4 30 didst break the violence of the mighty
2 Ma 1 7 in the trouble and v. that came upon us
4 40 began to use violence, one Tyrannus
9 7 as he was going with v. that he fell
15 1 purposed to set upon him with all v.
Mat 11 12 kingdom of heaven suffereth violence
Mark 5 13 the herd with great v. was carried
Luke 3 14 do violence to no man; neither
16 16 every one useth violence towards it
Acts 5 26 and brought them without violence
21 35 because of the violence of the people
24 7 with great v. took him away out of our
27 41 hinder part was broken with the violence
Heb 11 34 quenched the violence of fire, escaped
2 P 3 10 heavens shall pass away with great v.
Apoc 18 21 with such v. as this shall Babylon
violent 3 K 22 32 making a violent assault they
2 Pa 16 12 of a most v. pain in his feet and yet
Jdth 6 1 Holofernes being in a violent passion
Job 1 19 a violent wind came on a sudden from
5 15 the poor from the hand of the violent
27 13 inheritance of the violent which they
34 6 my arrow is violent without any sin
20 take away the violent without hand
36 9 deeds, because they have been violent
38 25 who gave a course to violent showers
Prov 28 3 the poor, is like a violent shower
Ecce 5 7 oppressions of the poor, and v. judgments
Eccu 46 7 he made a v. assault against the nation
Isa 9 5 violent taking of spoils, with tumult
59 19 he shall come as a violent stream which
Jer 30 23 his fury going forth, a v. storm, it
Eze 38 22 with v. rain and vast hailstones: I
Mat 11 12 violence, and the violent bear it away
violently Gen 19 9 they pressed very v. upon Lot
Lev 25 53 he shall not afflict him violently
2 Pa 20 12 multitude, which cometh v. upon us
Job 20 19 he hath violently taken away a house
24 9 they have v. robbed the fatherless
Prov 30 33 he that violently bloweth his nose
Isa 47 11 calamity shall fall v. upon thee, which
Eze 13 11 cause great hailstones to fall v. from
Dan 14 29 saw that they pressed upon him v.: and
Mich 3 2 that v. pluck off their skins from
2 Ma 11 11 rushing v. upon the enemy like lions
Mat 8 32 the herd ran violently down. Luke 8:33
Luke 11 53 the lawyers began v. to urge him and
Acts 7 56 with one accord ran violently upon him
violet Exod 25 4 violet and purple and scarlet. 26:1, 31, 36; 27:16; 28:5, 6, 8, 15, 33; 35:6, 23, 25; 36:8, 35, 37; 38:18, 23; 39:1, 2, 8, 22, 28; 2 Pa 3:14
Exod 25 5 skins dyed red, and v. skins and
26 4 thou shalt make loops of violet in
14 another cover of violet colored skins
28 28 rings of the ephod with a violet fillet
31 tunick of the ephod all of v. 39:20
37 thou shalt tie it with a violet fillet
35 7 dyed red, and violet colored skins. 23
36 11 made also loops of violet in the edge
19 another cover over that of violet skins
39 19 rings, which a violet fillet joined
30 to the miter with a violet fillet
33 and the other cover of violet skins
Lev 8 7 putting on him the violet tunick
Num 4 6 cover it again with a cover of v. skins
6 spread over it a cloth all of violet
7 table of proposition in a cloth of v.
8 cover with a covering of violet skins
9 they shall take also a cloth of violet
10 shall put a cover of violet skins
11 golden altar also in a cloth of violet
11 over it a cover of violet skins. 12
12 they shall wrap up in a cloth of violet
14 with a covering of violet skins and
25 the violet covering over all, and the
2 Pa 2 14 how to work . . . in purple also and v.
Esth 8 15 apparel, to wit, of v. and sky color
Jer 10 9 violet and purple is their clothing
Eze 16 10 shod thee with violet colored shoes
viper Isa 30 6 the viper and the flying basilisk
Acts 28 3 viper coming out of the heat, fastened
viper's Job 20 16 the v. tongue shall kill him
vipers Mat 3 7 ye brood of v., who hath showed
Mat 12 34 generation of vipers, how can you speak
23 33 you serpents, generation of vipers, how
Luke 3 7 ye offspring of vipers, who hath
virgin Gen 24 16 maid and a most beautiful v.
Gen 24 43 the virgin that shall come out to draw
34 2 and lay with her, ravishing the virgin
Lev 21 13 he shall take a virgin unto his wife
Deut 22 14 in to her, I found her not a virgin
17 I found not thy daughter a virgin: and
19 defamed by a very ill name a virgin
23 espoused a damsel that is a virgin
32 25 the young man and virgin, the sucking

2 K 13 2 as she [Thamar] was a virgin, he thought
3 K 1 2 seek for our lord the king a young v.
4 K 19 21 the v. the daughter of Sion. Isa 37:22
Tob 6 22 thou shalt take the v. with the fear
8 4 then Tobias exhorted the virgin and said
Jdth 9 2 uncovered the virgin unto confusion
Job 31 1 would not so much as think upon a v.
Eccu 15 2 receive him as a wife married of a v.
30 21 as an eunuch embracing a virgin and
Isa 7 14 a virgin shall conceive and bear a son
23 12 shalt glory no more, O virgin daughter
47 1 virgin daughter of Babylon, sit on
62 5 young man shall dwell with the virgin
Jer 2 32 will a virgin forget her ornament
14 17 v. daughter of my people is afflicted
18 13 as the v. of Israel hath done to excess
31 4 thou shalt be built, O virgin of Israel
13 then shall the v. rejoice in the dance
21 v. of Israel, return to these thy cities
46 11 take balm, O virgin daughter of Egypt
51 22 in pieces the young man and the virgin
Lam 1 15 winepress for the v. daughter of Juda
2 2 the strongholds of the virgin of Juda
13 comfort thee, O virgin daughter of Sion
Joel 1 8 lament like a v. girded with sackcloth
Amos 5 2 the virgin of Israel is cast down upon
Mat 1 23 behold a virgin shall be with child
Luke 1 27 a virgin espoused to a man whose name
1 C 7 28 if a virgin marry, she hath not sinned
34 unmarried woman and the v. thinketh on
36 with regard to his virgin, for that she
37 his heart, to keep his virgin, doth well
38 he that giveth his virgin in marriage
2 C 11 2 present you as a chaste virgin to Christ
virginity Deut 22 15 with them the tokens of her v.
Deut 22 17 the tokens of my daughter's virginity
20 virginity be not found in the damsel
Judg 11 37 and may bewail my virginity with my
38 she mourned her v. in the mountains
Eccu 42 10 in her virginity, lest she should be
Jer 3 4 art my father, the guide of my virginity
Eze 23 3 teats of their virginity were bruised
8 they bruised the breasts of her v.
21 and the paps of thy virginity broken
Luke 2 36 seven years from her virginity. And
virgin's Esth 2 12 when every virgin's turn came
Luke 1 27 and the virgin's name was Mary. And
virgins Exod 22 17 which v. are wont to receive
Num 31 18 that are virgins save for yourselves
Judg 21 11 kill, but the virgins you shall save
12 found of Jabes Galaad 400 virgins
2 K 13 18 the king's daughters that were virgins
Jdth 15 15 rejoiced, with the women and virgins
16 6 infants a prey, and my virgins captives
Esth 2 2 for the king, virgins and beautiful
3 to look for beautiful maidens and v.
8 beautiful virgins were brought to Susan
11 in which the chosen virgins were kept
15 Egeus the eunuch the keeper of the v.
19 and when the virgins were sought the
Ps 44 15 shall virgins be brought to the king
Isa 23 4 young men, nor brought up virgins
Lam 1 4 her virgins are in affliction and she
18 my virgins and my young men are gone
2 10 v. of Jerusalem hang down their heads
21 my virgins and my young men are fallen
5 11 Sion and the v. in the cities of Juda
Eze 44 22 they shall take virgins of the seed of
Amos 8 13 fair virgins and young men shall faint
Zach 9 17 elect, and wine springing forth virgins
1 Ma 1 27 v. and the young men were made feeble
2 Ma 3 19 the virgins also that were shut up came
5 13 and killing of virgins and infants. And
Mat 25 1 like to ten virgins, who taking their
7 all those virgins arose and trimmed
11 at last came also the other virgins
Acts 21 9 four daughters, v., who did prophesy
1 C 7 25 concerning v., I have no commandment of
Apoc 14 4 they are virgins. They follow the Lamb
virtue Ruth 4 11 she may be an example of virtue
Jdth 10 4 not proceed from sensuality, but from v.
16 26 chastity was joined to her virtue
Ps 83 8 they shall go from virtue to virtue
Wisd 5 13 been able to show no mark of virtue
19 19 fire had power in water above its own v.
Eccu 24 25 in me is all hope of life and of virtue
38 6 the virtue of these things is come to
44 6 rich men in v. studying beautifulness
2 Ma 6 31 for an example of virtue and fortitude
Mark 5 30 the virtue that had proceeded from him
Luke 6 19 v. went out from him and healed all
8 46 I know that virtue is gone out from me
Rom 15 19 by the virtue of signs and wonders, in
1 C 15 24 brought to nought all . . . power and v.
Eph 1 21 above all principality and power and v.
Phil 4 8 if there be any virtue, if any praise
2 P 1 3 by his own proper glory and virtue
5 minister in your faith, virtue; and in virtue, knowledge
virtues 2 Pa 9 5 in my country of thy v. and wisdom
2 Pa 9 6 hast exceeded the same with thy virtues
Wisd 7 17 world and the virtues of the elements
20 of plants and the virtues of roots
8 7 her labors have great virtues; for she
Eccu 16 25 virtues that God hath put upon his works
2 Ma 15 12 from a child was exercised in virtues
1 P 2 9 that you may declare his virtues, who
3 22 the angels and powers and virtues
virtuous Ruth 3 11 thou art a virtuous woman
Tob 7 7 the son of a good and most virtuous man
Eccu 26 2 a v. woman rejoiceth her husband and
2 Ma 15 12 a good and virtuous man, modest in
visage Isa 52 14 so shall his v. be inglorious
visible Col 1 16 visible and invisible, whether
Heb 11 3 from invisible things v. things might
vision Gen 15 1 word of Lord came to Abram by v.
Gen 22 2 lovest and go into the land of vision
46 2 he heard him by a vision in the night
Num 12 6 Lord, I will appear to him in a vision
24 4 that hath beheld the v. of the Almighty
1 K 3 1 those days, there was no manifest vision
15 Samuel feared to tell the v. to Heli
2 K 7 17 according to all this vision. 17:15
2 Pa 9 29 and in the vision of Addo the seer
Job 4 13 in the horror of a vision by night
20 8 he shall pass as a vision of the night
33 15 by a dream in a vision by night, when
Ps 88 20 thou spokest in a vision to thy saints
Prov 30 1 the vision which the man spoke with
31 1 vision wherewith his mother instructed
Eccu 34 3 the vision of dreams is the resemblance
6 except it be a vision sent forth from
40 7 is troubled in the vision of his heart
49 10 Ezechiel that saw the glorious vision
Isa 1 1 the vision of Isaias the son of Amos
6 9 see the vision, and know it not. Blind
21 2 a grievous vision is told me: he that
22 1 the burden of the valley of vision
5 in the valley of vision, searching
29 7 shall be as the dream of a vision by
11 the vision of all shall be unto you as
Jer 14 14 they prophesy unto you a lying vision
23 16 they speak a vision of their own heart
Lam 2 9 her prophets have found no vision from
Eze 1 13 this was the vision running to and fro
2 1 v. of the likeness of the glory of Lord

7 13 v. which regardeth all the multitude
26 they shall seek a vision of the prophet
8 3 brought me in the vision of God into
4 the vision which I had seen in the plain
11 24 to them of the captivity, in vision
24 the vision which I had seen was taken
12 22 prolonged, and every vision shall fail
23 at hand, and the effect of every vision
27 the vision that this man seeth, is for
13 7 have you not seen a vain vision and
43 3 and I saw the vision according to the
3 according to the v. which I had seen
Dan 2 19 to Daniel by a vision in the night
4 7 this was the vision of my head in my bed
10 I saw in the vision of my head upon
7 1 the vision of his head was upon his bed
2 I saw in my v. by night and behold
7 I beheld in the v. of the night. 13
8 1 a vision appeared to me. I Daniel, after
2 saw in my v. when I was in the castle
2 I saw in the vision that I was over
13 how long shall be the v. concerning
15 I Daniel saw the vision and sought
16 make this man to understand the vision
17 of the end the v. shall be fulfilled
26 the v. of the evening and the morning
26 thou therefore seal up the vision
27 I was astonished at the vision and
9 21 Gabriel, whom I had seen in the vision
23 mark the word, and understand the v.
24 and v. and prophecy may be fulfilled
10 1 there is need of understanding in a v.
7 I Daniel alone saw the vision: for the
8 I being left alone saw this great vision
14 days, for as yet the vision is for days
11 14 lift up themselves to fulfil the v.
Osee 10 4 you speak words of an unprofitable v.
Abdi 1 the vision of Abdias. Thus saith the
Mich 3 6 night shall be to you instead of vision
Nah 1 1 the book of the vision of Nahum the
Haba 2 2 write the vision, and make it plain
3 as yet the vision is far off and it
Zach 13 4 confounded, every one by his own vision
2 Ma 15 12 the vision was in this manner: Onias
Mat 17 9 tell the vision to no man till the Son
Luke 1 22 that he had seen a v. in the temple
24 23 they had also seen a vision of angels
Acts 9 10 Lord said to him in a vision: Ananias
10 3 this man saw in a vision manifestly
17 what the v. that he had seen should mean
19 as Peter was thinking of the vision
11 5 I saw in an ecstasy of mind a vision
12 9 [Peter] thought he saw a vision. And
16 9 a v. was showed to Paul in the night
10 and as soon as he had seen the vision
18 9 said to Paul in the night, by a vision
26 19 I was not incredulous to the heavenly v.
Apoc 9 17 thus I saw the horses in the vision
visions Num 24 16 seeth the v. of the Almighty
Deut 4 34 stretched out arm, and horrible visions
Job 7 14 with dreams and terrify me with v.
Wisd 17 4 sad v. appearing to them affrighted
18 17 visions of evil dreams troubled them
19 visions that troubled them foreshowed
Eccu 34 2 man that giveth heed to lying visions
Isa 29 10 your prophets and princes, that see v.
Eze 1 1 opened and I saw the visions of God
12 24 there shall be no more any vain visions
13 16 that see visions of peace for her: and
40 2 in the visions of God he brought me
Dan 1 17 the understanding also of all visions
2 28 v. of thy head upon thy bed, are these
4 2 the visions of my head troubled me. 7:15
6 tell me the visions of my dreams that
Osee 12 10 and I have multiplied visions and I
Joel 2 28 and your young men shall see visions
Mich 3 7 they shall be confounded that see v.
Acts 2 17 your young men shall see visions, and
2 C 12 1 I will come to visions and revelations
visit Gen 50 23 God will visit you after my death
Gen 50 24 God will visit you, carry my bones
Exod 13 19 God shall visit you, carry out my bones
32 34 will visit this sin also of theirs. The
Lev 18 25 abominations of which I will visit
26 16 I will quickly visit you with poverty
Deut 11 12 Lord thy God doth always visit it and
Judg 15 1 Samson came, meaning to visit his wife
2 K 13 5 when thy father shall come to v. thee
6 when the king came to visit him, Amnon
4 K 8 29 went down to visit Joram. 2 Pa 22:6
9 16 king of Juda was come down to v. Joram
1 Es 7 14 to visit Judea and Jerusalem according
Jdth 4 16 that he would visit his people Israel
16 20 in the day of judgment he will v. them
Job 2 11 together and v. him and comfort him
Ps 26 4 of the Lord, and may visit his temple
58 6 attend to visit all the nations: have no
79 15 and see, and visit this vineyard: and
88 33 I will v. their iniquities with a rod
105 4 people: visit us with thy salvation
Eccu 7 39 be not slow to visit the sick: for
Isa 10 12 I will visit the fruit of the proud
13 11 I will visit the evils of the world
23 17 the Lord will visit Tyre and will bring
24 21 the Lord shall visit upon the host of
26 21 to v. the iniquity of the inhabitant
27 1 shall visit leviathan the bar serpent
Jer 5 9 shall I not v. for these things. 29
9 9 shall I not visit them for these things
25 I will visit upon every one that hath
11 22 behold I will visit upon them: their
13 21 thou say when he shall visit thee? for
14 10 their iniquities, and visit their sins
15 3 I will visit them with four kinds, saith
15 remember me and visit me and defend
21 14 I will visit upon you according to
23 2 I will visit upon you for the evil
34 I will visit upon that man and upon
27 8 I will visit upon that nation with
29 10 I will visit you: and I will perform
32 behold I will visit upon Semeias
30 20 I will visit against all that afflict
32 5 he shall be there till I visit him
44 13 I will visit them that dwell in the
46 25 behold I will visit upon the tumult of
50 18 I will visit the king of Babylon and his
51 44 I will visit against Bel in Babylon
47 and I will visit the idols of Babylon
52 I will visit her graven things and in
Eze 34 11 seek my sheep and will visit them. As
12 will I visit my sheep and will deliver
Osee 1 4 I will visit the blood of Jezrahel
2 13 I will visit upon her the days of Baalim
4 9 I will visit their ways upon them and I
14 I will not visit upon your daughters
8 13 iniquity, and will visit their sins
9 9 iniquity, and will visit their sin
Amos 3 2 will I v. upon you all your iniquities
14 to visit the transgressions of Israel
14 I will visit upon him and upon the
Soph 1 8 I will visit upon the princes and
9 I will visit in that day upon every
12 will visit upon the men that are settled
2 7 the Lord their God will visit them
Zach 10 3 I will visit upon the buck goats: for
11 16 who shall not visit what is forsaken

Mat 25 43 and in prison, and you did not visit me
Acts 7 23 into his heart to visit his brethren
15 36 let us return and visit our brethren
James 1 27 to visit the fatherless and widows in
visitation Job 10 12 v. hath preserved my spirit
Wisd 3 13 she shall have fruit in the visitation
Eccu 2 21 will have patience even until his v.
Isa 10 3 what will you do in the day of v. and
15 7 greatness of their work, is their v.
29 6 a v. shall come from the Lord of hosts
60 17 I will make thy visitation peace and thy
Jer 6 15 time of their v. they shall fall. 8:12
10 15 in time of their v. they shall perish
11 23 men of Anathoth, the year of their v.
23 12 evils upon them, the year of their v.
27 22 shall be until the day of their v.
46 21 upon them, the time of their visitation
48 44 upon Moab the year of their visitation
49 8 upon him, the time of his visitation
50 27 is come, the time of their visitation
31 is come, the time of thy visitation
51 18 in time of their v. they shall perish
Osee 9 7 the days of visitation are come, the
12 2 with Juda and visitation for Jacob
Mich 7 4 day of thy inspection, thy v. cometh
Luke 19 44 hast not known the time of thy v.
1 P 2 12 glorify God in the day of visitation
5 6 he may exalt you in the time of v.
visitations Eze 9 1 v. of the city are at hand
visited Gen 21 1 the Lord v. Sara, as he had
Exod 3 16 visiting I have visited you: and I have
4 31 Lord had visited the children of Israel
Num 16 29 and if they be visited with a plague
29 wherewith others also are wont to be v.
1 K 2 21 the Lord visited Anna and she conceived
Ps 16 3 proved my heart and visited it by night
64 10 thou hast visited the earth and hast
Prov 19 23 in fulness without being v. with evil
Eccu 49 18 his bones were visited, and after death
Isa 24 22 after many days they shall be visited
26 14 hast thou visited and destroyed them
Jer 3 16 remember it, neither shall it be v.
6 6 Jerusalem: this is the city to be v.
23 2 and have not visited them: behold I
44 13 as I have visited Jerusalem by the
50 18 as I have visited the king of Assyria
Lam 4 22 captivity: he hath visited thy iniquity
Eze 38 8 after many days thou shalt be v.: at the
Soph 3 7 things wherein I have visited her: but
Zach 10 3 Lord of hosts hath v. his flock
Mat 25 36 covered me: sick, and you visited me
Luke 1 68 because he hath visited and wrought
78 the Orient from on high hath v. us
7 16 us: and God hath visited his people
Acts 15 14 Simon hath related how God first v. to
visitest Num 14 18 who v. the sins of the fathers
Job 7 18 thou visitest him early in the morning
Ps 8 5 son of man that thou v. him. Heb 2:6
visiteth Eze 34 12 as the shepherd v. his flock
visiting Exod 3 16 visiting I have visited you
Exod 20 5 v. the iniquity of fathers. Deut 5:9
Job 5 24 visiting thy beauty thou shalt not sin
2 Ma 3 8 under a color of visiting the cities
Acts 9 32 Peter, as he passed through, visiting
visitor 2 Ma 3 39 v. and protector of that place
vital Lev 3 14 covereth all the vital parts
2 Pa 21 15 till thy vital parts come out by little
vitals Lev 3 10 covereth the belly and all the v.
vocation 1 C 1 26 for see your vocation, brethren
Eph 4 1 you walk worthy of the vocation in which
Phil 3 14 to the prize of the supernal vocation
2 Th 1 11 make you worthy of his vocation, and
Heb 3 1 partakers of the heavenly vocation

voice Mat 2 18 a voice in Rama was heard, lamentation
Mat 3 3 v. of one crying in the desert. Mark 1:3
17 a voice from heaven, saying: This is
17 5 voice out of the cloud, saying: This
24 31 with a trumpet and a great voice: and
Mark 1 11 there came a voice from heaven: Thou
9 6 a v. came out of the cloud. Luke 9:35
Luke 1 44 as soon as the voice of thy salutation
3 4 voice of one crying in the wilderness
22 a voice came from heaven. John 12:28
9 36 whilst the voice was uttered, Jesus
11 27 lifting up her voice, said to him
17 13 lifted up their voice, saying: Jesus
John 1 23 I am the voice of one crying out in
3 29 joy because of the bridegroom's voice
5 25 shall hear the voice of the Son. 28
10 5 they know not the voice of strangers
12 30 this voice came not because of me
Acts 4 24 lifted up their voice to God and said
7 31 voice of the Lord came unto him
8 32 like a lamb without voice before his
9 4 falling on the ground, he heard a voice
7 hearing indeed a v., but seeing no man
10 13 came a voice to him: Arise, Peter; kill
15 v. spoke to him again the second time
11 7 I heard also a voice saying to me
9 the voice answered again from heaven
12 14 as soon as she knew Peter's voice
22 it is the voice of a god, and not of
14 10 lifted up their voice in the Lycaonian
19 34 with one voice, for space of about two
22 7 I heard a voice saying to me: Saul, Saul
9 they heard not the v. of him that spoke
14 shouldst hear the voice from his mouth
22 and then lifted up their voice, saying
24 21 except it be for this one voice only
26 13 I heard v. speaking to me in the Hebrew
1 C 14 10 this world; and none is without voice
11 if then I know not the power of the v.
1 Th 4 15 with the voice of an archangel, and with
Heb 12 19 sound of a trumpet and the v. of words
26 whose voice then moved the earth; but
2 P 1 17 this voice coming down to him from
18 this voice we heard brought down from
2 16 speaking with a man's voice, forbade
Apoc 1 10 heard behind me a great voice, as of
12 I turned to see the voice that spoke
4 1 the first voice which I heard, as it
5 11 I heard the voice of many angels round
6 1 as it were the voice of thunder, saying
6 a voice in the midst of the four living
7 heard the voice of the fourth living
8 13 heard the voice of one eagle flying
9 13 I heard a voice from the four horns of
10 4 I heard a v. from heaven. 8; 14:2, 13
7 days of the voice of the seventh angel
11 12 they heard a great voice from heaven
12 10 I heard a loud voice in heaven, saying
14 2 and as the voice of great thunder; and
2 the voice which I heard was as the voice of harpers
16 1 I heard a great voice out of the
17 came a great voice out of the temple
18 2 he cried out with a strong voice saying
4 I heard another voice from heaven
22 the voice of harpers and of musicians
23 voice of the bridegroom and the bride
19 1 the voice of much people in heaven
5 and a voice came out from the throne
6 I heard as it were the voice of a
6 as the voice of many waters and as the voice of great thunders
21 3 I heard a great voice from the throne

his voice Mat 12 19 neither shall any man hear his voice
John 3 8 and thou hearest his voice, but thou
5 37 neither have you heard his voice at
10 3 sheep hear his voice: and he calleth
4 him, because they know his voice
Acts 2 14 lifted up his voice and spoke to them
Heb 3 7 today if you shall hear his v. 15; 4:7
Apoc 1 15 his voice as the sound of many waters
my voice John 10 16 they shall hear my voice, and there
John 10 27 my sheep hear my voice: and I know
18 37 that is of the truth, heareth my voice
Gal 4 20 present with you now, and change my v.
Apoc 3 20 if any man shall hear my voice and
voices Judg 21 2 evening, lifted up their voices
1 K 11 4 all the people lifted up their voices
30 4 were with him, lifted up their voices
Esth 11 5 behold there were voices and tumults
Ps 18 4 where their voices are not heard. Their
73 23 forget not the voices of thy enemies
103 12 they shall give forth their voices
Eccu 47 11 by their voices he made sweet melody
50 20 the singers lifted up their voices and
Luke 23 23 but they were instant with loud voices
23 crucified; and their voices prevailed
Acts 13 27 not knowing him, nor the voices of
Apoc 4 5 proceeded lightnings and voices and
8 5 there were thunders and voices and
13 by reason of the rest of the voices of
10 3 seven thunders uttered their voices
4 seven thunders had uttered their voices
11 15 and there were great voices in heaven
19 there were lightnings and voices. 16:18
void Gen 1 2 and the earth was void and empty
Lev 26 15 by me, and to make void my covenant
44 and I should make void my covenant with
Num 30 3 he shall not make his word void but shall
6 her vows and her oaths shall be void
Deut 31 16 will make void the covenant which I have
20 despise me and make void my covenant
Judg 2 1 that I would not make void my covenant
2 Pa 21 19 as to void his very bowels, his disease
Job 40 3 wilt thou make void my judgment: and
Ps 88 35 from my mouth I will not make void
131 11 and he will not make it void: of the
Prov 28 16 a prince void of prudence shall oppress
29 7 the wicked is void of knowledge. Corrupt
Eccu 23 13 if he make it void, his sin shall be
34 1 a man that is void of understanding
Isa 44 25 that make void the tokens of diviners
55 11 it shall not return to me void, but
Jer 4 23 beheld the earth, and lo it was void
Zach 11 10 asunder to make void my covenant which
1 Ma 14 45 or shall make void any of these things
2 Ma 14 28 he should make void the articles that
Mark 7 9 well do you make void the commandment
13 making void the word of God by your
1 C 9 15 that any man should make my glory void
15 10 his grace in me hath not been void, but
Eph 2 15 making void the law of commandments
Heb 10 28 a man making void the law of Moses
made void Num 6 12 the former days be made void
Num 15 31 word of the Lord and m. v. his precept
Josu 21 43 promised to perform unto them was m. v.
Judg 2 20 this nation hath made void my covenant
Job 15 4 thou hast made void fear and hast taken
Eccu 2 8 your reward shall not be made void
Isa 33 8 the covenant is made void, he hath
Jer 11 10 have made void my covenant, which I
31 32 the covenant which they made void and
33 20 my covenant with the day can be m. v.
21 covenant with David . . . may be m. v.
Eze 17 16 whose oath he hath made void and whose
Zach 11 11 it was made void in that day and so the
Mala 2 8 have made void the covenant of Levi
Mat 15 6 you have made void the commandment of
Rom 4 14 heirs, faith is made void, the promise
1 C 1 17 lest cross of Christ should be made void
13 8 whether prophesies shall be made void
2 C 3 7 of his countenance, which is made void
13 on the face of that which is made void
14 away, because in Christ it is made void
9 3 you, be not made void in this behalf
Gal 5 4 you are made void of Christ, you who
11 then is the scandal of cross made void
1 Tim 5 12 they have made void their first faith
voluble Eze 10 13 these wheels he called voluble
volume Deut 17 18 Deuteronomy of this law in a v.
Deut 28 58 this law, that are written in this v.
61 not written in the volume of this law
29 20 curses that are written in this v. 27
31 24 wrote the words of this law in a volume
Josu 24 26 in the volume of the law of the Lord
Esth 9 26 contained in the volume of this epistle
Jer 36 6 read out of v. which thou hast written
8 reading out of the volume the words
10 Baruch read out of the volume the words
13 when Baruch read out of the volume
14 in thy hand the v. in which thou hast
14 took the volume in his hand and came to
18 and I wrote in a volume with ink. And
20 they laid up the volume in the chamber
21 sent Judi that he should take the v.
23 till all the volume was consumed with
27 after that the king had burnt the volume
28 take thee again another volume: and write
28 that were in the first v. which Joakim
29 thou hast burnt that volume, saying
32 Jeremias took another volume and gave
Zach 5 1 I saw, and behold a volume flying
2 I said: I see a volume flying: the
voluntarily Lev 22 23 thou mayst offer voluntarily
Lev 23 38 which you shall give to the Lord v.
Num 15 3 paying your vows, or v. offering gifts
Deut 12 17 and that thou wilt offer voluntarily
2 Ma 6 19 went forward v. to the torment. And
1 P 5 2 not for filthy lucre's sake, but v.
voluntary Exod 35 29 dedicated v. offerings to
Num 29 39 besides your vows and v. oblations for
Deut 16 10 a voluntary oblation of thy hand which
Eze 46 12 prince shall offer a v. holocaust or
12 voluntary peace offerings to the Lord
Philem 14 not be as it were of necessity, but v.
vomit Lev 18 25 it may v. out its inhabitants
Lev 18 28 lest in like manner it vomit you also
20 22 to dwell therein, vomit you also out
Job 20 15 which he hath swallowed, he shall v. up
Prov 23 8 hadst eaten, thou shall vomit up: and
25 16 being glutted therewith, thou v. it up
26 11 as a dog that returneth to his vomit
Eccu 31 25 eat much, arise, go out, and vomit
Isa 28 8 all tables were full of vomit and filth
Jer 25 27 drink ye and be drunken, and vomit
48 26 Moab shall dash his hand in his own v.
2 P 2 22 the dog is returned to his vomit: and
Apoc 3 16 I will begin to vomit thee out of my
vomited Lev 18 28 as it v. out the nation that
Jon 2 11 and it v. out Jonas upon the dry land
Vomiter Prov 30 1 words of Gatherer the son of V.
vomiteth Isa 19 14 drunken man staggereth and v.
vomiting Haba 2 16 shameful v. shall be on thy
vouchsafe Ruth 2 10 shouldst v. to take notice
Tob 12 4 that he would vouchsafe to accept. 5
Jdth 5 5 if thou vouchsafe, my lord, to hear
vow Gen 28 20 he [Jacob] made a vow, saying: If
Gen 31 13 anoint the stone and make a vow to me
Lev 7 16 if any man by vow or of his own accord

22 23 a vow may not be paid with them. You
23 38 things that you offer by vow or which
27 2 the man that shall have made a vow and
9 if any one shall vow, shall be holy
11 if any man shall vow, shall be brought
14 if a man shall vow his house, and
16 if he vow the field of his possession
17 if he vow his field immediately from
26 the Lord, no man may sanctify and vow
Num 6 2 shall make a vow to be sanctified and
4 consecrated to the Lord by vow: they
13 days which he had determined by vow
15 8 sacrifice of oxen, to fulfil thy vow or
18 11 which the children of Israel shall vow
14 children of Israel shall give by vow
21 2 Israel binding himself by v. to the Lord
30 3 if any man make a vow to the Lord or
4 if a woman vow anything and bind herself
4 if her father knew the vow that she hath
4 she shall be bound by the vow. 8
7 have a husband and shall vow anything
10 shall fulfil whatsoever they vow. If
11 hath bound herself by vow and by oath
Deut 12 11 gifts which you shall vow to the Lord
23 21 when thou hast made a vow to the Lord
Judg 11 30 he [Jephte] made a vow to the Lord
1 K 1 11 she [Anna] made a vow, saying: O Lord
21 Lord the solemn sacrifice and his vow
2 K 15 8 made a vow when he was in Gessur of
24 23 the Lord thy God receive thy vow. And
Ps 64 2 a vow shall be paid to thee in Jerusalem
75 12 vow ye, and pay to the Lord your God
131 2 he vowed a vow to the God of Jacob: if
Ecce 5 4 and it is much better not to vow, than
4 than after a vow not to perform the
Mala 1 14 making a vow offereth in sacrifice
Acts 18 18 for he had a vow. And he came to
21 23 we have 4 men, who have a vow on them
vowed Lev 27 15 if he that v. will redeem it
Lev 27 19 if he that had vowed will redeem his
20 he that vowed it may not redeem it but
23 he that had vowed, shall give that to
Num 6 21 when he hath vowed his oblation to the
21 which he had vowed in his mind so shall
30 15 whatsoever she had vowed and promised
Deut 12 26 hast sanctified and vowed to the Lord
23 18 whatsoever it be that thou hast vowed
Judg 11 39 and he did to her as he had vowed
17 3 I have consecrated and v. this silver
2 K 15 7 which I have vowed to the Lord in Hebron
3 K 15 15 father had dedicated and he had vowed
2 Pa 5 1 things which David his father had vowed
15 18 the things which his father had vowed
18 he himself had vowed, he brought into
31 6 which they had vowed to the Lord their
12 and the tithes and all they had vowed
35 8 willingly offered what they had vowed
Ps 131 2 he vowed a vow to the God of Jacob
Prov 7 14 I vowed victims for prosperity, this
Ecce 5 3 if thou hast vowed anything to God
3 but whatsoever thou hast vowed, pay it
Eze 44 29 every v. thing in Israel shall be theirs
Jon 2 10 I will pay whatsoever I have vowed for
vowest Deut 12 17 nor anything that thou vowest and
vows Exod 36 3 daily in morning offered their vows
Lev 22 18 his oblation, either paying his vows or
21 to the Lord, either paying his vows
Num 15 3 paying your v. or voluntarily offering
29 39 besides your v. and voluntary oblations
30 6 her vows and her oaths shall be void
Deut 12 6 firstfruits of your hands and your vows
2 K 15 7 let me go and pay my vows which I have
Jdth 16 22 they all offered holocausts and vows
Job 22 27 will hear thee and thou shalt pay vows
Ps 21 26 I will pay my vows in the sight of them
49 14 pay thy vows to the most High. And
55 12 in me, O God, are vows to thee, which
60 9 that I may pay my vows from day to day
65 13 offerings: I will pay thee my vows which
115 14 I will pay my vows to the Lord. 18
Prov 7 14 prosperity, this day I have paid my v.
15 8 the vows of the just are acceptable
20 25 holy ones and after vows to retract
31 2 what, O the beloved of my vows? Give
Isa 19 21 they shall make vows to the Lord and
Jer 33 11 of them that shall bring their vows
44 25 let us perform our vows which we have
25 you have fulfilled your vows and have
Amos 5 22 neither will I regard the vows of your
Jon 1 16 victims to the Lord, and made vows
Nah 1 15 keep thy festivals and pay thy vows
2 Ma 3 35 sacrifice to God, and made great vows
Acts 24 17 to bring alms . . . and offerings and vows
voyage Wisd 14 1 beginning to make his voyage
Acts 21 7 we having finished the voyage by sea
27 10 I see that the voyage beginneth to be
vulgar Acts 17 5 some wicked men of the v. sort
vulture Lev 11 14 and the kite and the vulture
Deut 14 13 ringtail and the vulture and the kite
Job 28 7 neither hath eye of vulture beheld it

W

wafer Exod 29 23 oil, a wafer out of the basket of
Lev 8 26 a cake tempered with oil and a wafer
Num 6 19 the basket, and one unleavened wafer
wafers Exod 29 2 w. also unleavened anointed with
Lev 2 4 unleavened wafers, anointed. Lev 7:12
Num 6 15 wafers without leaven anointed with
wag Job 16 5 and would wag my head over you
Jer 18 16 shall be astonished and wag his head
Soph 2 15 by her, shall hiss and wag his hand
wage 1 Ma 9 51 they might wage war against
wages Gen 29 15 shalt thou serve me without wages
Gen 29 15 tell me what wages thou wilt have. Now
30 28 appoint thy wages which I shall give
32 as among the goats, shall be my wages
31 7 and hath changed my wages ten times
8 said: The speckled shall be thy wages
8 take all the white ones for thy wages
41 hast changed also my wages ten times
Exod 2 9 him for me: I will give thee thy w.
Lev 19 13 the wages of him that hath been hired
25 53 his wages being allowed for which
Deut 15 18 years according to wages of a hireling
Tob 4 15 let not the wages of thy hired servant
12 2 father, what wages shall we give him
Wisd 2 22 nor hoped for the wages of justice
10 17 to the just the wages of their labors
Jer 22 13 cause, and will not pay him his wages
Eze 29 19 and it shall be wages for his army
Mich 1 7 all her wages shall be burnt with fire
Agge 1 6 he that hath earned wages, put them
Zach 11 12 good in your eyes, bring hither my w.
12 they weighed for my wages thirty pieces
Mala 3 5 that oppress the hireling in his wages
1 Ma 14 32 men of his nation, and gave them wages
John 4 36 he that reapeth receiveth wages and
Rom 6 23 for the wages of sin is death. But the
2 C 11 8 receiving w. of them for your ministry
2 P 2 15 who loved the wages of iniquity, but
wagged 4 K 19 21 wagged her head behind thy back
Ps 21 8 spoken with the lips, and w. the head
Isa 37 22 hath wagged the head after thee. Whom
Lam 2 15 have hissed, and wagged their heads
wagging Tob 11 9 by his fawning and w. his tail

Mat 27 39 w. their heads and saying. Mark 15:29
waging Gen 49 5 Simeon and Levi . . . waging war
wagon Num 7 3 two princes offered one wagon
wagons Gen 45 19 orders also that they take w.
Gen 45 21 Joseph gave them wagons according to
27 when he saw the wagons and all that
46 5 in the wagons which Pharao had sent
Num 7 3 their gifts before the Lord, six w.
6 receiving the wagons and the oxen
7 two wagons and four oxen he gave to the
8 the other 4 wagons and 8 oxen he
9 to the sons of Caath he gave no wagons
wail Job 35 9 shall wail for the violence of the
wailing Esth 4 3 with fasting, w., and weeping
Jer 9 19 voice of wailing is heard out of Sion
20 and teach your daughters wailing
Amos 5 16 in every street there shall be wailing
17 in all vineyards there shall be wailing
Mich 1 8 I will make wailing like the dragons
Mark 6 38 and people weeping and wailing much
wain 2 K 24 22 oxen for a holocaust, and the wain
Isa 25 10 as straw is broken in pieces with the w.
41 15 have made thee as a new thrashing wain
Amos 2 13 as a wain screaketh that is laden with
wains Amos 1 3 have thrashed Galaad with iron w.
wait Gen 3 15 thou shalt lie in wait for her heel
Exod 18 14 all the people wait from morning till
21 31 he that did not lie in wait for him
14 purpose and by lying in wait for him
24 14 wait ye here till we return to you
34 24 no man shall lie in wait against thy
Deut 19 11 lie in wait for his life and rise and
Judg 6 18 he answered: I will wait thy coming
Ruth 1 13 if you would wait till they were grown
3 18 wait, my daughter, till we see what end
1 K 10 8 seven days shalt thou wait, till I come
23 22 that I lie craftily in wait for him
24 12 but thou liest in wait for my life
2 K 19 31 ready also to wait on him beyond the
1 Es 8 31 and of such as lay in wait by the way
2 Es 12 24 of God, and to wait equally in order
Jdth 7 23 let us wait these five days for mercy
8 20 let us humbly wait for his consolation
Job 6 19 ways of Saba, and wait a little while
17 13 if I wait hell is my house, and I have
30 13 they have lain in wait against me and
31 9 if I have laid wait at my friend's door
16 have made the eyes of the widow wait
38 40 in the dens and lie in wait in holes
Ps 9 9 he lieth in wait in secret like a lion
24 3 none of them that wait on thee shall
26 14 courage, and wait thou for the Lord
36 9 that wait upon the Lord, they shall
51 11 I will wait on thy name, for it is good
141 8 the just wait for me until thou reward
Prov 1 11 let us lie in wait for blood, let us
18 lie in wait for their own blood and
7 12 now lying in wait near the corners
12 6 words of the wicked lie in wait for
20 22 wait for the Lord and he will deliver
23 28 she lieth in wait in the way as a
24 15 lie not in wait nor seek after
Wisd 2 12 let us therefore lie in w. for the just
8 12 they shall wait for me when I hold my
Eccu 2 3 wait on God with patience: join
7 fear the Lord, wait for his mercy
6 19 soweth, and wait for her good fruits
11 33 lieth in wait and turneth good into
34 a sinful man lieth in wait for blood
12 15 in his heart he lieth in wait to throw
13 9 thyself to God, and wait for his hands
27 11 the lion always lieth in wait for prey
31 vengeance as a lion shall lie in wait
28 30 thy enemies who lie in wait for thee
34 22 is only for them that wait upon him
36 18 reward them that patiently w. for thee
51 12 deliverest them that wait for thee
Isa 8 17 I will wait for the Lord, who hath hid
30 18 blessed are all they that wait for him
42 4 the islands shall wait for his law
49 23 not be confounded that wait for him
51 5 and shall patiently wait for my arm
60 9 the islands wait for me, and the ships
64 4 prepared for them that wait for thee
Jer 5 26 wicked men, that lie in w. as fowlers
9 8 and secretly he lieth in wait for him
Lam 3 10 is become to me as a bear lying in wait
24 my soul: therefore will I wait for him
26 it is good to wait with silence for the
4 19 they lay in w. for us in the wilderness
Osee 3 3 thou shalt wait for me many days: thou
3 no man's, and I also will wait for thee
Mich 7 2 they all lie in wait for blood, every
7 I will wait for God my Savior: my God
Haba 2 3 if it make any delay, wait for it: for
1 Ma 1 38 to lie in wait against the sanctuary
5 4 by lying in wait for them in the way
2 Ma 9 25 wait for opportunities and expect what
Mark 3 9 that a small ship should wait on him
Luke 11 54 lying in wait for him and seeking to
12 36 like to men who wait for their lord
Acts 1 4 wait for the promise of the Father
9 24 their laying in wait was made known
20 3 spent 3 months, the Jews laid wait for
23 and afflictions wait for me at Jerusalem
23 16 had heard, of their lying in wait, he
21 for there lie in wait for him more than
25 3 laying wait to kill him in the way. But
Rom 8 25 we see not, we wait for it with patience
1 C 11 33 together to eat, wait for one another
Gal 5 5 we in spirit, by faith, w. for the hope
Eph 4 14 by which they lie in wait to deceive
1 Th 1 10 we wait for his son from heaven
waited Gen 8 10 having w. yet seven other days
Judg 9 25 while they waited for his coming, they
1 K 2 22 women that waited at the door of the
13 8 he [Saul] waited seven days according
4 K 5 2 maid, and she waited upon Naaman's wife
1 Pa 9 18 the sons of Levi waited by their turns
28 1 captains . . . who waited on the king
Job 29 21 that heard me, waited for my sentence
23 they waited for me as for rain, and
30 26 I waited for light, and darkness broke
32 4 so Eliu waited while Job was speaking
11 I have waited for your words, I have
16 because I have waited and they have
Ps 24 5 on thee have I waited all the day long
21 to me: because I have waited on thee
39 2 with expectation I have waited for the
54 9 I waited for him that hath saved me
55 7 as they have waited for my soul, for
105 13 and they waited not for his counsel
118 95 the wicked have w. for me to destroy
129 4 thy law, I have waited for thee, O Lord
Isa 25 9 this is our God, we have waited for him
9 we have patiently waited for him, we
26 8 we have patiently waited for thee: thy
33 2 we have waited for thee: be thou our
Acts 10 24 Cornelius waited for them, having called
17 16 whilst Paul waited for them at Athens
27 33 is the 14th day that you have waited
1 P 3 20 when they waited for the patience of
waiters Mat 22 13 the king said to the waiters
John 2 5 his mother saith to the waiters
9 but the waiters knew who had drawn the
waiteth Ps 32 20 our soul waiteth for the Lord

Prov 8 34 and waiteth at the posts of my doors
Isa 30 18 the Lord waiteth that he may have mercy
Dan 12 12 blessed is he that waiteth and cometh
13 59 angel of the Lord waiteth with a sword
Mich 5 7 which waiteth not for man nor tarrieth
Rom 8 19 waiteth for revelation of sons of God
James 5 7 husbandman w. for the precious fruit
waiting Judg 3 25 w. a long time till they were
Judg 18 17 the 600 valiant men waiting not far
Jdth 10 6 and the ancients of the city waiting
Jer 3 2 waiting for them as a robber in the
Luke 1 21 the people were waiting for Zachary
2 25 waiting for the consolation of Israel
8 40 him: for they were all waiting for him
John 5 8 waiting for the moving of the water
Rom 8 23 waiting for the adoption of sons of God
1 C 1 7 waiting for the manifestation of our
2 P 3 14 waiting for these things, be diligent
Jude 21 waiting for the mercy of our Lord
waiting-maids 1 K 25 42 went with her, her w.
Esth 2 9 deck out both her and her waiting-maids
waked Zach 4 1 w. me as a man that is wakened
wakened Zach 4 1 as a man that is w. out of his
wakeneth Isa 50 4 he w. in the morning, in the morning he w. my ear
waketh Eccu 42 9 the father w. for the daughter
waking Luke 9 32 waking, they saw his glory
walk Mat 9 5 or to say, Arise and w. Luke 5:23
Mat 11 5 the blind see, the lame walk. Luke 7:22
15 31 seeing the dumb speak, the lame walk
Mark 2 9 take up thy bed and w. John 5:8, 11, 12
7 5 do not thy disciples walk according
12 38 beware of the scribes, who love to w.
Luke 11 44 men that walk over are not aware
13 33 I must walk today and tomorrow, and
20 46 who desire to walk in long robes and
24 17 as you walk and are sad? And one of
John 7 1 for he would not walk in Judea because
11 9 man walk in the day, he stumbleth not
10 if he walk in the night, he stumbleth
12 35 walk whilst you have the light, that
21 18 and didst walk where thou wouldst
Acts 3 6 arise and walk. And taking him by the
12 power we had made this man to walk
14 15 suffered all nations to walk in their
21 21 nor walk according to the custom. What
Rom 6 4 so we also may walk in newness of life
8 1 who walk not according to the flesh. 4
13 13 let us walk honestly, as in the day: not
1 C 3 3 not carnal, and walk according to man
7 17 hath called every one, so let him walk
2 C 5 7 for we walk by faith, and not by sight
6 16 will dwell in them, and walk among them
12 18 did we not walk with the same spirit
Gal 5 16 walk in the spirit, and you shall not
25 Spirit, let us also walk in the Spirit
Eph 2 10 God hath prepared that we should walk in
4 1 that you walk worthy of the vocation in
17 you walk not as also the Gentiles walk
5 2 walk in love, as Christ also hath loved
8 walk then as children of the light. For
Phil 3 18 many walk, of whom I have told you often
Col 1 10 that you may walk worthy of God, in all
2 6 Jesus Christ, the Lord, walk ye in him
4 5 walk with wisdom towards them that are
1 Th 2 12 that you would walk worthy of God, who
4 1 how you ought to walk, and to please
1 so also you would walk, that you may
11 that you walk honestly towards them that
2 Th 3 11 some among you who walk disorderly
Heb 13 9 not profited those that walk in them
2 P 2 10 who walk after the flesh in the lust
1 J 1 6 with him, and walk in darkness, we
7 but if we walk in the light, as he
2 6 ought also to walk, even as he walked
2 J 6 charity, that we walk according to his
6 you should walk in the same. For many
3 J 4 to hear that my children walk in truth
Apoc 3 4 and they shall walk with me in white
9 20 neither can see nor hear nor walk
16 15 lest he walk naked and they see his
21 24 the nations shall walk in the light of
walked Mat 14 29 walked upon the water to come
Mark 2 23 Lord walked through the corn fields on
5 42 the damsel rose up and walked: and she
Luke 9 57 as they walked in the way, that a
19 1 entering in, he walked through Jericho
John 5 9 and he took up his bed and walked
6 67 back; and walked no more with him
7 1 Jesus walked in Galilee; for he would
10 23 and Jesus walked in the temple, in
11 54 Jesus walked no more openly among the
Acts 3 8 he leaping up, stood and walked and
14 7 his mother's womb, who never had w.
9 feet. And he leaped up, and walked
2 C 10 2 as if we walked according to the flesh
Gal 2 14 when I saw that they w. not uprightly
Eph 2 2 you walked according to the course of
Col 3 7 in which you also walked some time, when
1 P 4 3 who have walked in riotousness, lusts
1 J 2 6 ought also to walk, even as he walked
walkest Acts 21 24 thou thyself also w. keeping
Rom 14 15 thou w. not now according to charity
3 J 3 even as thou walkest in the truth
walketh Mat 12 43 he walketh through dry places
Luke 11 24 walketh through places without water
John 8 12 followeth me, walketh not in darkness
12 35 he that walketh in darkness, knoweth
1 J 2 11 is in darkness, and w. in darkness
Apoc 2 1 who w. in the midst of the seven golden
walking Mat 4 18 Jesus walking by the sea of
Mat 14 25 came to them w. upon the sea. Mark 6:48
26 seeing him w. upon the sea. Mark 6:49
Mark 8 24 I see men as it were trees, walking
11 27 when he was walking in the temple
16 12 another shape to two of them walking
Luke 1 6 walking in all the commandments and
John 1 36 beholding Jesus walking, he saith
6 19 they see Jesus walking upon the sea
Acts 3 8 walking and leaping and praising God
9 all the people saw him walking and
9 31 edified, walking in fear of the Lord
2 C 4 2 dishonesty, not walking in craftiness
Col 2 18 walking in the things which he hath not
2 Th 3 6 from every brother walking disorderly
2 P 3 3 scoffers, w. after their own lusts
2 J 4 of thy children walking in truth, as
Jude 16 w. according to their own desires. 18
wall Gen 49 6 they undermined a wall. Cursed be
Gen 49 22 daughters run to and fro upon the wall
Exod 14 22 the water was as a wall on their right
29 waters . . . as a wall on the right hand
Num 22 25 thrust herself close to the wall and
Josu 2 15 for her house joined close to the wall
1 K 6 18 to the village that was without wall
18 11 thinking to nail David to the wall
19 10 endeavored to nail David to the wall
10 missed him and was fastened in the wall
20 25 his chair . . . which was beside the wall
25 16 they were a wall unto us both by night
22 any that pisseth against the wall. 34
31 10 his body they hung on wall of Bethsan
12 took the body . . . from the wall of
2 K 11 20 approach so near to the wall to fight
20 are thrown from above off the wall
21 piece of millstone upon him from wall

21 why did you go near the wall. Thou
24 at thy servants from off the wall above
18 24 on the top of the gate upon the wall
20 21 his head shall be thrown . . . from wall
22 30 in my God I will leap over the wall
3 K 3 1 and the wall of Jerusalem round about
4 33 unto the hyssop that cometh out of wall
6 5 upon wall of the temple he built floors
18 no stone could be seen in the wall at
27 wing of the one touched one wall and
27 of other cherub touched the other wall
29 as it were . . . coming forth from the w.
9 15 to build . . . the wall of Jerusalem
14 10 him that pisseth against the wall. 21:21; 4 K 9:8
16 11 not one thereof to piss against a wall
20 30 w. fell upon seven and twenty thousand
21 4 he turned away his face to the wall
4 K 3 27 him for a burnt offering upon the wall
6 26 king of Israel was passing by the wall
30 king . . . passed by upon the wall. And
9 33 the wall was sprinkled with her blood
14 13 he broke down the wall of Jerusalem
18 26 of the people that are upon the wall
27 to the men that sit upon the wall
20 2 and he turned his face to the wall
2 Pa 3 11 and reached to the wall of the house
12 the wing . . . reached to the wall
16 1 Baasa . . . built a wall about Rama
26 6 broke down the wall of Geth and the wall of Jabnia and the wall of Azotus
9 the rest in the same side of the wall
27 3 on the wall of Ophel he built much
32 5 he built up also . . . all the wall
5 and built . . . another wall without
33 14 built a wall without the city of David
36 19 and broke down the wall of Jerusalem
2 Es 1 3 wall of Jerusalem is broken down and
2 13 and I viewed the wall of Jerusalem which
15 I went up . . . and viewed the wall and
3 8 unto the wall of the broad street. And
13 thousand cubits in the wall unto the gate
27 built . . . unto the wall of the temple
4 1 heard that we were building the wall he
3 he will leap over their stone wall. Hear
6 so we built the wall and joined it all
9 and set watchmen upon the wall day and
10 we shall not be able to build the wall
13 the people in the place behind the wall
17 of them that built on the wall and
19 we are separated on the wall one far
5 16 I built in the work of the wall, and I
6 1 heard that I had built the wall, and
6 and therefore thou buildest the wall
15 wall was finished the five and twentieth
7 1 after the wall was built, and I had set
12 27 and at the dedication of the wall of
30 purified . . . the gates and the wall. And
31 upon the wall toward the dunghill gate
31 princes of Juda go up upon the wall and
36 at the going up of the w. of the house
37 the half of the people upon the wall
37 the furnaces, even to the broad wall and
13 21 why stay you before the wall? If you
Tob 2 10 cast himself down by the wall and slept
Jdth 5 12 waters . . . firm as a wall on either side
Job 30 14 upon me, as when a wall is broken and a
Ps 17 30 through my God I shall go over a wall
61 4 you were thrusting down a leaning wall
143 14 there is no breach of wall nor passage
Prov 18 11 as a strong wall compassing him about
24 31 and the stone wall was broken down. Which
Cant 2 9 behold he standeth behind our wall
14 in the hollow places of the wall, show
8 9 if she be a wall: let us build upon it
10 I am a wall: and my breasts are as a
Wisd 13 15 setting it in a wall and fastening it
Isa 2 15 tower and upon . . . every fenced wall
5 5 I will break down the wall thereof and
15 1 the wall of Moab is destroyed in the
16 11 parts [shall sound] for the brick wall
22 5 searching the wall, and magnificent
6 shield was taken down from the wall. And
10 broken down houses to fortify the wall
25 4 like a whirlwind beating against a wall
26 1 wall and a bulwark shall be set therein
30 13 and is found wanting in a high wall
36 11 of the people that are upon the wall
12 rather to the men that sit on the wall
38 2 Ezechias turned his face toward the w.
59 10 we have groped for the wall, and like
Jer 1 18 a wall of brass, over all the land, to
15 20 to this people as a strong w. of brass
39 8 they threw down the wall of Jerusalem
43 9 the vault that is under the brick wall
48 31 for the men of the brick wall that. 36
49 27 a fire in the wall of Damascus, and it
51 44 the wall also of Babylon shall fall. Go
58 broad wall of Babylon shall be utterly
52 14 broke down all the wall of Jerusalem
Lam 2 8 to destroy the wall of daughter of Sion
8 the wall hath been destroyed together
Eze 4 3 set it for a wall of iron between thee
8 7 I saw, and behold a hole in the wall
8 son of man, dig in the wall. And when
8 when I had digged in the wall, behold
10 were painted on the w. all round about
12 5 dig thee a way through the wall before
7 I digged through the wall with my hand
12 they shall dig through the w. to bring
13 5 nor have you set up a w. for the house
10 the people built up a wall and they
12 when the wall is fallen: shall it not
14 I will break down the w. that you have
15 will accomplish my wrath upon the wall
15 will say to you: The wall is no more
23 14 she had seen men painted on the wall
38 11 up to the land which is without a wall
11 all these dwell without a wall, they
20 every wall shall fall to the ground
40 5 was a wall on the outside of the house
41 5 the wall of the house six cubits, and
6 they might enter in through the wall
6 not to touch the wall of the temple
9 thickness of wall for the side chamber
12 wall of the building, five cubits thick
17 and without all the wall round about
20 palm trees wrought in w. of the temple
42 7 the outward wall . . . fifty cubits long
10 in the breadth of the outward wall of
20 by the four winds he measured the wall
43 8 was but a wall between me and them
46 23 there was a wall round about compassing
Dan 5 5 upon the surface of the wall of the
Osee 2 6 I will stop it up with a wall, and she
Joel 2 7 like men of war they shall scale the w.
9 they shall run upon the wall, they
Amos 1 7 I will send a fire on the wall of Gaza
10 I will send a fire upon the wall of Tyre
14 I will kindle a fire in the w. of Rabba
5 19 and lean with his hand upon the wall
7 7 Lord was standing upon a plastered wall
Haba 2 11 the stone shall cry out of the wall
Zach 2 5 I will be to it . . . a wall of fire
1 Ma 1 35 city of David with great and strong w.
6 62 commandment to throw down the wall

12 37 for the wall that was upon the brook
13 45 their wives and children upon the wall
2 Ma 5 5 the citizens ran together to the wall
10 35 approached manfully to the wall, and
14 43 he ran boldly to the wall and manfully
Acts 9 25 conveyed him away by the wall, letting
23 3 God shall strike thee, thou whited wall
2 C 11 33 in a basket was I let down by the wall
Eph 2 14 breaking down middle wall of partition
Apoc 21 12 it had a wall great and high, having
14 wall of the city had 12 foundations
15 and the gates thereof and the wall
17 measured the wall thereof 144 cubits
18 the building of the wall thereof was
19 foundations of the wall of the city
walled Num 13 20 cities, walled or without walls
Num 13 29 and the cities are great and walled
32 17 all we have shall be in walled cities
Deut 1 28 great and walled up to the sky. 9:1
3 K 9 19 and were not walled, he fortified
2 Pa 8 5 walled cities, with gates and bars and
11 5 Jerusalem, and built w. cities in Juda
23 of Benjamin and in all the w. cities
16 4 and all the walled cities of Nephtali
17 12 houses like towers and walled cities
19 others whom he put in the w. cities
wallet Jdth 13 11 and bade her put it into her w.
Jdth 13 19 head of Holofernes out of the wallet
wallow Eccu 23 16 and they shall not w. in sins
wallowing Jdth 14 4 without his head, w. in his
2 P 2 22 washed, to her wallowing in the mire
walls Exod 30 3 as the walls round about and the
Lev 14 37 if he see in the w. thereof as it were
44 the walls full of spots, it is a lasting
25 29 selleth a house within the walls of a
31 house be in a village that hath no w.
Num 13 20 manner of cities, walled or without w.
22 24 in a narrow place between two walls
35 4 which suburbs shall reach from the w.
Deut 3 5 cities were fenced with very high walls
5 innumerable towns that had no walls
28 52 thy strong and high walls be brought
Josu 6 5 and the walls of the city shall fall
20 the walls forthwith fell down, and
2 K 5 11 and carpenters and masons for walls
20 15 labored to throw down the walls. And
24 7 they passed near the walls of Tyre and
3 K 4 13 threescore great cities with walls and
6 5 in the walls of the house round about
6 not be fastened in walls of the temple
15 and he built the walls of the house
15 to the top of the w. and to the roofs
29 walls of temple round about he carved
7 9 from foundation to top of the walls
4 K 3 25 so that brick walls only remained: and
25 4 the two walls by the king's garden
10 broke down the walls of Jerusalem
1 Pa 29 4 to overlay the walls of the temple
2 Pa 3 7 and he graved cherubims on the walls
11 11 when he had enclosed them with walls
14 7 and compass them with walls and fortify
24 13 the breach of the walls was closed up
25 23 and broke down the walls thereof from
26 15 towers, and in the corners of the walls
32 18 to the people that sat on the walls
1 Es 4 12 ramparts thereof and repairing the w.
13 built up, and the w. thereof repaired
16 built, and the walls thereof repaired
5 3 house, and to repair the walls thereof
8 timber is laid in the walls: and this
9 this house, and to repair these walls
2 Es 2 8 the house, and the walls of the city
17 let us build up the walls of Jerusalem
3 15 and the walls of the pool of Siloe
4 7 that the walls of Jerusalem were made
15 and we returned all of us to the walls
Tob 13 21 walls thereof round about of precious
Jdth 1 2 the walls thereof seventy cubits broad
4 4 they compassed their towns with walls
7 7 were springs not far from the walls
13 13 cried to the watchmen upon the walls
14 1 hang ye up this head upon our walls
7 the head of Holofernes upon the walls
Ps 50 20 the walls of Jerusalem may be built
54 11 shall iniquity surround it upon its w.
Prov 9 3 the tower and to the walls of the city
25 28 as a city . . . not compassed with walls
Cant 5 7 keepers of the walls took away my veil
Eccu 14 25 fastening a pin in her walls shall set
23 26 the walls cover me, and no man seeth me
49 15 who raised up for us our walls that
50 2 building and the high w. of the temple
Isa 16 7 them that rejoice upon the brick walls
22 11 you made a ditch between the two walls
25 12 bulwarks of thy high walls shall fall
49 16 thy walls are always before my eyes
56 5 to them in my house and within my walls
60 10 of strangers shall build up thy walls
18 and salvation shall possess thy walls
62 6 upon thy walls, O Jerusalem, I have
Jer 1 15 upon all the walls thereof round about
5 10 scale the walls thereof and throw
21 4 that besiege you round about the walls
39 4 by gate that was between the two walls
50 15 are fallen, her walls are thrown down
51 12 upon the walls of Babylon set up the
52 7 the gate that is between the two walls
Lam 2 5 hath overthrown all the walls thereof
7 hath delivered the walls of the towers
18 heart cried to the Lord upon the walls
Eze 26 4 they shall break down the walls of Tyre
9 and battering rams against thy walls
10 thy walls shall shake at the noise
12 they shall destroy thy walls and pull
27 11 Arad were with thy army upon thy walls
11 hung up their quivers on thy walls
33 30 that talk of thee by the walls and
36 4 to desolate places and ruinous walls
41 13 walls thereof, 100 cubits in length
22 and the walls thereof were of wood
25 trees, like as were made on the walls
26 house, and the breadth of the walls
Dan 9 25 and the walls in straitness of times
Amos 9 11 I will close up the breaches of the w.
Mich 7 11 come, that thy walls may be built up
Nah 2 5 they shall quickly get upon the walls
3 8 is its riches, the waters are its walls
Zach 2 4 Jerusalem shall be inhabited without w.
1 Ma 1 33 and threw down . . . the walls thereof
4 60 mount Sion with high walls and strong
5 65 burnt the walls thereof and the towers
6 7 about the sanctuary with high walls
8 10 their land and threw down their walls
9 50 with high walls and gates and bars
54 commanded the walls of the inner court
10 11 he ordered workmen to build the walls
45 building also of the walls of Jerusalem
45 for the building of the walls in Judea
12 36 and to build up walls in Jerusalem
13 10 to finish all the walls of Jerusalem
33 with high towers and great walls and
14 37 and he raised up the walls of Jerusalem
16 23 the building of the walls which he made
2 Ma 3 19 some to Onias and some to the walls
6 10 threw down headlong from the walls
11 9 the fiercest beasts and walls of iron

12 13 city, encompassed with bridges and w.
14 trusting in the strength of the walls
15 of war threw down the walls of Jericho
15 Machabeus . . . fiercely assaulted the w.
27 stout young men standing upon the walls
Heb 11 30 by faith the walls of Jericho fell down
wand Eccu 33 25 wand and a burden are for an ass
wander Num 14 33 shall wander in the desert forty
Deut 27 18 he that maketh the blind to wander out
Ps 106 40 he caused them to wander where there
Prov 21 16 a man that shall w. out of the way of
Cant 1 6 lest I begin to wander after the flocks
Eccu 9 7 nor wander up and down in the streets
Isa 16 3 and betray not them that wander about
Jer 50 6 have made them wander in the mountains
wandered Gen 21 14 wandered in the wilderness of
1 K 23 13 w. up and down uncertain where they
Ps 106 4 they w. in a wilderness, in a place
Eccu 29 24 and they have w. in strange countries
51 18 was yet young, before I wandered about
Isa 16 8 they have wandered in the wilderness
Lam 4 14 they have wandered as blind men in the
Eze 34 6 my sheep have w. in every mountain and
44 10 and have w. from me after their idols
Heb 11 37 they wandered about in sheepskins, in
wanderers Osee 9 17 shall be w. among the nations
wandereth Prov 27 8 a bird that w. from her nest
wandering Gen 37 15 him there w. in the field
Lev 13 57 spot, a flying and wandering leprosy
Job 38 41 w. about because they have no meat
Prov 5 6 her steps are w. and unaccountable
7 10 deceive souls; talkative and wandering
Wisd 4 12 wandering of concupiscence overturneth
Isa 57 17 and he went away w. in his own heart
Jer 14 9 why wilt thou be as a wandering man
31 22 wilt thou be dissolute . . . w. daughter
Heb 11 38 w. in deserts, in mountains, and in
Jude 13 w. stars, to whom the storm of darkness
want Gen 33 15 I want nothing else but only to
Gen 41 57 to seek some relief of their want
42 2 live and not be consumed with want
43 22 money besides, to buy what we want
Exod 17 3 were thirsty there for want of water
Deut 8 3 he afflicted thee with want, and gave
9 without any want thou shalt eat thy
28 22 Lord afflict thee with miserable want
48 nakedness and in want of all things
55 nothing else in the siege and the want
57 shall eat them secretly for the want
Judg 18 10 in which there is no want of anything
19 19 with me: we want nothing but lodging
Ruth 4 14 not suffered thy family to want a
2 Pa 2 16 out of Libanus, as thou shalt want
Tob 1 17 he saw Gabelus in want, who was one
Job 20 10 his children shall be oppressed with w.
30 3 barren with want and hunger, who
31 19 that was perishing for want of clothing
41 13 dwell, and want goeth before his face
Ps 22 1 ruleth me: and I shall want nothing
33 10 there is no want to them that fear him
43 24 forgettest our want and our trouble
106 10 of death: bound in want and in iron
Prov 3 33 want is from the Lord in the house of
6 11 and want shall come upon thee as a
11 want shall flee far from thee. A
10 19 of words there shall not want sin: but
21 shall die in the want of understanding
11 24 not their own, and are always in want
14 23 many words, there is oftentimes want
21 5 but every sluggard is always in want
17 loveth good cheer, shall be in want
28 27 that giveth to the poor, shall not want
31 7 let them drink and forget their want
Ecce 5 13 son who shall be in extremity of want
Wisd 16 3 after suffering want for a short time
Eccu 4 2 and provoke not the poor in his want
11 11 sorrow and is so much the more in want
19 25 hindered from sinning for want of power
20 23 is hindered from sinning through want
29 33 I want my house, my brother being to
36 27 no wife, he mourneth that is in want
40 27 there is no w. in the fear of the Lord
29 for it is better to die than to want
43 29 say much, and yet shall want words
Isa 50 2 fishes shall rot for want of water and
Jer 9 11 desolate, for want of an inhabitant
Lam 4 9 being consumed for want of the fruits
Amos 4 6 want of bread in all your places: yet
Mala 3 9 you are cursed with want, and you
2 Ma 2 15 if you want these things, send some
8 26 they came back for want of time: for it
Mark 12 44 she of her want cast in all she had
Luke 15 14 country: and he began to be in want
21 4 of her want, hath cast in all the
22 35 and shoes, did you want anything
2 C 8 14 let your abundance supply their want
14 their abundance also may supply your w.
15 and he that had little, had no want. And
9 12 not only supply the want of the saints
Phil 4 11 I speak not as it were for want. For I
19 and may my God supply all your want
1 Th 4 11 and that you want nothing of any man's
Heb 11 37 being in want, distressed, afflicted
James 1 5 if any of you want wisdom, let him ask
2 15 and want daily food: and one of you
wanted Gen 47 14 when the buyers wanted money, all
Num 33 14 where the people wanted water to drink
Deut 2 7 forty years, and thou hast w. nothing
Ps 33 11 rich have wanted, and have suffered
Jer 44 18 we have wanted all things and have been
1 C 12 24 giving to that which wanted the more
2 C 11 9 when I was present with you, and wanted
wantest Eccu 13 7 and will say: What wantest thou
2 Ma 14 35 Lord of all things, who wantest nothing
wanteth Gen 34 21 large and wide w. men to till
Deut 23 20 thou shalt lend that which he wanteth
2 K 3 29 falleth by the sword, or that w. bread
4 K 12 5 shall see anything that w. repairing
Job 32 19 belly is as new wine which wanteth vent
Prov 10 13 rod on the back of him that w. sense
12 9 than he that is glorious and w. bread
Ecce 6 2 his soul w. nothing of all that he
Eccu 10 30 that boasteth himself and wanteth bread
11 12 is an inactive man that wanteth help
16 23 he that wanteth understanding thinketh
19 21 less wisdom and wanteth understanding
wanting Gen 44 30 our father, and the boy be w.
Exod 39 40 nothing was wanting of the vessels that
Num 20 2 the people wanting water, came together
31 49 and not so much as one was wanting
Deut 15 11 there will not be wanting poor in the
Judg 21 5 whosoever were wanting should be slain
2 K 2 30 were w. of David's servants 19 men
3 K 11 22 what is wanting to thee with me, that
4 K 10 19 let none be wanting, for I have a great
19 whosoever shall be wanting shall not
2 Es 9 21 desert, and nothing was wanting to them
Ps 38 5 that I may know what is wanting to me
Cant 7 2 like a round bowl never wanting cups
Wisd 19 4 up what was wanting to their torments
Eccu 7 38 be not w. in comforting them that weep
19 20 man that is foolish, wanting in wisdom
Isa 30 13 and is found wanting in a high wall
34 16 not one of them was wanting, one hath
Jer 23 4 none shall be wanting of their number
35 19 shall not be wanting a man of the race

Dan 5 27 in the balance and art found wanting
Mat 19 20 my youth, what is yet wanting to me
Luke 18 22 yet one thing is w. to thee. Mark 10:21
1 C 1 7 that nothing is w. to you in any grace
16 17 which was w. on your part. Phil 2:30
2 C 11 9 for that which was wanting to me, the
Col 1 24 fill up those things that are wanting
1 Th 3 10 accomplish those things that are wanting
Titus 1 5 set in order the things that are wanting
3 13 care, that nothing be wanting to them
Heb 4 1 you should be thought to be wanting
12 15 lest any man be wanting to the grace
wanton 1 Pa 13 9 the oxen being w. had made it
Prov 7 22 as a lamb playing the wanton and not
Isa 3 16 and wanton glances of their eyes and
Osee 4 16 hath gone astray like a wanton heifer
Amos 6 4 ivory, and are wanton on your couches
1 Tim 5 11 when they have grown wanton in Christ
wants Ps 9 1 why dost thou slight us in our wants
Phil 2 25 and he that hath ministered to my wants
war Gen 49 5 vessels of iniquity, waging war. Let
Exod 1 10 if any war shall rise against us
15 3 the Lord is as a man of war, Almighty
17 16 war of the Lord shall be against Amalec
Num 1 3 the men of Israel fit for war and you
20 that were able to go forth to war. 22, 24, 26, 30, 32, 36, 40, 42, 45
28 all that could go forth to war. 34
10 9 if you go forth to war out of your
26 2 all that are able to go forth to war
31 4 men be chosen . . . to be sent to the war
27 that fought and went out of the war
32 20 go on well appointed for war before
29 if the children of Gad . . . armed for war
Deut 2 14 generation . . . fit for war was consumed
24 make war against him [Sehon]. This day
20 1 thou go out to war against thy enemies
7 lest he die in the war and another
12 if they . . . shall begin war against thee
23 9 when thou goest out to war and another
24 5 he shall not go out to war, neither
Josu 5 4 all the men fit for war, died in desert
Judg 1 1 and shall be the leader of the war
3 2 and to be trained up to war: the five
5 20 war from heaven was made against them
11 27 by declaring an unjust war against me
18 11 furnished with arms for war. 1 Pa 12:37
20 2 met . . . 400,000 footmen fit for war
46 fighting men, most valiant for war
21 22 took them not away as by right of war
1 K 4 1 went out to war against the Philistines
14 52 was a great war against the Philistines
52 to be a valiant man and fit for war
16 18 of great strength and a man fit for war
19 8 the war began again, and David went out
28 1 to be prepared for war against Israel
1 thou shalt go out with me to the war
2 K 1 27 and the weapons of war perished
3 1 war between the house of Saul. 6
11 1 at the time when kings go forth to war
7 people, and how the war was carried on
25 for various is the event of war: and
22 35 he teacheth my hands to war: and maketh
3 K 2 5 and shed the blood of war in peace
5 put the blood of war on his girdle
8 44 if thy people go out to war against
9 22 they were men of war and his servants
12 21 gathered . . . chosen men for war, to
14 30 was war between Roboam and Jeroboam. 15:6; 2 Pa 12:15
15 7 was war between Abiam and Jeroboam
16 was war between Asa and Baasa. 15:32
22 1 without war between Syria and Israel
4 K 13 25 which he had taken . . . by war, three
14 7 and took the rock by war and called
24 16 that were valiant men and fit for war
26 4 all the men of war fled in the night
19 who was captain over the men of war
1 Pa 5 18 sons of Ruben . . . that went out to war
7 4 most valiant men ready for war: for
5 valiant men for war. 9; 12:25; Jer 41:16
11 and two hundred fit to go out to war
40 of the age that was fit for war
12 24 sons . . . 6,800 well appointed to war
33 well appointed with armor for war
38 all these men of war well appointed
20 4 after this there arose a war at Gazer
28 3 because thou art a man of war, and
2 Pa 6 34 if thy people go out to war against
8 9 for they were men of war and chief
13 2 was war between Abia and Jeroboam
3 also chosen and most valiant for war
15 19 and there was no war unto the five
17 10 durst not make war against Josaphat
18 with him 180,000 ready for war
18 3 and we will be with thee in the war
26 11 his fighting men, that went out to war
13 who were fit for war and fought for
28 12 against them that came from the war
32 2 whole force of the war was turning
Jdth 2 2 he called . . . his officers of war
3 8 valiant men, and chosen for war. And so
4 4 together corn for provision for war
5 27 and without skill in the art of war
7 5 taking their arms of war, they posted
Job 6 4 the terrors of the Lord war against me
10 17 wrath upon me, and pains war against me
20 23 and rain down his war upon him. He
38 23 against the day of battle and war
Ps 55 3 they are many that make war against me
143 1 my hands to fight, and my fingers to war
Prov 24 6 war is managed by due ordering: and
Ecce 3 8 a time of war and a time of peace
8 8 neither . . . to rest when war is at hand
9 18 better is wisdom than weapons of war
Cant 3 8 holding swords, and most expert in war
Wisd 8 15 shall be found good, and valiant in war
12 9 the wicked under the just by war
14 22 they lived in a great war of ignorance
Eccu 26 26 a man of war fainting through poverty
37 12 nor with a coward concerning war
46 1 valiant in war was Jesus son of Nave
Isa 2 4 they be exercised any more to war
3 2 the strong man and the man of war
13 4 hath given charge to the troops of war
36 5 strength dost thou prepare for war
41 12 the men that war against thee. For I
42 13 as a man of war shall he stir up zeal
Jer 6 4 prepare ye war against her: arise, and
23 upon horses, prepared as men for war
21 2 Nabuchodonosor . . . maketh war against us
4 I will turn back the weapons of war
28 8 prophesied . . . of war and of affliction
38 4 weakeneth the hands of the men of war
39 4 and all the men of war saw them, they
42 14 where we shall see no war, nor hear
49 2 noise of the war to be heard in Rabbath
26 all the men of war shall be silent
50 22 a noise of war in the land, and a great
30 her men of war shall hold their peace
51 20 thou dashest . . . the weapons of war
32 and the men of war are affrighted. For
52 7 men of war fled and went out of city
25 that was chief over the men of war
Bar 3 26 of great stature, expert in war. The
6 14 but cannot save himself from war, or

48 when war cometh upon them or evils
49 can neither deliver themselves from war
55 they cannot withstand a king and war
Eze 26 9 and he shall set engines of war and
27 27 thy men of war also . . . shall fall
39 20 all the men of war, saith the Lord God
Dan 9 26 after the end of the war the appointed
Osee 2 18 I will destroy . . . war out of the land
Joel 2 7 like men of war they shall scale the
3 9 prepare war, rouse up the strong: let
9 let all the men of war come up. Cut
Mich 2 8 passed harmless you have turned to war
3 5 they prepare war against him. Therefore
4 3 neither shall they learn war any more
Zach 9 8 with them that serve me in war, going
10 the bow for war shall be broken: and he
1 Ma 2 66 he shall manage the war of the people
3 10 from Samaria to make war against Israel
19 success of war is not in the multitude
4 7 and these were trained up to war. And
17 spoils: for there is war before us
5 19 make no war against the heathens till
8 24 if there come first any war upon the
27 if war shall come first upon the nation
32 and will make war against thee by sea
9 51 that they might wage war against Israel
10 71 with me is the strength of war. Ask
11 20 made many engines of war against it
12 44 the people, whereas we have no war
54 let us make war upon them and take
13 10 gathering together all the men of war
54 John his son was a valiant man for war
14 9 put on them glory and the robes of war
15 3 great army, and have built ships of war
13 above Dora with 120,000 men of war
39 and to war against the people. But
2 Ma 1 11 as we have been in war with such a king
2 14 such things as were lost by the war
8 9 of great experience in matters of war
10 15 the Jews . . . attempted to make war
12 15 without any rams or engines of war
27 place there were many engines of war
Luke 14 31 what king, about to go to make war
2 C 10 3 we do not war according to the flesh
1 Tim 1 18 that thou war in them a good warfare
James 4 1 which war in your members? You covet
2 you contend and war, and you have not
1 P 2 11 desires which war against the soul
Apoc 11 7 shall make war against them and shall
12 17 to make war with the rest of her seed
13 7 it was given unto him to make war with
19 19 to make war with him that sat upon the
ward 2 K 20 3 concubines . . . and put them in ward
1 Pa 26 16 way of the ascent, ward against ward
Isa 21 8 I am upon my ward, standing whole
Acts 12 10 passing through the first and second w.
wardens Osee 10 5 the wardens of its temple that
Soph 1 4 names of the wardens of the temples
wardrobe 4 K 10 22 to them that were over the w.
4 K 22 14 son of Araas keeper of the wardrobe
2 Pa 34 22 son of Hasra keeper of the wardrobe
wards 1 Pa 26 12 the chiefs of the wards as well as
Eze 40 45 that watch in the wards of the temple
wares 2 Es 3 30 of the sellers of small wares
2 Es 13 16 brought fish and all manner of wares
20 and they that sold all kinds of wares
Amos 8 5 be over, and we shall sell our wares
Jon 1 5 they cast forth the wares that were in
warfare Jdth 5 3 who is the king over their w.
Job 7 1 the life of man upon earth is a warfare
14 14 all the days in which I am now in w.
2 C 10 4 the weapons of our w. are not carnal
1 Tim 1 18 that thou war in them a good warfare
warily 1 Ma 6 40 they marched on w. and orderly
warlike Job 17 1 father of Galaad who was a w. man
Jdth 2 8 he made all his warlike preparations
1 Ma 3 3 as a giant and girt his warlike armor
warm 3 K 1 1 covered with clothes, he was not w.
3 K 1 2 sleep in his bosom and warm our lord
4 K 4 34 and the child's flesh grew warm. Then
Job 39 14 thou perhaps wilt warm them in the dust
Ecce 4 11 lie together, they shall w. one another
Eccu 3 17 as the ice in the fair warm weather
Isa 44 16 aha, I am warm, I have seen the fire
warmed Job 31 20 if he were not warmed with the
Ecce 4 11 how shall one alone be warmed? And if
Wisd 16 27 being warmed with a little sunbeam
Isa 44 15 he took thereof and warmed himself
16 was filled and was warmed, and said
47 14 no coals wherewith they may be warmed
Agge 1 6 clothed yourselves but have not been w.
Mark 14 54 at the fire, and warmed himself. And
John 18 18 and warmed themselves. And with them
James 2 16 go in peace, be ye warmed and filled
warming Mark 14 67 she had seen Peter w. himself
John 18 18 Peter also, standing and w. himself. 25
warn Eze 3 21 but if thou warn the just man
Eze 33 8 dost not speak to warn the wicked man
warned Exod 21 29 warned his master, and he did
Eze 3 21 live, because thou hast warned him
2 Ma 2 4 how the prophet, being warned by God
Mat 2 22 being warned in sleep, retired into the
warning Ps 59 6 a w. to them that fear thee: that
Eze 3 19 if thou give warning to the wicked
20 because thou hast not given him warning
2 Ma 6 17 few words for a warning to the readers
warp Lev 13 48 shall have the leprosy in the warp
Lev 13 59 leprosy . . . in the warp or woof, or
warred 4 K 6 8 king of Syria w. against Israel
warrior Judg 11 1 most valiant man and a warrior
1 K 17 33 but he is a warrior from his youth
2 K 17 8 thy father is a warrior and will not
Eccu 47 6 to take away the mighty warrior and
Jer 20 11 the Lord is with me as a strong warrior
warriors Josu 10 7 the army of the w. with him
Judg 8 10 120,000 warriors that drew the sword
2 K 10 7 sent Joab and whole army of warriors
11 25 encourage thy warriors against the city
15 18 and all the Gethites, valiant warriors
16 6 all the warriors walked on the right
4 K 25 5 w. that were with him were scattered
1 Pa 7 7 five chiefs . . . most valiant warriors
12 1 most valiant men and excellent w. 8
2 Pa 11 1 chosen men and warriors, to fight
17 13 and he had warriors and valiant men
32 21 cut off all stout men and the warriors
Jdth 9 6 horsemen and in a multitude of w.
Jer 8 16 sound of the neighing of his warriors
42 1 all the captains of the w. and Jonathan
Haba 3 14 his scepters, the head of his warriors
wars Exod 13 17 if they should see wars arise
Lev 26 37 their brethren as fleeing from wars
Num 21 14 in the book of the wars of the Lord
Josu 11 23 and the land rested from wars. 14:15
Judg 3 1 not known the wars of the Chanaanites
5 8 the Lord chose new wars, and he
3 K 5 3 because of the wars that were round
1 Pa 26 27 out of the wars and the spoils won
2 Pa 14 6 there had no wars risen in his time
7 while all is quiet from wars because
16 9 this time wars shall arise against thee
27 7 the acts of Joatham and all his wars
1 Es 4 15 and that wars were raised therein
19 seditions and wars have been raised
Jdth 9 10 who destroyest wars from the beginning
16 3 the Lord putteth an end to wars, the

Ps 45 10 making wars to cease even to the end
67 31 thou the nations that delight in wars
Prov 20 18 wars are to be managed by governments
1 Ma 9 22 rest of the words of the wars of Judas
12 13 we have had many troubles and wars on
14 of our allies and friends in these wars
14 28 have often been wars in our country
16 23 rest of the acts of John and his wars
2 Ma 2 21 as also the wars against Antiochus
10 10 the evils that happened in the wars
14 6 nourish wars and raise seditions and
Mat 24 6 hear of w. and rumors of w. Mark 13:7
Luke 21 9 you shall hear of wars and seditions
James 4 1 whence are wars and contentions among
was Apoc 1 4 that is and that was and that is to
Apoc 1 8 who is and who was and who is to come
4 8 who was and who is and who is to come
wash Gen 18 4 wash ye your feet, and rest ye
Gen 19 2 wash your feet, and in the morning
24 32 water to wash his feet and the feet of
49 11 he shall wash his robe in wine and his
Exod 2 5 came down to wash herself in the river
19 10 and let them wash their garments
30 18 brazen laver with its foot, to wash in
19 Aaron and his sons shall wash their
Lev 1 13 entrails and the feet they shall wash
11 25 shall wash his clothes. 28, 40; 13:6; 14:47; 15:5, 6, 7, 8, 10, 11, 22, 23, 27; 16:26, 28; 17:15
13 54 they shall wash that part wherein the
58 he shall wash with water the parts
15 16 shall wash all his body with water
17 weareth, he shall wash with water
16 24 shall wash his flesh in the holy place
17 16 if he do not wash his clothes and his
Num 5 23 shall w. them out with the most bitter
19 8 shall wash his garments and his. 21
19 shall w. both himself and his garments
31 24 and you shall wash your garments the
Deut 21 6 shall wash their hands over the heifer
Ruth 3 3 wash thyself therefore and anoint thee
1 K 25 41 to wash the feet of the servants of my
2 K 11 8 go into thy house and wash thy feet
4 K 5 10 go, and wash seven times in the Jordan
12 that I may wash in them and be made
13 thee: Wash, and thou shalt be clean
2 Pa 4 6 to wash in them all such things as they
6 the sea was for the priests to wash in
Tob 6 2 and he went out to wash his feet, and
Ps 6 7 every night I will wash my bed: I will
25 6 will wash my hands among the innocent
50 4 wash me yet more from my iniquity, and
9 shalt wash me, and I shall be made
57 11 shall wash his hands in the blood of
Isa 1 16 wash yourselves, be clean, take away
4 4 if the Lord shall wash away the filth
4 shall wash away the blood of Jerusalem
Jer 2 22 though thou wash thyself with niter
4 14 wash thy heart from wickedness, O
Eze 23 40 for whom thou didst wash thyself and
Dan 13 15 desirous to wash herself in the orchard
17 doors of the orchard, that I may wash
Mat 6 17 anoint thy head and wash thy face
15 2 they wash not their hands when they
Luke 7 38 she began to wash his feet with tears
John 9 7 go, wash in the pool of Siloe, which
11 go to the pool of Siloe and wash
13 5 began to wash the feet of the disciples
6 to him: Lord, dost thou wash my feet
8 thou shalt never wash my feet. Jesus
8 if I wash thee not, thou shalt have
10 needeth not but to wash his feet, but
14 also ought to wash one another's feet
Acts 22 16 and be baptized, and wash away thy sins
Apoc 22 14 that wash their robes in the blood of
washed Gen 43 24 water, and they w. their feet
Gen 43 31 when he had washed his face, coming
Exod 19 14 when they had washed their garments
29 4 hast washed the father and his sons
17 having washed his entrails and feet
40 12 having washed them with water, thou
29 his sons washed their hands and feet
Lev 1 9 the entrails and feet being washed
6 27 it shall be washed in a holy place
28 shall be scoured and washed with water
8 6 when he [Moses] had washed them, he
21 having first washed the entrails. 9:14
13 34 clothes being washed he shall be clean
56 after the garment is washed he shall
14 8 when the man hath washed his clothes
8 body, and shall be washed with water
9 having washed again his clothes and
15 5 being washed with water, he shall be
6 w. with water, shall be unclean. 11
7 being himself washed with water shall
8 being w. with water, he shall be. 10
11 not having washed his hands before
12 if a vessel of wood, it shall be washed
13 having washed his clothes and all his
18 shall be washed with water and shall be
22 being himself washed with water, shall
23 himself being washed with water. 27
16 4 he shall put on, after he is washed
22 6 when he hath washed his flesh with
Num 8 7 they shall have washed their garments
21 were purified and washed their garments
19 10 hath washed his garments, he shall be
Deut 23 11 shall not return before he be washed
Judg 19 21 after they had washed their feet, he
2 K 12 20 David arose from the ground and washed
19 24 he had neither washed his feet . . . nor washed his garments
3 K 22 38 they washed his chariot in the pool of
38 his blood, and they washed the reins
4 K 5 14 and washed in the Jordan seven times
2 Es 4 23 stripped himself when he was to be w.
Jdth 10 3 washed her body and anointed herself
12 7 washed herself in a fountain of water
Job 9 30 if I be washed as it were with snow
14 19 ground by little and little is w. away
29 6 when I washed my feet with butter, and
Ps 72 13 and washed my hands among the innocent
Prov 30 12 are not washed from their filthiness
Cant 5 3 I have washed my feet, how shall I
12 which are washed with milk, and sit
Eze 16 4 neither wast thou washed with water
9 I washed thee with water and cleansed
Mat 27 24 washed his hands before the people
Mark 7 4 unless they be washed, they eat not
Luke 7 44 she with tears hath washed my feet
11 38 why he was not washed before dinner
John 9 7 he went therefore, and washed, and
11 I washed, and I see. 15
13 10 he that is washed, needeth not but to
12 then after he had washed their feet
14 have washed your feet; you also ought
Acts 9 37 when they had washed, they laid her
16 33 washed their stripes, and himself was
1 C 6 11 but you are w., but you are sanctified
1 Tim 5 10 if she have washed the saints' feet, if
Heb 10 28 and our bodies washed with clean water
2 P 2 22 sow that was washed, to her wallowing
Apoc 1 5 loved us and washed us from our sins in
7 14 have washed their robes and have made
washeth Ecclu 34 30 that w. himself after touching
washing Num 19 7 after w. his garments and body

2 K 11 2 he saw . . . a woman washing herself
Cant 4 2 shorn, which come up from the washing
6 5 sheep, which come up from the washing
Eccu 34 30 him again, what doth his washing avail
Dan 13 17 bring me oil and washing balls and
Zach 13 1 for the washing of the sinner and of
Mark 7 3 eat not without often w. their hands
Luke 5 2 and were washing their nets. And
washings Mark 7 4 w. of cups and of pots. 8
Heb 9 10 divers washings, and justices of the
wasps Wisd 12 8 didst send wasps, forerunners of
wast Apoc 11 17 who art and who wast and who art
Apoc 16 5 who art and who wast, the Holy One
waste Gen 9 11 henceforth a flood to w. the earth
Lev 26 16 heat, which shall waste your eyes and
Num 24 17 shall waste all the children of Seth
24 and shall waste the Hebrews and at the
33 52 statues and waste all their high places
Judg 11 12 art come against me, to waste my land
3 K 17 14 the pot of meal shall not waste, nor
1 Pa 17 9 shall the children of iniquity w. them
2 Pa 6 28 or if their enemies waste the country
26 10 plains and in the waste of the desert
Ps 38 12 thou has made his soul to waste away
Isa 34 10 generation to generation it shall lie w.
Eccu 21 5 injuries and wrongs will waste riches
Isa 34 10 it shall lie waste, none shall pass
49 17 that destroy thee and make thee waste
61 4 build the places that have been waste
Jer 1 10 to pull down and to waste and to
30 16 they that waste thee shall be wasted
44 6 they are turned to desolation and waste
48 2 Oronaim: waste and great destruction
49 28 and waste the children of the east
50 10 all that waste her shall be filled
21 waste, and destroy all behind them
Eze 14 15 beasts also upon the land to waste it
26 12 they shall waste thy riches, they shall
32 12 they shall waste the pride of Egypt
33 29 when I shall have made their land waste
35 3 I will make thee desolate and waste
7 and I will make mount Seir waste and
36 34 shall be tilled, which before was waste
38 so shall the waste cities be full of
38 8 which have been continually waste: but
Dan 9 26 and the end thereof shall be waste
Amos 5 9 the strong, and waste upon the mighty
Mat 26 8 to what purpose is this waste? For
Mark 14 4 why was this w. of the ointment made
laid waste; *see* **laid**
lay waste; *see* **lay**
wasted Num 32 39 went into Galaad and wasted it
Deut 28 39 because it shall be wasted with worms
Josu 10 42 lands he took and wasted at one onset
Judg 6 4 w. all things as they were in the blade
10 9 children of Ammon . . . wasted Juda and
1 K 27 9 David wasted all the land and left
2 K 12 28 when the city shall be wasted by me
3 K 17 16 the pot of meal wasted not, and the
1 Pa 20 1 w. the land of the children of Ammon
2 Pa 21 17 into the land of Juda and wasted it
19 being wasted with a long consumption
Job 17 1 my spirit shall be wasted, my days
18 12 let his strength be wasted with famine
Ps 30 11 my life is wasted with grief: and my
Wisd 19 20 the flames wasted not the flesh of
Isa 1 7 desolate as when wasted by enemies
5 5 hedge thereof, and it shall be wasted
6 11 he said: Until the cities be wasted
17 14 portion of them that have wasted us
19 5 and the river shall be wasted and dry
42 22 is a people that is robbed and wasted
60 12 Gentiles shall be w. with desolation
Jer 9 19 how are we w. and greatly confounded
25 36 the Lord hath wasted their pastures
30 16 they that waste thee shall be wasted
47 4 the Lord hath wasted the Philistines
48 20 tell ye it in Arnon, that Moab is w.
49 3 howl, O Hesebon, for Hai is wasted
Lam 1 13 me desolate, wasted with sorrow all
3 51 my eye hath wasted my soul because
Eze 29 10 utterly desolate and w. by the sword
30 7 midst of the cities that are wasted
38 12 hand upon them that had been wasted
Osee 7 13 they shall be wasted because they have
Joel 1 10 for the corn is wasted, the wine is
1 Ma 15 29 their borders you wasted, and you
Luke 15 13 there wasted his substance, living
16 1 that he had wasted his goods. And he
Gal 1 13 I persecuted church of God, and w. it
wastes Isa 44 26 I will raise up the w. thereof
Jer 49 13 her cities shall be everlasting wastes
wasteth Prov 18 9 of him that w. his own works
Eccu 38 29 vapor of the fire w. his flesh and
wasting Gen 34 28 w. all they had in their houses
Exod 10 15 face of the earth, wasting all things
Deut 3 4 wasting all his cities at one time
Judg 6 5 wasting whatsoever they touched. And
9 27 into the fields, wasting the vineyards
Isa 59 7 w. and destruction are in their ways
60 18 wasting nor destruction in thy borders
watch Exod 14 24 now the morning watch was come
Num 1 53 they shall keep watch and guard the
3 6 let them watch, and observe whatsoever
32 that w. for the guard of the sanctuary
18 3 Levites shall watch to do thy commands
4 watch in the charge of the tabernacle
5 watch ye in the charge of the sanctuary
31 30 Levites that watch in the charge of
Judg 7 11 where was the watch of men in arms
19 at the beginning of the midnight watch
1 K 11 11 midst of camp in the morning watch
19 11 guards to David's house to watch him
2 K 13 34 and the young man that kept the watch
3 K 14 27 them that kept watch before the gate
4 K 11 6 and keep the watch of the king's house
6 keep the watch of the house of Messa
7 keep the watch of the house of the Lord
2 Pa 20 24 and when Juda came to the watch tower
1 Es 8 29 w. ye and keep them, till you deliver
2 Es 12 38 they stood still in the watch gate
44 they kept the watch of their God and
Jdth 4 5 keep watch where the way was narrow
7 11 when they had kept this watch for full
13 5 without before the chamber and to w.
Jon 21 32 and shall watch in the heap of the dead
Ps 36 12 the sinner shall watch the just man
55 7 hide themselves: they will w. my heel
62 2 to thee do I watch at break of day
89 4 and as a watch in the night, things
129 6 from the morning watch even until night
140 3 set a watch, O Lord, before my mouth
Prov 8 17 that in the morning early watch for me
Eccu 1 38 watch over them, lest thou fall, and
4 13 that watch for her, shall embrace her
19 9 hearken to thee and will watch thee
26 13 on a daughter . . . set a strict watch
37 18 that sit in a high place to watch. But
40 6 sleep, as in the day of keeping watch
42 11 keep a sure watch over a shameless
Isa 26 9 the morning early I will watch to thee
Jer 1 12 I will watch over my word to perform
31 28 so will I watch over them, to build
44 27 I will watch over them for evil and
51 12 set up the standard, strengthen the w.
Eze 40 45 priests that watch in the wards of the

46 priests that watch over the ministry
Nah 2 1 watch the way, fortify thy loins
Haba 2 1 I will stand upon my watch and fix
1 I will watch to see what will be said
1 Ma 12 27 commanded his men to watch and to be
Mat 14 25 fourth watch of the night. Mark 6:48
24 42 w. ye therefore, because you know. 25:13
43 would come, he would certainly watch
26 38 you here and watch with me. Mark 14:34
40 could you not watch one hour with me
41 w. ye and pray that ye enter. Mark 14:38
Mark 13 33 take ye heed, watch and pray. For ye
34 and commanded the porter to watch
35 watch ye, therefore, for you know not
37 what I say to you, I say to all: Watch
14 37 couldst thou not watch one hour? Watch
Luke 12 38 if he shall come in the second watch
38 or come in the third watch, and find
39 he would surely watch and would not
20 20 being upon the watch, they sent spies
21 36 watch ye, therefore, praying at all
Acts 20 31 watch, keeping in memory, that for three
1 C 16 13 watch ye, stand fast in the faith, do
1 Th 5 6 do; but let us watch and be sober. For
10 that, whether we watch or sleep, we may
Heb 13 17 they w. as being to render an account
1 P 4 7 prudent therefore, and w. in prayers
5 8 be sober and watch: because your
Apoc 3 3 if then thou shalt not watch, I will
watched Exod 38 8 the women that w. at the door
Num 31 47 Levites that watched in the tabernacle
Tob 11 6 and while she watched his coming from
Ps 58 1 when Saul sent and watched his house
70 10 they that watched my soul have consulted
101 8 I have w. and am become as a sparrow
Isa 29 20 all cut off that watched for iniquity
Jer 31 28 as I have watched over them, to pluck
Lam 1 14 the yoke of my iniquities hath watched
Bar 2 9 Lord hath watched over us for evil
Dan 9 14 the Lord hath watched upon the evil
13 12 they watched carefully every day to see
15 as they watched a fit day, she went in
Osee 5 1 them whom you should have watched over
2 Ma 14 29 he watched an opportunity to comply
Mat 27 36 and they sat and watched him. And they
Mark 3 2 they watched him whether he would heal
Luke 6 7 w. if he would heal on the sabbath
14 1 they watched him. And behold, there
Acts 9 24 they w. the gates also day and night
watcher Dan 4 10 a w. and a holy one came down
Dan 4 20 the king saw a watcher and a holy one
watchers Dan 4 14 by the sentence of the w. and
watches Lev 8 35 observing the w. of the Lord
Num 9 19 kept the watches of the Lord. 23
1 Pa 9 27 and they abode in their watches round
2 Pa 23 6 people keep the watches of the Lord
Ps 76 5 my eyes prevented the watches. I was
Wisd 14 23 or keep watches full of madness. So
43 11 and shall never fail in their watches
Lam 2 19 night, in the beginning of the watches
Bar 3 34 the stars have given light in their w.
Luke 2 8 keeping the night w. over their flock
watcheth Ps 36 32 the wicked watcheth the just man
Ps 126 1 he watcheth in vain that keepeth it
Prov 8 34 and that watcheth daily at my gates
Cant 5 2 I sleep, and my heart watcheth: the
Wisd 6 16 w. for her, shall quickly be secure
Jer 5 6 a leopard watcheth for their cities
Apoc 16 15 blessed is he that watcheth and keepeth
watchful Apoc 3 2 be w. and strengthen the
watchfulness Prov 4 23 with all w. keep thy heart
watching Judg 16 2 and w. there all the night in
1 K 4 13 upon a stool over against the way w.
Job 24 5 by w. for a prey they get bread for
Eccu 31 1 w. for riches consumeth the flesh, and
23 w. and choler and gripes are with an
38 28 by his watching shall finish the work
31 watching to polish them to perfection
34 his watching to make clean the furnace
Jer 1 11 and I said: I see a rod watching. And
Dan 6 11 those men carefully watching him, found
2 Ma 2 27 a business full of watching and sweat
Mat 27 54 that were with him watching Jesus
Luke 2 8 in the same country shepherds w. and
12 37 when he cometh, shall find watching
Eph 6 18 in the same watching with all instance
Col 4 2 prayer; watching in it with thanksgiving
watchings 2 C 6 5 in labors, in w., in fastings
2 C 11 27 in much watchings, in hunger and thirst
watchman 2 K 18 24 w. that was on the top of gate
2 K 18 26 the watchman saw another man running
27 w. said: The running of the foremost
4 K 9 17 watchman . . . saw the troop of Jehu
18 w. told, saying: The messenger came
20 w. told, saying: He came even to them
Isa 21 6 Lord said to me: Go and set a watchman
11 watchman, what of the night? Watchman
12 the watchman said: The morning cometh
Eze 3 17 made thee a w. to house of Israel. 33:7
33 2 and make him a watchman over them: and
6 if the w. see the sword coming, and
6 his blood at the hand of the watchman
Osee 9 8 the w. of Ephraim was with my God: the
watchmen Judg 7 19 w. being alarmed, they began
1 K 14 16 the watchmen of Saul, who were in Gabaa
4 K 17 9 from the tower of the watchmen. 18:8
2 Es 4 9 and set watchmen upon the wall day and
23 the watchmen that followed me did not
7 3 I set watchmen of the inhabitants of
Jdth 10 11 the watchmen of the Assyrians met her
13 13 cried to the watchmen upon the walls
14 3 the watchmen must needs run to awake
Cant 3 3 the watchmen who keep the city found me
Eccu 37 18 more than seven watchmen that sit in
Isa 52 8 voice of thy watchmen: they have lifted
56 10 his watchmen are all blind, they are
62 6 I have appointed watchmen all the day
Jer 6 17 I appointed watchmen over you, saying
31 6 w. on mount Ephraim shall cry: Arise
51 12 set up the w., prepare the ambushes
watchtower Isa 21 5 in the w. them that eat and
Isa 21 8 and a lion cried out: I am upon the w.
Jer 31 21 set thee up a watchtower, make to thee
watchword 2 Ma 8 23 for a w., The help of God
2 Ma 13 15 for a watchword, The victory of God
water Mat 3 11 I indeed baptize you in water unto
Mat 3 16 forthwith came out of the water: and
8 18 gave orders to pass over the water
28 come on the other side of the water
9 1 he passed over the water and came into
10 42 a cup of cold water only in the name
14 22 to go before him over the water, till
29 walked upon the water to come to Jesus
16 5 disciples were come over the water
17 14 into the fire, and often into the water
27 24 taking water washed his hands before
Mark 1 8 I have baptized you with water; but
10 coming out of the water, he saw the
6 45 might go before him over the water to
8 13 passed to the other side of the water
9 40 to drink a cup of water in my name
14 13 man carrying a pitcher of w. Luke 22:10
Luke 3 16 I indeed baptize you with water; but
7 44 thou gavest me no water for my feet
8 24 the wind and the rage of the water
11 24 walketh through places without water

13 15 the manger, and lead them to water
16 24 may dip the tip of his finger in water
John 1 26 I baptize with water; but there hath
31 am I come baptizing with water. And
33 he who sent me to baptize with water
2 7 fill the waterpots with water. And
9 had tasted the water made wine, and
9 waiters knew who had drawn the water
3 5 unless a man be born again of water
23 because there was much water there
4 7 a woman of Samaria to draw water
10 he would have given thee living water
11 whence then hast thou living water
13 drinketh of this water, shall thirst
13 the water that I will give him. 14
14 shall become in him a fountain of w.
15 give me this water, that I may not
46 where he made the water wine. And
5 3 waiting for the moving of the water
4 the water was moved. And he that went
4 pond after the motion of the water
7 have no man, when the water is troubled
7 38 shall flow rivers of living water
13 5 he putteth water into a basin and
19 34 there came out blood and water. And
Acts 1 5 John indeed baptized with water. 11:16
8 36 they came to a certain water; and the
36 see, here is water: what doth hinder
38 they went down into the water, both
39 when they were come up out of the water
10 47 can any man forbid water, that these
Eph 5 26 by the laver of w. in the word of life
1 Tim 5 23 do not still drink water, but use a
9 19 goats, with water and scarlet wool and
10 22 and our bodies washed with clean water
James 3 11 the same hole, sweet and bitter water
12 neither can the salt water yield sweet
1 P 3 20 eight souls, were saved by water
2 P 2 17 these are fountains without water and
3 5 the earth out of w. and through w.
6 being overflowed with water, perished
1 J 5 6 that came by water and blood, Jesus
6 not by w. only, but by w. and blood
8 the spirit and the water and the blood
Jude 12 clouds without water, which are carried
Apoc 12 15 out of his mouth after the woman, water
16 12 and dried up the water thereof, that a
21 6 of the fountain of the water of life
22 1 he showed me a river of water of life
17 let him take the water of life, freely
watered Gen 13 10 which was watered throughout
Gen 24 46 I drank, and she watered the camels
29 2 the beasts were watered out of it, and
3 after the sheep were watered, to put
11 having watered the flock, he kissed her
Exod 2 17 defending the maids, w. their sheep
Num 24 6 as watered gardens near the rivers
Josu 15 19 give me also a land that is watered
Ps 64 10 the earth, and hast plentifully w. it
Eccu 39 28 and as a flood hath watered the earth
Isa 58 11 thou shalt be like a watered garden
Jer 31 12 their soul shall be as a watered garden
Eze 31 14 any of them that are watered stand up
1 C 3 6 I have planted, Apollo watered, but God
waterest Ps 103 13 w. the hills from thy upper
watereth Josu 13 3 troubled river, that w. Egypt
Job 5 10 and watereth all things with waters
1 C 3 7 planteth is anything, nor he that w.
8 he that planteth, and he that w., are
watering Gen 2 6 w. all the surface of the
waterpot John 4 28 left her w. and went her way
waterpots John 2 6 there six waterpots of stone
John 2 7 fill the waterpots with water. And
waters Mat 8 32 they perished in the waters. And they
Mat 14 28 bid me come to thee upon the waters
Mark 9 21 fire and into waters to destroy him
2 C 11 26 in journeying often, in perils of waters
Apoc 1 15 his voice as the sound of many w.
7 17 to the fountains of the waters of life
8 10 rivers and upon the fountains of waters
11 part of the waters became wormwood
11 many men died of the waters, because
11 6 they have power over waters to turn
14 2 as the noise of many waters and as
14 7 the sea and the fountains of waters
16 4 the rivers and the fountains of waters
5 I heard the angel of the waters saying
17 1 harlot, who sitteth upon many waters
17 15 the waters which thou sawest where the
19 6 as the voice of many waters, and as the
waterside Num 24 6 as cedars by the waterside
watery Josu 15 19 upper and the nether w. ground
Judg 1 15 dry land: give me also a watery land
Isa 19 10 and its watery places shall be dry
wave Eccu 29 23 tossed them as a wave of the sea
Jer 51 55 their wave shall roar like many waters
James 1 6 is like a wave of the sea, which is
waver Ps 54 23 shall not suffer the just to w.
Isa 29 9 and wonder, waver and stagger: be drunk
wavereth James 1 6 that w. is like a wave of the
wavering Heb 10 23 of our hope without wavering
James 1 6 let him ask in faith, nothing wavering
waves Exod 14 27 them up in the middle of the w.
Job 9 8 and walketh upon the waves of the sea
30 12 have overwhelmed me . . . as with waves
31 23 feared God, as waves swelling over me
38 11 here thou shalt break thy swelling w.
Ps 64 8 depth of the sea, the noise of its w.
87 8 all thy waves thou hast brought in upon
88 10 and appeasest the motion of the waves
92 3 the floods have lifted up their waves
106 25 and the waves thereof were lifted up
29 into a breeze: and its waves were still
Wisd 5 10 as a ship that passeth through the w.
14 1 his voyage through the raging waves
3 and a most sure path among the waves
Eccu 24 8 have walked in the waves of the sea
Isa 48 18 thy justice as the waves of the sea
51 15 the sea, and the waves thereof swell
57 20 waves thereof cast up dirt and mire
Jer 5 22 the waves thereof shall toss themselves
31 35 the sea, and the waves thereof roar
46 8 waves thereof shall be moved as rivers
51 42 is covered with the multitude of the w.
Eze 26 3 to thee as the waves of the sea rise up
Jon 2 4 and thy waves have passed over me
Zach 10 11 and shall strike the waves in the sea
2 Ma 9 8 to command even the waves of the sea
Mat 8 24 so that the boat was covered with waves
14 24 was tossed with the waves: for the wind
Mark 4 37 and the waves beat into the ship, so
Luke 21 25 roaring of the sea and of the waves
Jude 13 raging waves of the sea, foaming out
wax Jdth 16 18 the rocks shall melt as wax before
Job 39 26 doth the hawk wax feathered by thy
Ps 21 15 my heart is become like wax melting
57 9 like wax that melteth, they shall be
67 3 as wax melteth before the fire, so let
96 5 the mountains melted like wax at the
Mich 1 4 shall be cleft, as wax before the fire
waxed Luke 2 40 the child grew, and waxed strong
way Mat 2 12 they went back another way into
Mat 3 3 prepare ye way of the Lord. Mark 1:13
4 15 the way of the sea beyond the Jordan
7 13 broad is the way that leadeth to
14 strait is the way that leadeth to life

8 28 so that none could pass by that way
10 5 ye not into the way of the Gentiles
11 7 when they went their way, Jesus began
20 5 and they went their way. And again he
22 16 teachest the way of God in truth. Mark 12:14; Luke 20:21
Mark 1 2 who shall prepare the way before thee
6 8 they should take nothing for the way
10 17 when he was gone forth into the way
11 4 going their way, they found the colt
12 12 and leaving him, they went their way
14 16 his disciples went their way and came
Luke 1 79 direct our feet into the way of peace
3 4 prepare ye the way of the Lord, make
5 19 they could not find by what way they
8 14 going their way, are choked with the
10 4 shoes; and salute no man by the way
31 certain priest went down the same way
15 20 when he was yet a great way off, his
19 4 see him; for he was to pass that way
32 they that were sent, went their way
John 1 23 make straight the way of the Lord
4 28 went her way into the city and saith
10 1 but climbeth up another way, the same
14 4 and the way you know. Thomas saith
5 goest; and how can we know the way
6 I am the way and the truth and the
18 8 you seek me, let these go their way
Acts 8 26 way that goeth down from Jerusalem
36 as they went on their way, they came
9 2 he found any men and women of this way
15 3 being brought on their way by church
16 17 who preach unto you way of salvation
18 26 expounded to him the way of the Lord
19 9 speaking evil of the way of the Lord
23 disturbance about the way of the Lord
21 5 they all bringing us on our way, with
22 4 who persecuted this way unto death
24 14 that according to the way, which they
22 certain knowledge of this way, saying
Rom 3 2 much every way. First indeed, because
12 all have turned out of the way; they are
17 the way of peace they have not known
14 13 or a scandal in your brother's way. I
15 24 be brought on my way thither by you, if
1 C 12 31 I show unto you yet a more excellent way
16 6 me on my way whithersoever I shall go
7 I will not see you now by the way, for
2 C 1 16 to be brought on my way towards Judea
12 11 for I have no way come short of them
Col 2 14 he hath taken the same out of the way
1 Th 3 11 Jesus Christ, direct our way unto you
Heb 9 8 the way into the holies was not yet made
10 20 Christ; a new and living way which he
12 13 no one, halting, may go out of the way
James 2 25 and sending them out another way? For
2 P 2 2 way of truth shall be evil spoken of
15 leaving the right way they have gone
15 having followed the way of Balaam of
21 not to have known the way of justice
3 1 I stir up by way of admonition your
3 J 6 do well to bring forward on their way
his way Mat 13 25 cockle among the wheat and went his way
Mat 13 46 went his way and sold all that he had
25 16 went his way and traded with the same
18 going his way digged into the earth and
27 60 of the monument, and went his way
Mark 2 12 taking up his bed, went his way in the
5 20 he went his way and began to publish
Luke 4 30 through midst of them, went his way
50 the man believed . . . and went his way
5 15 the man went his way and told the Jews
Acts 8 39 and he went on his way rejoicing. But
9 17 Ananias went his way, and entered
20 38 they brought him on his way to the ship
1 C 16 11 but conduct ye him on his way in peace
James 1 24 he beheld himself and went his way
5 20 converted from the error of his way
in the way Mat 5 25 whilst thou art in the way. Luke 12:58
Mat 15 32 fasting, lest they faint in the way
21 8 spread their garments i. . . . Mark 11:8
8 trees and strewed them i. . . . Mark 11:8
32 John came to you in the way of justice
Mark 8 3 their home, they will faint in the way
27 in the way he asked his disciples
9 32 what did you treat of in the way
33 in the way they had disputed among
10 32 were in the way going up to Jerusalem
52 he saw, and followed him in the way
Luke 9 57 as they walked i. . . . that a certain
19 36 their clothes underneath in the way
24 32 within us, whilst he spoke in the way
35 told what things were done in the way
Acts 9 17 he that appeared to thee in the way as
18 25 instructed in the way of the Lord; and
25 3 laying wait to kill him in the way. But
26 13 I saw in the way light from heaven above
Jude 11 for they have gone in the way of Cain
thy way Mat 11 10 who shall prepare thy way
Mat 20 14 take what is thine, and go thy way
Mark 7 29 for this saying go thy way, the devil
10 52 go thy way, thy faith hath made thee
Luke 7 27 who shall prepare thy way before thee
8 48 made thee whole; go thy way in peace
17 19 go thy way, thy faith hath made thee
John 4 50 go thy way; thy son liveth. The man
Acts 9 15 the Lord said to him: Go thy way; for
24 25 for this time, go thy way: but when I
wayfaring Jer 9 2 a lodging place of w. men
Jer 14 8 and as a w. man turning in to lodge
ways Mat 22 5 they neglected, and went their w.
Mat 22 10 his servants going forth into the ways
22 leaving him, went their ways. That day
Mark 11 4 without, in the meeting of two ways
Luke 1 76 face of the Lord to prepare his ways
3 5 straight; and the rough ways plain
Acts 2 28 hast made known to me the ways of life
13 10 pervert the right ways of the Lord
14 15 suffered . . . to walk in their own ways
Rom 3 16 destruction and misery in their ways
11 33 and how unsearchable his ways! For who
1 C 4 17 who will put you in mind of my ways
Heb 3 10 and they have not known my ways
James 1 8 is inconstant in all his ways. But let
11 the rich man fade away in his ways
Apoc 15 3 just and true are thy ways, O king of
wayside Ps 139 6 a stumblingblock by the w.
Mat 13 4 some fell by the w. Mark 4:4; Luke 8:5
19 he that received the seed by the w.
20 30 two blind men sitting by the wayside
21 19 fig tree by the wayside, he came to it
Mark 4 15 these are they by the wayside, where
10 46 sat by the wayside begging. Luke 18:35
Luke 8 12 they by the wayside are they that
weak Lev 25 35 impoverished and weak of hand
Num 13 19 whether they be strong or weak: few in
Judg 16 7 moist, I shall be weak like other men
11 I shall be weak and like other men
13 it in the ground, I shall be weak
17 I shall become weak and shall be like
20 36 they saw themselves to be too weak
1 K 2 4 and the weak are girt with strength
2 K 17 2 for he is now weary and weak handed
4 K 19 26 inhabitants of them were weak of hand

2 Pa 34 10 the temple, and mend all that was weak
Job 26 2 art thou? Is it of him that is weak
Ps 6 3 mercy on me, O Lord, for I am weak
63 9 tongues against them are made weak. All
Prov 30 26 the rabbit, a weak people, which maketh
Wisd 9 5 a weak man and of short time, and
13 18 he maketh supplication to the weak
Eccu 11 12 is very weak in ability and full of
30 14 a rich man who is weak and afflicted
Isa 35 3 hands, and confirm the weak knees. Say
37 27 inhabitants of them were weak of hand
Jer 15 9 that hath borne seven is become weak
20 11 shall fall and shall be weak: they
Bar 6 35 nor save the weak from the mighty
Eze 34 4 the weak you have not strengthened
16 will strengthen that which was weak
21 struck all the weak cattle with your
Joel 3 10 spears. Let the weak say: I am strong
Mich 1 12 for she is become weak unto good that
Mat 26 41 is willing, but the flesh w. Mark 14:38
Acts 20 35 so laboring you ought to support weak
Rom 4 19 he was not weak in faith; neither did
5 6 when as yet we were weak, according to
8 3 in that it was weak through the flesh
14 1 him that is weak in faith, take unto you
2 but he that is weak, let him eat herbs
21 or scandalized or made weak. Hast thou
15 1 to bear the infirmities of the weak, and
1 C 1 27 the weak things of world hath God chosen
4 10 we are weak, but you are strong; you
8 7 and their conscience, being weak, is
9 liberty become stumblingblock to weak
10 shall not his conscience, being weak, be
11 the weak brother perish for whom Christ
12 and wound their weak conscience, you sin
9 22 to the weak I became weak, that I might gain the weak
11 30 are there many infirm and weak among you
2 C 10 10 but his bodily presence is weak, and his
11 21 we had been weak in this part. Wherein
29 who is weak, and I am not weak? Who is
12 10 for when I am weak, then am I powerful
13 3 in me, who towards you is not weak, but
4 for we also are weak in him: but we
9 we rejoice that we are weak, and you are
Gal 4 9 how turn you again to the weak and needy
1 Th 5 14 support the weak, be patient towards all
Heb 5 11 because you are become weak to hear
weakened Deut 32 36 shall see that their hand is w.
1 K 2 5 she that had many children is weakened
2 K 4 1 and his hands were weakened, and all
2 Pa 15 7 and let not your hands be weakened
Jdth 16 8 weakened him with the beauty of her face
Ps 9 4 they shall be w. and perish before thy
17 37 steps under me: and my feet are not w.
25 1 in the Lord, and shall not be weakened
26 2 have themselves been w. and have fallen
30 11 my strength is w. through poverty, and
57 8 he hath bent his bow till they be w.
67 10 was w., but thou hast made it perfect
106 12 they were w., and there was none to
108 24 my knees are weakened through fasting
Isa 24 4 earth . . . faded away and is weakened
4 height of the people of the earth is w.
38 14 my eyes are weakened looking upward
Jer 51 56 are taken and their bow is weakened
Lam 1 14 my strength is weakened: the Lord hath
Eze 19 5 seeing herself weakened and that her
Soph 3 16 to Sion: Let not thy hand be weakened
weakenest Eze 29 7 brokest and w. all their loins
weakeneth Jer 38 4 w. the hands of the men of war
weaker Gen 42 9 are come to view the w. parts
Eccu 24 38 a weaker shall not search her out
1 P 3 7 to the female as to the weaker vessel
weakness Ecce 10 18 through w. of hands, the house
Isa 8 22 and behold . . . weakness and distress
1 C 1 25 and the w. of God is stronger than men
2 3 and I was with you in weakness, and in
15 43 it is sown in w., it shall rise in
2 C 13 4 he was crucified through weakness, yet
Heb 7 18 because of the w. and unprofitableness
11 34 recovered strength from w., became
wealth 2 Pa 1 11 hast not asked riches and wealth
2 Pa 1 12 and I will give thee riches and wealth
Job 21 13 they spend their days in wealth, and
Ps 111 3 glory and wealth shall be in his house
Prov 24 4 with all precious and most beautiful w.
Ecce 2 8 and the wealth of kings and provinces
Eccu 10 33 a man that is honored for his wealth
34 in poverty, how much more in wealth
34 glorified in w., let him fear poverty
wealthy Job 16 13 that was formerly so wealthy
Isa 32 18 of confidence and in wealthy rest. But
Amos 6 1 woe to you that are wealthy in Sion
Zach 1 15 great anger with the wealthy nations
7 7 as yet was inhabited and was wealthy
Apoc 3 17 thou sayest: I am rich and made wealthy
wean 1 K 1 23 stay till thou wean him [Samuel]
weaned Gen 21 8 the child grew and was weaned
1 K 1 22 I will not go till the child be weaned
23 gave her son suck, till she weaned him
24 after she had weaned him, she carried
Job 39 4 their young are weaned and go to feed
Ps 130 2 as a child that is weaned is towards
Isa 11 8 the weaned child shall thrust his hand
28 9 them that are weaned from the milk
Osee 1 8 w. her that was called Without mercy
weaning Gen 21 8 feast on the day of his weaning
weapon Isa 54 17 no weapon that is formed against
Eze 9 1 every one hath a destroying weapon
2 each one had his weapon of destruction
weapons 1 K 21 8 sword nor my own w. with me
2 K 1 27 fallen, and the weapons of war perished
4 K 11 8 having weapons in your hands: and if
11 every one their weapons in their hands
Job 20 24 he shall flee from weapons of iron
Ps 45 10 shall destroy the bow and break the w.
56 5 whose teeth are weapons and arrows
Ecce 9 18 better is wisdom than weapons of war
Jer 21 4 I will turn back the weapons of war
22 7 against thee the destroyer and his w.
50 25 brought forth the weapons of his wrath
51 20 dashest together for me the w. of war
Eze 32 27 that went down to hell with their w.
39 9 shall set on fire and burn the weapons
10 they shall burn the weapons with fire
1 Ma 5 43 they threw away their w. and fled. 7:44
9 39 and musical instruments and many w.
16 16 and his men rose up and took their w.
2 Ma 8 18 they trust in their weapons and in
John 18 3 with lanterns and torches and weapons
2 C 10 4 the w. of our warfare are not carnal
wear Exod 29 30 sanctuary, shall w. it seven days
Exod 39 1 for Aaron to wear when he ministered
Lev 19 10 thou shalt not wear a garment that is woven of. Deut 22:11
Judg 8 24 were accustomed to wear golden earlets
1 K 2 28 and to wear the ephod before me: and I
Job 14 19 waters wear away the stones, and with
Eccu 6 36 let thy foot wear the steps of his
Isa 4 1 own bread, and wear our own apparel
14 23 I will sweep it and wear it out with
Eze 44 20 shave their heads, nor wear long hair
1 Ma 11 58 purple, and to wear a golden buckle
14 44 purple, or to wear a buckle of gold
weareth Lev 15 17 the garment or skin that he w.

Eccu 40 4 from him that weareth purple and
wearied Judg 16 16 soul fainted away and was w.
1 K 14 31 the people were wearied exceedingly
Tob 2 10 being wearied with burying, he came to
Jdth 7 9 being wearied out they will yield up
22 when being wearied with these cries
9 7 over their camp and darkness w. them
Job 3 17 there the w. in strength are at rest
Wisd 5 7 we w. ourselves in the way of iniquity
Eccu 22 16 shalt not be w. out with his folly
Isa 16 12 when it is seen that Moab is wearied
33 1 being w. thou shalt cease to despise
43 23 oblations, nor w. thee with incense
24 hast wearied me with thy iniquities
57 10 hast been wearied in the multitude of
Jer 12 5 if thou hast been wearied with running
20 9 I was wearied, not being able to bear
45 3 I am wearied with my groans, and I
Mala 2 17 you have wearied the Lord with your
17 wherein have we wearied him? In that
1 Ma 10 82 the horsemen were wearied: and they
John 4 6 wearied with his journey, sat thus on
Heb 12 3 be not wearied, fainting in your minds
5 neither be thou wearied whilst thou
weariness Isa 46 1 of heavy weight even unto w.
wearing 1 P 3 3 the w. of gold or the putting
wearisome Job 7 3 numbered to myself w. nights
Phil 3 1 to you, to me indeed is not wearisome
weary Gen 27 46 I am weary of my life because of
Exod 17 12 his hands were not weary until sunset
Num 21 4 began to be weary of their journey and
30 they came weary to Nophe and unto
Deut 25 18 who sat down, being weary, when thou
Judg 8 4 were so w. that they could not pursue
15 to the men that are weary and faint
1 K 30 9 and some being weary stayed there
10 being w. could not go over the torrent
21 who being weary had stayed and were
2 K 16 14 and all the people with him came w.
17 2 for he [David] is now weary and weak
23 10 till his hand was weary and grew stiff
4 K 10 32 the Lord began to be weary of Israel
Job 4 3 thou hast strengthened the weary hands
9 21 ignorant of and I shall be w. of my life
10 1 my soul is weary of my life, I will
22 7 thou hast not given water to the weary
Prov 24 10 being weary in the day of distress
Ecce 2 17 and therefore I was weary of my life
Eccu 23 24 he will not be weary of sinning unto
43 34 all your strength, and be not weary
Isa 1 14 I am weary of bearing them. And when
28 12 this is my rest, refresh the weary, and
40 29 he that giveth strength to the weary
31 they shall run and not be weary, they
44 12 shall drink no water and shall be weary
50 4 to uphold by word him that is weary
Jer 6 11 I am weary with holding in: pour it
15 6 I am weary of entreating thee. And I
31 25 for I have inebriated the weary soul
Lam 5 5 we were weary and no rest was given
2 Ma 12 36 had fought long and were weary, Judas
Luke 18 5 lest continually coming, she weary me
2 C 1 8 so that we were weary even of life. But
2 Th 3 13 brethren, be not weary in well doing
weasel Lev 11 29 the weasel and the mouse and the
weather Prov 25 20 looseth his garment in cold w.
Eccu 3 17 as the ice in the fair warm weather
Dan 13 15 in the orchard: for it was hot weather
Mat 16 2 you say, It will be fair weather
weave Exod 35 35 linen and to weave all things
weaver Job 7 6 than the web is cut by the w.
Isa 38 12 my life is cut off, as by a weaver
weaver's 1 K 17 7 spear was like a weaver's beam. 2 K 21:19; 1 Pa 20:5
1 Pa 11 23 who had a spear like a weaver's beam
weaving Tob 2 19 Anna his wife went daily to w.
Isa 19 9 flax, combing and weaving fine linen
web Job 7 6 than the web is cut by the weaver
Job 8 14 trust shall be like the spider's web
Isa 25 7 the web that he began over all nations
30 1 would begin a web, and not by my spirit
webs Judg 16 12 broke the bands like threads of w.
Isa 59 5 and have woven the webs of spiders
6 their webs shall not be for clothing
Osee 8 6 shall be turned to spiders' webs. For
wedding Judg 14 15 have you called us to the w.
Tob 9 3 and desire him to come to my wedding
7 made him come with him to the wedding
Esth 2 18 for the marriage and wedding of Esther
Mat 22 11 man who had not on a wedding garment
12 not having on a wedding garment? But he
Luke 12 36 when he shall return from the wedding
14 8 when thou art invited to a wedding
wedlock Ruth 1 12 with age, and not fit for w.
Tob 8 4 over, we will be in our own wedlock
weed Eccu 40 16 the weed growing over every water
week Gen 29 27 the week of days of this match
Gen 29 28 after the week was past, he married
Lev 23 16 unto the morrow after the seventh week
2 Pa 23 8 to succeed one another every week
Ps 23 8 on the first day of the week, a psalm
47 1 of Core, on the second day of the week
93 1 himself on the fourth day of the week
Dan 9 27 the covenant with many, in one week
27 in the half of the week the victim
Mat 28 1 first day of the w. Mark 16:2, 9; Luke 24:1; John 20:1; Acts 20:7; 1 C 16:2
Luke 18 12 I fast twice in a week: I give tithes
John 20 19 that same day, the first of the week
weeks Exod 34 22 shalt keep the feast of weeks
Lev 12 5 she shall be unclean two w. according
23 15 of the firstfruits, seven full weeks
25 7 number to thee seven weeks of years
Num 28 26 when after the weeks are accomplished
Deut 16 9 shalt number unto thee seven weeks
10 shalt celebrate the festival of weeks
16 unleavened bread in the feast of weeks
2 Pa 8 13 bread and in the feast of weeks and
Tob 8 23 adjured Tobias to abide with him two w.
Dan 9 24 seventy weeks are shortened upon thy
25 there shall be 7 weeks and 62 weeks
26 after 62 weeks Christ shall be slain
10 2 I Daniel mourned the days of 3 weeks
3 till the days of three weeks were
2 Ma 12 31 the feast of the weeks being at hand
weep Gen 23 2 Abraham came to mourn and weep for
Num 11 13 they weep against me, saying: Give us
Judg 21 2 and began to lament and weep, saying
Ruth 1 9 lifted up their voice and began to w. 14
1 K 11 5 what aileth the people that they weep
2 K 1 24 ye daughters of Israel, weep over Saul
12 21 thou didst fast and weep for the child
4 K 8 12 why doth my lord weep? And he said
2 Es 8 9 do not mourn nor weep: for all the
Tob 5 23 his mother began to weep and to say
26 weep not, our son will arrive thither
10 3 and they began both to weep together
11 11 his wife, and they began to weep for joy
Job 27 15 in death, and his widows shall not weep
30 31 organ into the voice of those that weep
Ps 94 6 and weep before the Lord that made us
Ecce 3 4 a time to weep and a time to laugh
Eccu 7 38 in comforting them that weep, and
22 10 weep for the dead, for his light hath

10 w. for the fool, for his understanding
11 weep but a little for the dead, for
31 15 shall it weep over all the face when
38 17 weep bitterly for a day, and then
Isa 22 4 depart from me, I will weep bitterly
30 19 thou shalt not weep, he will surely
33 7 the angels of peace shall weep bitterly
Jer 9 1 and I will weep day and night for the
13 17 my soul shall weep in secret for your
17 weeping it shall weep, and my eyes
22 10 weep not for him that is dead nor
48 32 of Sabama, I will weep for thee with
Lam 1 16 therefore do I weep, and my eyes run
Eze 24 16 thou shalt not lament nor weep: neither
23 you shall not lament nor weep, but you
27 31 and they shall weep for thee with
Joel 1 5 awake, ye that are drunk, and weep and
2 17 priests the Lord's ministers shall weep
Zach 7 3 must I weep in the fifth month or must
Mich 1 10 it not in Geth, weep ye not with tears
Mark 5 39 why make you this ado and weep? The
14 72 thrice deny me. And he began to weep
Luke 6 21 blessed are ye that weep now: for
25 laugh: for you shall mourn and weep
7 13 towards her, he said to her: Weep not
8 52 weep not; the maid is not dead, but
23 28 w. not over me; but w. for yourselves
John 11 31 she goeth to the grave to weep there
16 20 you shall lament and weep, but the
Rom 12 15 that rejoice; weep with them that weep
1 C 7 30 they that weep, as though they wept not
James 4 9 be afflicted and mourn and weep: let
5 1 weep and howl in your miseries, which
Apoc 5 5 weep not; behold the lion of the tribe
18 9 shall weep and bewail themselves over
11 the merchants of the earth shall weep
weepers Judg 2 1 from Galgal to the place of w.
Judg 2 5 was called, The place of weepers or of
weepest 1 K 1 8 Anna, why weepest thou and why
John 20 13 woman, why weepest thou. 15
weepeth Eccu 12 16 an enemy w. with his eyes: but
weeping Gen 35 8 place was called, The oak of w.
Gen 37 35 whilst he [Jacob] continued weeping
45 2 he lifted up his voice with weeping
50 1 father's face, weeping and kissing him
Num 11 4 burned with desire, sitting and weeping
10 Moses heard the people weeping by
25 6 w. before the door of the tabernacle
2 K 3 16 her husband followed her [Michol], w.
15 30 going up and weeping, walking barefoot
30 went up with their heads covered w.
4 K 20 3 and Ezechias wept with much weeping
1 Es 3 13 the noise of the weeping of the people
10 1 praying and beseeching and weeping
Tob 3 22 after tears and weeping thou pourest
5 28 mother ceased w. and held her peace
7 7 with tears, and weeping upon his neck
Jdth 6 14 all of them together mourning and w.
16 when their weeping was ended and the
7 18 there was great weeping and lamentation
14 14 with weeping, and rent his garments
Esth 4 3 with fasting, wailing, and weeping
14 2 garments suitable for w. and mourning
Job 16 17 my face is swollen with weeping, and
Ps 6 9 Lord hath heard the voice of my weeping
29 6 in the evening weeping shall have place
101 10 bread, and mingled my drink with w.
Isa 15 3 all shall howl and come down weeping
5 the ascent of Luith they shall go up w.
16 9 I will lament with the weeping of Jazer
22 5 of treading down and of weeping to
12 shall call to weeping and to mourning

30 19 weeping thou shalt not weep, he will
38 3 and Ezechias wept with great weeping
65 19 the voice of weeping shall no more
Jer 3 21 weeping and howling of the children of
9 10 for the mountains I will take up w.
13 17 weeping it shall weep, and my eyes
31 9 they shall come with weeping: and I
15 of lamentation, of mourning and w.
15 of Rachel weeping for her children
16 let thy voice cease from weeping, and
41 6 to meet them, w. all along as he went
48 5 shall the mourner go up with weeping
50 4 weeping they shall make haste and
Lam 1 2 weeping she hath wept in the night and
2 11 my eyes have failed with weeping, my
Bar 4 11 but I sent them away with weeping and
23 I sent you forth with mourning and w.
Eze 27 31 bitterness of soul, with most bitter w.
Dan 13 35 she weeping looked up to heaven, for
Joel 2 12 all your heart, in fasting and in w.
Mala 2 13 altar of the Lord with tears, with w.
1 Ma 7 36 weeping, they said: Thou, O Lord, hast
2 Ma 13 12 with w. and fasting, lying prostrate
Mat 8 12 shall be w. and gnashing of teeth. 13:42, 50; 22:13; 24:51; 25:30; Luke 13:28
Mark 5 38 he seeth a tumult, and people weeping
16 10 who were mourning and weeping. And
John 11 33 when he saw her weeping, and the Jews
33 Jews that were come with her, weeping
20 11 Mary stood at the sepulcher without, w.
11 as she was w., she stooped down and
Acts 9 39 stood about him weeping, and showing
20 37 there was much w. among them all; and
21 13 what do you mean weeping and afflicting
Phil 3 18 you often, and now tell you weeping
Apoc 18 15 w. and mourning and saying: Alas. 19
weepings Jdth 7 22 tired with these w., they held
weigh Job 31 6 let him w. me in a just balance
Isa 46 6 and weigh out silver in the scales
Eze 5 1 take thee a balance to weigh in and
2 Ma 9 8 to weigh the heights of the mountains
weighed Gen 23 16 w. out the money that Ephron
Exod 37 24 the vessels thereof w. a talent of gold
1 K 17 7 head of his spear weighed 600 sicles
2 K 14 26 w. the hair of his head at 200 sicles
21 16 the iron of whose spear w. 300 ounces
3 K 7 47 multitude the brass could not be w.
1 Es 8 25 weighed unto them the silver and gold
26 I weighed to their hands 650 talents
33 vessels were w. in the house of our
Job 6 2 my sins . . . were weighed in a balance
28 15 neither shall silver be w. in exchange
25 and weighed the waters by measure
Eccu 21 28 of the wise shall be w. in a balance
Isa 40 12 and weighed the heavens with his palm
12 and weighed the mountains in scales
Jer 32 9 I weighed him the money, seven staters
10 I w. him the money in the balances
Dan 5 27 thou art weighed in the balance, and
Zach 11 12 they weighed for my wages 30 pieces of
weigher Prov 6 2 the Lord is the w. of spirits
weigheth Prov 21 2 but the Lord w. the hearts
weighing Gen 24 22 golden earrings, w. two sicles
Num 7 13 a silver dish weighing 130 sicles. 19, 25, 31, 37, 43, 49, 55, 61, 67, 73, 79
20 mortar of gold weighing 10 sicles. 26, 32, 38, 44, 50, 56, 62, 68, 74, 80
85 each dish weighing 130 sicles of silver
86 mortars . . . weighing ten sicles apiece
Ecce 7 28 weighing one thing after another, that
weight Gen 24 22 bracelets of ten sicles weight
Gen 43 21 have now brought again in the same w.

Exod 25 39 the whole weight of the candlestick
30 24 by the weight of the sanctuary. Num 7:25, 43, 61, 85, 86; 18:16
34 frankincense, all shall be of equal w.
Lev 5 15 according to the weight of the sanctuary. Num 3:47, 50; 7:13, 19, 31, 49, 55, 67, 73, 79
19 35 do not any unjust thing . . . in weight
26 26 in one oven, and give it out by weight
27 3 after the w. of the sanctuary. Num 7:37
Num 11 11 laid the w. of all this people upon me
31 52 the gold . . . in weight 16,750 sicles
Deut 25 15 shalt have a just and a true weight
Judg 8 26 weight of the earlets that he requested
9 4 and they gave him 70 weight of silver
1 K 17 5 and the weight of his coat of mail was
31 3 weight of battle was turned upon Saul
2 K 12 30 weight of which was a talent of gold
14 26 sicles, according to the common weight
3 K 10 14 the weight of the gold that was brought
4 K 21 13 and the weight of the house of Achab
25 16 of all these vessels was without weight
1 Pa 20 2 found in it a talent weight of gold
21 25 six hundred sicles of gold of just w.
22 3 joinings, and of brass an immense w.
14 of brass and of iron there is no weight
23 29 and of every weight and measure. And
28 14 gold by weight for every vessel for
14 silver by weight according to the
15 also he gave silver by weight for the
17 he gave by weight, for every lion. In
17 he set aside different weight of silver
2 Pa 3 9 weight of every nail was fifty sicles
4 18 the weight of the brass was not known
9 13 weight of the gold that was brought to
10 11 yoke, and I will add more weight to it
1 Es 8 29 till you deliver them by weight before
30 received the weight of the silver and
34 according to the number and weight of
34 all the weight was written at that time
Job 23 6 me with the weight of his greatness
28 25 who made a weight for the winds and
31 23 and his weight I was not able to bear
Prov 11 1 the Lord: and a just weight is his will
16 11 weight and balance are judgments of the
Wisd 11 21 things in measure and number and weight
Eccu 6 15 no weight of gold and silver is able
42 7 deliver all things in number and weight
Isa 28 17 I will set judgment in w., and justice
46 1 your burdens of heavy weight even unto
Jer 52 20 no w. of the brass of all these vessels
Eze 4 10 shall be in weight twenty staters a day
16 they shall eat bread by weight and with
45 11 their weight shall be equal according
1 Ma 14 24 shield . . . of the w. of 1,000 pounds
John 19 39 aloes, about an hundred pound weight
2 C 4 17 exceedingly an eternal weight of glory
Heb 12 1 laying aside every weight and sin

weightier Mat 23 23 left the w. things of the law

weights Lev 19 36 balance be just and w. equal
Deut 25 13 thou shalt not have divers weights
Prov 16 11 his work all the weights of the bag
20 10 diverse weights . . . are abominable
23 diverse weights are an abomination
Eccu 42 4 of exactness of balance and weights
Mich 6 11 and the deceitful weights of the bag

weighty Prov 27 3 a stone is heavy, and sand w.
2 C 10 10 his epistle . . . are weighty and strong

welcome Eccu 41 3 death, thy sentence is w. to

welfare 2 K 11 11 thy w. and by the w. of thy soul
Esth 2 11 having a care for Esther's welfare
10 3 which were for the welfare of his seed
Wisd 6 26 is the welfare of the whole world
2 Ma 1 10 that are in Egypt, health and welfare
9 19 wisheth much health and welfare and
13 3 not for the w. of his country, but in
14 14 to be the welfare of their affairs

well Mat 3 17 Son, in whom I am well pleased. 17:5; 2 P 1:17
Mat 12 18 in whom my soul hath been well pleased
15 7 well hath Isaias prophesied of you
25 21 well done, good and faithful servant. 23
Mark 1 11 in thee I am well pleased. Luke 3:22
2 17 they that are well have no need of a
5 15 sitting, clothed, and well in his wits
7 6 well did Isaias prophesy of you
9 well do you make void the commandment
37 saying: He hath done all things well
12 28 seeing that he had answered them well
32 well, Master, thou hast said in truth
Luke 1 7 they both were well advanced in years
19 17 well done, thou good servant, because
20 39 to him: Master, thou hast said well
John 2 10 when men have well drunk, then that
4 6 Jacob's well was there. Jesus therefore
6 [Jesus] sat thus on the well. It was
11 wherein to draw, and the well is deep
12 our father Jacob, who gave us the well
17 thou hast said well, I have no husband
8 48 do not we say well that thou art a
11 12 Lord, if he sleep, he shall do well
13 13 Master and Lord; and you say well, for
18 23 but if well, why strikest thou me
Acts 10 33 and thou hast done well in coming. Now
47 received the Holy Ghost, as well as we
15 8 unto them Holy Ghost, as well as to us
25 with our w. beloved Barnabas and Paul
29 you shall do well. Fare ye well. They
25 10 no injury, as thou very well knowest
28 25 well did Holy Ghost speak to our fathers
Rom 11 20 well: because of unbelief they were
1 C 7 37 his heart, to keep his virgin, doth well
38 giveth his virgin in marriage, doth well
9 5 as well as the rest of the apostles, and
10 5 with most of them God was not w. pleased
14 17 for thou indeed givest thanks well, but
16 2 laying up what it shall well please him
Gal 4 17 they are zealous in your regard not well
5 7 you did run well, who hath hindered you
Eph 5 10 proving what is well pleasing to God
6 3 that it may be well with thee, and thou
Phil 4 14 you have done well in communicating to
Col 1 19 in him, it hath well pleased the Father
3 20 for this is well pleasing to the Lord
2 Th 3 13 brethren, be not weary in well doing
1 Tim 3 4 one that ruleth well his own house
12 who rule well their children, and their
13 for they that have ministered well
5 17 the priests that rule well, be esteemed
2 Tim 1 18 me at Ephesus, thou very well knowest
Titus 2 3 not given to much wine, teaching well
Heb 13 18 to behave ourselves well in all things
21 which is well pleasing in his sight
James 2 3 sit thou here well; but say to the
8 thy neighbor as thyself; you do well
19 that there is one God. Thou dost well
1 P 2 15 by doing well you may put to silence
20 but if doing well you suffer patiently
3 6 you are, doing well and not fearing any
17 it is better doing well, if such be
2 P 1 19 whereunto you do well to attend, as to
3 J 2 fare well as thy soul doth prosperously
6 shalt do well to bring forward on

well's Gen 29 8 the stone from the well's mouth

wells Num 21 22 will not drink waters of the w.
Eccu 50 3 in his days the wells of water flowed

weltering Jdth 14 14 without the head, w. in his
went Mat 2 9 having heard the king, went their way
Mat 2 12 they went back another way into their
3 5 then went out to him Jerusalem and all
4 24 his fame went throughout all Syria
5 1 he went up into a mountain, and when
Luke 16 30 if one went to them from the dead
wept Gen 21 16 she lifted up her voice and wept
Gen 27 38 when he [Esau] wept with a loud cry
29 11 kissed her and, lifting up his voice, w.
33 4 about the neck, and kissing him, wept
42 24 himself away a little while and wept
43 30 and going into his chamber, he wept
45 14 he [Joseph] embraced him and wept
14 Benjamin . . . wept also on his neck
15 and wept upon every one of them: after
46 29 upon his neck, and embracing him w.
50 17 and when Joseph heard this, he wept
Num 11 20 and have wept before him, saying: Why
14 1 whole multitude crying wept that night
Deut 1 45 when you returned and wept before the
Judg 2 4 they lifted up their voice and wept
14 16 she wept before Samson and complained
17 she wept before him the seven days
20 23 and wept before the Lord until night
26 wept before the Lord: and they fasted
1 K 1 7 but Anna wept and did not eat. Then
11 4 people lifted up their voices and wept
20 41 they wept together, but David more
24 17 Saul lifted up his voice and wept
30 4 and wept till they had no more tears
2 K 1 12 they mourned and wept and fasted until
3 32 wept at the grave of Abner: and all the people also wept
34 the people repeating it wept over him
12 22 yet alive, I fasted and wept for him
13 36 they lifted up their voice and wept
36 and the king also . . . wept very much
15 23 and they all wept with a loud voice
18 33 high chamber over the gate and wept
19 1 that the king wept and mourned for his
4 K 8 11 as to blush: and the man of God wept
13 14 and Joas . . . wept before him, and said
20 3 and Ezechias wept with much weeping
22 19 rent thy garments and wept before me. 2 Pa 34:27
1 Es 3 12 the priests . . . wept with a loud voice
10 1 the people wept with much lamentation
2 Es 1 4 sat down and wept and mourned for many
8 9 all the people wept when they heard the
Tob 7 8 wife and Sara their daughter wept
19 her daughter in thither and she wept
9 8 Gabelus wept and blessed God and said
10 4 mother wept and was quite disconsolate
Job 2 12 they wept and rending their garments
30 25 I wept heretofore for him that was
Ps 125 6 going they went and wept, casting their
136 1 rivers of Babylon, there we sat and wept
Isa 38 3 and Ezechias wept with great weeping
Lam 1 2 weeping she hath wept in the night and
Bar 1 5 when they heard it they w. and fasted
Dan 13 33 friends and all her acquaintance wept
Osee 12 4 he wept and made supplication to him
Mat 26 75 and going forth, he wept bitterly
Luke 7 32 have mourned, and you have not wept
8 52 all wept and mourned for her. But he
19 41 seeing the city, he wept over it
22 62 and Peter going out, wept bitterly
John 11 35 and Jesus wept. The Jews therefore
1 C 7 30 they that weep, as though they wept not
Apoc 5 4 I wept much because no man was found
west Gen 12 8 his tent, having Bethel on the west
Gen 13 14 look . . . to the east and to the west
28 14 thou shalt spread abroad to the west
Exod 10 19 very strong wind to blow from the west
27 12 of the court, that looketh to the west
36 27 against the west, to wit, at that side
Num 3 23 pitch behind the tabernacle on the west
35 5 sea also, which looketh to the west
Deut 3 27 cast thy eyes round about to the west
Josu 11 3 on the east and on the west, and the
16 and the plains and the west country
15 8 is over against Geennom to the west
22 7 brethren beyond the Jordan to the west
3 K 7 25 and three towards the west, and three
1 Pa 12 15 toward the east and toward the west
26 16 to Sephim and Hosa towards the west
18 porters toward the west four in the way
2 Pa 4 4 north, and other three toward the west
32 30 toward the west of the city of David
Tob 1 1 beyond the way that leadeth to the west
Jdth 2 5 against all the kingdoms of the west
Job 23 8 if to the west, I shall not understand
Ps 67 5 for him who ascendeth upon the west
74 7 neither from the east nor from the west
102 12 as far as the east is from the west
Isa 9 12 and the Philistines from the west
43 5 the east and gather thee from the west
45 6 sun, and they who are from the west
59 19 they from the west shall fear the name
Jer 25 24 Arabia, and all the kings of the west
Bar 4 37 together from the east even to the west
Eze 42 19 toward the west he measured 500
45 7 from the west border to the east border
46 19 there was a place bending to the west
48 18 and 10,000 toward the west, shall be as
Dan 8 4 pushing with his horns against the west
5 behold a he goat came from the west
Zach 14 4 to the west with a very great opening
Mat 8 11 from the east and the west. Luke 13:29
24 27 and appeareth even into the west: so
Luke 12 54 you see a cloud rising from the west
Apoc 21 13 gates: and on the west, three gates
west side Exod 26 22 west side of the tabernacle
Exod 26 27 as many at the west side: and they
36 32 five other bars at the west side of the
Num 2 18 on the west side shall be the camp of
34 6 w. s. shall begin from the great sea
Josu 8 9 on the west side of the city of Hai
12 Hai, on the west side of the same city
13 reached to the west side of the city
12 7 beyond the Jordan on the west side
Judg 20 34 to march from the west side of the city
2 Pa 33 14 the west side of Gihon in the valley
Eze 48 16 on the west side 4,500. And the suburbs
23 from the east side to the west side. 24, 25, 26
34 at the west side, 4,500, and their three
western Deut 11 24 unto the w. sea shall be your
westward Josu 5 1 who dwelt beyond the Jordan w.
Josu 15 10 it compasseth from Baala westward unto
11 and is bounded w. with the great sea
16 3 westward, by the border of Jephleti
18 12 going up westward to the mountains
14 this is their coast towards the sea w.
19 34 border returneth w. to Azanotthabor
34 to Zabulon southward and to Asar w.
1 Pa 7 28 and eastward Noran and westward Gazer
26 30 over Israel beyond the Jordan westward
wet Judg 6 39 and all the ground wet with dew
Job 24 8 who are wet with the showers of the
Dan 4 12 let it be wet with the dew of heaven
22 shalt be wet with the dew of heaven
30 his body was wet with the dew. 5:21
wethers Tob 8 22 and four wethers to be killed
whale Job 7 12 am I a sea or a whale, that thou
Isa 27 1 shall slay the whale that is in the

whale's Mat 12 40 as Jonas was in the w. belly
whales Gen 1 21 God created the great whales
Eccu 43 27 and the monstrous creatures of whales
Dan 3 79 ye whales and all that move in the
wheat Gen 30 14 out in the time of the w. harvest
Gen 41 49 there was so great abundance of wheat
42 2 have heard that wheat is sold in Egypt
25 servants to fill their sacks with wheat
44 2 the price which he gave for the wheat
25 go again and buy us a little wheat
45 23 carrying wheat and bread for the journey
Exod 9 32 the wheat and other winter corn
34 22 of the corn of thy wheat harvest and
Deut 8 8 land of wheat and barley and vineyards
28 51 will leave thee no wheat nor wine nor
32 14 and goats with the marrow of wheat
Judg 6 11 son was threshing and cleansing wheat
15 1 days of the wheat harvest were at hand
Ruth 2 23 till all the barley and the wheat were
1 K 6 13 the Bethsamites were reaping wheat
12 17 is it not wheat harvest today? I will
2 K 4 5 cleansing wheat, was fallen asleep
17 28 w. and barley and meal and parched corn
3 K 5 11 allowed Hiram 20,000 measures of wheat
1 Pa 21 20 at that time he was thrashing wheat
23 wood, and the wheat for the sacrifice
2 Pa 2 10 for their food 20,000 cores of wheat
15 the wheat therefore and the barley and
27 5 of silver and 10,000 measures of wheat
1 Es 6 9 wheat, salt, wine, and oil according
7 22 and unto a hundred cores of wheat
Job 5 26 heap of wheat is brought in its season
31 40 thistles grow up to me instead of w.
Ps 80 17 he fed them with the fat of wheat
Cant 7 2 thy belly is like a heap of wheat, set
Isa 28 25 put wheat in order, and barley and
Jer 12 13 they have sown wheat, and reaped thorns
23 28 what hath the chaff to do with the w.
41 8 we have stores in the field, of wheat
Eze 4 9 take to thee wheat and barley and
45 13 sixth part of an ephi of a core of w.
Osee 7 14 they have thought upon wheat and wine
14 8 they shall live upon wheat, and they
Joel 1 11 the vinedressers have howled for the w.
2 24 the floors shall be filled with wheat
1 Ma 8 26 or furnish them with wheat or arms or
28 wheat or arms or money or ships
Mat 3 12 and gather his wheat into the barn
13 25 oversowed cockle among the wheat and
29 you root up the wheat also together
30 the wheat gather ye into my barn
Luke 3 17 will gather the wheat into his barn
12 42 to give them their measure of wheat
16 7 said: An hundred quarters of wheat
22 31 that he may sift you as wheat: but I
John 12 24 unless the grain of wheat falling into
Acts 27 38 ship, casting the wheat into the sea
1 C 14 37 but bare grain, as of w., or of some of
Apoc 6 6 two pounds of wheat for a penny, and
18 13 wine and oil and fine flour and wheat
wheaten Exod 29 2 shalt make them all of wheaten
wheel 3 K 7 32 height of a w. was a cubit and
Ps 76 19 the voice of thy thunder in a wheel
82 14 make them like a w.; and as stubble
Prov 20 26 and bringeth over them the wheel. The
Ecce 12 6 the wheel be broken upon the cistern
Eccu 33 5 heart of a fool is as a wheel of a cart
38 32 turning the wheel about with his feet
Isa 28 27 neither shall the cart wheel turn about
28 neither shall the cart wheel hurt it
Jer 18 3 behold he was doing a work on the wheel
Eze 1 15 creatures one wheel with four faces
16 a w. in the midst of a w. 10:10
10 6 he went in and stood beside the wheel
9 one w. by one cherub, and another w. by
23 24 well appointed with chariot and wheel
James 3 6 inflameth the wheel of our nativity
wheels Exod 14 25 overthrew the w. of the chariots
3 K 7 30 every base had four w. and axletrees
32 four w. which were at the four corners
33 w. as are used to be made in a chariot
Isa 5 28 their w. like the violence of a tempest
Jer 47 3 chariots, and the multitude of his w.
Nah 3 2 the noise of the rattling of the wheels
Eze 1 16 the appearance of the wheels and the
18 the wheels had also a size and a
19 the wheels also went together by them
19 the w. also were lifted up. 20, 21
20 spirit of life was in the wheels. 21
3 13 and the noise of the wheels following
10 2 go in between the wheels that are under
6 take fire from the midst of the wheels
9 were four wheels by the cherubims
9 appearance of the w. was to the sight
12 of eyes, round about the four wheels
13 and these wheels he called voluble
16 went, the wheels also went by them
16 the wheels stayed not behind, but were
19 they went out, the wheels also followed
11 22 lifted up their wings and the wheels
26 10 at the noise of the horsemen and wheels
Dan 7 9 the wheels of it like a burning fire
whelp Gen 49 9 Juda is a lion's whelp: to the
Isa 31 4 as the lion roareth, and the lion's w.
Osee 5 14 like a lion's w. to the house of Juda
Joel 1 6 his cheek teeth as of a lion's whelp
Amos 3 4 will the lion's w. cry out of his den
1 Ma 3 4 like a lion's w. roaring for his prey
whelps 2 K 17 8 when her whelps are taken away
Job 4 10 teeth of the whelps of lions are broken
38 39 and satisfy the appetite of her whelps
Prov 17 12 to meet a bear robbed of her whelps
Eze 19 2 bring up her whelps in the midst of
3 she brought out one of her whelps, and
Osee 13 8 as a bear that is robbed of her whelps
Nah 2 12 the lion caught enough for his whelps
Mat 15 27 the whelps also eat of the crumbs that
Mark 7 28 the whelps also eat under the table
whet Deut 32 41 if I shall whet my sword as the
whether Mat 9 5 whether is easier, to say, Thy
Mat 23 17 whether is greater, the gold or temple
19 w. is greater, the gift or the altar
27 21 whether will you of the two to be
whetted Ps 63 4 have w. their tongues like a
while Judg 15 1 a while after, when the days of
1 K 9 27 stand thou still a while, that I may
25 7 the while they were with us in Carmel
Jdth 10 18 worth our w. for their sakes to fight
13 11 after a w. she went out and delivered
Job 32 22 after a while my Maker may take me away
Osee 8 10 shall rest a while from the burden
2 Ma 5 17 consider that God was angry for a w.
7 17 stay patiently a while, and thou shalt
Mark 14 70 after a while they that stood by said
Luke 8 13 they believe for a while, and in time
little while; *see* **little**
whip Prov 26 3 whip for a horse, and a snaffle
Eccu 28 21 stroke of a whip maketh a blue mark
Nah 3 2 the noise of the whip, and the noise
whips Exod 5 16 thy servants are beaten with w.
3 K 12 11 my father beat you with whips. 14
2 Ma 7 1 were tormented with whips and scourges
whirled 1 K 25 29 of thy enemies shall be w.
whirling 1 K 25 29 violence and w. of a sling
whirlwind 4 K 2 1 up Elias into heaven by a w.
4 K 2 11 Elias went up by a whirlwind into heaven

Job 3 6 let a darksome w. seize upon that night
9 17 he shall crush me in a whirlwind and
21 18 as ashes which the whirlwind scattereth
27 21 and as a whirlwind shall snatch him
38 1 Lord answered Job out of a whirlwind
40 1 Lord answering Job out of the whirlwind
Wisd 5 24 as a whirlwind shall divide them
Eccu 11 36 and he shall overthrow thee with a w.
43 18 so doth the northern storm and the w.
48 9 wast taken up in a whirlwind of fire
13 Elias was indeed covered with the w.
Isa 4 6 for a security and covert from the w.
17 13 and as a whirlwind before a tempest
25 4 a refuge from the whirlwind, a shadow
4 blast of the mighty is like a whirlwind
28 2 a destroying w., as the violence of
29 6 and with a great noise of whirlwind
30 30 he shall crush to pieces with whirlwind
40 24 w. shall take them away as stubble
41 16 and the whirlwind shall scatter them
66 15 and his chariots are like a whirlwind
Jer 23 19 w. of the Lord's indignation shall come
25 32 great w. shall go forth from the ends
30 23 behold the whirlwind of the Lord, his
Eze 1 4 a whirlwind came out of the north: and
Osee 8 7 they shall sow wind, and reap a w.
13 3 as the dust that is driven with a w.
Amos 1 14 with a whirlwind in the day of trouble
Nah 1 3 Lord's ways are in a tempest and a w.
Haba 3 14 that came out as a w. to scatter me
Zach 9 14 trumpet, and go in the w. of the south
Heb 12 18 a burning fire and a w. and darkness
whirlwinds Isa 21 1 as w. come from the south
Joel 2 2 a day of clouds and w. Soph 1:15
2 P 2 17 and clouds tossed with whirlwinds, to
whisper Job 4 12 received the veins of its w.
Eccu 12 19 clap his hands and whisper much
whispered Ps 40 8 all my enemies whispered together
whisperer Lev 19 16 nor a w. among the people
Eccu 5 16 be not called a whisperer and be not
17 to the whisperer hatred and enmity
28 15 the whisperer and the double tongued
whisperers Rom 1 29 full of envy, murder, . . . w.
whispering 2 K 12 19 David saw his servants w.
whisperings 2 C 12 20 w., swellings, seditions
whistle Isa 5 26 will whistle to them from the
Zach 10 8 I will whistle for them and I will
whistling 3 K 19 12 after the fire a w. of a
Wisd 17 17 whether it were a whistling wind or
whit Exod 5 19 shall not a whit be diminished
white Gen 30 35 that is, of w. and black fleece
Gen 30 40 the white and the black were Laban's
31 8 thou shalt take all the white ones
8 all the flocks brought forth white ones
Exod 16 31 and it was like coriander seed white
Lev 13 3 in his skin, and the hair turned white
10 when there shall be a white color in
19 ulcer, there appeareth a white scar
20 other flesh, and the hair turned white
24 is healed hath a white or a red scar
25 view it, and if he see it turned white
39 not the leprosy, but a white blemish
42 there be risen a white or reddish color
49 be infected with a white or red spot
Num 12 10 appeared white as snow with a leprosy
4 K 5 27 out from him a leper as w. as snow
Tob 6 9 eyes, in which there is a white speck
11 14 and a white skin began to come out of
13 22 be paved with white and clean stones
Ecce 9 8 at all times let thy garments be white
Cant 5 10 my beloved is white and ruddy, chosen
Isa 1 18 they shall be made white as snow: and
18 crimson, they shall be white as wool
Bar 6 70 they are no better than a white thorn
Dan 7 9 his garment was as white as snow, and the
11 35 may be chosen and made white even
Joel 1 7 the branches thereof are made white
Zach 1 8 were horses, red, speckled, and white
6 3 and in the third chariot white horses
6 and the white went forth after them
2 Ma 11 8 going before them in white clothing
Mat 5 36 not make one hair white or black
17 2 and his garments became white as snow
Mark 9 2 shining and exceeding white as snow so as
no fuller upon earth can make white
16 5 right side, clothed with a white robe
Luke 9 29 raiment became white and glittering
23 11 putting on him a white garment and sent
John 4 35 for they are white already to harvest
20 12 she saw two angels in white, sitting
Acts 1 10 two men stood by them in w. garments
10 30 a man stood before me in white apparel
Apoc 1 14 his hairs were as white as white wool
2 17 and will give him a white counter, and
3 4 and they shall walk with me in white
5 clothed in white garments. 18; 4:4
6 2 behold a white horse, and he. 19:11
11 white robes were given to every one of
7 9 clothed with white robes and palms in
13 these that are clothed in white robes
14 made them white in the blood of the
14 14 a white cloud; and upon the cloud one
15 6 clothed with clean and white linen
19 8 with fine linen, glittering and white
14 followed him on white horses, clothed in fine
linen, white and clean
20 11 I saw a great white throne and one
whited Ps 67 15 shall be w. with snow in Selmon
Mat 23 27 you are like to whited sepulchers
Acts 23 3 God shall strike thee, thou whited wall
whiter Gen 49 12 and his teeth whiter than milk
Ps 50 9 and I shall be made whiter than snow
Lam 4 7 her Nazarites were whiter than snow
whiteness Gen 30 37 were pilled, there appeared w.
Lev 13 4 if there be a shining w. in the skin
13 because it is all turned into whiteness
16 if again it be turned into whiteness
28 if the whiteness stay in its place
38 if a whiteness appear in the skin of
39 find that a darkish whiteness shineth
Eccu 43 20 admireth at the beauty of the whiteness
whole Mat 8 32 whole herd ran violently down
Mat 8 34 the whole city went out to meet Jesus
9 22 thy faith hath made thee whole. Mark 5:34;
10:53; Luke 8:48; 17:19; 18:42
22 the woman was made whole from that
13 33 until the w. was leavened. Luke 13:21
14 36 many as touched were made w. Mark 6:56
21 10 the whole city was moved, saying: Who
22 37 whole heart and with thy whole soul. Mark
12:30; Luke 10:27
37 whole soul and with thy whole mind
40 dependeth the w. law and the prophets
26 59 the whole council sought false witness
27 25 the whole people answering, said: His
27 together unto him the whole band. And
Mark 5 28 touch but his garment, I shall be whole
34 and be thou whole of thy disease. While
6 55 running through that whole country
11 18 whole multitude was in admiration at
12 30 thy w. soul and with thy w. mind and thy
w. strength
33 he should be loved with the whole heart and
with whole understanding and with the
whole soul and with the whole strength
44 in all she had, even her whole living

15 1 and the scribes and the whole council
16 they called together the whole band
Luke 4 14 went out through the whole country
5 31 that are whole need not the physician
6 12 passed the whole night in the prayer
7 10 found the servant whole who had been
8 39 and he went through the whole city
11 36 the whole shall be lightsome; and as
19 37 the whole multitude of his disciples
20 6 the whole people will stone us: for
23 1 whole multitude of them rising up, led
18 whole multitude together cried out
John 5 4 was made whole of whatsoever infirmity
6 to him: Wilt thou be made whole
9 immediately the man was made whole
11 he that made me whole, he said to me
14 behold thou art made whole: sin no more
15 it was Jesus who had made him whole
7 23 because I have healed the whole man on
11 50 and that the whole nation perish not
Acts 2 2 it filled the whole house where they
4 9 by what means he hath been made whole
10 this man standeth here before you w.
11 26 they conversed there . . . a w. year
13 6 they had gone through the whole island
44 w. city almost came together, to hear
49 published throughout the w. country
14 6 Lycaonia, and to w. country round about
17 26 dwell upon the w. face of the earth
19 29 the whole city was filled with confusion
20 28 heed to yourselves, and to whole flock
21 30 the whole city was in an uproar: and the
28 30 he remained two whole years in his own
1 C 5 6 leaven corrupteth the w. lump. Gal 5:9
12 17 if the whole were hearing, where would
Gal 5 3 that he is a debtor to do the whole law
23 your whole spirit and soul and body, may
Titus 1 11 be reproved, who subvert whole houses
James 2 10 whosoever shall keep the whole law
Apoc 6 12 and the whole moon became as blood
whole body; *see* **body**
whole church; *see* **church**
whole earth Gen 1 26 dominion over . . . w. e.
Gen 7 3 be saved upon the face of the w. e.
8 9 the waters were upon the whole earth
9 19 all mankind spread over the whole e.
11 9 language of whole earth was confounded
19 31 after the manner of the whole earth
Num 14 21 whole earth shall be filled with the
Josu 3 13 Lord the God of the whole earth
Jdth 5 25 we shall be a reproach to the w. e.
6 4 Nabuchodonosor is lord of the w. e.
Ps 8 2 admirable is thy name in the whole e.
47 3 with the joy of the whole earth
71 19 w. e. shall be filled with his majesty
Isa 14 7 the whole earth is quiet and still
25 8 shall take away from off the w. earth
Jer 50 23 the hammer of the whole earth broken
51 25 which corruptest the whole earth
Eze 35 14 when the whole earth shall rejoice
Dan 2 35 mountain, and tilled the whole earth
6 25 to all people . . . in the whole earth
7 23 and shall devour the whole earth
8 5 from the west on face of the w. earth
14 42 inhabitants of the w. earth fear the
Mich 4 13 to the Lord of the whole earth
Zach 4 10 that run to and fro through w. earth
14 stand before the Lord of the w. earth
Mat 27 45 darkness over w. earth. Mark 15:33; Luke 27:44
Luke 21 35 that sit upon face of the whole earth
whole land Gen 13 9 the whole land is before thee
Gen 19 28 Gomorrha and the w. l. of that country
41 29 years of great plenty in the whole land
41 appointed thee over the w. l. of Egypt
43 governor over the whole land of Egypt
45 9 me lord of the whole land of Egypt
47 26 in the whole land of Egypt, the fifth
Exod 8 21 the whole land wherein they shall be
9 9 boils . . . in the whole land of Egypt
22 be hail in the whole land of Egypt
24 never . . . seen in the w. l. of Egypt
10 14 and they came up over the whole land
32 13 this whole land . . . I will give to your
Deut 29 2 to Pharao . . . and to his whole land. 34:11
2 K 24 8 having gone through the whole land
Isa 13 5 of his wrath, to destroy the whole land
Jer 51 47 her whole land shall be confounded
wholesome Tob 1 15 and gave them w. admonitions
Eccu 15 3 him the water of w. wisdom to drink
31 24 sound and w. sleep with a moderate man
35 2 it is a w. sacrifice to take heed
2 Ma 12 46 and w. thought to pray for the dead
wholly Lev 6 22 shall be w. burnt on the altar
Josu 3 16 until they w. failed. And the people
2 Pa 20 3 betook himself wholly to pray to the
Job 10 8 and fashioned me wholly round about
Ecce 6 4 and his name shall be wholly forgotten
Eccu 23 11 nameth, shall not be w. pure from sin
Isa 22 1 that thou too art wholly gone up to
Jer 50 13 inhabited, but shall be wholly desolate
2 Ma 4 21 that he was wholly excluded from the
7 40 died undefiled, wholly trusting in the
Luke 5 9 he was wholly astonished, and all
John 9 34 thou wast wholly born in sins, and
13 10 to wash his feet, but is clean wholly
Acts 17 16 seeing city wholly given to idolatry
1 Tim 4 15 these things, be wholly in these things
whore Deut 22 21 to play the w. in her father's
Deut 23 17 no whore among the daughters of Israel
whoredom Lev 21 9 of a priest be taken in w.
Apoc 17 2 drunk with the wine of her whoredom
whoremonger Deut 23 17 nor w. among the sons of
whoremongers Apoc 21 8 w. and sorcerers and
wicked Mat 12 45 more w. than himself. Luke 11:26
Mat 12 45 shall it be also to this w. generation
13 49 separate the wicked from among the just
16 4 a wicked and adulterous generation
18 32 thou wicked servant, I forgave thee all
25 26 wicked and slothful servant, thou
Mark 15 28 and with the wicked he was reputed
Luke 11 29 this generation is a wicked generation
19 22 I judge thee, thou wicked servant
23 37 and with the wicked was he reckoned
Acts 2 23 you by the hands of wicked men have
17 5 and taking unto them some wicked men
19 12 the wicked spirits went out of them. Now
15 the wicked spirit, answering, said to
16 the man in whom the wicked spirit was
Gal 1 4 deliver us from this present w. world
1 Tim 1 9 for sinners, for the wicked and defiled
2 Tim 3 2 disobedient to parents, ungrateful, w.
James 4 16 all such rejoicing is wicked. To him
2 P 2 7 and lewd conversation of the wicked
1 J 3 12 because his own works were wicked: and
2 J 11 communicateth with his wicked works
wicked one Mat 13 19 there cometh the wicked one
Mat 13 38 are the children of the wicked one
Eph 6 16 the fiery darts of the most wicked one
2 Th 2 8 then that wicked one shall be revealed
1 J 2 13 you have overcome the wicked one. 14
3 12 as Cain, who was of the wicked one
5 18 and the wicked one toucheth him not
wickedly Deut 9 5 but because they have done w.
Deut 31 29 you will do wickedly and will quickly
Judg 19 23 do not so, my brethren, do not so w.

1 K 3 13 he knew that his sons did wickedly
12 25 if you will still do wickedly, both
2 K 22 22 have not wickedly departed from my God
24 17 am he that have sinned, I have done w.
3 K 16 25 Amri . . . acted w. above all that were
2 Pa 6 37 we have sinned, we have done wickedly
22 3 mother pushed him on to do wickedly
36 14 and the people wickedly transgressed
2 Es 9 33 hast done truth, but we have done w.
Ps 17 22 have not done wickedly against my God
43 18 we have not done w. in thy covenant
73 3 see what things the enemy hath done w.
74 5 I said to the wicked: Do not act w.
Prov 12 2 trusteth in his own devices doth w.
16 12 that act w. are abominable to the king
Wisd 11 15 his being wickedly exposed to perish
Eccu 1 40 because thou camest to the Lord w.
15 21 he hath commanded no man to do w., and
19 23 one that humbleth himself wickedly
Isa 58 4 and strife, and strike with the fist w.
Jer 5 28 have most w. transgressed my words
12 1 all them that transgress and do w.
Lam 3 42 we have done wickedly and provoked thee
Bar 2 12 we have sinned, we have done wickedly
Eze 16 52 sins, doing more wickedly than they
22 11 hath w. defiled his daughter-in-law
Dan 9 5 we have done w. and have revolted
11 32 such as deal w. against the covenant
12 10 and the wicked shall deal wickedly
Amos 4 4 come ye to Bethel, and do wickedly
Mich 3 4 have behaved wickedly in their devices
Mala 4 1 and all that do w. shall be stubble
2 Ma 4 17 acting wickedly against the laws of
2 P 2 6 to those that should after act w.
wickedness Gen 6 5 God seeing that the w. of
Gen 19 15 lest thou also perish in the wickedness
50 17 forget the wickedness of thy brethren
17 also pray thee to forgive . . . this w.
Exod 32 12 be appeased upon the w. of thy people
34 7 who takest away iniquity and wickedness
Lev 19 29 land be defiled and filled with w.
Num 14 18 taking away iniquity and wickedness
25 13 hath made atonement for the wickedness
Deut 9 4 are destroyed for their wickedness
27 nor on their wickedness and sin: lest
19 15 whatsoever the sin or wickedness be
25 1 to be wicked, they shall condemn of w.
Josu 7 12 destroy him that is guilty of this w.
13 that is defiled with this wickedness
15 and hath done wickedness in Israel
22 20 he alone had perished in his wickedness
29 God keep us from any such wickedness
24 19 and will not forgive your w. and sins
Judg 19 25 and abandoned her to their wickedness
20 3 how so great a w. had been committed
10 and render to it for its w. what it
1 K 17 28 thy pride and the w. of thy heart
24 14 from the wicked shall w. come forth
25 39 returned the w. of Nabal upon his head
2 K 3 39 that doth evil according to his w.
3 K 2 44 hath returned thy w. upon thy own head
8 47 unjustly, we have committed wickedness
2 Pa 6 23 by making his wickedness fall upon
29 9 led away captives for this wickedness
Esth 16 23 are destroyed for their wickedness
Job 4 18 and in his angels he found wickedness
22 5 and not for thy manifold wickedness
34 10 far from God be wickedness and iniquity
35 8 thy w. may hurt a man that is like thee
15 neither doth he revenge w. exceedingly
Ps 7 10 the w. of sinners shall be brought to
27 4 according to the w. of their inventions
31 5 thou hast forgiven the w. of my sin
54 16 there is wickedness in their dwellings
63 6 will not fear: they are resolute in w.
72 6 covered with their iniquity and their w.
8 have thought and spoken wickedness
106 34 for the w. of them that dwell therein
Prov 8 7 and my lips shall hate wickedness. All
10 2 treasures of w. shall profit nothing
11 5 wicked man shall fall by his own w.
12 3 men shall not be strengthened by w.
13 6 wickedness overthroweth the sinner
14 32 shall be driven out in his wickedness
21 27 because they are offered of wickedness
24 15 nor seek after wickedness in the house
25 5 take away w. from the face of the king
Ecce 7 16 wicked man liveth a long time in his w.
26 to know the wickedness of the fool
8 8 neither shall w. save the wicked. All
Wisd 4 6 witnesses of w. against their parents
11 lest w. should alter his understanding
5 13 but are consumed in our wickedness
24 w. shall overthrow the thrones of the
10 5 conspired together to consent to w.
7 land for a testimony of their w. is
12 2 that leaving their w., they may believe
20 might be changed from their wickedness
14 9 the wicked and his w. are hateful alike
17 10 for whereas wickedness is fearful, it
19 12 justly according to their own w. For
Eccu 3 30 the plant of w. shall take root in them
12 10 as a brass pot his wickedness rusteth
14 6 this is the reward of his wickedness
7 and at the last he discovereth his w.
19 6 he that is delighted with wickedness
19 learning of wickedness is not wisdom
20 there is a subtle wickedness, and the
25 17 the wickedness of a woman is all evil
19 and any w., but the w. of a woman
24 the w. of a woman changeth her face
29 10 have refused to lend, not out of w.
46 23 blot out the wickedness of the nation
49 3 he took away the abominations of w.
Isa 9 18 for wickedness is kindled as a fire
10 25 my wrath shall be upon their wickedness
47 10 thou hast trusted in thy wickedness
53 8 for the w. of my people have I struck
58 6 loose the bands of wickedness, undo the
Jer 1 16 touching all their wickedness, who
2 19 thy own wickedness shall reprove thee
3 2 with thy fornications and with thy w.
4 4 because of the w. of your thoughts
14 wash thy heart from w., O Jerusalem
18 this is thy w., because it is bitter
6 7 so hath she made her wickedness cold
7 12 did to it for the w. of my people Israel
11 15 hath wrought much w. in my house
12 4 for the w. of them that dwell therein
13 27 the w. of thy fornication: and thy
14 16 I will pour out their own w. upon them
20 we acknowledge, O Lord, our w., the
22 22 confounded and ashamed of all thy w.
23 11 in my house I have found their w.
26 3 unto them for the w. of their doings
33 5 from this city because of all their w.
44 3 because of w. which they have committed
Eze 3 19 and he be not converted from his w.
16 23 came to pass after all thy wickedness
58 thou hast borne thy wickedness and thy
18 20 the w. of the wicked shall be upon him
27 turneth himself away from his w. which
22 9 have committed w. in the midst of thee
23 21 thou hast renewed the w. of thy youth
27 I will put an end to thy wickedness
29 shall be discovered, thy wickedness

35 bear thou also thy wickedness and thy
48 I will take away w. out of the land
48 not to do according to the w. of them
49 and they shall render your w. upon you
31 11 I have cast him out according to his w.
33 12 w. of the wicked shall not hurt him
12 day soever he shall turn from his w.
19 when wicked shall depart from his w.
39 24 according to their uncleanness and w.
Dan 13 38 seeing this wickedness, ran up to them
57 of Juda would not abide your w. Now
Osee 6 9 of Sichem: for they have wrought w.
7 1 was discovered, and the w. of Samaria
2 that I remember all their wickedness
3 have made the king glad with their w.
9 15 all their wickedness is in Galgal, for
15 for the w. of their devices I will cast
10 13 you have plowed w., you have reaped
Joel 3 13 run over: for their w. is multiplied
Jon 1 2 the w. thereof is come up before me
Mich 1 5 for the wickedness of Jacob is all this
5 what is the wickedness of Jacob? Is it
3 8 to declare unto Jacob his wickedness
6 7 shall I give my firstborn for my w.
Nah 3 19 for upon whom hath not thy w. passed
Zach 5 8 he said: This is w. And he cast her
Mala 1 4 they shall be called the borders of w.
3 15 they that work wickedness are built up
1 Ma 7 42 and judge thou him according to his w.
2 Ma 4 13 and unheard of wickedness of Jason
12 3 were guilty of this kind of wickedness
Mat 22 18 Jesus knowing their wickedness, said
Mark 7 22 thefts, covetousness, w., deceit
Acts 3 26 convert himself from his wickedness
8 22 do penance therefore for this thy w.
Rom 1 29 being filled with all . . . wickedness
1 C 5 8 nor with leaven of malice and wickedness
Eph 4 14 of doctrine by the wickedness of men
6 12 against the spirits of wickedness in
1 J 5 19 the whole world is seated in wickedness
wickednesses Ps 5 11 the multitude of their w.
Eze 16 47 less than they according to their w.
44 13 shall bear their shame and their w.
wickets Eze 41 24 two w. on both sides of the
wide Gen 34 21 and wide wanteth men to till it
Josu 5 6 of the journey in the wide wilderness
2 Es 4 19 the work is great and wide and we are
7 4 the city was very wide and great, and
Ps 34 21 they opened their mouth wide against
80 11 open thy mouth wide, and I will fill
103 25 sea which stretcheth wide its arms
Prov 20 19 deceitfully, and openeth wide his lips
Isa 30 33 Topheth is prepared . . . deep and wide
57 4 have you opened your mouth wide and
Jer 22 14 I will build me a wide house and large
Eze 23 32 drink thy sister's cup, deep and wide
Nah 3 13 shall be set wide open to thy enemies
Mat 7 13 wide is the gate, and broad is the way
widow Gen 38 11 remain a w. in thy father's house
Exod 22 22 you shall not hurt a w. or an orphan
Lev 21 14 a w. or one that is divorced or defiled
22 13 but if she be a widow or divorced
Num 30 10 the widow and she that is divorced
Deut 10 18 judgment to the fatherless and the w.
14 29 stranger and the fatherless and the widow. 16:11, 14; 24:19, 20, 21; 26:12, 13; 27:19; Jer 7:6; 22:3
2 K 14 5 answered: Alas, I am a widow woman
3 K 7 14 the son of a widow woman of the tribe
11 26 mother was named Sarua, a w. woman
17 9 commanded a widow woman there to feed
10 saw the widow woman gathering sticks
20 hast thou afflicted also the widow
Jdth 8 1 when Judith a widow had heard these
4 Judith his relict was widow now three
9 3 assist . . . O Lord God, me a widow. For
Job 24 21 and to the widow he hath done no good
29 13 and I comforted the heart of the widow
31 16 have made the eyes of the widow wait
Ps 93 6 have slain the widow and the stranger
108 9 be fatherless, and his wife a widow
131 15 blessing I will bless her widow: I
145 9 will support the fatherless and the w.
Prov 15 25 will strengthen the borders of the w.
Wisd 2 10 just man, and not spare the widow
Eccu 35 17 the widow, when she poureth out her
Isa 1 17 judge for the fatherless, defend the w.
47 8 I shall not sit as a widow, and I shall
Jer 5 28 have not judged the cause of the widow
Lam 1 1 mistress of the Gentiles become as a w.
Bar 4 12 let no man rejoice over me, a widow
16 carried away the beloved of the widow
6 37 they shall not pity the widow nor do
Eze 22 7 grieved the fatherless and w. in thee
44 22 neither shall they take to wife a widow
22 they may take a widow . . . the widow of a priest
Zach 7 10 oppress not the w. and the fatherless
Mark 12 42 and there came a certain poor widow
43 this poor w. hath cast in. Luke 21:3
Luke 2 37 she was a widow until fourscore and
4 26 to Sarepta of Sidon, to a w. woman
7 12 of his mother; and she was a widow
18 3 was a certain widow in that city
5 this widow is troublesome to me, I
21 2 and he saw also a certain poor widow
1 Tim 5 4 but if any widow have children, or
5 but she that is a widow indeed, and
9 w. be chosen of no less than threescore
Apoc 18 7 I sit a queen, and am no widow; and
widowhood Gen 38 14 put off the garments of her widowhood. Jdth 16:9
Gen 38 19 put on the garments of her widowhood
2 K 20 3 unto day of their death living in w.
Jdth 10 2 put away the garments of her widowhood
Isa 47 9 in one day barrenness and widowhood
54 4 remember no more the reproach of thy w.
widow's Deut 24 17 away the w. raiment for a pledge
Job 24 3 taken away the widow's ox for a pledge
Eccu 35 18 do not the widow's tears run down
Isa 1 23 widow's cause cometh not in to them
widows Exod 22 24 and your wives shall be widows
Job 22 9 thou hast sent widows away empty, and
27 15 in death, and his widows shall not weep
Ps 67 6 father of orphans and the judge of w.
77 64 sword: and their widows did not mourn
Isa 9 17 mercy on their fatherless and widows
10 2 that widows might be their prey, and
Jer 15 8 their widows are multiplied unto me
18 21 wives be bereaved of children and w.
49 11 thy widows shall hope in me. For thus
Lam 5 3 without a father: our mothers are as w.
Eze 19 7 he learned to make widows and to lay
22 25 they have made many widows in the
Mala 3 5 wages, and widows and the fatherless
2 Ma 3 10 for the subsistence of the widows and
8 28 the feeble and the orphans and the w.
30 the feeble, the fatherless, and the w.
Mat 23 14 devour the houses of widows. Mark 12:40; Luke 20:47
Luke 4 25 there were many widows in the days of
Acts 6 1 that their widows were neglected in
9 39 widows stood about him weeping, and
41 and the widows, he presented her alive
1 C 7 8 I say to unmarried, and to the widows
1 Tim 5 3 honor widows that are widows indeed

11 but the younger widows avoid. For when
16 if any of the faithful have widows, let
16 sufficient for them that are w. indeed
James 1 27 to visit the fatherless and widows in
wife Mat 1 6 that had been the wife of Urias
Mat 1 20 not to take unto thee Mary thy wife
14 3 of Herodias, his brother's w. Luke 3:19
19 28 left . . . wife or children. Luke 10:29
22 25 the first having married a wife, died
28 whose wife of the seven shall she be
Mark 6 17 Herodias the wife of Philip his brother
18 for thee to have thy brother's wife
10 12 and if the wife shall put away her
12 20 first took a wife and died. Luke 20:29
23 whose wife shall she be of them? For
23 the seven had her to wife. Luke 20:33
Luke 1 13 thy wife Elizabeth shall bear thee a
18 and my wife is advanced in years. And
8 3 Joanna the wife of Chusa, Herod's
14 20 I have married a wife, and therefore
17 32 not return back. Remember Lot's wife
20 28 any man's brother die, having a wife
28 his brother should take her to wife
30 and the next took her to wife, and he
33 whose wife of them shall she be? For
1 C 5 1 that one should have his father's wife
7 2 let every man have his own w., and let
3 wife also in like manner to the husband
4 w. hath not power of her own body, but
4 not power of his own body, but the wife
10 the wife depart not from her husband
12 if any brother hath wife that believeth
14 husband is sanctified by believing wife
14 and the unbelieving wife is sanctified
16 for how knowest thou, O wife, whether
16 O man, whether thou shalt save thy wife
27 art thou bound to a wife? seek not to
27 thou loosed from wife? seek not a wife
28 if thou take a w., thou hast not sinned
32 that is without a wife, is solicitous
33 he that is with a wife, is solicitous
Eph 5 23 the husband is the head of the wife, as
33 and let the wife fear her husband
1 Tim 3 2 blameless, the husband of one wife
12 let deacons be the husbands of one wife
5 9 who hath been the wife of one husband
Titus 1 6 husband of one wife, having faithful
Apoc 21 9 thee the bride, the wife of the Lamb
his wife Mat 1 24 took unto him his wife
Mat 5 31 whosoever shall put away his wife. 32; 19:9; Mark 10:11
18 25 that he should be sold, and his wife
19 3 lawful . . . to put away his w. Mark 10:2
5 shall cleave to his wife. Mark 10:7; Eph 5:31
10 if the case of a man with his wife be
22 24 his brother shall marry his wife and
25 issue, left his wife to his brother
27 19 his wife sent to him, saying: Have
Mark 12 19 die, and leave his wife behind him
19 his brother should take his wife and
Luke 1 5 his w. was of the daughters of Aaron
24 Elizabeth his wife conceived, and hid
2 5 with Mary his espoused wife, who was
14 26 and hate not his . . . wife and children
16 18 every one that putteth away his wife
Acts 5 1 Ananias, with Saphira his wife, sold
2 land, his wife being privy thereunto
7 when his wife, not knowing what had
18 2 come from Italy, with Priscilla his w.
24 24 Felix, coming with Drusilla his wife
1 C 7 3 husband render the debt to his wife
11 let not the husband put away his wife
33 the world, how he may please his wife
Eph 5 28 he that loveth his wife, loveth himself
33 particular love his wife as himself
Apoc 19 7 and his wife hath prepared herself
wife's Gen 39 19 too much credit to his w. words
Lev 18 11 nakedness of thy father's w. daughter
18 thou shalt not take thy wife's sister
Tob 11 18 an abundance of money of his wife's
Mat 8 14 he saw his wife's mother lying and
Mark 1 30 Simon's wife's mother lay in a fit of a
Luke 4 38 Simon's wife's mother was taken with
wild Gen 16 12 he shall be a wild man: his hand
Gen 37 33 an evil wild beast hath eaten him
Exod 12 8 unleavened bread with wild lettuce
Lev 17 13 if . . . he take a wild beast or a bird
Num 9 11 with unleavened bread and wild lettuce
Deut 14 5 chamois, the pygarg, the wild goat
20 20 trees that are not fruitful, but wild
1 K 24 3 which are accessible only to wild goats
4 K 4 39 into the field to gather wild herbs
39 he found something like a wild vine
39 gathered of it w. gourds of the field
Job 6 5 will the wild ass bray when he hath
11 12 himself born free like a w. ass's colt
24 5 like wild asses in the desert go forth
39 1 when the wild goats bring forth among
5 who hath sent out the wild ass free
Ps 79 14 a singular wild beast hath devoured it
103 11 the wild asses shall expect in their
Eccu 13 23 the wild ass is the lion's prey in the
Isa 5 2 it brought forth wild grapes. And how
4 and it hath brought forth wild grapes
17 11 shall be the wild grape, and in the
32 14 a joy of wild asses, the pastures of
51 20 ways, as the wild ox that is snared
Jer 2 24 wild ass accustomed to the wilderness
14 6 the wild asses stood upon the rocks
Dan 5 21 his dwelling was with the wild asses
Osee 8 9 to Assyria, a wild ass alone by himself
Amos 7 14 but I am a herdsman plucking wild figs
Mat 3 4 his meat was locusts and wild honey
Mark 1 6 and he ate locusts and wild honey
Rom 11 17 being wild olive, art ingrafted in them
24 if thou wert cut out of wild olive tree
wild beasts; *see* **beasts**
wilderness Gen 14 6 of Pharan, which is in the w.
Gen 16 7 her by a fountain of water in the w.
21 14 wandered in the wilderness of Bersabee
20 he grew and dwelt in the wilderness
21 he dwelt in the wilderness of Pharan
36 24 that found the hot waters in the w.
37 22 this pit, that is in the wilderness
47 19 the land be turned into a wilderness
Exod 3 18 three days' journey into the w. 5:3; 8:27
8 28 to sacrifice to Lord your God in the w.
13 20 in the utmost coasts of the wilderness
14 11 thou hast brought us to die in the w.
12 to serve them than to die in the w.
15 22 went forth into the wilderness of Sur
22 marched three days through the w.
16 2 against Moses and Aaron in the w.
10 they looked towards the wilderness
14 it appeared in the wilderness small
32 wherewith I fed you in the wilderness
19 1 they came into the wilderness of Sinai
23 29 lest the land be brought into a w.
Lev 16 10 and let him go into the wilderness
26 31 I will bring your cities to be a w.
Num 10 12 the cloud rested in the w. of Pharan
31 what places we should encamp in the w.
14 3 would God we may die in this vast w.
16 therefore did he kill them in the w.
22 that I have done in Egypt and in the w.
25 return into the w. by the way of the

		29	in the wilderness shall your carcasses
		32	your carcasses shall lie in the w.
		35	in this wilderness shall it faint away
	15	32	the children of Israel were in the w.
	20	4	out the church of the Lord into the w.
	21	5	out of Egypt, to die in the wilderness
		11	their tents in Jeabarim in the w. that
		18	they marched from the w. to Mathana
	23	28	Phogor, which looketh towards the w.
	26	65	foretold that they should die in the w.
	32	15	he will leave the people in the w.
	33	8	through midst of the sea into the w.
	34	3	side shall begin from the w. of Sin
Deut	1	1	beyond the Jordan, in the plain w.
		19	through the terrible and vast wilderness
		31	in the wilderness . . . God hath carried in the w. (as thou hast seen) the Lord
		40	return you and go into the w. by the
	2	1	we came into the w. that leadeth to
		7	thou hast passed through this great w.
		26	sent messengers from the w. of Cademoth
	3	17	the plain of the w. and the Jordan and
	4	43	Bosor in the w. which is situate in
		49	the east side unto the sea of the w.
	8	15	thy leader in the great and terrible w.
		16	fed thee in the wilderness with manna
	9	7	the Lord thy God to wrath in the w.
		28	that he might kill them in the w., who
	11	5	what he hath done to you in the w.
	32	10	in a place of horror and of vast w.
Josu	3	16	down into the sea of the wilderness
	5	6	years of the journey in the wide w.
	8	15	fleeing by the way of the wilderness
		20	were going toward the w., turned back
		24	after Israel in his flight to the w.
	12	1	east country that looketh towards the w.
		3	from the w. to the sea of Ceneroth . . . and to the sea of the w.
		8	in Asedoth and in the w. and in the
	14	10	when Israel journeyed through the w.
	16	1	the w. which goeth up from Jericho to
	18	12	reaching to the wilderness of Bethaven
	20	8	which is upon the plain of the w. of
	21	36	Bosor in the wilderness, one of the
	24	7	and you dwelt in the w. a long time
Judg	1	16	into the wilderness of his lot which is
	11	22	and from the wilderness to the Jordan
	20	45	saw this, they fled into the w. and
		47	were able to escape and flee to the w.
1 K	23	25	and abode in the wilderness of Maon
		25	pursued after David in the wilderness
	25	1	David . . . went down into w. of Pharan
		2	certain man in the wilderness of Maon
		4	when David heard in the wilderness
		14	David sent messengers out of the w. to
		21	belonged to this man in the wilderness
	26	1	Hachila, which is over against the w.
		2	Saul arose and went down to the w. of
		2	to seek David in the wilderness of Ziph
		3	Hachila, which was over against the w.
		3	the way: and David abode in the w.
		3	Saul was come after him into the w.
2 K	2	24	by the way of the wilderness in Gabaon
	4	7	went off by the way of the wilderness
	15	28	I will lie hid in the plains of the w.
	17	16	this night in the plains of the w.
		29	faint with hunger and thirst in the w.
3 K	9	18	Palmira in the land of the wilderness
4 K	14	25	Emath unto the sea of the wilderness
	25	4	leadeth to the plains of the wilderness
1 Pa	6	78	Bosor in the w. with its suburbs, and
	12	8	to David, when he lay hid in the w.
2 Pa	1	3	where was the tabernacle . . . in the w.
	20	16	over against the wilderness of Jeruel
	26	10	he built towers in the w. and dug
Job	30	3	who gnawed in the w., disfigured with
	38	26	on the earth without man in the w.
	39	6	to whom I have given a house in the w.
Ps	54	8	off flying away: and I abode in the w.
	64	13	the beautiful places of the wilderness
	77	15	he struck the rock in the wilderness
		19	can God furnish a table in the w.
		52	guided them in the w. like a flock
	94	9	the day of temptation in the wilderness
	101	7	like to a pelican of the wilderness
	105	9	led them through the depths as in a w.
	106	4	they wandered in a wilderness, in a
		33	hath turned rivers into a wilderness
		35	turned wilderness into pools of waters
Prov	21	19	it is better to dwell in a wilderness
Wisd	18	20	disturbance of the multitude in the w.
Eccu	6	3	thou be left as a dry tree in the w.
	43	23	devour the mountains and burn the w.
	45	22	compassed him about in the wilderness
Isa	14	17	that made the world a wilderness and
	16	8	they have wandered in the wilderness
	27	10	be forsaken and shall be left as a w.
	32	16	judgment shall dwell in the wilderness
	35	1	the wilderness shall rejoice and shall
		6	in the desert, and streams in the w.
	40	3	make straight in the w. the paths of
	41	19	I will plant in the w. the cedar and
	43	19	I will make a way in the wilderness
		20	I have given waters in the wilderness
	51	3	and her w. as the garden of the Lord
	63	13	a horse in the w. that stumbleth not
Jer	2	15	they have made his land a wilderness
		24	wild ass accustomed to the wilderness
		31	am I become a wilderness to Israel
	3	2	waiting for them as a robber in the w.
	4	26	and behold Carmel was a wilderness
	9	2	who will give me in the wilderness
		12	perished, and is burnt up like a w.
	12	10	delightful portion into a desolate w.
		12	are come upon all the ways of the w.
	22	6	surely I will make thee a wilderness
	48	6	your lives: and be as heath in the w.
	50	12	a wilderness unpassable and dry
	52	7	went by the way that leadeth to the w.
Lam	4	19	they lay in wait for us in the w.
Eze	15	8	and I shall have made their land a w.
	20	18	I said to their children in the w.
		23	I lifted up my hand upon them in the w.
		35	I will bring you into the w. of people
	29	9	of Egypt shall become a desert and a w.
	33	28	I will make the land a wilderness and
	34	25	that dwell in the w. shall sleep secure
	35	14	shall rejoice, I will make thee a w.
Osee	2	3	I will make her as a w. and will set
		14	and will lead her into the wilderness
	13	5	thee in the desert in the land of the w.
Joel	1	19	the beautiful places of the w. 20
	2	3	behind it a desolate w., neither is
		22	beautiful places of the w. are sprung
	3	19	Edom a wilderness destroyed: because
Amos	2	10	I led you forty years through the w.
Soph	2	13	he will make the beautiful city a w.
Zach	7	14	changed the delightful land into a w.
Mala	1	3	I have made his mountains a wilderness
1 Ma	1	41	her sanctuary was desolate like a w.
	2	31	away into the secret places in the w.
Mark	8	4	fill them here with bread in the w.
Luke	3	4	voice of one crying in the w. John 1:23
Acts	7	38	was in the church in the wilderness
2 C	11	26	in perils in the wilderness, in perils
Apoc	12	6	and the woman fled into the wilderness

wildernesses Wisd 11 2 they went through w. that
wile Mark 14 1 how they might by some wile lay
wilful Eccu 20 4 so thou shalt escape wilful sin
wilfully Heb 10 26 if we sin w. after having the
2 Ma 14 3 had wilfully defiled himself in the time
2 P 3 5 this they are wilfully ignorant of
wiliness Mark 12 15 knowing their w., saith to
willows Lev 23 40 trees, and w. of the brook
Job 40 17 willows of the brook shall compass him
Ps 136 2 on the willows in the midst thereof
Isa 15 7 lead them to the torrent of the w.
44 4 as willows beside the running waters
wills Ps 102 7 his w. to the children of Israel
Ps 110 2 sought out according to all his wills
Mich 6 16 hast walked according to their wills
Acts 13 22 own heart, who shall do all my wills
wind Gen 8 1 brought a wind upon the earth, and
Exod 10 19 and he made a very strong wind to blow
15 10 thy wind blew and the sea covered them
Num 11 31 a wind going out from the Lord, taking
2 K 22 11 and slid upon the wings of the wind
3 K 18 45 heavens grew dark with clouds and wind
19 11 great and strong wind before the Lord
11 the Lord is not in the wind, and after the wind an earthquake
4 K 3 17 you shall not see wind nor rain: and
Job 1 19 a violent wind came on a sudden from
4 16 the voice as it were of a gentle wind
6 26 and you utter words to the wind. You
7 7 remember that my life is but wind, and
8 2 words of thy mouth be like a strong w.
13 25 leaf that is carried away with the wind
15 2 as if he were speaking in the wind
21 18 as chaff before the face of the wind
30 15 as a w. thou hast taken away my desire
22 and set me as it were upon the wind
37 17 when south wind blows upon the earth
21 the wind shall pass and drive them away
Ps 1 4 like the dust, which the wind driveth
17 43 as small as the dust before the wind
34 5 let them become as dust before the wind
47 8 with a vehement wind thou shalt break
77 26 he removed the south wind from heaven
26 power brought in the southwest wind
39 a wind that goeth and returneth not
82 14 as stubble before the wind. As fire
106 25 word, and there arose a storm of wind
147 18 his wind shall blow, and the waters
Prov 25 14 as clouds and wind, when no rain
23 the north wind driveth away rain, as
27 16 is as he that would hold the wind and
30 4 who hath held the wind in his hands
Ecce 5 15 him that he hath labored for the wind
11 4 that observeth the wind, shall not sow
Cant 4 16 arise, O north w., and come, O south w.
Wisd 4 4 they shall be shaken with the wind
5 15 dust which is blown away with the wind
15 that is scattered abroad by the wind
24 a mighty wind shall stand up against
13 2 imagined either the fire or the wind
Eccu 5 11 winnow not with every wind, and go not
17 17 whether it were a whistling wind or
22 21 will not stand against face of the wind
34 2 shadow, and followeth after the wind
43 17 at his will the south wind shall blow
22 the cold north wind bloweth, and the
25 at his word the wind is still, and with
Isa 7 2 of the woods are moved with the wind
17 13 dust of the mountains before the wind
26 18 in labor, and have brought forth wind
32 2 be as when one is hid from the wind
41 2 as stubble driven by the wind, to his
16 and the wind shall carry them away
29 vain: their idols are wind and vanity
57 13 the wind shall carry them all off
58 5 to wind his head about like a circle
64 6 iniquities, like the wind, have taken
Jer 2 24 snuffed up the wind of his love: none
4 12 full wind from these places shall come
5 13 the prophets have spoken in the wind
10 13 forth the wind out of his treasures
13 24 which is carried away by the wind
14 6 they snuffed up the wind like dragons
22 22 the wind shall feed all thy pastors
49 32 I will scatter into every wind them
51 1 a pestilential wind against Babylon
16 forth the wind out of his treasures
Bar 6 60 the wind bloweth in every country. And
Eze 5 2 third part thou shalt scatter in the w.
10 thy whole remnant into every wind
12 of thee will I scatter into every wind
12 14 his troops I will scatter into every w.
13 11 and a stormy wind to throw it down
13 I will cause a stormy wind to break
17 21 shall be scattered into every wind
27 26 the south wind hath broken thee in the
Dan 2 35 they were carried away by the wind
3 50 like the blowing of a wind bringing dew
Osee 4 19 the wind hath bound them up in its
8 7 shall sow wind, and reap a whirlwind
12 1 Ephraim feedeth on the wind and
Amos 4 13 the mountains and createth the wind
Jon 1 4 the Lord sent a great wind into the sea
Agge 2 18 I struck you with a blasting wind
Zach 5 9 two women, and wind was in their wings
Mat 11 7 a reed shaken with the wind. Luke 7:24
14 24 the waves: for the wind was contrary
30 seeing the wind strong, he was afraid
32 the wind ceased. Mark 4:39; 6:51
Mark 4 37 there arose a great storm of wind
39 he rebuked the wind. Luke 8:24
40 that both wind and sea obey him? And
6 48 for the wind was against them, and
8 23 there came down a storm of wind upon
12 55 when ye see the south wind blow, you
John 6 18 by reason of a great wind that blew
Acts 2 2 as of a mighty wind coming, and it
27 7 the wind not suffering us, we sailed
13 south w. gently blowing, thinking that
14 arose against it a tempestuous wind
15 and could not bear up against the wind
40 hoisting up the mainsail to the wind
28 13 after one day, the south wind blowing
Eph 4 14 carried about with every w. of doctrine
James 1 6 is moved and carried about by the wind
Apoc 6 13 figs when it is shaken by a great wind
burning wind Gen 41 27 that were blasted with the burning wind
Exod 10 13 the Lord brought a burning w. all that
13 the burning wind raised the locusts
14 21 took it away by a strong and burning w.
Job 27 21 a burning wind shall take him up and
Jer 4 11 a burning wind is in the ways that are
18 17 as a burning wind will I scatter them
Eze 17 10 when the burning wind shall touch it
19 12 the burning wind dried up her fruit
Osee 13 15 the Lord will bring a burning wind
Amos 4 9 I struck you with a burning wind and
Jon 4 8 Lord commanded a hot and burning wind
Haba 1 9 prey, their face is like a burning wind
winding 3 K 6 8 by w. stairs they went up to
Job 26 13 hand brought forth the winding serpent
Eze 41 7 going up by winding stairs, and it
John 11 44 feet and hands with winding bands
window Gen 6 16 thou shalt make a w. in the ark
Gen 8 6 Noe, opening the window of the ark

26 8 Abimelech . . . looking out through a w.
Josu 2 15 let them down with a cord out of a w.
18 a sign, and thou tie it in the window
21 hung the scarlet cord in the window
Judg 5 28 his mother looked out at a window and
1 K 19 12 she let him down through a window. And
2 K 6 16 Michol . . . looking out through a w.
4 K 9 30 but Jezabel . . . looked out of a window
32 Jehu lifted up his face to the window
13 17 and said: Open the window to the east
1 Pa 15 29 looking out at a window, saw king David
Prov 7 6 I look out of the window of my house
Eccu 21 26 a fool will peep through the window
Soph 2 14 voice of the singing bird in the window
Acts 20 9 Eutychus, sitting on the window, being
2 C 11 33 through a window in a basket was I let
windows 3 K 6 4 made in the temple oblique w.
Cant 2 9 our wall, looking through the windows
Eccu 14 24 he who looketh in at her windows and
Isa 60 8 clouds, and as doves to their windows
Jer 9 21 death is come up through our windows
22 14 who openeth to himself windows, and
Eze 40 16 slanting w. in the little chambers
16 there were also in the porches windows
22 the windows thereof and the porch. 29
25 windows thereof and the porches. 33
25 as the other w.: the length was 50
36 the porch thereof and the windows
41 16 the thresholds and the oblique windows
16 the ground was up to the w., and the w. were shut over the doors
26 upon which were the oblique windows
Dan 6 10 opening the w. in his upper chamber
Joel 2 8 they shall fall through the windows
9 they shall come in at the windows
2 Ma 3 19 and others looked out of the windows
winds Job 28 25 who made a weight for the winds
Ps 10 7 storms of winds shall be the portion
17 11 he flew upon the wings of the winds
103 3 walkest upon the wings of the winds
134 7 bringeth forth winds out of his stores
148 8 fire, hail, snow, ice, stormy winds
Prov 10 4 that trusteth to lies feedeth the winds
11 29 his own house, shall inherit the winds
Wisd 4 4 through the force of winds they shall
7 20 rage of wild beasts, the force of winds
Jer 49 36 I will bring upon Elam the four winds
36 I will scatter them into all these w.
Eze 37 9 come, spirit, from the four winds
42 20 by the four winds he measured the wall
Dan 7 2 the four winds of the heaven strove
8 8 under it towards the four w. of heaven
11 4 it shall be divided towards the four w.
Zach 2 6 scattered you into the four winds of
6 5 these are the four winds of the heaven
Mat 7 25 the floods came, and the winds blew. 27
8 26 he commanded the winds and the sea
27 for the winds and the sea obey him
24 31 gather together his elect from the four winds. Mark 13:27
Luke 8 25 commandeth both the winds and the sea
Acts 27 4 Cyprus, because the winds were contrary
15 giving up the ship to the winds, we
James 3 4 and are driven by strong winds, yet
Jude 12 which are carried about by winds, trees
Apoc 7 1 holding the four winds of the earth
windy Job 16 3 shall windy words have no end
wine Gen 9 21 Noe . . . drinking of the wine, was
Gen 9 24 Noe awakening from the wine, when he
14 18 bringing forth bread and wine, for he
19 32 let us make him drunk with wine and
34 let us make him drink wine also tonight
35 made their father drink wine. 19:35
27 25 he [Jacob] offered him wine also
28 God give . . . abundance of corn and wine
37 established him with corn and wine
49 11 he shall wash his robe in wine and his
12 his eyes are more beautiful than wine
Exod 29 40 wine for libation of the same measure. Num 15:10
Lev 10 9 you shall not drink wine nor anything
23 13 libations also of wine, the fourth part
Num 6 3 they shall abstain from wine and from
3 they shall not drink vinegar of wine
20 after this the Nazarite may drink wine
15 5 he shall give the same measure of wine
7 same measure of wine for the libation
18 12 all the best of the oil and of the wine
28 7 for a libation you shall offer of wine
14 these shall be the libations of wine
Deut 11 14 that you may gather in . . . your wine
12 17 not eat . . . of thy corn and thy wine
14 23 shalt eat . . . of thy corn and thy wine
26 shalt buy . . . wine also and strong
18 4 firstfruits also of corn, of wine, and
28 39 shalt not drink the wine nor gather any
51 will leave thee no wheat or wine nor
29 6 nor have you drunk wine or strong drink
32 33 their wine is the gall of dragons
38 drank the w. of their drink offerings
33 28 eye of Jacob in land of corn and wine
Josu 9 4 wine bottles rent and sewed up again
13 these bottles of wine when we filled
Judg 9 13 can I forsake my wine, that cheereth
13 4 drink no wine nor strong drink. 7
14 neither let her drink wine or strong
19 19 we have . . . bread and wine for the use
1 K 1 14 digest a little the wine, of which
15 and have drunk neither wine nor any
24 bushels of flour, and a bottle of wine
10 3 and another carrying a bottle of wine
16 20 laden with bread, and a bottle of wine
25 18 and took . . . two vessels of wine and
37 when Nabal had digested his wine, his
2 K 13 28 when Amnon shall be drunk with wine
16 1 cakes of figs, and a vessel of wine
2 the wine to drink if any man be faint
4 K 18 32 a fruitful land, and plentiful in wine
1 Pa 9 29 charge of the fine flour and wine and
12 40 meal, figs, raisins, wine, oil and oxen
27 27 and over the wine cellars, Zabdias an
2 Pa 2 10 I will give . . . 20,000 measures of wine
15 and the wine . . . send to thy servants
11 11 provisions, that is, of oil and of wine
31 5 offered . . . firstfruits of corn, wine
32 28 storehouses also of corn, of wine
1 Es 6 9 wine and oil . . . be given them day by
7 22 and unto a hundred bates of wine, and
2 Es 2 1 wine was before him, and I took up the wine and gave it to the king
5 11 restore . . . and of the corn, the wine
15 took of them in bread and wine and in
8 10 eat fat meats and drink sweet wine
10 39 firstfruits of corn, of wine, and of
13 5 the tithes of the corn, of the wine
12 brought tithe of the corn and the wine
15 lading asses with wine and grapes and
Tob 4 18 lay out thy bread and thy wine upon the
Jdth 10 5 she gave to her maid a bottle of wine
11 12 consecrated things . . . in corn, wine
12 12 she may eat with him and drink wine
20 and drank exceeding much wine, so much
13 2 they were all overcharged with wine
Esth 1 7 wine also in abundance and of the best
10 king . . . was well warmed with wine
5 6 after he had drunk wine plentifully

7 2 after he was warm with wine: What is
14 17 that I have not drunk the wine of the
Job 1 13 were eating and drinking wine in. 18
32 19 my belly is as new wine which wanteth
Ps 4 8 by the fruit of their corn, their wine
59 5 hast made us drink the wine of sorrow
68 13 they that drank wine made me their song
74 9 a cup of strong wine full of mixture
77 65 that hath been surfeited with wine
103 15 that wine may cheer the heart of man
Prov 3 10 thy presses shall run over with wine
4 17 and drink the wine of iniquity. But the
9 2 she hath . . . mingled her wine, and set
5 drink the wine which I have mingled
12 11 delighted in passing his time over wine
20 1 fools. Wine is a luxurious thing and
21 17 that loveth wine . . . shall not be rich
23 30 they that pass their time in wine, and
31 look not upon the w. when it is yellow
35 when shall I awake and find wine again
31 4 give not wine to kings: because there
6 wine to them that are grieved in mind
Ecce 2 3 to withdraw my flesh from wine, that
8 and vessels to serve to pour out wine
9 7 and drink thy wine with gladness
10 19 and wine, that the living may feast
Cant 1 1 thy breasts are better than wine. 4:10
3 remembering thy breasts more than wine
2 4 he brought me into the cellar of wine
5 1 I have drunk my wine with my milk
7 9 thy throat like the best wine, worthy
8 2 I will give thee a cup of spiced wine and new wine of my pomegranates
Wisd 2 7 let us fill ourselves with costly wine
Eccu 9 13 strive not with her over wine, lest thy
15 a new friend is as new wine: it will
19 2 wine and women make wise men fall off
31 22 how sufficient is a little wine for a
30 challenge not them that love wine: for
30 wine hath destroyed very many. Fire
31 wine drunk to excess shall rebuke the
32 wine taken with sobriety is equal life
33 his life, who is diminished with wine
35 wine was created from the beginning to
36 wine drunken with moderation is the joy
38 w. drunken with excess raiseth quarrels
39 wine drunken with excess is bitterness
41 rebuke not thy neighbor in banquet of w.
32 7 a concert of music in a banquet of wine
8 music with pleasant and moderate wine
40 20 wine and music rejoice the heart, but
49 2 as music at a banquet of wine. He was
Isa 1 22 thy wine is mingled with water. Thy
5 11 the evening, to be inflamed with wine
12 the pipe and wine are in your feasts
22 you that are mighty to drink wine
16 10 he shall not tread out w. in the press
22 13 eating flesh and drinking wine: let
24 9 shall not drink wine with a song: the
11 shall be a crying for w. in the streets
25 6 shall make . . . a feast of wine, of fat
6 of wine purified from the lees. And
27 2 be singing to the vineyard of pure wine
28 1 the fat valley, staggering with wine
7 also have been ignorant through wine
7 they are swallowed up with wine, they
29 9 be drunk, and not with wine: stagger
36 17 away to . . . a land of corn and of wine
49 26 drunk . . . as with new wine: and all
51 21 thou that art drunk but not with wine
55 1 buy wine and milk without money, and
56 12 let us take wine, and be filled with
62 8 shall not drink thy wine for which
Jer 13 12 every bottle shall be filled with wine
23 9 I am become . . . as a man full of wine
25 15 take the cup of wine of this fury at
31 12 the corn and wine and oil and the
35 2 and thou shalt give them wine to drink
5 I set . . pots full of wine, and cups
5 and I said to them: Drink ye wine
6 they answered: We will not drink wine
6 you shall drink no wine, neither you
8 so as to drink no wine all our days
14 commanded his sons not to drink wine
40 12 gathered wine and a very great harvest
48 33 taken away the wine out of the presses
51 7 the nations have drunk of her wine
Lam 2 12 where is corn and wine? When they
Eze 27 18 thy merchants . . . in rich wine, in wool
44 21 no priest shall drink wine when he is
Dan 1 5 of the wine of which he drank himself
8 nor with the wine which he drank
16 and the wine that they should drink
5 4 they drank wine and praised their gods
10 3 nor wine entered into my mouth, neither
14 2 forty sheep and sixty vessels of wine
10 and make ready the wine and shut the
Osee 2 8 not know that I gave her corn and wine
9 will I return and take away . . . my wine
22 earth shall hear the corn and the wine
4 11 and wine . . . take away the understanding
7 5 the princes began to be mad with wine
14 they have thought upon wheat and wine
9 2 the wine shall deceive them. They
4 they shall not offer wine to the Lord
14 8 shall be as the wine of Libanus. Ephraim
Joel 1 5 that take delight in drinking sweet w.
10 the wine is confounded, the oil hath
2 19 I will send you corn and wine and oil
24 presses shall overflow with wine and
3 3 the girl they have sold for wine, that
Amos 2 8 and drank the wine of the condemned
12 you will present wine to the Nazarites
5 11 and shall not drink the wine of them
6 6 that drink wine in bowls and anoint
9 14 vineyards, and drink the wine of them
Mich 2 11 I will let drop to thee of wine and
6 15 thou shalt tread . . . the new wine, but shalt not drink the wine
Haba 2 5 as wine deceiveth him that drinketh it
Soph 1 13 and shall not drink the wine of them
Agge 1 11 I called for a drought . . . upon the w.
2 13 and touch with his skirt . . . wine or
Zach 9 15 shall be inebriated as it were with w.
17 wine springing forth virgins? Ask
10 7 their heart shall rejoice as through w.
2 Ma 15 40 as it is hurtful to drink always wine
Mat 9 17 neither do they put new wine into old
17 break, and the wine runneth out and
17 new wine they put into new bottles
11 19 that is a glutton and a wine drinker
27 34 they gave him wine to drink mingled
Mark 2 22 no man putteth new w. into. Luke 5:37
22 the wine will burst the bottles, and
22 the wine will be spilled, and the
22 new wine must be put into new bottles. Luke 5:38
15 23 him to drink wine mingled with myrrh
Luke 1 15 shall drink no wine nor strong drink
5 37 otherwise the new wine will break
7 33 neither eating bread nor drinking wine
34 that is a glutton and a drinker of w.
10 34 his wounds, pouring in oil and wine
John 2 3 the wine failing, the mother of Jesus
3 saith to him: They have no wine. And
9 had tasted the water made wine, and

10 at first setteth forth good wine, and
10 thou hast kept the good wine until now
4 46 where he made the water wine. And
Acts 2 13 said: These men are full of new wine
Rom 14 21 not to eat flesh, and not to drink wine
Eph 5 18 be not drunk with w., wherein is luxury
1 Tim 3 3 bishop . . . not given to w. Titus 1:7
8 tongued, not given to much wine, not
5 23 use a little wine for thy stomach's sake
Titus 2 3 not given to much wine, teaching well
1 P 4 3 in riotousness, lusts, excess of wine
Apoc 6 6 see thou hurt not the wine and the oil
14 8 w. of the wrath of her fornication. 18:3
10 shall drink of the wine of the wrath
10 which is mingled with pure wine in the
16 19 wine of the indignation of his wrath
17 2 drunk with the wine of her whoredom
winefat Mark 12 1 dug a place for the winefat
winepress Num 18 30 of the barnfloor and the w.
Deut 15 14 and out of thy barnfloor and thy w.
16 13 thy fruit of the barnfloor and of the w.
Judg 6 11 and cleansing wheat by the winepress
7 25 and Zeb in the winepress of Zeb. And
4 K 6 27 out of the barnfloor or out of the w.
Eccu 33 17 gathereth grapes, have I filled the w.
Isa 5 2 set up a winepress therein: and he
63 2 like theirs that tread in the winepress
3 I have trodden the winepress alone
Lam 1 15 the Lord hath trodden the winepress
Osee 9 2 and the winepress shall not feed them
Apoc 19 15 he treadeth the w. of the fierceness
winepresses Num 18 27 the barnfloors as of the w.
Job 24 11 having trodden the w. suffer thirst
80 1 for the w., a psalm for Asaph himself
83 1 for the w., a psalm for the sons of
Zach 14 10 of Hananeel even to the king's w.
wines 2 Es 5 18 I gave store of divers wines
wing 3 K 6 24 w. of cherub was five cubits, and
3 K 6 24 of one w. to extremity of the other w.
27 the wing of the one touched one wall
27 the wing of the other cherub touched
2 Pa 3 11 so that one wing was five cubits long
11 reached to the wing of the other cherub
12 in like manner the wing of other cherub
12 his other wing was five cubits long
12 touched the wing of the other cherub
Job 39 13 wing of the ostrich is like the wings
Isa 10 14 there was none that moved the wing
1 Ma 9 1 the right wing of his army with them
12 and Bacchides was in the right wing
15 the right wing was discomfited by them
16 that were in the left wing saw that the right wing was discomfited
winged Gen 1 21 every w. fowl according to its
wings Exod 19 4 carried you upon w. of eagles
Exod 25 20 spreading their wings and covering. 37:9
Deut 14 19 and hath little wings shall be unclean
32 11 he spread his wings and hath taken him
Ruth 2 12 and under whose wings thou art fled
2 K 22 11 and slid upon the wings of the wind
3 K 6 27 cherubims stretched forth their wings
27 other wings . . . touched one another
8 6 under the w. of the cherubims. 2 Pa 5:7
7 the cherubims spread forth their wings
1 Pa 28 18 the cherubims spreading their wings
2 Pa 3 11 wings of the cherubims were extended
13 wings of the two cherubims were spread
5 8 the cherubims spread their wings over
Job 39 13 ostrich is like the wings of the heron
18 she setteth up her wings on high: she
26 spreading her wings to the south? Will
Ps 16 8 protect me under the shadow of thy w.
17 11 he flew upon the wings of the winds
35 8 their trust under the covert of thy w.
54 7 who will give me wings like a dove
56 2 in the shadow of thy wings will I hope
60 5 protected under the covert of thy wings
62 8 I will rejoice under covert of thy w.
67 14 as wings of a dove covered with silver
90 4 and under his wings thou shalt trust
103 3 walkest upon the wings of the winds
138 9 if I take my wings early in the morning
Prov 1 17 before the eyes of them that have wings
23 5 they shall make themselves wings like
Ecce 10 20 he that hath wings will tell what thou
Wisd 5 11 only the sound of the wings beating
11 she moved her wings, and hath flown
Isa 6 2 one had six w. and the other had six w.
8 8 stretching out of his wings shall fill
40 31 they shall take wings as eagles, they
Jer 48 40 shall stretch forth his wings to Moab
49 22 he shall spread his wings over Bosra
Eze 1 6 four faces, and every one four wings
8 the hands of a man under their wings
8 had faces and wings on the four sides
9 w. of one were joined to w. of another
11 and their wings were stretched upward
11 two wings of every one were joined
23 under the firmament were their wings
23 every one with two wings covered his
24 and I heard the noise of their wings
24 they stood, their wings were let down
25 they stood, and let down their wings
3 13 noise of the w. of the living creatures
10 5 the sound of the wings of the cherubims
8 likeness of man's hand under their wings
12 their w. and the circles were full of
16 cherubims lifted up their w. 11:22
19 the cherubims lifting up their wings
21 four faces, and each one had four w.
21 of man's hand was under their wings
11 22 the cherubims lifted up their wings
17 3 a large eagle with great wings
7 another large eagle, with great wings
Dan 7 4 lioness, and had the wings of an eagle
4 I beheld her till her w. were plucked
6 had upon it four wings as of a fowl
Osee 4 19 wind hath bound them up in its wings
Zach 5 9 wind was in their wings, and they had wings like the wings of a kite
Mala 4 2 shall arise, and health in his wings
1 Ma 6 38 at the two wings, with trumpets to
Mat 23 37 gather her chickens under her wings
Luke 13 34 bird doth her brood under her wings
Apoc 4 8 had each of them six wings; and round
9 9 the noise of their wings was as the
12 14 two wings of a great eagle, that she
wink Ps 34 19 without cause, and w. with the eyes
Eccu 30 11 youth, and wink not at his devices
winked Acts 17 30 w. at the times of this
winketh Prov 6 13 he w. with the eyes, presseth
Prov 10 10 he that w. with the eye shall cause
Eccu 27 25 he that w. with the eye forgeth wicked
winks Prov 6 25 be not caught with her winks
winning Wisd 4 2 w. reward of undefiled conflicts
winnow Eccu 5 11 w. not with every wind, and go
winnowed Isa 30 24 provender as it was w. in the
winnoweth Ruth 3 2 this night he w. barley in
winter Gen 8 22 cold and heat, summer and w.
Exod 9 32 and other winter corn were not hurt
Job 37 6 the winter rain and the shower of his
Cant 2 11 winter is now past, the rain is over
Eccu 21 9 himself stones to build in the winter
Isa 18 6 of the earth shall winter upon them
Jer 36 22 now the king sat in the winter house
Amos 3 15 I will strike the winter house with

Zach 14 8 they shall be in summer and in winter
Mat 24 20 that your flight be not in the winter
Mark 13 18 that these things happen not in winter
John 10 22 at Jerusalem: and it was winter. And
Acts 27 12 it was not a commodious haven to w. in
12 they might reach Phenice to winter there
1 C 16 6 I shall abide, or even spend the winter
2 Tim 4 21 make haste to come before w. Eubulus
Titus 3 12 for there I have determined to winter
wintered Acts 28 11 that had w. in the island
winter's Wisd 16 29 shall melt away as the w. ice
wipe 2 Es 13 14 and wipe not out my kindnesses
Prov 20 30 blueness of a wound shall w. away evils
Isa 25 8 Lord God shall wipe away tears from
Bar 6 12 they wipe their face because of the
23 except a man wipe off the rust, they
Luke 10 11 cleaveth to us, we wipe off against
John 13 5 and to wipe them with the towel
Apoc 7 17 God shall wipe away all tears from. 21:4
wiped 3 K 20 41 wiped off the dust from his face
Luke 7 38 and wiped them with the hairs of her
44 and with her hairs hath wiped them
John 11 2 and wiped his feet with her hair. 12:3
wipeth Prov 30 20 who eateth and wipeth her mouth
wisdom Mat 11 19 wisdom is justified by her children. Luke 7:35
Mat 12 42 to hear the w. of Solomon. Luke 11:31
13 54 how came this man by this wisdom and
Mark 6 2 what wisdom is this that is given to
Luke 1 17 incredulous to the wisdom of the just
2 40 waxed strong, full of wisdom; and the
47 astonished at his w. and his answers
52 Jesus advanced in wisdom and age and
11 49 the wisdom of God said: I will send
21 15 I will give you a mouth and wisdom
Acts 6 3 full of the Holy Ghost and wisdom
10 were not able to resist the wisdom
7 10 he gave him favor and wisdom in the
22 instructed in all the wisdom of the
Rom 8 6 the w. of the flesh is death; but the w. of the spirit is life and peace
7 wisdom of the flesh is an enemy to God
11 33 O the depth of the riches of the w. and
1 C 1 17 not in w. of speech, lest the cross of
19 I will destroy the wisdom of the wise
20 God made foolish the w. of this world
21 for seeing that in the wisdom of God
21 the world, by wisdom, knew not God, it
22 and the Greeks seek after wisdom: but
24 power of God, and the wisdom of God
30 who of God is made unto us wisdom, and
2 1 came not in loftiness of speech or of w.
4 in persuasive words of human wisdom, but
5 faith might not stand on the w. of men
6 we speak wisdom among the perfect: yet
6 yet not wisdom of this world, neither
7 we speak the w. of God in a mystery, a w. which is hidden
13 not in learned words of human wisdom
3 19 the wisdom of this world is foolishness
11 8 by Spirit, is given the word of wisdom
2 C 1 12 not in carnal wisdom, but in the grace
Eph 1 8 hath superabounded in us in all wisdom
17 may give unto you the spirit of wisdom
3 10 that the manifold wisdom of God may be
Col 1 9 the knowledge of his will, in all wisdom
28 teaching every man in all wisdom, that
2 3 in whom are hid all the treasures of w.
23 which things have indeed a show of w.
3 16 dwell in you abundantly, in all wisdom
4 5 walk with wisdom towards them that are
James 1 5 if any of you want wisdom, let him ask
3 13 his work in the meekness of wisdom
15 this is not wisdom, descending from
17 the wisdom that is from above, first
2 P 3 15 Paul, according to the w. given him
Apoc 5 12 to receive power and divinity and w.
7 12 and glory and wisdom and thanksgiving
13 18 here is w. He that hath understanding
17 9 is the understanding that hath wisdom
wise Gen 39 8 he in no wise consenting to that
Gen 41 15 I have heard that thou art very wise
33 king provide a wise and industrious man
Exod 23 8 bribes, which even blind the wise and
28 3 shalt speak to all the wise of heart
35 10 whosoever of you is wise, let him come
36 8 all the men that were wise of heart
Deut 1 13 among you wise and understanding men
15 of your tribes men wise and honorable
4 6 behold a wise and understanding people
16 19 for gifts blind the eyes of the wise
32 29 O that they would be wise, and would
2 K 14 2 and fetched from thence a wise woman
20 but thou, my lord, O king, art wise
20 16 a wise woman cried out from the city
3 K 3 12 thee a wise and understanding heart
2 Pa 2 12 king David a wise and knowing son
Job 5 13 catcheth the wise in their craftiness
9 4 he is wise in heart and mighty in
37 24 all that seem to themselves to be wise
Ps 48 11 when he shall see the wise dying: the
93 8 people: and, you fools, be wise at last
106 43 who is wise and will keep these things
Prov 1 6 words of the wise and their mysterious
3 7 be not wise in thy own conceit: fear
35 the wise shall possess glory: the
8 33 hear instruction and be wise, and
9 12 if thou be wise, thou shalt be so to
10 8 the wise of heart receiveth precepts
13 in the lips of the wise is wisdom found
19 that refraineth his lips is most wise
11 29 winds: and the fool shall serve the wise
30 and he that gaineth souls, is wise
12 15 that is wise hearkeneth unto counsels
16 he that dissembleth injuries is wise
13 14 law of the wise is a fountain of life
20 walketh with the wise, shall be wise
14 1 a wise woman buildeth her house: but
3 the lips of the wise preserve them
6 the learning of the wise is easy. Go
15 but the wise servant shall prosper in
24 the crown of the wise is their riches
35 wise servant is acceptable to the king
15 2 tongue of the wise adorneth knowledge
7 lips of wise shall disperse knowledge
12 reproveth him: nor will he go to the w.
14 heart of the wise seeketh instruction
24 the path of life is above for the wise
31 shall abide in the midst of the wise
16 23 heart of the wise shall instruct his
17 2 a wise servant shall rule over foolish
24 wisdom shineth in the face of the wise
27 bounds to his words, is knowing and w.
28 hold his peace, will be counted wise
18 15 a wise heart shall acquire knowledge
15 ear of the wise seeketh instruction
19 20 thou mayst be wise in thy latter end
20 1 delighted therewith shall not be wise
26 a wise king scattereth the wicked
21 11 if he follow the wise, he will receive
22 17 thy ear, and hear the words of the wise
23 15 if thy mind be wise, my heart shall
19 hear thou, my son, and be wise: and
24 23 these things also to the wise: It is
25 12 pearl, so is he that reproveth the wise
26 5 lest he imagine himself to be wise

12 thou seen a man wise in his own conceit
27 19 hearts of men are laid open to the wise
28 11 the rich man seemeth to himself wise
30 24 they are wiser than the wise: the ants
Ecce 2 16 remembrance of the wise no more than
4 13 better is a child that is poor and w.
7 5 heart of w. is where there is mourning
8 oppression troubleth the wise, and
17 and be not more wise than is necessary
20 wisdom hath strengthened the wise more
24 I have said: I will be wise: and it
9 11 nor bread to the wise, nor riches to
15 was found in it a man poor and wise
17 words of the wise are heard in silence
12 9 and whereas Ecclesiastes was very wise
11 the words of the wise are as goads and
Wisd 6 26 multitude of the wise is the welfare
26 w. king is the upholding of the people
7 15 wisdom and the director of the wise
Eccu 3 31 heart of the w. is understood in wisdom
32 w. heart and which hath understanding
4 29 and learning by the word of the wise
5 15 honor and glory is in word of the wise
6 24 give ear, my son, and take w. counsel
33 apply thy mind, thou shalt be wise
34 thou love to hear, thou shalt be wise
35 multitude of ancients that are wise
7 5 desire not to appear wise before the
21 depart not from a wise and good wife
23 let a wise servant be dear to thee
8 9 of them that are ancient and wise
9 21 and treat with the wise and prudent
10 1 a wise judge shall judge his people
28 shall serve a servant that is wise
16 5 by one that is wise a country shall
19 28 that holdeth his peace, he is wise
20 5 holdeth his peace, that is found wise
13 a man wise in words shall make himself
21 14 he that is not wise in good, will not
18 will praise every wise word he shall
19 in the lips of the wise, grace shall be
28 the words of the wise shall be weighed
22 4 w. daughter shall bring an inheritance
20 thought of him that is wise at all
25 11 is he that dwelleth with a wise woman
26 18 such is a wise and silent woman, and
36 21 and the wise heart false speeches
37 25 wise man that is wise to his own soul
38 35 and every one is wise in his own art
40 25 but wise counsel is above them both
50 30 in his heart, shall be wise always
47 15 how wise wast thou in thy youth. And
Isa 5 21 to you that are wise in your own eyes
19 11 wise counsellors of Pharao have given
11 to Pharao: I am the son of the wise
27 11 it is not a wise people, therefore he
31 2 he that is the wise one hath brought
44 25 that turn the wise backward and that
Jer 4 22 they are wise to do evil, but to do
8 8 how do you say: We are wise, and the
9 17 and send to them that are wise women
18 18 nor counsel from the wise, nor the word
23 5 a king shall reign and shall be wise
Dan 2 21 giveth wisdom to the w., and knowledge
Osee 14 10 who is wise, and he shall understand
Abdi 8 destroy the wise out of Edom, and
Zach 9 2 taken to themselves to be exceeding w.
Mat 1 18 generation of Christ was in this wise
10 16 be ye therefore wise as serpents and
11 25 hid these things from the w. Luke 10:21
24 45 is a faithful and wise servant, whom
25 2 five of them were foolish and five wise
4 but the wise took oil in their vessels
8 the foolish said to the wise: Give us
9 the wise answered, saying: Lest perhaps
Luke 12 42 is the faithful and wise steward
Rom 1 14 to wise and to unwise, I am a debtor
22 for professing themselves to be wise
11 25 you should be wise in your own conceits
12 3 not to be more w. than it behoveth to be w., but to be w. unto sobriety
16 be not wise in your own conceits. To no
16 19 but I would have you to be wise in good
27 to God the only wise, through Jesus
1 C 1 19 I will destroy the wisdom of the wise
20 where is the wise? Where is the scribe
26 there are not many wise according to the
27 chosen, that he may confound the wise
3 10 as w. architect, I have laid foundation
18 if any man among you seem to be wise in
18 him become a fool, that he may be wise
19 catch the wise in their own craftiness
20 the Lord knoweth the thoughts of the w.
4 10 but you are wise in Christ; we are weak
2 C 11 19 the foolish; whereas yourselves are wise
23 I speak as one less wise: I am more; in
Eph 5 16 but as wise: redeeming the time, because
Titus 2 4 teach the young women to be wise, to

wise man Exod 36 1 every w. man to whom the
2 K 13 3 the brother of David, a very wise man
3 K 2 9 but thou art a wise man and knowest
1 Pa 26 14 Zacharias, a very wise and learned man
27 32 a counsellor, a wise and learned man
2 Pa 2 13 Hiram, a wise and most skilful man
Tob 4 19 seek counsel always of a wise man
Prov 9 8 rebuke a w. man, and he will love thee
14 16 a wise man feareth and declineth from
Ecce 2 14 the eyes of a wise man are in his head
19 whether he will be a wise man or a fool
6 8 what hath the w. man more than the fool
7 6 is better to be rebuked by a wise man
30 who is as the wise man? And who hath
8 5 the heart of a wise man understandeth
17 yea, though the wise man shall say
10 2 heart of a wise man is in his right
12 words of the mouth of a wise man are
Eccu 7 27 great work, and give her to a wise man
19 26 a wise man, when thou meetest him
20 7 a wise man will hold his peace till he
29 a wise man shall advance himself with
21 8 a wise man knoweth to slip by him
16 knowledge of a wise man shall abound
23 but a wise man will scarce laugh low
27 a wise man will be grieved with the
31 silent and wise man shall be honored
33 2 a wise man hateth not the commandments
37 25 wise man that is wise to his own soul
26 wise man instructeth his own people
27 wise man shall be filled with blessings
29 a wise man shall inherit honor among
38 4 and a wise man will not abhor them
39 1 the wise man will seek out the wisdom
45 12 purple, a woven work of a wise man
Jer 9 12 who is the w. man, that may understand
23 let not the w. man glory in his wisdom
Dan 2 10 such a thing of any diviner or w. man
2 Ma 2 9 like a w. man, he offered the sacrifice
Mat 7 24 a wise man that built his house upon
1 C 6 5 there is not among you any one wise man
James 3 13 who is a wise man and endued with

wise men Deut 1 13 wise and understanding men
1 Es 8 16 and Joiarib and Elnathan, wise men
Job 13 5 you might be thought to be wise men
15 18 wise men confess and hide not their
Prov 10 14 wise men lay up knowledge: but the
Ecce 9 1 there are just men and wise men, and

Eccu 21 29 mouth of wise men is in their heart
Isa 19 12 where are now thy wise men? Let them
29 14 wisdom shall perish from their w. men
Jer 8 9 the wise men are confounded, they are
10 7 among all the wise men of the nations ·
50 35 upon her princes, and upon her wise men
51 57 her princes drunk, and her wise men
Eze 27 8 thy wise men, O Tyre, were thy pilots
9 ancients of Gebal and the wise men
Dan 1 20 than all the diviners and wise men
2 2 together the diviners and the wise men
12 all the wise men of Babylon should
13 the wise men were slain: and Daniel
14 forth to kill the wise men of Babylon
18 with the rest of the w. men of Babylon
24 destroy not the wise men of Babylon
24 given orders to destroy the wise men of
27 to know, none of the wise men or the
48 over all the wise men of Babylon. And
4 3 that all the wise men of Babylon should
4 came in the diviners, the wise men
15 wise men of my kingdom are not able
5 7 out aloud to bring in the wise men
7 and said to the wise men of Babylon
8 then came in all the king's wise men
11 appointed him prince of the wise men
15 the wise men the magicians have come
Mat 2 1 there came wise men from the east to
7 Herod, privately calling the wise men
16 that he was deluded by the wise men
16 diligently inquired of the wise men
23 34 I send to you prophets and wise men
1 C 10 15 idols. I speak as to wise men: judge ye
wise son 3 K 5 7 given to David a very w. son
Prov 10 1 a wise son maketh the father glad: but
5 gathered in the harvest, is a wise son
13 1 a wise son heareth the doctrine of his
15 20 a wise son maketh a father joyful
23 24 that hath begotten a wise son, shall
28 7 he that keepeth the law is a wise son
Eccu 47 14 after him arose up a wise son and
wisely Gen 40 16 seeing that he had w. interpreted
Exod 1 10 let us wisely oppress them, lest they
1 K 18 14 David behaved wisely in all his ways
30 David behaved himself more wisely than
2 K 20 22 to all the people and spoke to them w.
4 K 18 7 he [Ezechias] behaved himself wisely
Ps 46 8 king of all the earth: sing ye wisely
57 6 nor of the wizard that charmeth wisely
Prov 17 8 turneth himself, he understandeth w.
28 26 he that walketh w., he shall be saved
Ecce 1 13 and search out wisely concerning all
16 mind hath contemplated many things w.
Eccu 13 27 is rebuked also: he hath spoken wisely
18 29 have also done wisely themselves: and
Mark 12 34 seeing that he had answered wisely
Luke 16 8 forasmuch as he had done wisely: for
wiser Judg 5 29 was w. than the rest of his wives
3 K 4 31 he was w. than all men: w. than Ethan
11 23 he was w. and mightier than all
Ps 118 98 hast made me wiser than my enemies
Prov 1 5 wise man shall hear and shall be wiser
19 25 the fool shall be wiser: but if thou
21 11 the little one will be wiser: and if
26 16 sluggard is wiser in his own conceit
30 24 they are wiser than the wise: the ants
Eze 28 3 thou art wiser than Daniel: no secret
Luke 16 8 children of this world are wiser in
1 C 1 25 the foolishness of God is w. than men
wisest 2 K 23 8 the wisest chief among the three
wish 4 K 5 3 I wish my master had been with the
Tob 5 24 I wish the money . . . had never been
Job 11 5 I wish that God would speak with thee
13 5 and I wish you would hold your peace
39 35 spoken, which I wish I had not said
Eccu 23 19 wish that thou hadst not been born
wished Gen 29 30 obtained the marriage he wished
Job 14 6 rest, until his wished for day come
Ps 106 30 to the haven which they wished for
Wisd 7 7 I wished, and understanding was given me
Acts 27 29 out of the stern, and wished for the day
Rom 9 3 for I w. myself to be an anathema from
wisheth 2 Ma 9 19 w. much health and welfare and
wishing Gen 24 60 w. prosperity to their sister
Job 31 30 to sin, by wishing a curse to his soul
witch 1 Pa 10 13 moreover consulted also a witch
witchcraft 1 K 15 23 like the sin of w., to rebel
Nah 3 4 harlot . . . that made use of witchcraft
witchcrafts Nah 3 4 families through her w.
Gal 5 19 immodesty, luxury, idolatry, witchcrafts
withal Mark 16 20 Lord working w. and confirming
Luke 6 38 measure that you shall mete withal
withdraw Josu 10 6 w. not thy hands from helping
Job 13 21 withdraw thy hand far from me, and let
33 17 that he may w. a man from the things
30 he may w. their souls from corruption
Prov 21 12 that he may w. the wicked from evil
25 17 w. thy foot from the house of thy
Ecce 2 3 to withdraw my flesh from wine, that I
7 19 and from him withdraw not thy hand
Wisd 1 5 will w. himself from thoughts that are
Eccu 13 12 by one that is mightier, w. thyself
32 15 to thy house, and there w. thyself
Mich 2 3 from which you shall not w. your necks
2 Th 3 6 that you withdraw yourselves from every
Heb 10 38 if he w. himself, he shall not please
withdraweth 2 Ma 6 16 never w. his mercy from us
withdrawing Eccu 38 20 w. aside sorrow remaineth
Heb 10 39 not the children of w. unto perdition
withdrawn Deut 13 10 he would have w. thee from
Deut 13 13 have w. the inhabitants of their city
Job 22 7 thou hast w. bread from the hungry
Wisd 4 2 they desire it when it hath w. itself
Lam 2 8 hath not w. his hand from destroying
Eze 18 8 hath withdrawn his hand from iniquity
Osee 5 6 shall not find him: he is w. from them
Joel 1 12 joy is w. from the children of men
2 Ma 2 10 the stars have w. their shining. 3:15
5 27 had w. himself into a desert place
Luke 22 41 he was w. away from them a stone's
withdrew 1 K 2 17 they w. men from the sacrifice
2 Es 9 29 they w. the shoulder and hardened their
1 Ma 9 6 many w. themselves out of the camp and
2 Ma 1 7 after Jason withdrew himself from the
Gal 2 12 he w. and separated himself, fearing
wither Job 15 32 and his hands shall wither away
Job 33 19 and he maketh all his bones to wither
Ps 36 2 they shall shortly w. away as grass
89 6 he shall fall, grow dry, and wither
Eccu 10 18 the roots of proud nations to wither
20 made some of them to wither away and
Isa 19 6 reed and the bulrush shall wither away
7 it shall wither away and shall be no
25 5 branch of the mighty to wither away
42 15 will make all their grass to wither
51 12 who shall wither away like grass? And
Jer 12 4 and the herb of every field wither for
Eze 17 9 hath shot forth, and make it wither
10 and shall it not wither in the furrows
Zach 11 17 his arm shall quite wither away, and
John 15 6 forth as a branch, and shall wither
withered 3 K 13 4 stretched forth against him w.
Job 7 5 my skin is withered and drawn together
Ps 101 5 as grass, and my heart is withered
12 shadow, and I am withered like grass
Wisd 2 8 with roses before they be withered

Isa 15 6 the grass is w. away, the spring is
37 27 which withered before it was ripe
40 7 grass is withered, and the flower. 8
24 they are w., and a whirlwind shall
Lam 4 8 stuck to their bones, it is withered
Eze 19 12 her strong rods are withered and dried
Joel 1 12 all the trees of the field are withered
Amos 1 2 and the top of Carmel is withered
4 7 piece whereupon I rained not, withered
Jon ·4 7 it struck the ivy and it withered
Mat 12 10 man who had a withered hand. Mark 3:1, 3; Luke 6:8
13 6 they had not root, they withered away
21 19 immediately the fig tree withered away
20 how is it presently withered away? And
Mark 4 6 it had no root, it withered away. And
11 21 thou didst curse, is withered away
Luke 6 6 a man whose right hand was withered
8 6 it w. away because it had no moisture
John 5 3 sick, of blind, of lame, of withered
1 P 1 24 the grass is withered, and the flower
withereth Job 8 12 it withereth before all herbs
Ps 128 6 which withereth before it be plucked up
withering Luke 21 26 men w. away from fear and
withheld Gen 20 6 w. thee from sinning against
Ecce 2 10 I withheld not my heart from enjoying
Eze 31 15 I withheld its rivers and restrained
withhold Exod 9 2 if thou refuse and w. them
2 Es 9 20 thy manna thou didst not w. from their
Job 4 2 who can w. the words he hath conceived
12 15 if he withhold the waters, all things
Ps 39 12 w. not thou, O Lord, thy tender mercies
Prov 3 27 do not withhold him from doing good
23 13 withhold not correction from a child
withholden 1 K 25 26 hath w. thee from coming to
1 K 25 34 who hath w. me from doing thee any evil
Ps 20 3 not w. from him the will of his lips
Jer 3 3 the showers were withholden and the
5 25 your sins have w. good things from you
Eze 18 16 nor withholden the pledge nor taken
Amos 4 7 I also have withholden the rain from
withholdeth Job 26 9 w. the face of his throne
Jer 48 10 be he that w. his sword from blood
2 Th 2 6 you know what w., that he may be
withholding Eccu 46 9 and w. the people from sins
withstand Num 22 32 I am come to w. thee [Balaam]
1 K 17 33 thou art not able to w. this Philistine
2 Pa 13 8 you say that you are able to withstand
Ecce 4 12 against one, two shall withstand him
Wisd 12 12 or who shall withstand thy judgment
Jer 7 16 do not w. me: for I will not hear thee
49 19 that can w. my countenance. 50:44
Bar 6 55 they cannot withstand a king and war
Dan 8 4 and no beasts could withstand him
7 and the ram could not withstand him
11 15 arms of the south shall not withstand
1 Ma 5 40 we shall not be able to withstand him
Acts 11 17 who was I, that could withstand God
withstood 2 Pa 26 18 withstood the king and said
Wisd 18 21 making supplication, w. the wrath and
2 Ma 8 5 he could not be w. by the heathens
Acts 13 8 Elymas . . . withstood them, seeking
Gal 2 11 I withstood him to the face, because he
2 Tim 4 15 he hath greatly withstood our words
witness Gen 31 47 Laban called it The w. heap
Gen 31 48 this heap shall be a witness between
48 Galaad, that is, The witness heap. The
50 none is witness of our speech but God
52 shall be a witness: this heap, I say
44 34 lest I be a witness of the calamity
Exod 20 16 thou shalt not bear false witness
23 1 join thy hand to bear false witness
Lev 5 1 the voice of one swearing, and is a w.
Deut 4 26 heaven and earth to w. 30:19; 31:28
17 6 when only one beareth witness against
19 15 one witness shall not rise up against
16 if a lying witness stand against a man
Judg 11 10 he himself is mediator and witness
1 K 12 5 the Lord is witness against you, and
5 and his anointed is witness this day
5 my hand. And they said: He is witness
3 K 21 13 bore w. against him before the people
Jdth 7 17 we call to witness this day heaven and
Job 16 20 behold my witness is in heaven, and he
29 11 the eye that saw me gave witness to me
Ps 88 38 and a faithful witness in heaven. But
Prov 6 19 a deceitful witness that uttereth lies
12 17 he that lieth, is a deceitful witness
19 hasty witness, frameth a lying tongue
14 5 a faithful witness will not lie: but a
5 but a deceitful witness uttereth a lie
25 a faithful witness delivereth souls
19 28 an unjust witness scorneth judgment
21 28 lying w. shall perish: an obedient man
24 28 be not witness without cause against
Wisd 1 6 God is witness of his reins, and he is
17 10 it beareth witness of its condemnation
Eccu 28 13 tongue that beareth w. bringeth death
Isa 55 4 I have given him for a witness to the
Jer 29 23 I am the judge and the witness, saith
Osee 11 12 Juda went down as a witness with God
Mich 1 2 let the Lord God be a witness to you
Mala 2 14 Lord hath been w. between thee and the
3 5 will be a speedy w. against sorcerers
1 Ma 2 56 for bearing w. before the congregation
2 Ma 9 8 bearing w. to the manifest power of God
Mat 26 62 things which these witness against thee
Mark 14 59 and their witness did not agree. And
John 1 7 this man came for a witness to give
15 John beareth w. of him and crieth out
5 31 if I bear w. of myself, my w. is not
32 another that beareth witness of me
32 w. which he witnesseth of me is true
Acts 1 22 one of these must be made a witness
20 26 I take you to witness this day, that I
22 15 thou shalt be his witness to all men
20 blood of Stephen thy witness was shed
26 16 I may make thee a minister and a w. of
Rom 1 9 for God is my witness. Phil 1:8
2 15 their conscience bearing w. to them
9 1 bearing me witness in the Holy Ghost
2 C 1 23 I call God to witness upon my soul, that
1 Th 2 5 occasion of covetousness, God is w.
Heb 2 4 God also bearing them witness by signs
7 8 there he hath witness, that he liveth
1 P 5 1 and a w. of the sufferings of Christ
Apoc 1 5 Jesus Christ, who is the faithful w.
2 13 when Antipas was my faithful witness
3 14 Amen, the faithful and true witness
bear witness; ***see*** **bear**
false witness; ***see*** **false**
witnessed Rom 3 21 being w. by the law and
witnesses Num 5 13 and cannot be proved by w.
Num 35 30 the murderer shall be punished by w.
Deut 17 6 by mouth of two or three w. shall he
7 hands of the witnesses shall be first
19 15 in the mouth of two or three w. every
Josu 24 22 you are witnesses, that you yourselves
22 and they answered: We are witnesses
Ruth 4 9 you are witnesses this day, that I have
10 you, I say, are witnesses of this thing
11 the ancients answered: We are witnesses
Job 10 17 thou renewest thy witnesses against me
Ps 26 12 unjust witnesses have risen up against
34 11 unjust witnesses rising up have asked
Wisd 4 6 w. of wickedness against their parents

Isa 8 2 I took unto me faithful w., Urias the
43 9 let them bring forth their witnesses
10 you are my witnesses. 12; 44:8
44 9 they are their witnesses, that they do
Jer 32 10 book and sealed it and took witnesses
12 in presence of the w. that subscribed
25 buy a field for money and take w.
44 sealed, and witnesses shall be taken
Dan 13 40 tell us: of this thing we are witnesses
Mat 18 16 in mouth of two or three w. 2 C 13:1
23 31 you are witnesses against yourselves
26 60 many false witnesses had come in. And
60 there came two false witnesses. And
65 what further need have we of witnesses
Mark 14 63 what need we any further witnesses
24 48 and you are witnesses of these things
Acts 1 8 you shall be w. unto me in Jerusalem
2 32 raised again, whereof all we are w.
3 15 from the dead, of which we are w. And
5 32 and we are witnesses of these things
6 13 they set up false witnesses, who said
7 57 w. laid down their garments at the
10 39 we are witnesses of all things that
41 w. preordained by God, even to us, who
13 31 this present are his w. to the people
1 C 15 15 yea, and we are found false witnesses
1 Th 2 10 you are w., and God also, how holily
1 Tim 5 19 under two or three witnesses. Heb 10:28
6 12 good confession before many witnesses
2 Tim 2 2 hast heard of me by many witnesses, the
Heb 12 1 so great a cloud of w. over our head
Apoc 11 3 I will give unto my two witnesses and
witnesseth John 5 32 which he w. of me is true
Acts 20 23 the Holy Ghost in every city w. to me
witnessing Acts 26 22 I stand unto this day, w.
wits Mark 5 15 clothed, and well in his wits
witty Wisd 8 19 I was a w. child and had received
wives Gen 4 19 Lamech, who took two wives: the
Gen 4 23 hear my voice, ye wives of Lamech
6 2 took to themselves wives of all which
18 wives of thy sons with thee. 8:16
7 7 the wives of his sons with him. 8:18
13 three wives of his sons with them went
11 29 and Abram and Nachor married wives
26 34 Esau being 40 years old, married w.
30 26 give me my wives and my children, for
31 50 if thou bring in other wives over them
34 21 we shall take their daughters for wives
36 2 Esau took wives of the daughters of
37 2 Bala and Zelpha his father's wives
46 26 out of his thigh, besides his sons' w.
Num 14 3 our wives and children be led away
32 26 we will leave our children and our w.
36 3 if men of another tribe take them to w.
7 shall marry wives of their own tribe
Deut 17 17 he shall not have many w., that may
21 15 if a man have two w., one beloved
Judg 3 6 they took their daughters to wives
8 30 seventy sons . . . for he had many wives
12 9 wives for his sons of the same number
21 7 whence shall they take wives? For we
14 w. were given them of the daughters
16 the rest that have not received wives
Ruth 1 4 they took wives of the women of Moab
1 K 1 2 he had two wives, the name of one
30 5 wives also of David were taken captives
2 K 5 13 David took more concubines and wives
12 8 and thy master's wives into thy bosom
11 I will take thy wives before thy eyes
11 he shall lie with thy w. in the sight
19 5 daughters and the lives of thy wives
3 K 11 3 he had seven hundred wives as queens
20 3 w. and thy goodliest children are mine
5 thy wives and thy children thou shalt
7 he sent to me for my wives and for
4 K 4 1 woman of the wives of the prophets
24 15 he carried away . . . the king's wives
1 Pa 4 5 had two wives, Halaa and Naara: and
7 4 for they had many wives and children
15 and Machir took wives for his sons
14 3 David took other wives in Jerusalem
2 Pa 11 21 [Roboam] had married eighteen wives
23 abundance, and he sought many wives
13 21 but Abia . . . took fourteen wives: and
21 14 wives and all thy substance. And thou
24 3 Joiada took for him [Joas] two wives
29 9 and wives are led away captives for
1 Es 10 2 taken strange wives of the people of
3 covenant . . . to put away all the wives
10 taken strange w., to add to the sins
14 them that have taken strange wives
17 the men that had taken strange wives
18 of priests that had taken strange w.
44 all these had taken strange wives, and
2 Es 13 23 Jews that married w., women of Azotus
Jdth 7 16 after we have seen our wives and our
Esth 1 18 all the wives of the princes of the
20 let all wives as well of the greater as
Jer 29 6 take ye wives and beget sons and
6 take wives for your sons, and give your
23 adultery with the w. of their friends
35 8 no wine . . . neither we nor our wives
38 23 thy w. and thy children shall be brought
Dan 5 23 thy w. and thy concubines have drunk
1 Ma 3 20 to destroy us and our wives and our
56 building houses or had betrothed wives
13 6 sanctuary and our children and wives
Luke 17 27 in the days of Noe . . . they married w.
20 35 neither be married nor take wives
1 C 7 29 that they also who have wives, be as
Col 3 18 wives, be subject to your husbands
1 P 3 1 let w. be subject to their. Eph 5:24
1 won . . . by the conversation of the w.
his wives Gen 4 23 Lamech said to his wives
Gen 31 17 his children and wives upon camels
32 22 rising early he took his two wives
36 6 Esau took his wives and his sons and
Judg 5 29 was wiser than the rest of his wives
1 K 25 43 and they were both of them his wives
27 3 David with his two wives, Achinoam the
30 18 and he [David] rescued his two wives
2 K 2 2 so David went up, and his two wives
3 K 11 8 did in this manner for all his wives
1 Pa 8 8 he sent away Husim and Bara his wives
2 Pa 11 21 loved Maacha . . . above all his wives
21 17 house, his sons also and his wives
Dan 5 2 his w. and his concubines might drink
3 his wives and his concubines, drank
their wives Gen 34 29 their children and wives they took captive
Gen 45 19 carriage of their children and their w.
46 5 their children and wives in the wagons
Num 16 27 entry of their pavilions with their w.
Judg 21 10 to the sword, with their w. and their
1 K 30 3 and that their wives and their sons
2 Pa 20 13 with their little ones and their wives
31 18 to their wives and to their children
1 Es 10 19 to put away their wives and to offer
2 Es 5 1 cry of the people and of their wives
10 28 their wives, their sons, and their
12 42 t. w. also and their children rejoiced
Jdth 4 7 and prayers, both they and their wives
9 made a prey, and their wives carried off
9 3 gavest their wives to be made a prey
Esth 8 11 enemies with their wives and children
13 6 destroyed . . . with their wives and

Wisd 3 12 their wives are foolish, and their
Isa 13 16 pillaged, and their w. shall be ravished
Jer 6 12 to others, with their lands and their w.
14 16 none to bury them: they and their wives
18 21 let their wives be bereaved of children
44 9 of Juda, and the evils of their wives
15 that their wives sacrificed to other
Bar 6 27 also their wives take part of them
32 clothe their wives and their children
Dan 6 24 into the lions' den . . . and their w.
14 9 priests of Bel were 70, besides their w.
14 to their custom, with their wives
20 he took the priests and their wives
1 Ma 2 30 they and their children and their wives
38 were slain with their wives and their
5 13 they have carried away their wives
23 in Arbatis with their w. and children
45 Judas gathered . . . and their wives and
8 10 they carried away their wives and their
13 45 went up with their wives and children
2 Ma 12 3 to go with their w. and children into
15 18 their concern was less for their wives
Acts 21 5 our way, with their wives and children
28 so also ought men to love their wives
your wives Exod 19 15 come not near your wives
Exod 22 24 your wives shall be widows, and your
32 2 earrings from the ears of your wives
Deut 3 19 leaving your wives and children and
29 11 your children and your wives and the
Josu 1 14 your wives and children and cattle
1 Es 10 11 separate . . . from your strange wives
2 Es 4 14 fight for . . . daughters and your wives
Jer 44 9 your evils and the evils of your w.
25 you and your wives have spoken with
Mat 19 8 permitted you to put away your wives
Eph 5 25 husbands, love your wives. Col 3:19
wives' 1 Tim 4 7 avoid foolish and old w. fables
wizard Deut 18 10 neither let there be any wizard
Ps 57 6 nor of the wizard that charmeth wisely
wizards Exod 22 18 w. thou shalt not suffer to
Lev 19 31 go not aside after wizards, neither
Isa 19 3 diviners and their w. and soothsayers
woe 1 K 4 8 sighing, they said: Woe to us: for
1 K 4 8 woe to us. Who shall deliver us from
Tob 10 4 woe, woe is me, my son: why did we
Jdth 16 20 woe be to the nation that riseth up
Job 10 15 if I be wicked, woe unto me: and if
Ps 119 5 woe is me, that my sojourning is
Prov 23 29 who hath woe? Whose father hath woe
Ecce 4 10 woe to him that is alone, for when
10 16 woe to thee, O land, when thy king is
Eccu 2 14 woe to them . . . of a double heart
15 woe to them that are fainthearted
16 woe to them that have lost patience
31 7 woe to them that eagerly follow after
41 11 woe to you, ungodly men, who have
Isa 1 4 woe to the sinful nation, a people
3 9 woe to their souls, for evils are
11 woe to the wicked unto evil: for the
5 8 woe to you that join house to house
11 woe to you that rise up early in the
18 woe to you that draw iniquity with
20 woe to you that call evil good and
21 woe to you that are wise in your own
22 woe to you that are mighty to drink
6 5 woe is me because I have held my peace
10 1 woe to them that make wicked laws
5 woe to the Assyrian, he is the rod
17 12 woe to the multitude of many people
18 1 woe to the land, the winged cymbal
24 16 my secret to myself, woe is me: the
28 1 woe to the crown of pride, to the
29 1 woe to Ariel, to Ariel the city which
15 woe to you that are deep of heart, to
30 1 woe to you, apostate children, saith
31 1 woe to them that go down to Egypt
33 1 woe to thee that spoilest, shalt not
45 9 woe to him that gainsayeth his maker
10 woe to him that saith to his father
Jer 4 13 woe unto us, for we are laid waste
31 woe is me, for my soul hath fainted
6 4 woe unto us, for the day is declined
10 19 woe is me for my destruction, my
13 27 woe to thee, Jerusalem, wilt thou not
15 10 woe is me, my mother: why hast thou
22 13 woe to him that buildeth up his house
23 1 woe to the pastors, that destroy and
45 3 woe is me, wretch that I am, for the
48 1 woe to Nabo, for it is laid waste
46 woe to thee, Moab, thou hast perished
50 27 woe to them, for their day is come
Lam 5 16 woe to us, because we have sinned
Eze 2 9 were written in it . . . canticles and woe
13 3 woe to the foolish prophets that follow
18 woe to them that sew cushions under
16 23 woe, woe to thee, saith the Lord
24 6 woe to the bloody city, to the. 9
9 woe to the bloody city, of which I
30 2 howl ye: Woe, woe to the day: for the
34 2 woe to the shepherds of Israel, that
Osee 7 13 woe to them, for they have departed
9 12 woe to them, when I shall depart from
Amos 5 18 woe to them that desire the day of
6 1 woe to you that are wealthy in Sion
Mich 2 1 woe to you that devise that which is
7 1 woe is me, for I am become as one
Nah 3 1 woe to thee, O city of blood, all full
Haba 2 6 woe to him that heapeth together that
9 woe to him that gathereth together
12 woe to him that buildeth a town with
15 woe to him that giveth drink to his
19 woe to him that saith to wood: Awake
Soph 2 5 woe to you that inhabit the seacoast
3 1 woe to the provoking and redeemed city
1 Ma 2 7 Mathathias said: Woe is me, wherefore
Mat 11 21 woe to thee, Corozain, woe to thee, Bethsaida. Luke 10:13
18 7 woe to the world because of scandals
7 woe to that man by whom the scandal
23 13 woe to you scribes and Pharisees. 14, 15, 23, 25, 27, 29
24 19 woe to them that are with child. Mark 13:17; Luke 21:23
26 24 woe to that man by whom. Luke 14:21; 22:22
Luke 6 24 woe to you that are rich: for you
25 woe to you that are filled: for you
25 woe to you that now laugh: for you
26 woe to you when men shall bless you
11 42 woe to you Pharisees. 43
44 woe to you, because you are as
46 woe to you lawyers. 52
47 woe to you who build the monuments of
17 1 woe to him through whom they come
1 C 9 16 for woe is unto me if I preach not the
Jude 11 woe unto them, for they have gone in
Apoc 8 13 woe, woe, woe to the inhabitants of
9 12 one woe is past, and behold there come
11 14 the second woe is past: and behold the
14 behold the third woe will come quickly
12 12 woe to the earth and to the sea, because
woes Apoc 9 12 come yet two woes more hereafter
wolf Gen 49 27 Benjamin a ravenous wolf, in
Eccu 13 21 if the wolf shall at any time have
Isa 11 6 the wolf shall dwell with the lamb
65 25 wolf and the lamb shall feed together

Jer 5 6 wolf in the evening hath spoiled them
John 10 12 seeth the wolf coming, and leaveth
12 the wolf catcheth and scattereth the
wolves Eze 22 27 like wolves ravening the prey
Haba 1 8 leopards, and swifter than evening w.
Soph 3 3 lions: her judges are evening wolves
Mat 7 15 inwardly they are ravening wolves
10 16 you as sheep in the midst of wolves
Luke 10 3 I send you as lambs among wolves
Acts 20 29 ravening w. will enter in among you
woman Mat 5 28 shall look on a woman to lust
Mat 9 20 a woman who was troubled with an issue
22 the woman was made whole from that
13 33 leaven which a woman took. Luke 13:21
15 22 a woman of Canaan who came out of
28 O woman, great is thy faith: be it
22 27 last of all the woman died also. Mark 12:22; Luke 20:32
26 7 w. having an alabaster box. Mark 14:3
10 why do you trouble this woman? For she
Mark 5 25 a woman who was under an issue of blood
33 but the woman fearing and trembling
7 25 a woman as soon as she heard of him
26 the w. was a Gentile, a Syrophenician
Luke 4 26 to Sarepta of Sidon, to a widow w.
7 37 a woman that was in the city, a sinner
39 and what manner of woman this is that
44 turning to the woman, he said unto
44 dost thou see this woman? I entered
50 he said to the woman: Thy faith hath
8 43 a certain woman having an issue of
47 the woman seeing that she was not hid
10 38 certain woman named Martha, received
11 27 a certain w. from the crowd, lifting
13 11 a w. who had a spirit of infirmity
12 woman, thou art delivered from thy
15 8 what woman having ten groats; if she
22 57 him, saying: Woman, I know him not
John 2 4 woman, what is that to me and to thee
4 7 there cometh a woman of Samaria to
9 Samaritan woman saith to him: How dost
9 to drink, who am a Samaritan woman
11 the woman saith to him. 15, 19, 25
17 the woman answered and said: I have no
21 woman, believe me, that the hour cometh
27 wondered that he talked with the w.
28 the woman therefore left her waterpot
39 word of the woman giving testimony
42 they said to the woman: We now believe
8 3 unto him a woman taken in adultery
4 this woman was even now taken in
9 and the woman standing in the midst
10 woman, where are they that accuse
16 21 a woman, when she is in labor, hath
19 26 to his mother: Woman, behold thy son
20 13 woman, why weepest thou. 15
Acts 5 8 tell me, woman, whether you sold the
9 36 this woman was full of good works and
16 1 Timothy, the son of a Jewish woman
14 certain woman named Lydia, a seller
17 34 w. named Damaris, and others with them
Rom 7 2 the woman that hath an husband, whilst
1 C 7 1 is good for a man not to touch a woman
2 let every woman have her own husband
13 if any w. hath a husband that believeth
34 unmarried w. and the virgin thinketh on
39 woman is bound by the law as long as her
9 5 have we not power to carry about woman
11 3 the head of the woman is the man; and
5 every woman praying or prophesying with
6 if a woman be not covered, let her be
6 if it be a shame to a woman to be shorn
7 the woman is the glory of the man. For
8 for the man is not of the w., but the w. of the man
9 the man was not created for the w., but the w. for the man
10 ought the woman to have a power over her
11 neither is the man without the w., nor w. without the man
12 as the woman is of the man, so also is the man by the woman
13 doth it become a woman, to pray unto God
15 if a woman nourish her hair, it is glory
14 35 it is a shame for w. to speak in church
Gal 4 4 God sent his Son, made of a woman, made
22 bondwoman, and the other by a free woman
23 but he of the free woman, was by promise
30 not be heir with son of the free woman
1 Tim 2 12 but I suffer not a woman to teach, nor
14 the woman being seduced, was in the
Apoc 2 20 thou sufferest the woman Jezabel, who
12 1 a woman clothed with the sun, and the
4 the dragon stood before the woman who
6 and the woman fled into the wilderness
13 woman who brought forth the man child
14 were given to the woman two wings of
15 cast out of his mouth after the woman
16 and the earth helped the woman, and
17 the dragon was angry against the woman
17 3 I saw a woman sitting upon a scarlet
4 the woman was clothed round about with
7 mystery of the woman and of the beast
9 mountains, upon which the w. sitteth
18 the woman which thou sawest is the
womankind Lev 18 22 lie with mankind as with w.
woman's Exod 21 22 as the w. husband shall require
Deut 22 5 neither shall a man use woman's apparel
Ruth 4 5 shalt buy the field at the w. hand
3 K 3 19 this woman's child died in the night
Eccu 25 28 look not upon a woman's beauty, and
29 a woman's anger and impudence and
Eze 16 7 and camest to woman's ornament: thy
2 Ma 7 21 joining a man's heart to a w. thought
womanservant Deut 15 17 in like manner to thy w.
womb Gen 20 18 the Lord had closed up every womb
Gen 25 22 the children struggled in her womb
23 two nations are in thy womb, and two
23 shall be divided out of thy womb
24 behold twins were found in her womb
29 31 that he despised Lia, opened her womb
30 2 deprived thee of the fruit of thy womb
22 Rachel, heard her and opened her womb
38 27 bed, there appeared twins in her womb
49 25 blessings of the breasts and of the w.
Exod 13 2 that openeth the womb. Num 3:12
12 all that openeth the womb. 15; 23:19
Num 5 22 may thy womb swell and thy thigh rot
8 16 of firstborn that openeth every womb
12 12 is cast forth from the mother's womb
Deut 7 13 and will bless the fruit of thy womb
28 4 blessed shall be the fruit of thy womb
11 abound . . . with fruit of thy womb
18 cursed shall be the fruit of thy womb
53 thou shalt eat the fruit of thy womb
30 9 abound . . . in the fruit of thy womb
Judg 13 5 Nazarite . . . from his mother's womb. 7
16 17 consecrated to God from my mother's womb
Ruth 1 11 have I any more sons in my womb, that
1 K 1 5 the Lord had shut up her womb. 6
4 K 4 16 thou shalt have a son in thy womb
Tob 4 4 perils she suffered for thee in her w.
Job 1 21 naked came I out of my mother's womb
3 10 the doors of the womb that bore me
11 why did I not die in the womb, why
10 18 thou bring me forth out of the womb

19 carried from the womb to the grave
15 35 iniquity, and his w. prepareth deceits
19 17 I entreated the children of my womb
31 15 did not he that made me in the womb
15 one and the same form me in the womb
18 came out with me from my mother's womb
38 8 broke forth as issuing out of the womb
29 out of whose womb came the ice and
Ps 21 10 that hast drawn me out of the womb
11 I was cast upon thee from the womb
11 from my mother's womb thou art my God
57 4 the wicked are alienated from the womb
4 they have gone astray from the womb
70 6 have I been confirmed from the womb
6 from my mother's womb thou art my
109 3 from the womb before the day star I
126 3 the reward, the fruit of the womb. As
131 11 of the fruit of thy womb I will set
138 13 hast protected me from my mother's womb
Prov 30 16 hell and the mouth of the womb and
31 2 what, O the beloved of my womb, what
Ecce 5 14 came forth naked from his mother's w.
11 5 bones are joined together in the womb
Wisd 7 1 in womb of my mother I was fashioned
Eccu 1 16 created with the faithful in the womb
40 1 their coming out of their mother's womb
49 9 a prophet from his mother's womb
50 24 increased our days from our mother's w.
Isa 13 18 no pity upon the sucklings of the womb
44 2 formed thee, thy helper from the womb
24 redeemer and thy maker, from the womb
46 3 are borne up by my womb. Even to your
48 8 called thee a transgressor from the w.
49 1 the Lord hath called me from the womb
5 that formed me from the womb to be
15 not to have pity on the son of her womb
Jer 1 5 before thou camest forth out of the w.
20 17 who slew me not from the womb, that
17 her womb an everlasting conception
18 why came I out of the womb, to see
Eze 20 26 they offered all that opened the womb
Osee 9 11 from the w. and from the conception
14 give them a womb without children, and
16 slay best beloved fruit of their w.
12 3 in the womb he supplanted his brother
2 Ma 7 22 not how you were formed in my womb
27 that bore thee nine months in my womb
Mat 19 12 were born so from their mother's womb
Luke 1 15 Ghost, even from his mother's womb
31 thou shalt conceive in thy womb, and
41 the infant leaped in her womb. And
42 and blessed is the fruit of thy womb
44 the infant in my womb leaped for joy
2 21 before he was conceived in the womb
23 every male opening the womb shall be
11 27 blessed is the womb that bore thee
John 3 4 second time into his mother's womb
Acts 3 2 who was lame from his mother's womb
14 7 cripple from his mother's womb, who
Rom 4 19 years old, nor the dead womb of Sara
Gal 1 15 who separated me from my mother's womb
wombs Luke 23 29 the wombs that have not borne and
women Mat 11 11 that are born of w. Luke 7:28
Mat 14 21 was 5,000 men, besides women and
15 38 4,000 men, besides children and women
24 41 two women shall be grinding. Luke 17:35
27 55 there were there many women afar off
28 5 said to the women: Fear not you; for
Mark 15 40 there were also women looking on afar
41 many other women that came up with
Luke 1 28 blessed art thou among women. 42
8 2 certain w. who had been healed of
23 27 women, who bewailed and lamented him
49 w. that had followed him from Galilee
55 the women that were come with him from
24 10 and the other w. that were with them
22 certain women also of our company
24 found it so as the women had said, but
Acts 1 14 one mind in prayer with the women and
5 14 of men and women who believed in the
8 3 and dragging away men and women
12 were baptized, both men and women
9 2 he found any men and women of this way
13 50 Jews stirred up religious . . . women
16 13 and sitting down, we spoke to the women
17 4 of noble women not a few. But the Jews
12 of honorable w. that were Gentiles
22 4 delivering into prisons both men and w.
Rom 1 26 their w. have changed the natural use
27 leaving the natural use of the women
1 C 14 34 let w. keep silence in the churches: for
Eph 5 22 let women be subject to their husbands
Phil 4 3 help those women who have labored with
1 Tim 2 9 like manner women also in decent apparel
10 as it becometh w. professing godliness
11 let the w. learn in silence, with all
3 11 the women in like manner chaste, not
5 2 old w., as mothers: young w., as sisters
2 Tim 3 6 lead captive silly women laden with sins
Titus 2 3 aged women, in like manner, in holy
4 teach the young women to be wise, to
Heb 11 35 women received their dead raised to
1 P 3 5 holy women also, who trusted in God
Apoc 9 8 and they had hair as the hair of women
14 4 they who were not defiled with women
women's Esth 2 3 let them receive w. ornaments
Esth 2 9 eunuch to fasten the women's ornaments
15 but she sought not women's ornaments
Eze 23 40 wast adorned with women's ornaments
womenservants Gen 24 35 gold, menservants and w.
Gen 32 5 and sheep and menservants and w.
1 Es 2 65 their menservants and w. 2 Es 7:67
Tob 10 10 all his substance in menservants and w.
won 1 Pa 26 27 and the spoils won in battles
Jer 48 41 taken, and the strongholds are won
2 Ma 10 17 won the holds, killed them that came
1 P 3 1 they may be won without the word by
wonder Deut 13 1 and he foretell a sign and a w.
4 K 22 19 that they should become a wonder and a
2 Pa 32 31 to inquire of the wonder that had
Job 33 7 but yet let not my wonder terrify thee
40 18 will drink up a river and not wonder
Ps 70 7 I am become unto many as a wonder
Ecce 5 7 wonder not at this matter: for he that
Wisd 8 11 the faces of princes shall w. at me
Eccu 16 11 is a w. if he had escaped unpunished
26 14 and wonder not if she slight thee
Isa 8 18 given me for a sign and for a wonder
20 3 shall be a sign and a wonder of three
21 4 Babylon my beloved is become a wonder
29 9 be astonished and wonder, waver and
60 5 thy heart shall wonder and be enlarged
Jer 44 12 for an execration and for a wonder
Eze 26 16 shall wonder at thy sudden fall. And
Haba 1 5 wonder and be astonished: for a work
Mark 7 37 and so much the more did they wonder
John 3 7 wonder not that I said to thee, you
5 20 will he show him, that you may wonder
28 wonder not at this; for the hour cometh
7 21 I have done; and you all wonder
Acts 3 10 and they were filled with wonder and
12 why wonder you at this? Or why look
13 41 ye despisers, and wonder, and perish
2 C 11 14 no w.: for Satan himself transformeth
Gal 1 6 I wonder that you are so soon removed
1 J 3 13 wonder not, brethren, if the world

Apoc 17 7 why dost thou wonder? I will tell thee
8 shall wonder, seeing the beast that
wondered Gen 43 33 and they wondered very much
Deut 1 37 against the people to be wondered at
1 K 16 4 and the ancients of the city wondered
Jdth 10 14 they wondered exceedingly at her beauty
Ps 47 6 they wondered, they were troubled, they
Eccu 11 13 many have wondered at him and have
47 18 the countries wondered at thee for
2 Ma 1 22 fire kindled, so that all wondered
7 12 wondered at the young man's courage
Mat 8 27 the men wondered, saying: What manner
9 33 multitudes w., saying, Never was the
13 54 they w. and said: How came this man
19 26 disciples w. very much, saying: Who
21 20 disciples seeing it wondered, saying
22 22 hearing this they wondered and leaving
27 14 so that the governor w. exceedingly
Mark 2 12 all wondered and glorified God, saying
5 20 had done for him: and all men wondered
6 6 he wondered because of their unbelief
10 26 who wondered the more, saying among
15 5 nothing; so that Pilate wondered. Now
44 w. that he should be already dead. And
Luke 1 21 they w. that he tarried so long in the
63 is his name. And they all wondered
2 18 all that heard, wondered; and at those
48 seeing him, they wondered. And his
4 22 they wondered at the words of grace
8 25 wondered, saying one to another: Who
9 44 while all wondered at all the things
24 41 believed not, and wondered for joy
John 4 27 they w. that he talked with the woman
7 15 the Jews wondered, saying: How doth
Acts 2 7 and they were all amazed and wondered
12 they were all astonished and wondered
4 13 they w.; and they knew them that they
7 31 Moses seeing it, wondered at the sight
8 13 w. to see the signs and exceeding
Apoc 17 6 and I wondered when I had seen her
wondereth Eccu 40 7 and w. that there is no fear
wonderful Exod 8 22 wherein my people is, w.
Exod 9 4 Lord will make a wonderful difference
11 7 how wonderful a difference the Lord
Judg 13 18 why askest thou my name, which is w.
19 the Lord, who doth wonderful things
3 K 7 17 work wreathed together with w. art
Tob 12 20 and publish all his wonderful works
13 4 you may declare his wonderful works
1 Pa 16 12 remember his wonderful works which he
Job 9 10 great and incomprehensible and w.
Ps 4 4 Lord hath made his holy one wonderful
15 3 hath made w. all my desires in them
16 7 show forth thy wonderful mercies: thou
30 22 hath shown his wonderful mercy to me
39 6 hast multiplied thy wonderful works
41 5 into the place of the w. tabernacle
64 6 holy is thy temple, w. in justice
67 36 God is wonderful in his saints: the God
70 17 till now I will declare thy w. works
71 18 who alone doth wonderful things. And
77 12 w. things did he do in the sight of
85 10 art great and dost wonderful things
92 4 the sea: wonderful is the Lord on high
117 23 Lord's doing: and it is w. in our eyes
118 129 thy testimonies are w.: therefore my
138 6 thy knowledge is become wonderful to me
14 w. are thy works, and my soul knoweth
Wisd 10 17 and conducted them in a wonderful way
16 17 which was wonderful, in water, which
Eccu 11 4 the works of the Highest only are w.
36 10 that they may declare thy w. works
39 25 there is nothing wonderful before him
43 27 there are great and wonderful works
32 far exceed, and his magnificence is w.
Isa 9 6 and his name shall be called Wonderful
25 1 for thou hast done wonderful things
28 29 of hosts, to make his counsel wonderful
29 14 by a great and wonderful miracle: for
64 3 when thou shalt do wonderful things
Jer 5 30 w. things have been done in the land
21 2 according to all his wonderful works
Dan 3 43 us according to thy wonderful works
7 7 fourth beast, terrible and wonderful
Mat 21 15 seeing the wonderful things that he
42 and it is w. in our eyes. Mark 12:11
Luke 5 26 we have seen wonderful things today
John 9 30 herein is a wonderful thing, that
Acts 2 11 our own tongues the w. works of God
2 Th 1 10 to be made wonderful in all them who
Apoc 15 1 sign in heaven, great and wonderful
3 great and wonderful are thy works
wonderfully Gen 24 35 hath blessed my master w.
Job 10 16 and returning thou tormentest me w.
37 5 God shall thunder w. with his voice
Ps 44 5 thy right hand shall conduct thee w.
75 5 enlightenest w. from the everlasting
Wisd 19 5 that thy people might w. pass through
Eccu 43 8 name, increasing w. in her perfection
Lam 1 9 she is wonderfully cast down, not
wondering Gen 27 33 w. beyond what can be believed
Luke 2 33 his father and mother were wondering
20 26 w. at his answer, they held their
24 12 and went away wondering in himself at
Acts 3 11 called Solomon's, greatly wondering
wonders Exod 3 20 strike Egypt with all my w.
Exod 4 21 thou do all the wonders before Pharao
7 3 multiply my signs and wonders in the
11 10 Moses and Aaron did all the wonders
14 13 and see the great wonders of the Lord
15 11 terrible and praiseworthy, doing w.
Deut 4 34 by temptations, signs, and wonders
6 22 he wrought signs and wonders great
7 19 signs and wonders and the strong hand
26 8 with great terror, with signs and w.
28 46 they shall be as signs and wonders
29 3 seen, those mighty signs and wonders
34 11 in all the signs and wonders, which he
Josu 3 5 tomorrow the Lord will do w. among you
24 5 I struck Egypt with many signs and w.
1 Pa 16 24 Gentiles: his wonders among all people
2 Es 9 10 showedst signs and wonders upon Pharao
17 they remembered not thy wonders which
Esth 10 9 hath wrought great signs and wonders
Ps 9 2 I will relate all thy wonders. I will
45 9 what wonders he hath done upon earth
76 12 I will be mindful of thy wonders from
15 thou art the God that dost wonders
77 4 and his wonders which he hath done
11 forgot his benefits and his wonders
43 and his wonders in the field of Tanis
87 11 wilt thou show wonders to the dead
13 shall thy wonders be known in the dark
88 6 the heavens shall confess thy wonders
95 3 Gentiles: his wonders among all people
104 5 his w. and the judgments of his mouth
27 and his wonders in the land of Cham
105 7 understood not thy wonders in Egypt
106 24 his wonders in the deep. He said the
134 9 he sent forth signs and wonders in
135 4 who alone doth great wonders: for his
Wisd 8 8 she knoweth signs and wonders before
10 16 stood against dreadful kings in wonders
19 8 hand, seeing thy miracles and wonders
Eccu 36 2 that they may show forth thy wonders
38 6 that he may be honored in his wonders

	45	24	he wrought wonders upon them, and
	48	15	in his life he did great wonders, and
Jer	23	32	to err by their lying and by their w.
	32	20	and wonders in the land of Egypt even
		21	with wonders and with a strong hand
Bar	2	11	with w. and with thy great power and
Dan	3	99	hath wrought signs and w. toward me
		100	his wonders, because they are mighty
	6	27	doing signs and wonders in heaven
	12	6	long shall it be to the end of these w.
	14	42	the Savior, working signs and wonders
Joel	2	26	who hath done wonders with you and
		30	I will show wonders in heaven; and in
Mich	7	15	land of Egypt I will show him wonders
2 Ma	15	21	called upon the Lord, that worketh w.
Mat	24	24	false Christs . . . shall show great signs and wonders. Mark 13:22
John	4	48	unless you see signs and wonders, you
Acts	2	19	I will show wonders in the heaven
		22	by miracles and wonders and signs
		43	many wonders also and signs were done
	4	30	hand to cures and signs and wonders
	5	12	were many signs and wonders wrought
	6	8	did great wonders and signs among the
	7	36	doing wonders and signs in the land
	14	3	granting signs and wonders to be done
	15	12	signs and wonders God had wrought
Rom	15	19	by the virtue of signs and wonders, in
2 C	12	12	in signs and wonders and mighty deeds
2 Th	2	9	in all power and signs and lying wonders
Heb	2	4	bearing them witness by signs and w.
wondrous Ps	25	7	tell of all thy wondrous works
Ps	74	2	we will relate thy wondrous works: when
	77	32	and they believed not for his w. works
Eccu	17	8	and glory in his wondrous acts, that
	48	4	was Elias magnified in his w. works
wont Gen	24	11	women are wont to come out to draw
Gen	40	13	office, as before thou wast wont to do
	44	5	and in which he is wont to divine
Exod	5	13	as before you were wont to do when
	16	5	double to that they were wont to gather
	21	7	out as bondwomen are wont to go out
		29	if the ox was wont to push with his
		36	if he knew that his ox was wont to push
	22	17	dowry which virgins are wont to receive
	28	32	as is wont to be made in the outmost
	33	11	as a man is wont to speak to his friend
Lev	1	16	the ashes are wont to be poured. 4:12
	4	24	where the holocaust is wont to be slain
		26	as is wont to be done with the victims
		31	as is wont to be taken away of the
		33	victims of holocausts are w. to be slain
		35	is wont to be taken away: and shall
	5	3	wherewith he is wont to be defiled
		10	holocaust, as is wont to be done: and
	6	3	things, wherein men are wont to sin
	14	13	where the victim for sin is wont to be
	22	13	as she was wont to do when she was a
Num	5	6	sins that men are wont to commit, and
	11	12	as the nurse is wont to carry the
	16	29	others also are wont to be visited
	22	4	as the ox is wont to eat the grass
	29	11	that are wont to be offered for sin
Deut	1	31	as a man is wont to carry his little
	28	29	as the blind is wont to grope in the
Josu	4	18	and ran as they were wont before. And
Judg	7	5	their tongues, as dogs are wont to lap
	8	21	camels of kings are wont to be adorned
		26	the kings of Madian were wont to use
	15	14	as the flax is wont to be consumed
1 K	14	14	which a yoke of oxen is wont to plow
	20	5	am wont to sit beside the king to eat
2 K	3	33	not as cowards are wont to die, hath
4 K	21	13	as tables are wont to be effaced, and
2 Es	5	11	which you were wont to exact of them
Job	4	13	when deep sleep is wont to hold men
Isa	16	10	the press that was wont to tread it out
	23	1	from whence they were wont to come
Eze	46	12	as it is w. to be done on the sabbath
wood Gen	22	3	had cut wood for the holocaust
Gen	22	6	he took the wood for the holocaust
		7	behold, saith he, fire and wood: where
		9	and laid the wood in order upon it
		9	him on the altar upon the pile of wood
Exod	7	19	both in vessels of wood and of stone
	31	5	precious stones and variety of wood
	38	23	was an excellent artificer in wood
Lev	1	7	before laid in order a pile of wood
		12	shall lay them upon the wood, under
		17	putting fire under the wood. 3:5
	4	12	he shall burn them upon a pile of wood
	6	12	putting wood on it every day in the
	11	32	whether it be a vessel of wood or a
	14	4	cedar wood and scarlet and hyssop
		6	he shall dip, with the cedar wood and
		49	shall take two sparrows and cedar wood
		51	he shall take the cedar wood and the
		52	sparrow, and with the cedar wood and
	15	12	if vessel of wood, it shall be washed
Num	19	6	the priest shall also take cedar wood
	31	20	the skins or hair of goats, or of wood
	35	18	if he that is struck with wood die
Deut	4	28	wood and stone, that neither see nor
	10	1	and thou shalt make an ark of wood
	19	5	gone with him to the wood to hew wood
	28	36	serve strange gods, wood and stone
		64	serve strange gods . . . wood and stone
	29	11	hewers of w. and them that bring water
Josu	9	21	in hewing wood and bringing in water
		23	your race shall always be hewers of w.
		27	hewing wood and carrying water, until
	17	18	and shalt cut down the wood and make
Judg	6	26	a holocaust upon a pile of the wood
1 K	6	14	they cut in pieces the wood of the cart
	22	6	Saul abode in Gabaa and was in the wood
	23	15	David was in desert of Ziph in a wood
		16	arose and went to David into the w.
		18	David abode in the wood; but Jonathan
		19	with us in the strongholds of the wood
	31	13	and buried them in the wood of Jabes
2 K	6	5	all manner of instruments made of wood
	17	8	as a bear raging in the wood when her
	23	8	most tender little worm of the wood
	24	22	and the yokes of the oxen for wood
3 K	5	6	a man that has skill to hew wood like
	7	7	and covered it with cedar wood from
	18	23	cut it in pieces and lay it upon wood
		23	the other bullock, and lay it on wood
		33	and he laid the wood in order and cut
		33	in pieces and laid it upon the wood
		34	upon the burnt offering and upon the w.
		38	consumed the holocaust and the wood
4 K	6	2	out of the wood every man a piece of
		4	come to the Jordan, they cut down wood
		6	he cut off a piece of wood and cast it
	19	18	works of men's hands of wood and stone
1 Pa	16	33	shall the trees of the wood give praise
	21	23	for a holocaust, and the drays for wood
	29	2	things of iron, wood for things of wood
2 Pa	9	16	armory, which was compassed with a wood
	25	18	beasts that were in the wood of Libanus
2 Es	8	4	stood upon a step of wood which he
		15	olive and branches of beautiful wood
	10	34	the people for the offering of wood
	13	31	the offering of wood at times appointed
Esth	1	5	court of the garden and of the wood

Job 41 18 iron as straw, and brass as rotten wood
Ps 73 5 as with axes in a wood of trees, they
79 14 boar out of the wood hath laid it waste
82 15 as fire which burneth the wood: and
131 6 have found it in the fields of the w.
Prov 25 20 a garment, and a worm by the wood
26 20 when the wood faileth, the fire shall
21 are to burning coals, and wood to fire
Ecce 2 6 therewith the wood of the young trees
Cant 3 9 him a litter of the wood of Libanus
Wisd 10 4 course of the just by contemptible wood
13 11 tree proper for his use in the wood
13 a crooked piece of wood, and full of
14 1 calleth upon a piece of wood more frail than the wood that carrieth him
5 trust their lives even to a little wood
7 blessed is the wood by which justice
21 incommunicable name to stones and wood
Eccu 8 4 and heap not wood upon his fire
22 19 a frame of wood bound together in the
28 12 as the wood of the forest is, so the
38 5 not bitter water made sweet with wood
Isa 10 15 staff exalt itself, which is but wood
30 33 nourishment thereof is fire and much w.
37 19 works of men's hands, of wood and stone
40 20 he hath chosen strong wood, and that
45 20 that set up the wood of their graven
60 17 for wood brass, and for stones iron
Jer 5 6 lion out of the wood hath slain them
14 as fire, and this people as wood, and
10 8 the doctrine of their vanity is wood
11 19 saying: Let us put wood on his bread
12 8 become to me as a lion in the wood
28 13 thou hast broken chains of wood, and
46 22 come against her, as hewers of wood
Lam 4 8 it is withered and is become like wood
5 4 for money: we have bought our wood
13 and the children fell under the wood
Bar 6 3 see in Babylon gods . . . of wood borne
29 gods of silver and of gold and of wood
38 their gods of wood and of stone and of
50 they are but of wood and laid over
54 upon the house of these gods of wood
56 neither are these gods of wood and of
69 so are their gods of wood and of silver
70 like manner also their gods of wood
Eze 15 2 shall be made of the wood of the vine
3 shall wood be taken of it, to do any
39 10 they shall not bring wood out of the
41 16 and floored with wood all round about
22 altar of wood was three cubits high
22 and the walls thereof were of wood
Dan 5 4 of iron and of wood and of stone. 23
Haba 2 19 woe to him that saith to wood: Awake
Zach 12 6 like a furnace of fire amongst wood
2 Ma 1 21 both the wood and the things that were
Luke 23 31 if in the green wood they do these
1 C 3 12 silver, precious stones, wood, hay
2 Tim 2 20 of silver, but also of w. and of earth
James 3 5 how small a fire kindleth a great wood
Apoc 9 20 idols of . . . brass and stone and wood
18 12 and all thyine wood and all manner of
setim wood; *see* **setim**
wooden 1 Ma 6 37 there were strong wooden towers
woodland Gen 14 3 came together into the w. vale
Gen 14 8 in battle array in the woodland vale
10 the woodland vale had many pits of
Josu 17 15 go up into the woodland, and cut
woodlands 2 K 24 6 they came into the w. of Dan
woods Josu 15 9 Cariathiarim . . . city of the w. 60
2 K 2 18 like one of roes that abide in the w.
Ps 28 9 he will discover the thick woods: and
49 10 all the beasts of the woods are mine
95 12 shall all the trees of the w. rejoice
103 20 shall all the beasts of the w. go about
Cant 2 3 apple tree among the trees of the woods
Isa 7 2 as the trees of the woods are moved
Bar 5 8 woods and every sweet-smelling tree
6 62 to consume mountains and woods, doth
Eze 15 2 out of all the trees of the woods that
1 Ma 9 45 side, and banks and marshes and woods
woody Num 13 21 barren, woody or without trees
Num 24 6 as woody valleys, as watered gardens
1 K 23 14 the desert of Ziph, in a woody hill
Eze 6 13 and under every woody tree and under
woof Gen 14 23 from the very woof thread unto
Exod 39 3 that they might be twisted with the w.
Lev 13 48 leprosy in the woof and the warp
59 garment, either in the warp or woof
wool Deut 18 4 of oil and a part of the wool
Judg 6 37 put this fleece of wool on the floor
Ps 147 16 who giveth snow like wool: scattereth
Prov 31 13 she hath sought wool and flax, and
Isa 1 18 crimson, they shall be white as wool
51 8 the moth shall consume them as wool
Eze 27 18 in rich wine, in wool of the best color
34 3 you clothed yourselves with the wool
Dan 7 9 the hair of his head like clean wool
Osee 2 5 my wool and my flax, my oil and my
9 I will set at liberty my wool and my
Heb 9 19 goats, with water and scarlet wool and
Apoc 1 14 his hairs were as white as white wool
woolen Lev 13 47 w. or linen garment that shall
Lev 13 59 leprosy of any woolen or linen garment
Deut 22 11 garment that is woven of w. and linen
Eze 44 17 neither shall any woolen come upon them
word Mat 2 8 found him, bring me word again
Mat 4 4 but in every word that proceedeth from
8 8 say the word, and my servant. Luke 7:7
12 32 shall speak a word against the Son of
36 every idle word that men shall speak
13 19 heareth the word of the kingdom and
20 heareth the word, and immediately
21 and persecution because of the word
22 is he that heareth the word, and the
22 of riches choketh up the word, and he
23 heareth the word and understandeth
15 23 who answered her not a word. And his
18 16 witnesses every word may stand. And
21 24 I also will ask you one w. Mark 11:29
22 46 no man was able to answer him a word
26 44 third time, saying the selfsame word
75 Peter remembered the word of Jesus
27 14 and he answered him to never a word
Mark 1 45 and to blaze abroad the word: so that
2 2 door, and he spoke to them the word
4 14 he that soweth, soweth the word. And
15 the wayside, where the word is sown
15 Satan cometh and taketh away the word
16 who when they have heard the word
17 and persecution ariseth for the word
18 that hear the word, and the cares of
19 choke the word, and it is made fruitless
20 who hear the word and receive it and
33 he spoke to them the word, according
5 36 Jesus having heard the word that was
8 32 he spoke the word openly. And Peter
9 9 and they kept the word to themselves
31 they understood not the w. Luke 2:50
13 31 but my word shall not pass away. But
14 72 remembered the word that Jesus had
16 20 confirming the word with signs that
Luke 1 2 eyewitnesses and ministers of the word
37 no word shall be impossible with God
2 17 they understood of the word that had
4 36 what word is this, for with authority

8 12 taketh the word out of their heart
13 they hear, receive the word with joy
15 hearing the word, keep it and bring
12 10 speaketh a word against the Son of man
24 19 mighty in work and word before God and
John 2 22 and the word that Jesus had said. Now
4 39 word of the woman giving testimony
50 the man believed the word which Jesus
51 brought word, saying, that his son
5 24 he who heareth my word and believeth
8 31 if you continue in my word, you shall
37 because my word hath no place in you
43 because you cannot hear my word. You
51 if any man keep my word, he shall. 52
12 48 the word that I have spoken, the same
14 23 love me, he will keep my word, and
24 the word which you have heard, is not
15 3 you are clean by reason of the word
20 my word that I said to you: The servant
20 if they have kept my word, they will
25 that the word may be fulfilled which
17 20 who through their word shall believe
18 9 that the word might be fulfilled which
32 that the word of Jesus might be
Acts 4 4 many of them who had heard the word
6 4 and to the ministry of the word. And
10 36 sent the word to the children of Israel
37 know the w. which hath been published
44 fell on all them that heard the word
11 19 speaking the w. to none, but to Jews
13 15 if you have any w. of exhortation to
26 to you the word of this salvation is
14 3 testimony to the word of his grace
15 7 Gentiles should hear the w. of gospel
27 themselves also will, by w. of mouth
16 6 forbidden . . . to preach word in Asia
17 11 who received word with all eagerness
18 15 if they be questions of word and names
20 24 ministry of the word which I received
32 I commend you to God, and to the word
38 most of all for word which he had said
Rom 9 9 this is the word of promise: According
28 a short word shall the Lord make upon
10 8 the word is nigh thee, even in thy mouth
8 this is the w. of faith, which we preach
17 and hearing by the word of Christ. But
15 18 obedience of the Gentiles, by w. and
1 C 1 18 the word of the cross, to them indeed
11 8 by Spirit, is given the word of wisdom
12 8 and to another, the word of knowledge
2 C 5 19 placed in us the word of reconciliation
6 7 in word of truth, in the power of God
8 7 things you abound in faith, and word
10 11 that such as we are in word by epistles
13 1 three witnesses shall every word stand
Gal 6 6 let him that is instructed in the word
Eph 1 13 after you had heard the word of truth
5 26 by the laver of water in word of life
Phil 2 16 holding forth the word of life to my
Col 1 5 you have heard in the word of the truth
3 16 let the word of Christ dwell in you
17 whatsoever you do in word or in work
1 Th 1 5 hath not been unto you in word only, but
6 receiving the word in much tribulation
2 13 when you had received of us the word
13 you received it not as the word of men
2 Th 2 2 neither by spirit nor by word nor by
14 whether by word or by our epistle. Now
16 confirm you in every good work and word
3 14 if any man obey not our word by this
1 Tim 4 12 an example of the faithful in word, in
5 17 they who labor in the word and doctrine
2 Tim 2 15 rightly handling the word of truth. But
4 2 preach the word: be instant in season
Titus 1 9 embracing that faithful word which is
2 8 sound word that cannot be blamed: that
3 1 to obey at a word, to be ready to every
Heb 1 3 upholding all things by the word of his
2 2 for if the word, spoken by angels
4 2 the word of hearing did not profit them
5 13 is unskilful in the word of justice: for
6 1 leaving the word of the beginning of
7 28 the word of the oath, which was since
12 19 that the word might not be spoken to
James 1 18 he begotten us by the word of truth
21 receive the ingrafted word, which is
22 be ye doers of the word, and not
23 if a man be a hearer of the word, and
3 2 if any man offend not in word, the
1 P 1 25 the word which by the gospel hath been
2 8 to them who stumble at the word
3 1 if any believe not the word, they may
1 they may be won without the word by
2 P 1 19 we have the more firm prophetical word
3 7 by the same word are kept in store
1 J 1 1 have handled, of the word of life
2 7 is the word which you have heard
3 18 let us not love in word nor in tongue
Apoc 3 8 hast kept my word, and hast not denied
10 thou hast kept the word of my patience
12 11 and by the word of the testimony, and

his word Mat 8 16 out the spirits with his word
Luke 10 39 at the Lord's feet, heard his word
20 26 they could not reprehend his word
John 4 41 in him because of his own word. And
5 38 you have not his word abiding in you
8 55 I do know him and do keep his word
Acts 2 41 that received his word, were baptized
Rom 9 28 for he shall finish his word, and cut
Titus 1 3 manifested his word in preaching, which
1 J 1 10 him a liar, and his word is not in us
2 5 that keepeth his word, in him in very

this word Mat 15 12 Pharisees, when they heard this word
Mat 19 11 all men take not this word, but they
22 when the young man had heard this word
28 15 this word was spread abroad among the
Luke 2 15 let us see this word that is come to
8 50 Jesus hearing this word, answered the
9 45 but they understood not this word
45 afraid to ask him concerning this word
18 34 and this word was hid from them, and
Acts 7 29 Moses fled upon this word and was a
17 18 what is it, that this w. sower would
22 22 they heard him until this word, and then
28 25 Paul speaking this one word: Well did
Rom 13 9 it is comprised in this word, Thou shalt
Heb 13 22 you suffer this word of consolation

thy word Luke 1 38 be it done to me according to thy word
Luke 2 29 Lord, according to thy word in peace
5 5 at thy word I will let down the net
John 17 6 them; and they have kept thy word
14 I have given them thy word, and the
17 thy word is truth. As thou hast sent
Acts 4 29 all confidence they may speak thy w.

word of God Gen 41 32 the w. . . . cometh to pass
Mark 7 13 making void the word of God by your
Luke 4 4 bread alone, but by every word of God
5 1 pressed upon him to hear the w. . . .
8 11 the seed is the word of God. And they
21 they who hear the word of God. 11:28
John 10 35 to whom the word of God was spoken
Acts 4 31 they spoke the w. . . . with confidence
6 2 that we should leave the word of God
8 4 went about preaching the word of God

14 heard that Samaria had received w. . . .
11 1 Gentiles also had received the w. . . .
13 5 they preached the w. . . . in synagogues
7 [Bar-jesu] desired to hear the w. . . .
44 city almost came together to hear w. . . .
46 it behoved us first to speak the w. . . .
17 13 had knowledge that the word of God
18 11 teaching among them the word of God
19 20 mightily grew the word of God, and was
Rom 9 6 as though word of God hath miscarried
1 C 14 36 did word of God come out from you? Or
2 C 2 17 as many, adulterating the word of God
4 2 nor adulterating the word of God; but
Eph 6 17 of the Spirit, which is the word of God
Phil 1 14 to speak the word of God without fear
Col 1 25 you, that I may fulfil the word of God
1 Th 2 13 but, as it is indeed, the word of God
2 Th 3 1 that the word of God may run, and may be
1 Tim 4 5 it is sanctified by the word of God and
2 Tim 2 9 but the word of God is not bound
Titus 2 5 that the word of God be not blasphemed
Heb 4 12 the word of God is living and effectual
6 5 have moreover tasted the good w. . . .
11 3 world was framed by the word of God
13 7 who have spoken the w. . . . to you
1 P 1 23 born again . . . by the word of God
2 P 3 5 consisting by the word of God, whereby
1 J 2 14 the word of God abideth in you, and
Apoc 1 2 who hath given testimony to the w. . . .
9 for the w. . . . and for the testimony of
6 9 that were slain for the word of God
20 4 of Jesus, and for the word of God
word of the Lord Luke 3 2 word of the Lord was made unto John
Luke 22 61 Peter remembered the word of the Lord
Acts 6 7 word of the Lord increased. 12:24
8 25 testified and preached the w. . . .
11 16 remembered the w. . . . , how that he said
13 48 were glad, and glorified the w. . . .
49 w. . . . was published throughout the
14 24 and having spoken the w. . . . in Perge
15 35 preaching, with many others, the w. . . .
36 preached the w. . . . , to see how they do
16 32 they preached the w. . . . to him and to
19 10 who dwelt in Asia, heard the w. . . .
20 35 remember the word of the Lord Jesus, how
1 Th 1 8 from you was spread abroad the w. . . .
4 14 we say unto you in the word of the Lord
1 P 1 25 the word of the Lord endureth forever
Word John 1 1 in the beginning was the Word, and the Word was with God, and the Word was God
John 1 14 and the Word was made flesh and dwelt
1 J 5 7 Father, the Word, and the Holy Ghost
Apoc 19 13 his name is called, The Word of God
word's 2 K 7 21 for thy word's sake, and according
Ps 118 154 quicken thou me for thy word's sake
words Mat 10 14 receive you nor hear your words
Mat 12 37 by thy words thou shalt be justified
37 by thy words thou shalt be condemned
Mark 14 39 he prayed, saying the same words. And
Luke 1 4 know the verity of those words in
4 22 they wondered at the words of grace
23 9 and he questioned him in many words
24 44 the words which I spoke to you while
John 3 34 hath sent, speaketh the words of God
6 64 the words that I have spoken to you
69 thou hast the words of eternal life
8 47 is of God, heareth the words of God
10 21 these are not the words of one that
14 10 the words that I speak to you, I speak
17 8 the words which thou gavest me, I have
Acts 2 40 with very many other words did he
5 20 to the people all the w. of this life
6 11 heard him speak words of blasphemy
13 to speak words against the holy place
7 38 received the words of life to give
10 22 his house, and to hear words of thee
11 14 who shall speak to thee words, whereby
15 15 to this agree the w. of the prophets
24 troubled you with words, subverting
32 with many w. comforted the brethren
20 2 had exhorted them with many words, he
24 4 thy clemency to hear us in few words
26 25 I speak words of truth and soberness
Rom 3 2 the words of God were committed to them
4 thou mayest be justified in thy words
10 18 their w. unto ends of the whole world
16 18 and by pleasing speeches and good words
1 C 2 4 preaching was not in the persuasive w.
13 speak, not in learned words of human
14 19 I had rather speak five words with my
19 you also; than 10,000 words in a tongue
2 C 12 4 into paradise, and heard secret words
Eph 3 3 as I have written above in a few words
5 6 let no man deceive you with vain words
Col 2 4 may deceive you by loftiness of words
1 Tim 4 6 nourished up in the words of faith, and
6 3 consent not to the sound words of our
4 sick about questions and strifes of w.
20 avoiding the profane novelties of words
2 Tim 1 13 hold the form of sound words, which thou
2 14 contend not in words, for it is to no
4 15 he hath greatly withstood our words
Heb 5 12 the first elements of the words of God
12 19 sound of a trumpet and the voice of w.
13 22 I have written to you in a few words
1 P 4 11 let him speak, as the words of God
2 P 2 3 with feigned words make merchandise of
3 2 those words which I told you before
3 J 10 with malicious w. prating against us
Jude 17 words which have been spoken before
Apoc 1 3 heareth the w. of this prophecy. 22:18
17 17 till the words of God be fulfilled
22 7 the words of the prophecy of this book
9 that keep the words of the prophecy
10 seal not the words of the prophecy of
19 the words of the book of this prophecy
his words Mark 10 24 were astonished at his w.
Mark 12 13 that they should catch him in his w.
Luke 7 1 when he had finished all his words
20 20 might take hold of him in his words
24 8 they remembered his words. And going
Acts 7 22 he was mighty in his words and in his
my words Mat 7 24 that heareth these my w. 26
Mat 24 35 but my w. shall not pass. Luke 21:33
Mark 8 38 be ashamed of me and of my w. Luke 9:26
Luke 1 20 thou hast not believed my words, which
6 47 cometh to me and heareth my words and
John 5 47 how will you believe my words? After
12 47 man hear my words and keep them not
48 and receiveth not my words, hath one
14 24 loveth me not, keepeth not my words
15 7 in me, and my words abide in you
Acts 2 14 and with your ears receive my words
these words Mat 7 28 when Jesus had fully ended these words
Mat 19 1 when Jesus had ended these words, he
26 1 when Jesus had ended all these words
Luke 2 19 Mary kept all these words, pondering
51 kept all these words in her heart
9 28 about eight days after these words
24 11 these words seemed to them as idle
John 7 40 when they had heard these words of
8 20 these words Jesus spoke in the
10 19 again among the Jews for these words
19 13 when Pilate had heard these words, he

Acts 2 22 ye man of Israel, hear these words
37 when they had heard these words, they
5 5 Ananias hearing these words, fell down
24 and the chief priest heard these w.
10 44 Peter was yet speaking these words
13 42 would speak unto them these words
16 36 keeper of prison told these words to
38 told these words to the magistrates
1 Th 4 17 comfort ye one another with these words
Apoc 19 9 to me: These words of God are true
21 5 for these words are most faithful. 22:6
wore 1 K 14 3 and Achias . . . wore the ephod. And
1 K 22 18 day 85 men that wore the linen ephod
2 K 8 7 which the servants of Adarezer wore
4 K 6 30 the haircloth which he wore within
Jdth 8 6 and she wore haircloth upon her loins
Wisd 18 24 in the priestly robe which he wore
1 Ma 8 14 none of all these wore a crown or
Luke 8 27 he wore no clothes, neither did he
work Mat 7 23 depart from me, you that work iniquity
Mat 13 41 scandals and them that work iniquity
21 28 son, go work today in my vineyard
Mark 13 12 the parents, and shall work their death
34 to his servants over every work, and
Luke 13 14 there are wherein you ought to work
24 19 mighty in work and word before God and
John 4 34 sent me that I may perfect his work
5 17 Father worketh until now; and I work
6 28 that we may work the works of God
29 this is the work of God, that you
30 believe thee? What dost thou work
7 21 one work I have done; and you all
9 4 I must work the works of him that
4 night cometh, when no man can work
17 4 I have finished the work which thou
Acts 5 38 if this council or this work be of men
13 2 the w. whereunto I have taken them
41 I w. a w. in your days, a w. which you will not believe
14 25 unto the w. which they accomplished
15 18 to the Lord was his own work known from
38 and not gone with them to the work
27 16 we had much work to come by the boat
Rom 2 15 who show the work of the law written in
7 5 did work in our members, to bring forth
15 for that which I work I understand not
8 28 all things work together unto good, to
14 20 destroy not the work of God for meat
1 C 3 13 every man's work shall be manifest; for
13 and the fire shall try every man's work
14 if any man's work abide, which he hath
15 if any man's work burn, he shall suffer
9 1 Lord? Are not you my work in the Lord
13 they who work in the holy place, eat
15 58 always abounding in the w. of the Lord
16 10 for he worketh the work of the Lord, as
Gal 6 4 let every one prove his own work, and
10 time, let us work good to all men, but
Eph 4 12 the saints, for the w. of the ministry
Phil 2 12 with fear and trembling work out your
30 for the work of Christ he came to the
Col 3 17 whatsoever you do in word or in work
1 Th 1 3 being mindful of the work of your faith
4 11 and work with your own hands, as we
2 Th 1 11 goodness and the w. of faith in power
3 10 if any man will not work, neither let
2 Tim 4 5 do the work of an evangelist, fulfil
18 delivered me from every evil work: and
Heb 6 10 that he should forget your work, and
James 1 4 patience hath a perfect work; that you
25 hearer, but a doer of the work; this
3 13 his work in the meekness of wisdom
16 is inconstancy and every evil work
1 P 1 17 judgeth according to every one's work
Apoc 18 17 as many as work in the sea, stood afar
good work Mat 26 10 she hath wrought a good work. Mark 14:6
John 10 33 for a good work we stone thee not, but
Rom 2 7 who according to patience in good work
13 3 princes are not a terror to good work
2 C 9 8 things, may abound to every good work
Phil 1 6 he who hath begun a good work in you
Col 1 10 being fruitful in every good work, and
2 Th 2 16 confirm you in every good work and word
1 Tim 3 1 office of bishop, he desireth a good w.
5 10 diligently followed every good work
2 Tim 2 21 prepared unto every good work. But flee
3 17 be perfect, furnished to every good w.
Titus 1 16 and to every good work reprobate. But
3 1 to be ready to every good work. To
Philem 6 every good w., that is in you in Christ
worked Mat 20 12 these last have w. but one hour
2 Th 3 8 we worked night and day, lest we should
worker Exod 38 23 and worker in tapestry and
Wisd 7 21 wisdom, which is the w. of all things
8 6 who is a more artful worker than she
Eccu 14 20 the worker thereof shall go with it
21 the worker thereof shall be honored
workers Wisd 15 9 to do like the workers in brass
Osee 6 8 Galaad is a city of workers of idols
1 C 12 30 are all workers of miracles? Have all
Phil 3 2 beware of dogs, beware of evil workers
workers of iniquity Ps 5 7 hatest all the w. . . .
Ps 6 9 depart from me, all ye w. . . . : for
27 3 and with the w. . . . destroy me not
35 13 there the w. . . . are fallen, they are
52 5 shall not all the w. . . . know, who eat
63 3 from the multitude of the w. . . .
91 8 all the w. of iniquity shall appear
10 and all the w. . . . shall be scattered
93 16 shall stand with me against the w. . . .
100 8 that I might cut off all the w. . . .
124 5 the Lord shall lead out with the w. . . .
1 Ma 3 6 and all the w. . . . were troubled: and
9 23 Israel, and all the w. . . . rose up
13 27 from me, all ye workers of iniquity
worketh Job 33 29 these things God w. three times
Ps 14 2 walketh without blemish and w. justice
100 7 he that worketh pride shall not dwell
Prov 10 23 a fool w. mischief as it were for sport
21 24 ignorant, who in anger worketh pride
26 28 and a slippery mouth worketh ruin
Wisd 15 11 inspired into him the soul that w.
Eccu 7 22 hurt not servant that w. faithfully
11 35 a mischievous man, for he w. evils
20 30 he that w. justice shall be exalted
33 26 he worketh under correction and seeketh
37 14 with him that worketh by the year
2 Ma 15 21 upon the Lord, that worketh wonders
John 5 17 my Father w. until now; and I work
Acts 10 35 he that feareth him, and w. justice
Rom 2 9 upon every soul of man that w. evil
10 peace to every one that worketh good
4 4 now to him that w., the reward is not
5 to him that w. not, yet believeth in him
15 for the law worketh wrath. For where
5 3 knowing that tribulation w. patience
13 10 love of our neighbor worketh no evil
15 18 which Christ worketh not by me, for the
1 C 12 6 but the same God, who worketh all in all
11 these things one and the same Spirit w.
16 10 for he worketh the work of the Lord, as
16 to every one that worketh with us, and
2 C 1 6 w. the enduring of the same sufferings
4 12 so then death w. in us, but life in you
17 w. for us above measure exceedingly an

7 10 w. penance, steadfast unto salvation
10 the sorrow of the world worketh death
11 how great carefulness it worketh in you
9 11 which w. through us thanksgiving to God
Gal 3 5 Spirit, and worketh miracles among you
5 6 but faith that worketh by charity. You
Eph 1 11 purpose of him who worketh all things
2 2 now worketh on the children of unbelief
3 20 according to the power that w. in us
Phil 2 13 it is God who worketh in you, both to
Col 1 29 which he worketh in me in power. For I
1 Th 2 13 who worketh in you that have believed
2 Th 2 7 the mystery of iniquity already worketh
James 1 3 the trying of your faith w. patience
20 of man worketh not the justice of God
Apoc 21 27 defiled or that worketh abomination
working Wisd 13 19 for getting and for w. and for
Eccu 6 20 in working about her thou shalt labor
Dan 14 42 he is the Savior, working signs and
Mark 16 20 the Lord working withal and confirming
Rom 1 27 men with men w. that which is filthy
1 C 4 12 we labor, working with our own hands
12 10 to another, the working of miracles; to
Eph 4 19 unto the working of all uncleanness
28 let him labor, working with his hands
Col 1 29 striving according to his working which
1 Th 2 9 working night and day, lest we should
2 Th 2 9 is according to the working of Satan
3 11 w. not at all, but curiously meddling
12 working with silence, they would eat
Apoc 16 14 the spirits of devils working signs
workman Cant 7 1 made by the hand of a skilful w.
Wisd 13 1 have acknowledged who was the workman
14 2 the workman built it by his skill
Eccu 19 1 a workman that is a drunkard shall
Isa 40 19 hath the workman cast a graven statue
20 skilful workman seeketh how he may set
Jer 10 3 the works of the hand of the workman
Osee 8 6 a workman made it, and it is no god
2 Tim 2 15 a w. that needeth not to be ashamed
Mat 10 10 for the workman is worthy of his meat
workman's Judg 5 26 her right hand to w. hammer
workmanship Exod 28 8 the very w. also and all
Exod 28 15 according to w. of the ephod, of gold
Eph 2 10 for we are his w., created in Christ
workmaster Eccu 38 28 every craftsman and w.
workmen Exod 36 4 the w. being constrained to
3 K 5 13 and king Solomon chose workmen out of
4 K 12 15 money to distribute it to the workmen
22 5 let it be given to the workmen by the
9 given it to be distributed to the w.
1 Pa 22 15 thou hast also workmen in abundance
2 Pa 2 10 I will give thy servants the workmen
24 13 and the workmen were diligent and
34 10 over the w. in the house of the Lord
12 now the overseers of the workmen were
17 overseers of the artificers and of w.
Bar 6 45 they are made by workmen and by
1 Ma 10 11 he ordered workmen to build the walls
Acts 19 25 together, with the w. of like occupation
2 C 11 13 for such false apostles are deceitful w.
work's 1 Th 5 13 in charity, for their w. sake
good works Mat 5 16 they may see your g. w.
John 10 32 many good works I have showed you from
Acts 9 36 this woman was full of good works and
Eph 2 10 created in Christ Jesus in good works
1 Tim 2 10 professing godliness, with good works
5 10 having testimony for her good works, if
6 18 to do good, to be rich in good works, to
Titus 2 7 show thyself an example of good works
14 acceptable, a pursuer of good works
3 8 may be careful to excel in good works
14 men also learn to excel in good works
Heb 10 24 provoke unto charity and to good works
1 P 2 12 the good works which they shall behold
2 P 1 10 by good works you may make sure your
works' John 14 12 believe for the very works' sake
world Gen 41 45 called him . . . savior of the w.
2 K 22 16 foundations of the world were laid open
1 K 2 8 and upon them he hath set the world
1 Pa 16 30 he hath founded the world immoveable
2 Es 1 9 away to the uttermost parts of the w.
Esth 13 2 brought all the w. under my dominion
Job 9 13 they stoop that bear up the world. What
18 18 and shall remove him out of the world
28 24 he beholdeth the ends of the world
34 13 whom hath he set over the world which
Ps 9 9 he shall judge the world in equity
17 16 foundations of the w. were discovered
18 5 their words unto the ends of the world
23 1 the w. and all they that dwell therein
32 8 the inhabitants of the world be in awe
48 2 give ear, all ye inhabitants of the w.
49 12 world is mine and the fulness thereof
72 12 sinners; and yet abounding in the world
76 19 thy lightnings enlightened the world
88 12 the world and the fulness thereof thou
89 2 before . . . earth and world was formed
92 1 for he hath established the world which
95 10 hath corrected the world, which shall
13 shall judge the w. with justice. 97:9
96 4 his lightnings have shone forth to w.
97 7 the world and they that dwell therein
Prov 8 26 not yet made . . . the poles of the w.
31 playing in the world; and my delights
Ecce 3 11 delivered world to their consideration
9 6 neither have they any part in this w.
Wisd 2 24 of the devil, death came into the w.
9 3 he should order the world according
9 present when thou madest the world
10 1 formed by God the father of the world
11 18 hand, which made the world of matter
13 2 to be the gods that rule the world
9 as to make a judgment of the world
14 6 left to the world seed of generation
6 hope of the world fleeing to a vessel
14 by vanity of men they came into the w.
16 17 for the world fighteth for the just
18 4 light of the law was to be given to w.
Eccu 1 2 who hath numbered . . . days of the w.
3 8 that brought him into the world. Honor
14 12 covenant of this world shall surely die
24 14 and before the world, was I created
14 unto the w. to come I shall not cease
26 21 as the sun when it riseth to the world
38 39 shall strengthen the state of the world
42 19 hath beheld the signs of the world
43 6 and the moon . . . a sign of the world
10 Lord enlighteneth the world on high
44 19 the covenants of the world were made
46 22 time of the end of his life in the w.
Isa 9 6 the Father of the world to come, the
13 11 I will visit the evils of the world
14 17 that made the world a wilderness and
21 nor fill face of the world with cities
18 3 all ye inhabitants of the world, who
23 17 with all the kingdoms of the world
24 4 and is weakened: the world faded away
26 9 inhabitants of the world shall learn
27 6 shall fill face of the world with seed
34 1 the world and everything that cometh
Jer 10 12 that prepareth the world by his wisdom
51 15 hath prepared the world by his wisdom
Lam 4 12 inhabitants of world would not have
Dan 2 39 which shall rule over all the world
3 45 God, and glorious over all the world

Nah 1 5 quaked at his presence, and the world
Haba 3 6 the hills of the world were bowed down
Zach 13 3 mother, that brought him into the world
2 Ma 2 23 most renowned temple in all the world
5 15 temple, the most holy in all the world
6 23 would rather be sent into the other w.
7 9 the King of the world will raise us up
23 Creator of the world, that formed the
12 15 calling upon the great Lord of the w.
13 14 all to God, the creator of the world
Mat 4 8 him all the kingdoms of the w. Luke 4:5
5 14 you are the light of the world. A city
12 32 in this world nor in the w. to come
13 22 the care of this world and the
38 the field is the world. And the good
39 the harvest is the end of the world
40 so shall it be at the end of the w. 49
18 7 woe to the world because of scandals
24 3 the consummation of the world. 28:20
Mark 4 19 the cares of the world and the
10 30 receive . . . in the world to come life everlasting. Luke 18:30
Luke 12 30 things do the nations of the w. seek
16 8 children of this world are wiser in
20 34 the children of this world marry and
35 be accounted worthy of that world and
John 1 9 every man that cometh into this world
10 he was in the world, and the world was made by him, and the world knew him not
29 who taketh away the sin of the world
3 16 God so loved the world as to give his
17 Son into the world to judge the world
17 that the world may be saved by him
19 the light is come into the world and
4 42 this is indeed the Savior of the world
6 14 prophet that is to come into the world
33 heaven, and giveth life to the world
52 is my flesh, for the life of the world
7 4 things, manifest thyself to the world
7 the world cannot hate you; but me it
8 12 I am the light of the world. 9:5
23 you are of this w., I am not of this w.
26 these same I speak in the world. And
9 39 for judgment I am come into this world
10 36 sanctified and sent into the world
11 9 because he seeth the light of this w.
27 who art come into this world. And when
12 25 he that hateth his life in this world
31 now is the judgment of the world: now
31 the prince of this world be cast out
46 I am come a light into the world; that
47 I came not to judge the world, but to save the world
13 1 that he should pass out of this world
1 loved his own who were in the world
14 17 whom the world cannot receive because
19 and the world seeth me no more. But
22 thyself to us, and not to the world
30 the prince of this world cometh, and
31 that the world may know, that I love
15 18 if the world hate you, know ye that
19 if you had been of the w., the w. would love its own: but because you are not of the w., but I have chosen you out of the w., therefore the w. hateth you
16 8 he will convince the world of sin and
11 prince of this world is already judged
20 and weep, but the world shall rejoice
21 joy that a man is born into the world
28 Father, and am come into the world
28 I leave the world, and I go to the
33 in the world you shall have distress
33 confidence, I have overcome the world
17 5 which I had, before the world was, with
6 thou hast given me out of the world
9 I pray not for the world, but for them
11 and now I am not in the world, and these are in the world
14 the world hath hated them, because
14 they are not of the w.; as I also am not of the w. 16
15 shouldst take them out of the world
18 as thou hast sent me into the world
18 I also have sent them into the world
21 that the world may believe that thou
23 world may know that thou hast sent me
24 loved me before the creation of the w.
25 the world hath not known thee; but I
18 20 I have spoken openly to the world: I
36 my kingdom is not of this world. If my kingdom were of this world
37 and for this came I into the world
21 25 the world itself, I think, would not
Acts 17 24 God, who made the world, and all things
31 he will judge the world in equity, by
19 27 whom all Asia and the world worshippeth
24 5 among all the Jews throughout the w.
Rom 1 20 things of him, from creation of the w.
3 6 otherwise how shall God judge this world
19 all the world may be made subject to God
4 13 that he should be heir of the world; but
5 12 as by one man sin entered into this w.
13 until the law sin was in the world; but
11 12 offence of them be the riches of the w.
15 loss of them be reconciliation of the w.
12 2 and be not conformed to this world; but
1 C 1 20 where is the disputer of this world
20 God made foolish the wisdom of this w.
21 the world, by wisdom, knew not God, it
27 foolish things of the w. hath God chosen
27 the weak things of world hath God chosen
28 base things of the world, and the things
2 6 yet not wisdom of this world, neither of the princes of this world
7 which God ordained before the world
8 which none of princes of this w. knew
12 we have received not spirit of this w.
3 18 seem to be wise in this world, let him
19 the wisdom of this world is foolishness
22 Cephas, or the world, or life, or death
4 9 we are made a spectacle to the world
13 we are made as the refuse of this world
5 10 not with the fornicators of this w.
10 you must needs go out of this world
6 2 that the saints shall judge this world
2 if the world shall be judged by you, are
3 how much more things of this world. If
4 things pertaining to this world, set
7 31 they that use this w., as if they used
31 the fashion of this world passeth away
33 is solicitous for things of the world
34 thinketh on the things of the world
8 4 we know that an idol is nothing in w.
10 11 upon whom the ends of the world are come
11 32 we be not condemned with this world
14 10 so many kinds of tongues in this world
2 C 1 12 we have conversed in this world: and
4 4 the god of this world hath blinded the
5 19 reconciling the world to himself, not
7 10 the sorrow of the world worketh death
Gal 1 4 deliver us from this present wicked w.
4 3 serving under the elements of the w.
6 14 by whom the w. is crucified to me, and I to the w.
Eph 1 21 not only in this w., but also in that
2 2 according to the course of this world

12 promise, and without God in this world
3 21 world without end. Phil 4:20
6 12 against the rulers of the world of this
Phil 2 15 among whom you shine as lights in the w.
Col 2 8 according to the elements of the world
20 Christ from the elements of this world
20 yet decree as though living in the w.
1 Tim 1 15 Jesus came into this w. to save sinners
3 16 is believed in the world, is taken up
6 7 we brought nothing into this world: and
2 Tim 1 9 Jesus before the times of the world
4 9 Demas hath left me, loving this world
Titus 1 2 promised before the times of the world
2 12 soberly and justly and godly in this w.
Heb 1 2 by whom also he made the world. Who
6 in the first begotten into the world
2 5 subjected unto angels the w. to come
6 5 and the powers of the world to come
9 26 often from the beginning of the world
10 5 when he cometh into the world, he saith
11 3 world was framed by the word of God
7 by the which he condemned the world; and
38 of whom the world was not worthy
James 1 27 one's self unspotted from this world
2 5 God chosen the poor in this world
3 6 tongue is a fire, a world of iniquity
4 4 friendship of this world is the enemy
4 will be a friend of this w., becometh
1 P 5 9 your brethren who are in the world
2 P 1 4 concupiscence which is in the world
2 5 and spared not the original world, but
5 flood upon the world of the ungodly
20 flying from the pollutions of the w.
3 6 whereby the world that then was, being
1 J 2 15 love not the world, nor the things
15 if any man love the world, the charity
16 for all that is in the world, is the
16 not of the Father, but is of the world
17 and the world passeth away, and the
3 1 the world knoweth not us, because it
13 wonder not . . . if the world hate you
17 that hath the substance of this world
4 1 prophets are gone out into the world
3 and he is now already in the world
4 in you, than he that is in the world
5 they are of the w.: therefore of the w. they speak, and the w. heareth them
9 his only begotten Son into the world
14 his Son to be the Savior of the world
17 as he is, we also are in this world
5 4 is born of God, overcometh the world
5 who is he that overcometh the world
2 J 7 many seducers are gone out into the w.
Apoc 11 15 the kingdom of this world is become
foundation of the world; *see* **foundation**
from the beginning of the world; *see* **beginning**
whole world Gen 41 54 famine prevailed in w. w.
Gen 47 13 in whole world there was want of bread
Jdth 11 6 and it is told through the whole world
Esth 9 28 all provinces in the whole world shall
13 4 scattered through the whole world
Wisd 1 7 spirit of Lord hath filled whole world
5 21 the whole world shall fight with him
6 26 is the welfare of the whole world
7 17 to know the disposition of the whole w.
11 23 whole world before thee is as the least
17 19 the whole world was enlightened with
18 24 which he wore, was the whole world
Bar 6 61 commandeth them to go over the w. w.
2 Ma 3 12 which is honored throughout the w. w.
8 18 can utterly destroy . . . the whole w.
Mat 16 26 if he gain the whole world. Mark 8:36; Luke 9:25
24 14 shall be preached in the whole world. 26:13; Mark 14:9
Mark 16 15 go ye into the whole world, and preach
Luke 2 1 that the whole world should be enrolled
21 26 shall come upon the whole w. Apoc 3:10
John 12 19 the whole world is gone after him
Acts 11 28 a great famine over the whole world
Rom 1 8 your faith is spoken of in whole world
10 18 their words unto ends of whole world
Col 1 6 unto you, as also it is in the whole w.
1 J 2 2 but also for those of the whole world
5 19 the whole world is seated in wickedness
Apoc 12 9 who seduceth the whole world; and he
worldly Titus 2 12 ungodliness and w. desires, we
Heb 9 1 divine service, and a worldly sanctuary
worlds Tob 13 6 extol the eternal King of worlds
worm Exod 16 24 neither was there w. found in it
2 K 23 8 was like the most tender little worm
Job 25 6 and the son of man who is a worm
Ps 21 7 I am a worm, and no man: the reproach
Prov 25 20 a garment, and a worm by the wood
Isa 41 14 fear not, thou worm of Jacob, you
51 8 worm shall eat them up as a garment
66 24 their w. shall not die, and their fire
Jon 4 7 but God prepared a worm, when the
Mark 9 43 where their worm dieth not. 45, 47
worms Exod 16 20 it began to be full of worms
Deut 28 39 because it shall be wasted with worms
Jdth 16 21 he will give fire and worms into their
Job 17 14 to worms, my mother and my sister
21 26 the dust, and worms shall cover them
24 20 may worms be his sweetness: let him
Eccu 7 19 flesh of the ungodly is fire and worms
10 13 inherit serpents and beasts and worms
19 3 rottenness and worms shall inherit him
Isa 14 11 strewed, and w. shall be thy covering
1 Ma 2 62 sinful man, for his glory is dung and w.
2 Ma 9 9 worms swarmed out of the body of this
Acts 12 23 [Herod] being eaten up by worms, he
wormwood Prov 5 4 her end is bitter as wormwood
Jer 9 15 I will feed this people with wormwood
23 15 I will feed them with wormwood and
Lam 3 15 he hath inebriated me with wormwood
19 and transgression, the w. and the gall
Amos 5 7 you that turn judgment into wormwood
6 13 the fruit of justice into w. you that
Apoc 8 11 name of the star is called Wormwood
11 the third part of the waters became w.
worn Deut 8 4 for age, and thy foot is not worn
Deut 29 5 your garments are not worn out neither
Josu 9 13 of the very long journey are worn out
2 Es 9 21 grow old and their feet were not worn
Eccu 11 5 would think on, hath worn the crown
Isa 51 6 the earth shall be worn away like a
Eze 23 43 that was worn out in her adulteries
worse Lev 27 10 neither a better for a worse, nor a worse for a better
Judg 2 19 did much worse things than their
2 K 19 7 that will be worse to thee than all the
Wisd 15 18 compared to these, are worse than they
17 6 thought things which they saw to be w.
19 14 in another respect also they were w.
Eccu 11 26 and what shall I be made worse by this
14 6 none worse than he that envieth himself
19 7 word, and thou shalt not fare the worse
22 12 of a wicked fool is worse than death
25 22 no head worse than head of a serpent
32 28 in him, shall fare never the worse
39 40 this is worse than that: for all shall
Jer 7 26 and have done worse than their fathers
16 12 you also have done worse than your
2 Ma 13 9 show himself worse to the Jews than
Mat 12 45 that man is made worse than the first

27 64 last error shall be w. than the first
Mark 5 26 nothing the better, but rather worse
Luke 11 26 of that man becomes w. than the first
John 2 10 then that which is worse. But thou
5 14 lest some worse thing happen to thee
1 C 11 17 not for the better, but for the worse
1 Tim 5 8 the faith, and is worse than an infidel
2 Tim 3 13 evil men and seducers shall grow worse
Heb 10 29 think he deserveth worse punishments
2 P 2 20 latter state is become unto them worse
worship Gen 27 29 serve thee, and tribes w. thee
Gen 37 10 mother and thy brethren worship thee
Exod 8 26 those things which the Egyptians w.
11 8 down to me and shall worship me, saying
Deut 12 30 their gods, so will I also worship
28 14 nor follow strange gods nor w. them
Josu 22 16 and revolting from the worship of him
3 K 9 6 but will go and worship strange gods
4 K 5 18 into the temple of Remmon to worship
10 18 but I will worship him [Baal] more
17 28 taught them how they should w. the Lord
35 nor shall you adore them nor w. them
38 neither shall you worship strange gods
18 22 you shall w. before this altar in
1 Pa 29 18 remain always for the worship of thee
2 Pa 14 2 destroyed the altars of foreign worship
29 11 to minister to him and to worship him
32 12 you shall worship before one altar
Tob 13 13 end of the earth shall worship thee
Jdth 5 8 consisted in the worship of many gods
17 departed from the worship of the Lord
19 revolted from the worship of their God
11 14 I thy handmaid worship God even now
Esth 8 17 joined themselves to their worship
Ps 5 8 I will worship towards thy holy. 137:2
Wisd 14 15 he began now to worship as a god, and
27 the w. of abominable idols is the cause
15 6 that love them and they that w. them
18 they w. also the vilest creatures: but
Eccu 1 32 w. of God is an abomination to a sinner
50 21 until the w. of the Lord was perfected
Isa 19 21 shall worship him with sacrifices and
36 7 you shall worship before this altar
45 14 they shall worship thee and shall make
46 6 a god: and they fall down and worship
49 23 they shall w. thee with their face
56 6 adhere to the Lord to worship him and
60 14 shall worship the steps of thy feet
Jer 35 15 follow not strange gods nor w. them
44 3 offer sacrifice and worship other gods
19 did we make cakes to worship her, to
Bar 6 25 be they confounded also that w. them
38 they that w. them shall be confounded
Eze 20 32 earth, to worship stocks and stones
Dan 3 12 they worship not thy gods nor do they
14 that you do not worship my gods nor
17 our God, whom we worship, is able to
18 we will not worship thy gods nor adore
33 servants and to them that w. thee
11 38 he shall worship the god Moazim in
38 he shall worship with gold and silver
14 4 I do not worship idols made with hands
Soph 1 5 them that worship the host of heaven
2 Ma 1 3 give you all a heart to worship him
Mat 15 9 in vain do they worship me. Mark 7:7
Acts 17 23 what . . . you worship, without knowing
18 13 men to worship God contrary to law
worshipped Gen 19 1 w. prostrate to the ground
Gen 22 5 after we have w., will return to you
Exod 18 7 and worshipped and kissed him: and
33 10 worshipped at the doors of their tents
Num 22 31 he worshipped him falling flat on the
Deut 12 2 w. their gods upon high mountains
30 as these nations have w. their gods
29 17 silver and gold, which they worshipped
32 17 whom their fathers worshipped not
Judg 10 13 me, and have worshipped strange gods
1 K 1 19 they rose in the morning and worshipped
24 9 worshipped, and said to Saul: Why
2 K 9 6 [Miphiboseth] fell on his face and w.
12 20 into the house of the Lord: and w.
14 4 worshipped and said: Save me, O king
24 21 he [Areuna] w. the king, bowing with
3 K 1 16 bowed herself and w. the king. And
23 before the king, and had w., bowing
31 w. the king, saying: May my lord David
53 going in he [Adonias] w. king Solomon
9 9 gods and adored them and w. them
11 5 Solomon w. Astarthe the goddess of the
19 18 that hath not w. him kissing the hands
22 54 he served also Baal, and w. him and
4 K 2 15 they w. him [Eliseus], falling to the
4 37 at his feet and w. upon the ground
10 18 Achab w. Baal a little, but I will
16 12 he saw the altar and worshipped it
17 7 and they worshipped strange gods. And
12 they w. abominations, concerning which
32 nevertheless they worshipped the Lord
33 when they w. the Lord, they served
19 37 as he was w. in the temple of Nesroch
1 Pa 29 20 and worshipped God and then the king
2 Pa 7 22 and adored them and worshipped them
24 17 of Juda went in and w. the king: and
33 3 host of heaven and he worshipped them
Jdth 5 9 they worshipped one God of heaven, who
18 own God, they worshipped any other
8 18 their God, and worshipped strange gods
21 whether they worshipped their God truly
Job 1 20 down upon the ground and worshipped
Wisd 11 16 worshipped dumb serpents and worthless
12 23 by the same things which they w. For
14 16 statues were w. by the commandment
Dan 2 46 fell on his face and w. Daniel, and
14 3 the king also worshipped him and went
22 and the Babylonians worshipped him
26 said: Behold him whom you worshipped
Osee 10 5 have w. the kine of Bethaven: for the
Acts 16 14 one that w. God, did hear: whose heart
18 7 one that w. God, whose house was
Rom 1 25 w. and served the creature rather than
2 Th 2 4 all that is called God, or that is w.
worshipper Acts 19 35 is a w. of the great Diana
worshippers Deut 4 3 hath destroyed all his w.
4 K 10 19 might destroy the worshippers of Baal
23 and said to the worshippers of Baal
2 Ma 1 19 the priests that then were w. of God
Heb 10 2 the w. once cleansed should have no
worshippeth Tob 3 21 is sure of that w. thee
Wisd 15 17 he is better than they whom he w.
Acts 19 27 whom all Asia and the world worshippeth
worshipping Gen 37 9 and eleven stars w. me
Gen 50 18 worshipping prostrate on the ground
Exod 18 20 ceremonies and the manner of w.
Josu 5 15 and w. said: What saith my lord
Ruth 2 10 and w. upon the ground, said to him
Wisd 14 18 and to the worshipping of these, the
Isa 37 38 he was w. in the temple of Nesroch
1 P 4 3 and unlawful worshipping of idols
worst 4 K 14 12 and Juda was put to the worst
Eze 7 24 will bring the worst of the nations
worth Gen 23 9 for as much money as it is worth
Gen 23 15 desirest is worth 400 sicles of silver
Lev 27 17 as much as it may be worth, at so much
3 K 21 2 I will give thee the worth of it in
1 Pa 21 22 take of me as much money as it is w.
24 give thee money as much as it is w.

Jdth 10 18 we should not think it w. our while
Prov 10 20 heart of the wicked is nothing worth
Wisd 2 11 feeble, is found to be nothing worth
Eccu 26 18 so much worth as a well instructed soul
37 17 no other thing of more worth to thee
worthily 2 Pa 1 10 can w. judge this the people
Job 37 23 we cannot find him w.: he is great
Wisd 16 1 they were worthily punished and were
worthless Wisd 11 16 dumb serpents and w. beasts
Wisd 12 24 for gods which are the most worthless
worthy Gen 32 10 I am not worthy of the least of
Exod 30 35 pure and most worthy of sanctification
Deut 25 2 that the offender be worthy of stripes
2 K 22 4 the Lord who is worthy to be praised
23 21 a man worthy to be a sight, having a
3 K 2 26 thou [Abiathar] art worthy of death
20 42 out of thy hand a man worthy of death
2 Pa 2 6 can be able to build him a w. house
Tob 3 19 or they perhaps were not worthy of me
9 2 I should not make a w. return for thy
12 2 or what can be worthy of his benefits
Job 3 7 night be solitary and not w. of praise
Ps 112 3 name of the Lord is worthy of praise
Prov 12 4 that doth things worthy of confusion
18 13 to be a fool and worthy of confusion
Ecce 9 1 whether he be worthy of love or hatred
Cant 7 9 wine, worthy for my beloved to drink
Wisd 1 16 they are w. to be of the part thereof
3 5 God hath tried them and found them w.
6 17 seeking such as are worthy of her and
7 15 to conceive thoughts worthy of those
9 12 shall be worthy of the throne of my
12 7 might receive a worthy colony of the
16 9 because they were w. to be destroyed
17 8 of a fear worthy to be laughed at. For
18 4 were worthy to be deprived of light
19 4 a necessity, of which they were worthy
Eccu 8 6 that we are all worthy of reproach
14 11 and offer to God worthy offerings
26 20 no price is worthy of a continent soul
Isa 32 8 such things as are worthy of a prince
Jer 51 18 vain works, and worthy to be laughed
Bar 6 43 was not thought as worthy as herself
Dan 3 26 and thy name is worthy of praise and
52 worthy to be praised and glorified
52 worthy to be praised and exalted. 55
56 worthy of praise and glorious forever
Mich 6 6 offer to the Lord that is worthy
Soph 2 1 O nation, not worthy to be loved
1 Ma 10 15 and the worthy acts that he and his
54 I will give . . . gifts worthy of thee
16 23 his wars and the worthy deeds which
2 Ma 3 2 the place worthy of the highest honor
4 25 nothing worthy of the high priesthood
6 27 shall show myself worthy of my old age
7 18 worthy of admiration are done to us
20 mother . . . worthy to be remembered
29 a worthy partner with thy brethren
8 33 a worthy reward for his impieties
9 15 not account worthy to be so much as
15 11 told them a dream w. to be believed
21 giveth victory to them that are worthy
Mat 3 8 fruit worthy of penance. Luke 3:8
11 whose shoes I am not worthy to bear
8 8 I am not w. that thou shouldst. Luke 7:6
10 10 for the workman is worthy of his meat
11 inquire who in it is worthy, and there
13 if that house be worthy, your peace
13 if it be not worthy, your peace shall
37 is not worthy of me. 38
22 8 they that were invited were not worthy
Mark 1 7 I am not worthy to loose. Luke 3:16; John 1:27; Acts 13:25
Luke 7 4 he is worthy that thou shouldest do
7 neither did I think myself worthy to
10 7 for the laborer is worthy of his hire
12 48 not, and did things worthy of stripes
15 19 I am not w. to be called thy son. 21
20 35 be accounted worthy of that world and
21 36 worthy to escape all these things
23 15 nothing worthy of death is done to him
Acts 5 41 w. to suffer reproach for the name
23 29 laid to his charge w. of death or of
25 11 have committed anything w. of death, I
25 that he hath committed w. of death. But
26 20 turn to God, doing works w. of penance
31 this man hath done nothing w. of death
Rom 1 32 who do such things, are worthy of death
8 18 the sufferings of this time are not w.
1 C 15 9 who am not w. to be called an apostle
Eph 4 1 you walk worthy of the vocation in which
Phil 1 27 your conversation be w. of the gospel
Col 1 10 that you may walk worthy of God, in all
12 who hath made us worthy to be partakers
1 Th 2 12 that you would walk worthy of God, who
2 Th 1 5 that you may be counted worthy of the
11 make you worthy of his vocation, and
1 Tim 1 15 worthy of all acceptation, that Christ
4 9 saying and worthy of all acceptation
5 17 be esteemed worthy of double honor
18 the laborer is worthy of his reward
6 1 count their masters worthy of all honor
Heb 3 3 this man was counted w. of greater glory
11 38 of whom the world was not worthy
3 J 6 on their way in a manner w. of God
Apoc 3 4 with me in white, because they are w.
4 11 thou art worthy, O Lord our God, to
5 2 who is worthy to open the book and to
4 worthy to open the book nor to see it
9 thou art worthy, O Lord, to take the
12 the Lamb that was slain is worthy to
16 6 blood to drink; for they are worthy
would to God Exod 16 3 would to God we had died by the hand of the Lord
Num 14 3 would God that we had died in Egypt
3 would God we may die in this vast
20 3 would God we had perished among our
Josu 7 7 would God we had stayed beyond the
22 20 would to God he alone had perished
Judg 9 29 would to God that some man would put
1 K 1 18 would to God thy handmaid may find grace
Acts 26 29 Paul said: I would to God, that both in
wound Gen 34 25 when pain of the w. was greatest
Exod 21 24 wound for wound, stripe for stripe
Lev 1 15 and breaking the place of the wound, he
Judg 3 22 went in after the blade into the wound
5 26 seeking in his head a place for the w.
20 31 so as to wound and kill some of them
2 K 20 10 gave him not a second w., and he died
3 K 8 38 when a man shall know the wound of his
22 35 and the blood ran out of the wound
Job 16 15 he hath torn me with wound upon wound
Prov 20 30 blueness of wound shall wipe away evils
Eccu 21 4 sword, there is no remedy for the wound
22 27 of secrets or a treacherous wound: for
27 28 the deceitful stroke will wound the
Isa 14 6 people in wrath with an incurable wound
12 the earth, that didst wound the nations
30 26 shall bind up the wound of his people
26 shall heal the stroke of their wound
38 21 lay it as a plaster upon the wound
Jer 8 22 the wound of the daughter of my people
10 19 destruction, my wound is very grievous
15 18 my wound desperate so as to refuse to
30 12 incurable, thy wound is very grievous
14 wounded thee with the wound of an enemy

Mich 1 9 because her wound is desperate, because
Nah 3 19 is not hidden, thy wound is grievous
2 Ma 14 43 missed of giving himself a sure wound
1 C 8 12 and wound their weak conscience, you
Apoc 13 3 and his death's wound was healed. And
12 beast, whose wound to death was healed
14 which had the wound by the sword and
16 2 there fell a sore and grievous wound
wounded Exod 22 2 and be wounded so as to die
1 K 17 52 fell many wounded of the Philistines
31 3 he was grievously w. by the archers
2 K 1 18 that are dead, w. on thy high places
11 15 that he [Urias] may be wounded and die
3 K 20 37 and he struck him and wounded him. So
22 34 out of the army, for I am grievously w.
4 K 8 28 the Syrians wounded Joram. 2 Pa 22:5
29 the Syrians had w. him in Ramoth when
9 15 for the Syrians had wounded him, when
1 Pa 10 1 and fell down wounded in mount Gelboe
3 the archers reached him and w. him
11 11 against 300 wounded by him at one time
2 Pa 13 17 there fell wounded of Israel 500,000
18 33 out of the battle, for I am wounded
35 23 and there he was wounded by the archers
23 of the battle for I am grievously w.
Jdth 6 4 and fall among the wounded of Israel
Job 16 14 he hath wounded my loins, he hath not
24 12 the soul of the wounded hath cried out
Prov 7 26 for she hath cast down many wounded
Ecce 10 9 cutteth trees, shall be wounded by them
Cant 4 9 thou hast wounded my heart, my sister
5 7 found me: they struck me and wounded me
Eccu 25 31 a heavy countenance and a w. heart
27 22 the snare: because his soul is wounded
Isa 14 10 thou also art wounded as well as we
51 9 the proud one and wounded the dragon
53 5 he was wounded for our iniquities
Jer 30 14 I have wounded thee with the wound of
37 9 should be left of them some wounded men
51 4 and the wounded in the regions thereof
52 in all her land the wounded shall groan
Lam 2 12 when they fainted away as the wounded
Eze 21 29 necks of the wicked that are wounded
30 4 when the wounded shall fall in Egypt
32 8 when thy w. shall fall in the midst
Dan 13 10 were both wounded with the love of her
Zach 13 6 with these I was wounded in the house
1 Ma 1 19 fled, and many were wounded unto death
9 17 there fell many wounded of the one side
40 there fell many wounded, and the rest
16 8 and there fell many of them wounded
9 Judas John's brother was wounded: but
2 Ma 3 16 of the high priest, was wounded in heart
4 42 many of them were wounded and some
8 24 having w. and disabled the greater
11 12 many of them being wounded, escaped
12 22 wounded with the strokes of their own
14 45 and he was grievously wounded, he ran
Mark 12 4 him they wounded in the head and used
Luke 10 30 having wounded him went away, leaving
20 12 they wounded him also, and cast him
Acts 19 16 fled out of that house naked and w.
woundeth Job 5 18 he w. and cureth: he striketh
wounding Gen 4 23 slain a man to the w. of myself
wounds 4 K 9 15 be healed in Jezrahel of his w.
2 Pa 22 6 for he received many wounds in the
Job 9 17 multiply my wounds even without cause
Ps 63 8 the arrows of children are their wounds
68 27 have added to the grief of my wounds
Prov 23 29 who hath wounds without cause? Who hath
27 6 better are the wounds of a friend than
Eccu 30 7 of his sons he shall blind up his wounds
31 40 lessening strength and causing wounds
Isa 1 6 wounds and bruises and swelling sores
Jer 30 17 scar, and will heal thee of thy wounds
33 6 I will close their wounds and give them
Eze 19 4 took him, but not without receiving w.
8 over him, in their wounds he was taken
Zach 13 6 what are these wounds in the midst of
Luke 10 34 bound up his wounds, pouring in oil
Apoc 16 11 because of their pains and wounds, and
wove 4 K 23 7 wove as it were little dwellings
woven Exod 28 32 a border round about it woven
Exod 38 16 hangings of the court were woven with
39 21 a woven border round about the hole
25 also fine linen tunicks with woven work
Lev 19 19 a garment that is woven of two sorts
Deut 22 11 garment that is w. of woolen and linen
Jdth 10 19 a canopy which was woven of purple and
Prov 7 16 I have woven my bed with cords, I have
Eccu 45 12 a woven work of a wise man, endued
Isa 59 5 and have woven the webs of spiders
Eze 27 7 linen from Egypt was woven for thy sail
John 19 23 woven from the top throughout. They
wrangle 2 Tim 2 24 servant of Lord must not w.
wrangling Prov 19 13 a w. wife is like a roof
wrap Num 4 5 wrap up the ark of the testimony
Num 4 7 they shall wrap up also the table of
11 they shall wrap up the golden altar
12 they shall wrap up in a cloth of violet
13 shall wrap it up in a purple cloth
wrapped Num 4 15 when Aaron and his sons have w.
Num 4 15 enter in to carry the things wrapped
20 sanctuary before they be wrapped up
1 K 21 9 wrapped up in a cloth behind the ephod
Job 3 5 and let it be wrapped up in bitterness
37 19 for we are wrapped up in darkness. Who
38 9 w. it in a mist as in swaddling bands
40 12 sinews of his testicles are w. together
Isa 9 18 and it shall be wrapped up in smoke
14 19 w. up among them that were slain by
Eze 27 24 were wrapped up and bound with cords
Soph 1 11 cut off that were wrapped up in silver
Mat 27 59 wrapped it up in a clean linen cloth
Mark 15 46 wrapped him up in the fine linen and
Luke 2 7 wrapped him up in swaddling clothes
12 you shall find the infant wrapped in
23 53 he wrapped him in fine linen and laid
John 20 7 but apart, wrapped up into one place
wrappeth Job 38 2 is this that w. up sentences
wrathful Ps 68 25 let thy w. anger take hold of
Eccu 45 23 consumed in his wrathful indignation
Eze 5 15 and in indignation and in w. rebukes
wraths Gal 5 20 wraths, quarrels, dissensions
wreath 2 Pa 4 13 were joined to each w. to cover
wreathed 3 K 7 17 and chain work w. together
wreaths 2 Pa 4 13 and two wreaths of network
wrest 2 P 3 16 the unlearned and unstable w.
wrestled Gen 32 24 man w. with him till morning
Eccu 51 25 my soul hath wrestled for her and
wrestling Eph 6 12 our w. is not against flesh
wretch Jdth 9 17 hear me a poor wretch, making
Isa 16 4 wretch is consumed, he hath failed
Jer 45 3 woe is me, wretch that I am, for the
2 Ma 4 13 Jason, that impious w. and no priest
38 the sacrilegious wretch should be put
13 6 the sacrilegious wretch to be thrown
wretched Num 20 5 brought us into this w. place
Judg 5 27 he [Sisara] lay lifeless and wretched
2 Pa 21 19 he died of a most wretched illness
Apoc 3 17 and knowest not that thou art wretched
wringing Judg 6 38 w. the fleece, he filled a
wrinkle Eph 5 27 church, not having spot or w.
wrinkles Job 16 9 my w. bear witness against me
write Exod 17 14 write this for a memorial in a
Exod 34 1 I will write upon them the words which

27 write thee these words by which I have
Num 5 23 the priest shall write these curses
17 2 w. the name of every man upon his rod
Deut 6 9 thou shalt write them in the entry and
10 2 I will write on the tables the words
11 20 thou shalt write them upon the posts
24 1 he shall write a bill of divorce and
27 3 mayst write on them all the words of
8 thou shalt write upon the stones all
31 19 write you this canticle and teach the
2 Es 9 38 we ourselves make a covenant and w. it
Job 31 35 himself that judgeth would write a book
Prov 3 3 write them in the tables of thy heart
7 3 write it upon the tables of thy heart
Isa 8 1 book, and write in it with a man's pen
10 1 and when they write, write injustice
19 a child shall write them down. And it
30 8 go in and write for them upon box and
Jer 22 30 write this man barren, a man that shall
30 2 write thee all the words that I have
31 33 and I will write it in their heart
36 2 thou shalt write in it all the words
17 how didst thou write all these words
28 write in it all the former words that
Eze 24 2 write thee the name of this day, on
37 16 take thee a stick: and write upon it
16 take another stick and write upon it
43 11 and thou shalt write it in their sight
Osee 8 12 I shall write to him my manifold laws
Haba 2 2 write the vision and make it plain
1 Ma 10 24 I also will write to them words of
12 22 well to write to us of your prosperity
13 37 to write to the king's chief officers
42 began to write in the instruments and
15 19 us to write to the kings and countries
2 Ma 11 37 make haste to write back, that we may
Mark 10 4 permitted to write a bill of divorce
Luke 1 3 to write to thee in order, most
16 6 and sit down quickly and write fifty
7 take thy bill and write eighty. And
John 1 45 of whom . . . the prophets did write
19 21 write not, the King of the Jews; but
Acts 15 20 we write unto them, that they refrain
25 26 have nothing certain to w. to my lord
26 being made, I may have what to write
1 C 4 14 I write not these things to confound you
14 37 let him know things that I write to you
2 C 1 13 for we write no other things to you
2 9 for to this end also did I write, that
9 1 it is superfluous for me to w. unto you
13 10 I write these things, being absent, that
Gal 1 20 now the things which I write to you
Phil 3 1 to write the same things to you, to me
1 Th 4 9 we have no need to write to you; for
5 1 need not, that we should write to you
2 Th 3 17 is the sign in every epistle. So I write
1 Tim 3 14 these things I write to thee, hoping
Heb 8 10 in their heart will I write them: and I
10 16 and on their minds will I write them
2 P 3 1 this second epistle I write to you
1 J 1 4 these things we write to you, that you
2 1 these things I write to you. 5:13
7 I write not a new commandment to you
8 a new commandment I write unto you
12 I write unto you, little children
13 I write unto you, fathers, because you
13 I write unto you, young men. 14
14 I write unto you, babes, because you
2 J 12 having more things to write unto you
3 J 13 I had many things to write unto thee
13 I would not by ink and pen w. to thee
Jude 3 taking all care to write unto you
3 I was under a necessity to w. unto you
Apoc 1 11 what thou seest, write in a book and
19 write therefore the things which thou
2 1 unto the angel of the church . . . w. 8, 12, 18; 3:1, 7, 14
3 12 I will write upon him the name of my
10 4 I was about to write: and I heard a
4 have spoken; and write them not. And
14 13 saying to me: Write: Blessed are the
19 9 write: Blessed are they that are called
21 5 write, for these words are most faithful
writer's Eze 9 2 had a writer's inkhorn at his. 3
writest Job 13 26 w. bitter things against me
writeth Ps 44 2 of a scrivener that w. swiftly
writhe Eccu 27 26 at the last he will w. his mouth
writing Exod 32 16 the w. also of God was graven
Josu 18 9 parts, writing them down in a book
2 K 11 15 w. in the letter: Set ye Urias in the
2 Pa 36 22 w. also, saying: Thus saith. 1 Es 1:1
1 Es 2 62 sought the writing of their genealogy
2 Es 7 64 they sought their writing in the record
Tob 7 16 they made a writing of the marriage
8 24 a writing, that the half that remained
Esth 9 27 which the writing testifieth, and
12 4 the memory of the thing to writing
Eccu 39 38 these things and left them in writing
42 7 put all in writing that thou givest out
Isa 38 9 the writing of Ezechias king of Juda
Eze 13 9 in the writing of the house of Israel
Dan 5 5 writing over against the candlestick
7 whosoever shall read this writing and
8 they could neither read the writing nor
15 in before me, to read this writing
15 declare to me the meaning of this w.
16 if thou art able to read the writing
17 the writing I will read to thee, O king
25 this is the writing that is written
7 1 writing the dream, he comprehended it
1 Ma 8 22 copy of the writing that they wrote
12 21 in writing concerning the Spartans
14 27 and this is a copy of the writing
48 commanded that this w. should be put
2 Ma 2 4 it was also contained in the same w.
Luke 1 63 demanding a writing table, he wrote
John 19 19 the writing was: Jesus of Nazareth
Acts 15 23 writing by their hands: The apostles
2 J 5 not as writing a new commandment to
writings Ps 86 6 the Lord shall tell in his w.
Jer 32 14 take these writings, this deed of
1 Ma 14 43 all the w. in the country should be
2 Ma 11 17 delivering your writings, requested
John 5 47 but if you do not believe his writings
written Exod 11 10 all the wonders that are w.
Exod 24 12 the commandments which I have written
31 18 testimony w. with the finger of God
32 15 two tables . . . written on both sides
32 32 out of the book that thou hast written
Num 5 30 to all things that are here written
Deut 9 10 of stone w. with the finger of God
10 4 according as he had written before
28 58 written in this volume. 29:20, 27
61 not written in the volume of this law
30 10 ceremonies which are w. in this law
32 46 fulfil all that is written in this law
Josu 1 8 do all things that are written in it
10 13 w. in the book of the just. 2 K 1:18
3 K 11 41 written in the book of the words. 14:19, 29; 15:7, 23, 31; 16:5, 14, 20, 27; 22:39, 46; 4 K 1:18; 8:23; 10:34; 12:19; 13:8, 12; 14:15, 18, 28; 15:6, 11, 15, 21, 26, 31, 36; 16:19; 20:20; 21:17, 25; 23:28; 24:5
21 11 as it was w. in the letters which she
4 K 22 13 book, to do all that is written for us
23 3 words . . . which were w. in that book

24 written in the book which Helcias
1 Pa 4 41 these whose names are written above
9 1 written in the book of the kings. 2 Pa 16:11; 25:26; 27:7; 28:26; 32:32; 35:27
16 40 w. in the law of the Lord, which he
28 19 came to me w. by the hand of the Lord
29 29 are w. in the book of Samuel the
2 Pa 9 29 are written in the words of Nathan
12 15 are w. in the books of Semeias the
13 22 of Abia . . . are written diligently in
20 34 are written in the words of Jehu the
21 12 from Elias . . . in which it was written
24 27 they are w. more diligently in the book
26 22 of Ozias . . . were written by Isaias
33 19 are written in the words of Hozai. And
34 21 do all things that are w. in this book
24 all the curses that are w. in this book
31 written in that book which he had read
35 4 and Solomon his son hath written. And
13 to that which is written in the law
25 is found written in the Lamentations
1 Es 4 7 letter of accusation was w. in Syriac
15 thou shalt find written in the records
5 7 letter . . . was written thus: To Darius
10 have w. the names of the men that are
6 2 book in which this record was written
8 34 all the weight was written at that time
2 Es 6 5 a letter in his hand w. in this manner
7 5 therein it was found written: These are
8 14 they found written in the law that the
12 23 were written in the book of Chronicles
13 1 therein was found w. that the Ammonites
Job 19 23 grant me that my words may be written
Ps 68 29 with the just let them not be written
101 19 let these things be w. unto another
138 16 and in thy book all shall be written
149 9 upon them the judgment that is written
Wisd 18 24 thy majesty was w. upon the diadem
Eccu 50 29 hath w. in this book the doctrine of
Jer 17 1 the sin of Juda is written with a pen
13 that depart from thee shall be w. in
25 13 all that is written in this book, all
32 44 deeds shall be written and sealed, and
36 6 which thou hast written from my mouth
27 the words that Baruch had written from
29 why hast thou written therein and said
45 1 when he had written these words in a
51 60 words that are written against Babylon
Eze 2 9 and it was written within and without
9 there were written in it lamentations
13 9 nor shall they be w. in the writing
37 20 the sticks whereon thou hast written
Dan 5 24 of the hand which hath written this
25 this is the writing that is written
12 1 that shall be found w. in the book
Zach 5 3 shall be judged as is there written
Mala 3 16 a book of remembrance was written
1 Ma 7 16 according to the word that is written
8 31 we have written to him [Demetrius]
9 22 the rest . . . are not written: for they
10 56 I will do to thee as thou hast written
11 31 which we have written to Lasthenes
12 23 and we also have written back to you
14 23 we have w. a copy of them to Simon
15 15 having letters written to the kings
22 were written to king Demetrius and to
16 24 these are written in the book of the
2 Ma 2 16 we have written unto you: and you
9 25 I have written to him what I have
11 16 letters w. to the Jews from Lysias
Mat 27 37 put over his head his cause written
Mark 11 17 is it not written: My house shall be
15 26 inscription of his cause was w. over
Luke 3 4 as it was written in the book of the
4 17 found the place where it was written
10 20 that your names are written in heaven
26 what is written in the law? How
18 31 which were written by the prophets
20 17 that is written, The stone which the
21 22 may be fulfilled that are written
22 37 that is written must yet be fulfilled
23 38 w. over him in letters of Greek and
24 44 which are written in the law of Moses
John 2 17 that it was written: The zeal of thy
10 34 is it not written in your law: I said
12 16 remembered that these things were w.
15 25 written in their law: They hated me
19 20 it was w. in Hebrew, in Greek, and in
22 what I have written, I have written
20 30 which are not written in this book
31 these are written that you may believe
21 25 if they were written every one, the
25 to contain the books that should be w.
Acts 13 29 fulfilled all things that were w. of him
33 in the second psalm also is written
17 23 found an altar also, on which was w.
21 25 we have w., decreeing that they should
24 14 believing all things which are written
Rom 2 15 show work of the law w. in their hearts
4 23 now it is not written only for him, that
15 4 for what things soever were w., were w. for our learning
15 but I have written to you, brethren
1 C 4 6 for another, above that which is written
5 11 I have w. to you, not to keep company
9 10 these things are written for our sakes
15 neither have I written these things
10 11 and they are written for our correction
15 54 come to pass the saying that is written
2 C 3 2 you are our epistle, w. in our hearts
3 w. not with ink, but with the Spirit
Gal 3 10 which are written in the book of the law
6 11 see what a letter I have written to you
Eph 3 3 as I have written above in a few words
Philem 19 I Paul have written it with my own hand
21 I have written to thee: knowing that
Heb 12 23 firstborn, who are w. in the heavens
13 22 I have written to you in a few words
1 P 5 12 I have written briefly: beseeching and
2 P 3 15 brother Paul . . . hath written to you
1 J 2 21 I have not written to you as to them
26 these things have I written to you
3 J 9 I had written perhaps to the church
Jude 4 who were w. of long ago unto this
Apoc 1 3 keepeth those things which are w. in it
2 17 in the counter, a new name written
5 1 a book written within and without
13 8 whose names are not w. in the book. 17:8
14 1 name of his Father written on their
17 5 and on her forehead a name was written
19 12 he had a name written, which no man
16 on his thigh written: King of kings
20 12 things which were written in the books
21 12 names written thereon, which are the
27 that are written in the book of life
22 18 the plagues written in this book. And
19 things that are written in this book

it is written Mat 2 5 for so i. . . . by the prophet. And thou Bethlehem
Mat 4 4 it is written, Not in bread alone doth
6 i. . . . : That he hath given. Luke 4:10
7 it is written again: Thou shalt not
11 10 of whom i. . . . : Behold I send. Luke 7:27
21 13 i. . . . My house shall be called the
26 24 Son of man indeed goeth, as i. . . . Mark 14:21

31 for i. . . . : I will strike the shepherd. Mark 14:27
Mark 1 2 as i. . . . in Isaias the prophet: Behold
7 6 as it is written: This people honoreth
9 11 as i. . . . of the Son of man, that he
12 as it is written of him. 14:21
Luke 2 23 it is w. in the law of the Lord. 24
4 4 i. . . . that man liveth not by bread
19 46 i. . . . My house is the house of prayer
24 46 thus i. . . . and thus it behoved Christ
John 6 31 as it is written: He gave them bread
45 i. . . . in the prophets: And they shall
8 17 i. . . . that the testimony of two men
12 14 as i. . . . Fear not, daughter of Sion
Acts 1 20 i. . . . in the book of Psalms: Let their
7 42 as i. . . . in the books of the prophets
15 15 words of the prophets, as it is written
23 5 for it is written: Thou shalt not speak
Rom 1 17 as it is written: The just man liveth
2 24 blasphemed among Gentiles, as it is w.
3 4 as it is written, That thou mayest be
10 as it is written: There is not any man
4 17 as it is written: I have made thee a
8 36 as it is written: For thy sake we are
9 13 as it is written: Jacob I have loved
33 as it is written: Behold I lay in Sion
10 15 as it is written: How beautiful are the
11 8 as it is written: God hath given them
26 as it is written: There shall come out
12 19 it is written: Revenge is mine, I will
14 11 it is written: As I live, saith the Lord
15 3 as it is written: The reproaches of them
9 it is written: Therefore will I confess
21 as it is written: They to whom he was
1 C 1 19 for it is written: I will destroy the
31 as it is written: He that glorieth, may
2 9 but, as it is written: That eye hath not
3 19 it is written: I will catch the wise in
9 9 for it is written in the law of Moses
10 7 as it is written: The people sat down
14 21 in law it is written: In other tongues
15 44 as it is written: The first man Adam was
2 C 4 13 as it is written: I believed, for which
8 15 as it is written: He that had much, had
9 9 as it is written: He hath dispersed
Gal 3 6 it is written: Abraham believed God, and
10 it is written: Cursed is every one. 13
4 22 it is written that Abraham had two sons
27 it is written: Rejoice, thou barren
Heb 10 7 it is written of me: that I should do
1 P 1 16 i. . . . : You shall be holy, for I am
wrong Gen 50 15 remember the w. he suffered, and
Exod 2 13 and he said to him that did the wrong
Deut 28 29 mayst thou at all times suffer wrong
2 K 19 43 why hast thou done me a wrong, and
1 Pa 16 21 he suffered no man to do them wrong
Ps 34 1 judge thou, O Lord, them that wrong me
102 6 and judgment for all that suffer wrong
145 7 judgment for them that suffer wrong
Eccu 4 9 deliver him that suffereth wrong out
9 17 be not pleased with the wrong done by
13 4 the rich man hath done wrong, and yet
Isa 41 29 they are all in the wrong, and their
Jer 51 35 the wrong done to me and my flesh
Haba 1 4 therefore wrong judgment goeth forth
1 Ma 2 67 revenge ye the wrong of your people
2 Ma 10 12 by reason of the wrong that had been
14 23 abode in Jerusalem and did no wrong
Mat 20 13 I do thee no wrong: didst thou not
Acts 7 24 he had seen one of them suffer wrong
1 C 6 7 why do you not rather take wrong? Why
8 but you do wrong and defraud, and that
2 C 7 12 it was not for his sake that did wrong
Col 3 25 for he that doth wrong, shall receive
wronged Lev 6 5 to the owner, whom he wronged
1 K 12 3 if I [Samuel] have wronged any man
4 hast not wronged us nor oppressed us
1 Es 4 14 we count it a crime to see the king w.
Wisd 18 2 they that before had been wronged, gave
Eccu 13 4 the poor is wronged and must hold his
35 16 hear the prayer of him that is wronged
Eze 18 7 and hath not wronged any man: but hath
Luke 19 8 if I have wronged any man of anything
Philem 18 if he hath wronged thee in anything, or
wrongest Judg 11 27 w. me by declaring an unjust
wrongfully Ps 34 19 enemies w. rejoice over me
Ps 37 20 that hate me wrongfully are multiplied
68 5 grown strong who have w. persecuted me
Eccu 34 21 that sacrificeth of a thing w. gotten
Lam 3 36 to destroy a man w. in his judgment
1 Ma 2 37 that you put us to death wrongfully
2 Ma 8 16 the enemies who came w. against them
Col 3 25 receive for that which he hath done w.
1 P 2 19 a man endure sorrows, suffering w.
wrongs Prov 19 11 and his glory is to pass over w.
Eccu 10 8 because of injustices and wrongs and
21 5 injuries and wrongs will waste riches
wrote Exod 24 4 Moses wrote all the words of the
Exod 34 28 he wrote upon the tables the ten words
39 29 they wrote on it with the engraving
Num 33 2 which Moses wrote down according to
Deut 4 13 that he wrote in two tables of stone
5 22 he wrote them in two tables of stone
10 4 he wrote in the tables according as
31 9 Moses wrote this law and delivered it
22 Moses therefore wrote the canticle
24 after Moses had wrote the words of
Josu 8 32 he wrote upon stones the Deuteronomy
24 26 he wrote all these things in the volume
1 K 10 25 wrote it in a book and laid it up
2 K 11 14 David wrote a letter to Joab: and sent
3 K 21 8 so she wrote letters in Achab's name
4 K 10 1 Jehu wrote letters and sent to Samaria
6 wrote letters the second time to them
17 37 commandment which he wrote for you
1 Pa 24 6 wrote them down before the king and
2 Pa 30 1 he w. letters to Ephraim and Manasses
32 17 wrote also letters full of blasphemy
1 Es 4 6 they wrote an accusation against the
7 in the council wrote to Artaxerxes
8 wrote a letter from Jerusalem to king
Jdth 4 5 and Eliachim the priest wrote to all
Ecce 12 10 and wrote words most right and full of
Jer 32 10 I wrote it in a book and sealed it and
36 4 Baruch wrote from the mouth of Jeremias
18 to me: and I wrote in a volume with ink
32 wrote in it from the mouth of Jeremias
51 60 Jeremias wrote in one book all the
Bar 1 1 which Baruch . . . wrote in Babylonia
Dan 5 5 beheld the joints of the hand that w.
6 25 king Darius w. to all people, tribes
1 Ma 1 43 Antiochus wrote to all his kingdom
53 he wrote to his whole kindom and he
8 22 writing that they wrote back again
10 17 he wrote a letter and sent it to him
25 he wrote to them in these words: King
59 w. to Jonathan that he should come
11 22 wrote to Jonathan, that he should not
29 he wrote letters to Jonathan of all
57 and young Antiochus wrote to Jonathan
12 5 which Jonathan wrote to the Spartans
13 35 wrote a letter in this manner: King
14 18 they wrote to him in tables of brass
15 24 they wrote a copy thereof to Simon
16 18 Ptolemee wrote these things and sent
2 Ma 1 7 we Jews wrote to you, in the trouble

8 8 then Philip . . . wrote to Ptolemee the
9 18 he wrote to the Jews in the manner of
11 15 Machabeus wrote to Lysias concerning
14 27 wrote Nicanor, signifying that he was
Mark 10 5 he wrote you that precept. But from
12 19 Moses wrote unto us, that if any man's brother. Luke 20:28
Luke 1 63 he wrote, saying: John is his name
John 5 46 believe me also; for he wrote of me
8 6 Jesus . . . wrote with his finger on
8 stooping down, he wrote on the ground
19 19 Pilate wrote a title also, and he put
Acts 18 27 brethren exhorting, w. to the disciples
23 25 and he wrote a letter after this manner
Rom 10 5 Moses w., that the justice which is of
16 22 I Tertius, who w. this epistle, salute
1 C 5 9 I wrote to you in an epistle, not to
7 1 things whereof you wrote to me: It is
2 C 2 3 I wrote this same to you; that I may not
4 I wrote to you with many tears: not that
7 12 although I wrote to you, it was not for
wrought Exod 4 30 w. the signs before the people
Exod 10 2 and wrought my signs amongst them: and
26 31 linen, wrought with embroidered work
28 28 that the joining artificially wrought
Num 14 11 signs that I have wrought before them
23 23 and to Israel what God hath wrought
26 10 and there was a great miracle wrought
Deut 6 22 he wrought signs and wonders, great and
Ruth 2 19 where hast thou wrought? Blessed be he
19 she told her with whom she had wrought
1 K 11 13 this day hath w. salvation in Israel
14 45 who hath wrought this great salvation
45 for he hath wrought with God this day
19 5 Lord wrought great salvation for all
2 K 23 10 the Lord wrought a great victory that
3 K 6 18 the joints thereof artfully wrought
7 14 to king Solomon, he w. all his work
35 so wrought that the laver might be set
4 K 12 11 masons that w. in house of the Lord
17 19 errors of Israel, which they had w.
1 Pa 4 21 the house of them that w. fine linen
2 Pa 3 14 and silk: and wrought in it cherubims
24 12 and such as wrought in iron and brass
31 20 wrought that which was good and right
33 6 he wrought many evils before the Lord
36 8 and his abominations, which he wrought
Jdth 14 6 that the God of Israel had wrought
Job 36 23 say to him: Thou hast wrought iniquity
Ps 30 20 which thou hast w. for them that hope
43 2 work thou hast wrought in their days
51 4 as a sharp razor, thou hast w. deceit
67 29 O God, what thou hast wrought in us
73 12 he hath wrought salvation in the midst
77 43 how he wrought his signs in Egypt
97 1 right hand hath w. for him salvation
105 6 acted unjustly, we have w. iniquity
117 16 right hand of the Lord hath w. strength
128 3 the wicked have wrought upon my back
Prov 10 4 the slothful hand hath wrought poverty
31 13 hath w. by the counsel of her hands
Ecce 2 11 the works which my hands had wrought
Wisd 3 14 the eunuch, that hath not w. iniquity
Eccu 44 2 Lord hath wrought great glory through
45 24 he w. wonders upon them and consumed
48 15 wonders, and in death he w. miracles
Isa 17 8 to the things that his fingers wrought
19 9 be confounded that wrought in flax
22 11 at a distance, that w. it long ago
26 12 thou hast wrought all our works for us
18 we have not wrought salvation on the
41 4 who hath wrought and done these things
44 12 the smith hath wrought with his file
12 hath w. with the strength of his arm
Jer 8 8 of the scribes hath wrought falsehood
11 15 beloved hath w. much wickedness in my
Eze 18 18 wrought evil in the midst of his people
19 the son hath w. judgment and justice
22 in his justice which he hath wrought
26 in the injustice that he hath wrought
27 his wickedness which he hath wrought
28 his iniquities which he hath wrought
20 22 hand, and wrought for my name's sake
27 19 set forth in thy marts wrought iron
41 18 were cherubims and palm trees wrought
20 palm trees wrought in the wall of the
25 cherubims also wrought in the doors
Dan 3 99 hath wrought signs and wonders toward
Osee 6 9 for they have wrought wickedness
Soph 2 3 you that have wrought his judgment
Mat 11 21 had been w. the miracles that have been w. in you. 23
13 58 he wrought not many miracles there
26 10 she hath wrought a good work upon me. Mark 14:6
Mark 6 2 mighty works as are w. by his hands
Luke 1 68 and w. the redemption of his people
10 13 if in Tyre and Sidon had been w. the mighty works that have been w. in you
23 8 hoped to see some sign wrought by him
Acts 4 22 that miraculous cure had been wrought
5 12 were many signs and wonders wrought
15 12 wonders God had w. among the Gentiles
19 11 God wrought by the hand of Paul more
21 19 related . . . what things God had wrought
Rom 7 8 w. in me all manner of concupiscence
13 that which is good, wrought death in me
2 C 12 12 been wrought on you, in all patience
Gal 2 8 wrought in Peter to the apostleship of
8 wrought in me also among the Gentiles
Eph 1 20 which he wrought in Christ, raising him
Heb 11 33 wrought justice, obtained promises
2 J 8 the things which you have wrought
Apoc 19 20 prophet who wrought signs before him

X

Xanthicus 2 Ma 11 30 day of the month of X. 33, 38

Y

yard Deut 23 1 yard cut off, shall not enter into
Acts 27 17 they let down the sail yard, and so
yea Gen 31 7 yea, your father also hath
Lev 7 18 yea rather whatsoever soul shall defile
1 K 14 15 yea and all the people of their
15 20 yea I have hearkened to the voice of
23 17 yea, and my father knoweth this. And
2 K 18 13 yea and if I should have acted boldly
19 30 yea, let him take all, forasmuch as my
3 K 3 13 yea, and the things also which thou
1 Pa 16 9 sing to him, yea, sing praises to him
2 Pa 26 20 yea, himself also being frightened
1 Es 7 25 yea and the ignorant teach ye freely
2 Es 9 18 yea when they had made also to
Job 35 14 yea when thou shalt say: He considereth
Ps 9 16 yea, forever and ever. 44:18; 51:10; 144:1, 2, 21
12 6 yea, I will sing to the name of the
28 5 yea, the Lord shall break the cedars
38 7 yea, and he is disquieted in vain
44 13 yea, all the rich among the people
64 14 shout, yea they shall sing a hymn
67 19 yea for those also that do not believe
70 24 yea and my tongue shall meditate on
82 9 yea, and the Assyrian also is joined

89 17 yea, the work of our hands do thou
104 2 sing to him, yea sing praises to him
12 were but a small number: yea very few
Ecce 7 19 yea, and from him withdraw not thy hand
8 17 yea, though the wise man shall say
10 3 yea, and the fool when he walketh in
Wisd 8 3 yea and the Lord of all things hath
11 21 yea and without these, they might
14 4 yea though a man went to sea without
15 12 yea and they have counted our life
19 yea, neither by sight can any man see
Isa 5 29 yea, they shall roar and take hold of
13 12 yea a man than the finest of gold
26 9 yea, and with my spirit within me
46 7 yea, when they shall cry also unto him
49 25 yea verily, even the captivity shall be
Jer 6 15 yea, rather they were not confounded
8 12 yea rather they are not confounded
14 5 yea, the hind also brought forth in
50 3 yea they are removed and gone away
Lam 3 8 yea, and when I cry and entreat, he
Bar 6 10 yea and they give thereof to
Eze 4 6 yea, a day for a year I have appointed
17 13 yea, and he shall take away the mighty
23 38 yea, and they have done this to me
30 3 yea the day of the Lord is near: a
33 13 yea, if I shall say to the just that
46 1 yea and on the day of the new moon
Dan 6 22 yea and before thee, O king, I have
11 22 yea also the prince of the covenant
Osee 4 3 yea, the fishes of the sea also shall
7 9 yea, gray hairs also are spread about
9 12 yea, and woe to them, when I shall
Joel 1 18 yea, and the flocks of sheep are
20 yea and the beasts of the field have
2 8 yea, and they shall fall through the
Amos 7 6 yea this also shall not be, said the
Mich 4 8 yea the first power shall come, the
Zach 6 13 yea, he shall build a temple to the
Mala 2 2 yea, I will curse them because you
1 Ma 5 27 yea, and that they were kept shut up
2 Ma 2 27 yea rather a business full of watching
8 30 the widows, yea and the aged also. And
9 17 yea also, that he would become a Jew
11 12 yea and Lysias himself fled away
Mat 5 37 your speech be yea, yea. James 5:12
9 28 unto you? They say to him, Yea, Lord
11 9 a prophet? Yea I tell you, and more
26 yea, Father; for so hath it seemed good
15 27 yea Lord; for the whelps. Mark 7:28
21 16 yea, have you never read: Out of the
26 35 yea, though I should die with thee
Luke 7 26 yea, I say to you. 11:51; 12:5
10 21 yea, Father, for so it hath seemed
11 28 yea rather, blessed are they who hear
12 7 yea, the very hairs of your head are
14 26 yea and his own life also, he cannot
24 22 yea and certain women also of our
John 11 27 yea, Lord, I have believed that thou
16 2 yea, the hour cometh, that whosoever
21 15 yea, Lord, thou knowest that I love. 16
Acts 5 8 much? And she said: Yea, for so much
19 27 reputed for nothing; yea, and her
22 27 art thou a Roman? But he said: Yea. And
Rom 8 34 Jesus that died, yea that is risen also
1 C 2 10 all things, yea, the deep things of God
12 22 yea, much more those that seem to be
15 15 yea, and we are found false witnesses
2 C 7 11 yea defence, yea indignation, yea fear
Phil 1 18 in this also I rejoice, yea, and will
2 17 yea, and if I be made a victim upon the
Philem 20 yea, brother. May I enjoy thee in the
Apoc 16 7 yea, O Lord God Almighty, true and

year Luke 3 1 fifteenth year of the reign of
Luke 4 19 preach the acceptable year of the Lord
13 8 let it alone this year also, until I
John 11 49 being the high priest that year. 51
18 13 who was the high priest of that year
Acts 11 26 they conversed there . . . a whole year
18 11 he stayed there a year and six months
2 C 8 10 do, but also to be willing, a year ago
9 2 Achaia also is ready from the year past
Heb 9 7 the high priest alone, once a year: not
James 4 13 city, and there we will spend a year
Apoc 9 15 prepared for . . . a month and a year
every year Exod 23 14 three times e. y. you shall
Deut 14 22 e. y. thou shalt set aside the tithes
15 20 shalt thou eat them every year in the
Judg 17 10 I will give thee every year ten pieces
1 K 1 7 thus she did every year, when the time
7 16 he went every year about to Bethel and
3 K 5 11 thus gave Solomon to Hiram every year
9 25 offered three times every y. holocausts
10 14 brought to Solomon e. y. 2 Pa 9:13
25 spices and horses and mules every year
4 K 17 4 Assyrians, as he had done every year
2 Pa 9 24 every year they brought him presents
2 Es 10 32 third part of a sicle every year for
1 Ma 7 49 that this day should be kept every year
8 4 the rest pay them tribute every year
16 their government to one man every year
10 40 I give every year 15,000 sicles of
42 every year shall also belong to the
11 34 the king received of them every year
13 52 these days should be kept every year
2 Ma 10 8 should keep those days every year
11 3 the high priesthood to sale every year
Luke 2 41 and his parents went every year to
Heb 9 25 every year with the blood of others: for
10 1 which they offer continually every year
3 made a commemoration of sins every year
fifth year Lev 19 25 in fifth year you shall eat
Lev 27 5 from the fifth year until the twentieth
6 from one month until the fifth year
3 K 14 25 f. y. of the reign of Roboam. 2 Pa 12:2
4 K 8 16 in the fifth year of Joram son of Achab
Jer 36 9 came to pass in fifth year of Joakim
Bar 1 2 in the fifth year, in the seventh day
Eze 1 2 same was the fifth y. of the captivity
2 Ma 4 18 the game that was used every fifth year
first year Lev 23 12 a lamb . . . of the first y.
Lev 23 18 lambs without blemish of the f. y.
19 and two lambs of the first year for
2 Pa 29 3 in the first y. and month of his reign
36 22 in the first year of Cyrus. 1 Es 1:1; 5:13; 6:3
Jer 25 1 same is first year of Nabuchodonosor
52 31 in the first year of his reign, lifted
Dan 1 21 even to the first year of king Cyrus
7 1 in the first year of Baltasar king of
9 1 in the first year of Darius the son of
2 the first year of his reign, I Daniel
11 1 from the first y. of Darius the Mede
1 Ma 13 42 first year of Simon the high priest
one year Exod 12 5 lamb . . . a male, of one y.
Exod 23 29 them out from thy face in one year
Lev 25 29 to redeem it, until one year be expired
Num 6 12 offering a lamb of one year for sin
Deut 24 5 that for one year he may rejoice with
1 K 13 1 Saul was a child of one year when he
4 K 8 26 reigned one y. in Jerusalem. 2 Pa 22:2
Eccu 33 7 and one year another year, when all
Jer 51 46 and a rumor shall come in one year
second year Gen 47 18 they came the second year
Exod 40 15 first month of s. y. the tabernacle
Num 1 1 second year of their going out of Egypt
10 11 second year in the second month, the

3 K 15 25 reigned over Israel second year of Asa
4 K 1 17 in the second year of Joram the son
14 1 in the second year of Joas son of
15 32 in the second year of Phacee the son
19 29 in second year, such things as spring
2 Pa 27 5 give him in the second and third year
1 Es 3 8 second y. of their coming to the temple
4 24 till second year of the reign of Darius
Esth 11 2 second year of the reign of Artaxerxes
Isa 37 30 in the second year eat fruits: but in
Dan 2 1 second year of reign of Nabuchodonosor
Agge 1 1 the s. y. of Darius. 2:1, 11; Zach 1:7
Zach 1 1 in the second year of king Darius
seventh year Exod 23 11 s. y. thou shalt let it
Lev 25 4 seventh year there shall be a sabbath
20 what shall we eat the seventh year
Deut 15 1 in s. y. thou shalt make a remission
9 seventh year of remission draweth nigh
12 seventh year thou shalt let him go free
4 K 11 4 in the seventh year Joiada sent, and
12 1 in seventh year of Jehu, Joas began to
18 9 which was the seventh year of Osee
2 Pa 23 1 in the seventh year Joiada being
1 Es 7 7 in the seventh year of Artaxerxes the
8 in the seventh year of the king. For
2 Es 10 31 that we would leave the seventh year
Esth 2 16 in the seventh year of his reign. And
Jer 52 28 in the seventh year, 3,023 Jews. In the
Eze 20 1 it came to pass in the seventh year
1 Ma 6 53 because it was the seventh year: and
third year Deut 14 28 t. y. thou shalt separate
Deut 26 12 in the third year of tithes thou shalt
3 K 15 28 in the third year of Asa. 33
18 1 came to Elias, in the third year
22 2 the third year Josaphat . . . came down
4 K 18 1 in the third year of Osee the son of
19 29 the third year sow and reap. Isa 37:30
2 Pa 17 7 in third year of his reign, he sent
27 5 give him in the second and third year
Tob 1 7 in the third y. he gave all his tithes
Esth 1 3 in the third year of his reign he made
Dan 1 1 third year of the reign of Joakim
8 1 third year of reign of king Baltasar
10 1 in the third year of Cyrus king of the
1 Ma 14 27 being the third year under Simon the
yearly Judg 21 19 there is a y. solemnity of the
1 Es 4 13 tribute nor toll nor yearly revenues
2 Es 5 14 did not eat the yearly allowance that
18 I did not require my yearly allowance
Jer 5 24 us the fulness of the yearly harvest
years Mat 9 20 issue of blood twelve y. Mark 5:25; Luke 8:43
Luke 1 7 they both were well advanced in years
18 and my wife is advanced in years. And
2 36 she was far advanced in years, and
37 a widow until fourscore and four years
3 23 about the age of 30 years; being, as
13 11 a spirit of infirmity eighteen years
16 hath bound, lo, these eighteen years
John 2 20 six and forty years was this temple
5 5 that had been eight and thirty years
Acts 7 6 bondage, and treat them evil 400 years
13 20 as it were, after 453 years: and after
28 30 he remained two whole years in his own
2 C 12 2 I know a man in Christ above 14 years
Gal 2 1 then, after fourteen years, I went up
3 17 the law which was made after 430 years
4 10 you observe days . . . and times and y.
1 Tim 5 9 of no less than threescore years of age
Heb 1 12 selfsame, and thy years shall not fail
2 P 3 8 is as a thousand years, and a thousand years as one day
Apoc 20 2 Satan, and bound him for 1,000 years
3 till the thousand years be finished
4 reigned with Christ a thousand years
5 till the thousand years were finished
6 shall reign with him a thousand years
7 when the thousand y. shall be finished
Acts 9 33 kept his bed for eight years, who was
forty years Gen 25 20 when he [Isaac] was f. y.
Gen 26 34 Esau being forty years old, married
Exod 16 35 children of Israel ate manna 40 years
Num 14 33 shall wander in the desert forty years
34 forty years you shall receive your
32 13 them about through the desert 40 years
Deut 2 7 this great wilderness for forty years
8 2 hath brought thee for forty y. through
29 5 brought you forty years through the
Josu 5 6 during the forty years of the journey
14 7 I was forty years old when Moses the
Judg 3 11 the land rested forty years. 5:32; 8:28
13 1 into hands of the Philistines 40 years
1 K 4 18 he [Heli] judged Israel forty years
2 K 2 10 Isobeth . . . was 40 years old when he
5 4 and he [David] reigned forty years
15 7 after 40 y., Absalom said to king David
3 K 2 11 David reigned in Israel were 40 years
11 42 that Solomon reigned . . . were 40 years
4 K 12 1 [Joas] reigned forty years. 2 Pa 24:1
1 Pa 29 27 reigned over Israel, were forty years
2 Pa 9 30 Solomon reigned . . . forty years. And he
2 Es 9 21 forty years didst thou feed them in the
Jdth 5 15 for forty years they received food from
Ps 94 10 forty years long was I offended with
Eze 29 11 nor shall it be inhabited during 40 y.
12 they shall be desolate for forty years
Amos 2 10 I led you forty years through the
5 25 to me in the desert for forty years
Acts 4 22 the man was above forty years old, in
7 23 when he was full forty years old, it
30 when forty years were expired, there
36 Red Sea and in the desert 40 years
42 and sacrifices to me for forty years
13 18 for the space of forty years endured
21 of the tribe of Benjamin, forty years
Heb 3 10 proved and saw my works, forty years
17 with whom was he offended forty years
many years Lev 25 51 there be m. y. that remain
1 Es 5 11 temple that was built these many years
2 Es 9 30 didst forbear with them for many years
Jdth 16 30 nor many years after her death. But
Ecce 6 3 live many years and attain to a great
11 8 if a man live many years and have
Bar 6 2 Babylon, you shall be there many years
Zach 7 3 as I have now done for many years
1 Ma 1 10 and their sons after them many years
2 Ma 1 20 when many years had passed, and it
Luke 12 19 much goods laid up for many years
15 29 for so many years do I serve thee
Acts 24 10 knowing that for many years thou hast
17 after many years, I came to bring alms
Rom 15 23 having a great desire these many years
seven years Gen 29 18 I will serve thee s. y.
Gen 29 20 Jacob served seven years for Rachel
27 thou shalt render me other seven years
30 served with him other seven years
41 26 seven full ears are seven y. of plenty
27 are seven years of famine to come
29 shall come seven years of great plenty
30 other seven years of so great scarcity
34 fruits during the seven fruitful years
36 against the famine of seven years to
47 fruitfulness of the seven years came
53 when the seven years of the plenty
54 seven years of scarcity, which Joseph
Num 13 23 Hebron was built seven y. before Tanis

Deut 31 10 after s. y., in the year of remission
Judg 6 1 into the hand of Madian seven years
25 and another bullock of seven years
12 9 he [Abesan] judged Israel seven years
2 K 2 11 of Juda was 7 years and 6 months
5 5 he reigned over Juda seven years
24 13 either seven years of famine shall come
3 K 2 11 in Hebron he reigned s. y. 1 Pa 29:27
6 38 and he was seven years in building it
4 K 8 1 it shall come upon the land seven y.
3 when the seven years were ended, the
11 21 Joas was s. y. old when he. 2 Pa 24:1
1 Pa 3 4 where he [David] reigned seven years
Jer 34 14 at the end of seven years, let ye go
Eze 39 9 shall burn them with fire seven years
Luke 2 36 with her husband 7 years from her
three years Gen 15 9 take me a cow of 3 y. old and a she goat of 3 y. and a ram of 3 y.
Lev 25 21 it shall yield the fruits of three y.
Judg 9 22 Abimelech reigned over Israel 3 years
2 K 13 38 come into Gessur, was there three years
21 1 there was a famine . . . for three years
3 K 2 39 it came to pass after three years
10 22 the king's navy, once in three years
15 2 [Abiam] reigned 3 years in Jerusalem
22 1 there passed three years without war
4 K 18 10 after three years, in the sixth year of
24 1 Joakim became his servant three years
2 Pa 9 21 servants of Hiram, once in three years
11 17 Roboam son of Solomon for 3 years
17 of David and of Solomon only 3 years
13 2 three years he reigned in Jerusalem
31 16 besides the males from three years
Isa 15 5 unto Segor a heifer of three years old
16 14 in 3 y., as the y. of a hireling, the
20 3 a wonder of three years upon Egypt
Jer 48 34 as a heifer of three years old: the
Dan 1 5 being nourished three years, afterwards
2 Ma 4 23 three years afterwards Jason sent
7 27 and gave thee suck three years and
14 1 after the space of three years, Judas
Luke 4 25 when heaven was shut up three years
13 7 for these three years I come seeking
Acts 20 31 keeping in memory, that for 3 years I
Gal 1 18 after three years, I went to Jerusalem
James 5 17 it rained not for three years and six
twenty years Gen 31 38 been with thee 20 years
Gen 31 41 I served thee in thy house 20 years
Exod 30 14 from twenty years and upwards. 38:25; Num chap. 1, *passim;* 14:29; 26:2, 4; 32:11; 1 Pa 23:24, 27; 2 Pa 25:5; 1 Es 3:8
Lev 27 3 from 20 years old unto 60 years old
Judg 4 3 for 20 years had grossly oppressed
15 20 he judged Israel . . . 20 years. 16:31
3 K 9 10 and when twenty years were ended after
4 K 15 27 over Israel in Samaria twenty years
16 2 Achaz was 20 years old when. 2 Pa 28:1
1 Pa 27 23 from twenty years old and under
two years Gen 11 10 two years after the flood
Gen 41 1 after two years Pharao had a dream
45 6 it is two years since the famine began
1 K 13 1 Saul . . . reigned two years over Israel
2 K 2 10 and he [Isboseth] reigned two years
13 23 after 2 y., that the sheep of Absalom
14 28 Absalom dwelt two years in Jerusalem
3 K 15 25 Nadab . . . reigned over Israel two y.
16 8 reigned over Israel in Thersa two years
22 52 Ochozias . . . reigned over Israel 2 y.
4 K 15 23 reigned Phaceia . . . in Samaria 2 y.
21 19 [Amon] reigned two years in Jerusalem
2 Pa 21 19 time rolled on, two whole years passed
Jer 28 3 as yet two years of days, and I will
11 after two full years from off the neck
Amos 1 1 two years before the earthquake. And
1 Ma 1 30 after two full years the king sent
9 57 the land was quiet for two years
2 Ma 10 3 they offered sacrifices after two years
Mat 2 16 from two years old and under, according
Acts 19 10 this continued for the space of 2 years
24 27 when two years were ended, Felix had
years old; *see* **old**
years' 1 Pa 21 12 either three years' famine: or
yellow Lev 13 30 hair yellow and thinner than
Lev 13 36 whether the hair be turned yellow
Prov 23 31 look not upon the wine when it is y.
Jer 30 6 and all faces are turned yellow? Alas
yes Mat 13 51 these things? They say to him: Yes
Mat 17 24 he [Peter] said: Yes. And when he was
Rom 3 28 the Gentiles? Yes, of the Gentiles also
10 18 yes, verily, their sound hath gone forth
yesterday Gen 31 29 of your father said to me y.
Gen 31 42 of my hands, and rebuked thee y.
Exod 2 14 as thou didst y. kill the Egyptian
5 14 task of bricks both y. and today
1 K 20 27 son of Isai to meat neither y. nor
2 K 15 20 yesterday thou [Ethai] camest, and
4 K 9 26 which I saw yesterday, saith the Lord
Job 8 9 we are but of y. and are ignorant
Ps 89 4 thousand years in thy sight are as y.
Eccu 38 23 yesterday for me, and today for thee
Isa 30 33 Topheth is prepared from yesterday
John 4 52 y. at the seventh hour the fever left
Acts 7 28 as thou didst y. kill the Egyptian
Heb 13 8 Jesus Christ y. and today and the same
yesterday and the day before Exod 4 10 I am not eloquent from y. . . .
Exod 21 29 was wont to push with his horn y. . . .
36 knew that his ox was wont to push y. . . .
Deut 19 4 have no hatred against him y. . . .
1 K 4 8 there was no such great joy y. . . .
10 11 and all that had known him y. . . .
14 21 had been with the Philistines y. . . .
19 7 was before him as he had been y. . . .
21 5 we have refrained ourselves from y. . . .
2 K 5 2 y. . . . when Saul was king. 1 Pa 11:2
4 K 13 5 dwelt in their pavilions as y. . . .
Dan 13 15 she went in on a time, as y. . . .
1 Ma 9 44 enemies: for it is not now as y. . . .
yield Gen 4 12 it shall not y. to thee its fruit
Gen 49 20 and he shall yield dainties to kings
Exod 23 2 neither shalt thou yield in judgment
Lev 25 19 the ground may yield you its fruits
21 shall yield the fruits of three years
26 20 nor the trees yield their fruit. If
Num 20 8 before them and it shall yield waters
Deut 1 45 neither would he yield to your voice
11 17 nor the earth yield her fruit, and you
Ruth 4 6 I yield up my right of next akin: for
3 K 12 7 if thou wilt yield to this people today
2 Pa 30 8 yield yourselves to the Lord and come
Jdth 7 9 wearied out they will y. up their city
15 yield ourselves all up to the people
10 12 would not of their own accord yield
Ps 84 13 and our earth shall yield her fruit
Prov 6 35 nor will he yield to any man's prayers
Cant 2 13 vines in flower yield their sweet smell
Eccu 39 19 yield a smell, and bring forth leaves
Isa 5 10 ten acres of vineyard shall yield one
10 30 bushels of seed shall y. 3 bushels
Eze 34 27 tree of the field shall yield its fruit
27 the earth shall yield her increase
36 8 yield your fruit to my people of
Osee 8 7 the bud shall yield no meal; and if
7 if it should yield, strangers shall
9 16 dried up, they shall yield no fruit
Haba 3 17 and the fields shall yield no food

Zach 8 12 the vine shall yield her fruit and
1 Ma 10 32 I yield up also the power of the
Mat 3 10 that doth not yield good fruit, shall
Mark 4 20 and yield fruit, the one thirty, another
Luke 8 14 of this life, and yield no fruit
Rom 6 13 yield ye your members as instruments of
16 know you not, that to whom you yield
19 now yield your members to serve justice
Heb 12 11 it will yield to them that are
James 3 12 neither can the salt water yield sweet
yielded Gen 29 28 he [Jacob] y. to his pleasure
Ruth 4 7 if at any time one yielded his right
Ps 66 6 thee: the earth hath yielded her fruit
106 37 and they yielded fruit of birth. And he
Eccu 24 20 I yielded a sweet odor like the best
Joel 2 22 the vine have yielded their strength
1 Ma 2 48 they y. not the horn to the sinner
9 24 and all their country y. to Bacchides
14 8 the land of Juda yielded her increase
Mat 27 50 with a loud voice yielded up the ghost
Mark 4 7 choked it, and it yielded no fruit
8 grew up and increased and yielded
Luke 8 8 yielded fruit a hundredfold. Saying
Rom 6 19 as you have y. your members to serve
Gal 2 5 to whom we yielded not by subjection
yieldeth Gen 1 12 such as y. seed according to
Prov 13 18 that y. to reproof, shall be glorified
15 32 that yieldeth to reproof possesseth
Mat 13 23 yieldeth the one an hundredfold and
yielding Gen 1 11 tree y. fruit after its kind
2 Pa 30 11 of Zabulon, yielding to counsel, came
Wisd 17 11 yielding up of the succors from thought
Agge 1 10 earth was hindered from y. her fruits
2 Ma 13 23 entreating the Jews and y. to them
Mat 21 43 to a nation yielding the fruits thereof
Apoc 22 2 yielding its fruits every month, and
yoke Gen 27 40 loose his yoke from thy neck. Esau
Num 19 2 and which hath not carried the yoke
21 30 their yoke is perished from Hesebon
Deut 21 3 that hath not drawn in the yoke nor
28 48 shall put an iron yoke upon thy neck
Judg 19 22 sons of Belial (that is, without yoke)
1 K 6 7 on which there hath come no yoke, tie
14 14 which a yoke of oxen is wont to plow
3 K 12 4 thy father laid a grievous yoke upon us
4 most heavy yoke which he put upon us
9 yoke which thy father put upon us
10 father made our yoke heavy. 2 Pa 10:10
11 my father put a heavy yoke upon you
11 you but I will add to your yoke. 14
14 my father made your yoke heavy, but
19 19 plowing with twelve yoke of oxen
21 took a yoke of oxen and killed them
2 Pa 10 3 oppressed us with a most grievous yoke
9 ease the yoke which thy father laid
11 my father laid upon you a heavy y. 14
Jdth 2 6 cities thou shalt bring under my yoke
5 24 brought under the yoke of thy power
Job 1 3 camels and five hundred yoke of oxen
42 12 camels and a thousand yoke of oxen
Ps 2 3 let us cast away their yoke from us
Eccu 26 10 as a yoke of oxen that is moved to and
28 23 that hath not drawn the yoke thereof
24 its yoke is a yoke of iron: and its
33 27 yoke and the thong bend a stiff neck
40 1 heavy yoke is upon the children of Adam
51 34 submit your neck to the yoke and let
Isa 9 4 the yoke of their burden, and the rod
10 27 his yoke from off thy neck, and the yoke shall putrify at the presence of
14 25 his yoke shall be taken away from them
47 6 upon the ancient thou hast laid thy y.
Jer 2 20 of old time thou hast broken my yoke
5 5 have altogether broken the yoke more
47 8 y. of king of Babylon. 11, 12; 28:2, 4
28 11 will I break the yoke of Nabuchodonosor
14 I have put a yoke of iron upon the neck
30 8 I will break his yoke from off thy neck
31 18 young bullock unaccustomed to the yoke
51 23 and his yoke of oxen, and with thee I
Lam 1 14 the yoke of my iniquities hath watched
3 27 he hath borne the y. from his youth
Eze 34 27 shall have broken the bonds of their y.
Osee 7 16 that they might be without yoke: they
11 4 that taketh off the yoke on the jaws
7 but a yoke shall be put upon them
1 Ma 8 18 off from them the yoke of the Grecians
31 why hast thou made thy yoke heavy upon
13 41 yoke of the Gentiles was taken off
Mat 11 29 take up my yoke upon you, and learn of
30 my yoke is sweet and my burden light
21 5 foal of her that is used to the yoke
Luke 14 19 I have bought five yoke of oxen and
Acts 15 10 why tempt you God to put a yoke upon
2 C 6 14 bear not the yoke with unbelievers. For
Gal 5 1 be not held again under y. of bondage
1 Tim 6 1 whosoever are servants under the yoke
2 P 2 16 the dumb beast used to the yoke, which
yoked 1 K 6 10 they yoked them to the cart and
yokes 2 K 24 22 the yokes of the oxen for wood
yonder Gen 22 5 will go with speed as far as y.
1 K 14 1 is on the other side of yonder place
Mat 26 36 you here, till I go yonder and pray
young Gen 19 4 beset the house, both y. and old
Gen 33 13 I have with me . . . kine with young
43 29 is this your young brother of whom
44 20 father an old man, and a young boy
Exod 10 9 we will go with our young and old
Lev 1 14 if the oblation . . . of young pigeons
5 7 not able to offer . . . two y. pigeons. 5:11
12 6 she shall bring . . . a young pigeon
8 she shall take . . . two young pigeons
14 22 two turtles or two young pigeons. 15:14, 29; Num 6:10
30 he shall offer a turtle or y. pigeon
Num 16 15 not taken of them so much as a y. ass
Deut 22 6 find . . . dam sitting upon the young
6 thou shalt not take her with her young
7 shalt let her go, keeping the young
32 11 as the eagle enticing her young to fly
33 22 Dan is a young lion, he shall flow
Josu 6 21 all that were in it . . . young and old
23 42 had bought . . . for 100 young ewes and
Judg 14 5 a young lion met him [Samson] raging
19 6 father of the young woman said to his
Ruth 4 12 Lord shall give thee of this y. woman
1 K 1 24 now the child was as yet very young
16 11 there remaineth yet a young one who
2 K 9 12 Miphiboseth had a young son . . . Micha
3 K 1 2 let us seek for our lord . . . a y. virgin
3 so they sought a beautiful young woman
4 K 25 19 captain . . . who exercised the y. soldiers
1 Pa 22 5 Solomon my son is very y. and tender. 29:1
Tob 2 20 received a y. kid and brought it home
4 11 the young lions are scattered abroad
39 3 bow themselves to bring forth young
4 their young are weaned and go to feed
Ps 16 12 as a y. lion dwelling in secret places
36 25 I have been young, and now am old: and
56 5 my soul from the midst of the y. lions
67 26 in the midst of young damsels playing on
68 32 please God better than a young calf
77 70 the ewes great with young. To feed
103 21 the young lions roaring after their prey
118 141 I am very young and despised; but I
143 13 their sheep fruitful in y., abounding

146 9 to the young ravens that call upon him
Prov 30 17 let . . . and the young eagles eat it
Ecce 2 6 water therewith the wood of the y. trees
Cant 1 2 therefore y. maidens have loved thee
2 9 my beloved is like a roe or a young hart
17 be like . . . to a roe or to a young hart
4 5 thy two breasts like two young roes
6 7 and young maidens without number. One
8 14 be like to the roe and to the young hart
Wisd 8 10 honor with the ancients, though I be y.
Eccu 20 2 shall deflower a young maiden: so
30 12 bow down his neck while he is young
42 9 away his sleep when she is young, lest
Isa 5 29 they shall roar like young lions: yea
7 21 a man shall nourish a young cow and
11 7 their young ones shall rest together
16 2 as young ones flying out of the nest
20 4 the captivity of Egypt, young and old
38 14 I will cry like a young swallow, I will
40 11 shall carry them that are with young
Jer 31 18 as a young bullock unaccustomed to
51 38 shake their manes like young lions
52 25 who exercised the young soldiers
Lam 4 3 they have given suck to their young
Eze 9 6 utterly destroy old and young, maidens
19 2 whelps in the midst of young lions
5 took one of her young lions and set
31 6 forth their young under his branches
Dan 13 45 raised up the holy spirit of a y. boy
Amos 2 7 have gone to the same young woman, to
Mich 5 8 as a young lion among the flocks of
Nah 2 11 feeding place of the young lions, to
11 the young lion, and there was none
13 sword shall devour thy young lions
3 10 her young children were dashed in
1 Ma 6 17 reign, whom he brought up young: and he
11 54 with him Antiochus the young boy, who
57 young Antiochus wrote to Jonathan
13 31 journey with the young king Antiochus
2 Ma 5 13 there was a slaughter of young and old
7 12 wondered at the young man's courage
Mark 10 13 they brought to him young children
Luke 2 24 of turtledoves or two young pigeons
John 12 14 Jesus found a young ass, and sat upon
1 Tim 5 2 young women, as sisters, in all chastity
Titus 2 4 teach the young women to be wise, to
young man Deut 32 25 the y. m. and the virgin
Judg 17 7 also another young man of Bethlehem
18 3 knowing the voice of the young man the
15 they went into house of the young man
19 9 the young man arose to set forward with
Ruth 2 5 and Booz said to the young man that
1 K 14 1 to the young man that bore his armor
6 Jonathan said to the young man that
17 42 he was a y. man, ruddy and of a comely
55 of what family is this y. man descended
58 young man, of what family art thou
30 13 he said: I am a young man of Egypt
Ps 118 9 by what doth a y. man correct his way
Prov 1 4 little ones to the y. man knowledge
7 7 I behold a foolish y. man who passeth
13 catching the young man, she kisseth
22 6 a young man according to his way, even
Ecce 4 15 second young man, who shall rise up
11 9 rejoice therefore, O young man, in thy
Eccu 32 10 young man, scarcely speak in thy own
Isa 62 5 young man shall dwell with the virgin
Jer 15 8 against the mother of the young man
51 22 I will break in pieces the young man
Dan 13 21 that a young man was with thee, and
37 a young man that was there hid came
40 we asked who the young man was, but
Zach 2 4 run, speak to this young man, saying
2 Ma 7 25 when the young man was not moved with
25 counselled her to deal with the y. m.
30 young man said: For whom do you stay
Mat 19 20 the young man saith to him: All these
22 when the young man had heard this word
Mark 14 51 and a certain young man followed him
16 5 they saw a young man sitting on the
Luke 7 14 said: Young man, I say to thee, arise
Acts 7 57 of a young man, whose name was Saul
20 9 certain y. man named Eutychus, sitting
23 17 bring this young man to the tribune, for
18 desired me to bring this young man unto
22 tribune . . . dismissed the young man
young men Josu 6 23 y. men went in and brought
Judg 14 10 Samson: for so the y. men used to do
Ruth 2 9 for I have charged my young men not
3 10 because thou hast not followed y. men
1 K 2 17 the sin of the young men was exceeding
8 16 your goodliest young men and your
21 4 if the young men be clean, especially
5 the vessels of the young men were holy
25 5 he sent ten young men and said to them
13 then David said to his young men: Let
27 give it to the young men that follow
30 17 young men who had gotten upon camels
2 K 2 14 let the young men arise and play
3 K 12 8 and consulted with the young men that
10 the young men that had been brought up
14 according to counsel of the young men
4 K 5 22 two young men of the sons of the
Jdth 15 6 sent their chosen young men armed
15 and y. men, playing on instruments
16 6 and kill my young men with the sword
8 mighty one did not fall by young men
Job 29 8 the young men saw me and hid themselves
Ps 77 63 fire consumed their young men: and
Prov 20 29 the joy of young men is their strength
Eccu 42 8 aged, that are judged by young men
Isa 9 17 shall have no joy in their young men
23 4 nor have I nourished up young men nor
31 8 and his young men shall be tributaries
40 30 and young men shall fall by infirmity
Jer 6 11 upon the council of the young men
9 21 without, the y. men from the streets
11 22 their young men shall die by the sword
18 21 let their young men be stabbed with
31 13 the dance, the young men and old men
48 15 her choice young men are gone down
49 26 her young men shall fall in her streets
50 30 shall her young men fall in her streets
51 3 spare not her young men, destroy all
Lam 1 18 my young men are gone into captivity
2 21 my virgins and my y. men are fallen
5 13 they abused the young men indecently
14 young men have ceased from the choir
Bar 3 20 young men have seen the light and
Eze 23 12 and to young men all of great beauty
23 the Assyrians, beautiful young men
20 17 the young men of Heliopolis and of
Dan 11 6 given up, and her y. men that brought
Joel 2 28 and your young men shall see visions
Amos 2 11 and of young men for Nazarites. Is it
4 10 I slew your young men with the sword
8 13 the young men shall faint for thirst
1 Ma 1 27 and the young men were made feeble
2 9 her young men are fallen by the sword
14 9 and the young men put on them glory
2 Ma 3 26 there appeared two other young men
33 same young men in the same clothing
6 28 an example of fortitude to young men
31 leaving not only to young men, but
10 35 twenty young men of them that were with
12 27 stout young men standing upon the walls

13 15 with most valiant chosen young men, he
15 17 strengthen the hearts of the young men
Acts 2 17 your young men shall see visions, and
5 6 the young men rising up, removed him
10 the young men coming in, found her
1 Tim 5 1 as a father: young men, as brethren
Titus 2 6 young men, in like manner, exhort that
1 P 5 5 young men, be subject to the ancients
1 J 2 13 I write unto you, young men. 14
young ones Lev 22 28 same day with their y. ones
Job 38 41 raven, when her young ones cry to God
39 16 she is hardened against her young ones
30 her young ones shall suck up blood
Ps 83 4 herself where she may lay her y. ones
Isa 34 15 ericius . . . brought up its young ones
younger Gen 9 24 what his younger son had done
Gen 19 31 elder said to the younger: Our father is
34 elder said to the younger: Behold I lay
35 the younger daughter went in and lay
38 the younger also bore a son, and she
25 23 and the elder shall serve the younger
29 16 Lia: the younger was called Rachel
18 seven years for Rachel thy y. daughter
26 to give the younger in marriage first
48 14 head of Ephraim the younger brother
19 this younger brother shall be greater
Josu 15 17 y. brother of Caleb. Judg 1:13; 3:9
Judg 15 2 sister, who is younger and fairer
1 K 14 49 and the name of the younger Michol
1 Pa 24 31 both the elder and the younger. The
25 8 the elder equally with the younger
Tob 1 4 when he was younger than any of the
Job 30 1 but now the younger in time scorn me
32 6 I am younger in days, and you are more
Ps 148 12 let the old with the younger, praise
Eze 16 61 thy sisters, thy elder and thy younger
23 4 elder, and Ooliba her younger sister
2 Ma 5 24 to sell the women and the younger sort
Luke 15 12 the younger of them said to his father
13 the y. son, gathering all together
22 26 let him become as the younger; and he
John 21 18 when thou wast younger, thou didst
Rom 9 12 her: The elder shall serve the younger
1 Tim 5 11 but the younger widows avoid. For when
14 the younger should marry, bear children
younger's Gen 44 2 in the mouth of the y. sack
youngest Gen 42 13 the y. is with our father
Gen 42 15 until your youngest brother come. Send
20 bring your youngest brother to me. 34
32 the youngest is with our father in the
43 3 unless you bring your youngest brother
5 not see my face without your y. brother
33 and the youngest according to his age
44 12 at the eldest and ending at the y.
23 except your youngest brother come with
26 if our youngest brother go down with us
Judg 9 5 Joatham the youngest son of Jerobaal
1 K 17 14 but David was the youngest. So the
3 K 16 34 in his youngest son Segub he set up
2 Pa 21 17 him but Joachaz, who was the youngest
22 1 made Ochozias his youngest son king
2 Ma 7 24 upbraider, when the y. was yet alive
youth Gen 8 21 are prone to evil from his youth
Gen 48 15 God that feedeth me from my youth
Deut 33 25 as the days of thy youth, so also shall
1 K 12 2 conversed with you from my youth unto
17 33 but he is a warrior from his youth
2 K 19 7 befallen thee from thy youth until now
Jdth 7 2 provinces and cities of all the youth
Job 13 26 wilt consume me for sins of my youth
20 11 be filled with the vices of his youth
29 4 as I was in the days of my youth, when
33 25 let him return to the days of his youth
Ps 24 7 sins of my youth and my ignorances
42 4 to God who giveth joy to my youth. To
67 28 there is Benjamin a youth, in ecstasy
70 5 my hope, O Lord, from my youth. By
17 hast taught me, O God, from my youth
87 16 poor and in labors from my youth: and
102 5 thy youth shall be renewed like the
128 1 fought against me from my youth. 2
143 12 sons are as new plants in their youth
Prov 2 17 and forsaketh the guide of her youth
5 18 rejoice with the wife of thy youth
30 19 sea, and the way of a man in youth
Ecce 11 9 rejoice therefore . . . in thy youth
9 which is good in the days of thy youth
10 flesh. For youth and pleasure are vain
12 1 remember thy Creator in days of thy y.
Wisd 2 6 us speedily use the creatures as in y.
4 16 youth soon ended, the long life of
8 2 and have sought her out from my youth
Eccu 6 18 from thy youth up receive instruction
25 5 thou hast not gathered in thy youth
30 11 give him not liberty in his youth, and
47 3 the lambs of the flock, in his youth
15 O how wise wast thou in thy youth
51 20 from my youth up I sought after her
Isa 47 12 which thou hast labored from thy youth
15 thy merchants from thy youth, every
54 4 shalt forget the shame of thy youth
6 and as a wife cast off from her youth
Jer 2 2 remembered thee, pitying thy youth
3 24 the labor of our fathers from our youth
25 from our youth even to this day, and
22 21 this hath been thy way from thy youth
31 19 I have borne the reproach of my youth
32 30 done evil in my eyes from their youth
48 11 Moab hath been fruitful from his youth
Lam 3 27 when he hath borne the yoke from his y.
Eze 16 22 not remembered the days of thy y. 43
60 covenant with thee in days of thy youth
23 3 in their y. they committed fornication
8 they also lay with her in her youth
19 remembering the days of her youth, in
21 hast renewed the wickedness of thy y.
Osee 2 15 according to the days of her youth
Joel 1 8 sackcloth for the husband of her y.
Zach 13 5 for Adam is my example from my youth
Mala 2 14 between thee and the wife of thy youth
15 and despise not the wife of thy youth
1 Ma 1 7 brought up with him from his youth
2 66 valiant and strong from his youth up
16 2 from our youth even to this day: and
2 Ma 4 9 place for exercise and a place for y.
Mat 19 20 have I kept from my y. Luke 18:21
Mark 10 20 things I have observed from my youth
Acts 20 12 they brought the youth alive, and were
26 4 my life indeed from my youth, which was
1 Tim 4 12 let no man despise thy youth: but be
youthful 2 Tim 2 22 but flee thou youthful desires
youths Isa 40 30 youths shall faint and labor and
Eze 23 6 princes and rulers, beautiful youths
Dan 1 10 leaner than those of the other youths
2 Ma 4 12 all the choicest youths in brothel

Z

Zabad 1 Pa 2 36 begot Z., and Z. begot Ophlal
1 Pa 7 20 Thahath his son, and his son Zabad
11 41 a Hethite, Zabad the son of Oholi
2 Pa 24 26 that conspired against him were Zabad
1 Es 10 27 of the sons of Zethua . . . Zabad and
33 of the sons of Hasom . . . Zabad
43 of the sons of Nebo . . . Zabad, Zabina
Zabadeans 1 Ma 12 31 Arabians that are called Z.

Zabadia 1 Pa 8 15 Z. and Arod and Heder and
1 Pa 8 17 Zabadia and Mosollam and Hezeci and
12 7 and Zabadia the sons of Jeroham of
Zabadias 1 Pa 26 2 sons of Meselemia . . . Zabadias
1 Pa 27 7 and Zabadias his son after him: and
2 Pa 17 8 Nathanias and Zabadias and Asael and
19 11 Zabadias the son of Ismahel, who is
Zabbai 1 Es 10 28 Hanania, Zabbai, Athalai: and
Zabdi Josu 7 1 Zabdi the son of Zare. 18
Josu 7 17 by the houses, he found it to be Zabdi
1 Pa 8 19 and Jacim and Zechri and Zabdi and
Zabdias 1 Pa 27 27 over the wine cellars, Zabdias
Zabdiel 1 Pa 27 2 Jesboam, the son of Zabdiel
2 Es 11 14 their ruler Zabdiel son of the mighty
1 Ma 11 17 Zabdiel . . . took off Alexander's head
Zabina 1 Es 10 43 of the sons of Nebo . . . Zabina
Zabud 3 K 4 5 Zabud the son of Nathan the priest
Zabulon Gen 30 20 she called his name Zabulon
Gen 35 23 Levi and Juda and Issachar and Zabulon. Exod 1:3; 1 Pa 2:1
46 14 the sons of Zabulon: Sared and Elon
49 13 Zabulon shall dwell on the seashore
Num 1 9 of Zabulon, Eliab the son of Helon
30 of the sons of Zabulon, by the
7 24 the prince of the sons of Zabulon
26 27 these are the kindreds of Zabulon
Deut 27 13 Ruben, Gad and Aser and Zabulon, Dan
33 18 to Zabulon he said: Rejoice, O Zabulon
Josu 19 10 third lot fell to children of Zabulon
16 inheritance of tribe of children of Z.
27 and passeth along to Zabulon. 34
21 7 of Ruben and of Gad and of Zabulon
Judg 1 30 Z. destroyed not the inhabitants of
4 6 of Nephtali and of the children of Z.
10 he called unto him Zabulon and Nephtali
5 14 out of Zabulon they that led the army
18 Z. and Nephtali offered their lives
6 35 other messengers into Aser and Zabulon
12 12 and he died and was buried in Zabulon
1 Pa 12 33 of Zabulon such as went forth to battle
40 even as far as Issachar and Zabulon
2 Pa 30 10 of Manasses, even to Zabulon, whilst
11 of Zabulon, yielding to the counsel
18 part of the people from . . . Zabulon
Ps 67 28 their leaders: the princes of Zabulon
Isa 9 1 land of Z. and the land of Nephtali
Eze 48 26 west side, one portion for Zabulon
27 by the border of Z., from the east side
33 Issachar one, the gate of Zabulon one
Mat 4 13 borders of Zabulon and of Nephthalim
15 land of Zabulon and land of Nephthalim
tribe of Zabulon Num 2 7 in the tribe of Zabulon the prince of Eliab. 10:16
Num 13 11 of the tribe of Zabulon, Geddiel the
34 25 of the tribe of Zabulon, Elisaphan the
Josu 21 34 of the tribe of Zabulon, Jecnam and
1 Pa 6 63 out of the tribe of Zabulon, they gave
77 out of the tribe of Zabulon, Remmono
Apoc 7 8 of the tribe of Zabulon, 12,000 signed
Zabulonite Judg 12 11 him succeeded Ahialon a Z.
Zabulonites 1 Pa 27 19 over the Z., Jesmaias the
Zacchur 1 Pa 24 27 Soam and Zacchur and Hebri
1 Pa 25 2 of the sons of Asaph: Zacchur and
Zachai 1 Es 2 9 children of Z., 760. 2 Es 7:14
2 Es 3 20 Baruch the son of Zachai built another
Zacharia 2 Es 8 4 Hasbadana, Z., and Mosollam
2 Es 12 16 of Adaia, Zacharia: of Genthon
40 Zacharia, Hanania with trumpets, and
Zacharias 4 K 14 29 Z. his son reigned in his
4 K 15 8 reigned Zacharias son of Jeroboam over
11 now the rest of the acts of Zacharias
18 2 mother was Abi the daughter of Z.
1 Pa 5 7 had for princes Jehiel and Zacharias
9 21 Z. the son of Mosollamia was porter
37 Gedor also and Ahio and Zacharias
15 18 in the second rank, Zacharias and Ben
20 Zacharias and Oziel and Semiramoth
24 Z. and Banaias and Eliezer the priests
16 5 chief, and next after him Zacharias
24 25 Jesia: and the son of Jesia, Zacharias
26 2 sons of Meselemia: Zacharias the
11 Tabelias the third, Zacharias the fourth
14 Zacharias, a very wise and learned man
27 21 in Galaad, Jaddo the son of Zacharias
2 Pa 17 7 Benhail and Abdias and Zacharias and
20 14 Jahaziel the son of Zacharias the son
21 2 Zacharias and Azaria and Michael and
24 20 spirit of God then came upon Zacharias
26 5 sought the Lord in days of Zacharias
29 1 mother was Abia the daughter of Z.
13 the sons of Asaph, Z. and Mathanias
34 12 Z. and Mosollam of the sons of Caath
35 8 Z. and Jahiel rulers of the house of
1 Es 5 1 Z. the son of Addo, prophesied to the
6 14 prophet, and of Z. the son of Addo
8 3 the son of Pharos, Zacharias, and with
11 of the sons of Bebai, Zacharias the
16 Zacharias and Mosollam, chief men
2 Es 11 4 Aziam the son of Zacharias the son of
5 son of Joiarib the son of Zacharias
12 the son of Amsi the son of Zacharias
12 34 with trumpets, Z. the son of Jonathan
Ps 111 1 of the returning of Aggeus and Z.
145 1 Alleluia, of Aggeus and Zacharias
Isa 8 2 the priest, and Z. the son of Barachias
Zach 1 1 word of the Lord came to Z. 7; 7:1, 8
1 Ma 5 18 Joseph the son of Zacharias. 56
Mat 23 35 unto the blood of Zacharias. Luke 11:51
Zachary Luke 1 5 a certain priest named Zachary
Luke 1 12 Zachary seeing him, was troubled and
13 fear not, Zachary, for thy prayer is
18 and Zachary said to the angel: Whereby
21 the people were waiting for Zachary
40 she entered into the house of Zachary
59 called him by his father's name Z.
67 Z. his father was filled with the Holy
3 2 made unto John, the son of Zachary
Zacher 1 Pa 8 31 Gedor and Ahio and Zacher and
Zacheus 2 Ma 10 19 left Simon and Joseph and Z.
Luke 19 2 a man named Zacheus, who was the chief
5 Zacheus, make haste and come down
8 Zacheus standing, said to the Lord
Zachur 1 Pa 4 26 Zachur his son, Semei his son
1 Pa 25 10 the third to Zachur, to his sons and
1 Es 8 14 of the sons of Begui, Uthai and Zachur
2 Es 3 2 next to them built Z. the son of Amri
10 12 Zachur, Serebia, Sabania, Odaia, Bani
13 13 next to them Hanan the son of Zachur
zain Ps 118 49 zain. Lam 1:7; 2:7; 3:19, 20, 21; 4:7
Zambri Num 25 14 Z. the son of Salu, a prince
3 K 16 9 his servant Zambri, who was captain
10 Zambri rushing in, struck him [Ela]
12 Zambri destroyed all the house of Baasa
15 Zambri reigned seven days in Thersa
16 when they heard that Z. had rebelled
18 Zambri seeing that the city was about
20 but the rest of the acts of Zambri
4 K 9 31 can there be peace for Z., that hath
Jer 25 25 all the kings of Zambri and all the
Zamira 1 Pa 7 8 the sons of Bechor were Zamira
Zamma 1 Pa 6 20 Jahath his son, Zamma his son
1 Pa 6 42 the son of Ethan the son of Zamma
Zamran Gen 25 2 who bore him Zamran and Jecsan
1 Pa 1 32 Zamran, Jecsan, Madan, Madian, Jesboc
Zamri 1 Pa 2 6 sons also of Zare: Z. and Ethan
1 Pa 8 36 begot Alamath and Azmoth and Z. 9:42

36 Zamri begot Mosa, and Mosa begot. 9:42
11 45 Jedihel the son of Zamri, and Joha
1 Ma 2 26 as Phinees did by Zamri the son of
Zanoa 2 Es 11 30 at Jerimuth, Zanoa, Odollam
Zanoe Josu 15 34 Zanoe and Engannim and Taphua
Josu 15 56 Jota, Jezrael and Jucadam and Zanoe
1 Pa 4 18 and Icuthiel the father of Zanoe
2 Es 3 13 Hanun built, and the inhabitants of Z.
Zara Gen 36 13 the sons of Rahuel were Nahath and Zara. 1 Pa 1:37
Gen 36 17 duke Zara, duke Samma, duke Meza. And
33 Jobab the son of Z. of Bosra reigned
38 30 scarlet thread: and she called him Z.
46 12 Onan and Sela and Phares and Zara
1 Pa 2 4 Thamar . . . bore him Phares and Zara
4 24 Namuel and Jamin, Jarib, Zara, Saul
6 21 Addo his son, Zara his son, Jethrai
41 Athanai the son of Zara the son of
9 6 of the sons of Zara: Jethuel, and their
2 Pa 14 9 Zara the Ethiopian came out against
2 Es 11 24 Mesezebel of the children of Zara
Mat 1 3 Judas begot Phares and Zara of Thamar
Zarahi 1 Pa 27 11 a Husathite of the race of Z.
Zarahia 1 Pa 6 51 Ozi his son, Zarahia his son
Zarahias 1 Es 7 4 Maraioth the son of Zarahias
Zarai 1 Pa 27 13 a Netophathite of the race of Z.
Zaraias 1 Pa 6 6 Ozi begot Z., and Z. begot
Zare Num 26 13 Zare, of him is the family. 20
Josu 7 1 son of Zare of the tribe of Juda. 18
17 it was found to be the family of Zare
24 Achan the son of Zare. 22:20
1 Pa 1 44 Jobab the son of Zare of Bosra reigned
2 6 the sons also of Zare: Zamri and
Zared Num 21 12 they came to the torrent Zared
Deut 2 13 rising up to pass the torrent Zared
14 till we passed over the torrent Zared
Zareha 1 Es 8 4 Eleoenai the son of Zareha, and
Zares Esth 5 10 to him his friends and Z. his wife
Esth 5 14 Z. his wife and the rest of his friends
6 13 he told Zares his wife and his friends
Zarites Num 26 13 is the family of the Zarites. 20
Zathan 1 Pa 26 22 sons of Jehieli: Z. and Joel
Zavan Gen 36 27 Balaan and Zavan and Acan. And
1 Pa 1 42 of Eser: Balaan and Zavan and Jacan
zeal Num 25 11 because he was moved with my zeal
Num 25 11 not destroy children of Israel in my z.
2 K 21 2 Saul sought to slay them out of zeal
3 K 19 10 with zeal have I been zealous for. 14
4 K 10 16 and see my zeal for the Lord. So he
19 31 zeal of the Lord of hosts shall do this
Jdth 9 3 who were zealous with thy zeal: assist
Ps 68 10 the zeal of thy house hath eaten me up
72 3 I had a zeal on occasion of the wicked
78 5 shall thy zeal be kindled like a fire
118 139 my zeal hath made me pine away
Wisd 5 18 his zeal will take armor, and he will
Eccu 51 24 I have a zeal for good and shall not
Isa 9 7 zeal of the Lord of hosts will perform
37 32 zeal of the Lord of hosts shall do this
42 13 as a man of war shall he stir up zeal
59 17 was clad with zeal as with a cloak
63 15 where is thy zeal and thy strength
Eze 5 13 I the Lord have spoken it in my zeal
36 5 in the fire of my zeal I have spoken
6 I have spoken in my zeal. 38:19
Zach 1 14 Jerusalem and Sion with a great zeal
1 Ma 2 26 showed zeal for the law, as Phinees
27 every one that hath zeal for the law
54 by being fervent in the zeal of God
58 Elias . . . full of zeal for the law
John 2 17 the zeal of thy house hath eaten me
Rom 10 2 they have zeal of God, but not according
2 C 7 7 desire, your mourning, your zeal for me
11 fear, yea desire, yea zeal, yea revenge
Phil 3 6 according to z., persecuting the church
James 3 14 if you have bitter zeal, and there
zealous Num 25 13 he hath been z. for his God
3 K 19 10 have I been zealous for the Lord. 14
Jdth 9 3 to thy servants, who were zealous with
Joel 2 18 the Lord hath been z. for his land
Zach 1 14 I am zealous for Jerusalem and Sion
1 Ma 2 50 be ye zealous for the law and give
2 Ma 4 2 and was zealous for the law of God
Acts 21 20 and they are all zealous for the law
22 3 fathers, zealous for the law, as also
1 C 12 31 but be zealous for the better gifts
14 1 after charity, be z. for spiritual gifts
12 as you are zealous of spirits, seek to
39 brethren, be zealous to prophesy; and
Gal 1 14 being more abundantly zealous for the
4 17 they are zealous in your regard not well
17 you, that you might be zealous for them
18 but be zealous for that which is good
1 P 3 13 hurt you if you be zealous of good
Apoc 3 19 be zealous therefore and do penance
Zeb Judg 7 25 two men of Madian, Oreb and Zeb
Judg 7 25 Zeb in the winepress of Zeb. And they
25 carrying the heads of Oreb and Zeb to
8 3 the princes of Madian, Oreb and Zeb
Ps 82 12 make their princes like Oreb and Zeb
Zebedee Mat 4 21 James the son of Z. 10:3; Mark 1:19; 3:17
Mat 4 21 in a ship with Zebedee their father
Mark 1 20 leaving their father Z. in the ship
sons of Zebedee Mat 20 20 the mother of the sons of Zebedee. 27:56
Mat 26 37 with him Peter and the two sons of Z.
Mark 10 35 s. . . . come to him, saying: Master, we
Luke 5 10 James and John the sons of Zebedee
John 21 2 and the s. . . . and two others of his
Zebedei 2 Es 11 17 Micha the son of Zebedei, the
Zebedia 1 Es 10 20 the sons of Emmer . . . Zebedia
Zebee Judg 8 5 that we may pursue Zebee and
Judg 8 6 palms of the hands of Z. and Salmana
7 when the Lord shall have delivered Z.
10 Zebee and Salmana were resting with all
12 Zebee and Salmana fled, and Gedeon
15 behold Zebee and Salmana, concerning
15 the hands of Zebee and Salmana are
18 he said to Zebee and Salmana: What
21 Zebee and Salmana said: Do thou rise
21 Gedeon rose up and slew Z. and Salmana
Ps 82 12 make their princes like . . . Zebee and
Zebida 4 K 23 36 name of his mother was Zebida
Zebodia 1 Es 8 8 of the sons of Saphatia, Z.
Zebul Judg 9 28 made Zebul his servant ruler over
Judg 9 30 Zebul the ruler of the city, hearing
36 said to Zebul: Behold a multitude
38 Zebul said to him: Where is now thy
41 Zebul drove Gaal and his companions
Zechri Exod 6 21 Core and Nepheg and Zechri. The
1 Pa 8 19 and Jacim and Zechri and Zabdi and
23 and Abdon and Zechri and Hanan and
27 Elia and Zechri, the sons of Jeroham
9 15 the son of Zechri the son of Asaph
26 25 Joram, and his son Zechri and his son
27 16 Eliezer the son of Zechri was ruler
2 Pa 17 16 after him was Amasias the son of Z.
23 1 Elisaphat the son of Zechri: and
28 7 Zechri a powerful man of Ephraim slew
2 Es 11 9 and Joel the son of Zechri their ruler
12 17 of Abia, Zechri: of Miamin and Moadia
Zechur Num 13 5 of Ruben, Sammua the son of Z.
2 Es 12 34 Michaia the son of Zechur the son of
Zelotes Luke 6 15 and Simon who is called Zelotes
Acts 1 13 where abode . . . Simon Zelotes and

Zelpha Gen 29 24 his daughter a handmaid named Z.
Gen 30 9 gave Zelpha her handmaid to her husband
12 Zelpha also bore another. And Lia
35 26 the sons of Zelpha, Lia's handmaid
37 2 was with the sons of Bala and of Z.
46 18 these are the sons of Zelpha, whom
Zemma 2 Pa 29 12 Joah the son of Zemma, and Eden
Zenas Titus 3 13 send forth Zenas, the lawyer
Zephrona Num 34 9 limits shall go as far as Z.
Zethan 1 Pa 7 10 Z. and Tharsis and Ahisahar
1 Pa 23 8 Jahiel and Zethan and Joel, three
Zethar Esth 1 10 Z. and Charcas, the 7 eunuchs
Zethu 2 Es 10 14 Elam, Zethu, Bani, Bonni, Azgad
Zethua 1 Es 2 8 the children of Zethua, 945
1 Es 10 27 of the sons of Zethua, Elioenai
2 Es 7 13 the children of Zethua, 845. The
Zie 1 Pa 5 13 Jacan and Zie and Heber, seven
Zio 3 K 6 1 Zio, the same is the second month
3 K 6 37 house of Lord founded in the month Zio
Ziph Josu 15 24 Ziph and Telem and Baloth, New
Josu 15 55 Maon and Carmel and Ziph and Jota
1 K 23 14 in a mountain of the desert of Ziph
15 and David was in the desert of Ziph
24 they arose and went to Ziph before Saul
26 1 the men of Ziph came to Saul in Gabaa
2 went down to the wilderness of Ziph
2 to seek David in the wilderness of Ziph
1 Pa 4 16 sons of Jaleleel: Ziph and Zipha
2 Pa 11 8 Geth and Maresa and Ziph and Aduram
Ps 53 2 when the men of Ziph had come and said
Zipha 1 Pa 4 16 sons of Jaleleel: Ziph and Zipha
Ziphites 1 K 23 19 the Z. went up to Saul in Gabaa
Ziza 1 Pa 2 33 Jonathan begot Phaleth and Ziza
1 Pa 4 37 Ziza also the son of Sephei the son
23 10 Ziza and Jaus and Baria: these were
11 Leheth was the first, Ziza the second
2 Pa 11 20 and Ethai and Ziza and Salomith. And
Zoheleth 3 K 1 9 by the stone of Zoheleth, which
Zoheth 1 Pa 4 20 sons of Jesi Zoheth and Benzoheth
Zomzommims Deut 2 20 whom the Ammonites call Z.
Zoom 2 Pa 11 19 Jehus and Somorias and Zoom. And
Zorobabel 1 Pa 3 19 of Phadaia were born Z. and
1 Pa 3 19 Zorobabel begot Mosollam, Hananias
1 Es 2 2 who came with Z., Josue. 2 Es 7:7
3 2 and his brethren the priests and Z.
8 in Jerusalem, the second month, Z.
4 2 they came to Zorobabel and the chief
3 Z. and Josue and the rest of the chiefs
5 2 then rose up Zorobabel the son of
2 Es 12 1 Levites, that went up with Zorobabel
46 all Israel, in the days of Zorobabel
Eccu 49 13 how shall we magnify Zorobabel? For
Agge 1 1 of Aggeus the prophet to Zorobabel
12 Z. the son of Salathiel, and Jesus
14 the Lord stirred up the spirit of Z.
2 3 the prophet, saying: Speak to Z.
5 yet now take courage, O Zorobabel
22 speak to Z. the governor of Juda
24 I will take thee, O Zorobabel the
Zach 4 6 this is the word of the Lord to Z.
7 art thou, O great mountain, before Z.
9 hands of Z. have laid the foundations
10 tin plummet in the hand of Zorobabel
Mat 1 12 Salathiel begot Z. and Z. begot Abiud
Luke 3 27 Reza, who was of Zorobabel, who was
Zuzim Gen 14 5 the Zuzim with them and the Emim

Numbers (Cardinal)

2 Gen 1 16 God made 2 great lights: a greater
Gen 2 24 wife: they shall be 2 in one flesh
4 19 Lamech: who took 2 wives: the name
6 19 shalt bring 2 of a sort into the ark
20 two of every sort shall go in with thee
7 3 the beasts that are unclean 2 and two
9 two and 2 went in to Noe into the ark
15 into the ark, 2 and 2 of all flesh
9 22 he told it to his 2 brethren without
15 10 laid the 2 pieces of each one against
19 1 the 2 angels came to Sodom in the
8 I have 2 daughters who as yet have
15 take thy wife and the 2 daughters
16 of his wife and of his 2 daughters
36 so the 2 daughters of Lot were with
22 6 as they 2 went on together, Isaac
24 22 golden earrings, weighing 2 sicles
25 23 two nations are in thy womb: and she
23 two peoples shall be divided out of thy
27 9 bring me 2 kids of the best, that I
29 16 he had 2 daughters . . . Lia . . . Rachel
32 7 divided the people . . . into 2 companies
10 and now I return with 2 companies
22 he took his 2 wives and his 2 handmaids
34 25 two of the sons of Jacob, Simeon and
40 1 two eunuchs, the butler and the baker
45 22 for every one of them 2 robes: but to
46 27 and the sons of Joseph . . . two souls
Exod 2 13 next day, he saw 2 Hebrews quarrelling
4 9 they will not even believe these 2 signs
16 22 that is, 2 gomors every man: and all
21 21 if the party remain alive a day or two
25 12 two rings be on the one side, and 2 on
18 thou shalt make also 2 cherubims of
18 gold, on the 2 sides of the oracle
22 and from the midst of the 2 cherubims
35 bowls under 2 branches in 3 places
26 17 of the boards shall be made 2 mortises
19 may be put 2 sockets at the 2 corners
21 two sockets shall be put under each
23 other 2 which shall be erected in the
24 the 2 boards that are to be put in the
25 reckoning 2 sockets for each board
27 6 two bars for the altar of setim wood
28 7 it shall have the 2 edges joined in the
9 and thou shalt take 2 onyx stones
14 two little chains of the purest gold
23 two rings of gold, which thou shalt put in the 2 ends at the top
25 thou shalt join together with 2 hooks
26 thou shalt make also 2 rings of gold
27 two rings of gold which are to be set
29 13 of the liver and the 2 kidneys. 22
38 two lambs of a year old every day
30 2 foursquare, and two [cubits] in height
4 two golden rings under the crown on
36 22 there were 2 mortises throughout every
24 two sockets were put under one board
24 on the 2 sides of the corners, where
26 of silver, 2 sockets for every board
28 and 2 others at each corner of the
30 to wit, 2 sockets under every board
37 3 two rings in one side and 2 in the other
7 two cherubims also of beaten gold
7 on the 2 sides of the propitiatory
8 two cherubims at the 2 ends of the
18 six branches on the 2 sides: three
21 bowls under 2 branches in 3 places
27 and 2 golden rings under the crown
38 15 for between the 2 he made the entry
39 4 two borders coupled one to the other
6 he prepared also 2 onyx stones, fast
16 two hooks and as many rings of gold
17 the 2 golden chains should hang, which
Lev 3 4 the 2 kidneys with the fat wherewith
4 of the liver with the 2 little kidneys
15 the 2 little kidneys with the caul

Book	Ch	V	Text
	4	9	the 2 little kidneys and the caul that
	5	7	two turtles or 2 young pigeons. 11; 12:8; 14:22; 15:14, 29; Num 6:10
		15	flocks, that may be bought for 2 sicles
	7	4	the 2 little kidneys, and the fat which
	8	2	a calf for sin, 2 rams, a basket with
		16	two little kidneys with their fat. 9:19
		25	the 2 kidneys with their fat, and with
	12	5	she shall be unclean 2 weeks, according
	14	4	to offer for himself 2 living sparrows
		10	the eighth day he shall take 2 lambs
		49	he shall take 2 sparrows, and cedar
	16	5	two buck goats for sin, and one ram
		7	he shall make the 2 buck goats to stand
	19	19	a garment that is woven of 2 sorts
	23	13	two tenths of flour tempered with oil. Num 28:9
		17	two loaves of the firstfruits, of 2 tenths of flour leavened, which
		18	one calf from the herd and 2 rams
		19	and 2 lambs of the first year for
	24	5	two tenths shall be in every loaf
Num	3	21	of Gerson were 2 families, the Lebnites
	7	3	two princes offered one wagon, and each
		7	two wagons and four oxen he gave to
		17	sacrifice of peace offerings, 2 oxen. 23, 29
		35	victims of peace offerings, 2 oxen
		41	sacrifices of peace offerings, 2 oxen. 47, 53, 59, 65, 71, 77, 83
		89	over the ark between the 2 cherubims
	10	2	make thee 2 trumpets of beaten silver
	11	19	not for one day nor 2, nor 5, nor ten
		26	there remained in the camp 2 of the men
	15	6	be a sacrifice of flour of 2 tenths
	22	22	the ass and had 2 servants with him
		24	stood in a narrow place between 2 walls
	28	3	two lambs of a year old without. 9
		11	two calves of the herd, one ram
		19	offer . . . two calves of the herd. 27
		20	two tenths [of flour] to every ram. 28
	29	3	calf, 2 tenths [of flour] to a ram. 9
		13	you shall offer . . . two rams. 17, 20, 23, 26, 29, 32
		14	two tenths to each ram, being 2 rams
	34	15	two tribes and a half, have received
Deut	3	8	out of the hand of the 2 kings of the
		21	your God hath done to these 2 kings
	4	42	was not his enemy a day or 2 before
		47	of the 2 kings of the Amorrhites, who
	14	6	beast that divideth the hoof in 2 parts
	17	6	by the mouth of 2 or 3 witnesses shall
	19	15	but in the mouth of 2 or 3 witnesses
	21	15	if a man have 2 wives, one beloved and
	32	30	how should . . . two chase ten thousand
Josu	2	10	and what things you did to the 2 kings
	9	10	and to the 2 kings of the Amorrhites
	14	3	to 2 tribes and a half Moses had given
		4	children of Joseph divided into 2 tribes
	15	60	Arebba: 2 cities and their villages
	21	16	suburbs: 9 cities out of the 2 tribes
		25	tribe of Manasses . . . 2 cities
		27	children of Gerson . . . 2 cities
	24	12	places, the 2 kings of the Amorrhites
Judg	5	16	why dwellest thou between 2 borders
	9	44	whilst the 2 other companies chased
	11	37	may go about the mountains for 2 months
		38	go, and he sent her away for 2 months
		39	and the 2 months being expired, she
	15	13	and they bound him with 2 new cords
	16	25	they made him stand between 2 pillars
		28	and for the loss of my 2 eyes I may
	19	3	having with him a servant and 2 asses
		10	leading with him 2 asses laden, and his
	20	31	whilst they fled by 2 highways, whereof
1 K	1	2	[Elcana] had 2 wives, the name of one
	2	21	and bore 3 sons and 2 daughters
	6	7	and 2 kine that have calved, on which
		10	taking 2 kine that had sucking calves
	10	4	and will give thee 2 loaves, and thou
	11	11	that 2 of them were not left together
	14	49	and the names of his 2 daughters, the
	18	21	in 2 things thou shalt be my son-in-law
	23	18	the 2 made a covenant before the Lord
	25	18	took 200 loaves and 2 vessels of wine
	27	3	David with his 2 wives, Achinoam the
	30	5	the 2 wives also of David were taken
		12	cake of figs and 2 bunches of raisins
		18	and he [David] rescued his 2 wives
2 K	2	2	so David went up, and his 2 wives
	8	2	he measured with 2 lines, one to put
	13	6	and make in my sight 2 little messes
	16	1	came to meet him with two asses, laden
	18	24	and David sat between 2 gates: and the
	23	20	he slew the 2 lions of Moab, and he
3 K	2	5	what he did to the 2 captains of the
	3	16	there came 2 women that were harlots
		18	with us in the house, only we two
		25	the living child in two and give half
	5	12	and they 2 made a league together
		14	so that 2 months they were at home
	6	23	he made in the oracle 2 cherubims, of
		32	two doors of olive tree: and he carved
		34	and 2 doors of fir tree, one of each
	7	15	and he cast 2 pillars in brass, each
		16	made also 2 chapiters of molten brass
		18	and 2 rows round about each network
		24	there were 2 rows cast of chamfered
		41	the 2 pillars and the 2 cords of the
		41	and the 2 networks to cover the 2 cords
		42	and 400 pomegranates for the 2 networks
		42	two rows of pomegranates for each
	9	10	after Solomon had built the 2 houses
	10	19	two hands on either side holding the
		19	and 2 lions stood, one at each hand
	11	29	and they 2 were alone in the field
	16	21	people of Israel divided into 2 parts
	17	12	I am gathering 2 sticks that I may go
	18	21	how long do you halt between 2 sides
		23	let 2 bullocks be given us, and let
		32	breadth of 2 furrows round about
	20	27	like 2 little flocks of goats: but the
4 K	1	14	and consumed the 2 first captains
	2	6	leave thee; and they 2 went on together
		7	but they 2 stood by the Jordan. And
		12	garments and rent them in 2 pieces
		24	there came forth 2 bears out of the
	5	17	from hence 2 mules' burden of earth
		22	give them . . . two changes of garments
		23	it is better that thou take 2 talents
		23	bound 2 talents of silver in 2 bags
		23	and 2 changes of garments, and laid
		23	and laid them upon 2 of his servants
	7	1	two bushels of barley for a stater. 16
		14	they brought therefore 2 horses, and
		18	two bushels of barley shall be for a
	9	32	and 2 or 3 eunuches bowed down to him
	10	4	two kings could not stand before him
		8	and he said: Lay ye them in 2 heaps by
	11	7	let 2 parts of you, all that go forth
	17	16	and made to themselves 2 molten calves
	23	12	had made in the 2 courts of the temple
	25	4	fled in the night between the 2 walls
		16	took away. That is, 2 pillars, one sea
1 Pa	4	5	Assur, the father of Thecua had 2 wives

11 22 he [Banaias] slew the 2 ariels of Moab
26 18 four in the way: and 2 at every cell
2 Pa 3 10 of holies 2 cherubims of image work
13 wings of the 2 cherubims were spread
15 before the doors of the temple 2 pillars
4 3 belly of the sea, as it were with 2 rows
12 the 2 pillars and the pommels and the
13 and 2 wreaths of network, so that two
9 18 a footstool . . . and 2 arms one on
18 side, and 2 lions standing by the arms
24 3 Joiada took for him 2 wives, by whom
33 5 in the 2 courts of the house of the
1 Es 8 27 two vessels of the best shining brass
10 13 it is not a work of one day or two
2 Es 12 31 and I appointed 2 great choirs to give
39 the 2 choirs of them that gave praise
Tob 8 19 hast taken pity upon 2 only children
22 he caused also 2 fat kine and four
23 Tobias to abide with him 2 weeks. And
9 6 and 2 camels and went to Rages the city
Jdth 13 12 and they 2 went out according to their
Job 13 20 two things only do not to me, and then
42 7 against thee and against thy 2 friends
Ps 61 12 these 2 things have I heard, that power
Prov 30 7 two things I have asked of thee, deny
15 the horseleech hath 2 daughters that
Ecce 4 9 that 2 should be together, than one
11 if 2 lie together, they shall warm one
12 against one, 2 shall withstand him: a
Cant 4 5 thy 2 breasts like 2 young roes that
7 3 thy 2 breasts are like 2 young roes
Wisd 14 30 for 2 things they shall be justly
Eccu 2 14 sinner that goeth on the earth 2 ways
3 28 a heart that goeth 2 ways shall not
26 25 at 2 things my heart is grieved, and
28 two sorts of callings have appeared
33 15 two and 2, and one against another
38 18 for a day or 2 for fear of detraction
46 5 and one day made as 2? He called upon
10 they 2 being appointed, were delivered
50 27 two nations which my soul abhorreth
Isa 6 2 with 2 they covered his face, and with
2 they covered his feet, and with 2 they flew
7 4 of the 2 tails of these firebrands
16 forsaken of the face of her 2 kings
21 shall nourish a young cow and 2 sheep
8 14 of offence to the 2 houses of Israel
17 6 two or 2 berries in the top of a bough
21 7 and he saw a chariot with 2 horsemen, a
9 rider upon the chariot with 2 horsemen
22 11 you made a ditch between the 2 walls
47 9 these 2 things shall come upon thee
51 19 two things that have happened to thee
Jer 2 13 my people have done 2 evils. They have
3 14 you, one of a city and 2 of a kindred
24 1 and behold 2 baskets full of figs, set
33 24 two families which the Lord had chosen
34 18 when they cut the calf in 2 and passed
39 4 gate that was between the 2 walls. 52:7
52 20 the 2 pillars, and one sea, and twelve
Eze 1 11 two wings of every one were joined, and
11 were joined, and 2 covered their bodies
23 every one with 2 wings covered his body
21 19 man, set thee 2 ways, for the sword of
21 in the highway, at the head of 2 ways
23 2 there were 2 women, daughters of one
35 10 the 2 nations and the 2 lands shall be
37 22 and they shall no more be 2 nations
22 be divided any more into 2 kingdoms
41 18 a cherub, and every cherub had 2 faces
23 there were 2 doors in the temple, and in
24 and in the 2 doors on both sides were
24 were 2 little doors, which were folded
24 for there were 2 wickets on both sides
Dan 8 3 having 2 high horns, and one higher
7 broke his 2 horns, and the ram could
11 27 the heart of the 2 kings shall be to do
12 5 behold as it were 2 others stood: one
13 5 and there were 2 of the ancients of the
15 and the day before, with 2 maids only
16 nobody there, but the 2 old men that
19 the 2 elders arose and ran to her, and
28 the 2 elders also came full of wicked
34 but the 2 elders rising up in the midst
36 alone, this woman came in with 2 maids
51 separate these 2 far from one another
55 sentence of him, shall cut thee in two
59 with a sword to cut thee in 2, and to
61 and they rose up against the 2 elders
14 31 them 2 carcasses every day and 2 sheep
Osee 10 10 be chastised for their 2 iniquities
Amos 3 3 shall 2 walk together except they be
12 get out of the lion's mouth 2 legs
4 8 and 2 and 3 cities went to one city to
Zach 4 3 and 2 olive trees over it: one upon the
11 what are these 2 olive trees upon the
12 what are the 2 olive branches that are
12 that are by the 2 golden beaks in which
5 9 and behold there came out 2 women, and
6 1 came out from the midst of 2 mountains
11 7 and I took unto me 2 rods, one I called
13 8 two parts in it shall be scattered and
1 Ma 1 17 that he might reign over 2 kingdoms
6 38 and on that side at the 2 wings, with
9 11 the horsemen were divided into 2 troops
12 and the legion drew near on 2 sides and
10 49 and the 2 kings joined battle, and the
60 he met there the 2 kings, and he gave
11 13 and set 2 crowns upon his head, that of
2 Ma 6 10 for 2 women were accused to have
10 22 death, and forthwith took the 2 towers
23 he slew more than 20,000 in the 2 holds
30 Jews: 2 of whom took Machabeus between
12 16 so that a pool adjoining of 2 furlongs
Mat 4 18 saw 2 brethren, Simon who is called
21 he saw other 2 brethren, James the son
5 41 thee one mile, go with him other two
6 24 no man can serve 2 masters. For either
8 28 met him 2 that were possessed with
9 27 followed him 2 blind men crying out
10 10 nor 2 coats nor shoes nor a staff; for
29 are not 2 sparrows sold for a farthing
11 2 sending 2 of his disciples, he said to
14 17 five loaves and 2 fishes. 19; Mark 6:41; Luke 9:13, 16
18 8 than having 2 hands or 2 feet to be
9 than having 2 eyes to be cast into hell
16 take with thee one or 2 more: that in
19 if 2 of you shall consent upon earth
20 where there are 2 or 3 gathered together
19 5 they 2 shall be in one flesh. Mark 10:8
6 they are not 2, but one flesh. Mark 10:8
20 24 with indignation against the 2 brethren
30 two blind men sitting by the wayside
21 1 Jesus sent 2 disciples, saying to them
31 which of the 2 did the father's will
22 40 on these 2 commandments dependeth
24 40 two shall be in the field: one shall be
41 two women shall be grinding at the mill
25 15 five talents, and to another 2, and to
17 had received the 2, gained other two
22 received the 2 talents came and said
22 thou deliveredst 2 talents to me: behold I have gained other two

26 60 there came 2 false witnesses. And they
27 21 of the 2 to be released unto you? But
38 were crucified with him 2 thieves: one
51 the veil of the temple was rent in two. Mark 15:38
Mark 6 7 and began to send them two and two and
9 that they should not put on 2 coats
38 they say: Five, and 2 fishes. And he
41 the 2 fishes he divided among them all
9 42 than having 2 hands to go into hell
44 than having 2 feet, to be cast into
46 than having 2 eyes to be cast into the
11 1 he sendeth 2 of his disciples. 14:13
4 gate without, in the meeting of 2 ways
12 42 poor widow, and she cast in 2 mites
15 27 and with him they crucify 2 thieves
16 12 in another shape to 2 of them walking
Luke 2 24 pair of turtle doves or 2 young pigeons
3 11 he that hath 2 coats, let him give to
5 2 saw 2 ships standing by the lake: but
7 19 John called to him 2 of his disciples
41 a certain creditor had 2 debtors, the
42 of the 2 loveth him most? Simon
9 3 bread nor money; neither have 2 coats
10 1 he sent them 2 and 2 before his face
35 he took out 2 pence and gave to the
12 6 not 5 sparrows sold for 2 farthings
52 three against 2, and 2 against three
16 13 no servant can serve 2 masters: for
17 35 two women shall be grinding together
19 29 he sent 2 of his disciples, saying: Go
21 2 poor widow casting in 2 brass mites
22 38 said: Lord, behold here are 2 swords
23 32 there were 2 other malefactors led with
24 13 two of them went the same day to a town
John 1 35 John stood, and 2 of his disciples
37 the 2 disciples heard him speak, and
40 was one of the 2 who had heard of John
2 6 containing 2 or 3 measures apiece
6 9 that hath 5 barley loaves and 2 fishes
19 18 crucified him, and with him 2 others
20 12 and she saw 2 angels in white, sitting
21 2 and 2 others of his disciples. Simon
Acts 1 23 and they appointed 2, Joseph, called
24 whether of these 2 thou hast chosen
10 7 he called 2 of his household servants
12 6 Peter was sleeping between 2 soldiers: bound with 2 chains
19 22 sending into Macedonia 2 of them that
34 for space of about 2 hours, cried out
21 33 commanded him to be bound with 2 chains
23 23 having called 2 centurions, he said to
27 41 fallen into a place where 2 seas met
28 30 he remained 2 whole years in his own
1 C 6 16 they shall be, saith he, 2 in one flesh
14 27 speak with a tongue, let it be by two
29 let the prophets speak, two or three
2 C 13 1 in the mouth of 2 or 3 witnesses shall
Gal 4 24 for these are the 2 testaments. The
Eph 2 15 that he might make the 2 in himself
5 31 wife, and they shall be 2 in one flesh
Phil 1 23 but I am straitened between 2: having
1 Tim 5 19 but under 2 or 3 witnesses. Them that
Heb 6 18 by 2 immutable things, in which it is
10 28 dieth . . . under 2 or 3 witnesses: how
Apoc 6 6 two pounds of wheat for a penny, and
6 thrice 2 pounds of barley for a penny
9 12 come yet 2 woes more hereafter. And
11 3 I will give unto my 2 witnesses and
4 these are the 2 olive trees and the
4 the 2 candlesticks that stand before
10 these 2 prophets tormented them that
12 14 two wings of a great eagle, that she
13 11 he had 2 horns, like a lamb, and he
19 20 these 2 were cast alive into the pool
2 cubits; *see* **cubits**
2 days Lev 19 7 if after two days any man eat
Num 9 22 if it remained . . . for two days or a
2 K 1 1 David . . . abode two days in Siceleg
Osee 6 3 he will revive us after two days: on
2 Ma 10 37 having for two days together pillaged
2 tables; *see* **tables**
2 men Gen 22 3 took with him two young men
Num 13 24 which two men carried upon a lever
Deut 25 11 if two men have words together and
Josu 2 1 Josue . . . sent from Setim two men to
6 22 two men that had been sent for spies
Judg 7 25 having taken two men of Madian, Oreb
1 K 10 2 shalt find two men by the sepulcher
28 8 he [Saul] went, and two men with him
2 K 4 2 the sons of Saul had two men captains
12 1 there were two men in one city, the one
3 K 2 32 because he [Joab] murdered two men
21 10 and suborn two men, sons of Belial
13 bringing two men, sons of the devil
4 K 5 22 there are come to me . . . two young men
2 Ma 3 26 there appeared two other young men
Luke 9 30 behold two men were talking with him
32 and the two men that stood with him
17 34 there shall be two men in one bed
35 two men shall be in the field; the
18 10 two men went up into the temple to
24 4 two men stood by them, in shining
John 8 17 that the testimony of two men is true
Acts 1 10 behold two men stood by them in white
9 38 sent unto him two men, desiring him
3 Gen 6 10 he [Noe] begot 3 sons, Sem, Cham, and
Gen 7 13 the 3 wives of his sons with them went
9 19 these 3 are the sons of Noe: and from
18 2 there appeared to him 3 men standing
6 temper together 3 measures of flour
29 2 three flocks of sheep lying by it: for
34 to me because I have borne him 3 sons
30 36 he set the space of 3 days' journey
38 24 after 3 months they told Juda, saying
40 10 a vine on which were 3 branches which
12 dream: the 3 branches are yet 3 days
16 I had 3 baskets of meal upon my head
18 the 3 baskets are yet 3 days: after
Exod 2 2 him a goodly child, hid him 3 months
3 18 we will go 3 days' journey. 8:27
5 3 go 3 days' journey into the wilderness
21 11 if he do not these 3 things, she shall
25 32 three out of the one side, and 3 out of
33 three cups as it were nuts to every
33 three cups likewise of the fashion of
35 under two branches in three places. 37:21
21 1 that is, foursquare, and 3 cubits high
14 three pillars and as many sockets. 15; 38:15
37 18 three branches on one side, and 3 on
19 three cups in manner of a nut on each
19 three cups of the fashion of a nut
38 1 five cubits square and 3 in height
14 with 3 pillars and their sockets. And
Lev 14 10 three tenths of flour tempered with
27 6 be given 5 sickles: for a female three
Num 10 33 so they marched . . . 3 days' journey
12 4 come out you 3 only to the tabernacle
15 9 give for every ox 3 tenths of flour
28 12 three tenths of flour . . . for every
29 3 three tenths of flour . . . to every calf. 9, 14, 20, 28
35 14 three shall be beyond the Jordan, and three in the land of Chanaan
Deut 4 41 set aside 3 cities beyond the Jordan

17 6 mouth of 2 or 3 witnesses. 19:15
19 2 thou shalt separate to thee 3 cities
3 thy land equally into 3 parts: that he
7 that thou separate 3 cities at equal
9 thou shalt add to thee other 3 cities
9 double the number of the 3 cities
Josu 15 14 out of it the 3 sons of Enac. Judg 1:20
18 4 choose of every tribe 3 men that I may
21 32 of tribe also of Nephtali . . . 3 cities
Judg 7 16 he divided the 300 men into 3 parts
20 sounded their trumpets in 3 places
9 43 army and divided it into 3 companies
Ruth 2 14 an ephi of barley, that is, 3 bushels
1 K 1 24 with 3 calves and 3 bushels of flour
2 13 a fleshhook of 3 teeth in his hand
21 and bore 3 sons and 2 daughters: and
10 3 shall meet thee 3 men going up to God
3 carrying 3 kids, and another 3 loaves
11 11 Saul put the people in 3 companies
13 17 Philistines 3 companies to plunder
17 13 his 3 eldest sons followed Saul to the
13 names of his 3 sons that went to the
14 the 3 eldest having followed Saul
20 20 I will shoot 3 arrows near it and will
30 12 nor drunk water 3 days and 3 nights
31 6 so Saul died, and his 3 sons, and his
8 they found Saul and his 3 sons lying
2 K 2 18 and there were the 3 sons of Sarvia
6 11 in the house of Obededom . . . 3 months
14 27 there were born to Absalom 3 sons: and
18 14 he [Joab] took 3 lances in his hand
23 8 was the wisest chief among the three
9 Eleazar . . . one of the 3 valiant men
13 the 3 who were princes among the 30
16 the 3 valiant men broke through the
17 drink. These things did these 3 mighty
18 the son of Sarvia was chief among 3
18 he [Abisai] was renowned among the 3
19 [Abisai] was . . . the noblest of the 3
23 was renowned among the 3 valiant men
23 but he attained not to the first three
24 12 I give thee thy choice of 3 things
13 or thou shalt flee 3 months before thy
3 K 6 36 court with 3 rows of polished stones
7 12 court . . . with 3 rows of hewed stones
25 three looked towards the north, and 3 towards the west, and 3 towards the south, and 3 towards the east
27 every base was . . . 3 cubits high. And
4 K 3 13 gathered together these 3 kings, to
9 32 two or 3 eunuchs bowed down to him
25 17 which was upon it was 3 cubits high
18 the second priest and 3 doorkeepers
1 Pa 2 3 these 3 were born to him [Juda] of the
16 Abisai, Joab, and Asael, three. And
3 23 the sons of Naaria . . . three. The
7 6 the sons of Benjamin were . . . three
11 12 Eleazar . . . was one of the 3 mighties
15 three of the thirty captains went down
18 these 3 broke through the midst of the
19 these things did the 3 most valiant
20 and Abisai . . . he was chief of three
20 and he was renowned among the three
21 and illustrious among the second three
21 yet he attained not to the first three
24 Banaias . . . was renowned among the 3
25 yet to the 3 he [Banaias] attained not
21 10 I give thee the choice of 3 things
23 8 the sons of Leedan . . . three. The
9 the sons of Semei . . . three. These were
23 the sons of Musi . . . three. These
25 5 gave to Heman 14 sons and 3 daughters
2 Pa 4 4 three of which looked toward the north, and other 3 toward the west: and other 3 toward the south
4 other 3 that remained toward the east
6 13 five cubits broad and 3 cubits high
1 Es 6 4 three rows of unpolished stones and
Tob 3 10 for 3 days and 3 nights did neither
8 4 for these 3 nights we are joined to God: and
12 22 they lying prostrate for 3 hours upon
Job 1 2 born to him 7 sons and 3 daughters
4 they called their 3 sisters to eat
17 the Chaldeans made 3 troops and have
2 11 when Job's 3 friends heard all the
32 1 so these 3 men ceased to answer Job
5 saw that the 3 were not able to answer
42 13 and he had 7 sons and 3 daughters
Prov 22 20 described it to thee 3 manner of ways
30 15 three things that never are satisfied
18 three things are hard to me, and the
21 by 3 things the earth is disturbed
29 there are 3 things which go well, and
Eccu 25 1 with 3 things my spirit is pleased, which
3 three sorts my soul hateth and I am
26 5 of 3 things my heart hath been afraid
Isa 5 10 bushels of seed shall yield 3 bushels
17 6 two or three berries in the top of
40 12 hath poised with 3 fingers the bulk of
Jer 36 23 Judi had read 3 or 4 pages, he cut it
52 24 priest, and the 3 keepers of the entry
Eze 14 14 if these 3 men, Noe, Daniel, and Job
16 if these 3 men shall be in it as I live
18 and these 3 men be in the midst thereof
40 10 three on this side and three on that
10 all 3 were of one measure and the fronts
21 chambers thereof three on this side and three on that side
48 three cubits on this side, and 3 cubits on
41 16 galleries round about on 3 sides
22 the altar of wood was 3 cubits high
42 6 for they were of 3 stories and had not
48 31 three gates on the north side, the gate
32 three gates, the gate of. 33, 34
Dan 3 51 then these 3 as with one mouth praised
91 did we not cast 3 men bound into the
6 2 three princes over them, of whom Daniel
7 5 and there were 3 rows in the mouth
8 three of the first horns were plucked
20 before which 3 horns fell: and of that
24 the former, he shall bring down 3 kings
10 2 I Daniel mourned the days of 3 weeks
3 ointment: till the days of 3 weeks were
11 2 there shall stand yet 3 kings in Persia
Amos 1 3 for 3 crimes of. 6, 9, 11, 13; 2:1, 4, 6
4 8 and 3 cities went to one city to drink
Jon 2 1 belly of the fish 3 days and 3 nights
3 3 a great city of 3 days' journey. And
Zach 11 8 and I cut off 3 shepherds in one month
1 Ma 5 24 went 3 days' journey through the desert
33 he came with 3 companies behind them
10 30 the 3 cities that are added. 38
11 28 the 3 governments and Samaria, and the
34 the borders of Judea and the 3 cities
2 Ma 4 44 three men were sent from the ancients
Mat 12 40 the whale's belly 3 days and 3 nights
13 33 hid in 3 measures of meal. Luke 13:21
17 4 let us make here 3 tabernacles. Mark 9:4; Luke 9:33
18 16 mouth of 2 or 3 witnesses. 2 C 13:1
20 where there are 2 or 3 gathered
Luke 1 56 Mary abode with her about 3 months
10 36 which of these 3, in thy opinion, was
11 5 to him: Friend, lend me 3 loaves
12 52 three against 2, and 2 against three
John 2 6 containing 2 or 3 measures apiece

Acts 5 7 about the space of 3 hours after, when
7 20 who was nourished 3 months in his
10 19 to him: Behold 3 men seek thee. Arise
11 11 three men come to the house wherein I
17 2 three sabbath days he reasoned with
19 8 spoke boldly for the space of 3 months
20 3 he had spent 3 months, the Jews laid
28 11 after 3 months, we sailed in a ship
15 as far as Apii Forum, and Three Taverns
1 C 13 13 faith, hope, and charity, these three
14 27 it be by 2, or at the most by three
29 let the prophets speak, 2 or three
1 Tim 5 19 but under 2 or 3 witnesses. Them that
Heb 10 28 dieth . . . under 2 or 3 witnesses: how
11 23 was hid 3 months by his parents because
1 J 5 7 there are 3 who give testimony. 8
7 these 3 are one. 8
Apoc 8 13 rest of the voices of the 3 angels
9 18 by these three plagues was slain the
16 13 three unclean spirits like frogs. For
19 great city was divided into 3 parts
21 13 on the . . . three gates: and on the

3 days Gen 40 12 the 3 branches are yet 3 days
Gen 40 18 the three baskets are yet three days
42 17 he put them in prison three days
Exod 10 22 horrible darkness . . . for three days
15 22 marched 3 days through the wilderness
Num 10 33 for three days providing a place for
33 8 marched three days through the desert
Josu 2 16 there lie ye hid three days, till they
22 mountains, and stayed there three days
3 1 they abode there for three days
9 16 three days after the league was made
20 5 his enemy two or three days before
Judg 14 14 could not in 3 days expound the riddle
19 4 in house of his father-in-law 3 days
1 K 9 20 asses which were lost three days ago
30 12 nor drunk water 3 days and 3 nights
13 I began to be sick three days ago
2 K 24 13 three days there shall be a pestilence
4 K 2 17 sought three days but found him not
1 Pa 12 39 they were there with David three days
21 12 three days to have the sword of Lord
2 Pa 10 5 come to me again after three days
20 25 nor in three days take away the spoils
1 Es 8 15 and we stayed there three days. 32
10 8 would not come within three days
9 together to Jerusalem within three days
2 Es 2 11 to Jerusalem, and was there three days
Tob 3 10 three days and three nights did neither
6 18 for three days keep thyself continent
Jdth 12 6 might go out and in . . . for three days
Esth 4 16 nor drink for three days and three
Jon 2 1 in the belly of the fish three days
1 Ma 10 34 and three days before the solemn day and three days after the solemn day
2 Ma 5 14 slain in the space of three whole days
13 12 prostrate on the ground for three days
Mat 12 40 in the whale's belly three days
40 in the heart of the earth three days and
15 32 they continue with me now three days
26 61 after three days to rebuild it
27 40 that . . . in three days dost rebuild
63 after three days I will rise again
Mark 8 2 have now been with me three days
31 and after three days rise again
14 58 within three days I will build another
15 29 in three days buildest it up again
Luke 2 46 after three days they found him in
John 2 19 in three days I will raise it up
20 wilt thou raise it up in three days
Acts 9 9 he was there [Damascus] three days
17 2 three sabbath days he reasoned with
25 1 after three days he went up to Jerusalem
28 7 Publius . . . for three days entertained
12 we tarried there [Syracusa] three days
Apoc 11 9 see their bodies for three days and a
11 after three days and a half, the spirit

4 Gen 2 10 from thence is divided into 4 heads
Gen 14 9 king of Pontus: 4 kings against five
47 24 the other 4 you shall have for seed
Exod 22 1 shall restore . . . 4 sheep for one
25 12 four golden rings, which thou shalt put
12 shalt put at the 4 corners of the ark
25 itself a polished crown, 4 inches high
26 thou shalt prepare also 4 golden rings
26 shalt put them in the 4 corners of the
34 in candlestick itself shall be 4 cups
26 2 cubits, the breadth shall be 4 cubits
8 the breadth [of curtain] 4 cubits
32 it up before 4 pillars of setim wood
27 2 there shall be horns at the 4 corners
4 at the 4 corners of which shall be 4 rings of brass
16 it shall have 4 pillars with as many
28 17 thou shalt set in it 4 rows of stones
36 9 one curtain . . . the breadth 4 [cubits]
15 thirty cubits long and 4 cubits broad
37 3 four rings of gold at the 4 corners
12 crown of gold of 4 fingers' breadth
13 he cast 4 rings of gold, which he put
13 which he put in the 4 corners at each
20 in the shaft itself were 4 cups after
38 5 casting 4 rings at the 4 ends of the net
19 and the pillars in the entry were four
39 10 he set 4 rows of precious stones in it
Lev 11 20 whatsoever goeth upon 4 feet, shall be
21 but whatsoever walketh upon 4 feet, but
23 whatsoever hath 4 feet only, shall be an
27 of all animals which go on all four
42 goeth upon the breast on 4 feet, or hath
Num 7 7 two wagons and 4 oxen he gave to the
8 the other 4 wagons and 8 oxen he gave
Deut 3 11 bed . . . 9 cubits long and 4 broad
22 12 in the hem at the 4 corners of thy cloak
Josu 19 7 Asan: 4 cities and their villages
21 18 their suburbs, 4 cities. 22, 24, 29, 31
35 four cities with their suburbs. 36, 37
Judg 9 34 laid ambushes near Sichem in 4 places
11 40 of Jephte the Galaadite for 4 days
19 2 abode with him 4 months. And her
20 47 abode in the rock Remmon 4 months
1 K 27 7 time that David dwelt . . . was 4 months
2 K 21 22 these 4 were born of Arapha in Geth
3 K 7 2 and 4 galleries between pillars of
19 of lily work in the porch, of 4 cubits
27 every base was 4 cubits in length and 4 cubits in breadth
30 every base had 4 wheels and axletrees
30 at the 4 sides were undersetters under
32 the 4 wheels which were at the 4 corners
34 the 4 undersetters that were at every
38 contained 4 bases and was of 4 cubits
10 29 a chariot of 4 horses came out of
18 34 fill 4 buckets with water and pour
4 K 7 3 there were 4 lepers at the entering
1 Pa 3 5 four of Bethsabee the daughter of Ammiel
7 1 now the sons of Issachar were . . . four
9 24 in 4 quarters were the porters: that is
26 to these 4 Levites were committed the
21 20 [Ornan] and his 4 sons hid themselves
23 10 these were the sons of Semei, four
26 17 towards the north 4 a day: and towards the south likewise 4 a day
18 in the cells . . . toward the west four
2 Pa 1 17 chariot of 4 horses for 600 pieces of

2 Es 6 4 to me according to this word, 4 times
9 3 they read . . . 4 times in the day, and 4 times they confessed
Tob 8 22 caused also 2 fat kine and 4 wethers
9 6 then Raphael took 4 of Raguel's servants
Job 1 19 shook the 4 corners of the house
Prov 30 24 there are 4 very little things of
Wisd 18 24 in the 4 rows of the stones the glory
Eccu 37 21 four manner of things arise, good
Isa 11 12 from the 4 quarters of the earth
17 6 four or five upon the top of the tree
Jer 15 3 and I will visit them with 4 kinds, saith
36 23 and when Judi had read 3 or 4 pages, he
49 36 I will bring upon Elam the 4 winds
36 four winds from the 4 quarters of
52 21 but the thickness thereof was 4 fingers
Eze 1 5 the likeness of 4 living creatures: and
6 four faces, and every one 4 wings
8 under their wings on their 4 sides
8 they had faces and wings on the 4 sides
10 on the . . . side of all the four
10 the face of an eagle over all the four
15 living creatures one wheel with 4 faces
16 the 4 had all one likeness: and their
17 they went by their 4 parts: and they
18 full of eyes round about all the four
7 2 end is come upon the 4 quarters of
10 9 there were 4 wheels by the cherubims
10 all 4 were alike: as if a wheel
11 they went by 4 ways: and they turned
12 of eyes, round about the 4 wheels
14 and every one had 4 faces: one face was
21 had 4 faces, and each one had 4 wings
14 21 my 4 grievous judgments, the sword and
37 9 come, spirit, from the 4 winds and blow
40 41 four tables were on this side, and 4 tables on that side
42 the 4 tables for the holocausts were
41 5 breadth of every side chamber 4 cubits
42 20 by the 4 winds he measured the wall
43 14 to the greater brim 4 cubits, and the
15 and the Ariel itself was 4 cubits: and
15 and from the Ariel upward were 4 horns
17 and 14 cubits broad in the 4 corners
20 shalt put it upon the 4 horns thereof
20 upon the 4 corners of the brim. 45:19
46 21 the 4 corners of the court. 22
22 broad, all the 4 were of one measure
23 about compassing the 4 little courts
Dan 3 92 I see 4 men loose, and walking in the
7 2 the 4 winds of the heaven strove upon
3 four great beasts, different one from
6 and it had upon it 4 wings as of a fowl
6 the beast had 4 heads, and power was
17 these 4 great beasts are 4 kingdoms
8 8 there came up 4 horns under it towards
22 was broken, there arose up 4 for it
22 four kings shall rise up of his nation
11 4 be divided towards the 4 winds of the
Amos 1 3 for 4 I will not convert it. 6, 9
11 for 4 I will not convert him. 13; 2:1, 4, 6
Zach 1 18 up my eyes and saw: and behold 4 horns
20 and the Lord showed me 4 smiths. And I
2 6 I have scattered you into the 4 winds
6 1 four chariots came out from the midst
5 these are the 4 winds of the heaven
1 Ma 11 57 I appoint thee ruler over the 4 cities
13 28 and his mother and his 4 brethren: and
2 Ma 10 33 laid siege to the fortress 4 days. But
Mat 24 31 his elect from the 4 winds. Mark 13:27
Mark 2 3 of the palsy, who was carried by four
Luke 2 37 a widow until fourscore and four years
John 4 35 you say, There are yet 4 months, and
11 17 had been 4 days already in the grave
39 he stinketh, for he is now of 4 days
19 23 they made 4 parts, to every soldier
Acts 10 11 linen sheet let down by 4 corners
30 said: Four days ago unto this hour, I
11 5 let down from heaven by 4 corners, and
12 4 delivering him to 4 files of soldiers
21 9 he had 4 daughters, virgins, who did
23 we have 4 men, who have a vow on them
27 29 they cast 4 anchors out of the stern
Apoc 4 6 were 4 living creatures, full of eyes
8 the 4 living creatures had each of
5 6 throne and of the 4 living creatures
8 the 4 living creatures and the four
14 the 4 living creatures said: Amen
6 1 heard one of the 4 living creatures
6 the midst of the 4 living creatures
8 over the 4 parts of the earth, to
7 1 saw 4 angels standing on the 4 corners
1 holding the 4 winds of the earth, that
2 four angels to whom it was given to
11 ancients and the 4 living creatures
9 13 I heard a voice from the 4 horns of
14 loose the 4 angels who are bound in
15 the 4 angels were loosed, who were
14 3 and before the 4 living creatures
15 7 one of the 4 living creatures
19 4 the 4 living creatures fell down
20 7 are over the 4 quarters of the earth

5 Gen 14 9 four kings against five. Now the
Gen 18 28 if there be 5 less than 50 just
43 34 Benjamin, so that it exceeded by 5 parts
45 6 and 5 years more remain, wherein there
11 are yet 5 years of famine remaining
22 of silver with 5 robes of the best
47 2 five men also the last of his brethren
Exod 22 1 he shall restore 5 oxen for one ox
26 3 five curtains shall be joined one to
3 the other 5 shall be coupled together
9 five of which thou shalt couple by
26 shalt make also 5 bars of setim wood
27 and 5 others on the other side, and as
37 thou shalt overlay with gold 5 pillars
36 10 he joined 5 curtains, one to another
10 other 5 he coupled one to another
16 five of which he joined apart, and the
31 five to hold together the boards of one
32 five others to join together the boards
32 five other bars at the west side of the
38 and 5 pillars with their heads, which
Lev 26 8 five of yours shall pursue a hundred
27 6 for a male shall be given 5 sicles
Num 3 47 shalt take 5 sicles for every head
7 17 two oxen, 5 rams, 5 he goats, 5 lambs
23 five rams, 5 buck goats, 5 lambs. 29, 35, 41, 47, 53, 59, 65, 71, 77, 83
11 19 not for one day nor 2 nor 5 nor 10, no
18 16 redemption . . . for 5 sicles of silver
31 8 five princes of the nation: Balaam
Josu 10 5 the 5 kings of the Amorrhites being
16 the 5 kings were fled and had hidden
17 that the 5 kings were found hidden
22 bring forth to me the 5 kings that lie
23 brought out to him the 5 kings out of
26 hanged them upon 5 gibbets, and they
14 10 it is 40 and 5 years since the Lord
Judg 3 3 the 5 princes of the Philistines and
18 2 children of Dan sent 5 most valiant
7 so the 5 men going on came to Lais: and
14 the 5 men that before had been sent
1 K 6 5 five golden emerods and 5 golden mice
16 the 5 princes of the Philistines saw
18 of the Philistines, of the 5 provinces

17 40 and chose him 5 smooth stones out of
21 3 though it were but 5 loaves, give
25 18 five sheep ready dressed and 5 measures of parched corn
42 and 5 damsels went with her [Abigail]
2 K 4 4 he was 5 years old when the tidings
21 8 five sons of Michol the daughter of Saul
3 K 6 31 of olive tree, and posts of 5 corners
7 39 bases, 5 on the right side of the temple, and 5 on the left
49 candlesticks, 5 on right . . . and 5 on
4 K 6 25 pigeon's dung, for 5 pieces of silver
7 13 us take 5 horses that are remaining in
13 19 if thou hadst smitten 5 or 6 or 7 times
25 19 five men of them that had stood before
1 Pa 2 4 so all the sons of Juda were five. And
6 the sons also of Zare . . . five in all
3 20 Hasaba also and . . . Josabhesed, five
4 32 towns also were Etam and . . . 5 cities
7 3 sons of Ozi . . . five all great men. And
7 the sons of Bela . . . 5 chiefs of their
2 Pa 4 6 five on right hand and 5 on left. 7
8 five on right side and 5 on the left
Jdth 7 23 and let us wait these 5 days for mercy
25 if after 5 days be past there come no
8 10 if within 5 days there come no aid to
32 in 5 days the Lord may look down upon
Isa 17 6 four or five upon the top of the tree
19 18 there shall be 5 cities in the land of
30 17 and for fear of 5 shall you flee, till
1 Ma 2 2 he had 5 sons: John who was surnamed
2 Ma 2 24 comprised in 5 books by Jason of Cyrene
10 29 from heaven 5 men upon horses, comely
11 5 the space of 5 furlongs from Jerusalem
Mat 14 17 we have not here but 5 loaves and two
19 he took the 5 loaves and the 2 fishes
16 9 the 5 loaves among 5,000 men, and how
25 2 five of them were foolish and 5 wise
3 the 5 foolish, having taken their lamps
15 one he gave 5 talents, and to another
16 he that had received the 5 talents. 20
16 traded with same and gained other five
20 brought other 5 talents, saying: Lord
20 didst deliver to me 5 talents, behold
20 I have gained other 5 over and above
Mark 6 38 they say: Five, and 2 fishes. And he
41 when he had taken the 5 loaves and the
8 19 when I broke the 5 loaves among 5,000
Luke 1 24 and hid herself 5 months, saying: Thus
9 13 we have no more than 5 loaves and two
16 taking the 5 loaves and the 2 fishes
12 6 are not 5 sparrows sold for 2 farthings
52 five in one house divided: 3 against
14 19 I have bought 5 yoke of oxen and I go
16 27 father's house, for I have 5 brethren
19 18 thy pound hath gained 5 pounds. And he
19 said to him: Be thou also over 5 cities
John 4 18 for thou hast had 5 husbands: and he
5 2 named Bethsaida, having 5 porches
6 9 hath 5 barley loaves and 2 fishes
13 fragments of the 5 barley loaves
Acts 20 6 came to them to Troas in 5 days, where
24 1 after 5 days high priest Ananias came
1 C 14 19 I had rather speak 5 words with my
2 C 11 24 of the Jews 5 times did I receive forthy
Apoc 9 5 they should torment them 5 months
10 their power was to hurt men 5 months
17 10 five are fallen, one is, and the other

5 cubits; *see* **cubits**

6 Gen 30 20 because I have borne him 6 sons
Gen 31 41 thy daughters, and 6 for thy flocks
Exod 25 32 six branches shall come out of the sides
33 such shall be work of the 6 branches
35 make 6 coming forth out of one shaft
26 9 six others thou shalt couple one to
22 on west side . . . shalt make 6 boards
28 10 six names on one stone, and the other six on the other
36 16 apart, and the other 6 [curtains] apart
27 against the west . . . he made 6 boards
37 18 six [branches] on the two sides: three
19 the work of the 6 branches that went
21 which together make 6 branches going
Lev 24 6 thou shalt set them 6 and 6 one against
Num 7 3 six wagons covered and 12 oxen. Two
35 6 six shall be separated for refuge
Josu 7 5 and there fell of them 6 and 30 men
15 59 six cities and their villages. 62
Ruth 3 15 he measured 6 measures of barley, and
17 he hath given me 6 measures of barley
1 K 17 4 whose height was 6 cubits and a span
2 K 2 11 David abode . . . 7 years and 6 months
5 5 reigned over Juda 7 years and 6 months
6 13 the ark of the Lord had gone 6 paces
21 20 that had 6 fingers on each hand and 6 toes
3 K 6 6 middle floor was 6 cubits in breadth
10 19 had 6 steps: and the top of the throne
20 little lions stood upon the 6 steps
11 16 Joab remained there 6 months with all
4 K 13 19 if thou hadst smitten 5 or 6 or 7 times
15 8 Zacharias . . . in Samaria 6 months
1 Pa 3 4 so 6 sons were born to him in Hebron
4 where he reigned 7 years and 6 months
22 Semeia whose sons were . . . 6 in number
4 27 sons of Semei were 16, and 6 daughters
8 38 Asel had 6 sons whose names. 9:44
20 6 six on each hand and foot: who also
25 3 and Hasabias and Mathathias, six
26 17 now towards the east were 6 Levites
2 Pa 9 18 and 6 steps to go up to the throne
2 Es 5 18 day by day one ox and 6 choice rams
Jdth 8 4 a widow now 3 years and 6 months
Job 5 19 in 6 troubles he shall deliver thee
Prov 6 16 six things there are which the Lord
Isa 6 2 had 6 wings, and the other had six
Eze 9 2 six men came from the way of the upper
40 5 reed of 6 cubits and a handbreadth
12 the little chambers were 6 cubits
41 1 six cubits broad on this side and 6 cubits on
3 the gate 6 cubits, and the breadth
5 measured the wall of the house 6 cubits
8 of a reed the space of 6 cubits: and
46 4 shall be 6 lambs without blemish, and a
6 the 6 lambs and the rams shall be
Dan 3 1 a statue of gold . . . 6 cubits broad
Luke 4 25 was shut up 3 years and 6 months
John 2 6 there were set there 6 waterpots
Acts 11 12 six brethren went with me also: and
18 11 he stayed there a year and 6 months
James 5 17 rained not for 3 years and 6 months
Apoc 4 8 had each of them 6 wings; and round

6 days Exod 16 26 gather it six days
Exod 20 9 six days shalt thou labor. Deut 5:13
11 in six days the Lord made. 31:17
23 12 six days thou shalt work. 34:21
24 16 covering it with a cloud six days
31 15 six days shall you do work. Lev 23:3
35 2 six days you shall do work
Deut 16 8 six days shalt thou eat unleavened
Josu 6 3 so shall ye do for six days
14 so they did six days. But the seventh
Eze 46 1 gate . . shall be shut the six days
Dan 14 30 den of lions, and he was there six days
Mat 17 1 after six days Jesus taketh. Mark 9:1
Luke 13 14 six days there are wherein . . . to work
John 12 1 six days before the pasch, came to

7 Gen 7 2 of all clean beasts take 7 and 7
Gen 7 3 of the fowls also of the air 7 and 7
21 28 Abraham set apart 7 ewe lambs of the
29 what mean these 7 ewe lambs which thou
30 thou shalt take 7 ewe lambs at my hand
41 2 came up 7 kine very beautiful and fat
3 other 7 also came up out of the river
5 seven ears of corn came up upon one
6 then 7 other ears sprung up thin and
18 seven kine came up out of the river
19 there followed these, other 7 kine
22 seven ears of corn grew upon one stalk
23 other 7 also thin and blasted sprung
26 the 7 beautiful kine and the 7 full ears are 7 years of plenty
27 the 7 lean and thin kine that came
27 the 7 thin ears that were blasted
46 25 she bore to Jacob; all the souls seven
Exod 2 16 the priest of Madian had 7 daughters
25 37 thou shalt make also 7 lamps, and shalt
37 23 he made also the 7 lamps with their
Lev 23 15 you shall count . . . 7 full weeks. Even
25 8 also number to thee 7 weeks of years
26 28 I will chastise you with 7 plagues
Num 8 2 when thou shalt place the 7 lamps
23 1 build me here 7 altars and prepare. 29
4 I have erected 7 altars, and have laid
14 Balaam built 7 altars, and laying on
18 you shall offer . . . 7 lambs. 28:11, 19, 27; 29:2, 8, 36
28 21 tenth of a tenth . . . to all the 7 lambs
29 which in all are 7 lambs. 29:4, 10
29 32 you shall offer 7 calves and 2 rams
Deut 7 1 seven nations much more numerous than
16 9 thou shalt number unto thee 7 weeks
28 7 seven ways shall they flee before thee
25 and flee 7 ways, and be scattered
Josu 6 4 the priests shall take the 7 trumpets
6 let 7 other priests take the 7 trumpets
8 the 7 priests blew the 7 trumpets
13 and 7 of them [took] 7 trumpets, which
18 2 but there remained 7 tribes of the
5 to yourselves the land into 7 parts
6 between these mark ye out into 7 parts
9 surveying it divided it into 7 parts
10 divided the land . . . into 7 parts
Judg 16 7 if I shall be bound with 7 cords
8 brought unto her 7 cords such as he
13 if thou plattest the 7 locks of my head
19 called a barber, and shaved his 7 locks
Ruth 4 15 to thee, than if thou hadst 7 sons
1 K 6 1 ark of God was in the land . . . 7 months
16 10 Isai therefore brought his 7 sons
2 K 6 12 and there were with David 7 choirs and
21 6 let 7 men of his children be delivered
9 these 7 died together in the first
3 K 6 6 the third floor was 7 cubits in breadth
7 17 7 rows of nets were on one chapiter, and 7 nets on the other chapiter
4 K 3 9 fetched a compass of 7 days' journey
1 Pa 3 24 the sons of Elioenai . . . seven
5 13 brethren according to the houses . . . 7
15 26 offered in sacrifice 7 oxen and 7 rams
2 Pa 13 9 a bullock of the herd and with 7 rams
29 21 they offered together 7 bullocks and 7 rams and 7 lambs and 7 he goats
1 Es 7 14 before the king and his 7 counsellors
Tob 3 8 she had been given to 7 husbands, and
10 as thou hast already killed 7 husbands
6 14 that she hath been given to 7 husbands
7 11 knowing what had happened to those 7
8 12 as it did to the other 7 husbands
12 15 I am the angel Raphael, one of the seven
14 5 Tobias and his children, 7 young men
Job 1 2 there were born to him 7 sons and three
2 3 on the ground 7 days and 7 nights
42 8 unto you therefore 7 oxen and 7 rams
13 he had 7 sons and 3 daughters. And he
Prov 9 1 house, she hath hewn her out 7 pillars
26 16 conceit, than 7 men that speak sentences
25 there are 7 mischiefs in his heart
Ecce 11 2 give a portion to 7 and also to 8
Eccu 37 18 more than 7 watchmen that sit in a high
Isa 4 1 seven women shall take hold of one man
11 15 shall strike it in the 7 streams
Jer 15 9 she that hath borne 7 is become weak
32 9 I weighed him the money, 7 staters
52 25 seven men of them that were near the
Bar 6 2 a long time, even to 7 generations
Eze 39 12 shall bury them for 7 months to cleanse
14 after 7 months they shall begin to seek
40 22 they went up to it by 7 steps, and a
26 and there were 7 steps to go up to it
41 3 and the breadth of the gate 7 cubits
45 23 to the Lord 7 calves and 7 rams without
Dan 9 25 there shall be 7 weeks and sixty-two
14 31 in the den there were 7 lions, and they
Mich 5 5 shall raise against him 7 shepherds
Zach 3 9 upon one stone there are 7 eyes: behold
4 2 and the 7 lights thereof upon it: and
2 and 7 funnels for the lights that were
10 these are the 7 eyes of the Lord that
1 Ma 13 28 and he set up 7 pyramids one against
2 Ma 7 1 seven brethren together with their
20 who beheld her 7 sons slain in the
Mat 12 45 taketh with him 7 other. Luke 11:26
15 34 they said: Seven, and a few little
36 taking the 7 loaves. Mark 8:6
37 they took up 7 baskets full, of what
16 10 the 7 loaves among 4,000 men. Mark 8:20
22 25 there were with us 7 brethren: and the
28 whose wife of the 7 shall she be? For
Mark 8 5 many loaves have ye? Who said: Seven
8 left of the fragments, 7 baskets. And
20 took you up? And they say to him: Seven
12 20 there were 7 brethren; and the first
22 the 7 all took her in like manner
23 the 7 had her to wife. Luke 20:33
16 9 out of whom he had cast 7 devils. She
Luke 8 2 out of whom 7 devils were gone forth
20 29 there were therefore 7 brethren: and
31 in like manner all the 7, and they left
Acts 6 3 look ye out among you 7 men of good
13 19 destroying 7 nations in the land of
19 14 certain men, 7 sons of Sceva, a Jew, a
21 8 one of 7, we abode with him. And he
Apoc 1 4 the 7 churches which are in Asia. 11
4 from the 7 spirits which are before
12 seven golden candlesticks. 13, 20; 2:1
16 he had in his right hand 7 stars. And
20 the 7 stars are angels of the 7 churches
20 the 7 candlesticks are the 7 churches
2 1 who holdeth the 7 stars in his right
3 1 he that hath the 7 spirits of God and
4 5 seven lamps burning before the throne
5 which are the 7 spirits of God. 5:6
5 1 and without, sealed with 7 seals. And
5 and to loose the 7 seals thereof. And
6 having 7 horns and 7 eyes: which are
6 1 had opened one of the 7 seals and
8 2 seven angels standing in the presence
2 there were given to them 7 trumpets
6 the 7 angels who had the 7 trumpets
10 3 seven thunders uttered their voices
4 when the 7 thunders had uttered their
4 which the 7 thunders have spoken; and

12 3 having 7 heads and 10 horns. 13:1; 17:3
3 and on his heads 7 diadems: and his
15 1 seven angels having 7 last plagues. 6
6 the 7 angels came out of the temple
7 gave to the 7 angels 7 golden vials
8 till the 7 plagues of the 7 angels were fulfilled
16 1 saying to the 7 angels: Go and pour out the 7 vials of the wrath of God
17 1 there came one of the 7 angels, who
7 which hath the 7 heads and 10 horns
9 the 7 heads are 7 mountains, upon
9 and they are 7 kings: 5 are fallen
11 is the eighth, and is of the 7 and
21 9 there came one of the 7 angels who had the vials full of the 7 last plagues
7 days Gen 7 4 after s. d. I will rain
Gen 7 10 after the 7 days . . . waters of the
8 10 having waited yet seven other days
12 [Noe] stayed yet other seven days
31 23 [Laban] pursued after him seven days
50 10 exequies . . . they spent full seven days
Exod 7 25 seven days were fully ended
12 15 s. d. shall you eat unleavened. Lev 23:6
19 seven days . . . not be found any leaven
13 6 seven days shalt thou eat unleavened. 23:15; 34:18
7 unleavened bread shall you eat 7 days
22 30 seven days let it be with its dam
29 30 shall wear it seven days
35 seven days . . . consecrate their hands
37 seven days shalt thou expiate the altar
Lev 8 33 not go out . . . for seven days
33 in 7 days the consecration is finished
12 2 shall be unclean seven days. 15:24; Num 19:14, 16
13 4 shall shut him up seven days. 21, 26, 31
5 shall shut him up again other 7 days
33 he shall be shut up other seven days
50 he shall . . . shut it up 7 days. 14:38
54 he shall shut it up other seven days
14 8 tarry without his own tent seven days
15 13 number 7 days after his cleansing
19 woman . . . shall be separated 7 days
28 shall count 7 days of her purification
22 27 shall be seven days under the udder
23 8 you shall offer sacrifice . . . 7 days
34 feast of tabernacles seven days
35 seven days you shall offer holocausts
39 celebrate the feast of the Lord 7 days
41 keep the solemnity thereof seven days
42 you shall dwell in bowers seven days
Num 12 14 have been ashamed for 7 days at least
14 let her be separated seven days
15 Mary . . . out of the camp seven days
19 11 is therefore unclean seven days
28 17 seven days shall they eat unleavened
24 shall you do every day of the 7 days
29 12 shall celebrate a solemnity . . . 7 days
31 19 stay without the camp seven days
Deut 16 3 s. d. shalt thou eat without leaven
4 no leaven shall be seen . . . for 7 days
13 solemnity of tabernacles seven days
15 seven days shalt thou celebrate
Judg 14 12 within the seven days of the feast
17 wept before him seven days of the feast
1 K 10 8 seven days shalt thou wait till I
11 3 allow us seven days that we may send
13 8 he [Saul] waited seven days
31 13 and fasted seven days. 1 Pa 10:12
3 K 8 65 feast . . . seven days and seven days
16 15 Zambri reigned seven days in Thersa
20 29 in array one against other seven days
2 Pa 7 8 the solemnity at that time seven days
9 celebrated the solemnity seven days
9 dedication of the altar seven days
30 21 feast of unleavened bread seven days
22 they ate during the seven days
23 pleased . . . to keep other seven days
35 17 feast of unleavened bread seven days. 1 Es 6:22
2 Es 8 18 they kept the solemnity seven days
Tob 11 18 after seven days Sara his son's wife
21 for 7 days they feasted and rejoiced
Jdth 16 29 all the people mourned for seven days
Esth 1 5 commanded a feast to be made 7 days
Job 2 13 sat with him on the ground seven days
Eccu 22 13 mourning for the dead is seven days
Isa 30 26 as the light of seven days
Eze 3 16 at the end of seven days the word of
Eze 3 15 I remained there seven days mourning
16 at the end of seven days the word of
43 25 seven days shalt thou offer a he goat
26 seven days shall they expiate the altar
44 26 they shall reckon unto him seven days
45 21 seven days unleavened bread shall be
23 in the solemnity of the seven days he
23 shall offer . . . daily for seven days
25 he shall do the like for the 7 days
Acts 20 6 Troas . . . where we abode seven days
21 4 we tarried there seven days
27 when the 7 days were drawing to an
28 14 were desired to tarry with them 7 days
Heb 11 30 by the going round them seven days
8 Gen 22 23 these 8 did Melcha bear to Nachor
Exod 26 25 they shall be in all 8 boards and their
36 30 so there were in all 8 boards and they
Num 7 8 the other 4 wagons and 8 oxen he gave
29 29 you shall offer 8 calves, 2 rams, and
1 K 17 12 Isai, who had 8 sons, and was an old
3 K 7 10 great stones of 10 cubits or 8 cubits
1 Pa 24 4 of the sons of Ithamar 8 by their
Ecce 11 2 give a portion to 7 and also to 8: for
Jer 41 15 Ismahel . . . fled with 8 men from the
Eze 40 9 measured the porch of the gate 8 cubits
31 there were 8 steps to go up to it. 49
34 the going up thereof was by 8 steps
37 and the going up to it was by 8 steps
41 at the sides of the gate were 8 tables
Mich 5 5 against him . . . eight principal men
1 P 3 20 wherein a few, that is, 8 souls, were
8 days Gen 17 12 infant of e. d. old shall
2 Pa 29 17 they purified the temple in eight days
1 Ma 4 56 dedication of the altar eight days
59 from year to year for eight days
2 Ma 2 12 celebrated the dedication eight days
10 6 they kept eight days with joy
Luke 2 21 after eight days were accomplished
9 28 about eight days after, he took Peter
John 20 26 after eight days . . . Jesus cometh
Acts 25 6 tarried no more than eight or ten days
9 Num 29 26 you shall offer 9 calves, 2 rams, and
Num 34 13 to be given to the 9 tribes and to the
Deut 3 11 his bed . . . being 9 cubits long and
Josu 13 7 land in possession to the 9 tribes
14 2 to the 9 tribes and the half tribe
15 44 nine cities, and their villages. 54
21 16 nine cities out of the two tribes
2 K 24 8 after 9 months and 20 days, they came
4 K 17 1 Osee the son of Ela . . . reigned 9 years
1 Pa 3 8 Jebaar also and . . . Elipheleth, nine
2 Es 11 1 and 9 parts in the other cities. And
Eccu 25 9 nine things that are not to be imagined
2 Ma 7 27 that bore thee 9 months in my womb
12 10 were now gone from thence 9 furlongs
Luke 17 17 ten made clean? And where are the nine

10 Gen 16 3 ten years after they first dwelt in
Gen 18 32 more: what if 10 should be found there
32 will not destroy it for the sake of ten
24 10 took 10 camels of his master's herd
22 as many bracelets of 10 sicles weight
55 let the maid stay at least 10 days
31 7 and hath changed my wages 10 times
41 hast changed also my wages 10 times
32 15 twenty she asses, and 10 of their foals
42 3 the 10 brethren of Joseph went down
45 23 adding besides 10 he asses to carry
Exod 26 1 thou shalt make 10 curtains of fine
27 12 and 10 pillars and as many sockets
34 28 he wrote upon the tables the 10 words
36 8 made 10 curtains of twisted fine linen
38 12 ten pillars of brass with their sockets
Lev 26 26 so that 10 women shall bake your bread
27 5 man shall give 20 sicles: a woman ten
7 shall give 15 sicles: a woman ten. If
Num 7 14 a little mortar of 10 sicles of gold
20 mortar of gold weighing 10 sicles. 26, 32, 38, 44, 50, 56, 62, 68, 74, 80, 86
11 19 not for one day nor 2 nor 5 nor ten
32 gathered together of quails . . . 10 cores
14 22 have tempted me now 10 times, and have
29 23 you shall offer 10 calves, 2 rams, and
Deut 4 13 the 10 words that he wrote in 2 tables
10 4 wrote in the tables . . . the 10 words
Josu 15 57 Thamna: ten cities and their villages
17 5 and there fell 10 portions to Manasses
21 5 tribe of Manasses, 10 cities. 1 Pa 6:61
26 all the cities were 10, with their
22 14 ten princes with him, one of every tribe
Judg 6 27 Gedeon taking 10 men of his servants
12 11 he [Ahialon] judged Israel 10 years
17 10 thee every year 10 pieces of silver
20 10 we will take 10 men of a hundred out of
Ruth 1 4 they dwelt there 10 years. And they
4 2 Booz taking 10 men of the ancients of
1 K 1 8 not I better to thee than 10 children
17 17 these 10 loaves, and run to the camp
18 carry these 10 little cheeses to the
18 7 David his ten thousands. 21:11; 29:5
8 they have given David 10 thousands
25 5 he sent 10 young men and said to them
38 and after 10 days had passed, the Lord
2 K 15 16 the king left 10 women his concubines
18 11 I would have given thee 10 sicles of
15 ten young men, armorbearers of Joab
19 43 I have 10 parts in the king more than
20 3 he took the 10 women his concubines
3 K 4 23 ten fat oxen and 20 out of the pastures
7 37 he made 10 bases, of one casting and
38 he made also 10 lavers of brass: one
38 upon every base in all 10 he put as
39 and he set the 10 bases, 5 on the right
43 the 10 bases and the 10 lavers on the
11 31 said to Jeroboam: Take to thee 10 pieces
31 and will give thee 10 tribes. 35
14 3 take also with thee 10 loaves and
4 K 5 5 took with him 10 talents of silver
5 pieces of gold and 10 changes of raiment
13 7 and 10 chariots and 10,000 footmen
15 17 reigned Manahem . . . 10 years in Samaria
20 9 that the shadow go forward 10 lines
10 for the shadow to go forward 10 lines
10 but let it return back 10 degrees
11 brought the shadow 10 degrees backwards
25 25 Ismael . . . came and 10 men with him
2 Pa 4 6 he made also 10 lavers: and he set five
7 and he made 10 golden candlesticks
8 also 10 tables: and he set them in the
14 1 in his days the land was quiet 10 years
36 9 he reigned 3 months and 10 days in
1 Es 8 24 and with them 10 of their brethren
2 Es 4 12 by them came and told us 10 times
5 18 once in 10 days I gave store of divers
11 1 one part in 10 to dwell in Jerusalem
Tob 1 16 and had 10 talents of silver of that
4 21 I lent 10 talents of silver while thou
Esth 9 6 besides the 10 sons of Aman the Agagite
Job 19 3 behold, these 10 times you confound me
Ps 32 2 instrument of 10 strings. 91:4; 143:9
67 18 of the Lord is attended by 10 thousands
Ecce 7 20 wise more than 10 princes of the city
Wisd 7 2 in the time of 10 months I was compacted
Eccu 41 6 whether ten or a hundred . . . years
Isa 5 10 ten acres of vineyard shall yield one
38 8 Achaz with the sun, 10 lines backward
8 sun returned 10 lines by the degrees
Jer 32 9 seven staters and 10 pieces of silver
41 1 that Ismahel . . . and 10 men with him
2 Ismahel arose . . . and the 10 men that
8 ten men were found among them, that
42 7 after 10 days, the word of the Lord
Bar 4 28 you shall seek him 10 times as much
Eze 45 14 and 10 bates make a core: for 10 bates
Dan 1 12 try . . . thy servants for 10 days, and
14 words, he tried them for 10 days. And
15 and after 10 days their faces appeared
20 them 10 times better than all the
7 7 had seen before it, and had 10 horns
20 concerning the 10 horns that he had
24 the 10 horns . . . shall be 10 kings
Amos 5 3 there shall be left in it 10, in the
6 9 if there remain 10 men in one house
Agge 2 17 heap of 20 bushels, and they became ten
Zach 8 23 wherein 10 men of all languages of the
Mat 20 24 the ten hearing it, were moved with
25 1 like to 10 virgins, who taking their
28 and give it him that hath 10 talents
Mark 10 41 the 10 hearing it, began to be much
Luke 15 8 what woman having 10 groats; if she
17 17 were not 10 made clean? And where are
19 13 calling his 10 servants, he gave
13 servants, he gave them 10 pounds and
16 Lord, thy pound hath gained 10 pounds
17 thou shalt have power over 10 cities
24 give it to him that hath 10 pounds
25 said to him: Lord, he hath 10 pounds
Acts 25 6 them no more than 8 or 10 days, he
Apoc 2 10 and you shall have tribulation 10 days
12 3 having seven heads and 10 horns. 13:1; 17:3
13 1 upon his horns 10 diadems, and upon
17 7 hath the 7 heads and 10 horns. The
12 the 10 horns . . . are 10 kings, who
16 the 10 horns which thou sawest in the

10 cubits; *see* **cubits**

11 Gen 32 22 with his 11 sons, and passed over the
Gen 37 9 the moon, and 11 stars worshipping me
Exod 26 7 thou shalt make also 11 curtains of
36 14 made also 11 curtains of goats' hair
Num 29 20 third day you shall offer 11 calves
Deut 1 2 eleven days' journey from Horeb by the
Josu 15 51 Gilo: eleven cities and their villages
4 K 23 36 reigned 11 years in Jerusalem. 24:18; 2 Pa 36:5, 11; Jer 52:1
Eze 40 49 of the porch . . . the breath 11 cubits
Mat 28 16 the eleven disciples went into Galilee
Mark 16 14 at length he appeared to the eleven
Luke 24 9 they told all these things to the e.
33 they found the e. gathered together
Acts 1 26 was numbered with the eleven apostles
2 14 Peter standing up with the eleven
1 C 15 5 by Cephas; and after that by the eleven

12 Gen 14 4 had served Chodorlahomor 12 years
Gen 17 20 he [Ismael] shall beget 12 chiefs
35 22 now the sons of Jacob were twelve
42 13 we thy servants are 12 brethren, the
32 we are 12 brethren born of one father
49 28 all these are the 12 tribes of Israel
Exod 15 27 where there were 12 fountains of water
24 4 12 titles according to the 12 tribes
28 21 with 12 names shall they be engraved
21 name of one according to the 12 tribes
39 14 the 12 stones were engraved with the
14 engraved with names of the 12 tribes
Lev 24 5 flour, and shalt bake 12 loaves thereof
Num 1 44 Aaron and the 12 princes of Israel
7 3 six wagons covered and 12 oxen. Two
84 12 dishes of silver: 12 silver bowls: 12 little mortars of gold
86 twelve little mortars of gold full of
87 twelve oxen out of the herd for a
87 twelve rams, 12 lambs of a year old
87 libations: 12 buck goats for sin
17 2 twelve rods, and write the name of
6 were 12 rods besides the rod of Aaron
29 17 you shall offer 12 calves of the herd
33 9 where there were 12 fountains of waters
Deut 1 23 I sent of you 12 men one of every tribe
Josu 3 12 prepare ye 12 men of the tribes of
4 2 choose 12 men, one of every tribe: and
3 twelve very hard stones, which you
4 Josue called 12 men whom he had chosen
8 carrying out . . . twelve stones, as the
9 Josue put other 12 stones in the midst
20 the 12 stones which they had taken
18 24 twelve cities and their villages. 19:15
21 7 of Gad and of Zabulon, 12 cities
38 cities of children of Merari . . . were 12
Judg 19 29 his wife with her bones into 12 parts
2 K 2 15 twelve in number of Benjamin . . . and 12 of the servants of David
3 K 4 7 Solomon had 12 governors over all Israel
7 15 a line of 12 cubits compassed both
25 it stood upon 12 oxen, of which three
44 one sea and 12 oxen under the sea
10 20 and 12 little lions stood upon the six
11 30 he was clad, divided it into 12 parts
16 23 Amri reigned over Israel 12 years
18 31 and he took 12 stones according to
19 19 that were plowing with 12 yoke of oxen
4 K 3 1 he [Joram] reigned 12 years. And he
21 1 Manasses was 12 years old when he began. 2 Pa 33:1
23 5 to the moon and to the 12 signs and
1 Pa 6 63 of Zabulon, they gave by lot 12 cities
25 9 and his sons and his brethren 12 (and thus throughout the rest of this chapter)
2 Pa 4 4 the sea itself was set upon the 12 oxen
15 one sea and 12 oxen under the sea
9 19 moreover 12 other little lions standing
1 Es 6 17 for a sin offering . . . 12 he goats
8 24 separated 12 of the chief of the priests
35 twelve calves for all the people of
35 seven lambs, and 12 he goats for sin
2 Es 5 14 for 12 years I and my brethren did not
Eccu 44 26 divided him his portion in 12 tribes
49 12 may the bones of the 12 prophets spring
Jer 52 20 twelve oxen of brass that were under
21 a cord of 12 cubits compassed it
Eze 43 16 Ariel was 12 cubits long and 12 cubits
47 13 according to the 12 tribes of Israel
Dan 4 26 at the end of 12 months he was walking
14 2 twelve great measures of fine flour
1 Ma 1 8 Alexander reigned 12 years, and he died
Mat 9 20 with an issue of blood 12 years, came
10 1 having called his 12 disciples
2 the names of the 12 apostles are: The
5 these 12 Jesus sent: commanding them
11 1 an end of commanding his 12 disciples
14 20 twelve full baskets. Mark 6:43
19 28 you also shall sit on 12 seats judging the 12 tribes of Israel
20 17 took the 12 disciples apart and said
26 14 then went one of the 12, who was called
20 he sat down with his 12 disciples. And
47 Judas, one of the 12, came and with
53 more than 12 legions of angels? How
Mark 3 14 he made that 12 should be with him
4 10 the 12 that were with him asked him
5 25 under an issue of blood 12 years and
42 walked: and she was 12 years old: and
6 7 he called the 12; and began to send
8 19 took you up? They say to him, Twelve
9 34 sitting down, he called the 12, and
10 32 taking again the 12, he began to tell
11 11 he went out to Bethania with the twelve
14 10 Iscariot, one of the t. 43; 22:3
17 was come, he cometh with the twelve
20 one of the 12 who dippeth with me his
Luke 2 42 when he was 12 years old, they going
6 13 he chose 12 of them, whom also he
8 1 and the 12 were with him: and certain
42 daughter almost 12 years old, and she
43 having an issue of blood 12 years, who
9 1 calling together the 12 apostles, he
12 the 12 came and said to him: Send away
17 that remained to them 12 baskets. And
18 31 Jesus took unto him the 12 and said
22 14 he sat down, and the 12 apostles with
30 judging the 12 tribes of Israel. And
47 Judas, one of the 12, went before them
John 6 13 filled 12 baskets with the fragments
68 Jesus said to the 12: Will you also go
71 have not I chosen you 12; and one of
72 him whereas he was one of the twelve
11 9 are there not 12 hours of the day? If
20 24 Thomas, one of the 12, who is called
Acts 6 2 the 12 calling together the multitude
7 8 and Jacob [begot] the 12 patriarchs
19 7 and all the men were about twelve. And
24 11 there are yet but 12 days since I
26 7 our 12 tribes, serving night and day
James 1 1 to the 12 tribes which are scattered
Apoc 12 1 on her head a crown of 12 stars: and
21 12 great and high, having 12 gates, and
12 in the gates 12 angels, and names
12 which are the names of the 12 tribes
14 wall of the city had 12 foundations
14 in them the 12 names of the 12 apostles
21 the 12 gates are 12 pearls, one to each
22 2 the tree of life, bearing 12 fruits
13 Gen 17 25 Ismael his son was full 13 years old
Num 29 13 thirteen calves of the herd, two rams
14 to every calf, being in all 13 calves
Josu 19 6 thirteen cities and their villages
21 4 Simeon, and of Benjamin, 13 cities
6 tribe of Manasses in Basan, 13 cities
19 all the cities . . . were thirteen. 33
3 K 7 1 Solomon built his own house in 13 years
1 Pa 6 60 all their cities . . . were thirteen
62 to the sons of Gerson . . . 13 cities
26 11 sons and the brethren of Hosa were 13
Eze 40 11 and the length of the gate 13 cubits
14 Gen 31 41 twenty years, 14 for thy daughters
Gen 46 22 sons of Rachel . . . all the souls 14
Num 29 13 and 14 lambs of a year old. 17, 20, 23, 26, 29, 32
15 to every lamb, being in all 14 lambs

Josu 15 36 14 cities and their villages. 18:28
3 K 8 65 7 days and 7 days, that is 14 days
1 Pa 25 5 gave to Heman 14 sons and 3 daughters
2 Pa 13 21 Abia . . . took 14 wives: and begot
Eze 43 17 brim was 14 cubits long and 14 cubits
Mat 1 17 are fourteen generations. And from
2 C 12 2 I know a man in Christ above 14 years
Gal 2 1 then, after fourteen years, I went up
15 Gen 7 20 the water was 15 cubits higher than
Exod 27 14 for one side hangings of 15 cubits
15 there shall be hangings of 15 cubits
38 14 fifteen cubits of which were on one side
15 were hangings equally of 15 cubits
Lev 27 7 old or upward shall give 15 sicles
2 K 9 10 and Siba and 15 sons and 20 servants
19 17 his 15 sons, and 20 servants were with
3 K 7 3 and one row had 15 pillars, set one
4 K 14 17 after the death of Joas . . . 15 years. 2 Pa 25:25
20 6 will add to thy days 15 years. Isa 38:5
Eze 45 12 and 20 sicles and 15 sicles make a mna
Osee 3 2 bought her to me for 15 pieces of silver
John 11 18 near Jerusalem, about 15 furlongs off
Acts 27 28 a little further, they found 15 fathoms
Gal 1 18 Peter, and I tarried with him 15 days
16 Gen 37 2 Joseph, when he was 16 years old, was
Gen 46 18 these she bore to Jacob, 16 souls
Exod 26 25 and their silver sockets 16, reckoning
36 30 they had 16 sockets of silver, to wit
Josu 15 41 16 cities, and their villages. 19:22
4 K 13 10 reigned . . . in Samaria 16 years
14 21 took Azarias, who was 16 years old
15 2 was 16 years old when he began to reign. 2 Pa 26:3
33 he reigned 16 years. 16:2; 2 Pa 27:1, 8; 28:1
1 Pa 4 27 sons of Semei were 16, and 6 daughters
24 4 of the sons of Eleazar 16 chief men
2 Pa 13 21 Abia . . . begot 22 sons and 16 daughters
26 1 took his son Ozias who was 16 years old
17 Gen 47 28 he [Israel] lived in it 17 years
3 K 14 21 he reigned 17 years. 4 K 13:1; 2 Pa 12:13
18 Judg 3 14 served Eglon king of Moab 18 years
Judg 10 8 they were afflicted . . . for 18 years
3 K 7 15 pillar was 18 cubits high. 4 K 25:17; Jer 52:21
4 K 24 8 Joachin was 18 years old when he began
1 Pa 26 9 and their brethren strong men were 18
2 Pa 11 21 for he [Roboam] had married 18 wives
1 Es 8 18 and Sarabias . . . and his brethren 18
Luke 13 4 those 18 upon whom the tower fell in
11 a spirit of infirmity 18 years: and
16 hath bound, lo, those 18 years, be
19 Josu 19 38 nineteen cities and their villages
2 K 2 30 were wanting of David's servants 19 men
20 Gen 18 31 what if 20 be found there? He said
Gen 18 31 will not destroy it for the sake of 20
32 14 20 he goats, 200 ewes, and 20 rams
15 40 kine, and 20 bulls, 20 she asses
37 28 the Ismaelites for 20 pieces of silver
Exod 26 18 twenty shall be in the south side
20 there shall be 20 boards, having 40
27 10 20 pillars with as many sockets. 11
30 13 a sicle hath 20 obols. Lev 27:25; Num 3:47; 18:16; Eze 45:12
36 23 twenty were at the south side southward
25 he made 20 boards. With 40 sockets
38 10 twenty pillars of brass with their
Lev 27 5 a man shall give 20 sicles: a woman ten
Num 11 19 not for one day . . . no nor for 20
Judg 11 33 till you come to Mennith, 20 cities
1 K 14 14 first slaughter . . . was of about 20 men
2 K 3 20 he came to David in Hebron with 20 men
9 10 and Siba had 15 sons and 20 servants
19 17 his 15 sons and 20 servants were with
24 8 after 9 months and 20 days, they came
3 K 4 23 ten fat oxen and 20 out of the pastures
5 11 and 20 measures of the purest oil
9 11 Solomon gave Hiram 20 cities in the
4 K 4 42 of the firstfruits, 20 loaves of barley
1 Es 8 19 Isaias . . . his brethren and his sons 20
27 and 20 cups of gold, of 1,000 solids
Jdth 1 2 side was extended the space of 20 feet
7 11 had kept this watch for full 20 days
Eze 4 10 shall be in weight 20 staters a day
45 12 now 20 sicles and 5 and 20 sicles
Agge 2 17 when you went to a heap of 20 bushels
17 fifty vessels, and they became 20
2 Ma 10 35 twenty young men of them that were
Acts 27 28 who also sounding, found 20 fathoms; and
20 cubits; *see* **cubits**
20 years; *see* **years**
21 4 K 24 18 Sedecias was one and 20 years old. 2 Pa 36:11; Jer 52:1
Dan 10 13 resisted me one and twenty days: and
22 Josu 19 30 twenty-two cities and their villages
Judg 10 3 who judged Israel for 2 and 20 years
3 K 14 20 Jeroboam reigned, were 2 and 20 years
16 29 over Israel in Samaria and 2 and 20 years
4 K 8 26 Ochozias was 2 and 20 years old when
21 19 two and 20 years old was Amon when he
1 Pa 12 28 house of his father, 22 principal men
2 Pa 13 21 begot 2 and 20 sons and 16 daughters
33 21 Amon was 2 and 20 years old when he
2 Ma 13 2 5,000 horsemen, 22 elephants, and
23 Judg 10 2 he judged Israel 3 and 20 years
4 K 23 31 Joachaz was 3 and 20 years. 2 Pa 36:2
1 Pa 2 22 he had 3 and 20 cities in the land of
24 Num 7 88 peace offerings, oxen 24, rams
2 K 21 20 toes on each foot, 4 and 20 in all
3 K 15 33 reigned . . . in Thersa 4 and 20 years
1 Pa 20 6 whose fingers and toes were 4 and 20
Apoc 4 4 about the throne were 4 and 20 seats
4 and upon the seats 4 and 20 ancients
10 the 4 and 20 ancients fell down. 5:8, 14
11 16 the 4 and 20 ancients who sit on their
19 4 the 4 and 20 ancients and the four
25 Num 8 24 from 25 years old and upwards. 1 Es 3:8
3 K 22 42 he reigned 5 and 20 years. 2 Pa 20:31
4 K 14 2 was 5 and 20 years old. 15:33; 18:2; 23:36; 2 Pa 25:1; 27:1, 8; 29:1; 36:5
Eze 8 16 about 5 and 20 men having their backs
11 1 in the entry of the gate 5 and 20 men
40 13 breadth 5 and 20 cubits. 25
21 the porch . . . 5 and 20 cubits. 29, 30, 33, 36
45 12 now 20 sicles and 5 and 20 sicles
John 6 19 five and twenty or thirty furlongs
28 Exod 26 2 of one curtain shall be 28 cubits
Exod 36 9 length of one curtain was 28 cubits
4 K 10 36 Jehu reigned . . . was 8 and 20 years
2 Pa 11 21 he [Roboam] begot 8 and 20 sons
1 Es 8 11 with him [Zacharias] 8 and 20 men
29 Exod 38 24 in gifts was 9 and 20 talents
Josu 15 32 all the cities 29, and their villages
4 K 14 2 9 and 20 years he [Amasias] reigned
18 2 reigned 9 and 20 years. 2 Pa 25:1; 29:1
1 Es 1 9 bowls of silver, 9 and 20 knives, 30 cups
30 Gen 6 15 the height of it 30 cubits. Thou
Gen 11 14 Sale also lived 30 years and begot
18 Phaleg also lived 30 years and begot
22 Sarug lived 30 years, and begot Nachor
18 30 speak: what if 30 shall be found there
30 I will not do it if I find 30 there
32 15 presents . . . 30 milch camels with
41 46 was 30 years old when he stood before
Exod 21 32 he shall give 30 sicles of silver to

26 8 of one hair curtain shall be 30 cubits
36 15 one curtain was 30 cubits long and four
Lev 27 4 if a woman, thirty. But from the
16 be sowed with 30 bushels of barley
Num 4 3 from 30 years old and upward. 23, 30, 35, 39, 43, 47
20 30 mourned for him [Aaron] thirty days
Deut 34 8 mourned for him [Moses] . . . thirty days
Judg 10 4 30 sons that rode on 30 ass colts
4 and were princes of 30 cities, which
12 9 he had 30 sons and as many daughters
14 had 40 sons, and of them 30 grandsons
14 11 they brought him 30 companions to be
12 I will give you 30 shirts, and as many
13 you shall give me 30 shirts and the same
19 down to Ascalon and slew there 30 men
20 31 to Gabaa, and they slew about 30 men
39 vigorously, killing 30 men of their army
1 K 9 22 for there were about 30 men. And
2 K 5 4 David was 30 years old when he began to
23 13 the three who were princes among the 30
23 were the most honorable among the 30
24 the brother of Joab was one of the 30
3 K 4 22 was 30 measures of fine flour, and
6 2 in breadth, and 30 cubits in height
7 2 fifty cubits, and the height 30 cubits
6 in length, and 30 cubits in breadth
23 a line of 30 cubits compassed it round
4 K 18 14 talents of silver and 30 talents of gold
1 Pa 11 11 Jesbaam . . . the chief among the thirty
15 three of the 30 captains went down to
25 [Banaias] and the first among the thirty
42 prince of the Rubenites and 30 with him
12 4 stoutest among the 30 and over the 30
18 came upon Amasai the chief among 30
23 3 were numbered from the age of 30 years
27 6 valiant among the 30 and above the 30
2 Pa 4 2 and a line of 30 cubits compassed it
1 Es 1 9 thirty bowls of gold, 1,000 bowls of
9 thirty cups of gold, silver cups of a
Jdth 1 2 walls thereof . . . thirty cubits high
3 15 and stayed there for 30 days, in which
15 13 and 30 days were scarce sufficient for
Isa 5 10 thirty bushels of seed shall yield
Jer 38 10 take from hence 30 men with thee and
Eze 40 17 thirty chambers encompassed the pavement
46 22 40 cubits long, and 30 broad, all the
Dan 6 7 petition of any god or man for 30 days
12 to any of the gods or men for 30 days
Zach 11 12 for my wages 30 pieces of silver. And
13 I took the 30 pieces of silver, and I
Mat 13 23 another sixty, and another thirty
26 15 appointed him thirty pieces of silver
27 3 brought back the 30 pieces of silver
Mark 4 8 one thirty, another sixty. 20
Luke 3 23 about the age of 30 years; being, as
31 Josu 12 24 Thersa one: all the kings 30 and one
4 K 22 1 reigned one and 30 years. 2 Pa 34:1
32 Gen 11 20 Reu lived 32 years and begot Sarug
Num 31 40 to the portion of the Lord, 32 souls
3 K 20 1 there were 2 and 30 kings with him
16 drinking . . . and the 2 and 30 kings
22 31 commanded the 2 and 30 captains of the
4 K 8 17 was 2 and 30 years old when. 2 Pa 21:5, 20
1 Ma 6 30 and 32 elephants trained to battle
37 and upon every one 32 valiant men
33 Gen 46 15 souls of her sons and daughters, 33
Lev 12 4 she shall remain 3 and 30 days in the
2 K 5 5 he reigned 3 and 30 years. 1 Pa 3:4
3 K 2 11 he reigned 7 years, in Jerusalem 33
1 Pa 29 27 years, and in Jerusalem 3 and 30 years
Eze 41 6 side chambers . . . twice thirty-three
34 Gen 11 16 Heber lived 34 years and begot Phaleg
35 Gen 11 12 Arphaxad lived 35 years and begot
3 K 22 42 was 5 and 30 years old. 2 Pa 20:31
2 Pa 3 15 pillars which were 5 and 30 cubits high
36 Josu 7 5 there fell of them 6 and 30 men
37 2 K 23 39 Urias the Hethite, 30 and 7 in all
38 Deut 2 14 that we journeyed . . . was 38 years
John 5 5 that had been eight and thirty years
40 Gen 7 4 upon the earth 40 days and 40 nights. 12
Gen 18 29 if 40 be found there, what wilt thou
29 will not destroy it for the sake of 40
32 15 milch camels with their colts, 40 kine
Exod 24 18 he was there 40 days and 40 nights
26 19 40 sockets of silver. 21; 36:24, 26
34 28 with the Lord 40 days and 40 nights
Deut 25 3 that they exceed not the number of 40
Judg 12 14 and he [Abdon] had 40 sons, and of them
3 K 6 17 temple itself . . . was 40 cubits long
4 K 8 9 the burdens of forty camels. And
2 Es 5 15 and in money every day 40 sicles: and
Eze 41 2 measured the length thereof 40 cubits
46 22 little courts disposed, 40 cubits long
Dan 14 2 forty sheep and sixty vessels of wine
Mat 4 2 had fasted 40 days and 40 nights
Acts 23 13 they were more than forty men that had
21 lie in wait for him more than 40 men
2 C 11 24 five times did I receive forty stripes
40 days Gen 7 4 I will rain upon the earth forty days and forty nights
Gen 7 12 rain fell . . . 40 days and 40 nights
17 flood was forty days upon the earth
8 6 after that forty days were passed, Noe
50 3 there passed forty days: for this was
Exod 24 18 he was there forty days and forty
34 28 with the Lord 40 days and 40 nights
Num 13 26 they . . . returned after forty days
14 34 forty days wherein you viewed the land
Deut 9 9 I continued in the mount 40 days and
11 when forty days were passed
18 forty days and nights neither eating
25 I lay prostrate . . . 40 days and nights
10 10 I stood in the mount . . . 40 days and
1 K 17 16 and presented himself forty days
3 K 19 8 in the strength of that food 40 days
Eze 4 6 iniquity of the house of Juda 40 days
Jon 3 4 forty days, and Ninive shall be
2 Ma 5 2 space of forty days there were seen
Mat 4 2 fasted forty days and forty nights
Mark 1 13 he was in the desert 40 days and 40
Luke 4 2 the desert for the space of 40 days
Acts 1 3 for forty days appearing to them
41 3 K 14 21 was one and 40 years old. 2 Pa 12:13
3 K 15 10 he [Asa] reigned one and forty years
4 K 14 23 reigned Jeroboam . . . one and 40 years
42 Num 35 6 there shall be other 42 cities, that
4 K 2 24 forest, and tore of them 2 and 40 boys
10 14 at the pit by the cabin, 2 and 40 men
2 Pa 22 2 Ochozias was 42 years old when he began
1 Es 2 24 the children of Azmaveth 42. The
2 Es 7 28 the men of Bethazomth 42. The men of
Tob 14 1 to his sight, he lived 2 and 40 years
Apoc 11 2 tread under foot two and forty months
13 5 to him to do two and forty months. And
45 Gen 18 28 wilt thou for 5 and 40 destroy the
Gen 18 28 I will not destroy it if I find 5 and 40
Josu 14 10 it is 40 and 5 years since the Lord
3 K 7 3 it was held up with 5 and 40 pillars
Tob 1 24 after 45 days, the king was killed
46 John 2 20 six and forty years was this temple
48 Num 35 7 in all 48 with their suburbs. And of
Josu 21 39 the cities of the Levites . . . were 48
49 Lev 25 8 which together make 49 years: and
Dan 3 47 above the furnace 9 and 40 cubits
50 Gen 18 24 if there be 50 just men in the city

Gen 18 24 that place for the sake of the 50 just
26 if I find in Sodom 50 just within the
28 if there be 5 less than 50 just
Exod 26 5 every curtain shall have 50 loops
6 shalt make also 50 rings of gold
10 thou shalt make also 50 loops in the
10 and 50 loops in the edge of the other
11 thou shalt make also 50 buckles of brass
36 13 whereupon also he cast 50 rings of gold
17 he made 50 loops in the edge of one
17 and 50 in the edge of another curtain
18 and 50 buckles of brass wherewith the
Lev 23 16 full weeks . . . that is to say 50 days
27 3 he shall give 50 sicles of silver
16 let it be sold for 50 sicles of silver
Num 4 3 from thirty . . . to fifty years old. 23, 30, 35, 39, 43, 47
Deut 22 29 father of the maid 50 sicles of silver
Josu 7 21 of silver, and a golden rule of 50 sicles
2 K 15 1 and 50 men to run before him. 24:24
24 24 and the oxen for 50 sicles of silver
3 K 18 4 by 50 and 50 in caves. 13
4 K 1 9 he sent to him a captain of 50, and the 50 men that were under him
10 said to the captain of fifty: If I
10 consume thee and thy fifty. 12
10 consumed him and the 50 that were with
11 captain of 50 men and his 50 with him
12 fire . . . consume him and his fifty
12 fire . . . consumed him and his fifty
13 captain of 50 men, and the 50 that were
14 consumed the two first captains of 50
2 7 and 50 men of the sons of the prophets
16 are with thy servants 50 strong men
17 they sent 50 men: and they sought three
13 7 left of the people than 50 horsemen
15 20 tax . . . each man 50 sicles of silver
25 50 men of the sons of the Galaadites
2 Pa 3 9 the weight of every nail was 50 sicles
1 Es 8 6 son of Jonathan, and with him 50 men
2 Es 7 70 50 bowls and 530 garments for priests
Isa 3 3 the captain over 50 and the honorable
Agge 2 17 to press out 50 vessels, and they
1 Ma 9 61 authors of the mischief, 50 men, and
Luke 7 41 owed 500 pence, and the other 50
16 6 and sit down quickly and write fifty
John 8 57 thou art not yet fifty years old, and
50 cubits; *see* **cubits**
52 4 K 15 2 reigned 2 and 50 years. 2 Pa 26:3
1 Es 2 29 the children of Nebo 52. The children
2 Es 6 15 wall was finished . . . in 2 and 50 days
7 33 the men of the other Nebo 52. The
55 4 K 21 1 [Manasses] reigned 5 and 50 years
2 Pa 33 1 [Manasses] reigned 55 years in Jerusalem
56 1 Es 2 22 the men of Netupha 56. The men
Tob 14 3 he was 6 and 50 years old when he lost
60 Gen 25 26 Isaac was threescore years old
Lev 27 2 from 20 years old unto 60 years old
7 a man that is 60 years old or upward
Num 7 88 peace offerings, rams 60, buck goats 60, lambs of a year old 60
Deut 3 4 sixty cities, all the country of Argob
Josu 13 30 which are in Basan, threescore towns
3 K 4 13 threescore great cities with walls
22 flour and threescore measures of meal
6 2 was threescore cubits in length
4 K 25 19 threescore men of the common people
1 Pa 2 21 wife when he was threescore years old
23 the villages thereof, threescore cities
2 Pa 3 3 length by the first measure 60 cubits
11 21 wives and threescore concubines
21 sons and threescore daughters. But
1 Es 6 3 support the height of threescore cubits and the breadth of threescore cubits
8 13 sons of Adonicam . . . with them 60 men
Tob 14 3 and 60 when he recovered it again
Cant 3 7 threescore valiant ones of the most
6 7 there are threescore queens and
Jer 52 25 threescore men of the people of the
Eze 40 14 he made also fronts of 60 cubits: and
Dan 3 1 a statue of gold of 60 cubits high
14 2 forty sheep and 60 vessels of wine
1 Ma 7 16 he took threescore of them and slew
Mat 13 23 one an hundredfold, and another sixty
Mark 4 8 one thirty, another sixty. 20
Luke 24 13 which was 60 furlongs from Jerusalem
1 Tim 5 9 of no less than threescore years of age
61 Num 31 39 out of the 30,500 asses, 61 asses
62 1 Pa 26 8 men for service, 62 of Obededom
Dan 5 31 being threescore and two years old
9 25 there shall be 7 weeks and 62 weeks
26 after 62 weeks Christ shall be slain
65 Gen 5 15 Malaleel lived 65 years and begot
Gen 5 21 Henoch lived 65 years and begot
Isa 7 8 within threescore and five years
66 Gen 46 26 that went with Jacob . . . sixty-six
Lev 12 5 the blood of her purification 66 days
67 2 Es 7 72 gave . . . 67 garments for priests
68 1 Pa 16 38 and Obededom, with his brethren 68
70 Gen 4 24 for Lamech seventy times sevenfold
Gen 5 12 Cainan lived 70 years and begot
11 26 Thare lived 70 years and begot Abram
46 27 that entered into Egypt were 70
50 3 and Egypt mourned for him 70 days
Exod 1 5 out of Jacob's thigh, were 70: but
15 27 fountains of water and 70 palm trees
24 1 and 70 of the ancients, and you
9 70 of the ancients of Israel went up
Num 7 13 a silver bowl of 70 sicles. 19, 25, 31, 37, 43, 49, 55, 61, 67, 73, 79
85 each bowl [weighing] 70 sicles, that is
11 16 gather unto me 70 men of the ancients
24 and assembled 70 men of the ancients
25 in Moses, and giving to the 70 men
33 9 fountains of waters and 70 palm trees
Deut 10 22 in 70 souls thy fathers went down
Judg 1 7 said: 70 kings having their fingers
8 30 he [Gedeon] had 70 sons, who came out
9 2 that 70 men all the sons of Jerobaal
4 and they gave him 70 weight of silver
5 brethren the sons of Jerobaal, 70 men
18 killed his sons 70 men upon one stone
24 the murder of the 70 sons of Jerobaal
56 Abimelech . . . killing his 70 brethren
12 14 grandsons, mounted upon 70 ass colts
1 K 6 19 and he slew of the people 70 men, and
4 K 10 1 Achab had 70 sons in Samaria: so Jehu
6 the king's sons, being 70 men, were
2 Pa 29 32 was 70 bullocks, 100 rams, and two
36 21 sabbath, till the 70 years were expired
1 Es 8 7 Athalias, and with him [Isaias] 70 men
14 Uthai and Zachur, and with them 70 men
Jdth 1 2 made the walls thereof 70 cubits broad
Ps 89 10 in them are threescore and ten years
Isa 23 15 O Tyre, shalt be forgotten 70 years
15 after 70 years, there shall be unto
17 after 70 years, that the Lord will
Jer 25 11 serve the king of Babylon 70 years
12 when the 70 years shall be expired
29 10 when the 70 years shall begin to be
Eze 8 11 and 70 men of the ancients of the
41 12 was 70 cubits broad: and the wall of
Dan 9 2 that 70 years should be accomplished
24 seventy weeks are shortened upon thy
14 9 the priests of Bel were 70, besides
Zach 7 5 for these 70 years: did you keep a

Mat 18 22 but till seventy times seven times
Acts 23 23 make ready . . . seventy horsemen, and 200
72 Num 31 38 out of the 36,000 oxen, 72 oxen
Luke 10 1 appointed also other 72 and he sent
17 the 72 returned with joy, saying: Lord
74 1 Es 2 40 children of Odovia 74. The singing
2 Es 7 44 sons of Oduia, 74. The singing men
75 Gen 12 4 Abram was 75 years old when he went
Acts 7 14 and all his kindred, 75 souls. So
77 Judg 8 14 and he described unto him 77 men
1 Es 8 35 77 lambs and 12 he goats for sin
80 Exod 7 7 Moses was 80 years old, and Aaron
Judg 3 30 Israel: and the land rested 80 years
2 K 19 32 Berzellai . . . fourscore years old, and
35 I am this day fourscore years old
4 K 6 25 was sold for fourscore pieces of silver
10 24 Jehu had prepared him fourscore men
1 Pa 15 9 Eliel the chief: and his brethren 80
1 Es 8 8 son of Michael, and with him 80 men
Ps 89 10 in the strong they be fourscore years
Cant 6 7 queens, and fourscore concubines and
Jer 41 5 fourscore men with their beards shaven
2 Ma 4 8 out of other revenues fourscore talents
11 4 horsemen and his fourscore elephants
Luke 16 7 take thy bill and write eighty. And
83 Exod 7 7 Moses was 80 years old, and Aaron 83
85 Josu 14 10 this day I am 85 years old, as strong
1 K 22 18 eighty-five men that wore the linen
90 Gen 5 9 Enos lived 90 years, and begot Cainan
Gen 17 17 shall Sara that is 90 years old bring
Eze 41 12 the wall . . . ninety cubits long. And
2 Ma 6 24 at the age of fourscore and ten years
8 11 should have 90 slaves for one talent
95 1 Es 2 20 the children of Gebbar 95. The
2 Es 7 25 the children of Gabaon 95. The
96 1 Es 8 35 96 rams, 77 lambs, and 12 he goats
Jer 52 23 there were 96 pomegranates hanging
98 1 K 4 15 Heli was 98 years old and his eyes
1 Es 2 16 of Ather who were of Ezechias, 98
2 Es 7 21 of Ater, children of Hezechias, 98
99 Gen 17 1 began to be 90 and 9 years old
Gen 17 24 Abraham was 90 and 9 years old when
Tob 14 16 after he had lived 99 years in the
Mat 18 12 doth he not leave the 99. Luke 15:4
13 than for the 99 that went not astray
Luke 15 7 more than upon 99 just who need not
100 Gen 11 10 Sem was 100 years old when he
Gen 17 17 be born to him that is 100 years old
21 5 when he was 100 years old: for at this
33 19 he bought that part . . . for 100 lambs
Exod 38 26 were moreover 100 talents of silver
27 100 sockets were made of 100 talents
Lev 26 8 five of yours shall pursue 100 others
8 and 100 of you [shall pursue] 10,000
Deut 22 19 condemning him besides in 100 sicles
Josu 24 32 had bought . . . for 100 young ewes
Judg 20 10 we will take 10 men of 100 . . . and 100 out of 1,000
1 K 18 25 only 100 foreskins of the Philistines
25 18 100 clusters of raisins and 200 cakes
2 K 3 14 whom I espoused to me for 100 foreskins
8 4 only reserved of them for 100 chariots
16 1 100 bunches of raisins, 100 cakes of
3 K 4 23 and 100 rams, besides venison of harts
7 2 the length of it was 100 cubits, and
18 4 he took 100 prophets and hid them by
13 how I hid 100 men of the prophets of
4 K 4 43 that I should set it before 100 men
23 23 fine upon the land, of 100 talents of
1 Pa 12 14 least of them was captain over 100
18 4 100 chariots, which he reserved for
21 3 the Lord make his people 100 times more
2 Pa 3 16 100 pomegranates which he put between
4 8 100 bowls of gold. He made also
25 6 valiant men for 100 talents of silver
9 will then become of the 100 talents
27 5 him at that time 100 talents of silver
29 32 70 bullocks, 100 rams and 200 lambs
36 3 condemned the land in 100 talents of
1 Es 2 69 and 100 garments for the priests
6 17 100 calves, 200 rams, and 400 lambs
7 22 without delay, unto 100 talents of silver and unto 100 cores of wheat and unto 100 bates of wine and unto 100 bates of oil
8 26 100 vessels of silver and 100 talents
Jdth 7 10 round about 100 men at every spring
Prov 17 10 wise man than 100 stripes with a fool
Ecce 6 3 if a man beget 100 children and live
8 12 but though a sinner do evil 100 times
Eccu 18 8 days of men at the most are 100 years
41 6 whether 10 or 100 or 1,000 years
Isa 65 20 child shall die 100 years old, and the sinner being 100 years old shall be
Jer 52 23 the pomegranates being 100 in all
Amos 5 3 there shall be left in it 100: and out of which there came 100
1 Ma 13 16 now send 100 talents of silver and his
19 sent the children and the 100 talents
15 35 for these we will give 100 talents
Mat 18 12 if a man have an hundred sheep, and
28 that owed him an hundred pence
Mark 4 8 another sixty, and another a h. 20
10 30 who shall not receive an h. times as
Luke 15 4 that hath an hundred sheep: and if
16 6 he said: An hundred barrels of oil
7 said: An hundred quarters of wheat
John 19 39 aloes, about an hundred pound weight
Rom 4 19 whereas he was almost an h. years old
100 cubits; *see* **cubits**
102 Tob 14 2 after he had lived 102 years, he
105 Gen 5 6 Seth also lived 105 years and begot
Jdth 16 28 her husband's house 105 years and
110 Gen 50 22 [Joseph] lived 110 years. And he saw
Gen 50 25 died being 110 years old. Josu 24:29; Judg 2:8
1 Es 8 12 Eccetan, and with him Joanan 110 men
112 1 Pa 15 10 the chief: and his brethren 112
1 Es 2 18 the children of Jora 112. The children
2 Es 7 24 children of Hareph 112. The children
119 Gen 11 25 Nachor lived . . . 119 years: and begot
120 Gen 6 3 and his days shall be 120 years
Num 7 86 in all 120 sicles of gold. 12 oxen out
Deut 31 2 I am this day 120 years old. I can no
34 7 Moses was 120 years old when he died
3 K 9 14 Hiram sent to king Solomon 120 talents
10 10 she gave the king 120 talents of gold
1 Pa 15 5 was the chief, and his brethren 120
2 Pa 3 4 the height was 120 cubits: and he
5 12 120 priests, sounding with trumpets
9 9 she gave to the king 120 talents of
Dan 6 1 over the kingdom 120 governors to be
1 Ma 8 6 against them, having 120 elephants
Acts 1 15 of persons together was about 120
122 1 Es 2 27 the men of Machmas 122. 2 Es 7:31
123 Num 33 39 when he [Aaron] was 123 years old
1 Es 2 21 the children of Bethlehem 123. The men
2 Es 7 32 the men of Bethel and Hai 123. The men
127 Gen 23 1 Sara lived 127 years. And she died
128 1 Es 2 23 the men of Anathoth 128. 2 Es 7:27
1 Es 2 41 singing men: the children of Asaph 128
2 Es 11 14 brethren who were very mighty 128
130 Gen 5 3 Adam lived 130 years and begot
Gen 47 9 days of my pilgrimage are 130 years
Num 7 13 a silver dish weighing 130 sicles. 19, 25, 31, 37, 43, 49, 55, 61, 67, 73, 79
85 each dish weighing 130 sicles of silver

1 Pa 15 7 Joel the chief, and his brethren 130
2 Pa 24 15 Joiada . . . died when he was 130 years
133 Exod 6 18 years of Caath's life were 133
137 Gen 25 17 years of Ismael's life were 137
Exod 6 16 years of the life of Levi were 137
20 the years of Amram's life were 137
138 2 Es 7 46 the children of Sobai: 138
139 1 Es 2 42 children of Sobai: in all 139
140 Job 42 16 lived after these things 140 years
144 Apoc 21 17 measured wall thereof 144 cubits
147 Gen 47 28 days of his life came to 147 years
148 2 Es 7 45 the children of Asaph 148. The
2 Ma 11 21 fare ye well. In the year 148. 33, 38
149 1 Ma 6 16 Antiochus died there in year 149
2 Ma 13 1 in the year 149, Judas understood
150 Gen 7 24 the waters prevailed . . . 150 days
Gen 8 3 they began to be abated after 150 days
3 K 10 29 silver, and a horse for 150. 2 Pa 1:17
1 Pa 8 40 many sons and grandsons, even to 150
1 Es 8 3 and with him were numbered 150 men
1 Ma 6 20 besieged them in the year 150, and they
2 Ma 4 9 he promised also 150 more if he might
14 4 came to king Demetrius in the year 150
153 1 Ma 9 54 in the year 153, the second month
John 21 11 full of great fishes, 153. And
156 1 Es 2 30 the children of Megbis 156. The
160 1 Es 8 10 and with him [Selomith] 160 men
1 Ma 10 21 the year one hundred and threescore
162 Gen 5 18 Jared lived 162 years and begot
165 1 Ma 10 67 in the year 165 Demetrius . . . came
169 2 Ma 1 7 Demetrius reigned in the year 169
170 1 Ma 13 41 in the year 170 the yoke of the
171 1 Ma 13 51 the second month in the year 171
172 2 Es 11 19 brethren, who kept the doors: 172
1 Ma 14 1 in the year 172, king Demetrius
27 of the month Elul, in the year 172
174 1 Ma 15 10 in the year 174 Antiochus entered
175 Gen 25 7 of Abraham's life were 175 years
177 1 Ma 16 14 the year 177, the eleventh month
180 Gen 35 28 the days of Isaac were 180 years
182 Gen 5 28 Lamech lived 182 years and begot
187 Gen 5 25 Mathusala lived 187 years and
188 2 Es 7 26 of Bethlehem and Netupha 188
2 Ma 1 10 in the year 188 the people that is
200 Gen 11 23 after he begot Nachor, 200 years
Gen 32 14 200 she goats, 20 he goats, 200 ewes
Josu 7 21 and 200 sicles of silver, and a golden
Judg 17 4 she took 200 pieces of silver and gave
1 K 18 27 he slew of the Philistines 200 men
25 13 and 200 remained with the baggage
18 Abigail made haste and took 200 loaves
18 and 200 cakes of dry figs and laid them
30 10 for 200 stayed, who being weary could
21 David came to the 200 men, who being
2 K 14 26 he weighed the hair . . . at 200 sicles
15 11 there went with Absalom 200 men out of
16 1 asses, laden with 200 loaves of bread
3 K 7 20 of pomegranates there were 200 in rows
10 16 Solomon made 200 shields of the purest
1 Pa 12 32 sons of Issachar . . . 200 principal men
15 8 Semeias the chief: and his brethren 200
2 Pa 9 15 and king Solomon made 200 golden spears
29 32 70 bullocks, 100 rams, and 200 lambs
1 Es 2 65 them singing men and singing women 200
6 17 they offered . . . 100 calves, 200 rams
8 4 of Zareha, and with him 200 men
Cant 8 12 and 200 for them that keep the fruit
Eze 45 15 and one ram out of a flock of 200
2 Ma 3 11 talents of silver, and 200 of gold
12 4 they drowned no fewer than 200 of them
Mark 6 37 let us go and buy bread for 200 pence
John 6 7 200 pennyworth of bread is not
21 8 the land, but as it were 200 cubits

Acts 23 23 make ready 200 soldiers to go as far as
23 ready . . . 200 spearmen for the third
205 Gen 11 32 days of Thare were 205 years
207 Gen 11 21 after he begot Sarug, 207 years
209 Gen 11 19 after he begot Ru, 209 years
212 1 Pa 9 22 porters at the gates, were 212
218 1 Es 8 9 son of Jahiel, and with him 218 men
220 1 Pa 15 6 Asaia the chief, and his brethren 220
1 Es 8 20 Nathinites 220: all these were called
223 1 Es 2 19 the children of Hasum 223. The
1 Es 2 28 the men of Bethel and Hai 223. The
232 3 K 20 15 the number of 232: and he mustered
240 2 Ma 12 9 seen at Jerusalem 240 furlongs off
242 2 Es 11 13 the chiefs of the fathers: 242
245 1 Es 2 66 their mules 245. 2 Es 7:68
2 Es 7 67 them singing men and singing women 245
250 Exod 30 23 of cinnamon . . . 250 sicles, of calamus
in like manner 250
Num 16 2 up against Moses, and with them 250
17 offering to the Lord 250 censers
35 destroyed the 250 men that offered
26 10 when the fire burned 250 men. And there
2 Pa 8 10 captains of king Solomon's army were 250
Eze 48 17 of the city shall be to the . . . 250
273 Num 3 46 for the price of the 273, of the
276 Acts 27 37 we were in all in ship, 276 souls
284 2 Es 11 18 Levites in the holy city were 284
288 1 Pa 25 7 all the teachers, were 288. And they
300 Gen 5 22 after he begot Methusala 300 years
Gen 6 15 length of the ark shall be 300 cubits
45 22 Benjamin he gave 300 pieces of silver
Judg 7 6 hand to their mouth, was 300 men
7 by the 300 men that lapped water I
8 with the 300 gave himself to the battle
16 he divided the 300 men into 3 parts
19 Gedeon and the 300 men that were with
22 the 300 men nevertheless persisted
8 4 he passed over it with the 300 men
11 36 cities near the Jordan for 300 years
15 4 caught 300 foxes and coupled them
2 K 21 16 iron of whose spear weighed 300 ounces
23 18 his spear against 300 whom he slew
3 K 5 16 and 300 that ruled over the people
10 17 and 300 targets of fine gold: 300 pounds
11 3 wives as queens, and 300 concubines
4 K 18 14 a tax . . . of 300 talents of silver
1 Pa 11 11 lifted up his spear against 300. 20
2 Pa 9 16 300 golden shields of 300 pieces of gold
14 9 of 1,000,000 men and with 30 chariots
35 8 phase 2,600 small cattle and 300 oxen
1 Es 8 5 and with him [Sechenias] 300 men
1 Ma 11 28 and he promised him 300 talents
2 Ma 4 19 men to carry 300 didrachmas of silver
24 more than Jason by 300 talents of
13 2 and 300 chariots armed with hooks
Mark 14 5 been sold for more than 300 pence and
John 12 5 this ointment sold for 300 pence, and
303 Gen 11 13 after he begot Sale, 303 years
318 Gen 14 14 servants born in his house, 318
320 1 Es 2 32 the children of Harim 320. The
2 Es 7 35 the children of Harem 320. The
323 1 Es 2 17 the children of Besai 323. The
324 2 Es 7 23 the children of Besai 324. The
328 2 Es 7 22 the children of Hasem 328. The
345 1 Es 2 34 children of Jericho 345. 2 Es 7:36
350 Gen 9 28 lived after the flood 350 years
360 2 K 2 31 with Abner 360, who all died
2 Ma 4 8 promising him 360 talents of silver
365 Gen 5 23 the days of Henoch were 365 years
372 1 Es 2 4 children of Sephatia 372. 2 Es 7:9
390 Eze 4 5 the number of the days 390 days
Eze 4 9 390 days shalt thou eat thereof
392 1 Es 2 58 the Nathinites . . . 392. 2 Es 7:60

400 Gen 15 13 shall . . . afflict them 400 years
Gen 23 15 is worth 400 sicles of silver: this is
16 weighed out . . . 400 sicles of silver
32 6 with speed to meet thee with 400 men
33 1 saw Esau coming, and with him 400 men
Exod 38 29 72,000 talents and 400 sicles besides
Judg 21 12 found of Jabes Galaad 400 virgins that
1 K 22 2 there were with him about 400 men
25 13 there followed David about 400 men
30 10 but David pursued, he and 400 men: for
17 but 400 young men who had gotten upon
3 K 7 42 400 pomegranates for the two networks
18 19 and the prophets of the groves 400
22 6 assembled the prophets, about 400 men
4 K 14 13 to the gate of the corner, 400 cubits
2 Pa 4 13 and 400 pomegranates, and 2 wreaths of
18 5 of the prophets 400 men, and he said
25 23 broke down the walls . . . 400 cubits
1 Es 6 17 they offered . . . 200 rams, 400 lambs
Jdth 5 9 Egypt, and there for 400 years were so
2 Ma 3 11 the whole was 400 talents of silver
12 33 with 3,000 footmen and 400 horsemen
Acts 5 36 to whom a number of men, about 400
7 6 bondage, and treat them evil 400 years
403 Gen 11 15 after he begot Heber 403 years
410 1 Es 1 10 silver cups of a second sort, 410
420 3 K 9 28 they brought . . . 420 talents of gold
430 Gen 11 17 after he begot Phaleg 430 years
Exod 12 40 abode . . . in Egypt was 430 years
Gal 3 17 the law which was made after 430 years
435 1 Es 2 67 their camels 435, their. 2 Es 7:69
450 3 K 18 19 and the prophets of Baal 450
2 Pa 8 18 they took thence 450 talents of gold
453 Acts 13 20 as it were, after 453 years: and
454 1 Es 2 15 the children of Adin 454. The
468 2 Es 11 6 were 468 valiant men. And these
500 Gen 5 31 Noe, when he was 500 years old
Gen 11 11 after he begot Arphaxad 500 years
Exod 30 23 principal and chosen myrrh 500 sicles
24 of cassia 500 sicles by the weight of
Num 31 28 one soul of 500 as well of persons as
1 Pa 4 42 of Simeon, 500 men, went into mount
2 Pa 35 9 phase 5,000 small cattle and 500 oxen
Job 1 3 500 yoke of oxen and 500 she asses
Eze 42 16 he measured . . . 500 reeds. 17, 18, 19
20 wall . . . 500 cubits long and 500
45 2 on every side 500 by 500, foursquare
1 Ma 6 35 and 500 horsemen set in order were
15 31 give me for them 500 talents of silver
31 tributes of the cities other 500 talents
2 Ma 12 10 and 500 horsemen of the Arabians
14 39 sent 500 soldiers to take him. For he
Luke 7 41 the one owed 500 pence, and the other
1 C 15 6 was he seen by more than 500 brethren
530 2 Es 7 70 to bowls and 530 garments for priests
550 3 K 9 23 were 550 chief officers set over
595 Gen 5 30 after he begot Noe 595 years
600 Gen 7 6 he [Noe] was 600 years old when the
Exod 14 7 he took 600 chosen chariots, and all
Judg 3 31 who slew of the Philistines 600 men
18 11 600 men, furnished with arms for war
16 the 600 men stood before the door
17 the 600 valiant men waiting not far
27 the 600 men took the priest, and the
20 47 only 600 men that were able to escape
1 K 13 15 were found with him, about 600 men
14 2 people with him were about 600 men
17 7 head of his spear weighed 600 sicles
23 13 David and his men, who were about 600
27 2 went away, both he and the 600 men
30 9 so David went, he and the 600 men that
2 K 15 18 warriors, 600 men who had followed him
3 K 10 16 he allowed 600 sicles of gold for the
29 a chariot . . . for 600 sicles of silver
1 Pa 21 25 Ornan for the place 600 sicles of gold
2 Pa 1 17 chariot of 4 horses for 600 pieces of
3 8 gold, amounting to about 600 talents
9 15 of the sum of 600 pieces of gold
29 33 they consecrated to the Lord 600 oxen
1 Ma 6 42 there fell of the king's army 600 men
2 Ma 10 31 were slain 20,500 and 600 horsemen
12 29 lieth 600 furlongs from Jerusalem
621 1 Es 2 26 the children of Rama and Gabaa 621
2 Es 7 30 the men of Rama and Geba 621. The men
623 1 Es 2 11 the children of Bebai 623. The
628 2 Es 7 16 the children of Bebai 628. The
642 1 Es 2 10 the children of Bani 642. The
2 Es 7 62 the children of Necoda 642. And of
648 2 Es 7 15 the children of Banni 648. The
650 1 Es 8 26 weighed to their hands 650 talents
652 1 Es 2 60 the children of Necoda 652. And of
2 Es 7 10 the children of Area 652. The
655 2 Es 7 20 the children of Adin 655. The
666 3 K 10 14 weight . . . was 666 talents. 2 Pa 9:13
1 Es 2 13 the children of Adonicam 666. The
Apoc 13 18 of a man: and the number is 666
667 2 Es 7 18 the children of Adonicam 667. The
675 Num 31 37 portion of the Lord . . . 675 sheep
690 1 Pa 9 6 Jehuel and their brethren, 690
700 Judg 20 16 who were 700 most valiant men
2 K 10 18 of the Syrians the men of 700 chariots
3 K 11 3 [Solomon] had 700 wives as queens
4 K 3 26 he took with him 700 men that drew the
2 Pa 15 11 that they had brought, 700 oxen
721 2 Es 7 37 of Lod, of Hadid and Ono, 721
725 1 Es 2 33 children of Lod, Hadid and Ono 725
730 Exod 38 24 was 9 and 20 talents and 730 sicles
736 1 Es 2 66 their horses 736. 2 Es 7:68
743 1 Es 2 25 of Cariathiarim . . . 743. 2 Es 7:29
745 Jer 52 30 carried away of the Jews 745 souls
750 2 Ma 12 17 they departed 750 furlongs and
760 1 Es 2 9 children of Zachai 760. 2 Es 7:14
775 1 Es 2 5 the children of Area 775. The
777 Gen 5 31 days of Lamech came to 777 years
782 Gen 5 26 and Mathusala lived . . . 782 years
800 Gen 5 4 after he begot Seth, were 800 years
Gen 5 19 after he begot Henoch 800 years
2 K 23 8 wood, who killed 800 men at one onset
1 Ma 3 24 there fell of them 800 men, and the
9 6 remained of them no more than 800 men
807 Gen 5 7 after he begot Enos, 807 years
815 Gen 5 10 he [Enos] lived 815 years and
822 2 Es 11 12 do the works of the temple: 822
830 Gen 5 16 after he begot Jared, 830 years
832 Jer 52 29 832 souls from Jerusalem. In the
840 Gen 5 13 after he begot Malaleel, 840 years
845 2 Es 7 13 the children of Zethua 845. The
895 Gen 5 17 days of Malaleel were 895 years
900 Judg 4 3 had 900 chariots set with scythes
Judg 4 13 he gathered together his 900 chariots
905 Gen 5 11 the days of Enos were 905 years
910 Gen 5 14 days of Cainan were 910 years
912 Gen 5 8 the days of Seth were 912 years
920 Gen 11 24 Nachor lived 920 years and begot
928 2 Es 11 8 after him Gebbai, Sellai, 928
930 Gen 5 5 that Adam lived came to 930 years
945 1 Es 2 8 the children of Zethua 945. The
950 Gen 9 29 in the whole, 950 years: and he died
956 1 Pa 9 9 and of the sons of Benjamin . . . 956
962 Gen 5 20 the days of Jared were 962 years
969 Gen 5 27 days of Mathusala were 969 years
973 1 Es 2 36 house of Josue, 973. 2 Es 7:39
1,000 Gen 20 16 brother a t. pieces of silver
Num 31 4 let a t. men be chosen out of every
31 5 and they gave a t. of every tribe, that
35 4 outward, a t. paces on every side

Deut 7 9 commandments unto a t. generations
32 30 how should one pursue after a t., and
Josu 23 10 one of you shall chase a t. men of the
Judg 9 49 with the fire a t. persons were killed
15 15 [Samson] slew therewith a t. men. And
16 destroyed them and have slain a t. men
20 10 a hundred out of a t., and a t. out of 10,000
1 K 13 2 and a t. with Jonathan in Gabaa of
18 8 and to me they have given but a t.
13 made him a captain over a t. men, and
25 2 he had 3,000 sheep and a t. goats; and
2 K 10 6 and of the king of Maacha a t. men and
18 12 down in my hands a t. pieces of silver
19 17 with a t. men of Benjamin, and Siba
3 K 3 4 a t. victims for holocausts did Solomon
4 K 15 19 Manahem gave Phul a t. talents of silver
24 16 and the artificers, and the smiths a t.
1 Pa 12 14 soldiers, and the greatest over a t.
34 of Nephtali a t. leaders: and with them
16 16 which he commanded to a t. generations
18 4 David took from him a t. chariots and
19 6 sent a t. talents of silver to hire
29 21 a t. bullocks, a t. rams, a t. lambs
2 Pa 1 6 and offered up on it a t. victims. And
30 24 to the multitude a t. bullocks and
24 had given the people a t. bullocks and
1 Es 1 9 bowls of gold, a t. bowls of silver
8 27 and 20 cups of gold, of a t. solids
2 Es 3 13 a t. cubits in the wall unto the gate
7 70 into the treasure a t. drams of gold
Job 9 3 he cannot answer him one for a t. He
42 12 a t. yoke of oxen and a t. she asses
Ps 89 4 for a t. years in thy sight are as
90 7 a t. shall fall at thy side, and 10,000
104 8 which he commanded to a t. generations
Ecce 7 29 one man among a t. I have found, a
Cant 4 4 a t. bucklers hang upon it, all the
8 11 for fruit thereof a t. pieces of silver
12 a t. are for thee, the peaceable, and
Eccu 6 6 but let one of a t. be thy counsellor
16 3 feareth God, than a t. ungodly children
39 15 he shall leave a name above a t.; and
41 6 whether ten or a hundred or a t. years
15 more than a t. treasures precious and
Isa 7 23 a t. vines at a t. pieces of silver
30 17 a t. men shall flee for fear of one
60 22 the least shall become a t., and a
Eze 47 3 he measured a t. cubits: and he brought
5 he measured a t., and he brought me
Dan 5 1 a great feast for a t. of his nobles
Amos 5 3 the city out of which came forth a t.
1 Ma 2 38 to the number of a t. persons. And
4 1 men, and a t. of the best horsemen
5 13 they have slain there almost a t. men
6 35 stood by every elephant a t. men in
9 49 fell of Bacchides' side that day a t.
10 79 in the camp a t. horsemen behind them
12 47 into Galilee, and one t. went with him
14 24 gold, of the weight of a t. pounds
15 18 a shield of gold of a t. pounds. It
2 Ma 5 5 with him no fewer than a t. men
8 34 brought a t. merchants to the sale
2 P 3 8 is as 1,000 years, and 1,000 years as
Apoc 20 2 Satan, and bound him for 1,000 years
3 till the thousand years be finished
4 reigned with Christ a thousand years
5 till the thousand years were finished
6 shall reign with him a thousand years
7 when the t. years shall be finished
1,005 3 K 4 32 and his poems were 1,005. And
1,017 1 Es 2 39 the children of Harim 1,017. The
2 Es 7 42 the children of Arem 1,017. The
1,050 2 Es 5 17 magistrates to number of 1,050

1,052 1 Es 2 37 children of Emmer 1,052. 2 Es 7:40
1,100 Judg 16 5 every one of us 1,100 pieces of
Judg 17 2 the 1,100 pieces of silver, which thou
1,200 2 Pa 12 3 [Sesac] with 1,200 chariots
1,222 1 Es 2 12 the children of Azgad 1,222. The
1,247 1 Es 2 38 children of Pheshur 1,247. 2 Es 7:41
1,254 1 Es 2 7 children of Elam 1,254. 2 Es 7:12
1 Es 2 31 the children of the other Elam 1,254.
7 34 the men of the other Elam 1,254. The
1,260 Apoc 11 3 they shall prophesy 1,260 days
1,290 Dan 12 11 there shall be 1,290 days. Blessed
1,335 Dan 12 12 and cometh unto 1,335 days
1,365 Num 3 50 the firstborn . . . 1,365 sicles
1,400 2 Pa 1 14 and he had 1,400 chariots
1,500 2 Ma 8 22 giving to each one 1,500 men
1,600 2 Ma 11 11 they slew . . . 1,600 horsemen
Apoc 14 20 horses' bridles, for 1,600 furlongs
1,700 Judg 8 26 of the earlets . . . 1,700 sicles
2 K 8 4 David took from him 1,700 horsemen
1 Pa 26 30 1,700 had the charge over Israel beyond
1,760 1 Pa 9 13 families 1,700 and threescore
1,775 Exod 38 28 the 1,775 he made the heads
1,800 2 Ma 5 21 out of the temple 1,800 talents
2,000 Num 35 5 the east shall be 2,000 cubits
Num 35 5 the south . . . shall be 2,000 cubits
Josu 3 4 and the ark the space of 2,000 cubits
7 3 let two or three thousand men go and
Judg 20 45 pursued them and slew also other 2,000
1 K 13 2 and 2,000 were with Saul in Machmas
3 K 7 26 crisped lily: it contained 2,000 bates
4 K 18 23 I will give you 2,000 horses and see
1 Pa 5 21 of asses 2,000 and of men 100,000 souls
2 Es 7 72 people gave . . . 2,000 pounds of silver
Ecce 6 6 although he lived 2,000 years and
Isa 36 8 I will give thee 2,000 horses, and thou
1 Ma 5 60 the people of Israel about 2,000 men
9 4 with 20,000 men and 2,000 horsemen
12 47 of whom he sent 2,000 into Galilee
15 26 Simon sent to him 2,000 chosen men
16 10 there fell of them 2,000 men, and he
2 Ma 8 10 king the tribute of 2,000 talents
Mark 5 13 into the sea, being about 2,000, and
2,056 1 Es 2 14 the children of Beguai 2,056. The
2,067 2 Es 7 19 the children of Beguai 2,067. The
2,172 1 Es 2 3 children of Pharos 2,172. 2 Es 7:8
2,200 2 Es 7 71 gave . . . 2,200 pounds of silver
2,300 Dan 8 14 evening and morning 2,300 days
2,322 2 Es 7 17 the children of Azgad 2,322. The
2,400 Num 7 85 all the vessels . . . 2,400 sicles
2,500 2 Ma 12 20 had with him . . . 2,500 horsemen
2,600 2 Pa 26 12 number of chiefs . . . were 2,600
2 Pa 35 8 2,600 small cattle and 300 oxen
2,630 Num 4 40 they were found 2,630. This is the
2,700 1 Pa 26 32 2,700 chiefs of families. And
2,750 Num 4 36 they were found 2,750. This is the
2,812 1 Es 2 6 children of Josue: Joab, 2,812
2,818 2 Es 7 11 of Josue and Joab, 2,818
3,000 Josu 7 3 let two or three thousand men
Josu 7 4 went up therefore 3,000 fighting men
Judg 15 11 wherefore 3,000 men of Juda went down
16 27 about 3,000 persons of both sexes
1 K 13 2 and Saul chose him 3,000 men of Israel
24 3 Saul therefore took 3,000 chosen men
25 2 and he had 3,000 sheep and a thousand
26 2 with him 3,000 chosen men of Israel
3 K 4 32 Solomon also spoke 3,000 parables
5 16 over every work, in number 3,000
1 Pa 12 29 and of the sons of Benjamin . . . 3,000
29 4 3,000 talents of gold of the gold of
2 Pa 4 5 it held 3,000 measures. He made also
25 13 having killed 3,000, took away much
29 33 to the Lord 600 oxen and 3,000 sheep
35 7 cattle 30,000, and of oxen 3,000

Job 1 3 was 7,000 sheep and 3,000 camels and
1 Ma 4 6 in the plain with 3,000 men only, who
15 fell of them to number of 3,000 men
5 20 now 3,000 men were allotted to Simon
22 fell of the heathens almost 3,000 men
7 40 pitched in Adarsa with 3,000 men
9 5 in Laisa, and 3,000 chosen men with
11 44 Jonathan sent him 3,000 valiant men
74 fell of the aliens . . . 3,000 men
12 47 but he kept with him 3,000 men
2 Ma 4 40 Lysimachus armed about 3,000 men
12 33 he came out with 3,000 footmen and
Acts 2 41 were added in that day about 3,000
3,023 Jer 52 28 in the seventh year, 3,023 Jews
3,200 Num 4 44 they were found 3,200. This is
3,600 2 Pa 2 2 and 3,600 to oversee them. He
2 Pa 2 18 and 3,600 to be overseers of the
3,630 1 Es 2 35 the children of Senaa 3,630. The
3,700 1 Pa 12 27 and Joiada . . . and with him 3,700
3,930 2 Es 7 38 the children of Senaa 3,930. The
4,000 1 K 4 2 were slain . . . about 4,000 men
1 Pa 23 5 moreover, 4,000 were porters
2 Ma 13 15 and slew 4,000 men in the camp
Mat 15 38 that did eat were 4,000 men, besides
16 10 seven loaves among 4,000. Mark 8:20
Mark 8 9 they that had eaten were about 4,000
Acts 21 38 didst lead forth into desert 4,000 men
4,500 Eze 48 16 on the . . . side 4,500
Eze 48 30 thou shalt measure 4,500. 33
32 at the . . . side 4,500. 34
4,600 1 Pa 12 26 of the sons of Levi, 4,600. And
Jer 52 30 all the souls were 4,600. And it came
5,000 Josu 8 12 he had chosen 5,000 men and set
Judg 20 45 ways, they slew of them 5,000 men
1 K 17 5 of his coat of mail was 5,000 sicles
1 Pa 29 7 gold, 5,000 talents and 10,000 solids
2 Pa 35 9 phase 5,000 small cattle and 500 oxen
1 Es 2 69 they gave . . . 5,000 pounds of silver
Eze 45 6 possession of the city 5,000 bread
48 15 the 5,000 that remain in the breadth
1 Ma 4 1 Gorgias took 5,000 men and 1,000
28 chosen men, and 5,000 horsemen, that
34 fell of the army of Lysias 5,000
10 42 the 5,000 sicles of silver which
2 Ma 12 10 5,000 footmen . . . of the Arabians
13 2 having with him . . . 5,000 horsemen
Mat 14 21 of them that did eat, was 5,000 men
16 9 the 5 loaves among 5,000 men, and how
Mark 6 44 and they that did eat were 5,000 men
8 19 I broke the five loaves among 5,000
Luke 9 14 there were about 5,000 men. And he
John 6 10 sat down, in number about 5,000. And
Acts 4 4 the number of the men was made 5,000
5,400 1 Es 1 11 vessels of gold and silver 5,400
6,000 1 K 13 5 30,000 chariots and 6,000 horsemen
4 K 5 5 took with him . . . 6,000 pieces of gold
1 Pa 23 4 and 6,000 were the overseers and judges
Job 42 12 he had 14,000 sheep and 6,000 camels
2 Ma 8 1 they assembled 6,000 men. And they
20 being in all but 6,000, when it came to
12 20 having set in order about him 6,000 men
6,200 Num 3 34 of the male kind . . . 6,200
6,720 1 Es 2 67 their asses 6,720. 2 Es 7:69
6,800 1 Pa 12 24 bearing shield and spear, 6,800
7,000 3 K 19 18 I will leave me 7,000 men in
3 K 20 15 mustered . . . children of Israel, 7,000
4 K 24 16 all the strong men 7,000, and the
1 Pa 18 4 David took from him . . . 7,000 horsemen
19 18 David slew of the Syrians 7,000 chariots
29 4 and 7,000 talents of refined silver
2 Pa 15 11 brought, 700 oxen and 7,000 rams
30 24 thousand bullocks and 7,000 sheep
Job 1 3 his possession was 7,000 sheep and
1 Ma 3 39 he sent with them . . . 7,000 horsemen
2 Ma 8 16 but Machabeus calling together 7,000
Rom 11 4 I have left me 7,000 men, that have not
Apoc 11 13 in the earthquake names of men 7,000
7,100 1 Pa 12 25 valiant men for war, 7,100
7,337 1 Es 2 65 of whom there were 7,337
2 Es 7 67 menservants and womenservants . . . 7,337
7,500 Num 3 22 of the male sex . . . 7,500
7,700 2 Pa 17 11 7,700 rams and as many he goats
8,000 1 Ma 5 20 and 8,000 to Judas to go into
1 Ma 5 34 of them in that day almost 8,000 men
10 85 that were burnt, were almost 8,000 men
15 13 men of war, and 8,000 horsemen
8,580 Num 4 48 carry the burdens, were in all 8,580
8,600 Num 3 28 of the male sex . . . 8,600
9,000 2 Ma 8 24 they slew above 9,000 men: and
10,000 Lev 26 8 and 100 of you 10,000
Deut 32 30 after a thousand, and two chase 10,000
Judg 1 4 they slew of them in Bezec 10,000
3 29 slew of the Moabites . . . about 10,000
4 6 take with thee 10,000 fighting men
10 went up with 10,000 fighting men
14 Barac . . . and 10,000 fighting with him
7 3 home, and only 10,000 remained. And
20 10 1,000 out of 10,000 to bring victuals
34 10,000 men chosen out of all Israel
21 10 they sent 10,000 of the most valiant
1 K 14 22 there were with Saul about 10,000 men
15 4 footmen and 10,000 of the men of Juda
2 K 18 3 thou alone art accounted for 10,000
3 K 5 14 them to Libanus, 10,000 every month
4 K 13 7 and 10 chariots and 10,000 footmen
14 7 [Amasias] slew of Edom . . . 10,000 men
24 14 to the number of 10,000 into captivity
1 Pa 29 7 of gold, 5,000 talents and 10,000 solids: of silver 10,000 talents
2 Pa 25 11 slew of the children of Seir 10,000
12 other 10,000 men the sons of Juda took
27 5 10,000 measures of wheat and as many
30 24 people 1,000 bullocks and 10,000 sheep
Ps 67 18 of the Lord is attended by 10,000
90 7 thy side, and 10,000 at thy right hand
Eze 45 1 length 25,000 and in breadth 10,000
5 and 10,000 of breadth shall be for
48 9 and the breadth of 10,000. And these
10 toward the sea 10,000 in breadth, and
10 toward the east also 10,000 in breadth
13 10,000 in breadth. All the length shall
13 the breadth 10,000. And they shall not
18 the residue . . . 10,000 toward the
Dan 7 10 and 10,000 times 100,000 stood before
1 Ma 4 29 and Judas met them with 10,000 men
10 74 he chose 10,000 men and went out of
2 Ma 12 19 slew them . . . to the number of 10,000
Mat 18 24 that owed him ten thousand talents
Luke 14 31 whether he be able with 10,000 to meet
1 C 4 15 if you have 10,000 instructors in Christ
14 19 you also; than 10,000 words in a tongue
Apoc 9 16 of horsemen was 20,000 times 10,000
11,000 2 Ma 11 11 they slew of them 11,000 footmen
12,000 Num 31 5 12,000 men well appointed for
Josu 8 25 12,000 persons all of the city of Hai
2 K 10 6 thousand men, and of Istob 12,000 men
17 1 I will choose me 12,000 men and I will
3 K 4 26 chariot horses, and 12,000 for the
10 26 chariots and 12,000 horsemen. 2 Pa 1:14
2 Pa 9 25 and Solomon had . . . 12,000 chariots
Jdth 2 7 on foot, and 12,000 archers, horsemen
Ps 59 2 in the vale of the saltpits, 12,000 men
2 Ma 12 43 he sent 12,000 drachms of silver
Apoc 7 5 of the tribe of . . . 12,000 signed. 6, 7, 8
21 16 with the golden reed for 12,000 furlongs
14,000 Job 42 12 had 14,000 sheep and 6,000 camels

14,700 Num 16 49 number . . . slain was 14,700 men
15,000 Judg 8 10 15,000 men were left of all the
1 Ma 10 40 I give every year 15,000 sicles of
16,000 Num 31 40 out of the 16,000 persons. 46
16,750 Num 31 52 in weight 16,750 sicles, from
17,200 1 Pa 7 11 valiant men, 17,200 fit to go
18,000 Judg 20 25 to kill 18,000 men that drew the
Judg 20 44 slain in the same place were 18,000
2 K 8 13 after taking Syria . . . killing 18,000
1 Pa 12 31 of the half tribe of Manasses 18,000
18 12 in the vale of the saltpits, 18,000
29 7 of brass 18,000 talents: and of iron
Eze 48 35 its circumference was 18,000: and the
20,000 2 K 8 4 from him . . . 20,000 footmen. 1 Pa 18:4
2 K 10 6 Syrians of Soba, 20,000 footmen
18 7 was made that day of 20,000 men
3 K 5 11 allowed Hiram 20,000 measures of wheat
2 Pa 2 10 for their food . . . 20,000 measures of
2 Es 7 71 20,000 drams of gold and. 72
1 Ma 6 30 20,000 horsemen and 32 elephants
9 4 and went to Berea with 20,000 men
16 4 then he chose . . . 20,000 fighting men
2 Ma 8 9 no fewer than 20,000 of them that
30 they slew above 20,000 of them that
10 17 and slew . . . no fewer than 20,000
23 he slew more than 20,000 in the two
Luke 14 31 to meet him that, with 20,000, cometh
Apoc 9 16 of horsemen was 20,000 times 10,000
20,200 1 Pa 7 9 most valiant men for war, 20,200
20,500 2 Ma 10 31 and there were slain 20,500
20,800 1 Pa 12 30 of the sons of Ephraim 20,800
22,000 Num 3 39 all the Levites . . . were 22,000
Judg 7 3 two and twenty thousand men went away
20 21 of Israel that day 2 and 20 thousand
2 K 8 5 slew of the Syrians 2 and 20 thousand
3 K 8 63 peace offerings . . . 22,000 oxen and
1 Pa 18 5 David slew . . . 2 and 20 thousand
2 Pa 7 5 offered a sacrifice of 22,000 oxen
Jdth 7 2 2 and 20 thousand horsemen besides
2 Ma 5 24 Apollonius with an army of 22,000 men
22,034 1 Pa 7 7 and their number was 22,034
22,200 Num 26 14 the whole number was 22,200
22,273 Num 3 43 and the males . . . were 22,273
23,000 Exod 32 28 that day about 3 and 20 thousand
Num 26 62 that were numbered were 23,000 males
24,000 Num 25 9 were slain 4 and 20 thousand
1 Pa 23 4 24,000 were chosen and distributed
27 2 and under him were 4 and 20 thousand
4 part of the army of 4 and 20 thousand
5 in his division were 4 and 20 thousand
7 in his company were 4 and 20 thousand. 8, 9, 10, 11, 12, 13, 14, 15
25,000 Judg 20 15 of Benjamin 5 and 20 thousand
Judg 20 46 slain of Benjamin . . . 5 and 20 thousand
Eze 45 1 in length 25,000, and in breadth
3 measure the length of 5 and 20 thousand
5 and 5 and 20 thousand of length and
6 and 5 and 20 thousand long according
48 8 apart, 5 and 20 thousand in breadth
9 be the length of 5 and 20 thousand
10 north 5 and 20 thousand in length
10 south 5 and 20 thousand in length
13 shall have . . . 5 and 20 thousand in
13 length shall be 5 and 20 thousand
15 over against the 5 and 20 thousand. 21
20 firstfruits, of 5 and 20 thousand by 5 and 20 thousand foursquare
2 Ma 12 26 where he slew 5 and 20 thousand
28 city; and slew 5 and 20 thousand
25,100 Judg 20 35 that day 5 and 20 thousand and 100
26,000 1 Pa 7 40 that was fit for war was 26,000
27,000 3 K 20 30 wall fell upon 7 and 20 thousand
28,600 1 Pa 12 35 of Dan also 28,600 prepared for
30,000 Josu 8 3 sent 30,000 chosen valiant men
1 K 4 10 there fell of Israel 30,000 footmen
11 8 and of the men of Juda 30,000. And
13 5 30,000 chariots and 6,000 horsemen
2 K 6 1 all the chosen men of Israel. 30,000
3 K 5 31 Israel, and the levy was of 30,000 men
2 Pa 35 7 and of other small cattle 30,000
1 Ma 10 36 to the number of 30,000 of the Jews
2 Ma 12 23 profane, of whom he slew 30,000 men
30,500 Num 31 39 out of the 30,500 asses. 45
32,000 Num 31 35 32,000 persons of the female
1 Pa 19 7 hired 2 and 30 thousand chariots
32,200 Num 1 35 the sons of Manasses . . . 32,200
Num 2 21 that were numbered, were 32,200
32,500 Num 26 37 whose number was 32,500. These
35,000 2 Ma 15 27 no less than 5 and 30 thousand
35,400 Num 1 37 the sons of Benjamin . . . 35,400
Num 2 23 that were reckoned up, were 35,400
36,000 Num 31 38 out of the 36,000 oxen. 44
1 Pa 7 4 6 and 30 thousand most valiant men
37,000 1 Pa 12 34 of Nephtali . . . 7 and 30 thousand
38,000 1 Pa 23 3 were found of them 38,000 men
40,000 Josu 4 13 40,000 fighting men by their
Judg 5 8 was not seen among 40,000 of Israel
2 K 10 18 slew of the Syrians . . . 40,000 horsemen
3 K 4 26 Solomon had 40,000 stalls of chariot
1 Pa 12 36 and of Aser 40,000 going forth to fight
19 18 slew of the Syrians . . . 40,000 footmen
2 Pa 9 25 Solomon had 40,000 horses in the stables
1 Ma 3 39 and he sent with them 40,000 men
12 41 to meet him with 40,000 men chosen
2 Ma 5 14 40,000 were made prisoners, and as
40,500 Num 1 33 of the sons of Joseph . . . 40,500
Num 2 19 that were numbered were 40,500
26 18 the whole number was 40,500. The sons
41,500 Num 1 41 of the sons of Aser . . . 41,500
Num 2 28 were numbered, were 41,500
42,000 Judg 12 6 at that time of Ephraim 42,000
42,360 1 Es 2 64 as one man were 42,360. 2 Es 7:66
43,730 Num 26 7 number was found to be 43,730
45,400 Num 26 50 whose number was 45,400
45,600 Num 26 41 whose number was 45,600
45,650 Num 1 25 of the sons of Gad . . . 45,650
Num 2 15 that were numbered were 45,650
46,500 Num 1 21 go forth to war were 46,500
Num 2 11 that were numbered were 46,500
50,000 1 Pa 5 21 camels 50,000 and of sheep 250,000
1 K 6 19 and 50,000 of the common people
1 Pa 12 33 of Zabulon . . . there came 50,000 to
19 19 found the money to be 50,000 pieces of
52,700 Num 26 34 the number of them 52,700
53,400 Num 1 43 the sons of Nephtali . . . 53,400
Num 2 30 of his fighting men, were 53,400
26 47 sons of Aser, and their number 53,400
54,400 Num 1 29 the sons of Issachar . . . 54,400
Num 2 6 of his fighting men were 54,400
57,400 Num 1 31 the sons of Zabulon . . . 57,400
Num 2 8 fighting men of his stock, were 57,400
58,000 2 K 10 19 fled away, 8 and 50 thousand men
59,300 Num 1 23 sons of Simeon . . . 59,300
Num 2 13 of his fighting men . . . were 59,300
60,000 2 Pa 12 3 threescore thousand horsemen
1 Ma 4 28 threescore thousand chosen men and
60,500 Num 26 27 whose number was 60,500
61,000 Num 31 34 72,000 oxen, 61,000 asses
1 Es 2 69 they gave . . . 61,000 solids of gold
62,700 Num 1 39 of the sons of Dan . . . 62,700
Num 2 26 that were numbered were 62,700
64,300 Num 26 25 the whole number was 64,300
64,400 Num 26 43 whose number was 64,400
70,000 2 K 24 15 there died . . . 70,000 men
3 K 5 15 Solomon had 70,000 to carry burdens
1 Pa 21 14 and there fell of Israel 70,000 men

2 Pa 2 2 numbered out 70,000 men to bear burdens
18 he set 70,000 of them to carry burdens
2 Ma 10 20 taking 70,000 didrachmas, let some
72,000 Exod 38 29 of brass also 72,000 talents
Num 31 33 sheep, 72,000 oxen, 61,000 asses
74,600 Num 1 27 of the sons of Juda . . . 74,600
Num 2 4 men of his stock, were 74,600
75,000 Esth 9 16 were killed amounted to 75,000
76,500 Num 26 22 the whole number was 76,500
80,000 3 K 5 15 80,000 to hew stones. 2 Pa 2:2, 18
2 Ma 5 14 were slain . . . fourscore thousand
11 2 together fourscore thousand men and
87,000 1 Pa 7 5 fourscore and seven thousand
100,000 3 K 20 29 of the Syrians 100,000 footmen
4 K 3 4 paid to the king of Israel 100,000 lambs and 100,000 rams
1 Pa 5 21 asses 2,000 and of men 100,000 souls
22 14 of gold a hundred thousand talents
29 7 and of iron a hundred thousand talents
2 Pa 25 6 of Israel a hundred thousand valiant
Dan 7 10 and 10,000 times 100,000 stood before
1 Ma 6 30 number of his army was 100,000 footmen
11 48 they slew in that day 100,000 men
108,100 Num 2 24 camp of Ephraim, were 108,100
110,000 2 Ma 13 2 having with him 110,000 footmen
120,000 Judg 8 10 120,000 warriors that drew the
3 K 8 63 peace offerings . . . 120,000 sheep
1 Pa 12 37 tribe of Manasses 120,000 furnished
2 Pa 7 5 of 22,000 oxen and 120,000 rams: and
28 6 Phacee . . . slew of Juda 120,000 in
Jdth 2 7 120,000 fighting men on foot and
7 2 in his troops 120,000 footmen, and
Jon 4 12 are more than 120,000 persons that
1 Ma 11 45 to the number of 120,000 men, and
15 13 camped above Dora with 120,000 men
2 Ma 8 20 in all but 6,000 . . . slew 120,000
144,000 Apoc 4 4 144,000 were signed, of every
Apoc 14 1 with him 144,000 having his name and
3 say the canticle but those 144,000 who
151,450 Num 2 16 camp of Ruben, were 151,450
153,600 2 Pa 2 17 and they were found 153,600
157,600 Num 2 31 the camp of Dan were 157,600
180,000 3 K 12 21 Benjamin a hundred and fourscore thousand chosen men. 2 Pa 11:1
2 Pa 17 18 Jozabad and with him 180,000 ready for
185,000 4 K 19 35 slew in camp of the Assyrians 185,000. Isa 37:36
1 Ma 7 41 an angel . . . slew of them 185,000
2 Ma 8 19 how . . . 185,000 had been destroyed
2 Ma 15 22 didst kill 185,000 of the army of
186,400 Num 2 9 the camp of Juda, were 186,400
200,000 1 K 15 4 200,000 footmen and 10,000 of
2 Pa 17 16 and with him were 200,000. 17
28 8 of their brethren 200,000 women, boys
220,600 1 Pa 7 2 220,600 most valiant men. The
250,000 1 Pa 5 21 of sheep 250,000 and of asses
280,000 2 Pa 14 8 and drew bows, 280,000
2 Pa 17 15 Johanan . . . and with him 280,000. And
300,000 1 K 11 8 the children of Israel 300,000
2 Pa 14 8 shields and spears, of Juda 300,000
17 14 Ednas . . . with him 300,000 most valiant
25 5 found 300,000 young men that could go
307,500 2 Pa 26 13 whole army under them 307,500
337,500 Num 31 36 half . . . to wit, 337,500 sheep
Num 31 43 out of the 337,500 sheep, and out of
400,000 Judg 20 2 400,000 footmen fit for war
Judg 20 17 were found 400,000 that drew swords
2 Pa 13 3 400,000 most valiant and chosen men
440,760 1 Pa 5 18 440,760 that went out to war
470,000 1 Pa 21 5 of Juda 470,000 fighting men
500,000 2 Pa 13 17 fell wounded of Israel 500,000
2 K 24 9 and of Juda 500,000 fighting men
600,000 Exod 12 37 about 600,000 men on foot
Num 11 21 are 600,000 footmen of this people
Eccu 16 11 so did he with the 600,000 footmen
601,730 Num 26 51 were reckoned up, 601,730
603,550 Exod 38 25 of 603,550 men able to bear
Num 1 46 able to go to war were 603,550
2 32 of the children of Israel . . . 603,550
675,000 Num 31 32 the spoil . . . 675,000 sheep
800,000 2 K 24 9 of Israel 800,000 valiant men
2 Pa 13 3 800,000 men, who were also chosen and
1,000,000 2 Pa 14 9 army of ten hundred thousand
1,100,000 1 Pa 21 5 was found to be 1,100,000

Numbers (Ordinal)

1st; *see* **first**
2nd Gen 1 8 and morning were the second day. God
Gen 2 13 name of the second river is Gehon
32 19 he commanded the second and the third
33 2 Lia and her children in the s. place
41 43 made him go up into his second chariot
Exod 26 20 in the s. side also of the tabernacle
28 18 in the second [row] a carbuncle. 39:11
Lev 8 22 he offered also the second ram, in the
Num 2 16 they shall march in the second place
7 18 the s. day Nathanael the son of Suar
10 6 at the second sounding and like noise
29 17 second day you shall offer 12 calves
Josu 5 4 is the cause of the s. circumcision
6 14 round about the city the second day
19 1 the second lot came forth for the
Judg 6 26 thou shalt take the second bullock
28 the second bullock laid upon the altar
20 30 as they had done the first and s. 31
Ruth 4 4 thee, who art first, and me, who am s.
1 K 8 2 the name of the second was Abia, judges
17 13 the second Abinadab and the third Samma
20 27 second day after new moon was come
34 did not eat bread on the second day
2 K 3 3 born to David . . . his second Cheleab
20 10 gave him [Amasa] not a second wound
21 18 there was also a second battle in Gob
3 K 6 25 the second cherub also was ten cubits
7 21 like manner he set up the second pillar
4 K 9 19 he sent a second chariot of horses
23 4 the priests of the s. order and the
25 17 the second pillar had the like adorning
18 chief priest and Sophonias the s. priest
1 Pa 2 13 second Abinadab and the third Simmaa
3 1 s. Daniel of Abigail the Carmelitess
15 sons of Josias were . . . the s. Joakim
7 15 the name of the second was Salphaad
8 1 born, Asbel the second, Ahara the third
39 Jehus the s. and Eliphalet the third
11 21 and illustrious among the second three
12 9 Ezer the chief, Obdias the s., Eliab the
15 18 in the second rank, Zacharias and Ben
23 19 Amarias the second, Jahaziel the third
20 Micha the first, Jesia the s. The sons
24 7 lot . . . to Joiarib, the s. to Jedei
23 Jeriau the first, Amarias the second
25 9 the second to Godolias, to him and
26 2 Jahidel the second, Zabadias the third
4 Jozabad the s., Joaha the third, Sachar
11 Helcias the second, Tabelias the third
2 Pa 34 22 dwelt in Jerusalem in the Second part
1 Es 1 10 silver cups of a second part, 410
2 Es 8 13 second day the chiefs of the families
11 9 Judas . . . was second over the city
17 man to praise . . . and Becbecia the s.
12 37 the s. choir of them that gave thanks
Tob 6 20 the second night thou shalt be admitted
Esth 7 2 king said to her against the s. day
15 2 because Aman the second after the king

Job 42 14 and the name of the second Cassia, and
Ps 47 1 of Core, on the second day of the week
Ecce 4 8 there is but one and he hath not a s.
15 with the s. young man, who shall rise
Jer 41 4 on the second day after he had killed
52 22 the same of the second pillar, and the
24 and Sophonias the second priest, and
Eze 10 14 the second face, the face of a man
43 22 in the second day thou shalt offer
Zach 6 2 in the second chariot black horses
11 14 I cut off my second rod that was called
2 Ma 5 1 prepared for a s. journey into Egypt
Mat 22 26 in like manner the second, and the
39 the second is like to this: Thou shalt
Mark 12 21 and the second took her, and died: and
31 the second is like to it: Thou shalt
Luke 6 1 to pass on the second first sabbath
12 38 if he shall come in the second watch
19 18 the second came, saying: Lord, thy
John 4 54 this is again the second miracle that
Acts 12 10 passing through first and second ward
13 33 in the s. psalm also is written: Thou
28 13 we came the second day to Puteoli; where
1 C 15 47 the second man, from heaven, heavenly
2 C 1 15 that you might have a second grace: and
Titus 3 10 after the first and s. admonition, avoid
Heb 8 7 a place have been sought for a second
9 3 after the second veil, the tabernacle
7 into the second, the high priest alone
2 P 3 1 this second epistle I write to you
Apoc 2 11 shall not be hurt by the second death
4 7 the second living creature like a calf
6 3 when he had opened the second seal, I
3 I heard the second living creature
8 8 the second angel sounded the trumpet
11 14 the second woe is past: and behold the
16 3 the second angel poured out his vial
20 6 in these the s. death hath no power
14 pool of fire. This is the second death
21 8 which is the second death. And there
19 was jasper: the second, sapphire: the
2nd month; *see* **month**
2nd time Gen 22 15 called to Abraham a s. t.
Gen 27 36 s. t. he hath stolen away my blessing
36 hath supplanted me lo this second time
41 32 didst see the second time a dream
43 10 we had been here again the second time
Lev 13 58 the second time and they shall be clean
Josu 5 2 circumcise the second time the children
1 K 26 8 there shall be no need of a second time
2 K 14 29 when he had sent the s. t., and he
3 K 9 2 Lord appeared to him the second time
18 34 he said: Do the same the second time
19 7 angel of Lord came again second time
4 K 10 6 he [Jehu] wrote letters the second time
1 Pa 29 22 they anointed the second time Solomon
Job 33 14 not the selfsame thing the second time
Esth 2 19 the virgins were sought a second time
Isa 11 11 Lord shall set his hand the second time
Jer 1 13 word of Lord came to me s. t. 13:3
33 1 came to Jeremias the second time, while
Jon 3 1 came to Jonas the second time, saying
Agge 2 21 came a second time to Aggeus in the
1 Ma 15 25 moved his camp to Dora the second time
Mat 26 42 the second time, he went and prayed
John 3 4 can he enter a second time into his
Acts 7 13 at the second time, Joseph was known
10 15 spoke to him again the second time
Heb 9 28 the second time he shall appear without
2nd year; *see* **year**
3d Gen 2 14 name of the third river is Tigris
Gen 6 16 and third stories shalt thou make it
32 19 he commanded the second and the third
38 5 she bore also a t.: whom she called
50 22 he saw . . . to the third generation
Exod 19 1 in the third month of the departure
20 5 unto the third and fourth generation. 34:7; Num 14:18; Deut 5:9; Tob 9:11
28 19 in the third a ligurius. 39:12
Num 2 24 they shall march in the third place
28 14 a third for a ram and a fourth for a
Deut 23 8 in the third generation shall enter
Josu 19 10 t. lot fell to the children of Zabulon
1 K 13 18 third turned to the way of the border
17 13 the second Abinadab and the third Samma
2 K 3 3 born to David . . . the third Absalom
21 19 there was a t. battle in Gob against the
3 K 6 6 third floor was seven cubits in breadth
8 room, and from the middle to the third
4 K 1 13 he sent a third captain of fifty men
1 Pa 2 13 second Abinadab and the third Simmaa
3 2 the third Absalom the son of Maacha
15 sons of Josias were . . . the t. Sedecias
8 39 Jehus the second and Eliphalet the t.
12 9 Obdias the second, Eliab the third
23 19 the second, Jahaziel the third. 24:23
24 8 the third to Harim, the fourth to Seorim
25 10 the third to Zachur, to his sons and
26 2 Jadihel the second, Zabadias the third
4 Jozabad the second, Joaha the third
11 Helcias the second, Tabelias the third
27 5 and the captain of the third company
2 Pa 23 5 and a third at the gate that is called
Tob 6 21 the third night thou shalt obtain a
22 and when the third night is past, thou
8 4 when the third night is over, we will
Job 42 14 and the name of the third Cornustibii
Eccu 23 21 the t. bringeth wrath and destruction
26 25 and the third bringeth anger upon me
28 16 tongue of a t. person hath disquieted
19 tongue of a third person hath cast
45 28 Phinees . . . is the third in glory
50 27 the third is no nation, which I hate
Isa 19 24 in that day shall Israel be the third
Jer 38 14 took Jeremias . . . to the third gate
Eze 10 14 in the third was the face of a lion
Dan 2 39 another third kingdom of brass, which
5 7 and shall be the t. man in my kingdom
16 shalt be the third prince in my kingdom
29 had power as the t. man in the kingdom
Zach 6 3 in the third chariot white horses
2 Ma 7 10 the third was made a mocking stock, and
Mat 20 3 going out about the third hour, he saw
22 26 like manner the second and the third
Mark 12 21 issue. And the third in like manner
15 25 it was the third hour, and they
Luke 12 38 or come in the third watch, and find
20 12 he sent the third; and they wounded
31 and the third took her. And in like
Acts 2 15 seeing it is but the third hour of the
20 9 fell from third loft down, and was taken
23 23 spearmen for third hour of the night
2 C 12 2 such a one caught up to the third heaven
Apoc 4 7 third living creature, having the face
6 5 when he had opened the third seal, I
5 I heard the third living creature
8 10 the third angel sounded the trumpet
11 14 behold the third woe will come quickly
14 9 the third angel followed them, saying
16 4 the third poured out his vial upon the
21 19 sapphire: the third, a chalcedony: the
3d day Gen 1 13 and morning were the t. d.
Gen 22 4 on the third day, lifting up his eyes
31 22 told Laban on t. d. that Jacob fled
34 25 third day, when the pain of the wound
40 20 third day . . . was birthday of Pharao

42 18 third day he brought them out of prison
Exod 19 11 let them be ready against the t. day
11 third day the Lord will come down in
15 be ready against the third day and come
16 now the third day was come, and the
Lev 7 17 whatsoever shall be found on the t. day
18 victims of peace offerings on the t. day
19 6 whatsoever shall be left until t. day
Num 7 24 third day the prince of the sons of
19 12 sprinkled with this water on the t. day
12 if he were not sprinkled on third day
19 unclean on the third and seventh day
29 20 third day you shall offer eleven calves
31 19 shall be purified the third day and the
Josu 1 11 after the third day you shall pass
9 17 came into their cities on the t. day
1 K 20 5 in the field till evening of third day
30 1 were come to Siceleg on the third day
2 K 1 2 on third day, there appeared a man
20 4 men of Juda against the third day and
3 K 3 18 third day, after that I was delivered
12 5 go till the third day and come to me
12 came to Roboam the third day, as the
12 come to me again the third day. And the
4 K 20 5 on third day thou shalt go up to the
8 to temple of the Lord the third day
2 Pa 10 12 came to Roboam the third day, as he
1 Es 6 15 until third day of the month of Adar
Tob 3 12 it came to pass on the third day when
Esth 5 1 on the third day Esther put on her
15 4 on the third day she laid away the
Osee 6 3 on the third day she laid away the
Mat 16 21 third day rise again. Luke 9:22; 24:7
17 72 third day he shall rise again. 20:19; Mark 10:34; Luke 18:33
27 64 sepulcher to be guarded until t. day
Mark 9 30 he shall rise again the third day. But
Luke 13 32 and the third day I am consummated
24 21 today is third day since these things
46 to rise again from the dead the t. day
John 2 1 third day there was a marriage in Cana
Acts 10 40 him God raised up the third day, and
13 30 God raised him up the third day: who
27 19 third day they cast out . . . tackling
28 17 after the third day, he called together
1 C 15 4 he rose again the third day, according
3d part; *see* **part**
4th Gen 1 19 and morning were the fourth day
Gen 2 14 the fourth river is Euphrates. And the
15 16 in the fourth generation they shall
29 35 the fourth time she conceived and bore
Exod 20 5 unto the third and fourth generation. 34:7; Num 14:18; Deut 5:9; Tob 9:11
28 20 in the fourth [row] a chrysolite. 39:13
29 40 fourth part of a hin. Num 15:4; 28:5, 7
Lev 19 24 in the fourth year, all their fruit
23 13 of wine, the fourth part of a hin
Num 7 30 fourth day the prince of the sons of
28 14 for a ram, a f. [of a hin] for a lamb
29 23 fourth day you shall offer ten calves
Josu 19 17 the fourth lot came out to Issachar
Judg 19 5 but on the fourth day arising early in
1 K 9 8 in my hand the fourth part of a sicle
2 K 3 4 born to David . . . the fourth Adonias
21 20 fourth battle was in Geth: where there
3 K 6 1 in the f. year of the reign of Solomon
37 fourth year was the house . . . founded
22 41 over Juda in the fourth year of Achab
4 K 6 25 fourth part of a cabe of pigeon's dung
10 30 throne of Israel to the f. generation
15 12 thy children to the f. generation shall
18 9 in the fourth year of king Ezechias
1 Pa 2 14 fourth Nathanael and the fifth Raddai
3 2 the fourth Adonias the son of Aggith
15 sons of Josias were . . . the f. Sellum
8 2 Nohaa the fourth and Rapha the fifth
12 10 Masmana the fourth, Jeremias the fifth
23 19 the third, Jecmaam the fourth. 24:23
24 8 third to Harim, the fourth to Seorim
25 11 the fourth to Isari, to his sons and
26 2 Jathanael the fourth, Elam the fifth
4 Sachar the fourth, Nathanael the fifth
11 Zacharias the f.: all these the sons
27 7 the f. for the f. month was Asahel
2 Pa 3 2 fourth year of his reign. Jer 51:59
20 26 on the fourth day they were assembled
1 Es 8 33 on the fourth day the silver and the
Jdth 12 10 and it came to pass on the fourth day
Job 42 16 he saw . . . unto the fourth generation
Ps 93 1 for David himself on the fourth day
Prov 30 15 the fourth never saith: It is enough
18 the fourth I am utterly ignorant of
21 disturbed, and the f. it cannot bear
29 and the fourth that walketh happily
Eccu 26 5 at the fourth my face hath trembled
Jer 25 1 fourth year of Joakim. 36:1; 45:1; 46:1
28 1 in the fourth year in the fifth month
39 2 year of Sedecias, in the f. month, the
52 6 in the fourth month, the ninth day
Eze 1 1 in the fourth month on the fifth day
10 14 in the fourth the face of an eagle
Dan 2 40 the fourth kingdom shall be as iron
3 92 form of the fourth is like the Son
7 7 a fourth beast, terrible and wonderful
19 learn concerning the fourth beast
23 f. beast shall be the f. kingdom
11 2 the f. shall be enriched exceedingly
Zach 6 3 in the fourth chariot grisled horses
7 1 in the fourth year of king Darius
1 in the fourth day of the ninth month
8 19 the fast of the fourth month and the
2 Ma 7 13 tormented the fourth in the like manner
Mat 14 25 in the f. watch of the night. Mark 6:48
Apoc 4 7 fourth living creature was like an eagle
6 7 when he had opened the fourth seal, I
7 heard the voice of the fourth living
8 12 the fourth angel sounded the trumpet
16 8 the fourth angel poured out his vial
21 19 the fourth, an emerald: the fifth
5th Gen 30 17 conceived and bore the fifth son
Num 33 38 fifth month, the first day of the month
Josu 19 24 the fifth lot fell to the tribe of
2 K 3 4 born to David . . . the fifth Saphathia
4 K 25 8 in the fifth month, the seventh day
1 Pa 2 14 fourth Nathanael and the fifth Raddai
3 3 the fifth Saphatias of Abital, the sixth
8 2 Nohaa the fourth and Rapha the fifth
12 10 Masmana the fourth, Jeremias the fifth
24 9 fifth to Melchia, the sixth to Maiman
25 12 the fifth to Nathania, to his sons
26 3 Jathanael the fourth, Elam the fifth
4 Sachar the fourth, Nathanael the fifth
27 8 the fifth captain for the fifth month
2 Es 6 5 sent his servant to me the fifth time
Tob 14 15 children's children to f. generation
Jer 1 3 Jerusalem captive, in the fifth month
28 1 in the fourth year in the fifth month
52 12 in the fifth month, the tenth day of
Zach 8 19 fourth month and the fast of the f.
2 Ma 7 15 when they had brought the fifth, they
Apoc 6 9 when he had opened the fifth seal, I
9 1 the fifth angel sounded the trumpet
16 10 the fifth angel poured out his vial
21 20 the fifth, sardonyx: the sixth
5th day; *see* **day**
5th part; *see* **part**

5th year; *see* **year**
6th Gen 1 31 and morning were the sixth day
Gen 30 19 conceived again and bore the sixth son
Exod 16 5 the sixth day let them provide for to
22 on the sixth day they gathered twice
29 the sixth day he giveth you a double
26 9 so as to double the sixth curtain
Lev 25 21 I will give you my blessing the s. year
Num 7 42 s. day the prince of the sons of Gad
29 29 sixth day you shall offer eight calves
Josu 19 32 sixth lot came out to sons of Nephtali
2 K 3 4 born to David . . . the sixth Jethraam
4 K 18 10 in the sixth year of Ezechias, that is
1 Pa 2 15 the sixth Asom, the seventh David. And
3 3 the sixth Jethrahem of Egla his wife
12 11 Ethi the sixth, Eliel the seventh
24 9 fifth to Melchia, the sixth to Maiman
25 13 the sixth to Bocciau, to his sons
26 3 Johanan the s., Elioenai the seventh
5 Ammiel the sixth, Issachar the seventh
27 9 the sixth for the sixth month was Hira
1 Es 6 15 sixth year of the reign of king Darius
2 Es 3 30 built . . . Hanun the sixth son of Seleph
Eze 4 11 water . . . the sixth part of a hin
8 1 in the sixth year, in the sixth month
45 13 the sixth part of an ephi. 46:14
Agge 1 1 in the sixth month. 2:1
2 Ma 7 18 after him they brought the sixth, and
Mat 20 5 he went out about the sixth and the
27 45 from the sixth hour there was darkness
Mark 15 33 when the sixth hour was come, there
Luke 1 26 in the sixth month the angel Gabriel
36 this is the sixth month with her that
23 44 and it was almost the sixth hour; and
John 4 6 the well. It was about the sixth hour
19 14 of the pasch, about the sixth hour
Acts 10 9 the house to pray, about the sixth hour
Apoc 6 12 when he had opened the sixth seal, and
9 13 the sixth angel sounded the trumpet
14 the sixth angel, who had the trumpet
16 12 the sixth angel poured out his vial
21 20 the sixth, sardius: the seventh
7th Exod 21 2 in the seventh he shall go out free
Exod 31 17 in the seventh he ceased from work
Lev 23 16 morrow after the s. week be expired
Num 19 12 sprinkled . . . on third day and on s.
12 he cannot be cleansed on the seventh
Deut 5 14 the seventh is the day of the sabbath
Josu 6 16 when in the seventh going about
19 40 the s. lot came out to the tribe of
3 K 8 2 Ethanim, the same is the seventh month
18 44 at the s. time, behold a little cloud
1 Pa 2 15 the sixth Asom, the seventh David
12 11 Ethi the sixth, Eliel the seventh
24 10 seventh to Accos, the eighth to Abia
25 14 the seventh to Isreela, to his sons
26 3 Elioenai the seventh. And the sons of
5 Ammiel the sixth, Issachar the seventh
Job 5 19 in the s., evil shall not touch thee
Prov 6 16 and the seventh his soul detesteth
Zach 8 19 and the fast of the seventh [month]
Mat 22 26 the third, and so on the seventh
John 4 52 at the seventh hour the fever left him
Jude 14 Enoch also, the seventh from Adam
Apoc 8 1 when he had opened the seventh seal
10 7 days of the voice of the seventh angel
11 15 the seventh angel sounded the trumpet
16 17 the seventh angel poured out his vial
21 20 sardius: the seventh, chrysolite
7th day Gen 2 2 on s. d. God ended his work
Gen 2 2 he rested on seventh day from all his
3 he blessed the s. day, and sanctified it
Exod 12 15 leavened, from first day until s. day
16 the seventh day shall be kept with the
13 6 on seventh day shall be the solemnity
16 26 the s. day is the sabbath. 20:10; 31:15
27 seventh day came; and some of the people
29 let none go forth . . . the seventh day
30 kept the sabbath on the seventh day
20 11 the Lord . . . rested on the seventh day
11 the Lord blessed the seventh day and
23 12 the seventh day thou shalt cease, that
24 16 s. day he called him out of the midst
34 21 seventh day thou shalt cease to plow
35 2 the seventh day shall be holy unto you
Lev 13 5 the seventh day he shall look on him. 6
27 on the seventh day he shall view him
32 seventh day he shall look upon it. If
34 if on s. day the evil seem to have
51 on seventh day when he looketh on it
14 9 on the seventh day he shall shave the
39 returning on the s. day, he shall look
23 3 seventh day, because it is the rest of
8 seventh day shall be more solemn and
Num 6 9 shave it . . . again on the seventh day
7 48 seventh day the prince of the sons of
19 19 unclean on third and on the s. day
19 being expiated the s. day, he shall
28 25 seventh day also shall be most solemn
29 32 s. day you shall offer seven calves
31 19 purified the third day and the s. day
24 wash your garments the seventh day
Deut 16 8 seventh day, because it is the assembly
Josu 6 4 on seventh day the priests shall take
15 the seventh day, rising up early, they
Judg 14 15 when seventh day came, they said to
17 on the s. day as she was troublesome
18 on s. day before the sun went down
2 K 12 18 on seventh day that the child died
3 K 20 29 on the s. day the battle was fought
4 K 25 8 fifth month, s. day of the month, that
Esth 1 10 seventh day, when the king was merry
Bar 1 2 s. day of the month. Eze 30:20; 45:20
Dan 14 39 upon s. day the king came to bewail
2 Ma 12 38 and when the seventh day came, they
Heb 4 4 he spoke of the seventh day thus: And
7th month; *see* **month**
8th Lev 25 22 the eighth year you shall sow
3 K 6 38 month Bul, which is the eighth month
12 32 appointed a feast in the eighth month
33 the fifteenth day of the eighth month
4 K 24 12 him in the eighth year of his reign
1 Pa 12 12 Johanan the eighth, Elzebad the ninth
24 10 seventh to Accos, the eighth to Abia
25 15 the eighth to Jesaia, to his sons
26 5 Phollathi the eighth: for the Lord had
27 11 the e. for the e. month was Sobochai
2 Pa 34 3 and in the eighth year of his reign
Zach 1 1 eighth month, in the second year of
2 P 2 5 but preserved Noe, the eighth person
Apoc 17 11 the same also is the eighth, and is
21 20 chrysolite: the eighth beryl: the
8th day Gen 21 4 circumcised him the e. day
Exod 22 30 eighth day thou shalt give it to me
Lev 9 1 when the eighth day was come, Moses
12 3 e. day the infant shall be circumcised
14 10 on eighth day he shall take two lambs
23 he shall offer them on the e. day of
15 14 on e. day he shall take two turtles
29 on the eighth day she shall offer for
22 27 the e. day and thenceforth, they may be
23 36 eighth day also shall be most solemn
39 first day and e. day shall be a sabbath
Num 6 10 on the e. day he shall bring two turtles
7 54 the e. day the prince of the sons of
29 35 the e. day, which is most solemn, you

3 K 8 66 eighth day he sent away the people
2 Pa 7 9 he made on the eighth day a solemn
29 17 e. day of the same month they came
2 Es 8 18 in the eighth day a solemn assembly
Eze 43 27 e. day and thenceforth the priests
Luke 1 59 e. day they came to circumcise the
Acts 7 8 circumcised him [Isaac] the e. day
Phil 3 5 more, being circumcised the eighth day
9th Lev 23 32 ninth day of the month. 4 K 25:3
Lev 25 22 of the old fruits, until the n. year
Num 7 60 ninth day the prince of the sons of
4 K 17 6 in the ninth year of Osee. 18:10
25 1 the ninth year of his reign. Jer 52:4
1 Pa 12 12 Johanan the eighth, Elzebad the ninth
24 11 ninth to Jesua, the tenth to Sechenia
25 16 the ninth to Mathanaias, to his sons
27 12 ninth for the ninth month was Abiezer
1 Es 10 9 in the ninth month, the twentieth day
Jer 36 9 year of Joakim . . . in the ninth month
22 in the winter house in the ninth month
39 1 in the ninth year of Sedecias king of
52 6 fourth month the n. day of the month
Eze 24 1 the ninth year in the tenth month
1 Ma 4 52 n. month, which is the month of Casleu
Mat 20 5 out about the sixth and the ninth hour
27 45 the whole earth, until the ninth hour
46 about the ninth hour Jesus cried with
Mark 15 33 the whole earth until the ninth hour
34 at the ninth hour, Jesus cried out
Luke 23 44 all the earth until the ninth hour
Acts 3 1 temple at the ninth hour of prayer
10 3 the ninth hour of the day, an angel
30 praying in my house, at the n. hour
Apoc 21 20 the ninth, a topaz: the tenth, a
10th Gen 8 5 decreasing until the tenth month
Gen 8 5 in the tenth month, the first day of
Exod 12 3 on the t. day of this month let every
Lev 16 29 the tenth day of the month, you shall
23 27 t. day of this seventh month. Num 29:7
25 9 the seventh month, the tenth day of the
27 32 rod, every tenth that cometh shall be
Num 7 66 t. day the prince of the sons of Dan
28 13 and the tenth of a tenth of flour
21 the t. of a t. to every lamb. 29; 29:10, 15
29 4 one tenth [of flour] to a lamb, which
Deut 23 2 not enter . . . until the t. generation
3 even after the tenth generation shall
Josu 4 19 the tenth day of the first month
1 K 8 15 he will take the tenth of your corn
4 K 25 1 the tenth month, the tenth day of the
1 Pa 12 13 Jeremias the tenth, Machbani the
24 11 ninth to Jesua, the tenth to Sechenia
25 17 the tenth to Semeias, to his sons and
27 13 the tenth for the tenth month was Marai
Eccu 25 9 the tenth I will utter to men with
Jer 32 1 in the tenth year of Sedecias king of
39 1 of Sedecias . . . in the tenth month
52 4 the tenth day of the month. 12; Eze 20:1; 24:1; 40:1
Bar 1 8 Juda the tenth day of the month Sivan
Eze 29 1 in the tenth year, the tenth month, the
Zach 8 19 and the fast of the tenth [month]
2 Ma 5 27 Judas Machabeus, who was the tenth
John 1 39 day: now it was about the tenth hour
Apoc 21 20 the tenth, a chrysoprasus: the
10th part; *see* part
11th Num 7 72 eleventh day the prince of the sons
Deut 1 3 in the fortieth year, the 11th month
3 K 6 38 in the 11th year in the month Bul
4 K 9 29 the 11th year of Joram the son of
25 2 till the 11th year of king Sedecias, the
1 Pa 12 13 Jerenias the tenth, Machbani the 11th
24 12 the 11th to Eliasib, the 12th to Jacim
25 18 the 11th to Azareel, to his sons and
27 14 11th for the 11th month was Banaias
Tob 11 1 they came to Charan . . . the 11th day
Jer 1 3 the end of the 11th year of Sedecias
39 2 and in the 11th year of Sedecias, in
52 5 until the 11th year of king Sedecias
Eze 26 1 in the 11th year, the first day of
29 1 tenth month, the 11th day of the month
30 20 in the 11th year, in the first month
31 1 in the 11th year, the third month
Zach 1 7 the 11th month which is called Sabath
1 Ma 16 14 in the year 177, the 11th month
Mat 20 6 about the eleventh hour he went out
9 that came about the eleventh hour, they
Apoc 21 20 the eleventh, a jacinth: the twelfth
12th Num 7 78 twelfth day the prince of the sons
4 K 8 25 in the 12th year of Joram son of Achab
17 1 in the 12th year of Achaz king of
25 27 in the 12th month the seven and
1 Pa 24 12 the 11th to Eliasib, the 12th to Jacim
25 19 the 12th to Hasabia, to his sons and
27 15 the 12th for the 12th month was Holdai
2 Pa 34 3 the 12th year after he began to reign
Jdth 1 5 now in the 12th year of his reign
Jer 52 31 of Joachin . . . in the 12th month
Eze 32 1 in the 12th year, in the 12th month
17 in the 12th year, in the 15th day of
33 21 in the 12th year of our captivity, in
Apoc 21 20 the twelfth, an amethyst. And the
13th Gen 14 4 in the 13th year they revolted
1 Pa 24 13 the 13th to Hoppha, the 14th to Isbaab
20 the 13th to Subael, to his sons and
Jdth 2 1 in the 13th year of the reign of
Jer 1 2 in the 13th year of his reign. And
25 3 from the 13th year of Josias the son
1 Ma 7 43 battle on the 13th day of the month
49 being the 13th of the month of Adar
2 Ma 15 37 the 13th day of the month of Adar
14th Gen 14 5 in 14th year came Chodorlahomor
4 K 18 13 14th year of Ezechias, Sennacherib
1 Pa 24 13 the 13th to Hoppha, the 14th to Isbaab
25 21 the 14th to Mathathias, to his sons
Isa 36 1 the 14th year of king Ezechias, that
Eze 40 1 14th year after the city was destroyed
Acts 27 27 after the 14th night was come, as we
14th day Exod 12 6 keep it until f. day
Exod 12 18 f. day of the month in evening. Num 9:11
Lev 23 5 f. day of the month, is the phase of
Num 9 3 the f. day of this month in the evening
5 f. day of the month at evening. Josu 5:10
28 16 f. day of the month shall be the phase
2 Pa 30 15 on fourteenth day of the second month
35 1 on f. day of the first month. 1 Es 6:19
Esth 9 15 on fourteenth day of the month Adar
17 on the fourteenth day they left off
18 thirteenth and fourteenth day of same
19 appointed the fourteenth day of the
21 fourteenth and fifteenth day of month
10 13 on f. and fifteenth day of same month
13 6 fourteenth day of the twelfth month
Acts 27 33 fourteenth day that you have waited
15th Exod 16 1 the 15th day of the second month
Lev 23 6 the 15th day of the same month
34 from 15th day of this same 7th month
39 15th day of the 7th month. Num 29:12
Num 28 17 on the 15th day the solemn feast
33 3 on the 15th day of the first month
3 K 12 32 8th month, on the 15th day of the month
33 on the 15th day of the eighth month
4 K 14 23 in the 15th year of Amasias son of
1 Pa 24 14 the 15th to Belga, the 16th to Emmer
25 22 the 15th to Jerimoth, to his sons and
2 Pa 15 10 in the 15th year of the reign of Asa

Eze 32 17 12th year, in the 15th day of the month
45 25 in the 15th day of the month, in the
1 Ma 1 57 on the 15th day of the month Casleu
2 Ma 11 33 15th day of the month of Xanthicus. 38
Luke 3 1 in the fifteenth year of the reign of
16th 1 Pa 24 14 15th to Belga, the 16th to Emmer
1 Pa 25 23 the 16th to Hananias, to his sons and
2 Pa 29 17 on the 16th day of the same month they
17th Gen 7 11 in the 17th day of the month
3 K 22 52 17th year of Josaphat king of Juda
4 K 16 1 in the 17th year of Phacee the son
1 Pa 24 15 the 17th to Hezir, the 18th to Aphses
25 24 the 17th to Jesbacassa, to his sons
18th 3 K 15 1 the 18th year of reign of Jeroboam
4 K 3 1 in the 18th year of Josaphat king of
22 3 in the 18th year of king Josias, 23:23
1 Pa 24 15 the 17th to Hezir, the 18th to Aphses
25 25 the 18th to Hanani, to his sons and
2 Pa 13 1 in the 18th year of king Jeroboam
34 8 now in the 18th year of his reign
35 19 in the 18th year of the reign of Josias
Jer 32 1 18th year of Nabuchodonosor. 52:29
1 Ma 14 27 the 18th day of the month Elul, in the
19th 4 K 25 8 the 19th year of the king of Babylon
1 Pa 24 16 19th to Pheteia, the 20th to Hezechiel
25 26 the 19th to Mellothi, to his sons and
Jer 52 12 the 19th year of Nabuchodonosor king
20th Lev 27 5 from the fifth year until the 20th
Num 10 11 the 20th day of the month, the cloud
1 K 7 2 for it was now the 20th year, and
3 K 15 9 in the 20th year of Jeroboam king of
4 K 15 30 in the 20th year of Joatham the son
1 Pa 24 16 19th to Pheteia, the 20th to Hezechiel
25 27 the 20th to Eliatha, to his sons and
2 Pa 31 17 Levites from the 20th year and upward
2 Es 1 1 the month of Casleu in the 20th year
2 1 in the 20th year of Artaxerxes the
21st Exod 12 18 until the one and twentieth day
1 Pa 24 17 the one and twentieth to Jachin
25 28 the one and twentieth to Othir
22nd 1 Pa 24 17 the two and twentieth to Gamul
1 Pa 25 29 the two and twentieth to Geddelthi
Jdth 2 1 the two and twentieth day of the
23d 4 K 12 6 the three and twentieth year. 13:1; Jer 25:3; 52:30
1 Pa 24 18 the three and twentieth to Dalaiau
25 30 the three and twentieth to Mahazioth
2 Pa 7 10 three and twentieth day. 1 Ma 13:51
24th 1 Pa 24 18 the four and twentieth to Maaziau
1 Pa 25 31 four and twentieth to Romemthiezer
2 Es 9 1 the four and twentieth day. Dan 10:4; Agge 2:1, 11, 19, 21; Zach 1:7; 2 Ma 11:21
25th 2 Es 6 15 the five and twentieth day. Jer 52:31; 1 Ma 1:62; 4:52, 59; 2 Ma 1:18; 10:5
Eze 40 1 in the five and twentieth year of our
26th 3 K 16 8 the six and twentieth year of Asa
27th Gen 8 4 seven and twentieth day of the month. 14; 4 K 25:27
3 K 16 10 seven and twentieth year of Asa. 15
4 K 15 1 seven and twentieth year of Jeroboam
Eze 29 17 the seven and twentieth year, in the
30th Eze 1 1 in the 30th year, in the fourth
2 Ma 11 30 until the 30th day of the month of
31st 3 K 16 23 the one and thirtieth year of Asa
32nd 2 Es 5 14 the two and thirtieth year of Artaxerxes. 13:6
35th 2 Pa 15 19 no war unto five and thirtieth year
36th 2 Pa 16 1 the six and thirtieth year of his
37th 4 K 13 10 seven and thirtieth year of Joas
4 K 25 27 the seven and thirtieth year of the captivity. Jer 52:31
38th 3 K 16 29 eight and thirtieth year of Asa
4 K 15 8 the eight and thirtieth year of Azarias
39th 4 K 15 13 nine and thirtieth year of. 17
2 Pa 16 12 sick in the nine and thirtieth year
40th Num 33 38 40th year of the coming forth
Deut 1 3 in the 40th year, the 11th month
8 4 is not worn, lo this is the 40th year
1 Pa 26 31 in the 40th year of the reign of David
41st 2 Pa 16 13 died in the one and fortieth year
50th Lev 25 10 thou shalt sanctify the 50th
Lev 25 11 it is the jubilee and the 50th year
Num 8 25 accomplished the 50th year of their age
31 30 shalt take the 50th head of persons
47 Moses took the 50th head and gave it
36 4 that is, the 50th year of remission
4 K 15 23 in the 50th year of Azarias king of
52nd 4 K 15 27 two and fiftieth year of Azarias
70th Zach 1 12 this is now the 70th year
137th 1 Ma 1 11 he reigned in the 137th year of
143d 1 Ma 1 21 ravaged Egypt in the 143d year
145th 1 Ma 1 57 month of Casleu in 145th year
146th 1 Ma 2 70 he died in the 146th year
147th 1 Ma 3 37 in the 147th year: and he passed
148th 1 Ma 4 52 month of Casleu, in 148th year
151st 1 Ma 7 1 in the 151st year Demetrius the
152nd 1 Ma 9 3 the first month of the 152nd year
160th 1 Ma 10 1 in the 160th year Alexander the
162nd 1 Ma 10 57 to Ptolemais in the 162nd year
167th 1 Ma 11 19 Demetrius reigned in 167th year
480th 3 K 6 1 480th year after the children of
600th Gen 7 11 600th year of the life of Noe
601st Gen 8 13 the 601st year, the first month